# THIS DICTIONARY

## headword
The **headword** is printed in **bold** type. Variant spellings or alternative forms are given before the definition.

## pronunciation
Guidance on **pronunciation** is given in a new user-friendly system. See pp. viii-ix for details. Only the pronunciations standard in Australian English are given.

## part of speech
The **part of speech** is given for all main entries and derivatives. A dash before the abbreviated part of speech indicates that the headword is used for more than one part of speech, and that these other parts of speech are listed later in the entry.

## inflection
**Inflections** which follow regular patterns receive no comment. Inflections which follow less regular patterns are always given. A doubled consonant in verbal inflections (e.g. *rubbed, rubbing*) is shown in the form (-bb-) etc.

## definition
**Definitions** are listed in order of familiarity and importance.

## illustrative usage
**Definitions** are often followed by **illustrative usages,** which indicate how a word is typically used in a particular sense. These are printed in *italic* type.

## sense
The different **senses** for each part of speech are numbered.

## subject and usage labels
**Usage labels** (e.g. *colloq.* (*colloquial*)) are used to clarify the particular context in which a word or phrase is normally used. Some **subject labels** are used to indicate the particular relevance of a term or subject with which it is associated (e.g. *Mus.*), but they are not used when this is clear from the definition itself.

## usage note
**Usage notes** found at the end of entries give guidance on the current norms of standard English, especially on points of disputed usage.

## phrases
**Phrasal verbs, idioms,** and occasionally some other forms are listed in alphabetical order after the treatment of the main word.

## derivative
**Derivatives** (words formed by adding a suffix to another word) are often listed at the end of the entry for the main word (e.g. **acidic, acidify, acidity,** and **acidly** at **acid**).

## etymology
**Etymology** is given in square brackets at the end of an entry.

## Aboriginal language
**Aboriginal languages** are marked on the map at the end of the dictionary.

## cross-reference
**Cross-reference** to main entries is indicated by SMALL CAPITALS. Cross-references in italics are to phrases etc. within a main entry.

# THE AUSTRALIAN POCKET OXFORD DICTIONARY

## FOURTH EDITION

*Edited by*
**Bruce Moore**

*Based on*
**The Australian Pocket
Oxford Dictionary**
Third Edition
*Edited by*
**Bruce Moore**

*and*
*Based on*
**The Pocket Oxford Dictionary
of Current English**
Eighth Edition
*Edited by*
**Della Thompson**

Melbourne
OXFORD UNIVERSITY PRESS
Oxford    Auckland    New York

# OXFORD
UNIVERSITY PRESS

253 Normanby Road, South Melbourne, Australia

Oxford University Press is a department of the University of Oxford.
It furthers the University's objective of excellence in research,
scholarship, and education by publishing worldwide in

Oxford  New York

Athens  Auckland  Bangkok  Bogotá  Buenos Aires  Calcutta
Cape Town  Chennai  Dar es Salaam  Delhi  Florence  Hong Kong
Istanbul  Karachi  Kuala Lumpur  Madrid  Melbourne  Mexico City
Mumbai  Nairobi  Paris  Port Moresby  São Paulo  Shanghai
Singapore  Taipei  Tokyo  Toronto  Warsaw

with associated companies in Berlin  Ibadan

First edition 1924
Second edition 1934
Third edition 1939
Fourth edition 1942
Fifth edition 1969
Sixth edition 1978
Seventh edition 1984
Eighth edition 1992

First Australian edition Grahame Johnston 1976
Second Australian edition George W. Turner 1984
Third Australian edition Bruce Moore 1993
Fourth Australian edition Bruce Moore 1996
Reprinted 1997, 1998, 1999 (twice), 2000 (twice)

National Library of Australia
Cataloguing-in-Publication data:
The Australian pocket Oxford dictionary.

4th ed.
ISBN 0 19 554015 8.

1. English language—Dictionaries. 2. English language—
Australia—Dictionaries. 3. Australian languages—Dictionaries.
I Moore, Bruce, 1947–.

423

Typeset by Egan-Reid Ltd, Auckland, New Zealand
Printed through Bookpac Production Services, Singapore

# Contents

# Biographical Notes

Professor Grahame Johnston, editor of the first edition of the *Australian Pocket Oxford Dictionary*, held posts at the Universities of Queensland, Melbourne (Robert Wallace Professor of English, 1963–65), and New South Wales (Professor of English and Head of the Department of Language and Literature, Royal Military College, Duntroon, 1968–76). He died in 1976.

George W. Turner was Reader in English at the University of Adelaide at the time of editing the second edition of the *Australian Pocket Oxford Dictionary*. He was a consultant on Australian and New Zealand words for the *Oxford English Dictionary* Second Supplement, and editor of the *Australian Concise Oxford Dictionary* (first edition). Since retirement from university teaching he has continued to be involved with lexicography, and in 1989 with his wife Beryl Turner edited the first edition of the *Oxford Australian Paperback Dictionary*.

Dr Bruce Moore, editor of the third and fourth editions of the *Australian Pocket Oxford Dictionary*, has taught in English Departments at the Universities of Melbourne, Sydney and Monash, and at the Royal Military College, Duntroon. At the time of editing the third edition he was a Senior Lecturer in the Department of English, Australian Defence Force Academy, University of New South Wales. He is now a Reader at the Australian National University and Head of the Australian National Dictionary Centre.

# Preface to the Fourth Edition

This fourth edition of the *Australian Pocket Oxford Dictionary* is based on the previous edition, and preserves the major features of that edition. There is comprehensive coverage of Australian English, drawing on the *Australian National Dictionary* and on the continually updated database of Australian English at the Australian National Dictionary Centre (established in 1988 by Oxford University Press Australia and the Australian National University to conduct research into Australian English and to produce the range of Oxford Australian dictionaries). There is also comprehensive coverage of international English, drawing on the 20 volume *Oxford English Dictionary* and on the continually updated database of this dictionary at Oxford.

For its Australian material the *Australian Pocket Oxford Dictionary* draws heavily on the *Australian National Dictionary* ed. W.S. Ramson (1988), on *Australian Aboriginal Words in English* by R.M.W. Dixon, W.S. Ramson, and Mandy Thomas (1990), and on the continuing research of the Australian National Dictionary Centre. This is reflected in the dictionary's comprehensive coverage of Australian colloquialisms, flora and fauna, terms of historical significance, borrowings from Aboriginal languages, and words from Aboriginal English.

The text has been updated to take account of new words and meanings, e.g. *cafetière, calicivirus, dot ball, ecotourism, goth, Internet, mad cow disease, mosh, political correctness, push polling, rollover, schoolies' week, snail mail, Wollemi pine*, etc. More importantly, this edition introduces two new features. First, in response to requests from users of the dictionary, the symbols of the International Phonetic Alphabet have been replaced by more recognisable symbols. Words are also divided into syllables in the pronunciation section in order to clarify how they are actually pronounced. This new pronunciation system is explained on pp. viii–ix. Secondly, guidance on grammar (e.g noun), syntax (e.g. clause), punctuation (e.g. hyphen), and style (e.g. metaphor) is provided in panels at the point in the dictionary where the relevant headword occurs.

Special thanks to Gavin Mercer, the Centre's systems analyst and programmer, who controlled the computer programming for the project, and to Hilary Kent and Frederick Ludowyk for lexicographical help.

# How to use this Dictionary

## 1 Headword

The headword is printed in bold type (**like this**). If the word is not completely naturalised in Australian English, it is printed in bold italic type (***like this***).

Variant spellings are given before the definition. The form given as the headword is the preferred form. Hence, **colour** *n.* (also **color**), **colourise** *v.* (also **color-, -ize**).

Words that are normally spelled with a capital initial letter are given in this form as the headword. When they are in some senses spelled with a small initial letter and in others with a capital, this is indicated by repetition of the full word in the appropriate form within the entry (as at **rock¹**).

## 2 Pronunciation

The pronunciation system used is explained on pp. viii–ix.

## 3 Part-of-speech label

This is given for all main entries and derivatives.

Different parts of speech of a single word are listed separately, and introduced by a dash.

Verbs, whether transitive, intransitive, or both, are given the simple designation *v.* The designation *absol.* (absolute) denotes use with an implied object (as at **abdicate**).

## 4 Inflections

Nouns that form their plural regularly by adding *s* (or *-es*) receive no comment (except where there may be uncertainty about the correct form). Irregular forms are always given, except where the word is a compound of obvious formation (e.g. **schoolhouse**).

Verbs that form their third person singular present forms by adding *-s* (or *-es*) to the stem, and their past tenses and past participles by adding *ed* to the stem, receive no comment. A doubled consonant in verbal inflections (e.g. *rubbed, rubbing, sinned, sinning*) is shown in the form (**-bb-, -nn-**, etc.).

The following regular forms for the comparative and superlative of adjectives and adverbs receive no comment: (a) words of one syllable ending in *-er* and *-est* (e.g. *greater, greatest*); (b) words of one syllable ending in silent *-e*, which drop the *-e* and add *-er* and *-est* (e.g. *braver, bravest*).

## 5 Definition

Definitions are listed in order of comparative familiarity and importance, with the most important and current senses first.

Round brackets enclose letters or words that are optional (as at **crash** *v.* where '(cause to) make a loud smashing noise' can mean either 'make a loud smashing noise' or 'cause to make a loud smashing noise') and indicate typical objects of transitive verbs (such as 'milk' and 'the skin' in two senses of **cream** *v.*)

## 6 Subject and Usage labels

Subject labels (e.g. *Computing, Mus.*) are used to help clarify the subject field to which a particular sense applies. They are not used when this is clear from the definition itself.

Words and phrases more common in informal spoken English than in formal written English are labelled *colloq.* ('colloquial'), e.g. **budgie**, **skite**. Two categories of usage are indicated by special markings: **1** *coarse colloq.* indicates a word that, although widely found, is still unacceptable to many people; **2** *offens.* ('offensive') indicates a use that is offensive because of what it implies about the members of a particular group in society, e.g. **wog**[1]. The inclusion of such terms does not in any way imply that their use is acceptable.

## 7 Phrases and Compounds

Phrases and idioms (and occasionally compounds) are grouped together in alphabetical order at the end of the main word. This section is introduced by the symbol □. The words *a, the, one,* and *person* do not count for purposes of alphabetical order. Compound terms forming one word (e.g. **bathroom**, **jellyfish**) are listed as main entries. Compounds consisting of two or more words (e.g. **chain reaction**) or joined by a hyphen (e.g. **half-brother**) are similarly listed as main entries (although occasionally it has proved more helpful to list them in the phrases block).

## 8 Derivatives

Words formed by adding a suffix to another word are in many cases listed at the end of the entry for the main word (e.g. **chalkiness** and **chalky** at **chalk**). This section is introduced by the symbol □. Derivatives are not defined since they can be understood from the sense of the main word and that given at the suffix concerned; when further definition is called for they are given main entries in their own right (e.g. **changeable**).

## 9 Etymology

This is given in square brackets [ ] at the end of the entry. In the space available it can only give the direct line of derivation. 'Old English' is used for words that are known to have been used before AD 1150. 'Anglo-French' denotes the variety of French current in England after the Norman Conquest (AD 1066). 'Latin' denotes Classical and Late Latin of the period up to about AD 600; 'medieval Latin' denotes that of the period about 600–1500; 'Anglo-Latin' denotes Latin as used in medieval England. Names of the rarer languages that have contributed to English (such as Balti at **polo**) are given in full without explanation; they may be found in larger dictionaries or in encyclopaedias.

Special attention is paid to borrowings from Australian Aboriginal languages. In this dictionary the particular Aboriginal language (where known) from which the word was borrowed is given; these languages have separate entries in the body of the dictionary, and their location is marked on the map provided on the back endpaper.

## 10 Usage notes

Usage notes found at the end of some entries give guidance on the current norms of standard Australian English, i.e. the form of written and spoken English most generally accepted as a normal basis of communication in everyday life in Australia. Some of the rules given may legitimately be broken in less formal Australian English, and especially in conversation.

## 11 Cross-references

A cross-reference to a main entry is indicated by small capitals (e.g. **sus** var. of SUSS; **put a person wise** see WISE). Cross-reference in italics to a defined phrase or compound refers to the entry for the first word unless another is specified.

# Pronunciation

A guide to pronunciation is given for any word that is difficult to pronounce, or difficult to recognise when read, or spelled the same as another word but pronounced differently. The pronunciation given represents standard Australian speech.

The sounds represented are as follows:

| | |
|---|---|
| a | *as in* **a**nd, b**a**t, c**a**t |
| ah | *as in* c**a**lm, p**a**th, **a**rm |
| air | *as in* f**air**, c**are**, th**ere** |
| aw | *as in* l**aw**, f**or**, s**ore** |
| ay | *as in* pl**ay**, **a**ge, f**a**ce |
| b | *as in* **b**ed |
| ch | *as in* **ch**in, **ch**urch, whi**ch** |
| d | *as in* **d**ay |
| e | *as in* b**e**d, t**e**n, **e**gg |
| ee | *as in* m**ee**t, m**ea**t, **ea**ch |
| eer | *as in* b**eer**, h**ere**, f**ear** |
| er | *as in* h**er**, b**ir**d |
| f | *as in* **f**at |
| g | *as in* **g**et, wa**g**on, do**g** |
| h | *as in* **h**at |
| i | *as in* p**i**n, s**i**t, **i**s |
| j | *as in* **j**am, **j**ob, en**j**oy |
| k | *as in* **k**ing, **c**at, pi**que** |
| l | *as in* **l**eg |
| m | *as in* **m**e |
| n | *as in* **n**ot |
| ng | *as in* si**ng**, thi**ng**, a**nx**ious |
| o | *as in* g**o**t, t**o**p, **o**n |
| oh | *as in* m**o**st, b**oa**t, g**o** |
| oi | *as in* j**oi**n, v**oi**ce, b**oy** |
| oo | *as in* s**oo**n, b**oo**t, **oo**ze |
| oor | *as in* t**our** |
| ow | *as in* c**ow**, h**ow**, **ou**t |
| owuh | *as in* h**our**, p**ower** |
| p | *as in* **p**eg |
| r | *as in* **r**ed |
| s | *as in* **s**it |
| sh | *as in* **sh**op, fi**sh**, **ch**arade |
| t | *as in* **t**op |
| th | *as in* **th**in, me**th**od, bo**th** |
| *th* | *as in* **th**is, ei**th**er, **th**ose |
| u | *as in* b**u**n, **u**p |
| uh | *as in* **a**bove, c**o**rrect, moth**er** |
| uu | *as in* b**oo**k, l**oo**k, p**u**ll |
| uy | *as in* cr**y**, l**igh**t |

| uyuh | *as in* **fi**re, **wi**re, sp**ire** |
| v | *as in* **v**an, ri**v**er |
| w | *as in* **w**as, **w**ish |
| x | *as in* Scottish lo**ch** |
| y | *as in* **y**ard, **y**es, **y**ou |
| yoo | *as in* f**ew**, d**ue**, b**eau**ty, t**u**ne |
| yoor | *as in* c**ure**, p**ure**, end**ure** |
| z | *as in* **z**oo, la**z**y, rai**s**e |
| *zh* | *as in* divi**si**on, vi**si**on, mea**su**re |

### Note

1  The pronunciation is shown within slashes, usually directly after the head-word e.g. **galah** /guh-**lah**/.

2  Words are broken up into syllables by means of hyphens, as an aid to correct pronunciation.

3  The main or primary stress of a word of two or more syllables is indicated in bold type, like **this**. Any secondary stress is shown by ˌ preceding the syllable. Thus in **mobilise** /**moh**-buh-ˌluyz/ the first syllable receives primary stress and the third syllable receives secondary stress.

4  Alternative pronunciations are separated by a comma within the slashes. Thus:

    **belief** /bee-**leef**, buh-/

  means that this word can be pronounced /bee-**leef**/ *or* /buh-**leef**/;

    **maladroit** /mal-uh-**droit**, mal-/

  means that this word can be pronounced /mal-uh-**droit**/ *or* /**mal**-uh-droit/;

    **blessed** /**bles**-uhd, blest/

  means that this word can be pronounced in either of those two ways;

    **fructose** /**fruuk**-tohz, -tohs, **fruk**-/

  means that this word can be pronounced /**fruuk**-tohz/ *or* /**fruuk**-tohs/ *or* /**fruk**-tohz/ *or* /**fruk**-tohs/.

# Abbreviations Used in the Dictionary

Abbreviations in general use (such as etc., i.e., the names of Australian States, etc.) are explained in the dictionary itself.

| | | | |
|---|---|---|---|
| abbr. | abbreviation | ellipt. | elliptical(ly) |
| absol. | absolute(ly) | emphat. | emphatic |
| adj. | adjective | esp. | especially |
| adv. | adverb | euphem. | euphemism |
| Aeron. | Aeronautics | Exod. | Exodus |
| Anat. | Anatomy | | |
| Anglo-Ind. | Anglo-Indian | fem. | feminine |
| Antiq. | Antiquity | foll. | followed |
| Archaeol. | Archaeology | Gen. | Genesis |
| Archit. | Architecture | Geol. | Geology |
| assim. | assimilated | Geom. | Geometry |
| Astrol. | Astrology | Gk | Greek |
| Astron. | Astronomy | Gram. | Grammar |
| Astronaut. | Astronautics | | |
| attrib. | attributive(ly) | Hist. | History |
| attrib. adj. | attributive adjective | hist. | with historical reference |
| aux. | auxiliary | | |
| Bibl. | Biblical | imper. | imperative |
| Biochem. | Biochemistry | Ind. | of the subcontinent comprising India, Pakistan and Bangladesh |
| Biol. | Biology | | |
| Bot. | Botany | | |
| Brit. | British | | |
| Chem. | Chemistry | infin. | infinitive |
| Cinematog. | Cinematography | int. | interjection |
| collect. | collective(ly) | interrog. | interrogative |
| colloq. | colloquial(ly) | interrog. adj. | interrogative adjective |
| comb. | combination; combining | interrog. pron. | interrogative pronoun |
| compar. | comparative | Ir. | Irish |
| compl. | complement | iron. | ironical |
| conj. | conjunction | | |
| contr. | contraction | joc. | jocular |
| | | Judg. | Judges |
| demons. adj | demonstrative adjective | Lev. | Leviticus |
| demons. pron. | demonstrative pronoun | masc. | masculine |
| derog. | derogatory | Math. | Mathematics |
| dial. | dialect | Matt. | Matthew |
| | | Mech. | Mechanics |
| Eccl. | Ecclesiastical | Med. | Medicine |
| Econ. | Economics | Meteorol. | Meteorology |
| Electr. | Electricity | Mil. | Military |

| | |
|---|---|
| Mineral. | Mineralogy |
| Mus. | Music |
| Mythol. | Mythology |
| n. | noun |
| Naut. | Nautical |
| neg. | negative |
| N.Engl. | Northern English |
| n.pl. | noun plural |
| NZ | New Zealand |
| obj. | objective (case) |
| offens. | offensive |
| opp. | as opposed to |
| orig. | originally |
| Parl. | Parliament(ary) |
| part. | participle |
| past part. | past participle |
| Pharm. | Pharmacy; Pharmacology |
| Philos. | Philosophy |
| Phonet. | Phonetics · |
| Photog. | Photography |
| phr. | phrase |
| Physiol. | Physiology |
| pl. | plural |
| poet. | poetical |
| Polit. | Politics |
| poss. | possessive (case) |
| poss. pron. | possessive pronoun |
| prec. | preceded |
| predic. | predicative(ly) |
| predic. adj. | predicative adjective |
| prep. | preposition |
| pres. | present |
| pres. part | present participle |
| pron. | pronoun |
| pronunc. | pronunciation |
| propr. | proprietary term |
| Psychol. | Psychological |
| RC Ch | Roman Catholic Church |
| ref. | reference |
| refl. | reflexive |
| rel. adj. | relative adjective |
| rel. adv. | relative adverb |
| rel. pron. | relative pronoun |
| Relig. | Religion |
| Rev. | Revelation |
| rhet. | rhetorical |
| Rom. | Roman |
| S.Afr. | South Africa |
| Scot. | Scottish |
| Sci. | Science |
| sing. | singular |
| Stock Exch. | Stock Exchange |
| superl. | superlative |
| symb. | symbol |
| Theatr. | Theatre |
| Theol. | Theology |
| US | American, in American use |
| usu. | usually |
| v. | verb |
| var. | variant(s) |
| v.aux. | auxiliary verb |
| v.refl. | reflexive verb |
| Zool. | Zoology |

## Note on Proprietary Status

This dictionary includes some words which are, or are asserted to be, proprietary names or trade marks. Their inclusion does not imply that they have acquired for legal purposes a non-proprietary or general significance, nor is any other judgment implied concerning their legal status. In cases where the editor has some evidence that a word is used as a proprietary name or trade mark this is indicated by the designation *propr.*, but no judgment concerning the legal status of such words is made or implied thereby.

# A

**A¹** /ay/ n. (pl. **As** or **A's**) **1** (also **a**) first letter of the alphabet. **2** Mus. sixth note of the diatonic scale of C major. **3** first hypothetical person or example. **4** highest category (of academic marks). **5** (usu. **a**) Algebra first known quantity. □**A1** /ay **wun**/ colloq. first-rate, excellent. **from A to B** from one place to another (means of getting from A to B). **from A to Z** from beginning to end.

**A²** abbr. (also **A.**) **1** ampere(s). **2** answer.

**a¹** /uh, ay/ adj. (also **an** /an, uhn/ before a vowel sound) (called the indefinite article) **1** one, some, any. **2** one like (a Judas). **3** one single (not a chance). **4** the same (all of a size). **5** per (twice a year; seven a side). [Old English ān one]

**a²** /uh/ prep. (usu. as prefix) **1** to, towards (ashore; aside). **2** (with verb in pres. part. or infin.) doing or being (a-hunting; abuzz). **3** on (afire). **4** in (nowadays). [Old English an, on, ON]

**Å** abbr. ångström(s).

**a-¹** prefix not, without (amoral; agnostic). [Greek]

**a-²** prefix implying motion onward or away, adding intensity to verbs of motion (arise; awake; amaze). [Old English]

**a-³** prefix to, at, or into a state (agree; amass; avenge). [Latin ad- to, at]

**a-⁴** prefix **1** from, away (abridge). **2** of (akin; anew). **3** out, utterly (abash; affray). **4** in, on, engaged in, etc. (see A²). [sense 1 from Latin ab; sense 2 from Old English; sense 3 from Latin ex]

**a-⁵** prefix assim. form of AD- before sc, sp, st.

**aardvark** /ahd-vahk/ n. African mammal with a tubular snout and a long tongue, feeding on termites. [Afrikaans]

**ab-** prefix off, away, from (abduct; abnormal). [Latin]

**aback** /uh-bak/ adv. □ **taken aback** surprised, disconcerted. [Old English: related to A²]

**abacus** /ab-uh-kuhs/ n. (pl. **-cuses**) **1** frame with wires along which beads are slid for calculating. **2** Archit. flat slab on top of a capital. [Latin from Greek from Hebrew]

**abaft** /uh-bahft/ Naut. — adv. in the stern half of a ship. — prep. nearer the stern than. [from A², -baft: see AFT]

**abalone** /ˌab-uh-loh-nee/ n. mollusc with edible flesh, having a shallow ear-shaped shell lined with mother-of-pearl. [Spanish]

**abandon** /uh-ban-duhn/ — v. **1** give up completely or before completion (abandoned hope; abandoned the game). **2** forsake, desert. **3** (often foll. by to; often refl.) yield to a passion, another's control, etc. (abandoned himself to despair; abandoned the town to the enemy). — n. freedom from inhibitions or restraint etc. (partying with abandon). □**abandonment** n. [French: related to AD-, BAN]

**abase** /uh-bays/ v. (-sing) (also refl.) humiliate, degrade (another person or oneself). □**abasement** n. [French: related to AD-, BASE²]

**abashed** /uh-basht/ predic. adj. embarrassed, disconcerted. [French es- EX-¹, baïr astound]

**abate** /uh-bayt/ v. (-ting) make or become less strong, severe, intense, etc.; diminish (the storm abated). □**abatement** n. [French abatre from Latin batt(u)o beat]

**abattoir** /ab-uh-ˌtwah/ n. (pl. **abattoirs**, often treated as sing.) place where animals are slaughtered for food. [French abatre fell, as ABATE]

**abbess** /ab-uhs, ab-es/ n. woman who is the head of certain communities of nuns. [Latin: related to ABBOT]

**abbey** /ab-ee/ n. (pl. **-s**) **1** building(s) occupied by a community of monks or nuns. **2** the community itself. [medieval Latin abbatia]

**abbot** /ab-uht/ n. man who is the head of a community of monks. [Old English from Latin abbas]

**abbreviate** /uh-bree-vee-ˌayt/ v. (-ting) shorten, esp. represent (a word etc.) by a part of it. □**abbreviation** /uh-ˌbree-vee-ay-shuhn/ n. [Latin: related to BRIEF]

**ABC¹** /ˌay-bee-see/ n. **1** the alphabet. **2** rudiments of a subject. **3** alphabetical guide.

**ABC²** abbr. Australian Broadcasting Corporation.

**abdicate** /ab-duh-ˌkayt/ v. (-ting) **1** (usu. absol.) give up or renounce (a throne). **2** renounce (a duty, right, etc.). □**abdication** /ˌab-duh-kay-shuhn/ n. [Latin dico declare]

**abdomen** /ab-duh-muhn/ n. **1** part of the body containing the stomach, bowels,

1

reproductive organs, etc. **2** the hinder part of an insect etc. □ **abdominal** /ab-**dom**-uh-nuhl/ *adj.* [Latin]

**abduct** /uhb-**dukt**, ab-/ *v.* carry off illegally, kidnap. □ **abduction** *n.* **abductor** *n.* [Latin *duco* lead]

**aberrant** /**ab**-uh-ruhnt/ *adj.* deviating from what is normal or accepted. [Latin: related to ERR]

**aberration** /ˌab-uh-**ray**-shuhn/ *n.* **1** aberrant behaviour; moral or mental lapse. **2** *Biol.* deviation from a normal type. **3** distortion of an image because of a defect in a lens or mirror.

**abet** /uh-**bet**/ *v.* (-**tt**-) (usu. in **aid and abet**) encourage or assist (an offender or offence). [French: related to AD-, BAIT]

**abeyance** /uh-**bay**-uhns/ *n.* (usu. prec. by *in, into*) temporary disuse or suspension. [French: related to AD-, *beer* gape]

**abhor** /uhb-**haw**/ *v.* (-**rr**-) detest; regard with disgust. [Latin: related to HORROR]

**abhorrence** /uhb-**ho**-ruhns/ *n.* disgust; detestation.

**abhorrent** /uhb-**ho**-ruhnt/ *adj.* **1** (often foll. by *to*) disgusting or hateful. **2** (foll. by *to*) strongly conflicting with (*abhorrent to the spirit of the law*).

**abide** /uh-**buyd**/ *v.* (-**ding**; *past* **abided** or rarely **abode** /uh-**bohd**/ ) **1** (usu. in *neg.*) tolerate, endure (*can't abide him*). **2** (foll. by *by*) **a** act in accordance with (*abide by the rules*). **b** keep (a promise). **3** *archaic* **a** remain, continue. **b** dwell. [A-², BIDE]

**abiding** *adj.* enduring, permanent (*an abiding sense of loss*).

**ability** /uh-**bil**-uh-tee/ *n.* (*pl.* -**ies**) **1** (often foll. by *to* + infin.) capacity or power (*has the ability to write good poetry*). **2** cleverness, talent. [French: related to ABLE]

**-ability** *suffix* forming nouns of quality from, or corresponding to, adjectives in *-able* (*capability; vulnerability*).

***ab initio*** /ab i-**nish**-ee-oh/ *adv.* from the beginning. [Latin]

**abiogenesis** /ˌay-buy-oh-**jen**-uh-suhs/ *n.* **1** formation of living organisms from non-living substances. **2** supposed spontaneous generation of living organisms. □ **abiogenic** *adj.* [A-¹, Greek *bios* life, GENESIS]

**abject** /**ab**-jekt/ *adj.* **1** miserable, wretched (*abject poverty*). **2** degraded; self-abasing (*abject apology*). **3** despicable. □ **abjection** /ab-**jek**-shuhn/ *n.* **abjectly** *adv.* **abjectness** *n.* [Latin *jacio -ject-* throw]

**abjure** /uhb-**joor**/ *v.* (-**ring**) renounce (an opinion, claim, cause, etc.) on oath. □ **abjuration** /ˌab-juh-**ray**-shuhn/ *n.* [Latin *juro* swear]

**ablative** /**ab**-luh-tiv/ *Gram.* — *n.* case (in Latin) of nouns and pronouns indicating an agent, instrument, or location. — *adj.* of or in the ablative. [Latin *ablatus* taken away]

**ablaze** /uh-**blayz**/ *predic. adj. & adv.* **1** on fire. **2** glittering, glowing (*after the rain the desert was ablaze with colour*). **3** greatly excited (*ablaze with anger*).

**able** /**ay**-buhl/ *adj.* (**abler, ablest**) **1** (often foll. by *to* + infin.; used esp. in *is able, will be able*, etc., replacing tenses of *can*) having the capacity or power (*not able to come*). **2** talented, clever (*an able student*). □ **ably** *adv.* [Latin *habilis*]

**-able** *suffix* forming adjectives meaning: **1** that may or must be (*eatable; payable*). **2** that can be made the subject of (*dutiable; objectionable*). **3** relevant to or in accordance with (*fashionable; seasonable*). **4** that may (*comfortable; suitable*). [Latin *-abilis*]

**able-bodied** *adj.* fit, healthy.

**abled** /**ay**-buhld/ *adj.* **1** able-bodied (opp. *disabled*). **2** having a particular range of physical abilities (as specified by preceding adverb) (*differently abled*).

**ablution** /uh-**bloo**-shuhn/ *n.* (usu. in *pl.*) **1** ceremonial washing of the hands, sacred vessels, etc. **2** *colloq.* **a** ordinary bodily washing. **b** place for this. [Latin *ablutio* from *luo lut-* wash]

**-ably** *suffix* forming adverbs corresponding to adjectives in *-able*.

**abnegate** /**ab**-nuh-gayt/ *v.* (-**ting**) give up or renounce (a pleasure or right etc.). [Latin *nego* deny]

**abnegation** /ˌab-nuh-**gay**-shuhn/ *n.* denial; renunciation of a doctrine.

**abnormal** /ab-**naw**-muhl/ *adj.* deviating from the norm; exceptional. □ **abnormality** /ˌab-naw-**mal**-uh-tee/ *n.* (*pl.* -**ies**). **abnormally** *adv.* [French: related to ANOMALOUS]

**Abo** /**ab**-oh/ (also **abo**) *colloq. offens.* — *n.* (*pl.* -**s**) an Aborigine — *adj.* Aboriginal. [abbreviation]

**aboard** /uh-**bawd**/ *adv. & prep.* on or into (a ship, aircraft, etc.). [from A²]

**abode¹** /uh-**bohd**/ *n.* dwelling-place. [related to ABIDE]

**abode²** see ABIDE.

**abolish** /uh-**bol**-ish/ *v.* put an end to the existence or practice of (esp. a custom or institution). [Latin *aboleo* destroy]

**abolition** /ˌab-uh-**lish**-uhn/ *n.* **1** act or process of abolishing or being abolished. **2** instance of this. □ **abolitionist** *n.*

**A-bomb** /**ay**-bom/ *n.* = ATOMIC BOMB. [A for ATOMIC]

**abominable** /uh-**bom**-uh-nuh-buhl/ *adj.* **1** detestable, loathsome; morally reprehensible. **2** *colloq.* very bad or unpleasant (*abominable weather*). □ **abominably** *adv.* [Latin *abominor* deprecate]

**Abominable Snowman** *n.* unidentified manlike or bearlike animal said to exist in the Himalayas.

**abominate** /uh-**bom**-uh-ˌnayt/ *v.* (**-ting**) detest, loathe. [Latin: related to ABOMIN-ABLE]

**abomination** /uh-ˌbom-uh-**nay**-shuhn/ *n.* **1** loathing. **2** odious or degrading habit or act. **3** (often foll. by *to*) object of extreme disgust.

**aboriginal** /ˌab-uh-**rij**-uh-nuhl/ — *adj.* **1** indigenous, inhabiting a land from the earliest times, esp. before the arrival of colonists. **2** (usu. **Aboriginal**) of Australian Aborigines. — *n.* **1** aboriginal inhabitant. **2** (usu. **Aboriginal**) aboriginal inhabitant of Australia. **3** *colloq.* an Australian Aboriginal language. [as ABORIGINE]

**Aboriginal English** *n.* English, as used by many Aborigines, often in combination with words and constructions from one or more Aboriginal languages.

**Aboriginalisation** /ˌab-uh-rij-uh-nuh-luy-**zay**-shuhn/ *n.* (also **-ization**) affirmative action to enable Aborigines to take up positions in organisations etc., esp. organisations dealing with Aboriginal affairs. □ **Aboriginalise** (also **-ize**) *v.*

**Aboriginality** /ˌab-uh-rij-uh-**nal**-uh-tee/ *n.* **1** the quality of being Aboriginal. **2** the culture of the Aboriginal people.

**aborigine** /ˌab-uh-**rij**-uh-nee/ *n.* (usu. in *pl.*) **1** aboriginal inhabitant. **2** (usu. **Aborigine**) aboriginal inhabitant of Australia. **3** aboriginal plant or animal. [Latin *ab origine* from the beginning]

■ **Usage** There is no consensus on the use of the terms *Aborigine*(s) and *Aboriginal*(s) to refer to the original people of Australia. Some people prefer *Aboriginal* for a single person and *Aborigines* for more than one. Others prefer to use *Aborigine* and *Aborigines* for the persons, and to use *Aboriginal* only ˈas an adjective, and that is the practice of this dictionary. See KOORI[1].

**abort** /uh-**bawt**/ *v.* **1 a** (of a woman) undergo abortion; miscarry. **b** (of a foetus) be subjected to abortion. **2 a** effect abortion of (a foetus). **b** effect abortion in (a mother). **3** end or cause (a project, space flight, computer project, etc.) to end before completion. [Latin *orior* be born]

**abortion** /uh-**baw**-shuhn/ *n.* **1** natural or (esp.) medically induced expulsion of a foetus from the womb before it is able to survive independently. **2** stunted or deformed creature or thing. **3** failed project or action. □ **abortionist** *n.*

**abortive** /uh-**baw**-tiv/ *adj.* fruitless, unsuccessful.

**abound** /uh-**bownd**/ *v.* **1** be plentiful (*kangaroos abound in Australia*). **2** (foll. by *in*, *with*) be rich; teem (*Australia still abounds in gold*; *the dam abounds with yabbies*). [Latin *unda* wave]

**about** /uh-**bowt**/ — *prep.* **1 a** on the subject of (*a book about birds*). **b** relating to (*something funny about this*). **c** in relation to (*symmetry about a plane*). **d** so as to affect (*can do nothing about it*). **2** at a time near to (*about six*). **3 a** in, round (*walked about the town*; *a scarf about her neck*). **b** all round from a centre (*look about you*). **4** here and there in; at points throughout (*toys strewn about the house*). **5** at a point or points near to (*fighting going on about us*). **6** carried with (*no money about me*). **7** occupied with (*she is about her business*). — *adv.* **1 a** approximately (*about ten miles*). **b** *colloq.* in an understatement (*just about had enough*). **c** *colloq.* almost (*we're about ready to leave*). **2** here and there; at points nearby; prevailing (as a disease) (*I've seen him about recently*; *a lot of flu about*). **3** in every direction (*look about*). **4** on the move; in action (*out and about*). **5** in partial rotation; from front to back or vice versa (*turned about to hide his face*). **6** in rotation or succession (*turn and turn about*). □ **be about** (or **all about**) *colloq.* have as its essential nature (*life is all about having fun*). **be about to** be on the point of (*was about to laugh*). [Old English]

**about-face** *n.* & *int.* = ABOUT-TURN.

**about-turn** — *n.* **1** turn made so as to face the opposite direction. **2** complete change of opinion or policy etc. — *v.* make an about-turn. — *int.* (**about turn!**) *Mil.* command to make an about-turn.

**above** /uh-**buv**/ — *prep.* **1** over; on the top of; higher than; over the surface of (*head above water*; *above the din*). **2** more than (*above twenty people*). **3** higher in rank, importance, etc., than. **4 a** too great or good for (*not above cheating*). **b** beyond the reach of (*above my understanding*; *above suspicion*). — *adv.* **1** at or to a higher point; overhead (*the floor above*; *the sky above*). **2** earlier on a page or in a book (*as noted above*). **3** in addition (*over and above*). — *adj.* preceding (*the above argument*). — *n.* (prec. by *the*) preceding text (*the above shows that . . .*). □ **above all** most of all, more than anything else. **above oneself** conceited, arrogant. [Old English: related to A[2]]

**above-board** *adj. & adv.* without concealment; open or openly.

**abracadabra** /ˌab-ruh-kuh-**dab**-ruh/ — *int.* supposedly magic word used in conjuring. — *n.* spell or charm. [Latin from Greek]

**abrade** /uh-**brayd**/ *v.* (-**ding**) scrape or wear away (skin, rock, etc.) by rubbing. [Latin *rado* scrape]

**abrasion** /uh-**bray**-zhuhn/ *n.* **1** scraping or wearing away (of skin, rock, etc.). **2** resulting damaged area.

**abrasive** /uh-**bray**-siv, -ziv/ — *adj.* **1 a** tending to rub or graze. **b** capable of polishing by rubbing or grinding. **2** harsh or hurtful in manner. — *n.* abrasive substance.

**abreast** /uh-**brest**/ *adv.* **1** side by side and facing the same way. **2** (foll. by *of*) up to date; well-informed (*keep abreast of all the changes*).

**abridge** /uh-**brij**/ *v.* (-**ging**) shorten (a book, film, etc.). □ **abridgment** (also **abridgement**) *n.* [Latin: related to ABBREVIATE]

**abroad** /uh-**brawd**/ *adv.* **1** in or to a foreign country or countries. **2** widely (*scattered the grain abroad*). **3** in circulation (*there is a rumour abroad*). **4** *archaic* out of doors.

**abrogate** /**ab**-ruh-ˌgayt/ *v.* (-**ting**) repeal, abolish (a law etc.). □ **abrogation** /ˌab-ruh-**gay**-shuhn/ *n.* [Latin *rogo* propose a law]

**abrupt** /uh-**brupt**/ *adj.* **1** sudden and unexpected; hasty (*abrupt end*). **2** (of speech, manner, etc.) lacking continuity, curt. **3** steep, precipitous (*an abrupt descent*). □ **abruptly** *adv.* **abruptness** *n.* [Latin: related to RUPTURE]

**abscess** /**ab**-suhs/ *n.* (*pl.* **abscesses**) swelling containing pus. [Latin: related to AB-, CEDE]

**abscissa** /uhb-**sis**-uh/ *n.* (*pl.* **abscissae** /-ee/ or **-s**) *Math.* (in a system of coordinates) shortest distance from a point to the vertical or *y* -axis, measured parallel to the horizontal or *x* -axis. [Latin *abscindo* cut off]

**abscond** /uhb-**skond**, ab-/ *v.* depart hurriedly and furtively, esp. to avoid arrest; escape. □ **absconder** *n.* [Latin *abscondo* secrete]

**abseil** /**ab**-sayl/ — *v.* descend by using a doubled rope coiled round the body and fixed at a higher point. — *n.* descent made by abseiling. [German *ab* down, *Seil* rope]

**absence** /**ab**-suhns/ *n.* **1** state of being away. **2** time or duration of this. **3** (foll. by *of*) non-existence or lack of (*absence of the usual symptoms*). □ **absence of mind** inattentiveness. [Latin *absentia*]

**absent** — *adj.* /**ab**-suhnt/ **1 a** not present. **b** (foll. by *from*) not present at or in. **2** not existing; lacking (*true leaves are absent in some wattles*). **3** inattentive (*became absent and withdrawn*). —*v.refl.* /ab-**sent**/ go, or stay, away (*absented herself from the session*). □ **absently** *adv.* (in sense 3 of *adj.*).

**absentee** /ˌab-suhn-**tee**/ *n.* person not present, esp. one who is absent from work or school.

**absenteeism** /ˌab-suhn-**tee**-iz-uhm/ *n.* absenting oneself from work or school etc., esp. frequently or illicitly.

**absent-minded** *adj.* forgetful or inattentive. □ **absent-mindedly** *adv.* **absent-mindedness** *n.*

**absinth** /**ab**-sinth/ *n.* **1** wormwood. **2** (usu. **absinthe**) aniseed-flavoured liqueur based on this. [French from Latin]

**abso-bloody-lutely** /ˌab-suh-blu-dee-**loot**-lee/ *adv. colloq.* emphatic form of ABSOLUTELY (see also TMESIS).

**absolute** /**ab**-suh-ˌloot/ — *adj.* **1** complete, utter (*absolute bliss*). **2** unconditional; unlimited (*absolute authority*). **3** despotic; ruling with unrestricted power (*absolute monarch*). **4** (of a standard or other concept) universally valid; not relative or comparative. **5** *Gram.* **a** (of a construction) syntactically independent of the rest of the sentence, as *dinner being over* in *dinner being over, we left the table*. **b** (of an adjective or transitive verb) used or usable without an expressed noun or object, e.g. *the deaf; guns kill*. **6** (of a legal decree etc.) final. — *n. Philos.* **1** value, standard, etc. which is objective and universally valid. **2** (prec. by *the*) that which can exist independently of anything else. [Latin: related to ABSOLVE]

**absolutely** /**ab**-suh-ˌloot-lee/ *adv.* **1** completely, utterly. **2** independently; in an absolute sense (*God exists absolutely*). **3** /ˌab-suh-**loot**-lee/ *colloq.* (used in reply) quite so; yes.

**absolute majority** *n.* majority over all rivals combined.

**absolute pitch** *n.* ability to recognise or sound any given note.

**absolute temperature** *n.* one measured from absolute zero.

**absolute zero** *n.* theoretical lowest possible temperature, at which the particles whose motion constitutes heat would be minimal, calculated as −273.15° C (or 0° K).

**absolution** /ˌab-suh-**loo**-shuhn/ *n.* **1** formal release from guilt, obligation, or punishment. **2** *Eccl.* formal declaration by a priest, in the sacrament of penance, that a penitent's sins are now forgiven.

**absolutism** /**ab**-suh-loo-tiz-uhm/ *n.* principle or practice of absolute government. □ **absolutist** *n.*

**absolve** /uhb-**zolv**/ *v.* (-**ving**) **1** (often foll. by *from, of*) set or pronounce free from blame or obligation etc. **2** *Eccl.* (of a priest in the confessional etc.) declare (to a penitent) that (his or her) sins are now forgiven. [Latin: related to SOLVE]

**absorb** /uhb-**sawb**, -**zawb**/ *v.* **1** incorporate as part of itself or oneself (*this nation has successfully absorbed its immigrants*). **2** take in, suck up (liquid, heat, knowledge, etc.) (*absorbed all she was taught*). **3** reduce the effect or intensity of; deal easily with (an impact, sound, difficulty, etc.) (*a high fence will absorb some of the street-noise*). **4** consume (resources etc.) (*debts absorb most of his income*). **5** engross the attention of. [Latin *sorbeo* suck in]

**absorbed** *adj.* intensely engaged or interested (*absorbed in his book*).

**absorbent** — *adj.* tending to absorb. — *n.* **1** absorbent substance. **2** any of the vessels in plants and animals (e.g. root tips) that absorb nutriment. □ **absorbency** *n.*

**absorbing** *adj.* engrossing; intensely interesting.

**absorption** /uhb-**sawp**-shuhn, -**zawp**-/ *n.* **1** process or action of absorbing or being absorbed. **2** mental engrossment. □ **absorptive** *adj.*

**abstain** /uhb-**stayn**/ *v.* **1** (usu. foll. by *from*) refrain from indulging (*abstained from smoking*). **2** decline to vote. [Latin *teneo tent-* hold]

**abstemious** /uhb-**stee**-mee-uhs/ *adj.* moderate or ascetic, esp. in eating and drinking. □ **abstemiously** *adv.* [Latin: related to AB-, *temetum* strong drink]

**abstention** /uhb-**sten**-shuhn/ *n.* act or instance of abstaining, esp. from voting. [Latin: related to ABSTAIN]

**abstinence** /**ab**-stuh-nuhns/ *n.* act of abstaining, esp. from food or alcohol. □ **abstinent** *adj.* [French: related to ABSTAIN]

**abstract** — *adj.* /**ab**-strakt/ **1 a** of or existing in thought or theory rather than matter or practice; not concrete (*abstract questions rarely concerned him*). **b** (of a word, esp. a noun) denoting a quality, condition, etc. (e.g. *love, thought*), not a concrete object. **2** abstruse; difficult to understand. **3** (of art) achieving its effect by form and colour rather than by realism. — *v.* **1** /uhb-**strakt**/ (often foll. by *from*) take out of; extract; remove.

**2** /**ab**-strakt/ summarise (an article, book, etc.). — *n.* /**ab**-strakt/ **1** summary. **2** abstract work of art. **3** abstraction or abstract term. □ **in the abstract** in theory rather than practice. [Latin: related to TRACT¹]

**abstracted** /uhb-**strak**-tuhd/ *adj.* inattentive, distracted; lost in thought. □ **abstractedly** *adv.*

**abstraction** /uhb-**strak**-shuhn/ *n.* **1** act or instance of abstracting or taking away. **2** abstract or visionary idea. **3** abstract qualities (esp. in art). **4** absent-mindedness.

**abstruse** /uhb-**stroos**/ *adj.* hard to understand; profound. [Latin *abstrudo -trus-* conceal]

**absurd** /uhb-**serd**, -**zerd**/ *adj.* **1** (of an idea etc.) wildly illogical or inappropriate. **2** (of a person) ridiculous. **3** (of a thing) ludicrous; incongruous (*the situation was becoming absurd; an absurd hat*). □ **absurdity** *n.* (*pl.* -**ies**). **absurdly** *adv.* [Latin: related to SURD]

**abundance** /uh-**bun**-duhns/ *n.* **1** plenty; more than enough; a lot (*food and drink in abundance*). **2** wealth. **3** wealth of emotion (*abundance of heart*). [Latin: related to ABOUND]

**abundant** *adj.* **1** plentiful. **2** (foll. by *in*) rich (*all wattles are abundant in flowers*). □ **abundantly** *adv.*

**abuse** — *v.* /uh-**byooz**/ (-**sing**) **1** use improperly, misuse (*abused his position of power*). **2** insult verbally. **3** maltreat. — *n.* /uh-**byoos**/ **1** incorrect or improper use. **2** insulting language. **3** unjust or corrupt practice. **4** maltreatment (*child abuse*). □ **abuser** /uh-**byoo**-zuh/ *n.* [Latin: related to USE]

**abusive** /uh-**byoo**-siv/ *adj.* insulting, offensive. □ **abusively** *adv.*

**abut** /uh-**but**/ *v.* (-**tt**-) **1** (foll. by *on*) (of land) border on. **2** (foll. by *on, against*) (of a building) touch or lean upon (another) (*the pergola abuts on the back verandah*). [Anglo-Latin *butta* strip of land: related to BUTT¹]

**abuzz** /uh-**buz**/ *adv.* & *adj.* in a state of excitement or activity.

**abysmal** /uh-**biz**-muhl/ *adj.* **1** *colloq.* extremely bad (*abysmal weather*). **2** profound, utter (*abysmal ignorance*). □ **abysmally** *adv.* [Latin: related to ABYSS]

**abyss** /uh-**bis**/ *n.* **1** deep chasm. **2** immeasurable depth (*abyss of despair*). **3** (prec. by *the*) primal chaos; hell. [Latin from Greek, = bottomless]

**AC** *abbr.* **1** (also **ac**) alternating current. **2** Companion of the Order of Australia.

**Ac** *symb.* actinium.

**ac-** *prefix* assim. form of AD- before *c, q* (*accuse*; *acquit*).

**-ac** *suffix* forming adjectives often (or only) used as nouns (*cardiac*; *maniac*). [Latin *-acus*, Greek *-akos*]

**acacia** /uh-**kay**-shuh/ *n.* any plant of the largest Australian plant genus *Acacia*, of which there are in Australia nearly 800 described species (see WATTLE). [Greek *akakía*]

**academia** /,ak-uh-**dee**-mee-uh/ *n.* the academic world.

**academic** /,ak-uh-**dem**-ik/ — *adj.* **1** scholarly; to do with learning. **2** of no practical relevance; theoretical (*an academic question*). — *n.* teacher or scholar in a university etc. □ **academically** *adv.*

**academician** /uh-,kad-uh-**mish**-uhn/ *n.* member of an Academy. [French *académicien*]

**academy** /uh-**kad**-uh-mee/ *n.* (*pl.* **-ies**) **1** place of specialised training (*Australian Defence Force Academy*). **2** (usu. **Academy**) society or institution of distinguished scholars, artists, scientists, etc. (*Academy of the Humanities*). [Greek *akadēmeia* the place in Athens where Plato taught]

**Academy Award** *n.* film award given annually by the American Academy of Motion Picture Arts and Sciences. □ **Academy Award job** *colloq.* exaggerated performance, e.g. a footballer 'playing' for a free kick. **deserve an Academy Award** *colloq. iron.* (of a person's behaviour, performance, etc.) warrant a prize for histrionics.

**-acal** *suffix* forming adjectives, often used to distinguish them from nouns in *-ac* (*maniacal*).

**acanthus** /uh-**kan**-thuhs/ *n.* (*pl.* **-thuses**) **1** herbaceous plant with spiny leaves of Australia, the Mediterranean regions, etc. **2** *Archit.* representation of its leaf. [Latin from Greek]

**a cappella** /,ah kuh-**pel**-uh, ,a kuh-**pel**-uh/ *adj. & adv.* (of choral music) unaccompanied. [Italian, = in church style]

**acca** /**ak**-uh/ (also **acker**) *colloq.* — *n.* an academic. — *adj.* academic. — *v.* study, cram (*I need to acca for tomorrow's exam*). [abbreviation]

**accede** /ak-**seed**/ *v.* (**-ding**) (foll. by *to*) **1** take office, esp. as monarch. **2** assent or agree (*acceded to the proposal*). **3** formally subscribe to a treaty or other agreement. [Latin: related to CEDE]

**accelerate** /uhk-**sel**-uh-,rayt, ak-/ *v.* (**-ting**) **1** (of a moving body, esp. a vehicle) move or cause to move more quickly. **2** (of a process) happen or cause to happen more quickly (*his growth accelerated; the sun can accelerate the ageing process of the skin*). □ **acceleration** /uhk-,sel-uh-**ray**-shuhn, ak-/ *n.* [Latin: related to CELERITY]

**accelerator** *n.* **1** device for increasing speed, esp. the pedal controlling the speed of a vehicle's engine. **2** *Physics* apparatus for imparting high speeds to charged particles.

**accent** — *n.* /**ak**-sent/ **1** particular (esp. local or national) mode of pronunciation (*New Zealand accent*). **2** distinctive feature or emphasis (*accent on speed*). **3** prominence given to a syllable by stress or pitch. **4** mark on a letter or word to indicate pitch, stress, or vowel quality. — *v.* /ak-**sent**/ **1** emphasise (a word or syllable etc.). **2** write or print accents on (words etc.). **3** accentuate. □ **accentual** /uhk-**sen**-choo-uhl/ *adj.* [Latin *cantus* song]

**accentuate** /ak-**sen**-choo-,ayt/ *v.* (**-ting**) emphasise, make prominent. □ **accentuation** /ak-,sen-choo-**ay**-shuhn/ *n.* [medieval Latin: related to ACCENT]

**accept** /uhk-**sept**/ *v.* **1** (also *absol.*) willingly receive (a thing offered). **2** (also *absol.*) answer affirmatively (an offer etc.). **3** regard favourably; treat as welcome (*felt accepted*). **4** believe, receive (an opinion, explanation, etc.) as adequate or valid (*would not accept his excuses*). **5** take as suitable (*does not accept cheques*). **6** undertake (an office or duty). **7** tolerate; submit to (*have to accept the umpire's decision*). [Latin *capio* take]

**acceptable** *adj.* **1 a** worthy of being accepted. **b** pleasing, welcome. **2** tolerable (*an acceptable risk*). □ **acceptability** /uhk-,sep-tuh-bil-uh-tee/ *n.* **acceptably** *adv.* [French: related to ACCEPT]

**acceptance** *n.* **1** willingness to accept. **2** affirmative answer to an invitation etc. **3** approval, belief (*found wide acceptance*).

**access** /**ak**-ses/ — *n.* **1** way of approach or entry (*shop with rear access*). **2 a** right or opportunity to reach or use or visit; admittance (*access to secret files*). **b** *Law* enforceable right, usu. of a non-custodial parent, to visit a child. **3** (*attrib.*) (of broadcasting) allowed to minority or special-interest groups to undertake (*access radio*). — *v.* *Computing* gain access to (data etc.). [French: related to ACCEDE]

**accessible** /uhk-**ses**-uh-buhl/ *adj.* (often foll. by *to*) **1** that can readily be reached, entered, or used. **2** (of a person) readily available (esp. to subordinates). **3** (in a form) easy to understand (*the arguments in this thesis are not very* *accessible*). □ **accessibility** /uhk-ˌses-uh-**bil**-uh-tee/ *n.*

**accession** /uhk-**sesh**-uhn/ — *n.* **1** taking office, esp. as monarch. **2** thing added (e.g. a book to a library); increase, addition. **3** assent; formal acceptance of a treaty etc. — *v.* record the addition of (a new item) to a library etc.

**accessory** /uhk-**ses**-uh-ree/ — *n.* (*pl.* **-ies**) **1** additional or extra thing. **2** (usu. in *pl.*) **a** smaller articles of (esp. a woman's) dress, as shoes, gloves, etc. **b** minor fittings or attachments for a motor vehicle etc. **3** (often foll. by *to*) person who abets or is privy to an (esp. illegal) act. — *adj.* additional; contributing or aiding in a minor way. □ **accessory before** (or **after**) **the fact** person who incites (or assists) another to commit a crime, or knowingly assists the perpetrator to evade apprehension. [medieval Latin: related to ACCEDE]

**access time** *n. Computing* time taken to retrieve data from storage.

**acciaccatura** /uh-ˌchahk-uh-**tyoor**-ruh/ *n. Mus.* grace-note performed as quickly as possible before an essential note of a melody. [Italian]

**accident** /**ak**-suh-duhnt/ *n.* **1** unfortunate esp. harmful event, caused unintentionally. **2** event that is unexpected or without apparent cause (*their early arrival was just an accident*). □ **by accident** unintentionally. [Latin *cado* fall]

**accidental** /ˌak-suh-**den**-tuhl/ — *adj.* **1** happening by chance, unintentionally, or unexpectedly. **2** not essential to a conception; subsidiary (*accidental benefits*). — *n.* **1** *Mus.* sign indicating a note's momentary departure from the key signature. **2** something not essential to a conception. □ **accidentally** *adv.*

**acclaim** /uh-**klaym**/ — *v.* **1** welcome or applaud enthusiastically. **2** hail as (*was acclaimed the winner*). — *n.* applause, welcome, public praise. [Latin *acclamo*: related to CLAIM]

**acclamation** /ˌak-luh-**may**-shuhn/ *n.* **1** loud and eager assent. **2** (usu. in *pl.*) shouting in a person's honour.

**acclimatise** /uh-**kluy**-muh-ˌtuyz/ *v.* (also **-ize**) (**-sing** or **-zing**) adapt to a new climate or conditions. □ **acclimatisation** /-**zay**-shuhn/ *n.* [French *acclimater*: related to CLIMATE]

**acclivity** /uh-**kliv**-uh-tee/ *n.* (*pl.* **-ies**) upward slope (opp. DECLIVITY). [Latin *clivus* slope]

**accolade** /**ak**-uh-ˌlayd/ *n.* **1** praise given; acknowledgement of merit. **2** touch made with a sword at the conferring of a knighthood. [Latin *collum* neck]

**accommodate** /uh-**kom**-uh-ˌdayt/ *v.* (**-ting**) **1** provide lodging or room for (*flat accommodates two*). **2** adapt, harmonise, reconcile (*must accommodate himself to new ideas*). **3 a** do favour to, oblige (a person) (*sorry I can't accommodate you*). **b** (foll. by *with*) supply (a person) with (*accommodated him with what he needed*). [Latin: related to COMMODE]

**accommodating** *adj.* obliging, compliant.

**accommodation** /uh-ˌkom-uh-**day**-shuhn/ *n.* **1** lodgings. **2** adjustment or adaptation to suit a special or different purpose. **3** convenient arrangement; settlement, compromise.

**accompaniment** /uh-**kum**-puh-nee-muhnt, uh-**kump**-nee-/ *n.* **1** instrumental or orchestral support for a solo instrument, voice, or group. **2** accompanying thing (*accompaniments for the curry included cucumber in yoghurt*). □ **accompanist** *n.* (in sense 1).

**accompany** /uh-**kum**-puh-nee/ *v.* (**-ies**, **-ied**) **1** go with; escort. **2** (usu. in *passive*; foll. by *with*, *by*) **a** be done or found with; supplement (*speech accompanied with gestures*). **b** have as a result (*pills accompanied by side-effects*). **3** *Mus.* support or partner (a performer) with accompaniment. [French: related to COMPANION]

**accomplice** /uh-**kum**-pluhs, -**kom**-/ *n.* partner in a crime etc. [Latin: related to COMPLEX]

**accomplish** /uh-**kum**-plish, uh-**kom**-/ *v.* succeed in doing; achieve, complete. [Latin: related to COMPLETE]

**accomplished** *adj.* **1** clever, skilled (*accomplished performer on the didgeridoo; an accomplished liar*). **2** completed.

**accomplishment** *n.* **1** fulfilment or completion (of a task etc.). **2** acquired, esp. social, skill. **3** thing achieved (*he's bred a true blue rose — a major accomplishment*).

**accord** /uh-**kawd**/ — *v.* **1** (often foll. by *with*) be consistent or in harmony (*your story doesn't accord with the facts*). **2** grant (permission, a request, etc.). **b** give (a welcome etc.) (*accorded them a ticker-tape parade*). — *n.* **1** agreement, consent (*the prices and incomes accord*). **2** *Mus.* & *Art etc.* harmony or harmonious correspondence in pitch, tone, colour, etc. □ **of one's own accord** on one's own initiative; voluntarily. **with one accord** unanimously. [Latin *cor cord-* heart]

**accordance** *n.* harmony; agreement. □ **in accordance with** in conformity to. □ **accordant** *adj.*

**according** *adv.* **1** (foll. by *to*) **a** as stated by or in (*according to Mary*; *work according to the rules*). **b** in proportion to (*lives according to his means*). **2** (foll. by *as* + clause) in a manner or to a degree that varies as (*pays according as he is able*).

**accordingly** *adv.* **1** as circumstances suggest or require (*silence is vital, so please act accordingly*). **2** consequently; therefore (*accordingly, he left the room*).

**accordion** /uh-**kaw**-dee-uhn/ *n.* musical reed instrument with concertina-like bellows, keys, and buttons. □ **accordionist** *n.* [Italian *accordare* to tune]

**accost** /uh-**kost**/ *v.* **1** approach and address (a person), esp. boldly. **2** (of a prostitute) solicit. [Latin *costa* rib]

**account** /uh-**kownt**/ — *n.* **1** narration, description (*an account of his trip*). **2** arrangement at a bank etc. for depositing and withdrawing money, credit, etc. (*open an account*). **3** record or statement of financial transactions with the balance (*kept detailed accounts*). — *v.* consider as (*account him a fool*). □ **account for 1** serve as or provide an explanation for (*that accounts for his mood*). **2** answer for (money etc. entrusted, one's conduct, etc.) (*cannot account for his whereabouts at the time of the murder*). **3** kill, destroy, defeat (*this famine has accounted for a million people already*). **4** make up a specified amount of (*rent accounts for 50% of expenditure*). **by all accounts** in everyone's opinion. **call** (or **bring**) **to account** require an explanation from. **give a good** (or **bad**) **account of oneself** impress (or fail to impress); be successful (or unsuccessful). **keep account of** keep a record of; follow closely. **leave out of account** fail or decline to consider. **of no account** unimportant. **of some account** important. **on account 1** (of goods) to be paid for later. **2** (of money) in part payment. **on one's account** on one's behalf (*not on my account*). **on account of** because of. **on no account** under no circumstances. **settle** (or **square**) **accounts with 1** receive or pay money etc. owed to. **2** have revenge on. **take account of** (or **take into account**) consider (*took their age into account*). **turn to account** (or **good account**) turn to one's advantage or profit. [French: related to COUNT¹]

**accountability** /uh-ˌkown-tuh-**bil**-uh-tee/ *n.* concept that public organisations, such as the police, the public service, etc., are accountable to the public, esp. to persons affected by their operations.

**accountable** *adj.* **1** responsible; required to account for one's conduct. **2** explicable; understandable.

**accountant** *n.* professional keeper or verifier of accounts. □ **accountancy** *n.* **accounting** *n.*

**accoutrements** /uh-**koo**-truh-muhnts/ *n.pl.* **1** equipment, trappings. **2** soldier's equipment excluding weapons and clothes. [French]

**accredit** /uh-**kred**-uht/ *v.* (**-t-**) **1** (foll. by *to*) attribute (a saying etc.) to (a person). **2** (foll. by *with*) credit (a person) with (a saying etc.) (*they accredit him with the rediscovery of Lasseter's Reef*). **3** (usu. foll. by *to* or *at*) send (an ambassador etc.) with credentials (*was accredited to the Vatican*). **4** gain influence for or make credible (an adviser, a statement, etc.). □ **accreditation** *n.* [French: related to CREDIT]

**accredited** *adj.* **1** (of a person or organisation) officially recognised. **2** (of a belief) generally accepted.

**accretion** /uh-**kree**-shuhn/ *n.* **1** growth or increase by accumulation, addition, or organic enlargement. **2** the resulting whole. **3 a** matter so added. **b** adhesion of this to the core matter. [Latin *cresco cret-* grow]

**accrue** /uh-**kroo**/ *v.* (**-ues, -ued, -uing**) (often foll. by *to*) come as a natural increase or advantage, esp. financial. □ **accrual** *n.* [Latin: related to ACCRETION]

**accumulate** /uh-**kyoo**-myuh-ˌlayt/ *v.* (**-ting**) **1** acquire an increasing number or quantity of; amass, collect. **2** grow numerous; increase (*her wealth accumulates rapidly*). [Latin: related to CUMULUS]

**accumulation** /uh-ˌkyoo-myuh-**lay**-shuhn/ *n.* **1** act or process of accumulating or being accumulated. **2** accumulated mass. **3** growth of capital by continued interest. □ **accumulative** /uh-**kyoo**-myuh-luh-tiv/ *adj.*

**accumulator** *n.* **1** rechargeable electric cell. **2** register in a computer used to contain the results of an operation.

**accuracy** /**ak**-yuh-ruh-see/ *n.* exactness or careful precision. [Latin *cura* care]

**accurate** /**ak**-yuh-ruht/ *adj.* **1** careful, precise; lacking errors. **2** conforming exactly with the truth or a standard. □ **accurately** *adv.*

**accursed** /uh-**ker**-suhd, uh-**kerst**/ *adj.* **1** under a curse. **2** *colloq.* detestable, annoying. [Old English *a-* intensive prefix, CURSE]

**accusal** /uh-**kyoo**-zuhl/ *n.* = ACCUSATION.

**accusation** /ˌak-yoo-**zay**-shuhn/ n. 1 act or process of accusing or being accused. 2 statement charging a person with an offence or crime. [French: related to ACCUSE]

**accusative** /uh-**kyoo**-zuh-tiv/ Gram. —n. case expressing the object of an action. —adj. of or in this case.

**accusatory** /uh-**kyoo**-zuh-tuh-ree, ˌak-yoo-**zay**-tuh-ree, -tree/ adj. of or implying accusation.

**accuse** /uh-**kyooz**/ v. (-**sing**) (often foll. by of) charge with a fault or crime; blame. [Latin accusare: related to CAUSE]

**accustom** /uh-**kus**-tuhm/ v. (foll. by to) make used to (accustomed him to hardship). [French: related to CUSTOM]

**accustomed** adj. 1 (usu. foll. by to) used to a thing (accustomed to hard work). 2 customary, usual (sneered in his accustomed manner).

**AC/DC** colloq. —adj. bisexual. —n. bisexual person. [jocular use of the abbreviations for ALTERNATING CURRENT and DIRECT CURRENT]

**ace** — n. 1 playing-card etc. with a single spot and generally signifying 'one'. 2 a person who excels in some activity. b pilot who has shot down many enemy aircraft. 3 (in tennis) unreturnable stroke (esp. a service). —adj. colloq. excellent. □ **on one's ace** colloq. alone. **within an ace of** on the verge of. [Latin as unity]

**acellular** /ay-**sel**-yuh-luh/ adj. having no cells; not consisting of cells.

**-aceous** suffix forming adjectives in the sense 'of the nature of', esp. in the natural sciences (herbaceous). [Latin -aceus]

**acerbic** /uh-**ser**-bik/ adj. 1 astringently sour; harsh-tasting. 2 bitter or biting, in speech, manner, or temper. □ **acerbity** n. (pl. -**ies**). [Latin acerbus sour]

**acetaldehyde** /ˌas-uh-**tal**-duh-ˌhuyd/ n. colourless volatile liquid aldehyde. [from ACETIC, ALDEHYDE]

**acetate** /**as**-uh-ˌtayt/ n. 1 salt or ester of acetic acid, esp. the cellulose ester used to make textiles, gramophone records, etc. 2 fabric made from this.

**acetic** /uh-**see**-tik/ adj. of or like vinegar. [Latin acetum vinegar]

**acetic acid** n. clear liquid acid giving vinegar its characteristic taste.

**acetone** /**as**-uh-ˌtohn/ n. colourless volatile liquid that dissolves organic compounds, esp. paints, varnishes, etc.

**acetylene** /uh-**set**-uh-ˌleen/ n. hydrocarbon gas burning with a bright flame, used esp. in welding.

**ache** /ayk/ — n. 1 continuous dull pain. 2 mental distress. — v. (-**ching**) 1 suffer from or be the source of an ache (I ached all over; my left leg ached). 2 (foll. by to + infin.) desire greatly (we ached to be home again). [Old English]

**achieve** /uh-**cheev**/ v. (-**ving**) 1 reach or attain, esp. by effort (achieved victory; achieved notoriety). 2 accomplish (a feat or task). [French achever: related to CHIEF]

**achievement** n. 1 something achieved. 2 act or instance of achieving.

**Achilles heel** /uh-**kil**-eez/ n. person's weak or vulnerable point. [Achilles, Greek hero in the Iliad, invulnerable except in the heel]

**Achilles tendon** n. tendon connecting the heel with the calf muscles.

**achromatic** /ˌa-kroh-**mat**-ik, ˌay-/ adj. Optics 1 transmitting light without separation into constituent colours. 2 without colour. □ **achromatically** adv. [French: related to A-¹, CHROME]

**achy** /**ay**-kee/ adj. (-**ier**, -**iest**) full of or suffering from aches.

**acid** /**as**-uhd/ — n. 1 a any of a class of substances that liberate hydrogen ions in water, are usu. sour and corrosive, turn litmus red, and have a pH of less than 7. b any compound or atom donating protons. 2 (in general use) any sour substance. 3 colloq. the drug LSD. —adj. 1 sour. 2 biting, sharp (an acid wit). 3 Chem. having the essential properties of an acid. □ **put the acid on** colloq. exert a pressure (on a person) which is difficult to resist; seek to extract a loan or favour from. □ **acidic** /uh-**sid**-ik/ adj. **acidify** /uh-**sid**-uh-ˌfuy/ v. (-**ies**, -**ied**) **acidity** /uh-**sid**-uh-tee/ n. **acidly** adv. [Latin aceo be sour]

**acid head** n. habitual user of the drug LSD.

**acid house** n. a type of synthesised music with a simple repetitive beat, often associated with hallucinogenic drugs.

**acid rain** n. acid, esp. from industrial waste gases, falling with rain.

**acid test** n. 1 severe or conclusive test. 2 test in which acid is used to test for gold etc.

**acidulous** /uh-**sid**-yuh-luhs, uh-**sij**-uh-luhs/ adj. somewhat acid.

**-acious** suffix forming adjectives meaning 'inclined to, full of' (vivacious; pugnacious; voracious; capacious). [Latin -ax -acis, -OUS]

**-acity** suffix forming nouns of quality or state corresponding to adjectives ending in -ACIOUS (vivacity; capacity). [Latin -acitas -tatis]

**acknowledge** /uhk-**nol**-ij/ v. (-**ging**) 1 recognise; accept the truth of (acknowledged *its failure*). **2** confirm the receipt of (a letter etc.). **3 a** show that one has noticed (*acknowledged my arrival with a grunt*). **b** express appreciation of (a service etc.) (*acknowledged her great help in his campaign*). **4** recognise the validity of, own (*the acknowledged queen of detective fiction*). [from AD-, KNOWLEDGE]

**acknowledgment** *n.* (also **acknowledgement**) **1** act or instance of acknowledging. **2 a** thing given or done in gratitude. **b** letter confirming receipt of something. **3** (usu. in *pl.*) author's statement of gratitude, prefacing a book.

**acme** /ak-mee/ *n.* highest point (of achievement etc.). [Greek]

**acne** /ak-nee/ *n.* skin condition, usu. of the face (but also on the back etc.), characterised by pimples. [Latin]

**acolyte** /ak-uh-ˌluyt/ *n.* **1** person assisting a priest, esp. at Mass; altar server. **2** assistant; beginner. [Greek *akolouthos* follower]

**aconite** /ak-uh-ˌnuyt/ *n.* **1** any of various poisonous plants, e.g. wolfsbane. **2** drug from these. [Greek *akoniton*]

**acorn** /ay-kawn/ *n.* fruit of the oak, with a smooth nut in a cuplike base. [Old English]

**acoustic** /uh-koo-stik/ *adj.* **1** of sound or the sense of hearing. **2** (of a musical instrument etc.) without electrical amplification (*acoustic guitar*). □ **acoustically** *adv.* [Greek *akouō* hear]

**acoustics** *n.pl.* **1** properties or qualities (of a room etc.) in transmitting sound. **2** (usu. as *sing.*) science of sound.

**acquaint** /uh-kwaynt/ *v.* (usu. foll. by *with*) make aware of or familiar with (*acquaint me with the facts*). □ **be acquainted with** have personal knowledge of; know slightly. [Latin: related to AD-, COGNISANCE]

**acquaintance** *n.* **1** (usu. foll. by *with*) slight knowledge (of a person or thing). **2** fact or process of being acquainted (*our acquaintance lasted for a year*). **3** person one knows slightly. □ **acquaintanceship** *n.*

**acquiesce** /ˌak-wee-es/ *v.* (**-cing**) **1** agree, esp. tacitly or through weakness etc. (*she acquiesced in his harsh treatment of their child*). **2** raise no objection. **3** (foll. by *in*) accept (an arrangement etc.). □ **acquiescence** *n.* **acquiescent** *adj.* [Latin: related to AD-, QUIET]

**acquire** /uh-kwuyur/ *v.* (**-ring**) gain for oneself; come into possession of. [Latin: related to AD-, *quaero quisit-* seek]

**acquired immune deficiency syndrome** see AIDS.

**acquired taste** *n.* **1** liking developed by experience. **2** object of this (*witchetty grubs are an acquired taste*).

**acquisition** /ˌak-wuh-zish-uhn/ *n.* **1** thing (or person) acquired, esp. when valuable (*he was a priceless acquisition to our staff*). **2** act or instance of acquiring or being acquired. [Latin: related to ACQUIRE]

**acquisitive** /uh-kwiz-uh-tiv/ *adj.* keen to acquire things; avaricious; materialistic. □ **acquisitively** *adv.* **acquisitiveness** *n.*

**acquit** /uh-kwit/ *v.* (**-tt-**) **1** (often foll. by *of*) declare not guilty. **2** *refl.* **a** behave or perform in a specified way (*acquitted herself well in the debate*). **b** (foll. by *of*) discharge (a duty or responsibility) (*acquitted himself of the burden of honouring their debts*). □ **acquittal** *n.* [Latin: related to AD-, QUIT]

**acre** /ay-kuh/ *n.* in the imperial system, a measure of land, 4,840 sq. yds., 0.405 ha. [Old English]

**acreage** /ay-kuh-rij/ *n.* a number of acres; extent of land.

**acrid** /ak-ruhd/ *adj.* (**-er, -est**) **1** bitterly pungent; irritating; corrosive. **2** corrosive in temper or manner (*acrid comments*). □ **acridity** /uh-krid-uh-tee/ *n.* [Latin *acer* keen, pungent]

**acrimonious** /ˌak-ruh-moh-nee-uhs/ *adj.* bitter in manner or temper (*acrimonious remarks*). □ **acrimony** /ak-ruh-muh-nee/ *n.*

**acrobat** /ak-ruh-ˌbat/ *n.* entertainer performing gymnastic feats. □ **acrobatic** /ˌak-ruh-bat-ik/ *adj.* **acrobatically** /ˌak-ruh-bat-i-kuh-lee, -klee/ *adv.* [Greek *akrobatēs* from *akron* summit, *bainō* walk]

**acrobatics** /ˌak-ruh-bat-iks/ *n.pl.* **1** acrobatic feats. **2** (as *sing.*) art of performing these. **3** skill requiring ingenuity (*mental acrobatics*).

**acronym** /ak-ruh-nim/ *n.* word formed from the initial letters of other words (e.g. *Anzac*; *laser*; *scuba*). [Greek *akron* end, *onoma* name]

**acrophobia** /ˌak-ruh-foh-bee-uh/ *n.* abnormal dread of heights.

**acropolis** /uh-krop-uh-luhs/ *n.* citadel of an ancient Greek city. [Greek *akron* summit, *polis* city]

**across** /uh-kros/ — *prep.* **1** to or on the other side of (*across the river*). **2** from one side to another side of (*spread across the floor*). **3** at or forming an angle with (*a stripe across the flag*). — *adv.* **1** to or on the other side (*ran across*). **2** from one side to another (*stretched across*). **3** (of a crossword clue or answer) read horizontally (*cannot solve nine across*). □ **across the board** applying to all. **come across** see COME. [French *à, en, croix*: related to CROSS]

**acrostic** /uh-**kros**-tik/ *n.* poem etc. in which certain letters (usu. the first and last in each line) form a word or words. [Greek *akron* end, *stikhos* row]

**acrylic** /uh-**kril**-ik/ — *adj.* of material made with a synthetic polymer derived from acrylic acid. — *n.* acrylic fibre or fabric. [Latin *acer* pungent, *oleo* to smell]

**acrylic acid** *n.* a pungent liquid organic acid.

**ACT** *abbr.* Australian Capital Territory.

**act** — *n.* **1** something done; a deed. **2** process of doing (*caught in the act*). **3** item of entertainment, usu. one of a series in a programme. **4** pretence; behaviour intended to deceive or impress (*all an act*). **5** main division of a play etc. **6 a** decree of a legislative body. **b** document attesting a legal transaction. — *v.* **1** behave (*acted wisely*). **2** perform an action or function; take action (*act as referee*; *brakes failed to act*; *he acted quickly*). **3** (also foll. by *on*) have an effect (*alcohol acts on the brain*). **4 a** perform a part in a play, film, etc. **b** pretend. **5 a** play the part of (*acted Othello*; *acts the fool*). **b** perform (a play etc.). **c** portray (an incident) by actions. □ **act** (or **be**) **one's age** behave in a manner appropriate to one's age. **act for** be the (esp. legal) representative of. **act of God** natural event, e.g. an earthquake. **act on** (or **upon**) perform or carry out; put into operation (*acted on my advice*). **act up** *colloq.* misbehave; give trouble (*car is acting up*). **get one's act together** *colloq.* become properly organised; prepare. **put on an act** *colloq.* make a pretence. [Latin *ago act-* do]

**acting** — *n.* art or occupation of an actor. — *attrib. adj.* serving temporarily or as a substitute (*acting manager*).

**actinide** /**ak**-tuh-₁nuyd/ *n.* any of the series of 15 radioactive elements having increasing atomic numbers from actinium to lawrencium.

**actinism** /**ak**-tuh-₁niz-uhm/ *n.* property of short-wave radiation that produces chemical changes, as in photography. [Greek *aktis* ray]

**actinium** /ak-**tin**-ee-uhm/ *n. Chem.* radioactive metallic element found in pitchblende. [as ACTINISM]

**action** /**ak**-shuhn/ *n.* **1** fact or process of doing or acting (*demanded action*). **2** forcefulness or energy (*a woman of action*). **3** exertion of energy or influence (*action of acid on metal*). **4** deed, act (*not aware of his actions*). **5** (**the action**)

**a** series of events in a story, play, etc. **b** *colloq.* exciting activity (*missed the action*). **6** battle, fighting (*killed in action*). **7 a** mechanism of an instrument (*explain the action of an air pump*). **b** style of movement of an animal or human (*a runner with good action*). **8** lawsuit. □ **out of action** not working. [Latin: related to ACT]

**actionable** *adj.* giving cause for legal action.

**activate** /**ak**-tuh-₁vayt/ *v.* (**-ting**) **1** make active. **2** *Chem.* cause reaction in. **3** *Physics* make radioactive.

**active** /**ak**-tiv/ — *adj.* **1** marked by action; energetic; diligent (*an active life*). **2** working, operative (*active volcano*). **3** not merely passive or inert; positive (*active support*; *active ingredients*). **4** radioactive. **5** *Gram.* designating the form of a verb whose subject performs the action (e.g. *saw* in *he saw a film*). **6** (of a religious order) engaged in activity outside the monastery (opp. contemplative). — *n. Gram.* active form or voice of a verb. □ **actively** *adv.* [Latin: related to ACT]

**activism** *n.* policy of vigorous action, esp. for a political cause. □ **activist** *n.*

**activity** /ak-**tiv**-uh-tee/ *n.* (*pl.* **-ies**) **1** being active; busy or energetic action. **2** (often in *pl.*) occupation or pursuit (*outdoor activities*). **3** = RADIOACTIVITY.

**actor** *n.* person, male or female, who acts in a play, film, etc. [Latin: related to ACT]

**actress** *n.* female actor.

**ACTU** *abbr.* Australian Council of Trade Unions.

**actual** /**ak**-choo-uhl/ *adj.* (usu. *attrib.*) **1** existing in fact; real. **2** current. [Latin: related to ACT]

**actuality** /₁ak-choo-**al**-uh-tee/ *n.* (*pl.* **-ies**) **1** reality; what is the case. **2** (in *pl.*) existing conditions.

**actually** /**ak**-choo-uh-lee, -chuh-lee/ *adv.* **1** as a fact, really (*not actually very rich*). **2** strange as it may seem (*he actually refused!*).

**actuary** /**ak**-choo-uh-ree/ *n.* (*pl.* **-ies**) statistician, esp. one calculating insurance risks and premiums. □ **actuarial** /₁ak-choo-**air**-ree-uhl/ *adj.* [Latin *actuarius* bookkeeper]

**actuate** /**ak**-choo-₁ayt/ *v.* (**-ting**) **1** cause (a machine etc.) to move or function. **2** cause (a person) to act. □ **actuation** *n.* **actuator** *n.* [Latin]

**acuity** /uh-**kyoo**-uh-tee/ *n.* sharpness, acuteness (of a needle, senses, understanding, etc.). [medieval Latin: related to ACUTE]

**acumen** /**ak**-yuh-muhn/ *n.* keen insight or discernment. [Latin, = ACUTE thing]

**acupressure** /ak-yuh-,presh-uh, ak-uh-/ *n.* = SHIATSU.

**acupuncture** /ak-yuh-,pungk-chuh, ak-uh-/ *n.* medical procedure (orig. Chinese) in which the tips of slender needles are inserted into the skin at key points in various parts of the body in order to stimulate nerve impulses and so treat various disorders, relieve pain, etc. □**acupuncturist** *n.* [Latin *acu* with needle]

**acute** /uh-**kyoot**/ — *adj.* (**acuter**, **acutest**) **1** serious, severe (*acute hardship*). **2** (of senses etc.) keen, penetrating. **3** shrewd, perceptive (*an acute critic*). **4** (of a disease) coming quickly to a crisis. **5** (of an angle) less than 90°. **6** (of a sound) high, shrill. — *n.* = ACUTE ACCENT. □**acutely** *adv.* [Latin *acutus* pointed]

**acute accent** *n.* diacritical mark (´) placed over certain letters in French etc., esp. to show pronunciation.

**-acy** *suffix* forming nouns of state or quality (*accuracy*; *piracy*), or an instance of it (*conspiracy*; *fallacy*). [French *-acie*, Latin *-acia*, *-atia*, Greek *-ateia*]

**AD** *abbr.* of the Christian era. [ANNO DOMINI]

**ad** *n. colloq.* advertisement. [abbreviation]

**ad-** *prefix* (also **a-** before *sc*, *sp*, *st*, **ac-** before *c*, *k*, *q*, **af-** before *f*, **ag-** before *g*, **al-** before *l*, **an-** before *n*, **ap-** before *p*, **ar-** before *r*, **as-** before *s*, **at-** before *t*) implying motion or direction to, reduction or change into, addition, adherence, increase, or intensification. [Latin]

**-ad** *suffix* forming nouns in collective numerals (*myriad*; *triad*). [Greek *-as* *-ada*]

**adage** /**ad**-ij/ *n.* traditional maxim, proverb. [French from Latin]

**adagio** /uh-**dah**-zhee-oh/ *Mus.* — *adv.* & *adj.* in slow time. — *n.* (*pl.* **-s**) such a movement or passage. [Italian]

**Adam** /**ad**-uhm/ *n.* (in Biblical and Koranic traditions) the first man. □ **not know a person from Adam** be unable to recognise a person. [Hebrew, = man]

**adamant** /**ad**-uh-muhnt/ — *adj.* stubbornly resolute; unyielding. — *n. archaic* diamond or other hard substance. □ **adamantine** /-**man**-tuyn/ *adj.* **adamantly** *adv.* [Greek *adamas adamant-* untameable]

**Adam's apple** *n.* projection of the thyroid cartilage at the front of the neck, esp. as prominent in males.

**adapt** /uh-**dapt**/ *v.* **1 a** (foll. by *to*) fit, adjust (one thing to another) (*this dictionary has been adapted to Australian needs*). **b** (foll. by *to*, *for*) make suitable for a purpose (*adapted the wine-*

*barrel for use as a planter*). **c** modify (esp. a text for broadcasting etc.) (*the novel has been adapted for radio by Jane Smith*). **2** (also *refl.*, usu. foll. by *to*) adjust to new conditions. □ **adaptable** *adj.* [Latin: related to AD-, APT]

**adaptation** /ad-ap-**tay**-shuhn, ad-uhp-/ *n.* **1** act or process of adapting or being adapted. **2** thing that has been adapted. **3** *Biol.* process by which an organism or species becomes suited to its environment. **4** *Sociology* slow modification of individual and social behaviour in a community as a result of cultural pressures.

**adapter** *n.* person who adapts (a book etc. or a thing).

**adaption** /uh-**dap**-shuhn/ *n.* = ADAPTATION (sense 4).

**adaptor** *n.* **1** device for making equipment compatible. **2** device for connecting several electrical plugs to one socket.

**add** *v.* **1** join (one thing to another) as an increase or supplement (*add your efforts to mine*; *add insult to injury*). **2** put together (numbers) to find their total. **3** say further (*added that I was wrong*). □ **add in** include. **add up 1** find the total of. **2** (foll. by *to*) amount to. **3** *colloq.* make sense (*this just doesn't add up*). [Latin *addo*]

**addendum** /uh-**den**-duhm/ *n.* (*pl.* **-da**) **1** thing (usu. something omitted) to be added. **2** material added at the end of a book.

**adder** *n.* small venomous snake, esp. the common European viper. [Old English, originally *nadder* (a *nadder* being wrongly divided as *an adder*: cf. APRON, AUGER, UMPIRE)]

**addict** /**ad**-ikt/ *n.* **1** person addicted, esp. to a drug. **2** *colloq.* devotee (*film addict*). [Latin: related to AD-, *dico* say]

**addicted** /uh-**dik**-tuhd/ *adj.* **1** (usu. foll. by *to*) dependent on a drug etc. as a habit (*addicted to smoking*). **2** devoted to an interest (*addicted to footy*). □ **addiction** /uh-**dik**-shuhn/ *n.*

**addictive** *adj.* (of a drug, habit, etc.) causing addiction or dependence.

**addition** /uh-**dish**-uhn/ *n.* **1** act or process of adding or being added. **2** person or thing added (*useful addition to the team*). □ **in addition** (often foll. by *to*) also, as well (as). [Latin: related to ADD]

**additional** *adj.* added, extra, supplementary. □ **additionally** *adv.*

**additive** /**ad**-uh-tiv/ *n.* (in full **food additive**) substance, esp. a chemical, added to food and drink to affect colour, flavour etc. or to preserve it. [Latin: related to ADD]

**addle** /ad-uhl/ — v. (-**ling**) **1** muddle, confuse (*the alcohol has addled his mind*). **2** (usu. as **addled** *adj.*) (of an egg) become rotten. — *adj.* muddled, unsound (*addle-brained*). [Old English, = filth]

**add-on** — *n.* something added to an existing object (a car, computer, etc.), esp. as an optional extra. — *adj.* designed for adding on (*add-on items; power steering is an add-on option with this model*).

**address** /uh-**dres**/ — *n.* **1 a** place where a person lives or an organisation is situated. **b** particulars of this, esp. for postal purposes. **c** *Computing* location of an item of stored information. **2** discourse delivered to an audience. — *v.* **1** write postal directions on (an envelope etc.). **2** direct (remarks, a protest, etc.) (*addressed his verbal broadside to the reporters*). **3** speak or write to, esp. formally (*addressed the audience; how does one address a Cardinal?*). **4** direct one's attention to (*we need to address this issue*). **5** *Golf* take aim at (the ball). □ **address oneself to 1** speak or write to. **2** attend to. [French: related to AD-, DIRECT]

**addressee** /ˌad-res-**ee**/ *n.* person to whom a letter etc. is addressed.

**adduce** /uh-**dyoos**/ *v.* (-**cing**) cite as an instance or as proof or evidence. □ **adducible** *adj.* [Latin: related to AD-, *duco* lead]

**-ade** *suffix* forming nouns: **1** action done (*blockade; tirade*). **2** body concerned in an action or process (*cavalcade*). **3** product or result of a material or action (*arcade; masquerade*). [ultimately from Latin *-ata*]

**Adelaide** /**ad**-uh-ˌlayd/ name of the capital city of the State of SA (former Aboriginal name of the site *Tandarnya* or *Tandaringa*). [*Adelaide*, wife of the British king William IV]

**adenoids** /**ad**-uh-ˌnoidz/ *n.pl.* area of enlarged lymphatic tissue between the nose and the throat, often hindering breathing in the young. □ **adenoidal** /-**noi**-duhl/ *adj.* [Greek *adēn* gland]

**adept** /**ad**-ept, uh-**dept**/ — *adj.* (foll. by *at, in*) skilful; thoroughly proficient. — *n.* skilled performer; expert. □ **adeptly** *adv.* **adeptness** *n.* [Latin *adipiscor adept-* attain]

**adequate** /**ad**-uh-kwuht/ *adj.* sufficient, satisfactory (often with the implication of being barely so). □ **adequacy** *n.* **adequately** *adv.* [Latin: related to AD-, EQUATE]

**adhere** /uhd-**heer**/ *v.* (-**ring**) **1** (usu. foll. by *to*) (of a substance) stick fast to a surface, another substance, etc. **2** (foll. by *to*) behave according to or follow in detail (a rule, undertaking, etc.) (*adhered to our plans*). **3** (foll. by *to*) give allegiance (to a party, a cause, etc.) (*many Aborigines adhere to the old ways*). [Latin *haereo* stick]

**adherent** — *n.* supporter (of a party, person, etc.). — *adj.* sticking, adhering. □ **adherence** *n.*

**adhesion** /uhd-**hee**-zhuhn/ *n.* **1** act or process of adhering. **2** *Med.* unnatural union of body tissues due to inflammation. **3** maintenance of contact between the wheels of a vehicle and the road.

**adhesive** /uhd-**hee**-siv, -ziv/ — *adj.* sticky, causing adhesion. — *n.* adhesive substance, esp. one used to stick other substances together. □ **adhesiveness** *n.*

**ad hoc** /ad **hok**/ *adv. & adj.* **1** for one particular occasion or purpose or use and no other (*an ad hoc committee was set up to deal with the issue*). **2** impromptu,

---

### Adjective

An adjective is a word that describes a noun or pronoun, e.g.
 *red, clever, Tasmanian, depressed, grilled, sticky, shining*
Most can be used either before a noun (in which position they are attributive), e.g.
 *the red house, a clever woman,*
or after a verb like be, seem, or call (in which position they are predicative), e.g.
 *The house is red. I wouldn't call him lazy.*
 *She seems very clever.*
Some can be used only before a noun, e.g.
 *the main reason* (one cannot say *the reason is main*).
In this dictionary such an adjective is labelled *attrib. adj.* i.e. *attributive adjective.*
Some can be used only after a verb, e.g.
 *The ship is still* afloat (one cannot say *an afloat ship*).
In this dictionary such an adjective is labelled *predic. adj.* i.e. *predicative adjective.*
A few can be used only immediately after a noun, e.g.
 *the president* elect (one cannot say either *an elect president* or *The president is elect*).

improvised on the spur of the moment (in response to a sudden need etc.) (*his ad hoc decision to scrap the tax was described as policy-making on the run*). [Latin, = to this]

**ad hominem** /ad **hom**-i-nem, **hom**-uh-nuhm/ *adv. & adj.* **1** attacking the person instead of his or her arguments. **2** (of an argument) appealing to the emotions and not to reason. [Latin, = to the person]

**adieu** /uh-**dyoo**/ *int.* goodbye. [French, = to God]

**ad infinitum** /ad ,in-fuh-**nuy**-tuhm/ *adv.* without limit; for ever. [Latin]

**adipose** /**ad**-uh-,pohz, -,pohs/ *adj.* of fat; fatty (*adipose tissue*). □ **adiposity** /-**pos**-uh-tee/ *n.* [Latin *adeps* fat]

**adjacent** /uh-**jay**-suhnt/ *adj.* (often foll. by *to*) lying near; adjoining. □ **adjacency** *n.* [Latin *jaceo* lie]

**adjective** /**aj**-uhk-tiv/ *n.* word used to describe or modify a noun or pronoun (see panel). □ **adjectival** /,aj-uhk-**tuy**-vuhl/ *adj.* [Latin *jaceo* lie]

**adjigo** /**aj**-i-goh, -,koh/ *n.* (also **adjiko**, **ijjecka**) native yam of near coastal, southwestern WA, the edible underground tubers of which supported large populations of Aborigines. [probably Nhanta *ajuga* vegetable food]

**adjoin** /uh-**join**/ *v.* be next to and joined with. [Latin *jungo* join]

**adjourn** /uh-**jern**/ *v.* **1** put off, postpone; break off (a meeting etc.) temporarily. **2** (of a meeting) break and disperse or (foll. by *to*) transfer to another place (*adjourned to the pub*). □ **adjournment** *n.* [Latin: related to AD-, *diurnum* day]

**adjudge** /uh-**juj**/ *v.* (**-ging**) **1** pronounce judgment on (a matter). **2** pronounce or award judicially. □ **adjudgment** *n.* (also **adjudgement**). [Latin *judex* judge]

**adjudicate** /uh-**joo**-duh-,kayt/ *v.* (**-ting**) **1** act as judge in a competition, court, etc. **2** adjudge. □ **adjudication** /-**kay**-shuhn/ *n.* **adjudicative** *adj.* **adjudicator** *n.*

**adjunct** /**aj**-ungkt/ *n.* **1** (foll. by *to, of*) subordinate or incidental thing. **2** assistant; subordinate person, esp. one with temporary appointment only. **3** *Gram.* word or phrase used to explain or amplify the predicate, subject, etc. [Latin: related to ADJOIN]

**adjure** /uh-**joor**/ *v.* (**-ring**) (usu. foll. by *to* + infin.) charge or request (a person) solemnly or earnestly, esp. under oath. □ **adjuration** /,aj-uh-**ray**-shuhn/ *n.* [Latin *adjuro* put to oath: related to JURY]

**adjust** /uh-**just**/ *v.* **1 a** arrange; put in the correct order or position. **b** regulate, esp. by a small amount (*adjusted the tension*).

**2** (usu. foll. by *to*) make suited (*adjust the penalty to the crime*). **3** settle (discrepancies etc.) (*adjusted the students' marks to achieve a higher pass-rate*). **4** assess (loss or damages). **5** (usu. foll. by *to*) become familiar with, adapt (*soon adjusted to his new surroundings*). □ **adjustable** *adj.* **adjustment** *n.* [Latin *juxta* near]

**adjutant** /**aj**-uh-tuhnt/ *n.* army officer assisting a superior in administrative duties. □ **adjutancy** *n.* [Latin: related to AD-, *juvo jut-* help]

**ad lib** /ad **lib**/ — *v.* (**-bb-**) speak or perform without formal preparation; improvise. — *adj.* improvised (*an ad lib performance*). — *adv.* as one pleases, to any desired extent (*provided beer ad lib*). **2** impromptu (*spoke ad lib*). — *n.* something spoken or played extempore. [abbreviation of Latin *ad libitum* according to pleasure]

**admin** /**ad**-min/ *colloq.* — *n.* administration. — *adj.* pertaining to administration (*admin building*). [abbreviation]

**administer** /uhd-**min**-uh-stuh, ad-/ *v.* **1** manage (business affairs, an estate, etc.). **2 a** deliver or dispense, esp. formally (a punishment, sacrament, etc.) (*administered extreme unction to the dying*). **b** (usu. foll. by *to*) direct the taking of (an oath). **3 a** provide, apply (a remedy). **b** give, deliver (a rebuke). **4** act as administrator. [Latin: related to AD-, MINISTER]

**administrate** /uhd-**min**-uh-,strayt, ad-/ *v.* (**-ting**) administer (esp. business affairs); act as an administrator.

**administration** /uhd-,min-uh-**stray**-shuhn/ *n.* **1 a** management of a business, university, etc. **b** people involved in this. **2** management of public affairs; government. **3** government in power. **4** *Law* management of another person's estate.

**administrative** /uhd-**min**-uh-struh-tiv/ *adj.* of the management of affairs.

**administrator** /uhd-**min**-uh-,stray-tuh/ *n.* manager of a business, public affairs, a person's estate, etc.

**admirable** /**ad**-muh-ruh-buhl/ *adj.* deserving admiration; excellent. □ **admirably** *adv.* [Latin: related to ADMIRE]

**admiral** /**ad**-muh-ruhl/ *n.* **1 a** commander-in-chief of a navy. **b** high-ranking naval officer, commander. **2** any of various butterflies (*Australian admiral*). [Arabic: related to AMIR]

**admiration** /,ad-muh-**ray**-shuhn/ *n.* **1** respect; warm approval or pleasure. **2** object of this (*was the admiration of the whole city*).

**admire** /uhd-**muyuh**/ *v.* (**-ring**) **1** regard

with approval, respect, or satisfaction.
**2** express admiration of. □ **admirer** *n.*
**admiring** *adj.* **admiringly** *adv.* [Latin:
related to AD-, *miror* wonder at]

**admissible** /uhd-**mis**-uh-buhl/ *adj.* **1** (of
an idea etc.) worth accepting or
considering. **2** *Law* allowable as
evidence. [Latin: related to ADMIT]

**admission** /uhd-**mish**-uhn/ *n.* **1** acknowledgment (*admission of error*). **2 a**
process or right of entering. **b** charge for
this (*admission is $5*). **3** person admitted
to hospital.

■ **Usage** The noun *admission* has more
general application in senses of *admit*
than the noun *admittance*.

**admit** /uhd-**mit**/ *v.* (**-tt-**) **1** (often foll. by
*to be*, or *that* + clause) acknowledge;
recognise as true (*admitted him to be the
true author; admitted that she was right;
admitted the validity of our claim*). **2** (foll.
by *to*) confess to (a deed, fault, etc.).
**3** allow (a person) entrance, access, etc.
(*admit him to year 12; this pass will
admit you to the restricted area*). **4** take
(a patient) into hospital. **5** (of an enclosed
space) accommodate. **6** (foll. by *of*) allow
as possible (*this rule admits of no
exceptions*). [Latin *mitto miss-* send]

**admittance** *n.* right or process of
admitting or being admitted, usu. to a
place.

■ **Usage** The noun *admittance* is more
formal and technical than *admission*.

**admittedly** *adv.* as must be admitted.
**admixture** /ad-**miks**-chuh, **ad**-/ *n.*
**1** thing added, esp. a minor ingredient.
**2** act of adding this.

**admonish** /uhd-**mon**-ish/ *v.* **1** reprove
(*admonished me mildly for my lateness*).
**2** warn (*admonished me against driving
in my condition*). □ **admonishment** *n.* **admonition** /,ad-muh-**nish**-uhn/ *n.* **admonit-
ory** *adj.* [Latin *moneo* warn]

**ad nauseam** /ad **naw**-zee-uhm, **naw**-
see-uhm/ *adv.* to an excessive or disgusting degree. [Latin, = to sickness]

**Adnyamathanha** /ad-nyu-mud-u-nu/ *n.*
an Aboriginal language actively spoken
and fostered in central SA.

**ado** /uh-**doo**/ *n.* fuss, busy activity;
trouble. □ **without more ado** immediately.
[from AT, DO¹: originally in *much ado* =
much to do]

**adobe** /uh-**doh**-bee, uh-**dohb**/ *n.* **1** sun-
dried brick. **2** clay for making these.
[Spanish]

**adolescent** /,ad-uh-**les**-uhnt/ — *adj.* between childhood and adulthood. — *n.* ado-

lescent person. □ **adolescence** *n.* [Latin
*adolesco* grow up]

**Adonis** /uh-**doh**-nuhs/ *n.* beautiful or
handsome young man. [Latin, name of a
youth loved by Venus]

**adopt** /uh-**dopt**/ *v.* **1** legally take (a
person) into a relationship, esp. another's
child as one's own. **2** choose (a course of
action etc.) (*adopted the safer alternative*). **3** take over (another's idea etc.).
**4** accept, formally approve (a report,
accounts, etc.). □ **adopter** *n.* **adoption** *n.*
[Latin: related to AD-, OPT]

**adoptee** /uh-**dop**-tee/ *n.* adopted
person.

**adoptive** *adj.* because of adoption
(*adoptive son*). [Latin: related to ADOPT]

**adorable** /uh-**daw**-ruh-buhl/ *adj.*
**1** deserving adoration. **2** *colloq.* delightful, charming.

**adore** /uh-**daw**/ *v.* (**-ring**) **1** love
intensely. **2** worship as divine. **3** *colloq.*
like very much. □ **adoration** /,ad-uh-**ray**-
shuhn/ *n.* **adorer** *n.* **adoring** *adj.* [Latin
*adoro* worship]

**adorn** /uh-**dawn**/ *v.* add beauty to;
decorate. □ **adornment** *n.* [Latin: related
to AD-, *orno* decorate]

**ADP** *abbr.* automatic data processing.

**adrenal** /uh-**dree**-nuhl/ — *adj.* **1** at or
near the kidneys. **2** of the adrenal glands.
— *n.* (in full **adrenal gland**) either of two
ductless glands above the kidneys,
secreting adrenalin. [from AD-, RENAL]

**adrenalin** /uh-**dren**-uh-luhn/ *n.* (also
**adrenaline**) **1** hormone, secreted by the
adrenal glands, affecting circulation and
muscular action, and causing excitement
and stimulation. **2** this extracted or
synthesised for medicinal use.

**adrift** /uh-**drift**/ *adv.* & *predic. adj.*
**1** drifting. **2** powerless; at the mercy of
circumstances. **3** *colloq.* **a** unfastened.
**b** out of order, wrong (*plans went adrift*).

**adroit** /uh-**droit**/ *adj.* dexterous, skilful.
[French *à droit* according to right]

**adsorb** /uhd-**sawb**/ *v.* (usu. of a solid)
hold (molecules of a gas or liquid etc.) to
its surface, forming a thin film. □ **adsorb-
ent** *adj.* & *n.* **adsorption** *n.* [from AD-,
ABSORB]

**adulation** /,ad-yoo-**lay**-shuhn/ *n.* obsequious flattery. [Latin *adulor* fawn on]

**adult** /ad-**ult**, uh-**dult**/ — *adj.* **1** mature,
grown-up. **2** (*attrib.*) **a** of or for adults
(*adult education*). **b** *euphem.* sexually
explicit; dealing in sexual products (*adult
films; adult shop*). — *n.* adult person.
□ **adulthood** *n.* [Latin *adolesco adultus*
grow up]

**adulterate** /uh-**dul**-tuh-,rayt/ *v.* (**-ting**)
debase (esp. foods) by adding other

substances. □ **adulterant** adj. & n. **adulteration** /-**ray**-shuhn/ n. [Latin adultero corrupt]

**adulterer** /uh-**dul**-tuh-ruh/ n. (fem. **adulteress**) person who commits adultery.

**adultery** n. voluntary sexual intercourse between a married person and a person other than his or her spouse. □ **adulterous** adj.

**adumbrate** /**ad**-uhm-,brayt/ v. (-**ting**) **1** indicate faintly or in outline. **2** foreshadow (many of Christ's actions are adumbrated in the Old Testament). **3** overshadow (building adumbrated by a huge tree). □ **adumbration** /-**bray**-shuhn/ n. [Latin: related to AD-, umbra shade]

**advance** /uhd-**vahns**, -**vans**/ — v. (-**cing**) **1 a** move or put forward (the enemy advanced; advanced the clock). **b** make progress (our campaign is advancing rapidly). **2** pay or lend (money) beforehand. **3** give active support to; promote (a person, cause, etc.) (your interests will not be advanced by this behaviour). **4** put forward (a suggestion etc.). **5** (as **advanced** adj.) **a** far on in progress (the work is well advanced). **b** socially progressive (advanced ideas). — n. **1** act of going forward; progress. **2** prepayment; loan. **3** (in pl.) amorous approaches (made advances to him). **4** rise in price. — attrib. adj. done, supplied, or going beforehand (advance warning; advance party). □ **advance on** approach threateningly. **in advance** ahead in place or time. [Latin: related to AB-, ante before]

**Advance Australia** patriotic catchphrase frequently used as a slogan etc. from the early nineteenth century to the present day.

**Advance Australia Fair** n. the national anthem of Australia, composed about 1878, and officially replacing 'God Save the Queen' in 1984.

**advancement** n. promotion of a person, cause, or plan.

**advantage** /uhd-**vahn**-tij, -**van**-tij/ — n. **1** beneficial feature (this proposal has the advantage of simplicity). **2** benefit, profit (is not to your advantage). **3** (often foll. by over) superiority. **4** (in tennis) the next point after deuce. — v. (-**ging**) benefit, favour. □ **take advantage of 1** make good use of. **2** exploit, esp. unfairly. **3** euphem. seduce. **to advantage** in a way which exhibits the merits (was seen to advantage). □ **advantageous** /,ad-vuhn-**tay**-juhs/ adj. [French: related to ADVANCE]

**Advent** /**ad**-vent/ n. **1** season before Christmas. **2** coming of Christ. **3** (**advent**) important arrival (awaiting the advent of spring). [Latin adventus from venio come]

**adventitious** /,ad-ven-**tish**-uhs/ adj. **1** accidental, casual. **2** added from outside. **3** Biol. formed accidentally or under unusual conditions or appearing in an unusual position (the aerial adventitious roots of the banyan tree). [Latin: related to ADVENT]

**adventure** /uhd-**ven**-chuh/ — n. **1** unusual and exciting experience. **2** a daring enterprise; hazardous activity. **3** enterprise (spirit of adventure). — v. (-**ring**) **1** dare to go or come. **2** dare to undertake. **3** engage in adventure. [Latin: related to ADVENT]

---

**Adverb**

An adverb is used:

**1** with a verb, to say:
   **a** how something happens, e.g. He walks quickly.
   **b** where something happens, e.g. I live here.
   **c** when something happens, e.g. They visited us yesterday.
   **d** how often something happens, e.g. We usually have coffee.
**2** to strengthen or weaken the meaning of:
   **a** a verb, e.g. He really meant it. I almost fell asleep.
   **b** an adjective, e.g. She is very clever. This is a slightly better result.
   **c** another adverb, e.g. It comes off terribly easily. The boys nearly always get home late.
**3** to add to the meaning of a whole sentence, e.g.
   He is probably our best player. Luckily, no one was hurt.
In writing or in formal speech, it is **incorrect** to use an adjective instead of an adverb. For example, use
   Do it properly.     and not     Do it proper.
but note that many words are both an adjective and an adverb, e.g.

| adjective | adverb |
|---|---|
| a fast horse | He ran fast. |
| a long time | Have you been here long? |

**adventurer** n. (fem. **adventuress**) **1**.person who seeks adventure, esp. for personal gain or enjoyment. **2** financial speculator.

**adventurous** adj. venturesome, enterprising. □ **adventurously** adv.

**adverb** /ˈad-verb/ n. word indicating manner, degree, circumstance, etc., used to modify an adjective, verb, or other adverb (see panel). □ **adverbial** /ˈad-ver-bee-uhl/ adj. [Latin: related to AD-, verbum word, VERB]

**adversarial** /ˌad-vuh-ˈsair-ree-uhl/ adj. **1** involving conflict or opposition. **2** opposed, hostile.

**adversary** /ˈad-vuh-suh-ree, -sree/ n. (pl. **-ies**) enemy, opponent.

**adverse** /ˈad-vers/ adj. **1** unfavourable; hostile (adverse criticism). **2** harmful (had an adverse effect). **3** opposing; contrary (sailed the sea of life against many adverse gales). □ **adversely** adv. [Latin: related to AD-, verto vers- turn]

**adversity** /uhd-ˈver-suh-tee/ n. misfortune, distress.

**advert** /uhd-ˈvert/ v. (foll. by to) literary refer in speaking or writing. [from ADVERSE]

**advertise** /ˈad-vuh-ˌtuyz/ v. (-sing) **1** promote (goods or services) publicly to increase sales. **2** make generally known. **3** (often foll. by for) seek by a notice in a newspaper etc. to buy, employ, sell, etc. [French avertir: related to ADVERSE]

**advertisement** /uhd-ˈver-tuhs-muhnt, -tuhz-muhnt/ n. **1** public announcement, esp. of goods etc. for sale or wanted, vacancies, etc. **2** act or process of advertising. [French avertissement: related to ADVERSE]

**advertorial** /ˌad-vuh-ˈtaw-ree-uhl/ n. commercial advertisement written in the form of a news item, editorial, etc. [blend of ADVER(TISEMENT) and (EDI)TORIAL]

**advice** /uhd-ˈvuys/ n. **1** recommendation on how to act. **2** information given; news. **3** formal notice of a transaction. □ **take advice** obtain a professional opinion from an expert, e.g. a lawyer etc.

**advisable** /uhd-ˈvuy-zuh-buhl/ adj. **1** (of a course of action etc.) to be recommended. **2** expedient (it would be advisable to hurry — the storm's about to break). □ **advisability** /-bil-uh-tee/ n.

**advise** /uhd-ˈvuyz/ v. (-sing) **1** (also absol.) give advice to. **2** recommend (advised me to rest). **3** (usu. foll. by of, or that + clause) inform (advised him of his rights). [Latin: related to AD-, video vis-see]

**advisedly** /uhd-ˈvuy-zuhd-lee/ adv. after due consideration; deliberately.

**adviser** n. (also **advisor**) person who advises, esp. officially.

■ **Usage** The variant advisor (probably influenced by the adjective advisory) is fairly common, but is considered incorrect by many people.

**advisory** adj. giving advice (advisory body).

**advocacy** /ˈad-vuh-kuh-see/ n. support or argument for a cause, policy, etc.

**advocate** — n. /ˈad-vuh-kuht/ **1** (foll. by of) person who supports or speaks in favour. **2** person who pleads for another. — v. /ˈad-vuh-ˌkayt/ (-ting) recommend by argument (advocated that Australia become a republic). [Latin: related to AD-, voco call]

**adze** /adz/ n. tool like an axe, with an arched blade at right angles to the handle. [Old English]

**aegis** /ˈee-juhs/ n. protection; support. □ **under the aegis of** under the auspices of. [Greek aigis shield of Zeus or Athene]

**aeolian harp** /ee-ˈoh-lee-uhn, ay-/ n. stringed instrument or toy sounding when the wind passes through it. [Latin Aeolus wind-god, from Greek]

**aeon** /ˈee-on/ n. (also **eon**) **1** long or indefinite period. **2** an age of the universe. [Latin from Greek]

**aerate** /ˈair-rayt/ v. (-ting) **1** charge (a liquid) with a gas, esp. carbon dioxide. **2** expose to air. □ **aeration** /-ray-shuhn/ n. [Latin aer AIR]

**aerial** /ˈair-ree-uhl/ — n. device for transmitting or receiving radio waves. — adj. **1** by or from the air; involving aircraft (aerial attack). **2** existing in the air (plant with aerial roots). **3 a** of or like air; ethereal. **b** immaterial; imaginary. [Greek: related to AIR]

**aerial ping-pong** n. joc. or derog. Australian Rules football (so called because the game is characterised by frequent exchanges of long and high kicks).

**aero-** comb. form air; aircraft. [Greek aero- from aēr air]

**aerobatics** /ˌair-ruh-ˈbat-iks/ n.pl. **1** spectacular flying of aircraft, esp. to entertain. **2** (as sing.) performance of these. [from AERO-, after ACROBATICS]

**aerobics** /air-ˈroh-biks/ n.pl. vigorous exercises designed to increase oxygen intake and heart-rate and improve physical fitness. □ **aerobic** adj. [from AERO-, Greek bios life]

**aerodrome** /ˈair-ruh-ˌdrohm/ n. small airport or airfield. [from AERO-, Greek dromos course]

**aerodynamics** /ˌair-roh-duy-**nam**-iks/ *n.pl.* (usu. treated as *sing.*) study of the interaction between the air and solid bodies moving through it. □ **aerodynamic** *adj.*

**aerofoil** /**air**-ruh-ˌfoil/ *n.* structure with curved surfaces (e.g. a wing, fin, or tailplane) designed to give lift in flight.

**aeronautics** /ˌair-ruh-**naw**-tiks, ˌair-ruh-/ *n.pl.* (usu. treated as *sing.*) science or practice of motion in the air. □ **aeronautic** *adj.* **aeronautical** *adj.* [from AERO-, NAUTICAL]

**aeroplane** /**air**-ruh-ˌplayn/ *n.* powered heavier-than-air flying vehicle with fixed wings. [French: related to AERO-, PLANE¹]

**aerosol** /**air**-ruh-ˌsol/ *n.* **1** pressurised container releasing a substance as a fine spray. **2** system of minute particles suspended in gas (e.g. fog or smoke). [from AERO-, SOL(UTION)]

**aerospace** /**air**-roh-ˌspays/ *n.* **1** earth's atmosphere and outer space. **2** aviation in this.

**aesthete** /ees-theet, es-theet, uhs-**theet**/ *n.* person who has or professes a special appreciation of beauty. [Greek *aisthanomai* perceive]

**aesthetic** /ees-**thet**-ik, uhs-/ — *adj.* **1** of or sensitive to beauty. **2** artistic, tasteful. — *n.* (in *pl.*) philosophy of beauty, esp. in art. □ **aesthetically** *adv.* **aestheticism** /-uh-ˌsiz-uhm/ *n.*

**aestivate** /**es**-tuh-ˌvayt/ *v. Zool.* spend the summer or dry season in a state of torpor (cf. HIBERNATE). □ **aestivation** *n.* [Latin, from *aestus* heat]

**aetiology** /ˌee-tee-**ol**-uh-jee/ *n.* (also **etiology**) study of causation or of the causes of disease. □ **aetiological** /-uh-loj-i-kuhl/ *adj.* [Greek *aitia* cause]

**afar** /uh-**fah**/ *adv.* at or to a distance.

**affable** /**af**-uh-buhl/ *adj.* **1** approachable and friendly. **2** kind and courteous, esp. to inferiors. □ **affability** /-**bil**-uh-tee/ *n.* **affably** *adv.* [Latin *affabilis*]

**affair** /uh-**fair**/ *n.* **1** matter, concern, or thing to be attended to (*that is my affair*). **2 a** celebrated or notorious happening. **b** *colloq.* thing or event (*puzzling affair*). **3** = LOVE AFFAIR. **4** (in *pl.*) **a** ordinary pursuits of life. **b** business dealings. **c** public matters (*current affairs*). [French *à faire* to do]

**affect** /uh-**fekt**/ *v.* **1 a** produce an effect on. **b** (of disease etc.) attack (*it affected his liver*). **2** move emotionally (*much affected by the film*). **3** pretend (*affected ignorance*). **4** pose as or use for effect (*affects the aesthete; affects fancy hats*). □ **affecting** *adj.* **affectingly** *adv.* [Latin *afficio affect-* influence]

■ **Usage** *Affect* should not be confused with *effect*, meaning 'to bring about'. Note also that *effect* is used as a noun as well as a verb.

**affectation** /ˌaf-ek-**tay**-shuhn/ *n.* **1** assumed or contrived manner of behaviour, esp. in order to impress. **2** (foll. by *of*) studied display (*vulgar affectation of wealth*). **3** pretence (*his concern for the poor is mere affectation*).

**affected** /uh-**fek**-tuhd/ *adj.* **1** in senses 1 and 2 of AFFECT. **2** pretended, artificial (*an affected air of innocence*). **3** full of affectation (*an affected pronunciation*).

**affection** /uh-**fek**-shuhn/ *n.* **1** love, fond feeling; goodwill. **2** mental state; emotion.

**affectionate** /uh-**fek**-shuh-nuht/ *adj.* loving, fond. □ **affectionately** *adv.*

**affiance** /uh-**fuy**-uhns/ *v.* (usu. in *passive*) *literary* promise in marriage. [Latin *fidus* trusty]

**affidavit** /ˌaf-uh-**day**-vuht/ *n.* written statement confirmed by oath. [Latin, = has stated on oath]

**affiliate** — *v.* /uh-**fil**-ee-ˌayt/ (**-ting**) (foll. by *to*, *with*) attach, adopt, or connect as a member or branch. — *n.* /uh-**fil**-ee-uht/ affiliated person etc. □ **affiliation** *n.* [Latin: related to FILIAL]

**affinity** /uh-**fin**-uh-tee/ *n.* (*pl.* **-ies**) **1 a** spontaneous liking for or attraction to a person or thing (*strong affinity between him and me*). **b** feeling of kinship. **2** relationship, esp. by marriage. **3** similarity of structure or character suggesting a relationship. **4** *Chem.* the tendency of certain substances to combine with others. [Latin *finis* border]

**affirm** /uh-**ferm**/ *v.* **1** assert strongly; state as a fact. **2** *Law* make a solemn declaration in place of an oath. □ **affirmation** /ˌaf-uh-**may**-shuhn/ *n.* [Latin: related to FIRM¹]

**affirmative** /uh-**fer**-muh-tiv/ — *adj.* **1** affirming; asserting that a thing is so. **2** (of a vote) expressing approval. — *n.* affirmative statement or word etc.

**affirmative action** *n.* action (esp. in employment, promotion, etc.) favouring those who often suffer from discrimination.

**affix** — *v.* /uh-**fiks**/ **1** attach, fasten. **2** add in writing (a signature or postscript). — *n.* /**af**-iks/ **1** appendage, addition. **2** *Gram.* prefix or suffix. [Latin: related to FIX]

**afflict** /uh-**flikt**/ *v.* distress physically or mentally. □ **afflicted with** suffering from. [Latin *fligo flict-* strike down]

**affliction** /uh-**flik**-shuhn/ *n.* **1** physical or mental distress, esp. pain or illness. **2** cause of this.

**affluent** /**af**-loo-uhnt/ *adj.* wealthy, rich. □ **affluent society** a society in which material wealth is widely distributed. □ **affluence** *n.* [Latin: related to FLUENT]

**afford** /uh-**fawd**/ *v.* **1** (prec. by *can* or *be able to*) **a** have enough money, time, etc., for; be able to spare. **b** be in a position to do something (esp. without risk of adverse consequences) (*can't afford to be critical*). **2** provide; give (*affords a view of the sea*). [Old English *ge-* prefix implying completeness, FORTH]

**afforest** /uh-**fo**-ruhst/ *v.* **1** convert into forest. **2** plant an area with trees, esp. softwoods and other trees not native to Australia. □ **afforestation** /-ruh-**stay**-shuhn/ *n.* [Latin: related to FOREST]

**affray** /uh-**fray**/ *n.* breach of the peace by fighting or rioting in public. [Anglo-French, = remove from peace]

**affricate** /**af**-ruh-kuht/ *n.* (also **affricative**) *Phonet.* combination of a plosive with an immediately following fricative or spirant, e.g. *ch.* [Latin *affricare* (as AD-, *fricare* rub)]

**affront** /uh-**frunt**/ — *n.* open insult. — *v.* **1** insult openly. **2** offend, embarrass. [Latin: related to FRONT]

**Afghan** /**af**-gan/ — *n.* **1 a** native or national of Afghanistan. **b** person of Afghan descent. **c** (also **Ghan**) esp. *hist.* immigrant to Australia from Afghanistan, Pakistan, etc., engaged esp. in camel-driving and camel-breeding in the outback, and also in storekeeping, vending wares on foot, etc. **2** official language of Afghanistan. — *adj.* of Afghanistan. [Pashto]

**aficionado** /uh-ˌfish-yuh-**nah**-doh/ *n.* (*pl.* **-s**) devotee of a sport or pastime. [Spanish]

**afield** /uh-**feeld**/ *adv.* to or at a distance (esp. *far afield*). [Old English: related to A²]

**AFL** *abbr.* Australian Football League (see AUSTRALIAN RULES).

**aflame** /uh-**flaym**/ *adv. & predic. adj.* **1** in flames. **2** very excited.

**afloat** /uh-**floht**/ *adv. & predic. adj.* **1** floating. **2** at sea; on board ship. **3** out of debt or difficulty. **4** in general circulation; current (*many rumours are afloat*). **5** full of or covered with a liquid; flooded (*the whole area was afloat*). [Old English: related to A²]

**afoot** /uh-**fuut**/ *adv. & predic. adj.* **1** in operation; progressing. **2** astir; on the move; happening (*let me know what's afoot in Canberra*).

**afore-** *comb. form* before, previously (*aforementioned*; *aforesaid*).

**aforethought** *adj.* premeditated (following a noun: *malice aforethought*).

**afraid** /uh-**frayd**/ *predic. adj.* alarmed, frightened. □ **be afraid** *colloq.* admit or declare with (real or politely simulated) regret (*I'm afraid we're late*). [originally past part. of AFFRAY]

**afresh** /uh-**fresh**/ *adv.* anew; with a fresh beginning. [earlier *of fresh*]

**African** /**af**-ri-kuhn/ — *n.* **1** native of Africa. **2** person of African descent. — *adj.* of Africa. [Latin]

**Afrikaans** /ˌaf-ri-**kahns**, -**kahnz**/ *n.* language derived from Dutch, used in S. Africa. [Dutch, = 'African']

**Afrikaner** /ˌaf-ri-**kah**-nuh/ *n.* Afrikaans-speaking White person in S. Africa, esp. of Dutch descent.

**afro** /**af**-roh/ — *adj.* (of hair) tightly-curled and bushy. — *n.* (*pl.* **-s**) afro hairstyle.

**Afro-** *comb. form* African.

**aft** /ahft/ *adv. Naut. & Aeron.* at or towards the stern or tail. [earlier *baft*]

**after** /**ahf**-tuh/ — *prep.* **1** following in time; later than (*after a week*). **2** in view of, in spite of (*after what you did, what do you expect?*; *after all my efforts I still lost*). **3** behind (*shut the door after you*). **4** in pursuit or quest of (*run after them*). **5** about, concerning (*asked after her*). **6** in allusion to (*named after his uncle*). **7** in imitation of (*a painting after Sidney Nolan*). **8** next in importance to (*best one after mine*). — *conj.* in or at a time later than that when (*left after they arrived*). — *adv.* **1** later in time (*soon after*). **2** behind (*followed on after*). — *adj.* **1** later, following (*in after years*). **2** *Naut.* nearer the stern (*after cabins*). □ **after all** in spite of everything (*after all, what does it matter?*). **after one's own heart** to one's taste or desire. [Old English]

**afterbirth** *n.* placenta etc. discharged from the womb after childbirth.

**after-effect** *n.* delayed effect following an accident, trauma, etc.

**afterglow** *n.* glow remaining after its source has disappeared.

**afterlife** *n.* **1** life after death. **2** life at a later time.

**aftermath** /**ahf**-tuh-ˌmath, -ˌmahth/ *n.* consequences, esp. unpleasant (*aftermath of war*). [from AFTER, *math* mowing]

**afternoon** /ˌahf-tuh-**noon**/ *attrib.* /**ahf**-/ *n.* time from noon to evening.

**afterpains** *n.pl.* pains caused by contraction of the womb after childbirth.

**afters** *n.pl. colloq.* = DESSERT 1.

**aftershock** *n.* lesser quake or shock following an earthquake.

**aftertaste** *n.* taste after eating or drinking (*this wine has a curious aftertaste*).

**afterthought** *n.* thing thought of or added too late or later.

**afterwards** /**ahf**-tuh-wuhdz/ *adv.* later, subsequently. [Old English: related to AFTER, -WARD]

**Ag** *symb.* silver. [Latin *argentum*]

**again** /uh-**gen**, uh-**gayn**/ *adv.* **1** another time; once more. **2** as previously (*home again; she's well again*). **3** in addition (*as much again*). **4** further, besides (*again, what about you?*). **5** on the other hand (*I might, and again I might not*). □ **again and again** repeatedly. [Old English]

**against** /uh-**genst**, uh-**gaynst**/ *prep.* **1** in opposition to (*fight against crime*). **2** in collision or in contact with (*lean against the wall*). **3** to the disadvantage of (*my age is against me*). **4** in contrast to (*against a dark background*). **5** in anticipation of or preparation for (*against his coming; against the cold*). **6** as a compensating factor to (*income against expenditure*). **7** in return for (*issued against payment of the fee*). □ **against the grain** see GRAIN. **against time** see TIME. [from AGAIN, with inflectional -*s*]

**agape**[1] /uh-**gayp**/ *predic. adj.* gaping, open-mouthed. [from A[2]]

**agape**[2] /**ag**-uh-,pay/ *n.* **1** early Christian Eucharistic feast. **2** *Theol.* Christian love. [Greek, = brotherly love]

**agar** /**ay**-gah/ *n.* (also **agar-agar, moss, moss-jelly**) gelatinous substance obtained from any of various kinds of red seaweed and used in food (esp. in Asia etc.), microbiological media, etc. [Malay]

**agaric** /**ag**-uh-rik/ *n.* fungus with a cap and stalk, e.g. the common edible mushroom. [Greek *agarikon*]

**agate** /**ag**-uht/ *n.* **1** hard usu. streaked chalcedony. **2** coloured toy marble resembling this. [Greek *akhatēs*]

**age** /ayj/ — *n.* **1 a** length of time that a person or thing has existed. **b** particular point in, or part of, one's life (*old age; voting age*). **2 a** *colloq.* (often in *pl.*) a long time (*waited for ages*). **b** distinct historical period (*Bronze Age*). **c** *Geol.* period of time. **3** old age (*the peevishness of age*). — *v.* (**ageing, aging**) **1** show or cause to show signs of advancing age (*has aged a lot recently*). **2** grow old. **3** mature (*the wine has aged well*). **4** cause or allow to age (*this fright has aged me ten years in ten minutes; this wine needs to be aged*). □ **act** (or **be**) **one's age** see ACT. **come**

**of age** reach adult status (esp. *Law* at 18, formerly 21). [Latin *aetas*]

**-age** *suffix* forming nouns denoting: **1** action (*breakage*). **2** condition (*bondage*). **3** aggregate or number (*coverage; acreage*). **4** cost (*postage*). **5** result (*wreckage*). **6** place or abode (*anchorage; orphanage*). [Latin *-aticus*]

**aged** *adj.* **1** /ayjd/ (*predic.*) of the age of (*aged 3*). **2** /**ay**-juhd/ old.

**ageism** /**ay**-jiz-uhm/ *n.* prejudice or discrimination against people solely on grounds of age.

**ageist** /**ay**-juhst/ — *adj.* expressing or revealing ageism. — *n.* person who has or shows prejudice against older persons.

**ageless** *adj.* **1** never growing or appearing old. **2** eternal.

**agency** /**ay**-juhn-see/ *n.* (*pl.* **-ies**) **1** business or premises of an agent (*employment agency*). **2** action; intervention (*fertilised by the agency of insects; by the agency of God*). [Latin: related to ACT]

**agenda** /uh-**jen**-duh/ *n.* (*pl.* **-s**) **1** list of items to be considered at a meeting. **2** things to be done.

**agent** /**ay**-juhnt/ *n.* **1 a** person who acts for another in business etc. **b** spy. **2** person or thing that exerts power or produces an effect. □ **agential** /uh-**jen**-shuhl, ay-/ *adj.*

**agent-general** *n.* official representative of an Australian state, usu. in London.

**agent orange** *n.* chemical defoliant, esp. as used by US forces during the Vietnam War.

**agent provocateur** /,azh-zhon pruh-,vo-kuh-**ter**/ *n.* (*pl.* **agents provocateurs** pronunc. same) person (e.g. a policeman in civilian clothing) used to tempt suspected offenders to self-incriminating action. [French, = provocative agent]

**age of consent** *n.* age at which consent to sexual intercourse is valid in law.

**age-old** *adj.* very long-standing.

**agglomerate** — *v.* (**-ting**) /uh-**glom**-uh-,rayt/ collect into a mass. — *n.* /uh-**glom**-uh-ruht/ mass, esp. of fused volcanic fragments. — *adj.* /uh-**glom**-uh-ruht/ collected into a mass. □ **agglomeration** /-**ray**-shuhn/ *n.* [Latin *glomus -meris* ball]

**agglutinate** /uh-**gloo**-tuh-,nayt/ *v.* (**-ting**) **1** stick as with glue. **2** *Biol.* cause or undergo adhesion (of bacteria etc.). □ **agglutination** /-**nay**-shuhn/ *n.* **agglutinative** /uh-**gloo**-tuh-nuh-tiv/ *adj.* [Latin: related to GLUTEN]

**aggrandise** /**ag**-ruhn-,duyz, uh-**gran**-duyz/ *v.* (also **-ize**) (**-sing** or **-zing**) **1** increase the power, rank, or wealth of (a person or nation). **2** cause to seem greater than is the case. □ **aggrandisement** /uh-**gran**-duhz-muhnt/ *n*. [French: related to GRAND]

**aggravate** /**ag**-ruh-ˌvayt/ *v*. (**-ting**) **1** make worse or more serious (*aggravated the injury by walking too soon*). **2** annoy (*stop aggravating me*). □ **aggravation** /-**vay**-shuhn/ *n*. [Latin *gravis* heavy]

■ **Usage** The use of *aggravate* in sense 2 is regarded by some people as incorrect, but it is common in informal use.

**aggregate** — *n*. /**ag**-ruh-guht/ **1** sum total, amount assembled. **2** crushed stone etc. used in making concrete. **3** rock formed of a mass of different particles or minerals. — *adj*. /**ag**-ruh-guht/ combined, collective, total. — *v*. /**ag**-ruh-ˌgayt/ (**-ting**) collect, combine into one mass. □ **in the aggregate** as a whole. □ **aggregation** /-**gay**-shuhn/ *n*. **aggregative** /**ag**-ruh-ˌgay-tiv/ *adj*. [Latin *grex greg-* flock]

**aggression** /uh-**gresh**-uhn/ *n*. **1 a** act or practice of attacking without provocation, esp. beginning a quarrel or war. **b** unprovoked attack. **2** hostile or destructive behaviour. [Latin *gradior gress-* walk]

**aggressive** /uh-**gres**-iv/ *adj*. **1** given to aggression; hostile. **2** forceful, self-assertive (*aggressive marketing of the product*). □ **aggressively** *adv*.

**aggressor** *n*. person or party that attacks without provocation.

**aggrieved** /uh-**greevd**/ *adj*. having a grievance. [French: related to GRIEF]

**aggro** /**ag**-roh/ *colloq*. — *n*. aggressive or hostile behaviour (*no need for all this aggro*). — *adj*. aggressive, hostile (*known for his aggro attitude*). [abbreviation of *aggravation* or AGGRESSION]

**aghast** /uh-**gahst**/ *predic. adj*. filled with dismay or consternation (*were aghast at the extent of the damage*). [past part. of obsolete (*a*)*gast* frighten]

**agile** /**aj**-uyl/ *adj*. quick-moving, nimble, active (*agile in his footwork; has an agile intellect*). □ **agility** /uh-**jil**-uh-tee/ *n*. [Latin *agilis*: related to ACT]

**agistment** /uh-**jist**-muhnt/ *n*. **1** taking in of livestock to feed at a rate of so much per head. **2** price paid for this. □ **agist** *v*.

**agitate** /**aj**-uh-ˌtayt/ *v*. (**-ting**) **1** disturb or excite (a person or feelings). **2** (often foll. by *for*, *against*) campaign, esp. politically (*agitated for tax reform*). **3** shake briskly. □ **agitation** /ˌaj-uh-**tay**-shuhn/ *n*. **agitator** *n*. [Latin *agito*: related to ACT]

**aglow** /uh-**gloh**/ *predic. adj*. glowing.

**agnail** /**ag**-nayl/ *n*. **1** piece of torn skin at the root of a fingernail. **2** soreness resulting from this. [Old English, = tight (metal) nail, hard excrescence in flesh]

**agnostic** /ag-**nos**-tik/ — *n*. person who believes that the existence of God is not provable. — *adj*. **1** of or relating to agnostics. **2** claiming lack of knowledge of and hence commitment to (a particular issue etc.) (*I'm agnostic about abortion*). □ **agnosticism** /-tuh-ˌsiz-uhm/ *n*. [from A-[1], GNOSTIC]

**ago** /uh-**goh**/ *adv*. (prec. by duration) earlier; in the past (*ten years ago*). [originally *agone* = gone by]

■ **Usage** Note the construction *it is ten years ago that* (not *since*) *I saw him*.

**agog** /uh-**gog**/ — *predic. adj*. eager, expectant. — *adv*. eagerly, expectantly. [French *gogue* fun]

**agonise** /**ag**-uh-ˌnuyz/ *v*. (also **-ize**) (**-sing** or **-zing**) **1** undergo (esp. mental) anguish (*agonised over the decision*). **2** suffer or cause to suffer agony. **3** (as **agonised** *adj*.) expressing agony (*an agonised look*).

**agony** /**ag**-uh-nee/ *n*. (*pl*. **-ies**) **1** extreme mental or physical suffering. **2** severe struggle. [Greek *agōn* struggle]

**agoraphobia** /ˌag-uh-ruh-**foh**-bee-uh/ *n*. abnormal fear of open spaces or public places. □ **agoraphobic** *adj. & n*. [Greek *agora* market-place]

**agrarian** /uh-**grair**-ree-uhn/ — *adj*. **1** of the land or its cultivation. **2** of landed property. — *n*. advocate of the redistribution of land. [Latin *ager* field]

**agree** /uh-**gree**/ *v*. (**-ees**, **-eed**, **-eeing**) **1** hold the same opinion (*I agree with you*). **2** consent (*agreed to go*). **3** (often foll. by *with*) **a** become or be in harmony (*the accounts all agree; your version agrees with mine*). **b** suit; be good for (*fish didn't agree with him*). **c** *Gram*. have the same number, gender, case, or person as. **4** (foll. by *on*) decide mutually on (*agreed on a compromise*). **5** (foll. by *that* + clause) concede (*I agree that our weather has been worsening of late, but ...*). □ **be agreed** be of one opinion. [Latin: related to AD-, *gratus* pleasing]

**agreeable** *adj*. **1** pleasing, pleasant (*agreeable climate*). **2** (often foll. by *to*) willing to agree (*was agreeable to going*). **3** (foll. by *to*) conformable (*is this agreeable to your specifications?*). □ **agreeably** *adv*.

**agreement** *n*. **1** act or state of agreeing; holding of the same opinion (*reached agreement*). **2** an arrangement or contract (*had an agreement with the trade union*). **3** *Gram*. having same number, gender, case, or person.

**agricultural shot** n. Cricket awkward stroke with the bat.

**agriculture** /ag-ruh-,kul-chuh/ n. science or practice of cultivating the soil and rearing animals. ◻ **agricultural** /-kul-chuh-ruhl/ adj. **agriculturalist** /-kul-chuh-ruh-luhst/ n. [Latin ager field]

**agronomy** /uh-**gron**-uh-mee/ n. science of soil management and crop production. ◻ **agronomical** /,ag-ruh-**nom**-i-kuhl/ adj. **agronomist** n. [Greek agros land]

**agro-politician** n. person who is politically active on behalf of the rural sector. ◻ **agro-politics** n.

**aground** /uh-**grownd**/ predic. adj. & adv. on or on to the bottom of shallow water (run aground).

**ague** /**ay**-gyoo/ n. **1** hist. malarial fever. **2** shivering fit. [Latin: related to ACUTE]

**ah** /ah/ int. expressing surprise, pleasure, realisation, etc. [French a]

**aha** /ah-**hah**, uh-**hah**/ int. expressing surprise, triumph, mockery, etc. [from AH, HA[1]]

**ahead** /uh-**hed**/ adv. **1** further forward in space or time. **2** in the lead (ahead on points). **3** in the line of one's forward motion (roadworks ahead). ◻ **get ahead** get in the lead; be successful.

**ahem** /uh-**huhm**, uh-**hem**/ int. used to attract attention, gain time, etc. [from HEM[2]]

**-aholic** suffix see -HOLIC.

**ahoy** /uh-**hoi**/ int. Naut. call used in hailing. [from AH, HOY[1]]

**aid** — n. **1** help. **2** financial or material help, esp. given by one country to another. **3** person or thing that helps (he is a teaching aid; he uses an electronic teaching aid). — v. **1** help. **2** promote (sleep will aid recovery). ◻ **in aid of 1** in support of. **2** colloq. for the purpose of (what's it all in aid of?). [Latin: related to AD-, juvo help]

**aide** /ayd/ n. **1** aide-de-camp. **2** assistant. [French]

**aide-de-camp** /,ayd-duh-**kong**/ n. (pl. **aides-de-camp** pronunc. same) officer assisting a senior officer. [French]

**AIDS**[1] n. (also **Aids**) acquired immune deficiency syndrome, an often fatal syndrome caused by a virus transmitted in the blood, marked by severe loss of resistance to infection. [abbreviation]

**AIDS**[2] n. a computer virus. [named after AIDS[1]]

**Aids-related complex** n. (also **ARC**) second stage of infection by the Aids virus in which fever, weight loss, and malaise become apparent; sometimes leading to the third stage, always ultimately fatal (FULL-BLOWN AIDS).

**Aids virus** n. = HIV.

**ail** v. **1** archaic (only in 3rd person interrog. or indefinite constructions) trouble or afflict (what ails him?). **2** (usu. **be ailing**) be ill. [Old English]

**aileron** /**ay**-luh-,ron/ n. hinged flap on an aeroplane wing, used to control lateral balance. [French aile wing]

**ailing** adj. **1** ill. **2** in poor condition (ailing economy).

**ailment** n. minor illness or disorder.

**aim** — v. **1** intend or try (aim at winning; aim to win). **2** (usu. foll. by at) direct or point (a weapon, remark, etc.) (aimed her barbs at me). **3** take aim. **4** (foll. by at, for) seek to obtain or achieve (aim for the presidency). — n. **1** purpose or object. **2** the directing of a weapon etc. at an object. ◻ **take aim** direct a weapon etc. at a target. [Latin aestimare reckon]

**aimless** adj. without aim or purpose. ◻ **aimlessly** adv.

**ain't** /aynt/ contr. colloq. **1** am, is, or are not. **2** have or has not.

---

■ **Usage** The use of ain't is regarded as unacceptable in spoken and written English.

---

**air** /air/ — n. **1** mixture mainly of oxygen and nitrogen surrounding the earth. **2** earth's atmosphere; open space in it. **3** a distinctive impression or manner (air of mystery; with a triumphant air). **b** (esp. in pl.) pretentiousness (gave himself airs). **4** tune. **5** light wind. — v. **1** expose (clothes, a room, etc.) to fresh air or warmth to remove damp. **2** express and discuss publicly (an opinion, question, grievance, etc.). ◻ **by air** by or in an aircraft. **in the air 1** (of opinions etc.) prevalent. **2** (also **up in the air**) (of plans etc.) uncertain. **on** (or **off**) **the air** being (or not being) broadcast. **tread** (or **walk on**) **air** feel elated. [Greek aēr]

**airbag** n. safety device that fills with air on impact to protect the occupants of a vehicle in a collision.

**air bladder** n. bladder or sac filled with air in fish or some plants.

**airborne** adj. **1** transported by air. **2** (of aircraft) in the air after taking off.

**air brake** n. **1** brake worked by air pressure. **2** movable flap or other device in an aircraft to reduce its speed.

**air chief marshal** n. RAAF officer, equivalent to general in the army or admiral in the navy.

**air commodore** n. RAAF officer above group captain.

**air-conditioner** n. apparatus for air-conditioning.

**air-conditioning** *n.* **1** system for regulating the humidity, ventilation, and temperature in a building or vehicle. **2** air-conditioner. □ **air-conditioned** *adj.*

**aircraft** *n.* (*pl.* same) machine capable of flight, esp. an aeroplane or helicopter.

**aircraft carrier** *n.* warship carrying and used as a base for aircraft.

**airfield** *n.* area with runway(s) for aircraft.

**air force** *n.* branch of the armed forces fighting in the air.

**airfreight** /'air-,frayt/ — *n.* cargo carried by an aircraft. — *v.* transport by air.

**airgun** *n.* gun using compressed air to fire pellets.

**airhead** *n. colloq.* stupid or foolish person.

**airing** /'air-ring/ *n.* **1** exposure to air for drying etc. **2** public expression of an opinion etc. (*the idea will get an airing at tomorrow's meeting*).

**airless** *adj.* stuffy; still, calm.

**airlift** — *n.* emergency transport of supplies etc. by air, esp. in a blockade or other emergency. — *v.* transport thus.

**airline** *n.* public air transport system or company.

**airliner** *n.* large passenger aircraft.

**airlock** *n.* **1** stoppage of the flow by an air bubble in a pump or pipe. **2** compartment permitting movement between areas at different pressures.

**airmail** — *n.* **1** system of transporting mail by air. **2** mail carried by air. — *v.* send (a letter etc.) by air.

**airman** *n.* pilot or member of an aircraft crew, esp. in an air force.

**airplay** *n.* broadcasting (of recorded music).

**air pocket** *n.* apparent vacuum causing an aircraft to drop suddenly.

**airport** *n.* airfield with facilities for passengers and goods.

**air raid** *n.* attack by aircraft on ground targets.

**air rifle** *n.* rifle using compressed air to fire pellets.

**airs and graces** *n.pl.* affected manner.

**airship** *n.* power-driven aircraft lighter than air.

**airspace** *n.* air above a country and subject to its jurisdiction.

**air speed** *n.* aircraft's speed relative to the air.

**airstrip** *n.* strip of ground for the take-off and landing of aircraft.

**air terminal** *n.* building at an airport with facilities for passengers etc.

**airtight** *adj.* **1** impermeable to air. **2** *colloq.* without any flaws (*an airtight alibi*).

**airwaves** *n.pl. colloq.* radio waves used in broadcasting.

**airy** *adj.* (**-ier, -iest**) **1** well-ventilated, breezy. **2** flippant, superficial (*an airy apology*). **3** light as air. **4** ethereal. □ **airily** *adv.* **airiness** *n.*

**airy-fairy** *adj. colloq.* unrealistic, impractical; foolishly idealistic.

**aisle** /uyl/ *n.* **1** the part of a church on either side of the nave, divided from it by pillars. **2** passage between rows of pews, seats, etc. □ **lay them in the aisles** *colloq.* make an audience laugh uncontrollably; be a great success. [Latin *ala* wing]

**aitch** /aych/ *n.* the letter H. [French *ache*]

■ **Usage** The pronunciation /haych/ is very common in Australian speech, but is regarded as incorrect by many people.

**ajar** /uh-'jah/ *adv. & predic. adj.* (of a door) slightly open. [from A², obsolete *char* from Old English *cerr* a turn]

**aka** /'ak-uh/ *abbr.* also known as.

**akimbo** /uh-'kim-boh/ *adv.* (of the arms) with hands on the hips and elbows turned outwards. [originally *in kenebowe*, probably from Old Norse]

**akin** /uh-'kin/ *predic. adj.* **1** related by blood. **2** similar.

**Akubra** /uh-'koo-bruh/ *n. propr.* wide-brimmed Australian hat.

**Al** *symb.* aluminium.

**-al** *suffix* **1** (also **-ial**) forming adjectives meaning 'relating to, of the kind of' (*central*; *tidal*; *dictatorial*). **2** forming nouns, esp. of verbal action (*removal*). [Latin *-alis*]

**à la** /'ah la/ *prep.* in the manner of (*à la russe*). [French]

**alabaster** /'al-uh-,bahs-tuh, -,bas-tuh/ — *n.* translucent usu. white form of gypsum, used for carving etc. — *adj.* **1** of alabaster. **2** white or smooth. [Greek *alabastros*]

**à la carte** /,ah la 'kaht/ *adv. & adj.* with individually priced dishes. [French]

**alacrity** /uh-'lak-ruh-tee/ *n.* briskness; cheerful readiness. [Latin *alacer* brisk]

**alarm** /uh-'lahm/ — *n.* **1** warning of danger etc. **2 a** warning sound or device. **b** alarm clock. **3** frightened expectation of danger or difficulty (*filled with alarm*). — *v.* **1** frighten or disturb. **2** arouse to a sense of danger. □ **alarming** *adj.* **alarmingly** *adv.* [Italian *all' arme!* to arms]

**alarmist** *n.* person given to stirring up needless alarm.

**alas** /uh-'las, uh-'lahs/ *int.* expressing grief, pity, or concern. [French: related to AH, Latin *lassus* weary]

**alb** *n.* long white vestment worn by Christian priests. [Latin *albus* white]

**Albany daisy** /al-buh-nee/ *n.* small Australian shrub with heath-like leaves and pink daisy-flowers. [*Albany* in south-western WA]

**Albany doctor** see DOCTOR *n.* 4.

**Albany pitcher plant** see PITCHER PLANT.

**albatross** /al-buh-ˌtros/ *n.* **1 a** any of various long-winged, stout-bodied sea birds. **b** source of frustration or guilt; an encumbrance. **2** *Golf* score of three strokes under par at any hole. [alteration of *alcatras*, from Spanish and Portuguese *alcatraz* from Arabic, = the jug]

**albeit** /awl-bee-it, al-/ *conj. literary* though (*he tried, albeit without success*). [*all be it*]

**Albert lyre-bird** *n.* (also **Albert's lyre-bird**) reddish-brown lyre-bird of eastern Australian rainforests. [*Albert*, husband (d. 1861) of Queen Victoria]

**albino** /al-bee-noh/ *n.* (*pl.* **-s**) **1** person or animal lacking pigment in the skin and hair (which are white), and the eyes (usu. pink). **2** plant lacking normal colouring. □ **albinism** /al-buh-ˌniz-uhm/ *n.* [Spanish and Portuguese: related to ALB]

**album** /al-buhm/ *n.* **1** book for photographs, stamps, etc. **2 a** long-playing gramophone record. **b** set of these. [Latin, = blank tablet, from *albus* white]

**albumen** /al-byuh-muhn/ *n.* **1** egg-white. **2** substance found between the skin and germ of many seeds, usu. the edible part. [Latin: related to ALBUM]

**albumin** /al-byuh-muhn/ *n.* water-soluble protein found in egg-white, milk, blood, etc. □ **albuminous** /al-byoo-muh-nuhs/ *adj.*

**alchemy** /al-kuh-mee/ *n.* medieval chemistry, esp. seeking to turn base metals into gold. □ **alchemist** *n.* [Arabic]

**Alcheringa** /ˌal-chuh-ring-guh/ *n.* (also **Alchuringa**) **1** the Dreamtime, that collection of events beyond living memory which shaped the physical, spiritual, and moral world of the Aborigines. **2** the era in which these events occurred. **3** an Aborigine's consciousness of the enduring nature of this era. [Aranda *aljerre* dream, -*nge* from, of, the combination meaning 'in the Dreamtime']

**alcohol** /al-kuh-ˌhol/ *n.* **1** (in full **ethyl alcohol**) colourless volatile inflammable liquid, esp. as the intoxicant in wine, beer, spirits, etc., and as a solvent, fuel, etc. **2** liquor containing this. **3** *Chem.* any of many organic compounds containing one or more hydroxyl groups attached to carbon atoms. [Arabic]

**alcoholic** /ˌal-kuh-hol-ik/ — *adj.* of, like, containing, or caused by alcohol. — *n.* person suffering from alcoholism.

**alcoholism** /al-kuh-ho-ˌliz-uhm/ *n.* condition resulting from addiction to alcohol.

**alcohol-related** *adj.* caused or affected by the consumption of alcohol (*alcohol-related car crashes*).

**alcove** /al-kohv/ *n.* recess, esp. in the wall of a room or of a garden. [Arabic, = the vault]

**aldehyde** /al-duh-ˌhuyd/ *n. Chem.* any of a class of compounds formed by the oxidation of alcohols. [from ALCOHOL, DE-, HYDROGEN]

**al dente** /ul den-tay/ *adj.* (of pasta, vegetables etc.) cooked so as to be still firm, not mushy, when bitten. [Italian, = 'to the tooth']

**alderman** /awl-duh-muhn/ *n.* (*fem.* **alderwoman**) elected local government councillor in some Australian States. □ **aldermanic** /-man-ik/ *adj.* [Old English *aldor* chief, MAN, WOMAN]

**ale** *n.* beer (usu. as a trade word). [Old English]

**aleatory** /ay-leer-tree, al-ee-ay-tuh-ree/ *adj.* depending on chance. [Latin *alea* DIE²]

**alec** /al-ik/ *n.* (also **aleck**) *colloq.* fool, stupid person. [shortened version of SMART ALEC]

**aleph** /ah-lef/ *n.* first letter of the Hebrew alphabet. [Hebrew, literally 'ox']

**alert** /uh-lert/ — *adj.* **1** watchful, vigilant; ready to take action. **2** nimble (esp. of mental faculties); attentive. — *n.* **1** warning call or alarm. **2** state or period of special vigilance. — *v.* (often foll. by *to*) warn (*alerted us to the danger*). □ **on the alert** on the lookout against danger or attack. [French *alerte* from Italian *all 'erta* to the watch-tower]

**Alexandra palm** /ˌal-uhg-zan-druh/ *n.* (also **king palm**) north Queensland single-stemmed palm having pinnate leaves (silvery beneath), creamy flowers, and red fruits. [*Alexandra* Princess of Wales (d. 1925)]

**alexandrine** /ˌal-uhg-zan-dreen, -druyn/ — *adj.* (of a line of verse) having six iambic feet. — *n.* alexandrine line. [French *Alexandre*, title of a romance using this metre]

**Alf** — *n.* derogatory term for the type of the (sometimes uneducated) unthinkingly conservative, anti-intellectual, heterosexual, Australian male who holds women in low esteem, despises culture, and is prejudiced against minority groups. — *adj.* of or pertaining to an Alf (*Alf attitudes*).

**alfalfa** /al-fal-fuh/ *n.* **1** = LUCERNE. **2** sprouted lucerne seed eaten as a salad vegetable. [Arabic, = a green fodder]

**alfresco** /al-**fres**-koh/ *adv. & adj.* in the open air. [Italian]

**alga** /**al**-guh/ *n.* (*pl.* **algae** /**al**-jee, **al**-gee**/**) (usu. in *pl.*) non-flowering stemless water-plant, esp. seaweed and plankton. □ **algal** *adj.* **algoid** *adj.* [Latin]

**algebra** /**al**-juh-bruh/ *n.* branch of mathematics that uses letters etc. to represent numbers and quantities. □ **algebraic** /ˌal-juh-**bray**-ik/ *adj.* [ultimately from Arabic *al-jabr*, = reunion of broken parts]

**-algia** /**al**-juh/ *comb. form Med.* denoting pain in a part specified by the first element (*neuralgia*). □ **-algic** *comb. form* forming adjectives (*neuralgic*). [Greek *algos* pain]

**algorithm** /**al**-guh-ˌrith-uhm/ *n.* (also **algorism**) **1** process or set of rules used for calculation etc., esp. with a computer. **2** Arabic or decimal notation of numbers. □ **algorithmic** /ˌal-guh-**rith**-mik/ *adj.* [Persian, name of a 9th-c. mathematician *al-Kuwārizmī*]

**alias** /**ay**-lee-uhs/ — *adv.* also named or known as. — *n.* false or assumed name. [Latin, = at another time]

**alibi** /**al**-uh-ˌbuy/ *n.* (*pl.* **-s**) **1** claim or proof that one was elsewhere when a crime etc. was committed. **2** *colloq.* excuse. [Latin, = elsewhere]

■ **Usage** The use of *alibi* in sense 2 is considered incorrect by some people.

**alien** /**ay**-lee-uhn/ — *adj.* **1** (often foll. by *to*) unfamiliar; unacceptable or repugnant (*army discipline was alien to him; struck an alien note*). **2** foreign (*alien customs*). **3** of beings from other worlds. — *n.* **1** foreign-born resident who is not naturalised. **2** being from another world (*the aliens have landed in Canberra*). [Latin *alius* other]

**alienable** *adj. Law* able to be transferred to new ownership.

**alienate** *v.* (**-ting**) **1 a** cause (a person) to become unfriendly or hostile (*he has alienated most of his friends*). **b** (often foll. by *from*) cause (a person) to feel isolated from (*friends, society, etc.*) (*his actions have alienated him from us all*). **c** estrange; turn away; transfer (*he succeeded in alienating her affections; alienate funds*). **2** transfer ownership of (property) to another person etc. □ **alienation** /ˌay-lee-uh-**nay**-shuhn/ *n.*

**alight¹** /uh-**luyt**/ *predic. adj.* **1** on fire (*the house was well alight*). **2** lit up; excited (*eyes alight with expectation*). [on *a light* (= lighted) *fire*]

**alight²** /uh-**luyt**/ *v.* **1 a** (often foll. by *from*) descend from a vehicle. **b** dismount

from a horse. **2** come to earth, settle (*waiting for the bird to alight*). **3** (foll. by *on*) find by chance; notice. [Old English]

**align** /uh-**luyn**/ *v.* **1** put in a straight line or bring into line (*books neatly aligned on the shelf*). **2** (usu. foll. by *with*) ally (oneself etc.) with (a cause, party, etc.) (*aligned himself with Labor*). □ **alignment** *n.* [French *à ligne* into line]

**alike** /uh-**luyk**/ — *adj.* (usu. *predic.*) similar, like one another; indistinguishable. — *adv.* in a similar way (*all were treated alike*).

**alimentary** /ˌal-uh-**men**-tuh-ree, -tree/ *adj.* of or providing food or nourishment. [Latin *alo* nourish]

**alimentary canal** *n.* passage along which food passes from the mouth to the anus during digestion.

**alimony** /**al**-uh-muh-nee/ *n.* money payable to a spouse or former spouse after separation or divorce.

■ **Usage** This term has been replaced by *maintenance*.

**aliphatic** /ˌal-uh-**fat**-ik/ *adj. Chem.* of organic compounds in which carbon atoms form open chains, not aromatic rings. [Greek *aleiphar -phat-* fat]

**aliquot** /**al**-uh-ˌkwot/ — *adj.* (of a part or portion) contained by the whole an integral or whole number of times (*4 is an aliquot part of 12*). — *n.* **1** aliquot part. **2** (in general use) any known fraction of a whole; sample. [Latin, = several]

**alive** /uh-**luyv**/ *adj.* (usu. *predic.*) **1** living. **2 a** continuing; in operation or action (*kept his interest alive*). **b** under discussion; provoking interest (*the issue is still very much alive today*). **3** lively, active. **4** charged with an electric current. **5** (foll. by *to*) aware of; alert (*alive to the danger*). **6** (foll. by *with*) swarming or teeming with. [Old English: related to A², LIFE]

**alkali** /**al**-kuh-ˌluy/ *n.* (*pl.* **-s**) **1 a** any of a class of substances that liberate hydroxide ions in water, usu. form caustic or corrosive solutions, turn litmus blue, and have a pH of more than 7, e.g. caustic soda. **b** similar but weaker substance, e.g. sodium carbonate. **2** *Chem.* any substance that reacts with or neutralises hydrogen ions. □ **alkaline** *adj.* **alkalinity** /ˌal-kuh-**lin**-uh-tee/ *n.* [Arabic, = the calcined ashes]

**alkaloid** /**al**-kuh-ˌloid/ *n.* nitrogenous organic compound of plant origin, e.g. morphine, quinine.

**alkane** /**al**-kayn/ *n. Chem.* saturated aliphatic hydrocarbon having the general formula $C_nH_{2n+2}$, including methane and ethane.

**alkene** /al-keen/ *n.* *Chem.* unsaturated aliphatic hydrocarbon containing a double bond and having the general formula $C_nH_{2n}$, including ethylene.

**alkyl** /al-kuhl/ *n.* (in full **alkyl radical**) *Chem.* any radical derived from an alkane by the removal of a hydrogen atom. [German: related to ALCOHOL]

**alkyne** /al-kuyn/ *n.* *Chem.* unsaturated aliphatic hydrocarbon containing a triple bond and having the general formula $C_nH_{2n-2}$, including acetylene.

**all** /awl/ — *adj.* **1** whole amount, quantity, or extent of (*all day; all his life; take it all*). **2** any whatever (*beyond all doubt*). **3** greatest possible (*with all speed*). — *n.* **1** all concerned; everything (*all were present; all is lost*). **2** (foll. by *of*) **a** the whole of (*take all of it*). **b** every one of (*all of us*). **c** *colloq.* as much as (*all of six feet*). **d** *colloq.* in a state of (*all of a dither*). **3** one's whole strength or resources (*prec. by my, your*, etc.) (*gave my all*). **4** (in games) each (*two goals all*). — *adv.* **1 a** entirely, quite (*dressed all in black*). **b** as an intensifier (*stop all this grumbling*). **2** *colloq.* very (*went all shy*). **3** (foll. by *the* + *compar.*) to that, or the utmost, extent (*if they go, all the better; that makes it all the worse*). □ **all about** (orig. Australian pidgin) *colloq.* **1** everywhere (*travellers are welcome all about in Australia*). **2** everyone. **all along** from the beginning. **all and sundry** everyone. **all but** very nearly. **all for** *colloq.* strongly in favour of. **all found** with board and lodging provided free. **all in all** everything considered. **all manner of** every kind of. **all of a sudden** suddenly. **all one** (or **the same**) (usu. foll. by *to*) a matter of indifference. **all out** using all one's strength (also (with hyphen) *attrib.*: *all-out effort*). **all over 1** completely finished. **2** in or on all parts of (*mud all over the carpet*). **3** *colloq.* typically (*you all over*). **4** *colloq.* effusively attentive to (a person) (*was all over him*). **all right** (*predic.*) **1** satisfactory; safe and sound; in good condition. **2** satisfactorily (*it worked out all right*). **3 a** expressing consent. **b** as an intensifier (*that's the one all right*). **c** plea for reasonableness (*all right you guys, can we have some quiet?*). **all round 1** in all respects. **2** for each person. **all the same** nevertheless. **all there** *colloq.* mentally alert or normal. **all the time** throughout (despite some contrary expectation etc.). **all together** all at once;

all in one place or in a group (*came all together*) (cf. ALTOGETHER). **all told** in all. **all up with** hopeless for (a person). **at all** (with *neg.* or *interrog.*) in any way; to any extent (*did not swim at all; did you like it at all?*). **in all** in total; altogether. [Old English]

■ **Usage** Note the differences in meaning between *all together* and *altogether*: see note at *altogether*. On *all right* and *alright* see note at *alright*

**Allah** /al-uh, uh-lah/ *n.* the Muslim and Arab name of God. [Arabic]

**all-Australian** *adj.* **1** representing the whole of Australia. **2** exclusively or distinctively Australian (*an all-Australian film*).

**allay** /uh-lay/ *v.* **1** diminish (fear, suspicion, etc.). **2** alleviate (pain etc.). [Old English *a*- intensive prefix, LAY[1]]

**All Blacks** *n.pl.* New Zealand international Rugby Union team.

**all-clear** *n.* **1** signal that danger etc. is over. **2** (also **all clear**) *Aust. Rules* field umpire's signal to the goal umpire that no infringement of the rules has occurred prior to the kicking of the goal or behind.

**all comers** *n.pl.* any who apply, take up a challenge, etc.

**allegation** /,al-uh-gay-shuhn/ *n.* **1** assertion, esp. unproved. **2** act or instance of alleging. [Latin *allego* adduce]

**allege** /uh-lej/ *v.* (-**ging**) **1** declare to be the case, esp. without proof. **2** advance as an argument or excuse. □ **alleged** *adj.* [Latin *lis lit-* lawsuit]

**allegedly** /uh-lej-uhd-lee/ *adv.* as is alleged or said to be the case.

**allegiance** /uh-lee-juhns/ *n.* **1** loyalty (to a person or cause etc.). **2** the duty of a subject or citizen to a country or government (*new citizens must swear or promise allegiance*). [French: related to LIEGE]

**allegory** /al-uh-guh-ree, al-uh-gree/ *n.* (*pl.* -**ies**) story etc. in which the meaning or message is represented symbolically. □ **allegorical** /,al-uh-go-ri-kuhl/ *adj.* **allegorise** /al-uh-guh-,ruyz/ *v.* (also -**ize**) (-**sing** or -**zing**). [Greek *allēgoria* other speaking]

**allegretto** /,al-uh-gret-oh/ *Mus.* — *adv.* & *adj.* in a fairly brisk tempo. — *n.* (*pl.* -**s**) such a passage or movement. [Italian, diminutive of ALLEGRO]

**allegro** /uh-lay-groh, uh-leg-/ *Mus.* — *adv.* & *adj.* in a brisk tempo. — *n.* (*pl.* -**s**) such a passage or movement. [Italian, = lively]

**alleluia** /,al-uh-loo-yuh/ (also **hallelujah**

/ˌhal-/ ) — *int.* God be praised. — *n.* **1** song or shout of praise to God. **2** *RC Ch.* part of the Mass including this. [Hebrew]

**allergen** /ˈal-uh-juhn/ *n.* any substance that causes an allergic reaction. □ **allergenic** /ˌal-uh-**jen**-ik/ *adj.* [ALLERGY, -GEN]

**allergic** /uh-**ler**-jik/ *adj.* **1** (foll. by *to*) **a** having an allergy to (*allergic to cats*). **b** *colloq.* having a strong dislike for (*allergic to door-knocking evangelists*). **2** caused by or relating to an allergy (*allergic reaction*).

**allergy** /**al**-uh-jee/ *n.* (*pl.* **-ies**) **1** adverse reaction to certain substances, esp. particular foods, pollen, fur, or dust. **2** *colloq.* antipathy. [Greek *allos* other]

**alleviate** /uh-**lee**-vee-ˌayt/ *v.* (**-ting**) make (pain, suffering, etc.) less severe (*nothing will alleviate my grief*). □ **alleviation** /-ay-shuhn/ *n.* [Latin *levo* raise]

**alley¹** /**al**-ee/ *n.* (*pl.* **-s**) **1** narrow street or passageway. **2** enclosure for skittles, bowling, etc. **3** walk or lane in a park etc. □ **up** (or **right up**) **one's alley** = *up one's street* (see STREET). [French *aller* go]

**alley²** *n.* (also **ally**) (in the game of marbles) marble of excellent quality. □ **make one's alley good** *colloq.* exploit a situation; improve one's position. **throw** (or **pass** or **toss** etc.) **in one's alley** *colloq.* die; acknowledge defeat. [related to ALABASTER]

**alliance** /uh-**luy**-uhns/ *n.* **1** union or agreement to cooperate, esp. of nations by treaty or families by marriage. **2** relationship resulting from shared interests, affinity, etc.; friendship (*the strange alliance of big business and trade unions to defeat the proposed tax*). [French: related to ALLY]

**allied** /**al**-uyd/ *adj.* **1** (also **Allied**) associated in an alliance. **2** connected or related (*studied medicine and allied subjects*).

**alligator** /**al**-uh-ˌgay-tuh/ *n.* **1** large reptile of the crocodile family native to S. America and China, with a head broader and shorter than a crocodile's. **2** (in general use) any of several large members of the crocodile family, including the two species of crocodile found in northern Australia. [Spanish *el lagarto* the lizard]

**alliteration** /uh-ˌlit-uh-**ray**-shuhn/ *n.* repetition of the same letter or sound at the beginning of adjacent or closely connected words (e.g. *cool, calm, and collected*) (cf. ASSONANCE). □ **alliterate** /uh-**lit**-uh-ˌrayt/ *v.* (**-ting**). **alliterative** /uh-**lit**-uh-ruh-tiv/ *adj.* [Latin: related to LETTER]

**allo-** *comb. form.* other (*allopathy*). [Greek *allos* other]

**allocate** /**al**-uh-ˌkayt/ *v.* (**-ting**) (usu. foll. by *to*) assign or devote to (a purpose, person, or place) (*allocated more funds to organisations helping the needy*). □ **allocation** /ˌal-uh-**kay**-shuhn/ *n.* [Latin: related to LOCAL]

**allopathy** /uh-**lop**-uh-thee/ *n.* treatment of disease by conventional means, i.e. with drugs having opposite effects to the symptoms (cf. HOMOEOPATHY). □ **allopathic** /ˌal-uh-**path**-ik/ *adj.* [Greek, as ALLO-, -PATHY]

**all ordinaries index** *n.* (also **all-ords**) on the Australian stock exchanges, the weighted average of certain ordinary share prices.

**allot** /uh-**lot**/ *v.* (**-tt-**) **1** apportion or distribute to (a person), esp. as a share or task (*they were allotted equal sums*). **2** (foll. by *to*) give or distribute officially (*a sum was allotted to each charity*). [French *a* to, LOT]

**allotment** *n.* **1** small piece of land; building block. **2** share. **3** action of allotting.

**allotrope** /**al**-uh-ˌtrohp/ *n.* any of two or more different physical forms in which an element can exist (*graphite, charcoal, and diamond are all allotropes of carbon*). [back-formation from ALLOTROPY]

**allotropy** /uh-**lot**-ruh-pee/ *n.* existence of two or more different physical forms of a chemical element. □ **allotropic** /ˌal-uh-**trop**-ik/ *adj.* [Greek *allos* different, *tropos* manner]

**allow** /uh-**low**/ *v.* **1** (often foll. by *to* + infin.) permit (*I allow you to go, but on one condition*). **2** assign a limited amount etc. (*was allowed $500*). **3** (usu. foll. by *for*) provide or set aside for a purpose; add or deduct in consideration (*allow $50 for expenses; allow for wastage*). **4** admit, concede (*he allowed that it was so*). □ **allowable** *adj.* **allowably** *adv.* [originally = commend, from French: related to AD-, Latin *laudo* praise, *loco* place]

**allowance** *n.* **1** amount or sum allowed, esp. regularly for a stated purpose. **2** amount allowed in reckoning. **3** *Mech.* (foll. by *of*) tolerance of. **4 a** deduction. **b** deduction from the weight a racehorse is required to carry. □ **make allowance**(**s**) (often foll. by *for*) **1** consider (mitigating circumstances) (*made allowances for his demented state*). **2** make excuses for (a person, bad behaviour, etc.).

**alloy** /**al**-oi/ — *n.* **1** mixture of two or more metals. **2** inferior metal mixed esp. with gold or silver. — *v.* **1** mix (metals). **2** debase (a pure substance) by admixture. **3** moderate (*pleasure alloyed with pain*). [French: related to ALLY]

**all-purpose** *attrib. adj.* having many uses.

**all-right** *attrib. adj. colloq.* acceptable (*an all-right guy*).

**all-rounder** *n.* **1** versatile person. **2** person skilled in a number of aspects of a sport.

**allspice** *n.* **1** aromatic spice obtained from the berry of the pimento plant. **2** the berry.

**all-time** *attrib. adj.* (of a record etc.) unsurpassed.

**allude** /uh-**lood**/ *v.* (**-ding**) (foll. by *to*) refer to, esp. indirectly or briefly. [Latin: related to AD-, *ludo* play]

**allure** /uh-**loor**, -**lyoor**/ — *v.* (**-ring**) attract, charm, or entice. — *n.* attractiveness, personal charm, fascination. □ **allurement** *n.* [French: related to AD-, LURE]

**allusion** /uh-**loo**-*zh*uhn/ *n.* (often foll. by *to*) passing or indirect reference (*made an allusion to Whitlam's speech when he was dismissed by Kerr*). □ **allusive** /uh-**loo**-siv/ *adj.* [Latin: related to ALLUDE]

■ **Usage** Sometimes confused with *illusion.*

**alluvial** /uh-**loo**-vee-uhl/ — *adj.* of alluvium. — *n.* alluvium, esp. containing a precious metal such as gold.

**alluvium** /uh-**loo**-vee-uhm/ *n.* (*pl.* **-via**) deposit of usu. fine fertile soil left behind by a flood, esp. in a river valley. [Latin *luo* wash]

**ally** /**al**-uy/ — *n.* (*pl.* **-ies**) nation, person, etc., formally cooperating or united with another, esp. (also **Ally**) in war. (also /uh-**luy**/ (**-ies, -ied**) (often *refl.* and foll. by *with*) combine in alliance. [Latin *alligo* bind]

**alma mater** /,al-muh **mah**-tuh, **may**-tuh/ *n.* one's university, school, or college. [Latin, = bounteous mother]

**almanac** /**awl**-muh-,nak, al-/ *n.* (also **almanack**) calendar, usu. with astronomical data. [medieval Latin from Greek]

**almighty** /awl-**muy**-tee/ *adj.* **1** having complete power. **2** (**the Almighty**) God. **3** *colloq.* very great (*almighty crash*). [Old English: related to ALL, MIGHTY]

**almond** /**ah**-muhnd/ *n.* **1** nutlike kernel of a fruit allied to the peach and plum. **2** tree bearing this. [Greek *amugdalē*]

**almoner** /**ah**-muh-nuh/ *n.* **1** social worker attached to a hospital. **2** *hist.* official distributor of alms. [French: related to ALMS]

**almost** /**awl**-mohst/ *adv.* all but; very nearly. [Old English: related to ALL, MOST]

**alms** /ahmz/ *n.pl. hist.* donation of money or food to the poor. [Greek *eleēmosunē* pity]

**aloe** /**al**-oh/ *n.* **1** plant of the lily family with toothed fleshy leaves. **2** (in *pl.*) (in full **bitter aloes**) strong laxative from aloe juice. [Old English from Greek]

**aloe vera** /,al-oh **veer**-ruh/ *n.* kind of aloe, the leaves of which yield a juice used in skin preparations, shampoos, etc.

**aloft** /uh-**loft**/ *predic. adj. & adv.* **1** high up, overhead. **2** upwards. [Old Norse *á lopti* in air]

**alone** /uh-**lohn**/ — *predic. adj.* **1** without the presence or help of others. **2** lonely (*felt alone*). — *adv.* only, exclusively (*you alone can help me*). [earlier *al one*: related to ALL, ONE]

**along** /uh-**long**/ — *prep.* **1** from one end to the other end of (*Australian flags along the route*). **2** on or through any part of the length of (*was walking along the road*). **3** beside or through the length of (*shelves stood along the wall*). — *adv.* **1** onward, into a more advanced state (*come along; getting along nicely*). **2** with oneself or others (*bring a book along*). **3** beside or through part or the whole length of a thing. □ **along with** in addition to; together with. **get along** see GET. **go along with** agree with. [Old English, originally adj. = facing against]

**alongside** /uh-long-**suyd**/ — *adv.* at or to the side (of a ship, pier, etc.). — *prep.* close to the side of.

**aloof** /uh-**loof**/ — *adj.* distant, unsympathetic (*his manner was aloof*). — *adv.* away, apart (*he kept aloof*). [originally *Naut.*, from A² + LUFF]

**aloud** /uh-**lowd**/ *adv.* audibly.

**ALP** *abbr.* Australian Labor Party.

**alp** *n.* **1** high mountain. **2** (**the Alps**) **a** high range of mountains in south-eastern Australia. **b** high range of mountains in Switzerland and adjoining countries. [originally *alps*, from Greek *alpeis*]

**alpaca** /al-**pak**-uh/ *n.* **1** shaggy S. American mammal related to the llama. **2** its wool; fabric made from this. [Spanish from Quechua]

**alpha** /**al**-fuh/ *n.* **1** first letter of the Greek alphabet (A, α). **2** first-class mark for a piece of work etc. **3** *Astron.* chief star in a constellation. □ **alpha and omega** beginning and end. **alpha to omega** from beginning to end. [Latin from Greek]

**alphabet** /**al**-fuh-,bet/ *n.* **1** set of letters, in a particular order, used in writing a language. **2** symbols or signs for these. □ **alphabetical** /,al-fuh-**bet**-i-kuhl/ *adj.* [Greek ALPHA, BETA]

**alphabetise** /**al**-fuh-buh-,tuyz/ *v.* (also

-ize) (**-sing** or **-zing**) arrange (words, names, etc.) in alphabetical order. □ **alphabetisation** n.

**alphanumeric** /ˌal-fuh-nyoo-**me**-rik/ adj. containing both letters and numbers.

**alpha particle** n. helium nucleus emitted by a radioactive substance.

**alpine** /**al**-puyn/ — adj. **1** of or relating to mountainous regions. **2** growing or found on high mountains. — n. plant growing in mountainous regions. [Latin: related to ALP]

**alpine ash** n. **1** tall eucalypt of mountains in south-eastern Australia. **2** its wood.

**already** /awl-**red**-ee/ adv. **1** before the time in question (I knew that already). **2** as early or as soon as this (is back already). [from ALL, READY]

**alright** /awl-**ruyt**/ adv. = all right (see ALL) (English teachers like to write 'alright is alwrong' on essays).

■ **Usage** Although widely used, alright is still non-standard and is considered incorrect by many people.

**Alsatian** /al-**say**-shuhn/ n. = GERMAN SHEPHERD. [Latin Alsatia Alsace]

**also** /**awl**-soh/ adv. in addition, besides. [Old English: related to ALL, SO[1]]

**also-ran** n. **1** loser in a race. **2** undistinguished person.

**altar** /**awl**-tuh, ol-/ n. **1** table or flat block for sacrifice or offering to a deity. **2 a** table used for Mass. **b** Communion table. □ **lead to the altar** marry. [Latin altus high]

**alter** /**awl**-tuh, ol-/ v. make or become different; change. □ **alterable** adj. **alteration** /-**ray**-shuhn/ n. [Latin alter other]

**altercate** /**awl**-tuh-ˌkayt, ol-/ v. (**-ting**) (often foll. by with) dispute hotly, wrangle. [Latin]

**altercation** /ˌawl-tuh-**kay**-shuhn, ol-/ n. dispute, wrangle.

**alter ego** /ˌal-tuh ee-goh, ˌawl-/ n. (pl. **-s**) **1** one's hidden or second self. **2** intimate friend. [Latin, = other self]

**alternate** — v. /**awl**-tuh-ˌnayt, ol-/ (**-ting**) **1** (often foll. by with) occur or cause to occur by turns (rain and sunshine alternated). **2** (foll. by between) go repeatedly from one to another (alternated between hope and fear). — adj. /awl-**ter**-nuht/ **1** (with noun in pl.) every other (on alternate days). **2** (of things of two kinds) alternating (alternate joy and misery). **3** Bot. (of leaves etc.) placed alternately on the two sides of the stem. □ **alternately** /awl-**ter**-nuht-lee, ol-/ adv. **alternation** /ˌawl-tuh-**nay**-shuhn, ˌol-/ n. [Latin alterno do by turns: related to ALTER]

■ **Usage** See note at alternative.

**alternating current** n. electric current reversing its direction at regular intervals.

**alternative** /awl-**ter**-nuh-tiv, ol-/ — adj. **1** available as another choice (alternative route). **2** offering a different approach from the conventional or established one; belonging to the counter-culture (alternative medicine; alternative lifestyle). — n. **1** any of two or more possibilities. **2** choice (had no alternative but to go). □ **alternatively** adv.

■ **Usage** The adjective alternative should not be confused with alternate, as in 'there will be a dance on alternate Saturdays'.

**alternator** /**awl**-tuh-ˌnay-tuh, ol-/ n. dynamo that generates an alternating current.

**although** /awl-**thoh**/ conj. = THOUGH. [from ALL, THOUGH]

**altimeter** /**al**-tuh-ˌmee-tuh/ n. instrument indicating altitude reached.

**altitude** /**al**-tuh-ˌtyood/ n. **1** height, esp. of an object above sea level or above the horizon. **2** Geom. length of the perpendicular from a vertex to the opposite side of a figure. [Latin altus high]

**alto** /**al**-toh/ n. (pl. **-s**) **1** = CONTRALTO. **2 a** highest adult male singing-voice, above tenor. **b** singer with this voice. **3** instrument pitched second- or third-highest in its family. [Italian alto (canto) high (singing)]

**alto clef** n. Mus. clef placing middle C on the middle line of the staff, used chiefly for viola music.

**altogether** /ˌawl-tuh-**geth**-uh/ adv. **1** totally, completely (you are altogether wrong). **2** on the whole (altogether we've had a good day). **3** in total. □ **in the altogether** colloq. naked. [from ALL, TOGETHER]

■ **Usage** Note that altogether means 'in total', whereas all together means 'all at once' or 'all in one place'. The phrases six rooms altogether (in total) and six rooms all together (in one place) illustrate the difference.

**altruism** /**al**-troo-ˌiz-uhm/ n. regard for others as a principle of action; unselfishness. □ **altruist** n. **altruistic** /ˌal-troo-**is**-tik/ adj. [Italian altrui somebody else]

**alum** /**al**-uhm/ n. double sulphate of aluminium and potassium. [Latin alumen -min-]

**alumina** /uh-**loo**-muh-nuh/ n. aluminium

oxide occurring naturally as corundum and emery.

**aluminise** /uh-**loo**-muh-ˌnuyz/ v. (also **-ize**) (**-sing** or **-zing**) coat with aluminium.

**aluminium** /ˌal-yuh-**min**-ee-uhm/ n. silvery light and malleable metallic element resistant to tarnishing by air.

**alumnus** /uh-**lum**-nuhs/ n. (pl. **alumni** /-nee/; fem. **alumna**, pl. **alumnae** /-nee/) former pupil or student. [Latin, = nursling, pupil]

**alunqua** /uh-**lung**-kwuh/ n. (also **bush cucumber**) **1** twining plant of drier Australia, the young fruit of which was an important food for Aborigines. **2** the fruit itself, bright green and resembling a mini-cucumber. [Aranda, the name of the fruit (the vine itself is called *aljeye*)]

**alveolar** /al-vee-**oh**-luh, ˌal-vee-uh-luh/ adj. **1** of an alveolus. **2** *Phonet.* (of a consonant) pronounced with the tip of the tongue in contact with the ridge of the upper teeth, e.g. *n*, *s*, *t*. [ALVEOLUS, -AR¹]

**alveolus** /al-vee-**oh**-luhs, ˌal-vee-uh-luhs/ n. (pl. **alveoli** /-luy, -lee/) **1** any of the many tiny air sacs of the lungs which allow for rapid gaseous exchange. **2** the bony socket for the root of a tooth. □ **alveolate** adj. [Latin diminutive of *alveus* cavity]

**always** /**awl**-wayz/ adv. **1** at all times; on all occasions (*they are always late*). **2** whatever the circumstances (*I can always sleep on the floor*). **3** repeatedly, often (*they are always complaining*). [from ALL, WAY]

**alyssum** /**al**-i-suhm, uh-**luy**-suhm/ n. (also **sweet Alice**) plant with small usu. white honey-fragrant flowers. [Greek, = curing madness]

**Alzheimer's disease** /alts-ˌhuy-muhz/ n. serious brain disorder manifesting itself in progressive disorientation and premature senility. [*Alzheimer*, name of a neurologist]

**AM** abbr. **1** Member of the Order of Australia. **2** amplitude modulation.

**Am** symb. americium.

**am** *1st person sing. present* of BE.

**a.m.** abbr. before noon. [Latin *ante meridiem*]

**amalgam** /uh-**mal**-guhm/ n. **1** mixture or blend. **2** alloy of mercury and another metal or metals, used esp. as a filling in dentistry. [Greek *malagma* an emollient]

**amalgamate** /uh-**mal**-guh-ˌmayt/ v. (**-ting**) **1** combine or unite to form one structure, organisation, etc. (*the two firms are to amalgamate*). **2** (of metals) alloy with mercury. □ **amalgamation** /-**may**-shuhn/ n. [medieval Latin: related to AMALGAM]

**amanuensis** /uh-ˌman-yoo-**en**-suhs/ n. (pl. **-enses** /-seez/) literary assistant, esp. writing from dictation. [Latin *a manu* 'at hand']

**amaranth** /**am**-uh-ˌranth/ n. **1** plant with small green, red, or purple tinted flowers. **2** imaginary unfading flower. **3** purple colour. □ **amaranthine** /ˌam-uh-**ran**-thuyn/ adj. [Greek *amarantos* unfading]

**amass** /uh-**mas**/ v. heap together; accumulate (*amassed a fortune*). [French: related to AD-, MASS¹]

**amateur** /**am**-uh-tuh/ n. **1** person who engages in a pursuit (e.g. an art or sport) as a pastime rather than a profession. **2** person who performs with limited skill. **3** (attrib.) **a** for or done by amateurs (*amateur athletics*). **b** amateurish (a *woefully amateur performance*). □ **amateurism** n. [Latin *amator* lover: related to AMATORY]

**amateurish** /ˌam-uh-tuh-rish/ adj. unskilful; inexperienced.

**amatory** /**am**-uh-tuh-ree, -tree/ adj. of or pertaining to a lover or to sexual love generally. [Latin *amo* love]

**amaze** /uh-**mayz**/ v. (**-zing**) surprise greatly, fill with wonder. □ **amazement** n. **amazing** adj. [earlier *amase* from Old English *āmasod*]

**Amazon** /**am**-uh-zuhn/ n. **1** (in Greek legend) female warrior of a mythical race in the Black Sea area. **2** (**amazon**) large, strong, or athletic woman. □ **Amazonian** /ˌam-uh-**zoh**-nee-uhn/ adj. [Latin from Greek, explained by the Greeks as 'breastless', but the word is probably of foreign origin]

**ambassador** /am-**bas**-uh-duh/ n. **1** diplomat sent to live abroad to represent his or her country's interests. **2** representative or promoter of a specified thing (*ambassador of peace*; *good ambassador for Australia*). □ **ambassadorial** /am-ˌbas-uh-**daw**-ree-uhl/ adj. [Latin *ambactus* servant]

**amber** — n. **1 a** yellow translucent fossilised resin used in jewellery. **b** colour of this. **2** yellow traffic-light meaning caution. — adj. of or like amber. [French from Arabic]

**amber fluid** n. colloq. beer.

**ambergris** /**am**-buh-ˌgrees, -ˌgris/ n. waxlike secretion of the intestine of the sperm whale, found floating in tropical seas and used in perfumes. [French, = grey amber]

**amberjack** /**am**-buh-jak/ n. brightly coloured marine fish found in tropical and subtropical Atlantic waters, and around the Great Barrier Reef.

**ambidextrous** /ˌam-bee-**deks**-truhs/ *adj.* able to use either hand equally well. [Latin *ambi-* on both sides, DEXTER]

**ambience** /**am**-bee-uhns/ *n.* surroundings or atmosphere; character, mood, etc. of a place. [Latin *ambio* go round]

**ambient** *adj.* surrounding.

**ambiguity** /ˌam-buh-**gyoo**-uh-tee/ *n.* (*pl.* **-ies**) **1** double meaning which is either deliberate or caused by inexactness of expression. **2** example of this. **3** an expression able to be interpreted more than one way (e.g. *free range eggs available here*). [as AMBIGUOUS]

**ambiguous** /am-**big**-yoo-uhs/ *adj.* **1** having an obscure or double meaning. **2** difficult to classify (*the results are ambiguous*). [Latin *ambi-* both ways, *ago* drive]

**ambit** /**am**-buht/ *n.* **1** scope, extent, or bounds of something. **2** precincts or environs. **3** definition of the limits of an industrial dispute. [Latin: related to AMBIENCE]

**ambit claim** *n.* claim, made by employees, which sets the boundaries of an industrial dispute.

**ambition** /am-**bish**-uhn/ *n.* **1** determination to achieve success or distinction, usu. in a chosen field. **2** object of this (*the headmastership was his ambition*). [Latin, = canvassing: related to AMBIENCE]

**ambitious** *adj.* **1** full of ambition or high aims. **2** showing ambition (*an ambitious attempt*).

**ambivalence** /am-**biv**-uh-luhns/ *n.* coexistence in one person of opposing feelings towards a person or thing. □ **ambivalent** *adj.* **ambivalently** *adv.* [Latin *ambo* both, EQUIVALENCE]

**amble** /**am**-buhl/ — *v.* (**-ling**) move at an easy pace. — *n.* such a pace. [Latin *ambulo* walk]

**ambrosia** /am-**broh**-zee-uh/ *n.* **1** (in classical mythology) the food of the gods. **2** sublimely delicious food etc. [Greek, = elixir of life]

**ambulance** /**am**-byuh-luhns/ *n.* vehicle equipped for conveying patients to hospital. [Latin: related to AMBLE]

**ambulant** /**am**-byuh-luhnt/ *adj. Med.* (of a patient) able to walk about, not confined to bed. [Latin: related to AMBLE]

**ambulatory** /**am**-byuh-luh-tuh-ree, -tree/ *adj.* **1** = AMBULANT. **2** of or for walking. [Latin: related to AMBLE]

**ambuscade** /ˌam-buhs-**kayd**/ *n. & v.* (**-ding**) = AMBUSH.

**ambush** /**am**-buush/ — *n.* **1** surprise attack by persons hiding. **2** hiding-place for this. — *v.* attack from an ambush; waylay. [French: related to IN-¹, BUSH¹]

**ameliorate** /uh-**mee**-lee-uh-ˌrayt, -lyuh-ˌrayt/ *v.* (**-ting**) make or become better; improve. □ **amelioration** /uh-ˌmee-lee-uh-**ray**-shuhn/ *n.* **ameliorative** *adj.* [from AD-, Latin *melior* better]

**amen** /ah-**men**, ay-/ *int.* (esp. at the end of a prayer etc.) so be it. [Church Latin from Hebrew, = certainly]

**amenable** /uh-**mee**-nuh-buhl, uh-**men**-uh-/ *adj.* **1** responsive; capable of being won over (*he's not amenable to reason*). **2** (often foll. by *to*) answerable to law etc. [French: related to AD-, Latin *mino* drive animals]

**amend** /uh-**mend**/ *v.* **1** make minor alterations in to improve (a bill, document, etc.). **2** correct an error or errors in (a document etc.). **3** make better; improve (*you'd better amend your ways*). [Latin: related to EMEND]

■ **Usage** *Amend* is often confused with *emend*, a more technical word used in the context of textual correction.

**amendment** *n.* minor alteration or addition in a document (esp. a legal or statutory one), resolution, etc.

**amends** *n.* □ **make amends** (often foll. by *for*) compensate or make up (for).

**amenity** /uh-**mee**-nuh-tee, uh-**men**-uh-tee/ *n.* (*pl.* **-ies**) **1** pleasant or useful feature or facility. **2** pleasantness (of a place etc.). **3** public toilet. [Latin *amoenus* pleasant]

**amenorrhoea** /ay-ˌmen-uh-**ree**-uh, uh-/ *n. Med.* absence of menstruation. [A-¹, Greek *mēn, mēnos* month, *-rrhoia* from *rheō* flow]

**American** /uh-**me**-ri-kuhn/ — *adj.* of America, esp. the United States. — *n.* **1** native, citizen, or inhabitant of America, esp. the US. **2** English as used in the US. □ **Americanise** *v.* (also **-ize**) (**-sing** or **-zing**). [name of navigator *Amerigo* Vespucci]

**Americanism** *n.* word etc. of US origin or usage.

**americium** /ˌam-uh-**ris**-ee-uhm/ *n.* artificial radioactive metallic element. [*America*, where first made]

**amethyst** /**am**-uh-thuhst/ *n.* semiprecious stone of a violet or purple variety of quartz. [Greek, = preventing drunkenness]

**amiable** /**ay**-mee-uh-buhl/ *adj.* (esp. of a person) friendly and pleasant, likeable. □ **amiably** *adv.* [Latin: related to AMICABLE]

**amicable** /**am**-i-kuh-buhl/ *adj.* (esp. of an arrangement, relations, etc.) friendly (*an amicable meeting*). □ **amicably** *adv.* [Latin *amicus* friend]

**amid** /uh-**mid**/ prep. in the middle of, among. [Old English: related to ON, MID]

**amidships** adv. in or into the middle of a ship. [from AMID, alternative form midships]

**amidst** var. of AMID.

**amine** /**ay**-meen, **am**-een/ n. compound formed from ammonia by replacement of one or more hydrogen atoms by an organic radical or radicals.

**amino acid** /uh-**mee**-noh/ n. Biochem. any of a group of nitrogenous organic acids occurring naturally in plant and animal tissues and forming the basic constituents of proteins. [from AMINE, ACID]

**amir** var. of EMIR.

**amiss** /uh-**mis**/ — predic. adj. wrong; out of order; faulty (knew something was amiss). — adv. wrong(ly), inappropriately (everything went amiss). □ **take amiss** be offended by (don't take my words amiss, but . . .). [Old Norse à mis so as to miss]

**amity** /**am**-uh-tee/ n. friendship. [Latin amicus friend]

**ammeter** /**am**-ee-tuh/ n. instrument for measuring electric current in amperes. [from AMPERE, -METER]

**ammo** /**am**-oh/ n. colloq. ammunition. [abbreviation]

**ammonia** /uh-**moh**-nee-uh/ n. 1 pungent strongly alkaline gas. 2 (in general use) solution of ammonia in water. □ **ammoniated** adj. [Latin]

**ammonite** /**am**-uh-nuyt/ n. coil-shaped fossil shell. [Latin, = horn of Jupiter Ammon]

**ammunition** /,am-yuh-**nish**-uhn/ n. 1 supply of bullets, shells, grenades, etc. 2 information usable in an argument. [French la MUNITION taken as l'ammu-]

**amnesia** /am-**nee**-zee-uh, am-**nee**-zhuh/ n. loss of memory. □ **amnesiac** /-zee-,ak/ n. [Latin from Greek]

**amnesty** /**am**-nuh-stee/ — n. (pl. -ies) general pardon, esp. for political offences. — v. (-ies, -ied) grant an amnesty to. [Greek amnēstia oblivion]

**amniocentesis** /,am-nee-oh-sen-**tee**-suhs/ n. (pl. -teses /-seez/ ) sampling of amniotic fluid to detect foetal abnormality. [from AMNION, Greek kentēsis pricking]

**amnion** /**am**-nee-uhn/ n. (pl. **amnia**) innermost membrane enclosing the embryo of a reptile, bird, or mammal. □ **amniotic** /,am-nee-**ot**-ik/ adj. [Greek, = caul]

**amoeba** /uh-**mee**-buh/ n. (pl. -s) microscopic aquatic one-celled organism capable of changing shape. □ **amoebic** adj. [Greek, = change]

**amok** /uh-**mok**/ adv. □ **run amok** (or **amuck**) run wild. [Malay]

**among** /uh-**mung**/ prep. (also **amongst**) 1 surrounded by, with (lived among the trees; be among friends). 2 included in (among us were dissidents). 3 an example of; in the category of (among his best works). 4 a between; shared by (divide it among you). b from the joint resources of (among us we can manage it). 5 with one another (talked among themselves). 6 as distinguished from; preeminent in the category of (she is one among many). [Old English, = in a crowd]

**amoral** /ay-**mo**-ruhl/ adj. 1 not concerned with or outside the scope of morality. 2 without moral principles.

**amorous** /**am**-uh-ruhs/ adj. of, showing, or feeling sexual love. [Latin amor love]

**amorphous** /uh-**maw**-fuhs/ adj. 1 of no definite shape. 2 vague. 3 Mineral. & Chem. non-crystalline. [Greek a- not, morphē form]

**amortise** /uh-**maw**-tuyz/ v. (also -ize) (-sing or -zing) gradually extinguish (a debt) by regular instalments. [Latin ad mortem to death]

**amount** /uh-**mownt**/ — n. quantity, esp. a total in number, size, value, extent, etc. (large amount of money; came to a considerable amount). — v. (foll. by to) be equivalent to in number, significance, etc. (amounted to $100; amounted to a disaster). [Latin ad montem upward]

**amp**[1] n. ampere. [abbreviation]

**amp**[2] n. colloq. amplifier. [abbreviation]

**amperage** /**am**-puh-rij/ n. strength of an electric current in amperes.

**ampere** /**am**-pair/ n. SI base unit of electric current. [Ampère, name of a physicist]

**ampersand** /**am**-puh-,sand/ n. the sign '&' (= and). [corruption of and PER SE and]

**amphetamine** /am-**fet**-uh-,meen, -muhn/ n. synthetic drug used esp. as a stimulant. [abbreviation of chemical name]

**amphibian** /am-**fib**-ee-uhn/ — adj. 1 living on land as well as in water. 2 of a class of vertebrates (e.g. frogs) with an aquatic larval stage followed by a terrestrial adult stage. — n. 1 vertebrate of this class. 2 vehicle able to operate both on land and in water. [Greek amphi- both, bios life]

**amphibious** adj. 1 living or operating on land and in water. 2 involving military forces landed from the sea.

**amphitheatre** /**am**-fee-,theer-tuh/ n. 1 esp. circular unroofed building with tiers of seats surrounding a central space. **2** semicircular gallery in a theatre. **3** scene of a contest. [Greek *amphi-* round]

**amphora** /am-fuh-ruh/ *n.* (*pl.* **-phorae** /-ˌree/ ) narrow-necked Greek or Roman vessel with two handles. [Greek *amphoreus*]

**ample** /am-puhl/ *adj.* (**ampler, amplest**) **1 a** plentiful, abundant, extensive. **b** *euphem.* (esp. of a person) large, stout. **2** more than enough. □ **amply** *adv.* [Latin *amplus*]

**amplifier** /am-pluh-ˌfuy-uh/ *n.* electronic device for increasing the strength of electrical signals, esp. for conversion into sound.

**amplify** /am-pluh-ˌfuy/ *v.* (**-ies, -ied**) **1** increase the strength of (sound, electrical signals, etc.). **2** add detail to, expand (a story etc.). □ **amplification** /-fuh-**kay**-shuhn/ *n.* [Latin: related to AMPLE]

**amplitude** /am-pluh-ˌchood, -tyood/ *n.* **1 a** *Physics* maximum extent of a vibration or oscillation from the position of equilibrium. **b** *Electr.* maximum departure of the value of an alternating current or wave from the average value. **2** spaciousness; abundance. [Latin: related to AMPLE]

**amplitude modulation** *n.* *Electr.* modulation of a wave by variation of its amplitude.

**ampoule** /am-pool/ *n.* small sealed capsule holding a solution for injection. [French: related to AMPULLA]

**ampster** /am-stuh/ *n.* (also **amster**) accomplice of a sideshow operator, salesman, etc. who pretends to be a purchaser of a ticket or article with the intention of luring others to do likewise. [from *Amsterdam* rhyming slang for *ram* such a decoy]

**ampulla** /am-**puul**-uh/ *n.* (*pl.* **-pullae** /-ee/ ) **1** Roman globular flask with two handles. **2** ecclesiastical vessel. **3** *Anat.* dilated end of a vessel or duct. [Latin]

**amputate** /am-pyuh-ˌtayt/ *v.* (**-ting**) cut off surgically (a limb etc.). □ **amputation** /-**tay**-shuhn/ *n.* [Latin *amb-* about, *puto* prune]

**amputee** /ˌam-pyuh-**tee**/ *n.* person who has lost a limb etc. by amputation.

**amuck** var. of AMOK.

**amulet** /am-yuh-luht/ *n.* charm worn against evil. [Latin]

**amulla** /uh-**mul**-uh/ *n.* shrub, *Myoporum debile*, of NSW and Queensland with pink or white fruit, an Aboriginal bush-food. [Darumbal, probably *ngamula*]

**amuse** /uh-**myooz**/ *v.* (**-sing**) **1** cause to laugh or smile. **2** interest or occupy; keep entertained (*who will amuse the children while I finish my assignment?*). □ **amusing** *adj.* [French *a* cause to, *muser* stare]

**amusement** *n.* **1** thing that amuses. **2** state of being amused. **3** mechanical device (e.g. a roundabout) for entertainment at a fairground etc.

**amygdaloid** /uh-ˌmig-duh-**loid**/ *adj.* almond-shaped. [Greek *amugdalē* almond]

**amygdaloid nucleus** *n.* roughly almond-shaped mass of grey matter deep inside each hemisphere of the brain, associated with the sense of smell.

**an** form of the indefinite article (see A[1]) used before words beginning with a vowel sound (*an egg; an hour*).

■ **Usage** Now less often used before aspirated words beginning with *h* (so *a hotel*, not *an hotel*).

**an-** see A-[1].

**-an** *suffix* (also **-ean, -ian**) forming adjectives and nouns, esp. from names of places, systems, zoological classes, or orders and founders (*Australian; Anglican; crustacean; Franciscan*). [French *-ain*, Latin *-anus*]

**ana-** *prefix* (usu. **an-** before a vowel) meaning 'up'; 'back'; 'again'; 'against' (*anachronism*). [Greek]

**-ana** *suffix* forming plural nouns meaning 'things associated with' (*Australiana; Victoriana*). [neuter plural of Latin adjectival ending *-anus*]

**anabolic steroid** /ˌan-uh-**bol**-ik/ *n.* synthetic steroid hormone used to increase muscle size.

**anabolism** /uh-ˌnab-uh-**liz**-uhm/ *n.* synthesis of complex molecules in living organisms from simpler ones together with the storage of energy. [Greek *anabolē* ascent]

**anabranch** /an-uh-ˌbrahnch, -ˌbranch/ *n.* arm of a river which separates from and later rejoins the main stream. [shortening of *anastomosing branch*, ANA-, Greek *stoma* mouth, BRANCH]

**anachronism** /uh-**nak**-ruh-ˌniz-uhm/ *n.* **1 a** attribution of a custom, event, etc., to the wrong period (*the worst anachronism in the film was Governor Phillip saying that a soldier was as game as Ned Kelly*). **b** thing thus attributed. **2** out-of-date person or thing (*chivalry is an anachronism these days*). □ **anachronistic** /-**nis**-tik/ *adj.* [Greek *ana-* against, *khronos* time]

**anaconda** /ˌan-uh-**kon**-duh/ *n.* large non-poisonous S. American snake killing its prey by constriction. [Sinhalese *henakandayā*, originally of a snake in Sri Lanka]

**anaemia** /uh-**nee**-mee-uh/ *n.* (also **anemia**) deficiency of red blood cells or their haemoglobin, causing pallor and weariness. [Greek, = want of blood]

**anaemic** /uh-**nee**-mik/ *adj.* (also **anemic**) **1** of or suffering from anaemia. **2** pale, listless; lacking in vitality (*anaemic complexion*; *gave an anaemic performance*).

**anaesthesia** /ˌan-uhs-**thee**-zee-uh, -thee-*zh*uh/ *n.* (also **anes-**) absence of sensation, esp. artificially induced before surgery. [Greek]

**anaesthetic** /ˌan-uhs-**thet**-ik/ (also **anes-**) — *n.* substance producing anaesthesia. — *adj.* producing anaesthesia.

**anaesthetise** /uh-**nees**-thuh-ˌtuyz/ *v.* (also **anes-**) (also **-ize**) (**-sing** or **-zing**) administer an anaesthetic to.

**anaesthetist** /uh-**nees**-thuh-tuhst/ *n.* (also **anes-**) specialist in the administration of anaesthetics.

**anagram** /**an**-uh-ˌgram/ *n.* word or phrase formed by transposing the letters of another, e.g. Pilate's question *Quid est veritas? (What is truth?)* is an anagram of *Vir est qui adest (It is the man before you).* □ **anagrammatic** (**al**) *adj.* **anagrammatise** *v.* [Greek *ana* again, *gramma* letter]

**anal** /**ay**-nuhl/ *adj.* relating to or in or near the anus. □ **anally** *adv.*

**analgesia** /ˌan-uhl-**jee**-zee-uh/ *n.* absence or relief of pain. [Greek]

**analgesic** — *adj.* relieving pain. — *n.* analgesic drug.

**analog** *adj.* (of a watch or clock) indicating time by the position of hour and minute hands (cf. DIGITAL). [variant of ANALOGUE]

**analogous** /uh-**nal**-uh-guhs/ *adj.* (usu. foll. by *to*) partially similar or parallel (*with the coming of whites to Australia, the plight of the Aborigines was analogous to that of the Red Indians*). [Greek *analogos* proportionate]

**analogue** /**an**-uh-ˌlog/ *n.* **1** analogous or parallel thing. **2** (*attrib.*) (usu. **analog**) (of a computer etc.) using physical variables which change over a continuum to represent numbers (cf. DIGITAL).

**analogy** /uh-**nal**-uh-jee/ *n.* (*pl.* **-ies**) **1** (usu. foll. by *to*, *with*, *between*) correspondence or partial similarity (*drew an analogy between the displacement of Aborigines and that of Red Indians*). **2** *Logic* process of arguing from similarity in known respects to similarity in other respects. □ **analogical** /ˌan-uh-**loj**-i-kuhl/ *adj.* [Greek *analogia* proportion]

**analyse** /**an**-uh-ˌluyz/ *v.* (**-sing**) **1** exam-ine in detail; find or show the essence or structure of; ascertain the constituents of (a substance, sentence, etc.) (*analysed the urine sample*; *analysed the novel*). **2** psychoanalyse.

**analysis** /uh-**nal**-uh-suhs/ *n.* (*pl.* **-lyses** /-ˌseez/) **1 a** detailed examination of elements or structure. **b** statement of the result of this. **2** *Chem.* determination of the constituent parts of a mixture or compound. **3** psychoanalysis. [ANA-, Greek *luō* loose]

**analyst** /**an**-uh-luhst/ *n.* **1** person skilled in (esp. chemical or systems) analysis. **2** psychoanalyst.

**analytic** /ˌan-uh-**lit**-ik/ *adj.* (also **analytical**) **1** of or using analysis. **2** *Logic* (of a statement etc.) such that its denial is self-contradictory; true by definition e.g. *she's a mother so she must be female*, but not *she's a woman so she must be a mother.*

**anandrous** /an-**an**-druhs/ *adj. Bot.* having no stamens. [Greek, = without males]

**Anangu** /**ah**-nahng-oo/ *n.* (*pl.* same) an Aborigine. [Western Desert language, = person]

■ **Usage** See KOORI[1].

**anapaest** /**an**-uh-ˌpeest, -ˌpest/ *n.* metrical foot (˘ ˘ –) consisting of two short or unstressed syllables followed by one long or stressed syllable. [Greek *anapaistos* reversed (dactyl)]

**anarchism** /**an**-uh-ˌkiz-uhm/ *n.* political theory that all government and laws should be abolished. [French: related to ANARCHY]

**anarchist** /**an**-uh-kuhst/ *n.* advocate of anarchism or of political disorder. □ **anarchistic** /-ˌkis-tik/ *adj.*

**anarchy** /**an**-uh-kee/ *n.* disorder, esp. political or social. □ **anarchic** /uh-**nah**-kik/ *adj.* [Greek *an-* without, *arkhē* rule]

**anathema** /uh-**nath**-uh-muh/ *n.* (*pl.* **-s**) **1** detested thing or person (*is anathema to me*). **2** ecclesiastical curse, excommunicating a person or denouncing a doctrine. □ **anathematise** /uh-**nath**-uh-muh-ˌtuyz/ *v.* (also **-ize**). [Greek, = thing devoted (i.e. to evil)]

**anatomy** /uh-**nat**-uh-mee/ *n.* (*pl.* **-ies**) **1** science of animal or plant structure. **2** such a structure. **3** *colloq.* a human body (*he has a great anatomy*). **4** analysis. **5** dissection of the human body, animals, or plants. □ **anatomical** /ˌan-uh-**tom**-i-kuhl/ *adj.* **anatomist** *n.* [Greek *ana-* up, *temnō* cut]

**-ance** *suffix* forming nouns expressing: **1** quality or state or an instance of one (*arrogance*; *resemblance*). **2** action (*assistance*). [French *-ance*, Latin *-antia*]

**ancestor** /**an**-ses-tuh/ *n.* **1** person, animal, or plant from which another has descended or evolved. **2** prototype or forerunner (*ancestor of the computer*). [Latin *ante-* before, *cedo* go]

**ancestral** /an-**ses**-truhl/ *adj.* belonging to or inherited from one's ancestors.

**ancestry** /**an**-ses-tree/ *n.* (*pl.* **-ies**) **1** family descent, lineage. **2** ancestors collectively.

**anchor** /**ang**-kuh/ — *n.* **1** heavy metal weight used to moor a ship or a balloon. **2** stabilising thing (*faith is her anchor in this turmoil*). **3** (in *pl.*) *colloq.* brakes (of a motor vehicle). — *v.* **1** secure with an anchor. **2** fix firmly. **3** be moored by an anchor. [Greek *agkura*]

**anchorage** *n.* **1** place for anchoring. **2** act of anchoring or lying at anchor. **3** anything dependable.

**anchorite** /**ang**-kuh-,ruyt/ *n.* hermit; religious recluse. [Greek *anakhōreō* retire]

**anchorman** *n.* **1** coordinator, esp. as compère in a broadcast. **2** person who plays a crucial part, esp. at the back of a tug-of-war team or as the last runner in a relay race.

**anchovy** /**an**-chuh-vee, an-**choh**-vee/ *n.* (*pl.* **-ies**) small strong-flavoured fish of the herring family. [Spanish and Portuguese *anchova*]

**ancient** /**ayn**-shuhnt/ *adj.* **1** of long ago, esp. before the fall of the Roman Empire in the West in AD 476. **2** having lived or existed long. □ **the ancients** people of ancient times, esp. the Greeks and Romans. [Latin *ante* before]

**ancillary** /an-**sil**-uh-ree/ — *adj.* **1** providing essential support to a central service or industry. **2** (often foll. by *to*) subordinate, subservient. — *n.* (*pl.* **-ies**) **1** ancillary worker. **2** auxiliary or accessory. [Latin *ancilla* handmaid]

**-ancy** *suffix* forming nouns denoting a quality (*constancy*) or state (*infancy*). [Latin *-antia*]

**and** /and, uhnd/ *conj.* **1 a** connecting words, clauses, or sentences, to be taken jointly (*you and I*). **b** implying progression (*better and better*). **c** implying causation (*she hit him and he cried*). **d** implying great duration (*cried and cried*). **e** implying a great number (*miles and miles*). **f** implying addition (*two and two*). **g** implying variety (*there are books and books*). **2** *colloq.* to (*try and come*). **3** in relation to (*Australia and the South Pacific*). □ **and/or** either or both of two stated alternatives. [Old English]

**andante** /an-**dan**-tee/ *Mus.* — *adv. & adj.* in a moderately slow tempo. — *n.* such a passage or movement. [Italian, = going]

**androgynous** /an-**droj**-uh-nuhs/ *adj.* **1** hermaphrodite. **2** *Bot.* with stamens and pistils in the same flower. **3** *colloq.* (of a person, dress, etc.) neither distinctively male nor distinctively female; sexually ambiguous (*many pop-stars cultivate an androgynous image*). [Greek *anēr andr-man*, *gunē* woman]

**android** /**an**-droid/ *n.* robot with a human appearance. [Greek *anēr andr-man*, *-OID*]

**anecdote** /**an**-uhk-,doht/ *n.* short account of an entertaining or interesting incident. □ **anecdotal** /-**doh**-tuhl/ *adj.* [Greek *anekdota* things unpublished]

**anemia** var. of ANAEMIA.

**anemic** var. of ANAEMIC.

**anemometer** /,an-uh-**mom**-uh-tuh/ *n.* instrument for measuring wind force. [Greek *anemos* wind]

**anemone** /uh-**nem**-uh-nee/ *n.* plant of the buttercup family, with vividly-coloured flowers. [Greek, = wind-flower]

**aneroid** /**an**-uh-,roid/ — *adj.* (of a barometer) measuring air-pressure by its action on the elastic lid of a box containing a vacuum. — *n.* aneroid barometer. [Greek *a-* not, *nēros* water]

**anesthesia** etc. var. of ANAESTHESIA etc.

**aneurism** /**an**-yuh-,riz-uhm/ *n.* (also **aneurysm**) excessive localised enlargement of an artery. [Greek *aneurunō* widen]

**anew** /uh-**nyoo**/ *adv.* **1** again. **2** in a different way. [earlier *of newe*]

**angel** /**ayn**-juhl/ *n.* **1 a** attendant or messenger of God. **b** representation of this in human form with wings. **2** virtuous or obliging person. **3** *colloq.* financial backer of a play etc. [Greek *aggelos* messenger]

**angel-fish** *n.* any of various fish, of tropical waters in Australia and elsewhere, with winglike fins.

**angelic** /an-**jel**-ik/ *adj.* of or like an angel. □ **angelically** *adv.*

**angelica** /an-**jel**-i-kuh/ *n.* aromatic plant or its candied stalks. [medieval Latin, = angelic (herb)]

**angelus** /**an**-juh-luhs/ *n.* **1** Roman Catholic prayers commemorating the Annunciation and the Incarnation, said at morning, noon, and sunset. **2** bell announcing this. [Latin *Angelus domini* (= the angel of the Lord), opening words]

**anger** /**ang**-guh/ — *n.* extreme or passionate displeasure. — *v.* make angry. [Old Norse *angr* grief]

**angina** /an-**juy**-nuh/ *n.* (in full **angina pectoris**) /**pek**-tuh-ruhs/ ) chest pain brought on by exertion, caused by an inadequate blood supply to the heart. [Greek *agkhonē* strangling]

**angiogram** /**an**-jee-uh-,gram/ *n.* photograph taken by radiography of blood vessels after radio-opaque dyes have been injected. [Greek *aggeion* vessel, -GRAM]

**angiosperm** /**an**-jee-uh-,sperm/ *n.* plant producing flowers and reproducing by seeds enclosed within a carpel, including herbaceous plants, grasses, and most trees (opp. GYMNOSPERM). □ **angiospermous** *adj.* [Greek *aggeion* vessel]

**Angle** /**ang**-guhl/ *n.* (usu. in *pl.*) member of a N. German tribe that settled in E. Britain in the 5th c. [Latin *Anglus*, from the name *Angul* in Germany]

**angle**[1] /**ang**-guhl/ — *n.* **1** space between two meeting lines or surfaces, esp. as measured in degrees. **2** corner. **3** point of view (*we need a new angle on this problem*). — *v.* (-**ling**) **1** move or place obliquely. **2** present (information) in a biased way (*the report was angled in favour of the guilty party*). [Latin *angulus*]

**angle**[2] /**ang**-guhl/ *v.* (-**ling**) **1** fish with hook and line. **2** (foll. by *for*) seek an objective by devious or calculated means (*angled for a loan*). □ **angler** *n.* [Old English]

**Anglican** /**ang**-gli-kuhn/ — *adj.* of the Church of England or any church in communion with it, as the Anglican Church of Australia. — *n.* member of an Anglican Church. □ **Anglicanism** *n.* [Latin *Anglicanus*: related to ANGLE]

**Anglicise** /**ang**-gluh-,suyz/ *v.* (also -**ize**) (-**sing** or -**zing**) make English in character etc.

**Anglo** — *n.* = ANGLO-CELT. — *adj.* = ANGLO-CELTIC.

**Anglo-** *comb. form* **1** English. **2** of English origin. **3** English or British and (*Anglo-Australian agreement*). [Latin: related to ANGLE]

**Anglo-Catholic** /,ang-gloh-**kath**-uh-lik, -**kath**-lik/ — *adj.* of a High Church Anglican wing emphasising its Catholic tradition. — *n.* member of this group.

**Anglo-Celt** *n.* Australian whose origin is Anglo-Celtic (opp. European, Asian, etc.).

**Anglo-Celtic** *adj.* of or pertaining to Australians whose origins were in Britain and/or Ireland.

**Anglo-Saxon** /,ang-gloh-**sak**-suhn/ — *adj.* of the English Saxons before the Norman Conquest. — *n.* **1** Anglo-Saxon person. **2** Old English.

**angophora** /ang-**gof**-uh-ruh/ *n.* any of about 8 species of tree, closely related to the eucalypt, occurring in south-eastern Australia and bearing usu. white flowers in great profusion. [Greek *aggos* jar, *phoros* bearing, alluding to the vase-like fruits]

**angora** /ang-**gaw**-ruh/ *n.* **1** fabric or wool from the hair of the angora goat or rabbit. **2** long-haired variety of cat, goat, or rabbit. [*Angora* (= Ankara) in Turkey]

**angry** /**ang**-gree/ *adj.* (-**ier**, -**iest**) **1** feeling or showing anger (*don't be angry with me; angry at the treatment she received*). **2** (of a wound etc.) inflamed, painful. **3** suggesting or seeming to show anger (*angry sky*). □ **angrily** *adv.*

**angst** /angst/ *n.* anxiety; neurotic fear; guilt, remorse. [German]

**angstrom** /**ang**-struhm/ *n.* unit of length equal to $10^{-10}$ metre. [*Ångström*, name of a physicist]

**anguish** /**ang**-gwish/ *n.* **1** severe mental suffering. **2** pain, agony. □ **anguished** *adj.* [Latin *angustia* tightness]

**angular** /**ang**-gyuh-luh/ *adj.* **1** having angles or sharp corners. **2** (of a person) **a** having sharp features; lean and bony. **b** awkward in manner; stiff and formal in character. **3** forming an angle. **4** measured by angle (*angular distance*). □ **angularity** /-la-ruh-tee/ *n.* [Latin: related to ANGLE[1]]

**anhydrous** /an-**huy**-druhs/ *adj. Chem.* without water, esp. water of crystalisation. [Greek *an-* without, *hudōr* water]

**anigozanthos** /,an-uh-goh-**zan**-thuhs/ *n.* any plant of the small genus *Anigozanthos* endemic to the south-west of WA (see KANGAROO PAW). [Greek]

**aniline** /**an**-uh-,leen, -luhn, -,luyn/ *n.* colourless oily liquid used in making dyes, drugs, and plastics. [German *Anil* indigo, former source]

**anima** /**an**-uh-muh/ *n.* **1** *Psychol.* inner personality (opp. PERSONA). **2** feminine part of a man's personality (opp. ANIMUS). [Latin, = mind, soul]

**animadvert** /,an-uh-mad-**vert**/ *v.* (foll. by *on*) *literary* criticise, censure. □ **animadversion** *n.* [Latin *animus* mind, ADVERSE]

**animal** /**an**-uh-muhl/ — *n.* **1** living organism which feeds and usu. has sense-organs and a nervous system and is able to respond rapidly to stimuli. **2** such an organism other than man. **3** brutish person. — *adj.* **1** of or like an animal. **2** bestial; carnal. [Latin *animalis* having breath]

**animal husbandry** n. science of breeding and caring for farm animals.

**animalise** /an-uh-muh-ˌluyz/ v. (also **-ize**) (**-sing** or **-zing**) make (a person) bestial; sensualise.

**animalism** n. **1** nature and activity of animals. **2** belief that humans are not superior to other animals. **3** concern with physical matters; sensuality.

**animalist** — n. = ANIMAL LIBERATIONIST. — adj. discriminating against animals. [-IST]

**animality** /ˌan-uh-**mal**-uh-tee/ n. **1** the animal world. **2** animal behaviour.

**animal lib** n. colloq. = ANIMAL LIBERATION.

**animal libber** n. colloq. = ANIMAL LIBERATIONIST.

**animal liberation** n. movement aimed at securing animal rights, esp. to ensure their well-being on farms etc. and to prevent them being used experimentally in scientific etc. research.

**animal liberationist** n. person who champions the cause of animal liberation.

**animate** — adj. /**an**-uh-muht/ **1** having life. **2** lively. — v. /**an**-uh-ˌmayt/ (**-ting**) **1** enliven; make lively. **2** give life to. **3** inspire, actuate (animated by anti-war zeal). **4** encourage. [Latin anima breath]

**animated** /ˌan-uh-**may**-tuhd/ adj. **1** lively, vigorous. **2** having life. **3** (of a film etc.) using animation. □ **animator** n.

**animated stick** n. stick-insect of the eastern Australian coast, the female (up to 220 mm) being one of the world's longest insects.

**animation** /ˌan-uh-**may**-shuhn/ n. **1** vivacity, ardour. **2** state of being alive. **3** technique of producing a moving picture from a sequence of drawings or puppet poses etc.

**animism** /**an**-uh-ˌmiz-uhm/ n. **1** belief that plants, inanimate objects, and natural phenomena have souls. **2** belief in a supernatural power that organises and animates the material world. □ **animist** n. **animistic** /-**mis**-tik/ adj.

**animosity** /ˌan-uh-**mos**-uh-tee/ n. (pl. **-ies**) spirit or feeling of strong hostility. [Latin: related to ANIMUS]

**animus** /**an**-uh-muhs/ n. **1** animosity, ill feeling. **2** motivating spirit or feeling. **3** Psychol. masculine part of a woman's personality (opp. ANIMA). [Latin, = spirit, mind]

**anion** /**an**-ˌuy-uhn/ n. negatively charged ion. □ **anionic** /ˌan-uy-**on**-ik/ adj. [Greek ANA-, ION]

**anise** /**an**-ees, **an**-uhs/ n. herb-like plant with aromatic seeds. [Greek anison]

**aniseed** /**an**-uh-ˌseed/ n. seed of the anise, used for flavouring.

**aniseed tree** n. Australian tree bearing masses of long-anthered white flowers and lance-shaped leaves heavily redolent of aniseed.

**ankh** /angk/ n. device like a cross with a loop on top, used in ancient Egypt as a symbol of life. [Egyptian, = life, soul]

**ankle** /**ang**-kuhl/ n. **1** joint connecting the foot with the leg. **2** this part of the leg. [Old Norse]

**ankle-biter** n. colloq. very small child.

**anklet** /**ang**-kluht/ n. ornament or fetter worn round the ankle.

**ankylosis** /ˌang-kuh-**loh**-suhs/ n. stiffening of a joint by fusion of the bones. □ **ankylotic** adj. [Greek agkulos crooked]

**annals** /**an**-uhlz/ n.pl. **1** narrative of events year by year. **2** historical records. □ **annalist** n. [Latin annus year]

**anneal** /uh-**neel**/ v. heat (metal or glass) and cool slowly, esp. to toughen it. [Old English ǣlan bake]

**annelid** /**an**-uh-lid/ n. segmented worm, e.g. the earthworm. [Latin anulus ring]

**annex** /**an**-eks, uh-**neks**/ v. **1** (often foll. by to) add as a subordinate part. **2** incorporate (territory) into one's own. **3** add as a condition or consequence. **4** colloq. take without right. □ **annexation** /-**say**-shuhn/ n. [Latin necto bind]

**annexe** /**an**-eks/ n. (also **annex**) **1** separate or added building, esp. for extra accommodation. **2** addition to a document.

**annihilate** /uh-**nuy**-uh-ˌlayt/ v. (**-ting**) **1** completely destroy (the saturation bombing annihilated the city). **2** defeat utterly; make insignificant or powerless. □ **annihilation** /uh-ˌnuy-uh-**lay**-shuhn/ n. [Latin nihil nothing]

**anniversary** /ˌan-uh-**ver**-suh-ree/ n. (pl. **-ies**) **1** date of an event in a previous year. **2** celebration of this. [Latin annus year, verto vers- turn]

**Anno Domini** /ˌan-oh **dom**-uh-ˌnuy, -ˌnee/ adv. in the year of the Lord, in the year of the Christian era. [Latin, = in the year of the Lord]

**annotate** /**an**-oh-tayt, **an**-uh-tayt/ v. (**-ting**) add explanatory notes to (annotated Shakespeare). □ **annotation** /-**tay**-shuhn/ n. [Latin nota mark]

**announce** /uh-**nowns**/ v. (**-cing**) **1** make publicly known. **2** make known the arrival or imminence of (a guest, dinner, etc.). **3** be a sign of (this new growth announces spring). □ **announcement** n. [Latin nuntius messenger]

**announcer** n. person who announces, esp. in broadcasting.

**annoy** /uh-**noi**/ v. **1** (often in *passive*) anger or distress slightly; irritate (*am annoyed with you*). **2** bother; pester. □**annoyance** n. [Latin *in odio* hateful]

**annual** /**an**-yoo-uhl/ — adj. **1** reckoned by the year (*annual subscription*). **2** occurring yearly (*annual general meeting*). **3** living or lasting (only) a year. — n. **1** book etc. published yearly. **2** plant that lives only a year. □ **annually** adv. [Latin *annus* year]

**annuity** /uh-**nyoo**-uh-tee/ n. (pl. **-ies**) **1** yearly grant or allowance. **2** investment yielding a fixed annual sum.

**annul** /uh-**nul**/ v. (**-ll-**) declare a (marriage, a contract, etc.) invalid; abolish. □**annulment** n. [Latin *nullus* none]

**annular** /**an**-yuh-luh/ adj. ring-shaped. [Latin *anulus* ring]

**annular eclipse** n. solar eclipse in which a ring of light remains visible.

**annulate** /**an**-yoo-luht, -,layt/ adj. marked with or formed of rings.

**annunciation** /uh-,nun-see-**ay**-shuhn/ n. **1** announcement, esp. (**Annunciation**) the announcing of the Incarnation, made by the angel Gabriel to Mary. **2** festival of this (25 March). **3** first joyful mystery of the rosary. [Latin: related to ANNOUNCE]

**anode** /**an**-ohd/ n. **1** positive electrode in an electrolytic cell etc. **2** negative terminal of a primary cell such as a battery (opp. CATHODE). [Greek *anodos* way up]

**anodise** /**an**-uh-,duyz/ v. (also **-ize**)(**-sing** or **-zing**) coat (metal) with a protective layer by electrolysis.

**anodyne** /**an**-uh-,duyn/ — adj. **1** painrelieving. **2** mentally soothing.— n. anodyne drug or medicine. [Greek *an*without, *odunē* pain]

**anoint** /uh-**noint**/ v. **1** apply holy oil or chrism to, esp. ritually (e.g. in the sacraments of baptism, holy orders, extreme unction). **2** (usu. foll. by *with*) smear. [Latin *inungo* anoint]

**anomalous** /uh-**nom**-uh-luhs/ adj. having an irregular or deviant feature; abnormal. [Greek *an*- not, *homalos* even]

**anomaly** /uh-**nom**-uh-lee/ n. (pl. **-ies**) anomalous thing; irregularity.

**anon** /uh-**non**/ adv. *archaic* or *literary* soon, shortly (*will say more of this anon*). [Old English *on ān* into one]

**anon.** /uh-**non**/ abbr. anonymous.

**anonymous** /uh-**non**-uh-muhs/ adj. **1** of unknown name or authorship (*anonymous letters*; *anonymous novel*). **2** without character; featureless; impersonal (*an anonymous style of writing*). □**anonymity** /,an-uh-**nim**-uh-tee/ n. [Greek *an*- without, *onoma* name]

**anopheles** /uh-**nof**-uh-,leez/ n. any mosquito of the genus of the same name, many of which are carriers of the malarial parasite. [Greek, = unprofitable]

**anorak** /**an**-uh-,rak/ n. waterproof usu. hooded jacket. [Eskimo]

**anorexia** /,an-uh-**rek**-see-uh/ n. lack of appetite, esp. (in full **anorexia nervosa** /ner-**voh**-suh/) an obsessive desire to lose weight by refusing to eat. □**anorectic** adj. & n. **anorexic** adj. & n. [Greek *an*without, *orexis* appetite]

**another** /uh-**nuth**-uh/ — adj. **1** an additional; one more (*another cake*). **2** person like (*another Hitler*). **3** a different (*quite another matter*). **4** some other (*another man's work*). — pron. **1** additional one (*have another*). **2** different one (*take this book away and bring me another*). **3** some or any other one (*I love another*). [earlier *an other*]

**anotherie** /uh-**nuth**-uh-ree/ n. (also **anothery**) colloq. another (one, thing, etc.) (*ta, mate, I'll have anotherie*).

**answer** /**ahn**-suh, **an**-suh/ — n. **1** something said or done in reaction to a question, statement, or circumstance (*got no answer to my letter*; *her answer was to slap my face*). **2** solution to a problem. — v. **1** make an answer or response (to) (*answer my question*; *answer the door*). **2** suit (a purpose or need) (*a piece of old pantihose answers very well for tying plants to stakes*). **3** (foll. by *to*, *for*) be responsible (*you will answer to me for your conduct*). **4** (foll. by *to*) correspond, esp. to a description (*he answers to the description*). **5** be satisfactory (*that will answer nicely*). □ **answer back** answer insolently. [Old English, = swear against (a charge)]

**answerable** adj. **1** (usu. foll. by *to*, *for*) responsible (*answerable to them for any accident*). **2** that can be answered.

**ant** n. small usu. wingless insect living in complex social colonies and proverbial for industry. [Old English]

**-ant** suffix **1** forming adjectives denoting attribution of an action (*repentant*) or state (*arrogant*). **2** forming agent nouns (*assistant*). [Latin *-ant-*, present participial stem of verbs]

**antacid** /ant-**as**-uhd/ — adj. preventing or correcting acidity, esp. in the stomach. — n. antacid agent.

**antagonise** /an-**tag**-uh-,nuyz/ v. (also **-ize**) (**-sing** or **-zing**) evoke hostility, enmity, or opposition in (*antagonised the audience with his racist remarks*). □**antagonisation** /-,zay-shuhn/ n. [Greek *antagōnizomai* (as ANTI-, *agōn* contest)]

**antagonism** /an-**tag**-uh-,niz-uhm/ *n.* active hostility or opposition.

**antagonist** *n.* opponent or adversary. □ **antagonistic** /-**nis**-tik/ *adj.*

**Antarctic** /ant-**ahk**-tik/ — *adj.* of the south polar regions. — *n.* this region. [Latin: related to ARCTIC]

**Antarctic beech** see BEECH.

**Antarctic Circle** *n.* parallel of latitude 66° 32′ S., forming an imaginary line round the Antarctic region.

**antbed** *n.* **1** earth mound built by termites to house their nests. **2** earth from termite mounds, esp. as used for floors (*antbed floor*).

**antbed parrot** *n.* = ANTHILL PARROT.

**ant cap** *n.* shield placed on top of a building-support (piers, stumps, etc.) to discourage termites from entering the building from below. □ **ant capping** *n.*

**ante** /**an**-tee/ — *n.* **1** stake put up by a player in poker etc. before receiving cards. **2** amount payable in advance. — *v.* (**-tes, -ted**) **1** put up as an ante. **2** a bet, stake. **b** (foll. by *up*) pay (see also ANTE-UP). □ **up** (or **raise**) **the ante 1** increase the amount. **2** increase the requirements (*the employer upped the ante by requiring extra qualifications*).

**ante-** *prefix* before, preceding (*antechamber; antediluvian*). [Latin, = before]

**anteater** *n.* any of various mammals feeding on ants and termites, esp. the ECHIDNA and the NUMBAT.

**antecedent** /,an-tuh-**see**-duhnt/ — *n.* **1** preceding thing or circumstance. **2** *Gram.* word or phrase etc. to which another word (esp. a relative pronoun) refers (*in 'the boy who cried wolf', the word 'boy' is the antecedent of 'who'*). **3** (in *pl.*) person's past history or ancestors. — *adj.* previous. [Latin *cedo* go]

**antechamber** /**an**-tee-,chaym-buh/ *n.* small room leading to a main one.

**antedate** /**an**-tee-,dayt/ *v.* (**-ting**) **1** precede in time (*Aboriginal occupation of Australia antedates white occupation by at least forty thousand years*). **2** assign an earlier date to (a document, event, etc.), esp. one earlier than its actual date.

**antediluvian** /,an-tee-duh-**loo**-vee-uhn/ — *adj.* **1** of the time before the Biblical Flood. **2** *colloq.* very old or out of date (*antediluvian ideas*). — *n. colloq.* extremely old-fashioned person. [from ANTE-, Latin *diluvium* deluge]

**antelope** /**an**-tuh-,lohp/ *n.* (*pl.* same or **-s**) swift-moving deerlike ruminant of Africa and Asia, e.g. the gazelle and gnu. [Greek *antholops*]

**antenatal** /,an-tee-**nay**-tuhl/ *adj.* **1** before birth. **2** of pregnancy.

**antenna** /an-**ten**-uh/ *n.* **1** (*pl.* **-tennae** /-nee/) each of a pair of feelers on the heads of insects, crustaceans, etc. **2** (*pl.* **-s**) = AERIAL *n.* [Latin, = sail-yard]

**anterior** /an-**teer**-ree-uh/ *adj.* **1** nearer the front (opp. POSTERIOR). **2** (often foll. by *to*) earlier, prior. □ **anteriority** /-ree-o-ruh-tee/ *n.* **anteriorly** *adv.* [Latin from *ante* before]

**ante-room** /**an**-tee-,room/ *n.* small room leading to a main one.

**ante-up** *v. colloq.* provide (money) in advance, esp. as a contribution to a collective expense (see also ANTE) (*made a donation of $100 and said he hoped the others would ante-up as well*).

**anthem** /**an**-thuhm/ *n.* **1** elaborate choral composition usu. based on a passage of scripture. **2** solemn hymn of praise etc., esp. = NATIONAL ANTHEM. [Latin: related to ANTIPHON]

**anther** /**an**-thuh/ *n.* part of a stamen containing pollen. [Greek *anthos* flower]

**anthill** *n.* **1** moundlike nest built by ants or termites. **2** a community teeming with people.

**anthill parrot** *n.* (also **antbed parrot**) any of three Australian parrots which make their nests in termites' mounds: the hooded parrot, the golden-shouldered parrot, and the paradise parrot.

**anthology** /an-**thol**-uh-jee/ *n.* (*pl.* **-ies**) collection of poems, essays, stories, etc. □ **anthologise** *v.* (also **-ize**). **anthologist** *n.* [Greek *anthos* flower, *-logia* collection]

**anthouse plant** /**ant**-,hows/ *n.* any of several Queensland epiphytic plants with tall, fleshy stems bearing long, shining leaves and white flowers: the stems spring from bloated bases, honeycombed within with passages which ants use as nests.

**anthracite** /**an**-thruh-,suyt/ *n.* hard type of coal burning with little flame and smoke. [Greek: related to ANTHRAX]

**anthrax** /**an**-thraks/ *n.* disease of sheep and cattle transmissible to humans. [Greek, = coal, carbuncle]

**anthropocentric** /,an-thruh-poh-**sen**-trik/ *adj.* regarding mankind as the centre of existence. [Greek *anthrōpos* man]

**anthropoid** /**an**-thruh-,poid/ — *adj.* **1** resembling a human in form. **2** *colloq.* (of a person) apelike. — *n.* a being that is human in form only, esp. an anthropoid ape.

**anthropology** /,an-thruh-**pol**-uh-jee/ *n.* the study of mankind, esp. its societies and customs. □ **anthropological** /-puh-**loj**-i-kuhl/ *adj.* **anthropologist** *n.*

**anthropomorphism** /ˌan-thruh-puh-**maw**-fiz-uhm/ n. attribution of human characteristics to a god, animal, or thing. □ **anthropomorphic** adj. [Greek morphē form]

**anthropomorphous** /ˌan-thruh-puh-**maw**-fuhs/ adj. human in form.

**anti** /**an**-tee/ — prep. (also absol.) opposed to (he's anti everything; she seems a bit anti to me). — n. (pl. **-s**) person opposed to a particular policy etc.

**anti-** prefix **1** opposed to (anti-nuclear). **2** preventing (antifreeze). **3** opposite of (anticlimax). **4** rival (antipope). **5** unlike the conventional form (anti-hero; anti-novel). **6** Physics antiparticle of a specified particle (antiproton). [Greek]

**anti-aircraft** /ˌan-tee-**air**-krahft/ adj. (of a gun or missile) used to attack enemy aircraft.

**antibiotic** /ˌan-tee-buy-**ot**-ik/ — n. substance (e.g. penicillin) that can inhibit or destroy susceptible micro-organisms. — adj. functioning as an antibiotic. [Greek bios life]

**antibody** /ˌan-tee-**bod**-ee/ n. (pl. **-ies**) a blood protein produced in response to and then counteracting antigens. [translation of German Antikörper]

**antibody negative** adj. not showing antibodies to the Aids virus, and therefore not indicating the presence of the virus in the body.

**antibody positive** adj. showing antibodies to the Aids virus, and therefore indicating the presence of the virus in the body.

**antic** /**an**-tik/ — n. (usu. in pl.) foolish behaviour or action. — adj. archaic grotesque; bizarre. [Italian antico ANTIQUE]

**anticipate** /an-**tis**-uh-ˌpayt/ v. (**-ting**) **1** deal with or use before the proper time (anticipated the vote-counting by claiming victory even before the polls closed). **2** expect, foresee (did not anticipate a problem). **3** forestall (a person or thing). **4** look forward to (eagerly anticipating her arrival). □ **anticipation** /an-ˌtis-uh-**pay**-shuhn/ n. **anticipatory** adj. [Latin anti- before, capio take]

■ **Usage** The use of anticipate in sense 2, 'expect', 'foresee', is well-established in informal use, but is regarded as incorrect by some people.

**anticlimax** /ˌan-tee-**kluy**-maks/ n. disappointingly trivial conclusion to something significant, dramatic, etc., esp. where a climax was expected. □ **anticlimactic** /-**mak**-tik/ adj.

**anticlockwise** /ˌan-tee-**klok**-wuyz/ adj.

& adv. moving in a curve opposite in direction to the hands of a clock.

**anticyclone** /ˌan-tee-**suy**-klohn/ n. system of winds rotating outwards from an area of high pressure, producing fine weather.

**antidepressant** /ˌan-tee-duh-**pres**-uhnt/ — n. drug etc. that alleviates depression. — adj. alleviating depression.

**antidote** /**an**-tee-ˌdoht/ n. **1** medicine etc. used to counteract poison. **2** anything counteracting something unpleasant. [Greek antidotos given against]

**antifreeze** /**an**-tee-ˌfreez/ n. substance added to water to lower its freezing-point, esp. in a vehicle's radiator.

**antigen** /**an**-tuh-juhn/ n. foreign substance (e.g. toxin) which causes the body to produce antibodies. [Greek -genēs of a kind]

**anti-hero** /**an**-tee-ˌheer-roh/ n. (pl. **-es**) central character in a story, lacking conventional heroic qualities.

**antihistamine** /ˌan-tee-**his**-tuh-ˌmeen/ n. drug that counteracts the effects of histamine, used esp. in treating allergies.

**antiknock** /**an**-tee-ˌnok/ n. substance added to motor fuel to prevent premature combustion.

**anti-lock** /**an**-tee-ˌlok/ attrib. adj. (of brakes) set up so as to prevent locking and skidding when applied suddenly.

**antilogarithm** /ˌan-tee-**log**-uh-ˌrith-uhm/ n. number to which a logarithm belongs.

**antimatter** /**an**-tee-ˌmat-uh/ n. Physics matter composed solely of antiparticles.

**antimony** /**an**-tuh-muh-nee/ n. brittle silvery metallic element used esp. in alloys. [medieval Latin]

**antinomy** /an-**tin**-uh-mee/ n. (pl. **-ies**) **1** contradiction between two reasonable beliefs or conclusions. **2** conflict between two laws or authorities.

**anti-novel** /**an**-tee-ˌnov-uhl/ n. novel avoiding the conventions of the form.

**anti-nuclear** /an-tee-**nyoo**-klee-uh/ adj. opposed to the development of nuclear weapons or power.

**antiparticle** /**an**-tee-ˌpah-ti-kuhl/ n. Physics elementary particle having the same mass as a given particle but opposite electric or magnetic properties.

**antipasto** /ˌan-tee-**pas**-toh/ n. (pl. **-s** or **antipasti**) hors d'oeuvre. esp. in an Italian meal. [Italian]

**antipathy** /an-**tip**-uh-thee/ n. (pl. **-ies**) (often foll. by to, for, between) strong or deep-seated aversion or dislike. □ **antipathetic** /ˌan-tee-puh-**thet**-ik/ adj. [Greek: related to PATHETIC]

**antiphon** /**an**-tuh-fuhn, -fon/ n. **1** hymn sung alternately by two groups.

**2** versicle or phrase from this. **3** sentence chanted or said before and after a psalm or canticle, e.g. in matins, vespers, etc. □ **antiphonal** /ˌan-**tif**-uh-nuhl/ adj.

**antiphony** n. [Greek *phōnē* sound]

**antipodean** /an-ˌtip-uh-**dee**-uhn/ — adj. Australian. — n. an Australian.

**antipodes** /an-**tip**-uh-ˌdeez/ n.pl. places diametrically opposite to one another on the earth, esp. (also **Antipodes**) Australasia in relation to Europe. [Greek, = having the feet opposite]

**antipope** /**an**-tee-ˌpohp/ n. pope set up in opposition to one chosen by canon law.

**antiproton** /ˌan-tee-**proh**-ton/ n. *Physics* negatively charged antiparticle of a proton.

**antipyretic** /ˌan-tee-puy-**ret**-ik/ — adj. preventing or reducing fever. — n. antipyretic drug.

**antiquarian** /ˌan-tuh-**kwair**-ree-uhn/ — adj. of or dealing in antiques or rare books. — n. antiquary. □ **antiquarianism** n.

**antiquary** /**an**-tuh-kwuh-ree/ n. (pl. **-ies**) student or collector of antiques etc. [Latin: related to ANTIQUE]

**antiquated** /**an**-tuh-ˌkway-tuhd/ adj. old-fashioned.

**antique** /an-**teek**/ — n. old object, esp. a piece of furniture, of high value. — adj. **1** of or from an early date. **2** old-fashioned. — v. (**antiqued**, **antiquing**) give an antique appearance to (furniture etc.) by artificial means. [Latin *antiquus*]

**antiquity** /an-**tik**-wuh-tee/ n. (pl. **-ies**) **1** ancient times, esp. before the Middle Ages. **2** great age (*a city of great antiquity*). **3** (usu. in *pl.*) relics from ancient times. [Latin: related to ANTIQUE]

**anti-Semite** /ˌan-tee-**sem**-uyt, -**see**-muyt/ n. person who is hostile to or prejudiced against Jews. □ **anti-Semitic** /-suh-**mit**-ik/ adj. **anti-Semitism** /-**sem**-uh-ˌtiz-uhm/ n.

**antiseptic** /ˌan-tee-**sep**-tik/ — adj. **1** counteracting sepsis, esp. by preventing the growth of disease-causing micro-organisms. **2** sterile, uncontaminated. **3** lacking character (*an antiseptic account*). — n. antiseptic agent.

**antiserum** /ˌan-tee-**seer**-ruhm/ n. serum containing antibodies against specific antigens, injected to treat or protect against specific diseases.

**antisocial** /ˌan-tee-**soh**-shuhl/ adj. **1** opposed or harmful to society. **2** not sociable.

**antithesis** /an-**tith**-uh-suhs/ n. (pl. **-theses** /-ˌseez/) **1** (foll. by *of*, *to*) direct opposite (*love is the antithesis of hate*). **2** contrast or opposition between two things (*the antithesis between creationism and evolution*). **3** contrast of ideas expressed by parallelism of strongly contrasted words. □ **antithetic** (**al**) /-**thet**-ik(-uhl)/ adj. [Greek *antitithēmi* set against]

**antitoxin** /ˌan-tee-**tok**-suhn/ n. antibody counteracting a toxin. □ **antitoxic** adj.

**antivenene** /ˌan-tee-vuh-**neen**/ n. (also **antivenin** /-**ven**-uhn/ ) = ANTIVENOM.

**antivenom** n. antiserum containing antibodies against specific poisons in the venom of esp. snakes, spiders, etc. (*funnel-web antivenom*; *tiger snake antivenom*).

**anti-viral** /-**vuy**-ruhl/ adj. effective against viruses.

**anti-virus program** n. *Computing* program designed to prevent or neutralise a virus.

**antler** n. branched horn of a stag or other deer. □ **antlered** adj. [French]

**antonym** /**an**-tuh-nim/ n. word opposite in meaning to another (e.g. *bad* and *good*) (opp. SYNONYM). [Greek *onoma* name]

**antrum** /**an**-truhm/ n. (pl. **antra**) natural cavity in the body, esp. in a bone. [Greek, = cave]

**anus** /**ay**-nuhs/ n. (pl. **anuses**) excretory opening at the end of the alimentary canal. [Latin]

**anvil** /**an**-vuhl/ n. iron block on which metals are worked in forging. [Old English]

**anvil bird** n. = NOISY PITTA.

**anxiety** /ang-**zuy**-uh-tee/ n. (pl. **-ies**) **1** state of being anxious. **2** worry or concern about an imminent danger, difficulty, etc. **3** eagerness, troubled desire (*anxiety for promotion*). **4** thing that causes anxiety (*her children are an anxiety to her*). **5** *Psychol.* nervous disorder characterised by a state of excessive uneasiness. [Latin *anxietas* from *ango* choke]

**anxious** /**angk**-shuhs, **ang**-shuhs/ adj. **1** mentally troubled. **2** causing or marked by anxiety (*anxious moment*). **3** (foll. by *for*, or *to* + infin.) earnestly or uneasily wanting or trying (*anxious for you to succeed*; *anxious to please*). □ **anxiously** adv. [Latin *anxius*]

**any** /**en**-ee/ — adj. **1 a** one, no matter which, of several (*cannot find any answer*). **b** some, no matter how much or many or of what sort (*if any books arrive*; *have you any sugar?*). **2** a minimal amount of (*hardly any difference*). **3** whichever is chosen (*any fool knows*). **4** an appreciable or significant (*did not stay for any length of time*; *has any amount of money*). — *pron.* **1** any one (*did not know any of them*). **2** any number or amount (*are any of them yours?*; *is there any left?*).

— *adv.* (usu. with *neg.* or *interrog.*) at all (*don't make it any larger*; *is that any good?*). [Old English *ænig*: related to ONE, -Y[1]]

**anybody** *n. & pron.* **1** any person. **2** person of importance (*is he anybody?*).

**anyhow** *adv.* **1** anyway. **2** in a disorderly manner or state (*does his work anyhow*).

**anyone** *pron.* anybody.

■ Usage *Anyone* is written as two words to emphasise a numerical sense, as in *any one of us can do it*.

**anything** *pron.* any thing; thing of any sort. □ **anything but** not at all (*was anything but honest*).

**anyway** *adv.* **1** in any way or manner. **2** at any rate. **3** to resume (*anyway, as I was saying*).

**anywhere** — *adv.* in or to any place. — *pron.* any place (*anywhere will do*).

**Anzac** /**an**-zak/ *n.* **1** soldier in the Australian and New Zealand Army Corps who served in the Gallipoli campaign during the First World War. **2** (in general use) an Australian (or New Zealand) soldier or ex-soldier. **3** used emblematically to reflect the traditional view of the virtues displayed by those who served in the Gallipoli campaign, esp. as these are seen as national characteristics (*the spirit of Anzac has not been weakened by the passing years*). **4** (*attrib.*) of or pertaining to the Gallipoli campaign or to the traditions of Anzac (*the Anzac campaign; the Anzac spirit*). [acronym]

**Anzac Day** *n.* April 25, the anniversary of the landing at Anzac Cove in the Gallipoli peninsula of Australian and New Zealand troops: a national public holiday commemorating all Australia's war dead (also *attrib.*: *Anzac Day march*).

**AO** *abbr.* Officer of the Order of Australia.

**aorta** /ay-**aw**-tuh/ *n.* (*pl.* **-s**) main artery, giving rise to the arterial network carrying oxygenated blood to the heart. □ **aortic** *adj.* [Greek *aeirō* raise]

**apace** /uh-**pays**/ *adv. literary* swiftly. [French *à pas*]

**Apache** /uh-**pach**-ee/ *n.* member of a N. American Indian tribe. [Mexican Spanish]

**apart** /uh-**paht**/ *adv.* **1** separately, not together (*keep your feet apart*). **2** in pieces (*came apart; took the clock apart*). **3** to or on one side (*put them apart from the others*). **4** to or at a distance (*a long way apart*). **5** aside (placed after noun: *joking apart, what are my chances?*). □ **apart from 1** excepting, not considering

(*apart from that, what are your objections?*). **2** in addition to (*apart from banksias we grow hakeas*). [French *à part* to one side]

**apartheid** /uh-**pah**-tayt/ *n.* (esp. formerly in S. Africa) racial segregation or discrimination. [Afrikaans]

**apartment** /uh-**paht**-muhnt/ *n.* **1** (in *pl.*) suite of rooms. **2** single room. **3** flat. [Italian *a parte*, apart]

**apathy** /**ap**-uh-thee/ *n.* lack of interest; indifference. □ **apathetic** /ˌap-uh-**thet**-ik/ *adj.* [Greek *a-* without, PATHOS]

**ape** — *n.* **1** tailless monkey-like primate, e.g. the gorilla, chimpanzee, orang-utan, or gibbon. **2** imitator. — *v.* (**-ping**) imitate, mimic (*it's pathetic the way he apes the boss*). □ **go ape** (often foll. by *over*) *colloq.* became crazy or greatly excited (*went ape over the new car*). □ **apelike** *adj.* [Old English]

**aperient** /uh-**peer**-ree-uhnt/ — *adj.* laxative. — *n.* laxative medicine. [Latin *aperio* open]

**aperitif** /uh-ˌpe-ruh-**teef**, uh-pe-ruh-**tif**/ *n.* alcoholic drink taken before a meal to stimulate the appetite. [Latin *aperio* open]

**aperture** /**ap**-uh-chuh/ *n.* opening or gap, esp. a variable opening in a camera for admitting light. [Latin *aperio* open]

**apex[1]** /**ay**-peks/ *n.* (*pl.* **-es** or **apices** /-puh-ˌseez/) **1** highest point. **2** climax; high point of achievement etc. (*at the apex of her career*). **3** vertex of a triangle or cone. **4** tip or pointed end. [Latin]

**apex[2]** /**ay**-peks/ *n.* (often *attrib.*) system of reduced fares for scheduled flights (*apex fare*). [advance purchase excursion]

**aphasia** /uh-**fay**-zee-uh, -*zh*uh/ *n.* loss of verbal understanding or expression, owing to brain damage. [Greek *aphatos* speechless]

**aphelion** /ap-**hee**-lee-uhn, uh-**fee**-lee-uhn/ *n.* (*pl.* **-lia**) point in a celestial body's orbit where it is furthest from the sun. [Greek *aph* ' *hēliou* from the sun]

**aphid** /**ay**-fuhd/ *n.* small insect which sucks sap from leaves, stems, etc., of plants. [back-formation from *aphides*: see APHIS]

**aphis** /**ay**-fuhs/ *n.* (*pl.* **aphides** /-ˌdeez/ ) aphid. [invented by Linnaeus: perhaps a misreading of Greek *koris* bug]

**aphorism** /**af**-uh-ˌriz-uhm/ *n.* short pithy maxim. □ **aphorist** *n.* **aphoristic** /-**ris**-tik/ *adj.* [Greek *aphorismos* definition]

**aphrodisiac** /ˌaf-roh-**diz**-ee-ˌak/ — *adj.* arousing sexual desire. — *n.* aphrodisiac substance. [Greek *Aphroditē* goddess of love]

**apiary** /ay-pee-uh-ree, -pyuh-ree/ *n.* (*pl.* **-ies**) place where bees are kept. □ **apiarist** *n.* [Latin *apis* bee]

**apical** /ay-pi-kuhl, ap-i-kuhl/ *adj.* of, at, or forming an apex.

**apiculture** /ay-pee-,kul-chuh/ *n.* bee-keeping. □ **apiculturist** /-kulch-uh-ruhst/ *n.* [Latin *apis* bee, CULTURE]

**apiece** /uh-pees/ *adv.* for each one; severally (*five dollars apiece*). [originally *a piece*]

**apish** /ay-pish/ *adj.* **1** of or like an ape. **2** foolishly imitating.

**aplomb** /uh-plom/ *n.* self-assurance; self-confidence. [French, = straight as a plummet]

**apocalypse** /uh-pok-uh-lips/ *n.* **1** violent or destructive event. **2** (**the Apocalypse**) Revelation, the last book of the New Testament. **3** revelation, esp. about the end of the world. □ **apocalyptic** /uh-,pok-uh-lip-tik/ *adj.* [Greek *apokaluptō* reveal]

**Apocrypha** /uh-pok-ruh-fuh/ *n.pl.* **1** books included in the Septuagint and Vulgate versions of the Old Testament but not in the Hebrew Bible. **2** (**apocrypha**) writings etc. not considered genuine. [Greek *apokruptō* hide away]

**apocryphal** *adj.* **1** of doubtful authenticity. **2** invented; mythical (*that story about him is surely apocryphal*).

**apogee** /ap-uh-,jee/ *n.* **1** highest point; climax. **2** point in a celestial body's orbit where it is furthest from the earth. [Greek *apogeion*]

**apolitical** /,ay-puh-lit-i-kuhl/ *adj.* not interested in or concerned with politics.

**apologetic** /uh-,pol-uh-jet-ik/ — *adj.* **1** showing or expressing regret. **2** diffident. **3** of reasoned defence or vindication. — *n.* (usu. in *pl.*) reasoned defence, esp. of Christianity. □ **apologetically** *adv.*

**apologia** /,ap-uh-loh-jee-uh/ *n.* formal defence of opinions or conduct. [Greek: see APOLOGY]

**apologise** /uh-pol-uh-,juyz/ *v.* (also **-ize**) (**-sing** or **-zing**) make an apology, express regret.

**apologist** /uh-pol-uh-juhst/ *n.* person who defends something by argument.

**apology** /uh-pol-uh-jee/ *n.* (*pl.* **-ies**) **1** statement of regret for an offence or failure. **2** explanation or defence. **3** (foll. by *for*) poor specimen of (*this apology for a letter*). [Greek *apologia* from *apologeomai* speak in defence]

**apophthegm** /ap-uh-,them/ *n.* = APHORISM. [Latin from Greek]

**apoplectic** /,ap-uh-plek-tik/ *adj.* **1** of or causing apoplexy. **2** *colloq.* enraged.

**apoplexy** /ap-uh-,plek-see/ *n.* sudden paralysis caused by blockage or rupture of a brain artery; stroke. [Greek *apoplēssō* disable by stroke]

**apostasy** /uh-pos-tuh-see/ *n.* (*pl.* **-ies**) renunciation of a belief or faith, abandoning of principles, etc. [Greek, = defection]

**apostate** /uh-pos-tayt/ *n.* person who renounces a former belief etc. □ **apostatise** *v.* (also **-ize**) (**-sing** or **-zing**).

**a posteriori** /,ay pos-,teer-ree-aw-ruy/ — *adj.* (of reasoning) proceeding from effects to causes; inductive, empirical (cf. A PRIORI). — *adv.* inductively. [Latin, = from what comes after]

**apostle¹** /uh-pos-uhl/ *n.* **1** (**Apostle**) any of the twelve men sent out by Christ to preach the gospel. **2** leader or outstanding figure, esp. of a new movement (*apostle of workers' rights*). [Greek *apostolos* messenger]

**apostle²** *n.* (also **apostle bird**) **1** = LOUSY JACK. **2** = HAPPY JACK.

**apostolic** /,ap-uh-stol-ik/ *adj.* **1** of the Apostles or their teaching. **2** of the Pope (*the Apostolic See*).

**apostolic succession** *n.* uninterrupted transmission of spiritual authority from the Apostles through successive popes and bishops.

**apostrophe** /uh-pos-truh-fee/ *n.* **1** punctuation mark (') indicating omission of letters or numbers, or possessive case (see panel). **2** exclamatory passage addressed to (an often absent) person or thing. □ **apostrophise** *v.* (also **-ize**) (**-sing** or **-zing**) (in sense 2). [Greek, = turning away]

**apothecary** /uh-poth-uh-kuh-ree, -kree/ *n.* (*pl.* **-ies**) *archaic* dispensing chemist. [Greek *apothēkē* storehouse]

**apotheosis** /uh-,poth-ee-oh-suhs/ *n.* (*pl.* **-theoses** /-seez/) **1** elevation to divine status, deification. **2** glorification of a thing; sublime example (*he is the apotheosis of chivalry*). [Greek *theos* god]

**appal** /uh-pawl/ *v.* (**-ll-**) **1** greatly dismay or horrify. **2** (as **appalling** *adj.*) *colloq.* very bad, shocking. [French *apalir* grow pale: related to PALE¹]

**apparatus** /,ap-uh-rah-tuhs, -ray-/ *n.* **1** equipment for a particular function, esp. scientific or technical. **2** political or other complex organisation (*the Labor apparatus vs. the Liberal machine*). [Latin *paro* prepare]

**apparel** /uh-pa-ruhl/ *n.* *formal* clothing, dress. □ **apparelled** *adj.* [Romanic, = make fit, from Latin *par* equal]

**apparent** /uh-pa-ruhnt/ *adj.* **1** readily visible; obvious (*pinpricks of green are* *now apparent where the seeds are starting to sprout; surely my meaning is apparent*). **2** seeming (*the earth's apparent fixity and the sun's apparent motion*). □ **apparently** *adv.* [Latin: related to APPEAR]

**apparition** /ˌap-uh-**rish**-uhn/ *n.* remarkable or unexpected thing that appears; ghost or phantom.

**appeal** /uh-**peel**/ — *v.* **1** request earnestly or formally; plead (*appealed for calm*; *appealed for donations*). **2** (usu. foll. by *to*) attract, be of interest (*the idea of Australia as a Republic appeals to us greatly*). **3** (foll. by *to*) resort to for support (*I appeal to the Oxford English Dictionary — you will find that it supports me completely*). **4** *Law* **a** (often foll. by *to*) apply (to a higher court) for reconsideration of a legal decision. **b** refer (a case) to a higher court. **5** *Cricket* call on the umpire to declare whether a batsman is out. — *n.* **1** act or instance of appealing. **2** request for public support, esp. financial (*doorknock appeal*). **3** *Law* referral of a case to a higher court. **4** attractiveness (*sex appeal*). [Latin *appello* address]

**appear** /uh-**peer**/ *v.* **1** become or be visible (*at last! — the sun appears*). **2** be evident (*a new problem then appeared*). **3** seem; have the appearance of being (*appeared unwell; you appear to be right*).

**4** present oneself publicly or formally, esp. on stage or as the accused or counsel in a lawcourt. **5** be published (*a new edition will appear*). [Latin *appareo*]

**appearance** /uh-**peer**-ruhns/ *n.* **1** act or instance of appearing. **2** outward form as perceived (whether correctly or not) (*appearance of prosperity*). **3** semblance (*cultivates the appearance of virtue*). □ **keep up appearances** maintain an impression or pretence of virtue, affluence, etc. **make** (or **put in**) **an appearance** be present, esp. briefly. **to all appearances** as far as can be seen; apparently.

**appease** /uh-**peez**/ *v.* (**-sing**) **1** make calm or quiet, esp. conciliate (a potential aggressor) by making concessions. **2** satisfy (an appetite, scruples). □ **appeasement** *n.* [French *à to, pais* PEACE]

**appellant** /uh-**pel**-uhnt/ *n.* person who appeals to a higher court. [Latin *appello* address]

**appellate** /uh-**pel**-uht/ *attrib. adj.* (esp. of a court) concerned with appeals.

**appellation** /ˌap-uh-**lay**-shuhn/ *n. formal* name or title; nomenclature.

**append** /uh-**pend**/ *v.* (usu. foll. by *to*) attach, affix, add, esp. to a written document. [Latin *appendo* hang]

**appendage** /uh-**pen**-dij/ *n.* thing attached; addition.

**appendectomy** /ˌap-en-**dek**-tuh-mee/ *n.* (also **appendicectomy** /-duh-**sek**-tuh-

---

**Apostrophe** '
This is used:
**1** to indicate possession:
with a singular noun:
  *a boy's book*; *a week's work*; *the boss's salary*.
with a plural already ending with s:
  *a girls' school*; *two weeks' newspapers*; *the bosses' salaries*.
with a plural not already ending with s:
  *the children's shoes*; *women's liberation*.
with a singular name:
  *Gavin's hat*; *Louise's coat*; *Thomas's* (or *Thomas'* ) *book*; *Keats' poems*.
with a name ending in -es that is pronounced -uhz:
  *Bridges' poems*: *Moses' mother*
and before the word sake:
  *for God's sake*; *for goodness' sake*; *for Nicholas' sake*.
but it is often omitted in a business or place name:
  *Smiths Bookshop*; *Crows Nest*.
**2** to mark an omission of one or more letters or numbers:
  *he's* (*he is* or *he has*)    *haven't* (*have not*)
  *can't* (*cannot*)    *we'll* (*we shall*)
  *won't* (*will not*)    *o'clock* (*of the clock*)
  *the summer of '68* (1968)
**3** when letters or numbers are referred to in plural form:
  *mind your p's and q's*; *find all the number 7's*.
  but it is unnecessary in, e.g.,
  *MPs*; *the 1940s*

mee/ ) (*pl.* **-ies**) surgical removal of the appendix. [from APPENDIX, -ECTOMY]

**appendicitis** /uh-,pen-duh-**suy**-tuhs/ *n.* inflammation of the appendix.

**appendix** /uh-**pen**-diks/ *n.* (*pl.* **-dices** /-duh-,seez/ ) **1** tissue forming a tube-shaped sac attached to the large intestine. **2** subsidiary matter at the end of a book etc. [Latin: related to APPEND]

**appertain** /,ap-uh-**tayn**/ *v.* (foll. by *to*) relate, belong, or be appropriate. [Latin: related to PERTAIN]

**appetiser** /**ap**-uh-,tuy-zuh/ *n.* (also **-izer**) small amount, esp. of food or drink, to stimulate the appetite.

**appetising** *adj.* (also **-izing**) stimulating the appetite, esp. for food; tasty.

**appetite** /**ap**-uh-,tuyt/ *n.* **1** natural craving, esp. for food or sexual activity. **2** (usu. foll. by *for*) inclination or desire. [Latin *peto* seek]

**applaud** /uh-**plawd**/ *v.* **1** express strong approval, esp. by clapping. **2** commend, approve (a person or action) (*we applaud this initiative*). [Latin *applaudo* clap hands]

**applause** /uh-**plawz**/ *n.* **1** approval shown by clapping the hands. **2** warm approval.

**apple** /**ap**-uhl/ *n.* **1 a** roundish firm fruit with crisp flesh. **b** tree bearing this. **2** any of several Australian trees or shrubs thought by early settlers to resemble an apple or apple tree (*apple box; apple bush; apple gum*), esp. trees of the genus *Angophora* (*broad-leaved apple; dwarf apple; rough-barked apple; smooth-barked apple*). □ **apple of one's eye** cherished person or thing. [Old English]

**apple berry** *n.* = APPLE DUMPLING.

**apple dumpling** *n.* (also **billardiera, purple apple-berry**) Australian climber bearing tubular cream flowers followed by fleshy, dumpling-like, edible fruit, and often used in garden cultivation.

**Apple Isle** *n.* (also **Apple Island**) Tasmania, so called because of its identification as an apple-growing region. □ **Apple Islander** *n.*

**apples** *n.pl.* □ **she's apples** (or **she'll be apples**) *colloq.* everything is (or will be) fine. [elliptical use of rhyming slang *apples and spice* nice]

**appliance** /uh-**pluy**-uhns/ *n.* device etc. for a specific (esp. household) task. [related to APPLY]

**applicable** /**ap**-lik-uh-buhl, uh-**plik**-uh-buhl/ *adj.* (often foll. by *to*) that may be applied; relevant; appropriate. □ **applicability** /-**bil**-uh-tee/ *n.* **applicably** *adv.* [medieval Latin: related to APPLY]

**applicant** /**ap**-luh-kuhnt/ *n.* person who applies for something, esp. a job.

**application** /,ap-luh-**kay**-shuhn/ *n.* **1** formal request, usu. in writing, for employment, membership, etc. **2** act of applying, esp. medical ointment etc. to the skin. **3** substance applied. **4 a** relevance (*this has no application to the present circumstances*). **b** use (*has many applications*). **5** sustained or concentrated effort; diligence (*he lacks application*).

**applicator** /**ap**-luh-,kay-tuh/ *n.* device for applying ointment etc.

**applied** /uh-**pluyd**/ *adj.* practical, not merely theoretical (*applied science*).

**appliqué** /**ap**-luh-kay/ — *n.* cutting out of fabric patterns and attaching them to another fabric. — *v.* (**-qués, -quéd, -quéing**) decorate with appliqué. [French, = applied]

**apply** /uh-**pluy**/ *v.* (**-ies, -ied**) **1** (often foll. by *for, to*, or *to* + infin.) formally request (*applied for the job*). **2** be relevant (*does not apply in this case*). **3 a** make use of; employ (*apply the rules; apply common sense*). **b** operate (*apply the brakes*). **4** (often foll. by *to*) put or spread on (*asked me to apply goanna oil to the cut, but I jibbed*). **5** *refl.* (often foll. by *to*) devote oneself (*applied myself to the task*). [Latin *applico* fasten to]

**appoggiatura** /uh-poj-uh-**tyoor**-ruh/ *n. Mus.* grace-note performed before an essential note of a melody and normally taking half its time-value. [Italian]

**appoint** /uh-**point**/ *v.* **1** assign a job or office to. **2** (often foll. by *for*) fix (a time, place, etc.) (*Wednesday was appointed for the meeting*). **3** (as **appointed** *adj.*) equipped, furnished (*well-appointed*). [French *à point* to a point]

**appointee** /uh-,poin-**tee**/ *n.* person appointed.

**appointment** *n.* **1** act or instance of appointing or being appointed. **2** arrangement for meeting or consultation. **3 a** post or office open to applicants or recently filled (*took up the appointment on Monday*). **b** person appointed. **4** (usu. in *pl.*) furniture, fittings; equipment.

**apportion** /uh-**paw**-shuhn/ *v.* (often foll. by *to*) share out; assign as a share (*apportioned the blame*). □ **apportionment** *n.* [medieval Latin: related to PORTION]

**apposite** /**ap**-uh-zuht/ *adj.* (often foll. by *to*) apt, appropriate; well expressed (*made a few apposite remarks*). [Latin *appono* apply]

**apposition** /,ap-uh-**zish**-uhn/ *n.* **1** juxtaposition. **2** *Gram.* placing of a word next to another, esp. the addition of one noun to another, in order to qualify or explain the first (e.g. *William the Conqueror*; *my friend Sue*). □ **appositional** *adj.*

**appraise** /uh-**prayz**/ *v.* (**-sing**) estimate the value or quality of. □ **appraisal** *n.* [earlier *apprize*, assimilated to PRAISE]

**appreciable** /uh-**pree**-shuh-buhl/ *adj.* significant, considerable (*made an appreciable difference*). [French: related to APPRECIATE]

**appreciate** /uh-**pree**-shee-ayt, -see-,ayt/ *v.* (**-ting**) **1 a** esteem highly; value. **b** be grateful for (*we appreciate your sympathy*). **2** understand, recognise (*appreciate the danger*). **3** (of property etc.) rise or raise in value. □ **appreciative** /-shuh-tiv/ *adj.* **appreciatory** /-shuh-tree/ *adj.* [Latin *pretium* price]

**appreciation** /uh-,pree-shee-**ay**-shuhn, uh-,pree-see-/ *n.* **1** favourable or grateful recognition. **2 a** sensitive estimation or judgment (*wrote an appreciation of her work*). **b** understanding of or reaction to (*a quick appreciation of the problem*). **3** rise in value. [French: related to APPRECIATE]

**apprehend** /,ap-ruh-**hend**/ *v.* **1** seize, arrest. **2** understand, perceive (*apprehend your meaning*). **3** anticipate with uneasiness or fear (*apprehending the results*). [Latin *prehendo* grasp]

**apprehensible** /,ap-ruh-**hen**-suh-buhl/ *adj.* capable of being understood by the senses or the intellect.

**apprehension** /,ap-ruh-**hen**-shuhn/ *n.* **1** uneasiness, dread. **2** understanding. **3** arrest, capture.

**apprehensive** /,ap-ruh-**hen**-siv/ *adj.* uneasily fearful. □ **apprehensively** *adv.*

**apprentice** /uh-**pren**-tuhs/ — *n.* **1** person learning a trade etc. by working in it for an agreed period. **2** novice. — *v.* (**-cing**) (usu. foll. by *to*) engage as an apprentice (*apprenticed to a builder*). □ **apprenticeship** *n.* [French *apprendre* learn]

**apprise** /uh-**pruyz**/ *v.* (**-sing**) *formal* inform. □ **be apprised of** be aware of. [French *appris(e)* learnt, taught]

**appro** /**ap**-roh/ *n. colloq.* □ **on appro** = *on approval* (see APPROVAL). [abbreviation]

**approach** /uh-**prohch**/ — *v.* **1** come near or nearer (to) in space or time (*approached the city*; *the hour approaches*). **2** make a tentative proposal or suggestion to (*approached me about a loan*). **3** be similar or approximate to (*doesn't approach her in talent*; *a population approaching 5 million*). **4** set about (a task etc.) (*approached the cleaning-up with dread*). — *n.* **1** act or

means of approaching (*made an approach*; *they lined the approach to parliament*). **2** approximation (*an approach to an apology*). **3** technique (*try a new approach*). **4** *Golf* stroke from the fairway to the green. **5** *Aeron.* part of a flight before landing. [Latin *prope* near]

**approachable** *adj.* **1** friendly, easy to talk to. **2** able to be approached.

**approbation** /,ap-ruh-**bay**-shuhn/ *n.* approval, consent. □ **approbative** *adj.* **approbatory** *adj.* [Latin *probo* test]

**appropriate** — *adj.* /uh-**proh**-pree-uht/ suitable, proper (*appropriate for evening wear*). — *v.* /uh-**proh**-pree-,ayt/ (**-ting**) **1** take, esp. without authority. **2** devote (money etc.) to special purposes (*appropriated funds for AIDS research*). □ **appropriately** *adv.* **appropriation** /uh-,proh-pree-**ay**-shuhn/ *n.* [Latin *proprius* own]

**approval** /uh-**proo**-vuhl/ *n.* **1** act of approving. **2** instance of this; consent; favourable opinion (*with your approval*; *he looked on him with approval*). □ **on approval** (of goods supplied) returnable if not satisfactory.

**approve** /uh-**proov**/ *v.* (**-ving**) **1** confirm, sanction (*approved the application*). **2** (often foll. by *of*) regard with favour (*I don't approve of smoking*). [Latin *probo* test]

**approx.** *abbr.* approximate(ly).

**approximate** — *adj.* /uh-**prok**-suh-muht/ fairly correct, near to the actual (*approximate price*). — *v.* /uh-**prok**-suh-,mayt/ (**-ting**) (often foll. by *to*) bring or come near (esp. in quality, number, etc.) (*approximates to the truth*). □ **approximately** *adv.* **approximation** /-**may**-shuhn/ *n.* [Latin *proximus* nearest]

**appurtenance** /uh-**per**-tuh-nuhns/ *n.* (usu. in *pl.*) belonging; accessory (*the appurtenances of his trade*). [Latin *pertineo* belong to]

**après-ski** /,ap-ray-**skee**/ — *n.* social activities following a day's skiing. — *attrib. adj.* (of clothes, drinks, etc.) suitable for these. [French]

**apricot** /**ay**-pree-,kot, **ay**-pruh-,kot/ — *n.* **1 a** small juicy soft orange-yellow peachlike fruit. **b** tree bearing it. **2** its colour. — *adj.* orange-yellow. [Portuguese and Spanish from Arabic, ultimately from Latin *praecox* early-ripe]

**April** /**ay**-pruhl/ *n.* fourth month of the year. [Latin]

**April Fool** *n.* person successfully tricked on 1 April.

**a priori** /,ay pruy-**aw**-ruy, pree-, -ree/ — *adj.* **1** (of reasoning) proceeding from causes to effects; deductive (cf. A POSTERIORI). **2** (of concepts etc.) logically independent of experience; not derived from experience (opp. EMPIRICAL). **3** assumed without investigation (*an a priori conjecture*). — *adv.* **1** deductively. **2** as far as one knows; presumptively. [Latin, = from what is before]

**apron** /**ay**-pruhn/ *n.* **1** garment for covering and protecting the front of the clothes. **2** *Theatr.* part of a stage in front of the curtain. **3** area on an airfield for manoeuvring or loading. □ **tied to a person's apron strings** dominated by or dependent on that person (usu. a woman). [originally *napron*, from French *nape* table-cloth]

**apropos** /**ap**-ruh-,poh, -**poh**/ — *adj.* **1** to the point; appropriate (*her comment was apropos*). **2** *colloq.* (often foll. by *of*) in respect of (*apropos the meeting*). — *adv.* **1** appropriately (*spoke apropos*). **2** (*absol.*) incidentally (*apropos, she's not going*). [French *à propos*]

**apse** /aps/ *n.* large arched or domed recess, esp. at the end of a church. [related to APSIS]

**apsis** /**ap**-suhs/ *n.* (*pl.* **apsides** /-suh-,deez/) either of two points on the orbit of a planet etc. nearest to or furthest from the body round which it moves. [Greek (*h*)*apsis* arch, vault]

**apt** *adj.* **1** appropriate, suitable. **2** having a tendency (*apt to break down*). **3** clever; quick to learn (*an apt pupil*). [Latin *aptus* fitted]

**apteryx** /**ap**-tuh-riks/ *n.* = KIWI. [Greek *a-* without, *pterux* wing]

**aptitude** /**ap**-tuh-,tyood/ *n.* **1** natural talent (*shows an aptitude for drawing*). **2** ability or fitness, esp. specified (*has no sporting aptitude whatever*). [French: related to APT]

**aqua** /**ak**-wuh/ *n.* the colour aquamarine. [abbreviation]

**aqualung** /**ak**-wuh-,lung/ *n.* portable breathing-apparatus for divers, consisting of cylinders of compressed air, strapped on the back, feeding air automatically through a mask or mouthpiece. [Latin *aqua* water]

**aquamarine** /,ak-wuh-muh-**reen**/ — *n.* **1** bluish-green beryl. **2** its colour. — *adj.* bluish-green. [Latin *aqua marina* sea water]

**aquanaut** /**ak**-wuh-,nawt/ *n.* underwater swimmer or explorer. [Latin *aqua* water, Greek *nautēs* sailor]

**aquaplane** /**ak**-wuh-,playn/ — *n.* board for riding on water, pulled by a speedboat. — *v.* (**-ning**) **1** ride on this.

**2** (of a vehicle) glide uncontrollably on a wet surface. [Latin *aqua* water, PLANE¹]

**aqua regia** /,ak-wuh **ree**-jee-uh/ *n.* highly corrosive mixture of acids, attacking many substances unaffected by other reagents. [Latin, = royal water]

**aquarium** /uh-**kwair**-ree-uhm/ *n.* (*pl.* **-s**) **1** tank of water for keeping and showing fish etc. **2** building containing a number of these for study, exhibition, etc. [Latin *aquarius* of water]

**Aquarius** /uh-**kwair**-ree-uhs/ *n.* (*pl.* **-es**) **1** constellation and eleventh sign of the zodiac (the Water-carrier). **2** person born when the sun is in this sign. [Latin: related to AQUARIUM]

**aquathon** /**ak**-wuh-,thon/ *n.* endurance event consisting of swimming, running, board paddling, etc. [Latin *aqua* water, -ATHON]

**aquatic** /uh-**kwot**-ik/ — *adj.* **1** growing or living in water. **2** (of a sport) played in or on water. — *n.* **1** aquatic plant or animal. **2** (in *pl.*) aquatic sports. [Latin *aqua* water]

**aqua vitae** /,ak-wuh **vee**-tay/ *n.* strong alcoholic spirit, esp. brandy. [Latin, = water of life]

**aqueduct** /**ak**-wuh-,dukt/ *n.* artificial channel for conveying water, esp. a bridge on columns across a valley. [Latin *aquae ductus* conduit]

**aqueous** /**ay**-kwee-uhs, **ak**-wee-/ *adj.* **1** of or like water. **2** *Geol.* produced by water (*aqueous rocks*). [Latin *aqua* water]

**aqueous humour** *n.* clear fluid in the eye between the lens and the cornea.

**aquiline** /**ak**-wuh-,luyn/ *adj.* **1** of or like an eagle. **2** (of a nose) curved like an eagle's beak. [Latin *aquila* eagle]

**Ar** *symb.* argon.

**-ar¹** *suffix* **1** forming adjectives (*angular; linear; nuclear*). **2** forming nouns (*scholar*). [Latin *-aris*]

**-ar²** *suffix* forming nouns (*pillar*). [Latin *-ar, -are,* neuter of *-aris*]

**-ar³** *suffix* forming nouns (*bursar; mortar; vicar*). [Latin *-arius, -arium*]

**-ar⁴** *suffix* assim. form of -ER¹, -OR (*liar; pedlar*).

**Arab** /**a**-ruhb/ — *n.* **1** member of a Semitic people originating in Saudi Arabia and neighbouring countries, now widespread throughout the Middle East. **2** horse of a breed orig. native to Arabia. — *adj.* of Arabia or the Arabs (esp. with ethnic reference). [Arabic *araps*]

**Arabana** /u-ru-bun-u/ *n.* an Aboriginal language spoken over a vast area west of Lake Eyre in the north-eastern region of SA: now extinct.

**arabesque** /ˌa-ruh-**besk**/ *n.* **1** *Ballet* posture with one leg extended horizontally backwards and arms outstretched. **2** design of intertwined leaves, scrolls, etc. **3** *Mus.* florid piece. [French from Italian from *arabo* Arab]

**Arabian** /uh-**ray**-bee-uhn/ — *adj.* of or relating to Arabia (esp. in geographical contexts)(*Arabian desert*). — *n.* native of Arabia.

■ **Usage** In the sense 'native of Arabia', the usual term is now *Arab*.

**Arabic** /a-ruh-bik/ — *n.* Semitic language of the Arabs. — *adj.* of the Arabs (esp. their language or literature).

**arabic numeral** *n.* any of the numerals 0-9.

**arable** /a-ruh-buhl/ *adj.* (of land) suitable for crop production. [Latin *aro* to plough]

**arachnid** /uh-**rak**-nid/ *n.* arthropod of a class comprising spiders, scorpions, etc., having four pairs of walking legs. [Greek *arakhnē* spider]

**arachnophobia** /uh-**rak**-nuh-ˌfoh-bee-uh/ *n.* abnormal fear of spiders. [Greek *arakhnē* spider, -PHOBIA]

**arak** var. of ARRACK (esp. in the Middle East).

**Aramaic** /ˌa-ruh-**may**-ik/ — *n.* branch of the Semitic family of languages, esp. the language of Syria used as a lingua franca in SW Asia from the sixth century BC. — *adj.* of or in Aramaic. [Greek *Aramaios* of Aram (Hebrew name of Syria)]

**Aranda** /u-**run**-tu, **a**-ruhn-du/ *n.* (also **Arrernte**) an Aboriginal language still spoken over 200,000 square kilometres in the southern part of the NT (just extending into SA and Queensland) which includes Alice Springs.

**arbiter** /**ah**-buh-tuh/ *n.* **1** arbitrator in a dispute. **2** person influential in a specific field (*arbiter of taste*). **3** person who has entire control of something. [Latin from *arbitror* to judge]

**arbitrary** /**ah**-buh-truh-ree, -tree/ *adj.* **1** based on or derived from uninformed opinion or random choice; capricious (*their interpretation is purely arbitrary*). **2** despotic (*the government's action has been arbitrary and harsh*). □ **arbitrarily** *adv.* **arbitrariness** *n.*

**arbitrate** /**ah**-buh-ˌtrayt/ *v.* (**-ting**) decide by arbitration.

**arbitration** /ˌah-buh-**tray**-shuhn/ *n.* settlement of a dispute by an impartial third party. □ **arbitral** *adj.*

**arbitration award** *n.* determination made by a court of industrial arbitration.

**arbitration court** *n.* tribunal for the resolution of industrial disputes etc.

**arbitration system** *n.* organisation and method of resolving industrial disputes, determining industrial awards, etc.

**arbitrator** *n.* person appointed to arbitrate.

**arbor**[1] /**ah**-buh/ *n.* axle or spindle. [Latin, = tree]

**arbor**[2] var. of ARBOUR.

**arboreal** /ah-**baw**-ree-uhl/ *adj.* of or living in trees. [Latin *arbor* tree]

**arboriculture** /uh-**bo**-ree-ˌkul-chuh/ *n.* cultivation of trees and shrubs. [Latin *arbor* tree, after *agriculture*]

**arbour** /**ah**-buh/ *n.* (also **arbor**) shady garden alcove enclosed by trees etc. [Latin *herba* herb: assimilated to Latin *arbor* tree]

**ARC** *abbr.* = AIDS-RELATED COMPLEX.

**arc** — *n.* **1** part of the circumference of a circle or other curve. **2** *Electr.* luminous discharge between two electrodes. — *v.* (**arced**; **arcing** /**ah**-king/ ) form an arc; move in a curve. [Latin *arcus* bow]

**arcade** /ah-**kayd**/ *n.* **1** covered walk, esp. lined with shops. **2** series of arches supporting or set along a wall. [Romanic: related to ARC]

**Arcadian** /ah-**kay**-dee-uhn/ — *n.* idealised country dweller. — *adj.* poetically rural. [Greek *Arkadia* in the Peloponnese]

**arcane** /ah-**kayn**/ *adj.* mysterious, secret. [Latin *arceo* shut up]

**arch**[1] — *n.* **1** curved structure as an opening, as a support for a bridge, floor, etc., or as an ornament. **2** any arch-shaped curve. — *v.* **1** provide with or form into an arch. **2** span like an arch (*rainbow arching across the sky*). **3** form an arch. [Latin *arcus* arc]

**arch**[2] *adj.* self-consciously or affectedly playful (*a manner sickeningly arch*). □ **archly** *adv.* [from ARCH-, originally in *arch rogue* etc.]

**arch-** *comb. form* **1** chief, superior (*archbishop*). **2** pre-eminent, esp. unfavourably (*arch-enemy*). [Greek *arkhos* chief]

**Archaean** /ah-**kee**-uhn/ — *adj.* of the earliest geological era. — *n.* this time. [Greek *arkhaios* ancient]

**archaeology** /ˌah-kee-**ol**-uh-jee/ *n.* (also **archeology**) study of ancient cultures, esp. by the excavation and analysis of physical remains. □ **archaeological** /-**loj**-i-kuhl/ *adj.* **archaeologist** *n.* [Greek *arkhaiologia* ancient history]

**archaeopteryx** /ˌah-kee-**op**-tuh-riks/ *n.* fossil bird with teeth, feathers, and a reptilian tail. [Greek *arkhaios* ancient, *pterux* wing]

**archaic** /ah-**kay**-ik/ *adj.* **1 a** antiquated. **b** (of a word etc.) no longer in ordinary use. **2** of an early period of culture. □ **archaically** *adv.* [Greek *arkhē* beginning]

**archaism** /**ah**-kay-,iz-uhm/ *n.* **1** use of the archaic esp. in language or art. **2** archaic word or expression. □ **archaistic** /-**is**-tik/ *adj.*

**archangel** /**ahk**-,ayn-juhl/ *n.* angel of the highest rank.

**archbishop** /,ahch-**bish**-uhp/ *n.* bishop of the highest rank.

**archdeacon** /,ahch-**dee**-kuhn/ *n.* Anglican cleric ranking below a bishop. □ **archdeaconry** *n.* (*pl.* **-ies**).

**archdiocese** /,ahch-**duy**-uh-suhs/ *n.* diocese of an archbishop. □ **archdiocesan** /,ahch-duy-**os**-uh-suhn/ *adj.*

**arch-enemy** /,ahch-**en**-uh-mee/ *n.* (*pl.* **-ies**) **1** chief enemy. **2** the Devil.

**archer** *n.* **1** person who shoots with a bow and arrows. **2** (**the Archer**) zodiacal sign or constellation Sagittarius. [Latin *arcus* bow]

**archer-fish** *n.* fish of Queensland and elsewhere that catches flying insects by shooting water at them from its mouth.

**archery** *n.* shooting with a bow and arrows, esp. as a sport.

**archetype** /**ah**-kuh-,tuyp/ *n.* **1** original model; prototype. **2** typical specimen (*he's the archetype of the little Aussie battler*). □ **archetypal** /-**tuy**-puhl/ *adj.* [Greek *tupon* stamp]

**archimandrite** /,ah-kee-man-druyt/ *n.* **1** superior of a large monastery in the Orthodox Church. **2** honorary title of a monastic priest. [Greek *arkhi-* chief, *mandritēs* monk]

**archipelago** /,ah-kuh-**pel**-uh-,goh/ *n.* (*pl.* **-s**) **1** group of islands. **2** sea with many islands. [Greek *arkhi-* chief, *pelagos* sea]

**architect** /**ah**-kuh-,tekt/ *n.* **1** designer of buildings etc., supervising their construction. **2** (foll. by *of*) person who brings about a specified thing (*architect of peace*). [Greek *arkhi-* chief, *tektōn* builder]

**architecture** /**ah**-kuh-,tek-chuh/ *n.* **1** design and construction of buildings. **2** style of a building. **3** buildings etc. collectively. **4** *Computing* conceptual structure and overall organisation of a computer. □ **architectural** /-**tek**-chuh-ruhl/ *adj.*

**architrave** /**ah**-kuh-,trayv/ *n.* **1** (in classical architecture) main beam resting across the tops of columns. **2** moulded frame around a doorway or window. [Italian *archi-* ARCH-, Latin *trabs* beam]

**archive** /**ah**-kuyv/ — *n.* (usu. in *pl.*) **1** collection of documents or records. **2** store for these. — *v.* (**-ving**) **1** place or store in an archive. **2** *Computing* transfer (data) to a less frequently used file. [Greek *arkheia* public records]

**archivist** /**ah**-kuh-vuhst/ *n.* keeper of archives.

**archway** *n.* arched entrance or passage.

**arc lamp** *n.* (also **arc light**) light using an electric arc.

**Arctic** /**ahk**-tik/ — *adj.* **1** of the north polar regions. **2** (**arctic**) *colloq.* very cold. — *n.* Arctic regions. [Greek *arktos* Great Bear]

**Arctic Circle** *n.* parallel of latitude 66° 33′ N, forming an imaginary line round the Arctic region.

**ardent** /**ah**-duhnt/ *adj.* eager, fervent, passionate (*ardent desire*). □ **ardently** *adv.* [Latin *ardeo* burn]

**ardour** /**ah**-duh/ *n.* (also **ardor**) zeal, enthusiasm, passion.

**arduous** /**ah**-dyoo-uhs/ *adj.* **1** hard to accomplish; laborious, strenuous. **2** steep, difficult (*an arduous climb*). [Latin, = steep]

**are**[1] *2nd sing. present & 1st, 2nd, 3rd pl. present of* BE.

**are**[2] /ah/ *n.* metric unit of measure, 100 square metres. [Latin: related to AREA]

**area** /**air**-ree-uh/ *n.* **1** extent or measure of a surface (*over a large area*). **2** region (*southern area*). **3** space for a specific purpose (*dining area*). **4** scope or range of an activity or study (*working in the area of Aboriginal linguistics*). [Latin, = vacant space]

**arena** /uh-**ree**-nuh/ *n.* **1** central part of an amphitheatre etc. where the contests take place. **2** scene of conflict; sphere of action or discussion (*the arena of war; the arena of politics*). [Latin, = sand]

**aren't** /ahnt/ *contr.* **1** are not. **2** (in *interrog.*) am not (*aren't I coming too?*).

**areola** /uh-**reer**-luh/ *n.* (*pl.* **-lae** /-lee/) circular pigmented area, esp. around a nipple. □ **areolar** *adj.* [Latin diminutive of AREA]

**arête** /a-**ret**, a-**rayt**/ *n.* sharp mountain ridge. [French from Latin *arista* spine]

**argent** /**ah**-juhnt/ *n. & adj. archaic* silver; silvery-white. [Latin *argentum*]

**Argentine ant** /**ah**-juhn-teen/ *n.* destructive South American ant now a pest in Australia.

**argon** /**ah**-gon/ *n.* inert gaseous element. [Greek *argos* idle]

**argosy** /**ah**-guh-see/ *n.* (*pl.* **-ies**) *poet.* large merchant ship. [Italian *Ragusea nave* ship of Ragusa (in Dalmatia)]

**argot** /**ah**-goh/ *n.* jargon of a group or class. [French]

**arguable** /**ah**-gyoo-uh-buhl/ *adj.* **1** that may be argued or reasonably proposed. **2** that is open to argument; doubtful. □ **arguably** *adv.*

**argue** /**ah**-gyoo/ *v.* (**-ues, -ued, -uing**) **1** (often foll. by *with, about*, etc.) exchange views forcefully or contentiously. **2** (often foll. by *that*) maintain by reasoning; indicate (*argued the inevitability of Australia becoming a Republic*). **3** (foll. by *for, against*) reason (*argued against joining*). **4** treat (a matter) by reasoning (*argue the point*). **5** (foll. by *into, out of*) persuade (*argued me into going with him*). □ **argue the toss** *colloq.* dispute a choice already made. [Latin *arguo* make clear, prove]

**argument** /**ah**-gyuh-muhnt/ *n.* **1** (esp. contentious) exchange of views; dispute. **2** (often foll. by *for, against*) reason given; reasoning process (*the arguments for abolition*). **3** summary of the subject matter or line of reasoning of a book etc.

**argumentation** /ah-gyuh-muhn-**tay**-shuhn/ *n.* **1** methodical reasoning. **2** debate or argument.

**argumentative** /ah-gyuh-**men**-tuh-tiv/ *adj.* given to arguing.

**argus** /**ah**-guhs/ *n.* watchful guardian. [Greek *Argos* mythical giant with 100 eyes]

**argy-bargy** /ah-jee-**bah**-jee/ *n.* (*pl.* **-ies**) *joc.* dispute, wrangle. [originally Scots]

**aria** /**ah**-ree-uh/ *n.* long accompanied solo song in an opera etc. [Italian]

**-arian** *suffix* forming adjectives and nouns meaning 'person' concerned with or believing in' (*antiquarian; vegetarian*). [Latin]

**arid** /**a**-ruhd/ *adj.* **1 a** dry, parched. **b** too dry to support vegetation; barren. **2** uninteresting (*arid lectures*). □ **aridity** /uh-**rid**-uh-tee/ *n.* [Latin *areo* be dry]

**Aries** /**air**-reez/ *n.* (*pl.* same) **1** constellation and first sign of the zodiac (the Ram). **2** person born when the sun is in this sign. [Latin, = ram]

**aright** /uh-**ruyt**/ *adv.* rightly.

**arise** /uh-**ruyz**/ *v.* (**-sing**; *past* **arose**; *past part.* **arisen** /uh-**riz**-uhn/) **1** begin to exist; originate (*some present Easter activities arose from pre-Christian spring fertility ceremonies*). **2** (usu. foll. by *from, out of*) result (*accidents often arise from carelessness*). **3** come to one's notice; emerge (*the question of payment arose*). **4** rise, esp. from the dead or from kneeling. [Old English *a*- intensive prefix]

**aristocracy** /a-ruh-**stok**-ruh-see/ *n.* (*pl.* **-ies**) **1** ruling class or élite; nobility. **2 a** government by an élite. **b** nation so governed. **3** (often foll. by *of*) best representatives (*aristocracy of intellect*). [Greek *aristokratia* rule by the best]

**aristocrat** /**a**-ruh-stuh-krat/ *n.* member of the aristocracy.

**aristocratic** /a-ruh-stuh-**krat**-ik/ *adj.* **1** of or like the aristocracy. **2 a** distinguished (*aristocratic bearing*). **b** grand, stylish, lavish (*aristocratic splendour*; *affects an aristocratic manner*).

**Aristotelian** /a-ruh-stuh-**tee**-lee-uhn/ — *n.* disciple or student of Aristotle. — *adj.* of Aristotle or his ideas. [Greek *Aristotelēs*, name of a Greek philosopher (4th-c. BC)]

**aristotle** /**a**-ruh-stot-uhl/ *n. colloq.* bottle. [rhyming slang]

**arithmetic** — *n.* /uh-**rith**-muh-tik/ **1** science of numbers. **2** use of numbers; computation (*a problem involving arithmetic*). — *adj.* /a-rith-**met**-ik/ (also **arithmetical**) of arithmetic. [Greek *arithmos* number]

**arithmetic mean** *n.* = AVERAGE 2.

**arithmetic progression** *n.* sequence of numbers with constant intervals (e.g. 9, 7, 5, 3, etc.).

**ark** *n.* ship in which Noah is said to have escaped the Flood with his family and animals. □ **out of the ark** *colloq.* very antiquated. [Old English from Latin *arca*]

**Ark of the Covenant** *n.* chest or cupboard containing the scrolls or tables of Jewish Law.

**arm**[1] *n.* **1** upper limb of the human body from shoulder to hand. **2** forelimb or tentacle of an animal. **3 a** sleeve of a garment. **b** arm support of a chair etc. **c** thing branching from a main stem (*an arm of the sea*). **d** control (*arm of the law*). □ **arm in arm 1** with arms linked. **2** in close cooperation. **at arm's length** at a distance. **with open arms** cordially. □ **armful** *n.* (*pl.* **-s**). [Old English]

**arm**[2] — *n.* **1** (usu. in *pl.*) weapon; firearm. **2** (in *pl.*) the military profession. **3** branch of the military (e.g. infantry, artillery). **4** (in *pl.*) heraldic devices (*coat of arms*). — *v.* **1** supply or equip with weapons, esp. in preparation for war. **2** supply with tools or other requisites or advantages (*armed with the truth*). □ **take up arms** go to war. **under arms** equipped for war. **up in arms** (usu. foll. by *against, about*) actively resisting, highly indignant. [Latin *arma* arms]

**armada** /ah-**mah**-duh/ *n.* fleet of

warships, esp. (**Armada**) that sent by Spain against England in 1588. [Spanish from Romanic]

**armadillo** /ˌah-muh-**dil**-oh/ n. (pl. **-s**) S. American mammal with a plated body and large claws. [Spanish *armado* armed man]

**Armageddon** /ˌah-muh-**ged**-uhn/ n. **1** (in the New Testament) last battle between good and evil before the Day of Judgment. **2** any bloody battle or struggle on a huge scale. [Rev. 16:16]

**armament** /**ah**-muh-muhnt/ n. **1** (often in *pl.*) military equipment. **2** process of equipping for war. **3** force equipped for war. [Latin: related to ARM²]

**armature** /**ah**-muh-chuh/ n. **1** *Electr.* **a** rotating coil or coils of a dynamo or electric motor. **b** iron bar placed across the poles of a horseshoe magnet to preserve its power. **2** protective covering of an animal or plant. **3** metal framework on which a sculpture is moulded. [Latin *armatura*, = armour]

**armchair** n. **1** chair with arm supports. **2** (*attrib.*) theoretical rather than active (*armchair critic*).

**armchair ride** n. *colloq.* easy or trouble-free progress.

**armistice** /**ah**-muh-stuhs/ n. stopping of hostilities by common agreement of the opposing sides; truce. [Latin *arma* arms, *sisto* make stand]

**armor** etc. var. of ARMOUR etc.

**armorial** /ah-**maw**-ree-uhl/ adj. of heraldry or coats of arms. [related to ARMOUR]

**armour** /**ah**-muh/ — n. **1** protective usu. metal covering formerly worn in fighting. **2 a** (in full **armour-plate**) protective metal covering for an armed vehicle, ship, etc. **b** armed vehicles collectively. **3** protective covering or shell of an animal or plant. — v. (usu. as **armoured** adj.) provide with protective covering, and often guns (*armoured car*; *armoured train*). [Latin *armatura*: related to ARM²]

**armourer** n. **1** maker of arms or armour. **2** official in charge of arms.

**armoury** n. (pl. **-ies**) arsenal.

**armpit** n. hollow under the arm at the shoulder.

**armrest** n. = ARM¹ 3b.

**arms race** n. competitive accumulation of weapons by nations.

**army** n. (pl. **-ies**) **1** organised armed land force. **2** (prec. by *the*) the military profession. **3** (often foll. by *of*) very large number (*army of locusts*). **4** organised civilian body regarded as fighting for a particular cause (*Salvation Army*). [French: related to ARM²]

**army disposal store** n. shop selling (to civilians) military clothing, camping equipment, etc., orig. from the army.

**aroma** /uh-**roh**-muh/ n. **1** esp. pleasing smell, often of food. **2** subtle pervasive quality. [Greek, = spice]

**aromatherapy** n. therapy (involving usu. inhalation, massage, etc.) using essential oils and other plant extracts to promote a person's health, well-being, etc. □ **aromatherapist** n.

**aromatic** /ˌa-ruh-**mat**-ik/ — adj. **1** fragrant, spicy. **2** *Chem.* of organic compounds having an unsaturated ring, esp. containing a benzene ring. — n. aromatic substance. [Latin: related to AROMA]

**arose** past of ARISE.

**around** /uh-**rownd**/ — adv. **1** on every side; all round; round about. **2** *colloq.* **a** in existence; available (*has been around for weeks*). **b** near at hand (*it's good to have you around*). **3** here and there (*shop around*). — prep. **1** on or along the circuit of (*put a fence around the swimming pool*). **2** on every side of (*drove around the block*). **3** here and there in or near (*chairs around the room*). **4 a** round (*church around the corner*). **b** at a time near to (*came around four o'clock*). □ **have been around** *colloq.* be widely experienced.

**arouse** /uh-**rowz**/ v. (**-sing**) **1** induce (esp. an emotion) (*aroused their deep suspicion*). **2** awake from sleep. **3** stir into activity. **4** stimulate a person sexually. □ **arousal** n. [a- intensive prefix]

**arpeggio** /ah-**pej**-ee-ˌoh/ n. (pl. **-s**) *Mus.* notes of a chord played in succession. [Italian *arpa* harp]

**arrack** /**a**-ruhk/ n. (also **arak**, esp. in the Middle East) alcoholic spirit, esp. from the nectar tapped from the flowers of the coconut or palmyrah palm or from rice. [Arabic]

**arraign** /uh-**rayn**/ v. **1** indict before a tribunal; accuse. **2** find fault with; call into question (an action or statement). □ **arraignment** n. [Latin *ratio* reason]

**arrange** /uh-**raynj**/ v. (**-ging**) **1** put into order; classify. **2** plan or provide for; take measures (*arranged a meeting*; *arrange to see him*; *arranged for a taxi*). **3** come to an agreement (*arranged with her to meet later*). **4** *Mus.* adapt (a composition) for a particular manner of performance. [French: related to RANGE]

**arrangement** n. **1** act or process of arranging or being arranged. **2** manner of this (*don't like the arrangement of the furniture*). **3** something arranged (*flower arrangement*). **4** (in *pl.*) plans, measures (*made my own arrangements*). **5** agreement; understanding (*came to an ar-rangement about the disputed property*). **6** *Mus.* composition adapted for performance in a particular way.

**arrant** /a-ruhnt/ *adj. literary* downright, utter (*arrant liar*; *arrant nonsense*). [var. of ERRANT, originally in *arrant* (= outlawed, roving) *thief* etc.]

**arras** /a-ruhs/ *n. hist.* rich tapestry or wall-hanging. [*Arras* in France]

**array** /uh-ray/ — *n.* **1** imposing or well-ordered series or display (*an array of articles for sale*). **2** ordered arrangement, esp. of troops (*battle array*). **3** *poet.* outfit or dress (*in fine array*). — *v.* **1** deck, adorn. **2** set in order; marshal (forces). [Latin *ad-*, READY]

**arrears** /uh-reerz/ *n.pl.* amount (esp. of work, rent, etc.) still outstanding or uncompleted. □ **in arrears** behind, esp. in payment. [medieval Latin *adretro* behindhand]

**Arrernte** /u-run-tu, a-ruhn-du/ var. of ARANDA.

**arrest** /uh-rest/ — *v.* **1** lawfully seize (a suspect etc.). **2** stop or check the progress of (*arrested his cancer*). **3** attract (a person's attention) (*his weird green hair arrested a lot of attention*). — *n.* **1** act of arresting or being arrested. **2** stoppage (*cardiac arrest*). [Latin *resto* remain]

**arrival** /uh-ruy-vuhl/ *n.* **1** act of arriving; appearance on the scene. **2** person or thing that has arrived (*the new arrivals were from Sri Lanka*).

**arrive** /uh-ruyv/ *v.* (-ving) **1** (often foll. by *at*, *in*) reach a destination. **2** (foll. by *at*) reach (a conclusion etc.). **3** *colloq.* become successful; establish one's reputation or position. **4** *colloq.* (of a child) be born. **5** (of a time) come (*the long-awaited day has finally arrived*). [Latin *ripa* shore]

**arrogant** /a-ruh-guhnt/ *adj.* aggressively assertive or presumptuous; extremely proud. □ **arrogance** *n.* **arrogantly** *adv.* [related to ARROGATE]

**arrogate** /a-ruh-,gayt/ *v.* (-ting) **1** (often foll. by *to* oneself) claim (power etc.) without right (*arrogated to himself total control of the board*). **2** (often foll. by *to*) attribute unjustly (to a person) (*arrogated the meanest of motives to her*). □ **arrogation** /-gay-shuhn/ *n.* [Latin *rogo* ask]

**arrow** /a-roh/ *n.* **1** pointed slender missile shot from a bow. **2** representation of this, esp. indicating direction. [Old English]

**arrowroot** *n.* **1** nutritious starch. **2** plant yielding this.

**arse** /ahs/ *coarse colloq.* — *n.* **1** buttocks. **2** impudence; cheek. **3** good fortune; luck. **4** nonsense. **5** dismissal (from employment etc.) (*gave him the arse after all these years*). — *v.* **1** (usu. foll. by *about*, *around*) play the fool. **2** dismiss without ceremony (*they arsed him the moment he walked in*). □ **arse about face** back to front. [Old English]

**arsehole** *coarse colloq.* — *n.* **1** anus. **2** *offens.* contemptible person. — *v.* dismiss (a person) from employment etc.

**arsenal** /ah-suh-nuhl/ *n.* **1** store, esp. of weapons. **2** place for the storage and manufacture of weapons and ammunition. [Arabic, = workshop]

**arsenic** — *n.* /ah-suh-nik/ **1** non-scientific name for arsenic trioxide, a highly poisonous white powder used in weed-killers etc. **2** *Chem.* brittle semi-metallic element. — *adj.* /ah-sen-ik/ of or containing arsenic. [French, ultimately from Persian *zar* gold]

**arsey** /ah-see/ *adj.* (also **arsie**, **arsy**) *colloq.* extremely lucky. [alteration of TIN ARSE]

**arson** /ah-suhn/ *n.* crime of deliberately setting fire to property. □ **arsonist** *n.* [Latin *ardeo ars-* burn]

**art** *n.* **1 a** human creative skill or its application. **b** work showing this. **2 a** (in *pl.*; prec. by *the*) branches of creative activity concerned with the production of imaginative designs, sounds, or ideas, e.g. painting, music, writing. **b** any one of these. **3** creative activity resulting in visual representation (*good at music but not art*). **4** human skill as opposed to nature (*art and nature had combined to make her a great beauty*). **5** (often foll. by *of*) **a** skill, knack (*has the art of choosing the right word*). **b** cunning; trick, stratagem (*the wily art of hoodwinking the gullible*). **6** (in *pl.*; usu. prec. by *the*) supposedly creative subjects (esp. languages, literature, and history) as opposed to scientific, technical, or vocational subjects. [Latin *ars art-*]

**art deco** /dek-oh/ *n.* decorative art style of 1910–30, with geometric motifs and strong colours.

**artefact** /ah-tuh-,fakt/ *n.* (also **artifact**) man-made object, esp. a tool or vessel as an archaeological item. [Latin *arte* by art, *facio* make]

**arterial** /ah-teer-ree-uhl/ *adj.* **1** of or relating to an artery (*arterial blood*). **2** (esp. of a road) main, important. [French: related to ARTERY]

**arteriosclerosis** /ah-,teer-ree-oh-skluh-roh-suhs/ *n.* loss of elasticity and thickening of artery walls, esp. in old age. [from ARTERY, SCLEROSIS]

**artery** /**ah**-tuh-ree/ n. (pl. **-ies**) **1** any of the blood-vessels carrying blood from the heart. **2** main road or railway line. [Greek, probably from airō raise]

**artesian bore** /ah-tee-zhuhn/ n. (also **artesian well**) well in which water rises to the surface by natural pressure through a vertically drilled hole. [Artois, old French province]

**artful** adj. crafty, deceitful. □ **artfully** adv.

**arthritis** /ah-**thruy**-tuhs/ n. inflammation of a joint or joints. □ **arthritic** /-**thrit**-ik/ adj. & n. [Greek arthron joint]

**arthropod** /**ah-thruh-**,pod/ n. invertebrate with a segmented body and jointed limbs, e.g. an insect, spider, or crustacean. [Greek arthron joint, pous pod- foot]

**artichoke** /**ah**-tuh-,chohk/ n. **1** plant allied to the thistle. **2** (in full **globe artichoke**) its partly edible flower-head (see also JERUSALEM ARTICHOKE). [Italian from Arabic]

**article** /**ah**-tuh-kuhl/ — n. **1** item or thing. **2** non-fictional journalistic essay. **3** clause or item in an agreement or contract. **4 a** = DEFINITE ARTICLE. **b** = INDEFINITE ARTICLE. — v. (**-ling**) employ under contract as a trainee. [Latin articulus from artus joint]

**articled clerk** n. trainee solicitor.

**articulate** — adj. /ah-**tik**-yuh-luht/ **1** fluent and clear in speech. **2** (of sound or speech) having clearly distinguishable parts. **3** having joints. — v. /ah-**tik**-yuh-,layt/ (**-ting**) **1 a** pronounce distinctly. **b** speak or express clearly. **2** (usu. in passive) connect by joints. **3** (often foll. by with) form a joint. □ **articulately** adv.

**articulated** adj. **1** (of insects, crustaceans, etc.) having the body and limbs composed of segments jointed together. **2** (of a bus, semi-trailer, etc.) with sections connected by a flexible joint.

**articulation** /ah-,tik-yuh-**lay**-shuhn/ n. **1 a** act of speaking or being spoken. **b** articulate utterance; speech. **2 a** act or mode of jointing. **b** joint. [Latin: related to ARTICULATE]

**artifact** var. of ARTEFACT.

**artifice** /**ah**-tuh-fuhs/ n. **1** trick or clever device. **2** cunning. **3** skill, ingenuity. [Latin ars art- art, facio make]

**artificer** /ah-**tif**-uh-suh/ n. **1** craftsman. **2** skilled military mechanic.

**artificial** /,ah-tuh-**fish**-uhl/ adj. **1** not natural (artificial lake). **2** imitating nature (artificial flowers). **3** affected, insincere (an artificial smile). □ **artifici-**

ality /-ee-**al**-uh-tee/ n. **artificially** adv. [Latin: related to ARTIFICE]

**artificial insemination** n. non-sexual introduction of semen into the vagina or uterus.

**artificial intelligence** n. use of computers for tasks normally regarded as needing human intelligence.

**artificial respiration** n. manual or mechanical stimulation of breathing.

**artillery** /ah-**til**-uh-ree/ n. (pl. **-ies**) **1** heavy guns used in land warfare. **2** branch of the army using these. □ **artilleryman** n. [French artiller equip]

**artisan** /,ah-tuh-**zan**, ah-tuh-zuhn/ n. skilled manual worker or craftsman. [Latin artio instruct in the arts]

**artist** /**ah**-tuhst/ n. **1** practitioner of any of the arts, esp. painting. **2** artiste. **3** person who works with the dedication and attributes associated with an artist (an artist in crime). **4** (as final element in comb.) (also **-artist**) colloq. habitual practiser of a specified (usu. reprehensible) activity (booze artist; bull-artist; con-artist; grog artist; etc.). □ **artistry** n. [French artiste from Italian]

**artiste** /ah-**teest**/ n. professional performer, esp. a singer or dancer.

**artistic** /ah-**tis**-tik/ adj. **1** having natural skill in art. **2** skilfully or tastefully done. **3** of art or artists. □ **artistically** adv.

**artless** adj. **1** guileless, ingenuous. **2** natural. **3** clumsy. □ **artlessly** adv.

**art nouveau** /noo-**voh**/ n. art style of the late 19th century, characterised by flowing lines and natural organic forms.

**art union** n. large-scale lottery organised to raise funds for a charity or public cause (orig. with a work of art as the prize).

**arty** adj. (**-ier**, **-iest**) colloq. pretentiously or affectedly artistic.

**arty-farty** adj. colloq. = ARTY.

**arvo** /**ah**-voh/ n. colloq. afternoon (see you this arvo). [abbreviation]

**-ary** suffix **1** forming adjectives (contrary; primary). **2** forming nouns (dictionary; January). [French -aire, Latin -ari(u)s]

**Aryan** /**air**-ree-uhn/ — n. **1** speaker of any of the languages of the Indo-European family. **2** improperly (in Nazi ideology) non-Jewish Caucasian. — adj. of Aryans. [Sanskrit āryas noble]

**As** symb. arsenic.

**as** /az, uhz/ — adv. & conj. (adv. as antecedent in main sentence; conj. in relative clause expressed or implied) to the extent to which . . . is or does etc. (as am as tall as he; am as tall as he is; (colloq.) am as tall as him; as recently as last week). — conj. (with relative clause expressed or implied) **1** (with antecedent *so*) expressing result or purpose (*came early so as to meet us*). **2** (with antecedent adverb omitted) although (*good as it is* = although it is good). **3** (without antecedent adverb) **a** in the manner in which (*do as you like; rose as one man*). **b** in the capacity or form of (*I speak as your friend; Olivier as Hamlet*). **c** while (*arrived as I was eating*). **d** since, seeing that (*as you are here, we can talk*). **e** for instance (*capital cities, as Canberra*). — *rel. pron.* (with verb of relative clause expressed or implied) **1** that, who, which (*I had the same trouble as you; he is a writer, as is his wife; such countries as Indonesia*). **2** (with a sentence as antecedent) a fact that (*he lost, as you know*). □ **as for** with regard to (*as for you, I think you are wrong*). **as from** on and after (a specified date). **as if** (or **though**) as would be the case if (*acts as if he were in charge*). **as it were** in a way; to some extent (*he is, as it were, infatuated*). **as long as** see LONG¹. **as much** see MUCH. **as of 1** = *as from*. **2** at (a specified time). **as per** see PER. **as regards** see REGARD. **as soon as** see SOON. **as such** see SUCH. **as though** see *as if*. **as to** with regard to. **as well 1** in addition; to an equal extent. **2** (also **just as well**) with equal reason; with no loss of advantage or need for regret (*may as well give up; it would be just as well to stop now*). **as well as** in addition to. **as yet** until now or up to a particular time (*have received no news as yet*). [Old English, = ALSO]

**asap** /ay-sap/ *abbr.* (also **a.s.a.p.**) as soon as possible.

**asbestos** /uhs-**bes**-tuhs, as-/ *n.* **1** fibrous silicate mineral. **2** this as a heat-resistant or insulating material. [Greek, = unquenchable]

**asbestosis** /ˌas-bes-**toh**-suhs/ *n.* serious lung disease resulting from the inhalation of asbestos particles.

**ascend** /uh-**send**/ *v.* **1** move or slope upwards, rise (*the road ascends quite steeply here*). **2** climb; go up (*ascended the mountain*). **3** (of sound) rise in pitch. [Latin *scando* climb]

**ascendancy** *n.* (also **ascendency**) (often foll. by *over*) superior or dominant condition or position.

**ascendant** — *adj.* **1** rising. **2** *Astron.* rising towards the zenith. **3** *Astrol.* just above the eastern horizon. **4** predominant. — *n. Astrol.* point of the sun's apparent path that is ascendant at a given time (*Aries in the ascendant*). □ **in the ascendant 1** supreme or dominant. **2** rising; gaining power or authority.

**ascension** /uh-**sen**-shuhn/ *n.* **1** ascent.

**2** (**Ascension**) ascent of Christ into heaven.

**ascent** /uh-**sent**/ *n.* **1** act or instance of ascending, rising, or progressing. **2** upward slope or path etc.

**ascertain** /ˌas-uh-**tayn**/ *v.* find out for certain. □ **ascertainment** *n.* [French: related to CERTAIN]

**ascetic** /uh-**set**-ik/ — *adj.* severely abstinent; self-denying. — *n.* ascetic, esp. religious, person. □ **asceticism** /-uh-ˌsiz-uhm/ *n.* [Greek *askeō* exercise]

**ASCII** /**as**-kee/ *abbr. Computing* American Standard Code for Information Interchange.

**ascorbic acid** /uh-**skaw**-bik/ *n.* vitamin C, found in citrus fruits and green vegetables, essential for maintaining healthy connective tissue, a deficiency of this vitamin resulting in scurvy. [from A-¹, SCORBUTIC]

**ascribe** /uh-**skruyb**/ *v.* (**-bing**) (usu. foll. by *to*) **1** attribute (*ascribes his health to exercise*). **2** regard as belonging (*these poems were formerly ascribed to Chaucer*). □ **ascription** /uh-**skrip**-shuhn/ *n.* [Latin *scribo* write]

**ASEAN** *abbr.* Association of South East Asian Nations.

**asepsis** /ay-**sep**-suhs, uh-/ *n.* **1** absence of sepsis or harmful micro-organisms. **2** method of achieving asepsis in surgery. □ **aseptic** *adj.*

**asexual** /ay-**sek**-shoo-uhl/ *adj.* **1** without sex, sexual organs, or sexuality. **2** (of reproduction) not involving the fusion of gametes. □ **asexually** *adv.*

**ash**¹ *n.* **1** (often in *pl.*) powdery residue left after burning. **2** (*pl.*) human remains after cremation. **3** ashlike material thrown out by a volcano. **4** (**the Ashes**) *Cricket* trophy (an urn containing the ashes of a cricket stump) competed for by Australia and England. [Old English]

**ash**² *n.* **1 a** tree of the Northern hemisphere with silver-grey bark. **b** its hard, pale wood. **2** any of many Australian trees (usu. eucalypts) having a similar wood (*alpine ash; mountain ash; red ash*). [Old English]

**ashamed** /uh-**shaymd**/ *adj.* (usu. *predic.*) **1** embarrassed by shame (*ashamed of myself*). **2** (foll. by *to* + infin.) hesitant, reluctant out of shame (*am ashamed to say*). [Old English *a-* intensive prefix]

**ashen** *adj.* like ashes, esp. grey or pale.

**ashore** /uh-**shaw**/ *adv.* towards or on the shore or land.

**ashram** /**ash**-ram, **ash**-ruhm, **ahsh**-ruhm/ *n.* place of religious retreat for Hindus. [Sanskrit]

**Ash Wednesday** n. first day of Lent (from the ritual of the priest marking the foreheads of penitents in church with ashes on that day).

**ashy** adj. (**-ier, -iest**) **1** = ASHEN. **2** covered with ashes.

**Asian** /ˈay-zhuhn, -shuhn/ — n. **1** native of Asia. **2** person of Asian descent. — adj. of Asia. [Latin from Greek]

**Asianisation** n. (also **-ization**) influence of Asian culture etc. on another culture (the increasing Asianisation of the Australian palate).

**Asiatic** /ˌay-zhee-**at**-ik, ˌay-shee-/ — n. offens. Asian person. — adj. Asian. [Latin from Greek]

**aside** /uh-**suyd**/ — adv. **1** to or on one side; away, apart (put it aside for a while). **2** out of consideration (placed after the noun: jokes aside, which do you really think?). — n. **1** words spoken aside, esp. confidentially to the audience by an actor. **2** any incidental remark.

**asinine** /ˈas-uh-ˌnuyn/ adj. like an ass, esp. stupid or stubborn. □ **asininity** /-ˈnin-uh-tee/ n. [Latin asinus ass]

**ASIO** /ˈay-zee-ˌoh/ abbr. Australian Security Intelligence Organisation.

**ask** /ahsk/ — v. **1** call for an answer to or about (ask her about it; ask him his name). **2** seek to obtain from someone (ask a favour of). **3** (usu. foll. by out, in, or over, or to (a function etc.) invite (must ask them over; asked her to dinner). **4** (foll. by for) seek to obtain, meet, or be directed to (ask for help; asking for you; ask for the bar). — n. colloq. task; requirement (an impossible ask, mate). □ **ask after** inquire about (esp. a person). **ask for it** colloq. invite trouble. **a big ask** colloq. difficult task (it's a big ask to expect Australia to win from here). **for the asking** (obtainable) for nothing. **I ask you!** exclamation of disgust, surprise, etc. **if you ask me** colloq. in my opinion. [Old English]

**askance** /uh-**skans**/ adv. sideways or squinting. □ **look askance at** regard suspiciously. [origin unknown]

**askew** /uh-**skyoo**/ — adv. awry, crookedly. — predic. adj. oblique; awry (your tie is askew).

**asking price** n. price of an object set by the seller.

**aslant** /uh-**slahnt**, -**slant**/ — adv. obliquely or at a slant. — prep. obliquely across.

**asleep** /uh-**sleep**/ predic. adj. & adv. **1 a** in or into a state of sleep. **b** inactive, inattentive (the nation is asleep to this danger). **2** (of a limb etc.) numb. **3** euphem. dead.

**asp** n. small venomous snake of North Africa or Southern Europe. [Greek aspis]

**asparagus** /uh-**spa**-ruh-guhs/ n. **1** plant of the lily family. **2** edible shoots of this. [Latin from Greek]

**aspect** /ˈas-pekt/ n. **1** viewpoint, feature, etc. to be considered (one aspect of the problem). **2** appearance or look (cheerful aspect). **3** side of a building or location facing a particular direction (southern aspect). [Latin adspicio look at]

**aspen** /ˈas-puhn/ n. poplar with very tremulous leaves. [Old English: originally adj.]

**asperity** /uh-**spe**-ruh-tee/ n. (pl. **-ies**) **1** sharpness of temper or tone (replied with some asperity). **2** roughness, unevenness of a surface etc. [Latin asper rough]

**aspersion** /uh-**sper**-shuhn, -zhuhn/ n. damaging charge or accusation. □ **cast aspersions on** attack the reputation of. [Latin aspergo besprinkle]

**asphalt** /ˈash-felt, -folt, as-/ — n. **1** dark bituminous pitch. **2** mixture of this with sand, gravel, etc., for surfacing roads etc. — v. surface with asphalt. [Latin from Greek]

**asphyxia** /as-**fik**-see-uh/ n. lack of oxygen in the blood, causing unconsciousness or death; suffocation. □ **asphyxiant** adj. & n. [Greek a- not, sphuxis pulse]

**asphyxiate** /as-**fik**-see-ˌayt/ v. (**-ting**) suffocate. □ **asphyxiation** /-ˌay-shuhn/ n.

**aspic** /ˈas-pik/ n. savoury jelly used esp. to contain meat, fish, eggs, etc. [French, = ASP, suggested by the colours of the jelly]

**aspidistra** /ˌas-puh-**dis**-truh/ n. houseplant with broad tapering leaves. [Greek aspis shield]

**aspirant** /ˈas-puh-ruhnt, uh-**spuyuh**-ruhnt/ — adj. aspiring. — n. person who aspires. [Latin: related to ASPIRE]

**aspirate** /ˈas-puh-ruht/ — adj. Phonet. **1** pronounced with an exhalation of breath. **2** blended with the sound of h. — n. **1** consonant pronounced in this way (the 't' in 'tone' is an aspirate, whereas the 't' in 'stone' is not). **2** sound of h. — v. /-ˌrayt/ (**-ting**) **1** pronounce with breath or with initial h. **2** draw (fluid) by suction from a cavity etc.

**aspiration** /ˌas-puh-**ray**-shuhn/ n. **1** strong desire to achieve an end; ambition. **2** act or process of drawing breath. **3** Phonet. action of aspirating.

**aspirator** /ˈas-puh-ˌray-tuh/ n. apparatus for aspirating fluid. [Latin: related to ASPIRE]

**aspire** /uh-**spuyuh**/ v. (**-ring**) (usu. foll. by to or after, or to + infin.) have ambition or a strong desire (*aspires to the leadership*; *aspires after knowledge*). [Latin *aspiro* breathe upon]

**aspirin** /**as**-pruhn/ *n.* (*pl.* same or **-s**) **1** white powder, acetylsalicylic acid, used to reduce pain and fever. **2** tablet of this. [German]

**ass** *n.* **1 a** four-legged long-eared mammal related to the horse. **b** (in general use) donkey. **2** stupid person. □ **make an ass of** make (a person) look absurd or foolish. [Old English from Latin]

**assail** /uh-**sayl**/ *v.* **1** attack physically or verbally. **2** tackle (a task) resolutely. □ **assailant** *n.* [Latin *salio* leap]

**assassin** /uh-**sas**-uhn/ *n.* killer, esp. of a political or religious leader. [Arabic, = hashish-eater]

**assassinate** /uh-**sas**-uh-,nayt/ *v.* (**-ting**) **1** kill for political or religious motives. **2** destroy or harm (a person's character or reputation). □ **assassination** /-**nay**-shuhn/ *n.*

**assault** /uh-**sawlt**, uh-**solt**/ — *n.* **1** violent physical or verbal attack. **2** *Law* threat or display of violence against a person. **3** vigorous start made to a lengthy or difficult task (*decided to make an assault on the mounting paperwork*). **4** final rush on a fortified place, esp. at the end of a prolonged attack. **5** (*attrib.*) relating to or used in an assault (*assault craft*; *assault troops*). **6** = INDECENT ASSAULT. — *v.* make an assault on. □ **assault and battery** *Law* threatening act resulting in physical harm to a person. [Latin: related to ASSAIL]

**assay** /uh-**say**, **as**-ay/ — *n.* testing of a metal or ore to determine its ingredients and quality. — *v.* **1** make an assay of (a metal or ore). **2** *archaic* attempt. [French, var. of *essai* ESSAY]

**assemblage** /uh-**sem**-blij/ *n.* **1** act or instance of assembling. **2** collection of things or a gathering of people. **3** work of art made by grouping together found or unrelated objects.

**assemble** /uh-**sem**-buhl/ *v.* (**-ling**) **1** gather together; collect; arrange in order (*assemble the students in the quadrangle*; *the people assembled to hear the Prime Minister*). **2** esp. *Mech.* fit together (components, a whole). [Latin *ad* to, *simul* together]

**assembler** /uh-**sem**-bluh/ *n.* **1** person who assembles a machine etc. **2** *Computing* **a** program translating assembly language into machine code. **b** = ASSEMBLY LANGUAGE.

**assembly** /uh-**sem**-blee/ *n.* (*pl.* **-ies**) **1** act or instance of assembling. **2** assembled group, esp. as a deliberative or legislative body (*House of Assembly*). **3** gathering of all the members of a school. **4** assembling of a machine or structure or its parts.

**assembly language** *n.* *Computing* low-level programming language, usu. machine specific, in which an instruction translates into one machine code instruction.

**assembly line** *n.* machinery arranged so that a product can be progressively assembled.

**assent** /uh-**sent**/ — *v.* (usu. foll. by *to*) **1** express agreement (*assented to my view*). **2** consent (*assented to my request*). — *n.* consent or approval, esp. official. □ **assenter** *n.* [Latin *sentio* think]

**assert** /uh-**sert**/ *v.* **1** declare, state clearly (*assert that it is so*). **2** *refl.* insist on one's rights or opinions; demand recognition (*asserted himself to be recognised by the chair*). **3** enforce a claim to (*assert one's rights*). [Latin *assero -sert-*]

**assertion** /uh-**ser**-shuhn/ *n.* declaration, forthright statement.

**assertive** /uh-**ser**-tiv/ *adj.* **1** tending to assert oneself; forthright, positive. **2** dogmatic. □ **assertively** *adv.* **assertiveness** *n.*

**assess** /uh-**ses**/ *v.* **1** estimate the size or quality of. **2** estimate the value of (property, income, etc.) for taxation. **3** fix the amount of (a tax, fine, damages, etc.). □ **assessable** *adj.* **assessment** *n.* [Latin *assideo -sess-* sit by]

**assessor** *n.* **1** person who assesses (esp. for tax or insurance). **2** legal adviser on technical questions.

**asset** /**as**-et/ *n.* **1** useful or valuable person or thing (*she's an asset to the company*; *fitness is an asset*). **2** (usu. in *pl.*) property and possessions, esp. that can be set against debts etc. [French *asez* from Latin *ad satis* to enough]

**asset-stripping** *n.* *Commerce* the taking over of a company and selling off of its assets to make a profit.

**asseverate** /uh-**sev**-uh-,rayt/ *v.* (**-ting**) declare solemnly. □ **asseveration** /-**ray**-shuhn/ *n.* [Latin *severus* serious]

**assiduous** /uh-**sid**-yoo-uhs/ *adj.* **1** persevering, hard-working (*assiduous application to his studies*). **2** attending closely; devoted (*assiduous care*). □ **assiduity** /,as-i-**dyoo**-uh-tee/ *n.* **assiduously** *adv.* [Latin: related to ASSESS]

**assign** /uh-**suyn**/ — *v.* **1** (usu. foll. by *to*) **a** allot as a share or responsibility (*assigned them their duties*). **b** appoint to a position, task, etc. (*assigned me to supervise the working party*). **c** *hist.* allocate the services of a convict to a settler. **2** fix (a time, place, etc.) for a specific purpose (*assigned the day and time for the meeting*). **3** (foll. by *to*) ascribe to (a reason, date, etc.) (*assigned the manuscript to 1832*). **4** (foll. by *to*) *Law* transfer formally (esp. property) to (another). **5** *Computing* dedicate part of a computing system, e.g. a tape drive, for use by a program. — *n.* assignee. □ **assignable** *adj.* **assigner** *n.* **assignor** *n. Law*. [Latin *assigno* mark out]

**assignation** /ˌas-ig-**nay**-shuhn/ *n.* **1** appointment to meet, esp. by lovers in secret. **2** act or instance of assigning or being assigned.

**assignee** /ˌas-uy-**nee**/ *n. Law* person to whom a right or property is assigned.

**assignment** /uh-**suyn**-muhnt/ *n.* **1 a** task or mission. **b** written task etc. required from a student. **2** act or instance of assigning or being assigned. **3** legal transfer. **4** *hist.* making over to a private individual of the services of a convict.

**assimilate** /uh-**sim**-uh-ˌlayt/ *v.* (**-ting**) **1 a** absorb and digest (food etc.) into the body. **b** absorb (information etc.) into the mind. **c** absorb (people) into a larger group. **2** (usu. foll. by *to, with*) make like; cause to resemble. □ **assimilable** *adj.* **assimilative** /-luh-tiv/ *adj.* **assimilator** *n.* [Latin *similis* like]

**assimilation** /uh-ˌsim-uh-**lay**-shuhn/ *n.* **1** act or process of assimilating. **2 a** acceptance by immigrant minorities of prevailing cultural values. **b** integration of such minorities into a society. **c** integration of Aborigines into white Australian society.

**assist** /uh-**sist**/ *v.* (often foll. by *in* + verbal noun) help. □ **assistance** *n.* [Latin *assisto* stand by]

**assistant** *n.* (often *attrib.*) person who helps, esp. as a subordinate.

**associate** — *v.* /uh-**soh**-shee-ˌayt, -see-ˌayt/ (**-ting**) **1** connect mentally (*associate the smell of gum leaves with Australia*). **2** join or combine, esp. for a common purpose. **3** *refl.* declare oneself or be in agreement (*associate ourselves with the plan*). **4** (usu. foll. by *with*) meet frequently or have dealings (*associates with some very strange people*). — *n.* /uh-**soh**-shee-uht, -see-uht/ **1** partner, colleague. **2** friend, companion. **3** subordinate member of a society etc. — *adj.* /uh-**soh**-shee-uht, -see-uht/ **1** joined or allied. **2** of lower status (*associate member; associate professor*). □ **associative** /uh-**soh**-shee-uh-tiv, uh-**soh**-see-/ *adj.* [Latin *socius* allied]

**association** /uh-ˌsoh-see-**ay**-shuhn/ *n.* **1** group organised for a joint purpose; society. **2** act or instance of associating or being associated. **3** companionship. **4** mental connection between ideas. [medieval Latin: related to ASSOCIATE]

**assonance** /ˈas-uh-nuhns/ *n.* resemblance of sound between two syllables in nearby words arising from: **1** rhyming of two or more accented vowels (but not consonants), e.g. *sonnet, porridge*. **2** use of identical consonants with different vowels, e.g. *killed, cold, culled* (cf. ALLITERATION). □ **assonant** *adj.* [Latin *sonus* sound]

**assorted** *adj.* **1** of various sorts, mixed. **2** sorted into groups. **3** matched (*ill-assorted pair*). [related to SORT]

**assortment** *n.* diverse group or mixture.

**assuage** /uh-**swayj**/ *v.* (**-ging**) **1** calm or soothe (a person, pain, etc.) (*assuaged his grief*). **2** appease (an appetite or desire) (*assuaged his thirst*). □ **assuagement** *n.* [Latin *suavis* sweet]

**assume** /uh-**syoom**/ *v.* (**-ming**) **1** (usu. foll. by *that*) take to be true (*even if we assume that the world will end tomorrow, that's no reason for not mowing the lawn*). **2** simulate or pretend (ignorance etc.) (*assumed a look of wide-eyed innocence*). **3** undertake (an office etc.) (*assumed the position of acting manager*). **4** take or put on (an aspect, attribute, etc.) (*the problem assumed immense proportions*). **5** (usu. foll. by *to*) usurp or seize (credit, power, etc.) (*assumed to himself the right of veto*). [Latin *sumo* take]

**assuming** *adj.* arrogant, presumptuous (*an assuming and self-righteous prig*).

**assumption** /uh-**sump**-shuhn, uh-**sum**-shuhn/ *n.* **1** act or instance of assuming. **2** something accepted without proof (*the assumption of his innocence*). **3** arrogance. **4 a** (**Assumption**) reception of the Virgin Mary bodily into heaven after she died. **b** feast in honour of this (15 August).

**assurance** /uh-**shaw**-ruhns/ *n.* **1** emphatic declaration; guarantee. **2** insurance, esp. life insurance. **3** certainty. **4** self-confidence; assertiveness.

**assure** /uh-**shaw**/ *v.* (**-ring**) **1** (often foll. by *of*) **a** convince (*assured him of his daughter's safety*). **b** tell (a person) confidently (*assured him all was well*). **2** ensure; guarantee (a result etc.) (*his fitness will assure our team's success*). **3** insure (esp. a life). **4** (as **assured** *adj.*) **a** guaranteed. **b** self-confident. [Latin *securus* safe]

**assuredly** /uh-**shaw**-ruhd-lee/ *adv.* certainly.

**astatine** /ˈas-tuh-ˌteen/ *n.* radioactive element, the heaviest of the halogens. [Greek *astatos* unstable]

**aster** *n.* plant with bright daisy-like flowers. [Greek, = star]

**asterisk** /**as**-tuh-risk/ — n. symbol (*) used to mark words or to indicate omission etc. — v. mark with an asterisk. [Greek, = little star]

**astern** /uh-**stern**/ adv. (often foll. by of) **1** in or to the rear of a ship or aircraft. **2** backwards.

**asteroid** /**as**-tuh-,royd/ n. any of the minor planets orbiting the sun, mainly between the orbits of Mars and Jupiter. [Greek: related to ASTER]

**asthma** /**as**-muh/ n. respiratory condition marked by wheezing. [Greek azō breathe hard]

**asthmatic** /as-**mat**-ik/ — adj. of or suffering from asthma. — n. asthmatic person.

**astigmatism** /uh-**stig**-muh-,tiz-uhm/ n. eye or lens defect resulting in distorted images. □ **astigmatic** /,as-tig-**mat**-ik/ adj. [from A-¹, STIGMA]

**astir** /uh-**ster**/ predic. adj. & adv. **1** in motion. **2** out of bed.

**astonish** /uh-**ston**-ish/ v. surprise greatly, amaze. □ **astonishment** n. [obsolete astone from Latin ex- forth, tono thunder]

**astound** /uh-**stownd**/ v. astonish greatly. [obsolete astoned: see ASTONISH]

**astraddle** /uh-**strad**-uhl/ adv. astride.

**astral** /**as**-truhl/ adj. **1** of or connected with the stars; starry. **2** relating to the supposed substance, a counterpart of the body, which exists after death (the medium conjured up his astral body). [Latin astrum star]

**astray** /uh-**stray**/ adv. & predic. adj. **1** in or into error or sin (esp. lead astray). **2** out of the right way. □ **go astray** be missing. [Latin extra away, vagor wander]

**astride** /uh-**struyd**/ — adv. **1** (often foll. by of) with a leg on each side. **2** with legs apart. — prep. astride of; extending across.

**astringent** /uh-**strin**-juhnt/ — adj. **1 a** causing the contracting of body tissues, esp. the skin. **b** checking bleeding. **2** severe, austere (he has a most astringent manner). — n. astringent substance. □ **astringency** n. [Latin astringo draw tight]

**astrology** /uh-**strol**-uh-jee/ n. study of the supposed influence of celestial bodies on human affairs (cf. ASTRONOMY). □ **astrologer** n. **astrological** /,as-truh-**loj**-i-kuhl/ adj. **astrologist** n. [Greek astron star]

**astroloma** /,as-truh-**loh**-muh/ see NATIVE CRANBERRY.

**astronaut** /**as**-truh-,nawt/ n. crew member of a spacecraft. [Greek astron star, nautēs sailor]

**astronautics** /,as-truh-**naw**-tiks/ n.pl. (treated as sing.) science of space travel. □ **astronautical** adj.

**astronomical** /,as-truh-**nom**-i-kuhl/ adj. (also **astronomic**) **1** of or relating to astronomy. **2** vast, gigantic. □ **astronomically** adv.

**astronomy** /uh-**stron**-uh-mee/ n. the scientific study of celestial bodies. □ **astronomer** n. [Greek astron star, nemō arrange]

**astrophysics** /,as-troh-**fiz**-iks/ n.pl. (treated as sing.) the study of the physics and chemistry of celestial bodies. □ **astrophysical** adj. **astrophysicist** /-uh-suhst/ n. [Greek astron star]

**astroturf** /**as**-troh-,terf/ n. propr. artificial grass surface, esp. for sports fields. [Astrodome, name of a sports stadium in Texas where it was first used, TURF]

**astute** /uh-**styoot**/ adj. shrewd. □ **astutely** adv. **astuteness** n. [Latin astus craft]

**asunder** /uh-**sun**-duh/ adv. literary apart; into pieces (the lovers were kept asunder; tore it asunder). [Old English]

**asylum** /uh-**suy**-luhm/ n. **1 a** sanctuary; protection, esp. for fugitives from the law (seek asylum). **b** = POLITICAL ASYLUM. **2** hist. institution for the mentally ill or destitute. [Greek a- not, sulon right of seizure]

**asymmetry** /ay-**sim**-uh-tree/ n. lack of symmetry. □ **asymmetric** /-**met**-rik/ adj. **asymmetrical** /-**met**-rik-uhl/ adj. [Greek]

**At** symb. astatine.

**at** /at, uht/ prep. **1** expressing position (wait at the corner; at school). **2** expressing a point in time (at dawn). **3** expressing a point in a scale (at boiling-point; at his best). **4** expressing engagement in an activity etc. (at war). **5** expressing a value or rate (sell at $10 each). **6 a** with or with reference to (annoyed at losing; came at a run). **b** by means of (starts at a touch). **7** expressing motion or aim towards (aim at the target; laughed at us). □ **at all** see ALL. **at home** see HOME. **at it 1** engaged in an activity; working hard. **2** colloq. repeating a habitual (usu. disapproved of) activity (found them at it again). **at once** see ONCE. **at that 1** moreover (a good one at that). **2** then (at that he left). **at times** see TIME. **be at** colloq. be engaged in; be concerned with (what is he at these days?). **be at a person** colloq. criticise or scold him or her (she's always at the kids).

**where it's at** *colloq.* fashionable scene or with-it activity. [Old English]

**atavism** /at-uh-ˌviz-uhm/ *n.* **1** reappearance of a remote ancestral characteristic; throwback. **2** reversion to an earlier type. □ **atavistic** /-vis-tik/ *adj.* [Latin *atavus* ancestor]

**ataxia** /uh-tak-see-uh/ *n. Med.* imperfect control of bodily movements. □ **ataxic** *adj.* [Greek *a-* without, *taxis* order]

**ate** *past* of EAT.

**-ate**[1] *suffix* **1** forming nouns denoting status, function, or office (*doctorate*; *consulate*). **2** forming nouns denoting the salt of an acid (*chlorate*; *nitrate*). [Latin]

**-ate**[2] *suffix* forming adjectives with the sense 'having, full of' (*foliate*; *passionate*). [Latin participial ending *-atus*]

**atheism** /ay-thee-ˌiz-uhm/ *n.* belief that there is no God. □ **atheist** *n.* **atheistic** /-is-tik/ *adj.* [Greek *a-* not, *theos* god]

**atherosclerosis** /ˌath-uh-roh-skluh-roh-suhs/ *n.* degeneration of the arteries caused by a build-up of fatty deposits. [Greek *athērē* groats]

**athlete** /ath-leet/ *n.* **1** person who engages in athletics, exercise, etc. **2** healthy person with a natural athletic ability. [Greek *athlon* prize]

**athlete's foot** *n.* fungal foot condition.

**athletic** /ath-let-ik/ *adj.* **1** of athletes or athletics. **2** physically strong or agile. □ **athletically** *adv.* **athleticism** /-let-uh-ˌsiz-uhm/ *n.* [Latin: related to ATHLETE]

**athletics** *n.pl.* (usu. treated as *sing.*) physical exercises, esp. track and field events.

**-athon** *suffix* (also **-thon** after a vowel which is sounded) indicating an extended activity usu. involving much endurance, as specified in the first part (such activities being used for fund-raising, breaking records, etc.) (*read-out-aloud-athon*; *reciteathon*; *sitathon*; *sleepathon*; *telethon*; etc.). [falsely derived from the *-athon* in MARATHON]

**-atic** *suffix* forming adjectives and nouns (*aquatic*; *fanatic*; *idiomatic*). [Greek *-atikos*]

**-ation** *suffix* **1** forming nouns denoting an action or an instance of it (*flirtation*; *hesitation*). **2** forming nouns denoting a result or product of action (*plantation*; *starvation*). [Latin *-atio*]

**-ative** *suffix* forming adjectives denoting a characteristic or propensity (*authoritative*; *imitative*; *pejorative*; *talkative*). [Latin *-ativus*]

**Atlantic** /uht-lan-tik/ *adj.* of or adjoining the ocean between Europe and Africa to the east and America to the west. [Greek: related to ATLAS]

**atlas** /at-luhs/ *n.* book of maps or charts. [Greek *Atlas*, the Titan who held up the universe]

**atmosphere** /at-muhs-ˌfeer/ *n.* **1 a** gases enveloping the earth, any other planet, etc. **b** air in a room etc., esp. if unpleasant. **2** pervading tone or mood of a place, situation, or work of art (*has an atmosphere of perfect calm*). **3** unit of pressure equal to mean atmospheric pressure at sea level, 101,325 pascals. □ **atmospheric** /-fe-rik/ *adj.* [Greek *atmos* vapour, SPHERE]

**atmospherics** /ˌat-muhs-fe-riks/ *n.pl.* **1** electrical atmospheric disturbance, esp. caused by lightning. **2** interference with telecommunications caused by this.

**atoll** /at-ol/ *n.* ring-shaped coral reef enclosing a lagoon. [Maldive]

**atom** /at-uhm/ *n.* **1 a** smallest particle of a chemical element that can take part in a chemical reaction. **b** this as a source of nuclear energy. **2** minute portion or thing (*not an atom of pity*). [Greek *atomos* indivisible]

**atom bomb** *n.* bomb in which energy is released by nuclear fission.

**atomic** /uh-tom-ik/ *adj.* **1** of or using atomic energy or atomic bombs. **2** of atoms.

**atomic bomb** *n.* = ATOM BOMB.

**atomic energy** *n.* nuclear energy.

**atomic mass** *n.* mass of an atom measured in atomic mass units.

**atomic mass unit** *n.* unit of mass used to express atomic and molecular weights, equal to one-twelfth of the mass of an atom of carbon-12.

**atomic number** *n.* number of protons in the nucleus of an atom.

**atomic theory** *n.* theory that all matter consists of atoms.

**atomic weight** *n.* = RELATIVE ATOMIC MASS.

**atomise** /at-uh-ˌmuyz/ *v.* (also **-ize**) (**-sing** or **-zing**) reduce to atoms or fine spray.

**atomiser** *n.* (also **-izer**) = AEROSOL 1.

**atonal** /ay-toh-nuhl, uh-/ *adj. Mus.* not written in any key or mode. □ **atonality** /-nal-uh-tee/ *n.*

**atone** /uh-tohn/ *v.* (**-ning**) (usu. foll. by *for*) make amends (for a wrong). [from ATONEMENT]

**atonement** *n.* **1** act or instance of atoning for a wrong or injury. **2** (**the Atonement**) **a** expiation by Christ of mankind's sins. **b** (in full **Day of Atonement**) the most solemn religious fast of the Jewish year, eight days after the Jewish New Year. [*at one* + -MENT]

**atrium** /ay-tree-uhm, at-ree-/ n. (pl. **-s** or **atria**) **1 a** central court of an ancient Roman house. **b** (usu. skylit) central court rising through several storeys. **2** each of the two upper cavities of the heart. [Latin]

**atrocious** /uh-**troh**-shuhs/ adj. **1** very bad or unpleasant (atrocious manners). **2** savage or wicked (atrocious cruelty). □ **atrociously** adv. [Latin atrox cruel]

**atrocity** /uh-**tros**-uh-tee/ n. (pl. **-ies**) **1** wicked or cruel act. **2** extreme wickedness. [Latin: related to ATROCIOUS]

**atrophy** /**at**-ruh-fee/ — n. wasting away through undernourishment, ageing, or lack of use; emaciation. — v. (**-ies, -ied**) suffer atrophy or cause atrophy in. [Greek a- without, trophē food]

**atropine** /**at**-ruh-,peen, -puhn/ n. poisonous alkaloid found in deadly nightshade, used in medicine and in association with pre-surgical anaesthetics etc. [Greek Atropos, the Fate who cut the thread of life]

**attach** /uh-**tach**/ v. **1** fasten, affix, join. **2** (in passive; foll. by to) be very fond of (I'm very attached to him). **3** attribute or be attributable; assign (can't attach a name to it; no blame attaches to us). **4** accompany; form part of (no conditions are attached). **5** refl. (usu. foll. by to) take part in; join (attached himself to the team). **6** appoint for special or temporary duties. **7** seize by legal authority. [French from Germanic]

**attaché** /uh-**tash**-ay/ n. specialist member of an ambassador's staff.

**attaché case** n. small rectangular document case.

**attachment** n. **1** thing attached or to be attached, esp. to a machine, device, etc., for a special function (an electric food-processor with six different attachments). **2** affection, devotion. **3** act or means of attaching or state of being attached. **4** legal seizure. **5** temporary position in an organisation.

**attack** /uh-**tak**/ — v. **1** try to hurt or defeat using force. **2** criticise adversely. **3** act harmfully upon (rust attacks metal). **4** vigorously apply oneself to (attacked the meal with gusto). **5** Sport try to gain ground or score (against). — n. **1** act or process of attacking. **2** offensive operation. **3** sudden onset of an illness. □ **attacker** n. [French from Italian]

**attain** /uh-**tayn**/ v. **1** reach, gain, accomplish (a goal etc.). **2** (foll. by to) arrive at by effort or development. [Latin attingo reach]

**attainment** n. **1** (often in pl.) accomplish-

ment or achievement. **2** act or instance of attaining.

**attar** /**at**-ah/ n. perfume made from rose-petals. [Persian]

**attempt** /uh-**tempt**/ — v. **1** (often foll. by to + infin.) try to do or achieve (attempted to explain). **2** try to climb or master (a mountain etc.) (will attempt Everest again next year). — n. (often foll. by at, on, or to + infin.) act of attempting; endeavour (made an attempt at winning; an attempt on his life). [Latin tempto try]

**attend** /uh-**tend**/ v. **1 a** be present (at) (attended the meeting). **b** go regularly to (attends church). **2** escort (the king was attended by soldiers). **3 a** (often foll. by to) turn or apply one's mind (attend to what I am saying). **b** (foll. by to) deal with (attend to the matter). **4** (usu. in passive) follow as a result of (the error was attended by serious consequences). [Latin tendo stretch]

**attendance** n. **1** act of attending or being present. **2** number present (high attendance).

**attendant** — n. person escorting or providing a service (cloakroom attendant). — adj. **1** accompanying (attendant costs). **2** (often foll. by on) waiting; serving (attendant on the queen).

**attention** /uh-**ten**-shuhn/ n. **1** act or faculty of applying one's mind; notice (attention wandered; attract his attention). **2 a** consideration (give attention to the problem). **b** care (give special attention to your handwriting). **3** (in pl.) **a** courtesies. **b** sexual advances (unwelcome attentions). **4** erect esp. military attitude of readiness (stood to attention).

**attentive** /uh-**ten**-tiv/ adj. **1** concentrating; paying attention. **2** polite. □ **attentively** adv. **attentiveness** n.

**attenuate** /uh-**ten**-yoo-,ayt/ v. (**-ting**) **1** make thin (the higher we climbed, the more attenuated was the atmosphere). **2** reduce in force, value, etc. (high living attenuated their resources). □ **attenuation** /-ay-shuhn/ n. [Latin tenuis thin]

**attest** /uh-**test**/ v. **1** certify the validity of. **2** (foll. by to) bear witness to (attested to his honesty). □ **attestation** /,at-es-**tay**-shuhn/ n. [Latin testis witness]

**Attic** /**at**-ik/ — adj. of ancient Athens or Attica, or the form of Greek used there. — n. Greek as used by the ancient Athenians. [Greek Attikos]

**attic** /**at**-ik/ n. space or room at the top of a house, usu. under the roof. [from ATTIC, with ref. to an architectural feature]

**attire** /uh-**tuyuh**/ formal — n. clothes, esp. formal. — v. (**-ring**) (usu. as **attired**

*adj.*) dress, esp. formally. [French *à tire in order*]

**attitude** /at-e-ˌtyood/ *n.* **1** settled opinion or way of thinking; behaviour reflecting this (*don't like his attitude*). **2** *colloq.* **a** aggressive or uncooperative behaviour; resentful or antagonistic manner. **b** self-possession; style, swagger. **3** bodily posture; pose (*strike an attitude*). **4** position of an aircraft etc. relative to given points. □ **attitudinal** /at-uh-**tyoo**-duh-nuhl/ *adj.* [Latin *aptus* fitted]

**attitudinise** /ˌat-uh-**tyoo**-duh-ˌnuyz/ *v.* (also **-ize**) (**-sing** or **-zing**) adopt (esp. affected) attitudes; pose.

**attorney** /uh-**ter**-nee/ *n.* (*pl.* **-s**) lawyer etc. appointed to act for another in business or legal matters. [French *atorner* assign]

**Attorney-General** *n.* (*pl.* **Attorneys-General**) **1** (chief) law minister in an Australian government. **2** chief legal officer in some countries.

**attract** /uh-**trakt**/ *v.* **1** draw or bring to oneself or itself (*he attracts many admirers; the building attracts much attention*). **2** be attractive to; fascinate (*chess attracts me greatly*). **3** (of a magnet, gravity, etc.) exert a pull on (an object) (also *absol.: opposites attract*). [Latin *traho* draw]

**attraction** /uh-**trak**-shuhn/ *n.* **1 a** act or power of attracting (*the attraction of Australian wildlife draws many foreign tourists*). **b** person or thing that attracts by arousing interest (*the science exhibition is a big attraction*). **2** *Physics* the force by which bodies attract or approach each other (opp. REPULSION). **3** *Gram.* influence exerted by one word on another which causes it to change to an incorrect form (e.g. *is* in *the wages of sin is death*).

**attractive** /uh-**trak**-tiv/ *adj.* **1** attracting (esp. interest or admiration) (*an attractive proposition*). **2** aesthetically pleasing; good-looking. □ **attractively** *adv.*

**attribute** — *v.* /uh-**trib**-yoot/ (**-ting**) (usu. foll. by *to*) **1** regard as belonging to, written or said by, etc. (*a poem attributed to Milton*). **2** ascribe to (a cause) (*delays attributed to bad weather*). — *n.* /**at**-ruh-ˌbjoot/ **1** esp. characteristic quality ascribed to a person or thing (*loyalty is one of her attributes*). **2** object symbolising or appropriate to a person, office, or status (*a big house is an attribute of wealth*). □ **attributable** /uh-**trib**-yuh-tuh-buhl/ *adj.* **attribution** /ˌat-ruh-byoo-shuhn/ *n.* [Latin *tribuo* allot]

**attributive** /uh-**trib**-yuh-tiv/ *adj. Gram.* (of an adjective or noun) preceding the word described, as *old* in *the old dog* (opp. PREDICATIVE).

**attrition** /uh-**trish**-uhn/ *n.* **1** gradual wearing down. **2** abrasion, friction. □ **war of attrition** war in which one side wins by gradually wearing the other down with repeated attacks etc. [Latin *tero trit-* rub]

**attune** /uh-**tyoon**/ *v.* (**-ning**) **1** (usu. foll. by *to*) adjust to a situation etc. (*not attuned to the latest trends*). **2** *Mus.* tune. [related to TUNE]

**atypical** /ay-**tip**-i-kuhl/ *adj.* not typical; not conforming to a type. □ **atypically** *adv.*

**Au** *symb.* gold. [Latin *aurum*]

**aubergine** /**oh**-buh-ˌzheen/ *n.* = EGGPLANT. [French, ultimately from Sanskrit]

**auburn** /**aw**-buhn/ *adj.* reddish-brown (usu. of hair). [originally = yellowish white: from Latin *albus* white]

**auction** /**ok**-shuhn, **awk**-/ — *n.* sale in which articles are sold to the highest bidder. — *v.* sell by auction. [Latin *augeo auct-* increase]

**auctioneer** /ˌok-shuh-**neer**, ˌawk-/ *n.* person who conducts auctions, esp. for a living.

**audacious** /aw-**day**-shuhs/ *adj.* **1** daring, bold (*an audacious attempt*). **2** impudent; presumptuously wicked (*an audacious liar*). □ **audacity** /aw-**das**-uh-tee/ *n.* [Latin *audax* bold]

**audible** /**aw**-duh-buhl/ *adj.* able to be heard. □ **audibility** /-**bil**-uh-tee/ *n.* **audibly** *adv.* [Latin *audio* hear]

**audience** /**aw**-dee-uhns/ *n.* **1 a** assembled listeners or spectators, esp. at a play, concert, etc. **b** people addressed by a film, book, etc. **2** formal interview with a superior (*had an audience with the Pope*). [Latin: related to AUDIBLE]

**audio** /**aw**-dee-oh/ *n.* (usu. *attrib.*) sound or its reproduction. [Latin *audio* hear]

**audio-** *comb. form* hearing or sound.

**audio frequency** *n.* frequency able to be perceived by the human ear.

**audiology** /ˌaw-dee-**ol**-uh-jee/ *n.* science of hearing.

**audiotape** *n.* (also **audio tape**) **1 a** magnetic tape for recording sound. **b** a length of this. **2** a sound recording on tape.

**audiovisual** /ˌaw-dee-oh-**vizh**-yoo-uhl/ *adj.* (of teaching methods etc.) using both sight and sound.

**audit** /**aw**-duht/ — *n.* official scrutiny of accounts. — *v.* (**-t-**) conduct an audit of.

**audition** /aw-**dish**-uhn/ — *n.* test of a performer's suitability or ability. — *v.* assess or be assessed at an audition. [Latin *audio* hear]

**auditor** n. **1** person who audits accounts. **2** listener. [French from Latin]

**auditorium** /ˌaw-duh-**taw**-ree-uhm/ n. (pl. **-s**) part of a theatre etc. for the audience. [Latin]

**auditory** /aw-duh-tuh-ree, -tree/ adj. **1** concerned with hearing. **2** received by the ear.

**au fait** /oh fay/ predic. adj. (usu. foll. by with) conversant (au fait with the rules). [French]

**Augean** /aw-**jee**-uhn/ adj. filthy. [Greek Augeas, a mythical king: his filthy stables were cleaned by Hercules diverting a river through them]

**auger** /aw-guh/ n. **1** tool with a screw point for boring in wood. **2** similar large tool for boring holes in the ground. [Old English]

**aught** /awt/ n. archaic anything. [Old English]

**augment** /awg-**ment**/ v. make or become greater; increase (augmented his income by working at night). □ **augmentation** /ˌawg-men-**tay**-shuhn, ˌawg-muhn-/ n. [Latin: related to AUCTION]

**augmented interval** n. Mus. perfect or major interval that is increased by a semitone.

**au gratin** /oh **grat**-uhn/ adj. cooked with a crust of breadcrumbs or melted cheese. [French]

**augur** /aw-guh/ — v. portend, serve as an omen (augur well or ill). — n. hist. Roman religious official interpreting natural phenomena in order to pronounce on proposed actions. [Latin]

**augury** /aw-gyuh-ree/ n. (pl. **-ies**) **1** omen. **2** interpretation of omens.

**August** /aw-guhst/ n. eighth month of the year. [Latin Augustus, first Roman emperor]

**august** /aw-**gust**/ adj. venerable, imposing. [Latin]

**Augustan** /aw-**gus**-tuhn/ adj. **1** of the reign of Augustus, esp. as a flourishing literary period. **2** (of literature) refined and classical in style. [Latin: see AUGUST]

**auk** /awk/ n. black and white sea bird of the Northern hemisphere, having short wings. [Old Norse]

**auld lang syne** /ˌohld lang **zuyn**/ n. times long past. [Scots, = old long since]

**au naturel** /ˌoh nat-yoo-**rel**, nach-uh-**rel**/ predic. adj. & adv. uncooked; (cooked) in the most natural or simple way. [French, = in the natural state]

**aunt** /ahnt/ n. **1** sister of one's father or mother. **2** uncle's wife. **3** colloq. (form of address by a child to) parent's female friend. [Latin amita]

**auntie** /**ahn**-tee/ n. (also **aunty**) (pl. **-ies**) **1** colloq. = AUNT. **2** (in Aboriginal English) respectful mode of address to an older woman. **3** (**Auntie**) institution considered to be conservative or cautious, esp. the ABC.

**Aunt Sally** n. **1** game in which sticks or balls are thrown at a wooden dummy. **2** target of general abuse or attack.

**aura** /aw-ruh/ n. (pl. **-s**) **1** distinctive atmosphere diffused by or attending a person, place, etc. (an aura of tranquillity). **2** (in mystic or spiritualistic use) supposed subtle emanation, visible as a sphere of light surrounding the body of a living creature. [Greek, = breeze]

**aural** /aw-ruhl/ adj. of the ear or hearing. □ **aurally** adv. [Latin auris ear]

**aureate** /aw-ree-uht/ adj. literary **1** golden. **2** resplendent. [Latin aurum gold]

**aureole** /aw-ree-ˌohl/ n. (also **aureola** /aw-**ree**-uh-luh, ˌaw-ree-**oh**-luh/) **1** halo or circle of light, esp. in a religious painting. **2** corona round the sun or moon. [Latin, = golden (crown)]

**au revoir** /ˌoh ruh-**vwah**/ int. & n. goodbye (until we meet again). [French]

**auricle** /aw-ri-kuhl/ n. **1** each atrium of the heart. **2** external ear of animals. [Latin auris ear]

**auricular** /aw-**rik**-yuh-luh/ adj. **1 a** of or relating to the ear or hearing. **b** spoken aloud to the hearing (auricular confession to a priest). **2** of or relating to the auricle of the heart. **3** shaped like an auricle.

**auriferous** /aw-**rif**-uh-ruhs/ adj. yielding gold. [Latin aurifer from aurum gold]

**aurora** /aw-**raw**-ruh, uh-/ n. (pl. **-s** or **aurorae** /-ree/) luminous electrical atmospheric phenomenon, usu. of streamers of light in the night sky above the southern or northern magnetic pole. [Latin, = dawn, goddess of dawn]

**aurora australis** /o-**strah**-luhs/ n. southern occurrence of the aurora; southern lights (irregularly visible esp. in the southern parts of Australia). [New Latin, = southern aurora]

**aurora borealis** /ˌbaw-ree-**ah**-luhs/ n. northern occurrence of the aurora; northern lights. [New Latin, = northern aurora]

**auscultation** /ˌaw-skuhl-**tay**-shuhn/ n. listening, esp. to sounds from the heart, lungs, etc., for purposes of diagnosis. [Latin ausculto listen]

**auspice** /aw-spuhs/ n. **1** (in pl.) patronage (esp. under the auspices of). **2** omen, premonition. [originally 'observation of bird-flight': Latin avis bird]

**auspicious** /aw-**spish**-uhs/ *adj.* promising well; favourable.

**AUSSAT** /**os**-at, **oz**-,sat/ *abbr.* Australia's domestic satellite system. [*Australia, satellite*]

**Aussie** /**oz**-ee/ *colloq.* — *n.* **1** an Australian. **2** Australia. **3** Australian English. — *adj.* Australian. [abbreviation]

**Aussie battler** *n.* (also **little Aussie battler**) *colloq.* typical (esp. working class) Australian who survives against any odds.

**Aussie Rules** *n.* = AUSTRALIAN RULES.

**austere** /o-**steer**/ *adj.* (**-terer, -terest**) **1** severely simple (*an austere account*). **2** morally strict; severe in self-discipline (*an austere religious order*). **3** stern, grim. [Greek *austēros*]

**austerity** /o-**ste**-ruh-tee/ *n.* (*pl.* **-ies**) **1** sternness; moral severity. **2** (also *attrib.*) severe simplicity, e.g. of nationwide economies (*austerity measures*). **3** (esp. in *pl.*) austere practice (*the austerities of a Trappist monk's life*).

**austral** /o-**struhl**/ *adj.* **1** southern. **2** (**Austral**) **a** of Australia or Australasia. **b** used as the first element in the names of various Australian plants (*Austral bluebell*; *Austral pincushion*). [Latin *auster* south]

**Australasia** /o-struh-**lay**-*zh*uh, -shuh/ *n.* Australia, New Zealand, and neighbouring islands of the SW Pacific. □ **Australasian** *adj.*

**Austral bluebell** see ROYAL BLUEBELL.

**Australia** /o-**stray**-lyuh, uh-/ *n.* the continent in the Southern hemisphere bounded by the Indian, Southern, and Pacific Oceans (in early use often restricted to the mainland or to NSW as the only known part of the mainland); the federated States and Territories which together make up the Commonwealth of Australia. [Anglicisation of Latin (*Terra*) *Australis* the southern land]

**Australia Day** *n.* 26 January, the day on which the landing of Governor Phillip at Sydney Cove in 1788 is commemorated.

**Australia Felix** /**fee**-liks/ *n. hist.* name given by the explorer Thomas Mitchell in 1836 to the region south of the Murray River which, in 1851, was separated from New South Wales and named Victoria. [Latin *felix* happy, productive, fertile]

**Australian** /o-**stray**-lee-uhn, uh-, -lyuhn/ — *n.* **1** *hist.* an Aborigine. **2** native or national of Australia. **3** person of Australian descent. **4** = AUSTRALIAN ENGLISH. — *adj.* **1** characteristic of or belonging to Australia. **2** used as the first element in the names of some fauna and flora.

**Australiana** /o-stray-lee-**ah**-nuh, uh-/ *n.* books, documents, artefacts, etc., relating to or characteristic of Australia and its history.

**Australian adjective** see GREAT AUSTRALIAN ADJECTIVE.

**Australian bindweed** *n.* trailing Australian convolvulus bearing many rounded rose-pink flowers in spring and summer.

**Australian Broadcasting Corporation** *n.* Australia's national and international broadcaster, a statutory authority responsible for a national television network, radio services both domestic and overseas, etc.

**Australian Capital Territory** *n.* federal territory in south-eastern Australia which includes Canberra, the Capital of Australia.

**Australian cattle dog** see BLUE HEELER.

**Australian crawl** *n.* fast swimming stroke in which the body is prone, the arms reach forward alternately in an overarm action and pull back through the water, and the legs maintain a flutter kick.

**Australian Democrats** *n.* political party espousing liberal principles, founded in 1977.

**Australian English** *n.* the dialect of English spoken by Australians.

**Australian Football League** *n.* **1** regulating body for Australian National Football. **2** national competition run by this organisation.

**Australian golden wattle** see GOLDEN WATTLE.

**Australianise** *v.* (also **-ize**) (**-sing** or **-zing**) render (a person, institution, etc.) Australian in character.

**Australianism** *n.* **1** distinctively Australian word or phrase. **2 a** pride in Australian nationalism. **b** character distinctively Australian.

**Australian Labor Party** see LABOR PARTY.

**Australian language** *n.* **1** an Aboriginal language. **2** Australian English.

**Australian National Football** *n.* = AUSTRALIAN RULES.

**Australianness** *n.* quality or character distinctive of Australia or of Australians.

**Australian Rules** *n.* form of football originating in the mid-nineteenth century in Victoria, played with an oval ball by teams of 18; properly entitled Australian National Football.

**Australian salute** see GREAT AUSTRALIAN SALUTE.

**Australian terrier** *n.* (also **Sydney silky**) small, sturdy terrier with long bluish hair.

**Australite** /os-truh-ˌluyt/ n. small piece of dark meteoric glass found in Australia.

**Austral ladies' tresses** n. Australian terrestrial orchid having numerous pink or white scented flowers wreathing around spiral spikes which resemble long plaits of hair interwoven with flowers.

**Australoid** /os-truh-ˌloid/ adj. of, allied to, or resembling the ethnological type of the Aborigines of Australia.

**Australorp** /os-truh-ˌlawp/ n. Australian breed of Orpington fowl. [*Orpington* in England]

**Austral pincushion** see PINCUSHION 2.

**autarchy** /aw-ˌtah-kee/ n. absolute rule; despotism. [Greek *autos* self, *arkhē* rule]

**autarky** /aw-ˌtah-kee/ n. self-sufficiency, esp. economic. [Greek *autos* self, *arkeō* suffice]

**authentic** /aw-then-tik/ adj. **1** of undisputed origin; genuine. **2** reliable, trustworthy. □ **authentically** adv. **authenticity** /ˌaw-then-tis-uh-tee/ n. [Greek *authentikos*]

**authenticate** /aw-then-tuh-ˌkayt/ v. (-ting) establish as true, genuine, or valid. □ **authentication** /-kay-shuhn/ n.

**author** /aw-thuh/ n. (fem. **authoress**) **1** writer, esp. of books. **2** originator of an idea, event, etc. (*author of all my woes*). [Latin *auctor*]

**authorise** /aw-thuh-ˌruyz/ v. (also **-ize**) (-sing or -zing) **1** officially approve, sanction. **2** (foll. by to + infin.) give authority to (a person to do a thing). □ **authorisation** /ˌaw-thuh-ruy-zay-shuhn/ n. **authorised** adj. **authoriser** n.

**authoritarian** /aw-ˌtho-ruh-tair-ree-uhn, uh-/ — adj. favouring or enforcing strict obedience to authority, as opposed to individual freedom. — n. authoritarian person.

**authoritative** /aw-tho-ruh-tuh-tiv, uh-/ adj. **1** reliable, esp. having authority. **2** official (*an authoritative document*).

**authority** /aw-tho-ruh-tee, uh-/ n. (pl. -ies) **1 a** power or right to enforce obedience. **b** (often foll. by for, or to + infin.) delegated power. **2** (esp. in pl.) person or body having authority. **3** influence based on recognised knowledge or expertise. **4** expert. [Latin *auctoritas*]

**authorship** n. **1** origin of a book etc. (*of unknown authorship*). **2** profession of an author.

**autism** /aw-tiz-uhm/ n. mental condition, usu. present from childhood, characterised by self-absorption and social withdrawal. □ **autistic** /aw-tis-tik/ adj. [related to AUTO-]

**auto**[1] /aw-toh/ n. automatic control. [abbreviation]

**auto**[2] attrib. adj. automobile (*auto electronics; auto parts; auto repairs*).

**auto**[3] n. colloq. car. [abbreviation of AUTOMOBILE]

**auto-** comb. form **1** self (*autism*). **2** one's own (*autobiography*). **3** by oneself or spontaneous (*auto-suggestion*). **4** by itself or automatic (*automobile*). [Greek *autos*]

**autobiography** /ˌaw-toh-buy-og-ruh-fee, aw-tuh-/ n. (pl. -ies) **1** written account of one's own life. **2** this as a literary genre. □ **autobiographer** n. **autobiographical** /-graf-i-kuhl/ adj.

**autochthon** /aw-tok-thun/ n. (pl. -s or -es /-thuh-ˌneez/) (in pl.) original or earliest known inhabitants of a country (*the Aborigines are Australia's autochthones*). □ **autochthonous** adj. [Greek, = sprung from the earth (as AUTO- *khthōn*, land)]

**autocracy** /aw-tok-ruh-see/ n. (pl. -ies) **1** rule by an autocrat. **2** dictatorship. [Greek *kratos* power]

**autocrat** /aw-tuh-ˌkrat/ n. **1** absolute ruler. **2** dictatorial person. □ **autocratic** /-krat-ik/ adj. **autocratically** /-krat-i-kuhlee, -klee/ adv.

**autocross** /aw-toh-ˌkros/ n. motor racing across country or on unmade roads.

**autocue** /aw-toh-ˌkyoo/ n. propr. screen etc. from which a speaker reads a television script.

**auto-erotism** /ˌaw-toh-e-ruh-ˌtiz-uhm/ n. (also **auto-eroticism** /-uh-rot-uh-ˌsiz-uhm/) sexual excitement brought about by stimulating one's own body; masturbation. □ **auto-erotic** /-uh-rot-ik/ adj.

**autograph** /aw-tuh-ˌgrahf, -graf/ — n. signature, esp. that of a celebrity. — v. sign or write on in one's own hand. [Greek *graphō* write]

**auto-immune** /ˌaw-toh-uh-myoon/ adj. (of a disease) caused by antibodies produced against substances naturally present in the body.

**automate** /aw-tuh-ˌmayt/ v. (-ting) convert to or operate by automation.

**automated teller machine** n. automatic machine from which customers of a bank etc. may withdraw cash, esp. by using a keycard.

**automatic** /ˌaw-tuh-mat-ik/ — adj. **1** (of a machine, device, etc.) working by itself, without direct human intervention. **2 a** done spontaneously (*automatic reaction*). **b** following inevitably (*automatic penalty*). **3** (of a firearm) able to be loaded and fired continuously. **4** (of a vehicle or its transmission) using gears that change automatically. — n. **1** automatic machine, firearm, or tool. **2** vehicle with automatic transmission. □ **automatically** adv. [related to AUTOMATON]

**automatic pilot** n. device for keeping an aircraft or ship on a set course.

**automation** /ˌaw-tuh-**may**-shuhn/ n. **1** use of automatic equipment in place of manual labour. **2** production of goods etc. by this.

**automaton** /aw-**tom**-uh-tuhn/ n. (pl. **-mata** or **-s**) **1** machine controlled automatically; robot. **2** person acting like a robot. [Greek, = acting of itself]

**automobile** /ˈaw-tuh-muh-ˌbeel/ n. motor car. [French]

**automotive** /ˌaw-tuh-**moh**-tiv/ adj. of motor vehicles.

**autonomous** /aw-**ton**-uh-muhs/ adj. **1** having self-government. **2** acting or free to act independently. [Greek nomos law]

**autonomy** n. **1** self-government. **2** personal freedom.

**autopsy** /**aw**-top-see/ n. (pl. **-ies**) post-mortem. [Greek autoptēs eye-witness]

**auto-suggestion** /ˌaw-toh-suh-**jes**-chuhn/ n. hypnotic or subconscious suggestion made to oneself.

**autumn** /**aw**-tuhm/ n. **1** (often attrib.) season between summer and winter. **2** time of maturity or incipient decline (in the autumn of his life). □ **autumnal** /aw-**tum**-nuhl/ adj. [Latin autumnus]

**autumn equinox** n. (also **autumnal equinox**) equinox about 21 March.

**auxiliary** /og-**zil**-yuh-ree, awg-/ — adj. **1** subsidiary, additional. **2** giving help. — n. (pl. **-ies**) **1** auxiliary person or thing. **2** (in pl.) foreign or allied troops in the service of a nation at war. **3** verb used to form tenses or moods of other verbs (see panel). [Latin auxilium help]

**avail** /uh-**vayl**/ — v. **1** help; be of use. **2** refl. (foll. by of) make use of, profit by. — n. use, profit (of no avail). [Latin valeo be strong]

**available** adj. **1** at one's disposal, obtainable. **2 a** (of a person) free, not committed. **b** able to be contacted. □ **availability** /-**bil**-uh-tee/ n.

**avalanche** /**av**-uh-ˌlahnsh, -ˌlansh/ n. **1** rapidly sliding mass of snow and ice on a mountain. **2** sudden abundance (avalanche of work). [French]

**avant-garde** /ˌav-on-**gahd**/ — n. pioneers or (esp. artistic) innovators. — adj. new; pioneering. [French, = vanguard]

**avarice** /**av**-uh-ruhs/ n. extreme greed for money or gain. □ **avaricious** /ˌav-uh-**rish**-uhs/ adj. [Latin avarus greedy]

**avatar** /**av**-uh-tah/ n. (in Hindu mythology) descent of a deity etc. to earth in bodily form. [Sanskrit, = descent]

**Ave** /**ah**-vay/ n. (in full **Ave Maria**) prayer to the Virgin Mary (Luke 1:28). [Latin, = hail]

**avenge** /uh-**venj**/ v. (**-ging**) **1** inflict retribution on behalf of. **2** take vengeance for (an injury). □ **be avenged** avenge oneself. [Latin vindico]

**avenue** /**av**-uh-ˌnyoo/ n. **1** road or street (often tree-lined). **2** way of approaching or dealing with something (explored every avenue). [French avenir come to]

**aver** /uh-**ver**/ v. (**-rr-**) formal assert, affirm. □ **averment** n. [Latin verus true]

**average** /**av**-uh-rij, **av**-rij/ — n. **1** usual amount, extent, or rate. **2** amount obtained by adding two or more numbers and dividing by how many there are. **3** (with ref. to speed etc.) ratio obtained by subtracting the initial from the final value of each element of the ratio (average of 60 kilometres per hour). — adj. **1 a** usual, ordinary. **b** mediocre (gave a very average performance). **2** constituting an average (the average age is 72). — v. (**-ging**) **1** amount on average to (sales averaged six a week). **2** do on average (average six hours' work a day). **3** estimate the average of. □ **average out** (at) result in an average (of). **law of**

---

### Auxiliary verb

An auxiliary verb is used in front of another verb to alter its meaning. Mainly, it expresses:

**1** when something happens, by forming a tense of the main verb, e.g. I shall go. He was going.

**2** permission, obligation, or ability to do something, e.g. They may go. You must go. I can't go.

**3** The likelihood of something happening, e.g. I might go. She would go if she could. The principal auxiliary verbs are:

| | | | |
|---|---|---|---|
| be | have | must | will |
| can | let | ought | would |
| could | may | shall | |
| do | might | should | |

**averages** principle that if one of two extremes occurs the other will also. **on** (or **on an**) **average** as an average rate or estimate. [French, = damaged goods]

**averse** /uh-**vers**/ *predic. adj.* (usu. foll. by *to*) opposed, disinclined (*was not averse to helping me*). [Latin *verto vers-* turn]

**aversion** /uh-**ver**-*zh*uhn, -shuhn/ *n.* **1** (usu. foll. by *to*, *for*) dislike or unwillingness (*has an aversion to hard work*). **2** object of this.

**avert** /uh-**vert**/ *v.* (often foll. by *from*) **1** turn away (one's eyes or thoughts). **2** prevent or ward off (esp. danger).

**aviary** /**ay**-vuh-ree, -vyuh-/ *n.* (*pl.* **-ies**) large cage or building for keeping birds. [Latin *avis* bird]

**aviation** /ˌay-vee-**ay**-shuhn/ *n.* science or practice of flying aircraft. [Latin: related to AVIARY]

**aviator** /**ay**-vee-ˌay-tuh/ *n.* person who flies aircraft.

**avid** /**av**-uhd/ *adj.* (often foll. by *for*) eager, greedy (*an avid reader*; *avid for power*). □ **avidity** /uh-**vid**-uh-tee/ *n.* **avidly** *adv.* [Latin *aveo* crave]

**avionics** /ˌay-vee-**on**-iks/ *n.pl.* (usu. treated as *sing.*) electronics as applied to aviation. [from AVIATION, ELECTRONICS]

**avocado** /ˌav-uh-**kah**-doh/ *n.* (*pl.* **-s**) **1** dark green edible pear-shaped fruit with yellowish-green creamy flesh. **2** tree bearing it. [Spanish from Aztec]

**avocet** /**av**-uh-ˌset/ *n.* **1** long-legged wading bird with an upward-curved bill. **2** (in full **red-necked avocet**) avocet of mainland Australia having a bright chestnut head and black and white body. [French from Italian]

**avoid** /uh-**void**/ *v.* **1** keep away or refrain from (*avoid fatty foods*). **2** escape; evade (*avoided his pursuers*). **3** *Law* quash, annul. □ **avoidable** *adj.* [French]

**avoidance** /uh-**voi**-duhns/ *n.* act of shunning or averting.

**avoidance relationship** *n.* association that is forbidden in traditional Aboriginal society, e.g. that between mother-in-law and son-in-law.

**avoidance rules** *n.pl.* laws governing an AVOIDANCE RELATIONSHIP.

**avoirdupois** /ˌav-uh-duh-**poiz**/ *n.* (in full **avoirdupois weight**) former system of weights based on a pound of 16 ounces or 7,000 grains. [French, = goods of weight]

**avow** /uh-**vow**/ *v. formal* **1** declare, confess. **2** (as **avowed** *adj.*) admitted (*the avowed author*). □ **avowal** *n.* **avowedly** /uh-**vow**-uhd-lee/ *adv.* [Latin *voco* call]

**avuncular** /uh-**vung**-kyuh-luh/ *adj.* like or of an uncle, esp. in manner. [Latin *avunculus* uncle]

**Awabakal** /u-**wub**-u-kul/ *n.* an Aboriginal language spoken in a large area of eastern NSW north of Sydney: the language and its speakers are now extinct.

**await** /uh-**wayt**/ *v.* **1** wait for. **2** (of an event or thing) be in store for (*a surprise awaits you*). [French: related to WAIT]

**awake** /uh-**wayk**/ — *v.* (**-king**; *past* **awoke**; *past part.* **awoken**) **1** cease to sleep or arouse from sleep. **2** (often foll. by *to*) become or make alert, aware, or active (*awoke me to the possibilities*). — *predic. adj.* **1** not asleep. **2** (often foll. by *to*) alert, aware (*they are awake to what is going on*). [Old English: related to A²]

**awaken** *v.* = AWAKE *v.*

■ **Usage** *Awake* and *awaken* are interchangeable but *awaken* is much rarer than *awake* as an intransitive verb.

**award** /uh-**wawd**/ — *v.* give or order to be given as a payment or prize (*awarded her the prize*; *awarded damages*). — *n.* **1** thing or amount awarded. **2 a** judicial decision. **b** determination of an industrial court or commission or tribunal. [French]

**award wage** *n.* amount fixed by an industrial tribunal etc. as remuneration to be paid to specified workers (in an occupation, industry, etc.).

**aware** /uh-**wair**/ *predic. adj.* **1** (often foll. by *of* or *that*) conscious; having knowledge (*aware of the real facts*). **2** well-informed. **3** (usu. with preceding adverb indicating the area of concern) **a** (of a person, social group, etc.) fully informed about current issues of concern in a particular field (*an environmentally aware industry*). **b** (of a product) designed, manufactured, or marketed in such a way as to take account of current concerns and attitudes (*an ecologically aware detergent*). □ **awareness** *n.* [Old English]

■ **Usage** *Aware* is also found used attributively in sense 2, as in '*a very aware person*', but this should be avoided in formal contexts.

**awash** /uh-**wosh**/ *predic. adj.* **1** level with the surface of, and just covered by, water. **2** flooded (*the room was awash*). **3** carried or washed by the waves. **4** (foll. by *with*) overflowing, abounding; full of (*his language was awash with Australianisms; the city was awash with tourists*).

**away** /uh-**way**/ — adv. **1** to or at a distance from the place, person, or thing in question (go, give, look, away; 5 kilometres away). **2** into non-existence (explain, fade, away). **3** constantly, persistently (work away). **4** without delay (ask away). — attrib. adj. Sport not played on one's own ground (away match). [Old English: related to A², WAY]

**awe** /aw/ — n. reverential fear or wonder. — v. (**awing**) inspire with awe (awed by the Aboriginal paintings). [Old Norse]

**aweigh** /uh-**way**/ predic. adj. (of an anchor) clear of the bottom.

**awe-inspiring** adj. causing awe or wonder; magnificent.

**awesome** /**aw**-suhm/ adj. inspiring awe; dreaded.

**awful** /**aw**-fuhl/ adj. **1** colloq. very bad or unpleasant (has awful writing; awful weather). **2** (attrib.) colloq. as an intensifier (awful lot of money). **3** poet. inspiring awe (the awful wrath of God).

**awfully** adv. **1** badly; unpleasantly (played awfully). **2** very (awfully pleased).

**awhile** /uh-**wuyl**/ adv. for a short time. [a while]

**awkward** /**aw**-kwuhd/ adj. **1** difficult to use or deal with. **2** clumsy, ungainly. **3 a** embarrassed (felt awkward about it). **b** embarrassing (an awkward situation). [obsolete awk perverse]

**awl** n. small tool for piercing holes, esp. in leather. [Old English]

**awn** n. bristly head of a sheath of barley and other grasses. [Old Norse]

**awning** n. sheet of canvas etc. stretched on a frame as a shelter against the sun or rain. [origin uncertain]

**awoke** past of AWAKE.

**awoken** past part. of AWAKE.

**AWOL** /**ay**-wol/ abbr. absent without leave.

**awry** /uh-**ruy**/ — adv. **1** crookedly, askew (looked awry). **2** amiss, wrong (his plans have gone awry). — predic. adj. crooked; unsound (his theory is awry).

**axe** /aks/ — n. **1** chopping-tool with a handle and heavy blade. **2** (**the axe**) dismissal (of employees); abandonment of a project etc. (got the axe). — v. (**axing**) **1** cut (esp. costs or staff) drastically; abandon (a project). **2** remove or dismiss (axed twenty workers). □ **an axe to grind** private ends to serve. [Old English]

**axial** /**ak**-see-uhl/ adj. of, forming, or placed round an axis.

**axil** /**ak**-suhl/ n. upper angle between a leaf and stem or between a branch and the trunk. [Latin axilla armpit]

**axiom** /**ak**-see-uhm/ n. **1** established or accepted principle. **2** self-evident truth. □ **axiomatic** /ˌak-see-uh-**mat**-ik/ adj. [Greek axios worthy]

**axis** /**ak**-suhs/ n. (pl. **axes** /-seez/) **1 a** imaginary line about which a body rotates. **b** line which divides a regular figure symmetrically. **2** Math. fixed reference line for the measurement of coordinates etc. **3 a** alliance between two or more countries forming a centre for an eventual larger grouping of nations sharing a similar ideal or objective. **b** (**the Axis**) alliance of Germany, Italy, and later Japan, in the war of 1939–45. [Latin, = axle]

**axle** /**ak**-suhl/ n. spindle on which a wheel is fixed or turns. [Old Norse]

**ayatollah** /ˌuy-uh-**tol**-uh/ n. Shiite religious leader in Iran. [Persian from Arabic, = token of God]

**aye** /uy/ — adv. archaic or Brit. dial. yes. — n. affirmative answer or vote (the ayes have it). [probably from I, expressing assent]

**azalea** /uh-**zay**-lee-uh, uh-**zay**-lyuh/ n. a kind of rhododendron with large showy flowers. [Greek azaleos dry]

**azimuth** /**az**-uh-muhth/ n. angular distance from a north or south point of the horizon to the intersection with the horizon of a vertical circle passing through a given celestial body. □ **azimuthal** /-**myooth**-uhl/ adj. [French from Arabic]

**azoic** /uh-**zoh**-ik/ adj. **1** having no trace of life. **2** (**Azoic**) Geol. (of an age etc.) having no organic remains. [Greek azōos without life]

**AZT** abbr. drug intended for use against the Aids virus. [from the chemical name]

**Aztec** /**az**-tek/ — n. **1** member of the native Mexican people overthrown by the Spanish in 1519. **2** language of this people. — adj. of the Aztecs or their language. [Nahuatl, = men of the north]

**azure** /**ay**-zhuh, **ayz**-yuh/ — n. **1** deep sky-blue colour. **2** poet. clear sky. — adj. deep sky-blue. [Arabic]

# B

**B¹** /bee/ *n.* (*pl.* **Bs** or **B's**) **1** (also **b**) second letter of the alphabet. **2** *Mus.* seventh note of the diatonic scale of C major. **3** second hypothetical person or example. **4** second highest category (of academic marks etc.). **5** (usu. **b**) *Algebra* second known quantity.

**B²** *symb.* boron.

**B³** *abbr.* (also **B.**) **1** black (pencil-lead). **2** Blessed.

**b.** *abbr.* **1** born. **2** *Cricket* **a** bowled by. **b** bye.

**BA** *abbr.* Bachelor of Arts.

**Ba** *symb.* barium.

**baa** /bah/ — *v.* (**baas, baaed** or **baa'd**) bleat. — *n.* sheep's cry. [imitative]

**Baagandji** /bah-gun-jee/ *n.* an Aboriginal language spoken over a vast area on both sides of the Darling River in NSW from Bourke to Menindee, and extending into SA: now extinct, the last speakers having been recorded in the 1970s.

**babble** /bab-uhl/ — *v.* (**-ling**) **1 a** talk, chatter, or say incoherently or excessively. **b** (of a stream etc.) murmur. **2** repeat or divulge (a secret etc.) foolishly. — *n.* **1 a** incoherent speech. **b** foolish or idle talk. **2** murmur of voices, water, etc. [imitative]

**babbler** /bab-luh/ *n.* **1** person who babbles. **2 a** any of a large group of birds with loud chattering voices. **b** any of several Australian birds of this group, brownish-grey in colour with white eyebrows and usu. white breast, and having down-curved bills and long tails (*chestnut-crowned babbler; grey-crowned babbler; white-browed babbler*). **3** *colloq.* a cook (see BABBLING BROOK).

**babbling brook** *n.* (also **babbler**) *colloq.* a cook. [rhyming slang]

**babe** *n.* **1** *literary* baby. **2** innocent or helpless person (*babes in the wood*). **3** *colloq.* young woman. **4** *colloq.* attractive young person of either sex. [as BABY]

**babel** /bay-buhl/ *n.* **1** confused noise, esp. of voices. **2** scene of confusion. [Hebrew, = Babylon (Gen. 11)]

**baboon** /buh-boon, ba-/ *n.* large long-nosed African and Arabian monkey. [French and medieval Latin]

**baby** /bay-bee/ — *n.* (*pl.* **-ies**) **1** very young child. **2** childish person. **3** youngest member of a family etc. **4** (often *attrib.*) **a** very young animal. **b** thing that is small of its kind (*baby car*). **5** *colloq.* sweetheart. **6** one's responsibility, invention, concern, etc., regarded in a personal way. — *adj.* of or befitting a baby; for a baby's use (*baby talk; baby clothes*). — *v.* (**-ies, -ied**) treat like a baby; pamper. □ **babyhood** *n.* **babyish** *adj.* [imitative of child's *ba ba*]

**baby boom** *n. colloq.* temporary increase in the birthrate.

**baby boomer** *n. colloq.* person born during a baby boom, esp. that which occurred after World War II.

**babysit** *v.* (**-tt-**; *past* and *past part.* **-sat**) look after a child while its parents are out. □ **babysitter** *n.*

**baccarat** /bak-uh-rah/ *n.* gambling card-game. [French]

**bacchanal** /bak-uh-nuhl/ — *n.* **1** drunken revelry or reveller. **2** priest or follower of Bacchus. — *adj.* (also **bacchic** /bak-ik/) **1** of or like Bacchus. **2** drunkenly riotous. [Latin *Bacchus* from Greek, god of wine]

**Bacchanalia** /bak-uh-nay-lee-uh/ *n.pl.* **1** Roman festival of Bacchus. **2** (**bacchanalia**) drunken revelry.

**bach** /bach/ var. of BATCH².

**bachelor** /bach-uh-luh/ *n.* **1** unmarried man. **2** person with a university first degree. □ **bachelorhood** *n.* [medieval Latin]

**bachelor's buttons** *n.* = BILLY BUTTONS.

**bacillus** /buh-sil-uhs/ *n.* (*pl.* **bacilli** /-uy/) rod-shaped bacterium, esp. one causing disease. □ **bacillary** *adj.* [Latin, diminutive of *baculus* stick]

**back** — *n.* **1 a** rear surface of the human body from shoulder to hip. **b** upper surface of an animal's body. **c** spine (*broke his back*). **d** keel of a ship. **2** backlike surface (*back of the head, chair, shirt*). **3** reverse or more distant part (*back of the room; sat in the back; back of the house; write it on the back*). **4** (in Australia) a part of the interior which is remote from settlements or from water. **5** defensive player in football etc. — *adv.* **1** to the rear (*go back a bit; looked back*). **2** in or into a previous state, place, or time (*came back; put it back; back in June*). **3** at a distance (*stand back*). **4** in return (*pay back*). **5** in check (*hold him back*). — *v.* **1 a** give moral or financial support to (*backed me* *to the hilt).* **b** bet on (a horse etc.). **2** (often foll. by *up*) move (a vehicle etc.) backwards. **3 a** put or serve as a back, background, or support to. **b** *Mus.* accompany. **4** lie at the back of (*beach backed by cliffs*). **5** (of the wind) move anticlockwise. **6** (of a sheepdog) run across the backs of yarded sheep to drive them in a particular direction. — *adj.* **1** situated to the rear; remote, subsidiary (*back teeth; backstreets; back country*). **2** past; not current (*back pay; back issue*). **3** reversed (*back flow*). ▫ **back and forth** to and fro. **back down** withdraw from confrontation. **the back of beyond** very remote place. **back of** (a place) behind, beyond (*back of Bourke*). **back off 1** draw back, retreat. **2** = *back down*. **back on to** have its back adjoining (*backs on to a field*). **back out 1** reverse (a car etc.). **2** (often foll. by *of*) withdraw from a commitment. **back-pedal** reverse one's action or opinion. **back to** (a place) used of a reunion of former residents or associates (*back to Yass*). **back to back 1** with backs adjacent and facing each other (*stood back to back*). **2** (**back-to-back**) consecutive (*back-to-back premierships*). **back up 1** give (esp. moral) support to. **2** *Computing* make a backup of (data, a disk, etc.). **3** (also **back-up for**) return for a second helping etc. **get** (or **put**) **a person's back up** annoy a person. **get off a person's back** stop troubling a person. **get on a person's back** annoy or harass a person. **put one's back into** approach (a task etc.) with vigour. **turn one's back on** abandon; ignore. ▫ **backer** *n.* (in sense 1 of *v.*). **backless** *adj.* [Old English]

**backbench** *n.* backbencher's seat in a parliament.

**backbencher** *n.* MP not holding a senior office.

**backbiting** *n.* malicious talk. ▫ **backbite** *v.*

**backblocks** *n.pl.* **1** land in the remote and sparsely inhabited interior. **2** outer suburbs of a city. **3** (*attrib.*) **a** located in a sparsely populated inland district (*a backblocks pub*). **b** characteristic of those who live in such a district (*backblocks customs*).

**backbone** *n.* **1** spine. **2** chief support. **3** firmness of character.

**back-breaking** *adj.* (esp. of manual work) extremely hard.

**backburn** *v.* burn undergrowth etc. in the path of a bushfire to stop its advance.

**backburner** *n.* (also **back burner**) ▫ **put on** (or **consign to**) **the backburner** assign a

relatively low priority to (*your plan has been put on the backburner*).

**backchat** *n.* *colloq.* verbal insolence.

**backcloth** *n.* = BACKDROP.

**back country** *n.* **1** sparsely populated country area remote from closely settled districts. **2** (*attrib.*) **a** located in such an area. **b** characteristic of those who live in such an area.

**backdate** *v.* (**-ting**) **1** make retrospectively valid. **2** put an earlier date to than the actual one.

**back-door** *attrib.adj.* clandestine; underhand (*did a back-door deal*).

**backdrop** *n.* **1** painted cloth at the back of a stage. **2** background to a scene or situation.

**backfill** — *v.* refill an excavated or mined hole with the material dug out of it. — *n.* this material.

**backfire** *v.* (**-ring**) **1** (of an engine or vehicle) ignite or explode too early in the cylinder or exhaust. **2** (of a plan etc.) rebound adversely on its originator; have the opposite effect to what was intended.

**back-formation** *n.* **1** formation of a word from its seeming derivative (e.g. *laze* from *lazy*). **2** word so formed.

**background** *n.* **1** part of a scene or picture furthest from the observer. **2** (often *attrib.*) inconspicuous position (*kept in the background; background music*). **3** person's education, social circumstances, etc. **4** explanatory or contributory information or events.

**backhand** — *n.* **1** stroke played with the back of the hand turned towards one's opponent. **2** (*attrib.*) of or made with a backhand (*backhand volley*). — *adj.* (of handwriting) with the letters sloping backwards.

**backhanded** /bak-**han**-duhd/ *adj.* **1** made with the back of the hand. **2** indirect; ambiguous (*backhanded compliment*).

**backhander** *n.* **1 a** backhand stroke. **b** backhanded blow. **2** *colloq.* bribe.

**backing** *n.* **1 a** support, esp. financial or moral. **b** material used for a thing's back or support. **2** musical accompaniment, esp. to a pop singer.

**backing dog** *n.* sheepdog that backs (sense 6 of BACK *v.*).

**backlash** *n.* **1** violent, usu. hostile, reaction. **2** sudden recoil in a mechanism.

**back-loading** *n.* freight carried on a return journey, after delivery of the principal load.

**backlog** *n.* arrears of uncompleted work etc.

**back number** n. **1** out-of-date issue of a periodical. **2** *colloq.* out-of-date person or thing.

**backpack** — n. rucksack. — v. travel or hike with this. □ **backpacker** n.

**back paddock** n. paddock distant from the station homestead.

**back passage** n. rectum.

**back-pedal** v. (**-ll-**) **1** pedal backwards on a bicycle etc. **2** reverse one's previous action or opinion.

**back pocket** see POCKET n. 6.

**back road** n. (also **back track**) little used, often indirect, road or track.

**back room** n. (often as **backroom** attrib.) place where secret work is done (*back-room boys*).

**back seat** n. less prominent or inferior position or status.

**back-seat driver** n. person eager to advise without taking responsibility.

**backside** n. *colloq.* buttocks.

**back slang** n. slang using words spelt backwards (e.g. *yob*).

**backslide** v. (**-ding**; past **-slid**; past part. **-slid** or **-slidden**) return to bad habits etc.

**backspace** v. (**-cing**) move a typewriter carriage etc. back one or more spaces.

**backspin** n. (in tennis, golf, etc.) backward spin making a ball slow down on hitting a surface.

**backstab** v. harm a person (esp. a trusting friend) treacherously, esp. in secret.

**backstage** adv. & adj. behind the scenes.

**backstairs** — n.pl. rear or side stairs of a building. — attrib. adj. (also **backstair**) underhand; secret.

**back station** n. = OUTSTATION 1.

**backstitch** n. sewing with each stitch starting behind the end of the previous one.

**back-stop** n. **1** *Cricket* etc. **a** position directly behind the wicket-keeper. **b** fielder in this position. **2** last resort.

**backstreet** n. side-street, alley.

**backstroke** n. swimming stroke done on the back.

**back teeth** n.pl. □ **fed up to the back teeth** utterly fed up. **thrilled to the back teeth**. utterly thrilled.

**back-to-back** adj. consecutive.

**back to front** adj. **1** with back and front reversed. **2** in disorder.

**backtrack** — v. **1** retrace one's steps. **2** reverse one's policy or opinion. — n. (**back track**) = BACK ROAD.

**backup** n. (often attrib.) **1** support; reserve (*backup team*). **2** *Computing* **a** making of spare copies of data for safety. **b** copy so made.

**backward** /bak-wuhd/ — adv. = BACKWARDS. — adj. **1** towards the rear or starting-point (*backward look*). **2** reversed (*backward roll*). **3** slow to develop or progress. **4** hesitant, shy.

**backwards** adv. **1** away from one's front (*lean backwards*). **2** **a** with the back foremost (*walk backwards*). **b** in reverse of the usual way (*count backwards*). **3** **a** into a worse state (*these new policies are taking us backwards*). **b** into the past (*looked backwards over the years*). **c** (of motion) back towards the starting-point (*roll backwards*). □ **backwards and forwards** to and fro. **bend** (or **fall** or **lean**) **over backwards** *colloq.* make every effort, esp. to be fair or helpful.

**backwash** n. **1** **a** receding waves made by a ship etc. **b** backward current of air created by a moving aircraft. **2** repercussions.

**backwater** n. **1** peaceful, secluded, or dull place. **2** stagnant water fed from a stream.

**backwoods** n.pl. **1** remote uncleared forest land. **2** remote region. □ **backwoodsman** n.

**backyard** — n. (also **back yard**) enclosure, usu. including a garden, at the back of a house. — attrib. adj. illicit, illegal (*backyard abortion*).

**backyard business** n. small-scale business conducted in domestic premises (sometimes with the implication of inferiority or illegality).

**bacon** /bay-kuhn/ n. cured meat from the back or sides of a pig. □ **bring home the bacon** *colloq.* succeed in one's undertaking. [French from Germanic]

**bacon-and-eggs** n. any of several Australian shrubs, widespread in the bush, bearing usu. yellow and reddy-brown pea-flowers (the colours which suggest the foods in question): see BOSSIAEA; DAVIESIA; DILLWYNIA; PULTENAEA.

**bacteriology** /bak-teer-ree-ol-uh-jee/ n. the study of bacteria.

**bacterium** /bak-**teer**-ree-uhm/ n. (pl. **-ria**) unicellular micro-organism lacking an organised nucleus, esp. of a kind causing disease. □ **bacterial** adj. [Greek, = little stick]

■ **Usage** A common mistake is the use of the plural form *bacteria* as the singular. This should be avoided.

**bad** — adj. (**worse**, **worst**) **1** inadequate, defective (*bad work; bad light*). **2** (often foll. by *at*) unskilled; lacking competence (*bad at cricket; bad at Geography*). **3** unpleasant; unwelcome (*bad weather; bad news*). **4** harmful (*is bad for you*). **5**

(of food) decayed. **6** *colloq.* ill, injured (*feeling bad today; a bad leg*). **7** *colloq.* regretful, guilty (*feels bad about it*). **8** serious, severe (*a bad headache; bad mistake*). **9 a** morally unacceptable (*bad man; bad language*). **b** naughty (*you bad boy!*). **10** not valid (*a bad cheque*). — *n.* **1** ill fortune (*must take the bad with the good*). **2** ruin; a degenerate condition (*go to the bad*). □ **not** (or **not so**) **bad** *colloq.* fairly good. **too bad** *colloq.* regrettable. [Old English]

**bad blood** *n.* ill feeling.

**bad books** see BOOK.

**baddy** *n.* (*pl.* **-ies**) *colloq.* villain in a story, film, etc.

**bade** see BID.

**badge** *n.* **1** small flat emblem worn to signify office, membership, etc., or as decoration. **2** thing that reveals a condition or quality (*suntan and bleached hair are the badge of a surfie*). [origin unknown]

**badger** — *n.* nocturnal burrowing mammal of Europe etc. with a black and white striped head. — *v.* pester, harass (*kept badgering me for a loan*). [origin uncertain]

**badinage** /**bad**-uh-ˌnahzh/ *n.* playful ridicule. [French]

**badly** *adv.* (**worse**, **worst**) **1** in a bad manner (*plays badly*). **2** *colloq.* very much (*wants it badly*). **3** severely (*badly defeated*).

**badminton** /**bad**-min-tuhn/ *n.* game with racquets and a shuttlecock. [*Badminton* in England]

**bad-mouth** *v. colloq.* abuse verbally, put down.

**bad news** *n. colloq.* person or thing causing, or expected to cause, trouble (*he's bad news — avoid him; this house has been bad news from day one*).

**baffle** /**baf**-uhl/ — *v.* (**-ling**) **1** confuse or perplex. **2** frustrate, hinder (*plans etc.*). — *n.* device that checks flow esp. of fluid or sound waves. □ **bafflement** *n.* [origin uncertain]

**bag** — *n.* **1** soft open-topped receptacle. **2 a** piece of luggage. **b** woman's handbag. **3** (in *pl.*; usu. foll. by *of*) *colloq.* large amount (*bags of time*). **4** *colloq. derog.* woman. **5** animal's sac. **6 a** amount of game shot by one person. **b** number of wickets taken by a bowler. **7** (usu. in *pl.*) baggy skin under the eyes. **8** *colloq.* particular interest (*folk music is not my bag*). — *v.* (**-gg-**) **1** *colloq.* **a** secure (*bagged the best seat*). **b** (often in phr. **bags** I) *colloq.* claim as being the first (*bags I go next*). **2** put in a bag. **3** (cause to) hang loosely; bulge. **4** *colloq.* criticise;

disparage. □ **bag** (or **whole bag**) **of tricks** *colloq.* everything; the whole lot. **in the bag** *colloq.* achieved, secured. **out of the bag** unexpected, surprising (*well, that win was out of the bag*). **rough as bags** see ROUGH. □ **bagful** *n.* (*pl.* **-s**). [origin unknown]

**bagatelle** /ˌbag-uh-**tel**/ *n.* **1** game in which small balls are struck into holes on a board. **2** mere trifle. **3** short piece of esp. piano music. [French from Italian]

**bagel** /**bay**-guhl/ *n.* ring-shaped bread roll. [Yiddish]

**baggage** /**bag**-ij/ *n.* **1** luggage. **2** portable army equipment. [French]

**baggy** *adj.* (**-ier**, **-iest**) hanging loosely. □ **baggily** *adv.* **bagginess** *n.*

**bagman** *n.* **1** swagman. **2** bookmaker's clerk. **3** *colloq.* agent who collects or distributes money for illicit purposes.

**bagpipe** *n.* (usu. in *pl.*) musical instrument consisting of a windbag connected to reeded pipes.

**bag wagga** /**wog**-uh/ *n.* quilt made of hessian bags and stuffed with any handy material (see WAGGA).

**Bahasa Indonesia** /bah-ˌhah-suh ˌin-duh-**nee**-zhuh/ *n.* official language of Indonesia. [Indonesian *bahasa* language, from Sanskrit]

**bail¹** — *n.* **1** security given for a released prisoner's return for trial. **2** person(s) giving this. — *v.* (usu. foll. by *out*) **1** release or secure the release of (a prisoner) on payment of bail. **2** release from a difficulty; rescue. □ **jump bail** *colloq.* fail to appear for trial after being released on bail. **on bail** released after payment of bail. [Latin *bajulus* carrier]

**bail²** — *n.* **1** *Cricket* either of two crosspieces bridging the stumps. **2** bar separating horses in an open stable. **3** framework for securing the head of a cow during milking. — *v.* (usu. foll. by *up*) **1 a** secure (a cow) during milking. **b** (**bail up!**) call with which a cow is encouraged into the bail. **2** *hist.* **a** (of a bushranger) make (a person) hold up his or her arms to be robbed (*bailed up several gentlemen in one afternoon*). **b** (**bail up!**) bushranger's challenge, requiring those addressed to submit without resistance to being robbed. **3** buttonhole (a person) (*was bailed up in the street by nuns collecting for charity*). **4 a** bring (an animal) to bay (*the dogs bailed up a kangaroo*). **b** (of an animal) stand at bay. [French]

**bail³** *v.* (also **bale**) **1** (usu. foll. by *out*) scoop water out of (a boat etc.). **2** scoop (water etc.) out. □ **bail out** var. of *bale out* 1 (see BALE¹). [French]

**bailiff** /**bay**-luhf/ *n.* sheriff's officer who executes writs and carries out distraints. [French: related to BAIL[1]]

**bailiwick** /**bay**-lee-wik/ *n.* **1** *Law* district of a bailiff. **2** *joc.* person's particular interest. [as BAILIFF, obsolete *wick* district]

**bail-out** *n.* financial assistance given to a failing business or economy by a government, bank, etc. so as to save it from collapse. □ **bail out** *v.* [BAIL[3]]

**bain-marie** /ˌban-muh-**ree**/ *n.* (*pl.* **bains-marie** pronunc. same) pan of hot water holding a pan containing sauce etc. for slow heating. [French, translation of medieval Latin *balneum Mariae* bath of Maria (a supposed alchemist)]

**bairn** *n. archaic* child. [Old English: related to BEAR[1]]

**bait** — *n.* **1** food used to entice prey. **2** food treated with poison to eradicate pests etc. **3** allurement; something intended to tempt or entice. — *v.* **1 a** harass or annoy (a person). **b** torment (a chained animal). **2 a** put bait on (a hook, trap, etc.). **b** add poison to food. [Old Norse]

**baize** *n.* usu. green woollen felted material, used for coverings, esp. of the tops of billiard-tables or card-tables. [French pl. *baies* chestnut-coloured]

**bake** *v.* (**-king**) **1** cook or become cooked by dry heat, esp. in an oven. **2** *colloq.* (usu. as **be baking**) (of weather, a person, etc.) be very hot. **3** harden by heat. [Old English]

**baker** *n.* person who bakes and sells bread, cakes, etc., esp. for a living.

**baker's dozen** *n.* thirteen.

**bakery** *n.* (*pl.* **-ies**) place where bread and cakes are made or sold.

**baking powder** *n.* mixture of sodium bicarbonate, cream of tartar, etc., as a raising agent.

**baking soda** *n.* sodium bicarbonate.

**baklava** /**buk**-luh-vuh, ˌbak-luh-**vah**, ˌbuk-/ *n.* rich sweetmeat of flaky pastry, honey, and nuts. [Turkish]

**baksheesh** /**bak**-sheesh/ *n.* gratuity, tip. [Persian]

**balaclava** /ˌbal-uh-**klah**-vuh/ *n.* (in full **balaclava helmet**) usu. woollen covering for the whole head and neck, except for the face. [*Balaclava* in the Crimea, the site of a battle in 1854]

**balalaika** /ˌbal-uh-**luy**-kuh/ *n.* guitar-like stringed instrument with a triangular body. [Russian]

**balance** /**bal**-uhns/ — *n.* **1 a** even distribution of weight or amount. **b** stability of body or mind. **2** apparatus for weighing, esp. one with a central pivot,

beam, and two scales. **3 a** counteracting weight or force. **b** (in full **balance-wheel**) regulating device in a clock etc. **4** decisive weight or amount (*balance of opinion*). **5 a** agreement or difference between credits and debits in an account. **b** amount still owing or outstanding (*will pay the balance*). **c** amount left over. **6 a** *Art* harmony and proportion. **b** *Mus.* relative volume of sources of sound (*bad balance between violins and trumpets*). **7** (**the Balance**) zodiacal sign or constellation Libra. — *v.* (**-cing**) **1** bring into, keep, or be in equilibrium (*balanced a book on her head; balanced on one leg*). **2** (often foll. by *with*, *against*) offset or compare (one thing) with another (*balance the pros and cons*). **3** counteract, equal, or neutralise the weight or importance of (*the positives balance the negatives*). **4** (usu. as **balanced** *adj.*) make well-proportioned and harmonious (*balanced diet; balanced opinion*). **5 a** compare and esp. equalise the debits and credits of (an account). **b** (of an account) have credits and debits equal. □ **in the balance** uncertain; at a critical stage. **on balance** all things considered. **strike a balance** choose a moderate course or compromise. [Latin *bilanx* scales]

**balance of payments** *n.* difference in value between payments into and out of a country.

**balance of power** *n.* **1** situation of roughly equal power among the chief nations of the world. **2** power held by a small group when larger groups are of equal strength.

**balance of trade** *n.* difference in value between imports and exports.

**balance sheet** *n.* statement giving the balance of an account.

**balander** /buh-**lan**-duh/ *n.* (also **balanda**) (in Aboriginal English) white man. [corruption of *Hollander* (cf. NEW HOLLAND)]

**balcony** /**bal**-kuh-nee/ *n.* (*pl.* **-ies**) **1** usu. balustraded platform on the outside of a building with access from an upper floor. **2** upper tier of seats in a theatre etc. □ **balconied** *adj.* [Italian]

**bald** /bawld/ *adj.* **1** (of a person) lacking some or all hair on the scalp. **2** (of an animal, plant, etc.) lacking the usual hair, feathers, leaves, etc. **3** *colloq.* with a worn surface (*bald tyre*). **4 a** plain, direct (*bald statement; bald style*). **b** undisguised (*bald effrontery*). **5** marked with white, esp. on the face (*bald horse; bald eagle*). □ **balding** *adj.* (in senses 1–3).

**baldly** *adv.* (in sense 4). **baldness** *n.* [Old English]

**balderdash** /**bawl**-duh-ˌdash/ *n.* nonsense. [origin unknown]

**baldy** (also **bally**) — *n.* **1** a Hereford. **2** any white-faced beast. — *adj.* **1** Hereford (*a mob of baldy bullocks*). **2** (of cattle) with white markings on the face. [British dial.]

**bale**[1] — *n.* **1** tightly bound bundle of merchandise or hay. **2** pack of compressed, usu. greasy, wool weighing 110–204 kg. — *v.* (**-ling**) make up into bales. □ **bale out 1** (also **bail out**) (of an airman) make an emergency parachute descent. **2** var. of BAIL[1] *v.* 2. [Dutch: related to BALL[1]]

**bale**[2] var. of BAIL[3].

**baleen** /buh-**leen**/ *n.* whalebone. [Latin *balaena* whale]

**baleful** /**bayl**-fuhl/ *adj.* **1** menacing in look, manner, etc. **2** malignant, destructive. □ **balefully** *adv.* [archaic *bale* evil]

**balk** var. of BAULK.

**Balkan** /**bawl**-kuhn/ *adj.* **1** of the region of SE Europe bounded by the Adriatic, Aegean, and Black Sea. **2** of its peoples or countries. [Turkish]

**ball**[1] /bawl/ — *n.* **1** hollow or solid sphere, esp. for use in a game. **2** a ball-shaped object; material in the shape of a ball (*ball of snow; ball of wool*). **b** rounded part of the body (*ball of the foot*). **3** cannon-ball. **4** single delivery or pass of a ball in cricket, baseball, football, etc. **5** (in *pl.*) *coarse colloq.* **a** testicles. **b** (usu. as *int.*) nonsense. **c** courage, 'guts'. — *v.* **1** form into a ball. □ **the ball is in your** etc. **court** you (etc.) must be next to act. **ball of muscle** very fit person. **balls up** *colloq.* bungle; make a mess of. **have the ball at one's feet** have one's best opportunity. **keep the ball rolling** maintain the momentum of an activity. **on the ball** *colloq.* alert. **start** etc. **the ball rolling** set an activity in motion; make a start. [Old Norse]

**ball**[2] /bawl/ *n.* **1** formal social gathering for dancing. **2** *colloq.* enjoyable time (esp. *have a ball*). [Greek *ballō* throw]

**ballad** /**bal**-uhd/ *n.* **1** poem or song narrating a popular story. **2** slow sentimental song. [Provençal: related to BALL[2]]

**ball-and-socket joint** *n.* joint in which a rounded end lies in a concave socket, allowing freedom of movement.

**ballart** /**bal**-aht/ see NATIVE CHERRY. [Kuurn Kopan Noot and other Victorian languages *balad*]

**ballast** /**bal**-uhst/ — *n.* **1** heavy material stabilising a ship, the car of a balloon, etc.

**2** coarse stone etc. as the bed of a railway track or road. **3** mixture of coarse and fine aggregate for making concrete. **4** anything that affords stability or permanence. — *v.* **1** provide with ballast. **2** afford stability or weight to. [Low German or Scandinavian]

**ball-bearing** *n.* **1** bearing in which the two halves are separated by a ring of small balls. **2** one of these balls.

**ballcock** *n.* floating ball on a hinged arm controlling the water level in a cistern.

**ballerina** /ˌbal-uh-**ree**-nuh/ *n.* female ballet-dancer. [Italian: related to BALL[2]]

**ballet** /**bal**-ay/ *n.* **1** dramatic or representational style of dancing to music. **2** particular piece or performance of ballet. **3** company performing ballet. □ **balletic** /buh-**let**-ik/ *adj.* [French: related to BALL[2]]

**ball game** *n.* **1** game played with a ball. **2** *colloq.* affair; matter (*a whole new ball game*).

**ballista** /buh-**lis**-tuh/ *n.* (*pl.* **-stae** /-stee/ ) (in ancient warfare) catapult for hurling large stones etc. [Latin from Greek *ballō* throw]

**ballistic** /buh-**lis**-tik/ *adj.* **1** of or relating to projectiles. **2** moving under the force of gravity only.

**ballistic missile** *n.* missile that is powered and guided but falls by gravity.

**ballistics** *n.pl.* (usu. treated as *sing.*) science of projectiles and firearms.

**balloon** /buh-**loon**/ — *n.* **1** small inflatable rubber toy or decoration. **2** large usu. round inflatable flying bag, often carrying a basket for passengers. **3** balloon shape enclosing dialogue etc. in a comic strip or cartoon. — *v.* **1** (cause to) swell out like a balloon. **2** travel by balloon. □ **balloonist** *n.* [French or Italian, = large ball]

**ballot** /**bal**-uht/ — *n.* **1** occasion or system of voting, in writing and usu. secret. **2** total of such votes. **3** paper etc. used in voting. — *v.* (**-t-**) **1** (usu. foll. by *for*) **a** hold a ballot; give a vote. **b** draw lots for precedence etc. **2** take a ballot of (*balloted the members*). [Italian *ballotta*: related to BALLOON]

**ballot paper** *n.* = BALLOT *n.* 3.

**ballpark** *n.* US **1** baseball ground. **2** *colloq.* sphere of activity, etc. **3** (*attrib.*) *colloq.* approximate.

**ballpoint** *n.* (in full **ballpoint pen**) pen with a tiny ball as its writing point.

**ballroom** *n.* large room for dancing.

**balls-up** *n. colloq.* bungle, mess.

**ball-up** *n. Aust. Rules* bouncing of the ball by the field umpire to start or restart play.

**ballyhoo** /ˌbal-ee-**hoo**/ n. **1** loud noise or fuss. **2** noisy publicity. [origin unknown]

**balm** /bahm/ n. **1** aromatic ointment for anointing, soothing, or healing. **2** fragrant oil or resin exuded from certain trees and plants. **3** thing that heals or soothes. **4** aromatic herb (lemon balm). [Latin: related to BALSAM]

**Balmain bug** /ˌbal-mayn **bug**/ n. edible marine crustacean of southern Australian waters, having an oddly flattened body (see also SHOVEL-NOSED LOBSTER). [Balmain, suburb of Sydney]

**balmy** /**bah**-mee/ adj. (-ier, -iest) **1** mild and fragrant; soothing. **2** colloq. = BARMY. □ **balmily** adv. **balminess** n.

**baloney** n. (also **boloney**) colloq. nonsense. [origin uncertain]

**balsa** /**bol**-suh, **bawl**-/ n. **1** (in full **balsa wood**) tough lightweight wood used for making models etc. **2** tropical American tree yielding it. [Spanish, = raft]

**balsam** /**bol**-suhm, **bawl**-/ n. **1** aromatic resin exuded from various trees and shrubs. **2** ointment, esp. one composed of a substance dissolved in oil or turpentine. **3** tree or shrub yielding balsam. **4** any of several exotic flowering plants. □ **balsamic** /-**sam**-ik/ adj. [Latin balsamum]

**balsamic vinegar** n. an Italian vinegar made from wines and musts and aged in wooden casks.

**baluster** /**bal**-uh-stuh/ n. short post or pillar supporting a rail. [Greek balaustion wild-pomegranate flower]

■ Usage Baluster is often confused with banister. A baluster is usually part of a balustrade whereas a banister supports a stair handrail.

**balustrade** /ˌbal-uh-**strayd**/ n. railing supported by balusters, esp. on a balcony. □ **balustraded** adj.

**Bama** /**bam**-uh/ n. (also **Pama** /**pam**-uh/) an Aborigine. [many north Queensland languages bama person, man]

■ Usage See KOORI[1]

**bamboo** /bam-**boo**/ n. **1 a** tropical giant woody grass. **b** its stem, used for canes, furniture, etc. **2** (esp. in northern Australia) didgeridoo. [Dutch from Malay]

**bamboo shoot** n. young shoot of bamboo, eaten as a vegetable.

**bamboozle** /bam-**boo**-zuhl/ v. (**-ling**) colloq. cheat; mystify (bamboozled him out of $10; bamboozled by all this new technology). □ **bamboozlement** n. [origin unknown]

**ban** — v. (**-nn-**) forbid, prohibit, esp. formally. — n. formal prohibition (ban on smoking). [Old English, = summon]

**banal** /buh-**nahl**/ adj. trite, commonplace. □ **banality** /-**nal**-uh-tee/ n. (pl. **-ies**). **banally** adv. [French, related to BAN: originally = compulsory, hence = common]

**banana** /buh-**nah**-nuh/ n. **1** long curved soft fruit with a yellow skin. **2** treelike plant bearing it. □ **go bananas** colloq. go mad. [Portuguese or Spanish, from an African name]

**banana bender** n. colloq. Queenslander (one who puts the bend in the bananas).

**Bananaland** n. (also **Banana State**) colloq. Queensland.

**Bananalander** n. (also **Banana-lander**) colloq. Queensland.

**banana prawn** n. large food-prawn of the Gulf of Carpentaria and other warm waters, having a yellow-cream body and a tail-fan of yellow, green, and brown, giving it a banana-like appearance.

**banana republic** n. derog. small nation, esp. one in Central America, having a backward economy and depending on the influx of foreign capital.

**band** — n. **1** flat, thin strip or loop of paper, metal, cloth, etc., put round something esp. to hold or decorate it. **2 a** strip of material on a garment. **b** stripe of a different colour or material on an object. **3** group of esp. non-classical musicians. **4** organised group of criminals etc. **5** range of frequencies, wavelengths, or values. **6** belt connecting wheels or pulleys. — v. **1** (usu. foll. by together) unite (band together for mutual protection). **2** put a band on. **3** mark with stripes. [Old Norse (related to BIND) and French]

**bandage** /**ban**-dij/ — n. strip of material used to bind a wound etc. — v. (**-ging**) bind with a bandage. [French: related to BAND]

**bandaid** adj. temporary; makeshift; of the nature of a patch-up (bandaid solutions to the unemployment crisis). [Band-Aid (propr.) small adhesive plaster or patch for superficial wounds]

**bandanna** /ban-**dan**-uh/ n. large patterned handkerchief or scarf. [Portuguese from Hindi]

**b & b** abbr. bed and breakfast.

**banded anteater** see NUMBAT.

**bandicoot** /**ban**-dee-ˌkoot/ — n. any of various cat-sized Australian marsupials with a long, pointed head, nocturnal in habit, and feeding on tubers, insects, etc.; often with distinguishing epithet (long-nosed bandicoot; rabbit-eared bandicoot; short-nosed bandicoot). — v. **1** steal (potatoes etc.) from the ground, leaving the tops undisturbed. **2** fossick, esp. in a previously worked mining area. □ **as bald as a bandicoot** totally bald. **as lousy as a bandicoot** stingy, utterly mean. **as miserable as a bandicoot** thoroughly wretched; destitute. [Telugu *pandikokku* pig-rat of India and Sri Lanka]

**bandit** /**ban**-duht/ *n.* robber or outlaw, esp. one attacking travellers etc. □ **banditry** *n.* [Italian]

**Bandjalang** /**ban**-ju-lang/ *n.* an Aboriginal language once spoken over a large area in north-eastern NSW and south-eastern Queensland: now actively spoken only by a dwindling number of elderly Bandjalang people.

**bandolier** /ban-duh-**leer**/ *n.* (also **bandoleer**) shoulder belt with loops or pockets for cartridges. [Dutch or French]

**bandsaw** *n.* mechanical saw with a blade formed by an endless toothed band.

**bandwagon** *n.* □ **climb** (or **hop** or **jump**) **on the bandwagon** join a party, cause, or group that seems likely to succeed; get in on the winning side.

**bandy¹** *adj.* (**-ier, -iest**) **1** (of the legs) curved so as to be wide apart at the knees. **2** (also **bandy-legged**) having bandy legs. [perhaps from obsolete *bandy* curved stick]

**bandy²** *v.* (**-ies, -ied**) **1** (often foll. by *about*) **a** pass (a story, rumour, etc.) to and fro. **b** discuss disparagingly (*bandied her name about*). **2** (often foll. by *with*) exchange (blows, insults, etc.) (*don't you bandy words with me!*). [perhaps from French]

**bandy-bandy** *n.* either of two small venomous Australian snakes patterned with black and white bands around the body. [probably Kattang *bandi-bandi*]

**bane** *n.* **1** cause of ruin or trouble. **2** *poet.* ruin. **3** *archaic* (except in *comb.*) poison (*ratsbane*). □ **baneful** *adj.* [Old English]

**bang** — *n.* **1** loud short sound. **2** sharp blow. **3** *coarse colloq.* act of sexual intercourse. — *v.* **1** strike or shut noisily (*banged the door*). **2** (cause to) make a bang. **3** *coarse colloq.* have sexual intercourse (with). — *adv.* **1** with a bang. **2** *colloq.* exactly (*bang in the middle*). □ **bang on** *colloq.* exactly right. **go bang 1** shut noisily. **2** explode. **3** (as **bang goes** etc.) *colloq.* be suddenly lost (*bang went my hopes*). **go with a bang** go successfully (*the party went with a bang*). [imitative]

**bangalay** /**bang**-guh-lay, ,bang-**gal**-ee/ *n.* (also **bastard mahogany**) medium-sized eucalypt of NSW and Victoria, commonly found on saline coastal soils. [probably from Dharawal]

**bangalow** /**bang**-guh-loh/ *n.* (also **piccabeen**) tall palm of NSW and

Queensland, having arching, feather-like fronds, lilac flowers, and bright red fruits. [Dharawal, probably *bangala*]

**banger** *n.* **1** *colloq.* sausage. **2** firework designed to go bang.

**Banggala** /**bung**-gu-lu/ *n.* an Aboriginal language spoken extensively in southern SA: now extinct.

**bangle** /**bang**-guhl/ *n.* rigid bracelet or anklet. [Hindi *bangri*]

**bangtail** /**bang**-tayl/ — *n.* **1** horse or bullock etc. with its tail cut straight across. **2** = *bangtail muster.* — *v.* bangtail horses or cattle as an aid in counting or identifying. □ **bangtail muster** counting of stock on a station during which each beast has its tail-end cut off to distinguish it from those still to be counted.

**banian** var. of BANYAN.

**banish** /**ban**-ish/ *v.* **1** condemn to exile. **2** dismiss (esp. from one's mind). □ **banishment** *n.* [Germanic: related to BAN]

**banister** /**ban**-uhs-tuh/ *n.* (also **bannister**) (usu. in *pl.*) uprights and handrail beside a staircase. [corruption of BALUSTER]

■ **Usage** See note at *baluster*.

**banjo** /**ban**-joh/ *n.* (*pl.* **-s** or **-es**) **1** guitar-like stringed instrument with a circular body. **2** used of objects shaped like a banjo, e.g. shovel, shoulder of mutton, etc. □ **swing the banjo** use a shovel, esp. vigorously. □ **banjoist** *n.* [US southern corruption of *bandore* from Greek *pandoura* lute]

**bank¹** — *n.* **1** sloping ground beside a river. **2** raised area, esp. an elevation in the sea or a river bed; slope. **3** mass of cloud, fog, snow, etc. — *v.* **1** (often foll. by *up*) heap or rise into banks. **2** pack (a fire) tightly for slow burning. **3 a** (of a vehicle, aircraft, etc.) round a curve with one side higher than the other. **b** cause to do this. □ **bank up** pile up, accumulate (*the traffic had banked up bumper to bumper because of the accident*). [Old Norse: related to BENCH]

**bank²** — *n.* **1 a** establishment for depositing, withdrawing, and borrowing money. **b** building in which this business takes place. **2** kitty in some gambling games. **3** storage place (*blood bank*). — *v.* **1** deposit (money etc.) in a bank. **2** (often foll. by *at, with*) keep money (at a bank). □ **bank on** *colloq.* rely on (*I'm banking on you*). [French *banque* or Italian *banca*: related to BANK¹]

**bank³** *n.* row of similar objects, e.g. lights, switches, oars. [French *banc* from Germanic: related to BANK¹]

**bankcard** *n.* credit card issued by a bank.

**banker¹** n. **1** owner or manager of a bank. **2** keeper of the bank in some gambling games.

**banker²** n. river flooded to the top of its banks. □ **run a banker** (of a river) swell to the top of, or over, its banks. [BANK¹]

**banking** n. business of running a bank.

**banknote** n. piece of paper money.

**bankrupt** /bang-krupt/ — adj. **1** legally declared insolvent. **2** (often foll. by of) exhausted or drained (of some quality etc.); deficient, lacking (bankrupt of ideas; morally bankrupt). — n. **1** insolvent person, esp. one whose assets are used to repay creditors. **2** person exhausted of or deficient in a certain attribute (a moral bankrupt). — v. make bankrupt. □ **bankruptcy** n. (pl. **-ies**). [Italian banca rotta broken bench: related to BANK²]

**banksia** /bangk-see-uh/ n. any tree or shrub of the Australian genus Banksia (over 60 species), having usu. leathery leaves in a wide variety of shapes and dense flower-spikes, varying in colour from greenish to yellow to red, forming thick woody cones as the fruits mature. [Joseph Banks, English naturalist (d. 1820)]

**banksia man** n. large woody cone of several Banksia species, orig. as a character in children's stories.

**banner** n. **1** large sign bearing a slogan or design, esp. in a demonstration or procession; flag. **2** slogan, esp. political. [Latin bandum standard]

**banner headline** n. large, esp. front-page, newspaper headline.

**bannister** var. of BANISTER.

**banns** n.pl. notice announcing an intended marriage, read out in a church. [pl. of BAN]

**banquet** /bang-kwuht/ — n. **1** sumptuous, esp. formal, feast or dinner. **2** set-priced meal for a group in a Chinese restaurant etc., allowing diners to sample a wide range of dishes. — v. (**-t-**) attend, or entertain with, a banquet; feast. [French diminutive of banc bench]

**banshee** /ban-shee, -shee/ n. wailing female spirit (of Irish and Scottish folk tradition) warning of death in a house. [Irish bean sidhe fairy woman]

**bantam** /ban-tuhm/ n. **1** a kind of small domestic fowl. **2** small but aggressive person. [apparently from Bāntān in Java]

**bantamweight** n. **1** weight in certain sports between flyweight and featherweight, in amateur boxing 51–4 kg. **2** sportsman of this weight.

**banter** — n. good-humoured teasing. — v. tease; exchange banter. [origin unknown]

**Bantu** /ban-too/ — n. (pl. same or **-s**) **1** (often offens.) member of a large group of central and southern African Blacks. **2** group of languages spoken by them. — adj. of these peoples or languages. [Bantu, = people]

**banyan** /ban-ee-uhn, **ban-yuhn**/ n. (also **banian**) any fig tree (see FICUS) having adventitious roots which form buttresses around the trunk. [Portuguese from Sanskrit, applied originally to one such tree under which Hindu traders had built a temple]

**baobab** /bay-oh-,bab/ n. (also **boab**) **1** tree of north-western Australia, having a trunk swollen at the base and bearing tangy, yellowish to blue, edible fruits. **2** related African tree. [probably African dial.]

**baptise** /bap-tuyz/ v. (also **-ize**) (**-sing** or **-zing**) **1** administer baptism to. **2** give a name or nickname to.

**baptism** /bap-tiz-uhm/ n. sacrament of symbolic admission to the Christian Church, with water and usu. name-giving. □ **baptismal** /-tiz-muhl/ adj. [Greek baptizō baptise]

**baptism of fire** n. **1** initiation into battle. **2** painful initiation into an activity.

**baptist** n. **1** person who baptises, esp. John the Baptist. **2** (**Baptist**) Christian advocating baptism by total immersion.

**bar¹** — n. **1** long piece of rigid material, used esp. as an obstruction, confinement, fastening, weapon, etc. **2 a** something of similar form (bar of soap; bar of chocolate). **b** band of colour or light. **c** heating element of an electric heater. **d** metal strip below the clasp of a medal, awarded as an extra distinction. **e** sandbank or shoal at the mouth of a harbour or an estuary. **3 a** counter for serving alcohol etc. on. **b** room or building containing it. **c** small shop or stall serving refreshments (snack bar). **4 a** barrier. **b** restriction (colour bar; bar to promotion). **5** prisoner's enclosure in a lawcourt. **6** any of the sections into which a piece of music is divided by vertical lines. **7** (**the Bar**) Law **a** barristers collectively. **b** profession of barrister. — v. (**-rr-**) **1 a** fasten with a bar or bars. **b** (usu. foll. by in, out) shut or keep in or out. **2** obstruct, prevent (barred his progress). **3** (usu. foll. by from) prohibit, exclude (barred from attending). **4** mark with stripes. — prep. except. □ **behind bars** in prison. **not have a bar of** colloq. be unable to tolerate (someone etc.); dislike intensely; reject utterly (a course of action). [French]

**bar²** n. esp. *Meteorol.* unit of pressure, $10^5$ newtons per square metre, approx. one atmosphere. [Greek *baros* weight]

**barb¹** — n. **1** secondary backward-facing projection from an arrow, fish-hook, etc. **2** hurtful remark. **3** beardlike filament at the mouth of some fish. — v. **1** fit with a barb. **2** (as barbed *adj.*) (of a remark etc.) deliberately hurtful. [Latin *barba* beard]

**barb²** n. black strain of kelpie. [individual dog's name]

**barbarian** /bah-**bair**-ree-uhn/ — n. **1** uncultured or brutish person. **2** member of a pre-literate tribe etc. — *adj.* **1** rough and uncultured. **2** uncivilised. [Greek *barbaros* foreign]

**barbaric** /bah-**ba**-rik/ *adj.* **1** rough and uncultured. **2** brutal, cruel (*flogging is a barbaric punishment*). **3** primitive.

**barbarism** /**bah**-buh-₁riz-uhm/ n. **1** barbaric state or act. **2** non-standard word or expression; solecism. **3** anything considered to be in bad taste.

**barbarity** /bah-**ba**-ruh-tee/ n. (pl. **-ies**) **1** savage cruelty. **2** an example of this.

**barbarous** /**bah**-buh-ruhs/ *adj.* = BARBARIC 1.

**barbecue** /**bah**-buh-₁kyoo/ — n. **1 a** meal cooked over charcoal etc. out of doors. **b** party for this. **2** grill etc. used for this. — v. (**-ues**, **-ued**, **-uing**) cook on a barbecue. [Spanish from Haitian]

**barbed wire** n. wire with interwoven sharp spikes, used in fences and barriers.

**barbei** /**bah**-buhl/ n. **1** freshwater fish with barbs. **2** = BARB¹ n. 3. [Latin: related to BARB¹]

**barbell** n. iron bar with removable weights at each end, used for weight-lifting.

**barber** n. person who cuts men's hair etc. by profession. [medieval Latin *barba* beard]

**barbican** /**bah**-buh-kuhn/ n. outer defence, esp. a double tower above a gate or drawbridge. [French]

**barbie** /**bah**-bee/ n. *colloq.* barbecue. [abbreviation]

**barbiturate** /bah-**bich**-uh-ruht/ n. soporific or sedative drug from barbituric acid. [German, from the name *Barbara*]

**barbituric acid** /₁bah-buh-**choor**-rik/ n. organic acid from which barbiturates are derived.

**barcarole** /**bah**-kuh-₁rohl/ n. **1** gondoliers' song. **2** music imitating this. [Italian *barca* boat]

**bar code** n. machine-readable striped code on supermarket goods, library books, etc.

**Barcoo** /bah-**koo**/ *adj.* of or relating to the remote inland of Australia, its people, and its living conditions. □ **Barcoo dog** any noise-making contraption (elaboration of a rattle) used to drive sheep when there are no dogs to work them. **Barcoo rot** form of scurvy characterised by chronic sores. **Barcoo salute** = GREAT AUSTRALIAN SALUTE. **Barcoo sandwich** any outback food considered to be less than gourmet (e.g. a curlew between two sheets of bark). **Barcoo sickness** illness marked by Barcoo spews. **Barcoo sore** ulcer characteristic of Barcoo rot. **Barcoo spew** *colloq.* attack of vomiting. [*Barcoo River* in western Queensland]

**bard** n. **1** *poet.* poet. **2** *hist.* Celtic minstrel. □ **bardic** *adj.* [Celtic]

**Bardi** /**bahr**-dee/ n. an Aboriginal language of northern WA.

**bardi** /**bah**-dee/ n. (also **bardie**, **bardee**) edible larva or pupa of a species of beetle or of various species of moth (cf. WITCHETTY). [Nyungar and many other languages in WA and SA]

**bare** — *adj.* **1** unclothed or uncovered. **2 a** (of a tree) leafless. **b** unfurnished; empty (*bare room*; *cupboard was bare*). **c** (of a floor) uncarpeted. **3** plain, unadorned (*the bare truth*; *bare facts*). **4** (*attrib.*) scanty, just sufficient (*a bare majority*; *bare necessities*). — v. (**-ring**) uncover, reveal (*bared his teeth*; *bared his soul*). [Old English]

**bareback** *adj.* & *adv.* without a saddle.

**bare-belly** n. sheep with bare belly and legs caused by a defect in the fibre structure of the wool. □ **bare-bellied** *adj.*

**barefaced** *adj.* undisguised; impudent (*barefaced lie*).

**barefoot** *adj.* & *adv.* (also **barefooted**) wearing nothing on the feet.

**barely** *adv.* **1** scarcely (*barely escaped*). **2** scantily (*barely furnished*).

**barf** /bahf/ *colloq.* — v. vomit. — n. attack of vomiting. [origin unknown]

**bargain** /**bah**-guhn/ — n. **1 a** agreement on the terms of a sale etc. **b** this from the buyer's viewpoint (*a bad bargain*). **2** something acquired or offered cheaply. — v. (often foll. by *with*, *for*) discuss the terms of a sale etc. (*bargained with me*; *bargain for the table*). □ **bargain for** (or *colloq.* **on**) be prepared for; expect (*I didn't bargain for being asked to make a speech*). **bargain on** rely on. **into the bargain** moreover; in addition to what was expected. **make** (or **strike**) **a bargain** agree on a transaction. [French from Germanic]

**barge** — n. **1** long flat-bottomed cargo boat on a canal or river. **2** long ornamental boat used for pleasure or ceremony. — v. (**-ging**) **1** (foll. by *in*, *into*) **a** intrude rudely or awkwardly (*barged in on him*). **b** collide with (*barged into her*). **2** (often foll. by *around*) move clumsily about. [French: related to BARQUE]

**bargepole** n. □ **would not touch with a bargepole** refuse to be associated or concerned with.

**baritone** /**ba**-ruh-,tohn/ n. **1 a** second-lowest adult male singing voice. **b** singer with this voice. **2** instrument pitched second-lowest in its family. [Greek *barus* heavy, *tonos* tone]

**barium** /**bair**-ree-uhm/ n. white soft metallic element. [from BARYTA]

**barium meal** n. mixture swallowed to reveal the digestive tract in X-rays.

**bark**[1] — n. **1** sharp explosive cry of a dog etc. **2** sound like this. — v. **1** (of a dog etc.) give a bark. **2** speak or utter sharply or brusquely. **3** colloq. cough harshly. □ **bark up the wrong tree** make false assumptions; be on the wrong track. [Old English]

**bark**[2] — n. **1** tough outer skin of tree-trunks, branches, etc. **2** (*attrib.*) *hist.* **a** applied to items made of bark by Aborigines (*bark canoe*; *bark shield*). **b** applied to dwellings or buildings made of bark (*bark gunyah*; *bark humpy*; *bark school*). — v. **1** graze (one's shin etc.). **2** strip bark from. [Scandinavian]

**barker** n. tout outside a nightclub, at a sideshow, etc. [from BARK[1]]

**bark hut** n. *hist.* **1** name given by colonists to a temporary shelter constructed by an Aborigine. **2** dwelling built by whites, the walls and roof of which are made of bark.

**barking lizard** n. any of several Australian lizards which make barking noises.

**barking owl** n. (also **screaming-woman bird**) owl, of all except the arid parts of Australia, having a call like a human scream or a hoarse bark.

**barking spider** n. Australian spider which utters a loud whistling sound and which is also reputed to bark.

**bark painting** n. picture painted on bark as part of the ceremonial of Arnhem Land Aborigines; now a widely practised Aboriginal art form.

**barley** /**bah**-lee/ n. **1** cereal used as food and in spirits. **2** (also **barleycorn**) its grain. [Old English]

**barm** n. froth on fermenting malt liquor. [Old English]

**bar mitzvah** /bah **mits**-vuh/ n. **1** religious initiation ceremony of a Jew-

ish boy at 13. **2** boy undergoing this. [Hebrew, = son of the commandment]

**barmy** /**bah**-mee/ adj. (**-ier**, **-iest**) colloq. crazy, stupid. [from BARM: earlier, = frothy]

**barn** n. large farm building for storing grain etc. [Old English, = barley house]

**barnacle** /**bah**-nuh-kuhl/ n. **1** marine crustacean clinging to rocks, ships' bottoms, etc. **2** tenacious attendant or follower. [French or medieval Latin]

**barney** /**bah**-nee/ — n. (*pl.* **-s**) colloq. noisy quarrel. — v. argue. [perhaps British dial.]

**barnstorm** v. tour rural areas as an actor or political campaigner. □ **barnstormer** n.

**barometer** /buh-**rom**-uh-tuh/ n. **1** instrument measuring atmospheric pressure, used in meteorology. **2** anything which reflects changes in circumstances, opinions, etc. □ **barometric** /,ba-ruh-**met**-rik/ adj. [Greek *baros* weight, -METER]

**baron** /**ba**-ruhn/ n. **1** member of the lowest order of the nobility. **2** powerful businessman, entrepreneur, etc. (*beer baron*; *newspaper baron*). □ **baronial** /buh-**roh**-nee-uhl/ adj. [medieval Latin, = man]

**baroness** /**ba**-ruh-nes/ n. **1** woman holding the rank of baron. **2** baron's wife or widow.

**baronet** /**ba**-ruh-nuht, -net/ n. member of the lowest hereditary titled British order. □ **baronetcy** n. (*pl.* **-ies**).

**baroque** /buh-**rok**, buh-**rohk** / — adj. **1** highly ornate and extravagant in style, esp. of European art, music, etc. of the 17th and 18th c. **2** of this period. — n. baroque style or art. [Portuguese, originally = misshapen pearl]

**barque** /bahk/ n. **1** sailing-ship with the rear mast fore-and-aft-rigged and other masts square-rigged. **2** poet. boat. [Provençal from Latin *barca*]

**barra** /**ba**-ruh/ n. colloq. barramundi. [abbreviation]

**barrack**[1] /**ba**-ruhk/ — n. (usu. in *pl.*, often treated as *sing.*) **1** housing for soldiers. **2** large building of bleak or plain appearance. — v. lodge (soldiers etc.) in barracks. [Italian or Spanish]

**barrack**[2] /**ba**-ruhk/ v. **1** shout or jeer at (players, a speaker, etc.). **2** (foll. by *for*) cheer for, encourage (a team etc.). □ **barracker** n. **barracking** n. [perhaps from Irish *barrack* brag]

**barracouta** /,ba-ruh-**koo**-tuh/ n. (*pl.* same or **-s**) long slender fish of southern oceans, including those of southern Australia. [var. of BARRACUDA]

**barracuda** /,ba-ruh-**koo**-duh/ n. (*pl.*

same or **-s**) large tropical marine fish. [Spanish]

**barrage** /ba-rah*zh*/ n. **1** concentrated artillery bombardment. **2** rapid succession of questions or criticisms. [French *barrer* BAR[1]]

**barramundi** /ˌba-ruh-**mun**-dee/ n. (pl. same or **-s**) any of various Australian freshwater fishes highly valued as food. [probably from an Aboriginal language of central Queensland]

**barre** /bah/ n. horizontal bar at waist level, used in dance exercises. [French]

**barrel** /ba-ruhl/ — n. **1** cylindrical usu. convex container. **2** its contents. **3** measure of capacity in the imperial system (30 to 40 gallons). **4** cylindrical tube forming part of an object, e.g. a gun or a pen. — v. (**-ll-**) **1** put into a barrel or barrels. **2** *colloq.* (often foll. by *along*) drive fast. **3** *colloq.* **a** fell or flatten (a person). **b** (often foll. by *away*) press, demand, etc. persistently (*need to keep barrelling away at the government to have this law repealed*). □ **over a barrel** *colloq.* helpless, at a person's mercy. [French]

**barrel organ** n. mechanical musical instrument with a rotating pin-studded cylinder.

**barren** /ba-ruhn/ adj. (**-er**, **-est**) **1 a** unable to bear young. **b** (of land, a tree, etc.) unproductive. **2** unprofitable, dull. **3** (foll. by *of*) lacking in (*barren of wit*). □ **barrenness** n. [French]

**barricade** /ˌba-ruh-**kayd**, ba-/ — n. barrier, esp. one improvised across a street etc. — v. (**-ding**) block or defend with this. [French *barrique* cask]

**barrier** /ba-ree-uh/ n. **1** fence etc. that bars advance or access. **2** obstacle or circumstance that keeps people or things apart, or prevents communication (*class barriers*; *language barrier*). [Romanic: related to BAR[1]]

**barrier reef** n. coral reef separated from the shore by a channel.

**barring** /bah-ring/ prep. except, not including.

**barrister** /ba-ruh-stuh/ n. person entitled to practise as an advocate in any court. [from BAR[1]: perhaps after MINISTER]

**barrow**[1] /ba-roh/ n. **1** two-wheeled handcart, used esp. by street vendors. **2** = WHEELBARROW. □ **push one's own barrow** *colloq.* advocate one's own interests. [Old English: related to BEAR[1]]

**barrow**[2] /ba-roh/ n. ancient grave-mound. [Old English]

**barter** — v. **1** trade in goods without using money. **2** exchange (goods). — n.

trade by bartering. [perhaps from French]

**baryon** /ba-ree-ˌon/ n. heavy elementary particle (i.e. a nucleon or a hyperon). [Greek *barus* heavy]

**baryta** /buh-**ruy**-tuh/ n. barium oxide or hydroxide. [from BARYTES]

**barytes** /buh-**ruy**-teez/ n. mineral form of barium sulphate. [Greek *barus* heavy]

**basal** /**bay**-suhl/ adj. **1** of, at, or forming a base. **2** fundamental.

**basalt** /bas-awlt, -olt/ n. a dark volcanic rock whose strata sometimes form columns. □ **basaltic** adj. [Latin *basaltes* from Greek]

**base**[1] — n. **1 a** part supporting from beneath or serving as a foundation. **b** notional support or foundation (*power base*). **2** principle; starting-point. **3** esp. *Mil.* headquarters. **4** main or important ingredient. **5** *Math.* number in terms of which other numbers or logarithms are expressed. **6** *Chem.* substance capable of combining with an acid to form a salt. **7** *Geom.* line or surface on which a figure is regarded as standing. **8** *Baseball etc.* each of the four stations on a pitch. — v. (**-sing**) **1** (usu. foll. by *on*, *upon*) found or establish (a theory, hope, etc.). **2** station (*troops based in Cambodia*). □ **get to first base** achieve the first step towards an objective. [Greek *basis* stepping]

**base**[2] adj. **1** cowardly, despicable. **2** menial. **3** not pure; alloyed (*base coin*). **4** (of a metal) low in value. [Latin *bassus*]

**baseball** n. **1** game played with a circuit of four bases which batsmen must complete. **2** ball used in this.

**baseless** adj. unfounded, groundless.

**baseline** n. **1** line used as a base or starting-point. **2** line marking each end of a tennis-court.

**basement** /**bays**-muhnt/ n. floor of a building below ground level.

**bases** pl. of BASE[1], BASIS.

**bash** — v. **1 a** strike bluntly or heavily. **b** (often foll. by *up*) *colloq.* attack violently. **c** (often foll. by *down*, *in*, etc.) damage or break by striking forcibly. **2** (foll. by *into*) collide with. **3** *colloq.* assault figuratively (see EARBASH; SCRUB-BASH; SPINE-BASH). **4** criticise strongly; denigrate; abuse (*he likes to bash Canberra at every opportunity*) (see also -BASHING). — n. **1** heavy blow. **2** *colloq.* attempt (*had a bash at painting*). **3** *colloq.* party or social event (*there's a bash on at Mick's*). □ **basher** n. **bashing** n. [imitative]

**bashful** /**bash**-fuhl/ adj. shy, diffident. □ **bashfully** adv. [as ABASHED]

**-bashing** comb. form **1** vehement verbal abuse directed at the target specified

(*Canberra-bashing*; *union-bashing*). **2** vehement physical attack (*poofter-bashing*).

**BASIC** /**bay**-sik/ *n.* computer programming language using familiar English words. [*Beginner's All-purpose Symbolic Instruction Code*]

**basic** /**bay**-sik/ — *adj.* **1** serving as a base; fundamental (*basic requirements*). **2 a** simplest or lowest in level (*basic pay*; *basic needs*). **b** vulgar (*basic humour*). — *n.* (usu. in *pl.*) fundamental facts or principles. □ **basically** *adv.*

**basic wage** *n.* minimum living wage for an adult unskilled worker as determined by an industrial tribunal.

**basil** /**baz**-uhl/ *n.* aromatic herb used as flavouring. [Greek *basilikos* royal]

**basilica** /buh-**zil**-i-kuh, -**sil**-/ *n.* **1** ancient Roman hall with an apse and colonnades, used as a lawcourt etc. **2 a** usu. large Christian church having special privileges from the Pope. **b** church, usu. early, often with the nave on a higher elevation than the aisles. [Greek *basilikē* (*stoa*) royal (portico)]

**basilisk** /**baz**-uh-lisk, **bas**-/ *n.* mythical reptile with lethal breath and glance. [Greek, diminutive of *basileus* king]

**basin** /**bay**-suhn/ *n.* **1** round open vessel for holding liquids or preparing food in. **2** wash-basin. **3** hollow depression. **4** sheltered mooring area. **5** round valley. **6** area drained by a river. □ **basinful** *n.* (*pl.* **-s**). [medieval Latin *ba(s)cinus*]

**basis** /**bay**-suhs/ *n.* (*pl.* **bases** /-seez/ ) **1** foundation or support of something, esp. an idea or argument. **2** main determining principle or ingredient (*on a purely friendly basis*). **3** starting-point for a discussion etc. [Greek: related to BASE[1]]

**bask** /bahsk/ *v.* **1** relax in warmth and light. **2** (foll. by *in*) revel in (*basking in glory*). [Old Norse: related to BATHE]

**basket** /**bahs**-kuht/ *n.* **1** container made of interwoven cane, reed, wire, etc. **2** amount held by this. **3** the goal in basketball, or a goal scored. **4** *Econ.* group or range (of currencies). [French]

**basketball** *n.* **1** team game in which goals are scored by putting the ball through high nets. **2** ball used in this.

**basket case** *n. colloq.* mentally disturbed or eccentric person.

**Basque** /bahsk/ — *n.* **1** member of a people of the Western Pyrenees area of Spain and France. **2** their language. — *adj.* of the Basques or their language. [Latin *Vasco*]

**bas-relief** /**bas**-ruh-,leef/ *n.* sculpture or carving with figures projecting slightly

from the background. [French and Italian]

**bass**[1] /bays/ — *n.* **1 a** lowest adult male singing voice. **b** singer with this voice. **2** instrument pitched lowest in its family. **3** *colloq.* bass guitar or double-bass. **4** low-frequency output of a radio, record-player, etc. — *adj.* **1** lowest in musical pitch. **2** deep-sounding. □ **bassist** *n.* (in sense 3). [from BASE[2] altered after Italian *basso*]

**bass**[2] /bas/ *n.* (*pl.* same or **-es**) **1** any of various Northern hemisphere fish of the perch family. **2** marine fish of eastern Australian waters. **3** freshwater fish of eastern Australia. [Old English]

**bass clef** *n.* clef placing F below middle C on the second highest line of the staff.

**bassinet** /,bas-uh-**net**/ *n.* child's cradle or carrying basket. [French diminutive of *bassin* BASIN]

**bassoon** /buh-**soon**/ *n.* bass instrument of the oboe family, with a double reed. □ **bassoonist** *n.* [Italian: related to BASS[1]]

**bast** /bast/ *n.* fibre from the inner bark of a tree (esp. the lime) used in matting etc. [Old English]

**bastard** /**bahs**-tuhd/ *often offens.* — *n.* **1** person born of an unmarried mother. **2** *colloq.* used variously of a person in Australia: sometimes *derog.* (but without any suggestion of illegitimacy), frequently good-humoured if sometimes edged, often even affectionate: **a** unpleasant or despicable person. **b** person of a specified kind (*poor bastard*; *lucky bastard*). **c** person. **d** mate (*c'mon, you bastard, let's get going*). **3** *colloq.* difficult or awkward or unpleasant thing (*can't get this bastard of a screw to shift*; *bit of a bastard having to work on Christmas day*). — *attrib. adj.* **1** illegitimate by birth. **2** (of a plant or animal in Australia) resembling another species (*bastard dory*; *bastard mahogany*). □ **bastardy** *n.* (in sense 1 of *n.*). [French from medieval Latin]

**bastardisation** /,bah-stuh-duy-**zay**-shuhn/ *n.* (in certain educational institutions, the armed services, etc.) ritual of physical and psychological harassment of those newly enrolled (usu. for a specified period).

**bastardise** *v.* (also **-ize**) (**-sing** or **-zing**) **1** corrupt, debase. **2** initiate into a school, regiment, etc., by practising bastardisation.

**bastardry** /**bahs**-tuh-dree/ *n.* cruel, despicable, or malicious behaviour.

**baste**[1] /bayst/ *v.* (**-ting**) moisten (meat) with fat etc. during cooking. [origin unknown]

**baste²** /bayst/ *v.* (**-ting**) sew with large loose stitches, tack. [French from Germanic]

**bastinado** /ˌbas-tuh-**nay**-doh/ — *n.* punishment by beating with a stick on the soles of the feet. — *v.* (**-es, -ed**) punish in this way. [Spanish *baston* stick]

**bastion** /**bas**-tee-uhn/ *n.* **1** projecting part of a fortification. **2** thing regarded as protecting (*bastion of freedom*). [Italian *bastire* build]

**bat¹** — *n.* **1** implement with a handle, used for hitting balls in games. **2** turn at using this. **3** batsman. — *v.* (**-tt-**) **1** hit with or as with a bat. **2** take a turn at batting. □ **go to** (or **go in to**) **bat for** *colloq.* take up a person's cause. **off one's own bat** unprompted, unaided. [Old English from French]

**bat²** *n.* mouselike nocturnal flying mammal. □ **have bats in the belfry** be eccentric or crazy. **like a bat out of hell** very fast. [Scandinavian]

**bat³** *v.* (**-tt-**) □ **not** (or **never**) **bat an eyelid** *colloq.* show no reaction or emotion. [var. of obsolete *bate* flutter]

**batch¹** — *n.* **1** number of things or persons forming a group or dealt with together. **2** instalment (*sent off the latest batch*). **3** loaves etc. produced at one baking. — *v.* arrange or deal with in batches. [related to BAKE]

**batch²** *v.* (also **bach, batch it**) live on one's own; provide for oneself (in a rough and ready way, without the usual domestic conveniences). [from BACHELOR]

**bated** /**bay**-tuhd/ *adj.* □ **with bated breath** very anxiously. [as ABATE]

**bath** /bahth/ — *n.* (*pl.* **-s** /bah*thz*/ (esp. sense 3), /bahths/) **1 a** (usu. plumbed-in) container for sitting in and washing the body. **b** its contents. **2** act of washing in it (*have a bath*). **3** (usu. in *pl.*) public building with baths or a swimming-pool. **4 a** vessel containing liquid for immersing something, e.g. a film for developing. **b** its contents. — *v.* wash (esp. a baby) in a bath. [Old English]

**bathe** /bayth/ *v.* (**-thing**) **1** immerse oneself in water, esp. to swim or wash oneself. **2** immerse in, wash, or treat with liquid (*bathed his sore eyes*). **3** (of sunlight etc.) envelop. [Old English]

**bathers** /**bay**-*th*uhz/ *n.pl.* swimming costume.

**bathos** /**bay**-thos/ *n.* lapse in mood from the sublime to the absurd or trivial; anticlimax. □ **bathetic** /buh-**thet**-ik/ *adj.* [Greek, = depth]

**bathroom** *n.* **1** room with a bath, wash-basin, etc. **2** room with a lavatory.

**Bathurst burr** *n.* South American plant introduced to Australia, having burrs that infest sheep's wool. [*Bathurst* in central NSW]

**bathyscaphe** /**bath**-uh-ˌskayf/ *n.* manned vessel for deep-sea diving. [Greek *bathus* deep, *skaphos* ship]

**bathysphere** /**bath**-uh-ˌsfeer/ *n.* vessel for deep-sea observation. [Greek *bathus* deep, SPHERE]

**batik** /buh-**teek**, **bah**-tik, **bah**-teek/ *n.* **1** method of dyeing textiles by applying wax to parts to be left uncoloured. **2** cloth so treated. [Javanese, = painted]

**batman** /**bat**-muhn/ *n.* army officer's servant. [*bat* pack-saddle, from French]

**baton** /**bat**-uhn, buh-**ton**/ *n.* **1** thin stick for conducting an orchestra etc. **2** short stick passed on in a relay race. **3** stick carried by a drum major. **4** staff of office or authority. **5** police officer's truncheon. [French from Latin]

**batrachian** /buh-**tray**-kee-uhn/ — *n.* amphibian that discards its gills and tail, esp. a frog or toad. — *adj.* of batrachians. [Greek *batrakhos* frog]

**bats** *predic. adj. colloq.* crazy. [originally pl. of BAT²]

**batsman** *n.* person who bats, esp. in cricket.

**batswing coral tree** *n.* (also **coral tree**) spectacular deciduous tree of open forest in Australia, having a thorny cork-like bark, trifoliate leaves resembling bats' wings, and masses of red pea-flowers when the tree is leafless.

**batt** /bat/ *n.* insulation material (e.g. fibreglass) packed into a usu. rect-angular shape ready for installation in ceilings etc.

**battalion** /buh-**tal**-yuhn/ *n.* **1** army unit usu. of 300–1000 men. **2** large group with a common aim. [Italian *battaglia* BATTLE]

**batten¹** /**bat**-uhn/ — *n.* **1 a** long flat strip of squared timber. **b** horizontal strip of wood to which laths, tiles, etc., are fastened. **2** strip for securing tarpaulin over a ship's hatchway. — *v.* strengthen or fasten with battens. □ **batten down the hatches 1** secure a ship's tarpaulins. **2** prepare for a difficulty or crisis. [French: related to BATTER]

**batten²** /**bat**-uhn/ *v.* (foll. by *on*) thrive at the expense of (another). [Old Norse]

**batter¹** *v.* **1 a** strike hard and repeatedly. **b** (often foll. by *against, at*, etc.) pound insistently (*batter at the door*). **2** (often in *passive*) subject to long-term violence (*battered baby*; *battered wife*). □ **batterer** *n.* [French *battre* beat: related to BATTLE]

**batter²** *n.* mixture of flour, egg, and milk or water, used for pancakes etc. [French: related to BATTER¹]

**battered** adj. coated in batter and deep-fried.

**battering ram** n. hist. heavy beam, orig. with the striking end in the form of a ram's head, used in breaching fortifications by battering them.

**battery** /bat-uh-ree, bat-ree/ n. (pl. -ies) 1 usu. portable container of an electrically charged cell or cells as a source of current. 2 (often attrib.) series of cages for the intensive breeding and rearing of poultry etc. (battery hen). 3 set of similar units of equipment; series, sequence. 4 a emplacement for heavy guns. b artillery unit of guns, vehicles, etc. 5 Law unlawful physical violence against a person. [Latin: related to BATTLE]

**battle** /bat-uhl/ — n. 1 prolonged fight between armed forces. 2 difficult struggle; contest (battle for supremacy; battle of wits). — v. (-ling) 1 engage in battle with; fight. 2 struggle persistently (battling against the elements; battling AIDS; battling for women's rights). □ **half the battle** key to the success of an undertaking. [Latin battuo beat]

**battleaxe** n. 1 large axe used in ancient warfare. 2 colloq. derog. formidable older woman.

**battleaxe block** n. battleaxe-shaped block of land, one lacking a frontage and accessible through a lane.

**battle-cry** n. cry or slogan used in a battle or contest.

**battlement** /bat-uhl-muhnt/ n. (usu. in pl.) recessed parapet along the top of a wall, as part of a fortification. [French batailler fortify]

**battler** n. 1 person who strives long and hard and doggedly against the odds (little Aussie battler). 2 swagman or itinerant worker. □ **battling** adj.

**battle royal** n. 1 battle of many combatants; free fight. 2 heated argument.

**battleship** n. heavily armoured warship.

**batty** /bat-ee/ adj. (-ier, -iest) colloq. crazy. [from BAT²]

**bauble** /baw-buhl/ n. 1 showy worthless trinket or toy. 2 baton formerly used as an emblem by jesters. [French ba(u)bel toy]

**bauera** /bow-uh-ruh/ n. any shrub of the Australian genus Bauera, having a spreading habit and often extremely showy flowers (see RIVER ROSE). [Austrian botanical artists Franz (d. 1840) and Ferdinand (d. 1826) Bauer]

**bauhinia** /boh-hin-ee-uh/ n. deciduous shrub or small tree of mainly Queensland, having masses of white flowers, when leafless, yielding a sweet nectar used as a drink by the Aborigines (now

transferred to the genus Lysiphyllum). [Swiss botanists Jean (d. 1613) and Gaspard (d. 1624) Bauhin]

**baulk** /bawk/ (also **balk**) — v. 1 (often foll. by at) refuse to go on; jib, hesitate (horse baulked at the fence; baulked at the idea). 2 a thwart, hinder (baulked in his ambition). b disappoint (her hopes were baulked). 3 miss, let slip (a chance etc.). — n. 1 hindrance; stumbling-block. 2 roughly-squared timber beam. [Old English]

**bauxite** /bawk-suyt/ n. claylike mineral, the chief source of aluminium. [French from Les Baux in S. France]

**baw-baw berry** n. low-spreading Victorian plant of the Epacris family, having dark green leaves, yellow-green flowers, and greeny-white berries. [Mount Baw Baw in Victoria]

**bawd** /bawd/ n. woman who runs a brothel. [French baudetrot procuress]

**bawdy** /baw-dee/ — adj. (-ier, -iest) humorously indecent. — n. such talk or writing. [BAWD, -Y¹]

**bawdy house** n. brothel.

**bawl** /bawl/ v. 1 speak or shout noisily. 2 weep loudly. □ **bawl out** colloq. reprimand angrily. [imitative]

**bay¹** n. broad curving inlet of the sea. [Spanish bahia]

**bay²** n. 1 European laurel with deep green leaves. 2 (in pl.) bay wreath, for a victor or poet. [Latin baca berry]

**bay³** n. 1 space created by a window-line projecting outwards from a wall. 2 recess; section of wall between buttresses or columns, esp. in the nave of a church etc. 3 compartment (bomb bay). 4 area specially allocated or marked off (loading bay; parking bay). [French baer gape]

**bay⁴** — adj. (esp. of a horse) dark reddish-brown. — n. bay horse. [Latin badius]

**bay⁵** — v. bark or howl loudly and plaintively. — n. sound of this, esp. of hounds in close pursuit. □ **at bay** cornered, unable to escape. **bring to bay** gain on in pursuit; trap. **keep at bay** hold off (a pursuer). [French bayer to bark]

**bay leaf** n. leaf of the bay-tree, used for flavouring.

**bayonet** /bay-uh-, net/ n. stabbing blade attachable to the muzzle of a rifle. — v. (-t-) stab with bayonet. [French, perhaps from Bayonne in SW France]

**bay window** n. window projecting outwards from a wall.

**bazaar** /buh-zah/ n. 1 oriental market. 2 fund-raising sale of goods, esp. for charity. [Persian]

**bazooka** /buh-zoo-kuh/ n. anti-tank rocket-launcher. [origin unknown]

**BC** *abbr.* before Christ.

**bdellium** /**del**-ee-uhm/ *n.* **1** tree of Africa etc. yielding a fragrant resin. **2** this used in perfumes. [Latin from Greek]

**Be** *symb.* beryllium.

**be** /bee/ *v.* (*sing. present* **am**; **are** /ah/; /iz/; *past* **was** /woz/; **were** /wer/; *pres. part.* **being**; *past part.* **been**) **1** exist, live (*I think, therefore I am; there is no God*). **2 a** occur; take place (*dinner is at eight*). **b** occupy a position (*he is in the garden*). **3** remain, continue (*let it be*). **4** linking subject and predicate, expressing: **a** identity (*she is the person*). **b** condition (*he is ill today*). **c** state or quality (*he is kind; they are my friends*). **d** opinion (*I am against hanging*). **e** total (*two and two are four*). **f** cost or significance (*it is $5 to enter; it is nothing to me*). **5** *v.aux.* **a** with a past participle to form the passive (*it was done; it is said*). **b** with a present participle to form continuous tenses (*we are coming; it is being cleaned*). **c** with an infinitive to express duty or commitment, intention, possibility, destiny, or hypothesis (*I am to tell you; we are to wait here; he is to come at four; it was not to be found; they were never to meet again; if I were to die*). □ **be** (or **act**) **one's age** see ACT. **be at** occupy oneself with (*what is he at?; mice have been at the food*). **be off** *colloq.* go away; leave. **-to-be** of the future (in *comb.*: *bride-to-be*). [Old English]

**be-** *prefix* forming verbs: **1** (from transitive verbs) **a** all over; all round (*beset*). **b** thoroughly, excessively (*begrudge*). **2** (from intransitive verbs) expressing transitive action (*bemoan*; *bestride*). **3** (from adjectives and nouns) expressing transitive action (*becalm*). **4** (from nouns) **a** affect with (*befog*). **b** treat as (*befriend*). **c** (forming adjectives in *-ed*) having (*bejewelled*). [Old English, = BY]

**beach** — *n.* sandy or pebbly shore esp. of the sea. — *v.* run or haul (a boat etc.) on to a beach. [origin unknown]

**beach bum** *n. colloq.* habitual frequenter of beaches, and therefore regarded as lazy etc.

**beachcomber** *n.* **1** person who searches beaches for articles of value. **2** long wave rolling in from the sea.

**beachhead** *n.* fortified position set up on a beach by landing forces.

**beacon** /**bee**-kuhn/ *n.* **1** fire or light set up high as a warning etc. **2** visible warning or guiding device (e.g. a lighthouse, navigation buoy, etc.). **3** radio transmitter whose signal helps fix the position of a ship or aircraft. **4** person or thing that guides or warns. [Old English]

**bead** — *n.* **1 a** small usu. rounded piece of glass, stone, etc., for threading to make necklaces etc., or sewing on to fabric, etc. **b** (in *pl.*) bead necklace; rosary. **2** drop of liquid (*beads of sweat on her brow*). **3** small knob in the foresight of a gun. **4** inner edge of a pneumatic tyre gripping the rim of the wheel. — *v.* **1** adorn with or as with beads. **2 a** form or grow into beads. **b** cover with beads (*sweat beaded her brow*). □ **draw a bead on** take aim at. **tell one's beads** pray, using a rosary. □ **beaded** *adj.* [Old English, = prayer, rosary bead]

**beading** *n.* **1** moulding or carving like a series of beads. **2** bead of a tyre.

**beadle** /**bee**-duhl/ *n. hist.* minor parish disciplinary officer. [French from Germanic]

**beady** *adj.* (**-ier**, **-iest**) (esp. of the eyes) small, round, and bright.

**beady-eyed** *adj.* **1** with beady eyes. **2** observant.

**beagle** /**bee**-guhl/ *n.* small short-haired hound used for hunting. [French]

**beak¹** *n.* **1 a** bird's horny projecting jaws. **b** similar jaw of a turtle, platypus, etc. **2** *colloq.* hooked nose. **3** *hist.* pointed prow of a warship. **4** spout. [French from Celtic]

**beak²** *n. colloq.* **1** magistrate or judge. **2** schoolmaster. [probably thieves' cant]

**beaked hakea** *n.* attractive hakea of southern Australia, having white flowers and large, unusual, beak-shaped fruits.

**beaker** *n.* **1** tall cup or tumbler. **2** lipped glass vessel for scientific experiments. [Old Norse]

**beakie** *n.* = GARFISH.

**be-all and end-all** *n. colloq.* (often foll. by *of*) whole being or essence (of a thing).

**beam** — *n.* **1** long sturdy piece of squared timber or metal used in house-building etc. **2** ray or shaft of light or radiation. **3** bright look or smile. **4** series of radio or radar signals as a guide to a ship or aircraft. **5** crossbar of a balance. **6 a** ship's breadth. **b** width of a person's hips (esp. *broad in the beam*). **7** (in *pl.*) horizontal cross-timbers of a ship. — *v.* **1** emit or direct (light, approval, etc.). **2 a** shine. **b** look or smile radiantly. □ **off** (or **off the**) **beam** *colloq.* mistaken. **on the beam** *colloq.* on the right track. [Old English, = tree]

**bean** — *n.* **1 a** leguminous plant with edible seeds in long pods. **b** seed or pod of this. **2** similar seed of coffee etc. **3** *colloq.* (person's) head. — *v. colloq.* hit on the head. □ **full of beans** *colloq.* lively, exuberant. **not a bean** *colloq.* no money. **spill the beans** see SPILL. [Old English]

**beanbag** n. **1** small bag filled with dried beans and used as a ball. **2** large bag filled usu. with polystyrene pieces and used as a chair.

**bean curd** n. jelly or paste made from soya beans, used esp. in Asian cookery.

**beanfeast** n. colloq. celebration.

**beanie** /bee-nee/ n. small close-fitting knitted cap. [perhaps from BEAN sense 3]

**bean shoot** n. (also **beansprout**) sprout of a bean seed, esp. of the mung bean, used as food.

**bear**¹ /bair/ v. (past bore; past part. borne or born) **1** carry, bring, or take (esp. visibly) (bear gifts). **2** show; have, esp. characteristically (bear marks of violence; bears no relation to the case; bore no name). **3 a** produce, yield (fruit etc.). **b** give birth to (has borne a son; was born last week). **4 a** sustain (a weight, responsibility, cost, etc.). **b** endure (an ordeal, difficulty, etc.) (bore the loss calmly). **5** (usu. with neg. or interrog.) **a** tolerate (can't bear him). **b** admit of; be fit for (does not bear thinking about). **6** carry mentally (bear a grudge). **7** veer in a given direction (bear left). **8** bring or provide (something needed) (bear him company). **9** refl. behave (in a certain way) (has borne himself well under pressure). □ **bear down** press downwards. bear down on approach rapidly or purposefully. bear on (or **upon**) be relevant to. bear out support or confirm as evidence. bear up not despair. bear with tolerate patiently. bear witness testify. bring to bear bring into effective operation; employ, exert (bring pressure to bear on him). [Old English]

■ **Usage** The past part. born is used with reference to birth (was born in July), although borne is used of the mother's role (she has borne a son). In all other contexts the past part. is borne.

**bear**² /bair/ n. **1** any of several large heavy mammals with thick fur. **2** rough or uncouth person. **3** person selling shares for future delivery in hope of buying more cheaply before then. □ **the Great Bear, the Little Bear** constellations near the North Pole. [Old English]

**bearable** adj. endurable.

**beard** /beerd/ — n. **1** facial hair on the chin etc. **2** similar tuft etc. on an animal (esp. a goat) or wheat etc. — v. oppose openly; defy (bearded him in the study). □ **bearded** adj. **beardless** adj. [Old English]

**bearded dragon** n. (also **jew lizard**) lizard of eastern Australia having large spiny scales on the throat pouch and other parts of the body.

**beardie** n. = LING (so called because of its beard-like barbels).

**bearer** n. **1** person or thing that bears, carries, or brings. **2** person who presents a cheque etc.

**bear-hug** n. tight embrace.

**bearing** n. **1** bodily attitude; general manner. **2** (foll. by on, upon) relevance to (has no bearing on it). **3** endurability (beyond bearing). **4** part of a machine supporting a rotating or other moving part. **5** direction or position relative to a fixed point. **6** (in pl.) **a** one's position relative to one's surroundings. **b** awareness of this; sense of one's orientation (get one's bearings; lose one's bearings). **7** Heraldry device or charge.

**bear market** n. Stock Exch. market with falling prices.

**bearpit** n. (also **bear-house**) place (esp. the floor of parliament) where intense debate etc. occurs (the PM is the best performer in Canberra's bearpit).

**bearskin** n. **1** skin of a bear, esp. as a wrap etc. **2** tall furry hat worn by some regiments.

**beast** n. **1** animal, esp. a wild mammal. **2 a** brutal person. **b** colloq. objectionable person or thing (he's a beast for not inviting her; a beast of a problem). **3** (prec. by the) the animal nature in man (the beast in him came out). [Latin bestia]

**beastly** — adj. (**-ier**, **-iest**) **1** colloq. objectionable, unpleasant. **2** like a beast; brutal. — adv. colloq. very, extremely. □ **beastliness** n.

**beat** — v. (past beat; past part. beaten) **1 a** strike persistently and violently. **b** strike (a carpet, drum, etc.) repeatedly. **2** (foll. by against, at, on, etc.) pound or knock repeatedly (waves beating against the shore; beat at the door). **3 a** overcome; surpass; win a victory over. **b** be too hard for; perplex (this puzzle beats me; beats me how you can take it lying down). **4** (often foll. by up) whisk (eggs etc.) vigorously. **5** (often foll. by out) shape (metal etc.) by blows. **6** (of the heart etc.) pulsate rhythmically. **7** (often foll. by out) **a** indicate (a tempo etc.) by tapping etc. **b** sound (a signal etc.) by striking a drum etc. (beat a tattoo). **8** move or cause (wings) to move up and down. **9** make (a path etc.) by (or as if by) trampling (the world will beat a path to her door). **10** strike (bushes etc.) to rouse game. — n. **1 a** main accent in music or verse. **b** rhythm indicated by a conductor. **c** (in popular music) strong rhythm. **2 a** stroke or blow or measured sequence of strokes (*the beat of waves on the rocks*). **b** throbbing movement or sound (*the beat of his heart*). **3 a** police officer's route or area. **b** person's habitual round. **c** *colloq.* habitual area for making sexual liaisons. — *adj.* **1** (*predic.*) *colloq.* exhausted, tired out (*I'm dead beat*). **2** (*attrib.*) of or relating to beatniks (*the beat generation*). □ **beat about the bush** not come to the point. **beat down 1** cause (a seller) to lower the price by bargaining. **2** strike to the ground (*beat the door down*). **3** (of the sun, rain, etc.) shine or fall relentlessly. **beat it** *colloq.* go away. **beat off** drive back (an attack etc.). **beat a person to it** arrive or do something before another person. **beat a retreat** withdraw. **beat up** beat, esp. with punches and kicks. **off the beaten track 1** in or into an isolated place. **2** unusual. □ **beatable** *adj.* **beaten** *adj.* **beating** *n.* [Old English]

**beater** *n.* implement for beating (esp. eggs).

**beatific** /bee-uh-**tif**-ik/ *adj.* **1** *colloq.* blissful (*beatific smile*). **2** making blessed. [Latin *beatus* blessed]

**beatify** /bee-**at**-uh-,fuy/ *v.* (**-ies, -ied**) **1** *RC Ch.* (of the Pope) formally declare (a dead person) to be 'blessed', often as a step towards canonisation. **2** make happy. □ **beatification** /bee-,at-uh-fuh-**kay**-shuhn/ *n.*

**beatitude** /bee-**at**-uh-,tyood/ *n.* **1** perfect bliss or happiness. **2** (in *pl.*) blessings in Matt. 5:3–11.

**beatnik** /**beet**-nik/ *n.* member of a movement of socially unconventional young people in the 1950s.

**beat-up** *colloq.* — *adj.* dilapidated (a *beat-up old car*). — *n.* highly exaggerated or manufactured newspaper report etc.

**beau** /boh/ *n.* (*pl.* **-x** or **-s** /bohz/ ) **1** admirer; boyfriend. **2** fop; dandy. [Latin *bellus* pretty]

**Beaufort scale** /**boh**-fuht/ *n.* scale of wind speed ranging from 0 (calm) to 12 (hurricane). [Sir F. *Beaufort*, name of an admiral]

**beaut** /byoot/ *colloq.* — *n.* excellent or admirable person or thing (*it's a beaut*). — *adj.* excellent; exciting admiration. — *int.* (also **you beaut!**) expressing admiration, praise, etc. [abbreviation]

**beauteous** /**byoo**-tee-uhs/ *adj. poet.* beautiful.

**beautician** /byoo-**tish**-uhn/ *n.* specialist in beauty treatment; worker in a beauty parlour.

**beautiful** /**byoo**-tuh-,fuhl/ *adj.* **1** having beauty, pleasing to the eye, ear, or mind etc. (*beautiful voice*). **2** pleasant, enjoy-

able (*had a beautiful time*). **3** excellent (*beautiful specimen*). □ **beautifully** *adv.*

**beautify** /byoo-tuh-,fuy/ *v.* (**-ies, -ied**) make beautiful; adorn. □ **beautification** /-fuh-**kay**-shuhn/ *n.*

**beauty** /**byoo**-tee/ — *n.* (*pl.* **-ies**) **1 a** combination of qualities such as shape, colour, sound, etc., that pleases the senses. **b** combination of qualities that pleases the intellect or moral sense (*the beauty of the argument*). **2** *colloq.* **a** (also **bewdy** /**byoo**-dee/ ) (esp. as an exclamation of approval) excellent specimen (*what a beauty!*; *that's a bewdy!*; *gave him a bewdy right in the eye*). **b** attractive feature; advantage (*that's the beauty of it!*). **3** beautiful woman. — *adj.* (also **bewdy**) *colloq.* excellent; highly pleasing (*bewdy bottler*). — *int.* (also **you bewdy!**) *colloq.* expressing admiration, praise, etc. [Latin *bellus* pretty]

**beauty parlour** *n.* (also **beauty salon**) establishment for cosmetic treatment.

**beauty spot** *n.* **1** place of scenic beauty. **2** small facial mark considered to enhance the appearance.

**beaux** *pl.* of BEAU.

**beaver** — *n.* **1** amphibious broad-tailed rodent of Europe etc. which cuts down trees with its teeth and dams rivers. **2** its fur. **3** hat of this. — *v. colloq.* (usu. foll. by *away*) work hard. [Old English]

**beaver rat** *n.* = WATER-RAT.

**bebop** /**bee**-bop/ *n.* type of jazz originating in the 1940s, with complex harmony and rhythms. [imitative]

**becalm** /bee-**kahm**, buh-/ *v.* (usu. in *passive*) deprive (a ship) of wind.

**became** *past* of BECOME.

**because** /bee-**koz**, -**kawz**, buh-/ *conj.* for the reason that; since. □ **because of** on account of; by reason of. [from BY, CAUSE]

**bêche-de-mer** /besh-duh-**mair**/ *n.* (*pl.* **bêches-de-mer** pronunc. same) kind of sea-cucumber. [pseudo-French from Portuguese *bicho do mar* worm of the sea]

**beck** *n.* □ **at a person's beck and call** subject to a person's constant orders. [from BECKON]

**beckon** /**bek**-uhn/ *v.* **1** (often foll. by *to*) summon by gesture. **2** entice. [Old English]

**become** /bee-**kum**, buh-/ *v.* (**-ming**; *past* **became**; *past part.* **become**) **1** begin to be (*became prime minister*; *became famous*). **2** (often as **becoming** *adj.*) **a** look well on; suit (*blue becomes him*). **b** befit (*it ill becomes you to complain*). **c** (as **becoming** *adj.*) flattering the appearance; suitable, decorous (*becoming modesty*). □ **become**

**of** happen to (*what became of her?*). [Old English: related to BE-]

**becquerel** /**bek**-uh-,rel/ *n.* SI unit of radioactivity. [*Becquerel*, name of a physicist]

**bed** — *n.* **1** piece of furniture for sleeping on. **2** any place used for sleep or rest. **3** garden plot, esp. for flowers. **4 a** bottom of the sea, a river, etc. **b** foundations of a road or railway. **5** stratum, such as a layer of oysters. — *v.* (**-dd-**) **1** (usu. foll. by *down*) put or go to bed. **2** *colloq.* have sexual intercourse with. **3** (usu. foll. by *out*) plant in a garden bed. **4** cover up or fix firmly. **5** arrange as a layer. □ **bed of roses** life of ease. **go to bed 1** retire to sleep. **2** (often foll. by *with*) have sexual intercourse. [Old English]

**bed and breakfast** *n.* **1** room and breakfast in a hotel, private house, etc. **2** establishment providing this.

**bedaub** /bee-**dawb**, buh-/ *v.* smear or daub.

**bedazzle** /bee-**daz**-uhl, buh-/ *v.* (**-ling**) **1** dazzle. **2** confuse.

**bedbug** *n.* wingless parasite infesting beds etc.

**bedclothes** *n.pl.* sheets, blankets, etc., for a bed.

**bedding** *n.* **1** mattress and bedclothes. **2** litter for animals. **3** *Geol.* stratification of rocks, esp. when clearly visible.

**bedeck** /bee-**dek**, buh-/ *v.* adorn.

**bedevil** /bee-**dev**-uhl, buh-/ *v.* (**-ll-**) **1** trouble, vex. **2** confound, confuse. **3** torment, abuse. □ **bedevilment** *n.*

**bedfellow** *n.* **1** person who shares a bed. **2** associate.

**bedlam** /**bed**-luhm/ *n.* uproar and confusion. [St Mary of *Bethlehem*, name of a hospital in London]

**Bedouin** /**bed**-uh-wuhn/ *n.* (also **Beduin**) (*pl.* same) **1** nomadic desert Arab. **2** wandering person. [Arabic, = dwellers in the desert]

**Bedourie** /buh-**doo**-ree/ *n.* **1** dust storm. **2** (also **Bedourie dish, Bedourie (camp)** oven) type of portable camp oven with a lid (which can be used as a frying pan). [*Bedourie*, town in south-western Queensland]

**bedpan** *n.* portable toilet for use in bed.

**bedraggled** /buh-**drag**-uhld/ *adj.* dishevelled, untidy.

**bedridden** *adj.* confined to bed by infirmity.

**bedrock** *n.* **1** solid rock underlying alluvial deposits etc. **2** basic principles.

**bedroom** *n.* room for sleeping in.

**bedside** *n.* space beside esp. a patient's bed. □ **bedside manner** (esp. doctor's) way with patients.

**bedsitter** *n.* (also **bedsitting room**) combined bedroom and sitting-room with cooking facilities.

**bedsore** *n.* sore developed by lying in bed.

**bedspread** *n.* cover for a bed.

**bedstead** *n.* framework of a bed.

**Beduin** var. of BEDOUIN.

**bedwetting** *n.* involuntary urination when asleep in bed.

**bee** *n.* **1** four-winged stinging insect, collecting nectar and producing wax and honey. **2** (usu. **busy bee**) busy person. **3** meeting for communal work (*working bee*). □ **a bee in one's bonnet** obsession. **the bee's knees** *colloq.* something outstandingly good (*thinks he's the bee's knees*). [Old English]

**beech** *n.* **1** any large European forest tree of the genus *Fagus* having smooth grey bark and glossy leaves. **2** any of several Australian trees of the genus *Nothofagus*, including: Antarctic beech, deciduous beech (or tanglefoot), myrtle, and niggerhead. **3** any of several Australian trees of the genus *Gmelina*, esp. white beech. **4** = BROWN BEECH. [Old English]

**bee-eater** *n.* any of many bright-plumaged insect-eating birds with a long, slender, curved bill, including the Australian RAINBOW BIRD.

**beef** — *n.* **1 a** flesh of the bull or cow for eating. **b** (in Aboriginal English) meat of any kind. **2** *colloq.* well-developed male muscle. **3** (*pl.* **beeves**) bull or cow bred for beef. **4** (*pl.* **-s**) *colloq.* complaint. — *v.* *colloq.* complain. □ **beef up** *colloq.* strengthen, reinforce; increase (*need to beef up the system*). [Latin *bos bovis* ox]

**beefcake** *n.* *colloq.* well-developed male muscle, esp. when displayed for admiration.

**beefeater** *n.* warder at the Tower of London.

**beefwood** *n.* **1** tree grevillea (to 12m) of drier Australia, having erect spikes of creamy flowers, and yielding a dark red, close-grained timber with purple tinges. **2** any of several other Australian trees with a similar beef-like wood.

**beefy** *adj.* (**-ier, -iest**) **1** like beef. **2** solid, muscular. □ **beefiness** *n.*

**beehive** *n.* **1** artificial shelter for a colony of bees. **2** busy place.

**beeline** *n.* straight line between two places. □ **make a beeline for** go directly to.

**Beelzebub** /bee-**el**-zuh-,bub/ *n.* the Devil. [Hebrew, = lord of the flies]

**been** *past part.* of BE.

**Been There, Done That** see BT, DT.

**beep** — *n.* sound of a (esp. motor-car) horn. — *v.* emit a beep. [imitative]

**beer** n. **1 a** alcoholic drink made from fermented malt etc., flavoured with hops. **b** glass of this. **2** any of several other fermented or flavoured drinks (*ginger beer*). □ **beer and skittles** amusement. [Old English]

**beer garden** n. garden where beer is sold and drunk.

**beer gut** n. colloq. (beer-drinker's) distended belly; pot.

**beer-up** n. colloq. beer-drinking party or session.

**beery** adj. (**-ier**, **-iest**) **1** affected by beer-drinking. **2** like beer.

**beeswax** n. **1** wax secreted by bees to make honeycombs. **2** this used to polish wood.

**beeswing** n. filmy second crust on old port.

**beet** n. plant with an edible root (see BEETROOT, SUGAR BEET). [Old English]

**beetle**[1] /**bee-tuhl**/ — n. **1** insect with hard protective outer wings. **2** any similar, usu. black, insect. — v. (**-ling**) colloq. **1** (foll. by *about, off, etc.*) hurry, scurry. **2** (foll. by *along*) move rapidly (*beetling along in her car*). [Old English: related to BITE]

**beetle**[2] /**bee-tuhl**/ — adj. projecting, shaggy, scowling (*beetle brows*). — v. (usu. as **beetling** adj.) (of brows, cliffs, etc.) project, overhang. [origin unknown]

**beetle-browed** adj. with shaggy, projecting, or scowling eyebrows.

**beetroot** n. beet with an edible dark-red root.

**beeves** pl. of BEEF.

**befall** /bee-**fawl**, buh-/ v. (*past* **befell**; *past part.* **befallen**) poet. happen; happen to. [Old English: related to BE-]

**befit** /bee-**fit**, buh-/ v. (**-tt-**) be appropriate for.

**befog** /bee-**fog**, buh-/ v. (**-gg-**) **1** confuse, obscure. **2** envelop in fog.

**before** /bee-**faw**, buh-/ — *conj.* **1** earlier than the time when (*see me before you go*). **2** rather than that (*would die before he stole*). — *prep.* **1** earlier than (*before noon*). **2 a** in front of, ahead of (*before her in the queue*). **b** in the face of (*recoil before the attack*). **c** awaiting (*the future before them*). **3** rather than (*death before dishonour*). **4 a** in the presence of (*appear before the judge*). **b** for the attention of (*put before the committee*). — *adv.* **1** previously; already (*happened long before; I've done it before*). **2** ahead (*go before*). **3** on the front (*hit before and behind*). [Old English: related to BY, FORE]

**beforehand** adv. in anticipation; in advance; in readiness (*had prepared the meal beforehand*).

**befriend** /bee-**frend**, buh-/ v. act as a friend to; help.

**befuddle** /bee-**fud**-uhl, buh-/ v. (**-ling**) **1** make drunk. **2** confuse.

**beg** v. (**-gg-**) **1 a** (usu. foll. by *for*) ask for (food, money, etc.). **b** live by begging. **2** ask earnestly, humbly, or formally (for) (*begged for mercy; beg your indulgence; beg leave*). **3** (of a dog etc.) sit up with the front paws raised expectantly. **4** (foll. by *to* + infin.) take leave (*I beg to differ*). □ **beg off** ask to be excused from something. **beg pardon** see PARDON. **beg the question** assume the truth of a proposition needing proof, without arguing it or proving it. **go begging** be unwanted or refused. [related to BID]

---

■ **Usage** The expression *beg the question* is often used incorrectly to mean (1) to avoid giving a straight answer, or (2) to invite the obvious question (that . . .). These uses should be avoided.

---

**began** *past* of BEGIN.

**beget** /bee-**get**, buh-/ v. (**-tt-**; *past* **begot**; *archaic* **begat**; *past part.* **begotten**) *literary* **1** father, procreate. **2** cause (*anger begets violence*). [Old English: related to BE-]

**beggar** /**beg**-uh/ — n. **1** person who lives by begging. **2** colloq. person (*cheeky beggar*). — v. **1** reduce to poverty. **2** be too extraordinary for (*it beggars description*). □ **beggars cannot be choosers** those without other resources must take whatever is offered. □ **beggarly** adj.

**beggar on (the) coals** n. small damper.

**begin** /bee-**gin**, buh-/ v. (**-nn-**; *past* **began**; *past part.* **begun**) **1** perform the first part of; start (*begin work; begin crying; begin to understand*). **2** come into being (*war began in 1939; Queensland begins here*). **3** (usu. foll. by *to* + infin.) start at a certain time (*soon began to feel ill*). **4** be begun (*meeting began at 7*). **5 a** start speaking (*'No,' he began*). **b** take the first step, be the first (*shall I begin?*). **6** (usu. with *neg.*) colloq. show any likelihood (*can't begin to compete*). [Old English]

**beginner** n. trainee, learner. □ **beginner's luck** supposed good luck of a beginner.

**beginning** n. **1** time or place at which anything begins. **2** source or origin. **3** first part.

**begone** /bee-**gon**, buh-/ int. poet. go away at once! [*be gone*]

**begonia** /buh-**goh**-nyuh/ n. garden plant with bright flowers and glossy leaves. [*Bégon*, name of a patron of science]

**begot** *past* of BEGET.

**begotten** *past part.* of BEGET.

**begrudge** /bee-**gruj**, buh-/ *v.* (**-ging**) **1** resent; be dissatisfied at (*begrudged paying the bill*). **2** envy (a person) the possession of (*did not begrudge his wife her success*). □ **begrudgingly** *adv.*

**beguile** /bee-**guyl**, buh-/ *v.* (**-ling**) **1** charm; amuse. **2** wilfully divert, seduce. **3** (usu. foll. by *of, out of,* or *into* + verbal noun) delude; cheat (*beguiled him into paying for them all*). □ **beguilement** *n.* **beguiling** *adj.*

**beguine** /bee-**geen**, buh-/ *n.* popular dance of W. Indian origin. [French *béguin* infatuation]

**begum** /**bay**-guhm/ *n.* in India or Pakistan: **1** Muslim woman of high rank. **2** (**Begum**) title of a married Muslim woman. [Turkish *bīgam* princess]

**begun** *past part.* of BEGIN.

**behalf** /bee-**hahf**, buh-/ *n.* □ **on behalf of** (or **on a person's behalf**) in the interests of; as representative of. [earlier *bihalve* on the part of]

**behave** /bee-**hayv**, buh-/ *v.* (**-ving**) **1** act or react (in a specified way) (*behaved well*). **2** (often *refl.*) conduct oneself properly (*behave yourself!*). **3** (of a machine etc.) work well (or in a specified way). [from BE-, HAVE]

**behaviour** /bee-**hay**-vyuh, buh-/ *n.* (also **behavior**) **1** way of behaving or acting. **2** *Psychol.* response (of a person, animal, etc.) to a stimulus. □ **behavioural** *adj.*

**behavioural science** *n.* (also **behavioral**) the study of human behaviour.

**behaviourism** *n.* (also **behaviorism**) *Psychol.* theory that human behaviour is determined by conditioned response to stimuli rather than by thoughts and feelings, and that psychological disorders are best treated by altering behaviour. □ **behaviourist** *n.*

**behead** /bee-**hed**, buh-/ *v.* cut the head off (a person), esp. as execution. [Old English: related to BE-]

**beheld** *past* and *past part.* of BEHOLD.

**behemoth** /bee-**hee**-moth, buh-/ *n.* huge creature or thing. [Hebrew (Job 40:15)]

**behest** /bee-**hest**, buh-/ *n. literary* command; request. [Old English]

**behind** /bee-**huynd**, buh-/ — *prep.* **1 a** in or to the rear of. **b** on the far side of (*behind the bush*). **c** hidden or implied by (*something behind that remark*). **2 a** in the past in relation to (*trouble is behind me now*). **b** late regarding (*behind schedule*). **3** inferior to; weaker than (*behind the others in maths*). **4 a** in support of (*she's right behind us in this*

*endeavour*). **b** responsible for (*the man behind the project*). **5** in the tracks of; following. — *adv.* **1 a** in or to the rear; further back (*the street behind; glance behind*). **b** on the further side (*wall with a field behind*). **2** remaining· after departure (*stay behind; left her purse behind*). **3** (usu. foll. by *with*) **a** in arrears (*behind with the rent*). **b** late in finishing a task etc. (*working too slowly and getting behind*). **4** in a weak position; backward (*behind in Latin*). **5** following (*dog running behind*). **6** (of a watch or clock) slow. — *n.* **1** *colloq.* buttocks. **2** *Aust. Rules* scoring kick that scores one point. □ **behind the scenes** see SCENE. **behind time** late. **behind the times** old-fashioned, antiquated. [Old English]

**behind post** *n. Aust. Rules* each of a pair of posts flanking the goal posts.

**behold** /bee-**hohld**, buh-/ *v.* (*past* and *past part.* **beheld**) (esp. in *imper.*) *literary* look at; take notice, observe. [Old English: related to BE-]

**beholden** *predic. adj.* (usu. foll. by *to*) under obligation.

**behove** /bee-**hohv**/ *v.* (**-ving**) *formal* **1** be incumbent on. **2** befit (*it ill behoves him to protest*). [Old English: related to BE, HEAVE]

**beige** /bayzh/ — *n.* pale sandy fawn colour. — *adj.* of this colour. [French]

**being** /**bee**-ing/ *n.* **1** existence. **2** nature or essence (of a person etc.) (*his whole being revolted*). **3** anything that exists or is imagined (*human being; weird beings from outer space*).

**bejewelled** /bee-**joo**-uhld, buh-/ *adj.* adorned with jewels.

**bel** *n.* unit of relative power level, esp. of sound, corresponding to an intensity ratio of 10 to 1 (cf. DECIBEL). [*Bell,* name of the inventor of the telephone]

**belabour** /bee-**lay**-buh, buh-/ *v.* (also **belabor**) **1** attack physically or verbally. **2** argue or elaborate (a subject) in excessive detail (*you don't need to belabour the point*).

**belah** /buh-**lah**/ *n.* any of several casuarinas with slender jointed branches and woody cones, esp. *Casuarina cristata* of drier regions of Australia. [Wiradhuri *bilaarr*]

**belated** /bee-**lay**-tuhd, buh-/ *adj.* coming late or too late. □ **belatedly** *adv.*

**belay** /bee-**lay**, buh-/ — *v.* secure (a rope) by winding it round a peg, rock, etc. — *n.* act of belaying. [Dutch *beleggen*]

**bel canto** /bel **kan**-toh/ *n.* lyrical rich-toned style of operatic singing. [Italian, = fine song]

**belch** — v. **1** emit wind noisily through the mouth. **2** (of a chimney, gun, etc.) send (smoke etc.) out or up. — n. act of belching. [Old English]

**beleaguer** /bee-**lee**-guh, buh-/ v. **1** besiege (*beleaguered city*). **2** vex; harass (*I'm beleaguered with bills*). [Dutch *leger* camp]

**belfry** /**bel**-free/ n. (pl. **-ies**) **1** bell tower. **2** space for bells in a church tower. [Germanic, probably = peace-protector]

**Belial** /**bee**-lee-uhl/ n. the Devil. [Hebrew, = worthless]

**belie** /bee-**luy**, buh-/ v. (**belying**) **1** give a false impression of (*its appearance belies its age*). **2** fail to fulfil or justify (*his present performance belies his earlier promise*). [Old English: related to BE-]

**belief** /bee-**leef**, buh-/ n. **1** firm opinion; acceptance (*that is my belief*). **2** religious conviction (*belief in the afterlife*; *has no belief*). **3** (usu. foll. by *in*) trust or confidence. [related to BELIEVE]

**believe** /bee-**leev**, buh-/ v. (**-ving**) **1** accept as true or as conveying the truth (*I believe it*; *don't believe him*). **2** think, suppose (*I believe it's going to rain*). **3** (foll. by *in*) **a** have faith in the existence of (*believes in God*). **b** have confidence in (*believes in homoeopathy*). **c** have trust in as a policy (*believes in telling the truth*). **4** have (esp. religious) faith. □ **believable** adj. **believer** n. [Old English]

**belittle** /bee-**lit**-uhl, buh-/ v. (**-ling**) disparage, make appear insignificant (*he belittles all she does*). □ **belittlement** n.

**bell**[1] — n. **1** hollow esp. cup-shaped usu. metal object sounding a note when struck (either externally or by means of a clapper inside). **2 a** such a sound, esp. as a signal. **b** (prec. by a numeral) *Naut.* time as indicated every half-hour of a watch by the striking of the ship's bell one to eight times. **3** anything that sounds like or functions as a bell, esp. an electronic device that rings etc. as a signal (*rang the front doorbell*). **4** any bell-shaped object or part. — v. provide with a bell. □ **give a person a bell** *colloq.* telephone a person. **with bells on** = *with knobs on* (see KNOB). [Old English]

**bell**[2] — n. cry of a stag. — v. make this cry. [Old English]

**belladonna** /bel-uh-**don**-uh/ n. **1** deadly nightshade. **2** drug from this. [Italian, = fair lady]

**bellbird** n. **1** any of various birds with a bell-like song. **2** bird of forests in south-eastern Australia, typically living in colonies and maintaining contact by frequent pure, penetrating, bell-like calls.

**belle** /bel/ n. beautiful or most beautiful woman. [French, feminine of BEAU]

**belles-lettres** /bel **letr**/ n.pl. (also treated as *sing.*) literary writings or studies. [French, = fine letters]

**bell-fruit mallee** see MALLEE 1 a.

**bellicose** /**bel**-uh-kohz, -_kohs/ adj. eager to fight; warlike. [Latin *bellum* war]

**bellies** n.pl. = BELLY WOOL.

**belligerence** /buh-**lij**-uh-ruhns/ n. **1** aggressive or war-like behaviour. **2** status of a belligerent.

**belligerent** — adj. **1** engaged in war or conflict. **2** given to constant fighting; pugnacious. — n. belligerent nation or person. [Latin *belligero* wage war]

**bell jar** n. bell-shaped glass cover or container for use in a laboratory.

**bell magpie** n. any of three species of currawong.

**bellow** /**bel**-oh/ — v. **1** emit a deep loud roar. **2** utter loudly. — n. loud roar. [origin uncertain]

**bellows** n.pl. (also treated as *sing.*) device with an air bag for driving air into or through something, esp. for blowing air onto a fire or powering a harmonium or small organ. [related to BELLY]

**bells and whistles** n.pl. **1** insignificant or superficial details (*said that the party's policy would stand, given a little adjustment to the bells and whistles*). **2** (also *attrib.*) (**bells-and-whistles**) insignificant, superficial (*made some bells-and-whistles changes*).

**bell-wether** n. **1** leading sheep of a flock. **2** ringleader.

**belly** /**bel**-ee/ — n. (pl. **-ies**) **1** trunk below the chest, containing the stomach and bowels. **2** stomach, esp. representing the body's need for food. **3** front of the body from waist to groin. **4** underside of an animal. **5** cavity or bulging part of anything. — v. (**-ies, -ied**) (often foll. by *out*) swell; bulge (*the wind is beginning to belly out the sails*; *sails bellying in the wind*). [Old English, = bag]

**bellyache** *colloq.* — n. **1** stomach pain; colic. **2** complaint, whinge. — v. (**-ching**) complain noisily or persistently.

**belly-buster** n. *colloq.* = BELLYFLOP.

**belly button** n. *colloq.* navel.

**belly dance** n. oriental dance performed by a woman, with voluptuous belly movements. □ **belly dancer** n. **belly dancing** n.

**bellyflop** n. *colloq.* dive with the belly landing flat on the water.

**bellyful** n. (pl. **-s**) **1** enough to eat. **2** *colloq.* more than one can tolerate.

**belly-laugh** n. loud unrestrained laugh.

**belly wool** n. (also **bellies** pl.) wool shorn from the belly of a sheep.

**belong** /bee-**long**, buh-/ v. **1** (usu. foll. by to) **a** be the property of (this dictionary belongs to me). **b** be correctly assigned to (his family prides itself on belonging to the convict aristocracy). **c** be a member of (a club, group, etc.). **2** fit socially (just doesn't belong). **3** (foll. by in, under) be correctly placed or classified; fit a particular environment (this belongs in the top drawer; that book belongs under 'Bush Tucker'). [from BE-, obsolete long belong]

**belonging** n. **1** affinity (esp. a sense of belonging). **2** (pl.) possessions or luggage.

**Belorussian** var. of BYELORUSSIAN.

**beloved** /bee-**luv**-uhd, -**luvd**, buh-/ — adj. much loved. — n. much loved person.

**below** /bee-**loh**, buh-/ — prep. **1** lower in position, amount, status, etc., than (below the level of the snowline; below freezing-point; a captain ranks below major). **2** beneath the surface of (head below water). **3** (more usu. expressed by BENEATH) unworthy of (he is below contempt). — adv. **1** at or to a lower point or level (went below). **2 a** downstairs (lives below). **b** downstream. **3** further forward on a page or in a book (as noted below). [be BY, LOW[1]]

**belt** — n. **1** strip of leather etc. worn esp. round the waist. **2** circular band in machinery; conveyor belt. **3** distinct strip of colour etc. **4** belt worn as a sign of rank or achievement (black belt in judo). **5** region or extent (wheat belt). **6** colloq. heavy blow. — v. **1** put a belt round; fasten (a sword etc.) with a belt. **2** colloq. hit hard. **3** colloq. rush, hurry (usu. with compl.: belted along; belted home). □ **below the belt** unfair(ly). **belt out** colloq. sing or play (music) loudly or vigorously. **belt up** colloq. **1** be quiet. **2** put on a seatbelt. **3** savagely attack (a person). **tighten one's belt** economise. **under one's belt 1** (of food) eaten (get this under your belt). **2** securely acquired (has a degree under her belt). [Old English]

**beltman** n. member of a surf life-saving team who has a line attached to his belt.

**bemoan** /bee-**mohn**, buh-/ v. lament; grieve over.

**bemuse** /bee-**myooz**, buh-/ v. (**-sing**) puzzle, bewilder. [from BE-, MUSE[1]]

**bench** n. **1** long seat of wood or stone. **2** strong work-table. **3** (prec. by the) **a** office of judge or magistrate. **b** judge's seat. **c** lawcourt. **d** judges and magistrates collectively. **4** Sport area to the side of a playing-field, with seating where coaches and players not taking part can watch the game. **5** Parl. seat appropriated as specified (front bench). [Old English]

**benchman** n. (in a sawmill) employee responsible for feeding in the length of timber to be sawn.

**benchmark** — n. **1** surveyor's mark cut in a wall etc. as a reference point in measuring altitudes. **2** standard or point of reference (a benchmark decision by the High Court). **3** means of testing a computer, usu. by a set of programs run on a series of different machines. — v. evaluate (a computer) by a benchmark.

**bench-top** adj. of or pertaining to an article designed to sit on top of a work bench (bench-top computer etc.) or be incorporated into a work bench etc. (bench-top hotplates etc.).

**bend** — v. (past and past part. **bent** except in bended knee) **1 a** force or adapt (something straight) into a curve or angle. **b** (of an object) be so altered. **2** (often foll. by down, over, etc.) curve, incline, or stoop (road bends; bent down to pick it up; bent her head). **3** interpret or modify (a rule) to suit oneself. **4** turn (one's steps, eyes, or energies) in a new direction. **5** (in passive; foll. by on) have firmly decided; be determined (was bent on selling; on pleasure bent). **6** submit or force to submit (bent them to his will). **7** Naut. attach (a sail or cable) with a knot. — n. **1** curve; departure from a straight course. **2** bent part of anything. **3** (in pl.; prec. by the) colloq. decompression sickness. □ **bend the elbow** drink (esp. beer). **bend over backwards** see BACKWARDS. **round the bend** colloq. crazy, insane. □ **bendable** adj. **bendy** adj. (**-ier**, **-iest**) [Old English]

**bendee** /**ben**-dee/ n. **1** (also **bendi**) wattle of Queensland and the NT, found on shallow stony soils and usu. having a deeply-fluted trunk. **2** its wood. [perhaps from an Aboriginal language]

**bender** n. colloq. wild drinking-spree. [from BEND]

**beneath** /bee-**neeth**, buh-/ — prep. **1** unworthy of; too demeaning for (beneath him to reply). **2** below, under. — adv. below, underneath. [Old English: related to BE-, NETHER]

**Benedictine** /ˌben-uh-**dik**-teen/ — n. monk or nun of an order following the rule of St Benedict established circa 540 AD — adj. of St Benedict or the Benedictines. [Latin Benedictus Benedict]

**benediction** /ˌben-uh-**dik**-shuhn/ n. **1** pronouncing of a blessing, esp. at the end of Mass or other religious service. **2** (**Benediction**) special Roman Catholic service in which the priest blesses the people with the Blessed Sacrament in a monstrance. **3** state of being blessed. □ **benedictory** adj. [Latin benedico bless]

**benefaction** /ˌben-uh-**fak**-shuhn/ n. **1** donation, gift. **2** act of giving or doing good. [Latin: related to BENEFIT]

**benefactor** /**ben**-uh-ˌfak-tuh/ n. (fem. **benefactress**) person giving (esp. financial) support.

**beneficent** /buh-**nef**-uh-suhnt/ adj. doing good; generous, kind. □ **beneficence** n.

**beneficial** /ˌben-uh-**fish**-uhl/ adj. advantageous; having benefits. □ **beneficially** adv.

**beneficiary** /ˌben-uh-**fish**-uh-ree/ n. (pl. **-ies**) person who benefits, esp. from a will.

**benefit** /**ben**-uh-fuht/ — n. **1** favourable or helpful factor or circumstance; advantage, profit (strength is a distinct benefit in this job; it will be to your benefit). **2** (often in pl.) insurance or social security payment (sickness benefit). **3** (also attrib.) public performance or game in aid of a charitable cause etc. (putting on a special benefit for the children's hospital; a benefit concert). — v. (**-t-**) **1** help; bring advantage to. **2** (often foll. by from, by) receive an advantage or gain. □ **the benefit of the doubt** concession that a person is innocent, correct, etc., although doubt exists. [Latin benefactum from bene well, facio do]

**benevolent** /buh-**nev**-uh-luhnt/ adj. **1** well-wishing; actively friendly and helpful. **2** charitable (benevolent fund). □ **benevolence** n. [French from Latin bene volens well wishing]

**benighted** /buh-**nuy**-tuhd/ adj. intellectually or morally ignorant.

**benign** /buh-**nuyn**/ adj. **1** gentle, mild, kindly (a benign act). **2** fortunate, salutary (a benign influence). **3** (of a tumour etc.) not malignant. □ **benignly** adv. [Latin benignus]

**benignity** /buh-**nig**-nuh-tee/ n. (pl. **-ies**) kindliness.

**Bennett's wallaby** n. brownish-grey wallaby of Tasmania and Bass Strait islands. [E.T. Bennett, secretary of the Zoological Society, London (d. 1836)]

**bent**[1] past and past part. of BEND v. — adj. **1** curved, angular. **2** colloq. dishonest, illicit. **3** colloq. different from the norm, esp. as regards sexual preference (opp. STRAIGHT). **4** (foll. by on) set on doing or having (bent on getting his way). — n. **1** inclination or bias (his mind has a frivolous bent). **2** (foll. by for) talent (a bent for mimicry).

**bent**[2] n. kind of grass, some species of which are used in lawns etc. [Old English]

**benumb** /bee-**num**, buh-/ v. **1** make numb; deaden. **2** paralyse (the mind or feelings).

**benzene** /**ben**-zeen/ n. colourless liquid found in coal tar, petroleum, etc. and used as a solvent and in the making of plastics etc. [ultimately from Arabic]

**benzine** /**ben**-zeen/ n. mixture of liquid hydrocarbons obtained from petroleum.

**benzol** /**ben**-zol/ n. benzene, esp. unrefined.

**bequeath** /bee-**kweeth**, buh-/ v. **1** leave to a person in a will. **2** hand down to posterity. [from BE-: related to QUOTH]

**bequest** /bee-**kwest**, buh-/ n. **1** act or instance of bequeathing; bestowal by will. **2** thing bequeathed. [from BE-, obsolete quiste saying]

**berate** /bee-**rayt**, buh-/ v. (**-ting**) scold, rebuke.

**Berber** /**ber**-buh/ — n. **1** member of the indigenous mainly Muslim Caucasian peoples of N. Africa. **2** language of these peoples. — adj. of the Berbers or their language. [Arabic]

**bereave** /bee-**reev**, buh-/ v. (**-ving**) (esp. as **bereaved** adj.) (often foll. by of) deprive of a relation, friend, etc., esp. by death. □ **bereavement** n. [Old English, from reave deprive of]

**bereft** /bee-**reft**, buh-/ adj. (foll. by of) deprived (bereft of hope). [past part. of BEREAVE]

**beret** /**be**-ray/ n. round flattish brimless cap of felt etc. [French: related to BIRETTA]

**beriberi** /ˌbe-ree-**be**-ree/ n. nervous disease caused by a deficiency of vitamin $B_1$. [Sinhalese beri weakness, reduplicated]

**berkelium** /ber-**kee**-lee-uhm, **ber**-klee-uhm/ n. artificial radioactive metallic element. [Berkeley in US, where first made]

**berley** /**ber**-lee/ — v. (also absol., as **berley-up**) scatter ground-bait on (the water) in order to attract fish. — n. ground-bait. [origin unknown]

**berry** n. (pl. **-ies**) **1** any small roundish juicy stoneless fruit. **2** Bot. fruit with its seeds enclosed in pulp (e.g. a banana or tomato). [Old English]

**berry saltbush** n. near prostrate Australian saltbush of all mainland States, bearing masses of vivid red fruits.

**berserk** /buh-**serk**, -**zerk**/ adj. (esp. in **go berserk**) wild, frenzied; in a rage. [originally = Norse warrior: Icelandic, = bear-coat]

**berth** — n. **1** bunk on a ship, train, etc. for sleeping in. **2** place for a ship to moor or be at anchor. **3** adequate room for a ship. — v. **1** moor (a ship); be moored. **2**

provide a sleeping place for. □ **give a wide berth to** stay away from. [probably from a special use of BEAR[1]]

**beryl** /**be**-ruhl/ n. **1** transparent precious stone, esp. pale green. **2** mineral species including this, emerald, and aquamarine. [Greek *bērullos*]

**beryllium** /buh-**ril**-ee-uhm/ n. hard white metallic element used in the manufacture of light corrosion-resistant alloys.

**beseech** /bee-**seech**, buh-/ v. (*past* and *past part.* **besought** /-**sawt**/ or **beseeched**) **1** (foll. by *for*, or *to* + infin.) entreat. **2** ask earnestly for. [from BE-, SEEK]

**beset** /bee-**set**, buh-/ v. (-**tt**-; *past* and *past part.* **beset**) **1** attack or harass persistently (*beset by worries*). **2** surround (a person etc.). □ **besetting sin** the sin that especially or most frequently tempts one. □ **besetment** n. [Old English: related to BE-]

**beside** /bee-**suyd**, buh-/ prep. **1** at the side of; near (*lie down beside me*). **2** compared with (*beside him I am an angel*). **3** irrelevant to (*beside the point*). □ **beside oneself** frantic with worry etc. [Old English: related to BY, SIDE]

**besides** — prep. in addition to; apart from. — adv. also; moreover.

**besiege** /bee-**seej**, buh-/ v. (-**ging**) **1** lay siege to (*troops besieged the town*). **2** crowd round eagerly (*besieged by his fans*). **3** harass with requests or inquiries.

**besmirch** /bee-**smerch**, buh-/ v. **1** soil, discolour. **2** dishonour (*our family name has been besmirched*).

**besom** /**bee**-zuhm/ n. broom of twigs. [Old English]

**besotted** /bee-**sot**-uhd, buh-/ adj. **1** infatuated (*besotted with his new girlfriend*). **2** intoxicated, stupefied.

**besought** *past* and *past part.* of BESEECH.

**bespeak** /bee-**speek**, buh-/ v. (*past* **bespoke**; *past part.* **bespoken** or as adj. **bespoke**) **1** engage in advance. **2** order (goods). **3** suggest; be evidence of (*his gift bespeaks a kind heart*).

**best** — adj. (superl. of GOOD) of the most excellent or desirable kind. — adv. (superl. of WELL[1]). **1** in the best manner (*does it best*). **2** to the greatest degree (*like it best*). **3** most usefully (*is best ignored*). — n. **1** that which is best (*the best is yet to come*). **2** chief merit or advantage (*brings out the best in him*). **3** (foll. by *of*) winning majority of (games played etc.) (*the best of five*). **4** one's best clothes. — v. colloq. defeat, outwit, outbid, etc. □ **all the best** expression used to wish a person

good fortune. **at best** on the most optimistic view. **best bib and tucker** one's best clothes. **the best part of** most of. **do one's best** do all one can. **get the best of** defeat, outwit. **had best** would find it wisest to. **make the best of** derive what limited advantage one can from. [Old English]

**bestial** /**bes**-tee-uhl/ adj. **1** brutish, cruel. **2** of or like a beast. [Latin: related to BEAST]

**bestiality** /ˌbes-tee-**al**-uh-tee/ n. **1** bestial behaviour. **2** sexual intercourse between a person and an animal.

**bestiary** /**bes**-tee-uh-ree/ n. (pl. -**ies**) moralising medieval treatise on real and imaginary beasts. [medieval Latin: related to BEAST]

**bestir** /bee-**ster**, buh-/ v.refl. (-**rr**-) exert or rouse oneself.

**best man** n. bridegroom's chief attendant.

**bestow** /bee-**stoh**/ v. (foll. by *on*, *upon*) confer (a gift, right, etc.). □ **bestowal** n. [Old English *stow* a place]

**bestrew** /bee-**stroo**, buh-/ v. (*past part.* **bestrewed** or **bestrewn**) **1** (usu. foll. by *with*) strew (a surface). **2** lie scattered over.

**bestride** /bee-**struyd**, buh-/ v. (-**ding**; *past* -**strode**; *past part.* -**stridden**) **1** sit astride on. **2** stand astride over.

**bet** — v. (-**tt**-; *past* and *past part.* **bet** or **betted**) **1** risk a sum of money on the result of a race, contest, etc. (*I don't bet on horses*). **2** risk (a sum) thus, or risk (a sum) against (a person) (*bet $10 on a horse*; *he bet me $10 I'd lose*). **3** colloq. feel sure (*bet they've forgotten it*). — n. **1** act of betting (*make a bet*). **2** money etc. staked (*put a bet on*). **3** colloq. opinion (*that's my bet*). **4** colloq. choice or possibility (*she's our best bet*). □ **you bet** colloq. you may be sure. [origin uncertain]

**beta** /**bee**-tuh/ — n. **1** second letter of the Greek alphabet (B, β). **2** second-class mark for a piece of work etc. **3** *Astron.* second brightest star in a constellation. — adj. propr. (**Beta**) pertaining to video equipment designed for the Beta format. [Latin from Greek]

**beta blocker** n. drug preventing unwanted stimulation of the heart, used to treat angina and high blood pressure.

**Beta format** n. a particular format for video cassette recorders.

**betake** /bee-**tayk**, buh-/ v.refl. (-**king**; *past* **betook**; *past part.* **betaken**) (foll. by *to*) go to (a place or person) (*betook himself to the priest for confession*).

**beta particle** *n.* fast-moving electron emitted by the radioactive decay of substances.

**betatron** /bee-tuh-ˌtron/ *n.* apparatus for accelerating electrons in a circular path. [from BETA, ELECTRON]

**betel** /bee-tuhl/ *n.* aromatic leaf of an Asian evergreen climber, widely chewed in tropical Asia together with shavings from the betel-nut. [Portuguese from Malayalam]

**betel-nut** *n.* (also **arecanut**) seed of the tropical areca palm.

*bête noire* /bayt **nwah**/ *n.* (*pl.* *bêtes noires* pronunc. same) person or thing one hates or fears. [French, literally = 'black beast']

**bethink** /bee-**thingk**, buh-/ *v.refl.* (*past* and *past part.* **bethought**) *formal* **1** reflect; stop to think. **2** be reminded by reflection. [Old English: related to BE-]

**betide** /bee-**tuyd**, buh-/ *v.* □ **woe betide a person** used as a warning (*woe betide us if we fail*). [from BE-, *tide* befall]

**betoken** /bee-**toh**-kuhn, buh-/ *v.* be a sign of; indicate. [Old English: related to BE-]

**betook** *past* of BETAKE.

**betray** /bee-**tray**, buh-/ *v.* **1** be disloyal or treacherous to (a friend, one's country, a person's trust, etc.). **2** reveal involuntarily or treacherously; be evidence of (*his shaking hand betrayed his fear*). □ **betrayal** *n.* [from BE-, obsolete *tray* from Latin *trado* hand over]

**betroth** /bee-**troh***th*, buh-/ *v.* (usu. as **betrothed** *adj.*) engage to marry. □ **betrothal** *n.* [from BE-, TRUTH]

**better** — *adj.* (*compar.* of GOOD). **1** of a more excellent or desirable kind. **2** partly or fully recovered from illness (*feeling better*). — *adv.* (*compar.* of WELL[1]). **1** in a better manner (*he sings better*). **2** to a greater degree (*I like it better*). **3** more usefully (*is better forgotten*). — *n.* **1** better thing etc. (*the better of the two*). **2** (in *pl.*) one's superiors. — *v.* **1** improve on; surpass (*I can better his offer*). **2** improve (*we can better our chances*). **3** *refl.* improve one's position etc. (*tried to better himself*). □ **better off** in a better (esp. financial) position. **the better part of** most of. **for better or for worse** on terms accepting all results; whatever the outcome. **get the better of** defeat, outwit; win an advantage over. **had better** would find it wiser to. [Old English]

**betterment** *n.* improvement.

**betting** *n.* **1** gambling by risking money on an unpredictable outcome. **2** odds offered on this. □ **what's the betting?**

*colloq.* it is likely or to be expected (*what's the betting he'll be late?*).

**bettong** /bet-ong/ *n.* any of three species of KANGAROO RAT (see also WOYLIE). [Dharuk *bidung*]

**between** /buh-**tween**/ — *prep.* **1 a** at a point in the area bounded by two or more other points in space, time, etc. (*between Dubbo and Orange*; *between now and Friday*). **b** along the extent of such an area (*no shops between here and the centre*; *numbers between 10 and 20*). **2** separating (*difference between right and wrong*). **3 a** shared by (*$50 between us*). **b** by joint action (*agreement between us*). **4** to and from (*runs between Launceston and Devonport*). **5** taking one of (*choose between them*). — *adv.* (also **in between**) at a point or in the area bounded by two or more other points (*not fat or thin but in between*). □ **between ourselves** (or **you and me**) in confidence. [Old English: related to BY, TWO]

**betwixt** /bee-**twikst**, buh-/ *adv.* □ **betwixt and between** *colloq.* neither one thing nor the other. [Old English]

**bevel** /bev-uhl/ — *n.* **1** slope from the horizontal or vertical in carpentry etc.; sloping surface or edge. **2** tool for marking angles. — *v.* (**-ll-**) **1** reduce (a square edge) to a sloping edge. **2** slope at an angle. [French]

**bevel gear** *n.* gear working another at an angle to it.

**beverage** /bev-uh-rij/ *n.* *formal* drink. [Latin *bibo* drink]

**bevy** /bev-ee/ *n.* (*pl.* **-ies**) company (of quails, larks, women, etc.). [origin unknown]

**bewail** /bee-**wayl**, buh-/ *v.* lament; wail over.

**beware** /bee-**wair**, buh-/ *v.* (only in *imper.* or *infin.*; often foll. by *of*) be cautious (of) (*beware of the dog*; *beware the Ides of March*). [from BE, *ware* cautious]

**bewdy** /byoo-dee/ *var.* of BEAUTY.

**bewdy bonzer** *adj.* *colloq.* magnificent; wonderful; dinkum Australian.

**bewilder** /bee-**wil**-duh, buh-/ *v.* utterly perplex or confuse. □ **bewildering** *adj.* **bewilderment** *n.* [from BE-, obsolete *wilder* lose one's way]

**bewitch** /bee-**wich**, buh-/ *v.* **1** enchant. **2** cast a spell on.

**beyond** /bee-**yond**, buh-/ — *prep.* **1** at or to the further side of (*beyond the river*). **2** outside the scope or understanding of (*beyond repair*; *it is beyond me*). **3** more than (*sold for a price beyond its value*; *prospered beyond all others*). **4** (of time) later than. — *adv.* **1** at or to the further side. **2** further on. — *n.* (prec. by *the*) the unknown after death. □**beyond the black stump** see BLACK STUMP. [Old English: related to BY, YON]

**bezel** /**bez**-uhl/ *n.* **1** sloped edge of a chisel. **2** oblique faces of a cut gem. **3** groove holding a watch-glass or gem. [French]

**Bi** *symb.* bismuth.

**bi-** *comb. form* (often bin - before a vowel) forming nouns, adjectives, and verbs, meaning: **1** division into two (*biplane*; *bisect*). **2 a** occurring twice in every one or once in every two (*bi-weekly*). **b** lasting for two (*biennial*). **3** *Chem.* substance having a double proportion of what is indicated by the simple word (*bicarbonate*). **4** *Bot. & Zool.* having divided parts which are themselves similarly divided (*bipinnate*). [Latin]

**biannual** /buy-**an**-yoo-uhl/ *adj.* occurring etc. twice a year.

**bias** /**buy**-uhs/ — *n.* **1** (often foll. by *towards*, *against*) predisposition or prejudice. **2** *Statistics* distortion of a statistical result due to a neglected factor. **3** edge cut obliquely across the weave of a fabric. **4** *Sport* **a** irregular shape given to a bowl. **b** oblique course this causes it to run. — *v.* (**-s-** or **-ss-**) **1** (esp. as **biased** *adj.*) influence (usu. unfairly); prejudice. **2** give a bias to. □ **on the bias** obliquely, diagonally. [French]

**bias binding** *n.* strip of fabric cut obliquely and used to bind edges.

**biathlon** /buy-**ath**-lon/ *n.* athletic contest in cycling and running or skiing and shooting. [from BI-, after PENTATHLON]

**bib** *n.* **1** piece of cloth etc. fastened round a child's neck while eating. **2** top front part of an apron, dungarees, etc. □ **keep one's bib out** *colloq.* refrain from interfering. **push** (or **put** or **stick**) **one's bib in** interfere. [origin uncertain]

**bib-cock** *n.* tap with a bent nozzle. [perhaps from BIB]

**Bible** /**buy**-buhl/ *n.* **1 a** Christian scriptures of Old and New Testaments. **b** Jewish scriptures. **c** (**bible**) copy of these. **2** (**bible**) *colloq.* authoritative book (*this will be the footy fan's bible*). □ **biblical** /**bib**-li-kuhl/ *adj.* [Greek *biblia* books]

**bible-bashing** *n.* (also **bible-thumping**) *colloq.* aggressive fundamentalist preaching; aggressive moralising or the attempt to force one's own moral views on everyone. □ **bible-bash** *v.* (also **-thump**). **bible-basher** *n.* (also **-thumper**).

**bibliography** /bib-lee-**og**-ruh-fee/ *n.* (*pl.* **-ies**) **1 a** list of books etc. referred to in a scholarly work, essay, etc. **b** list of the books etc. by a particular author or on a specific subject; book containing this. **2** the study of books, their authorship, editions, etc. □ **bibliographer** *n.* **bibliographical** /-uh-**graf**-i-kuhl/ *adj.* [Greek: related to BIBLE]

**bibliophile** /**bib**-lee-oh-,fuyl/ *n.* lover or collector of books.

**bibulous** /**bib**-yuh-luhs/ *adj.* tending to drink alcohol. [Latin *bibo* drink]

**bicameral** /buy-**kam**-uh-ruhl/ *adj.* (of a parliament or legislative body) having two chambers. [from BI-, Latin *camera* chamber]

**bicarb** /**buy**-kahb/ *n.* *colloq.* = BICARBONATE 2. [abbreviation]

**bicarbonate** /buy-**kah**-buh-nuht/ *n.* **1** any acid salt of carbonic acid. **2** (in full **bicarbonate of soda**) sodium bicarbonate used as an antacid or in baking-powder.

**bicentenary** /,buy-sen-**tee**-nuh-ree/ *n.* (*pl.* **-ies**) **1** two-hundredth anniversary. **2** celebration of this.

**bicentennial** /,buy-sen-**ten**-ee-uhl/ — *n.* bicentenary. — *adj.* occurring every two hundred years.

**biceps** /**buy**-seps/ *n.* (*pl.* same) muscle with two heads or attachments, esp. that bending the elbow. [Latin *caput* head]

**bicker** *v.* argue pettily. [origin unknown]

**bickie** /**bik**-ee/ *n.* *colloq.* (also **bikkie**) biscuit. □ **big bickies** large sum of money (opp. **small bickies**). [abbreviation]

**bicuspid** /buy-**kus**-puhd/ — *adj.* having two cusps or points. — *n.* **1** the premolar tooth in humans. **2** tooth with two cusps. [from BI-, CUSP]

**bicycle** /**buy**-si-kuhl/ — *n.* pedal-driven two-wheeled vehicle. — *v.* (**-ling**) ride a bicycle. [Greek *kuklos* wheel]

**bicycle lizard** *n.* (also **cycling lizard**) name for any of several dragon lizards (esp. the frill-necked lizard), so called from their habit of using only their hind legs for movement.

**bid** — *v.* (**-dd-**; *past* **bid**, *archaic* **bade** /bayd, bad/; *past part.* **bid**, *archaic* **bidden**) **1** (*past* and *past part.* **bid**) **a** (esp. at an auction) make an offer (of) (*bid for the vase; bid $20*). **b** offer a service for a stated price. **2** *literary* command; invite (*bid the soldiers shoot; bade her start*). **3** *literary* utter (a greeting or farewell) to (*I bade him welcome*). **4** (*past* and *past part.* **bid**) *Cards* state before play how many tricks one intends to make. — *n.* **1** act of bidding. **2** amount bid. **3** attempt; effort (*made a bid for power*). □ **bidder** *n.* [Old English]

**biddable** *adj.* obedient.

**bidding** *n.* **1** command, request, or invitation. **2** bids at an auction or in a card-game.

**biddy** n. (pl. **-ies**) colloq. woman (esp. old biddy). [a form of the name Bridget]

**biddy bush** n. Australian shrub having aromatic leaves and plumes of fawn flowers.

**bide** v. (**-ding**) □ **bide one's time** wait for a good opportunity. [Old English]

**bidet** /bee-day/ n. low oval basin, with running water, for sitting on to wash the genital area. [French, = pony]

**biennale** /bee-uh-**nah**-lee/ n. exhibition of art etc. held every two years. [Italian]

**biennial** /buy-**en**-ee-uhl/ — adj. lasting, or recurring every, two years. — n. plant that grows from seed one year and flowers and dies the following. [Latin annus year]

**bier** /beer/ n. movable frame on which a coffin or corpse rests. [Old English]

**biff** colloq. — n. sharp blow. — v. strike (a person). [imitative]

**bifid** /buy-fuhd/ adj. divided by a deep cleft into two parts. [Latin findo cleave]

**bifocal** /buy-**foh**-kuhl/ — adj. having two focuses, esp. of a lens with a part for distant and a part for near vision. — n. (in pl.) bifocal spectacles.

**bifurcate** /buy-fuh-,kayt/ — v. (**-ting**) divide into two branches; fork. — adj. forked; branched. □ **bifurcation** /,buy-fuh-**kay**-shuhn/ n. [Latin furca fork]

**big** — adj. (**bigger, biggest**) **1 a** of considerable size, amount, intensity, etc. **b** of a large or the largest size (big toe). **2** important (my big day). **3** adult, elder (big sister). **4** colloq. **a** boastful (big words). **b** often iron. generous (big of him). **c** ambitious (big ideas). **5** (usu. foll. by with) advanced in pregnancy (big with child). — adv. colloq. impressively or grandly (think big). □ **big on** colloq. enthusiastic about; expert on. **in a big way** colloq. with great enthusiasm, display, etc. □ **biggish** adj. [origin unknown]

**Bigambil** /**big**-ahm-bil/ n. an Aboriginal language spoken over a vast area of the Darling Downs region of Queensland and north-eastern NSW: now extinct.

**bigamy** /**big**-uh-mee/ n. (pl. **-ies**) crime of marrying while still married to another person. □ **bigamist** n. **bigamous** adj. [Greek gamos marriage]

**big bang theory** n. theory that the universe began with the explosion of dense matter.

**Big Brother** n. supposedly benevolent watchful dictator.

**big deal** — n. colloq. fuss; commotion (no need to make such a big deal about it). — int. I am not impressed (I got the opposition leader's autograph. — Big deal!).

**big dipper** n. roller-coaster.

**big dry** n. dry season in any part of Australia.

**big end** n. (in a vehicle) end of the connecting-rod, encircling the crankpin.

**bight** /buyt/ n. **1** bay, inlet, etc. **2** loop of rope. [Old English]

**big league** n. senior level in any field (promoted to the big league).

**big mob** n. (orig. Australian pidgin) **1** large number (of animals or people) (big mob of galahs; a big mob turned up for the funeral). **2** colloq. large amount (it'll take a big mob of sweat to grub that paddock, mate).

**big money** n. large amounts of money.

**big mouth** colloq. — n. **1** person who boasts; braggart. **2** person who talks excessively. **3** person who cannot keep a secret. — v. boast, brag.

**big noise** n. (also **big shot**) colloq. = BIGWIG.

**big-note** v. colloq. **1** display one's wealth ostentatiously. **2** (refl.) promote or talk big about (oneself), esp. offensively or tediously (big-notes himself at every opportunity).

**bigot** /**big**-uht/ n. obstinate believer in a religion, political theory, etc. who is intolerant of others and tries to impose his or her views on others. □ **bigoted** adj. **bigotry** n. [French]

**big picture** n. overall or long-term view.

**big smoke** n. any large Australian city. [Australian pidgin]

**big stick** n. colloq. display of force.

**big sticks** n. pl. Aust. Rules the goal posts.

**Big Sunday** n. (in Aboriginal English) a major religious ceremony.

**big time** n. (prec. by the) colloq. success, esp. in show business. □ **big-timer** n.

**big top** n. main tent in a circus.

**big wet** n. wet season in any part of Australia.

**big wheel** n. **1** = BIG DIPPER. **2** = BIGWIG.

**bigwig** n. colloq. important person.

**bike** colloq. — n. bicycle or motor cycle. — v. (**-king**) ride a bike. □ **get off one's bike** colloq. become angry. [abbreviation]

**biker** /**buy**-kuh/ n. colloq. motor cyclist who does not belong to a motor cycle gang.

**bikie** /**buy**-kee/ colloq. — n. member of a gang of motor cyclists. — adj. of or pertaining to a bikie (bikie gangs).

**bikini** /buh-**kee**-nee/ n. (pl. **-s**) two-piece swimsuit for women. [Bikini, Pacific atoll]

**bilabial** /buy-**lay**-bee-uhl/ — adj. Phonet. (of a sound etc.) made with closed or nearly closed lips. — n. such a sound (e.g. p, b, m, w).

**bilateral** /buy-**lat**-uh-ruhl/ *adj.* **1** of, on, or with two sides. **2** affecting or between two parties, countries, etc. (*bilateral negotiations*). □ **bilaterally** *adv.*

**bilby** /**bil**-bee/ *n.* (also **dalgite, pinky, rabbit-eared bandicoot, rabbit rat**) **1** small burrowing marsupial bandicoot of drier mainland Australia. **2** smaller animal of the same genus, now rare and possibly extinct. [Yuwaalaraay *bilbi*]

**bile** *n.* **1** bitter greenish-brown digestive fluid secreted by the liver. **2** bad temper; peevish anger. [Latin *bilis*]

**bilge** /bilj/ *n.* **1 a** the almost flat part of a ship's bottom. **b** (in full **bilge water**) filthy water that collects there. **2** *colloq.* nonsense. [probably var. of BULGE]

**bilingual** /buy-**ling**-gwuhl/ — *adj.* **1** able to speak two languages. **2** spoken or written in two languages. — *n.* bilingual person. □ **bilingualism** *n.* [Latin *lingua* tongue]

**bilious** /**bil**-yuhs/ *adj.* **1** affected by a disorder of the bile. **2** bad-tempered. □ **biliously** *adv.* **biliousness** *n.* [Latin: related to BILE]

**bilk** *v. colloq.* **1** cheat. **2** give the slip to; elude. **3** avoid paying (a creditor or debt). [origin uncertain]

**bill¹** — *n.* **1** statement of charges for goods or services. **2** draft of a proposed law. **3** poster, placard. **4** programme of entertainment. **5** banknote (*ten-dollar bill*). — *v.* **1** send a statement of charges to. **2** put in the programme; announce (*billed to perform tonight only*). **3** (foll. by *as*) advertise as. [medieval Latin *bulla* seal]

**bill²** — *n.* **1** bird's beak. **2** muzzle of a platypus. — *v.* (of doves etc.) stroke bills. □ **bill and coo** exchange caresses. [Old English]

**billabong** /**bil**-uh-ˌbong/ *n.* **1** arm of a river, made by water flowing from the mainstream, usu. only in time of flood, to form a backwater, blind creek, anabranch or, when the water level falls, a pool or lagoon (often of considerable extent). **2** dry bed of such a formation. [Wiradhuri *bilabang*]

**billardiera** /ˌbil-ah-dee-uh-ruh/ *n.* any of more than 20 Australian climbers of the genus of the same name, often cultivated as ornamentals (see APPLE DUMPLING). [*Labillardière*, field botanist]

**billboard** *n.* large outdoor advertising hoarding.

**billet¹** /**bil**-uht/ — *n.* **1** place where troops etc. are lodged, usu. with civilians. **2 a** temporary lodging in a household for a member of a sporting team etc. **b** person so billeted. **3** *colloq.* job, situation in employment. — *v.* (**-t-**) **1** (usu. foll. by

on, *in*, *at*) quarter (soldiers etc.). **2** (of a householder) provide (a soldier, member of a sporting team, etc.) with board and lodging. [Anglo-French diminutive of BILL¹]

**billet²** /**bil**-uht/ *n.* **1** thick piece of firewood. **2** small metal bar. [French diminutive of *bille* tree-trunk]

**billiards** /**bil**-yuhdz/ *n.* **1** game played on a table, with three balls struck with cues. **2** (**billiard**) (in *comb.*) used in billiards (*billiard-ball*). [French: related to BILLET²]

**billion** /**bil**-yuhn/ *adj. & n.* (*pl.* same or (in sense 3) **-s**) **1** a thousand million ($10^9$). **2** (now less often) a million million ($10^{12}$). **3** (in *pl.*) *colloq.* a very large number (*billions of years*). □ **billionth** *adj. & n.* [French]

**billionaire** /ˌbil-yuh-**nair**/ *n.* person who has over a billion dollars etc. [after MILLIONAIRE]

**bill of exchange** *n.* written order to pay a sum of money on a given date to the drawer or to a named payee.

**bill of fare** *n.* menu.

**bill of rights** *n.* statement of the rights of the people of a nation.

**bill of sale** *n.* certificate of transfer of personal property, esp. as a security against debt.

**billow** /**bil**-oh/ — *n.* **1** wave. **2** any large soft mass (*a billow of smoke*). — *v.* rise, fill, or surge in billows. □ **billowy** *adj.* [Old Norse]

**billposter** *n.* (also **billsticker**) person who pastes up advertisements on hoardings.

**billy¹** /**bil**-ee/ *n.* (*pl.* **-ies**) (in full **billycan**) **1** cylindrical tin or enamel outdoor cooking-pot with a lid and wire handle, used esp. for boiling water, making tea, etc., over an open fire in the bush (also *attrib.*: *billy tea*). **2** = BILLY TEA. □ **boil the billy** brew tea. **sling** (or **swing**) **the billy** prepare to make tea, esp. as an act of hospitality for visitors etc. [Scottish *billy-pot* cooking utensil]

**billy²** /**bil**-ee/ *n.* (*pl.* **-ies**) (in full **billy-goat**) male goat. [from the name *Billy*]

**billy-boy** *n.* boy who makes the tea for outdoor workers etc.; general rouseabout.

**billy buttons** *n.* (also **bachelor's buttons**) Australian herbaceous plant having heads of globular or button-like yellow flowers springing from a rosette of light green leaves. [from the name *Billy*]

**billycan** *n.* = BILLY¹ (also *attrib.*: *my first taste of billycan tea*).

**billycart** *n.* **1** small handcart. **2** = GO-KART. [BILLY²]

**billyful** *n.* a (usu. small) quantity (*a*

billyful of stew; gathered only a billyful of pipis).

**billy-o** /**bil**-ee-oh/ n. (also **billy-oh**) colloq. □ **go to billy-o!** go to blazes!; get lost! **gone** (or **off**) **to billy-o** lost, astray, disappeared (my pen's gone to billy-o). **like billy-o** very much, hard, strongly, etc. (ran like billy-o; raining like billy-o).

**billy tea** n. (also **billy**) tea brewed in a billy.

**bimble** /**bim**-buhl/ n. (in full **bimble box**) poplar-like eucalypt of NSW and Queensland, having a fibrous brownish-grey bark and glossy green leaves. [Wiradhuri bimbil]

**bimbo** /**bim**-boh/ n. (pl. **-s** or **-es**) colloq. derog. attractive but unintelligent young woman. [Italian, = little child]

**bin** — n. **1** large receptacle for rubbish or storage. **2** wine of a particular bottling. — v. (**-nn-**) store or put in a bin. [Old English]

**binary** /**buy**-nuh-ree/ — adj. **1** of two parts, dual. **2** of the binary system. — n. (pl. **-ies**) **1** something having two parts. **2** binary number. [Latin bini two together]

**binary code** n. Computing coding system using a string of binary digits to represent a letter, digit, or other character in a computer.

**binary fission** n. division of a cell or organism into two parts.

**binary number** n. (also **binary digit**) one of two digits (usu. 0 or 1) in a binary system of notation.

**binary star** n. system of two stars orbiting each other.

**binary system** n. system using the digits 0 and 1 to code information, esp. in computing.

**bind** /buynd/ — v. (past and past part. bound) **1** tie or fasten tightly (bind the parcel securely). **2** restrain forcibly (gagged and bound him). **3** (cause to) cohere; fasten (bind the ingredients with egg yolk; the glue will bind in 24 hours). **4** (as bound adj.) constricted, obstructed (snowbound; housebound). **5** compel; impose a duty on (bound him to silence). **6 a** edge with braid etc. **b** fasten (the pages of a book) in a cover. **7** constipate. **8** ratify (a bargain, agreement, etc.). **9** (in passive) be required by obligation or duty (am bound to report what you've done to the police). **10** (often foll. by up) put a bandage or other covering round. — n. colloq. nuisance; restriction (homework's a real bind). □ **bind over** Law order (a person) to do something, esp. keep the peace. **in a bind** in trouble; in a dilemma or fix. [Old English]

**binder** n. **1** cover for loose papers etc. **2** substance that binds things together. **3** hist. reaping-machine that binds grain into sheaves. **4** bookbinder.

**bindi-eye** /**bin**-dee-uy/ n. (also **bindy-eye**) **1** any of several Australian plants bearing barbed fruits. **2** the fruit of these plants. [Kamilaroi and Yuwaalaraay bindayaa]

**binding** — n. thing that binds, esp. the covers, glue, etc., of a book. — adj. obligatory.

**bindweed** n. **1** convolvulus. **2** honeysuckle or other climber.

**bine** n. **1** twisting stem of a climbing plant, esp. the hop. **2** flexible shoot. [British dial. form of BIND]

**binge** /binj/ colloq. — n. bout of excessive eating, drinking, etc.; spree (also attrib.: binge-drinking; binge-eating). — v. (**-ging**) indulge in a binge. [probably British dial., = soak]

**binghi** /**bing**-gee/ n. offens. term for an Aborigine. [Awabakal, = (elder) brother]

**bingle** n. colloq. **1** collision (stacked the car — his third bingle for the day). **2** fight or skirmish. [British dial. bing thump, blow]

**bingo** /**bing**-goh/ — n. gambling game in which each player has a card with numbers to be marked off as they are called. — int. **1** exclamation made by a person winning a game of bingo. **2** exclamation of triumph, success, etc. in other contexts. [origin uncertain]

**bingoholic** /**bing**-guh-hol-ik/ n. colloq. person addicted to playing bingo. [-HOLIC]

**bingy** /**bin**-jee/ n. (also **bingie**) colloq. stomach, belly. [Dharuk bindhi belly]

**binocular** /buy-**nok**-yuh-luh, buh-/ adj. for both eyes. [Latin bini two together, oculus eye]

**binoculars** /buh-**nok**-yuh-luhz/ n.pl. instrument with a lens for each eye, for viewing distant objects.

**binomial** /buy-**noh**-mee-uhl/ — n. **1** algebraic expression of the sum or the difference of two terms. **2** a two-part name, esp. in taxonomy (e.g. Eucalyptus ficifolia). — adj. consisting of two terms. [Greek nomos part]

**binomial theorem** n. formula for finding any power of a binomial.

**bio-** comb. form **1** life (biography). **2** biological; of living things (biophysics). [Greek bios life]

**biochemistry** /buy-oh-**kem**-uh-stree/ n. the study of the chemistry of living organisms. □ **biochemical** adj. **biochemist** n.

**biodegradable** /buy-oh-duh-**gray**-duh-buhl/ adj. capable of being decomposed by bacteria or other living organisms.

**bioengineering** /ˌbuy-oh-ˌen-juh-**neer**-ring/ *n.* **1** the application of engineering techniques to biological processes. **2** the use of artificial tissues, organs, etc. to replace parts of the body, e.g. artificial limbs, pacemakers, etc.

**bioethics** /ˌbuy-oh-**eth**-iks/ *n.pl.* (treated as *sing.*) the ethics of medical and biological research.

**biogenesis** /ˌbuy-oh-**jen**-uh-suhs/ *n.* **1** hypothesis that a living organism arises only from a similar living organism. **2** synthesis of substances by living organisms.

**biogeography** /ˌbuy-oh-jee-**og**-ruh-fee/ *n.* scientific study of the geographical distribution of plants and animals.

**biography** /buy-**og**-ruh-fee/ *n.* (*pl.* **-ies**) **1** account of a person's life, written usu. by another. **2** these as a literary genre. □ **biographer** *n.* **biographical** /ˌbuy-uh-**graf**-i-kuhl/ *adj.* [French: related to BIO-]

**biological** /ˌbuy-uh-**loj**-i-kuhl/ *adj.* of biology or living organisms. □ **biologically** *adv.*

**biological clock** *n.* innate mechanism controlling an organism's rhythmic physiological activities.

**biological warfare** *n.* use of toxins or micro-organisms against an enemy.

**biology** /buy-**ol**-uh-jee/ *n.* the study of living organisms. □ **biologist** *n.* [German: related to BIO-]

**biome** /**buy**-ohm/ *n.* **1** large, naturally occurring community of fauna and flora adapted to the particular conditions in which they occur, e.g. an Australian rainforest. **2** the geographical region containing such a community.

**bionic** /buy-**on**-ik/ *adj.* **1** relating to bionics. **2** having electronically operated body parts or the resulting superhuman powers. [from BIO- after ELECTRONIC]

**bionics** *n.pl.* (treated as *sing.*) the study of mechanical systems that function like living organisms or parts of living organisms.

**biophysics** /ˌbuy-oh-**fiz**-iks/ *n.pl.* (treated as *sing.*) science of the application of the laws of physics to biological phenomena. □ **biophysical** *adj.* **biophysicist** *n.*

**biopic** /**buy**-oh-ˌpik/ *n.* film biography for television or cinema.

**biopsy** /**buy**-op-see/ *n.* (*pl.* **-ies**) examination of tissue removed from a living body to discover the presence, cause, or extent of a disease. [Greek *bios* life, *opsis* sight]

**biorhythm** /**buy**-oh-ˌrith-uhm/ *n.* any recurring biological cycle thought to affect one's physical, emotional, or intellectual state.

**biosphere** /**buy**-oh-ˌsfeer/ *n.* regions of the earth's crust and atmosphere occupied by living things. [German: related to BIO-]

**biosynthesis** /ˌbuy-oh-**sin**-thuh-suhs/ *n.* production of organic molecules by living organisms. □ **biosynthetic** /-**thet**-ik/ *adj.*

**biotechnology** /ˌbuy-oh-tek-**nol**-uh-jee/ *n.* branch of technology exploiting biological processes, esp. using micro-organisms, in industry, medicine, etc.

**biotin** /**buy**-uh-tuhn/ *n.* vitamin of the B complex, found in egg-yolk, liver, and yeast. [Greek *bios* life]

**bipartisan** /ˌbuy-pah-tuh-**zan**, buy-**pah**-tuh-zuhn/ *adj.* of or involving two (esp. political) parties.

**bipartite** /buy-**pah**-tuyt/ *adj.* **1** of two parts. **2** shared by or involving two parties. [Latin *bipartio* divide in two]

**biped** /**buy**-ped/ — *n.* two-footed animal. — *adj.* two-footed. □ **bipedal** /-**pee**-duhl/ *adj.* [Latin *bipes -edis*]

**biplane** /**buy**-playn/ *n.* aeroplane with two sets of wings, one above the other.

**bipolar** /buy-**poh**-luh/ *adj.* having two poles or extremities.

**birch** — *n.* **1** tree of Europe etc. with pale hard wood and thin peeling bark, bearing catkins. **2** bundle of birch twigs used for flogging. — *v.* beat with a birch. [Old English]

**bird** *n.* **1** two-legged feathered winged vertebrate, egg-laying and usu. able to fly. **2** *colloq.* **a** young woman. **b** girlfriend. **3** *colloq.* person (usu. as specified) (*strange bird*). **4** *colloq.* prison; prison sentence. **5** = DEAD BIRD. □ **a bird in the hand** something secured or certain. **the birds and the bees** *euphem.* sexual activity and reproduction. **birds of a feather** similar people. **for** (or **strictly for**) **the birds** *colloq.* trivial, uninteresting. [Old English]

**birdbrain** *n. colloq.* stupid or flighty person. □ **birdbrained** *adj.*

**birdcage** *n.* **1** cage for birds. **2** enclosure at a racecourse in which jockeys mount and dismount.

**bird-eating spider** *n.* gigantic, venomous, Australian spider (the female having a body often larger than a mouse) which captures large prey such as birds, frogs, lizards, etc.

**bird flower** *n.* WA shrub with soft, jade-green leaves and greeny-yellow pea-flowers bird-like in shape.

**birdie** *n.* **1** *colloq.* little bird. **2** *Golf* hole played in one under par.

**birdlime** *n.* sticky substance spread to trap birds.

**birdlime tree** see PISONIA.

**bird of paradise** n. any bird of the family Paradisaeidae of Australia and New Guinea, the male of which has brilliant plumage, esp. the VICTORIA RIFLE-BIRD.

**bird of passage** n. **1** migrant bird. **2** habitual traveller.

**bird orchid** n. any of six Australian terrestrial orchids having green, reddish-brown or rich purple bird-like flowers (*green bird-orchid*; *bronze bird-orchid*; *autumn bird-orchid*).

**bird's-eye view** n. general view from above.

**bird's nest fern** n. Australian rainforest fern having long, light green fronds radiating outwards from a central base and forming a bowl-shaped whole: often used in cultivation.

**Birdsville** /**berdz**-vuhl/ n. (in full **Birdsville disease**) condition of horses (caused by eating a central Australian indigofera) characterised by staggering, convulsions, etc. [town in south-western Queensland]

**birdwing** n. (also **bird's wing**) any of several large colourful butterflies occurring in north-eastern coastal Australia.

**biretta** /buh-**ret**-uh/ n. square usu. black cap with three flat projections on top, worn by Roman Catholic priests. [Latin *birrus* cape]

**biriani** /ˌbi-ree-**yah**-nee/ n. (also **buriani** /ˌbuu-ree-/ ) orig. Indian dish made with highly seasoned rice and meat (usu. lamb) etc.

**biro** /**buy**-roh/ n. (pl. **-s**) propr. a kind of ball-point pen. [*Biró*, name of its inventor]

**birth** — n. **1** emergence of a baby or young from its mother's body. **2** beginning (*birth of civilisation*). **3 a** ancestry (*of noble birth*). **b** high or noble birth; inherited position. — v. **1** give birth (to) (*she's determined to birth at home; the husband is often present when the wife births their baby*). **2** assist (a woman) to give birth. □ **give birth to 1** produce (young). **2** be the cause of (*what gave birth to this rumour?*). [Old Norse]

**birth certificate** n. official document detailing a person's birth.

**birth control** n. contraception.

**birthday** n. **1** day on which one was born. **2** anniversary of this.

**birthday suit** n. state of nudity. □ **in one's birthday suit** in the nude.

**birthmark** n. unusual coloured mark on one's body or from birth.

**birthplace** n. place where one was born.

**birth rate** n. number of live births per thousand of population per year.

**birthright** n. inherited, esp. property, rights.

**birthstain** n. hist. stigma once attached to convict ancestry in Australia (*the Earl of Beauchamp informed Australians that they had turned their birthstains to good*).

**birthstone** n. gem popularly associated with the month of one's birth.

**biscuit** /**bis**-kuht/ n. **1** flat thin un-leavened cake, usu. crisp and sweet. **2** fired unglazed pottery. **3** light brown colour. **4** small flat bundle of hay. [Latin *bis* twice, *coquo* cook]

**bisect** /buy-**sekt**/ v. divide into two (strictly, equal) parts. □ **bisection** n. **bisector** n. [from BI-, Latin *seco sect-* cut]

**bisexual** /buy-**sek**-shoo-uhl/ — adj. **1** feeling or involving sexual attraction to people of both sexes. **2** Biol. having characteristics of both sexes; herm-aphrodite. — n. bisexual person. □ **bisexuality** /-al-uh-tee/ n.

**bishop** /**bish**-uhp/ n. **1** senior Christian clergyman, usu. in charge of a diocese, and empowered to confer holy orders. **2** mitre-shaped chess piece. [Greek *episkopos* overseer]

**bishopric** /**bish**-uhp-rik/ n. office or diocese of a bishop. [Old English, = bishop's realm]

**bismuth** /**biz**-muhth/ n. **1** reddish-white metallic element used in alloys etc. **2** compound of it used medicinally. [German]

**bison** /**buy**-suhn/ n. (pl. same) wild hump-backed ox of Europe or N. America. [Latin from Germanic]

**bisque** /bisk/ n. rich shellfish soup, esp. of lobster. [French]

**bistro** /**bis**-troh/ n. (pl. **-s**) **1** small informal restaurant. **2** wine bar. [French]

**bit¹** — n. **1** small piece or quantity. **2** (prec. by *a*) fair amount (*sold quite a bit; needed a bit of persuading*). **3** short time or distance (*wait a bit; move up a bit*). — adv. somewhat (*am a bit tired*). □ **bit by bit** gradually. **bit of all right** colloq. pleasing person or thing, esp. a woman. **bit rough** colloq. **1** (of language, a joke, etc.) indecent; not seemly in the circum-stances. **2** unjust; unfair. **do one's bit** colloq. make a useful contribution. [Old English]

**bit²** past of BITE.

**bit³** n. **1** metal mouthpiece of a bridle, used to control a horse. **2** tool or piece for boring or drilling. **3** cutting or gripping part of a plane, pincers, etc. □ **take the bit between one's teeth 1** take decisive personal action. **2** escape from control. [Old English]

**bit⁴** n. Computing unit of information expressed as a choice between two possibilities; a 0 or 1 in binary notation. [BINARY, DIGIT]

**bitch** — n. **1** female dog or other canine animal. **2** colloq. offens. spiteful woman. **3** colloq. unpleasant or difficult thing or situation (this machine's a real bitch; had a bitch of a day). **4** complaint; whinge (what's your bitch?). — v. **1** speak scathingly or spitefully. **2** complain; whinge (always bitching about something). [Old English]

**bitchy** adj. (**-ier**, **-iest**) colloq. spiteful; malicious. □ **bitchily** adv. **bitchiness** n.

**bite** — v. (**-ting**; past **bit**; past part. **bitten**) **1** cut or puncture with the teeth. **2** (foll. by off, away, etc.) detach thus. **3 a** (of an insect, snake, etc.) wound with a sting, fangs, etc. **b** (of a sword etc.) cut into; penetrate. **c** (of an acid etc.) eat into; corrode. **4** (of a wheel, screw, etc.) grip, penetrate. **5** accept bait or an inducement. **6** be harsh in effect, esp. intentionally (his words bit). **7** (in passive) **a** swindle (was bitten by a con-man). **b** (foll. by by, with, etc.) be infected by (enthusiasm etc.) (bitten by love; bitten by the ballroom dancing fad). **8** colloq. cadge; borrow money from. **9** colloq. worry, perturb (what's biting you?). **10** cause smarting pain (biting wind; frostbitten). **11** be sharp or effective (biting wit). **12** (foll. by at) snap at. — n. **1** act of biting. **2** wound etc. made by biting. **3 a** mouthful of food. **b** snack. **4** taking of bait by a fish. **5** pungency (esp. of flavour). **6** incisiveness, sharpness (his speech lacked bite). **7** position of the teeth when the jaws are closed. **8** colloq. **a** cadger (he's the biggest bite this side of the black stump). **b** act of cadging. **c** victim of cadging. □ **bite the bullet** colloq. behave bravely or stoically. **bite the dust** colloq. **1** die. **2** fail (another of his projects bites the dust). **bite a person's head off** colloq. respond angrily. **bite one's lip** repress emotion etc. **a good bite** colloq. an easy victim (esp. of cadging). **put the bite on** colloq. borrow or extort money from. □ **biter** n. [Old English]

**bit part** n. minor role.

**bitser** n. (also **bitzer**) colloq. mongrel dog. [abbreviation of bits (and pieces)]

**bitter** — adj. **1** having a sharp pungent disagreeable taste; not sweet. **2 a** causing, showing, or feeling mental pain or resentment (bitter memories). **b** difficult to accept (a bitter disappointment). **3 a** harsh; virulent (bitter animosity). **b** piercingly cold. — n. **1** beer flavoured with hops and tasting slightly bitter. **2** (in pl.) liquor flavoured esp. with wormwood, used in cocktails. □ **to the bitter end** to the very end in spite of difficulties. □ **bitterly** adv. **bitterness** n. [Old English]

**bitter bark** n. (also **fever tree**, **fever bark**) any of several Australian trees having an extremely bitter-tasting bark (formerly used to reduce fever) (see also QUININE TREE).

**bittern** /**bit**-uhn/ n. **1** any of a group of wading birds of the heron family. **2** any of a number of Australian birds of this group, usu. feeding at night (black bittern; mangrove bittern; yellow bittern). [French butor from Latin butio]

**bitter-sweet** adj. **1** sweet with a bitter aftertaste. **2** arousing pleasure tinged with pain or sorrow.

**bitty** adj. (**-ier**, **-iest**) made up of bits; scrappy.

**bitumen** /**bich**-uh-muhn/ n. **1** tarlike mixture of hydrocarbons derived from petroleum and used for road surfacing etc. **2 a** tarred road. **b** Stuart Highway between Darwin and Alice Springs. □ **bituminous** adj. [Latin]

**bitzer** var. of BITSER.

**bivalve** /**buy**-valv/ — n. aquatic mollusc with a hinged double shell, e.g. the oyster and mussel. — adj. with such a shell.

**bivouac** /**biv**-oo-ak/ — n. temporary open encampment without tents, esp. of soldiers. — v. (**-ck-**) make, or camp in, a bivouac. [French, probably from German]

**biz** n. colloq. business. [abbreviation]

**bizarre** /buh-**zah**/ adj. strange; eccentric; grotesque. [French]

**Bk** symb. berkelium.

**blab** v. (**-bb-**) **1** talk foolishly or indiscreetly. **2** reveal (a secret etc.); confess. [imitative]

**blabber** — n. (also **blabbermouth**) person who blabs. — v. (often foll. by on) talk foolishly or inconsequentially.

**blachan** /**blah**-chahn/ n. dried shrimp paste, used esp. in Asian cooking.

**black** — adj. **1** reflecting no light, colourless from lack of light (like coal or soot); completely dark. **2** (**Black**) **a** of the human group with dark-coloured skin, esp. of Aboriginal or African descent. **b** of or relating to Black people (Black rights). **3** (of the sky etc.) heavily overcast. **4 a** angry; gloomy (black look; black mood). **b** sad; tragic (this is a black day for Australia). **5** implying disgrace etc. (in his black books; black mark). **6** wicked, sinister, deadly (black-hearted). **7** portending trouble (things look black). **8** (of hands, clothes, etc.) dirty (your fingernails are absolutely black). **9** comic but sinister (black comedy). **10** (of tea or coffee) without milk. **11** (of a company etc.) boycotted, esp. by a trade union in a strike etc. **12** used as a distinguishing epithet in the names of Australian fauna and flora (*black bream*; *black-breasted buzzard*; *black-faced wood swallow*; *black trevally*; *black apple*; *black oak*). — *n.* **1** black colour or pigment. **2** black clothes or material (*dressed in black*). **3 a** (in a game) black piece, ball, etc. **b** player of this. **4** credit side of an account (*in the black*). **5** (**Black**) member of a dark-skinned race, esp. an Aborigine or an African. — *v.* **1** make black (*blacked his boots*). **2** declare (goods etc.) 'black'. □ **black out 1** lose memory or consciousness. **2** suppress the release of information. **3 a** extinguish or cover lights as a precaution against air-raids. **b** cause the supply of electrical power to cease (*the storm blacked out half of Sydney*). **c** darken a theatre stage. [Old English]

**black and blue** *adj.* bruised.

**black and white** — *n.* recorded in writing or printing (*I have it in black and white*). — *adj.* **1** (of a film etc.) not in colour. **2** consisting of extremes only, oversimplified (*interpreted the problem in black and white terms*).

**black apple** *n.* tall tree of Queensland and NSW, having a ridged trunk, shining leaves, and black, plum-shaped, edible fruit (see also BURSARIA).

**black art** *n.* = BLACK MAGIC.

**blackball** *v.* **1** reject (a candidate) in a ballot (orig. by voting with a black ball). **2** ostracise or keep (a person) out of a club, group, etc.

**black ban** — *n.* **1** refusal (by suppliers, trade unions, etc.) to supply or provide goods or services, usu. as part of an industrial or political dispute or protest. **2** prohibition (esp. as imposed by a trade union) which prevents work (on a site etc.) from proceeding (usu. as part of industrial action) (cf. GREEN BAN). — *v.* (of a trade union) declare (a company etc.) black (*adj.* 11).

**black bean** see MORETON BAY CHESTNUT.

**black belt** *n.* **1** highest grade of proficiency in judo, karate, etc. **2** holder of this grade, entitled to wear a black belt.

**blackberry** *n.* (*pl.* **-ies**) black fleshy edible fruit of the bramble.

**blackbird**[1] *n.* common European thrush, introduced into Australia.

**blackbird**[2] *n. hist.* **1** an Aborigine (esp. in the phrase *blackbird shooting*, the practice whereby parties of whites would go out to hunt and murder Aborigines, often on a large scale) (see also BLACK

CROW; BLACK GAME). **2** a Pacific Islander as victim of kidnapping and enslavement by white Australians.

**blackbirding** *n. hist.* act or practice of kidnapping Pacific Islanders and selling them as slave labour, mainly for the Queensland cotton and sugar plantations.

**blackboard** *n.* board with a smooth dark surface for writing on with chalk.

**black box** *n.* flight-recorder.

**blackboy** *n.* = XANTHORRHOEA.

**blackbutt** *n.* any of several eucalypts with characteristic fire-charred fibrous bark on the lower trunk, esp. *E. pillularis* of Queensland and NSW.

**black cockatoo** *n.* any of several large Australian crested parrots with predominantly black plumage (*long-billed black cockatoo*; *red-tailed black cockatoo*; *yellow-tailed black cockatoo*).

**black crow** *n. hist.* an Aborigine (esp. in the phrase **black crow shooting** the practice by whites of shooting Aborigines for sport).

**blackcurrant** *n.* **1** cultivated flowering shrub. **2** its small dark edible berry.

**black economy** *n.* goods and services paid for by cash, which cash is not declared as part of taxable income.

**blacken** *v.* **1** make or become black or dark. **2** defame, slander.

**black eye** *n.* bruised skin around the eye.

**black-eyed Susan** see TETRATHECA.

**blackfellow** *n.* (also **blackfella**, **blackfeller** /blak-fel-uh/ )(in white use largely *hist.*) an Aborigine. □ **blackfellow law** = LAW 11.

**blackfish** *n.* any of several dark-coloured marine and freshwater food-fish of south-eastern Australia, esp. LUDERICK.

**Black Friar** *n.* Dominican friar.

**black game** *n. hist.* an Aborigine regarded by whites as an animal to be shot as a trophy or for sport (*as late as 1895 A.C. Bicknell wrote: 'I might get a brace or two of black game before the morning'*).

**blackguard** /blag-ahd, blag-uhd/ *n.* villain, scoundrel. □ **blackguardly** *adj.* [originally = menial]

**blackhead** *n.* black-topped pimple on the skin.

**black hole** *n.* region of space, resulting from the collapse of a star, from which matter and radiation cannot escape.

**blackjack** *n.* **1** tall, buttressed, rainforest tree of NSW and Queensland. **2** = PONTOON[1].

**black kangaroo-paw** see MACROPIDIA.

**blackleg** — *n. derog.* = SCAB 2. — *v.* (**-gg-**) act as a blackleg.

**black line** n. hist. (also **black war**) dragnet operation in 1830 in which the military and police, aided by settlers and their convict servants, moved systematically across eastern Tasmania in an attempt to round up the Aboriginal population, an action leading to their effective extermination.

**blacklist** — n. list of people in disfavour etc. — v. put on a blacklist.

**black magic** n. magic supposed to invoke evil spirits.

**blackmail** — n. **1 a** extortion of payment in return for silence. **b** payment so extorted. **2** use of threats or moral pressure. — v. **1** (try to) extort money etc. from by blackmail. **2** threaten, coerce. □ **blackmailer** n. [obsolete *mail* rent]

**black market** n. illicit trade in rationed, prohibited, or scarce commodities. □ **black marketeer** n.

**Black Mass** n. sacrilegious travesty of the Roman Catholic Mass, in worship of Satan.

**blackout** n. **1** temporary loss of consciousness or memory. **2** loss of electric power, radio reception, etc. **3** compulsory darkness as a precaution against air raids. **4** temporary suppression of news. **5** sudden darkening of a theatre stage.

**black plum** n. small tree of Queensland and NSW bearing black, oval, edible fruit.

**Black Power** n. movement for Black rights and political power.

**black prince** n. large black cicada (with green markings) of NSW and Queensland.

**black pudding** n. sausage of pork, dried pig's blood, suet, etc.

**black sassafras** see SASSAFRAS.

**black sheep** n. colloq. member of a family, group, etc. regarded as a disgrace or failure.

**blackshirt** n. hist. member of a Fascist organisation.

**blacksmith** n. smith who works in iron.

**black snake** n. either of two highly venomous Australian snakes, the red-bellied of south-eastern Australia and coastal eastern Queensland, and the spotted of south-eastern Queensland and north-eastern NSW.

**black spot** n. **1** place of danger or difficulty, esp. on a road (an accident black spot). **2** fungal plant disease producing black spots on leaves (e.g. on roses).

**black stump** n. imaginary marker at the limits of settled (and, by implication,

civilised) country in Australia. □ **beyond the black stump** in the remote outback. **this side of the black stump** in the world known to the speaker.

**black tea** n. tea that is fully fermented before drying (cf. GREEN TEA).

**blackthorn** n. thorny Australian shrub having dark green leaves and a dense profusion of white flowers followed by brown fruits.

**black tie** n. **1** black bow-tie worn with a dinner jacket. **2** colloq. man's formal evening dress.

**black tracker** n. Aborigine employed by the police to track down a person.

**blackwattle** n. tall Australian shrub or small tree, quite unrelated to the true wattle, having masses of creamy, bell-shaped, wattle-like flowers: early settlers used this shrub for their wattle-and-daub huts.

**black widow** n. venomous American spider of which the female devours the male immediately after mating has taken place.

**blackwood** n. **1** tall (to 30m) wattle of eastern and southern mainland Australia and Tasmania, having cream ball-flowers. **2** its reddish-brown wood.

**bladder** n. **1 a** sac in some animals which serves as the receptacle of the urine secreted by the kidneys. **b** any similar sac in the animal body containing liquid or gas (gall-bladder). **2** inflated sac in seaweed etc. **3** inflatable inner lining of a football. [Old English]

**bladder saltbush** n. silvery Australian saltbush having unusual fruits with large, inflated appendages.

**blade** n. **1 a** cutting part of a knife etc. **b** = RAZOR-BLADE. **2** flattened part of an oar, propeller, etc. **3 a** flat narrow leaf of grass etc. **b** broad thin part of a leaf. **4** flat bone, e.g. in the shoulder. [Old English]

**blady grass** n. (also bladey grass) any of several Australian grasses, the mature blades of which are stiff and have very sharp edges.

**blame** — v. (**-ming**) **1** assign fault or responsibility to (blamed me). **2** (foll. by on) fix responsibility for (an error etc.) on (blamed it on his brother). — n. **1** responsibility for an error etc. (must share the blame equally). **2** act of blaming or attributing of responsibility (got all the blame). □ **be to blame** be responsible; deserve censure (the weather's to blame; you are to blame). □ **blameable** adj. **blameless** adj. **blameworthy** adj. [French: related to BLASPHEME]

**blanch** /blahnch, blanch/ v. **1 a** make or

become white or pale by extracting colour. **b** grow or make pale from shock, fear, etc. (*he blanched when he saw the extent of her injuries*). **2 a** peel (almonds etc.) by scalding. **b** immerse (vegetables etc.) briefly in boiling water. **3** whiten (a plant) by depriving it of light. [French: related to BLANK]

**blancmange** /bluh-**monzh**, -**monj**/ *n.* sweet opaque jelly of flavoured cornflour and milk. [French, = white food]

**bland** *adj.* **1 a** mild, not irritating (*a bland comment*). **b** tasteless; insipid (*bland food*). **2** gentle in manner; suave. □ **blandly** *adv.* **blandness** *n.* [Latin *blandus* smooth]

**blandish** /**blan**-dish/ *v.* flatter; coax. □ **blandishment** *n.* (usu. in *pl.*). [Latin: related to BLAND]

**blank** — *adj.* **1 a** (of paper) not written or printed on. **b** (of a document) with spaces left for a signature or details. **2 a** empty (*blank space*). **b** unrelieved; sheer (*blank wall*). **3 a** without interest, result, or expression (*blank face*). **b** having (temporarily) no knowledge etc. (*mind went blank*). **4** complete (*a blank refusal; blank despair*). — *n.* **1 a** unfilled space, esp. in a document. **b** document having blank spaces. **2** (in full **blank cartridge**) cartridge containing gunpowder but no bullet. **3 a** dash written instead of a word or letter (*told him to — off*). **b** *euphem.* used in place of a word regarded as coarse (*told him to blank off*). **4** empty space or period of time (*the whole evening was a blank to me*). — *v.* (usu. foll. by *off, out*) screen, obscure. □ **draw a blank** get no response; fail. □ **blankly** *adv.* **blankness** *n.* [French *blanc* white, from Germanic]

**blank cheque** *n.* **1** cheque left for the payee to fill in. **2** *colloq.* unlimited freedom of action.

**blanket** /**blang**-kuht/ — *n.* **1** large esp. woollen sheet used as a bed-covering etc. **2** thick covering mass or layer (*blanket of fog; blanket of silence*). — *attrib. adj.* covering everything; inclusive (*blanket condemnation*). — *v.* (*-t-*) **1** cover (*snow blanketed the land*). **2** stifle, suppress (*blanketed all discussion*). [French: related to BLANK]

**blank verse** *n.* unrhymed verse, usu. iambic pentameters.

**blare** — *v.* (*-ring*) **1** sound or utter loudly. **2** make the sound of a trumpet. — *n.* blaring sound. [Low German or Dutch, imitative]

**blarney** /**blah**-nee/ — *n.* cajoling talk; flattery. — *v.* (*-eys, -eyed*) flatter, cajole. [*Blarney*, castle near Cork in Ireland]

**blasé** /**blah**-zay/ *adj.* bored or indifferent through over-familiarity. [French]

**blaspheme** /blas-**feem**/ *v.* (*-ming*) **1** use religious names irreverently; treat a religious or sacred subject irreverently. **2** talk irreverently about; use blasphemy against. [Greek *blasphēmeō*]

**blasphemy** /**blas**-fuh-mee/ *n.* (*pl.* -ies) **1** irreverent talk or treatment of a religious or sacred thing. **2** instance of this. □ **blasphemous** *adj.*

**blast** /blahst/ — *n.* **1** strong gust of air. **2 a** explosion. **b** destructive wave of air from this. **3** loud note from a wind instrument, car horn, etc. **4** *colloq.* severe reprimand or criticism. **5** strong current of air used in smelting etc. — *v.* **1** blow up (rocks etc.) with explosives. **2 a** wither, blight (a plant, animal, limb, etc.) (*blasted oak*). **b** destroy, ruin (*blasted her hopes*). **3** (cause to) make a loud noise (*blasted away on his trumpet*). **4** *colloq.* reprimand or criticise severely. — *int.* expressing annoyance. □ **at full blast** *colloq.* at maximum volume, speed, etc. **blast off** take off from a launching site. [Old English]

**blasted** *colloq.* — *attrib. adj.* damned; annoying (*that blasted nuisance!*). — *adv.* damned; extremely (*it's blasted cold*).

**blast furnace** *n.* smelting furnace into which hot air is driven.

**blast-off** *n.* launching of a rocket etc.

**blatant** /**blay**-tuhnt/ *adj.* **1** flagrant, unashamed (*blatant attempt to steal; blatant lie*). **2** loudly obtrusive. □ **blatantly** *adv.* [coined by Spenser]

**blather** /**bla**th-uh/ (also **blether**) — *n.* foolish talk. — *v.* talk foolishly.

**blaze¹** — *n.* **1** bright flame or fire. **2** violent outburst (of passion etc.) (*a blaze of patriotic fervour*). **3** brilliant display (*blaze of scarlet; blaze of glory*). — *v.* (*-zing*) **1** burn with a bright flame. **2** be brilliantly lighted. **3** show bright colours (*blazing with jewels*). **4** be consumed with anger, excitement, etc. □ **blaze away** (often foll. by *at*) **1** shoot continuously. **2** work vigorously. **go to blazes** *colloq.* go to hell!; get lost! **like blazes** *colloq.* **1** with great energy. **2** very fast. **what the blazes** *colloq.* what the hell (*what the blazes are you up to?*). [Old English, = torch]

**blaze²** — *n.* **1** white mark on an animal's face. **2** mark cut on a tree, esp. to show a route. — *v.* (*-zing*) mark (a tree or a path) with blazes. □ **blaze a trail** show the way for others. [origin uncertain]

**blaze³** *v.* (*-zing*) proclaim. □ **blaze abroad** spread (news) about. [Low German or Dutch, related to BLOW]

**blazer** *n.* jacket without matching trousers, often part of a uniform of schoolchildren, sporting teams, etc. [from BLAZE[1]]

**blazon** /blay-zuhn/ — *v.* **1** proclaim (esp. *blazon abroad*). **2** *Heraldry* describe or paint (arms). — *n.* **1** *Heraldry* shield or coat of arms. □ **blazonment** *n.* **blazonry** *n.* [French, originally = shield]

**bleach** — *v.* whiten in sunlight or by a chemical process. — *n.* bleaching substance or process. [Old English]

**bleak** *adj.* **1** bare, exposed; windswept (*bleak landscape*). **2** dreary, grim (*bleak prospects*). [Old Norse]

**blear** /bleer/ — *v.* make dim or obscure; blur. — *n.* a blur. [origin uncertain]

**bleary** /bleer-ree/ *adj.* (**-ier**, **-iest**) **1** (of the eyes or mind) dim; blurred. **2** indistinct (*bleary shapes of trees in the mist*). □ **blearily** *adv.*

**bleary-eyed** *adj.* having dim sight; lacking perception.

**bleat** — *v.* **1** (of a sheep, goat, or calf) make a wavering cry. **2** (often foll. by *out*) speak or say plaintively. — *n.* bleating cry. [Old English]

**bleed** — *v.* (*past* and *past part.* **bled**) **1** emit blood. **2** draw blood from surgically. **3** *colloq.* extort money from. **4** (often foll. by *for*) suffer wounds or violent death (*bled for his country*). **5 a** (of a plant) emit sap. **b** (of dye) come out in water. **6** empty (a system) of excess air or fluid (*tried bleeding the hydraulic system*). — *n.* act of bleeding. □ **one's heart bleeds** usu. *iron.* one is very sorrowful. [Old English]

**bleeder** *n. colloq.* a haemophiliac.

**bleeding** *adj. & adv. colloq. euphem.* = BLOODY (*adj.* 3; *adv.*) (*bleeding nuisance*; *bleeding awful*).

**bleeding heart** *n.* Australian shrub or small tree, having long, ovate, (fancifully, heart-shaped) leaves which colour a bloody red before they fall.

**bleep** — *n.* intermittent high-pitched electronic sound. — *v.* **1** make a bleep. **2** summon with a bleeper. [imitative]

**bleeper** *n.* small electronic device bleeping to contact the carrier.

**blemish** /blem-ish/ — *n.* flaw, defect, or stain. — *v.* spoil, mark, or stain. [French]

**blench** *v.* flinch, quail. [Old English]

**blend** — *v.* **1 a** mix (esp. sorts of tea, spirits, wine, etc.) together to produce a desired flavour etc. **b** produce by this method (*blended whisky*). **2 a** mix or combine (ingredients etc.) thoroughly. **b** do this with a blender. **3** form a harmonious compound; become one (*the instruments of the orchestra blended perfectly*). **4** (often foll. by *with*, *in*) mingle or be mingled (*truth blended with lies*; *blends in well with the locals*). **5** (esp. of colours) **a** pass imperceptibly into each other (*the blue blends into the green*). **b** go well together; harmonise (*the lounge suite blends well with the curtains*). — *n.* **1** mixture (*a blend of assorted nuts*). **2** = PORTMANTEAU WORD. [Old Norse]

**blender** *n.* machine for liquidising, chopping, or puréeing food.

**blenny** /blen-ee/ *n.* (*pl.* **-ies**) any of many small spiny-finned scaleless marine fish of Australian coastal waters and elsewhere. [Greek *blennos* mucus]

**bless** *v.* (*past* and *past part.* **blessed**, *poet.* **blest**) **1 a** (of a priest etc.) pronounce words, esp. in a religious rite, asking for divine favour, esp. by making the sign of the cross over. **b** ask God to look favourably on (*bless this house*). **2** sanctify (esp. the bread and wine at Mass etc. before the consecration). **3** glorify (God). **4** attribute one's good luck to (an auspicious time, one's fate, etc.); thank (*bless the day I met her*; *bless my lucky stars*). **5** (usu. in *passive*) make happy or successful (*blessed with children*; *blessed with peace for thirty years*). □ **bless me** or **my soul** exclamation of surprise etc. **bless you!** exclamation of endearment, gratitude, etc., or to a person who has just sneezed. [Old English]

**blessed** /bles-uhd, blest/ *adj.* (also *poet.* **blest**) **1 a** consecrated (*Blessed Sacrament*). **b** revered (*of blessed memory*). **2** fortunate; bringing happiness (*blessed with good health*). **3** *euphem.* cursed (*blessed nuisance!*). **4** *RC Ch.* beatified. **5** bringing happiness; blissful (*blessed ignorance*). □ **blessedness** *n.*

**blessing** *n.* **1** act of declaring, seeking, or bestowing (esp. divine) favour (*sought God's blessing*; *mother gave them her blessing*). **2** grace said at a meal. **3** gift of God, nature, etc.; thing one is glad of (*count your blessings*; *it was a blessing he turned up*).

**blew** *past* of BLOW[1].

**blight** /bluyt/ — *n.* **1** plant disease caused by fungi, insects, etc. **2** insect etc. causing such a disease. **3** = SANDY BLIGHT. **4** harmful or destructive force. — *v.* **1** affect with blight. **2** harm, destroy (*blighted my hopes*). **3** spoil. [origin unknown]

**blimp** *n.* **1** small non-rigid airship. **2** soundproof cover for a cine-camera. [origin uncertain]

**blind** /bluynd/ — *adj.* **1 a** lacking the power of sight. **b** (*absol.*; prec. by *the*) those who are blind. **c** of, pertaining to, or for the use of the blind (*blind school*).

**2 a** without adequate foresight, discernment, or information (*blind effort*). **b** (often foll. by *to*) unwilling or unable to appreciate a factor etc. (*blind to argument*). **3** not governed by purpose or reason (*blind forces*). **4** reckless (*blind hitting*). **5 a** concealed (*blind corner*). **b** closed at one end (*blind alley*). **6** (of flying) using instruments only. — *v.* **1** deprive of sight, permanently or temporarily. **2** rob of judgment; deceive; overawe (*greed blinded them to the danger; blinded by success*). — *n.* **1** screen for a window; awning. **2** thing used to hide the truth (*he's a spy, and his job is just a blind*). **3** obstruction to sight or light. — *adv.* blindly (*fly blind*). □ **blind to** incapable of appreciating. **turn a blind eye to** pretend not to notice. □ **blinding** *adj.* **blindly** *adv.* **blindness** *n.* [Old English]

**blind alley** *n.* **1** alley closed at one end. **2** futile course.

**blind date** *n. colloq.* date between two people who have not previously met.

**blind drunk** *adj. colloq.* extremely drunk.

**blinder** *n. colloq.* **1** excellent piece of play in a game (*took a blinder of a catch*). **2** bout of drinking to excess.

**blindfold** — *v.* cover the eyes of (a person) with a tied cloth etc. — *n.* cloth etc. so used. — *adj. & adv.* **1** with eyes covered. **2** without due care (*went into it blindfold*). [originally *blindfelled* = struck blind]

**blind Freddy** *n. colloq.* a most unperceptive person (*even blind Freddy could have seen that*).

**blind grass** *n.* a WA grass reputed to cause blindness in stock.

**blind man's buff** *n.* game in which a blindfold player tries to catch others.

**blind spot** *n.* **1** point on the retina insensitive to light. **2** area in which a person lacks understanding, impartiality, etc. (*religion is his blind spot*).

**blind-your-eye** *n.* = MILKY MANGROVE.

**blink** — *v.* **1** shut and open the eyes quickly. **2** (often foll. by *back*) prevent (tears) by blinking. **3** shine unsteadily, flicker. — *n.* **1** act of blinking. **2** momentary gleam or glimpse. □ **blink at 1** look at while blinking. **2** ignore; shirk; condone (*he should have taken a stand, but blinked at what was going on*). **on the blink** *colloq.* not working properly; out of order. [Dutch, var. of BLENCH]

**blinker** — *n.* **1** (usu. in *pl.*) each of two screens on a bridle preventing lateral vision. **2** device that blinks, esp. a car's indicators. — *v.* **1** obscure with blinkers. **2** (as **blinkered** *adj.*) having narrow and prejudiced views.

**blip** — *n.* **1** minor deviation or error; temporary problem (*the fall in the government's popularity was merely a blip*). **2** quick popping sound. **3** small image of an object on a radar screen. — *v.* (**-pp-**) **1** (of figures, an economic indicator, etc.) suffer a temporary movement (esp. in an unwelcome direction) (*the dollar has begun to blip*). **2** make a blip. [imitative]

**bliss** *n.* **1** perfect joy or happiness. **2** being in heaven. □ **blissful** *adj.* **blissfully** *adv.* [Old English]

**blister** — *n.* **1** small bubble on the skin filled with watery fluid and caused by heat or friction. **2** similar swelling on plastic, wood, etc. — *v.* **1** come up in blisters. **2** raise a blister on. □ **blistery** *adj.* [origin uncertain]

**blistering** *adj.* sharp; intense; severely critical (*blistering heat; blistering attack on their arguments*).

**blithe** /bluyth/ *adj.* **1** cheerful, happy. **2** careless, casual (*with blithe indifference*). □ **blithely** *adv.* **blitheness** *n.* **blithesome** /-suhm/ *adj.* [Old English]

**blithering** /bli*th*-uh-ring/ *attrib. adj. colloq.* hopeless; contemptible (*in blithering idiot*). [*blither*, var. of BLATHER]

**blitz** /blits/ *colloq.* — *n.* **1 a** intensive or sudden (esp. aerial) attack. **b** any intensive attack (*police blitz on drink-driving*). **c** intensive period of work etc. (*must have a blitz on this room*). **2** (**the Blitz**) German air raids on London in 1940. — *v.* **1** inflict a blitz on (*city was blitzed by enemy aircraft*). **2** *colloq.* defeat convincingly (*blitzed his opponent in the third set*). [abbreviation of BLITZKRIEG]

**blitzkrieg** /blits-kreeg/ *n.* intense military campaign intended to bring about a swift victory. [German, = lightning war]

**blizzard** /bliz-uhd/ *n.* severe snowstorm. [origin unknown]

**bloat** — *v.* **1** inflate, swell. **2** (as **bloated** *adj.*) inflated with pride, wealth, or food. **3** cure (a herring) by salting and smoking lightly. — *n.* (also **bloating**) disease of livestock characterised by an accumulation of gases in the stomach, usu. caused by eating too much green fodder. [Old Norse]

**blob** *n.* small drop or spot. [imitative]

**bloc** *n.* group of governments etc. sharing a common purpose. [French: related to BLOCK]

**block** — *n.* **1** solid piece of hard material, esp. stone or wood. **2 a** this as a base for chopping etc. **b** (in Queensland) one of the long piles supporting an above-ground house. **3 a** large building, esp.

when subdivided (*block of flats*). **b** group of buildings between streets. **c** group of city or suburban buildings bounded by four streets (*go for a walk round the block*). **d** large tract of land in a rural area. **e** building allotment in a suburb etc. **f** small holding, esp. an irrigated orchard or vineyard, or a hobby farm. **4 a** obstruction (*a block in the pipe*). **b** *Sport* action which obstructs the progress of an opponent. **5** two or more pulleys mounted in a case. **6** piece of wood or metal engraved for printing. **7** *colloq.* head (*knock his block off*). **8 a** (often *attrib.*) number of things as a unit, e.g. shares, theatre seats (*block booking*). **b** set of data or instructions treated as a single unit by a computer. **9** (in *pl.*) any of a set of solid cubes etc., used as a child's toy. **10** = STARTING-BLOCK. — *v.* **1 a** (often foll. by *up*) obstruct (*nose was blocked up*; *blocking my view*). **b** impede (*blocked his progress*). **2** restrict the use of (*blocked his funds*). **3** *Cricket* stop (a ball) with a bat defensively. □ **block in 1** sketch roughly; plan. **2** confine. **block out 1** shut out (light, noise, a memory, view, etc.). **2** sketch roughly; plan. **do** (or **lose**) **one's block** *colloq.* lose one's temper. **off one's block** *colloq.* mad, crazy. [Low German or Dutch]

**blockade** /blo-**kayd**/ — *n.* surrounding or blocking of a place by an enemy to prevent entry and exit. — *v.* (**-ding**) subject to a blockade.

**blockage** *n.* obstruction.

**block and tackle** *n.* system of pulleys and ropes, esp. for lifting.

**blockbuster** *n.* *colloq.* **1** thing of great power, esp. a very successful film, book, etc. **2** bomb capable of destroying a whole block of buildings.

**block capitals** *n.pl.* (also **block letters**) letters printed without serifs, or written with each letter separate and in capitals.

**blocker** *n.* proprietor of a small holding, esp. an orchard or vineyard.

**blockie** *n.* *colloq.* = BLOCKER.

**bloke** *n.* *colloq.* man, fellow. [Shelta, the ancient secret language of Irish gypsies etc.]

**blond** (of a woman usu. **blonde**) — *adj.* (of a person, hair, or complexion) light-coloured, fair. — *n.* blond person. [Latin *blondus* yellow]

**blood** /blud/ — *n.* **1** usu. red fluid circulating in the arteries and veins of animals. **2** bloodshed, esp. killing. **3** passion, temperament (*his blood is up*). **4** race, descent, parentage (*of the same blood*). **5** relationship; relations (*blood is thicker than water*). — *v.* initiate (a

person) by experience. □ **in one's blood** inherent in one's character. [Old English]

**blood bank** *n.* store of blood for transfusion.

**bloodbath** *n.* massacre.

**blood count** *n.* number of corpuscles in a specific amount of blood.

**blood-curdling** *adj.* horrifying.

**blood donor** *n.* person giving blood for transfusion.

**blooded** *adj.* **1** initiated. **2** (in *comb.*) having blood or a disposition of a specified kind (*cold-blooded*; *red-blooded*).

**blood group** *n.* any of the types of human blood determining compatibility in transfusion.

**blood-heat** *n.* normal human temperature, about 37 °C or 98.4 °F.

**bloodhound** *n.* large keen-scented dog used in tracking.

**bloodless** *adj.* **1** without blood. **2** without bloodshed (*bloodless coup*). **3** unemotional; cold. **4** pale; anaemic. **5** feeble; lifeless.

**blood money** *n.* **1** money paid as compensation for a death. **2** money paid to a killer.

**blood poisoning** *n.* diseased condition caused by micro-organisms in the blood.

**blood pressure** *n.* pressure of the blood in the arteries etc., measured for diagnosis.

**blood relation** *n.* (also **blood relative**) relative by birth.

**bloodshed** *n.* killing.

**bloodshot** *adj.* (of an eyeball) inflamed.

**blood sport** *n.* sport involving the killing or wounding of animals.

**bloodstain** *n.* stain caused by blood. □ **bloodstained** *adj.*

**bloodstream** *n.* blood in circulation.

**bloodsucker** *n.* **1** animal or insect that sucks blood, esp. a leech. **2** extortioner. □ **bloodsucking** *adj.*

**blood sugar** *n.* amount of glucose in the blood.

**bloodthirsty** *adj.* (**-ier**, **-iest**) eager for bloodshed.

**blood vessel** *n.* vein, artery, or capillary carrying blood.

**bloodwood** *n.* **1** any of many eucalypts, typically having a rough, tessellated, persistent bark and bleeding a viscous reddish kino when damaged. **2** = BRUSH BLOODWOOD.

**bloody** — *adj.* (**-ier**, **-iest**) **1** of, like, running with, or smeared with blood. **2 a** involving bloodshed. **b** bloodthirsty, cruel. **3** *colloq.* expressing annoyance or antipathy, or as an intensifier expressing approval or disapproval (*bloody idiot*; *a* *bloody marvel; a bloody sight better*) (see also GREAT AUSTRALIAN ADJECTIVE; TMESIS). **4** red. — *adv. colloq.* as an intensifier (*bloody awful; you'd bloody well better*). — *v.* (**-ies, -ied**) stain with blood.

**bloody-minded** *adj. colloq.* deliberately uncooperative.

**bloom** — *n.* **1 a** a flower, esp. cultivated. **b** state of flowering (*in bloom*). **2** state of perfection or loveliness (*in the full bloom of youth*). **3 a** healthy glow of the complexion. **b** fine powder on fresh fruit and leaves. — *v.* **1** bear flowers; be in flower. **2** be in one's prime; flourish. □ **blooming** *adj.* [Old Norse]

**bloomer** *n.* **1** *colloq.* blunder. **2** plant that blooms in a specified way (*autumn bloomer*).

**blossom** /blos-uhm/ — *n.* **1** flower or mass of flowers, esp. of a fruit-tree. **2** promising stage (*blossom of youth*). — *v.* **1** open into flower. **2** mature, thrive. [Old English]

**blot** — *n.* **1** spot or stain of ink etc. **2** blemish or defect in an otherwise good character; stain on a person's reputation. — *v.* (**-tt-**) **1** make a blot on, stain. **2** dry with blotting paper. □ **blot one's copybook** damage one's reputation. **blot out 1** obliterate. **2** obscure (a view, sound, etc.). [probably Scandinavian]

**blotch** — *n.* **1** discoloured or inflamed patch on the skin. **2** irregular patch of colour. — *v.* cover with blotches. □ **blotchy** *adj.* (**-ier, -iest**). [obsolete *plotch*, BLOT]

**blotting paper** *n.* absorbent paper for drying wet ink.

**blouse** /blowz/ — *n.* **1** woman's garment like a shirt. **2** upper part of a military uniform. — *v.* (**-sing**) make (a bodice etc.) full like a blouse. [French]

**blouson** /bloo-zon/ *n.* short blouse-shaped jacket. [French]

**blow¹** /bloh/ — *v.* (*past* **blew**; *past part.* **blown**) **1** direct a current of air (at) esp. from the mouth. **2** drive or be driven by blowing (*blew the door open*). **3** (esp. of the wind) move rapidly. **4** expel by breathing (*blew smoke*). **5** sound or be sounded by blowing (*blew the trumpet; whistle blew*). **6** (*past part.* **blowed**) *colloq.* (esp. in *imper.*) curse, confound (*I'm blowed if I know; blow it!*). **7** clear (the nose) by blowing. **8** puff, pant. **9** *colloq.* depart suddenly (from) (*he blew town yesterday*). **10** shatter etc. by an explosion. **11** make or shape (glass or a bubble) by blowing. **12 a** melt from overloading (*the fuse has blown*). **b** break or burst suddenly (*blew a tyre; tyre blew*). **13** (of a whale) eject air and water. **14** break into with explosives. **15** *colloq.* **a** squander

(*blew \$20*). **b** bungle (an opportunity etc.) (*blew his chance*). **c** fail (an examination etc.). **d** reveal (a secret etc.) (*blew their cover*). **16** (of flies) deposit eggs in (meat etc.). **17** *colloq.* boast. **18** register (a reading of one's blood-alcohol level) by blowing into a breathalyser (*he blew .06*). — *n.* **1** act of blowing. **2 a** gust of wind or air. **b** exposure to fresh air. □ **be blowed if one will** *colloq.* be unwilling to. **blow a gasket** *colloq.* lose one's temper. **blow hot and cold** *colloq.* vacillate. **blow in 1** break inwards by an explosion. **2** *colloq.* arrive unexpectedly. **blow a person's mind** *colloq.* cause to have hallucinations etc.; astound. **blow out 1** extinguish by blowing. **2** send outwards by an explosion. **3** *Econ.* (of expenditure estimates, a budget deficit, etc.) increase in size. **blow over** (of trouble, a storm, etc.) fade away. **blow through** *colloq.* depart suddenly. **blow one's top** *colloq.* explode in rage. **blow up 1** explode. **2** *colloq.* rebuke strongly. **3** inflate (a tyre etc.). **4** *colloq.* **a** enlarge (a photograph). **b** exaggerate. **5** *colloq.* arise, happen. **6** *colloq.* lose one's temper. [Old English]

**blow²** /bloh/ *n.* **1** hard stroke with a hand or weapon. **2** sudden shock or misfortune. **3** *Shearing* stroke of the shears. [origin unknown]

**blow-by-blow** *attrib. adj.* (of a narrative etc.) detailed.

**blowey** var. of BLOWIE.

**blowfish** *n.* marine fish (of Australia and elsewhere) able to inflate its body and having potentially highly poisonous flesh.

**blowfly** *n.* any of various large flies, esp. those which lay eggs in meat, wounds, the flesh of animals, etc.

**blow-hole** *n.* **1** nostril of a whale. **2 a** (in coastal rock) hole through which air or water rushes in response to the action of waves. **b** (in inland Australia) vent through which air passes out forcefully from an underground air reservoir. **3** hole (esp. in ice) for breathing or fishing through.

**blowie** /bloh-ee/ *n.* (also **blowey**) *colloq.* = BLOWFLY.

**blow-in** *n.* *colloq.* newcomer or recent arrival; intruder.

**blowlamp** *n.* device with a very hot flame for burning off paint etc.

**blown** *past part.* of BLOW¹.

**blown away** *adj. colloq.* astounded; overjoyed (*blown away when she saw what her present was*).

**blow-out** *n.* *colloq.* **1** burst tyre. **2** melted fuse. **3** *Econ.* increase in a budget deficit, expenditure estimates, etc.

**blowpipe** *n.* **1** tube for blowing air through, esp. to intensify a flame or to blow glass. **2** tube for propelling poisoned darts etc. by blowing.

**blow-up** *n.* **1** *colloq.* enlargement (of a photograph etc.). **2** explosion.

**blowy** /**bloh**-ee/ *adj.* (**-ier, -iest**) windy.

**blubber** — *n.* whale fat. — *v.* **1** sob loudly. **2** sob out (words). — *adj.* swollen, thick. [probably imitative]

**bludge** *colloq.* — *v.* **1** evade one's responsibilities. **2** (foll. by *on*) live off the efforts of others; impose on others. **3** avoid work, idle, usu. (by implication) at someone else's expense. **4** cadge or scrounge (money, food, etc.). — *n.* **1** an undemanding job. **2** (usu. foll. by *on*) act or instance of imposing on (a person). □**bludging** *adj. & n.* [back-formation from BLUDGER]

**bludgeon** /**bluj**-uhn/ — *n.* heavy club. — *v.* **1** beat with this. **2** coerce. [origin unknown]

**bludger** /**bluj**-uh/ *n. colloq.* **1** *hist.* man who lives on the earnings of a prostitute. **2** person who lives off the efforts of others. **3** idler, loafer. **4** person who cadges (money etc.) or who does not contribute his or her fair share (of a cost, of work, etc.). **5** person engaged in non-manual work, a white-collar worker. **6** generalised term of abuse. [originally English slang, = pimp]

**blue** /bloo/ — *adj.* (**bluer, bluest**) **1** having the colour of a clear sky. **2** sad, depressed. **3** pornographic (*a blue film*). **4** used as a distinguishing epithet in the names of Australian fauna and flora (*blue crane*; *blue mallee*). **5** with bluish skin through cold, fear, anger, etc. — *n.* **1** blue colour or pigment. **2** blue clothes or material (*dressed in blue*). **3** *colloq.* argument, row, fight. **4** *colloq.* mistake, blunder. **5** award for achievement in a university sport. **6** (as a nickname) red-headed person. — *v.* (**blues, blued, bluing** or **blueing**) **1** make blue. **2** *colloq.* squander (*blued his wages at the pub*). □ **once in a blue moon** very rarely. **out of the blue** unexpectedly. **stack** (or **bung**) **on a blue** *colloq.* create a disturbance. [French from Germanic]

**blue baby** *n.* baby with a blue complexion due to a congenital heart defect.

**bluebeard** see BLUE FAIRIES.

**bluebell** *n.* **1** any of various plants with bell-shaped blue flowers. **2** (also **Austral bluebell**) see ROYAL BLUEBELL; WAHLENBERGIA.

**blueberry** *n.* (pl. **-ies**) small blue-black edible fruit of various plants.

**blueberry ash** *n.* medium tree of eastern Australia bearing a profusion of fringed bell-flowers in white or pink, followed by blue fruits.

**blue-billed duck** *n.* diving duck of southern Australia, so called because the bill of the male turns blue in summer.

**blue blood** *n.* noble birth.

**blue bonnet** *n.* **1** = RED-COLLARED LORIKEET. **2** parrot of drier areas in southern Australia, having predominantly olive-brown plumage, bright colourings on wings, and a blue face.

**bluebottle** see PORTUGUESE MAN-OF-WAR.

**blue-collar** *attrib. adj.* (of a worker or work) manual; industrial.

**blue devil** *n.* shrub of grasslands in all Australian States, having a branched, metallic blue flower-stem and bearing many metallic blue flowers surrounded by long, extremely prickly bracts.

**blue fairies** *n.pl.* (also **bluebeard**) Australian terrestrial orchid bearing a deep blue flower (a colour rare in the orchid family) with a labellum or lip that may be said to resemble a blue beard.

**blue flyer** *n.* adult female red kangaroo.

**bluegrass** *n.* **1** any of several Australian perennial grasses having flower-head spikes of a blue or purple colour. **2** a kind of instrumental country-and-western music.

**blue-green algae** *n.* poisonous bacterium (not an alga) which infests rivers etc. with a mantle of blue-green scum.

**blue gum** *n.* any of several eucalypts having a smooth bluish-grey bark or bluish-grey juvenile foliage (*southern blue gum*; *Sydney blue gum*; *Tasmanian blue gum*).

**blue heeler** *n.* (also **blue cattle dog, Australian cattle dog**) breed of highly intelligent cattle (or sheep) dog having a blue or red-flecked coat, developed in Australia in the 19th century by crossing native dingo with merle collie from Scotland and subsequently with dalmatian and black-and-tan kelpie.

**blue metal** *n.* crushed bluestone used for road-making.

**blue pincushion** see PINCUSHION 2.

**blueprint** *n.* **1** photographic print of plans in white on a blue background. **2** detailed plan.

**blue ribbon** — *n.* high honour; prize. — *adj.* (**blue-ribbon**) **1** *Polit.* relating to an electorate which is held very comfortably by a particular political party (*blue-ribbon Labor seat*). **2** prize-winning.

**blue-ringed octopus** *n.* very small

highly venomous octopus of Australian coasts, having bands of bluish-purple on the tentacles.

**blues** *n.pl.* **1** (prec. by *the*) bout of depression. **2 a** (prec. by *the*; often treated as *sing.*) melancholic music of Black American origin, usu. in a twelve-bar sequence. **b** (*pl.* same) (as *sing.*) piece of such music (*played a blues*).

**bluestocking** *n.* usu. *derog.* intellectual or literary woman. [18th-c. Blue Stocking Society]

**bluestone** *n.* in eastern Australia, a blue-grey basalt used for building, road-making etc.; in SA, a dark-coloured type of stone used in building etc.

**blue swimmer** *n.* (also **sandie**) edible blue crab widely distributed in sheltered estuaries and inlets of Australia.

**blue tinsel lily** see TINSEL LILY.

**blue-tongue** *n.* (also **blue-tongued lizard**) any of several large Australian lizards with a broad blue tongue prominent when the animal is threatened.

**blue whale** *n.* rorqual, the largest known living mammal.

**blue wren** *n.* any of several Australian wrens, the adult male having bright blue on the crown and other parts of the body, esp. the superb blue wren.

**bluey** /*bloo*-ee/ *n.* **1 a** a swag (so called because the outer covering was traditionally a blue blanket). **b** luggage. **2** swagman's (usu. blue) blanket. **3** heavy grey-blue woollen outer garment or coat. **4** nickname for a red-haired person. **5 a** familiar form of any of a number of names for birds, animals, etc., usu. beginning with the word 'blue'. **b** familiar name for any bird, animal, or thing predominantly blue in colour.

**bluff¹** — *v.* pretend strength, confidence, etc., in order to gain an advantage. — *n.* act of bluffing. □ **call a person's bluff** challenge a person to prove a claim. [Dutch *bluffen* brag]

**bluff²** — *adj.* **1** blunt, frank, hearty. **2** vertical or steep and broad in front. — *n.* steep cliff or headland. [origin unknown]

**bluish** /*bloo*-ish/ *adj.* fairly blue.

**blunder** — *n.* serious or foolish mistake. — *v.* **1** make a blunder. **2** move clumsily; stumble. [probably Scandinavian]

**blunderbuss** /*blun*-duh-,bus/ *n. hist.* short large-bored gun. [Dutch *donderbus* thunder gun]

**blunt** — *adj.* **1** (of a knife, pencil, etc.) not sharp or pointed. **2** direct, outspoken. — *v.* **1** make blunt or less sharp. **2** weaken the force or effect of (*his tears blunted her anger*). □ **bluntly** *adv.* (in sense 2 of *adj.*).

**bluntness** *n.* [probably Scandinavian]

**blur** /bler/ — *v.* (**-rr-**) make or become unclear or less distinct; smear. — *n.* blurred object, sound, memory, etc. [perhaps related to BLEARY]

**blurb** *n.* promotional description, esp. as printed on the jacket of a book. [coined by G. Burgess 1907]

**blurt** *v.* (usu. foll. by *out*) utter abruptly, thoughtlessly, or tactlessly. [imitative]

**blush** — *v.* **1 a** become pink in the face from embarrassment or shame. **b** (of the face) redden thus. **2** feel embarrassed or ashamed. **3** redden. — *n.* **1** act of blushing. **2** pink tinge. [Old English]

**bluster** — *v.* **1** behave pompously or boisterously. **2** (of the wind etc.) blow fiercely. — *n.* noisily self-assertive talk; empty threats. □ **blustery** *adj.* [imitative]

**BMX** /,bee-em-**eks**/ *n.* **1** organised bicycle-racing on a dirt-track. **2** bicycle used for this. [abbreviation of *bicycle moto-cross*]

**BO** /,bee-**oh**/ *abbr. colloq.* body odour.

**boa** /**boh**-uh/ *n.* **1** large snake which kills by crushing and suffocating. **2** long stole of feathers or fur. [Latin]

**boab** /**boh**-ab/ *n.* = BAOBAB.

**boa constrictor** *n.* species of boa of tropical America and the West Indies.

**boar** /baw/ *n.* uncastrated male pig. [Old English]

**board** /bawd/ — *n.* **1 a** a flat thin piece of sawn timber, usu. long and narrow. **b** material resembling this, of compressed fibres. **c** thin slab of wood etc., often with a covering, used for any of various purposes (*chessboard; ironing board; notice-board*). **d** thick stiff card used in bookbinding. **2** provision of regular meals, usu. with accommodation, for payment. **3** directors of a company; official administrative body, e.g. a group of examiners. **4** (in *pl.*) stage of a theatre. **5** side of a ship. **6** the part of the floor of a shearing shed upon which sheep are shorn. **7** = SURFBOARD. — *v.* **1** go on board (a ship, train, etc.). **2** receive, or provide with, meals and usu. lodging. **3** (usu. foll. by *up*) cover with boards; seal or close. □ **across the board** see ACROSS. **go by the board** be neglected or discarded. **on board** on or on to a ship, aircraft, oil rig, etc. **sweep the board** see SWEEP. **take on board** consider, take notice of; accept. [Old English]

**boarder** *n.* **1** person who boards, esp. at a boarding-school. **2** person who boards a ship, esp. an enemy.

**board game** *n.* game played on a board.

**boardie** /**baw**-dee/ *n. colloq.* surfboard rider.

**boarding school** n. school in which pupils live in term-time.

**boardroom** n. room in which a board of directors etc. meets regularly.

**board-shorts** n.pl. long shorts, orig. as used by surfboard riders.

**boarfish** n. any of several deep-sea fish of Australian waters with an elongated snout resembling that of a boar.

**boast** — v. **1** declare one's virtues, wealth, etc. with excessive pride. **2** own or have with pride (*hotel boasts a ballroom*).— n. **1** act of boasting. **2** thing one is proud of. [Anglo-French]

**boastful** adj. given to boasting. □ **boastfully** adv.

**boat** — n. **1** small vessel propelled by water by an engine, oars, or sails. **2** any ship. **3** long low jug for sauce etc. — v. go in a boat, esp. for pleasure. □ **in the same boat** having the same problems. □ **boating** n. [Old English]

**boater** n. flat-topped straw hat with a brim.

**boat people** n.pl. refugees travelling by sea.

**boat race** n. colloq. team-competition which involves a race to drink quantities of beer etc.

**boatswain** /boh-suhn/ n. (also **bosun**, **bo'sun**) ship's officer in charge of equipment and crew.

**bob**[1] — v. (**-bb-**) **1** move quickly up and down. **2** (usu. foll. by *back*, *up*) bounce or emerge buoyantly or suddenly. **3** cut (the hair) in a bob. **4** curtsy. — n. **1** jerking or bouncing movement, esp. upward. **2** hairstyle with the hair hanging evenly above the shoulders. **3** weight on a pendulum etc. **4** horse's docked tail. **5** curtsy. [imitative]

**bob**[2] n. (pl. same) hist. colloq. shilling. [origin unknown]

**bob**[3] n. □ **bob's your uncle** colloq. expression of completion or success. [pet form of *Robert*]

**bobbin** /bob-uhn/ n. spool or reel for thread etc. [French]

**bobble** /bob-uhl/ n. small woolly ball on a hat etc. [diminutive of BOB[1]]

**bobby-dazzler** n. colloq. remarkable or excellent person or thing. [British dial., related to DAZZLE]

**bobcat** n. **1** small N. American wild cat. **2** small four-wheeled earth-moving machine.

**bob-sleigh** — n. mechanically-steered and -braked sledge used for racing down a steep ice-covered run. — v. race in a bob-sleigh.

**bobtail** n. **1** docked tail. **2** horse or dog with this. **3** (also **shingleback**, **stumpy tail**) slow-moving lizard of southern mainland Australia, having large ridged scales on the back and a short rounded tail (see also SLEEPY LIZARD).

**bobuck** /boh-buk/ n. possum of mountain forests in mainland south-eastern Australia. [perhaps from a NSW Aboriginal language]

**bod** n. colloq. **1** body. **2** person. [shortening of BODY]

**bode** v. (**-ding**) be a sign of, portend. □ **bode well** (or **ill**) be a good (or bad) sign. [Old English]

**bodgie**[1] /boj-ee/ — n. something flawed or worthless. — adj. **1** worthless; flawed; inferior; false (*bodgie second-hand car with bodgie number plates*). **2** (of names) assumed. [British dial. *bodge* work clumsily]

**bodgie**[2] n. male Australian youth, esp. of the 1950s, as distinguished by his conformity to American fashions and larrikin behaviour. [perhaps from BODGIE[1], in the sense 'pseudo' (American)]

**bodice** /bod-uhs/ n. **1** part of a woman's dress above the waist. **2** woman's vest-like undergarment. [originally *pair of bodies*]

**bodily** /bod-uh-lee/ — adj. of or concerning the body. — adv. **1** as a whole body (*threw them bodily*). **2** in the flesh, in person.

**bodkin** /bod-kuhn/ n. blunt thick needle for drawing tape etc. through a hem. [origin uncertain]

**body** /bod-ee/ — n. (pl. **-ies**) **1 a** whole physical structure, including the bones, flesh, and organs, of a person or an animal, whether dead or alive. **b** physical aspects of a human being (opp. SOUL). **2** = TRUNK 2. **3 a** main or central part (*body of the car*). **b** bulk or majority (*body of opinion*). **4 a** group regarded as a unit (*governing body*). **b** (usu. foll. by *of*) collection (*body of facts*). **5** quantity (*body of water*). **6** piece of matter (*heavenly body*). **7** colloq. person. **8** full or substantial quality of flavour, tone, etc. (*this wine lacks body*). — v. (**-ies**, **-ied**) (usu. foll. by *forth*) give body or substance to. □ **in a body** all together. [Old English]

**body blow** n. severe setback.

**bodybuilder** n. person who develops the muscles of the body by systematic exercise.

**bodyguard** n. person or group escorting and protecting another.

**body language** n. communication through gestures and poses.

**body odour** n. smell of the human body, esp. when unpleasant.

**body politic** n. nation as a corporate body.

**body surf** v. ride a wave towards the beach, streamlining the body and holding it rigid like a board. □ **body surfer** n.

**bodywork** n. outer shell of a vehicle.

**Boer** /boh-uh, baw/ — n. South African of Dutch descent. — adj. of the Boers. [Dutch, = farmer]

**boffin** /bof-uhn/ n. colloq. person expert in some field, esp. a research scientist. [origin unknown]

**bog** — n. **1 a** wet spongy ground. **b** stretch of this. **2** colloq. toilet. — v. (**-gg-**) (often foll. by down; usu. in passive) impede; become stuck (car is bogged in the mud; was bogged down by difficulties). □ **bog in** (or into) colloq. engage in (a task or activity) with vigour or enthusiasm (esp. begin eating). □ **boggy** adj. (**-ier, -iest**). [Irish or Gaelic bogach]

**bogan** /boh-guhn/ n. colloq. person who is not 'with it' in terms of behaviour and appearance, and hence perceived as not being 'one of us'; contemptible person. [origin unknown]

**bogey**[1] /boh-gee/ n. (pl. **-eys**) Golf score of one stroke more than par at any hole. [perhaps from Bogey, as an imaginary player]

**bogey**[2] /boh-gee/ n. (also **bogy**) (pl. **-eys** or **-ies**) **1** evil or mischievous spirit; devil. **2** awkward thing or circumstance. [originally (Old) Bogey the Devil]

**bogey**[3] (also **bogie**) — n. **1** a swim or bathe. **2** (in full **bogey hole**) swimming hole. — v. swim, bathe. [Dharuk bugi swim or dive]

**bogeyman** n. (also **bogyman**) person (real or imaginary) causing fear etc.

**boggi** /bog-uy/ n. (also **bog-eye, bogghi**) **1** = SLEEPY LIZARD. **2** handpiece of a shearing machine. [Wiradhuri, probably bugay]

**boggle** /bog-uhl/ v. (**-ling**) colloq. be startled or baffled (esp. the mind boggles). [probably British dial. boggle BOGEY[2]]

**bogie**[1] /boh-gee/ n. **1** wheeled undercarriage below a locomotive etc. **2** small truck used for carrying coal, rubble, etc. [origin unknown]

**bogie**[2] var. of BOGEY[3].

**bogong** /boh-gong/ n. (in full **bogong moth**) large brown moth which breeds on plains in southern Australia; the adults, which migrate to hills where they collect in rock crevices, were eaten by Aborigines. [Ngarigo bugung]

**bogus** /boh-guhs/ adj. sham, spurious. [origin unknown]

**bohemian** /boh-**hee**-mee-uhn/ — n. socially unconventional person, esp. an artist or writer. — adj. socially unconventional. □ **bohemianism** n. [French, = gypsy]

**boil**[1] — v. **1 a** (of a liquid) start to bubble up and turn into vapour; reach a temperature at which this happens. **b** (of a vessel) contain boiling liquid (kettle is boiling). **2 a** bring to boiling point. **b** cook in boiling liquid. **c** subject to boiling water, e.g. to clean. **3 a** (of the sea etc.) move or seethe like boiling water. **b** be very angry. **4** colloq. feel or be very hot (I'm boiling). — n. act or process of boiling; boiling point (on the boil; bring to the boil). □ **boil down 1** reduce in volume by boiling. **2** reduce to essentials. **3** hist. reduce (animal carcases) by boiling to produce tallow. **4** (foll. by to) amount to (it all boils down to this . . .). **boil over 1** spill over in boiling. **2** lose one's temper. [Latin bullio to bubble]

**boil**[2] n. inflamed pus-filled swelling under the skin. [Old English]

**boiler** n. **1** apparatus for heating a hot-water supply. **2** tank for heating water or turning it to steam. **3** fowl etc. suitable for cooking only by boiling.

**boiler maker** n. person who makes boilers; metalworker in heavy industry.

**boiler suit** n. protective outer garment of trousers and jacket in one.

**boiling point** n. **1** temperature at which a liquid begins to boil. **2** great excitement or tension (feelings reached boiling point at the meeting).

**boilover** n. orig. Horse-racing surprise result; unexpected defeat of a favourite.

**boisterous** /**boi**-stuh-ruhs/ adj. **1** (of a person) noisily exuberant, rough. **2** (of the sea etc.) stormy, rough. [origin unknown]

**bold** /bohld/ adj. **1** confidently assertive; adventurous, brave. **2** forthright; impudent (bold as brass in his denial). **3** vivid (bold colours; bold imagination). **4** Printing (in full **boldface** or **-faced**) printed in a thick black typeface. □ **make** (or **be**) **so bold as to** presume to; venture to. □ **boldly** adv. **boldness** n. [Old English]

**bole** n. trunk of a tree. [Old Norse]

**bolero** n. (pl. **-s**) **1** /buh-**lair**-roh/ Spanish dance, or the music for it, in triple time. **2** also /**bol**-uh-roh/ woman's short open jacket. [Spanish]

**boll** /bohl/ n. round seed-vessel of cotton, flax, etc. [Dutch]

**bollard** /**bol**-ahd/ n. **1** short post in the road, esp. on a traffic island. **2** short post on a quay or ship for securing a rope. [perhaps related to BOLE]

**bollocks** /**bol**-uhks/ n. coarse colloq. **1** (usu. as int.) nonsense. **2** testicles. [Old English: related to BALL¹]

**bollocky** /**bol**-uh-kee/ adj. (also **bollicky**) (of a person) naked. [bollock naked, -Y¹]

**boloney** var. of BALONEY.

**Bolshevik** /**bol**-shuh-vik/ — n. **1** hist. member of the radical faction of the Russian Social Democratic Party becoming the Communist Party in 1918. **2** Russian Communist. **3** (in general use) any revolutionary socialist. — adj. **1** of the Bolsheviks. **2** Communist. □ **Bolshevism** n. **Bolshevist** n. [Russian, = member of the majority]

**bolster** /**bohl**-stuh/ — n. long cylindrical pillow. — v. (usu. foll. by up) encourage, support, prop up (bolstered up our spirits). [Old English]

**bolt** /bohlt/ — n. **1** sliding bar and socket used to fasten a door etc. **2** large metal pin with a thread, usu. used with a nut, to hold things together. **3** discharge of lightning. **4** act of bolting (cf. sense 4 of v.). **5** roll of fabric. — v. **1** fasten with a bolt. **2** (foll. by in, out) keep (a person etc.) in or out by bolting a door. **3** fasten together with bolts. **4 a** dash off suddenly, esp. to escape. **b** (of a horse) suddenly gallop out of control. **5** gulp down (food) unchewed. **6** (of a plant) run to seed. — adv. (usu. in **bolt upright**) rigidly, stiffly. □ **bolt from the blue** complete surprise. **bolt** (**it**) **in** colloq. win easily. [Old English]

**bolter** n. **1** hist. runaway convict. **2** colloq. **a** horse with only a remote chance of winning a race; outsider (he doesn't have a bolter's chance). **b** horse that races well clear of the field, esp. at an early stage of a race. **c** unexpected winner of a horse-race.

**bolwarra** /bol-**wo**-ruh/ n. (also **native guava**) small tree of Victoria, NSW, and Queensland, having shiny leaves (red when young), cream flowers, and aromatic, edible fruit. [probably from an Aboriginal language]

**bomb** /bom/ — n. **1** container filled with explosive, incendiary material, etc., designed to explode and cause damage. **2** (prec. by the) the atomic or hydrogen bomb. **3** colloq. **a** old or unreliable motor vehicle. **b** anything in a dilapidated condition. **c** complete failure (the party was a real bomb). — v. **1** attack with bombs; drop bombs on. **2** colloq. fail badly (the show bombed). □ **bomb out** colloq. fail (bombed out in Maths). **like a bomb** colloq. **1** very successfully (party went like a bomb). **2** very fast (car goes like a bomb). [Greek bombos hum]

**bombard** /bom-**bahd**/ v. **1** attack with

heavy guns or bombs etc. **2** (often foll. by with) question or abuse persistently. **3** Physics direct a stream of high-speed particles at. □ **bombardment** n. [Latin: related to BOMB]

**bombardier** /,bom-buh-**deer**/ n. non-commissioned officer in the artillery.

**bombast** /**bom**-bast/ n. pompous language; hyperbole. □ **bombastic** /-**bas**-tik/ adj. [earlier bombace cotton wool]

**bombax** /**bom**-baks/ n. tall deciduous spiny tree of northern Australia, having large (10 cm in diameter) brilliant red flowers when leafless, making the tree spectacular when in flower. [Bombax plant genus, from Greek bombux silk]

**Bombay duck** /bom-**bay**/ n. dried fish as a relish, esp. with rice and curry. [corruption of bombil, native name of fish]

**bombed** adj. colloq. **1** drugged. **2** drunk.

**bomber** /**bom**-uh/ n. **1** aircraft equipped to drop bombs. **2** person using bombs, esp. illegally.

**bombora** /bom-**baw**-ruh/ n. **1** dangerous stretch of broken water forming over a submerged offshore reef or rock. **2** the reef or rock itself. [perhaps Dharuk bumbora]

**bombshell** n. **1** overwhelming surprise, shock, or disappointment (his announcement came as a bombshell). **2** artillery bomb.

**bommie** /**bom**-ee/ n. submerged coral reef; bombora. [BOM(BORA), -Y²]

**bona fide** /,boh-nuh **fuy**-dee/ — adj. genuine; sincere. — adv. genuinely; sincerely. [Latin, ablative singular of BONA FIDES]

**bona fides** n. **1** esp. Law honest intention; sincerity. **2** (as pl.) colloq. documentary evidence of acceptability (his bona fides are in order). [Latin, = good faith]

**bonanza** /buh-**nan**-zuh/ n. source of wealth, prosperity, good luck, etc. [Spanish, = fair weather]

**bon-bon** n. **1** = CRACKER¹. **2** lolly, sweet. [French bon good]

**bond** — n. **1** thing or force that unites or (usu. in pl.) restrains (sisterly bond; broke his bonds). **2** binding agreement. **3** Commerce certificate issued by a government or a company promising to repay borrowed money at a fixed rate of interest. **4** adhesiveness. **5** Law **a** deed binding a person to make payment to another. **b** term(s) under which a person is released by a court, e.g. a good behaviour bond. **6** (in full **bond money**) amount payable at the beginning of a tenancy to insure against damage to the property by the tenant or non-payment of rent. **7** *Chem.* linkage between atoms in a molecule. **8** *Building* laying of bricks in one of various patterns in order to ensure strength. — *v.* **1** hold or tie together. **2** connect or reinforce with a bond. **3** place (goods) in bond. **4** become emotionally attached. □ **in bond** (of imported goods) stored until duty is paid. [var. of BAND]

**bondage** *n.* **1** slavery. **2** subjection to constraint etc. **3** sado-masochistic practices involving constraint. [Anglo-Latin: related to BONDSMAN]

**bonded** *adj.* **1** (of goods) placed in bond. **2** (of a debt) secured by bonds. **3** (of material) reinforced by or cemented to another.

**Bondi** /bon-duy/ *n.* □ **shoot through like a Bondi tram** *colloq.* depart hastily. [suburb of Sydney]

**bondi** /bon-duy, -dee/ *n.* heavy Aboriginal club with a knob on the end. □ **give someone bondi** *colloq.* attack savagely. [Wiradhuri *bundi*]

**bonding** *n.* **1** process by which a mother becomes emotionally attached to her child. **2** process by which any couple or members of a group become emotionally attached one to the other(s) (*male bonding*).

**bond paper** *n.* high-quality writing-paper.

**bondsman** *n.* (also **bondman**) serf, slave. [Old English *bonda* husbandman]

**bone** — *n.* **1** any piece of hard tissue making up the skeleton in vertebrates. **2** (in *pl.*) **a** skeleton, esp. as remains. **b** body, esp. as a seat of intuitive feeling (*feel it in my bones*). **3** material of bones or similar material, e.g. ivory. **4** thing made of bone. **5** (in *pl.*) essentials (*the bare bones of an agreement*). **6** (in Aboriginal ritual practice) bone pointed at someone whose death is wished. — *v.* (**-ning**) **1** remove the bones from (*boned the chicken*). **2** *colloq.* steal. **3** (also **point the bone**) (in Aboriginal ritual practice) influence (a person at whom a bone is pointed) with the intention of causing the person's death. □ **bone up** (often foll. by *on*) *colloq.* study intensively. **have a bone to pick** (usu. foll. by *with*) have cause for dispute (with a person). **make no bones about 1** be frank about. **2** not hesitate or scruple. **point the bone** see POINT. □ **boneless** *adj.* [Old English]

**bone china** *n.* fine china made of clay mixed with bone ash.

**bone marrow** *n.* = MARROW 2.

**bone of contention** *n.* source of dispute.

**boner** /boh-nuh/ *n. colloq.* stupid mistake.

**boneseed** *n.* South African shrub introduced to Victoria in 1858, now naturalised and regarded as a noxious weed in southern Australia including Tasmania.

**bonfire** *n.* large open-air fire, esp. for burning rubbish or as part of a celebration. [from BONE (because bones were once used), FIRE]

**bongo** /bong-goh/ *n.* (*pl.* **-s** or **-es**) either of a pair of small drums usu. held between the knees and played with the fingers. [American Spanish]

**bonhomie** /bon-o-mee/ *n.* good-natured friendliness. [French]

**bonk** — *v.* **1** bang, bump. **2** *coarse colloq.* have sexual intercourse (with). — *n.* instance of bonking (*bonk on the head*). [imitative]

**bonkers** /bong-kuhz/ *predic. adj. colloq.* crazy. [origin unknown]

**bon mot** /bon moh/ *n.* (*pl.* **bons mots** /-mohz/ ) witty saying. [French]

**bonnet** /bon-uht/ *n.* **1** woman's or child's hat tied under the chin. **2** hinged cover over a vehicle's engine. [French]

**bonny** /bon-ee/ *adj.* (**-ier, -iest**) esp. *Scot.* **1** physically attractive; healthy looking. **2** good, pleasant. [perhaps from French *bon* good]

**bonsai** /bon-suy/ *n.* (*pl.* same) **1** dwarfed tree or shrub. **2** art of growing these. [Japanese]

**bonus** /boh-nuhs/ *n.* **1** extra benefit or payment. **2 a** (also **bonus issue**) extra issue of shares to the shareholders of a company. **b** distribution of profits to holders of an insurance policy. [Latin, = good]

**bon voyage** /bon-voi-yahzh/ *int.* expression of good wishes to a departing traveller. [French]

**bony** /boh-nee/ *adj.* (**-ier, -iest**) **1** thin with prominent bones. **2** having many bones. **3** of or like bone. □ **boniness** *n.*

**bonzer** /bon-zuh/ *colloq.* — *n.* something or someone that excites admiration. — *adj.* excellent, first-rate. [origin uncertain]

**boo** — *int.* **1** expression of disapproval etc. **2** sound intended to surprise. — *n.* utterance of *boo*, esp. to a performer etc. — *v.* (**boos, booed**) **1** utter boos. **2** jeer at by booing. [imitative]

**boob** *colloq.* — *n.* **1** (also **boo-boo**) silly mistake. **2** foolish person. — *v.* make a silly mistake. [shortening of BOOBY]

**boobialla** /ˌboo-bee-**al**-uh/ n. (also **boobyalla**) (some shrubby varieties also called **cockatoo bush**) any of several Australian plants (genus MYOPORUM) varying in form from ground-covers to tall shrubs or small trees, having usu. highly glossy leaves and purplish fruits, and usu. highly resistant to salt spray. [from the Aboriginal language of south-eastern Tasmania *bubiala*]

**boobook** /boo-buuk/ n. (also **boobook owl, mopoke**) smallest and most widespread of the Australian owls, having a characteristic two-note call. [Dharuk *bug bug*]

**booby** n. (pl. **-ies**) stupid or childish person. [Spanish *bobo*]

**booby prize** n. prize given for coming last.

**booby trap** n. 1 practical joke in the form of a trap, e.g. an object placed on top of a door ajar. 2 disguised explosive device triggered by the unknowing victim.

**boodie** n. (also **Lesueur's kangaroo-rat**) burrowing kangaroo-rat, formerly widespread on mainland Australia but now rare or extinct except on islands off the WA coast. [Nyungar *burdi*]

**boofhead** /buuf-hed/ n. *colloq.* 1 fool, simpleton. 2 person or animal having a large head. □ **boofheaded** adj. **boofheadedness** n. [probably from *bufflehead* (literally = bullock head) a fool]

**boogie** /boo-gee/ v. (**-ies, -ied, -ieing**) *colloq.* dance to pop music.

**boogie-woogie** /ˌboo-gee-**woo**-gee/ n. style of playing blues or jazz on the piano. [origin unknown]

**boojeree** var. of BUDGEREE.

**book** /buuk/ — n. 1 a written or printed work with pages bound along one side. b work intended for publication. 2 bound blank sheets for notes, records, etc. 3 bound set of tickets, stamps, matches, etc. 4 (in *pl.*) set of records or accounts. 5 main division of a large literary work. 6 libretto, script, etc. 7 record of bets made by a bookmaker. — v. 1 a (also *absol.*) reserve (a seat, a room, etc.) in advance. b engage (an entertainer etc.). 2 take the personal details of (an offender or rule-breaker). □ **book in** register at a hotel etc. **bring to book** call to account. **go by the book** proceed by the rules. **in a person's good** (or **bad**) **books** in (or out of) favour with a person. **in my book** in my opinion. **take a leaf out of a person's book** imitate a person. **throw the book at** *colloq.* charge or punish to the utmost. [Old English]

**bookcase** n. cabinet of shelves for books.

**bookie** /buuk-ee/ n. *colloq.* = BOOKMAKER. [abbreviation]

**booking** n. reservation or engagement.

**bookish** adj. 1 studious; fond of reading. 2 having knowledge mainly from books. □ **bookishness** n.

**bookkeeper** n. person who keeps accounts, esp. for a living. □ **bookkeeping** n.

**bookmaker** n. professional taker of bets. □ **bookmaking** n.

**bookworm** n. 1 *colloq.* devoted reader. 2 larva feeding on the paper and glue in books.

**boom**[1] — n. deep resonant sound. — v. make or speak with a boom. [imitative]

**boom**[2] — n. period of economic prosperity or activity. — v. be suddenly prosperous. [perhaps from BOOM[1]]

**boom**[3] n. 1 pivoted spar to which a sail is attached. 2 long pole carrying a microphone, camera, etc. 3 barrier across a harbour etc. [Dutch, = BEAM]

**boomalli** /boo-**mal**-ee/ v. beat (esp. an animal). [probably from an Aboriginal language]

**boomer** /boo-muh/ n. 1 large adult male kangaroo. 2 anything exceptionally large or outstanding of its kind (*a boomer of a day; that wave was a boomer; a boomer of a crisis brewing*). [British dial.]

**boomerang** /boo-muh-rang/ — n. 1 curved flat hardwood missile used by Aborigines in hunting prey, in warfare, and in recreation, and often of a kind able to return in flight to the thrower. 2 plan or scheme that recoils on its originator. 3 thing (esp. a book) lent or borrowed which the lender insists has to be returned (*I'll lend you the book, but remember it's a boomerang*). 4 dud cheque (which is returned to the sender). — v. 1 act as a boomerang (*the golf ball boomeranged off the tree; the cheque boomeranged*). 2 (of a plan etc.) backfire (*his innuendos boomeranged and the biter was bit*). [Dharuk, probably *bumaring*]

**boon**[1] n. advantage; blessing. [Old Norse]

**boon**[2] adj. intimate, favourite (usu. *boon companion*). [French *bon* from Latin *bonus* good]

**boonaree** /boo-nuh-ree/ n. (also **boonery, rosewood**) shrub or small tree of inland Australia, valued as a source of fodder. [probably Kamilaroi *bunari*]

**boondie** var. of BONDI.

**boong** /buung/ n. *offens.* 1 an Aborigine. 2 any dark-skinned person. [origin uncertain]

**boongarry** /buung-guh-ree/ n. = TREE-KANGAROO. [Warrgamay *bulnggarri*]

**boor** n. rude, ill-mannered person. □ **boorish** adj. [Low German or Dutch]

**boorie** /**buu**-ree/ *n. derog.* name for an Aborigine. [Wiradhuri (and neighbouring languages) *buray* boy, child]

**boost** *colloq.* — *v.* **1** promote or encourage (*boosted his spirits*). **2** increase, assist (*boost sales*). **3** push from below (*boosted me up the tree*). — *n.* act or result of boosting. [origin unknown]

**booster** *n.* **1** device for increasing power or voltage. **2** auxiliary engine or rocket for initial speed. **3** dose, injection, etc. renewing the effect of an earlier one.

**boot**[1] — *n.* **1** outer foot-covering reaching above the ankle. **2** luggage compartment of a car. **3** *colloq.* **a** firm kick. **b** (prec. by *the*) dismissal (*got the boot*). — *v.* **1** kick. **2** (often foll. by *out*) eject forcefully. **3** (usu. foll. by *up*) make (a computer) ready. □ **boots and all** without reservation; with no holds barred. **put** (or **sink**) **the boot in 1** kick brutally. **2** attack savagely (verbally or physically), esp. when the opponent is disadvantaged. [Old Norse]

**boot**[2] *n.* □ **to boot** as well, in addition. [Old English]

**bootee** /boo-**tee**/ *n.* (also **bootie**) baby's soft shoe.

**booth** /boo*th*, boo*th*/ *n.* **1** small temporary structure used esp. as a market stall. **2** enclosure for telephoning, voting, etc. [Old Norse]

**bootleg** — *adj.* (esp. of alcohol) smuggled, illicit. — *v.* (**-gg-**) illicitly make or deal in (alcohol etc.). □ **bootlegger** *n.* [from the smugglers' practice of concealing bottles in their boots]

**bootlicker** *n. colloq.* toady.

**boot-scooting** *n.* LINE-DANCING

**bootstrap** *n.* **1** loop used to pull a boot on. **2** technique for building up a computer system from simple, preliminary instructions. □ **pull oneself up by one's bootstraps** better oneself.

**booty** /**boo**-tee/ *n.* **1** loot, spoil. **2** *colloq.* prize or gain. [German]

**booyong** /**boo**-yong/ *n.* any of several ornamental and timber trees of the same genus, occurring in NSW and Queensland, esp. the *tulip oak*. [Bandjalang *buyang*]

**booze** *colloq.* — *n.* alcoholic drink. — *v.* (**-zing**) drink alcohol, esp. to excess. □ **boozy** *adj.* (**-ier**, **-iest**). [Dutch]

**booze bus** *n. colloq.* police vehicle carrying equipment for the random breath-testing of motorists.

**boozer** *n. colloq.* **1** habitual drinker. **2** hotel.

**booze-up** *n. colloq.* drinking bout.

**bop**[1] *colloq.* — *n.* **1 a** spell of dancing, esp.

to pop music. **b** social occasion for this. **2** = BEBOP. — *v.* (**-pp-**) dance, esp. to pop music. □ **bopper** *n.* [abbreviation]

**bop**[2] *colloq.* — *v.* (**-pp-**) hit or punch, esp. lightly. — *n.* esp. light blow or hit. [imitative]

**bora** /**baw**-ruh/ *n.* **1** initiation ceremony by which an Aboriginal boy is admitted to the privileges as well as the responsibilities of manhood. **2** (also **bora-circle**, **bora-ground**, **bora-ring**) sacred site at which the bora is performed. [Kamilaroi *buuru*]

**boracic** /buh-**ras**-ik/ *adj.* of borax.

**boracic acid** *n.* = BORIC ACID.

**borak** /**baw**-rak/ — *adv. obsolete* no; not. — *n.* nonsense; rubbish; derision (*not going to take any more borak from you lot*). □ **poke borak at** make fun of. [Wathawurung *burag* no; not]

**borax** /**baw**-raks/ *n.* salt used in making glass and china, and as an antiseptic. [French ultimately from Persian]

**border** — *n.* **1** edge or boundary, or the part near it. **2 a** line or region separating two countries. **b** boundary between two states in Australia. **3** esp. ornamental strip round an edge. **4** long narrow flower-bed (*herbaceous border*). — *v.* **1** be a border to. **2** provide with a border. **3** (usu. foll. by *on*, *upon*) adjoin; come close to being (*that borders on the truth*). [French from Germanic: related to BOARD]

**borderline** — *n.* **1** line dividing two (often extreme) conditions, e.g. decency and indecency, pass and fail. **2** line marking a boundary. — *adj.* **1** on the borderline. **2** verging on an extreme condition; barely acceptable (*that joke was very borderline*).

**bore**[1] — *v.* (**-ring**) **1** make (a hole), esp. with a revolving tool. **2** make a hole in, hollow out. — *n.* **1** hollow of a firearm barrel or of a cylinder in an internal-combustion engine. **2** diameter of this. **3 a** deep hole made esp. to find water. **b** = ARTESIAN BORE. □ **bore it up** (or **into**) *colloq.* attack vigorously (physically or esp. verbally) (*bored it right up him*; *bored it into them, the slackers*). [Old English]

**bore**[2] — *n.* tiresome or dull person or thing. — *v.* (**-ring**) weary by tedious talk or dullness. □ **bored** *adj.* **boring** *adj.* [origin unknown]

**bore**[3] *past* of BEAR[1].

**boredom** *n.* state of being bored. [from BORE[2]]

**boree** /**baw**-ree, baw-**ree**/ *n.* **1** any of several wattles, esp. *Acacia tephrina*, the phyllodes of which are covered with short white hairs. **2** = MYALL[2]. [Wiradhuri and Kamilaroi *burrii*]

**borer** /baw-ruh/ n. **1** any of several insects, insect larvae, etc., which bore into wood, other plant material, etc. **2** tool for boring.

**boric acid** /baw-rik/ n. acid derived from borax, used as an antiseptic and in the manufacture of heat-resistant glass and enamels.

**born** adj. **1** existing as a result of birth. **2 a** of natural ability or quality (a born leader). **b** (usu. foll. by to + infin.) destined (born lucky; born to be king). **3** (in comb.) of a certain status by birth (Australian-born; well-born). □ **not born yesterday** colloq. not stupid. [past part. of BEAR[1]]

**born-again** attrib. adj. **1** converted (esp. to fundamentalist Christianity). **2** (often iron.) full of the enthusiastic zeal of one recently converted or reconverted to a cause (odd to see yesterday's log-chip baron emerging as today's born-again environmentalist; born-again student).

**borne** /bawn/ past part. of BEAR[1]. — adj. (in comb.) carried by (airborne).

**boron** /baw-ron/ n. non-metallic usu. crystalline element. [from BORAX, after carbon]

**boronia** /buh-roh-nee-uh/ n. any of about 70 species of the genus of the same name endemic to Australia, most being small shrubs with usu. aromatic foliage, and flowers (usu. pink or mauve, but also blue, yellow, and dark brown) often highly and headily perfumed (see BROWN BORONIA). [Francesco Borone, Italian botanist (d. 1794)]

**borough** /bu-ruh/ n. urban local government area in Victoria. [Old English]

**borrow** /bo-roh/ v. **1 a** acquire temporarily, promising or intending to return. **b** obtain money thus. **2 a** use (an idea, invention, etc.) originated by another. **b** adopt (words, customs, etc.) from another language or people (Australian English has borrowed many words from Aboriginal languages). □ **borrower** n. [Old English]

**bortsch** /bawch/ n. Russian soup of beetroot, cabbage, etc. [Russian]

**bosh** n. & int. colloq. nonsense. [Turkish, = empty]

**bosom** /buuz-uhm/ — n. **1 a** person's (esp. woman's) breast. **b** colloq. each of a woman's breasts. **c** enclosure formed by the breast and arms. **2** emotional centre (bosom of one's family). — adj. intimate (bosom buddy). [Old English]

**boss**[1] colloq. — n. employer, manager, or supervisor. — v. (usu. foll. by about, around) give orders to; order about. [Dutch baas]

**boss**[2] n. **1** round knob, stud, etc., esp. on the centre of a shield. **2** Archit. ornamental carving etc. at the junction of the ribs in a vault. [French]

**boss cocky** n. **1** person who assumes or who is accorded (often grudgingly) authority over others (what makes him think he's the boss cocky?). **2** small farmer who can afford to employ labour to supplement his own.

**bossiaea** /bos-ee-uh/ n. (also **bacon-and-eggs** for the species bearing yellow-and-brown flowers) any of about 50 species of Australian bush shrubs bearing yellow, yellow-and-brown, yellow-and-red, orange, or, in one instance, vivid red pea-flowers.

**bossy** adj. (-ier, -iest) colloq. domineering. □ **bossiness** n.

**bosun** (also **bo'sun**) var. of BOATSWAIN.

**bot** — n. **1** any of various parasitic larvae infesting horses, sheep, etc. **2** colloq. person who persistently borrows or cadges from others. — v. colloq. **1** cadge. **2** 'borrow' (can I bot a drink? — I'm parched). [origin uncertain]

**botany** /bot-uh-nee/ n. **1** the study of plants. **2** the plant-life of a particular area or time. □ **botanic** /buh-tan-ik/ adj. **botanical** /buh-tan-i-kuhl/ adj. **botanist** n. [Greek botanē plant]

**Botany Bay** n. hist. **1** name used variously to refer to Port Jackson, to New South Wales, and to other Australian Colonies, individually and collectively. **2** penal servitude; a penal colony. [Botany Bay, NSW, named from the variety of its flora]

**botch** (also **bodge**) — v. **1** (also **botch-up**) bungle; do badly. **2** patch clumsily. — n. (also **botch-up**) bungled or spoilt work. [origin unknown]

**both** /bohth/ — adj. & pron. the two, not only one (both boys; both the boys; both of the boys; I like both). — adv. with equal truth in two cases (is both hot and dry). □ **have it both ways** alternate between two incompatible points of view to suit the needs of the moment. [Old Norse]

---

■ **Usage** Widely used with of, especially when followed by a pronoun (both of us) or a noun implying separate rather than collective consideration, e.g. both of the boys suggests each boy rather than the two together.

---

**bother** /both-uh/ — v. **1** trouble; worry,

disturb. **2** (often foll. by *about, with,* or *to* + infin.) take the time or trouble (*didn't bother to tell me; shan't bother with dessert*). — *n.* **1 a** person or thing that bothers. **b** minor nuisance. **2** trouble, worry. — *int.* expressing irritation. [Irish *bodhraim* deafen]

**bothersome** /*both*-uh-suhm/ *adj.* causing bother; troublesome.

**bo-tree** /*boh*-tree/ *n.* species of fig-tree sacred to Buddhists. [representing Sinhalese *bo gaha* tree of knowledge, the Buddha's enlightenment having occurred beneath such a tree]

**botrytis** /buh-*truy*-tuhs/ *n.* a fungus that sometimes attacks grapes and causes a condition, noble rot, which concentrates the sugar-content of the fruit, enabling the production from them of a sweet, valuable dessert wine.

**bottle** /*bot*-uhl/ — *n.* **1** container, esp. glass or plastic, for storing liquid. **2** amount filling it. **3** baby's feeding-bottle. **4** metal cylinder for liquefied gas. **5** (in Aboriginal English) glass. — *v.* (**-ling**) **1** put into, or preserve in, bottles or jars. **2** (foll. by *up*) conceal or restrain (esp. a feeling). □ **full bottle on** *colloq.* expert in (*he's full bottle on Aboriginal languages*). **hit the bottle** *colloq.* drink heavily. [medieval Latin: related to BUTT⁴]

**bottlebrush** *n.* **1** any shrub or small tree of the Australian genus *Callistemon*, the flower-spikes of which are shaped like a cylindrical brush. **2** (in general use) any of several other Australian plants with similar flowers, esp. of the genera *Melaleuca* and *Banksia*.

■ **Usage** The application of the term 'bottlebrush' to plants other than the callistemons is considered incorrect.

**bottle-feed** *v.* feed (a baby) from a bottle as opposed to the breast.

**bottleneck** *n.* **1** point at which the flow of traffic, production, etc., is constricted or slowed down. **2** narrow place causing constriction.

**bottler** /*bot*-luh/ *n. colloq.* excellent person or thing (*it's been a bottler of a day*).

**bottle shop** *n.* shop (or section of a hotel) which sells beer, wine, etc. to be taken away.

**bottle tree** *n.* **1** Queensland tree (related to the kurrajong and the flame tree) which develops a large swollen trunk (widest at the base and gradually narrowing upwards) resembling a bottle. **2** = BAOBAB.

**bottom** /*bot*-uhm/ — *n.* **1 a** lowest point or part (*lived at the bottom of a well*). **b** base (*bottom of the saucepan*). **c** underneath part (*scraped the bottom of the car*). **d** furthest or inmost part (*fairies at the bottom of the garden*). **2** *colloq.* **a** buttocks. **b** seat of a chair etc. **3 a** less honourable or important end of a table, class, etc. (*a rubber duck's at the very bottom of my list of requirements*). **b** person occupying this (*he's bottom of the class*). **4** ground below water (*swam until he touched the bottom*). **5** basic or fundamental part (*from the bottom of my heart*). **6** mineral-bearing stratum. — *adj.* **1** lowest (*bottom button*). **2** last (*got the bottom score*). — *v.* **1** put a bottom to (a chair etc.). **2** find the extent of (*have not yet bottomed the corruption in the force*). **3** touch the bottom or lowest point (of) (*his hopes have bottomed*). **4 a** excavate to the level of a mineral-bearing stratum. **b** (with *on*) strike gold. □ **at bottom** basically (*at bottom he's honest*). **be at the bottom of** have caused (*he's at the bottom of the strife*). **bottom out** reach the lowest level. **get to the bottom of** fully investigate and explain. [Old English]

**bottomless** *adj.* **1** without a bottom. **2** (of a supply etc.) inexhaustible.

**bottom line** *n. colloq.* underlying truth; ultimate, esp. financial, criterion; indispensable requirement.

**botulism** /*boch*-uh-liz-uhm/ *n.* poisoning caused by a bacillus in badly preserved food. [Latin *botulus* sausage]

**boudoir** /*boo*-dwah/ *n.* woman's private room. [French *bouder* sulk]

**boudoir bandicoot** *n. colloq. derog.* sexually promiscuous male.

**bougainvillea** /,boh-guhn-*vil*-ee-uh/ *n.* (also **-llaea**) tropical plant with large coloured bracts. [*Bougainville*, name of a navigator]

**bough** /bow/ *n.* branch of a tree, esp. a main one. [Old English]

**bought** *past* and *past part.* of BUY.

**bouillon** /*boo*-yon/ *n.* clear broth or stock. [French *bouillir* to boil]

**boulder** /*bohl*-duh/ *n.* large smooth rock. [Scandinavian]

**boulevard** /*boo*-luh-,vahd/ *n.* broad tree-lined avenue. [French from German]

**bounce** — *v.* (**-cing**) **1** (cause to) rebound. **2** *colloq.* (of a cheque) be returned by a bank when there are no funds to meet it. **3** (foll. by *about, up, in, out,* etc.) jump, move, or rush boisterously. **4** *Aust. Rules* bounce the ball in a ball-up, esp. with reference to the beginning of the game. **5** *colloq.* catch (a person) doing something illegal; arrest. — *n.* **1 a** rebound. **b** power of rebounding. **2** *colloq.* **a** swagger, self-confidence. **b** liveliness. **3** *Aust. Rules* = BALL-UP. □ **bounce back** recover well after a setback. □ **bouncy** *adj.* (**-ier**, **-iest**). [imitative]

**bouncer** *n.* **1** *colloq.* strong-arm man employed to eject troublemakers from a nightclub etc. **2** = BUMPER 3.

**bouncing** *adj.* (esp. of a baby) big and healthy.

**bound¹** — *v.* **1** spring, leap. **2** (of a ball etc.) bounce. — *n.* springy leap. [French *bondir* from Latin *bombus* hum]

**bound²** — *n.* (usu. in *pl.*) **1** limitation; restriction (*beyond the bounds of possibility*). **2** border, boundary. — *v.* **1** limit (*views bounded by prejudice*). **2** be the boundary of. □ **out of bounds 1** outside a permitted area. **2** beyond what is acceptable. [French from medieval Latin]

**bound³** *adj.* **1** (usu. foll. by *for*) starting or having started (*bound for stardom*). **2** (in *comb.*) in a specified direction (*north-bound*). [Old Norse, = ready]

**bound⁴** *past* and *past part.* of BIND. □ **bound to** certain to (*he's bound to come*). **bound up with** closely associated with.

**boundary** /**bown**-duh-ree, -dree/ *n.* (*pl.* **-ies**) **1** line marking the limits of an area etc. **2** *Cricket* hit crossing the limits of the field, scoring 4 or 6 runs. [related to BOUND²]

**boundary rider** *n.* person employed to ride round the fences etc. of a cattle or sheep station and keep them in good order. □ **boundary-ride** *v.*

**boundary umpire** *n. Aust. Rules* umpire on the sidelines who signals when a ball is out.

**bounden duty** /**bown**-duhn/ *n. formal* solemn responsibility. [archaic past part. of BIND]

**boundless** *adj.* unlimited.

**bounteous** /**bown**-tee-uhs/ *adj. poet.* = BOUNTIFUL. [French: related to BOUNTY]

**bountiful** /**bown**-tuh-ˌfuhl/ *adj.* **1** generous. **2** ample.

**bounty** /**bown**-tee/ *n.* (*pl.* **-ies**) **1** generosity. **2** reward, esp. from a government. **3** gift. [French from Latin *bonus* good]

**bouquet** /boo-**kay**, boh-/ *n.* **1** bunch of flowers, esp. professionally arranged. **2** scent of wine etc. [French *bois* wood]

**bouquet garni** /ˌboo-kay **gah**-nee, ˌgah-nee/ *n.* (*pl.* **bouquets garnis** pronunc. the same) bunch or bag of herbs (usu. including bay leaf, parsley, thyme) for seasoning.

**bourbon** /**ber**-buhn/ *n.* whisky from maize and rye. [*Bourbon* County, Kentucky]

**bourgeois** /**boor**-*zh*wah/ often *derog.* — *adj.* **1 a** conventionally middle-class. **b** selfishly materialistic. **2** capitalist. — *n.* (*pl.* same) bourgeois person. [French]

**bourgeoisie** /ˌboor-*zh*wah-**zee**/ *n.* **1** capitalist class. **2** middle class. [French]

**Bourke** /berk/ *n.* □ **back of Bourke** the remote and sparsely populated inland of Australia. [*Bourke* town in north-western NSW]

**bourn** /bawn/ *n.* (also **bourne**) *archaic* or *poet.* **1** goal, destination. **2** realm, territory. **3** a limit. [French *borne*]

**bourse** /boors/ *n.* **1** (**Bourse**) Paris Stock Exchange. **2** money-market. [French: related to PURSE]

**bout** /bowt/ *n.* **1** (often foll. by *of*) **a** spell (of work or activity). **b** period or attack (of illness). **2** wrestling- or boxing-match. [obsolete *bought* bending]

**boutique** /boo-**teek**/ *n.* **1** small shop selling esp. fashionable clothes. **2** (*attrib.*) (business) producing individual or high-class products (*boutique brewery; boutique winery*). [French]

**bouzouki** /buh-**zoo**-kee/ *n.* (*pl.* **-s**) Greek form of mandolin. [modern Greek]

**bovine** /**boh**-vuyn/ *adj.* **1** of or relating to cattle. **2** stupid, dull. [Latin *bos* ox]

**bovine spongiform encephalopathy** see BSE.

**bow¹** /boh/ — *n.* **1 a** slip-knot with a double loop. **b** ribbon etc. so tied. **2** curved piece of wood etc. with a string stretched across its ends, for shooting arrows. **3** rod with horsehair stretched along its length, for playing the violin etc. **4** curve or bend thing of this form. — *v.* (also *absol.*) use a bow on (a violin etc.). [Old English]

**bow²** /bow/ — *v.* **1** incline the head or body, esp. in greeting or acknowledgment. **2** submit (*bowed to the inevitable*). **3** cause (the head etc.) to incline (*bowed his head; bowed his will to hers*). — *n.* act of bowing. □ **bow and scrape** behave obsequiously. **bow down 1** bend or kneel esp. in submission or reverence. **2** make stoop; crush (*bowed down by care*). **bow out 1** exit (esp. formally). **2** withdraw retire. **take a bow** acknowledge applause [Old English]

**bow³** /bow/ *n.* **1** (often in *pl.*) front end of a boat. **2** rower nearest this. [Low German or Dutch: related to BOUGH]

**bowdlerise** /**bowd**-luh-ˌruyz/ *v.* (also **-ize**) (**-sing** or **-zing**) expurgate (a book etc.). □ **bowdlerisation** /-**zay**-shuhn/ *n.* [*Bowdler,* name of an expurgator of Shakespeare]

**bowel** /bow-uhl/ n. **1** (often in pl.) part of the alimentary canal below the stomach; intestine (also attrib.: bowel cancer). **2** (in pl.) innermost parts (bowels of the earth). [Latin botulus sausage]

**bower** /bow-uh/ n. **1** arbour; secluded place, esp. in a garden, enclosed by foliage. **2** poet. inner room; boudoir. [Old English, = dwelling]

**bowerbird** n. **1** any of various birds of Australia (and New Guinea), the males of which construct elaborate bowers decorated with feathers, grasses, shells, etc. during courtship (great bowerbird; spotted bowerbird; western bowerbird). **2 a** person who collects (useless) objects, ideas, etc. **b** thief.

**bowie** /boh-ee/ n. (in full **bowie knife**) a kind of long hunting-knife. [Bowie, name of an American soldier]

**bowl¹** /bohl/ n. **1 a** usu. round deep basin for food or liquid. **b** contents of a bowl. **2 a** any deep-sided container shaped like a bowl (toilet bowl). **b** hollow part of a tobacco-pipe, spoon, etc. **c** bowl-shaped region or building, esp. an amphitheatre (Myer Music Bowl). □ **bowlful** n. (pl. **-s**). [Old English]

**bowl²** /bohl/ — n. **1** hard heavy ball, made with a bias to run in a curve. **2** (in pl.; usu. treated as sing.) game played with these on grass. **3** ball used in tenpin bowling. **4** spell or turn of bowling in cricket. — v. **1 a** roll (a ball etc.). **b** play bowls. **2** (also absol.) Cricket etc. **a** deliver (a ball, over, etc.). **b** (often foll. by out) dismiss (a batsman) by knocking down the wicket with a ball. **3** (often foll. by along) go along rapidly (bowling along the highway in my new car). □ **bowl out** Cricket etc. dismiss (a batsman or a side). **bowl over 1** knock down. **2** colloq. impress greatly, overwhelm. [Latin bulla bubble]

**bow-legs** n.pl. bandy legs. □ **bow-legged** adj.

**bowler¹** n. **1** Cricket etc. player who bowls. **2** bowls-player.

**bowler²** n. (in full **bowler hat**) man's hard round felt hat. [Bowler, name of a hatter]

**bowline** /boh-luhn, boh-luyn/ n. **1** rope from a ship's bow keeping the sail taut against the wind. **2** knot forming a non-slipping loop at the end of a rope.

**bowser** /bow-zuh/ n. **1** petrol pump. **2** tanker used for fuelling aircraft etc. [originally a proprietary term]

**bowsprit** /boh-sprit/ n. spar running forward from a ship's bow.

**bow tie** n. necktie in the form of a bow.

**bowyang** /boh-yang/ n. **1** either of a pair of bands or straps worn round the trouser-legs below the knee. **2** (attrib.) used as a symbol of the manual worker (opp. white-collar worker, intellectual, etc.) (true-blue bowyang Labor man). [origin unknown]

**box¹** — n. **1** container, usu. flat-sided and firm. **2** amount contained in a box. **3** compartment for a small group in a theatre or at a sporting venue, for witnesses in a lawcourt, for horses in a stable, etc. **4 a** receptacle or enclosure for a special purpose (often in comb.: money box; post-office box; telephone box). **b** (also **caravan**) hist. movable box-like prison (a little more than 2m wide) in which up to 28 convicts were confined at night. **5** facility at a newspaper office for receiving replies to an advertisement. **6** (prec. by the) colloq. television. **7** protective casing for a piece of machinery. **8** area of print enclosed by a border. **9** = CHRISTMAS-BOX. **10** light shield for the genitals in cricket etc. **11** coachman's seat. — v. **1** put in or provide with a box. **2** (foll. by in, up) confine. **3** (foll. by up) mix up (different flocks of sheep). □ **out of the box** unusually good. **whole box and dice** everything. [Latin buxis: related to BOX³]

**box²** — v. **1 a** take part in boxing. **b** fight (an opponent) at boxing. **2** slap (esp. a person's ears). — n. hard slap, esp. on the ears. □ **box on** colloq. persevere; fight on. [origin unknown]

**box³** n. **1** any of several Australian trees of the family Myrtaceae, esp. of the genus Eucalyptus, having close-grained timber resembling that of the European Buxus and (usu.) a fibrous bark (apple box; brush box; red box; yellow box; etc.). **2 a** small evergreen European tree of the genus Buxus with dark green leaves. **b** its fine hard wood. [Latin buxus, Greek puxos]

**boxer** n. **1** person who boxes, esp. as a sport. **2** person in charge of a game of two-up.

**boxer shorts** n.pl. men's loose underpants like shorts.

**box girder** n. hollow girder square in cross-section.

**boxing** n. fighting with the fists, esp. as a sport.

**Boxing Day** n. day after Christmas. [from BOX¹, from the custom of giving Christmas-boxes]

**box jellyfish** n. jelly-like sea animal with a box-shaped body and stinging tentacles.

**box number** n. **1** address for a post-office box. **2** number for replies to a private advertisement in a newspaper.

**box office** n. **1** ticket-office at a theatre etc. **2** commercial aspect of the arts and entertainment (often *attrib.*: *box-office failure*).

**box seat** n. best or most favoured position.

**boxwood** n. = BOX³ 2 b.

**boy** — n. **1** male child, son. **2** young man. **3** male servant etc. **4** (in *pl.*) *colloq.* a man's male friends (*out with the boys again*). — *int.* expressing pleasure, surprise, etc. □ **boyhood** n. **boyish** *adj.* [origin uncertain]

**boycott** /boi-kot/ — v. **1** refuse to have social or commercial relations with (a person, country, etc.). **2** refuse to handle or buy (goods). — n. such a refusal. [Capt. *Boycott*, so treated from 1880]

**boyfriend** n. person's regular male companion or lover.

**boylya** /boi-lyuh/ n. **1** = KORADJI. **2** Aboriginal sorcerer or wizard. [Nyungar, probably *bulya* sorcery]

**boy next door** — n. the ordinary average youth. — *adj.* (**boy-next-door**) typifying such a youth (*seeking a wholesome boy-next-door type for the film*).

**boy scout** n. = SCOUT¹ n. 4.

**Br** *symb.* bromine.

**bra** /brah/ n. undergarment worn by women to support the breasts. [abbreviation of *brassiere*]

**brace** — n. **1** device that clamps or fastens tightly. **2** timber etc. strengthening a framework. **3** (in *pl.*) straps supporting trousers from the shoulders. **4** wire device for straightening the teeth. **5** (*pl.* same) pair (esp. of game). **6** rope for trimming a sail. **7** connecting mark { or } in printing. — v. (**-cing**) **1** make steady by supporting. **2** fasten tightly to make firm. **3** (esp. as **bracing** *adj.*) invigorate, refresh. **4** (often *refl.*) prepare for a difficulty, shock, etc. [Latin *bracchia* arms]

**brace and bit** n. revolving tool for boring, with a D-shaped central handle.

**bracelet** /brays-luht/ n. ornamental band or chain worn on the wrist or arm.

**bracelet honey-myrtle** n. extremely common melaleuca of Queensland, NSW, and Victoria, rounded and spreading in form, and having white bottlebrush-like flowers: often used as a windbreak.

**brachiosaurus** /ˌbray-kee-uh-**saw**-ruhs, ˌbrak-/ n. (*pl.* **-ruses**) plant-eating dinosaur with forelegs longer than its hind legs. [Latin from Greek *brakhiōn* arm, *sauros* lizard]

**brachycome** /ˌbrak-ee-**koh**-mee/ n. any of several small, hardy, extremely showy Australian plants bearing masses of usu. blue daisy-flowers and often used in cultivation, esp. the SWAN RIVER DAISY.

**bracken** /**brak**-uhn/ n. **1** large coarse perennial fern widespread in Australia. **2** mass of these. [Old Norse]

**bracket** /**brak**-uht/ — n. **1** (esp. angled) support projecting from a vertical surface. **2** shelf fixed to a wall with this. **3** each of a pair of marks ( ) [ ] { } enclosing words or figures (see panel). **4** group or classification (*income bracket*). — v. (**-t-**) **1** enclose in brackets. **2** group or classify together. [Latin *bracae* breeches]

**bracket creep** n. situation in which a wage-increase pushes a wage-earner into a higher marginal tax bracket which, with the effects of inflation, reduces or cancels the increase.

**brackish** /**brak**-ish/ *adj.* (of water etc.) slightly salty. [Low German or Dutch]

**bract** n. leaf-like and often brightly coloured part of a plant, growing before the flower. [Latin *bractea* thin sheet]

**brag** — v. (**-gg-**) talk boastfully. — n. boastful statement or talk. [origin unknown]

**braggart** /**brag**-uht/ n. boastful person.

**Brahma** /**brah**-muh/ n. **1** Hindu Creator.

---

**Brackets ( ) [ ]**

Round brackets, also called parentheses, are used mainly to enclose explanations and extra information or comment, e.g.

*Myanmar (formerly Burma)*
*He is (as he always was) a rebel.*
*This is done using integrated circuits (see page 38).*

In this dictionary round brackets enclose letters or words that are optional (as at *crash v.* where '(cause to) make a loud smashing noise' can mean either 'make a loud smashing noise' or 'cause to make a loud smashing noise'), and indicate typical objects of transitive verbs (such as '*milk*' and '*the skin*' in two senses of *cream v.*)

Square brackets are used mainly to enclose:
**1** words added by someone other than the original writer or speaker, e.g.
*Then the man said, 'He [the police officer] can't prove I did it.'*
**2** various special types of information, such as stage directions, e.g.
HEDLEY: Goodbye! [EXIT].

**2** supreme divine Hindu reality. [Sanskrit, = creator]

**Brahman** /brah-muhn/ n. (also **brahman**) (pl. **-s**) **1** (also **Brahmin**) member of the highest or priestly Hindu caste. **2** = BRAHMA 2. **3** animal of a breed of cattle developed from the zebu. □ **Brahmanic** /-man-ik/ adj. **Brahmanism** n.

**braid** — n. **1** woven band as edging or trimming. **2** plait of hair. — v. **1** plait. **2** trim with braid. □ **braiding** n. [Old English]

**braille** /brayl/ — n. system of writing and printing for the blind, with patterns of raised dots. — v. (**-ling**) print or transcribe in braille. [Braille, name of its inventor]

**brain** — n. **1** organ of soft nervous tissue in the skull of vertebrates, the centre of sensation and of intellectual and nervous activity. **2 a** colloq. intelligent person. **b** (often in pl.) intelligence. **3** (usu. in pl.; prec. by the) colloq. cleverest person in a group; mastermind. **4** electronic device functioning like a brain. — v. **1** dash out the brains of. **2** colloq. strike hard on the head. □ **on the brain** colloq. obsessively in one's thoughts. [Old English]

**brainchild** n. colloq. person's clever idea or invention.

**brain death** n. irreversible brain damage causing the end of independent respiration, regarded as indicative of death. □ **brain-dead** adj.

**brain drain** n. loss of skilled personnel by emigration.

**brain-fever bird** n. = PALLID CUCKOO.

**brainless** adj. foolish.

**brainpower** n. mental ability or intelligence.

**brainstorm** n. **1** sudden mental disturbance. **2** brainwave.

**brainwash** v. implant ideas or esp. ideology into (a person) by repetition etc. □ **brainwashing** n.

**brainwave** n. **1** (usu. in pl.) electrical impulse in the brain. **2** colloq. sudden bright idea.

**brainy** adj. (**-ier**, **-iest**) intellectually clever.

**braise** /brayz/ v. (**-sing**) stew slowly with a little liquid in a closed container. [French braise live coals]

**brake¹** — n. **1** (often in pl.) device for stopping or slowing a wheel, vehicle, etc. **2** thing that impedes (shortage of money was a brake on their enjoyment). — v. (**-king**) **1** apply a brake. **2** slow or stop with a brake. [probably obsolete brake = curb]

**brake²** — n. **1** toothed instrument for crushing flax and hemp. **2** (in full **brake harrow**) heavy harrow. — v. (**-king**) crush (flax or hemp). [Low German or Dutch: related to BREAK]

**brake³** n. thicket of brushwood, bushes, etc. [Old English]

**bramble** /bram-buhl/ n. wild thorny shrub, esp. the blackberry. □ **brambly** adj. [Old English]

**bran** n. grain husks separated from flour. [French]

**branch** /brahnch, branch/ — n. **1** limb of a tree or bough. **2** lateral extension or subdivision, esp. of a river, road, or railway. **3** subdivision of a family, knowledge, etc. **4** local office etc. of a large business. — v. (often foll. by off) **1** diverge. **2** divide into branches. □ **branch out** extend one's field of interest. [Latin branca paw]

**branchlet** n. small branch of a tree etc.

**brand** — n. **1 a** particular make of goods. **b** identifying trade mark, label, etc. **2** (usu. foll. by of) characteristic kind (brand of humour). **3** identifying mark burned esp. on livestock. **4** iron used for this. **5** piece of burning or charred wood. **6** stigma; mark of disgrace. **7** poet. torch. — v. **1** mark with a hot iron. **2** stigmatise; mark with disgrace (branded him a liar). **3** impress unforgettably on one's mind. **4** assign a trademark etc. to. [Old English]

**brandish** /bran-dish/ v. wave or flourish as a threat or display. [French from Germanic]

**brand new** adj. (also **brand-spanking new** colloq.) completely new.

**brandy** /bran-dee/ n. (pl. **-ies**) strong alcoholic spirit distilled from wine or fermented fruit juice. [Dutch brandewijn]

**brash** adj. vulgarly self-assertive; impudent. □ **brashly** adv. **brashness** n. [British dial.]

**brass** /brahs/ — n. **1** yellow alloy of copper and zinc. **2** brass objects collectively. **3** brass wind instruments. **4** colloq. money. **5** brass memorial tablet. **6** colloq. effrontery. **7** = TOP BRASS. — adj. made of brass. □ **brassed off** colloq. fed up. [Old English]

**brasserie** /bras-uh-ree/ n. restaurant, orig. one serving beer with food, now one which serves simple meals. [French brasser brew]

**brassiere** /braz-ee-uh, bras-ee-,air/ n. = BRA. [French]

**brass monkey** n. coarse colloq. used in various phrases to indicate extreme cold.

**brass razoo** n. = RAZOO.

**brass tacks** n.pl. colloq. essential details.

**brassy** /brah-see/ adj. (**-ier**, **-iest**) **1** of or like brass. **2** impudent. **3** vulgarly showy.

**brat** *n.* usu. *derog.* child, esp. an ill-behaved one. [origin unknown]

**bravado** /bruh-**vah**-doh/ *n.* show of boldness put on to impress. [Spanish]

**brave** — *adj.* **1** able or ready to face and endure danger or pain. **2** *formal* splendid, spectacular (*wattles making a brave show*). — *n.* American Indian warrior. — *v.* (**-ving**) face bravely or defiantly. □ **brave it out** endure defiantly under suspicion, blame, etc. □ **bravely** *adv.* **braveness** *n.* **bravery** *n.* [ultimately Latin *barbarus* barbarian]

**bravo** /brah-**voh**/ — *int.* expressing approval. — *n.* (*pl.* **-s**) cry of 'bravo'. [French from Italian]

**bravura** /bruh-**vyoo**-ruh/ *n.* **1** brilliant or ambitious action or display. **2** (often *attrib.*) passage of (esp. vocal) music requiring brilliant technique. [Italian]

**brawl** — *n.* noisy quarrel or fight. — *v.* **1** engage in a brawl. **2** (of a stream) run noisily. [Provençal]

**brawn** *n.* **1** muscular strength. **2** muscle; lean flesh. **3** jellied meat made from a pig's head. □ **brawny** *adj.* (**-ier**, **-iest**). [French from Germanic]

**bray** — *n.* **1** cry of a donkey. **2** harsh sound like this, e.g. that of a harshly-played brass instrument. — *v.* **1** make a bray. **2** utter harshly. [French *braire*]

**braze** *v.* (**-zing**) solder with an alloy of brass and zinc. [French *braser*]

**brazen** /**bray**-zuhn/ — *adj.* **1** shameless; insolent. **2** of or like brass. **3** harsh in sound. — *v.* (foll. by *out*) face or undergo defiantly (*brazen it out*). □ **brazenly** *adv.* [Old English]

**brazier** /**bray**-zee-uh/ *n.* metal pan or stand holding burning coals etc. [French: related to BRAISE]

**brazil** /bruh-**zil**/ *n.* **1** tall S. American tree. **2** (in full **brazil nut**) its large three-sided nut. [*Brazil* in S. America]

**breach** — *n.* **1** (often foll. by *of*) breaking or non-observation of a law, contract, etc. **2** breaking of relations; quarrel. **3** opening, gap, esp. one made by artillery in fortifications. — *v.* **1** break through; make a gap in. **2** break (a law, contract, etc.). □ **step into the breach** help in a crisis, esp. as a replacement. [Germanic: related to BREAK]

**breach of the peace** *n.* crime of causing a public disturbance.

**bread** /bred/ *n.* **1** baked dough of flour and water, usu. leavened with yeast. **2** necessary food; livelihood. **3** *colloq.* money. □ **cast one's bread upon the waters** do good without expecting gratitude or reward. [Old English]

**bread and butter** — *n.* one's livelihood. — *attrib. adj.* (**bread-and-butter**) done or produced to earn a basic living.

**breadfruit** *n.* **1** fruit which becomes soft like new bread when roasted. **2** tropical evergreen tree bearing it.

**breadline** *n.* **1** subsistence level (esp. *on the breadline*). **2** queue of needy people waiting to receive free food.

**breadth** /bredth/ *n.* **1** distance or measurement from side to side of a thing. **2** freedom from prejudice or intolerance (esp. *breadth of mind* or *view*). [Old English: related to BROAD]

**breadwinner** *n.* person who works to support a family.

**break** /brayk/ — *v.* (*past* **broke**; *past part.* **broken** /**broh**-kuhn/ ) **1 a** separate into pieces under a blow or strain; shatter. **b** make or become inoperative (*the toaster has broken*). **c** break a bone in or dislocate (part of the body). **2 a** interrupt (*broke our journey*; *the spell was broken*). **b** have an interval (*broke for lunch*). **3** fail to keep (a law, promise, etc.). **4 a** make or become subdued or weak; (cause to) yield; destroy (*broke his spirit*; *he broke under the strain*). **b** weaken the effect of (a fall, blow, etc.). **c** = *break in* 3c. **d** (of an employer) defeat the object of (a strike), e.g. by engaging other workers; (of an employee) fail to observe a strike. **5** surpass (a record). **6** (foll. by *with*) end a friendship with (a person etc.). **7 a** be no longer subject to (a habit). **b** (foll. by *of*) free (a person) from a habit (*broke them of their addiction*). **8** reveal or be revealed (*broke the news*; *story broke*). **9 a** (of fine weather) change suddenly. **b** (of waves) curl over and foam. **c** (of the day) dawn. **d** (of clouds) move apart. **e** (of a storm) begin violently. **10** *Electr.* disconnect (a circuit). **11 a** (of the voice) change with emotion. **b** (of a boy's voice) change at puberty. **12** (often foll. by *up*) divide (a set etc.) into parts, e.g. by selling to different buyers. **13** ruin financially (see also BROKE *adj.*). **14** penetrate (e.g. a safe) by force. **15** decipher (a code). **16** make (a way, path, etc.) by force. **17** burst forth (*sun broke through*). **18 a** (of troops) disperse in confusion. **b** make a rupture in (ranks). **19 a** (usu. foll. by *free*, *loose*, *out*, etc.) escape by a sudden effort. **b** escape or emerge from (prison, bounds, cover, etc.). **20** (of stock) stampede. **21** unfurl (a flag etc.). **22** *Tennis etc.* win a game against (an opponent's service). **23** (of boxers etc.) come out of a clinch. **24** *Billiards etc.* disperse the balls at the start of a game. **25** *Cricket* **a** (of a ball) change direction on bouncing. **b** (in full **break the wicket**) dislodge the bails in stumping or running out a batsman. **26** (of a race) get off the mark prematurely. **27** (of a horse, esp. in trotting and pacing) change gait. — *n.* **1 a** act or instance of breaking. **b** point of breaking; gap. **2** interval, interruption; pause (*a break for morning tea; having a three-week break from work*). **3** sudden dash (esp. to escape). **4** *colloq.* piece of luck; fair chance (*what a break!; give me a break*). **5** *Cricket* deflection of a bowled ball on bouncing. **6** *Billiards etc.* **a** series of points scored during one turn. **b** opening shot dispersing the balls. **7** (in jazz or rock music) short unaccompanied passage for a soloist. **8** (in cycling, running, etc.) lead (*has a ten-minute break on the rest of the field*). □ **break away** make or become free or separate. **break the back of** do the hardest or greatest part of. **break down 1 a** fail mechanically; cease to function. **b** (of human relationships etc.) fail, collapse. **c** fail in (esp. mental) health. **d** collapse in tears or emotion. **2 a** demolish, destroy. **b** suppress (resistance). **c** force to yield. **3** analyse into components. **break even** make neither profit nor loss. **break a person's heart** see HEART. **break the ice** begin to overcome formality or shyness. **break in 1** enter by force, esp. with criminal intent. **2** interrupt. **3 a** accustom to a habit etc. **b** wear etc. until comfortable. **c** tame (an animal); accustom (a horse) to a saddle etc. **d** bring (virgin land) into cultivation. **break in on** disturb; interrupt. **break into 1** enter forcibly. **2 a** burst forth with (a song, laughter, etc.). **b** change pace for (a faster one) (*broke into a gallop*). **3** interrupt. **4** enter (a business venture, show business, etc.) successfully. **break off 1** detach by breaking. **2** bring to an end. **3** cease talking etc. **break open** open forcibly. **break out 1** escape by force, esp. from prison. **2** begin suddenly. **3** (foll. by *in*) become covered in (a rash etc.). **4** exclaim. **break up 1** break into small pieces. **2** disperse; disband. **3** end the school term. **4** (cause to) terminate a relationship; disband. **5** burst into laughter. **break wind** release gas from the anus. **those are the breaks** *colloq.* that's the way life is. [Old English]

**breakable** — *adj.* easily broken. — *n.* (esp. in *pl.*) breakable thing.

**breakage** *n.* **1 a** broken thing. **b** damage caused by breaking. **2** act or instance of breaking.

**breakaway** *n.* **1** (often *attrib.*) act or

instance of breaking away; secession (*breakaway group*). **2** stampede of cattle, esp. at the sight of water.

**break-dancing** *n.* acrobatic style of street-dancing. □ **break-dance** *n.* **break-dancer** *n.*

**breakdown** *n.* **1 a** mechanical failure. **b** loss of (esp. mental) health. **2** collapse (*breakdown of communication*). **3** analysis of statistics etc.

**breaker** *n.* heavy breaking wave.

**breakfast** /brek-fuhst/ — *n.* first meal of the day. — *v.* have breakfast.

**break-in** *n.* illegal forced entry, esp. with criminal intent.

**breaking and entering** *n.* (formerly) the illegal entering of a building with intent to commit a crime.

**breaking point** *n.* point of greatest strain.

**breakneck** *attrib. adj.* (of speed) dangerously fast.

**break out** *n.* forcible escape (e.g. from gaol).

**breakthrough** *n.* **1** major advance or discovery. **2** act of breaking through an obstacle etc.

**breakup** *n.* **1** disintegration or collapse. **2** dispersal.

**breakwater** *n.* barrier breaking the force of waves.

**breakwind** *n.* an Aboriginal shelter.

**bream** /brim/ *n.* (*pl.* same) **1** /brim/ **a** any of several Australian marine fish, valued for sport and eating (*southern bream; yellowfin bream*). **b** (popular name for) any of several Australian freshwater perch, e.g. the SILVER PERCH. **2** /breem/ **a** freshwater fish of Europe etc. **b** (in full **sea bream**) similar marine fish of Europe etc. [French from Germanic]

**breast** /brest/ — *n.* **1 a** either of two milk-secreting organs on a woman's chest. **b** corresponding part of a man's body. **2 a** chest (*beat his breast*). **b** corresponding part of an animal. **3** part of a garment that covers the breast. **4** breast as a source of nourishment or emotion. — *v.* **1** face; meet in full opposition (*breast the wind; breasted his opponents*). **2** contend with (*breast it out against difficulties*). **3** reach the top of (a hill) (*breasted the summit*). □ **make a clean breast of** confess fully. [Old English]

**breastbone** *n.* thin flat vertical bone in the chest between the ribs.

**breastfeed** *v.* feed (a baby) from the breast.

**breastplate** *n.* armour covering the breast.

**breaststroke** n. swimming stroke made by extending both arms forward and sweeping them back.

**breath** /breth/ n. **1 a** air drawn into or expelled from the lungs. **b** one respiration of air. **c** breath as perceived by the senses (*her breath steaming in the cold air*; *bad breath*). **2 a** slight movement of air. **b** whiff (of perfume etc.). **3** whisper, murmur (esp. of scandal). □ **catch one's breath 1** cease breathing momentarily in surprise etc. **2** rest to restore normal breathing. **out of breath** gasping for air, esp. after exercise. **take one's breath away** surprise, delight, etc. **under one's breath** in a whisper. [Old English]

**breathalyser** /breth-uh-luy-zuh/ n. instrument for measuring alcohol levels in the exhaled breath into it. □ **breath-alyse** v. [from BREATH, ANALYSE]

**breathe** /breeth/ v. (-**thing**) **1** draw air into and expel it from the lungs. **2** be or seem alive (*is she breathing?*). **3 a** utter or sound (esp. quietly). **b** express (*breathed defiance*). **4** take breath; pause. **5** send out or take in (as if) with the breath (*breathed new life into them*; *breathed whisky*). **6** (of wine etc.) be exposed to the air. □ **breathe again** (or **freely**) feel relief.

**breather** /bree-thuh/ n. **1** colloq. brief pause for rest. **2** brief period in the fresh air.

**breathing-space** n. time to recover; pause.

**breathless** adj. **1** panting, out of breath. **2** holding the breath. **3** still, windless. □ **breathlessly** adv.

**breathtaking** adj. astounding; awe-inspiring. □ **breathtakingly** adv.

**breath test** — n. test with a breath-alyser. — v. (**breath-test**) breathalyse.

**bred** past and past part. of BREED.

**breech** n. **1** back part of a rifle or gun barrel. **2** archaic buttocks. [Old English]

**breech birth** n. (also **breech delivery**) delivery of a baby with the buttocks or feet foremost.

**breeches** /brich-uhz/ n.pl. **1** short trousers, esp. fastened below the knee (e.g. in ceremonial and riding costume). **2** colloq. trousers.

**breed** — v. (past and past part. **bred**) **1** (of animals) produce young. **2** propagate; raise (animals). **3** yield; result in (*war breeds famine*). **4** arise; spread (*disease breeds in the slums*). **5** bring up; train (*Hollywood breeds stars*). **6** create (fissile material) by nuclear reaction. — n. **1** stock of similar animals or plants within a species, usu. developed by deliberate selection. **2** race; lineage. **3** sort, kind. □ **breeder** n. [Old English]

**breeder reactor** n. nuclear reactor that can create more fissile material than it consumes.

**breeding** n. **1** process of developing or propagating (animals, plants, etc.). **2** social behaviour; ancestry.

**breeze** — n. **1** gentle wind. **2** colloq. easy task. — v. (-**zing**) (foll. by in, out, along, etc.) colloq. come or go in a casual or lighthearted manner. □ **breeze through** perform (a task) easily or with minimum effort. [probably Spanish and Portuguese briza]

**breezy** adj. (-**ier**, -**iest**) **1** slightly windy. **2** colloq. cheerful, light-hearted, casual.

**brekkie** /brek-ee/ n. (also **brekky**) colloq. breakfast.

**brethren** see BROTHER.

**Breton** /bret-uhn/ — n. **1** native of Brittany. **2** Celtic language of Brittany. — adj. of Brittany, its people, or language. [French, = BRITON]

**breve** n. **1** Mus. note twice the length of a semibreve. **2** mark (˘) indicating a short or unstressed vowel. [var. of BRIEF]

**breviary** /bree-vyuh-ree, brev-yuh-/ n. (pl. -**ies**) book containing the Roman Catholic daily office required to be read or recited daily by those in orders. [Latin: related to BRIEF]

**brevity** /brev-uh-tee/ n. **1** economy of expression; conciseness. **2** shortness (of time etc.) (*the brevity of happiness*). [Anglo-French: related to BRIEF]

**brew** /broo/ — v. **1 a** make (beer etc.) by infusion, boiling, and fermentation. **b** make (tea etc.) by infusion. **2** undergo these processes. **3** gather force; threaten (*mischief was brewing*; *storm is brewing*). **4** concoct (a plan etc.). — n. **1** liquid or amount brewed; concoction. **2** process of brewing. □ **brewer** n. [Old English]

**brewery** /broo-uh-ree/ n. (pl. -**ies**) factory for brewing beer etc.

**briar¹** /bruyuh/ n. wild rose of Europe etc. or other prickly bush. [Old English]

**briar²** n. **1** white heath of S. Europe. **2** tobacco pipe made from its root. [French bruyère]

**bribe** — v. (-**bing**) (often foll. by to + infin.) persuade to act improperly in one's favour by a gift of money etc. — n. money or services offered in bribing. □ **bribery** n. [French briber beg]

**bric-a-brac** /brik-uh-brak/ n. miscellaneous, often old, ornaments, trinkets, etc. of no great value. [French, = at random]

**brick** — n. **1 a** small usu. rectangular

block of fired or sun-dried clay used in building. **b** material of this. **2** child's toy block. **3** brick-shaped thing. **4** *colloq.* generous or loyal person. — *v.* (foll. by *in*, *up*) close or block with brickwork. — *adj.* **1** built of brick (*brick wall*). **2** (also **brick-red**) dull red. □ **be a brick short of a load** *colloq.* be mentally deficient. **thick as a brick** see THICK. [Low German or Dutch]

**brickbat** *n.* **1** piece of brick, esp. as a missile. **2** insult; criticism.

**brickfielder** *n.* **1** hot, dry, north wind. **2** *hist.* (in Sydney) sudden squally wind from the south, usu. accompanied by a dust-storm. [*Brickfield* Hill in Sydney where there was a brickfield]

**brickie** *n. colloq.* bricklayer.

**bricklayer** *n.* person who builds with bricks, esp. for a living. □ **bricklaying** *n.*

**brick veneer** *n.* (house with) timber frame and a brick exterior that is not part of the structure.

**bridal** /**bruy**-duhl/ *adj.* of or concerning a bride or wedding. [Old English]

**bride** *n.* woman on her wedding day and during the period just before and after it. [Old English]

**bridegroom** *n.* man on his wedding day and during the period just before and after it. [Old English]

**bridesmaid** *n.* girl or unmarried woman attending a bride at her wedding.

**bridge**¹ — *n.* **1 a** structure providing a way across a river, road, railway, etc. **b** thing joining or connecting (*English is a bridge between nations*). **c** device that interconnects two computer networks. **2** operational superstructure on a ship. **3** upper bony part of the nose. **4** piece of wood on a violin etc. over which the strings are stretched. **5** = BRIDGEWORK. — *v.* (**-ging**) **1** be or make a bridge over. **2** reduce (a gap, deficiency, etc.). [Old English]

**bridge**² *n.* card-game derived from whist. [origin unknown]

**bridgework** *n. Dentistry* dental structure covering a gap, joined to the teeth on either side.

**bridging loan** *n.* loan to cover the interval between buying a house etc. and selling another.

**bridle** /**bruy**-duhl/ — *n.* **1** headgear for controlling a horse, including reins and bit. **2** restraining thing (*put a bridle on your tongue*). — *v.* (**-ling**) **1** put a bridle on. **2** curb, restrain. **3** (often foll. by *up*) express anger, offence, etc., esp. by throwing up the head and drawing in the chin (*he bridled at the remark*). [Old English]

**bridled nail-tailed wallaby** see NAIL-TAILED WALLABY.

**brie** /bree/ *n.* a kind of soft cheese. [*Brie* in N. France]

**brief** — *adj.* **1** of short duration. **2 a** concise in expression. **b** abrupt, brusque (*was rather brief with me*). **3** scanty (*brief skirt*). — *n.* **1** (in *pl.*) **a** women's brief pants. **b** men's close-fitting underpants covering only the genitals and buttocks. **2 a** summary of a case drawn up for counsel. **b** piece of work for a barrister. **3** instructions for a task. **4** papal letter on an issue of discipline. — *v.* **1** instruct (a barrister) by brief. **2** inform or instruct in advance (*briefed him for the interview*). □ **hold a brief for** argue in favour of. **in brief** to sum up. □ **briefly** *adv.* **briefness** *n.* [Latin *brevis* short]

**briefcase** *n.* flat document case.

**brig** *n.* two-masted square-rigged ship. [abbreviation of BRIGANTINE]

**brigade** /bruh-**gayd**/ *n.* **1** military unit, usu. three battalions, as part of a division. **2** group organised for a special purpose (*fire brigade*). [Italian *briga* strife]

**brigadier** /,brig-uh-**deer**/ *n.* **1** officer commanding a brigade. **2** staff officer of similar standing.

**brigalow** /**brig**-uh-,loh/ *n.* **1** any of several wattles, esp. the NSW and Queensland wattle *Acacia harpophylla*, having a dark, furrowed bark and silver foliage. **2** (**the brigalow** or **brigalow country**) large areas of country dominated by brigalow. [perhaps from Kamilaroi *buriigal*]

**brigand** /**brig**-uhnd/ *n.* member of a robber band; bandit. □ **brigandage** *n.* [Italian *brigante*: related to BRIGADE]

**brigantine** /**brig**-uhn-,teen/ *n.* two-masted ship with a square-rigged fore-mast and a fore-and-aft rigged main-mast. [French or Italian: related to BRIGAND]

**bright** /bruyt/ — *adj.* **1** emitting or reflecting much light; shining. **2** (of colour) intense, vivid. **3** clever. **4** cheerful. **5** hopeful, encouraging, promising (*our chances of winning are bright*; *bright prospects*). — *adv.* esp. *poet.* brightly. □ **brightly** *adv.* **brightness** *n.* [Old English]

**brighten** *v.* make or become brighter.

**Bright's disease** /bruyts/ *n.* kidney disease. [*Bright*, name of a physician]

**brilliant** /**bril**-yuhnt/ — *adj.* **1** very bright; sparkling. **2** outstandingly talented or intelligent. **3** *colloq.* excellent, superb. — *n.* diamond of the finest cut with many facets. □ **brilliance** *n.* **brilliantly** *adv.* [French *briller* shine, from Italian]

**brim** — n. **1** edge or lip of a vessel. **2** projecting edge of a hat. — v. (**-mm-**) fill or be full to the brim. □ **brim over** overflow. [origin unknown]

**brim-full** adj. (also **brimful**) filled to the brim.

**brimstone** n. archaic sulphur. [from BURN, STONE]

**brindled** /brin-duhld/ adj. (esp. of domestic animals) brown or tawny with streaks of another colour. [Scandinavian]

**brine** n. **1** water saturated or strongly impregnated with salt. **2** sea water. [Old English]

**bring** v. (past and past part. **brought** /brawt/) **1 a** come carrying; lead, accompany; convey (brought gifts; brought all the children; brought news). **b** cause to come or be present (what brings you here?). **2** cause or result in (war brings misery). **3** be sold for; produce as income (brought a good price). **4** a prefer (a charge). **b** initiate (legal action). **5** cause to become or to reach a state (jazz brings me alive; cannot bring myself to agree). **6** adduce (evidence, an argument, etc.) (brought many arguments to bear against the decision). □ **bring about** cause to happen. **bring back** call to mind (that brings back many memories). **bring down 1** cause to fall. **2** lower (a price). **3** humble, abase. **bring forth 1** give birth to. **2** cause. **bring forward 1** move to an earlier date or time. **2** transfer from the previous page or account. **3** draw attention to; adduce. **bring home to** cause to realise fully. **bring the house down** receive rapturous applause. **bring in 1** introduce. **2** yield as income or profit. **bring off** achieve successfully. **bring on** cause to happen, appear, or make progress (glare brought on a migraine). **bring out 1** emphasise; make evident. **2** publish. **bring over** convert to one's own side. **bring round 1** restore to consciousness. **2** persuade. **bring through** aid (a person) through adversity, esp. illness. **bring to** restore to consciousness (brought him to). **bring up 1** rear (a child). **2** vomit. **3** call attention to (brought up a few difficulties with the plan). **4** (absol.) stop suddenly. **bring your own** see BYO. [Old English]

**brinjal** /brin-jawl/ n. = EGGPLANT. [Portuguese berinjela]

**brink** n. **1** extreme edge of land before a precipice, river, etc. **2** furthest point before danger, discovery, etc. □ **on the brink of** about to experience or suffer; in imminent danger of. [Old Norse]

**brinkmanship** n. pursuit of danger etc. to the brink of catastrophe before desisting.

**briny** — adj. (**-ier, -iest**) of brine or the sea; salty. — n. (prec. by the) colloq. the sea.

**briquette** /bri-ket/ n. block of compressed coal-dust as fuel. [French diminutive: related to BRICK]

**Brisbane** /briz-buhn/ n. name of the capital city of the State of Queensland. [Thomas Brisbane, governor of NSW 1821–25]

**brisk** — adj. **1** quick, lively, keen (brisk pace; brisk trade). **2** enlivening (brisk wind). — v. (often foll. by up) make or grow brisk. □ **briskly** adv. **briskness** n. [probably French BRUSQUE]

**brisket** /bris-kuht/ n. animal's breast, esp. as a joint of meat. [French]

**bristle** /bris-uhl/ — n. **1** short stiff hair, esp. one on an animal's back. **2** this, or a man-made substitute, used in brushes. — v. (**-ling**) **1 a** (of hair) stand upright. **b** make (hair) do this. **2** show irritation (he bristled at the suggestion). **3** (usu. foll. by with) be covered or abundant (in). □ **bristly** adj. (**-ier, -iest**). [Old English]

**bristlebird** n. any of three species of brownish-coloured birds of certain coastal areas of mainland Australia, having prominent bristles on the face (eastern bristlebird; rufous bristlebird; western bristlebird).

**Brit** colloq. — n. **1** British person (the Brits are having a rough time). **2** Britain. — adj. British. [abbreviation]

**British** /brit-ish/ — adj. of Britain, the British Commonwealth, or their people. — n. (prec. by the; treated as pl.) British people. [Old English]

**Briton** /brit-uhn/ n. **1** inhabitant of S. Britain before the Roman conquest. **2** native or inhabitant of Britain. [Latin Britto -onis]

**brittle** /brit-uhl/ adj. hard and fragile; apt to break. □ **brittlely** adv. (also **brittly**). [Old English]

**brittle gum** n. any of several eucalypts having brittle timber, esp. E. mannifera of NSW and the ACT, having beautiful smooth white multistemmed trunks (see also SNAPPY GUM).

**broach** — v. **1** raise (a subject) for discussion. **2** pierce (a cask) to draw liquor. — n. **1** bit for boring. **2** roasting-spit. [Latin broccus projecting]

**broad** /brawd/ — adj. **1** large in extent from one side to the other; wide. **2** in breadth (two metres broad). **3** extensive (broad plain). **4** full and clear (broad daylight). **5** explicit (broad hint). **6** general (broad intentions; broad facts). **7** tolerant, liberal (broad view). **8** coarse (broad humour). **9** (of an accent) markedly regional. — *n.* broad part (*broad of the back*). □ **broadly** *adv.* **broadness** *n.* [Old English]

**broad Australian** *n.* that pronunciation of Australian English which most vigorously exhibits distinctive Australian features.

**broadcast** — *v.* (*past* and *past part.* **broadcast**) **1** transmit by radio or television. **2** take part in such a transmission. **3** scatter (seed etc.). **4** disseminate (information) widely. **5** transmit (a message) to all nodes in a computer network. — *n.* radio or television programme or transmission. □ **broadcaster** *n.* **broadcasting** *n.*

**broaden** *v.* make or become broader.

**broad-leaved apple** *n.* angophora of Queensland and NSW (to 30m) with rough bark, heart-shaped leaves clasping the stem, and a profusion of cream flowers.

**broadloom** *adj.* (esp. of carpet) woven in broad widths.

**broad-minded** *adj.* tolerant, liberal.

**broadsheet** *n.* **1** large-sized newspaper. **2** large sheet of paper printed on one side only, esp. with information.

**broadside** *n.* **1** vigorous verbal attack. **2** simultaneous firing of all guns from one side of a ship. **3** side of a ship above the water between the bow and quarter.

**broadsword** *n.* broad-bladed sword, for cutting rather than thrusting.

**brocade** /bruh-**kayd**/ — *n.* rich fabric woven with a raised pattern. — *v.* (**-ding**) weave in this way. [Italian *brocco* twisted thread]

**broccoli** /**brok**-uh-lee/ *n.* plant related to the cabbage, having greenish flowerheads, used as a vegetable. [Italian]

**brochure** /**broh**-shuh, bruh-**shoor**/ *n.* pamphlet or booklet, esp. with descriptive information. [French *brocher* stitch]

**brogue**[1] /brohg/ *n.* **1** strong outdoor shoe with ornamental perforations. **2** rough shoe of untanned leather. [Gaelic and Irish *bróg* from Old Norse]

**brogue**[2] /brohg/ *n.* marked accent, esp. Irish. [perhaps related to BROGUE[1]]

**broil** *v.* **1** esp. *US* grill (meat). **2** make or become very hot, esp. from the sun. [French *bruler* burn]

**broke** *past* of BREAK. — *predic. adj. colloq.* having no money. □ **go for broke** *colloq.* risk everything.

**broken** *past part.* of BREAK. — *adj.* **1** having been broken; out of order. **2** (of a person) reduced to despair; beaten. **3** (of language) badly spoken, esp. by a foreigner. **4** interrupted (*broken sleep*).

**broken-down** *adj.* **1** worn out by age, use, etc. **2** not functioning.

**broken-hearted** *adj.* overwhelmed with grief.

**broken home** *n.* family disrupted by divorce or separation.

**broker** *n.* **1** agent who buys and sells for others; middleman. **2** = STOCKBROKER. □ **broking** *n.* [Anglo-French]

**brokerage** *n.* broker's fee or commission.

**brolga** /**brol**-guh/ *n.* large crane living near water in eastern and northern Australia, having grey plumage and red skin on its head. [Kamilaroi (and other languages across to Lake Eyre) *burralga*]

**brolly** /**brol**-ee/ *n.* (*pl.* **-ies**) *colloq.* umbrella. [abbreviation]

**bromide** /**broh**-muyd/ *n.* **1** any binary compound of bromine. **2** *Pharm.* preparation of non-potassium bromide, used as a sedative. **3** reproduction or proof on paper coated with silver bromide emulsion.

**bromine** /**broh**-meen/ *n.* poisonous liquid element with a choking smell, used in the manufacture of chemicals for photography or medicine. [Greek *brōmos* stink]

**bronchial** /**brong**-kee-uhl/ *adj.* of the bronchi (see BRONCHUS) or of the smaller tubes into which they divide.

**bronchitis** /brong-**kuy**-tuhs/ *n.* inflammation of the mucous membrane in the bronchial tubes.

**bronchus** /**brong**-kuhs/ *n.* (*pl.* **-chi** /-kuy/) either of the two main divisions of the windpipe. [Latin from Greek]

**bronco** /**brong**-koh/ *n.* (*pl.* **-s**) wild or half-tamed horse of the western US. [Spanish, = rough]

**brontosaurus** /ˌbron-tuh-**saw**-ruhs/ *n.* (*pl.* **-ruses**) large plant-eating dinosaur with a long whiplike tail. [Greek *brontē* thunder, *sauros* lizard]

**bronze** — *n.* **1** alloy of copper and tin. **2** its brownish colour. **3** thing of bronze, esp. a sculpture. — *adj.* made of or coloured like bronze. — *v.* (**-zing**) **1** make or become brown; tan. **2** (as **bronzed** *adj.*) pertaining to (the stereotype of) the sun-loving, healthy, Australian male (*bronzed Aussie*). [French from Italian]

**Bronze Age** *n.* *Archaeol.* period when weapons and tools were usu. made of bronze.

**bronze cuckoo** *n.* any of several species of cuckoo in the same genus, having more or less bronze-coloured feathers on various parts of the body and occurring in Australia and nearby regions (*little bronze cuckoo*; *shining bronze cuckoo*).

**bronze medal** n. medal, usu. awarded as third prize.

**bronze-wing** n. any of several Australian pigeons having bronze-coloured markings on the wings (*brush bronze-wing*; *common bronze-wing*).

**brooch** /brohch/ n. ornament fastened to clothing with a hinged pin. [French *broche*: related to BROACH]

**brood** /brood/ — n. **1** young (of esp. a bird) born or hatched at one time. **2** (*attrib.*) kept for breeding (*brood mare*). — v. **1** worry or ponder (esp. resentfully). **2** (of a bird) sit on eggs to hatch them. [Old English]

**broody** adj. (**-ier, -iest**) **1** (of a hen) wanting to brood. **2** sullenly thoughtful or depressed.

**brook¹** /bruuk/ n. small stream. [Old English]

■ **Usage** In Australia (except WA) *brook* has been replaced by *creek*.

**brook²** /bruuk/ v. (usu. with *neg.*) *literary* tolerate, allow. [Old English]

**broom** /broom/ n. **1** long-handled brush for sweeping. **2 a** (in full native broom) small Australian tree having drooping, apparently leafless branches and masses of yellow pea-flowers in spring. **b** unrelated European shrub with bright yellow flowers, often cultivated in Australia. [Old English]

**broomie** /broo-mee/ n. *colloq.* person employed to sweep in a shearing shed.

**Bros.** *abbr.* Brothers (esp. in the name of a firm).

**broth** n. thin soup of meat or fish stock. [Old English]

**brothel** /broth-uhl/ n. **1** premises for prostitution. **2** untidy or messy room etc. (*this room is a real brothel*). [originally = worthless fellow, from Old English]

**brother** /bruth-uhr/ n. **1** man or boy in relation to his siblings. **2** (often as a form of address) **a** close male friend or associate. **b** male fellow-member of a trade union. **3** (*pl.* also **brethren** /**breth**-ruhn/) member of a male religious order, esp. a monk or one not yet in holy orders (*lay brother*). **4** fellow human being. □ **brotherly** adj. [Old English]

**brother german** see GERMAN.

**brotherhood** n. **1** relationship between brothers. **2** association of people with a common interest. **3** community of feeling between human beings.

**brother-in-law** n. (*pl.* **brothers-in-law**) **1** one's wife's or husband's brother. **2** one's sister's or sister-in-law's husband.

**brought** *past* and *past part.* of BRING.

**brouhaha** /broo-hah-,hah/ n. commotion; sensation. [French]

**brow** /brow/ n. **1** (often in *pl.*) forehead (*knit one's brows*). **2** eyebrow. **3** summit of a hill etc. **4** edge of a cliff etc. [Old English]

**browbeat** v. (*past* **-beat**; *past part.* **-beaten**) intimidate, bully.

**brown** — adj. **1** having the colour produced by mixing red, yellow, and black, as of dark wood or rich soil. **2** dark-skinned or suntanned. **3** (of bread) made from wholemeal or wheatmeal flour. **4** used as a distinguishing epithet in the names of Australian fauna and flora (*brown bittern*; *brown-headed honeyeater*; *brown treecreeper*; *brown beech*). — n. **1** brown colour or pigment. **2** brown clothes or material. — v. make or become brown. □ **browned off** *colloq.* fed up, disheartened. □ **brownish** adj. [Old English]

**brown beech** n. tall tree of rainforests in Queensland and NSW, having somewhat glaucous leaves and black berries.

**brown boronia** /buh-roh-nee-uh/ n. WA shrub (to about 1m) bearing masses of small cup-shaped flowers, dark brown on the outside and old-gold within, which have, arguably, the strongest and headiest fragrance of any flower in the world.

**brown coal** n. = LIGNITE.

**brownie** n. **1** benevolent elf said to haunt houses and do household work secretly. **2** (**Brownie**) junior Guide. **3 a** small square of chocolate cake with nuts. **b** sweetened currant bread.

**brownie point** n. *colloq.* notional mark awarded for good conduct etc.

**brown rice** n. unpolished rice.

**brown snake** n. any of several Australian, more or less brown, highly venomous snakes.

**brown sugar** n. unrefined or partially refined sugar.

**brown tulip oak** see BOOYONG.

**browse** /browz/ — v. (**-sing**) **1** read desultorily or look over goods for sale. **2** (often foll. by *on*) feed on (leaves, twigs, etc.). — n. act of browsing. □ **browser** n. [French *brost* bud]

**brucellosis** /,broo-suh-loh-suhs/ n. bacterial disease causing abortion in cattle and fever in humans. [Sir D. *Bruce*, name of a physician]

**bruise** /brooz/ — n. **1** discoloration of the skin caused esp. by a blow. **2** similar damage on a fruit etc. — v. (**-sing**) **1 a** inflict a bruise on. **b** hurt mentally (*the rejection bruised his ego*). **2** be susceptible to bruising (*he bruises easily*). [originally = crush, from Old English]

**bruiser** n. colloq. **1** large tough-looking person. **2** professional boxer.

**bruit** /broot/ v. (often foll. by *abroad*, *about*) spread (a report or rumour). [French, = noise]

**brumby** /brum-bee/ n. wild unbroken horse. [origin uncertain: possibly from an Aboriginal language of southern Queensland or northern NSW]

**brummy** /brum-ee/ adj. colloq. counterfeit; cheaply or shoddily made. [*Brumm(agem)* (dialect form of *Birmingham*) counterfeit coin etc., -y¹]

**brunch** n. combined breakfast and lunch. [portmanteau word]

**brunette** /broo-net/ n. woman with dark brown hair. [French diminutive]

**brunt** n. chief impact of an attack, task, etc. (esp. *bear the brunt of*). [origin unknown]

**brush¹** — n. **1** implement with bristles, hair, wire, etc. set into a block, for cleaning, painting, arranging the hair, etc. **2** act of brushing. **3** (usu. foll. by *with*) short esp. unpleasant encounter (*a brush with the law*). **4** fox's bushy tail. **5** piece of carbon or metal as an electrical contact esp. with a moving part. — v. **1** sweep, scrub, treat, or tidy with a brush. **2** remove or apply with a brush. **3** graze or touch in passing. □ **brush aside** dismiss (a person, idea, etc.) curtly or lightly (*brushed his objections aside*). **brush off** dismiss abruptly. **brush up 1** clean up or smarten. **2** (also **brush up on**) revise one's former knowledge of (a subject) (*must brush up my Old English grammar*). [French]

**brush²** n. **1** tract of dense natural vegetation (orig. applied chiefly to the understorey, later to forest, esp. rainforest). **2** = SCRUB¹ 1. **3** = BRUSHWOOD 2. [French]

**brush bloodwood** n. medium-sized tree of NSW and Queensland rainforests, having white flowers and exuding a blood-coloured sap when the bark is cut or injured.

**brush box** n. any of several trees (family Myrtaceae) of Queensland and NSW, having twisted trunks with pinkish-grey scaly bark, shining leaves, and feathery white flowers.

**brush fence** n. fence made of sections of brushwood wired together.

**brush kangaroo** n. = BRUSH WALLABY.

**brush-off** n. abrupt dismissal.

**brush-tailed phascogale** n. arboreal marsupial (see PHASCOGALE) widespread in wooded country of mainland Aus-

tralia, having a bushy, bottle-brush tail (see also TUAN).

**brush-tailed possum** n. (also **brush-tail**) common possum, a widespread arboreal marsupial found in all Australian States, cat-sized with a long prehensile tail.

**brush-tailed rock wallaby** n. wallaby with a bushy dark tail, widespread in rocky places of mainland Australia.

**brush turkey** n. large, mound-building bird of eastern Australia, having a bare red head and neck, yellow or bluish-white wattles at the base of the neck, and otherwise mainly black plumage.

**brush wallaby** n. (also **brush kangaroo**) any of several macropods, usu. larger wallabies, of coastal scrubs and more open inland forests of Australia.

**brushwood** n. **1** undergrowth, thicket. **2** dead or felled vegetation used for building purposes, esp. the construction of fences.

**brushwork** n. **1** use of the brush in painting. **2** painter's style in this.

**brusque** /bruusk, brusk/ adj. abrupt or offhand in manner or speech. □ **brusquely** adv. **brusqueness** n. [Italian *brusco* sour]

**brussels sprout** /brus-uhlz/ n. **1** plant of the cabbage family with small cabbage-like buds on a stem. **2** such a bud used as a vegetable. [*Brussels* in Belgium]

**brutal** /broo-tuhl/ adj. **1** savagely cruel. **2** harsh, merciless (*the brutal truth*). □ **brutality** /-tal-uh-tee/ n. (pl. -ies). **brutally** adv. [French: related to BRUTE]

**brutalise** /broo-tuh-,luyz/ v. (also -ize) (-sing or -zing) **1** make brutal. **2** treat brutally.

**brute** /broot/ — n. **1 a** brutal or violent person. **b** unpleasant person or difficult thing. **2** animal. — attrib. adj. **1** unthinking (*brute force*). **2** cruel; animal-like. □ **brutish** adj. **brutishly** adv. **brutishness** n. [Latin *brutus* stupid]

**B.Sc.** abbr. Bachelor of Science.

**BSE** abbr. bovine spongiform encephalopathy, a usu. fatal cattle disease, affecting the nervous system.

**BT, DT** /,bee-tee dee-tee/ abbr. of 'Been There, Done That!', an expression (usu. in response to a suggestion that something be done etc.) indicating bored rejection = I've experienced it already.

**bub** n. (also **bubbie**) colloq. young child. [abbreviation of BABY]

**bubble** /bub-uhl/ — n. **1 a** thin sphere of liquid enclosing air etc. **b** air-filled cavity in a liquid or solidified liquid such as glass or amber. **2** transparent domed canopy. **3** visionary or unrealistic project. — v. (-ling) **1** rise in or send up bubbles. **2**

make the sound of boiling. □ **bubble over** (often foll. by *with*) be exuberant (*bubbling over with excitement*). [imitative]

**bubbler** /bub-luh/ *n*. drinking fountain.

**bubbly** — *adj*. (**-ier**, **-iest**) **1** having or like bubbles. **2** exuberant. — *n*. *colloq*. champagne.

**bubo** /byoo-boh/ *n*. (*pl*. **-es**) inflamed swelling in the armpit or groin. [Greek *boubōn* groin]

**bubonic plague** /byoo-**bon**-ik/ *n*. contagious disease, spread by rats, and characterised by fever, delirium, and the formation of buboes.

**buccaneer** /,buk-uh-**neer**/ *n*. **1** pirate. **2** unscrupulous adventurer. □ **buccaneering** *n*. & *adj*. [French]

**buck**[1] — *n*. **1** male deer, hare, rabbit, etc. **2** young man. **3** act or instance of bucking; a buckjump. — *v*. **1** (of a horse) jump upwards with its back arched. **2** (usu. foll. by *off*) throw (a rider) in this way. **3** oppose; resist (*buck the system*). **4** (usu. foll. by *up*) *colloq*. **a** cheer up (*bucked him up no end*). **b** hurry up; make an effort (*buck up! — we haven't got all day*). [Old English]

**buck**[2] *n*. *colloq*. dollar. [origin unknown]

**buck**[3] *n*. *colloq*. (in poker) article placed as a reminder before the next dealer. □ **the buck stops here** *colloq*. this is where the ultimate responsibility lies. **pass the buck** *colloq*. shift responsibility (to another). [origin unknown]

**buckee** var. of BUGEEN.

**bucket** /buk-uht/ — *n*. **1 a** round open container with a handle, for carrying or drawing water etc. **b** amount contained in this. **2** (in *pl*.) *colloq*. large quantities, esp. of rain or tears (*wept buckets*). **3** scoop in a water wheel, dredger, etc. **4** ice cream carton. — *v*. (**-t-**) *colloq*. **1** (often foll. by *down*) (esp. of rain) pour heavily. **2** *colloq*. denigrate (a person etc.) (*the national pastime of bucketing Canberra*). □ **drop** (or **tip**) **the bucket on** *colloq*. make damaging revelations about (e.g. a political opponent). [Anglo-French]

**bucket seat** *n*. seat with a rounded back for one person, esp. in a car.

**buckjump** — *v*. (of a horse) leap with head down, legs drawn together, and back arched in an attempt to throw the rider. — *n*. **1** act or instance of buckjumping. **2** buckjumping event (*won the buckjump*).

**buckjumper** *n*. horse which buckjumps habitually.

**buckle** /buk-uhl/ — *n*. clasp with a hinged pin for securing a belt, strap, etc. — *v*. (**-ling**) **1** (often foll. by *up*, *on*, etc.) fasten with a buckle. **2 a** (often foll. by *up*)

(cause to) crumple under longitudinal pressure. **b** (foll. by *up*) put on one's seatbelt. □ **buckle down** make a determined effort. **buckle to** (or **down to**) set about (work etc.); make a vigorous start to. **buckle under** give way to pressure, yield. [Latin *buccula* cheek-strap]

**bucklee** /buk-lee/ — *n*. (also **bucklegarroo**) Aboriginal initiation rite. — *v*. initiate (an Aboriginal boy). [Yindjibarndi *bagarli*]

**buckler** *n*. *hist*. small round shield.

**Buckley's** /buk-leez/ *n*. (in full **Buckley's chance**) *colloq*. little or no chance (*he's got Buckley's of getting the job*). [origin uncertain]

**buckram** /buk-ruhm/ *n*. coarse linen etc. stiffened with paste etc. [French *boquerant*]

**buckshot** *n*. coarse lead shot.

**buckskin** *n*. **1 a** skin of a buck. **b** leather made from this. **2** leather from a sheepskin.

**buck's party** *n*. party for males only given for a bridegroom, usu. on the eve of his wedding, by his male friends.

**buck spinifex** /spin-uh-,feks/ *n*. Australian grass with rigid, needle-sharp, pointed blades.

**buck-tooth** *n*. upper projecting tooth.

**buckwheat** *n*. seed of a plant related to rhubarb, used to make flour, or as an alternative to rice. [Dutch, = beech-wheat]

**bucolic** /byoo-**kol**-ik/ — *adj*. of shepherds; rustic, pastoral. — *n*. (usu. in *pl*.) pastoral poem or poetry. [Greek *boukolos* herdsman]

**bud**[1] — *n*. **1 a** knoblike shoot from which a stem, leaf, or flower develops. **b** flower or leaf not fully open. **2** asexual outgrowth from an organism separating to form a new individual. — *v*. (**-dd-**) **1** form buds. **2** begin to grow or develop (*budding artist*). **3** graft a bud of (a plant) on to another. [origin unknown]

**bud**[2] *colloq*. (as a form of address, often *derog*.) mate (*just watch it, bud!*).

**Buddha** /buud-uh/ *n*. **1** title of the Indian philosopher Gautama (5th-c. BC) and his successors. **2** sculpture etc. of Buddha. [Sanskrit, = enlightened]

**buddha** /buud-uh/ *n*. (also **budda**, **budtha**) any of several shrubs or small trees of inland Australia, the leaves and timber of which have a strong aroma resembling that of sandalwood; the wood of this plant. [Wiradhuri and Yuwaalaraay *budaa*]

**Buddhism** /buud-iz-uhm/ *n*. Asian religion or philosophy founded by Gautama Buddha. □ **Buddhist** *n*. & *adj*.

**buddy** /bud-ee/ — n. (pl. **-ies**) colloq. friend or mate. [perhaps from BROTHER]

**budge** v. (**-ging**) (usu. with neg.) **1** move slightly (this screw won't budge). **2** (cause to) change an opinion (he won't budge an inch). [French bouger]

**budgeree** /buj-uh-ree, buuj-uh-ree/ adj. (also **boodgery**, **boojeree**, **budgeri**) (orig. in Australian pidgin) good. [Dharuk bujiri]

**budgerigar** /buj-uh-ree-,gah/ n. small green and yellow Australian parrot, occurring in drier mainland areas, often in large flocks, and a popular cage-bird. [perhaps an alteration of Kamilaroi gijirrigaa]

**budget** /buj-uht/ — n. **1** amount of money needed or available for a specific item etc. **2 a** (**the Budget**) government's annual estimate or plan of revenue and expenditure. **b** similar estimate by a company, household, etc. **3** (attrib.) inexpensive (budget prices). — v. (**-t-**) (often foll. by for) allow or arrange for in a budget. □ **budgetary** adj. [Latin bulga bag]

**budgie** /buj-ee/ n. colloq. = BUDGERIGAR. [abbreviation]

**buff** — adj. of a yellowish beige colour (buff envelope). — n. **1** this colour. **2** (in comb.) colloq. enthusiast (railway buff). **3** velvety dull-yellow ox-leather. — v. **1** polish (metal etc.). **2** make (leather) velvety. □ **in the buff** colloq. naked. [originally = buffalo, from French buffle; sense 2 of n. originally from the buff uniforms formerly worn by New York volunteer firemen, applied to enthusiastic fire-watchers]

**buffalo** /buf-uh-,loh/ n. (pl. same or **-es**) **1** wild ox of Africa or Asia. **2** N. American bison. [Greek boubalos ox]

**buffalo grass** n. grass introduced to Australia, cultivated as a coarse lawn grass esp. in hot areas.

**buffel grass** /buf-uhl/ n. tussocky perennial African grass introduced to Australia and valued as a forage plant and soil stabiliser. [Dutch buffel buffalo]

**buffer** — n. **1** device on the front and rear of a railway vehicle, or at the end of a track, that deadens impact. **2** person or thing that protects against or reduces the effect of (damage, hostile forces, etc.) (a buffer against inflation.). **3** substance that maintains the constant acidity of a solution. **4** Computing temporary memory area or queue for data. — v. act as a buffer to. [imitative]

**buffer State** n. small State between two larger ones, potentially hostile to each other, regarded as reducing the likelihood of open hostilities.

**buffet¹** /buuf-ay, buf-ay/ n. **1** room or counter where refreshments are sold. **2** self-service meal of several dishes set out at once. **3** sideboard. [French, = stool]

**buffet²** /buf-uht/ — v. (**-t-**) **1 a** strike repeatedly (wind buffeted the trees). **b** strike with the hand or fist. **2** (of fate etc.) treat badly; plague (buffeted by misfortune). **3** struggle, fight one's way (through difficulties etc.). — n. **1** blow, esp. of the hand. **2** shock. [French diminutive of bufe blow]

**buffet car** n. railway coach serving refreshments.

**buffoon** /buh-foon/ n. **1** clown; jester. **2** stupid person. □ **buffoonery** n. [Latin buffo clown]

**bug** — n. **1 a** any of various insects with mouthparts modified for piercing and sucking. **b** any small insect. **2** colloq. virus; infection. **3** colloq. concealed microphone. **4** colloq. error in a computer program or system etc. **5** colloq. obsession, enthusiasm, etc. — v. (**-gg-**) **1** colloq. conceal a microphone in (bugged the room). **2** colloq. annoy (he really bugs me). [origin unknown]

**bugbear** n. **1** cause of annoyance. **2** object of baseless fear. [bug = bogey]

**bugeen** /bug-een/ n. (also **buckee**, **buggeen**) devil or evil spirit. [probably from Wiradhuri baginny evil spirit; but cf. British dial. bugan evil spirit]

**bugger** /bug-uh/ coarse colloq. (except in sense 2 of n. and 3 of v.) — n. **1 a** unpleasant or awkward person or thing. **b** person of a specified kind (clever bugger!). **2** person who commits buggery. — v. **1** as an exclamation of annoyance (bugger it!). **2 a** (often foll. by up) ruin; spoil. **b** exhaust. **3** commit buggery with. — int. expressing annoyance. □ **bugger all** nothing. **bugger about** (or **around**) (often foll. by with) mess about. **bugger off** (often in imper.) go away. **play silly buggers** fool about. [Latin Bulgarus Bulgarian heretic, buggery being one of the charges made against the Bulgarian heretics.]

**buggery** n. **1** anal intercourse. **2** = BESTIALITY 2. **3** (in various coarse colloq. usages) = HELL (go to buggery!; hurt like buggery).

**buggy** /bug-ee/ n. (pl. **-ies**) **1** small, sturdy, esp. open, motor vehicle (beach buggy). **2** light, horse-drawn vehicle for one or two people. [origin unknown]

**bugle** /byoo-guhl/ — n. brass military instrument like a small trumpet. — v. (**-ling**) **1** sound a bugle. **2** sound (a call etc.) on a bugle. □**bugler** *n*. [Latin *buculus* young bull]

**build** /bild/ — *v*. (*past* and *past part*. built /bilt/) **1** construct or cause to be constructed. **2 a** (often foll. by *up*) establish or develop (*built the business up*). **b** (often foll. by *on*) base (hopes, theories, etc.). **3** (as built *adj*.) of specified build (*sturdily built*). — *n*. **1** physical proportions (*slim build*). **2** style of construction; make. □ **build in** incorporate. **build on** add (an extension etc.). **build up 1** increase in size or strength. **2** praise; boost. **3** gradually become established. [Old English]

**builder** *n*. person who builds, esp. a building contractor.

**building** *n*. **1** permanent fixed structure e.g. a house, factory, or stable. **2** constructing of these.

**building society** *n*. public finance company paying interest to investors and lending capital for mortgages etc.

**build-up** *n*. **1** favourable advance publicity. **2** gradual approach to a climax. **3** accumulation or increase. **4** (in northern Australia) period of increasing humidity which precedes the wet season.

**built** *past* and *past part*. of BUILD.

**built-in** *adj*. integral.

**built-up** *adj*. **1** (of a locality) densely developed. **2** increased in height etc. by addition.

**bulb** *n*. **1 a** globular base of the stem of some plants, sending roots downwards and leaves upwards. **b** plant grown from this, e.g. a daffodil. **2** light globe. **3** object or part shaped like a bulb. [Latin *bulbus* from Greek, = onion]

**bulbous** *adj*. **1** bulb-shaped; fat or bulging. **2** having a bulb or bulbs; growing from a bulb.

**bulbul** /buul-buul/ *n*. songbird of Africa and Asia, usu. with distinctive crest, one species of which has been introduced into Australia (*red-whiskered bulbul*). [Arabic]

**bulge** — *n*. **1** irregular swelling. **2** *colloq*. temporary increase in quantity or number (*baby bulge*). — *v*. (**-ging**) swell outwards. □ **bulgy** *adj*. [Latin *bulga* bag]

**bulimia** /byoo-**lim**-ee-uh, buh-/ *n*. (in full **bulimia nervosa**) disorder in which overeating alternates with self-induced vomiting, fasting, etc. □ **bulimic** *adj*. & *n*. [Greek *bous* ox, *limos* hunger]

**bulk** — *n*. **1 a** size; magnitude (esp. large). **b** large mass, body, or person (*the jacket barely covered his bulk*). **c** large quantity (*struggling to pay a bulk of bills*). **2** (treated as *pl*. & usu. prec. by *the*) greater part or number (*the bulk of the applicants are women*). — *v*. seem (in size or importance) (*bulks large*). — *adj*. *colloq*. many; a lot of (*bulk people at the party*). □ **in bulk 1** in large quantities. **2** (of cargo) loose, not packaged. [Old Norse]

**bulk-bill** *v*. (of a medical practitioner) bill (the health insurance agency) for treatment of a number of patients at the scheduled fee. □ **bulk-billing** *n*.

**bulk buying** *n*. buying in quantity at a discount.

**bulkhead** *n*. upright partition in a ship, aircraft, etc.

**bulky** *adj*. (**-ier, -iest**) awkwardly large. □ **bulkiness** *n*.

**bull¹** /bull/ *n*. **1 a** uncastrated male bovine animal. **b** male of the whale, elephant, etc. **2** (**the Bull**) zodiacal sign or constellation Taurus. **3** *Stock Exch*. market with shares rising in price. □ **take the bull by the horns** face danger or a challenge boldly. □ **bullish** *adj*. [Old Norse]

**bull²** /buul/ *n*. formal papal edict. [Latin *bulla* seal]

**bull³** /buul/ *n*. **1** *colloq*. nonsense; exaggeration. **2** trivial or insincere talk or writing. [probably an abbreviation of BULLSHIT]

**Bullamakanka** /ˌbuul-uh-muh-**kang**-kuh/ *n*. imaginary place in Australia, remote and backward (see also WOOP WOOP).

**bullan-bullan¹** /buul-uhn-ˌbuul-uhn/ *n*. (also **buln-buln**) = RINGNECK. [Yuwaalaraay *bulun-bulun*]

**bullan-bullan²** *n*. (also **buln-buln**) the superb lyrebird. [Wuywurung *bulenbulen*]

**bull ant** *n*. = BULLDOG ANT.

**bull-artist** *n*. *colloq*. person noted for boasting, exaggeration, etc. [BULL³, -ARTIST]

**bull bar** *n*. = KANGAROO BAR.

**bull bird** *n*. (also **boomer**) Australian bittern, a swamp bird with a deep booming call, occurring in southern Australia.

**bulldog** *n*. **1** short-haired heavy-jowled sturdy dog. **2** tenacious and courageous person.

**bulldog ant** *n*. (also **bull ant**) large Australian ant capable of inflicting a painful sting.

**bulldoze** *v*. (**-zing**) **1** clear with a bulldozer. **2** *colloq*. **a** intimidate (*was bulldozed into agreeing*). **b** make (one's way) forcibly; force, push (*bulldozed his way through the crowd*; *bulldozed the bill through parliament*).

**bulldozer** *n*. powerful tractor with a broad vertical blade at the front for clearing ground.

**bulldust** n. **1** kind of fine powdery dust found in inland Australia. **2** euphem. = BULLSHIT.

**bullet** /buul-uht/ n. small pointed missile fired from a rifle, revolver, etc. □ **get the bullet** colloq. get the sack. [French diminutive of boule ball]

**bulletin** /buul-uh-tuhn/ n. **1** short official news report. **2** regular list of information etc. issued by an organisation or society. [Italian diminutive: related to BULL[2]]

**bullfight** n. public baiting, and usu. killing, of bulls. □ **bullfighter** n. **bullfighting** n.

**bullfrog** n. any of several large Australian frogs, having a booming croak.

**bullhead** n. (also **bull head burr, bull burr**) any of several unrelated Australian plants bearing spiny fruits, esp. DOUBLEGEE.

**bull-headed** adj. obstinate; blundering. □ **bull-headedly** adv. **bull-headedness** n.

**bullion** /buul-yuhn/ n. gold or silver in bulk before coining, or valued by weight. [French: related to BOIL[1]]

**bull mallee** n. **1** form of growth of mallee eucalypts in which they develop only 1–3 stems (cf. WHIPSTICK). **2** any of several mallee eucalypts with this form of growth.

**bull market** n. Stock Exch. market with shares rising in price.

**bull Mitchell** see MITCHELL.

**bull oak** n. (also **buloke**) any of several Australian trees, esp. the CASUARINA.

**bullock** /buul-uhk/ — n. castrated male of domestic cattle. — v. work tirelessly (like a bullock) (bullocked away for hours). □ **bullocking** n. [Old English diminutive of BULL[1]]

**bullocky** /buul-uh-kee/ — n. driver of a team of bullocks. — adj. of or pertaining to bullock driving or rural life generally (the bullocky life; bullocky yarns).

**bullring** n. arena for bullfights.

**bullroarer** /buul-,raw-ruh/ n. sacred object of Aboriginal ritual, a carved, flat, oval piece of wood tied to a string at one end and whirled round and round to produce a loud roaring noise.

**bull rout** n. any of several eastern Australian fish of coastal waters and freshwater streams, having venomous spines on the head.

**bull's-eye** n. **1** centre of a target. **2** hard minty sweet. **3** hemispherical ship's window. **4** small circular window. **5 a** hemispherical lens. **b** lantern with this. **6** boss of glass at the centre of a blown glass sheet.

**bullsh** /buulsh/ n. colloq. = BULLSHIT.

**bullshit** coarse colloq. — n. (often as int.) **1** nonsense, rubbish. **2** trivial or insincere talk or writing. — v. (**-tt-**) talk nonsense or as if one has specialist knowledge (to); bluff. □ **bullshitter** n. [from BULL[3]]

**bullswool** n. (also **bull's wool**) **1** fibrous bark, esp. that of some stringybarks. **2** euphem. = BULLSHIT.

**bully[1]** /buul-ee/ — n. (pl. **-ies**) person coercing others by fear. — v. (**-ies, -ied**) persecute or oppress by force or threats. — int. (foll. by for) often iron. expressing approval (bully for you). [Dutch]

**bully[2]** /buul-ee/ (in full **bully off**) — n. (pl. **-ies**) start of play in hockey in which two opponents strike each other's sticks three times and then go for the ball. — v. (**-ies, -ied**) start play in this way. [origin unknown]

**bully[3]** /buul-ee/ n. (in full **bully beef**) corned beef. [French: related to BOIL[1]]

**buln-buln** var. of BULLAN-BULLAN.

**bulrush** /buul-rush/ n. **1** a kind of tall rush used for weaving. **2** Bibl. papyrus. [perhaps from BULL[1] = coarse + RUSH[2]]

**bulwaddy** /buul-wod-ee/ n. tree of northern Australia that forms dense thickets. [probably from a NT Aboriginal language]

**bulwark** /buul-wuhk/ n. **1** defensive wall, esp. of earth. **2** protecting person or thing. **3** (usu. in pl.) ship's side above deck. [Low German or Dutch]

**bum[1]** n. colloq. buttocks. [origin uncertain]

**bum[2]** colloq. — n. loafer or tramp; dissolute person. — v. (**-mm-**) **1** (often foll. by around) loaf or wander around. **2** cadge; live off (another person). — attrib. adj. of poor quality. [German Bummler loafer]

**bumbag** n. small bag or pouch worn on a belt around the waist.

**bumble** /bum-buhl/ v. (**-ling**) **1** (foll. by on) speak in a rambling way. **2** (often as **bumbling** adj.) be inept; blunder. [from BOOM[1]]

**bumble-bee** n. large bee with a loud hum.

**bumble tree** n. (also **bumble**) = NATIVE ORANGE. [Kamilaroi and nearby languages bambul]

**bum chum** n. colloq. intimate male friend of a male.

**bumf** n. colloq. usu. derog. papers, documents. [abbreviation of bum-fodder = toilet-paper]

**bummer** /bum-uh/ n. colloq. unpleasant occurrence; disappointment (party was a bummer; I've had a bummer of a day).

**bump** — n. **1** dull-sounding blow or collision. **2** swelling or dent so caused. **3** uneven patch on a road etc. **4** prominence on the skull. — v. **1 a** hit or come against with a bump. **b** (often foll. by *against, into*) collide. **2** (often foll. by *against, on*) hurt or damage by striking (*bumped my head; bumped the car*). **3** (usu. foll. by *along*) move along with jolts. — adv. with a bump; suddenly; violently. □ **bump into** *colloq.* meet by chance. **bump off** *colloq.* murder. **bump up** *colloq.* increase (prices etc.). □ **bumpy** *adj.* (**-ier, -iest**). [imitative]

**bumper** n. **1** (in full **bumper bar**) horizontal bar at the front or back of a motor vehicle, reducing damage in a collision. **2** (usu. *attrib.*) unusually large or fine example (*bumper crop*). **3** *Cricket* ball rising high after pitching.

**bumpkin** /**bump**-kuhn/ n. rustic or socially inept person. [Dutch]

**bumptious** /**bump**-shuhs/ adj. offensively self-assertive or conceited. [from BUMP, after *fractious*]

**bun** n. **1** small sweet bread roll or cake, often with dried fruit. **2** hair coiled and pinned to the head. **3** (**buns**) *colloq.* buttocks. [origin unknown]

**bunch** — n. **1** things growing or festooned together (*bunch of grapes; bunch of keys*). **2** collection; lot (*best of the bunch*). **3** *colloq.* group; gang. — v. **1** make into a bunch; gather into close folds. **2** form into a group or crowd. □ **bunchy** *adj.* [origin unknown]

**bunchy top** n. viral disease affecting bananas.

**bundle** /**bun**-duhl/ — n. **1** things tied or fastened together. **2** set of nerve fibres etc. **3** *colloq.* large amount of money. — v. (**-ling**) **1** (usu. foll. by *up*) tie or make into a bundle. **2** (usu. foll. by *into*) throw or push, esp. quickly or confusedly (*bundled the papers into the drawer*). **3** (usu. foll. by *out, off, away*, etc.) send away hurriedly (*bundled him off*). □ **be a bundle of nerves** (or **fun** etc.) be extremely nervous (or amusing etc.). **bundle up** dress warmly. **drop one's bundle** give up hope; go to pieces mentally. [Low German or Dutch]

**bundy**[1] n. any of several eucalypts of south-eastern Australia. [probably Dharuk *bunda*]

**bundy**[2] n. (also **Bundy**) *propr.* time clock which employees activate to record the time they start and finish work.

**bun fight** n. *colloq.* disorderly social gathering; argument.

**bung**[1] — n. stopper, esp. for a cask. — v. **1** stop with a bung. **2** *colloq.* throw, toss (*bung them in the washing-machine;*

*bung some more sausages on the barbie*). □ **bunged up** blocked up. **bung it on** assume (a style of speech or behaviour which is pretentious or ostentatious) (*bunging it on like a pom — who does he think he is?*). [Dutch]

**bung**[2] adj. broken down; useless (*the telly's bung*). □ **go bung 1** break down (*the telly's gone bung*). **2** fail; go bankrupt. [originally Australian pidgin, = dead; probably Yagara]

**bungalow** /**bung**-guh-ˌloh/ n. cottage; shack; sleepout. [Gujarati, = of Bengal]

**bungarra** /bun-**ga**-ruh/ n. widespread Australian monitor lizard, usu. having a dark horizontal stripe through the eye, bordered by pale lines. [Nhanta, probably *bangarra*]

**bungee** /**bun**-jee/ n. (in full **bungee cord, bungee rope**) elasticated cord or rope used for securing baggage or in bungee jumping. [origin uncertain]

**bungee jumping** n. sport of jumping from a height while secured by a bungee from the ankles or a harness.

**bunger** /**bung**-uh/ n. firework that explodes with a loud report. [variant of BANGER]

**bungle** /**bung**-guhl/ — v. (**-ling**) **1** mismanage or fail at (a task). **2** work badly or clumsily. — n. bungled attempt or work. [imitative]

**bungwall** /**bung**-wawl/ n. Australian fern of swampy land, the root of which is an important traditional Aboriginal food. [Yagara *bangwal*]

**bunion** /**bun**-yuhn/ n. swelling on the foot, esp. on the big toe. [French]

**bunji-man** /**bun**-juh-ˌman/ n. white man with a predilection for Aboriginal women. [perhaps from a WA Aboriginal language; perhaps from English *fancyman*]

**bunk**[1] — n. **1** shelflike bed against a wall, esp. in a ship. **2** each of two or more beds one above the other, forming a unit. — v. (usu. foll. by *down*) *colloq.* lie down to sleep. [origin unknown]

**bunk**[2] *colloq.* — v. (often foll. by *off*) play truant (from). — n. (in **do a bunk**) leave or abscond hurriedly. [origin unknown]

**bunk**[3] n. *colloq.* nonsense, humbug. [shortening of BUNKUM]

**bunker** n. **1** container for fuel. **2** reinforced underground shelter. **3** sandy hollow in a golf-course. [origin unknown]

**bunkum** /**bung**-kuhm/ n. nonsense, humbug. [*Buncombe* in US]

**bunny** /**bun**-ee/ n. (pl. **-ies**) **1** child's name for a rabbit. **2** victim or dupe; scapegoat. [British dial. *bun* rabbit]

**Bunsen burner** /bun-suhn/ *n.* small adjustable gas burner used in a laboratory. [*Bunsen*, name of a chemist]

**bunting** /bun-ting/ *n.* **1** flags and other decorations. **2** loosely-woven fabric for these. [origin unknown]

**bunya** /bun-yuh/ *n.* (also **bunya bunya**) **1** tall, straight, Queensland tree, the cones of which contain seeds which are eaten raw, roasted, or pounded to a flour. **2** (also **bunya nut**) the seed of this tree. [Yagara *bunya-bunya*; Gabi-gabi and Waga-waga *bunyi*]

**bunyip** /bun-yip/ *n.* **1** fabulous Australian monster inhabiting swamps and lagoons. **2** impostor. **3** *attrib.* pertaining to Australians who consider themselves aristocrats (*even some of the bunyip aristocracy admit that Australia will be a republic*). [Wemba-wemba *banib*]

**buoy** /boi/ — *n.* **1** anchored float as a navigation mark etc. **2** lifebuoy. — *v.* **1** (usu. foll. by *up*) **a** keep afloat. **b** sustain the courage or spirits of (a person etc.); encourage, uplift. **2** (often foll. by *out*) mark with a buoy. [Dutch, perhaps from Latin *boia* collar]

**buoyant** /boi-uhnt/ *adj.* **1** able or apt to keep afloat. **2** resilient; exuberant. □**buoyancy** *n.* [French or Spanish: related to BUOY]

**burble** /ber-buhl/ — *v.* **1** talk ramblingly. **2** make a bubbling sound. — *n.* **1** burbling noise. **2** rambling speech. [imitative]

**Burdekin duck** /ber-duh-kuhn/ *n.* (also **rajah shieldrake**) **1** shelduck of northern Australia, having a white head, neck and underparts except for a chestnut band across the breast. **2** slice of meat battered and fried. [river in north-eastern Queensland]

**Burdekin plum** *n.* tree of Queensland rainforests, having pinnate leaves and purple-black plum-like fruits palatable only when very ripe.

**burden** /ber-duhn/ — *n.* **1** load, esp. a heavy one. **2** oppressive duty, expense, emotion, etc. **3** bearing of loads (*beast of burden*). **4 a** refrain of a song. **b** chief theme of a speech, book, etc. (*the burden of his reply was that . . .*). — *v.* load with a burden; oppress. □**burdensome** *adj.* [Old English: related to BIRTH]

**bureau** /byoo-roh, -roh/ *n.* (*pl.* **-x** or **-s** /-z/) **1** desk with drawers and usu. an angled hinged top. **2 a** office or department for specific business. **b** government department. [French, originally = baize]

**bureaucracy** /byoo-rok-ruh-see/ *n.* (*pl.* **-ies**) **1 a** government by central administration. **b** nation etc. so governed. **2** government officials, esp. regarded as oppressive and inflexible. **3** conduct typical of these.

**bureaucrat** /byoo-ruh-krat/ *n.* **1** official in a bureaucracy. **2** inflexible or insensitive administrator. □ **bureaucratic** /-krat-ik/ *adj.* **bureaucratically** /-krat-i-kuh-lee, -klee/ *adv.*

**burette** /byoo-ret/ *n.* graduated glass tube with an end-tap for measuring liquid in chemical analysis. [French]

**burgeon** /ber-juhn/ *v. literary* grow rapidly; flourish. [Latin *burra* wool]

**burgher** /ber-guh/ *n.* **1** citizen, esp. of a town in continental Europe. **2 a** descendant of a Dutch colonist in Sri Lanka, esp. as settled in Australia. **b** (*attrib.*) of or pertaining to such a descendant. [Dutch or German]

**burglar** /ber-gluh/ *n.* person who commits burglary. [Anglo-French]

**burglary** *n.* (*pl.* **-ies**) **1** illegal entry with intent to commit theft, do bodily harm, or do damage. **2** instance of this.

**burgle** /ber-guhl/ *v.* (**-ling**) commit burglary (on).

**burgundy** /ber-guhn-dee/ *n.* (*pl.* **-ies**) **1** (also **Burgundy**) **a** red or white wine from Burgundy in France. **b** similar wine from elsewhere. **2** dark red colour of this.

**burial** /be-ree-uhl/ *n.* **1 a** burying of a corpse. **b** funeral. **2** *Archaeol.* grave or its remains.

**burin** /byoo-ruhn/ *n.* **1** tool for engraving copper or wood. **2** *Archaeol.* chisel-pointed flint tool. [French]

**burl** /berl/ *n. colloq.* try, attempt. □**give it a burl** venture an attempt, have a go. [British dial. *birl* spin, twirl]

**burlesque** /ber-lesk/ — *n.* **1** comic imitation, parody. **2** this as a genre. — *adj.* of or using burlesque. — *v.* (**-ques, -qued, -quing**) parody. [Italian *burla* mockery]

**burly** /ber-lee/ *adj.* (**-ier, -iest**) large and sturdy. [Old English]

**Burmese** /ber-meez/ — *n.* **1 a** native or national of Burma (now officially Myanmar) in SE Asia. **b** person of Burmese descent. **2** member of the largest ethnic group of Burma. **3** language of this group. — *adj.* of or relating to Burma or its people or language.

**burn** — *v.* (*past* and *past part.* **burnt** or **burned**) **1** (cause to) be consumed or destroyed by fire. **2** blaze or glow with fire. **3** (cause to) be injured or damaged by fire, heat, radiation, acid, etc. **4** use or be used as a source of heat, light, or other energy. **5** char or scorch in cooking. **6** produce (a hole, mark, etc.) by fire or heat. **7 a** heat (clay, chalk, etc.). **b** harden (bricks) by fire. **8** colour, tan, or parch with heat or light (*surfies were burned brown by the sun*). **9** (be) put to death by fire. **10** (often foll. by *off*) clear land of vegetation by burning. **11** cauterise, brand. **12** make, be, or feel hot, esp. painfully. **13** (often foll. by *with*) (cause to) feel great emotion or passion (*burn with shame*). **14** *colloq.* drive fast. — *n.* **1** mark or injury caused by burning. **2** (also **burn-off**) forest area cleared by burning. **3** *colloq.* fast drive (*went for a burn*). □ **burn one's boats** (or **bridges**) commit oneself irrevocably. **burn the candle at both ends** work etc. excessively. **burn down** destroy or be destroyed by burning. **burn one's fingers** suffer for meddling or rashness. **burn the midnight oil** read or work late. **burn out 1** be reduced to nothing by burning. **2** (cause to) fail by burning. **3** (usu. *refl.*) suffer physical or emotional exhaustion. **burn up 1** get rid of by fire. **2** begin to blaze. **3** *colloq.* consume (*this car sure burns up the petrol*). [Old English]

**burning** *adj.* **1** ardent, intense (*burning passion*). **2** hotly discussed, vital, urgent (*burning question*).

**burnish** /**ber**-nish/ *v.* polish by rubbing. [French *brunir* from *brun* brown]

**burn-out** *n.* physical or emotional exhaustion, usu. caused by stress at work. □ **burnt-out** *adj.*

**burnt** see BURN.

**burnt ochre** *n.* (also **burnt sienna** or **umber**) pigment darkened by burning.

**burp** *colloq.* — *v.* **1** belch. **2** make (a baby) belch, usu. by patting its back. — *n.* belch. [imitative]

**burr¹** /ber/ *n.* **1 a** prickly clinging seed-case or flower-head. **b** any plant having these. **c** clinging person. [Scandinavian]

**burr²** — *n.* **1 a** whirring sound. **b** rough sounding of the letter *r*. **2** (also **bur**) **a** rough edge on metal or paper. **b** surgeon's or dentist's small drill. — *v.* make a burr. [imitative]

**burrawang** /**bu**-ruh-,wang/ see MACROZAMIA. [Dharuk *buruwan*]

**burrow** /**bu**-roh/ — *n.* hole or tunnel dug by a rabbit etc. as a dwelling or shelter. — *v.* **1** make a burrow. **2** make (a hole, one's way, etc.) (as) by digging. **3** (foll. by *into*) investigate, search. [apparently var. of BOROUGH]

**bursar** /**ber**-suh/ *n.* **1** treasurer, esp. of a college. **2** holder of a bursary. [medieval Latin *bursarius* from *bursa* purse]

**bursaria** /ber-**sair**-ree-uh/ *n.* any species of the Australian genus of the same name, prickly shrubs or small trees, esp.

sweet bursaria, having masses of sweetly-scented white flowers (see BLACKTHORN). [from Latin *bursa* purse, referring to the bag-like fruit capsules]

**bursary** *n.* (*pl.* **-ies**) grant, esp. a scholarship. [medieval Latin: related to BURSAR]

**burst** — *v.* (*past* and *past part.* **burst**) **1** (cause to) break suddenly and violently apart by expansion of contents or internal pressure. **2 a** (usu. foll. by *in, out*) make one's way suddenly or by force (*he burst into my bedroom*). **b** break away from or through (*river burst its banks*). **3** be full to overflowing (*bag was bursting at the seams*; *bursting with pride*). **4** appear or come suddenly (*burst into flame*). **5** (foll. by *into*) suddenly begin to shed or utter (*he burst into tears*; *she burst into an angry denunciation*). **6** seem about to burst from effort, excitement, etc. **7** suffer bursting (*burst a blood-vessel*). — *n.* **1** act or instance of bursting. **2** sudden issue or outbreak (*burst of flame*; *burst of applause*). **3** sudden effort, spurt (*put on a final burst and won*). □ **burst out 1** suddenly begin (*burst out laughing*). **2** exclaim. [Old English]

**bury** /**be**-ree/ *v.* (**-ies**, **-ied**) **1** place (a corpse) in the earth, a tomb, or the sea. **2** lose by death (*buried two sons*). **3 a** put or hide under ground. **b** cover up; conceal (*he buried his face in his hands*). **4** consign to obscurity; forget (*the idea was buried after brief discussion*). **5** (*refl.* or *passive*) involve deeply (*buried in a book*). **6** cause to penetrate (*she buried the knife in his breast*). □ **bury the hatchet** forget grievances; make peace. [Old English]

**bus** — *n.* (*pl.* **buses**) **1** large esp. public passenger vehicle, usu. travelling a fixed route. **2** *colloq.* car, aeroplane, etc. **3** *Computing* signal route which allows for direct communication between components of a computer. — *v.* (**buses**, **bussed**, **bussing**) **1** go by bus. **2** transport by bus. [abbreviation of OMNIBUS]

**bush¹** /buush/ — *n.* **1** shrub or clump of shrubs with stems of moderate length. **2** thing like a bush; clump of hair or fur. **3 a** natural vegetation. **b** tract of land covered in this. **4** country in its natural uncultivated state. **5** rural as opposed to urban life; country as opposed to town or city. — *adj.* **1 a** of or pertaining to natural vegetation or to a tract of land covered in this (*bush-covered hills*; *bush suburb*). **b** (of artefacts) made with branches, saplings, etc. (*bush gate*; *bush poles*). **2** (of Aborigines) living outside white society. **3 a** (of Australian fauna and flora) indigenous (*bush animal*; *bush food*). **b**

(of domestic animals) having become wild (*bush cattle*; *bush pig*). **4** of or pertaining to rural, as opposed to urban, life (*bush race-meeting*). **5** (in Aboriginal English) traditional or Aboriginal as opposed to European. □ **go bush 1** escape or disappear from one's usual haunts. **2** (of Aborigines) return to traditional life. **3** leave urban life for that of the country; visit the country. **4** (of fauna and flora) become wild (*brumbies are horses that had gone bush*). take to the bush **1** (orig. of convicts) escape from custody; run away. **2** (of animals) run wild. [Old English and Old Norse]

**bush²** /buush/ — *n.* **1** metal lining for a hole enclosing a revolving shaft etc. **2** sleeve giving electrical insulation. — *v.* fit with a bush. [Dutch *busse* box]

**bush ballad** *n.* folk-song of the bush.

**bush band** *n.* band which specialises in Australian folk-music, and which uses distinctively Australian instruments, e.g. the lagerphone.

**bush-bash** *v.* = SCRUB-BASH.

**bush bread** *n.* damper.

**bush capital** *n.* Canberra.

**bush carpenter** *n.* amateur, rough-and-ready carpenter.

**bush craft** *n.* knowledge of how to live or survive in the bush.

**bush cucumber** see ALUNQUA.

**bush cure** *n.* traditional or household remedy (*goanna oil, the famed bush cure*).

**bushed** *adj. colloq.* **1** lost in the bush. **2** tired out, exhausted. **3** bewildered (*problem has me bushed*).

**bushel** /buush-uhl/ *n.* measure of capacity for corn, fruit, etc. in the imperial system (8 gallons or 36.4 litres). [French]

**bushfire** *n.* fire which burns through (often extensive) areas of natural vegetation, often causing loss of life and property. □ **get on like a bushfire** *colloq.* get on or communicate extremely well.

**bushfire brigade** *n.* volunteer fire-fighting organisation.

**bush fly** *n.* small fly which settles persistently on the eyes, mouth, etc., of humans and animals.

**bush food** *n.* traditional Aboriginal food, esp. if hunted or gathered in traditional fashion.

**bush hay** *n.* hay made from native grasses.

**bush house** *n.* **1** roughly-built dwelling in the country. **2** dwelling occupied by a rural commune.

**bushie** /buush-ee/ (also **bushy**) — *adj.*

countrified; lacking the (supposed) refinements of urban life. — *n.* person who lives in the country as opposed to the town; person whose manner or appearance indicates this.

**bush kangaroo** *n.* medium-sized kangaroo.

**bush lawyer** *n.* **1** person claiming legal knowledge without qualifications for it. **2** argumentative person who offers seemingly legal arguments in support of a case.

**bushman** *n.* **1** person skilled and experienced in travelling through bush country. **2** person who lives in the bush. **3** unskilled country labourer. **4** (**Bushman**) member or language of a S.African aboriginal people. □ **bushmanship** *n.*

**bushman's clock** *n.* = KOOKABURRA.

**bush medicine** *n.* traditional Aboriginal medicine.

**bush mile** *n.* approximate and, because of the winding nature of roads or tracks in the bush, usu. underestimated measurement.

**bush mouse** *n.* any of many small Australian mammals, esp. the marsupial hopping mouse.

**bush name** *n.* Aboriginal language name (for a place etc.).

**bushrange** *v.* hold up and rob (travellers, dwellings, etc.). [back-formation from BUSHRANGER]

**bushranger** *n.* **1** *hist.* person who engages in armed robbery, escaping into, or living in, the bush in the manner of an outlaw. **2** person or business etc. seen as making extortionate demands, charging exorbitant prices, etc. (*those bushrangers in the income-tax department*). □ **bushranging** *n.*

**bush rat** *n.* any of several rat-sized Australian marsupials and rodents.

**bush sickness** *n.* disease of animals due to a lack of cobalt in the soil.

**bush telegraph** — *n.* **1** *hist.* person who alerts a bushranger to police movements or to a potential victim. **2 a** (also **mulga wire**) informal network by which information is conveyed in remote areas. **b** the information so conveyed; rumour. **3 a** (also **mulga wire**) means of very effective long-distance communication used by Aborigines, usu. employing smoke signals. **b** the message so conveyed. — *v.* communicate (information) by means of a bush telegraph. □ **bush telegraphy** /tuh-**leg**-ruh-fee/ *n.*

**bush tucker** *n.* traditional Aboriginal food.

**bush turkey** *n.* = BRUSH TURKEY.

**bush walk** — *n.* **1** (of an Aborigine) = WALKABOUT *n.* **2.** **2** a hike in the bush, esp. including camping out etc. — *v.* **1** (of an Aborigine) go walkabout. **2** take a (usu. extended) hike in the bush. □ **bushwalker** *n.* **bushwalking** *n.*

**bush week** *n.* **1** (fictitious) time when people from the country come to town and are easy targets for con-men etc. **2** (at some universities) period of student festivity, pranks, etc. □ **what do you think this is — bush week?** response to a request etc., implying that one is being unfairly imposed upon or taken for a (rustic) fool.

**bushwhack** *v.* **1** clear ground in bush country. **2** live or travel in bush country. **3** (as **bushwhacked** *adj.*) utterly exhausted. □ **bushwhacking** *n.* [back-formation from BUSHWHACKER]

**bushwhacker** /buush-ˌwak-uh/ *n.* **1** person who clears land in bush country by felling etc. **2** person who lives or travels in bush country; BUSHIE. [BUSH, WHACK]

**bushy** *adj.* (**-ier**, **-iest**) **1** covered with bush. **2** growing thickly like a bush. **3** having many bushes. **4** = BUSHIE.

**bushy yate** *n.* WA eucalypt, rounded in form, having large ball-shaped clusters of green flowers and large fruit (see YATE).

**business** /biz-nuhs/ *n.* **1** one's regular occupation or profession. **2** one's own concern. **3** task or duty. **4** serious work or activity. **5** (in Aboriginal English) traditional lore and ritual (see also SUNDAY BUSINESS). **6** (difficult or unpleasant) matter or affair (*sick of the whole business*). **7** thing(s) needing attention or discussion (*the business of the day*). **8** buying and selling; trade. **9** commercial firm. **10** *Theatr.* action on stage. □ **mean business** *colloq.* be in earnest. **mind one's own business** not meddle. [Old English: related to BUSY]

**business ground** *n.* (in Aboriginal English) ceremonial site (see BUSINESS 5).

**businesslike** *adj.* efficient, systematic.

**businessman** *n.* (*fem.* **businesswoman**) man or woman engaged in trade or commerce.

**busk** *v.* perform esp. music in the street etc. for tips. □ **busker** *n.* [obsolete *busk* peddle]

**bust**[1] *n.* **1** human chest, esp. of a woman; bosom. **2** sculpture of a person's head, shoulders, and chest. □ **busty** *adj.* (**-ier**, **-iest**). [French from Italian]

**bust**[2] *colloq.* — *v.* (*past* and *past part.* **busted** or **bust**) **1** break, burst. **2** (esp. of the police) **a** raid, search. **b** arrest. **3** gatecrash (a party etc.). **4** break, tame (a brumby etc.). — *n.* **1** police raid. **2** sudden failure; bankruptcy. — *adj.* (also **busted**) **1** broken, burst. **2** bankrupt. □ **be busting 1** be hard pressed to urinate. **2** be very keen to do something (*am busting to go on the trip*). **bust up 1** bring or come to collapse; explode. **2** (esp. of a couple in a relationship) quarrel and separate. **3** wreck. **4** disrupt (a meeting, a gathering, etc.). [var. of BURST]

**bustard** /bus-tuhd/ *n.* **1** large land bird of Europe and Asia that can run very fast. **2** Australian bird of the same family, also known as PLAIN TURKEY. [Latin *avis tarda* slow bird ('slow' unexplained)]

**buster**[1] *n. colloq.* (often *derog.*) mate; fellow. [from BUST[2]]

**buster**[2] *n.* strong squally wind, esp. from the south. [abbreviation of SOUTHERLY BUSTER]

**-buster** *comb. form* indicating that which: **1** eradicates (*dirt-buster; ghost-buster*). **2** destroys (*crime-buster; the post-Christmas sale was a door-buster*). **3** stretches to the full (*brain-buster; back-buster*).

**bustier** /bus-tee-uh/ *n.* strapless close-fitting bodice. [French]

**bustle**[1] /bus-uhl/ — *v.* (**-ling**) **1** (often foll. by *about*) (cause to) move busily and energetically. **2** (as **bustling** *adj.*) active, lively. — *n.* excited or energetic activity [perhaps from obsolete *busk* prepare]

**bustle**[2] /bus-uhl/ *n. hist.* padding worn under a skirt to puff it out behind. [origin unknown]

**bust-up** *n. colloq.* **1** violent quarrel. **2** (esp. of a couple in a relationship) acrimonious separation. **3** (of a business etc.) collapse. **4** wild party.

**busy** /biz-ee/ — *adj.* (**-ier**, **-iest**) **1** occupied or engaged in work etc. **2** full of activity (*busy evening; busy street*). **3** (of a telephone line) engaged. — *v.* (**-ies**, **-ied**) (often *refl.*) keep busy; occupy (*busied himself sorting out his notes*). □ **busily** *adv.* [Old English]

**busybody** *n.* (*pl.* **-ies**) meddlesome person.

**but** /but, buht/ — *conj.* **1 a** nevertheless however (*tried but failed; I am old, but I am not feeble*). **b** on the other hand; on the contrary (*I am old but you are young*). **2** except, otherwise than (*cannot choose but do it; what could we do but run?*). **3** without the result that (*it never rains but it pours*). — *prep.* except; apart from other than (*all cried but me; nothing but trouble*). — *adv.* **1** only; no more than only just (*we can but try; is but a child had but arrived*). **2** in emphatic repetition; definitely (*would see nobody, but* *nobody*). **3** *colloq.* at the end of a phrase or sentence) though; however; no doubt about it (*I didn't like it, but*). — *rel. pron.* who not; that not (*not a man but feels pity*). — *n.* objection (*ifs and buts*). □ **all but** see ALL. **but for** without the help or hindrance etc. of (*but for you I'd be rich*). **but one** (or **two** etc.) excluding one (or two etc.) from the number (*next door but one; last but one*). **but then** however (*I won, but then I am older*). [Old English]

●**utane** /ˈbyoo-tayn, byoo-ˈtayn/ *n.* gaseous alkane hydrocarbon, used in liquefied form as fuel. [from BUTYL]

●**utch** /buuch/ *adj. colloq.* masculine; tough-looking. [origin uncertain]

●**utcher** /ˈbuuch-uh/ — *n.* **1 a** person who deals in meat. **b** person who slaughters animals for food. **2** brutal murderer. — *v.* **1** slaughter or cut up (an animal) for food. **2** kill wantonly or cruelly. **3** *colloq.* ruin through incompetence (*butchered the piece he played on the violin*). [French *boc* BUCK[1]]

●**utcherbird** *n.* any of several birds of Australia and New Zealand, having black and white plumage and hook-tipped bills, noted for their predatory habits (including impaling lizards etc. on twigs in order to tear them apart) (*black butcherbird; pied butcherbird*).

●**utchery** *n.* (*pl.* **-ies**) **1** needless or cruel slaughter (of people). **2** butcher's trade.

●**utler** *n.* principal male servant of a household. [French *bouteille* bottle]

●**utt**[1] — *v.* **1** push or strike with the head or horns. **2** project, jut out. — *n.* a push with the head or horns. □ **butt in** interrupt, meddle. **butt out** *colloq.* cease to interfere or meddle (*asked him to butt out of her affairs*). [French from Germanic]

●**utt**[2] *n.* **1** (often foll. by *of*) object of ridicule etc. (*you're the butt of all his jokes*). **2 a** mound behind a target. **b** (in *pl.*) shooting-range. [French *but* goal]

●**utt**[3] *n.* **1** thicker end, esp. of a tool or weapon. **2** stub of a cigarette etc. **3** *colloq.* buttocks. [Dutch]

●**utt**[4] *n.* cask. [Latin *buttis*]

●**utter** — *n.* **1** solidified churned cream, used as a spread and in cooking. **2** substance of similar texture (*peanut butter*). — *v.* spread, cook, or serve with butter. □ **butter up** *colloq.* flatter. [Greek *bouturon*]

●**uttercup** *n.* (also **ranunculus**) plant of all States except WA, having many bright usu. buttery-yellow cup-shaped flowers.

●**utter-fingers** *n. colloq.* person prone to drop things.

●**utterfish** see MULLOWAY.

**butterfly** *n.* (*pl.* **-flies**) **1** insect with four usu. brightly coloured wings. **2** (in *pl.*) *colloq.* nervous sensation in the stomach. **3** = BUTTERFLY STROKE.

**butterfly nut** *n.* a kind of wing-nut.

**butterfly stroke** *n.* stroke in swimming, with arms raised and lifted forwards together.

**buttermilk** *n.* **1** liquid left after churning butter. **2** (in full **cultured buttermilk**) low-fat fermented milk beverage.

**butternut** *n.* a kind of pumpkin.

**butterscotch** *n.* brittle toffee made from butter, brown sugar, etc.

**buttock** /ˈbut-uhk/ *n.* **1** each of the two fleshy protuberances on the lower part of the human body. **2** corresponding part of an animal. [*butt* ridge]

**button** /ˈbut-uhn/ — *n.* **1** small disc etc. sewn to a garment as a fastener or worn as an ornament. **2** small round knob etc. pressed to operate electronic equipment. — *v.* = *button up* 1. □ **button up 1** fasten with buttons. **2** *colloq.* complete satisfactorily. **3** *colloq.* be silent. [French from Germanic]

**button grass** *n.* **1** large, tufted sedge bearing button-like flowers on tall thin stalks and forming distinctive plains esp. in western Tasmania. **2** short-lived annual grass of mainland Australia.

**buttonhole** — *n.* **1** slit in cloth for a button. **2** flower etc. worn in a lapel buttonhole. — *v.* (**-ling**) *colloq.* accost and detain (a reluctant listener).

**button quail** *n.* either of two quail-like Australian birds (related to the true quail of Australia, but smaller in size and lacking a hind toe): the painted button-quail and the chestnut-backed button-quail.

**buttress** /ˈbut-ruhs/ — *n.* **1** projecting support built against a wall. **2** source of help etc. — *v.* (often foll. by *up*) **1** support with a buttress. **2** support by argument etc. (*buttressed by facts*). [related to BUTT[1]]

**butyl** /ˈbyoo-tuhl/ *n.* the univalent alkyl radical $C_4H_9$. [Latin *butyrum* BUTTER]

**buxom** /ˈbuk-suhm/ *adj.* (esp. of a woman) plump and healthy-looking; having a big bust. [earlier = *pliant*: related to BOW[2]]

**buy** /buy/ — *v.* (**buys, buying**; *past* and *past part.* **bought** /bawt/ ) **1 a** obtain for money etc. **b** serve to obtain (*money can't buy happiness; the best that money can buy*). **2 a** procure by bribery etc. (*bought his silence*). **b** bribe. **3** get by sacrifice, great effort, etc. (*dearly bought*). **4** *colloq.* believe in, accept (*he bought the story, he's so gullible*). **5** be a buyer for a store etc. — *n. colloq.* purchase. □ **buy in** buy a stock of. **buy into 1** pay for a share in (an enterprise). **2** (also **buy in**) *colloq.* involve oneself in (an activity). **buy off** pay to get rid of. **buy out** pay (a person) for ownership, an interest, etc. **buy up 1** buy as much as possible of. **2** absorb (a firm etc.) by purchase. [Old English]

**buyer** *n.* **1** person employed to purchase stock for a large store etc. **2** purchaser, customer.

**buzz** — *n.* **1** hum of a bee etc. **2** sound of a buzzer. **3 a** low murmur as of conversation. **b** stir; hurried activity (*buzz of excitement*). **4** *colloq.* telephone call. **5** *colloq.* thrill. **6** *colloq.* rumour. — *v.* **1** hum. **2 a** summon with a buzzer. **b** *colloq.* telephone. **3 a** (often foll. by *about*) move busily. **b** (of a place) appear busy or full of excitement. **4** *Aeron. colloq.* fly (an aircraft) fast and very close to. □ **buzz off** *colloq.* go or hurry away. [imitative]

**buzzard** /**buz**-uhd/ *n.* large bird of the hawk family. [Latin *buteo* falcon]

**buzzer** *n.* electrical buzzing device as a signal.

**buzz-saw** *n.* circular saw.

**buzzword** *n. colloq.* fashionable technical or specialist word; catchword.

**by** /buy/ — *prep.* **1** near, beside (*sit by me*; *path by the river*). **2** through the agency or means of (*by proxy*; *poem by Judith Wright*; *by bus*; *by cheating*; *divide by two*; *killed by robbers*). **3** not later than (*by next week*). **4 a** past, beyond (*drove by the church*). **b** through; via (*went by Paris*). **5** during (*by day*; *by daylight*). **6** to the extent of (*missed by a foot*; *better by far*). **7** according to; using as a standard or unit (*judge by appearances*; *paid by the hour*). **8** with the succession of (*worse by the minute*; *day by day*). **9** concerning; in respect of (*did our duty by them*; *Smith by name*). **10** used in mild oaths (*by God*). **11** expressing dimensions of an area etc. (*three metres by two*). **12** avoiding, ignoring (*passed us by*). **13** inclining to (*north by north-west*). — *adv.* **1** near (*sat by*). **2** aside; in reserve (*put $100 by*). **3** past (*marched by*). — *n.* (*pl.* **byes**) = BYE¹. □ **by and by** before long; eventually. **by and large** on the whole. **by the by** (or **bye**) incidentally. **by oneself 1** unaided. **2** alone. [Old English]

**by-** *prefix* subordinate, incidental (*by-effect*; *byroad*).

**bye¹** /buy/ *n.* **1** *Cricket* run scored from a ball that passes the batsman without being hit. **2 a** status of an unpaired

competitor in a sport, who proceeds to the next round by default. **b** (in a competition with an uneven number of teams) status of a team not having a match in a particular round (*the Raiders have a bye this week*). [from BY as a noun]

**bye²** /buy/ *int.* (also **bye-bye**) *colloq.* = GOODBYE. [abbreviation]

**by-election** *n.* election to fill a vacancy arising between general elections.

**Byelorussian** /byel-oh-**rush**-uhn/ — *n.* native or language of Byelorussia in eastern Europe. — *adj.* of Byelorussia, its people, or language. [Russian from *belyĭ* white, *Russiya* Russia]

**bygone** — *adj.* past, antiquated. — *n.* (in phr. **let bygones be bygones**) forgive and forget past quarrels.

**by-law** *n.* regulation made by a local government authority or corporation. [obsolete *by* town]

**byline** *n.* **1** line naming the writer of a newspaper article etc. **2** secondary line of work. **3** goal-line or touch-line.

**BYO** /bee-wuy-**oh**/ *abbr.* bring-your-own. **1 a** intimation to patrons of an unlicensed restaurant that they may bring their own liquor. **b** such a restaurant. **2** pertaining to a barbecue, party, etc. to which people bring their own liquor (*BYO barbie at Bob's*).

**bypass** — *n.* **1** main road passing round a town or its centre. **2 a** secondary channel or pipe etc. used in emergencies. **b** alternative passage, provided by surgery for the circulation of blood through the heart. — *v.* avoid, go round (a town, difficulty, etc.).

**by-product** *n.* **1** incidental product made in the manufacture of something else. **2** secondary result.

**bystander** *n.* person present but not taking part; onlooker.

**byte** /buyt/ *n. Computing* group of eight binary digits, often representing one character. [origin uncertain]

**byway** *n.* **1** little used or secluded road or path. **2** minor activity.

**byword** *n.* **1** person or thing as a notable example (*is a byword for luxury*). **2** familiar saying.

**Byzantine** /biz-uhn-,teen, -,tuyn, bi-**zan**-,tuyn, buy-/ — *adj.* **1** of Byzantium or the E. Roman Empire. **2** of its highly decorated style of architecture. — *n.* citizen of Byzantium or the E. Roman Empire. □ **Byzantinism** *n.* **Byzantinist** *n.* [Latin *Byzantium*, now Istanbul]

# C

**C¹** /see/ *n.* (*pl.* **Cs** or **C's**) **1** (also **c**) third letter of the alphabet. **2** *Mus.* first note of the diatonic scale of C major. **3** third hypothetical person or example. **4** third highest category (of academic marks etc.). **5** *Algebra* (usu. **c**) third known quantity. **6** (as a Roman numeral) 100. **7** (also ©) copyright.

**C²** *symb.* carbon.

**C³** *abbr.* (also **C.**) **1** Celsius, Centigrade. **2** coulomb(s), capacitance.

**c.** *abbr.* **1** century. **2** cent(s).

**c.** *abbr. circa.*

**Ca** *symb.* calcium.

**ca.** *abbr. circa.*

**cab** *n.* **1** taxi. **2** driver's compartment in a truck, train, or crane, etc. □ **first cab off the rank** *colloq.* first to seize an opportunity; first to do something. [abbreviation of *cabriolet* two-wheeled one-horse carriage]

**cabal** /kuh-**bahl**, kuh-**bal**/ *n.* **1** secret intrigue. **2** political clique or faction. [French from Latin]

**cabana¹** /kuh-**bah**-nuh/ *n.* hut or shelter at a beach or swimming-pool. [Spanish]

**cabana²** *n.* spicy sausage, eaten cold. [origin unknown]

**cabanossi** /kab-uh-**nos**-ee/ *n.* spicy sausage, eaten cold. [origin unknown]

**cabaret** /**kab**-uh-,ray/ *n.* **1** entertainment in a nightclub or restaurant. **2** such a nightclub etc. [French, = tavern]

**cabbage** /**kab**-ij/ *n.* **1** vegetable with a round head and green or purple leaves. **2** *colloq.* person who is inactive or lacks interest. [French *caboche* head]

**cabbage gum** *n.* any of several eucalypts and angophoras (so called because of the softness of the timber, or because of the smell of the tree).

**cabbage tree** *n.* (also **cabbage-tree palm**) any of several palms of northern and central Australia, the young growing shoots or central mass of which are edible.

**cabbage-tree hat** *n. hist.* wide-brimmed hat woven from cabbage-tree leaves, a symbol of distinctive Australianness.

**cabbage-tree mob** *n. hist.* collective term for a class of young urban larrikins in colonial Australia, distinguished by their wearing of cabbage-tree hats as an emblem of pride.

**cabbala** /kuh-**bah**-luh, **kab**-uh-luh/ *n.* (also **cabala**) **1** Jewish mystical tradition. **2** any esoteric doctrine or occult lore. □ **cabbalism** *n.* **cabbalist** *n.* **cabbalistic** *adj.* [Rabbinical Hebrew, = tradition]

**cabernet sauvignon** /,kab-uh-nay **soh**-vi-nyon/ *n.* kind of grape used in making a claret-type wine.

**cabin** /**kab**-uhn/ *n.* **1** small shelter or house, esp. of wood. **2** room or compartment in an aircraft or ship for passengers or crew. **3** driver's cab. [French from Latin]

**cabinet** /**kab**-uh-nuht/ *n.* **1** cupboard or case for storing or displaying things. **2** (**Cabinet**) committee of senior ministers in a government. [diminutive of CABIN]

**cabinet-maker** *n.* skilled joiner.

**cable** /**kay**-buhl/ — *n.* **1** encased group of insulated wires for transmitting electricity etc. **2** (also **cable TV**) = CABLE TELEVISION. **3** thick rope of wire or hemp. **4** cablegram. **5** (in full **cable stitch**) knitting stitch resembling twisted rope. — *v.* (**-ling**) transmit (a message) or inform (a person) by cablegram. [Latin *caplum* halter, from Arabic *ḥabl*]

**cable car** *n.* small cabin suspended on a looped cable, for carrying passengers up and down a mountain etc.

**cablegram** *n.* telegraph message sent by undersea cable.

**cable television** *n.* **1** television transmission by cable to subscribers. **2** the stations and programmes that make use of this system.

**caboodle** /kuh-**boo**-duhl/ *n.* □ **the whole caboodle** (also **the whole kit and caboodle**) *colloq.* the whole lot. [origin uncertain]

**caboose** /kuh-**boos**/ *n.* kitchen on a ship's deck. [Dutch]

**cacao** /kuh-**kay**-oh/ *n.* (*pl.* **-s**) **1** seed from which cocoa and chocolate are made. **2** tree bearing these. [Spanish from Nahuatl]

**cachalot** /**kash**-uh-,lot, -,loht/ *n.* sperm whale. [French from Spanish and Portuguese]

**cache** /kash/ — *n.* **1** hiding-place for treasure, stores, guns, etc. **2** things so hidden. **3** (in full **cache memory**) high-speed computer memory used to improve performance. — *v.* (**-ching**) **1** put in a cache. **2** *Computing* put in cache memory. [French *cacher* hide]

141

**cachet** /**kash**-ay/ n. **1** prestige. **2** distinguishing mark or seal. [French *cacher* press]

**cack-handed** /kak-**han**-duhd/ adj. colloq. **1** clumsy. **2** left-handed. [British dial. *cack* excrement]

**cackle** /**kak**-uhl/ — n. **1** clucking of a hen etc. **2** raucous laugh. **3** noisy inconsequential chatter. — v. (**-ling**) **1** emit a cackle. **2** chatter noisily. [imitative]

**cacophony** /kuh-**kof**-uh-nee/ n. (pl. **-ies**) harsh discordant sound. □ **cacophonous** adj. [Greek *kakos* bad, *phōnē* sound]

**cactus** /**kak**-tuhs/ n. (pl. **-ti** /-tuy/ or **cactuses**) plant with a thick fleshy stem and usu. spines but no leaves, and brilliantly coloured flowers. □ **in the cactus** colloq. in difficulty. [Latin from Greek]

**cad** n. man who behaves dishonourably. □ **caddish** adj. [abbreviation of CADDIE]

**cadaver** /kuh-**dah**-vuh, -**dav**-uh/ n. esp. Med. corpse. [Latin *cado* fall]

**cadaverous** /kuh-**dav**-uh-ruhs/ adj. corpselike; very pale and thin.

**caddie** /**kad**-ee/ (also **caddy**) — n. (pl. **-ies**) person who carries a golfer's clubs during play. — v. (**-ies, -ied, caddying**) act as a caddie. [French CADET]

**caddy**[1] /**kad**-ee/ n. (pl. **-ies**) small container for tea. [Malay]

**caddy**[2] var. of CADDIE.

**cadence** /**kay**-duhns/ n. **1** rhythm; the measure or beat of a sound or movement. **2** fall in pitch of the voice. **3** tonal inflection. **4** close of a musical phrase. [Latin *cado* fall]

**cadenza** /kuh-**den**-zuh/ n. virtuoso passage for a soloist, usu. near the close of a movement of a concerto. [Italian: related to CADENCE]

**cadet** /kuh-**det**/ n. **1** young trainee for the armed services, police force, journalism, etc. **2** member of a military training corps in a secondary school. □ **cadetship** n. [French, ultimately from Latin *caput* head]

**cadge** v. (**-ging**) colloq. get or seek by begging or 'borrowing'. [origin unknown]

**cadmium** /**kad**-mee-uhm/ n. soft bluish-white metallic element used in the manufacture of solders and in electro-plating. [Greek *kadmia* Cadmean (earth)]

**cadre** /**kah**-duh/ n. basic unit, esp. of servicemen, forming a nucleus for expansion when necessary. [French from Latin *quadrus* square]

**caecum** /**see**-kuhm/ n. (pl. **-ca**) blind-ended pouch at the junction of the small and large intestines. [Latin *caecus* blind]

**Caenozoic** var. of CENOZOIC.

**Caesar** /**see**-zuh/ n. **1** title of Roman emperors. **2** autocrat. [Latin (C. Julius) *Caesar*]

**Caesarean** /suh-**zair**-ree-uhn/ — adj. (of birth) effected by Caesarean section. — n. Caesarean section. [from CAESAR: Julius Caesar was supposedly born this way]

**Caesarean section** n. delivery of a child by cutting through the mother's abdomen.

**caesium** /**see**-zee-uhm/ n. (also **cesium**) soft silver-white element. [Latin *caesius* blue-grey]

**caesura** /suh-**zyoor**-uh/ n. (pl. **-s**) pause in a line of verse. □ **caesural** adj. [Latin *caedo caes-* cut]

**café** /**kaf**-ay/ n. small coffee-house or restaurant. [French]

**caffe latte** /ˌkaf-ay **lah**-tay/ n. coffee with milk, white coffee. [Italian]

**cafeteria** /ˌkaf-uh-**teer**-ree-uh/ n. self-service restaurant. [American Spanish, = coffee-shop]

**cafetière** /ˌkaf-uh-tee-**air**/ n. coffee pot with a plunger for pressing grounds to the bottom.

**caffeine** /**kaf**-een/ n. alkaloid stimulant in tea-leaves and coffee beans. [French *café* coffee]

**caftan** /**kaf**-tan/ n. (also **kaftan**) **1** long tunic worn by men in SW Asia. **2** long loose dress or shirt. [Turkish]

**cage** — n. **1** structure of bars or wires, esp. for confining animals or birds. **2** similar open framework, esp. a lift in a mine etc. — v. (**-ging**) place or keep in a cage. [Latin *cavea*]

**cagey** /**kay**-jee/ adj. (also **cagy**) (**-ier, -iest**) colloq. cautious and non-committal. □ **cagily** adv. **caginess** n. [origin unknown]

**cahoots** /kuh-**hoots**/ n.pl. □ **in cahoots** colloq. in collusion. [origin uncertain]

**Cain** □ **raise Cain** colloq. make a disturbance; create trouble. [*Cain*, eldest son of Adam (Gen. 4)]

**Cainozoic** var. of CENOZOIC.

**cairn** n. mound of stones as a monument or landmark. [Gaelic]

**caisson** /**kay**-suhn/ n. watertight chamber for underwater construction work. [Italian *cassone*]

**cajole** /kuh-**johl**/ v. (**-ling**) persuade by flattery, deceit, etc. □ **cajolery** n. [French]

**cake** — n. **1** mixture of flour, butter, eggs, sugar, etc., baked in the oven and often iced and decorated. **2** other food in a flat round shape (*fish cake*). **3** flattish compact mass (*cake of soap*). — v. (**-king**)

**1** form into a compact mass. **2** (usu. foll. by *with*) cover (with a hard or sticky mass). □ **have one's cake and eat it** *colloq.* enjoy both of two mutually exclusive alternatives. **a piece of cake** *colloq.* something easily achieved. **sell** (or **go**) **like hot cakes** *colloq.* be sold (or go) quickly; be popular. **take the cake** see TAKE. [Old Norse]

**cake-hole** *n. colloq.* mouth.

**Cal** *abbr.* large calorie(s).

**cal** *abbr.* small calorie(s).

**calabash** /kal-uh-ˌbash/ *n.* **1** gourd-bearing tree of tropical America. **2** such a gourd, esp. as a vessel for water, etc. [French from Spanish]

**caladenia** /kal-uh-dee-nee-uh/ *n.* any of nearly 70 species of terrestrial orchid endemic to Australia, having extremely showy flowers (some species being known also as spider orchids) (*blue caladenia; Blubeard caladenia; black-tongue caladenia; bronze caladenia;* etc.).

**calamari** /ˌkal-uh-mah-ree/ *n.* any mollusc with a long, tapering, pen-like, horny shell, esp. a squid; used as a food. [Italian, from Latin *calamus* pen]

**calamine** /kal-uh-ˌmuyn/ *n.* powdered form of zinc carbonate and ferric oxide used as a skin lotion. [French from Latin]

**calamity** /kuh-lam-uh-tee/ *n.* (*pl.* **-ies**) disaster, great misfortune. □ **calamitous** *adj.* [French from Latin]

**calcareous** /kal-kair-ree-uhs/ *adj.* of or containing calcium carbonate. [related to CALX]

**calces** *pl.* of CALX.

**calciferol** /kal-sif-uh-ˌrol/ *n.* vitamin (D₂) promoting calcium deposition in the bones. [related to CALX]

**calciferous** /kal-sif-uh-ruhs/ *adj.* yielding calcium salts, esp. calcium carbonate.

**calcify** /kal-suh-ˌfuy/ *v.* (**-ies, -ied**) **1** harden by the depositing of calcium salts. **2** convert or be converted to calcium carbonate. □ **calcification** /-fuh-kay-shuhn/ *n.*

**calcine** /kal-suhn, -suyn/ *v.* (**-ning**) decompose or be decomposed by strong heat. □ **calcination** /-nay-shuhn/ *n.* [French or medieval Latin: related to CALX]

**calcite** /kal-suyt/ *n.* natural crystalline calcium carbonate. [Latin: related to CALX]

**calcium** /kal-see-uhm/ *n.* soft grey metallic element occurring in limestone, marble, chalk, etc. [related to CALX]

**calcium carbide** *n.* greyish solid used in the production of acetylene.

**calcium carbonate** *n.* white insoluble solid occurring as chalk, marble, etc.

**calcium hydroxide** *n.* white crystalline powder used in the manufacture of mortar.

**calcium oxide** *n.* white crystalline solid from which many calcium compounds are manufactured.

**calculate** /kal-kyuh-ˌlayt/ *v.* (**-ting**) **1** ascertain or forecast esp. by mathematics or reckoning. **2** plan deliberately. **3** (foll. by *on*) rely on; reckon on (*calculated on a quick response*). □ **calculable** *adj.* [Latin: related to CALCULUS]

**calculated** *adj.* **1** (of an action) done deliberately or with foreknowledge (*a calculated risk*). **2** (foll. by *to* + infin.) designed or suitable; intended (*calculated to offend*).

**calculating** *adj.* (of a person) scheming, mercenary.

**calculation** /ˌkal-kyuh-lay-shuhn/ *n.* act, process, or result of calculating. [Latin: related to CALCULUS]

**calculator** *n.* device (esp. a small electronic one) for making mathematical calculations.

**calculus** /kal-kyuh-luhs/ *n.* (*pl.* **-luses** or **-li** /-ˌluy/) **1** particular method of mathematical calculation or reasoning. **2** stone or mineral mass formed within the body. [Latin, = small stone (used on an abacus)]

**caldron** var. of CAULDRON.

**calendar** /kal-uhn-duh/ *n.* **1** system fixing the year's beginning, length, and subdivision. **2** chart etc. showing such subdivisions. **3** timetable of dates, events, etc. [ultimately from Latin *Kalendae* first day of a month]

**calendar year** *n.* period from 1 Jan. to 31 Dec. inclusive.

**calender** /kal-uhn-duh/ — *n.* machine in which cloth, paper, etc. is rolled to glaze or smooth it. — *v.* press in a calender. [French]

**calf¹** /kahf/ *n.* (*pl.* **calves** /kahvz/) **1** young cow or bull. **2** young of other animals, e.g. the elephant, deer, and whale. [Old English]

**calf²** /kahf/ *n.* (*pl.* **calves**) fleshy hind part of the human leg below the knee. [Old Norse]

**calf love** *n.* = PUPPY LOVE.

**calibrate** /kal-uh-ˌbrayt/ *v.* (**-ting**) **1** mark (a gauge) with a scale of readings. **2** correlate the readings of (an instrument or system of measurement) with a standard. **3** determine the calibre of (a gun). □ **calibration** /-bray-shuhn/ *n.*

**calibre** /kal-uh-buh/ *n.* **1 a** internal diameter of a gun or tube. **b** diameter of a bullet or shell. **2** strength or quality of character; ability, importance (*the job* *needs someone of your calibre*). [French from Italian from Arabic *kālib* mould]

**calices** pl. of CALIX.

**calicivirus** /kuh-**lee**-see/ n. any of a number of viruses characterised by having cup-like indentations, e.g. feline calicivirus (which causes an influenza-like disease in cats), rabbit calicivirus (which kills rabbits). [Latin *calix* cup, chalice]

**calico** /**kal**-i-,koh/ — n. (pl. **-es** or **-s**) cotton cloth, esp. plain white or un-bleached. — adj. of calico. [*Calicut* in India]

**californium** /,kal-uh-**faw**-nee-uhm/ n. artificial radioactive metallic element. [*California* in US, where first made]

**caliper** var. of CALLIPER.

**caliph** /**kay**-luhf/ n. esp. *hist.* chief Muslim civil and religious ruler. □ **caliphate** n. [Arabic, = successor (of Muhammad)]

**calisthenics** var. of CALLISTHENICS.

**calix** /**kay**-liks, **kal**-iks/ n. (pl. **calices** /-luh-,seez/) cup-like cavity or organ. [Latin *calix* cup]

**call** /kawl/ — v. **1 a** (often foll. by *out*) cry, shout; speak loudly. **b** (of a bird etc.) emit its characteristic sound. **2 a** communicate with by telephone or radio. **b** broadcast a description of a race as it is being run. **3 a** summon (*will you call the children?*). **b** arrange for (a person or thing) to come or be present (*called a taxi*). **4** (often foll. by *at, in, on*) pay a brief visit. **5 a** order to take place (*called a meeting*). **b** direct to happen; announce (*call a halt*). **6** name; describe as. **7** regard as (*I call that silly*). **8** rouse from sleep (*call me at 8*). **9** (foll. by *for*) order; demand (*called for silence*). **10** (foll. by *on, upon*) invoke; appeal to; request or require (*called on us to be quiet*). **11** name (a suit) in bidding at cards. **12** guess the outcome of tossing a coin etc. — n. **1** shout, cry. **2** characteristic cry of a bird etc. **3** brief visit. **4 a** act of telephoning. **b** telephone conversation. **5 a** invitation, summons. **b** vocation; appeal or invitation (from a specific source or discerned by a person's conscience etc.) to follow a certain profession, set of principles, etc. (*call of the sea; obeyed the call to be a Jesuit; heard God's call for her to be a priest*). **6** need, occasion (*no call for rudeness*). **7** demand (*a call on one's time*). **8** signal on a bugle etc. **9** option of buying stock at a fixed price at a given date. **10** *Cards* **a** player's right or turn to make a bid. **b** bid made. **11** broadcast description of a race in progress. □ **call in 1** withdraw from circulation. **2** seek the advice or services of (*called in a plumber*). **call off 1** cancel

(an arrangement). **2** order (an attacker or pursuer) to desist. **call out 1** summon to action. **2** order (workers) to strike. **call the shots** (or **tune**) *colloq.* be in control; take the initiative. **call up 1** telephone. **2** imagine, recollect. **3** summon to military service. **on call 1** (of a doctor etc.) available if required. **2** (of money lent) repayable on demand. [Old English from Old Norse]

**caller** n. **1** person who calls, esp. one who pays a visit or makes a telephone call. **2** person who broadcasts a description of a race as it is being run.

**call-girl** n. prostitute accepting appointments by telephone.

**calligraphy** /kuh-**lig**-ruh-fee/ n. **1** handwriting, esp. when fine. **2** art of this. □ **calligrapher** n. **calligraphic** /-**graf**-ik/ adj. **calligraphist** n. [Greek *kallos* beauty]

**calling** n. **1** profession or occupation. **2** inwardly felt call or summons; vocation.

**calliper** /**kal**-uh-puh/ n. (also **caliper**) **1** (in pl.) compasses for measuring diameters etc. **2** metal splint to support the leg. [var. of CALIBRE]

**callistemon** /kuh-**lis**-tuh-muhn/ n. = BOTTLEBRUSH 1. [Greek, = beautiful thread]

**callisthenics** /,kal-uhs-**then**-iks/ n.pl. (also **calisthenics**) exercises for fitness and grace. □ **callisthenic** adj. [Greek *kallos* beauty, *sthenos* strength]

**Callitris** /kuh-**luy**-truhs/ n. mainly Australian genus of coniferous trees (see CYPRESS PINE). [Greek, = beauty-three, referring to the arrangement of the leaves in whorls of three]

**callop** /**kal**-uhp/ n. (in SA) = YELLOWBELLY. [perhaps from a SA Aboriginal language]

**callosity** /kuh-**los**-uh-tee/ n. (pl. **-ies**) area of hard thick skin. [Latin: related to CALLOUS]

**callous** /**kal**-uhs/ adj. **1** unfeeling, insensitive. **2** (also **calloused**) (of skin) hardened. □ **callously** adv. **callousness** n. [Latin: related to CALLUS]

**callow** /**kal**-oh/ adj. inexperienced, immature. [Old English, = bald]

**call-up** n. summons to do military service.

**callus** /**kal**-uhs/ n. (pl. **calluses**) **1** area of hard thick skin or tissue. **2** hard tissue formed round bone ends after a fracture. [Latin]

**calm** /kahm/ — adj. **1** tranquil, quiet, windless. **2** serene; not agitated. — n. calm condition or period. — v. (often foll. by *down*) make or become calm. □ **calmly** adv. **calmness** n. [Greek *kauma* heat]

**caloric** /**kal**-uh-rik, kuh-**lo**-rik/ adj. of heat or calories.

**calorie** /**kal**-uh-ree/ n. (pl. **-ies**) unit of

quantity of heat, the amount needed to raise the temperature of one gram (**small calorie**) or one kilogram (**large calorie**) of water by 1°C, often used to measure the energy value of foods. [Latin *calor* heat]

**calorific** /ˌkal-uh-**rif**-ik/ *adj.* producing heat.

**calorimeter** /ˌkal-uh-**rim**-uh-tuh/ *n.* instrument for measuring quantity of heat.

**calothamnus** /ˌkal-oh-**tham**-nuhs/ *n.* (also **one-sided bottlebrush**) any of about 25 species of the genus of the same name, small to medium shrubs endemic to WA, having bright red or yellow flowers resembling those of the bottlebrush but on one side only of the stem.

**calumniate** /kuh-**lum**-nee-ˌayt/ *v.* (**-ting**) slander. [Latin]

**calumny** /**kal**-uhm-nee/ *n.* (*pl.* **-ies**) slander; malicious representation. □ **calumnious** /kuh-**lum**-nee-uhs/ *adj.* [Latin]

**calve** /kahv/ *v.* (-ving) give birth to a calf. [Old English: related to CALF[1]]

**calves** *pl.* of CALF[1], CALF[2].

**Calvinism** /**kal**-vuh-ˌniz-uhm/ *n.* theology of Calvin or his followers, stressing predestination. □ **Calvinist** *n. & adj.* **Calvinistic** /-**nis**-tik/ *adj.* [*Calvin*, name of a theologian (d. 1564)]

**calx** /kalks/ *n.* (*pl.* **calces** /**kal**-seez/ ) powdery substance formed when an ore or mineral has been heated. [Latin *calx calc-* lime]

**calypso** /kuh-**lip**-soh/ *n.* (*pl.* **-s**) W. Indian song with improvised usu. topical words and a syncopated rhythm. [origin unknown]

**calyx** /**kay**-liks, **kal**-iks/ *n.* (*pl.* **calyces** /-luh-ˌseez/ *or* **-es**) **1** sepals forming the protective case of a flower in bud. **2** = CALIX. [Greek, = husk]

**cam** *n.* projection on a wheel etc., shaped to convert circular into reciprocal or variable motion. [Dutch *kam* comb]

**camaraderie** /ˌkam-uh-**rah**-duh-ree/ *n.* friendly comradeship. [French]

**camber** — *n.* convex or arched shape of the surface of a road, ship's deck, etc. — *v.* build with a camber. [Latin *camurus* curved]

**Cambrian** /**kam**-bree-uhn/ — *adj.* **1** Welsh. **2** *Geol.* of the first period in the Palaeozoic era. — *n.* this period. [Welsh: related to CYMRIC]

**cambric** /**kam**-brik, **kaym**-/ *n.* fine linen or cotton fabric. [*Cambrai* in France]

**camcorder** /**kam**-ˌkaw-duh/ *n.* combined video camera and sound recorder. [CAM(ERA), (RE)CORDER]

**came** *past* of COME.

**camel** /**kam**-uhl/ *n.* **1** long-legged ruminant with one hump (**Arabian camel**) or two humps (**Bactrian camel**). **2** fawn colour. [Greek]

**camel-hair** *n.* fine soft hair used in artists' brushes or for fabric.

**camellia** /kuh-**meel**-yuh, **mee**-lee-uh/ *n.* any of several evergreen shrubs, native to E. Asia, with shiny leaves and showy flowers, the tea bush being one of the species. [*Camellus* or *Kamel*, Jesuit botanist (d. 1706)]

**camel poison** *n.* any of several extremely poisonous trees or shrubs of northern Australia.

**camembert** /**kam**-uhm-ˌbair/ *n.* a kind of soft creamy pungent cheese. [*Camembert* in France]

**cameo** /**kam**-ee-ˌoh/ *n.* (*pl.* **-s**) **1** small piece of hard stone carved in relief with a background of a different colour. **2 a** short descriptive literary sketch or acted scene. **b** small character part in a play or film, usu. brief and played by a distinguished actor. [French and medieval Latin]

**camera** /**kam**-ruh, -uh-ruh/ *n.* **1** apparatus for taking photographs or moving film. **2** equipment for converting images into electrical signals. □ **in camera** *Law* in private. [Latin: related to CHAMBER]

**camisole** /**kam**-uh-ˌsohl/ *n.* woman's lightweight vest. [Italian or Spanish: related to CHEMISE]

**camomile** /**kam**-uh-ˌmuyl, -ˌmeel/ *n.* (also **chamomile**) aromatic plant with daisy-like flowers used esp. to make tea. [Greek, = earth-apple]

**camouflage** /**kam**-uh-ˌflah*zh*/ — *n.* **1 a** disguising of soldiers, tanks, etc. so that they blend into the background. **b** such a disguise. **2** the natural blending colouring of an animal. **3** misleading or evasive precaution or expedient (*his friendliness is all camouflage*). — *v.* (**-ging**) hide by camouflage. [French *camoufler* disguise]

**camp**[1] — *n.* **1** place where troops are lodged or trained. **2 a** temporary accommodation of huts, tents, etc., for detainees, holiday-makers, etc. **b** complex of buildings for holiday accommodation, usu. with recreational facilities. **3** an Aboriginal living place, temporary or permanent. **4** assembly place of sheep or cattle. **5** supporters of a particular party or cause etc. regarded collectively (*the Labor camp was ecstatic about the election result*). — *v.* **1** set up or spend time in a camp. **2** (often foll. by *out*) lodge in temporary quarters or in the open. **3** (of sheep or cattle) flock together, esp. for rest. [Latin *campus* level ground]

**camp²** *colloq.* — *adj.* **1** affected, effeminate, theatrically exaggerated. **2** homosexual. — *n.* camp manner or style. — *v.* behave or do in a camp way. □ **camp it up** deliberately overact; behave affectedly. □ **campy** *adj.* (**-ier, -iest**). [origin uncertain]

**campaign** /kam-**payn**/ — *n.* **1** organised course of action, esp. to arouse public interest (e.g. before a political election). **2** military operations towards a particular objective. — *v.* take part in a campaign. □ **campaigner** *n.* [Latin: related to CAMP¹]

**campanology** /ˌkam-puh-**nol**-uh-jee/ *n.* **1** the study of bells. **2** art or practice of bell-ringing. □ **campanologist** *n.* [Latin *campana* bell]

**camp bed** *n.* portable folding bed.

**camper** *n.* **1** person who camps. **2** (also **campervan**) large motor vehicle with beds etc.

**camp follower** *n.* **1** civilian worker in a military camp. **2** disciple or adherent.

**camphor** /**kam**-fuh/ *n.* pungent white crystalline substance, obtained from camphor laurel, used in making celluloid, medicine, and mothballs. [French ultimately from Sanskrit *karpūram*]

**camphor laurel** *n.* tree of E. Asia (and introduced into Australia) from which camphor is obtained.

**camphorwood** *n.* fragrant wood of the camphor laurel (and of several other trees with a similarly fragrant wood).

**camp oven** *n.* heavy, iron, three-legged cooking vessel which stands in a fire and has a flat, usu. recessed, lid on top of which hot coals can be placed (cf. COLONIAL OVEN).

**campus** /**kam**-puhs/ *n.* (*pl.* **-es**) **1** grounds of a university or college. **2** (of a university with branches at different geographical locations) branch; part of a university (*the meeting is at the Kensington campus of the University of New South Wales*). [Latin, = field]

**camshaft** *n.* shaft with one or more cams.

**can¹** /kan, kuhn/ *v.aux.* (*3rd sing.* present can; *past* could /kuud/ ) **1 a** be able to; know how to (*I can run fast; can you speak Bahasa Indonesia?*). **b** be potentially capable of (*these storms can last for hours*). **2** be permitted to (*can we go to the party?*). [Old English, = know]

**can²** — *n.* **1** metal vessel for liquid. **2** sealed tin container for the preservation of food or drink. **3** (in *pl.*) *colloq.* headphones. **4** (prec. by *the*) *colloq.* prison. — *v.* (**-nn-**) **1** put or preserve in a can. **2** *colloq.* disparage; criticise (*critics canned his latest film*). **3** *colloq.* cancel;

shelve (*they've decided to can tonight's meeting*). □ **carry the can see** CARRY. **in the can** *colloq.* completed, ready (orig. of filmed or recorded material). [Old English]

**canagong** /kan-uh-jong/ *n.* = PIGFACE. [from a Tasmanian Aboriginal language, probably *ganajang*]

**canal** /kuh-**nal**/ *n.* **1** artificial waterway for inland navigation or irrigation. **2** tubular duct in a plant or animal for carrying food, liquid, or air. [Latin *canalis*]

**canapé** /**kan**-uh-pay/ *n.* small piece of bread or pastry with a savoury topping. [French]

**canard** /kuh-**nahd**, **kan**-ahd/ *n.* unfounded rumour or story. [French, = duck]

**canary** /kuh-**nair**-ree/ *n.* (*pl.* **-ies**) **1** small songbird with yellow feathers. **2** *hist.* **a** a convict in Australia (from the yellow clothing worn). **b** punishment of one hundred lashes (as meted out in Australia). [*Canary* Islands]

**canasta** /kuh-**nas**-tuh/ *n.* card-game using two packs and resembling rummy. [Spanish, = basket]

**Canberra** /**kan**-buh-ruh, -bruh/ *n.* name of the capital city of Australia and of the Australian Capital Territory. [from an Aboriginal language, possibly = 'woman's breasts' with reference to the peaks of Mount Ainslie and Black Hill; possibly *Nganbirra* meeting place; possibly *Kembery* or *Gnabra*, supposed Aboriginal names for the area.]

**cancan** /**kan**-kan/ *n.* lively stage-dance with high kicking. [French]

**cancel** /**kan**-suhl/ *v.* (**-ll-**) **1** revoke or discontinue (an arrangement) (*cancelled the wedding*). **2** delete (writing etc.). **3** mark or pierce (a ticket, stamp, etc.) to invalidate it. **4** annul; make void; abolish. **5** (often foll. by *out*) (of one factor or circumstance) neutralise or counterbalance (another). **6** *Math.* strike out (an equal factor) on each side of an equation etc. □ **cancellation** /ˌkan-suh-**lay**-shuhn/ *n.* [Latin: related to CHANCEL]

**cancer** *n.* **1 a** malignant tumour of body cells. **b** disease caused by this. **2** evil influence or corruption spreading uncontrolled (*the cancer of racial hatred*). **3** (**Cancer**) **a** constellation and fourth sign of the zodiac (the Crab). **b** person born when the sun is in this sign. □ **cancerous** *adj.* **cancroid** *adj.* [Latin, = crab]

**candela** /kan-**dee**-luh, -**day**-luh/ *n.* SI unit of luminous intensity. [Latin, = candle]

**candelabrum** /ˌkan-duh-**lah**-bruhm/ *n.*

(also **-bra**) (*pl.* **-bra**) large branched candlestick or lamp-holder. [Latin: related to CANDELA]

■ **Usage** The form *candelabra* is, strictly speaking, the plural. However, *candelabra* (singular) and *candelabras* (plural) are often found in informal use.

**candescent** /kan-**des**-uhnt/ *adj.* glowing with, or as with, white heat. □ **candescence** *n.* [Latin *candeo* be brilliant, shine]

**candid** /**kan**-duhd/ *adj.* **1** frank; not hiding one's thoughts. **2** (of a photograph) taken informally, usu. without the subject's knowledge. □ **candidly** *adv.* **candidness** *n.* [Latin *candidus* white]

**candidate** /**kan**-duh-duht, -,dayt/ *n.* **1** person nominated for or seeking office, an award, etc. **2** person or thing likely to gain some distinction or position. **3** *colloq.* likely prospect (*smoking as much as he does, he's a candidate for lung cancer*). **4** person entered for an examination. □ **candidacy** *n.* **candidature** *n.* [Latin, = white-robed]

**candied** /**kan**-deed/ *adj.* preserved or encrusted with sugar (*candied peel*).

**candle** /**kan**-duhl/ *n.* cylinder or block of wax or tallow with a central wick which gives light when burning. □ **cannot hold a candle to** is much inferior to. [Latin *candela*]

**candlebark** *n.* any of several eucalypts having a smooth white bark which frequently develops reddish patches before the bark is shed.

**Candlemas** /**kan**-duhl-muhs, -,mas/ *n.* feast of the Purification of the Virgin Mary (2 Feb.). [Old English: related to MASS²]

**candlenut** *n.* tree of Queensland and the Pacific Islands yielding a hard, oily, edible nut used, when grated, to thicken some Asian curries (and formerly to provide a candle-like light when burned).

**candlepower** *n.* unit of luminous intensity.

**candlestick** *n.* holder for one or more candles.

**candour** /**kan**-duh/ *n.* (also **candor**) frankness; openness. [Latin *candor*]

**candy** /**kan**-dee/ — *n.* (*pl.* **-ies**) (in full **sugar-candy**) sugar crystallised by repeated boiling and slow evaporation. — *v.* (**-ies**, **-ied**) (usu. as **candied** *adj.*) preserve (fruit etc.) in candy. [French from Arabic *ḳand* sugar]

**cane** — *n.* **1 a** hollow jointed stem of giant reeds or grasses (*bamboo cane*). **b** solid stem of slender palms. **2** = SUGAR CANE. **3** cane used for wickerwork etc. **4** cane used as a walking-stick, plant support, for punishment, etc. — *v.* (**-ning**) **1** beat with a cane. **2** weave cane into (a chair etc.). [Greek *kanna* reed]

**cane beetle** *n.* beetle, the larva of which attacks sugar-cane roots.

**cane cocky** *n.* proprietor of a sugar-cane farm.

**cane-cutter** *n.* itinerant worker employed in the harvesting of sugar-cane.

**cane toad** *n.* (also **Queensland cane toad**) very large toad, native to S. America, introduced into north-eastern Australia to combat the cane beetle, now a serious pest.

**canine** /**kay**-nuyn, **kan**-uyn/ — *adj.* **1** of a dog or dogs. **2** of or belonging to the animal family which includes dingoes, dogs, wolves, foxes, etc. — *n.* **1** dog. **2** (in full **canine tooth**) pointed tooth between incisors and premolars. [Latin *canis* dog]

**caning** *n.* **1** beating with a cane. **2** verbal attack or rebuff (*he'll get a real caning when the boss hears about this*). **3** overwhelming defeat (*the Canberra Raiders gave Manly an absolute caning*).

**canister** /**kan**-uh-stuh/ *n.* **1** small container for tea etc. **2** cylinder of shot, tear-gas, etc., exploding on impact. [Greek *kanastron* wicker basket]

**canker** — *n.* **1 a** destructive fungus disease of trees and plants. **b** open wound in the stem of a tree or plant. **2** ulcerous ear disease of animals, esp. cats and dogs. **3** corrupting influence (*a canker in society*). — *v.* **1** infect with canker. **2** corrupt. **3** (as **cankered** *adj.*) soured, malignant (*he has a cankered outlook*). □ **cankerous** *adj.* [Latin: related to CANCER]

**cannabis** /**kan**-uh-buhs/ *n.* **1** hemp plant. **2** parts of it used as a narcotic; marijuana. [Latin from Greek]

**canned** *adj.* **1** pre-recorded (*canned music*). **2** sold in a can (*canned beer*). **3** *colloq.* drunk. **4** *colloq.* cancelled.

**cannelloni** /,kan-uh-**loh**-nee/ *n.pl.* tubes of pasta stuffed with a savoury mixture. [Italian]

**cannery** /**kan**-uh-ree/ *n.* (*pl.* **-ies**) canning-factory.

**cannibal** /**kan**-uh-buhl/ *n.* person or animal that eats its own species. □ **cannibalise** *v.* **cannibalism** *n.* **cannibalistic** /-buh-**lis**-tik/ *adj.* [Spanish from Carib]

**cannon** /**kan**-uhn/ — *n.* **1** *hist.* (*pl.* usu. same) large heavy esp. mounted gun. **2** automatic gun on an aircraft, firing shells. **3** *Billiards* hitting of two balls successively by the player's ball. **4** (in full **cannon-bit**) smooth round bit for a horse.

— v. (usu. foll. by *against*, *into*) collide. [Italian: related to CANE]

**cannon fodder** n. soldiers regarded as expendable.

**cannot** /**kan**-ot, ka-**not**/ v.aux. can not.

**canny** /**kan**-ee/ adj. (**-ier**, **-iest**) shrewd, worldly-wise; thrifty. □ **cannily** adv. **canniness** n. [from CAN¹]

**canoe** /kuh-**noo**/ — n. **1** small narrow boat with pointed ends, usu. paddled. **2** hist. name given by the colonists to any Aboriginal boat. — v. (**-noes**, **-noed**, **-noeing**) travel in a canoe. □ **canoeist** n. [Spanish and Haitian]

**canon** /**kan**-uhn/ n. **1 a** general law, rule, principle, or criterion. **b** church decree or law. **2 a** member of certain Roman Catholic religious orders. **b** member of a cathedral chapter. **3 a** body of sacred writings accepted as genuine (*Biblical canon*). **b** recognised genuine works of a particular author (*Shakespearean canon*). **4 a** the part of the Roman Catholic Mass containing the words of consecration. **b** list of canonised saints. **5** *Mus.* piece with different parts taking up the same theme successively. [Greek *kanōn* rule]

**canonical** /kuh-**non**-i-kuhl/ — adj. (also **canonic**) **1 a** according to or authorised by canon law. **b** included in the Biblical canon. **2** authoritative, standard, accepted. — n. (in pl.) canonical dress of clergy. [medieval Latin: related to CANON]

**canonise** /**kan**-uh-₍nuyz/ v. (also **-ize**) (**-sing** or **-zing**) **1** (of the Pope) declare officially to be a saint, usu. with a ceremony. **2** regard as saintly, revere. □ **canonisation** /-₍zay-shuhn/ n. [medieval Latin: related to CANON]

**canon law** n. **1** church law as laid down by decrees of the popes, councils of the Church, etc. **2** laws of any Church.

**canoodle** /kuh-**noo**-duhl/ v. (**-ling**) *colloq.* kiss and cuddle. [origin unknown]

**canopy** /**kan**-uh-pee/ — n. (pl. **-ies**) **1 a** covering suspended over a throne, bed, etc. **b** sky. **c** overhanging shelter. **2** *Archit.* rooflike projection over a niche etc. **3** uppermost layers of foliage etc. in a forest. **4** expanding part of a parachute. — v. (**-ies**, **-ied**) supply or be a canopy to. [Greek, = mosquito-net]

**canst** *archaic* 2nd person sing. of CAN¹.

**cant¹** /kant/ — n. **1** insincere pious or moral talk. **2** language peculiar to a class, profession, etc.; jargon. — v. use cant. [probably from Latin: related to CHANT]

**cant²** — n. **1** slanting surface, bevel. **2** oblique push or jerk that upsets or partly upsets something. **3** tilted position. — v. push or pitch out of level; tilt. [Low German or Dutch, = edge]

**can't** /kahnt/ contr. can not.

**cantabile** /kan-**tah**-buh-lee, -lay/ *Mus.* — adv. & adj. in smooth flowing style. — n. cantabile passage or movement. [Italian, = singable]

**cantaloupe** /**kan**-tuh-₍lohp, -loop/ n. (also **cantaloup**) = ROCK MELON. [*Cantaluppi* papal estate near Rome, where it was first grown in Europe]

**cantankerous** /kan-**tang**-kuh-ruhs/ adj. bad-tempered, quarrelsome. □ **cantankerously** adv. **cantankerousness** n. [origin uncertain]

**cantata** /kan-**tah**-tuh/ n. *Mus.* composition with vocal solos and usu. choral and orchestral accompaniment. [Italian: related to CHANT]

**canteen** /kan-**teen**/ n. **1 a** restaurant for employees in an office, factory, etc. **b** shop for provisions in a barracks or camp. **c** school shop selling lunches etc. **2** case of cutlery. **3** soldier's or camper's water-flask. [Italian, = cellar]

**canter** — n. horse's pace between a trot and a gallop. — v. go or make go at a canter. [*Canterbury gallop* of medieval pilgrims]

**canticle** /**kan**-ti-kuhl/ n. song or chant with a biblical text. [Latin *canticum* CHANT]

**cantilever** /**kan**-tuh-₍lee-vuh/ n. **1** bracket or beam etc. projecting from a wall to support a balcony etc. **2** beam or girder fixed at one end only. □ **cantilevered** adj. [origin unknown]

**cantilever bridge** n. bridge made of cantilevers projecting from piers and connected by girders.

**canto** /**kan**-toh/ n. (pl. **-s**) division of a long poem. [Latin *cantus*: related to CHANT]

**canton** n. /**kan**-ton/ subdivision of a country, esp. of Switzerland. [French, = corner: related to CANT²]

**Cantonese** /₍kan-tuh-**neez**/ — n. dialect of Chinese spoken in SE China and Hong Kong. — adj. of this dialect or this region (*Cantonese cooking*). [*Canton* in China]

**cantor** /**kan**-taw/ n. **1** precentor in a synagogue. **2** church choir leader. [Latin, = singer]

**canvas** /**kan**-vuhs/ — n. **1** strong coarse cloth used for sails and tents etc. and for oil-painting. **2** a painting on canvas, esp. in oils. **3** open kind of canvas used as a basis for tapestry and embroidery. **4** a racing boat's covered end. — v. (**-ss-**) cover with canvas. □ **by a canvas** (in boat-racing) by a small margin. **under canvas 1** in tents. **2** with sails spread. [Latin: related to CANNABIS]

**canvass** /**kan**-vuhs/ v. **1** solicit votes, esp. from an electorate. **2 a** ascertain the opinions of. **b** seek custom from. **3** propose (an idea or plan etc.). □ **canvasser** n. [originally = toss in a sheet, agitate, from CANVAS]

**canyon** /**kan**-yuhn/ n. deep gorge. [Spanish *cañón* tube]

**cap** — n. **1 a** soft brimless hat, usu. with a peak. **b** head-covering worn in a particular profession (*nurse's cap*). **c** cap as a sign of membership of a sports team. **2 a** cover like a cap (*kneecap*). **b** top for a bottle, jar, pen, camera lens, etc. **3** = DIAPHRAGM 2. **4** = PERCUSSION CAP. **5** dental crown. **6** head of a mushroom. — v. (-**pp-**) **1 a** put a cap on. **b** cover the top or end of. **c** set a limit to. **2** award a sports cap to. **3** form the top of. **4** surpass, excel. □ **cap in hand** humbly. **if the cap fits** (of a remark) if it applies to you, so be it. **to cap it all** after everything else. [Latin *cappa*]

**capability** /ˌkay-puh-**bil**-uh-tee/ n. (pl. -**ies**) **1** ability, power. **2** undeveloped or unused faculty.

**capable** /**kay**-puh-buhl/ adj. **1** competent, able, gifted. **2** (foll. by *of*) **a** having the ability, fitness, etc. for (*is she capable of painting this portrait?*; *he's capable of such a crime*). **b** admitting of (explanation, improvement, etc.). □ **capably** adv. [Latin *capio* hold]

**capacious** /kuh-**pay**-shuhs/ adj. roomy. □ **capaciousness** n. [Latin *capax*: related to CAPABLE]

**capacitance** /kuh-**pas**-uh-tuhns/ n. **1** ability to store electric charge. **2** ratio of change in the electric charge in a system to the corresponding change in its electric potential.

**capacitor** /kuh-**pas**-uh-tuh/ n. device able to store electric charge.

**capacity** /kuh-**pas**-uh-tee/ n. (pl. -**ies**) **1 a** power to contain, receive, experience, or produce (*capacity for heat, pain*, etc.). **b** maximum amount that can be contained or produced etc. **c** (*attrib.*) fully occupying the available space etc. (*capacity crowd*). **2** mental power. **3** position or function (*in my capacity as critic*). **4** legal competence. □ **to capacity** fully. [Latin: related to CAPACIOUS]

**caparison** /kuh-**pa**-ruh-suhn/ *literary* — n. **1** (usu. in *pl.*) horse's trappings. **2** equipment, finery. — v. adorn. [Spanish, = saddle-cloth]

**cape**¹ n. **1** sleeveless cloak. **2** this worn over or as part of a longer cloak or coat. [Latin *cappa* CAP]

**cape**² n. **1** headland, promontory. **2** (**the Cape**) the Cape of Good Hope. [Latin *caput* head]

**Cape Barren goose** n. grey waterfowl breeding mainly on islands off the mainland southern coast of Australia. [*Cape Barren Island* in Bass Strait.]

**caper**¹ — v. jump or run playfully. — n. **1** playful leap. **2 a** prank. **b** *colloq.* any activity or occupation. □ **cut a caper** frolic. [abbreviation of Italian *capriola* a leap, from Latin *caper -pri* goat]

**caper**² n. **1** bramble-like shrub. **2** (in *pl.*) its pickled buds used esp. in a sauce. [Greek *kapparis*]

**capillarity** /ˌkap-uh-**la**-ruh-tee/ n. the rise or depression of a liquid in a narrow tube. [French: related to CAPILLARY]

**capillary** /kuh-**pil**-uh-ree/ — *attrib. adj.* **1** of or like a hair, esp. (of a tube) of very small diameter. **2** of the branching blood-vessels connecting arteries and veins. — n. (*pl.* -**ies**) **1** capillary tube. **2** capillary blood vessel. [Latin *capillus* hair]

**capillary action** n. = CAPILLARITY.

**capital** /**kap**-uh-tuhl/ — n. **1** chief town or city of a country or region, usu. its seat of government and administrative centre. **2 a** money etc. with which a company starts in business. **b** accumulated wealth, esp. as used in further production. **3** capitalists collectively. **4** capital letter. **5** head of a column or pillar. — *adj.* **1 a** principal, most important. **b** *colloq.* excellent. **2 a** involving punishment by death. **b** (of an error etc.) vitally harmful, fatal. **3** (of letters of the alphabet) large in size, used to begin sentences and names etc. □ **make capital out of** use to one's advantage. [Latin *caput -itis* head]

**capital gain** n. profit from the sale of investments or property.

**capital goods** *n.pl.* machinery, plant, etc., used in producing commodities (opp. CONSUMER GOODS).

**capitalise** v. (also -**ize**) (-**sing** or -**zing**) **1** (foll. by *on*) use to one's advantage; profit from (*failed to capitalise on the opportunity offered*). **2** convert into or provide with capital. **3 a** write (a letter of the alphabet) as a capital. **b** begin (a word) with a capital letter. □ **capitalisation** n. [French: related to CAPITAL]

**capitalism** n. **1** economic system in which the production and distribution of goods depend on invested private capital and profit-making. **2** *Polit.* dominance of private owners of capital and production for profit.

**capitalist** — n. **1** person investing or possessing capital. **2** advocate of capitalism. **3** usu. *derog.* rich person. — *adj.* of or favouring capitalism. □ **capitalistic** /-**lis**-tik/ adj.

**capitation** /ˌkap-uh-**tay**-shuhn/ n. tax or fee paid per person. [Latin: related to CAPITAL]

**capitulate** /kuh-**pich**-uh-ˌlayt/ v. (**-ting**) surrender, esp. on stated conditions. □ **capitulation** /kuh-ˌpich-uh-**lay**-shuhn/ n. [medieval Latin, = put under headings]

**capon** /**kay**-pon/ n. rooster castrated and fattened for eating. [Latin *capo*]

**cappuccino** /ˌkap-uh-**chee**-noh/ n. (pl. **-s**) coffee with milk made frothy with pressurised steam. [Italian, = CAPUCHIN]

**capriccio** /kuh-**prich**-ee-oh/ n. lively and usu. short musical composition. [Italian, = sudden start]

**caprice** /kuh-**prees**/ n. **1 a** unaccountable or whimsical change of mind or conduct. **b** tendency to this. **2** lively or fanciful work of art, music, etc. [Italian *capriccio* sudden start]

**capricious** /kuh-**prish**-uhs/ adj. subject to whims; unpredictable. □ **capriciously** adv. **capriciousness** n.

**Capricorn** /**kap**-ruh-ˌkawn/ n. **1** constellation and tenth sign of the zodiac (the Goat). **2** person born when the sun is in this sign. [Latin *caper -pri* goat, *cornu* horn]

**capsicum** /**kap**-suh-kuhm/ n. **1** plant with edible fruits, esp. any of several varieties of pepper. **2** red, green, or yellow fruit of these. [Latin *capsa* case]

**capsize** /kap-**suyz**/ v. (**-zing**) (of a boat etc.) be overturned; overturn. [Spanish *capuzar* sink]

**capstan** /**kap**-stuhn/ n. **1** thick revolving cylinder for winding a cable etc. **2** revolving spindle carrying the spool on a tape recorder. [Provençal]

**capsule** /**kap**-shool, -shuhl, -syool/ n. **1** small edible soluble case enclosing medicine. **2** detachable compartment of a spacecraft or nose of a rocket. **3** enclosing membrane in the body. **4 a** dry fruit that releases its seeds when ripe. **b** spore-producing part of mosses etc. **5** (*attrib.*) concise; condensed (*a capsule history of atrocities against Aborigines by white colonists*). □ **capsular** adj. [Latin *capsa* case]

**capsulise** v. (also **-ize**) (**-sing** or **-zing**) = ENCAPSULATE 2.

**Capt.** abbr. Captain.

**captain** /**kap**-tuhn/ — n. **1 a** chief, leader. **b** leader of a team. **2 a** commander of a ship. **b** pilot of a civil aircraft. — v. be captain of; lead. □ **captaincy** n. (pl. **-ies**) [Latin *caput capit-* head]

**Captain Cook** n. rhyming slang for 'look' (*took a Captain Cook at the files*). [James Cook, navigator and explorer (d. 1779)]

**caption** /**kap**-shuhn/ — n. **1** wording appended to an illustration, cartoon, etc. **2** wording on a cinema or television screen. **3** heading of a chapter, article etc. — v. provide with a caption. [Latin *capio capt-* take]

**captious** /**kap**-shuhs/ adj. given to finding fault or raising petty objections. [Latin: related to CAPTIVE]

**captivate** /**kap**-tuh-ˌvayt/ v. (**-ting**) fascinate; charm. □ **captivation** /-**vay**-shuhn/ n. [Latin: related to CAPTIVE]

**captive** /**kap**-tiv/ — n. confined or imprisoned person or animal. — adj. **1** taken prisoner; restrained. **2** unable to escape (*captive audience*). □ **captivity** /kap-**tiv**-uh-tee/ n. [Latin *capio capt-* take]

**captor** /**kap**-tuh, -taw/ n. person who captures. [Latin: related to CAPTIVE]

**capture** /**kap**-chuh/ — v. (**-ring**) **1 a** take prisoner; seize. **b** obtain by force or trickery. **2** portray; record on film etc (*could not capture his likeness*). **3** Physics absorb (a subatomic particle). **4** record (data) for use in a computer. — n. **1** act of capturing. **2** thing or person captured. [Latin: related to CAPTIVE]

**Capuchin** /**kap**-yuh-chuhn/ n. Franciscan friar of the new Rule of 1529. [Italian *cappuccio* cowl]

**car** n. **1** (in full **motor car**) motor vehicle for a driver and small number of passengers. **2** (in *comb.*) road vehicle or railway carriage esp. of a specified kind (*tramcar, dining-car*). **3** passenger compartment of a lift, balloon, etc. [French from Latin or Old Celtic origin]

**carafe** /kuh-**rahf**, -**raf**/ n. glass container for water or wine. [French from Arabic]

**caramel** /**ka**-ruh-muhl/ n. **1 a** burnt sugar or syrup as a flavouring or colouring. **b** a kind of soft toffee. **2** light brown colour. □ **caramelise** /-muh-ˌluyz/ v. (also **-ize**) (**-sing** or **-zing**). [French from Spanish]

**carapace** /**ka**-ruh-ˌpays/ n. upper shell of a tortoise or crustacean. [French from Spanish]

**carat** /**ka**-ruht/ n. **1** unit of weight for precious stones (200 mg). **2** measure of purity of gold (pure gold = 24 carats). [French ultimately from Greek *keration* horn]

**caravan** /**ka**-ruh-ˌvan/ — n. **1** vehicle equipped for living in and usu. towed by a car. **2** people travelling together, esp. across a desert in Asia or N. Africa. **3** BOX[1] n. 4 b. — v. (**-nn-**) travel or live in caravan. □ **caravanner** n. [French from Persian]

**caravanserai** /ˌka-ruh-**van**-suh-ˌruy, -ˌray/ *n*. inn with a central court where caravans (see CARAVAN 2) may rest. [Persian, = caravan place]

**caraway** /**ka**-ruh-ˌway/ *n*. plant with tiny white flowers. [Spanish from Arabic]

**caraway seed** *n*. fruit of the caraway as flavouring and a source of oil.

**carbeen** /**kah**-been/ *n*. = MORETON BAY ASH. [Kamilaroi and Yuwaalaraay *gaabiin*]

**carbide** /**kah**-buyd/ *n*. **1** binary compound of carbon. **2** = CALCIUM CARBIDE.

**carbie** /**kah**-bee/ *n*. (also **carby**) *colloq*. carburettor. [abbreviation]

**carbine** /**kah**-buyn, **kah**-buhn/ *n*. short rifle orig. for cavalry use. [French]

**carbohydrate** /ˌkah-buh-**huy**-drayt/ *n*. energy-producing organic compound of carbon, hydrogen, and oxygen (e.g. starch, sugar).

**carbolic** /kah-**bol**-ik/ *n*. (in full **carbolic acid**) phenol. [from CARBON]

**carbon** /**kah**-buhn/ *n*. **1** non-metallic element occurring naturally as diamond, graphite, and charcoal, and in all organic compounds. **2 a** = CARBON COPY. **b** = CARBON PAPER. **3** rod of carbon in an arc lamp. [Latin *carbo* charcoal]

**carbon-14** *n*. radioisotope of mass 14, used in carbon dating.

**carbon-12** *n*. stable isotope of carbon, used in calculations of atomic mass units.

**carbonaceous** /ˌkah-buh-**nay**-shuhs/ *adj*. **1** consisting of or containing carbon. **2** of or like coal or charcoal.

**carbonate** — *n*. /**kah**-buh-ˌnayt, -nuht/ *Chem*. salt of carbonic acid. — *v*. /-ˌnayt/ **-ting**) impregnate (e.g. a soft drink) with carbon dioxide; aerate. [French: related to CARBON]

**carbon copy** *n*. **1** copy made with carbon paper. **2** exact copy.

**carbon dating** *n*. determination of the age of an organic object from the ratio of isotopes, which changes as carbon-14 decays.

**carbon dioxide** *n*. colourless odourless gas occurring naturally in the atmosphere and formed by respiration.

**carbonic acid** *n*. weak acid formed from carbon dioxide in water.

**carboniferous** /ˌkah-buh-**nif**-uh-ruhs/ — *adj*. **1** producing coal. **2** (**Carboniferous**) of the fifth period in the Palaeozoic era, with evidence of the first reptiles and extensive formation of coal. — *n*. (**Carboniferous**) this period.

**carbonise** /**kah**-buh-ˌnuyz/ *v*. (also **-ize**) **-sing** or **-zing**) **1** convert into carbon. **2** reduce to charcoal or coke. **3** coat with carbon. □ **carbonisation** /-**zay**-shuhn/ *n*.

**carbon monoxide** *n*. toxic gas formed by the incomplete burning of carbon.

**carbon paper** *n*. thin carbon-coated paper used for making copies.

**carbon tetrachloride** *n*. colourless liquid used as a solvent.

**carborundum** /ˌkah-buh-**run**-duhm/ *n*. compound of carbon and silicon used esp. as an abrasive. [from CARBON, CORUNDUM]

**carbuncle** /**kah**-bung-kuhl/ *n*. **1** severe skin abscess. **2** bright-red gem. [Latin: related to CARBON]

**carburettor** /ˌkah-byuh-**ret**-uh, ˌkah-buh-/ *n*. apparatus in an internal-combustion engine for mixing petrol and air to make an explosive mixture.

**carcass** /**kah**-kuhs/ *n*. (also **carcase**) **1** dead body of an animal, esp. as meat. **2** bones of a cooked bird. **3** *colloq*. human body; corpse. **4** skeleton, framework, of a building, ship, etc. **5** worthless remains. [French]

**carcinogen** /kah-**sin**-uh-juhn/ *n*. substance producing cancer. □ **carcinogenic** /ˌkah-sin-uh-**jen**-ik/ *adj*. [related to CARCINOMA]

**carcinoma** /ˌkah-suh-**noh**-muh/ *n*. (*pl*. **-s** or **-mata**) cancerous tumour. [Greek *karkinos* crab]

**card**[1] *n*. **1** thick stiff paper or thin pasteboard. **2 a** piece of this for writing or printing on, esp. to send greetings, to identify a person, or to record information. **b** small rectangular piece of plastic issued by a bank etc. with personal (often machine-readable) data on it, chiefly to obtain cash or credit (*credit-card*). **3 a** = PLAYING-CARD. **b** (in *pl*.) card-playing. **4** programme of events at a race-meeting etc. **5** *colloq*. odd or amusing person. □ **card up one's sleeve** plan or secret weapon in reserve. **on the cards** possible or likely. **put** (or **lay**) **one's cards on the table** reveal one's resources, intentions, etc. [Greek *khartēs* papyrus-leaf]

**card**[2] — *n*. toothed instrument, wire brush, etc., for raising a nap on cloth or for disentangling fibres before spinning. — *v*. brush or comb with a card. [Latin *caro* card (v.)]

**cardamom** /**kah**-duh-muhm/ *n*. seeds of an aromatic plant of Sri Lanka, India, etc., used as a spice. [Latin from Greek]

**cardboard** — *n*. pasteboard or stiff paper, esp. for making boxes. — *adj*. **1** made of cardboard. **2** flimsy, insubstantial.

**card-carrying** *adj*. registered as a member (esp. of a political party or trade union).

**cardiac** /**kah**-dee-ˌak/ *adj*. of or relating to the heart. [Greek *kardia* heart]

**cardigan** /**kah**-di-guhn/ *n*. knitted

jacket fastening down the front. [Earl of *Cardigan*]

**cardinal** /**kah**-duh-nuhl/ — *adj.* **1** chief, fundamental. **2** deep scarlet. — *n.* (as a title **Cardinal**) leading Roman Catholic dignitary, one of the Sacred College electing the Pope. [Latin *cardo -din- hinge*]

**cardinal number** *n.* number denoting quantity (1, 2, 3, etc.), as opposed to an ordinal number (first, second, third, etc.).

**cardinal points** *n.pl.* four main points of the compass (N., S., E., W.).

**cardinal virtues** *n.pl.* justice, prudence, temperance, and fortitude.

**card index** *n.* index with a card for each entry.

**cardiogram** /**kah**-dee-oh-,gram, -uh- ,gram/ *n.* record of heart movements, made by a cardiograph. [Greek *kardia* heart]

**cardiograph** /**kah**-dee-oh-,grahf, -uh- ,grahf, -,graf/ *n.* instrument recording heart movements. □ **cardiographer** /-og- ruh-fuh/ *n.* **cardiography** /-og-ruh-fee/ *n.*

**cardiology** /,kah-dee-**ol**-uh-jee/ *n.* branch of medicine concerned with the heart. □ **cardiologist** *n.*

**cardiovascular** /,kah-dee-oh-**vas**-kyuh- luh/ *adj.* of the heart and blood-vessels.

**cardphone** *n.* public telephone operated by a machine-readable card instead of money.

**card-sharp** *n.* (also **card-sharper**) swindler at card-games.

**care** — *n.* **1** worry, anxiety. **2** cause of this. **3** serious attention; caution (*assembled with care*; *proceed with care*). **4** pro- tection, looking after, charge (*in the care of his uncle*). — *v.* (**-ring**) **1** (usu. foll. by *about, for, whether*) feel concern or interest. **2** (usu. foll. by *for*) like, be fond of (*don't care for jazz*). **3** (foll. by *to* + infin.) wish or be willing (*would you care to try?*). □ **care for** provide for; look after. **care of** (also **c/-**) at the address of. **couldn't care less** *colloq.* expression of complete indifference. **have a care** take care; be careful. **not care a damn** etc. = *not give a damn* etc. (see GIVE). **take care 1** be careful. **2** (foll. by *to* + infin.) not fail or neglect. **take care of 1** look after. **2** deal with; dispose of. [Old English, = sorrow]

**careen** /kuh-**reen**/ *v.* **1** turn (a ship) on one side for repair etc. **2** tilt, lean over. **3** swerve about. [Latin *carina* keel]

■ **Usage** Sense 3 of *careen* is influenced by the verb *career*.

**career** /kuh-**reer**/ — *n.* **1** one's profes- sional etc. progress through life. **2** profession or occupation, esp. as offering advancement. **3** (*attrib.*) **a** pursuing ( wishing to pursue a career (*caree woman*). **b** working permanently in specified profession (*career diplomat* **4** swift course (*in full career*). — *v.* **1** mov or swerve about wildly. **2** go swiftl [Latin: related to CAR]

**careerist** *n.* person predominantl concerned with personal advancement

**carefree** *adj.* free from care responsibility; joyous.

**careful** *adj.* **1** painstaking, thorough. cautious. **3** taking care; not neglectin (*careful to remind them*). **4** (foll. by *for, o* concerned for; taking care of (*he is alwa; careful of our feelings*). □ **carefully** *ad* **carefulness** *n.*

**careless** *adj.* **1** not taking care or payir attention. **2** unthinking, insensitive. done without care; inaccurate. **4** ligh hearted. **5** (foll. by *of*) not concerned abou taking no heed of (*careless of our feelings* □ **carelessly** *adv.* **carelessness** *n.*

**carer** *n.* person who cares for a sick elderly person, esp. a relative at home.

**caress** /kuh-**res**/ — *v.* touch or strol gently or lovingly; kiss. — *n.* loving gentle touch or kiss. [Latin *carus* dear

**caret** /**ka**-ruht/ *n.* mark (^, ⋏) indicatin a proposed insertion in printing writing. [Latin, = is lacking]

**caretaker** *n.* **1** person employed to loo after a house, building, etc. **2** (*attri* exercising temporary authority (*car taker government*).

**careworn** *adj.* showing the effects prolonged worry.

**cargo** /**kah**-goh/ *n.* (*pl.* **-es** or **-s**) goo carried on a ship or aircraft. [Spanis related to CHARGE]

**Carib** /**ka**-rib/ — *n.* **1** indigeno inhabitant of the southern W. Indies adjacent coasts. **2** their language. — *a* of the Caribs. [Spanish from Haitian]

**Caribbean** /,ka-ruh-**bee**-uhn, kuh-**ri** ee-uhn/ *adj.* of the Caribs or the W. Ind generally.

**caribou** /**ka**-ruh-,boo/ *n.* (*pl.* sam N. American reindeer. [French fro American Indian]

**caricature** /**ka**-ruh-kuh-tyoor, -choc — *n.* **1** grotesque usu. comically e aggerated representation esp. of person. **2** ridiculously poor or absu imitation or version. — *v.* (**-ring**) ma or give a caricature of. □ **caricaturist** [Italian *caricare* exaggerate]

**caries** /**kair**-reez/ *n.* (*pl.* same) decay a tooth or bone. [Latin]

**carillon** /kuh-**ril**-yuhn/ *n.* **1** set of be (in a tower) sounded either from keyboard or mechanically. **2** tune played on bells. [French]

**caring** *adj.* **1** kind, humane; committed, compassionate (*a caring society*; *he is caring in his outlook*). **2** (*attrib.*) concerned with looking after people (*the caring professions*).

**cark¹** /kahk/ *v.* **1** (of a crow) caw. **2** (of a person) speak raucously. [imitative]

**cark²** var. of KARK.

**Carmelite** /kah-muh-ˌlyt/ — *n.* **1** friar of the order of Our Lady of Mount Carmel, following a Rule of extreme asceticism; White Friar. **2** nun of a similar order. — *adj.* of the Carmelites. [Mt. *Carmel* in Palestine, where the order was founded in the 12th c.]

**carminative** /kah-muh-nuh-tiv/ — *adj.* relieving flatulence. — *n.* carminative drug. [Latin *carmino* heal by CHARM]

**carmine** /kah-muyn/ — *adj.* of vivid crimson colour. — *n.* **1** this colour. **2** carmine pigment made from cochineal. [probably from Latin *carmesinum* CRIMSON]

**carn** /kahn/ *v. colloq.* (in barracking at sporting fixtures) 'come on!'. [alteration of *come on*]

**carnage** /kah-nij/ *n.* great slaughter, esp. in battle. [Latin: related to CARNAL]

**carnal** /kah-nuhl/ *adj.* of the body or flesh; worldly. **2** sensual, sexual. □ **carnality** /-nal-uh-tee/ *n.* [Latin *caro carn-* flesh]

**carnal knowledge** *n. Law* sexual intercourse.

**carnation** /kah-nay-shuhn/ — *n.* **1** clove-scented pink with variously coloured flowers. **2** rosy-pink colour. — *adj.* rosy-pink. [Italian: related to CARNAL because of the flesh-colour]

**carnelian** var. of CORNELIAN.

**carnival** /kah-nuh-vuhl/ *n.* **1 a** annual festivities including a parade through the streets in fancy dress. **b** festival preceding Lent. **2** merrymaking. **3** series of sporting events (*swimming carnival*; *surf carnival*). [Latin *carnem levo* put away meat]

**carnivore** /kah-nuh-ˌvaw/ *n.* carnivorous animal or plant, esp. a mammal of the order including cats, dogs, and bears.

**carnivorous** /kah-niv-uh-ruhs/ *adj.* (of an animal or plant) feeding on flesh. [Latin: related to CARNAL, *voro* devour]

**carob** /ka-ruhb/ *n.* seed pod of a Mediterranean tree used as a chocolate substitute. [Arabic *ḳarrūba*]

**carol** /ka-ruhl/ — *n.* joyous song, esp. a Christmas hymn. — *v.* (**-ll-**) **1** sing carols. **2** sing joyfully. [French]

**carotene** /ka-ruh-ˌteen/ *n.* orange-coloured pigment found in carrots, tomatoes, etc., acting as a source of vitamin A. [Latin: related to CARROT]

**carotenoid** /kuh-rot-uh-ˌnoid/ *n.* any of a group of yellow, orange, or brown pigments giving characteristic colour to plant organs, e.g. ripe tomatoes, carrots, autumn leaves.

**carotid** /kuh-rot-uhd/ — *n.* each of the two main arteries carrying blood to the head and neck. — *adj.* of these arteries. [Latin from Greek]

**carouse** /kuh-rowz/ — *v.* (**-sing**) have a lively drinking-party. — *n.* such a party. □ **carousal** *n.* **carouser** *n.* [German *gar aus* (drink) right out!]

**carousel** /ˌka-ruh-sel, ka-ruh-sel/ *n.* **1** merry-go-round. **2** rotating luggage delivery system at an airport etc. [French from Italian]

**carp¹** *n.* (*pl.* same) freshwater fish often bred for food, introduced into Australian rivers. [Provençal or Latin]

**carp²** *v.* find fault; complain pettily. □ **carper** *n.* [Old Norse, = brag]

**carpal** /kah-puhl/ — *adj.* of the bones in the wrist. — *n.* wrist-bone. [from CARPUS]

**carpel** /kah-puhl/ *n.* female reproductive organ of a flower. [Greek *karpos* fruit]

**carpenter** /kah-puhn-tuh/ — *n.* person skilled in woodwork, esp. of a structural kind. — *v.* **1** make or construct in wood. **2** construct; fit together. □ **carpentry** *n.* [Latin *carpentum* wagon]

**carpet** /kah-puht/ — *n.* **1 a** thick fabric for covering floor or stairs. **b** piece of this. **2** thing resembling this etc. (*carpet of snow*). — *v.* (**-t-**) **1** cover with or as with carpet. **2** *colloq.* reprimand. □ **on the carpet** *colloq.* **1** being reprimanded. **2** under consideration. **sweep under the carpet** conceal (a problem or difficulty). [Latin *carpo* pluck]

**carpet-bagger** *n. colloq.* **1** esp. *US* political candidate etc. without local connections (orig. a northerner in southern US after the Civil War). **2** unscrupulous opportunist.

**carpet shark** *n.* (also **wobbegong**) any of several slow-moving, bottom-dwelling, eastern Australian sharks, having variegated patterning on its skin.

**carpet snake** *n.* python (growing to 4m) with variegated skin patterning, widespread in Australia.

**car phone** *n.* radio-telephone for use in a car etc.

**carport** *n.* roofed open-sided shelter for a car.

**carpus** /**kah**-puhs/ n. (pl. **-pi** /-puy/) small bones forming the wrist in humans and similar parts in other mammals. [Latin from Greek]

**carrel** /**ka**-ruhl, ,kuh-**rel**/ n. small cubicle for a reader in a library. [French from medieval Latin]

**carriage** /**ka**-rij/ n. **1** railway passenger vehicle. **2** wheeled horse-drawn passenger vehicle. **3 a** conveying of goods. **b** cost of this. **4** carrying part of a machine (e.g. a typewriter). **5** gun-carriage. **6** bearing, deportment. [French: related to CARRY]

**carriageway** n. the part of a road intended for vehicles.

**carrier** /**ka**-ree-uh/ n. **1** person or thing that carries. **2** transport or freight company. **3** person who transports goods etc. **4** framework on a bicycle for luggage or a passenger. **5** person or animal that may transmit disease etc. without suffering from it. **6** = AIRCRAFT-CARRIER.

**carrier pigeon** n. pigeon trained to carry messages.

**carrier wave** n. high-frequency electromagnetic wave modulated in amplitude or frequency to convey a signal.

**carrion** /**ka**-ree-uhn/ — n. **1** dead putrefying flesh. **2** something vile or filthy. — adj. rotten; loathsome. [Latin caro flesh]

**carrot** /**ka**-ruht/ n. **1 a** plant with a tapering orange-coloured root. **b** this as a vegetable. **2** means of enticement or persuasion. □ **carroty** adj. [Greek karōton]

**carry** /**ka**-ree/ — v. (**-ies, -ied**) **1** support or hold up, esp. while moving. **2** convey with one or have on one's person (I don't carry any money). **3** conduct or transmit (pipe carries water). **4** (often foll. by to) take (a process etc.) to a specified point; continue; prolong (carry into effect; carry a joke too far). **5** involve, imply (carries a two-year guarantee; principles carry consequences). **6** Math. transfer (a figure) to a column of higher value. **7** hold in a specified way (carry oneself erect). **8 a** (of a newspaper etc.) publish; include in its contents. **b** (of a radio or television station) broadcast. **9** keep a regular stock of. **10 a** (of sound) be audible at a distance. **b** (of a missile or gun etc.) travel or propel to a specified distance. **11 a** win victory or acceptance for (a proposal, motion, etc.). **b** win acceptance from (carried the audience with her). **c** win, capture (a prize, fortress, etc.). **12 a** endure the weight of; support (columns carry the dome). **b** be the driving force in (you carry the department). **13** be pregnant with. — n. (pl. **-ies**) **1** act of carrying. **2** Golf distance a ball travels before

reaching the ground. □ **carry away 1** remove. **2** inspire; affect emotionally or spiritually. **3** deprive of self-control (got carried away). **carry the can** colloq. bear the responsibility or blame. **carry the day** be victorious or successful. **carry forward** transfer to a new page or account. **carry it off** do well under difficulties. **carry off 1** take away, esp. by force. **2** win (a prize). **3** (esp. of a disease) kill. **carry on 1** continue. **2** engage in (conversation or business). **3** colloq. behave strangely or excitedly. **4** (often foll. by with) colloq. flirt or have a love affair. **carry out** put (an idea, instructions, etc.) into practice. **carry over 1** = carry forward. **2** postpone (work etc.). **carry through 1** complete successfully. **2** bring safely out of difficulties. **carry weight** be influential or important. [Anglo-French: related to CAR]

**carryings-on** n.pl. = CARRY-ON.

**carry-on** n. colloq. **1** fuss, excitement. **2** questionable behaviour. **3** flirtation or love affair.

**car seat** n. child's seat, offering protection in the event of an accident.

**carsick** adj. nauseous from car travel. □ **carsickness** n.

**cart** — n. **1** open usu. horse-drawn vehicle for carrying loads. **2** light vehicle for pulling by hand. — v. **1** convey in a cart. **2** colloq. carry or convey with effort. □ **put the cart before the horse** get one's priorities wrong; reverse the proper order or procedure. [Old English and Old Norse]

**carte blanche** /kaht **blonsh**/ n. full discretionary power. [French, = blank paper]

**cartel** /kah-**tel**/ n. informal association of manufacturers or suppliers etc. to control prices. [Italian diminutive: related to CARD¹]

**Cartesian** /kah-**tee**-zhuhn/ — adj. of Descartes or his philosophy. — n. follower of Descartes. [Latin Cartesius Descartes, French philosopher and mathematician (d. 1650)]

**Cartesian coordinates** n.pl. system for locating a point by reference to its distance from two or more axes intersecting at right angles.

**Carthusian** /kah-**thyoo**-zee-uhn/ — n. monk of a contemplative order founded by St Bruno in 1084. — adj. of this order. [Latin: related to CHARTREUSE]

**cartilage** /**kah**-tuh-lij, **kaht**-lij/ n. gristle, a firm flexible connective tissue, mainly replaced by bone in adulthood. □ **cartilaginous** /-**laj**-uh-nuhs/ adj. [French from Latin]

**cartography** /kah-**tog**-ruh-fee/ n. science or art of map-drawing. □ **cartographer** n.

**cartographic** /-tuh-**graf**-ik/ adj. [French carte map]

**carton** /**kah**-tuhn/ n. light esp. cardboard box or container. [French: related to CARTOON]

**cartoon** /kah-**toon**/ n. **1** humorous, topical, drawing in a newspaper etc. **2** sequence of drawings telling a story. **3** animated sequence of these on film. **4** full-size preliminary design for a painting, tapestry, etc. □ **cartoonist** n. [Italian: related to CARD¹]

**cartridge** /**kah**-trij/ n. **1** case containing an explosive charge or bullet for firearms or blasting. **2** sealed container of film, magnetic tape, etc. **3** component carrying the stylus on a record-player. **4** ink-container for insertion in a pen. [French: related to CARTOON]

**cartridge paper** n. thick rough paper for drawing etc.

**cartwheel** n. **1** wheel of a cart. **2** circular sideways handspring with arms and legs extended.

**carve** v. (**-ving**) **1** produce or shape by cutting. **2 a** cut patterns etc. in. **b** (foll. by into) form a pattern etc. from (carved it into a bust). **3** (absol.) cut (meat etc.) into slices. □ **carve out 1** take from a larger whole. **2** establish (a career etc.) purposefully. **carve up 1** divide into several pieces or parts; subdivide (territory etc.). **2** colloq. defeat soundly (our team was carved up by the opposition). □ **carver** n. [Old English]

**carvery** n. (pl. **-ies**) buffet or restaurant with joints displayed for carving.

**carve-up** n. colloq. sharing-out, esp. of spoils.

**carving** n. carved object, esp. as a work of art.

**Casanova** /kas-uh-**noh**-vuh/ n. notorious womaniser. [Italian adventurer (d. 1798)]

**cascade** /kas-**kayd**/ — n. **1** small waterfall, esp. one in a series, or part of a large broken waterfall. **2** thing falling or arranged like a cascade. — v. (**-ding**) fall in or like a cascade. [Latin: related to CASE¹]

**case¹** n. **1** instance of something occurring. **2** hypothetical or actual situation. **3** a person's illness, circumstances, etc., as regarded by a doctor, social worker, etc. **b** such a person. **4** matter under esp. police investigation. **5** suit at law. **6 a** sum of the arguments on one side, esp. in a lawsuit. **b** set of arguments (have a good case). **c** valid set of arguments (have no case). **7** Gram. **a** relation of a word to other words in a sentence. **b** form of a noun, adjective, or pronoun expressing

this. **8** colloq. **a** comical person. **b** person as specified (a hard case). □ **in any case** whatever the truth is; whatever may happen. **in case 1** in the event that; if. **2** lest; in provision against a possibility (took it in case). **in case of** in the event of. **is** (or **is not**) **the case** is (or is not) so. [Latin casus from cado fall]

**case²** — n. **1** container or enclosing covering. **2** this with its contents. **3** protective outer covering of a watch, seed-vessel, sausage, etc. **4** item of luggage, esp. a suitcase. **5** Printing partitioned receptacle for type, with the capitals in the upper part (thus UPPER CASE) and the simple letters in the lower part (thus LOWER CASE). — v. (**-sing**) **1** enclose in a case. **2** (foll. by with) surround. **3** colloq. reconnoitre (a house etc.) before burgling it. [Latin capsa box]

**case history** n. record of a person's life or medical history for use in professional treatment.

**casein** /**kay**-see-uhn, **kay**-seen/ n. the main protein in milk and cheese. [Latin caseus cheese]

**case law** n. law as established by decided cases.

**casement** /**kays**-muhnt/ n. window or part of a window hinged to open like a door. [Anglo-Latin: related to CASE²]

**case moth** n. any of several Australian moths whose larvae make and inhabit cases of silk.

**cash** — n. **1** money in coins or notes, as distinct from a cheque. **2** (also **cash down**) full payment at the time of purchase, as distinct from credit. **3** colloq. wealth. — v. give or obtain cash for (a note, cheque, etc.). □ **cashed up** colloq. well supplied with money. **cash in 1** obtain cash for. **2** colloq. (usu. foll. by on) profit (from); take advantage (of). [Latin: related to CASE²]

**cash book** n. book for recording receipts and cash payments.

**cash economy** n. = BLACK ECONOMY.

**cashew** /**kash**-oo/ n. **1** evergreen tree, native to Central and S. America, bearing kidney-shaped nuts attached to fleshy, edible fruit. **2** (in full **cashew apple**) this fruit. **3** (in full **cashew nut**) this edible nut. [Portuguese from Tupi (a) caju]

**cash flow** n. movement of money into and out of a business, as a measure of profitability.

**cashier¹** /ka-**sheer**, ka-**sheer**/ n. person dealing with cash transactions in a shop, bank, etc.

**cashier²** /ka-**sheer**/ v. dismiss from service, esp. with disgrace. [French: related to QUASH]

**cashmere** /**kash**-meer/ n. **1** fine soft wool, esp. that of a Kashmir goat. **2** material made from this. [*Kashmir* in Asia]

**cash register** n. till recording sales, totalling receipts, etc.

**cash-strapped** adj. colloq. short of cash.

**casing** /**kay**-sing/ n. **1** protective or enclosing cover. **2** material for this.

**casino** /kuh-**see**-noh/ n. (pl. **-s**) public room or building for gambling. [Italian diminutive of *casa* house]

**cask** /kahsk/ n. **1 a** (in full **wine cask**) plastic or foil-lined container for table wine, enclosed within a cardboard pack, and having a spigot so that wine not drawn off remains under a vacuum (also *attrib.*: *cask wine*). **b** such a container for fruit juice etc. **2 a** barrel, esp. for alcohol. **b** its contents. [French *casque* or Spanish *casco* helmet]

**casket** /**kahs**-kuht/ n. **1** small often ornamental box for jewels etc. **2** coffin. [Latin: related to CASE²]

**Cassandra** /kuh-**san**-druh/ n. prophet of disaster, esp. if disregarded. [name of a Trojan prophetess]

**cassata** /kuh-**sah**-tuh/ n. ice-cream containing fruit and nuts. [Italian]

**cassava** /kuh-**sah**-vuh/ n. **1** plant with starchy roots. **2** starch or flour from these, used e.g. in tapioca. [Taino]

**casserole** /**kas**-uh-ˌrohl/ — n. **1** covered dish, usu. of earthenware or glass, for cooking food in the oven. **2** food cooked in this. — v. (**-ling**) cook in a casserole. [Greek *kuathion* little cup]

**cassette** /kuh-**set**, ka-/ n. sealed case containing magnetic tape, film, etc., ready for insertion in a tape recorder, camera, etc. [French diminutive: related to CASE²]

**cassia** /**kas**-ee-uh/ n. **1** any of about 30 Australian species of the genus of this name, varying in size from low shrubs to large trees, all having attractive pinnate leaves and golden flowers which make the plant spectacular when in bloom. **2** tree of the same genus, native to Sudan, from the leaves of which senna is extracted. **3** cinnamon-like bark of an unrelated tree (*Cinnamomum cassia*) used as a spice. [Greek *kasia* from Hebrew]

**cassock** /**kas**-uhk/ n. long usu. black or red garment worn by priests, altar-servers, etc. □ **cassocked** adj. [French from Italian]

**cassowary** /**kas**-uh-ˌwuh-ree/ n. (pl. **-ies**) any of several large flightless Australasian birds with heavy body, stout legs, a wattled neck, and a bony crest on the forehead; the Australian cassowary is black with a bare blue neck and red wattles, and inhabits rainforest areas of northern Queensland. [Malay]

**cast** /kahst/ — v. (*past* and *past part.* **cast**) **1** throw, esp. deliberately or forcefully. **2** (often foll. by *on*, *over*) **a** direct or cause (one's eyes, a glance, light, a shadow, a spell, etc.) to fall. **b** express (doubts, aspersions, etc.). **3** throw out (a fishing-line etc.) into the water. **4** let down (an anchor etc.). **5 a** throw off, get rid of. **b** shed or lose (horns, skin, a horseshoe, etc.). **6** register (a vote). **7 a** shape (molten metal etc.) in a mould. **b** make (a product) in this way. **8 a** (usu. foll. by *as*) assign (an actor) to a role. **b** allocate roles in (a play etc.). **9** (foll. by *in*, *into*) arrange (facts etc.) in a specified form. **10** reckon, add up (accounts or figures). **11** calculate (a horoscope). **12** (in mustering) direct (a sheepdog) to make a wide sweep. — n. **1** throwing of a missile, dice, line, net, etc. **2 a** object made in a mould. **b** moulded mass of solidified material, esp. plaster for a broken limb. **3** actors in a play etc. **4** form, type, or quality (*cast of mind*). **5** tinge or shade of colour (*has a reddish cast*). **6** slight squint. **7 a** mass of earth excreted by a worm. **b** mass of indigestible food thrown up by a magpie, owl, etc. □ **cast about** (or **around**) search. **cast adrift** leave to drift. **cast aside** abandon. **cast loose** detach (oneself). **cast lots** see LOT. **cast off 1** abandon. **2** finish a piece of knitting. **3** set a ship free from a quay etc. **cast on** make the first row of a piece of knitting. **cast up 1** deposit on the shore. **2** add up (figures etc.). [Old Norse]

**castanet** /ˌkas-tuh-**net**/ n. (usu. in pl.) each of a pair of hand-held pieces of wood etc., clicked together as an accompaniment, esp. by Spanish dancers. [Latin: related to CHESTNUT]

**castaway** /**kahst**-uh-ˌway/ — n. ship-wrecked person. — adj. shipwrecked.

**caste** /kahst/ n. **1** any of the Hindu hereditary classes whose members have no social contact with other classes. **2** any exclusive social class or system of classes. [Spanish and Portuguese: related to CHASTE]

**castellated** /**kas**-tuh-ˌlay-tuhd/ adj. **1** having battlements. **2** castle-like. □ **castellation** /-**lay**-shuhn/ n. [medieval Latin: related to CASTLE]

**caster** var. of CASTOR.

**caster sugar** n. (also **castor sugar**) finely granulated white sugar.

**castigate** /**kas**-tuh-ˌgayt/ v. (**-ting**) rebuke or punish severely. □ **castigation**

/**-gay**-shuhn/ n. **castigator** n. [Latin *castus* pure]

**casting** /**kahs**-ting/ n. **1** cast, esp. of molten metal. **2** process of choosing actors for a film etc.

**casting vote** n. deciding vote when the votes on two sides are equal. [from an obsolete sense of *cast*, = turn the scale]

**cast iron** n. hard alloy of iron, carbon, and silicon cast in a mould.

**cast-iron** adj. **1** of cast iron. **2** very strong; rigid; unchallengeable (*must have a cast-iron stomach; cast-iron alibi*).

**castle** /**kah**-suhl, **kas**-uhl/ — n. **1** large fortified building with towers and battlements. **2** *Chess* = ROOK[2]. — v. (**-ling**) *Chess* move a rook next to the king and the king to the other side of the rook. □ **castles in the air** day-dream; impractical scheme. [Latin *castellum*]

**cast-off** — adj. abandoned, discarded. — n. cast-off thing, esp. a garment.

**castor** /**kah**-stuh/ n. (also **caster**) **1** small swivelled wheel on the leg or underside of a piece of furniture. **2** small perforated container for sprinkling sugar, flour, etc. [from CAST]

**castor oil** /**kah**-stuh/ n. oil from the seeds of a tropical plant, used as a purgative and lubricant. [origin uncertain]

**castrate** /kas-**trayt**, kah-**strayt**/ v. (**-ting**) **1** remove the testicles of; geld. **2** deprive of vigour (*editor castrated my article by cutting out so much*). □ **castration** n. [Latin *castro*]

**castrato** /ka-**strah**-toh/ n. (*pl.* **-ti** /-tee/) *hist.* male singer castrated in boyhood so as to retain a soprano or alto voice. [Italian: related to CASTRATE]

**casual** /**kazh**-yoo-uhl/ — adj. **1** accidental; chance. **2** not regular or permanent (*casual work*). **3 a** unconcerned (*was very casual about it*). **b** made or done without great care or thought (*a casual remark*). **4** (of clothes) informal. — n. **1** casual worker. **2** (usu. in *pl.*) casual clothes or shoes. □ **casually** adv. **casualness** n. [French and Latin: related to CASE[1]]

**casual sex** n. sexual activity between persons who are not regular or established sexual partners.

**casualty** /**kazh**-yoo-uhl-tee, **kazh**-uhl-tee/ n. (*pl.* **-ies**) **1** person killed or injured in a war or accident. **2** thing lost or destroyed. **3** = CASUALTY DEPARTMENT. **4** accident, mishap. [medieval Latin: related to CASUAL]

**casualty department** n. part of a hospital where casualties are dealt with.

**casuarina** /**kazh**-yuh-**ree**-nuh/ n. (also **she-oak**) any of about 30 Australian species, ranging from shrubs to tall trees, of the genus of the same name, having distinctive foliage consisting of whorls of minute teeth-like leaves on very slender jointed branchlets, resembling gigantic horsetails. [from modern Latin *casuarius* cassowary (from the fancied resemblance between branches and feathers)]

**casuist** /**kaz**-yoo-uhst/ n. **1** person who uses clever but false reasoning in matters of conscience etc. **2** sophist, quibbler. □ **casuistic** /-**is**-tik/ adj. **casuistry** n. [Latin: related to CASE[1]]

**CAT** /kat/ abbr. (in full **computerised axial tomography**) a medical technology which provides a series of cross-sectional pictures of internal organs and builds these up into a detailed picture using an x-ray machine controlled by a computer (used *attrib.*: *CAT scan; CAT scanner; CAT scanning*).

**cat**[1] n. **1** small soft-furred four-legged domesticated animal. **2** wild animal of the same family, e.g. lion, tiger. **3** *colloq.* malicious or spiteful woman. **4** = CAT-O'-NINE-TAILS. **5** *colloq.* jazz enthusiast. □ **the cat's whiskers** *colloq.* excellent person or thing. **let the cat out of the bag** reveal a secret. **like a cat on hot bricks** very agitated. **put** (or **set**) **the cat among the pigeons** cause trouble. **rain cats and dogs** see RAIN. [Latin *cattus*]

**cat**[2] n. *colloq.* catamaran. [abbreviation]

**cata-** *prefix* **1** down (*catarrh*). **2** wrongly (*catachresis*). [Greek *kata* down]

**catabolism** /kuh-**tab**-uh-,liz-uhm/ n. breakdown of complex molecules in living organisms to release energy; destructive metabolism. □ **catabolic** /,kat-uh-**bol**-ik/ adj. [Greek *katabolē* throwing down]

**catachresis** /,kat-uh-**kree**-suhs/ n. (*pl.* **-chreses** /-seez/) incorrect use of words. □ **catachrestic** /-**kree**-stik, -**kres**-tik/ adj. [Greek *khraomai khres-* use]

**cataclysm** /**kat**-uh-,kliz-uhm/ n. **1 a** violent, esp. social or political, upheaval or disaster. **b** great change. **2** great flood or deluge. □ **cataclysmic** /-**kliz**-mik/ adj. [Greek *kluzō -klusm-* wash]

**catacomb** /**kat**-uh-,kohm, -,koom/ n. (often in *pl.*) **1** underground cemetery, esp. Roman, with tunnels, recesses for tombs. **2** any similar underground construction. [French from Latin]

**catafalque** /**kat**-uh-,falk/ n. decorated framework for supporting the coffin of a distinguished person during a funeral or while lying in state. [French from Italian]

**Catalan** /**kat**-uh-lan, -luhn/ — n. native or language of Catalonia in Spain. — adj. of Catalonia. [French from Spanish]

**catalepsy** /kat-uh-,lep-see/ *n.* trance or seizure with unconsciousness and rigidity of the body. □ **cataleptic** /-lep-tik/ *adj. & n.* [Greek *lēpsis* seizure]

**catalogue** /kat-uh-,log/ — *n.* **1** complete alphabetical or otherwise ordered list of items, often with a description of each. **2** extensive list (*catalogue of disasters*). — *v.* (**-logues, -logued, -loguing**) **1** make a catalogue of. **2** enter in a catalogue. [Greek *legō* choose]

**catalyse** /kat-uh-,luyz/ *v.* (also **-yze**) (**-sing** or **-zing**) produce (a reaction) by catalysis.

**catalysis** /kuh-tal-uh-suhs/ *n.* (*pl.* **-lyses** /-,seez/) acceleration of a chemical reaction by a catalyst. [Greek *luō* set free]

**catalyst** /kat-uh-luhst/ *n.* **1** substance that does not itself change, but speeds up a chemical reaction. **2** person or thing that precipitates change.

**catalytic** /,kat-uh-lit-ik/ *adj.* of or involving catalysis.

**catalytic converter** *n.* device incorporated in a vehicle's exhaust system, with a catalyst for converting pollutant gases into harmless products.

**catamaran** /,kat-uh-muh-ran/ *n.* **1** boat with parallel twin hulls. **2** raft of yoked logs or boats. [Tamil]

**catamite** /kat-uh-,muyt/ *n.* passive partner (esp. a boy) in homosexual practices. [Latin, = Ganymede, boy abducted by the god Zeus to be his cup-bearer]

**cat-and-dog** *adj.* (of a relationship etc.) quarrelsome.

**catapult** /kat-uh-,pult/ — *n.* **1** forked stick etc. with elastic for shooting stones. **2** *Mil. hist.* machine for hurling large stones etc. **3** device for launching a glider, an aircraft from the deck of a ship, etc. — *v.* **1 a** hurl from or launch with a catapult. **b** fling forcibly. **2** leap or be hurled forcibly. [Latin from Greek]

**cataract** /kat-uh-,rakt/ *n.* **1 a** large waterfall. **b** downpour; rush of water. **2** eye condition in which the lens becomes progressively opaque, resulting in blurred vision. [Greek *katarrhaktēs*, = down-rushing]

**catarrh** /kuh-tah/ *n.* **1** inflammation of the mucous membrane of the nose, air-passages, etc. **2** mucus caused by this. □ **catarrhal** *adj.* [Greek *katarheō* flow down]

**catastrophe** /kuh-tas-truh-fee/ *n.* **1** great and usu. sudden disaster. **2** dénouement of a drama. □ **catastrophic** /-strof-ik/ *adj.* **catastrophically** /-strof-i-kuh-lee, -klee/ *adv.* [Greek *strephō* turn]

**catatonia** /,kat-uh-toh-nee-uh/ *n.* **1** schizophrenia with intervals of catalepsy and sometimes violence. **2** catalepsy. □ **catatonic** /-ton-ik/ *adj. & n.* [Greek: related to CATA-, TONE]

**catbird** *n.* any of several Australian rainforest birds with a miaow-like call (*green catbird*; *spotted catbird*; *tooth-billed catbird*).

**cat burglar** *n.* burglar who enters by climbing to an upper storey.

**catcall** — *n.* shrill whistle of disapproval. — *v.* make a catcall.

**catch** — *v.* (*past* and *past part.* **caught** /kawt/) **1** lay hold of so as to restrain or prevent from escaping; capture in a trap, one's hands, etc. **2** detect or surprise (esp. a guilty person) (*caught him smoking*). **3 a** intercept and hold (a moving thing) in the hands etc. (*caught the ball*; *a bowl to catch the drips*). **b** *Cricket* dismiss (a batsman) by catching the ball before it reaches the ground. **4 a** contract (a disease) from an infected person. **b** acquire (a quality etc.) from another (*caught her enthusiasm*). **5 a** reach in time and board (a train, bus, etc.). **b** be in time to see etc. (a person or thing about to leave or finish) (*caught the end of the performance*). **6 a** apprehend with the senses or mind (esp. a thing occurring quickly or briefly) (*didn't catch what you said*). **b** watch (a play, television programme, etc.); listen to (a concert etc.) (*catch the footy replay on telly tonight*). **7** (of an artist etc.) reproduce faithfully. **8 a** (cause to) become fixed, entangled, or checked (*the bolt began to catch*; *caught his jumper on a nail*). **b** (often foll. by *on*) hit, deal a blow to (*caught his elbow on the table*). **9** draw the attention of; captivate (*caught his eye*; *caught her fancy*). **10** begin to burn (*the fire hasn't caught yet*; *the gravy's beginning to catch*). **11** reach or overtake (a person etc. ahead). **12** (foll. by *at*) try to grasp. **13** check suddenly (*caught his breath*). — *n.* **1 a** act of catching. **b** *Cricket* etc. chance or act of catching the ball. **2 a** amount of a thing caught, esp. of fish. **b** thing or person caught or worth catching, esp. in marriage (*he's quite a catch*). **3 a** question, trick, etc., intended to deceive, incriminate, etc. (*what's the catch?*). **b** unexpected or hidden difficulty or disadvantage (*there's a catch — we have to submit the proposal within the hour*). **4** device for fastening a door or window etc. □ **catch fire** see FIRE. **catch hold of** grasp, seize. **catch it** *colloq.* be punished or in trouble. **catch on** *colloq.* **1** become popular. **2** understand what is meant. **catch out 1** detect in a mistake etc. **2** take unawares. **3** = sense 3b of *v*. **catch up 1 a** (often foll. by *with*) reach a person etc. ahead (*caught us up; caught up with us*). **b** (often foll. by *with, on*) make up arrears (*caught up on my correspondence; caught up on some sleep*). **2** pick up hurriedly (*caught up the first shirt that came to hand*). **3** (often in *passive*) **a** involve; entangle (*caught up in crime; caught up in peak-hour traffic*). **b** fasten up (*hair caught up in a ribbon*). [Latin *capto* try to catch]

**catch-all** *n*. (often *attrib*.) thing designed to be all-inclusive (*catch-all remedies rarely catch anything*).

**catching** *adj*. **1 a** (of a disease, practice, etc.) infectious. **b** (of a practice etc.) likely to be imitated. **2** attractive; captivating.

**catching pen** *n*. pen in a shearing shed from which the shearer takes the sheep to be shorn.

**catchment** *n*. collection of rainfall.

**catchment area** *n*. **1** area served by a school, hospital, etc. **2** area from which rainfall flows into a river etc.

**catch-phrase** *n*. phrase in frequent use.

**catch-22** *n*. (often *attrib*.) *colloq*. unresolvable situation containing conflicting or mutually dependent conditions.

**catchword** *n*. **1** phrase, word, or slogan in frequent current use. **2** *Printing* first word of a page given at the foot of a previous one.

**catchy** *adj*. (**-ier, -iest**) **1** (of a tune) easy to remember, attractive. **2** that snares or entraps; deceptive.

**catechise** /kat-uh-ˌkuyz/ *v*. (also **-ize**) (**-sing** or **-zing**) instruct by using a catechism. [Greek *katēkheō* cause to hear]

**catechism** /kat-uh-ˌkiz-uhm/ *n*. **1 a** principles of a religion in the form of questions and answers. **b** book containing this. **2** series of questions. [Church Latin: related to CATECHISE]

**catechist** /kat-uh-kuhst/ *n*. religious teacher, esp. one using a catechism.

**catechumen** /ˌkat-uh-kyoo-muhn/ *n*. Christian convert under instruction before baptism. [Church Latin *catechumenus*]

**categorical** /ˌkat-uh-go-ri-kuhl/ *adj*. unconditional, absolute; explicit (*a categorical refusal*). □ **categorically** *adv*. [related to CATEGORY]

**categorise** /kat-uh-guh-ˌruyz/ *v*. (also **-ize**) (**-sing** or **-zing**) place in a category. □ **categorisation** /-zay-shuhn/ *n*.

**category** /kat-uh-guh-ree, -gree/ *n*. (*pl*. **-ies**) class or division (of things, ideas, etc.). [Greek, = statement]

**cater** /kay-tuh/ *v*. **1** supply food. **2** (foll. by *for*) provide what is needed or desired (*caters for all tastes*). **3** (foll. by *to*) pander to (esp. low tastes) (*many TV shows cater only to kidults*). [Anglo-French *acatour* buyer, from Latin *capto*: related to CATCH]

**caterer** *n*. professional supplier of food for social events.

**caterpillar** /kat-uh-ˌpil-uh/ *n*. **1** larva of a butterfly or moth. **2** (**Caterpillar**) **a** (in full **Caterpillar track** or **tread**) *propr*. steel band passing round the wheels of a tractor etc. for travel on rough ground. **b** vehicle with these. [Anglo-French, = hairy cat]

**caterpillar flower** *n*. handsome flax-like Australian plant having long (to 2 m) narrow leaves and small flowers in clustered spikes foll. by bluish berries (also once called 'settlers' twine' since the leaves yield a coarse fibre).

**caterwaul** /kat-uh-ˌwawl/ — *v*. **1** make the shrill howl of a cat. **2** be as noisy (in quarrelling etc.) as cats fighting. — *n*. this noise. [from CAT, -*waul* etc. imitative]

**catfish** *n*. (*pl*. same) any of various marine and freshwater fish in Australia, having whisker-like barbels round the mouth and harmful spines (*long-tailed catfish; white-lipped catfish*).

**catgut** *n*. material used for the strings of musical instruments and surgical sutures, made of intestines of the sheep, horse, etc. (but not cat).

**catharsis** /kuh-**thah**-suhs/ *n*. (*pl*. **catharses** /-ˌseez/) **1** emotional release in drama or art. **2** *Psychol*. freeing and elimination of repressed emotion. **3** emptying of the bowels. [Greek from *kathairō* cleanse]

**cathartic** /kuh-**thah**-tik/ — *adj*. **1** effecting catharsis. **2** laxative. — *n*. laxative.

**cat head** *n*. any of several Australian plants having spiny fruits.

**cathedral** /kuh-**thee**-druhl/ *n*. principal church of a diocese, containing the bishop's throne. [Greek *kathedra* seat]

**catherine wheel** /kath-ruhn/ *n*. flat coiled firework spinning when lit. [St *Catherine*, who was martyred on a spiked wheel]

**catheter** /kath-uh-tuh/ *n*. tube inserted into a body cavity for introducing or removing fluid. [Greek *kathiēmi* send down]

**cathode** /kath-ohd/ *n*. *Electr*. **1** negative electrode in an electrolytic cell. **2** positive terminal of a battery etc. [Greek *kathodos* way down]

**cathode ray** *n*. beam of electrons from the cathode of a vacuum tube.

**cathode ray tube** n. vacuum tube in which cathode rays produce a luminous image on a fluorescent screen.

**catholic** /**kath**-uh-lik, **kath**-lik/ — adj. **1** all-embracing; of wide sympathies or interests (has catholic tastes). **2** of interest or use to all; universal. **3** (**Catholic**) Roman Catholic. — n. (**Catholic**) Roman Catholic. □ **Catholicism** /kuh-**thol**-uh-,siz-uhm/ n. **catholicity** /,kath-uh-**lis**-uh-tee/ n. [Greek kata in respect of, holos whole]

**Catholic Church** n. Christian Church maintaining apostolic succession with the Pope as its head.

**cation** /**kat**-,uy-uhn/ n. positively charged ion. □ **cationic** /,kat-uy-**on**-ik/ adj. [from CATA-, ION]

**catkin** n. small spike of usu. hanging flowers on a willow, hazel, etc. [Dutch, = kitten]

**catnap** — n. short sleep. — v. (**-pp-**) have a catnap.

**cat-o'-nine-tails** n. hist. whip with nine knotted lashes for flogging sailors, convicts, etc.

**CAT scan** see CAT.

**cat's-eye** n. **1** precious stone. **2** reflector stud set into a road.

**cat's-paw** n. **1** person used as a tool by another. **2** slight breeze. **3** any of the smaller WA herbs of the genus Anigozanthos, having a claw-like flower with a furry appearance (see KANGAROO PAW).

**cat's whiskers** n. (also **cat's pyjamas**) colloq. excellent person or thing.

**cattle** /**kat**-uhl/ n.pl. large ruminant animals with horns and cloven hoofs, esp. bred for milk or meat. [Anglo-French catel: related to CAPITAL]

**cattle dog** n. dog bred and trained to work with cattle, such as the BLUE HEELER.

**cattle duff** v. steal cattle. □ **cattle duffer** n.

**cattle grid** n. grid over a ditch, allowing people and vehicles but not livestock to pass over.

**cattle run** see RUN n. 13.

**cattle station** n. large cattle-raising establishment.

**catty** adj. (**-ier, -iest**) spiteful. □ **cattily** adv. **cattiness** n.

**catwalk** n. **1** narrow footway along a bridge, above a theatre stage, etc. **2** narrow platform used in fashion shows etc.

**Caucasian** /kaw-**kay**-zhuhn/ — adj. **1** of the so-called white or light-skinned race. **2** of the Caucasus. — n. Caucasian person. [Caucasus in southern Russia]

**Caucasoid** /**kaw**-kuh-,zoid/ adj. of Caucasians.

**caucus** /**kaw**-kuhs/ n. (pl. **-es**) **1** meeting of the parliamentary members of a political party. **2** collectively, those eligible to attend such a meeting. [perhaps from Algonquian]

**caudal** /**kaw**-duhl/ adj. **1** of or like a tail. **2** of the posterior part of the body. [Latin cauda tail]

**caudate** /**kaw**-dayt/ adj. tailed.

**caught** past and past part. of CATCH.

**caul** /kawl/ n. **1** membrane enclosing a foetus. **2** part of this occasionally found on a child's head at birth. [French]

**cauldron** /**kawl**-druhn/ n. (also **caldron**) large deep vessel used for boiling. [Latin caldarium hot bath]

**cauli** /**kol**-ee/ n. colloq. cauliflower. [abbreviation]

**cauliflower** /**kol**-ee-,flowuh/ n. cabbage with a large white flower-head. [French chou fleuri flowered cabbage]

**cauliflower ear** n. ear thickened by repeated blows, esp. in boxing.

**caulk** /kawk/ v. (also **calk**) **1** stop up (the seams of a boat etc.). **2** make (esp. a boat) watertight. [Latin calco tread]

**causal** /**kaw**-zuhl/ adj. **1** of or forming a cause. **2** relating to cause and effect. □ **causally** adv.

**causality** /kaw-**zal**-uh-tee/ n. **1** relation of cause and effect. **2** principle that everything has a cause.

**causation** /kaw-**zay**-shuhn/ n. **1** act of causing. **2** = CAUSALITY.

**causative** /**kaw**-zuh-tiv/ adj. acting as or expressing a cause.

**cause** /kawz/ — n. **1 a** thing that produces an effect, or gives rise to an action, phenomenon, or condition. **b** person or thing that occasions or produces something. **c** reason or motive (has no cause for complaint). **2** adequate reason (show cause). **3** principle, belief, or purpose (loyal to the cause). **4 a** matter to be settled at law. **b** case offered at law (plead a cause). — v. (**-sing**) be the cause of, produce, make happen. [Latin causa]

**cause célèbre** /,kawz suh-**leb**-ruh/ n. (pl. **causes célèbres** pronunc. same) lawsuit or issue that attracts much interest. [French]

**causeway** /**kawz**-way/ n. raised road across low or wet ground or water. [Anglo-French caucée from Latin CALX]

**caustic** /**kos**-tik/ — adj. **1** corrosive; burning. **2** sarcastic, biting. — n. caustic substance. □ **caustically** adv. **causticity** /-**tis**-uh-tee/ n. [Greek kaiō burn]

**caustic soda** n. sodium hydroxide.

**auterise** /**kaw**-tuh-,ruyz/ v. (also **-ize**) (**-sing** or **-zing**) burn or coagulate (tissue) with a heated instrument or caustic substance, esp. to stop bleeding. [French: related to CAUSTIC]

**aution** /**kaw**-shuhn/ — n. **1** attention to safety; prudence, carefulness. **2 a** Law warning, esp. a formal one. **b** warning and reprimand. **3** colloq. amusing or surprising person or thing. — v. **1** warn or admonish. **2** issue a caution to. [Latin caveo caut- take heed]

**autionary** adj. giving or serving as a warning.

**autious** adj. having or showing caution. □ **cautiously** adv. **cautiousness** n.

**avalcade** /,kav-uhl-**kayd**/ n. procession or assembly of riders, vehicles, etc. [Italian: related to CHEVALIER]

**avalier** /,kav-uh-**leer**/ — n. **1** courtly gentleman. **2** archaic horseman. — adj. offhand, supercilious, curt (a cavalier response to our submission). [related to CAVALCADE]

**avalry** /**kav**-uhl-ree/ n. (pl. **-ies**) (usu. treated as pl.) soldiers on horseback or in armoured vehicles. [related to CAVALCADE]

**ave** — n. large hollow in the side of a cliff, hill, etc., or underground. — v. (**-ving**) explore caves. □ **cave in 1** (cause to) subside or collapse. **2** yield, give up. [Latin cavus hollow]

**aveat** /**kav**-ee-uht, **kay**-vee-uht/ n. **1** warning, proviso. **2** Law process in court to suspend proceedings. [Latin, = let him beware]

**aveat emptor** /,kav-ee-uht **emp**-taw, ,kay-vee-uht/ n. principle that the buyer alone is responsible if dissatisfied. [Latin, = let the buyer beware]

**aveman** n. **1** prehistoric person living in caves. **2** crude or old-fashioned person.

**avern** /**kav**-uhn/ n. cave, esp. a large or dark one. □ **cavernous** adj. [Latin caverna: related to CAVE]

**aviar** /**kav**-ee-ah, ,kav-ee-**ah**/ n. (also **caviare**) pickled roe of sturgeon or other large fish. [Italian from Turkish]

**avil** /**kav**-uhl/ — v. (**-ll-**) (usu. foll. by at, about) make petty objections; carp. — n. trivial objection. [Latin cavillor]

**avity** /**kav**-uh-tee/ n. (pl. **-ies**) **1** hollow within a solid body. **2** decayed part of a tooth. [Latin: related to CAVE]

**avity wall** n. double wall with a space between.

**avort** /kuh-**vawt**/ v. caper excitedly. [origin uncertain]

**aw** — n. harsh cry of a crow etc. — v. utter this cry. [imitative]

**cayenne** /kay-**en**/ n. (in full **cayenne pepper**) powdered hot red pepper. [Tupi]

**Cazaly** /kuh-**zay**-lee/ n. □ **up there Cazaly!** colloq. (orig. in Australian Rules and now also elsewhere) cry of encouragement. [Roy Cazaly Australian Rules footballer (1921–26) with a reputation for taking very high marks (d. 1963)]

**CB** abbr. citizens' band.

**cc** abbr. (also **c.c.**) **1** cubic centimetre(s). **2** copy or copies (to).

**CD** abbr. compact disc.

**Cd** symb. cadmium.

**cd** abbr. candela.

**CD-ROM** /,see-dee-**rom**/ abbr. Computing compact disc read-only memory.

**CD video** /,see-dee-**vid**-ee-oh/ n. (pl. **-s**) **1** system of simultaneously reproducing high-quality sound and video pictures from a compact disc. **2** such a compact disc.

**Ce** symb. cerium.

**cease** formal — v. (**-sing**) stop; bring or come to an end. — n. (in **without cease**) unending. [Latin cesso]

**ceasefire** n. **1** period of truce. **2** order to stop firing.

**ceaseless** adj. without end. □ **ceaselessly** adv.

**cedar** /**see**-duh/ n. **1 a** spreading evergreen conifer of Europe etc. **b** its hard fragrant wood. **2** any of several Australian trees resembling the cedar in the colour, grain, or fragrance of the wood, esp. the rainforest tree red cedar (*Toona australis*), now rare because of indiscriminate logging for its attractive deep red timber. [Greek *kedros*]

**cedar wattle** n. tall wattle of NSW and Victoria, having dark green true leaves and creamy ball-flowers in profusion.

**cede** v. (**-ding**) formal give up one's rights to or possession of. [Latin cedo cess- yield]

**cedilla** /suh-**dil**-uh/ n. **1** mark written under c, esp. in French, to show it is sibilant (as in façade). **2** similar mark under s in Turkish etc. [Spanish diminutive of zeda Z]

**ceiling** /**see**-ling/ n. **1** upper interior surface of a room or other compartment. **2** upper limit on prices, wages, etc. **3** maximum altitude a given aircraft can reach. [origin uncertain]

**celebrant** /**sel**-uh-bruhnt/ n. person who performs a rite, esp. the priest at Mass etc., or a secular person authorised to conduct civil marriages or funerals.

**celebrate** /**sel**-uh-,brayt/ v. (**-ting**) **1** mark with or engage in festivities. **2** perform (a rite or ceremony). **3** praise

**celebrity** /suh-**leb**-ruh-tee/ n. (pl. **-ies**) **1** well-known person. **2** fame. [Latin: related to CELEBRATE]

**celerity** /suh-**le**-ruh-tee/ n. archaic or literary swiftness. [Latin celer swift]

**celery** /**sel**-uh-ree/ n. plant with crisp long whitish-green leaf-stalks used as a vegetable. [Greek selinon parsley]

**celery-top pine** n. **1** Tasmanian rainforest tree having branchlets the upper parts of which have fern-like leaves resembling the foliage of celery. **2** the timber of this tree, valued for its durability and resistance to chemicals.

**celesta** /suh-**les**-tuh/ n. small keyboard instrument with steel plates struck to give a bell-like sound. [French: related to CELESTIAL]

**celestial** /suh-**les**-tee-uhl/ adj. **1** of the sky or heavenly bodies. **2** heavenly; divinely good; sublime. [Latin caelum sky]

**celestial equator** n. the great circle of the sky in the plane perpendicular to the earth's axis.

**celestial sphere** n. imaginary sphere, of any radius, of which the observer is the centre and in which celestial bodies are represented as lying.

**celibate** /**sel**-uh-buht/ — adj. **1** unmarried or committed to sexual abstention, esp. for religious reasons (celibate priesthood). **2** having no sexual relations. — n. celibate person. □ **celibacy** n. [Latin caelebs unmarried]

**cell** /sel/ n. **1** small room, esp. in a prison or monastery. **2** small compartment, e.g. in a honeycomb. **3** small, active, esp. subversive, political group. **4 a** smallest structural and functional unit of living matter, consisting of cytoplasm and a nucleus enclosed in a membrane. **b** enclosed cavity in an organism etc. **5** vessel containing electrodes for current-generation or electrolysis. [Latin cella]

**cellar** /**sel**-uh/ — n. **1** storage room below ground level in a house. **2** stock of wine in a cellar. — v. store in a cellar. [Latin cellarium: related to CELL]

**cello** /**chel**-oh/ n. (pl. **-s**) bass instrument of the violin family, held between the legs of the seated player. □ **cellist** n. [abbreviation of VIOLONCELLO]

**cellophane** /**sel**-uh-,fayn/ n. propr. thin transparent viscose wrapping material. [from CELLULOSE: cf. DIAPHANOUS]

**cellphone** n. small portable radio-telephone (see CELLULAR TELEPHONE).

**cellular** /**sel**-yuh-luh/ adj. consisting o cells; of open texture, porous. □ **cellularit** /-la-ruh-tee/ n. [French: related to CELL

**cellular telephone** n. hand-held mobil radio-telephone, portable or for use in car, which sends or receives signals via series of computer-linked transmitters each being responsible for particular area or 'cell'.

**cellulite** /**sel**-yuh-,luyt/ n. lumpy fat, esp on the hips and thighs of women [French: related to CELL]

**celluloid** /**sel**-yuh-,loid/ n. **1** plasti made from camphor and cellulos nitrate. **2** cinema film.

**cellulose** /**sel**-yuh-,lohz, -,lohs/ n. carbohydrate forming plant-cell walls used in textile fibres. **2** (in general use paint or lacquer consisting of esp cellulose acetate or nitrate in solution [Latin: related to CELL]

**Celsius** /**sel**-see-uhs/ adj. of a scale o temperature on which water freezes at 0 and boils at 100°. [name of a Swedis astronomer (d. 1744)]

■ **Usage** See note at centigrade.

**Celt** /kelt/ n. (also **Kelt**) member of a ethnic group, including the inhabitant of Ireland, Wales, Scotland, Cornwall and Brittany. [Latin from Greek]

**Celtic** /**kel**-tik, **sel**-tik/ — adj. of the Celts. — n. group of Celtic languages including Gaelic and Irish, Welsh Cornish, and Breton.

**cement** /suh-**ment**/ — n. **1** powdery substance of calcined lime and clay mixed with water to form mortar or use in concrete (see also PORTLAND CEMENT). **2** any similar substance that hardens and fastens on setting. **3** uniting factor o principle. **4** substance used in fillin teeth, doing hip replacements, etc. ■ colloq. concrete. — v. **1 a** unite with or a with cement. **b** establish or strengthen (a friendship etc.). **2** apply cement to. **3** lin or cover with cement. □ **cementation** /,see-men-**tay**-shuhn/ n. [Latin caedo cut

**cemetery** /**sem**-uh-tree/ n. (pl. **-ies** public burial ground. [Greek koimaō pu to sleep]

**cenobite** var. of COENOBITE.

**cenotaph** /**sen**-uh-,tahf, -,taf/ n. tomb like monument to a person whose body i elsewhere. [Greek kenos empty, tapho tomb]

**Cenozoic** /,see-nuh-**zoh**-ik/ (als **Cainozoic** /,kuy-nuh-/ ) — adj. of the mos recent geological era, marked by the evolution and development of mammals etc. — n. this era. [Greek kainos new zōion animal]

**censer** /**sen**-suh/ n. vessel for burning incense, esp. during High Mass or other religious ceremony. [Anglo-French: related to INCENSE¹]

**censor** /**sen**-suh/ — n. official authorised to suppress or expurgate books, films, news, etc., on grounds of obscenity, threat to security, etc. — v. **1** act as a censor of. **2** make deletions or changes in. □ **censorial** /-**saw**-ree-uhl/ adj. [Latin censeo assess]

■ **Usage** As a verb, censor is often confused with censure.

**censorious** /sen-**saw**-ree-uhs/ adj. severely critical. □ **censoriously** adv.

**censorship** /**sen**-suh-,ship/ n. act or instance of censoring.

**censure** /**sen**-shuh/ — v. (**-ring**) criticise harshly; reprove. — n. hostile criticism; disapproval. [Latin: related to CENSOR]

■ **Usage** As a verb, censure is often confused with censor.

**census** /**sen**-suhs/ n. (pl. **-suses**) official count of population etc., often with various statistics noted. [Latin: related to CENSOR]

**cent** n. **1 a** one-hundredth of a dollar or other decimal currency unit. **b** coin of this value. **2** colloq. very small amount. [Latin centum 100]

**centaur** /**sen**-taw/ n. creature in Greek mythology with the head, arms, and torso of a man and the body and legs of a horse. [Latin from Greek]

**centenarian** /,sen-tuh-**nair**-ree-uhn/ — n. person a hundred or more years old. — adj. a hundred or more years old.

**centenary** /sen-**tee**-nuh-ree, -**ten**-uh-ree/ — n. (pl. **-ies**) **1** hundredth anniversary. **2** celebration of this. — adj. **1** of a centenary. **2** occurring every hundred years. [Latin centeni 100 each]

**centennial** /sen-**ten**-ee-uhl/ adj. **1** lasting for a hundred years. **2** occurring every hundred years. **3** completing or marking a hundred years. [Latin centum 100, annus year]

**centesimal** /sen-**tes**-uh-muhl/ adj. reckoning or reckoned by hundredths. [Latin centum 100]

**centi-** comb. form **1** one-hundredth. **2** hundred. [Latin centum 100]

**centigrade** /**sen**-tuh-,grayd/ adj. **1** = CELSIUS. **2** having a scale of a hundred degrees. [Latin gradus step]

■ **Usage** In sense 1, Celsius is usually preferred in technical contexts.

**centigram** /**sen**-tuh-,gram/ n. (also **centigramme**) metric unit of mass, equal to 0.01 gram.

**centilitre** /**sen**-tuh-,lee-tuh/ n. 0.01 litre.

**centimetre** /**sen**-tuh-,mee-tuh/ n. 0.01 metre.

**centipede** /**sen**-tuh-,peed/ n. arthropod with a segmented wormlike body and many legs. [Latin pes ped- foot]

**central** /**sen**-truhl/ adj. **1** of, at, or forming the centre. **2** from the centre. **3** chief, essential, most important. □ **centrality** /-**tral**-uh-tee/ n. **centrally** adv.

**central heating** n. method of heating a building by pipes, radiators, etc., fed from a central source.

**Centralia** /sen-**tray**-lee-uh/ n. region around Alice Springs. □ **Centralian** adj. & n. [portmanteau word: Cen (tral) (Aus) tralia]

**centralise** v. (also **-ize**) (**-sing** or **-zing**) **1** concentrate (esp. administration) at a single centre. **2** subject (a nation) to this system. □ **centralisation** /-**zay**-shuhn/ n.

**centralism** n. system that centralises (esp. administration). □ **centralist** n.

**central nervous system** n. brain and spinal cord.

**central processor** n. (also **central processing unit**) principal operating part of a computer.

**centre** /**sen**-tuh/ — n. **1** middle point. **2** pivot or axis of rotation. **3 a** place or buildings forming a central point or a main area for an activity (shopping centre; town centre). **b** (with a preceding word) equipment for a number of connected functions (music centre). **c** (prec. by the) (also **Red Centre**) Central Australia. **4** point of concentration or dispersion; nucleus, source. **5** political party or group holding moderate opinions. **6** filling in chocolate etc. **7** Sport **a** middle player in a line in some field games. **b** kick or hit from the side to the centre of a pitch. **c** (in Australian Rules) player occupying the position in the centre of the field. **d** (in two-up) central part of the ring where the spinner stands. **8** (attrib.) of or at the centre. — v. (**-ring**) **1** (foll. by in, on, round) have as its main centre. **2** place in the centre. **3** (foll. by in etc.) concentrate. [Greek kentron sharp point]

■ **Usage** The use of the verb in sense 1 with round is common and used by good writers, but is still considered incorrect by some people.

**centreboard** n. board lowered through a boat's keel to prevent leeway.

**centreboard shed** *n.* shearing shed in which shearing takes place in the middle rather than along each side (cf. SIDE-BOARD).

**centrefold** *n.* centre spread of a magazine etc., esp. with nude photographs.

**centre half-back** *n.* *Aust. Rules* player occupying the position between the centre and full-back positions.

**centre half-forward** *n.* *Aust. Rules* player occupying the position between the centre and full-forward positions.

**centre of gravity** *n.* (also **centre of mass**) point at which the weight of a body may be considered to act.

**centrepiece** *n.* **1** ornament for the middle of a table. **2** principal item.

**centric** *adj.* **1** at or near the centre. **2** from a centre. □ **centrical** *adj.* **centrically** *adv.*

**centrifugal** /ˌsen-truh-**fyoo**-guhl, sen-**trif**-uh-guhl/ *adj.* moving or tending to move from a centre. □ **centrifugally** *adv.* [from CENTRE, Latin *fugio* flee]

**centrifugal force** *n.* apparent force that acts outwards on a body moving about a centre.

**centrifuge** /**sen**-truh-ˌfyooj, -ˌfyoozh/ *n.* rapidly rotating machine designed to separate liquids from solids etc.

**centripetal** /sen-**trip**-uh-tuhl/ *adj.* moving or tending to move towards a centre. □ **centripetally** *adv.* [Latin *peto* seek]

**centripetal force** *n.* force acting on a body causing it to move towards a centre.

**centuple** /**sen**-chuh-puhl/ — *n.* a hundredfold amount. — *adj.* increased a hundredfold. — *v.* multiply by a hundred; increase a hundredfold. [ecclesiastical Latin *centuplus* from Latin *centum* hundred]

**centurion** /sen-**tyoo**-ree-uhn, -**choo**-/ *n.* commander of a century in the ancient Roman army. [Latin: related to CENTURY]

**century** /**sen**-chuh-ree/ *n.* (*pl.* -**ies**) **1 a** 100 years. **b** any century reckoned from the birth of Christ (*twentieth century* = 1901–2000; *fifth century* BC = 500–401 BC). **2** score etc. of 100 esp. by one batsman in cricket. **3** company in the ancient Roman army, orig. of 100 men. [Latin *centuria*: related to CENT]

■ **Usage** Strictly speaking, since the first century ran from the year 1–100, the first year of a given century should be that ending in 01. However, in popular use this has been moved back a year, and so the twenty-first century will commonly be regarded as running from 2000–2099.

**cephalic** /suh-**fal**-ik, ke-/ *adj.* of or in the head. [Greek *kephalē* head]

**cephalopod** /**sef**-uh-luh-ˌpod/ *n.* mollusc with a distinct tentacled head e.g. the octopus. [from CEPHALIC, Greek *pous pod-* foot]

**ceramic** /suh-**ram**-ik, kuh-/ — *adj.* **1** made of (esp.) baked clay. **2** of ceramics — *n.* ceramic article or product. [Greek *keramos* pottery]

**ceramics** *n.pl.* **1** ceramic products collectively. **2** (usu. treated as *sing.*) art of making ceramic articles.

**cereal** /**seer**-ree-uhl/ — *n.* **1 a** grain used for food. **b** wheat, maize, rye, etc. producing this. **2** breakfast food made from a cereal. — *adj.* of edible grain [Latin *Ceres* goddess of agriculture]

**cerebellum** /ˌse-ruh-**bel**-uhm/ *n.* (*pl.* -**s** or -**bella**) part of the brain, at the back of the skull, which coordinates and regulates muscular activity. [Latin diminutive of CEREBRUM]

**cerebral** /se-ruh-**bruhl**/ *adj.* **1** of the brain. **2** intellectual rather than emotional. [related to CEREBRUM]

**cerebral palsy** *n.* paralysis resulting from brain damage before or at birth, involving spasm of the muscles and involuntary movements.

**cerebration** /ˌse-ruh-**bray**-shuhn/ *n.* working of the brain.

**cerebrospinal** /ˌse-ruh-broh-**spuy**-nuhl/ *adj.* of the brain and spine.

**cerebrum** /se-ruh-**bruhm**/ *n.* (*pl.* -**bra**) principal part of the brain in vertebrates, located at the front of the skull, which integrates complex sensory and neural functions. [Latin]

**ceremonial** /ˌse-ruh-**moh**-nee-uhl/ — *adj.* **1** of or with ritual or ceremony. **2** formal (*a ceremonial bow*). — *n.* **1** system of rites etc. to be used esp. at a formal or religious occasion. **2** formalities or behaviour proper to any occasion (*with all due ceremonial*). □ **ceremonially** *adv.*

**ceremonious** /ˌse-ruh-**moh**-nee-uhs/ *adj.* **1** characterised by ceremony; formal. **2** excessively polite. □ **ceremoniously** *adv.*

**ceremony** /se-ruh-muh-nee/ *n.* (*pl.* -**ies**) **1** formal procedure, esp. at a public event or anniversary. **2** formalities, esp. ritualistic. **3** excessively polite behaviour (*bowed low with great ceremony*). □ **stand on ceremony** insist on formality. [Latin *caerimonia* worship]

**cerise** /suh-**rees**, -**reez**/ *n.* light clear red. [French: related to CHERRY]

**cerium** /**seer**-ree-uhm/ *n.* silvery metallic element of the lanthanide series. [*Ceres*, name of an asteroid]

**cert** /sert/ n. (esp. **dead cert**) colloq. a certainty. [abbreviation]

**cert.** abbr. **1** certificate. **2** certified.

**certain** /ser-tuhn/ — adj. **1 a** confident, convinced (I'm certain that I put it here). **b** indisputable (it is certain that he is guilty). **2** (often foll. by to + infin.) sure; destined (it is certain to rain; certain to win). **3** unerring, reliable (his touch is certain). **4** that need not be specified or may not be known to the reader or hearer (of a certain age; a certain John Smith). **5** some but not much (a certain reluctance). — pron. (as pl.) some but not all (certain of them knew). □ **for certain** without doubt. [Latin certus]

**certainly** adv. **1** undoubtedly. **2** (in answer) yes; by all means.

**certainty** n. (pl. **-ies**) **1 a** undoubted fact. **b** indubitable prospect (his return is a certainty). **2** absolute conviction (I can say that with certainty). **3** thing or person that may be relied on (a certainty to win the Cup).

**certifiable** /ser-tuh-**fuy**-uh-buhl/ adj. **1** able or needing to be certified. **2** colloq. insane.

**certificate** /suh-**tif**-uh-kuht/ — n. **1** formal document attesting a fact, esp. birth, marriage, or death, a medical condition, or a qualification. **2** hist. document issued at the expiry of a convict's term of penal servitude. — v. /-kayt/ (**-ting**) (esp. as **certificated** adj.) provide with, license, or attest by a certificate. □ **certification** /ser-tuh-fuh-**kay**-shuhn/ n. [Latin: related to CERTIFY]

**certified mail** n. Post Office service in which the despatch and receipt of a letter or parcel are recorded.

**certify** /ser-tuh-fuy/ v. (**-ies**, **-ied**) **1** attest; attest to esp. formally. **2** declare by certificate (that a person is qualified or competent). **3** officially declare insane. [Latin certus]

**certitude** /ser-tuh-tyood/ n. feeling of absolute certainty or conviction. [Latin: related to CERTAIN]

**cerulean** /suh-**roo**-lee-uhn/ adj. & n. literary deep sky-blue. [Latin caeruleus]

**cerumen** /suh-**roo**-muhn/ n. yellow-brown waxy substance in the outer ear; earwax.

**cervical** /ser-**vuy**-kuhl, **ser**-vi-kuhl/ adj. **1** of or relating to the neck (cervical vertebrae). **2** of or relating to the cervix (cervical cancer). [related to CERVIX]

**cervical smear** n. (also **pap smear**, **smear test**) specimen from the neck of the womb for examination.

**cervix** /ser-viks/ n. (pl. **cervices** /-vuh-seez/) **1** necklike structure, esp. the neck of the womb. **2** the neck. [Latin]

**CES** abbr. Commonwealth Employment Service.

**cesium** var. of CAESIUM.

**cessation** /se-**say**-shuhn/ n. ceasing or pause (cessation of hostilities). [Latin: related to CEASE]

**cession** /sesh-uhn/ n. (often foll. by of) the ceding or giving up (of rights, property, territory). [Latin: related to CEDE]

**cesspit** /ses-pit/ n. (also **cesspool**) **1** covered pit for the temporary storage of liquid waste or sewage. **2** centre of corruption, depravity, etc. (cesspit of vice). [origin uncertain]

**cetacean** /suh-**tay**-shuhn/ — n. marine mammal with streamlined hairless body and dorsal blowhole for breathing, e.g. the whale, dolphin, and porpoise. — adj. of cetaceans. [Greek kētos whale]

**cetane** /see-tayn/ n. liquid hydrocarbon used in standardising ratings of diesel fuel. [from SPERMACETI]

**Ceylonese** /sel-uh-**neez**, see-uh-luh-/ — n. a Sri Lankan. — adj. of or pertaining to Sri Lanka. [Ceylon former name of Sri Lanka]

**Ceylon moss** /suh-**lon**/ n. type of red seaweed from which is extracted a gelatinous substance used in desserts etc. (cf. AGAR). [Ceylon, now Sri Lanka]

**Cf** symb. californium.

**cf.** abbr. compare. [Latin confer]

**CFC** abbr. chloro-fluorocarbon, a usu. gaseous compound of carbon, hydrogen, chlorine, and fluorine, used in refrigerants, aerosol propellants, etc., and opposed as harmful to the ozone layer in the earth's atmosphere.

**cg** abbr. centigram(s).

**chablis** /**shah**-blee, **shab**-lee/ n. (pl. same /-leez/) very dry white wine orig. from Chablis in France.

**chafe** — v. (**-fing**) **1** make or become sore or damaged by rubbing. **2** make or become annoyed; fret. **3** rub (esp. the skin to restore warmth or sensation). — n. sore caused by rubbing. [Latin calefacio make warm]

**chafer** n. large slow-moving beetle. [Old English]

**chaff** /chahf/ — n. **1** separated husks of corn etc. **2** chopped hay or straw. **3** light-hearted teasing. **4** worthless things; rubbish. — v. tease, banter. [Old English]

**chagrin** /**shag**-ruhn, shuh-**green**/ — n. acute annoyance or disappointment. — v. affect with chagrin. [French]

**chain** — *n.* **1 a** connected flexible series of esp. metal links. **b** thing resembling this (*formed a human chain*) fetters; restraining force. **3** sequence, series, or set (*chain of events; mountain chain*). **4** group of associated hotels, shops, etc. **5** badge of office in the form of a chain worn round the neck. **6** (in the imperial system) unit of length (66 ft., 20.1168 m). **7** *Chem.* group of (esp. carbon) atoms bonded in sequence in a molecule. — *v.* **1** (often foll. by *up*) secure or confine with a chain. **2** confine or restrict (a person) (*is chained to the office*). □ **drag the chain** lag behind one's fellow workers or companions in an activity (see CHAIN-GANG). **on** (or **upon**) **the chain** *hist.* (of a convict) secured with a chain. [Latin *catena*]

**chain gang** *n. hist.* party of convicts in Australia assigned to hard labour in chains, such ankles usu. being ankle fetters joined by a chain which, to allow some freedom of movement, was tied to the belt (convicts wearing irons were also chained together when moving from place to place — see IRONED GANG).

**chain-mail** *n.* armour made of interlaced rings.

**chain reaction** *n.* **1** *Physics* self-sustaining nuclear reaction, esp. one in which a neutron from a fission reaction initiates a series of these reactions. **2** *Chem.* self-sustaining molecular reaction in which intermediate products initiate further reactions. **3** series of events, each caused by the previous one.

**chainsaw** *n.* motor-driven saw with teeth on a revolving chain.

**chain-smoke** *v.* smoke continually, esp. by lighting the next cigarette etc. from the previous one. □ **chain-smoker** *n.*

**chain store** *n.* one of a series of similar shops owned by one firm.

**chair** — *n.* **1** seat for one person, of various forms, usu. with a back and four legs. **2** professorship. **3 a** (non-sexist way of saying) chairman or chairwoman; chairperson (*resigned as chair of the society*). **b** seat or office of a chairperson. — *v.* **1** preside over (a meeting). **2** carry (a person) aloft in triumph. □ **take the chair** preside over a meeting. [Greek *kathedra*]

**chairlift** *n.* series of chairs on a looped cable, for carrying passengers up and down a mountain etc.

**chairman** *n.* (*fem.* also **chairwoman**) **1** person chosen to preside over a meeting. **2** permanent president of a committee, board of directors, etc.

**chairperson** *n.* chairman or chairwoman.

**chaise** /shayz/ *n.* esp. *hist.* horse-drawn usu. open carriage for one or two persons. [French]

**chaise longue** /shayz long/ *n.* (*pl.* **chaise longues** or **chaises longues** pronunc. same) sofa with only one arm rest. [French, = long chair]

**chalcedony** /kal-sed-uh-nee/ *n.* (*pl.* **-ies**) type of quartz with many varieties, e.g. onyx. [Latin from Greek]

**chalet** /shal-ay/ *n.* **1** Swiss mountain hut or cottage with overhanging eaves. **2** house in a similar style. **3** dwelling in a holiday camp etc., esp. at a ski resort. [Swiss French]

**chalice** /chal-uhs/ *n.* **1** cup for the wine at Mass or (in non-Catholic Churches) for Communion. **2** *literary* goblet. [Latin CALIX]

**chalk** /chawk/ — *n.* **1** white soft limestone formed from the skeletal remains of sea creatures. **2 a** similar substance, sometimes coloured, for writing or drawing. **b** piece of this. — *v.* **1** rub, mark, draw, or write with chalk. **2** (foll. by *up*) **a** write or record with chalk. **b** register or gain (success etc.). □ **as different as chalk and cheese** fundamentally different. **by a long chalk** by far. □ **chalky** *adj.* (**-ier**, **-iest**). **chalkiness** *n.* [Latin CALX]

**chalkie** /chaw-kee/ *n. colloq.* school-teacher. [CHALK, -Y²]

**challenge** /chal-uhnj/ — *n.* **1 a** summons to take part in a contest etc. **b** summons to prove or justify something. **2** demanding or difficult task. **3** objection made to a jury member. **4** call to respond, esp. a sentry's call for a password etc. — *v.* (**-ging**) **1** issue a challenge to. **2** dispute, deny. **3** (as **challenging** *adj.*) stimulatingly difficult. **4** object to (a jury member, evidence, etc.). □ **challenger** *n.* [Latin *calumnia* calumny]

**chamber** /chaym-buh/ *n.* **1 a** hall used by a legislative or judicial body. **b** body that meets in it, esp. any of the houses of a parliament. **2** (in *pl.*) **a** rooms used by a barrister or barristers. **b** judge's room for hearing cases not needing to be taken in court. **3** *archaic* room, esp. a bedroom. **4** *Mus.* (*attrib.*) of or for a small group of instruments (*chamber music*). **5** cavity or compartment in the body, machinery, etc. (esp. the part of a gun-bore that contains the charge). [Greek *kamara* vault]

**chamberlain** /chaym-buh-luhn/ *n.* officer managing a royal or noble household. [Germanic: related to CHAMBER]

**chambermaid** *n.* woman who cleans hotel bedrooms.

**chamber pot** *n.* receptacle for urine etc., used in the bedroom.

**chameleon** /kuh-**mee**-lee-uhn/ *n.* **1** small lizard able to change colour for camouflage. **2** variable or inconstant person. [Greek, = ground-lion]

**chamfer** /**cham**-fuh/ — *v.* bevel symmetrically (a right-angled edge or corner). — *n.* bevelled surface at an edge or corner. [French *chant* edge, *fraint* broken]

**chamois** *n.* **1** /**sham**-wah/ (*pl.* same /-wahz/ ) agile European and Asian mountain antelope. **2** /**sham**-ee/ (*pl.* same /-meez/ ) (in full **chamois leather**) **a** soft leather from sheep, goats, deer, etc. **b** piece of this. [French]

**champ**[1] — *v.* munch or chew noisily. — *n.* chewing noise. □ **champ at the bit** be restlessly impatient. [imitative]

**champ**[2] *n. colloq.* champion. [abbreviation]

**champagne** /sham-**payn**/ *n.* **1 a** white sparkling wine from Champagne. **b** similar wine from elsewhere. **2** pale cream colour. [*Champagne*, former province in E. France]

**champignon** /**sham**-pin-yong/ *n.* = BUTTON MUSHROOM.

**champion** /**cham**-pee-uhn, **cham**-pyuhn/ — *n.* **1** (often *attrib.*) person or thing that has defeated or surpassed all rivals. **2** person who fights or argues for a cause or another person. — *v.* support the cause of, defend. — *adj. colloq.* first class, splendid. [medieval Latin *campio* fighter]

**championship** *n.* **1** (often in *pl.*) contest to decide the champion in a sport etc. **2** position of champion.

**chance** /chahns, chans/ — *n.* **1** possibility (*just a chance we will catch the train*). **2** (often in *pl.*) probability (*the chances are against it*). **3** unplanned occurrence (*just a chance that they met*). **4** opportunity (*didn't have a chance to speak to him*). **5** fortune; luck (*we'll leave it to chance*). **6** (often **Chance**) course of events regarded as a power; fate. — *attrib. adj.* fortuitous, accidental (*a chance meeting*). — *v.* (**-cing**) **1** *colloq.* risk (*we'll chance it and go*). **2** happen (*I chanced to find it*). □ **by any chance** perhaps. **by chance** fortuitously. **chance one's arm** try though unlikely to succeed. **chance on** (or **upon**) happen to find, meet, etc. **game of chance** one decided by luck, not skill. **on the off chance** just in case (the unlikely occurs). **stand a chance** have a prospect of success etc. **take a chance** (or **chances**) risk failure; behave riskily. **take a** (or **one's**) **chance on** (or

**with**) risk the consequences of. [Latin *cado* fall]

**chancel** /**chahn**-suhl, **chan**-suhl/ *n.* part of a church near the altar. [Latin *cancelli* grating]

**chancellery** /**chahn**-suhl-ree, **chan**-/ *n.* (also **chancelry**) (*pl.* **-ies**) **1** position of chancellor. **2 a** chancellor's department or staff. **b** building or office containing these.

**chancellor** /**chahn**-suh-luh, **chan**-/ *n.* **1** chiefly *Brit.* government or legal official. **2** head of government in some European countries. **3** honorary head of a university. [Latin *cancellarius* secretary]

**chancre** /**chang**-kuh/ *n.* painless ulcer developing in venereal disease etc. [French: related to CANCER]

**chancy** /**chahn**-see, **chan**-/ *adj.* (**-ier**, **-iest**) uncertain; risky. □ **chancily** *adv.*

**chandelier** /ˌshan-duh-**leer**/ *n.* ornamental branched hanging support for lighting. [French: related to CANDLE]

**chandler** /**chahn**-dluh, **chan**-/ *n.* dealer in candles, oil, soap, paint, etc. [French: related to CANDLE]

**change** /chaynj/ — *n.* **1 a** act or instance of making or becoming different. **b** alteration or modification. **2 a** money exchanged for money in larger units or a different currency. **b** money returned as the balance of that given in payment. **c** = SMALL CHANGE. **3** new experience; variety (*need a change*). **4** substitution of one thing for another (*change of scene*; *change of clothes*). **5** (usu. in *pl.*) one of the different orders in which bells can be rung. — *v.* (**-ging**) **1** undergo, show, or subject to change; make or become different. **2 a** take or use another instead of; go from one to another (*change one's socks*; *changed trains*). **b** (usu. foll. by *for*) give up or get rid of in exchange (*changed the car for a van*). **3** give or get money in exchange for. **4** put fresh clothes or coverings on. **5** (often foll. by *with*) give and receive, exchange (*changed places with him*). **6** change trains etc. **7** (of the moon) arrive at a fresh phase. □ **change down** engage a lower gear. **change gear** engage a different gear. **change hands 1** pass to a different owner. **2** substitute one hand for the other. **change one's mind** adopt a different opinion or plan. **change over** change from one system or situation to another. **change one's tune** voice a different opinion from before. **2** become more respectful. **change up** engage a higher gear. **ring the changes** (**on**) vary the ways of expressing, arranging, or doing something. □ **changeful** *adj.* **changeless** *adj.* [Latin *cambio* barter]

**changeable** *adj.* **1** irregular; inconstant. **2** that can change or be changed.

**changeling** *n.* child believed to be substituted for another, esp. an elf-child left by fairies.

**change of heart** *n.* conversion to a different view.

**change of life** *n. colloq.* menopause.

**changeover** *n.* change from one system to another.

**channel** /**chan**-uhl/ — *n.* **1** piece of water wider than a strait, joining esp. two seas. **2** medium of communication; agency (*through the usual channels*). **3** band of frequencies used in radio and television transmission, esp. by a particular station. **4** course in which anything moves. **5 a** natural or artificial hollow bed of water. **b** navigable part of a waterway. **6** tubular passage for liquid. **7** lengthwise strip on recording tape etc. **8** groove. **9** *Computing* information route in input/output operations or data transmission. — *v.* (**-ll-**) **1** guide, direct. **2** form channel(s) in. [Latin: related to CANAL]

**channel-billed cuckoo** *n.* grey cuckoo of north-eastern Australia, having a channel or groove on each side of its large beak, and a call which traditionally presages rain.

**channel country** *n.* area in the south-west of Queensland and the north of SA, as characterised by the inland river system esp. after summer rains.

**chant** /chahnt, chant/ — *n.* **1** spoken singsong phrase, esp. one performed in unison by a crowd etc. **2 a** simple tune used for singing unmetrical words, e.g. psalms. **b** the psalm etc. so sung. **c** song, esp. monotonous or repetitive. — *v.* **1** talk or repeat monotonously. **2** sing or intone (a psalm etc.). [Latin *canto* from *cano* sing]

**chantry** /**chahn**-tree, **chan**-/ *n.* (*pl.* **-ies**) **1** endowment for the singing of masses. **2** priests, chapel, etc., so endowed. [French: related to CHANT]

**chaos** /**kay**-os/ *n.* **1** utter confusion. **2** formless matter supposed to have existed before the creation of the universe. □ **chaotic** /kay-**ot**-ik/ *adj.* **chaotically** /-ot-i-kuh-lee, -klee/ *adv.* [Latin from Greek]

**chap**[1] *n. colloq.* man, boy, fellow. [abbreviation of obsolete *chapman* (related to CHEAP, MAN) pedlar]

**chap**[2] — *v.* (**-pp-**) **1** (esp. of the skin) develop cracks or soreness. **2** (of the wind, cold, etc.) cause to chap. — *n.* (usu. in *pl.*) crack in the skin etc. [origin uncertain]

**chapati** /chuh-**pah**-tee/ *n.* (also **chapatti**) (*pl.* **-s**) flat thin cake of unleavened bread. [Hindi]

**chapel** /**chap**-uhl/ *n.* **1 a** place for private Christian worship in a Cathedral or large church, with its own altar. **b** this attached to a school etc. **2** members or branch of a printers' trade union at a place of work. [medieval Latin *cappa* cloak: the first chapel was a sanctuary in which St Martin's cloak (*cappella*) was preserved]

**chaperone** /**shap**-uh-,rohn/ (also **chaperon**) — *n.* person, esp. an older woman, ensuring propriety by accompanying a young unmarried woman on social occasions. — *v.* act as chaperone to. □ **chaperonage** *n.* [French from *chape* cope: related to CHAPEL]

**chaplain** /**chap**-luhn/ *n.* member of the clergy attached to a private chapel, institution, ship, regiment, etc. □ **chaplaincy** *n.* (*pl.* **-ies**). [Latin: related to CHAPEL]

**chaplet** /**chap**-luht/ *n.* **1** garland or circlet for the head. **2** short string of beads; rosary. [Latin: related to CAP]

**chapter** *n.* **1** main division of a book. **2** period of time (in a person's life etc.). **3 a** canons of a cathedral or members of a religious community. **b** meeting of these. [Latin diminutive of *caput* head]

**chapter and verse** *n.* exact reference or details.

**char** *v.* (**-rr-**) **1** make or become black by burning; scorch. **2** burn to charcoal. [from CHARCOAL]

**character** /**ka**-ruhk-tuh/ *n.* **1** collective qualities or characteristics that distinguish a person or thing. **2 a** moral strength (*has a weak character*). **b** reputation; esp. good reputation. **3 a** person in a novel, play, etc. **b** part played by an actor; role. **4** *colloq.* person, esp. an interesting or eccentric one. **5 a** printed or written letter, symbol, etc. **b** letter, digit, etc., as used in a computer. **6** characteristic (esp. of a biological species). □ **in** (or **out of**) **character** consistent (or inconsistent) with a person's character. □ **characterless** *adj.* [Greek *kharaktēr*]

**characterise** /**ka**-ruhk-tuh-,ruyz/ *v.* (also **-ize**) (**-sing** or **-zing**) **1 a** describe the character of. **b** (foll. by *as*) describe as (*characterised them as dangerous bigots*). **2** be characteristic of. **3** impart character to. □ **characterisation** /-zay-shuhn/ *n.*

**characteristic** /,ka-ruhk-tuh-**ris**-tik/ — *adj.* typical, distinctive. — *n.* **1** characteristic feature or quality. **2** *Math.* whole number or integral part of a logarithm. □ **characteristically** *adv.*

**charade** /shuh-**rahd**, -**rayd**/ n. **1** (usu. in pl., treated as sing.) game of guessing a word from acted clues. **2** absurd pretence. [Provençal charra chatter]

**charcoal** /**chah**-kohl/ n. **1 a** form of carbon consisting of black residue from partially burnt wood etc. **b** piece of this for drawing. **c** a drawing in charcoal. **2** (in full **charcoal grey**) dark grey. [origin unknown]

**chardonnay** /**shah**-duh-,nay/ n. **1** variety of white grape. **2** wine made from this. [French]

**charge** — v. (**-ging**) **1 a** ask (an amount) as a price (charged $10). **b** ask (a person) for an amount as a price (charged him $10). **2 a** (foll. by to, up to) debit the cost of to (a person or account). **b** debit (a person or account). **3 a** (often foll. by with) accuse (of an offence) (charged him with rape). **b** (foll. by that + clause) make an accusation that (charged that we were speeding). **4** (foll. by to + infin.) instruct or urge (I charge you to see that it is done). **5** (foll. by with) entrust with (charged her with the responsibility). **6 a** make a rushing attack (on) (charged their fortification). **b** Aust. Rules attack and push (a player) illegally. **7** (often foll. by up) **a** give an electric charge to. **b** store energy in (a battery). **8 a** fill (a glass). **b** (often foll. by with) load or fill (a gun etc.) to the full or proper extent. **9** (usu. as **charged** adj.) **a** (foll. by with) saturated with (air charged with vapour). **b** (usu. foll. by with) pervaded (with strong feelings etc.) (atmosphere charged with emotion). — n. **1 a** price asked for services or goods. **b** financial liability or commitment. **2** accusation, esp. against a prisoner brought to trial. **3 a** task, duty, commission. **b** care, custody (he's in my charge). **c** person or thing entrusted. **4 a** impetuous rush or attack, esp. in battle. **b** signal for this. **c** Aust. Rules act of attacking and pushing illegally. **5** appropriate amount of material to be put into a receptacle, mechanism, etc. at one time, esp. of explosive for a gun. **6 a** property of matter causing electrical phenomena. **b** quantity of this carried by the body. **c** energy stored chemically for conversion into electricity. **7** exhortation; directions, orders. **8** heraldic device or bearing. **9** (also **charge-on**) colloq. glass of alcoholic drink, esp. spirits. **10** colloq. thrill, 'kick' (gets a charge out of surfing). □ **in charge** having command. **take charge** (often foll. by of) assume control. □ **chargeable** adj. [Latin carrus CAR]

**chargé d'affaires** /,shah-zhay duh-**fair**/ n. (pl. **chargés** pronunc. same) **1** ambassador's deputy. **2** envoy to a minor country. [French]

**charger** n. **1** cavalry horse. **2** apparatus for charging a battery.

**chariot** /**cha**-ree-uht/ n. hist. two-wheeled vehicle drawn by horses, used in ancient warfare and racing. [French: related to CAR]

**charioteer** /,cha-ree-uh-**teer**/ n. chariot-driver.

**charisma** /kuh-**riz**-muh/ n. **1** power to inspire or attract others; exceptional charm. **2** divinely conferred power or talent. □ **charismatic** /,ka-ruhz-**mat**-ik/ adj. [Greek kharis grace]

**charitable** /**cha**-ruh-tuh-buhl/ adj. **1** generous in giving to those in need. **2** of or relating to a charity or charities. **3** generous in judging others. □ **charitably** adv.

**charity** /**cha**-ruh-tee/ n. (pl. **-ies**) **1** giving voluntarily to those in need. **2** organisation set up to help those in need or for the common good. **3 a** kindness, benevolence. **b** tolerance in judging others. **c** love of fellow human beings. [Latin caritas from carus dear]

**charlatan** /**shah**-luh-tuhn/ n. person falsely claiming knowledge or skill. □ **charlatanism** n. [Italian, = babbler]

**charleston** /**chahl**-stuhn/ n. (also **Charleston**) lively dance of the 1920s with side-kicks from the knee. [Charleston in S. Carolina]

**charlie**[1] /**chah**-lee/ n. colloq. **1** fool. **2** (in pl.) woman's breasts. [diminutive of the name Charles]

**charlie**[2] n. colloq. girl, woman. [rhyming slang for 'sheila', after Charles Wheeler Australian painter of the nude (d. 1977)]

**charm** — n. **1** power or quality of delighting, arousing admiration, or influencing; fascination, attractiveness. **2** trinket on a bracelet etc. **3** object, act, or word(s) supposedly having magic power. — v. **1** delight, captivate. **2** influence or protect as if by magic (a charmed life). **3** obtain or gain by charm (charmed agreement out of him). □ **charmer** n. [Latin carmen song]

**charming** adj. **1** delightful. **2** (often as int.) iron. expressing displeasure or disapproval. □ **charmingly** adv.

**charnel house** /**chah**-nuhl ,hows/ n. repository of corpses or bones. [Latin: related to CARNAL]

**chart** — n. **1** geographical map or plan, esp. for navigation. **2** sheet of information in the form of a table, graph, or diagram. **3** (usu. in pl.) colloq. listing of the currently best-selling pop records. — v. make a chart of, map. [Latin charta: related to CARD[1]]

**charter** — n. **1 a** document granting rights, issued esp. by a sovereign or legislature. **b** written constitution or description of an organisation's functions etc. **2** contract to hire an aircraft, ship, etc., for a special purpose. — v. **1** grant a charter to. **2** hire (an aircraft, ship, etc.). [Latin *chartula*: related to CHART]

**chartered** *attrib. adj.* (of an accountant etc.) qualified member of a professional body that has a royal charter.

**charter flight** *n.* flight by chartered aircraft.

**chartreuse** /shah-**trerz**/ *n.* **1** pale green or yellow brandy-based liqueur. **2** pale yellow or pale green colour of this. [*Chartreuse*, monastery in S. France]

**charwoman** *n. Brit.* woman employed as a cleaner in a house or offices.

**chary** /**chair**-ree/ *adj.* (**-ier, -iest**) **1** cautious, wary (*chary of employing such people*). **2** sparing; ungenerous (*chary of giving praise*). [Old English: related to CARE]

**Charybdis** see SCYLLA AND CHARYBDIS.

**chase¹** — v. (**-sing**) **1** run after; pursue. **2** (foll. by *from, out of, to*, etc.) force to run away or flee. **3 a** (foll. by *after*) hurry in pursuit of. **b** (foll. by *round* etc.) *colloq.* act or move about hurriedly. **4** (usu. foll. by *up*) *colloq.* **a** pursue (a thing overdue). **b** try to locate; look for (*is chasing up some references in the library*). **5** *colloq.* **a** try to attain (*chasing gold at the Olympics*). **b** court persistently (*has been chasing her for months*). — n. **1** pursuit. **2** (prec. by *the*) hunting, esp. as a sport. [Latin *capio*: related to CATCH]

**chase²** *v.* (**-sing**) emboss or engrave (metal). [French: related to CASE²]

**chaser** *n. colloq.* drink taken after another of a different kind, e.g. beer after spirits.

**chasm** /**kaz**-uhm/ *n.* **1** deep cleft or opening in the earth, rock, etc. **2** wide difference of feeling, interests, etc. [Latin from Greek]

**chassis** /**shaz**-ee, shas-/ *n.* (pl. same /-eez/) **1** base-frame of a motor vehicle, carriage, etc. **2** frame to carry radio etc. components. [Latin: related to CASE²]

**chaste** /chayst/ *adj.* **1** abstaining from sexual intercourse. **2** (of behaviour, speech, etc.) pure, virtuous. **3** (of artistic style etc.) simple, unadorned. □ **chastely** *adv.* **chasteness** *n.* [Latin *castus*]

**chasten** /**chay**-suhn/ *v.* **1** (esp. as **chastening, chastened** *adjs.*) subdue, restrain (*a chastening experience*). **2** discipline, punish.

**chastise** /chas-**tuyz**/ *v.* (**-sing**) **1** rebuke severely. **2** punish, esp. by beating. □ **chastisement** *n.*

**chastity** /**chas**-tuh-tee/ *n.* being chaste.

**chasuble** /**chaz**-yuh-buhl/ *n.* loose sleeveless usu. ornate outer vestment worn by a priest celebrating Mass or a minister (e.g. in some Anglican churches) celebrating the Eucharist. [Latin *casubla*]

**chat¹** — v. (**-tt-**) talk in a light familiar way. — n. pleasant informal talk. □ **chat up** *colloq.* chat to, esp. flirtatiously or with an ulterior motive. [shortening of CHATTER]

**chat²** *n.* **1** any of various small and colourful Australian birds with a metallic ringing or chattering call (*crimson chat; gibber chat; yellow chat;* etc.). **2** any of various small birds of Europe etc. with harsh calls.

**chat³** *colloq.* — n. **1** a louse. **2** debased person; a drunk. — v. remove lice from one's person. [British slang *chat* louse]

**chat⁴** *n. colloq.* small potato. [British dial.]

**chateau** /**sha**-toh/ *n.* (also **château**) (pl. **-x** /-tohz/) large French country house or castle. [French: related to CASTLE]

**chat show** *n.* television or radio broadcast in which celebrities are interviewed informally.

**chattel** /**chat**-uhl/ *n.* (usu. in *pl.*) movable possession. [French: related to CATTLE]

**chatter** — v. **1** talk quickly, incessantly, trivially, or indiscreetly. **2** (of a bird, monkey, etc.) emit short quick sounds. **3** (of teeth) click repeatedly together. — n. chattering talk or sounds. [imitative]

**chatterbox** *n.* talkative person.

**chatty** *adj.* (**-ier, -iest**) **1** fond of chatting. **2** resembling chat; informal and lively (*a chatty letter*). **3** *colloq.* afflicted with lice (see CHAT³). □ **chattily** *adv.* **chattiness** *n.*

**chauffeur** /**shoh**-fuh, -**fer**/ — n. person employed to drive a car. — v. drive (a car or person) as a chauffeur. [French, = stoker]

**chauvinism** /**shoh**-vuh-ˌniz-uhm/ *n.* **1** exaggerated or aggressive patriotism. **2** excessive or prejudiced support or loyalty for one's cause or group or sex (*male chauvinism*). [*Chauvin*, name of a character in a French play 1831]

**chauvinist** /**shoh**-vuh-nist/ *n.* **1** person exhibiting chauvinism. **2** (in full **male chauvinist**) man who shows prejudice against women. □ **chauvinistic** /-nis-tik/ *adj.* **chauvinistically** /-nis-ti-kuh-lee, -klee/ *adv.*

**cheap** /cheep/ — *adj.* **1** low in price;

worth more than its cost. **2** charging low prices; offering good value (*a cheap restaurant*). **3** of poor quality; inferior (*cheap housing*). **4 a** costing little effort, or acquired by discreditable means, and hence of little worth (*cheap popularity*; *a cheap joke*). **b** contemptible; despicable (*a cheap act of revenge*). — *adv.* cheaply. □ **on the cheap** cheaply. □ **cheaply** *adv.* **cheapness** *n.* [Old English, = price, bargain]

**cheapen** *v.* **1** make or become cheap. **2** depreciate, degrade (*your behaviour cheapens you*).

**cheapie** /chee-pee/ *n. colloq.* any cheap article, esp. a car.

**cheapo** see EL CHEAPO.

**cheapskate** *n. colloq.* stingy person.

**cheat** — *v.* **1 a** (often foll. by *into, out of*) deceive or trick. **b** (foll. by *of*) deprive of (*cheated him of his rights*). **2** gain an unfair advantage by deception or breaking rules. **3** avoid (something undesirable) by luck or skill (*cheated death*). — *n.* **1** person who cheats. **2** trick, deception. □ **cheat on** *colloq.* be sexually unfaithful to. [Middle English]

**check** — *v.* **1 a** examine the accuracy, quality, or condition of (*check these figures*; *check the tyres*). **b** make sure, verify (*checked that the doors were locked*). **2** stop or slow the motion of; curb (*progress was checked by bad weather*). **3** *Chess* directly threaten (the opposing king). **4** agree or correspond when compared (*your account doesn't check with mine*). **5** *Aust. Rules* keep a close watch etc. on an opposing player to stop him gaining the ball etc. **6** (usu. in *imper.*) *colloq.* look at, notice (*check the socks that guy's wearing!*). — *n.* **1** means or act of testing or ensuring accuracy, quality, etc. **2 a** stopping or slowing of motion. **b** rebuff. **c** person or thing that restrains. **3 a** pattern of small squares. **b** fabric so patterned. **c** (*attrib.*) so patterned. **4** (also *as int.*) *Chess* exposure of a king to direct attack. □ **check in 1** arrive or register at a hotel, airport, etc. **2** record the arrival of. **check in** register one's arrival at (a hotel etc.). **check off** mark on a list etc. as having been examined or dealt with. **check on** examine, verify, keep watch on. **check out 1** (often foll. by *of*) leave a hotel etc. with due formalities. **2** investigate; examine for authenticity or suitability (*had to check out his credentials*). **check up** make sure, verify. **check up on** = *check on*. **check** under control; restrained. [Persian, = king]

**check digit** *n.* (also **check character**) *Computing* extra digit which when added to a sequence enables the accuracy of the sequence to be validated.

**checked** *adj.* having a check pattern.

**checker**[1] *n.* person etc. that examines, esp. in a factory etc.

**checker**[2] *n.* var. of CHEQUER.

**check-in** *n.* act or place of checking in.

**checkmate** — *n.* **1** (also as *int.*) *Chess* check from which a king cannot escape. **2** final defeat or deadlock. — *v.* (**-ting**) **1** *Chess* put into checkmate. **2** defeat; frustrate. [French: related to CHECK, Persian *māt* is dead]

**checkout** *n.* **1** act of checking out. **2** pay-desk in a supermarket etc.

**checkpoint** *n.* **1** place, esp. a barrier or entrance, where documents, vehicles, etc., are inspected. **2** point in a computer process where interim results are stored, and at which reprocessing may be started.

**check-up** *n.* thorough (esp. medical) examination.

**cheddar** /ched-uh/ *n.* a kind of firm smooth cheese. □ **stiff cheddar** see STIFF. [*Cheddar* in England]

**cheek** — *n.* **1 a** side of the face below the eye. **b** side-wall of the mouth. **2 a** impertinence; cool confidence. **b** impertinent speech. **3** *colloq.* buttock. — *v.* be impertinent to. □ **cheek by jowl** close together; intimate. **turn the other cheek** accept attack etc. meekly; refuse to retaliate. [Old English]

**cheekbone** *n.* bone below the eye.

**cheeky** *adj.* (**-ier, -iest**) impertinent. **2** (in Aboriginal English) threatening or dangerous. □ **cheekily** *adv.* **cheekiness** *n.*

**cheep** — *n.* weak shrill cry of a young bird. — *v.* make such a cry. [imitative]

**cheer** — *n.* **1** shout of encouragement or applause. **2** mood, disposition (*full of good cheer*). **3** (in *pl.*; as *int.*) *colloq.* **a** expressing good wishes on parting or before drinking. **b** expressing gratitude. — *v.* **1 a** applaud with shouts. **b** (usu. foll. by *on*) urge with shouts. **2** shout for joy. **3** gladden; comfort (*this cheers my heart*). □ **cheer up** make or become less depressed. [Latin *cara* face, from Greek]

**cheerful** *adj.* **1** in good spirits, noticeably happy (*a cheerful disposition*). **2** bright, pleasant (*a cheerful room*). □ **cheerfully** *adv.* **cheerfulness** *n.*

**cheerio**[1] /cheer-ree-**oh**/ *int. colloq.* expressing good wishes on parting.

**cheerio**[2] /cheer-ree-oh/ *n. colloq.* (esp. in Queensland) small sausage of the frankfurter type.

**cheer-leader** *n.* person who leads cheers of applause etc.

**cheerless** *adj.* gloomy, dreary.

**cheery** *adj.* (**-ier**, **-iest**) in good spirits; cheerful. □ **cheerily** *adv.* **cheeriness** *n.*

**cheese** /cheez/ *n.* **1** food made from curds of milk. **2** cake of this with rind. □ **say cheese!** smile (for the camera). **stiff** (or **hard**) **cheese** see STIFF. [Latin *caseus*]

**cheesecake** *n.* **1** tart filled with sweetened curds etc. **2** *colloq.* portrayal of women in a sexually stimulating manner (cf. BEEFCAKE).

**cheesecloth** *n.* thin loosely-woven cloth (orig. used for wrapping cheese).

**cheesed** /cheezd/ *adj. colloq.* (often foll. by *off*) bored, fed up. [origin unknown]

**cheese-paring** *adj.* stingy.

**cheese tree** *n.* tree of Queensland and NSW, having lance-shaped leaves and fruit said to resemble small cheeses.

**cheesy** *adj.* (**-sier**, **-siest**) like cheese in taste, smell, appearance, etc. □ **cheesy smile** (or **grin**) forced or artificial smile (or grin).

**cheetah** /**chee**-tuh/ *n.* swift-running spotted leopard-like feline of Africa and western Asia. [Hindi *cītā*]

**chef** /shef/ *n.* cook, esp. the chief cook in a restaurant. [French]

**chef's hat correa** /ko-**ree**-uh/ *n.* NSW correa having dark green shiny leaves and light green flowers with an unusual calyx that gives each flower the appearance of a chef's traditional hat.

**chemical** /**kem**-i-kuhl/ — *adj.* of, made by, or employing chemistry or chemicals. — *n.* substance obtained or used in chemistry. □ **chemically** *adv.* [French or medieval Latin: related to ALCHEMY]

**chemical engineering** *n.* creation and operation of industrial chemical plants.

**chemical reaction** *n.* process that involves change in the structure of atoms, molecules, or ions.

**chemical warfare** *n.* warfare using poison gas and other chemicals.

**chemise** /shuh-**meez**/ *n. hist.* woman's loose-fitting undergarment or dress. [Latin *camisia* shirt]

**chemist** /**kem**-uhst/ *n.* **1 a** authorised dispenser of medicinal drugs. **b** shop at which a chemist operates and which also has cosmetics etc. for sale. **2** expert in chemistry. [French: related to ALCHEMY]

**chemistry** /**kem**-uh-stree/ *n.* (*pl.* **-ies**) **1** branch of science dealing with the elements and the compounds they form and the reactions they undergo. **2** chemical composition and properties of a substance. **3** *colloq.* sexual attraction.

**chemo-** /**kee**-moh/ *comb. form* chemical.

**chemosynthesis** /,kee-moh-**sin**-thuh-suhs/ *n.* synthesis of organic compounds by energy derived from chemical reactions.

**chemotherapy** /,kee-moh-**the**-ruh-pee, ,kem-oh-/ *n.* treatment of disease, esp. cancer, by chemical substances.

**chemurgy** /**kem**-er-jee/ *n.* chemical and industrial use of organic raw materials. □ **chemurgic** *adj.* [CHEMO-, after *metallurgy*]

**chenille** /shuh-**neel**/ *n.* **1** tufty velvety cord or yarn. **2** fabric of this. [French, = hairy caterpillar, from Latin *canicula* little dog]

**cheque** /chek/ *n.* **1** written order to a bank to pay the stated sum from the drawer's account. **2** printed form on which this is written. **3** total sum received by a rural worker at the end of a seasonal contract (*he drank the entire cheque*). □ **chequed up** in possession of a cheque (sense 3) and ready to spend it. [from CHECK]

**chequer** /**chek**-uh/ — *n.* (often in *pl.*) pattern of squares often alternately coloured. — *v.* **1** mark with chequers. **2** variegate; break the uniformity of. **3** (as **chequered** *adj.*) with varied fortunes (*chequered career*). [from EXCHEQUER]

**cherish** /**che**-rish/ *v.* **1** protect or tend lovingly. **2** hold dear, cling to (hopes, feelings, etc.). [French *cher* dear, from Latin *carus*]

**cheroot** /shuh-**root**/ *n.* cigar with both ends open. [French from Tamil]

**cherry** /**che**-ree/ — *n.* (*pl.* **-ies**) **1 a** small soft round stone-fruit. **b** any of several trees of the genus *Prunus* bearing this or grown for its ornamental flowers. **c** its wood. **2** light red colour. — *adj.* of light red colour. [Greek *kerasos*]

**cherry ballart** see NATIVE CHERRY.

**cherry nose** *n.* (also **whisky drinker**) dark-coloured Australian cicada with a bright red nose.

**cherry picker** *n. colloq.* crane for raising and lowering people.

**cherry tomato** *n.* miniature tomato with a strong flavour.

**cherub** /**che**-ruhb/ *n.* **1** (*pl.* **-im**) angelic being of the second order of the celestial hierarchy. **2 a** representation of a winged child or its head. **b** beautiful or innocent child. □ **cherubic** /chuh-**roo**-bik/ *adj.* [ultimately from Hebrew]

**cheshire** /**chesh**-uh/ *n.* a kind of firm crumbly cheese. □ **like a Cheshire cat** with a broad fixed grin. [*Cheshire* in England]

**chess** *n.* game for two with 16 pieces each, played on a chessboard. [French related to CHECK]

**chessboard** n. chequered board of 64 squares on which chess and draughts are played.

**chessman** n. any of the 32 pieces and pawns with which chess is played.

**chest** n. **1** large strong box. **2 a** part of the body enclosed by the ribs. **b** front surface of the body from the neck to the bottom of the ribs. **3** small cabinet for medicines etc. □ **get a thing off one's chest** colloq. disclose a secret etc. to relieve one's anxiety about it. [Latin cista]

**chestnut** /ches-nut/ — n. **1 a** glossy hard brown edible nut. **b** tree bearing it. **2** chestnut wood. **3** horse of a reddish-brown colour. **4** colloq. stale joke etc. **5** reddish-brown. — adj. reddish-brown. [Greek kastanea nut]

**chestnut-breasted shelduck** n. = MOUNTAIN DUCK.

**chevalier** /shuh-val-yay, shev-uh-leer/ n. **1** member of certain orders of knighthood (e.g. conferred by the Pope), or of the French Legion of Honour etc. **2** hist. knight. [medieval Latin caballarius horseman]

**chèvre** /shair-vruh/ n. cheese made from goat's milk. [French, = goat, she-goat]

**chevron** /shev-ruhn/ n. V-shaped line or stripe, esp. as a badge on a uniform indicating rank etc. [Latin caper goat]

**chew** /choo/ — v. **1** work (food etc.) between the teeth. **2** (foll. by up) damage, destroy (the machine chewed up my credit card). — n. act of chewing. □ **chew on 1** work continuously between the teeth. **2** think about (I'll chew on that for a while). **chew over 1** discuss, talk over (we need to chew this over). **2** think about. [Old English]

**chewie** var. of CHEWY n.

**chewing gum** n. flavoured gum for chewing.

**chewy** — adj. (-ier, -iest) **1** needing much chewing. **2** suitable for chewing. — n. (also **chewie**) colloq. (piece of) chewing gum. □ **chewie on your boot** barracker's call intended to discourage or deride a player. □ **chewiness** n.

**chez** /shay/ prep. at the home of. [Latin casa cottage]

**chi** /kuy/ n. twenty-second letter of the Greek alphabet (X, χ). [Greek]

**chiack** /chuy-ak/ (also **chyack**) — v. taunt, barrack, or tease (a person). — n. barracking. □ **chiacking** n. [British slang]

**chiaroscuro** /kee-ah-ruh-skyoo-roh/ n. **1** treatment of light and shade in drawing and painting. **2** use of contrast in literature etc. [Italian, = clear dark]

**chic** /sheek/ — adj. (**chic-er, chic-est**) stylish, elegant. — n. stylishness, elegance. [French]

**chicane** /shuh-kayn/ — n. **1** artificial barrier or obstacle on a motor racecourse etc. **2** chicanery. — v. (-ning) archaic **1** use chicanery. **2** (usu. foll. by into, out of, etc.) cheat (a person). [French]

**chicanery** /shuh-kay-nuh-ree/ n. (pl. -ies) **1** clever but misleading talk. **2** trickery, deception. [French]

**chick** /chik/ n. **1** young bird. **2** colloq. young woman. [Old English: related to CHICKEN]

**chicken** /chik-uhn/ — n. **1 a** domestic fowl. **b** its flesh as food. **2** young bird of a domestic fowl. **3** youthful person (is no chicken). **4** colloq. coward. — adj. colloq. cowardly. — v. (foll. by out) colloq. withdraw through cowardice. □ **chicken-and-egg problem** unresolved question as to which of two things caused the other. **play chicken** perform a dare. [Old English]

**chicken feed** n. **1** food for poultry. **2** colloq. trivial amount, esp. of money.

**chickenpox** n. infectious disease, esp. of children, with a rash of small blisters.

**chicken-wire** n. light wire netting with a hexagonal mesh.

**chick-pea** n. **1** leguminous plant with yellow pea-like seeds used as a vegetable. **2** these seeds. [Latin cicer]

**chicle** /chik-uhl/ n. milky juice of a tropical tree, used in chewing-gum. [Spanish from Nahuatl]

**chicory** /chik-uh-ree/ n. (pl. -ies) **1** plant with leaves used in salads. **2** its root, roasted and ground and used with or instead of coffee. [Greek kikhorion]

**chide** v. (past **chided** or **chid**; past part. **chided** or **chidden**) scold, rebuke. [Old English]

**chief** — n. **1 a** leader or ruler. **b** head of a tribe, clan, etc. **c** hist. = KING⁴. **2** head of a department; highest official. — adj. **1** first in position, importance, influence, etc. **2** prominent, leading. [Latin caput head]

**chiefly** adv. above all; mainly but not exclusively.

**chieftain** /cheef-tuhn/ n. leader of a tribe, clan, etc. □ **chieftaincy** n. (pl. -ies). [Latin: related to CHIEF]

**chiffon** /shif-on, shuh-fon/ n. light diaphanous fabric of silk, nylon, etc. [French chiffe rag]

**chignon** /shee-nyon/ n. coil of hair at the back of a woman's head. [French]

**chihuahua** /chuh-wah-wuh/ n. dog of a very small smooth-haired breed. [Chihuahua in Mexico]

**chilblain** /chil-blayn/ n. painful itching swelling on a hand, foot, etc., caused by exposure to cold and by poor circulation. [from CHILL, *blain* inflamed sore, blister]

**child** /chuyld/ n. (pl. **children** /chil-druhn/) **1 a** young human being below the age of puberty. **b** unborn or newborn human being. **2** one's son or daughter. **3** (foll. by *of*) descendant, follower, or product of (*children of Israel; child of nature*). **4** childish person. □ **childless** adj. [Old English]

**child abuse** n. maltreatment of a child, esp. by emotional or physical violence or sexual interference.

**childbirth** n. giving birth to a child.

**child care** n. the care of children, esp. in a crèche etc.

**childhood** n. state or period of being a child. □ **second childhood** person's dotage.

**childish** adj. **1** of, like, or proper to a child. **2** immature, silly. □ **childishly** adv. **childishness** n.

**childlike** adj. having the good qualities of a child, such as innocence, frankness, etc.

**childproof** adj. that cannot be damaged or operated by a child.

**children's python** n. small nocturnal python of northern Australia. [J.G. *Children* naturalist (d. 1852)]

**child's play** n. easy task.

**Child Support Scheme** n. means by which the transfer of child maintenance from the non-custodial to the custodial parent is implemented.

**chili** var. of CHILLI.

**chill** — n. **1 a** unpleasant cold sensation; lowered body temperature. **b** feverish cold (*catch a chill*). **2** unpleasant coldness (of air, water, etc.). **3** depressing influence (*cast a chill over the celebration*). **4** coldness of manner. — v. **1** make or become cold. **2** depress; horrify. **3** cool (food or drink). **4** harden (molten metal) by contact with cold material. — adj. *literary* chilly. [Old English]

**chilli** /chil-ee/ n. (pl. **-es**) small hot-tasting green or red pod of a variety of capsicum, used fresh (*green chilli; red chilli*) or dried (usu. in powdered form) in curries etc. [Spanish from Aztec]

**chilli con carne** /kon kah-nee/ n. dish of chilli-flavoured mince and beans.

**chillied** /chil-eed/ adj. having chilli as a main ingredient (*chillied prawns*).

**chilly** adj. (**-ier, -iest**) **1** (of the weather or an object) somewhat cold. **2** (of a person or animal) feeling somewhat cold; sensitive to the cold. **3** unfriendly; unemotional (*a chilly reception; chilly manner*).

**chime** /chuym/ — n. **1** set of attuned bells. **2** sounds made by this. **3** (often in *pl.*) set of attuned bells as a doorbell. — v. (**-ming**) **1** (of bells) ring. **2** show (the time) by chiming. **3** (usu. foll. by *together*, *with*) be in agreement (*your version doesn't chime with mine*). □ **chime in 1** interject a remark. **2** join in harmoniously. **3** (foll. by *with*) agree with. [Old English: related to CYMBAL]

**chimera** /kuh-meer-ruh/ n. **1** (in Greek mythology) monster with a lion's head, goat's body, and serpent's tail. **2** fantastic or grotesque product of the imagination; bogey. □ **chimerical** /-me-ri-kuhl/ adj. [Latin from Greek]

**chimney** /chim-nee/ n. (pl. **-s**) **1** channel conducting smoke etc. up and away from a fire, furnace, etc. **2** part of this above a roof. **3** glass tube protecting the flame of a lamp. **4** narrow vertical crack in a rock-face, often used by mountaineers to ascend. [Latin *caminus* oven, from Greek]

**chimney stack** n. number of chimneys grouped in one structure.

**chimney sweep** n. person who removes soot from inside chimneys.

**chimp** n. *colloq.* = CHIMPANZEE. [abbreviation]

**chimpanzee** /ˌchim-pan-zee/ n. small African ape. [French from Kongo]

**chin** n. front of the lower jaw. □ **keep one's chin up** *colloq.* remain cheerful, esp. in adversity. **take on the chin** suffer a severe blow from; endure courageously. [Old English]

**china** /chuy-nuh/ — n. **1** fine white or translucent ceramic ware, porcelain, etc. **2** things made of this. **3** *rhyming slang* mate (short for *china plate*). — adj. made of china. [*China* in Asia]

**china clay** n. kaolin.

**chinchilla** /chin-chil-uh/ n. **1 a** small S. American rodent. **b** its soft grey fur. **2** breed of cat or rabbit. [Spanish *chinche* bug]

**chine** /chuyn/ — n. **1 a** backbone. **b** joint of meat containing all or part of this. **2** ridge (of land). — v. (**-ning**) cut (meat) through the backbone. [Latin *spina* SPINE]

**Chinese** /chuy-neez/ — adj. of China. — n. **1** Chinese language. **2** (pl. same) **a** native or national of China. **b** person of Chinese descent.

**Chinese cabbage** n. lettuce-like cabbage.

**Chinese gooseberry** n. = KIWI FRUIT.

**Chinese lantern** n. collapsible paper lantern.

**Chink** *n. colloq. offens.* a Chinese. [abbreviation]

**chink**[1] *n.* narrow opening; slit. [related to *chine* narrow ravine]

**chink**[2] — *v.* (cause to) make a sound like glasses or coins striking together. — *n.* this sound. [imitative]

**chintz** /chints/ *n.* printed multicoloured usu. glazed cotton fabric. [Hindi from Sanskrit]

**chintzy** *adj.* (-ier, -iest) 1 like chintz. 2 gaudy, cheap.

**chinwag** *colloq.* — *n.* talk or chat. — *v.* (-gg-) chat. □ **chinwagger** *n.* **chinwagging** *n.*

**chip** — *n.* 1 small piece removed by chopping etc. 2 place or mark where a piece has been broken off. 3 a strip of potato, usu. deep-fried. b potato crisp. 4 counter used in some gambling games to represent money. 5 = MICROCHIP. 6 *Soccer* etc. & *Golf* short kick, pass, or shot, with the ball describing an arc. — *v.* (-pp-) 1 (often foll. by *off*, *away*) cut or break (a piece) from a hard material. 2 (often foll. by *at*, *away at*) cut pieces off (a hard material) to alter its shape etc. 3 be apt to break at the edge (*will chip easily*). 4 make (potatoes) into chips. 5 *Soccer* etc. & *Golf* kick or strike (the ball) with a chip (cf. sense 6 of *n.*). 6 dig or harrow ground with a hoe etc. □ **chip in** *colloq.* 1 interrupt. 2 contribute (money etc.). **a chip off the old block** child resembling its parent, esp. in character. **a chip on one's shoulder** *colloq.* inclination to feel resentful or aggrieved. **when the chips are down** *colloq.* when it comes to the point. [Old English]

**chipboard** *n.* board made from compressed wood chips.

**chip heater** *n.* domestic water-heater which uses small pieces of wood as fuel.

**chipmunk** /chip-mungk/ *n.* striped N. American ground squirrel. [Algonquian]

**chipolata** /chip-uh-lah-tuh/ *n.* small thin sausage. [French from Italian]

**chippie** /chip-ee/ *n.* (also **chippy**) (*pl.* -ies) *colloq.* carpenter.

**chiro-** *comb. form* hand. [Greek *kheir*]

**chiromancy** /kuy-roh-man-see/ *n.* palmistry. [Greek *mantis* seer]

**chiropody** /kuh-rop-uh-dee/ *n.* treatment of the feet and their ailments. □ **chiropodist** *n.* [Greek *pous podos* foot]

**chiropractic** /kuy-roh-prak-tik/ *n.* treatment of disease by manipulation of esp. the spinal column. □ **chiropractor** /kuy-ruh-prak-tuh/ *n.* [Greek *prattō* do]

**chirp** — *v.* 1 (of small birds, grasshoppers, etc.) utter a short sharp note. 2 speak or utter merrily. — *n.* chirping sound. [imitative]

**chirpy** *adj. colloq.* (-ier, -iest) cheerful, lively. □ **chirpily** *adv.* **chirpiness** *n.*

**chirrup** /chi-ruhp/ — *v.* (-p-) chirp, esp. repeatedly. — *n.* chirruping sound. [imitative]

**chisel** /chiz-uhl/ — *n.* hand tool with a squared bevelled blade for shaping wood, stone, or metal. — *v.* 1 (-ll-) cut or shape with a chisel. 2 (as **chiselled** *adj.*) (of facial features) clear-cut, fine. 3 *colloq.* cheat. [Latin *caedo* cut]

**chit**[1] *n.* 1 *derog.* or *joc.* young small woman (esp. *a chit of a girl*). 2 young child. [originally = whelp, cub]

**chit**[2] *n.* 1 note of requisition, of a sum owed, esp. for food or drink. 2 note or memorandum. [Hindi from Sanskrit]

**chit-chat** — *n. colloq.* light conversation; gossip. — *v.* (-tt-) engage in this. [reduplication of CHAT]

**chitin** /kuy-tin/ *n.* horny substance forming the major constituent in the exoskeleton of insects, certain shellfish, etc. □ **chitinous** *adj.* [Greek *khitōn* tunic]

**chivalrous** /shiv-uhl-ruhs/ *adj.* 1 gallant, honourable. 2 of or showing chivalry. □ **chivalrously** *adv.* [Latin: related to CHEVALIER]

**chivalry** /shiv-uhl-ree/ *n.* 1 medieval knightly system with its religious, moral, and social code. 2 honour, courtesy, and readiness to help the weak. □ **chivalric** /shuh-val-rik/ *adj.*

**chive** /chuyv/ *n.* small plant with long onion- or garlic-flavoured leaves. [Latin *cepa* onion]

**chivvy** /chiv-ee/ *v.* (-ies, -ied) urge persistently, nag. [probably from ballad of *Chevy Chase*]

**chlamydia** /kluh-mid-ee-uh/ *n.* (*pl.* **chlamydiae** /-ee-ee/) a virus-like parasitic bacterium of the genus *Chlamydia*, which causes diseases such as trachoma, psittacosis, and non-specific urethritis. [Greek *khlamus, -udos* cloak]

**chloral** /klaw-ruhl/ *n.* 1 colourless liquid aldehyde used in making DDT. 2 (in full **chloral hydrate**) *Pharm.* crystalline solid made from this and used as a sedative. [French: related to CHLORINE, ALCOHOL]

**chloride** /klaw-ruyd/ *n.* 1 compound of chlorine and another element or group. 2 bleaching agent containing this.

**chlorinate** /klaw-ruh-nayt, klo-ruh-/ *v.* (-ting) impregnate or treat with chlorine. □ **chlorination** /klaw-ruh-nay-shuhn, klo-ruh-/ *n.*

**chlorine** /klaw-reen/ *n.* poisonous gaseous element used for purifying water, bleaching, etc. [Greek *khlōros* green]

**chloro-** *comb. form* (also **chlor-** esp. before a vowel) **1** *Bot. & Mineral.* green. **2** *Chem.* chlorine. [Greek *khlōros* green]

**chloro-fluorocarbon** see CFC.

**chloroform** /klo-ruh-,fawm/ — *n.* colourless volatile liquid formerly used as a general anaesthetic. — *v.* render unconscious with this. [from CHLORINE, FORMIC ACID]

**chlorophyll** /klo-ruh-fil/ *n.* green pigment found in most plants, responsible for light absorption to provide energy for photosynthesis. [Greek CHLORO-, *phullon* leaf]

**chlorosis** /kluh-**roh**-suhs/ *n.* *Bot.* reduction or loss of the normal green coloration of plants, caused by iron deficiency in the soil. □ **chlorotic** /kluh-**rot**-ik/ *adj.* [CHLORO-, -OSIS]

**chock** — *n.* block or wedge to check the motion of a wheel etc. — *v.* make fast with chocks. [French]

**chock-a-block** *predic. adj.* (often foll. by *with*) crammed together or full.

**chock-and-log** *n.* (in full **chock-and-log fence**) kind of fence built of logs resting on transversely placed blocks of wood.

**chock-full** *predic. adj.* (often foll. by *of*) crammed full.

**chocolate** /chok-uh-luht, chok-luht/ — *n.* **1 a** food preparation in the form of a paste or solid block made from ground cacao seeds and usu. sweetened. **b** sweet made of or coated with this. **c** drink containing this. **2** deep brown. — *adj.* **1** made from chocolate. **2** deep brown. [Aztec *chocolatl*]

**chocolate lily** *n.* Australian perennial herb of the lily family, having grass-like leaves and showy purple flowers giving off a strong sweet chocolate scent; the tubers are an Aboriginal bush food.

**choice** — *n.* **1 a** act or instance of choosing. **b** thing or person chosen (*not a good choice*). **2** range from which to choose (*a wide choice of books for sale*). **3** power or opportunity to choose (*what choice have I?*). — *adj.* of superior quality; carefully chosen (*the choicest cuts of meat*). [Germanic: related to CHOOSE]

**choir** /kwuyuh/ *n.* **1** regular group of singers, esp. in a church. **2** part of a cathedral or large church between the altar and nave. [Latin: related to CHORUS]

**choirboy** *n.* (*fem.* **choirgirl**) boy soprano or alto in a church choir.

**choke** — *v.* (**-king**) **1** stop the breathing of (a person or animal), esp. by constricting the windpipe or (of gas, smoke, etc.) by being unbreathable. **2** suffer a stoppage of breath. **3 a** make or become speechless from emotion. **b** (often foll. by *up*) be overcome with emotion. **4** retard the growth of or kill (esp. plants) by depriving of light etc. (*weeds choking the seedlings*). **5** (often foll. by *back*) suppress (feelings) with difficulty (*choked back her anger*). **6** block or clog (a passage, tube, etc.). — *n.* **1** valve in a carburettor controlling the intake of air, esp. to enrich the fuel mixture. **2** device for smoothing the variations of an alternating current. [Old English]

**choker** *n.* close-fitting necklace.

**choko** /choh-koh/ *n.* succulent green pear-shaped vegetable like a cucumber in flavour. [Brazilian Indian]

**cholecalciferol** /,kol-uh-kal-**sif**-uh-,rol/ *n.* a vitamin (D₃) produced by the action of sunlight on a steroid in the skin. [from CHOLER, CALCIFEROL]

**choler** /kol-uh/ *n.* **1** *hist.* one of the four humours, bile. **2** *poet.* or *archaic* anger, irascibility. [Greek *kholē* bile]

**cholera** /kol-uh-ruh/ *n.* infectious often fatal bacterial disease of the small intestine, resulting in severe vomiting and diarrhoea. [related to CHOLER]

**choleric** /kol-uh-rik/ *adj.* irascible, angry.

**cholesterol** /kuh-les-tuh-,rol/ *n.* sterol found in most body tissues, including the blood where high concentrations promote arteriosclerosis. [from CHOLER, Greek *stereos* stiff]

**chomp** *v.* = CHAMP¹. [imitative]

**choof** /chuuf/ *v.* *colloq.* go or move (*time to choof*). □ **choof off** leave, depart (*if that's the way you feel, I'll choof off*). [figurative use of CHUFF]

**chook** /chuuk/ *n.* **1** chicken or fowl. **2** *colloq. offens.* older woman. [British dial. *chuck* chicken]

**choom** /chuum/ *n.* *colloq.* a pom. [reproducing a British dial. pronunciation of CHUM]

**choose** /chooz/ *v.* (**-sing**; *past* **chose** /chohz/; *past part.* **chosen**) **1** select out of a greater number. **2** (usu. foll. by *between* / *from*) take or select one or another (*you have to choose between us*). **3** (usu. foll. by *to* + infin.) decide, be determined (*chose to ignore the warnings against smoking*). **4** select as (*was chosen leader*). [Old English]

**choosy** /choo-zee/ *adj.* (**-ier**, **-iest**) *colloq.* fastidious. □ **choosiness** *n.*

**chop¹** — *v.* (**-pp-**) **1** (usu. foll. by *off*, *down* etc.) cut or fell by the blow of an axe etc. **2** (often foll. by *up*) cut into small pieces. **3** strike (esp. a ball) with a short heavy edgewise blow. — *n.* **1** cutting blow, esp with an axe. **2** event or series of events in which axemen compete in a contest of speed. **3** thick slice of meat (esp. pork or lamb) usu. including a rib. **4** *colloq.* share (usu. of winnings) (*he'll be in for his chop*). **5** short chopping stroke in cricket etc. **6** (prec. by *the*) *colloq.* **a** dismissal from employment (*poor Bill's got the chop*). **b** action of killing or being killed. **7** broken motion of water, usu. owing to the action of wind against the tide. [related to CHAP²]

**chop²** *n.* (usu. in *pl.*) jaw. [origin unknown]

**chop³** *v.* (-pp-) □ **chop and change** vacillate; change direction frequently. **chop logic** argue pedantically. [perhaps related to CHEAP]

**chop⁴** *adj.* □ **not much chop** no good; not up to much. [Hindi *chāp* seal, stamp of quality]

**chopper** *n.* **1 a** short axe with a large blade. **b** butcher's cleaver. **2** *colloq.* helicopter. **3** *colloq.* type of bicycle or motor cycle with high handlebars. **4** (in *pl.*) *colloq.* teeth. **5** *colloq.* = ROCK-CHOPPER.

**choppy** *adj.* (-ier, -iest) (of the sea etc.) fairly rough. □ **choppily** *adv.* **choppiness** *n.* [from CHOP¹]

**chopstick** *n.* each of a pair of sticks held in one hand as eating utensils by the Chinese, Japanese, etc. [pidgin English from Chinese, = nimble ones]

**chop suey** /chop-**soo**-ee/ *n.* (*pl.* -s) Chinese-style dish of meat fried with vegetables and rice. [Cantonese, = mixed bits]

**choral** /**kaw**-ruhl, **ko**-ruhl/ *adj.* of, for, or sung by a choir or chorus. [medieval Latin: related to CHORUS]

**chorale** /kuh-**rahl**/ *n.* simple stately hymn tune; harmonised form of this. [German: related to CHORAL]

**chord¹** /kawd/ *n.* group of notes (usu. three or more) sounded together. [originally *cord* from ACCORD]

**chord²** /kawd/ *n.* **1** *Math. & Aeron. etc.* straight line joining the ends of an arc, the wings of an aeroplane, etc. **2** *Engin.* one of the two principal members, usu. horizontal, of a truss. **3** *poet.* string of a harp etc. □ **strike a chord** elicit sympathy. [var. of CORD]

**chordate** /**kaw**-dayt/ — *n.* animal having a cartilaginous skeletal rod at some stage of its development. — *adj.* of chordates. [Latin *chorda* CHORD² after VERTEBRATE]

**chore** /chaw/ *n.* tedious or routine task, esp. domestic. [Old English]

**choreograph** /**ko**-ree-uh-,grahf, -,graf/ *v.* compose choreography for (a ballet etc.). □ **choreographer** /-ee-og-ruh-fuh/ *n.*

**choreography** /,ko-ree-**og**-ruh-fee/ *n.*

design or arrangement of a ballet etc. □ **choreographic** /,ko-ree-uh-**graf**-ik/ *adj.* [Greek *khoreia* dance]

**chorister** /**ko**-ruh-stuh/ *n.* member of a choir, esp. a choirboy. [French: related to CHOIR]

**chortle** /**chaw**-tuhl/ — *n.* gleeful chuckle. — *v.* (-ling) utter or express with a chortle. [probably from CHUCKLE, SNORT]

**chorus** /**kaw**-ruhs/ — *n.* (*pl.* -es) **1** group of singers; choir. **2** music composed for a choir. **3** refrain or main part of a song, in which a chorus participates. **4** simultaneous utterance (*chorus of disapproval*). **5** group of singers and dancers performing together in musical comedy etc. **6** *Gk Antiq.* **a** group of performers who comment on the action in a Greek play. **b** utterance made by it. **7** character speaking the prologue in a play. — *v.* (-s-) speak or utter simultaneously. [Latin from Greek]

**chose** *past* of CHOOSE.

**chosen** *past part.* of CHOOSE.

**chough** /chuf/ *n.* **1** (in full **white-winged chough**) bird of eastern Australia with black plumage and white wing markings. **2** bird of Europe etc. [imitative]

**choux pastry** /shoo/ *n.* very light pastry enriched with eggs. [French]

**chow** /chow/ *n.* **1** *colloq.* food. **2** *colloq. offens.* a Chinese. [Chinese]

**chowchilla** /chow-**chil**-uh/ *n.* (also **log-runner**) dark-coloured perching bird whose distinctive call is heard at dusk and dawn in the rainforest of north-eastern Queensland. [Dyirbal and Yidiny *jawujala*]

**chow-chow** /**chow**-chow/ *n.* Chinese preserve of ginger, carrot, etc. in a sugar syrup, used in Christmas cake etc. [pidgin English]

**chowder** /**chow**-duh/ *n.* soup or stew usu. of fresh fish, clams, corn, with bacon, onions, etc. [perhaps from French *chaudière* pot]

**chow mein** /chow **ming**, -**min**/ *n.* Chinese-style dish of fried noodles with shredded meat or shrimps etc. and vegetables. [Chinese *chao mian* fried flour]

**chrism** /**kriz**-uhm/ *n.* consecrated oil, esp. for anointing in Catholic and Greek Orthodox rites and sacraments. [Latin *chrisma* from Greek]

**Chrissie** /**kris**-ee/ *n.* (also **Chrissy**) *colloq.* Christmas (also *attrib.*: *Chrissie presents*).

**Christ** /kruyst/ — *n.* **1** title, also now treated as a name, given to Jesus. **2** Messiah as prophesied in the Old Testament. — *int. colloq.* expressing surprise, anger, etc. [Greek, = anointed]

**christen** /**kris**-uhn/ v. **1** baptise, and give a name to, as a sign of admission to the Christian Church. **2** give a name to anything, esp. with ceremony (*christened the ship 'Australia'*). **3** *colloq.* use for the first time (*let's christen our new spa*). □ **christening** n. [Latin: related to CHRISTEN]

**Christendom** /**kris**-uhn-duhm/ n. Christians worldwide.

**Christian** /**kris**-chuhn/ — adj. **1** of Christ's teaching. **2** believing in or following the religion of Christ. **3** showing the qualities associated with Christ's teaching. **4** *colloq.* kind, fair, decent. — n. adherent of Christianity. [Latin *Christianus* of CHRIST]

**Christianity** /ˌkris-tee-**an**-uh-tee/ n. **1** Christian religion. **2** being a Christian; Christian quality or character.

**Christian name** n. forename, esp. as given at baptism.

**Christmas** /**kris**-muhs/ n. **1** (also **Christmas Day**) annual festival of Christ's birth, celebrated on 25 December. **2** period around this. **3** *attrib.* associated with Christmas (*Christmas dinner*; *Christmas presents*). □ **Christmassy** adj. [Old English: related to CHRIST, MASS[2]]

**Christmas beetle** n. any of several Australian scarab beetles, so called because the adults emerge in summer.

**Christmas bells** n. any of four species of the Australian genus *Blandfordia*, having grass-like leaves and bright red and yellow flowers usu. appearing in summer.

**Christmas box** n. present or gratuity given at Christmas.

**Christmas bush** n. (also **New South Wales Christmas bush**) **1** shrub with white flowers, the calyx lobes of which enlarge and turn red in summer. **2** any of several unrelated Australian trees or shrubs known for their decorative qualities esp. at Christmas time.

**Christmas Eve** n. 24 December.

**Christmas tree** n. **1** evergreen tree (usu. pine) or imitation of this set up and decorated at Christmas. **2** see NUYTSIA.

**chromatic** /kruh-**mat**-ik/ adj. **1** of or produced by colour; in (esp. bright) colours. **2** *Mus.* **a** of or having notes not belonging to a particular diatonic scale. **b** (of a scale) ascending or descending by semitones. □ **chromatically** adv. [Greek *khrōma -mat-* colour]

**chromatin** /**kroh**-muh-tin/ n. chromosome material in a cell nucleus which stains with basic dyes. [Greek: related to CHROME]

**chromatography** /ˌkroh-muh-**tog**-ruh-

fee/ n. separation of the components of a mixture by slow passage through or over material which adsorbs them differently. [Greek: related to CHROME]

**chrome** /krohm/ n. **1** chromium, esp. as plating. **2** (in full **chrome yellow**) yellow pigment got from a certain compound of chromium. [Greek *khrōma* colour]

**chrome steel** n. hard fine-grained steel containing much chromium and used for tools etc.

**chromite** /**kroh**-muyt/ n. mineral of chromium and iron oxides.

**chromium** /**kroh**-mee-uhm/ n. hard metallic element used as a shiny decorative or protective coating.

**chromium plate** n. protective coating of chromium.

**chromosome** /**kroh**-muh-ˌsohm/ n. threadlike structure, usu. found in the cell nucleus of animals and plants, that carries the genetic information in the form of genes. [Greek: related to CHROME, *sōma* body]

**chronic** /**kron**-ik/ adj. **1** (esp. of an illness) long-lasting (*chronic depression*). **2** having a chronic complaint (*chronic bed-wetter*). **3** *colloq.* very bad; intense, severe (*chronic film*; *chronic headache*). **4** *colloq.* habitual, inveterate (*a chronic liar*). □ **chronically** adv. [Greek *khronos* time]

■ **Usage** The use of *chronic* in sense 3 is very informal, and its use in sense 4 is considered incorrect by some people.

**chronicle** /**kron**-i-kuhl/ — n. register of events in order of occurrence. — v. (**-ling**) record (events) thus. [Greek *khronika*: related to CHRONIC]

**chronological** /ˌkron-uh-**loj**-i-kuhl/ adj. **1** (of a number of events) arranged according to order of occurrence. **2** of or relating to chronology. □ **chronologically** adv.

**chronology** /kruh-**nol**-uh-jee/ n. (pl. **-ies**) **1** study of historical records to establish the dates of past events. **2 a** arrangement of events etc. in order of occurrence. **b** table or document displaying this. [Greek *khronos* time, -LOGY]

**chronometer** /kruh-**nom**-uh-tuh/ n. time-measuring instrument, esp. one used in navigation. [from CHRONOLOGY, -METER]

**chrysalis** /**kris**-uh-luhs/ n. (pl. **-lises**) **1** pupa of a butterfly or moth. **2** case enclosing it. [Greek *khrusos* gold]

**chrysanthemum** /kruh-**san**-thuh-muhm/ n. garden plant of the daisy family having brightly coloured flowers. [Greek, = gold flower]

**chrysolite** /kris-uh-ˌluyt/ n. precious variety of olivine. [Greek *khrusos* gold, *lithos* stone]

**chrysoprase** /kris-uh-ˌprayz/ n. apple-green variety of chalcedony. [Greek *khrusos* gold, *prason* leek]

**chubby** adj. (-ier, -iest) plump and rounded. [*chub* thick-bodied European fish]

**chuck¹** — v. 1 colloq. fling or throw carelessly or casually (*chucked it away*). 2 (often foll. by *in*, *up*) colloq. give up; reject (*chucked in my job*). 3 touch playfully, esp. under the chin. 4 (often foll. by *up*) colloq. vomit. 5 (foll. by *in*) contribute (*if each of us chucks in ten dollars*). 6 colloq. perform with vigour, speed, etc. (*chuck a uey*). — n. 1 playful touch under the chin. 2 toss. □ **the chuck** colloq. dismissal; rejection. **chuck it in** colloq. stop; cease work. **chuck off** (often foll. by *at*) colloq. ridicule; criticise. **chuck out** colloq. 1 expel (a person) from a gathering etc. 2 get rid of, discard. [perhaps from French *chuquer* knock]

**chuck²** — n. 1 cut of beef from neck to ribs. 2 device for holding a workpiece or bit. — v. fix to a chuck. [var. of CHOCK]

**chuckle** /chuk-uhl/ — v. (-ling) laugh quietly or inwardly. — n. quiet or suppressed laugh. [*chuck* cluck]

**chuditch** /choo-dich/ n. the western quoll, a native cat once widely distributed across the continent but now found only in the south-western corner of Australia. [Nyungar *judij*]

**chuff** /chuf, chuuf/ v. (of an engine etc.) work with a regular sharp puffing sound. [imitative]

**chuffed** /chuft/ adj. colloq. delighted. [British dial. *chuff*]

**chug** — v. (-gg-) 1 emit a regular muffled explosive sound, as of an engine running slowly. 2 move with this sound. — n. chugging sound. [imitative]

**chukker** n. (also **chukka**) period of play in polo. [Sanskrit *cakra* wheel]

**chum** n. 1 close friend. 2 British immigrant to Australia: see NEW CHUM. □ **chum up** (-mm-) (often foll. by *with*) become a close friend (of). □ **chummy** adj. (-ier, -iest). **chummily** adv. **chumminess** n. [abbreviation of *chamber-fellow*]

**chump** n. 1 colloq. foolish person. 2 thick end of a loin of lamb or mutton (*chump chop*). 3 short thick block of wood. [blend of CHUNK, LUMP¹]

**chunder** /chun-duh/ v. & n. colloq. vomit. □ **chunderous** adj. [rhyming slang *Chunder Loo of Akim Foo* for spew, after a cartoon figure drawn by the Australian artist Norman Lindsay]

**chunk** n. 1 thick piece cut or broken off. 2 substantial amount. [var. of CHUNK²]

**chunky** adj. (-ier, -iest) 1 consisting of or resembling chunks; thick, substantial. 2 small and sturdy. □ **chunkiness** n.

**church** n. 1 building for public Christian worship. 2 public worship (*met after church*). 3 (**Church**) **a** body of all Christians. **b** clergy or clerical profession (*went into the Church*). **c** organised Christian society of any time, country, or distinct principles of worship (*the early Church*; *High Church*). **d** institutionalised religion as a political or social force (*Church and State*). [Greek *kuriakon* Lord's (house)]

**Church of England** n. English Protestant Church, recognised by the State and having the sovereign as its head.

**Church of England in Australia** n. official title (until 1981) of the Anglican Church of Australia.

**Church of Rome** n. = CATHOLIC CHURCH.

**churchyard** n. enclosed ground around a church used for burials.

**churinga** /chuh-ring-guh/ n. (also **tjuringa**, **churinga stone**) sacred object, normally carved or painted, of Aboriginal ceremonial. [Aranda *jwerrenge* object from the Dreaming]

**churl** n. 1 ill-bred person. 2 archaic peasant. [Old English = man]

**churlish** adj. surly; mean. □ **churlishly** adv. **churlishness** n. [from CHURL]

**churn** — n. 1 large milk-can. 2 machine for making butter, ice-cream, etc. — v. 1 agitate (milk or cream) in a churn. 2 produce (butter) in a churn. 3 (usu. foll. by *up*) cause distress to; upset; agitate (*my stomach churns at the sight of blood*; *all churned up about the loss*). 4 (of a liquid) seethe, foam violently (*the churning sea*). □ **churn out** produce in large quantities. [Old English]

**chute¹** /shoot/ n. 1 sloping channel or slide for sending things to a lower level. 2 slide into a swimming-pool. 3 narrow passage or enclosure for cattle or sheep. [Latin *cado* fall]

**chute²** /shoot/ n. colloq. parachute. [abbreviation]

**chutney** /chut-nee/ n. (pl. -s) pungent orig. Indian condiment of fruits, vinegar, chillies, spices, sugar, etc. [Hindi]

**chutty** /chut-ee/ n. colloq. chewing-gum. [origin unknown]

**chutzpah** /chuts-pah/ n. colloq. shameless audacity. [Yiddish]

**chyack** var. of CHIACK.

**chyle** /kuyl/ n. milky fluid of food materials formed in the intestine after digestion. [Greek *khulos* juice]

**chyme** /kuym/ n. acid pulp formed from partly-digested food. [Greek *khumos* juice]

**ciao** /chow/ int. colloq. **1** goodbye. **2** hello. [Italian]

**ciborium** /suh-**baw**-ree-uhm/ n. (pl. **ciboria** /-ree-uh/) sacred vessel with an arched cover used to hold the consecrated hosts. [Greek *kibōrion*]

**cicada** /suh-**kah**-duh, -**kay**-duh/ n. large transparent-winged insect making a rhythmic chirping sound. [Latin]

**cicatrice** /**sik**-uh-truhs/ n. (also **cicatrix** /**sik**-uh-triks/) scar left by a wound. [Latin]

**-cide** /suyd/ suffix **1** person or substance that kills (*regicide*; *insecticide*). **2** killing of (*infanticide*). [Latin *caedo* kill]

**cider** /**suy**-duh/ n. drink of fermented apple juice. [Hebrew, = strong drink]

**cider gum** n. any of several eucalypts yielding a sweet sap which is drinkable, and which can be fermented.

**cig** /sig/ n. colloq. cigarette. [abbreviation]

**cigar** /suh-**gah**/ n. tight roll of tobacco-leaves for smoking. [French or Spanish]

**cigarette** /ˌsig-uh-**ret**/ n. finely cut tobacco rolled in paper for smoking. [French diminutive]

**cilium** /**sil**-ee-uhm/ n. (pl. **cilia**) **1** minute hairlike structure on the surface of many animal cells. **2** eyelash. □ **ciliary** adj. **ciliate** adj. [Latin, = eyelash]

**cinch** /sinch/ n. colloq. **1** sure thing; certainty. **2** easy task. [Spanish *cincha* saddle-girth]

**cincture** /**singk**-chuh/ n. **1** literary girdle, belt, or border. **2** white rope worn round the waist by a priest at Mass. [Latin *cingo* gird]

**cinder** n. **1** residue of coal or wood etc. after burning. **2** (in pl.) ashes. [Old English *sinder* = slag]

**cinderella** /ˌsin-duh-**rel**-uh/ n. person or thing of unrecognised or disregarded merit or beauty. [name of a girl in a fairy tale]

**cine-** /**sin**-ee/ comb. form cinematographic (*cine-camera*). [abbreviation]

**cinema** /**sin**-uh-ˌmuh/ n. **1** theatre where films are shown. **2 a** films collectively. **b** art or industry of producing films. □ **cinematic** /ˌsin-uh-**mat**-ik/ adj. [French: related to KINEMATIC]

**cinematography** /ˌsin-uh-muh-**tog**-ruh-fee/ n. art of making films. □ **cinematographer** n. **cinematographic** /-ˌmat-uh-**graf**-ik/ adj.

**cineol** /**sin**-ee-ol/ n. colourless terpene ether found in oil extracted from eucalypts, used in medicine etc. [Latin]

**cineraria** /ˌsin-uh-**rair**-ree-uh/ n. plant of the Canary Islands with bright flowers and ash-coloured down on its leaves, often found in garden cultivation. [Latin *cinis -ner-* ashes]

**cinnabar** /**sin**-uh-ˌbah/ n. **1** bright red mercuric sulphide. **2** vermilion. [Latin from Greek]

**cinnamon** /**sin**-uh-muhn/ n. **1** aromatic spice from the peeled, rolled, and dried bark of a tree *Cinnamomum zeylanicum* native to Sri Lanka, or from other related species (see CASSIA). **2** this tree. **3** yellowish-brown. [Greek *kinnamon*]

**cinnamon bells** n. saprophytic terrestrial orchid of all Australian States, having numerous brown and white bell-flowers strongly scented of cinnamon.

**cinquefoil** /**singk**-foil/ n. **1** plant with compound leaves of five leaflets. **2** Archit. five-cusped ornament in a circle or arch. [Latin *quinque* five, *folium* leaf]

**cipher** /**suy**-fuh/ (also **cypher**) — n. **1 a** secret or disguised writing. **b** thing so written. **c** key to it. **2** arithmetical symbol (0) used to occupy a vacant place in decimal etc. numeration. **3** any Arabic numeral. **4** person or thing of no importance. — v. write in cipher. [Arabic]

**circa** /**ser**-kuh/ prep. (preceding a date) about. [Latin]

**circadian** /ser-**kay**-dee-uhn/ adj. Physiol. occurring about once per day. [from CIRCA, Latin *dies* day]

**circle** /**ser**-kuhl/ — n. **1** round plane figure whose circumference is everywhere equidistant from its centre. **2** circular or roundish enclosure, structure, or road. **3** curved upper tier of seats in a theatre etc. (*dress circle*). **4** circular route. **5** persons grouped round a centre of interest (*sewing circle*). **6** set or restricted group (*not done in the best circles*). **7** = VICIOUS CIRCLE. — v. (**-ling**) **1** (often foll. by *round*, *about*) move in a circle. **2 a** revolve round. **b** form a circle round. □ **come full circle** return to the starting-point. [Latin diminutive: related to CIRCUS]

**circlet** /**ser**-kluht/ n. **1** small circle. **2** circular band, esp. as an ornament.

**circuit** /**ser**-kuht/ n. **1** line or course enclosing an area; the distance round. **2 a** path of an electric current. **b** apparatus through which a current passes. **3 a** judge's itinerary in non-metropolitan areas to hold courts. **b** the areas covered. **4** motor-racing track. **5** itinerary or specific sphere of operation (*election* *circuit; cabaret circuit*). **6** sequence of sporting events or athletic exercises (*tennis circuit*). **7** roundabout journey. **8** street which is circular. [Latin: related to CIRCUM-, *eo it-* go]

**circuit-breaker** *n.* automatic device for interrupting an electric circuit.

**circuitous** /ser-**kyoo**-uh-tuhs/ *adj.* **1** indirect. **2** going a long way round.

**circuitry** /**ser**-kuh-tree/ *n.* (*pl.* **-ies**) **1** system of electric circuits. **2** equipment forming this.

**circular** /**ser**-kyuh-luh/ — *adj.* **1 a** having the form of a circle. **b** moving (roughly) in a circle, finishing at the starting-point (*circular walk*). **2** (of reasoning) using the point it is trying to prove as evidence for its conclusion, hence invalid. **3** (of a letter etc.) distributed to a number of people. — *n.* circular letter, leaflet, etc. □ **circularity** /-**la**-ruh-tee/ *n.* [Latin: related to CIRCLE]

**circularise** *v.* (also **-ize**) (**-sing** or **-zing**) distribute circulars to.

**circular saw** *n.* power saw with a rapidly rotating wheel disc.

**circulate** /**ser**-kyuh-,layt/ *v.* (**-ting**) **1** be in circulation; spread. **2 a** put into circulation. **b** send circulars to. **3** move about among guests etc. □ **circulatory** *adj.* [Latin: related to CIRCLE]

**circulation** /,ser-kyuh-**lay**-shuhn/ *n.* **1** movement to and fro, or from and back to a starting-point, esp. that of the blood from and to the heart. **2 a** transmission or distribution (of news, ideas, books, etc.). **b** number of copies sold, esp. of journals and newspapers. □ **in** (or **out of**) **circulation** active (or not active) socially.

**circum-** *comb. form* round, about. [Latin]

**circumcise** /**ser**-kuhm-,suyz/ *v.* (**-sing**) **1** cut off the foreskin, as an Aboriginal, Jewish or Muslim rite or a surgical operation. **2** cut off the clitoris, usu. as a religious rite. □ **circumcision** /,ser-kuhm-**sizh**-uhn/ *n.* [Latin *caedo* cut]

**circumference** /suh-**kum**-fuh-ruhns/ *n.* **1** enclosing boundary, esp. of a circle. **2** distance round. □ **circumferential** /,suh-kum-fuh-**ren**-shuhl/ *adj.* [Latin *fero* carry]

**circumflex** /**ser**-kuhm-,fleks/ *n.* (in full **circumflex accent**) mark (ˆ) placed over a vowel to show contraction, length, etc. [Latin: related to FLEX[1]]

**circumlocution** /,ser-kuhm-luh-**kyoo**-shuhn/ *n.* **1 a** roundabout expression. **b** evasive talk. **2** verbosity. □ **circumlocutory** /-**lok**-yuh-tuh-ree, -tree/ *adj.*

**circumnavigate** /,ser-kuhm-**nav**-uh-,gayt/ *v.* (**-ting**) sail round (esp. the world). □ **circumnavigation** /-**gay**-shuhn/ *n.*

**circumscribe** /**ser**-kuhm-,skruyb/ *v.* (**-bing**) **1** (of a line etc.) enclose or outline. **2** lay down the limits of; confine, restrict (*our sight-seeing was circumscribed by lack of time*). **3** *Geom.* draw (a figure) round another, touching it at points but not cutting it. □ **circumscription** /-**skrip**-shuhn/ *n.* [Latin *scribo* write]

**circumspect** /**ser**-kuhm-,spekt/ *adj.* cautious; taking everything into account (*we need to be circumspect about this, not just rush in blindly*). □ **circumspection** /-**spek**-shuhn/ *n.* **circumspectly** *adv.* [Latin *specio spect-* look]

**circumstance** /**ser**-kuhm-stuhns, -stans/ *n.* **1 a** fact, occurrence, or condition, esp. (in *pl.*) all the factors connected with or influencing an event (*we need to know all the circumstances before we can judge*). **b** (in *pl.*) external conditions that affect or might affect an action (*he's a victim of circumstances*). **2** incident, occurrence, or fact, as needing consideration (*the circumstance that he left early is surely suspicious*). **3** (in *pl.*) one's financial or material condition (*in reduced circumstances*). **4** ceremony, fuss (*pomp and circumstance*). □ **in** (or **under**) **the circumstances** the state of affairs being what it is. **in** (or **under**) **no circumstances** not at all; never. □ **circumstanced** *adj.* [Latin *sto* stand]

**circumstantial** /,ser-kuhm-**stan**-shuhl/ *adj.* **1** giving full details (*circumstantial account*). **2** (of evidence etc.) indicating a conclusion by inference from known facts hard to explain otherwise. □ **circumstantiality** /-shee-**al**-uh-tee/ *n.*

**circumvent** /,ser-kuhm-**vent**/ *v.* **1** evade (a difficulty); find a way round (*circumvented the problem; we'll have to circumvent that billabong*). **2** baffle, outwit (*they'll try to circumvent the law*). □ **circumvention** *n.* [Latin *venio vent-* come]

**circus** /**ser**-kuhs/ *n.* (*pl.* **-es**) **1** travelling show of performing acrobats, clowns, animals, etc. **2** *colloq.* scene of lively or disorderly action. **3** chiefly *Brit.* open space in a town, where several streets converge. **4** *Rom. Antiq.* arena for sports and games. [Latin, = ring]

**cirrhosis** /si-**roh**-suhs, suh-/ *n.* chronic liver disease, as a result of alcoholism, hepatitis, etc. □ **cirrhotic** /-**rot**-ik/ *adj.* [Greek *kirrhos* tawny]

**cirrus** /**si**-ruhs/ *n.* (*pl.* **cirri** /-ruy/) **1** white wispy cloud at high altitude. **2** tendril or appendage of a plant or animal. [Latin, = curl]

**cissy** var. of SISSY.

**Cistercian** /suhs-**ter**-shuhn/ — *n.* monk or nun of the order founded in 1098 as a stricter branch of the Benedictines. — *adj.* of the Cistercians. [French *Cîteaux* in France]

**cistern** /**sis**-tuhn/ *n.* tank for storing water. [Latin *cista* box, from Greek]

**citadel** /sit-uh-ˌdel/ *n.* fortress, usu. on high ground, protecting or dominating a city. [French *citadelle*]

**citation** /suy-**tay**-shuhn/ *n.* **1** citing of a book or other source; passage cited. **2** *Mil.* mention in dispatches. **3** description of the reasons for an award.

**cite** *v.* (**-ting**) **1** mention as an example etc. **2** quote (a book etc.) in support of an argument etc. **3** *Mil.* mention in dispatches. **4** summon to appear in court. [Latin *cieo* set in motion]

**citizen** /**sit**-uh-zuhn/ *n.* **1** member of a nation, either native or naturalised. **2** inhabitant of a city. □ **citizenry** *n.* **citizenship** *n.* [Anglo-French: related to CITY]

**citizens' band** *n.* system of local inter-communication by individuals on special radio frequencies.

**citrate** /**sit**-rayt/ *n.* a salt of citric acid.

**citric** /**sit**-rik/ *adj.* derived from citrus fruit.

**citric acid** *n.* sharp-tasting acid in citrus fruits.

**citron** /**sit**-ruhn/ *n.* **1** tree with large lemon-like fruits. **2** this fruit. [French from Latin CITRUS]

**citronella** /ˌsit-ruh-**nel**-uh/ *n.* **1** a fragrant oil. **2** grass from S. Asia yielding it.

**citrus** /**sit**-ruhs/ *n.* (*pl.* **-es**) **1** tree of a group including the lemon, orange, and grapefruit. **2** (in full **citrus fruit**) fruit of such a tree. [Latin]

**city** /**sit**-ee/ *n.* (*pl.* **-ies**) **1 a** large town. **b** town qualified for city status (on the basis of population etc., requirements varying from State to State). **c** similar area within a large city, e.g. the city of Dandenong within the Melbourne metropolitan area. **2 a** business part of a city. **b** commercial circles. **3** inhabitants of a city (*almost the entire city turned up to watch*). [Latin *civitas*: related to CIVIC]

**city slicker** *n.* usu. *derog.* smart and sophisticated city-dweller.

**city state** *n.* esp. *hist.* city that with its surrounding territory forms an independent State (*Vatican City is a city-state*).

**civet** /**siv**-uht/ *n.* **1** (in full **civet cat**) catlike animal of Central Africa. **2** strong musky perfume obtained from it. [French ultimately from Arabic]

**civic** /**siv**-ik/ *adj.* **1** of a city. **2** of citizens or citizenship (*civic virtues*). □ **civically** *adv.* [Latin *civis* citizen]

**civil** /**siv**-uhl/ *adj.* **1** of or belonging to citizens. **2** of ordinary citizens; non-military. **3** polite, obliging, not rude. **4** *Law* concerning private rights and not criminal offences. □ **civilly** *adv.* [Latin *civilis*: related to CIVIC]

**civil defence** *n.* organising of civilians for protection during wartime attacks.

**civil disobedience** *n.* refusal to comply with certain laws as a peaceful protest.

**civil engineer** *n.* one who designs or maintains roads, bridges, dams, etc. □ **civil engineering** *n.*

**civilian** /suh-**vil**-yuhn/ — *n.* person not in the armed services or police force. — *adj.* of or for civilians.

**civilisation** /ˌsiv-uh-luy-**zay**-shuhn/ *n.* (also **-ization**) **1** advanced stage or system of social development. **2** peoples of the world that are regarded as having this. **3** a people or nation (esp. of the past) regarded as an element of social evolution (*Inca civilisation*).

**civilise** /**siv**-uh-ˌluyz/ *v.* (also **-ize**) (**-sing** or **-zing**) **1 a** bring out of a barbarous or primitive stage of society. **b** impose upon (esp. an indigenous people) a way of life alien to them. **2** enlighten; refine and educate. [French: related to CIVIL]

**civility** /suh-**vil**-uh-tee/ *n.* (*pl.* **-ies**) **1** politeness. **2** act of politeness. [Latin related to CIVIL]

**civil law** *n.* law concerning private rights (opp. criminal law).

**civil liberty** *n.* (often in *pl.*) freedom of action and speech subject to the law.

**civil marriage** *n.* one solemnised without religious ceremony.

**civil rights** *n.pl.* rights of citizens to political and social freedom and equality.

**civil war** *n.* war between citizens of the same country.

**civvies** *n.pl. colloq.* civilian clothes [abbreviation]

**civvy street** *n. colloq.* civilian life [abbreviation]

**Cl** *symb.* chlorine.

**clack** — *v.* **1** make a sharp sound as of boards struck together. **2** chatter. — *n.* clacking noise or talk. [imitative]

**clad** *adj.* **1** clothed. **2** provided with cladding. [past part. of CLOTHE]

**cladding** *n.* covering or coating on a structure or material etc.

**cladistics** /kluh-**dis**-tiks/ *n.pl.* (usu. treated as *sing.*) *Biol.* method of classifying animals and plants on the basis of shared characteristics. [Greek *klado* branch]

**cladode** /klad-ohd/ n. flattened stem which looks like a leaf. [Greek *klados* shoot]

**claim** — v. **1** state, declare, assert (*claimed that he knew*). **2** demand as one's due or property (*claimed that he was entitled to the house*). **3** represent oneself as having or achieving (*claim victory*). **4** (foll. by to + infin.) profess (*claimed to be the owner*). **5** have as an achievement or consequence (*could then claim five wins*; *fire claimed two victims*). **6** (of a thing) deserve (attention etc.) (*her achievement claims our utmost respect*). — n. **1 a** demand or request for a thing considered one's due (*lay claim to*; *put in a claim*). **b** application for compensation under the terms of an insurance policy. **2** (foll. by to, on) right or title to a thing (*his only claim to fame*). **3** assertion (*your claim lacks credibility*). **4** thing claimed. **5** *Mining* piece of land formally claimed and taken for mining purposes. [Latin *clamo* call out]

**claimant** n. person making a claim, esp. in a lawsuit.

**claim jumper** n. person who occupies or takes summary possession of another's mining claim.

**clairvoyance** /klair-**voi**-uhns/ n. supposed faculty of perceiving the future or things beyond normal sensory perception. □ **clairvoyant** n. & adj. [French: related to CLEAR, *voir* see]

**clam** — n. **1** edible bivalve mollusc. **2** *colloq.* shy or withdrawn or secretive person. — v. (**-mm-**) (foll. by up) *colloq.* refuse to talk. [related to CLAMP]

**clamber** — v. climb laboriously using hands and feet. — n. difficult climb. [from CLIMB]

**clammy** /**klam**-ee/ adj. (**-ier**, **-iest**) unpleasantly damp and sticky. □ **clammily** adv. **clamminess** n. [*clam* to daub]

**clamour** /**klam**-uh/ (also **clamor**) — n. **1** loud or vehement shouting or noise. **2** protest or complaint; appeal or demand (*a clamour for justice*). — v. **1** make a clamour. **2** utter with a clamour. □ **clamorous** adj. [Latin: related to CLAIM]

**clamp** — n. **1** device, esp. a brace or band of iron etc., for strengthening or holding things together. **2** (in full **wheel-clamp**) device for immobilising an illegally parked vehicle. — v. **1** strengthen or fasten with a clamp; fix firmly. **2** immobilise (a vehicle) by attaching a wheel-clamp to it. □ **clamp down** (usu. foll. by on) become stricter (about); suppress. [Low German or Dutch]

**clamp-down** n. sudden policy of suppression.

**clan** n. **1** group of people with a common ancestor, esp. among Aboriginal groups and in the Scottish Highlands. **2** large family as a social group. [Gaelic]

**clandestine** /klan-**des**-tuhn/ adj. surreptitious, secret. □ **clandestinely** adv. [Latin]

**clang** — n. loud resonant metallic sound. — v. (cause to) make a clang. [imitative: cf. Latin *clango* resound]

**clanger** /**klang**-uh/ n. *colloq.* mistake, blunder. □ **drop a clanger** commit a conspicuous indiscretion.

**clangour** /**klang**-guh, **klang**-uh/ n. (also **clangor**) prolonged or repeated clanging noise. □ **clangorous** adj.

**clank** — n. sound as of heavy pieces of metal meeting or a chain rattling. — v. (cause to) make a clank. [imitative]

**clannish** adj. often *derog.* (of a family or group) associating closely with each other; inward-looking.

**clap¹** — v. (**-pp-**) **1 a** strike the palms of one's hands together, esp. repeatedly as applause. **b** strike (the hands) together in this way. **2** applaud thus. **3** put or place quickly or with determination (*clapped him in prison*; *clapped a tax on books*). **4** (foll. by on) give a friendly slap (*clapped him on the back*). — n. **1** act of clapping, esp. as applause. **2** explosive sound, esp. of thunder. **3** slap, pat. □ **clap eyes on** *colloq.* see. **clap on** *colloq.* increase (*clapped on the speed*). [Old English]

**clap²** n. *colloq.* venereal disease, esp. gonorrhoea. [French]

**clapped out** adj. *colloq.* worn out; exhausted.

**clapper** n. tongue or striker of a bell.

**clapperboard** n. device in film-making of hinged boards struck together to synchronise the starting of picture and sound machinery.

**clap stick** n. (also **music stick**) Aboriginal percussion instrument consisting of two sticks of resonant wood clapped rhythmically together.

**claptrap** n. insincere or pretentious talk, nonsense.

**claret** /**kla**-ruht/ n. **1 a** red wine from Bordeaux in France. **b** similar wine from elsewhere. **2** purplish-red. [French: related to CLARIFY]

**claret ash** n. ornamental ash tree, orig. cultivated in SA, having purplish-red autumn leaves.

**clarify** /**kla**-ruh-fuy/ v. (**-ies**, **-ied**) **1** make or become clearer. **2 a** free (liquid, butter, etc.) from impurities. **b** make transparent. □ **clarification** /-fuh-**kay**-shuhn/ n. [Latin: related to CLEAR]

**clarinet** /ˌkla-ruh-**net**/ n. woodwind instrument with a single reed. □ **clarinettist** n. [French diminutive of *clarine*, a kind of bell]

**clarion** /**kla**-ree-uhn/ — n. **1** clear rousing sound. **2** hist. shrill wartrumpet. — adj. clear and loud. [Latin: related to CLEAR]

**clarity** /**kla**-ruh-tee/ n. clearness.

**clash** — n. **1 a** loud jarring sound as of metal objects struck together. **b** collision. **2 a** conflict or disagreement. **b** discord of colours etc. — v. **1** (cause to) make a clashing sound. **2** collide; coincide awkwardly (*the concert clashes with mum's birthday*). **3** (often foll. by *with*) **a** come into conflict or be at variance (*my wishes always clash with yours*). **b** (of colours) be discordant (*purple clashes with green*). [imitative]

**clasp** /klahsp, klasp/ — n. **1** device with interlocking parts for fastening. **2 a** embrace. **b** grasp, handshake. — v. **1** fasten with or as with a clasp. **2 a** grasp, hold closely. **b** embrace. [Old English]

**class** /klahs/ — n. **1** any set of persons or things grouped together, or graded or differentiated from others esp. by quality (*first class*; *economy class*). **2** division or order of society (*middle class*). **3** colloq. distinction, high quality; stylishness (*he has a lot of class*). **4 a** group of students taught together. **b** occasion when they meet. **c** their course of instruction. **5** division of candidates by merit in an examination. **6** Biol. next grouping of organisms below a division or phylum. — v. **1** assign to a class or category. **2** grade (*fleeces in a shearing shed*). □ **in a class of** (or **on**) **its** (or **one's**) **own** unequalled. □ **classer** n. (in sense 2 of v.). **classless** adj. [Latin *classis* assembly]

**class action** n. legal action brought on behalf of all members of a group with a common interest or grievance.

**class-conscious** adj. aware of social divisions or one's place in them. □ **class-consciousness** n.

**classic** /**klas**-ik/ — adj. **1** first-class; of lasting value and importance. **2** remarkably typical; outstandingly important (*a classic case*). **3 a** of ancient Greek and Latin literature, art, etc. **b** (of style in art, music, etc.) simple, harmonious, well-proportioned. **4** (of clothes) made in a simple elegant style not much affected by changes in fashion. — n. **1** classic writer, artist, work, or example. **2** (in pl.) ancient Greek and Latin. [Latin *classicus*: related to CLASS]

**classical** adj. **1 a** of ancient Greek or Roman literature or art. **b** (of a language)

having the form used by ancient standard authors. **c** based on the study of ancient Greek and Latin (*a classical education*). **2** (of music) serious or conventional, or of the period from c. 1750–1800. **3** restrained in style. □ **classicality** /-**kal**-uh-tee/ n. **classically** adv.

**classicism** /**klas**-uh-ˌsiz-uhm/ n. **1** following of a classic style. **2** classical scholarship. **3** ancient Greek or Latin idiom. □ **classicist** n.

**classified** /**klas**-uh-ˌfuyd/ adj. **1** arranged in classes or categories. **2** (of information etc.) designated as officially secret. **3** (of newspaper advertisements) arranged in columns according to various categories.

**classify** /**klas**-uh-ˌfuy/ v. (-ies, -ied) **1 a** arrange in classes or categories. **b** assign to a class or category. **2** designate as officially secret or not for general disclosure. □ **classifiable** adj. **classification** /-fuh-**kay**-shuhn/ n. **classificatory** /-**kay**-tuh-ree, -tree/ adj. [French: related to CLASS]

**classy** adj. (-ier, -iest) colloq. superior, stylish. □ **classily** adv. **classiness** n.

**clatter** — n. sound as of hard objects struck together. — v. (cause to) make a clatter. [Old English]

**clause** /klawz/ n. **1** Gram. part of a sentence, including a subject and predicate (see panel). **2** single statement or part in a treaty, law, contract, etc. □ **clausal** adj. [Latin *clausula*: related to CLOSE]

**claustrophobia** /ˌklos-truh-**foh**-bee-uh ˌklaw-struh-/ n. abnormal fear of confined places. □ **claustrophobic** adj. [Latin *claustrum* CLOISTER, -PHOBIA]

**clavichord** /**klav**-uh-ˌkawd/ n. small keyboard instrument with a very soft tone. [medieval Latin: related to CLAVICLE]

**clavicle** /**klav**-i-kuhl/ n. collar-bone [Latin *clavis* key]

**claw** — n. **1 a** pointed nail on an animal's foot. **b** foot armed with claws. **2** pincers of a shellfish. **3** device for grappling holding, etc. — v. scratch, maul, or pull with claws or fingernails. [Old English]

**claw back** — v. **1** regain laboriously or gradually. **2** recover (money paid out from another source (e.g. taxation). — n. (**clawback**) **1** act of clawing back. **2** money recovered in this way.

**claw flower** n. WA melaleuca with branches weeping to the ground and masses of large (the largest of any melaleuca) mauve, claw-shaped flowers

**claw hammer** n. hammer with one side of the head forked for extracting nails.

**clay** n. **1** stiff sticky earth, used for making bricks, pottery, etc. **2** poet. substance of the human body. □ **clayey** adj. [Old English]

**claypan** n. natural hollow in clay soil, retaining water after rain.

**clay pigeon** n. breakable disc thrown up from a trap as a target for shooting.

**Clayton's** /klay-tuhnz/ n. propr. something which is largely illusory or exists in name only; imitation (Australian English is not a Clayton's English). [from the advertising slogan used by the manufacturer of a non-alcoholic drink: 'It's the drink I have when I'm not having a drink']

**-cle** suffix forming (orig. diminutive) nouns (article; particle). [as -CULE]

**clean** /kleen/ — adj. **1** free from dirt or impurities, unsoiled. **2** clear; unused; pristine (clean air; clean page). **3** not obscene or indecent (good clean fun). **4** attentive to personal hygiene and cleanliness. **5** entire, complete, clear-cut (clean sweep; clean break). **6** showing no record of crime, disease, drug use, etc. **7** fair (a clean fight). **8 a** (of a ship, aircraft, or car) streamlined. **b** well-formed, slender and shapely (clean-limbed Aussie surfies; the car has clean lines). **9** (of timber) free from knots. **10** adroit, skilful (a clean bit of fielding). **11** (of a nuclear weapon etc.) producing relatively little radioactivity or fallout. — adv. **1** completely, outright, simply (cut clean through; clean bowled; clean forgot). **2** in a clean manner. — v. make or become clean. — n. act or process of cleaning (gave it a good clean). □ **clean out 1** clean thoroughly. **2** colloq. empty or deprive (esp. of money). **clean up 1 a** clear away (a mess). **b** (also absol.) put (things) tidy. **c** make (oneself) clean. **2** restore order or morality to (cleaned up his act). **3** colloq. acquire as or make a profit. **4** colloq. defeat thoroughly (cleaned them up in the final quarter). **come clean** colloq. confess fully. **make a clean breast of** see BREAST. [Old English]

**clean bill of health** n. declaration that there is no disease or defect.

**clean-bowl** v. Cricket bowl out (a batsman) with a ball that hits the wicket without having touched the bat or body of the batsman.

**clean-cut** adj. sharply outlined or defined (he has clean-cut features).

**cleaner** n. **1** person employed to clean rooms etc. **2** (usu. in pl.) establishment for cleaning clothes etc. **3** device or substance for cleaning. □ **take a person to the cleaners** colloq. **1** defraud or rob a person. **2** criticise severely.

**cleanliness** /klen-lee-nuhs/ n. state of being personally clean, attentive to personal hygiene.

**cleanly¹** /kleen-lee/ adv. **1** in a clean way (made the break cleanly). **2** efficiently; without difficulty.

**cleanly²** /klen-lee/ adj. (-ier, -iest) habitually clean; with clean habits.

**cleanse** /klenz/ v. (-sing) make clean or pure. □ **cleanser** n.

**clean-shaven** adj. without beard or moustache.

**clean sheet** n. (also **clean slate**) freedom from commitments or imputations; removal of these from one's record.

**cleanskin** n. **1** unbranded animal. **2 a** person who has no criminal record. **b** person new to (a situation or activity) and lacking experience. **3** colloq. unlabelled bottle of wine.

**clean-up** n. act of cleaning up.

**clear** — adj. **1** free from dirt or contamination or blemishes etc. (clear complexion). **2** (of weather, the sky, etc.) not dull or cloudy. **3 a** transparent. **b** lustrous; shining. **4 a** easily perceived; distinct; evident (a clear voice; it is clear that . . .). **b** easily understood (make a thing clear). **c** not confused or doubtful (clear evidence). **5** discerning readily and accurately (clear mind; clear thinking). **6** confident, convinced, certain (I am clear on that point; it is clear that he will die). **7** (of a conscience) free from guilt. **8** (of a road etc.) unobstructed. **9 a** net, without deduction ($1000 clear). **b** complete (three clear days). **10** (often foll. by of) free, unhampered; unencumbered (clear of debt). — adv. **1** clearly (speak loud and

---

**Clause**

A clause is a group of words that includes a finite verb. If it makes complete sense by itself, it is known as a main clause, e.g.

*The sun came out.*

Otherwise, although it makes some sense, it must be attached to a main clause. This is known as a subordinate clause, e.g.

*when the sun came out*
(as in *When the sun came out, we went outside.*)

*clear*). **2** completely (*got clear away*). **3** apart, out of contact (*keep clear*). — *v.* **1** make or become clear. **2 a** (often foll. by *of*) make or become free from obstruction etc. **b** free (land) for cultivation or building by cutting down trees etc. **c** cause people to leave (a room etc.) (*police moved in to clear the street*). **3** (often foll. by *of*) show (a person) to be innocent (*cleared him of complicity*). **4** approve (a person etc.) for a special duty, access to information, etc. **5** pass over or by, safely or without touching, esp. by jumping. **6** make (an amount of money) as a net gain or to balance expenses. **7** pass (a cheque) through a clearing-house. **8** pass through (customs etc.). **9** disappear (*mist cleared*). □ **clear the air** remove suspicion, tension, etc. **clear away 1** remove (esp. dishes etc.). **2** disappear. **clear the decks** prepare for action. **clear off** *colloq.* go away. **clear out 1** empty, tidy by emptying. **2** remove. **3** *colloq.* go away. **clear a thing with** get approval or authorisation for it from (a person). **clear up 1** tidy up. **2** solve. **3** (of weather) become fine. **4** disappear (*his cold has cleared up*). **in the clear** free from suspicion or difficulty. □ **clearly** *adv.* **clearness** *n.* [Latin *clarus*]

**clearance** *n.* **1** removal of obstructions etc. **2** space allowed for the passing of two objects or parts in machinery etc. **3** special authorisation or permission, e.g. for an aircraft to take off or land, for access to information, etc. **4 a** clearing of a person, ship, etc. by customs. **b** certificate showing this. **5** clearing of cheques. **6** clearing out.

**clear-cut** *adj.* sharply defined.

**clear-headed** *adj.* thinking clearly, sensible.

**clearing** *n.* open area in a forest.

**clearing bank** *n.* bank which is a member of a clearing house.

**clearing house** *n.* **1** bankers' establishment where cheques and bills are exchanged. **2** agency for collecting and distributing information etc.

**clearing sale** *n.* **1** sale, esp. of surplus stock, farm machinery, etc. at a rural property. **2** retailer's sale of superseded merchandise.

**clear-sighted** *adj.* seeing, thinking, or understanding clearly.

**clearway** *n.* road on which vehicles, at stated times, may not stop.

**cleat** *n.* **1** piece of metal, wood, etc., bolted on for fastening ropes to, or to strengthen woodwork etc. **2** projecting piece on a spar, gangway, etc., to prevent slipping. [Old English]

**cleavage** /klee-vij/ *n.* **1** hollow between a woman's breasts. **2** division, splitting. **3** line along which rocks, crystals, etc split.

**cleave**[1] *v.* (**-ving**; *past* **clove** or **cleft** or **cleaved**; *past part.* **cloven** or **cleft** or **cleaved**) *literary* **1** chop or break apart, split, esp. along the grain or line of cleavage. **2** make one's way through (air, water, etc.). [Old English]

**cleave**[2] *v.* (**-ving**) (foll. by *to*) *literary* stick fast; adhere (*I shall cleave to my principles*; *will cleave to him through thick and thin*). [Old English]

**cleaver** *n.* butcher's heavy chopping tool.

**clef** *n. Mus.* symbol indicating the pitch of notes on a staff. [Latin *clavis* key]

**cleft**[1] *adj.* split, partly divided. [past part. of CLEAVE[1]]

**cleft**[2] *n.* split, fissure. [Old English: related to CLEAVE[1]]

**cleft palate** *n.* congenital split in the roof of the mouth.

**clematis** /kluh-**may**-tuhs/ *n.* any climbing plant of the genus *Clematis* including five Australian species having profuse creamy flowers foll. by attractive flossy fruits (see OLD MAN'S BEARD). [Greek]

**clement** /**klem**-uhnt/ *adj.* **1** (of weather) mild. **2** merciful. □ **clemency** *n.* [Latin *clemens*]

**clench** — *v.* **1** close (the teeth, fingers, etc.) tightly. **2** grasp firmly. — *n.* clenching action; clenched state. [Old English]

**clerestory** /**kleer**-stuh-ree, - **staw**-ree/ *n.* (*pl.* **-ies**) upper row of windows in a cathedral or large church, above the level of the aisle roofs. [*clear storey*]

**clergy** /**kler**-jee/ *n.* (*pl.* **-ies**) (usu. treated as *pl.*) those ordained for religious duties. [French (related to CLERIC) and Church Latin]

**clergyman** *n.* member of the clergy.

**cleric** /**kle**-rik/ *n.* member of the clergy. [Greek *klērikos* from *klēros* lot, heritage]

**clerical** *adj.* **1** of clergy or clergymen. **2** of or done by clerks.

**clerk** /klahk/ — *n.* **1** person employed to keep records, accounts, etc. **2** secretary or agent of a local council, court, etc. **3** lay officer of a church. — *v.* work as clerk. [Old English and French: related to CLERIC]

**clever** /**klev**-uh/ *adj.* (**-er**, **-est**) **1** skilful, talented; quick to understand and learn. **2** adroit, dexterous. **3** (of the doer or the thing done) ingenious, cunning. **4** (in Aboriginal English) wise, learned in traditional lore, and spiritually powerful. **5** oversmart; cocky (*don't you get clever with me, mate!*). □ **cleverly** *adv.* **cleverness** *n.* [Old English]

**clever man** n. (in Aboriginal English) an Aborigine with recognised skills in traditional medicine and (frequently) a role in ceremonial life.

**clianthus** /klee-**an**-thuhs/ n. = STURT'S DESERT PEA.

**cliché** /klee-shay/ n. **1** hackneyed phrase or opinion. **2** metal casting of a stereotype or electrotype. □ **clichéd** adj. [French]

**click¹** — n. slight sharp sound (click of the switch; click of the latch). — v. **1** (cause to) make a click (door clicked shut; clicked his heels). **2** colloq. **a** become clear or understood (it suddenly all clicked). **b** be popular (the new TV quiz hasn't quite clicked with the viewers). **c** strike up a strong rapport with a person (he and I clicked from the moment we met). **3** Computing **a** press a button on a mouse. **b** select (an item represented on-screen, a particular function, etc.) by so doing. [imitative]

**click²** n. (also **klick**) colloq. kilometre.

**client** /**kluy**-uhnt/ n. **1** person using the services of a lawyer, architect, or other professional person. **2** customer. [Latin cliens]

**clientele** /ˌkluy-uhn-**tel**, ˌklee-uhn-/ n. **1** clients collectively. **2** customers. [French and Latin: related to CLIENT]

**cliff** n. steep rock-face, esp. on a coast. [Old English]

**cliff-hanger** n. **1** story etc. with a strong element of suspense. **2** sporting contest, election, etc. in which the result is very close.

**cliftie** /**klif**-tee/ v. colloq. steal (cliftied a hundred garden gnomes). [Greek kleptēs thief]

**climacteric** /ˌkluy-**mak**-tuh-rik, ˌkluy-muhk-**te**-rik/ n. period of life when fertility and sexual activity are in decline. [Greek: related to CLIMAX]

**climate** /**kluy**-muht/ n. **1** prevailing weather conditions of an area. **2** region with particular weather conditions (has a mild climate all year). **3** prevailing trend of opinion or public feeling. □ **climatic** /-**mat**-ik/ adj. **climatically** /-mat-i-kuh-lee, -klee/ adv. [Greek klima]

**climax** /**kluy**-maks/ — n. **1** event or point of greatest intensity or interest; culmination. **2** sexual orgasm. **3** Ecology state of equilibrium reached by a plant community. — v. colloq. reach or bring to a climax. □ **climactic** /kluy-**mak**-tik/ adj. [Greek, = ladder]

**climb** /kluym/ — v. **1** (often foll. by up) ascend, mount, go or come up. **2** grow up a wall etc. by clinging or twining. **3** progress, esp. in social rank. **4** slope upwards (the road climbs sharply here). — n. **1** ascent by climbing. **2** hill etc. climbed or to be climbed. □ **climb down 1** descend, esp. using hands. **2** withdraw from a stance taken up in an argument etc. □ **climber** n. [Old English]

**climb-down** n. withdrawal from a stance taken up.

**clime** n. literary **1** region. **2** climate. [Latin: related to CLIMATE]

**clinch** — v. **1** confirm or settle (an argument, bargain, etc.) conclusively. **2** (of boxers etc.) become too closely engaged. **3** secure (a nail or rivet) by driving the point sideways when through. — n. **1 a** clinching action. **b** clinched state. **2** colloq. embrace. [var. of CLENCH]

**clincher** n. colloq. point or remark that settles an argument etc.

**cline** /kluyn/ n. Biol. graded sequence of differences within a species etc. [Greek klinō slope]

**cling** v. (past and past part. **clung**) **1** (often foll. by to) adhere, stick to. **2** (foll. by to) be unwilling to give up; be emotionally dependent on (a habit, idea, friend, etc.). **3** (often foll. by to) maintain grasp; keep hold; resist separation. □ **clingy** adj. (**-ier**, **-iest**). [Old English]

**clinic** /**klin**-ik/ n. **1** private or specialised hospital. **2** place or occasion for giving medical treatment or specialist advice. **3** gathering at a hospital bedside for medical teaching. [Greek klinē bed]

**clinical** adj. **1** of or for the treatment of patients. **2** dispassionate, coolly detached. **3** (of a room, building, etc.) bare, functional. □ **clinically** adv. [Greek: related to CLINIC]

**clinical death** n. death judged by professional observation of a person's condition.

**clink¹** — n. sharp ringing sound. — v. (cause to) make a clink. [Dutch: imitative]

**clink²** n. colloq. prison. [origin unknown]

**clinker** n. **1** mass of slag or lava. **2** stony residue from burnt coal. **3** (in full **clinker brick**) hard brick used esp. for paving. [Dutch: related to CLINK¹]

**clip¹** — n. **1** device for holding things together or for attaching something (paper-clip). **2** piece of jewellery fastened by a clip. **3** set of attached cartridges for a firearm. — v. (**-pp-**) fix with a clip. [Old English]

**clip²** — v. (**-pp-**) **1** cut (hair, wool, etc.) short with shears or scissors. **2** trim or remove the hair or wool of. **3** colloq. hit smartly (clipped him on the ear). **4 a** omit (a letter etc.) from a word. **b** omit letters or syllables of (words uttered). **5** punch a hole in (a ticket) to show it has been used. **6** cut from a newspaper etc. **7** *colloq.* swindle, rob. — *n.* **1** act of clipping. **2** *colloq.* smart blow. **3 a** sequence from a motion picture. **b** = VIDEO CLIP. **4** yield of wool from a sheep, flock, season, etc.; wool clip. **5** *colloq.* speed, esp. rapid. [Old Norse]

**clipboard** *n.* small board with a spring clip for holding papers etc.

**clip joint** *n. colloq.* club etc. charging exorbitant prices.

**clipper** *n.* **1** (usu. in *pl.*) instrument for clipping hair, hedges, etc. **2** *hist.* fast sailing-ship.

**clipping** *n.* piece clipped, esp. from a newspaper.

**clique** /kleek, klik/ *n.* small exclusive group of people. □ **cliquey** *adj.* (**cliquier, cliquiest**). **cliquish** *adj.* [French]

**clitoris** /klit-uh-ruhs/ *n.* small erectile part of the female genitals at the upper end of the vulva. □ **clitoral** *adj.* [Latin from Greek]

**cloaca** /kloh-ay-kuh/ *n.* (*pl.* **-cae** /-kee/) genital and excretory cavity at the end of the intestinal canal in birds, reptiles, etc. □ **cloacal** *adj.* [Latin, = sewer]

**cloak** — *n.* **1** outdoor usu. long and sleeveless over-garment. **2** covering (*cloak of snow*). — *v.* **1** cover with a cloak. **2** conceal, disguise (*cloaked his real intention*). □ **under the cloak of** using as pretext. [ultimately from medieval Latin *clocca* bell]

**cloak-and-dagger** *adj.* involving intrigue and espionage.

**cloakroom** *n.* room where outdoor clothes or luggage may be left.

**clobber¹** *v. colloq.* **1** hit; beat up. **2** defeat. **3** criticise severely. [origin unknown]

**clobber²** *n. colloq.* clothing, belongings. [origin unknown]

**clock** — *n.* **1** instrument for measuring and showing time. **2 a** any measuring device resembling this. **b** *colloq.* speedometer, taximeter, or stopwatch. **3** time taken as an element in competitive sports etc. (*race against the clock*). — *v.* **1** *colloq.* **a** (often foll. by *up*) attain or register (a stated time, distance, or speed). **b** time (a race) with a stopwatch. **2** *colloq.* hit (*clocked him one*). □ **clock in** (or **on**) register one's arrival at work. **clock off** (or **out**) register one's departure from work. **round the clock** all day and (usu.) night. [medieval Latin *clocca* bell]

**clockwise** *adj. & adv.* in a curve corresponding in direction to that of the hands of a clock.

**clockwork** *n.* **1** mechanism like that of a clock, with a spring and gears. **2** (*attrib.*) driven by clockwork. □ **like clockwork** smoothly, regularly, automatically.

**clod** *n.* **1** lump of earth, clay, etc. **2** *colloq.* foolish person. [var. of CLOT]

**cloddish** *adj.* loutish, foolish, clumsy.

**clodhopper** *n. colloq.* **1** (usu. in *pl.*) large heavy shoe. **2** foolish or clumsy person.

**clog** — *n.* **1** shoe with a thick wooden sole. **2** block of wood to impede an animal's movement. — *v.* (**-gg-**) **1** (often foll. by *up*) obstruct or become obstructed; choke (*my nose is all clogged up*). **2** impede. [origin unknown]

**cloister** — *n.* **1** covered walk round a quadrangle, esp. in a convent, monastery, college, etc. **2 a** monastery or convent. **b** monastic life or seclusion. — *v.* seclude in, or as if in, a monastery or convent (*cloisters himself in his home*). □ **cloistered** *adj.* **cloistral** *adj.* [Latin *claustrum* related to CLOSE²]

**clomp** var. of CLUMP *v.* 2.

**clone** — *n.* **1 a** group of organisms produced asexually from one stock or ancestor. **b** one such organism. **2** *colloq.* person or thing regarded as identical to another. — *v.* (**-ning**) propagate as a clone. □ **clonal** *adj.* [Greek *klōn* twig]

**clonk** — *n.* abrupt heavy sound of impact. — *v.* **1** make this sound. **2** *colloq.* hit. [imitative]

**close¹** /klohs/ — *adj.* **1** (often foll. by *to*) situated at a short distance or interval. **2 a** having a strong or immediate relation or connection (*close friend*). **b** in intimate friendship or association (*we were very close*). **c** corresponding almost exactly (*close resemblance*). **3** in or almost in contact (*close combat*). **4** dense, compact with no or only slight intervals (*close formation*; *close thicket*). **5** (of a contest etc.) in which competitors are almost equal. **6** leaving no gaps or weaknesses rigorous (*close reasoning*). **7** concentrated, searching (*close examination*; *close attention*). **8** (of air etc.) stuffy humid. **9** closed, shut. **10** hidden, secret (*very close about what he does*). **11** niggardly (*close with his money*). **12** (of a danger etc.) directly threatening narrowly avoided (*that was close*; *a close call*). — *adv.* at only a short distance or interval. — *n.* **1** street closed at one end. **2** precinct of a cathedral. □ **at close quarters** very close together. **close up** (in Aboriginal English) near; nearby. □ **closely** *adv.* **closeness** *n.* [Latin *clausus* from *claudo* shut]

**close²** /klohz/ — *v.* (**-sing**) **1 a** shut (a lid door, room, etc.). **b** be shut (*the door* *closed slowly*). **c** deny access to (*the library is closed this weekend*). **d** block up (*closed the gap with rubble*). **2 a** bring or come to an end (*closed the account; this discussion is now closed*). **b** finish speaking (*closed with a few words of thanks*). **c** settle (a bargain etc.) (*closed the deal*). **3 a** end the day's business (*we close at 5*). **b** end the day's business at (a shop, office, etc.) (*we intend closing the stall at 5*). **4** bring or come closer or into contact (*closed ranks*). **5** make (an electric circuit etc.) continuous. **6** (foll. by *with*) express agreement with (an offer, terms, or the person offering them) (*closed with him after hours of negotiation*). **7** (often foll. by *with*) come within striking distance; grapple (*closed with the enemy forces*). **8** (foll. by *on*) (of a hand, box, etc.) grasp or entrap. — *n.* conclusion, end. □ **close down** (of a shop etc.) discontinue business. **close in 1** enclose. **2** come nearer. **3** (of days) get successively shorter. **close up 1** (often foll. by *to*) move closer. **2** shut. **3** block up. **4** (of an aperture) grow smaller. [Latin: related to CLOSE¹]

**closed book** *n.* subject one does not understand (*grammar's a closed book to me*).

**closed-circuit** *adj.* (of television) transmitted by wires to a restricted set of receivers.

**closed shop** *n.* business etc. where employees must belong to a specified trade union.

**close-knit** *adj.* tightly interlocked; closely united in friendship.

**close shave** *n.* (also **close thing**) *colloq.* narrow escape.

**closet** /kloz-uht/ — *n.* **1** small room. **2** cupboard. **3** = WATER-CLOSET. **4** (*attrib.*) secret (*closet homosexual*). — *v.* (**-t-**) shut away, esp. in private conference or study. [French diminutive: related to CLOSE²]

**close-up** *n.* photograph etc. taken at close range.

**closure** /kloh-zhuh/ *n.* **1** act or process of closing. **2** closed state. **3** procedure for ending a debate and taking a vote, esp. in parliament. [Latin: related to CLOSE²]

**clot** — *n.* **1** thick mass of coagulated liquid etc., esp. of blood. **2** *colloq.* foolish person. — *v.* (**-tt-**) form into clots. [Old English]

**cloth** *n.* **1** woven or felted etc. fabric from wool, cotton, silk, synthetic fibres, etc., used for clothing and a variety of other purposes. **2** piece of this, esp. for a specified purpose; tablecloth, dishcloth, etc. **3** (prec. by *the*) the clergy. [Old English]

**clothe** /klohth/ *v.* (**-thing**; *past* and *past part.* **clothed** or *formal* **clad**) **1** put clothes on; provide with clothes. **2** cover as with clothes. [Old English]

**clothes** /klohthz/ *n.pl.* **1** garments worn to cover the body and limbs. **2** bedclothes. [Old English]

**clothes hoist** *n.* rotary clothes drier consisting of a square frame between the arms of which run lengths of clothes-line, turning about a central pole and adjustable in height.

**clothes horse** *n.* frame for airing washed clothes.

**clothes line** *n.* rope, wire, etc. on which clothes are hung to dry.

**clothing** /kloh-thing/ *n.* clothes collectively.

**cloud** — *n.* **1** visible mass of condensed watery vapour floating high above the ground. **2** mass of smoke or dust. **3** (foll. by *of*) large mass of insects, birds, etc., moving together. **4 a** state of gloom, trouble, or suspicion. **b** frowning or depressed look (*a cloud on his brow*). — *v.* **1** cover or darken with clouds or gloom or trouble. **2** (often foll. by *over*, *up*) become overcast or gloomy. **3** make unclear (*you are clouding the issue*). □ **on cloud nine** *colloq.* extremely happy. **under a cloud** out of favour, under suspicion. **with one's head in the clouds** daydreaming. □ **cloudless** *adj.* [Old English]

**cloudburst** *n.* sudden violent rainstorm.

**cloud chamber** *n.* device containing vapour for tracking the paths of charged particles, X-rays, and gamma rays.

**cloud-cuckoo-land** *n.* fanciful or ideal place. [translation of Greek *Nephelokokkugia* in Aristophanes' *Birds*]

**cloudy** *adj.* (**-ier**, **-iest**) **1** (of the sky, weather) covered with clouds, overcast. **2** not transparent; unclear (*cloudy liquid*). □ **cloudily** *adv.* **cloudiness** *n.*

**clout** — *n.* **1** heavy blow. **2** influence, power of effective action, esp. in politics or business. — *v.* hit hard. [Old English]

**clove**¹ *n.* dried bud of a tropical plant used as a spice. [Latin *clavus* nail (from its shape)]

**clove**² *n.* small segment of a compound bulb, esp. of garlic. [Old English: related to CLEAVE¹]

**clove**³ *past* of CLEAVE¹.

**cloven** /kloh-vuhn/ *adj.* split, partly divided. [past part. of CLEAVE¹]

**cloven hoof** *n.* (also **cloven foot**) divided hoof, esp. of oxen, sheep, or goats, or of the Devil.

**clover** *n.* fodder plant having dense flower-heads and leaves consisting of usu. three leaflets. □ **in clover** in ease and luxury. [Old English]

**clover fern** see NARDOO.

**clown** — n. **1** comic entertainer, esp. in a circus. **2** foolish or playful person. — v. (often foll. by *about*, *around*) behave like a clown; act foolishly or playfully. □ **clownery** n. **clownish** adj. **clownishly** adv. **clownishness** n. [origin uncertain]

**cloy** v. satiate or sicken with an excess of sweetness, richness, sentimentality, etc. □ **cloying** adj. **cloyingly** adv. [obsolete *acloy* from Anglo-French: related to ENCLAVE]

**club** — n. **1** heavy stick with a thick end, esp. as a weapon. **2** stick used in a game, esp. a stick with a head used in golf. **3** association of persons meeting periodically for a shared activity. **4** organisation or premises offering members social amenities, meals, etc. **5 a** playing-card of the suit denoted by a black trefoil. **b** (in *pl.*) this suit. **6** commercial organisation offering subscribers special deals (*book club*). — v. (**-bb-**) **1** beat with or as with a club. **2** (foll. by *together*, *with*) combine, esp. to raise a sum of money for a purpose. [Old Norse]

**club foot** n. congenitally deformed foot.

**clubhouse** n. premises of a (usu. sporting) club.

**club moss** n. moss-like plant of tropical Australia and elsewhere, having upright stems a metre or more high, and nearly identical with fossils 400 million years old.

**cluck** — n. guttural cry like that of a hen. — v. emit cluck(s). [imitative]

**clucky** /kluk-ee/ adj. **1** (of a hen) sitting on eggs. **2** (of a woman) wanting to have a baby; broody.

**clue** /kloo/ — n. **1** fact or idea that serves as a guide, or suggests a line of inquiry, in a problem or investigation. **2** piece of evidence etc. in the detection of a crime. **3** verbal formula as a hint to what is to be inserted in a crossword. — v. (**clues**, **clued**, **cluing** or **clueing**) provide a clue to. □ **clue a person in** (or **up**) colloq. inform; provide him or her with the facts. **not have a clue** colloq. be ignorant or incompetent. [var. of Old English *clew*]

**cluey** /kloo-ee/ adj. colloq. knowledgable; alert (to the possibilities of a situation).

**clump** — n. (foll. by *of*) cluster or mass, esp. of trees or shrubs. — v. **1 a** form a clump. **b** heap or plant together. **2** (also **clomp**) walk with a heavy tread. [Low German or Dutch]

**clumsy** /klum-zee/ adj. (**-ier**, **-iest**) **1** awkward in movement or shape; ungainly; lacking in skill. **2** difficult to handle or use. **3** tactless. □ **clumsily** adv.

**clumsiness** n. [obsolete *clumse* be num▮ with cold]

**clung** past and past part. of CLING.

**clunk** — n. dull sound as of thick piece of metal meeting. — v. make such ▮ sound. [imitative]

**cluster** — n. close group or bunch o▮ similar people or things growing o▮ occurring together. — v. **1** bring into come into, or be in cluster(s). **2** (foll. b▮ *round*, *around*) gather. [Old English]

**cluster headache** n. intense recurrin▮ headache behind one eye or temple occurring in a cluster of several days o▮ weeks, followed by several weeks o▮ remission.

**cluster house** n. any of several houses i▮ a cluster housing complex.

**cluster housing complex** n. group o▮ several detached houses on a single larg▮ site with shared private roads and ope▮ space, the entire site having bee▮ developed as a single entity.

**clutch**[1] — v. **1** seize eagerly; grasp tightl▮ **2** (foll. by *at*) try desperately to seize — n. **1** tight grasp. **2** (in *pl.*) graspin▮ hands; cruel or relentless grasp or contro▮ (*I've been in his clutches for a long while*▮ **3 a** (in a vehicle) device for connectin▮ and disconnecting the engine and th▮ transmission. **b** pedal operating thi▮ [Old English]

**clutch**[2] n. **1** set of eggs for hatching. ▮ brood of chickens. [Old Norse, = hatch]

**clutter** — n. **1** crowded and untid▮ collection of things. **2** untidy state. — v▮ (often foll. by *up*, *with*) crowd untidily, fi▮ with clutter. [related to CLOT]

**Cm** symb. curium.

**cm** abbr. centimetre(s).

**CO** abbr. Commanding Officer.

**Co** symb. cobalt.

**Co.** abbr. company.

**co-** prefix added to: **1** nouns, with the sense 'joint, mutual, common' (*co-author*; *coequality*). **2** adjectives and adverbs, with the sense 'jointly, mutually' (*coequal*). **3** verbs, with the sense 'together with another or others' (*cooperate*). [var. of COM-]

**c/o** abbr. (also **c/-**) care of.

**coach** — n. **1** bus, usu. comfortably equipped for long journeys. **2** railway carriage. **3** closed horse-drawn carriage **4 a** instructor or trainer in a sport. **b** private tutor. **5** = COACHER. — v. **1 a** trai▮ or teach as a coach. **b** give hints to (*don'▮ coach the contestant*). **2** use tame cattl▮ etc. as a lure for wild cattle etc. [French from Magyar]

**coacher** n. tame beast used as a lure fo▮ others, esp. wild cattle or brumbies.

**coachwood** *n.* **1** any of several Australian trees with close-grained wood suitable for cabinet making etc. (so called from the use of the timber in coach-building), esp. the rainforest tree *Ceratopetalum apetalum* of Queensland and NSW. **2** wood of these trees.

**coagulate** /koh-**ag**-yuh-ˌlayt/ *v.* (**-ting**) **1** change from a fluid to a semisolid. **2** clot, curdle. □ **coagulant** *n.* **coagulation** /ˌkoh-ag-yuh-**lay**-shuhn/ *n.* [Latin *coagulum* rennet]

**coal** *n.* **1** hard black or blackish rock, mainly carbonised plant matter, found underground and used as a fuel. **2** piece of this, esp. one that is burning. □ (**carry**) **coals to Newcastle** take something to a place where it is already plentiful (since Newcastle in England used to be a coal-mining area). **haul over the coals** reprimand. [Old English]

**coalesce** /ˌkoh-uh-**les**/ *v.* (**-cing**) come together and form a whole. □ **coalescence** *n.* **coalescent** *adj.* [Latin *alo* nourish]

**coalface** *n.* **1** exposed working surface of coal in a mine. **2** *colloq.* any place where work is performed (esp. in practice as opposed to theory etc.).

**coal gas** *n.* mixed gases formerly extracted from coal and used for lighting and heating.

**coalition** /ˌkoh-uh-**lish**-uhn/ *n.* **1** temporary alliance, esp. of political parties. **2** fusion into one whole. [medieval Latin: related to COALESCE]

**coalmine** *n.* mine in which coal is dug. □ **coalminer** *n.*

**coal-scuttle** *n.* container for coal for a domestic fire.

**coal tar** *n.* thick black oily liquid distilled from coal and used as a source of benzene.

**coarse** /kaws/ *adj.* **1** rough or loose in texture; made of large particles. **2** (of a person's features) rough or large. **3** lacking refinement; crude, obscene (*coarse humour*). □ **coarsely** *adv.* **coarseness** *n.* [origin unknown]

**coarsen** *v.* make or become coarse.

**coast** /kohst/ — *n.* border of land near the sea; seashore. — *v.* **1** ride or move, usu. downhill, without the use of power. **2** (often foll. by *along*) make progress without much effort. □ **the coast is clear** there is no danger of being observed or caught. □ **coastal** *adj.* [Latin *costa* side]

**coaster** *n.* **1** ship that travels along the coast from port to port. **2** small tray or mat for a bottle or glass.

**coastguard** *n.* **1** member of a group of people employed to keep watch on coasts

to save life, prevent smuggling, etc. **2** such a group.

**coastline** *n.* line of the seashore, esp. with regard to its shape.

**coat** — *n.* **1** outer garment with sleeves, usu. extending below the hips; overcoat or jacket. **2 a** animal's fur or hair. **b** bark, skin, rind, or husk. **3** covering of paint etc. laid on a surface at one time. — *v.* **1** (usu. foll. by *with, in*) cover with a coat or layer. **2** (of paint etc.) form a covering to. [French from Germanic]

**coat-hanger** *n.* **1** = HANGER 2. **2** (Coat-hanger) name for the Sydney Harbour Bridge (from its resemblance to the shape of a coat-hanger).

**coating** *n.* layer of paint etc.

**coat of arms** *n.* heraldic bearings or shield of a person, family, or corporation.

**coat of mail** *n.* jacket of mail armour.

**coat-tail** *n.* each of the flaps formed by the back of a tailcoat.

**co-author** /ˌkoh-**aw**-thuh/ — *n.* joint author. — *v.* be a joint author of.

**coax** /kohks/ *v.* **1** persuade gradually or by flattery. **2** (foll. by *out of*) obtain (a thing from a person) thus (*coaxed the information out of him*). **3** manipulate (a thing) carefully or slowly (*coaxed it into its slot*). [obsolete *cokes* a fool]

**coaxial** /koh-**ak**-see-uhl/ *adj.* **1** having a common axis. **2** *Electr.* (of a cable or line) transmitting by means of two concentric conductors separated by an insulator.

**cob** *n.* **1** roundish lump of coal etc. **2** = CORN-COB. **3** sturdy riding-horse with short legs. **4** male swan. [origin unknown]

**cobalt** /**koh**-bawlt, -bolt/ *n.* **1** silvery-white metallic element. **2 a** pigment made from this. **b** its deep-blue colour. [German, probably = *kobold* demon in mines]

**cobber** — *n.* (often used as a mode of address) companion, friend, mate. — *v.* (often foll. by *up*) make friends with. □ **cobber-dobber** *colloq.* person who informs on a colleague. [perhaps related to English dial. *cob* take a liking to]

**cobble**¹ /**kob**-uhl/ — *n.* (in full **cobble-stone**) small rounded stone used for paving. — *v.* (**-ling**) pave with cobbles. [from COB]

**cobble**² /**kob**-uhl/ *v.* (**-ling**) **1** mend or patch up (esp. shoes). **2** (often foll. by *together*) join or assemble roughly. [from COBBLER]

**cobbler** *n.* **1** person who mends shoes professionally. **2** stewed fruit topped with a crust. **3** iced drink of wine, sugar, etc. **4** sheep which is difficult to shear and therefore the last to be shorn. **5 a**

freshwater catfish of WA, having harmful spiny fins. **b** marine fish of SA with similar fins. **6** (in *pl.*) *colloq.* nonsense (*a load of cobblers*). [origin unknown; sense 4 is a shortened form of *cobbler's last* as a pun on *last*]

**COBOL** /koh-bol/ *n.* computer language for use in commerce. [*common business oriented language*]

**cobra**[1] /**kob**-ruh, **koh**-bruh/ *n.* venomous hooded snake of Africa and Asia. [Latin *colubra* snake]

**cobra**[2] /**kob**-ruh/ *n.* shipworm, a mollusc native to mangroves, boring into wood in brackish or sea water and traditionally eaten by Aborigines. [probably from Djangati *gabara*]

**cobweb** *n.* **1** fine network spun by a spider from liquid it secretes. **2** thread of this. **3** anything compared with a cobweb, esp. in flimsiness of texture. □ **cobwebby** *adj.* [obsolete *coppe* spider]

**coca** /**koh**-kuh/ *n.* **1** S. American shrub. **2** its dried leaves, chewed as a stimulant. [Spanish from Quechua]

**cocaine** /koh-**kayn**/ *n.* drug from coca or prepared synthetically, used as a local anaesthetic and as a stimulant.

**coccyx** /**kok**-siks/ *n.* (*pl.* **coccyges** /-**suy**-, jeez/ ) small triangular bone at the base of the spinal column. [Greek, = cuckoo (from shape of its bill)]

**cochineal** /ˌkoch-uh-**neel**/ *n.* **1** scarlet dye used esp. for colouring food. **2** Mexican insects whose dried bodies yield this. [Latin *coccinus* scarlet, from Greek]

**cochlea** /**kok**-lee-uh/ *n.* (*pl.* **cochleae** /-lee-ee/ ) spiral cavity of the inner ear. [Latin, = snail-shell, from Greek *kokhlias*]

**cock** — *n.* **1** male bird, esp. of the domestic fowl. **2** *colloq.* (as a form of address) friend; fellow. **3** *coarse colloq.* penis. **4** *colloq.* nonsense. **5 a** firing lever in a gun, raised to be released by the trigger. **b** cocked position of this. **6** tap or valve controlling flow. — *v.* **1** raise or make upright or erect. **2** turn or move (the eye or ear) attentively or knowingly. **3** set aslant; turn up the brim of (a hat). **4** raise the cock of (a gun). □ **at half cock** only partly ready. **cock a snook** see SNOOK 1. **cock up** *colloq.* bungle; make a mess of. [Old English and French]

**cockade** /ko-**kayd**/ *n.* rosette etc. worn in the hat as a badge. [French: related to COCK]

**cock-a-doodle-doo** *n.* cock's crow.

**cock-a-hoop** *adj.* exultant.

**cock and bull story** *n.* absurd or incredible account.

**cockatiel** /ˌkok-uh-**teel**/ *n.* (also

**cockateel**) small crested Australian parrot, predominantly grey with a yellow face and orange earpatch; QUARRION, WEERO. [Dutch *kaketielje*]

**cockatoo** /ˌkok-uh-**too**/ — *n.* **1** any of several parrots of Australia etc. having powerful beaks and erectile crests including the galah, gang-gang cockatoo, Major Mitchell cockatoo, and sulphur-crested cockatoo. **2** look-out posted by those engaged in an illegal activity. **3** farmer with a small holding. **4** *hist.* convict serving a sentence on Cockatoo Island in Sydney Harbour (formerly a prison for intractable convicts); person who had served such a sentence. — *v.* act as a look-out. [Malay *kakatua*]

**cockatoo bush** *n.* = BOOBIALLA.

**cockatoo fence** *n.* fence improvised from logs and branches.

**cockatrice** /**kok**-uh-truhs, -truys/ *n.* **1** = BASILISK. **2** fabulous animal, hatched by a snake from an egg laid by a cock, having the body of a serpent with the head, wings, and legs of a cock, and a glance that instantly kills. [Middle English from Latin]

**cock crow** *n.* dawn.

**cockerel** /**kok**-uh-ruhl/ *n.* young male bird. [diminutive of COCK]

**cock-eyed** *adj. colloq.* **1** crooked, askew. **2** absurd, not practical. **3** drunk. [from COCK]

**cock-eyed bob** *n.* (chiefly in WA) sudden violent but short-lived storm or squall.

**cockie** /**kok**-ee/ *n. colloq.* cockroach. [abbreviation]

**cockle** /**kok**-uhl/ *n.* **1 a** edible bivalve shellfish of Europe. **b** its shell. **2** (in full **cockle-shell**) small shallow boat. **3** pucker or wrinkle in paper, glass, etc. □ **warm the cockles of one's heart** make one contented. [French *coquille* from Greek: related to CONCH]

**cockney** /**kok**-nee/ — *n.* (*pl.* **-s**) **1** native of London, esp. one born within hearing of Bow Bells. **2** dialect or accent used by cockneys. **3** young snapper. — *adj.* of cockneys or their dialect or accent [*cokeney* 'cock's egg']

**cockpit** *n.* **1** compartment for the pilot (and crew) of an aircraft or spacecraft. **2** driver's seat in a racing car. **3** space for the helmsman in some yachts.

**cockroach** /**kok**-rohch/ *n.* flat dark brown beetle-like insect infesting kitchens, bathrooms, etc. [Spanish *cucaracha*]

**cockscomb** /**koks**-kohm/ *n.* fleshy crest of a cock.

**cocksure** /ˌkok-**shaw**/ *adj.* arrogantly confident. [from COCK]

**cocktail** /**kok**-tayl/ n. **1** drink made of various spirits, fruit juices, etc. **2** appetiser containing shellfish or fruit. **3** any hybrid mixture. **4** (*attrib.*) small; suitable for a cocktail stick (*cocktail onion; cocktail sausage*). [origin unknown]

**cocktail stick** n. small pointed stick for serving an olive, cherry, etc.

**cock-up** n. colloq. muddle or mistake.

**cocky¹** adj. (**-ier, -iest**) colloq. conceited, arrogant. □ **cockily** adv. **cockiness** n. [from COCK]

**cocky²** n. (pl. **-ies**) colloq. = COCKATOO. [abbreviation]

**cocky³** — n. **1** farmer with a small holding (*cow cocky; fruit cocky*). **2** (now often applied to) a substantial farmer or the rural interests generally (also *attrib.*: *the cocky vote*). — v. farm in a small way.

**cocky apple** n. tree of northern Australia having an edible egg-shaped greenish fruit (often eaten by cockatoos).

**cocky gate** n. (also **cocky's gate**) improvised gate.

**cocky's joy** n. (also **cocky's delight**) treacle or golden syrup.

**coco** /**koh**-koh/ n. (pl. **-s**) coconut palm. [Portuguese and Spanish, = grimace]

**cocoa** /**koh**-koh/ n. **1** powder made from crushed cacao seeds, often with other ingredients. **2** drink made from this. [altered from CACAO]

**cocoa bean** n. cacao seed.

**coconut** /**koh**-kuh-,nut/ n. **1** large brown seed of the coco, with a hard shell and edible white lining enclosing a sweetish pale grey water. **2** (in Aboriginal English) an Aborigine living in a manner perceived as repudiating Aboriginal identity (*a coconut is brown on the outside and white underneath*).

**coconut milk** n. thick milky juice squeezed from the grated flesh of the coconut and used in cooking, esp. in curries (cf. COCONUT WATER).

**coconut water** n. drinkable sweetish watery liquid exuded when the coconut is cracked (cf. COCONUT MILK).

**cocoon** /kuh-**koon**/ — n. **1** silky case spun by insect larvae for protection as pupae. **2** protective covering. — v. wrap or coat in, or as if in, a cocoon (*a sheltered life, cocooned from the world*). [Provençal *coca* shell]

**COD** abbr. cash on delivery.

**cod¹** n. (pl. same) **1** any of a number of large sea fish such as the Atlantic cod, used as food, including the bearded rock-cod and the beardie (or ling) of southern Australian waters. **2** any of several unrelated Australian fish such as the Murray cod. [origin unknown]

**cod²** n. (usu. in pl.) colloq. scrotum; testicles. [Middle English]

**coda** /**koh**-duh/ n. **1** Mus. final additional passage of a piece or movement. **2** concluding section of a ballet. [Latin *cauda* tail]

**coddle** /**kod**-uhl/ v. (**-ling**) **1** treat as an invalid; protect attentively; pamper. **2** cook (an egg) in water below boiling point. □ **coddler** n. [a British dialect form of *caudle* invalids' gruel]

**code** — n. **1** system of words, letters, symbols, etc., used to represent others for secrecy or brevity. **2** system of pre-arranged signals used to ensure secrecy in transmitting messages. **3** Computing piece of program text. **4** systematic set of laws etc. **5** prevailing standard of moral behaviour (*code of honour*). — v. (**-ding**) put into code. [Latin CODEX]

**codeine** /**koh**-deen/ n. alkaloid derived from morphine, used to relieve pain. [Greek *kōdeia* poppy-head]

**codex** /**koh**-deks/ n. (pl. **codices** /**koh**-duh-,seez, kod-uh-/) **1** ancient manuscript text in book form. **2** collection of descriptions of drugs etc. [Latin, = tablet, book]

**codger** /**koj**-uh/ n. (usu. in **old codger**) colloq. person, esp. an old or strange one. [origin uncertain]

**codicil** /**koh**-duh-sil, kod-uh-/ n. addition to a will. [Latin diminutive of CODEX]

**codify** /**koh**-duh-,fuy, kod-/ v. (**-ies, -ied**) arrange (laws etc.) systematically into a code. □ **codification** /-fuh-**kay**-shuhn/ n. **codifier** n.

**codlin** /**kod**-luhn/ n. (also **codling**) **1** a kind of cooking apple. **2** (in full **codlin moth**) moth whose larva feeds on apples. [Anglo-French *quer de lion* lion-heart]

**codpiece** n. hist. appendage like a small bag or flap at the front of a man's breeches to enclose the genitals. [cod scrotum]

**codswallop** /**kodz**-,wol-uhp/ n. colloq. nonsense. [origin unknown]

**coed** /koh-**ed**/ colloq. — n. school for both sexes. — adj. coeducational. [abbreviation]

**coeducation** /,koh-ed-yuh-**kay**-shuhn, -ej-uh-/ n. education of pupils of both sexes together. □ **coeducational** adj.

**coefficient** /,koh-uh-**fish**-uhnt/ n. **1** Math. quantity placed before and multiplying an algebraic expression. **2** Physics multiplier or factor by which a property is measured (*coefficient of expansion*). [related to CO-, EFFICIENT]

**coelacanth** /see-luh-,kanth/ n. large sea fish formerly thought to be extinct. [Greek *koilos* hollow, *akantha* spine]

**coelenterate** /suh-**len**-tuh-,rayt, -tuh-ruht/ n. marine animal with a simple tube-shaped or cup-shaped body, e.g. jellyfish, corals, and sea anemones. [Greek *koilos* hollow, *enteron* intestine]

**coeliac disease** /see-lee-ak/ n. disease of the small intestine, brought on by contact with dietary gluten. [Latin *coeliacus* from Greek *koilia* belly]

**coenobite** /see-nuh-,buyt/ n. (also **cenobite**) member of a monastic community. [Greek *koinos bios* common life]

**coerce** /koh-**ers**/ v. (**-cing**) persuade or restrain by force (*coerced him into signing*). □ **coercible** adj. **coercion** /koh-er-shuhn/ n. **coercive** adj. [Latin *coerceo* restrain]

**coeval** /koh-ee-vuhl/ formal — adj. **1** of the same age or date of origin. **2** existing at the same time; contemporary. — n. coeval person or thing. □ **coevally** adv. [Latin *aevum* age]

**coexist** /,koh-uhg-**zist**/ v. (often foll. by *with*) **1** exist together. **2** (esp. of nations) exist in mutual tolerance of each other's ideologies etc. □ **coexistence** n. **coexistent** adj.

**coffee** /kof-ee/ n. **1 a** drink made from roasted and ground beanlike seeds of a tropical shrub. **b** cup of this. **2 a** shrub. **b** its seeds. **3** pale brown colour. [Turkish from Arabic]

**coffer** n. **1** large strong box for valuables. **2** (in pl.) treasury, funds. **3** sunken panel in a ceiling etc. [Latin *cophinus* basket]

**coffer-dam** n. watertight enclosure pumped dry to permit work below the waterline, e.g. building bridges etc. or repairing a ship.

**coffin** /kof-uhn/ n. box in which a corpse is buried or cremated. [Latin: related to COFFER]

**cog** n. **1** each of a series of projections on the edge of a wheel or bar transferring motion by engaging with another series. **2** unimportant member of an organisation etc. (*I'm just a small cog in a large machine*). [probably Scandinavian]

**cogent** /koh-juhnt/ adj. (of an argument etc.) convincing, compelling. □ **cogency** n. **cogently** adv. [Latin *cogo* drive]

**cogitate** /koj-uh-,tayt/ v. (**-ting**) ponder, meditate. □ **cogitation** /-tay-shuhn/ n. **cogitative** /-tuh-tiv/ adj. [Latin *cogito*]

**cognac** /kon-yak/ n. high-quality brandy, properly that distilled in Cognac in France.

**cognate** /kog-nayt/ — adj. **1** related to or descended from a common ancestor. **2** (of a word) having the same linguistic family or derivation (e.g. English *father*, German *Vater*, Sanskrit *pitr*, Latin *pater*, Sinhalese *pitha*, etc.). — n. **1** relative. **2** cognate word. [Latin *cognatus*]

**cognate object** n. *Gram.* object related in origin and sense to its verb (as in *live a good life*).

**cognisance** /**kog**-nuh-zuhns, **kon**-uh-/ n. formal knowledge or awareness; perception, notice (*take cognisance of these issues*). [Latin *cognosco* get to know]

**cognisant** adj. (foll. by *of*) formal having knowledge or being aware of (*I am cognisant of your request*).

**cognition** /kog-**nish**-uhn/ n. **1** knowing, perceiving, or conceiving as an act or faculty distinct from emotion and volition. **2** result of this. □ **cognitional** adj. **cognitive** /kog-nuh-tiv/ adj. [Latin *cognitio*: related to COGNISANCE]

**cognomen** /kog-**noh**-muhn/ n. **1** nickname. **2** ancient Roman's third or fourth name designating a branch of a family, as in Marcus Tullius *Cicero*, or as an epithet, as in Publius Cornelius Scipio *Africanus*. [Latin]

**cognoscente** /,kon-yuh-**shen**-tee/ n. (pl. **-ti** /-tee/) connoisseur. [Italian]

**cohabit** /koh-**hab**-uht/ v. (**-t-**) (esp. of an unmarried couple) live together as husband and wife. □ **cohabitation** /-tay-shuhn/ n. **cohabitee** /-tee/ n. [Latin *habito* dwell]

**cohere** /koh-**heer**/ v. (**-ring**) **1** (of parts or a whole) stick together, remain united. **2** (of reasoning etc.) be logical or consistent. [Latin *haereo haes-* stick]

**coherent** adj. **1** (of a person) intelligible and articulate. **2** (of an argument etc.) consistent; easily followed. **3** cohering; sticking together. **4** *Physics* (of waves) having a constant phase relationship. □ **coherence** n. **coherently** adv.

**cohesion** /koh-hee-*zh*uhn/ n. **1** act or condition of sticking together. **2** *Chem.* force with which molecules cohere. □ **cohesive** adj.

**cohort** /**koh**-hawt/ n. **1** ancient Roman military unit, one-tenth of a legion. **2** band of warriors. **3 a** persons banded together, esp. in a common cause. **b** group of persons with a common statistical characteristic. [Latin]

**coif** /koif/ n. *hist.* close-fitting cap. [Latin *cofia* helmet]

**coiffure** /kwah-**fyoor**/ n. hairstyle. [French]

**coign** /koin/ n. □ **coign of vantage** favourable position for observation or action. [old form of COIN]

**coil** /koil/ — v. **1** arrange or be arranged in spirals or concentric rings (*the cobra coiled and raised its hood*; *coiled the rope*). **2** move sinuously (as a snake). — n. **1** coiled arrangement. **2** coiled length of rope etc. **3** single turn of something coiled. **4** flexible loop placed in the uterus as a contraceptive device. **5** coiled wire for the passage of an electric current and acting as an inductor. [Latin: related to COLLECT[1]]

**coin** /koin/ — n. **1** stamped disc of metal as official money. **2** (*collect.*) metal money. — v. **1** make (coins) by stamping. **2** make (metal) into coins. **3** invent (esp. a new word or phrase). □ **coin money** make much money quickly. **to coin a phrase** *iron.* introducing a banal remark or cliché. [Latin *cuneus* wedge]

**coinage** n. **1** act or process of coining. **2 a** coins. **b** system of coins in use (*decimal coinage*). **3** invention, esp. of a word.

**coincide** /,koh-uhn-**suyd**/ v. (**-ding**) **1** occur at the same time. **2** occupy the same portion of space. **3** (often foll. by *with*) agree or be identical (*my opinion coincides with yours*). [Latin: related to INCIDENT]

**coincidence** /koh-**in**-suh-duhns/ n. **1** occurring or being together. **2** remarkable concurrence of events or circumstances, apparently by chance. □ **coincident** *adj.*

**coincidental** /koh-,in-suh-**den**-tuhl/ *adj.* in the nature of or resulting from a coincidence. □ **coincidentally** *adv.*

**coir** /**koi**-uh/ n. coconut fibre used for ropes, matting, etc. [Malayalam *kāyar* cord]

**coition** /koh-**ish**-uhn/ n. = COITUS. [Latin *coitio* from *eo* go]

**coitus** /**koh**-uh-tuhs/ n. sexual intercourse. □ **coital** *adj.* [Latin: related to COITION]

**coitus interruptus** /,in-tuh-**rup**-tuhs/ n. sexual intercourse with withdrawal of the penis before ejaculation.

**coke[1]** — n. solid substance left after gases have been extracted from coal. — v. (**-king**) convert (coal) into coke. [British dial. *colk* core]

**coke[2]** n. *colloq.* cocaine. [abbreviation]

**Col.** *abbr.* Colonel.

**col** n. **1** depression in the summit-line of a chain of mountains. **2** *Meteorol.* low-pressure region between anticyclones. [Latin *collum* neck]

**col.** *abbr.* column.

**col-** see COM-.

**cola** /**koh**-luh/ n. (also **kola**) **1** W. African tree bearing seeds containing caffeine. **2** carbonated drink usu. flavoured with these. [West African]

**colander** /**kul**-uhn-duh, **kol**-/ n. perforated vessel used to strain off liquid in cookery. [Latin *colo* strain]

**colane** /kuh-**layn**, **kol**-ayn/ n. = EMU APPLE 1. [Wiradhuri, probably *galayin*]

**cold** /kohld/ — *adj.* **1** of or at a low temperature, esp. when compared with the human body (*your feet are cold*). **2** not heated; cooled after heat (*my tea's cold*). **3** feeling cold. **4** lacking ardour, friendliness, or affection (*why are you cold towards me?*). **5 a** depressing, dispiriting (*the cold facts*). **b** (of colour) suggestive of cold (*cold blues*). **6 a** dead (*cold in the grave*). **b** *colloq.* unconscious (*knocked him cold*). **7** (of a scent in hunting) grown faint. **8** (in games) far from finding what is sought. — n. **1 a** prevalence of low temperature. **b** cold weather or environment. **2** infection of the nose or throat with sneezing, catarrh, etc. — *adv.* unrehearsed (*I can't do it cold*). □ **in cold blood** without emotion, deliberately. **leave a person cold** see LEAVE[1]. **out in the cold** ignored, neglected. **throw** (or **pour**) **cold water on** be discouraging about. □ **coldly** *adv.* **coldness** n. [Old English]

**cold-blooded** *adj.* **1** having a body temperature varying with that of the environment. **2** callous; deliberately cruel. □ **cold-bloodedly** *adv.* **cold-bloodedness** n.

**cold chisel** n. chisel for cutting metal, stone, or brick.

**cold comfort** n. poor consolation.

**cold feet** *n.pl. colloq.* loss of nerve.

**cold front** n. forward edge of an advancing mass of cold air.

**cold fusion** n. nuclear fusion at room temperature, esp. as a possible energy source.

**cold-hearted** *adj.* lacking sympathy or kindness. □ **cold-heartedly** *adv.* **cold-heartedness** n.

**coldie** /**kohl**-dee/ n. *colloq.* = COLD ONE.

**cold one** n. *colloq.* glass, bottle, or can of chilled beer.

**cold shoulder** — n. (prec. by *the*) intentional unfriendliness. — v. (**cold-shoulder**) be deliberately unfriendly towards.

**cold sore** n. inflammation and blisters in and around the mouth, caused by the *herpes simplex* virus.

**cold storage** n. **1** storage in a refrigerator. **2** temporary putting aside (of an idea etc.), postponement (*I've put the plan into cold storage*).

**cold sweat** *n.* sweating induced by fear or illness.

**cold turkey** *n. colloq.* abrupt withdrawal from addictive drugs.

**cold war** *n.* hostility between nations without actual fighting.

**coleopteron** /ˌkol-ee-**op**-tuh-ˌron/ *n.* insect with front wings serving as sheaths, e.g. the beetle and weevil. □ **coleopterous** *adj.* [Greek *koleon* sheath, *pteron* wing]

**coleslaw** /**kohl**-slaw/ *n.* dressed salad of sliced raw cabbage etc. [from *cole*, Dutch *sla* salad]

**colic** /**kol**-ik/ *n.* severe spasmodic abdominal pain. □ **colicky** *adj.* [Latin: related to COLON²]

**colitis** /kuh-**luy**-tuhs/ *n.* inflammation of the lining of the colon.

**collaborate** /kuh-**lab**-uh-ˌrayt/ *v.* (**-ting**) (often foll. by *with*) **1** work together. **2** cooperate with an enemy. □ **collaboration** /-ray-shuhn/ *n.* **collaborative** /-ruh-tiv/ *adj.* **collaborator** *n.* [Latin: related to LABOUR]

**collage** /**kol**-ah*zh*, kuh-**lah*zh***/ *n.* form or work of art in which various materials are arranged and fixed to a backing. [French, = gluing]

**collagen** /**kol**-uh-juhn/ *n.* protein found in animal connective tissue, yielding gelatine on boiling. [Greek *kolla* glue]

**collapse** /kuh-**laps**/ — *n.* **1** falling down or in of a structure; folding up; giving way (*collapse of the roof*; *bank is facing collapse*). **2** sudden failure of a plan etc. (*collapse of all my hopes*). **3** physical or mental breakdown; exhaustion (*he's near collapse*). — *v.* (**-sing**) **1** (cause to) undergo collapse (*the roof collapsed*; *this has collapsed my hopes*; *he collapsed and died*). **2** *colloq.* lie or sit down and relax, esp. after prolonged effort (*collapsed into a chair*). **3** (of furniture etc.) **a** be foldable into a small space (*this bed collapses*). **b** cause to fold into a small space (*why can't I collapse this table?*). □ **collapsible** *adj.* [Latin *labor laps-* slip]

**collar** /**kol**-uh/ — *n.* **1** that part of a shirt, dress, etc. that goes round the neck, upright or turned over. **2** band of leather etc. round an animal's neck. **3** restraining or connecting band or ring or pipe in machinery. **4** coloured marking resembling a collar round the neck of a bird or animal. — *v.* **1** capture, seize; gain control over (*have managed to collar the market in cherry pits*). **2** *colloq.* accost (*collared him as he was sneaking out the back way*). [Latin *collum* neck]

**collarbone** *n.* bone joining the breastbone and shoulder-blade.

**collared sparrowhawk** *n.* predominantly brown bird of prey having a rufous mark round the neck, widespread in Australia.

**collate** /kuh-**layt**, ko-/ *v.* (**-ting**) **1** assemble and arrange systematically (e.g. pages in their correct order prior to binding). **2** compare (texts, statements, etc.) to identify points of agreement and difference. □ **collator** *n.* [Latin: related to CONFER]

**collateral** /kuh-**lat**-uh-ruhl/ — *n.* **1** security pledged as a guarantee for the repayment of a loan. **2** person having the same ancestor as another but by a different line. — *adj.* **1** descended from the same ancestor but by a different line. **2** side by side; parallel (*collateral roads, one major, the other minor*). **3 a** additional but subordinate (*that was a collateral result of white settlement in Australia*). **b** contributory (*excessive felling of trees was a collateral cause of soil degradation*). **c** connected but aside from the main subject, course, etc. (*devoted part of his speech to the collateral issue of the power of the Senate to block supply*). □ **collaterally** *adv.* [Latin: related to LATERAL]

**collation** /kuh-**lay**-shuhn/ *n.* **1** act or instance of collating. **2** thing collated. **3 a** *RC Ch.* light meal allowed during a fast. **b** any light meal. [Latin: related to CONFER: sense 3 from *Collationes Patrum* (= *Lives of the Fathers*) read by Benedictine monks preceding a light meal]

**colleague** /**kol**-eeg/ *n.* fellow worker, esp. in a profession or business. [Latin *collega*]

**collect¹** /kuh-**lekt**/ *v.* **1** bring or come together; assemble, accumulate (*crowds collected in the main square*; *collect all these papers in a neat pile*). **2** systematically seek and acquire, esp. as a hobby (*collects stamps*). **3 a** gather (contributions etc.) from a number of people (*am collecting for Red Cross*). **b** gather or obtain (money) for (taxes, rent, winning bets, etc.) (*collecting rent from the tenants*; *went to collect his winnings*). **c** *colloq.* win (in a lottery etc.) (*with this lucky ticket I'm bound to collect*). **4** call for; fetch (*went to collect the kids*). **5 a** *refl.* regain control of oneself, esp. after a shock (*give him time to collect himself*). **b** concentrate (one's thoughts etc.) (*need to collect my wits*). **c** (as **collected** *adj.*) calm and cool; not perturbed or distracted. **6** *colloq.* (esp. of a motor vehicle) collide with (*lost control of the ute and collected two cats and a cow*). [Latin *lego lect-* pick]

**collect²** /kol-ekt/ n. prayer or set of short prayers said at Mass etc. in the Catholic and Anglican Churches. [Latin *collecta*: related to COLLECT¹]

**collectable** /kuh-**lek**-tuh-buhl/ (also **collectible**) — adj. worth collecting. — n. item sought by collectors.

**collection** /kuh-**lek**-shuhn/ n. **1** act or process of collecting or being collected. **2** things collected, esp. systematically (a *stamp collection*). **3** (foll. by *of*) accumulation; mass or pile (a *collection of dust*). **4 a** collecting of money, esp. at a church service or for a charitable cause. **b** the amount so collected.

**collective** /kuh-**lek**-tiv/ — adj. of, by, or relating to a group or society as a whole; joint; shared (*our collective opinion*). — n. **1 a** cooperative enterprise (*women's collective*). **b** its members. **2** = COLLECTIVE NOUN. □ **collectively** adv.

**collective bargaining** n. negotiation of wages etc. by an organised body of employees.

**collective noun** n. singular noun denoting a collection or number of individuals (e.g. *assembly*, *family*, *troop*).

**collectivism** n. theory and practice of collective ownership of land and the means of production. □ **collectivist** n. & adj.

**collector** n. **1** person who collects things of interest. **2** person who collects money etc. due (*rent collector; ticket collector*).

**college** /**kol**-ij/ n. **1** establishment for further, higher, or professional education. **2** college premises (*lived in college*). **3** students and teachers in a college. **4 a** upper secondary school. **b** private school. **5** organised body of persons with shared functions and privileges (*College of Physicians*). [Latin: related to COLLEAGUE]

**College of Cardinals** n. (in full **Sacred College of Cardinals**) **1** all the cardinals of the Catholic Church as constituting the Pope's council. **2** those cardinals (under a certain age) eligible to elect a new pope from among their number.

**collegiate** /kuh-**lee**-juht/ adj. of, or constituted as, a college; corporate.

**collide** /kuh-**luyd**/ v. (**-ding**) (often foll. by *with*) come into collision or conflict. [Latin *collido -lis-* clash]

**collie** /**kol**-ee/ n. sheepdog of an orig. Scottish breed. [perhaps from *coll* COAL]

**collier** /**kol**-ee-uh/ n. **1** coalminer. **2 a** coal ship. **b** member of its crew. [from COAL]

**colliery** n. (pl. **-ies**) coalmine and its buildings.

**collimate** /**kol**-uh-ˌmayt/ v. **1** adjust the line of sight of (a telescope etc.). **2** make (telescopes or rays) accurately parallel. □ **collimation** /-**may**-shuhn/ n. [Latin *collimare*, erroneous for *collineare* align]

**Collins Street cocky** see PITT STREET FARMER.

**collision** /kuh-**lizh**-uhn/ n. **1** violent impact of a moving body with another or with a fixed object. **2** clashing of interests etc. [Latin: related to COLLIDE]

**collocate** /**kol**-uh-ˌkayt/ v. (**-ting**) **1 a** place together or side by side. **b** arrange; set in a particular place. **2** *Linguistics* juxtapose (a word etc.) with another so as to form a collocation. [Latin: related to LOCUS]

**collocation** /ˌkol-uh-**kay**-shuhn/ n. **1** act, state, or result of collocating. **2** *Linguistics* **a** customary juxtaposition or association of a particular word with other particular words, e.g. *bold as brass; take a look*. **b** short group of words (*the collocation 'a round square' seems to make no sense*).

**colloid** /**kol**-oid/ n. **1** substance consisting of ultramicroscopic particles. **2** mixture of such particles dispersed in another substance. □ **colloidal** /kuh-**loi**-duhl/ adj. [Greek *kolla* glue]

**colloquial** /kuh-**loh**-kwee-uhl/ adj. of ordinary or familiar conversation, informal; not to be used in formal speech or writing. □ **colloquially** adv. [Latin: related to COLLOQUY]

**colloquialism** n. **1** colloquial word or phrase. **2** use of these.

**colloquium** /kuh-**loh**-kwee-uhm/ n. (pl. **-s** or **-quia**) academic conference or seminar. [Latin: related to COLLOQUY]

**colloquy** /**kol**-uh-kwee/ n. (pl. **-quies**) *literary* conversation, talk. [Latin *loquor* speak]

**collude** /kuh-**lood**/ v. (**-ding**) come to an understanding or conspire together, esp. for a fraudulent purpose (*colluded with his accountant to cheat on tax*). □ **collusion** n. **collusive** adj. [Latin *ludo lus-* play]

**collywobbles** /**kol**-ee-ˌwob-uhlz/ n.pl. *colloq.* **1** rumbling or pain in the stomach. **2** apprehensive feeling. [from COLIC, WOBBLE]

**cologne** /kuh-**lohn**/ n. eau-de-Cologne or similar toilet water. [abbreviation]

**colon¹** /**koh**-luhn/ n. punctuation mark (:), used esp. to introduce a quotation or a list of items or to mark antithesis (see panel). [Greek, = clause]

**colon²** /**koh**-luhn/ n. lower and greater part of the large intestine. [Latin from Greek]

**colonel** /**ker**-nuhl/ n. army officer in command of a regiment, ranking next below brigadier. □ **colonelcy** n. (pl. **-ies**). [Italian *colonnello*: related to COLUMN]

**colonial** /kuh-**loh**-nee-uhl/ — adj. **1** of, relating to, or characteristic of a colony or colonies. **2** of colonialism. **3** hist. **a** of, belonging to, or characteristic of one of the Australian Colonies before Federation, or of these Colonies collectively. **b** Australian, usu. as distinct from British. **c** (esp. of architecture or furniture) of, belonging to, or characteristic of Australia before Federation. — n. **1** inhabitant of a colony. **2** chiefly hist. person born in Australia of immigrant descent (as opposed to an immigrant from Britain).

**colonial experience** n. hist. **1** first-hand knowledge of life in outback Australia. **2** (also **colonial experiencer**) British youth acquiring this.

**colonial goose** n. boned and stuffed roast leg of mutton.

**colonialism** n. **1** policy of acquiring or maintaining colonies. **2** derog. exploitation of colonies. □ **colonialist** n. & adj.

**colonial oven** n. oblong wrought-iron box with a door in front, open fire on top (for boiling etc.), and a fire underneath as well (for roasting, baking, etc.); successor to the CAMP OVEN.

**colonial youth** n. hist. young person born in Australia of immigrant descent; (collect.) young persons of this category (heated contests between colonial youth and natives of England, currency vs. sterling).

**colonise** /**kol**-uh-nuyz/ v. (also **-ize**) (**-sing** or **-zing**) **1** establish a colony in. **2** join a colony. **3** (of plants and animals) become established in an area. □ **colonisation** /-zay-shuhn/ n.

**colonist** /**kol**-uh-nuhst/ n. settler in or inhabitant of a colony.

**colonnade** /,kol-uh-**nayd**/ n. row of columns, esp. supporting an entablature or roof. □ **colonnaded** adj. [French: related to COLUMN]

**colony** /**kol**-uh-nee/ n. (pl. **-ies**) **1 a** settlement or settlers in a new country, fully or partly subject to the mother country. **b** their territory. **2 a** hist. (prior to Federation) one of the British Colonies in Australia or the Australian Colonies collectively. **b** (after Federation) used loosely of Australia as a former British Colony or as one of a number of British Colonies. **3 a** people of one nationality, occupation, etc., esp. forming a community in a city. **b** separate or segregated group (nudist colony). **4** group of animals, plants, etc., living close together. [Latin *colonia* farm]

**colophon** /**kol**-uh-,fon, -fuhn/ n. **1** publisher's imprint, esp. on the title-page. **2** tailpiece in a manuscript or book, giving the writer's or printer's name, date, etc. [Greek, = summit]

**color** etc. var. of COLOUR etc.

**coloration** /,kul-uh-**ray**-shuhn/ n. (also **colouration**) **1** appearance as regards colour. **2** act or mode of colouring. [Latin: related to COLOUR]

**coloratura** /,kol-uh-ruh-**too**-ruh, -tyoo-ruh/ n. **1** (also attrib.) elaborate ornamentation of a vocal melody. **2** soprano skilled in this. [Italian: related to COLOUR]

**colossal** /kuh-**los**-uhl/ adj. **1** of immense size; huge. **2** colloq. splendid. □ **colossally** adv. [related to COLOSSUS]

**colossus** /kuh-**los**-uhs/ n. (pl. **-ssi** /-uy/ or **-ssuses**) **1** statue much bigger than life size. **2** gigantic or remarkable person etc. [Latin from Greek]

**colostomy** /kuh-**los**-tuh-mee/ n. (pl. **-ies**) operation on the colon to make an opening in the abdominal wall to provide an artificial anus. [from COLON²]

**colour** /**kul**-uh/ (also **color**) — n. **1** sensation produced on the eye by rays of light when resolved as by a prism into different wavelengths. **2** one, or any mixture, of the constituents into which light can be separated as in a spectrum or rainbow, sometimes including (loosely) black and white. **3** colouring substance, esp. paint. **4** use of all colours in photography, television, etc. **5 a** pigmentation of the skin, esp. when dark. **b** this as ground for prejudice or discrimination. **6**

---

**Colon :**

This is used:

**1** between two main clauses of which the second explains, enlarges on, or follows from the first, e.g.

  *It was not easy: to begin with I had to find the right house.*

**2** to introduce a list of items (a dash should not be added), and after expressions such as *namely, to resume, to sum up,* and *the following,* e.g.

  *You will need: a tent, a sleeping bag, cooking equipment, and insect repellent.*

**3** before a quotation, e.g.

  *The anthem begins: 'Australians all, let us rejoice.'*

ruddiness of complexion (*a healthy colour*). **7** (in *pl.*) appearance or aspect (*saw them in their true colours*). **8** (in *pl.*) **a** coloured ribbon or uniform etc. worn to signify membership of a school, club, team, etc. **b** flag of a regiment or ship. **9** quality, mood, or variety in music, literature, etc. **10** show of reason; pretext (*lend colour to*; *under colour of*). **11** *Mining* **a** trace or particle of gold. **b** (usu. in *pl.*) indication of the presence of opal. — *v.* **1** apply colour to, esp. by painting, dyeing, etc. **2** influence (*an attitude coloured by experience*). **3** misrepresent, exaggerate (*a highly coloured account*). **4** take on colour; blush. □ **off colour** unwell. **show one's true colours** reveal one's true character or intentions. **with flying colours** see FLYING. [Latin *color*]

**colouration** var. of COLORATION.

**colour bar** *n.* racial discrimination against non-White people.

**colour-blind** *adj.* unable to distinguish certain colours. □ **colour-blindness** *n.*

**coloured** (also **colored**) — *adj.* **1** having colour. **2** (**Coloured**) wholly or partly of non-White descent. — *n.* **1** (**Coloured**) Coloured person. **3** (in *pl.*) coloured clothing etc. for washing.

**colourful** *adj.* (also **color-**) **1** full of colour; bright. **2** full of interest; vivid. □ **colourfully** *adv.*

**colouring** *n.* (also **color-**) **1** appearance as regards colour, esp. facial complexion. **2** use or application of colour. **3** substance giving colour.

**colourise** *v.* (also **color-**, **-ize**) (**-sing** or **-zing**) add colour to a black and white film by means of a computer process.

**colourless** *adj.* (also **color-**) **1** without colour. **2** lacking character or interest (*a colourless personality*).

**colour-sergeant** *n.* senior sergeant of an infantry company.

**colposcopy** /ˌkol-**pos**-kuh-pee/ *n.* examination of the vagina and neck of the womb. □ **colposcope** /**kol**-puh-ˌskohp/ *n.* [Greek *kolpos* womb]

**colt** *n.* **1** young male horse (up to and including the age of 3). **2** *Sport* inexperienced player. □ **coltish** *adj.* [Old English]

**columbine** /**kol**-uhm-ˌbuyn/ *n.* garden plant with purple-blue etc. flowers like a cluster of doves. [Latin *columba* dove]

**column** /**kol**-uhm/ *n.* **1** upright cylindrical pillar, often slightly tapering, and with a base and capital. **2** column-shaped object. **3** vertical cylindrical mass of liquid or vapour (*column of smoke*). **4** vertical division of a printed page. **5** part of a newspaper etc. regularly devoted to

a particular subject (*gossip column*). **6** vertical row of figures in accounts etc. **7** narrow-fronted arrangement of troops or armoured vehicles in successive lines. □ **columnar** /kuh-**lum**-nuh/ *adj.* **columned** *adj.* [French and Latin]

**columnist** /**kol**-uhm-nuhst/ *n.* journalist contributing regularly to a newspaper etc.

**com-** *prefix* (also **co-**, **col-**, **con-**, **cor-**) with, together, jointly, altogether. [Latin *com-*, *cum* with]

■ **Usage** *Com-* is used before *b*, *m*, *p*, and occasionally before vowels and *f*; *co-* esp. before vowels, *h*, and *gn*; *col-* before *l*, *cor-* before *r*, and *con-* before other consonants.

**coma** /**koh**-muh/ *n.* (*pl.* **-s**) prolonged deep unconsciousness. [Latin from Greek]

**comatose** /**koh**-muh-ˌtohz, -ˌtohs/ *adj.* **1** in a coma. **2** drowsy, sleepy.

**comb** /kohm/ — *n.* **1 a** toothed strip of rigid material for tidying the hair. **b** similar curved decorative strip worn in the hair. **2** thing like a comb, esp. a device for tidying and straightening wool etc. **3** red fleshy crest of a fowl, esp. a cock. **4** honeycomb. **5** lower, fixed, and toothed part of the cutting-piece of a shearing machine, either of the standard breadth of 63.5 mm (*narrow comb*) or of greater breadth (*wide comb*). — *v.* **1** draw a comb through (the hair). **2** dress (wool etc.) with a comb. **3** *colloq.* search (a place) thoroughly (*combed the bush for the missing boy*). □ **comb out 1** arrange the hair loosely by combing. **2** remove with a comb. **3** search out and get rid of. [Old English]

**combat** /**kom**-bat/ — *n.* fight, struggle, contest. — *v.* (also /kuhm-**bat**/) (**-t-**) **1** engage in combat (with). **2** oppose; strive against. [Latin: related to BATTLE]

**combatant** /**kom**-buh-tuhnt/ — *n.* person engaged in fighting. — *adj.* **1** fighting. **2** for fighting.

**combative** /**kom**-buh-tiv/ *adj.* pugnacious.

**comber** /**koh**-muh/ *n.* **1** person or thing that combs. **2** long curling wave; a breaker.

**combi** /**kom**-bee/ *n.* (in full **combivan**) /**kom**-bee-ˌvan/) *colloq.* small light van. [from *Kombivan* proprietary term]

**combination** /ˌkom-buh-**nay**-shuhn/ *n.* **1** act or instance of combining or process of being combined. **2** combined set of things or people. **3** sequence of numbers or letters used to open a combination lock. [Latin: related to COMBINE]

**combination lock** n. lock that can be opened only by a specific sequence of movements.

**combine** — v. /kuhm-**buyn**/ (-**ning**) **1** join together; unite for a common purpose. **2** possess (qualities usually distinct) together (*combining charm and authority*). **3 a** (cause to) coalesce in one substance. **b** form or cause to form a chemical compound. — n. /**kom**-buyn/ **1** combination of esp. commercial interests. **2** = COMBINE HARVESTER. [Latin *bini* a pair]

**combine harvester** n. machine that reaps and threshes in one operation.

**combining form** n. linguistic element used in combination with another to form a word (e.g. *Anglo-* = English, *bio-* = life, *-graphy* = writing).

■ **Usage** In this dictionary, *combining form* is used of an element that contributes to the particular sense of words (as with both elements of *biography*), as distinct from a prefix or suffix that adjusts the sense of or determines the function of words (as with *un-*, *-able*, and *-ation*).

**combo** /**kom**-boh/ n. (pl. -**s**) colloq. **1** small jazz or dance band. **2 a** white man who lives with an Aboriginal woman. **b** white man who sexually exploits Aboriginal women. [abbreviation of COMBINATION]

**combustible** /kuhm-**bus**-tuh-buhl/ — adj. capable of or used for burning. — n. combustible substance. □ **combustibility** /-bil-uh-tee/ n. [Latin *comburo -bust-* burn up]

**combustion** /kuhm-**bus**-chuhn/ n. **1** burning. **2** *Chem* development of light and heat from the chemical combination of a substance with oxygen.

**come** /kum/ — v. (-**ming**; past **came**; past part. **come**) **1** move, be brought towards, or reach a place. **2** reach a specified situation or result (*came to no harm*). **3** reach or extend to a specified point (*the road comes to within a kilometre of us*). **4** traverse or accomplish (with compl.: *have come a long way*). **5** occur, happen; (of time) arrive in due course (*how did you come to break your leg?; the day soon came*). **6** take or occupy a specified position in space or time (*Nero came after Claudius; it does not come within the scope of this inquiry*). **7** become perceptible or known (*the church came into sight; it will come to me in a moment or two*). **8** be available (*comes in three sizes*). **9** become (*come loose*). **10** (foll. by *from, of*) **a** be descended from (*comes of an old convict family*). **b** be or have been a native or resident of (*I come from Sri Lanka; she comes from Koo-wee-rup*). **c** be the result of (*that comes of complaining*). **11** colloq. play the part of; behave like (*don't come the raw prawn with me!; don't come the bully with me*). **12** (also **cum**) coarse colloq. have an orgasm; ejaculate semen. **13** (in *subjunctive*) colloq. when a specified time is reached (*come next month*). **14** (as *int.*) expressing mild protest or encouragement (*come, it cannot be that bad*). — n. (also **cum**) coarse colloq. semen ejaculated. □ **come about** happen. **come across 1** meet or find by chance. **2** colloq. be effective or understood; give a specified impression (*she came across well; he comes across as a bit of a dill*). **3** (often foll. by *with*) colloq. hand over, contribute (money, information, etc.) (*will he come across, do you think?*). **come again** colloq. **1** make a further effort. **2** (as *imper.*) what did you say? **come along 1** make progress. **2** (as *imper.*) hurry up. **come at 1** attack (*came at me with a knife*). **2** reach, get access to (*I can't come at my files at the moment*). **3** colloq. accept; agree with; agree to undertake (*I can't come at that*). **come away 1** become detached. **2** (foll. by *with*) be left with (an impression etc.). **come back 1** return. **2** recur to one's memory. **3** (often foll. by *in*) become fashionable or popular again (*long hair's coming back for guys*). **4** reply, retort. **come before** be dealt with by (a judge etc.). **come between 1** interfere with the relationship of. **2** separate; prevent contact between. **come by 1** call on a visit. **2** obtain (*how did you come by that?*). **come clean** see CLEAN. **come a cropper** see CROPPER. **come down 1** lose position or wealth. **2** be handed down by tradition. **3** be reduced; show a downward trend (*prices are coming down*). **4** (foll. by *against, in favour of*) reach a decision. **5** (foll. by *to*) amount basically (*it comes down to who is willing to go*). **6** (foll. by *on*) criticise harshly; rebuke, punish (*came down on him like a ton of bricks*). **7** (foll. by *with*) begin to suffer from (a disease). **8** (of a river) be in flood. **come for 1** come to collect. **2** attack (*came for me with a hammer*). **come forward 1** advance. **2** offer oneself for a task, post, etc. **come in 1** enter. **2** take a specified position in a race etc. (*came in third*). **3** become fashionable or seasonable. **4** (with compl.) prove to be (useful etc.) (*came in handy*). **5** have a part to play (*where do I come in?*). **6** be received (*news has just come in*). **7** begin speaking, esp. in radio transmission. **8** (foll. by *for* receive (*came in for much criticism*). **9** (foll. by *on*) join (an enterprise, deal, etc.) (*will you come in on the deal?*). **10** (of a train etc.) approach its destination. **come in spinner** invitation to toss the coins in two-up. **come into 1** enter, be brought into (collision, prominence, etc.). **2** receive, esp. as an heir. **come of age** see AGE. **come off 1** (of an action) succeed, occur. **2** fare (badly, well, etc.). **3** be detached or detachable (from). **4** = *v.* 12. **come off it** *colloq.* expression of disbelief, disapproval, etc. **come on 1** advance, esp. to attack. **2** make progress (*it's really coming on*). **3** appear on a stage, field of play, etc. **4** (as *imper.*) expressing encouragement or disbelief. **5** = *come upon*. **come out 1** emerge; become known. **2** be published. **3 a** declare oneself (*came out in favour of the plan*). **b** openly declare that one is a homosexual (*came out to his family and friends*). **4** go on strike. **5** (of a photograph or thing photographed) be produced satisfactorily and clearly. **6** attain a specified result in an examination etc. **7** (of a stain etc.) be removed. **8** make one's début in society etc. **9** (foll. by *in*) become covered with (*came out in spots*). **10** (of a problem) be solved. **11** (foll. by *with*) declare openly; disclose. **come out of the closet** stop concealing the fact that one is homosexual. **come over 1 a** come from some distance to visit etc. **b** come nearer. **2** change sides or one's opinion. **3 a** (of a feeling etc.) overtake or affect (a person) (*what's come over you?*). **b** *colloq.* feel suddenly (*came over faint*). **4** appear or sound in a specified way (*you came over very well*). **come round 1** pay an informal visit. **2** recover consciousness. **3** be converted to another person's opinion. **4** (of a date or regular occurrence) recur; be imminent again. **come a stumer** *colloq.* suffer a serious (esp. financial) setback. **come through** survive. **come to 1** recover consciousness. **2** amount to (*comes to $17; it comes to this: you're fired*). **3** have as a destiny (*what's the world coming to?*). **come to one's senses** see SENSE. **come to that** *colloq.* in fact; if that is the case. **come up 1** arise; present itself; be mentioned or discussed. **2** attain position or wealth. **3** (often foll. by *to*) approach. **4** (foll. by *to*) match (a standard etc.). **5** (foll. by *with*) produce (an idea etc.). **6** (of a plant etc.) spring up out of the ground. **7** become brighter (e.g. with polishing). **come up against** be faced with or opposed by. **come upon 1** meet or find by chance. **2** attack by surprise. **have it coming to one** *colloq.* be about to get

one's just deserts. **how come?** *colloq.* how did that happen? [Old English]

**comeback** *n.* **1** return to a previous (esp. successful) state. **2** *colloq.* retaliation or retort. **3** sheep bred from crossbred and purebred parents for both wool and meat.

**comedian** /kuh-**mee**-dee-uhn/ *n.* **1** humorous entertainer. **2** comedy actor. **3** *colloq.* buffoon. [French]

**comedienne** /kuh-ˌmee-dee-**en**/ *n.* female comedian. [French feminine]

**comedown** *n.* **1** loss of status. **2** disappointment.

**comedy** /**kom**-uh-dee/ *n.* (*pl.* **-ies**) **1 a** play, film, etc., of amusing character, usu. with a happy ending. **b** such works as a dramatic genre (opp. TRAGEDY). **2** amusing or farcical incident or series of incidents in everyday life. □ **comedic** /kuh-**mee**-dik/ *adj.* [Greek *kōmōidia* from *kōmōidos* comic poet: see also COMIC]

**come-hither** *attrib. adj. colloq.* flirtatious, inviting.

**comely** /**kum**-lee/ *adj.* (**-ier**, **-iest**) *literary* handsome, good-looking. □ **comeliness** *n.* [Old English]

**come-on** *n. colloq.* lure or enticement.

**comer** /**kum**-uh/ *n.* person who comes as an applicant etc. (*offered it to the first comer*).

**comestibles** /kuh-**mes**-tuh-buhlz/ *n.pl. formal* or *joc.* food. [French from Latin]

**comet** /**kom**-uht/ *n.* hazy object moving in a path about the sun, usu. with a nucleus of ice surrounded by gas and with a tail pointing away from the sun. [Greek *komētes*]

**comeuppance** /kum-**up**-uhns/ *n. colloq.* deserved punishment. [*come up*, -ANCE]

**comfort** /**kum**-fuht/ — *n.* **1 a** state of physical well-being. **b** (usu. in *pl.*) things that make life easy or pleasant. **2** relief of suffering or grief, consolation. **3** person or thing giving consolation. — *v.* soothe in grief; console. [Latin *fortis* strong]

**comfortable** *adj.* **1** giving ease (*comfortable pair of shoes*). **2** free from discomfort; at ease (*I'm quite comfortable, thank you*). **3** having an easy conscience (*did not feel comfortable about refusing him*). **4 a** having an adequate standard of living; free from financial worry. **b** sufficient (*comfortable income*). **5 a** with a wide margin (*comfortable win*). **b** appreciable (*comfortable margin*). □ **comfortably** *adv.*

**comforter** *n.* **1** person who comforts. **2** *archaic* woollen scarf.

**comfy** /**kum**-fee/ *adj.* (**-ier**, **-iest**) *colloq.* comfortable. [abbreviation]

**comic** /**kom**-ik/ — *adj.* **1** of or like comedy. **2** funny. — *n.* **1** comedian. **2** periodical in the form of comic strips. □ **comical** *adj.* **comically** *adv.* [Greek *kōmos* revel]

**comic strip** *n.* sequence of drawings telling a story.

**coming** /**kum**-ing/ — *attrib. adj.* **1** approaching, next (*the coming week*). **2** of potential importance (*coming man*). — *n.* arrival.

**comma** /**kom**-uh/ *n.* punctuation mark (,) indicating a pause or break between parts of a sentence etc. (see panel). [Greek, = clause]

**command** /kuh-**mahnd**, -**mand**/ — *v.* **1** (often foll. by *to* + infin., or *that* + clause) give a formal order or instruction to (*I command you to go*; *commands that it be done*). **2** (also *absol.*) have authority or control over (*who commands here?*). **3** have at one's disposal or within reach (a skill, resources, etc.) (*commands a wide knowledge of history*; *commands a salary of $1000 a week*). **4** deserve and get (sympathy, respect, etc.). **5** *Mil.* dominate (a strategic position) from a superior height; look down over. — *n.* **1** authoritative order; instruction. **2** mastery, control, possession (*a good command of languages*; *has command of the resources*). **3** exercise or tenure of authority, esp. naval or military. **4 a** body of troops etc. **b** district under a commander. **5** *Computing* **a** instruction causing a computer to perform one of its basic functions. **b** signal initiating such an operation. [Latin: related to MANDATE]

**commandant** /**kom**-uhn-,dant, -,dahnt/ *n.* commanding officer, esp. of a military academy. [French or Italian or Spanish: related to COMMAND]

---

**Comma ,**

The comma marks a slight break between words, phrases, etc. In particular, it is used:

**1** to separate items in a list, e.g.
　　*red, white, and blue* or *red, white and blue*
　　*We bought some shoes, socks, gloves, and handkerchiefs.*
　　*potatoes, peas or carrots* or *potatoes, peas or carrots*

**2** to separate adjectives that describe something in the same way, e.g.
　　*It is a hot, dry, dusty place.*
　　but not if they describe it in different ways, e.g.
　　*a distinguished foreign author*
　　or if one adjective adds to or alters the meaning of another, e.g.
　　*a bright red tie*

**3** to separate main clauses, e.g.
　　*Cars will park here, and buses will turn left.*

**4** to separate a name or word used to address someone, e.g.
　　*David, I'm here.*
　　*Well, Mr Jones, we meet again.*
　　*Have you seen this, my friend?*

**5** to separate a phrase, e.g.
　　*Having had lunch, we went back to work.*
　　especially in order to clarify meaning, e.g.
　　*In the valley below, the town looked very small.*

**6** after words that introduce direct speech, or after direct speech where there is no question mark or exclamation mark, e.g.
　　*They answered, 'Here we are.'*
　　*'Here we are,' they answered.*

**7** after *Dear Sir*, *Dear Sarah*, etc., and *Yours faithfully*, *Yours sincerely*, etc. in letters.

**8** to separate a word, phrase, or clause that is secondary or adds information or a comment, e.g.
　　*I am sure, however, that it will not happen.*
　　*Fred, who is bald, complained of the cold.*
　　but not with a relative clause (one usually beginning with *who*, *which*, or *that*) that restricts the meaning of the noun it follows, e.g.
　　*Men who are bald should wear hats.*
　　No comma is needed between a month and a year in dates, e.g.
　　*in December 1996*
　　or between a number and a road in addresses, e.g.
　　*17 Warangamba Drive*

**commandeer** /ˌkom-uhn-**deer**/ v. **1** seize (goods or men) for military use. **2** take arbitrary possession of. [Afrikaans *kommanderen*]

**commander** /kuh-**mahn**-duh, -**man**-duh/ n. **1** person who commands. **2** naval officer next below captain.

**commander-in-chief** n. (pl. **commanders-in-chief**) supreme commander, esp. of a nation's forces.

**commanding** adj. **1** exalted, impressive (*has a commanding presence*). **2** (of a position) giving a wide view (*the house is in a commanding position above the valley*). **3** (of an advantage etc.) substantial (*commanding lead*).

**commandment** n. divine command.

**command module** n. control compartment in a spacecraft.

**commando** /kuh-**mahn**-doh, -**man**-doh/ n. (pl. **-s**) **1** unit of shock troops specially trained for carrying out raids into enemy territory etc. **2** member of this. [Portuguese: related to COMMAND]

**commemorate** /kuh-**mem**-uh-ˌrayt/ v. (**-ting**) **1** preserve in memory by a celebration or ceremony. **2** be a memorial of. □ **commemoration** /kuh-ˌmem-uh-**ray**-shuhn/ n. **commemorative** /kuh-**mem**-uh-ruh-tiv/ adj. [Latin: related to MEMORY]

**commence** /kuh-**mens**/ v. (**-cing**) *formal* begin. [Latin: related to COM-, INITIATE]

**commencement** n. *formal* beginning.

**commend** /kuh-**mend**/ v. **1** praise (*commended her for her efforts*). **2** entrust, commit (*commends his soul to God*). **3** recommend (*the method commends itself*). □ **commendation** /ˌkom-en-**day**-shuhn/ n. [Latin: related to MANDATE]

**commendable** adj. praiseworthy. □ **commendably** adv.

**commensurable** /kuh-**men**-shuh-ruh-buhl/ adj. **1** (often foll. by *with*, *to*) measurable by the same standard. **2** (foll. by *to*) proportionate to. **3** *Math.* (of numbers) in a ratio equal to the ratio of integers. □ **commensurability** /-**bil**-uh-tee/ n. [Latin: related to MEASURE]

**commensurate** /kuh-**men**-shuh-ruht/ adj. **1** (usu. foll. by *with*) having the same size, duration, etc.; coextensive. **2** (often foll. by *to*, *with*) proportionate.

**comment** /**kom**-ent/ — n. **1** brief critical or explanatory remark or note; opinion. **2** commenting; criticism (*aroused much comment; his art is a comment on society*). — v. (**1** often foll. by *on* or *that*) make (esp. critical) remarks. **2** (often foll. by *on*, *upon*) write explanatory notes. □ **no comment** *colloq.* I decline to answer your question. [Latin]

**commentary** /**kom**-uhn-tuh-ree, -tree/ n. (pl. **-ies**) **1** descriptive spoken esp. broadcast account of an event or performance as it happens. **2** set of explanatory notes on a text etc. [Latin]

**commentate** /**kom**-uhn-ˌtayt/ v. (**-ting**) act as a commentator.

**commentator** n. **1** person who provides a commentary. **2** person who comments on current events. [Latin]

**commerce** /**kom**-ers/ n. financial transactions, esp. buying and selling of merchandise, on a large scale; trading. [Latin: related to MERCER]

**commercial** /kuh-**mer**-shuhl/ — adj. **1** of or engaged in commerce (*commercial law; commercial motor vehicle*). **2** having financial profit as its primary aim rather than artistic etc, value; viewed as a matter of business (*a commercial success; need you be so sordidly commercial?*). **3** (of chemicals) supplied in bulk more or less unpurified. — n. television or radio advertisement. □ **commercially** adv.

**commercial broadcasting** n. broadcasting financed by advertising.

**commercialise** v. (also **-ize**) (**-sing** or **-zing**) **1** exploit or spoil for profit (*Christmas has become so commercialised*). **2** make commercial. □ **commercialisation** /-**zay**-shuhn/ n.

**commercialism** n. **1** commercial practices. **2** emphasis on financial profit.

**commercial traveller** n. firm's representative visiting shops etc. to get orders.

**commie** /**kom**-ee/ n. & adj. *colloq.* communist. [abbreviation]

**commination** /ˌkom-uh-**nay**-shuhn/ n. *literary* threatening of divine vengeance. □ **comminatory** /**kom**-uh-nuh-tuh-ree, -tree/ adj. [Latin: related to MENACE]

**commingle** /kuh-**ming**-guhl/ v. (**-ling**) *literary* mingle together.

**comminute** /**kom**-uh-ˌnyoot/ v. (**-ting**) **1** reduce to small fragments. **2** divide (property) into small portions. □ **comminution** /-**nyoo**-shuhn/ n. [Latin: related to MINUTE²]

**comminuted fracture** n. fracture producing multiple bone splinters.

**commiserate** /kuh-**miz**-uh-ˌrayt/ v. (**-ting**) (usu. foll. by *with*) express or feel sympathy. □ **commiseration** /-**ray**-shuhn/ n. [Latin: related to MISER]

**commissar** /**kom**-uh-ˌsah/ n. *hist.* **1** official of the Soviet Communist Party responsible for political education and organisation. **2** head of a government department in the USSR before 1946. [Latin: related to COMMIT]

**commissariat** /ˌkom-uh-**sair**-ree-uht, -ree-ˌat/ *n.* **1** esp. *Mil.* **a** department for the supply of food etc. **b** food supplied. **2** *hist.* government department of the USSR. [related to COMMISSARY]

**commissary** /**kom**-uh-suh-ree/ *n.* (*pl.* **-ies**) **1** deputy, delegate. **2** *Mil.* officer responsible for the supply of food etc. to soldiers. [Latin: related to COMMIT]

**commission**[1] /kuh-**mish**-uhn/ — *n.* **1 a** authority to perform a task etc. **b** person(s) entrusted with such authority (*set up a commission to investigate the allegations*). **c** task etc. given to such person(s). **2** government utility. **3** order for something, esp. a work of art, to be produced specially. **4 a** warrant conferring the rank of officer in the armed forces. **b** rank so conferred. **5** pay or percentage paid to an agent (*the wages are low but he gets a 20% commission*; *foreign exchange dealers always charge a commission*). **6** act of committing (a crime etc.). — *v.* **1** empower by commission. **2 a** give (an artist etc.) a commission for a piece of work. **b** order (a work) to be written etc. **3 a** give (an officer) command of a ship. **b** prepare (a ship) for active service. **4** bring (a machine etc.) into operation. □ **in** (or **out of**) **commission** ready (or not ready) for service or use. [Latin: related to COMMIT]

**commission**[2] *attrib. adj.* (in some States) of or pertaining to government-owned housing etc. for people on low incomes (*commission houses*). [abbreviation of *Housing Commission*]

**commissionaire** /kuh-ˌmish-uh-**nair**/ *n.* uniformed door-attendant at a theatre etc. [French: related to COMMISSIONER]

**commissioner** *n.* **1** person appointed by a commission to perform a specific task, e.g. the head of a police force etc. **2** member of a government commission. **3** representative of government in a district, department, etc. [medieval Latin: related to COMMISSION[1]]

**commit** /kuh-**mit**/ *v.* (**-tt-**) **1** do or make (a crime, blunder, etc.). **2** (usu. foll. by *to*) entrust or consign for: **a** safe keeping (*I commit him to your care*). **b** treatment, usu. destruction (*committed the book to the flames*). **3 a** send (a person) to prison etc. **b** (foll. by *for*) order an accused person to be tried by jury. **4** pledge or bind (esp. oneself) to a certain course or policy (*committed himself to further the republican cause in Australia*). **5** (as **committed** *adj.*) (often foll. by *to*) **a** dedicated (a *committed Christian*; *committed to retaining the Queen as Head of Aus-*

*tralia*). **b** obliged (*felt committed to stay*). □ **commit to memory** memorise. **commit to paper** write down. [Latin *committo -miss-*]

**commitment** *n.* **1** engagement or (esp. financial) obligation. **2** process or instance of committing or being committed. **3** dedication; committing oneself; pledge or undertaking (*commitment to the cause of Aboriginal land rights*).

**committal** *n.* **1** (in full **committal hearing**) proceedings before a magistrate to determine whether there is sufficient evidence to warrant a trial by jury. **2** act of committing, esp. to prison or a psychiatric institution. **3** burial of a dead body.

**committee** /kuh-**mit**-ee/ *n.* **1** body of persons appointed for a special function by (and usu. out of) a larger body. **2** (**Committee**) the whole House of Representatives when sitting as a committee during the committee stage of a bill. [from COMMIT, -EE]

**committee stage** *n.* stage of a bill's progress through parliament, following its second reading, when it may be considered in detail and amendments may be made.

**commo** /**kom**-oh/ *n.* *colloq.* a communist. [abbreviation]

**commode** /kuh-**mohd**/ *n.* chamber-pot in a chair with a cover. [Latin *commodus* convenient]

**commodious** /kuh-**moh**-dee-uhs/ *adj.* roomy and comfortable (*commodious living quarters*).

**commodity** /kuh-**mod**-uh-tee/ *n.* (*pl.* **-ies**) **1** article of trade, esp. a raw material or product as opposed to a service. **2** useful thing. [Latin: related to COMMODE]

**commodore** /**kom**-uh-ˌdaw/ *n.* **1** naval officer. **2** commander of a squadron or other division of a fleet. **3** president of a yacht-club. [French: related to COMMANDER]

**common** /**kom**-uhn/ *adj.* (**-er, -est**) **1 a** occurring often (*a common mistake*). **b** ordinary; without special rank or position (*the common people*). **2 a** shared by (or coming from) more than one (*common knowledge*; *by common consent*). **b** belonging to the whole community; public (*common land*). **3** *derog.* low-class; vulgar; inferior (*a common little man*). **4** of the most familiar type (*common cold*). **5** *Math.* belonging to two or more quantities (*common denominator*). **6** *Gram.* (of gender) referring to individuals of either sex (e.g. teacher). □ **in common 1** in joint use; shared. **2** of joint interest. **in common with** in the same way as. [Latin *communis*]

**commonality** /ˌkom-uh-**nal**-uh-tee/ *n.* (*pl.* **-ies**) **1** sharing of an attribute. **2** common occurrence. **3** = COMMONALTY. [var. of COMMONALTY]

**commonalty** /**kom**-uh-nuhl-tee/ *n.* (*pl.* **-ies**) **1** the common people. **2** the general body (esp. of mankind). [medieval Latin: related to COMMON]

**common denominator** *n.* **1** *Math.* common multiple of the denominators of several fractions. **2** common features, interest, etc. of the members of a group.

**commoner** *n.* one of the common people. [medieval Latin: related to COMMON]

**common ground** *n.* point or argument accepted by both sides in a dispute.

**common heath** *n.* small epacris (to 1m) bearing profuse dangling tube-like flowers all the year in colours ranging from white to deepest red, with the commonest colour being pink: the floral emblem of Victoria.

**common law** *n.* law based on custom and judicial precedent rather than statutes.

**commonly** *adv.* usually, frequently; ordinarily.

**Common Market** *n.* the European Community.

**common noun** *n. Gram.* name denoting a class of objects or a concept, not a particular individual.

**common or garden** *adj. colloq.* ordinary.

**commonplace** — *adj.* lacking originality; trite; ordinary. — *n.* **1** event, topic, etc. that is ordinary or usual. **2** everyday saying; platitude (*uttered a commonplace about the weather*). [translation of Latin *locus communis*]

**common room** *n.* room for the social use of students or teachers at a college etc.

**commonsense** *n.* (also **common sense**) sound practical sense.

**commonsensical** /ˌkom-uhn-**sen**-si-kuhl/ *adj.* (also **commonsense**) having or marked by commonsense.

**common time** *n. Mus.* four crotchets in a bar.

**commonwealth** *n.* **1** independent nation or community, esp. a democratic republic. **2** (**the Commonwealth**) **a** title of the federated States and Territories of Australia; the government of this federation (also *attrib.*). **b** loose international association, the members of which are nations that were previously part of the British Empire, as well as the United Kingdom.

**commotion** /kuh-**moh**-shuhn/ *n.* **1** con-

fused and noisy disturbance, uproar. **2** civil insurrection. [COM-, Latin *motio*]

**comms** /komz/ *abbr. Computing* communications.

**communal** /**kom**-yuh-nuhl, kuh-**myoo**-nuhl/ *adj.* shared among members of a group or community; for common use (*communal playground*). □ **communally** *adv.* [Latin: related to COMMUNE¹]

**commune¹** /**kom**-yoon/ *n.* **1** group of people sharing living accommodation, goods, etc., esp. as a political act. **2** communal settlement, esp. for the pursuit of shared interests. [medieval Latin: related to COMMON]

**commune²** /kuh-**myoon**/ *v.* (**-ning**) (usu. foll. by *with*) **1** speak intimately (*communed together about their loss*). **2** feel in close touch (*with nature etc.*) (*communing with the spirit of Uluru at dawn*). [French: related to COMMON]

**communicable** /kuh-**myoo**-ni-kuh-buhl/ *adj.* (esp. of a disease) able to be passed on. [Latin: related to COMMUNICATE]

**communicant** /kuh-**myoo**-nuh-kuhnt/ *n.* **1** person who receives Holy Communion. **2** person who imparts information. [related to COMMUNICATE]

**communicate** /kuh-**myoo**-nuh-ˌkayt/ *v.* (**-ting**) **1** impart, transmit (news, heat, motion, feelings, disease, ideas, etc.) (*communicated her thoughts; wide windows communicating warmth and light; communicated his affection*). **2** succeed in conveying information, evoking understanding etc. (*she communicates well*). **3** (often foll. by *with*) relate socially; share feelings or understanding (*communicates well with the neighbours*). **4** be connected (*my bedroom communicates with yours*). **5** receive Holy Communion. □ **communicator** *n.* **communicatory** *adj.* [Latin: related to COMMON]

**communication** /kuh-ˌmyoo-nuh-**kay**-shuhn/ *n.* **1 a** act of imparting, esp. news. **b** instance of this. **c** information etc. communicated. **d** letter, message, etc. **2** means (such as a door, passage, road, or railway) of connecting different places. **3** social intercourse (*it was difficult to maintain communication in the uproar*). **4** (in *pl.*) science and practice of transmitting information, esp. by electronic or mechanical means.

**communication(s) satellite** *n.* artificial satellite used to relay telephone circuits or broadcast programmes.

**communicative** /kuh-**myoo**-nuh-kuh-tiv/ *adj.* ready to talk and impart information.

**communion** /kuh-**myoo**-nyuhn/ n. **1** sharing, esp. of thoughts etc.; fellowship (*their minds were in communion*). **2** participation; sharing in common (*communion of interests*). **3** (**Communion** or **Holy Communion**) Eucharist. **4** Christian denomination (*the Methodist communion*). [Latin: related to COMMON]

**communiqué** /kuh-**myoo**-nuh-ˌkay/ n. official communication, esp. a news report. [French, = communicated]

**communism** /**kom**-yuh-ˌniz-uhm/ n. **1 a** social system in which most property is publicly owned and each person works for the common benefit. **b** political theory advocating this. **2** (usu. **Communism**) the form of socialist society established in Cuba, China, etc., and previously, the USSR. [French: related to COMMON]

**communist** /**kom**-yuh-nuhst/ — n. **1** person advocating communism. **2** (usu. **Communist**) supporter of Communism or member of a Communist Party. — adj. **1** of or relating to communism. **2** (usu. **Communist**) of Communists or a Communist party. □ **communistic** /-nis-tik/ adj.

**Communist Party** n. political party advocating communism or Communism.

**community** /kuh-**myoo**-nuh-tee/ n. (pl. **-ies**) **1 a** body of people living in one place, district, or country. **b** (*attrib.*) of, for, or relating to a community (*community service*; *community spirit*). **2** body of people having religion, ethnic origin, profession, etc., in common (*Melbourne's large Greek community*). **3** fellowship (*community of interest*). **4** monastic etc. body practising common ownership (*community of nuns*). **5** Ecol. group of animals or plants living or growing together in the same area. [Latin: related to COMMON]

**community language** n. any language (other than English or an Aboriginal language) spoken by Australians, e.g. Greek, Italian, Vietnamese, Yiddish, etc.

**community service** n. unpaid work in the community, esp. by an offender.

**commute** /kuh-**myoot**/ v. (**-ting**) **1** travel some distance to and from work. **2** Law (usu. foll. by *to*) change (a punishment) to one less severe. **3** (often foll. by *into*, *for*) change (one kind of payment or obligation) for another. □ **commutable** adj. **commutation** /ˌkom-yoo-**tay**-shuhn/ n. [Latin *muto* change]

**commuter** n. person who commutes to and from work.

**compact¹** — adj. /kuhm-**pakt**, **kom**-pakt/ **1** closely or neatly packed together.

**2** small and economically designed. **3** (of style etc.) concise. **4** (of a person) small but well-proportioned. — v. /kuhm-**pakt**/ **1** join or press firmly together. **2** condense. — n. /**kom**-pakt/ (in full **powder compact**) small flat case for face-powder. □ **compacted** adj. **compaction** n. **compactly** adv. **compactness** n. [Latin *pango* fasten]

**compact²** /**kom**-pakt/ n. agreement, contract. [Latin: related to PACT]

**compact disc** /ˌkom-pakt **disk**/ n. disc on which information or sound is recorded digitally and reproduced by reflection of laser light.

**compact-disc player** n. instrument which 'reads' and reproduces the information recorded on a compact disc.

**companion** /kuhm-**pan**-yuhn/ n. **1 a** person who accompanies or associates with another. **b** (foll. by *in*, *of*) partner, sharer (*companion in misfortune*). **c** person employed to live with and assist another. **2** handbook or reference book (*Oxford Companion to Australian Literature*). **3** thing that matches another (*the companion of this book-end is lost*). **4** (**Companion**) member of the highest General or Military Division of the Order of Australia. **5** euphem. person's lover. [Latin *panis* bread]

**companionable** adj. sociable, friendly. □ **companionably** adv.

**companion planting** n. the practice of growing side by side plants of different species which are supposed to benefit one another when so grown.

**companionship** n. state of being a companion; friendship; being together.

**company** /**kum**-puh-nee/ n. (pl. **-ies**) **1 a** number of people assembled. **b** guest(s). **2** state of being a companion; companionship, esp. of a specific kind (*enjoys low company*; *do not care for his company*). **3 a** commercial business. **b** partners in this. **4** actors etc. working together. **5** subdivision of an infantry battalion. **6** body of people combined for a common purpose (*the ship's company*). **7** being with another or others. □ **in company with** together with. **keep a person company** remain with a person to be sociable. **part company** (often foll. by *with*) cease to associate; separate; disagree. [French: related to COMPANION]

**comparable** /**kom**-puh-ruh-buhl, -pruh-buhl/ adj. **1** (often foll. by *with*) able to be compared (*the treatment of Australian Aborigines by white settlers is comparable with that of the American Indians*). **2** (often foll. by *to*) fit to be compared; worth comparing (*Australian fashions* *are comparable to those of France).* □ **comparability** /-bil-uh-tee/ *n.* **comparably** *adv.* [Latin: related to COMPARE]

■ **Usage** Use of *comparable* with *to* and *with* corresponds to the senses of *compare*: *to* is more common.

**comparative** /kuhm-**pa**-ruh-tiv/ — *adj.* **1** perceptible or estimated by comparison; relative (*in comparative comfort; the comparative merits of the two ideas*). **2** of or involving comparison (*a comparative study*). **3** *Gram.* (of an adjective or adverb) expressing a higher degree of a quality (e.g. *braver, more quickly*) (cf. POSITIVE; SUPERLATIVE). — *n. Gram.* comparative expression or word. □ **comparatively** *adv.* [Latin: related to COMPARE]

**compare** /kuhm-**pair**/ — *v.* (**-ring**) **1** (usu. foll. by *to*) express similarities in; liken (*compared the painting to a dog's breakfast*). **2** (often foll. by *to, with*) estimate the similarity or dissimilarity of; assess the relation between (*compared radio with television; that lacks quality compared to this*). **3** (often foll. by *with*) bear comparison (*compares favourably with the rest*). **4** *Gram.* form comparative and superlative degrees of (an adjective or adverb). — *n. literary* comparison (*beyond compare*). □ **compare notes** exchange ideas or opinions. [Latin *compar* equal]

■ **Usage** In current use, *to* and *with* are generally interchangeable, but *with* often implies a greater element of formal analysis.

**comparison** /kuhm-**pa**-ruh-suhn/ *n.* **1** act or instance of comparing. **2** illustration or example of similarity. **3** capacity for being likened (*there's no comparison*). **4** (in full **degrees of comparison**) *Gram.* positive, comparative, and superlative forms of adjectives and adverbs. □ **bear** (or **stand**) **comparison** (often foll. by *with*) be able to be compared favourably. **beyond comparison 1** totally different in quality. **2** greatly superior; excellent.

**compartment** /kuhm-**paht**-muhnt/ *n.* **1** space within a larger space, separated by partitions, e.g. in a railway carriage, wallet, desk, etc. **2** administrative unit of a forest. **3** watertight division of a ship. **4** area of activity etc. kept apart from others in a person's mind. [Latin: related to PART]

**compartmental** /ˌkom-paht-**men**-tuhl/ *adj.* of or divided into compartments or categories.

**compartmentalise** *v.* (also **-ize**) (**-sing** or **-zing**) divide into compartments or categories.

**compass** /**kum**-puhs/ *n.* **1** instrument showing the direction of magnetic north and bearings from it. **2** (usu. in *pl.*) instrument for taking measurements and describing circles, with two arms connected at one end by a hinge. **3** circumference or boundary. **4** area, extent; scope; range (e.g. of knowledge or experience) (*that's beyond my compass*). [Latin *passus* pace]

**compass bush** *n.* WA casuarina, often forming large stands in which these shrubs never grow vertically but always slant in the same direction, hence the common name.

**compassion** /kuhm-**pash**-uhn/ *n.* pity inclining one to help or be merciful. [Church Latin: related to PASSION]

**compassionate** /kuhm-**pash**-uh-nuht/ *adj.* showing compassion, sympathetic. □ **compassionately** *adv.*

**compassionate leave** *n.* leave granted on grounds of bereavement etc.

**compass rose** *n.* circle drawn (often with artistic embellishment) on a map etc. in order to show the direction of north.

**compatible** /kuhm-**pat**-uh-buhl/ *adj.* **1 a** able to coexist; well-suited (*a compatible couple*). **b** (often foll. by *with*) consistent (*their views are not compatible with their actions*). **2** (of equipment etc.) able to be used in combination. □ **compatibility** /-bil-uh-tee/ *n.* [medieval Latin: related to PASSION]

**compatriot** /kuhm-**pat**-ree-uht, -**pay**-tree-uht/ *n.* fellow countryman or countrywoman. [Latin *compatriota*]

**compel** /kuhm-**pel**/ *v.* (**-ll-**) **1 a** force, constrain (*compelled them to submit*). **b** bring about by force (*compel submission*). **2** arouse irresistibly (*compels admiration*). **3** (as **compelling** *adj.*) rousing strong interest, conviction, or admiration (*a compelling performance by the young Australian pianist*). □ **compellingly** *adv.* [Latin *pello puls-* drive]

**compendious** /kuhm-**pen**-dee-uhs/ *adj.* comprehensive but brief. [Latin: related to COMPENDIUM]

**compendium** /kuhm-**pen**-dee-uhm/ *n.* (*pl.* **-s** or **-dia**) concise summary or abridgment. [Latin]

**compensate** /**kom**-puhn-ˌsayt/ *v.* (**-ting**) **1 a** (often foll. by *for*) recompense (a person) (*compensated him for his loss*). **b** recompense (loss, damage, etc.). **2** (usu. foll. by *for* a thing) make amends (*compensated for the insult*). **3** counterbalance; make up for (*her natural skill* *should compensate for her lack of training; a shrub very difficult to grow, but its beauty amply compensates).* **4** *Mech.* provide (a pendulum etc.) with extra or less weight etc. to neutralise the effects of temperature etc. **5** *Psychol.* offset disability or frustration by development in another direction. □ **compensator** *n.* **compensatory** /-puhn-**say**-tuh-ree, -tree/ *adj.* [Latin *pendo pens*-weigh]

**compensation** /ˌkom-puhn-**say**-shuhn/ *n.* **1** act of compensating or the process of being compensated. **2** money etc. given as recompense. **3** *Psychol.* **a** act of compensating. **b** result of compensating. **4** = WORKERS' COMPENSATION.

**compère** /**kom**-pair/ — *n.* person who introduces a variety show etc. — *v.* (**-ring**) act as compère (to). [French, = godfather]

**compete** /kuhm-**peet**/ *v.* (**-ting**) **1** take part in a contest etc. **2** (often foll. by *with*, *against* a person, *for* a thing) strive for superiority or supremacy. [Latin *peto* seek]

**competence** /**kom**-puh-tuhns/ *n.* (also **competency**) **1** ability; state of being competent. **2** income large enough to live on. **3** legal capacity (of a court etc.) to deal with a matter.

**competent** *adj.* **1** adequately qualified or capable (*not competent to drive*). **2** effective (*a competent batsman*). **3** *Law* **a** (of a judge or court) authorised to deal with a matter. **b** (of a person) having legal capacity and qualification. □ **competently** *adv.* [Latin: related to COMPETE]

**competition** /ˌkom-puh-**tish**-uhn/ *n.* **1** (often foll. by *for*) competing (*competition for the job was fierce*). **2** event in which people compete. **3** the other people or trade competing; the opposition. [Latin: related to COMPETE]

**competitive** /kuhm-**pet**-uh-tiv/ *adj.* **1** of or involving competition. **2** (of prices etc.) comparing favourably with those of rivals. **3** having a strong urge to win. □ **competitiveness** *n.*

**competitor** /kuhm-**pet**-uh-tuh/ *n.* person who competes; rival, esp. in business.

**compile** /kuhm-**puyl**/ *v.* (**-ling**) **1 a** collect and arrange (material) into a list, book, etc. **b** produce (a book etc.) thus. **2** accumulate (a large number of) (*compiled a score of 160*). **3** *Computing* translate (a programming language) into machine code. □ **compilation** /ˌkom-puh-**lay**-shuhn/ *n.* [Latin *compilo* plunder]

**compiler** *n.* **1** person who compiles. **2** *Computing* program for translating a high-level programming language into machine code.

**complacent** /kuhm-**play**-suhnt/ *adj.* **1** smugly self-satisfied. **2** calmly content. □ **complacence** *n.* **complacency** *n.* **complacently** *adv.* [Latin *placeo* please]

■ *Usage* *Complacent* is often confused with *complaisant*.

**complain** /kuhm-**playn**/ *v.* **1** express dissatisfaction. **2** (foll. by *of*) **a** say that one is suffering from (an ailment) (*complained of a pain in the chest*). **b** state a grievance concerning (*complained of the delay*). [Latin *plango* lament]

**complainant** *n.* plaintiff in certain lawsuits.

**complaint** *n.* **1** act of complaining. **2** grievance, cause of dissatisfaction. **3** ailment. **4** *Law* process of initiating certain lawsuits, usu. civil actions.

**complaisant** /kuhm-**play**-suhnt, -**play**-zuhnt/ *adj. formal* **1** politely deferential. **2** willing to please; acquiescent. □ **complaisance** *n.* [French: related to COMPLACENT]

■ *Usage* *Complaisant* is often confused with *complacent*.

**complement** — *n.* /**kom**-pluh-muhnt/ **1 a** thing that completes. **b** one of a pair, or one of two things that go together. **2** (often **full complement**) full number needed (to man a ship, fill a conveyance, etc.). **3** word(s) added to a verb to complete the predicate of a sentence. **4** amount by which an angle is less than 90°. **5** *Math.* any element not belonging to a specified set or class. — *v.* /**kom**-pluh-ˌment/ **1** complete. **2** form a complement to (*the scarf complements her dress*). [Latin *compleo* fill up]

■ *Usage* *Complement* is often confused with *compliment*, especially in writing.

**complementary** /ˌkom-pluh-**men**-tuh-ree, -tree/ *adj.* **1** completing; forming a complement. **2** (of two or more things) complementing each other.

**complete** /kuhm-**pleet**/ — *adj.* **1** having all its parts; entire. **2** finished. **3** total, in every way (*a complete surprise*). — *v.* (**-ting**) **1** finish. **2 a** make whole or perfect. **b** make up the amount of (*completes the quota*). **3** fill in (a form etc.). □ **complete with** having (as an important feature) (*comes complete with instructions*). □ **completely** *adv.* **completeness** *n.* **completion** *n.* [Latin: related to COMPLEMENT]

**complex** /**kom**-pleks/ — *n.* **1** building,

series of rooms, etc., made up of related parts (*shopping complex*). **2** *Psychol.* group of usu. repressed feelings or thoughts which cause abnormal behaviour or mental states (*inferiority complex*; *Oedipus complex*). **3** (in general use) preoccupation; feeling of inadequacy (*has a complex about his legs being skinny*). — *adj.* **1** complicated (*a complex problem*). **2** consisting of related parts; composite. □ **complexity** /kuhm-**plek**-suh-tee/ *n.* (*pl.* **-ies**). [Latin *complexus*]

**complexion** /kuhm-**plek**-shuhn/ *n.* **1** natural colour, texture, and appearance of the skin, esp. of the face. **2** aspect, character (*puts a different complexion on the matter*). [Latin: related to COMPLEX]

**compliance** /kuhm-**ply**-uhns/ *n.* **1** obedience to a request, command, etc. **2** unworthy acquiescence. □ **in compliance with** according to.

**compliant** *adj.* obedient; yielding. □ **compliantly** *adv.*

**complicate** /**kom**-pluh-ˌkayt/ *v.* (**-ting**) **1** make difficult or complex. **2** (as **complicated** *adj.*) complex; intricate. [Latin *plico* to fold]

**complication** /ˌkom-pluh-**kay**-shuhn/ *n.* **1 a** involved or confused condition or state. **b** complicating circumstance; difficulty. **2** (often in *pl.*) disease or condition aggravating or arising out of a previous one. [Latin: related to COMPLICATE]

**complicity** /kuhm-**plis**-uh-tee/ *n.* partnership in wrongdoing. [French: related to COMPLEX]

**compliment** — *n.* /**kom**-pluh-muhnt/ **1 a** polite expression of praise. **b** act or circumstance implying praise (*their success was a compliment to their dedicated training*). **2** (in *pl.*) **a** formal greetings accompanying a present etc. **b** praise. — *v.* /**kom**-pluh-ˌment/ (often foll. by *on*) congratulate; praise. [Latin: related to COMPLEMENT]

■ **Usage** *Compliment* is often confused with *complement*, especially in writing.

**complimentary** /ˌkom-pluh-**men**-tuh-ree, -tree/ *adj.* **1** expressing a compliment. **2** given free of charge.

**compline** /**kom**-pluhn, -pluyn/ *n.* **1** *RC Church* **a** last of the seven canonical hours of the breviary. **b** service for this, said or chanted after vespers. **2** similar service in some other Churches. [Latin: related to COMPLY]

**comply** /kuhm-**ply**/ *v.* (**-ies, -ied**) (often foll. by *with*) act in accordance (with a request or command). [Latin *compleo* fill up]

**compo** /**kom**-poh/ *n.* *colloq.* payment or series of payments made under a workers' compensation scheme. □ **on compo** in receipt of workers' compensation. [abbreviation]

**component** /kuhm-**poh**-nuhnt/ — *n.* part of a larger whole, e.g. part of a motor vehicle. — *adj.* being part of a larger whole (*assembled the component parts*). [Latin: related to COMPOUND[1]]

**comport** /kuhm-**pawt**/ *v.refl. literary* conduct oneself; behave (*I would comport myself hysterically were I an early Christian contemplating a lion*). □ **comport with** suit, befit (*such behaviour does not comport with your principles*). □ **comportment** *n.* [Latin *porto* carry]

**compose** /kuhm-**pohz**/ *v.* (**-sing**) **1** create in music or writing. **2** constitute; make up (*a footy team is composed of eighteen players*). **3** arrange artistically, neatly, or for a specified purpose. **4 a** (often *refl.*) calm; settle. **b** (as **composed** *adj.*) calm, self-possessed. **5** *Printing* **a** set up (type). **b** arrange (an article etc.) in type. □ **composed of** made up of, consisting of. □ **composedly** /-zuhd-lee/ *adv.* [French: related to POSE]

■ **Usage** See note at *comprise*.

**composer** *n.* person who composes (esp. music).

**composite** /**kom**-puh-zuht/ — *adj.* **1** made up of parts. **2** of mixed Ionic and Corinthian style. **3** (of a plant) having a head of many flowers forming one bloom (e.g. the daisy). — *n.* composite thing or plant. [Latin: related to COMPOSE]

**composition** /ˌkom-puh-**zish**-uhn/ *n.* **1 a** act or method of putting together; composing. **b** thing composed, esp. music. **2** constitution of a substance (*the composition is two parts oil to one part vinegar*). **3** school essay. **4** artistic arrangement (of the parts of a picture, subjects for a photograph, etc.). **5** compound artificial substance, esp. one serving the purpose of a natural one. **6** mental constitution; character (*jealousy is not in his composition*). **7** *Printing* the setting-up of type. □ **compositional** *adj.*

**compositor** /kuhm-**poz**-uh-tuh/ *n.* person who sets up type for printing. [Latin: related to COMPOSE]

**compos mentis** /ˌkom-pos **men**-tis/ *adj.* sane. [Latin]

**compost** /**kom**-post/ — *n.* mixture of decayed organic matter used for enriching soil. — *v.* **1** treat with compost. **2** make into compost. [Latin: related to COMPOSE]

**composure** /kuhm-**poh**-*zh*uh/ *n.* tranquil manner. [from COMPOSE]

**compote** /**kom**-pot, -poht/ *n.* fruit preserved or cooked in syrup. [French: related to COMPOSE]

**compound¹** /**kom**-pownd/ — *n.* **1** mixture of two or more things, qualities, etc. **2** word made up of two or more existing words, e.g. *spaceship*. **3** substance formed from two or more elements chemically united in fixed proportions. — *adj.* made up of two or more ingredients or parts (*compound word; compound leaf*). — *v.* /kuhm-**pownd**/ **1** mix or combine (ingredients or elements) (*grief compounded with fear*). **2** increase or complicate (difficulties etc.) (*your anxiety is only compounding the problem*). **3** make up (a composite whole). **4** settle (a matter) by mutual agreement. **5** *Law* condone or conceal (a liability or offence) for personal gain. **6** (usu. foll. by *with*) *Law* come to terms with a person. [Latin *compono -pos-* put together]

**compound²** /**kom**-pownd/ *n.* **1** enclosure or fenced-in space. **2** enclosure, esp. in India, China, etc., in which a factory or house stands. [Malay *kampong*]

**compound eye** *n.* eye consisting of numerous visual units, as found in insects and crustaceans.

**compound fracture** *n.* fracture complicated by a skin wound.

**compound interest** *n.* interest payable on capital and its accumulated interest.

**compound leaf** *n.* leaf consisting of many leaflets.

**compound sentence** *n.* sentence with more than one subject or predicate.

**comprehend** /ˌkom-pruh-**hend**/ *v.* **1** grasp mentally; understand. **2** include; take in (*this new TV documentary will comprehend many aspects of multicultural Australia*). [Latin *comprehendo* seize]

**comprehensible** *adj.* that can be understood. [Latin: related to COMPREHEND]

**comprehension** *n.* **1 a** act or capability of understanding. **b** text set as a test of understanding. **2** inclusion.

**comprehensive** — *adj.* **1** including all or nearly all, inclusive (*comprehensive grasp of the subject*). **2** (of motor insurance) providing protection against most risks. — *n.* (in full **comprehensive school**) secondary school for children of all abilities. □ **comprehensively** *adv.* **comprehensiveness** *n.*

**compress** — *v.* /kuhm-**pres**/ **1** squeeze together. **2** bring into a smaller space or shorter time. — *n.* /**kom**-pres/ pad of lint

etc. pressed on to part of the body to relieve inflammation, stop bleeding, etc. □ **compressible** /kuhm-**pres**-uh-buhl/ *adj.* [Latin: related to PRESS¹]

**compression** /kuhm-**presh**-uhn/ *n.* **1** act of compressing or being compressed. **2** reduction in volume of the fuel mixture in an internal-combustion engine before ignition.

**compressor** /kuhm-**pres**-uh/ *n.* machine for compressing air or other gases.

**comprise** /kuhm-**pruyz**/ *v.* (**-sing**) **1** include (*in her own single person she could have comprised the duties of a prime minister and a superintendent of police*). **2** consist of. **3** make up, compose. [French: related to COMPREHEND]

■ **Usage** The use of this word in sense 3 is considered incorrect and *compose* is generally preferred. Thus, while *a football team comprises eighteen players* (sense 2) is acceptable, *a football team is comprised of eighteen players* (sense 3) is considered unacceptable.

**compromise** /**kom**-pruh-ˌmuyz/ — *n.* **1** settlement of a dispute by mutual concession. **2** (often foll. by *between*) intermediate state between conflicting opinions, actions, etc. (*a compromise between ideals and material necessity*). — *v.* (**-sing**) **1 a** settle a dispute by mutual concession. **b** modify one's opinions, demands, etc. **2** bring into disrepute or danger by indiscretion or folly (*compromised his reputation by conversing with a woman taken in adultery*). [Latin: related to PROMISE]

**comptroller** /kuhn-**troh**-luh, komp-/ *n.* controller (used in the title of some financial officers). [var. of CONTROLLER]

**compulsion** /kuhm-**pul**-shuhn/ *n.* **1** obligation; constraint (*I'm under no compulsion to suffer fools gladly*). **2** *Psychol.* irresistible urge to a form of behaviour, esp. against one's conscious wishes. [Latin: related to COMPEL]

**compulsive** /kuhm-**pul**-siv/ *adj.* **1** compelling (*compulsive reasons*). **2 a** resulting or acting (as if) from compulsion (*compulsive gambler*). **b** *Psychol.* resulting or acting from compulsion against one's better wishes. irresistible (*this novel makes for compulsive reading*). □ **compulsively** *adv.* [medieval Latin: related to COMPEL]

**compulsory** /kuhm-**pul**-suh-ree/ *adj.* **1** required by law or a rule. **2** essential; necessary. □ **compulsorily** *adv.*

**compulsory conference** *n.* meeting of parties in an industrial dispute, summoned compulsorily by an industrial tribunal.

**compulsory unionism** *n.* requirement that people are members of the relevant trade union as a precondition of employment.

**compunction** /kuhm-**pungk**-shuhn/ *n.* **1** pricking of conscience. **2** slight regret; scruple (*I had no compunction in refusing him*). [Church Latin: related to POINT]

**compute** /kuhm-**pyoot**/ *v.* (**-ting**) **1** reckon or calculate. **2** use a computer. □ **computation** /‚kom-pyoo-**tay**-shuhn/ *n.* [Latin *puto* reckon]

**computer** *n.* electronic device, usu. digital, for storing and processing data, making calculations, or controlling machinery.

**computerise** *v.* (also **-ize**) (**-sing** or **-zing**) **1** equip with a computer. **2** store, perform, or produce by computer. □ **computerisation** /-**zay**-shuhn/ *n.*

**computer-literate** *adj.* familiar with the operation of computers and hence able to use them efficiently.

**computer science** *n.* the study of the principles and use of computers.

**computer virus** *n.* self-replicating code maliciously introduced into a computer program and intended to corrupt the system or destroy data.

**comrade** /**kom**-rayd, -ruhd/ *n.* **1** associate or companion in some activity; friend, mate. **2** fellow socialist or Communist; fellow member of the Australian Labor Party (often as a form of address). □ **comradely** *adj.* **comradeship** *n.* [Spanish: related to CHAMBER]

**con**[1] *colloq.* — *n.* confidence trick. — *v.* (**-nn-**) swindle; deceive, trick (*he conned me into doing it*). [abbreviation]

**con**[2] — *n.* (usu. in *pl.*) reason against (*the pros and cons*). — *prep. & adv.* against (cf. PRO[2]). [Latin *contra* against]

**con**[3] *n. colloq.* convict. [abbreviation]

**con**[4] *v.* (**-nn-**) *archaic* study, learn by heart (*he conned his part well*). [from CAN[1]]

**con-** see COM-.

**con-artist** *n.* = CON MAN.

**concatenate** /kuhn-**kat**-uh-‚nayt/ — *v.* link together (a chain of events, things, computer data, etc.). — *adj.* joined; linked. □ **concatenation** *n.* [Latin *catena* chain]

**concave** /**kon**-kayv/ *adj.* curved like the interior of a circle or sphere (cf. CONVEX). □ **concavity** /-**kav**-uh-tee/ *n.* [Latin: related to CAVE]

**conceal** /kuhn-**seel**/ *v.* **1** keep secret (*concealed his true motives*). **2** hide (*concealed the letter in his pocket*). □ **concealment** *n.* [Latin *celo* hide]

**concede** /kuhn-**seed**/ *v.* (**-ding**) **1** admit to be true (*conceded that he was at fault*). **2** admit defeat (in) (*with 70% of the votes counted, the Leader of the Opposition has conceded the election; has he conceded yet?*). **3** grant, yield, or surrender (a right, privilege, etc.) (*conceded the point to his opponent*). **4** *Sport* allow an opponent to score (a goal) or to win (a match). [Latin: related to CEDE]

**conceit** /kuhn-**seet**/ *n.* **1** personal vanity; pride. **2** *literary* **a** far-fetched comparison; complex or surprising metaphor (*'the Antipodes in shoes / Have shod their heads in their canoes' is a conceit that doesn't work*). **b** fanciful notion. [from CONCEIVE]

**conceited** *adj.* vain, proud. □ **conceitedly** *adv.*

**conceivable** /kuhn-**see**-vuh-buhl/ *adj.* capable of being grasped or imagined; understandable. □ **conceivably** *adv.*

**conceive** /kuhn-**seev**/ *v.* (**-ving**) **1** become pregnant (with). **2 a** (often foll. by *of*) imagine, think (*can't conceive of that ever happening*). **b** (usu. in *passive*) formulate (a belief, plan, etc.) (*the plan was conceived in too much haste*). [Latin *concipio -cept-*]

**concelebrate** /kon-**sel**-uh-‚brayt/ *v. RC Ch* **1** (of two or more priests) celebrate the Mass together. **2** (esp. of a newly ordained priest) celebrate the Mass with the ordaining bishop. □ **concelebrant** /-**bruhnt**/ *n.* **concelebration** /-**bray**-shuhn/ *n.* [COM-, CELEBRATE]

**concentrate** /**kon**-suhn-‚trayt/ — *v.* (**-ting**) **1** (often foll. by *on*) focus one's attention or thought (*I can't concentrate; concentrated on the problem*). **2** bring together (troops, power, attention, etc.) to one point; focus (*he concentrated all his energy on the problem*). **3** increase the strength of (a liquid etc.) by removing water etc. **4** (as **concentrated** *adj.*) intense, strong. — *n.* concentrated substance. [Latin: related to CENTRE]

**concentration** /‚kon-suhn-**tray**-shuhn/ *n.* **1 a** act or power of concentrating (*needs to develop concentration*). **b** instance of this; mental attention (*interrupted my concentration*). **2** something concentrated (*a concentration of resources*). **3** weight of a substance in a given amount of material.

**concentration camp** *n.* camp where political prisoners, racial groups, etc., are detained, esp. in Nazi Germany for the mass extermination of Jews etc.

**concentric** /kuhn-**sen**-trik/ *adj.* (esp. of circles) having a common centre. □ **concentrically** *adv.* **concentricity** /‚kon-sen-**tris**-uh-tee/ *n.* [French or medieval Latin: related to CENTRE]

**concept** /**kon**-sept/ *n.* **1** general notion; abstract idea (*the concept of evolution*). **2** *colloq.* idea or invention to help sell or publicise a commodity (*a new concept in swimwear*). [Latin: related to CONCEIVE]

**conception** /kuhn-**sep**-shuhn/ *n.* **1** act or instance of conceiving or the process of being conceived. **2** idea, plan (*the whole conception showed originality*). **3** understanding (*has no conception*). □ **conceptional** *adj.* **conceptive** *adj.* [French from Latin: related to CONCEPT]

**conceptual** /kuhn-**sep**-choo-uhl/ *adj.* of mental conceptions or concepts. □ **conceptually** *adv.*

**conceptualise** /kuhn-**sep**-choo-uh-,luyz/ *v.* (also -**ize**) (-**sing** or -**zing**) form a concept or idea of. □ **conceptualisation** /-**zay**-shuhn/ *n.*

**concern** /kuhn-**sern**/ — *v.* **1 a** be relevant or important to (*this concerns you*). **b** relate to; be about. **2** (*refl.*; often foll. by *with*, *about*, *in*) interest or involve oneself (*don't concern yourself with my problems*). **3** worry, affect (*it concerns me that he is always so tired*). — *n.* **1** anxiety, worry. **2 a** matter of interest or importance to one (*no concern of mine*). **b** interest, connection (*has a concern in politics*). **3** business, firm (*a prosperous concern*). [Latin *cerno* sift]

**concerned** *adj.* **1** involved, interested (*the people concerned; concerned with proving his innocence*). **2** troubled, anxious (*concerned about him*). □ **be concerned** (often foll. by *in*) take part.

**concerning** *prep.* about, regarding.

**concert** /**kon**-suht/ — *n.* **1 a** musical performance of usu. several separate compositions. **b** series of entertainments including musical items, comedy sketches, etc. (*school concert*). **2** agreement, accord, harmony. — *v.* /kuhn-**sert**/ arrange (by mutual agreement or coordination) (*concerted their efforts to get the project completed in time*). □ **in concert 1** (often foll. by *with*) acting jointly. **2** (*predic.*) (of a musician) in a performance. [Italian: related to CONCERTO]

**concerted** /kuhn-**ser**-tuhd/ *adj.* **1** jointly arranged or planned (*a concerted effort*). **2** *Mus.* arranged in parts for voices or instruments.

**concertina** /,kon-suh-**tee**-nuh/ — *n.* **1** musical instrument like an accordion but smaller. **2** *colloq.* a side of lamb. — *v.* (-**nas**, -**naed** /-nuhd/ -**naing**) compress or collapse in folds like those of a concertina.

**concertise** /**kon**-ser-tuyz/ *v.* (also -**ize**) (-**sing** or -**zing**) give a concert-performance of music (*he has concertised in Australia as well as in Europe*).

**concerto** /kuhn-**sher**-toh, -**cher**-toh/ *n.* (*pl.* -**s** or -**ti** /-tee/) composition for solo instrument(s) and orchestra. [Italian]

**concert pitch** *n.* **1** pitch internationally agreed whereby A above middle C = 440 Hz. **2** state of unusual readiness, efficiency, and keenness (for action etc.).

**concession** /kuhn-**sesh**-uhn/ *n.* **1 a** act or instance of conceding (*made no concession that we were right*). **b** thing conceded. **2** reduction in price for a certain category of persons. **3 a** right to use land etc. **b** right to sell goods in a particular territory. □ **concessionary** *adj.* [Latin: related to CONCEDE]

**concessive** /kuhn-**ses**-iv/ *adj. Gram.* (of a preposition or conjunction) introducing a phrase or clause which contrasts with the main clause (e.g. *in spite of*, *although*). [Latin: related to CONCEDE]

**conch** /konch/ *n.* **1** thick heavy spiral shell of various marine gastropod molluscs. **2** any such gastropod. [Latin *concha*]

**conchie** /**kon**-chee/ *n.* (also **conchy**) (*pl.* -**ies**) *colloq. derog.* conscientious objector. [abbreviation]

**conchology** /kong-**kol**-uh-jee/ *n.* the study of shells. [from CONCH]

**concierge** /,kon-see-**airzh**/ *n.* (esp. in France) door-keeper or porter of a block of flats etc. [French]

**conciliate** /kuhn-**sil**-ee-,ayt/ *v.* (-**ting**) **1** make calm and amenable; pacify; gain the goodwill of. **2** reconcile. **3** (esp. in a dispute between employers and employees) attempt to bring disputing parties to an agreement. □ **conciliation** /kuhn-,sil-ee-**ay**-shuhn/ *n.* **conciliator** *n.* **conciliatory** /-**sil**-yuh-tuh-ree, -tree/ *adj.* [Latin: related to COUNCIL]

**concise** /kuhn-**suys**/ *adj.* brief but comprehensive in expression and treatment (*a concise statement of our aims*; *The Australian Concise Oxford Dictionary*). □ **concisely** *adv.* **conciseness** *n.* **concision** /kuhn-**sizh**-uhn/ *n.* [Latin *caedo* cut]

**conclave** /**kon**-klayv/ *n.* **1** private meeting. **2** *RC Ch.* **a** assembly of cardinals for the election of a pope. **b** meeting-place for this, a building etc. into which the cardinals are locked until the new pope is elected. [Latin *clavis* key]

**conclude** /kuhn-**klood**/ *v.* (-**ding**) **1** bring or come to an end. **2** (often foll. by *from* or *that*) infer (*concluded from the evidence that he had been mistaken*). **3**

settle, arrange (a treaty etc.). [Latin *concludo*: related to CLOSE[1]]

**conclusion** /kuhn-**kloo**-*zh*uhn/ *n.* **1** an ending, end; final result. **2** judgment reached by reasoning. **3** summing-up of an argument, book, etc. **4** settling (of peace etc.). **5** *Logic* proposition reached from given premises. □ **in conclusion** lastly, to conclude. [Latin: related to CONCLUDE]

**conclusive** /kuhn-**kloo**-siv/ *adj.* decisive, convincing (*conclusive proof*). □ **conclusively** *adv.* [Latin: related to CONCLUDE]

**concoct** /kuhn-**kokt**/ *v.* **1** make by mixing ingredients (*concocted a stew*). **2** invent (a story, lie, etc.). □ **concoction** /-**kok**-shuhn/ *n.* [Latin *coquo coct-* cook]

**concomitance** /kuhn-**kom**-uh-tuhns/ *n. Theol.* doctrine that both the body and the blood of Christ are present in the consecrated bread as well as in the consecrated wine.

**concomitant** /kuhn-**kom**-uh-tuhnt/ — *adj.* (often foll. by *with*) associated; accompanying; occurring together (*concomitant circumstances*; *malnutrition as concomitant with poverty*). — *n.* accompanying thing (*luxury is a concomitant of wealth*). □ **concomitance** *n.* [Latin *comes comit-* companion]

**concord** /**kon**-kawd, **kong**-/ *n.* agreement, harmony. □ **concordant** /kuhn-**kaw**-duhnt/ *adj.* [Latin *cor cord-* heart]

**concordance** /kuhn-**kaw**-duhns, -kuhng-/ *n.* **1** agreement. **2** alphabetical index of words used in a book or by an author. □ **concordant** *n.* [medieval Latin: related to CONCORD]

**concordat** /kuhn-**kaw**-dat, kong-/ *n.* agreement, esp. between the Vatican and a nation. [Latin: related to CONCORD]

**concourse** /**kon**-kaws, kong-/ *n.* **1** crowd, gathering. **2** a coming together (*a concourse of ideas*). **3** open central area in a large public building, a railway station, etc. [Latin: related to CONCUR]

**concrete** /**kon**-kreet, **kong**-/ — *adj.* **1 a** existing in a material form; real. **b** specific, definite (*concrete evidence*; *a concrete proposal*). **2** *Gram.* (of a noun) denoting a material object as opposed to an abstract quality, state, or action. — *n.* often *attrib.*) mixture of gravel, sand, cement, and water, used for building. — *v.* (**-ting**) **1** cover with or embed in concrete. **2** form into a mass; solidify. Latin *cresco cret-* grow]

**concretion** /kuhn-**kree**-shuhn/ *n.* **1 a** hard solid mass. **b** forming of this by coalescence. **2** *Geol.* small round mass of

rock particles embedded in limestone or clay. [Latin: related to CONCRETE]

**concubine** /**kong**-kyoo-,buyn/ *n.* **1** *literary* or *joc.* mistress. **2** (among polygamous peoples) secondary wife. □ **concubinage** /kuhn-**kyoo**-buh-nij, kon-/ *n.* [Latin *cubo* lie]

**concupiscence** /kon-**kyoo**-puh-suhns/ *n. formal* lust. □ **concupiscent** *adj.* [Latin *cupio* desire]

**concur** /kuhn-**ker**/ *v.* (**-rr-**) **1** (often foll. by *with*) have the same opinion. **2** happen together; coincide. [Latin *curro* run]

**concurrent** /kuhn-**ku**-ruhnt/ *adj.* **1** (often foll. by *with*) existing or in operation at the same time or together (*the judge ordered him to serve two concurrent sentences*). **2** *Geom.* (of three or more lines) meeting at or tending towards one point. **3** agreeing, harmonious. □ **concurrence** *n.* **concurrently** *adv.*

**concuss** /kuhn-**kus**, kuhng-/ *v.* subject to concussion. [Latin *quatio* shake]

**concussion** /kuhn-**kush**-uhn, kuhng-/ *n.* **1** temporary unconsciousness or incapacity due to a blow to the head, a fall, etc. **2** violent shaking.

**condemn** /kuhn-**dem**/ *v.* **1** express utter disapproval of (*condemned smoking in public places*). **2 a** find guilty; convict. **b** (usu. foll. by *to*) sentence to (a punishment). **3** pronounce (a building etc.) unfit for use. **4** (usu. foll. by *to*) doom or assign (to something unpleasant) (*condemned to spending hours at the kitchen sink*). □ **condemnation** /,kon-dem-**nay**-shuhn/ *n.* **condemnatory** /kuhn-**dem**-nuh-tuh-ree, kon-dem-**nay**-tuh-ree, -tree/ *adj.* [Latin: related to DAMN]

**condensation** /,kon-den-**say**-shuhn/ *n.* **1** act of condensing or being condensed. **2** condensed liquid (esp. water on a cold surface). **3** abridgment. **4** *Chem.* combination of molecules with the elimination of water or other small molecules. [Latin: related to CONDENSE]

**condense** /kuhn-**dens**/ *v.* (**-sing**) **1** make denser or more concentrated. **2** express in fewer words. **3** reduce or be reduced from a gas or vapour to a liquid. [Latin: related to DENSE]

**condenser** *n.* **1** apparatus or vessel for condensing vapour. **2** *Electr.* = CAPACITOR. **3** lens or system of lenses for concentrating light.

**condescend** /,kon-duh-**send**/ *v.* **1** be gracious enough (to do a thing) esp. while showing one's sense of dignity or superiority (*condescended to attend*). **2** (foll. by *to*) pretend to be on equal terms with (an inferior), usu. while maintaining an attitude of superiority. **3** (as

**condescending** *adj.*) patronising. □ **condescendingly** *adv.* **condescension** /ˌkon-duh-**sen**-shuhn/ *n.* [Latin: related to DESCEND]

**condign** /kuhn-**duyn**/ *adj.* (of a punishment etc.) severe and well-deserved. [Latin *dignus* worthy]

**condiment** /**kon**-duh-muhnt/ *n.* seasoning or relish for food. [Latin *condio* pickle]

**condition** /kuhn-**dish**-uhn/ — *n.* **1** stipulation; thing upon the fulfilment of which something else depends. **2 a** state of being or fitness of a person or thing (*arrived in bad condition*). **b** ailment, abnormality (*heart condition*). **3** (in *pl.*) circumstances, esp. those affecting the functioning or existence of something (*good working conditions*). — *v.* **1 a** bring into a good or desired state (*his trainer has conditioned him well for the fight*). **b** make fit (esp. dogs or horses). **2** teach or accustom to adopt certain habits etc. (*conditioned by society*). **3** govern; influence (*his behaviour was conditioned by his drunkenness*). **4 a** impose conditions on. **b** be essential to (*the two things condition each other*). □ **in** (or **out of**) **condition** in good (or bad) condition. **on condition that** with the stipulation that. [Latin *dico* say]

**conditional** *adj.* **1** (often foll. by *on*) dependent; not absolute; containing a condition (*a conditional offer*). **2** *Gram.* (of a clause, mood, etc.) expressing a condition. □ **conditionally** *adv.* [Latin: related to CONDITION]

**conditional emancipation** *n.* (also **conditional pardon**) *hist.* remission of a convict's sentence subject to certain conditions, but always precluding return to the British Isles until the expiration of the original sentence.

**conditioned reflex** *n.* reflex response to a non-natural stimulus, established by training.

**conditioner** *n.* agent that conditions, esp. the hair.

**condole** /kuhn-**dohl**/ *v.* (**-ling**) (foll. by *with*) express sympathy with (a person) over a loss etc. □ **condolatory** /kuhn-**doh**-luh-tuh-ree, -tree/ *adj.* **condolingly** *adv.* [Latin *condoleo* grieve with another]

■ **Usage** Condole is often confused with *console*[1].

**condolence** *n.* (often in *pl.*) expression of sympathy.

**condom** /**kon**-dom/ *n.* rubber etc. sheath worn on the penis during sexual intercourse as a contraceptive or to prevent infection. [origin unknown]

**condominium** /ˌkon-duh-**min**-ee-uhm/ *n.* **1 a** joint control of a nation's affairs by other nations. **b** joint rule or sovereignty. **2** building containing individually owned flats. [Latin *dominium* lordship]

**condone** /kuhn-**dohn**/ *v.* (**-ning**) **1** forgive or overlook (an offence or wrongdoing) (*I cannot condone what you did*). **2** approve or sanction, usu. reluctantly (*condoned the use of force against the demonstrators*). [Latin *dono* give]

**condor** /**kon**-daw/ *n.* large S. American vulture. [Spanish from Quechua]

**conduce** /kuhn-**dyoos**/ *v.* (**-cing**) (foll. by *to*) contribute to (a result) (*practices such as walking which conduce to health*). [Latin: related to CONDUCT]

**conducive** *adj.* (often foll. by *to*) contributing or helping (toward something) (*smoking is not conducive to good health*).

**conduct** — *n.* /**kon**-dukt/ **1** behaviour (esp. in its moral aspect). **2** activity or manner of directing or managing (a business, war, etc.) (*cut many corners in the conduct of his affairs*). — *v.* /kuhn-**dukt**/ **1** lead or guide. **2** direct or manage (a business etc.). **3** (also *absol.*) be the conductor of (an orchestra etc.). **4** transmit (heat, electricity, etc.) by conduction. **5** *refl.* behave (*it all depends on how you conduct yourself*). [Latin *duct-* duct- lead]

**conductance** /kuhn-**duk**-tuhns/ *n.* power of a specified material to conduct electricity.

**conduction** /kuhn-**duk**-shuhn/ *n.* transmission of heat, electricity, etc. through a substance. [Latin: related to CONDUCT]

**conductive** /kuhn-**duk**-tiv/ *adj.* transmitting (esp. heat, electricity, etc). □ **conductivity** /ˌkon-duk-**tiv**-uh-tee/ *n.*

**conductor** *n.* **1** person who directs an orchestra etc. **2** person who collects fares in a bus etc. **3** thing that conducts heat or electricity. [Latin: related to CONDUCT]

**conduit** /**kon**-dit, **kon**-joo-uht/ *n.* **1** channel or pipe conveying liquids. **2** tube or trough protecting insulated electric wires. [medieval Latin: related to CONDUCT]

**cone** *n.* **1** solid figure with a circular (or other curved) plane base, tapering to a point. **2** thing of similar shape (*ice-cream cone*). **3** dry fruit of a conifer. **4** any of the minute cone-shaped structures in the retina. [Latin from Greek]

**conesticks** *n.* any of about 40 species of plants in the endemic WA genus *Petrophile*, having extremely showy flowers in colours of cream, pink, and yellow, foll. by striking woody cones.

**confabulate** /kuhn-**fab**-yoo-ˌlayt/ v. (**-ting**) converse, chat. □ **confabulation** /-**lay**-shuhn/ n. [Latin: related to FABLE]

**confection** /kuhn-**fek**-shuhn/ n. dish or delicacy made with sweet ingredients. [Latin *conficio* prepare]

**confectioner** n. maker or retailer of confectionery.

**confectionery** n. confections, esp. sweets.

**confederacy** /kuhn-**fed**-uh-ruh-see/ n. (*pl.* **-ies**) **1** league or alliance, esp. of confederate States. **2** league for an unlawful or evil purpose. [French: related to CONFEDERATE]

**confederate** /kuhn-**fed**-uh-ruht/ — *adj.* esp. *Polit.* allied. — *n.* ally, esp. (in a bad sense) accomplice. — *v.* /-ˌrayt/ (**-ting**) (often foll. by *with*) bring or come into alliance. [Latin: related to FEDERAL]

**confederation** /kuhn-ˌfed-uh-**ray**-shuhn/ n. **1** union or alliance, esp. of States. **2** act or instance of confederating or the state of being confederated.

**confer** /kuhn-**fer**/ v. (**-rr-**) **1** (often foll. by *on, upon*) grant or bestow (*conferred on her the degree of Doctor of Laws*). **2** (often foll. by *with*) converse, consult (*I need to confer with you about this case*). □ **conferrable** *adj.* [Latin *confero* collat- bring together]

**conference** /**kon**-fuh-ruhns/ n. **1** consultation. **2** meeting for discussion. □ **conferential** /ˌkon-fuh-**ren**-shuhl/ *adj.* [French or medieval Latin: related to CONFER]

**conferment** /kuhn-**fer**-muhnt/ n. conferring of a degree, honour, etc.

**confess** /kuhn-**fes**/ v. **1 a** (also *absol.*) acknowledge or admit (a fault, crime, etc.) (*I confess; he confessed his guilt*). **b** (foll. by *to*) admit to (*confessed to having lied*). **2** admit reluctantly (*confessed it would be difficult*). **3 a** (also *absol.*) declare (one's sins) to a priest in the sacrament of penance (*confessed to Fr. Smith*). **b** (of a priest) hear the confession of (*Fr. Smith confessed me this morning*). [Latin *confiteor -fess-*]

**confessedly** /kuhn-**fes**-uhd-lee/ *adv.* by one's own or general admission.

**confession** /kuhn-**fesh**-uhn/ n. **1 a** act of confessing (*the suspect has made a full confession*). **b** thing confessed. **2 a** the sacrament of penance (*went to confession at Our Lady's*). **b** act of confessing to a priest as part of this sacrament. **3** (in full **confession of faith**) declaration of one's beliefs or principles.

**confessional** — n. enclosed stall in a church in which the priest hears confessions. — *adj.* of or relating to confession.

**confessor** n. **1** *Eccl.* priest who hears confessions and is empowered to give absolution. **2** person who confesses to a crime.

**confetti** /kuhn-**fet**-ee/ n. small bits of coloured paper thrown by wedding guests at the bride and groom. [Italian]

**confidant** /ˌkon-fuh-**dant**, **kon**-/ n. (*fem.* **confidante** pronunc. same) person trusted with knowledge of one's private affairs. [related to CONFIDE]

**confide** /kuhn-**fuyd**/ v. (**-ding**) **1** (foll. by *in*) talk confidentially to (*confided in her*). **2** (usu. foll. by *to*) tell (a secret etc.) in confidence. **3** (foll. by *to*) entrust (an object of care, a task, etc.) to. [Latin *confido* trust]

**confidence** /**kon**-fuh-duhns/ n. **1** firm trust. **2 a** feeling of reliance or certainty. **b** sense of self-reliance; boldness. **3** something told as a secret. □ **in confidence** as a secret. **in a person's confidence** trusted with a person's secrets. **take into one's confidence** confide in. [Latin: related to CONFIDE]

**confidence man** n. man who robs by means of a confidence trick.

**confidence trick** n. swindle in which the victim is persuaded to trust the swindler. □ **confidence trickster** n.

**confident** *adj.* **1** feeling or showing confidence; bold (*spoke with a confident air*). **2** assured, trusting (*confident of your support; confident that he will come*). □ **confidently** *adv.* [Italian: related to CONFIDE]

**confidential** /ˌkon-fuh-**den**-shuhl/ *adj.* **1** spoken or written in confidence. **2** entrusted with secrets (*confidential secretary*). **3** confiding (*spoke in a quiet and confidential tone*). □ **confidentiality** /-shee-al-uh-tee/ n. **confidentially** *adv.*

**configuration** /kuhn-ˌfig-yoo-**ray**-shuhn, -uh-**ray**-shuhn/ n. **1** arrangement in a particular form. **2** form or figure resulting from this. **3** relative position of planets etc. **4** fixed three-dimensional relationship of the atoms in a molecule. **5** *Computing* hardware and its arrangement of connections etc. □ **configurational** *adj.* **configure** v. (**-ring**). [Latin: related to FIGURE]

**confine** — v. /kuhn-**fuyn**/ (**-ning**) **1** keep or restrict (within certain limits) (*confined the fire to that one building*; *is confined to bed*). **2** hold captive; imprison. — n. /**kon**-fuyn/ (usu. in *pl.*) limit, boundary (*within the confines of the town*). [Latin *finis* limit]

**confinement** n. **1** act or instance of confining or state of being confined. **2** time of childbirth.

**confirm** /kuhn-**ferm**/ v. **1** provide support for the truth or correctness of (*confirmed my suspicions*). **2** (foll. by *in*) encourage (a person) in (an opinion etc.) (*it merely confirmed him in his obstinacy*). **3** establish more firmly (power, possession, etc.) (*her success has confirmed her control of the board*). **4** make (a treaty, agreement, etc.) formally valid. **5** administer the religious rite of confirmation to. [Latin: related to FIRM[1]]

**confirmation** /ˌkon-fuh-**may**-shuhn/ n. **1** act or instance of confirming or state of being confirmed. **2 a** sacrament or rite, administered by a bishop in some Churches, confirming a baptised person, esp. at the age of discretion, as a member of a particular Christian Church. **b** ceremony of confirming persons of about this age in the Jewish faith.

**confirmed** adj. firmly settled in some habit or condition (*confirmed bachelor; confirmed in his ways*).

**confiscate** /**kon**-fuhs-ˌkayt/ v. (**-ting**) take or seize by authority. □ **confiscation** /-**kay**-shuhn/ n. [Latin: related to FISCAL]

**conflagration** /ˌkon-fluh-**gray**-shuhn/ n. great and destructive fire. [Latin: related to FLAGRANT]

**conflate** /kuhn-**flayt**/ v. (**-ting**) blend or fuse together (esp. two variant texts into one). □ **conflation** /-**flay**-shuhn/ n. [Latin *flo flat*- blow]

**conflict** — n. /**kon**-flikt/ **1 a** state of opposition (*parent-child conflicts*). **b** fight, struggle (*conflict in the Middle East*). **2** (often foll. by *of*) clashing of opposed interests, principles, etc. — v. /kuhn-**flikt**/ **1** clash; be incompatible. **2** (as **conflicting** adj.) contradictory (*gave conflicting accounts*). [Latin *fligo flict*-strike]

**confluence** /**kon**-floo-uhns/ n. **1** place where two rivers meet. **2 a** coming together. **b** crowd of people. □ **confluent** adj. [Latin *fluo* flow]

**conform** /kuhn-**fawm**/ v. **1** comply with rules or general custom. **2** (foll. by *to, with*) comply with; be in accordance with (*what you've knitted doesn't conform to the pattern*). **3** (often foll. by *to*) be or make suitable. [Latin: related to FORM]

**conformable** adj. **1** (often foll. by *to*) similar. **2** (often foll. by *with*) consistent. **3** (often foll. by *to*) adaptable.

**conformation** /ˌkon-fuh-**may**-shuhn/ n. way a thing is formed; shape.

**conformist** /kuhn-**faw**-muhst/ — n. person who conforms to an established practice; conventional person. — adj. conforming, conventional. □ **conformism** n.

**conformity** n. **1** accordance with established practice. **2** agreement, suitability.

**confound** /kuhn-**fownd**/ — v. **1** perplex, baffle (*confounded by conflicting instructions*). **2** mix up; confuse (in one's mind) (*confounding truth with falsehood*). **3** archaic defeat, overthrow (*his hopes were quite confounded*). — int. expressing annoyance (*confound you!*). [Latin *confundo -fus-* mix up]

**confounded** attrib. adj. colloq. damned.

**confront** /kuhn-**frunt**/ v. **1 a** face in hostility or defiance (*he confronted the angry mob*). **b** face up to and deal with (*confronted the problem squarely*). **2** (of a difficulty etc.) present itself to (*countless obstacles confronted us*). **3** (foll. by *with*) bring (a person) face to face with (an accusation etc.) (*confronted him with the charge*). **4** meet or stand facing. □ **confrontation** /ˌkon-fruhn-**tay**-shuhn/ n. **confrontational** /ˌkon-fruhn-**tay**-shuh-nuhl/ adj. [French from medieval Latin]

**Confucian** /kuhn-**fyoo**-shuhn/ adj. of Confucius or his philosophy □ **Confucianism** n. [*Confucius*, name of a Chinese philosopher]

**confuse** /kuhn-**fyooz**/ v. (**-sing**) **1** perplex, bewilder (*the shouting confused her*). **2** mix up in the mind; mistake (one for another) (*he always confuses me with my brother*). **3** make indistinct (*that point confuses the issue*). **4** (often as **confused** adj.) throw into disorder (a confused jumble of clothes). □ **confusedly** /kuhn-**fyoo**-zuhd-lee/ adv. **confusing** adj. [related to CONFOUND]

**confusion** n. **1 a** act of confusing (*the confusion of fact and fiction*). **b** an instance of this; a misunderstanding (*confusions arise from a lack of communication*). **2 a** confused state; disorder (*thrown into confusion by his words*). **b** (foll. by *of*) disorderly jumble (*a confusion of ideas*). **3 a** civil commotion (*confusion broke out at the announcement*). **b** instance of this.

**confute** /kuhn-**fyoot**/ v. (**-ting**) prove (a person or argument) to be in error □ **confutation** /ˌkon-fyoo-**tay**-shuhn/ n. [Latin]

**conga** /**kong**-guh/ n. **1** Latin-American dance, with a line of dancers one behind the other. **2** tall narrow drum beaten with the hands. [Spanish *conga* (feminine), = of the Congo]

**congeal** /kuhn-**jeel**/ v. **1** make or become semi-solid by cooling. **2** (of blood etc.

coagulate. □ **congealment** n. **congelation** /ˌkon-juh-**lay**-shuhn/ n. [French from Latin *gelo* freeze]

**congener** /kuhn-**jee**-nuh, **kon**-juh-nuh/ n. thing or person of the same kind or category as another, esp. animals or plants of a specified genus. □ **congeneric** /ˌkon-juh-**ne**-rik/ [Latin: related to GENUS]

**congenial** /kuhn-**jee**-nee-uhl/ adj. **1** pleasant because akin to oneself in temperament or interests (*congenial companions*). **2** (often foll. by *to*) suited or agreeable (*found Canberra congenial to them*). □ **congeniality** /-al-uh-tee/ n. **congenially** adv. [from COM-, GENIAL]

**congenital** /kuhn-**jen**-uh-tuhl/ adj. **1** (esp. of disease) existing from birth. **2** as (or as if) such from birth (*congenital liar*). □ **congenitally** adv. [Latin: related to COM-]

**conger** /**kong**-guh/ n. large marine eel. [Greek *goggros*]

**congest** /kuhn-**jest**/ v. (esp. as **congested** adj.) affect with congestion (*congested streets*; *congested lungs from smoking*). [Latin *congero* -*gest*- heap together]

**congestion** /kuhn-**jes**-chuhn/ n. abnormal accumulation or obstruction, esp. of traffic etc. or of blood or mucus in part of the body.

**conglomerate** /kuhn-**glom**-uh-ruht/ — adj. **1** gathered into a rounded mass. **2** *Geol.* (of rock) made up of small stones held together. — n. **1** number of things or parts forming a heterogeneous mass. **2** group or corporation of merged firms. **3** *Geol.* conglomerate rock. — v. /kuhn-**glom**-uh-ˌrayt/ (-**ting**) collect into a coherent mass. □ **conglomeration** /kuhn-ˌglom-uh-**ray**-shuhn/ n. [Latin *glomus* -*eris* ball]

**congolli** /kuhng-**goh**-lee/ n. = TUPONG. [probably from an Aboriginal language]

**congratulate** /kuhn-**grach**-uh-ˌlayt, kuhng-/ v. (-**ting**) (often foll. by *on*) **1** express pleasure at the happiness, good fortune, or excellence of (a person). **2** *refl.* think oneself fortunate or clever. □ **congratulatory** /-uh-luh-tree, -uh-**lay**-tuh-ree/ adj. [Latin *gratus* pleasing]

**congratulation** /kuhn-ˌgrach-uh-**lay**-shuhn, kuhng-/ n. **1** congratulating. **2** (usu. in *pl.*) expression of this (*congratulations on winning!*).

**congregate** /**kong**-gruh-ˌgayt/ v. (-**ting**) collect or gather into a crowd. [Latin *grex greg-* flock]

**congregation** /ˌkong-gruh-**gay**-shuhn/ n. **1** process of congregating; collection into a crowd or mass. **2** gathering of people, esp. for religious worship. **3** body of persons regularly attending a particular church etc. **4** committee of the College

of Cardinals. [Latin: related to CONGREGATE]

**congregational** adj. **1** of a congregation. **2** (**Congregational**) of or adhering to Congregationalism.

**Congregationalism** n. system whereby individual Protestant congregations are largely self-governing. □ **Congregationalist** n.

**congress** /**kong**-gres/ n. formal meeting of delegates (from societies, nations, etc.) for discussion. □ **congressional** /kuhn-**gresh**-uh-nuhl/ adj. [Latin *gradior gress-* walk]

**congruent** /**kong**-groo-uhnt/ adj. **1** (often foll. by *with*) suitable, agreeing. **2** *Geom.* (of figures) coinciding exactly when superimposed. □ **congruence** n. **congruency** n. [Latin *congruo* agree]

**congruous** /**kong**-groo-uhs/ adj. (often foll. by *with*) suitable, agreeing; fitting. □ **congruity** /-**groo**-uh-tee/ n. [Latin: related to CONGRUENT]

**conic** /**kon**-ik/ adj. of a cone. [Greek: related to CONE]

**conical** adj. cone-shaped.

**conifer** /**kon**-uh-fuh/, n. evergreen tree usu. bearing cones, including pines, firs, cedars, etc. □ **coniferous** /kuh-**nif**-uh-ruhs, ko-/ adj. [Latin: related to CONE]

**conjectural** /kuhn-**jek**-chuh-ruhl/ adj. based on conjecture.

**conjecture** /kuhn-**jek**-chuh/ — n. **1** formation of an opinion on incomplete information; guessing. **2** opinion or conclusion reached in this way; guess. — v. (-**ring**) guess. [Latin *conjectura* from *jacio* throw]

**conjoin** /kuhn-**join**/ v. *formal* join, combine.

**conjoint** /kuhn-**joint**/ adj. *formal* associated, conjoined.

**conjugal** /**kon**-juh-guhl/ adj. of marriage or the relationship of husband and wife. [Latin *conjux* -*jug*- consort]

**conjugate** — v. /**kon**-juh-ˌgayt/ (-**ting**) **1** *Gram.* list the different forms of (a verb). **2 a** unite sexually. **b** (of gametes) become fused. — adj. /**kon**-juh-guht/ **1** joined together, paired. **2** fused. [Latin *jugum* yoke]

**conjugation** /ˌkon-juh-**gay**-shuhn/ n. *Gram.* system of verbal inflection.

**conjunct** /kuhn-**jungkt**, kon-/ adj. joined together; combined; associated. [Latin from *junctus* joined]

**conjunction** /kuhn-**jungk**-shuhn/ n. **1** action of joining or condition of being joined; connection. **2** *Gram.* word used to connect clauses or sentences or words in the same clause (see panel). **3** combination (of events or circumstances). **4**

alignment of two bodies in the solar system so that they have the same longitude as seen from earth.

**conjunctiva** /ˌkon-jungk-**tuy**-vuh/ *n.* (*pl.* **-s**) mucous membrane covering the front of the eye and the lining inside the eyelids.

**conjunctive** /kuhn-**jungk**-tiv/ *adj.* **1** serving to join. **2** *Gram.* of the nature of a conjunction.

**conjunctivitis** /kuhn-ˌjungk-tuh-**vuy**-tuhs/ *n.* inflammation of the conjunctiva.

**conjure** /**kun**-juh/ *v.* (**-ring**) **1** perform tricks which are seemingly magical, esp. by movements of the hands. **2** (usu. foll. by *out of, away, to,* etc.) cause to appear or disappear as if by magic (*conjured a rabbit out of a hat; his pain was conjured away*). **3** summon (a spirit or demon) to appear. **4** /kuhn-**joor**/ *formal* appeal solemnly to (*conjured them to keep the peace*). □ **conjure up 1** produce as if by magic. **2** evoke. [Latin *juro* swear]

**conjuror** /**kun**-juh-ruh/ *n.* (also **conjurer**) performer of conjuring tricks.

**conk**[1] *v.* (usu. foll. by *out*) *colloq.* **1** (of a machine etc.) break down. **2** (of a person) become exhausted and give up; fall asleep; faint; die (*he conked out on the sofa*). [origin unknown]

**conk**[2] *colloq.* — *n.* **1** nose or head. **2** punch on the nose or head. — *v.* hit on the nose or head (*I'll conk you one*). [perhaps = CONCH]

**conkerberry** /**kong**-kuh-be-ree/ *n.* either of two spiny shrubs or small trees of the genus *Carissa,* occurring mostly in northern regions of Australia, having round leaves, perfumed flowers, and sweet, black, edible berries. [Mayi-Yapi and Mayi-Kulan *ganggabarri*]

**con man** *n.* confidence trickster.

**connect** /kuh-**nekt**/ *v.* **1** (often foll. by *to, with*) join (two things, or one thing with another) (*a bush track connects the two small settlements; connected the hose to the tap*). **2** be joined or joinable (*the two parts do not connect*). **3** (often foll. by *with*) associate mentally or practically (*never connected her with the theatre*). **4** (foll. by *with*) (of a train etc.) be timed to arrive with another, so passengers can transfer. **5** put into communication by telephone. **6 a** (usu. in *passive;* foll. by *with*) associate with others in relationships etc. (*is connected with some influential people*). **b** be meaningful or relevant. **7** *colloq.* hit or strike effectively. [Latin *necto nex-* bind]

**connecting-rod** *n.* rod between the piston and crankpin etc. in an internal combustion engine.

**connection** /kuh-**nek**-shuhn/ *n.* (also **connexion**) **1** act or instance of connecting or state of being connected. **2** point at which two things are connected (*broke at the connection*). **3** link, esp. by telephone. **4** connecting train etc. **5** (often in *pl.*) **a** relative or associate, esp. one with influence. **b** owners etc. of a racehorse etc. **6** relation of ideas; context (*in this connection I have to disagree*). □ **in connection with** with reference to.

**connective** *adj.* connecting, esp. of body tissue connecting, separating, etc., organs etc.

**connector** *n.* thing that connects.

**conning tower** *n.* **1** superstructure of a submarine containing the periscope. **2** armoured pilot-house of a warship. [from *con* direct the steering]

**connive** /kuh-**nuyv**/ *v.* (**-ving**) **1** (foll. by *at*) disregard or tacitly consent to (a wrongdoing) (*clearly you connived at what was going on*). **2** (usu. foll. by *with*) conspire (*connived with them to rob the bank*). □ **connivance** *n.* [Latin *conniveo* shut the eyes]

**connoisseur** /ˌkon-uh-**ser**/ *n.* (often foll. by *of, in*) expert judge in matters of taste

---

## Conjunction

A conjunction is used to join parts of sentences which usually, but not always, contain their own verbs, e.g.

> *He found it difficult* but *I helped him.*
> *They made lunch for Alice* and *Mary.*
> *I waited* until *you came.*

The most common conjunctions are:

| | | | |
|---|---|---|---|
| *after* | *for* | *since* | *unless* |
| *although* | *if* | *so* | *until* |
| *and* | *in order that* | *so that* | *when* |
| *as* | *like* | *than* | *where* |
| *because* | *now* | *that* | *whether* |
| *before* | *once* | *though* | *while* |
| *but* | *or* | *till* | |

(in fine wines, in art, etc.). [French *connaître* know]

**connotation** /ˌkon-uh-**tay**-shuhn/ *n.* **1** that which is implied by a word etc. in addition to the literal or primary meaning (*his letter has sinister connotations*). **2** act of connoting or implying.

**connote** /kuh-**noht**/ *v.* (**-ting**) **1** (of a word etc.) imply in addition to the literal or primary meaning. **2** mean, signify. □ **connotative** /**kon**-uh-ˌtay-tiv, kuh-**noh**-tuh-tiv/ *adj.* [medieval Latin: related to NOTE]

**connubial** /kuh-**nyoo**-bee-uhl/ *adj.* of marriage or the relationship of husband and wife. [Latin *nubo* marry]

**conquer** /**kong**-kuh/ *v.* **1 a** overcome and control militarily. **b** be victorious. **2** overcome (a habit, emotion, disability, etc.) by effort (*conquered his fears*). **3** climb (a mountain) successfully. □ **conqueror** *n.* [Latin *conquiro* win]

**conquest** /**kong**-kwest/ *n.* **1** act or instance of conquering or state of being conquered. **2 a** conquered territory. **b** something won. **3** person whose affection has been won.

**conquistador** /kon-**kwis**-tuh-ˌdaw/ *n.* (*pl.* **conquistadores** /-reez/ or **conquistadors**) a conqueror, esp. one of the Spanish conquerors of Mexico and Peru in the 16th century. [Spanish]

**consanguineous** /ˌkon-sang-**gwin**-ee-uhs/ *adj.* descended from the same ancestor; akin. □ **consanguinity** *n.* [Latin *sanguis* blood]

**conscience** /**kon**-shuhns/ *n.* moral sense of right and wrong, esp. as affecting behaviour. □ **in all conscience** *colloq.* by any reasonable standard. **on one's conscience** causing one feelings of guilt. **prisoner of conscience** person imprisoned for his or her political or religious views. [Latin: related to SCIENCE]

**conscientious** /ˌkon-shee-**en**-shuhs/ *adj.* diligent and scrupulous. □ **conscientiously** *adv.* **conscientiousness** *n.* [medieval Latin: related to CONSCIENCE]

**conscientious objector** *n.* person who for reasons of conscience objects to military service etc.

**conscious** /**kon**-shuhs/ — *adj.* **1** awake and aware of one's surroundings and identity. **2** (usu. foll. by *of* or *that*) aware, knowing (*conscious of his failings*). **3** (of actions, emotions, etc.) realised or recognised by the doer; intentional (*made a conscious effort not to laugh*). **4** (in *comb.*) aware of; concerned with (*fashion-conscious*). — *n.* (prec. by *the*) the conscious mind. □ **consciously** *adv.* [Latin *scio* know]

**consciousness** /**kon**-shuhs-nuhs/ *n.* **1** state of being conscious (*lost consciousness during the fight*). **2 a** awareness, perception (*had no consciousness of being ridiculed*). **b** (in *comb.*) awareness of (*class-consciousness*). **3** totality of a person's thoughts and feelings, or of a class of these (*moral consciousness*).

**consciousness-raising** *n.* activity of increasing esp. social or political sensitivity or awareness.

**conscript** — *v.* /kuhn-**skript**/ summon for compulsory (esp. military) service. — *n.* /**kon**-skript/ conscripted person. □ **conscription** /kuhn-**skrip**-shuhn/ *n.* [Latin *scribo* write]

**consecrate** /**kon**-suh-ˌkrayt/ *v.* (**-ting**) **1** make or declare sacred; dedicate formally to religious or divine purpose (*consecrated the altar*). **2** (in Christian belief) transform (the substance of the bread and wine) into the substance of the body and blood of Christ. **3** (foll. by *to*) devote to (a purpose) (*consecrated her life to serving the sick and the dying*). **4** ordain (a priest) as bishop. □ **consecration** /-**kray**-shuhn/ *n.* [Latin: related to SACRED]

**consecutive** /kuhn-**sek**-yuh-tiv/ *adj.* **1 a** following continuously. **b** in an unbroken or logical order. **2** *Gram.* expressing a consequence. □ **consecutively** *adv.* [Latin *sequor secut-* follow]

**consecutive intervals** *n. Mus.* intervals of the same kind (esp. fifths or octaves), occurring in succession between two voices or parts in harmony.

**consensus** /kuhn-**sen**-suhs/ *n.* (often foll. by *of*; often *attrib.*) general agreement or opinion. [Latin: related to CONSENT]

**consent** /kuhn-**sent**/ — *v.* (often foll. by *to*) express willingness, give permission, agree. — *n.* voluntary agreement, permission. □ **age of consent** age at which consent to sexual intercourse is valid in law. [Latin *sentio* feel]

**consequence** /**kon**-suh-kwuhns/ *n.* **1** result or effect of what has gone before. **2** importance (*it is of no consequence; a person of some consequence*). □ **in consequence** as a result. **take the consequences** accept the results of one's choice or action. [Latin: related to CONSECUTIVE]

**consequent** *adj.* **1** (often foll. by *on, upon*) following as a result or consequence. **2** logically consistent.

**consequential** /ˌkon-suh-**kwen**-shuhl/ *adj.* **1** following as a result or consequence. **2** resulting indirectly (*consequential damage*).

**consequently** /**kon**-suh-ˌkwent-lee/ *adv. & conj.* as a result; therefore.

**conservation** /ˌkon-suh-**vay**-shuhn/ *n.* **1** preservation of the natural environment. **2** preservation of works of art, documents, etc. [Latin: related to CONSERVE]

**conservationist** *n.* supporter of environmental conservation.

**conservative** /kuhn-**ser**-vuh-tiv/ — *adj.* **1 a** averse to change, esp. if rapid; tending to want to maintain existing institutions etc. **b** (of views, taste, etc.) moderate, avoiding extremes (*conservative in his dress*). **2** (of an estimate etc.) purposely low. — *n.* **1** conservative person. **2** person having conservative political views. □ **conservatism** *n.* [Latin: related to CONSERVE]

**conservatorium** /kuhn-ˌser-vuh-taw-ree-uhm/ *n.* school of music. [from Italian *conservatorio*]

**conservatory** /kuhn-**ser**-vuh-tuh-ree, -tree/ *n.* (*pl.* -ies) greenhouse for tender plants. [Latin and Italian: related to CONSERVE]

**conserve** — *v.* /kuhn-**serv**/ (-**ving**) keep from harm or damage, esp. for later use. — *n.* /**kon**-serv/ jam made of fresh fruit. [Latin *servo* keep]

**consider** /kuhn-**sid**-uh/ *v.* **1** contemplate mentally, esp. in order to reach a conclusion. **2** examine the merits of (a course of action, a candidate, a claim, etc.). **3** look attentively at. **4** take into account; show consideration or regard for (*you might consider my feelings*). **5** (foll. by *that*) have the opinion (*he considers that the earth is flat after all*). **6** regard as (*consider it settled*). **7** (as **considered** *adj.*) formed after careful thought (*a considered opinion*). □ **all things considered** taking everything into account. [French from Latin]

**considerable** *adj.* **1** much; a lot of (*considerable pain*). **2** notable, important. □ **considerably** *adv.*

**considerate** /kuhn-**sid**-uh-ruht/ *adj.* thoughtful towards others; careful not to cause hurt or inconvenience. □ **considerately** *adv.* [Latin: related to CONSIDER]

**consideration** /kuhn-ˌsid-uh-**ray**-shuhn/ *n.* **1** careful thought. **2** thoughtfulness for others; being considerate. **3** fact or thing taken into account in deciding or judging something. **4** compensation; payment or reward. □ **in consideration of** in return for; on account of. **take into consideration** include as a factor, reason, etc.; make allowance for. **under consideration** being considered.

**considering** — *prep. & conj.* in view of; taking into consideration. — *adv. colloq.* taking everything into account (*not so bad, considering*).

**consign** /kuhn-**suyn**/ *v.* (often foll. by *to*) **1** hand over; deliver. **2** assign; commit (*consign it to the rubbish bin*). **3** transmit or send (goods). □ **consignee** /ˌkon-suy-**nee**/ *n.* **consignor** *n.* [Latin: related to SIGN]

**consignment** *n.* **1** act or instance of consigning or process of being consigned. **2** goods consigned.

**consist** /kuhn-**sist**/ *v.* **1** (foll. by *of*) be composed; have as ingredients (*his sandwich-filling consists of live witchetty grubs and tomato sauce*). **2** (foll. by *in, of*) have its essential features as specified (*its beauty consists in its use of colour*). [Latin *sisto* stop]

**consistency** /kuhn-**sis**-tuhn-see/ *n.* (*pl.* -ies) **1** degree of density, firmness, or viscosity, esp. of thick liquids. **2** state of being consistent; conformity with other or earlier attitudes etc. **3** state or quality of holding or sticking together and retaining shape. [Latin: related to CONSIST]

**consistent** *adj.* **1** (usu. foll. by *with*) compatible or in harmony; not contradictory. **2** (of a person) constant to the same principles of thought or action. □ **consistently** *adv.* [Latin: related to CONSIST]

**consistory** /kuhn-**sis**-tuh-ree/ *n.* (*pl.* -ies) *RC Ch.* council of cardinals (with or without the pope). [Latin: related to CONSIST]

**consolation** /ˌkon-suh-**lay**-shuhn/ *n.* **1** act or instance of consoling or state of being consoled. **2** consoling thing or person. □ **consolatory** /kuhn-**sol**-uh-tuh-ree/ /-tree/ *adj.*

**consolation prize** *n.* prize given to a competitor who just fails to win a main prize.

**console¹** /kuhn-**sohl**/ *v.* (-**ling**) comfort, esp. in grief or disappointment. [Latin: related to SOLACE]

■ **Usage** *Console* is often confused with *condole*, which is different in that it is always followed by *with*.

**console²** /**kon**-sohl/ *n.* **1 a** panel for switches, controls, etc. **b** workstation from which the operation of a computer system can be monitored and controlled. **2** cabinet for a television etc. **3** cabinet with the keyboards and stops of an organ. **4** bracket supporting a shelf etc. [French]

**consolidate** /kuhn-**sol**-uh-ˌdayt/ *v.* (-**ting**) **1** make or become strong or secure. **2** combine (territories, companies, debts, etc.) into one whole. □ **consolidation**

/kuhn-ˌsol-uh-**day**-shuhn/ n. **consolidator** n. [Latin: related to SOLID]

**consolidated revenue** n. main fund operated by a government into which tax revenue is paid.

**consommé** /**kon**-suh-may, kuhn-**soh**-may/ n. clear soup from meat stock. [French]

**consonance** /**kon**-suh-nuhns/ n. agreement, harmony, esp. of a combination of notes in music. [Latin *sono* SOUND¹]

**consonant** — n. 1 speech sound in which the breath is at least partly obstructed (e.g. *p*, *g*, — opp. VOWEL) and which forms a syllable by combining with a vowel. 2 letter(s) representing this. — adj. 1 (foll. by *with*, *to*) consistent; in agreement or harmony. 2 similar in sound. □ **consonantal** /-**nan**-tuhl/ adj.

**consort¹** — n. /**kon**-sawt/ wife or husband, esp. of royalty. — v. /kuhn-**sawt**/ 1 (usu. foll. by *with*, *together*) keep company (*consorting with criminals*). 2 harmonise. [Latin: related to SORT]

**consort²** /**kon**-sawt/ n. *Mus.* small group of players, singers, or instruments. [var. of CONCERT]

**consortium** /kuhn-**saw**-tee-uhm, -shee-uhm/ n. (pl. **-tia** or **-s**) association, esp. of several business companies. [Latin: related to CONSORT¹]

**conspicuous** /kuhn-**spik**-yoo-uhs/ adj. 1 clearly visible; attracting notice. 2 noteworthy (*conspicuous extravagance*). □ **conspicuously** adv. [Latin *specio* look]

**conspiracy** /kuhn-**spi**-ruh-see/ n. (pl. **-ies**) 1 secret plan to commit a crime; plot. 2 act of conspiring. [Latin: related to CONSPIRE]

**conspirator** /kuhn-**spi**-ruh-tuh/ n. person who takes part in a conspiracy. □ **conspiratorial** /-**taw**-ree-uhl/ adj.

**conspire** /kuhn-**spuyuh**/ v. (**-ring**) 1 combine secretly for an unlawful or harmful act. 2 (of events) seem to be working together, esp. disadvantageously. [Latin *spiro* breathe]

**constable** /**kun**-stuh-buhl/ n. police officer of the lowest rank. [Latin *comes stabuli* count of the stable]

**constabulary** /kuhn-**stab**-yuh-luh-ree/ n. (pl. **-ies**) police force. [medieval Latin: related to CONSTABLE]

**constancy** /**kon**-stuhn-see/ n. quality of being unchanging and dependable; faithfulness. [Latin: related to CONSTANT]

**constant** — adj. 1 continuous (*needs constant attention*). 2 occurring frequently (*constant complaints*). 3 unchanging, faithful, dependable. — n. 1 anything that does not vary. 2 *Math.* & *Physics* quantity or number that remains

the same. □ **constantly** adv. [Latin *sto* stand]

**constellation** /ˌkon-stuh-**lay**-shuhn/ n. 1 group of fixed stars whose outline is traditionally regarded as forming a particular figure, e.g. the Southern Cross. 2 group of associated persons noteworthy in some way (*a constellation of young Australian musicians*). [Latin *stella* star]

**consternation** /ˌkon-stuh-**nay**-shuhn/ n. anxiety or dismay causing mental confusion. [Latin *sterno* throw down]

**constipate** /**kon**-stuh-ˌpayt/ v. (**-ting**) (esp. as **constipated** adj.) affect with constipation. [Latin *stipo* cram]

**constipation** /ˌkon-stuh-**pay**-shuhn/ n. condition with hardened faeces and difficulty in emptying the bowels.

**constituency** /kuhn-**stich**-oo-uhn-see/ n. (pl. **-ies**) 1 = ELECTORATE. 2 body of customers, supporters, etc.

**constituent** /kuhn-**stich**-oo-uhnt/ — adj. 1 composing or helping to make a whole. 2 able to make or change a constitution (*constituent assembly*). 3 appointing or electing. — n. 1 member of a constituency. 2 component part. [Latin: related to CONSTITUTE]

**constitute** /**kon**-stuh-ˌtyoot/ v. (**-ting**) 1 be the components or essence of; compose. 2 a amount to (*this constitutes a warning*). b formally establish (*constitutes a precedent*). 3 give legal or constitutional form to. [Latin *constituo* establish]

**constitution** /ˌkon-stuh-**tyoo**-shuhn/ n. 1 act or method of constituting; composition (of something). 2 body of fundamental principles by which a nation or other body is governed. 3 person's inherent state of health, strength, etc. [Latin: related to CONSTITUTE]

**constitutional** — adj. 1 of or in line with a political constitution. 2 inherent (*constitutional weakness*). — n. walk taken regularly as healthy exercise. □ **constitutionality** /-**nal**-uh-tee/ n. **constitutionally** adv.

**constitutive** /**kon**-stuh-ˌtyoo-tiv/ adj. 1 able to form or appoint. 2 component (*constitutive parts of the drama*). 3 essential.

**constrain** /kuhn-**strayn**/ v. 1 compel (*I am constrained to agree*). 2 a confine forcibly; imprison. b restrict severely (*the injury constrains his freedom of movement*). 3 (as **constrained** adj.) forced, embarrassed (*a constrained voice*; *his manner was most constrained*). [Latin *stringo strict-* tie]

**constraint** /kuhn-**straynt**/ n. **1** act or result of constraining or being constrained. **2** restriction. **3** restraint of natural feelings or their expression.

**constrict** /kuhn-**strikt**/ v. make narrow or tight; compress. □ **constriction** n. **constrictive** adj. [Latin: related to CONSTRAIN]

**constrictor** n. **1** snake (esp. a boa) that kills by compressing. **2** muscle that contracts an organ or part of the body.

**construct** — v. /kuhn-**strukt**/ **1** make by fitting parts together; build, form. **2** Geom. delineate (a figure), esp. accurately to given conditions. — n. /**kon**-strukt/ thing constructed, esp. by the mind. □ **constructor** /kuhn-**struk**-tuh/ n. [Latin struo struct- build]

**construction** /kuhn-**struk**-shuhn/ n. **1** act or mode of constructing or being constructed. **2** thing constructed. **3** interpretation or explanation (they put a generous construction on his action). **4** syntactical arrangement of words. □ **constructional** adj.

**constructive** /kuhn-**struk**-tiv/ adj. **1** tending to form a basis for ideas (constructive criticism). **2** helpful, positive (a constructive approach). □ **constructively** adv.

**construe** /kuhn-**stroo**/ v. (**-strues**, **-strued**, **-struing**) **1** interpret (their action can be construed in many ways). **2** (often foll. by with) combine (words) grammatically ('rely' is construed with 'on'). **3** analyse the syntax of (a sentence). **4** translate literally. [Latin: related to CONSTRUCT]

**consul** /**kon**-suhl/ n. **1** official appointed by a nation to protect its citizens and interests in a foreign city. **2** hist. either of two chief magistrates in ancient Rome. □ **consular** /**kon**-syuh-luh/ adj. **consulship** n. [Latin]

**consulate** /**kon**-syuh-luht/ n. **1** official building of a consul. **2** position of consul.

**consult** /kuhn-**sult**/ v. **1** seek information or advice from. **2** (often foll. by with) refer to a person for advice etc. **3** take into account (feelings, interests, etc.). □ **consultative** adj. [Latin consulo consult-take counsel]

**consultancy** n. (pl. **-ies**) practice or position of a consultant.

**consultant** n. **1** person providing professional advice etc., esp. for a fee. **2** senior medical specialist in a hospital.

**consultation** /ˌkon-suhl-**tay**-shuhn/ n. **1** meeting arranged to consult, esp. with a doctor. **2** act or process of consulting. **3** lottery.

**consume** /kuhn-**syoom**/ v. (**-ming**) **1** eat or drink. **2** completely destroy (fire consumed the building). **3** preoccupy, possess (consumed with rage). **4** use up (time, energy, etc.). □ **consumable** adj. & n. [Latin consumo -sumpt-]

**consumer** n. **1** person who consumes, esp. one who uses a product. **2** purchaser of goods or services.

**consumer goods** n.pl. goods for consumers, not for producing other goods.

**consumerism** n. **1** protection of consumers' interests in relation to the producer. **2** (often derog.) continual increase in the consumption of goods. □ **consumerist** adj.

**consumer price index** n. measure of the cost of living based on a standard set of prices.

**consummate** — v. /**kon**-suh-ˌmayt, **kon**-syoo-ˌmayt/ (**-ting**) **1** complete; make perfect. **2** complete (a marriage) by sexual intercourse. — adj. /kuhn-**sum**-uht, **kon**-syoo-muht/ complete, perfect; fully skilled (a consummate craftsman). □ **consummation** /ˌkon-suh-**may**-shuhn/ n. [Latin summus utmost]

**consumption** /kuhn-**sump**-shuhn/ n. **1** act or instance of consuming or process of being consumed. **2** amount consumed. **3** use by a particular group (a film unsuitable for children's consumption). **4** archaic tuberculosis of the lungs. **5** purchase and use of goods etc. [French: related to CONSUME]

**cont.** abbr. **1** contents. **2** continued.

**contact** /**kon**-takt/ — n. **1** state or condition of touching, meeting, or communicating. **2** person who is or may be communicated with for information, assistance, etc. **3** connection for the passage of an electric current. **4** person likely to carry a contagious disease through being near an infected person. **5** (in full **contact period**) period when Aborigines and Europeans first interacted in a particular place. — v. (also /kuhn-**takt**/) **1** get in touch with (a person). **2** begin correspondence or personal dealings with. [Latin tango tact-touch]

**contact lens** n. small lens placed directly on the eyeball to correct vision.

**contagion** /kuhn-**tay**-juhn/ n. **1 a** spreading of disease by bodily contact. **b** contagious disease. **2** contagious or harmful influence. **3** moral corruption. [related to CONTACT]

**contagious** /kuhn-**tay**-juhs/ adj. **1 a** (of a person) likely to transmit a disease by contact. **b** (of a disease) transmitted in this way. **2** (of emotions etc.) likely to spread (*contagious enthusiasm*).

**contain** /kuhn-**tayn**/ v. **1** hold or be capable of holding within itself; include, comprise. **2** (of measures) consist of or be equal to (*a tablespoon contains 20 ml*). **3** prevent (an enemy, difficulty, etc.) from moving or extending. **4** control or restrain (feelings etc.) (*contained his anger with difficulty*). **5** (of a number) be divisible by (a factor) without a remainder. [Latin *teneo* hold]

**container** n. **1** box, jar, etc., for holding things. **2** large metal box for transporting goods (also *attrib.*: *container ship*).

**containerise** v. (also **-ize**) (**-sing** or **-zing**) pack in or transport by container. □ **containerisation** n.

**containment** n. action or policy of preventing the expansion of a hostile country or influence.

**contaminate** /kuhn-**tam**-uh-ˌnayt/ v. (**-ting**) **1** pollute, esp. with radioactivity. **2** infect. □ **contaminant** n. **contamination** /-**nay**-shuhn/ n. **contaminator** n. [Latin *contamino -taminat-* related to *tango* touch]

**contemplate** /**kon**-tuhm-ˌplayt/ v. (**-ting**) **1** survey visually or mentally. **2** regard (an event) as possible. **3** intend (*he is not contemplating retiring*). **4** meditate. □ **contemplation** /-**play**-shuhn/ n. [Latin]

**contemplative** /kuhn-**tem**-pluh-tiv/ — adj. of or given to (esp. religious) contemplation; thoughtful. — n. *Eccl.* person devoted to religious contemplation, esp. a monk or nun of one of the contemplative Orders of the Church. [Latin: related to CONTEMPLATE]

**contemplative Order** n. religious Order of monks or nuns (e.g. the Trappist Order, the Carmelite Order) in which religious contemplation is central to the life led (opp. the active Orders).

**contemporaneous** /kuhn-ˌtem-puh-**ray**-nee-uhs/ adj. (usu. foll. by *with*) existing or occurring at the same time. □ **contemporaneity** /-ruh-**nee**-uh-tee/ n. [Latin: related to COM-, *tempus* time]

**contemporary** /kuhn-**tem**-puh-ruh-ree, -puh-ree, -pree/ — adj. **1** living or occurring at the same time. **2** of approximately the same age. **3** modern in style or design. — n. (pl. **-ies**) contemporary person or thing. [medieval Latin: related to CONTEMPORANEOUS]

**contempt** /kuhn-**tempt**/ n. **1** feeling that a person or thing is beneath consideration or worthless, or deserving scorn or extreme reproach. **2** condition of being held in contempt. **3** (in full **contempt of court**) disobedience to or disrespect for a court of law. [Latin *temno tempt-* despise]

**contemptible** adj. deserving contempt; despicable. □ **contemptibly** adv.

**contemptuous** adj. (often foll. by *of*) feeling or showing contempt; scornful; insolent. □ **contemptuously** adv.

**contend** /kuhn-**tend**/ v. **1** (usu. foll. by *with*) fight, argue. **2** compete (*contending emotions*). **3** assert, maintain. □ **contender** n. [Latin: related to TEND[1]]

**content[1]** /kuhn-**tent**/ — predic. adj. **1** satisfied; adequately happy. **2** (foll. by *to* + infin.) willing. — v. make content; satisfy (*the response contented them all*). — n. contented state; satisfaction. □ **to one's heart's content** as much as one wishes. [Latin: related to CONTAIN]

**content[2]** /**kon**-tent/ n. **1** (usu. in pl.) what is contained, esp. in a vessel, book, or house. **2** amount (of a constituent) contained (*high fat content*). **3** substance (of a speech etc.) as distinct from form. **4** capacity or volume of a thing. [medieval Latin: related to CONTAIN]

**contented** /kuhn-**ten**-tuhd/ adj. showing or feeling content; happy, satisfied. □ **contentedly** adv. **contentedness** n.

**contention** /kuhn-**ten**-shuhn/ n. **1** dispute or argument; rivalry. **2** point contended for in an argument (*it is my contention that you are wrong*). [Latin: related to CONTEND]

**contentious** /kuhn-**ten**-shuhs/ adj. **1** quarrelsome. **2** likely to cause an argument; controversial.

**contentment** n. satisfied state; tranquil happiness.

**conterminous** /kon-**ter**-muh-nuhs/ adj. (often foll. by *with*) **1** having a common boundary. **2** coextensive, coterminous. □ **conterminously** adv. [COM-, TERMINUS]

**contest** — n. /**kon**-test/ **1** process of contending; strife. **2** a competition. — v. /kuhn-**test**/ **1** dispute (a decision etc.). **2** contend or compete for; compete in (an election). [Latin *testis* witness]

**contestant** /kuhn-**tes**-tuhnt/ n. person taking part in a contest.

**context** /**kon**-tekst/ n. **1** parts that surround a word or passage and clarify its meaning. **2** circumstances relevant to something under consideration (*must be seen in context*). □ **in** (or **out of**) **context** with (or without) the surrounding words or circumstances. □ **contextual** /kuhn-**teks**-choo-uhl/ adj. **contextualise** /kuhn-**teks**-choo-uh-ˌluyz/ v. (also **-ize**) (**-sing** or **-zing**). [Latin: related to TEXT]

**contiguous** /kuhn-**tig**-yoo-uhs/ *adj.* (usu. foll. by *with, to*) touching, esp. along a line; in contact (*NSW and Victoria are contiguous States*). □ **contiguity** /ˌkon-tuh-**gyoo**-uh-tee/ *n.* [Latin: related to CONTACT]

**continent¹** /**kon**-tuh-nuhnt/ *n.* **1** any of the world's seven main continuous expanses of land (Africa, N. and S. America, Antarctica, Asia, Australia, Europe). **2** (**the Continent**) the mainland of Europe. [Latin: related to CONTAIN]

**continent²** /**kon**-tuh-nuhnt/ *adj.* **1** able to control one's bowels and bladder. **2** exercising self-restraint, esp. sexually. □ **continence** *n.* [Latin: related to CONTAIN]

**continental¹** /ˌkon-tuh-**nen**-tuhl/ *adj.* **1** of or characteristic of a continent. **2** (**Continental**) of or characteristic of mainland Europe.

**continental²** *n. US hist.* currency note issued during the American War of Independence (and which depreciated sharply afterwards). □ **not to give** (or **care**) **a continental** *colloq.* not to care at all; not give a damn.

**continental breakfast** *n.* light breakfast of coffee, rolls, etc.

**continental drift** *n. Geol.* hypothesis that the continents are moving slowly over the surface of the earth on a deep-lying plastic sub-stratum.

**continental shelf** *n.* area of shallow seabed bordering a continent.

**contingency** /kuhn-**tin**-juhn-see/ *n.* (*pl.* -**ies**) **1** future event or circumstance regarded as likely to occur, or as influencing present action. **2** something dependent on another uncertain event. **3** uncertainty of occurrence. [Latin: related to CONTINGENT]

**contingent** — *adj.* **1** (usu. foll. by *on, upon*) conditional, dependent (on an uncertain event or circumstance). **2 a** that may or may not occur. **b** fortuitous; occurring by chance. — *n.* **1** body (of troops, ships, etc.) forming part of a larger group. **2** group of people sharing an interest, origin, etc. [Latin: related to CONTACT]

**continual** /kuhn-**tin**-yoo-uhl/ *adj.* constantly or frequently recurring; always happening. □ **continually** *adv.* [French: related to CONTINUE]

■ **Usage** *Continual* is often confused with *continuous*. *Continual* is used of something that happens very frequently (e.g. *there were continual interruptions*) while *continuous* is used of something that happens without a pause (e.g. *continuous rain all day*).

**continuance** /kuhn-**tin**-yoo-uhns/ *n.* **1** state of continuing in existence or operation. **2** duration.

**continuation** /kuhn-ˌtin-yoo-**ay**-shuhn/ *n.* **1** act or instance of continuing or process of being continued. **2** part that continues something else (*proposed continuation of the railway line*).

**continue** /kuhn-**tin**-yoo/ *v.* (-**ues**, -**ued** -**uing**) **1** persist in; maintain; not stop (an action etc.) (*continued to read*). **2** (also *absol.*) resume or prolong (a narrative, journey, etc.). **3** be a sequel to. **4** remain, stay (*will continue as manager; weather continued fine*). [Latin: related to CONTAIN]

**continuity** /ˌkon-tuh-**nyoo**-uh-tee/ *n.* (*pl.* -**ies**) **1** state of being continuous. **2** a logical sequence. **3** detailed scenario of a film or broadcast. **4** linking of broadcast items.

**continuo** /kuhn-**tin**-yoo-oh/ *n.* (*pl.* -**s**) *Mus.* accompaniment (played usu. on a keyboard instrument, e.g. a harpsichord) providing a bass line in Baroque music. [Italian]

**continuous** /kuhn-**tin**-yoo-uhs/ *adj.* **1** uninterrupted, connected throughout in space or time. **2** *Gram.* = PROGRESSIVE. □ **continuously** *adv.* [Latin: related to CONTAIN]

■ **Usage** See note at *continual.*

**continuum** /kuhn-**tin**-yoo-uhm/ *n.* (*pl.* -**nua**) thing having a continuous structure. [Latin: related to CONTINUOUS]

**contort** /kuhn-**tawt**/ *v.* twist or force out of its normal shape. □ **contortion** *n.* [Latin *torqueo tort-* twist]

**contortionist** /kuhn-**taw**-shuhn-uhst/ *n.* entertainer who adopts contorted postures.

**contour** /**kon**-toor/ — *n.* **1 a** outline, esp. representing or bounding the shape or form of something. **b** outline of a natural feature, e.g. a coast or mountain mass. **2** (in full **contour line**) line on a map joining points of equal altitude. — *v.* mark with contour lines. [Italian *contornare* draw in outline]

**contra-** *comb. form* against, opposite. [Latin]

**contraband** /**kon**-truh-ˌband/ — *n.* **1** smuggled goods. **2** smuggling; illegal trade. — *adj.* forbidden to be imported or exported. [Spanish from Italian]

**contraception** /ˌkon-truh-**sep**-shuhn/ *n.* prevention of pregnancy; use of contraceptives. [from CONTRA-, CONCEPTION]

**contraceptive** /ˌkon-truh-**sep**-tiv/ — *adj.* preventing pregnancy. — *n.* contraceptive device or drug.

**contract** — n. /**kon**-trakt/ **1** written or spoken agreement, esp. one enforceable by law. **2** document recording this. — v. /kuhn-**trakt**/ **1** make or become smaller. **2 a** (usu. foll. by *with*) make a contract. **b** (often foll. by *out*) arrange (work) to be done by contract. **3** become affected by (a disease). **4** enter into (marriage). **5** incur (a debt etc.). **6** draw together (the muscles, brow, etc.), or be drawn together. **7** shorten (a word or words) by combination or elision, e.g. *couldn't* (could not), *Halloween* (Hallow even). □ **contract in** (or **out**) choose to enter (or not to enter) a scheme or commitment. [Latin *contractus*: related to TRACT[1]]

**contractable** *adj.* (of a disease) that can be contracted.

**contract bridge** *n.* bridge in which only tricks bid and won count towards the game.

**contractible** *adj.* that can be shrunk or drawn together.

**contraction** /kuhn-**trak**-shuhn/ *n.* **1** act of contracting or state of being contracted. **2** *Med.* shortening of the uterine muscles during childbirth. **3** shrinking, diminution. **4** shortened form of a word or words (e.g. *he's*).

**contractor** /kuhn-**trak**-tuh/ *n.* person who makes a contract, esp. to conduct building operations.

**contractual** /kuhn-**trak**-choo-uhl/ *adj.* of, or in the nature of, a contract. □ **contractually** *adv.*

**contradict** /ˌkon-truh-**dikt**/ *v.* **1** deny or express the opposite of (a statement) (*contradicted his assertion*). **2** deny or express the opposite of a statement made by (a person) (*I will not have you contradict me*). **3** be in opposition to or conflict with (*this new evidence contradicts the theory*). □ **contradiction** *n.* **contradictory** *adj.* [Latin *dico dict-* say]

**contradistinction** /ˌkon-truh-duhs-**tingk**-shuhn/ *n.* distinction made by contrasting.

**contralto** /kuhn-**trahl**-toh, -**tral**-/ *n.* (*pl.* **-s**) **1** lowest female singing-voice. **2 a** singer with this voice. **b** part written for this voice. [Italian: related to CONTRA-, ALTO]

**contraption** /kuhn-**trap**-shuhn/ *n.* machine or device, esp. a strange or cumbersome one. [origin unknown]

**contrapuntal** /ˌkon-truh-**pun**-tuhl/ *adj.* *Mus.* of or in counterpoint. □ **contrapuntally** *adv.* [Italian]

**contrariwise** /**kon**-truh-ree-ˌwuyz/ *adv.* **1** on the other hand. **2** in the opposite way. **3** /kuhn-**trair**-ree-ˌwuyz/ perversely.

**contrary** /**kon**-truh-ree/ — *adj.* **1** (usu. foll. by *to*) opposed in nature or tendency; diametrically different (*put forward a contrary argument*; *the twins have contrary dispositions*). **2** /kuhn-**trair**-ree/ perverse, self-willed (*contrary behaviour*; *a contrary child*). **3** (of a wind) unfavourable, impeding. **4** opposite in position or direction (*took a contrary route*). — *n.* (prec. by *the*) the opposite (*the contrary is true*). — *adv.* (foll. by *to*) in opposition or contrast (*contrary to expectations*). □ **on the contrary** expressing denial of what has just been implied or stated. **to the contrary** to the opposite effect. □ **contrarily** /**kon**-truh-ruh-lee/ *adv.* (/kuhn-**trair**-ruh-lee/ in sense 2 of *adj.*) **contrariness** /**kon**-truh-ree-nuhs/ *n.* (/kuhn-**trair**-ree-nuhs/ in sense 2 of *adj.*) [Latin: related to CONTRA-]

**contrast** — *n.* /**kon**-trahst/ **1 a** juxtaposition or comparison showing differences (*contrast between light and shade*). **b** difference so revealed. **2** (often foll. by *to*) thing or person having different qualities (*he's a complete contrast to his twin*). **3** degree of difference between the tones in a television picture or photograph. — *v.* /kuhn-**trahst**/ (often foll. by *with*) **1** set together so as to reveal a contrast (*contrast his earlier style with his later*). **2** have or show a contrast (*his brutality to his wife contrasts with his caringness towards his mates*). [Italian from Latin *sto* stand]

**contravene** /ˌkon-truh-**veen**/ *v.* (**-ning**) **1** infringe (a law etc.). **2** (of things) conflict with. □ **contravention** /ˌkon-truh-**ven**-shuhn/ *n.* [Latin *venio* come]

**contretemps** /**kon**-truh-tong/ *n.* (*pl.* same) **1** unfortunate occurrence. **2** unexpected mishap. [French]

**contribute** /kuhn-**trib**-yoot/ *v.* (**-ting**) (often foll. by *to*) **1** give (time, money, etc.) towards a common purpose (*contributed $10 to the cause*). **2** help to bring about a result etc. (*contributed to their downfall*). **3** (also *absol.*) supply (an article etc.) for publication with others in a journal etc. □ **contributor** /kuhn-**trib**-yoo-tuh/ *n.* [Latin: related to TRIBUTE]

**contribution** /ˌkon-truh-**byoo**-shuhn/ *n.* **1** act of contributing. **2** thing contributed.

**contributory** /kuhn-**trib**-yoo-tuh-ree, -tree/ *adj.* **1** that contributes (*contributory negligence*). **2** using contributions.

**contrite** /**kon**-truyt, kuhn-**truyt**/ *adj.* penitent, feeling great guilt. □ **contritely** *adv.* **contrition** /kuhn-**trish**-uhn/ *n.* [Latin: related to TRITE]

**contrivance** /kuhn-**truy**-vuhns/ *n.* **1** something contrived, esp. a plan or mechanical device. **2** act of contriving, esp. deceitfully. **3** inventive capacity.

**contrive** /kuhn-**truyv**/ v. (**-ving**) **1** devise; plan or make resourcefully or with skill. **2** (often foll. by *to* + infin.) manage (*contrived to make matters worse*). [French from Latin]

**contrived** adj. planned so carefully as to seem unnatural; artificial, forced (*the plot seemed contrived*).

**control** /kuhn-**trohl**/ — n. **1** power of directing, command (*under the control of*). **2** power of restraining, esp. self-restraint (*has no control over his drinking*). **3** means of restraint (*what controls are there over those who exploit the weak?*). **4** (usu. in *pl.*) means of regulating prices etc. (*price controls*). **5** (usu. in *pl.*) switches and other devices by which a machine is controlled (also *attrib.*: *control panel*). **6** place where something is controlled or verified. **7** standard of comparison for checking the results of an experiment. — v. (**-ll-**) **1** have control of, regulate (*control the driving wheel*). **2** hold in check, restrain (*told him to control himself*). **3** check, verify (*we need another group to control the results of this experiment*). □ **in control** (often foll. by *of*) directing an activity. **out of control** no longer manageable. **under control** being controlled; in order. □ **controllable** adj. **controller** n. [medieval Latin, = keep copy of accounts: related to CONTRA-, ROLL]

**control panel** n. = CONTROL n. 5.

**control rod** n. rod of neutron-absorbing material used to vary the output power of a nuclear reactor.

**control tower** n. tall building at an airport etc. from which air traffic is controlled.

**control unit** n. *Computing* part of a central processing unit.

**controversial** /ˌkon-truh-**ver**-shuhl/ adj. causing or subject to controversy. [Latin: related to CONTROVERT]

**controversy** /kon-truh-ˌver-see, kuhn-**trov**-uh-see/ n. (pl. **-ies**) prolonged argument or dispute, esp. when conducted publicly. [Latin: related to CONTROVERT]

■ **Usage** The second pronunciation, stressed on the second syllable, is considered incorrect by some people.

**controvert** /**kon**-truh-ˌvert, -**vert**/ v. dispute, deny. [Latin *verto vers-* turn]

**contumacious** /ˌkon-choo-**may**-shuhs, -tyoo-/ adj. stubbornly or wilfully disobedient. □ **contumacy** /**kon**-choo-muh-see, -tyoo-/ n. (pl. **-ies**). [Latin *tumeo* swell]

**contumely** /**kon**-tyoo-muh-lee, -choo-/ n. **1** insolent language or treatment. **2** disgrace. [Latin: related to CONTUMACIOUS]

**contuse** /kuhn-**tyooz**/ v. (**-sing**) injure without breaking the skin; bruise. □ **contusion** /-tyoo-*zh*uhn/ n. [Latin *tundo tus-* thump]

**conundrum** /kuh-**nun**-druhm/ n. **1** riddle, esp. one with a pun in its answer. **2** hard or puzzling question [origin unknown]

**conurbation** /ˌkon-er-**bay**-shuhn/ n. extended urban area, esp. consisting of several towns and merging suburbs. [Latin *urbs* city]

**convalesce** /ˌkon-vuh-**les**/ v. (**-cing**) recover health after illness. [Latin *valeo* be well]

**convalescent** — adj. recovering from an illness. — n. convalescent person. □ **convalescence** n.

**convection** /kuhn-**vek**-shuhn/ n. **1** heat transfer by upward movement of a heated and less dense medium. **2** *Meteorol.* transfer of heat by the upward flow of hot air or downward flow of cold air. [Latin *veho vect-* carry]

**convector** /kuhn-**vek**-tuh/ n. heating appliance that circulates warm air by convection.

**convene** /kuhn-**veen**/ v. (**-ning**) **1** summon or arrange (a meeting etc.). **2** assemble. □ **convenor** n. (also **convener**). [Latin *venio vent-* come]

**convenience** /kuhn-**vee**-nee-uhns/ n. **1** state of being convenient; suitability. **2** useful thing, esp. an installation or piece of equipment. **3** advantage (*a great convenience*). **4** toilet, esp. a public one. □ **at one's convenience** at a time or place that suits one. [Latin: related to CONVENE]

**convenient** adj. **1 a** serving one's comfort or interests (*a dishwasher would be convenient*; *a convenient excuse*). **b** suitable (*will tomorrow be convenient?*). **c** free of trouble or difficulty (*it's not convenient for me to come*). **2** available or occurring at a suitable time or place (*a convenient thunderstorm saved us from certain defeat*). **3** well situated (*convenient for the shops*). □ **conveniently** adv.

**convent** /**kon**-vuhnt/ n. **1** religious community, esp. of nuns, under vows. **2** premises occupied by this. **3** (in full **convent school**) school attached to and run by a convent. [Latin: related to CONVENE]

**convention** /kuhn-**ven**-shuhn/ n. **1 a** general agreement on social behaviour etc. by implicit majority consent. **b** a custom or customary practice (*it's a convention that the audience at Handel's 'Messiah' should stand for the Hallelujah Chorus*). **2** conference of people with a common interest. **3** a formal agreement, esp. between nations. [Latin: related to CONVENE]

**conventional** *adj.* **1** depending on or according to convention. **2** (of a person) bound by social conventions. **3** usual; of agreed significance (*conventional wisdom has it that . . .*). **4** not spontaneous or sincere or original (*a very conventional production of the play*). **5** (of weapons etc.) non-nuclear. □ **conventionalism** *n.* **conventionality** /-**nal**-uh-tee/ *n.* (*pl.* **-ies**). **conventionally** *adv.*

**converge** /kuhn-**verj**/ *v.* (**-ging**) **1** come together or towards the same point. **2** (foll. by *on, upon*) approach from different directions. **3** *Math.* (of a series) approximate in the sum of its terms towards a definite limit. □ **convergence** *n.* [Latin *vergo* incline]

**convergent** /kuhn-**ver**-juhnt/ *adj.* **1** converging. **2** *Biol.* (of unrelated organisms) having the tendency to become similar while adapting to the same environment.

**conversant** /kuhn-**ver**-suhnt, **kon**-vuh-suhnt/ *adj.* (foll. by *with*) well acquainted with (*I'm not conversant with the local customs*). [French: related to CONVERSE[1]]

**conversation** /kon-vuh-**say**-shuhn/ *n.* **1** informal spoken communication. **2** instance of this. [Latin: related to CONVERSE[1]]

**conversational** *adj.* **1** of or in conversation. **2** colloquial. □ **conversationally** *adv.*

**conversationalist** *n.* person good at or fond of conversation.

**converse[1]** /kuhn-**vers**/ *v.* (**-sing**) (often foll. by *with*) talk. [Latin: related to CONVERT]

**converse[2]** /**kon**-vers/ — *adj.* opposite, contrary, reversed. — *n.* something, esp. a statement or proposition, that is opposite or reversed. □ **conversely** *adv.* [Latin: related to CONVERT]

**conversion** /kuhn-**ver**-shuhn, -*zh*uhn/ *n.* **1** act or instance of converting or process of being converted, esp. in belief or religion. **2** transformation of fertile into fissile material in a nuclear reactor. **3** *Rugby* scoring of points by a successful kick at goal after scoring a try. [Latin: related to CONVERT]

**convert** — *v.* /kuhn-**vert**/ **1** (usu. foll. by *into*) change in form or function. **2** cause (a person) to change belief, religion, etc. **3** change (moneys, stocks, units in which a quantity is expressed, etc.) into others of a different kind. **4** be converted or convertible (*the sofa converts into a bed*). **5** (also *absol.*) *Rugby* score extra points from (a try) by a successful kick at the goal. — *n.* /**kon**-vert/ (often foll. by *to*) person converted to a different belief, religion, etc. [Latin *verto vers-* turn]

**converter** /kuhn-**ver**-tuh/ *n.* (also **convertor**) **1** person or thing that converts. **2 a** *Electr.* electrical apparatus for the interconversion of alternating current and direct current. **b** *Electronics* apparatus for converting a signal from one frequency to another.

**converter reactor** *n.* nuclear reactor that converts fertile material into fissile material.

**convertible** /kuhn-**ver**-tuh-buhl/ — *adj.* **1** able to be converted. **2** (of currency etc.) that may be converted into other forms. **3** (of a car) having a folding or detachable roof. — *n.* car with a folding or detachable roof. □ **convertibility** /-**bil**-uh-tee/ *n.* [Latin: related to CONVERT]

**convertible note** *n.* unsecured note paying fixed interest and convertible on maturity to cash or ordinary shares.

**convex** /**kon**-veks/ *adj.* curved like the exterior of a circle or sphere (cf. CONCAVE). □ **convexity** /-**vek**-suh-tee/ *n.* [Latin]

**convey** /kuhn-**vay**/ *v.* **1** transport or carry (goods, passengers, etc.). **2** communicate (an idea, meaning, etc.). **3** *Law* transfer the title to (a property). **4** transmit (sound etc.). □ **conveyable** *adj.* [Latin *via* way]

**conveyance** *n.* **1 a** act or process of conveying or being conveyed. **b** communication (of ideas etc.). **2** means of transport; vehicle. **3** *Law* **a** transfer of property. **b** document effecting this. □ **conveyancer** *n.* (in sense 3). **conveyancing** *n.* (in sense 3).

**conveyor** *n.* (also **conveyer**) person or thing that conveys.

**conveyor belt** *n.* endless moving belt for conveying articles, esp. in a factory.

**convict** — *v.* /kuhn-**vikt**/ **1** (often foll. by *of*) prove to be guilty (of a crime etc.). **2** declare guilty by a legal process. — *n.* /**kon**-vikt/ **1** person found guilty of a criminal offence. **2** *hist.* person sentenced in the British Isles to a term of penal servitude in an Australian Colony. **3** (*attrib.*) of or relating to a convict or convicts (sense 2) (*convict element*; *convict clothing*; *convict labour*). [Latin *vinco vict-* conquer]

**convict colony** *n. hist.* an Australian Colony regarded primarily as a place of penal servitude for British convicts.

**conviction** /kuhn-**vik**-shuhn/ *n.* **1 a** act or process of proving or finding guilty. **b** instance of this (*has two previous convictions*). **2 a** action or resulting state of being convinced. **b** firm belief. [Latin: related to CONVICT]

**convict settlement** *n.* = CONVICT STATION.

**convict settler** *n. hist.* person transported as a convict who has subsequently taken up land in Australia.

**convict station** *n. hist.* outpost of an Australian Colony established for the confinement of convicts and for the employment of convict labour on public works.

**convict system** *n. hist.* transportation of convicts to Australia and treatment of them during confinement.

**convince** /kuhn-**vins**/ *v.* (**-cing**) **1** persuade (a person) to believe or realise. **2** (as **convinced** *adj.*) firmly persuaded (*a convinced Australian republican*). □ **convincible** *adj.* **convincing** *adj.* **convincingly** *adv.* [Latin: related to CONVICT]

**convivial** /kuhn-**viv**-ee-uhl/ *adj.* **1** fond of good company; sociable and lively. **2** festive (*a convivial atmosphere*). □ **conviviality** /-al-uh-tee/ *n.* [Latin *vivo* live]

**convoke** /kuhn-**vohk**/ *v.* (**-king**) *formal* call together; summon to assemble. □ **convocation** /ˌkon-vuh-**kay**-shuhn/ *n.* [Latin *voco* call]

**convoluted** /ˌkon-vuh-ˌloo-tuhd/ *adj.* **1** coiled, twisted. **2** complex, intricate (*a convoluted style of writing*). [Latin *volvo volut-* roll]

**convolution** /ˌkon-vuh-**loo**-shuhn/ *n.* **1** coiling, twisting. **2** coil or twist. **3** complexity. **4** sinuous fold in the surface of the brain.

**convolvulus** /kuhn-**vol**-vyuh-luhs/ *n.* (*pl.* **-luses**) **1** see AUSTRALIAN BINDWEED. **2** (also **bindweed, morning glory**) any of many twining plants having trumpet-shaped flowers. [Latin]

**convoy** /**kon**-voi/ — *n.* group of ships, vehicles, etc., travelling together or under escort. — *v.* escort, esp. with armed force. □ **in convoy** as a group. [French: related to CONVEY]

**convulse** /kuhn-**vuls**/ *v.* (**-sing**) **1** (usu. in *passive*) affect with convulsions. **2** cause to laugh uncontrollably. **3** shake violently; agitate, disturb. □ **convulsive** *adj.* **convulsively** *adv.* [Latin *vello vuls-* pull]

**convulsion** /kuhn-**vul**-shuhn/ *n.* **1** (usu. in *pl.*) violent irregular motion of the limbs or body caused by involuntary contraction of muscles, esp. as a disorder of infants. **2** violent natural disturbance, esp. an earthquake. **3** violent social or political agitation. **4** (in *pl.*) uncontrollable laughter.

**convulsive** /kuhn-**vul**-siv/ *adj.* **1** characterised by or affected with convulsions. **2** producing convulsions (see also ELECTROCONVULSIVE THERAPY). □ **convulsively** *adv.*

**coo** — *n.* soft murmuring sound as of a dove. — *v.* (**coos, cooed**) **1** emit a coo. **2** talk or say in a soft or amorous voice. □ **cooingly** *adv.* [imitative]

**cooba** /**koo**-buh/ *n.* (also **willow wattle**) any of several Australian wattles having a willow-like pendulous foliage, esp. *Acacia salicina* of drier mainland Australia. [Wiradhuri *gubaa*]

**cooboo** /**koo**-boo/ *n.* baby, esp. an Aboriginal baby. [possibly Martuthunira *gubuyu* small]

**cooee** /**koo**-ee/ — *n. colloq.* long loud call ending on a shrill, rising jerk on the 'ee', used to attract attention, esp. in the bush and at a distance (orig. a call used by an Aborigine to communicate with a distant person, later adopted by settlers and now widely used). — *int.* /koo-**ee**/ utterance of such a call. — *v.* /koo-**ee**/ (**cooees, cooeed, cooeeing**) utter such a call. □ **not** (**come**) **within** (**a**) **cooee** (**of**) not (come) near achieving something desired (*didn't come within a cooee of getting elected*). **within cooee** (or **a cooee of**) very near to. [Dharuk *guuu-wi* come here]

**cooee bird** *n.* = KOEL.

**cook** /kuuk/ — *v.* **1** prepare (food) by heating it. **2** (of food) undergo cooking. **3** *colloq.* falsify (accounts etc.); alter to produce a desired result (*cooked the books*). **4** (as **be cooking**) *colloq.* be happening or about to happen (*went to find out what was cooking*). — *n.* person who cooks, esp. professionally or in a specified way (*a good cook*). □ **cook a person's** (or **one's**) **goose** see GOOSE. **cook up** *colloq.* concoct (a story, excuse, etc.). [Latin *coquus*]

**cooker** *n.* appliance or vessel for cooking food.

**cookery** *n.* art or practice of cooking.

**cookie** /**kuuk**-ee/ *n.* **1** esp. *US* sweet biscuit. **2** *colloq.* person (*a tough cookie*). □ **the way the cookie crumbles** *colloq.* how things turn out; the unalterable state of affairs. [Dutch *koekje*]

**Cooktown orchid** *n.* Australian epiphytic (or lithophytic) orchid, *Dendrobium bigibbum*, having brilliant purple flowers; the floral emblem of Queensland. [*Cooktown* in northern Queensland]

**cool** — *adj.* **1** of or at a fairly low temperature, fairly cold (*a cool day*). **2** suggesting or achieving coolness (*cool colours*; *cool clothes*). **3** calm, unexcited (*need to have a cool head*). **4** lacking enthusiasm (*a bit cool about the project*). **5** unfriendly (*a cool reception*). **6** calmly audacious (*a cool customer*). **7** (prec. by *a*) *colloq.* at least (*cost a cool thousand*). **8** *colloq.* **a** excellent; marvellous (*the party was cool*). **b** stylish; fashionable (*cool clothes*). — *n.* **1** coolness (*feeling the cool*). **2** cool air or place (*cool of the evening*). **3** *colloq.* calmness, composure (*keep one's cool*). — *v.* (often foll. by *down*, *off*) **1** make or become cool. **2** lose the heat of anger etc.; become calm. □ **cool one's heels** see HEEL[1]. **cool it** *colloq.* relax, calm down. **that's cool with me** *colloq.* that's fine as far as I am concerned. □ **coolly** /**kool**-lee/ *adv.* **coolness** *n.* [Old English]

**coolabah** var. of COOLIBAH.

**coolah grass** /**koo**-luh/ *n.* any of several Australian grasses, having wide-spreading multi-branched seed-heads used by Aborigines as food. [Wiradhuri and Kamilaroi, probably *gulu*]

**coolamon** /**koo**-luh-muhn/ *n.* (also **pitchi**) basin-like vessel of wood or bark used by Aborigines to hold water and other liquids, and for a variety of other purposes such as carrying a baby. [Kamilaroi and nearby languages *gulaman*]

**coolant** *n.* cooling agent, esp. fluid, to remove heat from an engine, nuclear reactor, etc.

**Coolgardie** /ˌkool-**gah**-dee/ *n.* (in full **Coolgardie safe**) safe, consisting of a frame covered with hessian etc. kept constantly wet with a water-drip system, used for keeping foodstuffs cool esp. in the outback. [town in WA]

**coolibah** /**koo**-luh-bah/ *n.* any of several eucalypts, esp. the blue-leaved *Eucalyptus microtheca* found across central and northern Australia in seasonally flooded areas. [Yuwaaliyaay and nearby languages *gulabaa*]

**coolie** /**koo**-lee/ *n.* unskilled native labourer in some Asian countries. [perhaps from *Kulī*, an indigenous tribe of Gujarat in India]

**cooling-off period** *n.* interval to allow for a change of mind.

**cooloolah** /**kuh**-**loo**-luh/ *n.* Australian cypress pine, *Callitris columellaris*, often used for telegraph poles. [Gabi-gabi *gululay*]

**Cooloola monster** /**kuh**-**loo**-luh/ *n.* large, cricket-like insect, discovered in the late 1970s in Cooloola National Park. [as COOLOOLAH]

**coomb** /koom/ *n.* chiefly *Brit.* valley on the side of a hill. [Old English]

**coop** — *n.* **1** cage for keeping poultry. **2** any small place of confinement. — *v.* (often foll. by *up*, *in*) confine (a person) in, or as if in, a very small space (*cooped up in the house with nowhere to go*). [Latin *cupa* cask]

**co-op** /**koh**-op/ *n. colloq.* cooperative society or shop. [abbreviation]

**cooper** *n.* maker or repairer of casks, barrels, etc. [Low German or Dutch: related to COOP]

**cooperate** /koh-**op**-uh-ˌrayt/ *v.* (also **co-operate**)(-**ting**) **1** (often foll. by *with*) work or act together. **2** be helpful and do as one is asked. □ **cooperation** /koh-ˌop-uh-**ray**-shuhn/ *n.* [Church Latin *cooperari* (as CO-, *operari* from *opus operis* work)]

**cooperative** /koh-**op**-uh-ruh-tiv, -**op**-ruh-tiv/ (also **co-operative**) — *adj.* **1** willing to cooperate. **2** of or characterised by cooperation. **3** (of a business) owned and run jointly by its members, with profits shared. — *n.* cooperative society, business, etc.

**co-opt** /koh-**opt**/ *v.* appoint to membership of a body by invitation of the existing members. □ **co-option** *n.* **co-optive** *adj.* [Latin *coopto* from *opto* choose]

**coordinate** /koh-**aw**-duh-ˌnayt/ — *v.* /koh-**aw**-duh-ˌnayt/ (-**ting**) **1** bring (various parts, movements, etc.) into a proper or required relation to ensure harmony or effective operation etc. **2** work or act together effectively. — *adj.* /koh-**aw**-duh-nuht/ **1** equal in rank or importance. **2** *Gram.* (of parts of a compound sentence) equal in status. — *n.* /koh-**aw**-duh-nuht/ **1** *Math.* each of a system of values used to fix the position of a point, line, or plane. **2** (in *pl.*) matching items of clothing. □ **coordinator** /-ˌnay-tuh/ *n.* [Latin *ordino*: related to ORDER]

**coordinate clause** *n.* (also **co-ordinate clause**) one of two or more clauses of equal status in a compound sentence, joined by a coordinating conjunction such as *and*, *but*, or *or* (cf. SUBORDINATE CLAUSE).

**coordination** /koh-ˌaw-duh-**nay**-shuhn/ *n.* (also **co-ordination**) **1** act or instance of coordinating. **2** harmonious combination of functions etc. towards the production of a result, esp. the action of muscles in the production of complex movements. □ **coordinated** *adj.*

**coot** *n.* **1** black aquatic bird with a white horny plate on its forehead. **2** *colloq.* stupid person. □ **bald as a coot** *colloq.* very bald. [probably Low German]

**coota** /koo-tuh/ n. (also **couta**) colloq. = BARRACOUTA. [abbreviation]

**Cootamundra** /koo-tuh-mun-druh/ n. (in full **Cootamundra wattle**) the wattle *Acacia baileyana*, having bluish-grey (occasionally purplish) true leaves and a brilliant display of fluffy golden ball-flowers, native to the area near the town of Cootamundra in NSW, now widely planted and naturalised elsewhere.

**cop** colloq. — n. 1 police officer. 2 capture or arrest (*it's a fair cop*). — v. (**-pp-**) 1 catch or arrest (an offender). 2 receive, suffer (*copped a lot of criticism for his action; copped a punch in the jaw for his efforts*). 3 take, seize (*copped the best bits for himself*). 4 put up with (*I'm not going to cop any more of his insults*). 5 (*imper.*) take note of (*cop the guy with the purple hair!*). □ **cop a blast** (or **the flak** or **some flak** or **a serve** or **some stick**) receive severe criticism or a tongue-lashing. **cop it sweet** be lucky. **cop out 1** withdraw; give up. **2** go back on a promise. **cop this!** look at this! **not much cop** of little value or use. **sure cop** a certainty. **sweet cop** easy task. [French *caper* seize]

**cope¹** v. (**-ping**) 1 (often foll. by *with*) deal effectively or contend successfully with a person or task. 2 manage; deal with a situation or problem (*found he could no longer cope*). [French: related to COUP]

**cope²** — n. *Eccl.* long cloaklike vestment worn by a priest or bishop at benediction, in processions, etc. — v. (**-ping**) cover with a cope or coping. [Latin *cappa* CAP]

**Copernican system** /kuh-per-ni-kuhn/ n. theory that the planets (including the earth) move round the sun. [*Copernicus*, name of an astronomer]

**copier** /kop-ee-uh/ n. machine that copies (esp. documents).

**coping** n. top (usu. sloping) course of masonry in a wall. [from COPE²]

**coping saw** n. D-shaped saw for cutting curves in wood. [from COPE¹]

**coping stone** n. stone used in coping.

**copious** /koh-pee-uhs/ adj. 1 abundant, plentiful (*copious supply of food*). 2 producing much (*this cow's a copious milker; a copious writer*). □ **copiously** adv. [Latin *copia* plenty]

**cop-out** n. cowardly evasion.

**copper¹** — n. 1 malleable red-brown metallic element, used for electrical cables and apparatus. 2 bronze coin. 3 large metal vessel for boiling esp. laundry. — adj. made of or coloured like copper. — v. cover with copper. [Latin *cuprum*]

**copper²** n. colloq. police officer. [from COP]

**copper cups** n.pl. (also **pileanthus**) any of five WA shrubs with distinctive cup-shaped orange-red, magenta, etc., flowers in profusion.

**copperhead** n. 1 highly venomous snake of south-eastern Australia, the bite of which can be fatal. 2 venomous viper of N. America.

**copperplate** n. 1 a polished copper plate for engraving or etching. b print made from this. 2 ornate style of handwriting resembling that orig. used in engravings.

**coppice** /kop-uhs/ — n. area of under-growth and small trees. — v. 1 cut back (trees) to stimulate growth. 2 (of a tree which has been cut back or, as with some eucalypts, cut down to stump level, etc.) put forth new growth. [medieval Latin: related to COUP]

**copra** /kop-ruh/ n. dried coconut-kernels. [Portuguese from Malayalam *koppara* coconut]

**copro-** comb. form dung, faeces. [Greek *kopros* dung]

**coprophagous** /kop-rof-uh-guhs/ adj. (of beetles etc.) dung-eating. [COPRO-, Greek *phag-* eat]

**coprophilia** /ˌkop-ruh-fil-ee-uh/ n. abnormal interest in faeces and defecation. [COPRO-]

**coprosma** /kuh-proz-muh/ n. small evergreen Australasian plant of the genus of the same name. [Greek *kopros* dung, *osmē* smell]

**copse** n. = COPPICE n. [shortened form]

**cop shop** n. colloq. police station.

**Copt** n. 1 native Egyptian in the Hellenistic and Roman periods. 2 native Christian of the independent Egyptian Church. [French from Arabic]

**Coptic** — n. language of the Copts. — adj. of or relating to the Copts.

**copula** /kop-yuh-luh/ n. (pl. **-s**) connecting word, esp. part of the verb *be* connecting subject and predicate. □ **copular** adj. [Latin (as CO-, *apere* fasten]

**copulate** /kop-yuh-ˌlayt/ v. (**-ting**) (often foll. by *with*) have sexual intercourse. [Latin *copulo copulat-* fasten together (as COPULA)]

**copulation** /ˌkop-yuh-lay-shuhn/ n. 1 sexual union. 2 grammatical or logical connection.

**copulative** /kop-yuh-luh-tiv/ adj. 1 serving to connect. 2 *Gram.* a (of a word) that connects words or clauses linked in sense. b connecting a subject and predicate. 3 relating to sexual union.

**copy** /kop-ee/ — n. (pl. **-ies**) 1 thing made to imitate or be identical with another. **2** single specimen of a publication or issue (*ordered twenty copies*). **3 a** material to be printed. **b** material for a newspaper or magazine article, esp. regarded as good etc. reading matter (*scandals make exciting copy*). — *v.* (**-ies, -ied**) **1 a** make a copy of. **b** (often foll. by *out*) transcribe. **2** make a copy, esp. clandestinely (*I'm sure he copied my essay*). **3** imitate, do the same as (*whatever I do, he copies it*). [Latin *copia* transcript]

**copybook** *n.* **1** book containing models of handwriting for learners to imitate. **2** (*attrib.*) exemplary (*scored a copybook century*). □ **blot one's copybook** see BLOT.

**copycat** *n. colloq.* person who copies another, esp. slavishly.

**copyist** *n.* person who makes (esp. written) copies.

**copyright** — *n.* exclusive legal right for a specified period to reproduce and control the use of literary, dramatic, musical, and artistic works, including sound recordings, films, television and radio broadcasts, and computer software. — *adj.* protected by copyright. — *v.* secure copyright for (material).

**copywriter** *n.* person who writes or prepares advertising copy for publication.

**coquette** /ko-**ket**, koh-**ket**/ *n.* woman who flirts. □ **coquetry** /**kok**-uh-tree, koh-**kuh**-/ *n.* (*pl.* **-ies**). **coquettish** *adj.* [French diminutive: related to COCK¹]

**cor-** see COM-.

**coracle** /**ko**-ruh-kuhl/ *n.* small boat of wickerwork covered with watertight material. [Welsh]

**coral** /**ko**-ruhl/ — *n.* hard red, pink, or white calcareous substance secreted by marine polyps for support and habitation. — *adj.* **1** red or pink, like coral. **2** made of coral. **3** used as a descriptive epithet for Australian fauna and flora with reference either to habitat or to a fancied resemblance (*coral fish; coral gum*). [Greek *korallion*]

**coral cod** *n.* = CORAL TROUT.

**coral fern** *n.* **1** any of several ferns of the genus *Gleichenia* having slender forked coral-like fronds and found in all Australian States. **2** = CLUB MOSS.

**coral gum** *n.* small eucalypt of WA having a profuse display of coral-pink flowers.

**coral island** *n.* island formed by the growth of coral.

**coralline** /**ko**-ruh-luyn/ — *n.* seaweed with a hard jointed stem. — *adj.* of or like coral. [French and Italian: related to CORAL]

**coral pea** *n.* **1** any of several climbing or trailing plants of the Australian genus *Kennedia* with red or purple flowers, esp. the dusky coral pea, *K. rubicunda*, having coral-red flowers. **2** = SCARLET RUNNING POSTMAN. **3** (also **false sarsaparilla, purple coral pea**) = HARDENBERGIA.

**coral reef** *n.* reef formed by the growth of coral.

**coral snake** *n.* small venomous Australian snake, reddish-brown in colour with delicate black and yellow bands.

**coral tree** *n.* any of several Australian trees of the genus *Erythrina* with bright red or yellowish flowers, esp. the BATSWING CORAL TREE.

**coral trout** *n.* (also **coral cod**) blue-spotted fish of northern Australian coastal waters, highly prized for eating.

**cor anglais** /kawr-**ahng**-glay/ *n.* (*pl.* **cors anglais** /kawz/) alto woodwind instrument of the oboe family. [French]

**corbel** /**kaw**-buhl/ *n.* projection of stone, timber, etc., jutting out from a wall to support a weight. [Latin *corvus* crow]

**cord** — *n.* **1 a** flexible material like thick string, made from twisted strands. **b** piece of this. **2** similar structure in the body (*spinal cord*). **3** ribbed fabric, esp. corduroy. **4** electric flex. **5** moral or emotional tie (*cords of affection; cords binding him to his mother's apron*). — *v.* **1** fasten or bind with cord. **2** (as **corded** *adj.*) (of cloth) ribbed. [Greek *khordē* string]

**cordate** /**kaw**-dayt/ *adj.* heart-shaped. [Latin *cor* heart- heart]

**cordial** /**kaw**-dee-uhl/ — *adj.* **1** heartfelt, sincere. **2** friendly, warm. — *n.* fruit-flavoured drink. □ **cordiality** /-al-uh-tee/ *n.* **cordially** *adv.* [Latin *cor* cordheart]

**cordie** /**kaw**-dee/ *n. colloq.* member of the Corps of Staff Cadets at the Royal Military College, Duntroon, in Canberra.

**cordite** /**kaw**-duyt/ *n.* smokeless explosive. [from CORD, because of its appearance]

**cordless** *adj.* (of a hand-held electrical device) usable without a power cable because working from an internal source of energy or battery.

**cordon** /**kaw**-duhn/ — *n.* **1** line or circle of police, soldiers, guards, etc., esp. preventing access. **2** ornamental cord or braid. **3** fruit-tree trained to grow as a single stem. — *v.* (often foll. by *off*) enclose or separate with a cordon of police etc. [Italian and French: related to CORD]

**cordon bleu** /ˌkaw-don **bler**/ *Cookery* — *adj.* of the highest class. — *n.* cook of this class. [French, = blue ribbon]

**cords** *n.pl. colloq.* corduroy trousers. [abbreviation]

**corduroy** /**kaw**-duh-ˌroi, -dyuh-ˌroi/ *n.* **1** thick cotton fabric with velvety ribs. **2** (in *pl.*) corduroy trousers. [*cord* = ribbed fabric]

**cordy** var. of CORDIE.

**core** — *n.* **1** horny central part of certain fruits, containing the seeds. **2** central or most important part of anything (also *attrib.*: *core curriculum*). **3** inner central region of the earth. **4** part of a nuclear reactor containing fissile material. **5** central part cut out (esp. of rock etc. in boring). **6** inner strand of an electric cable. **7** piece of soft iron forming the centre of an electromagnet or induction coil. — *v.* (**-ring**) remove the core from. □ **corer** *n.* [origin unknown]

**corella** /kuh-**rel**-uh/ *n.* either of two large white Australian parrots, the little corella of western, eastern, and northern Australia, and the long-billed corella of central and western Victoria and surrounding areas. [Wiradhuri, probably *garila*]

**coriander** /ˌko-ree-**an**-duh/ *n.* **1** aromatic plant with leaves used for flavouring in eastern dishes, and small round fruit. **2** its powdered seeds used for flavouring in curries and as the largest ingredient in Sri Lankan etc. curry powder. [Greek *koriannon*]

**Corinthian** /kuh-**rin**-thee-uhn/ *adj.* **1** of ancient Corinth in southern Greece. **2** *Archit.* of the order characterised by ornate decoration and acanthus leaves. [Latin from Greek]

**cork¹** /**kawk**/ — *n.* **1** buoyant light-brown bark of a S. European oak. **2** bottle-stopper of cork or other material. **3** float of cork used in fishing etc. **4** (*attrib.*) made of cork. — *v.* (often foll. by *up*) **1** stop or confine. **2** restrain (feelings etc.). □ **put a cork in it** *colloq.* stop talking, shut up. **cork up!** *colloq.* shut up! [Spanish *alcorque*]

**cork²** *v.* bruise (*corked his thigh playing footy*). □ **corked** *adj.*

**corkage** *n.* charge made by a restaurant etc. for serving a customer's own wine etc.

**corkbark** *n.* any of several Australian shrubs or trees having a thick, rough, and corky bark, esp. of the genus *Hakea*.

**corked** *adj.* **1** stopped with a cork. **2** (of wine) spoilt by a decayed cork. **3** *colloq.* drunk.

**corker** *n. colloq.* excellent person or thing.

**corkie** /**kaw**-kee/ *n. colloq.* bad bruise (esp. on the thigh) (*received a corkie playing footy*). [CORK²]

**corkscrew** — *n.* **1** spiral device for extracting corks from bottles. **2** (often *attrib.*) thing with a spiral shape. — *v.* move spirally; twist.

**corkscrew grass** *n.* any of several Australian grasses bearing sharp pointed fruits with spirally twisted awns.

**corkwood** *n.* Australian shrub or small tree (genus *Duboisia*, from the leaves of which the important alkaloid *duboisine* is extracted), having a rough corky bark and shiny leaves: the leaves of a closely related plant were chewed by Aborigines for the narcotic effect (see PITURI).

**corm** *n.* underground swollen stem base of some plants. [Greek *kormos* lopped tree-trunk]

**cormorant** /**kaw**-muh-ruhnt/ *n.* any of various diving waterbirds having black or pied plumage, including the Australian little black cormorant and pied cormorant. [Latin *corvus marinus* sea-raven]

**corn¹** *n.* **1 a** maize or Indian corn. **b** chiefly *Brit.* wheat or oats. **c** cereal before or after harvesting, esp. the chief crop of a region. **d** grain or seed of a cereal plant. **2** *colloq.* something corny or trite. [Old English]

**corn²** *n.* small tender area of horny skin, esp. on the toe. [Latin *cornu* horn]

**corn cob** *n.* cylindrical centre of a maize ear on which the grains grow.

**corncrake** *n.* bird (a rail) of Australia and elsewhere, inhabiting grassland and nesting on the ground.

**cornea** /**kaw**-nee-uh/ *n.* transparent circular part of the front of the eyeball. □ **corneal** *adj.* [medieval Latin: related to CORN²]

**corned** *adj.* (esp. of beef) preserved in salt or brine. [from CORN¹]

**cornelian** /kaw-**nee**-lee-uhn/ *n.* (also **carnelian** /kah-/) dull red variety of chalcedony. [French]

**corner** — *n.* **1** place where converging sides or edges meet. **2** projecting angle, esp. where two streets meet. **3** internal space or recess formed by the meeting of two sides, esp. of a room. **4** difficult position, esp. one with no escape (*driven into a corner*). **5** secluded place (*some dark corner of the mind*; *given to whispering in corners*). **6** region or quarter, esp. a remote one (*from the four corners of the earth*). **7** action or result of buying or controlling the whole stock of a commodity. **8** *Boxing* & *Wrestling* corner of the ring where a contestant rests between rounds. **9** *Soccer* & *Hockey* free kick or hit from the corner of a pitch. **10** (**Corner**) = CORNER COUNTRY. — *v.* **1** force into a difficult or inescapable position (*the police have him cornered*). **2** establish a corner (*n.* sense 7) in (a commodity) (*have cornered the market*). **3** (esp. of or in a vehicle) go round a corner. □ **cut corners** see CUT. **round the corner 1** nearby; a short distance away. **2** at hand; about to occur or be realised (*said that the End of the World was round the corner*). **turn the corner** begin to improve; start recovering from an illness. [Latin: related to CORN²]

**Corner Country** *n.* (also **the Corner**) area in which the borders of NSW, Queensland, and SA meet.

**cornerstone** *n.* **1 a** stone in the projecting angle of a wall. **b** foundation-stone. **2** indispensable part or basis.

**cornet** /**kaw**-nuht/ *n.* **1** brass instrument resembling a trumpet but shorter and wider. **2** conical wafer for holding ice-cream. □ **cornetist** /kaw-**net**-uhst, **kaw**-nuh-tuhst/ *n.* (also **cornettist**). [Latin *cornu*: related to CORN²]

**cornflour** *n.* fine-ground flour, esp. of maize or rice.

**cornice** /**kaw**-nuhs/ *n.* ornamental moulding, esp. round a room just below the ceiling or as the topmost part of an entablature. [French from Italian]

**Cornish** /**kaw**-nish/ — *adj.* of Cornwall in England. — *n.* Celtic language of Cornwall.

**cornstalk** *n.* **1** *hist.* nickname for a non-Aboriginal native-born Australian (as opposed to a recent British immigrant), the Australians purportedly being remarkable for their tall height and leanness. **2** nickname for a person native to or resident in NSW.

**cornucopia** /ˌkaw-nyuh-**koh**-pee-uh/ *n.* **1** goat's horn overflowing with flowers, fruit, and corn, as a symbol of plenty. **2** abundant supply. □ **cornucopian** *adj.* [Latin: related to CORN², COPIOUS]

**corny** *adj.* (**-ier, -iest**) *colloq.* **1** banal, trite, hackneyed (*a corny joke*). **2** tiresomely or ridiculously old-fashioned or sentimental. □ **cornily** *adv.* **corniness** *n.* [from CORN¹]

**corolla** /kuh-**roh**-luh/ *n.* whorl of petals forming the inner envelope of a flower. [Latin diminutive of CORONA]

**corollary** /kuh-**rol**-uh-ree/ *n.* (*pl.* **-ies**) **1** proposition that follows from one already

proved. **2** (often foll. by *of*) natural consequence or result. [Latin, = gratuity: related to COROLLA]

**corona** /kuh-**roh**-nuh/ *n.* (*pl.* **-nae** /-nee/) **1 a** small circle of light round the sun or moon. **b** gaseous envelope of the sun, seen as an area of light around the moon during a total solar eclipse. **2** *Anat.* crownlike structure. **3** *Bot* crownlike outgrowth from the inner side of a corolla. **4** glow around an electric conductor. □ **coronal** *adj.* [Latin, = crown]

**coronary** /**ko**-ruh-nuh-ree, -ruhn-ree/ — *adj.* *Anat.* (of blood-vessels etc.) resembling or encircling like a crown. — *n.* (*pl.* **-ies**) = CORONARY THROMBOSIS. [Latin: related to CORONA]

**coronary artery** *n.* artery supplying blood to the heart.

**coronary thrombosis** *n.* blockage caused by a blood clot in a coronary artery.

**coronation** /ˌko-ruh-**nay**-shuhn/ *n.* ceremony of crowning a sovereign or consort. [medieval Latin: related to CORONA]

**coroner** /**ko**-ruh-nuh/ *n.* official holding inquests on deaths thought to be violent or accidental. [Anglo-French: related to CROWN]

**coronet** /**ko**-ruh-net/ *n.* **1** small crown. **2** circlet of precious materials, esp. as a headdress. [French diminutive: related to CROWN]

**coronial** /kuh-**roh**-nee-uhl/ *adj.* of or relating to a coroner.

**corpora** *pl.* of CORPUS.

**corporal¹** /**kaw**-puh-ruhl/ *n.* army or air force NCO below sergeant. [French from Italian]

**corporal²** /**kaw**-puh-ruhl/ *adj.* of the human body. □ **corporality** /ˌkaw-puh-**ral**-uh-tee/ *n.* [Latin *corpus* body]

**corporal punishment** *n.* physical punishment.

**corporate** /**kaw**-puh-ruht/ *adj.* **1** forming a corporation (*body corporate*). **2** of, belonging to, or united in a group (*corporate responsibility*). [Latin: related to CORPORAL²]

**corporation** /ˌkaw-puh-**ray**-shuhn/ *n.* **1** group of people authorised to act as an individual and recognised in law as a single entity, esp. in business. **2** *joc.* large stomach.

**corporeal** /kaw-**paw**-ree-uhl/ *adj.* bodily, physical, material, as distinct from *spiritual*. □ **corporeality** /-al-uh-tee/ *n.* **corporeally** *adv.* [Latin: related to CORPORAL²]

**corps** /kaw/ n. (pl. **corps** /kawz/ ) **1 a** body of troops with special duties (*intelligence corps*). **b** main subdivision of an army in the field. **2** body of people engaged in a special activity (*diplomatic corps*). [French: related to CORPSE]

**corps de ballet** /ˌkaw duh **bal**-ay/ n. group of ensemble dancers in a ballet. [French]

**corpse** n. dead body. [Latin: related to CORPUS]

**corpulent** /**kaw**-pyuh-luhnt/ adj. physically bulky; fat. □ **corpulence** n. [Latin: related to CORPUS]

**corpus** /**kaw**-puhs/ n. (pl. **-pora**) body or collection of writings, texts, etc. [Latin, = body]

**corpuscle** /**kaw**-puh-suhl/ n. minute body or cell in an organism, esp. (in pl.) the red or white cells in the blood of vertebrates. □ **corpuscular** /kaw-**pus**-kyuh-luh/ adj. [Latin diminutive of CORPUS]

**corpus delicti** /ˌkaw-puhs duh-**lik**-tuy/ n. Law facts and circumstances constituting a breach of a law. [Latin, = body of offence]

**corral** /ko-**rahl**/ — n. **1** pen for cattle, horses, etc. **2** enclosure for capturing wild animals. — v. (**-ll-**) put or keep in a corral. [Spanish and Portuguese]

**correa** /ko-**ree**-uh/ n. any shrub of the Australian genus of the same name, confined mainly to south-eastern Australia, bearing decorative, usu. tubular flowers of yellow, red, green, or a mixture of these, e.g. native fuchsia (*Correa reflexa*) with green-yellow or deep red flowers with yellow tips (see also CHEF'S HAT CORREA). [J.F. *Correia* da Serra, Portuguese botanist (d. 1823)]

**correct** /kuh-**rekt**/ — adj. **1** true, accurate (*the answer is correct*). **2** proper, in accordance with taste or a standard (*correct manners*). — v. **1** set right; amend (an error, omission, etc., or the person responsible for it). **2** mark errors in (written or printed work etc.). **3** substitute what is right for the errors or faults in (writing, a printer's proofs, etc.). **4 a** admonish or rebuke (a person) (*corrected him when he swore in front of the vicar*). **b** punish (a person or fault) (*parents have the right to correct their children when they do wrong*). **5** counteract (a harmful quality) (*correct the imbalance*). **6** adjust (an instrument etc.) to function accurately or accord with a standard. □ **correctly** adv. **correctness** n. **corrector** n. [Latin *rego rect-* guide]

**correction** /kuh-**rek**-shuhn/ n. **1 a** act or process of correcting. **b** instance of this.

**2** thing substituted for what is wrong; emendation (in writing, a printer's proofs, etc.). **3** *archaic* punishment (*house of correction*). □ **correctional** adj. [Latin: related to CORRECT]

**correctitude** /kuh-**rek**-tuh-ˌtyood/ n. consciously correct behaviour. [from CORRECT, RECTITUDE]

**corrective** — adj. serving to correct or counteract something harmful or undesired. — n. corrective measure or thing. [Latin: related to CORRECT]

**correlate** /**ko**-ruh-ˌlayt/ — v. (**-ting**) (usu. foll. by *with, to*) have or bring into a mutual relation or dependence (*we need to correlate our expenditure with our income*). — n. each of two related or complementary things (esp. so related that one implies the other) (*liver damage is a correlate of alcohol abuse*). □ **correlation** /ˌko-ruh-**lay**-shuhn/ n. [medieval Latin *correlatio*]

**correlative** /ko-**rel**-uh-tiv, kuh-/ — adj. **1** (often foll. by *with, to*) having a mutual relation. **2** (of words) corresponding to each other and used together (as *neither* and *nor*). — n. correlative word or thing.

**correspond** /ˌko-ruh-**spond**/ v. **1 a** (usu. foll. by *to*) be similar or equivalent (*the Australian Senate does not correspond to the British House of Lords*). **b** (usu. foll. by *with, to*) be in agreement, not contradict (*his account corresponds with yours*). **2** (usu. foll. by *with*) communicate by interchange of letters. □ **correspondingly** adv. [French from medieval Latin]

**correspondence** n. **1** agreement or similarity. **2 a** exchange of letters. **b** letters.

**correspondent** n. **1** person who writes letters. **2** person employed to write or report for a newspaper or for broadcasting etc.

**corridor** /**ko**-ruh-ˌdaw/ n. **1** passage giving access into rooms. **2** passage in a train giving access into compartments. **3** strip of territory of one nation passing through that of another, esp. securing access to the sea. **4** route which an aircraft must follow, esp. over a foreign country. [French from Italian]

**corrigendum** /ˌko-ruh-**gen**-duhm/ n. (pl. **-da**) error to be corrected. [Latin *corrigo*: related to CORRECT]

**corrigible** /**ko**-ruh-juh-buhl/ adj. **1** able to be corrected. **2** (of a person) submissive; open to correction. □ **corrigibly** adv. [medieval Latin: related to CORRIGENDUM]

**corroborate** /ko-**rob**-uh-ˌrayt/ v. (**-ting**) confirm or give support to (a statement or belief, or the person holding it), esp. in relation to witnesses in a law court (*his* *story was fully corroborated by the evidence*). □ **corroboration** /-**ray**-shuhn/ *n.* **corroborative** /-ruh-tiv/ *adj.* **corroborator** *n.* [Latin *robur* strength]

**corroboree** /kuh-**rob**-uh-ree/ — *n.* **1** Aboriginal dance ceremony, of which song and rhythmical musical accompaniment are an integral part, and which may be sacred and ritualised or non-sacred, occasional, and informal. **2** loosely, in extended senses, esp. with reference to an Aboriginal meeting or assembly, or to Aboriginal festivity generally. **3** in transferred senses (*a dozen magpies sitting on my fence and holding a corroboree of warbling; the weird, wonderful corroboree which takes place each year at Flemington to celebrate the Melbourne Cup*). **4** *colloq.* any noisy party or gathering. — *v.* **1** (of Aborigines) perform a corroboree. **2** in transferred senses (*surfies corroboreeing on the beach around a bonfire; mozzies corroboreed around my ears all night*). [Dharuk *garabari* a style of dancing]

**corroboree frog** *n.* small frog *Pseudophryne corroboree* of mountainous southern NSW, with black and yellow markings thought to resemble Aboriginal body-painting.

**corrode** /kuh-**rohd**/ *v.* (**-ding**) **1 a** wear away, esp. by chemical action. **b** decay. **2** destroy gradually (*his hopes have been corroded by recent misfortunes*). [Latin *rodo ros-* gnaw]

**corrosion** /kuh-**roh**-zhuhn/ *n.* **1** process of corroding, esp. of a rusting metal. **2 a** damage caused by corroding. **b** corroded area. □ **corrosive** *adj. & n.* [as CORRODE]

**corrugate** /**ko**-ruh-,gayt/ *v.* (**-ting**) (esp. as **corrugated** *adj.*) form into alternate ridges and grooves, esp. to strengthen (*corrugated iron*). □ **corrugation** /-**gay**-shuhn/ *n.* [Latin *ruga* wrinkle]

**corrupt** /kuh-**rupt**/ — *adj.* **1** dishonest, esp. using bribery. **2** immoral; wicked. **3** (of a text, computer data, etc.) made unreliable by errors or alterations. **4** rotten. — *v.* **1** make or become corrupt or depraved. **2** affect or harm by errors or alterations. **3** infect, taint. □ **corruptible** *adj.* **corruptibility** /-**bil**-uh-tee/ *n.* **corruptive** *adj.* **corruptly** *adv.* **corruptness** *n.* [Latin *rumpo rupt-* break]

**corruption** /kuh-**rup**-shuhn/ *n.* **1** moral deterioration, esp. widespread. **2** use of corrupt practices, esp. bribery or fraud (*alleged corruption in the police force*). **3 a** irregular alteration (of a text, computer data, etc.) from its original state. **b** an irregular altered form of a word. **4**

decomposition, esp. of a corpse or other organic matter.

**corsage** /kaw-**sahzh**/ *n.* small bouquet worn by women. [French: related to CORPSE]

**corsair** /**kaw**-sair/ *n.* **1** pirate ship. **2** pirate. [French: related to COURSE]

**corset** /**kaw**-suht/ *n.* closely-fitting undergarment worn to shape the body or to support it after injury. □ **corsetry** *n.* [French diminutive: related to CORPSE]

**cortège** /kaw-**tayzh**/ *n.* **1** procession, esp. for a funeral. **2** group of attendants. [French]

**cortex** /**kaw**-teks/ *n.* (*pl.* **-tices** /-tuh-,seez/ ) outer part of an organ, esp. of the brain or kidneys. □ **cortical** /**kaw**-tuh-kuhl/ *adj.* [Latin, = bark]

**cortisone** /**kaw**-tuh-,zohn/ *n.* hormone from the adrenal cortex used esp. in treating inflammation and allergy. [abbreviation of its chemical name]

**corundum** /kuh-**run**-duhm/ *n.* extremely hard crystallised alumina, used esp. as an abrasive, and varieties of which, e.g. ruby and sapphire, are used for gemstones. [Tamil *kurundam* from Sanskrit *kuruvinda* ruby]

**coruscate** /**ko**-ruh-,skayt/ *v.* (**-ting**) give off flashing light; sparkle. □ **coruscation** /-**skay**-shuhn/ *n.* [Latin]

**corvette** /kaw-**vet**/ *n.* **1** small naval escort-vessel. **2** *hist.* warship with one tier of guns. [French from Dutch]

**corymb** /**ko**-rimb, **ko**-rim/ *n.* flat-topped cluster of flowers with the flower-stalks proportionally longer lower down the stem. [Latin from Greek]

**cos**[1] /kos, koz/ *n.* lettuce with crisp narrow leaves. [*Kōs*, Greek island]

**cos**[2] /koz/ *abbr.* cosine.

**cos**[3] /koz, kuhz/ *conj. colloq.* because. [abbreviation]

**cosec** /**koh**-sek/ *abbr.* cosecant.

**cosecant** /koh-**see**-kuhnt/ *n. Math.* ratio of the hypotenuse (in a right-angled triangle) to the side opposite an acute angle.

**cosh** *colloq.* — *n.* heavy blunt weapon. — *v.* hit with a cosh. [origin unknown]

**co-signatory** /koh-**sig**-nuh-tuh-ree, -tree/ *n.* (*pl.* **-ies**) person or nation signing a treaty etc. jointly with others.

**cosine** /**koh**-suyn/ *n.* ratio of the side adjacent to an acute angle (in a right-angled triangle) to the hypotenuse.

**cosmetic** /koz-**met**-ik/ — *adj.* **1** intended to enhance or beautify the body, esp. the face. **2** intended to improve only appearances; superficially improving or beneficial (*these are only cosmetic* *changes to the rules).* **3** (of surgery or a prosthesis) imitating, restoring, or enhancing normal appearance. — *n.* cosmetic preparation, esp. for the face. □ **cosmetically** *adv.* [Greek *kosmētikos* from *kosmeō* adorn from *kosmos* order, adornment]

**cosmic** /**koz**-mik/ *adj.* **1** of the universe or cosmos or its scale; universal *(of cosmic significance).* **2** of or for space travel.

**cosmic rays** *n.pl.* high-energy radiations from space that reach the earth from all directions, usu. with high energy and penetrative power.

**cosmogony** /koz-**mog**-uh-nee/ *n.* (*pl.* **-ies**) **1** origin of the universe. **2** theory about this. [from COSMOS, Greek *-gonia* -begetting]

**cosmography** /koz-**mog**-ruh-fee/ *n.* (*pl.* **-ies**) description or mapping of general features of the universe (including the earth). □ **cosmographer** *n.* **cosmographic** /-muh-**graf**-ik/ *adj.* **cosmographical** /-muh-**graf**-i-kuhl/ *adj.* [from COSMOS, -GRAPHY]

**cosmology** /koz-**mol**-uh-jee/ *n.* science or theory of the universe. □ **cosmological** /-muh-**loj**-i-kuhl/ *adj.* **cosmologist** *n.* [from COSMOS, -LOGY]

**cosmonaut** /**koz**-muh-nawt/ *n.* Russian astronaut. [from COSMOS, Greek *nautēs* sailor]

**cosmopolitan** /ˌkoz-muh-**pol**-uh-tuhn/ — *adj.* **1 a** of, from, or knowing many parts of the world. **b** consisting of people from many or all parts *(Sydney is a very cosmopolitan city).* **2** free from national limitations or prejudices. **3** *Ecology* (of a plant, animal, etc.) widely distributed. — *n.* cosmopolitan person. □ **cosmopolitanism** *n.* [from COSMOS, Greek *politēs* citizen]

**cosmos** /**koz**-mos/ *n.* the universe, esp. as a well-ordered whole. [Greek, = order, adornment]

**Cossack** /**kos**-ak/ *n.* member of a people of southern Russia, noted for their horsemanship, and formerly famous for their military skill under the tsars. [Turki *quzzāq* nomad, adventurer]

**cosset** /**kos**-uht/ *v.* (**-t-**) pamper. [British dial. *cosset* = pet lamb, probably from Old English, = cottager]

**cossie** /**koz**-ee/ *n.* (also **cossy**) *colloq.* swimming costume. [abbreviation]

**cost** — *v.* (*past* and *past part.* **cost**) **1** be obtainable for (a sum of money); have as a price *(costs $200).* **2** involve as a loss or sacrifice *(cost them much effort; it cost him his life).* **3** (*past* and *past part.* **costed**) fix or estimate the cost of *(costed the repairs at $500).* **4** *colloq.* **a** be costly to *(it'll cost you).* **b** be costly *(I think it's going to cost).* — *n.* **1** what a thing costs; price. **2** loss or sacrifice; an expenditure of time, effort, etc. **3** (in *pl.*) legal expenses, esp. those allowed in favour of the winning party or against the losing party in a suit. □ **at all costs** (or **at any cost**) whatever the cost or risk may be. [Latin *consto* stand at a price]

**costal** /**kos**-tuhl/ *adj.* of the ribs. [Latin *costa* rib]

**cost-effective** *adj.* (also **cost-efficient**) effective or productive in relation to its cost.

**costing** *n.* estimation of cost(s).

**costive** /**kos**-tiv/ *adj.* constipated. [Latin: related to CONSTIPATE]

**costly** *adj.* (**-ier**, **-iest**) costing much; expensive. □ **costliness** *n.*

**cost of living** *n.* level of prices esp. of basic necessities.

**cost price** *n.* price paid for a thing by one who later sells it.

**costume** /**kos**-tyoom/ — *n.* **1** style of dress, esp. of a particular place or time. **2** set of clothes. **3** clothing for a particular activity, social occasion, etc. *(swimming-costume; fancy-dress costume; Father Christmas costume).* **4** actor's clothes for a part. — *v.* (**-ming**) provide with a costume. [Latin: related to CUSTOM]

**costume jewellery** *n.* artificial jewellery.

**costumier** /kos-**tyoo**-mee-uh/ *n.* person who makes or deals in costumes. [French: related to COSTUME]

**cosy** /**koh**-zee/ — *adj.* (**-ier**, **-iest**) comfortable and warm; snug. — *n.* (*pl.* **-ies**) cover to keep a teapot etc. hot. □ **cosily** *adv.* **cosiness** *n.* [origin unknown]

**cot**¹ *n.* **1** small bed with high sides for a baby. **2** small light bed. [Hindi *khāt* bedstead, hammock]

**cot**² *n. poet.* cottage. [Old English]

**cot**³ *abbr.* cotangent.

**cotangent** /koh-**tan**-juhnt/ *n.* ratio of the side adjacent to an acute angle (in a right-angled triangle) to the opposite side.

**cot-case** *n.* **1** person too ill to leave his or her bed. **2** *colloq.* person incapacitated by drink. **3** *colloq.* eccentric or mad person.

**cot death** *n.* (also **Sudden Infant Death Syndrome** or **SIDS**) unexplained death of a sleeping baby.

**cote** *n.* shelter for animals or birds. [Old English]

**coterie** /**koh**-tuh-ree/ *n.* exclusive group of people sharing interests. [French]

**coterminous** /koh-**ter**-muh-nuhs/ *adj.* (often foll. by *with*) having the same boundaries or extent (in space, time, or meaning). [CO-, *terminus* boundary]

**cotoneaster** /kuh-,toh-nee-**as**-tuh/ *n.* shrub (of Europe etc.) bearing usu. bright red berries; often cultivated as an ornamental in Australia, and becoming a serious pest in native forests etc. [Latin *cotoneum* QUINCE]

**cottage** /**kot**-ij/ *n.* **1** small simple house, esp. in the country. **2** detached, single-storeyed suburban house. [Anglo-French: related to COT², COTE]

**cottage cheese** *n.* soft white lumpy cheese made from skimmed milk curds.

**cottage industry** *n.* business activity carried on at home.

**cotter** *n.* **1** bolt or wedge for securing parts of machinery etc. **2** (in full **cotter pin**) split pin that can be opened after passing through a hole. [origin unknown]

**cotton** /**kot**-uhn/ *n.* **1** soft white fibrous substance covering the seeds of certain plants. **2** such a plant. **3** thread or cloth from this. □ **cotton on** (often foll. by *to*) *colloq.* begin to understand. □ **cottony** *adj.* [French from Arabic *ḳuṭn*]

**cotton bud** *n. propr.* small stick with cotton wool at each end, suitable for applying medication to the mouth, nostril, etc.

**cottonbush** *n.* any of several Australian shrubs bearing white cotton-like clusters.

**cotton tree** *n.* **1** any of several Australian plants, esp. *Hibiscus tiliaceus*, a small tree with large round leaves and very large yellow flowers with a red heart. **2** = KAPOK TREE.

**cottonwood** *n.* small tree of NSW, the ACT, and Victoria, having a white woolly down on the leaves.

**cotton wool** *n.* fluffy wadding of a kind orig. made from raw cotton. □ **keep** (or **wrap**) **in cotton wool** coddle or pamper (a person) as if fragile.

**cottony cushion scale** *n.* Australian scale insect which infests fruit trees, wattles, etc., covering its eggs with a white wax-like substance.

**cotyledon** /kot-uh-**lee**-duhn/ *n.* embryonic leaf in seed-bearing plants. [Greek *kotulē* cup]

**coucal** /**koo**-kal/ *n.* = PHEASANT COUCAL.

**couch¹** /kowch/ — *n.* **1** upholstered piece of furniture for several people; sofa. **2** long padded seat with a headrest at one end, esp. one on which a psychiatrist's or doctor's patient reclines during examination. — *v.* **1** (foll. by *in*) express in (certain terms) (*couched it in language all could understand*). **2** lay on, or as on, a couch

(*couched his head on my breast*). **3** *archaic* (of an animal) lie, esp. in its lair. **4** lower (a spear etc.) to the position for attack. **5** *Med.* treat (a cataract) by displacing the lens of the eye. [Latin *colloco* lay in place]

**couch²** /kooch/ *n.* (in full **couch grass**) any of several grasses with long creeping roots, often used in lawns. [Old English, perhaps related to QUICK]

**couch potato** /kowch/ *colloq.* — *n.* person who spends leisure time passively (e.g. by sitting watching television or videos), eats junk food, and takes little or no physical exercise (cf. NORM). — *v.* (couch-potato) behave as a couch potato does (*parents should take action if they notice that their children are couch-potatoing*).

**cougar** /**koo**-guh/ *n. US* puma. [French from Guarani]

**cough** /kof/ — *v.* **1** expel air etc. from the lungs with a sudden sharp sound. **2** (of an engine etc.) make a similar sound. — *n.* **1** act of coughing. **2** condition of respiratory organs causing coughing. □ **cough up 1** eject with coughs. **2** *colloq.* bring out or give (money or information), esp. reluctantly. [imitative, related to Dutch *kuchen*]

**could** /kuud/ *past* of CAN¹. — *v. colloq.* feel inclined to (*I could murder him*).

**couldn't** /**kuud**-uhnt/ *contr.* could not.

**coulomb** /**koo**-lom/ *n.* SI unit of electric charge, equal to the quantity of electricity conveyed in one second by a current of one ampere. [*Coulomb*, name of a French physicist (d. 1806)]

**council** /**kown**-suhl/ *n.* **1 a** advisory, deliberative, or administrative body. **b** meeting of such a body. **2 a** local administrative body of a town etc. **b** (*attrib.*) provided by a local council (*council road*). [Latin *concilium*]

**councillor** *n.* member of a (esp. local) council.

**counsel** /**kown**-suhl/ — *n.* **1** advice, esp. formally given. **2** consultation, esp. to seek or give advice. **3** (*pl.* same) legal adviser, esp. a barrister; body of these advising in a case. **4** plan of action. — *v.* (**-ll-**) **1** advise (a person) (*counselled me to stay away from him*). **2** give esp. professional advice to (a person) on personal problems. **3** recommend (a course of action). □ **keep one's own counsel** not confide in others. **take counsel** (usu. foll. by *with*) consult. □ **counselling** *n.* [Latin *consilium*]

**counsellor** *n.* **1** adviser. **2** person giving professional guidance on personal problems (*marriage guidance counsellor*).

**count¹** — v. **1** determine the total number of, esp. by assigning successive numbers. **2** repeat numbers in ascending order. **3** (often foll. by *in*) include or be included in one's reckoning or plan (*you can count me in; fifteen people, not counting the guide*). **4** consider or regard to be (lucky etc.) (*you can count yourself lucky you weren't killed*). **5** (often foll. by *for*) have value; matter (*my opinion counts for little*). — n. **1 a** act of counting or being counted. **b** sum total of a reckoning (*blood count; pollen count*). **2** *Law* each charge in an indictment (*guilty on ten counts*). □ **count against** be reckoned to the disadvantage of. **count one's blessings** be grateful for what one has. **count on** (or **upon**) rely on; expect confidently (*we're counting on your help*). **count out 1** count while taking from a stock. **2** complete a count of ten seconds over (a fallen boxer etc.). **3** *colloq.* exclude, disregard (*you can count me out*). **4** count (sheep or cattle) as they leave a pen or paddock. **count up** find the sum of. **keep count** take note of how many there have been etc. **lose count** forget the number etc. counted. **out for the count** *Boxing* defeated by being unable to rise within a count of ten. **2 a** defeated, demoralised. **b** unconscious; asleep. [Latin: related to COMPUTE]

**count²** n. nobleman (in some European countries) corresponding to a British earl. [Latin *comes* companion]

**countdown** n. **1** act of counting backwards to zero, esp. at the launching of a rocket etc. **2** period immediately before an event (*countdown to the Grand Final*).

**countenance** /kown-tuh-nuhns/ — n. **1** the face or facial expression. **2** composure (*keep one's countenance*). **3** moral support (*I shall lend no countenance to such a scheme*). — v. (**-cing**) **1** give approval to (an act etc.) (*cannot countenance this breach of the rules*). **2** (often foll. by *in*) encourage (a person or practice) (*countenanced him in his crusade against smoking; if you don't act against him, you'll be countenancing fraud*). [French: related to CONTAIN]

**counter¹** n. **1** long flat-topped fitment in a shop etc., across which business is conducted. **2 a** small disc for playing or scoring in board-games etc. **b** token representing a coin. **3** apparatus for counting. □ **under the counter** surreptitiously, esp. illegally. [related to COUNT¹]

**counter²** — v. **1 a** oppose, contradict (*countered our proposal with their own*). **b** meet by a countermove (*countered my move by taking my knight*). **c** make an opposing statement (*'I shall!' he countered*). **2** *Boxing* give a return blow while parrying. — adv. **1** in the opposite direction (*ran counter to the dingo*). **2** contrary (*his action was counter to my instructions*). — adj. opposite; opposed. — n. **1** parry; countermove. **2** something opposite or opposed. [related to COUNTER-]

**counter-** comb. form denoting: **1** retaliation, opposition, or rivalry (*counterthreat*). **2** opposite direction (*counterclockwise*). **3** correspondence (*counterpart; countersign*). [Latin *contra* against]

**counteract** /kown-tuh-**rakt**/ v. hinder or neutralise by contrary action (*this pill should counteract the fever*). □ **counteraction** n. **counteractive** adj.

**counter-attack** — n. attack in reply to a preceding attack (by an enemy or opponent). — v. attack in reply.

**counterbalance** — n. **1** weight balancing another. **2** argument, force, influence, etc. balancing another. — v. (**-cing**) act as a counterbalance to.

**counter-clockwise** /kown-tuh-**klok**-wuyz/ adv. & adj. = ANTICLOCKWISE.

**counter-culturalist** /kown-tuh-,kul-chuh-ruh-luhst/ n. person who follows the counter-culture.

**counter-culture** n. radical, alternative culture, esp. among young people, that seeks out new values to replace the established and conventional values of society (see also ALTERNATIVE adj. 2).

**counter-espionage** n. action taken against enemy spying.

**counterfeit** /kown-tuh-fuht, -feet/ — adj. (of a coin, writing, etc.) made in imitation; not genuine; forged. — n. a forgery or imitation. — v. **1 a** imitate fraudulently; forge. **b** make an imitation of. **2** simulate (feeling etc.) (*counterfeited interest in her tale*). [French]

**counterfoil** n. part of a cheque, receipt etc., retained by the payer as a record [from FOIL²]

**counter-intelligence** /,kown-tuh-in-**tel**-uh-juhns/ n. = COUNTER-ESPIONAGE.

**counter lunch** n. usu. cheap but substantial meal in a local hotel or pub (orig. at the bar or counter).

**countermand** /kown-tuh-**mahnd**-mand/ — v. **1** revoke (a command). **2** recall by a contrary order. — n. order revoking a previous one. [Latin: related to MANDATE]

**countermeasure** n. action taken to counteract a danger, threat, etc.

**countermove** n. move or action in opposition to another.

**counter-offensive** n. **1** Mil. attack made from a defensive position in order to effect an escape. **2** any attack made from a defensive position.

**counterpane** /**kown**-tuh-,payn/ n. bedspread. [medieval Latin culcita puncta quilted mattress]

**counterpart** n. **1** person or thing extremely like another. **2** person or thing forming a natural complement or equivalent to another.

**counterpoint** /**kown**-tuh-,point/ — n. **1** Mus. **a** art or technique of setting, writing, or playing a melody or melodies in conjunction with another, according to fixed rules. **b** melody played in conjunction with another. **2** contrasting argument, plot, literary theme, etc., used to set off the main element. — v. **1** Mus. add counterpoint to. **2** set (an argument, plot, etc.) in contrast to (a main element). [medieval Latin contrapunctum marked opposite, i.e. to the original melody]

**counterpoise** /**kown**-tuh-,poiz/ — n. **1** counterbalance. **2** state of equilibrium. — v. (**-sing**) counterbalance. [Latin pensum weight]

**counter-productive** /,kown-tuh-pruh-**duk**-tiv/ adj. having the opposite of the desired effect.

**counter-revolution** /,kown-tuh-,rev-uh-**loo**-shuhn/ n. revolution opposing a former one or reversing its results.

**countersign** — v. add a signature to (a document already signed by another). — n. **1** password spoken to a person on guard. **2** mark used for identification etc. [Italian: related to SIGN]

**counter tea** n. usu. cheap but substantial evening meal in a local hotel or pub (orig. at the bar or counter).

**counter-tenor** n. **1** male alto singing-voice. **2** singer with this voice. [Italian: related to CONTRA-]

**countervail** /,kown-tuh-**vayl**, kown-/ v. literary **1** counterbalance. **2** (often foll. by against) oppose forcefully and usu. successfully (your bare assertion cannot countervail against the evidence of your guilt). [Latin valeo have worth]

**counterweight** n. counterbalancing weight.

**countess** /**kown**-tes/ n. **1** wife or widow of a count or earl. **2** woman holding the rank of count or earl. [Latin comitissa: related to COUNT²]

**countless** adj. too many to be counted.

**count noun** n. Gram. any noun that can form a plural or be used with the indefinite article (e.g. book, kindness).

**countrified** /**kun**-truh-,fuyd/ adj. often derog. rural or rustic, esp. in manners, appearance, etc.

**country** /**kun**-tree/ n. (pl. **-ies**) **1** territory of a nation with its own government; sovereign State. **2** (often attrib.) rural districts as opposed to towns or the capital (a holiday house in the country; country town). **3** land of a person's birth or citizenship. **4** region with regard to its aspect, associations, etc. (mountainous country; central Australia, typical Namatjira country). **5** national population, esp. as voters (the country won't stand for it). **6** traditional territory of an Aboriginal people. □ **go** (or **appeal**) **to the country** test public opinion by dissolving parliament and holding a general election. [medieval Latin contrata (terra) (land) lying opposite]

**country and western** n. type of folk music originated by Whites in the southern US.

**countryman** n. (fem. **countrywoman**) **1** person living in a rural area. **2** (also **fellow-countryman**) person of one's own country. **3 a** person from an Aborigine's own country (see COUNTRY 6). **b** person(s) with whom an Aborigine has extremely close ritual etc. bonding, involving responsibility of one for the other.

**country music** n. = COUNTRY AND WESTERN.

**countryside** n. rural areas.

**country-wide** adj. & adv. extending throughout a nation.

**county** /**kown**-tee/ n. (pl. **-ies**) **1** territorial division for the establishment and description of land titles. **2** territorial division in some countries, usu. forming the chief unit of local administration. [Latin comitatus: related to COUNT²]

**county council** n. **1** local government body performing specified function(s) for a group of other local government bodies. **2** elected governing body of an administrative county.

**County Court** n. (in Victoria) = DISTRICT COURT.

**coup** /koo/ n. (pl. **-s** /kooz/ ) **1** successful stroke or move. **2** coup d'état. [medieval Latin colpus blow]

**coup de grâce** /,koo duh **grahs**/ n. **1** finishing stroke to kill a wounded animal or person. **2** action etc. that settles or puts an end to something (the coup de grâce was the producing of the incriminating letter). [French]

**coup d'état** /,koo day-**tah**/ n. (pl. **coups d'état** pronunc. same) violent or illegal seizure of power. [French]

**coupe** /koop/ n. area of a forest set aside for felling. [French couper to cut]

**coupé** /**koo**-pay/ *n.* car with a hard roof, esp. one with two seats and a sloping rear. [French *couper* cut]

**couple** /**kup**-uhl/ — *n.* **1 a** two (*a couple of girls*). **b** about two (*see you in a couple of hours*). **2 a** two people who are married to, or in a sexual relationship with, each other. **b** pair of partners in a dance etc. **3** *Mech.* pair of equal and parallel forces acting in opposite directions, and tending to cause rotation about an axis perpendicular to the plane containing them. — *v.* (**-ling**) **1** fasten or link together; connect, e.g. railway carriages. **2** associate in thought or speech (*the newspapers coupled their names*). **3** copulate. [Latin COPULA]

**couplet** /**kup**-luht/ *n.* two successive lines of verse, usu. rhyming and of the same length. [French diminutive: related to COUPLE]

**coupling** /**kup**-ling/ *n.* **1** link connecting railway carriages etc. **2** device for connecting parts of machinery. **3** act or instance of joining or linking together in a pair.

**coupon** /**koo**-pon/ *n.* **1** form etc. in a newspaper, magazine, etc., which may be filled in and sent as an application for a purchase, information, etc. **2** entry form for a competition etc. **3** discount voucher given with a purchase. **4** ticket entitling the holder to a ration of food, clothes, petrol, etc., esp. in wartime. [French *couper* cut]

**courage** /**ku**-rij/ *n.* ability to disregard fear; bravery. □ **courage of one's convictions** courage to act on one's beliefs. [Latin *cor* heart]

**courageous** /kuh-**ray**-juhs/ *adj.* brave, fearless. □ **courageously** *adv.*

**courgette** /kaw-**zhet**/ *n.* = ZUCCHINI. [French]

**courier** /**kuu**-ree-uh/ *n.* **1** person employed to guide and assist tourists. **2** special messenger; person who works for a courier service. [Latin *curro curs-* run]

**courier service** *n.* branch of the post office or a private firm which picks up and delivers parcels etc., esp. with speedy service.

**course** /kaws/ — *n.* **1** continuous onward movement or progression (*the course of history*; *during the course of the proceedings*). **2 a** direction taken (*changed course*; *the course of the winding river*). **b** correct or intended direction or line of movement (*steer a straight course*). **c** direction taken by a ship or aircraft etc. (*traced the course of the missile*). **3 a** stretch of land or water for races. **b** golf-course. **4 a** series of

lessons etc. in a particular subject (*science course*). **b** book for such a course (*A Modern French Course*). **5** each successive part of a meal (*served fillets of kangaroo for the second course*). **6** sequence of medical treatment etc. (*prescribed a course of antibiotics*). **7** line of conduct (*disappointed by the course he took*). **8** continuous horizontal layer of masonry, brick, etc. **9** channel in which water flows. — *v.* (**-sing**) **1** (esp. of liquid) run, esp. fast (*the blood coursing through his veins*). **2** (also *absol.*) use hounds to hunt (by sight rather than scent). □ **in the course of** during. **in due course 1** at about the appropriate time (*will do it in due course*). **2** in the natural order. **of course** naturally; as is or was to be expected; admittedly. **on** (or **off**) **course** following (or deviating from) the desired direction or goal. **run** (or **take**) **its course** (esp. of an illness) complete its natural development. [Latin *cursus*: related to COURIER]

**courser** *n. poet.* swift horse.

**court** /kawt/ — *n.* **1** (in full **court of law**) **a** judicial body hearing legal cases. **b** = COURTROOM. **2** quadrangular area for games (*tennis-court*; *squash-court*). **3 a** short street. **b** = COURTYARD. **4 a** the residence, retinue, and courtiers of a sovereign. **b** sovereign and councillors, constituting the ruling power. **c** assembly held by a sovereign. **5** attention paid to a person whose favour etc. is sought (*paid court to her*). — *v.* **1 a** try to win affection or favour of. **b** pay amorous attention to. **2** seek to win (applause, fame, etc.). **3** invite (misfortune) by one's actions (*courting fate*). □ **go to court** take legal action. **out of court 1** without reaching trial (*was settled out of court*). **2** not worthy of consideration (*that suggestion is quite out of court*). [Latin: related to COHORT]

**court card** *n.* playing-card that is a king, queen, or jack.

**courteous** /**ker**-tee-uhs/ *adj.* polite, considerate, well-mannered. □ **courteously** *adv.* **courteousness** *n.* [French: related to COURT]

**courtesan** /**kaw**-tuh-zan/ *n.* prostitute, esp. one with wealthy or upper-class clients. [Italian: related to COURT]

**courtesy** /**ker**-tuh-see/ *n.* (*pl.* **-ies**) **1** courteous behaviour; good manners. **2** courteous act. □ **by courtesy of** with the formal permission of. [French: related to COURTEOUS]

**courthouse** *n.* building in which a judicial court is held.

**courtier** /**kaw**-tee-uh/ *n.* person who

attends a sovereign's court. [Anglo-French: related to COURT]

**courtly** adj. (**-ier**, **-iest**) dignified, refined. □ **courtliness** n.

**court martial** /ˌkawt **mah**-shuhl/ — n. (pl. **courts martial**) judicial court trying members of the armed services. — v. (**court-martial**) (**-ll-**) try by court martial.

**Court of Appeal** n. court hearing appeals against judgments made in lower courts of the States.

**Court of Disputed Returns** n. court for determining disputes about elections.

**Court of Petty Sessions** n. inferior State court of summary jurisdiction, usu. presided over by a magistrate.

**court of summary jurisdiction** n. court having the authority to use summary proceedings and arrive at a judgment or conviction.

**court order** n. direction issued by a court or judge.

**courtroom** n. room in which a court of law meets.

**courtship** n. **1** courting, wooing. **2** courting behaviour of animals, birds, etc.

**court shoe** n. woman's light, usu. high-heeled, shoe with a low-cut upper.

**courtyard** n. area enclosed by walls or buildings.

**couscous** /koos-koos/ n. N.African dish of crushed wheat or coarse flour steamed over broth, often with meat or fruit added. [French from Arabic]

**cousin** /kuz-uhn/ n. **1 a** (also **first cousin**) child of one's uncle or aunt. **b** (in Aboriginal English) any of several more distant relatives. **2** person of a kindred race or nation (our British cousins). [Latin consobrinus]

■ **Usage** There is often some confusion as to the difference between cousin, first cousin, second cousin, first cousin once removed, etc. For definitions see cousin, second cousin and remove v. 5.

**couture** /koo-tyoor/ n. design and manufacture of fashionable clothes. [French]

**couturier** /koo-tyoor-ree-ˌay, koo-too-ree-uh/ n. fashion designer.

**covalency** /koh-vay-luhn-see/ n. Chem. **1** linking of atoms by a covalent bond. **2** number of pairs of electrons an atom can share with another. □ **covalent** adj.

**covalent bond** n. Chem. bond formed by the sharing of electrons, usu. in pairs by two atoms in a molecule.

**cove**[1] — n. **1** small bay or creek. **2** sheltered recess. **3** moulding, esp. at the junction of a wall and a ceiling. — v.

(**-ving**) provide (a room etc.) with a cove. [Old English]

**cove**[2] n. colloq. man, bloke, chap. [cant: origin unknown]

**coven** /kuv-uhn/ n. assembly of witches. [related to CONVENT]

**covenant** /kuv-uh-nuhnt/ — n. **1** agreement; contract. **2** Law sealed contract, esp. a deed of covenant. **3** (**Covenant**) Bibl. agreement between God and the Israelites. — v. agree, esp. by legal covenant. [French: related to CONVENE]

**Coventry** /kuv-uhn-tree/ n. □ **send a person to Coventry** refuse to associate with or speak to a person. [Coventry in England]

**cover** /kuv-uh/ — v. **1** (often foll. by with) protect or conceal with a cloth, lid, etc. **2 a** extend over; occupy the whole surface of (covered in dirt: covered with writing). **b** (often foll. by with) strew thickly or thoroughly (covered the floor with straw). **c** lie over; be a covering to (the blanket scarcely covered him). **3 a** protect; clothe (cover the furniture while we're away on holiday). **b** (as **covered** adj.) wearing a hat; having a roof. **c** envelop (covered in confusion; this will cover us in glory). **4** include; comprise; deal with (this book covers all the main topics). **5** travel (a specified distance) (covered sixty kilometres). **6** describe or investigate as a reporter (who is to cover this story?). **7** be enough to defray expenses, a bill, etc. ($20 should cover it). **8** a refl. take measures to protect oneself (had covered myself by saying I might be late). **b** (absol.; esp. foll. by for) stand in for (will you cover for me?). **9 a** aim a gun etc. at (covered him and said 'Bail up!'). **b** (of a fortress, guns, etc.) command (territory). **c** protect (an exposed person etc.) by being able to return fire (he covered me as I ran towards the gunman). **10 a** esp. Cricket stand behind (another player) to stop any missed balls. **b** mark (an opposing player). **11** (of a stallion etc.) copulate with. — n. **1** thing that covers, esp.: **a** lid. **b** book's binding. **c** either board of this binding. **d** envelope or wrapping (under separate cover). **2** hiding place; shelter (ran for cover). **3 a** pretence; screen (under cover of humility; under cover of darkness). **b** spy's pretended identity or activity, intended as a concealment (blew his cover). **c** Mil. supporting force protecting an advance party from attack. **4 a** funds, esp. obtainable from insurance to meet a liability or secure against loss. **b** insurance protection (third-party cover). **5** person acting as a substitute. **6** *Cricket* = COVER-POINT. □ **cover up 1** completely cover or conceal (*you'd better cover up your nakedness*). **2** conceal (circumstances etc., esp. illicitly) (*tried to cover up the embezzlement; refused to cover up for them*). **take cover** find shelter. [Latin *cooperio, coopert-* cover]

**coverage** *n.* **1** area or amount covered. **2** amount of publicity received by an event etc.

**cover charge** *n.* service charge per head in a restaurant, nightclub, etc.

**covering letter** *n.* (also **covering note**) explanatory letter sent with an enclosure.

**coverlet** /kuv-uh-luht/ *n.* bedspread. [Anglo-French: related to COVER, *lit* bed]

**cover note** *n.* temporary certificate of insurance.

**cover point** *n. Cricket* **1** fielding position covering point. **2** fielder at this position.

**cover story** *n.* **1** news story in a magazine that is advertised etc. on the front cover. **2** main story in a television current affairs programme.

**covert** /koh-vert, kuv-uht/ — *adj.* secret or disguised (*covert glance; covert operations*). — *n.* shelter, esp. a thicket; hiding place. □ **covertly** *adv.* [French: related to COVER]

**cover-up** *n.* concealment of facts or circumstances, esp. illicitly.

**covet** /kuv-uht/ *v.* (-t-) desire greatly (esp. a thing belonging to another person) (*coveted his huge collection of CDs; thou shalt not covet thy neighbour's wife*). [French: related to CUPID]

**covetous** /kuv-uh-tuhs/ *adj.* (usu. foll. by *of*) **1** greatly desirous (esp. of another's property). **2** grasping; avaricious. □ **covetously** *adv.*

**covey** /kuv-ee/ *n.* (*pl.* **-s**) **1** brood of partridges. **2** small group of people or things. [Latin *cubo* lie]

**cow**[1] *n.* **1** fully grown female of any esp. domestic bovine animal, used as a source of milk and beef. **2** female of other large animals, esp. the elephant, whale, and seal. **3** *derog. colloq.* woman. **4** *colloq.* term of abuse applied to any person, animal, situation, or thing to which the speaker takes violent exception (cf. BASTARD) (*it's a cow of a job; a horse has been known to commit suicide and a dog to run amok after being called a cow*). □ **till the cows come home** *colloq.* an indefinitely long time. [Old English]

**cow**[2] *v.* intimidate or dispirit (*cowed by ill-treatment*). [Old Norse]

**cowabunga** /ˌkow-uh-**bung**-guh/ *int. colloq.* exclamation of exhilaration or satisfaction. [originally Kawabonga etc., an exclamation of anger in a 1950s US cartoon; it has been suggested that the word came from a NSW Aboriginal language (*kauwul* big, *bong* death, *gubba* good) and migrated to the US through surfing contacts]

**cowal** /kow-uhl/ *n.* tree-covered swampy depression in the red country. [Kamilaroi, probably *guwal* gully]

**coward** /kow-uhd/ *n.* person who is easily frightened or intimidated by danger or pain. [Latin *cauda* tail]

**cowardice** /kow-uh-duhs/ *n.* lack of bravery.

**cowardly** *adj.* **1** of or like a coward; lacking courage. **2** (of an action) done against one who cannot retaliate.

**cow bail** *n.* = BAIL[2] *n.* 3.

**cowboy** *n.* **1** (*fem.* **cowgirl**) person who tends cattle, esp. in the western US. **2** *colloq.* unscrupulous or reckless person in business (*the cowboys of the money exchange markets*).

**cow cocky** *n.* dairy farmer.

**cower** /kow-uh/ *v.* crouch or shrink back in fear or distress; cringe. [Low German]

**cowhide** *n.* **1** cow's hide. **2** leather or whip made from this.

**cow juice** *n.* (also **moo juice**) *colloq.* milk.

**cowl** *n.* **1 a** hood of a monk's habit. **b** monk's hooded habit. **2** hood-shaped covering of a chimney or ventilating shaft. [Latin *cucullus*]

**cow-lick** *n.* projecting lock of hair, esp. over the forehead.

**cowling** *n.* removable cover of a vehicle or aircraft engine.

**co-worker** /koh-**wer**-kuh/ *n.* person who works with another.

**cow-pat** *n.* flat round piece of cow-dung.

**cowpox** *n.* disease of cows, whose virus was formerly used in smallpox vaccination.

**cowrie** /kow-ree/ *n.* **1** tropical mollusc with a bright shell. **2** its shell, esp. used as money in parts of Africa and S. Asia, and as ornament. [Urdu and Hindi]

**co-write** /koh-**ruyt**/ *v.* write with another person. □ **co-writer** *n.*

**cowslip** /kow-slip/ *n.* English primula with small yellow flowers. [obsolete *slyppe* dung]

**cowslip orchid** *n.* terrestrial orchid of south-western WA, bearing bright yellow flowers.

**cox** — *n.* coxswain, esp. of a racing-boat. — *v.* act as cox (of). [abbreviation]

**coxcomb** /koks-kohm/ *n.* ostentatiously conceited man. □ **coxcombry** *n.* (*pl.* **-ies**). [= *cock's comb*]

**coxswain** /**kok**-suhn, -swayn/ — n. **1** person who steers, esp. a rowing-boat. **2** senior petty officer in a small ship. — v. act as coxswain (of). [*cock ship's boat*, SWAIN]

**coy** adj. **1** affectedly shy. **2** irritatingly reticent (*always coy about her age*). □ **coyly** adv. **coyness** n. [French: related to QUIET]

**coyote** /kuy-**oh**-tee, **koi**-oht/ n. (pl. same or -**s**) N. American wolflike wild dog. [Mexican Spanish]

**coz** /kuz/ n. (*archaic* except in Aboriginal English) cousin.

**cozen** /**kuz**-uhn/ v. *literary* **1** (often foll. by *of, out of*) cheat, defraud. **2** (often foll. by *into*) beguile; persuade. **3** act deceitfully. □ **cozenage** n. **cozener** n. [cant]

**cozzie** var. of COSSIE.

**CPI** abbr. Consumer Price Index.

**Cpl.** abbr. Corporal.

**cps** abbr. (also **c.p.s.**) **1** *Computing* characters per second. **2** *Sci.* cycles per second.

**CPU** abbr. *Computing* central processing unit.

**Cr** symb. chromium.

**crab¹** n. **1 a** ten-footed crustacean, with the first pair of legs as pincers. **b** crab as food. **2** (**Crab**) sign or constellation Cancer. **3** (in full **crab-louse**) (often in pl.) parasitic louse transmitted sexually to esp. pubic hair. **4** machine for hoisting heavy weights. □ **catch a crab** *Rowing* jam an oar or miss the water. **draw the crabs** *colloq.* attract unwanted attention. □ **crablike** adj. [Old English]

**crab²** n. **1** (in full **crab apple**) small sour apple. **2** (in full **crab tree**) or (**crab-apple tree**) tree (esp. uncultivated) bearing this. **3** sour person. [origin unknown]

**crab³** v. (**-bb-**) *colloq.* **1** criticise; grumble. **2** act so as to spoil (*the mistake crabbed his chances*). [Low German *krabben*]

**crabbed** /krabd, **krab**-uhd/ adj. **1** = CRABBY. **2** (of handwriting) ill-formed; illegible. [from CRAB²]

**crabby** adj. (**-ier, -iest**) irritable, morose. □ **crabbily** adv. **crabbiness** n.

**crabhole** n. **1** a hole in the ground made by a land crab. **b** any similar hole. **2** depression in heavy clay soils, a form of GILGAI.

**crabwise** adv. & attrib. adj. (of movement) sideways or backwards like a crab.

**crack** — n. **1 a** sharp explosive noise (*the crack of a whip*). **b** sudden harshness or change in vocal pitch (*had a crack in his voice*). **2** sharp blow (*a crack on the head*). **3 a** narrow opening formed by a break

(*entered through a crack in the wall*). **b** partial fracture, with the parts still joined (*cup has a crack in it*). **c** chink (*looked through the crack formed by the door; a crack of light*). **4** *colloq.* joke or malicious remark. **5** *colloq.* attempt (*I'll have a crack at it*). **6** exact moment (*at the crack of noon*). **7** first-rate player, horse, etc. **8** *colloq.* highly addictive crystalline form of cocaine broken into small pieces and inhaled or smoked. — v. **1** break without separating the parts (*cracked the window*). **2** make or cause to make a sharp explosive sound (*the rifle cracked; cracked the whip*). **3** break or cause to break with a sharp sound. **4** give way or cause to give way (under torture etc.). **5** (of the voice, esp. of an adolescent boy or a person under strain) change pitch sharply; break. **6** *colloq.* find the solution to (*I've cracked the code*). **7** tell (a joke etc.). **8** *colloq.* hit sharply (*cracked her head on the door-frame; the batsman cracked the ball for a six*). **9** (as **cracked** adj.) crazy. **10** break (wheat) into coarse pieces. **11 a** break open (*they cracked the safe*). **b** open and consume (a bottle of wine, a can of beer, etc.) (*let's crack a few tinnies*). **12** *colloq.* obtain (*did you crack an invite to the party?*). **13** *Surfing* catch and ride (a wave). — attrib. adj. *colloq.* excellent; first-rate (*crack shot*). □ **crack down on** *colloq.* take severe measures against. **crack hardy** *colloq.* put on a brave front; feign equanimity. **crack it** *colloq.* succeed (in an enterprise etc.). **crack of dawn** daybreak. **crack on to** *colloq.* pursue with amorous intent. **crack up** *colloq.* **1** collapse under strain. **2** praise (*not what it's cracked up to be*). **3** laugh uncontrollably. **get cracking** *colloq.* **1** begin promptly and vigorously. **2** get a move on, depart. [Old English]

**crack-brained** adj. crazy.

**crackdown** n. *colloq.* severe measures (esp. against law-breakers).

**cracker¹** n. **1** paper cylinder pulled apart, esp. at Christmas, with a sharp noise and releasing a hat, joke, etc. **2** loud firework. **3** (in pl.) instrument for cracking. **4** thin dry savoury biscuit. **5** *colloq.* **a** a person or thing that is exceptionally attractive, fine, etc. **b** cracking or rattling pace (*the pace is a cracker*). **6** smallest imaginable amount of money (*stranded in the back of Bourke without a cracker*). □ **not worth a cracker** *colloq.* of no value whatsoever.

**cracker²** n. strip of horsehair, silk, etc. attached to the tip of a stockwhip to make a cracking sound.

**crack.er.jack** — *colloq. n.* **1** something that is exceptionally fine or splendid. **2** person who is exceptionally skilful or expert. — *adj.* exceptionally fine or good (*she's a crackerjack rider*).

**crackers** *predic. adj. colloq.* crazy.

**cracking** *colloq.* — *adj.* **1** excellent. **2** (*attrib.*) fast and exciting (*set a cracking pace*). — *adv.* outstandingly (*is cracking good at it*).

**crackle** /krak-uhl/ — *v.* (**-ling**) make a repeated slight cracking sound (*radio crackled; fire was crackling*). — *n.* such a sound. □ **crackly** *adj.* [from CRACK]

**crackling** /krak-ling/ *n.* crisp skin of roast pork.

**crackpot** *colloq.* — *n.* eccentric person. — *adj.* mad, unworkable (*a crackpot scheme*).

**crack-up** *n. colloq.* mental breakdown.

**-cracy** *comb. form* denoting a particular form of government, rule, or influence (*democracy; bureaucracy*). [Latin *-cratia*]

**cradle** /kray-duhl/ — *n.* **1 a** a baby's bed or cot, esp. on rockers. **b** place in which something begins, esp. civilisation (*cradle of democracy*). **2** supporting framework or structure, esp.: **a** that on which a ship, a boat, etc., rests during construction or repairs. **b** that on which a worker is suspended to work on a ceiling, the vertical side of a building, etc. **c** part of a telephone on which the receiver rests when not in use. **3** box-like apparatus for separating gold from sand, gravel, etc. — *v.* (**-ling**) **1** contain or shelter as in a cradle. **2** place in a cradle. **3** wash (gold-containing gravel etc.) in a miner's cradle. [Old English]

**cradle-snatcher** *n. colloq.* admirer or lover of a much younger person.

**craft** /krahft/ — *n.* **1** special skill or technique. **2** (often in *comb.*) occupation etc. needing this (*statecraft; handicraft; the craft of pottery*). **3** (*pl.* **craft**) **a** boat or vessel. **b** aircraft or spacecraft. **4** cunning or deceit (*he's full of craft*). — *v.* make in a skilful way (*crafted a poem; a well-crafted piece of work*). [Old English]

**craftsman** *n.* (*fem.* **craftswoman**) **1** skilled worker. **2** person who practises a craft. □ **craftsmanship** *n.*

**crafty** *adj.* (**-ier, -iest**) cunning, artful, wily. □ **craftily** *adv.* **craftiness** *n.*

**crag** *n.* steep or rugged rock. [Celtic]

**craggy** *adj.* (**-ier, -iest**) **1** (esp. of facial features) rugged; rough-textured. **2** (of a landscape) having crags. □ **cragginess** *n.*

**crake** *n.* any of various birds of the rail family inhabiting esp. reedbeds and swamps (*Australian crake; Baillon's crake*). [Old Norse, imitative of cry]

**cram** *v.* (**-mm-**) **1 a** fill to bursting; stuff. **b** (foll. by *in, into*; also *absol.*) force (a thing) in or into. **2** prepare intensively for an examination. **3** (often foll. by *with*) feed (poultry etc.) to excess. **4** *colloq.* eat greedily. □ **cram in** squeeze in (*crammed in another five minute's work*). [Old English]

**cramp** — *n.* **1** painful involuntary muscular contraction. **2** (also **cramp-iron**) metal bar with bent ends for holding masonry etc. together. — *v.* **1** affect with cramp. **2** (often foll. by *up*) confine narrowly (*we're really cramped up in this tiny house*). **3** restrict (*cramped by all these petty regulations*). **4** fasten with a cramp. □ **cramp a person's style** prevent a person from acting freely or naturally. [Low German or Dutch]

**cramped** *adj.* **1** (of a space) too small. **2** (of handwriting) small and with the letters close together.

**cranberry** /kran-buh-ree/ *n.* (*pl.* **-ies**) **1** shrub with small red acid berries. **2** this berry used in cookery. **3** = NATIVE CRANBERRY. [German *Kranbeere* craneberry]

**crane** — *n.* **1** machine with a long projecting arm for moving heavy objects. **2** any of various tall wading birds with long legs, neck, and bill, including the BROLGA. — *v.* (**-ning**) (also *absol.*) stretch out (one's neck) in order to see something. [Old English]

**cranium** /kray-nee-uhm/ *n.* (*pl.* **-s** or **-nia**) **1** skull. **2** part of the skeleton enclosing the brain. □ **cranial** *adj.* **craniology** /,kray-nee-ol-uh-jee/ *n.* [medieval Latin from Greek]

**crank** — *n.* **1** part of an axle or shaft bent at right angles for converting reciprocal into circular motion or vice versa. **2** eccentric person, esp. one obsessed by a particular theory or fad (*health-food crank*). — *v.* cause to move by means of a crank. □ **crank up** start (a car engine) with a crank. [Old English]

**crankcase** *n.* case enclosing a crankshaft.

**crankpin** *n.* pin by which a connecting-rod is attached to a crank.

**crankshaft** *n.* shaft driven by a crank.

**cranky** *adj.* (**-ier, -iest**) **1** *colloq.* eccentric, esp. obsessed with a particular idea; silly (*he has really cranky ideas about women; crankiest plan I ever heard!*). **2** working badly; shaky. **3** ill-tempered or crotchety. **4** (in Aboriginal English) mad, crazy. □ **crankily** *adv.* **crankiness** *n.*

**cranky fan** *n.* predominantly grey fantail, widespread throughout Aus tralia, so called because of its rapid changes of direction as it flies after insects.

**cranny** /kran-ee/ n. (pl. **-ies**) chink, crevice. □ **crannied** adj. [French]

**crap** coarse colloq. — n. **1** (often as int. or attrib.) nonsense, rubbish. **2** faeces. **3** odds and ends; things (don't leave your crap lying around the house). — v. (**-pp-**) defecate. □ **crap a person off** annoy or disgust him or her. **crap on** talk nonsense. □ **crappy** adj. (**-ier, -iest**). [Dutch]

**craps** n.pl. (also **crap game**) gambling dice game. [origin uncertain]

**crapulent** /krap-yuh-luhnt/ adj. suffering the effects of drunkenness. □ **crapulence** n. **crapulous** adj. [Latin crapula inebriation]

**crash** — v. **1** (cause to) make a loud smashing noise (the cymbals crashed; crashed the plates together in his rage). **2** throw, drive, move, or fall with a loud smash (the dishes crashed to the floor). **3** (often foll. by into) **a** collide or cause (a vehicle etc.) to collide violently; overturn at high speed (the car crashed into a fence; crashed his fist into the window; the truck crashed). **b** fall or cause (an aircraft) to fall violently on to the land or sea (crashed the plane; the pilot crashed into the sea). **4** collapse financially (the bank is about to crash). **5** colloq. gatecrash. **6** colloq. be heavily defeated (crashed to a 142–0 defeat). **7** Computing (of a machine or system) (cause to) fail unexpectedly. **8** colloq. **a** (often foll. by out) sleep, esp. on a floor etc. **b** collapse into sleep, esp. following a period of prolonged exertion or alcoholic indulgence. — n. **1** loud and sudden smashing noise. **2** violent collision or fall, esp. of a vehicle. **3** ruin, esp. financial. **4** Computing unexpected failure of a machine or system. **5** (attrib.) done rapidly or urgently (crash course in first aid; crash diet). — adv. with a crash (went crash — and that was it!). [imitative]

**crash barrier** n. barrier at the side or centre of a road etc.

**crash-dive** — v. **1 a** (of a submarine or its pilot) dive hastily in an emergency. **b** (of an aircraft or airman) dive and crash. **2** cause to crash-dive. — n. such a dive.

**crash helmet** n. helmet worn by motor cyclists, cyclists, etc.

**crash hot** adj. colloq. excellent.

**crashing** adj. colloq. overwhelming (crashing bore).

**crash-land** v. land or cause (an aircraft etc.) to land hurriedly with a crash. □ **crash landing** n.

**crass** adj. **1** grossly stupid (a crass idea). **2** gross (crass stupidity). □ **crassly** adv. crassness n. [Latin crassus thick]

**-crat** comb. form member or supporter of a type of government etc. (autocrat; democrat).

**crate** — n. **1** slatted wooden case etc. for conveying esp. fragile goods. **2** colloq. old aircraft or other vehicle. — v. (**-ting**) pack in a crate. [perhaps from Dutch]

**crater** — n. **1** mouth of a volcano. **2** bowl-shaped cavity, esp. that made by a shell or bomb. **3** hollow on the surface of a planet or moon, caused by the impact of a meteorite. — v. form a crater in. [Greek, = mixing-bowl]

**-cratic** comb. form (also **-cratical**) denoting a type of government or rule (autocratic; democratic). □ **-cratically** comb. form forming adverbs. [Latin: related to -CRACY]

**cravat** /kruh-vat/ n. man's scarf worn inside an open-necked shirt. [Serbo-Croatian Hrvat = Croat]

**crave** v. (**-ving**) (often foll. by for) long or beg for (craves affection; craves a blessing). [Old English]

**craven** /kray-vuhn/ adj. (of a person, behaviour, etc.) cowardly, abject. [probably French cravanté defeated]

**craving** n. strong desire or longing.

**craw** n. crop of a bird or insect. □ **stick in one's craw** be unacceptable. [Low German or Dutch]

**crawl** — v. **1 a** move slowly, esp. on hands and knees. **b** (of an insect, snake, etc.) move slowly with the body close to the ground etc. **2** walk or move slowly (the train crawled into the station; time crawls). **3** colloq. behave obsequiously; toady (it's sick the way he crawls to the boss). **4** (often foll. by with) be or appear to be covered or filled with crawling or moving things or people (crawling with spiders; shopping centre crawling with people). **5** (esp. of the skin) feel a creepy sensation (he makes my skin crawl). — n. **1** act of crawling. **2** slow rate of movement (traffic's at a crawl). **3** = AUSTRALIAN CRAWL. [origin unknown]

**crawler** /kraw-luh/ n. **1** colloq. person who behaves obsequiously in the hope of advantage; toady. **2** anything that crawls, esp. an insect.

**cray** /kray/ n. = CRAYFISH.

**crayfish** /kray-fish/ n. (pl. same) **1** small lobster-like freshwater crustacean esteemed as food (e.g. YABBY, MARRON). **2** any of several Australian elongated decapod crustaceans, esp. marine, esteemed as food (e.g. ROCK LOBSTER). [French crevice]

**crayon** /**kray**-on/ — n. **1** stick or pencil of coloured chalk, wax, etc. used for drawing. **2** drawing made with this. — v. draw with crayons. [French *craie* chalk]

**craze** — v. (**-zing**) **1** (usu. as **crazed** adj.) make insane (*crazed with grief*). **2** produce fine surface cracks on (pottery glaze etc.); develop such cracks. — n. **1** usu. temporary enthusiasm (*craze for skateboarding*). **2** object of this. [perhaps from Old Norse]

**crazy** adj. (**-ier, -iest**) **1** colloq. insane or mad; foolish. **2** (usu. foll. by *about*) colloq. extremely enthusiastic; extravagantly in love with (*crazy about hang-gliding*; *crazy about him*). **3** (*attrib.*) (of paving etc.) made up of irregular pieces. □ **crazily** adv. **craziness** n.

**creak** — n. harsh scraping or squeaking sound (*I heard a creak downstairs*). — v. **1** make a creak (*this door creaks*). **2** move stiffly or with a creaking noise. **b** be poorly constructed (*the plot of this play creaks*). [imitative]

**creaky** adj. (**-ier, -iest**) **1** liable to creak. **2 a** stiff or frail (*creaky joints*). **b** (of a practice, institution, etc.) decrepit, outmoded. □ **creakiness** n.

**cream** — n. **1** fatty part of milk. **2** its yellowish-white colour. **3** creamlike preparation, esp. a cosmetic (*hand cream*). **4 a** food or drink like or containing cream. **b** biscuit with a creamy filling. **5** (usu. prec. by *the*) best part of something (*the cream of the nation's youth*). — v. **1** take cream from (milk). **2** make creamy (*cream the butter and sugar together*). **3** treat (the skin etc.) with cosmetic cream. **4** (of milk or any other liquid) form a cream or scum. **5** colloq. defeat thoroughly (esp. in a sporting context) (*we creamed the opposition*). — adj. pale yellowish white. □ **cream off** take (esp. the best part) from a whole. [Latin *cramum* and Church Latin *chrisma* oil for anointing]

**cream cheese** n. soft rich cheese made from cream and unskimmed milk.

**cream of tartar** n. purified tartar, used in medicine, baking powder, etc.

**creamy** adj. (**-ier, -iest**) **1** like cream in consistency or colour. **2** rich in cream. □ **creamily** adv. **creaminess** n.

**crease** — n. **1 a** line caused by folding or crushing. **b** line ironed into the legs of a pair of trousers. **2** *Cricket* line marking the position of a bowler or batsman. — v. (**-sing**) **1** make creases in. **2** develop creases (*linen creases badly*). [from CREST]

**create** /kree-**ayt**/ v. (**-ting**) **1 a** (of natural or historical forces) bring into existence; cause (*poverty creates resentment*). **b** (of a person or persons) make or cause (*create a diversion*; *create a work of art*; *create a good impression*). **2** originate (*actor creates a part*). **3** invest with rank (*created him a lord*). **4** colloq. make a fuss. [Latin *creo, creat-*]

**creatine** /**kree**-uh-tuhn/ n. product of protein metabolism found in the muscles of vertebrates. [Greek *kreas* meat]

**creation** /kree-**ay**-shuhn/ n. **1 a** act of creating. **b** instance of this. **2 a** (usu. **the Creation**) God's creating of the universe. **b** (usu. **Creation**) all created things, the universe. **3** product of human intelligence, esp. of imaginative thought or artistic ability.

**creationism** /kree-**ay**-shuh-,niz-uhm/ n. theory attributing all matter, biological species, etc., to separate acts of creation by God, rather than to evolution. □ **creationist** n. & adj.

**creative** adj. **1** inventive, imaginative. **2** able to create. □ **creatively** adv. **creativeness** n. **creativity** /-tiv-uh-tee/ n.

**creative accounting** n. exploitation of loopholes in financial legislation to gain maximum advantage or present figures in a misleadingly favourable light.

**creator** n. **1** person who creates. **2** (as **the Creator**) God.

**creature** /**kree**-chuh/ n. **1** any living being, esp. an animal. **2** person of a specified kind (*poor creature*). **3** subservient person. □ **creaturely** adj. [French from Latin: related to CREATE]

**creature comforts** n.pl. material comforts such as good food, warmth, etc.

**crèche** /kraysh, kresh/ n. day nursery. [French]

**credence** /**kree**-duhns/ n. belief. □ **give credence to** believe. [medieval Latin: related to CREDO]

**credential** /kruh-**den**-shuhl/ n. (usu. in pl.) **1** evidence of a person's achievements, trustworthiness, etc., usu. in the form of certificates, references, etc. **2** letter(s) of introduction. [medieval Latin: related to CREDENCE]

**credibility** /,kred-uh-**bil**-uh-tee/ n. **1** condition of being credible or believable. **2** reputation, status.

**credibility gap** n. apparent difference between what is said and what is true.

**credible** /**kred**-uh-buhl/ adj. believable or worthy of belief. [Latin: related to CREDO]

■ **Usage** *Credible* is sometimes confused with *credulous*.

**credit** /**kred**-uht/ — n. **1** source of honour, pride, etc. (*is a credit to the* school). **2** acknowledgment of merit (*must give him credit for consistency*). **3** good reputation (*his credit with the community is high*). **4 a** belief or trust (*I place no credit in the promises of some politicians*). **b** credibility; trustworthiness (*that statement lacks any credit*). **5 a** person's financial standing, esp. as regards money in the bank etc. **b** power to obtain goods etc. before payment. **6** (usu. in *pl.*) acknowledgment of a contributor's services to a film etc., shown at the start or the end of a film. **7** grade above pass in an examination. **8** reputation for solvency and honesty in business. **9 a** entry in an account of a sum paid into it. **b** sum entered. **c** side of an account recording such entries. **10** official recognition of a course of study a student has completed in the process of gaining a degree. — *v.* (**-t-**) **1** believe (*I cannot credit it*). **2 a** (usu. foll. by *to*, *with*) enter on the credit side of an account. **b** (foll. by *with*) acknowledge a person as having (*credit me with at least a modicum of commonsense*). □ **do credit to** (or **do a person credit**) enhance the reputation of (*this does you great credit*). **on credit** with an arrangement to pay later. **to one's credit** in one's favour (*to his credit, he refused the offer*). [Italian or Latin: related to CREDO]

**creditable** *adj.* bringing credit or honour (*a creditable achievement*). □ **creditably** *adv.*

**credit card** *n.* plastic card from a bank etc., identifying the user as entitled to credit, usu. to a stated amount.

**credit note** *n.* note with a specific monetary value given by a shop etc. for goods returned.

**creditor** *n.* **1** person or company to whom a debt is owing. **2** person or company that gives credit for money or goods. [Latin: related to CREDIT]

**credit rating** *n.* estimate of a person's suitability for commercial credit.

**credit union** *n.* non-profit-making organisation which handles some of the functions of a bank, usu. for a group of employees.

**creditworthy** *adj.* considered suitable to receive commercial crawlit. □ **creditworthiness** *n.*

**credo** /**kray**-doh, **kree**-/ *n.* (*pl.* **-s**) **1** (**Credo**) statement of religious belief; a Creed. **2** musical setting of a Creed, e.g. in a Mass. **3** any creed (*his credo is 'Look after myself and let the devil take the rest'*). [Latin, = I believe]

**credulous** /**kred**-yuh-luhs/ *adj.* **1** too ready to believe; gullible. **2** (of behaviour)

showing such gullibility. □ **credulity** /kruh-**dyoo**-luh-tee/ *n.* **credulously** *adv.* [Latin: related to CREDO]

■ **Usage** *Credulous* is sometimes confused with *credible*.

**creed** *n.* **1** set of principles or beliefs, esp. as a philosophy of life (*his creed is moderation in everything*). **2** system of religious belief. **3 a** (often **the Creed**) formal summary of Christian doctrine (*Apostles' Creed*; *Nicene Creed*). **b** the Creed as part of the Mass. □ **credal** /**kree**-duhl/ *adj.* **creedal** *adj.* [Latin: related to CREDO]

**creek** *n.* watercourse, esp. a stream or tributary of a river. □ **up the creek** *colloq.* **1** in difficulties. **2** crazy. [Old Norse and Dutch]

**creel** *n.* fisherman's large wicker basket. [origin unknown]

**creep** — *v.* (*past* and *past part.* **crept**) **1** move with the body prone and close to the ground. **2** move stealthily or timidly (*crept up on the enemy*; *crept out without being seen*). **3** advance very gradually (*a feeling crept over her*). **4** *colloq.* act obsequiously in the hope of advancement. **5** (of a plant) grow along the ground or up a wall etc. **6** (as **creeping** *adj.*) developing slowly and steadily (*creeping inflation*). **7** (of flesh) shiver or shudder from fear, horror, etc. — *n.* **1** act or spell of creeping. **2** (in *pl.*; prec. by *the*) *colloq.* feeling of revulsion or fear (*gives me the creeps*). **3** *colloq.* unpleasant person. **4** (of metals etc.) gradual change of shape under stress. [Old English]

**creeper** *n.* **1** climbing or creeping plant. **2** bird that climbs, esp. a treecreeper.

**creeping boobialla** *n.* Australian prostrate ground-cover having white or blue star-flowers and showy purple, red, or green fruits (see BOOBIALLA).

**creepy** *adj.* (**-ier**, **-iest**) *colloq.* **1** feeling or causing horror or fear (*a creepy film*). **2** (of a person) unpleasant; sinister. □ **creepily** *adv.* **creepiness** *n.*

**creepy-crawly** /kree-pee-**kraw**-lee/ *n.* (*pl.* **-ies**) *colloq.* **1** small crawling insect etc. **2** (in *pl.*) feeling of fear or revulsion (*that guy gives me the creepy-crawlies*).

**cremate** /kruh-**mayt**/ *v.* (**-ting**) burn (a corpse etc.) to ashes. □ **cremation** *n.* [Latin *cremo* burn]

**crematorium** /,krem-uh-**taw**-ree-uhm/ *n.* (*pl.* **-ria** or **-s**) place where corpses are cremated.

**crème** /krem/ *n.* **1** = CREAM *n.* 4a. **2** liqueur (*crème de menthe*). [French, = cream]

**crème de la crème** /ˌkrem duh lah **krem**/ *n.* the best part; the élite.

**crème de menthe** /ˌkrem duh **month**, **mont**/ *n.* peppermint liqueur.

**crenate** /**kree**-nayt/ *adj. Bot.* (of a leaf) having a scalloped margin with projections like rounded teeth. □ **crenated** *adj.* **crenation** /kruh-**nay**-shuhn/ *n.* **crenature** /**kren**-uh-ˌchoor, **kree**-nuh-/ *n.* [Latin *crenatus* from *crena* notch]

**crenellate** /**kren**-uh-ˌlayt/ *v.* (**-ting**) provide (a tower etc.) with battlements. □ **crenellation** /-**lay**-shuhn/ *n.* [French *crenel* embrasure]

**Creole** /**kree**-ohl/ — *n.* **1 a** descendant of European settlers in the W. Indies or Central or S. America. **b** White descendant of French settlers in the southern US. **c** person of mixed European and Black descent. **2** (also **creole**) language formed from a European language and another (esp. African) language, as Torres Strait Creole (see KRIOL). — *adj.* **1** of or relating to a Creole or Creoles. **2** (usu. **creole**) of Creole origin etc. (*creole cooking*). [French from Spanish]

**creosote** /**kree**-uh-ˌsoht/ — *n.* **1** dark-brown oil distilled from coal tar, used as a wood-preservative. **2** oily fluid distilled from wood tar, used as an antiseptic. — *v.* (**-ting**) treat with creosote. [Greek *kreas* flesh, *sōtēr* preserver, because of its antiseptic properties]

**crêpe** /krayp/ *n.* (also **crepe**) **1** fine gauzy wrinkled fabric. **2** thin pancake with a savoury or sweet filling. **3** (also **crêpe rubber**) hard-wearing wrinkled sheet rubber used for the soles of shoes etc. **4** crêpe paper. □ **crêpey** *adj.* **crêpy** *adj.* [Latin: related to CRISP]

**crêpe de Chine** /duh **sheen**/ *n.* fine silk crêpe.

**crepe myrtle** *n.* (also **native crepe myrtle**) small deciduous tree of northern Queensland, having extremely showy deep pink or red flowers.

**crêpe paper** *n.* thin crinkled paper.

**crêpe Suzette** /soo-**zet**/ *n.* small dessert pancake flamed in alcohol.

**crepitate** /**krep**-uh-ˌtayt/ *v.* (**-ting**) make a crackling sound. □ **crepitation** /ˌkrep-uh-**tay**-shuhn/ *n.* [Latin *crepito* creak]

**crepitus** /**krep**-uh-tuhs/ *n.* **1** *Med.* grating noise from the ends of a fractured bone rubbing together. **2** similar sound heard from the chest in pneumonia etc. [Latin *crepitus* rattle]

**crept** *past* and *past part.* of CREEP.

**crepuscular** /kruh-**pus**-kyuh-luh/ *adj.* **1 a** of twilight. **b** dim. **2** *Zool.* appearing

or active in twilight. [Latin *crepusculum* twilight]

**Cres.** *abbr.* Crescent.

**cresc.** *abbr.* (also **cres.**) *Mus.* = CRESCENDO.

**crescendo** /kruh-**shen**-doh/ — *n.* (*pl.* **-s**) **1** *Mus.* gradual increase in loudness. **2** progress towards a climax (*a crescendo of passion*). — *adv.* & *adj.* increasing in loudness. [Italian, = increasing, growing, from Latin *cresco* grow]

■ **Usage** *Crescendo* is sometimes wrongly used to mean the climax itself (e.g. *reached a crescendo and then died away*) rather than progress towards it.

**crescent** /**kres**-uhnt, **krez**-/ — *n.* **1** curved sickle shape as of the waxing or waning moon. **2** thing of this shape, esp. a street forming an arc. — *adj.* crescent-shaped. [Latin *cresco* grow]

**crescent nail-tailed wallaby** see WURRUNG.

**cress** *n.* any of various plants with pungent edible leaves. [Old English]

**crest** — *n.* **1 a** comb or tuft etc. on a bird's or animal's head. **b** anything resembling this, esp. a plume of feathers on a helmet. **c** helmet; top of a helmet. **2** top of a mountain, wave, roof, etc. **3** *Heraldry* **a** device above a coat of arms. **b** such a device as used by schools, colleges, etc. (*the school crest*). — *v.* **1** reach the crest of (a hill, wave, etc.). **2** provide with a crest or serve as a crest to. **3** (of a wave) form a crest. □ **on the crest of a wave** at the most favourable time in one's progress. [Latin *crista*]

**crested** *adj.* **1** having a crest. **2** as a distinguishing epithet in the names of some Australian birds (*crested bell-bird*; *crested hawk*; *crested pigeon*).

**crestfallen** *adj.* dejected, dispirited.

**cretaceous** /kruh-**tay**-shuhs/ — *adj.* **1** of or like chalk. **2** (**Cretaceous**) *Geol.* of the last period of the Mesozoic era, with deposits of chalk. — *n.* (**Cretaceous**) *Geol.* this era or system. [Latin *creta* chalk]

**cretin** /**kret**-uhn/ *n.* **1** deformed and mentally retarded person, esp. as the result of thyroid deficiency. **2** *colloq.* stupid person. □ **cretinism** *n.* **cretinous** *adj.* [French *crétin*: related to CHRISTIAN]

**cretonne** /kre-**ton**, **kree**-ton/ *n.* (often *attrib.*) heavy cotton upholstery fabric, usu. with a floral pattern. [*Creton* in Normandy]

**Creutzfeldt-Jakob Disease** *n.* degenerative disease affecting nerve cells in the brain. [H.G. *Creutzfeldt* (d. 1964) and A. *Jakob* (d. 1931), German physicians]

**crevasse** /kruh-**vas**/ *n.* deep open crack, esp. in a glacier. [French: from Latin *crepo* crack]

**crevice** /**krev**-uhs/ *n.* narrow opening or fissure, esp. in rock etc. [French: related to CREVASSE]

**crew**[1] /kroo/ — *n.* (often treated as *pl.*) **1 a** people manning a ship, aircraft, train, etc. **b** these as distinct from the captain or officers. **c** people working together; team. **2** *colloq.* company of people; gang (*as motley a crew as ever I saw; had the whole crew from the shop over for lunch*). — *v.* **1** supply or act as a crew or crew member for. **2** act as a crew. [Latin *cresco* increase]

**crew**[2] *past* of CROW[2].

**crew-cut** *n.* close-cropped hairstyle.

**crewel** /**kroo**-uhl/ *n.* thin worsted yarn for tapestry and embroidery. [origin unknown]

**crewel work** *n.* design in crewel.

**crew neck** *n.* round close-fitting neckline, esp. on a sweater.

**crib** — *n.* **1 a** baby's small bed or cot. **b** model of the Nativity with a manger as a bed. **2** rack for animal fodder. **3** *colloq.* **a** translation of a text for the (esp. surreptitious) use of students. **b** plagiarised work etc. **4** framework lining the shaft of a mine. **5** heavy crossed timbers used in foundations in loose soil etc. **6 a** light meal or refreshment, packed to be eaten during a break from work. **b** the break itself. — *v.* (**-bb-**) (also *absol.*) **1** *colloq.* copy unfairly; plagiarise (*he cribbed from me, not me from him*). **2** confine in a small space (*I am cabined, cribbed, confined*). [Old English]

**cribbage** /**krib**-ij/ *n.* card-game for up to four players. [origin unknown]

**crick** — *n.* sudden painful stiffness, esp. in the neck. — *v.* produce a crick in (the neck etc.). [origin unknown]

**cricket**[1] /**krik**-uht/ *n.* team game played on a grass pitch with two teams of eleven players, one team taking turns to bowl at a wicket defended by a batting player of the other team. □ **not cricket** *colloq.* unfair behaviour. □ **cricketer** *n.* [origin uncertain]

**cricket**[2] /**krik**-uht/ *n.* grasshopper-like chirping insect. [French, imitative]

**cri de cœur** /,kree duh **ker**/ *n.* (*pl.* **cris de cœur** pronunc. same) passionate appeal, protest, etc. [French, = cry from the heart]

**cried** *past* and *past part.* of CRY.

**crier** /**kruyuh**/ *n.* (also **cryer**) **1** person who cries. **2** *hist.* official making public announcements (*town crier*). [related to CRY]

**crikey** /**kruy**-kee/ *int. colloq.* expression of astonishment. [euphemism for CHRIST]

**crim** *n.* & *adj. colloq.* = CRIMINAL. [abbreviation]

**crime** *n.* **1 a** offence punishable by law. **b** illegal acts as a whole (*resorted to crime*). **2** evil act (*crime against humanity*). **3** *colloq.* shameful act (*it's a crime to tease them*). [Latin *crimen*]

**crimean shirt** /,kruy-mee-uhn **shert**/ *n. hist.* coloured flannel shirt formerly popular among workers in the bush. [from the name of the Black Sea peninsula, probably with reference to the warmth of the material]

**criminal** /**krim**-uh-nuhl/ — *n.* person guilty of a crime. — *adj.* **1** of, involving, or concerning crime (*criminal records*). **2** guilty of crime. **3** *Law* of or concerning criminal offences (*criminal code; criminal lawyer*). **4** *colloq.* scandalous, deplorable (*it's criminal that he's allowed to act that way*). □ **criminality** /-**nal**-uh-tee/ *n.* **criminally** *adv.* [Latin: related to CRIME]

**criminology** /,krim-uh-**nol**-uh-jee/ *n.* the scientific study of crime. □ **criminologist** *n.*

**crimp** — *v.* **1** press into small folds; corrugate. **2** make waves in (hair). — *n.* crimped thing or form. [Low German or Dutch]

**crimson** /**krim**-zuhn/ — *adj.* **1** of a rich deep red. **2** used as a distinguishing epithet in the names of Australian fauna and flora (*crimson chat; crimson sun orchid*). — *n.* this colour. [ultimately from Arabic]

**crimson bottlebrush** *n.* commonest callistemon in cultivation, a shrub bearing crimson bottlebrush-flowers in profusion, and occurring in Queensland, NSW, and Victoria.

**crimson rosella** *n.* crimson and vivid blue parrot of eastern Australia.

**cringe** /krinj/ — *v.* (**-ging**) **1 a** shrink in fear; cower (*the child cringed when it saw the strap*). **b** shrink in sheer embarrassment and distaste. **2** (often foll. by *to*) behave obsequiously. — *n.* act or instance of cringing. [Old English *cringan* fall in battle, originally 'curl up']

**crinkle** /**kring**-kuhl/ — *n.* wrinkle or crease. — *v.* (**-ling**) form crinkles (in). □ **crinkly** *adj.* [related to CRINGE]

**crinkle-cut** *adj.* (of vegetables) with wavy edges.

**crinoline** /**krin**-uh-luhn/ *n.* **1** *hist.* stiffened or hooped petticoat. **2** stiff fabric of horsehair etc. used for linings, hats, etc. [French from Latin *crinis* hair, *linum* thread]

**cripes** /kruyps/ *int. colloq.* expressing astonishment. [perversion of CHRIST]

**cripple** /**krip**-uhl/ — n. **1** permanently lame person. **2** person disabled in a way as specified (*emotional cripple*). — v. (**-ling**) **1** make a cripple of; lame. **2** disable, weaken, or damage seriously (*crippled by strikes*). [Old English]

**crisis** /**kruy**-suhs/ n. (pl. **crises** /-seez/ ) **1** time of danger or great difficulty (*the economy is in crisis*). **2** decisive moment (*our marriage has reached a crisis*). **3** turning-point, in a serious illness, between recovery and death. [Greek, = decision]

**crisp** — adj. **1 a** hard but brittle. **b** firm and fresh (*crisp lettuce*). **2 a** (of air) bracing. **b** (of style or manner) lively, brisk and decisive. **c** (of features etc.) neat, clear-cut. **d** (of paper) stiff and crackling. **e** (of hair) closely curling. — n. **1** (in full **potato crisp**) potato sliced thinly, fried, and sold in packets. **2** thing overdone in roasting etc. (*burnt to a crisp*). — v. make or become crisp. □ **crisply** adv. **crispness** n. [Latin *crispus* curled]

**crispy** adj. (**-ier, -iest**) crisp. □ **crispiness** n.

**criss-cross** — n. pattern of crossing lines. — adj. crossing; in cross lines. — adv. crosswise; at cross purposes. — v. **1 a** intersect repeatedly. **b** move crosswise. **2** mark or make with a criss-cross pattern. [*Christ's cross*]

**criterion** /kruy-**teer**-ree-uhn/ n. (pl. **-ria**) principle or standard by which a thing is judged (*the sole criterion is 'will it work?'*). [Greek, = means of judging]

■ **Usage** The plural form of *criterion*, *criteria*, is often used incorrectly as the singular. In the singular *criterion* should always be used.

**criterium** /kruy-**teer**-ree-uhm/ n. cycling race of multiple laps of a circuit, often as a stage in a touring race. [French]

**critic** /**krit**-ik/ n. **1** person who reviews literary, artistic, musical, etc. works, esp. regularly or professionally. **2** person who censures, finds fault. [Latin *criticus* from Greek *kritēs* judge]

**critical** adj. **1 a** fault-finding, censorious. **b** expressing or involving criticism (*a critical assessment of the situation*; *a critical evaluation of the short stories of Henry Lawson*). **2** skilful at or engaged in criticism. **3** providing textual criticism (*critical edition of Henry Lawson*). **4 a** of or at a crisis; dangerous, risky (*in a critical condition*; *critical shortage of medicine*). **b** decisive, crucial (*at the critical moment*). **5 a** *Math.* & *Physics* marking a transition from one state etc. to another (*critical angle*). **b** (of a nuclear reactor) maintaining a self-sustaining chain reaction. □ **critically** adv. **criticalness** n.

**critical mass** n. *Physics* amount of fissile material needed to maintain a nuclear chain reaction.

**critical path** n. most important sequence of stages in an operation, determining the time needed for the whole operation.

**critical pressure** n. *Physics* & *Chem.* pressure required to liquefy a gas at its critical temperature.

**critical state** n. *Physics* & *Chem.* state of a substance when it is at its critical temperature and critical pressure.

**critical temperature** n. *Physics* & *Chem.* temperature above which a gas cannot be liquefied.

**critical volume** n. *Physics* & *Chem.* volume of unit mass of a substance at its critical temperature and pressure.

**criticise** /**krit**-uh-,suyz/ v. (also **-ize**) (**-sing** or **-zing**) (also *absol.*) **1** find fault with; censure. **2** discuss critically.

**criticism** /**krit**-uh-,siz-uhm/ n. **1 a** fault-finding; censure. **b** statement or remark expressing this. **2 a** work of a critic. **b** analytical article, essay, etc.

**critique** /kri-**teek**, kruh-**teek**/ n. critical essay or analysis; an instance or the process of formal criticism. [French: related to CRITIC]

**critter** /**krit**-uh/ n. mainly *US colloq.* creature. [perversion of CREATURE]

**croak** — n. deep hoarse sound, esp. of a frog. — v. **1** utter or speak with a croak or in a dismal manner. **2** *colloq.* die. [imitative]

**croaky** adj. (**-ier, -iest**) (of a voice) croaking; hoarse. □ **croakily** adv. **croakiness** n.

**Croat** /**kroh**-at/ — n. **1 a** native of Croatia. **b** person of Croatian descent. **2** Slavonic dialect of the Croats. — adj. of the Croats or their dialect. [Serbo-Croatian *Hrvat*]

**croc** /krok/ n. *colloq.* crocodile. [abbreviation]

**crochet** /**kroh**-shay, -shuh/ — n. needlework in which yarn is hooked to make a lacy patterned fabric. — v. (**crocheted** /-shayd/) (also *absol.*) make using crochet. [French: related to CROTCHET]

**crock**[1] n. *colloq.* old or worn-out person, horse, vehicle, etc. [originally Scots]

**crock**[2] n. **1** earthenware pot or jar. **2** broken piece of this. [Old English]

**crockery** n. earthenware or china dishes, plates, etc. [related to CROCK[2]]

**crocodile** /**krok**-uh-,duyl/ n. **1 a** large tropical amphibious reptile with thick scaly skin, a long tail, and long jaws. **b**

(often *attrib.*) its skin. **2** *colloq.* line of schoolchildren etc. walking in pairs. [Greek *krokodilos*]

**crocodile tears** *n.pl.* insincere grief (from the belief that crocodiles wept while devouring or alluring their prey).

**crocus** /kroh-kuhs/ *n.* (*pl.* **-cuses**) small plant with white, yellow, or purple flowers, growing from a corm, the stigmas of *Crocus sativus* yielding the spice saffron. [Latin from Greek]

**Croesus** /kree-suhs/ *n.* person of great wealth. [name of a king of ancient Lydia]

**croissant** /krwah-song/ *n.* light, crescent-shaped breakfast roll made of rich yeast pastry. [French: related to CRESCENT]

**Cro-Magnon** /kroh-man-yon, -mag-nuhn/ *adj. Anthropology* of a tall broad-faced European race of late palaeolithic times. [name of a hill in France, where remains were found in 1868]

**crone** *n.* withered old woman. [Dutch *croonje* carcass]

**cronk** /krongk/ *adj. colloq.* **1** unfit; unsound; liable to collapse. **2** fraudulent. [perhaps from British dial. *crank* weak, shaky]

**crony** /kroh-nee/ *n.* (*pl.* **-ies**) close friend, companion. [Greek *khronios* long-lasting]

**crook** /kruuk/ — *n.* **1** hooked staff of a shepherd; a bishop's crosier. **2 a** bend, curve, or hook (*in the crook of his arm*). **b** hooked or curved thing. **3** *colloq.* **a** rogue; swindler. **b** professional criminal. — *v.* bend, curve (*crooked his finger to summon me*). — *adj. colloq.* **1** (of a person) unwell; injured (*feeling a bit crook*; *he's got a crook back*). **2** (of circumstances, the weather, objects, etc.) bad; unpleasant; unsatisfactory (*things are really crook on the land*). **3** out of order, broken (*the telly's crook*). **4** bad-tempered, angry (*he's in a really crook mood*). **5** dishonest; unscrupulous (*involved in some crook dealings*; *there may be some crook cops*). □ **crook on** (also **crooked on**) *colloq.* infuriated with; hostile to (*he's crook on the way he's been treated*; *some people are crooked on the idea of Australia becoming a republic*). **go crook** *colloq.* **1** (usu. foll. by *at*, *on*) lose one's temper; become angry (*went crook at me for wearing his shirt*). **2** go out of order, cease functioning (*telly's gone crook again*). [Old Norse]

**crooked** /kruuk-uhd/ *adj.* (**-er**, **-est**) **1** not straight or level; bent. **2** *colloq.* not straightforward; dishonest; criminal. □ **crookedly** *adv.* **crookedness** *n.*

**croon** — *v.* sing, hum, or say in a low

sentimental voice. — *n.* such singing etc. □ **crooner** *n.* [Low German or Dutch]

**crop** — *n.* **1 a** produce of cultivated plants, esp. cereals. **b** season's yield (*a good crop*). **2** group, yield, etc., of one time or place (*a new crop of students*). **3** handle of a whip. **4 a** very short haircut. **b** cropping of hair. **5** pouch in a bird's gullet where food is prepared for digestion. — *v.* (**-pp-**) **1 a** cut off. **b** (of animals) bite off (the tops of plants) (*cows cropping the grass*). **2** cut (hair, cloth, etc.) short. **3** (foll. by *with*) sow or plant (land) with a crop. **4** (of land) bear a crop. □ **crop out** *Geol.* appear at the surface. **crop up 1** occur unexpectedly (*something must have cropped up to delay him*). **2** *Geol.* appear at the surface. [Old English]

**crop-dusting** *n.* spraying of insecticide on crops, esp. from the air. □ **crop-dust** *v.* **crop-duster** *n.*

**crop-eared** *adj.* with the ears (esp. of animals) or hair cut short.

**cropper** *n.* crop-producing plant of a specified quality (*a good cropper*). □ **come a cropper** *colloq.* **1** fall heavily. **2** fail badly.

**croppy** /krop-ee/ *n. hist.* **1** Irish convict, esp. one transported to Australia for taking part in the 1798 rebellion. **2** any convict. [obsolete *croppy* person who has the hair cut short]

**croquet** /kroh-kay/ *n.* lawn game in which wooden balls are driven through hoops with mallets. [perhaps a British dial. form of French *crochet* hook]

**croquette** /kroh-ket/ *n.* ball of breaded and fried mashed potato, minced meat, etc. [French *croquer* crunch]

**crosier** /kroh-zee-uh/ *n.* (also **crozier**) ceremonial hooked staff carried by a bishop or a mitred abbot as a symbol of pastoral office. [French *croisier* cross-bearer and *crossier* crook-bearer]

**cross** — *n.* **1** upright post with a transverse bar, as used in antiquity for crucifixion. **2 a** (**the Cross**) cross on which Christ was crucified. **b** representation of this as an emblem of Christianity. **c** sign of the cross. **3** staff surmounted by a cross, carried in a religious procession. **4** thing or mark like a cross, esp. two short intersecting lines (+ or x). **5** cross-shaped military etc. decoration. **6 a** intermixture of animal breeds or plant varieties. **b** animal or plant resulting from this; hybrid. **7** (foll. by *between*) mixture of or compromise between two things (*he's an appealing cross between a larrikin and a dandy*). **8** *Soccer etc.* a pass of the ball across the direction of play. **9** trial or affliction; something to be endured (*bear* one's crosses). **10 a** (**Cross**) = SOUTHERN CROSS. **b** (**the Cross**) abbr. of King's Cross, a district of Sydney noted for its cosmopolitan character. — v. **1** (often foll. by *over*) go across or to the other side of (a road, river, sea, etc.). **2** intersect (*the roads cross near the bridge*). **b** place crosswise (*cross one's legs*). **3 a** draw line(s) across. **b** mark (a cheque) with two parallel lines to indicate that it cannot be cashed. **4** (foll. by *off, out, through*) cancel etc. by drawing lines across (*cross out the last three names*). **5** (often *refl.*) make the sign of the cross on or over (*he crossed himself*). **6 a** pass in opposite or different directions. **b** (of letters between two correspondents) each be dispatched before receipt of the other. **c** (of telephone lines) be connected to an unwanted conversation. **7 a** cause to interbreed. **b** cross-fertilise (plants). **8** oppose or thwart (*crossed in love*). — adj. **1** (often foll. by *with*) peevish, angry. **2** (usu. *attrib.*) transverse; reaching from side to side (*crossbar*). **3** (usu. *attrib.*) intersecting (*crossroad*). **4** (usu. *attrib.*) contrary, opposed, reciprocal (*crosswind*; *crossfire*). **5** of mixed breed; hybrid. □ **at cross purposes** misunderstanding; conflicting. **cross one's fingers** (or **keep one's fingers crossed**) **1** put one finger across another to ward off bad luck. **2** trust in good luck. **cross the floor** (in parliament or a debating-assembly) vote with the opposing side. **cross one's heart** make a solemn pledge, esp. by crossing one's front. **cross one's mind** occur to one, esp. transiently. **cross swords** (often foll. by *with*) argue or dispute. **cross wires** (or **get one's wires crossed**) **1** become wrongly connected by telephone. **2** have a misunderstanding. □ **crossly** adv. **crossness** n. [Latin *crux*]

**cross-** comb. form **1** denoting movement or position across something (*cross-country*). **2** denoting interaction (*cross-cultural*; *cross-fertilise*). **3 a** passing from side to side; transverse (*cross-current*). **b** having a transverse part (*crossbow*). **4** describing the form or figure of a cross (*crossroads*).

**crossbar** n. horizontal bar, esp. that on a man's bicycle.

**cross-bench** n. seat in a parliamentary chamber occupied by a member of a minor party or an independent. □ **cross-bencher** n.

**crossbones** see SKULL AND CROSSBONES.

**crossbow** n. bow fixed on a wooden stock, with a groove for an arrow.

**cross-breed** — n. **1** hybrid breed of animals or plants. **2** individual hybrid. — v. produce by crossing.

**cross-check** — v. check by a second or alternative method, or by several methods. — n. such a check.

**cross-country** — adj. & adv. **1** across paddocks or open country (*cross-country skiing*). **2** not keeping to main roads. — n. (pl. **-ies**) cross-country race.

**cross-cut** — adj. cut across the main grain. — n. diagonal cut, path, etc.

**cross-cut saw** n. saw for cross-cutting.

**cross-dressing** n. practice of dressing in the clothes of the opposite sex. □ **cross-dress** v.

**cross-examine** v. question (esp. an opposing witness in a lawcourt) to check or extend testimony already given. □ **cross-examination** n.

**cross-eyed** /kros-uyd/ adj. having one or both eyes turned inwards.

**cross-fertilisation** n. (also **-ization**) **1** fertilisation of an animal or plant from another of the same species (opp. SELF-FERTILISATION). **2** help by the interchange of ideas etc. □ **cross-fertilise** v. **cross-fertile** adj. **cross-fertilising** adj.

**crossfire** n. **1** firing of weapons in two crossing directions simultaneously. **2 a** attack or criticism from all sides. **b** combative exchange of views etc.

**cross-grain** n. grain in timber, running across the regular grain.

**crossing** n. **1** place where things (esp. roads) cross. **2** place for crossing a street etc. (*pedestrian crossing*). **3** journey across water (*had a smooth crossing*). **4** intersection of a church nave and transepts.

**cross-legged** /kros-leg-uhd, legd, kros-/ adj. (sitting) with legs folded one across the other.

**crossover** — n. **1** point or place of crossing. **2 a** process of crossing over, esp. from one style or genre to another, or from one culture to another. **b** something or someone that has done this. — attrib. adj. that crosses over, esp. from one style or genre to another.

**crosspatch** n. colloq. bad-tempered person.

**crosspiece** n. transverse beam etc.

**cross-pollination** n. pollination of one plant from another (opp. SELF-POLLINA-TION). □ **cross-pollinate** v. **cross-pollinating** adj.

**cross-question** v. = CROSS-EXAMINE.

**cross-refer** v. (**-rr-**) refer from one part of a book etc. to another.

**cross-reference** — n. reference from one part of a book etc. to another. — v. provide with cross-references.

**crossroad** n. (usu. in pl.) intersection of

two or more roads. □ **at the crossroads** at the critical point.

**cross-section** *n.* **1 a** a cutting of a solid at right angles to an axis. **b** plane surface so produced (*counting the annual rings in this cross-section from the tree-trunk enables us to estimate its age*). **c** drawing etc. of this. **2** representative sample, esp. of people (*in this jury we have a good cross-section of the Bendigo community*). □ **cross-sectional** *adj.*

**cross-stitch** *n.* cross-shaped stitch.

**crosstalk** *n.* **1** unwanted signals between communication channels. **2** witty repartee.

**crossways** *adv.* = CROSSWISE.

**crosswise** *adj. & adv.* **1** in the form of a cross; intersecting. **2** diagonal or diagonally.

**crossword** *n.* (also **crossword puzzle**) printed grid of squares and blanks for vertical and horizontal words to be filled in from clues.

**crotch** *n.* place where something forks, esp. the human body between the legs, or a pair of trousers (cf. CRUTCH). [related to CROOK]

**crotchet** /**kroch**-uht/ *n. Mus.* note equal to a quarter of a semibreve and usu. one beat. [French diminutive of *croc*: related to CROOK]

**crotchety** *adj.* peevish, irritable.

**crouch** — *v.* lower the body with limbs close to the chest, esp. for concealment, or (of an animal) before pouncing; be in this position. — *n.* act of crouching; crouching position. [Old Norse: related to CROOK]

**croup**[1] /kroop/ *n.* childhood inflammation of the larynx etc., with a hard cough and difficulty in breathing. [imitative]

**croup**[2] /kroop/ *n.* rump, esp. of a horse. [French: related to CROP]

**croupier** /**kroo**-pee-uh, -pee-,ay/ *n.* person running a gaming-table, raking in and paying out money etc. [French: related to CROUP[2]]

**crouton** /**kroo**-ton/ *n.* small cube of fried or toasted bread served with soup etc. [French: related to CRUST]

**crow**[1] /kroh/ *n.* **1** any of various large black birds with a powerful black beak, including two Australian species, the little crow and the Terresian crow. **2** similar bird, e.g. the raven, rook, and jackdaw. □ **as the crow flies** in a straight line. **starve the crows** see STARVE. **stone the crows** see STONE. [Old English]

**crow**[2] /kroh/ — *v.* (*past* **crowed**) **1** (*past* also **crew** /kroo/) (of a rooster) utter a loud cry. **2** (of a baby) utter happy cries. **3** (usu. foll. by *over*) express unrestrained gleeful satisfaction; gloat; boast. — *n.* **1** cry of a rooster. **2** happy cry of a baby. [Old English]

**crowbar** *n.* iron bar with a flattened end, used as a lever.

**crowd** — *n.* **1** large gathering of people. **2** spectators; audience. **3** *colloq.* particular set of people (*met the crowd from the sales department*). **4** (*prec. by the*) majority (*go along with the crowd*). — *v.* **1 a** come together in a crowd (*they were crowding in the streets to watch the Mardi Gras*). **b** cause to do this (*crowded them into the room*). **c** force one's way (*crowded into the cinema*). **2 a** (foll. by *into*) force or compress into a confined space (*crowded all his clothes into the suitcase*). **b** (often foll. by *with*; usu. in *passive*) fill or make full of (*the place was crowded with tourists*). **3** *colloq.* **a** (of a number of people) come aggressively close to (*crowded him, demanding an answer*). **b** harass or pressure (a person) (*stop crowding me, mate*). □ **crowd out** exclude by crowding (*the weeds are crowding out my seedlings*). □ **crowdedness** *n.* [Old English]

**crowea** /**kroh**-ee-uh/ *n.* any of three species of the Australian genus of the same name, woody shrubs with extremely showy five-petalled star-flowers in white to deep rose. [James *Crowe*, English botanist (d. 1807)]

**croweater** *n. colloq.* person resident in or native to SA.

**crown** — *n.* **1** monarch's jewelled headdress. **2** (**the Crown**) **a** monarch as head of State, e.g. in Britain, or in a nation, such as Australia, under a monarchy. **b** power or authority of the monarchy. **3 a** wreath for the head as an emblem of victory. **b** award or distinction, esp. in sport. **4** crown-shaped ornament etc. **5** top part of the head, a hat, etc. **6 a** highest or central part (*crown of the road*). **b** thing that completes or forms a summit (*this was the crown of his achievements*). **7 a** part of a tooth visible outside the gum. **b** artificial replacement for this. **8** *hist.* Australian coin worth five shillings. — *v.* **1** put a crown on (a person or head). **2** invest with a royal crown or authority. **3** be a crown to; rest on top of. **4 a** (often as **crowning** *adj.*) (cause to) be the reward, summit, or finishing touch to (*crowning glory*). **b** bring to a happy outcome. **5** fit a crown to (a tooth). **6** *colloq.* hit on the head. **7** promote (a piece in draughts) to king. **8** (of a bushfire) move (rapidly) through the tops of trees (*the fire is beginning to crown*). [Latin *corona*]

**crown fire** n. bushfire which moves through the tops of trees.

**crown land** n. 1 unalienated land; land owned by the government. 2 *Brit.* land belonging to the Crown.

**crown of thorns starfish** n. spiny coral-eating starfish of tropical regions including the Great Barrier Reef, so called because of a fancied resemblance to Christ's crown of thorns.

**crown wheel** n. wheel with teeth at right angles to its plane, esp. in the gears of motor vehicles.

**crow's ash** n. (also **teak**) tall rainforest tree (to 40m) of Queensland and NSW (*Flindersia australis*), having sprays of white flowers, curious fruits which open into long boat-shaped segments, and a durable timber said to resemble true teak.

**crow's-foot** n. wrinkle near the eye.

**crow shrike** see PIED CURRAWONG.

**crow's-nest** n. shelter at a sailing-ship's masthead for a lookout man.

**crozier** var. of CROSIER.

**cruces** pl. of CRUX.

**crucial** /kroo-shuhl/ adj. 1 decisive, critical (*the experiment is at a crucial stage*). 2 very important (*it is crucial that I should go*). □ **crucially** adv. [Latin *crux crucis* cross]

■ **Usage** The use of *crucial* in sense 2 should be restricted to informal contexts.

**crucible** /kroo-suh-buhl/ n. melting-pot for metals etc. [medieval Latin: related to CRUCIAL]

**cruciferous** /kroo-**sif**-uh-ruhs/ adj. having flowers with four petals arranged in a cross. [Latin: related to CRUCIAL]

**crucifix** /kroo-suh-fiks/ n. model of a cross with the figure of Christ on it. [Latin *cruci fixus* fixed to a cross]

**crucifixion** /,kroo-suh-**fik**-shuhn/ n. 1 a crucifying or being crucified. b instance of this. 2 (**Crucifixion**) crucifixion of Christ. [Church Latin: related to CRUCIFIX]

**cruciform** /kroo-suh-,fawm/ adj. cross-shaped. [Latin *crux crucis* cross]

**crucify** /kroo-suh-,fuy/ v. (-**ies**, -**ied**) 1 put to death by fastening to a cross. 2 persecute, torment (*his conscience was crucifying him*). 3 *colloq.* defeat thoroughly in an argument, match, etc.; humiliate (*the prime minister crucified the opposition at question time*). [French: related to CRUCIFIX]

**crud** n. *colloq.* 1 deposit of grease, dirt, etc. 2 unpleasant person. 3 nonsense (*don't give me that crud*). [var. of CURD]

**cruddy** /krud-ee/ adj. (-**ier**, -**iest**) *colloq.*

1 dirty; unsavoury (*a cruddy room*; *a cruddy character*). 2 of inferior quality; shoddy (*bought this really cruddy watch*).

**crude** /krood/ — adj. 1 a in the natural state; not refined (*crude oil*). b unpolished; lacking finish (*written in a crude style*; *a crude carving*). 2 a (of an action, statement, or manners) rude, blunt. b offensive, indecent (*made a crude gesture*). 3 a *Statistics* (of figures) not adjusted or corrected. b rough (*a crude estimate*). — n. natural mineral oil. □ **crudely** adv. **crudeness** n. **crudity** n. [Latin *crudus* raw]

**cruel** /krool/ — adj. (**crueller, cruellest** or **crueler, cruelest**) 1 causing pain or suffering, esp. deliberately. 2 harsh, severe (*a cruel blow*). — v. (-**ll**-) *colloq.* spoil (an opportunity etc.); ruin (the chances of a person or an enterprise succeeding) (*cruelled his chances by laughing when the manager fell off his chair*). □ **cruelly** adv. **cruelness** n. **cruelty** n. (pl. -**ies**). [Latin: related to CRUDE]

**cruet** /kroo-uht/ n. 1 set of small salt, pepper, etc. containers for use at table. 2 such a container. □ **do one's cruet** *colloq.* lose one's temper. [Anglo-French diminutive: related to CROCK²]

**cruise** /krooz/ — v. (-**sing**) 1 a travel by sea for pleasure, calling at ports. b sail about. 2 (of a motor vehicle or aircraft) travel at a relaxed or economical speed. 3 achieve an objective, esp. win a race etc. with ease. 4 *colloq.* search for a sexual (esp. homosexual) partner in bars, streets, etc. — n. cruising voyage. □ **be cruising** *colloq.* doing or performing effortlessly (*How are the exams going? — I'm cruising, mate*). [Dutch: related to CROSS]

**cruise missile** n. one able to fly low and guide itself.

**cruiser** n. high-speed warship.

**crumb** /krum/ — n. 1 a small fragment, esp. of bread. b small particle (*crumb of comfort*). 2 soft inner part of a loaf of bread (i.e. without crusts). 3 *colloq.* objectionable person. — v. cover with or break into breadcrumbs. □ **pick up** (or **gather) the crumbs** *Aust. Rules* pick up a loose ball. [Old English]

**crumble** /krum-buhl/ — v. (-**ling**) 1 break or fall into small fragments. 2 (of power, a reputation, etc.) gradually disintegrate (*his prestige is crumbling*). — n. dish of stewed fruit with a crumbly topping (*apple crumble*).

**crumbly** adj. (-**ier**, -**iest**) consisting of, or apt to fall into, crumbs or fragments. □ **crumbliness** n.

**crumhorn** var. of KRUMMHORN.

**crummy** adj. (-ier, -iest) colloq. dirty, squalid; inferior, worthless. □ **crumminess** n. [var. of crumby covered in crumbs]

**crumpet** /**krum**-puht/ n. 1 soft flat yeasty cake toasted and buttered. 2 colloq. offens. **a** a sexually attractive woman. **b** women regarded collectively, esp. as objects of male sexual desire. □ **not worth a crumpet** colloq. worthless. [origin uncertain]

**crumple** /**krum**-puhl/ — v. (-ling) (often foll. by up) 1 crush or become crushed into creases or wrinkles. 2 collapse, give way. — n. crease or wrinkle. [obsolete crump curl up]

**crunch** — v. 1 **a** crush noisily with the teeth. **b** grind under foot, wheels, etc. 2 (often foll. by up, through) make a crunching sound in walking, moving, etc. — n. 1 crunching; crunching sound. 2 colloq. decisive event or moment (when it comes to the crunch, he's never there). [imitative]

**crunchy** adj. (-ier, -iest) hard and crisp. □ **crunchiness** n.

**crupper** n. 1 strap looped under a horse's tail to hold the harness back. 2 hindquarters of a horse. [French: related to CROUP²]

**crural** /**kroor**-uhl/ adj. of the leg. [from Latin crus crur- leg]

**crusade** /kroo-**sayd**/ — n. 1 hist. any of several medieval military expeditions made by Europeans to recover the Holy Land from the Muslims. 2 vigorous campaign for a cause (crusade against smoking). — v. (-ding) engage in a crusade. □ **crusader** n. [French: related to CROSS]

**crush** — v. 1 compress with force or violence, so as to break, bruise, etc. 2 reduce to powder by pressure (a machine to crush rocks). 3 crease or crumple (her dress was all crushed). 4 defeat or subdue completely (crushed their enemies; idealism crushed by bitter experience). — n. 1 act of crushing. 2 crowded mass of people. 3 narrow passage in a stockyard through which animals can pass only in single file. 4 drink from the juice of crushed fruit. 5 (usu. foll. by on) colloq. infatuation (has a crush on him). [French]

**crust** — n. 1 **a** hard outer part of bread. **b** hard dry scrap of bread. **c** colloq. livelihood (what do you do for a crust?). 2 pastry covering of a pie. 3 hard casing over a soft thing, e.g. a harder layer over soft snow. 4 Geol. outer portion of the earth. — v. cover or become covered with or form into a crust. [Latin crusta rind, shell]

**crustacean** /krus-**tay**-shuhn/ — n. esp. aquatic arthropod with a hard shell, e.g. the crab, lobster, shrimp, and yabby. — adj. of crustaceans.

**crusty** adj. (-ier, -iest) 1 having a crisp crust. 2 irritable, curt. □ **crustily** adv. **crustiness** n.

**crutch** — n. 1 usu. T-shaped support for a lame person fitting under the armpit. 2 support, prop. 3 crotch. 4 hindquarters of a sheep. — v. remove wool from about the tail of a sheep to prevent fouling, and esp. to prevent blowfly strike. [Old English]

**crutchings** n.pl. wool clipped from the hindquarters of a sheep.

**crux** n. (pl. **cruxes** or **cruces** /**kroo**-seez/ ) decisive point at issue. [Latin, = cross]

**cry** /kruy/ — v. (**cries, cried**) 1 (often foll. by out) make a loud or shrill sound, esp. to express pain, grief, etc., or to appeal for help. 2 shed tears; weep. 3 (often foll. by out) say or exclaim loudly or excitedly. 4 (foll. by for) appeal, demand, or show a need for. 5 (of an animal, esp. a bird) make a loud call. — n. (pl. **cries**) 1 loud shout or scream of grief, pain, etc. 2 spell of weeping. 3 loud excited utterance. 4 urgent appeal. 5 **a** public demand or opinion (the general cry was that the country should stay out of the war). **b** rallying call. 6 call of an animal. □ **cry down** disparage, belittle (cried down the opposition's solution). **cry off** withdraw from an undertaking. **cry out for** need as an obvious requirement or solution. **cry wolf** see WOLF. **a far cry** 1 a long way (it's quite a far cry away). 2 a very different thing (liberty is a far cry from licence). **for crying out loud** colloq. exclamation of surprise or annoyance. [Latin quirito]

**cryer** var. of CRIER.

**crying** attrib. adj. (of injustice etc.) flagrant, demanding redress (a crying need; a crying shame).

**cryo-** /**kruy**-oh/ comb. form (extreme) cold. [Greek kruos frost]

**cryogen** /**kruy**-oh-juhn/ n. freezing-mixture; substance used to produce very low temperatures.

**cryogenics** /ˌkruy-oh-**jen**-iks/ n. branch of physics dealing with very low temperatures. □ **cryogenic** adj.

**cryolite** /**kruy**uh-luyt/ n. lustrous mineral of sodium-aluminium fluoride, used in the manufacture of aluminium.

**cryonics** /kruy-**on**-iks/ n. use of extreme cold to preserve living tissue.

**cryosurgery** /ˌkruy-oh-**ser**-juh-ree/ n. surgery using the local application of intense cold for anaesthesia or therapy.

**crypt** /kript/ n. vault, esp. beneath a church, used usu. as a burial-place. [Latin *crypta* from Greek *kruptos* hidden]

**cryptic** /krip-tik/ adj. **1** obscure in meaning. **2** (of a crossword clue etc.) indirect; indicating the solution in a way that is not obvious. **3** secret, mysterious. □ **cryptically** adv.

**crypto-** /krip-toh/ comb. form concealed, secret (*he's a crypto-neo-Nazi*). [as CRYPT]

**cryptogam** /krip-tuh-,gam/ n. plant with no true flowers or seeds, e.g. ferns, mosses, and fungi. □ **cryptogamous** /-tog-uh-muhs/ adj. [as CRYPT, Greek *gamos* marriage]

**cryptogram** /krip-tuh-,gram/ n. text written in cipher. [related to CRYPT]

**cryptography** /krip-tog-ruh-fee/ n. art of writing or solving ciphers. □ **cryptographer** n. **cryptographic** /-tuh-graf-ik/ adj.

**crystal** /kris-tuhl/ — n. **1 a** transparent colourless mineral, esp. rock crystal. **b** piece of this. **2 a** highly transparent glass. **b** articles of this. **3** *Electronics* crystalline piece of semiconductor. **4** *Chem.* aggregation of molecules with a definite internal structure and the external form of a solid enclosed by symmetrically arranged plane faces. — adj. (usu. attrib.) made of, like, or clear as crystal. [Greek *krustallos*]

**crystal ball** n. glass globe used in supposed foretelling of the future.

**crystalline** /kris-tuh-,luyn/ adj. **1** of, like, or clear as crystal. **2** having the structure and form of a crystal. □ **crystallinity** /-lin-uh-tee/ n.

**crystallise** /kris-tuh-,luyz/ v. (also **-ize**) (**-sing** or **-zing**) **1** form into crystals. **2** (often foll. by *out*) (of ideas or plans) make or become definite (*his vague notions were beginning to crystallise*). **3** make or become coated or impregnated with sugar (*crystallised fruit*). □ **crystallisation** /-zay-shuhn/ n.

**crystallography** /,kris-tuh-log-ruh-fee/ n. science of crystal formation and structure. □ **crystallographer** n.

**crystalloid** /kris-tuh-,loid/ — adj. **1** crystal-like. **2** having a crystalline structure. — n. substance that in solution is able to pass through a semipermeable membrane.

**Cs** symb. caesium.

**c/s** abbr. cycles per second.

**CSIRO** abbr. Commonwealth Scientific and Industrial Research Organisation.

**Cu** symb. copper. [Latin *cuprum*]

**cu.** abbr. cubic.

**cub** — n. **1** young of a fox, bear, lion, etc. **2** (**Cub**) (in full **Cub Scout**) junior Scout.

**3** *colloq.* young newspaper reporter. — v. (**-bb-**) (also *absol.*) give birth to (cubs). [origin unknown]

**cubby hole** n. **1** very small room. **2** snug space. [Low German]

**cubby house** n. a child's playhouse.

**cube** — n. **1** solid contained by six equal squares. **2** cube-shaped block (e.g. a sugar-cube). **3** *Math.* product of a number multiplied by its square. — v. (**-bing**) **1** find the cube of (a number). **2** cut (food etc.) into small cubes. [Latin from Greek]

**cube root** n. number which produces a given number when cubed.

**cubic** adj. **1** cube-shaped. **2** of three dimensions. **3** involving the cube (and no higher power) of a number (*cubic equation*).

**cubical** adj. cube-shaped.

**cubicle** /kyoo-bi-kuhl/ n. small partitioned space, screened for privacy. [Latin *cubo* lie]

**cubic metre** etc. n. volume of a cube whose edge is one metre etc.

**cubism** /kyoo-biz-uhm/ n. style in art, esp. painting, in which objects are represented as an assemblage of geometrical forms. □ **cubist** n. & adj.

**cubit** /kyoo-buht/ n. ancient measure of length, approximating to the length of a forearm. [Latin *cubitum* elbow]

**cuboid** /kyoo-boid/ — adj. cube-shaped; like a cube. — n. *Geom.* rectangular parallelepiped.

**cuckold** /kuk-uhld/ — n. husband of an adulteress. — v. make a cuckold of. □ **cuckoldry** n. [French]

**cuckoo** /kuu-koo/ — n. any of various birds (including a number of Australian species) having a characteristic cry, and often laying its eggs in the nests of small birds (*brush cuckoo*; *fantailed cuckoo*; *pallid cuckoo*). — predic. adj. colloq. crazy. [French, imitative]

**cuckoo clock** n. clock with the figure of a cuckoo emerging to make a call on the hour.

**cuckoo-shrike** n. any of several birds of Australia and elsewhere, having predominantly grey plumage with black markings.

**cuckoo-spit** n. froth exuded by insect larvae on leaves, stems, etc.

**cucumber** /kyoo-kum-buh/ n. **1** long green fleshy fruit, used in salads. **2** climbing plant yielding this. [French from Latin]

**cucurbit** /kyoo-ker-buht/ n. any of various climbing or trailing plants of the gourd family, including melons, pumpkins, ornamental gourds, etc. [Latin *cucurbita*]

**cud** *n.* half-digested food returned to the mouth of ruminants for further chewing. [Old English]

**cuddle** /**kud**-uhl/ — *v.* (**-ling**) **1** hug, fondle. **2** nestle together, lie close and snug. — *n.* prolonged and fond hug. □ **cuddlesome** *adj.* [origin uncertain]

**cuddly** *adj.* (**-ier, -iest**) **1** (of a person, toy, etc.) soft and yielding. **2** given to cuddling.

**cudgel** /**kuj**-uhl/ — *n.* short thick stick used as a weapon. — *v.* (**-ll-**) beat with a cudgel. □ **cudgel one's brains** think hard about a problem. **take up the cudgels** (often foll. by *for*) make a vigorous defence. [Old English]

**cudgerie** /**kuj**-uh-ree/ *n.* any of several Australian rainforest trees, esp. bumpy ash (*Flindersia schottiana*). [probably from Bandjalang *gajari*]

**cue**[1] /kyoo/ — *n.* **1 a** last words of an actor's speech as a signal to another to enter or speak. **b** similar signal to a musician etc. **2 a** stimulus to perception etc. **b** signal for action. **c** hint on appropriate behaviour (*just stay behind me and take your cue from what I do*). **3** cueing audio equipment (see sense 2 of *v.*). — *v.* (**cues, cued, cueing** or **cuing**) **1** give a cue to. **2** put (audio equipment) in readiness to play a particular section. □ **cue in 1** insert a cue for. **2** give information to. **on cue** at the correct moment. [origin unknown]

**cue**[2] *Billiards etc.* — *n.* long rod for striking a ball. — *v.* (**cues, cued, cueing** or **cuing**) strike (a ball) with or use a cue. [var. of QUEUE]

**cue**[3] — *n.* shoe of a bullock with a flattened hollow heel and pointed, turned toe. — *v.* shoe (a bullock) with a cue. [British dial.]

**cue ball** *n.* ball to be struck with a cue.

**cuff**[1] *n.* **1** end part of a sleeve. **2** trouser turn-up. **3** (in *pl.*) *colloq.* handcuffs. □ **off the cuff** *colloq.* without preparation, extempore. [origin unknown]

**cuff**[2] — *v.* strike with an open hand. — *n.* such a blow. [perhaps imitative]

**cuff-link** *n.* two joined studs etc. for fastening a cuff (sense 1).

**cuirass** /kwuh-**ras**/ *n.* armour breastplate and back-plate fastened together. [Latin *corium* leather]

**cuisine** /kwuh-**zeen**/ *n.* style or method of cooking. [French]

**cul-de-sac** /**kul**-duh-,sak/ *n.* (*pl.* **culs-de-sac** pronunc. same or **cul-de-sacs**) **1** road etc. with a dead end. **2** route or course leading nowhere; position from

which one cannot escape. [French, = sack-bottom]

**-cule** *suffix* forming (orig. diminutive) nouns (*molecule*). [Latin *-culus*]

**culinary** /**kul**-uh-nuh-ree, -nree/ *adj.* of or for cooking. [Latin *culina* kitchen]

**cull** — *v.* **1** select or gather (*knowledge culled from books*). **2** gather (flowers etc.). **3 a** select (animals), esp. for killing. **b** reduce the population of (an animal) by selective slaughter (*culling kangaroos*). **4** select and destroy surplus or duplicate data. — *n.* **1** act or instance of culling or being culled. **2** animal(s) culled (*incinerated the cull*). [French: related to COLLECT[1]]

**cully** /**kuul**-ee/ *n.* (*pl.* **-ies**) *colloq.* (esp. as a form of address) mate. [origin unknown]

**culminate** /**kul**-muh-,nayt/ *v.* (**-ting**) (usu. foll. by *in*) reach its highest or final point (*culminate in war*). □ **culmination** /-**nay**-shuhn/ *n.* [Latin *culmen* top]

**culottes** /kuh-**lots**/ *n.pl.* women's trousers cut like a skirt. [French, = kneebreeches]

**culpable** /**kul**-puh-buhl/ *adj.* deserving blame. □ **culpability** /-**bil**-uh-tee/ *n.* [Latin *culpo* blame]

**culprit** /**kul**-pruht/ *n.* guilty person. [perhaps from Anglo-French *culpable*: see CULPABLE]

**cult** *n.* **1** religious system, sect, etc., esp. ritualistic. **2 a** quasi-religious devotion to a person or thing (*cult of Elvis Presley*; *cult of aestheticism*). **b** popular fashion, esp. followed by a specific section of society. **c** (*attrib.*) fashionable (*cult film*; *cult figure*). □ **cultic** *adj.* **cultism** *n.* **cultist** *n.* [Latin: related to CULTIVATE]

**cultivar** /**kul**-tuh-,vah/ *n.* plant variety produced by cultivation. [from CULTIVATE, VARIETY]

**cultivate** /**kul**-tuh-,vayt/ *v.* (**-ting**) **1 a** prepare and use (soil etc.) for crops or gardening. **b** break up (the ground) with a cultivator. **2 a** raise (crops). **b** culture (bacteria etc.). **3 a** (often as **cultivated** *adj.*) improve (the mind, manners, etc.). **b** nurture (a person, friendship, etc.). □ **cultivable** *adj.* **cultivation** /-**vay**-shuhn/ *n.* [Latin *colo cult-* till, worship]

**Cultivated Australian English** *n.* prestige pronunciation of Australian English.

**cultivator** *n.* **1** mechanical implement for breaking up the ground etc. **2** person or thing that cultivates.

**cultural** /**kul**-chuh-ruhl/ *adj.* of or relating to intellectual or artistic matters, or to a specific culture. □ **culturally** *adv.*

**cultural cringe** n. (Australian) attitude characterised by deference to the cultural achievements of other countries and disparagement of Australian culture.

**culture** /**kul**-chuh/ — n. **1 a** intellectual and artistic achievement or expression (*city lacking in culture*). **b** refined appreciation of the arts etc. (*person of culture*). **2** customs, achievements, etc. of a particular civilisation or group (*Chinese culture*). **3** improvement by mental or physical training. **4** cultivation of plants; rearing of bees etc. **5** quantity of micro-organisms and nutrient material supporting their growth. — v. (**-ring**) maintain (bacteria etc.) in suitable growth conditions. [Latin: related to CULTIVATE]

**cultured** adj. having refined taste etc.

**cultured pearl** n. pearl formed by an oyster after the insertion (by a person) of a foreign body into its shell.

**culture shock** n. disorientation felt by a person subjected to an unfamiliar way of life.

**culture vulture** n. colloq. person eager for cultural pursuits.

**culvert** /**kul**-vuht/ n. underground channel carrying water under a road etc. [origin unknown]

**cum** prep. (usu. in comb.) with, combined with, also used as (*bedroom-cum-study*). [Latin]

**cumbersome** /**kum**-buh-suhm/ adj. (also **cumbrous** /**kum**-bruhs/) inconveniently bulky etc.; unwieldy. [*cumber* hinder]

**cumbungi** /kum-**bun**-gee/ n. tall, vigorous, reed-like plant with spear-like flower spikes, found in or near water in all Australian States. [Wemba-wemba *gambong*]

**cumin** /**kum**-uhn/ n. (also **cummin**) **1** plant with aromatic seeds. **2** these as flavouring, esp. ground and used in curry powder. [Greek *kuminon*]

**cummerbund** /**kum**-uh-,bund/ n. waist sash. [Hindustani and Persian *kamarband* loin-band]

**cumquat** /**kum**-kwot/ n. (also **kumquat**) **1** small orange-like fruit with sweet rind and acid pulp, used in preserves etc. **2** shrub or small tree of the genus *Fortunella* yielding this. [Cantonese variant of Chinese *kin kü* gold orange]

**cumulative** /**kyoo**-myuh-luh-tiv/ adj. **1** increasing or increased progressively in amount, force, etc. (*cumulative evidence*). **2** formed by successive additions (*learning is a cumulative process*). **3** (of two or more gaol sentences) required to be served one after another (instead of concurrently). □ **cumulatively** adv.

**cumulus** /**kyoo**-myuh-luhs/ n. (pl. **-li** /-,luy/) cloud formation of rounded masses heaped up on a flat base. [Latin, = heap]

**cuneiform** /**kyoo**-nuh-,fawm/ — adj. **1** wedge-shaped. **2** of or using the wedge-shaped writing impressed usu. in clay in ancient Babylonian etc. inscriptions. — n. cuneiform writing. [Latin *cuneus* wedge]

**cunjevoi¹** /**kun**-juh-,voi/ n. sea-squirt occurring on intertidal rocks in southern Australia, the flesh of which is used as bait. [probably from a NSW Aboriginal language]

**cunjevoi²** n. rainforest plant of NSW and Queensland, having extremely large leaves and greenish, arum-lily-like flowers, the stem-tissue of the plant providing a staple food for Aborigines after it had been repeatedly pounded and baked to rid it of its very high toxicity. [probably from Bandjalang]

**cunji** /**kun**-jee/ n. (also **cunjy**) = CUNJEVOI¹ & CUNJEVOI². [abbreviation]

**cunmerrie** /**kun**-muh-ree/ n. (in Aboriginal lore) a huge winged spirit which carries off people and animals. [Pitta-pitta (and other languages) *ganmarri*]

**cunnilingus** /,kun-uh-**ling**-guhs/ n. oral stimulation of the female genitals. [Latin *cunnus* vulva, *lingo* lick]

**cunning** — adj. (**-er, -est**) **1** deceitful, clever, or crafty. **2** ingenious (*cunning device*). — n. **1** craftiness; deception. **2** skill, ingenuity. □ **cunningly** adv. [Old Norse: related to CAN¹]

**cup** — n. **1** small bowl-shaped container for drinking from. **2 a** its contents. **b** = CUPFUL. **3** cup-shaped thing, esp. the calyx of a flower or the socket of a bone. **4** flavoured wine, cider, etc., usu. chilled. **5** cup-shaped trophy as a prize (*the Melbourne Cup*). **6** one's fate or fortune (*a bitter cup*). — v. (**-pp-**) **1** form (esp. the hands) into the shape of a cup. **2** take or hold as in a cup. □ **one's cup of tea** colloq. what interests or suits one. **in one's cups** drunk. [medieval Latin *cuppa*]

**cupboard** /**kub**-uhd/ n. recess or piece of furniture with a door and (usu.) shelves, in which things are stored.

**cupful** n. (pl. **-s**) **1** amount held by a cup, esp. as a measure (250 ml) in cookery. **2** cup full of a substance (*drank a cupful of water*).

■ **Usage** A *cupful* is a measure, and so *three cupfuls* is a quantity regarded in terms of a cup; *three cups full* denotes the actual cups as in *brought us three cups full of water*.

**Cupid** /kyoo-puhd/ *n.* **1** Roman god of love, represented as a naked winged boy archer. **2** (also **cupid**) representation of Cupid. [Latin *cupio* desire]

**cupidity** /kyoo-**pid**-uh-tee/ *n.* greed; avarice. [Latin: related to CUPID]

**cupola** /kyoo-puh-luh/ *n.* **1** dome forming or adorning a roof. **2** revolving dome protecting mounted guns. **3** furnace for melting metals. □ **cupolaed** /-luhd/ *adj.* [Italian from Latin *cupa* cask]

**cuppa** /kup-uh/ *n. colloq.* **1** cup of. **2** cup of tea. [corruption]

**cupreous** /kyoo-pree-uhs/ *adj.* of or like copper. [Latin: related to COPPER¹]

**cupric** /kyoo-prik/ *adj.* of copper.

**cupro-nickel** /ˌkyoo-proh-**nik**-uhl/ *n.* alloy of copper and nickel.

**cur** /ker/ *n.* **1** mangy ill-tempered dog. **2** contemptible person. [perhaps from Old Norse *kurr* grumbling]

**curable** /kyoo-ruh-buhl/ *adj.* able to be cured. □ **curability** /-bil-uh-tee/ *n.*

**curaçao** /kyoo-ruh-**soh**/ *n.* (*pl.* **-s**) orange-flavoured liqueur. [*Curaçao*, Caribbean island]

**curacy** /kyoo-ruh-see/ *n.* (*pl.* **-ies**) curate's office or tenure of it.

**curare** /kyoo-**rah**-ree/ *n.* extract of various plants, paralysing the motor nerves, used by S. American Indians to poison arrows. [Carib]

**curate** /kyoo-ruht/ *n.* assistant to a parish priest. [medieval Latin *curatus*: related to CURE]

**curate's egg** *n.* thing that is partly good and partly bad.

**curative** /kyoo-ruh-tiv/ — *adj.* tending or able to cure. — *n.* curative agent. [medieval Latin: related to CURATE]

**curator** /kyoo-**ray**-tuh/ *n.* keeper or custodian of a museum, art collection, etc. □ **curatorship** *n.* [Anglo-Latin: related to CURE]

**curb** — *n.* **1** check, restraint (*need to put a curb on inflation*). **2** strap etc. passing under a horse's lower jaw, used as a check. **3** enclosing border, e.g. the frame round a well or a fender round a hearth. **4** = KERB. — *v.* **1** restrain (*need to curb their enthusiasm*). **2** put a curb on (a horse). [French: related to CURVE]

**curd** *n.* (often in *pl.*) **1** coagulated acidic milk product made into cheese or eaten as food. **2** any similar substance (*bean curd*; *lemon-curd*). [origin unknown]

**curdle** /ker-duhl/ *v.* (**-ling**) form into curds; congeal. □ **make one's blood curdle** horrify one. [from CURD]

**cure** — *v.* (**-ring**) **1** (often foll. by *of*) restore to health; relieve (*cured of pleurisy*). **2** eliminate (disease, evil, etc.). **3** preserve (meat, fruit, etc.) by salting, drying, etc. **4** vulcanise (rubber); harden (plastic etc.). — *n.* **1** restoration to health. **2** thing effecting a cure. **3** course of medical or healing treatment. **4 a** office or function of a curate. **b** parish or other sphere of spiritual ministration. [Latin *cura* care]

**cure-all** *n.* panacea; universal remedy.

**curette** /kyoo-**ret**/ — *n.* surgeon's small scraping-instrument. — *v.* (**-tting**) clean or scrape with this. □ **curettage** /kyoo-ret-ij, -ruh-**tahj**/ *n.* [French: related to CURE]

**curfew** /**ker**-fyoo/ *n.* **1 a** regulation restricting or forbidding the public circulation of people, esp. requiring people to remain indoors between specified hours, usu. at night. **b** the hour designated as the beginning of such a restriction. **2** *hist.* signal for extinction of fires at a fixed hour. [French: related to COVER, Latin FOCUS]

**Curia** /**kyoo**-ree-uh/ *n.* (also **curia**) papal court; the various government departments of the Vatican. [Latin]

**curie** /kyoo-ree/ *n.* unit of radioactivity. [P. *Curie*, name of a scientist]

**curio** /kyoo-ree-oh/ *n.* (*pl.* **-s**) rare or unusual object. [abbreviation of CURIOSITY]

**curiosity** /ˌkyoo-ree-**os**-uh-tee/ *n.* (*pl.* **-ies**) **1** eager desire to know; inquisitiveness. **2** strange, rare, etc., object. [Latin: related to CURIOUS]

**curious** /kyoo-ree-uhs/ *adj.* **1** eager to learn; inquisitive (*a curious child*). **2** strange, surprising, odd (*a curious coincidence*). □ **curiously** *adv.* [Latin: related to CURE]

**curium** /kyoo-ree-uhm/ *n.* artificial radioactive metallic element. [M. and P. *Curie*, name of scientists]

**curl** — *v.* **1** (often foll. by *up*) bend or coil into a spiral. **2** move in a spiral form (*smoke curling upwards*). **3 a** (of the upper lip) be raised contemptuously. **b** cause (the lip) to do this. — *n.* **1** lock of curled hair. **2** anything spiral or curved inwards. **3 a** curling movement. **b** state of being curled. □ **curl one's lip** express scorn. **curl up** lie or sit with the knees drawn up. **2** *colloq.* writhe in embarrassment etc. **make a person's hair curl** *colloq.* shock or horrify a person. [Dutch]

**curler** *n.* pin or roller etc. for curling the hair.

**curlew** /**ker**-loo/ *n.* **1** any of various wading birds, usu. with a long slender down-curved bill. **2** either of two similar ground-nesting birds formerly widespread in Australia but no longer found in closely settled areas. [French]

**curl flower** *n.* (also **ivory curl flower**) small rainforest tree of Queensland, having long lance-leaves and a profusion of ivory-coloured curling spikes of pendulous flowers.

**curlicue** /ker-lee-,kyoo/ *n.* decorative curl or twist. [from CURLY, CUE[2] or Q]

**curling** *n.* Scottish game resembling bowls, played on ice with round flat stones.

**curl the mo** *colloq.* — *v.* succeed brilliantly. — *adj.* (**curl-the-mo**) impressive; outstanding. [origin uncertain]

**curly** *adj.* (**-ier**, **-iest**) **1** having or arranged in curls. **2** moving in curves. □ **curliness** *n.*

**curly Mitchell** see MITCHELL.

**curly wigs** *n.* unusual Australian sedge having tall stems on the tops of which are clumps of leaves which look like curly wigs.

**currant** /ku-ruhnt/ *n.* **1** small seedless dried grape. **2 a** any of various shrubs of the genus *Ribes* producing red, white, or black berries. **b** such a berry. [Anglo-French from *Corinth* in Greece]

**currawong** /ku-ruh-,wong/ *n.* (also **bell magpie**) any of three species of birds of the Australian genus *Strepera*, having predominantly black or grey plumage, yellow eyes, and a loud, melodious, ringing call: black currawong, grey currawong, pied currawong. [probably from Yagara (and neighbouring languages) *garrawan*, or perhaps from Dharuk *gurawarun*]

**currency** /ku-ruhn-see/ *n.* (*pl.* **-ies**) **1 a** money in use in a country. **b** other commodity used as money. **2** *hist.* **a** money other than sterling circulating in the Australian Colonies and discounted against sterling. **b** (also *attrib.*) native-born Australian as opposed to a British immigrant (dubbed *sterling*). **3 a** being current; prevalence (e.g. of words or ideas). **b** the time during which something is current.

**currency boy** var. of CURRENCY LAD.

**currency lad** *n.* *hist.* (*fem.* **currency lass**) native-born Australian as opposed to a British-born immigrant. [CURRENCY 2]

**current** — *adj.* **1** belonging to the present; happening now (*current events*; *the current week*). **2** (of money, opinion, rumour, etc.) in general circulation or use. — *n.* **1** body of moving water, air, etc., esp. passing through still water etc. **2 a** ordered movement of electrically charged particles. **b** quantity representing the intensity of this. **3** (usu. foll. by *of*) general tendency or course (*the current of*

public opinion runs in favour of an Australian Republic). □ **currentness** *n.* [Latin *curro curs-* run]

**current account** *n.* **1** instantly accessible bank account. **2** transactions in goods etc. that make up a part of a country's balance of payments.

**currently** *adv.* at the present time; now.

**curriculum** /kuh-**rik**-yuh-luhm/ *n.* (*pl.* **-la**) subjects included in a course of study. [Latin, = course]

**curriculum vitae** /kuh-,rik-yuh-luhm vee-tuy/ *n.* brief account of one's education, career, etc.

**curry**[1] /**ku**-ree/ — *n.* (*pl.* **-ies**) Asian dish of meat, vegetables, etc., cooked in a spicy-hot sauce, usu. served as the main accompaniment to rice. — *v.* (**-ies**, **-ied**) cook (meat etc.) in a curry sauce. □ **give a person curry** *colloq.* make life difficult or 'hot' for a person, esp. attack (a person) physically or verbally. [Tamil *kari*]

**curry**[2] /**ku**-ree/ *v.* (**-ies**, **-ied**) **1** groom (a horse) with a curry-comb. **2** treat (tanned leather) to improve it. □ **curry favour** ingratiate oneself. [Germanic: related to READY]

**curry-comb** *n.* metal serrated device for grooming horses.

**curry powder** *n.* mixture of powdered coriander, chilli, cumin, fennel, and other spices, for making curry.

**curse** — *n.* **1** solemn utterance intended to invoke a supernatural power to inflict destruction or punishment on a person or thing. **2** supposed resulting evil. **3** violent or profane exclamation or oath. **4** thing causing evil or harm. **5** (prec. by *the*) *colloq.* menstruation. — *v.* (**-sing**) **1 a** utter a curse against. **b** (in *imper.*) may God curse. **2** (usu. in *passive*; foll. by *with*) afflict with (*cursed with blindness*). **3** swear profanely. [Old English]

**cursed** /ker-suhd, kerst/ *attrib. adj.* damned.

**cursive** /ker-siv/ — *adj.* (of writing) with joined characters. — *n.* cursive writing. [medieval Latin, = running: related to CURRENT]

**cursor** /ker-suh/ *n.* **1** *Math. etc.* transparent slide with a hairline, forming part of a slide-rule. **2** *Computing* indicator on a display screen identifying esp. the position that the program will operate on with the next keystroke. [Latin, = runner: related to CURSIVE]

**cursory** /ker-suh-ree/ *adj.* hasty, hurried (*a cursory glance*). □ **cursorily** *adv.* **cursoriness** *n.* [Latin: related to CURSOR]

**curt** *adj.* (of speech, manner, etc.)

noticeably or rudely brief. □ **curtly** *adv.*
**curtness** *n.* [Latin *curtus* short]

**curtail** /ker-**tayl**/ *v.* cut short; reduce.
□ **curtailment** *n.* [corruption of obsolete
adj. *curtal*: related to CURT]

**curtain** /**ker**-tuhn/ — *n.* **1** piece of cloth
etc. hung as a screen, esp. at a window. **2
a** rise or fall of a stage curtain between
acts or scenes. **b** = CURTAIN CALL. **3**
partition or cover. **4** (in *pl.*) *colloq.* the end
(*it's curtains for him if his father finds
out*). — *v.* **1** provide or cover with
curtain(s). **2** (foll. by *off*) shut off with
curtain(s). [Latin *cortina*]

**curtain call** *n.* audience's applause
summoning actors to take a bow.

**curtain-raiser** *n.* **1** short play before the
main performance. **2** preliminary event.

**curtsy** /**kert**-see/ (also **curtsey**) — *n.* (*pl.*
**-ies** or **-eys**) bending of the knees and
lowering the body made by a girl or
woman in acknowledgment of applause
or as a respectful greeting etc. — *v.* (**-ies**,
**-ied** or **-eys**, **-eyed**) make a curtsy. [var. of
COURTESY]

**curvaceous** /ker-**vay**-shuhs/ *adj. colloq.*
(esp. of a woman) having a shapely
figure. [Latin *curva*]

**curvature** /**ker**-vuh-chuh/ *n.* **1** act or
state of curving. **2** curved form or condition (*curvature of the spine*). **3** *Geom.*
deviation of a curve or curved surface
from a plane. [French from Latin: related
to CURVE]

**curve** — *n.* **1** line or surface having along
its length a regular deviation from being
straight or flat. **2** curved form or thing. **3**
curved line on a graph. — *v.* (**-ving**) bend
or shape to form a curve. □ **curved** *adj.*
**curvy** *adj.* [Latin *curvus* curved]

**curvilinear** /ˌker-vuh-**lin**-ee-uh/ *adj.*
contained by or consisting of curved lines.
□ **curvilinearly** *adv.* [from CURVE after
*rectilinear*]

**cuscus** /**kus**-kuhs/ *n.* any of several
nocturnal, usu. arboreal, marsupial
mammals of northern Australia and New
Guinea. [probably from a New Guinea
language]

**cushion** /**kuush**-uhn/ — *n.* **1** bag stuffed
with soft material, for sitting or leaning
on etc. **2** protection against shock;
measure to soften a blow (*a cushion
against inflation*). **3** padded rim of a
billiard-table etc. **4** air supporting a
hovercraft etc. — *v.* **1** provide or protect
with cushion(s). **2** mitigate the adverse
effects of (*cushioned the blow*). [Latin
*culcita* mattress]

**cushion bush** *n.* rounded, cushion-like
shrub of southern Australia, having

silvery foliage, often cultivated as an
ornamental.

**cushy** /**kuush**-ee/ *adj.* (**-ier**, **-iest**) *colloq.*
(of a job etc.) easy and pleasant;
comfortable. [Hindi *khūsh* pleasant]

**cusp** /kusp/ *n.* **1** apex or peak. **2** point at
which two curves meet, e.g. the horn of a
crescent moon etc. **3** *Astrol.* initial point
of a house. **4** *Bot.* pointed end, esp. of a
leaf. **5** cone-shaped prominence on the
surface of a tooth, esp. a molar or premolar. □ **cuspate** /-spayt/ *adj.* **cusped**
*adj.* **cuspidal** *adj.* [Latin *cuspis -id-* point,
apex]

**cuss** *colloq.* — *n.* **1** curse. **2** usu. *derog.*
person; creature (*queer cuss*). — *v.* curse.
[variant of CURSE]

**cussed** /**kus**-uhd/ *adj. colloq.* awkward
and stubborn. □ **cussedness** *n.*

**custard** /**kus**-tuhd/ *n.* pudding or sweet
sauce of eggs or flavoured cornflour and
milk. [obsolete *crustade*: related to CRUST]

**custard apple** *n.* fruit with a sweet
yellow pulp.

**custodian** /kus-**toh**-dee-uhn/ *n.* guardian
or keeper. □ **custodianship** *n.*

**custody** /**kus**-tuh-dee/ *n.* **1** guardianship; protective care. **2** imprisonment.
□ **take into custody** arrest. □ **custodial**
/kus-**toh**-dee-uhl/ *adj.* [Latin *custos -od-*
guard]

**custom** /**kus**-tuhm/ *n.* **1 a** usual or
conventional way of behaving or acting (*a
slave to custom*). **b** particular established
way of behaving (*our customs seem
strange to foreigners*). **2** *Law* established
usage having the force of law. **3** business
patronage; regular dealings or customers
(*has lost a lot of custom*). **4** (in *pl.*; also
treated as *sing.*) **a** duty on imports and
exports. **b** official department administering this. **c** area at a port, frontier,
etc., dealing with customs etc. [Latin
*consuetudo*]

**customary** *adj.* in accordance with
custom, usual. □ **customarily** *adv.*
**customariness** *n.* [medieval Latin:
related to CUSTOM]

**customary law** *n.* Aboriginal traditional
practices.

**custom-built** *adj.* (also **custom-made**)
made to order.

**customer** *n.* **1** person who buys goods or
services from a shop or business. **2** *colloq.*
person of a specified kind (*awkward
customer*; *cool customer*). [Anglo-French:
related to CUSTOM]

**customise** *v.* (also **-ize**) (**-sing** or **-zing**)
make to order or modify according to
individual requirements; personalise.

**cut** — v. (**-tt-**; past and past part. **cut**) **1 a** penetrate or wound with a sharp-edged instrument (*cut his finger*). **b** (of a cutting instrument) perform (as specified) (*this knife cuts well*). **c** admit of being cut (*this wood cuts easily*). **2** (often foll. by *into*) divide or be divided with a knife etc. (*cut the cake*). **3 a** shorten, reduce, or detach by cutting off a portion (*cut his hair; cut some flowers*). **b** shorten (a play, speech, etc.) by omitting portions. **4** (foll. by *loose, open*, etc.) loosen, open, etc. by cutting. **5** (esp. as **cutting** adj.) cause sharp physical or mental pain (*a cutting wind; cutting remark*). **6** (often foll. by *down*) reduce (wages, time, etc.) or cease (services etc.). **7 a** make (a coat, gem, key, etc.) by cutting. **b** make (a path, tunnel, etc.) by removing material. **c** record (a song or album). **8** perform, make (*cut a caper; cut a sorry figure*). **9** (also *absol.*) cross, intersect (*the line cuts the circle at two points*). **10** (foll. by *across, through,* etc.) traverse, esp. as a shorter way (*cut across the paddock*). **11 a** deliberately ignore (a person one knows) (*cut him completely*). **b** renounce (a connection) (*cut all ties with his friends*). **12** deliberately miss (a class etc.). **13** *Cards* **a** divide (a pack) into two parts. **b** do this to select a dealer etc. **14 a** edit (film or tape). **b** (often in *imper.*) stop filming or recording. **c** (foll. by *to*) go quickly to (another shot) (*the film cuts from the whites merrymaking to Aborigines being massacred*). **15** (in Aboriginal English) ritually circumcise (a boy) to initiate into manhood. **16** castrate, neuter (an animal). **17** *Cricket* (of the ball) turn sharply on pitching. **18** hit (a ball) with a chopping motion. **19** switch off (an engine etc.). — n. **1** act of cutting. **2** division or wound made by cutting. **3 a** stroke with a knife, whip, etc. **b** (in *pl.*) caning or strapping (*got the cuts*). **4 a** reduction (in wages etc.). **b** cessation (of power supply etc.). **5** removal of lines etc. from a play, film, etc. **6** wounding remark or act. **7** style of hair, garment, etc. achieved by cutting. **8** particular piece of butchered meat. **9** *colloq.* commission; share of profits (*I'm here for my cut*). **10** *Cricket* etc. stroke made by cutting. **11** deliberate ignoring of a person. **12** harvest, esp. of sugar cane etc. — adj. **1** gashed or wounded with a sharp instrument (*a cut finger*). **2 a** formed, shaped, or made by cutting (*cut glass*). **b** divided into pieces by cutting (*cut firewood*). **3** (of leaves etc.) having margins deeply indented. **4** shortened, lessened, or reduced by, or as by, cutting (*cut prices*). **5 a** castrated, neutered. **b**

*colloq.* circumcised. **6** *colloq.* drunk. **7** hurt (*quite cut by his rude remarks*). □ a **cut above** *colloq.* noticeably superior to. **be cut out** (foll. by *for*, or *to* + infin.) be suited (*was not cut out to be a teacher*). **cut across 1** transcend (normal limitations etc.). **2** see sense 10 of v. **cut and run** *colloq.* run away. **cut back 1** reduce (expenditure etc.). **2** prune (a tree etc.). **cut both ways 1** serve both sides of an argument etc. **2** (of an action) have both good and bad effects. **cut a corner** go across it. **cut corners** do perfunctorily or incompletely, esp. to save time. **cut a dash** make a brilliant show. **cut a person dead** deliberately ignore (a person one knows). **cut down 1** bring or throw down by cutting (*cut down some trees*). **b** kill by sword etc. or by disease (*cut down in the prime of youth*). **2** see sense 6 of v. **3** reduce the length of (*cut down trousers to make shorts*). **4** (often foll. by *on*) reduce consumption (*cut down on beer*). **cut a person down to size** deflate a person's pretensions. **cut in 1** interrupt. **2** pull in too closely in front of another vehicle (esp. having overtaken it). **3** interrupt a dancing couple to take over from one partner. **cut it fine** allow very little margin of time etc. **cut it out** (usu. in *imper.*) *colloq.* stop doing that. **cut loose 1** begin to act freely. **2** see sense 4 of v. **cut one's losses** abandon an unprofitable scheme or situation. **cut no ice** *colloq.* have no influence (*your promises cut no ice with me*). **cut off 1** remove by cutting. **2 a** (often in *passive*) bring to an abrupt end or (esp. early) death. **b** intercept, interrupt (*cut them off at the pass; cut off the gas supply*). **c** disconnect (a person on the telephone). **3 a** prevent from travelling (*was cut off by the snow*). **b** (as **cut off** adj.) isolated or remote (*felt cut off in the outback*). **4** disinherit. **cut out 1** remove from inside by cutting. **2** make by cutting from a larger whole. **3** omit. **4** *colloq.* stop doing or using (something) (*cut out chocolate; cut out the rough stuff*). **5** (cause to) cease functioning (*engine cut out*). **6** outdo or supplant (a rival). **7** separate (animals) from a mob. **8 a** finish shearing. **b** *colloq.* come to an end; be expended or exhausted (*the road cuts out in about two kilometres; the party ended when the grog cut out*). **cut short** interrupt; terminate. **cut one's teeth on** acquire experience from (*this grazier cut his teeth on jackerooing in the outback*). **cut a tooth** have it appear through the gum. **cut up 1** cut into pieces. **2** (usu. in *passive*) distress greatly. **cut up rough** *colloq.* show anger or resentment. [Old English]

**cut and dried** *adj.* **1** completely decided; inflexible. **2** (of opinions etc.) ready-made, lacking freshness.

**:ut and paste** *Computing* — *n.* facility to select text and copy or move it to another position or program. — *v.* use such a facility.

**:ut and thrust** *n.* lively argument etc.

**:utaneous** /kyoo-**tay**-nee-uhs/ *adj.* of the skin. [Latin: related to CUTICLE]

**:utaway** *attrib. adj.* (of a diagram etc.) with parts of the exterior left out to reveal the interior.

**:utback** *n.* cutting back, esp. a reduction in expenditure.

**:ute** /kyoot/ *adj. colloq.* **1** attractive, sexy (*he's really cute*). **2** (often sarcastic) clever, ingenious (*a cute move*; *who's the cute bastard who put itching powder in my jocks?*). □ **cutely** *adv.* **cuteness** *n.* [shortening of ACUTE]

**:ut glass** *n.* (often hyphenated when *attrib.*) glass with patterns cut on it.

**:uticle** /**kyoo**-ti-kuhl/ *n.* **1 a** dead skin at the base of a fingernail or toenail. **b** the epidermis or other superficial skin. **2** *Bot.* thin surface film on plants. [Latin diminutive of *cutis* skin]

**:utie** /**kyoo**-tee/ *n. colloq.* person who is CUTE (sense 1).

**:utis** /**kyoo**-tuhs/ *n.* true skin, beneath the epidermis. [Latin]

**:utlass** /**kut**-luhs/ *n. hist.* short sword with a slightly curved blade. [ultimately from Latin *culter* ploughshare, knife]

**:utlery** /**kut**-luh-ree/ *n.* knives, forks, and spoons for use at table. [Anglo-French]

**:utlet** /**kut**-luht/ *n.* **1** neck-chop of mutton or lamb. **2** small piece of veal etc. for frying. **3** fish steak. [French diminutive from Latin *costa* rib]

**:ut-off** *n.* **1** (often *attrib.*) point at which something is cut off (*cut-off point*). **2** device for stopping a flow.

**:ut-offs** *n.pl. colloq.* jeans which have been roughly cut above the knee and left to fray.

**:ut-out** *n.* **1** figure cut out of paper etc. **2** device for automatic disconnection, the release of exhaust gases, etc. **3** end of a shearing contract or season.

**:ut-price** *adj.* (also **cut-rate**) at a reduced price.

**:utter** *n.* **1 a** person or thing that cuts, e.g. a shearer, cane-cutter, timber-getter, etc. **b** (in *pl.*) cutting tool. **2 a** small fast sailing-ship. **b** small boat carried by a large ship. **3** *Cricket* ball turning sharply on pitching.

**:ut-throat** — *n.* **1** murderer. **2** (in full

**cut-throat razor**) razor with a long unguarded blade set in a handle. — *adj.* **1** (of competition) ruthless and intense. **2** (of a card-game) three-handed.

**cutting** — *n.* **1** piece cut from a newspaper etc. **2** piece cut from a plant for propagation. **3** excavated channel in a hillside etc. for a railway or road. — *adj.* see CUT *v.* 5. □ **cuttingly** *adv.*

**cutting edge** *n.* □ **be at the cutting edge** be at the forefront (of some activity, development, etc.).

**cutting grass** *n.* any of several Australian sedges with sharp-edged blades.

**cuttle-bone** *n.* internal shell of the cuttlefish, crushed and used for polishing, or as a supplement to the diet of a cage-bird.

**cuttlefish** /**kut**-uhl-,fish/ *n.* (*pl.* same or **-es**) mollusc with ten arms and ejecting a black fluid when threatened. [Old English]

**cutworm** *n.* any of several caterpillars that eat through the stems of young plants level with the ground.

**cuvée** /kyoo-**vay**/ *n.* blend or batch of wine. [French, = vatful]

**CV** *abbr.* curriculum vitae.

**cwt.** *abbr.* hundredweight.

**-cy** *suffix* denoting state, condition, or status (*idiocy*; *captaincy*). [Latin *-cia*, Greek *-kia*]

**cyanic acid** /suy-**an**-ik/ *n.* unstable colourless pungent acid gas. [Greek *kuanos* a blue mineral]

**cyanide** /**suy**-uh-,nuyd/ *n.* highly poisonous substance used in the extraction of gold and silver.

**cyanosis** /,suy-uh-**noh**-suhs/ *n.* bluish skin due to oxygen-deficient blood.

**cyathea** /,suy-uh-**thee**-uh/ *n.* any of several Australian tree-ferns, having tall, usu. very slender, trunks and long fronds radiating from the summit of the trunk.

**cybernetics** /,suy-buh-**net**-iks/ *n.pl.* (usu. treated as *sing.*) science of communications and control systems in machines and living things. □ **cybernetic** *adj.* [Greek *kubernētēs* steersman]

**cyberpunk** /**suy**-buh-,pungk/ *n.* science fiction writing combining high-tech plots with unconventional or nihilistic social values. [from CYBERNETICS, PUNK]

**cyberspace** *n.* **1** notional space within which electronic communication occurs, esp. when represented as the inside of a computer system. **2** space perceived as such by an observer but generated by a computer system and having no real existence; the space of virtual reality.

**cycad** /suy-kad/ n. palmlike plant often growing to a great height. [Greek *koix* Egyptian palm]

**cyclamate** /suy-kluh-, mayt/ n. former artificial sweetener. [chemical name]

**cyclamen** /suy-kluh-muhn, sik-luh-/ n. 1 plant with pink, red, or white flowers with backward-turned petals. 2 shade of colour of the red or pink flower. [Latin from Greek]

**cycle** /suy-kuhl/ — n. 1 a recurrent round or period (of events, phenomena, etc.). b time needed for this. 2 a *Physics etc.* recurrent series of operations or states. b *Electr.* = HERTZ. 3 series of related songs, poems, etc. 4 bicycle, tricycle, etc. — v. (-ling) 1 ride a bicycle etc. 2 move in cycles. [Greek *kuklos* circle]

**cyclic** /suy-klik, sik-lik/ adj. (also **cyclical** /suy-kli-kuhl, sik-luh-/) 1 a recurring in cycles. b belonging to a chronological cycle. 2 *Chem.* with constituent atoms forming a ring. 3 (of a flower) with its parts arranged in whorls.

**cyclist** /suy-kluhst/ n. rider of a bicycle.

**cyclo-** comb. form circle, cycle, or cyclic.

**cycloid** /suy-kloid/ n. *Math.* curve traced by a point on a circle when the circle is rolled along a straight line.

**cyclone** /suy-klohn/ n. 1 winds rotating inwards to an area of low barometric pressure; depression. 2 violent hurricane of limited diameter. □ **cyclonic** /-klon-ik/ adj. [Greek *kuklōma* wheel]

**cyclone fence** n. propr. fence made with interlocking wire in metal frames.

**cyclotron** /suy-kluh-, tron/ n. apparatus for the acceleration of charged atomic and subatomic particles revolving in a magnetic field.

**cygnet** /sig-nuht/ n. young swan. [Latin *cygnus* swan from Greek]

**cylinder** /sil-uhn-duh/ n. 1 uniform solid or hollow body with straight sides and a circular section. 2 thing of this shape, e.g. a container for liquefied gas. 3 cylinder-shaped part of various machines, esp. a piston-chamber in an engine. □ **cylindrical** /-lin-dri-kuhl/ adj. [Latin *cylindrus* from Greek]

**cymbal** /sim-buhl/ n. concave disc, struck usu. with another to make a ringing sound. □ **cymbalist** n. [Latin from Greek]

**cymbidium** /sim-bid-ee-uhm/ n. tropical orchid of the genus of the same name (three species being endemic to Australia) having large and showy flowers with a recess in the flower lip. [Greek *kumbē* cup]

**cyme** /suym/ n. *Bot.* flowering section of a plant in which the main stem bears a single terminal flower that develops first, followed by flowers on secondary and other stems (cf. RACEME). □ **cymose** adj. [Greek *kuma* wave]

**Cymric** /kim-rik/ adj. Welsh. [Welsh *Cymru* Wales]

**cynic** /sin-ik/ n. 1 person with a pessimistic view of human nature and little faith in human sincerity and goodness. 2 (**Cynic**) one of a school of ancient Greek philosophers showing contempt for ease and pleasure. □ **cynical** adj. **cynically** adv. **cynicism** /-, siz-uhm/ n. [Greek *kuōn* dog, nickname for a Cynic]

**cynosure** /sin-uh-, shoor, -, zhoor/ n. centre of attraction or admiration (*she was the cynosure of all eyes*). [Greek, = dog's tail (name for Ursa Minor)]

**cypher** var. of CIPHER.

**cypress** /suy-pruhs/ n. conifer with hard wood and dark foliage. [Greek *kuparissos*]

**cypress pine** n. 1 any of several Australian trees of the genus *Callitris*. 2 wood of these trees, often termite-resistant.

**Cypriot** /sip-ree-uht/ — n. native or national of Cyprus. — adj. of Cyprus. [*Cyprus* in E. Mediterranean]

**Cyrillic** /suh-ril-ik/ — adj. of the alphabet used by the Slavonic peoples of the Orthodox Church, now used esp. for Russian and Bulgarian. — n. this alphabet. [St *Cyril* (d. 869)]

**cyst** /sist/ n. *Med.* 1 morbid sac formed in the body, containing matter, a parasitic larva, etc. 2 *Biol.* hollow organ, bladder, etc., in an animal or plant, containing a liquid secretion. [Greek *kustis* bladder]

**cystic** adj. 1 of the bladder. 2 like a cyst.

**cystic fibrosis** n. hereditary disease usu. with respiratory infections.

**cystitis** /sis-tuy-tuhs/ n. inflammation of the bladder usu. causing frequent painful urination.

**-cyte** comb. form mature cell (*leucocyte*). [Greek *kutos* vessel]

**cyto-** /suy-toh/ comb. form cells or a cell. [as -CYTE]

**cytogenetics** /, suy-toh-juh-net-iks/ n. study of inheritance in relation to the structure and function of cells.

**cytology** /suy-tol-uh-jee/ n. the study of cells. □ **cytological** /, suy-tuh-loj-i-kuhl/ adj. **cytologist** n. [Greek *kutos* vessel]

**cytoplasm** /suy-toh-, plaz-uhm/ n. protoplasmic content of a cell apart from its nucleus. □ **cytoplasmic** /-plaz-mik/ adj.

**czar** var. of TSAR.

**Czech** /chek/ — n. 1 native or national of the Czech Republic in what was formerly Czechoslovakia. **2** official language of this Republic. — *adj.* of the Czech Republic, its people, or language. [Bohemian *Čech*]

**Czechoslovak** /ˌchek-uh-**sloh**-vak/ *hist.* — *n.* native or national of the former Czechoslovakia. — *adj.* of the former Czechoslovakia. [from CZECH, SLOVAK]

# D

**D[1]** /dee/ *n.* (also **d**) (*pl.* **Ds** or **D's**) **1** fourth letter of the alphabet. **2** *Mus.* second note of the diatonic scale of C major. **3** (as a Roman numeral) 500. **4** fourth highest class or category (of academic marks etc.).

**D[2]** *symb.* deuterium.

**d.** *abbr.* **1** died. **2** departs. **3** daughter. **4** *hist.* (pre-decimal) penny. [sense 4 from Latin DENARIUS]

**'d** *v. colloq.* (usu. after pronouns) had, would (*I'd; he'd*). [abbreviation]

**dab** — *v.* (**-bb-**) **1** (often foll. by *at*) repeatedly press briefly and lightly with a cloth etc. (*dabbed at her eyes*). **2** press (a cloth etc.) thus. **3** (foll. by *on*) apply by dabbing (*dab some lotion on the rash*). **4** (often foll. by *at*) aim a feeble blow; strike lightly. — *n.* **1** act or process of dabbing. **2** small amount thus applied (*dab of paint*). **3** light blow. [imitative]

**dabble** /dab-uhl/ *v.* (**-ling**) **1** (usu. foll. by *in*, *at*) engage (in an activity etc.) superficially. **2** move the feet, hands, etc. in esp. shallow liquid. **3** wet partly; stain, splash. □ **dabbler** *n.* [from DAB]

**dab hand** *n.* (usu. foll. by *at*) *colloq.* expert. [*dab* adept, origin unknown]

**da capo** /dah **kah**-poh/ *adv. Mus.* repeat from the beginning. [Italian]

**dachshund** /**daks**-huund, **dash**-huhnd/ *n.* dog of a short-legged long-bodied breed. [German, = badger-dog]

**dacks** *n.* = DAKS.

**dactyl** /**dak**-til/ *n.* metrical foot consisting of one long syllable followed by two short syllables (-˘˘). □ **dactylic** /dak-**til**-ik/ *adj.* [Greek, = finger]

**dad** *n. colloq.* father. [imitative of a child's *da da*]

**Dad and Dave** *adj.* of or pertaining to, esp. comic, bush matters. [characters in the stories of Steele Rudd]

**daddy** /**dad**-ee/ *n.* (*pl.* **-ies**) *colloq.* father. □ **the** (or **a**) **daddy of** the most notable; the biggest (*he was the daddy of all liars; had a daddy of a headache*). [from DAD]

**daddy-long-legs** *n.* (*pl.* same) **1** small spider with very long legs. **2** *colloq.* tall person. **3** Australian terrestrial orchid, a spider orchid, having usu. deep crimson flowers, the segments of which are thin, long (up to 12 cm) and often hairy, hence the common name.

**dado** /**day**-doh/ *n.* (*pl.* **-s**) **1** lower, differently decorated, part of an interior wall. **2** plinth of a column. **3** cube of a pedestal between the base and the cornice. [Italian: related to DIE[2]]

**daemon** /**dee**-muhn/ **1** dormant computer program invoked to perform a particular system task when specified conditions occur. **2** var. of DEMON 4.

**daffodil** /**daf**-uh-dil/ *n.* **1** spring bulb with a (usu. yellow) trumpet-shaped flower. **2** pale yellow colour. [related to *asphodel*, type of lily]

**daffy** /**daf**-ee/ *adj.* (**-ier**, **-iest**) *colloq.* = DAFT. [*daff* simpleton]

**daft** /dahft/ *adj. colloq.* silly, foolish, crazy. [Old English, = meek]

**dag[1]** — *n.* (usu. in *pl.*) lump of matted wool and dung hanging from the hinder parts of a sheep; such a lump cut from a sheep. — *v.* (**-gg-**) **1** remove dags from (a sheep). **2** castrate baby rams with a knife. □ **rattle one's dags** *colloq.* hurry up. [originally English dial.]

**dag[2]** *n. colloq.* **1** person who is eccentric but entertainingly so; a character. **2** person who is conservative, unfashionable, behind the times. **3** untidy or dirty-looking person. **4** socially awkward adolescent. [English dial. *dag* a dare, challenge]

**dagger** *n.* **1** short pointed knife used as a weapon. **2** *Printing* = OBELUS. □ **(at) daggers drawn** in bitter enmity. **look daggers at** glare angrily at. [origin uncertain]

**daggy** /**dag**-ee/ *adj.* **1** (of a sheep) fouled with dags. **2** (of a person) *colloq.* **a** unkempt, slovenly. **b** unfashionable; lacking style. **c** eccentric; stupid.

**dago** /**day**-goh/ *n.* (*pl.* **-s**) *colloq. offens.* foreigner, esp. an Italian (also *attrib. dago language*). [Spanish *Diego* = James]

**dag-picker** *n.* person employed in a shearing shed to pick over dags in order to separate wool from dung. □ **dag-picking** *n.* [DAG[1]]

**dag-rattler** *n. colloq.* a sheep. [DAG[1]]

**dahlia** /**day**-lee-uh/ *n.* large-flowered showy garden plant of Mexican origin. [*Dahl*, name of a Swedish botanist (d. 1789)]

**daily** /**day**-lee/ — *adj.* done, produced, or occurring every day or every weekday — *adv.* **1** every day. **2** constantly. — *n.* (*pl.* **-ies**) *colloq.* daily newspaper.

**dainty** /**dayn**-tee/ — adj. (**-ier**, **-iest**) **1** delicately pretty. **2** delicate or small. **3** (of food) choice. **4** fastidious; having delicate taste and sensibility. — n. (pl. **-ies**) choice delicacy. □ **daintily** adv. **daintiness** n. [Latin *dignitas* DIGNITY]

**dairy** /**dair**-ree/ n. (pl. **-ies**) **1** place for processing, distributing, or selling milk and its products. **2** (*attrib.*) of, containing, or used for, dairy products (*dairy cow*). □ **dairying** n. [Old English]

**dais** /**day**-uhs/ n. low platform, usu. at the upper end of a hall and used to support a table, lectern, etc. [Latin DISCUS disc, (later) table]

**daisy** /**day**-zee/ n. (pl. **-ies**) **1** small plant bearing composite flowers, each consisting of a central yellow disc (made up of many small flowers) surrounded by white rays. **2** any plant with similar flowers. □ **pushing up (the) daisies** *colloq.* dead and buried. [Old English, = *day's eye*]

**daisy bush** n. any of about 80 species of the genus *Olearia* endemic to Australia, having usu. masses of blue, pink, purple, or white daisy-flowers.

**daisy cutter** n. (in cricket, Australian Rules, etc.) ball bowled or kicked so as to skim along the ground.

**daks** /daks/ n.pl. propr. colloq. trousers.

**Dalai Lama** /dal-uy **lah**-muh/ n. spiritual head of Tibetan Buddhism. [Mongolian *dalai* ocean]

**dale** n. chiefly *Brit.* valley. [Old English]

**dalgite** /**dal**-guyt/ n. (also **dalgyte**) Western Australian name for the bilby. [Nyungar *dalgaj*]

**dally** /**dal**-ee/ v. (**-ies**, **-ied**) **1** delay; waste time. **2** (often foll. by *with*) flirt, trifle (*dallied with her affections*). □ **dalliance** n. [French]

**Dalmatian** /dal-**may**-shuhn/ n. large white short-haired dog with dark spots. [*Dalmatia* region on the eastern Adriatic coast]

**dal segno** /dal **sayn**-yoh/ adv. Mus. repeat from the point marked by a sign. [Italian, = from the sign]

**dam¹** — n. **1** barrier across a river etc., forming a reservoir or preventing flooding. **2** artificial pond or reservoir for the storage of water, usu. run-off rainwater, esp. to provide water for stock. — v. (**-mm-**) **1** provide or confine with a dam. **2** (often foll. by *up*) block up; obstruct. [Low German or Dutch]

**dam²** n. female parent, esp. of a four-footed animal. [var. of DAME]

**damage** /**dam**-ij/ — n. **1** harm or injury impairing the value or usefulness of something, or the health or normal function of a person (*serious damage to his lungs from smoking*). **2** (in pl.) *Law* financial compensation for loss or injury. **3** (prec. by *the*) *colloq.* cost (*what's the damage?*). — v. (**-ging**) **1** inflict damage on. **2** (esp. as **damaging** adj.) detract from the reputation of (*a most damaging admission*). [Latin *damnum*]

**damask** /**dam**-uhsk/ — n. reversible figured woven fabric, esp. white table linen. — adj. **1** made of damask. **2** coloured like a damask rose, velvety pink or vivid red. — v. weave with figured designs. [*Damascus* in Syria]

**damask rose** n. old sweet-scented rose used to make attar.

**dame** n. **1** (**Dame**) a title given to a woman with the rank of knight in the Order of Australia (no longer awarded), or in comparable British orders. **b** woman holding this title. **2** comic middle-aged female pantomime character, usu. played by a man. **3** *colloq.* woman. [Latin *domina* lady]

**damn** /dam/ — v. **1** (often *absol.* or as *int.* of anger or annoyance, = *may God damn*) curse (a person or thing). **2** doom to hell; cause the damnation of. **3** condemn, censure (*review damning the book*). **4 a** (often as **damning** adj.) (of circumstance, evidence, etc.) show or prove to be guilty. **b** be the ruin of. — n. **1** uttered curse. **2** colloq. negligible amount (*not worth a damn*). — adj. & adv. colloq. = DAMNED. □ **damn all** colloq. nothing at all. **damn well** colloq. (for emphasis) simply (*damn well do as I say*). **damn with faint praise** commend feebly, and so imply disapproval. **I'm (or I'll be) damned if** colloq. I certainly do not, will not, etc. **not give a damn** see GIVE. **well I'm (or I'll be) damned** colloq. exclamation of surprise etc. [Latin *damnum* loss]

**damnable** /**dam**-nuh-buhl/ adj. hateful, annoying. □ **damnably** adv.

**damnation** /dam-**nay**-shuhn/ — n. eternal punishment in hell. — int. expressing anger, annoyance, etc.

**damned** /damd/ colloq. — attrib. adj. damnable. — adv. extremely (*damned hot*). □ **damned well** = *damn well*. **do one's damnedest** do one's utmost.

**damp** — adj. slightly wet. — n. moisture in the air, on a surface, or in a solid, esp. as a source of inconvenience or danger. — v. **1** make damp; moisten. **2** (often foll. by *down*) **a** take the force or vigour out of; mute (*damps my enthusiasm*). **b** make (a fire) burn less strongly by reducing the flow of air to it. **3** reduce or stop the vibration of (esp. strings of a musical instrument). □ **damp off** (of a plant) die from a fungus attack in damp conditions. □ **damply** adv. **dampness** n. [Low German]

**damp course** n. (also **damp-proof course**) layer of waterproof material in a wall near the ground, to prevent rising damp.

**dampen** v. **1** make or become damp. **2** (often foll. by *down*) = DAMP v. 2a.

**damper**[1] n. **1** discouraging person or thing. **2** device that reduces shock or noise. **3** metal plate in a flue to control the draught. **4** *Mus.* pad silencing a piano string. □ **put a damper on** take the vigour or enjoyment out of; discourage.

**damper**[2] n. simple kind of bread, traditionally unleavened, baked in the ashes of an outdoor fire. [specialised use of British *damper* something which takes the edge off the appetite]

**dampiera** /dam-pee-**air**-ruh/ n. any of about 60 species of the endemic Australian genus of the same name, being small shrubs or ground-covers bearing bright blue to deep purple flowers in profusion. [William *Dampier*, English explorer (d. 1715)]

**damp squib** n. unsuccessful attempt to impress etc.; plan, enterprise, etc., that fails.

**damsel** /**dam**-zuhl/ n. *archaic* or *literary* young unmarried woman. [French diminutive: related to DAME]

**dan** n. **1** grade of proficiency in judo. **2** holder of such a grade. [Japanese]

**dance** /dahns, dans/ — v. (**-cing**) **1** move rhythmically, usu. to music. **2** move in a lively way; skip or jump about. **3** perform (a specified dance, role, etc.). — n. **1 a** dancing as an art form. **b** style or form of this. **2** social gathering for dancing. **3** single round or turn of a dance. **4** music for dancing to. **5** lively motion. □ **dance attendance on** serve obsequiously. **lead a person a dance** (or **merry dance**) cause a person much trouble. □ **danceable** adj. **dancer** n. [French]

**dancing orchid** n. Australian terrestrial orchid having large red-striped lime-green (or wholly reddish maroon) flowers, segments of which are spread out above and below the labellum and resemble the arms and legs of a ballet-dancer, the fringed labellum itself resembling a tutu.

**d. and c.** n. dilatation (of the cervix) and curettage (of the uterus).

**dandelion** /**dan**-duh-,luy-uhn/ n. weed with deeply indented leaves, a yellow flower, and a fluffy seed-head. [French *dent-de-lion*, = lion's tooth, alluding to the indented leaves]

**dandle** /**dan**-duhl/ v. (**-ling**) bounce (a child) on one's knees etc. [origin unknown]

**dandruff** /**dan**-druf/ n. **1** flakes of dead skin in the hair. **2** this as a condition [origin uncertain]

**dandy** /**dan**-dee/ — n. (pl. **-ies**) **1** man greatly devoted to style and fashion. **2** *colloq.* excellent thing. **3** (esp. in SA small container of ice-cream. — adj. (**-ier -iest**) *colloq.* splendid (often iron.: *that' just dandy!*). [perhaps from the nam *Andrew*]

**Dane** n. **1** native or national of Denmark **2** *hist.* Viking invader of England in th 9th–11th c. [Old Norse]

**danger** /**dayn**-juh/ n. **1** liability o exposure to harm. **2** person or thing tha causes or may cause harm. □ **in danger o** likely to incur or to suffer from. [earlier = 'power', from Latin *dominus* lord]

**dangerous** adj. involving or causin danger. □ **dangerously** adv.

**dangle** /**dang**-guhl/ v. (**-ling**) **1** be loosel suspended and able to sway. **2** hold o carry loosely suspended. **3** hold ou (hope, temptation, etc.) enticingl [imitative]

**Danish** /**day**-nish/ — adj. of or relatin to Denmark or the Danes. — n. **1** Danis language. **2** (prec. by *the*; treated as *pl.* the Danish people. [Latin: related t DANE]

**dank** adj. disagreeably damp and cold □ **dankly** adv. **dankness** n. [probabl Scandinavian]

**danthonia** /dan-**thoh**-nee-uh/ n. = WALLABY GRASS. [Latinised form of E *Danthoine* French botanist]

**daphne** /**daf**-nee/ n. any of variou flowering shrubs of the genus *Daphne* with highly scented flowers. [Greek]

**dapper** adj. **1** neat and precise, esp. ir dress. **2** sprightly. [Low German or Dutc] *dapper* strong]

**dapple** /**dap**-uhl/ — v. (**-ling**) mark o become marked with spots of colour o shade. — n. **1** dappled effect. **2** dapple animal, esp. a horse. [origin unknown]

**dare** /dair/ — v. (**-ring**; *3rd sing. presen* usu. dare before an expressed or implie infinitive without *to*) **1** (foll. by infin. wit or without *to*) have the courage o impudence (to) (*dare he do it?*; *if they dar to come*; *how dare you?*). **2** (usu. foll. by t + infin.) defy or challenge (*I dare you t own up*). — n. **1** act of daring. **2** chal lenge, esp. to prove courage. □ **I dare sa 1** (often foll. by *that*) it is probable. **2** probably; I grant that much (*I dare say but you are still wrong*). [Old English]

**daredevil** — *n.* recklessly daring person. — *adj.* recklessly daring. □ **daredevilry** *n.*

**darg** /dahg/ *n.* **1** a day's work. **2** definite amount of work; a task. [British dial. *daywerk* or *daywark* from Old English *dægweorc*]

**daring** — *n.* adventurous courage. — *adj.* adventurous, bold; prepared to take risks. □ **daringly** *adv.*

**dark** — *adj.* **1** with little or no light. **2** of deep or sombre colour. **3** (of a person) with brown or black hair or complexion. **4** gloomy, dismal (*dark thoughts*). **5** evil, sinister (*dark deeds*). **6 a** sullen, angry (*a dark mood*). **b** (*predic.*) *colloq.* angry, irate; in a glowering mood (*he's really dark about it*). **7** remote; secret, mysterious (*the dark and distant past*; *keep it dark*). — *n.* **1** absence of light (*don't go out after dark*). □ **dark on** *colloq.* angry with (*dark on her for standing him up*). **in the dark 1** lacking information (*we're being deliberately kept in the dark*). **2** with no light. □ **darkish** *adj.* [Old English]

**Dark Ages** *n.pl.* (also **Dark Age**) **1** period of European history from the 5th–10th c. **2** period of supposed unenlightenment.

**darken** *v.* make or become dark or darker. □ **never darken a person's door** keep away permanently. □ **darkener** *n.*

**dark horse** *n.* **1** little-known person who is unexpectedly successful. **2** little-known person who is considered (by some) to be a potential success.

**darkie** *n.* (also **darky**) *colloq. offens.* **1** dark-complexioned person. **2** an Aborigine.

**darkroom** *n.* darkened room for photographic work.

**dark star** *n.* invisible star known to exist from the reception of physical data other than light.

**darky** var. of DARKIE.

**darl** /dahl/ *n. colloq.* = DARLING. [abbreviation]

**darling** /**dah**-ling/ — *n.* **1** beloved, lovable, or endearing person or thing. **2** favourite. — *adj.* **1** beloved, lovable. **2** *colloq.* charming or pretty. [Old English: related to DEAR]

**Darling lily** *n.* Australian perennial plant bearing spectacular cream or white, scented, trumpet-shaped flowers. [*Darling* River in western NSW]

**Darling pea** *n.* **1** handsome perennial (*Swainsona galegifolia*) of SA, Queensland, and NSW, bearing profuse sprays of pea-flowers in colours ranging from white to vivid red. **2 a** any plant of the genus *Swainsona*, some of which can cause stock poisoning. **b** such poisoning (*the sheep have got Darling pea*).

**Darling shower** *n.* a dust-storm.

**darn**[1] — *v.* mend (cloth etc.) by filling a hole with stitching. — *n.* darned area. [origin uncertain]

**darn**[2] *v., int., adj., & adv. colloq.* = DAMN (in imprecatory senses). [corruption]

**darned** *adj. & adv. colloq.* = DAMNED.

**darning** *n.* **1** act of darning. **2** things to be darned.

**dart**[1] — *n.* **1** small pointed missile. **2** (in *pl.*; usu. treated as *sing.*) indoor game of throwing darts at a dartboard to score points. **3** sudden rapid movement. **4** dartlike structure, e.g. an insect's sting. **5** tapering tuck in a garment. **6** (**Dart**) = OLD DART. — *v.* (often foll. by *out, in, past*, etc.) move, send, or go suddenly or rapidly (*she darted out a moment ago*). [French from Germanic]

**dart**[2] *n.* any of several fish of warmer Australian waters (*common dart*; *snub-nosed dart*).

**dartboard** *n.* circular target in darts.

**darter** /**dah**-tuh/ *n.* any of various large water-birds having a narrow head and long thin neck (*Australian darter*).

**Darwin** /**dah**-wuhn/ *n.* name of the capital city of the Northern Territory. [Charles *Darwin*, English naturalist]

**darwinia** /dah-**win**-ee-uh/ *n.* any of 35 species of shrub of the Australian genus *Darwinia* (nearly all from WA) having attractive usu. red flower-heads, often

---

**Dash —**
This is used:
1  to mark the beginning and end of an interruption in the structure of a sentence:
   *My son—where has he gone?—would like to meet you.*
2  to show faltering speech in conversation:
   *Yes—well—I would—only you see—it's not easy.*
3  to show other kinds of breaks in a sentence, where a comma, semicolon, or colon would traditionally be used, e.g.
   *Come tomorrow—if you can.*
   *The most important thing is this—don't rush the work.*
   A dash is not used in this way in formal writing.

with highly colourful bracts. [Charles *Darwin*, English naturalist (d.1882)]

**Darwinian** /dah-**win**-ee-uhn/ — *adj.* of or relating to Darwin's theory of the evolution of species by the action of natural selection (cf. CREATIONISM). — *n.* adherent of this theory. □ **Darwinism** /dah-/ *n.* **Darwinist** /dah-/ *n.* [Charles *Darwin*, English naturalist (d. 1882)]

**Darwin rig** *n.* semi-formal male attire (in Darwin): long-sleeved white shirt with or without tie, long trousers or shorts with long white socks, no coat.

**Darwin stubby** *n.* a very large bottle of beer (usu. 2.25 litres) (cf. STUBBY *n.* 1).

**dash** — *v.* **1** rush (*dashed off in a tearing hurry*). **2** strike or fling forcefully, esp. so as to shatter (*dashed it to the ground*). **3** frustrate, dispirit (*dashed their hopes*). **4** *colloq.* (esp. **dash it** or **dash it all**) = DAMN *v.* 1. — *n.* **1** rush or onset; sudden advance (*made a dash for shelter*). **2** horizontal stroke (–) in writing or printing to mark a pause etc. (see panel). **3** impetuous vigour; capacity for or appearance of this (*has a lot of dash*). **4** sprinting-race. **5** longer signal of two in Morse code (cf. DOT *n.* 2). **6** slight admixture, esp. of a liquid (*add a dash of wine; a dash of salt*). **7** = DASHBOARD. □ **dash off** write or draw hurriedly. **do one's dash** exhaust one's energies or opportunities. [imitative]

**dashboard** *n.* instrument panel of a vehicle or aircraft.

**dashing** *adj.* **1** spirited, lively. **2** showy. □ **dashingly** *adv.* **dashingness** *n.*

**dastardly** /**das**-tuhd-lee/ *adj.* cowardly, despicable. □ **dastardliness** *n.* [origin uncertain]

**dasyure** /**das**-ee-,yoor, daz-/ *n.* any of various small carnivorous marsupials, including the Australian native cats. [Greek *dasus* rough, *oura* tail]

**data** /**day**-tuh, **dah**-tuh/ *n.pl.* (also treated as *sing.*, as in *that is the only data we have*, although the singular form is strictly *datum*) **1** known facts used for inference or in reckoning. **2** quantities or characters operated on by a computer etc. [Latin *data* from *do* give]

■ **Usage** (1) In scientific, philosophical, and general use, this word is usually considered to denote a number of items and is thus treated as plural with *datum* as the singular. (2) In computing and allied subjects (and sometimes in general use), it is treated as a mass (or collective) noun and used with words like *this, that,* and *much*, with singular verbs, e.g. *useful data has been collected*. Some people consider use (2) to be incorrect but

it is more common than use (1). However, *data* is not a singular countable noun and cannot be preceded by *a, every, each, either,* or *neither,* or be given a plural form *datas*.

**data bank** *n. Computing* **1** store or source of data usu. on a particular topic as available to a wide user community. **2** = DATABASE.

**database** *n.* structured set of data held in a computer, esp. one that is accessible in various ways.

**datable** /**day**-tuh-buhl/ *adj.* (often foll. by *to*) capable of being dated.

**data bus** *n.* signal route used to transmit data in parallel from one part of a computer to another.

**data processing** *n.* series of operations on large quantities of data, esp. by a computer. □ **data processor** *n.*

**date**¹ /dayt/ — *n.* **1** day of the month, esp. as a number. **2** particular day or year, esp. when a given event occurred. **3** day, month, and year of writing etc., at the head of a document etc. **4** period to which a work of art etc. belongs. **5** time when an event happens or is to happen. **6** *colloq.* **a** appointment, esp. social with a person of the opposite sex. **b** person to be met at this. — *v.* (**-ting**) **1** mark with a date. **2 a** assign a date to (an object, event, etc.) (*has this antique clock been dated?*). **b** (foll. by *to*) assign to a particular time, period, etc. (*dated the clock to the eighteenth century*). **3** (often foll. by *from, back to,* etc.) have its origins at a particular time (*dates back to medieval times*). **4** appear or expose as old-fashioned (*design that does not date, that hat dates you*). **5** *colloq.* **a** make a date with. **b** go out together as sexual partners. □ **out of date** (*attrib.* (**out-of-date**) old-fashioned, obsolete. **to date** until now. **up to date** (*attrib.* (**up-to-date**) modern; fashionable; current. [French: related to DATA]

**date**² *n.* **1** dark oval single-stoned fruit. **2** (in full **date-palm**) tree bearing it. [Greek: related to DACTYL, from the shape of the leaf]

**date-line** *n.* **1** north-south line partly along the meridian 180° from Greenwich (in England), to the east of which the date is a day earlier than to the west. **2** date and place of writing at the head of a newspaper article etc.

**date rape** *n.* rape committed on a person who has accepted a social invitation for a date.

**dative** /**day**-tiv/ *Gram.* — *n.* case expressing the indirect object or recipient. — *adj.* of or in this case. [Latin: related to DATA]

**datum** /**day**-tuhm, **dah**-tuhm/ see DATA.

**daub** /dawb/ — *v.* **1** spread (paint, plaster, or some other thick substance) crudely or roughly on a surface (*daubed paint on the fence*). **2** coat or smear (a surface) with paint etc. (*daubed her face with bottled mud*). **3** paint crudely or unskilfully. — *n.* **1** paint etc. daubed on a surface. **2** plaster, clay, etc., esp. coating laths or wattles to form a wall. **3** a crude painting. [Latin: related to DE-, ALB]

**daughter** /**daw**-tuh/ *n.* **1** girl or woman in relation to her parent(s). **2** female descendant. **3** (foll. by *of*) female member of a family etc. **4** (foll. by *of*) female descendant or inheritor of a quality etc. (*true daughter of the revolution*). □ **daughterly** *adj.* [Old English]

**daughter-in-law** *n.* (*pl.* **daughters-in-law**) wife of one's son.

**daunt** /dawnt/ *v.* discourage, intimidate. □ **daunting** *adj.* [Latin *domito* from *domo* tame]

**dauntless** *adj.* intrepid, persevering.

**dauphin** /**daw**-fuhn, doh-**fan**/ *n. hist.* eldest son of the King of France. [French from Latin *delphinus* DOLPHIN, as a family name]

**Davidson plum** *n.* small rainforest tree of Queensland and NSW (*Davidsonia pruriens*) having bluish-purple edible fruit.

**daviesia** /day-vee-zee-uh/ *n.* (also **bacon-and-eggs** for the species bearing yellow-and-brown flowers) any of 70 or more Australian shrubs of the genus of the same name, bearing bright red or, more usu., yellow-and-brown pea-flowers in masses.

**davit** /**dav**-uht/ *n.* small crane on board ship, esp. for moving or holding a lifeboat. [French diminutive of *David*]

**Davy** /**day**-vee/ *n.* (*pl.* **-ies**) (in full **Davy lamp**) miner's safety lamp. [name of its inventor]

**Davy Jones** /,day-vee **johnz**/ *n. colloq.* (in full **Davy Jones's locker**) bottom of the sea, esp. as the sailors' graveyard. [origin unknown]

**dawdle** /**daw**-duhl/ *v.* (**-ling**) **1** walk slowly and idly. **2** waste (time); procrastinate. [origin unknown]

**dawn** — *n.* **1** daybreak. **2** beginning or birth of something. — *v.* **1** (of a day) begin; grow light. **2** (often foll. by *on*, *upon*) begin to become obvious (to) (*it finally dawned on him that ...*). [Old English]

**dawn parade** *n.* (also **dawn service**) memorial service at dawn on Anzac Day.

**day** *n.* **1** time between sunrise and sunset. **2 a** 24 hours as a unit of time, corresponding to a complete revolution of the earth on its axis. **b** corresponding period on other planets (*Martian day*). **3** daylight (*clear as day*). **4** time during which work is normally done (*eight-hour day*). **5 a** (also *pl.*) historical period (*in those days*). **b** (prec. by *the*) present time (*issues of the day*). **6** prime of a person's life (*have had my day; in my day*). **7** a future time (*will do it one day*). **8** date of a specific festival or event etc. (*graduation day; Christmas day*). **9** day's endeavour, or the period of an endeavour, esp. as bringing success (*win the day*). □ **all in a day's work** part of the normal routine. **at the end of the day** when all is said and done. **call it a day** end a period of activity. **day after day** without respite. **day and night** all the time. **day by day** gradually. **day in, day out** routinely, constantly. **not one's day** day when things go badly (for a person). **one of these days** soon. **one of those days** day when things go badly. **that will be the day** *colloq.* that will never happen. [Old English]

**daybreak** *n.* first light in the morning.

**day care** *n.* care of young children, the elderly, the handicapped, etc. during the working day.

**daydream** — *n.* pleasant fantasy or reverie. — *v.* indulge in this. □ **daydreamer** *n.*

**daylight** *n.* **1** light of day. **2** dawn. **3** visible gap, e.g. between boats in a race. **4** (usu. in *pl.*) *colloq.* life or consciousness, esp. as representing vulnerability to fear, attack, etc. (*scared the daylights out of me; beat the living daylights out of them*). □ **see daylight** begin to understand what was previously obscure.

**daylight robbery** *n. colloq.* blatantly excessive price or charge.

**daylight saving** *n.* longer summer evening daylight, achieved by putting clocks forward.

**daytime** *n.* part of the day when there is natural light.

**day-to-day** *adj.* mundane, routine.

**day-trip** *n.* trip completed in one day. □ **day-tripper** *n.*

**daze** — *v.* (**-zing**) stupefy, bewilder. — *n.* state of bewilderment. [Old Norse]

**dazzle** /**daz**-uhl/ — *v.* (**-ling**) **1** blind or confuse temporarily with a sudden bright light. **2** impress or overpower with knowledge, ability, etc. — *n.* bright confusing light. □ **dazzling** *adj.* **dazzlingly** *adv.* [from DAZE]

**dazzler** /**daz**-luh/ *n. colloq.* anything exceptionally good, brilliant, etc.

**dB** *abbr.* decibel(s).

**DC** *abbr.* **1** (also **dc**) direct current. **2** da capo.

**D-Day** /dee-day/ *n.* **1** day (6 June 1944) on which Allied forces invaded N. France. **2** important or decisive day. [*D* for *day*]

**DDT** *abbr.* colourless chlorinated hydrocarbon used as insecticide. [from the chemical name]

**de-** *prefix* **1** forming verbs and their derivatives: **a** down, away (*descend*; *deduct*). **b** completely (*denude*). **2** added to verbs and their derivatives to form verbs and nouns implying removal or reversal (*de-ice*; *decentralisation*). [Latin]

**deacon** /dee-kuhn/ *n.* **1** *RC Ch.* **a** man ordained to the diaconate as the final step before ordination to the priesthood. **b** (in full **permanent deacon**) man ordained to the diaconate as a vocation in itself. **c** major assistant to the celebrant at High Mass. **d** (**Cardinal Deacon**) cardinal acting as major assistant to the Pope when he celebrates High Mass. **2** (in the Anglican Church) man or woman ranking below a priest and awaiting ordination to the priesthood. **3** (in Nonconformist churches) lay officer. **4** (in the early Church) an appointed minister of charity. □ **deaconess** /ˌdee-kuh-**nes**, **dee**-kuh-nuhs/ woman deacon (in sense 3). [Greek *diakonos* servant]

**deactivate** /dee-**ak**-tuh-ˌvayt/ *v.* (**-ting**) make inactive or less reactive.

**dead** /ded/ — *adj.* **1** no longer alive. **2** *colloq.* extremely tired or unwell. **3** numb (*fingers are dead*). **4** (foll. by *to*) unappreciative or unconscious of; insensitive to (*dead to any sense of shame*). **5** no longer effective or in use; extinct (*dead languages*). **6** (of a match, coal, etc.) extinguished. **7** inanimate (*dead matter*). **8 a** lacking force or vigour (*dead colour*; *a dead description*). **b** (esp. of turf) lacking resiliency or springiness (*dead pitch*; *dead track*). **c** (of sound) not resonant. **9** quiet; lacking activity (*dead season*). **10 a** (of a microphone, telephone, etc.) not transmitting sounds. **b** (of a circuit, conductor, etc.) carrying or transmitting no current; not connected to a source of electricity (*dead battery*). **11** (of a ball in a game) out of play. **12** abrupt, complete, exact, unqualified, unrelieved (*come to a dead stop*; *a dead faint*; *a dead calm*; *in dead silence*; *a dead certainty*). — *adv.* **1** absolutely, exactly, completely (*dead on target*; *dead level*; *dead tired*). **2** *colloq.* very, extremely (*dead easy*). — *n.* **1** (prec. by *the*) (treated as *pl.*) those who have died. **2** time of silence or inactivity (*dead of night*). □ **as dead as the** (or **a**)

**dodo 1** completely and unmistakably dead. **2** entirely obsolete. **dead as a doornail** completely or unmistakably dead. **dead cert** see CERT. **dead from the neck up** *colloq.* stupid. **dead ringer** see RINGER¹. **dead to the world** *colloq.* fast asleep; unconscious. **leave a person** (or **thing**) **for dead** completely outclass. **wouldn't be seen dead in** *colloq.* shall refuse to wear, be seen in, etc. **wouldn't be seen dead with** *colloq.* shall have nothing to do with. □ **deadness** *n.* [Old English]

**dead beat** *adj. colloq.* exhausted.

**deadbeat** *n. colloq.* derelict, tramp.

**dead bird** *n. Horse-racing colloq.* a certainty.

**dead centre 1** exact centre. **2** position of a crank etc. in line with the connecting-rod and not exerting torque. **3** (also **Dead Centre**) = DEAD HEART.

**dead duck** *n. colloq.* unsuccessful or useless person or thing.

**deaden** *v.* **1** deprive of or lose vitality, force, brightness, sound, feeling, etc. **2** (foll. by *to*) make insensitive.

**dead end** *n.* **1** closed end of a road, passage, etc. **2** (often, with hyphen, *attrib.*) situation, job, etc. offering no prospects of progress or advancement.

**dead finish** *n.* **1** small wattle of drier Australia which can form tangled prickly thickets. **2** *colloq.* limit; end (*any higher waves and it would have been the dead finish of them*).

**dead-head** — *n.* faded flower-head. — *v.* remove deadheads from (a plant).

**dead heart** *n.* (also **Dead Heart**, **dead centre**) the arid interior of Australia (see also RED CENTRE, RED HEART).

**dead heat** *n.* **1** race in which competitors tie. **2** result of such a race.

**dead language** *n.* language no longer spoken, e.g. Latin.

**dead letter** *n.* **1** law or practice no longer observed or recognised. **2** letter which lies unclaimed at a post-office or which cannot be delivered because of a faulty or inadequate address etc.

**deadline** *n.* time-limit for the completion of an activity etc.

**deadlock** — *n.* **1** state of unresolved conflict. **2** lock requiring a key to open or close it. — *v.* bring or come to a standstill.

**dead loss** *n. colloq.* **1** total failure. **2** totally worthless or useless person or thing.

**deadly** — *adj.* (**-ier**, **-iest**) **1 a** causing or able to cause fatal injury or serious damage. **b** poisonous (*deadly snake*). **2** intense, extreme (*deadly dullness*). **3** (of aim etc.) extremely accurate or effective.

**4** *colloq.* dreary, dull (*the party was really deadly*). **5** implacable (*a deadly enemy*). **6** (in Aboriginal English) fantastic, terrific (*a deadly shirt*). — *adv.* **1** like death; as if dead (*deadly faint*). **2** extremely (*deadly serious*).

**deadly nightshade** *n.* poisonous plant with purple-black berries.

**deadly sin** *n.* **1** = MORTAL SIN. **2** one of the seven deadly sins regarded as leading to damnation, i.e. pride, covetousness, lust, gluttony, envy, anger, and sloth.

**dead man's handle** *n.* (also **dead man's pedal**) controlling device on an electric train, allowing power to be connected only as long as the operator presses on it.

**dead marines** *n.pl. colloq.* = DEAD MEN.

**dead men** *n.pl. colloq.* bottles after the contents (the 'spirits') have been drunk.

**dead men's graves** *n.pl. colloq.* mounds occurring in heavy clay soils, a form of GILGAI.

**dead on** *adj.* exactly right.

**deadpan** *adj. & adv.* lacking expression or emotion.

**dead reckoning** *n.* calculation of a ship's position from the log, compass, etc., when visibility is bad.

**dead set** — *n.* determined attack. — *adj.* (also **dead-set**) genuine; absolute (*he's the dead-set image of his father*). — *adv.* (also **dead-set**) truly; really (*am dead-set worried*). □ **be dead set against** strongly oppose. **be dead set on** be determined to do or get.

**dead weight** *n.* (also **dead-weight**) **1 a** inert mass. **b** heavy burden. **2** total weight carried on a ship.

**dead wood** *n. colloq.* useless person(s) or thing(s).

**deaf** /def/ *adj.* **1** wholly or partly unable to hear. **2** (foll. by *to*) refusing to listen or comply (*deaf to all entreaties*). □ **turn a deaf ear** (usu. foll. by *to*) be unresponsive. □ **deafness** *n.* [Old English]

**deafen** *v.* (often as **deafening** *adj.*) overpower with noise or make deaf by noise, esp. temporarily. □ **deafeningly** *adv.*

**deaf mute** *n.* deaf and dumb person.

**deal**[1] — *v.* (*past* and *past part.* **dealt** /delt/) **1** (foll. by *with*) **a** take measures concerning (a problem, person, etc.), especially in order to put something right. **b** do business with; associate with. **c** discuss or treat (a subject). **2** (often foll. by *by, with*) behave in specified way (*dealt honourably by them*). **3** (foll. by *in*) sell or be concerned with commercially (*deals in insurance*). **4** (often foll. by *out, round*) distribute to several people etc. **5** (also *absol.*) distribute (cards) to players. **6**

administer (*was dealt a blow*). **7** assign, esp. providentially (*were dealt much happiness*). **8** (foll. by *in*) *colloq.* include (a person) in an activity (*you can deal me in*). — *n.* **1** (usu. **a good** or **great deal**) *colloq.* **a** large amount (*good deal of trouble*). **b** considerably (*great deal better*). **2** *colloq.* **a** business arrangement; transaction. **b** private or secret arrangement in commerce or politics entered into by parties for their mutual benefit. **3** specified treatment (*a rough deal; a fair deal*). **4 a** dealing of cards. **b** player's turn to do this. [Old English]

**deal**[2] *n.* **1** fir or pine timber, esp. as boards of a standard size. **2** board of this. [Low German]

**dealer** *n.* **1** trader in (esp. retail) goods (*car-dealer; dealer in antiques*). **2** player dealing at cards. **3** trafficker in drugs.

**dealings** *n.pl.* contacts, conduct, or transactions.

**dealt** *past* and *past part.* of DEAL[1].

**dean** *n.* **1 a** college or university official with disciplinary and advisory functions. **b** head of a university faculty or department or of a medical school. **2** head of a cathedral chapter etc. [Latin *decanus*]

**dear** — *adj.* **1** beloved or much esteemed (*a dear friend*). **2** as a formula of address, esp. beginning a letter (*Dear Sir*). **3** (often foll. by *to*) precious; cherished (*these books are very dear to me*). **4** (usu. in *superl.*) earnest, deeply felt (*my dearest wish*). **5 a** expensive. **b** having high prices. — *n.* (esp. as a form of address) dear person. — *adv.* at great cost (*will pay dear*). — *int.* expressing surprise, dismay, pity, etc. (*dear me!; oh dear!*). □ **for dear life** desperately. □ **dearly** *adv.* [Old English]

**Dear John** *n. colloq.* letter terminating a personal relationship (*received a Dear John this morning*).

**dearth** /derth/ *n.* scarcity or lack, esp. of food.

**death** /deth/ *n.* **1** irreversible ending of life; fact or process of dying or being killed. **2** instance of this. **3** destruction; ending (*death of our hopes*). **4** fact or state of being dead (*eyes closed in death*). **5** (usu. **Death**) personification of death, esp. as a skeleton. **6** lack of spiritual life. □ **at death's door** close to death. **be the death of 1** cause the death of. **2** be annoying or harmful to. **catch one's death** *colloq.* catch a serious chill etc. **do to death 1** kill. **2** overdo. **fate worse than death** *colloq.* very unpleasant experience. **like death warmed up** *colloq.* very tired or ill. **like grim death** see GRIM. **put to death** kill or cause to be killed. **to death** to the utmost, extremely (*bored to death*). □ **deathlike** *adj.* [Old English]

**death adder** *n.* any of three species of venomous snake of Australia and Papua New Guinea.

**death blow** *n.* **1** blow etc. causing death. **2** event etc. that destroys or ends something.

**death certificate** *n.* official statement of a person's death.

**death duty** *n.* property tax levied after death.

**deathly** — *adj.* (**-ier, -iest**) suggestive of death (*deathly silence*). — *adv.* in a deathly way (*deathly pale*).

**death mask** *n.* cast taken of a dead person's face.

**death penalty** *n.* punishment by death.

**death rate** *n.* number of deaths per thousand of population per year.

**death rattle** *n.* gurgling in the throat sometimes heard at death.

**death row** *n.* *US* part of a prison for those sentenced to death.

**death seat** *n. colloq.* **1** (in a trotting race) position (on the outside of the leader) from which it is difficult to win a race (because of the extra distance covered etc.). **2** seat beside the driver of a motor vehicle.

**death trap** *n. colloq.* dangerous building, vehicle, etc.

**death warrant** *n.* **1** order of execution. **2** anything that causes the end of an established practice etc.

**death wish** *n. Psychol.* alleged usu. unconscious desire for death.

**deb** *n. colloq.* débutante. [abbreviation]

**debacle** /day-**bah**-kuhl, duh-/ *n.* (also **débâcle**) **1 a** utter defeat or failure. **b** sudden collapse or downfall. **2** confused rush or rout. [French]

**debar** /dee-**bah**, duh-/ *v.* (**-rr-**) (foll. by *from*) exclude; prohibit (*debarred from the club*). □ **debarment** *n.* [French: related to BAR[1]]

**debase** /dee-**bays**, duh-/ *v.* (**-sing**) **1** lower in quality, value, or character. **2** depreciate (a coin) by alloying etc. □ **debasement** *n.* [from DE-, (A)BASE]

**debatable** /duh-**bay**-tuh-buhl/ *adj.* questionable; disputable. [related to DEBATE]

**debate** /duh-**bayt**-/ — *v.* (**-ting**) **1** (also *absol.*) discuss or dispute, esp. formally. **2** consider aspects of (a question); ponder (*debated whether he should go*). — *n.* **1** formal discussion on a particular matter, esp. in a legislative assembly etc. **2** discussion (*open to debate*). [French: related to BATTLE]

**debauch** /duh-**bawch**/ — *v.* **1** (as **debauched** *adj.*) dissolute. **2** corrupt, deprave. **3** debase (taste or judgment). — *n.* bout of sensual indulgence. [French]

**debauchery** *n.* excessive sensual indulgence.

**debenture** /duh-**ben**-chuh/ *n.* acknowledgment of indebtedness, esp. a company bond providing for payment of interest at fixed intervals. [Latin *debentur* are owed]

**debil debil** *n.* **1** = DEVIL-DEVIL. **2** = GILGAI (esp. *attrib.*: *debil debil country*).

**debilitate** /duh-**bil**-uh-,tayt/ *v.* (**-ting**) enfeeble, enervate. □ **debilitation** /-**tay**-shuhn/ *n.* [Latin *debilis* weak]

**debility** /duh-**bil**-uh-tee/ *n.* feebleness, esp. of health.

**debit** /**deb**-uht/ — *n.* **1** entry in an account recording a sum owed. **2** sum recorded. **3** total of such sums. **4** debit side of an account. — *v.* (**-t-**) **1** (foll. by *against, to*) enter on the debit side of an account (*debit $50 to my account*). **2** (foll. by *with*) charge (a person) with a debt (*debited me with $500*). [Latin *debitum* DEBT]

**debonair** /,deb-uh-**nair**/ *adj.* **1** cheerful, self-assured. **2** pleasant-mannered. [French]

**debouch** /duh-**bowch, -boosh**/ *v.* **1** (of troops or a stream) come out into open ground. **2** (often foll. by *into*) (of a river, road, etc.) merge into a larger body or area. □ **debouchment** *n.* [French *bouche* mouth]

**debrief** /dee-**breef**/ *v. colloq.* question (a diplomat, pilot, etc.) about a completed mission or undertaking. □ **debriefing** *n.*

**debris** /**deb**-ree, **day**-bree/ *n.* **1** scattered fragments, esp. of wreckage. **2** accumulation of loose rock etc. [French *briser* break]

**debt** /det/ *n.* **1** money etc. owed (*debt of gratitude*). **2** state of owing (*in debt; get into debt*). □ **in a person's debt** under obligation to a person. [Latin *debeo debit- owe*]

**debt of honour** *n.* debt not legally recoverable, esp. a sum lost in gambling.

**debtor** *n.* person owing money etc.

**debug** /dee-**bug**/ *v.* (**-gg-**) *colloq.* **1** remove concealed microphones from (a room etc.). **2** remove defects from (a computer program etc.). **3** = DELOUSE.

**debunk** /dee-**bungk**/ *v. colloq.* expose (a person, claim, etc.) as spurious or false. □ **debunker** *n.*

**debut** /**day**-byoo, duh-**byoo**, duh-**boo**/ — *n.* (also **début**) **1 a** first public appearance of a performer etc. **b** first presentation of a show etc. **2** first appearance of a debutante in society. — *v.* make a debut. [French]

**debutante** /**deb**-yoo,tont, **day**-byoo-/ *n.* (also **débutante**) young woman making her social debut.

**deca-** *comb. form* ten. [Greek *deka* ten]

**decade** /**dek**-ayd, duh-**kayd**/ *n.* **1** a period of ten years. **2** a set, series, or group of ten. □ **decadal** /**dek**-uh-duhl/ *adj.* [Greek: related to DECA-]

■ **Usage** The second pronunciation given, with the stress on the second syllable, is considered incorrect by some people.

**decadence** /**dek**-uh-duhns/ *n.* **1** moral or cultural decline, esp. after a peak or culmination of achievement. **2** immoral behaviour. □ **decadent** *adj.* & *n.* **decadently** *adv.* [Latin: related to DECAY]

**decaffeinated** /dee-**kaf**-uh-,nay-tuhd, duh-/ *adj.* (usu. of coffee) with caffeine removed or reduced.

**decagon** /**dek**-uh-guhn, -gon/ *n.* plane figure with ten sides and angles. □ **decagonal** /duh-**kag**-uh-nuhl/ *adj.* [Greek: related to DECA-, *-gōnos* -angled]

**decahedron** /,dek-uh-**hee**-druhn/ *n.* solid figure with ten faces. □ **decahedral** *adj.* [after POLYHEDRON]

**decalitre** /**dek**-uh-,lee-tuh/ *n.* metric unit of capacity, equal to 10 litres.

**Decalogue** /**dek**-uh-,log/ *n.* Ten Commandments. [Greek: related to DECA-, *logos* word, reason]

**decametre** /**dek**-uh-,mee-tuh/ *n.* metric unit of length, equal to 10 metres.

**decamp** /dee-**kamp**/ *v.* **1** depart suddenly; abscond. **2** break up or leave camp. □ **decampment** *n.* [French: related to CAMP[1]]

**decant** /duh-**kant**/ *v.* gradually pour off (liquid, esp. wine or a solution), from one container to another, esp. leaving the sediment behind. [Greek *kanthos* lip of jug]

**decanter** *n.* stoppered glass container for decanted wine or spirit.

**decapitate** /dee-**kap**-uh-,tayt, duh-/ *v.* (**-ting**) behead. □ **decapitation** /-**tay**-shuhn/ *n.* [Latin: related to CAPITAL]

**decapod** /**dek**-uh-,pod/ *n.* **1** crustacean with ten limbs for walking, e.g. crabs, prawns, and crayfish. **2** ten-tentacled mollusc, e.g. the squid. [Greek: related to DECA-, *pous pod-* foot]

**decarbonise** /dee-**kah**-buh-,nuyz/ *v.* (also **-ize**) (**-sing** or **-zing**) remove the carbon etc. from (an internal-combustion engine etc.). □ **decarbonisation** /-**zay**-shuhn/ *n.*

**decasyllable** /**dek**-uh-,sil-uh-buhl/ *n.* metrical line of ten syllables. □ **deca-syllabic** /-suh-**lab**-ik/ *adj.* & *n.*

**decathlon** /duh-**kath**-lon/ *n.* athletic contest of ten events for all competitors. □ **decathlete** /-leet/ *n.* [from DECA-, Greek *athlon* contest]

**decay** /duh-**kay**/ — *v.* **1** (cause to) rot or decompose. **2** decline or cause to decline in quality, power, energy, beauty, etc. **3** *Physics* **a** (of radioactivity) gradually diminish in intensity. **b** (of a substance) suffer a gradual decrease in radioactive power. **c** (of a radioactive substance etc.) change or disintegrate into one or more different substances. — *n.* **1** rotten or ruinous state; process of wasting away. **2** decline in health, quality, etc. **3** *Physics* **a** gradual decrease in the radioactivity of a substance. **b** spontaneous transformation of a single atomic nucleus or elementary particle into one or more different nuclei or particles. **4** decayed tissue. [Latin *cado* fall]

**decease** /duh-**sees**/ *formal* esp. *Law* — *n.* death. — *v.* (**-sing**) die. [Latin *cedo* go]

**deceased** *formal* — *adj.* dead. — *n.* (usu. prec. by *the*) person who has died, esp. recently.

**deceit** /duh-**seet**/ *n.* **1** deception, esp. by concealing the truth. **2** dishonest trick. **3** willingness to deceive. [Latin *capio* take]

**deceitful** *adj.* **1** (of a person) using deceit, esp. habitually. **2** (of an act, practice, etc.) intended to deceive. □ **deceitfully** *adv.* **deceitfulness** *n.*

**deceive** /duh-**seev**/ *v.* (**-ving**) **1** make (a person) believe what is false; purposely mislead. **2** be unfaithful to, esp. sexually (*is deceiving his wife*). **3** use deceit. □ **deceive oneself** persist in a mistaken belief. □ **deceiver** *n.*

**decelerate** /dee-**sel**-uh-,rayt/ *v.* (**-ting**) (cause to) reduce speed. □ **deceleration** /-**ray**-shuhn/ *n.* [from DE-, ACCELERATE]

**December** /duh-**sem**-buh/ *n.* twelfth month of the year. [Latin *decem* ten, originally 10th month of Roman year]

**decency** /**dee**-suhn-see/ *n.* (*pl.* **-ies**) **1** correct and tasteful standards of behaviour as generally accepted. **2** conformity with current standards of behaviour or propriety. **3** avoidance of obscenity. **4** (in *pl.*) the requirements of correct behaviour. **5** generosity, fairness (*had the decency to admit that the mistake was his*). [Latin: related to DECENT]

**decennial** /duh-**sen**-ee-uhl/ *adj.* **1** lasting ten years. **2** recurring every ten years. [Latin *decem* ten, *annus* year]

**decent** /**dee**-suhnt/ *adj.* **1 a** conforming with current standards of behaviour and propriety. **b** avoiding obscenity. **2**

respectable (*he comes from a decent background*). **3** acceptable, good enough (*a decent job; a decent pass in English*). **4** kind, obliging, generous (*was decent enough to apologise*). □ **decently** *adv.* [Latin *decet* is fitting]

**decentralise** /dee-**sen**-truh-,luyz/ *v.* (also **-ize**) (**-sing** or **-zing**) **1** transfer (power etc.) from a central to a local authority or government. **2** reorganise to give greater local autonomy. **3** shift (industry, population, etc.) from major cities to smaller cities, country areas, etc. □ **decentralisation** /-**zay**-shuhn/ *n.*

**deception** /duh-**sep**-shuhn/ *n.* **1** act or instance of deceiving or process of being deceived. **2** thing that deceives; trick or sham. [Latin: related to DECEIT]

**deceptive** /duh-**sep**-tiv/ *adj.* likely to deceive; misleading. □ **deceptively** *adv.* **deceptiveness** *n.*

**deci-** *comb. form* one-tenth. [Latin *decimus* tenth]

**decibel** /**des**-uh-,bel/ *n.* unit used in the comparison of sound levels or power levels of electrical signals.

**decide** /duh-**suyd**/ *v.* (**-ding**) **1** (usu. foll. by *to, that,* or *on, about*) resolve after consideration (*decided to stay; decided quickly; weather decided me; decided on a blue hat*). **2** resolve or settle (an issue etc.) (*that decides the matter*). **3** (usu. foll. by *between, for, against, in favour of,* or *that*) give a judgment (*decided in favour of the plaintiff*). □ **decidable** *adj.* [Latin *caedo* cut]

**decided** *adj.* **1** (usu. *attrib.*) definite, unquestionable (*decided tilt*). **2** (of a person, esp. as a characteristic) having clear opinions, wilful, resolute.

**decidedly** *adv.* undoubtedly, undeniably.

**decider** *n.* **1** game, race, etc., as a tie-break. **2** person or thing that decides.

**deciduous** /duh-**sid**-yoo-uhs/ *adj.* **1** (of a tree) shedding leaves annually. **2** (of leaves, horns, teeth, etc.) shed periodically. [Latin *cado* fall]

**deciduous beech** see BEECH 2.

**decigram** /**des**-uh-,gram/ *n.* (also **decigramme**) metric unit of mass, equal to 0.1 gram.

**decile** /**des**-uyl/ *n. Statistics* any of the nine values of a random variable which divide a frequency distribution into ten groups, each containing one-tenth of the total population. [French *décile* from Latin *decem* ten]

**decilitre** /**des**-ee-,lee-tuh/ *n.* metric unit of capacity, equal to 0.1 litre.

**decimal** /**des**-uh-muhl/ — *adj.* **1** (of a system of numbers, weights, measures,

etc.) based on the number ten. **2** of tenths or ten; reckoning or proceeding by tens (*decimal currency*). — *n.* decimal fraction. [Latin *decem* ten]

**decimal fraction** *n.* fraction expressed in tenths, hundredths, etc., esp. by units to the right of the decimal point (e.g. 0.61).

**decimalise** *v.* (also **-ize**) (**-sing** or **-zing**) **1** express as a decimal. **2** convert to a decimal system (esp. of coinage). □ **decimalisation** *n.*

**decimal point** *n.* dot placed before the fraction in a decimal fraction.

**decimate** /**des**-uh-,mayt/ *v.* (**-ting**) **1** destroy a large proportion of. **2** orig. *Rom. Hist.* kill or remove one in every ten of. □ **decimation** /-**may**-shuhn/ *n.*

■ **Usage** Sense 1 is now the usual sense, but it is considered inappropriate by some people. This word should not be used to mean 'defeat utterly'.

**decimetre** /**des**-uh-,mee-tuh/ *n.* metric unit of length, equal to 0.1 metre.

**decipher** /duh-**suy**-fuh/ *v.* **1** convert (coded information) into intelligible language. **2** determine the meaning of (unclear handwriting etc.). □ **decipherable** *adj.*

**decision** /duh-**sizh**-uhn/ *n.* **1** act or process of deciding. **2** resolution made, esp. as to future action, after consideration (*made my decision*). **3** (often foll. by *of*) **a** settlement of a question (*must accept the umpire's decision*). **b** formal judgment (*the decision of the court*). **4** tendency to decide firmly; resoluteness (*acted with decision*). [Latin: related to DECIDE]

**decisive** /duh-**suy**-siv/ *adj.* **1** conclusive, settling an issue. **2** (of a person, esp. as a characteristic) able to decide quickly and effectively. □ **decisively** *adv.* **decisiveness** *n.* [medieval Latin: related to DECIDE]

**deck** — *n.* **1 a** platform in a ship serving as a floor. **b** the accommodation on a particular deck of a ship. **2 a** usu. wooden-floored outdoor living space attached to the side of a dwelling. **b** anything compared to a ship's deck, e.g. the floor of a pier or a bus etc. **3** section for playing discs or tapes etc. in a sound system. **4** pack of cards. **5** *colloq.* the ground (*hit the deck*). — *v.* **1** (often foll. by *out*) decorate; dress (*decked out in all her finery*). **2** provide with or cover as a deck. **3** *colloq.* floor (a person) by hitting (*decked him*). □ **below deck** (**s**) in or into the space below the main deck. **clear the decks** see CLEAR. **on deck** *colloq.* ready for action, work, etc. (*am back on deck*). [Dutch, = cover]

**deckchair** n. folding chair of wood etc. and canvas.

**-decker** comb. form having a specified number of decks or layers (double-decker).

**deckhand** n. cleaner on a ship's deck.

**deckie** n. colloq. deck-hand. [abbreviation]

**decking** n. 1 planking etc. forming the deck of a ship. 2 anything compared to this, e.g. the floor of a pergola.

**declaim** /duh-**klaym**/ v. 1 speak or say as if addressing an audience. 2 (foll. by against) protest forcefully. □ **declamation** /,dek-luh-**may**-shuhn/ n. **declamatory** /duh-**klam**-uh-tuh-ree, -tree/ adj. [Latin: related to CLAIM]

**declaration** /,dek-luh-**ray**-shuhn/ n. 1 act or process of declaring. 2 a formal, emphatic, or deliberate statement. b statement asserting or protecting a legal right. 3 Cricket act of declaring an innings closed. 4 (in full **declaration of the poll**) public official announcement of the votes cast for candidates in an election. [Latin: related to DECLARE]

**declare** /duh-**klair**/ v. (-**ring**) 1 announce openly or formally (declare war). 2 pronounce (declared it invalid). 3 (usu. foll. by that) assert emphatically. 4 acknowledge possession of (dutiable goods, income, etc.) to customs. 5 (as **declared** adj.) admitting to be such (a declared atheist). 6 (also absol.) Cricket close (an innings) voluntarily before the team is out. 7 (of things) make evident, prove (your actions declare your honesty). □ **declare oneself** reveal one's intentions or identity. □ **declarative** /-**kla**-ruh-tiv/ adj. **declaratory** /-**kla**-ruh-tuh-ree, -tree/ adj. **declarer** n. [Latin clarus clear]

**declassify** /dee-**klas**-uh-,fuy/ v. (-**ies**, -**ied**) declare (information etc.) to be no longer secret. □ **declassification** /-fuh-**kay**-shuhn/ n.

**declension** /duh-**klen**-shuhn/ n. 1 Gram. a variation of the form of a noun, pronoun, or adjective to show its grammatical case etc. b class of nouns with the same inflexions. 2 a deterioration (gradual declension of his mental faculties). b a declining or bending downwards. [Latin: related to DECLINE]

**declination** /,dek-luh-**nay**-shuhn/ n. 1 downward bend or turn. 2 angular distance of a star etc. north or south of the celestial equator. 3 deviation of a compass needle from true north. □ **declinational** adj. [Latin: related to DECLINE]

**decline** /duh-**kluyn**/ — v. (-**ning**) 1 deteriorate; lose strength or vigour;

decrease (he is declining fast; the price of gold has declined sharply). 2 (also absol.) politely refuse (an invitation, challenge, etc.) (I must decline; declined to be made use of). 3 slope or bend downwards, droop. 4 Gram. state the forms of (a noun, pronoun, or adjective). — n. 1 gradual loss of vigour or excellence (he's on the decline). 2 deterioration (decline in living standards). [Latin clino bend]

**declivity** /duh-**kliv**-uh-tee/ n. (pl. -**ies**) downward slope. [Latin clivus slope]

**declutch** /dee-**kluch**/ v. disengage the clutch of a motor vehicle.

**decoction** /duh-**kok**-shuhn/ n. 1 boiling down to extract an essence. 2 the resulting liquid. [Latin coquo boil]

**decode** /dee-**kohd**/ v. (-**ding**) convert a coded message, computer data, etc. into intelligible language. □ **decoder** n.

**décolleté** /day-**kol**-tay/ adj. (also **décolletée**) (of a dress, woman, etc.) having or wearing a low neckline. [French collet collar]

**decolonise** /dee-**kol**-uh-,nuyz/ v. (also -**ize**) (of a nation) withdraw from (a colony) leaving it independent. □ **decolonisation** /-**zay**-shuhn/ n.

**decommission** /,dee-kuh-**mish**-uhn/ v. 1 close down (a nuclear reactor etc.). 2 take (a ship) out of service.

**decompose** /,dee-kuhm-**pohz**/ v. (-**sing**) 1 rot. 2 separate (a substance, light, etc.) into its elements. □ **decomposition** /,dee-kom-puh-**zish**-uhn/ n.

**decompress** /,dee-kuhm-**pres**/ v. subject to decompression.

**decompression** /,dee-kuhm-**presh**-uhn/ n. 1 release from compression. 2 gradual reduction of air pressure on a person who has been subjected to high pressure, esp. deep under water.

**decompression chamber** n. enclosed space for decompression.

**decompression sickness** n. condition caused by the sudden lowering of air pressure and formation of bubbles in the blood.

**decongestant** /,dee-kuhn-**jes**-tuhnt/ n. medicine etc. that relieves nasal congestion.

**deconstruction** /,dee-kuhn-**struk**-shuhn/ n. 1 action of undoing the construction of a thing. 2 Philos. & Literary Theory strategy of critical analysis directed towards exposing unquestioned meta-physical assumptions and internal contradictions in philosophical and literary language. □ **deconstruct** v. **deconstructionism** n. **deconstructionist** adj. & n.

**decontaminate** /,dee-kuhn-**tam**-uh-

‚nayt/ v. (**-ting**) remove contamination from (an area, person, clothes, etc.). □ **decontamination** /-**nay**-shuhn/ n.

**decor** /**day**-kaw/ n. (also **décor**) furnishing and decoration of a room, stage set, etc. [French: related to DECORATE]

**decorate** /**dek**-uh-‚rayt/ v. (**-ting**) **1** beautify, adorn. **2** paint, wallpaper, etc. (a room or building). **3** give a medal or award to. [Latin *decus -oris* beauty]

**decoration** /‚dek-uh-**ray**-shuhn/ n. **1** process or art of decorating. **2** thing that decorates or serves as an ornament. **3** medal etc. worn as an honour. **4** (in *pl.*) flags, tinsel, etc., put up on a festive occasion.

**decorative** /**dek**-uh-ruh-tiv/ adj. **1** serving to decorate. **2** pleasing merely in appearance; superficial. □ **decoratively** adv.

**decorator** n. **1** person who paints or papers houses professionally. **2** person who offers professional advice on the décor for rooms etc.

**decorous** /**dek**-uh-ruhs/ adj. having or showing good taste or propriety. □ **decorously** adv. **decorousness** n. [Latin *decorus* seemly]

**decorum** /duh-**kaw**-ruhm/ n. **1** seemliness, propriety. **2** polite dignified behaviour. [as DECOROUS]

**découpage** /‚day-koo-**pahzh**/ n. decoration of surfaces with paper cut-outs. [French]

**decoy** — n. /**dee**-koi/ person or thing used to lure an animal or person into a trap or danger; bait, enticement. — v. /duh-**koi**/ lure, esp. using a decoy. [Dutch]

**decrease** — v. /duh-**krees**/ (**-sing**) make or become smaller or fewer. — n. /**dee**-krees/ **1** act or instance of decreasing. **2** amount of this. □ **decreasingly** adv. [Latin: related to DE-, *cresco* grow]

**decree** /duh-**kree**/ — n. **1** official legal order. **2** legal judgment or decision. — v. (**-ees**, **-eed**, **-eeing**) ordain by decree. [Latin *decretum* from *cerno* sift]

**decree absolute** n. final order for completion of a divorce.

**decree nisi** /**nuy**-suy/ n. provisional order for divorce, made absolute usu. after a period of one month. [Latin *nisi* unless]

**decrepit** /duh-**krep**-uht/ adj. **1** weakened by age or infirmity. **2** worn out by long use; dilapidated. □ **decrepitude** n. [Latin *crepo* creak]

**decrescendo** /‚dee-kre-**shen**-doh/ adv., adj., & n. (*pl.* **-s**) = DIMINUENDO. [Italian: related to DECREASE]

**decretal** /duh-**kree**-tuhl/ n. **1** papal decree. **2** (in *pl.*) collection of these, forming part of canon law. [Latin: related to DECREE]

**decriminalise** /dee-**krim**-uh-nuh-‚luyz/ v. (also **-ize**) (**-sing** or **-zing**) cease to treat as criminal (*should the use of marijuana be decriminalised?*). □ **decriminalisation** /-**zay**-shuhn/ n.

**decry** /duh-**kruy**/ v. (**-ies**, **-ied**) disparage, belittle.

**dedicate** /**ded**-uh-‚kayt/ v. (**-ting**) (often foll. by *to*) **1** devote (esp. oneself) to a special task or purpose. **2** address (a book etc.) to a friend etc. (*dedicated the novel to his wife*). **3** devote (a building etc.) to a deity, saint, etc. (*dedicated the church to St. Francis Xavier*). **4** (as **dedicated** adj.) **a** (of a person) single-mindedly loyal to an aim, vocation, etc. **b** (of equipment, esp. a computer) designed for or assigned to a specific task. □ **dedicator** n. **dedicatory** adj. [Latin *dico* declare]

**dedication** /‚ded-uh-**kay**-shuhn/ n. **1** act or instance of dedicating or the process of being dedicated. **2** words with which a book etc. is dedicated. [Latin: related to DEDICATE]

**deduce** /duh-**dyoos**/ v. (**-cing**) (often foll. by *from*) infer logically. □ **deducible** adj. [Latin *duco duct-* lead]

**deduct** /duh-**dukt**/ v. (often foll. by *from*) subtract, take away, or withhold (an amount, portion, etc.). [related to DEDUCE]

**deductible** adj. that may be deducted, esp. from tax or taxable income.

**deduction** /duh-**duk**-shuhn/ n. **1 a** act of deducting. **b** amount deducted. **2 a** inferring of particular instances from a general law or principle. **b** conclusion deduced. [Latin: related to DEDUCE]

**deductive** adj. of deduction or of reasoning by deduction. □ **deductively** adv. [medieval Latin: related to DEDUCE]

**deed** n. **1** thing done intentionally or consciously. **2** brave, skilful, or conspicuous act. **3** action (*kind in word and deed*). **4** legal document used esp. for transferring ownership of property. [Old English: related to DO¹]

**deed poll** n. deed made by one party only, esp. to change one's name.

**deem** v. **1** calculate income to determine eligibility for social security benefits by assuming a prescribed rate of return on assets. **2** *formal* consider, judge (*deem it my duty*). □ **deeming** n. [Old English]

**deener** /**dee**-nuh/ n. *colloq.* **1** *hist.* Australian shilling coin. **2** small sum of money. [British slang *deaner*, probably ultimately from DENARIUS]

**deep** — *adj.* **1** extending far down or in (*deep water*; *deep wound*; *deep shelf*). **2** (*predic.*) **a** to or at a specified depth (*water 6 metres deep*). **b** in a specified number of ranks (*soldiers drawn up six deep*). **3 a** situated far down or back or in (*hands deep in his pockets*). **b** coming or brought from far down or in (*deep breath*). **4** low-pitched, full-toned (*deep voice*). **5** intense, vivid, extreme (*deep sleep*; *deep colour*; *deep interest*). **6** (*predic.*) fully absorbed or overwhelmed (*deep in a book*; *deep in debt*). **7** profound; difficult to understand (*a deep thinker*; *too deep for me*). **8** *colloq.* cunning or secretive (*he's a deep one*). — *n.* **1** (prec. by *the*) *poet.* sea, esp. when deep. **2** abyss, pit, cavity. **3** (prec. by *the*) *Cricket* position of a fielder distant from the batsman. **4** deep state (*deep of the night*). — *adv.* deeply; far down or in (*dig deep*). □ **go off the deep end** *colloq.* give way to anger or emotion. **in deep water** in trouble or difficulty. □ **deeply** *adv.* [Old English]

**deepen** *v.* make or become deep or deeper.

**deep-freeze** — *n.* cabinet for freezing and keeping food for long periods. — *v.* freeze or store in a deep-freeze. □ **give a person the deep-freeze** *colloq.* act coldly towards.

**deep-fry** *v.* immerse in boiling fat to cook.

**Deep North** *n.* Queensland. [by analogy with US *Deep South* the conservative southern States]

**deep-rooted** *adj.* (also **deep-seated**) (esp. of convictions) firmly established, profound.

**deer** *n.* (*pl.* same) four-hoofed grazing animal, the male of which usu. has antlers. [Old English]

**deerskin** *n.* (often *attrib.*) leather from a deer's skin.

**deerstalker** *n.* soft cloth peaked cap with ear-flaps.

**de-escalate** /dee-es-kuh-ˌlayt/ *v.* make or become less intense. □ **de-escalation** /-ˈlay-shuhn/ *n.*

**deface** /dee-ˈfays, duh-/ *v.* (**-cing**) spoil the appearance of; disfigure. □ **deface-ment** *n.* [French: related to FACE]

**de facto** /dee ˈfak-toh, day/ — *adv.* in fact (whether by right or not). — *adj.* that exists or is such in fact (*a de facto ruler*). — *n.* (in full **de facto wife** or **husband**) person living with another as if married (*he's my de facto*). [Latin]

**defalcate** /dee-ˈfal-ˌkayt/ *v.* (**-ting**) *formal* misappropriate, esp. money. □ **defalcator** *n.* [Latin *defalcare* lop, from *falx* sickle]

**defalcation** /ˌdee-fal-ˈkay-shuhn/ *n. formal*

**1 a** misappropriation of money. **b** amount misappropriated. **2** shortcoming.

**defame** /dee-ˈfaym/ *v.* (**-ming**) attack the good reputation of; libel; slander; speak ill of. □ **defamation** /ˌdef-uh-ˈmay-shuhn/ *n.* **defamatory** /duh-ˈfam-uh-tuh-ree, -tree/ *adj.* [Latin *fama* report]

**default** /duh-ˈfolt, -ˈfawlt/ — *n.* **1** failure to appear (e.g. in court on the day assigned), pay (a debt), or act as one should. **2** preselected option adopted by a computer program when no alternative is specified. — *v.* **1** fail to fulfil an obligation, esp. to pay money or appear in a lawcourt. **2 a** fail to take part as scheduled in a sporting match etc. **b** lose a match in this way. □ **by default** because of lack of an alternative or opposition. **in default of** because of the absence of. **win by default** win because an opponent fails to be present. □ **defaulter** *n.* [French: related to FAIL]

**defeat** /duh-ˈfeet/ — *v.* **1** overcome in battle, a contest, etc. **2** frustrate, baffle (*this crossword puzzle defeats me*). **3** reject (a motion etc.) by voting. — *n.* act or process of defeating or being defeated. [Latin: related to DIS-, FACT]

**defeatism** *n.* excessive readiness to accept defeat. □ **defeatist** *n.* & *adj.*

**defecate** /ˈdef-uh-ˌkayt/ *v.* (**-ting**) evacuate the bowels. □ **defecation** /-ˈkay-shuhn/ *n.* [Latin *faex faecis* dregs]

**defect** — *n.* /ˈdee-fekt, duh-ˈfekt/ fault, imperfection, shortcoming. — *v.* /duh-ˈfekt/ abandon one's country or cause for another. □ **defection** *n.* **defector** *n.* [Latin *deficio -fect-* fail]

**defective** /duh-ˈfek-tiv/ *adj.* **1** having defect(s); imperfect. **2** mentally sub-normal. □ **defectiveness** *n.* [Latin: related to DEFECT]

**defence** /duh-ˈfens/ *n.* **1** act of defending from or resisting attack. **2 a** means of resisting attack. **b** thing that protects. **c** military reserves of a country. **3** (in *pl.*) fortifications. **4 a** justification, vindica-tion. **b** speech or piece of writing to this end. **5** defendant's case or counsel in a lawsuit. **6** defending play or players. □ **defenceless** *adj.* **defencelessly** *adv.* **defencelessness** *n.* [related to DEFEND]

**defence mechanism** *n.* **1** body's resistance to disease. **2** usu. unconscious mental process to avoid conscious conflict or anxiety.

**defend** /duh-ˈfend/ *v.* (also *absol.*) **1** (often foll. by *against*, *from*) resist an attack made on; protect. **2** uphold by argument. **3** conduct a defence in a lawsuit. **4** compete to retain (a title etc.)

in a contest. □ **defender** n. [Latin *defendo -fens-*]

**defendant** n. person etc. sued or accused in a lawcourt. [French: related to DEFEND]

**defensible** /duh-**fen**-suh-buhl/ adj. **1** justifiable; supportable by argument. **2** able to be defended militarily. □ **defensibility** /-**bil**-uh-tee/ n. **defensibly** adv. [Latin: related to DEFEND]

**defensive** adj. **1** done or intended for defence. **2** over-reacting to criticism. □ **on the defensive 1** expecting criticism. **2** *Mil* ready to defend. □ **defensively** adv. **defensiveness** n. [medieval Latin: related to DEFEND]

**defer¹** /duh-**fer**/ v. (**-rr-**) postpone. □ **deferment**. **deferral** n. [originally the same as DIFFER]

**defer²** /duh-**fer**/ v. (**-rr-**) (foll. by *to*) yield or make concessions to (*you must defer to him on this since he knows better*). [Latin *defero* carry away]

**deference** /**def**-uh-ruhns/ n. **1** courteous regard, respect. **2** compliance with another's wishes. □ **in deference to** out of respect for.

**deferential** /,def-uh-**ren**-shuhl/ adj. respectful. □ **deferentially** adv.

**defiance** /duh-**fuy**-uhns/ n. open disobedience; bold resistance. [French: related to DEFY]

**defiant** adj. showing defiance; disobedient. □ **defiantly** adv.

**deficiency** /duh-**fish**-uhn-see/ n. (pl. **-ies**) **1** state or condition of being deficient. **2** (usu. foll. by *of*) lack or shortage. **3** thing lacking. **4** deficit, esp. financial.

**deficient** adj. (often foll. by *in*) incomplete or insufficient in quantity, quality, etc. [Latin: related to DEFECT]

**deficit** /**def**-uh-suht/ n. **1** amount by which a thing (esp. money) is too small. **2** excess of liabilities over assets. [French from Latin *deficit*]

**defile¹** /duh-**fuyl**/ v. (**-ling**) **1** make dirty; pollute. **2** desecrate, profane. □ **defilement** n. [earlier *defoul*, from French *defouler* trample down]

**defile²** /duh-**fuyl**/ — n. narrow gorge or pass. — v. (**-ling**) march in file. [French: related to FILE¹]

**define** /duh-**fuyn**/ v. (**-ning**) **1** give the meaning of (a word etc.). **2** describe or explain the scope of (*define one's position*). **3** outline clearly (*well-defined image*). **4** mark out the boundary of. □ **definable** adj. [Latin *finis* end]

**definite** /**def**-uh-nuht/ adj. **1** certain, sure (*she's quite definite that she saw you*). **2** clearly defined; not vague; precise (*your instructions need to be more definite than that*). □ **definitely** adv. [Latin: related to DEFINE]

■ **Usage** See note at *definitive*.

**definite article** n. the word (*the* in English) preceding a noun and implying a specific instance.

**definition** /,def-uh-**nish**-uhn/ n. **1 a** act or process of defining. **b** statement of the meaning of a word or the nature of a thing. **2** distinctness in outline, esp. of a photographic image (*the picture lacks definition*). [Latin: related to DEFINE]

**definitive** /duh-**fin**-uh-tiv/ adj. **1** (of an answer, verdict, etc.) decisive, unconditional, final. **2** (of an edition of a book etc.) most authoritative. □ **definitively** adv.

■ **Usage** In sense 1, this word is often confused with *definite*, which does not imply authority and conclusiveness. A *definite no* is a firm refusal, while a *definitive no* is an authoritative judgment or decision that something is not the case.

**deflate** /duh-**flayt**/ v. (**-ting**) **1** empty (a tyre, balloon, etc.) of air, gas, etc.; be so emptied. **2** (cause to) lose confidence or conceit (*he was quite deflated by her wit*). **3 a** subject (a currency or economy) to deflation. **b** pursue this as a policy. [from DE-, INFLATE]

**deflation** /duh-**flay**-shuhn/ n. **1** act or process of deflating or being deflated. **2** reduction of money in circulation intended to combat inflation. **3** *Geol.* removal of particles of rock etc. by the wind. □ **deflationary** adj.

**deflect** /duh-**flekt**/ v. **1** bend or turn aside from a course or purpose. **2** (often foll. by *from*) (cause to) deviate (*nothing will deflect me from my search for the truth*). □ **deflection** n. (also **deflexion**) **deflector** n. [Latin *flecto* bend]

**deflower** /dee-**flowuh**/ v. *literary* **1** deprive of virginity. **2** ravage, spoil [Latin: related to FLOWER]

**defoliant** /duh-**foh**-lee-uhnt/ n. chemical used to destroy the leaves of trees or plants.

**defoliate** /dee-**foh**-lee-,ayt/ v. (**-ting**) destroy the leaves of (trees or plants), esp as a military tactic. □ **defoliation** /-ay shuhn/ n. [Latin *folium* leaf, related to FOIL²]

**deforest** /dee-**fo**-ruhst/ v. clear of forests or trees. □ **deforestation** /-**tay**-shuhn/ n.

**deform** /duh-**fawm**/ v. make ugly or misshapen, disfigure. □ **deformation** /,dee-faw-**may**-shuhn/ n. [Latin: related to FORM]

**deformed** *adj.* (of a person or limb) misshapen.

**deformity** *n.* (*pl.* **-ies**) **1** state of being deformed. **2** malformation, esp. of a body or limb.

**defraud** /duh-**frawd**/ *v.* (often foll. by *of*) cheat by fraud. [Latin: related to FRAUD]

**defray** /duh-**fray**/ *v.* provide money for (a cost or expense). □ **defrayal** *n.* **defrayment** *n.* [medieval Latin *fredum* fine]

**defrock** /dee-**frok**/ *v.* deprive (esp. a priest) of office. [French: related to DE-, FROCK]

**defrost** /dee-**frost**, duh-/ *v.* **1** remove frost or ice from (a refrigerator, windscreen, etc.). **2** unfreeze (frozen food). **3** become unfrozen.

**deft** *adj.* neat; dexterous; adroit. □ **deftly** *adv.* **deftness** *n.* [var. of DAFT = 'meek']

**defunct** /dee-**fungkt**/ *adj.* **1** no longer existing or used. **2** dead or extinct. □ **defunctness** *n.* [Latin *fungor* perform]

**defuse** /dee-**fyooz**/ *v.* (**-sing**) **1** remove the fuse from (a bomb etc.). **2** reduce tension etc. in (a crisis, difficulty, etc.).

**defy** /duh-**fuy**/ *v.* (**-ies**, **-ied**) **1** resist openly; refuse to obey. **2** (of a thing) present insuperable obstacles to (*defies solution*). **3** (foll. by *to* + infin.) challenge (a person) to do or prove something. [Latin *fides* faith]

**degauss** /dee-**gows**/ *v.* remove unwanted magnetism from (esp. a television set) by encircling with a conductor carrying electric current.

**degenerate** — *adj.* /duh-**jen**-uh-ruht/ **1** having lost its usual or good qualities; immoral, degraded. **2** *Biol.* having changed to a lower type. **3** *Physics* (of a system of particles or gas) having properties which depart markedly from those described by classical statistical mechanics. — *n.* /duh-**jen**-uh-ruht/ degenerate person or animal; person of debased moral constitution. — *v.* /dee-**jen**-uh-,rayt, duh-/ (**-ting**) become degenerate. □ **degeneracy** *n.* [Latin *genus* race]

**degeneration** /duh-,jen-uh-**ray**-shuhn/ *n.* **1 a** process of becoming degenerate. **b** state of being degenerate. **2** *Med.* morbid deterioration of body tissue or change in its structure. [Latin: related to DEGENERATE]

**degradable** /duh-**gray**-duh-buhl/ *adj.* (of waste products etc.) capable of being broken down by chemical or biological means.

**degrade** /duh-**grayd**/ *v.* (**-ding**) **1** bring into dishonour or contempt. **2** reduce to a lower rank, esp. as a punishment. **3** *Geol.* wear down (rocks etc.) by disin-

tegration. **4** (of soils) reduce to a lower quality (due to erosion, overuse, etc.). **5** *Chem.* reduce to a simpler molecular structure. □ **degradation** /,deg-ruh-**day**-shuhn/ *n.* **degrading** *adj.* [Latin: related to GRADE]

**degree** /duh-**gree**/ *n.* **1** stage in a scale, series, or process. **2** stage in intensity or amount (*in some degree*). **3** unit of measurement of an angle or arc. **4** unit in a scale of temperature, hardness, etc. **5** extent of burns (*third-degree burns*). **6** academic rank conferred by a university etc. **7** *US* grade of crime (*first-degree murder*). **8** step in direct genealogical descent. **9** social rank (*person of high degree*). □ **by degrees** gradually. **to a degree** *colloq.* considerably; to a certain extent (*I'm with you to a degree*). [Latin *gradus* step]

**degrees of comparison** see COMPARISON 4.

**dehisce** /dee-**his**, duh-/ *v.* (**-cing**) (esp. of a pod, cut, etc.) gape or burst open. □ **dehiscence** *n.* **dehiscent** *adj.* [Latin *hio* gape]

**dehumanise** /dee-**hyoo**-muh-,nuyz/ *v.* (also **-ize**) (**-sing** or **-zing**) **1** take human qualities away from. **2** make impersonal or machine-like. □ **dehumanisation** /-**zay**-shuhn/ *n.*

**dehydrate** /dee-**huy**-drayt, ,dee-huy-**drayt**/ *v.* (**-ting**) **1** remove water from (esp. foods). **2** make or become dry, esp. make (the body) deficient in water. □ **dehydration** /-**dray**-shuhn/ *n.* [Greek *hudōr* water]

**de-ice** /dee-**uys**/ *v.* **1** remove ice from. **2** prevent the formation of ice on.

**deictic** /**duyk**-tik/ *Philology & Gram.* — *adj.* pointing, demonstrative. — *n.* a deictic word. [Greek, from *deiktos* capable of proof]

**deify** /**dee**-uh-,fuy, **day**-/ *v.* (**-ies**, **-ied**) **1** make a god of. **2** regard or worship as a god (*deifies wealth*). □ **deification** /-fuh-**kay**-shuhn/ *n.* [Latin *deus* god]

**deign** /dayn/ *v.* (foll. by *to* + infin.) think fit, condescend (*deigned to notice our presence*). [Latin *dignus* worthy]

**deinstitutionalise** /dee-,in-stuh-**tyoo**-shuh-nuh-,luyz/ *v.* (also **-ize**) (**-sing** or **-zing**) (usu. as **deinstitutionalised** *adj.*) remove from an institution or help recover from the effects of institutional life. □ **deinstitutionalisation** /-**zay**-shuhn/ *n.*

**deism** /**dee**-iz-uhm, **day**-/ *n.* belief in the existence of a god arising from reason rather than revelation (cf. THEISM). □ **deist** *n.* **deistic** /-**is**-tik/ *adj.* [Latin *deus* god]

**deity** /**dee**-uh-tee, **day**-/ *n.* (*pl.* **-ies**) **1** god or goddess. **2** divine status or nature. **3**

(**the Deity**) God. [French from Church Latin]

**déjà vu** /ˌday-zhah **voo**/ —n. feeling of having already experienced the present situation. —adj. tediously familiar. [French, = already seen]

**deject** /duh-**jekt**/ v. (usu. as **dejected** adj.) make sad or dispirited; depress. □ **dejectedly** adv. **dejection** n. [Latin jacio throw]

**de jure** /dee **joor**-ree, day **yoor**-ray/ —adj. rightful (which one is the de jure pope and which one the antipope?). —adv. rightfully; by right. [Latin]

**dekko** /**dek**-oh/ n. (pl. **-s**) colloq. look, glance (take a dekko at this, will you?). [Hindi dekho, imperative of dekhnā look]

**delay** /duh-**lay**/ —v. **1** postpone; defer (delayed his decision). **2** make late (was delayed by flooding across the road). **3** loiter; be late (don't delay!). —n. **1** act or instance of delaying or the process of being delayed. **2** time lost by this. [French]

**delayed-action** attrib. adj. (esp. of a bomb, camera, etc.) operating after a set interval.

**delectable** /duh-**lek**-tuh-buhl/ adj. esp. literary delightful, delicious. □ **delectably** adv. [Latin: related to DELIGHT]

**delectation** /ˌdee-lek-**tay**-shuhn/ n. literary pleasure, enjoyment.

**delegate** —n. /**del**-uh-guht/ **1** elected representative sent to a conference. **2** member of a committee or delegation. —v. /**del**-uh-ˌgayt/ (**-ting**) **1** (often foll. by to) **a** commit (power etc.) to an agent or deputy. **b** entrust (a task) to another. **2** send or authorise (a person) as a representative. [Latin: related to LEGATE]

**delegation** /ˌdel-uh-**gay**-shuhn/ n. **1** group representing others. **2** act or process of delegating or being delegated.

**delete** /duh-**leet**/ v. (**-ting**) **1** remove (a letter, word, etc.), esp. by striking out. **2** Computing remove or overwrite a record or item of data. □ **deletion** n. [Latin deleo]

**deleterious** /ˌdel-uh-**teer**-ree-uhs/ adj. harmful (to the mind or body). [Latin from Greek]

**deli** /**del**-ee/ n. (pl. **-s**) colloq. delicatessen. [abbreviation]

**deliberate** —adj. /duh-**lib**-uh-ruht/ **1 a** intentional (a deliberate foul). **b** considered; careful (made a deliberate choice). **2** slow in deciding; cautious (a ponderous and deliberate mind). **3** (of movement) leisurely and unhurried. —v. /duh-**lib**-uh-ˌrayt/ (**-ting**) **1** think carefully; take counsel (the jury deliberated for an hour). **2** consider; discuss carefully (deliberated the question). □ **deliberately** /duh-**lib**-uh-ruht-lee/ adv.

**deliberateness** /duh-**lib**-uh-ruht-nuhs/ n.

**deliberator** /duh-**lib**-uh-ˌray-tuh/ n. [Latin libra balance]

**deliberation** /duh-lib-uh-**ray**-shuhn/ n. **1** careful consideration. **2 a** discussion of reasons for and against. **b** debate or discussion. **3 a** caution and care. **b** (of movement) careful slowness.

**deliberative** /duh-**lib**-uh-ruh-tiv/ adj. (esp. of an assembly etc.) of or for deliberation or debate.

**delicacy** /**del**-uh-kuh-see/ n. (pl. **-ies**) **1** being delicate (in all senses). **2** a choice or expensive food. [from DELICATE]

**delicate** /**del**-uh-kuht/ adj. **1 a** fine in texture, quality, etc. (delicate silk). **b** soft, slender, or slight (delicate ferns). **c** of exquisite quality or workmanship (delicate carving). **d** (of a colour, flavour, etc.) subtle, hard to discern (a delicate blue light; a delicate taste of saffron in the food). **2 a** so fine or tender as to be easily damaged; fragile (delicate figurine). **b** (of a person) easily injured; susceptible to illness (he has a delicate constitution). **3 a** requiring tact; tricky (delicate situation). **b** (of an instrument) highly sensitive. **4** deft (delicate touch). **5** (of a person) avoiding the immodest or offensive. □ **delicately** adv. [Latin]

**delicatessen** /ˌdel-uh-kuh-**tes**-uhn/ n. shop or part of a supermarket selling cooked meats, cheeses, etc. [French: related to DELICATE]

**delicious** /duh-**lish**-uhs/ adj. highly enjoyable, esp. to taste or smell. □ **deliciously** adv. [Latin deliciae delights]

**delight** /duh-**luyt**/ —v. **1** (often as **delighted** adj.) please greatly (her singing delighted us; delighted to help). **2** (foll. by in) take great pleasure in (delights in surprising everyone). —n. **1** great pleasure. **2** thing that delights. □ **delighted** adj. **delightful** adj. **delightfully** adv. [Latin delecto]

**delimit** /dee-**lim**-uht/ v. (**-t-**) fix the limits or boundary of. □ **delimitation** /-**tay**-shuhn/ n. [Latin: related to LIMIT]

**delineate** /duh-**lin**-ee-ˌayt/ v. (**-ting**) portray by drawing etc. or in words. □ **delineation** /-**ay**-shuhn/ n. [Latin: related to LINE¹]

**delinquent** /duh-**ling**-kwuhnt/ —n. offender (juvenile delinquent). —adj. **1** guilty of a minor crime or misdeed. **2** failing in one's duty. □ **delinquency** n. [Latin delinquo offend]

**deliquesce** /ˌdel-i-**kwes**/ v. (**-cing**) **1** become liquid, melt. **2** Chem. dissolve in water absorbed from the air. □ **deliquescence** n. **deliquescent** adj. [Latin: related to LIQUID]

**delirious** /duh-**li**-ree-uhs, duh-**leer**-/ *adj.* **1** affected with delirium. **2** wildly excited, ecstatic. □ **deliriously** *adv.*

**delirium** /duh-**leer**-ree-uhm/ *n.* **1** disorder involving incoherent speech, hallucinations, etc., caused by intoxication, fever, etc. **2** great excitement, ecstasy. [Latin *lira* ridge between furrows]

**delirium tremens** /**trem**-enz, -uhnz/ *n.* psychosis of chronic alcoholism involving tremors and hallucinations.

**deliver** /duh-**liv**-uh/ *v.* **1 a** distribute (letters, goods, etc.) to their destination(s). **b** (often foll. by *to*) hand over. **2** (often foll. by *from*) save, rescue, or set free. **3 a** give birth to (*delivered a girl*). **b** assist at the birth of or in giving birth (*delivered six babies*). **4 a** utter (an opinion, speech, etc.). **b** (of a judge or jury) pronounce (a judgment). **5** (often foll. by *up, over*) abandon; resign (*delivered his soul up*). **6** launch or aim (a blow, a ball, an attack, etc.). **7** *colloq.* = *deliver the goods* (*will he ever deliver?*). □ **be delivered of** give birth to. **deliver the goods** *colloq.* carry out an undertaking. [Latin *liber* free]

**deliverance** *n.* act or instance of rescuing or process of being rescued.

**delivery** — *n.* (*pl.* **-ies**) **1** act or instance of delivering or process of being delivered. **2** regular distribution of letters etc. (*two deliveries a day*). **3** thing delivered. **4** childbirth. **5** deliverance. **6** act or style of throwing a ball. **7** act or style of delivering a speech, etc. **8** act of giving or surrendering (*delivery of the town to the enemy*). — *attrib. adj.* of or relating to a person or thing that makes a delivery (*delivery man; delivery van*). [Anglo-French: related to DELIVER]

**dell** *n.* small usu. wooded valley. [Old English]

**delouse** /dee-**lows**/ *v.* (**-sing**) rid (a person or animal) of lice.

**Delphic** /**del**-fik/ *adj.* (also **Delphian** /-fee-uhn/) **1** obscure, ambiguous, or enigmatic. **2** of the ancient Greek oracle at Delphi.

**delta** /**del**-tuh/ *n.* **1** triangular area of earth, alluvium etc. at the mouth of a river, formed by its diverging outlets. **2 a** fourth letter of the Greek alphabet (Δ, δ). **b** fourth-class mark for work etc. [Greek]

**delta rays** *n.pl. Physics* rays of low penetrative power consisting of slow electrons ejected from an atom by the impact of ionising radiation.

**deltoid** /**del**-toid/ — *adj.* triangular; like a river delta. — *n.* (in full **deltoid muscle**) thick triangular muscle covering the

shoulder joint and used for raising the arm away from the body. [Greek, = delta-shaped]

**delude** /duh-**lood**/ *v.* (**-ding**) deceive, mislead. [Latin *ludo* mock]

**deluge** /**del**-yooj/ — *n.* **1** great flood. **2** (**the Deluge**) biblical Flood (Gen. 6–8). **3** overwhelming rush (*a deluge of enquiries*). **4** heavy fall of rain. — *v.* (**-ging**) flood or inundate (*deluged with complaints*). [Latin *diluvium*]

**delusion** /duh-**loo**-*zh*uhn/ *n.* **1** false belief or impression. **2** *Psychol.* this as a symptom or form of mental disorder. □ **delusive** *adj.* **delusory** *adj.* [related to DELUDE]

**de luxe** /duh **luks**/ *adj.* luxurious; superior; sumptuous. [French, = of luxury]

**delve** *v.* (**-ving**) **1** (often foll. by *in, into*) search or research energetically or deeply (*delved into his pocket; delved into his family history*). **2** *poet.* dig. [Old English]

**demagogue** /**dem**-uh-,gog/ *n.* political agitator appealing to mob instincts. □ **demagogic** /-**gog**-ik/ *adj.* **demagogy** *n.* [Greek, = leader of the people]

**demand** /duh-**mahnd**, -**mand**/ — *n.* **1** insistent and peremptory request, made as a right. **2** desire for a commodity (*no demand for fur coats*). **3** urgent claim (*makes demands on her*). — *v.* **1** (often foll. by *of, from*, or *to* + infin., or *that* + clause) ask for insistently and urgently (*demanded to know*). **2** require (*task demanding skill*). **3** insist on being told (*demanded her age*). **4** (as **demanding** *adj.*) requiring skill, effort, attention, etc. (*demanding job; demanding child*). □ **in demand** sought after. **on demand** as soon as requested (*payable on demand*). [French from Latin: related to MANDATE]

**demarcation** /,dee-mah-**kay**-shuhn/ *n.* **1** act of marking a boundary or limits. **2** trade-union practice of restricting a specific job to one union. □ **demarcate** /**dee**-/ *v.* (**-ting**). [Spanish *marcar* MARK]

**dematerialise** /,dee-muh-**teer**-ree-uh-,luyz/ *v.* (also **-ize**) (**-sing** or **-zing**) make or become non-material; vanish. □ **dematerialisation** /-z**ay**-shuhn/ *n.*

**demean** /duh-**meen**/ *v.* (usu. *refl.*) lower the dignity of (*would not demean myself*). [from MEAN²]

**demeanour** /duh-**mee**-nuh/ *n.* (also **demeanor**) outward behaviour or bearing. [Latin *minor* threaten]

**demented** /duh-**men**-tuhd/ *adj.* mad. □ **dementedly** *adv.* [Latin *mens* mind]

**dementia** /duh-**men**-shuh/ *n.* chronic

disorder of the mental processes marked by memory disorders, personality changes, etc., due to brain disease or injury. [Latin: related to DEMENTED]

**dementia praecox** /pree-koks/ n. *formal* schizophrenia. [Latin, = premature dementia]

**demerit** /dee-me-ruht/ n. **1** fault; blemish. **2** mark awarded against an offender.

**demesne** /duh-meen, -mayn/ n. **1 a** territory; domain. **b** land attached to a mansion etc. **c** landed property. **2** (usu. foll. by *of*) region or sphere. **3** *Law hist.* possession (of real property) as one's own. [Latin *dominicus* from *dominus* lord]

**demi-** *prefix* half; partly. [Latin *dimidius* half]

**demigod** /dem-ee-,god/ n. **1 a** partly divine being. **b** child of a god or goddess and a mortal. **2** *colloq.* godlike person.

**demilitarise** /dee-mil-uh-tuh-,ruyz/ v. (also **-ize**) (**-sing** or **-zing**) remove an army etc. from (a frontier, zone, etc.). □ **demilitarisation** /-zay-shuhn/ n.

**demi-monde** /dem-ee-,mond/ n. **1** class of women considered to be of doubtful morality. **2** any group considered to be on the fringes of respectable society. [French, = half-world]

**demise** /duh-muyz/ — n. **1** death; termination. **2** *Law* transfer of an estate, title, etc. by demising. — v. (**-sing**) *Law* transfer (an estate, title, etc.) by will, lease, or death. [Anglo-French: related to DISMISS]

**demisemiquaver** /dem-ee-sem-ee-,kway-vuh, dem-/ n. *Mus.* note equal to half a semiquaver.

**demist** /dee-mist/ v. clear mist from (a windscreen etc.). □ **demister** n.

**demo** /dem-oh/ n. (*pl.* **-s**) *colloq.* **1** public display of interest in a cause, usu. as a procession or mass-meeting (*huge demo outside parliament house*). **2** (*attrib.*) pertaining to such a demo (*demo arrests*). **3** = DEMONSTRATION 3, 4. [abbreviation of DEMONSTRATION]

**demob** /dee-mob/ *colloq.* — v. (**-bb-**) demobilise. — n. demobilisation. [abbreviation]

**demobilise** /dee-moh-buh-,luyz/ v. (also **-ize**) (**-sing** or **-zing**) disband (troops, ships, etc.). □ **demobilisation** /-zay-shuhn/ n.

**democracy** /duh-mok-ruh-see/ n. (*pl.* **-ies**) **1 a** government by the whole population, usu. through elected representatives. **b** nation so governed. **2** classless and tolerant society. [Greek *dēmokratia* rule of the people]

**democrat** /dem-uh-,krat/ n. **1** advocate of democracy. **2** (**Democrat**) member of the Australian Democrats. **3** deep crimson variety of apple, grown chiefly in Tasmania.

**democratic** /,dem-uh-krat-ik/ adj. **1** of, like, practising, or being a democracy. **2** favouring social equality. □ **democratically** adv.

**democratise** /duh-mok-ruh-,tuyz/ v. (also **-ize**) (**-sing** or **-zing**) make democratic. □ **democratisation** /-zay-shuhn/ n.

**demography** /duh-mog-ruh-fee/ n. the study of the statistics of births, deaths, disease, etc. □ **demographic** /,dem-uh-graf-ik/ adj. **demographically** /,dem-uh-graf-i-kuh-lee, -klee/ adv. [Greek *dēmos* the people, -GRAPHY]

**demolish** /duh-mol-ish/ v. **1 a** pull down (a building). **b** destroy. **2** overthrow (an institution). **3** refute (an argument, theory, etc.). **4** *joc.* eat up voraciously. □ **demolition** /,dem-uh-lish-uhn/ n. [Latin *moles* mass]

**demon** /dee-muhn/ n. **1 a** evil spirit or devil. **b** personification of evil passion. **2** (often *attrib.*) forceful or skilful performer (*demon player*). **3** cruel person. **4** (also **daemon**) supernatural being in ancient Greece. **5** *colloq.* police officer, esp. a detective or motor-cycle policeman. □ **demon for work** *colloq.* person who works strenuously. □ **demonic** /duh-mon-ik/ adj. [Greek *daimōn* deity]

**demonetise** /dee-mun-uh-,tuyz/ v. (also **-ize**) (**-sing** or **-zing**) withdraw (a coin etc.) from use. □ **demonetisation** /-zay-shuhn/ n. [French: related to DE-, MONEY]

**demoniac** /duh-moh-nee-,ak/ — adj. **1** fiercely energetic or frenzied. **2** supposedly possessed by an evil spirit. **3** of or like demons. — n. person possessed by an evil spirit. □ **demoniacal** /,dee-muh-nuy-uh-kuhl/ adj. **demoniacally** /,dee-muh-nuy-uh-kuh-lee, -klee/ adv. [Church Latin: related to DEMON]

**demonology** /,dee-muh-nol-uh-jee/ n. the study of demons etc.

**demonstrable** /duh-mon-struh-buhl, dem-uhn-struh-buhl/ adj. able to be shown or proved. □ **demonstrably** adv.

**demonstrate** /dem-uhn-,strayt/ v. (**-ting**) **1** show (feelings etc.). **2 a** describe and explain by experiment, practical use, etc. **b** show, perform, etc., to display a talent etc. (*demonstrated his skill in playing gumleaves; demonstrated his fine physique*). **3** logically prove or be proof of the truth or existence of. **4** take part in a public demonstration. **5** act as a demonstrator. [Latin *monstro* show]

**demonstration** /ˌdem-uhn-**stray**-shuhn/ n. **1** (foll. by *of*) show of feeling etc. **2** (esp. political) public meeting, march, etc. **3 a** the exhibiting etc. of specimens or experiments in esp. scientific teaching. **b** a showing, a performance, which evidences a skill etc. **4** (also *attrib.*) exhibiting of products for sale (*demonstration model*). **5** proof by logic, argument, etc. **6** *Mil.* display of military force.

**demonstrative** /duh-**mon**-struh-tiv/ — adj. **1** showing feelings readily; affectionate (*very demonstrative for a man*). **2** (usu. foll. by *of*) logically conclusive; giving proof (*demonstrative of their skill*). **3** *Gram.* (of an adjective or pronoun) indicating the person or thing referred to (e.g. *this, that, those*). — n. *Gram.* demonstrative adjective or pronoun. □ **demonstratively** adv. **demonstrativeness** n.

**demonstrator** n. **1** person who demonstrates politically etc. **2** person who demonstrates machines etc. to prospective customers. **3** person who teaches by esp. scientific demonstration.

**demoralise** /dee-mo-ruh-ˌluyz/ v. (also **-ize**)(**-sing** or **-zing**) destroy the morale of; dishearten. □ **demoralisation** /-zay-shuhn/ n. [French]

**demote** /dee-**moht**, duh-/ v. (**-ting**) reduce to a lower rank or class. □ **demotion** /-**moh**-shuhn/ n. [from DE-, PROMOTE]

**demotic** /duh-**mot**-ik/ — n. **1** colloquial form of a language. **2** simplified form of ancient Egyptian writing (opp. HIERATIC). — adj. **1** (esp. of language) of the people; colloquial. **2** of ancient Egyptian or modern Greek demotic. [Greek *dēmos* the people]

**demotivate** /ˌdee-moh-tuh-ˌvayt/ v. (**-ting**) (also *absol.*) cause to lose motivation or incentive. □ **demotivation** /-vay-shuhn/ n.

**demur** /duh-**mer**/ — v. (**-rr-**) **1** (often foll. by *to, at*) raise objections (*demurred at the cost*). **2** *Law* put in a demurrer. — n. (usu. in *neg.*) objection; act or process of objecting (*agreed without demur*). [Latin *moror* delay]

**demure** /duh-**myoor**/ adj. (**demurer, demurest**) **1** quiet, reserved; modest. **2** affectedly shy and quiet; coy. □ **demurely** adv. **demureness** n. [French: related to DEMUR]

**demurrer** /duh-**mu**-ruh/ n. *Law* objection raised or exception taken.

**demystify** /dee-**mis**-tuh-ˌfuy/ v. (**-ies, -ied**) remove the mystery from; clarify (*court procedures need to be demystified*). □ **demystification** /-fuh-**kay**-shuhn/ n.

**den** n. **1** wild animal's lair. **2** place of crime or vice (*den of iniquity*). **3** small private room. [Old English]

**denarius** /duh-**nair**-ree-uhs, duh-**nah**-/ n. (*pl.* **denarii** /-ree-ˌuy/) ancient Roman silver coin. [Latin *deni* by tens]

**denary** /**dee**-nuh-ree/ adj. of ten; decimal.

**denationalise** /dee-**nash**-uh-nuh-ˌluyz/ v. (also **-ize**) (**-sing** or **-zing**) transfer (an industry etc.) from public to private ownership. □ **denationalisation** /-zay-shuhn/ n.

**denature** /dee-**nay**-chuh/ v. (**-ring**) **1** change the properties of (a protein etc.) by heat, acidity, etc. **2** make (alcohol) undrinkable. [French]

**dendrite** /**den**-druyt/ n. *Geol.* **a** stone or mineral with natural tree-like markings. **b** such marks on stones or minerals. **2** *Chem.* crystal with branching tree-like growth. **3** *Zool. & Anat.* branching process of a nerve-cell carrying signals to a cell body. [Greek, = tree-like, from *dendron* tree]

**dendrobium** /den-**droh**-bee-uhm/ n. **1** any of a large genus (about 1,400 species) of epiphytic or lithophytic orchids in SE Asia, India, and Australia (which has about 50 species) (see COOKTOWN ORCHID). **2** = ROCK ORCHID.

**dendrochronology** /ˌden-droh-kruh-**nol**-uh-jee/ n. **1** dating of trees by their annual growth rings. **2** the study of these. [Greek *dendron* tree]

**dendrocnide** /ˌden-droh-**knuy**-dee/ n. any tree or shrub of the genus of the same name, having large leaves covered in stinging hairs (which cause severe pain and glandular swelling), and showy, edible, and very tasty fruit: four species are recorded for Australia, the best known being the GYMPIE. [Greek *dendron* tree, *knidē* nettle]

**dendrology** /den-**drol**-uh-jee/ n. the study of trees. □ **dendrological** /-druh-**loj**-i-kuhl/ adj. **dendrologist** n. [Greek *dendron* tree]

**dengue** /**deng**-gee/ n. infectious tropical viral disease causing a fever and acute pains in the joints. [W. Indian Spanish from Swahili]

**deniable** /duh-**nuy**-uh-buhl/ adj. that may be denied.

**denial** /duh-**nuy**-uhl/ n. **1** act or instance of denying the truth or existence of a thing. **2** refusal of a request or wish. **3** disavowal of a leader etc. **4** = SELF-DENIAL.

**denigrate** /**den**-uh-ˌgrayt/ v. (**-ting**) defame or disparage the reputation of. □ **denigration** /-**gray**-shuhn/ n. **denigrator** n. **denigratory** /-**grayt**-uh-ree/ adj. [Latin *niger* black]

**denim** /**den**-uhm/ n. **1** (often *attrib.*) hard-wearing usu. blue cotton twill used for jeans, overalls, etc. **2** (in *pl.*) *colloq.* jeans etc. made of this. [French *de* of, *Nîmes* in France]

**denizen** /**den**-uh-zuhn/ n. **1** (usu. foll. by *of*) *poet.* inhabitant or occupant (*denizens of the outback*). **2** foreigner having certain rights in an adopted country. **3** naturalised foreign word, animal, or plant. [Latin *de intus* from within]

**denominate** /duh-**nom**-uh-,nayt/ v. (**-ting**) give a name to, call, describe as. [Latin: related to NOMINATE]

**denomination** /duh-,nom-uh-**nay**-shuhn/ n. **1** Church or religious sect. **2** class of units within a range or sequence of numbers, weights, money, etc. (*money of small denominations*). **3** name, esp. a characteristic or class name. □ **denominational** *adj.* [Latin: related to DENOMINATE]

**denominator** /duh-**nom**-uh-,nay-tuh/ n. number below the line in a vulgar fraction; divisor. [Latin *nomen* name]

**denotation** /,dee-noh-**tay**-shuhn/ n. **1** act of denoting; sign. **2** that which a word denotes; measuring or signification of a term (opp. CONNOTATION). □ **denotative** /-**noh**-tuh-tiv/ *adj.* [Latin: related to DENOTE]

**denote** /duh-**noht**/ v. (**-ting**) **1** (often foll. by *that*) be a sign of; indicate; mean (*an arrow denotes direction*). **2** stand as a name for; signify. [Latin: related to NOTE]

**denouement** /day-**noo**-mon, duh-/ n. (also **dénouement**) **1** final unravelling of a plot or complicated situation. **2** final scene (in a play, novel, etc.), in which the plot is resolved. [French, = unknot, from Latin *nodus* knot]

**denounce** /duh-**nowns**/ v. (**-cing**) **1** accuse publicly; condemn (*denounced him as a traitor*). **2** inform against (*denounced her to the police*). **3** announce withdrawal from (an armistice, treaty, etc.). □ **denouncement** n. [Latin *nuntius* messenger]

**dense** *adj.* **1 a** closely compacted in substance; thick (*dense fog*). **b** crowded together (*the population is less dense on the outskirts*). **2** *colloq.* stupid. □ **densely** *adv.* **denseness** n. [Latin *densus*]

**density** n. (*pl.* **-ies**) **1** denseness of thing(s) or a substance. **2** *Physics* degree of consistency measured by the quantity of mass per unit volume. **3** opacity of a photographic image.

**dent** — n. **1** slight hollow as made by a blow or pressure. **2** noticeable adverse effect (*made a dent in our funds*). — v. **1** mark with a dent. **2** adversely affect. [from INDENT]

**dental** /**den**-tuhl/ *adj.* **1** of or relating to the teeth or dentistry. **2** (of a consonant) produced with the tongue-tip against the upper front teeth (as *th*) or the ridge of the teeth (as *n, s, t*). [Latin *dens dent-* tooth]

**dental technician** n. person who makes and repairs artificial teeth.

**dentate** /**den**-tayt/ *adj. Bot.* & *Zool.* toothed; with toothlike notches.

**dentine** /**den**-teen/ n. hard dense tissue forming the bulk of a tooth.

**dentist** /**den**-tuhst/ n. person qualified to treat, extract, etc., teeth. □ **dentistry** n.

**dentition** /den-**tish**-uhn/ n. **1** type, number, and arrangement of teeth in a species etc. **2** teething.

**denture** /**den**-chuh/ n. removable artificial tooth or teeth.

**denuclearise** /dee-**nyoo**-kleer-,ruyz/ v. (also **-ize**) (**-sing** or **-zing**) remove nuclear weapons from (a country etc.). □ **denuclearisation** /-**zay**-shuhn/ n.

**denude** /duh-**nyood**/ v. (**-ding**) **1** make naked or bare (*grubs have denuded the shrub*). **2** (foll. by *of*) strip of (covering, property, etc.) (*was denuded of his privileges*). □ **denudation** /,den-yoo-**day**-shuhn/ n. [Latin *nudus* naked]

**denunciation** /dee-,nun-see-**ay**-shuhn, duh-/ n. act of denouncing (a person, policy, etc.); public condemnation. □ **denunciative** /-**nun**-see-uh-tiv/ *adj.* **denunciator** /-**nun**-see-,ay-tuh/ n. **denunciatory** /-**nun**-see-uh-tuh-ree, -tree/ *adj.* [Latin: related to DENOUNCE]

**deny** /duh-**nuy**/ v. (**-ies, -ied**) **1** declare untrue or non-existent (*denied the charge*). **2** repudiate or disclaim (*denied his faith*). **3** (often foll. by *to*) refuse (a person or thing, or something to a person) (*denied him the satisfaction; this was denied to me*). □ **deny oneself** be abstinent. [Latin: related to NEGATE]

**deodorant** /dee-**oh**-duh-ruhnt/ n. (often *attrib.*) substance applied to the body or sprayed into the air to conceal smells. [related to ODOUR]

**deodorise** /dee-**oh**-duh-,ruyz/ v. (also **-ize**) (**-sing** or **-zing**) remove or destroy the smell of. □ **deodorisation** /-**zay**-shuhn/ n.

**deoxyribonucleic acid** /,dee-ok-see-,ruy-boh-**nyoo**-klee-ik/ see DNA. [from DE-, OXYGEN, RIBONUCLEIC (ACID)]

**dep.** *abbr.* **1** departs. **2** deputy.

**depart** /duh-**paht**/ v. **1 a** (often foll. by *from*) go away; leave (*the train departs from this platform*). **b** (usu. foll. by *for*) start; set out (*trains depart for Geelong every hour*). **2** (usu. foll. by *from*) deviate (*departs from good taste*). **3** esp. *formal* or *literary* leave by death; die (*departed this life*). [Latin *dispertio* divide]

**departed** — adj. bygone (departed greatness). — n. (prec. by the) euphem. dead person or people.

**department** n. **1** separate part of a complex whole, esp.: **a** a branch of administration (Department of Defence). **b** a division of a school, university, etc., by subject (English Department). **c** a section of a large store (hardware department). **2** colloq. area of special expertise (that's not my department). [French: related to DEPART]

**departmental** /ˌdee-paht-**men**-tuhl/ adj. of a department. □ **departmentally** adv.

**department store** n. large shop with many departments.

**departure** /duh-**pah**-chuh/ n. **1** act or instance of departing. **2** (often foll. by from) deviation (from the truth, a standard, etc.). **3** (often attrib.) departing of a train, aircraft, etc. (departure lounge). **4** new course of action or thought (driving is rather a departure for him).

**depend** /duh-**pend**/ v. **1** (often foll. by on, upon) be controlled or determined by (it depends on luck). **2** (foll. by on, upon) **a** be unable to do without (depends on his car). **b** rely on (I'm depending on good weather). □ **it** (or **it all** or **that**) **depends** expressing uncertainty or qualification in answering a question (Will they come? – It depends). [Latin pendeo hang]

**dependable** adj. reliable. □ **dependability** /-**bil**-uh-tee/ n. **dependableness** n. **dependably** adv.

**dependant** n. person supported, esp. financially, by another. [French: related to DEPEND]

**dependence** n. **1** state of being dependent, esp. on financial or other support. **2** reliance; trust; confidence (shows great dependence on her judgment). **3** relation of anything subordinate to that from which it receives support etc.; subjection (opp. INDEPENDENCE).

**dependency** n. (pl. **-ies**) **1** country or province controlled by another. **2** anything dependent or subordinate.

**dependent** adj. **1** (usu. foll. by on, upon) depending, conditional, or subordinate. **2** unable to do without (esp. a drug). **3** maintained at another's cost. **4** (of a clause etc.) subordinate to a sentence or word.

**depict** /duh-**pikt**/ v. **1** represent in drawing or painting etc. **2** portray in words; describe (the play depicts him as a tool of the Nazis). □ **depicter** n. (also **-tor**). **depiction** n. [Latin: related to PICTURE]

**depilate** /**dep**-uh-ˌlayt/ v. (**-ting**) remove hair from. □ **depilation** /-**lay**-shuhn/ n. [Latin pilus hair]

**depilatory** /duh-**pil**-uh-tuh-ree, -tree/ — adj. removing unwanted hair. — n. (pl. **-ies**) depilatory substance.

**deplete** /duh-**pleet**/ v. (**-ting**) (esp. in passive) **1** reduce in numbers or quantity (depleted forces). **2** empty out; exhaust (their energies were depleted). □ **depletion** n. [Latin pleo fill]

**deplorable** /duh-**plaw**-ruh-buhl/ adj. **1** exceedingly bad (a deplorable meal). **2** to be lamented; sad, wretched (a deplorable fate). □ **deplorably** adv.

**deplore** /duh-**plaw**/ v. (**-ring**) **1** regret deeply; grieve over (deplore this tragic loss). **2** be scandalised by; find exceedingly bad (deplore the sale of cigarettes to minors). [Latin ploro wail]

**deploy** /duh-**ploi**/ v. **1** spread out (troops) into a line ready for action. **2** use (arguments, forces, resources, etc.) effectively. □ **deployment** n. [Latin plico fold]

**depoliticise** /ˌdee-puh-**lit**-uh-ˌsuyz/ v. (also **-ize**) (**-sing** or **-zing**) make non-political (depoliticised the debate about Australia becoming a Republic). □ **depoliticisation** /-**zay**-shuhn/ n.

**deponent** /duh-**poh**-nuhnt/ n. person making a deposition under oath. [Latin depono put down, lay aside]

**deport** /duh-**pawt**/ v. **1** remove forcibly or exile to another country; banish. **2** refl. behave (in a specified manner) (deported himself well). □ **deportation** /ˌdee-paw-**tay**shuhn/ n. (in sense 1). [Latin porto carry]

**deportee** /ˌdee-paw-**tee**/ n. deported person.

**deportment** /duh-**pawt**-muhnt/ n. bearing, demeanour, or manners, esp. of a cultivated kind. [French: related to DEPORT]

**depose** /duh-**pohz**/ v. (**-sing**) **1** remove from office, esp. dethrone. **2** Law (usu. foll. by to, or that + clause) testify, esp. on oath. [French from Latin: related to DEPOSIT]

**deposit** /duh-**poz**-uht/ — n. **1 a** money in a bank account. **b** anything stored for safe keeping, usu. in a bank. **2 a** payment made as a pledge for a contract or as an initial part payment for a thing bought. **b** returnable sum paid on the hire of an item. **3 a** natural layer of sand, rock, coal, etc. **b** layer of accumulated matter on a surface. — v. (**-t-**) **1 a** put or lay down (deposited the book on the shelf). **b** (of water, wind, etc.) leave (matter etc.) lying in a displaced position. **2 a** store or entrust for keeping. **b** pay (a sum of money) into a bank account. **3** pay (a sum) as part of a larger sum or as a pledge for a contract. [Latin *pono posit-* put]

**depositary** n. (pl. **-ies**) person to whom a thing is entrusted; trustee. [Latin: related to DEPOSIT]

**deposition** /ˌdep-uh-**zish**-uhn, ˌdee-puh-/ n. **1** act or instance of deposing, esp. dethronement. **2** sworn evidence; giving of this. **3** (**the Deposition**) taking down of Christ from the Cross. **4** act or instance of depositing or being deposited. [Latin: related to DEPOSIT]

**depositor** n. person who deposits money, property, etc.

**depository** n. (pl. **-ies**) **1 a** storehouse. **b** store (of wisdom, knowledge, etc.) (*this book is a depository of wit*). **2** = DEPOSITARY. [Latin: related to DEPOSIT]

**depot** /**dep**-oh/ n. **1 a** storehouse, esp. for military supplies. **b** headquarters of a regiment. **2** place where vehicles, e.g. buses or trams, are kept. [French: related to DEPOSIT]

**deprave** /duh-**prayv**/ v. (**-ving**) corrupt, esp. morally. □ **depravation** /ˌdep-ruh-**vay**-shuhn/ n. [Latin *pravus* crooked]

**depraved** /duh-**prayvd**-/ adj. morally bad; corrupt, wicked.

**depravity** /duh-**prav**-uh-tee/ n. (pl. **-ies**) moral corruption; wickedness.

**deprecate** /**dep**-ruh-ˌkayt/ v. (**-ting**) express disapproval of; deplore (*deprecate hasty action*). □ **deprecation** /-**kay**-shuhn/ n. **deprecatory** /-**kay**-tuh-ree/ adj. [Latin: related to PRAY]

---

■ **Usage** *Deprecate* is often confused with *depreciate*.

---

**depreciate** /duh-**pree**-shee-ˌayt, -see-ˌayt/ v. (**-ting**) **1** diminish in value (*the car has depreciated greatly in the two days since we bought it*). **2** disparage; belittle (*they are always depreciating his taste in ties*). **3** reduce the purchasing power of (money). □ **depreciatory** /duh-**pree**-shee-uh-tuh-ree, -tree/ adj. [Latin: related to PRICE]

---

■ **Usage** *Depreciate* is often confused with *deprecate*.

---

**depreciation** /duh-ˌpree-shee-**ay**-shuhn, -see-/ n. **1 a** decline in value, esp. due to wear and tear. **b** allowance made for this. **2** act or instance of depreciating; belittlement. **3** decrease in the value of a currency.

**depredation** /ˌdep-ruh-**day**-shuhn/ n. (usu. in pl.) despoiling, ravaging (*the depredations of war; the depredations of time have blurred his beauty*). [Latin: related to PREY]

**depress** /duh-**pres**/ v. **1** make dispirited

or dejected. **2** push down; lower (*depressed the lever*). **3** reduce the activity of (esp. trade). **4** (as **depressed** adj.) **a** miserable. **b** *Psychol.* suffering from depression. □ **depressing** adj. **depressingly** adv. [Latin: related to PRESS[1]]

**depressant** — adj. reducing activity, esp. of a body function; sedative. — n. **1** *Med.* agent, esp. a drug, that sedates. **2** influence that depresses.

**depression** /duh-**presh**-uhn/ n. **1** *Psychol.* extreme dejection or morbidly excessive melancholy, often with a reduction in vitality and physical symptoms. **2** *Econ.* long period of financial and industrial decline, with high unemployment etc. **3** lowering of atmospheric pressure; winds etc. caused by this. **4** hollow on a surface.

**depressive** — adj. **1** tending to depress (*depressive drug; depressive influence*). **2** *Psychol.* of or tending towards depression (*depressive illness*). — n. *Psychol.* person suffering from depression.

**deprivation** /ˌdep-ruh-**vay**-shuhn/ n. act or instance of depriving or state of being deprived (*deprivation of liberty; suffered many deprivations*).

**deprive** /duh-**pruyv**/ v. (**-ving**) **1** (usu. foll. by *of*) strip, dispossess; prevent from having or enjoying (*illness deprived him of success*). **2** (as **deprived** adj.) lacking what is needed for well-being; underprivileged. □ **deprival** n. [Latin: related to PRIVATION]

**Dept.** abbr. Department.

**depth** n. **1 a** deepness (*the depth is not great at the edge*). **b** measurement from the top down, from the surface inwards, or from front to back (*the depth of the drawer is 20 cm*). **2** difficulty; abstruseness (*theology has too much depth for my poor brain*). **3 a** wisdom (*a mind of great depth*). **b** intensity of emotion etc. (*the poem has little depth; in the depths of despair*). **4** intensity of colour, darkness, etc. **5** (usu. in pl.) **a** deep water or place; abyss. **b** low, depressed state (*out of the depths I cried unto thee, O Lord*). **c** lowest, central, or inmost part (*depths of the country; depth of winter*). □ **in depth** comprehensively, thoroughly (*studied it in depth*). **out of one's depth 1** in water over one's head. **2** engaged in a task etc. too difficult for one. [related to DEEP]

**depth charge** n. bomb exploding under water, esp. on a submerged submarine etc.

**deputation** /ˌdep-yoo-**tay**-shuhn/ n. group of people appointed to represent others, usu. for a specific purpose; delegation. [Latin: related to DEPUTE]

**depute** /duh-**pyoot**/ *v.* (**-ting**) (often foll. by *to*) **1** delegate (a task, authority, etc.) (*deputed the leadership to her*). **2** authorise as representative. [Latin *puto* think]

**deputise** /**dep**-yuh-tyuz/ *v.* (also **-ize**) (**-sing** or **-zing**) (usu. foll. by *for*) act as deputy.

**deputy** /**dep**-yuh-tee/ *n.* (*pl.* **-ies**) **1** person appointed to act for another (also *attrib.*: *deputy manager*). **2** parliamentary representative in some countries. [var. of DEPUTE]

**derail** /dee-**rayl**/ *v.* (usu. in *passive*) cause (a train etc.) to leave the rails. □ **derailment** *n.* [French: related to RAIL[1]]

**derange** /duh-**raynj**/ *v.* (**-ging**) **1** throw into confusion; disorganise; cause to act irregularly. **2** (esp. as **deranged** *adj.*) make insane (*deranged by the tragic events*). □ **derangement** *n.* [French: related to RANK[1]]

**derby** /**dah**-bee/ *n.* (*pl.* **-ies**) **1** major annual race for three-year-old horses. **2** important sporting contest. [Earl of *Derby*, founder of the English Derby (after which similar races elsewhere are named)]

**deregulate** /dee-**reg**-yoo-layt/ *v.* (**-ting**) remove (esp. government) regulations from (an industry, a commercial enterprise, etc.). □ **deregulation** /-**lay**-shuhn/ *n.*

**derelict** /**de**-ruh-likt/ — *adj.* **1** (esp. of a property) dilapidated. **2** abandoned, ownerless (esp. of a ship at sea or an empty decrepit property). — *n.* **1** person without a home, a job, or property. **2** abandoned property. [Latin: related to RELINQUISH]

**dereliction** /,de-ruh-**lik**-shuhn/ *n.* **1** (usu. foll. by *of*) neglect; failure to carry out obligations (*dereliction of duty*). **2** act or instance of abandoning or state of being abandoned.

**derestrict** /,dee-ruh-**strikt**/ *v.* remove restrictions (esp. speed limits) from. □ **derestriction** *n.*

**deride** /duh-**ruyd**/ *v.* (**-ding**) laugh scornfully at; mock. □ **derision** /duh-**rizh**-uhn/ *n.* [Latin *rideo* laugh]

**de rigueur** /duh ri-**ger**/ *predic. adj.* required by fashion or custom or etiquette (*evening dress is de rigueur*; *drugs were de rigueur*). [French]

**derisive** /duh-**ruy**-siv/ *adj.* = DERISORY. □ **derisively** *adv.* [from DERIDE]

**derisory** /duh-**ruy**-suh-ree/ *adj.* **1** scoffing, ironical (*derisory cheers*). **2** ridiculously small (*derisory offer*).

**derivation** /,de-ruh-**vay**-shuhn/ *n.* **1** act or instance of deriving or obtaining from a source, or the process of being derived. **2 a** formation of a word from another or from a root (e.g. *quickly* from *quick*). **b** tracing of the origin of a word. **c** statement or account of this. □ **derivational** *adj.*

**derivative** /duh-**riv**-uh-tiv/ — *adj.* derived from another source; not original (*his music is derivative*). — *n.* **1** word derived from another word or from a root. **2** chemical compound that is derived from another. **3** *Math.* quantity measuring the rate of change of another.

**derive** /duh-**ruyv**/ *v.* (**-ving**) **1** (usu. foll. by *from*) get or trace from a source (*derived satisfaction from work*). **2** (foll. by *from*) arise from, originate in (*happiness derives from many things*). **3** gather or deduce (*derived the information from the clues*). **4** (usu. foll. by *from*) show or state the origin or formation of (a word etc.) (*the word 'anaconda' derives from the Sinhalese word 'henakandayā'*). [Latin *rivus* stream]

**dermatitis** /,der-muh-**tuy**-tuhs/ *n.* inflammation of the skin. [Greek *derma* skin, -ITIS]

**dermatology** /,der-muh-**tol**-uh-jee/ *n.* the study of skin diseases. □ **dermatological** /-tuh-**loj**-i-kuhl/ *adj.* **dermatologist** *n.* [from DERMATITIS, -LOGY]

**dermis** /**der**-muhs/ *n.* **1** (in general use) the skin. **2** the true skin, the thick layer of living tissue below the epidermis. [from EPIDERMIS]

**dero** /**de**-roh/ *n.* (also **derro**) *colloq.* vagrant, esp. one dependent upon alcohol. [abbreviation of DERELICT]

**derogate** /**de**-ruh-,gayt/ *v.* (**-ting**) (foll. by *from*) *formal* detract from (merit, right, etc.) (*this new regulation is not intended to derogate from the right to free speech*). □ **derogation** /,de-ruh-**gay**-shuhn/ *n.* [Latin *rogo* ask]

**derogatory** /duh-**rog**-uh-tuh-ree, -tree/ *adj.* disparaging; insulting (*derogatory remark*). □ **derogatorily** *adv.*

**derrick** /**de**-rik/ *n.* **1** crane for heavy weights, with a movable pivoted arm. **2** framework over an oil well etc., holding the drilling machinery. [*Derrick*, name of an English hangman]

**derrière** /,de-ree-**air**/ *n. colloq. euphem.* buttocks. [French, = behind]

**derris** /**de**-ruhs/ *n.* **1** tropical climbing plant. **2** insecticide made from its root. [Latin from Greek]

**derry** /**de**-ree/ *n.* □ **have a derry on** *colloq.* be prejudiced against (*Melburnians and Sydney-siders have a derry on each other*). [perhaps from the song refrain *derry down*]

**dervish** /**der**-vish/ *n.* member of a

Muslim fraternity vowed to poverty and austerity, and which uses wild dancing etc. as part of its ceremonies. [Turkish from Persian, = poor]

**desalinate** /dee-**sal**-uh-,nayt/ v. (**-ting**) remove the salt from (esp. sea water). □ **desalination** /-**nay**-shuhn/ n. [from SALINE]

**descant** — n. /**des**-kant/ **1** harmonising treble melody above the basic melody, esp. of a hymn tune. **2** poet. melody; song. — v. /des-**kant**/ (foll. by on, upon) talk lengthily, esp. in praise of (descanting on the charms of the Apple Isle). [Latin cantus song: related to CHANT]

**descend** /duh-**send**/ v. **1** go or come down (a hill, stairs, etc.). **2** sink, fall (rain descended heavily). **3** slope downwards (paddock descending to the beach). **4** (usu. foll. by on) **a** make a sudden attack. **b** make an unexpected and usu. unwelcome visit (hope they don't descend on us at the weekend). **5** (of property etc.) be passed on by inheritance. **6 a** sink in rank, quality, etc. **b** (foll. by to) stoop to (an unworthy act) (you mustn't descend to violence). □ **be descended from** have as an ancestor. □ **descendent** adj. [Latin scando climb]

**descendant** n. person or thing descended from another. [French: related to DESCEND]

**descent** /duh-**sent**/ n. **1** act or way of descending (the descent was difficult). **2** downward slope (a steep descent). **3** lineage, family origin (of convict descent). **4** decline; fall (sudden descent into obscurity). **5** sudden violent attack.

**describe** /duh-**skruyb**/ v. (**-bing**) **1 a** state the characteristics, appearance, etc. of. **b** (foll. by as) assert to be; call (described him as a liar). **2 a** draw (esp. a geometrical figure). **b** move in (a specified way, esp. a curve) (described a parabola through the air). [Latin scribo write]

**description** /duh-**skrip**-shuhn/ n. **1 a** act or instance of describing or process of being described. **b** representation, esp. in words. **2** sort, kind (no food of any description). [Latin: related to DESCRIBE]

**descriptive** /duh-**skrip**-tiv/ adj. **1** describing, esp. vividly. **2** Linguistics describing a language without comparing, endorsing, or condemning particular usage, vocabulary, etc. **3** Gram. (of an adjective) describing the noun, rather than its relation, position, etc., e.g. blue as distinct from few. [Latin: related to DESCRIBE]

**descry** /duh-**skruy**/ v. (**-ies, -ied**) literary catch sight of; discern. [French: related to CRY]

**desecrate** /**des**-uh-,krayt/ v. (**-ting**) violate (a sacred place etc.) with violence, profanity, etc. □ **desecration** /-**kray**-shuhn/ n. **desecrator** n. [from DE-, CONSECRATE]

**desensitise** /dee-**sen**-suh-,tuyz/ v. (also **-ize**) (**-sing** or **-zing**) reduce or destroy the sensitivity of (photographic materials, an allergic person, etc.) (it is argued that people are desensitised to violence by watching violence). □ **desensitisation** /-**zay**-shuhn/ n.

**desert¹** /duh-**zert**/ v. leave without intending to return (deserted the sinking ship). **2** (esp. as **deserted** adj.) forsake, abandon (deserted his wife and children; a deserted house). **3** run away (esp. from military service). □ **deserter** n. (in sense 3). **desertion** n. [Latin desero -sert- leave]

**desert²** /**dez**-uht/ — n. **1** area of land, characteristically waterless and without vegetation; dry barren, esp. sandy, tract. **2** uninteresting or barren subject, period, etc. (a cultural desert). — adj. **1** of, like, or relating to a desert. **2** uninhabited, desolate, barren. **3** used as a descriptive epithet in the names of Australian flora inhabiting arid areas (desert gum; desert oak). [Latin desertus: related to DESERT¹]

**desert³** /duh-**zert**/ n. (in pl.) deserved reward or punishment (got his deserts). [French: related to DESERVE]

**desert boot** n. suede etc. ankle-high boot.

**desert chat** n. = GIBBER BIRD.

**desert gum** n. any of several eucalypts occurring in drier Australia, esp. the GHOST GUM.

**desertification** /duh-,zer-tuh-fuh-**kay**-shuhn/ n. changing of fertile land into desert or arid waste, esp. as a long-term result of human activity.

**desert lime** n. Australian shrub of the citrus family (Eremocitrus glauca), bearing edible lime-like fruit (see also the related FINGER LIME).

**desert oak** n. any of several trees of drier Australia, esp. the wattle Acacia coriacea and the casuarina Allocasuarina decaisneana.

**desert pea** n. = STURT'S DESERT PEA.

**desert rat** n. colloq. any Allied soldier who fought in the African desert campaign of 1941-2. [from the jerboa or desert rat, used as a badge by the 7th British armoured division]

**desert rose** n. = STURT'S DESERT ROSE.

**deserve** /duh-**zerv**/ v. (**-ving**) (often foll. by to + infin.) be worthy of (a reward, punishment, etc.) (deserves a prize). □ **deservedly** /-vuhd-lee/ adv. [Latin servio serve]

**deserving** adj. (often foll. by of) worthy (esp. of help, praise, etc.). □ **deservingly** adv. **deservingness** n.

**desex** /dee-**seks**/ v. 1 castrate or spay (an animal). 2 (esp. as **desexing** adj.) deprive of sexual qualities or attractions (the desexing effect of some clothes).

**desiccate** /**des**-uh-,kayt/ v. (-ting) 1 remove moisture from (esp. food) (desiccated coconut). 2 dry completely, dry up (am feeling desiccated in this heat). 3 become dry (the leaves are desiccating). □ **desiccation** /-**kay**-shuhn/ n. [Latin siccus dry]

**desideratum** /duh-,zid-uh-**rah**-tuhm, -**ray**-tuhm/ n. (pl. **-ta**) something lacking but needed or desired (privacy is a desideratum in this house). [Latin: related to DESIRE]

**design** /duh-**zuyn**/ — n. 1 a preliminary plan or sketch for making something. b art of producing these. 2 lines or shapes forming a pattern or decoration. 3 plan, purpose, or intention (my design is to make a million by the time I'm fifty). 4 a arrangement or layout of a product. b established version of a product (one of our most popular designs). — v. 1 produce a design for (a building, machine, etc.). 2 intend or plan (designed for beginners). 3 be a designer (he designs for a living). □ **by design** on purpose. **have designs on** plan to appropriate, seduce, etc. [Latin signum mark]

**designate** — v. /**dez**-ig-,nayt/ (-ting) 1 (often foll. by as) appoint to an office or function (designated his own successor). 2 specify (designated times). 3 (often foll. by as) describe as; style (it is designated 'a desirable riverside residence', but where's the river?). 4 serve as the name or symbol of (English uses French words to designate ballet steps). — adj. /**dez**-ig-nuht, -nayt/ (after the noun) appointed to office but not yet installed (bishop designate). [Latin: related to DESIGN]

**designation** /,dez-ig-**nay**-shuhn/ n. 1 name, description, or title. 2 act or process of designating.

**designedly** /duh-**zuy**-nuhd-lee/ adv. on purpose.

**designer** n. 1 person who designs e.g. clothing, machines, theatre sets; draughtsman. 2 (attrib.) a bearing the label of a famous designer; prestigious. b fashionable; marked with the label of a designing company (designer jeans).

**designer drug** n. synthetic analogue of an illegal drug, esp. one using a structure which is not yet illegal but which mimics the chemistry and effects of the illegal drug.

**designing** adj. crafty, scheming.

**desirable** /duh-**zuy**yuh-ruh-buhl/ — adj. 1 worth having or doing (it is desirable that nobody should smoke). 2 sexually attractive. — n. desirable person or thing. □ **desirability** /-**bil**-uh-tee/ n. **desirableness** n. **desirably** adv.

**desire** /duh-**zuy**yuh/ — n. 1 a unsatisfied longing or wish. b expression of this; request (expressed a desire to visit Ireland). 2 sexual appetite. 3 something desired (achieved his heart's desire). — v. (-ring) 1 (often foll. by to + infin., or that + clause) long for; wish (desires to see the Sphinx). 2 request (desires a cup of tea). [Latin desidero long for]

**desirous** predic. adj. 1 (usu. foll. by of) desiring, wanting (desirous of stardom). 2 wishful; hoping (desirous to do the right thing).

**desist** /duh-**zist**/ v. (often foll. by from) abstain; cease (please desist from interrupting; when requested, he desisted). [Latin desisto]

**desk** n. 1 piece of furniture with a surface for writing on, and often drawers. 2 counter in a hotel, bank, etc. (information desk). 3 specialised section of a newspaper office etc. (sports desk). [Latin: related to DISCUS]

**desktop** n. 1 working surface of a desk. 2 (attrib.) (esp. of a microcomputer) suitable for use on an ordinary desk.

**desktop publishing** n. production of professional quality printed matter with a desktop computer and high-quality printer.

**desolate** — adj. /**des**-uh-luht/ 1 left alone; solitary (lives a desolate life). 2 uninhabited, ruined, dreary (a desolate landscape; desolate remains of an outback house). 3 forlorn; wretched (was left weeping and desolate). — v. /**des**-uh-,layt/ (-ting) 1 depopulate, devastate; lay waste. 2 (esp. as **desolated** adj.) make wretched (desolated by grief). □ **desolately** /-luht-lee/ adv. **desolateness** /-luht-nuhs/ n. [Latin solus alone]

**desolation** /,des-uh-**lay**-shuhn/ n. 1 act of desolating or process of being desolated. 2 loneliness, grief, etc., esp. caused by desertion. 3 neglected, ruined, or empty state.

**despair** /duh-**spair**/ — n. 1 complete loss or absence of hope. 2 cause of this (he is my despair). — v. (often foll. by of) lose or be without hope (despaired of ever winning). [Latin spero hope]

**despatch** var. of DISPATCH.

**desperado** /,des-puh-**rah**-doh/ n. (pl. **-es**) desperate or reckless criminal etc. [as DESPERATE]

**desperate** /**des**-puh-ruht/ adj. **1** reckless from despair; violent and lawless (made a desperate attempt to escape his kidnappers; a desperate criminal). **2 a** extremely dangerous, serious, or bad (desperate situation). **b** staking all on a small chance (desperate remedy). **3** (usu. foll. by for) needing or desiring very much (desperate for recognition). □ **desperately** adv. **desperateness** n. **desperation** /-**ray**-shuhn/ n. [Latin: related to DESPAIR]

**despicable** /duh-**spik**-uh-buhl, **des**-pik-/ adj. vile; contemptible, esp. morally. □ **despicably** adv. [Latin specio spect- look at]

**despise** /duh-**spuyz**/ v. (-**sing**) regard as inferior, worthless, or contemptible. [Latin: related to DESPICABLE]

**despite** /duh-**spuyt**/ prep. in spite of. [Latin: related to DESPICABLE]

**despoil** /duh-**spoil**/ v. literary (often foll. by of) plunder; rob; deprive. □ **despoliation** /duh-,spoh-lee-**ay**-shuhn/ n. [Latin: related to SPOIL]

**despondent** /duh-**spon**-duhnt/ adj. in low spirits, dejected. □ **despondence** n. **despondency** n. **despondently** adv. [Latin: related to SPONSOR]

**despot** /**des**-pot/ n. **1** absolute ruler. **2** tyrant. □ **despotic** /des-**pot**-ik/ adj. **despotically** /-**pot**-i-kuh-lee, -klee/ adv. [Greek despotēs master]

**despotism** /**des**-puh-,tiz-uhm/ n. **1** rule by a despot; tyranny. **2** country ruled by a despot.

**dessert** /duh-**zert**/ n. **1** sweet course of a meal. **2** fruit, nuts, etc., served at the end of a meal. [French: related to DIS-, SERVE]

**dessertspoon** n. **1** medium-sized spoon used for dessert and as a measurement in cooking etc. **2** amount held by this (10 ml or 2 teaspoons). □ **dessertspoonful** n. (pl. -**s**).

**destabilise** /dee-**stay**-buh-,luyz/ v. (also **-ize**) (-**sing** or -**zing**) **1** make unstable. **2** subvert (esp. a foreign government). □ **destabilisation** /-**zay**-shuhn/ n.

**destination** /,des-tuh-**nay**-shuhn/ n. place to which a person or thing is going. [Latin: related to DESTINE]

**destine** /**des**-tuhn/ v. (-**ning**) (often foll. by to, for, or to + infin.) set apart; appoint; preordain; intend (destined him for the navy). □ **be destined to** be fated or preordained to (was destined to be a star). [French from Latin]

**destiny** /**des**-tuh-nee/ n. (pl. -**ies**) **1 a** fate. **b** this regarded as a power. **2** particular person's fate etc. (it was their

destiny to be rejected). [French from Latin]

**destitute** /**des**-tuh-,tyoot/ adj. **1** without food, shelter, etc. **2** (usu. foll. by of) lacking (destitute of friends). □ **destitution** /-**tyoo**-shuhn/ n. [Latin]

**destroy** /duh-**stroi**/ v. **1** pull or break down; demolish (destroyed the bridge). **2** end the existence of (the accident destroyed his confidence). **3** kill (esp. an animal). **4** make useless; spoil (heavy rain has destroyed this year's crop). **5** ruin, esp. financially. **6** defeat (destroyed the enemy). [Latin struo struct- build]

**destroyer** n. **1** person or thing that destroys. **2** fast armed warship escorting other ships.

**destruct** /duh-**strukt**/ esp. Astronaut. — v. destroy (one's own rocket etc.) or be destroyed deliberately, esp. for safety. — n. act of destructing.

**destructible** adj. able to be destroyed. [Latin: related to DESTROY]

**destruction** /duh-**struk**-shuhn/ n. **1** act or instance of destroying or process of being destroyed. **2** cause of this (greed was their destruction). [Latin: related to DESTROY]

**destructive** adj. **1** (often foll. by to, of) destroying or tending to destroy (destructive of his peace of mind; destructive to organisms). **2** negatively critical (opp. CONSTRUCTIVE). □ **destructively** adv. **destructiveness** n.

**desuetude** /duh-**syoo**-uh-,tyood/ n. formal state of disuse (the house has fallen into desuetude). [Latin suesco be accustomed]

**desultory** /**dez**-uhl-tuh-ree, **des**-, -tree/ adj. **1** constantly turning from one subject to another, esp. in a half-hearted way (a desultory conversation). **2** disconnected; unmethodical; superficial (made desultory attempts to study for the exam). □ **desultorily** adv. [Latin desultorius superficial]

**detach** /duh-**tach**/ v. **1** (often foll. by from) unfasten or disengage and remove. **2** send (troops etc.) on a separate mission. **3** (as **detached** adj.) **a** impartial; unemotional. **b** (esp. of a house) standing separate. □ **detachable** adj. [French: related to ATTACH]

**detachment** n. **1** aloofness; indifference. **2** impartiality. **3** act or process of detaching or being detached. **4** troops etc. detached for a specific purpose. [French: related to DETACH]

**detail** /**dee**-tayl/ — n. **1 a** small particular; item. **b** such a particular, considered (ironically) to be unimportant (the truth of the statement is just a detail).

**2 a** small items or particulars (esp. in an artistic work) regarded collectively (*an eye for detail*). **b** treatment of them (*the detail was insufficient*). **3** (often in *pl.*) number of particulars; aggregate of small items (*filled in the details on the form*). **4 a** minor decoration on a building, in a picture, etc. **b** small part of a picture etc. shown alone. **5** *Mil.* small detachment of soldiers etc. for special duty. — *v.* **1** give particulars of (*detailed his plans*). **2** relate circumstantially (*detailed the anecdote about . . .*). **3** assign for special duty. **4** (as **detailed** *adj.*) **a** (of a picture, story, etc.) containing many details. **b** itemised (*detailed list*). **5** refurbish etc. (a motor vehicle) with particular attention to detail. □ **in detail** item by item, minutely. [French: related to *tail* limitation of ownership]

**detailing** *n.* process by which a new car is given extras to enhance its appearance or durability (e.g. rust proofing, fabric protection) or an old car is refurbished (e.g. the cleaning of upholstery, buffing and polishing).

**detain** /duh-**tayn**/ *v.* **1** keep waiting; delay. **2** keep in custody, lock up. □ **detainment** *n.* [Latin *teneo* hold]

**detainee** /,dee-tay-**nee**, duh-**tay**-nee/ *n.* person kept in custody, esp. for political reasons.

**detect** /duh-**tekt**/ *v.* **1** discover or perceive (*detected a note of sarcasm*; *detected a smell of burning*). **2** (often foll. by *in*) discover (a criminal); solve (a crime). □ **detectable** *adj.* **detector** *n.* [Latin *tego tect-* cover]

**detection** /duh-**tek**-shuhn/ *n.* **1** act or instance of detecting or process of being detected. **2** work of a detective.

**detective** /duh-**tek**-tiv/ *n.* person, esp. a police officer, investigating crimes (also *attrib.*: *detective story*).

**détente** /**day**-tont/ *n.* (also **detente**) easing of strained, esp. international, relations. [French, = relaxation]

**detention** /duh-**ten**-shuhn/ *n.* **1** detaining or being detained. **2** being kept late in school as a punishment. **3** custody; confinement. [Latin: related to DETAIN]

**deter** /duh-**ter**/ *v.* (**-rr-**) (often foll. by *from*) **1** discourage or prevent (a person) through fear or dislike of the consequences. **2** discourage, check, or prevent (a thing, process, etc.). □ **determent** *n.* [Latin *terreo* frighten]

**detergent** /duh-**ter**-juhnt/ — *n.* synthetic cleansing agent used with water. — *adj.* cleansing. [Latin *tergeo* wipe]

**deteriorate** /duh-**teer**-ree-uh-,rayt/ *v.* (**-ting**) make or become bad or worse (*her*

*health is deteriorating*). □ **deterioration** /-**ray**-shuhn/ *n.* [Latin *deterior* worse]

**determinant** /duh-**ter**-muh-nuhnt/ — *adj.* serving to determine or define. — *n.* **1** determining factor etc. **2** *Math.* quantity obtained by the addition of products of the elements of a square matrix according to a given rule. [Latin: related to DETERMINE]

**determinate** /duh-**ter**-muh-nuht/ *adj.* **1** limited in time, space, or character. **2** of definite scope or nature. □ **determinacy** *n.* **determinateness** *n.*

**determination** /duh-,ter-muh-**nay**-shuhn/ *n.* **1** firmness of purpose; resoluteness (*she showed grit and determination*). **2** process of deciding or determining or calculating. **3 a** conclusion of a dispute by the decision of an arbitrator. **b** decision so reached. **4** judicial decision or sentence.

**determine** /duh-**ter**-muhn/ *v.* (**-ning**) **1** find out or establish precisely (*have to determine the extent of the problem*). **2 a** decide or settle (*determined who should go*). **b** settle or resolve (a dispute, argument), esp. by means of an arbitrator. **3** be the decisive factor in regard to (*demand determines supply*). **4** *Geom.* fix or define the position of. □ **be determined** be resolved. [Latin *terminus* boundary]

**determined** *adj.* showing determination; resolute, unflinching (*made a determined attempt*). □ **determinedly** *adv.*

**determiner** *n.* **1** person or thing which determines or decides something. **2** *Gram.* modifying word (e.g. *the, his, some*) which limits the application or reference of the noun modified.

**determinism** *n.* doctrine that human actions, events, etc. are determined by causes external to the will. □ **determinist** *n.* & *adj.* **deterministic** *adj.* **deterministically** *adv.*

**deterrent** /duh-**te**-ruhnt/ — *n.* deterrent thing or factor, esp. nuclear weapons regarded as deterring an enemy from attack. — *adj.* deterring. □ **deterrence** *n.*

**detest** /duh-**test**/ *v.* hate violently, loathe. □ **detestation** /,dee-tes-**tay**-shuhn/ *n.* [Latin *detestor* from *testis* witness]

**detestable** *adj.* intensely disliked; hateful.

**dethatch** *v.* remove a matted layer of plant debris (from a lawn) in order to improve aeration and water penetration.

**dethatcher** *n.* machine with hooked blades which rotate vertically, removing matted plant debris from a lawn.

**dethrone** /dee-**throhn**/ *v.* (**-ning**) remove from a throne, depose. □ **dethronement** *n.*

**detonate** /**det**-uh-,nayt/ *v.* (**-ting**) set off (an explosive charge); be set off.

□ **detonation** /ˌdet-uh-**nay**-shuhn/ n. [Latin *tono* thunder]

**detonator** n. device for detonating explosives.

**detour** /**dee**-toor/ — n. divergence from a usual route; roundabout course. — v. make or cause to make a detour. [French: related to TURN]

**detoxify** /dee-**tok**-suh-ˌfuy/ v. (**-ies, -ied**) remove poison or harmful substances from. □ **detoxification** /-fuh-**kay**-shuhn/ n. [Latin *toxicum* poison]

**detract** /duh-**trakt**/ v. (foll. by *from*) take away (a part); diminish; make seem less valuable or important (*his tantrums and bad sportsmanship during the tennis match detracted from his victory*). [Latin *traho tract-* draw]

**detractor** n. person who criticises unfairly. □ **detraction** n.

**detribalise** /dee-**truy**-buh-luyz/ v. (also **-ize**) (**-sing** or **zing**) destroy or distance (a person's) cultural, social, etc. connections with a tribe, esp. through contact with different cultures (*many Aborigines in the cities have been virtually detribalised*).

**detriment** /**det**-ruh-muhnt/ n. **1** harm, damage (*his racist remarks were more to his own detriment than to that of his fellow-Australians he slurred*). **2** cause of this. □ **detrimental** /ˌdet-ruh-**men**-tuhl/ adj. [Latin: related to TRITE]

**detritus** /duh-**truy**-tuhs/ n. gravel, sand, etc. produced by erosion; debris. □ **detrital** adj. [Latin: related to DETRIMENT]

**de trop** /duh **troh**/ predic. adj. not wanted, unwelcome, in the way (*racist remarks are decidedly de trop*). [French, = excessive]

**deuce**[1] /dyoos/ n. **1** two on dice or playing-cards. **2** *Tennis* score of 40 all, at which two consecutive points are needed to win. [Latin *duo duos* two]

**deuce**[2] /dyoos/ n. misfortune, the Devil, esp. as an exclamation of surprise or annoyance (*who the deuce are you?*). □ **the deuce to pay** trouble to be expected. [Low German *duus* two (being the worst throw at dice)]

**deus ex machina** /ˌday-uus eks **mak**-i-nuh/ n. unlikely agent resolving a seemingly hopeless situation, esp. in a play or novel (also attrib.: *a deus ex machina ending*). [Latin, = god from the machinery, i.e. in a theatre]

**deuterium** /dyoo-**teer**-ree-uhm/ n. stable isotope of hydrogen with a mass about double that of the usual isotope. [Greek *deuteros* second]

**Deutschmark** /**doich**-mahk/ n. (also

**Deutsche Mark** /**doich**-uh mahk/) chief monetary unit of Germany. [German: related to MARK[2]]

**devalue** /dee-**val**-yoo/ v. (**-ues, -ued, -uing**) **1** reduce the value of. **2** reduce the value of (a currency) in relation to others or to gold. □ **devaluation** /-ay-shuhn/ n.

**devastate** /**dev**-uh-ˌstayt/ v. (**-ting**) **1** lay waste; cause great destruction to. **2** (often in *passive*) overwhelm with shock or grief. □ **devastation** /-**stay**-shuhn/ n. [Latin *vasto* lay waste]

**devastating** adj. **1** crushingly effective; overwhelming (*a devastating attack*). **2** (frequently *figurative*, esp. in trivial or hyperbolic use) very effective or upsetting; astounding, overwhelming, 'stunning' (*a devastating bore; it came to him with devastating certainty*). □ **devastatingly** adv.

**devein** /dee-**vayn**/ v. remove the dorsal vein from (a prawn or shrimp).

**develop** /duh-**vel**-uhp/ v. (**-p-**) **1 a** make or become bigger, fuller, more elaborate, etc. (*the new suburb developed rapidly*). **b** bring or come to an active, visible, or mature state (*developed a plan of action*). **2** begin to exhibit or suffer from (*the car has developed a rattle; developed a rash*). **3 a** build on (land). **b** convert (land) to new use. **4** treat (photographic film etc.) to make the image visible. **5** *Mus.* elaborate (a theme) by modification of the melody, harmony, rhythm, etc. □ **developer** n. [French]

**developing country** n. poor country that is developing better economic and social conditions.

**development** n. **1** act or instance of developing or process of being developed. **2 a** stage of growth or advancement. **b** thing that has developed; new event or circumstance etc. (*latest developments*). **3** full-grown state. **4** developed land; group of buildings. **5** *Mus.* elaboration of a theme or themes, esp. in the middle section of a sonata movement.

**developmental** /duh-ˌvel-uhp-**men**-tuhl/ adj. **1** incidental to growth (*developmental diseases*). **2** evolutionary.

**deviant** /**dee**-vee-uhnt/ — adj. deviating from what is regarded by most as normal, esp. sexually. — n. deviant person or thing. □ **deviance** n. **deviancy** n.

**deviate** /**dee**-vee-ˌayt/ — v. (**-ting**) (often foll. by *from*) turn aside or diverge (from a course of action, rule, truth, etc.); digress (*this deviates from the usual pattern; stick to the point — don't deviate*). — n. /**dee**-vee-uht/ = DEVIANT n. □ **deviator** n. **deviatory** /-vee-uh-tuh-ree, -tree/ adj.

**deviation** /ˌdee-vee-**ay**-shuhn/ *n.* **1 a** deviating, digressing. **b** instance of this. **2** *Statistics* amount by which a single measurement differs from the mean.

**device** /duh-**vuys**/ *n.* **1** thing made or adapted for a special purpose (*labour-saving device*). **2** plan, scheme, or trick. **3** design, esp. heraldic. **4** *euphem.* bomb (*police located a device in the super-market*). □ **leave a person to his or her own devices** leave a person to do as he or she wishes. [French: related to DEVISE]

**devil** /**dev**-uhl/ — *n.* **1** (usu. **the Devil**) (in Christian and Jewish belief) supreme spirit of evil; Satan. **2 a** (the) evil spirit; demon. **b** personified evil. **3 a** wicked person. **b** mischievously energetic, clever, or self-willed person. **4** *colloq.* person of a specified kind (*lucky devil*). **5** fighting spirit, mischievousness (*devil is in him tonight*). **6** *colloq.* awkward thing (*this door's a devil to open*). **7** (**the devil** or **the Devil**) *colloq.* used as an exclamation of surprise or annoyance (*who the devil are you?*). **8** literary hack exploited by an employer. **9** = TASMANIAN DEVIL. — *v.* (**-ll-**) **1** cook (food) with chilli or other hot seasoning. **2 a** work as a novice barrister for an experienced barrister who takes the responsibility for the work and pays the novice. **b** (of a writer) work in a similar relationship with an author. □ **between the devil and the deep blue sea** in a dilemma. **a devil of** *colloq.* considerable, difficult, or remarkable (*a devil of a job; a devil of a time to come visiting*). **devil's own** *colloq.* very difficult or unusual (*the devil's own job*). **the devil to pay** trouble to be expected. **like the devil** with great energy or speed (*worked like the devil*). **speak** (or **talk**) **of the devil** said when a person appears just after being mentioned. [Greek *diabolos* accuser, slanderer]

**devil-devil** *n.* **1** (in Aboriginal belief) evil spirit; manifestation of evil. **2** = GILGAI. [originally Australian pidgin]

**devilish** — *adj.* **1** of or like a devil; wicked. **2** mischievous. — *adv. colloq.* very. □ **devilishly** *adv.*

**devil-may-care** *adj.* cheerful and reckless.

**devilment** *n.* mischief, wild spirits.

**devil-on-the-coals** *n.* small damper hastily baked on hot ashes.

**devilry** *n.* (*pl.* **-ies**) **1** wickedness; reckless mischief. **2** black magic.

**devil's advocate** *n.* **1** *RC Ch.* person who presents and argues the case against a dead person's canonisation or beatification (opp. POSTULATOR). **2** person who argues against a proposition to test it.

[translation of *advocatus diaboli* in the Catholic Church]

**devil's twine** *n.* = DODDER-LAUREL.

**devious** /**dee**-vee-uhs/ *adj.* **1** (of a person etc.) not straightforward; underhand (*a devious plan devised by a devious mind*). **2** winding, circuitous. □ **deviously** *adv.* **deviousness** *n.* [Latin *via* way]

**devise** /duh-**vuyz**/ *v.* (**-sing**) **1** carefully plan or invent. **2** *Law* leave (real estate) by will. [Latin: related to DIVIDE]

**devoid** /duh-**void**/ *predic. adj.* (foll. by *of*) lacking or free from (*he is devoid of commonsense*). [French: related to VOID]

**devolute** /**dee**-vuh-ˌloot/ *v.* transfer by devolution.

**devolution** /ˌdee-vuh-**loo**-shuhn/ *n.* **1** delegation of power, esp. by central government to local or regional administration. **2 a** descent or passing on through a series of stages. **b** descent by natural or due succession from one to another of property or qualities. **3** *Biol.* degeneration (opp. EVOLUTION). □ **devolutionary** *adj.* **devolutionist** *n.* & *adj.* [Latin: related to DEVOLVE]

**devolve** /duh-**volv**/ *v.* (**-ving**) **1** (foll. by *on, upon,* etc.) **a** pass (work or duties) to (a deputy etc.). **b** (of work or duties) pass to (a deputy etc.) (*the responsibility for supervising seventy children at the picnic devolved on me*). **2** (foll. by *on, to, upon*) (of property etc.) descend to. □ **devolvement** *n.* [Latin *volvo volut-* roll]

**devon** /**dev**-uhn/ *n.* (also **fritz**) large bland sausage eaten cold. [*Devon* county in England]

**Devonian** /duh-**voh**-nee-uhn/ — *adj.* of the fourth period of the Palaeozoic era with evidence of the first amphibians and tree forests. — *n.* this period. [*Devon* in England]

**devonshire tea** *n.* scones with jam and cream served with tea or coffee etc. [*Devonshire* in England, TEA (sense 4)]

**devote** /duh-**voht**/ *v.* (**-ting**) (often *refl.*; foll. by *to*) apply or give over to (a particular activity etc.) (*devoted their time to reading; devoted himself to the cause*). [Latin *voveo vot-* vow]

**devoted** *adj.* loving; loyal. □ **devotedly** *adv.*

**devotee** /ˌdev-uh-**tee**/ *n.* **1** (usu. foll. by *of*) zealous enthusiast or supporter. **2** zealously pious or fanatical person.

**devotion** /duh-**voh**-shuhn/ *n.* **1** (usu. foll. by *to*) great love or loyalty (to a person or cause). **2 a** religious worship; form of prayer (*the devotion known as the Way of the Cross*). **b** (in *pl.*) prayers. □ **devotional** *adj.* [Latin: related to DEVOTE]

**devour** /duh-**vowuh**/ v. **1** eat hungrily or greedily. **2** (of fire etc.) engulf, destroy. **3** take in eagerly (*devoured book after book*). **4** preoccupy (*devoured by fear*). [Latin *voro* swallow]

**devout** /duh-**vowt**/ adj. **1** earnestly religious (*a devout Buddhist*). **2** earnestly sincere (*devout hope*). □ **devoutly** adv. **devoutness** n. [Latin: related to DEVOTE]

**dew** n. **1** condensed water vapour forming on cool surfaces at night. **2** similar glistening moisture, e.g. tears. □ **dewy** adj. (**-ier, -iest**). [Old English]

**Dewey system** /**dyoo**-ee/ n. decimal system of library classification. [*Dewey*, name of the librarian who devised it (d. 1931)]

**dewlap** n. loose fold of skin hanging from the throat of cattle, dogs, etc. [from DEW, LAP¹]

**dew point** n. temperature at which dew forms.

**dexter** adj. esp. *Heraldry* on or of the right-hand side (observer's left) of a shield etc. [Latin, = on the right]

**dexterity** /dek-**ste**-ruh-tee/ n. **1** skill in using one's hands. **2** mental adroitness. [Latin: related to DEXTER]

**dexterous** /**deks**-truhs/ adj. (also **dextrous**) having or showing dexterity. □ **dexterously** adv. **dexterousness** n.

**dextrose** /**dek**-strohs/ n. form of glucose. [Latin *dextra* on or to the right]

**dhal** /dahl/ n. (also **red lentils**) **1** a kind of split pulse common in India, Sri Lanka, etc. **2** dish made with this. [Hindi]

**Dharawal** /**du**-ru-wol/ n. an Aboriginal language spoken in the Illawarra region of NSW, from the southern shore of Botany Bay to Jervis Bay, including the modern towns of Wollongong and Nowra: now extinct.

**dharma** /**dah**-muh/ n. *Ind.* **1** social custom; correct behaviour. **2** the Buddhist truth. **3** the Hindu moral law. [Sanskrit, = decree, custom]

**Dharuk** /**du**-ruuk/ n. an Aboriginal language of the Sydney region, from Port Jackson to the north side of Botany Bay, and inland at least as far as Camden and Penrith: now extinct.

**dhobi** /**doh**-bee/ n. (pl. **-s**) (in India and Sri Lanka) person who washes clothes for a living. [Hindi]

**dhoti** /**doh**-tee/ n. (pl. **-s**) loincloth worn by male Hindus. [Hindi]

**dhow** /dow/ n. lateen-rigged ship used on the Arabian Sea. [origin unknown]

**dhufish** /**dyoo**-fish/ n. = JEWFISH.

**Dhurga** /**duur**-gu/ n. an Australian Aboriginal language of NSW, spoken over a wide area from Jervis Bay to Lake Wallaga: now extinct.

**di-¹** comb. form two-, double. [Greek *dis* twice]

**di-²** prefix = DIS-.

**di-³** prefix form of DIA- before a vowel.

**dia.** abbr. diameter.

**dia-** prefix (also **di-** before a vowel) **1** through (*diaphanous*). **2** apart (*diacritical*). **3** across (*diameter*). [Greek *dia* through]

**diabetes** /duy-uh-**bee**-teez/ n. **1** any disorder of the metabolism with excessive thirst and the production of large amounts of urine. **2** (in full **diabetes mellitus**) the commonest form of diabetes in which sugar and starch are not properly absorbed from the blood, with thirst, emaciation, and excessive excretion of urine with glucose. **3** (in full **diabetes insipidus**) rare metabolic disorder due to a pituitary deficiency, with excessive urination and thirst. [originally = siphon: Latin from Greek from *diabainō* go through]

**diabetic** /duy-uh-**bet**-ik/ — adj. **1** of or having diabetes. **2** for use by diabetics. — n. person suffering from diabetes.

**diabolical** /duy-uh-**bol**-i-kuhl/ adj. (also **diabolic**) **1** of the Devil. **2** devilish; inhumanly cruel or wicked. **3** extremely bad, clever, or annoying. □ **diabolically** adv. [Latin: related to DEVIL]

**diachronic** /duy-uh-**kron**-ik/ adj. *Linguistics* etc. concerned with the historical development of a subject (esp. a language) (opp. SYNCHRONIC). □ **diachronically** adv. [from DIA- (sense 1), Greek *khronos* time]

**diaconal** /duy-**ak**-uh-nuhl/ adj. of a deacon. [from DIA- (sense 1), Church Latin: related to DEACON]

**diaconate** /duy-**ak**-uh-ˌnayt, -nuht/ n. **1** the Order of deacons. **2** body of deacons.

**diacritic** /duy-uh-**krit**-ik/ n. sign (e.g. an accent or cedilla) indicating different sounds or values of a letter (e.g. *ü* has the diacritic ¨ to distinguish it from *u*). [Greek: related to CRITIC]

**diacritical** — adj. distinguishing, distinctive. — n. (in full **diacritical mark** or **sign**) = DIACRITIC.

**diadem** /**duy**-uh-ˌdem/ n. crown or headband, usu. as a sign of sovereignty. [Greek *deō* bind]

**diaeresis** /duy-**eer**-ruh-suhs, -e-ruh-suhs/ n. (pl. **diaereses** /-ˌseez/) (also **dieresis**) mark (as in *naïve*) over a vowel to indicate that it is sounded separately. [Greek, = separation]

**diagnose** /**duy**-uhg-ˌnohz/ v. (**-sing**) make a diagnosis of (a disease, fault, etc.).

**diagnosis** /ˌduy-uhg-**noh**-suhs/ *n.* (*pl.* **diagnoses** /-ˌseez/ ) **1 a** identification of a disease from its symptoms. **b** formal statement of this. **2** identification of the cause of a mechanical fault etc. **3** distinctive characterisation in precise terms of a genus, species, etc. [Greek *gignōskō* recognise]

**diagnostic** /ˌduy-uhg-**nos**-tik/ — *adj.* of or assisting diagnosis. — *n.* symptom. □ **diagnostically** *adv.* **diagnostician** /-nos-**tish**-uhn/ *n.* [Greek: related to DIAGNOSIS]

**diagnostics** *n.* **1** (treated as *pl.*) *Computing* programs etc. used to identify faults in hardware or software. **2** (treated as *sing.*) science of diagnosing disease.

**diagonal** /duy-**ag**-uh-nuhl/ — *adj.* **1** crossing a straight-sided figure from corner to corner. **2** slanting, oblique. — *n.* straight line joining two opposite corners. □ **diagonally** *adv.* [Greek *gōnia* angle]

**diagram** /**duy**-uh-ˌgram/ *n.* **1** drawing showing the general scheme or outline of an object and its parts. **2** graphic representation of the course or results of an action or process. □ **diagrammatic** /-gruh-**mat**-ik/ *adj.* **diagrammatically** /-gruh-**mat**-i-kuh-lee, -klee/ *adv.* [Greek: related to -GRAM]

**dial** /**duy**-uhl/ — *n.* **1** face of a clock or watch, marked to show the hours etc. **2** similar flat plate marked with a scale for measuring weight, volume, etc., indicated by a pointer. **3** movable numbered disc on a telephone for making connection. **4 a** plate or disc etc. on a radio or television for selecting a wavelength or channel. **b** similar device on other equipment. **5** *colloq.* person's face (*wipe that smile off your dial!*). — *v.* (**-ll-**) **1** (*also absol.*) select (a telephone number) with dial. **2** measure, indicate, or regulate with dial. [medieval Latin *diale* from *dies* day]

**dialect** /**duy**-uh-ˌlekt/ *n.* **1** form of speech peculiar to a particular region or social group. **2** variety of language with non-standard vocabulary, pronunciation, or grammar. □ **dialectal** /-**lek**-tuhl/ *adj.* [Greek *legō* speak]

**dialectic** /ˌduy-uh-**lek**-tik/ *n.* **1** art of investigating the truth by discussion and logical argument. **2** process whereby contradictions merge to form a higher truth. **3** any situation or discussion involving the juxtaposition or conflict of opposites. [Greek: related to DIALECT]

**dialectical** *adj.* of dialectic. □ **dialectically** *adv.*

**dialectical materialism** *n.* Marxist theory that political and historical events

are due to the conflict of social forces arising from economic conditions.

**dialectics** *n.* (treated as *sing.* or *pl.*) = DIALECTIC *n.* 1.

**dialogue** /**duy**-uh-ˌlog/ *n.* **1 a** conversation. **b** this in written form (in a play or novel etc.). **2 a** discussion between the representatives of two nations, groups, etc. with different opinions (*dialogue between the Catholic and Anglican Churches on reunion*). **b** valuable or constructive criticism or communication. [Greek *legō* speak]

**dialysis** /duy-**al**-uh-suhs/ *n.* (*pl.* **dialyses** /-ˌseez/ ) **1** *Chem.* separation of particles in a liquid by differences in their ability to pass through a membrane into another liquid. **2** *Med.* **a** (in cases of kidney failure) purification of the blood by this technique, esp. outside the body in an artificial kidney. **b** occasion of undergoing this process. [Greek *luō* set free]

**diamanté** /duy-uh-**mon**-tee, dee-uh-/ *adj.* decorated with synthetic diamonds or another sparkling substance. [French *diamant* diamond]

**diameter** /duy-**am**-uh-tuh/ *n.* **1** straight line passing through the centre of a circle or sphere to its edges; length of this. **2** transverse measurement; width, thickness. **3** unit of linear magnifying power. [Greek: related to -METER]

**diametrical** /ˌduy-uh-**met**-ri-kuhl/ *adj.* (also **diametric**) **1** of or along a diameter. **2** (of opposites etc.) absolute. □ **diametrically** *adv.* [Greek: related to DIAMETER]

**diamond** /**duy**-uh-muhnd, **duy**-muhnd/ *n.* **1** very hard transparent precious stone of pure crystallised carbon. **2** figure shaped like the cross-section of a diamond; rhombus. **3 a** playing-card of the suit denoted by a red rhombus. **b** (in *pl.*) this suit. **4** *Baseball* baseball field. [Greek: related to ADAMANT]

**diamond bird** *n.* (also **spotted pardalote**) small bird of south-western WA and eastern Australia, having many white or yellow spots.

**diamond dove** *n.* small grey pigeon of northern and central Australia, having white spots on its wings.

**diamond firetail** *n.* (also **Java sparrow**) finch of south-eastern mainland Australia, having white-spotted black flanks.

**diamond snake** *n.* **1** greenish-black Australian python with diamond-shaped markings. **2** = COPPERHEAD 1.

**diamond sparrow** *n.* **1** = DIAMOND BIRD. **2** = DIAMOND FIRETAIL. **3** = ZEBRA FINCH.

**diamond wedding** n. 60th (or 75th) wedding anniversary.

**dianthus** /duy-**an**-thuhs/ n. flowering plant of the genus *Dianthus* including the carnation. [Greek, = flower of Zeus]

**diapason** /ˌduy-uh-**pay**-zuhn, -suhn/ n. **1** compass of a voice or musical instrument. **2** fixed standard of musical pitch. **3** either of two main organ-stops. [Greek, = through all (notes)]

**diaper** /**duy**-uh-puh/ n. US baby's nappy. [Greek *aspros* white]

**diaphanous** /duy-**af**-uh-nuhs/ adj. (of fabric etc.) light, delicate, and almost transparent. [Greek *phainō* show]

**diaphragm** /**duy**-uh-ˌfram/ n. **1** muscular partition between the thorax and abdomen in mammals. **2** thin contraceptive cap fitting over the cervix. **3 a** *Photog.* plate or disc pierced with a circular hole to cut off marginal beams of light. **b** vibrating disc in a microphone, telephone, loudspeaker, etc. **4** device for varying the lens aperture in a camera etc. [Greek *phragma* fence]

**diarist** /**duy**-uh-ruhst/ n. person who keeps a diary.

**diarrhoea** /ˌduy-uh-**ree**-uh/ n. condition of excessively frequent and loose bowel movements. □ **diarrhoeal** adj. **diarrhoeic** adj. [Greek *rheō* flow]

**diary** /**duy**-uh-ree/ n. (pl. -ies) **1** daily record of events or thoughts. **2** book for this or for noting future engagements. [Latin *dies* day]

**Diaspora** /duy-**as**-puh-ruh/ n. **1** the dispersion of the Jews after their exile in 538 BC. **2** the dispersed Jews. [Greek]

**diastole** /duy-**as**-tuh-lee/ n. period between two contractions of the heart when the heart muscle relaxes and allows the chambers to fill with blood (cf. SYSTOLE). □ **diastolic** /ˌduy-uh-**stol**-ik/ adj. [Greek *stellō* place]

**diatom** /**duy**-uh-tuhm/ n. one-cell alga found as plankton and forming fossil deposits. [Greek, = cut in half]

**diatomic** /ˌduy-uh-**tom**-ik/ adj. consisting of two atoms.

**diatonic** /ˌduy-uh-**ton**-ik/ adj. *Mus.* (of a scale, interval, etc.) involving only notes belonging to the prevailing key without chromatic variation. [Greek: related to TONIC]

**diatribe** /**duy**-uh-ˌtruyb/ n. forceful verbal attack or criticism; invective. [Greek *tribō* rub]

**diazepam** /duy-**az**-uh-ˌpam/ n. a tranquillising drug. [benzo *diaze*pine + *am*]

**dibbler** /**dib**-luh/ n. small, spotted, Australian marsupial mouse, once numerous in the extreme south-west but now almost extinct. [dialect of Nyungar, probably *dibala*]

**dibs** n.pl. colloq. **1** marbles. **2** money (*he's in the dibs*). □ **lose one's dibs** lose one's marbles, i.e. the use of one's sanity. **play for dibs** play for keeps. [earlier sense 'pebbles (for a game)', also *dib-stones*]

**dice** — n.pl. **1 a** small cubes with faces bearing 1–6 spots, used in games or gambling. **b** (treated as *sing.*) one of these cubes (see DIE[2]). **2** game played with dice. — v. (**-cing**) **1** take great risks, gamble (*dicing with death*). **2** cut (food) into small cubes. **3** colloq. reject; leave alone; abandon (*she's diced me*). □ **no dice** colloq. no success or prospect of it. [pl. of DIE[2]]

■ **Usage** See note at DIE[2].

**dicey** adj. (**dicier, diciest**) colloq. risky, unreliable.

**dichotomy** /duy-**kot**-uh-mee/ n. (pl. -ies) division into two (esp. sharply defined) parts or kinds. [Greek *dikho-* apart: related to TOME]

■ **Usage** The use of *dichotomy* to mean *dilemma* or *ambivalence* is considered incorrect in standard English.

**dick[1]** colloq. n. **1** (in certain set phrases) person (*clever dick*). **2** penis. **3** = DICKHEAD. □ **have had the dick** be finished; be irreparably damaged. [*Dick*, pet form of *Richard*]

**dick[2]** n. colloq. detective. [perhaps an abbreviation]

**dicken** /**dik**-uhn/ int. colloq. expression of disgust or disbelief. [variant of DICKENS]

**dickens** /**dik**-uhnz/ n. (usu. prec. by *how, what, why*, etc., *the*) colloq. (esp. in exclamations) deuce; the Devil (*what the dickens is it?*). [probably the name *Dickens*]

**Dickensian** /duh-**ken**-zee-uhn/ adj. **1** of the 19th-c. novelist Dickens or his work. **2** resembling situations in Dickens's work, esp. poverty.

**dickhead** n. coarse colloq. idiot, fool. [from DICK[1] sense 2]

**dicky** /**dik**-ee/ adj. (-ier, -iest) colloq. **1** unsound; unhealthy (*has a dicky heart*). **2** difficult; awkward; tricky (*this leaves us in a dicky situation*). [*Dicky*, pet form of *Richard*]

**dicotyledon** /ˌduy-kot-uh-**lee**-duhn/ n. flowering plant having two cotyledons. □ **dicotyledonous** adj.

**dicta** pl. of DICTUM.

**dictaphone** /**dik**-tuh-ˌfohn/ n. *propr.* machine for recording and playing back dictated words. [from DICTATE, PHONE]

**dictate** — v. /dik-**tayt**/ (**-ting**) **1** say or read aloud (material to be written down or recorded). **2** state or order authoritatively or peremptorily. — n. /**dik**-tayt/ (usu. in *pl.*) authoritative instruction or requirement (*dictates of conscience; dictates of fashion*). □ **dictation** /dik-**tay**-shuhn/ n. [Latin *dicto* from *dico* say]

**dictator** /dik-**tay**-tuh/ n. **1** usu. unelected ruler with unrestricted power. **2** omnipotent person in any sphere. **3** domineering person. **4** (in ancient Rome) chief magistrate with absolute power, appointed in an emergency. [Latin: related to DICTATE]

**dictatorial** /ˌdik-tuh-**taw**-ree-uhl/ adj. **1** of or like a dictator. **2** overbearing. □ **dictatorially** adv. [Latin: related to DICTATOR]

**dictatorship** n. **1** nation ruled by a dictator. **2** rule etc. by a dictator. **3** absolute authority in any sphere.

**diction** /**dik**-shuhn/ n. **1** manner of enunciation in speaking or singing. **2** choice of words or phrases in speech or writing. [Latin *dictio* from *dico dict-* say]

**dictionary** /**dik**-shuh-nuh-ree, -shuhn-ree/ n. (pl. **-ies**) **1** book that lists (usu. alphabetically) and explains the words of a language or gives corresponding words in another language. **2** reference book on any subject, the items of which are arranged in alphabetical order. [medieval Latin: related to DICTION]

**dictum** /**dik**-tuhm/ n. (pl. **dicta** or **-s**) **1** formal expression of opinion. **2** a saying or maxim. [Latin, neuter past part. of *dico* say]

**did** past of DO[1].

**didactic** /duy-**dak**-tik, duh-/ adj. **1** meant to instruct. **2** (of a person) tediously pedantic. □ **didactically** adv. **didacticism** /-tuh-ˌsiz-uhm/ n. [Greek *didaskō* teach]

**diddle** /**did**-uhl/ v. (**-ling**) colloq. swindle. [probably from *Diddler*, name of a character in a 19th-c. play]

**didgeridoo** /ˌdij-uh-ree-**doo**/ n. long, wooden, tubular Aboriginal wind instrument that produces a low-pitched, resonant sound with complex, rhythmic patterns but little tonal variation. [although it has been suggested that this must be a borrowing from an Australian language, it is not: the name probably evolved from white people's *ad hoc* imitation of the sound of the instrument]

**didn't** /**did**-uhnt/ contr. did not.

**die**[1] /duy/ v. (**dies, died, dying** /**duy**-ing/) **1** cease to live; expire (*many died of hunger; the plant has died*). **2 a** come to an end, fade away (*his interest died; the*

recipe for peanut wine has died with him). **b** cease to function (*the engine died*). **c** (of a flame) go out (*has the fire died?*). **3** (foll. by on) die or cease to function while in the presence or charge of (a person) (*she died on me; the drier's died on me*). **4** (usu. foll. by of, from, with) be exhausted or tormented (*nearly died of boredom; am dying from this heat*). **5** suffer (a specified death) (*died a natural death*). **6** experience an extreme of embarrassment, mortification, etc. (*I nearly died when he pointed to me in the audience and asked me to sing*). □ **be dying** (foll. by for, or to + infin.) wish for longingly or intently (*was dying for a drink*). **die away** fade to the point of extinction. **die back** (of a plant) decay from the tip towards the root. **die down** become fainter or weaker. **die hard** die reluctantly (*old habits die hard*). **die off** die one after another. **die out** become extinct, cease to exist. [Old Norse]

**die**[2] /duy/ n. **1** = DICE 1b. **2** (pl. **dies**) **a** engraved device for stamping coins, medals, etc. **b** device for stamping, cutting, or moulding material. □ **the die is cast** an irrevocable step has been taken. [Latin *datum* from *do* give]

■ **Usage** *Dice*, rather than *die*, is now the standard singular as well as plural form in the games sense (*one dice, two dice*).

**die-back** n. plant disease involving progressive decay from the leaf-tips down to the roots.

**die-casting** n. process or product of casting from metal moulds.

**diehard** n. conservative or stubborn person.

**dielectric** /ˌduy-uh-**lek**-trik/ — adj. not conducting electricity. — n. dielectric substance.

**dieresis** var. of DIAERESIS.

**diesel** /**dee**-zuhl/ n. **1** (in full **diesel engine**) internal-combustion engine in which heat produced by the compression of air in the cylinder ignites the fuel. **2** vehicle driven by a diesel engine. **3** fuel for a diesel engine. [R. *Diesel*, German engineer (d. 1913)]

**diesel oil** n. heavy petroleum fraction used in diesel engines.

**Dies irae** /ˌdee-ez **ee**-ray/ n. Latin SEQUENCE sung in a solemn Mass for the dead, the melody of which had often been used by composers to evoke desolation etc. in their works. [Latin (the hymn's first words), = day of wrath (i.e. the Day of Judgment)]

**diet**[1] /**duy**-uht/ — n. **1** range of foods

habitually eaten by a person or animal. **2** special course of food to which a person is restricted, esp. for medical reasons or to control weight. **3** thing regularly offered (*diet of half-truths*). — *v.* (**-t-**) restrict oneself to a special diet, esp. to slim. □ **dietary** *adj.* **dieter** *n.* [Greek *diaita* way of life]

**diet²** /**duy**-uht/ *n.* legislative assembly in certain countries. [Latin *dieta*]

**dietary fibre** *n.* (also **fibre**) food material such as bran and cellulose that is not broken down by the process of digestion; roughage.

**dietetic** /ˌduy-uh-**tet**-ik/ *adj.* of diet and nutrition. [Greek: related to DIET¹]

**dietetics** *n.pl.* (usu. treated as *sing.*) the study of diet and nutrition.

**dietitian** /ˌduy-uh-**tish**-uhn/ *n.* (also **dietician**) expert in dietetics.

**dif-** *prefix* = DIS-.

**diff** *n. colloq.* **1** = DIFFERENCE (*what's the diff?*). **2** = DIFFERENTIAL GEAR. [abbreviation]

**differ** *v.* **1** (often foll. by *from*) be unlike or distinguishable. **2** (often foll. by *with*) disagree (*I beg to differ; I differ with you on the need for cutting expenses*). [Latin *differo, dilat-* bring apart]

**difference** /**dif**-ruhns/ *n.* **1** state or condition of being different or unlike. **2** point in which things differ; distinction (*the difference between Marxism and socialism*). **3** degree of this (*there's a world of difference between life in the city and life in the bush*). **4 a** quantity by which amounts differ (*will have to make up the difference*). **b** remainder left after subtraction. **5 a** disagreement, dispute. **b** grounds of disagreement (*put aside their differences*). **make a** (or **all the, no,** etc.) **difference** have a significant (or a very significant, or no) effect. **with a difference** having a new or unusual feature.

**different** *adj.* **1** (often foll. by *from* or *to*) unlike, of another nature (*your conclusion is quite different from mine*). **2** distinct, separate (*a different issue altogether*). **3** unusual (*I must say this music's certainly different*). □ **differently** *adv.*

■ **Usage** In sense 1, *different from* is more widely acceptable than *different to*, which is common in less formal use.

**differential** /ˌdif-uh-**ren**-shuhl/ — *adj.* **1 a** of, exhibiting, or depending on a difference. **b** varying according to circumstances. **2** *Math.* relating to infinitesimal differences. **3** constituting a specific difference; distinctive; relating to specific differences (*differential diagnosis*). **4** *Physics & Mech.* concerning the difference of two or more motions, pressures, etc. — *n.* **1** difference between things of the same kind. **2** difference in wages between industries or categories of employees in the same industry (*wage differential*). **3** *Math.* **a** infinitesimal difference between successive values of a variable. **b** function expressing this as a rate of change with respect to another variable. **4** = DIFFERENTIAL GEAR.

**differential calculus** *n. Math.* method of calculating rates of change, maximum or minimum values, etc.

**differential equation** *n. Math.* equation involving differentials among its quantities.

**differential gear** *n.* gear enabling a vehicle's rear wheels to revolve at different speeds in cornering.

**differentiate** /ˌdif-uh-**ren**-shee-ˌayt/ *v.* (**-ting**) **1** constitute a difference between or in (*its strong perfume differentiates the scented sun orchid from other Australian sun orchids*). **2** recognise as different; distinguish (*can you differentiate between irony and sarcasm?*). **3** (of species, word-forms, etc.) make or become different in the process of growth or development. **4** *Math.* calculate the derivative of. □ **differentiation** /-ˌay-shuhn/ *n.*

**difficult** /**dif**-uh-kuhlt/ *adj.* **1 a** needing much effort or skill (*a difficult essay to write*). **b** troublesome, perplexing (*a difficult position to be in*). **2** (of a person) demanding; not easy to please; uncooperative. **3** characterised by hardship or problems (*a difficult period of his life*).

**difficulty** *n.* (*pl.* **-ies**) **1** state or condition of being difficult. **2 a** difficult thing, problem, hindrance. **b** (often in *pl.*) distress, esp. financial (*in difficulties*). [Latin *difficultas*: related to FACULTY]

**diffident** /**dif**-uh-duhnt/ *adj.* shy, lacking self-confidence; excessively reticent. □ **diffidence** *n.* **diffidently** *adv.* [Latin *diffido* distrust]

**diffract** /duh-**frakt**/ *v.* break up (a beam of light) into a series of dark and light bands or coloured spectra, or (a beam of radiation or particles) into a series of high and low intensities. □ **diffraction** *n.* **diffractive** *adj.* [Latin *diffringo*: related to FRACTION]

**diffuse** — *adj.* /duh-**fyoos**/ **1** (of light inflammation, etc.) spread out, not concentrated. **2** (of prose, speech, etc.) not concise, wordy. — *v.* /duh-**fyooz**/ (**-sing 1** disperse or spread widely. **2** *Physics* (esp. of fluids) intermingle by diffusion

□ **diffusible** /duh-**fyooz**-uh-buhl/ *adj.*
**diffusive** /duh-**fyoo**-siv/ *adj.* [Latin: related to FOUND³]

**diffusion** /dif-**fyoo**-*zh*uhn/ *n.* **1** act or instance of diffusing or process of being diffused. **2** *Physics & Chem.* interpenetration of substances by natural movement of their particles. [Latin: related to DIFFUSE]

**dig** — *v.* (-**gg**-; *past* and *past part.* **dug**) **1** (also *absol.*) break up and remove or turn over (ground etc.). **2** (foll. by *up*) break up the soil of (fallow land). **3** make (a hole, tunnel, etc.) by digging. **4** (often foll. by *up, out*) **a** obtain by digging (*digging up potatoes*; *dug up an Aboriginal artefact*). **b** (foll. by *up, out*) find or discover (*managed to dig up some interesting facts*). **c** (foll. by *into*) search for information in (a book etc.). **5** (also *absol.*) excavate (an archaeological site). **6** *colloq.* **a** like (*she really digs sci-fi*). **b** understand (*I didn't dig a single word*). **c** look at; take notice of (*dig that guy with the tattoos on his nose!*). **7** (foll. by *in, into*) **a** thrust (a sharp object) (*carelessly dug the awl into his hand*). **b** eat (*dig into this while it's hot*). **c** (often foll. by *in*) prod or nudge (*stop digging me*; *dug him in the ribs*). **8** (foll. by *into, through, under*) make one's way by digging. — *n.* **1** piece of digging. **2** thrust or poke (*a dig in the ribs*). **3** *colloq.* pointed or critical remark (*had a dig at him about his body odour*). **4** archaeological excavation. **5** (in *pl.*) *colloq.* lodgings. **6** = DIGGER 3b. □ **dig one's heels in** be obstinate. **dig in 1** firmly establish one's position. **2** *Mil.* prepare a defensive trench or pit. **3** *Cricket* consolidate one's position in batting. **4** *colloq.* begin eating etc. [Old English]

**digest** — *v.* /duy-**jest**/ **1** assimilate (food) in the stomach and bowels. **2** understand and assimilate mentally. **3** reduce to a systematic or convenient form; summarise. — *n.* /**duy**-jest/ **1** periodical synopsis of current literature or news. **2** methodical summary, esp. of laws. □ **digestible** *adj.* [Latin *digero -gest-*]

**digestion** /duy-**jes**-chuhn, duh-/ *n.* **1** process of digesting. **2** capacity to digest food (*has a weak digestion*).

**digestive** — *adj.* of or aiding digestion. — *n.* substance aiding digestion.

**digger** *n.* **1** person or machine that digs, esp. a mechanical excavator. **2** miner, esp. a gold-digger of the Australian goldfields. **3 a** soldier (esp. a private) from Australia or New Zealand (increasingly, an Australian soldier exclusively). **b** (also **dig**) (as a form of address, orig.

to a fellow-soldier, later also more generally) mate, fellow.

**digger's delight** *n.* species of speedwell, so called from the supposition that the plant grows only on gold-bearing soil.

**digger's hat** *n.* felt slouch hat worn as part of the Australian soldier's uniform.

**diggings** *n.pl.* **1** (also **diggins**) Australian goldfield. **2** a mine. **3** material dug out of a mine etc.

**digging-stick** *n.* = YAM-STICK.

**diggins** var. of DIGGINGS 1.

**digit** /**dij**-uht/ *n.* **1** any numeral from 0 to 9. **2** finger or toe. [Latin, = finger, toe]

**digital** /**dij**-uh-tuhl/ *adj.* **1** of or using digits. **2** (of a clock, watch, etc.) giving a reading by displayed digits. **3** (of a computer) operating on data represented by a series of usu. binary digits. **4** (of a recording) with sound-information represented by digits for more reliable transmission. □ **digitally** *adv.* [Latin: related to DIGIT]

**digital audio tape** *n.* magnetic tape on which sound is recorded digitally.

**digitalis** /‚dij-uh-**tay**-luhs, -**tah**-luhs/ *n.* drug prepared from foxgloves, used to stimulate the heart. [related to DIGIT, from the form of the flowers]

**digital to analog converter** *n.* *Computing* device for converting digital values to analog form.

**digitise** *v.* (also **-ize**) (**-sing** or **-zing**) convert (data etc.) into digital form, esp. for processing by a computer. □ **digitisation** /-zay-shuhn/ *n.* **digitiser** *n.*

**dignified** /**dig**-nuh-‚fuyd/ *adj.* having or showing dignity; noble or stately in appearance or manner.

**dignify** /**dig**-nuh-‚fuy/ *v.* (**-ies, -ied**) **1** confer dignity on; ennoble. **2** give a fine name to (*dignified the house with the name of mansion*). [Latin *dignus* worthy]

**dignitary** /**dig**-nuh-tuh-ree, -tree/ *n.* (*pl.* **-ies**) person of high rank or office. [from DIGNITY]

**dignity** /**dig**-nuh-tee/ *n.* (*pl.* **-ies**) **1** composed and serious manner. **2** worthiness, nobleness (*dignity of work*). **3** high rank or position. □ **beneath one's dignity** not worthy enough for one (*it's beneath my dignity to respond to such insults*). **stand on one's dignity** insist on being treated with respect. [Latin *dignus* worthy]

**digraph** /**duy**-grahf, -graf/ *n.* two letters representing one sound, e.g. *ph*, *ey* as in *ph*one, k*ey*. [from DI-¹, -GRAPH]

■ **Usage** *Digraph* is sometimes confused with *ligature*, which means two or more letters joined together.

**digress** /duy-**gres**/ v. depart from the main subject in speech or writing. □ **digression** n. [Latin *digredior -gress-*]

**digs** see DIG n. 5.

**dike**[1] var. of DYKE[1].

**dike**[2] var. of DYKE[2].

**diktat** /**dik**-tat/ n. categorical statement or decree. [German, = DICTATE]

**dilapidated** /duh-**lap**-uh-,day-tuhd/ adj. in disrepair or ruin. □ **dilapidation** n. /duh-,lap-uh-**day**-shuhn/ n. [Latin: related to DI-[2], *lapis* stone]

**dilatation** /,duy-luh-**tay**-shuhn/ n. 1 dilating of the cervix, e.g. for surgical curettage. 2 dilation. [from DILATE]

**dilate** /duy-**layt**/ v. (**-ting**) 1 make or become wider or larger (*the pupils of his eyes are dilated*). 2 (often foll. by *on, upon*) speak or write at length (*dilating on the virtues of vegetarianism*). □ **dilation** n. [Latin *latus* wide]

**dilatory** /**dil**-uh-tuh-ree, -tree/ adj. given to or causing delay. [Latin *dilatorius*: related to DIFFER]

**dildo** /**dil**-doh/ n. (pl. **-s**) artificial erect penis for sexual stimulation. [origin unknown]

**dilemma** /duh-**lem**-uh, duy-/ n. 1 situation in which a choice has to be made between two equally undesirable alternatives. 2 difficult situation, predicament. [Greek *lēmma* premise]

■ **Usage** The use of *dilemma* in sense 2 is considered incorrect by some people.

**dilettante** /,dil-uh-**tan**-tee/ — n. (pl. **dilettanti** /-tee/ or **-s**) 1 person who studies a subject or area of knowledge superficially; dabbler. 2 person who enjoys the arts. — adj. trifling, not thorough; amateurish. □ **dilettantism** n. [Italian *dilettare* DELIGHT]

**diligent** /**dil**-uh-juhnt/ adj. 1 hardworking. 2 showing care and effort. □ **diligence** n. **diligently** adv. [French from Latin *diligo* love]

**dill**[1] n. herb with aromatic leaves and seeds. [Old English]

**dill**[2] n. colloq. fool, simpleton. [from DILLY[1]]

**dillon bush** /**dil**-uhn/ n. salt-tolerant plant of all mainland States but not the NT, a rigid spreading shrub bearing edible fruits. [Wemba-wemba *dilany*]

**dillwynia** /dil-**win**-ee-uh/ n. (also **bacon-and-eggs** for the red-and-yellow species) any of 20 or more species of the Australian genus of the same name, bearing yellow or red-and-yellow pea-flowers in profusion. [L.W. *Dillwyn*, English botanist (d. 1853)]

**dilly**[1] /**dil**-ee/ adj. colloq. 1 odd or eccentric. 2 foolish, stupid; mad. [British dial.]

**dilly**[2] colloq. — adj. remarkable or excellent. — n. remarkable or excellent person or thing (*that's a dilly*). [from *delightful* or *delicious*]

**dillybag** n. (formerly **dilly**) 1 Aboriginal bag or basket made from woven vine, grass, or fibre. 2 bag of any sort, usu. small, and usu. for carrying provisions etc. [Yagara *dili* coarse grass or reeds; a bag woven of this]

**dilly-dally** /,dil-ee-**dal**-ee/ v. (**-ies, -ied**) colloq. 1 dawdle, loiter. 2 vacillate. [reduplication of DALLY]

**dilute** /duy-**lyoot**, -**loot**/ — v. (**-ting**) 1 reduce the strength of (a fluid) by adding water etc. 2 weaken or reduce in effect. — adj. (also /**duy**-/) (esp. of a fluid) diluted, weakened. □ **dilution** n. [Latin *diluo -lut-* wash away]

**diluvial** /duy-**loo**-vee-uhl, duh-/ adj. of a flood, esp. of the Flood in Genesis. [Latin: related to DELUGE]

**dim** — adj. (**dimmer, dimmest**) 1 a only faintly luminous or visible; not bright (*the light's very dim; dim hallway*). b obscure; indistinct (*dim shapes in the mist*). 2 not clearly perceived or remembered (*only a dim recollection of what happened*). 3 colloq. stupid (*he's utterly dim*). 4 (of the eyes) not seeing clearly. — v. (**-mm-**) make or become dim. □ **take a dim view of** colloq. disapprove of. □ **dimly** adv. **dimness** n. [Old English]

**dim.** abbr. diminuendo.

**dime** n. US ten-cent coin. □ **dime-a-dozen** very cheap or commonplace. [Latin *decima* tenth (part)]

**dimension** /duh-**men**-shuhn/ — n. 1 measurable extent, as length, breadth, depth, etc. 2 (in pl.) size (*of huge dimensions*). 3 aspect, facet (*gained a new dimension*). — v. (usu. as **dimensioned** adj.) mark dimensions on (a diagram etc.). □ **dimensional** adj. [Latin *metior mens-* measure]

**diminish** /duh-**min**-ish/ v. 1 make or become smaller or less. 2 (often as **diminished** adj.) lessen the reputation or influence of (a person). □ **law of diminishing returns** fact that expenditure etc. beyond a certain point ceases to produce a proportionate yield. [Latin: related to MINUTE[1]]

**diminished** adj. 1 reduced; made smaller or less. 2 *Mus.* (of an interval, usu. a seventh or a fifth) less by a semitone than the corresponding minor or perfect interval.

**diminished responsibility** n. Law limitation of criminal responsibility on the ground of mental weakness or abnormality.

**diminuendo** /duh-ˌmin-yoo-**en**-doh/ Mus. — n. (pl **-s**) gradual decrease in loudness. — adv. & adj. decreasing in loudness. [Italian: related to DIMINISH]

**diminution** /ˌdim-uh-**nyoo**-shuhn/ n. **1** diminishing or being diminished. **2** decrease. [Latin: related to DIMINISH]

**diminutive** /duh-**min**-yuh-tiv/ — adj. **1** tiny. **2** (of a word or suffix) implying smallness, affection, etc. (e.g. -let in 'streamlet', -kins in 'How's my Johnny-kins?'; also -y, -ie, etc., in such words as Bluey (for a red-head), matey, footy, tinnie, etc.). — n. diminutive word or suffix.

**dimmer** n. (in full **dimmer switch**) device for varying the brightness of an electric light.

**dimorphic** /duy-**maw**-fik/ adj. (also **dimorphous** /-**maw**-fuhs/) Biol., Chem., & Mineral. exhibiting, or occurring in, two distinct forms. □ **dimorphism** n. [DI-¹, Greek morphē form]

**dimple** /**dim**-puhl/ — n. small hollow, esp. in the cheek or chin. — v. (**-ling**) form dimples (in). □ **dimply** adj. [probably Old English]

**dim sum** /dim sum/ n. (also **dim sim**) **1** meal or course of savoury Cantonese-style snacks. **2** (now usu. **dim sim**) small roll of seasoned meat etc. wrapped in thin dough and steamed or fried. [Cantonese dim-sām, literally 'dot of the heart']

**dimwit** n. colloq. stupid person. □ **dimwitted** adj.

**DIN** n. any of a series of technical standards originating in Germany and used internationally, esp. to designate electrical connections, film speeds, and paper sizes. [German, from Deutsche Industrie-Norm]

**din** — n. prolonged loud confused noise. — v. (**-nn-**) **1** (foll. by into) force (information) into a person by constant repetition. **2** make a din. [Old English]

**dine** v. (**-ning**) **1 a** eat the main meal of the day, the evening meal; have dinner. **b** (foll. by on, upon) eat for dinner (dined on barramundi). **2** (esp. in phr. wine and dine) entertain with food. □ **dine out** dine away from home. [French diner as DIS-, Latin jejunus fasting]

**diner** n. **1** person who dines. **2** dining-car. **3** small restaurant.

**ding¹** — v. make a ringing sound. — n. ringing sound. [imitative]

**ding²** n. colloq. party or celebration, esp. a wild one. [perhaps from DING-DONG]

**ding³** colloq. — n. **1** minor collision of motor vehicles etc. **2** dent (in a surfboard, motor vehicle, etc.). — v. damage; smash (dinged the car). [imitative]

**dingbat** n. colloq. **1** stupid or eccentric person. **2** (in pl.) **a** madness. **b** discomfort, unease. □ **be** (or **have the**) **dingbats** be mad, stupid, eccentric, etc. **give a person the dingbats** inflict a feeling of discomfort or irritation upon (your singing is giving me the dingbats). [perhaps from ding to beat, BAT¹]

**ding-dong** — n. **1** sound of two chimes, esp. as a doorbell. **2** colloq. heated argument or fight (had a ding-dong with his wife). — adj. (of a contest etc.) evenly matched and intensely waged (it was a ding-dong battle all the way). [imitative]

**dinge** /dinj/ n. = DING³ n. 2

**dinghy** /**ding**-gee/ n. (pl. **-ies**) **1** small boat carried by a ship. **2** small pleasure-boat. **3** small inflatable rubber boat. [Hindi, originally a rowing-boat used on Indian rivers]

**dingo** /**ding**-goh/ — n. (pl. **-es**) **1** (also **warrigal**) wolf-like native dog, Canis familiaris dingo of mainland Australia, typically tawny yellow, apparently introduced by the Aborigines. **2** person who displays characteristics popularly attributed to the dingo, esp. cowardice and treachery. — v. behave in a cowardly manner. □ **dingo it** act the coward; back away (he didn't dingo it but stood and fought). **dingo on a person** betray, let down him or her. [Dharuk din-gu or dayn-gu domesticated dingo]

**dingy** /**din**-jee/ adj. (**-ier**, **-iest**) dirty-looking, drab. □ **dingily** adv. **dinginess** n. [origin uncertain; perhaps ultimately from Old English dynge DUNG]

**dink¹** /dingk/ colloq. (also **double dink**) — n. a lift on a bicycle etc. ridden by another. — v. carry (a passenger) on a bicycle etc. (he dinked me to school). [origin uncertain]

**dink²** abbr. (also **dinks**) = DINKUM (find out if he's dink or not; fair dinks).

**dink³** n. colloq. either partner of a career couple with no children, both of whom work and who are therefore viewed as affluent consumers. [double (or dual) income, no kids]

**dinkum** /**ding**-kuhm/ colloq. — n. **1** obsolete work, labour. **2** hist. member of the 2nd Division of the Australian Imperial Forces in the war of 1914–18. — adj. reliable, genuine, honest, true (if you're dinkum, I'll help you; the kangaroo is a dinkum Aussie; dinkum digger). — adv. really, truly; really?, truly? (it's dinkum good stuff, goanna oil is; It *was truly like that? — Yes, dinkum!; 'He wanted one that would bend.' — 'Dinkum?' the clerk asked. — 'My oath!' — 'Kinky!' said the clerk.*). □ **dinkum oil** the honest truth (*what's the dinkum oil on this banana business?*). **fair dinkum** (frequently as *int.*) **1** fair play (*let's have fair dinkum here*). **2** genuine(ly), honest(ly), true, truly (*he's a fair dinkum bushie; It's god's own truth. — Fair dinkum? — Fair dinkum!*). [origin unknown]

**dinky-di** /ding-kee-duy/ *adj., adv., & int.* (also **dinkie-di, dinky-die**) = DINKUM in all senses (*a dinky-di Aussie; dinky-di, I kid you not; dinky-di?* etc.).

**dinner** *n.* **1** main meal of the day, either at midday, or esp., in the evening. **2** meal eaten at midday, but not the principal meal of the day; lunch. **3** (in full **dinner party**) formal evening meal, esp. with guests. □ **do like a dinner** *colloq.* defeat; outwit (*our team was done like a dinner*). [French: related to DINE]

**dinner-camp** — *n.* (in stock droving) **1** mid-day break. **2** place where such a break is taken. — *v.* break for dinner at mid-day (*dinner-camped beside the billabong*).

**dinnyhaser** /din-ee-hay-zuh/ *n.* **1** knockout-blow. **2** (figurative) (*a dinnyhaser of a storm; party was a dinnyhaser*). [origin unknown]

**dinosaur** /duy-nuh-ˌsaw/ *n.* **1** extinct, often enormous, reptile of the Mesozoic era. **2** unwieldy system or organisation, esp. one not adapting to new conditions. [Greek *deinos* terrible, SAURIAN]

**dint** — *n.* dent. — *v.* mark with dints. □ **by dint of** by force or means of. [Old English and Old Norse]

**diocese** /duy-uh-suhs/ *n.* district under the pastoral care of a bishop. □ **diocesan** /duy-os-uh-suhn/ *adj.* [Greek *dioikēsis* administration]

**diode** /duy-ohd/ *n.* **1** semiconductor allowing the flow of current in one direction only and having two terminals. **2** thermionic valve having two electrodes. [from DI-¹, ELECTRODE]

**dioecious** /duy-ee-shuhs/ *adj. Bot.* having male and female organs on separate plants. [DI-¹, Greek *-oikos* -housed]

**Dionysian** /ˌduy-uh-nis-ee-uhn, -niz-/ *adj.* (also **Dionysiac**) wildly sensual; unrestrained. [Greek *Dionusos* god of wine]

**dioptre** /duy-op-tuh/ *n.* unit of refractive power of a lens. [Greek: related to DIA-, *opsis* sight]

**diorama** /ˌduy-uh-rah-muh/ *n.* **1** scenic painting lit to simulate sunrise etc. **2** small scene with three-dimensional figures, viewed through a window etc. **3** small-scale model or film-set. [from DIA-, Greek *horaō* see]

**dioxide** /duy-ok-suyd/ *n.* oxide containing two atoms of oxygen which are not linked together (*carbon dioxide*).

**dioxin** /duy-ok-suhn/ *n.* any of several chemical compounds, derivatives of which are used in herbicides.

**dip** — *v.* (**-pp-**) **1** put or lower briefly into liquid etc.; immerse (*don't dip your biscuit in your coffee*). **2 a** go below a surface or level (*the sun dipped below the horizon*). **b** (of income, activity, etc.) decline slightly, esp. briefly (*profits dipped in May*). **3** slope or extend downwards (*road dips*). **4** go under water and emerge quickly. **5** (foll. by *into*) look cursorily into (a book, subject, etc.). **6 a** (foll. by *into*) put a hand, ladle, etc., into (a container) to take something out (*she dipped into her handbag for a tissue*). **b** use part of (one's resources) (*dipped into our savings*). **7** lower or be lowered, esp. in salute (*dipped the flag*). **8** lower the beam of (headlights) to reduce dazzle. **9** colour (a fabric) by immersing it in dye. **10** wash (sheep) by immersion in a vermin-killing liquid. — *n.* **1** act of dipping or being dipped. **2** liquid for dipping (*sheep dip*). **3** brief bathe in the sea etc. **4** downward slope or hollow in a road, skyline, etc. **5** sauce or semi-liquid savoury mixture into which food is dipped before being eaten. **6** *Astron. & Surveying* apparent depression of the horizon from the line of observation, due to the curvature of the earth. **7** *Physics* angle made with the horizontal at any point by the earth's magnetic field. **8** *Geol.* angle a stratum makes with the horizon. □ **dip one's lid** (now chiefly figurative) raise one's hat as a mark of respect. **dip out** (**on**) *colloq.* fail; miss an opportunity. [Old English]

**diphtheria** /dif-theer-ree-uh/ *n.* acute infectious bacterial disease with inflammation of a mucous membrane esp. of the throat. [Greek *diphthera* skin, hide]

■ **Usage** The pronunciation /dip-theer-ree-uh/ is sometimes heard, but is considered incorrect.

**diphthong** /dif-thong/ *n.* **1** speech sound in one syllable in which the articulation begins as for one vowel and moves as for another (e.g. the glide from *o* to *i* in coin, *o* to *u* in loud, *o* to *y* in toy). **2 a** a digraph representing the sound of a diphthong or single vowel (e.g. *ea* in *feat*). **b** a compound vowel character; a ligature (as æ). □ **diphthongal** /-**thong**-guhl/ *adj.* [DI-¹, Greek *phthoggos* voice]

**diplodocus** /dip-**lod**-uh-kuhs, ˌdip-loh-**doh**-kuhs/ *n.* (*pl.* **-cuses**) giant plant-eating dinosaur with a long neck and tail. [Greek *diplous* double, *dokos* wooden beam]

**diploid** /**dip**-loyd/ *Biol.* — *adj.* (of an organism or cell) having two complete sets of chromosomes per cell. — *n.* diploid cell or organism. [Greek *diplous* double, -OID]

**diploma** /duh-**ploh**-muh/ *n.* **1** certificate of qualification awarded by a college etc. **2** document conferring an honour or privilege. [Greek, = folded paper, from *diplous* double]

**diplomacy** /duh-**ploh**-muh-see/ *n.* **1 a** management of international relations. **b** skill in this. **2** adroitness in personal relationships; tact. [French: related to DIPLOMATIC]

**diplomat** /**dip**-luh-ˌmat/ *n.* **1** official representing a country abroad; member of a diplomatic service. **2** tactful person.

**diplomatic** /ˌdip-luh-**mat**-ik/ *adj.* **1** of or involved in diplomacy. **2** tactful. □ **diplomatically** *adv.* [French: related to DIPLOMA]

**diplomatic corps** *n.* body of diplomats representing other countries at a seat of government.

**diplomatic immunity** *n.* exemption of diplomatic staff abroad from arrest, taxation, etc.

**diplomatic service** *n.* branch of the civil service concerned with the representation of a country abroad.

**diplomatist** /duh-**ploh**-muh-tuhst/ *n.* diplomat.

**dipole** /**duy**-pohl/ *n.* **1** *Physics* two equal and oppositely charged or magnetised poles separated by a distance. **2** *Chem.* molecule in which a concentration of positive charges is separated from a concentration of negative charges. **3** aerial consisting of a horizontal metal rod with a connecting wire at its core. □ **dipolar** /duy-**poh**-luh/ *adj.*

**dipper** *n.* ladle.

**dippy** /**dip**-ee/ *adj.* (**-ier**, **-iest**) *colloq.* crazy, silly. [origin uncertain]

**diprotodon** /duy-**proh**-tuh-don/ *n.* extinct, gigantic, herbivorous, quadruped marsupial of the Australian genus of the same name, having two prominent incisors in the lower jaw. [DI-¹, PROTO-, Greek *odous odont-* tooth]

**dipso** /**dip**-soh/ *n.* (*pl.* **-s**) *colloq.* alcoholic. [abbreviation]

**dipsomania** /ˌdip-suh-**may**-nee-uh/ *n.* alcoholism. □ **dipsomaniac** /-**may**-nee-ˌak/ *n.* [Greek *dipsa* thirst]

**dipstick** *n.* **1** rod for measuring the depth of esp. oil in a vehicle's engine. **2** *colloq.* fool; crazy or unliked person.

**dipterous** /**dip**-tuh-ruhs/ *adj.* **1** (of an insect) having two wings, e.g. the fly or mosquito. **2** *Bot.* having two winglike appendages. [DI-¹, Greek *pteron* wing]

**diptych** /**dip**-tik/ *n.* painting, esp. an altarpiece, on two hinged panels closing like a book. [Greek, = pair of writing-tablets, from *ptukhē* fold]

**dire** /duyuh/ *adj.* **1 a** calamitous, dreadful (*in dire straits*). **b** ominous (*dire warnings*). **c** (*predic.*) *colloq.* very bad (*this party is dire*). **2** urgent (*in dire need*). [Latin]

**direct** /duh-**rekt**, duy-/ — *adj.* **1** extending or moving in a straight line or by the shortest route; not crooked or circuitous. **2** straightforward; frank. **3** with nothing or no-one in between; personal (*direct line*). **4** (of descent) lineal, not collateral. **5** complete, greatest possible (*the direct opposite*). — *adv.* **1** in a direct way or manner (*dealt with them direct*). **2** by the direct route (*sent direct to Darwin*). — *v.* **1** control; govern or guide (*duty directs me*). **2** (foll. by *to* + infin., or *that* + clause) order (a person) to (*I direct you to do it; directed that it be done at once*). **3** (foll. by *to*) **a** address (a letter etc.). **b** tell or show (a person) the way to (a place). **4** (foll. by *at, to, towards*) point, aim, or turn (a blow, attention, or remark) (*are you directing that innuendo at me?*). **5** (also *absol.*) supervise the performing, staging, etc., of (a film, play, etc.). □ **directness** *n.* [Latin *dirigo* from *rego rect-* guide]

**direct access** *n.* facility of retrieving data immediately from any part of a computer file.

**direct action** *n.* action (such as a strike) directly affecting employers, a government, etc. and meant to reinforce demands made by a trade union or other large organised group.

**direct billing** *n.* system (put in place under MEDICARE) by which doctors choosing to do so invoice Medicare for the services they have given to patients instead of invoicing the patients themselves. □ **direct bill** *v.*

**direct current** *n.* electric current flowing in one direction only.

**direction** /duh-**rek**-shuhn, duy-/ *n.* **1** act or process of directing; supervision. **2** (usu. in *pl.*) order or instruction (*just follow the directions*). **3** line along which, or point to or from which, a person or thing moves or looks (*sailed in an easterly direction*). **4** tendency or scope of a theme, subject, or inquiry.

**directional** *adj.* **1** of or indicating direction. **2** *Electronics* **a** sending or receiving radio or sound waves in one particular direction. **b** (of equipment) designed to receive radio or sound waves from a particular direction or directions and not others.

**directive** /duy-**rek**-tiv, duh-/ — *n.* order from an authority. — *adj.* serving to direct.

**directly** — *adv.* **1 a** at once; without delay, immediately (*directly after lunch*). **b** presently, shortly (*be with you directly*). **2** exactly (*directly opposite*). **3** in a direct manner (*spoke very directly*). — *conj.* *colloq.* as soon as (*will tell you directly they come*).

**direct object** *n.* primary object of the action of a transitive verb (e.g. 'bone' in *gave the dog a bone*, 'the dog' being the indirect object of 'gave').

**director** *n.* **1** person who directs or controls, esp. a member of the board of a company. **2** person who directs a film, play, etc. □ **directorial** *adj.* **directorship** *n.*

**directory** /duh-**rek**-tuh-ree, duy-, -tree/ *n.* (*pl.* **-ies**) book with a list of telephone subscribers, inhabitants of a district, or members of a profession etc. [Latin: related to DIRECT]

**direct speech** *n.* words actually spoken, not reported.

**direct tax** *n.* tax that one pays directly to the government, esp. on income.

**dirge** *n.* **1** lament for the dead, esp. forming part of a funeral service. **2** any mournful song or lament. [Latin imperative *dirige* = direct, the first word in the Latin antiphon (from Psalm 5:8) in the Matins part of the Catholic Office for the Dead]

**dirigible** /di-rij-uh-buhl, duh-**rij**-/ — *adj.* capable of being guided. — *n.* dirigible balloon or airship. [related to DIRECT]

**dirk** *n.* short dagger. [origin unknown]

**dirt** *n.* **1** unclean matter that soils. **2 a** earth, soil. **b** earth, cinders, etc., used to make the surface for a road etc. (usu. *attrib.*: *dirt track*). **3** foul or malicious words or talk. **4** person or thing considered worthless. **5** excrement. □ **eat dirt** *colloq.* suffer insults etc. without retaliating. **treat like dirt** treat with contempt. [Old Norse *drit* excrement]

**dirt cheap** *adj.* & *adv. colloq.* extremely cheap.

**dirty** — *adj.* (**-ier**, **-iest**) **1** soiled, unclean. **2** causing dirtiness (*dirty job*). **3** sordid,

lewd, obscene. **4** unpleasant, dishonourable, unfair (*dirty trick*). **5** (of weather) rough, squally. **6** (of colour) muddied, dingy. **7** *colloq.* (of a nuclear weapon) producing considerable radioactive fallout. **8** *colloq.* resentful; angry. — *adv. colloq.* **1** very (*a dirty great diamond*). **2** in a dirty manner (*talk dirty*; *act dirty*) (esp. in senses 3 and 4 of *adj.*). — *v.* (**-ies**, **-ied**) make or become dirty. — *n. colloq.* **1** (in full **dirty weekend**) weekend etc. spent secretly with a lover. **2** = DIRTY DANCING. □ **dirty on** *colloq.* angry with; resentful of (*he's dirty on you for what you said*). **do the dirty on** *colloq.* play a mean trick on. □ **dirtily** *adv.* **dirtiness** *n.*

**dirty dancing** *n.* (also **dirty**) form of dancing to pop music with much suggestive body contact.

**dirty linen** *n.* (also **dirty washing**) *colloq.* intimate secrets, esp. of a scandalous nature.

**dirty look** *n. colloq.* look of disapproval or disgust.

**dirty word** *n.* **1** offensive or indecent word. **2** word for something disapproved of (*profit is a dirty word*).

**dirty work** *n.* dishonourable or illegal activity, esp. done clandestinely (*some dirty work going on*).

**dis-** *prefix* forming nouns, adjectives, and verbs implying: **1** negation or direct opposite (*dishonest*; *discourteous*). **2** reversal (*disengage*; *disorientate*). **3** removal of a thing or quality (*dismember*; *disable*). **4** separation (*distinguish*). **5** completeness or intensification (*disgruntled*). **6** expulsion from (*disaffiliate*). [French *des-* or Latin *dis-*]

**disability** /,dis-uh-**bil**-uh-tee/ *n.* (*pl.* **-ies**) **1** permanent physical or mental incapacity. **2** lack of some capacity etc., preventing action.

**disable** /dis-**ay**-buhl/ *v.* (**-ling**) **1** deprive of an ability or function. **2** (often as **disabled** *adj.*) physically incapacitate. □ **disablement** *n.*

**disablist** /dis-**ay**-bluhst/ — *adj.* showing discrimination or prejudice against disabled people. — *n.* person who shows such prejudice etc.

**disabuse** /,dis-uh-**byooz**/ *v.* (**-sing**) (usu. foll. by *of*) free from a mistaken idea etc. (*disabused him of his belief that he is God's gift to women*).

**disadvantage** /,dis-uhd-**vahn**-tij, -**van**-tij/ — *n.* **1** unfavourable circumstance or condition. **2** damage to one's interest or reputation. — *v.* (**-ging**) cause disadvantage to. □ **at a disadvantage** in an unfavourable position or aspect.

□ **disadvantageous** /dis-,ad-vuhn-**tay**-juhs/ *adj.*

**disadvantaged** *adj.* lacking normal opportunities through poverty, disability, etc.

**disaffected** /,dis-uh-**fek**-tuhd/ *adj.* discontented (esp. politically); no longer loyal or friendly. □ **disaffection** *n.*

**disaffiliate** /,dis-uh-**fil**-ee-,ayt/ *v.* **1 a** end the affiliation of (*the Perth branch was disaffiliated from the Society*). **b** end one's affiliation (*the Perth branch decided to disaffiliate*). **2** detach. □ **disaffiliation** /-ay-shuhn/ *n.*

**disagree** /,dis-uh-**gree**/ *v.* (**-ees**, **-eed**, **-eeing**) (often foll. by *with*) **1** hold a different opinion. **2** (of factors) not correspond. **3** quarrel. **4** upset (*onions disagree with me*). □ **disagreement** *n.*

**disagreeable** *adj.* **1** unpleasant, not to one's liking. **2** quarrelsome, rude, or bad-tempered. □ **disagreeably** *adv.*

**disallow** /,dis-uh-**low**/ *v.* refuse to allow or accept as valid; prohibit.

**disappear** /,dis-uh-**peer**/ *v.* **1** cease to be visible (*the ghost disappeared; my car-keys have disappeared again*). **2** cease to exist or be in circulation or use (*some Australian fauna and flora have become extinct: many have all but disappeared*). **3** (of a person) go missing. **4** *colloq.* leave. □ **disappearance** *n.*

**disappoint** /,dis-uh-**point**/ *v.* **1** fail to fulfil the desire or expectation of (a person) (*you have disappointed us greatly*). **2** frustrate (a hope etc.); cause the failure of (a plan etc.). □ **disappointed** *adj.* **disappointing** *adj.*

**disappointment** *n.* **1** person or thing that disappoints. **2** feeling of distress, vexation, etc., resulting from this (*I cannot hide my disappointment*).

**disapprobation** /dis-,ap-ruh-**bay**-shuhn/ *n. formal* disapproval.

**disapprove** /,dis-uh-**proov**/ *v.* (**-ving**) (usu. foll. by *of*) have or express an unfavourable opinion. □ **disapproval** *n.*

**disarm** /dis-**ahm**/ *v.* **1** take weapons etc. away from. **2** reduce or give up one's own weapons. **3** defuse (a bomb etc.). **4** make less angry, hostile, etc; charm, win over (*disarmed me with his smile*). □ **disarming** *adj.* (in sense 4). **disarmingly** *adv.*

**disarmament** /dis-**ahm**-uh-muhnt/ *n.* reduction by a nation of its military forces and weapons.

**disarray** /,dis-uh-**ray**/ — *n.* disorder. — *v.* throw into disorder.

**disassociate** /,dis-uh-**soh**-shee-,ayt, -see,ayt/ *v.* (**-ting**) = DISSOCIATE. □ **disassociation** /-ay-shuhn/ *n.*

**disaster** /duh-**zah**-stuh/ *n.* **1** great or sudden misfortune; catastrophe. **2** *colloq.* complete failure (*the negotiations were a disaster*). □ **disastrous** *adj.* **disastrously** *adv.* [DIS-, Latin *astrum* star]

**disavow** /,dis-uh-**vow**/ *v.* disclaim knowledge of or responsibility for. □ **disavowal** *n.*

**disband** /dis-**band**/ *v.* break up; disperse. □ **disbandment** *n.*

**disbelieve** /,dis-buh-**leev**/ *v.* (**-ving**) be unable or unwilling to believe; be sceptical. □ **disbelief** *n.* **disbelievingly** *adv.*

**disburse** /dis-**bers**/ *v.* (**-sing**) pay out (money). □ **disbursal** *n.* **disbursement** *n.* [Old French: related to DIS-, medieval Latin *bursa* purse]

**disc** *n.* (also **disk** in sense 4) **1 a** flat thin circular object. **b** round flat or apparently flat surface or mark (*disc of the sun*). **2** layer of cartilage between vertebrae. **3** gramophone record. **4** (usu. **disk**) **a** computer storage device in the form of one or more rotatable platters where data is stored, either magnetically or optically. **b** = FLOPPY *n.* [Latin DISCUS]

**discalced** /dis-**kalst**/ *adj.* (of a friar or nun) barefoot or wearing only sandals (*the Order of discalced Carmelites*). [DIS-, Latin *calceus* shoe]

**discard** — *v.* **1** reject as unwanted. **2** *Cards* remove or put aside (a card). — *n.* /**dis**-kahd/ discarded item or person. [from DIS-, CARD¹]

**disc brake** *n.* brake employing the friction of pads against a disc.

**discern** /duh-**sern**/ *v.* **1** perceive clearly with the mind or senses. **2** make out by thought or by gazing, listening, etc. □ **discernible** *adj.* [Latin *cerno cret-* separate]

**discerning** *adj.* having good judgment. □ **discerningly** *adv.* **discernment** *n.*

**discharge** — *v.* /dis-**chahj**/ (**-ging**) **1** release (a prisoner); allow (a patient, jury) to leave. **2** dismiss from office or employment. **3** fire (a gun etc.). **4** throw; eject (*discharged a stone at the cat*). **5** emit, pour out (pus etc.). **6** (foll. by *into*) (of a river etc.) flow into (esp. the sea). **7 a** carry out (a duty or obligation) (*discharged her responsibilities*). **b** relieve oneself of (a debt etc.). **c** relieve (a bankrupt) of residual liability. **8** *Law* cancel (an order of court). **9** release an electrical charge from (*discharge a battery*). **10 a** relieve (a ship etc.) of cargo. **b** unload (cargo). — *n.* /**dis**-chahj/ **1** act or instance of discharging or process of being discharged. **2** certificate of release, dismissal, etc. **3** matter discharged; pus etc. **4** act of firing a gun etc. **5** release of an electric charge, esp. with a spark.

**disciple** /duh-**suy**-puhl/ *n.* **1** follower of a leader, teacher, etc. **2** any early believer in Christ, esp. one of the twelve apostles. [Latin *disco* learn]

**disciplinarian** /,dis-uh-pluh-**nair**-ree-uhn/ *n.* enforcer of or believer in firm discipline.

**disciplinary** /**dis**-uh-pluh-nuh-ree, -pluh-ree/ *adj.* of or enforcing discipline.

**discipline** /**dis**-uh-pluhn/ — *n.* **1 a** control or order exercised over people or animals, e.g. over members of an organisation. **b** system of rules for this. **c** behaviour of groups subjected to such rules (*poor discipline in the ranks*). **2 a** mental, moral, or physical training. **b** adversity as used to bring about such training (*left the course because he couldn't take the discipline*). **3** branch of learning (*philosophy is a hard discipline*). **4** punishment. **5** *Eccl.* mortification by physical self-punishment. — *v.* (-**ning**) **1** punish. **2** control by training in obedience. □ **disciplinable** *adj.* **disciplinal** /,dis-uh-**pluy**-nuhl, **dis**-uh-pluh-nuhl/ *adj.* **discipliner** *n.* [Latin *disciplina* from *disco* learn]

**disc jockey** *n.* presenter of recorded pop music.

**disclaim** /dis-**klaym**/ *v.* **1** deny or disown (*disclaim all responsibility*). **2** renounce legal claim to.

**disclaimer** *n.* renunciation or disavowal; statement disclaiming something.

**disclose** /dis-**klohz**/ *v.* (-**sing**) **1** make known; reveal (*disclosed the truth*). **2** remove the cover from; expose to view (*removed the lid and disclosed the grisly contents*). □ **disclosure** *n.*

**disco** /**dis**-koh/ *colloq.* — *n.* (*pl.* -**s**) discothèque. — *v.* (-**es**, -**ed**) dance to disco music. [abbreviation]

**discolour** /dis-**kul**-uh/ *v.* (also **discolor**) cause to change from its normal colour; stain; tarnish. □ **discoloration** /-**ray**-shuhn/ *n.*

**discomfit** /dis-**kum**-fit, -fuht/ *v.* (-**t**-) disconcert, baffle, frustrate (*the candidate was quite discomfited by the question put to him at the interview*). □ **discomfiture** *n.* [French: related to DIS-, CONFECTION]

■ **Usage** *Discomfit* is sometimes confused with *discomfort*.

**discomfort** /dis-**kum**-fuht/ — *n.* **1** lack of comfort; slight pain (*a tight collar caused him much discomfort*). **2** mental uneasiness (*his presence caused her discomfort*). — *v.* make uncomfortable ('*These wads of wool in your mouth,*' said the dentist, '*may discomfort you a bit.*').

■ **Usage** As a verb, *discomfort* is sometimes confused with *discomfit*.

**discommode** /,dis-kuh-**mohd**/ *v.* inconvenience (a person etc.). □ **discommodious** *adj.* [from French]

**discompose** /,dis-kuhm-**pohz**/ *v.* (-**sing**) disturb the composure of; agitate. □ **discomposure** *n.*

**disco music** *n.* popular dance music with a heavy bass rhythm.

**disconcert** /,dis-kuhn-**sert**/ *v.* **1** disturb the composure of; fluster (*disconcerted by his expression*). **2** spoil or upset (plans etc.). □ **disconcerted** *adj.* **disconcerting** *adj.*

**disconnect** /,dis-kuh-**nekt**/ *v.* **1** break the connection of. **2** put (an electrical device) out of action by disconnecting the parts, esp. by pulling out the plug. □ **disconnection** *n.*

**disconnected** *adj.* **1** not connected. **2** (of speech, writing, argument, etc.) incoherent and illogical.

**disconsolate** /dis-**kon**-suh-luht/ *adj.* forlorn, unhappy, disappointed. □ **disconsolately** *adv.* [Latin: related to DIS-, SOLACE]

**discontent** /,dis-kuhn-**tent**/ — *n.* lack of contentment; dissatisfaction, grievance. — *v.* (esp. as **discontented** *adj.*) make dissatisfied. □ **discontentment** *n.*

**discontinue** /,dis-kuhn-**tin**-yoo/ *v.* (-**ues**, -**ued**, -**uing**) **1** come or bring to an end (*a discontinued line*). **2** give up, cease from (doing something) (*discontinued her subscription*; *discontinued his visits*). □ **discontinuance** *n.*

**discontinuous** *adj.* lacking continuity; intermittent. □ **discontinuity** /-,kon-tuh-**nyoo**-uh-tee/ *n.*

**discord** /**dis**-kawd/ *n.* **1** disagreement; strife. **2** harsh noise; clashing sounds. **3** *Mus.* lack of harmony in a chord. [Latin: related to DIS-, *cor cord*- heart]

**discordant** /dis-**kaw**-duhnt/ *adj.* **1** disagreeing. **2** not in harmony; dissonant. □ **discordance** *n.* **discordantly** *adv.*

**discotheque** /**dis**-kuh-,tek/ *n.* **1** nightclub etc. for dancing to pop records. **2** professional lighting and sound equipment used for this. **3** party with such equipment. [French, = record-library]

**discount** /**dis**-kownt/ — *n.* amount deducted from a full or normal price, esp. for prompt or advance payment or to a special class of buyers (*employees receive a discount*; also *attrib.*: *discount store*; *discount rate*). — *v.* **1** /dis-**kownt**/ disregard as unreliable or unimportant (*discounted his story*). **2** deduct an amount from (a price etc.). **3** give or get the present worth of (an investment certificate which has yet to mature). □ **at a discount** below the usual price or true value.

**discountenance** /dis-**kown**-tuh-nuhns/ *v.* (**-cing**) **1** (esp. in *passive*) disconcert (*was discountenanced by his stare*). **2** refuse to countenance or approve of.

**discourage** /dis-**ku**-rij/ *v.* (**-ging**) **1** deprive of courage or confidence. **2** dissuade, deter (*discouraged him from trying to parachute off the skyscraper*). **3** show disapproval of (*smoking is discouraged*). □ **discouragement** *n.*

**discourse** — *n.* /**dis**-kaws/ **1** *literary* conversation. **2** dissertation on an academic subject. **3** lecture, speech. **4** *Linguistics etc.* connected series of utterances; a text. — *v.* /dis-**kaws**/ (**-sing**) **1** converse. **2** speak or write at length on a subject. [Latin *curro curs-* run]

**discourteous** /dis-**ker**-tee-uhs/ *adj.* lacking courtesy; rude. □ **discourteously** *adv.* **discourtesy** *n.* (*pl.* **-ies**).

**discover** /duh-**skuv**-uh/ *v.* **1 a** find out or become aware of, by intention or chance. **b** be first to find or find out (*who discovered America?*). **2** (in show business) find and promote as a new performer. □ **discoverer** *n.* [Latin *discooperio*: related to DIS-, COVER]

**discovery** *n.* (*pl.* **-ies**) **1** act or process of discovering or being discovered. **2** person or thing discovered.

**discredit** /dis-**kred**-uht/ — *n.* **1** harm to reputation (*brought discredit on the firm*). **2** person or thing causing this (*he is a discredit to the family*). **3** lack of credibility (*threw discredit on her story*). — *v.* (**-t-**) **1** harm the good reputation of. **2** cause to be disbelieved (*this new information discredits her story*). **3** refuse to believe (*I discredit it utterly*).

**discreditable** *adj.* bringing discredit; shameful. □ **discreditably** *adv.*

**discreet** /dis-**skreet**/ *adj.* (**-er, -est**) **1 a** circumspect in speech or action, esp. to avoid social disgrace or embarrassment. **b** tactful; judicious, prudent (*was most discreet in his questioning*). **2** unobtrusive (*a discreet touch of rouge*). □ **discreetly** *adv.* **discreetness** *n.* [Latin: related to DISCERN]

**discrepancy** /dis-**skrep**-uhn-see/ *n.* (*pl.* **-ies**) **1** difference; failure to correspond; inconsistency (*there is a discrepancy between the two sets of figures*). **2** instance of this (*the discrepancy is in the supposed time of departure*). □ **discrepant** *adj.* [Latin *discrepo* be discordant]

**discrete** /dis-**kreet**/ *adj.* individually distinct; separate, discontinuous. □ **discreteness** *n.* [Latin: related to DISCERN]

**discretion** /duh-**skresh**-uhn/ *n.* **1** being discreet (*treats confidences with discretion*). **2** prudence; good judgment (*discretion is the better part of valour*). **3** freedom or authority to act according to one's judgment (*I leave it entirely to your discretion as to what action to take*). □ **at one's discretion** as one pleases. **at the discretion of** to be settled or disposed of according to the judgment or choice of. **use one's discretion** act according to one's own judgment. □ **discretionary** *adj.* [Latin: related to DISCERN]

**discriminate** /duh-**skrim**-uh-,nayt/ *v.* (**-ting**) **1** (often foll. by *between*) make or see a distinction (*cannot discriminate between right and wrong*). **2** (usu. foll. by *against* or *in favour of*) treat unfavourably or favourably, esp. on the basis of race, gender, etc. (*the hotel was accused of discriminating against Aborigines*). □ **discriminatory** /-nuh-tuh-ree, -tree/ *adj.* [Latin *discrimino*: related to DISCERN]

**discriminating** *adj.* showing good judgment or taste.

**discrimination** /duh-,skrim-uh-**nay**-shuhn/ *n.* **1** unfavourable treatment based on racial, sexual, etc. prejudice (*discrimination against gays; discrimination against women*). **2** good taste or judgment in artistic matters etc. **3** power of discriminating or observing differences.

**discursive** /dis-**ker**-siv/ *adj.* tending to digress, rambling. [Latin *curro curs-* run]

**discus** /**dis**-kuhs/ *n.* (*pl.* **-cuses**) heavy thick-centred disc thrown in athletic events. [Latin from Greek]

**discuss** /duh-**skus**/ *v.* **1** talk about (*discussed their holidays*). **2** talk or write about (a subject) in detail. □ **discussion** *n.* [Latin *discutio -cuss-* disperse]

**disdain** /dis-**dayn**/ — *n.* scorn, contempt. — *v.* **1** regard with disdain. **2** refrain or refuse out of disdain (*disdained his offer*). □ **disdainful** *adj.* **disdainfully** *adv.* [Latin: related to DE-, DEIGN]

**disease** /duh-**zeez**/ *n.* **1** unhealthy condition of the body or mind, plants, society, etc. **2** particular kind of disease. □ **diseased** *adj.* [French: related to DIS-, EASE]

**disembark** /,dis-uhm-**bahk**/ *v.* put or go ashore; get off an aircraft, bus, etc. □ **disembarkation** /-**kay**-shuhn/ *n.*

**disembodied** /,dis-uhm-**bod**-eed/ *adj.* **1** (of the soul etc.) freed from the body or concrete form. **2** lacking a body (*disembodied spectre*). □ **disembodiment** *n.*

**disembowel** /,dis-uhm-**bow**-uhl/ *v.* (**-ll-**)

remove the bowels or entrails of.
□ **disembowelment** n.

**disenchant** /ˌdis-uhn-**chahnt**, -**chant**/ v.
disillusion. □ **disenchantment** n.

**disenfranchise** /ˌdis-uhn-**fran**-chuyz/ v.
(also **disfranchise**) (**-sing**) **1** give of the
right to vote or to be represented. **2**
deprive of rights as a citizen or of a
franchise held. □ **disenfranchisement** n.

**disengage** /ˌdis-uhn-**gayj**/ — v. (**-ging**) **1**
detach, loosen, release (disengaged the
clutch). **2** remove (troops) from battle etc.
**3** become detached. **4** (as **disengaged**
adj.) **a** at leisure. **b** uncommitted, esp.
politically. □ **disengagement** n.

**disentangle** /ˌdis-uhn-**tang**-guhl/ v.
(**-ling**) free or become free of tangles or
complications. □ **disentanglement** n.

**disestablish** /ˌdis-uh-**stab**-lish/ v. **1**
deprive (a Church) of government
support. **2** terminate the establishment
of. □ **disestablishment** n.

**disfavour** /dis-**fay**-vuh/ (also **disfavor**)
— n. **1** disapproval or dislike (views Australia's links with the monarchy with
disfavour). **2** being disliked (he's in
disfavour with the government). — v.
regard or treat with disfavour.

**disfigure** /dis-**fig**-uh/ v. (**-ring**) spoil the
appearance of. □ **disfigurement** n.

**disfranchise** var. of DISENFRANCHISE.

**disgorge** /dis-**gawj**/ v. (**-ging**) **1** eject
from the throat (the magpie disgorged
a pellet of undigested matter). **2** pour
forth (tourist buses disgorging tourists 'cameraed' to the eyebrows).
□ **disgorgement** n.

**disgrace** /dis-**grays**/ — n. **1** loss of
reputation; shame; ignominy. **2** shameful
or very bad person or thing (bus service
is a disgrace). — v. (**-cing**) bring shame or
discredit on. □ **in disgrace** out of favour.
[Latin: related to DIS-, GRACE]

**disgraceful** adj. shameful; causing
disgrace. □ **disgracefully** adv.

**disgruntled** /dis-**grun**-tuhld/ adj. discontented; sulky. □ **disgruntlement** n.
[from DIS-, GRUNT]

**disguise** /dis-**guyz**, duhs-/ — v. (**-sing**) **1**
alter the appearance etc. of, so as to
conceal the identity or make unrecognis-
able (disguised himself as a policewoman; disguised the taste by adding
sugar). **2** misrepresent or cover up (disguised the truth; disguised my anger).
— n. **1 a** costume, make-up, etc., used to
disguise. **b** action, manner, etc., used to
deceive (his friendliness was all a
disguise). **2** disguised state (in disguise).
**3** act or practice of disguising; concealment of reality. [French desguis(i)er (as
DIS-, GUISE)]

**disgust** /dis-**gust**/ — n. strong aversion;
repugnance. — v. cause disgust in.
□ **disgusting** adj. **disgustingly** adv.
[French or Italian: related to DIS-, GUSTO]

**dish** — n. **1 a** shallow flat-bottomed
container for food. **b** its contents (all the
dishes were delightful). **c** particular kind
of food or food prepared to a particular
recipe (meat dish). **2** (in pl.) crockery,
pans, etc. after a meal (wash the dishes).
**3** vessel in which alluvial soil, gravel, etc.,
is washed to separate out gold. **4 a** dish-
shaped object or cavity. **b** = SATELLITE DISH.
**5** colloq. sexually attractive person. — v.
= dish up **1**. □ **dish it out (to)** colloq. **1** deal
out punishment, reprimands, etc. (really
dished it out to them). **2** fight hard (he can
dish it out with the best of them). **dish out**
colloq. distribute. **dish up 1** put (food) in
dishes for serving (I'm ready to dish up
now). **2** colloq. seek to present (facts,
arguments, etc.) attractively. [Old
English from Latin DISCUS]

**disharmony** /dis-**hah**-muh-nee/ n. lack
of harmony; discord. □ **disharmonious**
/-**moh**-nee-uhs/ adj.

**dishcloth** n. cloth for washing dishes.

**dishearten** /dis-**hah**-tuhn/ v. cause
to lose courage, hope, or confidence.
□ **disheartenment** n.

**dishevelled** /di-**shev**-uhld/ adj. (of the
hair, a person, etc.) untidy; ruffled.
□ **dishevel** v. (**-ll-**). **dishevelment** n. [from
DIS-, chevel 'hair', from Latin capillus]

**dishonest** /dis-**on**-uhst/ adj. fraudulent
or insincere. □ **dishonestly** adv. **dishonesty** n.

**dishonour** /dis-**on**-uh/ (also **dishonor**)
— n. **1** state of shame or disgrace;
discredit. **2** thing causing this (he's a
dishonour to his profession). — v. **1**
disgrace (dishonoured his name). **2**
refuse to accept or pay (a cheque etc.).

**dishonourable** adj. (also **dishonorable**) **1**
causing disgrace; ignominious. **2**
unprincipled. □ **dishonourably** adv.

**dishwasher** n. machine or person that
washes dishes.

**dishwater** n. **1** water in which dishes
have been washed. **2** colloq. anything
purportedly resembling this, esp. a weak
drink of coffee etc. □ **dull as dishwater**
colloq. extremely dull or boring.

**dishy** adj. (**-ier**, **-iest**) colloq. sexually
attractive.

**disillusion** /ˌdis-uh-**loo**-zhuhn/ — v. free
from an illusion or mistaken belief. — n.
disillusioned state. □ **disillusionment** n.

**disincentive** /ˌdis-in-**sen**-tiv/ n. **1** thing
discouraging action, effort, etc. **2** Econ.
source of discouragement to productivity
or progress.

**disincline** /ˌdis-in-**kluyn**/ v. (**-ning**) make unwilling or reluctant (*the glorious weather outside has disinclined us for work; this information disinclines me to support them any longer*). □ **disinclination** /ˌdis-in-kluh-**nay**-shuhn/ n.

**disinfect** /ˌdis-in-**fekt**/ v. cleanse of infection, esp. with disinfectant. □ **disinfection** n.

**disinfectant** — n. substance that destroys germs etc. — adj. disinfecting.

**disinformation** /ˌdis-in-fuh-**may**-shuhn/ n. false information, propaganda.

**disingenuous** /ˌdis-in-**jen**-yoo-uhs/ adj. insincere, not candid. □ **disingenuously** adv.

**disinherit** /ˌdis-in-**he**-ruht/ v. (**-t-**) reject as one's heir; deprive of the right of inheritance. □ **disinheritance** n.

**disintegrate** /dis-**in**-tuh-ˌgrayt/ v. (**-ting**) **1** separate into component parts or fragments, break up. **2** colloq. break down, esp. mentally. **3** (of an atomic nucleus) emit particles or divide into smaller nuclei. □ **disintegration** /dis-ˌin-tuh-**gray**-shuhn/ n.

**disinter** /ˌdis-in-**ter**/ v. (**-rr-**) dig up (esp. a corpse). □ **disinterment** n.

**disinterested** /dis-**in**-truh-stuhd/ adj. not influenced by one's own advantage; impartial (*his ruling was completely disinterested and fair*). **2** colloq. uninterested (*I'm disinterested in opera and all that jazz*). □ **disinterest** n. **disinterestedly** adv.

■ **Usage** Use of *disinterested* in sense 2 is common in informal use, but is widely regarded as incorrect. The use of the noun *disinterest* to mean 'lack of interest' is also objected to but it is rarely used in any other sense and the alternative *uninterest* is rare.

**disjoint** /dis-**joint**/ v. **1** take apart at the joints (*disjointed the chook*). **2** (as **disjointed** adj.) (esp. of conversation) incoherent; disconnected. **3** disturb the working of; disrupt.

**disjunction** /dis-**jungk**-shuhn/ n. separation.

**disjunctive** /dis-**jungk**-tiv/ adj. **1** involving separation. **2** (of a conjunction) expressing an alternative, e.g. *or* in *is it wet or dry?*

**disk** var. of DISC (*Computing*).

**disk drive** n. *Computing* mechanism for rotating a disk and reading or writing data from or to it.

**diskette** /dis-**ket**/ n. *Computing* = FLOPPY n.

**dislike** /dis-**luyk**/ — v. (**-king**) have an aversion to; not like (*I dislike rabbit-food,*

*meaning salad*). — n. **1** feeling of repugnance or not liking (*I've taken a strong dislike to door-knockers who try to bible-bash me*). **2** object of this.

**dislocate** /**dis**-luh-ˌkayt/ v. (**-ting**) **1** disturb the normal connection of (esp. a joint in the body). **2** disrupt; put out of order. □ **dislocation** /ˌdis-luh-**kay**-shuhn/ n.

**dislodge** /dis-**loj**/ v. (**-ging**) remove from an established or fixed position (*dislodged a brick from the fence; was dislodged from his directorship*). □ **dislodgement** n.

**disloyal** /dis-**loi**-uhl/ adj. not loyal; unfaithful; treacherous. □ **disloyally** adv. **disloyalty** n.

**dismal** /**diz**-muhl/ adj. **1** gloomy; miserable. **2** colloq. feeble, inept (*dismal attempt*). □ **dismally** adv. [medieval Latin *dies mali* unlucky days]

**dismantle** /dis-**man**-tuhl/ v. (**-ling**) **1** take to pieces; pull down. **2** deprive of defences or equipment.

**dismay** /dis-**may**/ — v. fill with consternation or anxiety; discourage or depress; reduce to despair. — n. **1** consternation or anxiety. **2** depression or despair. [French from Germanic: related to DIS-, MAY]

**dismember** /dis-**mem**-buh/ v. **1** remove the limbs from. **2** partition or divide up. □ **dismemberment** n.

**dismiss** /dis-**mis**/ v. **1** send away, esp. from one's presence; disperse. **2** terminate the employment of, esp. as the result of a dishonourable action etc.; sack. **3** put from one's mind or emotions (*dismissed it from my memory*). **4** consider not worth talking or thinking about; treat summarily (*dismissed his objection*). **5** *Law* refuse further hearing to (a case). **6** *Cricket* put (a batsman or side) out (usu. for a stated score). □ **dismissal** n. [Latin *mitto miss-* send]

**dismissive** adj. dismissing rudely or casually; disdainful. □ **dismissively** adv. **dismissiveness** n.

**dismount** /dis-**mownt**/ v. **1 a** alight from a horse, bicycle, etc. **b** (usu. in *passive*) throw from a horse; unseat. **2** remove (a thing) from its mounting (esp. a gun from its carriage).

**disobedient** /ˌdis-uh-**bee**-dee-uhnt/ adj. disobeying; rebellious. □ **disobedience** n. **disobediently** adv.

**disobey** /ˌdis-uh-**bay**/ v. refuse or fail to obey.

**disoblige** /ˌdis-uh-**bluyj**/ v. (**-ging**) **1** refuse to help or cooperate with (a person). **2** (as **disobliging** adj.) uncooperative.

**disorder** /dis-**aw**-duh/ — n. **1** lack of order; confusion. **2** public disturbance; riot. **3** usu. minor ailment or disease. — v. **1** throw into confusion; disarrange. **2** put out of good health; upset. □ **disordered** adj.

**disorderly** adj. **1** untidy; confused. **2** riotous, unruly. **3** Law contrary to public order or morality. □ **disorderliness** n.

**disorganise** /dis-**aw**-guh-,nuyz/ v. (also **-ize**) (**-sing** or **-zing**) **1** throw into confusion or disorder. **2** (as **disorganised** adj.) badly organised; untidy. □ **disorganisation** /-**zay**-shuhn/ n.

**disorient** /dis-**o**-ree-uhnt/ v. = DISORIENTATE.

**disorientate** /dis-**o**-ree-uhn-,tayt/ v. (also **disorient**) (**-ting**) confuse (a person), esp. as to his or her bearings. □ **disorientation** /-**tay**-shuhn/ n.

**disown** /dis-**ohn**/ v. deny or give up any connection with; repudiate, renounce.

**disparage** /dis-**pa**-rij/ v. (**-ging**) **1** criticise; belittle. **2** bring discredit on. □ **disparagement** n. [French: related to DIS-, parage rank]

**disparate** /**dis**-puh-ruht/ adj. essentially different; not comparable. □ **disparateness** n. [Latin disparo separate]

**disparity** /dis-**pa**-ruh-tee/ n. (pl. **-ies**) inequality; difference; incongruity.

**dispassionate** /dis-**pash**-uh-nuht/ adj. free from emotion; impartial. □ **dispassionately** adv.

**dispatch** /dis-**pach**, duh-**spach**/ (also **despatch**) — v. **1** send off to a destination or for a purpose (dispatched him with the message). **2** perform (a task etc.) promptly; finish off (dispatched the day's business by noon). **3** kill, execute (dispatched him with a boomerang). **4** colloq. eat quickly. — n. **1** act or instance of dispatching or being dispatched. **2** a official written message, esp. military. **b** news report to a newspaper etc. **3** promptness, efficiency (done with dispatch). [Italian dispacciare or Spanish despachar]

**dispel** /dis-**pel**/ v. (**-ll-**) drive away; scatter (fears etc.). [Latin pello drive]

**dispensable** /dis-**pen**-suh-buhl/ adj. that can be done without; unnecessary.

**dispensary** /dis-**pen**-suh-ree/ n. (pl. **-ies**) place where medicines are dispensed.

**dispensation** /,dis-pen-**say**-shuhn/ n. **1** act or instance of dispensing or distributing. **2 a** exemption from a penalty, rule, etc.; instance of this. **b** (in the Catholic Church) exemption from a religious observance on a particular occasion; instance of this. **3** religious or political system obtaining in a nation etc. (the Christian dispensation).

**dispense** /dis-**pens**/ v. (**-sing**) **1** distribute; deal out. **2** administer (a sacrament, justice, etc.). **3** make up and give out (medicine etc.) according to a doctor's prescription. **4** (foll. by with) do without; make unnecessary (let's dispense with formalities). [French from Latin pendo pens- weigh]

**dispersal** /dis-**per**-suhl, duh-**sper**-/ n. hist. euphemistic name given by whites to: **1** the forced expulsion of Aborigines from their traditional territories. **2** the pursuit and mass slaughter of Aborigines.

**disperse** /dis-**pers**, duh-**spers**/ v. (**-sing**) **1** go, send, drive, or scatter widely or in different directions. **2** (of people at a meeting etc.) leave and go their various ways. **3** hist. (of whites) **a** forcibly drive Aborigines away from an area they possessed. **b** seek out and kill a group or tribe of Aborigines; exterminate. **4** send to or station at different points. **5** put in circulation; disseminate. **6** Chem. distribute (small particles) in a medium. **7** Physics divide (white light) into its coloured constituents. □ **dispersive** adj. [Latin: related to DIS-, SPARSE]

**dispersion** /dis-**per**-shuhn/ n. **1** act or instance of dispersing or process of being dispersed. **2** (**the Dispersion**; also **Diaspora**) the Jews dispersed among the Gentiles after the Captivity in Babylon. **3** Chem. mixture of one substance dispersed in another. **4** Physics. separation of white light into colours or of any radiation according to wavelength. **5** Statistics extent to which values of a variable differ from the mean.

**dispirit** /di-**spi**-ruht/ v. (esp. as **dispiriting**, **dispirited** adjs.) make despondent, deject.

**displace** /dis-**plays**/ v. (**-cing**) **1** move from its place. **2** remove from office. **3** take the place of; oust.

**displaced person** n. refugee in war etc., or from persecution.

**displacement** n. **1** act or instance of displacing or process of being displaced. **2** amount of fluid displaced by an object floating or immersed in it. **3** Psychol. **a** substitution of one idea or impulse for another. **b** unconscious transfer of strong unacceptable emotions from one object to another. **4** amount by which a thing is shifted from its place.

**display** /dis-**play**/ — v. **1** exhibit; show. **2** reveal; betray (displayed his ignorance). — n. **1** act or instance of displaying. **2 a** exhibition or show. **b**

thing(s) displayed. **3** ostentation; flashiness. **4** mating rituals of some birds etc. **5 a** temporary presentation of signals or data on a screen etc. **b** the information so presented. [Latin *plico* fold]

**displease** /dis-**pleez**/ *v.* (**-sing**) make upset or angry; annoy. □ **displeasure** /dis-**plezh**-uh/ *n.*

**disport** /dis-**pawt**/ *v.* (often *refl.*) play, frolic, enjoy oneself. [Anglo-French *porter* carry, from Latin]

**disposable** /duh-**spohz**-uh-buhl, dis-**pohz**-/ — *adj.* **1** intended to be used once and discarded. **2** able to be disposed of. — *n.* disposable article.

**disposable income** *n.* income after tax and other fixed payments.

**disposal** /duh-**spoh**-zuhl, dis-**pohz**-/ *n.* act or instance of disposing of something. □ **at one's disposal 1** available for one's use. **2** subject to one's orders or decisions.

■ **Usage** *Disposal* is the noun corresponding to the verb *dispose of* (get rid of, deal with, etc.). *Disposition* is the noun from *dispose* (arrange, incline).

**disposals store** *n.* = ARMY DISPOSAL STORE.
**dispose** /duh-**spohz**, dis-**pohz**-/ *v.* (**-sing**) **1** (usu. foll. by *to*, or *to* + infin.) **a** make willing; incline (*was disposed to agree*). **b** tend (*wheel was disposed to buckle*). **2** arrange suitably (*disposed the pictures in sequence*). **3** (as **disposed** *adj.*) have a specified inclination (*ill-disposed*; *well-disposed*). **4** determine events (*man proposes, God disposes*). □ **dispose of 1 a** deal with. **b** get rid of. **c** finish. **d** kill. **2** sell. **3** prove (an argument etc.) incorrect. [French: related to POSE]

**disposition** /ˌdis-puh-**zish**-uhn/ *n.* **1** natural tendency; temperament (*a disposition to overeat*; *a happy disposition*). **2 a** placing in order; arranging. **b** relative position of parts; arrangement. **3** (usu. in *pl.*) **a** *Mil.* stationing of troops ready for attack or defence. **b** preparations; plans. **4 a** bestowal by deed or will. **b** control; power of disposing.

■ **Usage** See note at *disposal*.

**dispossess** /ˌdis-puh-**zes**/ *v.* **1** (usu. foll. by *of*) (esp. as **dispossessed** *adj.*) deprive (a person) of. **2** dislodge; oust (a person). □ **dispossession** /-**zesh**-uhn/ *n.*

**disproportion** /ˌdis-pruh-**paw**-shuhn/ *n.* lack of proportion; being out of proportion. □ **disproportional** *adj.* **disproportionally** *adv.*

**disproportionate** *adj.* **1** out of proportion. **2** relatively too large or small etc. □ **disproportionately** *adv.*

**disprove** /dis-**proov**/ *v.* (**-ving**) prove false; refute.

**disputable** /dis-**pyoo**-tuh-buhl, dis-**pyuh**-/ *adj.* open to question; uncertain. □ **disputably** *adv.*

**disputant** /dis-**pyoo**-tuhnt/ *n.* person in a dispute.

**disputation** /ˌdis-pyoo-**tay**-shuhn/ *n.* **1** debate, esp. formal. **2** argument; controversy.

**disputatious** *adj.* argumentative.

**dispute** /duh-**spyoot**, dis-**pyoot**-/ — *v.* (**-ting**) **1** debate, argue. **2** discuss, esp. heatedly; quarrel. **3** question the truth or validity of (a statement etc.). **4** contend for (*disputed territory*). **5** resist, oppose (a landing, advance of an enemy, etc.). — *n.* **1** controversy; debate. **2** quarrel. **3** disagreement leading to industrial action. □ **in dispute 1** being argued about. **2** (of a workforce) involved in industrial action. [Latin *puto* reckon]

**disqualify** /dis-**kwol**-uh-ˌfuy/ *v.* (**-ies, -ied**) **1** debar from a competition or pronounce ineligible as a winner because of an infringement of the rules etc. **2** make or pronounce ineligible, unsuitable, or unqualified (*disqualified from driving*). □ **disqualification** /dis-ˌkwol-uh-fuh-**kay**-shuhn/ *n.*

**disquiet** /dis-**kwuy**-uht/ — *v.* deprive of peace; make anxious. — *n.* anxiety; uneasiness.

**disquietude** *n.* disquiet.

**disquisition** /ˌdis-kwuh-**zish**-uhn/ *n.* long or elaborate treatise or discourse on a subject. [Latin *quaero quaesit-* seek]

**disregard** /ˌdis-ruh-**gahd**/ — *v.* **1** ignore. **2** treat as unimportant. — *n.* indifference; neglect.

**disrepair** /ˌdis-ruh-**pair**/ *n.* poor condition due to lack of repairs.

**disreputable** /dis-**rep**-yuh-tuh-buhl/ *adj.* **1** of bad reputation. **2** not respectable in character or appearance. □ **disreputably** *adv.*

**disrepute** /ˌdis-ruh-**pyoot**/ *n.* lack of good reputation; discredit.

**disrespect** /ˌdis-ruh-**spekt**/ *n.* lack of respect; discourtesy. □ **disrespectful** *adj.* **disrespectfully** *adv.*

**disrobe** /dis-**rohb**/ *v.* (**-bing**) *literary* undress.

**disrupt** /dis-**rupt**/ *v.* interrupt the continuity of; bring disorder to. □ **disruption** *n.* **disruptive** *adj.* **disruptively** *adv.* [Latin: related to RUPTURE]

**dissatisfy** /dis-**sat**-uhs-ˌfuy/ *v.* (**-ies, -ied**) make discontented; fail to satisfy. □ **dissatisfaction** /-**fak**-shuhn/ *n.*

**dissect** /duy-**sekt**, duh-/ *v.* **1** cut into pieces, esp. for examination or post mortem. **2** analyse or criticise in detail. □ **dissection** n. [Latin: related to SECTION]

**dissemble** /duh-**sem**-buhl/ v. (-**ling**) **1** be hypocritical or insincere. **2 a** disguise or conceal (a feeling, intention, etc.). **b** simulate (*he dissembled grief in public*). [Latin *simulo* SIMULATE]

**disseminate** /duh-**sem**-uh-ˌnayt/ v. (-**ting**) scatter about, spread (esp. ideas) widely. □ **dissemination** /-**nay**-shuhn/ n. [Latin: related to DIS-, SEMEN]

**dissension** /duh-**sen**-shuhn/ n. angry disagreement. [Latin: related to DISSENT]

**dissent** /duh-**sent**/ — v. (often foll. by *from*) **1** think differently; disagree, esp. openly. **2** differ in religious opinion, esp. from the doctrine of an established church. — n. **1 a** difference of opinion. **b** expression of this. **2** refusal to accept the doctrines of an established church; nonconformity. □ **dissenter** n. [Latin: related to DIS-, *sentio* feel]

**dissentient** /di-**sen**-shuhnt/ — adj. disagreeing with the established or official view. — n. person who dissents.

**dissertation** /ˌdis-uh-**tay**-shuhn/ n. detailed discourse, esp. one submitted towards an academic degree; thesis. [Latin *disserto* discuss]

**disservice** /dis-**ser**-vuhs/ n. an ill turn; an injury, esp. done when trying to help (*I did her a disservice when I tried to reconcile her with her husband*).

**dissident** /**dis**-uh-duhnt/ — adj. disagreeing, esp. with the established government, system, etc. — n. dissident person. □ **dissidence** n. [Latin: related to DIS-, *sedeo* sit]

**dissimilar** /di-**sim**-uh-luh/ adj. unlike, not similar. □ **dissimilarity** /-la-ruh-tee/ n. (pl. -**ies**).

**dissimulate** /duh-**sim**-yuh-ˌlayt/ v. (-**ting**) dissemble. □ **dissimulation** /-**lay**-shuhn/ n. [Latin: related to DISSEMBLE]

**dissipate** /**dis**-uh-ˌpayt/ v. (-**ting**) **1** disperse, disappear, dispel (*the darkness dissipated*; *tried to dissipate their fears*). **2** squander or fritter away (money, energy, etc.). **3** (as **dissipated** adj.) given to dissipation; dissolute. [Latin *dissipo -pat-*]

**dissipation** /ˌdis-uh-**pay**-shuhn/ n. **1** act or instance of dissipating or state of being dissipated. **2** intemperate, dissolute, or debauched living. **3** (usu. foll. by *of*) wasteful expenditure (*dissipation of resources*).

**dissociate** /di-**soh**-shee-ˌayt, -see-ˌayt/ v. (-**ting**) **1** (usu. foll. by *from*) disconnect or become disconnected; separate. **2** *Chem.* (of compound substances) separate into their primary elements or less complex

compounds. □ **dissociate oneself from 1** declare oneself unconnected with. **2** decline to support or agree with (a proposal etc.). □ **dissociation** /di-ˌsoh-see-**ay**-shuhn, -shee-/ n. **dissociative** /-uh-tiv/ adj. [Latin: related to DIS-, ASSOCIATE]

**dissoluble** /di-**sol**-yuh-buhl/ adj. that can be dissolved, disintegrated, loosened or disconnected; soluble.

**dissolute** /**dis**-uh-ˌloot/ adj. lax in morals; licentious. [Latin: related to DISSOLVE]

**dissolution** /ˌdis-uh-**loo**-shuhn/ n. **1** disintegration; decomposition. **2** (usu. foll. by *of*) undoing or relaxing of a bond, esp. a marriage, partnership, or alliance. **3** dismissal or dispersal of an assembly, esp. of a parliament at the end of its term. **4** death. **5** bringing or coming to an end; fading away.

**dissolve** /duh-**zolv**/ v. (-**ving**) **1** make or become liquid, esp. by immersion or dispersion in a liquid. **2** (cause to) disappear gradually (*he walked away from me and dissolved into the gloom*). **3** dismiss (an assembly, esp. a parliament). **4** annul or put an end to (a partnership, marriage, etc.). **5** (often foll. by *into*) be overcome (by tears, laughter, etc.). [Latin: related to DIS-, *solvo solut-* loosen]

**dissonant** /**dis**-uh-nuhnt/ adj. **1** *Mus.* harsh-toned; unharmonious. **2** incongruous; clashing (*wore dissonant colours*). □ **dissonance** n. [Latin: related to DIS-, *sono* SOUND[1]]

**dissuade** /di-**swayd**/ v. (-**ding**) (often foll. by *from*) discourage (a person); persuade against. □ **dissuasion** /-**sway**-zhuhn/ n. **dissuasive** adj. [Latin: related to DIS-, *suadeo* advise]

**dissyllable** var. of DISYLLABLE.

**distaff** /**dis**-tahf/ n. cleft stick holding wool or flax for spinning by hand. [Old English]

**distance** /**dis**-tuhns/ — n. **1** condition of being far off; remoteness. **2 a** space between two things. **b** length of this (*distance of twenty metres*). **3** gap or gulf (*there's quite a distance between living frugally and being destitute*). **4** ground (literal and figurative) (*covered a lot of distance in just two hours*; *my son's gone quite a distance towards walking again since he began physiotherapy*). **5** distant point or place (*came from a distance*). **6** aloofness; reserve (*there was a certain distance between them*). **7** remoter field of vision (*in the distance*). **8** interval of time (*can't remember what happened at this distance*). — v. (-**cing**) (often *refl.*) **1** place or cause to seem far off; be aloof (*distanced himself from them*). **2** leave far behind in a race etc. □ **at a distance** far off. **go the distance 1** *Boxing* complete a fight without being knocked out. **2** complete, esp. a hard task; endure an ordeal. **keep one's distance** remain aloof. [Latin: related to DIS-, *sto* stand]

**distant** *adj.* **1** far away; at a specified distance (*three kilometres distant*). **2** remote or far apart in position, time, relationship, etc. (*distant prospect; distant relation*). **3** aloof (*his manner was distant*). **4** abstracted (*distant stare*). **5** faint, vague (*he was a distant memory to her*). □ **distantly** *adv.*

**distaste** /dis-**tayst**/ *n.* (usu. foll. by *for*) dislike; aversion. □ **distasteful** *adj.* **distastefully** *adv.* **distastefulness** *n.*

**distemper**[1] /dis-**tem**-puh/ —*n.* paint using glue or size as a base, for use on walls. —*v.* paint with this. [Latin, = soak: see DISTEMPER[2]]

**distemper**[2] /dis-**tem**-puh/ *n.* viral disease of esp. dogs, with coughing and weakness. [Latin: related to DIS-, *tempero* mingle]

**distend** /dis-**tend**/ *v.* swell out by pressure from within (*distended stomach*). □ **distensible** /-**ten**-suh-buhl/ *adj.* **distension** /-**ten**-shuhn/ *n.* [Latin: related to TEND[1]]

**distich** /**dis**-tik/ *n.* verse couplet. [Greek *stikhos* line]

**distil** /duh-**stil**/ *v.* (-**ll**-) **1** purify or extract the essence from (a substance) by vaporising and condensing it and collecting the resulting liquid. **2** extract the essential meaning of (an idea etc.). **3** make (whisky, essence, etc.) by distilling raw materials. **4** fall or cause to fall in drops. □ **distillation** /dis-tuh-**lay**-shuhn/ *n.* [Latin: related to DE-, *stillo* drip]

**distillery** *n.* (*pl.* **-ies**) place where alcoholic liquor is distilled.

**distinct** /dis-**tingkt**, duh-**stingkt**/ *adj.* **1** (often foll. by *from*) not identical; separate; different (*the two wattles are quite distinct from each other*). **2** clearly perceptible (*the rash is becoming quite distinct*). **3** unmistakable, decided (*distinct advantage*). □ **distinctly** *adv.* [Latin: related to DISTINGUISH]

**distinction** /dis-**tingk**-shuhn, duh-**stingt**-/ *n.* **1** act or instance of discriminating or distinguishing. **2** difference between two things (*there is a clear distinction between the true leaves and the phyllodes of a wattle*). **3** thing that differentiates or distinguishes, esp. a mark, name, or title. **4** special consideration or honour (*treat with distinction*). **5** distinguished character; excellence (*person of distinction*). **6** grade

in an examination denoting great excellence (*passed with distinction*). [Latin: related to DISTINGUISH]

**distinctive** *adj.* distinguishing, characteristic. □ **distinctively** *adv.* **distinctiveness** *n.*

**distinguish** /dis-**ting**-gwish, duh-**sting**-/ *v.* **1** (often foll. by *from, between*) differentiate; see or draw distinctions (*you can distinguish the male from the female by their colouring; distinguish between right and wrong*). **2** be a mark or property of; characterise (*distinguished by his greed*). **3** discover by listening, looking, etc. (*could distinguish two voices*). **4** (usu. *refl.*; often foll. by *by*) make prominent (*distinguished himself by winning*). □ **distinguishable** *adj.* [Latin: related to DIS-, *stinguo* stinct- extinguish]

**distinguished** *adj.* **1** eminent; famous. **2** dignified.

**distort** /dis-**tawt**, duh-**stawt**/ *v.* **1** pull or twist out of shape. **2** misrepresent (facts etc.). **3** transmit (sound etc.) inaccurately. □ **distortion** *n.* [Latin *torqueo tort-* twist]

**distract** /dis-**trakt**, duh-**strakt**/ *v.* **1** (often foll. by *from*) draw away the attention of (*this is distracting me from my work*). **2** bewilder, perplex. **3** (as **distracted** *adj.*) confused, mad, or angry (*distracted by grief*). **4** amuse, esp. to divert from pain etc. (*these colouring books may distract him*). [Latin: related to DIS-, *traho tract-* draw]

**distraction** /dis-**trak**-shuhn, duh-**strak**-/ *n.* **1 a** act of distracting or being distracted. **b** thing that distracts; interruption. **2** relaxation; amusement. **3** confusion; frenzy, madness (*your whistling is driving me to distraction*).

**distrain** /dis-**trayn**, duh-**strayn**/ *v.* (usu. foll. by *upon*) impose distraint (on a person, goods, etc.). [Latin: related to DIS-, *stringo strict-* draw tight]

**distraint** /dis-**traynt**, duh-**straynt**/ *n.* seizure of goods to enforce payment.

**distraught** /dis-**trawt**, duh-**strawt**/ *adj.* distracted with worry, fear, etc.; extremely agitated. [related to DISTRACT]

**distress** /duh-**stres**/ —*n.* **1** anguish or suffering caused by pain, sorrow, worry, etc. **2** lack of money or comforts; poverty. **3** *Law* = DISTRAINT. —*v.* cause distress to, make unhappy. □ **in distress 1** suffering or in distress. **2** (of a ship, aircraft, etc.) in danger or damaged. □ **distressful** *adj.* [Romanic: related to DISTRAIN]

**distressed** *adj.* **1** suffering from distress. **2** impoverished.

**distribute** /dis-**trib**-yoot, duh-**strib**-/ *v.* (-**ting**) **1** give shares of; deal out. **2 a**

scatter; put at different points (*distributed the seeds evenly over the garden*). **b** (usu. in *passive*) occur; be dispersed (*mammals are distributed over the entire earth*). **3** divide and place in classes; arrange; classify (*plants of this region are distributed into three distinct classes*). [Latin *tribuo -but-* assign]

**distributed system** *n.* cooperation among a number of independent, interconnected computers.

**distribution** /ˌdis-truh-**byoo**-shuhn/ *n.* **1** act or instance of distributing or process of being distributed. **2 a** commercial dispersal of goods etc. **b** extent to which different groups etc. share in a nation's total wealth etc. **3** *Statistics* way in which a characteristic is spread over members of a class.

**distributive** /dis-**trib**-yuh-tiv, duh-**strib**-/ — *adj.* **1** of or produced by distribution. **2** *Logic* & *Gram.* referring to each individual of a class, not to the class collectively (e.g. *each*, *either*). — *n. Gram.* distributive word.

**distributor** *n.* **1** person or thing that distributes, esp. goods. **2** device in an internal-combustion engine for passing current to each spark-plug in turn. **3** main road carrying traffic from a busy centre and leading to several minor roads.

**district** /**dis**-trikt/ *n.* **1** (often *attrib.*) area marked off as an administrative unit (*postal district*). **2** area which has common characteristics; region (*wine-growing district*). [Latin: related to DISTRAIN]

**District Court** *n.* (in NSW, Queensland, and WA) intermediate State court between Courts of Petty Sessions and Supreme Court, presided over by a judge.

**distrust** /dis-**trust**/ — *n.* lack of trust; suspicion. — *v.* have no trust or confidence in; doubt. □ **distrustful** *adj.* **distrustfully** *adv.*

**disturb** /dis-**terb**, duh-**sterb**/ *v.* **1** break the rest, calm, or quiet of. **2** agitate; worry (*your story disturbs me*). **3** move from a settled position (*disturbed my papers*). **4** (as **disturbed** *adj.*) emotionally or mentally unstable. [Latin: related to DIS-, *turba* tumult]

**disturbance** *n.* **1** act or instance of disturbing or process of being disturbed. **2** tumult; uproar. **3** agitation; worry. **4** interruption.

**disunion** /dis-**yoo**-nyuhn/ *n.* lack of union; separation; dissension.

**disunite** /dis-yoo-**nuyt**/ *v.* (**-ting**) **1** remove the unity from. **2** separate. □ **disunity** /-**yoo**-nuh-tee/ *n.*

**disuse** — *n.* /dis-**yoos**/ disused state. — *v.* /dis-**yooz**/ (**-sing**) cease to use.

**disyllable** /duy-**sil**-uh-buhl/ *n.* (also **dissyllable**) *Prosody* word or metrical foot of two syllables. □ **disyllabic** /-**lab**-ik/ *adj.*

**ditch** — *n.* **1** long narrow excavation for drainage or irrigation. **2** watercourse, stream, etc. — *v.* **1** make or repair ditches. **2** *colloq.* abandon; discard (*ditched her boyfriend*; *the plans have been ditched*). **3 a** bring (an aircraft) down on the sea in an emergency. **b** (of an aircraft) make a forced landing on the sea. □ **dull as ditchwater** extremely dull [Old English]

**dither** /**dith**-uh/ — *v.* hesitate; be indecisive. — *n. colloq.* state of agitation or hesitation. □ **ditherer** *n.* **dithery** *adj.* [var. of *didder* DODDER[1]]

**dithyramb** /**dith**-uh-ˌram, -ˌramb/ *n.* **1** wild choral hymn in ancient Greece. **2** passionate or inflated poem etc. □ **dithyrambic** /-**ram**-bik/ *adj.* [Latin from Greek]

**ditto** /**dit**-oh/ *n.* (*pl.* **-s**) **1** (in accounts, inventories, etc.) the aforesaid, the same. **2** *colloq.* (used to avoid repetition) the same (*came late today and ditto yesterday*). [Latin DICTUM]

■ **Usage** In sense 1, the word *ditto* is often replaced by " under the word or sum to be repeated.

**ditty** /**dit**-ee/ *n.* (*pl.* **-ies**) short simple song. [Latin: related to DICTATE]

**diuretic** /ˌduy-yoo-**ret**-ik/ — *adj.* causing increased output of urine. — *n.* diuretic drug. [Greek: related to DIA-, *ouresis* urinate]

**diurnal** /duy-**er**-nuhl/ *adj.* **1** of the day or daytime. **2** daily. **3** *Astron.* occupying one day. **4** *Zool.* (of animals) active in the daytime. □ **diurnally** *adv.* [Latin *diurnalis* from *dies* day]

**diva** /**dee**-vuh/ *n.* (*pl.* **-s**) great woman opera singer; prima donna. [Italian from Latin, = goddess]

**divalent** /duy-**vay**-luhnt/ *adj. Chem.* having a valency of two.

**divan** /duh-**van**/ *n.* low couch or bed without a back or ends. [ultimately from Persian *dīvān* bench]

**dive** — *v.* (**-ving**) **1** plunge head first into water. **2** (of an aircraft, person, etc.) plunge steeply downwards. **3** (foll. by *into*) *colloq.* put one's hand into (a pocket, handbag, etc.). **4** move suddenly (*dived into a shop*). — *n.* **1** act of diving; plunge. **2** steep descent or fall (*share prices took a dive*). **3** *colloq.* disreputable nightclub, bar, etc. [Old English]

**Usage** In some parts of North America the past tense is *dove* rather than *dived*. *Dove* is not acceptable in Australian English.

**ive-bomb** v. bomb (a target) from a living aircraft. □ **dive-bomber** n.

**iver** n. **1** person who dives, esp. working under water. **2** diving bird.

**iverge** /duy-**verj**/ v. (**-ging**) **1 a** spread out from a central point, become dispersed (*diverging rays; the path diverges here*). **b** take different courses (*their interests diverged*). **2 a** (often foll. from) depart from a set course (*diverged from the track*). **b** (of opinions etc.) differ. □ **divergence** n. **divergent** adj. [Latin: related to DI-², *vergo* incline]

**ivers** /duy-verz/ adj. archaic various; several. [Latin: related to DIVERSE]

**iverse** /duy-vers, duy-vers, duh-/ adj. varied. [Latin: related to DI-², *verto* versturn]

**iversify** /duy-ver-suh-,fuy, duh-/ v. (**-ies, -ied**) **1** make diverse; vary. **2** spread investment) over several enterprises, esp. to reduce the risk of loss. **3** (often foll. by *into*) expand one's range of products. □ **diversification** /-fuh-**kay**-shuhn/ n.

**iversion** /duy-ver-*zh*uhn, -shuhn, duh-/ n. **1** act or process of diverting or process of being diverted; deviation. **2 a** diverting of attention. **b** stratagem for this (*created a diversion to secure their escape*). **3** recreation, pastime. **4** alternative route when a road is temporarily closed; detour. □ **diversionary** adj.

**iversity** /duy-ver-suh-tee, duh-/ n. variety.

**ivert** /duy-vert, duh-/ v. **1 a** turn aside from a proper direction or course; deflect (*diverted the stream; traffic was diverted around the accident area*). **b** distract (attention). **2** (often as **diverting** adj.) entertain; amuse. [Latin: related to DIVERSE]

**livest** /duy-vest/ v. (usu. foll. by *of*) **1** unclothe; strip. **2** deprive, rid (*cannot divest himself of the belief that he is Cleopatra's crocodile*). [Latin: related to VEST]

**livide** /duh-**vuyd**/ — v. (**-ding**) **1** (often foll. by *in, into*) separate into parts; break up; split (*the river divides into two; divide them into three groups*). **2** (often foll. by *out*) distribute; deal; share (*divide it between you*). **3 a** separate (one thing) from another (*divide the sheep from the goats*). **b** classify into parts or groups (*the ruler is divided into centimetres*). **4** cause to disagree (*religion divided them*). **5 a** find how many times (a number)

contains or is contained in another (*divide 20 by 4; divide 4 into 20*). **b** (of a number) be contained in (a number) without remainder (*4 divides into 20*). **6** *Parl.* **a** (of a legislative assembly etc.) part into two groups for voting (*the House divided*). **b** so divide (a parliament etc.) for voting. — n. **1** dividing or boundary line (*the divide between rich and poor*). **2** watershed. [Latin *divido -vis-*]

**divided road** n. dual carriageway.

**dividend** /**div**-uh-,dend/ n. **1 a** sum of money to be divided among a number of persons, esp. that paid by a company to shareholders. **b** similar sum payable in a totalisator pool, to creditors of a liquidated company, etc. **2** *Math.* number to be divided by a divisor. **3** benefit from an action (*their long training paid dividends*). [Anglo-French: related to DIVIDE]

**divider** n. **1** screen etc. dividing a room. **2** (in *pl.*) measuring-compasses.

**dividing range** n. stretch of high country forming a division between adjacent river systems.

**divination** /,div-uh-**nay**-shuhn/ n. supposed supernatural insight into the future etc. [Latin: related to DIVINE]

**divine** /duh-**vuyn**/ — adj. (**diviner, divinest**) **1 a** of, from, or like God or a god. **b** sacred (*the divine office*). **2** more than humanly excellent, gifted, or beautiful (*possessed of a divine talent; divine beauty*). **3** *colloq.* excellent; delightful (*that outfit is simply divine*). — v. (**-ning**) **1** discover by intuition, guessing, inspiration, or magic. **2** foresee, predict, conjecture. **3** practise divination. **4** search for underground water or minerals by holding a Y-shaped stick or rod (which is supposed to dip abruptly over the right spot). □ **divinely** adv. [Latin *divinus*]

**divine office** see OFFICE 9 a.

**diviner** n. person who practises divination.

**divine right of kings** n. doctrine that monarchs derive their sovereignty and authority from God, not from their subjects.

**diving bell** n. open-bottomed enclosure, supplied with air, for descent into deep water.

**diving board** n. elevated board for diving from.

**diving suit** n. watertight suit, usu. with helmet and air-supply, for work under water.

**divining rod** n. rod used to divine (sense 4).

**divinity** /duh-**vin**-uh-tee/ n. (*pl.* **-ies**) **1** state or quality of being divine. **2** god; godhead. **3** theology.

**divisible** /duh-**viz**-uh-buhl/ *adj.* capable of being divided. □ **divisibility** /-**bil**-uh-tee/ *n.*

**division** /duh-**vizh**-uhn/ *n.* **1** act or instance of dividing or process of being divided. **2** *Math.* dividing one number by another. **3** disagreement (*division of opinion*). **4** *Parl.* separation of members for counting votes. **5** one of two or more parts into which a thing is divided. **6** something that divides or that marks separation; dividing line, boundary. **7** unit of administration, esp.: **a** group of army brigades or regiments. **b** *Sport* grouping of teams within a competition, usu. by ability. **c** section within an industry, business, etc. (*I'll put you through to the marketing division*). □ **divisional** *adj.*

**divisional van** *n.* (in Victoria) police van (used by a particular division of the police force).

**division sign** *n.* sign (÷) indicating that one quantity is to be divided by another.

**divisive** /duh-**vuy**-siv/ *adj.* causing disagreement. □ **divisively** *adv.* **divisiveness** *n.* [Latin: related to DIVIDE]

**divisor** /duh-**vuy**-zuh/ *n.* number by which another is divided.

**divorce** /duh-**vaws**/ — *n.* **1** legal dissolution of a marriage. **2** separation (*divorce between thought and feeling*). — *v.* (**-cing**) **1 a** (usu. as **divorced** *adj.*) (often foll. by *from*) legally dissolve the marriage of. **b** separate by divorce. **c** end one's marriage with. **2** separate (*divorced from reality*). [Latin: related to DIVERSE]

**divorcee** /ˌduh-vaw-**see**/ *n.* divorced person.

**divot** /**div**-uht/ *n.* piece of turf cut out by a blow, esp. by the head of a golf club. [origin unknown]

**divulge** /duy-**vulj**, duh-/ *v.* (**-ging**) disclose, reveal (a secret etc.). □ **divulgence** *n.* [Latin *divulgo* publish]

**divvy** /**div**-ee/ *colloq.* — *n.* (*pl.* **-ies**) dividend. — *v.* (**-ies, -ied**) (often foll. by *up*) **1** share out (*divvied up the spoils*). **2** (often foll. by *with*) share (*I'll divvy with you*). [abbreviation]

**Dixie** /**dik**-see/ *n.* southern States of the US. [origin uncertain]

**dixie** /**dik**-see/ *n.* **1** large iron cooking-pot used by campers etc. **2** utensil used by a soldier in the field as a plate, cooking vessel, etc. **3** (chiefly in Victoria) small carton of ice-cream. [Hindustani *degchī* cooking pot]

**Dixieland** *n.* **1** = DIXIE. **2** traditional kind of jazz.

**Diyari** /**deer**-ree/ *n.* an Aboriginal language spoken over a large region of east central SA: now extinct, the last

speakers having been recorded in th 1970s.

**dizzy** /**diz**-ee/ — *adj.* (**-ier, -iest**) **1** giddy. **b** feeling confused. **2** causin giddiness (*dizzy heights*). **3** *colloq.* stupi — *v.* (**-ies, -ied**) **1** make dizzy. **2** bewilde □ **dizzily** *adv.* **dizziness** *n.* [Old English

**DJ** *abbr.* disc jockey.

**Djangati** /**jung**-u-tee/ *n.* an Aborigina language of north-eastern NSW: no extinct.

**Djaru** /**jah**-roo/ *n.* an Aborigina language spoken over a large area north-eastern WA.

**djellaba** /**jel**-uh-buh/ *n.* (also **jellaba** loose hooded cloak (as) worn by Ara men. [Arabic]

**Djingulu** /**jing**-uu-loo/ *n.* an Aborigina language spoken over a vast area of th central region of the NT.

**djinn** var. of JINNEE.

**dl** *abbr.* decilitre(s).

**D-layer** *n.* lowest layer of the ionospher [*D* arbitrary]

**dm** *abbr.* decimetre(s).

**DNA** *abbr.* deoxyribonucleic acid, the sel replicating material (present in nearl all living organisms, esp. as a constituer of chromosomes) which is the carrier c genetic information.

**D-notice** *n.* government notice to new editors not to publish items on specifie subjects, for security reasons. [*defence* NOTICE]

**do**[1] /doo/ — *v.* (*3rd sing. pres.* **does** /duz past **did**; *past part.* **done** /dun/; *pres. par* **doing**) **1** perform, carry out, achiev complete (work etc.) (*did his homewor a lot to do*). **2** produce, make, provid (*doing a painting*; *we do lunches*). grant; impart; have a specified effect o (*do me a favour*; *does you good*). **4** ac behave, proceed (*do as I do*; *would do we to wait*). **5** work at; study (*do carpentr do chemistry*). **6** be suitable or acceptable satisfy (*will never do*; *will do me nicely* **7** deal with; attend to (*do one's hair*; *d the dishes*). **8** fare; get on (*did badly in th test*). **9 a** solve; work out (*did the sum*). (*prec. by can or be able to*) be competen at (*can you do cartwheels?*). **10 a** travers (a certain distance) (*did 50 kilometre today*). **b** travel at a specified speed (*wa doing eighty*). **11** *colloq.* act or behav like; play the part of (*did a Melba*; *I'm doing Lady Macbeth*). **12** produce (a pla opera, etc.) (*we're doing 'Dimboola'*). **13 a** *colloq.* finish (*have you done annoyin me yet?*). **b** (as **done** *adj.*) be finished (*da is done*). **14** cook, esp. completely (*do it i the oven*; *potatoes aren't done*). **15** be i progress (*what's doing?*). **16** *colloq.* visi (*did the museums*). **17** *colloq.* **a** (often as **done** *adj.*) exhaust; tire out. **b** beat up; defeat; kill (*did him like a dinner*). **c** ruin (*if we can't find the error, we're done*). **d** act so as to bring trouble or retribution on oneself (*now you've done it*). **18** (foll. by *into*) translate or transform (*do this German bit into English for me*). **19** *colloq.* **a** rob (*did a big bank*). **b** swindle (*did us for $200*). **20** *colloq.* charge; prosecute, convict (*done for shoplifting*). **21** *colloq.* undergo (a term of imprisonment) (*did six months*). **22** *colloq.* spend one's available money completely (*did all his money on the pokies*). — *v.aux.* **1** in questions and negative statements or commands (*do you understand?*; *I don't smoke*; *don't be silly*). **2** ellipt. or in place of a verb (*you know her better than I do*; *I wanted to go and I did*; *tell me, do!*). **3** for emphasis (*I do want to*; *do tell me*; *they did go*). **4** in inversion for emphasis (*rarely does it happen*; *did he but know it*). — *n.* (*pl.* **dos** or **do's**) *colloq.* elaborate party, operation, etc. (*it's going to be a really big do*). □ **be done with** see DONE. **be nothing to do with 1** be no business of (*this is nothing to do with you*). **2** be unconnected with (*his depression is nothing to do with his father's death*). **be to do with** be concerned or connected with (*the argument was to do with money*). **do away with** *colloq.* **1** get rid of; abolish. **2** kill. **do down** *colloq.* **1** cheat, swindle. **2** overcome. **do for 1** be satisfactory or sufficient for (*that'll do for me, thanks*). **2** *colloq.* (esp. as **done for** *adj.*) destroy, ruin, kill (*he knew he was done for*). **3** *colloq.* **a** act as cleaner etc. for. **b** see *v.* 20. **do in 1** *colloq.* **a** kill. **b** ruin. **2** *colloq.* exhaust, tire out (*I'm all done in*). **do justice to** see JUSTICE. **do nothing for** (or **to**) *colloq.* not flatter or enhance (*that hat does nothing for you*). **do or die** persist recklessly. **do out** *colloq.* clean or redecorate (a room). **do a person out of** *colloq.* cheat of. **do over** *colloq.* **1** attack; beat up. **2** redecorate, refurbish (*need to do over the lounge*). **do proud** see PROUD. **dos and don'ts** rules of behaviour. **do something for** (or **to**) *colloq.* enhance the appearance or quality of. **do up 1** fasten. **2** *colloq.* **a** refurbish, renovate. **b** adorn, dress up. **do with** (prec. by *could*) would be glad of; would profit by (*could do with a rest*). **do without** manage without; forgo. **have nothing to do with 1** have no connections or dealings with (*after the row he had nothing to do with his father*). **2** be no business or concern of (*the decision has nothing to do with him*). **have to do** (or **something to do**) **with** have a connection with (*his limp has to do with*

a car accident; *what has this to do with the price of eggs?*). □ **doable** *adj.* [Old English]

**do²** var. of DOH.

**do.** *abbr.* ditto.

**dob** *v.* (**-bb-**) *Aust. Rules* kick (esp. a goal) (*dobbed the ball through the centre*). □ **dob in** *colloq.* **1** incriminate (a person) by informing on him or her. **2** impose (a responsibility) upon (*dobbed him in to do the cleaning*). **3** contribute (money) towards a common cause (*everyone dobbed in a few dollars to help him out*). **dob on** *colloq.* inform on; betray. □ **dobber** *n.* [British dial. *dob* put down, throw down]

**doc** *n. colloq.* doctor. [abbreviation]

**docile** /**doh**-suyl/ *adj.* submissive, easily managed. □ **docilely** *adv.* **docility** /-**sil**-uh-tee/ *n.* [Latin *doceo* teach]

**dock¹** — *n.* **1** enclosed harbour for the loading, unloading, and repair of ships. **2** (in *pl.*) docks with wharves and offices. **3** = DRY DOCK. — *v.* **1** bring or come into dock. **2 a** join (spacecraft) together in space. **b** be joined thus. [Dutch *docke*]

**dock²** *n.* enclosure in a criminal court for the accused. [Flemish *dok* cage]

**dock³** *n.* weed with broad leaves. [Old English]

**dock⁴** *v.* **1** cut short (an animal's tail). **2** take away part of, reduce (wages, supplies, etc.). [Old English]

**docker** *n.* person employed to load and unload ships.

**docket** /**dok**-uht/ — *n.* document or label listing goods delivered, jobs done, contents of a package, or recording payment of customs dues etc. — *v.* (**-t-**) label with, or enter on, a docket. [origin unknown]

**dockland** *n.* district near docks or former docks.

**dockyard** *n.* area with docks and equipment for building and repairing ships.

**doctor** /**dok**-tuh/ — *n.* **1** qualified practitioner of medicine; physician. **2 a** person who holds a doctorate from a university. **b** (**Doctor**) the title for such a person. **3** *colloq.* person who carries out repairs (*tree doctor*). **4** cool, refreshing sea breeze (*Albany doctor*; *Fremantle doctor*). **5** (in Aboriginal English) = CLEVER MAN. — *v. colloq.* **1** treat medically. **2** castrate or spay. **3** patch up (machinery etc.). **4** adulterate (*doctor a person's drink*). **5** tamper with, falsify (*doctor the accounts*). □ **go for the doctor** *colloq.* **1** make an all-out effort. **2** bet all one has. **what the doctor ordered** *colloq.* something welcome. [Latin *doceo* teach]

**doctoral** adj. of or for the degree of doctor (*writing my doctoral thesis*).

**doctorate** /**dok**-tuh-ruht/ n. highest university degree in any faculty, sometimes honorary.

**doctrinaire** /ˌdok-truh-**nair**/ adj. applying theory or doctrine dogmatically in all circumstances. [French: related to DOCTRINE]

**doctrine** /**dok**-truhn/ n. **1** what is taught; body of instruction (*religious doctrine*; *Marxist doctrine*). **2 a** principle of religious or political etc. belief (*doctrine of Transubstantiation*). **b** set of such principles; dogma. □ **doctrinal** /dok-**truy**-nuhl, **dok**-truh-nuhl/ adj. [Latin: related to DOCTOR]

**docudrama** /**dok**-yoo-ˌdrah-muh/ n. television drama based on real events. [from DOCUMENTARY, DRAMA]

**document** — n. /**dok**-yuh-muhnt/ thing providing a record or evidence of events, agreement, ownership, identification, etc. — v. /**dok**-yoo-ˌment/ **1** prove by or support with documents (*well documented research*). **2** record in a document. [Latin: related to DOCTOR]

**documentary** /ˌdok-yoo-**men**-tuh-ree, -tree/ — adj. **1** consisting of documents (*documentary evidence*). **2** providing a factual record or report. — n. (pl. **-ies**) documentary film etc.

**documentation** /ˌdok-yoo-men-tay-shuhn/ n. **1 a** collection and classification of information. **b** material so collected. **2** material used to prove or support an argument etc. (*this essay has inadequate documentation*). **3** collection of documents relating to a process or event, esp. the written specifications and instructions accompanying a computer program.

**dodder**[1] v. tremble or totter, esp. from age. □ **dodderer** n. **doddery** adj. [obsolete British dial. *dadder*]

**dodder**[2] n. **1** threadlike climbing parasitic plant. **2** = DODDER-LAUREL. [origin uncertain]

**dodder-laurel** n. (also **devil's twine**) any of several parasitic perennial climbers (of all Australian States) belonging to the genus *Cassytha*.

**dodecagon** /doh-**dek**-uh-guhn/ n. plane figure with twelve sides. [Greek *dōdeka* twelve, -*gōnos* angled]

**dodecahedron** /ˌdoh-dek-uh-**hee**-druhn/ n. solid figure with twelve faces. [from DODECAGON, Greek *hedra* base]

**dodge** — v. (**-ging**) **1** (often foll. by *about, behind, round*) move quickly to elude a pursuer, blow, etc. **2** evade by cunning or trickery (*dodged paying the fare*). **3** *colloq.* acquire dishonestly. — n. **1** quick movement to avoid something. **2** clever trick or expedient. [origin unknown]

**dodgem** /**doj**-uhm/ n. small electrically-driven car in an enclosure at a funfair bumped into others for fun. [from DODGE 'EM]

**dodger** /**doj**-uh/ n. **1** person who dodges, esp. an artful or elusive person. **2** *colloq.* bread.

**dodgy** adj. (**-ier, -iest**) *colloq.* **1** awkward, unreliable, risky. **2** cunning, artful.

**dodo** /**doh**-doh/ n. (pl. **-s**) **1** large extinct bird of Mauritius etc. **2** old-fashioned or stupid person. □ **dead as a dodo** see DEAD. [Portuguese *doudo* simpleton]

**doe** n. (pl. same or **-s**) female fallow deer, kangaroo, reindeer, hare, or rabbit. [Old English]

**doer** /**doo**-uh/ n. **1** person who does something. **2** person who acts rather than theorising. **3** (in full **hard-doer**) eccentric or amusing person.

**does** see DO[1].

**doesn't** /**duz**-uhnt/ contr. does not.

**doff** v. remove (a hat or clothes). [from *do off*]

**dog** — n. **1** four-legged flesh-eating animal akin to the fox and wolf, and of many breeds. **2** male of this, or of the fox or wolf. **3** *colloq.* a despicable person. **b** person of a specified kind (*lucky dog*). **c** informer; traitor. **4** mechanical device for gripping. **5** (in pl.; prec. by *the*) *colloq.* greyhound-racing. — v. (**-gg-**) **1** follow closely; pursue, track (*this weirdo dogged my heels all the way home*). **2** annoy, trouble; plague (*this project has been dogged by misfortune from the start*). **3** hunt dingoes. □ **dog poor** *colloq.* in a very poor condition. **go to the dogs** *colloq.* deteriorate, be ruined. **not a dog's chance** no chance at all. **turn dog on** *colloq.* inform on; betray. [Old English]

**dog box** n. *colloq.* compartment in a railway carriage without a corridor.

**dog collar** n. **1** collar for a dog. **2** *colloq.* clerical collar.

**doge** /dohj/ n. *hist.* chief magistrate of Venice or Genoa. [Italian from Latin *dux* leader]

**dog-eared** adj. (of a book etc.) with bent or worn corners. □ **dog-ear** v.

**dog-eat-dog** adj. *colloq.* ruthlessly competitive.

**dogfight** n. **1** close combat between fighter aircraft. **2** rough fight.

**dogfish** n. (pl. same or **-es**) a kind of small shark.

**dogged** /**dog**-uhd/ adj. tenacious, grimly persistent. □ **doggedly** adv. **doggedness** n.

**dogger** /dog-uh/ n. person who hunts dingoes.

**doggerel** /dog-uh-ruhl/ n. poor or trivial verse. [apparently from DOG]

**doggie** /dog-ee/ n. see MAYFLY ORCHID. [from DOG]

**doggo** /dog-oh/ adv. □ **lie doggo** colloq. lie motionless or hidden.

**doggy** — adj. **1** of or like a dog. **2** devoted to dogs (a doggy person). — n. (also **doggie**) (pl. **-ies**) pet name for a dog.

**doggy bag** n. bag for leftovers given to a customer in a restaurant etc.

**doghouse** n. dog's kennel. □ **in the doghouse** colloq. in disgrace.

**dog-leg** adj. (also **dog-legged**) bent like a dog's hind leg.

**dog-leg-fence** n. fence made from logs laid horizontally on crossed supports.

**dog licence** n. (also **dog certificate, dog ticket**) hist. certificate exempting an Aborigine from legislation pertaining specifically to Aborigines only, esp. that prohibiting the sale of alcohol to Aborigines.

**dogma** /dog-muh/ n. **1** principle, tenet, or system of these, esp. of a Church or political party. **2** arrogant declaration of opinion. [Greek, = opinion]

**dogman** n. (pl. **-men**) worker who rides on the hook of a crane (or on a girder etc. being lifted by a crane) and gives signals to the crane-operator.

**dogmatic** /dog-mat-ik/ adj. **1** asserting or imposing personal opinions; intolerantly authoritative; arrogant. **2** of or in the nature of dogma; doctrinal. □ **dogmatically** adv.

**dogmatise** /dog-muh-tyuz/ v. (also **-ize**) (**-sing** or **-zing**) **1** speak dogmatically. **2** express (a principle etc.) as dogma.

**dogmatism** /dog-muh-tiz-uhm/ n. tendency to be dogmatic. □ **dogmatist** n.

**do-gooder** n. well-meaning but unrealistic or patronising philanthropist or reformer.

**dog-paddle** — n. elementary swimming stroke like that of a dog. — v. swim using this stroke.

**dog rose** n. = RIVER ROSE.

**dogsbody** n. (pl. **-ies**) colloq. drudge.

**dog's breakfast** n. (also **dog's dinner**) colloq. mess.

**dog's life** n. life of misery etc.

**dog-star** n. chief star of the constellation Canis Major or Minor, esp. Sirius.

**dog-tired** adj. tired out.

**dog-tooth** n. V-shaped pattern or moulding; chevron.

**dogwood** n. **1** any of various shrubs of Europe etc., belonging to the genus *Cornus*. **2** any of several unrelated Australian shrubs or trees, esp.: **a** ELLANGOWAN POISON BUSH. **b** STINKWOOD.

**doh** /doh/ n. (also **do**) Mus. first note of a major scale. [Italian *do*]

**doily** /doi-lee/ n. (also **doyley**) (pl. **-ies** or **-eys**) small ornamental mat of lace, paper, etc., used on a plate for cakes etc. [Doiley, name of a draper]

**doing** /doo-ing/ pres. part. of DO[1]. — n. **1 a** action (famous for his doings). **b** effort (takes a lot of doing). **2** (in pl.) colloq. necessary things, ingredients (have we got all the doings?). **3** colloq. scolding; beating.

**doing-over** n. colloq. attack, beating-up.

**do-it-yourself** — adj. (of work) done or to be done by a householder etc. — n. such work.

**Dolby** /dol-bee/ n. propr. electronic noise-reduction system used esp. in tape-recording to reduce hiss. [name of its inventor]

**doldrums** /dol-druhmz/ n.pl. (usu. prec. by the) **1** low spirits; feeling of boredom or depression. **2** period of inactivity. **3** equatorial ocean region with little or no wind. [perhaps after dull, tantrum]

**dole** — n. **1** (usu. prec. by the) unemployment benefit. **2 a** charitable distribution. **b** thing given sparingly or reluctantly. — v. (**-ling**) (usu. foll. by out) distribute sparingly. □ **on the dole** receiving unemployment benefit. [Old English]

**dole-bludger** /dohl-bluj-uh/ n. colloq. **1** person who exploits the system of unemployment benefits by avoiding gainful employment. **2** person who allegedly prefers the dole to work. □ **dole-bludging** n. & adj.

**doleful** /dohl-fuul/ adj. **1** mournful, sad. **2** dreary, dismal. □ **dolefully** adv. **dolefulness** n. [Latin doleo grieve]

**doley** /doh-lee/ n. (pl. **-s** or **dolies**) colloq. person receiving the dole.

**doll** — n. **1** small model of esp. a baby or child as a child's toy. **2** colloq. **a** pretty but silly young woman. **b** attractive person of either sex (formerly only of a woman). **3** ventriloquist's dummy. — v. (foll. by up) colloq. dress smartly (all dolled up and nowhere to go). [pet form of Dorothy]

**dollar** /dol-uh/ n. **1** chief monetary unit in Australia since 1966. **2** chief monetary unit in the US, Canada, various countries in SE Asia, etc. [Low German daler from German Taler]

**dollop** /dol-uhp/ — n. shapeless lump of food etc. — v. (**-p-**) (usu. foll. by out) serve in dollops. [perhaps from Scandinavian]

**dolly** n. (pl. **-ies**) **1** child's name for a doll.

**2** apparatus for crushing auriferous quartz in order to extract the gold. **3** movable platform for a cine-camera etc. **4** easy catch in cricket. **5** = DOLLY-BIRD.

**dolly-bird** *n. colloq.* attractive and stylish young woman.

**dolma** /**dol**-muh, -mah/ *n.* (*pl.* **-s** or **dolmades** /-**mah**-deez/ ) E. European delicacy of spiced rice or meat etc. wrapped in vine or cabbage leaves. [modern Greek]

**dolmen** /**dol**-muhn/ *n.* megalithic tomb with a large flat stone laid on upright ones. [French]

**dolomite** /**dol**-uh-,muyt/ *n.* mineral or rock of calcium magnesium carbonate. [de *Dolomieu*, name of a French geologist]

**dolour** /**do**-luh/ *n.* (also **dolor**) *literary* sorrow, distress. □ **dolorous** *adj.* [Latin *dolor* pain]

**dolphin** /**dol**-fuhn/ *n.* large porpoise-like sea mammal with a slender pointed snout. [Greek *delphis -in-*]

**dolt** /dohlt/ *n.* stupid person. □ **doltish** *adj.* [apparently related to obsolete *dol* = DULL]

**Dom** *n.* title of some Catholic dignitaries, and of Benedictine and Carthusian monks. [Latin *dominus* master]

**-dom** *suffix* forming nouns denoting: **1** condition (*freedom*). **2** rank, domain (*earldom*; *kingdom*). **3** class of people (or associated attitudes etc.) regarded collectively (*officialdom*). [Old English]

**domain** /duh-**mayn**/ *n.* **1** area under one rule; realm. **2** sphere of control or influence (*he's in his own domain*). **3** sphere of thought or action; scope of an area of knowledge (*the domain of science*). **4** *Math.* the set of possible values of an independent variable. **5** *Physics* discrete region of magnetism in ferromagnetic material. [French: related to DEMESNE]

**dome** — *n.* **1** rounded (usu. hemispherical) vault forming a roof. **2** dome-shaped thing. — *v.* (**-ming**) (usu. as **domed** *adj.*) cover with or shape as a dome. [Latin *domus* house]

**domestic** /duh-**mes**-tik/ — *adj.* **1** of the home, household, or family affairs. **2** of one's own country, not foreign or international. **3** (of an animal) tamed, not wild. **4** fond of home life. — *n.* **1** household servant. **2** domestic disturbance, esp. an argument or fight between a husband and wife etc. (*police don't like being called to domestics*). □ **domestically** *adv.* [Latin *domus* home]

**domesticate** /duh-**mes**-tuh-,kayt/ *v.* (**-ting**) **1** tame (an animal) to live with

humans. **2** accustom to housework etc. □ **domestication** /-**kay**-shuhn/ *n.* [medieval Latin: related to DOMESTIC]

**domesticity** /,do-mes-**tis**-uh-tee, ,doh-/ *n.* **1** state of being domestic. **2** domestic or home life.

**domestic science** *n.* = HOME ECONOMICS.

**domicile** /**dom**-uh-,suyl/ — *n.* **1** dwelling-place. **2** *Law* **a** place of permanent residence. **b** fact of residing. — *v.* (**-ling**) (usu. as **domiciled** *adj.*) (usu. foll. by *at*, *in*) settle in a place. □ **domiciliary** *adj.* [Latin *domus* home]

**dominant** /**dom**-uh-nuhnt/ — *adj.* **1** dominating, prevailing, most influential, most important. **2** (of a high place) prominent, overlooking others. **3** (of an inherited characteristic) appearing in offspring even when the opposite characteristic is also inherited. — *n. Mus.* fifth note of the diatonic scale of any key. □ **dominance** *n.* **dominantly** *adv.*

**dominate** /**dom**-uh-,nayt/ *v.* (**-ting**) **1** command, control. **2** be the most influential or obvious. **3** (of a high place) overlook. □ **domination** /,dom-uh-**nay**-shuhn/ *n.* **dominator** *n.* [Latin *dominor* from *dominus* lord]

**domineer** /,dom-uh-**neer**/ *v.* (often as **domineering** *adj.*) behave arrogantly or tyrannically. [French: related to DOMINATE]

**Dominican** /duh-**min**-i-kuhn/ — *adj.* of St Dominic or his order (which he founded in 1215–16). — *n.* Dominican friar or nun. [Latin *Dominicus* Dominic]

**dominion** /duh-**min**-yuhn/ *n.* **1** sovereignty, control. **2** realm; domain. **3** *hist.* self-governing territory of the British Commonwealth. [Latin *dominus* lord]

**domino** /**dom**-uh-,noh/ *n.* (*pl.* **-es**) **1** any of 28 small oblong pieces marked with 0–6 pips in each half. **2** (in *pl.*) game played with these. [French, probably as DOMINION]

**domino effect** *n.* (also **domino theory**) effect whereby (or theory that) one event precipitates others in causal sequence, like a row of falling dominoes, esp. the notion that a political event etc. in one country will cause similar events in neighbouring countries.

**don**[1] *n.* **1** university teacher. **2** (**Don**) Spanish title prefixed to a forename. [Spanish from Latin *dominus* lord]

**don**[2] *v.* (**-nn-**) put on (clothing). [= *do on*]

**donate** /doh-**nayt**/ *v.* (**-ting**) give (money etc.), esp. to charity. [from DONATION]

**donation** /doh-**nay**-shuhn/ *n.* **1** act or instance of donating. **2** thing, esp. money, donated. [Latin *donum* gift]

**done** /dun/ *adj.* **1** completed. **2** cooked. **3** *colloq.* socially acceptable (*the done thing*). **4** (often with *in*) *colloq.* tired out. **5** (esp. as *int.* in reply to an offer etc.) accepted. □ **be done with** have or be finished with. **done for** *colloq.* **1** in serious trouble. **2** ruined, esp. financially. **3** utterly exhausted. **4** dead; on the verge of death. **have done with** be rid of; finish dealing with. [past part. of DO¹]

**doner kebab** /don-uh, doh-nuh/ *n.* spiced lamb cooked on a spit and served in slices, often with pitta bread. [Turkish: related to KEBAB]

**dong** — *n.* **1** deep sound of a large bell. **2** *colloq.* heavy blow. **3** (also **donger**) *coarse colloq.* penis. — *v.* **1** make the deep sound of a large bell. **2** *colloq.* hit, punch (*donged him one*). [imitative]

**donga** /dong-guh/ *n.* **1** dry watercourse. **2** broad, shallow, often circular depression most often found in dry country. **3** makeshift or temporary dwelling. [Zulu]

**Don Juan** /,don joo-uhn, ,don **wahn**/ *n.* seducer of women. [name of a legendary Spanish nobleman]

**donkey** /dong-kee/ — *n.* (*pl.* -**s**) **1** domestic ass. **2** *colloq.* stupid or utterly stubborn person. **3** (in SA) = DINK¹ *n.* — *v.* (in SA) = DINK¹ *v.* □ **talk the hind legs off a donkey** *colloq.* talk excessively or persistently. [perhaps from *Duncan*: cf. NEDDY]

**donkey engine** *n.* small auxiliary engine.

**donkey lick** *v.* (also **donkey-wallop**) *colloq.* defeat resoundingly.

**donkey orchid** *n.* Australian terrestrial orchid of all States, having strikingly large, usu. rich gold and brown flowers, the upper two petals of which resemble a donkey's ears.

**donkey's years** *n.pl. colloq.* very long time. [pun on *donkey's ears*]

**donkey vote** *n.* **1** vote recorded by unthinkingly allocating preferences according to the order in which candidates are listed on the ballot paper. **2** such votes viewed collectively.

**donkey work** *n.* laborious part of a job; drudgery.

**donks** *n.* □ **in** (or **for**) **donks** *colloq.* in (or for) a very long time (*haven't seen him in donks*). [abbreviation of DONKEY'S YEARS]

**Donna** /don-uh/ *n.* title of an Italian, Spanish, or Portuguese lady. [Latin *domina* mistress]

**donnybrook** /don-ee-,bruuk/ *n.* fight; scene of uproar. [*Donnybrook* in Ireland]

**donor** /doh-nuh/ *n.* **1** person who donates (e.g. to charity). **2** person who provides blood, semen, or an organ or tissue for medical use. **3** *Chem.* atom or molecule that provides a pair of electrons in forming a coordinate bond. **4** *Physics* impurity atom in a semiconductor which contributes a conducting electron to the material.

**don't** /dohnt/ — *contr.* do not. — *n.* prohibition (*dos and don'ts*).

**doodle** /doo-duhl/ — *v.* (-**ling**) scribble or draw, esp. absent-mindedly. — *n.* such a scribble or drawing. □ **doodler** *n.* [originally = foolish person]

**doom** — *n.* **1 a** grim fate or destiny. **b** death or ruin. **2** condemnation. — *v.* **1** (usu. foll. by *to*) condemn or destine (*Australian animals doomed to extinction by the commercial destruction of their habitats*). **2** (esp. as **doomed** *adj.*) consign to misfortune or destruction (*the project's doomed*). [Old English, = STATUTE]

**doomsday** *n.* day of the Last Judgment. □ **till doomsday** for ever.

**doona** /doo-nuh/ *n. propr.* thick soft quilt with a detachable cover, used instead of an upper sheet and blankets.

**door** *n.* **1 a** esp. hinged barrier for closing and opening the entrance to a building, room, cupboard, etc. **b** this as representing a house etc. (*lives two doors away*). **2 a** entrance or exit; doorway. **b** means of access. □ **close** (or **open**) **the door to** exclude (or create) an opportunity for. [Old English]

**doorknock** — *n.* (also *attrib.*) **1** appeal in which agents for a (charitable) cause go from house to house soliciting contributions. **2** campaign in support of a political party. — *v.* engage in door-knocking.

**doormat** *n.* **1** mat at an entrance, for wiping shoes. **2** *colloq.* feebly submissive person.

**doorstep** *n.* **1** step or area in front of the outer door of a house etc. **2** *colloq.* thick slice of bread. □ **on one's doorstep** very near.

**doorstop** — *n.* device for keeping a door open or to prevent it from striking the wall. — *v.* wait at the entrance of a building for (a person) in order to interview (him or her).

**door-to-door** *adj.* (of selling etc.) done at each house in turn.

**doorway** *n.* opening filled by a door.

**doover** /doo-vuh/ *n. colloq.* thing-ummyjig. [origin uncertain]

**dope** — *n.* **1 a** *colloq.* narcotic. **b** drug etc. given to a horse, athlete, etc., to improve performance. **2** *colloq.* stupid person. **3** *colloq.* information. — *v.* (-**ping**) give or add a drug to. [Dutch, = sauce]

**dopey** adj. (also **dopy**) (**dopier, dopiest**) colloq. **1** half asleep or stupefied as if by a drug. **2** stupid. □ **dopily** adv. **dopiness** n.

**doppelgänger** /**dop**-uhl-ˌgeng-uh/ n. apparition or double of a living person. [German, = double-goer]

**Doppler effect** n. increase (or decrease) in the frequency of sound, light, etc. waves caused by moving nearer to (or further from) the source. [Doppler, name of a physicist (d. 1853)]

**Doric** /**do**-rik/ adj. Archit. of the oldest, sturdiest, and simplest of the Greek orders. [from Dōris in Greece]

**dork** /dawk/ n. colloq. stupid or ineffectual person. [US dork penis]

**dormant** /**daw**-muhnt/ adj. **1** lying inactive; sleeping. **2** (of a volcano etc.) temporarily inactive. **3** (of plants) alive but not actively growing. □ **dormancy** n. [Latin dormio sleep]

**dormer** n. (in full **dormer window**) projecting upright window in a sloping roof. [French: related to DORMANT]

**dormitory** /**daw**-muh-tuh-ree, -tree/ n. (pl. **-ies**) sleeping-room with several beds, esp. in a school or institution. [Latin: related to DORMER]

**dormouse** /**daw**-mows/ n. (pl. **-mice**) small mouselike hibernating rodent. [origin unknown]

**Dorothy Dix** /ˌdo-ruh-thee **diks**/ n. (also **Dorothy Dixer**) a prearranged parliamentary question asked so as to allow a minister to deliver a prepared speech. [Dorothy Dix US writer of a question-and-answer column (d. 1951)]

**dorsal** /**daw**-suhl/ adj. of or on the back (dorsal fin; dorsal petal). [Latin dorsum back]

**dory** /**daw**-ree/ n. (pl. same or **-ies**) any of various edible marine fish, esp. the John Dory. [French dorée = gilded]

**DOS** /dos/ n. Computing controlling software usu. used with microcomputers. [disk operating system]

**dosage** /**doh**-sij/ n. **1** size of a dose. **2** giving of a dose.

**dose** — n. **1** amount of medicine for taking at one time. **2** quantity or experience of something regarded as analogous in some way to a dose of medicine, esp. something unpleasant (dose of flu). **3** amount of ionising radiation received or absorbed at one time or over a specified period. **4** colloq. venereal infection. — v. (**-sing**) treat with or give doses of medicine to. [Greek dosis gift]

**dosh** n. colloq. money. [origin unknown]

**doss** v. (often foll. by down) colloq. sleep,

esp. roughly or in cheap lodgings. [probably originally = 'seat-back cover': from Latin dorsum back]

**dossier** /**dos**-ee-uh, -eeˌay/ n. set of documents, esp. a file containing information about a person, event, etc. [French]

**dot** — n. **1 a** small spot or mark. **b** this as part of i or j, as a decimal point, full stop, etc. **2** shorter signal of the two in Morse code. **3** Mus. dot used to denote the lengthening of a note or rest, or to indicate staccato. **4** tiny or apparently tiny object (a dot on the horizon). — v. (**-tt-**) **1 a** mark with dot(s). **b** place a dot over (a letter). **2** (often foll. by about) scatter like dots. **3** partly cover as with dots (sea dotted with ships). **4** colloq. hit (dotted him one). □ **dot the i's and cross the t's** colloq. **1** be minutely accurate. **2** add the final touches to a task etc. **on the dot** exactly on time. **the year dot** colloq. far in the past. [Old English]

**dotage** n. feeble-minded senility (in his dotage).

**dotard** /**doh**-tuhd/ n. senile person.

**dot ball** n. Cricket bowled ball, esp. in the last hour of a one-day match, from which no run is scored. [indicated by a DOT on the scoreboard]

**dote** v. (**-ting**) (foll. by on) be excessively fond of. □ **dotingly** adv. [origin uncertain]

**dot painting** n. style of Aboriginal art from central Australia.

**dotted line** n. line of dots on a document etc., esp. for writing a signature on.

**dotterel** /**dot**-uh-ruhl/ n. any of various small wading birds (often also called plovers), in Australia both resident and migrant (hooded dotterel; inland dotterel; red-kneed dotterel). [from DOTE, named from the ease with which it is caught, taken to indicate stupidity]

**dotty** adj. (**-ier, -iest**) colloq. **1** crazy; eccentric. **2** (foll. by about) infatuated with. □ **dottiness** n.

**double** /**dub**-uhl/ — adj. **1** consisting of two parts or things; twofold. **2** twice as much or many (double thickness; double the number). **3** having twice the usual size, quantity, strength, etc. (double bed). **4** (of a flower) with two or more circles of petals. **5** ambiguous, deceitful (double meaning; a double life). **6** Mus. lower in pitch by an octave (double bassoon). — adv. **1** at or to twice the amount etc. (counts double). **2** two together (sleep double). — n. **1** double quantity (of spirits etc.) or thing; twice as much or many. **2** counterpart; person who looks exactly like another. **3** (in pl.) game between two pairs of players. **4** pair of victories. **5** bet in which winnings and stake from the first bet are transferred to the second (*daily double*). **6** (at a motel etc.) room for two. — *v.* (**-ling**) **1** make or become double; increase twofold; multiply by two. **3** amount to twice as much as. **3** fold or bend over on itself; become folded. **4 a** act (two parts) in the same play etc. **b** (often foll. by *for*) be understudy etc. **5** (usu. foll. by *as*) play a twofold role. **6** turn sharply in flight or pursuit. **7** increase a bid (in cards) or bet etc. twofold. □ **at** (or **on**) **the double** running, hurrying; quickly. **bent double** stooping. **double back** turn back in the opposite direction. **double bank** = DINK[1]. **double or quits** gamble to decide whether a player's loss or debt be doubled or cancelled. **double up 1** (cause to) bend or curl up with pain or laughter. **2** share or assign to a shared room, quarters, etc. □ **doubly** *adv.* [Latin *duplus*]

**double agent** *n.* spy working simultaneously for rival countries.

**double-barrelled** *adj.* **1** (of a gun) having two barrels. **2** (of a surname) hyphenated. **3** having a twofold purpose, meaning, etc. (*double-barrelled question*).

**double bass** *n.* largest instrument of the violin family.

**double blind** — *adj.* (of a test or experiment) in which neither the tester nor the subject has knowledge of identities etc. which might lead to bias. — *n.* such a test or experiment.

**double bluff** *n.* genuine action or statement disguised as a bluff.

**double-breasted** *adj.* (of a coat etc.) having two fronts overlapping across the body.

**double chin** *n.* chin with a fold of loose flesh below it.

**double-cross** — *v.* deceive or betray (a supposed ally). — *n.* act of doing this. □ **double-crosser** *n.*

**double-dealing** — *n.* deceit, esp. in business. — *adj.* practising deceit.

**double-decker** *n.* **1** bus having an upper and lower deck. **2** *colloq.* sandwich with two layers of filling.

**double decomposition** *n.* chemical reaction involving exchange of radicals between two reactants.

**double-dipping** *n.* practice by which a retired person draws income from two publicly funded sources.

**double dissolution** *n.* simultaneous dissolution of the upper and lower houses of a parliament preparatory to an election.

**double drummer** *n.* large black and yellow cicada of southern and eastern

Australia, so called from the two large organs which produce its characteristic sound (cf. DRUM *n.* 8).

**double dutch** *n. colloq.* gibberish, nonsense.

**double-edged** *adj.* **1** presenting both a danger and an advantage. **2** (of a knife etc.) having two cutting-edges.

**double entendre** /,doo-buhl ahn-**tahn**-druh, on-**ton**-druh/ *n.* ambiguous phrase open to usu. indecent interpretation. [obsolete French]

**double-faced** *adj.* **1** insincere. **2** (of a fabric or material) finished on both sides so that either may be used as the right side.

**double figures** *n.pl.* numbers from 10 to 99.

**doublegee** /dub-uhl-**jee**/ *n.* **1** (also **prickly jack, spiny emex, three-cornered jack**) naturalised South African herb of all mainland States, bearing a fruit with three rigid spines; the fruit itself. **2** any of several other plants bearing a similarly spiny fruit; the fruit of these plants. [Afrikaans *dubbel* double, *-tjie* diminutive suffix]

**double-glazing** *n.* two layers of glass in a window.

**double header** *n.* **1** *Sport* two matches etc. in succession between the same opponents or between different opponents. **2** coin with a head on both sides.

**double helix** *n.* pair of parallel helices with a common axis, esp. in the structure of a DNA molecule.

**double-jointed** *adj.* having joints that allow unusual bending.

**double negative** *n. Gram.* negative statement containing two negative elements (e.g. *he didn't say nothing*).

■ **Usage** The double negative is considered incorrect in standard English.

**double pneumonia** *n.* pneumonia affecting both lungs.

**double quick** *adj. & adv. colloq.* very quick or quickly.

**double standard** *n.* rule or principle applied more strictly to some people than to others (or to oneself).

**doublet** /**dub**-luht/ *n.* **1** *hist.* man's short close-fitting jacket. **2** one of a pair of similar things, esp. either of two words of the same or related derivation but different sense (e.g. *fashion* and *faction*, *shirt* and *skirt*). [French: related to DOUBLE]

**double take** *n.* delayed reaction to a situation etc.

**double-talk** *n.* (usu. deliberately) ambiguous or misleading speech.

**double-think** *n.* capacity to accept contrary opinions or beliefs at the same time.

**double time** *n.* wages paid at twice the normal rate.

**double whammy** /**wam**-ee/ *n. colloq.* stroke of good or (more usu.) extremely bad fortune which has two parts to it or comes in two stages etc.

**doubloon** /dub-**loon**/ *n. hist.* Spanish gold coin. [French or Spanish: related to DOUBLE]

**doubt** /dowt/ — *n.* **1** uncertainty; undecided state of mind (*be in no doubt about*). **2** inclination to disbelieve (*have one's doubts about*). **3** uncertain state (*all is in doubt*). **4** lack of full proof or clear indication (*benefit of the doubt*). — *v.* **1** feel uncertain or undecided about. **2** hesitate to believe. **3** call in question. □ **in doubt** open to question. **no doubt** certainly; admittedly. **without doubt** (or **a doubt**) certainly. [Latin *dubito* hesitate]

**doubtful** *adj.* **1** feeling doubt or misgivings. **2** causing doubt; ambiguous. **3** unreliable (*a doubtful ally*). □ **doubtfully** *adv.* **doubtfulness** *n.*

**doubtless** *adv.* certainly; probably.

**douche** /doosh/ — *n.* **1** jet of liquid applied onto or into part of the body for cleansing or medicinal purposes. **2** device for producing such a jet. — *v.* (**-ching**) **1** treat with a douche. **2** use a douche. [Latin: related to DUCT]

**dough** /doh/ *n.* **1** thick mixture of flour etc. and liquid for baking. **2** *colloq.* money. □ **doughy** *adj.* (**-ier, -iest**). [Old English]

**doughboy** *n.* flour dumpling, usu. boiled or fried.

**doughnut** *n.* small fried cake of sweetened dough, usu. in the shape of a ring or ball.

**doughty** /**dow**-tee/ *adj.* (**-ier, -iest**) *archaic* valiant. □ **doughtily** *adv.* **doughtiness** *n.* [Old English]

**dour** /door/ *adj.* severe, stern, sullenly obstinate. [probably Gaelic *dúr* dull, obstinate]

**douse** *v.* (also **dowse**) (**-sing**) **1 a** throw water over. **b** plunge into water. **2** extinguish (a light). [origin uncertain]

**dove** /duv/ *n.* **1** any of various birds of the pigeon family having short legs, a small head, and a large breast, including the native Australian *diamond dove*, *emerald dove*, and *peaceful dove*, and the introduced *spotted turtle-dove*. **2** gentle or innocent person. **3** advocate of peace or peaceful policies (opp. HAWK). [Old Norse]

**dovecote** /**duv**-kot/ *n.* (also **dovecot**)

shelter with nesting-holes for domesticated pigeons.

**dovetail** — *n.* mortise and tenon joint shaped like a dove's spread tail. — *v.* **1** join with dovetails. **2** fit together combine neatly or compactly (*your stor dovetails with hers*).

**dowager** /**dow**-uh-juh/ *n.* **1** widow with a title or property from her late husband (*dowager duchess*). **2** *colloq.* dignifie elderly woman. [French: related t DOWER]

**dowak** /**dow**-uhk/ *n.* weapon used by Aborigines, a wooden club abruptly pointed at each end. [Nyungar, probably *duwag*]

**dowdy** /**dow**-dee/ *adj.* (**-ier, -iest**) **1** (o clothes) unattractively dull; unfashion able. **2** dressed dowdily. □ **dowdily** *adv* **dowdiness** *n.* [origin unknown]

**dowel** /**dow**-uhl/ — *n.* cylindrical peg fo holding structural components together — *v.* (**-ll-**) fasten with a dowel. [Lov German]

**dowelling** *n.* rods for cutting into dowels

**dower** *n.* **1** widow's share for life of husband's estate. **2** *archaic* dowry. [Latin *dos* dowry]

**Dow-Jones index** /dow-**johnz**/ *n.* (als **Dow-Jones average**) a figure indicating the relative price of shares on the New York Stock Exchange. [*Dow* and *Jones*, names of American economists]

**down¹** — *adv.* **1** into or towards a lowe place, esp. to the ground (*fall down*). **2** in a lower place or position (*blinds were down*). **3** to or in a place regarded a lower, esp.: **a** southwards. **b** away from major city (*travelling down from Melbourne*). **4 a** in or into a low or weaker position or condition (*hit a man when he's down*; *down with a cold*). **b** losing by (*three goals down*; *$5 down*). **c** (of computer system) out of action or un available for use (esp. temporarily). **5** from an earlier to a later time (*custom handed down*; *down to 1600*). **6** to a fine or thinner consistency or smaller amoun or size (*grind down*; *water down*; *boi down*). **7** cheaper; lower in price or valu (*bread is down*; *shares are down*). **8 a** int a more settled state (*calm down*). **b** int a quieter or milder state (*turn down th volume*; *tone down your criticism*). **9** i writing or recorded form (*copy it down down on tape*; *down to speak next*). **10** paid or dealt with as a deposit or part (*$ down, $20 to pay*; *three down, six to go*) **11** *Naut.* with the current or wind. **12** (o a crossword clue or answer) read vertic ally (*five down*). — *prep.* **1** downward along, through, or into. **2** from the top t the bottom of. **3** along (*walk down the road*). **4** at or in a lower part of (*situated down the river*). — *adj.* **1** directed downwards (*a down draught*). **2** from a capital or centre (*down train*; *down platform*). **3** *colloq.* depressed; miserable (*am feeling down*). — *v. colloq.* **1** knock or bring down. **2** swallow; drink (*down the medicine in one gulp*; *down a few tinnies*). — *n.* **1** act of putting down. **2** reverse of fortune (*ups and downs*). **3** *colloq.* period of depression. **4** *colloq.* feeling of dislike or hostility; grudge. □ **be** (or **have a**) **down on** *colloq.* disapprove of; show animosity towards (*he is down on Asians*; *he has a down on Aborigines*). **be down to 1** be the responsibility of (*it's down to you now*). **2** have nothing left but (*down to my last cent*). **3** be attributable to (*it is down to sheer good luck that you weren't killed*). **come down** (of a watercourse) flood, be in spate. **down and out 1** penniless; destitute. **2** *Boxing* unable to resume the fight. **down at** (or **to**) **1** at or to (*works down at the pub*; *gone down to the coast*). **2** (with ellipsis of the preposition *at* or *to*) (*works down the pub weekends*; *going down the pub for a beer?*). **down on one's luck** *colloq.* temporarily unfortunate. **down tools** *colloq.* cease work, go on strike. **down with** expressing rejection of a specified person or thing. [earlier *adown*: related to DOWN³]

**down²** *n.* **1 a** first covering of young birds. **b** bird's under-plumage. **c** fine soft feathers or hairs. **2** fluffy substance. [Old Norse]

**down³** *n.* (often in *pl.* and usu. prec. by *the*) open rolling land (*the Darling Downs*). [Old English]

**down-and-out** *n.* destitute person.

**downbeat** — *n. Mus.* accented beat, usu. the first of the bar. — *adj.* **1** pessimistic, gloomy. **2** relaxed.

**downcast** *adj.* **1** dejected. **2** (of eyes) looking downwards.

**down country** *adj.* of or pertaining to the more closely settled areas of Australia.

**downer** *n. colloq.* **1** depressant or tranquillising drug. **2** depressing person or experience; failure. **3** = DOWNTURN.

**downfall** *n.* **1 a** fall from prosperity or power. **b** cause of this. **2** sudden heavy fall of rain etc.

**downgrade** — *v.* (**-ding**) **1** reduce in rank or status. **2** speak disparagingly of. — *n.* downward slope. □ **on the downgrade** in decline.

**downhearted** *adj.* dejected. □ **downheartedly** *adv.* **downheartedness** *n.*

**downhill** — *adv.* in a descending direction. — *adj.* sloping down, declining. — *n.* **1** downhill race in skiing. **2** down-

ward slope. □ **go downhill** *colloq.* deteriorate.

**down in the mouth** *adj.* looking unhappy.

**download** *v. Computing* transfer (data) from a central storage device or controlling system to another (esp. a smaller remote one).

**downmarket** *adj. & adv. colloq.* of or to the cheaper sector of the market (opp. UPMARKET).

**down payment** *n.* partial initial payment.

**downpipe** *n.* pipe to carry rainwater from a roof.

**downpour** *n.* heavy fall of rain.

**downright** — *adj.* **1** plain, straightforward. **2** utter; complete (*downright nonsense*). — *adv.* thoroughly (*downright rude*).

**Down's syndrome** *n.* congenital disorder with mental retardation and physical abnormalities. [*Down*, name of a physician (d. 1896)]

**downstage** *adv.* nearer the front of a theatre stage.

**downstairs** — *adv.* **1** down the stairs. **2** to or on a lower floor. — *attrib. adj.* (also **downstair**) situated downstairs. — *n.* lower floor.

**downstream** *adv. & adj.* in the direction in which a stream etc. flows.

**down time** *n.* time during which a machine, esp. a computer, is out of action or unavailable for use.

**down-to-earth** *adj.* practical, realistic.

**downtown** — *attrib. adj.* of the lower or more central part of a town or city. — *n.* downtown area. — *adv.* in or into the downtown area.

**downtrodden** *adj.* oppressed; badly treated.

**downturn** *n.* decline, esp. in economic activity.

**down under** *colloq.* — *adv.* in or to the antipodes, esp. Australia. — *n.* Australia (and sometimes New Zealand) (also *attrib.*: *he had the pommy mannerisms which down under people dislike*).

**downward** /**down**-wuhd/ — *adv.* (also **downwards**) towards what is lower, inferior, less important, or later. — *adj.* moving or extending downwards.

**downwind** *adj. & adv.* in the direction in which the wind is blowing.

**downy** *adj.* (**-ier, -iest**) **1** of, like, or covered with down. **2** soft and fluffy.

**dowry** /**dowuh**-ree, **dow**-ree/ *n.* (*pl.* **-ies**) property or money brought by a bride to her husband. [Anglo-French = French *douaire* DOWER]

**dowse¹** /dowz/ v. (**-sing**) = DIVINE v. 4.
□ **dowser** n. [origin unknown]

**dowse²** var. of DOUSE.

**dowsing rod** n. = DIVINING ROD.

**doxology** /dok-**sol**-uh-jee/ n. (pl. **-ies**) liturgical hymn etc. of praise to God, esp. the *gloria Patri* ... or *glory be to the Father* ... □ **doxological** /-suh-**loj**-i-kuhl/ adj. [Greek *doxa* glory]

**doyen** /**doi**-uhn/ n. (fem. **doyenne** /doi-**en**/) senior member of a group. [French: related to DEAN]

**doyley** var. of DOILY.

**doz.** abbr. dozen.

**doze** — v. (**-zing**) sleep lightly; be half asleep. — n. short light sleep. □ **doze off** fall lightly asleep. [origin unknown]

**dozen** /**duz**-uhn/ n. **1** (prec. by a or a number) (pl. **dozen**) twelve (*a dozen eggs; two dozen eggs*). **2** set of twelve (*sold in dozens*). **3** (in pl.; usu. foll. by of) colloq. very many (*dozens of errors*). □ **talk nineteen to the dozen** talk incessantly. [Latin *duodecim* twelve]

**Dr** abbr. **1** Doctor. **2** Drive.

**drab** adj. (**drabber**, **drabbest**) **1** dull, uninteresting. **2** of a dull brownish colour. □ **drably** adv. **drabness** n. [obsolete *drap* cloth]

**drachm** /dram/ n. weight formerly used by apothecaries, = ⅛ ounce. [Latin from Greek]

**drachma** /**drak**-muh/ n. (pl. **-s**) **1** chief monetary unit of Greece. **2** silver coin of ancient Greece. [Greek *drakhmē*]

**drack** /drak/ colloq. — adj. **1** (of a person) unattractive; dressed in a slovenly way. **2** dreary, dull. — n. unattractive or slovenly person. [origin uncertain]

**draconian** /druh-**koh**-nee-uhn/ adj. (of laws) very harsh, cruel. [*Drakōn*, name of an Athenian lawgiver]

**draft** /drahft/ — n. **1** preliminary written version of a speech, document, etc., or outline of a scheme. **2 a** written order for payment of money by a bank. **b** drawing of money by this. **3 a** party detached from a larger group for a special duty or service. **b** animal or number of animals separated from the main flock or herd for a specific purpose. **4** conscription. — v. **1** prepare a draft of (a document, scheme, etc.). **2** select for a special duty or purpose. **3** conscript. □ **drafting** n. [phonetic spelling of DRAUGHT]

**draft dodger** n. colloq. person who evades military conscription.

**drafting yard** n. (often in pl.) enclosure in which animals are drafted.

**draftsman** n. **1** person who drafts documents. **2** = DRAUGHTSMAN 1. [phonetic spelling of DRAUGHTSMAN]

**drag** — v. (**-gg-**) **1** pull along with effort. **2 a** trail or allow to trail along the ground. **b** (often foll. by on) (of time, a meeting, etc.) go or pass slowly or tediously. **3 a** use a grapnel or drag (to find a drowned person or lost object). **b** search the bottom of (a river etc.) with grapnels, nets, etc. **4** (often foll. by to) colloq. take (an esp. unwilling person) with one (*dragged him with me to the party*). **5** (foll. by on, at) draw on (a cigarette etc.). **6** colloq. take part in a drag-race. — n. **1 a** obstruction to progress (*he was a real drag on her career*). **b** Aeron. longitudinal retarding force created by air. **c** slow motion; impeded progress. **2** colloq. boring or tiresome person, duty, etc. **3** apparatus for dredging or recovering drowned persons etc. from under water. **4** = DRAG-NET. **5** colloq. inhalation of a cigarette etc. **6** colloq. **a** women's clothes worn by men. **b** party at which these are worn. **7** colloq. street or road (*the main drag*). **8** = DRAG-RACE. □ **drag the chain** see CHAIN. **drag one's feet** be deliberately slow or reluctant to act. **drag in** introduce (an irrelevant subject). **drag out** protract. **drag up** colloq. introduce or revive (an unwelcome subject). [Old English or Old Norse]

**draggle** /**drag**-uhl/ v. (**-ling**) **1** make dirty, wet, or limp by trailing. **2** hang trailing. [from DRAG]

**dragnet** n. **1** net drawn through a river or across the ground to trap fish or game or to find a drowned person etc. **2** systematic hunt for criminals etc.

**dragon** /**drag**-uhn/ n. **1** mythical usu. winged monster like a reptile, able to breathe fire. **2** any of various lizards of Australia (and of New Guinea, Africa, etc.) often having crests, spines, and neck frills (*bearded dragon; mallee dragon*). **3** fierce woman. [Greek *drakōn* serpent]

**dragonet** /**drag**-uh-nuht/ n. any of various spiny marine fish, the males often being brightly coloured, including Australian species (*fingered dragonet; rough-headed dragonet*). [diminutive of DRAGON]

**dragonfly** n. large insect with a long body and two pairs of transparent wings.

**dragoon** /druh-**goon**/ — n. cavalryman. — v. (foll. by into) coerce or bully into (*dragooned him into going to the opera*). [French *dragon*: related to DRAGON]

**drag queen** n. colloq. derog. male homosexual transvestite.

**drag-race** n. acceleration race between cars, usu. over a set distance.

**dragster** /**drag**-stuh/ n. car built or modified to take part in drag-races. [DRAG, (ROAD)STER]

**drain** — v. **1** draw off liquid from, esp.: **a** make (land etc.) dry by providing an outflow for moisture. **b** (of a river) carry off the superfluous water (of a district). **c** remove purulent matter from (an abscess). **2** draw off (liquid) esp. by a pipe. **3** flow or trickle away. **4** (of washed dishes etc.) dry or become dry as liquid flows away. **5** exhaust (a person or thing) of strength or resources. **6 a** drink to the dregs. **b** empty (a glass etc.) by drinking the contents. — n. **1 a** channel, conduit, or pipe carrying off liquid, sewage, etc. **b** tube for drawing off discharge etc. **2** constant outflow or expenditure (*a great drain on my resources*). □ **down the drain** *colloq.* lost, wasted. [Old English: related to DRY]

**drainage** n. **1** process or means of draining. **2** system of drains. **3** what is drained off.

**drainpipe** n. **1** pipe for carrying off water etc. **2** (*attrib.*) (of trousers) very narrow. **3** (in *pl.*) very narrow trousers.

**drake** n. male duck. [origin uncertain]

**dram** n. **1** small drink of spirits, esp. whisky. **2** = DRACHM. [Latin *drama*: related to DRACHM]

**drama** /drah-muh/ n. **1** play for stage or broadcasting. **2** art of writing, acting, and presenting plays. **3** exciting or emotional event, set of circumstances, etc. **4** dramatic quality (*the drama of the situation*). [Latin from Greek *draō* do]

**dramatic** /druh-**mat**-ik/ adj. **1** of drama or the study of drama. **2** sudden and exciting or unexpected. **3** vividly striking. **4** (of a gesture etc.) theatrical. □ **dramatically** adv. [Greek: related to DRAMA]

**dramatic irony** see IRONY.

**dramatics** n.pl. (often treated as *sing.*) **1** performance of plays. **2** exaggerated behaviour.

**dramatise** /dram-uh-ˌtuyz/ v. (also **-ize**) (**-sing** or **-zing**) **1** turn (a novel etc.) into a play. **2** make a dramatic scene of. **3** express or react to in a dramatic way. □ **dramatisation** /-zay-shuhn/ n.

**dramatis personae** /ˌdram-uh-tuhs per-**soh**-nuy, -nee/ n.pl. **1** characters in a play. **2** list of these. [Latin, = persons of the drama]

**dramatist** /**dram**-uh-tuhst/ n. writer of dramas.

**drank** *past of* DRINK.

**drape** — v. (**-ping**) **1** hang or cover loosely, adorn with cloth etc. **2** arrange (hangings etc.) esp. in folds. **3** position (one's limbs etc.) loosely or casually (*draped himself on the sofa*). — n. (in *pl.*) curtains. [Latin *drappus* cloth]

**draper** n. dealer in textile fabrics.

**drapery** n. (*pl.* **-ies**) **1** clothing or hangings arranged in folds. **2** draper's trade or fabrics.

**drastic** /**dras**-tik/ adj. far-reaching in effect; severe. □ **drastically** adv. [Greek *drastikos*: related to DRAMA]

**drat** *colloq.* — v. (**-tt-**) (usu. as *int.*) curse (*drat the thing!*). — *int.* expressing anger or annoyance. □ **dratted** adj. [(G)od rot]

**draught** /drahft/ — n. **1** current of air in a room or chimney etc. **2** pulling, traction. **3** depth of water needed to float a ship. **4** drawing of liquor from a cask etc. **5 a** single act of drinking or inhaling. **b** amount drunk thus. **6** (in *pl.*) game for two with 12 pieces each on a draughtboard. **7** a drawing in of a fishing-net. **8** fish so caught. **8** = DRAFT (esp. n. **1**). — v. = DRAFT (esp. v. **1**). □ **feel the draught** *colloq.* suffer from esp. financial hardship. [related to DRAW]

**draught beer** n. **1** beer from the cask, not bottled or canned. **2** beer with the properties etc. of draught beer sold in bottles or cans.

**draughtboard** n. = CHESSBOARD.

**draught horse** n. horse for heavy work.

**draughtsman** n. **1** person who makes drawings, plans, or sketches. **2** piece in draughts. □ **draughtsmanship** n.

**draughty** adj. (**-ier**, **-iest**) (of a room etc.) letting in sharp currents of air. □ **draughtiness** n.

**Dravidian** /druh-**vid**-ee-uhn/ — n. **1** member of an indigenous people of South India and Sri Lanka (including the Tamils and Kanarese) (see TAMIL). **2** any of the group of languages spoken by this people. — adj. of or relating to this people or group of languages. [Sanskrit *Dravida*, a province of S. India]

**draw** — v. (*past* **drew** /droo/; *past part.* **drawn**) **1** pull or cause to move towards or after one. **2** pull (a thing) up, over, or across. **3** pull (curtains etc.) open or shut. **4** take (a person) aside. **5** attract; bring; take in (*drew a deep breath; felt drawn to her; drew my attention; drew a crowd*). **6** (foll. by *at*, *on*) inhale from (a cigarette, pipe, etc.). **7** (also *absol.*) take out; remove (a tooth, gun, cork, card, etc.). **8** obtain or take from a source (*draw a salary; draw inspiration; drew $100 from my account*). **9 a** (also *absol.*) make (a line or mark). **b** produce (a picture) thus. **c** represent (something) thus. **10** (also *absol.*) finish (a contest or game) with equal scores. **11** make one's or its way; proceed; move, come (*drew near the bridge; draw to a close; drew level; the time draws near*). **12** infer (a conclusion). **13 a** elicit, evoke (*draw criticism*). **b** induce (a person) to reveal facts etc. (*refused to be drawn on that matter*). **14** haul up (water) from a well. **15** bring out (liquid from a tap etc. or blood from a wound). **16** extract a liquid essence from. **17** (of a chimney etc.) promote or allow a draught. **18** (of tea) infuse. **19** obtain by lot (*drew the winner*). **20** (foll. by *on*) call on (a person or a person's skill, memory, imagination, etc.). **21** write out (a cheque) (*drew a cheque on the bank*). **22** formulate or perceive (a comparison or distinction). **23** disembowel. **24** protract, stretch, elongate (*long-drawn agony*). **25 a** *Golf* drive (the ball) to the left (or, of a left-handed player, the right) esp. purposely. **b** *Bowls* cause (a ball) to travel in a curve to the desired point. — *n.* **1** act of drawing. **2** person or thing attracting custom, attention, etc. (*she will be the big draw at our concert*). **3** drawing of lots, raffle. **4** drawn game. **5** inhalation of smoke etc. **6** act of removing a gun from a holster in order to shoot (*quick on the draw*). □ **draw back** withdraw from an undertaking. **draw a bead on** see BEAD. **draw a blank** see BLANK. **draw in 1** (of days) become shorter. **2** persuade to join. **3** (of a train) arrive at a station. **draw in one's horns** become less assertive or ambitious. **draw the line at** set a limit of tolerance etc. at. **draw lots** see LOT. **draw on 1** approach, come near. **2** lead to. **3** allure. **4** put (gloves, boots, etc.) on. **draw out 1** prolong. **2** elicit. **3** induce to talk. **4** (of days) become longer. **5** (of a train) leave a station. **draw stumps** *Cricket* take the stumps out of the ground at close of play. **draw up 1** draft (a document etc.). **2** bring into order. **3** come to a halt. **4** make (oneself) erect. **quick on the draw** quick to react. [Old English]

**drawback** *n.* **1** disadvantage. **2** inhaling cigarette smoke into the lungs.

**drawbridge** *n.* hinged retractable bridge, esp. over a moat.

**drawcard** *n.* person, event, etc. that attracts a large audience.

**drawer** /**draw**-uh/ *n.* **1** person or thing that draws, esp. a cheque etc. **2** (also /draw/) lidless boxlike storage compartment, sliding in and out of a table etc. (*chest of drawers*). **3** (in *pl.*) knickers, underpants.

**drawing** /**draw**-ing/ *n.* **1** art of representing by line with a pencil etc. **2** picture etc. made thus.

**drawing board** *n.* board on which paper is fixed for drawing on. □ **back to the drawing board** *colloq.* (after the failure of an enterprise, plan, etc.) we have to start again.

**drawing-pin** *n.* flat-headed pin for fastening paper etc. to a surface.

**drawing room** *n.* **1** room in a private house for sitting or entertaining in. **2** (*attrib.*) restrained, polite (*drawing-room manners*). [earlier *withdrawing-room*]

**drawl** — *v.* speak with drawn-out vowel sounds. — *n.* drawling utterance or way of speaking. [Low German or Dutch]

**drawn** *adj.* looking strained and tense.

**drawstring** *n.* string or cord threaded through a waistband, bag opening, etc.

**dray** *n.* low cart without sides for heavy loads. [related to DRAW]

**dread** /dred/ — *v.* fear greatly, esp. in advance. — *n.* great fear or apprehension. — *adj.* **1** dreaded. **2** *archaic* awe-inspiring, dreadful. [Old English]

**dreadful** *adj.* **1** terrible; inspiring fear or awe (*a dreadful cataclysm*). **2** *colloq.* very annoying, very bad (*had a dreadful time at the party*). □ **dreadfully** *adv.*

**dreadlocks** *n.pl.* Rastafarian hairstyle with hair hanging in tight braids on all sides.

**dream** — *n.* **1** series of scenes or feelings in the mind of a sleeping person. **2** daydream or fantasy. **3** ideal, aspiration, or ambition (*his dream is to be a pop-star*). **4** beautiful or ideal person or thing. **5** state of mind without proper perception of reality (*goes about in a dream*). — *v.* (*past* and *past part.* **dreamt** /dremt/ or **dreamed**) **1** experience a dream. **2** imagine as in a dream. **3** (with *neg.*) consider possible (*never dreamt that he would come*; *would not dream of it*). **4** (foll. by *away*) waste (time). **5** be inactive or unpractical. □ **dream up** imagine, invent. **like a dream** *colloq.* easily, effortlessly. □ **dreamer** *n.* [Old English]

**dreamboat** *n.* *colloq.* sexually attractive or ideal person.

**Dreaming** *n.* = DREAMTIME, esp. as manifested in the natural world and celebrated in Aboriginal ritual; the spiritual identification of an Aborigine with a place, species of plant or animal, etc.; a place, species, or being so regarded; the spiritual significance of a place (often *attrib.* as *Dreaming place*; *Dreaming site*; *Dreaming track*).

**Dreamtime** *n.* (in Aboriginal belief) a collection of events beyond living memory which shaped the physical, spiritual, and moral world; the era in which these occurred; an Aborigine's consciousness of the enduring nature of that era even in the present day. [translation of ALCHERINGA]

**dreamy** *adj.* (**-ier**, **-iest**) **1** given to daydreaming or fantasy. **2** dreamlike; vague.

**3** *colloq.* delightful; marvellous (*he's dreamy*). □ **dreamily** *adv.* **dreaminess** *n.*

**dreary** *adj.* (**-ier**, **-iest**) dismal, dull, gloomy. □ **drearily** *adv.* **dreariness** *n.* [Old English]

**dredge**[1] — *n.* apparatus used to scoop up oysters etc., or to clear mud etc., from a river or sea bed. — *v.* (**-ging**) **1** (often foll. by *up*) **a** bring up or clear (mud etc.) with a dredge. **b** bring up (something forgotten) (*why dredge up the past?*). **c** *colloq.* find or locate with difficulty (*have to dredge up $500 by tomorrow*; *where did you dredge up that excuse?*). **2** clean with or use a dredge. [origin uncertain]

**dredge**[2] *v.* (**-ging**) sprinkle with flour, sugar, etc. [earlier = sweetmeat, from French]

**dregs** *n.pl.* **1** sediment; grounds, lees. **2** = SCUM *n.* 2 (*dregs of humanity*). [Old Norse]

**drench** — *v.* **1** wet thoroughly. **2** force (an animal) to take medicine. — *n.* **1** soaking; downpour. **2** dose of medicine for an animal. [Old English]

**dress** — *v.* **1 a** (also *absol.*) put clothes on. **b** have and wear clothes (*dresses well*). **2** put on evening dress (*dress for dinner*). **3** arrange or adorn (hair, a shop window, etc.). **4** treat (a wound) esp. with a dressing. **5 a** prepare (poultry, crab, etc.) for cooking or eating. **b** add dressing to (a salad etc.). **6** apply manure etc. to a paddock, garden, etc. **7** finish the surface of (fabric, leather, stone, etc.). **8** correct the alignment of (troops). — *n.* **1** woman's garment of a bodice and skirt. **2 a** clothing, esp. a whole outfit (*fussy about his dress*). **b** clothing of a period (*medieval dress*). **3** formal or ceremonial costume (*evening dress*). **4** external covering; outward form (*birds in their winter dress*). □ **dress down** *colloq.* **1** reprimand or scold. **2** dress informally. **dressed** (**up**) **to the nines** dressed very elaborately. **dress up 1** dress (oneself or another) elaborately for a special occasion. **2** put on fancy dress. **3** make (a thing) more attractive or interesting (*the food needs to be dressed up a bit*). [French *dresser*, ultimately related to DIRECT]

**dressage** /dres-ah*zh* / *n.* training of a horse in obedience and deportment; display of this. [French]

**dress circle** *n.* first gallery in a theatre (in which evening dress was formerly required).

**dresser**[1] *n.* kitchen sideboard with shelves for plates etc. [French *dresser* prepare]

**dresser**[2] *n.* **1** person who helps to dress actors or actresses. **2** surgeon's assistant

in operations. **3** person who dresses in a specified way (*snappy dresser*).

**dressing** *n.* **1** putting one's clothes on. **2 a** sauce, esp. of oil and vinegar etc., for salads (*French dressing*). **b** sauce or stuffing etc. for food. **3** bandage, ointment, etc., for a wound. **4** size or stiffening used to coat fabrics. **5** (also **top-dressing**) compost, loam, etc. spread over land.

**dressing down** *n.* *colloq.* scolding; thrashing.

**dressing gown** *n.* loose robe worn when one is not fully dressed.

**dressing room** *n.* room for changing one's clothes, esp. in a theatre or sports ground, or attached to a bedroom.

**dressing shed** *n.* changing room at a swimming pool etc.

**dressing table** *n.* table with a flat top, mirror, and drawers, used while applying make-up etc.

**dressmaker** *n.* person who makes women's clothes, esp. for a living. □ **dressmaking** *n.*

**dress rehearsal** *n.* final rehearsal (of a play etc.) in full costume.

**dressy** *adj.* (**-ier**, **-iest**) *colloq.* (of clothes or a person) smart, elaborate, elegant. □ **dressiness** *n.*

**drew** *past* of DRAW.

**dribble** /**drib**-uhl/ — *v.* (**-ling**) **1** allow saliva to flow from the mouth. **2** flow or allow to flow in drops. **3** (also *absol.*) esp. *Soccer & Hockey* move (the ball) forward with slight touches of the feet or stick. — *n.* **1** act or instance of dribbling. **2** small trickling flow. [obsolete *drib* = DRIP]

**driblet** /**drib**-luht/ *n.* small quantity.

**dribs and drabs** *n.pl.* *colloq.* small scattered amounts (*did the work in dribs and drabs*).

**dried** *past* and *past part.* of DRY.

**drier**[1] *compar.* of DRY.

**drier**[2] /**druy**-uh/ *n.* (also **dryer**) device for drying hair, laundry, etc.

**driest** *superl.* of DRY.

**drift** — *n.* **1 a** slow movement or variation (*a steady drift of people moving from the country to the city*; *the drift of public opinion*). **b** this caused by a current (*drifts of seaweed*). **2** intention, meaning, etc., of what is said etc. (*I didn't catch his drift*). **3** large mass of sand etc. accumulated by wind or water. **4 a** slow deviation of a ship, aircraft, etc., from its course, due to currents, winds, etc. **b** controlled slide of a racing car etc. **5** tool for enlarging or shaping a hole in metal. **6** fragments of rock heaped up (*glacial drift*). **7** large mass of esp. flowering plants (*a drift of purple wax-lip orchids*).

— v. **1** be carried by or as if by a current of air or water. **2** progress casually or aimlessly (*drifted into teaching*). **3** pile or be piled into drifts. **4** (of a current) carry, cause to drift. [Old Norse and Germanic *trift* movement of cattle]

**drifter** n. **1** aimless or rootless person. **2** boat used for drift-net fishing.

**drift-net** n. net for sea fishing, allowed to drift.

**driftwood** n. wood floating on moving water or washed ashore.

**drill**¹ — n. **1** tool or machine for boring holes, sinking wells, etc. **2** instruction in military exercises (e.g. marching, use of weapons, etc.). **3** routine procedure in an emergency (*fire-drill*). **4** thorough training, esp. by repetition. **5** *colloq.* recognised procedure (*what's the drill?*). — v. **1 a** make a hole in or through with a drill. **b** make (a hole) with a drill. **2** train or be trained by drill. **3** *colloq.* shoot with a gun (*drilled him full of holes*). [Dutch]

**drill**² — n. **1** machine for making furrows, sowing, and covering seed. **2** small furrow. **3** row of seeds sown by a drill. — v. plant in drills. [origin unknown]

**drill**³ n. coarse twilled cotton or linen fabric. [Latin *trilix* having three threads]

**drily** / **druy**-lee/ adv. (also **dryly**) (said) in a dry manner; with restrained humour.

**drink** — v. (past **drank**; past part. **drunk**) **1 a** (also *absol.*) swallow (liquid) (*drink your medicine*). **b** swallow the contents of (a vessel) (*drank the cup to the dregs*). **2** take alcohol, esp. to excess (*I'm afraid he drinks*). **3** (of a plant, sponge, etc.) absorb (moisture). **4** bring (oneself etc.) to a specified condition by drinking (*drank himself into a stupor*). **5** wish (a person good health etc.) by drinking (*drank his health*). — n. **1 a** liquid for drinking. **b** draught or specified amount of this (*had a drink of milk*). **2 a** alcoholic liquor. **b** portion, glass, etc. of this. **c** excessive use of alcohol (*took to drink*). **3** (**the drink**) *colloq.* the sea. □ **drink in** listen eagerly to. **drink to** toast; wish success to. **drink a person under the table** *colloq.* remain sober longer than one's drinking companion. **drink up** (also *absol.*) drink all or the remainder of. **drink with the flies** *colloq.* drink alone. □ **drinkable** adj. **drinker** n. [Old English]

**drink-driver** n. person who drives with excess alcohol in the blood. □ **drink-driving** n.

**drip** — v. (-**pp**-) **1** fall or let fall in drops. **2** (often foll. by *with*) be so wet as to shed drops. — n. **1 a** liquid falling in drops (*steady drip of rain*). **b** drop of liquid. **c** sound of dripping. **2** *colloq.* dull or

ineffectual person. **3** = DRIP-FEED. □ **be dripping with** be full of or covered with. **dripping wet** very wet. [Danish: cf. DROP]

**drip-dry** — v. dry or leave to dry crease-free when hung up. — adj. able to be drip-dried.

**drip-feed** — v. feed intravenously in drops. — n. **1** feeding thus. **2** apparatus for doing this.

**drip irrigation** n. drip by drip form of localised watering of plants.

**dripping** n. fat melted from roasted meat.

**drippy** adj. (-**ier**, -**iest**) *colloq.* (of a person) ineffectual; sloppily sentimental.

**drive** — v. (-**ving**; past **drove**; past part. **driven** / **driv**-uhn / ) **1** (usu. foll. by *away*, *back*, *down*, *in*, *off*, *on*, *out*, *up*, etc., defining the direction) urge in some direction, esp. forcibly (*drove the cattle into the paddock*; *drove the dingoes back*). **2 a** compel or constrain forcibly (*was driven to complain*; *drove her to stealing*). **b** force into a specified state (*drove him mad*). **c** (often *refl.*) urge to overwork (*drives herself too hard*). **3 a** operate and direct (a vehicle, locomotive, etc.). **b** convey or be conveyed in a vehicle (*drove them to the station*; *drove to the station in a bus*). **c** be competent to drive (a vehicle) (*does he drive?*). **d** travel in a private vehicle (*drove throughout the countryside sightseeing*). **e** (also *absol.*) urge and direct the course of (an animal etc.). **f** chase (animals, an enemy in warfare, etc.) from a large area to a smaller, to kill or capture; corner. **3** (of wind etc.) carry along, propel, esp. rapidly (*driven snow*; *driving rain*). **5 a** (often foll. by *into*) force (a stake, nail, etc.) into place by blows. **b** *Mining* bore (a tunnel etc.). **6** effect or conclude forcibly (*drove a hard bargain*; *drove his point home*). **7** (of electricity or other power) set or keep (machinery) going. **8** (usu. foll. by *at*) work hard; dash; rush (*still driving away at his fantasy trilogy*). **9** hit (a ball) forcibly. — n. **1** journey or excursion in a vehicle (*let's go for a drive*; *lives an hour's drive from us*). **2 a** (esp. scenic) street or road. **b** private road through a garden to a house. **3 a** capacity for achievement; motivation and energy (*lacks the drive needed to succeed*). **b** *Psychol.* inner urge to attain a goal or satisfy a need (*unconscious emotional drives*; *sex-drive*). **4** forcible stroke of a bat etc. **5** organised effort (for a fund-raising purpose etc.) (*membership drive*; *lamington drive*). **6 a** transmission of power to machinery, wheels, etc. (*front-wheel drive*). **b** position of the steering-wheel in a vehicle (*left-hand drive*). **c** *Computing* = DISK DRIVE. **7** felling of a number of trees which have been only partly cut through, the impetus or 'drive' being given by the felling of a larger tree (or one uphill of the others) against them. ◻ **drive at** seek, intend, or mean (*what is he driving at?*). [Old English]

**drive-in** *—attrib. adj.* (of a cinema, bottle-shop, etc.) used while sitting in one's car. *— n.* such a cinema, bottle-shop, etc.

**drivel** /driv-uhl/ *— n.* silly talk; nonsense. *— v.* (**-ll-**) **1** talk drivel. **2** run at the mouth or nose. [Old English]

**driven** *past part.* of DRIVE.

**driver** *n.* **1** person who drives a vehicle. **2** golf-club for driving from a tee.

**drivetime** *adj.* (of a radio programme) intended for people driving home from work in the evening.

**driveway** *n.* **1** = DRIVE *n.* 2b. **2** area in front of a service station (also *attrib.*: *driveway service*).

**driving wheel** *n.* wheel communicating motive power in machinery.

**drizzle** /driz-uhl/ *— n.* very fine rain. *— v.* (**-ling**) (of rain) fall in very fine drops. ◻ **drizzly** *adj.* [Old English]

**droll** /drohl/ *adj.* quaintly amusing; strange, odd. ◻ **drollery** *n.* (*pl.* **-ies**). **drolly** *adv.* [French]

**dromedary** /drom-uh-duh-ree, drum-/ *n.* (*pl.* **-ies**) one-humped (esp. Arabian) camel bred for riding. [Greek *dromas -ados* runner]

**drone** *— n.* **1** non-working male of the honey-bee, whose sole function is to mate with fertile females. **2** idler. **3** deep humming sound. **4** monotonous speaking tone. **5** bass-pipe of bagpipes or its continuous note. *— v.* (**-ning**) **1** make a deep humming sound. **2** speak or utter monotonously. [Old English]

**drongo** /drong-goh/ *n.* (*pl.* **-os** or **-oes**) **1** any of various black birds of India, Africa, and Australia, having elongated tail feathers like a fish's tail (see SPANGLED DRONGO). **2** *colloq.* fool, simpleton. [Malagasy]

**droob** *n. colloq.* hopeless-looking ineffectual person. ◻ **drooby** *adj.* [perhaps from DROOP]

**drool** *v.* **1** slobber, dribble. **2** (often foll. by *over*) admire extravagantly. [from DRIVEL]

**droop** *— v.* **1** bend or hang down, esp. from weariness; sag. **2** (of the eyes) look downwards. **3** lose heart or be dejected. *— n.* **1** drooping attitude. **2** loss of spirit or enthusiasm. ◻ **droopy** *adj.* [Old Norse: related to DROP]

**drop** *— n.* **1 a** globule of liquid that hangs, falls, or adheres to a surface. **b** very small

amount of liquid (*just a drop left*). **c** glass etc. of alcohol. **2 a** abrupt fall or slope. **b** amount of this (*drop of fifteen metres*). **c** act of falling or dropping. **d** fall in prices, temperature, etc. **e** deterioration (*drop in status*). **3** drop-shaped thing, esp. a pendant or sweet. **4** curtain or scenery let down on to a stage. **5** (in *pl.*) liquid medicine used in drops (*eye drops*). **6** minute quantity (*not a drop of pity*). **7** number of lambs or calves born on a station in a season. **8** *colloq.* hiding-place for stolen goods etc. **9** *Cricket* fall of a wicket (*came in first drop*). **10** act of delivering goods (*this is our last drop for the day*). *— v.* (**-pp-**) **1** fall or let fall in drops, shed (tears), blood). **2** fall or allow to fall; let go. **3 a** sink or cause to sink or fall to the ground from exhaustion, a blow, a wound, etc. (*dropped with weariness*; *dropped him with a savage blow*). **b** fall naturally (*drop asleep*; *drop into the habit*). **4 a** (cause to) cease or lapse; abandon, be done with (*the project has been dropped*; *drop everything and come at once*). **b** *colloq.* break off acquaintance or association with (*has dropped her latest boyfriend*). **c** cease to discuss (*let's drop the subject*). **5** set down (a passenger etc.) (*drop me here*). **6** utter or be uttered casually (*dropped a hint*). **7** send casually (*drop me a line*). **8 a** fall or allow to fall in direction, amount, condition, degree, pitch, etc. (*voice dropped*; *wind dropped*; *we dropped the price*). **b** (of a person) jump down lightly; let oneself fall. **c** allow (trousers etc.) to fall to the ground. **9** omit (a letter) in speech (*drop one's h's*). **10** (as **dropped** *adj.*) in a lower position than usual (*dropped handle-bars*; *dropped waist*). **11** give birth to (esp. a lamb). **12** lose (a game, point, etc.) (*dropped three service games*). **13** deliver by parachute etc. **14** *Rugby* send (a ball), or score (a goal), by a drop-kick. **15** *colloq.* dismiss or omit (*dropped from the team*). **16** *colloq.* do, perform (*drop a uey*; *drop a wheelie*). ◻ **at the drop of a hat** given the slightest excuse or provocation; on the spur of the moment (*they stop work at the drop of a hat*). **drop back** (or **behind**) fall back; get left behind. **drop a brick** (or a **clanger**) *colloq.* make an indiscreet or embarrassing remark. **drop** (or **tip**) **the bucket on** *colloq.* **1** disgrace or incriminate another by revealing facts. **2** criticise a person scathingly. **drop one's bundle** see BUNDLE. **drop in** *colloq.* **1** (also **drop by**) visit casually. **2** *Surfing* **a** (also **drop in on**) obstruct another surfer by beginning one's surf ride in his or her path. **b** slide down the face of a wave immediately after take-off. **a drop in the bucket** (or **in the ocean**) very small amount, esp. compared with what is needed or expected. **drop it!** *colloq.* stop it!; leave off!; drop the subject! **drop off 1** fall asleep. **2** drop (a passenger). **3** decline gradually (*sales have dropped off*). **drop out** *colloq.* cease to participate; opt out from society. **for the drop 1** *hist.* for execution by hanging. **2** *colloq.* for the sack etc. (*he's heading for the drop*). **get** (or **have**) **the drop on** *colloq.* get (or have) a person at a disadvantage (esp. because of what one knows about him or her). **have had a drop too much** *colloq.* be slightly drunk. □ **droplet** *n.* [Old English]

**drop curtain** *n.* painted curtain lowered on to a stage.

**drop-kick** *n.* **1** *Aust. Rules* & *Rugby* kick as the ball touches the ground having been dropped. **2** *colloq.* contemptible person.

**drop-out** *n.* *colloq.* person who has dropped out of conventional society, a course of study, etc.

**dropper** *n.* **1** device for releasing liquid in drops. **2** vertical batten placed at regular intervals between the posts of a wire fence to keep the wires braced.

**droppings** *n.pl.* **1** dung of animals or birds. **2** thing that falls or has fallen in drops.

**drop punt** *n.* *Aust. Rules* kick made with the ball held vertically before dropping it onto the foot.

**drop scone** *n.* = PIKELET.

**drop-shot** *n.* (in tennis) shot dropping abruptly over the net.

**dropsy** /**drop**-see/ *n.* = OEDEMA. □ **dropsical** *adj.* [earlier *hydropsy* from Greek *hudrōps*: related to HYDRO-]

**drosophila** /druh-**sof**-uh-luh/ *n.* fruit fly used in genetic research. [Greek, = dew-loving]

**dross** *n.* **1** rubbish. **2 a** scum from melted metals. **b** impurities. [Old English]

**drought** /drowt/ *n.* prolonged absence of rain. [Old English]

**Droughtmaster** *n.* breed of cattle developed in Australia having not less than ⅜ or more than ½ Brahman blood and bred to withstand dry conditions.

**drove**[1] *past* of DRIVE.

**drove**[2] — *n.* **1 a** moving crowd. **b** (in *pl.*) *colloq.* great number (*people arrived in droves*). **2** herd or flock driven or moving together. — *v.* drive (a herd or flock), esp. over a great distance (*she droved the cattle overland for 3,000 kilometres*). [Old English: related to DRIVE]

**drover** *n.* person who drives a herd or flock, esp. over a great distance.

**drover's dog** *n.* person who earns no respect; a drudge (*even a drover's dog could have won the election, but he lost it*).

**droving** *n.* **1** act of driving a herd or flock over a great distance. **2** occupation of a drover.

**drown** *v.* **1** kill or die by submersion in liquid. **2** submerge; flood; drench (*drowned the yard in a metre of water*). **3** deaden (grief etc.) by drinking (*drowned his sorrows*). **4** (often foll. by *out*) overpower (sound) with louder sound. [probably Old English]

**drowse** /drowz/ *v.* (**-sing**) be lightly asleep. [from DROWSY]

**drowsy** /**drow**-zee/ *adj.* (**-ier, -iest**) very sleepy, almost asleep. □ **drowsily** *adv.* **drowsiness** *n.* [probably Old English]

**drub** *v.* (**-bb-**) **1** beat, thrash. **2** defeat thoroughly. □ **drubbing** *n.* [Arabic *ḍaraba* beat]

**drudge** — *n.* person who does dull, laborious, or menial work. — *v.* (**-ging**) work laboriously, toil. □ **drudgery** *n.* [origin uncertain]

**drug** — *n.* **1** medicinal substance. **2** (esp. addictive) narcotic, hallucinogen, or stimulant. — *v.* (**-gg-**) **1** add a drug to (food or drink). **2 a** give a drug to. **b** stupefy. [French]

**druggie** /**drug**-ee/ *n. colloq.* drug-addict.

**Druid** /**droo**-uhd/ *n.* **1** priest of an ancient Celtic religion. **2** member of a modern Druidic order. □ **Druidic** /-**id**-ik/ *adj.* **Druidism** *n.* [Latin from Celtic]

**drum** — *n.* **1** hollow esp. cylindrical percussion instrument covered at the end(s) with plastic etc. **2** (often in *pl.*) percussion section of an orchestra etc. **3** sound made by a drum. **4** thing resembling a drum, esp. a container, etc. **5** swagman's bundle of possessions; swag. **6** segment of a pillar. **7** eardrum. **8** *Zool.* natural organ by which an animal produces a loud or bass sound. **9** (also **the drum**) *colloq.* piece of reliable information, esp. a racing tip. — *v.* (**-mm-**) **1** play a drum. **2** beat or tap continuously with the fingers etc. **3** (of a bird or insect) make a loud noise with the wings. **4** *colloq.* provide with (reliable) information. □ **drum into** drive (a lesson or facts) into (a person) by persistence. **drum out** dismiss with ignominy. **drum up** summon or get by vigorous effort (*drum up support*). **run a drum** *colloq.* (of a racehorse) perform as tipped. [Low German]

**drum brake** *n.* brake in which brake shoes on a vehicle press against the brake drum on a wheel.

**drum major** *n.* leader of a marching band.

**drum majorette** *n.* female baton-twirling member of a parading group.

**drummer** *n.* **1** player of drums. **2** any of several Australian marine fish able to make a drumming noise (*Queensland drummer*; *silver drummer*).

**drummy** /drum-ee/ *adj.* (of certain terrain in Australia, of rock) hollow-sounding.

**drumstick** *n.* **1** stick for beating drums. **2** lower leg of a dressed fowl.

**drumsticks** see ISOPOGON.

**drunk** — *adj.* **1** lacking control from drinking alcohol. **2** (often foll. by *with*) overcome with joy, success, power, etc. — *n.* person who is drunk, esp. habitually. [past part. of DRINK]

**drunkard** /drungk-uhd/ *n.* person who is habitually drunk.

**drunken** *adj.* (usu. *attrib.*) **1** = DRUNK 1. **2** caused by or involving drunkenness (*drunken brawl*). **3** often drunk. □ **drunkenly** *adv.* **drunkenness** *n.*

**drupe** /droop/ *n.* fleshy stone-fruit, e.g. the olive and plum. [Latin from Greek]

**druthers** /druth-uhz/ *n.pl. colloq.* choice, preference (*if I had my druthers I'd leave immediately*). [alteration of *I* (etc.) *would rather*]

**dry** /druy/ — *adj.* (**drier**; **driest**) **1** free from moisture, esp.: **a** with moisture having evaporated, drained away, etc. (*clothes are not dry yet*; *sheep are dry enough for shearing*). **b** (of eyes) free from tears. **c** (of a climate etc.) with insufficient rain; not rainy (*dry spell*). **d** (of a river, well, etc.) dried up. **e** using or producing no moisture (*dry shampoo*; *dry cough*). **2** (of wine) not sweet (*dry sherry*). **3 a** plain, unelaborated (*dry facts*). **b** uninteresting (*dry book*). **4** (of a sense of humour) subtle, ironic, understated. **5** prohibiting the sale of alcohol; without alcohol (*a dry area*; *a dry wedding-breakfast*). **6** (of bread) without butter etc. (*dry toast*). **7** (of provisions etc.) solid, not liquid (*dry goods*). **8** impassive; unsympathetic; hard; cold. **9** (of a cow) not yielding milk. **10** *colloq.* thirsty or thirst making (*feel dry*; *this is really dry work*). **11** of, or being, a political 'dry' (opp. WET *adj.* 6). — *v.* (**dries, dried**) **1** make or become dry. **2** (usu. as **dried** *adj.*) preserve (food etc.) by removing moisture (*dried fruit*; *dried flowers*). **3** (often foll. by *up*) *Theatr. colloq.* forget one's lines. — *n.* (*pl.* **dries**) **1** process or an instance of drying. **2** politician who advocates individual responsibility, free trade, economic stringency, etc., and opposes high government spending on social welfare etc. (opp. WET *n.* 4). **3** (prec. by *the*)

**a** (in northern and central Australia) the dry season (opp. the WET). **b** desert area; waterless country. **4** dry ginger ale. **5** dry place (*come into the dry*). □ **dried out 1** (of land) parched. **2** (of people) driven off drought-stricken land. **dry out 1** make or become fully dry. **2** treat or be treated for alcoholism. **dry up 1** make or become utterly dry. **2** dry dishes. **3** *colloq.* (esp. in *imper.*) cease talking. **4** become unproductive. **5** (of supplies) run out. □ **dryness** *n.* [Old English]

**dryad** /druy-ad, -uhd/ *n.* wood nymph. [Greek *drus* tree]

**dryandra** /druy-**an**-druh/ *n.* any plant of the genus of shrubs and small trees *Dryandra* (of the same family as the banksia) endemic to south-western WA, notable for its large and spectacular flowers. [Jonas *Dryander*, Swedish botanist and librarian to Joseph Banks (d. 1810)]

**dry battery** *n.* (also **dry cell**) electric battery or cell in which electrolyte is absorbed in a solid.

**dry bible** *n.* condition of cattle in which the omasum (third stomach) becomes dry and jammed with food, its folds resembling the pages of a book, the affliction being occasioned esp. by drought.

**dryblow** /druy-ˌbloh/ *v.* separate (particles of a mineral, esp. gold) from the surrounding material, using a current of air. □ **dryblowing** *n.*

**dryblower** *n.* **1** person who uses the method of dryblowing to separate gold etc. from its surrounding material. **2** apparatus consisting of a series of sieves mounted one over the other and shaken while attached bellows provide wind: used for dryblowing gold-bearing material.

**dry-clean** *v.* clean (clothes etc.) with solvents without water. □ **dry-cleaner** *n.* **dry-cleaning** *n.*

**dry country** *n.* area with very low rainfall.

**dry digging** *n.* (also **dry diggings**) place removed from running water where gold is found on or near the surface.

**dry dock** *n.* dock that can be pumped dry for building or repairing ships.

**dryer** var. of DRIER[2].

**dry farmer** *n.* person who farms in dry country. □ **dry farming** *n.*

**dry heart** *n.* central Australia.

**dry ice** *n.* solid carbon dioxide used as a refrigerant.

**dry land** *n.* land as distinct from sea etc.

**dryly** var. of DRILY.

**dry rot** n. decayed state of unventilated wood; fungi causing this.

**dry run** n. colloq. rehearsal.

**dry season** n. (also **dry spell**) period of low rainfall; drought (opp. WET SEASON).

**dry-shod** adj. & adv. without wetting one's shoes.

**dry track** n. track through waterless country.

**DT** abbr. (also **DT's** /dee-teez/) delirium tremens.

**dual** /dyoo-uhl/ —adj. **1** in two parts; twofold. **2** double (dual ownership). —n. Gram. dual number or form. □ **duality** /-al-uh-tee/ n. [Latin duo two]

**dual carriageway** n. road with a dividing strip between traffic flowing in opposite directions.

**dualism** /dyoo-uh-liz-uhm/ n. **1** being twofold; duality. **2** Philos. theory that in any domain of reality there are two independent underlying principles, e.g. mind and matter, form and content. **3** Theol. theory that the forces of good and evil are equally balanced in the universe. □ **dualist** n. **dualistic** /-lis-tik/ adj.

**dub**[1] v. (**-bb-**) **1** make (a person) a knight by touching the shoulders with a sword. **2** give (a person) a name, nickname, etc. **3** smear (leather) with grease. [French]

**dub**[2] v. (**-bb-**) **1** provide (a film etc.) with an, esp. translated, alternative soundtrack. **2** add (sound effects or music) to a film or broadcast. **3** transfer or make a copy of (recorded sound or images). [abbreviation of DOUBLE]

**dubbo** /dub-oh/ colloq. —n. **1** person who appears to be a bit of a country bumpkin. **2** idiot; imbecile. —adj. loutish; imbecilic. [Dubbo country town in NSW]

**dubiety** /dyoo-buy-uh-tee/ n. literary doubt. [Latin: related to DUBIOUS]

**dubious** /dyoo-bee-uhs/ adj. **1** hesitating, doubtful (dubious about going). **2** of questionable truth or value (a dubious claim). **3** unreliable; suspicious (dubious company). **4** of doubtful result (a dubious undertaking at best). □ **dubiously** adv. **dubiousness** n. [Latin dubium doubt]

**ducal** /dyoo-kuhl/ adj. of or like a duke. [French: related to DUKE]

**ducat** /duk-uht/ n. gold coin, formerly current in most of Europe. [medieval Latin ducatus DUCHY]

**duchess** /duch-uhs, -es/ —n. **1** duke's wife or widow. **2** woman holding the rank of duke. **3** stately or imposing woman. **4** (esp. in Queensland) dressing table with a pivoting mirror. —v. **1** entertain (esp. a visiting dignitary) lavishly and

with ceremony. **2** colloq. fawn on, treat obsequiously in order to curry favour etc. [medieval Latin ducissa: related to DUKE]

**duchy** /duch-ee/ n. (pl. **-ies**) territory of a duke or duchess. [medieval Latin ducatus: related to DUKE]

**duck**[1] —n. (pl. same or **-s**) **1 a** any of various swimming-birds, esp. the domesticated form of the mallard or wild duck, and including many wild Australian species (freckled duck; wood duck). **b** female of this. **c** its flesh as food. **2** score of 0 in cricket. —v. **1** bob down, esp. to avoid being seen or hit. **2 a** dip one's head briefly under water. **b** plunge (a person) briefly in water. **3** colloq. dodge (a task etc.). □ **duck into** (or **out**) colloq. go in(to) (or out) for a brief time (I'll just duck into this shop; I'm ducking out for a few minutes). **like a duck to water** adapting very readily. **like water off a duck's back** colloq. producing no effect. [Old English]

**duck**[2] n. strong linen or cotton fabric. [Dutch]

**duck**[3] n. colloq. amphibious military landing-craft. [DUKW, its official designation]

**duckbill** n. (also **duck-billed platypus**) = PLATYPUS.

**duckling** n. young duck.

**duck-shove** v. colloq. evade (responsibilities); avoid (an issue). □ **duck-shoving** n.

**duckweed** n. any of various plants growing on the surface of still water.

**duco** /dyoo-koh/ —n. propr. kind of paint, used esp. on the body of a motor vehicle. —v. paint (a motor vehicle) with duco.

**duct** —n. channel or tube for conveying a fluid, cable, bodily secretions, etc. (tear ducts). —v. convey through a duct. [Latin ductus from duco duct- lead]

**ductile** /duk-tuyl/ adj. **1** (of metal) capable of being drawn into wire; pliable. **2** (of a substance) easily moulded. **3** (of a person) docile; gullible. □ **ductility** /-til-uh-tee/ n. [Latin: related to DUCT]

**ductless gland** n. gland secreting directly into the bloodstream.

**dud** colloq. —n. **1** useless or broken thing. **2** counterfeit article. **3** (in pl.) trousers; clothes. —adj. useless, defective. [origin unknown]

**dude** /dyood, dood/ n. colloq. **1** person, guy, fellow (wouldn't have anything to do with those dudes if I were you). **2** (as a form of address) friend, mate. □ **cool dude** 'with it', fashionable, or otherwise attractive or desirable person (esp. a male). [originally US, from German dial. dude fool]

**dudgeon** /duj-uhn/ *n.* resentment, indignation. □ **in high dudgeon** very angry. [origin unknown]

**due** /dyoo/ — *adj.* **1** owing or payable (*our thanks are due to him; rent is due on Friday*). **2** (often foll. by *to*) merited; appropriate (*her due reward; received the praise due to a hero*). **3** (foll. by *to*) that ought to be given or ascribed to (a person, cause, etc.) (*first place is due to Shakespeare; difficulty due to ignorance*). **4** (often foll. by *to* + infin.) expected or under an obligation at a certain time (*due to speak tonight; train due at 7.30*). **5** suitable, right, proper (*in due time; after due consideration*). — *n.* **1** what one owes or is owed (*give him his due*). **2** (usu. in *pl.*) fee or amount payable. — *adv.* (of a compass point) exactly, directly (*went due east*). □ **due to** because of (*he was late due to an accident*). [French from Latin *debeo* owe]

---

■ **Usage** The use of *due to* to mean 'because of' as in the example given is regarded as unacceptable by some people and could be avoided by substituting *his lateness was due to an accident*. Alternatively, *owing to* could be used.

---

**duel** /dyoo-uhl/ — *n.* **1** armed contest between two people, usu. to the death. **2** two-sided contest (*duel of wits*). — *v.* (**-ll-**) fight a duel. □ **duellist** *n.* [Latin *duellum* war]

**duet** /dyoo-et/ *n.* musical composition for two performers. □ **duettist** *n.* [Latin *duo* two]

**duff** *v.* **1** steal and alter brands on (cattle etc.). **2** pasture (stock) illegally on another's land. **3** alter the appearance etc. of stolen goods. □ **duffing** *n.* [DUFFER²]

**duffer¹** *n. colloq.* inefficient or stupid person; dunce. [origin uncertain]

**duffer²** — *n.* **1** person who steals stock and alters brand marks. **2** unproductive mine or claim. — *v.* (of a mine etc.) prove unproductive; peter out. [British slang *duffer* person who deals in counterfeit goods; that which is counterfeit or 'no good']

**duffle-coat** *n.* hooded overcoat fastened with toggles. [*duffel* heavy woollen cloth (from *Duffel* in Belgium)]

**dug¹** *past* and *past part.* of DIG.

**dug²** *n.* udder, teat. [origin unknown]

**dugite** /doo-guyt/ *n.* highly venomous, predominantly grey, olive, or brown snake of south-western Australia. [Nyungar, probably *dugaj*]

**dugong** /doo-gong/ *n.* (*pl.* same or **-s**) Asian sea-mammal; sea cow. [Malay]

**dugout** *n.* **1 a** roofed shelter, esp. for troops in trenches. **b** underground air-raid or nuclear shelter. **2** canoe made from a hollowed tree-trunk.

**duke** /dyook/ *n.* **1** person holding the highest hereditary title of the nobility. **2** sovereign prince ruling a duchy or small nation. **3** (usu. in *pl.*) (also **dooks**) *colloq.* hand; fist (*put up your dukes*). □ **dukedom** *n.* [Latin *dux* leader]

**dulcet** /dul-suht/ *adj.* sweet-sounding. [Latin *dulcis* sweet]

**dulcimer** /dul-suh-muh/ *n.* metal stringed instrument struck with two hand-held hammers. [Latin: related to DULCET, *melos* song]

**dull** — *adj.* **1** tedious; not interesting. **2** (of the weather) overcast. **3** (of colour, light, sound, etc.) not bright, vivid, or clear. **4** (of a pain) indistinct; not acute (*a dull ache*). **5** slow-witted; stupid. **6** (of a knife-edge etc.) blunt. **7 a** (of trade etc.) sluggish, slow. **b** listless; depressed (*he's been a dull chap since the accident*). **8** (of the ears, eyes, etc.) lacking keenness. — *v.* make or become dull (*his memory dulled by drink*). □ **dullness** *n.* **dully** /dul-lee/ *adv.* [Low German or Dutch]

**dullard** /dul-uhd/ *n.* stupid person.

**duly** /dyoo-lee/ *adv.* **1** in due time or manner. **2** rightly, properly.

**dumb** /dum/ *adj.* **1 a** unable to speak, usu. because of a congenital defect or deafness. **b** (of an animal) naturally dumb. **2** silenced by surprise, shyness, etc. (*struck dumb by the revelation*). **3** taciturn or reticent, esp. insultingly (*dumb insolence*). **4** suffered or done in silence (*dumb agony*). **5** *colloq.* stupid; ignorant. **6** disenfranchised; inarticulate (*dumb masses*). **7** (of a computer terminal etc.) able only to transmit data or receive data from a computer; not programmable (opp. INTELLIGENT). **8** giving no sound (*some keys on this piano are dumb*). [Old English]

**dumb-bell** *n.* **1** short bar with a weight at each end, for muscle-building etc. **2** *colloq.* stupid person.

**dumbfound** /dum-fownd/ *v.* nonplus, make speechless with surprise. [from DUMB, CONFOUND]

**dumbo** /dum-boh/ *n.* (*pl.* **-s**) *colloq.* stupid person. [from DUMB, -O]

**dumbshow** *n.* gestures; mime.

**dumbstruck** *adj.* speechless with surprise.

**dumb waiter** *n.* small hand-operated lift for conveying food from kitchen to dining-room.

**dumdum** /dum-dum/ *n.* (in full **dumdum bullet**) soft-nosed bullet that expands on impact. [*Dum-Dum* in India]

**dum-dum** — *n. colloq.* stupid person. — *adj.* stupid. [DUMB]

**dummy** /ˈdum-ee/ — *n.* (*pl.* **-ies**) **1** model of a human figure, esp. as used to display clothes or by a ventriloquist or as a target. **2** (often *attrib.*) imitation object used to replace a real or normal one. **3** baby's rubber or plastic teat. **4** *colloq.* stupid person. **5** person taking no significant part; figurehead. **6** *Cards* player whose cards are exposed and usu. played by a partner etc. **7** (also **dummy pass**) *Rugby* pretended pass or move. — *attrib. adj.* sham; imitation. — *v.* (**-ies**, **-ied**) make a pretended pass or swerve in rugby etc. □ **spit the dummy** see SPIT[1]. [from DUMB]

**dummy run** *n.* trial attempt; rehearsal.

**dump**[1] — *n.* **1** place or heap for depositing rubbish. **2** *colloq.* unpleasant or dreary place. **3** temporary store of ammunition etc. **4** *Computing* **a** printout of stored data. **b** process or result of dumping data. — *v.* **1** put down firmly or clumsily (*dumped the shopping on the table*). **2** deposit as rubbish. **3** *colloq.* abandon or get rid of (*she's dumped him for good this time*). **4** send (goods unsaleable at a high price in the home market) to a foreign market for sale at a low price, to keep up the price at home, and to capture a new market. **5** *Computing* **a** copy (stored data) to a different location. **b** reproduce the contents of (a store) externally. **6** (of a wave) break suddenly and violently into shallow water, throwing (a surfer) down, often against the bottom. □ **dump on** *colloq.* criticise or abuse; get the better of. [origin uncertain]

**dump**[2] *n. hist.* colonial coin struck from the centre of a Spanish dollar, circulating in NSW from 1813 (see also HOLEY DOLLAR). [British *dump* rough-cast leaden counter used by children in games]

**dumper** /ˈdump-uh/ *n.* **1** person or thing that dumps. **2** large wave which crashes down as it breaks, driving a surfer towards the shore. **3** *colloq.* = TIPPER.

**dumpling** /ˈdump-ling/ *n.* **1** ball of dough boiled in stew or containing apple etc. **2** small fat person. [*dump* small round object]

**dumps** *n.pl.* (usu. in **down in the dumps**) *colloq.* low spirits. [Low German or Dutch: related to DAMP]

**dumpy** *adj.* (**-ier**, **-iest**) short and stout. □ **dumpily** *adv.* **dumpiness** *n.* [related to DUMPLING]

**dun**[1] — *adj.* greyish-brown. — *n.* dun colour. [Old English]

**dun**[2] — *n.* demand for payment. — *v.*

(**-nn-**) importune for payment of a debt; pester. [obsolete *dunkirk* privateer]

**dunce** *n.* person slow at learning; dullard. [John *Duns* Scotus, Franciscan scholastic theologian (d. 1308), whose followers were ridiculed by 16th-c. humanists and Protestants]

**dunce's cap** *n.* paper cone formerly put on the head of a dunce at school as a mark of disgrace.

**dunderhead** /ˈdun-duh-ˌhed/ *n.* stupid person. [origin unknown]

**dune** *n.* drift of sand etc. formed by the wind. [Dutch: related to DOWN[3]]

**dung** *n.* excrement of animals; manure. [Old English]

**dungaree** /ˌdung-guh-ˈree/ *n.* **1** coarse cotton cloth. **2** (in *pl.*) overalls or trousers of this. [Hindi *dungri*]

**dung-beetle** *n.* beetle whose larvae develop in dung.

**dungeon** /ˈdun-juhn/ *n.* underground prison cell. [earlier *donjon* keep of a castle; ultimately from Latin *dominus* lord]

**dunghill** *n.* heap of dung or refuse.

**dunk** *v.* **1** dip (food) into liquid before eating. **2** immerse (*dunked him in the river*). [German *tunken* dip]

**dunnart** /ˈdun-aht/ *n.* any of the narrow-footed marsupial or 'pouched' mice of all Australian States (see also MARSUPIAL MOUSE, POUCHED MOUSE). [Nyungar *dunard*]

**dunny** /ˈdun-ee/ *n. colloq.* **1** (orig.) unsewered outdoor toilet. **2** any toilet. □ **all alone like a country dunny** solitary, quite alone. [British dial. *dunnekin* privy (*dunna* faeces, *ken* house)]

**dunny can** *n.* removable receptacle in an outdoor toilet.

**dunny cart** *n.* (esp. in unsewered areas and formerly) vehicle for the collection and disposal of human excrement.

**duo** /ˈdyoo-oh/ *n.* (*pl.* **-s**) **1** pair of performers. **2** duet. [Italian from Latin, = two]

**duodecimal** /ˌdyoo-oh-ˈdes-uh-muhl/ *adj.* **1** of twelfths or twelve. **2** in or by twelves. [Latin *duodecim* twelve]

**duodenum** /ˌdyoo-uh-ˈdee-nuhm/ *n.* (*pl.* **-s**) first part of the small intestine immediately below the stomach. □ **duodenal** *adj.* [medieval Latin: related to DUODECIMAL, from its length of about 12 fingers' breadth]

**duologue** /ˈdyoo-uh-ˌlog/ *n.* dialogue between two people. [from DUO, MONOLOGUE]

**dupe** /dyoop/ — *n.* victim of deception. — *v.* (**-ping**) deceive, trick. □ **dupable** *adj.* **duper** *n.* [French]

**duple** /**dyoo**-puhl/ adj. of two parts. [Latin duplus]

**duple time** n. Mus. rhythm with two beats to the bar.

**duplex** /**dyoo**-pleks/ — n. (often attrib.) **1** building with a flat on the ground floor and a flat above. **2** (in some areas) one of two semi-detached houses. — adj. **1** of two parts. **2** (also **full-duplex**) Computing (of a circuit) allowing simultaneous two-way transmission of signals. [Latin, = double]

**duplicate** — adj. /**dyoo**-pluh-kuht/ **1** exactly like something already existing; copied (esp. in large numbers). **2 a** existing in two examples; paired. **b** twice as large or many; doubled. **3** (of card-games) with the same hands played by different players. — n. /**dyoo**-pluh-kuht/ identical thing, esp. a copy. — v. /**dyoo**-pluh-,kayt/ (**-ting**) **1** multiply by two; double. **2** make or be an exact copy of. **3** repeat (an action etc.), esp. unnecessarily. □ **in duplicate** in two exact copies. □ **duplicable** /-kuh-buhl/ adj. **duplication** /-**kay**-shuhn/ n. [Latin: related to DUPLEX]

**duplicity** /dyoo-**plis**-uh-tee/ n. double-dealing; deceitfulness. □ **duplicitous** adj. [Latin: related to DUPLEX]

**durable** /**dyoo**-ruh-buhl/ — adj. **1** lasting; hard-wearing. **2** (of goods) with a relatively long useful life. — n. (in pl.) durable goods. □ **durability** /-**bil**-uh-tee/ n. [Latin durus hard]

**dura mater** /,dyoo-ruh **mah**-tuh/ n. tough outermost membrane enveloping the brain and spinal cord. [medieval Latin = hard mother, translation of Arabic]

**duration** /dyoo-**ray**-shuhn/ n. **1** time taken by an event. **2** specified length of time (duration of a minute). □ **for the duration 1** until the end of an event. **2** for a very long time. [medieval Latin: related to DURABLE]

**duress** /dyoo-**res**, **dyoo**-/ n. **1** compulsion, esp. illegal use of threats or violence (under duress). **2** imprisonment. [Latin durus hard]

**during** /**dyoo**-ring/ prep. **1** throughout the course or duration of (read during the meal). **2** at some point in the duration of (came in during the evening). [Latin: related to DURABLE]

**durry** /**du**-ree/ n. colloq. cigarette. [origin unknown]

**dusk** n. darker stage of twilight. [Old English]

**dusky** adj. (**-ier, -iest**) **1** shadowy; dim. **2** dark-coloured; darkish. □ **duskily** adv. **duskiness** n.

**dusky coral pea** see CORAL PEA.

**dust** — n. **1 a** finely powdered earth, dirt, etc., or fine powder of other material (pollen dust). **b** cloud of this. **2** anything reduced by disintegration or decay, esp. a dead person's remains. **3** confusion, turmoil (raised quite a dust). **4** the ground (kissed the dust). **5** colloq. gold dust. **6** colloq. silicosis. — v. **1** wipe the dust from (furniture etc.). **2 a** sprinkle (a thing) with powder, sugar, etc. (dust the cake with icing sugar). **b** sprinkle (sugar, powder, etc.) (dust icing sugar on the cake). **3** (usu. in passive) colloq. defeat thoroughly, thrash (our team got dusted). □ **bite the dust** see BITE. **dust down 1** dust the clothes of. **2** colloq. reprimand. **3** = dust off. **dust off 1** remove the dust from. **2** use again after a long period (thinking of dusting off my golf clubs). **hit the dust** fall, or throw oneself, to the ground. **lick the dust 1** colloq. take a heavy fall; be injured or killed. **2** toady, grovel. **raise** (or **kick up** or **stir up**) **the dust** colloq. create commotion or a disturbance; make a fuss. **throw dust in a person's eyes** confuse, mislead, or dupe a person. **when the dust settles** when things quieten down. [Old English]

**dust bowl** n. desert made by drought or erosion.

**dusted** adj. colloq. suffering from silicosis.

**duster** n. cloth for dusting furniture etc.

**dusting** n. colloq. sound defeat; thrashing (our team got a dusting).

**dust jacket** n. (also **dust cover**) paper cover on a hardback book.

**dustpan** n. pan into which dust is brushed from the floor.

**dust storm** n. storm with clouds of dust gathered in the air.

**dust-up** n. colloq. fight, disturbance.

**dusty** adj. (**-ier, -iest**) **1** full of or covered with dust. **2** (of a colour) dull or muted. □ **dustily** adv. **dustiness** n.

**dusty miller** n. Australian shrub with rounded leaves and white flowers surrounded by very large white leaf-like bracts which look as if they have been dusted with flour.

**Dutch** — adj. of the Netherlands or its people or language. — n. **1** the Dutch language. **2** (prec. by the; treated as pl.) the people of the Netherlands. □ **go Dutch** share expenses on an outing etc. [Dutch]

**Dutch auction** n. one in which the price is progressively reduced.

**Dutch cap** n. dome-shaped contraceptive device fitting over the cervix.

**Dutch courage** n. courage induced by alcohol.

**Dutch elm disease** n. fungus disease of elms, first found in the Netherlands.

**Dutch oven** n. 1 metal box with the open side facing a fire. 2 covered cooking-pot for braising etc.

**Dutch treat** n. party, outing, etc., at which people pay for themselves.

**Dutch uncle** n. kind but firm adviser.

**duteous** /dyoo-tee-uhs/ adj. literary dutiful. □ **duteously** adv.

**dutiable** /dyoo-tee-uh-buhl/ adj. requiring the payment of duty.

**dutiful** /dyoo-tuh-ful/ adj. doing one's duty; obedient. □ **dutifully** adv.

**duty** /dyoo-tee/ n. (pl. **-ies**) 1 a moral or legal obligation; responsibility (it's my duty to report it). b binding force of what is right (has a strong sense of duty). 2 a tax levied on certain goods, imports, etc. b tax levied on the transfer of property, legal recognition of documents, etc. 3 job or function arising from a business or office (playground duty). □ **do duty for** serve as or pass for (something else). **on** (or **off**) **duty** working (or not working). [Anglo-French: related to DUE]

**duty-bound** adj. obliged by duty.

**duvet** /doo-vay/ n. = DOONA. [French]

**dux** /duks/ n. top pupil in a class or in a school. [Latin = leader]

**dwarf** /dwawf/ — n. (pl. **-s** or **dwarves** /dwawvz/ ) 1 person, animal, or plant much below normal size. 2 small mythological being, often with magical powers. 3 small usu. dense star. — v. 1 stunt in growth. 2 make seem small (efforts dwarfed by their rivals' achievements). □ **dwarfish** adj. [Old English]

■ **Usage** In sense 1, with regard to people, the term person of restricted growth is now often preferred.

**dwarf apple** n. shrub or small tree (Angophora cordifolia) of NSW (see also ANGOPHORA, APPLE 2).

**dweeb** n. colloq. contemptible or boring person, esp. one who is studious, puny, or unfashionable. [origin unknown]

**dwell** v. (past and past part. **dwelt** or **dwelled**) live, reside. □ **dwell on** (or **upon**) think, write, or speak at length on; brood or harp on (always dwelling on his grievances). □ **dweller** n. [Old English, = lead astray]

**dwelling** n. house, residence.

**dwindle** /dwin-duhl/ v. (**-ling**) 1 become gradually less or smaller. 2 lose importance; decline. [Old English]

**Dy** symb. dysprosium.

**dye** /duy/ — n. 1 substance used to change the colour of hair, fabric, etc. 2

colour so produced. — v. (**dyeing, dyed**) 1 colour with dye. 2 dye a specified colour (dyed it yellow). □ **dyer** n. [Old English]

**dyed-in-the-wool** adj. (usu. attrib.) out and out; unchangeable (dyed-in-the-wool monarchist).

**dying** /duy-ing/ attrib. adj. of, or at the time of, death (dying words).

**Dyirbal** /jeer-bahl/ n. an Aboriginal language of northern Queensland spoken, with dialectal variants, over a vast area from Cardwell to beyond Innisfail along the coast, and inland to Malanda and Herberton: still actively spoken.

**dyke**[1] /duyk/ (also **dike**) — n. 1 embankment built to prevent flooding. 2 low wall of turf or stone. 3 Geol. intrusion of igneous rock across sedimentary strata. 4 colloq. toilet. — v. (**-king**) provide or protect with dyke(s). [related to DITCH]

**dyke**[2] /duyk/ n. (also **dike**) colloq. lesbian. [origin unknown]

**dynamic** /duy-**nam**-ik/ adj. 1 energetic; active. 2 Physics a of motive force. b of force in actual operation. 3 of dynamics. 4 Computing capable of change while the system or program continues to run. □ **dynamically** adv. [Greek dunamis power]

**dynamics** n.pl. 1 (usu. treated as sing.) a Mech. branch of mechanics concerned with the motion of bodies under the action of forces. b branch of any science in which forces or changes are considered (aerodynamics; population dynamics). 2 motive forces, physical or moral, affecting behaviour and change in any sphere. 3 Mus. varying degree of volume of sound in musical performance.

**dynamism** /duy-nuh-,miz-uhm/ n. 1 energy; dynamic power. 2 Philos. theory that phenomena of matter or mind are due to the action of forces (rather than to motion or matter).

**dynamite** /duy-nuh-,muyt/ — n. 1 high explosive mixture containing nitroglycerine mixed with an absorbent. 2 potentially dangerous person, situation, etc. — v. (**-ting**) charge or blow up with dynamite.

**dynamo** /duy-nuh-,moh/ n. (pl. **-s**) 1 machine converting mechanical into electrical energy, esp. by rotating coils of copper wire in a magnetic field. 2 colloq. energetic person. [abbreviation of dynamo-electric machine]

**dynamometer** /,duy-nuh-**mom**-uh-tuh/ n. instrument measuring energy expended. [Greek: related to DYNAMIC]

**dynasty** /**din**-uh-stee/ *n.* (*pl.* **-ies**) **1** line of hereditary rulers. **2** succession of leaders in any field. □ **dynastic** /duh-**nas**-tik/ *adj.* [Latin from Greek]

**dyne** /duyn/ *n. Physics* force required to give a mass of one gram an acceleration of one centimetre per second per second. [Greek *dunamis* force]

**dys-** *prefix* bad, difficult. [Greek]

**dysentery** /**dis**-uhn-tree/ *n.* inflammation of the intestines, causing severe diarrhoea with blood and mucus. [Greek *entera* bowels]

**dysfunction** /dis-**fungk**-shuhn/ *n.* abnormality or impairment of functioning.

**dyslexia** /dis-**lek**-see-uh/ *n.* abnormal difficulty in reading and spelling, caused by a condition of the brain. □ **dyslectic** /-**lek**-tik/ *adj.* & *n.* **dyslexic** *adj.* & *n.* [Greek *lexis* speech]

**dysmenorrhoea** /dis-men-uh-**ree**-uh/ *n.* painful or difficult menstruation.

**dyspepsia** /dis-**pep**-see-uh/ *n.* indigestion. □ **dyspeptic** *adj.* & *n.* [Greek *peptos* digested]

**dysphasia** /dis-**fay**-zee-uh/ *n.* lack of coordination in speech, owing to brain damage. [Greek *dusphatos* hard to utter]

**dysprosium** /dis-**proh**-zee-uhm/ *n.* metallic element of the lanthanide series. [Greek *dusprositos* hard to get at]

**dystrophy** /**dis**-truh-fee/ *n.* defective nutrition. [Greek *-trophē* nourishment]

# E

**E¹** /ee/ n. (also **e**) (pl. **Es** or **E's**) **1** fifth letter of the alphabet. **2** Mus. third note of the diatonic scale of C major.

**E²** abbr. (also **E.**) east, eastern.

**e-** prefix see EX-¹ before some consonants.

**each** /eech/ — adj. every one of two or more persons or things, regarded separately (five in each class). — pron. each person or thing (each of us; cost a dollar each). [Old English]

**each other** pron. one another (they hate each other).

**each way** adj. (of a bet) backing a horse etc. either to win or to come second or third.

**eager** /ee-guh/ adj. keen, enthusiastic (eager to learn; eager for news). □ **eagerly** adv. **eagerness** n. [Latin acer keen]

**eager beaver** n. colloq. very diligent person.

**eagle** /ee-guhl/ n. **1 a** any of various large birds of prey with keen vision and powerful flight. **b** = WEDGE-TAILED EAGLE. **2** score of two strokes under par at any hole in golf. [Latin aquila]

**eagle eye** n. keen sight, watchfulness. □ **eagle-eyed** adj.

**eagle hawk** — n. = WEDGE-TAILED EAGLE. — v. (**eaglehawk**) pluck wool from a dead sheep.

**eaglet** /ee-gluht/ n. young eagle.

**ear¹** /eer/ n. **1** organ of hearing, esp. its external part. **2** faculty for discriminating sounds (an ear for music). **3** attention, esp. sympathetic (give ear to; have a person's ear). □ **all ears** listening attentively. **by ear** (performance of music) without reference to the written score etc. **have** (or **keep**) **an ear to the ground** be alert to rumours or trends. **out on one's ear** dismissed in disgrace. **play by ear** see PLAY. **up to one's ears** (often foll. by in) colloq. deeply involved or occupied. [Old English]

**ear²** n. seed-bearing head of a cereal plant. [Old English]

**earbash** v. (also **ear-bash**) subject a person to a torrent of words; talk at great length to; harangue. □ **earbasher** n. **earbashing** n.

**eardrum** n. membrane of the middle ear.

**earful** n. (pl. **-s**) colloq. **1** prolonged amount of talking. **2** strong reprimand (gave me an earful when I got home late).

**earl** /erl/ n. (in the UK) male ranking between marquis and viscount. □ **earldom** n. [Old English]

**early** /er-lee/ — adj. & adv. (**-ier, -iest**) **1** before the due, usual, or expected time. **2 a** not far on in the day or night, or in time (early evening; at the earliest opportunity). **b** prompt (early payment appreciated). **3 a** not far on in a period, development, or process of evolution; being the first stage (early Christians; early spring). **b** of the distant past (early man). **c** not far on in a sequence or serial order (the early chapters; appears early in the list). **d** used with reference to the earliest period of white settlement in Australia (early settlers). **4** forward in flowering, ripening, etc. (early peaches). — n. (pl. **-ies**) **1** (usu. in pl.) early fruit or vegetable. **2** (in pl.) the early years of white settlement in Australia (many Aborigines were systematically massacred by whites in the earlies). □ **early** (or **earlier**) **on** at an early (or earlier) stage □ **earliness** n. [Old English: related to ERE]

**early days** n.pl. too soon to expect results etc.

**early mark** n. approval to leave work early as a reward.

**early Nancy** n. bulbous Australian plant of the lily family occurring in all States having rounded white flowers blotched with purple appearing early in spring.

**earmark** — n. **1** owner's mark on the ear of an animal. **2** any identifying mark — v. **1** set aside for a special purpose (funds earmarked for AIDS research). **2** mark (sheep etc.) with an identifying mark.

**earn** /ern/ v. **1 a** bring in as income in the form of money in return for labour or services (earn a weekly wage). **b** (of capital invested) bring in as interest or profit. **2 a** deserve; be entitled to or obtain as the reward for work or merit (have earned a holiday). **b** incur (a reproach, reputation, etc.) (he earned the reputation for being a cheat). □ **earner** n. [Old English]

**earnest¹** /er-nuhst/ adj. intensely serious. □ **in earnest** serious, seriously, with determination. □ **earnestly** adv. **earnestness** n. [Old English]

**earnest²** /er-nuhst/ n. **1** money paid as an instalment, esp. to confirm a contract etc. **2** token or foretaste. [Latin arr(h)a pledge]

342

**earnings** *n.pl.* money earned.

**earphone** *n.* device applied to the ear to aid hearing or receive radio or telephone communications.

**earpiece** *n.* part of a telephone etc. applied to the ear.

**ear-piercing** *adj.* shrill. — *n.* piercing of the ears for wearing earrings.

**earplug** *n.* piece of wax etc. placed in the ear to protect against water, noise, etc.

**earring** *n.* jewellery worn on (esp. the lobe of) the ear.

**earshot** *n.* hearing-range (*within ear-shot*).

**ear-splitting** *adj.* excessively loud.

**earth** /erth/ — *n.* **1 a** (also **Earth**) one of the planets of the solar system orbiting about the sun between Venus and Mars; the planet on which we live. **b** land and sea, as distinct from sky. **2 a** dry land; the ground (*fell to earth*). **b** soil. **3** *Relig.* this world, as distinct from heaven or hell. **4** connection to the earth as the completion of an electrical circuit. **5** hole of a fox etc. **6** (prec. by *the*) *colloq.* huge sum; everything (*cost the earth*; *want the earth*). — *v.* connect (an electrical circuit) to the earth. □ **come back** (or **down**) **to earth** return to realities. **gone to earth** in hiding. **on earth** *colloq.* **1** existing anywhere (*the happiest man on earth*; *looked like nothing on earth*). **2** used as an intensifier (*what on earth have you done?*). **run to earth** find after a long search. □ **earthward** *adj. & adv.* **earthwards** *adv.* [Old English]

**earthbound** *adj.* **1** attached to the earth or earthly things. **2** moving towards the earth.

**earthen** /er-thuhn, er-thuhn/ *adj.* made of earth or baked clay.

**earthenware** *n.* pottery made of fired clay.

**earthling** /erth-ling/ *n.* inhabitant of the earth, esp. in science fiction.

**earthly** *adj.* **1** of the earth or human life on it; terrestrial. **2** (usu. with *neg.*) *colloq.* remotely possible or conceivable (*is no earthly use; there wasn't an earthly reason*).

**earthquake** *n.* convulsion of the earth's surface as a result of faults in strata or volcanic action.

**earth sciences** *n.pl.* sciences concerned with the earth or part of it.

**earth-shattering** *adj. colloq.* traumatic, devastating. □ **earth-shatteringly** *adv.*

**earthworm** *n.* common worm living in the ground.

**earthy** *adj.* (**-ier, -iest**) **1** of or like earth or soil. **2** coarse, crude (*earthy humour*). □ **earthiness** *n.*

**ear-trumpet** *n.* trumpet-shaped device formerly used as a hearing-aid.

**earwig** *n.* **1** small insect with pincers at its rear end. **2** *colloq.* eavesdropper. [Old English, from EAR[1], *wicga* probably related to WIGGLE, because earwigs were once thought to enter the head through the ear]

**ease** /eez/ — *n.* **1** absence of difficulty; facility, effortlessness (*did it with ease*). **2 a** freedom or relief from pain or trouble. **b** freedom from embarrassment or awkwardness. **c** freedom or relief from constraint or formality (*his ease of manner put us at our ease*). — *v.* (**-sing**) **1** relieve from pain or anxiety (*eased my mind*). **2** (often foll. by *off, up*) **a** become less burdensome or severe (*has the pain eased up yet?*). **b** relax; begin to take it easy. **c** slow down; moderate one's behaviour etc. (*ease up, mate, or you'll have a heart attack*). **3 a** relax; slacken; make a less tight fit (*ease the tension on the wire or it will snap*). **b** move or be moved carefully into place (*eased it into position*). □ **at ease 1** free from anxiety or constraint. **2** *Mil.* **a** in a relaxed attitude, with the feet apart. **b** the order to stand in this way. [Latin: related to ADJACENT]

**easel** /ee-zuhl/ *n.* stand for an artist's work, a blackboard, etc. [Dutch *ezel* ass]

**easement** *n.* legal right of way or similar right over another's land. [French: related to EASE]

**easily** /ee-zuh-lee/ *adv.* **1** without difficulty. **2** by far (*easily the best*). **3** very probably (*it could easily snow*).

**east** /eest/ — *n.* **1 a** point of the horizon where the sun rises at the equinoxes (cardinal point 90° to the right of north). **b** compass point corresponding to this. **c** direction in which this lies. **2** (usu. **the East**) countries situated in this direction. **3** eastern part of a country, town, etc. — *adj.* **1** towards, at, near, or facing the east. **2** from the east (*east wind*). — *adv.* **1** towards, at, or near the east. **2** (foll. by *of*) further east than. □ **to the east** (often foll. by *of*) in an easterly direction. [Old English]

**Easter** *n.* **1** festival (held on a variable Sunday in March or April) commemorating Christ's resurrection. **2** season in which this occurs, esp. the weekend from Good Friday to Easter Monday. [Old English, apparently from *Eostre* goddess of dawn whose festival was kept at the vernal equinox]

**easterly** — *adj. & adv.* **1** in an eastern position or direction. **2** (of a wind) from the east. — *n.* (*pl.* **-ies**) such a wind.

**eastern** *adj.* of or in the east. □ **east-ernmost** *adj.*

**Eastern Church** *n.* Orthodox Church.

**easterner** *n.* native or inhabitant of the east.

**eastern grey** *n.* (in full **eastern grey kangaroo**) = GREAT GREY KANGAROO.

**Eastern Standard Time** *n.* standard time used in eastern Australia.

**Eastern States** *n.* Australia, excluding Western Australia (and sometimes South Australia). □ **Eastern Stater** *n.pl.*

**eastward** — *adj. & adv.* (also **eastwards**) towards the east. — *n.* eastward direction or region.

**easy** /ee-zee/ — *adj.* (**-ier**, **-iest**) **1** not difficult; not requiring great effort. **2 a** free from pain, trouble, or anxiety. **b** comfortably off, affluent (*easy circum-stances*). **3** free from constraint; relaxed and pleasant (*an easy manner*). **4** compliant; obliging; easily persuaded (*she's an easy touch*; *he's easy game*). **5** *colloq.* of loose morals; promiscuous. — *adv.* with ease; in an effortless or relaxed manner. — *int.* go or move carefully. □ **easy come, easy go** *colloq.* what is easily got is soon lost or spent. **easy does it** *colloq.* go carefully. **easy on the eye** (or **ear** etc.) *colloq.* pleasant to look at (or listen to etc.). **go easy** (foll. by *with*, *on*) **1** be sparing or cautious (*go easy on the chilli*). **2** be lenient; not be harsh. **I'm easy** *colloq.* I'm ready to comply (with whatever is proposed); I have no preference. **take it easy 1** proceed gently. **2** relax; work less. □ **easiness** *n.* [French: related to EASE]

**easygoing** *adj.* placid and tolerant.

**Easy Street** *n. colloq.* affluence.

**easy touch** *n. colloq.* person who is easily duped, tricked, etc.

**easy wicket** *n. colloq.* comfortable circumstances; well-paid undemanding job etc. (*he's on an easy wicket*).

**eat** /eet/ — *v.* (*past* **ate** /et, ayt/; *past part.* **eaten**) **1 a** take into the mouth, chew, and swallow (food). **b** consume food; take a meal. **c** devour (*eaten by a lion*). **2** (foll. by *away*, *at*, *into*) **a** destroy gradually, esp. by corrosion, erosion, disease, etc. **b** begin to consume or diminish (resources etc.) (*I'm eating into my capital*). **3** *colloq.* trouble, vex (*what's eating you?*). — *n.* (in *pl.*) *colloq.* food. □ **eat one's heart out** be gnawed by emotion, esp. by envy or longing. **eat out** have a meal away from home, esp. in a restaurant. **eat out of a person's hand** be entirely submissive to a person. **eat up 1** eat completely. **2** use or deal with rapidly or wastefully (*eats up petrol*). **3** preoccupy

(*eaten up with envy*). **eat one's words** admit that one was wrong. [Old English]

**eatable** — *adj.* fit to be eaten. — *n.* (usu. in *pl.*) food.

**eat crow** *v.* submit to humiliation, eat humble pie.

**eater** *n.* person who eats (*a big eater*).

**eau de Cologne** /ˌoh-duh-kuh-**lohn**/ *n.* perfume of a kind orig. from Cologne. [French, = water of Cologne]

**eaves** /eevz/ *n.pl.* underside of a projecting roof. [Old English]

**eavesdrop** *v.* (**-pp-**) listen to a private conversation. □ **eavesdropper** *n.* [*eaves-dropper* originally 'person who listens under walls']

**ebb** — *n.* **1** movement of the tide out to sea (also *attrib.*: *ebb tide*). **2** flowing away; decline; change from a better to a worse state (*the ebb of all my hopes*). — *v.* (often foll. by *away*) **1** flow out to sea; recede. **2** decline; run low (*life was ebbing away*). [Old English]

**Ebola virus** /uh-**boh**-luh/ *n.* virus which causes uncontrollable internal and external bleeding in humans and usu. death. [named after a river in Zaire]

**ebonite** /**eb**-uh-ˌnuyt/ *n.* vulcanite. [from EBONY]

**ebony** /**eb**-uh-nee/ — *n.* heavy hard dark wood of a tropical tree. — *adj.* **1** made of ebony. **2** black like ebony. [Greek *ebenos* ebony tree]

**ebony heart** *n.* northern Queensland rainforest tree having cream bell-flowers, green fruits, and a hard dark timber.

**ebullient** /uh-**buul**-ee-uhnt, uh-**bul**-/ *adj.* exuberant; high-spirited. □ **ebullience** *n.* **ebulliency** *n.* **ebulliently** *adv.* [Latin: related to BOIL¹]

**EC** *abbr.* European Community.

**ecad** /**ee**-kad/ *n. Ecology* an organism modified by its environment. [Greek *oikos* house]

**eccentric** /uhk-**sen**-trik, ek-/ — *adj.* **1** odd, irregular, or capricious in behaviour or appearance (*eccentric person*; *eccentric conduct*). **2** (also **excentric**) **a** not placed, not having its axis placed, centrally. **b** (often foll. by *to*) (of a circle) not concentric (to another). **c** (of an orbit) not circular. — *n.* **1** eccentric person (*this place is full of eccentrics*). **2** disc at the end of a shaft for changing rotatory into backward-and-forward motion. □ **eccentrically** *adv.* **eccentricity** /ˌek-sen-**tris**-uh-tee/ *n.* [Greek: related to CENTRE]

**ecclesiastic** /uh-ˌklee-zee-**as**-tik/ — *n.* priest or clergyman. — *adj.* = ECCLESI-ASTICAL. [Greek *ekklēsia* church]

**ecclesiastical** *adj.* of the Church or clergy.

**ECG** *abbr.* electrocardiogram.

**echelon** /**esh**-uh-,lon/ *n.* **1** level in an organisation, in society, etc.; those occupying it (often in *pl.*: *upper echelons*). **2** wedge-shaped formation of troops, aircraft, etc. [French, = ladder, from Latin *scala*]

**echidna** /uh-**kid**-nuh/ *n.* (also **spiny ant eater**) any of several egg-laying pouch-bearing mammals native to Australia (and New Guinea), with a covering of spines, and having a long snout and long claws. [Greek, = viper (alluding to the tongue, which resembles that of a snake)]

**echinoderm** /uh-**kuy**-nuh-,derm, **ek**-uh-nuh-/ *n.* (usu. spiny) sea animal of the group including the starfish and sea urchin. [Greek *ekhinos* sea-urchin, *derma* skin]

**echo** /**ek**-oh/ — *n.* (*pl.* **-es**) **1 a** repetition of a sound by the reflection of sound waves. **b** sound so produced. **2** reflected radio or radar beam. **3** close imitation or imitator. **4** circumstance or event reminiscent of an earlier one. **5** *Computing* reflection of transmitting data back to its source. — *v.* (**-es, -ed**) **1 a** (of a place) resound with an echo. **b** (of a sound) be repeated; resound. **c** (of rumour, memory, etc.) be repeated (as if by echoing) (*his fame will echo down the years; his voice still echoes in my mind*). **2** repeat (a sound) thus. **3 a** repeat (another's words) (*you needn't echo everything I say*). **b** imitate the words, opinions, or actions, etc. of (*children echo their parents*). [Latin from Greek]

**echo chamber** *n.* enclosure with sound-reflecting walls.

**echoic** /e-**koh**-ik/ *adj.* (of a word) imitating the sound it represents; onomatopoeic (e.g. *boom*).

**echo sounder** *n.* depth-sounding device using timed echoes.

**éclair** /ay-**klair**, uh-**klair**/ *n.* small elongated iced cake of choux pastry filled with cream. [French, = lightning]

**eclampsia** /uh-**klamp**-see-uh/ *n.* convulsive condition occurring esp. in pregnant women. [ultimately from Greek]

**éclat** /ay-**klah**, **ay**-klah/ *n.* **1** brilliant display (*she played the piano concerto with verve and éclat*). **2** social distinction; conspicuous success; universal applause (*was received with great éclat*). [French]

**eclectic** /ek-**lek**-tik/ — *adj.* selecting ideas, style, etc., from various sources. — *n.* eclectic person or philosopher. □ **eclectically** *adv.* **eclecticism** /-,siz-uhm/ *n.* [Greek *eklegō* pick out]

**eclipse** /uh-**klips**, ee-**klips**/ — *n.* **1** obscuring of light from one heavenly body by another. **2** loss of light, importance, or prominence. — *v.* (**-sing**) **1** (of a heavenly body) cause the eclipse of (another). **2** outshine, surpass (*her skill eclipses that of her competitors*). [Greek *ekleipsis*]

**ecliptic** /uh-**klip**-tik, ee-/ — *n.* sun's apparent path among the stars during the year. — *adj.* of an eclipse or the ecliptic.

**eclogue** /**ek**-log/ *n.* short pastoral poem. [Greek: related to ECLECTIC]

**eco-** *comb. form* ecology, ecological (*ecoclimate*).

**ecology** /ee-**kol**-uh-jee, uh-/ *n.* **1** the study of the relations of organisms to one another and to their surroundings. **2** (in full **human ecology**) the study of the interaction of people with their environment. □ **ecological** /,ee-kuh-**loj**-i-kuhl/ *adj.* **ecologically** /,ee-kuh-**loj**-i-kuh-lee, -klee/ *adv.* **ecologist** *n.* [Greek *oikos* house]

**econocrat** /uh-**kon**-uh-krat, ee-/ *n.* person, esp. in government, who believes that a nation's economy must be paramount and override all other considerations including the immediate welfare of its citizens. □ **econocracy** /,ee-kuh-**nok**-ruh-see/ *n.* [ECONOMY, -CRAT]

**economic** /,ee-kuh-**nom**-ik, ,ek-uh-/ *adj.* **1** of or relating to economics. **2** profitable (*not economic to run buses on a Sunday*). **3** practical; studied with regard to human needs (*economic geography*). □ **economically** *adv.* [Greek: related to ECONOMY]

**economical** *adj.* sparing in the use of resources; avoiding waste. □ **economically** *adv.*

**economics** *n.pl.* (as *sing.*) **1** science of the production and distribution of wealth. **2** application of this to a particular subject (*the economics of publishing*).

**economise** /uh-**kon**-uh-,muyz/ *v.* (also **-ize**) (**-sing** or **-zing**) **1** be economical; make economies; reduce expenditure. **2** (foll. by *on*) use sparingly; spend less on (*we need to economise on food*).

**economist** /uh-**kon**-uh-muhst/ *n.* expert on or student of economics.

**economy** /uh-**kon**-uh-mee/ *n.* (*pl.* **-ies**) **1 a** wealth and resources of a community, esp. in terms of the production and consumption of goods and services. **b** particular kind of this (*a capitalist economy*). **c** administration or condition of this. **2 a** careful management of (esp. financial) resources; frugality. **b** instance of this (*made many economies*). **3** sparing or careful use (*economy of language*). [Greek *oikonomia* household management]

**economy class** n. cheapest class of air etc. travel.

**ecosphere** /ee-koh-ˌsfeer, ek-oh-/ n. region of space including planets where conditions are such that living things can exist.

**ecosystem** /ee-koh-ˌsis-tuhm, ek-oh-/ n. biological community of interacting organisms and their physical environment.

**ecotourism** n. a form of tourism which uses but does not exploit ecologically sensitive areas. [eco(logical) + TOURISM]

**ecstasy** /ek-stuh-see/ n. (pl. -ies) 1 overwhelming joy or rapture. 2 Psychol. emotional or religious frenzy or trance-like state. 3 colloq. type of hallucinogenic drug. □ **ecstatic** /ek-stat-ik/ adj. **ecstatically** /-stat-i-kuh-lee, -klee/ adv. [Greek ekstasis standing outside oneself]

**ECT** abbr. electroconvulsive therapy.

**ecto-** comb. form outside. [Greek ektos]

**ectoderm** /ek-toh-ˌderm/ n. Biol. outermost layer of an animal embryo in early development. □ **ectodermal** /-der-muhl/ adj.

**-ectomy** comb. form denoting the surgical removal of part of the body (appendectomy). [Greek ektomē excision]

**ectopic** /ek-top-ik/ adj. Med. in an abnormal place or position. [Greek ektopos out of place]

**ectopic pregnancy** n. pregnancy occurring outside the womb.

**ectoplasm** /ek-toh-ˌplaz-uhm, ek-tuh-/ n. supposed viscous substance exuding from the body of a spiritualistic medium during a trance. [from ECTO-, PLASMA]

**ecu** /ay-kyoo/ n. (also **Ecu**) (pl. -s) European Currency Unit. [abbreviation]

**ecumenical** /ˌee-kyoo-men-uh-kuhl, ek-yoo-/ adj. (also **ecumenic**) 1 of or representing the whole Christian world. 2 seeking worldwide Christian unity. □ **ecumenically** adv. **ecumenism** /ee-kyoo-muh-ˌniz-uhm/ n. [Greek oikoumenikos of the inhabited earth]

**Ecumenical Council** n. assembly of the bishops of the world convened by the Pope to consider questions of doctrine and practice, the conclusions of such a Council being binding upon the whole Church.

**eczema** /ek-suh-muh/ n. inflammation of the skin, with itching and discharge. [Latin from Greek]

**ed.** abbr. 1 edited by. 2 edition. 3 editor. 4 educated.

**-ed¹** suffix forming adjectives: 1 from nouns, meaning 'having, wearing, etc.' (talented; trousered). 2 from phrases of adjective and noun (good-humoured). [Old English]

**-ed²** suffix forming: 1 past tense and past participle of weak verbs (needed). 2 participial adjectives (escaped prisoner). [Old English]

**edam** /ee-dam, ee-duhm/ n. round orig. Dutch cheese with a red rind. [Edam in Holland]

**eddy** /ed-ee/ — n. (pl. -ies) 1 circular movement of water causing a small whirlpool. 2 movement of wind, smoke, etc. resembling this. — v. (-ies, -ied) whirl round in eddies. [Old English ed- again, back]

**edelweiss** /ay-duhl-ˌvuys/ n. plant with white flowers, growing in the European Alps. [German, = noble-white]

**Eden** /ee-duhn/ n. place or state of great happiness, with reference to the abode of Adam and Eve at the Creation. [Hebrew, originally = delight]

**edge** — n. 1 boundary-line or margin of an area or surface. 2 narrow surface of a thin object. 3 meeting-line of surfaces. 4 a sharpened side of a blade etc. b sharpness of this (the knife has lost its edge). 5 brink of a precipice (edge of the cliff). 6 edge-like thing, esp. the crest of a ridge. 7 effectiveness, incisiveness; excitement (the argument had real edge to it). — v. (-ging) 1 advance or move, esp. gradually or furtively (edged it into the corner; began to edge towards the exit). 2 a provide with an edge or border. b form a border to. 3 sharpen (a tool etc.). 4 Cricket strike (the ball) with the edge of the bat. □ **have the edge on** (or **over**) have a slight advantage over. **on edge** tense and irritable. **over the edge 1** insane. 2 outside the bounds of reasonableness or decency. **set a person's teeth on edge** (of taste or sound) cause an unpleasant nervous sensation. **take the edge off** make less intense (that's taken the edge off my appetite). [Old English]

**edgeways** adv. (also **edgewise**) with edge uppermost or foremost. □ **get a word in edgeways** contribute to a conversation when the dominant speaker pauses.

**edging** n. thing forming an edge or border.

**edgy** adj. (-ier, -iest) irritable; anxious. □ **edgily** adv. **edginess** n.

**edible** /ed-uh-buhl/ — adj. fit to be eaten. — n. (in pl.) food. □ **edibility** /-bil-uh-tee/ n. [Latin edo eat]

**edict** /ee-dikt/ n. order proclaimed by authority. [Latin edico proclaim]

**edifice** /ed-uh-fuhs/ n. building, esp. an imposing one. [Latin aedis dwelling]

**edify** /ed-uh-ˌfuy/ v. (**-ies, -ied**) improve morally or intellectually. □ **edification** /ˌed-fuh-**kay**-shuhn/ n. [Latin *aedifico* build]

**edit** /**ed**-uht/ v. (**-t-**) **1 a** assemble, prepare, or modify (written material for publication). **b** prepare an edition of (an author's work). **2** be editor of (a newspaper etc.). **3** take extracts from and collate (a film etc.) to form a unified sequence. **4 a** prepare (data) for processing by a computer. **b** alter (a text entered in a word processor etc.). **5 a** reword in order to correct, or to alter the emphasis. **b** (foll. by *out*) remove (a part) from a text etc. [Latin *edo edit-* give out]

**edition** /uh-**dish**-uhn/ n. **1** edited or published form of a book etc. **2** copies of a book, newspaper, etc. issued at one time. **3** instance of a regular broadcast (*the Sunday edition*). **4** person or thing similar to another (*a miniature edition of her mother*).

**editor** n. **1** person who edits material for publication or broadcasting. **2** person who directs the preparation of a newspaper or broadcast news programme or a particular section of one (*sports editor*). **3** person who selects or commissions material for publication. **4** person who edits films, sound track, etc. **5** computer program for entering and modifying textual data. □ **editorship** n.

**editorial** /ˌed-uh-**taw**-ree-uhl/ adj. **1** of or concerned with editing or editors. **2** written or approved by an editor. — n. article giving a newspaper's views on a current topic. □ **editorially** adv.

**EDP** abbr. electronic data processing.

**educate** /**ed**-yuh-ˌkayt/ v. (**-ting**) **1** give intellectual, moral, and social instruction to. **2** provide education for. **3** train or instruct for a particular purpose. **4** train (a person, a particular mental or physical faculty or organ), so as to develop some special aptitude, taste, etc. (*his ear needs educating; educating myself to like cheese that smells of dirty socks*). □ **educable** /-kuh-buhl/ adj. **educability** /-kuh-**bil**-uh-tee/ n. **educative** /-kuh-tiv/ adj. **educator** n. [Latin *educo -are educat-* rear]

**educated** adj. **1** having had an (esp. good) education. **2** resulting from this (*educated feel for Australian history*). **3** based on experience or study (*educated guess*). **4** trained (to appreciate art, good food, etc.) (*an educated eye and ear; an educated palate*). **5** hist. (of a convict) fitted by training or experience (prior to transportation to Australia) for professional or clerical employment (see GENTLEMAN CONVICT).

**education** /ˌed-yuh-**kay**-shuhn/ n. **1** act or process of educating or being educated; systematic instruction. **2** particular kind of or stage in education (*a classical education; further education*). **3 a** development of character or mental powers. **b** stage in or aspect of this (*a trip to the outback will be an education for him*). □ **educational** adj. **educationally** adv.

**educationist** n. (also **educationalist**) expert in educational methods.

**educe** /ee-**dyoos**, uh-/ v. (**-cing**) *literary* bring out or develop from latent or potential existence; elicit. □ **eduction** /ee-**duk**-shuhn, uh-/ n. [Latin *educo -ere educt-* draw out]

**Edwardian** /ed-**waw**-dee-uhn/ — adj. of or characteristic of the reign of the British king Edward VII (1901–10). — n. person of this period.

**-ee** suffix forming nouns denoting: **1** person affected by the verbal action (*employee; payee*). **2** person concerned with or described as (*absentee; refugee*). **3** object of smaller size (*bootee*). [French *-é* in past participle]

**EEC** abbr. European Economic Community.

**EEG** abbr. electroencephalogram.

**eel** n. any of various snakelike fish having slippery skins, and in Australia varying in length from a few centimetres to more than two metres. [Old English]

**EEO** /ˌee-ee-**oh**/ abbr. government policy that people should be employed, promoted, etc., on merit alone and without regard to factors such as sex, race, physical disability, etc. (also *attrib.: EEO policy*). [*Equal Employment Opportunity*]

**EEO officer** n. person employed or appointed to ensure the implementation etc. of EEO policy.

**-eer** suffix forming: **1** nouns meaning 'person concerned with' (*auctioneer*). **2** verbs meaning 'be concerned with' (*electioneer*). [French *-ier* from Latin *-arius*]

**eerie** /**eer**-ree/ adj. (**eerier, eeriest**) gloomy and strange; weird (*eerie silence*). □ **eerily** adv. **eeriness** n. [Old English]

**ef-** see EX-[1].

**efface** /uh-**fays**/ v. (**-cing**) **1** rub or wipe out (a mark, recollection, etc.) (*effaced it from his memory*). **2** surpass, eclipse (*all previous attempts have been effaced by this success*). **3** refl. (usu. as **self-effacing** adj.) treat oneself as unimportant. □ **effacement** n. [French: related to FACE]

**effect** /ee-**fekt**, uh-/ — n. **1** result or consequence of an action etc. **2** efficacy (*had little effect*). **3** impression produced on a spectator, hearer, etc. (*lights gave a pretty effect; said it just for effect*). **4** (in *pl.*) personal property. **5** (in *pl.*) lighting, sound, etc., giving realism to a play, film, etc. **6** physical phenomenon (*greenhouse effect*). — *v.* bring about; accomplish (a change, cure, etc.) (*effected a cure using traditional Aboriginal medical lore*). □ **bring** (or **carry**) **into effect** accomplish. **give effect to** make operative. **in effect** for practical purposes. **take effect** become operative (*has the medicine taken effect yet?*). **take** (or **come into**) **effect** (of a law etc.) come into force. **to the effect that** the general substance or gist being that. **to that effect** having that result or implication. **with effect from** coming into operation at (a stated time). [Latin: related to FACT]

■ **Usage** *Effect* should not be confused with *affect* which, as a verb, has more meanings and is more common, but which does not exist as a noun. *Effected the cure* means 'brought about the cure; cured', but *affected the cure* means 'had an effect on a cure' (which was already in place).

**effective** *adj.* **1** producing a definite or desired result. **2** impressive, striking (*an effective display*). **3** actual (*took effective control in their absence*). **4** operative (*effective as from 1 May*). □ **effectively** *adv.* **effectiveness** *n.*

**effectual** /ee-**fek**-choo-uhl, uh-/ *adj.* capable of producing the required effect; answering its purpose. **2** valid (*an effectual agreement*). □ **effectually** *adv.*

**effeminate** /ee-**fem**-uh-nuht, uh-/ *adj.* (of a man) feminine in appearance or manner; unmasculine. □ **effeminacy** *n.* **effeminately** *adv.* [Latin *femina* woman]

**effervesce** /,ef-uh-**ves**/ *v.* (**-cing**) **1** give off bubbles of gas. **2** (of a person) be lively or energetic. □ **effervescence** *n.* **effervescent** *adj.* [Latin: related to FERVENT]

**effete** /uh-**feet**/ *adj.* **1** feeble, languid. **2** worn out; exhausted of vitality. □ **effeteness** *n.* [Latin *effetus* worn out by bearing young (as EX-, FOETUS)]

**efficacious** /,ef-uh-**kay**-shuhs/ *adj.* producing the desired effect. □ **efficacy** /**ef**-uh-kuh-see/ *n.* [Latin *efficax*: related to EFFICIENT]

**efficient** /uh-**fish**-uhnt, ee-/ *adj.* **1** productive with minimum waste or effort. **2** (of a person) capable; acting effectively. □ **efficiency** *n.* **efficiently** *adv.* [Latin *facio* make]

**effigy** /**ef**-uh-jee/ *n.* (*pl.* **-ies**) sculpture or model of a person. □ **burn in effigy** burn a

model of a person to express dislike etc. [Latin *effigies* from *fingo* fashion]

**effloresce** /,ef-law-**res**, ,ef-luh-/ *v.* (**-cing**) **1** burst into flower. **2 a** (of a substance) turn to a fine powder on exposure to air. **b** (of salts) come to the surface and crystallise. **c** (of a surface) become covered with salt particles. □ **efflorescence** *n.* **efflorescent** *adj.* [Latin *flos flor-* FLOWER]

**effluence** /**ef**-loo-uhns/ *n.* **1** flowing out of light, electricity, etc. **2** that which flows out. [Latin *fluo flux-* flow]

**effluent** — *adj.* flowing out. — *n.* **1** sewage or industrial waste discharged into a river etc. **2** stream or lake flowing from a larger body of water.

**effluvium** /uh-**floo**-vee-uhm/ *n.* (*pl.* **-via**) unpleasant or noxious odour or exhaled substance. [Latin: related to EFFLUENCE]

**effort** /**ef**-uht/ *n.* **1** use of physical or mental energy (*required much effort*). **2** determined attempt (*made an effort to reach the top*). **3** *colloq.* result of an attempt; something accomplished (*not bad for a first effort*). [Latin *fortis* strong]

**effortless** *adj.* easily done, requiring no effort. □ **effortlessly** *adv.* **effortlessness** *n.*

**effrontery** /uh-**frun**-tuh-ree, ee-/ *n.* (*pl.* **-ies**) **1** shameless insolence; impudent audacity (esp. *have the effrontery to*). **2** instance of this. [Latin *frons front-* forehead]

**effulgent** /uh-**ful**-juhnt, ee-/ *adj. literary* radiant; shining brilliantly. □ **effulgence** *n.* [Latin *fulgeo* shine]

**effuse** /uh-**fyooz**, ee-/ *v.* (**-sing**) **1** pour forth (liquid, light, etc.). **2** give out (ideas etc.). [Latin *fundo fus-* pour]

**effusion** /ee-**fyoo**-*zh*uhn, uh-/ *n.* **1** outpouring. **2** *derog.* unrestrained flow of words. [Latin: related to EFFUSE]

**effusive** /uh-**fyoo**-siv, -ziv, ee-/ *adj.* gushing, over-demonstrative, unrestrained (*effusive praise*). □ **effusively** *adv.* **effusiveness** *n.*

**EFT** *abbr.* electronic funds transfer.

**EFTPOS** /**eft**-pos/ *abbr.* electronic funds transfer at point of sale.

**e.g.** *abbr.* for example. [Latin *exempli gratia*]

**egalitarian** /uh-,gal-uh-**tair**-ree-uhn, ee-/ — *adj.* of or advocating equal rights and opportunities for all. — *n.* egalitarian person. □ **egalitarianism** *n.* [French *égal* EQUAL]

**egg**[1] *n.* **1 a** body produced by females of birds, insects, etc. and capable of developing into a new individual. **b** egg of the domestic hen, used for food. **2** *Biol.* female reproductive cell in animals and plants. **3** *colloq.* person or thing of a specified kind (*tough egg*). □ **with egg on one's face** *colloq.* looking foolish. □ **eggy** *adj.* [Old Norse]

**egg²** *v.* (foll. by *on*) urge. [Old Norse: related to EDGE]

**egg-flip** *n.* (also **egg-nog**) drink of alcoholic spirit with beaten egg, milk, etc.

**egghead** *n. colloq.* intellectual; expert.

**eggplant** *n.* (also **aubergine**) (plant bearing) purple or white egg-shaped fruit used as a vegetable.

**eggs-and-bacon** *n.* = BACON-AND-EGGS.

**eggshell** — *n.* shell of an egg. — *adj.* **1** (of china) thin and fragile. **2** (of paint) with a slight gloss.

**egg white** *n.* white part round the yolk of an egg; albumen.

**ego** /ee-goh/ *n.* (*pl.* **-s**) **1** the self; the part of the mind that reacts to reality and has a sense of individuality. **2** (in general use) idealisation of oneself; self-conceit (*has a swollen ego*). **3** *Psychol.* the part of the mind developed from the ego by an awareness of social standards. [Latin, = I]

**egocentric** /ˌee-goh-**sen**-trik/ *adj.* self-centred.

**egoism** /ee-goh-ˌiz-uhm/ *n.* **1** self-interest as the moral basis of behaviour. **2** systematic selfishness. **3** = EGOTISM. □ **egoist** *n.* **egoistic** /-**is**-tik/ *adj.* **egoistical** /-**is**-ti-kuhl/ *adj.* **egoistically** /-**is**-ti-kuh-lee, -klee/ *adv.*

■ **Usage** The senses of *egoism* and *egotism* overlap, but *egoism* alone is used as a term in philosophy and psychology to mean self-interest (often contrasted with *altruism*).

**egotism** /ee-guh-ˌtiz-uhm/ *n.* **1** excessive use of 'I' and 'me'. **2** practice of talking about oneself; self-conceit. **3** selfishness. □ **egotist** *n.* **egotistic** /-**tis**-tik/ *adj.* **egotistical** /-**tis**-ti-kuhl/ *adj.* **egotistically** /-**tis**-ti-kuh-lee, -klee/ *adv.*

■ **Usage** See note at *egoism*.

**ego trip** *n. colloq.* activity to boost one's own self-esteem or self-conceit.

**egregious** /uh-**gree**-juhs/ *adj.* **1** extremely bad; shocking (*egregious folly*). **2** *archaic* remarkable. [Latin *grex greg-* flock]

**egress** /**ee**-gres/ *n. formal* **1** exit. **2** right of going out. [Latin *egredior -gress-* walk out]

**egret** /**ee**-gruht/ *n.* any of various herons having long white feathers in the breeding season, including several Australian species (*cattle egret*; *great egret*; *little egret*; *plumed egret*). [French *aigrette*]

**Egyptian** /ee-**jip**-shuhn, uh-/ — *adj.* of or relating to Egypt. — *n.* **1** native of Egypt. **2** language of the ancient Egyptians.

**Egyptology** /ˌee-jip-**tol**-uh-jee/ *n.* the study of the language, history, and culture of ancient Egypt. □ **Egyptologist** *n.*

**eh** /ay/ *int. colloq.* **1** expressing enquiry or surprise. **2** inviting assent. **3** asking for repetition or explanation. [instinctive exclamation]

**eider** /**uy**-duh/ *n.* any of various large ducks of the Northern hemisphere. [Icelandic]

**eiderdown** *n.* quilt stuffed with down (orig. from the eider) or some other soft material.

**eight** /ayt/ *adj. & n.* **1** one more than seven. **2** symbol for this (8, viii, VIII). **3** eight-oared rowing-boat or its crew. **4** eight o'clock. [Old English]

**eight ball** *n. US* black ball, numbered eight, in the US variety of pool. □ **behind the eight ball** at a disadvantage; 'snookered'.

**eighteen** /ay-**teen**/ *adj. & n.* **1** one more than seventeen. **2** symbol for this (18, xviii, XVIII). **3** set or team of eighteen individuals. □ **eighteenth** *adj. & n.* [Old English]

**eightfold** *adj. & adv.* **1** eight times as much or as many. **2** consisting of eight parts.

**eighth** *adj. & n.* **1** next after seventh. **2** one of eight equal parts of a thing. □ **eighthly** *adv.*

**eight, ten, two, and a quarter** *n. hist.* a week's ration of food (as issued to a hand on a rural property) consisting of 8 pounds of flour, 10 pounds of meat, 2 pounds of sugar, and a quarter pound of tea.

**eighty** /**ay**-tee/ *adj. & n.* (*pl.* **-ies**) **1** eight times ten. **2** symbol for this (80, lxxx, LXXX). **3** (in *pl.*) numbers from 80 to 89, esp. the years of a century or of a person's life. □ **eightieth** *adj. & n.* [Old English]

**einsteinium** /uyn-**stuy**-nee-uhm/ *n.* artificial radioactive metallic element. [A. *Einstein*, German-American physicist (d. 1955)]

**eisteddfod** /uh-**sted**-fuhd/ *n.* (*pl.* **-s** or **eisteddfodau** /-fuh-duy/) **1** congress of Welsh poets and musicians. **2** any festival for musical competitions etc. [Welsh]

**either** /**uy**-thuh, **ee**-thuh/ — *adj. & pron.* **1** one or the other of two (*either of you can go*; *you may have either book*). **2** each of two (*houses on either side of the road*). — *adv. & conj.* **1** as one possibility (*is* *either right or wrong*). **2** as one choice or alternative; which way you will (*either come in or go out*). **3** (with *neg.*) **a** any more than the other (*if you do not go, I shall not either*). **b** moreover (*there is no time to lose, either*). [Old English]

**ejaculate** /ee-**jak**-yuh-ˌlayt, uh-/ *v.* (**-ting**) (also *absol.*) **1** utter suddenly; exclaim. **2** emit (semen) in orgasm. □ **ejaculation** /-**lay**-shuhn/ *n.* **ejaculatory** *adj.* [Latin *ejaculor* dart out]

**eject** /ee-**jekt**, uh-/ *v.* **1** expel, compel to leave. **2** (of a pilot etc.) cause oneself to be propelled from an aircraft as an emergency measure. **3** cause to be removed, drop out, or pop up automatically from a gun, cassette-player, etc. **4** dispossess (a tenant). **5** emit, send out. □ **ejection** *n.* **ejective** *adj.* [Latin *ejicio eject-* throw out]

**eke** /eek/ *v.* (**eking**) □ **eke out 1** (foll. by *with*, *by*) supplement (income etc.) (*eked out his meagre income by doing odd jobs after work*). **2** make (a living) or support (an existence) with difficulty (*eked out a scanty livelihood from the stony soil*). **3** make (scanty resources, food, etc.) last by economy, partial use of substitutes, addition, etc. (*eked out the children's milk by watering it*). [Old English]

**elaborate** — *adj.* /uh-**lab**-uh-ruht, ee-/ **1** minutely worked out (*elaborate detail*). **2** complicated (*elaborate plot*). — *v.* /uh-**lab**-uh-ˌrayt, ee-/ (**-ting**) **1** work out or explain in detail (*elaborated on his plan for saving the world*). **2** (*absol.*) go into details (*I need not elaborate*). □ **elaborately** /-ruht-lee/ *adv.* **elaborateness** /-ruht-nuhs/ *n.* **elaboration** /-ray-shuhn/ *n.* [Latin: related to LABOUR]

**élan** /ay-**lan**/ *n.* vivacity, dash. [French]

**eland** /**ee**-luhnd/ *n.* (*pl.* same or **-s**) large African antelope. [Dutch]

**elapse** /ee-**laps**, uh-/ *v.* (**-sing**) (of time) pass by. [Latin *elabor elaps-* slip away]

**elastic** /ee-**las**-tik, uh-/ — *adj.* **1** able to resume its normal bulk or shape after contraction, dilation, or distortion. **2** springy. **3** flexible, adaptable (*elastic conscience*). — *n.* elastic cord or fabric, usu. woven with strips of rubber. □ **elastically** *adv.* **elasticity** *n.* [Greek *elastikos* propulsive]

**elastic sides** *n.pl.* = 'LASTIC-SIDES.

**elate** /ee-**layt**, uh-/ *v.* (**-ting**) (esp. as **elated** *adj.*) make delighted or proud (*elated by his victory*). □ **elatedly** *adv.* **elation** *n.* [Latin *effero elat-* raise]

**elbow** /**el**-boh/ — *n.* **1 a** joint between the forearm and the upper arm. **b** part of a sleeve covering the elbow. **2** elbow-shaped bend etc. — *v.* (foll. by *in*, *out*, *aside*, etc.) **1** jostle or thrust (a person or oneself). **2**

make (one's way) thus. □ **give a person the elbow** *colloq.* dismiss or reject a person. [Old English: related to ELL, BOW¹]

**elbow grease** *n.* *colloq.* vigorous polishing; hard work.

**elbow room** *n.* sufficient room to move or work in.

**el cheapo** /ˌel **chee**-poh/ *colloq.* — *adj.* cheap, inferior (*buy an el cheapo watch and you get an el cheapo watch*). — *n.* thing (e.g. a restaurant) that is el cheapo (*a bit broke, so we ate out at an el cheapo*).

**elder** — *attrib. adj.* (of persons, esp. when related) senior; of greater age. — *n.* **1** older of two persons (*is my elder by ten years*). **2** (in *pl.*) persons of greater age or venerable because of age (*respect your elders*). **3** official in the early Christian Church and some modern Churches. **4** person of recognised authority in an Aboriginal community. [Old English: related to OLD]

**elderly** *adj.* rather old; past middle age.

**eldest** *adj.* first-born; oldest surviving.

**eldorado** /ˌel-duh-**rah**-doh/ *n.* (*pl.* **-s**) **1** imaginary land of great wealth. **2** place of abundance or opportunity. [Spanish *el dorado* the gilded]

**eldritch** /**el**-drich/ *adj.* (orig. *Scot.*) **1** weird. **2** hideous (*an eldritch shriek in the night*). [origin uncertain]

**elect** /ee-**lekt**, uh-/ — *v.* (usu. foll. by *to* + infin.) **1** choose (*the principles they elected to follow*). **2** choose by voting (*elected a new chairperson*). — *adj.* **1** chosen. **2** select, choice. **3** (after the noun) chosen but not yet in office (*president elect*). **4** *Theol.* chosen by God. — *n.* person or persons chosen by God (*the elect*). [Latin *eligo elect-* pick out]

**election** /ee-**lek**-shuhn, uh-/ *n.* **1** process of electing or being elected. **2** occasion of this.

**electioneer** /ee-ˌlek-shuh-**neer**, uh-/ *v.* take part in an election campaign.

**elective** /ee-**lek**-tiv, uh-/ — *adj.* **1** chosen by or derived from election. **2** (of a body) having the power to elect. **3** (of a course of study) chosen by the student; optional. **4** (of a surgical operation etc.) optional; not urgently necessary. — *n.* elective course of study.

**elector** *n.* person who has the right to vote in an election. □ **electoral** *adj.*

**electoral roll** *n.* register of those entitled to vote in an electorate.

**electorate** /ee-**lek**-tuh-ruht, uh-/ *n.* **1** body of all electors. **2** area represented by one member of parliament.

**Electra complex** /ee-**lek**-truh, uh-/ *n.* *Psychol.* a daughter's subconscious sexual attraction to her father and hostility towards her mother, corresponding to the Oedipus complex in a son. [*Electra* in Greek tragedy, who caused her mother to be murdered for having murdered Electra's father]

**electric** /uh-**lek**-trik, ee-/ *adj.* **1** of, worked by, or charged with electricity; producing or capable of generating electricity. **2** causing or charged with excitement (*the news had an electric effect*). [Greek *ēlektron* amber]

**electrical** *adj.* of electricity. □ **electrically** *adv.*

**electric chair** *n.* (in the US) electrified chair used for capital punishment.

**electric eel** *n.* **1** eel-like fish able to give an electric shock. **2** device for clearing drainage pipes of blockages.

**electric eye** *n.* *colloq.* photoelectric cell operating a relay when a beam of light is broken.

**electric guitar** *n.* guitar with a solid body and built-in electrical sound pick-up rather than a soundbox.

**electrician** /ee-lek-**trish**-uhn, el-, uh-/ *n.* person who installs or maintains electrical equipment for a living.

**electricity** /ee-lek-**tris**-uh-tee, el-, uh-/ *n.* **1** form of energy resulting from the existence of charged particles (electrons, protons, etc.), either statically as an accumulation of charge or dynamically as a current. **2** branch of physics dealing with electricity. **3** supply of electricity. **4** excitement.

**electric shock** *n.* effect of a sudden discharge of electricity through the body of a person etc.

**electrify** /uh-**lek**-truh-,fuy, ee-/ *v.* (**-ies**, **-ied**) **1** charge with electricity. **2** convert to the use of electric power. **3** cause sudden excitement (*news was electrifying*). □ **electrification** /-fuh-**kay**-shuhn/ *n.*

**electro-** *comb. form* of, by, or caused by electricity.

**electrocardiogram** /ee-lek-troh-**kah**-dee-uh-,gram, uh-/ *n.* record traced by an electrocardiograph. [German: related to ELECTRO-]

**electrocardiograph** /ee-lek-troh-**kah**-dee-uh-,grahf, uh-, -,graf/ *n.* instrument recording the electric currents generated by a heartbeat.

**electroconvulsive therapy** /ee-lek-troh-kuhn-**vul**-siv, uh-/ *n.* (*abbr.* **ECT**) treatment of mental illness by the application of an electric shock to the central nervous system.

**electrocute** /uh-**lek**-truh-,kyoot, ee-/ *v.* (**-ting**) kill by electric shock. □ **electrocution** /-**kyoo**-shuhn/ *n.* [from ELECTRO-, after *execute*]

**electrode** /uh-**lek**-trohd, ee-/ *n.* conductor through which electricity enters or leaves an electrolyte, gas, vacuum, etc. [from ELECTRIC, Greek *hodos* way]

**electrodynamics** /ee-lek-troh-duy-**nam**-iks, uh-/ *n.pl.* (usu. treated as *sing.*) the study of electricity in motion. □ **electrodynamic** *adj.*

**electroencephalogram** /ee-lek-troh-en-**sef**-uh-luh-,gram, -**kef**-uh-luh-, uh-/ *n.* record traced by an electroencephalograph. [German: related to ELECTRO-]

**electroencephalograph** /ee-lek-troh-en-**sef**-uh-luh-,grahf, uh-, -,graf, -**kef**-uh-luh-/ *n.* instrument that records the electrical activity of the brain.

**electrolyse** /uh-**lek**-truh-,luyz, ee-/ *v.* (**-sing**) subject to or treat by electrolysis.

**electrolysis** /ee-lek-**trol**-uh-suhs/ *n.* **1** decomposition of a substance by the application of an electric current. **2** destruction of tumours, hair-roots, etc., by this process. □ **electrolytic** /ee-,lek-truh-**lit**-ik, uh-/ *adj.*

**electrolyte** /uh-**lek**-truh-,luyt, ee-/ *n.* **1** substance which conducts electricity when molten or in solution, esp. in an electric cell or battery. **2** a solution of this.

**electromagnet** /ee-lek-troh-**mag**-nuht, uh-/ *n.* soft metal core made into a magnet by passing an electric current through a coil surrounding it.

**electromagnetic** /ee-lek-troh-mag-**net**-ik, uh-/ *adj.* having both electrical and magnetic properties. □ **electromagnetically** *adv.*

**electromagnetism** /ee-lek-troh-**mag**-nuh-,tiz-uhm, uh-/ *n.* **1** magnetic forces produced by electricity. **2** the study of these.

**electrometer** /ee-lek-**trom**-uh-tuh, el-/ *n.* instrument for measuring electrical potential without drawing any current from the circuit. □ **electrometric** /-**met**-rik/ *adj.* **electrometry** /-**trom**-uh-tree/ *n.*

**electromotive** /ee-lek-troh-**moh**-tiv, uh-/ *adj.* producing or tending to produce an electric current.

**electromotive force** *n.* force set up in an electric circuit by a difference in potential.

**electron** /ee-**lek**-tron, uh-/ *n.* stable elementary particle with a charge of negative electricity, found in all atoms and acting as the primary carrier of electricity in solids.

**electronic** /ee-lek-**tron**-ik/ *adj.* **1 a** produced by or involving the flow of electrons. **b** of or relating to electrons or electronics. **2** (of music) produced by electronic means and usu. recorded on tape. □ **electronically** *adv.*

**electronic funds transfer** *n.* computerised bank system for the transfer of funds.

**electronic mail** *n.* (also **email**) messages distributed by a computer system.

**electronic media** *n.* radio and television (opp. PRINT MEDIA).

**electronics** *n.pl.* (treated as *sing.*) science of the movement of electrons in a vacuum, gas, semiconductor, etc., esp. in devices in which the flow is controlled and utilised.

**electronic tagging** *n.* the attaching of electronic markers to people or goods, enabling them to be tracked down.

**electron lens** *n.* device for focusing a stream of electrons by means of electric or magnetic fields.

**electron microscope** *n.* microscope with high magnification and resolution, using electron beams instead of light.

**electronvolt** *n.* a unit of energy, the amount gained by an electron when accelerated through a potential difference of one volt.

**electroplate** /uh-**lek**-truh-,playt, ee-/ — *v.* (**-ting**) coat with a thin layer of chromium, silver, etc., by electrolysis. — *n.* electroplated articles.

**electroscope** /uh-**lek**-truh-,skohp, ee-/ *n.* instrument for detecting and measuring electricity, esp. as an indication of the ionisation of air by radioactivity. □ **electroscopic** /-**skop**-ik/ *adj.*

**electro-shock** /uh-**lek**-troh-,shok, ee-/ *attrib. adj.* (of therapy) by means of electric shocks.

**electrostatic** /uh-**lek**-troh-,stat-ik, uh-/ *adj.* of electricity at rest.

**electrostatics** *n.pl.* (treated as *sing.*) the study of electricity at rest.

**electrotechnology** /ee-,lek-troh-tek-**nol**-uh-jee, uh-/ *n.* science of the application of electricity in technology.

**electrotherapy** /ee-,lek-troh-**the**-ruh-pee, uh-/ *n.* treatment of diseases by use of electricity.

**elegant** /**el**-uh-guhnt/ *adj.* **1** tasteful, refined, graceful. **2** ingeniously simple. □ **elegance** *n.* **elegantly** *adv.* [Latin: related to ELECT]

**elegant parrot** *n.* grass-parrot of southwestern and southern central Australia, having mainly green plumage with some blue and yellow colouring.

**elegiac** /,el-uh-**juy**-ik/ — *adj.* **1** (of a metre) used for elegies. **2** mournful. — *n.* (in *pl.*) elegiac verses. □ **elegiacally** *adv.*

**elegy** /**el**-uh-jee/ *n.* (*pl.* **-ies**) **1** sorrowful poem or song, esp. for the dead. **2** poem in elegiac metre (a metrical form used in

Greek and Latin verse). [Latin from Greek]

**element** /**el**-uh-muhnt/ *n.* **1** component part; contributing factor. **2** any of the substances that cannot be resolved by chemical means into simpler substances. **3 a** any of the four substances (earth, water, air, and fire) in ancient and medieval philosophy. **b** any of these as a being's natural abode or environment. **4** *Electr.* wire that heats up in an electric heater, kettle, etc. **5** (in *pl.*) atmospheric agencies, esp. wind and storm. **6** (in *pl.*) rudiments of learning or of an art etc. **7** the bread and the wine of the Eucharist, each element being changed at the Consecration into the substance of the body and blood of Christ, or a representation of that body and blood. □ **in one's element** in one's preferred situation, doing what one does well and enjoys. [French from Latin]

**elemental** /,el-uh-**men**-tuhl/ — *adj.* **1** of the four elements. **2** of the powers of nature. **3** comparable to a force of nature (*elemental grandeur*). **4** uncompounded (*elemental oxygen*). **5** essential. — *n.* an entity or force which manifests itself in physical form (through magic etc.).

**elementary** /,el-uh-**men**-tuh-ree, -tree/ *adj.* **1 a** dealing with the simplest facts of a subject; rudimentary, introductory. **b** simple (*Elementary, my dear Watson!*). **2** *Chem.* not decomposable.

**elementary particle** *n.* *Physics* subatomic particle, esp. one not known to consist of simpler ones.

**elephant** /**el**-uh-fuhnt/ *n.* (*pl.* same or **-s**) largest living land animal, with a trunk and ivory tusks. [Middle English *olifaunt* etc., from Greek *elephas -phantos*]

**elephant beetle** *n.* any of several Australian weevils with a head structure resembling that of an elephant.

**elephantiasis** /,el-uh-fuhn-**tuyuh**-suhs/ *n.* skin disease causing gross enlargement of limbs etc.

**elephantine** /,el-uh-**fan**-tuyn/ *adj.* **1** of elephants. **2 a** huge. **b** clumsy (*elephantine movements*; *elephantine humour*).

**elevate** /**el**-uh-,vayt/ *v.* (**-ting**) **1** raise, lift up. **2** *Eccl.* raise up (the Host, and then the chalice, immediately after Consecration) for adoration. **3** raise, lift (one's spirits etc.). **4** exalt in rank etc. **5** (usu. as **elevated** *adj.*) raise morally or intellectually (*elevated style*). [Latin *levo* lift]

**elevation** /,el-uh-**vay**-shuhn/ *n.* **1 a** process of elevating or being elevated. **b** angle with the horizontal, esp. of a gun or of the direction of a heavenly body. **c** height above sea level etc. **d** high place or position. **2 a** drawing or diagram made by projection on a vertical plane. **b** flat drawing or diagram showing one side of a building. **3** *Eccl.* (**Elevation**) the raising up for adoration of the Host and then the chalice immediately after Consecration. **4** *Ballet* **a** capacity of a dancer to attain height in springing movements. **b** action of tightening the muscles and uplifting the body.

**elevator** *n.* **1 a** lift (sense 3a). **b** moving platform for raising or lowering persons or things to different floors of a building or different levels of a mine etc. **2** movable part of a tailplane for changing an aircraft's altitude. **3** hoisting machine. **4** place for lifting and storing quantities of grain.

**eleven** /uh-**lev**-uhn, ee-/ *adj. & n.* **1** one more than ten. **2** symbol for this (11, xi, XI). **3** team of eleven players at cricket, soccer, etc. **4** eleven o'clock. [Old English]

**elevenfold** *adj. & adv.* **1** eleven times as much or as many. **2** consisting of eleven parts.

**eleventh** *adj. & n.* **1** next after tenth. **2** each of eleven equal parts of a thing. □ **eleventh hour** last possible moment.

**elf** *n.* (*pl.* **elves** /elvz/) **1** mythological being that is small and mischievous. **2** (in recent fantasy literature) human-sized being of great beauty, wisdom, etc., belonging to a magical non-human race. □ **elfish** *adj.* **elvish** *adj.* [Old English]

**elfin** *adj.* of elves; elflike.

**elicit** /uh-**lis**-uht/ *v.* (**-t-**) draw out (facts, a response, etc.), esp. with difficulty. □ **elicitation** /-tay-shuhn/ *n.* [Latin *elicio*]

**elide** /uh-**luyd**/ *v.* (**-ding**) omit (a vowel or syllable) in pronunciation. [Latin *elido elis-* crush out]

**eligible** /**el**-uh-juh-buhl/ *adj.* **1** (often foll. by *for*) fit or entitled to be chosen (*eligible for a rebate*). **2** desirable or suitable, esp. for marriage. □ **eligibility** /-**bil**-uh-tee/ *n.* [Latin: related to ELECT]

**eliminate** /uh-**lim**-uh-nayt, ee-/ *v.* (**-ting**) **1** remove, get rid of. **2** exclude from consideration. **3** exclude from a further stage of a competition through defeat etc. **4** *Physiol.* discharge (waste matter) from the body; excrete. **5** *Algebra* remove (a quantity) by combining equations. □ **elimination** /-**nay**-shuhn/ *n.* **eliminator** *n.* [Latin *limen limin-* threshold]

**elision** /uh-**lizh**-uhn/ *n.* omission of a vowel or syllable in pronunciation (e.g. in *we'll*). [Latin: related to ELIDE]

**elite** /ay-**leet**, uh-, ee-/ (also **élite**) — *n.* **1** (prec. by *the*) the best (of a group). **2** select group or class. — *adj.* of or belonging to

an elite; exclusive; first-class. [French: related to ELECT]

**elitism** *n.* (also **élitism**) **1** recourse to or advocacy of leadership or dominance by a select group. **2** sense of belonging to a select group. □ **elitist** *n. & adj.*

**elixir** /uh-**lik**-suh/ *n.* **1 a** alchemist's preparation supposedly able to change metals into gold or (in full **elixir of life**) to prolong life indefinitely. **b** remedy for all ills. **2** aromatic medicinal drug. [Latin from Arabic]

**Elizabethan** /uh-liz-uh-**bee**-thuhn, ee-/ — *adj.* of the time of Elizabeth I, queen of England 1558–1603 (*Elizabethan drama*). — *n.* person of this time.

**elk** *n.* (*pl.* same or **-s**) large deer of northern parts of Europe, N. America, and Asia. [Old English]

**elkhorn** /**elk**-hawn/ *n.* large epiphytic fern of Queensland and NSW, forming often enormous clumps on trees and rocks, and having large lobed fronds resembling the horns of an elk (cf. STAGHORN).

**ell** *n. hist.* measure = 114 cm (45 in.). [Old English, = forearm]

**Ellangowan poison bush** /el-uhn-**gow**-uhn/ *n.* (also **dogwood**, **turkey bush**) small, much-branched eremophila of drier mainland Australia, sometimes poisonous to stock. [Mount *Ellangowan* in south-eastern Queensland]

**ellipse** /uh-**lips**, ee-/ *n.* regular oval, traced by a point moving in a plane so that the sum of its distances from two other points is constant, or resulting when a cone is cut obliquely by a plane. [Greek *elleipsis* deficit]

**ellipsis** /uh-**lip**-suhs, ee-/ *n.* (*pl.* **ellipses** /-seez/) **1** omission of words needed to complete a construction or sense. **2** set of three dots etc. indicating omission.

**ellipsoid** /uh-**lip**-soid, ee-/ *n.* solid of which all the plane sections through one axis are circles and all the other plane sections are ellipses.

**elliptical** /uh-**lip**-ti-kuhl, ee-/ *adj.* (also **elliptic**) **1 a** of, relating to, or having the form of an ellipsis. **b** of or in the form of an ellipse. **2** (of speech, style, etc.) concise, condensed (often to the point of producing ambiguity etc.). □ **elliptically** *adv.*

**elm** *n.* tree (of Europe etc.) with rough serrated leaves. [Old English]

**El Niño** /el **nin**-yoh/ *n.* an irregular warming of the southern Pacific Ocean surface that causes far-reaching changes in weather. [shortening of Spanish *El Niño de Navidad* the Christmas Child, in allusion to the appearance of the current off the coast of Peru shortly after Christmas]

**elocution** /ˌel-uh-**kyoo**-shuhn/ n. art of clear and expressive speech, esp. of distinct pronunciation and articulation. [Latin *loquor locut-* speak]

**elongate** /ee-long-ˌgayt/ v. (**-ting**) lengthen, extend. □ **elongation** /ˌee-long-**gay**-shuhn/ n. [Latin *longus* long]

**elope** /ee-**lohp**, uh-/ v. (**-ping**) run away to marry secretly. □ **elopement** n. [Anglo-French]

**eloquence** /**el**-uh-kwuhns/ n. fluent, powerful, and effective use of language. [Latin *loquor* speak]

**eloquent** adj. **1** having or showing eloquence (*an eloquent speaker; made an eloquent oration*). **2** (often foll. by *of*) clearly expressive or indicative (*an eloquent glance that spoke volumes; her entire attitude was eloquent of discouragement*). □ **eloquently** adv.

**else** adv. **1** (prec. by indefinite or interrog. pron.) besides (*someone else; nowhere else; who else?*). **2** instead (*what else could I say?*). **3** otherwise; if not (*run, (or) else you will be late*). □ **or else** see OR[1]. [Old English]

**elsewhere** adv. in or to some other place.

**elucidate** /uh-**loo**-suh-ˌdayt, ee-/ v. (**-ting**) throw light on; explain. □ **elucidation** /-**day**-shuhn/ n. **elucidatory** adj. [Latin: related to LUCID]

**elude** /uh-**lood**, ee-/ v. (**-ding**) **1** escape adroitly from (danger, pursuit, etc.); dodge. **2** avoid compliance with (a law etc.) or fulfilment of (an obligation). **3** (of a fact, solution, etc.) escape from or baffle (a person or memory etc.) (*the name eludes me at the moment*). □ **elusion** /-**loo**-zhuhn/ n. [Latin *ludo lus-* play]

**elusive** /uh-**loo**-siv, ee-/ adj. **1** difficult to find or catch. **2** difficult to remember. **3** (of an answer) avoiding the point raised. □ **elusiveness** n.

**elven** /**el**-vuhn/ adj. of or pertaining to an elf (sense 2).

**elves** pl. of ELF.

**elvish** see ELF.

**Elysium** /uh-**liz**-ee-uhm, ee-/ n. **1** (also **Elysian Fields**) (in Greek mythology) abode of the blessed after death. **2** place of ideal happiness. □ **Elysian** adj. [Latin from Greek]

**em** n. *Printing* unit of measurement equal to the width of an M. [name of the letter *M*]

**em-**[1,2] see EN-[1,2].

**'em** /uhm/ pron. *colloq.* them.

**emaciate** /ee-**may**-see-ˌayt, uh-/ v. (**-ting**) (esp. as **emaciated** adj.) make abnormally thin or feeble. □ **emaciation** /-ay-shuhn/ n. [Latin *macies* leanness]

**email** /**ee**-mayl/ n. (also **e-mail**) = ELECTRONIC MAIL.

**emanate** /**em**-uh-ˌnayt/ v. (**-ting**) (usu. foll. by *from*) issue or originate (from a source) (*light emanating from above; the rumours emanate from him*). □ **emanation** /ˌem-uh-**nay**-shuhn/ n. [Latin *emano emanat-* flow out]

**emancipate** /uh-**man**-suh-ˌpayt, ee-/ v. (**-ting**) **1** free from social or political restraint. **2** (usu. as **emancipated** adj.) free from the inhibitions of moral or social conventions. **3** free from slavery. **4** *hist.* (usu. as **emancipated** adj.) discharge as free (a convict who has received a pardon). □ **emancipatory** adj. [Latin, = free from possession, from *manus* hand, *capio* take]

**emancipation** /uh-ˌman-suh-**pay**-shuhn/ n. **1** emancipating. **2 a** setting free, esp. from slavery. **b** *hist.* act of setting free a convict who has received a pardon.

**emancipist** /uh-**man**-suh-ˌpuhst, ee-/ n. *hist.* convict who has been pardoned or whose sentence has expired.

**emasculate** — v. /ee-**mas**-kyuh-ˌlayt, uh-/ (**-ting**) **1** deprive of force or vigour. **2** castrate. — adj. /ee-**mas**-kyuh-luht, uh-/ **1** deprived of force. **2** castrated. **3** effeminate. □ **emasculation** /-**lay**-shuhn/ n. [Latin: related to MALE]

**embalm** /em-**bahm**/ v. preserve (a corpse) from decay, orig. with spices, now by means of arterial injection. □ **embalmment** n. [French: related to BALM]

**embankment** /em-**bangk**-muhnt/ n. earth or stone bank constructed to keep back water or carry a road, railway, etc.

**embargo** /em-**bah**-goh/ — n. (pl. **-es**) **1** order forbidding foreign ships to enter, or any ships to leave, a country's ports. **2** official suspension of commerce or other activity (*be under embargo*). — v. (**-es**, **-ed**) place under embargo. [Spanish: related to BAR[1]]

**embark** /em-**bahk**/ v. **1** (often foll. by *for*) put or go on board a ship or aircraft (to a destination). **2** (foll. by *on, in*) begin an activity or undertaking (*embarked on a new career*). □ **embarkation** /ˌem-bah-**kay**-shuhn/ n. (in sense 1). [French: related to BARQUE]

**embarrass** /em-**ba**-ruhs/ v. **1** make (a person) feel awkward or self-conscious or ashamed. **2** (as **embarrassed** adj.) encumbered with debts. □ **embarrassment** n. [Italian *imbarrare* bar in]

**embassy** /**em**-buh-see/ n. (pl. **-ies**) **1 a** residence or offices of an ambassador. **b** ambassador and staff. **2** deputation to a foreign government. [French: related to AMBASSADOR]

**embattled** /em-**bat**-uhld/ adj. **1** prepared or arrayed for battle. **2** fortified with battlements. **3** under heavy attack or involved in trying circumstances.

**embed** /em-**bed**/ v. (also **imbed**) (**-dd-**) (esp. as **embedded** adj.) fix firmly in a surrounding mass.

**embellish** /em-**bel**-ish/ v. **1** beautify, adorn. **2** add interest to (a narrative) with fictitious additions. □ **embellishment** n. [French bel, BEAU]

**ember** n. (usu. in pl.) small piece of glowing coal etc. in a dying fire. [Old English]

**embezzle** /em-**bez**-uhl/ v. (**-ling**) divert (money etc.) fraudulently to one's own use. □ **embezzlement** n. **embezzler** n. [Anglo-French]

**embitter** /em-**bit**-uh/ v. arouse bitter feelings in. □ **embitterment** n.

**emblazon** /em-**blay**-zuhn/ v. **1** portray or adorn conspicuously. **2** adorn (a heraldic shield). □ **emblazonment** n.

**emblem** /em-**bluhm**/ n. **1** symbol or representation typifying or identifying an institution, quality, etc. **2** (foll. by of) type, embodiment (the very emblem of courage). **3** heraldic or representative device. **4** see FAUNAL EMBLEM, FLORAL EMBLEM. □ **emblematic** /-**mat**-ik/ adj. [Greek, = insertion]

**embody** /em-**bod**-ee/ v. (**-ies**, **-ied**) **1** make (an idea etc.) actual or discernible. **2** (of a thing or person) be a tangible expression of (courage embodied in heroic actions). **3** include, comprise (embodies all the latest developments). **4** provide (a spirit) with a bodily form. □ **embodiment** n.

**embolden** /em-**bohl**-duhn/ v. make bold; encourage.

**embolism** /em-buh-**liz**-uhm/ n. obstruction of an artery by a clot, air-bubble, etc. [Latin from Greek]

**embolus** /em-buh-luhs/ n. (pl. **-li** /-,luy/) object causing an embolism.

**emboss** /em-**bos**/ v. carve or decorate with a design in relief. □ **embossment** n. [related to BOSS²]

**embouchure** /om-buu-,**shoor**/ n. way of applying the mouth to the mouthpiece of a musical instrument. [French: related to EN-¹, bouche mouth]

**embrace** /em-**brays**/ — v. (**-cing**) **1 a** hold closely in the arms. **b** (absol., of two people) embrace each other. **2** clasp, enclose. **3** accept eagerly (an offer etc.) (embraced the opportunity). **4** adopt (a cause, idea, etc.) (embraced Buddhism). **5** include, comprise (this new plan embraces several features of the previous one). **6** take in with the eye or mind. — n. act of embracing, clasp. □ **embraceable** adj.

**embrasure** /em-**bray**-zhuh/ n. **1** bevelling of a wall at the sides of a window etc. **2** opening in a parapet for a gun etc. □ **embrasured** adj. [French embraser splay]

**embrocation** /,em-bruh-**kay**-shuhn/ n. liquid for rubbing on the body to relieve muscular pain. [Greek embrokhē lotion]

**embroider** /em-**broi**-duh/ v. **1** decorate (cloth etc.) with needlework. **2** embellish (a narrative) with fictitious additions. □ **embroiderer** n. [Anglo-French from Germanic]

**embroidery** n. (pl. **-ies**) **1** art of embroidering. **2** embroidered work. **3** unnecessary ornament. **4** fictitious additions (to a story etc.).

**embroil** /em-**broil**/ v. (often foll. by with) involve (a person etc.) in a conflict or difficulties. □ **embroilment** n. [French brouiller mix]

**embryo** /em-**bree**-oh/ n. (pl. **-s**) **1 a** unborn or unhatched offspring. **b** human offspring in the first eight weeks from conception. **2** rudimentary plant in a seed. **3** thing in a rudimentary stage. **4** (attrib.) undeveloped, immature. □ **in embryo** undeveloped. □ **embryonic** /,em-bree-**on**-ik/ adj. [Greek bruō grow]

**embryology** /,em-bree-**ol**-uh-jee/ n. the study of embryos.

**emend** /ee-**mend**, uh-/ v. edit (a text etc.) to make corrections. □ **emendation** /,ee-men-**day**-shuhn/ n. [Latin menda fault]

■ **Usage** See note at **amend**.

**emerald** /em-uh-ruhld/ — n. **1** brightgreen gem. **2** colour of this. — adj. bright green. [Greek smaragdos]

**Emerald Isle** n. Ireland.

**emerge** /ee-**merj**, uh-/ v. (**-ging**) **1** come up or out into view (emerged from the cave). **2** (of facts etc.) become known, be revealed, esp. as a result of inquiry etc. **3** become recognised or prominent (emerged as a leading contender). **4** (of a question, difficulty, etc.) become apparent. **5** survive (an ordeal etc.) with a specified result (emerged unscathed). □ **emergence** n. **emergent** adj. [Latin: related to MERGE]

**emergency** /ee-**mer**-juhn-see, uh-/ n. (pl. **-ies**) **1** sudden state of danger etc., requiring immediate action. **2 a** medical condition requiring immediate treatment. **b** patient with this. **3** (attrib.) for use in an emergency. **4 a** Sport reserve player. **b** Horse Racing reserve runner. [medieval Latin: related to EMERGE]

**emeritus** /ee-**me**-ruh-tuhs, uh-/ *adj.* retired but retaining one's title as an honour (*emeritus professor*). [Latin *mereor* earn]

**emery** /**em**-uh-ree/ *n.* coarse corundum for polishing metal etc. [Greek *smēris* polishing powder]

**emery board** *n.* emery-coated nail-file.

**emetic** /uh-**met**-ik/ — *adj.* that causes vomiting. — *n.* emetic medicine. [Greek *emeō* vomit]

**emf** *abbr.* (also **e.m.f.**) electromotive force.

**emigrant** /**em**-uh-gruhnt/ — *n.* person who emigrates. — *adj.* emigrating.

**emigrate** /**em**-uh-grayt/ *v.* (**-ting**) leave one's own country to settle in another. □ **emigration** /-**gray**-shuhn/ *n.* [Latin: related to MIGRATE]

**émigré** /**em**-uh-gray/ *n.* (also **emigre** /**uh**-meer/) emigrant, esp. a political exile. [French]

**eminence** /**em**-uh-nuhns/ *n.* **1** distinction; recognised superiority. **2** piece of rising ground. **3** (**Eminence**) title used in addressing or referring to a cardinal (*Your Eminence; His Eminence Edward Cardinal Clancy*). [Latin: related to EMINENT]

**éminence grise** /ˌay-muh-ˌnons **greez**/ *n.* (*pl.* **éminences grises** pronunc. same) person who exercises power or influence without holding office. [French, = grey cardinal (orig. of Richelieu's secretary)]

**eminent** /**em**-uh-nuhnt/ *adj.* distinguished, notable, outstanding. [Latin *emineo* jut out]

**emir** /e-**meer**, uh-**meer**/ *n.* (also **amir** /uh-**meer**/) title of various Muslim rulers. [French from Arabic]

**emirate** /**em**-uh-ruht/ *n.* rank, domain, or reign of an emir.

**emissary** /**em**-uh-suh-ree/ *n.* (*pl.* **-ies**) person sent on a special (usu. diplomatic) mission. [Latin: related to EMIT]

**emission** /ee-**mish**-uhn, uh-/ *n.* **1** (often foll. by *of*) process or act of emitting. **2** thing emitted. **3** discharge of a fluid from the body, esp. semen (*nocturnal emission*). [as EMIT]

**emission control** *n.* control (by government regulation) of the release of air-borne pollutants from cars, factories, incinerators, etc.

**emit** /ee-**mit**, uh-/ *v.* (**-tt-**) give or send out (heat, light, a smell, sound, etc.); discharge. [Latin *emitto emiss-*]

**emollient** /ee-**mol**-ee-uhnt, uh-, -**moh**-lee-/ — *adj.* that softens or soothes the skin, feelings, etc. — *n.* emollient substance. [Latin *mollis* soft]

**emolument** /ee-**mol**-yuh-muhnt, uh-/ *n.* fee from employment, salary. [Latin]

**emote** /ee-**moht**, uh-/ *v.* (**-ting**) show excessive emotion.

**emotion** /ee-**moh**-shuhn, uh-/ *n.* **1** strong instinctive feeling such as love or fear. **2** emotional intensity or sensibility (*spoke with emotion*). [French: related to MOTION]

**emotional** *adj.* **1** of or relating to the emotions. **2** especially liable to emotion (*is a very emotional person*). **3** expressing or based on emotion (*became very emotional; an emotional appeal*). **4** arousing emotion (*a highly emotional issue*). □ **emotionalism** *n.* **emotionally** *adv.*

■ **Usage** See note at *emotive*.

**emotive** /ee-**moh**-tiv, uh-/ *adj.* **1** arousing emotion. **2** of or characterised by emotion. **3** (of language etc.) arousing feeling; not purely descriptive. [Latin: related to MOTION]

■ **Usage** Although the senses of *emotive* and *emotional* overlap, *emotive* is more common in the sense 'arousing emotion', as in *an emotive issue*, and is not used at all in sense 2 of *emotional*.

**empanel** /em-**pan**-uhl/ *v.* (also **impanel**) (**-ll-**) enter (a jury) on a panel.

**empathise** /**em**-puh-ˌthyuz/ *v.* (also **-ize**) (**-sing** or **-zing**) (usu. foll. by *with*) exercise empathy (*I can empathise with you*).

**empathy** /**em**-puh-thee/ *n. Psychol.* the power of identifying oneself mentally with (and so fully comprehending) a person or object of contemplation. □ **empathetic** /-**thet**-ik/ *adj.* **empathetically** /-**thet**-i-kuh-lee, -klee/ *adv.* **empathic** /-**path**-ik/ *adj.* **empathically** /-**path**-i-kuh-lee, -klee/ *adv.* [as PATHOS]

**emperor** /**emp**-uh-ruh/ *n.* **1** sovereign of an empire. **2** any of several tropical Australian fish. [Latin *impero* command]

**emperor gum moth** *n.* large moth of eastern Australia, having a conspicuous spot on each wing, the large larvae of the moth feeding mainly on eucalypts.

**emperor penguin** *n.* largest Antarctic penguin.

**emphasis** /**em**-fuh-suhs/ *n.* (*pl.* **emphases** /-ˌseez/) **1** importance or prominence attached to a thing, fact, idea, etc. (*emphasis on economy*). **2** stress laid on a word or syllable to make the meaning clear or show importance. **3** vigour or intensity of expression, feeling, etc. [Latin from Greek]

**emphasise** /**em**-fuh-ˌsuyz/ *v.* (also **-ize**) (**-sing** or **-zing**) put emphasis on, stress.

**emphatic** /em-**fat**-ik/ *adj.* **1** (of language, tone, or gesture) forcibly expressive. **2** of words: **a** bearing the stress. **b** used to give emphasis. **3** expressing oneself with emphasis (*he was most emphatic about it*). □ **emphatically** *adv.*

**emphysema** /ˌem-fuh-**see**-muh/ *n.* **1** disease involving enlargement of the air sacs of the lungs causing breathlessness. **2** swelling caused by the presence of air in the connective tissues of the body. [Greek *emphusaō* puff up]

**empire** /**em**-puyuh/ *n.* **1** large group of countries under a single authority, esp. an emperor. **2** supreme dominion. **3** large commercial organisation etc. owned or directed by one person. [Latin *imperium* dominion]

**empirical** /em-**pi**-ri-kuhl/ *adj.* (also **empiric**) based on observation, experience, or experiment, not on theory. □ **empirically** *adv.* **empiricism** /-ˌsiz-uhm/ *n.* **empiricist** /-sist/ *n.* [Greek *empeiria* experience]

**empirical formula** *n. Chem.* formula showing the constituents of a compound but not their configuration.

**employ** /em-**ploi**/ — *v.* **1** use the services of (a person) in return for payment. **2** use (a thing, time, energy, etc.) to good effect. **3** keep (a person) occupied. — *n.* (in phr. **in the employ of**) employed by. □ **employable** *adj.* **employer** *n.* [Latin *implicor* be involved]

**employee** /ˌem-ploi-**ee**, em-**ploi**-ee/ *n.* person employed for wages.

**employment** *n.* **1** act of employing or state of being employed. **2** person's trade or profession.

**emporium** /em-**paw**-ree-uhm/ *n.* (*pl.* **-s** or **-ria**) **1** large retail store selling a wide variety of goods. **2** centre of commerce, market. [Greek *emporos* merchant]

**empower** /em-**powuh**/ *v.* **1** authorise, license. **2** give power to.

**empress** /**em**-pruhs/ *n.* **1** wife or widow of an emperor. **2** woman emperor. [French: related to EMPEROR]

**empty** /**emp**-tee, em-**tee**/ — *adj.* (**-ier**, **-iest**) **1** containing nothing. **2** (of a house etc.) unoccupied or unfurnished. **3** (of a vehicle etc.) without passengers etc. **4 a** meaningless, hollow, insincere (*an empty gesture; empty threats; an empty promise*). **b** without purpose (*an empty existence*). **c** vacuous; foolish (*an empty head*). **5** *colloq.* hungry. — *v.* (**-ies**, **-ied**) **1** remove the contents of. **2 a** (often foll. by *into*) transfer (the contents of a container). **b** (often foll. by *of*) deprive of certain contents (*empty the room of its chairs*). **3** become empty. **4** (of a river) discharge itself (into the sea etc.). — *n.* (*pl.* **-ies**) *colloq.* empty bottle etc. □ **emptiness** *n.* [Old English]

**empty-handed** *adj.* (usu. *predic.*) **1** bringing or taking nothing. **2** having achieved nothing.

**empty-headed** *adj.* foolish; lacking sense.

**empyrean** /ˌem-puy-**ree**-uhn, -**pi**-ree-/ — *n.* **1** the highest heaven, as the sphere of fire in ancient cosmology or the abode of God in early Christianity. **2** the visible heavens. — *adj.* of the empyrean. □ **empyreal** *adj.* [Greek *pur* fire]

**emu** /**ee**-myoo/ *n.* (*pl.* **-s**) **1** large flightless Australian bird up to 2m tall, capable of running at high speed, and having exposed blue skin on the neck and long grey-brown feathers on the back. **2** *colloq.* person who collects discarded betting tickets at racecourses etc. in the hope of finding a winning ticket. [Portuguese *ema*]

**emu apple** *n.* **1 a** (also **colane**, **sourplum**) small tree, *Owenia acidula*, of central Australia. **b** its edible apple-like fruit with bitter red flesh, so called because eaten by emus. **2** any of several other similar Australian plants.

**emu-bob** *v.* **1** pick up pieces of timber, roots, etc., after clearing or burning. **2** collect litter. □ **emu-bobber** *n.* **emu-bobbing** *n.*

**emu bush** *n.* **1** any of many shrubs of the mainland Australian genus *Eremophila*, some species of which bear fruits eaten by the emu. **2** = PITURI.

**emu dance** *n.* Aboriginal dance in which the movements of the emu are emulated.

**emulate** /**em**-yoo-ˌlayt, em-yuh-ˌlayt/ *v.* (**-ting**) **1** try to equal or excel. **2** imitate zealously. □ **emulation** /-lay-shuhn/ *n.* **emulative** /-luh-tiv/ *adj.* **emulator** *n.* **emulous** /**em**-yuh-luhs/ *adj.* [Latin *aemulus* rival]

**emulsifier** /uh-**mul**-suh-fuyuh/ *n.* **1** any substance that stabilises an emulsion, esp. a food additive used to stabilise processed foods. **2** apparatus for producing an emulsion.

**emulsify** /ee-**mul**-suh-ˌfuy, uh-/ *v.* (**-ies**, **-ied**) convert into an emulsion. □ **emulsification** /-fuh-**kay**-shuhn/ *n.*

**emulsion** /ee-**mul**-shuhn, uh-/ *n.* **1** fine dispersion of one liquid in another, esp. as paint, medicine, etc. **2** mixture of a silver compound in gelatine etc. for coating photographic plate or film. **3** emulsion paint. [Latin *mulgeo mulsmilk*]

**emu parade** *n.* assembly, esp. of soldiers, for the purpose of picking up litter etc. (cf. EMU-BOB).

**emu wren** n. any of several long-tailed birds of southern Australia (*mallee emu wren*; *southern emu wren*) or of central Australia (*rufous-crowned emu wren*), so called because its long tail-feathers resemble the feathers of an emu.

**en** n. *Printing* unit of measurement equal to half an em. [name of the letter *N*]

**en-**[1] *prefix* (also **em-** before *b*, *p*) forming verbs, = IN-[2]: **1** from nouns, meaning 'put into or on' (*engulf*; *entrust*; *embed*). **2** from nouns or adjectives, meaning 'bring into the condition of' (*enslave*); often with the suffix *-en* (*enlighten*). **3** from verbs: **a** in the sense 'in, into, on' (*enfold*). **b** as an intensifier (*entangle*). [French *en-*, Latin *in-*]

**en-**[2] *prefix* (also **em-** before *b*, *p*) in, inside (*energy*; *enthusiasm*). [Greek]

**-en**[1] *suffix* forming verbs: **1** from adjectives, usu. meaning 'make or become so or more so' (*deepen*; *moisten*). **2** from nouns (*happen*; *strengthen*). [Old English]

**-en**[2] *suffix* (also **-n**) forming adjectives from nouns, meaning: **1** made or consisting of (often with extended and figurative senses) (*wooden*). **2** resembling; of the nature of (*golden*; *silvern*). [Old English]

**-en**[3] *suffix* (also **-n**) forming past participles of strong verbs: **1** as a regular inflection (*spoken*; *sworn*). **2** with restricted sense (*drunken*). [Old English]

**-en**[4] *suffix* forming the plural of a few nouns (*children*; *brethren*; *oxen*). [Middle English reduction of Old English *- an*]

**-en**[5] *suffix* forming diminutives of nouns (*chicken*; *maiden*). [Old English]

**-en**[6] *suffix* **1** forming feminine nouns (*vixen*). **2** forming abstract nouns (*burden*). [Old English]

**enable** /en-ay-buhl, uh-nay-/ v. (**-ling**) **1** (foll. by *to* + infin.) give (a person etc.) the means or authority. **2** make possible. **3** esp. *Computing* make (a device) operational; switch on.

**enact** /en-akt/ v. **1 a** ordain, decree. **b** make (a bill etc.) law. **2** play (a part on stage or in life). □ **enactive** *adj*.

**enactment** n. **1** law enacted. **2** process of enacting.

**enamel** /uh-nam-uhl, e-/ — n. **1** glass-like opaque ornamental or preservative coating on metal etc. **2 a** smooth hard coating. **b** a kind of hard gloss paint. **c** cosmetic simulating this, esp. nail varnish. **3** hard coating of a tooth. **4** painting done in enamel. — v. (**-ll-**) inlay, coat, or portray with enamel. [Anglo-French from Germanic]

**enamour** /e-nam-uh/ v. (also **enamor**) (usu. in *passive*; foll. by *of*) inspire with love or delight (*I am enamoured of him*;

*enamoured of antique French clocks*). [French *amour* love]

**en bloc** /on blok/ *adv.* in a block; all at the same time. [French]

**encamp** /en-kamp/ v. settle in a (esp. military) camp. □ **encampment** n.

**encapsulate** /en-kap-syuh-,layt, -kap-shuh-/ v. (**-ting**) **1** enclose in or as in a capsule. **2** express briefly, summarise. □ **encapsulation** /-lay-shuhn/ n. [related to CAPSULE]

**encase** /en-kays/ v. (**-sing**) enclose in or as in a case. □ **encasement** n.

**-ence** *suffix* forming nouns expressing: **1** a quality or state or an instance of this (*patience*; *an impertinence*). **2** an action (*reference*). [French *-ence*, Latin *-ens*]

**encephalitis** /en-,sef-uh-luy-tuhs, en-kef-/ n. inflammation of the brain. [Greek *egkephalos* brain]

**encephalogram** /en-sef-uh-luh-,gram, en-kef-/ n. = ELECTROENCEPHALOGRAM.

**encephalograph** /en-sef-uh-luh-,grahf, en-kef-, -,graf/ n. = ELECTROENCEPHALOGRAPH.

**encephalopathy** /en-,sef-uh-lop-uh-thee, en-kef-/ n. a disease of the brain.

**enchant** /en-chahnt, -chant/ v. **1** charm, delight. **2** bewitch, cast a magic spell over. □ **enchantedly** *adv.* **enchanting** *adj.* **enchantingly** *adv.* **enchantment** n.

**enchanter** n. (*fem.* **enchantress**) person who enchants, esp. by using magic.

**encircle** /en-ser-kuhl/ v. (**-ling**) **1** surround. **2** form a circle round. □ **encirclement** n.

**enclave** /en-klayv/ n. **1** territory of one nation surrounded by that of another. **2** group of people who are culturally, intellectually, or socially distinct from those surrounding them. [Latin *clavis* key]

**enclitic** /en-klit-ik/ — *adj.* (of a word) pronounced with so little emphasis that it forms part of the preceding word. — n. such a word, e.g. *not* in *cannot*. [Greek *klinō* lean]

**enclose** /en-klohz/ v. (**-sing**) **1 a** surround with a wall, fence, etc. **b** shut in. **2** put in a receptacle (esp. in an envelope with a letter). **3** (usu. as **enclosed** *adj.*) seclude (a religious community) from the outside world (*an enclosed Order*). [Latin: related to INCLUDE]

**enclosure** /en-kloh-zhuh/ n. **1** act of enclosing. **2** enclosed space or area, esp. for a special class of persons at a sporting event. **3** thing enclosed with a letter. [French: related to ENCLOSE]

**encode** /en-kohd/ v. (**-ding**) put into code.

**encomium** /en-koh-mee-uhm/ n. (*pl.* **-s**)

formal or high-flown praise. [Greek *kōmos* revelry]

**encompass** /en-**kum**-puhs/ v. **1** contain; include (*this book encompasses all aspects of the subject*). **2** surround, or form a circle about, esp. to protect or attack (*I am encompassed by idiots*).

**encore** /**ong**-kaw/ — n. **1** audience's demand for the repetition of an item, or for a further item. **2** such an item. — v. (**-ring**) **1** call for the repetition of (an item). **2** call back (a performer) for this. — int. also /'-**kaw**/ again, once more. [French, = once again]

**encounter** /en-**kown**-tuh/ — v. **1** meet unexpectedly. **2** meet as an adversary. — n. meeting by chance or in conflict. [Latin *contra* against]

**encourage** /en-**ku**-rij/ v. (**-ging**) **1** give courage, confidence, or hope to. **2** urge, advise (*encouraged him to see the doctor*). **3** promote or assist (an enterprise, opinion, etc.). □ **encouragement** n. [French: related to EN-¹]

**encroach** /en-**krohch**/ v. **1** (foll. by *on*, *upon*) intrude on another's territory etc. (*your fence encroaches on my property*). **2** (often foll. by *on*, *upon*) advance gradually beyond due limits (*the sea constantly encroaching on more and more land*; *you are encroaching on personal matters*). □ **encroachment** n. [French *croc* CROOK]

**encrust** /en-**krust**/ v. (also **incrust**) **1** cover with or form a crust. **2** overlay with an ornamental crust of precious material (*encrusted with pearls*). [French: related to EN-¹, CRUST]

**encrustation** /,en-krus-**tay**-shuhn/ n. (also **incrustation**) **1** process of encrusting or state of being encrusted. **2** crust or hard coating. **3** deposit on a surface (*an encrustation of salt on the soil*).

**encumber** /en-**kum**-buh/ v. **1** be a burden to. **2** hamper, impede. **3** burden (a person or estate) with debts, esp. mortgages. **3** (usu. as **encumbered** adj.) subject (ownership of vehicle etc.) to financial obligation. [French from Romanic]

**encumbrance** /en-**kum**-bruhns/ n. **1** burden. **2** impediment. **3** mortgage or other charge on a property. **4** an annoyance. □ **without encumbrance** having no children.

**-ency** suffix forming nouns denoting quality or state (*efficiency*; *fluency*; *presidency*). [Latin *-entia*]

**encyclical** /en-**sik**-li-kuhl/ — n. formal epistle from the Pope to all bishops of the Catholic Church. — adj. for wide circulation. [Greek: related to CYCLE]

**encyclopaedia** /en-,suy-kluh-**pee**-dee-

uh/ n. (also **-pedia**) book, often in a number of volumes, giving information on many subjects, or on many aspects of one subject. [Greek *egkuklios* all-round, *paideia* education]

**encyclopaedic** adj. (also **-pedic**) (of knowledge or information) comprehensive.

**end** — n. **1 a** extreme limit; point beyond which a thing does not continue (*the end of the road*). **b** extremity; furthest point (*to the ends of the earth*). **2** extreme part or surface of a thing (*strip of wood with a nail in one end*). **3 a** finish (*no end to his misery*). **b** latter or final part (*towards the end of his reign*). **c** death, destruction, downfall (*met an untimely end*). **d** result, outcome (*what was the end of your discussions?*). **4** goal, purpose (*will do anything to achieve his ends*; *to what end?*). **5** remnant (*cigarette-end*). **6** (prec. by *the*) colloq. the limit of endurability. **7** half of a sports pitch etc. occupied by one team or player. **8** part with which a person is concerned (*no problem at my end*). — v. **1** bring or come to an end, finish. **2** (foll. by *in*) result (*ended in disaster*). □ **end it all** (or **end it**) colloq. commit suicide. **end on** with the end facing one, or adjoining the end of the next object. **end to end** with the end of one adjoining the end of the next in a series. **end up** reach a specified state or action eventually (*ended up a drunkard*; *ended up making a fortune*). **in the end** finally. **keep one's end up** do one's part despite difficulties. **make ends** (or **both ends**) **meet** live within one's income. **no end of** colloq. much or many of. **on end 1** upright (*hair stood on end*). **2** continuously (*for three weeks on end*). **put an end to** stop, abolish, destroy. [Old English]

**endanger** /en-**dayn**-juh/ v. place in danger.

**endangered species** n. species in danger of extinction.

**endear** /en-**deer**/ v. (usu. foll. by *to*) make dear to or beloved by (*endeared himself to everyone he met*). □ **endearing** adj.

**endearment** n. **1** an expression of affection. **2** liking, affection.

**endeavour** /en-**dev**-uh/ (also **endeavor**) — v. (foll. by *to* + infin.) try earnestly. — n. earnest attempt. [from EN-¹, French *devoir* owe]

**endemic** /en-**dem**-ik/ — adj. (often foll. by *to*) regularly or only found among a particular people or in a particular region. — n. endemic disease or plant. □ **endemically** adv. [Greek *en-* in, *dēmos* the people]

**ending** n. **1** end or final part, esp. of a story. **2** inflected final part of a word.

**endive** /en-duyv, -div/ n. curly-leaved plant used in salads. [Greek *entubon*]

**endless** adj. **1** infinite; without end. **2** continual (*endless complaints*). **3** interminable (*an endless sermon*). **4** colloq. innumerable. **5** (of a belt, chain, etc.) having the ends joined for continuous action over wheels etc. □ **endlessly** adv. [Old English: related to END]

**endmost** adj. nearest the end.

**endo-** comb. form internal. [Greek *endon* within]

**endocrine** /en-doh-ˌkruyn, -ˌkreen/ adj. (of a gland) secreting directly into the blood; ductless. [Greek *krinō* sift]

**endocrinology** /ˌen-doh-kruh-**nol**-uh-jee/ n. study of the structure and physiology of the endocrine glands.

**endoderm** /en-doh-ˌderm/ n. Biol. innermost layer of an animal embryo in early development. [Greek *derma* skin]

**endogamy** /en-**dog**-uh-mee/ n. **1** Anthropology marrying within the same tribe. **2** Bot. pollination from the same plant. [Greek *gamos* marriage]

**endogenous** /en-**doj**-uh-nuhs/ adj. growing or originating from within.

**endometrium** /ˌen-doh-**mee**-tree-uhm/ n. membrane lining the womb. [Greek *mētra* womb]

**endorphin** /en-**daw**-fuhn/ n. Biochem. any of a group of peptide neurotransmitters occurring naturally in the brain and having pain-relieving properties. [French: related to ENDOGENOUS, MORPHINE]

**endorse** /en-**daws**/ v. (also **indorse**) (**-sing**) **1 a** approve (*I endorse what you've said*). **b** select as a candidate for an election (*the endorsed candidate for Wills*). **2** sign or write on (a document), esp. sign the back of (a cheque). **3** enter details of a conviction for an offence on (a driving-licence). □ **endorsement** n. [Latin *dorsum* back]

**endoscope** /en-doh-ˌskohp/ n. instrument for viewing internal parts of the body.

**endoskeleton** /en-doh-ˌskel-uh-tuhn/ n. internal skeleton, as found in vertebrates (opp. EXOSKELETON).

**endothelium** /ˌen-doh-**thee**-lee-uhm/ n. layer of cells lining the blood-vessels, heart, and lymphatic vessels. [Greek *thēlē* teat]

**endow** /en-**dow**/ v. **1** bequeath or give a permanent income to (a person, institution, etc.). **2** (esp. as **endowed** adj.) (usu. foll. by *with*) provide with talent, ability, etc. [Anglo-French: related to DOWER]

**endowment** n. **1** act or instance of endowing. **2** endowed income. **3** (usu. in pl.) skill, talent, etc., with which a person is endowed.

**endpaper** n. either of the blank leaves of paper at the beginning and end of a book.

**end product** n. final product of manufacture etc.

**endue** /en-**dyoo**/ v. (also **indue**) (**-dues, -dued, -duing**) (foll. by *with*) provide (a person) with (qualities, powers, etc.) (*endued with herculean strength*). [Latin *induo* put on clothes]

**endurance** /en-**dyoo**-ruhns/ n. **1** power of enduring (*it's beyond endurance*). **2** ability to withstand prolonged strain (*the racing-car showed great endurance*) (also attrib.: *endurance test*). [French: related to ENDURE]

**endure** /en-**dyoor**/ v. (**-ring**) **1** undergo (a difficulty etc.) (*endured much pain*). **2** tolerate (*cannot endure him*). **3** last (*your luck will not endure for ever*). □ **endurable** adj. [Latin *durus* hard]

**endways** adv. (also **endwise**) **1** with end uppermost or foremost. **2** end to end.

**enema** /en-uh-muh/ n. **1** introduction of fluid etc. into the rectum, esp. to flush out its contents. **2** fluid etc. used for this. [Greek *hiēmi* send]

**enemy** /en-uh-mee/ n. (pl. **-ies**) **1** person actively hostile to another, or to a cause, etc. **2 a** hostile nation or army (often attrib.: *destroyed by enemy action*). **b** member of this. **3** adversary or opponent (*enemy of progress*). [Latin: related to IN-², *amicus* friend]

**energetic** /ˌen-uh-**jet**-ik/ adj. full of energy, vigorous. □ **energetically** adv. [Greek: related to ENERGY]

**energise** /en-uh-ˌjuyz/ v. (also **-ize**) (**-sing** or **-zing**) **1** give energy to. **2** provide (a device) with energy for operation.

**energy** /en-uh-jee/ n. (pl. **-ies**) **1** capacity for activity; intensity of action (*these kids have great energy*). **2** (in pl.) power displayed or exerted (*threw all their energies into the project*). **3** force or vigour of expression (*writes with great energy*; *I admire the energy of his style*). **4** Physics capacity of matter or radiation to do work. [Greek *ergon* work]

**enervate** /en-uh-ˌvayt/ v. (**-ting**) deprive of vigour or vitality (*an enervated style of writing*). □ **enervation** /ˌen-uh-vay-shuhn/ n. [Latin: related to NERVE]

**en famille** /ˌon fa-**mee**-yuh/ adv. in or with one's family (*I'm dining en famille*). [French, = in family]

**enfant terrible** /ˌon-fon tuh-**ree**-bluh/ n. (*pl.* **enfants terribles** pronunc. same) indiscreet or unruly person. [French, = terrible child]

**enfeeble** /en-**fee**-buhl/ v. (**-ling**) make feeble; weaken. □ **enfeeblement** n.

**enfold** /en-**fohld**/ v. **1** (usu. foll. by *in*, *with*) wrap; envelop (*enfolded him in his blanket*). **2** clasp, embrace (*enfolded him in his arms*).

**enforce** /en-**faws**/ v. (**-cing**) **1** compel observance of (a law etc.) (*enforced the regulation concerning dogs*). **2** (foll. by *on*) impose (an action or one's will, etc.) on (*enforced his interpretation on them all*). **3** persist in (a demand or argument). □ **enforceable** adj. **enforcement** n. **enforcer** n. [Latin: related to FORCE]

**enfranchise** /en-**fran**-chuyz/ v. (**-sing**) **1** give (a person) the right to vote. **2** *hist.* free (a slave etc.). □ **enfranchisement** /-uhz-muhnt/ n. [French: related to FRANK¹]

**engage** /en-**gayj**/ v. (**-ging**) **1** employ or hire (a person). **2 a** (usu. in *passive*) employ busily; occupy (*are you engaged tomorrow?*). **b** hold fast (a person's attention). **3** (usu. in *passive*) bind by a promise, esp. of marriage. **4** arrange beforehand to occupy (a room, seat, etc.). **5 a** interlock (parts of a gear etc.). **b** (of a gear etc.) become interlocked. **6 a** come into battle with. **b** bring (troops) into battle with. **c** come into battle with (an enemy etc.). **7** take part (*engage in politics*). **8** (foll. by *that* + clause or *to* + infin.) undertake (*engaged to get the matter attended to*). [French: related to GAGE]

**engaged** adj. **1** pledged to marry. **2** (of a person) occupied, busy. **3** (of a telephone line, toilet, etc.) in use.

**engagement** n. **1** act or state of engaging or being engaged. **2** appointment with another person. **3** betrothal. **4** battle.

**engaging** adj. attractive, charming. □ **engagingly** adv.

**engender** /en-**jen**-duh/ v. give rise to; produce (a feeling etc.) (*engendered hostility in his audience*). [related to GENUS]

**engine** /**en**-juhn/ n. **1** mechanical contrivance of parts working together, esp. as a source of power (*steam engine*). **2** railway locomotive. [Latin *ingenium* device]

**engineer** /ˌen-juh-**neer**/ — n. **1** person skilled in a branch of engineering. **2** person who makes or is in charge of engines etc. (*ship's engineer*). **3** person who designs and constructs military works; soldier so trained. **4** skilful or artful contriver (*the engineer of our*

*misfortune*). — v. **1** contrive, bring about. **2** act as an engineer. **3** construct or manage as an engineer. [medieval Latin: related to ENGINE]

**engineering** n. application of science to the design, building, and use of machines, constructions, etc. (*civil engineering*).

**English** /**ing**-glish/ — adj. of England or its people or language. — n. **1** language of England, now used in the UK, US, and most Commonwealth countries, and often internationally. **2** (prec. by *the*; treated as *pl.*) the people of England. [Old English]

**engorge** /en-**gawj**/ v. **1** (in *passive*) **a** be crammed full (*engorged with food*). **b** be congested with fluid, esp. blood (*the penis when engorged becomes erect*). **2** devour greedily. [French: related to EN-¹, GORGE]

**engraft** /en-**grahft**/ v. (also **ingraft**) **1** *Bot.* (usu. foll. by *into*, *on*) insert (a scion of one tree into another). **2** (usu. foll. by *in*) implant (principles etc.) in a person's mind. **3** (usu. foll. by *into*) incorporate.

**engrave** /en-**grayv**/ v. (**-ving**) **1** (often foll. by *on*) carve (a text or design) on a hard surface. **2** inscribe (a surface) thus. **3** (often foll. by *on*) impress deeply (on a person's memory). □ **engraver** n. [from GRAVE³]

**engraving** n. print made from an engraved plate.

**engross** /en-**grohs**/ v. **1** absorb the attention of; occupy fully (*the problem engrossed him for hours*). **2** write out (a document etc.) in larger letters or in larger format. □ **engrossment** n. [Anglo-French: related to EN-¹]

**engulf** /en-**gulf**/ v. flow over and swamp; overwhelm. □ **engulfment** n.

**enhance** /en-**hahns**, -**hans**/ v. (**-cing**) intensify (qualities, powers, etc.); improve (something already good) (*enhanced his knowledge of the topic*). □ **enhancement** n. [Anglo-French from Latin *altus* high]

**enigma** /uh-**nig**-muh/ n. **1** puzzling thing or person. **2** riddle or paradox. □ **enigmatic** /ˌen-ig-**mat**-ik/ adj. **enigmatically** /ˌen-ig-**mat**-i-kuh-lee, -klee/ adv. [Latin from Greek]

**enjoin** /en-**join**/ v. **1** command or order (a person) (*I enjoin you to keep the peace*). **2** (often foll. by *on*) impose (an action or conduct) (*enjoined on them the need for secrecy*). **3** (usu. foll. by *from*) *Law* prohibit by injunction (from doing a thing). [Latin *injungo* attach]

**enjoy** /en-**joi**/ v. **1** take pleasure in. **2** have the use or benefit of (*enjoys a very privileged position in society*). **3** experience (*enjoy good health*). □ **enjoy oneself** experience pleasure. □ **enjoyment** n. [French]

**enjoyable** *adj.* pleasant; giving enjoyment. □ **enjoyably** *adv.*

**enkephalin** /en-**kef**-uh-luhn/ *n.* either of two morphine-like peptides in the brain thought to control levels of pain. [Greek *egkephalos* brain]

**enkindle** /en-**kin**-duhl/ *v.* (**-ling**) cause to flare up, arouse.

**enlarge** /en-**lahj**/ *v.* (**-ging**) **1** make or become larger or wider. **2** (often foll. by *on, upon*) describe in greater detail (*enlarged upon his experiences in the outback*). **3** reproduce a photograph on a larger scale. □ **enlargement** *n.* [French: related to LARGE]

**enlighten** /en-**luy**-tuhn/ *v.* **1** (often foll. by *on*) inform (about a subject). **2** (as **enlightened** *adj.*) free from prejudice or superstition; progressive.

**enlightenment** *n.* **1** act or instance of enlightening or state of being enlightened. **2** (**the Enlightenment**) 18th-c. philosophy of reason and individualism.

**enlist** /en-**list**/ *v.* **1** enrol in the armed services. **2** secure as a means of help or support. □ **enlistment** *n.*

**enliven** /en-**luy**-vuhn/ *v.* make lively or cheerful; brighten (a picture etc.); give life or spirit to. □ **enlivenment** *n.*

**en masse** /on **mas**/ *adv.* all together. [French]

**enmesh** /en-**mesh**/ *v.* entangle in or as in a net.

**enmity** /**en**-muh-tee/ *n.* (*pl.* **-ies**) **1** state of being an enemy. **2** hostility. [Romanic: related to ENEMY]

**ennoble** /e-**noh**-buhl/ *v.* (**-ling**) **1** make noble; elevate (*her courage has ennobled her*). **2** make (a person) a noble. □ **ennoblement** *n.* [French: related to EN-¹]

**ennui** /on-**wee**/ *n.* mental weariness from idleness or lack of interest; boredom. [French: related to ANNOY]

**enormity** /ee-**naw**-muh-tee, uh-/ *n.* (*pl.* **-ies**) **1** monstrous wickedness; monstrous crime. **2** great size (*amazed at the enormity of Uluru*). [Latin *enormitas*]

■ **Usage** Sense 2 is commonly found, but is regarded as incorrect by some people.

**enormous** /ee-**naw**-muhs, uh-/ *adj.* extremely large. □ **enormously** *adv.* [Latin *enormis*: related to NORM]

**enough** /ee-**nuf**, uh-/ — *adj.* as much or as many as required (*enough cake; enough apples*). — *n.* sufficient amount or quantity (*we have enough*). — *adv.* **1** to the required degree; adequately (*warm enough*). **2** fairly (*sings well enough*). **3** quite (*you know well enough what I mean*). — *int.* that is enough (in

various senses, esp. to put an end to an action, a thing said, etc.). □ **enough's enough** *colloq.* exclamation indicating that one will not tolerate any more. **have had enough of** want no more of; be satiated with. **sure enough** as expected. [Old English]

**en passant** /,on pa-**son**/ *adv.* in passing; casually (*mentioned it en passant*). [French, = in passing]

**enquire** /in-**kwuyuh**, en-/ *v.* (**-ring**) **1** seek information; ask; ask a question. **2** = INQUIRE. **3** (foll. by *after, for*) ask about (a person, a person's health, etc.). □ **enquirer** *n.* [Latin *quaero quaesit-* seek]

**enquiry** *n.* (*pl.* **-ies**) **1** act or instance of asking or seeking information. **2** = INQUIRY.

**enrage** /en-**rayj**/ *v.* (**-ging**) make furious. [French: related to EN-¹]

**enrapture** /en-**rap**-chuh/ *v.* (**-ring**) delight intensely.

**enrich** /en-**rich**/ *v.* **1** make rich or richer. **2** make more nutritive (*fertiliser enriches the soil; drink enriched with vitamin C*). **3** endow with mental or spiritual wealth (*reading enriches the mind*). **4** make splendid or more valuable with decoration (*the scabbard was enriched with precious gems*). **5** increase the quality or size of (a language) (*Australian English has been enriched with borrowings from Aboriginal languages*). **6** make richer in quality, flavour, colour, content, etc. **7** increase the content of an isotope in (material), esp. enrich uranium with isotope U-235. □ **enrichment** *n.* [French: related to EN-¹]

**enrol** /en-**rohl**/ *v.* (**-ll-**) **1** enlist. **2 a** write the name of (a person) on a list. **b** incorporate as a member of a society etc. **c** enrol oneself, esp. for a course of study. □ **enrolment** *n.* [French: related to EN-¹]

**en route** /on **root**/ *adv.* on the way. [French]

**ensconce** /en-**skons**/ *v.* (**-cing**) (usu. *refl.* or in *passive*) establish or settle comfortably or safely (*ensconced himself in his favourite armchair*). [from *sconce* small fortification]

**ensemble** /on-**som**-buhl/ *n.* **1 a** thing viewed as the sum of its parts. **b** general effect of this. **2** set of clothes worn together. **3** group of actors, dancers, musicians, etc., working together. **4** *Mus.* concerted passage for an ensemble. [Latin *simul* at the same time]

**enshrine** /en-**shruyn**/ *v.* (**-ning**) **1** enclose in a shrine. **2** preserve or cherish (*enshrined in her memory*). □ **enshrinement** *n.*

**enshroud** /en-**shrowd**/ *v. literary* **1**

cover with or as with a shroud. **2** cover completely; hide from view.

**ensign** /**en**-suyn, -suhn/ n. **1** banner or flag, esp. the military or naval flag of a nation. **2** standard-bearer. [French: related to INSIGNIA]

**enslave** /en-**slayv**/ v. (**-ving**) make (a person) a slave. □ **enslavement** n.

**ensnare** /en-**snair**/ v. (**-ring**) catch in or as in a snare; entrap. □ **ensnarement** n.

**ensue** /en-**syoo**/ v. (**-sues, -sued, -suing**) **1** happen afterwards (*what ensued?*). **2** occur as a result (*a brawl ensued from his drunken taunts*). [Latin *sequor* follow]

**en suite** /on **sweet**/ n. bathroom leading off a bedroom. [French, = in sequence]

**ensure** /en-**shaw, -shoor**/ v. (**-ring**) **1** make certain. **2** (usu. foll. by *against*) make safe (*ensure against risks*). □ **ensurer** n. [Anglo-French: related to ASSURE]

**ENT** abbr. ear, nose, and throat.

**-ent** suffix **1** forming adjectives denoting attribution of an action (*consequent*) or state (*existent*). **2** forming agent nouns (*president*). [Latin *-ent-* present participial stem of verbs]

**entablature** /en-**tab**-luh-chuh/ n. upper part of a classical building supported by columns including an architrave, frieze, and cornice. [Italian: related to TABLE]

**entail** /en-**tayl**/ — v. **1** necessitate or involve unavoidably (*entails much effort*). **2** *Law* bequeath (an estate) to a specified line of beneficiaries so that it cannot be sold or given away. — n. *Law* **1** entailed estate. **2** succession to such an estate. [related to *tail* limitation of ownership]

**entangle** /en-**tang**-guhl/ v. (**-ling**) **1** catch or hold fast in a snare, tangle, etc. **2** involve in difficulties or illicit activities. □ **entanglement** n.

**entente** /on-**tont**/ n. friendly understanding between nations. [French]

**enter** v. **1** go or come in or into. **2** come on stage (also as a direction:*enter Macbeth*). **3** penetrate (*bullet entered his arm*). **4** write (name, details, etc.) in a list, book, etc. **5** register, record the name of as a competitor (*entered for the long jump*). **6 a** become a member of (a society or profession) (*entered a Dominican monastery*). **b** enrol in a school etc. **7** make known; present for consideration (*enter a protest*). **8** record formally (before a court of law etc.). **9** (foll. by *into*) **a** engage in (conversation etc.). **b** subscribe to; bind oneself by (an agreement, contract, etc.). **c** form part of (a calculation, plan, etc.) (*this did not enter into my calculations*). **d** sympathise with (feelings) (*you must*

*enter into the spirit of the occasion*). **10** (foll. by *on, upon*) **a** begin; begin to deal with (*entered on the long process of negotiation*). **b** assume the functions of (an office) (*entered on his third term as chairman*). **c** *Law* assume possession (of land etc.). [Latin *intra* within]

**enteric** /en-**te**-rik/ adj. of the intestines. □ **enteritis** /,en-tuh-**ruy**-tuhs/ n. [Greek *enteron* intestine]

**enterprise** /**en**-tuh-,pruyz/ n. **1** undertaking, esp. a challenging one. **2** readiness to engage in such undertakings (*he has no enterprise*). **3** business firm. [Latin *prehendo* grasp]

**enterprise bargaining** n. negotiations on wages and conditions conducted between employer and employees of a particular enterprise (see ENTERPRISE 3), any agreement reached being confined to that enterprise, with no flow-on to other enterprises.

**enterprising** adj. showing enterprise; resourceful, imaginative, energetic. □ **enterprisingly** adv.

**entertain** /,en-tuh-**tayn**/ v. **1** amuse; occupy agreeably. **2 a** receive as a guest. **b** receive guests (*they entertain a great deal*). **3** cherish, consider (an idea etc.) (*don't even begin to entertain that idea!*). [Latin *teneo* hold]

**entertainer** n. person who entertains, esp. professionally.

**entertaining** adj. amusing, diverting. □ **entertainingly** adv.

**entertainment** n. **1** act or instance of entertaining or process of being entertained. **2** thing that entertains; performance.

**enthral** /en-**thrawl**/ v. (**-ll-**) captivate, please greatly. □ **enthralment** n. [from EN-¹, THRALL]

**enthrone** /en-**throhn**/ v. (**-ning**) place (a king, bishop, etc.) on a throne, esp. ceremonially. □ **enthronement** n.

**enthuse** /en-**thooz, -thyooz**/ v. (**-sing**) *colloq.* be or make enthusiastic.

**enthusiasm** /en-**thoo**-zee-,az-uhm, -**thyooz**-/ n. (often foll. by *for, about*) strong interest or admiration, great eagerness. [Greek *entheos* inspired by a god]

**enthusiast** n. person full of enthusiasm. [Church Latin: related to ENTHUSIASM]

**enthusiastic** /en-,thoo-zee-**as**-tik, -,thyoo-/ adj. having enthusiasm. □ **enthusiastically** adv.

**entice** /en-**tuys**/ v. (**-cing**) attract by the offer of pleasure or reward. □ **enticement** n. **enticing** adj. **enticingly** adv. [French *enticier* probably from Romanic]

**entire** /en-**tuyuh**/ adj. **1** whole, complete (*the entire audience was enthralled*). **2** not broken or decayed (*the ancient fortifications are still entire*). **3** unqualified, absolute (*an entire success*). **4** in one piece; continuous. **5** not castrated (*an entire horse*). [Latin: related to INTEGER]

**entirely** adv. **1** wholly, completely (*the stock is entirely exhausted*). **2** solely (*did it entirely for my benefit*).

**entirety** /en-**tuyuh**-ruh-tee/ n. (pl. **-ies**) **1** completeness. **2** (usu. foll. by *of*) sum total. □ **in its entirety** in its complete form.

**entitle** /en-**tuy**-tuhl/ v. (**-ling**) **1** (usu. foll. by *to*) give (a person) a just claim or right. **2** give a title to (*the book is entitled 'Understanding Shakespeare' by E.F.C. Ludowyk*). □ **entitlement** n. [Latin: related to TITLE]

**entity** /en-tuh-tee/ n. (pl. **-ies**) **1** thing with distinct existence, as opposed to a quality or relation. **2** thing's existence in itself. [Latin *ens ent-* being]

**entomb** /en-**toom**/ v. place in, or as in, a tomb. □ **entombment** n. [French: related to TOMB]

**entomology** /,en-tuh-**mol**-uh-jee/ n. the study of insects. □ **entomological** /-muh-**loj**-i-kuhl/ adj. **entomologist** n. [Greek *entomon* insect]

**entourage** /,on-toor-**rahzh**/ n. people attending an important person. [French]

**entr'acte** /**on**-trakt/ n. **1** interval between acts of a play. **2** music or dance performed during this. [French]

**entrails** /en-traylz/ n.pl. **1** bowels, intestines. **2** innermost parts of a thing (*went down into the entrails of the earth*). [Latin *inter* among]

**entrance¹** /en-truhns/ n. **1** place for entering. **2** act or instance of going or coming in. **3** right of admission (*the sign says 'No entrance'*). **4** coming of an actor on stage. **5** (in full **entrance fee**) admission fee. [French: related to ENTER]

**entrance²** /en-**trahns**, **-trans**/ v. (**-cing**) **1** enchant, delight. **2** put into a trance. □ **entrancement** n. **entrancing** adj. **entrancingly** adv.

**entrant** /**en**-truhnt/ n. person who enters (an examination, profession, competition, etc.). [French: related to ENTER]

**entrap** /en-**trap**/ v. (**-pp-**) **1** catch in or as in a trap. **2** beguile or trick (a person). □ **entrapment** n. [related to EN-¹]

**entreat** /en-**treet**/ v. ask earnestly, beg. [related to EN-¹]

**entreaty** n. (pl. **-ies**) earnest request.

**entrée** /**on**-tray/ n. **1** dish served before the main course of a meal, or between the fish and meat courses. **2** right or privilege of admission. [French]

**entrench** /en-**trench**/ v. **1 a** establish firmly (in a position, office, etc.). **b** (as **entrenched** adj.) (of an attitude etc.) not easily modified. **2** surround with a trench as a fortification. □ **entrenchment** n.

**entrepreneur** /,on-truh-pruh-**ner**/ n. **1** person who undertakes a commercial venture, esp. one with the chance of great profit or great loss. **2** contractor acting as an intermediary. □ **entrepreneurial** adj. **entrepreneurialism** n. (also **entrepreneurism**). [French: related to ENTERPRISE]

**entropy** /**en**-truh-pee/ n. **1** Physics measure of the disorganisation or degradation of the universe, resulting in a decrease in available energy. **2** Physics measure of the unavailability of a system's thermal energy for conversion into mechanical work. [Greek: related to EN-², *tropē* transformation]

**entrust** /en-**trust**/ v. (also **intrust**) **1** (foll. by *to*) give (a person or thing) into the care of a person. **2** (foll. by *with*) assign responsibility for (a person or thing) to (a person) (*entrusted him with my camera*).

**entry** /**en**-tree/ n. (pl. **-ies**) **1 a** act or instance of going or coming in. **b** coming of an actor on stage. **c** ceremonial entrance (*made a grand entry*). **d** liberty to go or come in (*he has entry any time he pleases*). **2** place of entrance; door, gate, etc. **3 a** item entered in a diary, list, etc. **b** recording of this. **4** person or thing competing in a race etc. **5** start or resumption of music for a particular instrument in an ensemble. [Romanic: related to ENTER]

**entwine** /en-**twuyn**/ v. (**-ning**) twine round, interweave.

**enumerate** /uh-**nyoo**-muh-,rayt, ee-/ v. (**-ting**) **1** specify (items) (*enumerated all their demands*). **2** count. □ **enumeration** /-ray-shuhn/ n. **enumerative** /-ruh-tiv/ adj. **enumerator** n. [Latin: related to NUMBER]

**enunciate** /uh-**nun**-see-,ayt, ee-/ v. (**-ting**) **1** pronounce (words) clearly. **2** express (a proposition or theory) in definite terms. **3** proclaim. □ **enunciation** /-ay-shuhn/ n. [Latin *nuntio* announce]

**enuresis** /,en-yoo-**ree**-suhs/ n. involuntary urination; bed-wetting. [Greek *enoureō* urinate in]

**envelop** /en-**vel**-uhp/ v. (**-p-**) **1 a** wrap up or cover completely. **b** make obscure; conceal (*was enveloped in mystery*). **2** Mil. completely surround (an enemy). □ **envelopment** n. [French]

**envelope** /**en**-vuh-,lohp, **on**-/ n. **1** folded paper container for a letter etc. **2** wrapper, covering. **3** gas container of a balloon or airship. **4** outer metal or glass housing of a vacuum tube, electric light, etc.

**envenom** /en-**ven**-uhm/ v. **1** put poison on or into; make poisonous (*the arrows were envenomed*). **2** infuse venom or bitterness into (feelings, words, or actions) (*an envenomed reply*). [EN-¹, VENOM]

**enviable** /**en**-vee-uh-buhl/ adj. likely to excite envy; desirable. □ **enviably** adv.

**envious** /**en**-vee-uhs/ adj. feeling or showing envy. □ **enviously** adv. [Anglo-French: related to ENVY]

**environment** /en-**vuy**-ruhn-muhnt/ n. **1** physical surroundings and conditions, esp. as affecting people's lives. **2** conditions or circumstances of living. **3** *Ecology* external conditions affecting the growth of plants and animals. **4** *Computing* overall structure within which a user, computer, or program operates. □ **environmental** /-**men**-tuhl/ adj. **environmentally** /-**men**-tuh-lee/ adv. [French *environ* surroundings]

**environmentalist** /en-,vuy-ruhn-**men**-tuh-luhst/ — n. person concerned with the protection of the natural environment. — adj. of or concerning the protection of the natural environment. □ **environmentalism** n.

**environs** /en-**vuy**-ruhnz/ n.pl. district round a town etc.

**envisage** /en-**viz**-ij, -uhj/ v. (**-ging**) **1** have a mental picture of (a thing not yet existing). **2** imagine as possible or desirable (*cannot envisage this plan being accepted*). [French: related to VISAGE]

**envoy** /**en**-voi/ n. **1** messenger or representative. **2** (in full **envoy extraordinary**) diplomatic agent ranking below ambassador. [French *envoyer* send, from Latin *via* way]

**envy** /**en**-vee/ — n. (pl. **-ies**) **1** discontent aroused by another's better fortune etc. **2** object of this feeling. — v. (**-ies**, **-ied**) feel envy of (a person etc.). [Latin *invidia*, from *video* see]

**Enzed** /en-**zed**/ n. colloq. **1** New Zealand. **2** a New Zealander. [pronunciation of *NZ*]

**Enzedder** /en-**zed**-uh/ n. colloq. a New Zealander.

**enzyme** /**en**-zuym/ n. protein catalyst of a specific biochemical reaction. [Greek *enzumos* leavened]

**Eocene** /**ee**-oh-,seen/ *Geol.* — adj. of the second epoch of the Tertiary period with evidence of an abundance of mammals including horses, bats, and whales. — n. this epoch. [Greek *ēōs* dawn, *kainos* new]

**eolian harp** var. of AEOLIAN HARP.

**eolithic** /,ee-uh-**lith**-ik/ adj. of the period preceding the palaeolithic age, thought to include the earliest use of flint tools. [Greek *ēōs* dawn, *lithos* stone]

**eon** var. of AEON.

**epacris** /uh-**pak**-ruhs/ n. any shrub of the south-eastern Australian genus *Epacris*, having attractive tube-shaped flowers (see COMMON HEATH, HEATH 2). [EPI-, Greek *akris* summit]

**epaulette** /**ep**-uh-let, ,ep-uh-**let**/ n. (also **epaulet**) ornamental shoulder-piece on a coat etc., esp. on a uniform. [French *épaule* shoulder]

**épée** /ay-**pay**, **ep**-ay/ n. sharp-pointed sword, used (with the end blunted) in fencing. [French: related to SPATHE]

**epeirogenesis** /ep-,uy-roh-**jen**-uh-suhs/ n. (also **epeirogeny** /-**roj**-uh-nee/) *Geol.* regional uplift of extensive areas of the earth's crust. [Greek *ēpeiros* mainland, GENESIS]

**ephedrine** /**ef**-uh-dreen, -druyn/ n. alkaloid drug used to relieve asthma, etc. [*Ephedra*, genus of plants yielding it]

**ephemera** /ee-**fem**-uh-ruh, uh-/ n.pl. things of only short-lived relevance. [Latin: related to EPHEMERAL]

**ephemeral** /ee-**fem**-uh-ruhl, uh-/ adj. lasting or of use for only a short time; transitory. [Greek: related to EPI-, *hēmera* day]

**ephod** /**ee**-fod/ n. Jewish priestly vestment. [Hebrew]

**epi-** prefix **1** upon. **2** above. **3** in addition. [Greek]

**epic** /**ep**-ik/ — n. **1** long poem narrating the adventures or deeds of one or more heroic or legendary figures. **2** book or film based on an epic narrative or heroic in type or scale. — adj. **1** of or like an epic. **2** grand, heroic. [Greek *epos* song]

**epicene** /**ep**-ee-,seen/ — adj. **1** of, for, denoting, or used by both sexes. **2** having characteristics of both sexes or of neither sex. **3** effete, effeminate. — n. epicene person. [Greek *koinos* common]

**epicentre** /**ep**-ee-,sen-tuh/ n. **1** point at which an earthquake reaches the earth's surface. **2** central point of a difficulty. [Greek: related to CENTRE]

**epicure** /**ep**-ee-,kyoor, **ep**-uh-/ n. person with refined tastes, esp. in food and drink. □ **epicurism** n. [medieval Latin: related to EPICUREAN]

**Epicurean** /,ep-ee-kyoo-**ree**-uhn, ,ep-uh-/ — n. **1** disciple or student of the Greek philosopher Epicurus. **2** (**epicurean**) devotee of (esp. sensual) enjoyment. — adj. **1** of Epicurus or his ideas. **2** (**epicurean**) characteristic of an epicurean. □ **Epicureanism** n. [Latin from Greek]

**epidemic** /,ep-uh-**dem**-ik/ — n. **1** widespread occurrence of a disease in a community at a particular time. **2** such a disease. **3** (foll. by *of*) wide prevalence of something usu. undesirable (*an epidemic of burglaries*). — adj. in the nature of an epidemic. [Greek *epi* against, *dēmos* the people]

**epidemiology** /,ep-uh-dee-mee-**ol**-uh-jee/ n. the study of the incidence and distribution of epidemic diseases, and of their control and prevention. □ **epidemiologist** n.

**epidermis** /,ep-ee-**der**-muhs, ,ep-uh-/ n. **1** outer cellular layer of the skin. **2** outer layer of cells of leaves, stems, roots, etc. □ **epidermal** adj. [Greek *derma* skin]

**epidiascope** /,ep-ee-**duy**-uh-,skohp/ n. optical projector capable of giving images of both opaque and transparent objects. [from EPI-, DIA-, -SCOPE]

**epididymis** /,ep-ee-**did**-uh-muhs, ,ep-uh-/ n. (pl. **epididymides** /-did-**im**-uh-deez, -duh-**dim**-uh-/) Anat. convoluted duct behind the testis, along which sperm passes to the vas deferens. [EPI-, Greek *didumoi* testicles]

**epidural** /,ep-ee-**dyoo**-ruhl/ — adj. (of an anaesthetic) introduced into the space around the dura mater of the spinal cord. — n. epidural anaesthetic, used esp. in childbirth. [from EPI-, DURA MATER]

**epiglottis** /,ep-ee-**glot**-uhs/ n. flap of cartilage at the root of the tongue, depressed during swallowing to cover the windpipe. □ **epiglottal** adj. [Greek *glōtta* tongue]

**epigram** /**ep**-ee-,gram, **ep**-uh-/ n. **1** short poem with a witty ending. **2** pointed saying. □ **epigrammatic** /-gruh-**mat**-ik/ adj. [Greek: related to -GRAM]

**epigraph** /**ep**-ee-,grahf, -,graf, **ep**-uh-/ n. inscription on a statue, quotation at the head of a chapter, etc. [Greek: related to -GRAPH]

**epilepsy** /**ep**-uh-,lep-see/ n. nervous disorder with convulsions and often loss of consciousness. [Greek *lambanō* take]

**epileptic** /,ep-uh-**lep**-tik/ — adj. of or relating to epilepsy. — n. person with epilepsy. [French: related to EPILEPSY]

**epilogue** /**ep**-ee-,log, **ep**-uh-/ n. **1** short piece ending a literary work. **2** speech addressed to the audience by an actor at the end of a play. [Greek *logos* speech]

**epiphany** /uh-**pif**-uh-nee/ n. (pl. **-ies**) **1** (**Epiphany**) **a** manifestation of Christ to the Magi. **b** festival of this on 6 January. **2** any manifestation of a god or demigod. [Greek *phainō* show]

**epiphyte** /**ep**-ee-,fuyt, **ep**-uh-/ n. plant growing but not parasitic on another, e.g. a moss, various Australian orchids growing on trees. □ **epiphytic** /-**fit**-ik/ adj. [EPI-, Greek *phuton* plant]

**episcopacy** /uh-**pis**-kuh-puh-see/ n. (pl. **-ies**) **1** government of a Church by bishops. **2** (prec. by *the*) the bishops.

**episcopal** /uh-**pis**-kuh-puhl/ adj. **1** of a bishop or bishops. **2** (of a Church) governed by bishops. □ **episcopally** adv. [Church Latin: related to BISHOP]

**episcopalian** /uh-,pis-kuh-**pay**-lee-uhn/ adj. of or advocating government of a Church by bishops.

**episcopate** /uh-**pis**-kuh-puht/ n. **1** the office or tenure of a bishop. **2** (prec. by *the*) the bishops collectively. [Church Latin: related to BISHOP]

**episiotomy** /e-,pee-zee-**ot**-uh-mee, uh-pee-/ n. (pl. **-ies**) surgical cut made at the vaginal opening during childbirth, to aid delivery. [Greek *epision* pubic region]

**episode** /**ep**-uh-,sohd/ n. **1** event or group of events as part of a sequence. **2** each of the parts of a serial story or broadcast. **3** incident or set of incidents in a narrative. **4** incident that is distinct but contributes to a whole (*a romantic episode in his life*). [Greek *eisodos* entry]

**episodic** /,ep-uh-**sod**-ik/ adj. **1** consisting of separate episodes. **2** irregular, sporadic. □ **episodically** adv.

**epistemology** /uh-,pis-tuh-**mol**-uh-jee/ n. philosophy of knowledge, esp. with regard to its methods and validation. □ **epistemological** /-muh-**loj**-i-kuhl/ adj. [Greek *epistēmē* knowledge]

**epistle** /uh-**pis**-uhl/ n. **1** formal or joc. letter. **2** (**Epistle**) **a** any of the apostles' letters in the New Testament. **b** extract from an Epistle read at Mass or other church service. **3** poem etc. in the form of a letter. [Greek *epistolē* from *stellō* send]

**epistolary** /uh-**pis**-tuh-luh-ree/ adj. of or in the form of a letter or letters. [Latin: related to EPISTLE]

**epitaph** /**ep**-uh-,tahf, -,taf/ n. words written in memory of a dead person, esp. as a tomb inscription. [Greek *taphos* tomb]

**epithalamium** /,ep-uh-thuh-**lay**-mee-uhm/ n. (pl. **epithalamiums** or **epithalamia** /-mee-uh/) song or poem celebrating a marriage. [Greek, = at the bridal chamber]

**epithelium** /,ep-ee-**thee**-lee-uhm/ n. (pl. **-s** or **-lia** /-lee-uh/) tissue forming the outer layer of the body and lining many hollow structures of the body. □ **epithelial** adj. [Greek *thēlē* teat]

**epithet** /**ep**-uh-,thet/ n. **1** adjective or

other descriptive word or phrase expressing a quality or attribute which is characteristic of the person or thing described (e.g. 'the Great' in *Alfred the Great*). **2** this as a term of abuse (*hurled some choice epithets at him*). [Greek *tithēmi* place]

**epitome** /uh-**pit**-uh-mee/ *n.* **1** person or thing embodying a quality, class, etc. (*the epitome of greed*). **2** summary of a written work; an abstract. [Greek *temnō* cut]

**epitomise** /uh-**pit**-uh-muyz/ *v.* (also **-ize**) (**-sing** or **-zing**) **1** make or be a perfect example of (a quality etc.); typify. **2** make an epitome of (a book etc.).

**EPNS** *abbr.* electroplated nickel silver.

**epoch** /**ee**-pok/ *n.* **1** period of history etc. marked by notable events. **2** beginning of an era. **3** *Geol.* division of a period, corresponding to a set of strata. □ **epochal** /**ep**-uh-kuhl/ *adj.* [Greek, = pause]

**epoch-making** *adj.* remarkable; very important.

**eponym** /**ep**-uh-nim/ *n.* **1** word, place-name, etc., derived from a person's name (e.g. the State of *Victoria* from Queen *Victoria*). **2** person whose name is used in this way. □ **eponymous** /uh-**pon**-uh-muhs/ *adj.* [Greek *onoma* name]

**epoxy** /ee-**pok**-see/ *adj.* relating to or derived from a compound with one oxygen atom and two carbon atoms bonded in a triangle. [from EPI-, OXYGEN]

**epoxy resin** *n.* synthetic thermosetting resin.

**epsilon** /**ep**-si-,lon/ *n.* fifth letter of the Greek alphabet (Ε, ε). [Greek]

**Epsom salts** /**ep**-suhm/ *n.* magnesium sulphate used as a purgative etc. [*Epsom* in England]

**equable** /**ek**-wuh-buhl/ *adj.* **1** even; not varying. **2** uniform and moderate (*equable climate*). **3** (of a person) not easily disturbed or angered (*he has an equable temperament*). □ **equably** *adv.* [related to EQUAL]

**equal** /**ee**-kwuhl/ — *adj.* **1** (often foll. by *to*, *with*) the same in quantity, quality, size, degree, level, etc. **2** having the necessary strength, ability, etc. (*he was equal to the task*). **3** evenly balanced (*an equal contest*). **4** having the same rights or status (*human beings are essentially equal*). — *n.* person or thing equal to another, esp. in rank or quality (*their treatment of the subject has no equal*; *is the equal of any person*). — *v.* (**-ll-**) **1** be (or become) equal to in number, quality, etc. (*one plus one equals two*; *my grief equals yours*). **2** achieve something that is equal to (*equalled the record*). □ **be equal to** have

the ability or resources for. [Latin *aequalis*]

**equalise** *v.* (also **-ize**) (**-sing** or **-zing**) **1** make or become equal. **2** reach one's opponent's score. □ **equalisation** /-zay-shuhn/ *n.*

**equaliser** *n.* (also **-izer**) equalising score or goal etc.

**equality** /ee-**kwol**-uh-tee, uh-/ *n.* state of being equal. [Latin: related to EQUAL]

**equally** *adv.* **1** in an equal manner (*treated them equally*). **2** to an equal degree (*equally important*).

■ **Usage** In sense 2, construction with *as* (e.g. *equally as important*) is often found, but is incorrect in standard English.

**equal opportunity** *n.* (often in *pl.*) opportunity or right to be employed, paid, etc., without discrimination on grounds of sex, race, etc.

**equal sign** *n.* (also **equals sign**) the symbol = used to indicate that two things are equal.

**equanimity** /,ek-wuh-**nim**-uh-tee, ,ee-kwuh-/ *n.* composure, evenness of temper, esp. in adversity. [Latin *aequus* even, *animus* mind]

**equate** /ee-**kwayt**, uh-/ *v.* (**-ting**) **1** (usu. foll. by *to*, *with*) regard as equal or equivalent. **2 a** (foll. by *with*) be equal or equivalent to. **b** agree or correspond (*your story does not equate with the facts*). □ **equatable** *adj.* [Latin *aequo aequat-*: related to EQUAL]

**equation** /ee-**kway**-*zh*uhn, uh-/ *n.* **1** process of equating or making equal; state of being equal. **2** statement that two mathematical expressions are equal (indicated by the sign =). **3** formula indicating a chemical reaction by means of symbols.

**equator** *n.* **1** imaginary line round the earth or other body, equidistant from the poles. **2** = CELESTIAL EQUATOR. [medieval Latin: related to EQUATE]

**equatorial** /,ek-wuh-**taw**-ree-uhl/ *adj.* of or near the equator.

**equerry** /**ek**-wuh-ree/ *n.* (*pl.* **-ies**) officer attending the British royal family. [French *esquierie* stable]

**equestrian** /uh-**kwes**-tree-uhn/ — *adj.* **1** of or relating to horse-riding. **2** on horseback. — *n.* rider or performer on horseback. □ **equestrianism** *n.* [Latin *equestris* from *equus* horse]

**equi-** *comb. form* equal. [Latin: related to EQUAL]

**equiangular** /,ee-kwee-**ang**-gyuh-luh, ,ek-wee-/ *adj.* having equal angles.

**equidistant** /ˌee-kwee-**dis**-tuhnt, ˌek-wee-/ *adj.* at equal distances.

**equilateral** /ˌee-kwuh-**lat**-uh-ruhl/ *adj.* having all its sides equal in length.

**equilibrium** /ˌee-kwuh-**lib**-ree-uhm, ˌek-wuh-/ *n.* (*pl.* **-ria** /-ree-uh/ or **-s**) **1** state of physical balance. **2** state of mental or emotional composure. **3** state in which the energy in a system is evenly distributed and forces, influences, etc., balance each other. [Latin *libra* balance]

**equine** /**ee**-kwuyn, **ek**-wuyn/ *adj.* of or like a horse. [Latin *equus* horse]

**equinoctial** /ˌee-kwuh-**nok**-shuhl, ˌek-wuh-/ — *adj.* happening at or near the time of an equinox. — *n.* (in full **equinoctial line**) = CELESTIAL EQUATOR. [Latin: related to EQUINOX]

**equinox** /**ee**-kwuh-ˌnoks, **ek**-wuh-/ *n.* time or date (twice each year) at which the sun crosses the celestial equator, when day and night are of equal length (about 20 March and 22 September). [Latin *nox noctis* night]

**equip** /ee-**kwip**, uh-/ *v.* (**-pp-**) supply with what is needed. [Old Norse *skipa* to man a ship]

**equipment** *n.* **1** articles, clothing, etc., necessary for a purpose. **2** process of equipping or being equipped. [French: related to EQUIP]

**equipoise** /**ek**-wuh-ˌpoiz, **ee**-kwuh-/ *n.* **1** equilibrium. **2** counterbalancing thing.

**equitable** /**ek**-wuh-tuh-buhl/ *adj.* **1** fair, just. **2** *Law* valid in equity as distinct from law. □ **equitably** *adv.* [French: related to EQUITY]

**equity** /**ek**-wuh-tee/ *n.* (*pl.* **-ies**) **1** fairness. **2 a** principles of justice used to correct or supplement the law. **b** *Law* body of principles and rules developed in England since medieval times and followed in Australia in contrast to the principles and rules of the common law. **3 a** value of the shares issued by a company. **b** (in *pl.*) stocks and shares not bearing fixed interest. **4** (**Equity**) actors' trade union. [Latin *aequitas*: related to EQUAL]

**equivalent** /ee-**kwiv**-uh-luhnt, uh-/ — *adj.* **1** (often foll. by *to*) equal in value, amount, importance, etc. **2** corresponding. **3** having the same meaning or result. — *n.* equivalent thing, amount, etc. □ **equivalence** *n.* [Latin: related to VALUE]

**equivalent weight** *n.* weight of a substance that can combine with or displace one gram of hydrogen or eight grams of oxygen.

**equivocal** /ee-**kwiv**-uh-kuhl, uh-/ *adj.* **1** of double or doubtful meaning (*tried to protect himself by giving equivocal answers*). **2** (of a person, character, etc.) questionable, suspect. □ **equivocally** *adv.* [Latin *voco* call]

**equivocate** /ee-**kwiv**-uh-ˌkayt, uh-/ *v.* (**-ting**) use ambiguity to conceal the truth. □ **equivocation** /-**kay**-shuhn/ *n.* **equivocator** *n.* [Latin: related to EQUIVOCAL]

**Er** *symb.* erbium.

**er** /er/ *int.* expressing hesitation. [imitative]

**-er¹** *suffix* forming nouns from nouns, adjectives, and verbs, denoting: **1** person, animal, or thing that performs the action or activity indicated (*executioner*; *poker*; *eye-opener*). **2** person or thing that has the attribute or form indicated (*foreigner*; *four-wheeler*; *second-rater*). **3** person concerned with the thing or subject indicated (*hatter*; *geographer*). **4** person belonging to the place or group indicated (*New Zealander*; *sixth-former*). [Old English]

**-er²** *suffix* forming the comparative of adjectives (*wider*) and adverbs (*faster*). [Old English]

**-er³** *suffix* used in a colloquial distortion of the root word (*soccer*). [probably an extension of -ER¹]

**-er⁴** *suffix* forming iterative and frequentative verbs (*blunder*; *glimmer*; *twitter*). [Old English]

**era** /**eer**-ruh/ *n.* **1** system of chronology reckoning from a noteworthy event (*Christian era*). **2** large period, esp. regarded historically (*pre-Roman era*). **3** date at which an era begins. **4** major division of geological time. [Latin, = number (pl. of *aes* money)]

**eradicate** /ee-**rad**-uh-ˌkayt, uh-/ *v.* (**-ting**) root out; destroy completely. □ **eradicable** *adj.* **eradication** /-**kay**-shuhn/ *n.* **eradicator** *n.* [Latin *radix -icis* root]

**erase** /ee-**rayz**, uh-/ *v.* (**-sing**) **1** rub out; obliterate. **2** remove all traces of (*erased it from my memory*). **3** remove recorded material from (magnetic tape or disk). □ **erasable** *adj.* **erasure** *n.* [Latin *rado ras-* scrape]

**eraser** *n.* thing that erases, esp. a piece of rubber etc. for removing pencil etc. marks.

**erbium** /**er**-bee-uhm/ *n.* metallic element of the lanthanide series. [*Ytterby* in Sweden]

**ere** /air/ *prep.* & *conj.* poet. or *archaic* before (of time) (*ere noon*; *ere they come*). [Old English]

**erect** /ee-**rekt**, uh-/ — *adj.* **1** upright, vertical. **2** (of the penis etc.) enlarged and rigid, esp. in sexual excitement. **3** (of hair) bristling. — v. **1** raise; set upright. **2** build. **3** establish (erect a theory). □ **erectly** adv. **erectness** n. [Latin erigere erect- set up]

**erectile** adj. that can become erect (esp. of body tissue in sexual excitement). [French: related to ERECT]

**erection** /ee-**rek**-shuhn, uh-/ n. **1** act or instance of erecting or state of being erected. **2** building or structure. **3** enlarged and erect state of erectile tissue, esp. of the penis.

**eremophila** /e-ruh-**mof**-uh-luh/ n. (also **emu bush**, **poverty bush**) any shrub or small tree of the large Australian genus Eremophila, esp. prevalent in dry inland WA, and bearing showy usu. tubular bellflowers in cream, pink, purple, and red. [Greek erēmos desert, phil- loving]

**erg** n. Physics unit of work or energy. [Greek ergon work]

**ergo** /**er**-goh/ adv. therefore. [Latin]

**ergonomics** /,er-guh-**nom**-iks/ n. the study of the relationship between people and their working environment. □ **ergonomic** adj. [Greek ergon work]

**erica** /e-**rik**-uh/ n. any of various shrubs or heaths (esp. from southern Africa) with small leathery leaves and bell-like flowers. [Greek ereikē heath]

**Erin** /e-rin, eer-rin/ n. poet. Ireland. [Irish]

**eriostemon** /e-ree-**os**-tuh-muhn/ n. (also **wax flower**) any of many species of the Australian genus Eriostemon, small to medium shrubs bearing profuse starflowers (often waxy in texture) in colours ranging from white through rose to mauve. [Greek erion wool, STAMEN]

**ermine** /**er**-muhn/ n. (pl. same or **-s**) **1** stoat, esp. when white in winter. **2** its white fur, used to trim robes etc. [French]

**erode** /e-**rohd**, ee-/ v. (**-ding**) wear away, destroy or be destroyed gradually (water has eroded the slope; his confidence was eroded by her laughter). □ **erosion** n. **erosive** adj. [Latin rodo ros- gnaw]

**erogenous** /uh-**roj**-uh-nuhs, ee-/ adj. **1** (of a part of the body) particularly sensitive to sexual stimulation. **2** giving rise to sexual desire or excitement. [Greek (as EROTIC), -GENOUS]

**erogenous zones** n.pl. those parts of the body which provide sexual pleasure when stimulated.

**eros** /**eer**-ros/ n. **1** (**Eros**) Greek god of sexual love. **2** earthly sexual love as a principle or phenomenon. **3** (in Freudian psychology) urge towards self-preservation and sexual pleasure.

**erotic** /uh-**rot**-ik, e-, ee-/ adj. of or causing

sexual love, esp. tending to arouse sexual desire or excitement. □ **erotically** adv. [Greek erōs sexual love]

**erotica** n.pl. erotic literature or art.

**eroticism** /uh-**rot**-uh-,siz-uhm, e-, ee-/ n. **1** erotic nature or character. **2** use of or response to erotic images or stimulation.

**erotogenic** /uh-,rot-oh-**jen**-ik, e-/ adj. = EROGENOUS.

**err** /er/ v. **1** be mistaken or incorrect. **2** do wrong; sin. [Latin erro stray]

**errand** /e-ruhnd/ n. **1** short journey, esp. on another's behalf, to take a message, collect goods, etc. **2** object of such a journey. [Old English]

**errant** /e-ruhnt/ adj. **1** erring; deviating from an accepted standard. **2** literary or archaic travelling in search of adventure (knight errant). □ **errantry** n. (in sense 2). [from ERR: sense 2 ultimately from Latin iter journey]

**erratic** /uh-**rat**-ik, ee-/ adj. **1** inconsistent in conduct, opinions, etc. **2** uncertain in movement (his progress down the street was erratic). □ **erratically** adv. [Latin: related to ERR]

**erratum** /uh-**rah**-tuhm, e-/ n. (pl. **errata**) error in printing or writing, esp. (in pl.) a list of corrected errors attached to a book etc. [Latin: related to ERR]

**erroneous** /uh-**roh**-nee-uhs, e-/ adj. incorrect; arising from error. □ **erroneously** adv. [Latin: related to ERR]

**error** /e-ruh/ n. **1** mistake. **2** condition of being wrong in conduct or judgment (led into error). **3** degree of inaccuracy in a calculation etc. (2% error). [Latin: related to ERR]

**error message** n. Computing message that reports a software, hardware, or operator error.

**ersatz** /**er**-zats, **er**-sats/ adj. & n. substitute, imitation (esp. of inferior quality) (ersatz coffee). [German]

**erstwhile** /**erst**-wuyl/ — adj. former, previous (his erstwhile lover). — adv. archaic formerly. [related to ERE]

**eructation** /,ee-ruk-**tay**-shuhn/ n. formal act or instance of belching. [Latin ructo belch]

**erudite** /e-roo-,duyt, e-ruh-/ adj. **1** (of a person) learned. **2** (of writing etc.) showing great learning. □ **erudition** /-**dish**-uhn/ n. [Latin eruditus instructed: related to RUDE]

**erupt** /ee-**rupt**, uh-/ v. **1** break out suddenly or dramatically (the crowd erupted into applause). **2** (of a volcano) eject lava etc. **3** (of a rash etc.) appear on the skin. □ **eruption** n. **eruptive** adj. [Latin erumpo erupt- break out]

**-ery** *suffix* (also **-ry**) forming nouns denoting: **1** class or kind (*greenery*; *machinery*; *citizenry*). **2** employment; state or condition (*dentistry*; *slavery*). **3** place of work or cultivation or breeding (*brewery*; *rookery*). **4** behaviour (*mimicry*). **5** often *derog*. all that has to do with (*tomfoolery*). [French *-erie*]

**erysipelas** /ˌe-ruh-**sip**-uh-luhs/ *n.* disease causing fever and a deep red inflammation of the skin. [Latin from Greek]

**erythrocyte** /uh-**rith**-roh-ˌsuyt/ *n.* red blood cell. [Greek *eruthros* red, -CYTE]

**Es** *symb.* einsteinium.

**escalate** /**es**-kuh-ˌlayt/ *v.* (**-ting**) **1** increase or develop (usu. rapidly) by stages. **2** make or become more intense (*fighting has escalated*). □ **escalation** /-**lay**-shuhn/ *n.* [from ESCALATOR]

**escalator** *n.* moving staircase consisting of a circulating belt forming steps. [Latin *scala* ladder]

**escalope** /**es**-kuh-ˌlop/ *n.* thin slice of boneless meat, esp. veal. [French, originally = shell]

**escapade** /**es**-kuh-ˌpayd, ˌes-kuh-**payd**/ *n.* piece of daring or reckless behaviour. [French from Provençal or Spanish: related to ESCAPE]

**escape** /uh-**skayp**/ — *v.* (**-ping**) **1** (often foll. by *from*) get free of restriction or control. **2** (of gas etc.) leak. **3** succeed in avoiding danger, punishment, etc.; get off safely (*escaped by the skin of my teeth*). **4** get free of (a person, grasp, etc.). **5** avoid (a commitment, danger, etc.) (*escaped doing the dishes*). **6** elude the notice or memory of (*nothing escapes you; name escaped me*). **7** (of words etc.) issue unawares from (a person etc.) (*a sigh escaped him*). — *n.* **1** act or instance of escaping; avoidance of danger, injury, etc. **2** means of escaping (often *attrib*.: *escape hatch*). **3** leakage of gas etc. **4** temporary relief from unpleasant reality or worry (*he daydreams as an escape*). [Latin *cappa* cloak]

**escape clause** *n. Law* clause specifying conditions under which a contracting party is free from an obligation.

**escapee** /ˌes-kuh-**pee**, e-**skay**-pee/ *n.* person who has escaped.

**escapement** *n.* part of a clock etc. that connects and regulates the motive power. [French: related to ESCAPE]

**escape velocity** *n.* minimum velocity needed to escape from the gravitational field of a body.

**escapism** *n.* pursuit of distraction and relief from (esp. unpleasant) reality, esp. through fantasising, immersing oneself in frivolous entertainments, etc. □ **escapist** *n. & adj.*

**escapology** /ˌes-kuh-**pol**-uh-jee/ *n.* techniques of escaping from confinement, esp. as entertainment. □ **escapologist** *n.*

**escarpment** /uh-**skahp**-muhnt/ *n.* long steep slope at the edge of a plateau etc. [French from Italian: related to SCARP]

**-esce** /es/ *suffix* forming verbs, usu. initiating action (*effervesce*). [Latin]

**-escence** /es-uhns/ *suffix* forming nouns denoting the beginning of a state or action, a state, etc. (*effervescence*).

**-escent** /es-uhnt/ *suffix* forming adjectives denoting the beginning of a state or action (*effervescent*).

**eschatology** /ˌes-kuh-**tol**-uh-jee/ *n.* the part of theology concerned with death and final destiny. □ **eschatological** /-tuh-**loj**-i-kuhl/ *adj.* [Greek *eskhatos* last]

**eschew** /es-**choo**, -uhs-/ *v. formal* avoid; abstain from (*eschewed fornication for Lent*). □ **eschewal** *n.* [Germanic: related to SHY[1]]

**escort** — *n.* /**es**-kawt/ **1** one or more persons, vehicles, etc., accompanying a person, vehicle, etc., for protection or as a mark of status. **2** person accompanying a person of the opposite sex socially. **3 a** person hired to accompany a person socially. **b** *euphem*. male or female prostitute. — *v.* /uh-**skawt**/ act as an escort to. [French from Italian]

**escritoire** /ˌes-kri-**twah**/ *n.* writing-desk with drawers etc. [French from Latin *scriptorium* writing-room]

**escutcheon** /uh-**skuch**-uhn/ *n.* shield or emblem bearing a coat of arms. [Latin *scutum* shield]

**-ese** /eez/ *suffix* forming adjectives and nouns denoting: **1** inhabitant or language of a country or city (*Japanese*; *Viennese*). **2** often *derog*. character or style, esp. of language (*officialese*).

**Eskimo** /**es**-kuh-ˌmoh/ — *n.* (*pl.* same or **-s**) **1** member of a people inhabiting N. Canada, Alaska, Greenland, and E. Siberia. **2** language of this people. — *adj.* of Eskimos or their language. [Algonquian, = eaters of raw flesh]

■ **Usage** The people themselves prefer the name *Inuit*.

**esky** /**es**-kee/ *n.* (*pl.* **-ies**) *propr.* portable insulated container for keeping food or drink cool. [probably from ESKIMO, with reference to their cold climate]

**esophagus** var. of OESOPHAGUS.

**esoteric** /ˌee-soh-**te**-rik, ˌes-uh-/ *adj.* **1** intelligible only to those with special knowledge (*esoteric jargon*). **2** (of a belief etc.) intended only for the initiated. □ **esoterically** *adv.* [Greek *esō* within]

**ESP** *abbr.* extrasensory perception.

**espadrille** /ˌes-puh-**dril**/ n. light canvas shoe with a plaited fibre sole. [Provençal]

**espalier** /es-**pal**-yuh/ n. **1** lattice-work along which the branches of a tree or shrub are trained to grow flat against a wall etc. **2** tree or shrub so trained. [French from Italian]

**especial** /uh-**spesh**-uhl/ adj. **1** notable; exceptional. **2** attributed or belonging chiefly to one person or thing (*your especial charm*). [Latin: related to SPECIAL]

**especially** adv. **1** in particular. **2** much more than in other cases. **3** particularly.

**Esperance wax** n. WA shrub of the family Myrtaceae, bearing many waxy white flowers in spring. [*Esperance* Bay in WA]

**Esperanto** /ˌes-puh-**ran**-toh/ n. an artificial language designed for universal use. [Latin *spero* hope]

**espionage** /es-pee-uh-ˌnah*zh*, -ˌnahj/ n. spying or use of spies, esp. by governments. [French: related to SPY]

**esplanade** /ˌes-pluh-**nahd**, -**nayd**/ n. long open level area (or street) for walking on, esp. beside the sea. [Latin *planus* level]

**espousal** /uh-**spow**-zuhl, es-**pow**-/ n. **1** (foll. by *of*) espousing of (a cause etc.). **2** *archaic* marriage, betrothal.

**espouse** /uh-**spowz**, es-**powz**/ v. (**-sing**) **1** adopt or support (a cause, doctrine, etc.). **2** *archaic* **a** (usu. of a man) marry. **b** (usu. foll. by *to*) give (a woman) in marriage. [Latin *spondeo* betroth]

**espresso** /es-**pres**-oh/ n. (also **expresso** /ek-**spres**-oh/) (pl. **-s**) strong black coffee made under steam pressure. [Italian, = pressed out]

**esprit** /es-**pree**, uh-/ n. sprightliness, wit. □ **esprit de corps** /duh **kaw**/ devotion to and pride in one's group. [French: related to SPIRIT]

**espy** /uh-**spuy**, es-**puy**/ v. (**-ies**, **-ied**) catch sight of. [French: related to SPY]

**Esq.** abbr. Esquire.

**-esque** suffix forming adjectives meaning 'in the style of' or 'resembling' (*Kafkaesque*; *statuesque*). [French from Latin *-iscus*]

**esquire** /es-**kwuyuh**/ n. **1** (usu. as abbr. **Esq.**) title added to a man's surname when no other title is used, esp. as a form of address for letters. **2** *archaic* = SQUIRE. [French from Latin *scutum* shield]

**-ess** suffix forming nouns denoting females (*hostess*; *lioness*). [Greek *-issa*]

■ **Usage** In many contexts, sex-based suffixes of this kind are no longer acceptable, e.g. *authoress*, *poetess*.

**essay** — n. /**es**-ay/ **1** short piece of writing on a given subject. **2** (also /uh-**say**/) (often foll. by *at*, *in*) formal attempt. — v. /uh-**say**/ attempt (*essayed the north face of the mountain*). □ **essayist** n. [Latin *exigo* weigh: cf. ASSAY]

**essence** /**es**-uhns/ n. **1** fundamental nature; inherent characteristics. **2 a** extract got by distillation etc. (*essence of vanilla*). **b** perfume. □ **of the essence** indispensable. **in essence** fundamentally. [Latin *esse* be]

**essential** /uh-**sen**-shuhl/ — adj. **1** necessary; indispensable. **2** of or constituting the essence of a person or thing. — n. (esp. in pl.) basic or indispensable element or thing. □ **essentially** adv. [Latin: related to ESSENCE]

**essential oil** n. volatile oil derived from a plant etc. with its characteristic odour.

**-est** suffix forming the superlative of adjectives (*widest*; *nicest*; *happiest*) and adverbs (*soonest*). [Old English]

**establish** /uh-**stab**-lish/ v. **1** set up (a business, system, etc.) on a permanent basis. **2** (foll. by *in*) settle (a person or oneself) in some capacity. **3** (esp. as **established** adj.) **a** achieve permanent acceptance for (a custom, belief, practice, etc.) (*establish a precedent*). **b** become recognised; gain a footing (*established himself as a writer*; *an established writer*). **c** place (a fact etc.) beyond dispute (*the police have established the fact that he was there*; *an established fact*). [Latin *stabilio* make firm]

**establishment** n. **1** act or instance of establishing or process of being established. **2 a** business organisation or public institution. **b** place of business. **c** residence. **3 a** staff of an organisation. **b** household. **4** any organised body permanently maintained for a purpose. **5** (**the Establishment**) powerful groups in society exercising a great deal of authority or influence (such as those controlling the public service, the armed services, the mainstream Churches, as well as the judiciary, etc.) and seen as conservative and resisting change.

**estate** /uh-**stayt**, es-**tayt**/ n. **1** property consisting of much land and usu. a large house. **2** modern residential or industrial area with an integrated design or purpose. **3** *Law* **a** interest in land measured by duration, such as fee simple or leasehold. **b** person's assets and liabilities, esp. at death. **4** property where rubber, tea, grapes, etc., are cultivated. **5** order or class forming (or regarded as) part of the body politic. **6** *archaic* or *literary* state or position in life (*the estate* *of holy matrimony*). [French *estat*, from Latin *sto stat-* stand]

**estate agent** *n.* person whose business is the sale or lease of buildings and land on behalf of others.

**esteem** /uh-**steem**/ — *v.* **1** (often in *passive*) have a high regard for; deeply respect (*I esteem him greatly*; *she was greatly esteemed*). **2** *formal* consider (*esteemed it an honour*). — *n.* high regard; favour (*held in high esteem*). [Latin: related to ESTIMATE]

**ester** /**es**-tuh/ *n. Chem.* a compound produced by replacing the hydrogen of an acid by an organic radical. [German]

**estimable** /**es**-tuh-muh-buhl/ *adj.* worthy of esteem; admirable. [Latin: related to ESTEEM]

**estimate** — *n.* /**es**-tuh-muht/ **1** approximate judgment, esp. of cost, value, size, etc. **2** statement of approximate charge for work to be undertaken. — *v.* /**es**-tuh-,mayt/ (**-ting**) (*also absol.*) **1** form an estimate or opinion of. **2** (foll. by *that*) make a rough calculation. **3** (often foll. by *at*) form an estimate; adjudge. □ **estimator** /-,may-tuh/ *n.* [Latin *aestimo* fix the price of]

**estimation** /,es-tuh-**may**-shuhn/ *n.* **1** process or result of estimating. **2** judgment of worth (*in my estimation*). [Latin: related to ESTIMATE]

**Estonian** /es-**toh**-nee-uhn/ — *n.* **1 a** native or national of Estonia in eastern Europe. **b** person of Estonian descent. **2** language of Estonia. — *adj.* of Estonia, its people, or language.

**estrange** /uh-**straynj**/ *v.* (**-ging**) **1** (usu. in *passive*; often foll. by *from*) alienate; make hostile or indifferent. **2** (as **estranged** *adj.*) (of a husband or wife) no longer living with his or her spouse. □ **estrangement** *n.* [Latin: related to STRANGE]

**estrogen** var. of OESTROGEN.

**estuary** /**es**-choo-ree/ *n.* (*pl.* **-ies**) wide tidal river mouth. □ **estuarine** *adj.* [Latin *aestus* tide]

**ET** *abbr.* extraterrestrial.

**-et** *suffix* forming nouns (orig. diminutives) (*baronet*; *bullet*; *sonnet*).

**ETA** *abbr.* estimated time of arrival.

**eta** /**ee**-tuh/ *n.* seventh letter of the Greek alphabet (Η, η). [Greek]

**et al.** /et **al**/ *abbr.* and others. [Latin *et alii*]

**etc.** *abbr.* = ET CETERA.

**et cetera** /et **set**-uh-ruh, **set**-ruh/ (*also* **etcetera**) — *adv.* **1** and the rest. **2** and so on. — *n.* (*in pl.*) the usual extras. [Latin]

**etch** *v.* **1 a** reproduce (a picture etc.) by engraving it on a metal plate with acid

(esp. to print copies). **b** engrave (a plate) in this way. **2** practise this craft. **3** (foll. by *on*, *upon*) impress deeply (esp. on the mind). □ **etcher** *n.* [Dutch *etsen*]

**etching** *n.* **1** print made from an etched plate. **2** art of producing these plates.

**eternal** /ee-**ter**-nuhl, uh-/ *adj.* **1** existing always; without an end or (usu.) beginning. **2** essentially unchanging (*eternal truths*). **3** *colloq.* constant; too frequent (*eternal nagging*). □ **eternally** *adv.* [Latin *aeternus*]

**eternal triangle** *n.* two people of one sex and one person of the other involved in a complex emotional relationship.

**eternity** /ee-**ter**-nuh-tee, uh-/ *n.* (*pl.* **-ies**) **1** infinite (esp. future) time. **2** endless life after death. **3** being eternal. **4** *colloq.* (often prec. by *an*) a very long time (*you're taking an eternity to finish that job*). [Latin: related to ETERNAL]

**eternity ring** *n.* finger-ring esp. set with gems all round, usu. given as a token of lasting affection.

**-eth** var. of -TH.

**ethanal** /**eth**-uh-,nal, ee-**thuh**-/ *n.* = ACETALDEHYDE.

**ethane** /**ee**-thayn, **eth**-ayn/ *n.* gaseous hydrocarbon of the alkane series, occurring in natural gas. [from ETHER]

**ethanol** /**eth**-uh-,nol/ *n. Chem.* = ALCOHOL 1. [ETHAN(E), (ALCOH)OL]

**ether** /**ee**-thuh/ *n.* **1** *Chem.* colourless volatile organic liquid used as an anaesthetic or solvent. **2** clear sky; upper regions of the air. **3** *hist.* **a** medium formerly assumed to permeate all space. **b** medium through which electromagnetic waves were formerly thought to be transmitted. [Greek *aithō* burn]

**ethereal** /ee-**theer**-ree-uhl, uh-/ *adj.* **1** light, airy. **2** highly delicate, esp. in appearance. **3** heavenly, celestial (*ethereal spirits*). **4** *Chem.* of or relating to ether. □ **ethereally** *adv.* [Greek: related to ETHER]

**ethic** /**eth**-ik/ — *n.* set of moral principles (*the Quaker ethic*). — *adj.* = ETHICAL. [Greek: related to ETHOS]

**ethical** *adj.* **1** relating to morals, esp. as concerning human conduct. **2** morally correct; honourable. □ **ethically** *adv.*

**ethics** *n.pl.* (*also treated as sing.*) **1** moral philosophy. **2 a** moral principles; rules of conduct. **b** set of these.

**Ethiopian** /,ee-thee-**oh**-pee-uhn/ — *n.* **1** native or national of Ethiopia in NE Africa. **2** person of Ethiopian descent. — *adj.* of Ethiopia.

**ethnic** /**eth**-nik/ — *adj.* **1 a** (of a social group) having common national, racial, cultural, religious, or linguistic characteristics; esp. (in Australia) designating a social group of migrants (or their descendants) whose original language is not English. **b** (of music, clothing, etc.) inspired by or resembling those of an exotic people (*ethnic dancing*). **2** of or pertaining to ethnic groups (*ethnic radio*). **3** denoting origin by birth or descent rather than nationality (*ethnic Turks*; *ethnic origins*). — *n.* member of an ethnic group. □ **ethnically** *adv.* [Greek *ethnos* nation]

**ethnic cleansing** *n. euphem.* massacre or mass expulsion of one ethnic or religious group by another.

**ethno** /*eth*-noh/ *n. colloq. offens.* person from an ethnic group.

**ethno-** /*eth*-noh/ *comb. form* ethnic, ethnological.

**ethnocentric** /ˌeth-noh-**sen**-trik/ *adj.* regarding one's own race or ethnic group as of supreme importance and superior to all others; evaluating other races and cultures by criteria specific to one's own. □ **ethnocentricity** /-**tris**-uh-tee/ *n.* **ethnocentrism** *n.*

**ethnography** /eth-**nog**-ruh-fee/ *n.* the scientific description of races and cultures of mankind. □ **ethnographer** *n.* **ethnographic** /-nuh-**graf**-ik/ *adj.* **ethnographical** *adj.*

**ethnology** /eth-**nol**-uh-jee/ *n.* the comparative scientific study of peoples. □ **ethnological** /-nuh-**loj**-i-kuhl/ *adj.* **ethnologist** *n.*

**ethos** /*ee*-thos/ *n.* characteristic spirit or attitudes of a community etc. [Greek *ēthos* character]

**ethyl** /*eth*-uhl/ *n.* (*attrib.*) a radical derived from ethane, present in alcohol and ether. [German: related to ETHER]

**ethylene** /*eth*-uh-ˌleen/ *n.* a hydrocarbon of the alkene series, occurring in natural gas and used in the manufacture of polythene.

**etiolate** /*ee*-tee-oh-ˌlayt/ *v.* (**-ting**) **1** make (a plant) pale by excluding light. **2** give a sickly colour to (a person). □ **etiolation** /-ˌlay-shuhn/ *n.* [Latin *stipula* straw]

**etiology** var. of AETIOLOGY.

**etiquette** /*et*-uh-ˌkuht, et-ee-/ *n.* conventional rules of social behaviour or professional conduct. [French: related to TICKET]

**Etruscan** /uh-**trus**-kuhn/ — *adj.* of ancient Etruria in Italy. — *n.* **1** native of Etruria. **2** language of Etruria. [Latin *Etruscus*]

**et seq.** *abbr.* and the following (pages etc.). [Latin *et sequentia*]

**-ette** *suffix* forming nouns meaning: **1** small (*kitchenette*). **2** imitation or substitute (*flannelette*). **3** female (*usherette*). [French]

**étude** /*ay*-tyood, -ˈtyood/ *n.* = STUDY *n.* 6. [French, = study]

**etymology** /ˌet-uh-**mol**-uh-jee/ *n.* (*pl.* **-ies**) **1 a** derivation and development of a word in form and meaning. **b** account of this (cf. FOLK ETYMOLOGY). **2** the study of word origins. □ **etymological** /-muh-**loj**-i-kuhl/ *adj.* **etymologist** *n.* [Greek *etumos* true]

**Eu** *symb.* europium.

**eu-** *comb. form* well, easily. [Greek]

**eucalypt** /*yoo*-kuh-lipt/ *n.* Australian tree of the genus *Eucalyptus* (also *attrib.*: *eucalypt forest*). [abbreviation]

**eucalyptol** /ˌyoo-kuh-**lip**-tol/ *n.* common (and formerly scientific) name for the volatile oil cineol, a principal component of pharmaceutical-grade eucalyptus oil.

**eucalyptus** /ˌyoo-kuh-**lip**-tuhs/ *n.* (*pl.* **-tuses** or **-ti** /-tuy/) (also **eucalypt** *pl.* **-s**) **1** essentially Australian genus (*Eucalyptus*) of trees (and some shrubs), consisting of some 600 classified species. **2** any tree (or shrub) of this genus, evergreen, cultivated for its timber and for the oil from its leaves (see also GUMTREE). [from EU-, Greek *kaluptos* covered: 'well-covered' referring to the fact that the flower before it opens is protected by a cap, the operculum]

**eucalyptus leaf** see GUMLEAF.

**eucalyptus oil** *n.* any of several volatile oils extracted from the leaves of certain eucalypts and valued for medicinal and germicidal properties, etc.

**Eucharist** /*yoo*-kuh-ruhst/ *n.* **1** Christian sacrament in which consecrated bread (or bread and wine) are consumed. **2** consecrated elements, esp. the bread. □ **Eucharistic** /-**ris**-tik/ *adj.* [Greek, = thanksgiving]

**euchre** /*yoo*-kuh/ — *n.* card-game. — *v.* **1** (in the card-game) gain the advantage over (another player) when that player fails to take three tricks. **2** *colloq.* outwit, deceive (a person). **3** (as **euchred** *adj.*) *colloq.* exhausted; finished. [origin unknown]

**eugenics** /yoo-**jen**-iks, -**jee**-niks/ *n.pl.* (also treated as *sing.*) improvement of the qualities of a race by control of inherited characteristics. □ **eugenic** *adj.* **eugenically** *adv.* [from EU-, Greek *gen-* produce]

**eulogise** /*yoo*-luh-ˌjuyz/ *v.* (also **-ize**) (**-sing** or **-zing**) praise in speech or writing. □ **eulogistic** /-**jis**-tik/ *adj.*

**eulogy** /*yoo*-luh-jee/ *n.* (*pl.* **-ies**) **1** speech or writing in praise of a person. **2** expression of praise. [Latin from Greek]

**eunuch** /**yoo**-nuhk/ *n.* **1** castrated man. **2** person lacking effectiveness (*political eunuch*). [Greek, = bedchamber attendant]

**euphemism** /**yoo**-fuh-,miz-uhm/ *n.* **1** mild or vague expression substituted for one thought to be too harsh or blunt or direct (e.g. *pass over* for *die*). **2** use of such expressions. □ **euphemistic** /-**mis**-tik/ *adj.* **euphemistically** /-**mis**-tik-uh-lee, -klee/ *adv.* [Greek *phēmē* speaking]

**euphonium** /yoo-**foh**-nee-uhm/ *n.* brass instrument of the tuba family. [related to EUPHONY]

**euphony** /**yoo**-fuh-nee/ *n.* (*pl.* **-ies**) **1** pleasantness of sound, esp. of a word or phrase. **2** pleasant sound. □ **euphonious** /yoo-**foh**-nee-uhs/ *adj.* [Greek *phōnē* sound]

**euphoria** /yoo-**faw**-ree-uh/ *n.* intense feeling of well-being and excitement, esp. one based on over-confidence or over-optimism. □ **euphoric** /-**fo**-rik/ *adj.* [Greek *pherō* bear]

**Eurasian** /yoo-**ray**-*zh*uhn/ — *adj.* **1** of mixed European and Asian parentage. **2** of Europe and Asia. — *n.* Eurasian person.

**eureka** /yoo-**ree**-kuh/ — *int.* I have found it! (announcing a discovery etc.). — *n.* **1** the exultant cry of 'eureka'. **2** (**Eureka**) *hist.* clash between gold-miners and the police and the military at Ballarat in 1854, now a symbol of republicanism. [Greek *heurēka*; sense 2 of *n.* from the name of a lead in the Ballarat goldfield]

**Eureka flag** *n.* blue flag bearing a white cross with a star at the end of each arm, first raised at the EUREKA STOCKADE; now associated with the Australian republican cause.

**Eureka stockade** *n.* site of the clash between gold-miners and the police and the military at Ballarat in 1854.

**eurhythmics** /yoo-**rith**-miks/ *n.pl.* (also treated as *sing.*) harmony of bodily movement, esp. as developed with music and dance into a system of education. [EU-, Greek *rhuthmos* proportion, rhythm]

**euro** /**yoo**-roh/ *n.* reddish, short-haired macropod of drier Australia west of the Great Dividing Range, a sub-species of WALLAROO. [Adnyamathanha *yuru*, *thuru*]

**Euro-** /**yoo**-roh/ *comb. form* Europe, European. [abbreviation]

**Eurocentric** /,yoo-roh-**sen**-trik/ *adj.* having things European (e.g. culture, literature, etc.) as the centre or focus of interest.

**European** /,yoo-ruh-**pee**-uhn/ — *adj.* **1** of or in Europe. **2** originating in, native to, or characteristic of Europe. — *n.* native or inhabitant of Europe. [Greek *Eurōpē* Europe]

**European community** *n.* economic and political association of certain European countries as a unit with internal free trade and common external tariffs.

**European wasp** *n.* (also **killer wasp**) dangerous, bee-sized wasp with yellow-and-black bands, able to sting repeatedly; orig. of Europe etc., but now well established in Australia.

**europium** /yuh-**roh**-pee-uhm/ *n.* metallic element of the lanthanide series. [from the name *Europe*]

**Eustachian tube** /yoo-**stay**-shuhn/ *n.* tube leading from the pharynx to the cavity of the middle ear, and equalising the pressure on each side of the eardrum. [*Eustachio*, name of an anatomist (d. 1574)]

**eustasy** /**yoo**-stuh-see/ *n.* change in sea level throughout the world caused by tectonic movements, the melting of glaciers, etc. □ **eustatic** /-**stat**-ik/ *adj.* [back-formation from German *eustatisch* (*adj.*) (as EU-, STATIC)]

**euthanasia** /,yoo-thuh-**nay**-*zh*ee-uh, -*zh*uh/ *n.* bringing about of a gentle and painless death in the case of incurable and painful disease. [EU-, Greek *thanatos* death]

**euthanise** /**yoo**-thuh-,nuyz/ *v.* **1** subject to euthanasia. **2** put (an animal) to death humanely.

**eV** *abbr.* electronvolt.

**evacuate** /ee-**vak**-yoo-,ayt, uh-/ *v.* (**-ting**) **1 a** remove (people) from a place of danger. **b** empty (a place) in this way. **2** make empty (a vessel of air etc.). **3** (of troops) withdraw from (a place). **4** empty (the bowels etc.). □ **evacuation** /-**ay**-shuhn/ *n.* [Latin *vacuus* empty]

**evacuee** /ee-,vak-yoo-**ee**, uh-/ *n.* person evacuated from a place of danger.

**evade** /ee-**vayd**, uh-/ *v.* (**-ding**) **1 a** escape from, avoid, esp. by guile or trickery. **b** avoid doing (one's duty etc.). **c** avoid answering (a question). **2** avoid paying (tax). **3** (of a thing) elude or baffle (a person) (*the answer evades me*). [Latin *evado evas-* escape]

**evaluate** /ee-**val**-yoo-,ayt, uh-/ *v.* (**-ting**) **1** assess, appraise. **2** *Math.* find or state the number or amount of. □ **evaluation** /-**ay**-shuhn/ *n.* [French: related to VALUE]

**evanesce** /,ee-vuh-**nes**, ,ev-/ *v.* (**-cing**) *literary* fade from sight. [Latin *vanus* empty]

**evanescent** /,ee-vuh-**nes**-uhnt, ,ev-uh-/ *adj.* quickly fading. □ **evanescence** *n.*

**evangelical** /,ee-van-**jel**-i-kuhl, -uh-**kuhl**/

— *adj.* **1** of or according to the teaching of the gospel. **2** of the Protestant school maintaining the doctrine of salvation by faith. — *n.* member of this. □ **evangelicalism** *n.* **evangelically** *adv.* [Greek: related to EU-, ANGEL]

**evangelise** *v.* (also **-ize**) (**-sing** or **-zing**) **1** (also *absol.*) preach the gospel to. **2** convert to Christianity. □ **evangelisation** /-zay-shuhn/ *n.*

**evangelism** /ee-van-juh-,liz-uhm, uh-/ *n.* preaching or spreading of the gospel.

**evangelist** *n.* **1** writer of one of the four Gospels. **2** preacher of the gospel. □ **evangelistic** /ee-,van-juh-lis-tik, uh-/ *adj.*

**evaporate** /ee-vap-uh-,rayt, uh-/ *v.* (**-ting**) **1** turn from solid or liquid into vapour. **2** (cause to) lose moisture as vapour. **3** (cause to) disappear (*our courage evaporated*). □ **evaporable** *adj.* **evaporation** /-ray-shuhn/ *n.* [Latin: related to VAPOUR]

**evaporated milk** *n.* unsweetened milk concentrated by evaporation.

**evasion** /ee-vay-*zh*uhn, uh-/ *n.* **1** act or means of evading. **2** evasive answer. [Latin: related to EVADE]

**evasive** /ee-vay-siv, uh-/ *adj.* **1** seeking to evade. **2** not direct in one's answers etc. **3** enabling or effecting evasion (*evasive action*). □ **evasively** *adv.* **evasiveness** *n.*

**eve** *n.* **1** evening or day before a festival etc. (*Christmas Eve*; *eve of the funeral*). **2** time just before an event (*eve of the election*). **3** *archaic* evening. [= EVEN²]

**even¹** /ee-vuhn/ — *adj.* (**evener, evenest**) **1** level; flat and smooth (*even ground*; *even surface*). **2 a** uniform in quality, constant (*even light*; *an even speed*). **b** equal in number or amount or value etc. (*use even amounts of flour and sugar*). **c** equally balanced (*the scales are even*; *an even contest*). **3** (of accounts, affairs, a reckoning) having no debt on either side; square (*now we're even*). **4** (usu. foll. by *with*) in the same plane or line (*try to get the edges even*). **5** (of a person's temper etc.) equable, calm. **6 a** (of a number such as 4, 6) divisible by two without a remainder. **b** bearing such a number (*no parking on even dates*). **c** not involving fractions; exact (*in even dozens*). — *adv.* **1** used to invite comparison of the stated assertion, negation, etc., with an implied one that is less strong or remarkable (*never even opened [let alone read] the letter*; *does he even suspect [not to say realise] the danger?*; *ran even faster [not just as fast as before]*). **2** introducing an extreme case (*even you must realise it*; *it might even cost $100 an hour*). — *v.* (often foll. by *up*) make or become even. □ **even**

**as** at the very moment that (*even as he was bucketing the bishop, he kicked the bucket*). **even now** now as well as before. **2** at this very moment. **even so** notwithstanding that; nevertheless. **even though** despite the fact that. **get** (or **be**) **even with** have one's revenge on. □ **evenly** *adv.* **evenness** *n.* [Old English]

**even²** /ee-vuhn/ *n.* *poet.* evening; eve. [Old English]

**even chance** *n.* equal chance of success or failure.

**even-handed** *adj.* impartial.

**evening** /eev-ning/ *n.* **1** end part of the day, esp. from about 6 p.m. to bedtime. **2** a time compared with this, esp. the last part of a person's life. [Old English: related to EVEN²]

**evening dress** *n.* formal dress for evening wear.

**evening primrose** *n.* plant with pale-yellow flowers that open in the evening.

**evening star** *n.* planet, esp. Venus, conspicuous in the west after sunset.

**even money** *n.* **1** betting odds offering the gambler the chance of winning the amount staked. **2** equally likely to happen or not (*it's even money he won't turn up*).

**evens** *n.pl.* = EVEN MONEY.

**evensong** *n.* service of evening prayer in the Anglican Church. [from EVEN²]

**even-stevens** *adj.* & *adv.* intensive form of 'even' in various senses; fifty-fifty (*my chances of getting the job are even-stevens*; *split the money even-stevens*).

**event** /ee-vent, uh-/ *n.* **1** thing that happens or takes place, esp. one of importance. **2** fact of a thing's occurring (*it's all very well to be wise after the event*). **3** item in a (esp. sports) programme. □ **at all events** (or **in any event**) whatever happens. **in the event** as it turns (or turned) out. **in the event of** if (a specified thing) happens. **in the event that** if it happens that. [Latin *venio vent-* come]

■ **Usage** The phrase *in the event that* is considered awkward by some people. It can usually be avoided by rephrasing, e.g. *in the event that it rains* can be replaced by *in the event of rain*.

**eventful** *adj.* marked by noteworthy events. □ **eventfully** *adv.*

**eventide** /ee-vuhn-,tuyd/ *n.* *archaic* or *poet.* = EVENING. [related to EVEN²]

**eventual** /ee-ven-choo-uhl, uh-/ *adj.* occurring in due course; ultimate (*what was the eventual result?*). □ **eventually** *adv.* [from EVENT]

**eventuality** /ee-,ven-choo-**al**-uh-tee, uh-/ *n.* (*pl.* **-ies**) possible event or outcome (*prepared for any eventuality*).

**eventuate** /ee-**ven**-choo-,ayt, uh-/ *v.* (**-ting**) **1** turn out in a specified way; come about (*what will eventuate if I press this button?*). **2** (often foll. by *in*) result (*eventuated in a tragic loss of life*).

**ever** /ev-uh/ *adv.* **1** at all times; always (*ever hopeful; ever after*). **2** at any time (*have you ever been to Baddaginnie?*; *nothing ever happens*). **3** (used for emphasis) in any way; at all (*how ever did you do it?*). **4** (in *comb.*) constantly (*ever-present*). **5** (foll. by *so, such*) *colloq.* very; very much (*ever so easy; thanks ever so*). **6** (foll. by *compar.*) constantly, increasingly (*grew ever larger*). □ **did you ever?** *colloq.* did you ever hear or see the like? **ever since** throughout the period since. [Old English]

■ **Usage** When *ever* is used with a question word for emphasis it is written separately (see sense 3). When used with a relative pronoun or adverb to give it indefinite or general force, *ever* is written as one word with the relative pronoun or adverb, e.g. *however it's done, it's difficult.*

**evergreen** — *adj.* **1** retaining green leaves all year round. **2** always fresh; popular for a long time (*evergreen song*). — *n.* **1** evergreen plant. **2** thing which remains popular for a long time (*that play's an evergreen*).

**everlasting** — *adj.* **1** lasting for ever or for a long time. **2** (of flowers) keeping their shape and colour when dried. — *n.* **1** eternity. **2** = PAPER DAISY.

**evermore** *adv.* for ever; always.

**every** /ev-ree/ *adj.* **1** each single (*heard every word*). **2** each at a specified interval in a series (*comes every four days*). **3** all possible (*every prospect of success*). □ **every bit as** *colloq.* (in comparisons) quite as (*every bit as good as his brother*). **every now and again** (or **then**) from time to time. **every other** each second in a series (*every other day*). **every so often** occasionally. **every which way** *colloq.* **1** in all directions. **2** in a disorderly manner. [Old English: related to EVER, EACH]

**everybody** *pron.* every person.

**everyday** *attrib. adj.* **1** occurring every day. **2** suitable for or used on ordinary days (*everyday clothes*). **3** commonplace, usual (*an everyday activity*).

**Everyman** *n.* ordinary or typical human being. [name of a character in a 15th-c. morality play]

**everyone** *pron.* everybody.

**every one** *n.* each one.

**everything** *pron.* **1** all things. **2** most important thing (*speed is everything*).

**everywhere** *adv.* **1** in or to every place (*God is everywhere, they say*). **2** *colloq.* in or to many places (*I've been everywhere except to Toogoolawah*).

**evict** /ee-**vikt**, uh-/ *v.* expel (a tenant etc.) by legal process. □ **eviction** *n.* [Latin *evinco evict-* conquer]

**evidence** /ev-uh-duhns/ — *n.* **1** (often foll. by *for, of*) available facts, circumstances, etc. indicating whether or not a thing is true or valid. **2** *Law* **a** information tending to prove a fact or proposition. **b** statements or proofs admissible as testimony in a lawcourt. — *v.* (**-cing**) be evidence of; attest (*this slipshod work evidences a lack of interest*). □ **in evidence** conspicuous. [Latin *video* see]

**evident** *adj.* plain or obvious; manifest. [Latin: related to EVIDENCE]

**evidential** /,ev-uh-**den**-shuhl/ *adj.* of or providing evidence.

**evidently** *adv.* **1** seemingly; as it appears (*he was evidently unwilling*). **2** as shown by evidence.

**evil** /ee-vuhl/ — *adj.* **1** morally bad; wicked. **2** harmful or tending to harm, esp. characteristically (*smoking is evil*). **3** disagreeable (*he has an evil temper*). **4** unlucky; causing misfortune (*evil days; evil omen*). — *n.* **1** evil thing; instance of something evil. **2** evil quality; wickedness; harm (*chose the lesser of two evils*). □ **evilly** *adv.* [Old English]

**evildoer** *n.* sinner. □ **evildoing** *n.*

**evil eye** *n.* gaze that is superstitiously believed to cause harm.

**evince** /ee-**vins**, uh-/ *v.* (**-cing**) indicate, display (a quality, feeling, etc.) (*evinced a desire to eat a witchetty grub*). [Latin: related to EVICT]

**eviscerate** /ee-**vis**-uh-,rayt, uh-/ *v.* (**-ting**) disembowel. □ **evisceration** /-ray-shuhn/ *n.* [Latin: related to VISCERA]

**evocative** /ee-**vok**-uh-tiv, uh-/ *adj.* tending to evoke (esp. feelings or memories) (*clothes evocative of the sixties*). □ **evocatively** *adv.* **evocativeness** *n.*

**evoke** /ee-**vohk**, uh-/ *v.* (**-king**) inspire or draw forth (memories, a response, etc.) (*evoked the past; his tears evoked no response from her*). □ **evocation** /,ev-uh-**kay**-shuhn/ *n.* [Latin *voco* call]

**evolution** /,ee-vuh-**loo**-shuhn, ,ev-uh-/ *n.* **1** gradual development, esp. from a simple to a more complex form (*the evolution of the computer*). **2** development of species from earlier forms, as an explanation of their origins. **3** unfolding of events etc. (*evolution of the plot*). **4** the giving off or evolving of gas, heat, etc. □ **evolutionary** *adj.* [Latin: related to EVOLVE]

**evolutionist** *n.* person who regards evolution as explaining the origin of species.

**evolve** /ee-**volv**, uh-/ *v.* (**-ving**) **1** develop gradually (a theory, plan, etc.) (*evolved a scheme to extract sunbeams from cucumbers*). **2** (of species) develop from lower to higher forms. **3** unfold; open out (*as the plot of the play evolved*). **4** give off (gas, heat, etc.). [Latin *volvo volut-* roll]

**ewe** /yoo/ *n.* female sheep. [Old English]

**ewer** /**yoo**-uh/ *n.* water-jug with a wide mouth. [Latin *aqua* water]

**ex¹** *prep.* **1** (of goods) sold from (*ex-warehouse*). **2** (of stocks or shares) without, excluding. [Latin, = out of]

**ex²** *n. colloq.* former husband or wife, boyfriend or girlfriend. [see EX-¹ 2]

**ex-¹** *prefix* (also before some consonants **e-**, **ef-** before *f*) **1** forming verbs meaning: **a** out, forth (*exclude; exit*). **b** upward (*extol*). **c** thoroughly (*excruciate*). **d** bring into a state (*exasperate*). **e** remove or free from (*expatriate; exonerate*). **2** forming nouns from titles of office, status, etc., meaning 'formerly' (*ex-convict; ex-president*). [Latin from *ex* out of]

**ex-²** *prefix* out (*exodus*). [Greek]

**exacerbate** /ek-**sas**-uh-,bayt, -zas-, uhg-/ *v.* (**-ting**) **1** make (pain, anger, etc.) worse. **2** irritate (a person). □ **exacerbation** /-**bay**-shuhn/ *n.* [Latin *acerbus* bitter]

**exact** /eg-**zakt**, uhg-/ — *adj.* **1** accurate, correct in all details (*exact description*). **2** precise (*that is my exact point*). — *v.* **1** demand and enforce payment of (money etc.). **2** demand; insist on; require (*exacted silence from the witnesses by threatening them with death*). □ **exactness** *n.* [Latin *exigo exact-* require]

**exacting** *adj.* **1** making great demands (*a very exacting teacher*). **2** requiring much effort (*a very exacting task*).

**exaction** /eg-**zak**-shuhn, uhg-/ *n.* **1** act or instance of exacting or process of being exacted. **2 a** illegal or exorbitant demand; extortion. **b** sum or thing exacted.

**exactitude** *n.* exactness, precision.

**exactly** *adv.* **1** precisely (*worked it out exactly*). **2** (said in reply) I quite agree. **3** just (*that's exactly what I like*).

**exaggerate** /eg-**zaj**-uh-,rayt, uhg-/ *v.* (**-ting**) **1** (also *absol.*) give an impression of (a thing), esp. in speech or writing, that makes it seem larger or greater etc. than it really is. **2** increase beyond normal or due proportions (*exaggerated politeness*). □ **exaggeratedly** *adv.* **exaggeratingly** *adv.* **exaggeration** /-**ray**-shuhn/ *n.* **exaggerative** /-ruh-tiv/ *adj.* **exaggerator** *n.* [Latin *agger* heap]

**exalt** /eg-**zawlt**, uhg-, -**zolt**/ *v.* **1** raise in rank or power etc. **2** praise highly. **3** (usu. as **exalted** *adj.*) make lofty or noble (*exalted aims; exalted style*). □ **exaltation** /-**tay**-shuhn/ *n.* [Latin *altus* high]

■ *Usage* Exalt is often confused with *exult*.

**exam** /eg-**zam**, uhg-/ *n.* = EXAMINATION 3.

**examination** /eg-,zam-uh-**nay**-shuhn, uhg-/ *n.* **1** act or instance of examining or state of being examined. **2** detailed inspection. **3** test of proficiency or knowledge by questions. **4** instance of examining or being examined medically. **5** formal questioning of a witness etc. in court.

**examine** /eg-**zam**-uhn, uhg-/ *v.* (**-ning**) **1** inquire into the nature or condition etc. of. **2** look closely or analytically at. **3** test the proficiency of, esp. by examination. **4** check the health of (a patient). **5** formally question in court. [Latin *examen* tongue of a balance]

**examinee** *n.* **1** person who is a candidate in an examination. **2** person under examination.

**examiner** *n.* **1** person appointed to examine a pupil, candidate, etc., or to set an examination. **2** person who inquires into facts or investigates the nature or condition of something.

**example** /eg-**zahm**-puhl, -zam-, uhg-/ *n.* **1** thing characteristic of its kind or illustrating a general rule. **2** person, thing, or piece of conduct, in terms of its fitness to be imitated (*must set him an example*; *you are a bad example to your children*). **3** circumstance or treatment seen as a warning to others; person so treated (*shall make an example of you*). **4** problem or exercise designed to illustrate a rule. □ **for example** by way of illustration. [Latin *exemplum*: related to EXEMPT]

**exasperate** /eg-**zah**-spuh-,rayt, -zas-puh-, uhg-/ *v.* (**-ting**) irritate intensely. □ **exasperation** /-**ray**-shuhn/ *n.* [Latin *asper* rough]

**ex cathedra** /,eks kuh-**thee**-druh/ *adj. & adv.* **1** (of a papal pronouncement) with full authority (involving infallibility as doctrinally defined). **2** (in an extended sense) authoritative(ly) (*some husbands try to lay down the law ex cathedra to their wives*). [Latin, = from the chair (of St. Peter)]

**excavate** /eks-kuh-ˌvayt/ v. (-ting) **1 a** make (a hole or channel) by digging. **b** dig out material from (the ground). **2** reveal or extract by digging. **3** (also *absol.*) *Archaeol.* dig systematically to explore (a site). □ **excavation** /-vay-shuhn/ n. **excavator** n. [Latin *excavo*: related to CAVE]

**exceed** /ek-seed, uhk-/ v. **1** (often foll. by *by* an amount) be more or greater than (in number, extent, etc.) (*exceeded the word limit by 5,000 words*). **2** go beyond or do more than is warranted by (a set limit, esp. of one's authority, instructions, or rights) (*exceeded his authority*). **3** surpass, excel (a person or achievement). [Latin *excedo* -*cess*- go beyond]

**exceedingly** /ek-see-ding-lee, uhk-/ adv. extremely.

**excel** /ek-sel, uhk-/ v. (-ll-) **1** be superior to; surpass. **2** be pre-eminent or the most outstanding (*excels at sports*). □ **excel oneself** surpass one's previous performance. [Latin *excello* be eminent]

**excellence** /ek-suh-luhns/ n. state of excelling; outstanding merit or quality. [Latin: related to EXCEL]

**Excellency** n. (pl. **-ies**) (usu. prec. by *Your, His, Her, Their*) title used in addressing or referring to certain high officials, e.g. ambassadors and governors.

**excellent** adj. extremely good; pre-eminent.

**excentric** var. of ECCENTRIC (in technical senses).

**except** /ek-sept, uhk-/ — v. (often as **excepted** adj. placed after the object) exclude from a general statement, condition, etc. (*excepted him from the amnesty; present company excepted*). — prep. (often foll. by *for*) not including; other than (*all failed except him; all here except for John; is all right except that it is too long*). — conj. archaic unless (*except he be born again*). [Latin *excipio* -*cept*- take out]

**excepting** prep. = EXCEPT prep.

■ **Usage** *Excepting* should be used only after *not* and *always*; otherwise, *except* should be used (*all are to blame, not excepting you*).

**exception** /ek-sep-shuhn, uhk-/ n. **1** act or instance of excepting or state of being excepted (*made an exception in my case*). **2** thing that has been or will be excepted. **3** instance that does not follow a rule. □ **take exception** (often foll. by *to*) object; be resentful (about) (*took exception to my dog's barking*). **with the exception of** except; not including.

**exceptionable** adj. open to objection (*your morals are exceptionable*).

■ **Usage** *Exceptionable* is sometimes confused with *exceptional*.

**exceptional** adj. **1** forming an exception; unusual (*exceptional circumstances*). **2** outstanding (*an exceptional athlete*). □ **exceptionally** adv.

■ **Usage** See note at *exceptionable*.

**excerpt** — n. /ek-serpt/ short extract from a book, film, musical composition, etc. — v. /ek-serpt/ (also *absol.*) take excerpts from (a book etc.). □ **excerption** /-serp-shuhn/ n. [Latin *carpo* pluck]

**excess** /uhk-ses, ek-ses/ — n. **1** state or instance of exceeding. **2** amount by which one thing exceeds another. **3 a** overstepping of accepted limits of moderation, esp. in eating or drinking. **b** (in *pl.*) outrageous or immoderate behaviour (*condemned their excesses*). **4** extreme or improper degree or extent (*an excess of cruelty*). **5** part of an insurance claim to be paid by the insured. — attrib. adj. usu. /ek-ses/ **1** that exceeds a limited or prescribed amount (*excess weight*). **2** required as extra payment (*excess postage*). □ **in** (or **to**) **excess** exceeding the proper amount or degree. **in excess of** more than; exceeding. [Latin: related to EXCEED]

**excessive** /ek-ses-iv, uhk-/ adj. too much or too great. □ **excessively** adv.

**exchange** /eks-chaynj, uhks-/ — n. **1** act or instance of giving of one thing (or person) and receiving of another in its place (*exchange of gifts; exchange of prisoners; exchange of blows*). **2** thing (or person) that is offered or given in exchange. **3** giving of money for its equivalent in the money of the same or another country. **4 a** centre where telephone connections are made. **b** office where information is given or a service provided. **5** place of exchange; place where merchants, bankers, etc. transact business. **6** system of settling debts without the use of money, by bills of exchange. **7** short conversation, esp. a disagreement or quarrel (*I came off worse in that exchange*). **8** (attrib.) forming part of an exchange, e.g. of personnel between institutions (*exchange student*). — v. (-ging) **1** (often foll. by *for*) give or receive (one thing) in place of another. **2** give and receive as equivalents (e.g. things or people, blows, greetings, information, etc.); give one and receive another of. **3** (often foll. by *with*) make an exchange. □ **in exchange** (often foll. by *for*) as a thing exchanged (for). □ **exchangeable** adj. [French: related to CHANGE]

**exchange rate** n. value of one currency in terms of another.

**exchequer** /eks-**chek**-uh/ n. **1** treasury of a nation. **2** money of a private individual or group. [medieval Latin *scaccarium* chessboard (its original sense, with reference to keeping accounts on a chequered cloth)]

**excise**[1] /**ek**-suyz, ek-**suys**/ — n. **1** tax on goods produced or sold within the country of origin. **2** tax on certain licences. — v. (**-sing**) charge excise on. [Dutch *excijs* from Romanic: related to Latin CENSUS tax]

**excise**[2] /ek-**suyz**/ v. (**-sing**) **1** remove (a passage from a book etc.). **2** cut out (an organ etc.) by surgery. □ **excision** /ek-**sizh**-uhn/ n. [Latin *excido* cut out]

**excitable** /ek-**suy**-tuh-buhl, uhk-/ adj. easily excited. □ **excitability** /-**bil**-uh-tee/ n. **excitably** adv.

**excite** /ek-**suyt**, uhk-/ v. (**-ting**) **1 a** rouse the emotions of (a person). **b** bring into play; rouse up (feelings etc.) (*the characters in this novel excite little interest*). **c** arouse sexually. **2** provoke (an action etc.) (*tried to excite an uprising*). **3** stimulate (an organism, tissue, etc.) to activity. **4** *Physics* **a** cause (a substance) to emit radiation. **b** put (an atom etc.) into a state of higher energy. □ **excitant** /ek-**suy**-tuhnt/ adj. & n. **excitation** /,ek-suy-**tay**-shuhn/ n. **excitative** /ek-**suy**-tuh-tiv/ adj. **excitatory** /ek-**suy**-tuh-tuh-ree, ek-suy-**tay**-tuh-ree, -tree/ adj. **excited** adj. **excitedly** adv. **exciter** n. (esp. in sense 4). [Latin *cieo cit-* stir up]

**excitement** n. **1** excited state of mind. **2** exciting thing.

**exciting** adj. arousing great interest or enthusiasm. □ **excitingly** adv.

**exclaim** /ek-**sklaym**/ v. **1** cry out suddenly, esp. in anger, surprise, pain, etc. **2** (foll. by *that*) utter by exclaiming. [Latin: related to CLAIM]

**exclamation** /,eks-kluh-**may**-shuhn/ n. **1** act or instance of exclaiming. **2** word(s) exclaimed. **3** strong sudden cry. [Latin: related to EXCLAIM]

**exclamation mark** n. punctuation mark (!) indicating exclamation (see panel).

**exclamatory** /eks-**klam**-uh-tuh-ree, -tree/ adj. of or serving as an exclamation.

**exclude** /ek-**sklood**, uhk-/ v. (**-ding**) **1** keep out (a person or thing) from a place, group, privilege, etc. **2** remove from consideration (*no theory can be excluded*). **3** make impossible, preclude (*excluded all doubt*). □ **exclusion** n. [Latin *excludo -clus-* shut out]

**exclusionist** /ek-**skloo**-zhuh-nuhst, uhk-/ — adj. **1** favouring exclusion, esp. from rights or privileges. **2** *hist.* opposed to the integration of ex-convicts into Australian society. — n. person favouring exclusion.

**exclusive** /ek-**skloo**-siv, uhk-/ adj. **1** excluding other things. **2** (*predic.*; foll. by *of*) not including; except for (*my price is exclusive of fees and other charges*). **3** tending to exclude others, esp. socially (*exclusive club*). **4** high-class (*exclusive restaurant*). **5 a** (of a commodity) not obtainable elsewhere. **b** (of a newspaper article, television programme, etc.) not published or broadcast elsewhere. **6** (foll. by *to*) restricted or limited to; existing or available in (*exclusive to our City store*). **7** (of terms, numbers, etc.) excluding what is specified (*bring me all issues of the journal, numbers 40–49 exclusive*). **8** employed or followed or held to the exclusion of all else; single, sole (*my exclusive occupation*; *exclusive rights*). — n. article published by only one newspaper etc. □ **exclusively** adv. **exclusiveness** n. **exclusivity** /-**siv**-uh-tee/ n. [medieval Latin: related to EXCLUDE]

**excommunicate** — v. /,eks-kuh-**myoo**-nuh-,kayt/ (**-ting**) officially exclude (a person) from membership and esp. sacraments of the Church. — adj. /,eks-kuh-**myoo**-ni-kuht/ excommunicated. — n. /,eks-kuh-**myoo**-ni-kuht/ excommunicated person. □ **excommunication** /-**kay**-shuhn/ n. [Latin: related to COMMON]

**excoriate** /ek-**skaw**-ree-,ayt/ v. (**-ting**) **1 a** remove skin from (a person etc.) by abrasion. **b** strip off (skin). **2** censure severely. □ **excoriation** /-**ay**-shuhn/ n. [Latin *corium* hide]

**excrement** /**eks**-kruh-muhnt/ n. waste discharged from the body, esp. faeces. □ **excremental** /-**men**-tuhl/ adj. [Latin: related to EXCRETE]

---

**Exclamation mark !**
This is used instead of a full stop at the end of a sentence to show that the speaker or writer is very angry, enthusiastic, insistent, disappointed, hurt, surprised, etc., e.g.

| | |
|---|---|
| *I am not pleased at all!* | *I wish I could have gone!* |
| *I just love lollies!* | *Ouch!* |
| *Go away!* | *He didn't even say goodbye!* |

**excrescence** /ek-**skres**-uhns/ n. **1** abnormal or morbid outgrowth on the body or a plant. **2** ugly addition (*this new house is an excrescence in our old street*). □ **excrescent** adj. [Latin *cresco* grow]

**excreta** /ek-**skree**-tuh/ n.pl. waste discharged from the body, esp. faeces and urine. [Latin: related to EXCRETE]

**excrete** /ek-**skreet**, uhk-/ v. (-**ting**) (of an animal or plant) expel (waste matter). □ **excretion** n. **excretory** adj. [Latin *cerno cret-* sift]

**excruciating** /ek-**skroo**-shee-,ay-ting, uhk-/ adj. causing acute mental or physical pain. □ **excruciatingly** adv. [Latin *crucio* torment]

**exculpate** /eks-kul-,payt/ v. (-**ting**) *formal* (often foll. by *from*) free from blame; clear of a charge. □ **exculpation** /-**pay**-shuhn/ n. **exculpatory** /-**kul**-puh-tuh-ree, -tree/ adj. [Latin *culpa* blame]

**excursion** /ek-**sker**-shuhn, uhk-/ n. **1** journey (usu. a day-trip) to a place and back, made for pleasure or other purpose. **2** a digression (*the physicist made a brief excursion into fantasy at the end of his lecture*). [Latin *excurro -curs-* run out]

**excursive** /ek-**sker**-siv, uhk-/ adj. *literary* digressive. □ **excursively** adv. **excursiveness** n.

**excuse** — v. /ek-**skyooz**, uhk-/ (-**sing**) **1** try to lessen the blame attaching to (a person, act, or fault). **2** (of a fact) serve as a reason to judge (a person or act) less severely. **3** (often foll. by *from*) release (a person) from a duty etc. **4** forgive (a fault or offence) (*please excuse my lateness*). **5** (foll. by *for*) forgive (a person) for (a fault) (*excuse me for being late*). **6** *refl.* apologise for leaving (*excused himself and left the meeting*). — n. /ek-**skyoos**, uhk-/ **1** reason put forward to mitigate or justify an offence. **2** apology (*made my excuses*). **3** (foll. by *for*) poor or inadequate example of (*this scrawl is a poor excuse for an essay*). □ **be excused** be allowed to leave the room etc. or be absent. **excuse me** polite preface to an interruption etc., or to disagreeing. □ **excusable** /-**skyoo**-zuh-buhl/ adj. [Latin *causa* accusation]

**execrable** /ek-suh-kruh-buhl/ adj. abominable, detestable (*execrable behaviour*). [Latin: related to EXECRATE]

**execrate** /ek-suh-,krayt/ v. (-**ting**) **1** express or feel abhorrence for. **2** (also *absol.*) curse (a person or thing). □ **execration** /-**kray**-shuhn/ n. **execrative** adj. **execratory** adj. [Latin *exsecror* curse: related to SACRED]

**execute** /ek-suh-,kyoot/ v. (-**ting**) **1 a** carry out, perform (a plan, duty, command, etc.). **b** *Computing* carry out (an instruction or program). **2 a** carry out a design for (a product of art or skill) (*executed the mural in three days*). **b** perform (a musical composition, dance, etc.). **3** carry out a death sentence on. **4** make (a legal instrument) valid by signing, sealing, etc. **5** put into effect (a judicial sentence, the terms of a will, etc.). □ **executable** adj. [Latin *sequor secut-* follow]

**execution** /,ek-suh-**kyoo**-shuhn/ n. **1** act or instance of carrying out or performing something; performance. **2** technique or style of performance in the arts, esp. music (*her execution was flawless*). **3** carrying out of a death sentence. [Latin: related to EXECUTE]

**executioner** n. person who carries out a death sentence.

**executive** /eg-**zek**-yuh-tiv, uhg-/ — n. **1** person or body with managerial or administrative responsibility in a business organisation etc. **2** branch of a government etc. concerned with executing laws, agreements, etc., or with other administration or management. — adj. concerned with executing laws, agreements, etc., or with other administration or management. [medieval Latin: related to EXECUTE]

**Executive Council** n. constitutional body in the Commonwealth of Australia (presided over by the Governor General and consisting of government ministers) responsible for the implementation of the laws.

**executor** /eg-**zek**-yuh-tuh, uhg-/ n. (*fem.* **executrix** /-triks/) person appointed by a testator to administer his or her will. □ **executorial** /-**taw**-ree-uhl/ adj. **executorship** n. **executory** adj.

**exegesis** /,ek-suh-**jee**-suhs/ n. (*pl.* **exegeses** /-seez/) critical explanation of a text, esp. of Scripture. □ **exegetic** /-**jet**-ik/ adj. **exegetical** adj. [Greek *hēgeomai* lead]

**exemplar** /eg-**zem**-pluh, -plah, uhg-/ n. **1** model or pattern. **2** typical or parallel instance. [Latin: related to EXAMPLE]

**exemplary** adj. **1** fit to be imitated; outstandingly good (*exemplary behaviour*). **2** serving as a warning (*exemplary punishment*). **3** illustrative; representative. [Latin: related to EXAMPLE]

**exemplify** /eg-**zem**-pluh-,fuy, uhg-/ v. (-**ies**, -**ied**) **1** illustrate by example (*you need to exemplify this point by quoting from the poem*). **2** be an example of (*this exemplifies the need for greater security*). □ **exemplification** /-fuh-**kay**-shuhn/ n.

**exemplum** /eg-**zem**-pluhm, uhg-/ n. (*pl.* **exempla** /-pluh/) example or model, esp.

a moralising or illustrative story (*Christ's exemplum of the Good Samaritan*). [Latin]

**exempt** /eg-**zempt**, uhg-/ — *adj.* (often foll. by *from*) free from an obligation, duty, liability, etc. imposed on others (*is exempt from military service*). — *v.* (foll. by *from*) make exempt. □ **exemption** *n.* [Latin *eximo -empt-* take out]

**exequies** /**ek**-suh-kweez/ *n.pl.* formal funeral rites. [Latin *exsequiae* from *exsequor* follow after]

**exercise** /**ek**-suh-ˌsuyz/ — *n.* **1** activity requiring physical effort, done as training or to sustain or improve health. **2** mental or spiritual activity, esp. as practice to develop a faculty (*spiritual exercises of St. Ignatius*). **3 a** (often in *pl.*) particular task or set of tasks devised as exercise, practice in a technique, etc. (*Czerny's piano exercises*). **b** short essay or translation written by students in a school etc. **4 a** use or application of a mental faculty, right, etc. (*an exercise in concentration*). **b** practice of an ability, quality, etc. (*the exercise of tolerance*). **5** (often in *pl.*) military drill or manoeuvres. **6** (foll. by *in*) process directed at or concerned with something specified (*was an exercise in public relations*). — *v.* (**-sing**) **1** use or apply (a faculty, right, influence, restraint, etc.) (*exercised his intuition*; *exercised his right to keep silent*; *exercised her authority*; *exercised all due care*). **2** perform (a function) (*exercised his duty as ombudsman*). **3 a** take (esp. physical) exercise. **b** provide (an animal) with exercise. **4 a** tax the powers of (*this problem will exercise their minds*). **b** perplex, worry (*was much exercised by fear for her safety*). [Latin *exerceo* keep busy]

**exert** /eg-**zert**, uhg-/ *v.* **1** bring to bear, use (a quality, force, influence, etc.) (*exerted pressure on the members*). **2** *refl.* (often foll. by *for*, or *to* + infin.) use one's efforts or endeavours; strive (*exerted herself to put the past behind her*). □ **exertion** *n.* [Latin *exsero exsert-* put forth]

**exeunt** /**ek**-see-ˌuunt/ *v.* (as a stage direction) (actors) leave the stage. [Latin, = they go out: related to EXIT]

**exfoliate** /eks-**foh**-lee-ˌayt/ *v.* (**-ting**) **1** (of bone, the skin, a mineral, etc.) come off in scales or layers. **2** (of a tree) throw off layers of bark. □ **exfoliation** /-**ay**-shuhn/ *n.* [Latin *folium* leaf]

**ex gratia** /eks **gray**-shuh/ — *adv.* as a favour; not from (esp. legal) obligation. — *attrib. adj.* granted on this basis (*ex gratia payment*). [Latin, = from favour]

**exhale** /eks-**hayl**/ *v.* (**-ling**) **1** breathe out (esp. air or smoke) from the lungs. **2** give off or be given off in vapour. □ **exhalation** /ˌeks-huh-**lay**-shuhn/ *n.* [French from Latin *halo* breathe]

**exhaust** /eg-**zawst**, uhg-/ — *v.* **1** consume or use up the whole of (*the entire stock is exhausted*). **2** (often as **exhausted** *adj.* or **exhausting** *adj.*) use up the strength or resources of; tire out (*he has exhausted my patience*; *this work is exhausting*). **3** study or expound (a subject) completely (*exhausted all the known sources*). **4** (often foll. by *of*) empty (a vessel etc.) of its contents. — *n.* **1** waste gases etc. expelled from an engine after combustion. **2** (also **exhaust pipe**) pipe or system by which these are expelled. **3** process of expulsion of these gases. □ **exhaustible** *adj.* [Latin *haurio haust-* drain]

**exhaustion** /eg-**zaws**-chuhn, uhg-/ *n.* **1** act or instance of exhausting or state of being exhausted. **2** total loss of strength.

**exhaustive** /eg-**zaws**-tiv, uhg-/ *adj.* thorough, comprehensive (*exhaustive research*). □ **exhaustively** *adv.* **exhaustiveness** *n.*

**exhibit** /eg-**zib**-uht, uhg-/ — *v.* (**-t-**) **1** show or reveal, esp. publicly (*exhibited her paintings*). **2** display (a quality etc.) (*exhibited great impatience*). — *n.* **1** thing or collection of things forming part or all of an exhibition. **2** document or other item or object produced in a lawcourt as evidence. □ **exhibitor** *n.* [Latin *exhibeo -hibit-*]

**exhibition** /ˌek-suh-**bish**-uhn/ *n.* **1** display (esp. public) of works of art, industrial products, etc. **2** act or instance of exhibiting or state of being exhibited. **3** scholarship, esp. from the funds of a school, college, etc. □ **make an exhibition of oneself** behave so as to appear ridiculous or foolish.

**exhibitionism** *n.* **1** tendency towards attention-seeking behaviour. **2** *Psychol.* mental condition characterised by the compulsion to display one's genitals in public. □ **exhibitionist** *n.*

**exhilarate** /eg-**zil**-uh-ˌrayt, uhg-/ *v.* (often as **exhilarating** *adj.* or **exhilarated** *adj.*) affect with great liveliness or joy; raise the spirits of. □ **exhilaration** /-**ray**-shuhn/ *n.* [Latin *hilaris* cheerful]

**exhort** /eg-**zawt**, uhg-/ *v.* (often foll. by *to* + infin.) urge strongly or earnestly. □ **exhortation** /ˌeg-zaw-**tay**-shuhn/ *n.* **exhortative** /-tuh-tiv/ *adj.* **exhortatory** /-tuh-tuh-ree, -**tay**-tuh-ree, -tree/ *adj.* [Latin *exhortor* encourage]

**exhume** /eks-**hyoom**/ *v.* (**-ming**) dig up (esp. a buried corpse). □ **exhumation** /-**may**-shuhn/ *n.* [Latin *humus* ground]

**exigency** /ek-suh-juhn-see, uhg-**zij**-uhn-/ *n. (pl.* **-ies**) (also **exigence**) **1** urgent need or demand (*the exigencies of the long-term unemployed*). **2** emergency (*we need quick help in this exigency*). □ **exigent** *adj.* [Latin *exigo* EXACT]

**exiguous** /eg-**zig**-yoo-uhs, uhg-/ *adj.* scanty, small (*trying to make do on an exiguous income*). □ **exiguity** /-**gyoo**-uh-tee/ *n.* **exiguousness** *n.* [Latin]

**exile** /ek-suyl, eg-zuyl/ — *n.* **1** expulsion from one's native land or (**internal exile**) native town etc. **2** long absence abroad, esp. enforced. **3** exiled person. — *v.* (**-ling**) send into exile. [French from Latin]

**exist** /eg-zist, uhg-/ *v.* **1** have a place in objective reality (*do ghosts exist?*). **2 a** have being under specified conditions (*air does not exist in a vacuum*). **b** (foll. by *as*) exist in the form of (*exists as a vapour*). **3** (of circumstances etc.) occur; be found (*as long as these conditions exist*). **4** live with no pleasure under adverse conditions; barely maintain life (*felt he was merely existing, not living*). **5** continue in being; maintain life (*we need food to exist*). **6** live (*how can you exist in this dirty, crowded city?*). [Latin *existo*]

**existence** *n.* **1** fact or condition of being or existing (*no longer in existence*). **2** continuance in life or being (*they depend on the dole for their existence*). **3** manner of one's existence or living, esp. under adverse conditions (*a wretched existence*). **4** all that exists. □ **existent** *adj.*

**existential** /,eg-zis-**ten**-shuhl/ *adj.* **1** of or relating to existence. **2** *Philos.* concerned with existence, esp. with human existence as viewed by existentialism. □ **existentially** *adv.*

**existentialism** *n.* philosophical theory emphasising the existence of the individual as a free and self-determining agent. □ **existentialist** *n. & adj.*

**exit** /eg-zuht, ek-suht/ — *n.* **1** passage or door by which to leave a room etc. **2** act or right of going out. **3** place where vehicles can leave a major road etc. **4** actor's departure from the stage. — *v.* (**-t-**) **1** go out of a room etc. **2** leave the stage (also as a direction: *exit Macbeth*). [Latin *exeo exit-* go out]

**exit poll** *n.* poll of people leaving a polling-station, asking how they voted.

**ex libris** /eks **lib**-ruhs/ *n. (pl.* same) a usu. decorated label bearing the owner's name, pasted into the front of a book. [Latin, = among the books (of)]

**exo-** *comb. form* external. [Greek *exō* outside]

**exocrine** /ek-soh-,kruyn/ *adj.* (of a gland) secreting through a duct. [Greek *krinō* sift]

**exodus** /ek-suh-duhs/ *n.* **1** mass departure. **2** (**Exodus**) Biblical departure of the Israelites from Egypt. [Greek *hodos* way]

**ex officio** /,eks uh-**fish**-ee-oh/ *adv. & attrib. adj.* by virtue of one's office. [Latin]

**exogamy** /ek-**sog**-uh-mee/ *n.* **1** custom by which a marriage partner is chosen from outside one's own tribe or group (opp. ENDOGAMY). **2** *Biol.* fusion of reproductive cells from distantly related or unrelated individuals. □ **exogamous** *adj.*

**exonerate** /eg-**zon**-uh-,rayt, uhg-/ *v.* (**-ting**) (often foll. by *from*) free or declare free from blame etc. □ **exoneration** /-,ray-shuhn/ *n.* [Latin *onus oner-* burden]

**exorbitant** /eg-**zaw**-buh-tuhnt, uhg-/ *adj.* (of a price, demand, etc.) grossly excessive. [Latin: related to ORBIT]

**exorcise** /ek-saw-,suyz/ *v.* (also **-ize**) (**-sing** or **-zing**) **1** expel (a supposed evil spirit) by prayers or other religious ritual etc. **2** (often foll. by *of*) free (a person or place) in this way. □ **exorcism** *n.* **exorcist** *n.* [Greek *horkos* oath]

**exordium** /ek-**saw**-dee-uhm/ *n. (pl.* **-s** or **-dia**) introductory part, esp. of a discourse or treatise. [Latin *exordior* begin]

**exoskeleton** /,ek-soh-**skel**-uh-tuhn/ *n.* rigid external covering for the body in certain animals, esp. arthropods (e.g. crustaceans), providing support and protection (opp. ENDOSKELETON). □ **exoskeletal** *adj.*

**exosphere** /ek-soh-,sfeer/ *n.* layer of atmosphere furthest from the earth.

**exotic** /eg-**zot**-ik, uhg-/ — *adj.* **1** introduced from a foreign country; not native (*exotic plant*). **2** attractively or remarkably strange or unusual. — *n.* exotic plant, person, or thing. □ **exotically** *adv.* [Greek *exō* outside]

**exotica** *n.pl.* strange or rare objects.

**expand** /ek-**spand**, uhk-/ *v.* **1** increase in size or bulk or importance (*air expands when warm*; *our trade with Asia is expanding*). **2** open or stretch out; unfold (*you need to expand the concertina more*; *the eagle expanded its wings*). **3** (often foll. by *on*) give a fuller account (*you need to expand the paragraph on Aboriginal hunting implements*; *expand on this theme*). **4** become more genial (*after a drink or two he began to expand*). **5** set or write out in full (something condensed or abbreviated). **6** spread out flat. □ **expandable** *adj.* [Latin *pando pans-* spread]

**expanse** /ek-**spans**, uhk-/ *n.* **1** wide continuous area of land, space, etc. **2** an amount of expansion. [as EXPAND]

**expansion** /ek-**span**-shuhn, uhk-/ n. **1** act or instance of expanding or state of being expanded. **2** enlargement of the scale or scope of (esp. commercial) operations. **3** increase in the amount of a nation's territory or area of control.

**expansionism** n. advocacy of expansion, esp. of a nation's territory. □ **expansionist** n. & adj.

**expansive** /ek-**span**-siv, uhk-/ adj. **1** able or tending to expand. **2** extensive, wide-ranging. **3** (of a person, feelings, or speech) effusive, open, not inhibited (was in an expansive mood). □ **expansively** adv. **expansiveness** n.

**expatiate** /ek-**spay**-shee-,ayt, uhk-/ v. (**-ting**) (usu. foll. by on, upon) speak or write at length (expatiated on the un-Australianness of racism). □ **expatiation** /-ay-shuhn/ n. **expatiatory** /-shee-uh-tuh-ree, -tree/ adj. [Latin spatium SPACE]

**expatriate** — adj. /eks-**pat**-ree-uht/ **1** living abroad. **2** exiled. — n. /eks-**pat**-ree-uht, -**pay**-tree-uht/ expatriate person. — v. /eks-**pat**-ree-,ayt/ (**-ting**) **1** expel (a person) from his or her native country. **2** refl. renounce one's citizenship. □ **expatriation** /-ay-shuhn/ n. [Latin patria native land]

**expect** /ek-**spekt**, uhk-/ v. **1 a** regard as likely; assume as a future event or occurrence (I expect that we will win the election). **b** look for as appropriate or one's due (I expect cooperation). **2** colloq. think, suppose (I expect we'll be on time). □ **be expecting** colloq. be pregnant (with). [Latin specto look]

**expectancy** /ek-**spek**-tuhn-see, uhk-/ n. (pl. **-ies**) **1 a** state of expectation. **b** thing expected (life expectancy). **2** prospect, esp. of future possession. **3** (foll. by of) prospective chance (the expectancy of a better life after death).

**expectant** /ek-**spek**-tuhnt, uhk-/ adj. **1** hopeful, expecting. **2** having an expectation. **3** having a baby (said of the mother or father). □ **expectantly** adv.

**expectation** /,ek-spek-**tay**-shuhn/ n. **1** act or instance of expecting or looking forward. **2** thing expected or hoped for. **3** (foll. by of) probability of an event. **4** (in pl.) one's prospects of inheritance.

**expectorant** /ek-**spek**-tuh-ruhnt/ — adj. causing the coughing out of phlegm etc. — n. expectorant medicine.

**expectorate** /ek-**spek**-tuh-,rayt/ v. (**-ting**) (also absol.) cough or spit out (phlegm etc.) from the chest or lungs. □ **expectoration** /-ray-shuhn/ n. [Latin pectus pector- breast]

**expedient** /ek-**spee**-dee-uhnt, uhk-/ — adj. advantageous; advisable on prac-

tical rather than moral grounds (it may be expedient to deny that you were there). — n. means of attaining an end; resource (when every expedient had been exhausted, he tried blackmail). □ **expedience** n. **expediency** n. [related to EXPEDITE]

**expedite** /**eks**-puh-,duyt/ v. (**-ting**) **1** assist the progress of; hasten (an action, process, etc.) (we need to expedite this matter). **2** accomplish (business) quickly. [Latin expedio from pes ped- foot]

**expedition** /,eks-puh-**dish**-uhn/ n. **1** journey or voyage for a particular purpose, esp. exploration or scientific research. **2** people etc. undertaking this. **3** speed (use all the expedition possible). [Latin: related to EXPEDITE]

**expeditionary** adj. of or used in an expedition.

**expeditious** /,eks-puh-**dish**-uhs/ adj. acting or done with speed and efficiency.

**expel** /ek-**spel**, uhk-/ v. (**-ll-**) (often foll. by from) **1** deprive (a person) of membership etc. of a school, society, etc. **2** force out, eject (a thing from its container etc.) (expelled the spent cartridge from the gun; expelled air from his lungs). **3** order or force to leave a building etc. [Latin pello puls- drive]

**expend** /ek-**spend**, uhk-/ v. spend or use up (money, time, etc.). [Latin pendo pens- weigh]

**expendable** adj. **1** that may be sacrificed or dispensed with, esp. to achieve a purpose (considered their lives expendable). **2** not regarded as worth preserving or saving.

**expenditure** /ek-**spen**-duh-chuh, uhk-/ n. **1** process or instance of spending or using up. **2** thing (esp. money) expended.

**expense** /ek-**spens**, uhk-/ n. **1** cost incurred; payment of money (the expense of feeding a family; went to great expense). **2** (usu. in pl.) **a** costs incurred in doing a job etc. (will pay your expenses). **b** amount paid to reimburse this (offered me $100 a day expenses). **3** thing on which money is spent (the car is a real expense). **4** expenditure (of other than money) (at great expense of time and energy). □ **at the expense of** so as to cause loss or harm to; costing. [Latin expensa: related to EXPEND]

**expensive** adj. **1** costing much. **2** making a high charge. **3** causing much expense (has expensive tastes). □ **expensively** adv. **expensiveness** n.

**experience** /ek-**speer**-ree-uhns, uhk-/ — n. **1** observation of or practical acquaintance with facts or events (has little experience of the real world; school has a work experience programme). **2**

knowledge or skill resulting from this (*most job advertisements ask for people with experience*). **3 a** event regarded as affecting one (*an unpleasant experience*). **b** fact or process of being so affected (*learnt by experience*). — *v.* (**-cing**) **1** have experience of; undergo (*he thinks he's experiencing a mid-life crisis*). **2** feel or be affected by (an emotion etc.) (*experienced sheer terror*). [Latin *experior -pert-* try]

**experienced** *adj.* **1** having had much experience. **2** skilled from experience (*experienced driver*).

**experiential** /ek-,speer-ree-**en**-shuhl, uhk-/ *adj.* involving or based on experience. □ **experientially** *adv.*

**experiment** /ek-**spe**-ruh-muhnt, uhk-, -,ment/ — *n.* **1** procedure adopted in the hope of success, or for testing a hypothesis etc., or to demonstrate a known fact. **2** act or instance of trying out something new. — *v.* (often foll. by *on*, *with*) make an experiment (*many detest the fact that some cosmetics manufacturers experiment on animals; many young people experiment with drugs*). □ **experimentation** /-men-**tay**-shuhn/ *n.* **experimenter** *n.* [Latin: related to EXPERIENCE]

**experimental** /ek-,spe-ruh-**men**-tuhl, uhk-/ *adj.* **1** based on or making use of experiment. **2** used in experiments. □ **experimentalism** *n.* **experimentally** *adv.*

**expert** /**ek**-spert/ — *adj.* **1** (often foll. by *at*, *in*) having special knowledge of or skill in a subject. **2** (*attrib.*) involving or resulting from this (*expert advice*). — *n.* **1** (often foll. by *at*, *in*) person with special knowledge or skill. **2** person responsible for the maintenance of machinery, esp. in a shearing shed. — *v.* maintain the machinery in a shearing shed. □ **expertly** *adv.* [Latin: related to EXPERIENCE]

**expertise** /**ek**-sper-,teez/ *n.* expert skill, knowledge, or judgment. [French]

**expert system** *n.* *Computing* system, used to simulate highly specialised tasks, which infers new facts from a given information base and which has the ability to explain its reasoning processes.

**expiate** /**eks**-pee-,ayt/ *v.* (**-ting**) pay the penalty for or make amends for (wrongdoing). □ **expiable** /**eks**-pee-uh-buhl/ *adj.* **expiation** /-**ay**-shuhn/ *n.* **expiatory** *adj.* [Latin *expio*: related to PIOUS]

**expire** /ek-**spuyuh**, uhk-/ *v.* (**-ring**) **1** (of a period of time, validity, etc.) come to an end. **2** (of a document, authorisation, etc.) cease to be valid. **3** die. **4** (also *absol.*) breathe out (air etc.). □ **expiration** /,ek-spuh-**ray**-shuhn/ *n.* **expiratory** *adj.* (in sense 4). [Latin *spirare* breathe]

**expiry** *n.* end of validity or duration (also *attrib.*: *expiry date*).

**explain** /ek-**splayn**, uhk-/ *v.* **1** (also *absol.*) make clear or intelligible with detailed information etc. (*explained the way it should be constructed; let me explain*). **2** (foll. by *that*) say by way of explanation (*explained that the train was an hour late*). **3** account for (one's conduct etc.). □ **explain away** minimise the significance of by explanation. **explain oneself 1** make one's meaning clear. **2** give an account of one's motives or conduct. [Latin *explano* from *planus* flat]

**explanation** /,ek-spluh-**nay**-shuhn/ *n.* **1** act or instance of explaining. **2** statement or circumstance that explains something.

**explanatory** /ek-**splan**-uh-tuh-ree, uhk-, -tree/ *adj.* serving or designed to explain.

**expletive** /ek-**splee**-tiv/ *n.* swear-word or exclamation. [Latin *expleo* fill out]

**explicable** /ek-**splik**-uh-buhl, uhk-/ *adj.* that can be explained.

**explicate** /**eks**-pluh-,kayt/ *v.* (**-ting**) **1** develop the meaning of (an idea etc.). **2** make clear, explain (esp. a literary text). □ **explication** /-**kay**-shuhn/ *n.* [Latin *explico -plicat-* unfold]

**explicit** /ek-**splis**-uht, uhk-/ *adj.* **1** expressly stated, not merely implied; stated in detail (*explicit instructions*). **2** (of knowledge, a notion, etc.) definite. **3** (of a person, book, etc.) expressing views unreservedly; outspoken. **4** graphic; leaving nothing to the imagination (*explicit sex scenes*). □ **explicitly** *adv.* **explicitness** *n.* [Latin: related to EXPLICATE]

**explode** /ek-**splohd**, uhk-/ *v.* (**-ding**) **1 a** (of gas, gunpowder, a bomb, etc.) expand suddenly with a loud noise owing to a release of internal energy. **b** cause (a bomb etc.) to explode. **2** give vent suddenly to emotion, esp. anger. **3** (of a population etc.) increase suddenly or rapidly. **4** show (a theory etc.) to be false or baseless (*exploded his contention that the holocaust never took place*). **5** (as **exploded** *adj.*) (of a drawing etc.) showing the components of a mechanism somewhat separated but in the normal relative positions. [Latin *explodo -plos-* hiss off the stage]

**exploit** — *n.* /**ek**-sploit/ bold or daring feat. — *v.* /ek-**sploit**/ **1** make use of (a resource etc.); derive benefit from. **2** usu. *derog.* utilise or take advantage of (esp. a person) for one's own ends (*the union prevented the workers from being exploited*). □ **exploitation** /,ek-sploi-**tay**-shuhn/ *n.* **exploitative** /ek-**sploi**-tuh-tiv/

*adj.* **exploiter** *n.* [Latin: related to EXPLICATE]

**exploratory** /ek-**splo**-ruh-tuh-ree, uhk-, -tree/ — *adj.* **1** (of discussion etc.) preliminary, serving to establish procedure etc. **2** of or concerning exploration or investigation (*an exploratory journey into the Nullarbor; exploratory surgery*).

**explore** /ek-**splaw**, uhk-/ *v.* (**-ring**) **1** travel through (a country etc.) to learn about it. **2** inquire into; investigate thoroughly (*must explore all avenues*). **3** *Surgery* examine (a part of the body) in detail. □ **exploration** /ek-spluh-**ray**-shuhn/ *n.* **explorer** *n.* [Latin *exploro* search out]

**explosion** /ek-**sploh**-zhuhn, uhk-/ *n.* **1** act or instance of exploding. **2** loud noise caused by this. **3** sudden outbreak of feeling, esp. anger. **4** rapid or sudden increase esp. of population (*an explosion in the rabbit population*). [Latin: related to EXPLODE]

**explosive** /ek-**sploh**-siv, uhk-/ — *adj.* **1** able, tending, likely to explode. **2** likely to cause a violent outburst etc.; dangerously tense (*an explosive situation*). — *n.* explosive substance. □ **explosiveness** *n.*

**Expo** /**ek**-spoh/ *n.* (also **expo**) (*pl.* **-s**) large international exhibition. [abbreviation of EXPOSITION 4]

**exponent** /ek-**spoh**-nuhnt, uhk-/ *n.* **1** person who favours or promotes an idea etc. (*an exponent of harsh censorship laws*). **2** practitioner of an activity, profession, etc. **3** person who explains or interprets something. **4** type or representative (*he's a perfect exponent of dullness*). **5** raised symbol beside a numeral indicating how many of the number are to be multiplied together (e.g. $2^3 = 2 \times 2 \times 2$). [Latin *expono* EXPOUND]

**exponential** /,eks-puh-**nen**-shuhl/ *adj.* **1** of or indicated by a mathematical exponent. **2** (of an increase etc.) more and more rapid.

**export** — *v.* /ek-**spawt**, uhk-, **ek**-/ sell or send (goods or services) to another country. — *n.* /**ek**-spawt/ **1** process of exporting. **2 a** exported article or service (also *attrib.*: *export quality beef*). **b** (in *pl.*) amount exported. □ **exportation** /-**tay**-shuhn/ *n.* **exporter** /-**spaw**-tuh/ *n.* [Latin *porto portat-* carry]

**expose** /ek-**spohz**, uhk-/ *v.* (**-sing**) (esp. as **exposed** *adj.*) **1** leave uncovered or unprotected. **2** esp. from the weather. **2** (foll. by *to*) put at risk of (*was exposed to great danger*). **3** (as **exposed** *adj.*) (foll. by *to*) open to; unprotected from (*exposed to the east*). **4** subject or lay open to (an influence etc.) (*Mozart was exposed to*

*music from infancy*). **5** *Photog.* subject (a film) to light, esp. by operation of a camera. **6** reveal the identity or fact of (*exposed their secret dealings to the press*). **7** exhibit, display (*exposed his paintings to the critics; exposed his teeth in a grin*). □ **expose oneself** display one's body, esp. one's genitals, indecently in public. [Latin *pono posit-* put]

**exposé** /,eks-poh-**zay**/ *n.* **1** orderly statement of facts. **2** revelation of something discreditable. [French]

**exposition** /,eks-puh-**zish**-uhn/ *n.* **1** explanatory statement or account. **2** explanation or commentary. **3** *Mus.* part of a movement in which the principal themes are presented. **4** large public exhibition. □ **expositional** *adj.* [Latin: related to EXPOUND]

**expostulate** /ek-**spos**-tyoo-,layt, uhk-/ *v.* (**-ting**) (often foll. by *with* a person) make a protest; remonstrate (*expostulated with him about his treatment of his wife*). □ **expostulation** /-**lay**-shuhn/ *n.* **expostulatory** /-luh-tuh-ree, -tree/ *adj.* [Latin: related to POSTULATE]

**exposure** /ek-**spoh**-zhuh, uhk-/ *n.* (foll. by *to*) **1** act or instance of exposing or being exposed (to air, cold, danger, etc.). **2** physical condition resulting from being exposed to the elements (*died from exposure*). **3** *Photog.* **a** exposing a film etc. to the light. **b** duration of this. **c** section of film etc. affected by it. **4** revelation of an identity or fact, esp. when concealed (*went into hiding following the exposure of his secret life*). **5** aspect or outlook (*has a fine southern exposure*).

**expound** /ek-**spownd**, uhk-/ *v.* **1** set out in detail (a doctrine, theory, etc.). **2** explain or interpret (*expounding the scriptures*). [Latin *pono posit-* place]

**express** /ek-**spres**, uhk-/ — *v.* **1** represent or make known in words or by gestures, conduct, etc. (*expresses her ideas well; expressed dissatisfaction; his body language expresses unease*). **2** *refl.* communicate what one thinks, feels, or means (*expressed himself of the view that Australia should be a Republic; expresses herself in her art*). **3** esp. *Math.* represent by symbols. **4** squeeze out (liquid or air) (*express the juice from the orange*). — *adj.* **1 a** operating at high speed (*express train*). **b** (of a train etc.) not stopping at intermediate or minor stations etc. **2** esp. /**ek**-spres/ definitely stated; explicit (*my express instructions were that you should not go*). **3** done, made, or sent for a special purpose (*did it with the express intention of humiliating his wife*). **4** delivered by a specially fast service (*express delivery*).

— *adv.* **1** at high speed. **2** by express messenger or train (*send it express*). — *n.* **1** express train etc. **2** service for the rapid transport of parcels etc. □ **expressible** *adj.* **expressly** *adv.* (in sense 2 of *adj.*). [Latin *exprimo -press-* squeeze out]

**expression** /ek-**spresh**-uhn, uhk-/ *n.* **1** act or instance of expressing or state of being expressed. **2** word or phrase expressed. **3** person's facial appearance or intonation of voice, esp. as indicating feeling. **4** conveying of feeling in music, speaking, dance, etc. **5** depiction of feeling etc. in art. **6** *Math.* collection of symbols expressing a quantity. □ **expressionless** *adj.* [French: related to EXPRESS]

**expressionism** *n.* style of painting, music, drama, etc., seeking to express emotional experience rather than impressions of the external world. □ **expressionist** *n.* & *adj.* **expressionistic** /-**nuh**-stik/ *adj.*

**expressive** /ek-**spres**-iv, uhk-/ *adj.* **1** full of expression (*expressive look*). **2** (foll. by *of*) serving to express (*words expressive of contempt*). □ **expressively** *adv.* **expressiveness** *n.*

**expresso** var. of ESPRESSO.

**expressway** *n.* road designed for fast traffic.

**expropriate** /eks-**proh**-pree-,ayt/ *v.* (**-ting**) **1** (esp. of a government) take away (property) from its owner. **2** (foll. by *from*) dispossess. □ **expropriation** /-**ay**-shuhn/ *n.* **expropriator** *n.* [Latin *proprium* property]

**expulsion** /ek-**spul**-shuhn, uhk-/ *n.* act or instance of expelling or process of being expelled. □ **expulsive** *adj.* [Latin: related to EXPEL]

**expunge** /ek-**spunj**/ *v.* (**-ging**) erase, remove (esp. a passage from a book etc. or a name from a list). [Latin *expungo* prick out (for deletion)] □ **expunction** /-**spung**-shuhn/ *n.* **expunger** *n.*

**expurgate** /**eks**-puh-,gayt/ *v.* (**-ting**) **1** remove objectionable matter from (a book etc.). **2** remove (such matter). □ **expurgation** /-**gay**-shuhn/ *n.* **expurgator** *n.* [Latin: related to PURGE]

**exquisite** /**eks**-kwuh-zuht, ek-**skwiz**-uht/ *adj.* **1** extremely beautiful or delicate. **2** keenly felt (*exquisite pleasure*). **3** highly sensitive or discriminating (*exquisite taste*). □ **exquisitely** *adv.* [Latin *exquiro -quisit-* seek out]

**extant** /ek-**stant**, **ek**-stuhnt/ *adj.* still existing, surviving (*the only extant manuscript*). [Latin *ex(s)to* exist]

**extemporaneous** /ek-,**stem**-puh-**ray**-nee-uhs, uhk-/ *adj.* spoken or done

without preparation. □ **extemporaneously** *adv.* [from EXTEMPORE]

**extemporary** /ek-**stem**-puh-ruh-ree, uhk-, -pruh-ree/ *adj.* = EXTEMPORANEOUS. □ **extemporarily** *adv.*

**extempore** /ek-**stem**-puh-ree, uhk-/ *adj.* & *adv.* without preparation. [Latin]

**extemporise** /ek-**stem**-puh-,ruyz, uhk-/ *v.* (also **-ize**) (**-sing** or **-zing**) compose or produce (music, a speech, etc.) without preparation; improvise. □ **extemporisation** /-**zay**-shuhn/ *n.*

**extend** /ek-**stend**, uhk-/ *v.* **1** lengthen or make larger in space or time. **2 a** stretch or lay out at full length. **b** stretch or continue for a specified distance (*the road extends for another five kilometres; his power extends from Moscow to London*). **3** (foll. by *to*, *over*) reach or be or make continuous over a specified area (*the fog extended over the entire valley*). **4** (foll. by *to*) have a specified scope (*permit does not extend to camping*). **5** offer or accord (an invitation, hospitality, kindness, etc.). **6** (usu. *refl.* or in *passive*) tax the powers of (an athlete, horse, etc.) (*you need to extend yourself to the utmost*). □ **extendible** *adj.* (also **extensible**). [Latin *extendo -tens-*: related to TEND¹]

**extended family** *n.* family including relatives in addition to parents and their children.

**extension** /ek-**sten**-shuhn, uhk-/ *n.* **1** act or instance of extending or process of being extended. **2** part enlarging or added on to a main building etc. **3** additional part of anything (*this instrument feels like an extension of my hand; considers himself an extension to the family*; also *attrib.*: *extension cord*). **4 a** subsidiary telephone on the same line as the main one. **b** its number. **5** additional period of time (*got an extension on my essay; extension on a loan*). **6** extramural instruction by a university or college (also *attrib.*: *extension classes*). □ **extensional** *adj.*

**extensive** /ek-**sten**-siv, uhk-/ *adj.* **1** covering a large area (*extensive areas of forest*). **2** having a wide scope; far-reaching (*extensive knowledge of music; extensive investigation*). □ **extensively** *adv.* **extensiveness** *n.* [Latin: related to EXTEND]

**extent** /ek-**stent**, uhk-/ *n.* **1** space over which a thing extends. **2** range, scope, degree (*the full extent of their power; to a great extent*). [Anglo-French: related to EXTEND]

**extenuate** /ek-**sten**-yoo-,ayt/ *v.* (often as **extenuating** *adj.*) make (guilt or an offence) seem less serious by reference to another factor (*extenuating circumstances*). □ **extenuation** /-ay-shuhn/ *n.* [Latin *tenuis* thin]

**exterior** /ek-**steer**-ree-uh, uhk-/ — *adj.* **1** of or on the outer side. **2** coming from outside (*exterior pressures*). — *n.* **1** outward aspect or surface of a building etc. **2** outward demeanour (*seemed calm on the exterior*). [Latin]

**exterminate** /ek-**ster**-muh-,nayt, uhk-/ *v.* (**-ting**) **1** destroy utterly (esp. a living thing). **2** get rid of; eliminate (a pest, disease, etc.). □ **extermination** /-**nay**-shuhn/ *n.* **exterminator** *n.* [Latin: related to TERMINAL]

**external** /ek-**ster**-nuhl, uhk-/ — *adj.* **1 a** of or on the outside or visible part (opp. INTERNAL). **b** coming from the outside or an outside source. **2** relating to a country's foreign affairs. **3** outside the conscious subject or mind (*the external world*). **4** (of medicine etc.) for use on the outside of the body. **5** for or concerning students taking the examinations of a university without attending it. — *n.* (in *pl.*) **1** outward features or aspect. **2** external circumstances. **3** inessentials. □ **externality** /,ek-ster-**nal**-uh-tee/ *n.* **externally** *adv.* [Latin *externus* outer]

**externalise** *v.* (also **-ize**) (**-sing** or **-zing**) give or attribute external existence to. □ **externalisation** /-**zay**-shuhn/ *n.*

**extinct** /ek-**stingkt**, uhk-/ *adj.* **1** (of a species, etc.) that has died out. **2 a** no longer burning. **b** (of a volcano) that no longer erupts. **3** (of life, hope, etc.) terminated, quenched. **4** (of an office etc.) obsolete. [Latin *ex(s)tinguo -stinct-* quench]

**extinction** /ek-**stingk**-shuhn, uhk-/ *n.* **1** act of making or state of being or process of becoming extinct. **2** act of extinguishing or state of being extinguished. **3** total destruction or annihilation.

**extinguish** /ek-**sting**-gwish, uhk-/ *v.* **1** cause (a flame, light, etc.) to die out. **2** make extinct; destroy (*programme to extinguish disease*). **3** put an end to; terminate (a feeling, quality, etc.) (*his hopes were extinguished*). □ **extinguishable** *adj.* [as EXTINCT]

**extinguisher** *n.* = FIRE-EXTINGUISHER.

**extirpate** /ek-stuh-,payt/ *v.* (**-ting**) root out; destroy completely. □ **extirpation** /-**pay**-shuhn/ *n.* [Latin *ex(s)tirpo* from *stirps* stem of tree]

**extol** /ek-**stohl**, uhk-/ *v.* (**-ll-**) praise enthusiastically. [Latin *tollo* raise]

**extort** /ek-**stawt**, uhk-/ *v.* obtain by force, threats, persistent demands, etc. [Latin *torqueo tort-* twist]

**extortion** /ek-**staw**-shuhn, uhk-/ *n.* **1** act or instance of extorting, esp. money. **2** illegal exaction. □ **extortioner** *n.* **extortionist** *n.*

**extortionate** /ek-**staw**-shuh-nuht, uhk-/ *adj.* **1** (of a price etc.) exorbitant. **2** using or given to extortion (*extortionate methods*). □ **extortionately** *adv.*

**extra** /**eks**-truh/ — *adj.* additional; more than usual or necessary or expected. — *adv.* **1** more than usually (*played extra well*). **2** additionally (*was charged extra*). — *n.* **1** extra thing. **2** thing for which an extra charge is made (*salad's an extra*). **3** person engaged temporarily for a minor part in a film. **4** lesson taken by a teacher for an absent colleague. **5** special issue of a newspaper etc. **6** *Cricket* run scored other than from a hit with the bat. [probably from EXTRAORDINARY]

**extra-** *comb. form* **1** outside, beyond (*extraterrestrial*). **2** beyond the scope of (*extra-curricular*). [Latin *extra* outside]

**extra cover** *n. Cricket* **1** fielding position on a line between cover-point and mid-off, but beyond these. **2** fielder at this position.

**extract** — *v.* /ek-**strakt**, uhk-/ **1** remove or take out, esp. by effort or force (*extract a tooth*). **2** obtain (money, an admission, etc.) against a person's will (*we'll extract the information from him somehow*). **3** obtain (a natural resource) from the earth. **4** select or reproduce for quotation or performance (*a passage of writing, music, etc.*). **5** obtain (juice etc.) by pressure, distillation, etc. **6** derive (pleasure etc.) (*extracted great satisfaction from his opponent's defeat*). **7** *Math.* find (the root of a number). — *n.* /**ek**-strakt/ **1** short passage from a book etc. **2** preparation containing a concentrated constituent of a substance (*malt extract*). [Latin *traho tract-* draw]

**extraction** /ek-**strak**-shuhn, uhk-/ *n.* **1** act or instance of extracting or process of being extracted. **2** removal of a tooth. **3** lineage, descent (*of Sri Lankan extraction*). [Latin: related to EXTRACT]

**extractor** /ek-**strak**-tuh, uhk-/ *n.* **1** person or machine that extracts. **2** (*attrib.*) (of a device) that extracts bad air etc. (*extractor fan*).

**extra-curricular** /,eks-truh-kuh-**rik**-yuh-luh/ *adj.* not part of the normal curriculum.

**extraditable** /**eks**-truh-,duy-tuh-buhl/ *adj.* **1** liable to extradition. **2** (of a crime) warranting extradition.

**extradite** /**eks**-truh-,duyt/ *v.* (**-ting**) hand over (a person accused or convicted of a crime) to the foreign country, State, etc. in which the crime was committed (*was*

**extradited** from Tasmania to Victoria). □ **extradition** /ˌek-struh-**dish**-uhn/ n. [French: related to TRADITION]

**extramarital** /ˌeks-truh-**ma**-ruh-tuhl/ adj. (esp. of sexual relations) occurring outside marriage.

**extramural** /ˌeks-truh-**myoo**-ruhl/ adj. additional to normal teaching or studies, esp. for non-resident students.

**extraneous** /ek-**stray**-nee-uhs, uhk-/ adj. 1 of external origin (a pearl is formed around an extraneous particle). 2 (often foll. by to) irrelevant, unrelated (these matters are extraneous to the topic). □ **extraneously** adv. **extraneousness** n. [Latin extraneus]

**extraordinaire** /ˌek-straw-duh-**nair**/ adj. (always following the noun) of exceptional skill or talent (a chef extraordinaire; a cryptic-crossword-solver extraordinaire).

**extraordinary** /ek-**straw**-duh-nuh-ree, uhk-, ˌek-struh-**aw**-duh-nuh-ree, -duhn-ree/ adj. 1 unusual or remarkable (extraordinary events). 2 unusually great (an extraordinary talent). 3 (of a meeting) specially convened. 4 (of an official etc.) additional; specially employed (envoy extraordinary). □ **extraordinarily** adv. **extraordinariness** n. [Latin]

**extrapolate** /ek-**strap**-uh-ˌlayt, uhk-/ v. (**-ting**) (also absol.) 1 calculate approximately from known values, data, etc. (other values, data, etc. which lie outside the range of those known). 2 calculate on the basis of (known facts) to estimate unknown facts, esp. extend (a curve) on a graph. 3 infer more widely from a limited range of known factors. □ **extrapolation** /-**lay**-shuhn/ n. [from EXTRA-, INTERPOLATE]

**extrasensory** /ˌeks-truh-**sen**-suh-ree/ adj. derived by means other than the known senses, e.g. by telepathy.

**extraterrestrial** /ˌeks-truh-tuh-**res**-tree-uhl/ — adj. outside the earth or its atmosphere. — n. (in science fiction) being from outer space.

**extra time** n. Sport 1 added playing time to make up for time lost through interruptions to play. 2 additional period of play to achieve a result.

**extravagant** /ek-**strav**-uh-guhnt, uhk-/ adj. 1 spending money excessively; wasteful in the use of resources. 2 excessive; unreasonable, absurd (extravagant claims). 3 flamboyant; showy (an extravagant display). 4 exorbitant; costing much (extravagant prices). □ **extravagance** n. **extravagantly** adv. [Latin vagor wander]

**extravaganza** /ek-ˌstrav-uh-**gan**-zuh, uhk-/ n. 1 spectacular theatrical or television production. 2 fanciful literary, musical, or dramatic composition. [Italian]

**extreme** /ek-**stream**, uhk-/ — adj. 1 of a high, or the highest, degree; exceedingly great or intense (extreme old age; extreme danger). 2 a severe; lacking restraint or moderation (extreme measures; extreme reaction). b (of a person, opinion, etc.) going to great lengths; advocating immoderate measures. 3 outermost (extreme edge). 4 on the far left or right of a political party. 5 utmost (outside the extreme range of our telescope). 6 last (extreme unction). — n. 1 (often in pl.) either of two things as remote or as different as possible (the extremes of hope and despair; avoid extremes). 2 thing at either end (a stick with a knob at each extreme). 3 highest degree (an extreme of excitement). 4 Math. first or last term of a ratio or series. □ **go to extremes** take an extreme course of action. **in the extreme** to an extreme degree. □ **extremely** adv. [French from Latin]

**extreme unction** n. sacrament of the last rites in the Catholic and Orthodox Churches, whereby a priest anoints a dying person with sacred oil (now also called 'the sacrament of the anointing of the sick' in the Catholic Church).

**extremist** n. (also attrib.) person with extreme or fanatical political or religious views, esp. one who resorts to or advocates extreme action. □ **extremism** n.

**extremity** /ek-**strem**-uh-tee, uhk-/ n. (pl. **-ies**) 1 extreme point of anything; very end of anything. 2 (in pl.) the hands and feet. 3 condition of extreme adversity or difficulty. [Latin: related to EXTREME]

**extricate** /**eks**-truh-ˌkayt/ v. (**-ting**) (often foll. by from) free or disentangle from a difficulty etc. □ **extricable** adj. **extrication** /-**kay**-shuhn/ n. [Latin tricae perplexities]

**extrinsic** /ek-**strin**-zik/ adj. 1 not inherent or intrinsic; not essential (opp. INTRINSIC). 2 (often foll. by to) extraneous; not belonging. □ **extrinsically** adv. [Latin extrinsecus outwardly]

**extrovert** /**eks**-truh-ˌvert/ — n. 1 outgoing or sociable person (opp. INTROVERT). 2 Psychol. person mainly concerned with external things rather than with the self. — adj. typical of or with the nature of an extrovert. □ **extroversion** /-**ver**-shuhn/ n. **extroverted** adj. [Latin verto turn]

**extrude** /ek-**strood**/ v. (**-ding**) 1 (foll. by from) thrust or force out. 2 shape metal, plastics, etc. by forcing them through a die. □ **extrusion** n. **extrusive** adj. [Latin extrudo -trus- thrust out]

**exuberant** /eg-zyoo-buh-ruhnt, uhg-/ adj. **1** lively, high-spirited. **2** (of a plant etc.) prolific. **3** (of feelings etc.) abounding, lavish, effusive. □ **exuberance** n. **exuberantly** adv. [Latin uber fertile]

**exude** /eg-zyood, uhg-/ v. (**-ding**) **1** ooze out. **2** emit (a smell). **3** display (an emotion etc.) freely or abundantly (exuding displeasure). □ **exudation** /-day-shuhn/ n. [Latin sudo sweat]

**exult** /eg-zult, uhg-/ v. **1** be greatly joyful (exulted in his freedom). **2** (often foll. by over) have a feeling of triumph (over a person) (exulted over their downfall). □ **exultation** /-tay-shuhn/ n. **exultant** adj. **exultantly** adv. [Latin ex(s)ulto from salio salt- leap]

■ **Usage** Exult is often confused with exalt.

**-ey** var. of -y².

**eye** /uy/ — n. **1** organ of sight. **2** eye characterised by the colour of the iris (see IRIS 1) (has blue eyes). **3** region round the eye (eyes swollen from weeping). **4** (in sing. or pl.) sight (demonstrate to the eye; needs perfect eyes to be a pilot). **5** particular visual ability; visual appreciation (a straight eye; cast an expert eye over). **6** (in sing. or pl.) a look, gaze, or glance, esp. as indicating the feeling of the viewer (a friendly eye). **7** thing like an eye, esp.: **a** a spot on a peacock's tail. **b** a leaf-bud of a potato. **8** centre of something circular, e.g. a flower or target. **9** calm region at the centre of a hurricane etc. **10** hole of a needle. — v. (**eyes, eyed, eyeing** or **eying**) watch or observe closely, esp. admiringly or with suspicion (eyed him with distaste). □ **all eyes** watching intently (go ahead! — I'm all eyes). **an eye for an eye** retaliation in kind. **eye off** colloq. watch closely (esp. with the intention of stealing) (eyeing off the jewellery in the display case). **get** (or **keep**) **one's eye in** accustom oneself (or keep oneself accustomed) to the conditions of play etc. so as to judge speed, distance, etc. **have an eye for** be discerning about; be able to appreciate (has an eye for beauty; has an eye for a bargain). **have one's eye on** wish or plan to procure (has his eye on a particular sports car). **have an eye to** be alert to (has an eye to the main chance). **have eyes for** be interested in (has eyes for no-one but me). **keep an eye on 1** watch. **2** look after. **keep an eye open** (or **out**) (often foll. by for) watch carefully. **keep one's eyes open** (or **peeled** or **skinned**) watch out; be on the alert. **make eyes** (or **sheep's eyes**) (foll. by at) look amorously or flirtatiously at. **one in the eye** (foll. by for) disappointment or setback. **pick the eyes out of** select the best parts of. **see eye to eye** (often foll. by with) agree. **set eyes on** see. **up to the** (or **one's**) **eyes** in deeply engaged or involved in. **with one's eyes open** deliberately; with full awareness. **with one's eyes shut** (or **closed**) with little effort (can do it with my eyes shut). **with an eye to** with a view to. [Old English]

**eyeball** — n. ball of the eye within the lids and socket. — v. look or stare (at).

**eyeball to eyeball** adv. colloq. confronting closely.

**eyebrow** n. line of hair on the ridge above the eye-socket. □ **raise one's eyebrows** show surprise, disbelief, or disapproval.

**eye-catching** adj. colloq. striking.

**eyeful** n. (pl. **-s**) colloq. **1** (esp. in phr. **get an eyeful (of)**) good look; as much as the eye can take in. **2** visually striking person or thing (he's quite an eyeful).

**eyeglass** n. lens to assist defective sight.

**eyelash** n. each of the hairs growing on the edges of the eyelids.

**eyelet** /uy-luht/ n. **1** small hole for string or rope etc. to pass through. **2** metal ring strengthening this. [French oillet from Latin oculus]

**eyelid** n. either of the folds of skin closing to cover the eye.

**eyeliner** n. cosmetic applied as a line round the eye.

**eye-opener** n. colloq. enlightening experience; unexpected revelation.

**eyepiece** n. lens or lenses to which the eye is applied at the end of an optical instrument.

**eye-shade** n. device to protect the eyes, esp. from strong light.

**eyeshadow** n. coloured cosmetic applied to the eyelids.

**eyesight** n. faculty or power of seeing.

**eyesore** n. visually offensive or ugly thing, esp. a building.

**eye strain** n. fatigue of the eye muscles.

**eye-tooth** n. canine tooth in the upper jaw just under the eye.

**eyewash** n. **1** lotion for the eyes. **2** colloq. nonsense; insincere talk.

**eyewitness** n. person who saw a thing happen and can tell of it (also attrib.: eyewitness account).

**eyrie** /eer-ree, air-ree/ n. **1** nest of a bird of prey, esp. an eagle, built high up. **2** house etc. perched high up. [French aire lair, from Latin agrum piece of ground]

# F

**F¹** /ef/ *n.* (also **f**) (*pl.* **Fs** or **F's**) **1** sixth letter of the alphabet. **2** *Mus.* fourth note of the diatonic scale of C major.

**F²** *abbr.* (also **F.**) **1** Fahrenheit. **2** farad(s). **3** fine (pencil-lead).

**F³** *symb.* fluorine.

**f** *abbr.* (also **f.**) **1** female. **2** feminine. **3** following page etc. **4** *Mus.* forte. **5** folio. **6** focal length. **7** *Math.* function (of).

**fa** var. of FAH.

**fab** *adj. colloq.* fabulous, marvellous. [abbreviation]

**fable** /**fay**-buhl/ *n.* **1 a** fictional, esp. supernatural, story. **b** moral tale, esp. with animals as characters. **2** legendary tales collectively (*in fable talking animals are accepted*). **3 a** lie. **b** thing only supposed to exist. [Latin *fabula* discourse]

**fabled** *adj.* celebrated; legendary.

**fabric** /**fab**-rik/ *n.* **1** woven material; cloth. **2** walls, floor, and roof of a building. **3** essential structure or essence of a thing (*the fabric of society*). [Latin *faber* metalworker]

**fabricate** /**fab**-ruh-ˌkayt/ *v.* (**-ting**) **1** construct, esp. from components. **2** invent (a story etc.). **3** forge (a document). □ **fabrication** /-**kay**-shuhn/ *n.* **fabricator** *n.* [Latin: related to FABRIC]

**fabulous** /**fab**-yuh-luhs/ *adj.* **1** incredible (*fabulous wealth*). **2** *colloq.* marvellous (*you look fabulous*). **3** legendary (*the fabulous bunyip*). □ **fabulously** *adv.* [Latin: related to FABLE]

**façade** /fuh-**sahd**/ *n.* **1** face or front of a building. **2** outward appearance, esp. a deceptive one. [French: related to FACE]

**face** — *n.* **1** front of the head from forehead to chin. **2** facial expression. **3** coolness, effrontery. **4** surface, esp.: **a** side of a mountain etc. (*north face*). **b** = COALFACE. **c** *Geom.* each surface of a solid. **d** façade of a building. **e** dial of a clock etc. **5** functional side of a tool etc. **6** front of a bushfire. **7** side of a mob of cattle etc. that is being worked. **8** = TYPEFACE. **9** aspect (*unacceptable face of capitalism*). — *v.* (**-cing**) **1** look or be positioned towards or in a certain direction. **2** be opposite (*facing page 20*). **3** meet resolutely. **4** confront (*faces us with a problem*). **5 a** coat the surface of (a thing). **b** put a facing on (a garment). □ **face the music** *colloq.* take unpleasant consequences without flinching. **face up** to accept bravely. **have**

the face be shameless enough. **in face** (or **the face**) **of** despite. **lose face** be humiliated. **on the face of it** apparently. **put a bold** (or **brave**) **face on it** accept difficulty etc. cheerfully. **save face** avoid humiliation. **set one's face against** oppose stubbornly. [Latin *facies*]

**-face** *comb. form* used with (usu.) offens. words to create terms of abuse.

**faceless** *adj.* **1** without identity; characterless. **2** purposely not identifiable.

**facelift** *n.* **1** cosmetic surgery to remove wrinkles etc. **2** improvement to appearance, efficiency, etc.

**facet** /**fas**-uht/ *n.* **1** aspect. **2** side of a cut gem etc. [French: related to FACT]

**facetious** /fuh-**see**-shuhs/ *adj.* intending or intended to be amusing, esp. inappropriately. □ **facetiously** *adv.* [Latin *facetia* jest]

**face to face** *adv.* & *adj.* (also **face-to-face**) when *attrib.*) (often foll. by *with*) facing; confronting each other.

**face value** *n.* **1** nominal value as printed on money. **2** superficial appearance or implication.

**face washer** *n.* = WASHER 3.

**facia** var. of FASCIA.

**facial** /**fay**-shuhl/ — *adj.* of or for the face. — *n.* beauty treatment for the face. □ **facially** *adv.*

**facile** /**fas**-uyl/ *adj.* usu. *derog.* **1** easily achieved or of little value. **2** glib, fluent. [Latin *facio* do]

**facilitate** /fuh-**sil**-uh-ˌtayt/ *v.* (**-ting**) make easy or less difficult or more easily achieved. □ **facilitation** /-**tay**-shuhn/ *n.* [Italian: related to FACILE]

**facility** /fuh-**sil**-uh-tee/ *n.* (*pl.* **-ies**) **1** ease; absence of difficulty. **2** fluency, dexterity (*facility of expression*). **3** (esp. in *pl.*) opportunity or equipment for doing something. [Latin: related to FACILE]

**facing** *n.* **1** layer of material covering part of a garment etc. for contrast or strength. **2** outer covering on a wall etc.

**facsimile** /fak-**sim**-uh-lee/ *n.* exact copy, esp. of writing, printing, a picture, etc. (see also FAX). [Latin, = make like]

**fact** *n.* **1** thing that is known to exist or to be true. **2** (usu. in *pl.*) item of verified information. **3** truth, reality. □ **as a matter of fact** actually. **before** (or **after**) **the fact** before (or after) the committing of a crime. **in** (or **in point of**) **fact 1** in reality. **2** in short. [Latin *factum* from *facio* do]

**fact-finding** *adj.* (of an inquiry, mission, delegation, etc.) inquiring into the facts, seeking information.

**faction** /fak-shuhn/ *n.* small organised dissentient group within a larger one, esp. in politics. □ **factional** *adj.* [Latin: related to FACT]

**-faction** *comb. form* forming nouns of action from verbs in *-fy* (*satisfaction*). [Latin *-factio*]

**factious** /fak-shuhs/ *adj.* of, characterised by, or inclined to faction. [Latin: related to FACTION]

**factitious** /fak-tish-uhs/ *adj.* **1** specially contrived, not genuine (*factitious value*). **2** artificial (*factitious joy*). [Latin: related to FACT]

**fact of life** *n.* something that must be accepted.

**factor** /fak-tuh/ *n.* **1** circumstance etc. contributing to a result. **2** *Math.* whole number etc. that when multiplied with another produces a given number. **3** business agent. □ **factor in** take account of. [Latin: related to FACT]

**factorial** /fak-taw-ree-uhl/ *Math.* — *n.* product of a number and all the whole numbers below it. — *adj.* of a factor or factorial.

**factorise** *v.* (also **-ize**) (**-sing** or **-zing**) *Math.* resolve into factors. □ **factorisation** /-zay-shuhn/ *n.*

**factory** /fak-tuh-ree, -tree/ *n.* (*pl.* **-ies**) building(s) in which goods are manufactured. [ultimately from Latin *factorium*]

**factory floor** *n.* workers in a factory or industry as opposed to the management.

**factotum** /fak-toh-tuhm/ *n.* (*pl.* **-s**) employee who does all kinds of work. [medieval Latin: related to FACT, TOTAL]

**facts and figures** *n.pl.* precise details.

**fact sheet** *n.* leaflet setting out relevant information.

**facts of life** *n.pl.* (prec. by *the*) information about sexual functions and practices.

**factual** /fak-choo-uhl/ *adj.* based on or concerned with fact. □ **factually** *adv.*

**faculty** /fak-uhl-tee/ *n.* (*pl.* **-ies**) **1** aptitude for a particular activity. **2** inherent mental or physical power. **3 a** group of related university departments. **b** academic staff of these departments. [Latin: related to FACILE]

**fad** *n.* **1** short-lived craze. **2** peculiar notion. □ **faddish** *adj.* [probably from *fiddle-faddle* trivial matters]

**fade** — *v.* (**-ding**) **1** lose or cause to lose colour, light, or sound; slowly diminish. **2** lose freshness or strength. **3** (foll. by *in*, *out*) *Cinematog.* etc. cause (a picture or sound) to appear or disappear, increase or decrease, gradually. **4** angle a surfboard towards the breaking part of a wave. — *n.* action of fading. □ **fade away** **1** *colloq.* languish, grow thin. **2** die gradually (*there was no pain, she just faded away*). **3** slowly disappear. [French *fade* dull]

**faeces** /fee-seez/ *n.pl.* waste matter discharged from the bowels. □ **faecal** /fee-kuhl, fee-suhl/ *adj.* [Latin]

**fag¹** *colloq.* — *n.* **1** tedious task. **2** cigarette. — *v.* (**-gg-**) (often foll. by *out*) exhaust. [origin unknown]

**fag²** *n. colloq. offens.* male homosexual. [abbreviation of FAGGOT]

**fag end** *n.* last bit; useless remnant.

**faggot** /fag-uht/ *n.* **1** bundle of sticks etc. **2** *colloq. offens.* male homosexual. [French from Italian]

**fah** /fah/ *n.* (also **fa**) *Mus.* fourth note of a major scale. [Latin *famuli*: see GAMUT]

**Fahrenheit** /fa-ruhn-huyt/ *adj.* of a scale of temperature on which water freezes at 32° and boils at 212°. [*Fahrenheit*, name of a physicist (d. 1736)]

**fail** — *v.* **1** not succeed (*failed to qualify*). **2** be or judge to be unsuccessful in (an examination etc.). **3** be unable; neglect (*I fail to see the point; failed to appear*). **4** disappoint; let down. **5** (of supplies, crops, etc.) be absent or insufficient. **6** become weaker; cease functioning (*health is failing; engine failed*). **7** become bankrupt. — *n.* failure in an examination. □ **without fail** for certain, whatever happens. [Latin *fallo* deceive]

**failed** *adj.* unsuccessful (*failed actor*).

**failing** — *n.* fault, weakness. — *prep.* in default of.

**fail-safe** *adj.* reverting to a safe condition when faulty etc.; foolproof.

**failure** /fay-lyuh/ *n.* **1** lack of success; failing. **2** unsuccessful person or thing. **3** non-performance. **4** breaking down or ceasing to function (*heart failure*; *computer failure*). **5** running short of supply etc. [Anglo-French: related to FAIL]

**faint** — *adj.* **1** indistinct, pale, dim. **2** weak or giddy. **3** slight (*a faint chance*). **4** feeble; half-hearted (*faint praise*). **5** timid (*a faint heart*). **6** (also **feint**) (of paper) with inconspicuous ruled lines. — *v.* **1** lose consciousness. **2** become faint. — *n.* act or state of fainting. □ **faintly** *adv.* **faintness** *n.* [French: related to FEIGN]

**faint-hearted** *adj.* cowardly, timid.

**fair¹** — *adj.* **1** just, equitable; in accordance with the rules. **2** blond; light or pale. **3 a** moderate in quality or amount (*it was a fair performance*). **b** considerable, satisfactory (*a fair chance of success*). **4** (of weather) fine; (of the wind) favourable. **5** clean, clear (*fair copy*). **6** *archaic* beautiful. — *adv.* **1** in a just manner. **2** *colloq.* exactly, completely (*I was fair taken by surprise*). □ **fair cop** *colloq.* discovery of someone caught in the act; caught redhanded. **fair cow** *colloq.* anything unpleasant or difficult (*a fair cow of a job*). **fair crack of the whip** *colloq.* = FAIR GO *int.* **fair enough** *colloq.* **1** acceptable; tolerably good (*a fair enough attempt*). **2** (expressing agreement etc.) okay. **fair's fair** *colloq.* plea for fair play. **fair suck (of the sauce bottle)** *colloq.* = FAIR GO *int.* **fair to middling** moderately good. **fair treat** *colloq.* excessively, lavishly (*she bucketed him a fair treat*). **in a fair way** to likely to. □ **fairness** *n.* [Old English]

**fair**² *n.* **1** stalls, amusements, etc., for public entertainment. **2** periodic gathering for the sale of goods (*book fair*). **3** exhibition, esp. commercial and international (*trade fair*). [Latin *feriae* holiday]

**fair and square** — *adj.* honest, just, straightforward. — *adv.* exactly; straightforwardly (*got him fair and square between the eyes*).

**fair dinkum** — *adj.* true, genuine, reliable, DINKUM — *int.* (also **fair dink**) an assertion of utter reliability (*I wouldn't lie to you, mate, fair dink!*).

**fair game** *n.* person or thing crying out for criticism (*after his obnoxiously racist remarks, he's fair game*).

**fair go** *colloq.* — *n.* fair chance; fair treatment. — *int.* (a plea for fair treatment) steady on!; be reasonable (*fair go, mate!*).

**fairly** *adv.* **1** in a fair manner. **2** moderately (*fairly good*). **3** quite, rather (*fairly narrow*).

**fair play** *n.* just treatment or behaviour.

**fairway** *n.* **1** part of a golf-course between a tee and its green, kept free of rough grass. **2** navigable channel.

**fair-weather** *adj.* reliable only when things go well, unreliable in times of trouble (*fair-weather friend*).

**fairy** *n.* (*pl.* **-ies**) **1** (often *attrib.*) small winged legendary being. **2** *colloq. offens.* **a** effeminate man. **b** effeminate male homosexual. [French: related to FAY, -ERY]

**fairy bread** *n.* bread buttered and sprinkled with hundreds and thousands.

**fairy floss** — *n.* **1** airy spun sugar on a stick. **2** inconsequential person or thing. — *adj.* lacking in substance, strength (of character) etc.; trivial; of no consequence.

**fairyland** *n.* **1** home of fairies. **2** enchanted region.

**fairy penguin** *n.* small penguin with steel-blue back and white front found on the southern coasts of Australia.

**fairy possum** *n.* small possum inhabiting tree-hollows in south-eastern Australia.

**fairy story** *n.* (also **fairy tale**) **1** tale about fairies. **2** incredible story; lie.

**fairy toast** *n.* = *Melba toast* (see MELBA).

**fairy wren** *n.* any of several Australian wrens, the breeding male having bright variously coloured plumage, e.g. the splendid wren, the variegated wren, the white-winged wren.

**fait accompli** /fayt uh-kom-**plee**/ *n.* thing that has been done and is not capable of alteration. [French]

**faith** *n.* **1** complete trust or confidence. **2** firm, esp. religious, belief not based on proof. **3** religion or creed (*Christian faith*). **4** loyalty, trustworthiness. [Latin *fides*]

**faithful** *adj.* **1** showing faith. **2** (often foll. by *to*) loyal, trustworthy. **3** maintaining sexual fidelity, having sex with no-one but one's lover or spouse. **4** accurate (*faithful account*). **5** (**the Faithful**) the believers in a religion. □ **faithfulness** *n.*

**faithfully** *adv.* in a faithful manner. □ **Yours faithfully** formula for ending a formal letter when it begins 'Dear Sir' or 'Dear Madam'.

**faithless** *adj.* **1** false, unreliable, disloyal. **2** without religious faith.

**fake** — *n.* false or counterfeit thing or person. — *adj.* counterfeit; not genuine. — *v.* (**-king**) **1** make a fake or imitation of (*faked my signature*). **2** feign (a feeling, illness, etc.). [German *fegen* sweep]

**fakir** /**fay**-keer, fuh-**keer**/ *n.* Muslim or (rarely) Hindu religious beggar or ascetic. [Arabic, = poor man]

**falcon** /**fawl**-kuhn, **fal**-kuhn/ *n.* small hawk sometimes trained to hunt. [Latin *falco*]

**falconry** *n.* breeding and training of hawks.

**fall** /fawl/ — *v.* (*past* **fell**; *past part.* **fallen**) **1** go or come down freely; descend (*fell from the top floor*; *the curtain fell*). **2** (often foll. by *over*) come suddenly to the ground from loss of balance etc. **3 a** (of hair, clothing, etc.) hang down. **b** (of ground etc.) slope. **c** (foll. by *into*) (of a river etc.) discharge into. **4 a** sink lower; decline, esp. in power, status, etc. **b** subside (*demand has fallen*). **5** occur (*falls on a Monday*). **6** (of the face) show dismay or disappointment. **7** yield to temptation. **8** take or have a particular direction or place (*his eye fell on me*; *accent falls on the first syllable*). **9 a** find a place; be naturally divisible (*the subject* *falls into three parts).* **b** (foll. by *under*, *within*) be classed among. **10** come by chance or duty (*it fell to me to answer*). **11 a** pass into a specified condition (*fell ill*). **b** become (*fall asleep*). **12** be defeated or captured. **13** die (*fall in battle*). **14** (foll. by *on*, *upon*) **a** attack. **b** meet with. **c** embrace or embark on avidly. **15** (foll. by *to* + verbal noun) begin (*fell to wondering*). — *n.* **1** act or instance of falling; sudden rapid descent. **2** that which falls or has fallen, e.g. snow. **3** recorded amount of rainfall etc. **4** overthrow; downfall (*fall of Rome*). **5 a** succumbing to temptation. **b** (**the Fall**) Adam's sin and its results. **6** (also **Fall**) *US* autumn. **7** (esp. in *pl.*) waterfall etc. **8** wrestling-bout; throw in wrestling. □ **fall about** *colloq.* be helpless with laughter. **fall away 1** (of a surface) incline abruptly. **2** become few or thin; gradually vanish. **3** desert; revolt. **fall back** retreat. **fall back on** have recourse to in difficulty. **fall behind 1** be outstripped; lag. **2** be in arrears. **fall down** (often foll. by *on*) *colloq.* fail; perform poorly. **fall flat** fail completely, miss the desired effect (*his joke fell flat*). **fall for** *colloq.* be captivated or deceived by. **fall foul of** come into conflict with. **fall in 1** take one's place in military formation. **2** collapse inwards. **fall in with 1** meet by chance. **2** agree with. **3** coincide with. **fall off 1** become detached. **2** decrease, deteriorate. **fall off the back of a truck** *colloq.* be stolen or otherwise dishonestly obtained (*that trannie you bought at the pub must have fallen off the back of a truck*). **fall out 1** quarrel. **2** (of the hair, teeth, etc.) become detached. **3** *Mil.* come out of formation. **4** result; occur. **fall over backwards** see BACKWARDS. **fall over oneself** *colloq.* **1** be eager. **2** stumble through haste, confusion, etc. **fall short 1** be deficient. **2** (of a missile etc.) not reach its target. **fall short of** fail to reach or obtain. **fall through** fail; miscarry. **fall to** begin, e.g. eating or working. [Old English]

**fallacy** /ˈfal-uh-see/ *n.* (*pl.* **-ies**) **1** mistaken belief. **2** faulty reasoning; misleading argument. □ **fallacious** /fuh-ˈlay-shuhs/ *adj.* [Latin *fallo* deceive]

**fallen** *past part* of FALL. — *adj.* **1** morally degraded. **2** slain in battle.

**fall guy** *n. colloq.* easy victim; scapegoat.

**fallible** /ˈfal-uh-buhl/ *adj.* capable of making mistakes. □ **fallibility** /-ˈbil-uh-tee/ *n.* **fallibly** *adv.* [medieval Latin: related to FALLACY]

**falling-out** *n. colloq.* breach of friendship, break in a relationship etc., esp. after a quarrel.

**falling star** *n.* meteor.

**Fallopian tube** /fuh-ˈloh-pee-uhn/ *n.* either of two tubes along which ova travel from the ovaries to the womb. [*Fallopius*, name of an anatomist (d. 1562)]

**fallout** *n.* **1** radioactive nuclear debris. **2** adverse side-effects of a situation etc.

**fallow**[1] /ˈfal-oh/ *adj.* (of land) ploughed but left unsown; uncultivated. [Old English]

**fallow**[2] *adj.* of a pale brownish or reddish yellow (*fallow deer*). [Old English]

**false** /fols, fawls/ *adj.* **1** wrong, incorrect (*a false idea*). **2 a** spurious, artificial (*false gods*; *false teeth*). **b** acting as such; appearing to be such, esp. deceptively (*false lining*). **3** improperly so called (*false acacia*). **4** deceptive. **5** (foll. by *to*) deceitful, treacherous, or unfaithful. □ **falsely** *adv.* **falseness** *n.* [Latin *falsus*: related to FAIL]

**false alarm** *n.* alarm given needlessly.

**falsehood** *n.* **1** untrue thing. **2 a** act of lying. **b** lie.

**false pretences** *n.pl.* misrepresentations made with intent to deceive (esp. *under false pretences*).

**false sarsaparilla** *n.* = HARDENBERGIA.

**falsetto** /fol-ˈset-oh, fawl-/ *n.* male singing voice above the normal range. [Italian diminutive: related to FALSE]

**falsify** /ˈfol-suh-ˌfuy, fawl-/ *v.* (**-ies**, **-ied**) **1** fraudulently alter. **2** misrepresent. □ **falsification** /-fuh-ˈkay-shuhn/ *n.* [French or medieval Latin: related to FALSE]

**falsity** *n.* state of being false, falseness.

**falter** /ˈfol-tuh, ˈfawl-/ *v.* **1** stumble; go unsteadily. **2** lose courage. **3** speak hesitatingly. [origin uncertain]

**fame** *n.* **1** renown; state of being famous. **2** *archaic* reputation (*house of ill fame*). [Latin *fama*]

**famed** *adj.* (usu. foll. by *for*) famous; much spoken of.

**familial** /fuh-ˈmil-yuhl/ *adj.* of a family or its members.

**familiar** /fuh-ˈmil-yuh/ — *adj.* **1 a** (often foll. by *to*) well known. **b** common, usual; often encountered or experienced. **2** (foll. by *with*) knowing a thing well. **3** (often foll. by *with*) well acquainted (with a person). **4** informal, esp. presumptuously so (*don't get familiar with the queen*). — *n.* close friend. □ **familiarity** /fuh-ˌmil-ee-a-ruh-tee/ *n.* **familiarly** *adv.* [Latin: related to FAMILY]

**familiarise** *v.* (also **-ize**) (**-sing** or **-zing**) (usu. foll. by *with*) make (a person or oneself) conversant or well acquainted. □ **familiarisation** /-ˌzay-shuhn/ *n.*

**family** /fam-uh-lee, fam-lee/ n. (pl. -ies) **1** set of relations, esp. parents and children. **2 a** members of a household. **b** person's children. **c** (attrib.) serving the needs of families; of or relating to a family (family doctor; family problems). **3 a** all the descendants of a common ancestor. **b** all the languages derived from a particular early language. **4** group of similar objects, people, etc. **5** group of related genera of animals or plants. □ **in the family way** colloq. pregnant. [Latin familia]

**family allowance** n. any of various government schemes offering financial assistance with the rearing of children.

**Family Court of Australia** n. court which administers family law.

**family planning** n. birth control.

**family reunion** n. **1** get together for extended members of a family. **2** immigration policy which favours immigrants who have members of their family already settled in Australia.

**family tree** n. chart showing a family's relationships and lines of descent; genealogical chart.

**famine** /fam-uhn/ n. extreme scarcity, esp. of food. [Latin fames hunger]

**famish** /fam-ish/ v. (usu. in passive) make or become extremely hungry. □ **be famished** (or **famishing**) colloq. be very hungry. [Romanic: related to FAMINE]

**famous** /fay-muhs/ adj. **1** (often foll. by for) celebrated; well-known. **2** colloq. excellent. □ **famously** adv. [Latin: related to FAME]

**fan**[1] — n. **1** apparatus, usu. with rotating blades, for ventilation etc. **2** folding semicircular device waved to cool oneself. **3** thing spread out like a fan, e.g. a bird's tail. — v. (-nn-) **1** blow air on, with or as with a fan. **2** (of a breeze) blow gently on. **3** (usu. foll. by out) spread out like a fan. [Latin vannus winnowing-basket]

**fan**[2] n. devotee of a particular activity, performer, etc. (footy fan). [abbreviation of FANATIC]

**fanatic** /fuh-nat-ik/ — n. person obsessively devoted to a belief, activity, etc. — adj. excessively enthusiastic. □ **fanatical** adj. **fanatically** adv. **fanaticism** n. [Latin fanum temple]

**fan belt** n. belt driving a fan to cool the radiator in a vehicle.

**fancier** /fan-see-uh/ n. connoisseur or follower of some activity or thing (dog-fancier).

**fanciful** /fan-suh-ˌfuhl/ adj. **1** imaginary. **2** indulging in fancies; whimsical. □ **fancifully** adv.

**fan club** n. organised group of devotees.

**fancy** /fan-see/ — n. (pl. -ies) **1** individual taste or inclination (take a fancy to). **2** whim or caprice. **3** supposition. **4 a** faculty of imagination. **b** mental image. — adj. (-ier, -iest) **1** ornamental; not plain. **2** whimsical; extravagant (at a fancy price). — v. (-ies, -ied) **1** (foll. by that) be inclined to suppose. **2** colloq. feel a desire for (fancy a drink?). **3** colloq. find sexually attractive. **4** colloq. value (oneself, one's ability, etc.) unduly highly. **5** (in imper.) exclamation of surprise (fancy their doing that!). **6** picture to oneself; imagine. □ **take a fancy to** become (esp. inexplicably) fond of. **take a person's fancy** suddenly attract or please. □ **fancily** adv. **fanciness** n. [contraction of FANTASY]

**fancy dress** n. costume for masquerading at a party.

**fancy-free** adj. without (esp. emotional) commitments.

**fandango** /fan-dang-goh/ n. (pl. -es or -s) **1** lively Spanish dance for two. **2** music for this. [Spanish]

**fanfare** /fan-fair/ n. short showy or ceremonious sounding of trumpets etc. [French]

**fan-flower** n. small Australian shrub or prostrate plant with profuse fan-shaped bluish or whitish flowers.

**fanfold** n. paper (for a computer-printer) the sheets of which are so folded that they fall in a zig-zag way like the folds of a fan.

**fan-forced** adj. (of a convection oven) fitted with a fan that distributes the heat evenly throughout.

**fang** — n. **1** canine tooth, esp. of a dog or wolf. **2** tooth (of a venomous snake) by which poison is injected. **3** root of a tooth or its prong. — v. colloq. borrow in a pressurising way (he fanged me for forty bucks). □ **put the fangs in** colloq. attempt to cadge or borrow; importune. [Old English]

**fanlight** n. small, orig. semicircular, window over a door or another window.

**fan palm** n. Queensland palm with large circular leaves.

**fantail** n. **1** pigeon with a fan-shaped tail. **2** flycatcher with a fan-shaped tail, including several Australian species (grey fantail; rufous fantail).

**fantasia** /fan-tay-zee-uh, -tay-zhuh/ n. free or improvisatory musical or other composition, or one based on familiar tunes. [Italian: related to FANTASY]

**fantasise** /fan-tuh-ˌsuyz/ v. (also -ize) (-sing or -zing) **1** day-dream. **2** imagine; create a fantasy about.

**fantastic** /fan-**tas**-tik/ adj. **1** colloq. excellent, extraordinary. **2** extravagantly fanciful; eccentric. **3** grotesque or quaint in design etc. □ **fantastically** adv. [Greek: related to FANTASY]

**fantasy** /**fan**-tuh-see, -zee/ — n. (pl. **-ies**) **1** imagination, esp. when unrelated to reality (lives in the realm of fantasy). **2** mental image, day-dream. **3** fantastic invention or composition. **4** special category of fiction concerned with imaginative, often magical worlds. — adj. dealing with imaginative, magical worlds (fantasy novel; fantasy literature). [Greek phantasia appearance]

**fanzine** /**fan**-zeen/ n. magazine containing information etc. about a fantasy writer, pop star, etc. [FAN², (MAGA)ZINE]

**far** (**further**, **furthest** or **farther**, **farthest**) — adv. **1** at, to, or by a great distance (far away; far off; far out). **2** a long way (off) in space or time (are you travelling far?). **3** to a great extent or degree; by much (far better; far too early). — adj. **1** remote; distant (far country). **2** more distant (far end of the hall). **3** extreme (far left). □ **as far as 1** right up to (a place). **2** to the extent that (travel as far as you like). **by far** by a great amount. **a far cry** a long way. **far from** very different from being; almost the opposite of (far from being fat). **go far 1** achieve much. **2** contribute greatly. **go too far** overstep the limit (of propriety etc.). **so far 1** to such an extent; to this point. **2** until now. **so** (or **in so**) **far as** (or **that**) to the extent that. **so far so good** satisfactory up to now. [Old English]

**farad** /**fa**-ruhd/ n. SI unit of capacitance, such that one coulomb of charge causes a potential difference of one volt. [Faraday, name of a physicist]

**faradaya** /**fa**-ruh-day-uh/ n. vigorous liana-forming climbing plant Faradaya splendida of Queensland rainforests, having jade-green heart-shaped leaves and large tube-shaped highly perfumed flowers followed by edible fruit.

**far and away** adv. by a very large amount.

**far and wide** adv. over a large area.

**faraway** adj. **1** remote. **2** (of a look or voice) dreamy, distant.

**farce** n. **1 a** low comedy with a ludicrously improbable plot. **b** this branch of drama. **2** absurdly futile proceedings; pretence. □ **farcical** adj. [Latin farcio to stuff, used metaphorically of interludes etc.]

**fare** — n. **1 a** price of a journey on public transport. **b** fare-paying passenger. **2** range of food. — v. (**-ring**) **1** progress; get on (how did you fare?). **2** happen; turn out. [Old English]

**farewell** /fair-**wel**/ — int. goodbye. — n. **1** leave-taking. **2** function organised to mark a person's departure. — adj. valedictory. — v. say goodbye to.

**far-fetched** adj. unconvincing, incredible.

**far-flung** adj. **1** widely scattered. **2** remote.

**far gone** adj. colloq. very ill, drunk, etc.

**farina** /fuh-**ree**-nuh/ n. **1** flour or meal of cereal, nuts, or starchy roots. **2** starch. □ **farinaceous** /ˌfa-ruh-**nay**-shuhs/ adj. [Latin]

**farm** — n. **1** land and its buildings under one management for growing crops, rearing animals, etc. **2** used land etc. for a specified purpose (trout-farm). — v. **1 a** use (land) for growing crops, rearing animals, etc. **b** be a farmer; work on a farm. **2** breed (fish etc.) commercially. **3** (often foll. by out) delegate or subcontract (work) to others. □ **buy back the farm** retrieve Australian land, companies, etc. from foreign ownership. **sell off the farm** sell the capital assets of Australia to foreign interests. □ **farming** n. [French ferme from Latin firma fixed payment]

**farmer** n. owner or manager of a farm, esp. one whose principal occupation is the cultivation of crops.

**farmhand** n. worker on a farm.

**farmhouse** n. house attached to a farm.

**farmstead** /**fahm**-sted/ n. farm and its buildings.

**far-off** adj. remote.

**far-out** adj. **1** distant. **2** colloq. avant-garde, unconventional. **3** colloq. fantastic, wonderful.

**farrago** /fuh-**rah**-goh/ n. (pl. **-s**) medley, hotchpotch. [Latin, = mixed fodder]

**far-reaching** adj. widely influential or applicable.

**farrier** /**fa**-ree-uh/ n. smith who shoes horses. [Latin ferrum iron, horseshoe]

**farrow** /**fa**-roh/ — n. **1** litter of pigs. **2** birth of a litter. — v. (also absol.) (of a sow) produce (pigs). [Old English]

**far-seeing** adj. showing foresight; wise.

**far-sighted** adj. having foresight, prudent.

**fart** colloq. — v. **1** emit wind from the anus. **2** (foll. by about, around) behave foolishly. — n. **1** an emission of wind from the anus. **2** unpleasant or foolish person. [Old English]

**farther** var. of FURTHER (esp. of physical distance).

**farthest** var. of FURTHEST (esp. of physical distance).

**farthing** /**fah**-thing/ n. **1** hist. coin and monetary unit worth a quarter of an old penny. **2** trifling amount (not worth a *farthing*). [Old English: related to FOURTH]

**fascia** /fay-shuh/ *n.* (also **facia**)(*pl.* **-s**) **1** stripe or band. **2 a** long flat surface in classical architecture. **b** flat surface, usu. of wood, covering the ends of rafters. **3** /**fash**-uh/ *Anat.* thin sheath of fibrous tissue. [Latin, = band, door-frame]

**fascinate** /**fas**-uh-,nayt/ *v.* (**-ting**) **1** capture the interest of; attract. **2** (esp. of a snake) paralyse (a victim) with fear. □ **fascination** /-**nay**-shuhn/ *n.* [Latin *fascinum* spell]

**Fascism** /**fash**-iz-uhm/ *n.* **1** extreme totalitarian right-wing nationalist movement in Italy (1922–43). **2** (also **fascism**) any similar movement. □ **Fascist** *n.* & *adj.* (also **fascist**). **Fascistic** /fa-**shis**-tik/ *adj.* (also **fascistic**). [Italian *fascio* bundle, organised group]

**fashion** /**fash**-uhn/ — *n.* **1** current popular custom or style, esp. in dress. **2** manner of doing something (*in a peculiar fashion*). — *adj.* pertaining to fashion (*a fashion show*). — *v.* (often foll. by *into*) make or form. □ **after** (or **in**) **a fashion** to some extent, barely acceptably. **in** (or **out of**) **fashion** fashionable (or not fashionable). [Latin *factio*: related to FACT]

**fashionable** *adj.* **1** following or suited to current fashion. **2** of or favoured by high society. □ **fashionableness** *n.* **fashionably** *adv.*

**fast¹** /fahst/ — *adj.* **1** rapid, quick-moving. **2** capable of or intended for high speed (*fast car; fast lane*). **3** (of a clock etc.) ahead of the correct time. **4 a** (of a pitch etc.) causing the ball to bounce quickly. **b** (of a racecourse) firm and dry, enabling fast times. **5** firm; firmly fixed or attached (*fast knot; fast friendship*). **6** (of a colour) not fading in light or when washed. **7** pleasure seeking, dissolute. **8** (of photographic film etc.) needing only short exposure. — *adv.* **1** quickly; in quick succession. **2** firmly, fixedly, tightly (*stand fast*). **3** soundly, completely (*fast asleep*). □ **pull a fast one** (or **a fastie** or **a swiftie**) *colloq.* perpetrate deceit. [Old English]

**fast²** /fahst/ — *v.* abstain from food, or certain food, for a time. — *n.* act or period of fasting. [Old English]

**fastback** *n.* **1** car with a sloping rear. **2** such a rear.

**fast breeder** *n.* (also **fast breeder reactor**) reactor using fast neutrons to produce the same fissile material as it uses.

**fast buck** *n. colloq.* money made quickly and usu. dishonestly.

**fasten** /**fah**-suhn/ *v.* **1** make or become

fixed or secure. **2** (foll. by *in, up*) lock securely; shut in. **3 a** (foll. by *on, upon*) direct (a look, thoughts, etc.) fixedly or intently. **b** focus or direct the attention fixedly upon (*fastened him with her eyes*). **4** (foll. by *on, upon*) fix (a designation or imputation etc.) (*fastened the guilt on him*). **5** (foll. by *on, upon*) **a** take hold of. **b** single out. **6** (foll. by *off*) fix with a knot or stitches. □ **fastener** *n.* [Old English: related to FAST¹]

**fastening** /**fah**-suh-ning/ *n.* device that fastens something; fastener.

**fast food** *n.* restaurant food that is quickly produced and served.

**fast forward** — *n.* switching device (on a video tape-recorder) which runs the tape forward swiftly. — *v.* run (a videotape) swiftly forward.

**fastidious** /fas-**tid**-ee-uhs/ *adj.* **1** excessively discriminatory; fussy. **2** easily disgusted; squeamish. □ **fastidiously** *adv.* **fastidiousness** *n.* [Latin *fastidium* loathing]

**fastie** *n. colloq.* deceitful act. □ **pull a fastie** perpetrate deceit.

**fast lane** *n.* **1** lane on a highway for overtaking or travelling fast. **2** quickest route to social and financial success. □ **life in the fast lane** life lived at a hectic pace.

**fast neutron** *n.* neutron with high kinetic energy.

**fast-talk** *v.* deceive by confusing the listener with rapid flow of talk. □ **fast-talk(ing)** *n.*

**fast-track** — *n.* = FAST LANE 2. — *v.* bring about the completion of something very speedily (*they wanted the government to fast-track the building of the bypass*).

**fat** — *n.* **1** natural oily or greasy substance found esp. in animal bodies. **2** part of meat etc. containing this. **3** excessive presence of fat in a person or animal; corpulence (*work off the fat*). **4** *coarse colloq.* erection of the penis. — *adj.* (**fatter**, **fattest**) **1** (of a person or animal) corpulent; plump. **2** (of an animal) made plump for slaughter; fatted. **3** containing much fat. **4** (of land or resources) fertile, rich. **5 a** thick (*fat book*). **b** substantial (*fat cheque*). **6** *colloq. iron.* very little; not much (*a fat chance*; *a fat lot*). — *v.* (**-tt-**) make or become fat. □ **the fat is in the fire** trouble is imminent. **live off** (or **on**) **the fat of the land** live luxuriously. □ **fatless** *adj.* **fatness** *n.* **fattish** *adj.* [Old English]

**fatal** /**fay**-tuhl/ *adj.* **1** causing or ending in death (*fatal accident*). **2** (often foll. by *to*) ruinous (*fatal mistake*). **3** fateful. □ **fatally** *adv.* [Latin: related to FATE]

**fatalism** /**fay**-tuh-liz-uhm/ *n.* **1** belief in

predetermination. **2** submissive attitude to events as being inevitable. □ **fatalist** n.

**fatalistic** /-tuh-**lis**-tik/ adj. **fatalistically** /-**lis**-ti-kuh-lee, -klee/ adv.

**fatality** /fuh-**tal**-uh-tee/ n. (pl. **-ies**) **1 a** death by accident or in war etc. **b** person killed in this way. **2** fatal influence. **3** predestined liability to disaster.

**fat cat** n. derog. **1** person who is accustomed to special privileges because of status or influence. **2** member of the higher echelons of the Public Service.

**fate** — n. **1** supposed power predetermining events. **2 a** the future so determined. **b** individual's destiny or fortune. **c** ultimate condition or end of a person or thing (*that sealed our fate*). **3** death, destruction. — v. (**-ting**) **1** (usu. in *passive*) preordain (*fated to win*). **2** (as **fated** adj.) doomed. □ **fate worse than death** see DEATH. [Italian and Latin *fatum*]

**fateful** adj. **1** important, decisive. **2** controlled by fate. □ **fatefully** adv.

**fat-headed** adj. stupid.

**father** /**fah**-thuh/ — n. **1** male parent. **2** (usu. in pl.) forefather. **3** originator, early leader. **4** (**Fathers** or **Fathers of the Church**) early Christian theologians. **5** (also **Father**) (often as a title or form of address) priest. **6** (**the Father**) (in Christian belief) first person of the Trinity. **7** (**Father**) venerable person, esp. as a title in personifications (*Father Time*). **8** (usu. in pl.) elders (*city fathers*). — v. **1 a** beget; be the father of. **b** behave as a father towards. **2** originate (a scheme etc.). □ **father of** (or **mother of**, or **father and mother of**) the greatest or biggest thing of a class (*the mother of all battles in Iraq*). □ **fatherhood** n. **fatherless** adj. **fatherly** adj. [Old English]

**father figure** n. older man respected and trusted like a father.

**father-in-law** n. (pl. **fathers-in-law**) father of one's husband or wife.

**fatherland** n. one's native country.

**Father's Day** n. day (usu. the first Sunday in September) on which fathers are honoured, given presents, etc.

**fathom** /**fa**-thuhm/ — n. (pl. often **fathom** when prec. by a number) measure of six feet (1.8288 m), esp. in depth soundings. — v. **1** grasp or comprehend (a problem or difficulty). **2** measure the depth of (water). □ **fathomable** adj. [Old English]

**fathomless** adj. too deep to fathom.

**fatigue** /fuh-**teeg**/ — n. **1** extreme tiredness. **2** weakness in metals etc. caused by repeated variations of stress,

e.g. cleaning. **3 a** non-military army duty. **b** (in pl.) clothing worn for this. — v. (**-gues**, **-gued**, **-guing**) cause fatigue in. [Latin *fatigo* exhaust]

**fatten** v. make or become fat.

**fatty** adj. (**-ier**, **-iest**) like or containing fat.

**fatty acid** n. organic compound consisting of a hydrocarbon chain and a terminal carboxyl group.

**fatuous** /**fa**-choo-uhs/ adj. vacantly silly; purposeless, idiotic. □ **fatuity** /fuh-**choo**-uh-tee/ n. (pl. **-ies**). **fatuously** adv. **fatuousness** n. [Latin *fatuus*]

**fatwa** /**fat**-wah/ n. legal decision or ruling by an Islamic religious leader. [Arabic]

**faucet** /**faw**-suht/ n. esp. US tap. [French *fausset* vent-peg]

**fault** /folt, fawlt/ — n. **1** defect or imperfection of character, structure, appearance, etc. **2** responsibility for wrongdoing, error, etc. (*your own fault*). **3** break in an electric circuit. **4** transgression, offence. **5 a** *Tennis etc.* incorrect service. **b** (in showjumping) penalty for error. **6** break in rock strata. — v. **1** find fault with; blame. **2** commit a fault. **3** *Geol.* **a** break the continuity of (strata). **b** show a fault. □ **at fault** guilty; to blame. **find fault** (often foll. by *with*) criticise; complain. **to a fault** excessively (*generous to a fault*). [Latin *fallo* deceive]

**faultless** adj. free from defect or error, perfect. □ **faultlessly** adv.

**faulty** adj. (**-ier**, **-iest**) having faults; imperfect, defective. □ **faultily** adv. **faultiness** n.

**faun** /fawn/ n. (in Roman mythology) rural deity with goat's horns, legs, and tail. [Latin *Faunus*]

**fauna** /**faw**-nuh/ n. (pl. **-s** or **-nae** /-nee/) animal life of a region or period. □ **faunal** adj. [Latin *Fauna*, name of a rural goddess]

**faunal emblem** n. an animal officially adopted by a country (and in Australia also by a State or Territory) as a symbol, e.g. the koala by Queensland.

**faux pas** /foh **pah**/ n. (pl. same /**pahz**/) tactless mistake; blunder; social indiscretion. [French, = false step]

**favour** /**fay**-vuh/ (also **favor**) — n. **1** kind act (*did it as a favour*). **2** approval, goodwill; friendly regard (*gained their favour*). **3** partiality; too generous or lenient treatment. **4** badge, ribbon, etc., as an emblem of support. — v. **1** regard or treat with favour or partiality. **2** support, promote, prefer. **3** be to the advantage of (a person); facilitate (a process etc.). **4** tend to confirm (an idea etc.). **5** (foll. by *with*) oblige (*favour me* *with a reply).* **6** (as **favoured** *adj.*) having special advantages. □ **in favour 1** approved of. **2** (foll. by *of*) **a** in support of. **b** to the advantage of. **out of favour** disapproved of. [Latin *faveo* be kind to]

**favourable** /fay-vuh-ruh-buhl/ *adj.* (also **favorable**) **1** well-disposed; propitious; approving. **2** promising, auspicious (*a favourable aspect*). **3** helpful, suitable. □ **favourably** *adv.*

**favourite** /fay-vuh-ruht/ (also **favorite**) — *adj.* preferred to all others (*favourite book*). — *n.* **1** favourite person or thing. **2** *Sport* competitor thought most likely to win. [Italian: related to FAVOUR]

**favouritism** *n.* (also **favoritism**) unfair favouring of one person etc. at the expense of another.

**fawn¹** — *n.* **1** deer in its first year. **2** light yellowish brown. — *adj.* fawn-coloured. — *v.* (also *absol.*) give birth to (a fawn). [Latin: related to FOETUS]

**fawn²** *v.* **1** (often foll. by *on, upon*) behave servilely, cringe. **2** (of esp. a dog) show extreme affection. [Old English]

**fax** — *n.* **1** transmission of an exact copy of a document etc. electronically. **2** copy produced by this. — *v.* transmit in this way. [abbreviation of FACSIMILE]

**fay** *n. literary* fairy. [Latin *fata* pl., = goddesses of destiny]

**faze** *v.* (**-zing**) (often as **fazed** *adj.*) *colloq.* disconcert, disorientate. [origin unknown]

**Fe** *symb.* iron. [Latin *ferrum*]

**fealty** /fee-uhl-tee/ *n.* (*pl.* **-ies**) **1** *hist.* fidelity to a feudal lord. **2** allegiance. [Latin: related to FIDELITY]

**fear** — *n.* **1** panic or distress caused by a sense of impending danger, pain, etc. **b** cause of this. **c** state of alarm (*in fear*). **2** (often foll. by *of*) dread, awe (towards) (*fear of heights*). **3** danger (*little fear of failure*). — *v.* **1** feel fear about or towards. **2** (foll. by *for*) feel anxiety about (*feared for my life*). **3** (often foll. by *that*) foresee or expect with unease, fear, or regret (*fear the worst; I fear that you are wrong*). **4** (foll. by verbal noun) shrink from (*feared meeting his ex-wife*). **5** revere (esp. God). □ **for fear of** (or **that**) to avoid the risk of (or that). **no fear** *colloq.* certainly not! **without fear or favour** impartially. [Old English]

**fearful** *adj.* **1** (usu. foll. by *of* or *that*) afraid. **2** terrible, awful. **3** *colloq.* extreme, esp. unpleasant (*fearful row*). □ **fearfully** *adv.* **fearfulness** *n.*

**fearless** *adj.* (often foll. by *of*) not afraid, brave. □ **fearlessly** *adv.* **fearlessness** *n.*

**fearsome** *adj.* frightening, esp. in appearance. □ **fearsomely** *adv.*

**feasible** /fee-zuh-buhl/ *adj.* practicable, possible; easily or conveniently done. □ **feasibility** /,fee-zuh-buhl-uh-tee/ *n.* **feasibly** *adv.* [Latin *facio* do]

■ **Usage** *Feasible* should not be used to mean 'possible' or 'probable' in the sense 'likely' (e.g. *it is feasible that it will rain*). 'Possible' or 'probable' should be used instead.

**feast** — *n.* **1** large or sumptuous meal. **2** sensual or mental pleasure. **3 a** (also **Feast**) annual religious celebration (*Feast of the Nativity*). **b** day dedicated to a particular saint. — *v.* (often foll. by *on*) partake of a feast; eat and drink sumptuously. □ **feast one's eyes on** look with pleasure at. [Latin *festus* joy]

**feat** *n.* remarkable act or achievement. [Latin: related to FACT]

**feather** /feth-uh/ — *n.* **1** one of the structures forming a bird's plumage, with a horny stem and fine strands. **2** (*collect.*) plumage. — *v.* **1** cover or line with feathers. **2** turn (an oar) edgeways through the air. □ **feather in one's cap** a personal achievement. **feather one's nest** enrich oneself. **in fine** (or **high**) **feather** *colloq.* in good spirits. **make the feathers fly** create turmoil. **show the white feather** show cowardice. □ **feathery** *adj.* [Old English]

**featherbed** *n.* bed with a feather-stuffed mattress.

**feather-bed** *v.* (**-dd-**) **1** provide with (esp. financial) advantages. **2** protect workers (in a factory etc.) by limiting the work to be done.

**featherbrain** *n.* silly or absent-minded person. □ **feather-brained** *adj.*

**feather flower** *n.* any plant of the Australian genus *Verticordia*.

**featherweight** *n.* **1 a** weight in certain sports between bantamweight and lightweight, in amateur boxing 54–7kg. **b** sportsman in this weight. **2** very light person or thing. **3** (usu. *attrib.*) unimportant thing.

**feature** /fee-chuh/ — *n.* **1** distinctive or characteristic part of a thing. **2** (usu. in *pl.*) part of the face. **3** (esp. specialised) article in a newspaper etc. **4** (in full **feature film**) main film in a cinema programme. — *v.* (**-ring**) **1** make a special display of; emphasise. **2** have as or be a central participant or topic in a film, broadcast, etc. □ **featureless** *adj.* [Latin *factura* formation: related to FACT]

**febrifuge** /feb-ruh-,fyooj/ *n.* medicine or treatment for fever. [Latin *febris* fever]

**febrile** /fee-bruyl, feb-ruyl/ *adj.* of or

relating to fever; feverish. [Latin *febris* fever]

**February** /**feb**-roo-uh-ree/ *n.* (*pl.* **-ies**) second month of the year. [Latin *februa* purification feast]

**fecal** var. of FAECAL.

**feces** var. of FAECES.

**feckless** /**fek**-luhs/ *adj.* **1** feeble, ineffective. **2** unthinking, irresponsible. [Scots *feck* from *effeck* var. of EFFECT]

**fecund** /**fee**-kuhnd, **fek**-uhnd/ *adj.* prolific, fertile. □ **fecundity** /fuh-**kun**-duh-tee/ *n.* [Latin]

**fed**[1] *past* and *past part.* of FEED. □ **fed up** (**to the back teeth**) (often foll. by **with**) discontented or frustrated.

**fed**[2] *n. colloq.* officer of the Australian Federal Police.

**federal** /**fed**-uh-ruhl/ *adj.* **1 a** of a system of government in which self-governing States unite for certain functions etc. **b** of or pertaining to the Commonwealth of Australia, as distinct from the States (*federal election*; *federal parliament*; *Canberra, the federal capital*). **2** of such a federation (*federal laws*). **3** of or favouring centralised government. **4** comprising an association of largely independent units. □ **federalise** *v.* (also **-ize**) (**-sing** or **-zing**). **federalisation** /-zay-shuhn/ *n.* **federalism** *n.* **federalist** *n.* **federally** *adv.* [Latin *foedus* covenant]

**federate** — *v.* /**fed**-uh-rayt/ (**-ting**) unite on a federal basis. — *adj.* /**fed**-uh-ruht/ federally organised. □ **federative** /**fed**-uh-ruh-tiv/ *adj.*

**federation** /ˌfed-uh-**ray**-shuhn/ *n.* **1** group (of States etc.) united on a federal basis. **2** act of federating. **3** (**Federation**) **a** association of the six Australian colonies in a federal union. **b** formation of the Commonwealth of Australia on 1 January 1901. [Latin: related to FEDERAL]

**federation style** *n.* **1** style of Australian domestic architecture flourishing between 1895 and 1915. **2** imitation of this.

**fee** *n.* **1** payment made for professional advice or services etc. **2 a** charge for a privilege, examination, admission to a society, etc. (*enrolment fee*). **b** money paid for the transfer to another employer of a footballer etc. **3** (in *pl.*) regular payments (esp. to a school). [medieval Latin *feudum*]

**feeble** /**fee**-buhl/ *adj.* (**feebler**, **feeblest**) **1** weak, infirm (*feeble of mind and body*). **2** lacking strength, energy, or effectiveness (*feeble effort*; *feeble joke*). **3** dim, indistinct (*feeble light*). □ **feebly** *adv.* [Latin *flebilis* lamentable]

**feeble-minded** *adj.* mentally deficient.

**feed** — *v.* (*past* and *past part.* **fed**) **1 a** supply with food. **b** put food into the mouth of. **2** give as food, supply to animals. **3** (usu. foll. by *on*) (esp. of animals, or *colloq.* of people) eat. **4** (often foll. by *on*) nourish or be nourished by; benefit from. **5 a** keep (a fire, machine, etc.) supplied with fuel etc. **b** (foll. by *into*) supply (material) to a machine etc. **c** (often foll. by *into*) (of a river etc.) flow into a lake etc. **d** keep (a meter) supplied with coins to ensure continuity. **6** *colloq.* supply (an actor etc.) with cues. **7** *Sport* send passes to (a player). **8** gratify (vanity etc.). **9** provide (advice, information, etc.) to. — *n.* **1** food, esp. for animals or infants. **2** act or instance of feeding; giving of food. **3** *colloq.* meal. **4 a** raw material for a machine etc. **b** provision of or device for this. □ **feed back** produce feedback. **feed up** fatten. [Old English]

**feedback** *n.* **1** public response to an event, experiment, etc. **2** *Electronics* **a** return of a fraction of an output signal to the input. **b** signal so returned.

**feeder** *n.* **1** person or thing that feeds, esp. in specified manner (*some plants are gross feeders*). **2** bib. **3** tributary stream. **4** branch road, railway line, etc. linking with a main system. **5** main carrying electricity to a distribution point. **6** feeding apparatus in a machine.

**feel** — *v.* (*past* and *past part.* **felt**) **1 a** examine or search by touch. **b** (*absol.*) have the sensation of touch (*unable to feel*). **2** perceive or ascertain by touch (*feel the warmth*). **3** experience, exhibit, or be affected by (an emotion, conviction, etc.) (*felt strongly about it*; *felt the rebuke*). **4** (foll. by *that*) have an impression (*I feel that I am right*). **5** consider, think (*I feel it useful to go*). **6** seem (*air feels chilly*). **7** be consciously; consider oneself (*I feel happy*; *I don't feel well*). **8** (foll. by *for*, *with*) have sympathy or pity. — *n.* **1** act or instance of feeling; testing by touch. **2** sensation characterising a material, situation, etc. **3** sense of touch. □ **feel like** have a wish or inclination for. **feel out** explore tentatively in order to judge possible reactions (*we need to feel out the Democrats before we make a move*). **feel up to** be ready to face or deal with. **feel one's way** proceed cautiously. **get the feel of** become accustomed to using. [Old English]

**feeler** *n.* **1** organ in certain animals for touching or searching for food. **2** tentative proposal or suggestion, esp. to elicit a response (*put out feelers*).

**feeling** — *n.* **1 a** capacity to feel; sense of

touch (*lost all feeling in his arm*). **b** physical sensation. **2 a** (often foll. by *of*) emotional reaction (*feeling of despair*). **b** (in *pl.*) emotional susceptibility or sympathies (*hurt my feelings; had strong feelings about it*). **3** particular sensitivity (*feeling for literature*). **4 a** opinion or notion (*had a feeling she would*). **b** general sentiment (*the feeling was against it*). **5** sympathy or compassion. **6** emotional sensibility or intensity (*played with feeling*). **7** (as **bad feelings**, **good feelings**) presentiments, good or bad (*I have bad feelings about this, really bad vibes*). — *adj.* sensitive, sympathetic; heartfelt. □ **feelingly** *adv.*

**feet** *pl.* of FOOT.

**feign** /fayn/ *v.* simulate; pretend (*feign madness*). [Latin *fingo fict-* mould, contrive]

**feint** /faynt/ — *n.* **1** sham attack or diversionary blow. **2** pretence. — *v.* make a feint. — *adj.* = FAINT *adj.* 6. [French: related to FEIGN]

**felafel** /fuh-**lah**-fuhl/ *n.* (also **falafel**) spicy dish of fried rissoles made from mashed chick peas, chillies, etc. [Arabic *falāfil*]

**feldspar** /**feld**-spah/ *n.* (also **felspar**) common aluminium silicate of potassium, sodium, or calcium. □ **feldspathic** /-**spath**-ik/ *adj.* [German *Feld* field, *Spat(h)* SPAR3]

**felicitate** /fuh-**lis**-uh-ˌtayt/ *v.* (**-ting**) *formal* congratulate. □ **felicitation** /-**tay**-shuhn/ *n.* (usu. in *pl.*). [Latin *felix felic-* happy]

**felicitous** /fuh-**lis**-uh-tuhs/ *adj. formal* apt; pleasantly ingenious; well-chosen.

**felicity** /fuh-**lis**-uh-tee/ *n.* (*pl.* **-ies**) *formal* **1** intense happiness. **2 a** capacity for apt expression. **b** well-chosen phrase. [Latin *felix* happy]

**feline** /**fee**-luyn/ — *adj.* **1** of or relating to the cat family. **2** catlike. — *n.* animal of the cat family. □ **felinity** /fuh-**lin**-uh-tee/ *n.* [Latin *feles* cat]

**fell**[1] *past* of FALL *v.*

**fell**[2] *v.* **1** cut down (esp. a tree). **2** strike or knock down. [Old English]

**fell**[3] *adj. poet.* or *rhet.* ruthless, destructive. □ **at** (or **in**) **one fell swoop** in a single (orig. deadly) action. [French: related to FELON]

**fella** *n.* = FELLOW 1 & 4.

**fell**[5] *n.* animal's hide or skin with its hair. [Old English]

**fellatio** /fuh-**lay**-shee-oh/ *n.* sexual practice in which a person stimulates the penis of another with lips, mouth, and tongue. [Latin *fello* suck]

**feller** *n.* = FELLOW 1 & 4.

**fellow** /**fel**-oh/ — *n.* **1** (also **fella**, **feller**) *colloq.* man or boy (*poor fellow!*). **2** *colloq.* boyfriend (*he's my fellow*). **3** (usu. in *pl.*) person in a group etc.; comrade (*separated from their fellows*). **4** (in Aboriginal English) (usu. as **fella** or **feller**) person. **5** counterpart; one of a pair. **6** equal; peer. **7** graduate paid to do research at a university etc. **8** (usu. **Fellow**) member of a learned society (*Fellow of the Royal Australasian College of Physicians*). — *adj.* of the same group etc. (*fellow-countryman*). [Old English from Old Norse]

**fellow feeling** *n.* sympathy.

**fellowship** *n.* **1** friendly association with others, companionship. **2** body of associates. **3** status or income of a fellow of a university etc.

**fellow-traveller** *n.* **1** person who travels with another. **2** sympathiser with the Communist Party.

**felon** /**fel**-uhn/ *n.* person who has committed a felony. [medieval Latin *fello*]

**felony** *n.* (*pl.* **-ies**) serious, usu. violent, crime. □ **felonious** /fuh-**loh**-nee-uhs/ *adj.*

**felspar** var. of FELDSPAR.

**felt**[1] — *n.* cloth of matted and pressed fibres of wool etc. — *v.* **1** make into felt; mat. **2** cover with felt. **3** become matted. [Old English]

**felt**[2] *past* and *past part.* of FEEL.

**felt-tipped pen** *n.* (also **felt-tip pen**) pen with a fibre point.

**female** /**fee**-mayl/ — *adj.* **1** of the sex that can give birth or produce eggs. **2** (of plants) fruit-bearing; having a pistil and no stamens. **3** of or consisting of women or female animals or plants. **4** (of a screw, socket, etc.) hollow to receive an inserted part. — *n.* female person, animal, or plant. [Latin diminutive of *femina* woman, assimilated to *male*]

**feminine** /**fem**-uh-nuhn/ — *adj.* **1** of or characteristic of women. **2** having womanly qualities. **3** *Gram.* of or denoting the female gender. — *n. Gram.* feminine gender or word. [Latin: related to FEMALE]

**feminism** /**fem**-uh-ˌniz-uhm/ *n.* advocacy of women's rights and sexual equality. □ **feminist** *n.* & *adj.*

**femme fatale** /ˌfem fuh-**tahl**/ *n.* (*pl.* **femmes fatales** pronunc. same) dangerously seductive woman. [French]

**femur** /**fee**-muh/ *n.* (*pl.* **-s** or **femora** /**fem**-uh-ruh/) thigh-bone. □ **femoral** /**fem**-uh-ruhl/ *adj.* [Latin]

**fen** *n. Brit.* low marshy land. [Old English]

**fence** — *n.* **1** barrier, railing, etc., enclosing a field, garden, etc. **2** large upright jump for horses. **3** *colloq.* receiver of stolen goods. **4** guard or guide in machinery. — *v.* (**-cing**) **1** surround with or as with a fence. **2** (foll. by *in, off, up*) enclose, separate, or seal, with or as with a fence. **3** practise fencing with a sword. **4** evade answering (a person or question). **5** *colloq.* deal in (stolen goods). □ **over the fence** *colloq.* unacceptable (*that remark was a bit over the fence*). **sit on the fence** remain neutral; be wary of committing oneself. □ **fencer** *n.* [from DEFENCE]

**fencing** *n.* **1** set of, or material for, fences. **2** sword-fighting, esp. as a sport.

**fend** *v.* **1** (foll. by *for*) look after (esp. oneself). **2** (usu. foll. by *off*) keep away; ward off (an attack etc.). [from DEFEND]

**fender** *n.* **1** low frame bordering a fireplace. **2** bumper bar of a car.

**fennel** /fen-uhl/ *n.* yellow-flowered fragrant herb used for flavouring and as an ingredient in curry-powder. [Latin *fenum* hay]

**fenugreek** /fen-yoo-,greek/ *n.* leguminous plant with aromatic seeds used for flavouring, esp. in curries. [Latin, *faenugraecum* 'Greek hay']

**feral** /fe-ruhl, feer-ruhl/ — *adj.* **1** wild; uncultivated. **2 a** (of an animal) escaped and living wild. **b** (of a plant) growing vigorously outside its normal habitat; invasive. **3 a** (of a young person) living outside the home environment, often as a 'street kid'. **b** = HIPPIE 2. — *n.* a feral animal, plant, or person. [Latin *ferus* wild]

**ferment** — *n.* /fer-ment/ **1** excitement, unrest. **2 a** fermentation. **b** fermenting-agent. — *v.* /fuh-**ment**/ **1** undergo or subject to fermentation. **2** excite; stir up. [Latin *fermentum*: related to FERVENT]

**fermentation** /,fer-men-**tay**-shuhn/ *n.* **1** breakdown of a substance by yeasts and bacteria etc., esp. of sugar in making alcohol. **2** agitation, excitement. □ **fermentative** /-**men**-tuh-tiv/ *adj.* [Latin: related to FERMENT]

**fermium** /fer-mee-uhm/ *n.* transuranic artificial radioactive metallic element. [*Fermi*, name of a physicist]

**fern** *n.* flowerless plant usu. having feathery fronds. □ **ferny** *adj.* [Old English]

**fern gully** *n.* small valley in a damp forest where tree-ferns flourish.

**fern root** *n.* edible root of two ferns of the *Blechnum* genus.

**ferocious** /fuh-**roh**-shuhs/ *adj.* fierce, savage; wildly cruel. □ **ferociously** *adv.* **ferocity** /fuh-ros-uh-tee/ *n.* [Latin *ferox*]

**-ferous** *comb. form* (usu. **-iferous**)

forming adjectives with the sense 'bearing', 'having' (*auriferous*; *odoriferous*). [Latin *fero* bear]

**ferret** /fe-ruht/ — *n.* **1** small polecat used in catching rabbits, rats, etc. **2** person who searches assiduously. — *v.* **1** hunt with ferrets. **2** (often foll. by *out, about*, etc.) rummage; search out (secrets, criminals, etc.). [Latin *fur* thief]

**ferric** /fe-rik/ *adj.* **1** of iron. **2** containing iron in a trivalent form. [Latin *ferrum* iron]

**ferro-** *comb. form* **1** iron. **2** (of alloys) containing iron. [related to FERRIC]

**ferroconcrete** /,fe-roh-**kong**-kreet/ — *n.* reinforced concrete. — *adj.* made of this.

**ferrous** /fe-ruhs/ *adj.* **1** containing iron. **2** containing iron in a divalent form.

**ferrule** /fe-rool/ *n.* **1** ring or cap on the lower end of a stick, umbrella, etc. **2** band strengthening or forming a joint. [Latin *viriae* bracelet]

**ferry** — *n.* (*pl.* **-ies**) **1** boat or aircraft etc. for esp. regular transport, esp. across water. **2** the service itself or the place where it operates. — *v.* (**-ies, -ied**) **1** convey or go in a ferry. **2** (of a boat etc.) cross water regularly. **3** transport, esp. regularly, from place to place. □ **ferryman** *n.* [Old Norse]

**fertile** /fer-tuyl/ *adj.* **1 a** (of soil) abundantly productive. **b** fruitful. **2 a** (of a seed, egg, etc.) capable of growth. **b** (of animals and plants) able to reproduce. **3** (of the mind) inventive. **4** (of nuclear material) able to become fissile by the capture of neutrons. □ **fertility** /-til-uh-tee/ *n.* [French from Latin]

**fertilise** /fer-tuh-,luyz/ *v.* (also **-ize**) (**-sing** or **-zing**) **1** make (soil etc.) fertile. **2** cause (an egg, female animal, etc.) to develop a new individual by introducing male reproductive material. □ **fertilisation** /,fer-tuh-luy-**zay**-shuhn/ *n.*

**fertiliser** *n.* (also **-izer**) substance added to soil to make it more fertile.

**fervent** /fer-vuhnt/ *adj.* ardent, intense (*fervent admirer*; *fervent hatred*). □ **fervency** *n.* **fervently** *adv.* [Latin *ferveo* boil]

**fervid** /fer-vuhd/ *adj.* **1** burning; intensely impassioned (*fervid love-making*). **2** *poet.* hot, glowing. □ **fervidly** *adv.* [Latin: related to FERVENT]

**fervour** /fer-vuh/ *n.* (also **fervor**) passion, zeal. [Latin: related to FERVENT]

**fescue** /fes-kyoo/ *n.* a pasture and lawn grass. [Latin *festuca* stalk, straw]

**-fest** *suffix* indicating a specific period for the festive celebration of something (*jazzfest*; *filmfest*). [German, = festival]

**festal** /fes-tuhl/ *adj.* **1** joyous, merry. **2**

of a feast or festival. □ **festally** *adv.* [Latin: related to FEAST]

**fester** *v.* **1** make or become septic. **2** cause continuing anger or bitterness. **3** rot, stagnate. [Latin FISTULA]

**festival** /fes-tuh-vuhl/ *n.* **1** day or period of celebration. **2** series of cultural events in a town etc. (*Adelaide Festival*). [French: related to FESTIVE]

**festive** /fes-tiv/ *adj.* **1** of or characteristic of a festival. **2** joyous. □ **festively** *adv.* **festiveness** *n.* [Latin: related to FEAST]

**festivity** /fes-tiv-uh-tee/ *n.* (*pl.* **-ies**) **1** gaiety, rejoicing. **2** (in *pl.*) celebration; party.

**festoon** /fes-toon/ — *n.* curved hanging chain of flowers, leaves, ribbons, etc. — *v.* (often foll. by *with*) adorn with or form into festoons; decorate elaborately. [Italian: related to FESTIVE]

**Festschrift** /fest-shrift/ *n.* (also **festschrift**) (*pl.* **-en** or **-s**) collection of writings published in honour of a scholar. [German, = festival-writing]

**feta** /fet-uh/ *n.* soft white esp. ewe's-milk cheese made esp. in Greece. [Greek *pheta*]

**fetch** — *v.* **1** go for and bring back (*fetch a doctor*). **2** be sold for (a price) (*fetched $10*). **3** cause (blood, tears, etc.) to flow (*a slap so hard it fetched tears*). **4** draw (breath), heave (a sigh). **5** *colloq.* give (a blow etc.) (*fetched him a slap*). — *n.* **1** act of fetching. **2** dodge, trick. □ **fetch and carry** do menial tasks. **fetch up** *colloq.* **1** arrive, come to rest, end up. **2** vomit. [Old English]

**fetching** *adj.* attractive. □ **fetchingly** *adv.*

**fete** /fayt/ (also **fête**) — *n.* **1** outdoor fund-raising event with stalls and amusements etc. **2** festival. **3** saint's day. — *v.* (**-ting**) honour or entertain lavishly. [French: related to FEAST]

**fetid** /fet-uhd, fee-tuhd/ *adj.* (also **foetid**) stinking. [Latin *feteo* stink]

**fetish** /fet-ish/ *n.* **1 a** *Psychol.* non-sexual object, e.g. underwear, or part of the body, e.g. feet, which arouses sexual desire. **b** sexual desire for such an object etc. (*fetish for feet*). **2 a** object worshipped by primitive peoples for its supposed inherent magical powers or as being inhabited by a spirit. **b** obsessional cause (*makes a fetish of punctuality*). □ **fetishism** *n.* **fetishist** *n.* **fetishistic** /-shis-tik/ *adj.* [Portuguese *feitiço* charm]

**fetlock** /fet-lok/ *n.* back of a horse's leg above the hoof with a tuft of hair. [ultimately related to FOOT]

**fetter** — *n.* **1** shackle for holding a prisoner by the ankles. **2** (in *pl.*) captivity.

**3** restraint or check. — *v.* **1** put into fetters. **2** restrict, restrain. [Old English]

**fettle** /fet-uhl/ *n.* condition or trim (*in fine fettle*). [Old English]

**feud**¹ /fyood/ — *n.* **1** prolonged hostility, esp. between families, tribes, etc. **2** prolonged or bitter quarrel or dispute. — *v.* conduct a feud. [Germanic: related to FOE]

**feud**² /fyood/ *n.* = FIEF. [medieval Latin *feudum* FEE]

**feudal** /fyoo-duhl/ *adj.* **1** of, like, or according to the feudal system. **2** reactionary (*feudal attitude*). □ **feudalism** *n.* **feudalistic** /-lis-tik/ *adj.* [medieval Latin *feudum* FEE]

**feudal system** *n.* medieval system of land tenure with allegiance and service due to the landowner.

**fever** — *n.* **1 a** abnormally high temperature, often with delirium etc. **b** disease characterised by this (*scarlet fever*). **2** nervous excitement; agitation. — *v.* (esp. as **fevered** *adj.*) affect with fever or excitement. [Latin *febris*]

**fever bark** *n.* (also **fever tree**) tree of north Queensland, the bitter bark of which was used by Aborigines to make a medicine.

**feverish** *adj.* **1** having symptoms of fever. **2** excited, restless. □ **feverishly** *adv.* **feverishness** *n.*

**fever pitch** *n.* state of extreme excitement.

**few** — *adj.* not many (*few professional footballers smoke*). — *n.* (as *pl.*) **1** (prec. by *a*) some but not many (*a few of his friends were there*). **2** not many (*few are chosen*). **3** (prec. by *the*) **a** the minority. **b** the elect. □ **a good** (or **fair**) **few** *colloq.* fairly large number. **no fewer than** as many as (a specified number). **not a few** a considerable number. **quite a few** = *a good few*. [Old English]

**few and far between** *predic. adj.* scarce.

**fey** /fay/ *adj.* **1 a** strange, other-worldly; whimsical. **b** clairvoyant. **2** *hist.* fated to die soon. [Old English, = doomed to die]

**fez** *n.* (*pl.* **fezzes**) man's flat-topped conical red cap worn by some Muslims. [Turkish]

**ff** *abbr. Mus.* fortissimo.

**ff.** *abbr.* and the following (pages etc.).

**fiancé** /fee-on-say/ *n.* (*fem.* **fiancée** pronunc. same) person one is engaged to. [French]

**fiasco** /fee-as-koh/ *n.* (*pl.* **-s**) ludicrous or humiliating failure or breakdown. [Italian, = bottle]

**fiat** /fee-at, fee-uht/ *n.* **1** authorisation. **2** decree. [Latin, = let it be done]

**fib** — *n.* trivial lie. — *v.* (**-bb-**) tell a fib.

□ **fibber** *n.* [perhaps from *fible-fable*, a reduplication of FABLE]

**fibre** /**fuy**-buh/ *n.* **1** thread or filament forming tissue or textile. **2** piece of threadlike glass. **3** substance formed of fibres, or able to be spun, woven, etc. **4** structure; character (*lacks moral fibre*). **5** dietary material that is resistant to the action of digestive enzymes; roughage. [French from Latin *fibra*]

**fibreboard** *n.* board of compressed wood or other plant fibres.

**fibreglass** *n.* **1** fabric made from woven glass fibres. **2** plastic reinforced by glass fibres.

**fibre optics** *n.pl.* optics using thin glass fibres, usu. for the transmission of modulated light to carry signals.

**fibril** /**fuy**-bruhl/ *n.* small fibre. [diminutive of FIBRE]

**fibro** — *n.* **1** = FIBRO-CEMENT. **2** house made of sheets of fibro. — *adj.* made of fibro (*a fibro house*).

**fibro-cement** *n.* mixture of asbestos and cement compressed into sheets for use as a building material.

**fibroid** /**fuy**-broid/ — *adj.* of, like, or containing fibrous tissue or fibres. — *n.* benign fibrous tumour growing in the womb.

**fibrosis** /fuy-**broh**-suhs/ *n.* thickening and scarring of connective tissue, usu. as a result of injury. [from FIBRE, -OSIS]

**fibrositis** /ˌfuy-bruh-**suy**-tuhs/ *n.* rheumatic inflammation of fibrous tissue. [from FIBRE, -ITIS]

**fibrous** /**fuy**-bruhs/ *adj.* consisting of or like fibres.

**fibula** /**fib**-yoo-luh, **fib**-yuh-luh/ *n.* (*pl.* **fibulae** /-ˌlee/ or **-s**) small outer bone between the knee and the ankle. □ **fibular** *adj.* [Latin, = brooch]

**-fic** *suffix* (usu. as **-ific**) forming adjectives meaning 'producing', 'making' (*prolific; pacific*). [Latin *facio* make]

**-fication** *suffix* (usu. as **-ification**) forming nouns of action from verbs in *-fy* (*purification; simplification*).

**fiche** /feesh/ *n.* (*pl.* same or **-s**) microfiche. [abbreviation]

**fickle** /**fik**-uhl/ *adj.* inconstant, changeable, disloyal. □ **fickleness** *n.* [Old English]

**fiction** /**fik**-shuhn/ *n.* **1** non-factual literature, esp. novels. **2** invented idea, thing, etc. **3** generally accepted falsehood (*polite fiction*). □ **fictional** *adj.* **fictionalise** *v.* (also **-ize**) (**-sing** or **-zing**). [Latin: related to FEIGN]

**fictitious** /fik-**tish**-uhs/ *adj.* imaginary, unreal; not genuine.

**ficus** /**fuy**-kuhs/ *n.* (also **fig**) any of several trees, shrubs, or vines of the large genus *Ficus*, having a milky sap, and tiny flowers and seeds inside a fruit-like receptacle called a fig, e.g. the banyan tree, the sacred bo tree, the rubber plant, and several Australian trees, e.g. Moreton Bay fig, Port Jackson fig, sandpaper fig.

**fiddle** /**fid**-uhl/ — *n.* **1** violin or other stringed instrument, esp. when played as a folk-instrument. **2** illegal or fraudulent scheme. — *v.* (**-ling**) **1 a** (often foll. by *with, at*) play restlessly. **b** (often foll. by *about*) move aimlessly; waste time. **c** (usu. foll. by *with*) adjust, tinker; tamper. **2** *colloq.* **a** cheat, swindle. **b** falsify. **c** get by cheating. **3** play (a tune) on the fiddle. □ **as fit as a fiddle** in very good health. **play second** (or **first**) **fiddle** take a subordinate (or leading) role. [Old English]

**fiddle-faddle** — *n.* trivial matters. — *v.* (**-ling**) fuss, trifle. — *int.* nonsense! [reduplication of FIDDLE]

**fiddler** *n.* **1** fiddle-player. **2** *colloq.* swindler, cheat. **3** any of several fish (rays) of Australian waters with a flattened, fiddle-shaped body.

**fiddling** *adj.* **1** petty, trivial. **2** *colloq.* = FIDDLY.

**fiddly** *adj.* (**-ier**, **-iest**) *colloq.* awkward or tiresome to do or use.

**fidelity** /fuh-**del**-uh-tee/ *n.* **1** faithfulness, loyalty. **2** strict conformity to truth or fact. **3** precision in sound reproduction (*high fidelity*). [Latin *fides* faith]

**fidget** /**fij**-uht/ — *v.* (**-t-**) **1** move or act restlessly or nervously. **2** be or make uneasy. — *n.* **1** person who fidgets. **2** (usu. in *pl.*) restless movements or mood. □ **fidgety** *adj.* [obsolete or British dial. *fidge* twitch]

**fiduciary** /fuh-**dyoo**-shuh-ree/ — *adj.* **1 a** of a trust, trustee, or trusteeship. **b** held or given in trust. **2** (of paper currency) dependent on public confidence or securities. — *n.* (*pl.* **-ies**) trustee. [Latin *fiducia* trust]

**field** — *n.* **1** area of esp. cultivated enclosed land. **2** area rich in some natural product (*gold field*). **3** land for a game etc. (*football field*). **4** participants in a contest, race, or sport, or all except those specified (*Smith and Jones were far ahead of the field*). **5** *Cricket* the side fielding. **6** expanse of ice, snow, sea, sky, etc. **7 a** battlefield. **b** (*attrib.*) (of artillery etc.) light and mobile. **8** area of activity or study (*in his own field*). **9** *Physics* **a** region in which a force is effective (*gravitational field*). **b** force exerted in this. **10** range of perception (*field of view*). **11** (*attrib.*) **a** (of an animal or plant) wild (*field mouse*). **b** in the natural environment, not in a laboratory etc. (*field trip*). **12 a** background of a picture, coin, flag, etc. **b** *Heraldry* surface of an escutcheon. **13** *Computing* part of a record representing an item of data. — *v.* **1 a** act as a fieldsman in cricket etc. **b** stop and return (the ball) in cricket etc. **2** select to play in a game. **3** deal with (questions, an argument, etc.). □ **play the field** date many partners. **take the field** begin a campaign. [Old English]

**field day** *n.* **1** exciting or successful time. **2** day set aside for the display of agricultural machinery. **3** military exercise or review.

**fielder** *n. Cricket, Baseball, etc.* member (other than the bowler or pitcher) of the fielding side.

**field events** *n.pl.* athletic events other than races.

**field goal** *n. Rugby* a goal scored with a drop-kick.

**field mouse** *n.* mouse which inhabits paddocks etc. (as distinct from the house mouse).

**fieldsman** *n.* = FIELDER.

**field umpire** *n. Aust. Rules* umpire (or one of three umpires in major games) in control of the match.

**fieldwork** *n.* **1** practical surveying, science, sociology, etc. conducted in the natural environment. **2** temporary fortification. □ **fieldworker** *n.*

**fiend** *n.* **1 a** evil spirit, demon. **b** (prec. by *the*) the Devil. **2 a** wicked or cruel person. **b** mischievous or annoying person. *colloq.* devotee (*fitness fiend*). **4** difficult or unpleasant thing. □ **fiendish** *adj.* **fiendishly** *adv.* [Old English]

**fierce** *adj.* (**fiercer, fiercest**) **1** violently aggressive or frightening (*fierce animal*). **2** eager, intense (*fierce competition*). **3** unpleasantly strong or intense (*fierce heat*). □ **fiercely** *adv.* **fierceness** *n.* [Latin *ferus* savage]

**fiery** /**fuyuh**-ree/ *adj.* (**-ier, -iest**) **1** consisting of or flaming with fire. **2** bright red. **3** hot; burning. **4 a** flashing, ardent (*fiery eyes*). **b** pugnacious; spirited (*fiery temper*). □ **fierily** *adv.* **fieriness** *n.*

**fiesta** /fee-**es**-tuh/ *n.* holiday, festivity, or religious festival. [Spanish]

**fife** *n.* small shrill flute used in military music. □ **fifer** *n.* [German *Pfeife* PIPE or French *fifre*]

**fifteen** /fif-**teen**, **fif**-/ *adj. & n.* **1** one more than fourteen. **2** symbol for this (15, xv, XV). **3** team of fifteen players, esp. in

Rugby. □ **fifteenth** *adj. & n.* [Old English: related to FIVE, -TEEN]

**fifth** *adj. & n.* **1** next after fourth. **2** any of five equal parts of a thing. **3** *Mus.* interval or chord spanning five consecutive notes in a diatonic scale (e.g. C to G). □ **fifthly** *adv.* [Old English: related to FIVE]

**fifth column** *n.* traitorous group within a country at war etc. □ **fifth columnist** *n.*

**fifty** /**fif**-tee/ *adj. & n.* (*pl.* **-ies**) **1** five times ten. **2** symbol for this (50, l, L). **3** (in *pl.*) numbers from 50 to 59, esp. the years of a century or of a person's life. □ **fiftieth** *adj. & n.* [Old English]

**fifty-fifty** *colloq.* — *adj.* equal. — *adv.* equally, half and half.

**fig** *n.* **1** soft pulpy fruit with many seeds. **2** (in full **fig-tree**) tree of the genus *Ficus* bearing figs. □ **not care** (or **give**) **a fig** not care at all. [Latin *ficus*]

**fig.** *abbr.* **1** figure. **2** figurative. **3** figuratively.

**fig-bird** *n.* greenish-coloured fruit-eating bird, usu. with red eye-patch, of eastern and northern Australia.

**fight** /fuyt/ — *v.* (*past* and *past part.* **fought** /fawt/) **1** (often foll. by *against, with*) contend or contend with in war, battle, single combat, etc. **2** engage in (a battle, duel, etc.). **3** contend (an election); maintain (a lawsuit, cause, etc.) against an opponent. **4** strive to achieve something or to overcome (disease, fire, fear, etc.). **5** make (one's way) by fighting. — *n.* **1 a** combat. **b** boxing match. **c** battle. **2** conflict, struggle, or effort. **3** power or inclination to fight (*no fight left*). □ **fight back 1** counter-attack. **2** suppress (tears etc.). **fight for 1** fight on behalf of. **2** fight to secure. **fight a losing battle** struggle without hope of success. **fight off** repel with effort. **fight out** (usu. **fight it out**) settle by fighting. **fight shy of** avoid. **put up a fight** offer resistance. [Old English]

**fighter** *n.* **1** person or animal that fights. **2** fast military aircraft designed for attacking other aircraft.

**fighting chance** *n.* slight chance of success if an effort is made.

**fighting fit** *adj.* fit and ready; at the peak of fitness.

**figment** /**fig**-muhnt/ *n.* invented or imaginary thing. [Latin: related to FEIGN]

**figuration** /fig-uh-**ray**-shuhn/ *n.* **1 a** act or mode of formation; form. **b** shape or outline. **2** ornamentation. [Latin: related to FIGURE]

**figurative** /**fig**-uh-ruh-tiv/ *adj.* **1** metaphorical, not literal. **2** characterised by

**figure** 405 **fillet**

figures of speech. **3** of pictorial or sculptural representation. □ **figuratively** *adv.* [Latin: related to FIGURE]

**figure** /fig-uh/ — *n.* **1** external form or bodily shape. **2 a** person as seen in outline but not identified (*saw a figure crouching by the door*). **b** person of a specified kind or appearance (*public figure*; *cut a poor figure*). **3 a** human form in drawing, sculpture, etc. **b** image or likeness. **4** two- or three-dimensional space enclosed by lines or surface(s), e.g. a triangle or sphere. **5 a** numerical symbol or number, esp. 0–9. **b** amount; estimated value (*cannot put a figure on it*). **c** (in *pl.*) arithmetical calculations. **6** diagram or illustration. **7** decorative pattern. **8** movement or sequence in a set dance etc. **9** *Mus.* short succession of notes producing a single impression, a brief melodic formula out of which longer passages are developed. **10** (in full **figure of speech**) recognised form of rhetorical expression, esp. metaphor or hyperbole. — *v.* (**-ring**) **1** appear or be mentioned, esp. prominently. **2** represent pictorially. **3** imagine; picture mentally. **4** embellish with a pattern etc. (*figured satin*). **5** calculate; do arithmetic. **6** symbolise. **7 a** understand, consider. **b** *colloq.* make sense; be likely (*that figures*). □ **figure on** count on, expect. **figure out** work out by arithmetic or logic. [Latin *figura*: related to FEIGN]

**figured bass** *n. Mus.* = CONTINUO.

**figurehead** *n.* **1** nominal leader or head without real power. **2** wooden bust or figure at a ship's prow.

**figure skating** *n.* skating in prescribed patterns. □ **figure skater** *n.*

**figurine** /fig-uh-**reen**/ *n.* small statue. [Italian: related to FIGURE]

**filament** /fil-uh-muhnt/ *n.* **1** threadlike body or fibre (esp. in animal or vegetable structures). **2** conducting wire or thread in an electric bulb etc. **3** *Bot.* the part of the stamen that supports the anther. □ **filamentary** /-men-tuh-ree, -tree/ *adj.* **filamentous** /-men-tuhs/ *adj.* [Latin *filum* thread]

**filch** *v.* pilfer, steal. [origin unknown]

**file¹** — *n.* **1** folder, box, etc., for holding loose papers. **2** papers kept in this. **3** *Computing* collection of (usu. related) data stored under one name. **4** line of people or things one behind another. — *v.* (**-ling**) **1** place (papers) in a file or among (esp. public) records. **2** submit (a petition for divorce, a patent application, etc.). **3** (of a reporter) send (copy) to a newspaper. **4** walk in a line. □ **on file**

placed in order for easy reference. [Latin *filum* thread]

**file²** — *n.* tool with a roughened surface for smoothing or shaping wood, fingernails, etc. — *v.* (**-ling**) smooth or shape with a file. [Old English]

**filial** /fil-ee-uhl/ *adj.* of or due from a son or daughter. □ **filially** *adv.* [Latin *filius, filia* son, daughter]

**filibuster** /fil-uh-,bus-tuh/ — *n.* **1** obstruction of progress in a legislative assembly, esp. by prolonged speaking. **2** esp. *US* person who engages in this. — *v.* act as a filibuster (against). □ **filibusterer** *n.* [Dutch: related to FREEBOOTER]

**filigree** /fil-uh-,gree/ — *n.* **1** fine ornamental work in gold etc. wire. **2** similar delicate work. — *adj.* made of or resembling filigree work. □ **filigreed** *adj.* [Latin *filum* thread, *granum* seed]

**filing** *n.* (usu. in *pl.*) particle rubbed off by a file.

**Filipino** /fil-uh-pee-noh/ — *n.* (*pl.* **-s**) native or national of the Philippines. — *adj.* of the Philippines or Filipinos. [Spanish, = Philippine]

**fill** — *v.* **1** (often foll. by *with*) make or become full. **2** occupy completely; spread over or through. **3** block up (a cavity in a tooth); drill and put a filling into (a decayed tooth). **4** appoint a person to hold or (of a person) hold (a post). **5** hold (an office). **6** carry out or supply (an order, commission, etc.). **7** occupy (vacant time). **8** (of a sail) be distended by wind. **9** (usu. as **filling** *adj.*) (esp. of food) satisfy, satiate. — *n.* **1** as much as one wants or can bear (*eat your fill*). **2** earth etc. used to fill a cavity. □ **fill the bill** be suitable or adequate. **fill in 1** complete (a form, document, etc.). **2 a** complete (a drawing etc.) within an outline. **b** fill (an outline) in this way. **3** fill (a hole etc.) completely. **4** (often foll. by *for*) act as a substitute. **5** occupy oneself during (spare time). **6** *colloq.* inform (a person) more fully. **fill out 1** enlarge to the required size. **2** become enlarged or plump. **3** fill in (a document etc.). **fill up 1** make or become completely full. **2** fill the petrol tank of (a car etc.). **fill a person's shoes** be an effective replacement for someone. [Old English]

**filler** *n.* **1** material used to fill a cavity or increase bulk. **2** paste or similar substance used to fill in holes or cracks prior to painting a surface. **3** small item filling space in a newspaper etc.

**fillet** /fil-uht/ — *n.* **1 a** boneless piece of meat or fish. **b** (in full **fillet steak**) undercut of a sirloin. **2** ribbon etc. binding the hair. **3** thin narrow strip or ridge. **4** narrow flat band between mouldings. — *v.*

**(-t-) 1** remove bones from (fish or meat) or divide into fillets. **2** bind or provide with fillet(s). [Latin *filum* thread]

**filling** *n.* material that fills a tooth, sandwich, pie, etc.

**fillip** /fil-uhp/ — *n.* **1** stimulus, incentive. **2** flick with a finger or thumb. — *v.* (**-p-**) **1** stimulate (*fillip one's memory*). **2** flick. [imitative]

**filly** /fil-ee/ *n.* (*pl.* **-ies**) **1** young female horse, usu. before it is four years old. **2** *colloq.* girl or young woman. [Old Norse]

**film** — *n.* **1** thin coating or covering layer. **2** strip or sheet of plastic etc. coated with light-sensitive emulsion for exposure in a camera. **3 a** story, episode, etc., on film, with the illusion of movement. **b** (in *pl.*) the cinema industry. **4** slight veil or haze etc. **5** dimness or morbid growth affecting the eyes. — *v.* **1** make a photographic film of (a scene, story, etc.). **2** cover or become covered with or as with a film. [Old English]

**filmstrip** *n.* series of transparencies in a strip for projection.

**filmy** *adj.* (**-ier**, **-iest**) **1** thin and translucent. **2** covered with or as with a film. □ **filmily** *adv.* **filminess** *n.*

**Filofax** /fuy-luh-faks/ *n. propr.* a type of loose-leaf personal organiser. [from FILE 1, FACT]

**filo pastry** /fee-loh, fuy-/ *n.* leaved tissue-thin pastry. [Greek *phúllon* leaf]

**filter** — *n.* **1** porous device for removing impurities or solid particles etc. from a liquid or gas passed through it. **2** screen or attachment for absorbing or modifying light, X-rays, etc. **3** device for suppressing unwanted electrical or sound waves. — *v.* **1** (cause to) pass through a filter. **2** (foll. by *through*, *into*, etc.) make way gradually. **3** (foll. by *out*) (cause to) leak. □ **filter out** (or **through**) become known gradually (*the news filtered through that . . .*). [Germanic: related to FELT 1]

**filth** *n.* **1** repugnant or extreme dirt. **2** vileness; obscenity. **3** foul or obscene language. [Old English: related to FOUL]

**filthy** — *adj.* (**-ier**, **-iest**) **1** extremely or disgustingly dirty. **2** obscene. **3** *colloq.* (of weather) very unpleasant. — *adv.* **1** filthily (*filthy dirty*). **2** *colloq.* extremely (*filthy rich*). □ **filthily** *adv.* **filthiness** *n.*

**filtrate** /fil-trayt/ — *v.* (**-ting**) filter. — *n.* filtered liquid. □ **filtration** /-tray-shuhn/ *n.* [related to FILTER]

**fin** *n.* **1** (usu. thin) flat external organ of esp. fish, for propelling, steering, etc. (*dorsal fin*). **2** similar stabilising projection on an aircraft, underneath a surfboard, etc. **3** underwater swimmer's flipper. □ **finned** *adj.* [Old English]

**finagle** /fuh-nay-guhl/ *v.* (**-ling**) *colloq.* act or obtain dishonestly. □ **finagler** *n.* [British dial. *fainaigue* cheat]

**final** /fuy-nuhl/ — *adj.* **1** situated at the end, coming last. **2** conclusive, decisive. — *n.* **1** last or deciding heat or game in sports etc. (*footie final*). **2** last daily edition of a newspaper. **3** (usu. in *pl.*) examinations at the end of a degree course. □ **finally** *adv.* [Latin *finis* end]

**finale** /fuh-nah-lee/ *n.* last movement or section of a piece of music or drama etc. [Italian: related to FINAL]

**finalise** *v.* (also **-ize**) (**-sing** or **-zing**) put into final form; complete. □ **finalisation** /-zay-shuhn/ *n.*

**finalist** *n.* competitor in the final of a competition etc.

**finality** /fuy-nal-uh-tee/ *n.* (*pl.* **-ies**) **1** quality or fact of being final. **2** final act etc. [Latin: related to FINAL]

**final solution** *n.* Nazi policy (1941–5) of exterminating European Jews.

**finance** /fuy-nans, fuh-nans/ — *n.* **1** management of (esp. public) money. **2** monetary support for an enterprise. **3** (in *pl.*) money resources of a nation, company, or person. — *v.* (**-cing**) provide capital for (a person or enterprise). [French: related to FINE 2]

**finance company** *n.* company providing money, esp. for hire-purchase transactions.

**financial** /fuy-nan-shuhl, fuh-/ *adj.* **1** of finance. **2** *colloq.* having ready money. **3** (of a club-member etc.) with fees or dues fully paid to date. □ **financially** *adv.*

**financial year** *n.* year as reckoned for taxing or accounting (in Australia 1 July to 30 June).

**financier** /fuy-nan-see-uh/ *n.* person engaged in large-scale financial operations. [French: related to FINANCE]

**finch** *n.* any of many small seed-eating Australian birds, often with brightly coloured plumage (*blue-faced finch*; *crimson finch*; *Gouldian finch*; *zebra finch*). [Old English]

**find** /fuynd/ — *v.* (*past* and *past part.* **found**) **1 a** discover or get by chance or effort (*found a key*). **b** become aware of. **2 a** obtain, succeed in obtaining; receive (*cannot find the money for the trip*; *idea found acceptance*). **b** summon up (*found courage*). **3** seek out and provide or supply (*will find you a book*; *finds his own meals*). **4** discover by study inquiry etc. (*find the answer*). **5 a** perceive or experience (*find no sense in it*; *find difficulty in breathing*). **b** (often in *passive*) discover to be present (*not found in Shakespeare*). **c** discover from experience (*finds Canberra* *too cold*). **6** *Law* (of a jury, judge, etc.) decide and declare (*found him guilty*). **7** reach by a natural process (*water finds its own level*). — *n.* **1** discovery of treasure etc. **2** valued thing or person newly discovered. □ **all found** (of wages) with board and lodging provided free. **find fault** see FAULT. **find favour** prove acceptable. **find one's feet 1** become able to walk. **2** develop independence. **find oneself 1** discover that one is (*found herself agreeing*). **2** discover one's vocation. **find out 1** discover or detect (a wrongdoer etc.). **2** (often foll. by *about*) get information. **3** discover (*find out where we are*). **4** (often foll. by *about*) discover the truth, a fact, etc. (*he never found out*). □ **finder** *n.* [Old English]

**finding** *n.* (often in *pl.*) conclusion reached by an inquiry etc.

**fine**[1] — *adj.* **1 a** of high quality; excellent (*fine painting*). **b** good, satisfactory (*that will be fine*). **2 a** pure, refined. **b** (of gold or silver) containing a specified proportion of pure metal. **3** imposing, dignified (*fine buildings*). **4** in good health (*I'm fine*). **5** (of weather etc.) bright and clear. **6 a** thin; sharp (*has a fine point*). **b** in small particles. **c** worked in slender thread. **d** (esp. of print) small. **7 a** capable of delicate perception or discrimination. **b** perceptible only with difficulty (*a fine distinction*). **8** delicate; subtle; exquisitely fashioned. — *adv.* **1** finely. **2** *colloq.* very well (*suits me fine*). — *v.* (**-ning**) **1** (often foll. by *away, down, off*) make or become finer, thinner, more tapering, or less coarse. **2** (foll. by *up*) become fine (esp. of weather). □ **not to put too fine a point on it** to speak bluntly. □ **finely** *adv.* **fineness** *n.* [French *fin* from Latin *finio* FINISH]

**fine**[2] — *n.* money to be paid as a penalty. — *v.* (**-ning**) punish by a fine (*fined him $50*). □ **in fine** in short. [French *fin* settlement of a dispute, from Latin *finis* end]

**fine arts** *n.pl.* poetry, music, and the visual arts, esp. painting, sculpture, and architecture.

**fine leg** *n.* *Cricket* position (of a player) on the leg-side behind the wicket.

**fine print** *n.* detailed printed information, esp. in legal documents etc.

**finery** /**fuy**-nuh-ree/ *n.* showy dress or decoration. [from FINE[1]]

**fine-spun** *adj.* **1** delicate. **2** (of theory etc.) too subtle, unpractical.

**finesse** /fuh-**nes**/ — *n.* **1** refinement. **2** subtle manipulation. **3** artfulness, esp. in handling a difficulty tactfully. **4** *Cards* attempt to win a trick with a card that is not the highest held. — *v.* (**-ssing**) **1** use

or achieve by finesse. **2** *Cards* **a** make a finesse. **b** play (a card) as a finesse. [French: related to FINE[1]]

**fine-tooth comb** *n.* comb with close-set teeth. □ **go over with a fine-tooth comb** check or search thoroughly.

**fine-tune** *v.* make small adjustments to (a mechanism etc.).

**fine-woolled** *adj.* (of a sheep etc.) having wool with fibres less than 18.05 microns thick.

**finger** /**fing**-guh/ — *n.* **1** any of the terminal projections of the hand (usu. excluding the thumb). **2** part of a glove etc. for a finger. **3** finger-like object or structure (*fish finger*). **4** *colloq.* small measure of liquor. — *v.* touch, feel, or turn about with the fingers. □ **burn one's fingers** suffer injury or loss by doing something. **get** (or **pull**) **one's finger out** *colloq.* start to act. **have a finger in the pie** be involved in the doing of something. **keep one's fingers crossed** hope for success. **lay a finger on** touch, however slightly. **not lift a finger** do nothing, make no effort. **put one's finger on** locate or identify exactly. **put the finger on** *colloq.* name or inform on someone to the police etc. **slip through one's fingers** escape or elude one. **snap one's fingers at** show defiance against or contempt for. **twist round one's little finger** have complete influence or dominance over. □ **fingerless** *adj.* [Old English]

**fingerboard** *n.* part of the neck of a stringed instrument on which the fingers press to vary the pitch.

**finger cherry** *n.* elongated cherry-like fruit of the Queensland tree *Rhodomyrtus macrocarpa*.

**finger flower** *n.* small Australian shrub having deep violet flowers with long gold anthers resembling fingers.

**fingering** *n.* **1** technique etc. of using the fingers, esp. in playing music. **2** indication of this in a musical score.

**finger lime** *n.* shrub or small tree of the citrus family (*Microcitrus australasica*) of rainforests in Queensland and NSW, bearing perfumed white flowers followed by long finger-like edible limes (see also DESERT LIME).

**fingerling** *n.* very young, fingersized fish, esp. a trout or salmon.

**fingernail** *n.* nail of each finger.

**fingerprint** — *n.* impression of a fingertip on a surface, used in detecting crime. — *v.* record the fingerprints of.

**finger-stall** *n.* protective cover for an injured finger.

**finger talk** *n.* an Aboriginal sign language.

**fingertip** *n.* tip of a finger. □ **have at one's**

**fingertips** be thoroughly familiar with (a subject etc.).

**finial** /**fin**-ee-uhl/ n. ornamental top or end of a roof, gable, etc. [Anglo-French: related to FINE¹]

**finicky** /**fin**-i-kee/ adj. (also **finical**, **finicking**) **1** over-particular, fastidious. **2** detailed; fiddly. □ **finickiness** n. [perhaps from FINE¹]

**finis** /**fin**-is, fi-**nis**/ n. end, esp. of a book. [Latin]

**finish** /**fin**-ish/ — v. **1 a** (often foll. by off) bring or come to an end or the end of; complete; cease. **b** (usu. foll. by off) kill; vanquish. **c** (often foll. by off, up) consume or complete consuming (food or drink). **d** treat the surface of (cloth, woodwork, etc.). — n. **1 a** end, last stage, completion. **b** point at which a race etc. ends. **2** method, material, etc. used for surface treatment of wood, cloth, etc. (mahogany finish). □ **finish up** (often foll. by in, by) end (finished up by crying). **finish with** have no more to do with, complete using, etc. [Latin finis end]

**finishing touch** n. (also **finishing touches**) final enhancing detail(s).

**finite** /**fuy**-nuyt/ adj. **1** limited; not infinite. **2** (of a part of a verb) having a specific number and person. [Latin: related to FINISH]

**fink** n. colloq. **1** despicable person, esp. one who goes back on his or her word. **2** strikebreaker, blackleg. [origin unknown]

**Finn** n. native or national of Finland; person of Finnish descent. [Old English]

**Finnish** — adj. of the Finns or their language. — n. language of the Finns.

**fiord** var. of FJORD.

**fipple** /**fip**-uhl/ n. plug at the mouth-end of a wind instrument. [origin unknown]

**fir** n. (in full **fir tree**) evergreen coniferous tree with needles growing singly on the stems. [Old Norse]

**fire** — n. **1 a** combustion of substances with oxygen, giving out light and heat. **b** flame or incandescence. **2** destructive burning (bushfire). **3** burning fuel in a grate, furnace, etc. **4 a** fervour, spirit, vivacity. **b** poetic inspiration. **5** burning heat, fever. — v. (**-ring**) **1** (often foll. by at, into, on) **a** shoot (a gun, missile, etc.). **b** shoot a gun or missile etc. **2** produce (a broadside, salute, etc.) by shooting guns etc. **3** (of a gun etc.) be discharged. **4** explode or kindle (an explosive). **5** deliver or utter rapidly (fired insults at us). **6** colloq. dismiss (an employee). **7 a** set fire to intentionally. **b** (esp. of Aborigines) set fire to the bush in order to trap animals or maintain grassland. **8** catch fire. **9** (of esp. an internal-combustion engine) undergo ignition. **10** supply (a furnace, engine, etc.) with fuel. **11** stimulate; enthuse. **12** bake, dry, or cure (pottery, bricks, tea, tobacco, etc.). **13** become or cause to become heated, excited, red, or glowing. □ **catch fire** begin to burn. **fire away** colloq. begin; go ahead. **on fire 1** burning. **2** excited. **set fire to** (or **set on fire**) ignite, kindle. **set the world on fire** do something remarkable or sensational. **under fire 1** being shot at. **2** being rigorously criticised or questioned. [Old English]

**firearm** n. (usu. in pl.) gun, pistol, or rifle.

**fireball** n. **1** large meteor. **2** ball of flame (esp. from a nuclear explosion or in a bushfire). **3** ball of lightning.

**fire-ban** n. official prohibition of the lighting of fires in the open on days of high fire-risk.

**firebrand** n. **1** piece of burning wood. **2** person causing trouble or unrest.

**firebreak** n. obstacle (esp. a strip that has been cleared) to the spread of fire in a forest etc.

**fire brigade** n. body of professional firefighters.

**firebug** n. colloq. person who deliberately sets fire to the bush on days of high fire-danger or sets buildings etc. alight.

**firecracker** n. explosive firework.

**firedamp** n. miners' name for methane, which is explosive when mixed with air.

**fire door** n. fire-resistant door preventing the spread of fire.

**firedrake** n. (also **firedragon**) fire-breathing dragon. [Old English]

**fire drill** n. rehearsal of the procedures to be used in case of fire.

**fire-eater** n. conjuror who appears to swallow fire.

**fire engine** n. vehicle carrying hoses, firefighters, etc.

**fire escape** n. emergency staircase etc. for use in a fire.

**fire-extinguisher** n. apparatus discharging foam etc. to extinguish a fire.

**firefighter** n. member of a team employed to put out fires, esp. bushfires.

**firefly** n. beetle emitting phosphorescent light, e.g. the glow-worm.

**fireguard** n. protective screen placed in front of a fireplace.

**fireirons** n.pl. tongs, poker, and shovel for a domestic fire.

**firelighter** n. inflammable material used to start a fire in a fireplace or barbecue.

**fireman** n. **1** member of a fire brigade. **2** person who tends a steam engine or steamship furnace.

**fireplace** *n.* **1 a** place for a domestic fire, esp. a recess in a wall. **b** structure surrounding this. **2** any structure provided at a picnic-place, rest-area, etc. in which a cooking fire may be lit.

**fireplough** *n.* implement that cuts a furrow wide enough to form a firebreak.

**firepower** *n.* destructive capacity of guns etc.

**fireproof** — *adj.* able to resist fire or great heat. — *v.* make fireproof.

**fire-risk** *n.* **1** likelihood of bushfires. **2** risk of the loss of property by fire. **3** building etc. which because of its condition is in danger of catching fire.

**fire screen** *n.* ornamental and/or protective screen for a fireplace.

**fire station** *n.* headquarters of a fire brigade.

**firestick** *n.* smouldering stick used to light a fire, esp. as carried by an Aborigine.

**firestick farming** *n.* method of vegetation control by selective burning, esp. as carried out by Aborigines.

**firetail** *n.* any of several often colourful Australian finches having red rumps.

**fire trail** *n.* permanent track through bush providing access for firefighters.

**fire trap** *n.* building without fire-escapes etc.

**fire watcher** *n.* person keeping watch for fires, esp. bushfires.

**fireweed** *n.* any of several plants, esp. of the genus *Senecio*, which appear rapidly after fire.

**firewheel tree** *n.* tree of eastern Australia remarkable for its whorls of fire-red flowers.

**firewood** *n.* wood as fuel.

**firework** *n.* **1** device that burns or explodes spectacularly when lit. **2** (in *pl.*) outburst of passion. esp. anger.

**firing** *n.* **1** discharge of guns. **2** fuel. **3** heating process which hardens clay into pottery etc.

**firing line** *n.* **1** front line in a battle. **2** centre of activity etc.

**firing squad** *n.* **1** soldiers ordered to shoot a condemned person. **2** group firing the salute at a military funeral.

**firm¹** — *adj.* **1 a** solid or compact. **b** fixed, stable, steady. **2 a** resolute, determined. **b** steadfast, constant (*firm belief; firm friend*). **3** (of an offer etc.) definite; not conditional. — *adv.* firmly (*stand firm*). — *v.* (often foll. by *up*) make or become firm, secure, compact, or solid. □ **firmly** *adv.* **firmness** *n.* [Latin *firmus*]

**firm²** *n.* business concern or its partners. [Latin *firma*: cf. FIRM¹]

**firmament** /**fer**-muh-muhnt/ *n. literary* the sky regarded as a vault or arch. [Latin: related to FIRM¹]

**firmware** *n. Computing* system software programmed into a read-only memory.

**first** — *adj.* **1** earliest in time or order (*took the first bus*). **2** foremost in rank or importance. **3** most willing or likely (*the first to admit it*). **4** basic or evident (*first principles*). — *n.* **1** (prec. by *the*) person or thing first mentioned or occurring. **2** first occurrence of something notable. **3** place in the first class in an examination. **4** first gear, usu. in a motor vehicle. **5 a** first place in a race. **b** winner of this. — *adv.* **1** before any other person or thing (*first of all; first and foremost*). **2** before someone or something else (*get this done first*). **3** for the first time (*when did you first see her?*). **4** in preference; rather (*will see him damned first*). □ **at first** at the beginning. **at first hand** directly from the original source. **first past the post** (of an electoral system) selecting a candidate or party by simple majority. **first up** first of all; at the first attempt. **from the first** from the beginning. **in the first place** as first consideration. [Old English]

**first aid** *n.* emergency medical treatment.

**First Australian** *n.* an Aborigine.

**firstborn** — *adj.* eldest. — *n.* person's eldest child.

**first class** — *n.* **1** best group or category. **2** best accommodation in a train, ship, etc. **3** highest division in an examination. — *adj. & adv.* (**first-class**) **1** of or by the first class. **2** excellent.

**first cousin** see COUSIN.

**first-day cover** *n.* envelope with stamps postmarked on their first day of issue.

**first-degree** *adj.* denoting non-serious surface burns.

**First Fleet** *n.* first British ships to bring convicts, civilians, marines, to Australia (1788).

**First Fleeter** *n.* **1** person who came to Australia with the First Fleet. **2** descendant of such a person.

**first floor** *n.* floor above the ground floor.

**first-fruit** *n.* (usu. in *pl.*) **1** first agricultural produce of a season, esp. as offered to God. **2** first results of work etc.

**first-hand** *adj. & adv.* from the original source; direct.

**first light** *n.* dawn.

**firstly** *adv.* in the first place, first (cf. FIRST *adv.*).

**first name** *n.* personal or Christian name.

**first offender** *n.* criminal without previous convictions.

**first person** see PERSON.

**first-rate** — adj. excellent. — adv. colloq. very well (feeling first-rate).

**first thing** adv. colloq. before anything else; very early.

**firth** n. (also **frith**) **1** narrow inlet of sea. **2** estuary. [Old Norse: related to FIORD]

**fiscal** /fis-kuhl/ adj. **1** of public revenue. **2** financial (fiscal year). [Latin fiscus treasury]

**fish** — n. (pl. same or **-es**) **1** vertebrate cold-blooded animal with gills and fins living wholly in water. **2** any of various non-vertebrate animals living wholly in water, e.g. the cuttlefish, shellfish, and jellyfish. **3** fish as food. **4** colloq. person of a specified kind (usu. used disparagingly) (an odd fish). **5** (**the Fish** or **Fishes**) sign or constellation Pisces. — v. **1** try to catch fish. **2** fish in (a certain river, lake, etc.). **3** (foll. by for) **a** search for. **b** seek indirectly (fishing for compliments). **4** (foll. by up, out, etc.) retrieve with effort. □ **drink like a fish** drink alcohol excessively. **fish out of water** person out of his or her element. **other fish to fry** other matters to attend to. [Old English]

**fisherman** n. person who catches fish as a livelihood or for sport.

**fishery** n. (pl. **-ies**) **1** place where fish are caught or reared. **2** industry of fishing or breeding fish.

**fish-eye lens** n. very wide-angle lens with a highly-curved front.

**fish finger** n. small oblong piece of fish in batter or breadcrumbs.

**fish-hook** n. barbed hook for catching fish.

**fishing** n. catching fish. □ **go on a fishing expedition** question or investigate in the hope of uncovering something detrimental (the royal commission was accused of going on a fishing expedition when it demanded that it be allowed to examine the bank accounts of various individuals).

**fishing rod** n. tapering usu. jointed rod for fishing.

**fishing weir** n. barrier built by Aborigines across a watercourse to catch fish.

**fishmonger** n. dealer in fish.

**fishnet** n. (often attrib.) open-meshed fabric (fishnet stockings).

**fishplate** n. flat piece of iron etc. connecting railway rails or positioning masonry.

**fishtail palm** n. tall palm of Queensland rainforests having leaves like fishtails and spikes of greeny-yellow and purple flowers.

**fishwife** n. coarse-mannered or noisy woman.

**fishy** adj. (**-ier, -iest**) **1** of or like fish. **2** colloq. dubious, suspect. □ **fishily** adv. **fishiness** n.

**fissile** /fis-uyl/ adj. **1** capable of undergoing nuclear fission. **2** tending to split. [Latin: related to FISSURE]

**fission** /fish-uhn/ — n. **1** splitting of a heavy atomic nucleus, with a release of energy. **2** Biol. cell division as a mode of reproduction. — v. (cause to) undergo fission. □ **fissionable** adj. [Latin: related to FISSURE]

**fission bomb** n. atomic bomb.

**fissure** /fish-uh/ — n. crack or split, usu. long and narrow. — v. (**-ring**) split, crack. [Latin findo fiss- cleave]

**fist** n. tightly closed hand. □ **make a good** (or **poor**) **fist of something** do something well (or badly). □ **fistful** n. (pl. **-s**). [Old English]

**fisticuffs** /fis-tee-kufs/ n.pl. fighting with the fists. [probably from obsolete fisty (from FIST), CUFF2]

**fistula** /fis-choo-luh/ n. (pl. **-s** or **-lae** /-lee/) abnormal or artificial passage between an organ and the body surface or between two organs. □ **fistular** adj. **fistulous** adj. [Latin, = pipe]

**fit¹** — adj. (**fitter, fittest**) **1 a** well suited. **b** qualified, competent, worthy. **c** in suitable condition, ready. **d** (foll. by for) good enough (fit for a king). **2** in good health or condition. **3** proper, becoming, right (it is fit that). — v. (**-tt-**) **1 a** (also absol.) be of the right shape and size for (dress fits her; key doesn't fit). **b** (often foll. by in, into) be correctly positioned (that bit fits here). **c** find room for (can't fit another on the bench). **2** make suitable or competent; adapt (fitted him to be a priest; fitted for battle). **3** (usu. foll. by with) supply (fitted the boat with a new rudder). **4** fix in place (fit a lock on the door). **5** = fit on. **6** befit, become (it fits the occasion). — n. way in which a garment, component, etc., fits (tight fit). — adv. (foll. by to + infin.) colloq. so that; likely (laughing fit to bust). □ **fit as a fiddle** (or **mallee bull**) colloq. very well, extremely healthy. **fit the bill** = fill the bill. **fit in 1** (often foll. by with) be (esp. socially) compatible; accommodate (doesn't fit in with the rest of the group; tried to fit in with their plans). **2** find space or time for (dentist fitted me in). **fit on** try on (a garment). **fit out** (or **up**) (often foll. by with) equip. **fit to be tied** colloq. extremely angry; ropeable. **see** (or **think**) **fit** (often foll. by to + infin.) decide or choose (a specified action). □ **fitly** adv. **fitness** n. [origin unknown]

**fit²** n. **1** sudden esp. epileptic seizure with unconsciousness or convulsions. **2** sudden brief bout or burst (*fit of giggles*; *fit of coughing*; *fit of rage*). □ **by** (or **in**) **fits and starts** spasmodically. **have a fit** *colloq.* be greatly surprised or outraged. **in fits** laughing uncontrollably. [Old English]

**fitful** *adj.* spasmodic or intermittent. □ **fitfully** *adv.*

**fitted** *adj.* **1** made to fit closely or exactly (*fitted carpet*). **2** provided with built-in fittings etc. (*fitted kitchen*). **3** built-in (*fitted cupboards*).

**fitted sheet** n. bed sheet with elastic at the corners to keep attachment to the mattress secure.

**fitter** n. **1** mechanic who fits together and adjusts machinery. **2** supervisor of the cutting, fitting, etc. of garments.

**fitting** — n. **1** trying-on of a garment etc. for adjustment before completion. **2** (in *pl.*) fixtures and furnishings of a building. — *adj.* proper, becoming, right. □ **fittingly** *adv.*

**five** *adj. & n.* **1** one more than four. **2** symbol for this (5, v, V). **3** set or team of five. **4** five o'clock (*is it five yet?*). □ **take five** *colloq.* take a short break. [Old English]

**five-eighth** n. *Rugby* either of two players between the scrum-half and the centre three-quarter.

**fivefold** *adj. & adv.* **1** five times as much or as many. **2** consisting of five parts.

**fix** — v. **1** make firm or stable; fasten, secure. **2** decide, settle, specify (a price, date, etc.). **3** mend, repair. **4** implant in the mind (*couldn't get the rules fixed in his head*). **5 a** (foll. by *on, upon*) direct (the eyes etc.) steadily, set. **b** attract and hold (the attention, eyes, etc.). **c** (foll. by *with*) single out with one's look etc. **6** place definitely, establish. **7** determine the exact nature, position, etc., of; refer (a thing) to a definite place or time; identify, locate. **8 a** make (the eyes, features, etc.) rigid. **b** (of eyes, features, etc.) become rigid. **9** *colloq.* prepare (food or drink). **10** congeal or become congealed. **11** *colloq.* punish, kill, deal with (a person). **12** *colloq.* **a** bribe or threaten into supporting. **b** gain a fraudulent result of (a race etc.). **13** *colloq.* inject a narcotic. **14** make (a colour, photographic image, microscope-specimen, etc.) fast or permanent. **15** (of a plant etc.) assimilate (nitrogen or carbon dioxide) by forming a non-gaseous compound. — n. **1** *colloq.* dilemma, predicament. **2 a** finding one's position by bearings etc. **b** position found in this way. **3** *colloq.* dose of an addictive drug. **4 a** dishonest act. **b** a bribe. □ **be fixed** (usu.

foll. by *for*) *colloq.* be situated (regarding) (*how is he fixed for money?*). **fix on** (or **upon**) choose, decide on. **fix up 1** arrange, organise. **2** accommodate. **3** (often foll. by *with*) provide (a person) (*fixed me up with a job*). □ **fixable** *adj.* [Latin *figo fix-*]

**fixate** /fik-sayt/ v. (**-ting**) **1** direct one's gaze on. **2** *Psychol.* (usu. in *passive*; often foll. by *on, upon*) cause (a person) to become abnormally attached to a person or thing. [Latin: related to FIX]

**fixation** /fik-say-shuhn/ n. **1** state of being fixated. **2** obsession, concentration on a single idea. **3** process of rendering solid; coagulation. **4** process of assimilating a gas to form a solid compound.

**fixative** /fik-suh-tiv/ — *adj.* tending to fix or secure. — n. substance used to fix colours, hair, microscope-specimens, etc.

**fixed interest** n. interest rate which does not vary over the term of a loan.

**fixedly** /fik-suhd-lee/ *adv.* intently.

**fixed star** n. *Astron.* seemingly motionless star.

**fixer** n. **1** person or thing that fixes. **2** *Photog.* substance for fixing a photographic image etc. **3** *colloq.* person who makes arrangements, esp. of an illicit kind.

**fixity** n. fixed state; stability; permanence.

**fixture** /fiks-chuh/ n. **1 a** something fixed in position. **b** *colloq.* person or thing confined to or established in a particular place (*he seems to be a fixture*). **2 a** sporting event, esp. a match, race, etc. **b** date agreed for this. **3** (in *pl.*) articles attached to a house or land and regarded as legally part of it.

**fizgig** n. police informer. [probably FIZZ, obsolete *gig* flighty girl]

**fizz** — v. **1** make a hissing or spluttering sound. **2** (of a drink) effervesce. — n. **1** effervescence. **2** *colloq.* effervescent drink, esp. champagne. [imitative]

**fizzer¹** n. *colloq.* **1** firecracker which does not explode. **2** failure, fiasco (*the party was a fizzer*).

**fizzer²** n. *colloq.* police informer. [from FIZGIG]

**fizzle** /fiz-uhl/ — v. (**-ling**) make a feeble hiss. — n. such a sound. □ **fizzle out** end feebly. [imitative]

**fizzy** *adj.* (**-ier, -iest**) effervescent. □ **fizziness** n.

**fjord** /fee-awd/ n. (also **fiord**) long narrow sea inlet, as in Norway. [Norwegian]

**fl.** *abbr.* **1** floruit. **2** fluid.

**flab** n. *colloq.* fat; flabbiness. [imitative, or from FLABBY]

**flabbergast** /flab-uh-,gahst, -,gast/ v. (esp. as **flabbergasted** *adj.*) *colloq.* astonish; dumbfound. [origin uncertain]

**flabby** /**flab**-ee/ adj. (**-ier, -iest**) **1** (of flesh etc.) hanging down; limp; flaccid. **2** (of language or character) feeble. □ **flabbiness** n. [alteration of *flappy*: related to FLAP]

**flaccid** /**flak**-suhd, **flas**-uhd/ adj. limp, flabby, drooping; not rigid or erect. □ **flaccidity** /-**sid**-uh-tee/ n. [Latin *flaccus* limp]

**flag¹** — n. **1** usu. oblong or square piece of cloth with particular colours and often symbols, used as a country's emblem or standard. **2** similar device for signalling or indicating (*goal umpire's flags*). **3** adjustable strip of metal etc. indicating a taxi's availability for hire. **4** (prec. by *the) Aust. Rules* flag awarded for winning the premiership; the premiership itself (*who will win the flag this year?*). — v. (**-gg-**) **1 a** grow tired; lag (*was soon flagging*). **b** hang down; droop. **2** mark out with or as if with a flag or flags. **3** inform, warn, give notice of, communicate, etc. by or as if by flag-signals. □ **bring up both flags** *Aust. Rules* score a goal (signalled by the goal umpire raising two small flags). **flag down** signal to stop. **flying the Australian flag** *colloq.* with shirt tail untucked and hanging out. **show the flag** rally round; make an appearance. [origin unknown]

**flag²** n. plant with a bladed leaf (esp. the iris). [origin unknown]

**flagellant** /**flaj**-uh-luhnt, fluh-**jel**-uhnt/ — n. person who scourges himself, herself, or others as a religious discipline or as a sexual stimulus. — adj. of flagellation. [Latin *flagellum* whip]

**flagellate** /**flaj**-uh-layt/ v. (**-ting**) scourge, flog. □ **flagellation** /-**lay**-shuhn/ n.

**flagellum** /fluh-**jel**-uhm/ n. (pl. **-gella**) long lashlike appendage on some microscopic organisms. [Latin, = whip]

**flageolet** /ˌflaj-uh-**let**/ n. small flute. [French from Provençal]

**flagfall** n. initial (pre-trip) charge for the hire of a taxi. [see FLAG¹ 3]

**flag of convenience** n. foreign flag under which a ship is registered, usu. to avoid regulations or financial charges.

**flagon** /**flag**-uhn/ n. **1** large bottle, esp. of wine etc. **2** large vessel for wine etc., usu. with a handle, spout, and lid. [Latin *flasco* FLASK]

**flagpole** n. = FLAGSTAFF.

**flagrant** /**flay**-gruhnt/ adj. blatant; notorious; scandalous. □ **flagrancy** n. **flagrantly** adv. [Latin *flagro* blaze]

**flagship** n. **1** ship with an admiral on board. **2** something that is held to be the best or most important of its kind; leader.

**flagstaff** n. pole on which a flag may be hoisted.

**flagstone** n. **1** flat usu. rectangular paving stone. **2** (in pl.) pavement of these.

**flag-waving** — n. populist agitation, chauvinism. — adj. aggressively patriotic, chauvinistic.

**flail** — n. wooden staff with a short heavy stick swinging from it, used for threshing. — v. **1** wave or swing wildly or erratically. **2** beat with or as with a flail. [Latin *flagellum* whip]

**flair** n. **1** natural talent in a specific area (*flair for languages*). **2** style, finesse. [French *flairer* to smell]

**flak** n. **1** anti-aircraft fire. **2** adverse criticism; abuse. □ **cop the** (or **some**) **flak** come in for heavy criticism or abuse. [German, *Fliegerabwehrkanone*, 'aviator-defence-gun']

**flake** — n. **1** small thin light piece of snow etc. **2** thin broad piece peeled or split off. **3** flesh of the school shark and other Australian sharks etc., sold (esp. in fish-and-chip shops) as food. — v. (**-king**) (often foll. by *away, off*) **1** take off or come away in flakes. **2** sprinkle with or fall in flakes. □ **flake out** *colloq.* fall asleep or drop from exhaustion; faint. □ **flaky** adj. [origin unknown]

**flambé** /**flom**-bay/ adj. (of food) covered with alcohol and set alight briefly (following a noun: *pancakes flambé*). [French: related to FLAME]

**flamboyant** /flam-**boi**-uhnt/ adj. **1** ostentatious; showy. **2** floridly decorated or coloured. □ **flamboyance** n. **flamboyantly** adv. [French *flamboyer* to flame]

**flame** — n. **1 a** ignited gas. **b** portion of this (*flame flickered*). **c** (usu. in pl.) visible combustion (*burst into flames*). **2 a** bright light or colouring. **b** brilliant orange-red colour. **3 a** brilliant flashes of red found in some opals. **b** such an opal. **4 a** strong passion, esp. love (*fan the flame*). **b** *colloq.* sweetheart. — v. (**-ming**) **1** (often foll. by *away, forth, out, up*) burn; blaze. **2** (often foll. by *out, up*) **a** (of passion) break out. **b** (of a person) become angry. **3** shine or glow like flame. [Latin *flamma*]

**flamenco** /fluh-**meng**-koh/ n. (pl. **-s**) **1** style of Spanish gypsy guitar music with singing. **2** dance performed to this. [Spanish, = Flemish]

**flame pea** n. mainly WA genus of shrubs or twining plants bearing masses of spectacular orange and red pea-flowers.

**flame-thrower** n. weapon for throwing a spray of flame.

**flame tree** n. (also **Illawarra flame tree**) deciduous eastern Australian tree with spectacular flame-coloured flowers.

**flaming** adj. **1** emitting flames. **2** very hot. **3** colloq. passionate (flaming row). **4** expressing annoyance, or as an intensifier; (euphem. for) bloody etc. (flaming idiot; stone the flaming crows). **5** bright-coloured.

**flamingo** /fluh-**ming**-goh/ n. (pl. **-s** or **-es**) tall long-necked wading bird with mainly pink plumage. [Provençal: related to FLAME]

**flammable** /**flam**-uh-buhl/ adj. inflammable. □ **flammability** /-bil-uh-tee/ n. [Latin: related to FLAME]

■ Usage Flammable is often used because inflammable can be mistaken for a negative (the true negative being non-flammable).

**flan** n. **1** pastry case with a savoury or sweet filling. **2** sponge base with a sweet topping. [medieval Latin flado -onis]

**flange** /flanj/ n. projecting flat rim etc., for strengthening or attachment. [origin uncertain]

**flank** — n. **1** side of a body between ribs and hip. **2** side of a mountain, building, etc. **3** right or left side of an army etc. **4** Aust. Rules outside position, e.g. half-forward flank. — v. (often in passive) be at or move along the side of (road flanked by mountains). [French from Germanic]

**flannel** /**flan**-uhl/ n. **1 a** woven woollen usu. napless fabric. **b** (in pl.) flannel garments, esp. trousers. **2** face-washer, esp. towelling. [Welsh gwlanen from gwlân wool]

**flannelette** /ˌflan-uh-**let**/ n. napped cotton fabric like flannel.

**flannel flower** n. Australian plant having divided silvery leaves and large white star-flowers with attractive flannel-like bracts.

**flap** — v. (**-pp-**) **1** move or be moved up and down like wings; beat. **2** colloq. be agitated or panicky. **3** sway; flutter (flags flapping in the wind). **4** strike with a flexible flat object (flapped him with the towel). **5** colloq. (of ears) listen intently. — n. **1** piece of cloth, wood, etc. attached by one side esp. to cover a gap, e.g. a pocket-cover, the folded part of an envelope, a table-leaf. **2** motion of a wing, arm, etc. **3** colloq. agitation; panic (in a flap). **4** aileron. **5** light blow with something flat and flexible. □ **flappy** adj. [probably imitative]

**flapjack** n. **1** small thick pancake; pikelet. **2** sweet oatcake.

**flapper** n. hist. (in the 1920s) young unconventional woman.

**flare** — v. (**-ring**) **1** widen gradually (flared trousers). **2** (cause to) burn brightly and unsteadily. **3** blaze suddenly. **4** (often foll. by up or out) burst into a sudden blaze, anger, activity, etc. — n. **1 a** dazzling irregular flame or light. **b** sudden outburst of flame. **2** flame or bright light used as a signal or to illuminate a target etc. **3 a** gradual widening, esp. of a skirt or trousers. **b** (in pl.) wide-bottomed trousers. [origin unknown]

**flare-path** n. line of lights on a runway to guide aircraft.

**flare-up** n. colloq. **1** violent row or argument. **2** outburst of flame, temper, activity, etc.

**flash** — v. **1** (cause to) emit a brief or sudden light; (cause to) gleam. **2** send or reflect like a sudden flame (eyes flashed fire). **3 a** burst suddenly into view or perception (answer flashed upon me). **b** move swiftly (train flashed past). **4 a** send (news etc.) by radio, telegraph, etc. **b** signal to (a person) with lights. **5** colloq. show ostentatiously (flashed her ring). **6** colloq. indecently expose oneself. — n. **1** sudden bright light or flame, e.g. of lightning. **2** an instant (in a flash). **3** sudden brief feeling, display of wit, etc. (flash of hope). **4** = NEWSFLASH. **5** Photog. = FLASHLIGHT. **6** Mil. coloured cloth patch on a uniform. **7** bright patch of colour. — adj. **1** rapid or sudden (flash flood). **2** colloq. gaudy; showy (flash car). **3** colloq. smart, with-it (flash jacket you're wearing). [imitative]

**flashback** n. scene set in an earlier time than the main action.

**flashbulb** n. Photog. bulb for a flashlight.

**flasher** n. **1** colloq. man who briefly exposes his private parts in public. **2** automatic device for switching lights rapidly on and off.

**flashgun** n. device operating a camera flashlight.

**flashing** n. (usu. metal) strip used to prevent water penetration at a roof joint etc. [British dial.]

**flash in the pan** n. promising start followed by failure.

**flashlight** n. light giving an intense flash, used for night or indoor photography.

**flashpoint** n. **1** temperature at which vapour from oil etc. will ignite in air. **2** point at which anger etc. is expressed.

**flashy** adj. (**-ier, -iest**) showy; gaudy; cheaply attractive. □ **flashily** adv. **flashiness** n.

**flask** /flahsk/ n. **1** narrow-necked bulbous bottle for wine etc. or used in chemistry. **2** = HIP FLASK. [Latin flasca, flasco: cf. FLAGON]

**flat¹** — *adj.* (**flatter, flattest**) **1 a** horizontally level (*a flat roof*). **b** even; smooth; unbroken; without projection or indentation (*a flat stomach*). **c** level and shallow (*flat cap*). **d** (of the heel of a shoe) low. **e** (of feet) with flattened arch. **2** unqualified; downright (*flat refusal*). **3 a** dull; lifeless; monotonous (*spoke in a flat tone*). **b** dejected. **4** (of a fizzy drink) having lost its effervescence. **5** (of paint) not glossy, having a matt finish. **6** (of a battery etc.) having exhausted its charge. **7** *Mus.* **a** below true or normal pitch (*violins are flat*). **b** (of a key) having a flat or flats in the signature. **c** (as B, E, etc. flat) semitone lower than B, E, etc. **8** (of a tyre) punctured; deflated. — *adv.* **1** at full length; spread out (*lay flat; flat against the wall*). **2** *colloq.* **a** completely, absolutely (*flat broke*). **b** exactly (*in five minutes flat*). **3** *Mus.* below the true or normal pitch (*sings flat*). — *n.* **1** flat part or thing (*flat of the hand*). **2** level ground, esp. a plain or swamp. **3** *Mus.* **a** note lowered a semitone below natural pitch. **b** sign (♭) indicating this. **4** *Theatr.* flat scenery on a frame. **5** *colloq.* flat tyre. □ **fall flat** fail to have the intended effect. **flat out 1** at top speed. **2** using all one's strength etc. **that's flat** *colloq.* that is definite. □ **flatly** *adv.* **flatness** *n.* **flattish** *adj.* [Old Norse]

**flat²** — *n.* set of rooms, usu. on one floor, as a residence. — *v.* live in a flat; share accommodation (with) (*I'm flatting by myself; she flats with her sister*). [obsolete *flet* floor, dwelling, from Germanic: related to FLAT¹]

**flatette** *n.* tiny flat.

**flatfish** *n.* sole, plaice, etc. with both eyes on one side of a flattened body.

**flatfoot** *n.* foot with a flattened arch.

**flat-footed** *adj.* **1** having flat feet. **2** *colloq.* **a** uninspired; clumsy. **b** unprepared (*their sudden arrival caught us flat-footed*).

**flathead** *n.* common food-fish with flattened head.

**flatmate** *n.* person sharing a flat, house, etc.

**flat racing** *n.* horse racing without jumps, over level ground.

**flat rate** *n.* unvarying rate or charge.

**flat spin** *n.* **1** *Aeron.* a nearly horizontal spin. **2** *colloq.* state of panic.

**flat strap** *adv.* (also **flat chat**) *colloq.* very fast (*he drove flat strap to get her to the hospital in time*).

**flatten** *v.* **1** make or become flat. **2** *colloq.* **a** humiliate. **b** knock down.

**flatter** *v.* **1** compliment unduly, esp. for gain or advantage. **2** (usu. *refl.*; usu. foll. by *that*) congratulate or delude (oneself etc.) (*he flatters himself that he can sing*). **3** (of colour, style, etc.) enhance the appearance of (*that blouse flatters you*). **4** (esp. of a portrait, a portrait-painter, etc.) represent too favourably. □ **flatterer** *n.* **flattering** *adj.* **flatteringly** *adv.* [French]

**flattery** *n.* exaggerated or insincere praise.

**flattie** *n. colloq.* **1** = FLATHEAD. **2** flat tyre. **3** (as flatties) low-heeled or heel-less shoes.

**flatulent** /**flach**-uh-luhnt, **flat**-yoo-/ *adj.* **1 a** causing intestinal wind. **b** caused by or suffering from this. **2** (of speech etc.) inflated, pretentious. □ **flatulence** *n.* [Latin *flatus* blowing]

**flatworm** *n.* worm with a flattened body, e.g. flukes, tapeworms.

**flaunt** *v.* (often *refl.*) display proudly; show off; parade. [origin unknown]

■ **Usage** *Flaunt* is often confused with *flout* which means 'to disobey contemptuously'.

**flautist** /**flaw**-tuhst/ *n.* flute-player. [Italian: related to FLUTE]

**flavour** /**flay**-vuh/ (also **flavor**) — *n.* **1** mingled sensation of smell and taste (*cheesy flavour*). **2** characteristic quality (*romantic flavour*). **3** (usu. foll. by *of*) slight admixture of a usu. undesirable quality (*a flavour of failure hangs over the enterprise*). — *v.* give flavour to; season. □ **flavourless** *adj.* **flavoursome** *adj.* [French]

**flavouring** *n.* (also **flavoring**) substance used to flavour food or drink.

**flavour of the month** *n.* (also **flavour of the week**) temporary trend or fashion.

**flaw** — *n.* **1** imperfection; blemish (*has a character without flaw*). **2** crack or similar fault (*this antique cup has a flaw*). **3** *Law* invalidating defect in a legal matter. — *v.* crack; damage; spoil. □ **flawless** *adj.* **flawlessly** *adv.* [Old Norse]

**flax** *n.* **1** blue-flowered plant cultivated for its textile fibre and its seeds. **2** flax fibres. [Old English]

**flaxen** *adj.* **1** of flax. **2** (of hair) pale yellow.

**flax lily** *n.* any of several Australian lilies having long flax-like leaves and vivid blue flowers with prominent gold anthers, followed by bright blue fruits.

**flay** *v.* **1** strip the skin or hide off, esp. by beating. **2** criticise severely (*the play was flayed by the critics*). **3** peel off (skin, bark, peel, etc.). [Old English]

**flea** *n.* small wingless jumping insect, feeding on human and other blood.

□ **a flea in one's ear** sharp reproof. [Old English]

**fleabag** *n. colloq.* **1** sleeping bag. **2** flea-ridden animal. **3** shabby or unattractive person or thing.

**flea-bitten** *adj.* **1** bitten by or infested with fleas. **2** shabby, tatty.

**flea market** *n.* (street) market selling second-hand goods etc.

**fleck** — *n.* **1** small patch of colour or light. **2** particle, speck. — *v.* mark with flecks. [Old Norse, or Low German or Dutch]

**fled** past and past part. of FLEE.

**fledge** *v.* (**-ging**) **1** provide or deck (an arrow etc.) with feathers. **2** bring up (a young bird) until it can fly. **3** (as **fledged** *adj.*) **a** able to fly. **b** independent; mature. [obsolete adj. *fledge* fit to fly]

**fledgling** /flej-ling/ *n.* (also **fledgeling**) **1** young bird. **2** inexperienced person.

**flee** *v.* (past and past part. **fled**) (often foll. by *from, before*) **1** run away (from); leave abruptly (*fled the room*). **2** seek safety by fleeing. [Old English]

**fleece** — *n.* **1 a** woolly coat of a sheep etc. **b** wool sheared from a sheep at one time. **2** thing resembling a fleece, esp. soft fabric for lining etc. — *v.* (**-cing**) **1** (often foll. by *of*) strip of money, valuables, etc.; swindle. **2** shear (sheep etc.). **3** cover as if with a fleece (*sky fleeced with clouds*). □ **fleecy** *adj.* (**-ier, -iest**). [Old English]

**fleece-picker** *n.* person who sorts skirtings into classes defined by the wool-classer.

**fleet** — *n.* **1 a** warships under one commander-in-chief. **b** (prec. by *the*) nation's warships etc.; navy. **2** number of ships, aircraft, buses, taxis, etc., operating together or owned by one proprietor. — *adj. poet. literary* swift, nimble. [Old English]

**fleeting** *adj.* transitory; brief. □ **fleetingly** *adv.*

**Fleming** /flem-ing/ *n.* **1** native of medieval Flanders. **2** member of a Flemish-speaking people of N. and W. Belgium. [Old English]

**Flemish** /flem-ish/ — *adj.* of Flanders. — *n.* language of the Flemings. [Dutch]

**flesh** *n.* **1 a** soft, esp. muscular, substance between the skin and bones of an animal or a human. **b** plumpness; fat (*has put on flesh*). **2** the body, as opposed to the mind or soul, esp. considered as sinful. **3** pulpy substance of a fruit etc. **4 a** visible surface of the human body. **b** (also **flesh colour**) yellowish pink colour. **5** animal or human life. □ **all flesh** all animate creation. **flesh out 1** make or become substantial. **2** expand, amplify. **in the flesh** in person.

**one's own flesh and blood** near relatives. **the way of all flesh** experience common to all human beings. [Old English]

**flesh and blood** — *n.* **1** the body or its substance. **2** humankind. **3** human nature, esp. as fallible. — *adj.* real, not imaginary.

**fleshly** *adj.* (**-lier, -liest**) **1** (of desire etc.) bodily; sensual (*fleshly lusts*). **2** mortal, not divine. **3** worldly.

**fleshpots** *n.pl.* places of luxurious living.

**flesh wound** *n.* superficial wound.

**fleshy** *adj.* (**-ier, -iest**) **1** of or like flesh. **2** plump, fat. **3** (of plant or fruit tissue) pulpy. □ **fleshiness** *n.*

**fleur-de-lis** /ˌfler-duh-lee/ *n.* (also **fleur-de-lys**) (*pl.* **fleurs-** pronunc. same) **1** iris flower. **2** *Heraldry* **a** lily of three petals. **b** former royal arms of France. [French, = flower of lily]

**flew** past of FLY[1].

**flews** *n.pl.* hanging lips of a bloodhound etc. [origin unknown]

**flex[1]** *v.* **1** bend (a joint, limb, etc.) or be bent. **2** move (a muscle) or (of a muscle) be moved to bend a joint. [Latin *flecto flex-* bend]

**flex[2]** *n.* flexible insulated electric cable. [abbreviation of FLEXIBLE]

**flex[3]** — *n.* = FLEXI. — *v.* (foll. by *off*) take time off from work under the flexitime system (*he's flexing off today*).

**flexi** *n. colloq.* flexiday (*having a flexi tomorrow*).

**flexible** /flek-suh-buhl/ *adj.* **1** capable of bending without breaking; pliable. **2** easily led; manageable. **3** adaptable; variable (*works flexible hours*). □ **flexibility** /-bil-uh-tee/ *n.* **flexibly** *adv.* [Latin *flexibilis*: related to FLEX[1]]

**flexiday** *n.* day taken off from work under the flexitime system.

**flexitime** /flek-see-,tuym/ *n.* system of flexible working hours. [from FLEXIBLE]

**flibbertigibbet** /flib-uh-tee-,jib-uht/ *n.* gossiping, frivolous, or restless person. [imitative]

**flick** — *n.* **1 a** light sharp blow with a whip etc. **b** sudden release of a bent finger or thumb, esp. to propel a small object. **2** sudden movement or jerk, esp. of the wrist in throwing etc. **3** *colloq.* **a** cinema film. **b** (in *pl.*; prec. by *the*) the cinema. — *v.* **1** (often foll. by *away, off*) strike or move with a flick (*flicked the ash off*). **2** give a flick with (a whip etc.). □ **flick through 1** turn over (cards, pages, etc.). **2 a** turn over the pages etc. of, by a rapid movement of the fingers. **b** glance through (a book etc.). **give a person the flick** *colloq.* reject; sack (*management gave him the flick*). [imitative]

**flicker** — v. **1** (of light or flame) shine or burn unsteadily. **2** (of a flag, eyelid, reptile's tongue, etc.) wave to and fro; flutter. **3** (of hope etc.) waver. — n. **1** flickering movement or light. **2** brief spell (of hope etc.). □ **flicker out** die away. [Old English]

**flick knife** n. knife with a blade that springs out when a button is pressed.

**flick pass** n. Aust. Rules handpass in which the ball is struck with the open hand (instead of a closed fist).

**flier** var. of FLYER.

**flight¹** /fluyt/ — n. **1 a** act or manner of flying. **b** movement or passage through the air. **2 a** journey through the air or in space. **b** timetabled airline journey. **3** flock of birds, insects, etc. **4** (usu. foll. by of) series, esp. of stairs. **5** imaginative excursion or sally (flight of fancy). **6** (usu. foll. by of) volley (flight of arrows). **7** tail of a dart. — v. **1** set flying, start in flight. **2** vary the trajectory and pace of (a cricket ball etc.). [Old English: related to FLY¹]

**flight²** /fluyt/ n. act or manner of fleeing; hasty retreat. □ **put to flight** cause to flee. **take** (or **take to**) **flight** flee. [Old English]

**flight attendant** n. steward or stewardess in an aircraft.

**flight deck** n. **1** deck of an aircraft-carrier. **2** control room of a large aircraft.

**flightless** adj. (of a bird etc.) unable to fly.

**flight lieutenant** n. RAAF officer next below squadron leader.

**flight path** n. planned course of an aircraft etc.

**flight recorder** n. device in an aircraft to record technical details during a flight, that may be used in the event of an accident to discover its cause.

**flighty** adj. (-ier, -iest) (usu. of a girl) frivolous, fickle, changeable. □ **flighti-ness** n.

**flimsy** /flim-zee/ adj. (-ier, -iest) **1** insubstantial, rickety (flimsy structure). **2** (of an excuse etc.) unconvincing. **3** (of clothing) thin. □ **flimsily** adv. **flimsiness** n. [origin uncertain]

**flinch** v. draw back in fear etc.; wince. [French from Germanic]

**Flinders grass** n. any of several Australian annual, or short-lived perennial, fodder grasses. [Matthew Flinders, English explorer (d. 1814)]

**fling** — v. (past and past part. **flung**) **1** throw or hurl forcefully or hurriedly. **2** refl. (usu. foll. by into) **a** rush headlong (into a person's arms etc.). **b** embark wholeheartedly (on an enterprise). **3** utter (words) forcefully (flung out the

accusation). **4** (foll. by on, off) put on or take off (clothes) carelessly or rapidly. **5** put or send suddenly or violently (was flung into jail). **6** rush, esp. angrily (flung out of the room). **7** (foll. by away) discard rashly. — n. **1** act or instance of flinging; throw. **2** spell of indulgence or wild behaviour. **3** attempt at something, esp. when uncertain of success (oh well, I'll give it a fling). **4** whirling Scottish dance, esp. the Highland fling. [Old Norse]

**flint** n. **1 a** hard grey siliceous stone. **b** piece of this, esp. as a primitive tool or weapon. **2** piece of hard alloy used to give a spark. **3** anything hard and unyielding. □ **flinty** adj. (-ier, -iest). [Old English]

**flintlock** n. hist. old type of gun fired by a spark from a flint.

**flip¹** — v. (-pp-) **1** flick or toss (a coin, pellet, etc.) so that it spins in the air. **2** turn (a small object) over; flick. **3** colloq. = flip one's lid. — n. **1** act of flipping. **2** somersault. — adj. colloq. glib; flippant. □ **flip one's lid** colloq. lose self-control; go mad. **flip over a person** (or **thing**) colloq. be passionately fond of. **flip a person for** colloq. toss a coin with a person for something or to determine an issue (I'll flip you for the front seat; flip you to see who mows the lawn). **flip through** = flick through. [probably from FILLIP]

**flip²** n. = EGG-FLIP.

**flippant** /flip-uhnt/ adj. lacking in seriousness; treating serious things lightly; disrespectful; offhand. □ **flippancy** n. **flippantly** adv. [from FLIP¹]

**flipper** n. **1** broad flat limb of a turtle, penguin, etc., used in swimming. **2** similar rubber foot attachment for underwater swimming. **3** Cricket top-spinner given an extra flip of the fingers.

**flipping** adj. & adv. colloq. expressing annoyance, or as an intensifier (flipping idiot).

**flip side** n. colloq. **1** reverse side of a gramophone record. **2** reverse or less important side of something.

**flirt** — v. **1** (usu. foll. by with) behave in a frivolously amorous or sexually enticing manner. **2** (usu. foll. by with) **a** superficially interest oneself (with an idea etc.) (flirted with politics). **b** trifle (with danger etc.). — n. person who flirts. □ **flirtation** /-tay-shuhn/ n. **flirtatious** /-tay-shuhs/ adj. **flirtatiously** /-tay-shuhs-lee/ adv. **flirtatiousness** /-tay-shuhs-nuhs/ n. [imitative]

**flit** — v. (-tt-) **1** move lightly, softly, or rapidly. **2** make short flights (flit from branch to branch). **3** colloq. disappear secretly to escape creditors etc. — n. act of flitting. □ **do a flit** depart surreptitiously. [Old Norse: related to FLEET]

**flitch** n. side of bacon. [Old English]

**flitter** v. flit about; flutter. [from FLIT]

**float** — v. **1 a** (cause to) rest or move on the surface of a liquid. **b** set (a stranded ship) afloat. **2** *colloq.* **a** move in a leisurely way (*floated about, humming quietly*). **b** (often foll. by *before*) hover before the eye or mind (*the prospect of lunch floated before them*). **3 a** move with a liquid or current of air; drift (*the clouds floated high up*). **b** (often foll. by *in*) move or be suspended freely in a liquid or gas. **4 a** start or launch (a company, scheme, etc.). **b** offer (stock, shares, etc.) on the stock market. **5** *Commerce* cause or allow to have a fluctuating exchange rate. **6** circulate or cause (a rumour or idea) to circulate. — n. **1** thing that floats, esp.: **a** a raft. **b** a light object as an indicator of a fish biting or supporting a fishing-net. **c** a hollow structure enabling an aircraft to float on water. **d** a floating device on water, petrol, etc., controlling the level. **2** decorated platform or tableau on a truck in a procession etc. **3** (in full **horse float**) closed vehicle for transporting a horse or horses. **4 a** supply of loose change in a shop, at a fête, etc. **b** petty cash. □ **floatable** adj. [Old English]

**floatation** var. of FLOTATION.

**floater** n. **1** person or thing that floats. **2** cheque that bounces. **3** person who frequently changes jobs. **4** (in two-up) coin that fails to spin when tossed. **5** piece of ore that has come to the surface. **6** (in SA) meat pie served floating in gravy and peas.

**floaties** /floh-teez/ n.pl. inflatable floats fixed on the arms of a child learning to swim.

**floating** adj. not settled; variable (*floating population*).

**floating dock** n. floating structure usable as a dry dock.

**floating kidney** n. abnormally movable kidney.

**floating rib** n. lower rib not attached to the breastbone.

**flocculent** /flok-yuh-luhnt/ adj. like or in tufts of wool etc.; downy. □ **flocculence** n. [related to FLOCK²]

**flock¹** — n. **1 a** number of animals of one kind, esp. birds, feeding or travelling together. **b** number of domestic animals, esp. sheep, goats, or geese, kept together. **2** large crowd of people. **3** people in the care of a priest or teacher etc. — v. (usu. foll. by *to, in, out, together*) congregate; mass; troop. [Old English]

**flock²** n. **1** lock or tuft of wool, cotton, etc. **2** (also in *pl.*; often *attrib.*) wool-refuse etc. used for quilting and stuffing. [Latin *floccus*]

**flock pigeon** n. **1** mainly brown nomadic pigeon of inland north Australia. **2** mainly grey pigeon of eastern Australian rainforests.

**floe** n. sheet of floating ice. [Norwegian]

**flog** v. (**-gg-**) **1 a** beat with a whip, stick, etc. **b** make work through violent effort (*flogged the engine*). **2** (often foll. by *off*) *colloq.* sell. **3** *colloq.* steal. □ **flog a dead horse 1** try to do something quite useless. **2** try to raise or revive interest in a dead issue etc. **flog to death** *colloq.* talk about or promote at tedious length. [origin unknown]

**flogger** /flog-uh/ n. (esp. in Australian Rules) streamers (in the colours of a team) attached to a rod and waved by cheerleaders and supporters.

**flood** /flud/ — n. **1 a** overflowing or influx of water, esp. over land; inundation. **b** the water that overflows. **2** outpouring; torrent (*flood of tears*). **3** inflow of the tide (also in *comb.*: *flood-tide*). **4** *colloq.* floodlight. **5** (**the Flood**) the flood described in Genesis. — v. **1 a** overflow, cover, or be covered with or as if with a flood (*bathroom flooded; flooded with enquiries*). **b** (of rain etc.) fill (a river) to overflowing. **c** (of a river) rise in height to overflowing. **2** irrigate (*flooded the paddy fields*). **3** deluge (a mine etc.) with water. **4** (often foll. by *in, through*) come in great quantities (*complaints flooded in*). **5** overfill (a carburettor) with petrol. [Old English]

**flooded gum** n. any of several eucalypts growing in moist places.

**flood fence** n. free-hanging fence across a creek etc., designed to float above an occasional flood.

**floodgate** n. **1** gate for admitting or excluding water, esp. in a lock. **2** (usu. in *pl.*) last restraint holding back tears, rain, anger, etc.

**floodlight** — n. large powerful light (usu. one of several) to illuminate a building, sports ground, etc. — v. illuminate with floodlights. □ **floodlit** adj.

**floodtide** n. exceptionally high tide caused esp. by the moon.

**floor** /flaw/ — n. **1** lower supporting surface of a room. **2 a** bottom of the sea, a cave, etc. **b** any level area. **3** all the rooms etc. on one level of a building; storey. **4 a** (in a legislative chamber) place where members sit and speak. **b** right to speak next in a debate (*gave him the floor*). **5** minimum of prices, wages, etc. **6** *colloq.*

ground. — v. **1** provide with a floor; pave. **2** knock or bring (a person) down. **3** *colloq.* confound, baffle (*was floored by the puzzle*). **4** *colloq.* get the better of; overcome. □ **from the floor** (of a speech etc.) given by a member of the audience. **take the floor 1** begin to dance. **2** speak in a debate. [Old English]

**floorboard** n. long wooden board used for flooring.

**flooring** n. **1** floor. **2** material of which a floor is made. **3** material with which a floor is covered.

**floor manager** n. stage-manager of a television production.

**floor plan** n. diagram of the rooms etc. on one storey.

**floor show** n. nightclub entertainment.

**flop** — v. (**-pp-**) **1** sway about heavily or loosely (*his hair flopped over his face*). **2** move in an ungainly way (*flopped along the beach in flippers*). **3** (often foll. by *down, on, into*) fall or sit etc. awkwardly or suddenly. **4** *colloq.* (esp. of a play, film, book, etc.) fail; collapse. **5** make a dull soft thud or splash. — n. **1** flopping movement or sound. **2** *colloq.* failure. — *adv.* with a flop. [var. of FLAP]

**floppy** — *adj.* (**-ier, -iest**) tending to flop; flaccid. — n. (*pl.* **-ies**) (in full **floppy disk**) *Computing* removable magnetic disc for the storage of data. □ **floppiness** n.

**flora** /**flaw**-ruh/ n. (*pl.* **-s** or **florae** /-ree/) **1** plant life of a region or period. **2** list or book of these. [Latin *Flora*, name of the goddess of flowers]

**floral** /**flo**-ruhl, **flaw**-/ *adj.* of, decorated with, or depicting flowers. □ **florally** *adv.* [Latin]

**floral emblem** n. plant officially adopted by a country (and in Australia also by a State or Territory) as a symbol, hence: **1** (of Australia) AUSTRALIAN GOLDEN WATTLE *Acacia pycnantha*. **2** (of the ACT) ROYAL BLUEBELL *Wahlenbergia gloriosa*. **3** (of the NT) STURT'S DESERT ROSE *Gossypium sturtianum*. **4** (of NSW) waratah (see WARATAH) *Telopea speciosissima*. **5** (of Queensland) COOKTOWN ORCHID *Dendrobium biggibum*. **6** (of SA) STURT'S DESERT PEA *Clianthus formosus*. **7** (of Tasmania) TASMANIAN BLUE GUM *Eucalyptus globulus*. **8** (of Victoria) COMMON HEATH *Epacris impressa*. **9** (of WA) RED-AND-GREEN KANGAROO PAW *Anigozanthos manglesii*.

**Florentine** /**flo**-ruhn-,tuyn/ — *adj.* of Florence in Italy. — n. native or citizen of Florence. [Latin]

**floret** /**flo**-ruht, **flaw**-/ n. **1** each of the small flowers making up a composite flower-head. **2** each stem of a head of cauliflower, broccoli, etc. **3** small flower. [Latin *flos* FLOWER]

**floribunda** /,flo-ruh-**bun**-duh, ,flaw-/ n. plant, esp. a rose, bearing dense clusters of flowers. [related to FLORET: cf. MORIBUND]

**florid** /**flo**-ruhd/ *adj.* **1** ruddy (*florid complexion*). **2** (of a book, picture, music, architecture, etc.) elaborately ornate; showy. □ **floridly** *adv.* **floridness** n. [Latin: related to FLOWER]

**florin** /**flo**-ruhn/ n. *hist.* silver two-shilling coin. [Italian *fiorino*: related to FLORIST]

**florist** /**flo**-ruhst/ n. person who deals in or sells flowers. □ **floristry** n. [Latin *flos* FLOWER]

**floruit** /**flo**-roo-uht, **flaw**-/ v. (*abbr.* **fl.**) flourished; lived and worked (of a painter, writer, etc., whose exact dates are unknown). [Latin, = he or she flourished]

**floss** — n. **1** rough silk of a silkworm's cocoon. **2** silk thread used in embroidery. **3** = DENTAL FLOSS. — v. (also *absol.*) clean (teeth) with dental floss. □ **flossy** *adj.* [French *floche*]

**flotation** /floh-**tay**-shuhn/ n. (also **floatation**) **1** act or state of floating. **2** launching or financing of a commercial enterprise etc. [from FLOAT]

**flotilla** /fluh-**til**-uh/ n. **1** small fleet. **2** fleet of small ships. [Spanish]

**flotsam** /**flot**-suhm/ n. wreckage found floating. [Anglo-French: related to FLOAT]

**flotsam and jetsam** n. **1** wreckage found floating as well as cast ashore. **2** odds and ends.

**flounce**[1] — v. (**-cing**) (often foll. by *away, about, off, out*) go or move angrily or impatiently (*flounced out in a huff*). — n. flouncing movement. [origin unknown]

**flounce**[2] — n. ornamental strip of material gathered and sewn to a dress, skirt, etc. — v. (**-cing**) trim with flounces. [alteration of *frounce* pleat, from French]

**flounder**[1] — v. **1** struggle helplessly as if wading in mud. **2** do a task clumsily. — n. act of floundering. [imitative]

**flounder**[2] n. (*pl.* same) any of various species of edible flatfish, including the species found in coastal Australian waters. [Anglo-French, probably Scandinavian]

**flour** — n. **1** meal or powder from ground wheat etc. **2** any fine powder. — v. sprinkle with flour. □ **floury** *adj.* (**-ier, -iest**). **flouriness** n. [different spelling of FLOWER 'best part']

**flourish** /**flu**-rish/ — v. **1** **a** grow vigorously; thrive. **b** prosper. **c** be in one's prime. **d** be in good health. **2** wave (a weapon, one's limbs, etc.) vigorously. **3** show ostentatiously (*flourished his cheque-book*). — *n.* **1** showy gesture (*removed his hat with a flourish*). **2** ornamental curve in handwriting. **3** *Mus.* ornate passage or fanfare. [Latin *floreo* from *flos* FLOWER]

**floury baker** *n.* (also **floury miller**) common cicada of coastal eastern Australia, having floury scales.

**flout** — *v.* disobey (the law etc.) contemptuously; mock; insult (*flouted convention by shaving her head*). — *n.* flouting speech or act. [Dutch *fluiten* whistle: related to FLUTE]

■ **Usage** *Flout* is often confused with *flaunt* which means 'to display proudly, show off'.

**flow** /floh/ — *v.* **1** glide along as a stream. **2** (of liquid, blood, etc.) gush out; be spilt. **3** (of blood, money, electric current, etc.) circulate. **4** move in large numbers or smoothly or steadily (*traffic flowed down the hill*). **5 a** (of talk, literary style, etc.) proceed easily and smoothly. **b** (of a garment, hair, etc.) hang gracefully. **6** (often foll. by *from*) be caused by (*his failure flows from his shyness*). **7** (esp. of the tide) be in flood. **8** (of wine etc.) be plentiful. **9** (foll. by *with*) *archaic* be plentifully supplied with (*flowing with milk and honey*). — *n.* **1 a** flowing movement or mass. **b** flowing liquid (*stop the flow*). **c** outpouring; stream (*flow of complaints*). **2** rise of a tide or river (*ebb and flow*). [Old English]

**flow chart** *n.* (also **flow diagram** or **flow sheet**) **1** diagram of the movement or action of persons engaged in a complex activity. **2** graphical representation of a computer program in relation to its sequence of functions (as distinct from the data it processes).

**flower** /flowuh/ — *n.* **1 a** part of a plant from which the fruit or seed is developed. **b** reproductive organ in a plant containing one or more pistils or stamens or both, and usu. a corolla and calyx. **2** blossom, esp. used for decoration. **3** plant cultivated for its flowers. — *v.* **1** bloom or cause (a plant) to bloom; blossom. **2** reach a peak. □ **the flower of** the best of. **in flower** blooming. □ **flowered** *adj.* [Latin *flos flor*]

**flowering gum** *n.* any of several eucalypts noted for their beauty while flowering, esp. the red-flowering gum (*Eucalyptus ficifolia*).

**flower people** *n.* hippies with flowers as symbols of peace and love.

**flower power** *n.* peace and love, esp. as a political idea.

**flowers of sulphur** *n.* fine powder produced when sulphur evaporates and condenses.

**flowery** *adj.* **1** decorated with flowers or floral designs. **2** (of style, speech, etc.) high-flown; ornate. **3** full of flowers. □ **floweriness** *n.*

**flowing** *adj.* **1** (of style etc.) fluent; easy. **2** (of a line, curve, etc.) smoothly continuous. **3** (of hair etc.) unconfined. □ **flowingly** *adv.*

**flown** *past part.* of FLY[1].

**flow-on** *n.* wage increase granted to other sections of the workforce because it had previously been granted to one section of it.

**flu** /floo/ *n. colloq.* influenza. [abbreviation]

**fluctuate** /fluk-choo-,ayt/ *v.* (**-ting**) vary irregularly; rise and fall. □ **fluctuation** /-ay-shuhn/ *n.* [Latin *fluctus* wave]

**flue** /floo/ *n.* **1** smoke-duct in a chimney. **2** channel for conveying heat. [origin unknown]

**fluent** /floo-uhnt/ *adj.* **1** (of speech, style, etc.) flowing, natural. **2** verbally facile, esp. in a foreign language (*fluent in German*). □ **fluency** *n.* **fluently** *adv.* [Latin *fluo* flow]

**fluff** — *n.* **1** soft fur, feathers, or fabric particles etc. **2** *colloq.* mistake in a performance etc. — *v.* **1** (often foll. by *up*) shake into or become a soft mass. **2** *colloq.* make a mistake (in a theatrical part, game, playing music, speech, etc.); bungle. □ **bit of fluff** *colloq. offens.* woman regarded as an object of sexual desire. □ **fluffy** *adj.* (**-ier**, **-iest**). **fluffiness** *n.* [probably British dial. alteration of *flue* fluff]

**fluid** /floo-uhd/ — *n.* **1** substance, esp. a gas or liquid, whose shape is determined by its confines. **2** fluid part or secretion. — *adj.* **1** able to flow and alter shape freely. **2** constantly changing or fluctuating (*situation is fluid*). □ **fluidity** /-id-uh-tee/ *n.* **fluidly** *adv.* **fluidness** *n.* [Latin: related to FLUENT]

**fluid ounce** *n. Brit.* one-twentieth, or *US* one-sixteenth, of a pint (approximately 0.028 litre).

**fluke[1]** /flook/ — *n.* **1** lucky accident (*won by a fluke*). **2** chance breeze. — *v.* (**-king**) achieve by a fluke. □ **fluky** *adj.* (also **flukey**) (**-ier**, **-iest**). [origin uncertain]

**fluke[2]** /flook/ *n.* **1** parasitic flatworm, e.g. the liver fluke. **2** flatfish, esp. a flounder. [Old English]

**fluke[3]** /flook/ *n.* **1** broad triangular plate on an anchor arm. **2** lobe of a whale's tail. [perhaps from FLUKE[2]]

**flummery** /flum-uh-ree/ *n.* (*pl.* **-ies**) **1**

flattery; nonsense. **2** sweet dish made with beaten eggs, sugar, etc. [Welsh *llymru*]

**flummox** /flum-uhks/ *v. colloq.* bewilder, disconcert. [origin unknown]

**flung** *past* and *past part.* of FLING.

**flunk** *v. colloq.* **1** fail (esp. an exam). **2** (foll. by *out*) give up, get out of (*he flunked out of the swimming trials*). [origin unknown]

**flunkey** /flung-kee/ *n.* (also **flunky**) (*pl.* **-eys** or **-ies**) usu. *derog.* **1** uniformed servant. **2** servile toady, crawler. [origin uncertain]

**fluoresce** /floor-res, fluh-/ *v.* (**-scing**) be or become fluorescent. [from FLUORESCENT]

**fluorescence** *n.* **1** light radiation from certain substances. **2** property of absorbing invisible light and emitting visible light. [from FLUORSPAR, after *opalescence*]

**fluorescent** *adj.* of, having, or showing fluorescence.

**fluorescent tube** *n.* (also **fluorescent lamp**) esp. tubular lamp or bulb radiating largely by fluorescence.

**fluoridate** /floor-ruh-, dayt, floo-/ *v.* (**-ting**) add fluoride to (drinking-water, toothpaste, etc.), esp. to prevent tooth decay. □ **fluoridation** /,floor-ruh-**day**-shuhn, ,floo-/ *n.*

**fluoride** /floor-ruyd, floo-/ — *n.* binary compound of fluorine. — *adj.* containing fluoride (*fluoride toothpaste*).

**fluorinate** /floor-ruh-,nayt, floo-/ *v.* (**-ting**) **1** = FLUORIDATE. **2** introduce fluorine into (a compound). □ **fluorination** /-**nay**-shuhn/ *n.*

**fluorine** /floor-reen, floo-/ *n.* poisonous pale-yellow gaseous element. [French: related to FLUORSPAR]

**fluorite** /floor-ruyt, floo-/ *n.* mineral form of calcium fluoride. [Italian: related to FLUORSPAR]

**fluorocarbon** /,floor-roh-**kah**-buhn/ *n.* compound of a hydrocarbon with fluorine atoms.

**fluorspar** /floor-spah/ *n.* = FLUORITE. [*fluor* a mineral used as flux, from Latin *fluo* flow]

**flurry** /flu-ree/ — *n.* (*pl.* **-ies**) **1** gust or squall (of snow, rain, etc.). **2** sudden burst of activity, excitement, etc.; commotion. — *v.* (**-ies**, **-ied**) confuse; agitate. [imitative]

**flush¹** — *v.* **1** blush, redden, glow warmly (*he flushed with embarrassment*). **2** (usu. as **flushed** *adj.*) cause to glow or blush (often foll. by *with*: *he was flushed with pride*). **3 a** cleanse (a drain, lavatory, etc.) by a flow of water. **b** (often foll. by *away*,

*down*) dispose of in this way. **4** rush out, spurt. — *n.* **1** blush or glow. **2 a** rush of water. **b** cleansing of a drain, toilet, etc. thus. **3** rush of esp. elation or triumph. **4** freshness; vigour (*in the first flush of manhood*). **5 a** (also **hot flush**) sudden feeling of heat during menopause. **b** feverish redness or temperature etc. — *adj.* **1** level, in the same plane (*fitted it flush with the wall*). **2** *colloq.* having plenty of money. — *adv.* squarely, directly (*punched him flush on the nose*). [perhaps = FLUSH³]

**flush²** *n.* hand of cards all of one suit, esp. in poker. [Latin *fluxus* FLUX]

**flush³** *v.* cause (esp. a game-bird) to fly up. □ **flush out 1** reveal; bring into the open. **2** drive out. [imitative]

**fluster** — *v.* **1** make or become nervous or confused (*he flusters easily*). **2** bustle. — *n.* confused or agitated state. [origin unknown]

**flute** /floot/ — *n.* **1 a** high-pitched woodwind instrument held sideways. **b** any similar wind instrument. **2** ornamental vertical groove in a column. — *v.* (**-ting**) **1** play, or play (a tune etc.) on the flute. **2** speak or sing etc. in a high voice. **3** make grooves in. □ **fluting** *n.* **fluty** *adj.* (in sense 1a of *n.*) [French]

**flutist** /floo-tuhst/ *n.* = FLAUTIST.

**flutter** — *v.* **1** flap (the wings) in flying or trying to fly. **2** fall quiveringly (*leaves fluttering to the ground*). **3** wave or flap quickly (*flags fluttered in the breeze*). **4** move about restlessly. **5** (of a pulse etc.) beat feebly or irregularly. — *n.* **1** act or instance of fluttering. **2** tremulous excitement (*caused a flutter*). **3** *colloq.* small bet, esp. on a horse. **4** abnormally rapid heartbeat. **5** rapid variation of pitch, esp. of recorded sound. □ **fluttery** *adj.* [Old English]

**fluvial** /floo-vee-uhl/ *adj.* of or found in rivers. [Latin *fluvius* river]

**fluvioglacial** /,floo-vee-oh-**glay**-shuhl, -see-uhl/ *adj.* of or caused by streams from glacial ice, or the combined actions of rivers and glaciers.

**flux** *n.* **1** process of flowing or flowing out. **2** discharge. **3** continuous change (*state of flux*). **4** substance mixed with a metal etc. to aid fusion. [Latin *fluxus* from *fluo flux-* flow]

**fly¹** /fluy/ — *v.* (**flies**; *past* **flew** /floo/; *past part.* **flown** /flohn/) **1 a** (of an aircraft, bird, etc.) move through the air or space under control, esp. with wings. **b** travel through the air or space. **2** control the flight of or transport in (esp. an aircraft). **3 a** cause to fly or remain aloft. **b** (of a flag, hair, etc.) wave or flutter. **4** pass, move, or rise quickly (*time flies*). **5 a** flee; flee from. **b** *colloq.* depart hastily. **6** be driven, forced, or scattered (*sent me flying*). **7** (foll. by *at, upon*) **a** hasten or spring violently. **b** (also foll. by *into*) attack or criticise fiercely. — *n.* (*pl.* -**ies**) **1** (usu. in *pl.*) **a** concealing flap, esp. over a trouser-fastening. **b** this fastening. **2** flap at a tent entrance. **3** (*in pl.*) space above a stage where scenery and lighting are suspended. **4** act or instance of flying. □ **fly high** be ambitious; prosper. **fly in the face of** disregard or disobey. **fly a kite** test opinion. **fly off the handle** *colloq.* lose one's temper. **let fly 1** throw or propel. **2** give free vent to. **3** burst out into a verbal attack (*let fly at all and sundry*). [Old English]

**fly²** /fluy/ *n.* (*pl.* **flies**) **1** insect with two usu. transparent wings. **2** other winged insect, e.g. a firefly. **3** (esp. artificial) fly as bait in fishing. □ **like flies** in large numbers (usu. of people dying etc.). **no flies on** (**him** etc.) *colloq.* (he is) very astute. [Old English]

**flyblown** *adj.* tainted, esp. by flies.

**fly-by-night** *colloq.* — *adj.* unreliable. — *n.* unreliable person.

**flycatcher** *n.* any of several birds catching insects during short flights from a chosen perch, including several Australian species (*leaden flycatcher*; *restless flycatcher*; *satin flycatcher*).

**flyer** *n.* (also **flier**) *colloq.* **1** airman or airwoman. **2** thing that flies in a specified way (*poor flyer*). **3** fast-moving animal (esp. a kangaroo) or vehicle. **4** ambitious or outstanding person. **5** small promotional handbill.

**flying** — *adj.* **1** fluttering, waving, or hanging loose. **2** hasty, brief (*flying visit*). **3** designed for rapid movement. **4** (of an animal) leaping with winglike membranes etc. — *n.* flight, esp. in an aircraft. □ **with flying colours** with distinction.

**flying boat** *n.* boatlike seaplane.

**flying buttress** *n.* (usu. arched) buttress running from the upper part of a wall to an outer support and transmitting the thrust of the roof or vault.

**flying doctor** *n.* doctor who uses an aircraft to visit patients.

**flying duck orchid** *n.* Australian terrestrial ground orchid having reddish brown flowers remarkably like a duck in flight, the glossy 'beak' being a very sensitive pollinating mechanism that snaps downward when touched.

**flying fish** *n.* tropical fish with winglike fins for gliding through the air.

**flying fox** *n.* **1** any of various fruit-eating bats of Australia and elsewhere with a foxlike head. **2** overhead cable and apparatus for the transport of materials etc. over difficult terrain.

**flying officer** *n.* RAAF rank next below flight lieutenant.

**flying possum** *n.* (also **flying phalanger**) any of several tree-climbing Australian marsupials, esp. one that glides through the air using flaps of skin between the fore and hind limbs as parachutes.

**flying saucer** *n.* supposed alien space-ship.

**flying squad** *n.* rapidly mobile police detachment etc.

**flying start** *n.* **1** start (of a race etc.) in which the starting-point is crossed at full speed. **2** *colloq.* distinct advantage (*his knowledge of Bahasa Indonesia gave him a flying start over the other applicants*).

**fly in the ointment** *n.* minor irritation or setback.

**flyleaf** *n.* blank leaf at the beginning or end of a book.

**fly on the wall** *n.* unnoticed observer.

**fly-past** *n.* ceremonial flight of aircraft.

**flyscreen** *n.* mesh-frame over a window or door to permit ventilation but exclude flies.

**flytrap** *n.* plant that catches flies.

**flyweight** *n.* **1** weight in certain sports between light flyweight and bantam-weight, in amateur boxing 48–51 kg. **2** sportsman of this weight.

**flywheel** *n.* heavy wheel on a revolving shaft to regulate machinery or accumulate power.

**FM** *abbr.* = FREQUENCY MODULATION.

**Fm** *symb.* fermium.

**f-number** /ef-num-buh/ *n.* ratio of the focal length to the effective diameter of a camera lens. [from *f*ocal]

**foal** — *n.* young of a horse or related animal. — *v.* give birth to (a foal). □ **in** (or **with**) **foal** (of a mare etc.) pregnant. [Old English]

**foam** — *n.* **1** mass of small bubbles formed on or in liquid by agitation, fermentation, etc. **2** froth of saliva or sweat. **3** substance resembling these, e.g. spongy rubber or plastic. — *v.* emit or run with foam; froth. □ **foam at the mouth** be very angry. □ **foamy** *adj.* (-**ier**, -**iest**). [Old English]

**foam bark** *n.* rainforest tree of Queensland and NSW, the bark of which contains a substance that foams in the water and was used by the Aborigines to stun fish.

**fob¹** *n.* **1** chain of a pocket-watch. **2** small pocket for a watch etc. **3** tab on a key-ring. [German]

**fob²** v. (**-bb-**) □ **fob off 1** (often foll. by *with*) put off or deter (a person) (*don't fob me off with fast-talk*). **2** (often foll. by *with* a thing) deceive into accepting something inferior. **3** (often foll. by *on* or *on to* a person) offload (an unwanted thing). [cf. obsolete *fop* dupe]

**focaccia** /fuh-**kah**-chuh/ n. type of flat savoury Italian bread made with yeast and oil and usu. seasoned with herbs etc. [Italian]

**focal** /**foh**-kuhl/ adj. of or at a focus. [Latin: related to FOCUS]

**focal length** n. distance between the centre of a mirror or lens and its focus.

**focal point** n. **1** = FOCUS n. 1. **2** centre of interest or activity.

**fo'c'sle** var. of FORECASTLE.

**focus** /**foh**-kuhs/ n. (pl. **focuses** or **foci** /**foh**-kuy/) **1 a** point at which rays or waves meet after reflection or refraction. **b** point from which rays etc. appear to proceed. **2 a** point at which an object must be situated for a lens or mirror to give a well-defined image (*bring into focus*). **b** adjustment of the eye or a lens to give a clear image (*the binoculars were not in focus*). **c** state of clear definition (*the photograph was out of focus*). **3** = FOCAL POINT 2. **4** principal site of an infection or disease. **5** place of origin of an earthquake. — v. (**-s-** or **-ss-**) **1** bring into focus. **2** adjust the focus of (a lens or eye). **3** concentrate or be concentrated on. **4** converge or make converge to a focus. [Latin, = hearth]

**fodder** n. dried hay or straw etc. as animal food. [Old English]

**foe** n. esp. *poet.* enemy. [Old English]

**foetid** var. of FETID.

**foetus** /**fee**-tuhs/ n. (also **fetus**) (pl. **-tuses**) unborn mammalian offspring, esp. a human embryo of eight weeks or more. □ **foetal** adj. [Latin *fetus* offspring]

**fog** — n. **1 a** thick cloud of water droplets or smoke suspended at or near the earth's surface. **b** obscurity in the atmosphere caused by this. **2** cloudiness on a photographic negative etc. **3** uncertain or confused position or state. — v. (**-gg-**) **1** cover or become covered with or as with fog. **2** bewilder or confuse (as if with a fog). [perhaps a back-formation from FOGGY]

**fogbound** adj. unable to travel because of fog.

**fogey** /**foh**-gee/ n. (also **fogy**) (pl. **-ies** or **-eys**) dull old-fashioned person (esp. *old fogey*). [origin unknown]

**foggy** adj. (**-ier**, **-iest**) **1** full of fog. **2** of or like fog. **3** vague, indistinct. □ **not have**

the foggiest *colloq.* have no idea at all. □ **fogginess** n. [perhaps from *fog* long grass]

**foghorn** n. **1** horn warning ships in fog. **2** *colloq.* loud penetrating voice.

**fogy** var. of FOGEY.

**foible** /**foi**-buhl/ n. minor weakness or idiosyncrasy. [French: related to FEEBLE]

**foil¹** v. frustrate, baffle, defeat (*foiled their plans*). [perhaps from French *fouler* trample]

**foil²** n. **1** metal rolled into a very thin sheet. **2** person or thing that enhances the qualities of another by contrast. [Latin *folium* leaf]

**foil³** n. light blunt fencing sword. [origin unknown]

**foist** v. (foll. by *on*) **1** force (a thing or oneself) on to an unwilling person. **2** (foll. by *in*, *into*) introduce surreptitiously or unwarrantably. [Dutch *vuisten* take in the hand]

**fold¹** /fohld/ — v. **1 a** bend or close (a flexible thing) over upon itself. **b** (foll. by *back*, *over*, *down*) bend part of (a thing) in the manner specified (*fold down the flap*). **2** become or be able to be folded. **3** (foll. by *away*, *up*) make compact by folding. **4** (often foll. by *up*) *colloq.* (of an enterprise) fail; go bankrupt. **5** enfold (esp. *fold in the arms* or *to the breast*). **6** (foll. by *about*, *round*) clasp (the arms). **7** (foll. by *in*) mix (an ingredient with others) gently. — n. **1** act or instance of folding. **2** line made by folding. **3** folded part. **4** hollow among hills. **5** curvature of geological strata. [Old English]

**fold²** /fohld/ — n. **1** enclosure for sheep. **2** religious group or congregation. — v. enclose (sheep) in a fold. [Old English]

**-fold** *suffix* forming adjectives and adverbs from cardinal numbers, meaning: **1** in an amount multiplied by (*repaid tenfold*). **2** with so many parts (*threefold blessing*). [originally = 'folded in so many layers']

**folder** n. folding cover or holder for loose papers.

**foliaceous** /ˌfoh-lee-**ay**-shuhs/ adj. **1** of or like leaves. **2** laminated. [Latin: related to FOIL²]

**foliage** /**foh**-lee-ij/ n. leaves, leafage. [French *feuillage* from *feuille* leaf]

**foliar** /**foh**-lee-uh/ adj. of or relating to leaves. [as FOLIATE]

**foliate** — adj. /**foh**-lee-uht/ **1** leaflike. **2** having leaves. — v. /**foh**-lee-ˌayt/ (**-ting**) split or beat into thin layers. □ **foliation** /-**ay**-shuhn/ n. [Latin *folium* leaf]

**folic acid** /**foh**-lik/ n. vitamin of the B complex, found in leafy green vegetables, liver, and kidney, a deficiency of which causes pernicious anaemia.

**folio** /foh-lee-oh/ — n. (pl. -s) **1** leaf of paper etc., esp. numbered only on the front. **2** sheet of paper folded once making two leaves of a book. **3** book of such sheets. — adj. (of a book) made of folios, of the largest size. □ **in folio** made of folios. [Latin, ablative of folium leaf]

**folk** /fohk/ n. (pl. same or **-s**) **1** (treated as pl.) people in general or of a specified class (few folk about; townsfolk). **2** (in pl.) (usu. **folks**) one's parents or relatives. **3** (treated as sing.) a people or nation. **4** (in full **folk music**) (treated as sing.) colloq. traditional music or modern music in this style. **5** (attrib.) of popular origin (folk art). [Old English]

**folk dance** n. dance of popular origin.

**folk etymology** n. **1** popular modifying of the form of a word or phrase to make it seem to be derived from a more familiar word, e.g. FORLORN HOPE. **2** spurious explanation of the origin of a word.

**folkie** n. colloq. player or follower of folk music.

**folklore** n. traditional beliefs and stories of a people; the study of these.

**folk singer** n. singer of folk songs.

**folk song** n. song of popular or traditional origin or style.

**folksy** /fohk-see/ adj. (**-ier, -iest**) **1** of or like folk art, culture, etc. **2** friendly, unpretentious. □ **folksiness** n.

**folk tale** n. traditional story.

**follicle** /fol-i-kuhl/ n. **1** small sac or vesicle in the body, esp. one containing a hair-root. **2** single-carpelled dry fruit opening on one side only to release its seeds. □ **follicular** /fo-lik-yuh-luh/ adj. [Latin diminutive of follis bellows]

**follow** /fol-oh/ v. **1** (often foll. by after) go or come after (a person or thing ahead). **2** go along (a road etc.). **3** come after in order or time (dessert followed; proceed as follows). **4** take as a guide or leader. **5** conform to (follow your example). **6** practise (a trade or profession). **7** understand (a speaker, argument, etc.). **8** take an interest in (current affairs etc.). **9** (foll. by with) provide with a sequel or successor. **10** happen after something else; ensue. **11 a** be necessarily true as a consequence. **b** (foll. by from) result. □ **follow on 1** continue. **2** (of a cricket team) have to bat twice in succession. **follow out** carry out (instructions etc.). **follow suit 1** play a card of the suit led. **2** conform to another's actions. **follow through 1** continue to a conclusion. **2** continue the movement of a stroke after hitting the ball. **follow up** (foll. by with) **1** develop,

supplement. **2** investigate further. [Old English]

**follower** n. **1** supporter or devotee. **2** person who follows. **3** Aust. Rules either of the two players who, with the rover, does not have a fixed position and so follows the play.

**following** — prep. after in time; as a sequel to. — n. supporters or devotees. — adj. that follows or comes after. □ **the following 1** what follows. **2** now to be given or named (answer the following).

**folly** n. (pl. **-ies**) **1** foolishness. **2** foolish act, behaviour, idea, etc. **3** fanciful ornamental building created for display. [French folie from fol mad, FOOL¹]

**foment** /fuh-ment, foh-/ v. **1** instigate or stir up (trouble, discontent, etc.). **2 a** bathe (a limb etc.) with warm or medicated liquid. **b** apply warmth (to a limb etc.). □ **fomentation** /ˌfoh-men-tay-shuhn/ n. [Latin foveo heat, cherish]

**fond** adj. **1** (foll. by of) having affection or liking for. **2 a** affectionate. **b** doting. **3** (of beliefs etc.) foolishly optimistic or credulous. □ **fondly** adv. **fondness** n. [obsolete fon fool, be foolish]

**fondant** /fon-duhnt/ n. soft sugary sweet. [French = melting: related to FUSE¹]

**fondle** /fon-duhl/ v. (**-ling**) touch or stroke lovingly; caress. [related to FOND]

**fondue** /fon-doo/ n. dish of flavoured melted cheese. [French, = melted: related to FUSE¹]

**font¹** n. receptacle in a church for baptismal water. [Latin fons font-fountain]

**font²** n. (also **fount** pronunc. same) set of printing type of the same face and size. [French: related to FOUND³]

**fontanelle** /ˌfon-tuh-nel/ n. membranous space in an infant's skull at the angles of the parietal bones. [Latin fontanella little FOUNTAIN]

**food** n. **1 a** substance taken in to maintain life and growth. **b** solid food (as opposed to drink). **2** mental stimulus (food for thought). [Old English]

**food additive** n. substance added to food to colour or flavour it etc.

**food chain** n. series of organisms each dependent on the next for food.

**food poisoning** n. illness due to bacteria etc. in food.

**food processor** n. machine for chopping and mixing food.

**foodstuff** n. substance used as food.

**fool¹** — n. **1** rash, unwise, or stupid person. **2** hist. jester; clown. **3** dupe. — v. **1** deceive. **2** (foll. by into or out of) trick;

cheat. **3** joke or tease. **4** (foll. by *about, around*) play or trifle. **5** (foll. by *around with*) dally sexually with. □ **act** (or **play**) **the fool** behave in a silly way. **be no** (or **nobody's**) **fool** be shrewd or prudent. **fool away** fritter away time, money, etc. **make a fool of** make (a person or oneself) look foolish; trick, deceive. [Latin *follis* bellows]

**fool²** *n.* dessert of fruit purée with cream or custard. [perhaps from FOOL¹]

**foolery** *n.* foolish behaviour.

**foolhardy** *adj.* (**-ier, -iest**) rashly or foolishly bold; reckless. □ **foolhardily** *adv.* **foolhardiness** *n.*

**foolish** *adj.* lacking good sense or judgment; unwise. □ **foolishly** *adv.* **foolishness** *n.*

**foolproof** *adj.* (of a procedure, mechanism, etc.) incapable of misuse or mistake.

**foolscap** /**foolz**-kap/ *n.* large size of paper, about 330 x 200 mm. [from a watermark of a *fool's cap*]

**fool's paradise** *n.* illusory happiness.

**foot** /fuut/ — *n.* (*pl.* **feet**) **1 a** part of the leg below the ankle. **b** part of a sock etc. covering this. **2 a** lowest part of a page, stairs, mountain, etc. **b** end of a bed where the feet rest. **c** base, often projecting, of anything extending vertically. **3** step, pace, or tread (*fleet of foot*). **4** (*pl.* **feet** or **foot**) linear measure (in the imperial system) of 12 inches (30.48 cm). **5** metrical unit of verse forming part of a line. — *v.* **1** pay (a bill). **2** (usu. as **foot it**) go or traverse on foot. □ **fall on one's feet** emerge unscathed (or with little damage) from misfortune or trouble. **feet of clay** fundamental weakness in a respected person. **have one's** (or **both**) **feet on the ground** be practical. **have one foot in the grave** be near death or very old. **my foot!** *int.* expressing strong contradiction. **on foot** walking. **put one's feet up** *colloq.* take a rest. **put one's foot down** *colloq.* **1** insist firmly. **2** accelerate a vehicle. **put one's foot in one's mouth** (or **in it**) *colloq.* make a tactless blunder. **under one's feet** in the way. **under foot** on the ground. □ **footless** *adj.* [Old English]

**footage** *n.* **1** a length of TV or cinema film etc. **2** length in feet.

**foot-and-mouth disease** *n.* **1** contagious viral disease of cattle etc. **2** (usu. **foot-in-mouth disease**) *colloq.* proneness to put one's foot in one's mouth.

**football** *n.* **1** large inflated ball of leather or plastic. **2** outdoor team game played with this. □ **footballer** *n.*

**football pools** *n.* (also **football pool**) large-scale organised gambling on the results of football matches.

**footbrake** *n.* foot-operated brake on a vehicle.

**footbridge** *n.* bridge for pedestrians.

**footer** *n.* **1** (in *comb.*) person or thing of so many feet in length or height (*six-footer*). **2** (in word-processing) words etc. programmed to appear at the foot of every page (opp. HEADER).

**footfall** *n.* sound of a footstep.

**foot-fault** *n.* (in tennis) placing of the foot over the baseline while serving.

**foothill** *n.* any of the low hills at the base of a mountain or range.

**foothold** *n.* **1** secure place for a foot when climbing etc. **2** secure initial position or advantage.

**footie** var. of FOOTY.

**footing** *n.* **1** foothold; secure position (*lost his footing*). **2** operational basis. **3** relative position or status (*on an equal footing*).

**footlights** *n.pl.* row of floor-level lights at the front of a stage.

**footling** /**foot**-ling/ *adj. colloq.* trivial, silly. [origin uncertain]

**footloose** *adj.* free to act as one pleases.

**footman** *n.* uniformed servant attending at the door, at table, etc.

**footnote** *n.* note printed at the foot of a page.

**footpath** *n.* path for pedestrians; pavement.

**footprint** *n.* impression left by a foot or shoe.

**footsie** /**fuut**-see/ *n. colloq.* foot. □ **play footsie(s)** *colloq.* (foll. by *with*) **1** touch someone secretly with one's feet, as part of amorous play. **2** flirt, have an affair.

**footsore** *adj.* with sore feet, esp. from walking.

**footstep** *n.* **1** step taken in walking. **2** sound of this. □ **follow in a person's footsteps** do as another did before.

**footstool** *n.* stool for resting the feet on when sitting.

**footwear** *n.* shoes, socks, etc.

**footwork** *n.* use or agility of the feet in sports, dancing, etc.

**footy** *n.* (also **footie**) **1** game of football, esp. Australian Rules. **2** a football, esp. the oval ball used in Australian Rules.

**fop** *n.* man obsessed with fashion, clothes, appearance, etc. □ **foppery** *n.* **foppish** *adj.* [perhaps from obsolete *fop* fool]

**for** /faw, fuh/ — *prep.* **1** in the interest or to the benefit of; intended to go to (*did it all for my country*; *these flowers are for you*). **2** in defence, support, or favour of (*fight for one's rights*). **3** suitable or appropriate to (*a dance for beginners*; *not for me to say*). **4** in respect of or with reference to; regarding (*usual for ties to be worn*; *ready for bed*). **5** representing or in place of (*MP for Corio*; *here for my uncle*). **6** in exchange with, at the price of, corresponding to (*swapped it for a cake*; *give me \$5 for it*; *bought it for \$5*; *word for word*). **7** as a consequence of (*fined for speeding*; *decorated for bravery*; *here's \$5 for your trouble*). **8 a** with a view to; in the hope or quest of; in order to get (*go for a walk*; *send for a doctor*; *did it for the money*). **b** on account of (*could not speak for laughing*). **9** to reach; towards (*left for Rome*). **10** so as to start promptly at (*meet at seven for eight*). **11** through or over (a distance or period); during (*walked for miles*). **12** as being (*for the last time*; *I for one refuse*). **13** in spite of; notwithstanding (*for all your fine words*). **14** considering or making due allowance in respect of (*good for a beginner*). — *conj.* because, since, seeing that. □ **be for it** *colloq.* be about to be punished etc. (*I'm for it this time*). **for all (that)** in spite of, although. **for ever** for all time (cf. FOREVER). [Old English reduced form of FORE]

**for-** *prefix* forming verbs etc. meaning: **1** away, off (*forget*; *forgive*). **2** prohibition (*forbid*). **3** abstention or neglect (*forgo*; *forsake*). [Old English]

**forage** /**fo**-rij/ — *n.* **1** food for horses and cattle. **2** searching for food. — *v.* **1** go searching; rummage (esp. for food). **2** collect food from. **3** get by foraging. [Germanic: related to FODDER]

**forasmuch as** /ˌfaw-ruhz-**much**/ *conj. archaic* because, since. [from *for as much*]

**foray** /**fo**-ray, **faw**-ray/ — *n.* sudden attack; raid. — *v.* make a foray. [French: related to FODDER]

**forbade** (also **forbad**) *past* of FORBID.

**forbear**[1] /faw-**bair**/ *v.* (*past* **forbore**; *past part.* **forborne**) *formal* abstain or desist (from) (*could not forbear (from) speaking out*; *forbore to mention it*). [Old English: related to BEAR[1]]

**forbear**[2] var. of FOREBEAR.

**forbearance** *n.* patient self-control; tolerance.

**forbid** /fuh-**bid**/ *v.* (**forbidding**; *past* **forbade** /-**bad**, -**bayd**/ or **forbad**; *past part.* **forbidden**) **1** (foll. by *to* + infin.) order not (*I forbid you to go*). **2** refuse to allow (a thing, or a person to have a thing). **3** refuse a person entry to (*the gardens are forbidden to children*). □ **God forbid!** may it not happen! [Old English: related to BID]

**forbidden fruit** *n.* something desired esp. because not allowed.

**forbidding** *adj.* stern, threatening. □ **forbiddingly** *adv.*

**forbore** *past* of FORBEAR[1].

**forborne** *past part.* of FORBEAR[1].

**force** — *n.* **1** power; strength, impetus; intense effort. **2** coercion, compulsion. **3 a** military strength. **b** organised body of soldiers, police, etc. **4 a** moral, intellectual, or legal power, influence, or validity. **b** person etc. with such power (*force for good*). **5** effect; precise significance (*the force of his words*). **6** *Physics* **a** influence tending to cause a change in the motion of a body. **b** intensity of this. — *v.* (**-cing**) **1** compel or coerce (a person) by force. **2** make a forcible entry into; break open by force. **3** drive or propel violently or against resistance (*forced it into the hole*). **4** make (a way) by force. **5** (foll. by *on*, *upon*) impose or press on (a person) (*forced their views on us*). **6** cause, produce, or attain by effort (*forced a smile*; *forced an entry*). **7** strain or increase to the utmost. **8** artificially hasten the growth of (a plant). **9** seek quick results from; accelerate the process of (*force the pace*). □ **force a person's hand** make a person act prematurely or unwillingly. **force the issue** make an immediate decision necessary. **in force 1** valid (*laws now in force*). **2** in great strength or numbers (*attacked in force*). [Latin *fortis* strong]

**forced labour** *n.* compulsory labour, esp. in prison.

**forced landing** *n.* emergency landing of an aircraft.

**forced march** *n.* long and vigorous march, esp. by troops.

**force-feed** *v.* force (esp. a prisoner) to take food.

**forceful** *adj.* vigorous, powerful, impressive. □ **forcefully** *adv.* **forcefulness** *n.*

**forcemeat** *n.* minced seasoned meat for stuffing or garnish. [related to FARCE]

**forceps** /**faw**-seps, -suhps/ *n.* (*pl.* same) surgical pincers. [Latin]

**forcible** *adj.* done by or involving force; forceful. □ **forcibly** *adv.* [French: related to FORCE]

**ford** — *n.* shallow place where a river or stream may be crossed by wading, in a vehicle, etc. — *v.* cross (water) at a ford. □ **fordable** *adj.* [Old English]

**fore** — *adj.* situated in front. — *n.* front part; bow of a ship. — *int.* (in golf) warning to a person in the path of a ball. □ **to the fore** in or into a conspicuous position. [Old English]

**fore-** *prefix* forming: **1** verbs meaning: **a** in front (*foreshorten*). **b** beforehand (*forewarn*). **2** nouns meaning: **a** situated in front of (*forecourt*). **b** front part of (*forehead*). **c** of or near the bow of a ship (*forecastle*). **d** preceding (*forerunner*).

**fore and aft** — *adv.* at bow and stern; all over the ship. — *adj.* (**fore-and-aft**) (of a sail or rigging) lengthwise.

**forearm**[1] /**faw**-rahm/ *n.* the arm from the elbow to the wrist or fingertips.

**forearm**[2] /fawr-**ahm**/ *v.* arm beforehand, prepare.

**forebear** /**faw**-bair/ *n.* (also **forbear**) (usu. in *pl.*) ancestor. [from FORE, obsolete *beer*: related to BE]

**forebode** /faw-**bohd**/ *v.* (**-ding**) **1** be an advance sign of, portend (an evil or unwelcome event). **2** (often foll. by *that*) have a presentiment of (usu. evil).

**foreboding** *n.* expectation of trouble or evil.

**forecast** — *v.* (*past* and *past part.* **-cast** or **-casted**) predict; estimate beforehand. — *n.* prediction, esp. of weather. ◻ **forecaster** *n.*

**forecastle** /**fohk**-suhl/ *n.* (also **fo'c'sle**) forward part of a ship, formerly the living quarters.

**foreclose** /faw-**klohz**/ *v.* (**-sing**) **1** stop (a mortgage) from being redeemable. **2** repossess the mortgaged property of (a person) when a loan is not duly repaid. **3** exclude, prevent. ◻ **foreclosure** *n.* [Latin *foris* outside, CLOSE[2]]

**forecourt** *n.* enclosed space in front of a large building.

**forefather** *n.* (usu. in *pl.*) ancestor of a family or people.

**forefinger** *n.* finger next to the thumb.

**forefoot** *n.* front foot of an animal.

**forefront** *n.* **1** leading position. **2** foremost part.

**forego** var. of FORGO.

**foregoing** /faw-**goh**-ing, **faw**-/ *adj.* preceding; previously mentioned.

**foregone conclusion** /**faw**-gon/ *n.* easily predictable result.

**foreground** *n.* **1** part of a view or picture nearest the observer. **2** most conspicuous position. [Dutch: related to FORE-, GROUND[1]]

**forehand** *n.* **1** (in tennis etc.) stroke played with the palm of the hand facing the opponent. **2** (*attrib.*) (also **forehanded**) of or made with a forehand.

**forehead** /**fo**-ruhd, **faw**-hed/ *n.* the part of the face above the eyebrows.

**foreign** /**fo**-ruhn/ *adj.* **1** of, from, in, or characteristic of, a country or language other than one's own. **2** dealing with other countries (*foreign affairs*). **3** of another district, society, etc. **4** (often foll. by *to*) unfamiliar, alien (*his behaviour is foreign to me*). **5** coming from outside (*a foreign body lodged in my eye*). ◻ **foreignness** *n.* [Latin *foris* outside]

**foreign affairs** *n.pl.* a nation's dealings with other nations (*Department of Foreign Affairs*).

**foreigner** *n.* person born in or coming from another country.

**foreign exchange** *n.* **1** currencies of other countries. **2** dealings in these.

**foreknow** /faw-**noh**/ *v.* (*past* **-knew**, *past part.* **-known**) *literary* know beforehand. ◻ **foreknowledge** /faw-**nol**-ij/ *n.*

**foreleg** *n.* front leg of an animal.

**forelimb** *n.* front limb of an animal.

**forelock** *n.* lock of hair just above the forehead.

**foreman** *n.* **1** worker supervising others. **2** member of a jury who presides over its deliberations and speaks on its behalf.

**foremast** *n.* mast nearest the bow of a ship.

**foremost** — *adj.* **1** most notable, best. **2** first, front. — *adv.* most importantly (*first and foremost*). [Old English]

**forename** *n.* person's personal name as distinct from the surname or family name; (among Christians) Christian name.

**forensic** /fuh-**ren**-sik, -**ren**-zik/ *adj.* **1** of or used in connection with legal problems, esp. for use in inquiries (*forensic science*; *forensic medicine*). **2** of or involving forensic science (*sent for forensic examination*). ◻ **forensically** *adv.* [Latin *forensis*: related to FORUM]

■ **Usage** Use of *forensic* in sense 2 is common but considered an illogical extension of sense 1 by some people.

**foreordain** /ˌfaw-raw-**dayn**/ *v.* destine beforehand.

**forepaw** *n.* front paw of an animal.

**foreplay** *n.* sexual stimulation preceding sexual intercourse.

**forerunner** *n.* **1** predecessor. **2** advance messenger.

**foresail** /**faw**-sayl, -suhl/ *n.* principal sail on a foremast.

**foresee** /faw-**see**/ *v.* (*past* **-saw**; *past part.* **-seen**) see or be aware of beforehand. ◻ **foreseeable** *adj.*

**foreshadow** /faw-**shad**-oh/ *v.* be a warning or indication of (a future event).

**foreshore** *n.* shore between high- and low-water marks.

**foreshorten** /faw-**shaw**-tuhn/ *v.* show or portray (an object) with the apparent shortening due to visual perspective. □ **foreshortening** n.

**foresight** n. **1** regard or provision for the future. **2** foreseeing.

**foreskin** n. retractable fold of skin covering the end of the penis; prepuce.

**forest** — n. **1 a** (often *attrib.*) large area of trees and undergrowth. **b** trees in this. **2** tract of open well-grassed land with occasional stands of trees. **3** large number or dense mass. — v. **1** plant with trees. **2** convert into a forest. □ **forested** adj. [Latin *forestis*: related to FOREIGN]

**forestall** /faw-**stawl**/ v. **1** prevent by advance action. **2** deal with beforehand. [from FORE-, STALL¹]

**forester** n. **1** person managing a forest or skilled in forestry. **2** eastern Australian grey kangaroo.

**forest oak** n. casuarina of eastern NSW and Queensland, having slender, drooping, reddening branchlets and red timber.

**forestry** n. science or management of forests.

**foretaste** /**faw**-tayst/ — n. small preliminary experience of something (*foretaste of the pleasure to come; a foretaste of hell*). — v. /faw-**tayst**/ taste beforehand; anticipate the experience of.

**foretell** /faw-**tel**/ v. (*past* and *past part.* -**told**) **1** predict, prophesy. **2** indicate the approach of; be a precursor of.

**forethought** n. **1** care or provision for the future. **2** previous thinking or devising. **3** deliberate intention.

**forever** /fuh-**rev**-uh/ adv. continually, persistently (*is forever complaining*) (cf. *for ever*).

**forewarn** /faw-**wawn**/ v. warn beforehand.

**foreword** n. introductory remarks at the beginning of a book, often not by the author.

**forfeit** /**faw**-fuht/ — n. **1** penalty. **2** thing surrendered as a penalty. — adj. lost or surrendered as a penalty. — v. (**-t-**) lose the right to, be deprived of, or surrender as a penalty. □ **forfeiture** n. [French *forfaire* transgress, from Latin *foris* outside, *facio* do]

**forgather** /faw-**gath**-uh/ v. assemble; associate. [Dutch]

**forgave** *past* of FORGIVE.

**forge¹** — v. (**-ging**) **1 a** make (money etc.) in fraudulent imitation. **b** write (a document or signature) in order to pass it off as written by another. **2** shape (metal) by heating and hammering. — n. **1** furnace or workshop etc. for melting or refining metal. **2** blacksmith's workshop; smithy.

□ **forger** n. [Latin *fabrica*: related to FABRIC]

**forge²** v. (**-ging**) move forward gradually or steadily. □ **forge ahead 1** take the lead. **2** progress rapidly. [perhaps an alteration of FORCE]

**forgery** /**faw**-juh-ree/ n. (pl. **-ies**) **1** act or instance of forging, counterfeiting, or falsifying a document etc. **2** forged document etc.

**forget** /fuh-**get**/ v. (**forgetting**; *past* **forgot**; *past part.* **forgotten**) **1** (often foll. by *about*) lose remembrance of; not remember (*forgot his name*). **2** neglect or overlook (*forgot to put out the washing*). **3** cease to think of (*forgive and forget*). □ **forget it 1** drop the subject. **2** don't mention it; you're welcome. **forget oneself 1** act without dignity. **2** act selflessly. □ **forgettable** adj. [Old English]

**forgetful** adj. **1** apt to forget, absent-minded. **2** (often foll. by *of*) neglectful. □ **forgetfully** adv. **forgetfulness** n.

**forget-me-not** n. plant with small blue flowers, so called because those wearing it were supposed never to be forgotten by their lovers.

**forgive** /fuh-**giv**/ v. (**-ving**; *past* **forgave**; *past part.* **forgiven**) **1** cease to feel angry or resentful towards; pardon. **2** remit (a debt). □ **forgivable** adj. [Old English]

**forgiveness** n. act of forgiving or state of being forgiven.

**forgiving** adj. inclined readily to forgive.

**forgo** /faw-**goh**/ v. (also **forego**) (**-goes**; *past* **-went**; *past part.* **-gone**) go without; relinquish. [Old English]

**forgot** *past* of FORGET.

**forgotten** *past part.* of FORGET.

**fork** — n. **1 a** pronged item of cutlery. **b** similar large tool used for digging, lifting, etc. **c** any pronged device or component (*tuning-fork*). **2** forked support for a bicycle wheel. **3 a** divergence of a branch, road, etc. into two parts. **b** place of this. **c** either of the two parts (*take the left fork*). — v. **1** form a fork or branch by separating into two parts. **2** take one road at a fork. **3** dig, lift, etc., with a fork. □ **fork out** (or **over** or **up**) colloq. pay, esp. reluctantly. [Latin *furca* pitchfork]

**forked lightning** n. lightning-flash in the form of a zigzag or branching line.

**forklift** n. (in full **forklift truck**) electric vehicle with a fork for lifting and carrying loads.

**forlorn** /fuh-**lawn**/ adj. **1** sad and abandoned. **2** in a pitiful state. **3** desperate, hopeless (*a forlorn attempt*). □ **forlornly** adv. [*lorn* = past part. of obsolete *leese* LOSE]

**forlorn hope** *n.* faint remaining hope or chance. [Dutch *verloren hoop* lost troop]

**form** — *n.* **1** shape; arrangement of parts; visible aspect. **2** person or animal as visible or tangible (*the familiar form of the policeman*). **3** mode of existence or manifestation (*took the form of a book*). **4** kind or variety (*a form of art*). **5** printed document with blank spaces for information to be inserted. **6** class in a school. **7** customary method (*common form*). **8** set order of words. **9** etiquette or specified adherence to it (*good or bad form*). **10** (prec. by *the*) correct procedure (*knows the form*). **11 a** (of an athlete, horse, etc.) condition of health and training (*in form; out of form*). **b** racing history of a horse etc. **12** general state or disposition (*in great form*). **13** reputation or record (including criminal). **14** any of the spellings, inflections, etc. of a word. **15** arrangement and style in a literary or musical composition. **16** long low bench. **17** hare's lair. — *v.* **1** make or be made (*formed a straight line; puddles formed*). **2** make up or constitute (*together they form a unit; forms part of the structure*). **3** develop or establish as a concept, institution, or practice (*form an idea; form a habit*). **4** (foll. by *into*) mould or organise to become (*formed ourselves into a circle*). **5** (often foll. by *up*) (of troops etc.) bring or move into formation. **6** train or instruct. [Latin *forma*]

**-form** *comb. form* (usu. as **-iform**) forming adjectives meaning: **1** having the form of (*cruciform*). **2** having so many forms (*uniform*).

**formal** /**faw**-muhl/ — *adj.* **1** in accordance with rules, convention, or ceremony (*formal dress; formal occasion*). **2** precise or symmetrical (*formal garden*). **3** prim or stiff in manner. **4** valid or correctly so called because of its form; explicit and definite (*formal vote; formal agreement*). **5** of or concerned with (outward) form, not content or matter (*formal logic*). **6** (of education) obtained in a recognised establishment. — *n.* official dance esp. to mark graduation from secondary school and at which usu. formal dress is to be worn. □ **formally** *adv.* [Latin: related to FORM]

**formaldehyde** /faw-**mal**-duh-ˌhuyd/ *n.* colourless pungent gas used as a disinfectant and preservative. [from FORMIC ACID, ALDEHYDE]

**formalin** /**faw**-muh-luhn/ *n.* solution of formaldehyde in water used as a preservative for biological specimens etc.

**formalise** *v.* (also **-ize**) (**-sing** or **-zing**) **1** give definite (esp. legal) form to. **2** make formal. □ **formalisation** /-ˌzay-shuhn/ *n.*

**formalism** *n.* strict adherence to external form without regard to content, esp. in art. □ **formalist** *n.*

**formality** /faw-**mal**-uh-tee/ *n.* (*pl.* **-ies**) **1 a** formal or ceremonial act, regulation, or custom (often with an implied lack of real significance). **b** thing done simply to comply with a rule. **2** rigid observance of rules or convention. **3** ceremony; elaborate procedure.

**format** /**faw**-mat/ — *n.* **1** shape and size (of a book etc.). **2** style or manner of procedure etc. **3** *Computing* defined structure for holding data etc. in a record for processing or storage. — *v.* (**-tt-**) **1** arrange or put into a format. **2** *Computing* prepare (a storage medium) to receive data. [Latin *formatus* shaped: related to FORM]

**formation** /faw-**may**-shuhn/ *n.* **1** act or instance of forming. **2** thing formed. **3** particular arrangement (e.g. of troops). **4** rocks or strata with a common characteristic. [Latin: related to FORM]

**formative** /**faw**-muh-tiv/ *adj.* serving to form or fashion; of formation (*formative years*).

**former** *attrib. adj.* **1** of the past, earlier, previous (*in former times*). **2** having been previously (*her former husband*). **3** (**the former**) (often *absol.*) the first or first-mentioned of two. [related to FOREMOST]

**-former** *comb. form* pupil in a specified form (*fourth-former*).

**formerly** *adv.* in former times.

**formica** /faw-**muy**-kuh/ *n. propr.* hard durable plastic laminate used for surfaces. [origin uncertain]

**formic acid** /**faw**-mik/ *n.* colourless irritant volatile acid contained in fluid emitted by ants; methanoic acid. [Latin *formica* ant]

**formidable** /**faw**-muh-duh-buhl, faw-**mid**-uh-buhl/ *adj.* **1** inspiring dread, awe, or respect. **2** hard to overcome or deal with. □ **formidably** *adv.* [Latin *formido* fear]

■ **Usage** The second pronunciation given, with the stress on the second syllable, is common but considered incorrect by some people.

**formless** *adj.* without definite or regular form. □ **formlessness** *n.*

**formula** /**faw**-myuh-luh/ *n.* (*pl.* **-s** or (esp. in senses 1, 2) **-lae** /-ˌlee/) **1** set of chemical symbols showing the constituents of a substance. **2** mathematical rule expressed in symbols. **3 a** fixed form of words, esp. one used on social or ceremonial occasions. **b** words used to formulate a treaty etc. **4** established and successful mode (*the film followed the usual formula: sex and violence*). **5** list of ingredients. **6** classification of a racing car, esp. by engine capacity. □ **formulaic** /-**lay**-ik/ *adj*. [Latin, diminutive of *forma* FORM]

**formulary** /**faw**-myuh-luh-ree/ *n*. (*pl.* **-ies**) **1** collection of esp. religious formulas or set forms. **2** *Pharm.* compendium of drug formulae. [French or medieval Latin: related to FORMULA]

**formulate** /**faw**-myuh-layt/ *v*. (**-ting**) **1** express in a formula. **2** express clearly and precisely. □ **formulation** /-lay-shuhn/ *n*.

**fornicate** /**faw**-nuh-kayt/ *v*. (**-ting**) *archaic* or *joc.* (of people not married to each other) have sexual intercourse. □ **fornication** /-**kay**-shuhn/ *n*. **fornicator** *n*. [Latin *fornix* brothel]

**forsake** /fuh-**sayk**, faw-/ *v*. (**-king**; *past* **forsook** /-**suuk**/; *past part.* **forsaken**) *literary* **1** give up; renounce. **2** desert, abandon. [Old English]

**forsooth** /fuh-**sooth**, faw-/ *adv. archaic* or *joc.* truly; no doubt. [Old English: related to FOR, SOOTH]

**forswear** /faw-**swair**/ *v*. (*past* **forswore**; *past part.* **forsworn**) **1** abjure; renounce an oath. **2** (as **forsworn** *adj.*) perjured. □ **forswear oneself** perjure oneself. [Old English]

**fort** *n*. fortified military building or position. □ **hold the fort** keep things going as normal (esp. in the absence of a person in charge). [Latin *fortis* strong]

**forte¹** /**faw**-tay, fawt/ *n*. person's strong point or speciality. [feminine of French FORT]

**forte²** /**faw**-tay/ *Mus.* — *adj.* loud. — *adv.* loudly. — *n.* loud playing or passage. [Italian: related to FORT]

**fortescue** /**faw**-tuh-skyoo/ *n*. fish of eastern Australian coasts, having venomous spines. [origin unknown]

**forth** *adv. archaic* except in set phrases **1** forward; into view (*bring forth; come forth*). **2** onwards in time (*from this time forth*). **3** forwards (*back and forth*). **4** out from a starting-point (*set forth*). □ **and so forth** see SO¹. [Old English]

**forthcoming** /fawth-**kum**-ing, fawth-/ *adj.* **1** coming or available soon. **2** produced when wanted (*no reply was forthcoming*). **3** (of a person) informative, responsive.

**forthright** *adj.* **1** outspoken; straightforward. **2** decisive, unhesitating. [Old English]

**forthwith** /fawth-**with**, -**with**/ *adv.* at once; without delay. [from FORTH]

**fortification** /ˌfaw-tuh-fuh-**kay**-shuhn/ *n*. **1** act or instance of fortifying. **2** (usu. in *pl.*) defensive works, walls, etc.

**fortify** /**faw**-tuh-fuy/ *v*. (**-ies**, **-ied**) **1** provide with fortifications. **2** strengthen physically, mentally, or morally. **3** strengthen (wine) with alcohol. **4** increase the nutritive value of (food, esp. with vitamins). [Latin *fortis* strong]

**fortissimo** /faw-**tis**-i-ˌmoh/ *Mus.* — *adj.* very loud. — *adv.* very loudly. — *n.* (*pl.* **-s** or **-mi** /-ˌmee/) very loud playing or passage. [Italian, superlative of FORTE²]

**fortitude** /**faw**-tuh-ˌtyood/ *n.* courage in pain or adversity. [Latin *fortis* strong]

**fortnight** *n.* two weeks. [Old English, = *fourteen nights*]

**fortnightly** — *adj.* done, produced, or occurring once a fortnight. — *adv.* every fortnight.

**Fortran** /**faw**-tran/ *n.* (also **FORTRAN**) computer language used esp. for scientific calculations. [from formula *translation*]

**fortress** /**faw**-truhs/ *n.* fortified building or town. [Latin *fortis* strong]

**fortuitous** /faw-**tyoo**-uh-tuhs/ *adj.* happening by esp. lucky chance; accidental. □ **fortuitously** *adv.* **fortuitousness** *n.* **fortuity** *n.* (*pl.* **-ies**). [Latin *forte* by chance]

**fortunate** /**faw**-chuh-nuht/ *adj.* **1** favoured by fortune; lucky. **2** auspicious, favourable. [Latin *fortunatus*: related to FORTUNE]

**fortunately** *adv.* **1** luckily, successfully. **2** (qualifying a whole sentence) it is fortunate that.

**fortune** /**faw**-choon, -chuhn/ *n.* **1 a** chance or luck in human affairs. **b** person's destiny. **2** (in *sing.* or *pl.*) luck that befalls a person or enterprise. **3** good luck. **4** prosperity. **5** (also *colloq.* (**small fortune**) great wealth. □ **make a** (or **one's**) **fortune** become very rich. [Latin *fortuna*]

**fortune-teller** *n.* person who claims to predict future events in a person's life. □ **fortune-telling** *n.*

**forty** /**faw**-tee/ *adj. & n.* (*pl.* **-ies**) **1** four times ten. **2** symbol for this (40, xl, XL). **3** (in *pl.*) numbers from 40 to 49, esp. the years of a century or of a person's life. □ **fortieth** *adj. & n.* [Old English: related to FOUR]

**forty winks** *n. colloq.* short sleep.

**forum** /**faw**-ruhm/ *n.* **1** place of or meeting for public discussion. **2** court or tribunal. **3** *hist.* public square in an ancient Roman city used for judicial and other business. [Latin]

**forward** /**faw**-wuhd/ — *adj.* **1** onward; towards the front. **2** lying in the direction in which one is moving. **3** precocious; bold; presumptuous. **4** relating to the future (*forward contract*). **5** approaching maturity or completion. — *n.* **1** attacking player near the front in soccer, hockey, etc. **2** *Aust. Rules* any of the six players (e.g. full forward) in a position to attack the goal. **3** *Rugby* any of the players who make up the scrum. — *adv.* **1** to the front; into prominence (*come forward*; *move forward*). **2** in advance; ahead (*sent them forward*). **3** onward so as to make progress (*no further forward*). **4** towards the future (*from this time forward*). **5** (also **forwards**) **a** towards the front in the direction one is facing. **b** in the normal direction of motion. **c** with continuous forward motion (*rushing forward*). — *v.* **1 a** send (a letter etc.) on to a further destination. **b** dispatch (goods etc.). **2** help to advance; promote. [Old English: related to FORTH, -WARD]

**forwent** *past* of FORGO.

**fossick** *v.* **1** search desultorily for gold etc., esp. in claims abandoned by others. **2** (often foll. by *about*) search likewise for anything (*fossick in the box for a needle*). □ **fossicker** *n.* **fossicking** *n.* [British dial.]

**fossil** /fos-uhl/ — *n.* **1** remains or impression of a (usu. prehistoric) plant or animal hardened in rock. **2** *colloq.* antiquated or unchanging person or thing. — *attrib. adj.* of or like a fossil (*fossil shells*). □ **fossilise** *v.* (also **-ize**) (**-sing** or **-zing**). **fossilisation** /-zay-shuhn/ *n.* [Latin *fodio foss-* dig]

**fossil fuel** *n.* natural fuel, such as oil or gas, formed in the past from the remains of living organisms.

**foster** — *v.* **1 a** promote the growth or development of. **b** encourage or harbour (a feeling). **2 a** bring up (another's child). **b** (often foll. by *out*) (of a government agency etc.) assign (a child) to be fostered. — *attrib. adj.* **1** having a family connection by fostering (*foster-brother*; *foster-parent*). **2** concerned with fostering a child (*foster care*; *foster home*). [Old English: related to FOOD]

**fought** *past* and *past part.* of FIGHT.

**foul** — *adj.* **1** offensive; loathsome, stinking. **2** soiled, filthy. **3** *colloq.* disgusting, awful. **4 a** noxious (*foul air*). **b** clogged, choked (*a foul drain*). **5** morally polluted; disgustingly abusive or offensive (*foul language*; *foul deeds*). **6** unfair; against the rules (*by fair means or foul*). **7** (of the weather) rough, stormy. **8** (of a rope etc.) entangled. — *n.* **1** *Sport* illegal stroke or play. **2** collision or entanglement, esp. in riding, rowing, or running. — *adv.* unfairly. — *v.* **1** make or become

foul. **2** (of an animal) foul with excrement. **3** *Sport* commit a foul against (a player). **4** (often foll. by *up*) **a** (cause to) become entangled or blocked. **b** spoil or bungle. **5** collide with. □ **foully** *adv.* **foulness** *n.* [Old English]

**foul-mouthed** *adj.* using obscene or offensive language.

**foul play** *n.* **1** unfair play in games. **2** treacherous or violent act, esp. murder.

**foul-up** *n.* muddle, bungle.

**found¹** *past* and *past part.* of FIND. □ **all found** with all necessities provided.

**found²** *v.* **1** establish (an institution etc.); initiate, originate. **2** be the original builder of (a town etc.). **3** lay the base of (a building). **4** (foll. by *on, upon*) construct or base (a story, theory, rule, etc.) on. [Latin *fundus* bottom]

**found³** *v.* **1 a** melt and mould (metal). **b** fuse (materials for glass). **2** make by founding. □ **founder** *n.* [Latin *fundo fuspour*]

**foundation** /fown-**day**-shuhn/ *n.* **1 a** solid base or base beneath a building. **b** (usu. in *pl.*) lowest part of a building, usu. below ground level. **2** body or ground on which other parts are overlaid. **3** basis, underlying principle. **4 a** act or instance of establishing (esp. an endowed institution, a State, etc.) (*holiday to celebrate the foundation of Western Australia*). **b** institution so founded. **5** cosmetic preparation used as a base and over which other facial make-up is applied. [Latin: related to FOUND²]

**foundation stone** *n.* **1** stone laid ceremonially at the founding of a building. **2** main ground or basis of something.

**founder¹** *n.* person who founds an institution etc.

**founder²** *v.* **1** (of a ship) fill with water and sink. **2** (of earth, a building, etc.) fall down or in; give way. **3** (of a plan etc.) fail. **4** (of a horse or its rider) stumble, fall lame, stick in mud etc. [related to FOUND²]

**foundling** /**fownd**-ling/ *n.* abandoned infant of unknown parentage. [related to FIND]

**foundry** /**fown**-dree/ *n.* (*pl.* **-ies**) workshop for or business of casting metal (cf. FOUND³).

**fount¹** *n. poet.* spring or fountain; source. [back-formation from FOUNTAIN]

**fount²** var. of FONT².

**fountain** /**fown**-tuhn/ *n.* **1 a** a spouting jet or jets of water as an ornament or for drinking. **b** structure for this. **2** natural spring of water. **3** (often foll. by *of*) source. [Latin *fontana* from *fons font-* spring]

**fountainhead** *n.* source.

**fountain pen** *n.* pen with a reservoir or cartridge for ink.

**four** /faw/ *adj. & n.* **1** one more than three. **2** symbol for this (4, iv, IV). **3** team or crew of four; four-oared rowing-boat. **4** four o'clock. □ **on all fours** on hands and knees. [Old English]

**fourfold** *adj. & adv.* **1** four times as much or as many. **2** of four parts.

**four-on-the-floor** *n. colloq.* (of a car) gearbox (with four forward gears) mounted on the floor instead of on the steering-column.

**four-poster** *n.* bed with four posts supporting a canopy.

**foursome** *n.* **1** group of four people. **2** golf match between two pairs.

**four-stroke** — *adj.* (of an internal-combustion engine) having a cycle of four strokes of the piston with the cylinder firing once. — *n.* four-stroke engine or vehicle.

**fourteen** /faw-**teen**/ *adj. & n.* **1** one more than thirteen. **2** symbol for this (14, xiv, XIV). □ **fourteenth** *adj. & n.* [Old English: related to FOUR, -TEEN]

**fourth** — *n.* **1** next after third. **2** any of four equal parts of a thing. **3** fourth (and often highest) in a sequence of gears. **4** *Mus.* **a** interval or chord spanning four consecutive notes in the diatonic scale (e.g. C to F). **b** note separated from another by this interval. — *adj.* that is the fourth. □ **fourthly** *adv.* [Old English: related to FOUR]

**fourth dimension** *n.* **1** postulated dimension additional to those determining area and volume. **2** time regarded as equivalent to linear dimensions.

**fourth estate** *n.* the press.

**fourth generation language** *n.* (usu. as **4GL**) *Computing* type of high-level programming language designed for non-programmers and used mainly for database and report generation applications.

**four-wheel drive** *n.* drive acting on all four wheels of a vehicle.

**fowl** — *n.* (*pl.* same or **-s**) **1** chicken kept for eggs and meat. **2** poultry as food. **3** *archaic* (except in *comb.*) bird (*guinea-fowl*; *wildfowl*). — *v.* catch or hunt wildfowl. [Old English]

**fox** — *n.* **1 a** wild canine animal (introduced into Australia) with a bushy tail and red or grey fur. **b** its fur. **2** cunning person. — *v.* **1** deceive, baffle, trick. **2** (usu. as **foxed** *adj.*) discolour (leaves of a book etc.) with brownish marks. □ **foxlike** *adj.* [Old English]

**foxglove** *n.* **1** tall European plant of the genus *Digitalis* with purple or white flowers like glove-fingers. **2** any plant of the endemic WA genus *Pityrodia* having very showy foxglove-like flowers.

**foxhole** *n. Mil.* hole in the ground used as a shelter etc. in battle.

**foxing** *n.* brownish discoloration (on leaves of a book etc.) caused by mildew.

**fox terrier** *n.* a kind of short-haired terrier.

**foxtrot** — *n.* **1** ballroom dance with slow and quick steps. **2** music for this. — *v.* (**-tt-**) perform this.

**foxy** *adj.* (**-ier, -iest**) **1** foxlike. **2** sly or cunning. **3** reddish-brown. **4** *colloq.* (of a woman) sexually attractive. □ **foxily** *adv.* **foxiness** *n.*

**foyer** /**foi**-uh/ *n.* entrance-hall in a hotel, theatre, etc. [French, = hearth, home, from Latin FOCUS]

**Fr** *symb.* francium.

**Fr.** *abbr.* **1** Father. **2** French.

**fracas** /**frak**-ah, **frak**-uhs/ *n.* (*pl.* same /-kahz/) noisy disturbance or quarrel. [French from Italian]

**fraction** /**frak**-shuhn/ *n.* **1** part of a whole number (e.g. Z\x, 0.5). **2** small part, piece, or amount. **3** portion of a mixture obtained by distillation etc. **4** act or instance of breaking. □ **fractional** *adj.* **fractionally** *adv.* [Latin *frango fract-* break]

**fractious** /**frak**-shuhs/ *adj.* irritable, peevish. [from FRACTION in obsolete sense 'brawling']

**fracture** /**frak**-chuh/ — *n.* breakage, esp. of a bone or cartilage. — *v.* (**-ring**) cause a fracture in; suffer fracture. [Latin: related to FRACTION]

**fragile** /**fraj**-uyl/ *adj.* **1** easily broken; weak. **2** delicate; not strong. □ **fragility** /fruh-**jil**-uh-tee/ *n.* [Latin: related to FRACTURE]

**fragment** — *n.* /**frag**-muhnt/ **1** part broken off. **2** extant remains or unfinished portion (of a book etc.). — *v.* /frag-**ment**/ break or separate into fragments. □ **fragmental** /-**men**-tuhl/ *adj.* **fragmentary** /**frag**-muhn-tuh-ree, -tree/ *adj.* [Latin: related to FRACTION]

**fragmentation** /ˌfrag-muhn-**tay**-shuhn/ *n.* **1** process or instance of breaking into fragments. **2** *Computing* **a** creation of many small often unusable areas of memory. **b** an instance of this.

**fragrance** /**fray**-gruhns/ *n.* **1** sweetness of smell. **2** sweet scent. [Latin *fragro* smell sweet]

**fragrant** *adj.* sweet-smelling.

**frail** *adj.* **1** fragile, delicate. **2** morally weak. □ **frailly** *adv.* **frailness** *n.* [Latin: related to FRAGILE]

**frailty** n. (pl. **-ies**) **1** frail quality. **2** weakness, foible.

**frame** — n. **1** case or border enclosing a picture, window, door, etc. **2** basic rigid supporting structure of a building, vehicle, etc. **3** (in pl.) structure of spectacles holding the lenses. **4** human or animal body, esp. as large or small (his whole frame shook with laughter). **5 a** established order or system (the frame of society). **b** construction, build, structure. **6** temporary state (esp. in **frame of mind**). **7** single complete image on a cinema film or transmitted in a series of lines by television. **8 a** triangular structure for positioning balls in snooker etc. **b** round of play in snooker etc. **9** colloq. = FRAME-UP. — v. (**-ming**) **1 a** set in a frame. **b** serve as a frame for. **2** construct, put together, devise. **3** (foll. by to, into) adapt or fit. **4** colloq. concoct a false charge or evidence against; devise a plot against. [Old English, = be helpful]

**frame of reference** n. **1** set of standards or principles governing behaviour, thought, etc. **2** Geom. system of geometrical axes for defining position.

**frame-up** n. colloq. conspiracy to convict an innocent person.

**framework** n. **1** essential supporting structure. **2** basic system.

**franc** n. unit of currency of France, Belgium, Switzerland, etc. [French: related to FRANK]

**franchise** /fran-chuyz/ — n. **1** right of a citizen to vote. **2** full membership of a corporation or nation; citizenship. **3** authorisation to sell a company's goods etc. in a particular area. **4** right or privilege granted to a person or corporation. — v. (**-sing**) grant a franchise to. [French franc FRANK]

**Franciscan** /fran-sis-kuhn/ — adj. of St Francis of Assisi (d. 1226) or his order. — n. Franciscan friar or nun. [Latin Franciscus Francis]

**francium** /fran-see-uhm/ n. radioactive metallic element. [France, the discoverer's country]

**Franco-** comb. form French and (Franco-German). [Latin: related to FRANK]

**franger** n. colloq. condom. [possibly a corruption of FRENCH LETTER]

**frangipani** /ˌfran-juh-**pa**-nee/ n. **1** (also **native frangipani**) small tree of rainforests in Queensland and NSW, having shiny leaves and fragrant cream flowers turning yellow as they age; often cultivated in gardens. **2 a** unrelated tropical American tree with clusters of fragrant cream, pink, or yellow flowers. **b** perfume made from this plant.

[probably from Marquis Frangipani, 16th-c. inventor of the perfume]

**Frank** n. member of the Germanic people that conquered Gaul in the 6th c. □ **Frankish** adj. [Old English]

**frank¹** — adj. **1** candid, outspoken (frank opinion). **2** undisguised (frank admiration). **3** ingenuous; open (a frank face). — v. mark (a letter) to record the payment of postage. — n. franking signature or mark. □ **frankly** adv. **frankness** n. [Latin francus free: related to FRANK]

**frank²** n. colloq. = FRANKFURT.

**Frankenstein** /**frang**-kuhn-ˌstuyn/ n. (in full **Frankenstein's monster**) thing that becomes terrifying to its maker; a monster. [Frankenstein, name of a character in and title of a novel (1818) by Mary Shelley]

**frankfurt** /**frangk**-ˌfert/ n. (also **frankfurter**, **frank**) seasoned smoked sausage. [German from Frankfurt in Germany]

**frankincense** /**frang**-kuhn-ˌsens/ n. aromatic gum resin burnt as incense. [French: related to FRANK in obsolete sense 'high quality', INCENSE¹]

**frantic** /**fran**-tik/ adj. **1** wildly excited; frenzied. **2** hurried, anxious; desperate, violent. **3** colloq. extreme. □ **frantically** adv. [Latin: related to FRENETIC]

**fraternal** /fruh-**ter**-nuhl/ adj. **1** of brothers, brotherly; comradely. **2** (of twins) developed from separate ova and not necessarily similar. □ **fraternally** adv. [Latin frater brother]

**fraternise** /**frat**-uh-ˌnuyz/ v. (also **-ize**) (**-sing** or **-zing**) (often foll. by with) **1** associate; make friends. **2** enter into friendly relations with enemies etc. □ **fraternisation** /-ˌzay-shuhn/ n. [French and Latin: related to FRATERNAL]

**fraternity** /fruh-**ter**-nuh-tee/ n. (pl. **-ies**) **1** religious brotherhood. **2** group with common interests, or of the same professional class (medical fraternity). **3** brotherliness. [Latin: related to FRATERNAL]

**fratricide** /**frat**-ruh-ˌsuyd/ n. **1** killing of one's brother or sister. **2** person who does this. □ **fratricidal** /-ˌsuy-duhl/ adj. [Latin frater brother]

**Frau** /frow/ n. (pl. **Frauen** /**frow**-uhn/) (often as a title) married or widowed German woman. [German]

**fraud** /frawd/ n. **1** deception; use of false representation to gain an unjust advantage. **2** dishonest artifice or trick. **3** person who, or thing which, is other than he, she, or it claims to be. [Latin fraus fraud-]

**fraudulent** /fraw-dyuh-luhnt/ *adj.* of, involving, or guilty of fraud. □ **fraudulence** *n.* **fraudulently** *adv.* [Latin: related to FRAUD]

**fraught** /frawt/ *adj.* **1** (foll. by *with*) filled or charged with (danger etc.). **2** *colloq.* causing or affected by great anxiety or distress. [Dutch *vracht* FREIGHT]

**Fräulein** /froi-luyn/ *n.* (often as a title or form of address) unmarried (esp. young) German woman. [German]

**fray¹** *v.* **1** wear through or become worn; esp. (of woven material) unravel at the edge. **2** (of nerves, temper, etc.) become strained. [Latin *frico* rub]

**fray²** *n.* **1** conflict, fight (*eager for the fray*). **2** noisy quarrel or brawl. [related to AFFRAY]

**frazzle** /fraz-uhl/ *colloq.* — *n.* worn, exhausted, or shrivelled state (*burnt to a frazzle*). — *v.* (-ling) (usu. as frazzled *adj.*) wear out; exhaust. [origin uncertain]

**freak** — *n.* **1** (often *attrib.*) monstrosity; abnormal person or thing (*freak storm*). **2** *colloq.* **a** unconventional person. **b** fanatic of a specified kind (*health freak*). **c** drug addict. — *v.* (often foll. by *out*) *colloq.* **1 a** experience (or cause another to experience) strong emotions, whether good or bad (*he'll freak (out) when we tell him he won the car; his failure freaked him out*). **b** get into a panic or rage. **2** (cause to) undergo hallucinations etc., esp. as a result of drug abuse. **3** adopt an unconventional lifestyle. □ **freakish** *adj.* **freaky** *adj.* (-ier, -iest). [probably from British dial.]

**freckle** /frek-uhl/ — *n.* **1** small light brown spot on the skin. **2** *coarse colloq.* anus. — *v.* (-ling) (usu. as freckled *adj.*) spot or be spotted with freckles. □ **freckly** *adj.* [Old Norse]

**free** — *adj.* (freer /free-uh/) **1 a** not a slave or under another's control; having personal rights and social and political liberty. **b** *hist.* (of a convict in Australia) released from penal servitude. **c** *hist.* (of a settler in Australia) not transported hither as a convict. **2** (of a nation, its citizens, etc.) autonomous; democratic (*free society*). **3 a** unrestricted; not confined or fixed. **b** not imprisoned. **c** released from duties etc. **d** independent (*free agent*). **4** (foll. by *of, from*) **a** exempt from (tax etc.). **b** not containing or subject to (*free of preservatives; free from disease*). **5** (foll. by *to* + infin.) permitted; at liberty to (*you are free to choose*). **6** costing nothing. **7 a** clear of duties etc. (*am free tomorrow*). **b** not in use (*bathroom is free*). **8** spontaneous, unforced (*free offer*). **9** available to all. **10** lavish (*free with their money*). **11** frank, unreserved (*a free disposition; too free with his tongue*). **12** (of literary style) informal, unmetrical (*free verse*). **13** (of translation) not literal. **14** familiar, impudent (*that child's too free with adults*). **15** *Chem.* not combined (*free oxygen*). **16** (of power or energy) disengaged, available. — *n. colloq.* = FREE KICK. — *adv.* **1** freely. **2** without cost or payment. — *v.* (**frees, freed**) **1** make free; liberate. **2** (foll. by *of, from*) relieve from (something undesirable). **3** disentangle, clear. □ **for free** *colloq.* free of charge, gratis. □ **freely** *adv.* [Old English]

**-free** ⌐ *comb. form* free of or from (*worry-free; duty-free*).

**free and easy** *adj.* informal, relaxed.

**freebie** /free-bee/ *n. colloq.* thing given free of charge.

**freebooter** *n.* pirate. [Dutch *vrijbuiter*: related to FREE, BOOTY]

**freeborn** *adj.* **1** not born a slave. **2** *hist.* (of a person born in an Australian colony) free of any association with the convict system.

**freedom** /free-duhm/ *n.* **1** condition of being free or unrestricted. **2** personal or civic liberty; absence of slave or convict status. **3** liberty of action (*freedom to leave*). **4** (foll. by *from*) condition of being exempt from or not subject to (a defect, burden, etc.). **5** (foll. by *of*) **a** honorary membership or citizenship (*freedom of the city*). **b** unrestricted use of (a house etc.). **6** facility or ease in action. [Old English]

**freedom fighter** *n.* person who takes part in violent resistance to an established political system etc.

**free enterprise** *n.* freedom of private business from government control.

**free fall** *n.* **1 a** movement under the force of gravity only. **b** period of descent by parachute before the parachute opens. **2** dramatic and uncontrollable fall in money and commodity values, stock market prices, etc.

**free-for-all** *n.* fight or brawl involving many; discussion, argument, etc. involving many and hence chaotic.

**free-form** *attrib. adj.* of irregular shape or structure.

**freehand** — *adj.* (of a drawing etc.) done by hand without special instruments or guides. — *adv.* in a freehand manner.

**free hand** *n.* freedom to act at one's own discretion.

**free-handed** *adj.* generous.

**freehold** — *n.* **1** complete ownership of property for an unlimited period (cf. LEASEHOLD). **2** such land or property. — *adj.* owned thus. □ **freeholder** *n.*

**free-kick** n. set kick in football (resulting from an infringement of the rules) allowed to be taken by one side without interference from the other.

**freelance** — n. 1 (also **freelancer**) person, usu. self-employed, working for several employers on particular assignments. 2 (attrib.) (freelance editor). — v. (-cing) act as a freelance. — adv. as a freelance. [free lance, a medieval mercenary]

**freeloader** n. colloq. person who eats or drinks at another's expense; sponger. □ **freeload** v.

**free love** n. sexual relations according to choice and unrestricted by marriage etc.; sexual freedom.

**free market** n. market governed by unrestricted competition.

**Freemason** /free-, may-suhn/ n. member of an international fraternity for mutual help and fellowship with elaborate secret rituals. □ **Freemasonry** n.

**freemasonry** n. fellowship, informal brotherhood.

**free port** n. 1 port without customs duties. 2 port open to all traders.

**freepost** n. system of business post where postage is paid by the recipient firm or business.

**free radical** n. Chem. atom or group of atoms with one or more unpaired electrons.

**free-range** adj. 1 (of hens etc.) roaming freely; not kept in a battery. 2 (of eggs) produced by such hens.

**free-selection** n. hist. scheme under which Australian land suitable for farming could be acquired on favourable terms (in contrast to land acquired by squatting or Crown grant). □ **free-select** v.

**free-selector** n. hist. small farmer who acquired a tract of land under a free-selection scheme.

**freesia** /free-zhuh/ n. African bulb with fragrant flowers. [Freese, name of a physician]

**free speech** n. right to express one's opinions.

**free spirit** n. independent or uninhibited person.

**free-spoken** adj. forthright.

**free-standing** adj. not supported by another structure.

**freestyle** n. 1 swimming race in which any stroke may be used. 2 wrestling allowing almost any hold.

**freethinker** n. person who rejects dogma or authority, esp. in religious belief. □ **freethinking** n. & adj.

**free trade** n. 1 international trade without restrictions on imports or exports, and without subsidies by producing nations. 2 trade without restrictions between Australian States.

**free vote** n. parliamentary vote not subject to party discipline.

**freeway** n. main road, with separate carriageways and limited access, designed for fast traffic.

**freewheel** — n. driving wheel of a bicycle, able to revolve with the pedals at rest. — v. 1 ride a bicycle with the pedals at rest. 2 act without constraint. □ **freewheeler** n. **freewheeling** adj.

**free will** n. 1 power of acting independently of necessity or fate. 2 ability to act without coercion (did it of my own free will).

**freeze** — v. (-zing; past **froze**; past part. **frozen**) 1 a turn into ice or another solid by cold. b make or become rigid from the cold (the pipes are frozen). 2 be or feel very cold. 3 cover or become covered with ice. 4 (foll. by to, together) adhere by frost (the curtains froze to the window). 5 refrigerate (food) below freezing point. 6 a make or become motionless through fear, surprise, etc. b (as **frozen** adj.) devoid of emotion (frozen smile). 7 make (assets etc.) unrealisable. 8 fix (prices, wages, etc.) at a certain level. 9 stop (the movement in a film). — n. 1 period or state of frost; period of the coming of frost or very cold weather. 2 fixing or stabilisation of prices, wages, etc. 3 (in full **freeze-frame**) still film-shot. □ **freeze out** exclude from business, society, etc., by severe competition, chilling behaviour, etc. [Old English]

**freeze-dry** v. preserve (food) by freezing and then drying in a vacuum.

**freezer** n. refrigerated cabinet etc. for preserving frozen food at very low temperatures.

**freezing point** n. temperature at which a liquid, esp. water, freezes.

**freezing works** n.pl. place where animals are slaughtered and carcases frozen, esp. for export.

**freight** /frayt/ — n. 1 transport of goods in containers or by water, land, or air. 2 goods transported; cargo, load. 3 charge for the transport of goods. — v. transport as or load with freight. [Low German or Dutch vrecht]

**freighter** n. 1 ship or aircraft for carrying freight. 2 person whose business it is to receive and forward freight.

**Fremantle doctor** see DOCTOR 4.

**French** — adj. 1 of France, its people, or language. 2 having French characteristics. — n. 1 the French language. 2 (the

**French** (*pl.*) the people of France. [Old English: related to FRANK]

**French bread** *n.* = FRENCH STICK.

**French dressing** *n.* salad dressing of seasoned vinegar and oil.

**French fries** *n.pl.* thin strips of fried potato.

**French horn** *n.* coiled brass wind instrument with a wide bell.

**French kiss** *n.* kiss in which one partner's tongue is inserted in the other's mouth.

**French letter** *n. colloq.* condom.

**French polish** *n.* shellac polish for wood. □ **French-polish** *v.*

**French stick** *n.* long roll of white bread with a crisp crust.

**French window** *n.* glazed door in an outside wall, serving both as door and as window.

**frenetic** /fruh-**net**-ik/ *adj.* (also **phrenetic**) frantic, frenzied. □ **frenetically** *adv.* [Greek *phrēn* mind]

**frenzy** /**fren**-zee/ — *n.* (*pl.* **-ies**) mental derangement; wild excitement, agitation, or fury. — *v.* (**-ies, -ied**) (usu. as **frenzied** *adj.*) drive to frenzy. □ **frenziedly** *adv.* [medieval Latin: related to FRENETIC]

**frequency** /**free**-kwuhn-see/ *n.* (*pl.* **-ies**) **1** commonness of occurrence. **2** frequent occurrence. **3** *Physics* rate of recurrence of a vibration, oscillation, etc.; number of repetitions in a given time, esp. per second. **4** *Statistics* ratio of the number of actual to possible occurrences of an event. [related to FREQUENT]

**frequency distribution** *n. Statistics* measurement of the frequency of occurrences of the values of a variable.

**frequency modulation** *n. Electronics* modulation by varying carrier-wave frequency.

**frequent** — *adj.* /**free**-kwuhnt/ **1** occurring often or in close succession. **2** habitual, constant (*a frequent caller*). — *v.* /fruh-**kwent**/ attend or go to habitually. □ **frequently** /**free**-kwuhnt-lee/ *adv.* [Latin *frequens -ent-* crowded]

**frequentative** /fruh-**kwen**-tuh-tiv/ *Gram.* — *adj.* (of a verb etc.) expressing frequent repetition or intensity ('*chatter*' *is a frequentative verb*). — *n.* frequentative verb etc.

**fresco** /**fres**-koh/ *n.* (*pl.* **-os** or **-oes**) **1** painting done in water-colour on a wall or ceiling before the plaster is dry. **2** (esp. as **in fresco**) this method of painting. [Italian, = fresh]

**fresh** — *adj.* **1** newly made or obtained (*fresh sandwiches*). **2 a** other, different; new (*start a fresh page; fresh ideas*). **b**

additional (*fresh supplies*). **3** (foll. by *from*) lately arrived from (a specified place or situation). **4** not stale, musty, or faded (*fresh flowers; fresh memories*). **5** (of food) not preserved; newly caught, grown, etc. **6** not salty (*fresh water*). **7 a** pure, untainted, refreshing (*fresh air*). **b** bright and pure in colour (*fresh complexion*). **8** (of wind) brisk. **9** cheeky; amorously impudent. **10** alert, vigorous (*never felt fresher*). **11** inexperienced. — *adv.* newly, recently (esp. in *comb.*: *fresh-baked*). □ **freshly** *adv.* **freshness** *n.* [Old English *fersc* and French *freis*]

**freshen** *v.* **1** make or become fresh. **2** (foll. by *up*) **a** wash, tidy oneself, etc. **b** revive, renew.

**fresher** *n.* first-year student at university.

**freshet** /**fresh**-uht/ *n.* **1** rush of fresh water flowing into the sea. **2** flood of a river.

**freshie** *n.* (also **freshy**) *colloq.* Australian freshwater crocodile.

**freshwater** *attrib. adj.* (of fish etc.) not of the sea.

**fret**[1] — *v.* (**-tt-**) **1** be worried or distressed (*is fretting over the missing cat*). **2** worry, vex. **3** wear or consume by gnawing or rubbing. — *n.* worry, vexation. [Old English: related to FOR, EAT]

**fret**[2] — *n.* ornamental pattern of straight lines joined usu. at right angles. — *v.* (**-tt-**) embellish with a fret or with carved or embossed work. [French *freter*]

**fret**[3] *n.* each of a series of bars or ridges on the finger-board of a guitar etc. to guide fingering. [origin unknown]

**fretful** *adj.* anxious, irritable. □ **fretfully** *adv.*

**fretsaw** *n.* narrow saw on a frame for cutting thin wood in patterns.

**fretwork** *n.* ornamental work in wood done with a fretsaw.

**Freudian** /**froi**-dee-uhn/ — *adj.* of or relating to the psychologist Sigmund Freud (d. 1939), his theories, or his method of psychoanalysis. — *n.* follower of Freud.

**Freudian slip** *n.* unintentional verbal error regarded as revealing subconscious feelings.

**friable** /**fruy**-uh-buhl/ *adj.* easily crumbled. □ **friability** /-bil-uh-tee/ *n.* [Latin *frio* crumble]

**friar** /**fruyuh**/ *n.* member of a male non-enclosed Roman Catholic order, e.g. Augustinians, Carmelites, Dominicans, and Franciscans. [Latin *frater* brother]

**friar-bird** *n.* any of four large Australian honeyeaters having bare skin on the head (suggesting a tonsured friar), a knob on the bill, and a raucous call (*helmeted friar-bird; noisy friar-bird*).

**friar's balsam** n. tincture of benzoin etc. used esp. as an inhalant.

**friary** /**fruy**-uh-ree/ n. (pl. **-ies**) monastery for friars.

**fricassee** /frik-uh-,see, -**see**/ — n. stewed or fried meat served in a thick white sauce. — v. (**fricassees, fricasseed**) make a fricassee of. [French]

**fricative** /**frik**-uh-tiv/ — adj. (of a consonant) sounded by friction of the breath in a narrow opening. — n. such a consonant (e.g. f, th). [Latin frico rub]

**friction** /**frik**-shuhn/ n. **1** action of one object rubbing against another. **2** the resistance encountered in so moving. **3** clash of wills, opinions, etc. □ **frictional** adj. [Latin: related to FRICATIVE]

**Friday** /**fruy**-day/ — n. day of the week following Thursday. — adv. colloq. **1** on Friday. **2** (**Fridays**) on Fridays; each Friday. [Old English (named after Frigg the wife of the Germanic god Odin)]

**fridge** n. colloq. = REFRIGERATOR. [abbreviation]

**friend** /frend/ n. **1** person one likes and chooses to spend time with (usu. without sexual or family bonds). **2** sympathiser, helper. **3** ally or neutral person (friend or foe?). **4** person already mentioned (our friend at the bank). **5** regular supporter of an institution (friends of the Australian Opera). **6** (**Friend**) Quaker. [Old English]

**friendly** — adj. (**-ier, -iest**) **1** outgoing, well-disposed, kindly. **2 a** (often foll. by with) on amicable terms. **b** not hostile. **3** (in comb.) not harming; helping (ozone-friendly; user-friendly). **4** = USER-FRIENDLY. — adv. in a friendly manner. □ **friendliness** n.

**friendly society** n. society for mutual insurance against illness or the effects of old age.

**friendship** n. friendly relationship or feeling.

**frier** var. of FRYER.

**Friesian** /**free**-zhuhn/ n. one of a breed of black and white dairy cattle orig. from Friesland.

**frieze** /freez/ n. **1** part of an entablature between the architrave and cornice. **2** horizontal band of sculpture filling this. **3** band of decoration, esp. at the top of a wall. [Latin Phrygium (opus) Phrygian (work)]

**frig¹** /frig/ v. (**-gg-**) colloq. **1** (usu. foll. by around) mess about; fool around. **2** (usu. foll. by up) confuse, mess up; break, damage (you've frigged the fridge up again with your tampering). **3** (foll. by off) go away, get lost. [perhaps imitative]

**frig²** /frij/ n. colloq. = REFRIGERATOR.

**frigate** /**frig**-uht/ n. naval escort-vessel. [French from Italian]

**fright** /fruyt/ n. **1 a** sudden or extreme fear. **b** instance of this (gave me a fright). **2** person or thing looking grotesque or ridiculous. □ **take fright** become frightened. [Old English]

**frighten** v. **1** fill with fright (the bang frightened me; frightened of dogs). **2** (foll. by away, off, out of, into) drive or force by fright (frightened it out of the room; frightened me into agreeing). □ **frightening** adj. **frighteningly** adv.

**frightful** adj. **1** dreadful, shocking, revolting. **2** colloq. extremely bad (a frightful idea). **3** colloq. very great; extreme (frightful rush). □ **frightfully** adv.

**frigid** /**frij**-uhd/ adj. **1** unfriendly, cold (frigid stare). **2** sexually unresponsive. **3** (esp. of a climate or air) cold. □ **frigidity** /-**jid**-uh-tee/ n. [Latin frigus (n.) cold]

**frigid zones** n. pl. parts of the earth south of the Antarctic Circle and north of the Arctic Circle.

**frill** — n. **1** strip of gathered or pleated material as an ornamental edging. **2** (in pl.) **a** unnecessary embellishments. **b** affectations. — v. decorate with a frill. □ **frilly** adj. (**-ier, -iest**). [origin unknown]

**frill-necked lizard** n. (also **frillie**) large northern Australian lizard with an erectile membrane around the neck.

**fringe** — n. **1 a** border of tassels or loose threads. **b** anything resembling this; any border or edging. **2** front hair hanging over the forehead. **3 a** outer limit of an area, population, etc. **b** (attrib.) existing on the edge or margin of an area, sphere of activity, etc. (fringe-dweller; fringe theatre). **4** area of sparse settlement bordering the arid Australian inland. **5** unimportant area or part. — v. (**-ging**) **1** adorn with a fringe. **2** serve as a fringe to. [Latin fimbria]

**fringe benefit** n. employee's benefit additional to salary.

**fringed lily** n. small Australian plant bearing blue or purple flowers with fringed margins.

**fringe-dweller** n. Aborigine who lives on the outskirts of a town.

**fringe medicine** n. systems of treatment of disease etc., not regarded as orthodox by the medical profession.

**frippery** /**frip**-uh-ree/ n. (pl. **-ies**) **1** showy finery, esp. in dress. **2** empty display in speech, literary style, etc. **3** (usu. in pl.) knick-knacks, trifles. [French friperie]

**frisbee** /**friz**-bee/ n. propr. concave

plastic disc for skimming through the air as an outdoor game. [perhaps from *Frisbie* bakery pie-tins]

**frisk** — v. **1** leap or skip playfully. **2** *colloq.* search (a person) for a weapon etc. by feeling. — n. **1** playful leap or skip. **2** *colloq.* frisking of a person. [French *frisque* lively]

**frisky** *adj.* (**-ier, -iest**) **1** lively, playful. **2** *colloq.* sexually aroused. □ **friskily** *adv.* **friskiness** n.

**frisson** /free-son, fris-on/ n. emotional thrill. [French]

**fritter**[1] v. (usu. foll. by *away*) waste (money, time, etc.) triflingly. [obsolete *fritter(s)* fragments]

**fritter**[2] n. fruit, meat, etc. coated in batter and fried. [French *friture* from Latin *frigo* FRY[1]]

**fritz** n. (also **devon, German sausage**) bland sausage usu. sliced and eaten cold.

**frivolous** /friv-uh-luhs/ *adj.* **1** not serious, silly, shallow (*a frivolous character*). **2** paltry, trifling (*arrested on a frivolous charge*). □ **frivolity** /-vol-uh-tee/ n. (*pl.* **-ies**). **frivolously** *adv.* **frivolousness** n. [Latin]

**frizz** — v. form (hair) into tight curls. — n. frizzed hair or state. [French *friser*]

**frizzle**[1] v. (**-ling**) **1** fry or cook with a sizzling noise. **2** (often foll. by *up*) burn or shrivel. [obsolete *frizz*: related to FRY[1], with imitative ending]

**frizzle**[2] /friz-uhl/ — v. (**-ling**) form into tight curls. — n. frizzled hair. [perhaps related to FRIZZ]

**frizzy** *adj.* (**-ier, -iest**) in tight curls.

**fro** *adv.* back (now only in *to and fro*: see TO). [Old Norse: related to FROM]

**frock** — n. **1** woman's or girl's dress. **2** monk's or priest's gown. **3** smock. — v. invest with priestly office (cf. DEFROCK). [French from Germanic]

**frog**[1] n. **1** small smooth tailless leaping amphibian. **2** (**Frog**) *colloq. offens.* Frenchman. □ **frog in one's throat** *colloq.* hoarseness. [Old English]

**frog**[2] n. ornamental coat-fastening of a button and loop. [origin unknown]

**frogman** n. person with a rubber suit, flippers, and an oxygen supply for underwater swimming.

**frogmarch** v. hustle (a person) forward with the arms pinned behind.

**frogmouth** n. any of various nocturnal Australian and Asian birds having large wide frog-like beaks and brown or grey marbled plumage (*marbled frogmouth*; *plumed frogmouth*).

**frolic** /frol-ik/ — v. (**-ck-**) play about cheerfully. — n. **1** cheerful play. **2** prank. [Dutch *vrolijk* (adj.) from *vro* glad]

**frolicsome** *adj.* merry, playful.

**from** /fruhm, from/ *prep.* expressing separation or origin, followed by: **1** person, place, time, etc., that is the starting-point of motion or action, or of extent in place or time (*rain comes from the clouds*; *dinner is served from 6*; *from start to finish*). **2** place, object, etc. at a specified distance etc. (*5 miles from Gundagai*; *far from sure*). **3 a** source (*gravel from a pit*; *quotations from Lawson*). **b** giver or sender (*presents from Father Christmas*; *not heard from her*). **4** thing or person avoided, deprived, etc. (*dissuaded him from folly*; *released him from prison*; *took his gun from him*). **5** reason, cause, motive (*died from fatigue*; *did it from jealousy*). **6** thing distinguished or unlike (*know black from white*). **7** lower limit (*from 10 to 20 boats*). **8** state changed for another (*from being poor he became rich*). **9** adverb or preposition of time or place (*from long ago*; *from abroad*; *from under the bed*). **10** position of a person who observes or considers (*saw it from the roof*; *from his point of view*). □ **from time to time** occasionally. [Old English]

**fromage frais** /from-ah*zh* fray/ n. smooth low-fat soft cheese, used esp. as a dessert. [French, = fresh cheese]

**frond** n. **1** leaflike part of a fern or palm. **2** leaflike structure of seaweed, algae, etc. [Latin *frons frond-* leaf]

**front** /frunt/ — n. **1** side or part most prominent or important, or nearer the spectator or direction of motion (*front of the house*). **2 a** line of battle. **b** ground towards an enemy. **c** scene of actual fighting (*went to the front*). **3 a** (with preceding epithet) organised sector of activity (compared to a military front) (*domestic front*; *home front*). **b** organised political group (*Popular Front for . . .*). **4** demeanour, bearing (*show a bold front*). **5** forward or conspicuous position (*come up to the front*). **6 a** bluff. **b** pretext. **7** person etc. as a cover for subversive or illegal activities. **8** land facing a road, river, the sea, etc. **9** forward edge of advancing cold or warm air. **10** forward edge of a bushfire. **11** auditorium of a theatre. **12** breast of a garment (*spilt food down his front*). — *attrib. adj.* **1** of the front. **2** situated in front. — v. **1** (foll. by *on, to, towards, upon*) have the front facing or directed towards. **2** (foll. by *for*) *colloq.* act as a front or cover for. **3** (often foll. by *up*) *colloq.* turn up, make an appearance (*he had to front up before the headmaster*). **4** lead (a band, organisation, etc.). □ **in front** in an advanced or facing position. **in front of 1** ahead of, in advance of. **2** in the presence of. **up front** in advance (*payment up front*). [Latin *frons front- face*]

**frontage** *n.* **1** front of a building. **2** land next to a street or water etc. **3** extent of a front (*the property has a small frontage*). **4 a** the way a thing faces. **b** outlook.

**frontal** *adj.* **1** of or on the front (*frontal view*; *fully frontal nudity*; *frontal attack*). **2** of the forehead (*frontal bone*).

**frontbench** — *n.* **1** seats in parliament occupied by leading members of the government and opposition. **2** the ministry. — *adj.* pertaining to the frontbench or frontbenchers.

**frontbencher** *n.* government minister or opposition shadow-minister occupying the frontbench.

**frontier** /frun-teer, -teer/ *n.* **1 a** border between two countries. **b** district on each side of this. **2** limits of attainment or knowledge in a subject (*the frontiers of science*). □ **frontiersman** *n.*

**frontispiece** /frun-tuhs-,pees/ *n.* illustration facing the title-page of a book. [Latin: related to FRONT, *specio* look]

**front line** — *n.* foremost part of an army or group under attack. — *adj.* (**front-line**) prominent; in the forefront.

**front runner** *n.* favourite in a race, election, etc.

**frost** — *n.* **1 a** frozen dew or vapour. **b** consistent temperature below freezing point. **2** cold dispiriting atmosphere. — *v.* **1** (usu. foll. by *over*, *up*) become covered with frost. **2 a** cover with or as with frost. **b** injure (a plant etc.) with frost. **3** make (glass) non-transparent by roughening its surface. [Old English: related to FREEZE]

**frostbite** *n.* injury to body tissues due to freezing and often resulting in gangrene. □ **frostbitten** *adj.*

**frostie** *n. colloq.* chilled can or bottle of beer.

**frosting** *n.* icing.

**frosty** *adj.* (**-ier**, **-iest**) **1** cold with frost. **2** covered with or as with frost. **3** unfriendly or cold in manner. □ **frostily** *adv.* **frostiness** *n.*

**froth** — *n.* **1** foam. **2 a** idle talk, ideas, etc. **b** anything unsubstantial or of little worth. — *v.* **1** emit or gather froth. **2** cause (beer etc.) to foam. □ **frothy** *adj.* (**-ier**, **-iest**). [Old Norse]

**frown** — *v.* **1** wrinkle one's brows, esp. in displeasure or concentration. **2** (foll. by *at*, *on*) disapprove of. — *n.* **1** act of frowning. **2** look of displeasure or concentration. [French]

**frowzy** /frow-zee/ *adj.* (also **frowsy**)(**-ier**, **-iest**) **1** fusty. **2** slatternly, dingy. [origin unknown]

**froze** *past* of FREEZE.

**frozen** *past part.* of FREEZE. — *adj.* **1** turned into or covered over with ice. **2** made stiff with or killed by cold. **3** (of food) preserved by refrigeration below freezing point. **4** very cold, chilled to the bone (*I'm frozen*). **5** devoid of emotion or icy in manner. **6** (of wages etc.) fixed at a certain level. **7** (of assets etc.) made unavailable.

**fructify** /fruk-tuh-,fuy/ *v.* (**-ies**, **-ied**) **1** bear fruit. **2** make fruitful. [Latin: related to FRUIT]

**fructose** /fruk-tohz, -tohs, fruuk-/ *n.* sugar in honey, fruits, etc. [Latin: related to FRUIT]

**frugal** /froo-guhl/ *adj.* **1** sparing or thrifty, esp. as regards food. **2** sparingly used or supplied, meagre, cheap. □ **frugality** /-gal-uh-tee/ *n.* **frugally** *adv.* [Latin]

**fruit** /froot/ — *n.* **1 a** seed-bearing part of a plant or tree; this as food. **b** these collectively. **2** (usu. in *pl.*) vegetables, grains, etc. as food (*fruits of the earth*). **3** (usu. in *pl.*) profits, rewards. **4** *colloq. offens.* homosexual male. — *v.* (cause to) bear fruit. [Latin *fructus* from *fruor* enjoy]

**fruitbat** *n.* any of various large bats (of Australia and elsewhere), including the flying fox, which feed on fruit.

**fruit cake** *n.* **1** cake containing dried fruit. **2** (**fruitcake**) *colloq.* eccentric or mad person.

**fruit cocky** *n.* fruit farmer

**fruit dove** *n.* any of several Australian fruit-eating pigeons, often found in rainforest areas (*rose-crowned fruit dove*; *purple-crowned fruit dove*).

**fruiterer** *n.* dealer in fruit.

**fruit fly** *n.* any of various flies which lay their eggs in fruit, esp. the Queensland fruit fly.

**fruitful** *adj.* **1** producing much fruit. **2** successful, profitable. □ **fruitfully** *adv.*

**fruition** /froo-ish-uhn/ *n.* **1** bearing of fruit. **2** realisation of aims or hopes. [Latin: related to FRUIT]

**fruitless** *adj.* **1** not bearing fruit. **2** useless, unsuccessful. □ **fruitlessly** *adv.*

**fruity** *adj.* (**-ier**, **-iest**) **1 a** of fruit. **b** tasting or smelling like fruit. **2** (of a voice etc.) deep and rich. **3** *colloq.* slightly indecent or sexually suggestive. □ **fruitily** *adv.* **fruitiness** *n.*

**frump** *n. offens.* dowdy unattractive woman. □ **frumpish** *adj.* **frumpy** *adj.* (**-ier**, **-iest**). [perhaps British dial. *frumple* wrinkle]

**frustrate** /frus-trayt/ v. (**-ting**) **1** make (efforts) ineffective. **2** prevent (a person) from achieving a purpose. **3** (as **frustrated** adj.) **a** discontented because unable to achieve one's aims. **b** sexually unfulfilled. □ **frustrating** adj. **frustratingly** adv. **frustration** n. [Latin frustra in vain]

**fry**[1] — v. (**fries, fried**) cook or be cooked in hot oil or fat. — n. (pl. **fries**) **1** offal, usu. eaten fried (lamb's fry). **2** fried food, esp. meat. [Latin frigo]

**fry**[2] n.pl. **1** young or newly hatched fishes. **2** young of other creatures produced in large numbers, e.g. bees or frogs. □ **small fry 1** people of no importance. **2** children. [Old Norse, = seed]

**fryer** n. (also **frier**) **1** person who fries. **2** vessel for frying esp. fish.

**frying pan** n. shallow pan used in frying. □ **out of the frying pan into the fire** from a bad situation to a worse one.

**frypan** n. **1** electric frying pan. **2** = FRYING PAN.

**ft** abbr. foot, feet.

**fuchsia** /fyoo-shuh/ n. shrub with drooping red, purple, or white flowers. [Fuchs, name of a botanist (d. 1566)]

**fuddle** /fud-uhl/ — v. (**-ling**) confuse or stupefy, esp. with alcohol. — n. **1** confusion. **2** intoxication. [origin unknown]

**fuddy-duddy** /fud-ee-ˌdud-ee/ colloq. — adj. old-fashioned or quaintly fussy. — n. (pl. **-ies**) such a person. [origin unknown]

**fudge** — n. **1** soft toffee-like sweet made of milk, sugar, butter, etc. **2** piece of dishonesty or faking. — v. (**-ging**) make or do clumsily or dishonestly; fake (fudge the results). [origin uncertain]

**fuehrer** /fyoo-ruh/ n. (also **führer**) tyrannical leader. [German]

**fuel** /fyoo-uhl, fyool/ — n. **1** material for burning or as a source of heat, power, or nuclear energy. **2** food as a source of energy. **3** thing that sustains or inflames passion etc. — v. (**-ll-**) **1** (often foll. by up) supply with, take in, or get, fuel (fuelled the car; will have to fuel up soon). **2** inflame (feeling etc.). [French from Latin]

**fuel cell** n. cell producing electricity direct from a chemical reaction.

**fug** n. colloq. close stuffy atmosphere. □ **fuggy** adj. [origin unknown]

**fugitive** /fyoo-juh-tiv/ — n. (often foll. by from) person who flees, e.g. from justice or an enemy. — adj. **1** fleeing. **2** transient, fleeting. [Latin fugio flee]

**fugue** /fyoog/ n. piece of music in which a short melody or phrase is introduced by one part and taken up and developed by others. □ **fugal** adj. [Latin fuga flight]

**führer** var. of FUEHRER.

**-ful** comb. form forming: **1** adjectives from **a** nouns, meaning full of or having qualities of (beautiful; masterful). **b** adjectives (direful). **c** verbs, meaning 'apt to' (forgetful). **2** nouns (pl. **-fuls**) meaning 'amount that fills' (handful; spoonful).

**fulcrum** /fuul-kruhm/ n. (pl. **-s** or **-cra**) point on which a lever is supported. [Latin fulcio to prop]

**fulfil** /fuul-fil/ v. (**-ll-**) **1** carry out (a task, prophecy, promise, etc.). **2 a** satisfy (conditions, a desire, prayer, etc.). **b** (as **fulfilled** adj.) completely happy. **3** answer (a purpose). □ **fulfil oneself** realise one's potential. □ **fulfilment** n. [Old English: related to FULL, FILL]

**full** /fuul/ — adj. **1** holding all it can (bucket is full; full of water). **2** having eaten all one can or wants. **3** abundant, copious, satisfying (a full life; full details). **4** (foll. by of) having an abundance of (full of vitality). **5** (foll. by of) engrossed in (full of himself). **6** complete, perfect (full membership; in full bloom). **7 a** (of tone) deep and clear. **b** (of motion etc.) vigorous (at full gallop). **8** plump, rounded (full figure). **9** (of clothes) ample, hanging in folds. **10** colloq. drunk. — adv. **1** very (knows full well). **2** quite, fully (full six kilometres). **3** exactly (full on the nose). □ **full up** colloq. completely full. **in full 1** without abridgment. **2** to or for the full amount. **in full view** entirely visible. **to the full** to the utmost extent. [Old English]

**full-back** n. defensive player near the goal in football, hockey, etc.

**full blood** n. **1** person of unmixed race. **2** pure-bred animal.

**full-blooded** adj. **1** vigorous, hearty, sensual. **2** not hybrid.

**full-blown** adj. fully developed.

**full-blown Aids** n. stage of Aids (reached by some persons who have been infected with the Aids virus) that is ultimately fatal and is characterised by the breaking down of the body's natural defences against infection and sometimes by the development of tumours etc. (see also AIDS1, AIDS-RELATED COMPLEX).

**full board** n. provision of bed and all meals at a hotel etc.

**full-bodied** adj. rich in quality, tone, etc.

**full forward** n. **1** (in Australian Rules) position in front of the goal on the forward line of the attacking team. **2** player in this position.

**full-frontal** adj. **1** (of a nude figure) turned front-on so that the genitals are fully exposed. **2** explicit, unrestrained.

**full house** n. **1** maximum attendance at a theatre etc. **2** hand in poker with three of a kind and a pair.

**full-length** adj. **1** not shortened. **2** (of a mirror, portrait, etc.) showing the whole figure. **3** (of skirt) covering body from waist to ankles.

**full moon** n. **1** moon with its whole disc illuminated. **2** time of this.

**fullness** n. being full. □ **the fullness of time** the appropriate or destined time.

**full-scale** adj. not reduced in size, complete.

**full stop** n. **1** punctuation mark (.) at the end of a sentence or an abbreviation (see panel). **2** complete cessation.

**full term** n. completion of a normal pregnancy.

**full-time** — adj. **1** for or during the whole of the working week (*full-time job*). **2** of or pertaining to the time a football etc. match is scheduled to end (*full-time siren*). — n. time a football etc. match is scheduled to end. — adv. on a full-time basis (*work full-time*).

**full toss** n. *Cricket* ball pitched right up to the batsman without touching the ground.

**fully** adv. **1** completely, entirely (*am fully aware*). **2** at least (*fully 60*).

**fulminant** /ful-muh-nuhnt, fuul-/ adj. **1** fulminating. **2** (of a disease etc.) developing suddenly. [Latin: related to FULMINATE]

**fulminate** /ful-muh-,nayt, fuul-/ v. (**-ting**) **1** (often foll. by *against*) criticise loudly and forcefully. **2** explode violently; flash. □ **fulmination** /-nay-shuhn/ n. [Latin *fulmen -min-* lightning]

**fulsome** /fuul-suhm/ adj. excessive, cloying, insincere (*fulsome praise*). □ **fulsomely** adv. [from FULL]

■ **Usage** The phrase *fulsome praise* is sometimes wrongly used to mean generous praise rather than excessive praise.

**fumble** /fum-buhl/ — v. (**-ling**) **1** use the hands awkwardly, grope about. **2** handle clumsily or nervously (*fumbled the ball*). — n. act of fumbling. [Low German *fummeln*]

**fume** — n. (usu. in *pl.*) exuded gas, smoke, or vapour, esp. when harmful or unpleasant. — v. (**-ming**) **1** emit fumes or as fumes. **2** be very angry. **3** subject (oak, film, etc.) to fumes to darken. [Latin *fumus* smoke]

**fumigate** /fyoo-muh-,gayt/ v. (**-ting**) disinfect or purify with fumes. □ **fumigation** /-gay-shuhn/ n. **fumigator** n. [Latin: related to FUME]

**fun** — n. **1** lively or playful amusement. **2** source of this. **3** mockery, ridicule (*figure of fun*). — attrib. adj. colloq. amusing, enjoyable (*a fun thing to do*). □ **for fun** (or **for the fun of it**) not for a serious purpose. **in fun** as a joke, not seriously. **like fun** (as *int.*) colloq. absolutely not! **make fun of** (or **poke fun at**) ridicule, tease. [obsolete *fun, fon*: related to FOND]

■ **Usage** The use of *fun* as an attributive adjective (e.g. *a fun party*) is common in informal use, but is considered incorrect by some people.

**function** /fungk-shuhn/ — n. **1** a proper

---

**Full stop .**
This is used:
1 at the end of a sentence, e.g.
    *I am going to the movies tonight.*
    *The film begins at seven.*
    The full stop is replaced by a question mark at the end of a question, and by an exclamation mark at the end of an exclamation.
2 After an abbreviation, e.g.
    *E.G. Whitlam*      *p. 19* (= *page 19*)      *Sun.* (= *Sunday*)
    *Ex. 6* (= *Exercise 6*).
Full stops are **not** used with:
  **a** numerical abbreviations, e.g. *1st, 2nd, 15th, 23rd*
  **b** acronyms, e.g. *ASEAN, UNESCO, ABC*
  **c** abbreviations that are used as ordinary words, e.g. *con, demo, recap*
  **d** chemical symbols, e.g. *Fe, K, $H_2O$*
Full stops are not essential for:
  **a** abbreviations consisting entirely of capitals, e.g. *SBS, AD, BC, CES*
  **b** *C* (= *Celsius*), *F* (= *Fahrenheit*)
  **c** measures of length, weight, time, etc., except for *in.* (= *inch*), *st.* (= *stone*)
  **d** *Dr, Revd* (but note *Rev.*), *Mr, Mrs, Ms, Mme, Mlle, St* (= *Saint*)

or necessary role, activity, or purpose. **b** official or professional duty. **2** public or social occasion. **3** *Math.* quantity whose value depends on the varying values of others. **4** *Computing* program unit that computes a single value. — *v.* **1** fulfil a function, operate; be in working order. **2** (foll. by *as*) do the work, perform the role (of someone or something else). [Latin *fungor funct-* perform]

**functional** *adj.* **1** of or serving a function. **2** practical rather than attractive. **3** in working order. **4** (esp. of a disease) affecting the function of a bodily organ but not its structure. □ **functionally** *adv.*

**functionalism** *n.* belief that a thing's function should determine its design. □ **functionalist** *n.* & *adj.*

**functionary** *n.* (*pl.* **-ies**) official performing certain duties.

**fund** — *n.* **1** permanently available stock (*fund of knowledge*). **2** sum of money, esp. set apart for a purpose. **3** (in *pl.*) money resources. — *v.* **1** provide with money. **2** convert (a floating debt) into a more or less permanent debt at fixed interest. [Latin *fundus* bottom]

**fundamental** /ˌfun-duh-**men**-tuhl/ — *adj.* of or being a base or foundation; essential, primary (*fundamental rules; a fundamental change*). — *n.* **1** (usu. in *pl.*) fundamental principle. **2** *Mus.* fundamental note. □ **fundamentally** *adv.* [Latin: related to FOUND²]

**fundamentalism** *n.* **1** strict maintenance of the belief that every detail of the Bible is literally true. **2** (in Islam) movement which demands rigorous adherence to Islamic laws. □ **fundamentalist** *n.* & *adj.*

**fundamental note** *n. Mus.* lowest note of a chord.

**fundamental particle** *n.* elementary particle.

**funeral** /**fyoo**-nuh-ruhl/ — *n.* **1** ceremonial burial or cremation of a corpse. **2** *colloq.* one's (usu. unpleasant) concern (*that's your funeral*). — *attrib. adj.* of or used at funerals. [Latin *funus funer-*]

**funeral director** *n.* undertaker.

**funeral parlour** *n.* **1** undertaker's establishment where corpses are prepared for funerals. **2** place where non-church funeral services are conducted.

**funerary** /**fyoo**-nuh-ruh-ree/ *adj.* of or used at funerals.

**funereal** /fyoo-**neer**-ree-uhl/ *adj.* **1** of or appropriate to a funeral. **2** dismal, dark. □ **funereally** *adv.*

**fungal** /**fung**-guhl/ *adj.* **1** of, relating to, or caused by a fungus (*fungal infection*). **2** like a fungus.

**fungicide** /**fung**-guh-ˌsuyd/ *n.* substance that kills fungi. □ **fungicidal** /-**suy**-duhl/ *adj.*

**fungoid** /**fung**-goid/ — *adj.* fungus-like. — *n.* fungoid plant.

**fungous** /**fung**-guhs/ *adj.* **1** = FUNGAL. **2** springing up like a mushroom; transitory.

**fungus** /**fung**-guhs/ *n.* (*pl.* **-gi** /-gee, -guy/ or **-guses**) mushroom, toadstool, or allied plant, including moulds, feeding on organic matter. □ **fungal** *adj.* [Latin]

**funicular** /fuh-**nik**-yuh-luh/ — *adj.* (of a mountain railway) operating by cable with ascending and descending cars counterbalanced. — *n.* funicular railway. [Latin *funiculus* diminutive of *funis* rope]

**funk¹** *colloq.* — *n.* **1** fear, panic. **2** coward. — *v.* **1** evade through fear. **2** be afraid (of). [origin uncertain]

**funk²** *n. colloq.* funky music. [origin uncertain]

**funky** *adj.* (**-ier, -iest**) *colloq.* **1** (esp. of jazz or rock music) earthy, bluesy, with a heavy rhythm. **2** exciting, excellent.

**funnel** /**fun**-uhl/ — *n.* **1** tube widening at the top, for pouring liquid etc. into a small opening. **2** metal chimney on a steam engine or steamship. — *v.* (**-ll-**) guide or move through or as through a funnel. [Provençal *fonilh* from Latin *(in)fundibulum*]

**funnel-web** *n.* large, aggressive, venomous spider of eastern Australia with a potentially fatal bite: it builds a funnel-shaped web.

**funny** /**fun**-ee/ — *adj.* (**-ier, -iest**) **1** amusing, comical. **2** strange, perplexing, hard to account for. **3** *colloq.* **a** slightly unwell. **b** eccentric. **c** impertinent (*don't be funny!*). — *n. colloq.* joke (*he's cracked a funny*). □ **funnily** *adv.* **funniness** *n.* [from FUN]

**funny bone** *n.* part of the elbow over which a very sensitive nerve passes.

**fun run** *n.* footrace, often including both serious competitors and those in it just for enjoyment, and often run to raise money for charity.

**fur** — *n.* **1 a** short fine soft animal hair. **b** hide with fur on it, used esp. for clothing. **2** garment of or lined with fur. **3** fur-like coating on the tongue, in a kettle, etc. — *v.* (**-rr-**) **1** (esp. as **furred** *adj.*) line or trim with fur. **2** (often foll. by *up*) (of a kettle etc.) become coated with fur. □ **make the fur fly** *colloq.* cause a disturbance, stir up trouble. [French from Germanic]

**furbish** /**fer**-bish/ *v.* (often foll. by *up*) = REFURBISH. [French from Germanic]

**furcate** /fer-kayt/ — adj. forked, branched. — v. (-ting) fork, divide. □ **furcation** /fer-kay-shuhn/ n. [Latin: related to FORK]

**furious** /fyoo-ree-uhs/ adj. **1** very angry. **2** raging, frantic (furious storm). □ **furiously** adv. [Latin: related to FURY]

**furl** v. **1** roll up and secure (a sail etc.). **2** become furled. [French ferler]

**furlong** /fer-long/ n. (in the imperial system) eighth of a mile (201.168 m). [Old English: related to FURROW, LONG¹]

**furlough** /fer-loh/ n. leave of absence, esp. military. [Dutch: related to FOR-, LEAVE¹]

**furnace** /fer-nuhs/ n. **1** enclosed structure for intense heating by fire, esp. of metals or water. **2** very hot place (this room is a furnace). [Latin fornax from fornus oven]

**furnish** /fer-nish/ v. **1** provide (a house, room, etc.) with furniture. **2** (often foll. by with) supply. [French from Germanic]

**furnished** adj. (of a house etc.) let with furniture.

**furnishings** n.pl. furniture and fitments in a house, room, etc.

**furniture** /fer-nuh-chuh/ n. **1** movable equipment of a house, room, etc., e.g. tables, beds. **2** Naut. ship's equipment. **3** accessories, e.g. the handles and lock on a door. [French: related to FURNISH]

**furore** /fyoo-raw, fyoo-raw-ree/ n. **1** uproar; fury. **2** wave of enthusiastic admiration; a craze. [Latin: related to FURY]

**furph** n. colloq. = FURPHY.

**furphy** □ (pl. -ies) **1** false report or rumour. **2** absurd story. [water and sanitary Furphy carts (centres of gossip during World War 1) made by the Australian firm J. Furphy & Sons]

**furrier** /fu-ree-uh/ n. dealer in or dresser of furs. [French]

**furrow** /fu-roh/ — n. **1** narrow trench made by a plough. **2** rut, groove, wrinkle. **3** ship's track. — v. **1** plough. **2** make furrows in. [Old English]

**furry** /fer-ree/ adj. (-ier, -iest) like or covered with fur.

**further** /fer-thuh/ — adv. (also **farther** /fah-thuh/) **1 a** more distant in space or time (unsafe to proceed further). **b** at a greater distance (nothing was further from my mind). **2** to a greater extent, more (will enquire further). **3** in addition (I may add further). — adj. (also **farther** /fah-thuh/) **1** more distant or advanced (on the further side). **2** more, additional (further details). — v. promote or favour

(a scheme etc.). [Old English: related to FORTH]

■ **Usage** The form farther is used esp. with reference to physical distance, although further is preferred by many people even in this sense.

**furtherance** n. furthering of a scheme etc.

**further education** n. education beyond secondary school.

**furthermore** /fer-thuh-maw/ adv. in addition, besides.

**furthest** /fer-thuhst/ — adj. most distant. — adv. to or at the greatest distance.

■ **Usage** The form farthest is used esp. with reference to physical distance, although furthest is preferred by many people even in this sense.

**furtive** /fer-tiv/ adj. sly, stealthy. □ **furtively** adv. **furtiveness** n. [Latin fur thief]

**fury** /fyoo-ree/ n. (pl. -ies) **1 a** wild and passionate anger. **b** fit of rage. **2** violence of a storm, disease, etc. **3** (**Fury**) (usu. in pl.) (in Greek mythology) avenging goddess. **4** avenging spirit. **5** angry or malignant person. □ **like fury** colloq. with great force or effort. [Latin furia]

**fuse¹** /fyooz/ — v. (-sing) **1** melt with intense heat. **2** blend into one whole by melting. **3** provide (an electric circuit) with a fuse. **4 a** (of an appliance) fail owing to the melting of a fuse. **b** cause to do this. — n. device with a strip or wire of easily melted metal placed in an electric circuit so as to interrupt an excessive current by melting. [Latin fundo fus- melt]

**fuse²** /fyooz/ (also **fuze**) — n. **1** device of combustible matter for igniting a bomb or explosive charge. **2** component made of this in a shell, mine, etc. — v. (-sing) fit a fuse to. [Latin fusus spindle]

**fuselage** /fyoo-zuh-lahzh, -lij/ n. body of an aeroplane. [French from fuseau spindle]

**fusible** /fyoo-zuh-buhl/ adj. that can be melted. □ **fusibility** /-bil-uh-tee/ n. [Latin: related to FUSE¹]

**fusil** /fyoo-zuhl/ n. hist. light musket. [Latin focus fire]

**fusilier** /fyoo-zuh-leer/ n. member of any of several British regiments formerly armed with fusils. [French: related to FUSIL]

**fusillade** /fyoo-zuh-layd/ n. **1** period of continuous discharge of firearms. **2** sustained outburst of criticism etc.

**fusion** /fyoo-*zh*uhn/ *n.* **1** act or instance of fusing or melting. **2** blending of different things into one. **3** = NUCLEAR FUSION. [Latin: related to FUSE[1]]

**fuss** — *n.* **1** excited commotion, bustle. **2** excessive concern about a trivial thing. **3** sustained protest or dispute. — *v.* **1** behave with nervous concern. **2** agitate, worry, bother. □ **make a fuss** complain vigorously. **make a fuss of** (or **over**) treat (a person or animal) affectionately. □ **fusser** *n.* [origin unknown]

**fussed** *adj.* worried, concerned, bothered (*I can't be fussed*).

**fusspot** *n. colloq.* person given to fussing.

**fussy** *adj.* (**-ier, -iest**) **1** inclined to fuss. **2** full of unnecessary detail or decoration. **3** fastidious. □ **fussily** *adv.* **fussiness** *n.*

**fusty** /*fus*-tee/ *adj.* (**-ier, -iest**) **1** musty, stuffy. **2** antiquated; old fashioned. □ **fustiness** *n.* [French *fust* cask, from Latin *fustis* cudgel]

**futile** /*fyoo*-tuyl/ *adj.* useless, ineffectual. □ **futility** /-til-uh-tee/ *n.* [Latin *futilis* leaky, futile]

**futon** /*foo*-ton/ *n.* Japanese quilted mattress used as a bed; this sold with a frame of wooden slats. [Japanese]

**future** /*fyoo*-chuh/ — *adj.* **1** about to happen, be, or become (*his future career*). **2 a** of time to come (*future years*). **b** *Gram.* (of a tense) describing an event yet to happen. — *n.* **1** time to come. **2** future events (*the future is certain*). **3** future condition of a person, country, etc. **4** prospect of success etc. (*there's no future in it*). **5** *Gram.* future tense. **6** (in *pl.*) *Stock Exch.* **a** goods etc. sold for future delivery. **b**

contracts for these. □ **in future** from now onwards. [Latin *futurus* future part. of *sum* be]

**future perfect** *n. Gram.* tense giving the sense 'will have done'.

**future shock** *n.* inability to cope with rapid technological etc. progress.

**futurism** *n.* early 20th-century artistic movement departing from traditional forms and celebrating technology and dynamism. □ **futurist** *n. & adj.*

**futuristic** /ˌfyoo-chuh-**ris**-tik/ *adj.* **1** suitable for the future; ultra-modern. **2** of futurism.

**futurity** /fyoo-**choo**-ruh-tee/ *n.* (*pl.* **-ies**) *literary* **1** future time. **2** (in *sing.* or *pl.*) future events.

**futurology** /ˌfyoo-chuh-**rol**-uh-jee/ *n.* forecasting of the future, esp. from present trends.

**fuzz** *n.* **1** fluff. **2** fluffy or frizzed hair. **3** *colloq.* **a** (prec. by *the*) the police. **b** police officer. [probably Low German or Dutch]

**fuzzy** *adj.* (**-ier, -iest**) **1** like fuzz, fluffy. **2** blurred, indistinct. □ **fuzzily** *adv.* **fuzziness** *n.*

**fuzzy wuzzy** *n. hist.* a New Guinean.

**fuzzy-wuzzy angel** *n. hist.* a New Guinean who helped Australian service personnel during World War II.

**-fy** *suffix* forming: **1** verbs from nouns, meaning: **a** make, produce (*pacify*). **b** make into (*deify*; *petrify*). **2** verbs from adjectives, meaning 'bring or come into a state' (*solidify*). **3** verbs in a causative sense (*horrify*; *stupefy*). [French *-fier* from Latin *facio* make]

# G

**G²** *abbr.* (also **G.**) **1** gauss. **2** giga-. **3** gravitational constant.

**g** *abbr.* (also **g.**) **1** gram(s). **2 a** gravity. **b** acceleration due to gravity.

**G7** *attrib. adj.* designating the world's seven richest nations. [*Group of Seven*]

**Ga** *symb.* gallium.

**gab** *colloq.* — *n.* **1** talk, idle chitchat. **2** fast-talking, smooth (perhaps suspicious) eloquence (*gift of the gab*). — *v.* talk idly, chitchat. [var. of GOB¹]

**gabardine** var. of GABERDINE.

**Gabba** /ˈga-buh/ *n.* (prec. by *the*) *colloq.* Queensland Cricket Association ground at Woolloongabba, Brisbane. [abbreviation]

**gabble** /ˈgab-uhl/ — *v.* (**-ling**) talk or utter unintelligibly or too fast. — *n.* fast unintelligible talk. □ **gabbler** *n.* [Dutch, imitative]

**gaberdine** /ˈgab-uh-ˌdeen, -ˈdeen/ *n.* (also **gabardine**) **1** twill-woven cloth, esp. of worsted. **2** raincoat etc. made of this. [French *gauvardine*]

**gabfest** /ˈgab-ˌfest/ *n.* = TALKFEST.

**Gabi-gabi** /ˈgub-ee-ˌgub-ee/ *n.* an Aboriginal language spoken in southeastern Queensland, north of Brisbane; now extinct.

**gable** /ˈgay-buhl/ *n.* **1** triangular upper part of a wall at the end of a ridged roof. **2** gable-topped wall. □ **gabled** *adj.* [Old Norse and French]

**gad** *v.* (**-dd-**) (foll. by *about*) go about idly or in search of pleasure. [obsolete *gadling* companion]

**gadabout** *n.* person who gads about.

**gadfly** *n.* **1** fly that bites cattle and horses. **2** stingingly critical and/or irritating person. [obsolete *gad* spike]

**gadget** /ˈgaj-uht/ *n.* small mechanical device or tool. □ **gadgetry** *n.* [origin unknown]

**gadolinium** /ˌgad-uh-ˈlin-ee-uhm/ *n.* metallic element of the lanthanide series. [*Gadolin*, Finnish mineralogist (d. 1852)]

**Gael** /gayl/ *n.* **1** Scottish Celt. **2** Gaelic-speaking Celt. [Gaelic *Gaidheal*]

**Gaelic** /ˈgay-lik, ˈgal-ik/ — *n.* Celtic language of Ireland and Scotland. — *adj.* of the Celts or the Celtic languages.

**gaff¹** — *n.* **1 a** stick with an iron hook for landing large fish. **b** barbed fishing-spear. **2** spar to which the head of a fore-and-aft sail is bent. — *v.* seize (a fish) with a gaff. [Provençal *gaf* hook]

**gaff²** *n. colloq.* □ **blow the gaff** reveal a plot or secret. [origin unknown]

**gaffe** /gaf/ *n.* blunder; indiscreet act or remark. [French]

**gaffer** /ˈgaf-uh/ *n.* chief electrician in a film or television production unit. [probably from GODFATHER]

**gag** — *n.* **1** thing thrust into or tied across the mouth, esp. to prevent speaking or crying out. **2** joke or comic scene. **3** government closure of debate in parliament when opposition members wish the debate to be prolonged. **4** thing restricting free speech. — *v.* (**-gg-**) **1** apply a gag to. **2** silence; deprive of free speech. **3** apply the gag in parliament. **4** choke, retch. [origin uncertain]

**gaga** /ˈgah-gah/ *adj. colloq.* **1** senile. **2** slightly crazed. **3** crazy (about), infatuated (*he's gone gaga over her*). [French]

**gage** *n.* **1** pledge; thing deposited as security. **2** symbol of a challenge to fight, esp. a glove thrown down. [Germanic: related to WED, WAGE]

**gaggle** /ˈgag-uhl/ *n.* **1** flock of geese. **2** *colloq.* disorganised group of people. [imitative]

**gaiety** /ˈgay-uh-tee/ *n.* **1** being merry; mirth. **2** merrymaking. **3** bright appearance. [French: related to GAY]

**gaily** *adv.* **1** in a merry or carefree manner (*gaily announced their departure*). **2** colourfully (*gaily decorated*).

**gain** — *v.* **1** obtain or win (*gain advantage; gain recognition*). **2** acquire as profits etc., earn. **3** (often foll. by *in*) get more of, improve (*gain momentum; gain in experience*). **4** benefit, profit. **5** (of a clock etc.) become fast; become fast by (a specified amount of time). **6** (often foll. by *on, upon*) come closer to a person or thing pursued. **7 a** reclaim (land from the sea). **b** win (a battle). **8** reach (a desired place). — *n.* **1** increase of wealth etc.; profit, improvement. **2** (in *pl.*) sums of money got by trade etc. **3** increase in amount. **4** *Electronics* **a** factor by which power etc. is increased. **b** logarithm of this. **5** volume of an amplifier. □ **gain ground 1** advance. **2** (foll. by *on*) catch up (a person pursued). [French from Germanic]

**gainful** *adj.* **1** (of employment) paid. **2** lucrative. □ **gainfully** *adv.*

**gainsay** /ˌgayn-ˈsay/ *v.* deny, contradict. [Old Norse: related to AGAINST, SAY]

444

**gait** n. **1** (of a person) manner of walking. **2** (of a horse) manner of forward motion, as trot, gallop, etc. [Old Norse]

**gala** /**gah**-luh/ — n. festive occasion (*the Geelong gala*). — adj. festive, celebratory (*gala occasion*). [ultimately from French *gale* rejoicing, from Germanic]

**galactic** /guh-**lak**-tik/ adj. of a galaxy or galaxies.

**galah** /guh-**lah**/ n. **1** grey-backed, pink-breasted cockatoo occurring in most parts of Australia. **2** *colloq.* fool, idiot. □ **mad as a gum-tree full of galahs** *colloq.* crazy. **make a proper galah of oneself** *colloq.* make a complete fool of oneself. [Yuwaalaraay *gilaa*]

**galangal** /guh-**lang**-guhl/ n. aromatic rhizome of certain plants of the ginger family, used in Asian cooking. [perhaps ult. from Chinese]

**galaxy** /**gal**-uhk-see/ n. (*pl.* **-ies**) **1** independent system of stars, gas, dust, etc., in space. **2** (**the Galaxy**) Milky Way. **3** (foll. by *of*) brilliant company (*galaxy of talent*). [Greek *gala* milk]

**gale** n. **1** very strong wind or storm. **2** outburst, esp. of laughter. [origin unknown]

**gall¹** /gawl/ n. **1** impudence. **2** rancour. **3** bitterness. **4** bile. [Old Norse]

**gall²** /gawl/ — n. **1** sore made by chafing. **2** mental soreness or its cause. **3** place rubbed bare. — v. **1** rub sore. **2** vex, humiliate. [Low German or Dutch *galle*]

**gall³** /gawl/ n. abnormal growth produced by insects, bacteria, etc. on plants and trees, esp. on eucalypts and wattles. [Latin *galla*]

**gallant** — adj. /**gal**-uhnt/ **1** brave. **2** fine, stately. **3** /guh-**lant**/ very attentive to women. — n. /guh-**lant**/ ladies' man. □ **gallantly** /**gal**-uhnt-lee/ adv. [French *galer* make merry]

**gallantry** /**gal**-uhn-tree/ n. (*pl.* **-ies**) **1** bravery. **2** devotion to women. **3** polite act or speech.

**gall bladder** n. organ storing bile.

**galleon** /**gal**-ee-uhn/ n. *hist.* warship (usu. Spanish). [French or Spanish: related to GALLEY]

**galleria** /,gal-uh-**ree**-uh/ n. collection of small shops under a single roof. [Italian]

**gallery** /**gal**-uh-ree/ n. (*pl.* **-ies**) **1** room or building for showing works of art. **2** balcony, esp. in a church, hall, etc. (*minstrels' gallery*). **3 a** highest balcony in a theatre containing the cheapest seats. **b** the audience seated there. **4** covered walk partly open at the side; colonnade. **5** long narrow room or passage (*shooting-gallery*). **6** horizontal underground passage in a mine etc. **7** group of spectators at a golf match etc. □ **play to the gallery** seek to win approval by appealing to popular taste. [French *galerie*]

**galley** /**gal**-ee/ n. (*pl.* **-s**) **1** *hist.* **a** long flat single-decked vessel usu. rowed by slaves or criminals. **b** ancient Greek or Roman warship. **2** ship's or aircraft's kitchen. **3** *Printing* (in full **galley proof**) proof in continuous form before division into pages. [Latin *galea*]

**galley slave** n. **1** *hist.* slave on a galley. **2** drudge, one who is overworked.

**Gallic** /**gal**-ik/ adj. **1** French or typically French. **2** of Gaul (the ancient region comprising France, Belgium, etc.) or its people. [Latin *Gallicus*]

**gallinaceous** /,gal-uh-**nay**-shuhs/ adj. of the order including domestic poultry, pheasants, etc. [Latin *gallina* hen]

**galling** /**gaw**-ling/ adj. mortifying; thoroughly exasperating.

**gallium** /**gal**-ee-uhm/ n. soft bluish-white metallic element. [Latin *Gallia* France: so named patriotically by its discoverer Lecoq]

**gallivant** /**gal**-uh-,vant/ v. gad about, esp. with amorous pleasure in mind (*gallivanting around the nightspots in town*). [origin uncertain]

**gallon** /**gal**-uhn/ n. **1** measure of capacity in the imperial system, equal to eight pints (approximately 4.5 litres). **2** (in *pl.*) *colloq.* large amount. [French]

**gallop** /**gal**-uhp/ — n. **1** fastest pace of a horse etc., with all the feet off the ground together in each stride. **2** a ride at this pace. — v. (**-p-**) **1 a** (of a horse etc. or its rider) go at a gallop. **b** make (a horse etc.) gallop. **2** read, talk, etc., fast. **3** progress rapidly (*galloping inflation*). [French: related to WALLOP]

**gallows** /**gal**-ohz/ *n.pl.* (usu. treated as *sing.*) **1** structure, usu. of two uprights and a crosspiece, for hanging criminals. **2** structure from which the carcase of a slaughtered beast is hung. [Old Norse]

**gallstone** n. small hard mass forming in the gall-bladder.

**gallup poll** /**gal**-uhp/ n. = OPINION POLL. [*Gallup*, US statistician (d. 1984)]

**galore** /guh-**law**/ adv. in plenty. [Irish]

■ **Usage** *Galore* always follows the noun, e.g. *whisky galore*; *parties galore*; *sales galore*.

**galoshes** /guh-**losh**-uhz/ *n.pl.* (also **goloshes**) overshoes, usu. of rubber. [French]

**galvanic** /gal-**van**-ik/ *adj.* **1 a** producing an electric current by chemical action. **b** (of electricity) produced by chemical action. **2 a** sudden and remarkable (*had a galvanic effect*). **b** stimulating; full of energy. □ **galvanically** *adv.*

**galvanise** /**gal**-vuh-‚nuyz/ *v.* (also **-ize**) (**-sing** or **-zing**) **1** (often foll. by *into*) rouse forcefully, esp. by shock or excitement (*was galvanised into action*). **2** stimulate by or as by electricity. **3** coat (iron) with zinc to protect against rust. □ **galvanisation** /-**zay**-shuhn/ *n.* [*Galvani*, Italian physiologist (d. 1798)]

**galvanised iron** *n.* zinc-coated sheets of corrugated iron used as a roofing, fencing, etc. material.

**galvanometer** /‚gal-vuh-**nom**-uh-tuh/ *n.* instrument for detecting and measuring small electric currents. □ **galvanometric** /-nuh-**met**-rik/ *adj.*

**galvo** /**gal**-voh/ *n. colloq.* = GALVANISED IRON.

**gambit** /**gam**-buht/ *n.* **1** chess opening in which a player sacrifices a piece or pawn to secure an advantage. **2** opening move in a discussion etc. **3** trick or device. [Italian *gambetto* tripping up]

**gamble** /**gam**-buhl/ — *v.* (**-ling**) **1** play games of chance for money. **2 a** bet (a sum of money) in gambling. **b** (often foll. by *away*) lose by gambling. **3** risk much in the hope of great gain. **4** (foll. by *on*) act in the hope of.... — *n.* **1** risky undertaking. **2** spell of gambling. □ **gambler** *n.* [obsolete *gamel* to sport, related to GAME[1]]

**gambol** /**gam**-buhl/ — *v.* (**-ll-**) skip or jump about playfully. — *n.* frolic, caper. [French *gambade* leap, from Italian *gamba* leg]

**game**[1] — *n.* **1** form of play or sport, esp. a competitive one with rules. **2** portion of play forming a scoring unit, e.g. in bridge or tennis. **3** (in *pl.*) series of athletic etc. contests (*Olympic Games*). **4** a piece of fun, jest (*didn't mean to upset you — it was only a game*). **b** (in *pl.*) dodges, tricks (*none of your games!*). **5** *colloq.* **a** scheme (*so that's your game*). **b** type of activity or business (*have been in the antiques game a long time*). **6 a** wild animals or birds hunted for sport or food. **b** their flesh as food. — *adj.* spirited; eager and willing (*are you game for a walk?*). — *v.* (**-ming**) gamble for money stakes. □ **easy game** easily hoodwinked or seduced. **game as Ned Kelly** see NED KELLY. **the game's up** scheme is revealed or foiled. **have the game by the throat** (or **sewn up**) *colloq.* have the upper hand; be in complete mastery. **lift one's game** perform better; try harder. **name of the game** main point;

salient aim (*winning votes is the name of the game in politics*). □ **gamely** *adv.* [Old English]

**game**[2] *adj. colloq.* (of a leg, arm, etc.) crippled. [origin unknown]

**gamelan** /**gam**-uh-‚lan/ *n.* **1** SE Asian orchestra mainly of percussion instruments. **2** type of xylophone used in this. [Javanese]

**gamesmanship** /**gaymz**-muhn-ship/ *n.* art of winning games by gaining psychological advantage.

**gamete** /**gam**-eet/ *n.* mature germ cell able to unite with another in sexual reproduction. □ **gametic** /guh-**met**-ik/ *adj.* [Greek, = wife]

**gaming** /**gay**-ming/ *n.* gambling.

**gamma** /**gam**-uh/ *n.* **1** third letter of the Greek alphabet (Γ, γ). **2** third-class mark for a piece of work etc. [Greek]

**gamma radiation** *n.* (also **gamma rays**) electromagnetic radiation of shorter wavelength than X-rays.

**gammon** /**gam**-uhn/ *n.* **1** bottom piece of a flitch of bacon including a hind leg. **2** ham of a pig cured like bacon. [French: related to JAMB]

**gammy** /**gam**-ee/ *adj.* (**-ier**, **-iest**) *colloq.* = GAME2. [British dial. form of GAME[2]]

**gamut** /**gam**-uht/ *n.* entire range or scope. □ **run the gamut of** experience or perform the complete range of. [Latin *gamma ut*, words arbitrarily taken as names of notes in music]

**Ganay** /**gun**-uy/ *n.* an Aboriginal language spoken over a very large area of south-eastern Victoria: now extinct.

**gander** *n.* **1** male goose. **2** *colloq.* look, glance (*take a gander*). [Old English]

**gang** *n.* **1** band of persons associating for some (usu. antisocial or criminal) purpose. **2** set of workers, slaves, or prisoners. □ **gang up** *colloq.* **1** (often foll. by *with*) act together. **2** (foll. by *on*) combine against. [Old Norse]

**gang-gang** /**gang**-gang/ *n.* grey cockatoo of south-east Australia, the male having an orange-red crest and head. [Wiradhuri, imitative]

**gangling** /**gang**-gling/ *adj.* (of a person) loosely built; lanky. [frequentative of Old English *gang* go]

**ganglion** /**gang**-glee-uhn/ *n.* (*pl.* **-lia** or **-s**) structure containing an assemblage of nerve cells. □ **ganglionic** /-**on**-ik/ *adj.* [Greek]

**gangly** /**gang**-glee/ *adj.* (**-ier**, **-iest**) = GANGLING.

**gangplank** *n.* movable plank for boarding or disembarking from a ship etc.

**gangrene** /**gang**-green/ n. death of body tissue, usu. resulting from obstructed circulation. □ **gangrenous** /**gang**-gruh-nuhs/ adj. [Greek *gaggraina*]

**gangster** n. member of a gang of violent criminals.

**gangway** n. 1 passage, esp. between rows of seats. 2 a opening in a ship's bulwarks. b bridge from ship to shore.

**gannet** /**gan**-uht/ n. any of various large diving sea birds, including the *Australian gannet*. [Old English]

**gantry** /**gan**-tree/ n. (pl. **-ies**) structure supporting a travelling crane, railway or road signals, rocket-launching equipment, etc. [probably *gawn*, a British dial. form of GALLON, + TREE]

**gaol** var. of JAIL.

**gap** n. 1 empty space, interval; deficiency. 2 breach in a hedge, fence, etc. 3 wide divergence in views etc. (*generation gap*). 4 gorge or pass; ravine. □ **gappy** adj. [Old Norse]

**gape** — v. (**-ping**) 1 a open one's mouth wide. b be or become wide open; split. 2 (foll. by *at*) stare at. — n. 1 open-mouthed stare; open mouth. 2 a rent or opening. [Old Norse]

**gap insurance** n. private medical insurance taken to bridge the gap between the Medicare pay-out and the scheduled fee for service by a doctor.

**garage** /**ga**-rah*zh*, guh-**rah**zh, -**rahj**/ — n. 1 building for housing a vehicle. 2 establishment selling petrol etc., and/or repairing motor vehicles. — v. (**-ging**) put or keep in a garage. [French]

**garage sale** n. sale (of miscellaneous household goods) held usu. in the garage of a private house.

**garam masala** /,ga-ruhm muh-**sah**-luh/ n. fragrant mixture of spices used esp. in Indian cooking. [Hindustani, = hot spices]

**garb** — n. 1 clothing, esp. of a distinctive kind. 2 external semblance; form. — v. (usu. in *passive* or *refl.*) dress. [Germanic: related to GEAR]

**garbage** /**gah**-bij/ n. 1 refuse, esp. kitchen waste. 2 *colloq.* a nonsense. b trash, worthless stuff. [Anglo-French]

**garbage man** n. person employed to clear household refuse left outside for disposal.

**garble** /**gah**-buhl/ v. (**-ling**) 1 (esp. as **garbled** adj.) unintentionally distort or confuse (facts, messages, etc.). 2 make a (usu. unfair) selection from (facts, statements, etc.). □ **garbler** n. [Italian from Arabic]

**garbo** /**gah**-boh/ n. *colloq.* = GARBAGE MAN.

**garden** /**gah**-duhn/ — n. 1 piece of ground for growing flowers, fruit, or vegetables, and as a place of recreation. 2 (esp. in *pl.*) grounds laid out for public enjoyment. 3 (*attrib.*) cultivated (*garden plants*). — v. cultivate or tend a garden. □ **lead a person up the garden path** swindle or hoodwink him or her. □ **gardening** n. [Germanic: related to YARD2]

**garden centre** n. place where plants and garden equipment are sold.

**gardener** /**gah**-duh-nuh, **gah**-duh-nuh/ n. person who gardens, esp. for a living.

**gardenia** /gah-**dee**-nyuh/ n. tree or shrub with large fragrant flowers. [A. *Garden*, naturalist (d. 1791)]

**garfish** /**gah**-fish/ n. (pl. same or **-es**) any of various fishes found in Australian waters and elsewhere, having a long spearlike snout. [Old English, = spearfish]

**gargantuan** /gah-**gan**-choo-uhn/ adj. gigantic. [from the name *Gargantua*, a giant in Rabelais]

**gargle** /**gah**-guhl/ — v. (**-ling**) wash (the throat) with a liquid kept in motion by breathing through it. — n. liquid for gargling. [French: related to GARGOYLE]

**gargoyle** /**gah**-goil/ n. grotesque carved face or figure, esp. as a spout from the gutter of a building. [French, = throat]

**garish** /**gair**-rish, **gah**-rish/ adj. obtrusively bright; showy; gaudy. □ **garishly** adv. **garishness** n. [obsolete *gaure* stare]

**garland** /**gah**-luhnd/ — n. wreath of flowers etc., worn as an honour or hung as a decoration. — v. adorn or crown with a garland or garlands. [French]

**garland lily** n. lily-like plant of inland river-banks in south-eastern Australia, bearing a dozen or more wine-red trumpet-flowers with a golden throat.

**garlic** /**gah**-lik/ — n. plant of the onion family with a pungent bulb used in cookery. — adj. containing garlic (*garlic bread*). □ **garlicky** adj. [Old English, = spear-leek]

**garment** /**gah**-muhnt/ n. 1 article of dress. 2 outward covering. [French: related to GARNISH]

**garner** /**gah**-nuh/ — v. 1 collect. 2 store. — n. *literary* storehouse or granary. [Latin: related to GRANARY]

**garnet** /**gah**-nuht/ n. glassy silicate mineral, esp. a red kind used as a gem. [medieval Latin *granatum* POMEGRANATE]

**garnish** /**gah**-nish/ — v. decorate (esp. food). — n. decoration, esp. to food. [French *garnir* from Germanic]

**garret** /**ga**-ruht/ *n.* attic or room in a roof. [French, = watch-tower: related to GARRISON]

**garrison** /**ga**-ruh-suhn/ — *n.* troops stationed in a town etc. to defend it. — *v.* (**-n-**) **1** provide with or occupy as a garrison. **2** place on garrison duty. [French *garir* defend, from Germanic]

**garrotte** /guh-**rot**/ (also **garotte**) — *v.* (**-ting**) execute or kill by strangulation, esp. with a wire collar. — *n.* device used for this. [French or Spanish]

**garrulous** /**ga**-ruh-luhs/ *adj.* talkative, esp. on trivial matters; wordy. □ **garrulity** /guh-**roo**-luh-tee/ *n.* **garrulousness** *n.* [Latin]

**garter** *n.* band worn to keep a sock or stocking up. [Old French *gartier*]

**garter stitch** *n.* plain knitting stitch.

**garuda** /guh-**roo**-duh/ *n.* **1** fabulous, partly human bird of Indian myth. **2** national emblem of Indonesia (hence *Garuda Airline*). [Sanskrit *garudá.*]

**gas** — *n.* (*pl.* **-es**) **1** any airlike substance (i.e. not solid or liquid) moving freely to fill any space available. **2** such a substance (esp. found naturally or extracted from coal) used as fuel (also *attrib.*: *gas cooker*; *gas industry*). **3** nitrous oxide or other gas as an anaesthetic. **4** poisonous gas used in war. **5** *colloq.* idle talk; boasting. **6** *colloq.* something wonderful, successful (*the barbie was a gas*). — *adj. colloq.* excellent (*that's a gas notion*). — *v.* (**gases, gassed, gassing**) **1** expose to gas, esp. to kill. **2** *colloq.* talk idly or boastfully. [Dutch invented word based on Greek *khaos* = CHAOS]

**gasbag** *n. colloq.* idle talker; empty boaster.

**gas chamber** *n.* room filled with poisonous gas to kill people or animals.

**gaseous** /**gas**-ee-uhs/ *adj.* of or like gas.

**gash** — *n.* long deep slash, cut, or wound. — *v.* make a gash in; cut. [French]

**gasket** /**gas**-kuht/ *n.* sheet or ring of rubber etc., shaped to seal the junction of metal surfaces. □ **blow a gasket** *colloq.* explode with anger. [French *garcette*]

**gas mask** *n.* respirator as a protection against poison gas.

**gasoline** /**gas**-uh-,leen/ *n.* (also **gasolene**) *US* petrol.

**gasometer** /ga-**som**-uh-tuh/ *n.* large tank from which gas is distributed by pipes. [French *gazomètre*: related to GAS, -METER]

**gasp** /gahsp, gasp/ — *v.* **1** catch one's breath with an open mouth as in exhaustion or astonishment. **2** utter with

gasps. **3** be filled with desire for, crave (*gasping for a drink*). — *n.* convulsive catching of breath. [Old Norse]

**gassy** *adj.* (**-ier, -iest**) **1** of or like gas. **2** full of gas.

**gastric** /**gas**-trik/ *adj.* of the stomach. [French: related to GASTRO-]

**gastric brooding frog** *n.* (also **platypus frog**) rare Queensland frog which swallows its fertilised eggs, turns its stomach into a uterus, and spits the fully formed young out of its mouth.

**gastric flu** *n. colloq.* intestinal disorder of unknown cause.

**gastric juice** *n.* digestive fluid secreted by the stomach glands.

**gastritis** /ga-**stry**-tuhs/ *n.* inflammation of the stomach.

**gastro-** *comb. form* stomach. [Greek *gastēr* stomach]

**gastroenteritis** /,gas-troh-,en-tuh-**ruy**-tuhs/ *n.* inflammation of the stomach and intestines.

**gastronome** /**gas**-truh-,nohm/ *n.* gourmet. [Greek *gastēr* stomach, *nomos* law]

**gastronomy** /gas-**tron**-uh-mee/ *n.* science or art of good eating and drinking. □ **gastronomic** /,gas-truh-**nom**-ik/ *adj.* **gastronomical** *adj.* **gastronomically** *adv.*

**gastropod** /**gas**-truh-,pod/ *n.* mollusc that moves by means of a ventral muscular organ, e.g. a snail. [from GASTRO-, Greek *pous pod-* foot]

**gasworks** *n.* place where gas is manufactured for lighting and heating.

**gate** *n.* **1** barrier, usu. hinged, used to close an opening made for entrance and exit through a wall, fence, etc. **2** such an opening. **3** means of entrance or exit. **4** numbered place of access to aircraft at an airport. **5** device regulating the passage of water in a lock etc. **6 a** number of people entering by payment at the gates of a sports ground etc. **b** (in full **gate money**) amount of money taken thus. **7 a** electrical signal that causes or controls the passage of other signals. **b** electrical circuit with an output that depends on the combination of several inputs. [Old English]

**-gate** *comb. form* denoting a scandal or corruption of some kind, esp. political (*Dianagate*; *Irangate*). [from *Watergate* the name of a building in Washington DC, where the headquarters of the US Democratic Party were burgled in 1972 by persons associated with the Republican Party, creating a major political scandal]

**gateau** /**gat**-oh/ *n.* (*pl.* **-s** or **-x** /-ohz/) large rich cake filled with cream etc. [French]

**gatecrasher** *n.* uninvited guest at a party etc. □ **gatecrash** *v.*

**gateway** *n.* **1** opening which can be closed with a gate. **2** means of access (*Wodonga, gateway to Victoria; gateway to success*). **3** *Computing* device that interconnects two networks and whose presence is visible to users.

**gather** /**gath**-uh/ — *v.* **1** bring or come together; accumulate. **2** pick or collect as harvest. **3** infer or deduce (*I gather that the Premier is set to resign*). **4 a** increase (*gather speed*). **b** collect (*gather dust*). **5** summon up (energy etc.). **6** draw together in folds or wrinkles. **7** (often as **gathering** *adj.*) come to a head (*gathering storm*). **8** develop a purulent swelling. — *n.* fold or pleat. □ **gather up** bring together; pick up from the ground; draw into a small compass. [Old English]

**gathering** *n.* assembly.

**GATT** /gat/ *abbr.* General Agreement on Tariffs and Trade.

**gauche** /gohsh/ *adj.* **1** socially awkward. **2** tactless. □ **gauchely** *adv.* **gaucheness** *n.* [French]

**gaucherie** /goh-shuh-‚ree/ *n.* gauche manners or act. [French: related to GAUCHE]

**gaucho** /**gow**-choh/ *n.* (*pl.* **-s**) cowboy from the S. American pampas. [Spanish from Quechua]

**gaudy** /**gaw**-dee/ *adj.* (**-ier, -iest**) tastelessly showy. □ **gaudily** *adv.* **gaudiness** *n.* [obsolete *gaud* ornament, from Latin *gaudeo* rejoice]

**gauge** /gayj/ — *n.* **1** standard measure, esp. of the capacity or contents of a barrel, fineness of a textile, diameter of a bullet, or thickness of sheet metal. **2** instrument for measuring pressure, width, length, thickness, etc. **3** distance between rails or opposite wheels. **4** capacity, extent. **5** criterion, test. **6** (usu. **gage**) *Naut.* position relative to the wind. — *v.* (**-ging**) **1** measure exactly. **2** measure the capacity or content of. **3** estimate (a person, situation, etc.). [French]

**gaunt** /gawnt/ *adj.* **1** lean, haggard. **2** grim, desolate. □ **gauntness** *n.* [origin unknown]

**gauntlet¹** /**gawnt**-luht/ *n.* **1** stout glove with a long loose wrist. **2** *hist.* armoured glove. □ **pick up** (or **take up**) **the gauntlet** accept a challenge. **throw down the gauntlet** issue a challenge. [French diminutive of *gant* glove]

**gauntlet²** /**gawnt**-luht/ *n.* □ **run the gauntlet 1** undergo harsh criticism. **2** pass between two rows of people and receive blows from them, as a punishment or ordeal. [Swedish *gatlopp* from *gata* lane, *lopp* course]

**Gaurna** /**gowuh**-nu/ *n.* an Aboriginal language spoken over a vast area of south-eastern SA, including what is now Adelaide (and hence referred to as 'the Adelaide language'): now extinct.

**gauss** /gows/ *n.* (*pl.* same) unit of magnetic flux density. [K. *Gauss*, German mathematician (d. 1855)]

**gauze** /gawz/ *n.* **1** thin transparent fabric of silk, cotton, etc. **2** fine mesh of wire etc. □ **gauzy** *adj.* (**-ier, -iest**). [French from *Gaza* in Palestine]

**gave** *past* of GIVE.

**gavel** /**gav**-uhl/ *n.* hammer used for calling attention by an auctioneer, chairman, or judge. [origin unknown]

**gavotte** /guh-**vot**/ *n.* **1** old French dance. **2** music for this. [French from Provençal]

**gawk** — *v. colloq.* gawp. — *n.* awkward or bashful person. [obsolete *gaw* GAZE]

**gawky** *adj.* (**-ier, -iest**) awkward or ungainly. □ **gawkily** *adv.* **gawkiness** *n.*

**gawp** *v. colloq.* stare stupidly or obtrusively. [related to YELP]

**gay** — *adj.* **1 a** homosexual. **b** intended for or used by homosexuals (*gay bar*). **2** light-hearted, cheerful. **3** brightly coloured. **4** *colloq.* careless, thoughtless (*gay abandon*). — *n.* (esp. male) homosexual (*many gays are open about their gayness*). □ **gayness** *n.* [French]

---

■ **Usage** Senses 2 and 3 have now been superseded by sense 1.

---

**gaze** — *v.* (**-zing**) (foll. by *at, into, on*, etc.) look fixedly. — *n.* intent look. [origin unknown]

**gazebo** /guh-**zee**-boh/ *n.* (*pl.* **-s**) freestanding garden structure, e.g. a summerhouse, affording an enjoyable view. [perhaps a fanciful formation from GAZE]

**gazelle** /guh-**zel**/ *n.* (*pl.* same or **-s**) small graceful antelope. [Arabic *ḡazāl*]

**gazette** /guh-**zet**/ — *n.* **1** newspaper (used in the title). **2** official government publication with announcements etc. — *v.* (**-tting**) announce or name in an official gazette. [French from Italian]

**gazetteer** /gaz-uh-**teer**/ *n.* geographical index. [Italian: related to GAZETTE]

**gazpacho** /guhz-**pah**-choh/ *n.* (*pl.* **-s**) cold Spanish soup with uncooked tomato, onion, cucumber, garlic, etc., and oil and vinegar. [Spanish]

**gazump** /guh-**zump**/ *v. colloq.* **1** raise the price of a property after accepting an offer from (a buyer). **2** swindle. [origin unknown]

**Gd** *symb.* gadolinium.

**g'day** /guh-**day**/ *contr.* = GOOD-DAY.

**GDP** *abbr.* gross domestic product.

**Ge** *symb.* germanium.

**gear** — *n.* **1** (often in *pl.*) **a** set of toothed wheels that work together, esp. those connecting the engine of a vehicle to the road wheels. **b** particular setting of these (*first gear*). **2 a** equipment, apparatus, or tackle. **b** personal belongings, esp. movable items. **3** *colloq.* clothing. — *v.* **1** (foll. by *to*) adjust or adapt to (*my business isn't geared to the mail-order market*). **2** (often foll. by *up*) equip with gears. **3** (foll. by *up*) make ready or prepared. **4** put in gear. [Old Norse]

**gearbox** *n.* **1** set of gears with its casing, esp. in a vehicle. **2** the casing itself.

**gearing** *n.* set or arrangement of gears.

**gearstick** *n.* (also **gearshift, gear lever**) lever used to engage or change gear.

**gecko** /**gek**-oh/ *n.* (*pl.* **-s**) small, tropical house-lizard. [Malay]

**gee** /jee/ *int.* (usu. foll. by *up*) command to a horse etc. to start or go faster. [origin unknown]

**geebung** /**jee**-bung/ *n.* **1** fruit (of any of several Australian shrubs or small trees of the genus *Persoonia*) having an edible fleshy layer around the stone. **2** this shrub or tree. [Dharuk, probably *jibung*]

**geek** *n.* **1** *colloq.* a look (*take a geek at that!*). **2** a dull or socially inept person. [British dial.]

**geese** *pl.* of GOOSE.

**geez** /jeez/ *int.* expression of surprise etc. [probably an abbreviation of *Jesus*]

**geezer** /**gee**-zuh/ *n.* *colloq.* **1** peculiar person. **2** person, bloke, etc. **3** an old man. [British dial. *guiser* mummer]

**Geiger counter** /**guy**-guh/ *n.* device for detecting and measuring radioactivity. [H. *Geiger*, German physicist (d. 1945)]

**geisha** /**gay**-shuh, **gee**-shuh/ *n.* (*pl.* same or **-s**) Japanese woman trained to entertain men. [Japanese]

**gel** /jel/ — *n.* **1** semi-solid jelly-like colloid. **2** jelly-like substance used for setting the hair. — *v.* (**-ll-**) **1** form a gel. **2** use gel (in hair) to create a hairdo. **3** = JELL 2. [from GELATINE]

**gelatine** /**jel**-uh-teen, jel-uh-**teen**/ *n.* transparent tasteless substance extracted from skin, tendons, etc., used in cookery, photography, etc. □ **gelatinise** /juh-**lat**-uh-ˌnuyz/ *v.* (also **-ize**) (**-sing** or **-zing**). [Italian: related to JELLY]

**gelatinous** /juh-**lat**-uh-nuhs/ *adj.* of a jelly-like consistency.

**gelato** /juh-**lah**-toh/ *n.* (*pl.* **-s** or **gelati** /juh-**lah**-tee/) kind of Italian ice-cream made with water (sometimes with milk). [Italian]

■ **Usage** The Italian *pl.* *gelati* is often treated as a *sing.* in Australian usage.

**geld** /geld/ *v.* castrate. [Old Norse]

**gelding** *n.* gelded animal, esp. a horse.

**gelignite** /**jel**-uhg-ˌnuyt/ *n.* explosive made from nitroglycerine. [from GELATINE, IGNEOUS]

**gelled** /jeld/ *adj.* (of hair) set with GEL (*boys with gelled hair in spikes*).

**gem** /jem/ *n.* **1** precious stone, esp. cut and polished or engraved. **2** thing or person of great beauty or worth. [Latin *gemma* bud, jewel]

**gemfish** *n.* (also **hake**) popular food fish, found off the coast of NSW and Victoria.

**geminate** — *adj.* /**jem**-uh-nuht/ combined in pairs. — *v.* /**jem**-uh-ˌnayt/ (**-ting**) **1** double, repeat. **2** arrange in pairs. □ **gemination** /-**nay**-shuhn/ *n.* [Latin: related to GEMINI]

**Gemini** /**jem**-uh-ˌnuy, -ˌnee/ *n.* (*pl.* **-s**) **1** constellation and third sign of the zodiac (the Twins). **2** person born when the sun is in this sign. [Latin, = twins]

**gemma** /**jem**-uh/ *n.* (*pl.* **gemmae** /-ee/) small cellular body in plants such as mosses, that separates from the mother-plant and starts a new one. [Latin, see GEM]

**gemmation** /juh-**may**-shuhn/ *n.* reproduction by gemmae.

**gemstone** *n.* precious stone used as a gem.

**gen** /jen/ *colloq.* — *n.* information. — *v.* (**-nn-**) (foll. by *up*) gain or give information. [probably *gen*eral information]

**-gen** *comb. form* *Chem.* that which produces (*hydrogen*; *antigen*). [Greek *-genes* born]

**gendarme** /**zhon**-dahm/ *n.* (in French-speaking countries) police officer. [French *gens d'armes* men of arms]

**gender** /**jen**-duh/ *n.* **1 a** classification roughly corresponding to the two sexes and sexlessness. **b** class of noun according to this classification (see MASCULINE, FEMININE, NEUTER). **2** a person's sex. [Latin GENUS]

**gender gap** *n.* purported divergence between males and females in customs, attitudes, patterns of behaviour, etc.

**gene** /jeen/ *n.* unit in a chromosome determining heredity. [German]

**genealogy** /ˌjee-nee-**al**-uh-jee/ *n.* (*pl.* **-ies**) **1** line of descent traced continuously from an ancestor. **2** study of lines of descent. **3** organism's line of development from earlier forms. □ **genealogical** /-uh-**loj**-i-kuhl/ *adj.* **genealogically** *adv.* **genealogist** *n.* [Greek *genea* race]

**genera** /**jen**-uh-ruh/ *pl.* of GENUS.

**general** /jen-ruhl, jen-uh-ruhl/ — *adj.* **1** including or affecting all or most parts or cases of things. **2** prevalent, usual (*the general feeling*). **3** not partial or particular or local. **4** not limited in application, true of all or nearly all cases (*as a general rule*). **5** not restricted or specialised (*general knowledge; general hospital*). **6** not detailed (*general idea*). **7** vague (*spoke only in general terms*). **8** chief, head; having overall authority (*general manager; Secretary-General*). — *n.* **1** commander of an army. **2** strategist (*a great general*). **3** head of a religious order, e.g. of Jesuits etc. □ **in general 1** as a normal rule; usually. **2** for the most part. [Latin *generalis*]

**general anaesthetic** *n.* anaesthetic affecting the whole body, usu. with loss of consciousness.

**General Australian** *n.* pronunciation of Australian English used by the majority of Australians.

**general election** *n.* national parliamentary election.

**generalise** /jen-ruh-ˌluyz, jen-uh-ruh-ˌluyz/ *v.* (also **-ize**) (**-sing** or **-zing**) **1 a** speak in general or indefinite terms. **b** form general notions. **2** reduce to a general statement. **3** infer (a rule etc.) from particular cases. **4** bring into general use. □ **generalisation** /-zay-shuhn/ *n.*

**generality** /ˌjen-uh-ral-uh-tee/ *n.* (*pl.* **-ies**) **1** general statement or rule. **2** general applicability. **3** lack of detail. **4** (foll. by *of*) main body or majority.

**generally** /jen-ruh-lee, jen-uh-ruh-lee/ *adv.* **1** usually; in most respects or cases (*generally get up early; was generally well-behaved*). **2** in a general sense; without regard to particulars or exceptions (*generally speaking*). **3** for the most part (*not generally known*).

**general meeting** *n.* meeting open to all the members of a society etc.

**general practitioner** *n.* (*abbr.* **GP**) community doctor treating cases of all kinds in the first instance, opp. a specialist.

**general store** *n.* shop which stocks a wide range of miscellaneous goods, esp. in a country town.

**general strike** *n.* simultaneous strike of workers in all or most trades and industries.

**generate** /jen-uh-ˌrayt/ *v.* (**-ting**) bring into existence; produce. [Latin: related to GENUS]

**generation** /ˌjen-uh-ray-shuhn/ *n.* **1** all the people born at about the same time. **2 a** single stage in a family history (*three generations were present in the photograph*). **b** stage in an immigrant family's lineage (*first generation Australian*). **3** stage in (esp. technological) development (*fourth-generation computers*). **4** average time in which children are ready to take the place of their parents (about 30 years). **5** production, esp. of electricity. **6** procreation. [Latin: related to GENERATE]

**generation gap** *n.* differences of outlook between different generations.

**generative** /jen-uh-ruh-tiv/ *adj.* **1** of procreation. **2** productive.

**generator** /jen-uh-ˌray-tuh/ *n.* **1** machine for converting mechanical into electrical energy. **2** apparatus for producing gas, steam, etc.

**generic** /juh-ne-rik/ — *adj.* **1** characteristic of or relating to a class; general, not specific or special. **2** *Biol.* characteristic of or belonging to a genus. **3** (of e.g. supermarket goods) having no brand name. — *n.* such a product (in e.g. a supermarket) sold under the name of the product itself (e.g. coffee) and not under a brand name. □ **generically** *adv.* [Latin: related to GENUS]

**generous** /jen-uh-ruhs, jen-ruhs/ *adj.* **1** giving or given freely. **2** magnanimous, unprejudiced. **3** abundant, copious. □ **generosity** /-ros-uh-tee/ *n.* **generously** *adv.* [Latin: related to GENUS]

**genesis** /jen-uh-suhs/ *n.* **1** origin; mode of formation. **2** (**Genesis**) first book of the Old Testament, with an account of the Creation. [Greek *gen-* be produced]

**gene therapy** *n.* introduction of normal genes into cells in place of defective or missing ones in order to correct genetic disorders.

**genetic** /juh-net-ik/ *adj.* **1** of genetics or genes. **2** of or in origin. □ **genetically** *adv.* [from GENESIS]

**genetic code** *n.* arrangement of genetic information in chromosomes.

**genetic engineering** *n.* manipulation of DNA to modify hereditary features.

**genetic fingerprinting** *n.* (also **genetic profiling**) identifying individuals by DNA patterns.

**genetics** *n.pl.* (treated as *sing.*) the study of heredity and the variation of inherited characteristics. □ **geneticist** /-tuh-suhst/ *n.*

**genial** /jee-nee-uhl/ *adj.* **1** jovial, sociable, kindly. **2** (of the climate) mild and warm; conducive to growth. **3** cheering. □ **geniality** /-al-uh-tee/ *n.* **genially** *adv.* [Latin: related to GENIUS]

**genie** /jee-nee/ n. (pl. **genii** /-nee-,uy/) (in Arabian tales) spirit or goblin with magical powers. [French *génie* GENIUS: cf. JINNEE]

**genital** /jen-uh-tuhl/ — adj. of animal reproduction or the reproductive organs. — n. (in pl.) reproductive organs, esp. the external sex organs. [Latin *gigno genit-* beget]

**genitalia** /,jen-uh-**tay**-lee-uh/ n.pl. genitals. [Latin, neuter pl. of *genitalis*: see GENITAL]

**genitive** /jen-uh-tiv/ n. Gram. case expressing possession or close association, corresponding to *of*, *from*, etc. [Latin: related to GENITAL]

**genius** /jee-nee-uhs/ n. (pl. **geniuses** for definitions 1, 4, 5; **genii** for definitions 2, 3) **1 a** exceptional intellectual or creative power or other natural ability or tendency. **b** person with this. **2** tutelary spirit of a person, place, etc. **3** spirit powerfully influencing a person for good or evil. **4** person powerfully influencing another for good or evil (*he is my evil genius*). **5** prevalent feeling or association etc. of a people or place. [Latin]

**genocide** /jen-uh-,suyd/ n. deliberate extermination of a people or nation. □ **genocidal** /-suy-duhl/ adj. [Greek *genos* race, -CIDE]

**genome** /jee-nohm/ n. **1** the haploid set of chromosomes of an organism. **2** the genetic material of an organism. [GENE, CHROMOSOME]

**-genous** comb. form forming adjectives meaning 'produced' (*endogenous*).

**genre** /zhon-ruh/ n. **1** kind or style (of literature, art, etc.). **2** painting depicting scenes from ordinary life. [French: related to GENDER]

**gent** n. colloq. (often joc.) **1** gentleman. **2** (**the gents**) colloq. men's public toilet. [shortening of GENTLEMAN]

**genteel** /jen-teel/ adj. **1 a** cultured, well-bred, well-mannered. **b** iron. of or appropriate to the upper classes. **2** affected, excessively refined or stylish. □ **genteelly** adv. [French *gentil*: related to GENTLE]

**gentile** /jen-tuyl/ — adj. not Jewish; heathen. — n. person who is not Jewish. [Latin *gentilis* from *gens* family]

**gentility** /jen-**til**-uh-tee/ n. **1** social superiority. **2** genteel manners or behaviour. [French: related to GENTLE]

**gentle** /jen-tuhl/ adj. (**gentler**, **gentlest**) **1** not rough or severe; mild, kind (*a gentle nature*). **2** moderate (*gentle breeze*). **3** (of birth, pursuits, etc.) honourable, of or fit for people of good social position. **4** quiet; requiring patience (*the gentle art of*

persuasion*). □ **gentleness** n. **gently** adv. [Latin: related to GENTILE]

**gentleman** n. **1** man (in polite or formal use). **2** chivalrous well-bred man. **3** man of good social position (*country gentleman*). **4** (in pl.) (as a form of address) male audience or part of this.

**gentleman convict** n. hist. convict in Australia fitted by prior training for employment in a clerical or professional capacity.

**gentlemanly** /jen-tuhl-,muhn-lee/ adj. like or befitting a gentleman.

**gentleman's agreement** n. (also **gentlemen's agreement**) agreement binding in honour but not legally enforceable.

**gentrification** /,jen-truh-fuh-**kay**-shuhn/ n. upgrading of a working-class urban area by the arrival of more affluent residents. □ **gentrify** /-,fuy/ v. (**-ies, -ied**).

**gentry** /jen-tree/ n.pl. **1** people on the upper levels of society. **2** Brit. people next below the nobility. [French: related to GENTLE]

**genuflect** /jen-yuh-,flekt/ v. bend the right knee (or both knees), esp. in worship. □ **genuflection** /-**flek**-shuhn/ n. (also **genuflexion**). [Latin *genu* knee, *flecto flex-* bend]

**genuine** /jen-yoo-uhn/ adj. **1** really coming from its reputed source etc. **2** properly so called; not sham; sincere. □ **genuinely** adv. **genuineness** n. [Latin]

**genus** /jee-nuhs/ n. (pl. **genera** /jen-uh-ruh/) **1** taxonomic category of animals or plants with common structural characteristics, usu. containing several species. **2** (in logic) kind of things including subordinate kinds or species. **3** kind, class. [Latin *genus -eris*]

**geo-** comb. form earth. [Greek *gē*]

**geocentric** /,jee-oh-**sen**-trik/ adj. **1** considered as viewed from the earth's centre. **2** having the earth as the centre. □ **geocentrically** adv.

**geode** /jee-ohd/ n. **1** cavity lined with crystals. **2** rock containing this. [Greek *geōdēs* earthy]

**geodesic** /,jee-oh-**dee**-zik/ adj. (also **geodetic** /-**det**-ik/) of geodesy.

**geodesic line** n. shortest possible line between two points on a curved surface.

**geodesy** /jee-**od**-uh-see/ n. the study of the shape and area of the earth. [Greek *geōdaisia*]

**geographical** /,jee-uh-**graf**-i-kuhl/ adj. (also **geographic**) of geography. □ **geographically** adv.

**geography** /jee-**og**-ruh-fee/ n. **1** science of the earth's physical features, resources, climate, population, etc.

**2** features or arrangement of an area, rooms, etc. □ **geographer** n. [Latin from Greek]

**geology** /jee-**ol**-uh-jee/ n. **1** science of the earth's crust, strata, origin of its rocks, etc. **2** geological features of a district. □ **geological** /,jee-uh-**loj**-i-kuhl/ adj. **geologically** /,jee-uh-**loj**-i-kuh-lee, -klee/ adv. **geologist** n.

**geometric** /,jee-uh-**met**-rik/ adj. (also **geometrical**) **1** of geometry. **2** (of a design etc.) with regular lines and shapes. □ **geometrically** adv.

**geometric progression** n. progression with a constant ratio between successive quantities (as 1, 3, 9, 27).

**geometry** /jee-**om**-uh-tree/ n. science of the properties and relations of lines, surfaces, and solids. □ **geometrician** /,jee-uh-muh-**trish**-uhn/ n. [from GEO-, -METRY]

**geophysics** /,jee-oh-**fiz**-iks/ n.pl. (treated as sing.) physics of the earth.

**Georgian** /**jaw**-juhn/ adj. of the time of the kings of England George I–IV or of George V and VI.

**Geraldton wax** /je-**ruhld**-tuhn/ n. spreading WA shrub of the family Myrtaceae, having hooked linear leaves and a profusion of large waxy flowers ranging in colour from white to pink to deep purple. [Geraldton in WA]

**geranium** /juh-**ray**-nee-uhm/ n. (pl. -s) **1** herb or shrub bearing fruit shaped like a crane's bill. **2** (in general use) cultivated pelargonium. [Greek geranos crane]

**gerbil** /**jer**-buhl/ n. (also **jerbil**) mouselike desert rodent with long hind legs. [French: related to JERBOA]

**geriatric** /,je-ree-**at**-rik/ — adj. **1** of or pertaining to GERIATRICS. **2** colloq. a offens. of old people. **b** old, outdated. — n. **1** old person under geriatric care. **2** colloq. offens. any elderly person. [Greek gēras old age, iatros doctor]

■ **Usage** The use of the adjective and noun geriatric in any sense other than the technical (see geriatrics) is considered offensive by most people.

**geriatrics** n.pl. (usu. treated as sing.) branch of medicine or social science dealing with the health and care of old people. □ **geriatrician** /-uh-**trish**-uhn/ n.

**germ** /jerm/ n. **1** micro-organism, esp. one causing disease. **2** portion of an organism capable of developing into a new one; rudiment of an animal or plant in seed (wheat germ). **3** original idea etc. from which something may develop; elementary principle. □ **germy** adj. (-ier, -iest). [Latin germen sprout]

**German** /**jer**-muhn/ — n. **1 a** native or national of Germany. **b** person of German descent. **2** language of Germany. — adj. of Germany or its people or language. [Latin Germanus]

**german** /**jer**-muhn/ adj. (placed after brother, sister, or cousin) having both parents the same, or both grandparents the same on one side (brother german; cousin german). [Latin germanus]

**germane** /jer-**mayn**/ adj. (usu. foll. by to) relevant (to a subject). [var. of GERMAN]

**Germanic** /jer-**man**-ik/ — adj. **1** having German characteristics. **2** hist. of the Germans. **3** of the Scandinavians, Anglo-Saxons, or Germans. — n. **1** the branch of Indo-European languages which includes English, German, Dutch, and the Scandinavian languages. **2** the primitive language of Germanic peoples.

**germanium** /jer-**may**-nee-uhm/ n. brittle greyish-white semi-metallic element. [related to GERMAN]

**German measles** n.pl. = RUBELLA.

**German sausage** n. = DEVON.

**German shepherd** n. large wolf-like dog, much used as a police-dog, guard-dog, etc.

**germicide** /**jer**-muh-,suyd/ n. substance that destroys germs. □ **germicidal** /-**suy**-duhl/ adj.

**germinal** /**jer**-muh-nuhl/ adj. **1** of germs. **2** in the earliest stage of development. **3** productive of new ideas. □ **germinally** adv. [related to GERM]

**germinate** /**jer**-muh-,nayt/ v. (-ting) **1** sprout, bud, or develop. **2** cause to do this. □ **germination** /-**nay**-shuhn/ n. **germinator** n. **germinative** adj. [Latin: related to GERM]

**germ warfare** n. use of germs to spread disease in war.

**gerontology** /,je-ruhn-**tol**-uh-jee/ n. the study of old age and the process of ageing. [Greek gerōn geront- old man]

**gerrymander** — v. /,je-ree-**man**-duh/ manipulate the boundaries of (an electorate etc.) to gain unfair electoral advantage. — n. /**je**-ree-,man-duh/ this practice. [Governor Gerry of Massachusetts, (SALA)MANDER, from the shape of one of the districts on a redrawn map of 1812]

**gerund** /**je**-ruhnd/ n. verbal noun, in English ending in -ing (e.g. do you mind my asking you?). [Latin]

**Gestapo** /guh-**stah**-poh/ n. hist. Nazi secret police. [German, from Geheime Staats polizei]

**gestation** /jes-**tay**-shuhn/ n. **1 a** process of carrying or being carried in the uterus between conception and birth. **b** this period. **2** development of a plan, idea, etc. □ **gestate** /jes-tayt/ v. (**-ting**). [Latin *gesto gestat-* carry]

**gesticulate** /jes-tik-yuh-ˌlayt/ v. (**-ting**) **1** use gestures instead of, or to reinforce, speech. **2** express thus. □ **gesticulation** /-ˌlay-shuhn/ n. [Latin: related to GESTURE]

**gesture** /jes-chuh/ — n. **1** significant movement of hands, head, body, etc. **2** use of such movements to convey a particular feeling. **3** action to evoke a response or convey intention, usu. friendly. **4** a token or not very committed response (*he made a gesture towards reconciliation*). — v. (**-ring**) gesticulate. [Latin *gestura* from *gero gest-* wield]

**get** v. (**getting**; *past* and *past part.* **got** (and in *comb.*) **1** come into possession of; receive or earn (*get a job; got $400 a week*). **2** fetch or procure (*get my book for me; got a new car*). **3** go to reach or catch (a bus, train, etc.). **4** prepare (a meal etc.). **5 a** (cause to) reach some state or become (*get rich; get married; got him into trouble*). **b** cause to happen (*got my legs waxed; got the fire going*). **6** obtain as a result of calculation (*if you take 3 from 10 you get 7*). **7** contract (a disease etc.). **8** establish contact by telephone etc. with; receive (a broadcast signal) (*get him on the phone; getting ABC FM clearly*). **9** experience or suffer; have inflicted on one; receive as one's lot or penalty (*got four years in prison*). **10 a** succeed in bringing, placing, etc. (*get it round the corner; get it on to the agenda*). **b** (cause to) succeed in coming or going (*will get you there somehow; got absolutely nowhere; got home*). **11** (prec. by *have*) **a** possess (*have not got a cent*). **b** (foll. by *to* + infin.) be bound or obliged (*have got to see you*). **12** (foll. by *to* + infin.) induce; prevail upon (*got them to help me*). **13** *colloq.* understand (a person or an argument) (*I get your point; do you get me?*). **14 a** *colloq.* harm, injure, kill, esp. in retaliation (*I'll get you for that*). **b** strike, hit (*the arrow got him in the neck*). **15** *colloq.* **a** annoy (*it gets me the way you pick your nose in public*). **b** affect emotionally (*Bach gets me*). **c** attract (*she gets me, fair dinkum, so how do I arrange to meet her?*). **16** (foll. by *to* + infin.) develop an inclination (*am getting to like it*). **17** (foll. by verbal noun) begin (*get going*). **18** establish (an idea etc.) in one's mind (*he's got it in his head that . . .*). **19** (esp. in *past* or *perfect*) catch in an argument; corner; puzzle (*that riddle's got me*). **20** *colloq.* be off; go away (*go on, get!*). □ **get about 1 a** travel extensively or fast; go from place to place. **b** (of news,

rumours, etc.) spread. **2** begin walking etc. (esp. after illness). **get across 1** communicate (an idea etc.). **2** (of an idea etc.) be communicated. **get ahead** make progress (esp. in a career etc.). **get along** (or **on**) (often foll. by *together*, *with*) live harmoniously. **get around** = *get about*. **get at 1** reach; get hold of. **2** *colloq.* imply (*what are you getting at?*). **3** *colloq.* nag, criticise. **4** *colloq.* corrupt, as by bribery etc. (*they say the jury was got at*). **get away 1 a** escape. **b** start (e.g. horses in a race). **2** (as *int.*) *colloq.* expressing disbelief or scepticism. **3** (foll. by *with*) escape blame or punishment for (*he's rich enough to get away with murder*). **get away from it all** leave behind the pressures of work, family, etc., by e.g. travelling. **get back 1** return; get in touch with again. **2** receive as profit etc. **get back at** *colloq.* retaliate against. **get by** *colloq.* manage, even if with difficulty. **get cracking** see CRACK. **get down 1** alight, descend (from a vehicle, ladder, etc.). **2** record in writing. **get a person down** depress, lower the spirits of him or her. **get down to** begin working on. **get the drop on a person** *colloq.* gain the upper hand over. **get even with** be revenged against. **get a hammering** (or **get hammered**) *colloq.* be soundly beaten (*our team got hammered yesterday*). **get hold of** grasp, secure, acquire, obtain; make contact with (a person). **get a hold on oneself** take control of oneself. **get in 1** arrive; obtain a place in a university etc. **2** be elected. **get in for one's chop** *colloq.* seek one's rightful share (or what one can contrive to get). **get in good with a person** *colloq.* wheedle one's way into favour, esp. in a crawling way. **get in on the act** (or **action**) *colloq.* involve oneself in. **get into** *colloq.* become deeply interested in (*I just can't get into classical music*). **get it** *colloq.* be punished. **get it (all) together** *colloq.* succeed in acquiring equilibrium of body, mind, will, etc.; become efficient. **get a kick out of** *colloq.* receive much satisfaction from. **get one's** (or **a**) **leg in the door** *colloq.* make a start towards succeeding in something. **get off 1** *colloq.* (cause to) be acquitted; escape with little or no punishment. **2** start. **3** alight from (a bus etc.). **4** (foll. by *with*, *together*) *colloq.* form an amorous relationship, esp. quickly. **get on 1** make progress; manage. **2** enter (a bus etc.). **3** = *get along*. **4** (usu. as **getting on**) grow old. **get on to** *colloq.* **1** make contact with. **2** understand; become aware of. **3** (as *imper.*) just look at! (*get on to that guy with the long hair!*). **get out 1** leave or escape or help to do this. **2** manage to go outdoors. **3** alight from a vehicle. **4** transpire; become known. **get out from under** extricate (oneself) from a situation which has collapsed (on one). **get out of** avoid or escape (a duty etc.). **get over 1** recover from (an illness, upset, etc.). **2** overcome (a difficulty). **3** =*get across*. **get a thing over** (or **over and done with**) complete a tedious task quickly. **get one's own back** *colloq.* have one's revenge. **get real** *colloq.* wake up (to oneself, to facts, etc.). **get rid of** see RID. **get round 1** coax or cajole (a person) esp. to secure a favour. **2** evade (a law etc.). **get round to** deal with (a task etc.) in due course. **get somewhere** make progress; be initially successful. **get stuck into a person** *colloq.* **1** verbally abuse. **2** attack physically. **get stuck into something** *colloq.* begin (working, eating, etc.) energetically. **get there** *colloq.* succeed. **get through 1** pass (an examination etc.). **2** finish or use up (esp. resources). **3** make contact by telephone, fax, etc. **4** (foll. by *to*) succeed in making (a person) understand. **get together** gather, assemble. **get up 1** rise from sitting etc., or from bed after sleeping etc. **2** (of wind etc.) begin to be strong. **3** prepare or organise. **4** produce or stimulate (*get up steam*). **5** (often *refl.*) dress or arrange elaborately; arrange the appearance of. **6** (foll. by *to*) *colloq.* indulge or be involved in (*always getting up to mischief*). **7** win a race etc. (*did your horse get up in the Melbourne Cup?*). **get with it** *colloq.* **1** become more aware of. **2** become more up-to-date. **get a person wrong** misunderstand (*don't get me wrong, but...*). [Old Norse]

**get-at-able** /get-at-uh-buhl/ *adj. colloq.* accessible.

**getaway** — *n.* **1** escape, esp. after a crime etc. **2** holiday involving travel. — *adj.* pertaining to a getaway (*getaway car; getaway holiday on the Gold Coast; getaway tours*).

**get-together** *n. colloq.* social gathering.

**get-up** *n. colloq.* **1 a** style or arrangement of dress etc. **b** clothing, outfit (*his get-up was weird*). **2** style or layout etc. of something (*the get-up of his kitchen was quite stunning*).

**get-up-and-go** *n.* *colloq.* energy, enthusiasm.

**geyser** /gee-zuh, guy-zuh/ *n.* intermittent hot spring. [Icelandic *Geysir* from *geysa* to gush]

**Ghan** /gahn/ *n.* **1** = AFGHAN. **2** (prec. by *the*) train running on the Central Australian Railway.

**ghastly** /gahst-lee/ *adj.* (**-ier**, **-iest**) **1** horrible, frightful. **2** *colloq.* terrible,

unpleasant. **3** deathlike, pallid. □ **ghastliness** *n.* [obsolete *gast* terrify]

**ghee** /gee/ *n.* Indian clarified butter. [Hindi *ghī*, from Sanskrit]

**gherkin** /ger-kuhn/ *n.* small pickled cucumber. [Dutch]

**ghetto** /get-oh/ *n.* (*pl.* **-s** or **-es**) **1** part of a city occupied by a minority group. **2** *hist.* Jewish quarter in a city. **3** segregated group or area. [Italian]

**ghetto blaster** *n. colloq.* large portable radio, esp. for playing loud pop music.

**ghost** /gohst/ — *n.* **1** supposed apparition of a dead person or animal; disembodied spirit. **2** shadow or semblance (*not a ghost of a chance*). **3** secondary image in a defective telescope or television picture. — *v.* (often foll. by *for*) act as ghost writer of (a work). □ **give up the ghost 1** die. **2** (of equipment etc.) cease functioning. □ **ghostliness** *n.* **ghostly** *adj.* (**-ier**, **-iest**). [Old English]

**ghost gum** *n.* northern Australian eucalypt with smooth, shimmering white bark.

**ghosting** *n.* appearance of a 'ghost' image in a television picture.

**ghost town** *n.* town with few or no remaining inhabitants.

**ghost writer** *n.* person who writes on behalf of the credited author.

**ghoul** /gool/ *n.* **1** person morbidly interested in death etc. **2** evil spirit or phantom. **3** spirit in Muslim folklore preying on corpses. □ **ghoulish** *adj.* **ghoulishly** *adv.* [Arabic *ghūl*]

**GI** /jee-uy/ *n.* (often *attrib.*) soldier in the US army. [abbreviation of *government* (or *general*) *issue*]

**giant** /juy-uhnt/ — *n.* **1** (*fem.* **giantess**) imaginary or mythical being of human form but superhuman size. **2** person or thing of great size, ability, courage, etc. — *attrib. adj.* **1** gigantic. **2** of a very large kind. [Greek *gigas gigant-*]

**giant lily** *n.* = GYMEA LILY.

**giant perch** *n.* = BARRAMUNDI.

**gibber**[1] /jib-uh/ *v.* jabber inarticulately. [imitative]

**gibber**[2] /gib-uh/ *n.* stone, rock, boulder. [Dharuk *giba* stone]

**gibber bird** *n.* (also **gibber chat**, **desert chat**) small yellow and brown bird inhabiting gibber country in central Australia.

**gibber country** *n.* = GIBBER PLAIN.

**gibberish** /jib-uh-rish/ *n.* unintelligible or meaningless speech; nonsense.

**gibber plain** /gib-uh/ *n.* arid, stony area of low relief in which stones form a surface layer.

**gibbet** /jib-uht/ — n. hist. **1 a** gallows. **b** post with an arm on which an executed criminal was hanged. **2** (prec. by the) death by hanging. — v. (-t-) **1** put to death by hanging. **2** expose or hang up on a gibbet. [French gibet]

**gibbon** /gib-uhn/ n. long-armed SE Asian anthropoid ape. [French]

**gibbous** /gib-uhs/ adj. **1** convex. **2** (of a moon or planet) having the bright part greater than a semicircle and less than a circle. **3** humpbacked. [Latin gibbus hump]

**gibe** /juyb/ (also **jibe**) — v. (-bing) (often foll. by at) jeer, mock. — n. jeering remark, taunt. [perhaps from French giber handle roughly]

**giblets** /jib-luhts/ n.pl. edible organs (heart, gizzard, liver) of a bird, removed and usu. cooked separately. [French gibelet game stew]

**gidday** /guh-day/ contr. colloq. = GOODDAY.

**giddy** /gid-ee/ adj. (-ier, -iest) **1** dizzy, tending to fall or stagger. **2 a** mentally intoxicated (giddy with success). **b** excitable, frivolous, flighty. **3** making dizzy (giddy heights). □ **giddily** adv. **giddiness** n. [Old English gidig insane, literally 'possessed by a god']

**gidgee** /gij-ee/ n. **1** wattle tree which at times emits a disagreeable smell, stinkwattle. **2** Aboriginal spear. [Yuwaalaraay gijir]

**gift** /gift/ n. **1** thing given; present. **2** natural ability or talent. **3** the power to give (in his gift). **4** giving. **5** colloq. easy task; anything easily or cheaply obtained. □ **have the gift of the gab** be endowed with fast-talking, smooth (perhaps suspect) eloquence. **look a gift-horse in the mouth** (usu. neg.) find fault with what has been freely given. [Old Norse: related to GIVE]

**gifted** adj. talented; intelligent.

**gift-wrap** — v. **1** wrap (a gift) in attractive paper etc. **2** present something inferior in an attractive way (his argument was gift-wrapped in fine-sounding words). — n. (**giftwrap**; also **gift-wrapping**) attractive covering for a gift etc.

**gig¹** /gig/ n. **1** light two-wheeled one-horse carriage. **2** light ship's boat for rowing or sailing. **3** rowing-boat esp. for racing. [probably imitative]

**gig²** /gig/ colloq. — n. engagement to play music etc., usu. for one night. — v. (-gg-) perform a gig. [origin unknown]

**gig³** /gig/ colloq. — n. **1** a fool or figure of fun (having a gig at the neighbours). — v. **1** mock or make fun of. **2** peek at inquisitively. [British dial.]

**giga-** comb. form one thousand million (10⁹). [Greek: related to GIANT]

**gigantic** /juy-gan-tik/ adj. huge, giant-like. □ **gigantically** adv. [Latin: related to GIANT]

**gigantic lily** n. = GYMEA LILY.

**giggle** /gig-uhl/ — v. (-ling) laugh in half-suppressed spasms. — n. **1** such a laugh. **2** colloq. amusing person or thing; joke (did it for a giggle). □ **giggler** n. **giggly** adj. (-ier, -iest). [imitative]

**gigolo** /jig-uh-loh, zhig-/ n. (pl. -s) **1** young man paid by an older woman to be her escort or lover. **2** colloq. a womaniser. [French]

**gild** /gild/ v. (past part. **gilded** or as adj. in sense 1 **gilt**) **1** cover thinly with gold. **2** tinge with a golden colour. **3** give a false brilliance to. □ **gild the lily** try to improve what is already satisfactory. [Old English: related to GOLD]

**gilgai** /gil-guy/ n. **1** low-relief terrain in inland Australia characterised by hollows and mounds formed by expansion and contraction of the surface. **2** a hollow in such a terrain in which water collects, waterhole. [Wiradhuri and Kamilaroi gilgaay]

**gilgie** /jil-gee/ n. (also **jilgie**) WA name for YABBY. [Nyungar jilgi]

**gill¹** /gil/ n. (usu. in pl.) **1** respiratory organ in a fish etc. **2** vertical radial plate on the underside of a mushroom etc. **3** flesh below a person's jaws and ears. □ **fed up to the gills** colloq. utterly discontented or frustrated. **green** (or **white**) **at** (or **about** or **around**) **the gills** colloq. **1** thoroughly nauseous and showing it. **2** inexperienced. [Old Norse]

**gill²** /jil, gil/ n. imperial unit of liquid measure equal to ¼ pint (142 ml). [French]

**gilt** /gilt/ — adj. **1** thinly covered with gold. **2** gold-coloured. — n. gold or gold-like material applied in gilding. [from GILD]

**gilt-edged** adj. (of securities, stocks, etc.) having a high degree of reliability.

**gimlet** /gim-luht/ n. **1** small tool with a screw-tip for boring holes. **2** slender WA eucalypt, the trunk of which is characteristically very twisted, shiny, and bronze-coloured. [French]

**gimlet eye** n. eye with a piercing glance.

**gimmick** /gim-ik/ n. trick or device to attract attention or publicity, or, esp., to deceive (the price is too good to be true — so what's the gimmick?). □ **gimmickry** n. **gimmicky** adj. [origin unknown]

**gin¹** /jin/ n. spirit made from grain or malt and flavoured with juniper berries. [Dutch geneva: related to JUNIPER]

**gin²** /jin/ *n.* (now *derog.*) Aboriginal woman. [Dharuk *diyin* woman, wife]

**gin³** — *n.* **1** snare, trap. **2** machine separating cotton from its seeds. **3** a kind of crane and windlass. — *v.* (**-nn-**) **1** treat (cotton) in a gin. **2** trap. [French: related to ENGINE]

**ging** /ging/ *n.* child's catapult, SHANGHAI. [origin uncertain]

**ginger** /jin-juh/ — *n.* **1 a** hot spicy root usu. powdered for use in cooking, or preserved in syrup, or candied. **b** plant having this root. **2** light reddish-yellow. **3** spirit, mettle. — *adj.* of a ginger colour. — *v.* **1** flavour with ginger. **2** (foll. by *up*) enliven. □ **gingery** *adj.* [Old English, ultimately from Sanskrit, = horn-body, referring to the antler-shape of the root]

**gingerbread** — *n.* ginger-flavoured treacle cake. — *attrib. adj.* gaudy, tawdry.

**ginger group** *n.* group urging a party or movement to stronger policy or action (*Labor ginger group in caucus*).

**gingerly** — *adv.* in a careful or cautious manner. — *adj.* showing great care or caution. [perhaps from French *gensor* delicate]

**gingham** /ging-uhm/ *n.* plain-woven cotton cloth, esp. striped or checked. [Dutch from Malay]

**gingivitis** /,jin-juh-**vuy**-tuhs/ *n.* inflammation of the gums. [Latin *gingiva* GUM², -ITIS]

**gink¹** /gingk/ *n.* colloq. fellow (*stupid gink*). [origin unknown]

**gink²** /gingk/ *n.* colloq. a scrutinising look. [probably an alteration of GEEK]

**ginkgo** /ging-koh/ *n.* (also **maidenhair tree**) (*pl.* **-s**) tree with fan-shaped leaves and yellow flowers. [Chinese, = silver apricot]

**ginormous** /juy-**naw**-muhs/ *adj.* colloq. enormous. [from GIGANTIC, ENORMOUS]

**ginseng** /jin-seng/ *n.* **1** plant found in E. Asia and N. America. **2** root of this used as a medicinal tonic. [Chinese]

**gipsy** /jip-see/ — *n.* (also **gypsy**) (*pl.* **-ies**) **1** (usu. **Gipsy**) member of a nomadic people of Europe and North America, of Hindu origin, with dark skin and hair. **2** one whose looks, lifestyle, etc. suggest a Gipsy. — *adj.* of or pertaining to the Gipsies. [from earlier *gipcyan* Egyptian]

**giraffe** /juh-**rahf**/ *n.* (*pl.* same or **-s**) large four-legged African animal with a spotted skin, long neck and forelegs. [French, ultimately from Arabic *zarāfa*]

**gird** /gerd/ *v.* (*past* and *past part.* **girded** or **girt**) **1** encircle, attach, or secure, with a belt or band. **2** enclose or encircle. **3** (foll. by *round*) place (a cord etc.) round.

**4** (often foll. by *up*) prepare for action. □ **gird** (or **gird up**) **one's loins** prepare for action. [Old English]

**girder** *n.* iron or steel beam or compound structure for bridge-building etc.

**girdle** /ger-duhl/ — *n.* **1** belt or cord worn round the waist. **2** corset. **3** thing that surrounds. **4** bony support for the limbs (*pelvic girdle*). — *v.* (**-ling**) surround with a girdle. [Old English]

**girl** /gerl/ *n.* **1** female child, daughter. **2** young woman. **3** *colloq.* girlfriend. **4** female servant. □ **the girls** a woman's close circle of female friends. □ **girlhood** *n.* **girlish** *adj.* **girly** *adj.* [origin uncertain]

**girlfriend** *n.* **1** person's regular female companion or lover. **2** female friend.

**girl guide** *n.* a member of the organisation known as the Girl Guides (see SCOUT¹ *n.* 4).

**girt** see GIRD.

**girth** /gerth/ *n.* **1** distance round a thing. **2** band round the body of a horse to secure the saddle etc. [Old Norse: related to GIRD]

**gismo** var. of GIZMO.

**gist** /jist/ *n.* substance or essence of a matter. [Latin *jaceo* LIE¹]

**give** /giv/ — *v.* (**-ving**; *past* **gave**; *past part.* **given** /**giv**-uhn/) **1** transfer the possession of freely; hand over as a present; donate (*gave her his collection of prints; gives generously to AIDS research*). **2 a** transfer temporarily; provide with (*gave him the dog to hold; gave her a new hip*). **b** administer (medicine). **c** deliver (a message) (*give her my best wishes*). **3** (usu. foll. by *for*) make over in exchange or payment (*gave him $30 for the bicycle*). **4 a** confer; grant (a benefit, honour, etc.). **b** accord; bestow (love, time, etc.). **c** award; administer (praise, blame, etc.) (*gave him the sack; give him my blessing; gave him a talking-to*). **d** pledge (*give his word*). **5 a** perform (an action etc.) (*gave a jump; gave a performance*). **b** utter; declare (*gave a shriek; gave the batsman out*). **6** (in *passive*; foll. by *to*) be inclined to or fond of (*is given to boasting; is given to strong drink*). **7** yield to pressure; collapse (*the tent's beginning to give*). **8** yield as a product or result (*this paddock gives feed for twenty cows; the lamp gives a poor light; gives an average of 7*). **9** (usu. foll. by *of*) grant; bestow (*gave freely of his time*). **10 a** consign, put (*gave him into custody*). **b** sanction the marriage of (a daughter etc.). **11** devote; dedicate (*gave his life to the cause*). **12** present; offer; show; hold out (*gives no sign of life; gave her his arm; give me an example*). **13** impart; be a source of;

cause (*gave him my sore throat; gave me trouble; gave much pain*). **14** concede (*I give you the benefit of the doubt*). **15** deliver (a judgment etc.) authoritatively (*gave his verdict*). **16** provide (a party, meal, etc.) as host. **17** (as *past part.*) assume or grant or specify (*given the circumstances; in a given situation; given that we earn so little*). **18** (*absol.*) *colloq.* tell what one knows (*you've got ten seconds: give!*). **19** *colloq.* take place; happen (*so what gives in your neck of the woods?*). **20** *colloq.* tell; mention as excuse or explanation (*don't give me that!*). — *n.* capacity to yield or comply; elasticity (*there's no give in his attitudes; this rubber band's lost its give*). □ **give and take 1** exchange of words, ideas, blows, etc. **2** ability to compromise. **give away 1** transfer as a gift. **2** hand over (a bride) to a bridegroom. **3** reveal (a secret etc.). **4** betray (*don't give me away*). **5** abandon (*he's had to give surfing away*). **give a person a break** *colloq.* cease pestering or importuning. **give a person the chop** (or **the boot**) *colloq.* sack unceremoniously; spurn decisively. **give a person the cold shoulder** *colloq.* snub by pointedly ignoring him or her. **give the dinkum oil** (or **the drum**) *colloq.* give the most accurate information. **give the game away 1** reveal a secret or intention. **2** abandon (something) (*after six years as a hairdresser, he gave the game away*). **give a person a go** *colloq.* be fair to. **give in 1** yield; acknowledge defeat. **2** hand in (a document etc.) to an official etc. **give it a bash** (or **whirl**) *colloq.* attempt, have a go at. **give it a go 1** *colloq.* = *give it a bash*. **2** (a plea for fair treatment) = FAIR GO *int.* (*give it a go, mate, he's too small for you to pick on*). **give it to a person** *colloq.* scold or punish. **give it to a person straight** *colloq.* tell the full, blunt truth with no evasion. **give me** I prefer (*give me Greece any day*). **give off** emit (fumes etc.). **give one's back teeth** (or **right arm**) **for** *colloq.* covet or wish for desperately. **give oneself away** disclose something about oneself unintentionally; make a FREUDIAN SLIP. **give oneself up to** abandon oneself to (despair etc.). **give on to** (or **into**) (of a window, corridor, etc.) overlook or lead into. **give or take** *colloq.* accepting as a margin of error in estimating (*took him ten years to build, give or take a few months*). **give out 1** announce; emit; distribute. **2** be exhausted. **3** run short. **give over 1** *colloq.* stop or desist. **2** hand over. **3** devote. **give rise to** cause. **give a person a serve** *colloq.* criticise or

censure severely. **give a person to understand** inform or assure. **give up 1** resign; surrender. **2** part with. **3** deliver (a wanted person etc.). **4** pronounce incurable or insoluble; renounce hope of. **5** renounce or cease (an activity). **give way** see WAY. **not give a damn** (or **a continental** or **a hang** or **two hoots** etc.) *colloq.* not care at all. □ **giver** *n.* [Old English]

**give-away** *n. colloq.* **1** unintentional revelation. **2** thing given as a gift or at a low price.

**gizmo** /giz-moh/ *n.* (also **gismo**) (*pl.* **-s**) *colloq.* gadget. [origin unknown]

**gizzard** /giz-uhd/ *n.* second part of a bird's stomach, for grinding food. [French]

**glacé** /glas-ay, glah-say/ *adj.* **1** (of fruit, esp. cherries) preserved in sugar. **2** (of cloth etc.) smooth; polished. [French]

**glacial** /glay-shuhl, -see-uhl/ *adj.* **1** of ice in masses. **2** *Geol.* characterised or produced by ice. **3** icy cold (*glacial temperatures*). **4** *Chem.* forming ice-like crystals on freezing (*glacial acetic acid*). [Latin *glacies* ice]

**glacial epoch** (or **period**) *n.* period when an exceptionally large area of the earth's surface was covered by ice; ice age.

**glaciated** /glay-see-,ay-tuhd, glay-shee-, glas-ee-/ *adj.* **1** marked or polished by the action of ice. **2** covered by glaciers or ice sheets. □ **glaciation** /-ay-shuhn/ *n.* [*glaciate* freeze, from Latin: related to GLACIAL]

**glacier** /glay-see-uh, glas-ee-uh/ *n.* mass of land ice formed by the accumulation of snow on high ground. [French: related to GLACIAL]

**glad**[1] *adj.* (**gladder, gladdest**) **1** (*predic.*) pleased. **2** expressing or causing pleasure (*glad cry; glad news*). **3** ready and willing (*am glad to help*). □ **be glad of** find useful, be grateful for (*I'd be glad of some company*). □ **gladly** *adv.* **gladness** *n.* [Old English]

**glad**[2] *n. colloq.* = GLADIOLUS. [abbreviation]

**gladden** /glad-uhn/ *v.* make or become glad.

**gladdie** *n. colloq.* = GLADIOLUS.

**glade** *n.* open space in a forest. [origin unknown]

**gladiator** /glad-ee-,ay-tuh/ *n. hist.* trained fighter in ancient Roman shows. □ **gladiatorial** /-ee-uh-taw-ree-uhl/ *adj.* [Latin *gladius* sword]

**gladiolus** /,glad-ee-oh-luhs/ *n.* (*pl.* **-li** /-luy/ **-luses** /-luhs-uhz/) plant of the lily family with sword-shaped leaves and flower-spikes. [Latin, diminutive of *gladius* sword]

**glad rags** *n.pl. colloq.* best clothes.

**gladsome** /**glad**-suhm/ *adj. poet.* cheerful, joyous.

**gladwrap** /**glad**-ˌrap/ *n. propr.* thin, transparent plastic sheeting used for wrapping food etc.

**glamorise** /**glam**-uh-ˌruyz/ *v.* (also **-ize**) (**-sing** or **-zing**) make glamorous or attractive.

**glamour** /**glam**-uh/ *n.* (also **glamor**) **1** physical, esp. cosmetic, attractiveness. **2** alluring or exciting beauty or charm. □ **glamorous** *adj.* **glamorously** *adv.* [var. of GRAMMAR in obsolete sense 'magic']

**glance** /glahns, glans/ — *v.* (**-cing**) **1** (often foll. by *down, up, over*, etc.) look briefly, direct one's eye. **2** strike at an angle and glide off an object (*glancing blow; ball glanced off his bat*). **3** (usu. foll. by *over*) refer briefly or indirectly to a subject or subjects. **4** (of light etc.) flash or dart. — *n.* **1** brief look. **2** flash or gleam. **3** glancing stroke in cricket. □ **at a glance** immediately upon looking. □ **glancingly** *adv.* [origin uncertain]

**gland** *n.* **1** organ or similar structure secreting substances for use in the body or for ejection. **2** *Bot.* similar organ in a plant. [Latin *glandulae* pl.]

**glandular** /**glan**-dyoo-luh, -juh-/ *adj.* of a gland or glands.

**glandular fever** *n.* infectious viral disease with swelling of the lymph glands.

**glans** /glanz/ *n.* (*pl.* **glandes** /**glan**-deez/) the rounded part forming the end of the penis or clitoris. [Latin, = acorn]

**glare** — *v.* (**-ring**) **1** look fiercely or fixedly. **2** shine dazzlingly or oppressively. — *n.* **1 a** strong fierce light, esp. sunshine. **b** oppressive public attention (*glare of publicity*). **2** fierce or fixed look. **3** tawdry brilliance. [Low German or Dutch]

**glaring** *adj.* **1** obvious, conspicuous (*glaring error*). **2** shining oppressively. □ **glaringly** *adv.*

**glasnost** /**glaz**-nost/ *n.* (in the former Soviet Union) policy of more open government and access to information. [Russian, = openness]

**glass** /glahs/ — *n.* **1 a** (often *attrib.*) hard, brittle, usu. transparent substance, made by fusing sand with soda and lime etc. **b** substance of similar properties. **2** glass objects collectively, glassware. **3 a** glass drinking vessel. **b** its contents. **4** mirror. **5** glazed frame for plants. **6** barometer. **7** covering of a watch-face. **8** lens. **9** (in *pl.*) **a** spectacles. **b** binoculars. — *adj.* of or made from glass. — *v.* (usu. as **glassed** *adj.*) fit with glass. □ **glassful** *n.* (*pl.* **-s**). [Old English]

**glass-blowing** *n.* blowing semi-molten glass to make glassware.

**glass ceiling** *n.* an unofficial or unacknowledged barrier to personal advancement, esp. of a woman or a member of an ethnic minority.

**glasshouse** *n.* = GREENHOUSE.

**glassware** *n.* articles made of glass.

**glassy** *adj.* (**-ier, -iest**) **1** like glass. **2** (of the eye, expression, etc.) abstracted; dull; fixed.

**glaucoma** /glaw-**koh**-muh/ *n.* eye-condition with increased pressure in the eyeball and gradual loss of sight. □ **glaucomatous** *adj.* [Greek *glaukos* greyish blue]

**glaze** — *v.* (**-zing**) **1** fit (a window etc.) with glass or (a building) with windows. **2 a** cover (pottery etc.) with a glaze. **b** fix (paint) on pottery thus. **3** cover (pastry, meat, etc.) with a glaze (sense 2). **4** cover a painted surface etc. with a glaze (sense 3). **5** (often foll. by *over*) (of the eyes) become glassy. **6** give a glassy surface to. — *n.* **1** vitreous substance for glazing pottery. **2** smooth shiny coating of milk, sugar, egg-white, etc. on food. **3** thin coat of transparent paint to modify underlying tone. **4** surface formed by glazing. [from GLASS]

**glazier** /**glay**-zee-uh/ *n.* person whose trade is glazing windows etc.

**gleam** — *n.* **1** faint or brief light. **2** faint, sudden or temporary show (*a gleam of hope*). — *v.* **1** emit gleams, shine. **2** (of a quality) be indicated (*fear gleamed in his eyes*). [Old English]

**glean** *v.* **1** acquire (facts etc.) in small amounts. **2** gather (corn left by reapers). [French]

**gleanings** *n.pl.* things gleaned, esp. facts.

**glee** *n.* **1** mirth; delight. **2** part-song for three or more (esp. male) voices. [Old English]

**gleeful** *adj.* joyful. □ **gleefully** *adv.* **gleefulness** *n.*

**glen** *n.* narrow valley. [Gaelic]

**glib** *adj.* (**glibber, glibbest**) speaking or spoken quickly or fluently but without sincerity. □ **glibly** *adv.* **glibness** *n.* [obsolete *glibbery* slippery, perhaps imitative]

**glide** — *v.* (**-ding**) **1** move smoothly and continuously. **2** (of an aircraft or pilot) fly without engine-power. **3** pass gradually or imperceptibly. **4** go stealthily. **5** cause to glide. — *n.* gliding movement. [Old English]

**glide path** *n.* aircraft's line of descent to land.

**glider** *n.* **1** person who or thing which glides. **2** light aircraft without an engine.

**3** any of various tree-dwelling Australian marsupials (e.g. flying possum, sugar glider, etc.) that glide through the air using flaps of skin between the fore and hind limbs as 'parachutes'.

**glimmer** — v. shine faintly or intermittently. — n. **1** feeble or wavering light. **2** (also **glimmering**) (usu. foll. by *of*) small sign (of hope etc.). [probably Scandinavian]

**glimpse** /glimps/ — n. (often foll. by *of*, *at*) **1** brief view or look. **2** faint transient appearance (*glimpses of the truth*). — v. (**-sing**) have a brief view of (*glimpsed his face in the crowd*). [related to GLIMMER]

**glint** — v. flash, glitter. — n. a brief flash, sparkle. [probably Scandinavian]

**glissade** /gli-**sahd**, -**sayd**/ — n. **1** controlled slide down a snow slope in mountaineering. **2** gliding step in ballet. — v. (**-ding**) perform a glissade. [French]

**glissando** /gli-**san**-doh/ n. (pl. **-di** /-dee/ or **-s**) *Mus.* continuous slide of adjacent notes. [French *glissant* sliding: related to GLISSADE]

**glisten** /**glis**-uhn/ — v. shine like a wet or polished surface. — n. glitter; sparkle. [Old English]

**glitch** n. *colloq.* sudden irregularity or malfunction (of equipment etc.). [origin unknown]

**glitter** — v. **1** shine with a bright reflected light; sparkle. **2** (usu. foll. by *with*) be showy or splendid. — n. **1** sparkle. **2** showiness. **3** tiny pieces of sparkling material as decoration etc. □ **glitteringly** adv. **glittery** adj. [Old Norse]

**glitterati** /ˌglit-uh-**rah**-tee/ n.pl. *colloq.* rich fashionable people. [from GLITTER, LITERATI]

**glitz** n. *colloq.* showy glamour, over-ostentatious display of luxury. □ **glitzy** adj. (**-ier**, **-iest**). [from GLITTER, RITZY]

**gloaming** /**gloh**-ming/ n. *Scot.* or *poet.* twilight. [Old English]

**gloat** — v. (often foll. by *over* etc.) look or consider with greed, malice, triumphant satisfaction, etc. — n. act of gloating. [origin unknown]

**glob** n. *colloq.* mass or lump of semi-liquid substance, e.g. mud. [perhaps from BLOB, GOB2]

**global** /**gloh**-buhl/ adj. **1** worldwide (*global conflict*). **2** all-embracing. **3** *Computing* relating to an entire program, set of data, etc. (*a global change*). □ **globally** adv. [French: related to GLOBE]

**global warming** n. increase in the temperature of the earth's atmosphere caused by the greenhouse effect.

**globe** /glohb/ n. **1 a** (prec. by *the*) the earth. **b** spherical representation of it with a map on the surface. **2** spherical object, e.g. a fish-bowl etc. **3** = LIGHT GLOBE. [Latin *globus*]

**globe-trotter** n. *colloq.* person who travels widely. □ **globe-trotting** n. & *attrib. adj.*

**globular** /**glob**-yuh-luh/ adj. **1** globe-shaped. **2** composed of globules.

**globule** /**glob**-yool/ n. small globe or round particle or drop. [Latin *globulus*]

**globulin** /**glob**-yuh-luhn/ n. molecule-transporting protein in plant and animal tissues.

**glockenspiel** /**glok**-uhn-ˌspeel, -ˌshpeel/ n. musical instrument with bells or metal bars or tubes struck by hammers. [German, = bell-play]

**gloom** — n. **1** darkness; obscurity. **2** melancholy; despondency. — v. **1** become dark or threatening; lour. **2** be melancholy or despondent; frown. [origin unknown]

**gloomy** adj. (**-ier**, **-iest**) **1** dark; unlit. **2** depressed or depressing. □ **gloomily** adv. **gloominess** n.

**glorify** /**glaw**-ruh-ˌfuy/ v. (**-ies**, **-ied**) **1** make glorious. **2** make seem better or more splendid than it is. **3** (as **glorified** adj.) invested with more attractiveness, importance, etc. than it has in reality (*I'm not an executive, just a glorified office-boy*). **4** extol. □ **glorification** /-fuh-**kay**-shuhn/ n. [Latin: related to GLORY]

**glorious** /**glaw**-ree-uhs/ adj. **1** possessing or conferring glory; illustrious. **2** *colloq.* often *iron.* splendid, excellent (*glorious day*; *glorious muddle*). □ **gloriously** adv.

**glory** /**glaw**-ree/ — n. (pl. **-ies**) **1** renown, fame; honour. **2** adoring praise. **3** resplendent majesty, beauty, etc. **4** thing that brings renown, distinction, or pride. **5** heavenly bliss and splendour. **6** *colloq.* state of exaltation, prosperity, etc. **7** halo of a saint etc. — v. (**-ies**, **-ied**) (often foll. by *in*) pride oneself, exult (*she glories in her skill*). [Latin *gloria*]

**glory box** n. young woman's collection of linen, clothes, and other household goods in anticipation of marriage.

**glory-hole** n. *colloq.* room, cupboard, etc., in which things can be bundled away out of sight.

**gloss¹** — n. **1** surface shine or lustre. **2** deceptively attractive appearance. **3** (in full **gloss paint**) paint giving a glossy finish. — v. make glossy. □ **gloss over** seek to conceal, esp. by mentioning only briefly. [origin unknown]

**gloss²** — n. **1** explanatory comment

added to a text, e.g. in the margin. **2** interpretation or paraphrase. — v. add a gloss to (a text, word, etc.). [Latin *glossa* tongue]

**glossary** /**glos**-uh-ree/ n. (pl. **-ies**) **1** list or dictionary of technical or special words. **2** collection of glosses. [Latin: related to GLOSS2]

**glossolalia** /ˌglos-uh-**lay**-lee-uh/ n. babbling, meaningless 'speech' associated with some schizophrenic disorders and certain religious states (e.g. in the modern phenomenon known as 'speaking with tongues'). [Greek *glōssa* tongue, *laléein* talk, babble]

**glossy** — adj. (**-ier, -iest**) **1** smooth and shiny (*glossy paper*). **2** printed on such paper. — n. (pl. **-ies**) *colloq.* glossy magazine or photograph. □ **glossily** adv. **glossiness** n.

**glottal stop** /**glot**-uhl/ n. sound produced by the sudden opening or shutting of the glottis.

**glottis** /**glot**-uhs/ n. opening at the upper end of the windpipe and between the vocal cords. □ **glottal** /**glot**-uhl/ adj. [Greek]

**glove** /gluv/ — n. **1** hand-covering for protection, warmth, etc., usu. with separate fingers. **2** boxing glove. — v. (**-ving**) cover or provide with gloves. [Old English]

**glovebox** n. recess for small articles in the dashboard of a car etc.

**glow** /gloh/ — v. **1 a** emit light and heat without flame. **b** shine as if heated in this way. **2** (often foll. by *with*) **a** (of the body) be heated. **b** show or feel strong emotion (*glowed with pride*). **3** show a warm colour. **4** (as **glowing** adj.) expressing pride or satisfaction (*glowing report*). — n. **1** glowing state. **2** bright warm colour. **3** feeling of satisfaction or well-being. [Old English]

**glower** /**glowuh**/ — v. **1** (often foll. by *at*) look angrily. **2** look dark or threatening. — n. glowering look. [origin uncertain]

**glow-worm** n. beetle whose wingless female emits light from the end of the abdomen.

**glucose** /**gloo**-kohz, -kohs/ n. sugar found in the blood or in fruit juice etc., and as a constituent of starch, cellulose, etc. [Greek *gleukos* sweet wine]

**glue** /gloo/ — n. any adhesive substance. — v. (**glues, glued, gluing** or **glueing**) **1** fasten or join with glue. **2 a** keep or put very close (*eye glued to the keyhole*). **b** stick fast (to something) through intense interest, habit, etc. (*glued to the telly; glued to his book*). □ **gluey** /**gloo**-ee/ adj.

(**gluier, gluiest**). [Latin *glus*: related to GLUTEN]

**glue ear** n. blocking of the Eustachian tube, esp. in children.

**glue-sniffing** n. inhalation of fumes from adhesives as an intoxicant. □ **glue-sniffer** n.

**gluggy** /**glug**-ee/ adj. *colloq.* gluey, sticky (*gluggy rice*).

**glum** adj. (**glummer, glummest**) dejected; sullen. □ **glumly** adv. **glumness** n. [var. of GLOOM]

**glut** — v. (**-tt-**) **1** feed (a person, one's stomach, etc.) or indulge (a desire etc.) to the full; satiate. **2** fill to excess. **3** overstock (a market). — n. **1** supply exceeding demand. **2** full indulgence; surfeit. [French *gloutir* swallow: related to GLUTTON]

**glutamate** /**gloo**-tuh-ˌmayt/ n. salt or ester of glutamic acid, esp. a sodium salt used to enhance the flavour of food.

**glutamic acid** /gloo-**tam**-ik/ n. amino acid normally found in proteins. [from GLUTEN, AMINE]

**gluten** /**gloo**-tuhn/ n. mixture of proteins present in cereal grains; sticky protein substance left when starch is washed out of flour. [Latin *gluten* -tin- glue]

**glutinous** /**gloo**-tuh-nuhs/ adj. sticky; like glue. [Latin: related to GLUTEN]

**glutton** /**glut**-uhn/ n. **1** greedy eater. **2** (often foll. by *for*) *colloq.* person insatiably eager (*glutton for punishment; glutton for work*). □ **gluttonise** v. **gluttonous** adj. **gluttonously** adv. [Latin *gluttio* SWALLOW1]

**gluttony** /**glut**-uh-nee/ n. greed or excess in eating. [French: related to GLUTTON]

**gluyas** /**gloo**-yuhs, **gluy**-yuhs/ n. drought-resistant Australian variety of wheat. [H.I. *Gluyas*, wheat-farmer]

**glycerine** /ˌglis-uh-**reen**, **glis**-uh-ruhn/ n. (also **glycerol**) thick sweet colourless liquid used as medicine, ointment, etc., and in explosives. [Greek *glukeros* sweet]

**glycerol** /**glis**-uh-ˌrol/ n. = GLYCERINE.

**glycogen** /**gluy**-kuh-juhn/ n. polysaccharide serving as a store of carbohydrates, esp. in animal tissues.

**glycolysis** /gluy-**kol**-uh-suhs/ n. breakdown of glucose by enzymes with the release of energy.

**gm** abbr. gram(s).

**GMT** abbr. Greenwich Mean Time.

**gnamma** /**nam**-uh/ n. (also **namma**; in full **gnamma hole**) hole (commonly in granite) in which rainwater collects. [Nyungar *ngama*]

**gnarled** /nahld/ adj. (of a tree, hands, etc.) knobbly, twisted, rugged. [var. of *knarled*: related to KNURL]

**gnash** /nash/ v. **1** grind (the teeth). **2** (of the teeth) strike together. [Old Norse]

**gnat** /nat/ n. small two-winged biting fly. [Old English]

**gnaw** /naw/ v. **1 a** (usu. foll. by *away* etc.) wear away by biting. **b** (often foll. by *at*, *into*) bite persistently. **2 a** corrode; wear away. **b** (of pain, fear, etc.) torment (*was gnawed by doubt*). **3** (as **gnawing** adj.) persistent, worrying. [Old English]

**gneiss** /nuys/ n. coarse-grained metamorphic rock of feldspar, quartz, and mica. [German]

**gnocchi** /**nok**-ee, **nyok**-ee/ n.pl. (in Italian cuisine) tiny dumplings made with mashed potato and flour etc., and eaten in a soup or with a sauce. [Italian]

**gnome** /nohm/ n. **1 a** dwarfish legendary spirit or goblin living underground. **b** figure of this as a garden ornament. **2** (esp. in pl.) colloq. person with sinister influence, esp. financial (*gnomes of Zurich*). □ **gnomish** adj. [French]

**gnomic** /**noh**-mik, **nom**-ik/ adj. of aphorisms; sententious. [Greek gnōmē opinion]

**gnomon** /**noh**-mon/ n. rod or pin etc. on a sundial, showing the time by its shadow. [Greek, = indicator]

**gnosis** /**noh**-suhs/ n. knowledge of spiritual mysteries. [Greek gnōsis knowledge]

**gnostic** /**nos**-tik/ — adj. **1** of knowledge; having special mystical knowledge. **2** (**Gnostic**) concerning the Gnostics. — n. (**Gnostic**) (usu. in pl.) early Christian heretic claiming mystical knowledge. □ **Gnosticism** /-tuh-,siz-uhm/ n. [Greek, related to GNOSIS]

**gnow** /now/ n. = MALLEE FOWL. [Nyungar ngow and ngowu]

**GNP** abbr. gross national product.

**gnu** /noo/ n. (pl. same or **-s**) oxlike antelope. [Bushman nqu]

**go** /goh/ — v. (3rd sing. present **goes** /gohz/; past **went**; past part. **gone** /gon/) **1 a** start moving or be moving from one place or point in time to another; travel, proceed. **b** (foll. by *and* + verb) colloq. expressing annoyance (*you went and told him*). **2** (foll. by verbal noun) make a special trip for; participate in (*went skiing; goes running*). **3** lie or extend in a certain direction (*the road goes to Geelong*). **4** leave; depart (*they had to go*). **5** move, act, work, etc. (*clock doesn't go*). **6 a** make a specified movement (*go like this with your foot*). **b** make a sound (often of a specified kind) (*gun went bang; door bell went*). **c** (of an animal) make (its characteristic cry) (*the cow went 'moo'*). **d** colloq. say (*so he goes to me 'Why didn't you like it?'*). **7** be in a specified state (*go hungry; went in fear of his life*). **8 a** pass into a specified condition (*gone bad; went to sleep*). **b** colloq. die. **c** proceed or escape in a specified condition (*poet went unrecognised*). **9** (of time or distance) pass, elapse; be traversed (*ten days to go before Easter; the last kilometre went quickly*). **10 a** (of a document, verse, song, etc.) have a specified content or wording (*the tune goes like this*). **b** be current or accepted (*so the story goes*). **c** be suitable; fit; match (*the shoes don't go with the hat; those pinks don't go*). **d** be regularly kept or put (*the forks go here*). **e** find room; fit (*this won't go into the cupboard*). **11 a** turn out, proceed; take a course or view (*things went well; Canberra went Labor*). **b** be successful (*make the party go*). **12 a** be sold (*went for $1; went cheap*). **b** (of money) be spent (*$200 went on a new jacket*). **13 a** be relinquished or abolished (*the fridge will have to go*). **b** fail, decline; give way, collapse (*his sight is going; the light globe has gone*). **14** be acceptable or permitted; be accepted without question (*anything goes; what I say goes*). **15** (often foll. by *by*, *with*, *on*, *upon*) be guided by; judge or act on or in harmony with (*have nothing to go on; a good rule to go by*). **16** attend regularly (*goes to school*). **17** (foll. by pres. part.) colloq. proceed (often foolishly) to do (*went running to the police; don't go making him angry*). **18** act or proceed to a certain point (*will go so far and no further; went as high as $100*). **19** (of a number) be capable of being contained in another (*6 into 5 won't go*). **20** (usu. foll. by *to*) be allotted or awarded; pass (*first prize went to the girl*). **21** (foll. by *to*, *towards*) amount to; contribute to (*100 centimetres go to make a metre; this will go towards your holiday*). **22** (in imper.) begin motion (a starter's order in a race) (*ready, steady, go!*). **23** (usu. foll. by *by*, *under*) be known or called (*goes by the name of Ocker*). **24** colloq. proceed to (*go jump in the lake*). **25** (foll. by *for*) apply to (*that goes for me too*). — n. (pl. **goes**) **1** mettle; animation (*has a lot of go in her*). **2** vigorous activity (*it's all go*). **3** colloq. success (*made a go of it*). **4** colloq. turn; attempt (*I'll have a go; he's had two goes already*). **5** bout (of illness) (*a bad go of flu*). **6** colloq. a fixture, definite arrangement (*next week's match against the Cats is now a go*). — adj. colloq. functioning properly (*all systems are go*). □ **all the go** colloq. in the height of current fashion, all the rage. **as a person** (or **thing**) **goes** as the average is (*he's a bit skinny* *as rugby players go*). **as** (or **so**) **far as it goes** an expression of caution against taking a statement too positively (*the work is good as far as it goes*). **give it a go** see GIVE. **go about 1** set to work at. **2** (foll. by pres. part.) make a habit of doing (*he goes about telling lies*). **go ahead 1** proceed without hesitation (*he went ahead with the project*). **2** proceed with the speaker's permission ('*Shall I do it then?*' — '*Go ahead!*'). **go all out** *colloq.* do one's utmost, give one's all. **go all the way** (foll. by *with*) agree or support unreservedly (*I go all the way with you on this*). **go along with** agree to or with. **go around 1** = *go about*. **2** suffice for everyone (*is there enough beer to go around?*). **3** (foll. by *with*) **a** be regularly in the company of (*he goes around with Johnno*). **b** have a romantic relationship with (*he goes around with Kylie*). **go at** take in hand energetically (*went at it with a will*). **go back on** fail to keep (a promise etc.). **go bananas** (or **batty** or **bonkers** or **crackers**, etc.) **1** become insane. **2** become extremely angry. **go begging** see BEG. **go bung** *colloq.* (of equipment etc.) break down, stop working (*the video's gone bung*). **go bush** *colloq.* **1** live in the country, having given up urban life. **2** retreat (usu. temporarily) to some place where one cannot be contacted. **go by 1** pass. **2** be dependent on; be guided by (*he goes by the book*). **go down 1** descend. **2** be defeated (*the Sydney Swans went down to the Cats*). **3 a** (of an amount) become less through use (*coffee bottle's gone down a lot*). **b** subside (*the flood's going down*). **c** decrease in price. **4 a** (of a ship) sink. **b** (of the sun) set. **c** (of a theatre curtain) fall. **5** deteriorate; (of a computer system etc.) cease to function. **6 a** be recorded in writing. **b** *colloq.* be remembered (*go down as the biggest ratbag in Oz*). **7** be swallowed. **8** (often foll. by *with*) find acceptance (*how do you think my speech went down?*). **9** *colloq.* be sent to prison. **go down** (or **over**) **like a lead balloon** *colloq.* fail dismally. **go down the gurgler** *colloq.* **1** fail completely. **2** (esp. of money) be completely lost. **go down with** become ill with (a disease). **go far** see FAR. **go for 1** go to fetch. **2** pass for or be accounted as (*your opinion goes for nothing*). **3** prefer; choose (*that's the one I go for*). **4** *colloq.* strive to attain (*go for it!*). **5** attack (*the dog went for him*). **go for broke** *colloq.* go all out (esp. with one's capital in gambling, investing, etc.). **go hell for leather** *colloq.* **1** move with utmost speed. **2** do, act, with all one's might etc. **go in 1** enter a room, house, etc. **2** (of the

sun etc.) become obscured by cloud. **go in for 1** enter as a competitor. **2** *colloq.* take as one's particular pursuit, interest, etc. (*goes in for abseiling*). **go into 1** enter (a profession, hospital, etc.). **2** investigate. **go it alone** work or act alone. **go like a bomb** *colloq.* be extremely successful (*the barbie went like a bomb*). **go a long way 1** (often foll. by *towards*) have a great effect. **2** (of food, money, etc.) last a long time, buy much. **3** = *go far*. **go missing** *colloq.* be lost. **go off 1** explode; discharge. **2** (of an actor in a play) make an exit. **3** wear off. **4 a** (esp. of foodstuffs) deteriorate. **b** lose popular appeal (*that café's gone off the last few weeks — it's no longer in*). **5** go to sleep. **6** *colloq.* begin to dislike (*I've gone off him*). **go off at** *colloq.* reprimand, scold. **go off one's head** (or **rocker** or **scone**) = *go bananas*. **go off the rails** = *go bananas*. **go off well** (or **badly** etc.) (of an enterprise etc.) be received or accomplished well (or badly etc.) (*the performance went off well*). **go on 1** (often foll. by pres. part.) continue, persevere (*decided to go on with it; went on trying*). **2** happen (*what went on at the meeting?*). **3** (of an actor in a play) make an entrance. **4** *colloq.* **a** talk at great length. **b** (foll. by *at*) nag. **5** (foll. by *to* + infin.) proceed (*went on to become a star*). **6** conduct oneself (*shameful the way they went on*). **7** (also **go upon**) use as evidence (*the police have nothing to go on*). **8** *colloq.* approach (*he's twelve going on thirteen; it must be going on noon*). **go one better** *colloq.* outdo (*tried to go one better than the guy next door*). **go out 1** leave a room, house, etc. **2** be extinguished (*fire's gone out*). **3** be broadcast. **4** (often foll. by *with*) be courting, regularly dating (*whom's he going out with?*). **5** cease to be fashionable (*floral ties are going out*). **6** *colloq.* lose consciousness (*went out like a light*). **7** (usu. foll. by *to*) (of the heart etc.) expand with sympathy etc. towards (*my heart goes out to them*). **8** (of a tide) ebb to low tide. **9** go on strike (*going out over unsafe working conditions*). **go over 1** inspect the details of; rehearse; retouch. **2** be received (as specified) (*the play went over very well in Cootamundra*). **3** change sides, loyalties, religion, etc. (*some city Liberals are going over to Labor*). **go overboard** *colloq.* act in an excessive manner. **go places** be successful. **go round 1** spin, revolve. **2** (of food etc.) suffice for everybody (*don't think the savs will go round*). **3** (usu. foll. by *to*) visit informally (*let's go round to Bill's*). **go slow** work slowly, as a form of industrial action. **go through 1** be dealt with or completed. **2** discuss or scrutinise in detail. **3** perform. **4** undergo; endure (*after what I've gone through, I've a right to be bitter*). **5** colloq. use up; spend (money etc.). **6** (of a book) be successfully published (in so many editions). **go through with 1** complete. **2** put up with, endure. **go too far** see FAR. **go to show** (or **prove**) serve to demonstrate (or prove). **go to town** colloq. **1** act without restraint or with unbridled enthusiasm. **2** have a wild celebration. **3** (foll. by on) censure or criticise savagely (*she really went to town on him for his behaviour*). **go to whoa** (from) start to finish. **go under** sink; fail; succumb. **go up 1** rise in price. **2** be consumed (in flames etc.); explode. **go walkabout 1** (of an Aborigine) wander into the bush (away from contact with whites) in order to re-establish contact with spiritual resources. **2** wander around casually. **3** lose concentration etc. (*he went walkabout halfway through the second set and lost it*). **4** colloq. (of an article) be lost (probably because of theft) (*okay, who's the culprit? — my wallet's gone walkabout*). **go with 1** be harmonious with; match (*this goes with that*). **2** be courting, dating, etc. (*he's going with Sally*). **go without** manage without; forgo (also *absol.*). **have a go** (foll. by *at*) attack, criticise. **2** (often foll. by *at*) attempt; try harder. **let go 1** release. **2** colloq. be uninhibited; loosen up (*let go, mate, and have some fun*). **let oneself go 1** neglect one's appearance etc., become slovenly. **2** = *let go* (sense 2). **make a go of** colloq. make a success of. **no go** colloq. impossible; not feasible; not on. **on the go** colloq. **1** in constant motion. **2** constantly working; extremely active, busy. **that's the way it goes** colloq. that's how things inevitably turn out. [Old English: *went* is originally a past of WEND]

**goad** /gohd/ — *v.* **1** urge on with a goad. **2** (usu. foll. by *on, into*) irritate; stimulate (*goaded him into retaliating; goaded me on to win*). — *n.* **1** spiked stick used for urging cattle forward. **2** anything that torments or incites. [Old English]

**go-ahead** — *n.* permission to proceed. — *adj.* enterprising.

**goal** /gohl/ — *n.* **1** object of ambition or effort; destination. **2 a** structure into or through which the ball has to be sent to score in certain games. **b** point(s) won. — *v.* score a goal. □ **goalless** *adj.* [origin unknown]

**goalie** /goh-lee/ *n. colloq.* = GOALKEEPER.

**goalkeeper** *n.* player defending a goal in sports such as soccer, hockey, etc.

**goal sneak** *n. Aust. Rules* player who adroitly sneaks in a goal, catching the opposing players by surprise.

**goal umpire** *n. Aust. Rules* one of two umpires (one at each goal) who judges when a goal or a behind is scored.

**goanna** /goh-an-uh/ *n.* any of various Australian monitor lizards, typically large and fast-moving. [corruption of IGUANA]

**goanna oil** *n.* oil from goanna fat, a bush panacea.

**goat** /goht/ *n.* **1** hardy domesticated cud-chewing mammal, with horns and (in the male) a beard. **2** lecherous man. **3** colloq. foolish person. **4** (**the Goat**) zodiacal sign or constellation Capricorn. □ **get** (or **on**) **a person's goat** colloq. irritate a person intensely. [Old English]

**goatee** /goh-tee/ *n.* small pointed beard.

**goatish** *adj.* goat-like; lustful. □ **goatishly** *adv.* **goatishness** *n.*

**gob**[1] *n. colloq.* mouth. [origin unknown]

**gob**[2] colloq. — *n.* clot of slimy matter. — *v.* (**-bb-**) spit. [French *go(u)be* mouthful]

**gobbet** /gob-uht/ *n.* **1** piece or lump of flesh, food, etc. **2** extract from a text, esp. one set for translation or comment. [French diminutive of *gobe* GOB[2]]

**gobble**[1] /gob-uhl/ *v.* (**-ling**) **1** eat hurriedly and noisily. **2** (usu. foll. by *up*) **a** take over, seize control of (*retail giants gobbling up the small shopkeepers*). **b** read eagerly, devour (a book etc.). [from GOB[2]]

**gobble**[2] /gob-uhl/ *v.* (**-ling**) **1** (of a turkey) make a characteristic guttural sound. **2** make such a sound when speaking. [imitative]

**gobbledegook** /gob-uhl-dee-gook, -guuk/ *n.* (also **gobbledygook**) colloq. pompous or unintelligible (esp. official) jargon. [probably imitative of a turkeycock]

**go-between** *n.* an intermediary.

**goblet** /gob-luht/ *n.* drinking-vessel with a foot and stem. [French diminutive of *gobel* cup]

**goblin** /gob-luhn/ *n.* mischievous ugly dwarflike creature of folklore. [Anglo-French]

**goby** /goh-bee/ *n.* (*pl.* **-ies**) small fish with ventral fins joined to form a disc or sucker. [Greek *kōbios* GUDGEON]

**go-cart** *n.* var. of GO-KART.

**god** *n.* **1 a** (in many religions) super-human being or spirit worshipped as having power over nature, human fortunes, etc. **b** image, idol, etc., symbolising a god. **2** (**God**) (in Christian and other monotheistic religions) creator and ruler of the universe. **3** adored or greatly admired person. **4** (in *pl.*) *Theatr.* gallery. **5** (**God!**) exclamation of surprise, anger, etc. □ **God forbid** may it not happen! **God knows 1** it is beyond all knowledge. **2** I call God to witness that. **God's gift** *colloq.* (usu. *iron.*) a godsend (*he thinks he's God's gift to women*). **God willing** if Providence allows. [Old English]

**godchild** *n.* person in relation to his or her godparent.

**god-daughter** *n.* female godchild.

**goddess** /god-**uhs**, god-**es**/ *n.* **1** female deity. **2** adored woman.

**godfather** *n.* **1** male godparent. **2** esp. *US* person directing an illegal organisation, esp. the Mafia.

**godforsaken** *adj.* dismal; inaccessible, remote.

**godhead** *n.* (also **Godhead**) **1 a** state of being God or a god. **b** divine nature. **2** deity. **3** (**the Godhead**) God.

**godless** /god-**luhs**/ *adj.* **1** impious; wicked. **2** without a god. **3** not recognising God. □ **godlessness** *n.*

**godlike** *adj.* resembling God or a god.

**godly** *adj.* (**-ier**, **-iest**) pious, devout. □ **godliness** *n.*

**godmother** *n.* female godparent.

**godparent** *n.* person who presents a child at baptism and responds on the child's behalf.

**godsend** *n.* unexpected but welcome event or acquisition.

**godson** *n.* male godchild.

**godspeed** /god-**speed**/ *int.* expression of good wishes to a person starting a journey.

**godwit** *n.* any of various wading birds with long legs and a long straight or slightly curved bill, some of which are summer migrants to Australia from Asia etc. (*bar-tailed godwit*). [origin unknown]

**Godzone** /god-**zohn**/ *n. joc.* God's Own Country (used esp. of Australia or New Zealand). [respelling]

**goer** *n.* **1** person or thing that goes (*slow goer*). **2** (often in *comb.*) person who attends, esp. regularly (*churchgoer*). **3** *colloq.* lively or persevering person. **4** *colloq.* project likely to be accepted or to succeed. **5** person or thing that goes very fast (*that horse in race three's a real goer*).

**gofer** /goh-**fuh**/ *n. colloq.* **1** one who does menial jobs for others, runs errands, etc. **2** toady, crawler. [alteration of *go for*; glancing at GOPHER[1]]

**go-getter** *n. colloq.* aggressively enterprising person.

**goggle** /gog-**uhl**/ — *v.* (**-ling**) **1 a** (often foll. by *at*) look with wide-open eyes. **b** (of the eyes) be rolled about; protrude. **2** roll (the eyes). — *adj.* (usu. *attrib.*) (of the eyes) protuberant or rolling. — *n.* (in *pl.*) special spectacles for protecting the eyes. [probably imitative]

**goggle-eyed** *adj.* having staring or protuberant eyes. — *adv.* with eyes opened wide from fear, astonishment, etc. (*gazed goggle-eyed at the ghost*).

**going** /goh-**ing**/ — *n.* **1** act or process of going. **2 a** condition of the ground for walking, riding, etc. **b** progress affected by this. — *adj.* **1** in or into action (*set the clock going*). **2** existing, available (*there's cold beef going*). **3** current, prevalent (*the going rate*). □ **get going** start steadily talking, working, etc. **going on fifteen** (etc.) approaching one's fifteenth (etc.) birthday. **going on** (**for**) approaching (a time, period, etc.) (*it's going on ten; must be going on for six years since I saw her last*). **going strong** continuing vigorously. **going to** intending to; about to. **to be going on with** to start with; for the time being. **while the going is good** while conditions are favourable.

**going concern** *n.* a thriving business.

**going-over** *n.* (*pl.* **goings-over**) **1** *colloq.* inspection or overhaul. **2** *colloq.* a thrashing.

**goings-on** *n.pl.* **1** (esp. morally suspect) behaviour. **2** current news etc. (*the goings-on in Bosnia*).

**going thing** *n.* (prec. by *the*) the latest craze, fad, or trend.

**goitre** /goi-**tuh**/ *n.* swelling of the neck resulting from enlargement of the thyroid gland. [Latin *guttur* throat]

**go-kart** *n.* (also **go-cart**) miniature racing car with a skeleton body.

**gold** — *n.* **1** precious yellow metallic element. **2** colour of gold. **3 a** coins or articles made of gold. **b** wealth. **4** something precious or beautiful. **5** = GOLD MEDAL (*going for gold at the Olympics*). — *adj.* **1** made wholly or chiefly of gold. **2** coloured like gold. [Old English]

**gold-digger** *n.* **1** person who digs for gold. **2** *colloq.* person who flirts with others to obtain money from them.

**golden** *adj.* **1 a** made or consisting of gold. **b** yielding gold. **2** coloured or shining like gold (*golden hair*). **3** precious; excellent.

**golden age** *n.* **1** a supposed past age when people were happy and innocent. **2** period of a nation's greatest prosperity, cultural merit, etc.

**golden handshake** *n. colloq.* payment given on redundancy or early retirement.

**golden jubilee** *n.* fiftieth anniversary.

**golden mean** *n.* **1** the principle of moderation. **2** = GOLDEN SECTION.

**golden moths** *n.pl.* (also **snake orchid**) Australian terrestrial orchid bearing golden moth-like flowers, marked with greeny-brown, on long slender (fancifully) snake-like stems.

**golden oldie** *n. colloq.* old hit record or film etc. that is still well known and popular.

**golden rule** *n.* basic principle of action, esp. 'do as you would be done by'.

**golden section** *n.* division of a line so that the whole is to the greater part as that part is to the smaller part.

**golden staph** *n.* virulent species of (the staphylococcus) bacterium which has developed a resistance to many antibiotics.

**golden wattle** *n.* heavily flowering small tree, the golden flower of which is popularly regarded as the floral emblem of Australia.

**golden wedding** *n.* fiftieth anniversary of a wedding.

**goldfield** *n.* district in which gold occurs naturally.

**goldfinch** *n.* European songbird with a yellow band across each wing, introduced into Australia and now common.

**goldfish** *n.* (*pl.* same or **-es**) small reddish-golden Chinese carp.

**goldfish bowl** *n.* **1** globular glass container for goldfish. **2** situation in which privacy is completely lacking.

**gold foil** *n.* gold beaten into a thin sheet.

**gold leaf** *n.* gold beaten into a very thin sheet.

**gold medal** *n.* medal of gold, usu. awarded as first prize.

**goldmine** *n.* **1** place where gold is mined. **2** *colloq.* source of great wealth.

**gold plate** *n.* **1** vessels made of gold. **2** material plated with gold.

**gold-plate** *v.* plate with gold.

**gold reserve** *n.* total quantity of gold coins or bullion held by a central bank etc. and used e.g. to maintain the value of coins and notes issued by the government.

**goldrush** *n.* rush to a newly discovered goldfield.

**goldsmith** *n.* worker in gold.

**gold standard** *n.* system by which the value of a currency is defined in terms of gold.

**golem** /goh-luhm/ *n.* **1** mannikin made of clay etc. and (according to Jewish legend) magically brought to life by human intervention. **2** robot; automaton. [Hebrew]

**golf** — *n.* game in which a small hard ball is driven with clubs into a series of 18 or 9 holes with the fewest possible strokes. — *v.* play golf. □ **golfer** *n.* [origin unknown]

**golliwog** /gol-ee-wog/ *n.* black-faced soft doll with fuzzy hair. [origin uncertain]

**gonad** /goh-nad/ *n.* animal organ producing gametes, esp. the testis or ovary. [Greek *gonē* seed]

**gondola** /gon-duh-luh/ *n.* **1** light flat-bottomed boat used on Venetian canals. **2** car suspended from an airship or balloon, or attached to a ski-lift. [Italian]

**gondolier** /,gon-duh-**leer**/ *n.* oarsman on a gondola. [Italian: related to GONDOLA]

**gone** /gon/ *adj.* **1** (of time) past (*it's gone nine*). **2 a** lost; hopeless. **b** dead. **3** *colloq.* pregnant for a specified time (*already three months gone*). **4** consumed, used up (*the butter's just about gone*). **5** *colloq.* completely enthralled or entranced, esp. by rhythmic music, drugs, etc. □ **be gone** depart; leave temporarily (*I'll be gone for about ten minutes, in case anyone rings*) (cf. BEGONE). **a bit gone** *colloq.* somewhat mad; eccentric (*he's a bit gone ever since the clock fell on his head*). **far gone** *colloq.* **1** thoroughly mad or insane. **2** totally drunk. **3** utterly weary. **4** near death. **5** in a state of terminal disrepair (*your fridge is far gone, mate — not worth fixing*). **6** far advanced. **gone missing** *colloq.* lost; not to be found (*he's gone missing since late yesterday arvo; my pen's gone missing again*). **gone on** *colloq.* infatuated with (*he's gone on heavy metal; gone on the girl next door*). **gone to billy-o** *colloq.* gone too far to recall; gone into oblivion. [past part. of GO]

**goner** /gon-uh/ *n. colloq.* person or thing that is doomed or irrevocably lost; dead.

**gong** *n.* **1** metal disc with a turned rim, giving a resonant note when struck. **2** saucer-shaped bell. [Malay]

**gonorrhoea** /,gon-uh-**ree**-uh/ *n.* (also **gonorrhea**) venereal disease with inflammatory discharge from the urethra or vagina. □ **gonorrhoeal** *adj.* [Greek, = semen-flux]

**goo** *n. colloq.* **1** sticky or slimy substance. **2** sickly sentiment. [origin unknown]

**good** /guud/ — *adj.* (**better**, **best**) **1** having the right or desired qualities (*good wine*); adequate (*his results were just good*). **2 a** (of a person) efficient, competent (*good at French; good driver*). **b** effective, reliable (*good brakes*). **c** (of health etc.) strong (*good eyesight*). **3 a** kind, benevolent (*good of you to come*). **b** morally excellent; virtuous (*good deed*). **c** well-behaved (*good child*). **d** loyal, reliable (*good friend*). **e** *colloq.* in good health (*'How's your wife?' — 'She's good,* *thanks.*'). **4** enjoyable, agreeable (*good party*; *good news*). **5** thorough, considerable (*gave the car a good wash*). **6 a** not less than (*waited a good hour*). **b** considerable in number, quality, etc. (*a good many people*). **7** beneficial (*milk is good for you*). **8 a** valid, sound (*good reason*). **b** financially sound (*his credit is good*). **9** in exclamations of surprise (*good grief!*). **10** right, expedient (*thought it good to have a try*). **11** fresh, untainted (*is the meat still good?*). **12** (sometimes patronising) commendable, worthy (*good old George*; *my regards to your good lady*; *good reputation*). **13** attractive (*good looks*). **14** suited to the purpose (*now's a good time to water the garden*). **15** in courteous greetings and farewells (*good morning*). — *n.* **1** (only in *sing.*) that which is good; what is beneficial or morally right (*only good can come of it*; *what good will it do?*). **2** (in *pl.*) **a** movable property or merchandise. **b** things to be transported. **c** (prec. by *the*) *colloq.* what one has undertaken to supply (*politicians promise the sky but rarely deliver the goods*). **d** (prec. by *the*) *colloq.* the real thing; the genuine article (*he's the goods*). **e** (prec. by *the*) *colloq.* incriminating evidence etc. (*the police have the goods on him*). — *adv. colloq.* well (*doing pretty good, thanks*). □ **all to the good** *colloq.* in (one's) best interests, to (one's) advantage (often used to justify an unpleasant occurrence) (*well, you didn't get the job, but it might be all to the good*). **as good as** practically (*he as good as told me*). **as good as they come** *colloq.* among the (the) very best. **come good** *colloq.* fulfil an expectation (*he'll come good in the end*); improve after an uncertain start (*the business finally came good*). **fat lot of good** *colloq.* no good whatever. **for good (and all)** finally, permanently; once and for all. **good and** *colloq.* used as an intensifier before an *adj.* or *adv.* (*raining good and hard*). **a good few** many (*a good few were uncertain how they would vote*). **good for 1** beneficial to; having a good effect on. **2** able to be trusted to pay. **3** *colloq.* reliably forthcoming, able to be counted on (*Mum's always good for a few bucks*). **4** inclined for; able to perform (*good for a 10-kilometre hike*). **5** valid (*your pass is good for another two trips*). **good graces** *colloq.* see GRACE. **good guts** *colloq.* = *good oil*. **good-oh!** *colloq.* exclamation of agreement, satisfaction, etc. **good oil** *colloq.* reliable information (*the good oil for the Melbourne Cup is . . .*). **good one!** *colloq.* **1** exclamation of

admiration, agreement, praise, etc. **2** ironical exclamation indicating that the recipient has just made a tactless remark, done something tactless, etc. (*good one, Bill! — didn't you know her husband's left her?*). **good on you!** (or **him!** or **her!** etc.) *colloq.* exclamation of approval and encouragement towards a person. **good question** *colloq.* extraordinarily difficult question to answer (*good question, mate! — no idea where the beer's all gone*). **good riddance** see RIDDANCE. **good show** *colloq.* reasonable chance (*she's got a good show of being the first woman to be trade union boss*). **good sort** *colloq.* **1** attractive person of either sex. **2** friendly, reliable person of either sex. **a good thing going** *colloq.* an extremely advantageous or satisfactory position, state, etc. **have a good mind** see MIND. **have the goods on a person** *colloq.* have information about a person, giving one an advantage over him or her. **in good time 1** with no risk of being late. **2** (also **all in good time**) in due course but without haste. **in good with a person** *colloq.* in his or her favour, good graces. **that's a good one!** *colloq.* expression of scepticism or disbelief. [Old English]

**goodbye** /guud-**buy**/ — *int.* expressing good wishes on parting, ending a telephone conversation, etc. — *n.* (*pl.* -**byes**) parting; farewell. [from *God be with you!*]

**good-day** (usu. ellipt. as **g'day** or **gidday**) familiar daytime greeting.

**good faith** *n.* sincerity of intention.

**good-for-nothing** — *adj.* worthless. — *n.* worthless person.

**Good Friday** *n.* Friday before Easter Sunday, commemorating the crucifixion of Christ.

**good-hearted** *adj.* kindly, well-meaning.

**good humour** *n.* genial mood.

**good-humoured** *adj.* cheerful, amiable. □ **good-humouredly** *adv.*

**goodie** *colloq.* — *n.* (also **goody**) (*pl.* -**ies**) **1** good or favoured person, esp. a hero in a film etc. **2** (usu. in *pl.*) something good or attractive, esp. to eat. **3** = GOODY-GOODY. — *int.* expressing childish or affected delight.

**goodish** /guud-ish/ *adj.* **1** fairly good. **2** somewhat considerable (*a goodish distance away*).

**good job** *n. colloq.* fortunate state of affairs (*good job you brought the tool-kit along*).

**good-looker** *n.* (also **looker**) *colloq.* good-looking person (male or female).

**good-looking** *adj.* handsome; physically attractive.

**good nature** n. friendly disposition.

**good-natured** adj. kind, patient; easy-going. □ **good-naturedly** adv.

**goodness** — n. **1** virtue; excellence. **2** kindness (*had the goodness to wait*). **3** what is beneficial in a thing (*vegies with all the goodness boiled out*). — int. (esp. as a substitution for 'God') expressing surprise, anger, etc. (*goodness me!*; *goodness knows*). [Old English]

**good-o** /guud-oh/ (also **good-oh**) colloq. — adj. pleasing; fine; satisfactory (*things are pretty good-o at present*). — adv. well; satisfactorily (*the barbie was going good-o until it began to rain*). — int. okay!; fine!

**goodwill** /guud-**wil**/ — n. **1** kindly feeling. **2** established reputation of a business etc. as enhancing its value. **3** cheerful consent or acquiescence; readiness (*he minded my kids all day for me with great goodwill*). — adj. showing or intending to foster goodwill (*a goodwill gesture*).

**goody-goody** colloq. — n. (pl. **-ies**) smug or obtrusively virtuous person. — adj. obtrusively or smugly virtuous.

**gooey** /goo-ee/ adj. (**gooier, gooiest**) colloq. **1** viscous, sticky. **2** sickly sentimental. [from GOO]

**goof** /goof, guuf/ colloq. — n. **1** foolish or stupid person. **2** mistake. — v. **1** bungle. **2** blunder. □ **goof around** fool around, act the clown. **goof up** bungle or mess (something) up (*goofed up the entire works with his carelessness*). [Latin *gufus* coarse]

**goofy** /goo-fee/ adj. (**-ier, -iest**) colloq. stupid; bungling. □ **goofiness** n.

**goog** /guug/ n. colloq. **1** egg. **2** idiot. □ **full as a goog 1** extremely full (*car was packed full as a goog*). **2** totally drunk. **3** (of a person) filled with food (*I'm as full as a goog — can't eat another crumb*). [abbreviation of GOOGIE]

**googie** /guug-ee/ n. colloq. an egg. [Scottish dial.]

**googly** /goo-glee/ n. (pl. **-ies**) Cricket ball bowled so as to bounce in an unexpected direction. [origin unknown]

**goolie** /goo-lee/ n. colloq. **1** pebble, stone. **2** (usu. in pl.) testicle. [origin uncertain]

**goon** /goon/ n. colloq. **1** stupid person. **2** ruffian hired by racketeers etc. to terrorise people. [origin uncertain]

**goose** n. (pl. **geese**) **1 a** large water-bird with webbed feet and a broad bill. **b** female of this (opp. GANDER 1). **c** flesh of a goose as food. **2** colloq. simpleton. □ **cook a person's goose** colloq. bring his or her

plans, hopes, etc. to naught. **one's goose is cooked** colloq. one is ruined, finished, done for. [Old English]

**gooseberry** /**guuz**-buh-ree/ n. (pl. **-ies**) **1** yellowish-green berry with juicy flesh. **2** thorny shrub bearing this. [origin uncertain]

**goose-flesh** n. (also **goose-bumps**, **goose pimples**) bristling state of the skin produced by cold, fright, etc.

**goose-step** n. military marching step in which the knees are kept stiff.

**gooya** /goo-yuh/ n. = EMU APPLE. [Yuwaalaraay *guuya*]

**gopher**[1] /**goh**-fuh/ n. American burrowing rodent, ground-squirrel, or burrowing tortoise. [origin uncertain]

**gopher**[2] n. colloq. = GOFER.

**Gordian** /**gaw**-dee-uhn/ adj. □ **cut the Gordian knot** solve a seemingly insoluble problem by force or by evasion. [*Gordius* king of Phrygia, who tied an extremely intricate knot later cut by Alexander the Great]

**gore**[1] /gaw/ n. blood shed and clotted. [Old English, = dirt]

**gore**[2] /gaw/ v. (**-ring**) pierce with a horn, tusk, etc. [origin unknown]

**gore**[3] /gaw/ — n. **1** wedge-shaped piece in a garment. **2** triangular or tapering piece in an umbrella etc. — v. (**-ring**) shape (a garment) with a gore. [Old English, = triangle of land]

**gorge** /gawj/ — n. **1** narrow opening between hills. **2** act of gorging; a feast. **3** contents of the stomach. **4** food-passage extending from the back of the throat to the stomach. — v. (**-ging**) **1** feed greedily (*don't gorge*). **2 a** (often refl.) glut, satiate (*gorged himself on meat-pies at the footy*). **b** devour greedily (*gorged the entire duck*). □ **one's gorge rises (at)** one is sickened (by). [French, = throat]

**gorgeous** /**gaw**-juhs/ adj. **1** richly coloured, sumptuous. **2** colloq. very pleasant, splendid (*gorgeous weather*). **3** colloq. strikingly beautiful. □ **gorgeously** adv. [French]

**gorgon** /**gaw**-guhn/ n. **1** (in Greek mythology) each of three snake-haired sisters (esp. Medusa) with the power to turn anyone who looked at them to stone. **2** frightening or repulsive woman. [Greek *gorgos* terrible]

**gorgonzola** /,gaw-guhn-**zoh**-luh/ n. type of rich cheese with bluish-green veins. [*Gorgonzola* in Italy]

**gorilla** /guh-**ril**-uh/ n. largest anthropoid ape, native to Africa. [Greek, perhaps from African = wild man]

**gormandise** /**gaw**-muhn-ˌduyz/ v. (also **-ize**) eat or devour voraciously. [from GOURMAND]

**gormless** /**gawm**-luhs/ adj. colloq. foolish, lacking sense. □ **gormlessly** adv. **gormlessness** n. [originally gaumless from British dial. gaum understanding]

**gorse** n. spiny yellow-flowered shrub; furze. □ **gorsy** adj. [Old English]

**gory** adj. (**-ier**, **-iest**) **1** involving bloodshed; bloodthirsty. **2** covered in gore. **3** colloq. nasty; unpleasant (filled us in on the row with his boss, down to the last gory detail). □ **gorily** adv. **goriness** n.

**gosh** int. expressing surprise. [euphemism for GOD]

**goshawk** /**gos**-hawk/ n. any of various large short-winged and long-tailed hawks, including some Australian species (brown goshawk; red goshawk). [Old English gōs-hafoc: related to GOOSE, HAWK[1]]

**gosling** /**goz**-ling/ n. young goose. [Old Norse: related to GOOSE]

**go-slow** n. **1** working slowly, as a form of industrial action. **2** = WORK TO RULE.

**gospel** /**gos**-puhl/ n. **1** teaching or revelation of Christ. **2** (**Gospel**) a record of Christ's life in the first four books of the New Testament. **b** each of these books. **c** portion from one of them read at a service. **3** (also **gospel truth**) thing regarded as absolutely true. **4** (in full **gospel music**) Black American religious singing. [Old English: related to GOOD, SPELL[1] = news]

**gossamer** /**gos**-uh-muh/ — n. **1** filmy substance of small spiders' webs. **2** delicate filmy material. — adj. light and flimsy as gossamer. [origin uncertain]

**gossip** /**gos**-uhp/ — n. **1 a** unconstrained talk or writing, esp. about persons or social incidents. **b** idle talk; groundless rumour. **2** person who indulges in gossip. — v. (**-p-**) talk or write gossip. □ **gossiper** n. **gossipy** adj. [Old English, originally 'godparent', hence 'familiar acquaintance']

**got** past and past part. of GET. □ **got Buckley's** colloq. not a chance; not a hope (beating me at golf? — you've got Buckley's!). **got into a person** colloq. causing a person to be short-tempered, irritable, etc. (what's got into you this past hour?). **got it in for a person** colloq. filled with spite, animosity, etc. (the teachers have got it in for me — failed me in every subject). **got it in one** to possessed with the ability, skill, potential, etc. to (he's got it in him to go to uni but he won't do the work). **got me** colloq. don't know; haven't

a clue (you've got me: so what is the capital of Sri Lanka?). **got a quid** colloq. very rich.

**Goth** /goth/ n. **1** member of a Germanic tribe that invaded the Roman Empire in the 3rd–5th c. **2** uncivilised or ignorant person. [Old English Gota and Greek Gothoi]

**goth** n. **1** style of rock music with an intense or droning blend of guitars, bass, and drums, often with apocalyptic or mystical lyrics. **2** performer or devotee of this music, or member of the subculture favouring black clothing and white-painted faces with black make-up.

**Gothic** /**goth**-ik/ — adj. **1** of the Goths. **2** in the style of architecture prevalent in W. Europe in the 12th–16th c., characterised by pointed arches. **3** (of a novel etc.) in a style popular in the 18th–19th c., with supernatural or horrifying events. **4** barbarous, uncouth. — n. **1** Gothic language. **2** Gothic architecture. [Latin: related to GOTH]

**gotten** US past part. of GET.

**gouache** /goo-**ahsh**/ n. **1** method of painting in opaque pigments ground in water and thickened with a gluelike substance. **2** these pigments. [French from Italian]

**gouda** /**gow**-duh, **goo**-duh/ n. flat round usu. Dutch cheese. [Gouda in Holland]

**gouge** /gowj/ — n. **1** chisel with a concave blade. **2** groove etc. made with such a tool. — v. (**-ging**) **1** cut with or as with a gouge. **2** (foll. by out) force out (esp. an eye with the thumb) with or as with a gouge. **3** dig for opal. [Latin gubia]

**gouging** n. (in football, esp. rugby) the infringement of incapacitating an opponent by poking a finger into his eye.

**goulash** /**goo**-lash/ n. highly-seasoned (orig. Hungarian) stew of meat and vegetables. [Magyar gulyás-hús, = herdsman's meat]

**gourd** /goord, gawd/ n. **1 a** fleshy usu. large fruit with a hard skin. **b** climbing or trailing plant of the cucumber family bearing this. **2** dried skin of the gourd-fruit, used as a drinking-vessel etc. [Latin cucurbita]

**gourmand** /gaw-**mond**, **gaw**-muhnd/ n. **1** glutton. **2** gourmet. [French]

■ **Usage** The use of gourmand in sense 2 is considered incorrect by some people.

**gourmet** /**gaw**-may, **goor**-/ n. connoisseur of good food. [French]

**gout** /gowt/ n. disease with inflammation of the smaller joints, esp. of the toe. □ **gouty** adj. [Latin gutta drop]

**govern** /**guv**-uhn/ v. **1** rule or control (a nation etc.) with authority; conduct the policy and affairs of. **2** influence or determine (a person or course of action) (*pride governs his behaviour*). **3** be a standard or principle for. **4** check or control (esp. passions). **5** *Gram.* (esp. of a verb or preposition) have (a noun or pronoun or its case) depending on it (*in 'he hit me', the verb 'hit' governs the objective case of the pronoun 'me'*). [Greek *kubernaō* steer]

**governance** /**guv**-uh-nuhns/ n. **1** act or manner of governing. **2** function of governing. [French: related to GOVERN]

**governess** /**guv**-uh-nuhs, **guv**-uh-nes/ n. woman employed to teach children in a private household.

**government** /**guv**-uhn-muhnt, **guv**-muhnt, **guv**-uh-muhnt/ — n. **1** act or manner of governing. **2** system by which a nation, State, etc. is governed. **3 a** body of persons governing a nation etc. **b** (usu. **Government**) particular ministry in office. **4** the State as an agent. — adj. of or pertaining to the government (*government department; government car*). □ **governmental** /-**men**-tuhl/ adj.

■ **Usage** The pronunciations /**guv**-muhnt, **guv**-uh-muhnt/ are extremely common in Australia, but are considered incorrect by some people.

**governor** /**guv**-uh-nuh, **guv**-nuh/ n. **1** anyone who governs. **2** representative of the Crown: **a** in each Australian State. **b** in a colony or former colony. **3** head or member of the governing body of an institution (*Governor of the Reserve Bank*). **4** official in charge of a prison. **5 a** *colloq.* one's employer. **b** *colloq.* one's father. **6** *Mech.* automatic regulator controlling the speed of an engine etc. □ **governorship** n.

**Governor-General** n. representative of the Crown: **a** in the Commonwealth of Australia. **b** in any other British Commonwealth country that regards the British monarch as Head of State.

**govie** /**guv**-ee/ colloq. (also **guvvie**) — adj. government (*govie car*). — n. (also **govie flat** or **house**) flat or house originally built or bought by the government for low-cost or subsidised rental.

**Gowar** /**guu**-wahr/ n. an Aboriginal language spoken on Moreton Island in Moreton Bay, Queensland: now extinct.

**gown** — n. **1** loose flowing garment, esp. a woman's long dress. **2** official robe of an alderman, judge, cleric, academic, etc. **3** surgeon's overall. — v. (usu. as **gowned**

adj.) attire in a gown (*gowned professors in procession*). [Latin *gunna* fur]

**goy** n. (pl. **-im** or **-s**) Jewish name for a non-Jew. [Hebrew, = people]

**GP** abbr. general practitioner.

**GPO** abbr. General Post Office.

**gr** abbr. (also **gr.**) **1** gram(s). **2** grains. **3** gross.

**grab** — v. (**-bb-**) **1** seize suddenly. **2** take greedily or unfairly. **3** colloq. attract the attention of, impress (*how did the rock concert grab you?*). **4** (foll. by *at*) snatch at. **5** (of brakes) act harshly or jerkily. — n. **1** sudden clutch or attempt to seize. **2** mechanical device for clutching. □ **up for grabs** colloq. easily obtainable; inviting capture. □ **grabber** n. [Low German or Dutch]

**grab bag** n. miscellaneous collection (*made a grab bag of promises*).

**grace** — n. **1** attractiveness, esp. in elegance of proportion or manner or movement. **2** courteous good will (*had the grace to apologise*). **3** attractive feature; accomplishment (*social graces*). **4 a** (in Christian belief) the unmerited favour of God. **b** state of receiving this. **5** goodwill, favour (*fall from grace*). **6** delay granted as a favour (*a year's grace*). **7** short thanksgiving before or after a meal. **8** (**Grace**) (in Greek mythology) each of three beautiful sister goddesses, bestowers of beauty and charm. **9** (**Grace**) (prec. by *His, Her, Your*) forms of description or address for a duke, duchess, or archbishop. — v. (**-cing**) (often foll. by *with*) add grace to; confer honour on (*graced us with his presence*). □ **in a person's good** (or **bad**) **graces** regarded by a person with favour (or disfavour) **put on airs and graces** show snobbish pride; display affected mannerisms. **with good** (or **bad**) **grace** as if willingly (or reluctantly). [Latin *gratia*]

**graceful** adj. having or showing grace or elegance. □ **gracefully** adv. **gracefulness** n.

**graceless** /**grays**-luhs/ adj. lacking grace, elegance, or charm; boorish.

**grace note** n. *Mus.* extra note as an embellishment.

**gracious** /**gray**-shuhs/ — adj. **1 a** kind **b** indulgent to inferiors (*the Queen being gracious to commoners*). **2** (of God) merciful, benign. — int. expressing surprise. □ **graciously** adv. **graciousness** n. [Latin: related to GRACE]

**gradate** /gruh-**dayt**/ v. (**-ting**) **1** (cause to) pass gradually from one shade to another. **2** arrange in steps or grades or size etc.

**gradation** /gruh-**day**-shuhn/ n. (usu. in pl.) **1** stage of transition or advance. **2 a** certain degree in rank, intensity, etc. **b** arrangement in such degrees. □ **gradational** adj. [Latin: related to GRADE]

**grade** — n. **1 a** certain degree in rank, merit, proficiency, etc. **b** class of persons or things of the same grade. **2** mark indicating the quality of a student's work. **3** class in school. **4** gradient, slope. — v. (-**ding**) **1** arrange in grades. **2** (foll. by *up*, *down*, *off*, *into*, etc.) pass gradually between grades, or into a grade. **3** give a grade to (a student). **4** reduce (a road etc.) to easy gradients. — adj. (of sports) organised in grades according to level of ability (*grade cricket*). [Latin *gradus* step]

**grader** n. **1** person or thing that grades. **2** wheeled, motor-driven machine for levelling the ground, esp. in roadmaking.

**gradient** /**gray**-dee-uhnt/ n. **1 a** stretch of road, railway, etc., that slopes. **b** amount of such a slope. **2** rate of rise or fall of temperature, pressure, etc., in passing from one region to another. [probably from GRADE after *salient*]

**gradual** /**graj**-oo-uhl/ — adj. **1** progressing by degrees. **2** not rapid, steep, or abrupt. — n. a response sung or recited between the Epistle and the Gospel in the Mass. □ **gradually** adv. [Latin: related to GRADE]

**graduate** — n. /**graj**-oo-uht/ person holding an academic degree. — v. /**graj**-oo-,ayt/ (-**ting**) **1** obtain an academic degree. **2** (foll. by *to*) move up to (a higher grade of activity etc.). **3** mark out in degrees or parts. **4** arrange in gradations; apportion (e.g. tax) according to a scale. □ **graduation** /,graj-oo-**ay**-shuhn/ n. [medieval Latin *graduor* take a degree: related to GRADE]

**Graeco-Roman** /,gree-koh-**roh**-muhn/ adj. **1** of the Greeks and Romans. **2** displaying Greek and Roman influences, e.g. in Roman sculpture.

**graffiti** /gruh-**fee**-tee/ n.pl. (*sing.* **graffito** /gruh-**fee**-toh/) writing or drawing scribbled, scratched, or sprayed on a surface. [Italian *graffio* a scratch]

■ **Usage** The singular or collective use of the form *graffiti* is considered incorrect by some people, but it is frequently found, e.g. *graffiti has appeared.*

**graft**[1] /grahft/ — n. **1** *Bot.* **a** shoot or scion inserted into a slit of stock, from which it receives sap. **b** place where a graft is inserted. **2** *Surgery* piece of living tissue, organ, etc., transplanted surgically. — v. **1** (often foll. by *into*, *on*, *together*, etc.) insert (a scion) as a graft. **2** transplant (living tissue). **3** (foll. by *in*, *on*) insert or fix (a thing) permanently to another. [Greek *graphion* stylus]

**graft**[2] /grahft/ *colloq.* — n. **1** practices, esp. bribery, used to secure illicit gains in politics or business. **2** such gains. — v. seek or make such gains. [origin unknown]

**graft**[3] *colloq.* — n. hard work. — v. work hard (*grafting for opals at Coober Pedy*).

**Grail** n. (in full **Holy Grail**) (in medieval legend) cup used by Christ at the Last Supper. [medieval Latin *gradalis* dish]

**grain** — n. **1** fruit or seed of a cereal. **2** (*collect.*) wheat or any allied grass used as food. **3** small hard particle of salt, gold, sand, etc. **4** unit of weight, 0.0648 gram. **5** smallest possible quantity (*not a grain of truth in it*). **6** roughness of surface. **7** texture of skin, wood, stone, etc. **8 a** pattern of lines of fibre in wood or paper. **b** lamination in stone etc. — v. **1** paint in imitation of the grain of wood etc. **2** give a granular surface to. **3** form into grains. □ **against the grain** contrary to one's natural inclination or feeling. **with a grain of salt** with some scepticism. □ **grainy** adj. (-**ier**, -**iest**). [Latin *granum*]

**gram**[1] /gram/ n. metric unit of mass equal to one-thousandth of a kilogram. [Greek *gramma* small weight]

**gram**[2] /gram/ n. any of various pulses used as food (*green gram*, *black gram*, etc.). [Portuguese *grão* from Latin *granum* grain]

**-gram**[1] *comb. form* **1** forming nouns denoting a thing written or recorded (often in a certain way) (*anagram*; *epigram*; *telegram*). **2** meaning *telegram* and denoting one intended to amuse or embarrass the receiver since it is delivered in public (e.g. at a birthday party) by a specified messenger, e.g. a clown, a singer, one who delivers with a kiss, a derelict, etc.; hence *clownogram*, *sing-a-gram*, *kissogram*, *dero-gram*, etc. [Greek *gramma* thing written]

**-gram**[2] *comb. form* denoting grams (*kilogram*).

**graminaceous** /,gram-uh-**nay**-shuhs/ adj. of or like grass. [Latin *gramen* grass]

**gramineous** /gruh-**min**-ee-uhs/ = GRAMINACEOUS.

**graminivorous** /,gram-uh-**niv**-uh-ruhs/ adj. feeding on grass, cereals, etc.

**gramma** /**gram**-uh/ n. variety of pumpkin with sweet orange flesh, used in the Australian version of the pumpkin-pie. [origin unknown]

**gramma pie** *n.* Australian pumpkin-pie.

**grammar** /**gram**-uh/ *n.* **1** the study or rules of a language's inflections or other means of showing the relation between words. **2** observance or application of the rules of grammar (*bad grammar*). **3** book on grammar. [Greek *gramma* letter]

**grammarian** /gruh-**mair**-ree-uhn/ *n.* expert in grammar or linguistics.

**grammar school** *n.* a private school.

**grammatical** /gruh-**mat**-i-kuhl/ *adj.* of or conforming to the rules of grammar. □ **grammatically** *adv.*

**gramme** var. of GRAM¹.

**gramophone** /**gram**-uh-ˌfohn/ *n.* = RECORD-PLAYER. [inversion of *phonogram*: as PHONO-, -GRAM]

**gramophone record** = RECORD *n.* 3.

**granary** /**gran**-uh-ree/ *n.* (*pl.* **-ies**) **1** storehouse for threshed grain. **2** region producing, and esp. exporting, much grain. [Latin: related to GRAIN]

**grand** — *adj.* **1** splendid, magnificent, imposing, dignified. **2** main; of chief importance (*grand final; grand prix*). **3** of the highest rank (*grand duke; grand master in chess*). **4** *colloq.* excellent, enjoyable. **5** (in *comb.*) (in names of family relationships) denoting the second degree of ascent or descent (*granddaughter*). **6** complete; full (*grand total*). — *n.* **1** = GRAND PIANO. **2** (*pl.* same) *colloq.* a thousand dollars. □ **grandly** *adv.* **grandness** *n.* [Latin *grandis* full-grown]

**grandchild** *n.* child of one's son or daughter.

**granddaughter** *n.* female grandchild.

**grandeur** /**gran**-juh/ *n.* **1** majesty, splendour; dignity of appearance or bearing. **2** high rank, eminence. **3** nobility of character. [French: related to GRAND]

**grandfather** *n.* male grandparent.

**grandfather clock** *n.* clock in a tall wooden case, driven by weights.

**grand final** *n.* concluding match of a competition.

**grandiloquent** /ˌgran-**dil**-uh-kwuhnt/ *adj.* pompous or inflated in language. □ **grandiloquence** *n.* [Latin: related to GRAND, *-loquus* from *loquor* speak]

**grandiose** /**gran**-dee-ˌohs/ *adj.* **1** producing or meant to produce an imposing effect. **2** planned on an ambitious scale. **3** pretentiously grand; pompous. □ **grandiosity** /-**os**-uh-tee/ *n.* [Italian: related to GRAND]

**grand mal** /gron **mal**/ *n.* serious form of epilepsy with loss of consciousness. [French, = great sickness]

**grandmother** *n.* female grandparent.

**grand opera** *n.* opera on a serious theme, or in which the entire libretto (including dialogue) is sung.

**grandparent** *n.* parent of one's father or mother.

**grand piano** *n.* large full-toned piano standing on three legs, with the strings arranged horizontally.

**grand prix** /gron **pree**/ — *n.* (*pl.* **grands prix**) **1** highest award in a show, competition, etc. **2** (usu. **Grand Prix**) any of several important international motor or motor-cycle racing events. [French, = great or chief prize]

**grand slam** *n.* **1** *Sport* winning of all of a group of matches etc. **2** *Bridge* winning of 13 tricks.

**grandson** *n.* male grandchild.

**grandstand** /**gran**-stand, **grand**-ˌstand/ — *n.* main stand for spectators at a racecourse etc. — *v.* act in an ostentatious, self-important manner in order to impress (*as soon as he noticed the TV cameras, he began to grandstand outrageously*). — *adj.* advantageous for observing (*from his second-floor window he had a grandstand view of the accident*). □ **grandstand finish** close and exciting finish to a race etc.

**grand total** *n.* sum of other totals.

**graniferous** /gruh-**nif**-uh-ruhs/ *adj.* producing grain or a grainlike seed. [Latin: related to GRAIN]

**granite** /**gran**-uht/ *n.* granular crystalline rock of quartz, mica, etc., used for building. [Italian *granito*: related to GRAIN]

**granivorous** /gruh-**niv**-uh-ruhs/ *adj.* feeding on grain. [Latin: related to GRAIN]

**granny** /**gran**-ee/ *n.* (also **grannie**) (*pl.* **-ies**) *colloq.* **1** grandmother. **2** (in Aboriginal English) an elderly relative or community elder. [diminutive of *grannam* from archaic *grandam*: related to GRAND, DAME]

**granny bonnet** *n.* (also **granny's bonnet**) **1** = COLUMBINE. **2** (also **pimelea**) eastern Australian shrub with showy heads of white flowers.

**granny flat** *n.* addition to (or part of) a house made into self-contained accommodation for an elderly parent etc.

**granny knot** *n.* reef-knot crossed the wrong way and therefore insecure.

**Granny Smith** *n.* Australian green variety of apple. [Maria Ann ('Granny') Smith who first produced them in Sydney (d. 1870)]

**grant** /grahnt, grant/ — *v.* **1 a** consent to fulfil (a request etc.) (*granted all he asked*). **b** allow (a person) to have (a thing) (*granted me my freedom*). **2** give formally; transfer legally. **3** (often foll. by *that*) admit as true; concede. — *n.* **1** process of granting. **2** sum of money given by the State. **3** legal conveyance by written instrument. □ **take for granted 1** assume something to be true or valid. **2** cease to appreciate through familiarity. □ **grantor** /-taw/ *n.* (esp. in sense 2 of *v.*). [French *gr(e)anter* var. of *creanter* from Latin *credo* entrust]

**granular** /**gran**-yuh-luh/ *adj.* **1** of or like grains or granules. **2** having a granulated surface or structure. □ **granularity** /-la-ruh-tee/ *n.* [Latin: related to GRANULE]

**granulate** /**gran**-yuh-layt/ *v.* (**-ting**) **1** form into grains (*granulated sugar*). **2** roughen the surface of. □ **granulation** /-lay-shuhn/ *n.*

**granule** /**gran**-yool/ *n.* small grain. [Latin diminutive of *granum*: related to GRAIN]

**grape** *n.* **1** berry (usu. green, purple, or black) growing in clusters on a vine, used as fruit and in making wine. **2** any vine bearing these berries. [French, probably from *grappe* hook]

**grapefruit** *n.* (*pl.* same) **1** large round usu. yellow citrus fruit with an acid juicy pulp. **2** tree bearing this fruit.

**grapevine** *n.* **1** vine. **2** *colloq.* the means of transmission of a rumour (*heard it on the grapevine*).

**graph** /grahf, graf/ — *n.* diagram showing the relation between variable quantities, usu. of two variables, each measured along one of a pair of axes. — *v.* plot or trace on a graph. [abbreviation of *graphic formula*]

**-graph** *comb. form* forming nouns and verbs meaning: **1** thing written or drawn etc. in a specified way (*photograph*). **2** instrument that records (*seismograph*).

**-grapher** *comb. form* forming nouns denoting a person concerned with a subject (*geographer*; *radiographer*). [Greek *-graphos* writer, -ER[1]]

**graphic** /**graf**-ik/ *adj.* **1** of or relating to the visual or descriptive arts, esp. writing and drawing. **2** vividly descriptive. □ **graphically** *adv.* [Greek *graphē* writing]

**-graphic** *comb. form* (also **-graphical**) forming adjectives corresponding to nouns in *-graphy*.

**graphic arts** *n.pl.* visual and technical arts involving design or the use of lettering.

**graphic novel** *n.* novel in comic-strip format.

**graphics** *n.pl.* (usu. treated as *sing.*) **1** products of the graphic arts. **2** use of diagrams in calculation and design. **3** (in full **computer graphics**) mode of processing and output in which a significant part of the information is in pictorial form.

**graphite** /**graf**-uyt/ *n.* crystalline allotropic form of carbon used as a lubricant, in pencils, etc. □ **graphitic** /-fit-ik/ *adj.* [German *Graphit* from Greek *graphō* write]

**graphology** /gruh-**fol**-uh-jee/ *n.* the study of handwriting, esp. as a supposed guide to character. □ **graphologist** *n.* [Greek: related to GRAPHIC]

**graph paper** *n.* paper printed with a network of lines as a basis for drawing graphs.

**-graphy** *comb. form* forming nouns denoting: **1** descriptive science (*geography*). **2** technique of producing images (*photography*). **3** style or method of writing etc. (*calligraphy*).

**grapnel** /**grap**-nuhl/ *n.* **1** device with iron claws, for dragging or grasping. **2** small anchor with several flukes. [French *grapon*: related to GRAPE]

**grapple** /**grap**-uhl/ — *v.* (**-ling**) **1** (often foll. by *with*) fight in close combat. **2** (foll. by *with*) try to manage (a difficult problem etc.). **3 a** grip with the hands; come to close quarters with. **b** seize with or as with a grapnel. — *n.* **1** hold or grip in or as in wrestling. **b** contest at close quarters. **2** clutching-instrument; grapnel. [French *grapil*: related to GRAPNEL]

**grappling iron** *n.* (also **grappling hook**) = GRAPNEL.

**grasp** /grahsp, grasp/ — *v.* **1 a** clutch at; seize greedily. **b** hold firmly. **2** (foll. by *at*) try to seize; accept avidly. **3** understand or realise (a fact or meaning). — *n.* **1** firm hold; grip. **2** (foll. by *of*) **a** mastery (*a grasp of the situation*). **b** mental hold (*maths was beyond his grasp*). □ **grasp at straws** see STRAW. **grasp the nettle** tackle a difficulty boldly. [earlier *grapse*: related to GROPE]

**grasping** *adj.* avaricious.

**grass** /grahs/ — *n.* **1 a** any of a group of wild plants with green blades that are eaten by ruminants. **b** plant of the family which includes cereals, reeds, and bamboos. **2** pasture land. **3** grass-covered ground, lawn (*keep off the grass*). **4** grazing (*out to grass*). **5** *colloq.* marijuana. **6** *colloq.* informer, esp. a police informer. — *v.* **1** cover with turf. **2** provide with pasture. **3** *colloq.* **a** betray, esp. to the police. **b** inform the police. □ **exciting as watching grass grow** *colloq.* utterly boring (*listening to his speech was just about as exciting as watching grass grow*). **not let the grass grow under one's**

**feet** be quick to act or seize an opportunity. **put out to grass 1** (of a racehorse) retire it from racing when it is past its prime. **2** *colloq.* retire a person. □ **grassy** *adj.* (**-ier, -iest**). [Old English]

**grass-fed** *adj.* (of a horse) inexperienced, not trained as a racehorse.

**grass fighter** *n. colloq.* one who fights with no holds barred.

**grasshopper** *n.* jumping and chirping plant-eating insect.

**grassland** *n.* large open area covered with grass, esp. used for grazing.

**grass parrot** *n.* (also **grass parakeet**) any of various Australian parrots frequenting grassy country and feeding mainly on grass seeds (e.g. the budgerigar).

**grassroots** — *n.pl.* **1** fundamental level or source. **2** ordinary people; rank and file of an organisation, esp. a political party. — *adj.* pertaining to or deriving from ordinary people etc. (*grassroots opposition to the new tax*).

**grass-tree** *n.* (also **blackboy, xanthorrhoea, yakka**) any of many small woody-trunked Australian trees bearing a very tall flowering spike arising from a crown of grass-like leaves, and yielding a yellowish resin.

**grass widow** *n.* (also **grass widower**) person whose husband (or wife) is away for a prolonged period.

**grass wren** *n.* any of several large ground-dwelling Australian wrens inhabiting mainly spinifex country.

**grate**[1] *v.* (**-ting**) **1** reduce to small particles by rubbing on a serrated surface. **2** (often foll. by *against, on*) rub with a harsh scraping sound. **3** utter in a harsh tone. **4** (often foll. by *on*) **a** sound harshly. **b** have an irritating effect. **5** grind (one's teeth). **6** creak. □ **grater** *n.* [French from Germanic]

**grate**[2] *n.* **1** fireplace or furnace. **2** metal frame confining fuel in this. [Latin *cratis* hurdle]

**grateful** /**grayt**-fuhl/ *adj.* **1** thankful; feeling or showing gratitude. **2** pleasant, acceptable (*a grateful breeze*). □ **gratefully** *adv.* [obsolete *grate* from Latin *gratus*]

**gratify** /**grat**-uh-₁fuy/ *v.* (**-ies, -ied**) **1 a** please, delight. **b** please by compliance. **2** yield to (a feeling or desire). □ **gratification** /-fuh-**kay**-shuhn/ *n.* [Latin: related to GRATEFUL]

**grating** *n.* **1** framework of parallel or crossed metal bars. **2** *Optics* set of parallel wires, lines ruled on glass, etc.

**gratis** /**grah**-tuhs/ *adv.* & *adj.* free; without charge. [Latin]

**gratitude** /**grat**-uh-₁tyood/ *n.* being

thankful; readiness to return kindness. [Latin: related to GRATEFUL]

**gratuitous** /gruh-**tyoo**-uh-tuhs/ *adj.* **1** given or done free of charge. **2** uncalled-for; lacking good reason (*a gratuitous insult*). □ **gratuitously** *adv.* **gratuitousness** *n.* [Latin, = spontaneous]

**gratuity** /gruh-**tyoo**-uh-tee/ *n.* (*pl.* **-ies**) = TIP[3] *n.* 1. [Latin: related to GRATEFUL]

**grave**[1] /grayv/ *n.* **1** trench dug in the ground for the burial of a corpse; mound or memorial stone placed over this. **2** (prec. by *the*) death. □ **dig one's own grave** be responsible for one's own downfall. **one foot in the grave** very old, very ill, or seeming so. **turn in one's grave** (of a dead person) be thought of as likely in certain circumstances to have been shocked or angry when alive. [Old English]

**grave**[2] — *adj.* /grayv/ **1 a** serious, weighty, important. **b** dignified, solemn, sombre. **2** extremely serious or threatening. — *n.* /grahv/ = GRAVE ACCENT. □ **gravely** *adv.* [Latin *gravis* heavy]

**grave**[3] /grayv/ *v.* (**-ving**; *past part.* **graven** or **graved**) **1** (foll. by *in, on*) fix indelibly (on one's memory). **2** *archaic* engrave, carve. [Old English]

**grave accent** /grahv/ *n.* a mark (`) placed over a vowel to denote pronunciation, length, etc.

**gravel** /**grav**-uhl/ — *n.* **1** mixture of coarse sand and small stones, used for paths etc. **2** *Med.* aggregations of crystals formed in the urinary tract. — *v.* (**-ll-**) lay or strew with gravel. [French diminutive, perhaps of *grave* brave]

**gravelly** *adj.* **1** of or like gravel. **2** (of a voice) deep and rough-sounding.

**graven** *past part.* of GRAVE[3].

**graveyard** *n.* burial-ground. □ **graveyard shift** *n.* work-shift scheduled for very late at night or at dawn.

**gravid** /**grav**-uhd/ *adj.* pregnant. [Latin *gravidus*: related to GRAVE[2]]

**gravimeter** /gruh-**vim**-uh-tuh, **grav**-uh-₁mee-tuh/ *n.* instrument measuring the difference in the force of gravity between two places. [Latin: related to GRAVE[2]]

**gravimetry** /gruh-**vim**-uh-tree/ *n.* measurement of weight. □ **gravimetric** /₁grav-uh-**met**-rik/ *adj.*

**gravitate** /**grav**-uh-₁tayt/ *v.* (**-ting**) **1** (foll. by *to, towards*) move or be attracted to (*gravitated towards the pub*). **2 a** move or tend by force of gravity towards. **b** sink by or as if by gravity. [related to GRAVE[2]]

**gravitation** /₁grav-uh-**tay**-shuhn/ *n.* *Physics* **1** force of attraction between any particle of matter in the universe and any other. **2** effect of this, esp. the falling of bodies to the earth. □ **gravitational** *adj.*

**gravity** /grav-uh-tee/ n. **1 a** force that attracts a body to the centre of the earth etc. **b** degree of intensity of this. **c** gravitational force. **2** property of having weight. **3 a** importance, seriousness (*the gravity of AIDS is not realised by many*). **b** solemnity. [Latin: related to GRAVE²]

**gravy** /gray-vee/ n. (pl. **-ies**) **1** juices exuding from meat during and after cooking. **2** sauce for food, made from these etc. [perhaps from a misreading of French *grané* from *grain* spice, GRAIN]

**gravy beef** n. lesser quality but flavoursome meat from shank or shin used for making stock, broth, etc.

**gravyboat** n. boat-shaped vessel for serving gravy.

**gravy train** n. *colloq*. source of easy financial benefit.

**grayling** n. (pl. same) silver-grey freshwater fish of south-eastern Australia. [from GREY, -LING]

**graze¹** v. (**-zing**) **1** (of cattle, sheep, etc.) eat growing grass. **2 a** feed (cattle etc.) on growing grass. **b** feed on (grass). **3** pasture cattle. [Old English: related to GRASS]

**graze²** — v. (**-zing**) **1** rub or scrape (part of the body, esp. the skin). **2 a** touch lightly in passing. **b** (foll. by *against*, *along*, etc.) move with a light passing contact. — n. abrasion. [perhaps from GRAZE¹, as if 'take off the grass close to the ground']

**grazier** /gray-zee-uh/ n. owner of a large-scale property on which sheep or cattle are raised. [from GRASS]

**grazier's alert** n. warning of cold weather ahead issued by the weather bureau to graziers, esp. when it is lambing season.

**grazing country** n. land suited to or used for the raising of sheep or cattle.

**grazing district** n. area in which sheep or cattle raising is the principal industry.

**grease** /grees/ — n. **1** oily or fatty matter, esp. as a lubricant. **2** melted fat of a dead animal. — v. (also /greez/) (**-sing**) smear or lubricate with grease. □ **grease the palm of** *colloq*. bribe. [Latin *crassus* (adj.) fat]

**greasepaint** n. make-up used by actors.

**greaseproof** adj. impervious to grease (*greaseproof paper*).

**greaser** /gree-zuh/ n. *colloq*. obsequious person, a crawler.

**greasies** /gree-zeez/ n.pl. *colloq*. **1** fish and chips. **2** any take-away food (esp. if oily).

**greasy** /gree-zee, gree-see/ — adj. (**-ier**, **-iest**) **1 a** of or like grease. **b** smeared or covered with grease. **c** containing or having too much grease. **2 a** slippery. **b** (of a person or manner) unpleasantly unctuous. — n. *colloq*. **1** person who cooks for a number, as an army cook. **2** shearer. □ **greasily** adv. **greasiness** n.

**great** /grayt/ — adj. **1 a** of a size, amount, extent, or intensity considerably above the normal or average (*a great hole*; *great fun*). **b** also with implied admiration, contempt, etc., esp. in exclamations (*you great idiot!*; *great stuff!*). **c** reinforcing other words denoting size, quantity, etc. (*great big hole*; *a great many*). **2** important, pre-eminent (*the great thing is not to get caught*). **3** grand, imposing (*great occasion*). **4** distinguished. **5** remarkable in ability, character, etc. (*great men*; *great thinker*). **6** (foll. by *at*, *on*) competent, well-informed (*great at chess*; *great on Aboriginal languages*). **7** fully deserving the name of; doing a thing extensively (*great reader*; *great believer in tolerance*). **8** (also **greater**) the larger of the name, species, etc. (*great grey kangaroo*; *greater glider*). **9** *colloq*. very enjoyable or satisfactory (*had a great time*). **10** (in *comb.*) (in names of family relationships) denoting one degree further removed upwards or downwards (*great-uncle*; *great-great-grandmother*). — n. great or outstanding person or thing. □ **go great guns** *colloq*. succeed, do well (*going great guns as a carpenter*). **great one for** *colloq*. very keen on; very skilled at (*he's a great one for computer games*). **greatest thing since sliced bread** *colloq*. wonderful, first rate. □ **greatness** n. [Old English]

**great Australian adjective** n. the epithet 'bloody'. [from ubiquitous use]

**great Australian salute** n. frequently seen wave of the hand brushing flies off the face.

**Great Bear** see BEAR².

**great circle** n. circle on the surface of a sphere whose plane passes through the sphere's centre.

**greatcoat** n. heavy overcoat.

**great deal** n. = DEAL¹ n. 1.

**greater glider** n. large gliding possum of mainland Australia.

**great grey kangaroo** n. (also **great kangaroo, eastern grey kangaroo**) extremely large kangaroo (the male may stand nearly 2 metres tall) of eastern Australia, with silvery grey fur.

**greatly** adv. much; by a considerable amount (*greatly admired*; *greatly superior*).

**Great War** n. world war of 1914–18.

**grebe** /greeb/ n. any of various diving

birds (of Europe, Australia, etc.) with a long neck, lobed toes, and almost no tail (*Australasian grebe*; *great crested grebe*; *hoary-headed grebe*). [origin unknown]

**Grecian** /**gree**-shuhn/ *adj.* pertaining to ancient Greece (esp. its art, architecture, etc.) (*Grecian urn*). [Latin *Graecia* Greece]

**Grecian nose** *n.* straight nose (as portrayed in ancient Greek statues etc.) that continues the line of the forehead without a dip.

**greed** *n.* excessive desire, esp. for food or wealth. [from GREEDY]

**greedy** *adj.* (**-ier, -iest**) **1** having or showing greed. **2** (foll. by *for*, or *to* + infin.) very eager. □ **greedily** *adv.* **greediness** *n.* [Old English]

**Greek** — *n.* **1 a** native or national of modern Greece; person of Greek descent. **b** native or citizen of any of the ancient States of Greece. **2** language of Greece. — *adj.* of Greece or its people or language; Hellenic. □ **Greek to me** *colloq.* incomprehensible to me. [Old English ultimately from Greek *Graikoi*]

**green** — *adj.* **1** of the colour between blue and yellow in the spectrum; coloured like grass. **2** covered with leaves or grass. **3** (of fruit etc. or wood) unripe or unseasoned. **4** not dried, smoked, or tanned. **5** uncooked (*green prawns*). **6** inexperienced, gullible. **7 a** (of the complexion) pale, sickly-hued. **b** jealous, envious. **8** young, flourishing. **9** not withered or worn out (*a green old age*). **10** (also **Green**) concerned with protection of the environment as a political principle; not harmful to the environment. — *n.* **1** green colour or pigment. **2** green clothes or material. **3 a** *Brit.* piece of public grassy land (*village green*). **b** grassy area used for a special purpose (*putting-green*). **4** (in *pl.*) green vegetables. **5** (also **Green**) supporter of an environmentalist group or party. — *v.* make or become green. □ **greenish** *adj.* **greenly** *adv.* **greenness** *n.* [Old English]

**green ban** *n.* **1** prohibition (esp. by a trade union) which prevents construction work from proceeding on a site within a GREEN BELT. **2** similar prohibition against the demolition or marring of e.g. a building of historical, cultural, etc. significance.

**green belt** *n.* area of open land round a city, designated for preservation.

**green drought** *n.* new but insubstantial growth (of forage) following rain.

**greenery** *n.* green foliage or growing plants.

**greenfinch** *n.* finch with green and

yellow plumage, related to the goldfinch, introduced to Australia.

**green fingers** *n. colloq.* skill in growing plants.

**greenfly** *n.* **1** green aphid. **2** these collectively.

**greengage** *n.* roundish green variety of plum. [W. *Gage*, botanist (d. 1727)]

**green gram** *n.* = MUNG.

**greengrocer** *n.* **1** retailer of fruit and vegetables. **2** species of large Australian cicada when in its green stage (cf. YELLOW MONDAY).

**greenhood** *n.* any of many species of terrestrial Australian orchid of the genus *Pterostylis*, having a hooded greenish (often translucent) flower.

**greenhorn** *n.* inexperienced person; new recruit.

**greenhouse** *n.* light structure with the sides and roof mainly of glass in order to trap heat from the sun, and used for rearing plants.

**greenhouse effect** *n.* trapping of the sun's warmth in the lower atmosphere of the earth, caused by an increase in carbon dioxide, methane, etc.

**greenhouse gas** *n.* any of the gases, esp. carbon dioxide and methane, that contribute to the greenhouse effect.

**greenie** /**gree**-nee/ *n. colloq.* member or supporter of an environmentalist group or party; conservationist.

**green leek** *n.* any of several predominantly green or green-faced Australian parakeets.

**green light** *n.* **1** signal to proceed on a road, railway, etc. **2** *colloq.* permission to proceed with a project.

**green mallee** *n.* small eucalypt of inland eastern Australia with very narrow vividly green leaves; one of the species used for the distillation of eucalyptus oil.

**green monday** *n.* = GREENGROCER 2.

**green pick** *n.* new growth (of forage) promoted by rain.

**green room** *n.* room in a theatre for actors who are off stage.

**green shoot** *n.* new growth (of vegetation) immediately after a bushfire.

**green-stick fracture** *n.* bone-fracture, esp. in children, in which one side of the bone is broken and one only bent.

**green tea** *n.* tea made from steam-dried leaves which have not been previously fermented.

**green tree ant** *n.* (also **green ant**) ant of northern Australia and elsewhere, having a green body and living in trees in which it makes large intricate nests from leaves.

**Greenwich Mean Time** /gren-ich/ *n.* local time on the meridian of Greenwich, used as an international basis of time-reckoning.

**greeny** /gree-nee/ — *adj.* greenish. — *n.* = GREENIE.

**greet** *v.* **1** address politely or welcomingly on meeting or arrival. **2** receive or acknowledge in a specified way (*greeted with derision*). **3** (of a sight, sound, etc.) become apparent to or noticed by (*laughter greeted his ears*). [Old English]

**greeting** *n.* **1** act or instance of welcoming etc. **2** words, gestures, etc., used to greet a person. **3** (often in *pl.*) expression of goodwill.

**gregarious** /gruh-**gair**-ree-uhs/ *adj.* **1** fond of company. **2** living in flocks or communities. □ **gregariousness** *n.* [Latin *grex gregis* flock]

**Gregorian calendar** /gruh-**gaw**-ree-uhn/ *n.* the calendar now in use introduced in 1582 by Pope Gregory XIII.

**Gregorian chant** *n.* plainsong ritual music, named after Pope Saint Gregory I (the Great), *circa* 540–604.

**gremlin** /**grem**-luhn/ *n. colloq.* imaginary mischievous sprite regarded as responsible for mechanical faults etc. [origin unknown]

**grenade** /gruh-**nayd**/ *n.* small bomb thrown by hand (**hand grenade**) or shot from a rifle. [French: related to POMEGRANATE]

**grevillea** /gruh-**vil**-ee-uh/ *n.* any shrub or tree of the large chiefly Australian genus of the same name, many of which have extremely showy flowers and are widely cultivated as ornamentals. [C.F. *Greville*, botanist (d. 1809)]

**grew** *past of* GROW.

**grey** /gray/ — *adj.* **1** of a colour intermediate between black and white. **2** dull, dismal (*grey skies*). **3 a** (of hair) turning white with age etc. **b** having grey hair. **4** anonymous, unidentifiable (*grey area*). — *n.* **1 a** grey colour or pigment. **b** grey clothes or material (*dressed in grey*). **2** grey or white horse. — *v.* make or become grey. □ **greyish** *adj.* **greyness** *n.* [Old English]

**grey area** *n.* situation or topic not clearly defined.

**grey box** *n.* any of several Australian eucalypts, some with a silvery grey shining bark, others with a rough grey bark.

**grey butcherbird** *n.* woodland bird, widespread in Australia, having black, grey, and white plumage, and noted for its predatory habits and beautiful song.

**grey currawong** see CURRAWONG.

**Grey Friar** *n.* Franciscan friar.

**greyhound** *n.* dog of a tall slender breed capable of high speed. [Old English, = bitch-hound]

**grey kangaroo** *n.* **1** = GREAT GREY KANGAROO. **2** = WESTERN GREY.

**grey matter** *n.* **1** the darker tissues of the brain and spinal cord. **2** *colloq.* intelligence.

**grey nurse** *n.* common shark of south-eastern Australian waters.

**grey power** *n.* influence (esp. political) exerted by senior citizens, esp. through organisations representing them.

**grey thrush** *n.* predominantly grey woodland bird of Australia (not a member of the thrush family) zoologically named *harmonica* after the beauty of its song.

**grey water** *n.* bath or laundry water, esp. as used for watering garden etc.

**grid** *n.* **1** a grating. **b** (in an opening in a fence) a set of metal rails fixed on the ground over a shallow trench, and so spaced as to prevent the passage of stock. **2** system of numbered squares printed on a map and forming the basis of map references. **3** network of lines, electric-power connections, gas-supply lines, etc. **4** pattern of lines marking the starting-places on a motor-racing track. **5** perforated electrode controlling the flow of electrons in a thermionic valve etc. **6** arrangement of town streets in a rectangular pattern. [from GRIDIRON]

**griddle** /**grid**-uhl/ *n.* circular iron plate placed over a source of heat for cooking etc. [Latin *cratis* hurdle]

**gridiron** /**grid**-uy-uhn/ *n.* **1** cooking utensil of parallel metal bars for broiling or grilling. **2** field (with parallel lines marking out the area of play) on which American football (a game evolved from Rugby) is played. [related to GRIDDLE]

**grief** *n.* **1** intense sorrow. **2** cause of this. □ **come to grief** meet with disaster. [French: related to GRIEVE]

**grievance** /**gree**-vuhns/ *n.* real or fancied cause for complaint. [French: related to GRIEF]

**grieve** *v.* (**-ving**) **1** cause grief to. **2** suffer grief. □ **griever** *n.* [Latin: related to GRAVE[2]]

**grievous** /**gree**-vuhs/ *adj.* **1** (of pain etc.) severe. **2** causing grief. **3** injurious. **4** flagrant, heinous. □ **grievously** *adv.* [French: related to GRIEF]

**grievous bodily harm** *n. Law* serious injury inflicted intentionally.

**griffin** /**grif**-uhn/ *n.* (also **gryphon**) fabulous creature with an eagle's head and wings and a lion's body. [Latin *gryphus* from Greek]

**grill** — n. **1 a** device in a cooker for radiating heat downwards. **b** = GRIDIRON. **2** food cooked on a grill. **3** (in full **grill room**) restaurant specialising in grilled food. — v. **1** cook or be cooked under a grill or on a gridiron. **2** subject or be subjected to extreme heat. **3** subject to severe questioning. □ **griller** n. **grilling** n. (in sense 3 of verb). [French: related to GRIDDLE]

**grille** n. (also **grill**) **1** grating or latticed screen, used as a partition etc. **2** metal grid protecting the radiator of a vehicle.

**grim** adj. (**grimmer**, **grimmest**) **1** of stern or forbidding appearance. **2** harsh, merciless (grim reality). **3** ghastly, joyless (has a grim truth in it). **4** unpleasant, unattractive (grim sense of humour). □ **like grim death** with utmost determination (held on like grim death). □ **grimly** adv. **grimness** n. [Old English]

**grimace** /grim-uhs, gruh-**mays**/ — n. distortion of the face made in disgust etc. or to amuse. — v. (**-cing**) make a grimace. [French from Spanish]

**grime** /gruym/ — n. soot or dirt ingrained in a surface. — v. (**-ming**) blacken with grime; befoul. □ **griminess** n. **grimy** adj. (**-ier**, **-iest**) [Low German or Dutch]

**grin** — v. (**-nn-**) **1 a** smile broadly, showing the teeth. **b** make a forced, unrestrained, or stupid smile. **2** express by grinning (grinned his satisfaction). — n. act of grinning. □ **grin and bear it** take pain etc. stoically. [Old English]

**grind** /gruynd/ — v. (past and past part. **ground**) **1** reduce to small particles or powder by crushing. **2 a** sharpen or smooth by friction (grind the axe). **b** rub or rub together gratingly (ground his teeth in rage). **3** (often foll. by down) oppress; harass with exactions (grinding poverty). **4 a** (often foll. by away) work or study hard. **b** (foll. by out) produce with effort (grinding out excuses). — n. **1** act or instance of grinding. **2** colloq. hard dull work or study (the daily grind). □ **grind to a halt** stop laboriously. [Old English]

**grinder** n. **1** person or thing that grinds, esp. a machine. **2** molar tooth.

**grindstone** n. **1** thick revolving disc used for grinding, sharpening, and polishing. **2** a kind of stone used for this. □ **keep one's nose to the grindstone** work hard and continuously.

**grip** — v. (**-pp-**) **1 a** grasp tightly. **b** take a firm hold, esp. by friction. **2** compel the attention of (the story gripped us). **3** (of a feeling or emotion) deeply affect (a person) (was gripped by fear). — n. **1 a** firm hold; tight grasp. **b** manner of grasping or holding. **2** power of holding attention. **3 a** intellectual mastery. **b** effective control of one's behaviour etc. (lose one's grip). **4 a** part of a machine that grips. **b** part by which a weapon etc. is held. **5** travelling bag. □ **come** (or **get**) **to grips with** approach purposefully; begin to deal with. [Old English]

**gripe** — v. (**-ping**) **1** colloq. complain. **2** affect with gastric pain. — n. **1** (usu. in pl.) colic. **2** colloq. complaint. [Old English]

**grisly** /griz-lee/ adj. (**-ier**, **-iest**) causing horror, disgust, or fear. □ **grisliness** n. [Old English]

**grist** n. corn to grind. □ **grist to the** (or **a person's**) **mill** source of profit or advantage. [Old English: related to GRIND]

**gristle** /gris-uhl/ n. tough flexible animal tissue; cartilage. □ **gristly** /gris-lee/ adj. [Old English]

**grit** — n. **1** particles of stone or sand, esp. as irritating or hindering. **2** coarse sandstone. **3** colloq. pluck, endurance. — v. (**-tt-**) **1** clench (the teeth). **2** make a grating sound. □ **gritty** adj. (**-ier**, **-iest**). [Old English]

**grizzle**[1] /griz-uhl/ v. (**-ling**) colloq. **1** (esp. of a child) cry fretfully. **2** complain whiningly, whinge. □ **grizzly** adj. [origin unknown]

**grizzle**[2] v. become or make grey. [grizzle grey, from French grisel]

**grizzled** /griz-uhld/ adj. **1** (of hair) grey or streaked with grey. **2** having grizzled hair.

**grizzle-guts** n. colloq. constant whinger, complainer.

**grizzly** /griz-lee/ — adj. (**-ier**, **-iest**) grey, grey-haired. — n. (pl. **-ies**) (in full **grizzly bear**) large variety of brown bear, found in N. America and N. Russia.

**groan** — v. **1 a** make a deep sound expressing pain, grief, or disapproval. **b** utter with groans. **2** (usu. foll. by under, beneath, with) be loaded or oppressed. — n. **1** sound made in groaning. **2** colloq. boring person or thing (he's such a groan; the party was a real groan). [Old English]

**grocer** /groh-suh/ n. dealer in food and household provisions. [Anglo-French grosser from Latin grossus GROSS]

**grocery** /groh-suh-ree/ n. (pl. **-ies**) **1** grocer's trade or shop. **2** (in pl.) goods, esp. food, sold by a grocer.

**grog** — n. **1 a** colloq. beer. **b** other alcoholic drinks. **2** hist. drink of rum (or other spirit) and water. — v. colloq. drink beer or some other alcoholic beverage. □ **grog on** colloq. engage in a prolonged drinking session. **on the grog 1** *colloq.* taken to drinking (*he's on the grog in spite of his doctor's warning*). **2** engaged in a bout of heavy drinking. [origin uncertain]

**grog-artist** *n. colloq.* heavy drinker (see ARTIST 4).

**groggy** *adj.* (**-ier, -iest**) **1** incapable or unsteady from being dazed etc. (*the boxer was groggy after the uppercut*). **2** *colloq.* drunk. □ **groggily** *adv.* **grogginess** *n.*

**grog-on** *n.* (also **grog-up**) *colloq.* prolonged drinking session.

**grog shanty** *n. hist.* roughly run (unlicensed) hotel, esp. on a goldfield.

**grog shop** *n. colloq.* shop selling alcohol.

**groin** — *n.* **1** depression between the belly and the thigh. **2** *Archit.* **a** edge formed by intersecting vaults. **b** arch supporting a vault. — *v. Archit.* build with groins. [origin uncertain]

**grommet** /**grom**-uht/ *n.* (also **grummet**) **1** metal, plastic, or rubber eyelet placed in a hole to protect or insulate a rope or cable etc. passed through it. **2** tube passed through the eardrum to make a communication with the middle ear. **3** (also **grom**) *colloq.* young, inexperienced surfie. [French]

**groom** /groom/ — *n.* **1** person employed to take care of horses. **2** = BRIDEGROOM. — *v.* **1 a** curry or tend (a horse). **b** give a neat appearance to (a person etc.). **2** (of an ape etc.) clean the fur of (its fellow) with its fingers. **3** prepare or train (a person) for a particular purpose or job. [origin unknown]

**groove** — *n.* **1** channel or elongated hollow, esp. one made to guide motion or receive a corresponding ridge. **2** habitual pattern, monotonous routine (*get into a groove*). **3** spiral track cut in a gramophone record. — *v.* (**-ving**) **1** make a groove or grooves in. **2** *colloq.* enjoy oneself. [Dutch]

**groovy** /**groo**-vee/ *adj.* (**-ier, -iest**) *colloq.* **1** excellent; exciting. **2** trendy.

**grope** — *v.* (**-ping**) **1** (usu. foll. by *for*) feel about or search blindly. **2** (foll. by *for, after*) search mentally. **3** feel (one's way) towards something. **4** *colloq.* fondle clumsily. — *n.* act of groping. [Old English]

**groper¹** /**groh**-puh/ *n.* any of several large Australian or New Zealand sea fish with heavy body, big head, and enormously wide mouth. [Portuguese *garupa*]

**groper²** *n. colloq.* = SANDGROPER. [abbreviation]

**gross** /grohs/ — *adj.* **1** overfed, bloated. **2** (of a person, manners, or morals)

coarse, unrefined, or indecent (*his behaviour was gross*). **3** flagrant (*gross negligence*). **4** total; not net (*gross income*). **5** (of the senses etc.) dull. **6** *colloq.* repulsive; off-putting (*wearing ties is really gross*). — *v.* produce as gross profit. — *n.* (*pl.* same) amount equal to twelve dozen. — *int. colloq.* exclamation indicating revulsion etc. □ **gross out** *colloq.* to disgust (*that grosses me out*). □ **grossly** *adv.* **grossness** *n.* [Latin *grossus*]

**gross domestic product** *n.* (*abbr.* **GDP**) total value of goods produced and services provided in a country in one year.

**gross national product** *n.* (*abbr.* **GNP**) gross domestic product plus the total of net income from abroad.

**grot** *n. colloq.* **1** dirt. **2** dirty person. [back-formation from GROTTY]

**grotesque** /groh-**tesk**/ — *adj.* **1** comically or repulsively distorted. **2** incongruous, absurd. — *n.* **1** decorative form interweaving human and animal features. **2** comically distorted figure or design. □ **grotesquely** *adv.* **grotesqueness** *n.* [Italian: related to GROTTO]

**grotto** /**grot**-oh/ *n.* (*pl.* **-es** or **-s**) **1** picturesque cave. **2** artificial ornamental cave. [Italian *grotta* from Greek *kruptē* CRYPT]

**grotty** /**grot**-ee/ *adj.* (**-ier, -iest**) *colloq.* unpleasant, dirty, shabby, unattractive. [shortening of GROTESQUE]

**grouch** *colloq.* — *v.* grumble; complain. — *n.* **1** discontented person. **2 a** fit of grumbling or the sulks. **b** complaint (*what's your grouch?*). □ **grouchy** *adj.* (**-ier, -iest**). [related to GRUDGE]

**ground¹** — *n.* **1 a** surface of the earth, esp. as contrasted with the air around it. **b** part of this specified in some way (*low ground*). **2** soil, earth (*stony ground*). **3 a** position, area, or distance on the earth's surface (*the explorers covered a lot of ground in inland Australia*). **b** extent of a subject dealt with (*this book covers a lot of ground*). **4** (often in *pl.*) reason, justification (*what are your grounds for saying this?*). **5** area of a special kind or use (often in *comb.*: *cricket-ground; fishing-grounds*). **6** (in *pl.*) enclosed land attached to a house etc. **7** area or basis for agreement etc. (*common ground*). **8** (in painting etc.) the surface giving the predominant colour. **9** (in *pl.*) solid particles, esp. of coffee, forming a residue. **10** *Electr.* = EARTH *n.* 4. **11** bottom of the sea. **12** (in full **ground bass**) *Mus.* short theme in the bass constantly repeated with the upper parts of the music varied.

**13** (*attrib.*) (of animals) living on or in the ground; typically seen on the ground (*ground parrot*); (of plants) dwarfish or trailing (*ground cover*). — *v.* **1** refuse authority for (a pilot or an aircraft) to fly. **2 a** run (a ship) aground; strand. **b** (of a ship) run aground. **3** (foll. by *in*) instruct thoroughly (in a subject). **4** (often as **grounded** *adj.*) (foll. by *on*) base (a principle, conclusion, etc.) on. **5** (often as **grounded adj.**) withdraw privileges etc. as a punishment. **6** *Electr.* = EARTH *v.* □ **break new** (or **fresh**) **ground** treat a subject previously not dealt with; do something not done before. **cut the ground from under a person's feet** anticipate and then undercut his or her arguments, plans, etc. **get in on the ground floor** become part of an enterprise in its early stages. **get off the ground** *colloq.* make a successful start. **give** (or **lose**) **ground 1** retreat, decline. **2** lose the advantage or one's position in an argument, contest, etc. **go to ground** retire from the public eye for a prolonged period. **hold** (or **stand**) **one's ground** not retreat or give way. **lose ground** retreat; give way; lose what one has gained. **old stamping ground** *colloq.* place one used to frequent, esp. in one's youth (*that games arcade was our old stamping ground*). **on the grounds of** because of (*retired on the grounds of ill-health*). **run a person** (or **thing**) **into the ground** *colloq.* overwork (or misuse) until exhausted (or beyond repair) (*running his workers into the ground; ran his car into the ground*). [Old English]

**ground²** *past* and *past part.* of GRIND.

**ground control** *n.* personnel directing the landing etc. of aircraft etc.

**ground cover** *n.* low-growing plant(s) covering the surface of the earth.

**ground floor** *n.* floor of a building at ground level.

**ground glass** *n.* **1** glass made non-transparent by grinding etc. **2** glass ground to a powder.

**grounding** *n.* basic training or instruction.

**groundless** *adj.* without motive or foundation (*our fears were groundless*).

**ground parrot** *n.* (also **ground parakeet**) any of several Australian parrots typically seen on the ground.

**ground plan** *n.* **1** plan of a building at ground level. **2** general outline of a scheme.

**ground rule** *n.* basic rule, code of conduct, etc. (*these are the ground rules for this excursion*).

**groundsel** /**grown**-suhl/ *n.* wild plant

with small yellow flowers, used as a food for cage-birds etc. [Old English]

**groundsheet** *n.* waterproof sheet for spreading on the ground.

**groundsman** /**growndz**-muhn/ *n.* person who maintains a sports ground.

**ground speed** *n.* aircraft's speed relative to the ground.

**ground state** *n. Physics.* lowest energy state of an atom etc.

**groundswell** *n.* **1** heavy sea caused by a distant or past storm or an earthquake. **2** increasingly forceful presence, esp. of public opinion (*a groundswell of support for a new flag*).

**ground thrush** *n.* any of several Australian birds typically seen on the ground and having a strong resemblance to the song thrush of Britain.

**groundwork** *n.* preliminary or basic work.

**ground zero** *n.* the point on the ground under an exploding (usu. nuclear) bomb.

**group** /groop/ — *n.* **1** number of persons or things located close together, or considered or classed together. **2** number of people working together etc. **3** number of commercial companies under common ownership. **4** ensemble of musicians (*pop group; jazz group*). **5** = BLOOD GROUP. — *v.* **1** form or be formed into a group. **2** (often foll. by *with*) place in a group or groups. [Italian *gruppo*]

**group captain** *n.* RAAF officer next below air commodore.

**group certificate** *n.* annual record of salary etc. and tax deducted, given to an employee for submission with a tax return.

**grouper** *n.* = GROPER¹

**groupie** *n. colloq.* ardent follower or fan (of pop groups, sports stars, etc.).

**group practice** *n.* medical practice in which several doctors are associated.

**group therapy** *n.* therapy in which people are brought together to assist one another psychologically.

**grouse¹** /grows/ *n.* (*pl.* same) **1** game-bird with a plump body and feathered legs. **2** its flesh as food. [origin uncertain]

**grouse²** /grows, growz/ *colloq.* — *v.* (**-sing**) grumble or complain. — *n.* complaint. [origin unknown]

**grouse³** /grows/ *adj. colloq.* very good of its kind (*that film was grouse*). □ **extra grouse** excellent, terrific. [origin unknown]

**grout** — *n.* thin fluid mortar for filling gaps between floor tiles, wall tiles, etc. — *v.* provide or fill with grout. □ **grouter** *n.* [origin uncertain]

**grouter** n. colloq. unfair advantage.
□ **come in on the grouter** start with an
unfair advantage. [origin uncertain]

**grove** n. small wood or group of trees. [Old
English]

**grovel** /grov-uhl/ v. (-**ll**-) **1** behave
obsequiously. **2** lie prone in abject
humility. □ **grovelling** adj. [obsolete
grovelling (adv.) from Old Norse á grúfu
face down]

**grow** /groh/ v. (past **grew**; past part.
**grown**) **1** increase in size, height,
quantity, degree, etc. **2** develop or exist as
a living plant or natural product. **3 a**
produce (plants etc.) by cultivation. **b**
allow (a beard etc.) to develop. **4 a** become
gradually (grow rich). **b** (foll. by to +
infin.) come by degrees (grew to like it). **5**
(foll. by on) become gradually more
favoured by (gardening has grown on
me). **6** (foll. by into) become large enough
for or suited to (will grow into the coat;
grew into her new job). **7** (in passive; foll.
by over etc.) be covered with a growth.
□ **grow out of 1** become too large to wear.
**2** become too mature to retain (a habit
etc.). **3** develop from. **grow up 1** advance
to maturity. **2** (of a custom) arise. **3** (in
Aboriginal English) rear, bring up (his
father grew me up). [Old English]

**grower** n. **1** (often in comb.) person
growing produce (fruit-grower). **2** plant
that grows in a specified way (fast
grower).

**growing pains** n.pl. **1** early difficulties in
the development of a project etc. **2**
neuralgic pain in children's legs due to
fatigue etc.

**growl** /growl/ — v. **1 a** (often foll. by at)
make a low guttural sound, usu. of anger.
**b** murmur angrily. **2** rumble (my
stomach's growling). **3 a** (often foll. by
out) utter with a growl. **b** (in Aboriginal
English) criticise or threaten. — n. **1**
growling sound. **2** angry murmur. **3**
rumble. □ **growlingly** adv. [probably
imitative]

**grown** /grohn/ past part. of GROW.

**grown-up** — adj. adult. — n. adult
person.

**growth** /grohth/ n. **1** act or process of
growing. **2** increase in size or value. **3**
something that has grown or is growing.
**4** Med. mass of diseased tissue, e.g. a
tumour.

**growth hormone** n. substance which
stimulates the growth of a plant or
animal.

**growth industry** n. industry that is
developing rapidly.

**groyne** n. (also **groin**) timber, stone, or
concrete wall built at right angles to the
coast to check beach erosion. [British
dial. groin snout, from French]

**grub** — n. **1 a** larva of an insect. **b** =
WITCHETTY. **2** colloq. food. **3** colloq. dirty or
untidy child. — v. (-**bb**-) **1** dig superficially, clear away roots etc. (grub that
paddock). **2** (foll. by up, out) **a** extract by
digging, uproot (grub up that gum-tree
stump). **b** extract (information etc.) by
searching in books etc. **3** rummage
(grubbing for scraps). **4** (foll. by on, along,
away) toil, plod. [Old English]

**grubber** n. **1** person or thing that grubs.
**2** Cricket ball that does not bounce but
speeds along the ground. **3** Rugby (also
**grubber kick**) deliberate kick, usu. to
touch, intended to send the ball end-for-
end (and hence slowly) along the ground.

**grubby** adj. (-**ier**, -**iest**) **1** dirty. **2** of or
infested with grubs. □ **grubbily** adv.
**grubbiness** n.

**grudge** — n. persistent feeling of ill will
or resentment. — v. (-**ging**) **1** be resentfully unwilling to give or allow. **2** (foll. by
verbal noun or to + infin.) be reluctant to
do. [French]

**grudge match** n. **1** game or contest in
which there is bitterness or personal
antipathy between the opponents. **2**
contest, game, etc. played to settle a
grudge.

**gruel** /groo-uhl/ n. liquid food of oatmeal
etc. boiled in milk or water. [French from
Germanic]

**gruelling** adj. extremely demanding or
tiring.

**gruesome** /groo-suhm/ adj. horrible,
grisly, disgusting. □ **gruesomely** adv.
[Scandinavian]

**gruff** adj. **1 a** (of a voice) low and harsh. **b**
(of a person) having a gruff voice. **2** surly.
□ **gruffly** adv. **gruffness** n. [Low German
or Dutch grof coarse]

**gruie** /groo-ee/ n. = EMU APPLE.
[Kamilaroi garuye]

**grumble** /grum-buhl/ — v. (-**ling**) **1**
complain peevishly. **2** rumble (my
stomach's grumbling). — n. **1** complaint.
**2** rumble. □ **grumbler** n. [obsolete
grumme]

**grummet** var. of GROMMET.

**grump** colloq. — n. **1** irritable, grumpy
person; a grouch. **2** (in pl.) fit of sulks.
— v. grumble, whinge, complain. [from
GRUMPY]

**grumpy** /grum-pee/ adj. (-**ier**, -**iest**)
morosely irritable. □ **grumpily** adv.
**grumpiness** n.

**grunge** n. colloq. **1** grime, dirt. **2** style of
rock music characterised by a raucous
guitar sound and lazy vocal delivery.

**3** style of dress characterised by untidy loose-fitting clothes etc. [origin uncertain]

**grunt** — *n.* **1** low guttural sound made by a pig. **2** similar sound. — *v.* **1** make a grunt. **2** make a similar sound, esp. to express discontent. **3** utter with a grunt. [Old English, imitative]

**grunter** *n.* **1** pig. **2** person or animal that grunts. **3** any of many Australian freshwater fish that grunt when caught, e.g. silver perch, spangled grunter.

**gruyère** /groo-**yair**, **groo**-yuh/ *n.* a firm pale cheese. [*Gruyère* in Switzerland]

**gryphon** var. of GRIFFIN.

**G-string** /**jee**-string/ *n.* **1** *Mus.* string sounding the note G. **2** narrow strip of cloth etc. covering only the genitals and attached to a string round the waist.

**GT** *n.* high-performance saloon car. [Italian *gran turismo* great touring]

**guano** /**gwah**-noh/ *n.* (*pl.* **-s**) **1** excrement of sea birds, used as manure. **2** artificial manure, esp. that made from fish. [Spanish from Quechua *huanu* dung]

**guarantee** /ˌga-ruhn-**tee**/ — *n.* **1 a** formal promise or assurance, esp. that something is of a specified quality and durability. **b** document giving such an undertaking. **2** = GUARANTY. **3 a** *Law* person to whom a guaranty is given. **b** (in popular use) person making a guaranty. **4** that which acts as does a guaranty (*hard work is a guarantee of success*). — *v.* (**-tees**, **-teed**) **1 a** give or serve as a guarantee for. **b** provide with a guarantee. **2** give a promise or assurance. **3** (foll. by *to*) secure the possession of (a thing) for a person. [related to WARRANT]

**guarantor** /ˌga-ruhn-**taw**/ *n.* person who gives a guarantee or guaranty.

**guaranty** /**ga**-ruhn-tee/ *n.* (*pl.* **-ies**) **1** written or other undertaking to answer for the payment of a debt or for the performance of an obligation by another person liable in the first instance. **2** thing serving as security.

**guard** /gahd/ — *v.* **1** (often foll. by *from*, *against*) watch over and defend or protect. **2** keep watch by (a door etc.) to control entry or exit. **3** supervise (prisoners etc.) and prevent from escaping. **4** keep (thoughts or speech) in check. **5** (foll. by *against*) take precautions. — *n.* **1** state of vigilance. **2** person who protects or keeps watch. **3** soldiers etc. protecting a place or person; escort. **4** official in general charge of a train. **5** part of an army detached for some purpose (*advance guard*). **6** thing that protects (*fire-guard*). **7** defensive

posture or motion in boxing etc. □ **be on** (or **keep** or **stand**) **guard** keep watch. **lower one's guard** reduce vigilance against attack. **off** (or **off one's**) **guard** unprepared for some surprise or difficulty. **on** (or **on one's**) **guard** prepared for all contingencies. [Germanic: related to WARD]

**guarded** *adj.* (of a remark etc.) cautious. □ **guardedly** *adv.*

**guardian** /**gah**-dee-uhn/ *n.* **1** protector, keeper. **2** person having legal custody of another, esp. a minor. □ **guardianship** *n.* [French: related to WARD, WARDEN]

**guard rail** *n.* a rail, e.g. a handrail, fitted as a support or to prevent an accident.

**guava** /**gwah**-vuh/ *n.* **1** edible pale orange fruit with pink flesh. **2** small tropical American tree bearing this. [Spanish]

**gubba** /**gub**-uh/ *n. colloq.* (also **gub**, **gubbar**, **gubber**) name given by Aborigines to a white person. [origin unknown]

**guck** *n. colloq.* dirt; slime. [origin unknown]

**gudgeon** /**guj**-uhn/ — *n.* **1** small easily caught freshwater fish of Europe. **2** any of several similar Australian fish. **3** credulous or easily fooled person. — *v.* fool, dupe. [French *goujon* from Latin *gobio* GOBY]

**Guernsey** /**gern**-zee/ *n.* (*pl.* **-s**) **1** one of a breed of dairy cattle from Guernsey in the Channel Islands. **2** (**guernsey**) **a** type of thick woollen sweater. **b** football jersey, esp. the (often sleeveless) jumper in team colours worn by a player of Australian Rules football. □ **get a** (or **the**) **guernsey 1** be selected for a football team. **2** approval, recognition, etc. (*in this list of Australia's best places to live, why didn't Canberra get a guernsey?*).

**guerrilla** /guh-**ril**-uh/ *n.* (also **guerilla**) member of a small independently acting (usu. political) group taking part in irregular fighting. [Spanish diminutive of *guerra*: related to WAR]

**guerrilla war** (or **warfare**) *n.* fighting by or with guerrillas.

**guess** /ges/ — *v.* **1** (often *absol.*) estimate without calculation or measurement (*guess what's in my hand*). **2** form a hypothesis or opinion about; conjecture; think likely (*guess at the clearance under that bridge*). **3** conjecture or estimate correctly (*cannot guess how you did it*). **4** (foll. by *at*) make a conjecture about (*he guessed at the weight after careful observation*). — *n.* estimate, conjecture. □ **I guess** *colloq.* I think it likely; I suppose. [origin uncertain]

**guesstimate** (also **guestimate**) *colloq.* — *n.* /**ges**-tuh-muht/ an estimate based on a mixture of guesswork and calculation. — *v.* /**ges**-tuh-ˌmayt/ estimate in this manner. [from GUESS, ESTIMATE]

**guesswork** *n.* process of or results got by guessing.

**guest** /gest/ *n.* **1** person invited to visit another's house or to have a meal etc. at another's expense. **2** person lodging at a hotel etc. **3** outside performer invited to take part with a regular body of performers. □ **be my guest** *colloq.* make what use you wish of the available facilities. [Old Norse]

**guff** *n. colloq.* empty talk; nonsense. [originally 'puff': imitative]

**guffaw** /gu-**faw**, guh-**faw**/ — *n.* coarse or boisterous laugh. — *v.* utter a guffaw. [imitative]

**guidance** /**guy**-duhns/ *n.* **1** advice or direction for solving a problem etc. **2** guiding or being guided.

**guide** /guyd/ — *n.* **1** person who leads or shows the way. **2** person who conducts tours. **3** adviser. **4** directing principle (*one's feelings are a bad guide*). **5** book with essential information on a subject, esp. = GUIDEBOOK. **6** thing marking a position or guiding the eye. **7** bar etc. directing the motion of something. **8** (**Guide**) member of a girls' organisation similar to the Scouts. — *v.* (**-ding**) **1** act as guide to. **2** be the principle or motive of (*anger guided his actions*). [French from Germanic]

**guidebook** *n.* book of information about a place for tourists etc.

**guided missile** *n.* missile under remote control or directed by equipment within itself.

**guide dog** *n.* dog trained to guide a blind person.

**guideline** *n.* principle guiding or directing action.

**guild** /gild/ *n.* (also **gild**) **1** association of people for mutual aid or the pursuit of a common goal. **2** medieval association of craftsmen or merchants. [Low German or Dutch *gilde*]

**guile** /guyl/ *n.* cunning or sly behaviour; treachery, deceit. □ **guileful** *adj.* **guileless** *adj.* [French from Scandinavian]

**guillotine** /**gil**-uh-ˌteen/ — *n.* **1** machine with a blade sliding vertically in grooves, used for beheading. **2** device for cutting paper etc. **3** method of preventing delay in the discussion of a legislative bill by fixing times at which various parts of it must be voted on. — *v.* (**-ning**) use the guillotine on. [*Guillotin*, French physician (d. 1814)]

**guilt** /gilt/ *n.* **1** fact of having committed a specified or implied offence. **2** feeling of having done wrong. [Old English]

**guiltless** *adj.* (often foll. by *of* an offence) innocent.

**guilty** *adj.* (**-ier**, **-iest**) **1** culpable of or responsible for a wrong. **2** conscious of or affected by guilt (*a guilty look*). **3** causing a feeling of guilt (*a guilty secret*). **4** (often foll. by *of*) having committed a (specified) offence (*guilty of murder*). □ **guiltily** *adv.* **guiltiness** *n.* [Old English: related to GUILT]

**guinea** /**gin**-ee/ *n.* **1** *hist.* sum of 21 shillings. **2** *hist.* former British gold coin first coined for the African trade. [*Guinea* in W. Africa]

**guinea-flower** *n.* any of many Australian plants of the genus *Hibbertia*, found in all States, and bearing showy, usu. gold, flowers.

**guinea fowl** *n.* African fowl with slate-coloured white-spotted plumage.

**guinea pig** *n.* **1** domesticated S. American cavy, kept as a pet or for research in biology etc. **2** person used in an experiment.

**guise** /guyz/ *n.* **1** assumed appearance; pretence (*in the guise of; under the guise of*). **2** external appearance. [Germanic: related to WISE²]

**guitar** /guh-**tah**/ *n.* usu. six-stringed musical instrument played with the fingers or a plectrum. □ **guitarist** *n.* [Greek *kithara* harp]

**gulf** — *n.* **1** stretch of sea consisting of a deep inlet with a narrow mouth. **2** (**the Gulf**) the Gulf of Carpentaria, Queensland. **3** deep hollow; chasm. **4** wide difference of feelings, opinion, etc.; wide separation (*the enormous gulf between the haves and the have-nots*). — *v.* = ENGULF. [Greek *kolpos*]

**Gulf fever** *n.* malaria.

**gull¹** *n.* any of various long-winged web-footed sea birds. [probably Welsh *gwylan*]

**gull²** — *v.* to dupe, fool. — *n.* a dupe, fool. [perhaps from obsolete *gull* yellow from Old Norse]

**gullet** /**gul**-uht/ *n.* **1** food-passage extending from the mouth to the stomach; oesophagus. **2** throat. [Latin *gula* throat]

**gullible** /**gul**-uh-buhl/ *adj.* easily persuaded or deceived. □ **gullibility** /-bil-uh-tee/ *n.* [from GULL²]

**gully** /**gul**-ee/ *n.* (pl. **-ies**) **1** water-worn ravine. **2** eroded watercourse; elongated water-worn depression; (small) river valley. **3** gutter or drain. **4** *Cricket* fielding position between point and slips. [French *goulet*: related to GULLET]

**gully-rake** *v.* **1** muster unbranded cattle from country not readily accessible. **2** steal such cattle. □ **gully-raker** cattle-thief.

**gully trap** *n.* (also **gulley trap**) water-sealed trap (against the return of gases) through which household drainage flows to outside drains.

**gulp** — *v.* **1** (often foll. by *down*) swallow hastily, greedily, or with effort. **2** swallow gaspingly or with difficulty; choke. **3** (foll. by *down*, *back*) suppress (esp. tears). — *n.* **1** act of gulping (*drained his glass at a gulp*). **2** large mouthful of a drink. [Dutch *gulpen*, imitative]

**gum¹** — *n.* **1 a** sticky substance oozing out of some trees and shrubs. **b** adhesive substance made from this. **2** = GUM-TREE, often with distinguishing *adj.*, as apple gum, blue gum, fluted gum, red gum, etc. **3** chewing gum. **4** = GUM ARABIC. **5** = GLUE. — *v.* (**-mm-**) **1** (usu. foll. by *down*, *together*, etc.) fasten with gum. **2** apply gum to. □ **gum up** *colloq.* interfere with the smooth running of. [Greek *kommi* from Egyptian *kemai*]

**gum²** *n.* (usu. in *pl.*) firm flesh around the roots of the teeth. [Old English]

**gum arabic** *n.* gum exuded by some kinds of acacia and used as a glue and in incense.

**gumboil** *n.* small abscess on the gum.

**gumboot** *n.* rubber boot; wellington.

**gumleaf** *n.* leaf of a gum-tree, esp. as used to make musical sounds (as a resonator when cupped in the hands and blown upon).

**gumleaf band** *n.* band of musicians playing gumleaves.

**gummy¹** *adj.* (**-ier**, **-iest**) **1** sticky. **2** exuding gum.

**gummy²** — *adj.* (**-ier**, **-iest**) toothless. — *n.* **1** (in full **gummy shark**) small shark with rounded teeth. **2** toothless sheep.

**gumnut** *n.* woody seed-case of the gum-tree: the large gumnut of the flowering gum (*Eucalyptus ficifolia*) is used by Australian scouts as a woggle.

**gumption** /**gump**-shuhn/ *n. colloq.* **1** resourcefulness, initiative. **2** common sense. [origin unknown]

**gumsucker** *n.* (mainly *hist.*) **1** nickname for a native-born, non-Aboriginal Australian (opp. esp. an immigrant from Britain). **2** a Victorian.

**gum tree** *n.* (also **gum**) **1** any tree of the large, chiefly Australian genus *Eucalyptus*, the dominant tree genus of Australian forests and woodlands, esp. those eucalypts which have a smooth

trunk (opp. rough-barked eucalypts such as the stringybark, box, etc.). **2** any other tree which exudes gum. □ **up a gum tree** *colloq.* **1** in great difficulties. **2** thoroughly baffled.

**gun** — *n.* **1** weapon consisting of a metal tube from which bullets or other missiles are propelled with great force, esp. by a contained explosion. **2** starting pistol. **3** device for discharging insecticide, grease, electrons, etc., in the required direction. **4** member of a shooting-party. **5** (in full **gun shearer**) shearer with a high daily tally of sheep shorn. — *v.* (**-nn-**) **1 a** (usu. foll. by *down*) shoot (a person) with a gun. **b** shoot at with a gun. **2** *colloq.* accelerate or rev (an engine or vehicle). **3** go shooting. **4** (foll. by *for*) seek out determinedly in order to attack or rebuke (*they are gunning for me*). — *adj.* pre-eminent (in an occupation or activity); exceptionally talented or skilled (*gun fencer*; *gun picker*; *gun surfer*; *gun entertainer*; *Victoria's gun batsman last summer*). □ **go great guns** see GREAT. **in the gun** *colloq.* in bad favour; likely to attract criticism or punishment (*don't get caught or we'll all be in the gun*). **stick to one's guns** *colloq.* maintain one's position under attack. [perhaps an abbreviation of the Scandinavian woman's name *Gunnhildr*, applied to cannon etc.]

**gunboat** *n.* small vessel with heavy guns.

**gunboat diplomacy** *n.* political negotiation backed by the threat of force.

**gun cotton** *n.* explosive made by steeping cotton in nitric and sulphuric acids.

**gundy¹** /**gun**-dee/ *n.* (also **goondie**) = GUNYAH. [Yuwaaliyaay and Kamilaroi *gundhi* house, hut; also Wiradhuri *gunday* stringybark, and a shelter made from this]

**gundy²** /**gun**-dee/ *n.* □ **no good to gundy** no good at all. [origin unknown]

**gunfire** *n.* firing of a gun or guns.

**gung-ho** /gung-**hoh**/ *adj.* zealous, arrogantly eager. [Chinese *gonghe* work together]

**gungurru** /gung-guh-**roo**/ *n.* (also **gungunnu** /gung-guh-**noo**/) small WA eucalypt with large spectacular gold-tipped pink flowers and powdery white drooping branches; often cultivated as an ornamental. [probably Kalaaku]

**gunk** /gungk/ *n. colloq.* **1** junk food, esp. foods filled with sugar. **2** nonsense (*don't give me all that gunk*). **3** sticky or viscous matter (ointment; face-creams; etc.) (*smeared her face with gunk*). [originally the proprietary name of a detergent]

**gunman** *n.* man armed with a gun, esp. when committing a crime.

**gunmetal** n. **1** a dull bluish-grey colour. **2** alloy formerly used for guns.

**gunnel** /gun-uhl/ var. of GUNWALE.

**gunner** n. **1** artillery soldier (esp. as an official term for a private). **2** member of an aircraft crew who operates a gun.

**gunnery** n. /gun-uh-ree/ **1** construction and management of large guns. **2** firing of guns.

**gunny** /gun-ee/ n. (pl. **-ies**) **1** coarse sacking, usu. of jute fibre. **2** (also **gunny-bag, gunny-sack**) sack made of this. [Hindi and Marathi *gōnī* sack]

**gunpoint** n. □ **at gunpoint** threatened with a gun or with an ultimatum etc.

**gunpowder** n. explosive made of saltpetre, sulphur, and charcoal.

**gunrunner** n. person engaged in the illegal sale or importing of firearms. □ **gunrunning** n.

**gunshot** n. **1** shot fired from a gun. **2** range of a gun (*within gunshot*).

**gunsmith** n. maker and repairer of small firearms.

**gunwale** /gun-uhl/ n. (also **gunnel**) upper edge of the side of a boat or ship. [from GUN, WALE (a plank), because it was formerly used to support guns]

**Gunwinygu** /guun-win-goo/ n. an Aboriginal language spoken in Arnhem Land in the north of the NT.

**Gunya** /gun-yu/ n. an Aboriginal language spoken over a vast region of southern Queensland: now extinct.

**gunyah** /gun-yuh/ n. a temporary shelter of the Aborigines, usu. a simple frame of branches covered with bark, leaves, or grass. [Dharuk *ganyi*]

**gunyang** /gun-yang/ n. (also **kangaroo apple**) any of several Australian plants bearing a green to ivory-coloured globular berry which is edible. [Ganay]

**guppy** /gup-ee/ n. (pl. **-ies**) freshwater fish (of the W. Indies and S. America) which gives birth to live young; frequently kept in aquariums. [*Guppy*, name of a clergyman]

**Gureng-gureng** /guu-reng guu-reng/ n. an Aboriginal language of south-eastern Queensland spoken in a large area including present-day Bundaberg: now extinct.

**gurgle** /ger-guhl/ — v. (**-ling**) **1** make a bubbling sound as of water from a bottle. **2** utter with such a sound. — n. gurgling sound. [probably imitative]

**gurgler** /ger-gluh/ n. colloq. plughole in sink; drain. □ **down the gurgler** down the drain; irretrievably lost.

**guru** /guu-roo, goo-roo/ n. (pl. **-s**) **1** Hindu spiritual teacher or head of a religious sect. **2** any influential or revered teacher (*Mrs Smith was my guru at uni*). [Hindi]

**gush** — v. **1** emit or flow in a sudden and copious stream. **2** speak or behave with excessive emotion. — n. **1** sudden or copious stream. **2** effusive or highly sentimental manner. □ **gushing** adj. **gushingly** adv. [probably imitative]

**gusher** n. **1** oil well from which oil flows without being pumped. **2** effusive person.

**gushy** /gush-ee/ adj. (**gushier, gushiest**) excessively emotional, effusive; highly sentimental. □ **gushily** adv. **gushiness** n.

**gusset** /gus-uht/ n. **1** piece let into a garment etc. to strengthen or enlarge it. **2** bracket strengthening an angle of a structure. [French]

**gust** — n. **1** sudden strong rush of wind. **2** burst of rain, smoke, emotion, etc. — v. blow in gusts. □ **gusty** adj. (**-ier, -iest**). [Old Norse]

**gusto** /gus-toh/ n. zest; enjoyment or vigour in doing something. [Latin *gustus* taste]

**gut** — n. **1** lower alimentary canal from stomach to anus; the intestine. **2** (in pl.) the bowel or entrails. **3** (in pl.) colloq. personal courage and determination; perseverance. **4** (in pl.) colloq. **a** a glutton. **b** greedy person (one who takes the lion's share of anything). **5** colloq. stomach, belly. **6** (in pl.) **a** essential components or contents (*tinkering with the guts of the clock*). **b** essence (of e.g. an issue or problem) (*get down to the guts of the matter*). **7 a** material for violin strings etc. **b** material for fishing-lines made from the silk-glands of silkworms. **8** (attrib.) **a** instinctive (*a gut reaction*). **b** fundamental (*a gut issue*). — v. (**-tt-**) **1** remove or destroy the internal fittings of (a house etc.) (*the shop was gutted by fire*). **2** remove the guts of (a fish etc.). — adj. (as **guts**) colloq. full of determination, vigour, etc. (*made a guts effort to win the cup*). □ **good guts** colloq. information, the facts (of a matter) (*gave us the good guts about their adventure in the Nullarbor*). **hate a person's guts** colloq. dislike a person intensely. **have a gutful** colloq. have as much as one can take (*I've had a gutful of your whingeing*). **rough as guts** colloq. lacking in refinement. **spill one's guts** colloq. confess; admit everything. **work one's guts out** colloq. work extremely hard. [Old English]

**gutless** adj. colloq. lacking courage or energy (*our representative was gutless; a gutless performance; this car's really gutless going up a hill*). □ **gutless wonder**

*colloq.* one who lacks courage or determination.

**gutser** var. of GUTZER.

**gutsy** /**gut**-see/ *adj.* (**-ier, -iest**) *colloq.* **1** courageous (*a gutsy effort*). **2** strong, full of character (*a gutsy soup, wine, etc.*). **3** greedy.

**gutta-percha** /ˌgut-uh-**per**-chuh/ *n.* tough rubbery substance obtained from latex. [Malay]

**gutter** — *n.* **1** shallow trough below the eaves of a house, or a channel at the side of a street, to carry off rainwater. **2** (prec. by *the*) poor or degraded background or environment (*your language is straight from the gutter*). **3** open conduit. **4** groove. **5** lowest part of a former watercourse, where gold is most likely to be concentrated. — *v.* **1** to furrow, channel (as water does). **2** (of a candle) burn unsteadily and melt away rapidly. [Latin *gutta* drop]

**guttering** /**gut**-uh-ring/ *n.* **1** gutters of a building etc. **2** material for gutters.

**gutter press** *n.* sensational journalism concerned esp. with the private lives of public figures, scandals, etc.

**guttersnipe** /**gut**-uh-ˌsnuyp/ *n.* **1** street urchin. **2** person who speaks or acts as a street urchin is supposed to do.

**guttural** /**gut**-uh-ruhl/ — *adj.* **1** throaty, harsh-sounding. **2** *Phonet.* (of a consonant) produced in the throat or by the back of the tongue and palate. **3** of the throat. — *n. Phonet.* guttural consonant (e.g. *k, g*). □ **gutturally** *adv.* [Latin *guttur* throat]

**gutzer** /**gut**-suh/ *n.* (also **gutser**) *colloq.* **1** a heavy fall. **2** a failure. □ **come a gutzer** fail as a result of miscalculation, 'come a cropper' (*the opposition has come an absolute gutzer on this issue*). [origin uncertain]

**Guugu Yimidhirr** /ˌgoo-goo **yim**-i-dee-r/ *n.* an Aboriginal language still actively spoken in the Cooktown region of far northern Queensland, this language contributing the first Aboriginal loan into English in 1770, *kangaroo*.

**guv** *n. colloq.* = GOVERNOR 5. [abbreviation]

**guvvie** var. of GOVIE.

**guy**[1] /guy/ — *n.* **1** *colloq.* man; fellow. **2** (usu. in *pl.*) *colloq.* any person, female as well as male (*'come on you guys!' he said to the girls and boys who were bickering*). **3** effigy of Guy Fawkes burnt on 5 November — *v.* ridicule. [*Guy* Fawkes, name of a conspirator]

**guy**[2] /guy/ — *n.* rope or chain to secure a tent or steady a crane-load etc. — *v.* secure with a guy or guys. [probably Low German]

**Guyani** /guu-yun-nee/ *n.* an Aboriginal language, a dialect of Adnyamathanha, still actively spoken and fostered in central SA between Lake Torrens and Lake Eyre.

**guzzle** /**guz**-uhl/ *v.* (**-ling**) eat or drink greedily. □ **guzzler** *n.* [probably French *gosiller* from *gosier* throat]

**gybe** /juyb/ *v.* (also **jibe**) (**-bing**) **1** (of a fore-and-aft sail or boom) swing across. **2** cause (a sail) to do this. **3** (of a ship or its crew) change course so that this happens. [Dutch *gijben*]

**gym** /jim/ — *n. colloq.* **1** gymnasium. **2** gymnastics. — *adj.* pertaining to gymnastics (*gym boots, gym shoes, gym gear*). [abbreviation]

**gymea lily** /**guy**-mee-uh/ *n.* (also **giant lily, gigantic lily**) spectacular eastern Australian plant with sword-like leaves 1m in length surrounding a 4m high flower spike bearing a huge cluster of scarlet flowers each 10 cms in width.

**gymkhana** /jim-**kah**-nuh/ *n.* **1** horse-riding events with races and various games, competitions, etc. **2** gymnastic and athletics meet. [Hindustani *gendkhāna* ball-house, assimilated to GYMNASIUM]

**gymnasium** /jim-**nay**-zee-uhm/ *n.* (*pl.* **-s** or **-sia**) room or building equipped for gymnastics. [Greek *gumnos* naked]

**gymnast** /**jim**-nast, -nuhst/ *n.* person who does gymnastics, esp. an expert. [Greek *gymnastēs* athlete-trainer, from *gumnos* naked]

**gymnastic** /jim-**nas**-tik/ *adj.* of or involving gymnastics. □ **gymnastically** *adv.*

**gymnastics** *n.pl.* (also treated as *sing.*) **1** exercises performed in order to develop or display physical agility. **2** other forms of physical or mental agility. [Greek *gumnastikos* from *gumnos* naked]

**gymnosperm** /**jim**-noh-ˌsperm/ *n.* any of a group of plants having seeds unprotected by an ovary, including conifers, cycads, and ginkgos (opp. ANGIOSPERM). [Greek *gumnos* naked]

**gympie** /**gim**-pee/ *n.* shrub of northern NSW and Queensland, the hairs of which inflict an extremely painful recurring sting. [Gabi-gabi *gimbi*]

**gynaecology** /ˌguy-nuh-**kol**-uh-jee/ *n.* (also **gynecology**) medical science dealing with the physiological functions and diseases of women. □ **gynaecological** /-kuh-**loj**-i-kuhl/ *adj.* **gynaecologist** *n.* [Greek *gunē gunaik*- woman, -LOGY]

**gyp**[1] /jip/ *colloq.* — *v.* defraud, cheat. — *n.* **1** a swindle. **2** swindler. [origin uncertain]

**gyp²** *n. colloq.* **1** pain or severe discomfort. **2** a scolding (*gave them gyp*). [origin uncertain]

**gypsum** /**jip**-suhm/ *n.* mineral used esp. to make plaster of Paris. [Greek *gupsos*]

**gypsy** var. of GIPSY.

**gyrate** /juy-**rayt**/ *v.* (**-ting**) move in a circle or spiral; revolve, whirl. □ **gyration** /-**ray**-shuhn/ *n.* **gyratory** *adj.* [Greek: related to GYRO-]

**gyro** /**juy**-roh/ *n.* (*pl.* **-s**) *colloq.* = GYROSCOPE. [abbreviation]

**gyro-** *comb. form* rotation. [Greek *guros* ring]

**gyrocompass** /**juy**-roh-ˌkum-puhs/ *n.* compass giving true north and bearings from it by means of a gyroscope.

**gyroscope** /**juy**-ruh-ˌskohp/ *n.* rotating wheel whose axis is free to turn but maintains a fixed direction unless perturbed, esp. used for stabilisation or with the compass in an aircraft, ship, etc. □ **gyroscopic** *adj.* [GYRO-, -SCOPE]

# H

**H¹** /aych/ n. (also **h**) (pl. **Hs** or **H's**) **1** eighth letter of the alphabet (see AITCH). **2** anything having the form of an H (esp. in comb.: H-girder).

**H²** abbr. (also **H.**) **1** (of a pencil-lead) hard. **2** colloq. heroin. **3** Electr. henry(s).

**H³** symb. hydrogen.

**h.** abbr. (also **h**) **1** hecto-. **2** (also **h**) height. **3** hot. **4** hour(s).

**Ha** symb. hahnium.

**ha¹** /hah/ (also **hah**) — int. expressing surprise, derision, triumph, etc. (cf. HA HA). — v. (in **hum and ha**): see HUM. [imitative]

**ha²** abbr. hectare(s).

**habeas corpus** /ˌhay-bee-uhs kaw-puhs/ n. writ requiring a person to be brought before a judge or into court, esp. to investigate the lawfulness of his or her detention. [Latin, = you must have the body]

**haberdasher** /ˈhab-uh-ˌdash-uh/ n. dealer in dress accessories and sewing-goods. □ **haberdashery** n. (pl. **-ies**). [probably Anglo-French]

**habit** /ˈhab-uht/ n. **1** settled or regular tendency or practice (often foll. by of + verbal noun: has a habit of ignoring me). **2** practice that is hard to give up (smoking's a deadly habit). **3** mental constitution or attitude. **4** dress, esp. of a religious order. [Latin habeo habit- have]

**habitable** /ˈhab-uh-tuh-buhl/ adj. suitable for living in. □ **habitability** /-ˈbil-uh-tee/ n. [Latin habito inhabit]

**habitat** /ˈhab-uh-ˌtat/ n. natural home of an animal or plant. [Latin, = it dwells]

**habitation** /ˌhab-uh-ˈtay-shuhn/ n. **1** process of inhabiting or living in (fit for human habitation). **2** house or home.

**habit-forming** adj. causing addiction.

**habitual** /huh-ˈbich-oo-uhl/ adj. **1** done constantly or as a habit. **2** regular, usual. **3** given to a (specified) habit (habitual smoker). □ **habitually** adv.

**habituate** /huh-ˈbich-oo-ˌayt/ v. (**-ting**) (often foll. by to) accustom. □ **habituation** /-ˈay-shuhn/ n. [Latin: related to HABIT]

**habitué** /huh-ˈbit-yoo-ˌay/ n. **1** habitual visitor to a place (habitués of the theatre). **2** a resident. [French]

**hachures** /ha-ˈshoor/ n.pl. parallel lines on a map indicating the degree of steepness of hills. [French: related to HATCH³]

**hack¹** — v. **1** cut or chop roughly. **2** Rugby etc. kick the shin of (an opponent). **3** (often foll. by at) deliver cutting blows. **4** savagely cut, shorten (a piece of writing etc.) (hacked my report to pieces). **5** cut (one's way) through foliage etc. **6** colloq. (often foll. by into) gain unauthorised access to (data in a computer network). **7** colloq. manage, cope with; tolerate (they couldn't hack the pace). **8** (as **hacking** adj.) (of a cough) short, dry, and frequent. — n. **1** kick given with the toe of a boot. **2** a gash or wound, esp. from a kick. **3** = HACKER 2b. **4 a** mattock. **b** miner's pick. [Old English]

**hack²** — n. **1 a** = HACKNEY. **b** horse let out for hire. **c** old or decrepit horse; jade. **2** person hired to do dull routine work, esp. writing. — attrib. adj. **1** used as a hack. **2** typical of a hack; commonplace (hack work). — v. ride on horseback on a road at an ordinary pace. [abbreviation of HACKNEY]

**hacker** n. **1** person or thing that hacks or cuts roughly. **2** colloq. **a** person whose hobby is computing or computer programming. **b** person who gains unauthorised access to a computer network and uses or alters data etc.

**hackle** /ˈhak-uhl/ n. **1 a** (in pl.) erectile hairs on an animal's neck, rising when it is angry or alarmed. **b** feather(s) on the neck of a domestic cock etc. **2** steel comb for dressing flax. □ **have one's hackles up** be extremely angry, fighting mad. **make one's hackles rise** cause one to be angry or indignant. [Old English]

**hackney** /ˈhak-nee/ n. (pl. **-s**) horse for ordinary riding. [Hackney in London, where horses were pastured]

**hackneyed** /ˈhak-need/ adj. (of a phrase etc.) made trite by overuse.

**hacksaw** n. saw with a narrow blade set in a frame, for cutting metal.

**hackwork** n. work (esp. artistic or literary) which is routine, uninspired (his latest novel is just hackwork).

**had** past and past part. of HAVE.

**haddock** /ˈhad-uhk/ n. (pl. same) N. Atlantic marine fish used as food. [probably French]

**Hades** /ˈhay-deez/ n. (in Greek mythology) the underworld. [Greek, originally a name of Pluto]

**hadn't** /ˈhad-uhnt/ contr. had not.

**haemal** /ˈhee-muhl/ adj. (also **hem-**) of the blood. [Greek haima blood]

488

**haematite** /hee-muh-ˌtuyt/ *n.* (also **hem-**) a ferric oxide ore; iron-ore. [Latin: related to HAEMAL]

**haematology** /ˌhee-muh-**tol**-uh-jee/ *n.* (also **hem-**) the study of the physiology of the blood. □ **haematologist** *n.*

**haemoglobin** /ˌhee-muh-**gloh**-buhn/ *n.* (also **hem-**) oxygen-carrying substance in the red blood cells of vertebrates. [from GLOBULIN]

**haemophilia** /ˌhee-muh-**fil**-ee-uh/ *n.* (also **hem-**) hereditary failure of the blood to clot normally with the tendency to bleed severely from even a slight injury. [Greek *haima* blood, *philia* loving]

**haemophiliac** *n.* (also **hem-**) person with haemophilia.

**haemorrhage** /**hem**-uh-rij/ (also **hem-**) — *n.* **1** profuse loss of blood from a ruptured blood-vessel. **2** damaging loss, esp. of people or assets. — *v.* (**-ging**) suffer a haemorrhage. [Greek *haima* blood, *rhēgnunai* burst]

**haemorrhoids** /**hem**-uh-ˌroidz/ *n.pl.* (also **hem-**) swollen veins in the wall of the anus; piles. [Greek *haima* blood, *-rhoos-* flowing]

**hafnium** /**haf**-nee-uhm/ *n.* silvery lustrous metallic element. [Latin *Hafnia* Copenhagen]

**haft** /hahft/ — *n.* handle of a dagger, knife, etc. — *v.* provide with a haft. [Old English]

**hag** *n.* **1** ugly old woman. **2** witch. □ **haggish** *adj.* [Old English]

**haggard** /**hag**-uhd/ *adj.* looking exhausted and distraught, esp. from worry, suffering, etc. [French *hagard*]

**haggis** /**hag**-is/ *n.* Scottish dish of offal boiled in a sheep's stomach with suet, oatmeal, etc. [origin unknown]

**haggle** /**hag**-uhl/ — *v.* (**-ling**) (often foll. by *about, over*) bargain persistently. — *n.* haggling. [Old Norse]

**hagio-** *comb. form* of saints. [Greek *hagios* holy]

**hagiography** /ˌhag-ee-**og**-ruh-fee/ *n.* writing about saints' lives. □ **hagiographer** *n.*

**hagiology** /ˌhag-ee-**ol**-uh-jee/ *n.* literature dealing with the lives and legends of saints.

**hag-ridden** *adj.* afflicted by nightmares or anxieties.

**hah** var. of HA[1].

**ha ha** /hah-**hah**/ *int.* representing laughter (*iron.* when spoken). [Old English]

**ha-ha**[1] /**hah**-hah/ *n.* ditch with a wall in it, forming a boundary or fence without interrupting the view. [French]

**ha-ha**[2] *n.* (also **ha-ha bird**) kookaburra, laughing jackass.

**hahnium** /**hah**-nee-uhm/ *n.* artificially produced radioactive element. [*Hahn*, name of a chemist]

**haiku** /**huy**-koo/ *n.* (*pl.* same) Japanese three-part poem of usu. 17 syllables. [Japanese]

**hail**[1] — *n.* **1** pellets of frozen rain. **2** (foll. by *of*) barrage or onslaught (*a hail of bullets*). — *v.* **1 a** (prec. by *it* as subject) hail falls (*if it hails*). **b** come down forcefully (*stones hailed down on us*). **2** pour down (blows, words, etc.) (*hailed blows on his body*). [Old English]

**hail**[2] — *v.* **1** signal to (a taxi etc.) to stop. **2** greet enthusiastically. **3** acclaim (*hailed him king*). **4** (foll. by *from*) originate or come (*hails from Geelong*). — *int. archaic* or *joc.* expressing greeting. — *n.* act of hailing. [Old Norse *heill*: related to WASSAIL]

**Hail Mary** *n.* the Ave Maria (see AVE).

**hailstone** *n.* pellet of hail.

**hailstorm** *n.* period of heavy hail.

**hair** *n.* **1 a** any of the fine threadlike strands growing from the skin of mammals, esp. from the human head. **b** these collectively (*has long hair*). **2** thing resembling a hair. **3** elongated cell growing from a plant. **4** very small quantity or extent (*won by a hair*; also *attrib.*: *hair crack*). □ **get in a person's hair** *colloq.* encumber or annoy a person. **have a person by the short hairs** (or **by the short and curlies**) *colloq.* have him or her completely in one's power. **(not) hide nor hair** *colloq.* (not) the slightest trace (*haven't seen hide nor hair of them since yesterday*). **keep one's hair on** *Brit. colloq.* keep calm; not get angry. **let one's hair down** *colloq.* enjoy oneself by abandoning restraint. **make one's hair curl** *colloq.* flabbergast one. **make one's hair stand on end** *colloq.* horrify one. **not turn a hair** remain unmoved or unaffected. **put hair on one's chest** *colloq.* (of food or drink) make one feel very much stronger (*get this inside you — it'll put hair on your chest*). □ **haired** *adj.* (also in *comb.*). **hairless** *adj.* **hairlike** *adj.* [Old English]

**haircloth** *n.* stiff cloth woven from hair.

**haircut** *n.* **1** act of cutting the hair. **2** style in which the hair is cut.

**hairdo** *n.* (*pl.* **-s**) style of or act of styling the hair.

**hairdresser** *n.* **1** person who cuts and styles the hair, esp. for a living. **2** hairdresser's shop. □ **hairdressing** *n.*

**hairline** *n.* **1** edge of a person's hair, esp. on the forehead. **2** very narrow line, crack (usu. **hairline crack**), etc.

**hairline fracture** *n.* fracture in bone, metal, etc. which shows itself as a hairline on the surface.

**hair of the dog** *n.* further alcoholic drink taken to cure the effects of drink.

**hairpiece** *n.* **1** wig worn to conceal baldness. **2** quantity or switch of detached hair worn to augment a person's natural hair for a particular style etc.

**hairpin** *n.* U-shaped pin for fastening the hair.

**hairpin bend** *n.* sharp U-shaped bend in a road.

**hair-raising** *adj.* extremely alarming; terrifying.

**hair's breadth** — *n.* a tiny amount or margin (*escaped death by a hair's breadth*). — *adj.* extremely close (*a hair's breadth brush with death*).

**hair shirt** *n.* shirt of haircloth, worn formerly by penitents and ascetics.

**hair-splitting** *adj. & n.* making overfine distinctions; quibbling. □ **hair-splitter** *n.*

**hairspring** *n.* fine spring regulating the balance-wheel in a watch.

**hairstyle** *n.* particular way of arranging the hair. □ **hairstylist** *n.*

**hair-trigger** — *n.* trigger of a firearm set for release at the slightest pressure. — *adj.* acting as a hair-trigger does, very quick (*he has hair-trigger reactions*).

**hairy** *adj.* (**-ier, -iest**) **1 a** covered with hair. **b** having the feel of hair. **2** *colloq.* frightening, dangerous (*a hairy ride in a car with no brakes*). **3** *colloq.* very difficult (*quite a hairy problem*). □ **hairiness** *n.*

**hairy man** *n.* = YOWIE.

**hairy-nosed wombat** *n.* either of two wombats of southern and eastern Australia with fine hairs on the snout.

**haka** /**hah**-kuh/ *n.* **1** Maori ceremonial war dance with chanting. **2** imitation of this by a sports team before a match. [Maori]

**hake** *n.* (*pl.* same) **1** marine fish resembling the cod, used as food. **2** = GEMFISH. [origin uncertain]

**hakea** /**hay**-kee-uh/ *n.* any shrub of the large Australian genus *Hakea* (belonging to the protea family), characterised by spiny (and usu. very showy) flower-heads and woody fruits with winged seeds. [Baron von *Hake*, patron of botany]

**halal** /hah-**lahl**, ha-**lal**/ *n.* (also **hallal**) (often *attrib.*) meat from an animal killed according to Muslim law. [Arabic]

**halberd** /**hal**-buhd/ *n. hist.* combined spear and battleaxe. [French from German]

**halcyon** /**hal**-see-uhn/ *adj.* calm, peaceful, happy (*halcyon days*). [Greek, =

kingfisher, because it was reputed to calm the sea at midwinter]

**hale¹** *adj.* strong and healthy (esp. in **hale and hearty**). [var. of WHOLE]

**hale²** *v.* drag or draw forcibly (*haled him into the room by the scruff of his neck*). [Old Norse]

**half** /hahf/ — *n.* (*pl.* **halves** /hahvz/) **1** either of two (esp. equal) parts into which a thing is divided. **2** *Sport* either of two equal periods of play. **3** *colloq.* = HALF-BACK. — *adj.* **1** amounting to half or nearly half (*half the men; spent half the time reading*). **2** forming a half (*a half share*). **3** incomplete; inadequate (*doesn't go in for half measures*). — *adv.* **1** (often in *comb.*) to the extent of half; partly (*half cooked*). **2** to some extent (esp. in idiomatic phrases: *half dead; am half convinced*). **3** (in reckoning time) by the amount of half (an hour etc.) (*half past two*). □ **and a half** *colloq.* (adding to the outstanding qualities of) and more, 'and then some' (*he's a statesman and a half*). **at half cock** see COCK. **by half** (prec. by *too* + adj.) excessively (*too clever by half*). **by halves** imperfectly or incompletely (*does nothing by halves*). **half the battle** see BATTLE. **half a chance** the slightest opportunity (esp. *given half a chance*). **half an eye** some degree of perceptiveness (*kept half an eye on the kids while he was cooking*). **half a mind** see MIND. **half a mo** *colloq.* a very short while; soon (*I'll do it in half a mo*). **the half of it** *colloq.* the rest or more important part of something (usu. after *neg.*: *you don't know the half of it*). **half the time** see TIME. **half your luck** *colloq.* I wish I had half your luck. **not half 1** *colloq.* extremely, violently (*he didn't half swear*). **2** not nearly (*not half long enough*). **3** *colloq.* not at all (*not half bad*). [Old English]

**half-back** *n. Sport* **1 a** position between the forwards and full back(s). **b** player in such a position. **2** *Rugby* player who places the ball in the scrum and tries to retrieve it when it emerges. **3** *Aust. Rules* **a** any of three positions between the back and centre lines. **b** player in such a position.

**half-back flanker** *n. Aust. Rules* player on either flank of the half-back line.

**half-baked** *adj. colloq.* **1** not thoroughly thought out; foolish (*half-baked schemes*). **2** (of enthusiasm etc.) only partly committed.

**half-blood** *n.* **1** person having one parent in common with another person. **2** this relationship. **3** = HALF-BREED.

**half-breed** *n. offens.* = HALF-CASTE.

**half-brother** *n.* brother related through one parent only.

**half-caste** *n. offens.* **1 a** person whose parents are of different races. **b** *hist.* child of an Aborigine and a European. **2** *colloq.* person with an admixture of Aboriginal blood.

**half-duplex** *n. Computing* (of a circuit) allowing the two-way transmission of signals but not simultaneously.

**half-forward** *n. Aust. Rules* **1** any of three positions between the forward and centre lines. **2** player in such a position.

**half-forward flanker** *n. Aust. Rules* player on either flank of the half-forward line.

**half-hearted** *adj.* not fully committed; lukewarm (*a half-hearted attempt to put things right*). □ **half-heartedly** *adv.* **half-heartedness** *n.*

**half hitch** *n.* knot formed by passing the end of a rope round its standing part and then through the loop.

**half-hour** *n.* **1** (also **half an hour**) period of 30 minutes. **2** point of time 30 minutes after any hour o'clock. □ **half-hourly** *adj.* & *adv.*

**half-life** *n.* time taken for radioactivity etc. to fall to half its original value.

**half mast** *n.* position of a flag halfway down a mast, as a mark of respect for a deceased person.

**half measures** *n.pl.* unsatisfactory compromise or inadequate policy.

**half moon** *n.* **1** moon when only half its surface is illuminated. **2** time when this occurs. **3** semicircular object.

**half nelson** see NELSON.

**halfpenny** /hayp-nee/ *n.* (*pl.* **-pennies** or **-pence** /hay-puhns/ ) former coin worth half a penny.

**half-sister** *n.* sister related through one parent only.

**half-stick** *n.* half-open position (of the lid of a grand piano) for performance.

**half-time** *n.* **1** mid-point of a game or contest. **2** short break occurring at this time.

**half-title** *n.* title or short title of a book printed on the front of the leaf preceding the title-page.

**halftone** *n.* photographic illustration in which various tones of grey are produced from small and large black dots.

**half-truth** *n.* statement that (esp. deliberately) conveys only part of the truth.

**half-volley** *n.* (in ball games) playing of the ball as soon as it bounces off the ground.

**halfway** — *adv.* **1** at a point midway between two others (*halfway to Melbourne*). **2** to some extent, more or less (*is halfway acceptable*). — *adj.* situated halfway (*reached a halfway point*). □ **meet a person halfway** reach a compromise with him or her.

**halfway house** *n.* **1** a compromise. **2** halfway point in a progression. **3** home in which ex-prisoners, mental patients, drug addicts, etc. can live until they are equipped to re-enter the outside world.

**halfwit** *n.* **1** foolish or stupid person. **2** *offens.* person who is mentally deficient. □ **half-witted** *adj.*

**halibut** /hal-uh-buht/ *n.* (*pl.* same) **1** large marine flat-fish used as food. **2** (also **Queensland halibut**) fine food-fish found in tropical Australian waters. [from HOLY (perhaps because eaten on holy days), *butt* flat-fish]

**halitosis** /hal-uh-toh-suhs/ *n.* bad breath. [Latin *halitus* breath]

**hall** /hawl/ *n.* **1 a** area into which the front entrance of a house etc. opens. **b** corridor or passage in a house or other building. **2** large room or building for meetings, concerts, etc. **3** *Brit.* large country house. **4** (in full **hall of residence**) residence for students. [Old English]

**hallelujah** var. of ALLELUIA.

**halliard** var. of HALYARD.

**hallmark** — *n.* **1** mark indicating the standard of purity of gold, silver, and platinum in articles made of these metals. **2** distinctive feature (*generosity was the hallmark of his life*). — *v.* stamp with a hallmark. [*mark* used orig. at Goldsmith's *Hall*, London]

**hallo** var. of HELLO.

**hallow** /hal-oh/ *v.* **1** make holy, consecrate. **2** honour as holy. [Old English: related to HOLY]

**Halloween** /hal-oh-een/ *n.* (also **Hallowe'en**) the eve of All Saints' Day, 31 October [*hallow* saint, *e'en* EVEN²]

**hallucinate** /huh-loo-suh-nayt/ *v.* (**-ting**) experience hallucinations. □ **hallucinant** *adj.* & *n.* **hallucinator** *n.* [Greek *alussō* be uneasy]

**hallucination** /huh-loo-suh-nay-shuhn/ *n.* illusion of seeing or hearing something not actually present. □ **hallucinatory** /huh-loo-suh-nuh-tuh-ree, -tree/ *adj.*

**hallucinogen** /huh-loo-suh-nuh-juhn/ *n.* drug causing hallucinations. □ **hallucinogenic** /-jen-ik/ *adj.*

**hallway** *n.* entrance-hall or corridor.

**halo** /hay-loh/ — *n.* (*pl.* **-es**) **1** disc or circle of light shown surrounding the head of a sacred person. **2** glory associated with an idealised person etc.

**3** circle of white or coloured light round a luminous body, esp. the sun or moon. — v. (**-es**, **-ed**) surround with a halo. [Greek *halōs* threshing-floor, disc of the sun or moon]

**halogen** /hal-uh-juhn/ n. any of the non-metallic elements (fluorine, chlorine, bromine, iodine, and astatine) which form a salt (e.g. sodium chloride) when combined with a metal. [Greek *hals halos* salt, -GEN]

**halon** /hay-lon/ n. any of various gaseous compounds of carbon, bromine, and other halogens, used to extinguish fires. [related to HALOGEN]

**halt¹** /holt, hawlt/ — n. **1** stop (usu. temporary) (*come to a halt*). **2** minor stopping-place on a local railway line. — v. stop; come or bring to a halt. □ **call a halt (to)** decide to stop. [German: related to HOLD]

**halt²** /holt, hawlt/ — v. (esp. as **halting** *adj.*) proceed hesitantly. — *adj. archaic* lame (*the halt and the blind*). □ **haltingly** *adv.* [Old English]

**halter** /hol-tuh, hawl-/ n. **1** headstall and rope for leading or tying up a horse etc. **2 a** rope with a noose for hanging a person. **b** death by hanging. **3 a** strap round the neck holding a dress etc. up and leaving the shoulders and back bare. **b** (also **halterneck**) dress etc. held by this. [Old English]

**halva** /hal-vuh/ n. (also **halwa**) confection of sesame flour and honey etc. [Yiddish from Turkish *helva* from Arabic *ḥalwa*]

**halve** /hahv/ v. (**-ving**) **1** divide into two halves or parts; share equally between two. **2** reduce by half. **3** *Golf* use the same number of strokes as one's opponent in (a hole or match).

**halves** *pl.* of HALF.

**halyard** /hal-yuhd/ n. (also **halliard**) rope or tackle for raising or lowering a sail, yard, etc. [HALE²]

**ham** — n. **1 a** upper part of a pig's leg salted and dried or smoked for food. **b** meat from this. **2** back of the thigh; thigh and buttock. **3** *colloq.* (often *attrib.*) inexpert or unsubtle actor or piece of acting. **4** *colloq.* operator of an amateur radio station. — v. (**-mm-**) (usu. in **ham it up**) *colloq.* overact. [Old English]

**ham-and-egg daisy** n. = POACHED EGG DAISY.

**hamburger** /ham-ber-guh/ n. small flat cake of seasoned minced beef, usu. fried or grilled and eaten in a soft bread roll. [*Hamburg* in Germany]

**ham-fisted** *adj.* (also **ham-handed**) *colloq.* clumsy.

**hamlet** /ham-luht/ n. small village. [French *hamelet* diminutive]

**hammer¹** — n. **1 a** tool with a heavy metal head at right angles to its handle, used for driving in nails etc. **b** similar device, as for exploding the charge in a gun, striking the strings of a piano, etc. **2** auctioneer's mallet. **3** metal ball attached to a wire for throwing in an athletic contest. — v. **1 a** hit or beat with or as with a hammer. **b** strike loudly. **2 a** drive in (nails) with a hammer. **b** fasten or secure by hammering (*hammered the lid down*). **3** (usu. foll. by *in*) inculcate (ideas, knowledge, etc.) forcefully or repeatedly (*he hammered in the facts until I knew them by heart*). **4** *colloq.* defeat utterly; beat up. **5** (foll. by *at, away at*) work hard or persistently at. □ **come** (or **go**) **under the hammer** be sold at auction. **hammer out 1** make flat or smooth by hammering. **2** work out details of (a plan etc.) laboriously. **3** play (a tune, esp. on the piano) loudly or clumsily. □ **hammering** n. (esp. in sense 4 of v.). [Old English]

**hammer²** n. *colloq.* a person's back. □ **on a person's hammer** in hot pursuit of him or her; hounding or pestering him or her. [abbreviation of *hammer and tack* rhyming slang for 'back']

**hammer and sickle** n. symbols of the industrial worker and peasant used as an emblem of the former USSR and international communism.

**hammer and tongs** *adv. colloq.* with great vigour and commotion.

**hammerhead** n. shark with a flattened head and with eyes in lateral extensions of it (thereby resembling a double-headed hammer).

**hammering** n. *colloq.* a thorough defeat.

**hammerlock** n. *Wrestling* hold in which the arm is twisted and bent behind the back.

**hammer-toe** n. deformity in which the toe is bent permanently downwards.

**hammock** /ham-uhk/ n. bed of canvas or rope network suspended by cords at the ends. [Spanish from Carib]

**hammy** /ham-ee/ *adj.* (**-ier**, **-iest**) *colloq.* over-theatrical.

**hamper¹** n. **1** large basket, usu. with a hinged lid, for containing food (*picnic hamper*). **2** a selection of food, drink, etc. for a special occasion (and often given as a present, or raffled, etc.) (*Christmas hamper*). [French *hanap* goblet]

**hamper²** v. prevent the free movement of; hinder. [origin unknown]

**hamster** /ham-stuh/ n. mouselike

rodent with a short tail and large cheek-pouches for storing food. [German]

**hamstring** /ham-ˌstring/ — n. 1 each of five tendons at the back of the human knee. 2 great tendon at the back of the hock in quadrupeds. — v. (past and past part. **-strung** or **-stringed**) 1 cripple by cutting the hamstrings of (a person or animal). 2 impair the activity or efficiency of (we were hamstrung by the lack of proper equipment).

**hand** — n. 1 a end part of the human arm beyond the wrist. b end part of a forelimb. 2 a (often in pl.) control, management, custody, disposal (is in good hands). b agency or influence (suffered at their hands). c share in an action; active support (had a hand in it; give me a hand). 3 thing like a hand, esp. the pointer of a clock. 4 right or left side or direction relative to a person or thing. 5 a skill (has a hand for making pastry). b person skilful in some respect (she's a deft hand at making pastry). 6 person who does or makes something, esp. distinctively (a painting by the same hand). 7 person's writing or its style (a legible hand). 8 person etc. as a source (at first hand). 9 pledge of marriage. 10 manual worker, esp. at a factory or farm; member of a ship's crew. 11 a playing-cards dealt to a player. b round of play. 12 colloq. burst of applause (got a big hand). 13 unit of measure of a horse's height, 10.16 cm (4 inches). 14 forehock of pork. 15 cluster or bunch (a hand of bananas). 16 (attrib.) a operated by or held in the hand (hand-drill). b done by hand, not machine (hand-knitted). — v. 1 a pass (hand me the scissors). b (foll. by in, to, over, etc.) deliver; transfer by hand or otherwise. 2 colloq. give away too readily (handed them the advantage). □ **all hands** entire crew or workforce. **at hand** 1 close by. 2 about to happen. **at the hand(s) of** through the action(s) of (suffered at the hands of the police). **by hand** 1 by a person, not a machine. 2 delivered privately, not by post. **dead hand at** colloq. expert at (dead hand at shearing). **declare one's hand** reveal one's intentions. **eat out of a person's hand** submissive to him or her. **a firm hand** strict authority, control. **from hand to mouth** satisfying only one's immediate needs (also attrib.: a hand-to-mouth existence). **get** (or **have** or **keep**) **one's hand in** become (or be or remain) in practice. **give** (or **lend**) **a hand** assist in an action or enterprise. **hand and foot** completely (waited on them hand and foot). **hand down 1** pass ownership or use

of to a later generation etc. **2** a transmit (a decision) from a higher court etc. b express (a decision or verdict). **hand it to** colloq. award deserved praise to (must hand it to them — they did a fine job). **hand on** pass (a thing) to the next in a series. **hand out 1** serve, distribute. **2** award, allocate (handed out stiff penalties). **hand over fist** rapidly; in quantity. **hand round** serve, distribute. **hands down** with no difficulty; completely (won hands down). **hand a person a line** colloq. deceive a person usu. by lying or falsifying. **have a hand in** have an involvement in. **have one's hands full** be fully occupied. **have one's hands tied** colloq. be unable to act. **heavy hand** see HEAVY. **hold the hand out** colloq. ask for and expect to gain welfare payments etc. **in hand 1** receiving attention (the matter is in hand). **2** in reserve; at one's disposal. **3** under control (we've got it in hand). **lay** (or **put**) **one's hands on** see LAY[1]. **off one's hands** no longer one's responsibility. **on hand** available. **on the one** (or **the other**) **hand** from one (or another) point of view. **out of hand 1** out of control. **2** peremptorily (refused out of hand). **out of one's hands** no longer one's responsibility; beyond one's ability to act upon. **put** (or **set**) **one's hand to** start work on; engage in. **take a hand in** participate in. **throw in one's hand** give up. **to hand** within easy reach; available. **turn one's hand to** undertake (as a new activity). □ **-handed** adj. (in comb.). [Old English]

**handbag** n. small bag carried esp. by a woman.

**handball** — n. 1 game with a ball thrown by hand among players or against a wall. 2 Aust. Rules = HANDPASS. 3 Soccer intentional touching of the ball, constituting a foul. — v. Aust. Rules = HANDPASS.

**handbill** n. printed notice usu. distributed by hand.

**handbook** n. short manual or guidebook.

**handbrake** n. brake operated by hand.

**handclap** n. clapping of the hands.

**handcraft** — n. = HANDICRAFT. — v. make by handicraft.

**handcuff** — n. each of a pair of linked metal rings for securing a prisoner's wrist(s). — v. put handcuffs on.

**handful** n. (pl. **-s**) 1 quantity that fills the hand. 2 small number or amount. 3 colloq. troublesome person or task.

**hand grenade** see GRENADE.

**handgun** n. small firearm held in and fired with one hand.

**handicap** /han-dee-ˌkap/ — n. 1 physical or mental disability (see note under HANDICAPPED). 2 thing that makes progress or success difficult. **3 a** disadvantage imposed on a superior competitor to make chances more equal. **b** race etc. in which this is imposed. **4** number of strokes by which a golfer normally exceeds par for a course. — *v.* (**-pp-**) **1** impose a handicap on. **2** place at a disadvantage. [*hand i'* (= in) *cap* describing a kind of sporting lottery]

**handicapped** *adj.* suffering from a physical or mental disability.

■ **Usage** A person with a disability is not necessarily unable to function effectively. The terms *handicap* and *handicapped* are offensive because they imply lack of ability and should (as with *disabled*) be avoided.

**handicraft** /**han**-dee-,krahft/ *n.* work requiring manual and artistic skill. [from earlier HANDCRAFT]

**hand in glove** *adj.* in collusion or association (*he was hand in glove with the bank robber*).

**hand in hand** *adv.* **1** in close association (*power and money go hand in hand*). **2** (**hand-in-hand**) holding hands.

**handiwork** /**han**-dee-,werk/ *n.* work done or a thing made by hand, or by a particular person. [Old English]

**handkerchief** /**hang**-kuh-cheef/ *n.* (*pl.* **-s** or **-chieves** /-,cheevz/ ) square of cloth for wiping one's nose etc.

**handle** /**han**-duhl/ — *n.* **1** part by which a thing is held, carried, or controlled. **2** fact that may be taken advantage of (*gave a handle to his critics*). **3** *colloq.* **a** a person's title, e.g. *Sir* Robert Menzies. **b** a person's name. — *v.* (**-ling**) **1** touch, feel, operate, or move with the hands. **2 a** manage, deal with (*can handle people; handles himself well in a crisis*). **b** cope with (*I can't handle all this aggression*). **3** deal in (goods) (*what merchandise do you handle?*). **4** discuss or write about (a subject) (*handled the topic well*). **5** respond (to one's handling) (*this car is old but handles really well*). □ **get a handle on** *colloq.* understand the basis of or reason for a situation etc. [Old English: related to HAND]

**handlebar** *n.* (usu. in *pl.*) steering-bar of a bicycle etc.

**handler** *n.* **1** person who handles or deals in something. **2** person who trains and looks after an animal (esp. a police dog).

**handmade** *adj.* made by hand (as opposed to machine).

**hand-me-down** *n.* article of clothing etc. passed on from another person (*have to wear my brother's hand-me-downs*).

**handout** *n.* **1** thing given free to a needy person. **2** statement given to the press etc.; notes given out in a class etc.

**hand over fist** *adv. colloq.* with rapid progress.

**handpass** *Aust. Rules* — *n.* pass (to a team mate) in which the ball is held in one hand and struck with the other. — *v.* deliver a handpass.

**hand-pick** *v.* choose carefully or personally.

**handrail** *n.* narrow rail for holding as a support.

**handsaw** *n.* saw worked by one hand.

**handset** *n.* telephone mouthpiece and earpiece as one unit.

**handshake** *n.* **1** clasping of a person's hand as a greeting etc. **2** *Computing* exchange of signals that establishes communication between two or more pieces of computer equipment.

**hands off** — *int.* warning not to touch or interfere with something. — *adj. & adv.* (**hands-off**) *Computing etc.* not requiring the manual use of controls.

**handsome** /**han**-suhm/ *adj.* (**handsomer**, **handsomest**) **1** (usu. of a man) good-looking. **2** (of an object) imposing, attractive. **3 a** generous, liberal (*handsome present*). **b** (of a price, fortune, etc.) considerable. □ **handsomely** *adv.*

**hands-on** — *adj. & adv. Computing etc.* of or requiring personal operation at a keyboard. — *attrib. adj.* practical rather than theoretical (*lacks hands-on experience*).

**handspring** *n.* gymnastic feat consisting of a handstand, somersaulting, and landing in a standing position.

**handstand** *n.* supporting oneself on one's hands with one's feet in the air.

**hand-to-hand** *adj.* (of fighting) at close quarters.

**handwriting** *n.* **1** writing done with a pen, pencil, etc. **2** person's particular style of this. □ **handwritten** *adj.*

**handy** *adj.* (**-ier**, **-iest**) **1** convenient to handle or use; useful. **2** ready to hand. **3** clever with the hands. □ **handily** *adv.* **handiness** *n.*

**handyman** /**han**-dee-,man/ *n.* person able to do occasional repairs etc.; odd-job man.

**hang** — *v.* (*past* and *past part.* **hung** except in sense 7) **1 a** secure or cause to be supported from above, esp. with the lower part free. **b** (foll. by *up*, *on*, *on to*, etc.) attach by suspending from the top. **2** set up (a door etc.) on hinges. **3** place (a picture) on a wall or in an exhibition. **4** attach (wallpaper) to a wall. **5** (foll. by *on*) *colloq.* blame (a thing) on (a person) (*can't* *hang that on me).* **6** (foll. by *with*) decorate by suspending pictures etc. (*hall hung with tapestries*). **7** (*past* and *past part.* **hanged**) **a** suspend or be suspended by the neck with a noosed rope until dead, esp. as a form of capital punishment (*they hanged him this morning*). **b** as a mild oath (*hang the expense; expenses be hanged!*). **8** let droop (*hang one's head*). **9** suspend (meat, bacon, etc.; game by the feet) from a hook and leave until cured or dry; or tender or high (HIGH 12 b). **10** be or remain hung (in various senses). **11** remain static in the air. **12** (often foll. by *over*) be present or imminent, esp. oppressively or threateningly (*a hush hung over the room*). **13** (foll. by *on*) be contingent or dependent on (*everything hangs on his reply*). **b** listen closely to (*hangs on my every word*). — *n.* **1** way a thing hangs or falls (*the hang of the drapes*). **2** *colloq.* (foll. by *of*) **a** meaning or sense (*can't get the hang of fluvial geomorphology*). **b** skill in handling (*can't get the hang of this knitting machine*). □ **hang about** (or **around**) **1 a** stand about or spend time aimlessly; not move away. **b** linger near (a person or place). **2** (often foll. by *with*) *colloq.* associate with (*he hangs around with Jeff*). **hang back** show reluctance to act or move. **hang fire** be slow in taking action or in progressing. **hang five** *colloq.* ride standing on the nose of a surfboard with the toes of one foot dangling over the edge. **hang heavily** (or **heavy**) (of time) seem to pass slowly. **hang in** *colloq.* **1** persist, persevere. **2** ride a surfboard close to the breaking part of a wave. **hanging in the balance** in a state of suspense with the outcome as yet unclear. **hang loose** *colloq.* be relaxed or uninhibited. **hang on 1** (often foll. by *to*) continue to hold or grasp. **2** (foll. by *to*) retain; fail to give back. **3** *colloq.* **a** wait for a short time. **b** (in telephoning) not ring off during a pause in the conversation. **4** *colloq.* continue; persevere. **hang out 1** suspend from a window, clothes-line, etc. **2 a** protrude downwards (*shirt hanging out*). **b** (foll. by *of*) lean out of (a window etc.). **3** *colloq.* **a** be frequently present at a place (*he hangs out at the games arcade*). **b** live in a place (*he hangs out somewhere near Wagga Wagga*). **hang out for** *colloq.* **1** hold on resolutely until one gets what one wants (*I'm hanging out for $1000, not a cent less*). **2** crave (*I'm hanging out for some Chinese food*). **hang ten** *colloq.* ride standing on the nose of a surfboard with the toes of both feet dangling over the edge. **hang together 1** be consistent; make sense (*this article on genetic engineering doesn't hang together at all*). **2** remain associated. **hang** (or **do**) **a uey** *colloq.* make a U-turn in a vehicle. **hang up 1** hang from a hook etc. **2** (often foll. by *on*) end a telephone conversation by replacing the receiver (*he hung up on me*). **3** (usu. in *passive*, foll. by *on*) *colloq.* have a psychological problem or an obsession for (*is hung up on her father*). **4** *colloq.* tether a horse. **let it all hang out** *colloq.* be uninhibited or relaxed. **not care** (or **give**) **a hang** *colloq.* not care at all. [Old English]

**hangar** /hang-uh/ *n.* building for housing aircraft etc. [French]

**hangdog** *adj.* shamefaced.

**hanger** *n.* **1** person or thing that hangs. **2** (in full **coat-hanger**) shaped piece of wood, wire, etc. for hanging clothes on.

**hanger-on** *n.* (*pl.* **hangers-on**) follower or dependant, esp. an unwelcome one.

**hang-glider** *n.* glider with a fabric wing on a light frame, from which the operator is suspended. □ **hang-glide** *v.* **hang-gliding** *n.*

**hanging** *n.* **1** execution by suspending by the neck. **2** (usu. in *pl.*) draperies hung on a wall etc.

**hangman** *n.* executioner who hangs condemned persons.

**hangnail** *n.* = AGNAIL.

**hang-out** *n.* *colloq.* place frequented by a person; haunt.

**hangover** *n.* **1** severe headache etc. from drinking too much alcohol. **2** survival from the past.

**hang-up** *n.* *colloq.* emotional problem or inhibition.

**hank** *n.* coil or skein of wool or thread etc. [Old Norse]

**hanker** *v.* (foll. by *for*, *after*, or *to* + infin.) long for; crave. □ **hankering** *n.* [from obsolete *hank*]

**hanky** /hang-kee/ *n.* (also **hankie**) (*pl.* **-ies**) *colloq.* handkerchief. [abbreviation]

**hanky-panky** /ˌhang-kee-**pang**-kee/ *n.* *colloq.* **1** naughtiness, esp. sexual. **2** double-dealing; trickery. [origin unknown]

**Hansard** /han-sahd/ *n.* **1** official verbatim printed record of debates and proceedings of the Australian Parliament. **2** similar record in Britain, New Zealand, and Canada. [*Hansard*, name of its first printer]

**Hansen's disease** /han-suhnz/ *n.* leprosy. [*Hansen*, name of a physician]

**Hanukkah** /hah-nuh-kuh, -xuh/ *n.* Jewish festival of lights, commemorating the purification of the Temple in 165 BC. [Hebrew *ḥānukkāh* consecration]

**haphazard** /hap-**haz**-uhd/ *adj.* done etc. by chance; random. □ **haphazardly** *adv.* [archaic *hap* chance, luck, from Old Norse *happ*]

**hapless** *adj.* unlucky.

**haploid** /**hap**-loid/ *adj.* (of an organism or cell) with a single set of chromosomes. [Greek *haplous* single, *eidos* form]

**happen** /**hap**-uhn/ *v.* **1** occur (by chance or otherwise). **2** (foll. by *to* + infin.) have the (good or bad) fortune to (*I happened to meet her*). **3** (foll. by *to*) be the (esp. unwelcome) fate or experience of (*what happened to you?*). **4** (foll. by *on*) encounter or discover by chance (*I happened on her at Tuggeranong*). □ **as it happens** in fact; in reality. [related to HAPHAZARD]

**happening** *n.* **1** event. **2** improvised or spontaneous theatrical etc. performance.

**happy** /**hap**-ee/ *adj.* (**-ier**, **-iest**) **1** feeling or showing pleasure or contentment. **2 a** fortunate; characterised by happiness. **b** (of words, behaviour, etc.) apt, pleasing (*has a happy turn of phrase*). **3** (in *comb.*) *colloq.* inclined to use excessively or at random (*trigger-happy*). □ **happy as Larry** *colloq.* extremely happy. □ **happily** *adv.* **happiness** *n.*

**happy family** *n.* = APOSTLE 2.

**happy-go-lucky** *adj.* cheerfully casual.

**happy hour** *n.* time of the day when goods, esp. drinks, are sold at reduced prices.

**happy jack** *n.* (also **apostle**) either of two Australian babblers (noisy, insect-eating birds of scrub and open forest), the grey-crowned babbler or the white-browed babbler.

**happy medium** *n.* compromise; avoidance of extremes.

**happy wanderer** *n.* common term for the HARDENBERGIA.

**hara-kiri** /ˌhah-ruh-**ki**-ree, ha-/ *n.* ritual suicide by disembowelment with a sword, formerly practised by samurai to avoid dishonour. [Japanese *hara* belly, *kiri* cutting]

**harangue** /huh-**rang**/ — *n.* a lengthy, ranting speech, often attacking the listeners. — *v.* (**-guing**) **1** make a harangue to; lecture. **2** scold, verbally abuse (*she harangued me for hours*). [French *arenge* from medieval Latin]

**harass** /**ha**-ruhs, huh-**ras**/ *v.* **1** trouble and annoy continually (*he keeps harassing me for a loan*). **2** make repeated attacks or raids on (*harassed the enemy outposts*). □ **harassment** *n.* [French]

■ **Usage** The second pronunciation given, with the stress on the second

syllable, is extremely common in Australia and elsewhere, but is considered incorrect by some people.

**harbinger** /**hah**-bin-juh/ *n.* **1** person or thing that announces or signals the approach of another. **2** forerunner; omen (*the comet was considered a harbinger of doom*). [Germanic: related to HARBOUR]

**harbour** /**hah**-buh/ (also **harbor**) — *n.* **1** place of shelter for ships (*Sydney harbour*). **2** shelter; refuge. — *v.* **1** give shelter to (esp. a criminal). **2** keep in one's mind (esp. resentment etc.) (*harboured ill-feeling towards me*). [Old English, = army shelter]

**hard** — *adj.* **1** (of a substance etc.) firm and solid. **2 a** difficult to understand, explain, or accomplish. **b** (foll. by *to* + infin.) not easy to (*hard to please*). **3** difficult to bear (*a hard life*). **4** unfeeling; severely critical (*a hard heart; a hard taskmaster*). **5** (of a season or the weather) severe (*a hard frost*). **6** unpleasant to the senses, harsh (*hard colours; a hard voice*). **7 a** strenuous, enthusiastic, intense (*a hard worker*). **b** severe, uncompromising (*a hard bargain*). **c** *Polit.* extreme; most radical (*the hard right*). **8 a** (of liquor) strongly alcoholic. **b** (of drugs) highly addictive and dangerous. **c** (of radiation) highly penetrating. **d** (of pornography) highly obscene. **9** (of water) containing mineral salts that make lathering difficult. **10** established; not disputable (*hard facts*). **11** (of a consonant) guttural (as *c* in *cat*, *g* in *go*). — *adv.* **1** strenuously, intensely, copiously (*try hard; raining hard*). **2** with difficulty or effort (*hard-earned*). □ **be hard on 1** be difficult for (*it's hard on her to bring up three children singlehanded*). **2** be severe in one's treatment or criticism of (*don't be too hard on him*). **3** be unpleasant to (the senses) (*that music's hard on my ears*). **be hard put to it** (usu. foll. by *to* + infin.) find it difficult (*I'm hard put to it to make ends meet*). **do (something) the hard way** choose a more difficult way of doing (something). **go hard with** turn out to (a person's) disadvantage (*it'll go hard with you if you don't hand in that essay by tomorrow*). **hard at it** *colloq.* busily working or occupied. **hard by** close by. **hard (or stiff) cheese** (or **cheddar**) ! *colloq.* **1** (sympathetic way of saying) bad luck! **2** (unsympathetic way of saying) that's your problem, not mine! **hard nut to crack** *colloq.* **1** difficult problem. **2** person or thing not easily understood or influenced. **hard on** (or **upon**) close to in pursuit etc. **put the hard word on a person** *colloq.* pressure a person for a favour. **put (something) in the too-hard basket** decide that (something) is much too difficult to do. □ **hardish** *adj.* **hardness** *n.* [Old English]

**hard and fast** *adj.* (of a rule or distinction) definite, unalterable, strict.

**hardback** *n.* book bound in boards covered with cloth etc. (opp. PAPERBACK).

**hardbitten** *adj. colloq.* tough and cynical.

**hardboard** *n.* stiff board made of compressed and treated wood pulp.

**hard-boiled** *adj.* **1** (of an egg) boiled until the white and yolk are solid. **2** *colloq.* (of a person) tough, shrewd.

**hard case** *n. colloq.* **1 a** a highly stubborn or intractable person. **b** hard-hearted person. **2** condition or instance of hardship.

**hard cash** *n.* coins and banknotes (opp. cheques, bankcard, etc.).

**hard copy** *n.* material printed by a computer on paper.

**hard core** *n.* **1** irreducible nucleus. **2** *colloq.* the most committed members of a society etc. (*the hard core of the ALP*).

**hard-core** *adj.* **1** forming a nucleus. **2** belonging to the hard core (*a member of the hard-core Left*). **3** (of pornography) explicit, obscene.

**hard disk** *n. Computing* large-capacity rigid usu. magnetic storage disk.

**hard-done-by** *adj.* harshly or unfairly treated.

**harden** *v.* **1** make or become hard or harder. **2** become, or make (one's attitude etc.), less sympathetic. □ **harden off** accustom (a plant) to the cold by gradually increasing its exposure.

**hardenbergia** /ˌhah-duhn-**ber**-jee-uh, -**ber**-gee-uh/ *n.* (also **purple coral pea, false sarsaparilla**) any species of the Australian genus *Hardenbergia* consisting of climbing or trailing plants with profuse masses of usu. purple pea-flowers completely hiding the foliage. [Countess von *Hardenberg*, Austrian patron of botany]

**hardening of the arteries** *n.* = ARTERIOSCLEROSIS.

**hard-gut** *n.* (in full **hard-gut mullet**) young sea-mullet of mainly southern Australian seas and estuaries.

**hard-headed** *adj.* practical; not sentimental. □ **hard-headedness** *n.*

**hard-hearted** *adj.* unfeeling. □ **hard-heartedness** *n.*

**hard-hit** *adj.* badly affected (*hard-hit by drought*).

**hard-hitting** *adj.* aggressively critical.

**hardihood** /hah-dee-ˌhuud/ *n.* boldness, daring.

**hard labour** *n.* heavy manual work as a punishment, esp. in a prison.

**hard line** — *n.* unyielding adherence to a policy (*he takes the hard line on drugs*). — *adj.* (**hardline**) sticking rigidly to a policy (*he has a hardline attitude to strikes*).

**hardliner** *n.* person (esp. a politician) who takes a hard line on an issue.

**hard luck** *n.* worse fortune than one deserves.

**hardly** *adv.* **1** scarcely; only just (*hardly knew me*). **2** only with difficulty (*can hardly see*). **3** surely not (*can hardly have realised*). □ **hardly any** almost no; almost none. **hardly ever** very seldom.

**hard-nosed** *adj. colloq.* realistic; ruthless; uncompromising.

**hard of hearing** *adj.* somewhat deaf.

**hard palate** *n.* front part of the palate.

**hard-pressed** *adj.* **1** closely pursued. **2** burdened with urgent business.

**hard rock** *n. colloq.* rock music with a heavy beat.

**hard sell** *n.* aggressive salesmanship.

**hardship** *n.* **1** severe suffering or privation. **2** circumstance causing this.

**hard up** *adj.* short of money.

**hardware** *n.* **1** tools and household articles of metal etc. **2** heavy machinery or armaments. **3** mechanical and electronic components of a computer etc. (opp. SOFTWARE).

**hard-wearing** *adj.* able to stand much wear.

**hardwood** *n.* wood from a eucalypt or deciduous broad-leaved tree.

**hard-working** *adj.* diligent.

**hardy** /**hah**-dee/ *adj.* (**-ier, -iest**) **1** robust; capable of enduring difficult conditions. **2** (of a plant) able to grow in the open air all year. □ **hardiness** *n.* [French *hardi* made bold]

**hard yakka** /**yak**-uh/ *n.* (also **yakker**) *colloq.* hard, tedious work (see YAKKA).

**hare** — *n.* mammal like a large rabbit, with long ears, short tail, and long hind legs. — *v.* (**-ring**) run rapidly. □ **run with the hare and hunt with the hounds** try to remain on good terms with both sides. [Old English]

**hare-brained** *adj.* rash, wild.

**harelip** *n.* congenital cleft in the upper lip.

**harem** /**hair**-ruhm, hah-**reem**/ *n.* **1** women of a Muslim household. **2** their quarters. [Arabic, = prohibited place]

**hare-wallaby** *n.* any of several small hare-like wallabies of mainland Australia.

**haricot** /ha-ruh-ˌkoh/ n. (in full **haricot bean**) variety of French bean with small white seeds dried and used as a vegetable. [French]

**hark** v. (usu. in *imper.*) *archaic* listen attentively. □ **hark back** revert to earlier topic. [Old English]

**harlequin** /hah-luh-kwuhn/ — n. **1** (**Harlequin**) name of a mute character in pantomime, usu. masked and dressed in a diamond-patterned costume. **2** highly prized form of opal. — *attrib. adj.* in varied colours. [French]

**harlot** /hah-luht/ n. *archaic* prostitute. □ **harlotry** n. [French, = knave]

**harm** — n. hurt, damage. — v. cause harm to. □ **out of harm's way** in safety. [Old English]

**harmful** adj. causing or likely to cause harm. □ **harmfully** adv. **harmfulness** n.

**harmless** adj. **1** not able or likely to cause harm. **2** inoffensive. □ **harmlessly** adv. **harmlessness** n.

**harmonic** /hah-**mon**-ik/ — adj. of or relating to harmony; harmonious. — n. *Mus.* overtone accompanying (and forming a note with) a fundamental at a fixed interval. □ **harmonically** adv.

**harmonica** n. small rectangular musical instrument played by blowing and sucking air through it.

**harmonious** /hah-**moh**-nee-uhs/ adj. **1** sweet-sounding; tuneful. **2** forming a pleasing or consistent whole. **3** free from disagreement or dissent. □ **harmoniously** adv.

**harmonise** /**hah**-muh-ˌnuyz/ v. (also **-ize**) (**-sing** or **-zing**) **1 a** add notes to (a melody) to produce harmony. **b** sing in harmony. **2** bring into or be in harmony. **3** make or form a pleasing or consistent whole. □ **harmonisation** /-**zay**-shuhn/ n.

**harmonium** /hah-**moh**-nee-uhm/ n. keyboard instrument in which the notes are produced by air driven through metal reeds by foot-operated bellows. [Latin: related to HARMONY]

**harmony** /**hah**-muh-nee/ n. (pl. **-ies**) **1** combination of simultaneously sounded musical notes to produce chords and chord progressions, esp. as creating a pleasing effect. **2 a** apt or aesthetic arrangement of parts. **b** pleasing effect of this. **3** agreement, concord. □ **in harmony 1** in agreement. **2** (of singing etc.) producing chords; not discordant. [Greek *harmonia* joining]

**harness** /**hah**-nuhs/ — n. **1** equipment of straps etc. by which a horse is fastened to a cart etc. and controlled. **2** similar arrangement for fastening a thing to a person's body. — v. **1 a** put a harness on. **b** (foll. by *to*) attach by harness to. **2** make use of (natural resources), esp. to produce energy. □ **in harness** in the routine of daily work. [French *harneis* military equipment]

**harp** — n. large upright triangular stringed instrument plucked with the fingers. — v. (foll. by *on*, *on about*) talk repeatedly and tediously about (*don't harp on about it*). □ **harpist** n. [Old English]

**harpoon** /hah-**poon**/ — n. barbed spearlike missile with a rope attached, for catching whales etc. — v. spear with a harpoon. [Greek *harpē* sickle]

**harpsichord** /**hahp**-suh-ˌkawd/ n. keyboard instrument with horizontal strings plucked mechanically. □ **harpsichordist** n. [Latin *harpa* harp, *chorda* string]

**harpy** /**hah**-pee/ n. (pl. **-ies**) **1** mythological monster with a woman's filthy head and body and a bird's wings and claws. **2** grasping unscrupulous person. [Greek *harpuiai* snatchers]

**harridan** /**ha**-ruh-duhn/ n. bad-tempered old woman. [origin uncertain]

**harrier** /**ha**-ree-uh/ n. **1** hound used for hunting hares. **2** group of cross-country runners. **3** any of various hawk-like birds of prey, including some Australian species (*spotted harrier*; *swamp harrier*). [from HARE, HARRY]

**harrow** /**ha**-roh/ — n. heavy frame with iron teeth dragged over ploughed land to break up clods etc. — v. **1** draw a harrow over (land). **2** (usu. as **harrowing** adj.) distress greatly (*was harrowed by guilt*). [Old Norse *hervi*]

**harry** /**ha**-ree/ v. (**-ies**, **-ied**) **1** ravage or despoil. **2** harass. [Old English]

**harsh** adj. **1** unpleasantly rough or sharp, esp. to the senses. **2** severe, cruel. □ **harshen** v. **harshly** adv. **harshness** n. [Low German]

**hart** n. (pl. same or **-s**) male of the (esp. red) deer, esp. after its 5th year. [Old English]

**harum-scarum** /ˌhair-ruhm-**skair**-ruhm/ *colloq.* — adj. wild and reckless. — n. such a person. [rhyming formation on HARE, SCARE]

**harvest** /**hah**-vuhst/ — n. **1 a** process of gathering in crops etc. **b** season of this. **2** season's yield. **3** product of any action. — v. gather as harvest, reap. [Old English]

**harvester** n. **1** reaper. **2** reaping machine, esp. with sheaf-binding.

**has** *3rd sing.* present of HAVE.

**has-been** n. *colloq.* person or thing that is no longer important or well-regarded.

**hash¹** — n. **1** dish of cooked meat cut into

**hash²** small pieces and reheated. **2 a** mixture; jumble. **b** mess. **3** recycled material. — *v.* (often foll. by *up*) recycle (old material). □ **make a hash of** *colloq.* make a mess of; bungle. **settle a person's hash** *colloq.* deal with and subdue a person. [French *hacher* cut up]

**hash²** *n. colloq.* hashish. [abbreviation]

**hashish** /*hash*-eesh/ *n.* resinous product of hemp, smoked or chewed as a narcotic. [Arabic]

**hasn't** /*haz*-uhnt/ *contr.* has not.

**hasp** /hasp, hahsp/ *n.* hinged metal clasp fitting over a staple and secured by a padlock. [Old English]

**hassle** /*has*-uhl/ *colloq.* — *n.* **1** trouble; problem. **2** argument; quarrel. — *v.* (**-ling**) harass, annoy. [originally a British dial. word]

**hassock** /*has*-uhk/ *n.* **1** thick firm cushion for kneeling on. **2** tuft of matted grass etc. [Old English]

**haste** /hayst/ — *n.* urgency of movement or action; excessive hurry. — *v.* (**-ting**) *archaic* = HASTEN 1. □ **in haste** quickly, hurriedly. **make haste** hurry; be quick. [French from Germanic]

**hasten** /*hay*-suhn/ *v.* **1** make haste; hurry. **2** cause to occur or be ready or be done sooner (*hasten the process*).

**hasty** /*hay*-stee/ *adj.* (**-ier, -iest**) **1** hurried; acting too quickly. **2** said, made, or done too quickly or too soon; rash. **3** quick-tempered. □ **hastily** *adv.* **hastiness** *n.*

**hat** *n.* **1** (esp. outdoor) covering for the head, often with a brim. **2** *colloq.* person's position, rank, etc. (esp. if one of several) (*wearing his managerial hat*). □ **eat one's hat** *colloq.* express firm conviction that what one says will happen will happen (*if he passes Maths I'll eat my hat!*). **keep it under one's hat** *colloq.* keep it secret. **pass** (or **hand**) **the hat around** collect contributions of money. **take one's hat off to** *colloq.* acknowledge admiration for. **talk through one's hat** *colloq.* speak nonsense (through ignorance of the facts). **throw one's hat in (first)** declare an intention in order to see what the response is; test the water. **throw one's hat in** (or **into**) **the ring** enter a contest; take up a challenge. **wear two hats** hold two official jobs at the same time. [Old English]

**hatch¹** *n.* **1 a** opening in a wall between a kitchen and dining-room for serving food. **b** opening or trapdoor in a floor, roof, etc. **c** cover for this. **2** opening or door in an aircraft etc. **3 a** = HATCHWAY. **b** cover for this (often in *pl.: batten the hatches*). □ **down the hatch** *colloq.* (as a toast) drink up, cheers! [Old English]

**hatch²** — *v.* **1 a** (often foll. by *out*) (of a young bird or fish etc.) emerge from the egg. **b** (of an egg) produce a young animal. **2** incubate (an egg). **3** (also foll. by *up*) devise (a plot etc.). — *n.* **1** act of hatching. **2** brood hatched. [earlier *hacche*, from Germanic]

**hatch³** *v.* mark with close parallel lines. □ **hatching** *n.* [French *hacher*: related to HASH¹]

**hatchback** *n.* car with a sloping back hinged at the top to form a door.

**hatchery** /*hach*-uh-ree/ *n.* place for hatching eggs, esp. of fish or poultry.

**hatchet** /*hach*-uht/ *n.* light short-handled axe. [French *hachette*]

**hatchet-faced** *adj.* sharp-featured or grim-looking.

**hatchet-job** *n.* fierce verbal attack on a person, esp. in print.

**hatchet man** *n. colloq.* **1** person hired by an employer to do unpleasant tasks on his or her behalf, such as firing employees, cutting costs, etc. **2** person hired to murder another.

**hatchway** *n.* opening in a ship's deck for raising and lowering cargo.

**hate** — *v.* (**-ting**) **1** dislike intensely. **2 a** dislike. **b** be reluctant (to do something) (*I hate to disturb you*). — *n.* **1** hatred. **2** *colloq.* hated person or thing (*that's my pet hate*). — *adj.* expressing hate (*a hate session*). [Old English]

**hateful** *adj.* arousing hatred; detestable.

**hatred** /*hay*-truhd/ *n.* extreme dislike or ill will.

**hatstand** *n.* stand with hooks for hanging hats etc. on.

**hatter** *n.* **1** person (esp. a miner or bushman) who lives alone. **2** maker or seller of hats. □ **mad as a hatter** quite crazy.

**hat-trick** *n.* **1** *Cricket* taking of three wickets by the same bowler with three successive balls. **2** three consecutive successes etc.

**haughty** /*haw*-tee/ *adj.* (**-ier, -iest**) arrogant and disdainful. □ **haughtily** *adv.* **haughtiness** *n.* [*haught, haut* from French, = high]

**haul** /hawl/ — *v.* **1** pull or drag forcibly. **2** transport by truck, cart, etc. **3** turn a ship's course. **4** *colloq.* (usu. foll. by *up*) bring for reprimand or trial (*hauled him up before the magistrate*). — *n.* **1** act of hauling. **2** amount gained or acquired (*good haul of fish*). **3** distance to be traversed (*a short haul*). □ **haul over the coals** see COAL. **in** (or **over**) **the short** (or **long**) **haul** in the short (or long) term (*in the short haul unemployment is not expected to decline*). [French *haler* from Old Norse *hala*]

**haulage** /**haw**-lij/ *n. Brit.* **1** commercial transport of goods. **2** charge for this.

**haulier** /**haw**-lee-uh/ *n.* person or firm engaged in the transport of goods.

**haunch** /hawnch/ *n.* **1** fleshy part of the buttock with the thigh. **2** leg and loin of an animal as food; hindquarter. [French from Germanic]

**haunt** /hawnt/ — *v.* **1** (of a ghost) visit (a place) regularly. **2** frequent (a place) (*he haunts the disco*). **3** linger in the mind (*that melody haunts me*). **4** distress; torment (*haunted by guilt*). **5** be often in the company of. — *n.* place frequented by a person or animal (*his favourite haunt*). [French from Germanic]

**haunting** *adj.* (of a memory, melody, etc.) tending to linger in the mind; poignant, evocative.

**haute couture** /,oht koo-**tyoor**/ *n.* high fashion; leading fashion houses or their products. [French]

**haute cuisine** /,oht kwuh-**zeen**/ *n.* high-class cookery. [French]

**hauteur** /oh-**ter**/ *n.* haughtiness. [French]

**have** /hav/ — *v.* (**-ving**; *3rd sing. present* **has** /haz/; *past* and *past part.* **had**) **1** as an auxiliary verb with *past part.* or *ellipt.*, to form the perfect, pluperfect, and future perfect tenses, and the conditional mood (*he has seen; he had seen; he will have seen; had I known, I would have gone; yes, I have*). **2** own or be able to use; be provided with (*has a car; had no time*). **3** hold in a certain relationship (*has a sister; had no equals*). **4** contain as a part or quality (*box has a lid; has big eyes*). **5 a** experience (*had a good time, a shock, a pain*). **b** be subjected to a specified state (*had my car stolen; book has a page missing*). **c** cause (a person or thing) to be in a particular state or take particular action (*had him sacked; had us worried; had my hair cut; had a copy made; had them to stay*). **6 a** engage in (an activity) (*have an argument, sex*). **b** hold (a meeting, party, etc.). **7** eat or drink (*had a beer*). **8** (usu. in *neg.*) accept or tolerate; permit to (do something) (*I won't have it; will not have you say such things*). **9 a** feel (*have no doubt; has no sympathy for them; has nothing against me*). **b** show (mercy, pity, etc.) (*have pity on him*). **c** (foll. by *to* + *infin.*) show by action that one is influenced by (a feeling, quality, etc.) (*have the sense to stop*). **10 a** give birth to (offspring) (*had twins*). **b** conceive mentally (an idea etc.) (*had a brainwave*). **11** receive, obtain (*had a letter from him; not a ticket to be had*). **12** be burdened with or committed to (*has a*

job to do). **13 a** have obtained (a qualification) (*has an English Honours degree*). **b** know (a language) (*has no Latin*). **14** *colloq.* **a** get the better of (*I had him there*). **b** (usu. in *passive*) cheat, deceive (*you were had*). — *n. colloq.* a swindle (*that was a real have*). □ **had best** see BEST. **had better** see BETTER. **had rather** see RATHER. **have done** (**with**) see DONE. **have got to** *colloq.* = *have to* (*I've got to go*). **have had** (**a person** or **thing**) *colloq.* be thoroughly fed up with. **have had it** *colloq.* **1** have missed one's chance. **2** have passed one's prime. **3** have been killed, defeated, etc. **4** be exhausted (*been at it since dawn — I've had it*). **5** be ruined or broken (*the telly's had it*). **have it 1** (foll. by *that*) maintain that (*he has it that the drought has been caused by pollution in the atmosphere*). **2** win a decision in a vote etc. (*the ayes have it*). **3** *colloq.* have found the answer etc. **have it coming** *colloq.* be due for retribution (*he has it coming to him for what he's done*). **have it easy** *colloq.* be well-off (*he's had it easy since he won the lottery*). **have it in for** *colloq.* be hostile or ill-disposed towards. **have it out** (often foll. by *with*) *colloq.* attempt to settle a dispute by argument. **have on 1** wear (clothes). **2** have (an engagement) (*what does he have on next Monday at 3?*). **3** *colloq.* tease, hoax (*he's having you on*). **have oneself on** *colloq.* be so conceited as to delude oneself. **the haves and the have-nots** *colloq.* the rich and the poor. **have something** (or **nothing**) **on a person 1** know something (or nothing) discreditable or incriminating about a person. **2** have an (or no) advantage or superiority over a person. **have to** be obliged to, must (*I have to go*). **have to do with** see DO[1]. **have up** *colloq.* bring (a person) before a judge, interviewer, etc. (*he was had up before the magistrate*). **have what it takes** *colloq.* have all the requirements for success. [Old English]

**haven** /**hay**-vuhn/ *n.* **1** refuge. **2** harbour, port. [Old English]

**haven't** /**hav**-uhnt/ *contr.* have not.

**haversack** /**hav**-uh-,sak/ *n.* stout canvas bag carried on the back or over the shoulder. [German *Habersack*, = oats-sack]

**havoc** /**hav**-uhk/ *n.* widespread destruction; great disorder. [French *havo(t)*]

**haw** see HUM.

**hawk**[1] — *n.* **1** bird of prey with a curved beak, rounded short wings, and a long tail. **2** *Polit.* person who advocates aggressive (esp. military) policies (opp.

DOVE). — *v.* hunt with a hawk. □ **hawkish**
*adj.* [Old English]

**hawk²** *v.* **1** carry about or offer (goods) for
sale. **2** (often foll. by *about*) spread (news,
gossip, etc.) freely. [back-formation from
HAWKER]

**hawk³** *v.* **1** clear the throat noisily. **2** (foll.
by *up*) bring (phlegm etc.) up from the
throat. [imitative]

**hawker** *n.* person who travels about
selling goods. [Low German or Dutch]

**hawk-eyed** *adj.* keen-sighted.

**hawser** /**haw**-zuh/ *n.* thick rope or cable
for mooring or towing a ship. [French,
*haucier* hoist, from Latin *altus* high]

**hawthorn** /**haw**-thawn/ *n.* thorny shrub
with small dark red berries. [Old
English]

**hay** *n.* grass cut and dried for fodder.
□ **hayed off** (of grass) dried while
standing. **make hay (while the sun shines)**
seize opportunities. [Old English]

**hay fever** *n.* allergy with asthmatic
symptoms etc., caused by pollen or dust.

**haystack** *n.* (also **hayrick**) packed pile of
hay with a pointed or ridged top.

**haywire** *adj. colloq.* **1** badly disorganised;
out of order. **2** out of control; berserk (*he
went haywire*).

**hazard** /**haz**-uhd/ — *n.* **1** danger or risk.
**2** source of this. **3** chance. **4** *Golf* obstacle,
e.g. a bunker. — *v.* **1** venture (*hazard a
guess*). **2** risk. [Arabic *az-zahr* chance,
luck]

**hazardous** *adj.* risky.

**haze¹** *n.* **1** thin atmospheric vapour. **2**
mental obscurity or confusion. [back-
formation from HAZY]

**haze²** *v.* **1** *Naut.* harass with overwork. **2**
subject (newcomers to a group, first-year
students at a university, etc.) to a period
of organised bullying, ridicule, abuse, etc.
as part of initiation. [origin uncertain]

**hazel** /**hay**-zuhl/ — *n.* **1** shrub or small
tree of Europe and America bearing
round brown edible nuts. **2** shrub or
small tree (*Pomaderris*) of eastern
Australia, with scented flowers and
rough wrinkled leaves, bearing some
resemblance to a hazel. — *adj.* greenish-
brown. [Old English]

**hazelnut** *n.* nut of the hazel.

**hazy** *adj.* (**-ier, -iest**) **1** misty. **2** vague,
indistinct. **3** confused, uncertain. □ **hazily**
*adv.* **haziness** *n.* [origin unknown]

**HB** *abbr.* (of pencil-lead) hard black.

**H-bomb** /**aych**-bom/ *n.* = HYDROGEN BOMB.
[from H³]

**HCF** *abbr.* highest common factor.

**He** *symb.* helium.

**he** /hee/ — *pron.* (*obj.* **him**; *poss.* **his**; *pl.*

they) **1** the man, boy, or male animal
previously named or in question. **2**
person etc. of unspecified sex (*if anyone
comes he will have to wait; he who
hesitates*). — *n.* (*pl.* **hes** /heez/ ) **1** male;
man. **2** (in *comb.*) male (*he-goat*). [Old
English]

**head** /hed/ — *n.* **1** upper part of the
human body, or foremost or upper part of
an animal's body, containing the brain,
mouth, and sense-organs. **2 a** seat of
intellect (*use your head*). **b** mental
aptitude or tolerance (*a good head for
business; no head for heights*). **3** thing
like a head in form or position, esp.: **a** the
operative part of a tool. **b** the top of a nail.
**c** the leaves or flowers at the top of a
stem. **d** foam on the top of a glass of beer
etc. **4 a** a person in charge, esp. the
principal teacher of a school. **b** position
of command. **5** front part of a queue etc.
**6** upper end of a table or bed etc. **7** top or
highest part of a page, stairs, etc. **8 a**
individual person as a unit (*$10 per
head*). **b** (*pl.* same) individual animal as
a unit (*20 head of cattle*). **9 a** side of a coin
bearing the image of a head. **b** (usu. in *pl.*)
this as a choice when tossing a coin. **10 a**
source of a river etc. **b** end of a lake at
which a river enters it. **11** height or
length of a head as a measure (*horse won
by a head; he's taller than I by a head*). **12**
part of a machine in contact with or very
close to what is being worked on, esp.: **a**
the part of a tape recorder that touches
the moving tape and converts signals. **b**
the part of a record-player that holds the
playing cartridge and stylus. **c** *Computing* (also **printhead**) the part of a disk
drive, tape drive, or printer that reads or
writes. **13** (usu. in phr. **come to a head**)
climax, crisis. **14** a confined body of water
or steam in an engine etc. **b** pressure
exerted by this. **15** promontory (esp. in
place-names) (*Barwon Heads*). **16** heading or headline. **17** fully developed top of
a boil etc. **18** *colloq.* headache. **19** (*attrib.*)
chief, principal (*head waiter*). — *v.* **1** be
at the head or front of (*heads the
procession*). **2** be in charge of (*headed a
small team*). **3** provide with a head or
heading. **4** (often foll. by *for*) face, move,
or direct in a specified direction (*is
heading for trouble*). **5** hit (a ball etc.)
with the head. □ **above** (or **over**) **one's
head** beyond one's understanding. **all in
the head** imagined, not real (*your
stomach-ache is all in the head*). **bury** (or
**hide**) **one's head in the sand** refuse to face
up to facts or realities. **come to a head**
reach a crisis. **get it into one's head** (foll.
by *that*) **1** adopt a mistaken idea (*got it*

*into his head that there were Martians in Canberra).* **2** (also foll. by *to* + infin.) form a definite plan (*got it into his head to pave over the lawn*). **give a person his** (or **her**) **head** allow a person to act freely. **go to one's head 1** (of liquor) make one slightly dizzy. **2** make one conceited. **have a good head on one's shoulders** be level-headed and sensible; be intelligent. **have one's head screwed on the right way** = *have a good head on one's shoulders.* **head and shoulders above** *colloq.* by a considerable amount (*his performance was head and shoulders above mine*). **head off 1** get ahead of so as to intercept and turn aside. **2** forestall. **head on down** go (*let's head on down to the beach.* **head over turkey** (or **head over heels**) **1** so as to turn completely over (*tumbled head over turkey down the stairs*). **2** completely, utterly (*head over turkey in love*). **head them** make both coins in the game of two-up land with head upwards; hence, play the game of two-up. **hold up one's head** be confident or unashamed. **keep** (or **lose**) **one's head** remain (or fail to remain) calm. **keep one's head above water 1** keep out of debt. **2** avoid succumbing to difficulties. **keep one's head down** *colloq.* **1** try to remain unnoticed in difficult situations. **2** work diligently. **make head or tail of** (usu. with *neg.* or *interrog.*) understand at all. **need one's head read** *colloq.* be crazy. **off one's head** *colloq.* crazy; crazed. **off the top of one's head** *colloq.* impromptu; unrehearsed. **on one's head** *colloq.* with the greatest ease (*did it on his head*). **on one's** (or **one's own**) **head** as one's own responsibility (*on your head be it*). **out of one's head 1** from one's memory or imagination. **2** *colloq.* crazy; crazed. **over one's head 1** beyond one's understanding. **2** without one's rightful knowledge or involvement, esp. of action taken by a subordinate consulting one's own superior (*he went over my head to the managing director*). **3** with disregard for one's own (stronger) claim (*was promoted over my head*). **put heads together** consult together. **take it into one's head** (foll. by *that* + clause or *to* + infin.) decide, esp. impetuously. **turn a person's head** make a person conceited. [Old English]

**-head¹** *suffix* = -HOOD.

**-head²** *suffix colloq.* indicating a person who has a certain character etc. (*thick-head* a fool), or who has a particular partiality to something (*waxhead* a surfing fanatic).

**headache** *n.* **1** continuous pain in the head. **2** *colloq.* worrying problem, person, or thing. □ **headachy** *adj.*

**headband** *n.* band worn round the head as decoration or to confine the hair.

**head-butt** — *n.* thrust with the head into the chin or body of another person. — *v.* attack with a head-butt.

**headcount** *n.* **1** a count of individual people. **2** total number of people, esp. employees.

**headdress** *n.* covering for the head.

**header** *n.* **1** *Soccer* shot or pass made with the head. **2** *colloq.* headlong fall or dive. **3** brick etc. laid at right angles to the face of a wall. **4** (in word-processing) heading programmed to appear at the top of every page (opp. FOOTER).

**head first** *adv.* **1** with the head foremost. **2** precipitately.

**headgear** *n.* hat or headdress.

**head-hunting** *n.* **1** (among certain tribes) collecting of the heads of dead enemies as trophies. **2** seeking to employ (esp. senior) staff by approaching people employed elsewhere. **3** getting rid of (esp. political) opponents. **4** seeking a scapegoat. □ **headhunt** *v.* **headhunter** *n.*

**heading** *n.* **1 a** title at the head of a page or section of a book etc. **b** section of a subject of discourse etc. **2** horizontal passage made in preparation for building a tunnel, or in a mine.

**headlamp** *n.* = HEADLIGHT.

**headland** *n.* promontory.

**headlight** *n.* **1** strong light at the front of a vehicle. **2** beam from this.

**headline** *n.* **1** heading at the top of an article or page, esp. in a newspaper. **2** (in *pl.*) summary of the most important items in a news bulletin.

**headlock** *n. Wrestling* hold with an arm round the opponent's head.

**headlong** *adv. & adj.* **1** with the head foremost. **2** in a rush.

**headmaster** *n.* (*fem.* **headmistress**) teacher in charge of a school.

**head-on** *adj. & adv.* **1** with the front foremost (*head-on crash*). **2** in direct confrontation.

**headphones** *n.pl.* set of earphones fitting over the head, for listening to audio equipment etc.

**headquarters** *n.* (as *sing.* or *pl.*) administrative centre of an organisation.

**headset** *n.* headphones, often with a microphone attached.

**headshrinker** *n.* **1** headhunter who shrinks human heads. **2** *colloq.* psychiatrist.

**head start** *n.* advantage granted or gained at an early stage.

**headstone** *n.* stone set up at the head of a grave.

**headstrong** *adj.* self-willed and obstinate.

**headwaters** *n.pl.* streams flowing from the sources of a river.

**headway** *n.* **1** progress. **2** ship's rate of progress.

**headwind** *n.* wind blowing from directly in front.

**headword** *n.* word beginning an entry in a dictionary or encyclopaedia.

**heady** *adj.* (**-ier, -iest**) **1** (of liquor) potent. **2** intoxicating, exciting. **3** impulsive, rash. **4** headachy. □ **headily** *adv.* **headiness** *n.*

**heal** *v.* **1** (often foll. by *up*) become sound or healthy again (*the cut is healing nicely*). **2** cause (a wound, disease, or person) to heal or be healed. **3** put right (differences etc.). **4** alleviate (sorrow etc.). □ **healer** *n.* [Old English: related to WHOLE]

**health** /helth/ *n.* **1** state of being well in body or mind. **2** person's mental or physical condition. **3** soundness, esp. financial or moral (*the health of the nation*). [Old English: related to WHOLE]

**health centre** *n.* building containing various local medical services and doctors' practices.

**health food** *n.* natural food, free from additives, thought to promote good health.

**health kick** *n. colloq.* an obsession with one's health (*he's on a health kick and eats only vegies*).

**healthy** *adj.* (**-ier, -iest**) **1** having, showing, or promoting good health. **2** indicative of (esp. moral or financial) health (*a healthy sign*). **3** substantial (*won by a healthy 40 seconds*). □ **healthily** *adv.* **healthiness** *n.*

**heap** — *n.* **1** disorderly pile. **2** (esp. in *pl.*) *colloq.* large number or amount. **3** *colloq.* dilapidated vehicle. — *v.* **1** (foll. by *up, together*, etc.) collect or be collected in a heap. **2** (foll. by *with*) load copiously with. **3** (foll. by *on, upon*) give or offer copiously (*heaped insults on them*). □ **give** (**a person** or **'em** or **them**) **heaps** *colloq.* oppose (an opponent, team, etc.) with vigour. [Old English]

**hear** *v.* (*past* and *past part.* **heard** /herd/) **1** (also *absol.*) perceive with the ear. **2** listen to (*heard them on the radio*). **3** listen judicially to (a case etc.). **4** be told or informed. **5** (foll. by *from*) be contacted by, esp. by letter or telephone. **6** be ready to obey (an order). **7** grant (a prayer). □ **have heard of** be aware of the existence of. **hear! hear!** *int.* expressing agreement.

**hear a person out** listen to all a person says. **hear things** imagine noises. **let's hear it for** (**a person**) give (a person) a round of applause. **will not hear of** will not allow. □ **hearer** *n.* [Old English]

**hearing** *n.* **1** faculty of perceiving sounds. **2** range within which sounds may be heard (*within hearing*). **3** opportunity to state one's case (*a fair hearing*). **4** trial of a case before a court.

**hearing aid** *n.* small device to amplify sound, worn by a partially deaf person.

**hearken** /**hah**-kuhn/ *v. archaic* (often foll. by *to*) listen. [Old English: related to HARK]

**hearsay** *n.* rumour, gossip.

**hearse** /hers/ *n.* vehicle for conveying the coffin at a funeral. [French *herse* harrow, from Latin *hirpex* large rake]

**heart** /haht/ *n.* **1** hollow muscular organ maintaining the circulation of blood by rhythmic contraction and dilation. **2** region of the heart; the breast (*clasped him to my heart*). **3 a** centre of thought, feeling, and emotion (esp. love). **b** capacity for feeling emotion (*has no heart*). **4 a** courage or enthusiasm (*take heart*). **b** mood or feeling (*change of heart*). **5 a** central or innermost part of something (*heart of the city*). **b** essence (*heart of the matter*). **6** compact tender inner part of a lettuce etc. **7 a** heart-shaped thing. **b** conventional representation of a heart with two equal curves meeting at a point at the bottom and a cusp at the top. **8 a** playing-card of the suit denoted by a red figure of a heart. **b** (in *pl.*) this suit. □ **all heart** completely kind-hearted, generous. **at heart 1** in one's inmost feelings. **2** basically. **break a person's heart** overwhelm a person with sorrow. **by heart** from memory. **close to one's heart 1** dear to one. **2** affecting one deeply. **cry one's heart out** cry bitterly; cry lengthily until exhausted. **from the heart** (or **the bottom of one's heart**) sincerely. **give** (or **lose**) **one's heart** (often foll. by *to*) fall in love (with). **have a change of heart** reverse a previous decision, attitude. **have a heart** be merciful. **have the heart** (usu. with *neg.*; foll. by *to* + infin.) be insensitive or hard-hearted enough (*didn't have the heart to scold him*). **have one's heart in one's mouth** be greatly frightened. **have one's heart in the right place** be sincere or well-intentioned. **heart and soul** totally. **in one's heart of hearts** in one's inmost feelings. **set a person's heart at rest** relieve his or her mind of worry etc. **set one's heart on** (**something**) yearn greatly to get or achieve (something). **take to heart 1** give serious consideration to (*took his doctor's warning to heart*). **2** be much affected by. **to one's heart's content** see CONTENT[1]. **with all one's heart** sincerely; with all goodwill. [Old English]

**heartache** *n.* mental anguish.

**heart attack** *n.* sudden occurrence of coronary thrombosis.

**heartbeat** *n.* pulsation of the heart.

**heartbreak** *n.* overwhelming distress. □ **heartbreaking** *adj.* **heartbroken** *adj.*

**heartburn** *n.* burning sensation in the chest from indigestion.

**hearten** *v.* make or become more cheerful. □ **heartening** *adj.*

**heart failure** *n.* failure of the heart to function properly, esp. as a cause of death.

**heartfelt** *adj.* sincere; deeply felt.

**hearth** /hahth/ *n.* **1** floor of a fireplace or the area in front of it. **2** this as a symbol of the home. [Old English]

**heartily** *adv.* **1** in a hearty manner. **2** very (*am heartily sick of it*).

**heartland** *n.* central part of an area.

**heartleaf** *n.* (in full **heartleaf poison bush**) any of several related and extremely attractive Australian shrubs with yellow and red, orange, or all red pea-flowers, and heart-shaped leaves which are extremely toxic to stock.

**heartless** *adj.* unfeeling, pitiless. □ **heartlessly** *adv.*

**heart-rending** *adj.* causing acute distress or mental anguish.

**heart-searching** *n.* examination of one's own feelings and motives (*after much heart-searching he decided to quit the job*).

**heartsick** *adj.* despondent.

**heartstrings** *n.pl.* one's deepest feelings (*the tale tugged at his heartstrings*).

**heart-throb** *n.* *colloq.* person for whom one has (esp. immature) romantic feelings.

**heart-to-heart** — *attrib. adj.* (of a conversation etc.) candid, intimate. — *n.* candid or personal conversation.

**heart-warming** *adj.* emotionally rewarding or uplifting.

**heartwood** *n.* dense inner part of a tree-trunk, yielding the hardest timber.

**hearty** *adj.* (**-ier, -iest**) **1** strong, vigorous. **2** (of a meal or appetite) large. **3** warm, friendly. □ **heartiness** *n.*

**heat** — *n.* **1** condition of being hot. **2** *Physics* form of energy arising from the motion of bodies' molecules. **3** hot weather. **4** warmth of feeling; anger or excitement (*replied with some heat*). **5** (foll. by *of*) most intense part or period of

activity (*heat of battle*). **6** (usu. preliminary or trial) round in a race etc. **7** *colloq.* intensive investigation, e.g. by the police (*the bank-robbers lay low while the heat was on*). **8 a** receptive period of the sexual cycle, esp. in female mammals. **b** sexual excitement during such a period. — *v.* **1** make or become hot or warm. **2** excite or inflame the mind, passions, etc. □ **on heat** (of mammals, esp. females) sexually receptive. **put the heat on a person** *colloq.* put pressure on. **turn the heat on** *colloq.* concentrate an attack or criticism on (a person). [Old English]

**heated** *adj.* angry; impassioned. □ **heatedly** *adv.*

**heater** *n.* stove or other heating device.

**heath** *n.* **1 a** area of flattish uncultivated land with low shrubs. **b** plant growing on a heath, esp. heather. **2** any of several plants occurring in the Australian bush, esp. the epacris, a low shrub bearing masses of attractive tube-shaped white, pink, or scarlet flowers, including *Epacris impressa*, the floral emblem of Victoria. [Old English]

**heathen** /hee-*th*uhn/ — *n.* **1** person who does not belong to a widely held religion (esp. one which proclaims that there is only one God) as regarded by those who do belong to such a religion; a pagan. **2** person regarded as lacking culture or moral principles. — *adj.* **1** of heathens; pagan. **2** having no proper religion; unenlightened. [Old English]

**heather** /*heth*-uh/ *n.* any of various European shrubs growing esp. on moors and heaths, e.g. Scotch heather. [origin unknown]

**heating** *n.* **1** imparting or generation of heat. **2** equipment used to heat a building etc.

**heatproof** — *adj.* able to resist great heat. — *v.* make heatproof.

**heat shield** *n.* device to protect (esp. a spacecraft) from excessive heat.

**heatwave** *n.* period of unusually hot weather.

**heave** — *v.* (**-ving**; *past* and *past part.* heaved or esp. *Naut.* hove /hohv/) **1** lift or haul with great effort. **2** utter with effort (*heaved a sigh*). **3** *colloq.* throw (*heave me the rope*). **4** rise and fall rhythmically or spasmodically. **5** *Naut.* haul by rope. **6** retch; vomit. — *n.* instance of heaving. □ **heave in sight** come into view. **heave (something) out** discard. **heave to** esp. *Naut.* bring or be brought to a standstill. [Old English]

**heaven** /*hev*-uhn/ *n.* **1** place regarded in some religions as the abode of God and the angels, and of the blessed after death, often characterised as above the sky. **2** place or state of supreme bliss. **3** *colloq.* something delightful (*this reclining chair is simply heaven*). **4** (usu. **Heaven**) God, Providence (often as an exclamation or mild oath: *Heavens!*). **5** (**the heavens**) esp. *poet.* the sky as seen from the earth, in which the sun, moon, and stars appear. □ **heaven (only) knows** no one knows. **to high heaven** to an extreme extent (*those prawns are off — they stink to high heaven*). □ **heavenward** *adv.* (also **heavenwards**). [Old English]

**heavenly** *adj.* **1** of heaven; divine. **2** of the heavens or sky. **3** *colloq.* very pleasing; wonderful.

**heavenly bodies** *n.pl.* the sun, stars, planets, etc.

**heaven-sent** *adj.* providential.

**heavy** /hev-ee/ — *adj.* (**-ier**, **-iest**) **1** of great or unusually high weight; difficult to lift. **2** of great density (*heavy metal*). **3** abundant, considerable (*heavy crop; heavy traffic*). **4 a** severe, intense, extensive (*heavy fighting; a heavy sleep*). **b** grave, serious (*a heavy responsibility*). **c** meaningful; intense (*a heavy session; a heavy discussion*). **5** doing a thing to excess (*heavy drinker*). **6** striking or falling with force; causing strong impact (*heavy blows; heavy rain; heavy sea; a heavy fall*). **7 a** (of machinery, artillery, etc.) very large of its kind; large in calibre etc. **b** concerned with the manufacture of large goods etc. (*heavy industry*). **8** needing much physical effort (*heavy work; heavy going*). **9** (of soldiers etc.) carrying heavy weapons (*the heavy brigade*). **10** (of a person, writing, music, etc.) serious or sombre in tone or attitude; dull, tedious. **11 a** (of food) hard to digest. **b** (of a book etc.) hard to read or understand. **12** (of bread etc.) too dense from not having risen. **13** (of ground) difficult to traverse or work; (of soil) very clayey. **14** oppressive; hard to endure (*heavy taxes; heavy demands*). **15 a** weighted down with care or grief (*my heart is heavy*). **b** oppressive (because of pain etc.) (*a heavy head*). **16 a** coarse, ungraceful (*heavy features*). **b** clumsy, unwieldy; ponderous (*has too heavy a foot to be a dancer*). **c** pronounced, marked (*a heavy accent*). **17** *colloq.* using physical and/or psychological pressure; intimidating. — *n.* (*pl.* **-ies**) **1** *colloq.* a large violent person; thug (esp. hired). **b** strong-arm man such as a bodyguard or a bouncer. **c** (usu. in *pl.*) policeman. **2 a** a villainous role in a film or play. **b** actor who plays such a role. **3** *colloq.* person at the top of a profession etc.; bigwig (*all the military heavies were*

there at the ceremony). **4** (in *pl.*) *colloq.* pressurising argument (*put the heavies on me to lend him the money*). **5** *colloq.* beer of full alcoholic strength (opp. LIGHT) (*he avoids heavies, sticks to lights*). — *adv.* heavily (esp. in *comb.*: *heavy-laden*). — *v.* put pressure on or harass (*heavied him into doing things their way*). □ **a heavy hand 1** severity (*dispensed justice with a heavy hand*). **2** excessive liberality (*peppered the soup with a heavy hand*). **heavy on** using a lot of (*heavy on petrol*). **make heavy weather of** see WEATHER. □ **heavily** *adv.* **heaviness** *n.* **heavyish** *adj.* [Old English]

**heavy-duty** *adj.* intended to withstand hard use.

**heavy going** *n.* slow or difficult progress.

**heavy-handed** *adj.* **1** clumsy. **2** over-bearing, oppressive. **3** excessively liberal with ingredients (*don't be heavy-handed with the brandy*). □ **heavy-handedly** *adv.* **heavy-handedness** *n.*

**heavy-hearted** *adj.* sad, doleful.

**heavy hydrogen** *n.* = DEUTERIUM.

**heavy industry** *n.* industry producing metal, machinery, etc.

**heavy-laden** *adj.* **1** carrying a heavy load. **2** burdened by care; extremely weary.

**heavy metal** *n.* **1** heavy guns. **2** metal of high density. **3** *colloq.* loud kind of rock music with a pounding rhythm.

**heavy water** *n.* water, composed of deuterium and oxygen, used in nuclear physics.

**heavyweight** *n.* **1 a** weight in certain sports, in amateur boxing over 81 kg. **b** sportsman of this weight. **2** person etc. of above average weight. **3** *colloq.* person of influence or importance (*the heavyweights of finance*).

**Hebraic** /hee-**bray**-ik/ *adj.* of Hebrew or the Hebrews.

**Hebrew** /**hee**-broo/ — *n.* **1** member of a Semitic people orig. centred in ancient Palestine. **2 a** their language. **b** modern form of this, used esp. in Israel. — *adj.* **1** of or in Hebrew. **2** of the Hebrews or the Jews. [Hebrew, = one from the other side of the river]

**heck** *int.* *colloq.* mild exclamation of surprise or dismay (*what the heck!*). □ **heck of a** *colloq.* **1** terrible (*had a heck of a time trying to prove his innocence*). **2** wonderful (*that's one heck of a car you've bought*). [a form of HELL]

**heckle** /**hek**-uhl/ — *v.* (**-ling**) interrupt and harass (a public speaker). — *n.* act of heckling. □ **heckler** *n.* [var. of HACKLE]

**HECS** *abbr.* Higher Education Contribution Scheme.

**hectare** /hek-tair/ *n.* metric unit of square measure, 100 ares (2.471 acres or 10,000 square metres). [French: related to HECTO-, ARE²]

**hectic** /hek-tik/ *adj.* **1** busy and confused; excited. **2** feverish. □ **hectically** *adv.* [Greek *hektikos* habitual]

**hecto-** *comb. form* hundred. [Greek *hekaton*]

**hector** /hek-tuh/ — *v.* bully, intimidate. — *n.* a bully. [from the name *Hector* in the *Iliad*]

**he'd** /heed/ *contr.* **1** he had. **2** he would.

**hedge** — *n.* **1** fence or boundary of dense bushes or shrubs. **2** protection against possible loss (*a hedge against inflation*). — *v.* (**-ging**) **1** (often foll. by *in, off,* etc.) surround or bound with a hedge. **2** (often foll. by *in, about*) enclose; surround; hem in (*the troubles hedging me; hedged in by creditors*). **3 a** reduce one's risk of loss on (a bet or speculation) by compensating transactions on the other side (*hedging his bets*). **b** avoid committing oneself; be evasive (*don't hedge — say exactly what you mean!*). [Old English]

**hedgehog** *n.* small insect-eating mammal with a piglike snout and a coat of spines, rolling itself up into a ball when attacked.

**hedgerow** *n.* row of bushes etc. forming a hedge.

**hedonism** /hee-duh-,niz-uhm, hed-uh-/ *n.* **1** belief in pleasure as the highest good and mankind's proper aim. **2** behaviour based on this. □ **hedonist** *n.* **hedonistic** /-nis-tik/ *adj.* [Greek *hēdonē* pleasure]

**heebie-jeebies** /,hee-bee-**jee**-beez/ *n.pl.* (prec. by *the*) *colloq.* **1** nervous anxiety, tension; fear, revulsion. **2** = DELIRIUM TREMENS. [origin unknown]

**heed** — *v.* attend to; take notice of. — *n.* careful attention. □ **heedful** *adj.* **heedless** *adj.* **heedlessly** *adv.* [Old English]

**hee-haw** /hee-haw/ — *n.* **1** bray of a donkey. **2** rude donkey-like laughter. — *v.* make a braying sound; bray with laughter. [imitative]

**heel¹** — *n.* **1** back of the foot below the ankle. **2** corresponding part in vertebrate animals. **3 a** part of a sock etc. covering the heel. **b** part of a shoe etc. supporting the heel. **4** thing like a heel in form or position (e.g. the part of the palm next to the wrist, the end of a violin bow at which it is held, etc.). **5** crust end of a loaf of bread. **6** *colloq.* person regarded with contempt. **7** (as *int.*) command to a dog to walk close to its owner's heel. **8** small fragment of the parent branch left at the end of a shoot taken as a cutting. — *v.* **1** fit or renew a heel on (a shoe etc.). **2** touch the ground with the heel as in dancing. **3** (foll. by *out*) *Rugby* pass the ball with the heel. **4** (usu. foll. by *in*) = HELE. □ **at heel 1** (of a dog) close behind. **2** (of a person etc.) under control. **at** (or **on**) **the heels of** following closely after (a person or event) (*hot on the heels of the bushfire came the floods*). **cool** (or **kick**) **one's heels** be kept waiting. **down at heel 1** (of a shoe) with the heel worn down. **2** (of a person) **a** shabby in dress etc. **b** impoverished. **kick up one's heels** have fun, have one's fling. **show a clean pair of heels** flee (faster than those pursuing). **take to one's heels** run away. **to heel 1** (of a dog) close behind. **2** (of a person etc.) under control. **turn on one's heel** turn sharply round. [Old English]

**heel²** — *v.* (often foll. by *over*) **1** (of a ship etc.) lean over, tilt. **2** cause (a ship etc.) to do this. — *n.* act or amount of heeling. [obsolete *heeld,* from Germanic]

**heel³** var. of HELE.

**heel cutting** *n.* **1** type of cutting (for plant propagation) in which a shoot is so removed that a fragment (the heel) of the parent branch is left at the base of the shoot. **2** a shoot or cutting removed in this way.

**heeler** /hee-luh/ *n.* = BLUE HEELER. [abbreviation]

**heft** *v.* lift (something heavy), esp. to judge its weight. [probably from HEAVE after *cleft, weft*]

**hefty** /hef-tee/ *adj.* (**-ier, -iest**) **1** (of a person) big and strong. **2** (of a thing) large, heavy, powerful. □ **heftily** *adv.* **heftiness** *n.* [*heft* weight: related to HEAVE]

**hegemony** /hej-uh-muh-nee, heg-, huh-gem-uh-nee/ *n.* **1** leadership, domination, esp. by one State of a confederacy over the others. **2** domination; predominance. □ **hegemonic** /hej-uh-**mon**-ik, heg-uh-/ *adj.* [Greek *hēgemōn* leader]

**heifer** /hef-uh/ *n.* **1** young cow, esp. one that has not had more than one calf. **2** female calf. [Old English]

**height** /huyt/ *n.* **1** measurement from base to top or (of a standing person) from head to foot. **2** elevation above the ground or a recognised level (usu. sea level). **3** considerable elevation (*situated at a height*). **4** high place or area. **5** top. **6 a** most intense part or period (*battle was at its height*). **b** extreme example (*the height of daring*). [Old English]

**heighten** *v.* make or become higher or more intense (*heightened the suspense by using eerie sound-effects*).

**heinous** /hay-nuhs, hee-nuhs/ *adj.* utterly odious or wicked (*a heinous crime*). [French *haïr* hate]

**heir** /air/ *n.* (*fem.* **heiress**) **1** person entitled to property or rank as the legal successor of its former holder (*heir to the throne*). **2** person, group, etc. deriving some quality from predecessors, or continuing some tradition etc. established earlier. [Latin *heres hered-*]

**heir apparent** *n.* heir whose claim cannot be set aside by the birth of another heir.

**heirloom** *n.* **1** piece of personal property that has been in a family for several generations. **2** piece of property as part of an inheritance.

**heir presumptive** *n.* heir whose claim may be set aside by the birth of another heir.

**heist** /huyst/ — *v.* = HOIST 3. — *n.* = HOIST 4. [variant pronunc. of *hoist*]

**held** *past* and *past part.* of HOLD[1].

**hele** /heel/ *v.* (**-ling**) (also commonly **heel**) (usu. foll. by *in*) preserve a plant or cutting by burying its rooting end in loose soil until one is ready to plant it in its permanent position. [Old English *helian*]

■ **Usage** The spelling 'heel' for this verb is etymologically incorrect, although its use is widespread.

**helical** /**hel**-i-kuhl/ *adj.* having the form of a helix.

**helices** *pl.* of HELIX.

**helichrysum** /ˌhel-ee-**kruy**-suhm/ *n.* any of about 100 endemic Australian shrubs and herbaceous plants, annual and perennial, most with large, extremely showy white, bright gold, or pink downy flowers and usu. silvery foliage. [Greek *helix* sun, *khrusos* gold]

**helicopter** /**hel**-ee-ˌkop-tuh, **hel**-uh-/ *n.* wingless aircraft obtaining lift and propulsion from horizontally revolving overhead blades. [Greek: related to HELIX, *pteron* wing]

**helio-** *comb. form* (also **heli-**) sun. [Greek *hēlios* sun]

**heliocentric** /ˌhee-lee-oh-**sen**-trik/ *adj.* **1** regarding the sun as centre. **2** considered as viewed from the sun's centre.

**heliograph** /**hee**-lee-uh-ˌgrahf, -ˌgraf/ — *n.* **1** signalling apparatus reflecting sunlight in flashes. **2** message sent by means of this. — *v.* send (a message) by heliograph.

**heliotrope** /**hee**-lee-uh-ˌtrohp, **hel**-ee-/ *n.* **1 a** European plant with fragrant purple flowers. **b** characteristic scent of these. **2** any plant that turns towards the sun. **3** light purple colour. **4** bloodstone. [Greek: related to HELIO-, *trepō* turn]

**heliotropism** /ˌhee-lee-**ot**-ruh-piz-uhm/

*n.* directional growth of a plant in response to sunlight (cf. PHOTOTROPISM). □ **heliotropic** /ˌhee-lee-uh-**trop**-ik/ *adj.*

**helipad** /**hel**-ee-ˌpad/ *n.* = HELIPORT.

**heliport** /**hel**-ee-ˌpawt/ *n.* place where helicopters take off and land.

**helipterum** /he-**lip**-tuh-ruhm/ *n.* any of several Australian everlastings or 'paper flowers' with a profusion of white, yellow, pink, or red flowers.

**helium** /**hee**-lee-uhm/ *n.* light inert gaseous element used in airships and as a refrigerant. [related to HELIO-]

**helix** /**hee**-liks/ *n.* (*pl.* **helices** /**hee**-luh-ˌseez, **hel**-uh-/) spiral curve (like a corkscrew) or coiled curve (like a watch spring). [Latin from Greek]

**hell** — *n.* **1** place (of fire and other torment) regarded in some religions as the abode of the dead, or of devils and condemned sinners. **2** place or state of misery or wickedness (*prison was sheer hell*). **3** anything that harasses, is extremely unpleasant, etc. (*driving in peak-hour traffic is hell; it's hell working outdoors in a Canberra winter*). — *int.* expressing anger, surprise, etc. □ **as much chance as a snowball in hell** *colloq.* no chance at all. **beat** etc. **the hell out of** *colloq.* beat etc. without restraint. **come hell or high water** no matter what the difficulties. **for the hell of it** *colloq.* for no particular reason; just for fun. **get hell** *colloq.* be severely scolded or punished. **give a person hell** *colloq.* scold or punish a person. **a** (or **one**) **hell of a** *colloq.* outstanding example of (*a hell of a mess; one hell of a party*). **the hell** (usu. prec. by *what, where, who,* etc.) expressing anger, disbelief, etc. (*who the hell told you that?; the hell you are!*). **hell to pay** *colloq.* serious consequences to face. **like hell** *colloq.* **1** not at all. **2** recklessly; exceedingly. **not a hope in hell** *colloq.* no chance at all. **play hell** (or **merry hell**) **with** *colloq.* be upsetting or disruptive to. **raise hell** raise pandemonium; cause a great deal of trouble. **what the hell** *colloq.* it is of no importance. [Old English]

**he'll** /heel/ *contr.* he will; he shall.

**hell-bent** *adj.* (foll. by *on*) recklessly determined.

**Hellene** /**hel**-een/ *n.* **1** native of modern Greece. **2** native of ancient Greece. □ **Hellenic** /he-**len**-ik, -**lee**-nik/ *adj.* [Greek]

**Hellenism** /**hel**-uh-ˌniz-uhm/ *n.* (esp. ancient) Greek character or culture. □ **Hellenist** *n.*

**Hellenistic** /ˌhel-uh-**nis**-tik/ *adj.* of Greek history, language, and culture of the late 4th to the late 1st c. BC.

**hellfire** *n.* fire(s) regarded as existing in hell.

**hell for leather** *adv.* at full speed.

**hell-hole** *n.* oppressive or unbearable place.

**hellish** — *adj.* **1** of or like hell. **2** *colloq.* extremely difficult or unpleasant. — *adv. colloq.* extremely (*hellish expensive*). □ **hellishly** *adv.*

**hello** /huh-**loh**, hu-**loh**/ (also **hallo, hullo**) — *int.* expression of informal greeting, or of surprise, or to call attention. — *n.* (*pl.* **-s**) cry of 'hello'. [var. of earlier *hollo*]

**hell's angel** *n.* (orig.) member of a gang of male motor-cycle enthusiasts notorious for violent and violent behaviour in the USA.

**hell, west and crooked** *adv. colloq.* all over the place (*the cattle stampeded hell, west and crooked*).

**helm** *n.* tiller or wheel for controlling a ship's rudder. □ **at the helm** in control; at the head of an organisation etc. [Old English]

**helmet** /**hel**-muht/ *n.* protective head-covering worn by soldiers, cyclists, motor cyclists, construction workers, etc. [French from Germanic]

**helmeted honeyeater** *n.* extremely rare nectar-eating bird occurring only in a small area east of Melbourne, and a faunal emblem of Victoria: it has olive-black colouring on its upper surface, and the yellow feathers on its head form what looks like a helmet.

**helmsman** /**helmz**-muhn/ *n.* person who steers a ship.

**help** — *v.* **1** provide with the means towards what is needed or sought (*helped me with my work; helped me (to) pay my debts; helped him on with his coat*). **2** (often *absol.*) be of use or service to (*does that help?*). **3** contribute to alleviating (a pain or difficulty). **4** prevent or remedy (*it can't be helped*). **5** (usu. with *neg.*) **a** refrain from (*can't help it; could not help laughing*). **b** *refl.* refrain from acting (*couldn't help himself*). **6** (often foll. by *to*) serve (a person with food) (*may I help you to more greens?*). — *n.* **1** helping or being helped (*need your help; came to our help*). **2** person or thing that helps. **3** *colloq.* domestic assistant or assistance. **4** remedy or escape (*there is no help for it*). □ **help oneself** (often foll. by *to*) **1** serve oneself (with food etc.). **2** take without permission. **help a person out** give a person help, esp. in difficulty. **so help me (God)** (as an invocation or oath) I am speaking the truth. □ **helper** *n.* [Old English]

**helpful** *adj.* giving help; useful. □ **helpfully** *adv.* **helpfulness** *n.*

**helping** — *n.* portion of food at a meal. — *adj.* providing support, aid, etc. (*a helping hand*).

**helpless** *adj.* **1** lacking help or protection; defenceless. **2** unable to act without help (*helpless invalid; don't be so helpless!*). □ **helplessly** *adv.* **helplessness** *n.*

**helpmate** *n.* helpful companion or partner (usu. a husband or wife).

**helter-skelter** /ˌhel-tuh-**skel**-tuh/ *adv. & adj.* in disorderly haste. [imitative]

**hem**[1] — *n.* border of cloth where the edge is turned under and sewn down. — *v.* (**-mm-**) turn down and sew in the edge of (cloth etc.). □ **hem in** confine; restrict the movement of (*enemy troops hemmed us in*). [Old English]

**hem**[2] — *int.* calling attention or expressing hesitation by a slight cough. — *n.* utterance of this. — *v.* (**-mm-**) say *hem*; hesitate in speech. □ **hem and haw** = *hum and haw* (see HUM[1]). [imitative]

**he-man** *n.* masterful or virile man.

**hemi-** *comb. form* half. [Greek, = Latin *semi-*]

**hemipterous** /huh-**mip**-tuh-ruhs/ *adj.* of the insect order including aphids, bugs, and cicadas, with piercing or sucking mouthparts. [Greek *pteron* wing]

**hemisphere** /**hem**-uh-ˌsfeer/ *n.* **1** half a sphere. **2** half of the earth, esp. as divided by the equator (into *northern* and *southern hemisphere*) or by a line passing through the poles (into *eastern* and *western hemisphere*). □ **hemispherical** /-sfe-ruh-kuhl/ *adj.* [Greek: related to HEMI-, SPHERE]

**hemlock** /**hem**-lok/ *n.* **1** poisonous plant with fernlike leaves and small white flowers. **2** poison made from this. [Old English]

**hemp** *n.* **1** (in full **Indian hemp**) Asian herbaceous plant. **2** its fibre used to make rope and stout fabrics. **3** any of several narcotic drugs made from the hemp plant (HASHISH, MARIJUANA). [Old English]

**hempen** *adj.* made of hemp.

**hen** *n.* female bird, esp. of a domestic fowl. □ **as rare** (or **scarce**) **as hen's teeth** *colloq.* extremely rare; nonexistent. [Old English]

**hen-and-chickens fern** *n.* eastern Australian fern very popular for cultivation: the parent plant (the hen) grows an abundance of plantlets (the chickens) at the ends of its leaves, and these can be removed and grown separately.

**hence** *adv.* **1** from this time (*two years*

hence). **2** for this reason (*the helmeted honeyeater exists only in a small area east of Melbourne and hence it is extremely rare*). **3** *archaic* from here. [Old English]

**henceforth** *adv.* from this time onwards.

**henchman** *n.* now usu. *derog.* trusted supporter. [Old English *hengst* horse, MAN]

**henna** /hen-uh/ — *n.* **1** tropical shrub. **2** reddish dye made from it and used to colour hair. — *v.* (**hennaed, hennaing**) dye with henna. [Arabic]

**henpeck** *v.* (of a wife) constantly nag and dominate her husband. □ **henpecked** *adj.*

**henry** /hen-ree/ *n.* (*pl.* **-s** or **-ies**) *Electr.* SI unit of inductance. [*Henry*, name of a physicist]

**hen's party** *n. colloq.* (also **hen-party**) social gathering of women only.

**he-oak** /hee-,ohk/ *n.* any of several trees of the *Casuarina* family (see SHE-OAK).

■ **Usage** The term *he-oak* is now infrequently used.

**hepatic** /huh-**pat**-ik/ *adj.* of the liver. [Greek *hēpar -atos* liver]

**hepatitis** /,hep-uh-**tuy**-tuhs/ *n.* inflammation of the liver; disease in which this occurs. □ **hepatitis A** viral form of hepatitis transmitted in food, causing fever and jaundice. **hepatitis B** severe viral form of hepatitis transmitted in infected blood, causing fever, debility, and jaundice. **hepatitis C** severe viral form of hepatitis transmitted in the same way as *hepatitis B*. [related to HEPATIC]

**hepta-** *comb. form* seven. [Greek]

**heptagon** /hep-tuh-guhn, -gon/ *n.* plane figure with seven sides and angles. □ **heptagonal** /-**tag**-uh-nuhl/ *adj.* [Greek: related to HEPTA-, *-gōnos* angled]

**heptathlon** /hep-**tath**-luhn/ *n.* athletic contest of seven events for all competitors. □ **heptathlete** /-leet/ *n.* [from HEPTA-, Greek *athlon* contest]

**her** — *pron.* **1** *objective case* of SHE (*I like her*). **2** *colloq.* she (*it's her all right*). — *poss. pron.* (*attrib.*) of or belonging to her or herself (*her house*). [Old English dative and genitive of SHE]

**herald** /he-ruhld/ — *n.* **1** official messenger bringing news. **2** forerunner, harbinger (*spring is the herald of summer*). **3 a** *hist.* officer responsible for official ceremonial and etiquette. **b** official concerned with pedigrees and coats of arms. — *v.* proclaim the approach of; usher in. □ **heraldic** /huh-**ral**-dik/ *adj.* [French from Germanic]

**heraldry** /he-ruhl-dree/ *n.* **1** art or knowledge of a herald (see HERALD 3). **2** coats of arms.

**herb¹** *n.* **1** any non-woody seed-bearing plant. **2** plant with leaves, seeds, or flowers used for flavouring, food, medicine, scent, etc. □ **herby** *adj.* (**-ier, -iest**). [Latin *herba*]

**herb²** *colloq.* — *n.* (always in *pl.*) horsepower of a car engine (*my new car has plenty of herbs*). — *v.* **1** drive (or travel in) a car fast (*herbing along the Hume highway*). **2** (foll. by *over*) hand (something) over (usu. at great speed, urgently) (*herb over a towel or something — the pan's on fire*). [origin unknown]

**herbaceous** /her-**bay**-shuhs/ *adj.* of or like herbs.

**herbage** /her-bij/ *n.* vegetation collectively, esp. as pasture.

**herbal** — *adj.* of herbs in medicinal and culinary use. — *n.* book describing the medicinal and culinary uses of herbs.

**herbalist** /her-buh-luhst/ *n.* **1** dealer in medicinal herbs. **2** writer on herbs.

**herbarium** /her-**bair**-ree-uhm/ *n.* (*pl.* **-ria**) **1** systematically arranged collection of dried plants. **2** book, room, etc. for these.

**herbicide** /her-buh-,suyd/ *n.* poison used to destroy unwanted vegetation.

**herbivore** /her-buh-,vaw/ *n.* animal that feeds on plants. □ **herbivorous** /-**biv**-uh-ruhs/ *adj.* [Latin *voro* devour]

**herculean** /,her-kyuh-lee-uhn, -**kyoo**-lee-uhn/ *adj.* having or requiring great strength or effort. [from the name *Hercules*, Latin alteration of Greek *Hēraklēs*]

**herd** — *n.* **1** a number of animals, esp. cattle, feeding or travelling or kept together. **2** (prec. by *the*) *derog.* large number of people; mob (*tends to follow the herd*). — *v.* **1** (cause to) go in a herd (*herded together for warmth*; *herded the cattle into the paddock*). **2** look after (sheep, cattle, etc.). [Old English]

**herd instinct** *n.* (prec. by *the*) tendency to think and act as a crowd.

**herdsman** *n.* man who owns or tends a herd.

**here** — *adv.* **1** in or at or to this place or position (*come here*; *sit here*). **2** indicating a person's presence or a thing offered (*my son here will show you*; *here is your coat*). **3** at this point in the argument, indication, etc. (*here I have a question*). — *n.* this place (*get out of here*; *lives near here*; *fill it up to here*). — *int.* **1** calling attention: short for *come here, look here*, etc. (*here, where are you going with that?*). **2** indicating one's presence in a roll-call: short for *I am here*. □ **here goes!** *colloq.* expression indicating the start of a bold act. **here's to** I drink to the health of. **here**

**we are** *colloq.* said on arrival at one's destination. **here we go again** *colloq.* the same, usu. undesirable, events are recurring. **here you are** said on handing something to somebody. **neither here nor there** of no importance. [Old English]

**hereabouts** /ˌheer-ruh-**bowts**/ *adv.* (also **hereabout**) near this place.

**hereafter** /heer-**ahf**-tuh/ — *adv.* from now on; in the future. — *n.* **1** the future. **2** life after death.

**here and now** *adv.* at this very moment; immediately.

**here and there** *adv.* in various places.

**hereby** /heer-**buy**/ *adv.* by this means; as a result of this.

**hereditary** /huh-**red**-uh-tuh-ree, -tree/ *adj.* **1** (of a disease, instinct, etc.) able to be passed down genetically from one generation to another. **2 a** descending by inheritance (*hereditary ownership*). **b** holding a position by inheritance (*hereditary owner*). **3** the same as or resembling what one's parents had; traditional (*hereditary hatred; a hereditary enemy*). [Latin: related to HEIR]

**heredity** /huh-**red**-uh-tee/ *n.* **1 a** passing on of physical or mental characteristics from parents to offspring. **b** these characteristics. **2** genetic constitution of an individual.

**Hereford** /**he**-ruh-fuhd/ *n.* animal of a breed of red and white beef cattle. [*Hereford* in England]

**herein** /heer-**in**/ *adv. formal* in this matter, book, etc.

**hereinafter** /ˌheer-rin-**ahf**-tuh/ *adv. esp. Law formal* **1** from this point on. **2** in a later part of this document etc.

**hereof** /heer-**ov**/ *adv. formal* of this.

**heresy** /**he**-ruh-see/ *n.* (*pl.* **-ies**) **1** esp. *RC Ch.* religious belief or practice contrary to orthodox doctrine. **2** opinion contrary to what is normally accepted or maintained. [Greek *hairesis* choice]

**heretic** /**he**-ruh-tik/ *n.* **1** person believing in or practising religious heresy. **2** holder of an unorthodox opinion. □ **heretical** /huh-**ret**-i-kuhl/ *adj.*

**hereto** /heer-**too**/ *adv. formal* to this matter.

**heretofore** /ˌheer-too-**faw**/ *adv. formal* before this time.

**hereupon** /ˌheer-ruh-**pon**/ *adv.* after this; in consequence of this.

**herewith** /heer-**with**/ *adv.* with this (esp. of an enclosure in a letter etc.).

**heritable** /**he**-ruh-tuh-buhl/ *adj.* **1** *Law* capable of being inherited or of inheriting. **2** *Biol.* genetically transmissible

from parent to offspring. [French: related to HEIR]

**heritage** /**he**-ruh-tij/ *n.* **1** what is or may be inherited. **2** inherited circumstances, benefits, etc. **3** a nation's historic buildings, monuments, countryside, etc., esp. when regarded as worthy of preservation.

**hermaphrodite** /her-**maf**-ruh-ˌduyt/ — *n.* person, animal, or plant having both male and female reproductive organs. — *adj.* combining both sexes. □ **hermaphroditic** /-**dit**-ik/ *adj.* [from *Hermaphroditus*, son of *Hermes* and *Aphrodite*, who became joined in one body to a nymph]

**hermetic** /her-**met**-ik/ *adj.* **1** with an airtight closure. **2** relating to alchemy, magic, etc. (*hermetic arts*). □ **hermetically** *adv.* [from the Greek god *Hermes*, regarded as the founder of alchemy]

**hermit** /**her**-muht/ *n.* **1** person who, esp. for religious reasons, lives in solitude and austerity. **2** any person living (and preferring to live) in solitude. □ **hermitic** /-**mit**-ik/ *adj.* [Greek *erēmos* solitary]

**hermitage** *n.* **1** hermit's dwelling. **2** monastery. **3** any secluded dwelling.

**hermit crab** *n.* crab that protects itself by living in a mollusc's cast-off shell.

**hernia** /**her**-nee-uh/ *n.* protrusion of part of an organ through the wall of the body cavity containing it, esp. of the abdomen. [Latin]

**hero** /**heer**-roh/ *n.* (*pl.* **-es**) **1** person noted or admired for nobility, courage, outstanding achievements, etc. **2** chief male character in a play, story, etc. [Greek *hērōs*]

**heroic** /huh-**roh**-ik/ — *adj.* of, fit for, or like a hero; very brave. — *n.* (in *pl.*) **1** high-flown language or sentiments. **2** (of poetry) dealing with the ancient heroes. **3** unduly bold behaviour. □ **heroically** *adv.*

**heroic couplet** *n.* two lines of rhyming iambic pentameters.

**heroic verse** *n.* type of verse used for heroic poetry, esp. the hexameter, the iambic pentameter, or the alexandrine.

**heroin** /**he**-roh-uhn/ *n.* dangerous and addictive analgesic drug derived from morphine, often used as a narcotic. [German: related to HERO, from the effect on the user's self-esteem]

**heroine** /**he**-roh-uhn/ *n.* **1** woman noted or admired for nobility, courage, outstanding achievements, etc. **2** chief female character in a play, story, etc. [Greek: related to HERO]

**heroism** /**he**-roh-ˌiz-uhm/ *n.* heroic conduct or qualities. [French *héroïsme*: related to HERO]

**heron** /**he**-ruhn/ n. any of various long-legged wading birds with a long S-shaped neck, including some Australian species. [French from Germanic]

**hero-worship** — n. idealisation of an admired person. — v. idolise.

**herpes** /**her**-peez/ n. virus disease causing skin blisters. □ **herpetic** adj. [Greek herpō creep]

**herpes simplex** n. 1 = COLD SORE. 2 form of herpes occurring on the genitals.

**herpes zoster** n. = SHINGLES.

**herpetology** /,her-puh-**tol**-uh-jee/ n. scientific study of reptiles. □ **herpetological** /,her-puh-tuh-**loj**-i-kuhl/ adj. **herpetologist** n. [Greek herpeton reptile]

**Herr** /hair/ n. (pl. **Herren** /**hair**-ruhn/) title of a German man; Mr. [German]

**herring** /**he**-ring/ n. (pl. same or **-s**) 1 N. Atlantic fish used as food. 2 name transferred to any of several similar Australian marine or freshwater fish as the tommy rough, cucumber fish, etc. [Old English]

**herringbone** n. stitch or weave consisting of a series of small 'V' shapes making a zigzag pattern.

**hers** /herz/ poss. pron. the one or ones belonging to or associated with her (it is hers; hers are over there). □ **of hers** of or belonging to her (friend of hers).

**herself** /huh-**self**/ pron. 1 a emphat. form of SHE or HER (she herself will do it). b refl. form of HER (she has hurt herself). 2 in her normal state of body or mind (does not feel quite herself today). □ **be herself** see ONESELF. **by herself** see by oneself. [Old English: related to HER, SELF]

**hertz** /herts/ n. (pl. same) SI unit of frequency, equal to one cycle per second. [Hertz, name of a physicist]

**he's** /heez/ contr. 1 he is. 2 he has.

**hesitant** /**hez**-uh-tuhnt/ adj. hesitating; irresolute. □ **hesitance** n. **hesitancy** n. **hesitantly** adv.

**hesitate** /**hez**-uh-,tayt/ v. (**-ting**) 1 show or feel indecision or uncertainty; pause in doubt (hesitated over her choice). 2 be reluctant (I hesitate to say so). □ **hesitation** /-**tay**-shuhn/ n. **hesitative** adj. [Latin haereo haes- stick fast]

**hessian** /**hesh**-uhn/ n. strong coarse sacking made of hemp or jute. [Hesse in Germany]

**hetero** /**het**-roh, **het**-uh-roh/ adj. & n. colloq. = HETEROSEXUAL. [abbreviation]

**hetero-** comb. form other, different (often opp. HOMO-). [Greek heteros other]

**heterodox** /**het**-uh-ruh-,doks/ adj. not orthodox. □ **heterodoxy** n. [from HETERO-, Greek doxa opinion]

**heterogeneous** /,het-uh-roh-**jee**-nee-uhs/ adj. 1 diverse in character. 2 varied in content. □ **heterogeneity** /-juh-**nee**-uh-tee/ n. [Latin from Greek genos kind]

**heteromorphic** /,het-uh-roh-**maw**-fik/ adj. (also **heteromorphous** /-**maw**-fuhs/) Biol. 1 of dissimilar forms. 2 (of insects) existing in different forms at different stages in their life cycle. □ **heteromorphism** n.

**heterosexual** /,het-uh-roh-**sek**-shoo-uhl/ — adj. feeling or involving sexual attraction to persons of the opposite sex. — n. heterosexual person. □ **heterosexuality** /-al-uh-**tee**/ n.

**het** /het/ predic. adj. colloq. excited, overwrought. [het, a British dial. word = heated]

**heuristic** /hyoo-**ris**-tik, hyoor-**ris**-tik/ adj. 1 allowing or assisting to discover. 2 proceeding to a solution by trial and error. [Greek heuriskō find]

**hew** v. (past part. **hewn** /hyoon/ or **hewed**) 1 chop or cut with an axe, sword, etc. 2 cut into shape. [Old English]

**hex** — v. 1 practise witchcraft. 2 bewitch. — n. magic spell. [German]

**hexa-** comb. form six. [Greek]

**hexadecimal** /,hek-suh-**des**-uh-muhl/ adj. esp. Computing of a system of numerical notation that has 16 (the figures 0 to 9 and the letters A to F) rather than 10 as a base.

**hexagon** /**hek**-suh-guhn, -gon/ n. plane figure with six sides and angles. □ **hexagonal** /-**sag**-uh-nuhl/ adj. [Greek: related to HEXA-, -gōnos angled]

**hexagram** /**hek**-suh-,gram/ n. 1 six-sided figure formed by two intersecting equilateral triangles. 2 figure of six lines.

**hexahedron** /,hek-suh-**hee**-druhn/ n. solid figure with six faces. □ **hexahedral** adj.

**hexameter** /hek-**sam**-uh-tuh/ n. line of verse with six metrical feet.

**hexham grey** /**hek**-suhm/ n. large, voracious, widespread, dappled grey mosquito, the largest biting mosquito in Australia. [Hexham, town near Newcastle, NSW]

**hey** /hay/ int. calling attention or expressing joy, surprise, inquiry, etc. [imitative]

**heyday** /**hay**-day/ n. time of greatest success or prosperity. [Low German]

**hey presto!** int. conjuror's phrase on completing a trick.

**Hf** symb. hafnium.

**Hg** symb. mercury.

**hi** /huy/ int. calling attention or as a greeting.

**hiatus** /**huy-ay**-tuhs/ n. (pl. **-tuses**) **1** break or gap in a series or sequence. **2** break between two vowels coming together but not in the same syllable, as in *though oft the ear*. □ **hiatal** adj. [Latin *hio* gape]

**hibbertia** /hi-**ber**-shuh/ n. any of several temperate Australian shrubs with masses of gold or orange flowers (see GUINEA-FLOWER). [George *Hibbert*, London merchant]

**hibernate** /**huy**-buh-,nayt/ v. (**-ting**) **1** (of an animal) spend the winter in a dormant state. **2** remain inactive or secluded. □ **hibernation** /-**nay**-shuhn/ n. [Latin *hibernus* wintry]

**Hibernian** /huy-**ber**-nee-uhn/ *archaic* poet. — adj. of Ireland. — n. native of Ireland. [Latin *Hibernia* Ireland]

**hibiscus** /huy-**bis**-kuhs/ n. (pl. **-cuses**) cultivated shrub with large bright-coloured flowers, some native to Australia. [Greek *hibiskos* mallow, a kind of plant]

**hiccup** /**hik**-up/ (also **hiccough**) — n. **1** involuntary spasm of the diaphragm causing a characteristic sound 'hic'. **2** temporary or minor stoppage or difficulty. — v. (**-p-**) make a hiccup. [imitative]

**hick** n. (often *attrib.*) *colloq.* country bumpkin, unsophisticated provincial person. [familiar form of *Richard*]

**hickory** /**hik**-uh-ree/ n. (pl. **-ies**) **1 a** N. American tree yielding wood and nutlike edible fruits (see PECAN). **b** the tough heavy wood of this. **2 a** any of several Australian trees, usu. of the wattle family (e.g. *hickory wattle*), yielding a tough, close-grained timber. **b** the wood of these trees. [Virginian *pohickery*]

**hid** past of HIDE¹.

**hidden** past part. of HIDE¹.

**hidden agenda** n. secret motivation behind a policy, statement, etc.; ulterior motive.

**hide¹** — v. (**-ding**; past **hid**; past part. **hidden**) **1** put or keep out of sight. **2** conceal oneself. **3** (usu. foll. by *from*) keep (a fact) secret (*hid his real motive from her*). **4** conceal a thing from sight intentionally or not (*trees hid the house*). — n. camouflaged shelter used for observing wildlife. □ **hide one's head** keep out of sight, esp. from shame. **hide one's light under a bushel** conceal one's merits. □ **hider** n. [Old English]

**hide²** n. **1** animal's skin, esp. when tanned or dressed. **2** *colloq.* the human skin, esp. the backside (*I'll tan your hide*). **3** *colloq.* impertinence, effrontery (*he's got a hide coming here after what he's done*). □ **neither hide nor hair** not a trace (*saw*

neither hide nor hair of him). **thick hide** *colloq.* insensitivity, esp. to criticism. [Old English]

**hideaway** n. hiding-place or place of retreat.

**hidebound** adj. **1** narrow-minded, bigoted. **2** (of the law, rules, etc.) constricted by tradition.

**hideous** /**hid**-ee-uhs/ adj. **1** very ugly, revolting. **2** *colloq.* unpleasant. □ **hideously** adv. **hideousness** n. [Anglo-French *hidous*]

**hide-out** n. hiding-place, esp. for those on the run from the law; refuge.

**hiding¹** n. **1** a thrashing, a belting. **2** a sound defeat (*the Australians gave the Brits a hiding in the last test*). [from HIDE²]

**hiding²** n. **1** act of hiding. **2** state of remaining hidden (*go into hiding*). [from HIDE¹]

**hiding place** n. place of concealment.

**hierarchy** /**huy**-uh-,rah-kee/ n. (pl. **-ies**) system in which grades of status or authority are ranked one above the other (*a cardinal ranks just below pope in the governing hierarchy of the Catholic Church*). □ **hierarchical** /-**rah**-ki-kuhl/ adj. [Greek *hieros* sacred, *arkhō* rule]

**hieratic** /,huy-uh-**rat**-ik/ adj. **1** of priests. **2** of the ancient Egyptian abridged hieroglyphic writing as used by priests (opp. DEMOTIC). [Greek *hiereus* priest]

**hieroglyph** /**huy**uh-ruh-glif/ n. **1** picture representing a word, syllable, or sound, as used in ancient Egyptian etc. **2** secret or enigmatic symbol. [Greek *hieros* sacred, *gluphō* carve]

**hieroglyphic** /,huy-uh-ruh-**glif**-ik/ — adj. **1** of or written in hieroglyphs. **2** symbolical. — n. (in *pl.*) **1** hieroglyphs; hieroglyphic writing. **2** *joc.* writing difficult to read (*doctor's hieroglyphics on a prescription*).

**hi-fi** /**huy**-fuy/ — adj. = HIGH FIDELITY. — n. high-quality record-player, amplifier, and speakers which reproduce the original sounds faithfully and with little distortion. [abbreviation]

**higgledy-piggledy** /,hig-uhl-dee-**pig**-uhl-dee/ adv. & adj. in confusion or disorder. [origin uncertain]

**high** /huy/ — adj. **1 a** of great vertical extent (*high building*). **b** (*predic.*; often in *comb.*) of a specified height (*one metre high*; *waist-high*). **2 a** far above ground or sea level etc. (*high altitude*). **b** inland, esp. when raised (*High Asia*). **3** extending above the normal level (*high boots*; *jersey with a high neck*). **4 a** of exalted quality (*high minds*; *high principles*). **b** lavish; superior (*high living*; *high fashion*). **5** of exalted rank (*high society*; *is high in the Government*).

**6 a** great; intense; extreme; powerful (*high praise; high temperature*). **b** greater than normal (*high prices*). **c** extreme or very traditional in religious opinion (*high Anglican*). **7** performed at, to, or from a considerable height (*high diving; high flying*). **8** (often foll. by *on*) *colloq.* intoxicated by alcohol or esp. drugs. **9** (of a sound etc.) of high frequency; shrill. **10** (of a period, age, time, etc.) at its peak (*high noon; high summer; High Renaissance*). **11** the most important; principal (*high altar; high table*). **12 a** (of meat etc.) beginning to go bad; off. **b** chiefly *Brit.* (of game) well-hung and slightly decomposed before cooking. — *n.* **1** high, or the highest, level or figure. **2** area of high pressure; anticyclone. **3** *colloq.* euphoric state, esp. drug-induced (*he's on a high*). **4** top gear of a motor vehicle (*shift to high*). **5** high school (*Bell Park High*). — *adv.* **1** far up; aloft (*flew the flag high*). **2** in or to a high degree. **3** at a high price. **4** (of a sound) at or to a high pitch (*can sing very high*). □ **on high** in or to heaven or a high place. **on one's high horse** *colloq.* acting arrogantly. [Old English]

**high altar** *n.* chief altar in a church, esp. a cathedral.

**high and dry** *adj.* stranded; aground.

**high and low** *adv.* everywhere (*searched high and low*).

**high and mighty** *adj. colloq.* arrogant.

**high-blocked** *adj.* (of a house) built on very high foundations, as in northern Australia.

**highbrow** *colloq.* — *n.* an intellectual; a highly cultured person. — *adj.* of or pertaining to highbrows; appealing to highbrows (*highbrow poetry*).

**High Church** *n.* (also **Anglo-Catholic Church**) section of the Anglican Church emphasising ritual, priestly authority, the sacraments, etc. (opp. LOW CHURCH). □ **High Church** *adj.*

**high-class** *adj.* of high quality.

**High Commission** *n.* embassy from one Commonwealth country to another. □ **High Commissioner** *n.*

**High Court** *n.* (in full **High Court of Australia**) supreme Federal Court established by the Constitution as the final arbiter of constitutional questions and final court of appeal from the Supreme Courts of the States and from Federal Courts.

**higher animal** *n.* (also **higher plant**) animal or plant evolved to a high degree.

**higher education** *n.* education continued beyond completed secondary schooling, e.g. at a university etc.

**high explosive** *n.* extremely explosive substance used in shells, bombs, etc.

**highfalutin** /ˌhuy-fuh-**loo**-tuhn/ *adj.* (also **highfaluting** /-ting/) *colloq.* pompous, pretentious. [origin unknown]

**high-fibre** *adj.* of or pertaining to foods which contain a high proportion of plant fibre for roughage (*high-fibre diet*).

**high fidelity** *adj.* (of an amplifier, speakers, etc.) giving high-quality sound reproduction with little distortion.

**high-flown** *adj.* (of language etc.) extravagant, bombastic.

**high-flyer** *n.* (also **high-flier**) **1** ambitious person. **2** person or thing of great potential for achievement etc. □ **high-flying** *adj.*

**high frequency** — *n.* frequency, esp. in radio, of 3 to 30 megahertz. — *adj.* (**high-frequency**) (of a sound) high in pitch.

**high gear** *n.* gear such that the driven end of a transmission revolves faster than the driving end.

**high-grade** *adj.* **1** of high quality. **2** (of ore) yielding a relatively high amount of metal.

**high-handed** *adj.* disregarding others' feelings; overbearing. □ **high-handedly** *adv.* **high-handedness** *n.*

**high jinks** *n.pl.* boisterous fun.

**high jump** *n.* **1** athletic event consisting of jumping as high as possible over a bar of adjustable height. **2** *colloq.* drastic punishment (*he's for the high jump*).

**highland** — *n.* (usu. in *pl.*) area of high land; mountainous region. — *adj.* of or in a highland. [Old English, = promontory: related to HIGH]

**high-level** *adj.* **1** (of negotiations etc.) conducted by high-ranking people. **2** *Computing* (of a programming language) not machine-dependent and usu. at a level of abstraction close to natural language.

**high life** *n.* (also **high living**) luxurious existence ascribed to the rich.

**highlight** — *n.* **1** moment or detail of vivid interest; outstanding feature (*the highlight of the celebration*). **2** (in a painting etc.) bright area, or one seeming to reflect light. **3** (usu. in *pl.*) light streak in the hair produced by bleaching. — *v.* **1** bring into prominence; draw attention to. **2** create a highlight. **3** mark with a highlighter.

**highlighter** *n.* marker pen for emphasising a printed word etc. by overlaying it with (usu. fluorescent) colour.

**highly** /**huy**-lee/ *adv.* **1** in a high degree (*highly amusing; commend it highly*). **2** favourably (*think highly of him*).

**highly-strung** adj. (also **high-strung**) very sensitive or nervous.

**High Mass** n. (esp. in *RC Church*) Mass celebrated by a priest, usu. attended by deacon and subdeacon, with ritual chanting of parts of the liturgy, the burning of incense, etc.

**high-minded** adj. having high moral principles. □ **high-mindedly** adv. **high-mindedness** n.

**highness** n. **1** state of being high (*highness of taxation*). **2** (**Highness**) title which could be used when addressing or referring to a prince or princess (*Her Highness*; *Your Royal Highness*).

**high-octane** adj. (of fuel used in internal-combustion engines) not detonating readily during the power stroke.

**high-pitched** adj. **1** (of a sound) high. **2** (of a roof) steep. **3** (of a quarrel, discussion, etc.) intense; very loud.

**high point** n. the maximum or best state reached.

**high-powered** adj. **1** having great power or energy (*high-powered car*; *high-powered election campaign*). **2** important or influential.

**high-pressure** adj. aggressive, vigorous, persistent (*high-pressure sales tactics*).

**high priest** n. (*fem.* **high priestess**) **1** chief priest, esp. Jewish. **2** head of a cult etc. (*high priest of rock-and-roll*). **3** person in a high position or exercising great power etc.

**high profile** — n. exposure to attention or publicity. — adj. (as **high-profile**) having a high profile (*high-profile politicians*).

**high-rise** — attrib. adj. (of a building) having many storeys. — n. such a building.

**high-risk** attrib. adj. involving or exposed to danger (*high-risk sports*).

**highroad** n. **1** main road; highway. **2** (usu. foll. by *to*) direct route (*highroad to success*).

**high school** n. secondary school. □ **high-schooler** n.

**high sea** n. (also **high seas**) open seas not under any country's jurisdiction.

**high season** n. busiest period at a resort etc.

**high-speed** attrib. adj. **1** operating at great speed. **2** (of photographic film) usable with short exposures under conditions of low light. **3** (of steel) suitable for cutting-tools even when red-hot.

**high-spirited** adj. vivacious; cheerful; lively. □ **high-spiritedness** n.

**high spot** n. important place or feature.

**high-stepping** adj. having a hectic or pleasure-filled lifestyle. □ **high-stepper** n.

**high table** n. dining-table for the most important guests or members.

**hightail** v. (usu. foll. by *it*) colloq. depart speedily (*hightailed it before the storm broke*).

**high-tech** adj. **1** employing, requiring, or involved in high technology. **2** imitating styles more usual in industry etc.

**high technology** n. advanced technological development, esp. in electronics.

**high tension** n. = HIGH VOLTAGE.

**high time** n. time that is overdue (*it is high time they arrived*).

**high treason** n. = TREASON.

**high-up** colloq. — n. (*pl.* **-ups**) person in an important position. — adj. holding an important position.

**high voltage** n. electrical potential large enough to injure or damage.

**high water** n. water at its highest level, e.g. in a river.

**high-water mark** n. **1** level reached at high water. **2** maximum recorded value or highest point of excellence.

**highway** n. **1 a** public road. **b** main route. **2** direct course of action (*on the highway to success*).

**highwayman** n. hist. robber of travellers etc., usu. mounted.

**high words** n.pl. angry talk, a row.

**hijack** /**huy**-jak/ — v. **1** seize control of (a loaded truck, an aircraft in flight, etc.), esp. to force it to a different destination. **2** seize (goods) in transit. **3** take control of (talks etc.) by force or subterfuge. — n. a hijacking. □ **hijacker** n. [origin unknown]

**hike** — n. **1** long walk, esp. in the country for pleasure. **2** rise in prices etc. (*another hike in the petrol-price*). — v. (**-king**) **1** go for a hike. **2** walk laboriously. **3** (usu. foll. by *up*) hitch up (clothing etc.); become hitched up. **4** (usu. foll. by *up*) raise (prices etc.). □ **hiker** n. [origin unknown]

**hilarious** /huh-**lair**-ree-uhs/ adj. **1** exceedingly funny. **2** boisterously merry. □ **hilariously** adv. **hilariousness** n. **hilarity** /-**la**-ruh-tee/ n. [Greek *hilaros* cheerful]

**hill** n. **1** naturally raised area of land, lower than a mountain. **2** (often in *comb.*) heap, mound (*anthill*). **3** sloping piece of road. **4** (**the hill**) uncovered area of rising ground for spectators at a sports ground. □ **as old as the hills** colloq. extremely old; stale (*that joke's as old as the hills*). **over the hill 1** past the prime of life; declining. **2** past the crisis. **take to the hills** run away into hiding. [Old English]

**hillite** /**hil**-uyt/ n. colloq. sports spectator who views from *the hill* (see HILL 4).

**hill kangaroo** n. = WALLAROO.

**hillock** /**hil**-uhk/ *n.* small hill, mound. □ **hillocky** *adj.*

**hilly** *adj.* (**-ier, -iest**) having many hills. □ **hilliness** *n.*

**hilt** *n.* handle of a sword, dagger, etc. □ **up to the hilt** completely. [Old English]

**hilum** /**huy**-luhm/ *n.* (*pl.* **hila** /-luh/) **1** *Bot.* point of attachment of a seed to its seed-vessel. **2** *Anat.* notch or indentation where a vessel enters an organ. [Latin, = little thing, trifle]

**him** *pron.* **1** objective case of HE (*I saw him*). **2** *colloq.* he (*it's him again*). [Old English, dative of HE]

**himself** /him-**self**/ *pron.* **1 a** *emphat.* form of HE or HIM (*he himself will do it*). **b** *refl.* form of HIM (*he has hurt himself*). **2** in his normal state of body or mind (*does not feel quite himself today*). □ **be himself** see ONESELF. **by himself** see *by oneself*. [Old English: related to HIM, SELF]

**hind**[1] /huynd/ *adj.* at the back (*hind leg*). [Old English *hindan* from behind]

**hind**[2] /huynd/ *n.* female (esp. red) deer, esp. in and after the third year. [Old English]

**hinder** /**hin**-duh/ *v.* impede; delay. [Old English]

**Hindi** /**hin**-dee/ *n.* **1** group of spoken dialects of N. India. **2** literary form of Hindustani, an official language of India. [Urdu *Hind* India]

**hindmost** /**huynd**-mohst/ *adj.* furthest behind.

**hindquarters** *n.pl.* hind legs and rump of a quadruped.

**hindrance** /**hin**-druhns/ *n.* **1** hindering; being hindered. **2** thing that hinders.

**hindsight** /**huynd**-suyt/ *n.* wisdom after the event.

**Hindu** /**hin**-doo, -**doo**/ — *n.* (*pl.* **-s**) follower of Hinduism. — *adj.* of Hindus or Hinduism. [Urdu *Hind* India]

**Hinduism** /**hin**-doo-ˌiz-uhm/ *n.* main religious and social system of India, including the belief in reincarnation, several gods, and a caste system.

**Hindustani** /ˌhin-doo-**stah**-nee/ *n.* language based on Hindi, used as a lingua franca in much of India. [from HINDU, *stān* country]

**hinge** /hinj/ — *n.* **1** movable joint on which a door, lid, etc., turns or swings. **2** principle on which all depends. — *v.* (**-ging**) **1** (foll. by *on*) depend (on a principle, an event, etc.) (*all hinges on his acceptance*). **2** attach or be attached by a hinge. □ **hinged** /hinjd/ *adj.* [related to HANG]

**hinny** /**hin**-ee/ *n.* (*pl.* **-ies**) offspring of a female donkey and a male horse. [Greek *hinnos*]

**hint** — *n.* **1** slight or indirect indication or suggestion. **2** small piece of practical information (*handy hints on cooking*). **3** very small trace; suggestion (*a hint of perfume*). — *v.* suggest slightly or indirectly. □ **hint at** give a hint of; refer indirectly to. **take a hint** heed a hint. [obsolete *hent* grasp]

**hinterland** /**hin**-tuh-ˌland/ *n.* **1** district beyond a coast or river's banks. **2** area served by a port or other centre. [German]

**hip**[1] *n.* **1** projection of the pelvis and the upper part of the thigh-bone. **2** (in *pl.*) circumference of the body at the buttocks (*has slim hips*). [Old English]

**hip**[2] *n.* fruit of a rose, esp. wild. [Old English]

**hip**[3] *int.* introducing a united cheer (*hip, hip, hooray*). [origin unknown]

**hip**[4] *adj.* (also **hep**) (**-pper, -ppest**) *colloq.* **1** trendy, stylish. **2** (often foll. by *to*) knowledgeable about; alert to (*hip to the latest trends in jazz*). [origin unknown]

**hip flask** *n.* small flask for spirits etc.

**hip hop** *n.* subculture combining rap music, graffiti art, and break-dancing. [from HIP[4]]

**hippie** /**hip**-ee/ *n.* (also **hippy**) (*pl.* **-ies**) **1** (esp. in the 1960s) person rejecting convention, typically with long hair, jeans, beads, etc., and taking hallucinogenic drugs. **2** person who rejects the values of conventional society and tries to live in accordance with principles of universal peace, love, etc. usu. in a back-to-nature environment. [from HIP[4]]

**hip pocket** — *n.* **1** trouser-pocket just behind the hip and where one's wallet usu. resides. **2** one's finances, bank-balance (*hit in the hip pocket by the latest budget*). — *adj.* pertaining to one's income (*voters are concerned about hip-pocket issues*).

**hip-pocket nerve** *n.* imaginary nerve which twinges sharply whenever demands are made on one's money (e.g. through proposed taxes etc.).

**Hippocratic oath** /ˌhip-uh-**krat**-ik/ *n.* statement of ethics of the medical profession. [*Hippocrates*, name of a Greek physician]

**hippodrome** /**hip**-uh-ˌdrohm/ *n.* **1** music-hall or dancehall. **2** (in classical antiquity) course for chariot races etc. [Greek *hippos* horse, *dromos* race]

**hippopotamus** /ˌhip-uh-**pot**-uh-muhs/ *n.* (*pl.* **-muses** or **-mi** /-ˌmuy/) large African mammal with short legs and thick skin, living by rivers, lakes, etc. [Greek *hippos* horse, *potamos* river]

**hippy** var. of HIPPIE.

**hipster** — *attrib. adj.* (of trousers, underpants, skirts, etc.) hanging from the hips rather than the waist. — *n.* (in *pl.*) trousers or underpants hanging from the hips.

**hire** /huyuh/ — *v.* (**-ring**) **1** purchase the temporary use of (a thing) (*hired a van*). **2** employ (a person). — *n.* **1** hiring or being hired. **2** payment for this. □ **for** (or **on**) **hire** ready to be hired. **hire out** grant the temporary use of (a thing) for payment. □ **hireable** *adj.* **hirer** *n.* [Old English]

**hireling** *n.* usu. *derog.* person who does anything (only) for money.

**hire purchase** *n.* system by which a person may purchase a thing by paying in instalments while having the use of it.

**hirsute** /her-syoot/ *adj.* hairy. □ **hirsuteness** *n.* [Latin]

**hirsutism** /her-syoo-tiz-uhm/ *n.* excessive growth of hair (esp. on legs, chest, back, etc.).

**his** /hiz/ *poss. pron.* **1** (*attrib.*) of or belonging to him or himself (*his house*; *his own business*). **2** the one or ones belonging to or associated with him (*it is his*; *his are over there*). □ **of his** of or belonging to him (*friend of his*). [Old English, genitive of HE]

**Hispanic** /his-**pan**-ik/ *adj.* **1** of Spain or Spain and Portugal. **2** of Spain and other Spanish-speaking countries. [Latin *Hispania* Spain]

**hiss** — *v.* **1** (of a person, snake, goose, etc.) make a sharp sibilant sound, as of the letter *s* (*the water hissed on the hotplate*). **2** express disapproval of by hisses (*audience booed and hissed*). **3** whisper urgently or angrily ('Where's the door?' he hissed). — *n.* **1** sharp sibilant sound as of the letter *s*. **2** *Electronics* interference at audio frequencies. [imitative]

**histamine** /his-tuh-meen/ *n.* chemical compound in body tissues etc., associated with allergic reactions. [from HISTOLOGY, AMINE]

**histogram** /his-tuh-gram/ *n.* statistical diagram of rectangles with areas proportional to the value of a number of variables. [Greek *histos* mast]

**histology** /his-tol-uh-jee/ *n.* the study of tissue structure. [Greek *histos* web]

**historian** /his-taw-ree-uhn/ *n.* **1** writer of history. **2** person learned in history.

**historic** /his-to-rik/ *adj.* famous or important in history or potentially so (*historic moment*).

**historical** *adj.* **1** of or concerning history (*historical evidence*). **2** (of the study of a subject) showing its development over a period. **3** factual, not fictional or legendary. **4** belonging to the past, not the present. **5** (of a novel etc.) dealing with historical events. □ **historically** *adv.*

**historicism** /his-to-ruh-siz-uhm/ *n.* **1** theory that social and cultural phenomena are determined by history. **2** belief that historical events are governed by laws.

**historicity** /his-tuh-**ris**-uh-tee/ *n.* historical truth or authenticity.

**historiography** /his-to-ree-**og**-ruh-fee/ *n.* **1** the writing of history. **2** the study of this. □ **historiographer** *n.*

**history** /his-tree, -tuh-ree/ *n.* (*pl.* **-ies**) **1** continuous record of (esp. public) events. **2 a** the study of past events, esp. human affairs. **b** total accumulation of past events, esp. relating to human affairs or a particular nation, person, thing, etc. **3** eventful past (*this house has a history*). **4** (foll. by *of*) past record (*had a history of illness*). **5 a** systematic or critical account of or research into past events etc. **b** similar record or account of natural phenomena. **6** historical play (*Shakespeare's histories*). □ **be history** *colloq.* **1** broken beyond repair (*my new car was history after the accident*). **2** damaged beyond recovery; finished (*their marriage is history; he's history now that his fingerprints have been found on the stolen car*). **3** dead. **make history** do something memorable. [Greek *historia* inquiry]

**histrionic** /his-tree-**on**-ik/ — *adj.* **1** of or concerning actors or acting. **2** (of behaviour) theatrical, dramatic. — *n.* (in *pl.*) insincere and dramatic behaviour designed to impress. [Latin *histrio* actor]

**hit** — *v.* (**-tt-**; *past* and *past part.* **hit**) **1 a** strike with a blow or missile. **b** (of a moving body) strike with force (*the plane hit the ground*). **c** reach (a target etc.) with a directed missile (*hit the wicket*). **2** cause to suffer; affect adversely (*the loss hit him hard*). **3** (often foll. by *at*, *against*) direct a blow. **4** (often foll. by *against*, *on*) knock (a part of the body) (*hit his head*). **5** achieve, reach (*hit the right tone in his apology*; *can't hit the high notes; Aussie swimmers hit the headlines*). **6 a** encounter; find (*hit a snag; hit the right road at last*). **b** arrive at (*hit town*). **7** *colloq.* indulge heavily in, esp. liquor etc. (*hit the bottle*). **8** *colloq.* rob or kill (*was hit by two masked men*). **9** *colloq.* demand or wrest money from (*the tax department has hit me for $2000*). **10** occur forcefully to (*it only hit him later*). **11 a** propel (a ball etc.) with a bat etc. to score runs or points. **b** score in this way (*hit a six*). — *n.* **1 a** blow, stroke. **b** collision. **2** shot etc. that hits its target. **3** *colloq.* a shot or dose of some drug. **4** a popular success (*the new song's a hit*). □ **hit back** retaliate. **hit below the belt 1** esp. *Boxing* give a foul blow. **2** treat or behave unfairly. **hit the ceiling** = *hit the roof*. **hit the deck 1** fall to the ground in self-protection. **2** *colloq.* arise, start the day (*I always hit the deck by 5 a.m.*). **hit the hay** (or **sack**) *colloq.* go to bed. **hit** (or **beat**) **one's head against a brick wall** do something completely futile or unavailing. **hit home** have a strong impact (*it hit home when he told me that if I didn't quit smoking I'd be dead within a year*). **hit it off** (often foll. by *with*, *together*) *colloq.* get on well (with a person). **hit me with** *colloq.* give me (*hit me with the latest news*). **hit the nail on the head** state the truth exactly. **hit on** (or **upon**) find by chance. **hit out** deal vigorous physical or verbal blows (*hit out at her enemies*). **hit the panic button** see PANIC BUTTON. **hit the road** *colloq.* depart. **hit rock bottom** *colloq.* reach the worst possible state in which to be (*our team's hit rock bottom*). **hit the roof** see ROOF. **hit the skids** *colloq.* **1** (of a motor vehicle) brake suddenly. **2** become destitute. **hit the ton** see TON. [Old English from Old Norse]

**hit-and-run** *attrib. adj.* **1** (of a driver, raider, etc.) causing death or injury and leaving the scene immediately. **2** (of an accident, attack, etc.) perpetrated by such a person or people.

**hitch** — *v.* **1** fasten or be fastened with a loop, hook, etc.; tether. **2** move (a thing) slightly or with a jerk (*hitched his pillow to a more comfortable position*). **3** *colloq.* **a** = HITCHHIKE. **b** obtain (a ride) by hitch-hiking. — *n.* **1** temporary obstacle or snag. **2** abrupt pull or push. **3** noose or knot of various kinds. **4** *colloq.* free ride in a vehicle. □ **get hitched** *colloq.* marry. **hitch up** lift (esp. clothing) with a jerk (*hitched up his trousers*). [origin uncertain]

**hitchhike** *v.* (**-king**) travel by seeking free lifts in passing vehicles. □ **hitchhiker** *n.*

**hi-tech** /huy-tek/ *adj.* = HIGH-TECH. [abbreviation]

**hither** /*hith*-uh/ *adv. formal* to or towards this place. [Old English]

**hither and thither** *adv.* to and fro.

**hitherto** /ˌhith-uh-too/ *adv.* until this time, up to now (*a problem hitherto unsolved*).

**hit list** *n. colloq.* list of prospective victims.

**hit man** *n. colloq.* hired assassin.

**hit-or-miss** *adj.* liable to error, random.

**hit parade** *n. colloq.* list of the current best-selling pop records.

**hit-up** *n.* brief practice or warm-up before a game (e.g. tennis) begins.

**HIV** *abbr.* human immunodeficiency virus, either of two retroviruses which cause a breakdown of the body's immune system, leading in some cases to the development of Aids.

**hive** — *n.* **1 a** beehive. **b** the bees in it. **2** busy swarming place (*a hive of industry*). **3** swarming multitude. — *v.* **1** place (bees) in a hive. **2** enter a hive. □ **hive off** (**-ving**) separate from a larger group. **hive up** hoard for future use. [Old English]

**hives** *n.pl.* skin-eruption, esp. nettle-rash. [origin unknown]

**Ho** *symb.* holmium.

**ho** /hoh/ *int.* expressing triumph, derision, etc., or calling attention. [natural exclamation]

**hoard** /hawd/ — *n.* **1** stock or store (esp. of money or food). **2** ancient store of treasure etc. — *v.* amass and store (esp. secretly). □ **hoarder** *n.* [Old English]

**hoarding** *n.* **1** large, usu. wooden, structure used to carry advertisements etc. **2** temporary fence round a building site etc. [obsolete *hoard* from French *hourd*]

**hoar frost** /haw/ *n.* frozen water vapour on vegetation etc. [Old English]

**hoarse** /haws/ *adj.* **1** (of the voice) rough and deep; husky, croaking. **2** having such a voice. □ **hoarsely** *adv.* **hoarsen** *v.* **hoarseness** *n.* [Old Norse]

**hoary** /haw-ree/ *adj.* (**-ier**, **-iest**) **1 a** (of hair) grey or white with age. **b** having such hair; aged. **2** old and trite (*hoary joke*). [Old English]

**hoax** /hohks/ — *n.* humorous or malicious deception; practical joke. — *v.* deceive (a person) with a hoax. □ **hoaxer** *n.* [probably a shortening of *hocus* in HOCUS-POCUS]

**hob** *n.* **1** flat heating surface with hotplates or burners, on a cooker or as a separate unit. **2** flat metal shelf at the side of a fireplace for heating a pan etc. [perhaps var. of HUB]

**Hobart** /hoh-baht/ *n.* name of the capital city of the State of Tasmania. [Robert *Hobart*, Britain's Secretary of State for War and the Colonies from 1801–04]

**hobbit** /hob-uht/ *n.* member of an imaginary race of half-sized people in stories by J.R.R. Tolkien. [an invented word]

**hobble** /hob-uhl/ — *v.* (**-ling**) **1 a** walk lamely; limp. **b** proceed haltingly in action or speech (*hobbled to his conclusion*). **2** tie the legs of (a horse etc.) loosely together to prevent it from straying. — *n.* **1** uneven or infirm gait. **2** rope etc. for hobbling a horse etc. [probably Low German]

**hobble chain** *n.* length of chain used to fetter an animal.

**hobby** /**hob**-ee/ *n.* (*pl.* **-ies**) leisure-time activity pursued for pleasure. [from the name *Robin*]

**hobby farm** *n.* farm maintained as a hobby, not as the main source of income. □ **hobby farmer** *n.*

**hobby horse** *n.* **1** child's toy consisting of a stick with a horse's head. **2** favourite or obsessive subject or idea.

**hobgoblin** /hob-,gob-luhn/ *n.* **1** mischievous imp. **2** bugbear. [from HOBBY, GOBLIN]

**hobnail** *n.* heavy-headed nail for boot-soles. [from HOB]

**hobnob** /**hob**-nob/ *v.* (**-bb-**) (usu. foll. by *with*) mix socially or informally (*people hobnobbing with the prime minister on the street*). [*hab nab* have or not have]

**hobo** /**hoh**-boh/ *n.* (*pl.* **-es** or **-s**) wandering worker; tramp. [origin unknown]

**Hobson's choice** /**hob**-suhnz/ *n.* choice of taking the thing offered or nothing. [*Hobson*, name of a carrier who let out horses thus]

**hock¹** *n.* joint of a quadruped's hind leg between the knee and the fetlock. [Old English]

**hock²** *n.* **1** Australian dry white wine. **2** white wine from the Rhineland. [*Hochheim* in Germany]

**hock³** *v.* *colloq.* **1** pawn. **2** sell, esp. illegally. □ **in hock 1** in pawn. **2** in debt. [Dutch]

**hockey** /**hok**-ee/ *n.* team game with hooked sticks and a small hard ball. [origin unknown]

**hocus-pocus** /,hoh-kuhs-**poh**-kuhs/ *n.* **1** deception; trickery. **2** typical verbal formula used in conjuring. [sham Latin]

**hod** *n.* **1** V-shaped trough on a pole used for carrying bricks etc. **2** portable receptacle for coal. [French *hotte* pannier]

**hoddie** /**hod**-ee/ *n.* bricklayer's labourer; hodman. [from HOD]

**hodgepodge** var. of HOTCHPOTCH.

**Hodgkin's disease** /**hoj**-kuhnz/ *n.* malignant disease of lymphatic tissues, usu. characterised by enlargement of the lymph nodes. [*Hodgkin*, name of a physician]

**hodman** /**hod**-muhn/ *n.* = HODDIE.

**hoe** /hoh/ — *n.* long-handled tool with a blade, used for weeding etc. — *v.* (**hoes, hoed, hoeing**) **1** weed (crops); loosen (earth); dig up with a hoe. **2** (foll. by *in*) *colloq.* **a** begin to eat eagerly. **b** begin working with vigour. **3** (foll. by *into*) *colloq.* **a** attack (one's food) (*hoed into the noodles like a starving man*). **b** attack (a task etc.) with vigour (*must hoe into all this paperwork*). **c** attack (a person) verbally (*the prime minister hoed into the leader of the opposition*). [French from Germanic]

**hog** — *n.* **1** castrated male pig. **2** *colloq.* greedy or selfish person. — *v.* (**-gg-**) *colloq.* take greedily, esp. more than one's fair share; hoard selfishly; monopolise. □ **go the whole hog** *colloq.* do something completely or thoroughly. □ **hoggish** *adj.* [Old English]

**hogget** /**hog**-uht/ *n.* **1** yearling sheep. **2** meat of this. [HOG]

**hogshead** *n.* **1** large cask. **2** liquid or dry measure (about 236 litres, 50 gallons). [from HOG: the reason for the name is unknown]

**hogtie** *v.* **1** secure by fastening the hands and feet or all four feet together. **2** restrain, impede (*all these rules have me hogtied*).

**hogwash** *n.* *colloq.* nonsense, rubbish.

**ho-hum** /hoh-**hum**/ *adj.* *colloq.* boring (*the lecture was utterly ho-hum*). [imitative of a yawn]

**hoick** /hoik/ *v.* (often foll. by *out*) lift or pull, esp. with a jerk (*hoicked him out of bed*). [perhaps var. of HIKE]

**hoi polloi** /,hoi puh-**loi**/ *n.* the masses; the common people. [Greek, = the many]

■ **Usage** This phrase is often preceded by *the*, which is, strictly speaking, unnecessary, since *hoi* means 'the'.

**hoist** — *v.* **1** raise or haul up. **2** raise by means of ropes and pulleys etc. **3** *colloq.* steal; shoplift. **4** *colloq.* throw (*hoisted it out of the window*). — *n.* **1** act of hoisting, lift. **2** apparatus for hoisting. **3** rotary clothes-hoist. **4** *colloq.* a theft. □ **hoist with one's own petard** caught by one's own trick etc. [earlier *hoise*, probably from Low German]

**hokum** /**hoh**-kuhm/ *n.* *colloq.* **1** bunkum; rubbish. **2** sentimental, sensational, or unreal material in a film or play etc. [origin unknown]

**hold¹** /hohld/ — *v.* (*past* and *past part.* **held**) **1 a** keep fast; grasp (esp. in the hands or arms). **b** (also *refl.*) keep or sustain (a thing, oneself, one's head, etc.) in a particular position (*hold it to the light; held himself erect*). **c** grip so as to control (*hold the reins*). **2** have the capacity for, contain (*holds two litres; the hall holds 900*). **3** possess, gain, or have, esp.: **a** be the owner or tenant of (land, property, stocks, etc.). **b** gain or have gained (a qualification, record, etc.) (*holds the long-jump record*). **c** have the position of (a job or office) (*holds the position of mayor*). **d** keep possession of (a place, a person's thoughts, etc.), esp. against attack (*held the fort against the enemy; continued to hold her affection*). **4** remain unbroken; not give way (*roof held under the storm*). **5** celebrate or conduct (a meeting, festival, conversation, etc.). **6 a** keep (a person etc.) in a place or condition (*held him in suspense*). **b** detain, esp. in custody (*hold him until I arrive*). **7 a** engross (*the book held him for hours*). **b** dominate (*held the stage*). **8** (foll. by *to*) keep (a person etc.) to (a promise etc.) (*I hold you to your word*). **9** (of weather) continue fine (*if the weather holds . . .*). **10** think, believe; assert (*held it to be plain; held that the earth was flat*). **11** regard with a specified feeling (*held him in contempt*). **12** cease; restrain (*hold your fire*). **13** keep or reserve (*please hold our seats*). **14** be able to drink (alcohol) without effect (*can't hold his drink*). **15** (of a judge, a court, etc.) lay down; decide (*held that there was no case to answer*). **16** *Mus.* sustain (a note). **17** = *hold the line. — n.* **1** (foll. by *on, over*) influence or power over (*has a strange hold over me*). **2** manner of holding in wrestling etc. **3** grasp (*take hold of him*). □ **hold (a thing) against (a person)** resent or regard it as discreditable to (a person). **hold aloof** avoid communication etc. with people, esp. out of pride or reserve. **hold back 1** impede the progress of; restrain. **2** keep for oneself. **3** (often foll. by *from*) hesitate; refrain. **hold one's breath** wait expectantly. **hold by** (or **to**) adhere to (a choice, purpose, etc.) (*he held to his decision*). **hold down 1** repress. **2** *colloq.* be competent enough to keep (one's job etc.). **hold the fort 1** act as a temporary substitute. **2** cope in an emergency. **hold forth** speak at length or tediously. **hold good** (or **true**) be valid. **hold one's ground** see GROUND¹. **hold one's head high** behave proudly and confidently. **hold one's horses** *colloq.* stop; slow down. **holding the ball** *Aust. Rules* not disposing of the ball after one has been seized by an opposing player, so incurring a penalty. **hold it** (or **everything**) cease action or movement. **hold the line** not ring off (in a telephone connection). **hold off 1** delay, not begin. **2** keep one's distance. **hold on 1** keep one's grasp on something. **2** wait a moment. **3** = *hold the line*. **hold out 1** stretch forth (a hand etc.). **2** offer (an inducement etc.). **3** maintain resistance. **4** persist or last (*will the cake hold out until he gets here?*). **hold out for** maintain one's stand etc. until one's demands are

met (*workers held out for more money*). **hold out on** *colloq.* refuse something to (a person). **hold over** postpone (*the meeting has been held over for a week*). **hold one's own** maintain one's position; not be beaten. **hold one's tongue** *colloq.* remain silent. **hold to ransom 1** keep prisoner until a ransom is paid. **2** demand concessions by threats. **hold up 1** support, sustain. **2** exhibit, display. **3** hinder, obstruct. **4** stop and rob by force. **hold water** (of reasoning) be sound, bear examination. **hold with** (usu. with *neg.*) approve of (*I don't hold with motor bikes*). **on hold 1** (of a telephone caller) kept waiting until the desired line is free. **2** in abeyance. **take hold** (of a custom or habit) become established. **with no holds barred** with no restrictions, all methods being permitted. □ **holdable** *adj.* **holder** *n.* [Old English]

**hold²** /hohld/ *n.* cavity in the lower part of a ship or aircraft for cargo. [Old English: related to HOLLOW]

**holdall** *n.* large soft travelling bag.

**holding** *n.* **1** tenure of land. **2** stocks, property, etc. held.

**holding company** *n.* company created to hold the shares of other companies, which it then controls.

**holding operation** *n.* manoeuvre designed to maintain the status quo.

**holding paddock** *n.* (also **holding pen**, **holding yard**) enclosure in which stock is kept for a special purpose.

**hold-up** *n.* **1** stoppage or delay. **2** robbery by force.

**hole** — *n.* **1 a** empty space in a solid body. **b** opening in or through something. **2** animal's burrow. **3** (in games) cavity or receptacle for a ball. **4** *colloq.* small or dingy place, town, etc. **5** *colloq.* awkward situation (*in a hole when our money ran out*). **6** *colloq.* aperture in the body (e.g. the mouth etc.). **7** *colloq.* flaw; fallacy (*your argument is full of holes*). **8** *Golf* **a** terrain or distance from tee to the hole in the putting green. **b** point scored by a player who gets the ball from tee to hole with the fewest strokes. — *v.* **1** make a hole or holes in. **2** pierce the side of (a ship). **3** put into a hole. □ **hole up** *colloq.* **1** (of an animal) go into its burrow. **2** hide oneself. **make a hole in** use a large amount of. □ **holey** *adj.* [Old English]

**hole-and-corner** *adj.* secret; underhand.

**hole-in-one** *n. Golf* shot that enters the hole from the tee.

**hole in the heart** *n. colloq.* congenital defect in the heart membrane.

**holey dollar** n. hist. (also **holy dollar**) coin made from a Spanish silver dollar by punching out its centre (or DUMP), used in Australia between 1814 and 1828.

**-holic** suffix. (or **-aholic**) colloq. addicted to (bingoholic; workaholic). [erroneously formed on alcoholic]

**holiday** /hol-uh-,day/ — n. **1** (often in pl.) extended period of recreation, esp. spent away from home or travelling; break from work. **2** day of festivity or recreation when no work is done, esp. a religious festival etc. — adj. **1 a** (of clothes etc.) suitable for a holiday. **b** festive (holiday mood; holiday atmosphere). **2** pertaining to a holiday (holiday home). — v. spend a holiday. [Old English: related to HOLY, DAY]

**holiday home** n. (also **holiday cottage, holiday house**) house (usu. located by the beach or at some popular holiday resort) used by the owners for their annual holiday and perhaps rented out for the rest of the year.

**holier-than-thou** adj. smugly self-righteous.

**holiness** /hoh-lee-nuhs/ n. **1** sanctity; state of being holy or sacred. **2** (**Holiness**) (prec. by His or Your) title used when addressing or referring to the Pope. [Old English: related to HOLY]

**holism** /hoh-liz-uhm/ n. (also **wholism**) **1** Philos. theory that certain wholes are greater than the sum of their parts. **2** Med. treating of the whole person rather than the symptoms of a disease. □ **holistic** /-lis-tik/ adj. [Greek holos whole]

**holland** /hol-uhnd/ n. smooth, hard-wearing, linen fabric. [Holland = Netherlands]

**holland blind** n. window blind made from holland (or some other strong material).

**hollandaise sauce** /,hol-uhn-dayz, hol-/ n. creamy sauce of melted butter, egg yolks, vinegar, etc. [French]

**hollow** /hol-oh/ — adj. **1 a** having a cavity within; not solid. **b** sunken (hollow cheeks). **2** (of a sound) echoing. **3** empty; hungry. **4** meaningless (hollow victory). **5** insincere (hollow laugh; hollow promises). — n. **1** hollow place; hole. **2** valley; basin. — v. (often foll. by out) make hollow; excavate. — adv. colloq. completely (beaten hollow). □ **have hollow legs** colloq. have an insatiable appetite. **in the hollow of one's hand** entirely subservient to one (she had him in the hollow of her hand). □ **hollowly** adv. **hollowness** n. [Old English]

**hollow-eyed** adj. with eyes deep sunk.

**holly** /hol-ee/ n. (pl. **-ies**) **1** evergreen European shrub with prickly leaves and red berries. **2** its branches or foliage used as a Christmas decoration. [Old English]

**hollyhock** /hol-ee-,hok/ n. tall plant with showy flowers. [from HOLY, obsolete hock mallow (a kind of plant)]

**holmium** /hol-mee-uhm/ n. metallic element of the lanthanide series. [Latin Holmia Stockholm]

**holocaust** /hol-uh-,kawst, -,kost/ n. **1** large-scale destruction, esp. by fire or nuclear war. **2** (**the Holocaust**) mass murder of the Jews by the Nazis 1939–45. **3** religious sacrifice (e.g. a lamb) wholly consumed by fire. [Greek holos whole, kaustos burnt]

**hologram** /hol-uh-,gram/ n. photographic pattern that gives a three-dimensional image when illuminated by coherent light. [Greek holos whole, -GRAM]

**holograph** /hol-uh-,grahf, -,graf/ — adj. wholly written by hand by the person named as the author. — n. holograph document. [Greek holos whole, -GRAPH]

**holography** /huh-**log**-ruh-fee/ n. the study or production of holograms.

**hols** /holz/ n.pl. colloq. holidays. [abbreviation]

**holster** /hohl-stuh/ n. leather case for a pistol or revolver, worn on a belt etc. [Dutch]

**holus-bolus** /,hoh-luhs-**boh**-luhs/ adv. all at once; altogether. [apparently sham Latin]

**holy** /hoh-lee/ adj. (**-ier, -iest**) **1** morally and spiritually excellent or perfect, and to be revered. **2** belonging to or devoted to God. **3** consecrated, sacred. [Old English: related to WHOLE]

**Holy Communion** see COMMUNION.

**holy cross toad** n. yellowish frog of inland south-eastern Australia with a warty cross on its back (also known as the Catholic frog).

**Holy Father** n. the Pope.

**Holy Ghost** n. = HOLY SPIRIT.

**Holy Grail** see GRAIL.

**Holy Land** n. area between the River Jordan and the Mediterranean Sea.

**holy of holies** n. **1** sacred inner chamber of the Jewish temple. **2** thing regarded as most sacred.

**holy orders** n.pl. **1** sacrament of ordination, esp. to the priesthood, conferred by a bishop. **2** the status of a bishop, priest, or deacon.

**Holy Roman Empire** n. Western part of the Roman Empire as revived by Charlemagne in 800 AD.

**Holy See** n. **1 a** the See of Rome. **b** jurisdiction and office of the Pope. **2** papacy or papal court.

**Holy Spirit** *n.* Third Person of the Trinity, God as spiritually acting.

**Holy Week** *n.* week before Easter.

**Holy Writ** *n.* holy writings, esp. the Bible.

**Holy Year** *n.* period of remission from the penal consequences of sin, granted by the Pope, under certain conditions, for a year usu. at intervals of 25 years.

**homage** /**hom**-ij/ *n.* tribute, expression of reverence (*pay homage to*). [Latin *homo* man]

**home** — *n.* **1 a** place where one lives; fixed residence. **b** dwelling-house. **2** family circumstances (*comes from a good home*). **3** native land. **4** institution caring for people or animals (*nursing home*). **5** place where a thing originates, is kept, or is native or most common. **6 a** finishing-point in a race. **b** (in games) place where one is safe; goal. — *attrib. adj.* **1** of or connected with one's home. **b** carried on, done, or made, at home. **2** in one's own country (*home industries; the home market*). **3** *Sport* played on one's own ground etc. (*home match*). — *adv.* **1** to, at, or in one's home or country (*go home; is he home yet?*). **2 a** to the point aimed at (*the thrust went home*). **b** as far as possible (*drove the nail home*). — *v.* (**-ming**) **1** (esp. of a trained pigeon) return home. **2** (often foll. by *on, in on*) (of a vessel, missile, etc.) be guided towards a destination or target. **3** send or guide homewards. □ **at home 1** in one's house or native land. **2** at ease (*make yourself at home*). **3** (usu. foll. by *in, on, with*) familiar or well informed (*thoroughly at home with maths*). **4** available to callers (*tell them I'm not at home*). **come** (or **bring**) **home** to become (or cause to become) fully realised by (*hasn't yet come home to him that his debts are so large; the police-siren brought it home to him that he had been speeding*). **come home to roost** SEE ROOST. **nothing to write home about** not worth paying attention to (*his so-called achievements are nothing to write home about*). [Old English]

**home and dry** *predic. adj.* = HOME AND HOSED.

**home and hosed** *predic. adj.* having achieved one's aim.

**home-brew** *n.* drink (esp. beer) brewed at home.

**home economics** *n.pl.* the study of household management.

**home help** *n.* person helping with housework etc., esp. one provided by a welfare agency.

**homeland** *n.* one's native land.

**homeland centre** *n.* traditional lands of an Aboriginal community to which that community has returned to live.

**homeland movement** *n.* the forming of homeland centres.

**homely** *adj.* (**-ier, -iest**) **1** simple, plain, unpretentious (*homely meal*). **2** (of facial appearance) plain, unattractive. **3** comfortable, cosy. □ **homeliness** *n.*

**homeopathy** var. of HOMOEOPATHY.

**home paddock** *n.* paddock adjacent to a homestead.

**Homeric** /hoh-**me**-rik/ *adj.* **1** of, or in the style of, the ninth century BC Greek poet Homer. **2** of Bronze Age Greece as described in Homer's poems.

**home rule** *n.* government of a country or region by its own citizens.

**homesick** *adj.* depressed by absence from home. □ **homesickness** *n.*

**homespun** — *adj.* **1** made of yarn spun at home. **2** plain, simple (*homespun philosophy*). — *n.* homespun cloth.

**home station** *n.* principal residence on a large stock-raising property.

**homestead** /**hohm**-sted/ *n.* **1** house, esp. a farmhouse, and outbuildings. **2** = HOME STATION. □ **homesteader** *n.*

**home stretch** *n.* (also **home straight**) **1** concluding stretch of a racecourse leading to the finishing line. **2** concluding stage of anything (*they are into the home stretch now with the new Yass bypass*).

**home truth** *n.* basic but unwelcome information about oneself.

**home unit** *n.* self-contained apartment (one of several in the same building) with separate title and usu. occupied by the owner.

**homeward** /**hohm**-wuhd/ — *adv.* (also **homewards**) towards home. — *adj.* going towards home.

**homework** *n.* **1** work to be done at home, esp. by a school pupil. **2** preparatory work or study (*did his homework well for the crucial board-meeting*).

**homey** *adj.* (also **homy**) (**-mier, -miest**) suggesting homeliness; cosy.

**homicide** /**hom**-uh-₁suyd/ *n.* **1** killing of a human being by another. **2** person who kills a human being. □ **homicidal** /-**suy**-duhl/ *adj.* [Latin *homo* man]

**homily** /**hom**-uh-lee/ *n.* (*pl.* **-ies**) **1** sermon. **2** tedious moralising discourse. □ **homiletic** /₁hom-uh-**let**-ik/ *adj.* [Greek *homilia*]

**homing** *attrib. adj.* **1** (of a pigeon) trained to fly home. **2** (of a device) for guiding to a target etc.

**hominid** /**hom**-uh-nid/ — *adj.* of the primate family including humans and their fossil ancestors. — *n.* member of this family. [Latin *homo homin-* man]

**hominoid** /**hom**-uh-,noid/ — *adj.* like a human. — *n.* animal resembling a human.

**homo** /**hoh**-moh/ *n.* (*pl.* **-s**) *colloq. offens.* homosexual. [abbreviation]

**homo-** *comb. form* same (opp. HETERO-). [Greek *homos* same]

**homoeopathy** /,hoh-mee-**op**-uh-thee, ,hom-ee-/ *n.* (also **homeopathy**) treatment of disease by minute doses of drugs that in a healthy person would produce symptoms of the disease. □ **homoeopath** /hoh-mee-oh-,path, hom-ee-/ *n.* **homoeopathic** /-**path**-ik/ *adj.* [Greek *homoios* like: related to PATHOS]

**homogeneous** /,hoh-muh-**jee**-nee-uhs, ,hom-uh-/ *adj.* **1** of the same kind. **2** consisting of parts all of the same kind; uniform. □ **homogeneity** /-juh-**nee**-uh-tee/ *n.* **homogeneously** *adv.* [from HOMO-, Greek *genos* kind]

■ **Usage** *Homogeneous* is often confused with *homogenous* which is a term in biology meaning 'similar owing to common descent'.

**homogenise** /huh-**moj**-uh-,nuyz/ *v.* (also **-ize**) (**-sing** or **-zing**) **1** make homogeneous. **2** treat (milk) so that the fat droplets are emulsified and the cream does not separate.

**homograph** /**hom**-uh-,grahf, -,graf/ *n.* word spelt like another but of different meaning or origin (e.g. POLE¹, POLE²).

**homologous** /huh-**mol**-uh-guhs/ *adj.* **1** **a** having the same relation, relative position, etc. **b** corresponding. **2** *Biol.* (of organs etc.) similar in position and structure but not necessarily in function. [from HOMO-, Greek *logos* ratio]

**homology** /huh-**mol**-uh-jee/ *n.* homologous state or relation; correspondence.

**homonym** /**hom**-uh-nim/ *n.* **1** word spelt or pronounced like another but of different meaning, e.g. *peal* and *peel*; *peer* (an equal) and *peer* (look closely); homograph or homophone. **2** namesake. [from HOMO-, Greek *onoma* name]

**homophobia** /,hoh-muh-**foh**-bee-uh, hom-uh-/ *n.* hatred or fear of homosexuals. □ **homophobe** /**hohm**-, hom-/ *n.* **homophobic** *adj.*

**homophone** /**hom**-uh-,fohn/ *n.* word pronounced like another but of different meaning or origin (e.g. *pair*, *pear*). [from HOMO-, Greek *phōnē* sound]

***Homo sapiens*** /,hoh-moh **sap**-ee-enz/ *n.* modern humans regarded as a species. [Latin, = wise man]

**homosexual** /,hoh-muh-**sek**-shoo-uhl, ,hom-uh-/ — *adj.* feeling or involving sexual attraction only to people of the same sex as oneself. — *n.* homosexual person. □ **homosexuality** /-al-uh-tee/ *n.* [from HOMO-, SEXUAL]

**hone** — *n.* whetstone, esp. for razors. — *v.* (**-ning**) sharpen on or as on a hone. [Old English]

■ **Usage** Frequently used in error, as *hone in*, for *home in* (see HOME *v.* 2).

**honest** /**on**-uhst/ — *adj.* **1** fair and just; not cheating or stealing. **2** free of deceit and untruthfulness; sincere. **3** fairly earned (*an honest living*). **4** blameless but undistinguished. — *adv. colloq.* genuinely, really (*'Won a million dollars.' — 'Honest?'*). [Latin *honestus*]

**honestly** *adv.* **1** in an honest way. **2** really (*I don't honestly know*). **3** expression of annoyance, exasperation, etc.

**honest to dinkum** (also **honest to God**) *colloq.* — *int.* I swear (*honest to God! — I'm innocent*). — *adj.* genuine (*this is an honest to dinkum chunk of Noah's Ark*).

**honesty** *n.* **1** being honest. **2** truthfulness. **3** exotic plant with purple or white flowers and flat round semi-transparent seed-pods.

**honey** /**hun**-ee/ *n.* (*pl.* **-s**) **1** sweet sticky yellowish fluid made by bees from nectar. **2** colour of this. **3 a** sweetness. **b** sweet thing. **4** (usu. as a form of address) darling, sweetheart. **5** *colloq.* person or thing exciting admiration (*he's a honey; my new car's a honey*). [Old English]

**honey ant** *n.* any of several Australian ants able to store a honey-like liquid in its crop: a delicacy for Aborigines who hold the living ant by its head and bite off the abdomen.

**honey-bag** *n.* (also **sugar-bag**) honeycomb of the wild Australian stingless bee.

**honey-bag ant** *n.* = HONEY-ANT.

**honey bee** *n.* common hive-bee.

**honeycomb** — *n.* **1** bees' wax structure of hexagonal cells for honey and eggs. **2** pattern arranged hexagonally. **3** honey-coloured brittle sweet, made by aerating boiled sugar and water etc. mixture. **4** tripe from the second stomach of a ruminant. — *v.* **1** fill with cavities or tunnels, undermine. **2** mark with a honeycomb pattern. [Old English]

**honeydew** *n.* **1** sweet sticky substance excreted by aphids on leaves and stems. **2** variety of melon with very sweet green flesh.

**honeyeater** *n.* any of numerous Australian birds having a long brush-tipped tongue for feeding on flower-nectar and other foods.

**honeyed** *adj.* (of words, flattery, etc.) sweet, sweet-sounding.

**honey flower** n. Australian native shrub (*lambertia*) with bizarre woody fruits and erect clusters of showy bright red flowers rich in nectar: also called *mountain devil* because of the horned fruits.

**honeymoon** — n. **1** holiday taken by a newly married couple. **2** initial period of enthusiasm or goodwill (*the honeymoon is over for the new government*). — v. spend a honeymoon. □ **honeymooner** n.

**honeysuckle** n. **1** exotic climbing shrub or upright with very fragrant yellow or pink flowers. **2** any of several Australian trees or shrubs bearing nectar-rich flowers, esp. the BANKSIA.

**honk** — n. **1** sound of a car horn. **2** cry of a wild goose. — v. (cause to) make a honk. [imitative]

**honky-tonk** /**hong**-kee-ˌtongk/ n. ragtime piano music. [origin unknown]

**honorarium** /ˌon-uh-**rair**-ree-uhm/ n. (pl. **-s** or **-ria**) fee, esp. a voluntary payment for professional services rendered without the normal fee. [Latin: related to HONOUR]

**honorary** /**on**-uh-ruh-ree/ adj. **1** conferred as an honour (*honorary degree*). **2** (of an office or its holder) unpaid.

**honorific** /ˌon-uh-**rif**-ik/ adj. **1** conferring honour. **2** (esp. of Oriental forms of speech) implying respect. **3** title of formal respect, as *Doctor, Professor*, etc.

**honour** /**on**-uh/ (also **honor**) — n. **1** high respect, public regard. **2** adherence to what is right or to an accepted standard of conduct. **3** nobleness of mind, magnanimity (*honour among thieves*). **4** thing conferred as a distinction, esp. an official award for bravery or achievement. **5** privilege, special right (*had the honour of being invited*). **6 a** exalted position. **b** (**Honour**) (prec. by *your*, *his*, etc.) title of a judge etc. **7** (foll. by *to*) person or thing that brings honour (*she is an honour to her profession*). **8 a** chastity (of a woman). **b** reputation for this. **9 a** (in *pl.*) special distinction in an examination (*got honours in English*). **b** course of degree studies more specialised than for an ordinary pass (*English Honours*). **10** (in card-games) the four or five highest-ranking cards. **11** *Golf* the right of driving off first. — v. **1** respect highly. **2** confer honour on (*honoured our city by his presence*). **3** accept or pay (a bill or cheque) when due (*didn't honour his cheque*). **4** fulfil (*I always honour my promises*). □ **do the honours** perform the duties of a host to guests etc. **in honour of** as a celebration of, in honour. **on one's honour** (usu. foll. by *to* + infin.) under a moral obligation. [Latin *honor* repute]

**honourable** adj. (also **honorable**) **1** deserving, bringing, or showing honour. **2** (**Honourable**) title indicating distinction, given to certain high officials and to members of parliament. □ **honourably** adv.

**honourable mention** n. award of merit to a candidate in an examination, a work of art, etc., not awarded a prize.

**hood** /huud/ — n. **1 a** covering for the head and neck, esp. as part of a garment. **b** separate hoodlike garment, worn over an academic gown, to indicate the wearer's degree and university. **2** folding top of a car etc. **3** hoodlike part of a cobra, seal, etc. **4** colloq. = HOODLUM. — v. cover with or as with a hood. [Old English]

**-hood** suffix forming nouns: **1** of condition or state (*childhood*; *falsehood*). **2** designating a group (*sisterhood*; *neighbourhood*). [Old English]

**hooded** adj. **1** having a hood. **2** (of an animal) having a hoodlike part (*hooded parrot*).

**hooded parrot** n. attractive NT parrot with a hooded crown.

**hooded robin** n. widespread black-and-white Australian bird.

**hoodlum** /**hood**-luhm/ n. **1** street hooligan, young thug. **2** gangster. [origin unknown]

**hoodoo** /**hoo**-doo/ — n. **1 a** bad luck. **b** thing or person that brings this. **2** voodoo. — v. **1** make unlucky (*he's hoodooed me*). **2** bewitch. [alteration of VOODOO]

**hoodwink** v. deceive, delude. [from HOOD: originally = 'blindfold']

**hooer** /hoor/ n. colloq. fool, idiot. [probably represents a British dial. pronunciation of WHORE]

**hooey** /**hoo**-ee/ n. & int. colloq. nonsense. [origin unknown]

**hoof** /huuf, hoof/ — n. (pl. **-s** or **hooves** /-vz/) **1** horny part of the foot of a horse etc. **2** colloq. human foot. — v. colloq. kick (*hoofed him out of the house*). □ **hoof it** colloq. go on foot. **hoof off** colloq. depart. **on the hoof** (of livestock) alive, not yet slaughtered. [Old English]

■ **Usage** The usual plural is *hoofs* which is preferable to *hooves*.

**hoo-ha** /**hoo**-hah/ n. colloq. commotion. [origin unknown]

**hook** /huuk/ — n. **1 a** bent or curved piece of metal etc. for catching hold of or for hanging things on. **b** (in full **fish-hook**) bent piece of wire for catching fish. **2** bend in a river or road, curved strip of land, etc. **3 a** *Cricket & Golf* hooking stroke (see sense 5 of v.). **b** *Boxing* short swinging blow with the elbow bent and rigid. **4** a trap, snare. **5** (in *pl.*) *colloq.* fingers (*keep your hooks off this — it's mine*). — *v.* **1** grasp or secure with hook(s). **2** (often foll. by *on*, *up*) **a** attach with or as with a hook (*hook this on to that*). **b** connect (apparatus etc.) to a power-source. **c** be or become attached with or as with a hook (*he's hooked on comics*). **3** catch with or as with a hook (*hooked a fish; she's hooked a husband*). **4** *colloq.* steal. **5** (in sports) send (the ball) in a curve or deviating path. **6** *Rugby* secure (the ball) and pass it backward with the foot in the scrum. □ **by hook or by crook** by one means or another, by fair means or foul. **hook it** *colloq.* run away, decamp. **off the hook 1** *colloq.* out of difficulty or trouble. **2** (of a telephone receiver) not on its rest. **3** (of clothes) ready-made. **put the hooks into** *colloq.* borrow or cadge (esp. money) from. [Old English]

**hookah** /**huuk**-uh/ *n.* oriental tobacco-pipe with a long tube by which smoke is drawn through water for cooling the smoke as it passes through. [Urdu from Arabic, = casket]

**hook and eye** *n.* small metal hook and loop as a fastener on a garment.

**hooked** *adj.* **1** hook-shaped (*hooked nose*). **2** furnished with a hook or hooks. **3** *colloq.* stolen. **4** (often foll. by *on*) *colloq.* addicted or captivated.

**hooker** *n.* **1** *Rugby* player in the front row of the scrum who tries to hook the ball. **2** *colloq.* prostitute.

**hook, line, and sinker** *adv.* entirely.

**hook-up** *n.* connection, esp. an interconnection of broadcasting equipment for special transmissions.

**hookworm** *n.* worm with hooklike mouthparts, infesting humans and animals.

**hooky** /**huuk**-ee/ *n.* (also **hookey**). □ **play hooky** *colloq.* play truant (esp. from school). [origin unknown]

**hooligan** /**hoo**-luh-guhn/ *n.* young ruffian. □ **hooliganism** *n.* [origin unknown]

**hoon** /hoon/ *n.* *colloq.* **1** = HOOLIGAN. **2** a show-off, exhibitionist. **3** = BLUDGER. [origin unknown]

**hoop** — *n.* **1** circular band of metal, wood, etc., esp. for encircling and binding the staves of barrels etc. **2** ring bowled along by a child, or for circus performers to jump through. — *v.* bind or encircle with hoop(s). □ **be put** (or **go**) **through the hoop** (or **hoops**) undergo rigorous testing. **jump through (the) hoops** obey without question (*the boss makes us all jump through hoops*). [Old English]

**hoopla** *n.* fairground game with rings thrown to encircle a prize.

**hoop pine** *n.* tall Australian conifer, so called from the hoops of bark which remain conspicuously on the forest floor.

**hooray¹** /huh-**ray**/ *int.* = HURRAH.

**hooray²** *int.* = HOOROO.

**hooroo** /**hoo**-roo/ *int. & n. colloq.* conventional form of farewell, goodbye ('*hooroo!*' *he said as he left; see my hooroos to all*).

**hoot** — *n.* **1** owl's cry. **2** sound made by a car's horn etc. **3** shout expressing scorn or disapproval. **4** *colloq.* **a** laughter. **b** cause of this. **5** (also **two hoots**) *colloq.* anything at all, in the slightest degree (*don't care a hoot; doesn't matter two hoots*). — *v.* **1** (of an owl, horn, etc.) utter or make hoot(s). **2** greet or drive away with scornful hoots. **3** laugh raucously (*hooted with laughter*). **4** sound (a car horn etc.). [imitative]

**hooter** *n.* **1** thing that hoots, esp. a car's horn or a factory siren. **2** *colloq.* nose.

**hoover** — *n. propr.* vacuum cleaner. — *v.* **1** (also *absol.*) clean with a vacuum cleaner. **2** (foll. by *up*) **a** suck up with a vacuum cleaner. **b** clean a room etc. with a vacuum cleaner. [name of the manufacturer of one brand of this]

**hooves** *pl.* of HOOF.

**hop¹** — *v.* (**-pp-**) **1** (of a bird, frog, etc.) spring with two or all feet at once. **2** (of a person) jump on one foot. **3** cross a ditch, fence, etc. by hopping (*hopped the fence*). **4** *colloq.* **a** go, esp. quickly (*hop over to the butcher's and get me some mince*). **b** take a quick flight or trip (*hopped over to Tassie for the day*). **5** *colloq.* **a** get into or out of (a car, train, etc.) (*hop in! —there's room for one more; I'm hopping off at Werribee*). **b** obtain a lift (*can I hop a ride with you?*) — *n.* **1** hopping movement. **2** *colloq.* informal dance. **3 a** short flight in an aircraft. **b** distance travelled by air without landing (*Melbourne to London in one hop*). **c** stage of a flight or journey (*our first hop's from Melbourne to Singapore*). □ **hop in for one's chop** *colloq.* make sure one gets one's fair share etc.; seize an opportunity. **hop into** *colloq.* **1** begin (a meal, activity, etc.) with alacrity (*hopped into the tucker*). **2** make a quick change of clothes (*hang on till I hop into my jeans!*). **hop it!** *colloq.* go away!, scram! **hop on (to) the bandwagon** see BANDWAGON. **hop to it** (usu. as *imper.*) get a move on; act immediately. **hop up and down** *colloq.* show impatience, rage, etc. **on the hop** *colloq.* **1** unprepared (*caught us on the hop*). **2** bustling busily about (*always on the hop*). [Old English]

**hop²** *n.* **1** climbing plant bearing cones. **2** (in *pl.*) **a** its ripe cones, used to give beer its bitter flavour. **b** beer. □ **on the hops** *colloq.* engaged in a drinking session. [Low German or Dutch]

**hop-bush** *n.* any shrub of the widespread Australian genus *Dodonaea*, with often highly coloured and showy three-angled fruits: the bitter fruits of some species were used by the early settlers as a substitute for hops in beer-making.

**hope** — *n.* **1** expectation and desire for a thing. **2** person or thing giving cause for hope (*he's the hope of our Olympic swimming team*). **3** what is hoped for. — *v.* (**-ping**) **1** feel hope. **2** expect and desire. **3** feel fairly confident. □ **hope against hope** cling to a mere possibility. **not a hope** no chance at all. **some hope!** = *not a hope*. [Old English]

**hopeful** — *adj.* **1** feeling hope. **2** causing or inspiring hope. **3** likely to succeed, promising. — *n.* person likely to succeed (*he's the young hopeful of our family*).

**hopefully** *adv.* **1** in a hopeful manner. **2** it is to be hoped (*hopefully, we will succeed*).

■ **Usage** The use of *hopefully* in sense 2 is common, but is considered incorrect by some people.

**hopeless** *adj.* **1** feeling no hope. **2** admitting no hope (*hopeless case*). **3** incompetent (*hopeless at tennis*). **4** not possible to solve or resolve (*hopeless mess*). □ **hopelessly** *adv.* **hopelessness** *n.*

**hopper** *n.* **1** person or animal that hops. **2** hopping insect, esp. a flea or young locust. **3** container (orig. having a hopping motion) tapering downward to an opening for discharging its contents.

**hopping mad** *predic. adj. colloq.* very angry.

**hopping mouse** *n.* any of several native mice of drier Australia having long hind legs and a rapid kangaroo-like hopping gait.

**hopscotch** *n.* children's game of hopping over squares marked on the ground to retrieve a stone etc. [from HOP¹, SCOTCH]

**hop, step, and jump** *n.* **1** = TRIPLE JUMP. **2** short distance (*lives only a hop, step, and jump away*).

**horde** *n.* usu. *derog.* **1** large group, multitude. **2** moving swarm or pack (of insects, animals). [Turkish *ordū* camp]

**horizon** /huh-**ruy**-zuhn/ *n.* **1** line at which the earth and sky appear to meet. **2** limit of mental perception, experience, interest, etc. □ **on the horizon** (of an event) just imminent or becoming apparent. [Greek *horizō* bound]

**horizontal¹** /ˌho-ruh-**zon**-tuhl/ — *adj.* **1** parallel to the plane of the horizon, at right angles to the vertical. **2** of or concerned with the same work, status, etc. (*it was a horizontal move rather than promotion*). — *n.* horizontal line, plane, etc. □ **horizontality** /-tal-uh-tee/ *n.* **horizontally** *adv.*

**horizontal²** *n.* (also **horizontal scrub**) small tree or shrub of Tasmania, the trunk of which grows horizontally on ageing, the branches doing likewise and interlocking, thus forming an impenetrable thicket.

**hormone** /**haw**-mohn/ *n.* **1** regulatory substance produced in an organism and transported in tissue fluids to stimulate cells or tissues into action. **2** similar synthetic substance. □ **hormonal** /haw-**moh**-nuhl/ *adj.* [Greek *hormaō* impel]

**hormone replacement therapy** *n.* treatment to relieve menopausal symptoms by boosting a woman's oestrogen levels.

**horn** *n.* **1 a** hard outgrowth, often curved and pointed, on the head of esp. hoofed animals. **b** each of two deciduous branched appendages on the head of (esp. male) deer. **c** hornlike projection on animals, e.g. a snail's tentacle. **2 a** substance of which true horns are made. **b** any similar substance, eg. corns, hoofs, toenails, etc. **3** *Mus.* **a** = FRENCH HORN. **b** horn player. **c** wind instrument played by lip vibration, orig. made of horn, now usu. of brass. **4** instrument sounding a warning (*foghorn; car horn*). **5** receptacle or instrument made of horn (*drinking horn*). **6** horn-shaped projection. **7** extremity of the moon or other crescent. **8** arm of a river etc. □ **horn in** *colloq.* intrude, interfere (*horned in on our tête-à-tête*). **lock horns with a person** enter into an argument, wrangle, etc. **on the horns of a dilemma** faced with a decision involving equally unfavourable alternatives. □ **horned** *adj.* **hornist** *n.* (in sense 3 of *n.*). [Old English]

**hornblende** /**hawn**-blend/ *n.* dark brown, black, or green mineral occurring in many rocks. [German]

**hornet** /**haw**-nuht/ *n.* large wasp capable of inflicting a serious sting. □ **mad as a hornet** *colloq.* in a rage. **stir up a hornet's nest** provoke or cause serious trouble or hostile opposition. [Low German or Dutch]

**horn of plenty** *n.* a cornucopia.

**hornpipe** *n.* **1** lively dance (esp. associated with sailors). **2** music for this.

**horn-rimmed** *adj.* (esp. of spectacles) having rims made of horn or a similar substance.

**horny** — adj. (**-ier, -iest**) **1** of or like horn. **2** hard like horn (horny-handed). **3** colloq. sexually excited. — n. bullock (milling mob of hornies). □ **horniness** n.

**horology** /huh-**rol**-uh-jee/ n. art of measuring time or making clocks, watches, etc. □ **horological** /ˌho-ruh-**loj**-i-kuhl/ adj. [Greek hōra time]

**horoscope** /**ho**-ruh-ˌskohp/ n. **1** forecast of a person's future from a diagram showing the relative positions of the stars and planets at his or her birth. **2** such a diagram. [Greek hōra time, skopos observer]

**horrendous** /huh-**ren**-duhs, ˌho-/ adj. horrifying. □ **horrendously** adv. [Latin: related to HORRIBLE]

**horrible** /**ho**-ruh-buhl/ adj. **1** causing or likely to cause horror. **2** colloq. unpleasant (horrible weather). □ **horribly** adv. [Latin horreo bristle, shudder at]

**horrid** /**ho**-ruhd/ adj. **1** horrible, revolting. **2** colloq. unpleasant (horrid weather).

**horrific** /huh-**rif**-ik, ho-/ adj. horrifying. □ **horrifically** adv.

**horrify** /**ho**-ruh-ˌfuy/ v. (**-ies, -ied**) arouse horror in; shock, scandalise. □ **horrifying** adj.

**horror** /**ho**-ruh/ — n. **1** painful feeling of loathing and fear. **2** (often foll. by of) intense dislike (a horror of being photographed). **3 a** person or thing causing horror. **b** colloq. bad or mischievous person etc. (he's a little horror). **4** (in pl.; prec. by the) **a** fit of disgust, terror, etc. (leeches give me the horrors). **b** = DELIRIUM TREMENS. **5** colloq. thing considered ugly, tasteless, etc. (that tie is a horror). — attrib. adj. (of films etc.) designed to interest to arousing feelings of horror.

**hors d'oeuvre** /aw-**derv**/ n. food served as an appetiser at the start of a meal. [French, = outside the work]

**horse** — n. **1 a** large four-legged mammal with flowing mane and tail, used for riding and to carry and pull loads. **b** adult male horse; stallion or gelding. **2** vaulting-block. **3** supporting frame (clothes-horse). — v. (**-sing**) (foll. by about, around) fool around; play or act roughly (stop horsing around). □ **back the wrong horse** give support to the wrong or losing side. **change horses in midstream** reverse a policy or a decision etc. after one has been acting on it. **flog a dead horse** see FLOG. **from the horse's mouth** (of information etc.) from the original or an authoritative source. **get on** (or **off**) **one's high horse** be (or cease to be) arrogant, pompous. **hold your horses** wait a bit; don't be im-

petuous. **horse of another** (or **different**) **colour** an altogether different matter; something else again. **look a gift-horse in the mouth** see GIFT. [Old English]

**horse duffer** n. hist. horse thief. □ **horse duffing** n.

**horseflesh** n. **1** flesh of a horse, esp. as food. **2** horses collectively.

**horse-float** n. closed trailer or van for transporting horse(s).

**horsehair** n. hair from the mane or tail of a horse, used for padding etc.

**horse laugh** n. loud, raucous (esp. jeering) laugh.

**horse mackerel** n. any of several marine fish, esp. the jack mackerel and the bonito, abundant along the east coast of Australia.

**horseman** n. (fem. **horsewoman**) **1** rider on horseback. **2** skilled rider. □ **horsemanship** n.

**horse-paddock** n. enclosure for horses, usu. small and for horses in regular use.

**horse plant** n. team of working horses.

**horseplay** n. boisterous play.

**horsepower** n. (pl. same) imperial unit of power (about 750 watts), esp. for measuring the power of an engine.

**horse race** n. race between horses with riders. □ **horse racing** n.

**horseradish** /**haws**-ˌrad-ish/ n. plant with a pungent root used to make a sauce.

**horseradish tree** n. tall, pyramidal tree of drier Australia with poplar-like leaves and green bell-shaped fruit: the bark and leaves have a pungent taste.

**horse sense** n. colloq. plain common sense.

**horseshoe** n. **1** U-shaped iron shoe for a horse. **2** thing of this shape.

**horsewhip** — n. whip for driving horses. — v. (**-pp-**) beat with a horsewhip.

**horsy** adj. (**-ier, -iest**) **1** of or relating to a horse (horsy smell). **2** concerned with or devoted to horses. **3** resembling a horse (with large face and teeth etc.). □ **horsiness** n.

**hortatory** /**haw**-tuh-tuh-ree, haw-**tay**-tuh-ree/ adj. (also **hortative** /**haw**-tuh-tiv/) tending or serving to encourage, exhort (gave the team a hortatory talk). [Latin hortor exhort]

**horticulture** /**haw**-tuh-ˌkul-chuh/ n. art of garden cultivation. □ **horticultural** /-**kul**-chuh-ruhl/ adj. **horticulturalist** n. **horticulturist** n. [Latin hortus garden, CULTURE]

**hosanna** /hoh-**zan**-uh/ n. & int. shout of adoration (Matt. 21:9, 15, etc.). [Hebrew]

**hose** /hohz/ — n. **1** (also **hosepipe**)

flexible tube for conveying water. **2 a** (*collect.*; as *pl.*) stockings and socks. **b** *hist.* breeches (*doublet and hose*). — *v.* (**-sing**) (often foll. by *down*) **1** water, spray, or drench with a hose. **2** *colloq.* reduce or defuse (*tried to hose down the agitators before the situation turned ugly*). [Old English]

**hosier** /hoh-zee-uh/ *n.* dealer in hosiery.

**hosiery** *n.* stockings and socks.

**hospice** /hos-puhs/ *n.* **1** home for people who are ill (esp. terminally) or destitute. **2** lodging for travellers, esp. one kept by a religious order. [Latin: related to HOST[2]]

**hospitable** /hos-**pit**-uh-buhl/ *adj.* **1** giving hospitality. **2** (foll. by *to*) open or receptive, esp. to new ideas etc. □ **hospitably** *adv.* [Latin *hospito* entertain: related to HOST[2]]

**hospital** /**hos**-puh-tuhl/ *n.* **1** institution providing medical and surgical treatment and nursing care for ill and injured people. **2** *hist.* hospice. [Latin: related to HOST[2]]

**hospitalise** /**hos**-puh-tuh-luyz/ *v.* (also **-ize**) (**-sing** or **-zing**) send or admit (a patient) to hospital. □ **hospitalisation** /-**zay**-shuhn/ *n.*

**hospitality** /ˌhos-puh-**tal**-uh-tee/ *n.* friendly and generous reception and entertainment of guests or strangers.

**host¹** /hohst/ *n.* (usu. foll. by *of*) large number of people or things (*host of matters to attend to*). [Latin *hostis* enemy, army]

**host²** /hohst/ — *n.* **1** person who receives or entertains another as a guest. **2** compère. **3** *Biol.* animal or plant having a parasite. **4** recipient of a transplanted organ etc. **5** (in full **host computer**) main or controlling computer in a network. — *v.* be host to (a person) or of (an event). [Latin *hospes hospitis* host, guest]

**host³** /hohst/ *n.* (usu. prec. by *the*; (often **Host**) bread consecrated in the sacrifice of the Mass. [Latin *hostia* victim]

**hostage** /**hos**-tij/ *n.* person seized or held as security for the fulfilment of a condition. [Latin *obses obsidis* hostage]

**hostel** /**hos**-tuhl, hos-**tel**/ *n.* **1** house of residence or lodging for students, nurses, etc. **2** = YOUTH HOSTEL. [medieval Latin: related to HOSPITAL]

**hostess** /**hohs**-tuhs, hohs-**tes**/ *n.* **1** woman who receives or entertains a guest. **2** woman employed to entertain customers at a nightclub etc. **3** female flight attendant. [related to HOST[2]]

**hostie** /**hohs**-tee/ *n.* *colloq.* female flight attendant. [abbreviation of HOSTESS]

**hostile** /**hos**-tuyl/ *adj.* **1** of an enemy (*hostile territory*). **2** (often foll. by *to*) unfriendly, opposed (*hostile mob; hostile to my wishes*). **3** *colloq.* angry (*hostile about the size of her pension*). □ **hostile on** *colloq.* angry with (*hostile on the neighbours for playing loud music at night*). **go hostile at** *colloq.* express anger or annoyance towards (*went all hostile at me for criticising his cat*). □ **hostilely** *adv.* [Latin: related to HOST[1]]

**hostility** /hos-**til**-uh-tee/ *n.* (*pl.* **-ies**) **1** being hostile, enmity. **2** state of warfare. **3** (in *pl.*) acts of warfare.

**hot** — *adj.* (**hotter**, **hottest**) **1** having a high temperature; giving off heat. **2** (of chilli, food, etc.) causing a burning sensation to the tongue (*red hot Sri Lankan curries*). **3** (of a person) feeling heat. **4** violent (*hot fighting*). **5** (of colours) with red predominating; intense (*hot pink*). **6** (of games etc.) close to what one is seeking (*you're getting hot*). **7 a** ardent, passionate, excited (*hot temper; hot embrace*). **b** (often foll. by *for*, *on*) eager, keen (*in hot pursuit*). **c** angry or upset. **d** *colloq.* exciting; trendy (*hot party; hot new clothes*). **8** (of news etc.) fresh, recent. **9** (of a trail, scent, etc.) fresh, recent. **10 a** (of a player, competitor, or feat) very skilful, formidable. **b** (of a competitor in a race etc.) strongly favoured to win (*hot favourite*). **11** (foll. by *on*) knowledgable about. **12** *colloq.* **a** (of goods) stolen. **b** (of persons) wanted by the police. **13** radioactive. **14** *colloq.* (of information) unusually reliable (*hot tip*). **15** (of motor cycles and cars) modified and tuned for high speed (*hot rod*). — *v.* (**-tt-**) (usu. foll. by *up*) **1** make or become hot. **2** make or become more active, exciting, or dangerous. **3** escalate or be escalated (*the war's hotting up*). **4** modify (a car etc.) to achieve high speed. □ **a bit hot** *colloq.* **1** unfair; a bit much. **2** overexpensive (*$10? — that's a bit hot*). **hot and bothered** agitated; flustered. **hot under the collar** angry, resentful, embarrassed. **like hot cakes** see CAKE. **make it (or things) hot for a person** persecute a person. **not so** (or **not too**) **hot** *colloq.* only mediocre; so-so. **running hot 1** achieving great success. **2** (of the telephone) ringing repeatedly. □ **hotly** *adv.* **hotness** *n.* **hottish** *adj.* [Old English]

**hot air** *n.* *colloq.* empty or boastful talk.

**hotbed** *n.* (foll. by *of*) environment conducive to (vice, intrigue, etc.).

**hot-blooded** *adj.* ardent, passionate; excitable.

**hotchpotch** /**hoch**-poch/ *n.* (also **hodgepodge** /**hoj**-poj/ ) confused mixture or jumble, esp. of ideas. [French *hochepot* shake pot]

**hot dog** *n. colloq.* frankfurt in a soft bread roll.

**hotel** /hoh-**tel**/ *n.* **1** public house, pub. **2** (usu. licensed) establishment providing accommodation and meals for payment. [French: related to HOSTEL]

**hotelier** /hoh-**tel**-ee-uh/ *n.* hotel-keeper.

**hot flush** see FLUSH[1].

**hotfoot** — *adv.* in eager haste. — *v.* hurry eagerly (esp. *hotfoot it*).

**hothead** *n.* impetuous or easily angered person. □ **hot-headed** *adj.* **hot-headedness** *n.*

**hothouse** — *n.* **1** heated (mainly glass) building for rearing tender plants. **2** environment conducive to the rapid growth or development of something. — *adj.* **1** of or relating to a tender plant needing hothouse treatment. **2** *derog.* (of a person) over-delicate; over-protected (*he's a real hothouse plant*).

**hotline** *n.* direct exclusive telephone etc. line, esp. for emergencies.

**hot money** *n.* capital frequently transferred.

**hotplate** *n.* electrically heated metal plate etc. (or a set of these) for cooking food or keeping it hot.

**hotpot** *n.* casserole of meat and vegetables (esp. potato).

**hot potato** *n. colloq.* contentious or highly controversial matter or person.

**hot rod** *n.* vehicle modified to have extra power and speed.

**hot seat** *n. colloq.* **1** position of difficult responsibility. **2** electric chair.

**hotshot** *colloq.* (often sarcastic) — *n.* important or exceptionally able person. — *attrib. adj.* important; able; expert; suddenly prominent.

**hot spot** *n.* **1** small region that is relatively hot. **2** lively or dangerous place.

**hot stuff** *n. colloq.* **1** formidably capable or important person or thing. **2** sexually attractive person.

**hot-tempered** *adj.* impulsively angry.

**hot water** *n. colloq.* difficulty, disgrace, or trouble.

**hot-water bottle** *n.* (usu. rubber) container filled with hot water to warm a bed.

**hot wind** *n.* extremely hot dry wind blowing periodically from the arid interior of Australia during summer.

**houmous** var. of HUMMUS.

**hound** — *n.* **1** dog used in hunting. **2** any dog. **3** *colloq.* despicable man. — *v.* harass or pursue. [Old English]

**hour** /owuh/ *n.* **1** twenty-fourth part of a day and night, 60 minutes. **2** time of day, point in time (*a late hour*; *what is the hour?*). **3** (in *pl.* with preceding numerals in form 18.00, 20.30, etc.) this number of hours and minutes past midnight on the 24-hour clock (*will assemble at 20.00 hours*). **4 a** period for a specific purpose (*lunch hour*; *keep regular hours*). **b** (in *pl.*) fixed working or open period (*office hours*; *opening hours*). **5** short period of time (*spent an idle hour browsing*). **6** special moment (*his hour has arrived*). **7** present time (*question of the hour*). **8** time for action etc. (*the hour has come*). **9** expressing distance by travelling time (*we are an hour from Brisbane*). **10** *RC Ch.* prayers to be said at one of seven fixed times of day (*book of hours*). **11** (prec. by *the*) each time o'clock of a whole number of hours (*buses leave on the hour*; *on the half hour*; *at a quarter past the hour*). □ **after hours** after closing-time. [Greek *hōra*]

**hourglass** *n.* two vertically connected glass bulbs containing sand taking an hour to pass from upper to lower bulb.

**houri** /**hoor**-ree, **hoo**-ree/ *n.* (*pl.* **-s**) beautiful young woman, esp. of the Muslim Paradise. [Persian from Arabic, = dark-eyed]

**hourly** — *adj.* **1** done or occurring every hour. **2** frequent. **3** reckoned hour by hour (*hourly wage*). — *adv.* **1** every hour. **2** frequently.

**house** — *n.* /hows/ (*pl.* /**how**-zuhz/) **1** building for human habitation. **2** building for a special purpose or for animals or goods (*opera-house*; *hen-house*). **3 a** religious community. **b** its buildings. **4** (prec. by *the*) principal residence on a rural property (as distinct from accommodation provided for employees). **5 a** body of pupils living in the same building at a boarding-school. **b** such a building. **c** division of a day-school for games, competitions, etc. **6** royal family or dynasty (*House of York*). **7 a** firm or institution (*the house of Chanel*). **b** its premises. **8 a** legislative or deliberative assembly (*House of Representatives*). **b** building for this. **9** audience or performance in a theatre etc. (*full house; second house starts at 7 p.m.*). **10** *Astrol.* twelfth part of the heavens. — *adj.* of or relating to a house (*house cat; house guest*). — *v.* /howz/ (**-sing**) **1** provide with a house or other accommodation. **2** store (goods etc.). **3** enclose or encase (a part or fitting). **4** fix in a socket, mortise, etc. □ **built like the side of a house** *colloq.* (of a person) **1** extremely large and strong. **2** obese. **keep house** provide for or manage a household. **like a house on fire 1** vigorously, fast. **2** successfully, excellently. **on the house** free. **put** (or **set**) **one's house in order** make necessary reforms. **run of the house** complete freedom of the home given to a guest. **safe as houses** thoroughly or completely safe. [Old English]

**house arrest** n. detention in one's own house, not in prison.

**houseboat** n. boat equipped for living in.

**housebound** adj. confined to one's house through illness etc.

**housebreaking** /hows-,bray-king/ n. act of breaking into a house, esp. to rob (amounting to a crime at common law). □ **housebreaker** n.

**housebroken** adj. (of animals) trained to be clean in the house.

**housecoat** n. woman's informal indoor coat or gown.

**housefly** n. common fly breeding in decaying organic matter and often entering houses.

**house guest** n. guest staying for some days in one's home.

**household** — n. **1** occupants of a house as a unit. **2** house and its affairs. — adj. **1** of or relating to a household (household expenses). **2** extremely well known; common (household word).

**householder** n. **1** person who owns or rents a house. **2** head of a household.

**household word** n. (also **household name**) **1** familiar name or saying. **2** familiar person or thing.

**house-husband** n. man who does a wife's traditional household duties.

**housekeeper** n. person, esp. a woman, employed to manage a household.

**housekeeping** n. **1** management of household affairs. **2** money allowed for this. **3** operations of maintenance, record-keeping, etc., in an organisation. **4** Computing actions performed within a program or system to maintain internal orderliness.

**house lights** n.pl. lights in a theatre auditorium.

**housemaid** n. female servant in a house.

**house mouse** n. common domestic mouse.

**House of Assembly** n. lower legislative house in SA and Tasmania.

**house of cards** n. insecure scheme etc.

**House of Representatives** n. lower legislative house of the federal parliament of Australia.

**house paddock** n. paddock adjacent to the house, usu. for horses.

**house-proud** adj. attentive to, or unduly preoccupied with, the care and appearance of the home.

**housetop** n. roof of a house. □ **shout** etc. **from the housetops** announce publicly.

**house-trained** adj. (of animals) trained to be clean in the house.

**house-warming** n. party celebrating a move to a new home.

**housewife** n. **1** woman who manages a household and usu. does not have a full-time paid job. **2** case for needles, thread, etc. □ **housewifely** adj. [from HOUSE, WIFE = woman]

**house wine** n. bulk wine selected by the management of a restaurant, hotel, etc. to be offered at a special price.

**housework** n. regular housekeeping work, e.g. cleaning and cooking.

**housey-housey** /,how-zee-**how**-zee/ n. (also **housie-housie**, **housie**) = BINGO.

**housing** /**how**-zing/ n. **1 a** dwelling-houses collectively. **b** provision of these. **2** shelter, lodging. **3** rigid casing for machinery etc. **4** hole or niche cut in one piece of wood for another to fit into.

**hove** past of HEAVE.

**hovea** /**hoh**-vee-uh/ n. any of twelve Australian shrubs bearing masses of purple or blue pea-flowers in spring. [A.P. Hove, Polish botanist (d. 1798)]

**hovel** /**hov**-uhl/ n. small miserable dwelling. [origin unknown]

**hover** /**hov**-uh/ — v. **1** (of a bird etc.) remain in one place in the air. **2** (often foll. by about, round) wait close at hand, linger. **3** waver (hovering between life and death). — n. **1** hovering. **2** state of suspense. [obsolete hove hover]

**hovercraft** n. (pl. same) vehicle travelling on a cushion of air provided by a downward blast.

**how** — interrog. adv. **1** by what means, in what way (how do you do it?; tell me how you do it; how could you?). **2** in what condition, esp. of health (how are you?; how do things stand?). **3 a** to what extent (how far is it?; how would you like to take my place?; how we laughed!). **b** to what extent good or well, what . . . like (how was the film?; how did they play?). — rel. adv. in whatever way, as (do it how you can). — conj. colloq. that (told us how he'd been in India). □ **and how!** colloq. (chiefly used ironically or intensively) very much so (she can sing — and how!). **how about** would you like (how about a quick swim?). **how about that!** exclamation indicating surprise or triumph, sometimes used ironically. **how are you going?** (in speech usu. how-ya-goin'?) (or **how goes it?**) informal version of how do you do? **how come?** colloq. why?; how did it come about that? (how come you weren't at the party last night?). **how do you do?**

a formal greeting. **how many** what number. **how much 1** what amount. **2** what price. **3** (as *interrog.*) *joc.* what?, come again? (*'She's a hedonist.' 'A how much?'*). **how's that? 1** what is your opinion or explanation of that? **2** (also **howzat?**) *Cricket* (said to an umpire) is the batsman out or not? **how's things** (or **tricks**)? informal version of *how do you do?* [Old English]

**howdah** /**how**-duh/ *n.* (usu. canopied) seat for riding on an elephant or camel. [Urdu *hawda*]

**how-do-you-do** *n.* (also **how-de-do**) (*pl.* **-dos**) awkward or tricky situation (*this is a fine how-de-do!*).

**however** /how-**ev**-uh/ — *adv.* **1 a** in whatever way (*do it however you want*). **b** to whatever extent (*must go however inconvenient*). **2** (as an emphatic) in what way, by what means (*however did that happen?*). — *conj.* nevertheless; and yet (*was very tired, however she kept on working*).

**howitzer** /**how**-it-suh/ *n.* short gun for the high-angle firing of shells. [Czech *houfnice* catapult]

**howl** — *n.* **1** long loud doleful cry of a dog etc. **2** prolonged wailing noise, e.g. as made by a strong wind. **3** loud cry of pain, rage, derision, or laughter. — *v.* **1** make a howl. **2** weep loudly. **3** utter with a howl. **4** drive away with howls (*howled him off the stage*). □ **howl down** prevent (a speaker) from being heard by howls of derision. [imitative]

**howler** *n. colloq.* glaring mistake.

**howsoever** /ˌhow-soh-**ev**-uh/ *adv. formal* **1** in whatsoever way. **2** to whatsoever extent.

**hoy**[1] *int.* used to call attention. □ **give a person a hoy** *colloq.* **1** attract his or her attention by calling out. **2** telephone him or her (*give me a hoy tomorrow*). [natural cry]

**hoy**[2] *n.* game of chance resembling bingo, using playing cards.

**hoya** /**hoi**-uh/ *n.* any of over 200 species of the genus *Hoya* native to tropical Asia and Australia, being climbers with fleshy leaves and clusters of thick, waxy, white, pink, yellow, or maroon flowers, sometimes scented. [F.T. *Hoy*, English gardener (d. 1821)]

**hoyden** /**hoi**-duhn/ *n.* boisterous girl. [Dutch *heiden*: related to HEATHEN]

**Hoyts** /hoits/ *n.* □ **the man outside Hoyts** *joc.* **1** mythical person who is the authority for reports, rumours, etc. (*must be true, but — heard it from the man outside Hoyts*). **2** important person. [orig. the commissionaire outside Hoyt's Theatre in Melbourne]

**h.p.** *abbr.* (also **hp**) **1** horsepower. **2** hire purchase.

**HQ** *abbr.* headquarters.

**HTML** *abbr. Computing* hypertext markup language.

**hub** *n.* **1** central part of a wheel, rotating on or with the axle. **2 a** centre of interest, activity, etc. **b** focal point, point of central importance (*Canberra, the hub of Australia*). [origin uncertain]

**hubbub** /**hub**-ub/ *n.* **1** confused noise of talking. **2** disturbance. [perhaps of Irish origin]

**hubris** /**hyoo**-bruhs/ *n.* arrogant pride or presumption. □ **hubristic** /-**bris**-tik/ *adj.* [Greek]

**huckster** /**huk**-stuh/ — *n.* aggressive salesman; hawker. — *v.* **1** haggle. **2** hawk (goods). [Low German]

**huddle** /**hud**-uhl/ — *v.* (**-ling**) **1** (often foll. by *up*) crowd together; nestle closely. **2** (often foll. by *up*) curl one's body into a small space. **3** heap together in a muddle. — *n.* **1** confused or crowded mass. **2** *colloq.* **a** close or secret conference (esp. in **go into a huddle**). **b** (in team games) a gathering of team members to receive instructions during a break in play. [perhaps from Low German]

**hue** /hyoo/ *n.* **1** colour, tint. **2** variety or shade of colour. [Old English]

**hue and cry** *n.* public clamour or outcry. [French *huer* shout]

**huff** — *n. colloq.* fit of petty annoyance (*got into a huff*). — *v.* **1** blow air, steam, etc. **2** (esp. **huff and puff**) bluster self-importantly but ineffectually. □ **in a huff** annoyed and offended (*walked off in a huff*). □ **huffish** *adj.* [imitative of blowing]

**huffy** *adj.* (**-ier, -iest**) **1** apt to take offence. **2** offended. □ **huffily** *adv.* **huffiness** *n.*

**hug** — *v.* (**-gg-**) **1** squeeze tightly in one's arms, esp. with affection. **2** (of a bear) squeeze (a person) between its forelegs. **3** keep close to (the shore, kerb, etc.). **4** fit tightly around (*a dress that hugs the body*). **5** cling to (prejudices etc.). — *n.* **1** strong clasp with the arms; an embrace. **2** squeezing grip in wrestling. [probably Scandinavian]

**huge** /hyooj/ *adj.* **1** extremely large; enormous. **2** (of an abstract thing) very great (*huge success*). □ **hugeness** *n.* [French *ahuge*]

**hugely** *adv.* **1** extremely (*hugely successful*). **2** very much (*enjoyed it hugely*).

**hugger-mugger** /**hug**-uh-ˌmug-uh/ — *adj. & adv.* **1** in secret. **2** confused; in confusion. — *n.* **1** secrecy. **2** confusion. [origin uncertain]

**Hughie** /**hyoo**-ee/ *n. joc.* the water god up above, as controlling rain and good waves for surfers (*surfing will be great — I've spoken to Hughie about it*). □ **send her down, Hughie!** let there be rain! **send 'em up** (or **whip 'em up**), **Hughie!** let the waves be awe-inspiring! [origin unknown]

**hula** /**hoo**-luh/ *n.* (also **hula-hula**) Polynesian dance performed by women, with flowing arm movements. [Hawaiian]

**hulk** *n.* **1** body of a dismantled ship. **2** *hist.* this as a prison for convicts. **3** large clumsy-looking person or thing. [Old English]

**hulking** *adj.* bulky; large and clumsy.

**hull¹** *n.* body of a ship, airship, etc. [perhaps related to HOLD²]

**hull²** — *n.* outer covering of a fruit, esp. the pod of peas and beans, the husk of grain, or the green calyx of a strawberry. — *v.* remove the hulls from (fruit etc.). [Old English]

**hullabaloo** /ˌhul-uh-buh-**loo**/ *n.* uproar. [reduplication of *hallo*, *hullo*, etc.]

**hullo** var. of HELLO.

**hum¹** — *v.* (**-mm-**) **1** make a low steady continuous sound like a bee. **2** sing with closed lips. **3** utter a slight inarticulate sound (in hesitation, embarrassment, etc.). **4** *colloq.* be active (*really made things hum*). **5** *colloq.* smell unpleasantly. — *int.* expressing hesitation or dissent. — *n.* **1** humming sound. **2** *colloq.* bad smell. □ **hum and haw** (or **ha**) hesitate; be indecisive. [imitative]

**hum²** *colloq.* — *n.* habitual borrower or scrounger. — *v.* cadge. □ **hummer** *n.* **humming** *n.* [origin unknown]

**human** /**hyoo**-muhn/ — *adj.* **1** of or belonging to the species *Homo sapiens*. **2** consisting of human beings (*the human race*). **3** of or characteristic of humankind, esp. as being weak, fallible, etc. (*is only human*). **4** showing warmth, sympathy, etc. (*is very human*). — *n.* human being. [Latin *humanus*]

**human being** *n.* man, woman, or child.

**humane** /hyoo-**mayn**/ *adj.* **1** benevolent, compassionate. **2** inflicting the minimum of pain. **3** (of learning) tending to civilise or confer refinement (*literature is one of the humane studies*). □ **humanely** *adv.* **humaneness** *n.*

**humanise** *v.* (also **-ize**) (**-sing** or **-zing**) make human or humane. □ **humanisation** /ˌ-**zay**-shuhn/ *n.* [French: related to HUMAN]

**humanism** /**hyoo**-muh-ˌniz-uhm/ *n.* **1** non-religious philosophy based on liberal human values. **2** (often **Humanism**) literary culture, esp. that of the Renaissance. □ **humanist** *n.* **humanistic** /-nis-tik/ *adj.*

**humanitarian** /hyoo-ˌman-uh-**tair**-ree-uhn/ — *n.* person who seeks to promote human welfare. — *adj.* of humanitarians. □ **humanitarianism** *n.*

**humanity** /hyoo-**man**-uh-tee/ *n.* (*pl.* **-ies**) **1 a** the human race. **b** human beings collectively. **c** being human. **2** humaneness, benevolence. **3** (in *pl.*) subjects concerned with human culture, e.g. language, literature, and history.

**humankind** *n.* human beings collectively.

**humanly** *adv.* **1** by human means (*if it is humanly possible*). **2** in a human manner.

**human nature** *n.* general characteristics and feelings of mankind.

**human rights** *n.pl.* rights held to be common to all human beings irrespective of race, status, etc.

**humble** /**hum**-buhl/ — *adj.* **1** meek; without pride. **2** having or showing low self-esteem. **b** offered with or affected by such an estimate (or pretence of such an estimate) (*if you want my humble opinion*). **3** of low social or political rank (*of humble origins*). **4** modest in size, pretensions, etc. (*humble cottage*; *humble volume of verse*). — *v.* (**-ling**) **1** bring low; abase. **2** lower the rank or status of. **3** make humble (*was humbled by the knowledge that he had erred*). □ **eat humble pie** apologise humbly; accept humiliation. □ **humbleness** *n.* **humbly** *adv.* [Latin *humilis*: related to HUMUS]

**humbug** — *n.* **1 a** lying or deception; hypocrisy; nonsense. **b** (in Aboriginal English) trouble, difficulty. **2** impostor. **3** hard-boiled striped peppermint sweet. — *v.* (**-gg-**) **1 a** be or behave like an impostor. **b** be sexually predatory (esp. of a white man with an Aboriginal woman). **2** deceive, hoax. □ **humbugger** *n.* **humbuggery** *n.* [origin unknown]

**humdinger** /**hum**-ˌding-uh/ *n. colloq.* excellent or remarkable person or thing. [origin unknown]

**humdrum** /**hum**-drum/ *adj.* commonplace, dull, monotonous. [a reduplication of HUM]

**humerus** /**hyoo**-muh-ruhs/ *n.* (*pl.* **-ri** /-ˌruy/) bone of the upper arm. □ **humeral** *adj.* [Latin, = shoulder]

**humid** /**hyoo**-muhd/ *adj.* (of the air or climate) warm and damp. [Latin *humidus*]

**humidifier** /hyoo-**mid**-uh-ˌfuy-uh/ *n.* device for keeping the atmosphere moist in a room etc.

**humidify** /hyoo-**mid**-uh-ˌfuy/ v. (**-ies**, **-ied**) make (air etc.) humid.

**humidity** /hyoo-**mid**-uh-tee/ n. (pl. **-ies**) **1** dampness. **2** degree of moisture, esp. in the atmosphere.

**humiliate** /hyoo-**mil**-ee-ˌayt/ v. (**-ting**) injure the dignity or self-respect of. □**humiliating** adj. **humiliation** /-ay-shuhn/ n. [Latin: related to HUMBLE]

**humility** /hyoo-**mil**-uh-tee/ n. **1** humbleness, meekness. **2** humble condition. [French: related to HUMILIATE]

**hummingbird** n. small tropical bird that makes a humming sound with its wings when it hovers.

**hummock** /**hum**-uhk/ n. hillock or hump. [origin unknown]

**hummus** /**huum**-uhs/ n. (also **houmous**) dip or appetiser made from ground chick-peas, sesame oil, lemon, and garlic. [Turkish]

**humorist** n. humorous writer, talker, or actor.

**humorous** /**hyoo**-muh-ruhs/ adj. showing humour or a sense of humour. □**humorously** adv.

**humour** /**hyoo**-muh/ (also **humor**) — n. **1 a** quality of being amusing or comic. **b** the expression of humour in literature, speech, etc. **2** (in full **sense of humour**) ability to perceive or express humour or take a joke. **3** mood or state of mind (bad humour). **4** inclination or whim (in the humour for fighting). **5** (in full **cardinal humour**) hist. each of the four fluids (blood, phlegm, choler, melancholy), thought to determine a person's physical and mental qualities. — v. gratify or indulge (a person or taste etc.) (humour me and do what I ask). □ **out of humour** displeased. □ **humourless** adj. [Latin humor moisture]

**hump** — n. **1** rounded protuberance on a camel's back, or as an abnormality on a person's back. **2** rounded raised mass of earth etc. **3** critical point in an under-taking. — v. **1 a** (often foll. by about) colloq. lift or carry (heavy objects etc.) with difficulty. **b** hoist up, shoulder (one's pack etc.). **2** make hump-shaped. □**hump it** colloq. travel on foot, carrying one's possessions. **hump one's swag** (or **bluey** or **Matilda**) colloq. = hump it. **over the hump** past the crisis; over the worst. [probably Low German or Dutch]

**humpback** n. **1 a** deformed back with a hump. **b** person with this. **2** whale with a dorsal fin forming a hump. □ **hump-backed** adj.

**humph** /humf/ int. & n. inarticulate sound of doubt or dissatisfaction. [imitative]

**humpy** /**hum**-pee/ n. (pl. **-ies**) **1** temporary bush shelter of the Aborigines made from saplings, boughs, etc.; GUNYAH. **2** any rough-and-ready bush hut etc. **3** colloq. oversmall or sub-standard house. [Yagara ngumbi]

**humus** /**hyoo**-muhs/ n. organic constituent of soil formed by the de-composition of vegetation. [Latin, = soil]

**Hun** n. **1** offens. German (esp. in military contexts). **2** member of a warlike Asiatic nomadic people who ravaged Europe in the 4th–5th c. **3** vandal. □ **Hunnish** adj. [Old English]

**hunch** — v. **1** bend or arch into a hump (hunched his back). **2** (usu. foll. by up) sit with the body hunched. — n. **1** intuitive feeling or idea (had a hunch that he would win). **2** hump. [origin unknown]

**hunchback** n. = HUMPBACK 1. □ **hunch-backed** adj.

**hundred** /**hun**-druhd/ adj. & n. (pl. **hundreds** or (in sense 1) **hundred**) (in sing., prec. by a or one) **1** ten times ten. **2** symbol for this (100, c, C). **3** (in sing. or pl.) a large number. **4** (in pl.) the years of a specified century (the seventeen hundreds). □ **hundredfold** adj. & adv. **hundredth** adj. & n. [Old English]

**hundreds and thousands** n.pl. tiny coloured sweets for decorating cakes etc.

**hundredweight** n. (pl. same or **-s**) **1** unit of weight in the imperial system equal to 112 lb (about 50.8 kg.). **2** (in full **metric hundredweight**) unit of weight equal to 50 kg.

**hung** past and past part. of HANG.

**Hungarian** /hung-**gair**-ree-uhn/ — n. **1 a** native or national of Hungary. **b** person of Hungarian descent. **2** language of Hungary. — adj. of Hungary or its people or language. [medieval Latin]

**hunger** /**hung**-guh/ — n. **1 a** lack of food. **b** feeling of discomfort or exhaustion caused by this. **2** (often foll. by for, after) strong desire (had a hunger for publicity). — v. **1** (often foll. by for, after) crave or desire. **2** feel hunger. [Old English]

**hunger strike** n. continuing refusal of food as a protest.

**hung-over** adj. suffering from a hang-over.

**hung parliament** n. parliament in which no party has a clear majority.

**hungry** /**hung**-gree/ adj. (**-ier**, **-iest**) **1** feeling or showing hunger; needing food. **2** inducing hunger (hungry work). **3** craving (hungry for news). **4** (of soil) poor, barren. □**hungrily** adv. [Old English]

**hung-up** adj. colloq. beset by worries; displaying acute inhibitions, anxieties, etc.

**hunk** n. **1** large piece cut off (*hunk of bread*). **2** colloq. physically attractive and desirable (usu. young) man. □ **hunky** adj. (**-ier, -iest**). [probably Dutch]

**hunky-dory** /ˌhung-kee-**daw**-ree/ adj. colloq. excellent. [origin unknown]

**hunt** — v. **1** (also absol.) **a** pursue and kill (wild animals or game) for sport or food. **b** (of an animal) chase (its prey). **2** (foll. by after, for) seek, search (hunting for a pen). **3** (foll. by away, from, etc.) drive off by pursuit (they were hunted from their tribal lands). **4** (as **hunted** adj.) (of a look etc.) terrified as if being hunted. — n. **1** practice or instance of hunting. **2** search. **3** pursuit. □ **hunt down** pursue and capture. **hunt up** search for; look up (in a book etc.) (hunted up the reference in the encyclopaedia). [Old English]

**hunter** n. **1 a** (fem. **huntress**) person or animal that hunts. **b** horse used in hunting. **2** person who seeks something (fortune-hunter). **3** pocket-watch with a hinged cover protecting the glass.

**hunting** n. **1** practice of pursuing and killing wild animals, esp. for sport. **2** stretch of country which is the hereditary possession of an Aboriginal community.

**huntsman**[1] n. hunter.

**huntsman**[2] n. (in full **huntsman spider**; also **tarantula, trantelope**) any of many large and flat-bodied hairy spiders which typically stalk and pounce upon their prey.

**huon pine** /**hyoo**-on/ n. tall conifer endemic in Tasmania, having weeping foliage and highly valued for its pale yellow timber. [named after the *Huon* river in Tasmania]

**hurdle** /**her**-duhl/ — n. **1 a** each of a series of light upright frames to be jumped over by athletes in a race. **b** (in pl.) hurdle-race. **2** obstacle or difficulty. **3** portable rectangular frame with bars, used as a temporary fence etc. — v. (**-ling**) **1** jump over a hurdle or anything else. **2** fence off etc. with hurdles. [Old English]

**hurdler** /**her**-dluh/ n. **1** athlete who runs in hurdle-races. **2** maker of hurdles.

**hurdy-gurdy** /**her**-dee-ˌger-dee/ n. (pl. **-ies**) **1** droning musical instrument played by turning a handle. **2** colloq. barrel-organ. [imitative]

**hurl** — v. **1** throw with great force. **2** utter (abuse etc.) vehemently. — n. forceful throw. [imitative]

**hurly-burly** /**her**-lee-ˌber-lee/ n. boisterous activity; commotion. [a reduplication of HURL]

**hurrah** /hoo-**rah**/ int. & n. (also **hurray** /huh-**ray**/) exclamation of joy or approval. [earlier *huzza*, origin uncertain]

**hurricane** /**hu**-ruh-kuhn, -ˌkayn/ n. **1** storm with a violent wind, esp. a cyclone. **2** Meteorol. wind of 65 knots (117 km/h) or more, force 12 on the Beaufort scale. [Spanish and Portuguese from Carib]

**hurricane-lamp** n. lamp with protected flame designed for use in windy conditions.

**hurry** /**hu**-ree/ — n. **1** great or eager haste. **2** (with neg. or interrog.) need for haste (there is no hurry; what's the hurry?). — v. (**-ies, -ied**) **1** move or act hastily. **2** cause to hurry. **3** (as **hurried** adj.) hasty; done rapidly. □ **hurry along** (or **up**) (cause to) make haste. **in a hurry 1** hurrying. **2** colloq. easily or readily (you will not beat that in a hurry). □ **hurriedly** adv. [imitative]

**hurry-up** — n. spur to action. — adj. providing a spur to action. □ **give a person a bit of a hurry-up** provide him or her with a spur to action.

**hurt** — v. (past and past part. **hurt**) **1** (also absol.) cause pain or injury to. **2** cause mental pain or distress to (a person, feelings, etc.). **3** suffer pain (my arm hurts). — n. **1** injury. **2** harm, wrong. **3** injured feelings (his hurt can be soothed by your apology). [French *hurter* knock]

**hurtful** adj. causing (esp. mental) hurt. □ **hurtfully** adv.

**hurtle** /**her**-tuhl/ v. (**-ling**) **1** move or hurl rapidly or noisily (rain came hurtling down). **2** come with a crash (hurtled into the barricade). [from HURT in the obsolete sense 'strike hard']

**husband** /**huz**-buhnd/ — n. married man, esp. in relation to his wife. — v. use (resources) economically; eke out. [Old English, = house-dweller]

**husbandry** n. **1** farming. **2** careful management of resources.

**hush** — v. make or become silent or quiet (hushed the child; hushed his fears). — int. calling for silence. — n. expectant stillness or silence. □ **hush up** suppress public mention of (an affair). [*husht*, an obsolete exclamation, taken as a past part.]

**hush-hush** adj. colloq. highly secret, confidential.

**hush money** n. colloq. money paid to ensure discretion.

**husk** — n. **1** dry outer covering of some fruits or seeds. **2** worthless outside part of a thing. — v. remove husk(s) from. [probably Low German]

**husky**[1] /**hus**-kee/ adj. (**-ier, -iest**) **1** (of a person or voice) dry in the throat; hoarse. **2** of or full of husks. **3** dry as a husk. **4** tough, strong, hefty. □ **huskily** adv. **huskiness** n.

**husky²** /**hus**-kee/ *n.* (*pl.* **-ies**) dog of a powerful breed used in the Arctic for pulling sledges. [perhaps from corruption of ESKIMO]

**hussar** /huu-**zah**, huh-**zah**/ *n.* soldier of a light cavalry regiment. [Magyar *huszár*]

**hussy** /**hus**-ee, **huz**-ee/ *n.* (*pl.* **-ies**) *derog.* impudent or promiscuous girl or woman. [contraction of HOUSEWIFE]

**hustings** /**hus**-tingz/ *n.* election campaign or proceedings. [Old English, = house of assembly, from Old Norse]

**hustle** /**hus**-uhl/ — *v.* (**-ling**) **1** jostle, bustle. **2** (foll. by *into, out of,* etc.) force, coerce, or hurry (*hustled them out of the room; was hustled into agreeing*). **3** *colloq.* solicit business aggressively. **4** *colloq.* obtain by energetic activity. — *n.* act or instance of hustling. □ **hustler** *n.* [Dutch]

**hut** — *n.* **1** small simple or crude house or shelter. **2** large house in ski-country for lodging skiers. **3** *hist.* **a** dwelling (not necessarily small) for employees on a cattle or sheep station. **b** dwelling for assigned convicts. — *v. hist.* place assigned convicts in huts. [French *hutte* from Germanic]

**hutch** *n.* box or cage for rabbits etc. [French *huche*]

**hut-keeper** *n. hist.* person who takes care of a hut, esp. occupied by convicts or employees (e.g. shearers etc.), providing meals etc. for the occupants and attending to certain menial tasks. □ **hut-keep** *v.*

**hut-mate** *n. hist.* fellow-dweller in a HUT (sense 3).

**hyacinth** /**huy**-uh-sinth/ *n.* **1** bulbous plant with racemes of bell-shaped (esp. purplish-blue) fragrant flowers. **2** purplish-blue. **3** orange variety of zircon used as a precious stone. [Greek *huakinthos*]

**hyacinth orchid** *n.* leafless Australian terrestrial orchid, living in symbiosis with a fungus at the roots of certain eucalypts, and having a tall stalk on which are up to 60 large, spectacular, deep pink flowers with darker pink spots.

**hyaena** var. of HYENA.

**hybrid** /**huy**-brid/ — *n.* **1** offspring of two plants or animals of different species or varieties. **2** thing composed of diverse elements, e.g. a word with parts taken from different languages. — *adj.* **1** bred as a hybrid. **2** heterogeneous. □ **hybridism** *n.* [Latin]

**hybridise** *v.* (also **-ize**) (**-sing** or **-zing**) **1** subject (a species etc.) to crossbreeding. **2 a** produce hybrids. **b** (of an animal or plant) interbreed. □ **hybridisation** *n.*

**hydra** /**huy**-druh/ *n.* **1** freshwater polyp with a tubular body and tentacles. **2** something hard to destroy. [Greek, a mythical snake with many heads that grew again when cut off]

**hydrangea** /huy-**drayn**-juh/ *n.* shrub with globular clusters of white, pink, or blue flowers. [Greek *hudōr* water, *aggos* vessel]

**hydrant** /**huy**-druhnt/ *n.* outlet (esp. in a street) with a nozzle for a hose, for drawing water from the main. [as HYDRO-]

**hydrate** /**huy**-drayt/ — *n.* compound in which water is chemically combined with another compound or an element. — *v.* (**-ting**) **1** combine chemically with water. **2** cause to absorb water. □ **hydration** /-**dray**-shuhn/ *n.* [French: related to HYDRO-]

**hydraulic** /huy-**dro**-lik/ *adj.* **1** (of water, oil, etc.) conveyed through pipes or channels. **2** (of a mechanism etc.) operated by liquid moving in this way (*hydraulic brakes*). □ **hydraulically** *adv.* [Greek *hudōr* water, *aulos* pipe]

**hydraulics** *n.pl.* (usu. treated as *sing.*) science of the conveyance of liquids through pipes etc., esp. as motive power.

**hydro** /**huy**-droh/ *n.* (*pl.* **-s**) hydroelectric power plant. [abbreviation]

**hydro-** *comb. form* **1** having to do with water (*hydroelectric*). **2** combined with hydrogen (*hydrochloric*). [Greek *hudro-* from *hudōr* water]

**hydrocarbon** /ˌhuy-droh-**kah**-buhn/ *n.* compound of hydrogen and carbon.

**hydrocephalus** /ˌhuy-druh-**kef**-uh-luhs, -**sef**-/ *n.* abnormal accumulation of fluid in the brain, esp. in young children, which makes the head enlarge. □ **hydrocephalic** /-kuh-**fal**-ik/ *adj.* [Greek *kephalē* head]

**hydrochloric acid** /ˌhuy-druh-**klaw**-rik, -**klo**-rik/ *n.* solution of the colourless gas hydrogen chloride in water.

**hydrocyanic acid** /ˌhuy-druh-suy-**an**-ik/ *n.* highly poisonous liquid smelling of bitter almonds; prussic acid.

**hydrodynamics** /ˌhuy-droh-duy-**nam**-iks/ *n.pl.* (usu. treated as *sing.*) science of forces acting on or exerted by fluids (esp. liquids). □ **hydrodynamic** *adj.*

**hydroelectric** /ˌhuy-droh-uh-**lek**-trik, ˌhuy-droh-uh-/ *adj.* **1** generating electricity by water-power. **2** (of electricity) so generated. □ **hydroelectricity** /-tris-uh-tee/ *n.*

**hydrofoil** /**huy**-druh-foil/ *n.* **1** boat equipped with planes for lifting its hull out of the water to increase its speed. **2** such a plane.

**hydrogen** /**huy**-druh-juhn/ *n.* tasteless odourless gas, the lightest element, occurring in water and all organic compounds. □ **hydrogenous** /-droj-uh-nuhs/ *adj.* [French: related to HYDRO-, -GEN]

**hydrogenate** /huy-**droj**-uh-,nayt, huy-druh-juh-,nayt/ *v.* (**-ting**) charge with or cause to combine with hydrogen. □ **hydrogenation** /-,nay-shuhn/ *n.*

**hydrogen bomb** *n.* immensely powerful bomb utilising the explosive fusion of hydrogen nuclei.

**hydrogen peroxide** *n.* viscous unstable liquid with strong oxidising properties.

**hydrogen sulphide** *n.* poisonous unpleasant-smelling gas formed by rotting animal matter.

**hydrography** /huy-**drog**-ruh-fee/ *n.* science of surveying and charting seas, lakes, rivers, etc. □ **hydrographer** *n.* **hydrographic** /,huy-druh-**graf**-ik/ *adj.*

**hydrology** /huy-**drol**-uh-jee/ *n.* science of the properties of water, esp. of its movement in relation to land. □ **hydrologist** *n.*

**hydrolyse** /**huy**-druh-,luyz/ *v.* (also **-lyze**) (**-sing** or **-zing**) decompose by hydrolysis.

**hydrolysis** /huy-**drol**-uh-suhs/ *n.* chemical reaction of a substance with water, usu. resulting in decomposition. [Greek *lusis* dissolving]

**hydrometer** /huy-**drom**-uh-tuh/ *n.* instrument for measuring the density of liquids.

**hydropathy** /huy-**drop**-uh-thee/ *n.* (medically unorthodox) treatment of disease by water. □ **hydropathic** /,huy-druh-**path**-ik/ *adj.* [related to PATHOS]

**hydrophilic** /,huy-druh-**fil**-ik/ *adj.* **1** having an affinity for water. **2** wettable by water. [Greek *philos* loving]

**hydrophobia** /,huy-druh-**foh**-bee-uh/ *n.* **1** aversion to water, esp. as a symptom of rabies in humans. **2** rabies, esp. in humans. □ **hydrophobic** *adj.*

**hydroplane** /**huy**-druh-,playn/ *n.* **1** light fast motor boat that skims over water. **2** finlike attachment enabling a submarine to rise and descend.

**hydroponics** /,huy-druh-**pon**-iks/ *n.* growing plants without soil, in sand, gravel, or liquid, with added nutrients. [Greek *ponos* labour]

**hydrosphere** /**huy**-druh-,sfeer/ *n.* waters of the earth's surface.

**hydrostatic** /,huy-druh-**stat**-ik/ *adj.* of the equilibrium of liquids and the pressure exerted by liquid at rest. [related to STATIC]

**hydrostatics** *n.pl.* (usu. treated as *sing.*) mechanics of the hydrostatic properties of liquids.

**hydrotherapy** /,huy-droh-**the**-ruh-pee/ *n.* use of water, esp. swimming, in the treatment of arthritis, paralysis, etc.

**hydrous** /**huy**-druhs/ *adj.* containing water. [related to HYDRO-]

**hydroxide** /huy-**drok**-suyd/ *n.* compound containing oxygen and hydrogen as either a hydroxide ion or a hydroxyl group.

**hydroxyl** /huy-**drok**-suhl/ *n.* (*attrib.*) univalent group containing hydrogen and oxygen.

**hyena** /huy-**ee**-nuh/ *n.* (also **hyaena**) doglike flesh-eating mammal. [Latin from Greek]

**hygiene** /**huy**-jeen/ *n.* **1** conditions or practices, esp. cleanliness, conducive to maintaining health. **2** science of maintaining health. □ **hygienic** /huy-**jee**-nik/ *adj.* **hygienically** /-jee-ni-kuh-lee, -klee/ *adv.* **hygienist** *n.* [Greek *hugiēs* healthy]

**hygrometer** /huy-**grom**-uh-tuh/ *n.* instrument for measuring the humidity of the air or a gas. [Greek *hugros* wet]

**hygroscope** /**huy**-gruh-,skohp/ *n.* instrument indicating but not measuring the humidity of the air.

**hygroscopic** /,huy-gruh-**skop**-ik/ *adj.* **1** of the hygroscope. **2** (of a substance) tending to absorb moisture from the air.

**hymen** /**huy**-men/ *n.* membrane at the opening of the vagina, usu. broken at the first occurrence of sexual intercourse. [Greek *humēn* membrane]

**hymenopterous** /,huy-muh-**nop**-tuh-ruhs/ *adj.* of an order of insects having four transparent wings, including bees, wasps, and ants. [Greek, = membrane-winged]

**hymenosporum** /,huy-muh-**nos**-puh-ruhm/ *n.* (also **native frangipani**) small rainforest tree of Queensland and NSW with shiny leaves and masses of fragrant creamy flowers ageing to yellow: often cultivated.

**hymn** /him/ — *n.* song of esp. Christian praise. — *v.* praise or celebrate in hymns. [Greek *humnos*]

**hymnal** /**him**-nuhl/ *n.* book of hymns. [medieval Latin: related to HYMN]

**hyoscine** /**huy**-uh-,seen/ *n.* poisonous alkaloid found in plants of the nightshade family, used to prevent motion sickness etc. [Greek *huoskuamos* henbane from *hus huos* pig, *kuamos* bean]

**hype** /huyp/ *colloq.* — *n.* **1** extravagant or intensive promotion of a product etc. **2** cheating; a swindle. — *v.* (**-ping**) promote with hype. [origin unknown]

**hyped up** *adj. colloq.* **1** nervously excited or stimulated. **2** (of a car etc. engine) modified and tuned to increase speed, power, etc. [shortening of HYPODERMIC]

**hyper** /**huy**-puh/ *adj. colloq.* hyper-active, highly-strung. [abbreviation of HYPERACTIVE]

**hyper-** *prefix* meaning: **1** over, beyond, above (*hypersonic*). **2** too (*hypersensitive*). [Greek *huper* over]

**hyperactive** /ˌhuy-puh-**rak**-tiv/ *adj.* (of a person) abnormally active.

**hyperbola** /huy-**per**-buh-luh/ *n.* (*pl.* **-s** or **-lae** /-ˌlee/) plane curve produced when a cone is cut by a plane that makes a larger angle with the base than the side of the cone makes. □ **hyperbolic** /ˌhuy-puh-**bol**-ik/ *adj.* [Greek *hyperbolē*, = excess: related to HYPER-, *ballō* throw]

**hyperbole** /huy-**per**-buh-lee/ *n.* exaggeration, esp. for effect. □ **hyperbolic** /-**bol**-ik/ *adj.* **hyperbolical** /-**bol**-i-kuhl/ *adj.*

**hyperbolic function** *n.* function related to a rectangular hyperbola, e.g. a hyperbolic cosine or sine.

**hypercritical** /ˌhuy-puh-**krit**-i-kuhl/ *adj.* excessively critical. □ **hypercritically** *adv.*

**hyperglycaemia** /ˌhuy-puh-gluy-**see**-mee-uh/ *n.* (also **hyperglycemia**) excess of glucose in the bloodstream. [from HYPER-, Greek *glukus* sweet, *haima* blood]

**hypermedia** /**huy**-puh-ˌmee-dee-uh/ *n.* provision of several media (e.g. audio, video, and graphics) on one computer system, with cross-references from one to another (often *attrib.*: *hypermedia database*).

**hypersensitive** /ˌhuy-puh-**sen**-suh-tiv/ *adj.* excessively sensitive. □ **hypersensitivity** /-tiv-uh-tee/ *n.*

**hypersonic** /ˌhuy-puh-**son**-ik/ *adj.* **1** of speeds of more than five times that of sound. **2** of sound-frequencies above about a thousand million hertz.

**hypertension** /ˌhuy-puh-**ten**-shuhn/ *n.* **1** abnormally high blood pressure. **2** great emotional tension.

**hypertext** /**huy**-puh-ˌtekst/ *n.* provision of several texts on one computer system, with cross-references from one to another.

**hyperthermia** /ˌhuy-puh-**ther**-mee-uh/ *n.* abnormally high body-temperature. [from HYPER-, Greek *thermē* heat]

**hyperthyroidism** /ˌhuy-puh-**thuy**-roi-ˌdiz-uhm/ *n.* overactivity of the thyroid gland, resulting in an increased rate of metabolism.

**hyperventilation** /ˌhuy-puh-ˌven-tuh-**lay**-shuhn/ *n.* abnormally rapid breathing. □ **hyperventilate** *v.* (**-ting**).

**hyphen** /**huy**-fuhn/ — *n.* sign (-) used to join or divide words (see panel). — *v.* = HYPHENATE. [Greek *huphen* together]

**hyphenate** /**huy**-fuh-ˌnayt/ *v.* (**-ting**) **1** write (a compound word) with a

---

**Hyphen -**

This is used:
1. to join two or more words so as to form a compound or single expression, e.g.
    *mother-in-law*, *non-stick*, *dressing-table*
    This use is growing less common; often you can do without such hyphens:
    *nonstick*, *treelike*, *dressing table*
2. to join words in an attributive compound (one put before a noun, like an adjective), e.g.
    *a well-known man* (but *the man is well known*)
    *an out-of-date list* (but *the list is out of date*)
3. to join a prefix etc. to a proper name, e.g.
    *anti-Darwinian*; *non-Aboriginal*; *neo-Nazi*; *ex-Premier*.
4. to make a meaning clear by linking words, e.g.
    *twenty-odd people* / *twenty odd people*
    or by separating a prefix, e.g.
    *re-cover/recover*; *re-present/represent*; *re-sign/resign*
5. to separate two identical letters in adjacent parts of a word, e.g.
    *pre-exist*, *co-opt*
6. to represent a common second element in the items of a list, e.g.
    *two-*, *three-*, or *fourfold*
7. to divide a word if there is no room to complete it at the end of the line, e.g.
    . . . *diction-*
    *ary* . . .
    The hyphen comes at the end of the line, not at the beginning of the next line. In general, words should be divided at the end of a syllable; *dicti-onary* would be quite wrong. In handwriting, typing and word-processing, it is safest (and often neatest) not to divide words at all.

hyphen. **2** join (words) with a hyphen. □ **hyphenation** /-**nay**-shuhn/ *n.*

**hypnosis** /hip-**noh**-suhs/ *n.* **1** state like sleep in which the subject acts only on external suggestion. **2** artificially produced sleep. [Greek *hupnos* sleep]

**hypnotherapy** /ˌhip-noh-**the**-ruh-pee/ *n.* treatment of disease etc. by hypnosis.

**hypnotic** /hip-**not**-ik/ — *adj.* **1** of or producing hypnosis. **2** inducing sleep. — *n.* hypnotic drug or influence. □ **hypnotically** *adv.* [Greek: related to HYPNOSIS]

**hypnotise** /hip-nuh-ˌtuyz/ *v.* (also **-ize**) (**-sing** or **-zing**) **1** produce hypnosis in. **2** fascinate; capture the mind of.

**hypnotism** /**hip**-nuh-ˌtiz-uhm/ *n.* the study or practice of hypnosis. □ **hypnotist** *n.*

**hypo¹** /**huy**-poh/ *n.* sodium thiosulphate (incorrectly called hyposulphite) used as a photographic fixer. [abbreviation]

**hypo²** /**huy**-poh/ *n.* (*pl.* **-s**) *colloq.* = HYPODERMIC *n.* [abbreviation]

**hypo-** *prefix* **1** under (*hypodermic*). **2** below normal (*hypotension*). **3** slightly. [Greek *hupo* under]

**hypocalymma** /ˌhuy-puh-kuh-**lim**-uh/ *n.* any of 13 small WA shrubs, all of which are very attractive, two in particular being used in cultivation: the *narrow-leaved hypocalymma*, a soft shrub with a profusion of white to pink flowers, and the *Swan River Myrtle*, with masses of deep rose flowers. [from HYPO-, Greek *kalumma* covering, hood (probably referring to the cap of the calyx in bud)]

**hypochondria** /ˌhuy-puh-**kon**-dree-uh/ *n.* abnormal and ill-founded anxiety about one's health. [Latin from Greek, = soft parts of the body below the ribs, where melancholy was thought to arise]

**hypochondriac** /ˌhuy-puh-**kon**-dree-ˌak/ — *n.* person given to hypochondria. — *adj.* of or affected by hypochondria.

**hypocrisy** /hi-**pok**-ruh-see/ *n.* (*pl.* **-ies**) **1** false claim to virtue; insincerity, pretence. **2** instance of this. [Greek, = acting, feigning]

**hypocrite** /**hip**-uh-krit/ *n.* person given to hypocrisy. □ **hypocritical** /-**krit**-i-kuhl/ *adj.* **hypocritically** /-**krit**-i-kuh-lee, -klee/ *adv.*

**hypodermic** /ˌhuy-puh-**der**-mik/ — *adj.* **1** of the area beneath the skin. **2 a** injected beneath the skin. **b** (of a syringe, etc.) used to do this. — *n.* hypodermic

injection or syringe. [from HYPO-, Greek *derma* skin]

**hypotension** /ˌhuy-poh-**ten**-shuhn/ *n.* abnormally low blood pressure.

**hypotenuse** /huy-**pot**-uh-ˌnyooz/ *n.* side opposite the right angle of a right-angled triangle. [Greek, = subtending line]

**hypothalamus** /ˌhuy-puh-**thal**-uh-muhs/ *n.* (*pl.* **-mi** /-ˌmuy/) region of the brain controlling body-temperature, thirst, hunger, etc. □ **hypothalamic** *adj.* [Latin: related to HYPO-, Greek *thalamos* inner room]

**hypothermia** /ˌhuy-poh-**ther**-mee-uh/ *n.* abnormally low body-temperature. [from HYPO-, Greek *thermē* heat]

**hypothesis** /huy-**poth**-uh-suhs/ *n.* (*pl.* **-theses** /-ˌseez/) **1** proposition or supposition made as the basis for reasoning or investigation. **2** a groundless assumption. [Greek, = foundation]

**hypothesise** /huy-**poth**-uh-ˌsuyz/ *v.* (also **-ize**) (**-sing** or **-zing**) form or assume a hypothesis.

**hypothetical** /ˌhuy-puh-**thet**-i-kuhl/ *adj.* **1** of, based on, or serving as a hypothesis. **2** supposed; not necessarily true. □ **hypothetically** *adv.*

**hypothyroidism** /ˌhuy-poh-**thuy**-roi-ˌdiz-uhm/ *n.* subnormal activity of the thyroid gland, resulting in cretinism. □ **hypothyroid** *n.* & *adj.*

**hypoventilation** /ˌhuy-poh-ˌven-tuh-**lay**-shuhn/ *n.* abnormally slow breathing.

**hyssop** /**his**-uhp/ *n.* small bushy aromatic herb, formerly used medicinally. [ultimately from Greek *hyssōpos*, of Semitic origin]

**hysterectomy** /ˌhis-tuh-**rek**-tuh-mee/ *n.* (*pl.* **-ies**) surgical removal of the womb. [Greek *hustera* womb, -ECTOMY]

**hysteresis** /ˌhis-tuh-**ree**-suhs/ *n.* phenomenon whereby changes in an effect lag behind changes in its cause. [Greek *husteros* coming after]

**hysteria** /his-**teer**-ree-uh/ *n.* **1** wild uncontrollable emotion or excitement. **2** functional disturbance of the nervous system, of psychoneurotic origin. [Greek *hustera* womb]

**hysteric** /his-**te**-rik/ *n.* **1** (in *pl.*) **a** fit of hysteria. **b** *colloq.* overwhelming laughter (*we were in hysterics*). **2** hysterical person.

**hysterical** *adj.* **1** of or affected with hysteria. **2** uncontrollably emotional. **3** *colloq.* extremely funny. □ **hysterically** *adv.*

**Hz** *abbr.* hertz.

# I

**I¹** /uy/ *n.* (also **i**) (*pl.* **Is** or **I's**) **1** ninth letter of the alphabet. **2** (as a Roman numeral) 1.

**I²** /uy/ *pron.* (*obj.* **me**; *poss.* **my, mine**; *pl.* **we**) used by a speaker or writer to refer to himself or herself. [Old English]

**I³** *symb.* iodine.

**I⁴** *abbr.* (also **I.**) **1** Island(s). **2** Isle(s).

**-ial** var. of -AL.

**iambic** /uy-**am**-bik/ *Prosody* — *adj.* of or using iambuses. — *n.* (usu. in *pl.*) iambic verse.

**iambic pentameter** *n.* line of poetry consisting of five iambuses.

**iambus** /uy-**am**-buhs/ *n.* (*pl.* **-buses** or **-bi** /-buy/) (also **iamb** /**uy**-amb, **uy**-am/) metrical foot consisting of one short followed by one long syllable (˘ ‾). [Greek, = lampoon]

**-ian** var. of -AN.

**Iberian** /uy-**beer**-ree-uhn/ — *adj.* of Iberia, the peninsula comprising Spain and Portugal; of Spain and Portugal. — *n.* native or language of Iberia. [Latin *Iberia*]

**ibid.** /**ib**-id/ *abbr.* in the same book or passage etc. [Latin *ibidem* in the same place]

**-ibility** *suffix* forming nouns from, or corresponding to, adjectives in -*ible*.

**ibis** /**uy**-buhs/ *n.* (*pl.* **-es**) **1** wading bird with a curved bill, long neck, and long legs. **2** any of three species of such birds native to Australia. [Greek, from Egyptian]

**-ible** *suffix* forming adjectives meaning 'that may or may be' (*forcible*; *possible*). [Latin]

**-ibly** *suffix* forming adverbs corresponding to adjectives in -*ible*.

**-ic** *suffix* **1** forming adjectives (*Arabic*; *classic*; *public*) and nouns (*critic*; *epic*; *mechanic*; *music*). **2** combined in higher valence or degree of oxidation (*ferric*; *sulphuric*). [Latin -*icus*, Greek -*ikos*]

**-ical** *suffix* forming adjectives corresponding to nouns or adjectives in -*ic* or -*y* (*classical*; *historical*).

**ice** — *n.* **1 a** frozen water. **b** sheet of this on water. **2** ice-cream or water-ice (*ate an ice*). — *v.* (icing) **1** mix with or cool in ice (*iced drinks*). **2** (often foll. by *over*, *up*) **a** cover or become covered with ice. **b** freeze. **3** cover (a cake etc.) with icing. □ **break the ice** see BREAK. **cut no ice with** see CUT. **on ice 1** performed by skaters. **2** *colloq.* in reserve; temporarily shelved (*our holiday plans had to be put on ice*). **on thin ice** in a risky situation. [Old English]

**ice age** *n.* glacial period.

**iceberg** *n.* **1** large floating mass of ice. **2** *colloq.* **a** cold, extremely unemotional person. **b** person who makes a practice of swimming in icy winter waters. □ **the tip of the iceberg** small perceptible part of something very large or complex. [Dutch]

**iceblock** *n.* confection of flavoured and frozen water.

**ice blue** *adj.* & *n.* (as adj. often hyphenated) very pale blue.

**ice-breaker** *n.* **1** ship designed to break through ice. **2** joke, incident, etc. that breaks the ice.

**ice cap** *n.* permanent covering of ice, esp. in polar regions.

**ice cream** *n.* sweet creamy frozen food, usu. flavoured.

**ice cube** *n.* small block of ice for drinks etc.

**ice hockey** *n.* form of hockey played on ice.

**Icelandic** /uys-**lan**-dik/ — *adj.* of Iceland. — *n.* language of Iceland.

**ice pack** *n.* **1** = PACK ICE. **2** ice applied to the body for medical purposes.

**ice pick** *n.* tool with a spike for splitting up ice.

**ice rink** *n.* = RINK *n.* 1.

**ice-skate** — *n.* boot with a blade beneath, for skating on ice. — *v.* skate on ice. □ **ice-skater** *n.*

**ichor** /**uy**-kaw/ *n. literary* blood.

**ichthyology** /,ik-thee-**ol**-uh-jee/ *n.* the study of fishes. □ **ichthyological** /-uh-**loj**-i-kuhl/ *adj.* **ichthyologist** *n.* [Greek *ikhthus* fish]

**ichthyosaurus** /,ik-thee-uh-**saw**-ruhs/ *n.* (also **ichthyosaur** /**ik**-thee-uh-,saw/) (*pl.* **-sauruses** or **-saurs**) extinct marine reptile with four flippers and usu. a large tail. [Greek *ikhthus* fish, *sauros* lizard]

**-ician** *suffix* forming nouns denoting persons skilled in subjects having nouns usu. ending in -*ic* or -*ics* (*magician*; *politician*). [French -*icien*]

**icicle** /**uy**-suh-kuhl/ *n.* hanging tapering piece of ice, formed from dripping water. [from ICE, obsolete *ickle* icicle]

**icing** *n.* **1** coating of sugar and water etc.

on a cake or biscuit. **2** formation of ice on a ship or aircraft. □ **icing on the cake** inessential though attractive addition or enhancement.

**icing sugar** *n.* finely powdered sugar.

**icon** /**uy**-kon/ *n.* (also **ikon**) **1** painting of Christ etc., esp. in the Orthodox Church. **2** image or statue. **3** symbol used in computer systems to represent a program, option, or window, esp. for selection. □ **iconic** /uy-**kon**-ik/ *adj.* [Greek *eikōn* image]

**iconoclast** /uy-**kon**-uh-ˌklast/ *n.* **1** person who attacks cherished beliefs. **2** *hist.* person destroying religious images. □ **iconoclasm** *n.* **iconoclastic** /-**klas**-tik/ *adj.* [Greek: related to ICON, *klaō* break]

**iconography** /ˌuy-kuh-**nog**-ruh-fee/ *n.* **1** the illustration of a subject by drawings or figures. **2** the study of portraits, esp. of an individual, or of artistic images or symbols. [Greek: related to ICON]

**-ics** *suffix* (treated as *sing.* or *pl.*) forming nouns denoting arts, sciences, etc. (*athletics*; *politics*).

**icy** /**uy**-see/ *adj.* (**-ier, -iest**) **1** very cold. **2** covered with or abounding in ice. **3** (of a tone or manner) unfriendly, hostile (*an icy stare*). □ **icily** *adv.* **iciness** *n.*

**icy pole** *n. propr.* = ICEBLOCK.

**ID** *abbr.* identification, identity (*can't get a passport without proper ID*).

**id** *n.* person's inherited unconscious psychological impulses. [Latin, = that]

**I'd** /uyd/ *contr.* **1** I had. **2** I should; I would.

**-ide** *suffix Chem.* forming nouns denoting binary compounds of an element (*sodium chloride*; *lead sulphide*; *calcium carbide*). [extended from OXIDE]

**idea** /uy-**deer**/ *n.* **1** plan etc. formed by mental effort (*an idea for a book*). **2 a** mental impression or concept. **b** vague belief or fancy (*had an idea you were married*). **3** intention or purpose (*the idea is to make money*). **4** archetype or pattern. **5** ambition or aspiration (*have ideas*; *had the idea to be a doctor*). □ **get** (*or* **have**) **ideas** be ambitious, rebellious, etc. **have no idea** *colloq.* **1** not know at all. **2** be completely incompetent; not have a clue. **not one's idea of** *colloq.* not what one regards as (*not my idea of a holiday*). **put ideas into a person's head** suggest ambitions, plans, etc. he or she would not otherwise have had. [Greek, = form, kind]

**ideal** /uy-**deel**/ — *adj.* **1 a** answering to one's highest conception. **b** perfect (*that's the ideal house for us*). **2** existing only in idea; visionary (*in an ideal world there would be no disease*). — *n.* perfect type, thing, concept, principle, etc., esp. as a standard to emulate. [French: related to IDEA]

**idealise** *v.* (also **-ize**) (**-sing** *or* **-zing**) **1** regard or represent as ideal or perfect. **2** regard or represent (esp. a person) as better than he or she really is. □ **idealisation** /-zay-shuhn/ *n.*

**idealism** *n.* **1** forming or pursuing ideals, esp. unrealistically. **2** representation of things in ideal form. **3** system of thought in which objects are held to be in some way dependent on the mind. □ **idealist** *n.* **idealistic** /-lis-tik/ *adj.* **idealistically** /-lis-ti-kuh-lee, -klee/ *adv.*

**ideally** *adv.* **1** in ideal circumstances. **2** according to an ideal.

**idée fixe** /ˌee-day **feeks**/ *n.* (*pl.* **idées fixes** pronunc. same) dominating idea; obsession. [French, = fixed idea]

**idem** /**id**-em, **uy**-dem/ — *adv.* in the same author as previously mentioned. — *n.* the same word or author as previously mentioned. [Latin]

**identical** /uy-**den**-ti-kuhl/ *adj.* **1** (often foll. by *with*) (of different things) absolutely alike. **2** one and the same. **3** (of twins) developed from a single ovum. □ **identically** *adv.* [Latin *identicus*: related to IDENTITY]

**identification** /uy-ˌden-tuh-fuh-**kay**-shuhn/ *n.* **1** act or instance of identifying. **2** means of identifying (*produced his passport as identification*) (also *attrib.*: *identification card*).

**identifier** *n.* **1** person or thing that identifies. **2** *Computing* sequence of characters used to identify or refer to an element of a program.

**identify** /uy-**den**-tuh-ˌfuy/ *v.* (**-ies, -ied**) **1** establish the identity of; recognise. **2** select or discover (*identify the best solution*). **3** (also *refl.*; foll. by *with*) associate inseparably or very closely (with a party, policy, etc.). **4** (often foll. by *with*) treat as identical. **5 a** (foll. by *with*) put oneself in the place of (another person). **b** (of a person of Aboriginal and European descent) associate oneself with those of Aboriginal descent. □ **identifiable** *adj.* [medieval Latin *identifico*: related to IDENTITY]

**identikit** /uy-**den**-tee-kit/ *n.* (often *attrib.*) *propr.* picture of esp. a wanted suspect assembled from standard components using witnesses' descriptions. [from IDENTITY, KIT]

**identity** /uy-**den**-tuh-tee/ *n.* (*pl.* **-ies**) **1 a** condition of being a specified person or thing. **b** individuality, personality (*felt he had lost his identity*). **2** identification or the result of it (*mistaken identity*; *identity* card). **3** absolute sameness (*identity of interests*). **4** *Algebra* **a** equality of two expressions for all values of the quantities. **b** equation expressing this. **5** *colloq.* **a** outstanding or well-known person (*several identities from the film world were present*). **b** (esp. as **old identity**) a local character, a long-standing resident of a place (*an old Ballarat identity*; *met several old identities in the country pub*). [Latin *identitas* from *idem* same]

**ideogram** /id-ee-oh-ˌgram/ *n.* character symbolising a thing without indicating the sounds in its name (e.g. a numeral, Chinese characters). [Greek *idea* form, -GRAM]

**ideograph** /id-ee-oh-ˌgrahf, -graf/ *n.* = IDEOGRAM. □ **ideographic** /-graf-ik/ *adj.* **ideography** /ˌid-ee-og-ruh-fee/ *n.*

**ideologue** /uy-dee-uh-ˌlog/ *n.* often *derog.* adherent of an ideology. [French: related to IDEA]

**ideology** /ˌuy-dee-ol-uh-jee, id-ee-/ *n.* (*pl.* -ies) **1** ideas at the basis of an economic or political theory (*Marxist ideology*). **2** characteristic thinking of a class etc. (*bourgeois ideology*). □ **ideological** /-uh-loj-i-kuhl/ *adj.* **ideologically** /-uh-loj-i-kuh-lee, -klee/ *adv.* **ideologist** *n.* [French: related to IDEA, -LOGY]

**ides** /uydz/ *n.pl.* day of the ancient Roman month (the 15th day of March, May, July, and October, the 13th of other months). [Latin *idus*]

**idiocy** /id-ee-uh-see/ *n.* (*pl.* -ies) **1** foolishness; foolish act. **2** extreme mental imbecility.

**idiom** /id-ee-uhm/ *n.* **1** phrase etc. established by usage and not immediately comprehensible from the words used (e.g. *over the moon, see the light*). **2** form of expression peculiar to a language etc. **3** language of a people or country. **4** characteristic mode of expression in art etc. (*idiom of the impressionists*). [Greek *idios* own]

**idiomatic** /ˌid-ee-oh-mat-ik/ *adj.* **1** relating or conforming to idiom. **2** characteristic of a particular language. □ **idiomatically** *adv.*

**idiosyncrasy** /ˌid-ee-oh-sing-kruh-see/ *n.* (*pl.* -ies) attitude, behaviour, or opinion peculiar to a person; anything highly individual or eccentric. □ **idiosyncratic** /-krat-ik/ *adj.* **idiosyncratically** /-krat-i-klee/ *adv.* [Greek *idios* private, *sun* with, *krasis* mixture]

**idiot** /id-ee-uht/ *n.* **1** stupid person. **2** mentally deficient person incapable of rational conduct. □ **idiotic** /-ot-ik/ *adj.*

**idiotically** /-ot-i-klee/ *adv.* [Greek *idiotēs*, = private citizen, ignorant person]

**idiot board** *n.* (also **idiot card**) *colloq.* board privately displaying to a television newsreader etc. the words to be said during the broadcast.

**idiot box** *n. colloq.* television set.

**idle** /uy-duhl/ — *adj.* (**idler, idlest**) **1** lazy, indolent. **2** not in use; not working (*idle machinery*; *idle employees*). **3** (of time etc.) unoccupied. **4** purposeless; groundless (*idle rumour*). **5** useless, ineffective (*idle protest*). — *v.* (-ling) **1** be idle. **2** run (an engine) or (of an engine) be run slowly without doing any work. **3** (foll. by *away*) pass (time etc.) in idleness. □ **the idle rich** the wealthy, esp. if their wealth has been inherited and so they do not need to work. □ **idleness** *n.* **idler** *n.* **idly** *adv.* [Old English]

**idle time** *n.* amount of time in a given period when a machine, esp. a computer, performs no useful function.

**idol** /uy-duhl/ *n.* **1** image of a deity etc. as an object of worship. **2** object of excessive or supreme adulation (*cinema idol*). [Greek *eidōlon* image, phantom]

**idolater** /uy-dol-uh-tuh/ *n.* **1** worshipper of idols. **2** devoted admirer. □ **idolatrous** *adj.* **idolatry** *n.* [related to IDOL, Greek *latreuō* worship]

**idolise** *v.* (also **-ize**) (**-sing** or **-zing**) **1** venerate or love excessively. **2** make an idol of. □ **idolisation** /-zay-shuhn/ *n.*

**idyll** /id-uhl, uy-duhl/ *n.* **1** short description, esp. in verse, of a peaceful or romantic, esp. rural, scene or incident. **2** such a scene or incident. [Greek *eidullion*]

**idyllic** /i-dil-ik, uy-dil-ik/ *adj.* **1** blissfully peaceful and happy. **2** of or like an idyll. □ **idyllically** *adv.*

**i.e.** *abbr.* that is to say. [Latin *id est*]

**-ie** see -Y[2].

**if** — *conj.* **1** introducing a conditional clause: **a** on the condition or supposition that; in the event that (*if he comes I will tell him*; *if you are tired we can rest*). **b** (with past tense) implying that the condition is not fulfilled (*if I knew I would say*). **2** even though (*I'll finish it, if it takes me all day*). **3** whenever (*if I am not sure I ask*). **4** whether (*see if you can find it*). **5** expressing a wish, surprise, or request (*if I could just try!*; *if it isn't my old hat!*; *if you wouldn't mind?*). **6** with implied reservation, = perhaps not (*very rarely if at all*). **7** despite being (*a useful if cumbersome device*). — *n.* **1** condition, supposition (*too many ifs about it*). **2** something doubtful (*the major if is the headmaster's attitude*). □ **if only 1** even if for no other reason than (*I'll come if only to see her*). **2** (often *ellipt.*) expression of regret; I wish that (*if only I had thought of it*). [Old English]

**iffy** *adj.* (**-ier**, **-iest**) *colloq.* uncertain; dubious.

**igloo** *n.* Eskimo dome-shaped dwelling, esp. of snow. [Eskimo, = house]

**igneous** /**ig**-nee-uhs/ *adj.* **1** of fire; fiery. **2** (esp. of rocks) volcanic. [Latin *ignis* fire]

**ignite** /ig-**nuyt**/ *v.* (**-ting**) **1** set fire to. **2** catch fire. **3** provoke or excite (feelings etc.). [Latin *ignio ignit-* set on fire]

**ignition** /ig-**nish**-uhn/ *n.* **1** mechanism for, or the action of, starting combustion in an internal-combustion engine. **2** igniting or being ignited.

**ignoble** /ig-**noh**-buhl/ *adj.* (**-bler**, **-blest**) **1** dishonourable. **2** of low birth, position, or reputation. □ **ignobly** *adv.* [Latin: related to IN-1, NOBLE]

**ignominious** /ˌig-nuh-**min**-ee-uhs/ *adj.* shameful, humiliating. □ **ignominiously** *adv.* [Latin: related to IGNOMINY]

**ignominy** /**ig**-nuh-muh-nee/ *n.* dishonour, infamy. [Latin: related to IN-1, Latin (*g*)*nomen* name]

**ignoramus** /ˌig-nuh-**ray**-muhs/ *n.* (*pl.* **-muses**) ignorant person. [Latin, = we do not know: related to IGNORE]

**ignorance** /**ig**-nuh-ruhns/ *n.* lack of knowledge. [French from Latin: related to IGNORE]

**ignorant** *adj.* **1** (often foll. by *of*, *in*) lacking knowledge (esp. of a fact or subject). **2** *colloq.* uncouth. □ **ignorantly** *adv.*

**ignore** /ig-**naw**/ *v.* (**-ring**) refuse to take notice of; intentionally disregard. [Latin *ignoro* not know]

**iguana** /ig-**wah**-nuh/ *n.* large American, W. Indian, or Pacific lizard with a dorsal crest. [Spanish from Carib *iwana*]

**iguanodon** /ig-**wah**-nuh-ˌdon/ *n.* large plant-eating dinosaur with small forelimbs. [from IGUANA, which it resembles, after *mastodon* etc.]

**ijjecka** var. of ADJIGO.

**ikebana** /ˌik-uh-**bah**-nuh/ *n.* art of Japanese flower arrangement. [Japanese, = living flowers]

**ikon** var. of ICON.

**il-** *prefix* assim. form of IN-1, IN-2 before *l*.

**ileum** /**il**-ee-uhm/ *n.* (*pl.* **ilea**) third and last portion of the small intestine. [Latin *ilium*]

**iliac** /**il**-ee-ˌak/ *adj.* of the lower body (*iliac artery*). [Latin *ilia* flanks]

**ilk** *n. colloq.* usu. *derog.* sort, family, class, etc. (*you and all your ilk ought to be prosecuted*). [Old English]

**ill** — *adj.* (*attrib.* except in sense 1) **1** (usu. *predic.*) not in good health; unwell. **2** wretched, unfavourable (*ill fortune*; *ill luck*). **3** harmful (*ill effects*). **4** hostile, unkind (*ill feeling*). **5** faulty, unskilful (*ill management*). **6** (of manners or conduct) improper. — *adv.* **1** badly, wrongly, imperfectly (*ill-matched*; *ill-provided*). **2** scarcely (*can ill afford it*). **3** unfavourably (*spoke ill of them*). — *n.* **1** injury, harm. **2** evil. □ **ill at ease** embarrassed, uneasy. [Old Norse]

**I'll** /uyl/ *contr.* I shall; I will.

**ill-advised** *adj.* foolish; imprudent.

**ill-assorted** *adj.* badly matched; mixed.

**Illawarra flame-tree** /ˌil-uh-**wo**-ruh/ *n.* = FLAME-TREE. [*Illawarra* coastal district south of Sydney]

**Illawarra shorthorn** *n.* popular breed of dairy cattle with a red coat developed in the Illawarra district south of Sydney.

**ill-behaved** *adj.* badly behaved.

**ill-bred** *adj.* badly brought up; rude.

**ill-defined** *adj.* not clearly defined; blurred.

**ill-disposed** *adj.* **1** (often foll. by *towards*) unfavourably disposed. **2** malevolent.

**illegal** /i-**lee**-guhl/ *adj.* **1** not legal. **2** criminal. □ **illegality** /-**gal**-uh-tee/ *n.* (*pl.* **-ies**). **illegally** *adv.*

**illegible** /i-**lej**-uh-buhl/ *adj.* not legible. □ **illegibility** /-bil-uh-tee/ *n.* **illegibly** *adv.*

**illegitimate** /ˌil-uh-**jit**-uh-muht/ *adj.* **1** born of parents not married to each other. **2** unlawful. **3** improper; not in good usage (*language illegitimate for the occasion*). **4** wrongly inferred (*illegitimate conclusion*). □ **illegitimacy** *n.* **illegitimately** *adv.*

**ill-equipped** *adj.* (often foll. by *to* + infin.) not adequately equipped or qualified.

**ill fame** *n.* bad or evil reputation.

**ill-fated** *adj.* destined to or bringing bad fortune (*ill-fated attempt to climb Everest*).

**ill-favoured** *adj.* unattractive (*ill-favoured person*).

**ill feeling** *n.* hostility; bad feeling.

**ill-founded** *adj.* (of an idea etc.) baseless (*ill-founded fears*).

**ill-gotten** *adj.* gained unlawfully or wickedly (*ill-gotten gains*).

**ill health** *n.* poor physical or mental condition.

**ill humour** *n.* irritability. □ **ill-humoured** *adj.*

**illiberal** /i-**lib**-uh-ruhl/ *adj.* **1** intolerant, narrow-minded. **2** without liberal culture; vulgar. **3** stingy; mean. □ **illiberality** /-ral-uh-tee/ *n.* **illiberally** *adv.*

**illicit** /i-**lis**-uht/ *adj.* unlawful, forbidden; unlicensed. □ **illicitly** *adv.*

**illiterate** /i-**lit**-uh-ruht/ — *adj.* **1** unable to read. **2** uneducated. — *n.* illiterate person. □ **illiteracy** *n.* **illiterately** *adv.*

**ill-mannered** *adj.* having bad manners; rude.

**ill-natured** *adj.* churlish, unkind.

**illness** *n.* **1** disease. **2** state of being ill.

**illogical** /i-**loj**-i-kuhl/ *adj.* devoid of or contrary to logic. □ **illogicality** /-**kal**-uh-tee/ *n.* (*pl.* **-ies**). **illogically** *adv.*

**ill-omened** *adj.* doomed.

**ill-starred** *adj.* = ILL-FATED.

**ill-tempered** *adj.* morose, irritable.

**ill-timed** *adj.* done or occurring at an inappropriate time.

**ill-treat** *v.* treat badly; abuse.

**illuminate** /i-**loo**-muh-,nayt/ *v.* (**-ting**) **1** light up; make bright. **2** decorate (buildings etc.) with lights. **3** decorate (a manuscript etc.) with gold, colour, etc. **4** help to explain (a subject etc.). **5** enlighten spiritually or intellectually. **6** shed lustre on. □ **illuminating** *adj.* **illumination** /-**nay**-shuhn/ *n.* **illuminative** *adj.* [Latin *lumen* light]

**illumine** /i-**loo**-muhn/ *v.* (**-ning**) *literary* **1** light up; make bright. **2** enlighten.

**ill-use** *v.* = ILL-TREAT.

**illusion** /i-**loo**-*zh*uhn/ *n.* **1** false impression or belief. **2** state of being deceived by appearances. **3** figment of the imagination. **4** = OPTICAL ILLUSION. □ **be under the illusion** (foll. by *that*) believe mistakenly. □ **illusive** *adj.* **illusory** *adj.* [Latin *illudo* mock]

**illusionist** *n.* conjuror.

**illustrate** /**il**-uh-,strayt/ *v.* (**-ting**) **1 a** provide (a book etc.) with pictures. **b** elucidate by drawings, pictures, examples, etc. **2** serve as an example of. □ **illustrator** *n.* [Latin *lustro* light up]

**illustration** /,il-uh-**stray**-shuhn/ *n.* **1** drawing or picture in a book, magazine, etc. **2** explanatory example. **3** act or instance of illustrating.

**illustrative** /**il**-uh-struh-tiv/ *adj.* (often foll. by *of*) explanatory; exemplary.

**illustrious** /i-**lus**-tree-uhs/ *adj.* distinguished, renowned. [Latin *illustris*: related to ILLUSTRATE]

**ill will** *n.* bad feeling; animosity.

**ill wind** *n.* unfavourable or untoward circumstance (with ref. to the proverb *it's an ill wind that blows nobody good*).

**illyari** /**il**-yuh-ree/ *n.* very showy small eucalypt with extremely large and striking budcaps, being bright scarlet, square, and topped with a cross (not unlike a cardinal's red biretta), foll. by large, bright yellow flowers with an emerald centre. [perhaps from an Aboriginal language]

**illywhacker** /i-lee-wak-uh/ *n.* small-time confidence trickster. [origin unknown]

**im-** *prefix* assim. form of IN-[1], IN-[2] before *b*, *m*, or *p*.

**I'm** /uym/ *contr.* I am.

**image** /**im**-ij/ — *n.* **1** representation of an object, e.g. a statue. **2** reputation or persona of a person, company, etc. (*the company's image is at risk*). **3** appearance as seen in a mirror or through a lens. **4** mental picture or idea. **5** simile or metaphor. **6** semblance, likeness. — *v.* (**-ging**) **1** make an image of; portray. **2** reflect, mirror. **3** describe or imagine vividly. □ **be the image of** be so like exactly like. **spitting image** exact copy or look-alike. [Latin *imago imagin-*]

**imagery** *n.* **1** figurative illustration, esp. in literature. **2** images; statuary, carving. **3** mental images collectively.

**imaginary** /i-**maj**-uh-ree/ *adj.* **1** existing only in the imagination. **2** *Math.* being the square root of a negative quantity. [Latin: related to IMAGE]

**imagination** /i-,maj-uh-**nay**-shuhn/ *n.* **1** mental faculty of forming images or concepts of objects or situations not existent or not directly experienced (*his imagination is playing tricks on him*; *beyond our imagination*). **2** mental creativity or resourcefulness (*hasn't enough imagination to succeed*).

**imaginative** /i-**maj**-uh-nuh-tiv/ *adj.* having or showing imagination. □ **imaginatively** *adv.* **imaginativeness** *n.*

**imagine** /i-**maj**-uhn/ *v.* (**-ning**) **1 a** form a mental image or concept of. **b** picture to oneself. **2** think of as probable (*can't imagine he'd be so stupid*). **3** guess (*can't imagine what he is doing*). **4** suppose (*I imagine you'll need help*). □ **imaginable** *adj.* [Latin *imaginor*]

**imago** /i-**may**-goh/ *n.* (*pl.* **-s** or **imagines** /i-**may**-uh-,neez/ ) fully developed stage of an insect, e.g. a butterfly. [Latin: see IMAGE]

**imam** /i-**mahm**/ *n.* **1** leader of prayers in a mosque. **2** title of various Muslim leaders. [Arabic]

**imbalance** /im-**bal**-uhns/ *n.* **1** lack of balance. **2** disproportion.

**imbecile** /**im**-buh-,seel, -,suyl/ — *n.* **1** *colloq.* stupid person. **2** person with a mental age of about five. — *adj.* mentally weak; stupid, idiotic. □ **imbecilic** /-**sil**-ik/ *adj.* **imbecility** /-**sil**-uh-tee/ *n.* (*pl.* **-ies**). [French from Latin]

**imbed** var. of EMBED.

**imbibe** /im-**buyb**/ *v.* (**-bing**) **1** drink (esp. alcohol). **2 a** assimilate (ideas etc.).

**b** absorb (moisture etc.). **3** inhale (air etc.). [Latin *bibo* drink]

**imbo** /im-boh/ *n. colloq.* gullible person, esp. the victim of an illywhacker etc.; a fool. [shortening of IMBECILE]

**imbroglio** /im-**broh**-lee-oh/ *n.* (*pl.* **-s**) **1** confused or complicated situation. **2** confused heap. [Italian: related to IN-[2], BROIL]

**imbue** /im-**byoo**/ *v.* (**-bues, -bued, -buing**) (often foll. by *with*) **1** inspire or permeate (with feelings, opinions, or qualities). **2** saturate. **3** dye. [Latin *imbuo*]

**imitate** /im-uh-,tayt/ *v.* (**-ting**) **1** follow the example of; copy. **2** mimic. **3** make a copy of. **4** be like. □ **imitable** *adj.* **imitator** *n.* [Latin *imitor -tat-*]

**imitation** /,im-uh-**tay**-shuhn/ *n.* **1** act or instance of imitating or being imitated. **2** something produced by this; a copy. **3** counterfeit (often *attrib.*: *imitation leather*). **4** the act of mimicking a person or thing for entertainment (*he does imitations*).

**imitative** /im-uh-tuh-tiv/ *adj.* **1** (often foll. by *of*) imitating; following a model or example. **2** (of a word) reproducing a natural sound (e.g. *fizz*), or otherwise suggestive (e.g. *blob*).

**immaculate** /i-**mak**-yoo-luht/ *adj.* **1** pure, spotless; perfectly clean and tidy. **2** perfect (*immaculate timing*). **3** innocent, faultless. □ **immaculately** *adv.* **immaculateness** *n.* [Latin: related to IN-[1], *macula* spot]

**Immaculate Conception** *n. RC Ch.* doctrine that God preserved the Virgin Mary from original sin from the moment she was conceived.

**immanent** /im-uh-nuhnt/ *adj.* **1** (often foll. by *in*) naturally present, inherent. **2** (of God) omnipresent. □ **immanence** *n.* [Latin: related to IN-[2], *maneo* remain]

**immaterial** /,im-uh-**teer**-ree-uhl/ *adj.* **1** unimportant; irrelevant. **2** not material; incorporeal. □ **immateriality** /-al-uh-tee/ *n.*

**immature** /,im-uh-**choor**/ *adj.* **1** not mature. **2** undeveloped, esp. emotionally. **3** unripe. □ **immaturely** *adv.* **immaturity** *n.*

**immeasurable** /i-**mezh**-uh-ruh-buhl/ *adj.* not measurable; immense. □ **immeasurably** *adv.*

**immediate** /i-**mee**-dee-uht/ *adj.* **1** occurring or done at once (*immediate reply*). **2** nearest, next; direct (*immediate vicinity; immediate future; immediate cause of death*). **3** most pressing or urgent (*our immediate concern*). □ **immediacy** *n.* **immediateness** *n.* [Latin: related to IN-[1], MEDIATE]

**immediately** — *adv.* **1** without pause or delay. **2** without intermediary. — *conj.* as soon as.

**immemorial** /,i-muh-**maw**-ree-uhl/ *adj.* ancient beyond memory or record (*from time immemorial*).

**immense** /i-**mens**/ *adj.* **1** extremely large; huge. **2** considerable (*immense difference*). **3** *colloq.* excellent (*immense idea*). □ **immenseness** *n.* **immensity** *n.* [Latin *metior mens-* measure]

**immensely** *adv.* **1** *colloq.* very much (*enjoyed myself immensely*). **2** to an immense degree (*immensely rich*).

**immerse** /i-**mers**/ *v.* (**-sing**) **1 a** (often foll. by *in*) dip, plunge. **b** submerge (a person). **2** (often *refl.* or in *passive*; often foll. by *in*) absorb or involve deeply (*immersed in his studies*). **3** (often foll. by *in*) bury, embed. [Latin *mergo mers-* dip]

**immersion** /i-**mer**-shuhn/ *n.* **1** act or instance of immersing or process of being immersed. **2** baptism by total bodily immersion. **3** mental absorption.

**immigrant** /im-uh-gruhnt/ — *n.* person who immigrates. — *adj.* **1** immigrating. **2** of immigrants.

**immigrate** /im-uh-,grayt/ *v.* come into a country and settle. □ **immigration** /-**gray**-shuhn/ *n.* [related to IN-[2], MIGRATE]

**imminent** /im-uh-nuhnt/ *adj.* impending; about to happen (*war is imminent*). □ **imminence** *n.* **imminently** *adv.* [Latin *immineo* be impending]

**immiscible** /i-**mis**-uh-buhl/ *adj.* (often foll. by *with*) not able to be mixed. □ **immiscibility** /-**bil**-uh-tee/ *n.*

**immobile** /i-**moh**-buyl/ *adj.* **1** not moving. **2** unable to move or be moved. □ **immobility** /-**bil**-uh-tee/ *n.*

**immobilise** /i-**moh**-buh-,luyz/ *v.* (also **-ize**) (**-sing** or **-zing**) **1** make or keep immobile. **2** keep (a limb or patient) still for healing purposes. □ **immobilisation** /-**zay**-shuhn/ *n.*

**immoderate** /i-**mod**-uh-ruht, i-**mod**-ruht/ *adj.* excessive; lacking moderation. □ **immoderately** *adv.*

**immodest** /i-**mod**-uhst/ *adj.* **1** lacking modesty; conceited. **2** shameless, indecent. □ **immodestly** *adv.* **immodesty** *n.*

**immolate** /im-uh-,layt/ *v.* (**-ting**) kill or offer as a sacrifice. □ **immolation** /-**lay**-shuhn/ *n.* [Latin, = sprinkle with meal]

**immoral** /i-**mo**-ruhl/ *adj.* **1** not conforming to accepted morality; morally wrong. **2** depraved, dissolute. □ **immorality** /,i-muh-**ral**-uh-tee/ *n.* (*pl.* **-ies**) **immorally** *adv.*

**immortal** /i-**maw**-tuhl/ — *adj.* **1 a** living for ever; not mortal. **b** divine. **2** unfading. **3** famous for all time. — *n.* **1 a** immortal being. **b** (in *pl.*) gods of antiquity. **2** person, esp. an author, remembered long after death. □ **immortalise** *v.* (also **-ize**) (**-sing** or **-zing**). **immortality** /ˌi-maw-**tal**-uh-tee/ *n.* **immortally** *adv.*

**immovable** /i-**moo**-vuh-buhl/ *adj.* (also **immoveable**) **1** not able to be moved. **2** steadfast, unyielding (*immovable beliefs*). **3** emotionless. **4** not subject to change (*immovable law*). **5** motionless. **6** (of property) consisting of land, houses, etc. □ **immovability** /-**bil**-uh-tee/ *n.* **immovably** *adv.*

**immune** /i-**myoon**/ *adj.* **1 a** (often foll. by *against*, *from*, *to*) protected against infection through inoculation etc. **b** relating to immunity (*immune system*). **2** (foll. by *from*, *to*) exempt or proof against a charge, duty, criticism, etc. [Latin *immunis* exempt]

**immunise** /**im**-yuh-ˌnuyz/ *v.* (also **-ize**) (**-sing** or **-zing**) make immune, usu. by inoculation. □ **immunisation** /-**zay**-shuhn/ *n.*

**immunity** *n.* (*pl.* **-ies**) **1** ability of an organism to resist infection by means of antibodies and white blood cells. **2** (often foll. by *from*) freedom or exemption.

**immunodeficiency** /ˌim-yuh-ˌnoh-duh-**fish**-uhn-see/ *n.* reduction in normal immune defences.

**immunoglobulin** /ˌim-yuh-noh-**glob**-yuh-luhn/ *n.* any of a group of related proteins functioning as antibodies.

**immunology** /ˌim-yoo-**nol**-uh-jee/ *n.* the scientific study of immunity. □ **immunological** /-nuh-**loj**-i-kuhl/ *adj.* **immunologist** *n.*

**immunotherapy** /ˌim-yuh-noh-**the**-ruh-pee/ *n.* prevention or treatment of disease with substances that stimulate the immune response.

**immure** /i-**myoor**/ *v.* (**-ring**) **1** imprison. **2** *refl.* shut oneself away. [Latin *murus* wall]

**immutable** /i-**myoo**-tuh-buhl/ *adj.* unchangeable. □ **immutability** /-**bil**-uh-tee/ *n.* **immutably** *adv.*

**imp** *n.* **1** mischievous child. **2** small devil or sprite. [Old English, = young shoot]

**impact** — *n.* /**im**-pakt/ **1** effect of sudden forcible contact between two solid bodies etc.; collision. **2** strong effect or impression. — *v.* /im-**pakt**/ **1** press or fix firmly. **2** (as **impacted** *adj.*) (of a tooth) wedged between another tooth and the jaw. **3** (often foll. by *on*) have an impact on. □ **impaction** /im-**pak**-shuhn/ *n.* [Latin: related to IMPINGE]

**impair** /im-**pair**/ *v.* damage, weaken. □ **impairment** *n.* [Latin, = make worse, from *pejor*]

**impale** /im-**payl**/ *v.* (**-ling**) transfix or pierce with a sharp stake etc. □ **impalement** *n.* [Latin *palus* PALE²]

**impalpable** /im-**pal**-puh-buhl/ *adj.* **1** not easily grasped by the mind; intangible. **2** imperceptible to the touch. **3** (of powder) very fine. □ **impalpability** /-**bil**-uh-tee/ *n.* **impalpably** *adv.*

**impanel** var. of EMPANEL.

**impart** /im-**paht**/ *v.* (often foll. by *to*) **1** communicate (news etc.). **2** give a share of (a thing). [Latin: related to PART]

**impartial** /im-**pah**-shuhl/ *adj.* treating all alike; unprejudiced, fair. □ **impartiality** /-shee-**al**-uh-tee/ *n.* **impartially** *adv.*

**impassable** /im-**pah**-suh-buhl/ *adj.* not able to be traversed (*road was impassable because of flooding*). □ **impassability** /-**bil**-uh-tee/ *n.* **impassableness** *n.* **impassably** *adv.*

**impasse** /**im**-pahs/ *n.* position from which progress is impossible; deadlock. [French: related to PASS¹]

**impassible** /im-**pas**-uh-buhl/ *adj.* **1** impassive. **2 a** incapable of feeling or emotion. **b** incapable of suffering injury. □ **impassibility** /-**bil**-uh-tee/ *n.* **impassibly** *adv.* [Latin *patior pass-* suffer]

**impassioned** /im-**pash**-uhnd/ *adj.* filled with passion; ardent. [Italian *impassionato*: related to PASSION]

**impassive** /im-**pas**-iv/ *adj.* incapable of or not showing emotion; serene. □ **impassively** *adv.* **impassiveness** *n.* **impassivity** /-**siv**-uh-tee/ *n.*

**impasto** /im-**pas**-toh/ *n. Art* technique of laying on paint thickly. [Italian]

**impatiens** /im-**pay**-shee-ˌenz/ *n.* any of several plants including the busy Lizzie. [Latin: related to IMPATIENT]

**impatient** /im-**pay**-shuhnt/ *adj.* **1** lacking or showing a lack of patience or tolerance. **2** restlessly eager. **3** (foll. by *of*) intolerant of (*he was impatient of our attempts to defend her*). □ **impatience** *n.* **impatiently** *adv.*

**impeach** /im-**peech**/ *v.* **1** charge with a crime against the nation, esp. treason. **2** call in question, disparage (a person's integrity etc.). □ **impeachable** *adj.* **impeachment** *n.* [French *empecher* from Latin *pedica* fetter]

**impeccable** /im-**pek**-uh-buhl/ *adj.* faultless, exemplary (*impeccable behaviour*). □ **impeccability** /-**bil**-uh-tee/ *n.* **impeccably** *adv.* [related to IN-¹, Latin *pecco* sin]

**impecunious** /ˌim-puh-**kyoo**-nee-uhs/ *adj.* having little or no money. □ **impecuniosity** /-os-uh-tee/ *n.* **impecuniousness** *n.* [related to PECUNIARY]

**impedance** /im-**pee**-duhns/ *n.* total effective resistance of an electric circuit etc. to an alternating current. [from IMPEDE]

■ *Usage* *Impedance* is sometimes confused with *impediment*, which means 'a hindrance' or 'a speech defect'.

**impede** /im-**peed**/ *v.* (**-ding**) obstruct; hinder. [Latin *impedio* from *pes ped-* foot]

**impediment** /im-**ped**-uh-muhnt/ *n.* **1** hindrance or obstruction. **2** speech defect, e.g. a stammer. [Latin: related to IMPEDE]

■ *Usage* See note at *impedance*.

**impel** /im-**pel**/ *v.* (**-ll-**) **1** drive, force, or urge. **2** propel. [Latin *pello* drive]

**impend** /im-**pend**/ *v.* (often foll. by *over*) **1** (of a danger, event, etc.) be threatening or imminent. **2** hang, be suspended; overhang. □ **impending** *adj.* [Latin *pendeo* hang]

**impenetrable** /im-**pen**-uh-truh-buhl/ *adj.* **1** not able to be penetrated. **2** inscrutable; unfathomable (*impenetrable look on his face*; *impenetrable problem*). **3** inaccessible to ideas, influences, etc. (*impenetrable ignorance*). □ **impenetrability** /-bil-uh-tee/ *n.* **impenetrableness** *n.* **impenetrably** *adv.*

**impenitent** /im-**pen**-i-tuhnt/ *adj.* not sorry, unrepentant. □ **impenitence** *n.*

**imperative** /im-**pe**-ruh-tiv/ — *adj.* **1** urgent; obligatory (*imperative need*). **2** commanding, peremptory (*imperative tone of voice*). **3** *Gram.* (of a mood) expressing a command (e.g. *come here!*). — *n.* **1** *Gram.* imperative mood. **2** a command. **3** essential or urgent thing (*to find water is our first imperative*). [Latin *impero* command]

**imperceptible** /,im-puh-**sep**-tuh-buhl/ *adj.* **1** not perceptible. **2** very slight, gradual, or subtle (*imperceptible decline*). □ **imperceptibility** /-bil-uh-tee/ *n.* **imperceptibly** *adv.*

**imperfect** /im-**per**-fuhkt/ — *adj.* **1 a** not perfect (*all men are imperfect*). **b** faulty, incomplete (*imperfect vision*). **2** *Gram.* (of a tense) denoting action in progress but not completed (e.g. *they were singing*). — *n.* imperfect tense. □ **imperfectly** *adv.*

**imperfection** /,im-puh-**fek**-shuhn/ *n.* **1** state of being imperfect. **2** fault, blemish.

**imperial** /im-**peer**-ree-uhl/ *adj.* **1** of or characteristic of an empire or similar sovereign State. **2 a** of an emperor. **b** majestic, august; authoritative. **3** (of non-metric weights and measures) statutory in the UK, esp. formerly (*imperial gallon*). □ **imperially** *adv.* [Latin *imperium* dominion]

**imperialism** *n.* **1** imperial rule or system. **2** usu. *derog.* policy of dominating other nations by acquiring dependencies etc. □ **imperialist** *n.* & *adj.* **imperialistic** /-lis-tik/ *adj.*

**imperil** /im-**pe**-ruhl/ *v.* (**-ll-**) endanger.

**imperious** /im-**peer**-ree-uhs/ *adj.* **1** overbearing, domineering (*has an imperious manner*). **2** urgent, imperative. □ **imperiously** *adv.* **imperiousness** *n.*

**imperishable** /im-**pe**-rish-uh-buhl/ *adj.* not able to perish, indestructible.

**impermanent** /im-**per**-muh-nuhnt/ *adj.* not permanent. □ **impermanence** *n.* **impermanency** *n.*

**impermeable** /im-**per**-mee-uh-buhl/ *adj.* not permeable, not allowing fluids to pass through. □ **impermeability** /-bil-uh-tee/ *n.*

**impermissible** /,im-puh-**mis**-uh-buhl/ *adj.* not allowable.

**impersonal** /im-**per**-suh-nuhl/ *adj.* **1** without personal reference; objective, impartial. **2** without human attributes; cold, unfeeling. **3** *Gram.* **a** (of a verb) used esp. with *it* as a subject (e.g. *it is snowing*). **b** (of a pronoun) = INDEFINITE. □ **impersonality** /-nal-uh-tee/ *n.* **impersonally** *adv.*

**impersonate** /im-**per**-suh-,nayt/ *v.* (**-ting**) **1** pretend to be (another person), esp. as entertainment or fraud. **2** act (a character). □ **impersonation** /-nay-shuhn/ *n.* **impersonator** *n.* [from IN-², Latin PERSONA]

**impertinent** /im-**per**-tuh-nuhnt/ *adj.* insolent, disrespectful. □ **impertinence** *n.* **impertinently** *adv.*

**imperturbable** /,im-puh-**ter**-buh-buhl/ *adj.* not excitable; calm. □ **imperturbability** /-bil-uh-tee/ *n.* **imperturbably** *adv.*

**impervious** /im-**per**-vee-uhs/ *adj.* (usu. foll. by *to*) **1** impermeable. **2** not responsive (to argument etc.) (*impervious to threats*).

**impetigo** /,im-puh-**tuy**-goh/ *n.* contagious skin infection forming pimples and sores. [Latin *impeto* assail]

**impetuous** /im-**pe**-choo-uhs, -**pet**-yoo-/ *adj.* **1** acting or done rashly or with sudden energy. **2** moving forcefully or rapidly. □ **impetuosity** /-os-uh-tee/ *n.* **impetuously** *adv.* **impetuousness** *n.* [Latin: related to IMPETUS]

**impetus** /im-puh-tuhs/ *n.* **1** force with which a body moves. **2** driving force or impulse. [Latin *impeto* assail]

**impiety** /im-**puy**-uh-tee/ *n.* (*pl.* **-ies**) **1** lack of piety or reverence. **2** act etc. showing this.

**impinge** /im-**pinj**/ v. (**-ging**) (usu. foll. by *on*, *upon*) **1** make an impact or effect. **2** encroach (*your statement impinges on the ridiculous*). □ **impingement** n. [Latin *pango pact-* fix]

**impious** /im-pee-uhs, im-**puy**-uhs/ adj. **1** not pious. **2** wicked, profane.

**impish** adj. of or like an imp; mischievous. □ **impishly** adv. **impishness** n.

**implacable** /im-**plak**-uh-buhl/ adj. unable to be appeased. □ **implacability** /-bil-uh-tee/ n. **implacably** adv.

**implant** — v. /im-**plahnt**, im-**plant**/ **1** (often foll. by *in*) insert or fix. **2** (often foll. by *in*) instil (an idea etc.) in a person's mind. **3** plant. **4 a** insert (tissue etc.) in a living body. **b** (in *passive*) (of a fertilised ovum) become attached to the wall of the womb. — n. /im-plahnt, im-plant/ thing implanted, esp. a piece of tissue. □ **implantation** /-tay-shuhn/ n. [Latin: related to PLANT]

**implausible** /im-**plaw**-zuh-buhl/ adj. not plausible. □ **implausibility** /-bil-uh-tee/ n. **implausibly** adv.

**implement** — n. /im-pluh-muhnt/ tool, instrument, utensil. — v. /im-pluh-ment/ put (a decision, plan, contract, etc.) into effect. □ **implementation** /im-pluh-men-tay-shuhn/ n. [Latin *impleo* fulfil]

**implicate** /im-pluh-kayt/ v. (**-ting**) **1** (often foll. by *in*) show (a person) to be involved (in a crime etc.). **2** imply. [Latin *plico* fold]

**implication** /im-pluh-**kay**-shuhn/ n. **1** thing implied. **2** act of implicating or implying.

**implicit** /im-**plis**-uht/ adj. **1** implied though not plainly expressed (*his guilt was implicit in his remarks*). **2** absolute, unquestioning (*implicit belief*). □ **implicitly** adv. [Latin: related to IMPLICATE]

**implode** /im-**plohd**/ v. (**-ding**) (cause to) burst inwards (opp. EXPLODE). □ **implosion** /im-**ploh**-zhuhn/ n. [from IN-², cf. EXPLODE]

**implore** /im-**plaw**/ v. (**-ring**) **1** (often foll. by *to* + infin.) entreat (a person). **2** beg earnestly for. [Latin *ploro* weep]

**imply** /im-**pluy**/ v. (**-ies, -ied**) **1** (often foll. by *that*) strongly suggest or insinuate without directly stating (*what are you implying?*). **2** signify, esp. as a consequence (*silence implies guilt*). [Latin: related to IMPLICATE]

**impolite** /im-puh-**luyt**/ adj. (**impolitest**) ill-mannered, uncivil, rude. □ **impolitely** adv. **impoliteness** n.

**impolitic** /im-**pol**-uh-tik/ adj. inexpedient, unwise. □ **impoliticly** adv.

**imponderable** /im-**pon**-duh-ruh-buhl, -druh-buhl/ — adj. **1** not able to be estimated. **2** very light; weightless. — n. (usu. in *pl.*) imponderable thing. □ **imponderability** /-bil-uh-tee/ n. **imponderably** adv.

**import** — v. /im-**pawt**, im-/ **1 a** bring in (esp. foreign goods or services) to a country. **b** *Computing* introduce data from an outside source. **2** imply, indicate, signify. — n. /im-pawt/ **1** (esp. in *pl.*) imported article or service. **2** importing. **3** what is implied; meaning (*what is the import of his remark?*). **4** importance. □ **importation** /im-paw-**tay**-shuhn/ n. **importer** /im-**paw**-tuh/ n. [Latin *importo* carry in]

**important** /im-**paw**-tuhnt/ adj. **1** (often foll. by *to*) of great effect or consequence; momentous (*your support is important to our cause*). **2** (of a person) having high rank or authority. **3** pompous. □ **importance** n. **importantly** adv. [Latin *importo* carry in, signify]

**importunate** /im-**paw**-chuh-nuht, -tyoo-nuht/ adj. **1** making persistent or pressing requests. **2** (of affairs, business, etc.) urgent. □ **importunity** /im-paw-**choo**-nuh-tee, -tyoo-/ n. [Latin *importunus* inconvenient]

**importune** /im-**paw**-tyoon, -**paw**-choon, -**tyoon**/ v. (**-ning**) pester (a person) with requests, demands, etc.

**impose** /im-**pohz**/ v. (**-sing**) **1** (often foll. by *on*, *upon*) lay (a tax, duty, charge, or obligation) on. **2** enforce compliance with. **3** also *refl.* (foll. by *on*, *upon*, or *absol.*) take advantage of (*will not impose on you any longer*). **4** (often foll. by *on*, *upon*) inflict (a thing) on (*imposed his presence upon us*). [Latin *impono*]

**imposing** adj. impressive, formidable, esp. in appearance.

**imposition** /im-puh-**zish**-uhn/ n. **1** imposing or being imposed. **2** unfair demand or burden. **3** tax, duty.

**impossible** /im-**pos**-uh-buhl/ adj. **1** not possible (*it is impossible to make time run backwards*). **2** (loosely) not easy, convenient, or believable (*it's impossible for me to listen to you now*). **3** *colloq.* (esp. of a person) outrageous, intolerable. □ **impossibility** /im-pos-uh-**bil**-uh-tee/ n. (*pl.* **-ies**). **impossibly** adv.

**impost** /im-pohst, -post/ n. tax, duty, or tribute. [Latin *impono impost-* impose]

**impostor** /im-**pos**-tuh/ n. (also **imposter**) **1** person who assumes a false character or pretends to be someone else. **2** swindler.

**imposture** /im-**pos**-chuh/ n. fraudulent deception.

**impotent** /im-puh-tuhnt/ adj. **1**

powerless; ineffective. **2** (of a male) unable to achieve an erection or orgasm. □ **impotence** n.

**impound** /im-**pownd**/ v. **1** confiscate. **2** take legal possession of. **3** shut up (animals) in a pound.

**impoverish** /im-**pov**-uh-rish/ v. **1** make poor. **2** exhaust the strength or natural fertility of (soil impoverished by bad management). □ **impoverishment** n. [French: related to POVERTY]

**impracticable** /im-**prak**-ti-kuh-buhl/ adj. not practicable. □ **impracticability** /-**bil**-uh-tee/ n. **impracticably** adv.

**impractical** /im-**prak**-ti-kuhl/ adj. not practical. □ **impracticality** /-**kal**-uh-tee/ n.

**imprecation** /,im-pruh-**kay**-shuhn/ n. formal spoken curse. □ **imprecate** /im-pruh-,kayt/ v. **imprecator** n. **imprecatory** adj. [Latin precor pray]

**imprecise** /,im-pruh-**suys**/ adj. not precise. □ **imprecisely** adv. **impreciseness** n. **imprecision** /-**sizh**-uhn/ n.

**impregnable** /im-**preg**-nuh-buhl/ adj. **1** strong enough to be secure against capture (an impregnable city). **2** resistant to attack or criticism (an impregnable argument). □ **impregnability** /-**bil**-uh-tee/ n. **impregnably** adv. [French: related to IN-¹, Latin prehendo take]

**impregnate** /im-**preg**-nayt/ v. (**-ting**) **1** (often foll. by with) fill or saturate. **2** (often foll. by with) imbue (with feelings etc.). **3 a** make (a female) pregnant. **b** fertilise (an ovum). □ **impregnation** /,im-preg-**nay**-shuhn/ n. [Latin: related to PREGNANT]

**impresario** /,im-pruh-**sah**-ree-oh/ n. (pl. **-s**) organiser of public entertainment, esp. a theatrical etc. manager. [Italian]

**impress** — v. /im-**pres**/ **1** (often foll. by with) **a** affect or influence deeply. **b** affect (a person) favourably (was most impressed by your efforts). **2** (often foll. by on) emphasise (an idea etc.) (must impress on you the need to be prompt). **3 a** (often foll. by on) imprint or make (a mark). **b** mark (a thing) with a stamp, seal, etc. — n. /**im**-pres/ **1** mark made by a seal, stamp, etc. **2** characteristic mark or quality. □ **impressible** /im-**pres**-uh-buhl/ adj. [French: related to PRESS¹]

**impression** /im-**presh**-uhn/ n. **1** effect (esp. on the mind or feelings). **2** notion or belief (esp. vague or mistaken). **3** imitation of a person or sound, esp. as entertainment. **4 a** impressing of a mark. **b** mark impressed. **5** unaltered reprint from standing type or plates (esp. as distinct from EDITION). **6** number of copies of a book etc. issued at one time. **7** print taken from a wood or copper engraving.

**impressionable** adj. easily influenced; able to be influenced. □ **impressionability** n. **impressionably** adv.

**impressionism** /im-**presh**-uh-,niz-uhm/ n. **1** style or movement in art concerned with conveying the effect of natural light on objects. **2** style of music or writing seeking to convey esp. fleeting feelings or experience. □ **impressionist** n. **impressionistic** /im-,presh-uh-**nis**-tik/ adj.

**impressive** /im-**pres**-iv/ adj. arousing respect, approval, or admiration. □ **impressively** adv. **impressiveness** n.

**imprimatur** /,im-pruh-**mah**-tuh, -**may**-tuh/ n. **1** RC Ch. licence to print (a religious book etc.). **2** official approval (the headmaster gave our project his imprimatur). [Latin, = let it be printed]

**imprint** — v. /im-**print**/ **1** (often foll. by on) impress firmly, esp. on the mind. **2 a** (often foll. by on) make a stamp or impression of (a figure etc.) on a thing. **b** make an impression on (a thing) with a stamp etc. — n. /**im**-print/ **1** impression, stamp. **2** printer's or publisher's name etc. printed in a book.

**imprinting** /im-**prin**-ting/ n. **1** in senses deriving from IMPRINT v. **2** Zool. development in a young animal of a pattern of recognition and trust for its own species.

**imprison** /im-**priz**-uhn/ v. **1** put in prison. **2** confine (imprisoned all day in the house). □ **imprisonment** n.

**improbable** /im-**prob**-uh-buhl/ adj. **1** unlikely. **2** difficult to believe. □ **improbability** /-**bil**-uh-tee/ n. **improbably** adv.

**impromptu** /im-**promp**-tyoo/ — adj. & adv. extempore, unrehearsed (made an impromptu speech; spoke impromptu). — n. (pl. **-s**) **1** extempore performance or speech. **2** short, usu. solo, instrumental composition, often improvisatory in style. [French from Latin in promptu in readiness]

**improper** /im-**prop**-uh/ adj. **1** unseemly; indecent. **2** inaccurate, wrong (improper use of the word 'infer'). □ **improperly** adv.

**improper fraction** n. fraction in which the numerator is greater than or equal to the denominator.

**impropriety** /,im-pruh-**pruy**-uh-tee/ n. (pl. **-ies**) **1** lack of propriety; indecency. **2** instance of this. **3** incorrectness.

**improve** /im-**proov**/ v. (**-ving**) **1 a** make or become better. **b** (foll. by on, upon) produce something better than (improved on his earlier attempt). **2** bring (land) into agricultural or pastoral use, so as to make it more productive and valuable. **3** (as **improving** *adj.*) giving moral benefit (*improving literature*). □ **on the improve** showing signs of betterment. □ **improvable** *adj.* **improved** *adj.* [Anglo-French *emprower* from French *prou* profit]

**improvement** *n.* **1** act or instance of improving or being improved. **2** something that improves, esp. an addition or alteration (to a house etc.) that adds to value. **3** bringing of land into agricultural or pastoral use.

**improvident** /im-**prov**-uh-duhnt/ *adj.* **1** lacking foresight. **2** profligate; wasteful. **3** incautious. □ **improvidence** *n.* **improvidently** *adv.*

**improvise** /**im**-pruh-,vuyz/ *v.* (**-sing**) (also *absol.*) **1** compose or perform (music, verse, etc.) extempore. **2 a** provide or construct from materials not intended for the purpose. **b** devise, invent, esp. on the spur of the moment. □ **improvisation** /-**zay**-shuhn/ *n.* **improvisational** /-**zay**-shuh-nuhl/ *adj.* **improvisatory** /-**zay**-tuh-ree/ *adj.* [Latin *improvisus* unforeseen]

**imprudent** /im-**proo**-duhnt/ *adj.* unwise, indiscreet. □ **imprudence** *n.* **imprudently** *adv.*

**impudent** /**im**-pyuh-duhnt/ *adj.* impertinent; shamelessly presumptuous. □ **impudence** *n.* **impudently** *adv.* [Latin *pudeo* be ashamed]

**impugn** /im-**pyoon**/ *v.* challenge or call in question (a statement, action, motives, etc.). □ **impugnment** *n.* [Latin *pugno* fight]

**impulse** /**im**-puls/ *n.* **1** sudden urge (*felt an impulse to laugh*). **2** tendency to follow such urges (*man of impulse*). **3** act or instance of impelling; a push (*he kept on swimming, driven by the impulse to survive*). **4** impetus. **5** *Physics* **a** large temporary force producing a change of momentum (e.g. a hammer-blow). **b** change of momentum so produced. **6** wave of excitation in a nerve. [Latin: related to PULSE[1]]

**impulse buying** *n.* purchasing goods on impulse and without prudent calculation. □ **impulse buyer** *n.*

**impulsive** /im-**pul**-siv/ *adj.* **1** tending to act on impulse. **2** done on impulse. **3** tending to impel. □ **impulsively** *adv.* **impulsiveness** *n.*

**impunity** /im-**pyoo**-nuh-tee/ *n.* exemption from punishment, bad consequences, etc. □ **with impunity** without punishment etc. (*taunted them with impunity*). [Latin *poena* penalty]

**impure** /im-**pyoor**/ *adj.* **1** adulterated; mixed with foreign matter. **2** unchaste (*impure thoughts*).

**impurity** *n.* (*pl.* **-ies**) **1** state of being impure. **2** impure thing or part.

**imputation** *n.* **1** an instance of imputing. **2** the allocation of tax paid at the company level to individual shareholders through credits attached to dividends.

**impute** /im-**pyoot**/ *v.* (**-ting**) (foll. by *to*) attribute (a fault etc.) to (*imputed his bankruptcy to mere bad luck*). [Latin *puto* reckon]

**In** *symb.* indium.

**in** — *prep.* **1** expressing inclusion or position within limits of space, time, circumstance, etc. (*in Australia; in bed; in 1993; in the rain*). **2 a** within (a certain time) (*finished it in two hours*). **b** after (a certain time) (*will be leaving in an hour*). **3** with respect to (*blind in one eye; good in parts*). **4** as a proportionate part of (*one in three failed; gradient of one in six*). **5** with the form or arrangement of (*packed in tens; falling in folds*). **6** as a member of (*in the army*). **7** involved with (*is in banking*). **8** as the content of (*there is something in what you say*). **9** within the ability of (*does he have it in him?*). **10** having the condition of; affected by (*in bad health; in danger*). **11** having as a purpose (*in search of; in reply to*). **12** by means of or using as material (*drawn in pencil; modelled in bronze*). **13 a** using as the language of expression (*written in French*). **b** (of music) having as its key (*symphony in C*). **14** (of a word) having as a beginning or ending (*words in un-*). **15** wearing (*in blue; in a suit*). **16** with the identity of (*found a friend in Mary*). **17** (of an animal) pregnant with (*in calf*). **18** into (with a verb of motion or change: *put it in the box; cut it in two*). **19** introducing an indirect object after a verb (*believe in; engage in; share in*). **20** forming adverbial phrases (*in any case; in reality; in short*). — *adv.* expressing position within limits, or motion to such a position: **1** into a room, house, etc. (*come in*). **2** at home, in one's office, etc. (*is not in*). **3** so as to be enclosed (*locked in*). **4** in a publication (*is the advert in?*). **5** in or to the inward side (*rub it in*). **6 a** in fashion or season (*long skirts are in*). **b** elected or in office (*an Australian Democrat got in*). **7** favourable (*their luck was in*). **8** *Cricket* (of a player or side) batting. **9** (of transport) at the platform etc. (*the train is in*). **10** (of a season, harvest, order, etc.) having arrived or been received (*avocados are in*). **11** (of a fire) continuing to burn. **12** denoting effective action (*join in*). **13** (of the tide) at the highest point. **14** (in *comb.*) *colloq.* denoting prolonged concerted action, esp. by large numbers (*sit-in*; *teach-in*). —*adj.* **1** internal; living in; inside (*in-patient*). **2** fashionable (*the in thing to do*). **3** confined to a small group (*in-joke*). □ **be in it** take part in (an activity etc.) with enthusiasm. **come in 1** come within the bounds of settled districts (*came in from the outback to stock up on supplies*). **2** be at a sheep or cattle station (*myalls came in on walkabout*). **count** (a **person**) **in** (or **out**) include (or exclude). **in all** see ALL. **in between** see BETWEEN *adv.* **in for 1** about to undergo or get (*in for a tongue-lashing*). **2** competing in or for. **in for it** about to be punished. **in on 1** sharing in (*he's in on the deal*). **2** privy to (a secret etc.). **ins and outs** (often foll. by *of*) all the details. **in so far as** see FAR. **in that** because; in so far as. **in with 1** (also **well in with**) on good terms with. **2** favourably placed for (*in with a chance*). [Old English]

**in-¹** *prefix* (also **il-, im-, ir-**) added to: **1** adjectives, meaning 'not' (*inedible*; *insane*). **2** nouns, meaning 'without, lacking (*inaction*). [Latin]

**in-²** *prefix* (also **il-, im-, ir-**) in, on, into, towards, within (*induce*; *influx*; *insight*; *intrude*). [from IN, or from Latin *in* (prep.)]

**inability** /,in-uh-**bil**-uh-tee/ *n.* **1** state of being unable. **2** lack of power or means.

**in absentia** /,in ab-**sen**-tee-uh, -**sen**-shuh/ *adv.* in (his, her, or their) absence. [Latin]

**inaccessible** /,in-ak-**ses**-uh-buhl/ *adj.* **1** not accessible. **2** (of a person) un-approachable. □ **inaccessibility** /-bil-uh-tee/ *n.*

**inaccurate** /in-**ak**-yuh-ruht/ *adj.* not accurate. □ **inaccuracy** *n.* (*pl.* **-ies**). **inaccurately** *adv.*

**inaction** /in-**ak**-shuhn/ *n.* lack of action.

**inactive** /in-**ak**-tiv/ *adj.* **1** not active. **2** not operating. **3** indolent. □ **inactivity** /-tiv-uh-tee/ *n.*

**inadequate** /in-**ad**-uh-kwuht/ *adj.* **1** not adequate; insufficient. **2** (of a person) incompetent; weak. □ **inadequacy** *n.* (*pl.* **-ies**). **inadequately** *adv.*

**inadmissible** /,in-uhd-**mis**-uh-buhl/ *adj.* that cannot be admitted or allowed (*inadmissible evidence*). □ **inadmissibility** /-bil-uh-tee/ *n.* **inadmissibly** *adv.*

**inadvertent** /,in-uhd-**ver**-tuhnt/ *adj.* **1** unintentional. **2** negligent, inattentive. □ **inadvertence** *n.* **inadvertently** *adv.* [from IN-¹, ADVERT]

**inadvisable** /,in-uhd-**vuy**-zuh-buhl/ *adj.* not advisable. □ **inadvisability** /-bil-uh-tee/ *n.*

**inalienable** /in-**ay**-lyuh-nuh-buhl/ *adj.* that cannot be transferred to another or taken away (*inalienable rights*).

**inane** /in-**ayn**/ *adj.* **1** silly, senseless (*inane chatter*). **2** empty, void. □ **inanely** *adv.* **inanity** /-**an**-uh-tee/ *n.* (*pl.* **-ies**). [Latin *inanis*]

**inanimate** /in-**an**-i-muht/ *adj.* **1** not endowed with, or deprived of, animal life (*an inanimate object*). **2** spiritless, dull.

**inapplicable** /in-uh-**plik**-uh-buhl/ *adj.* (often foll. by *to*) not applicable or relevant. □ **inapplicability** /-bil-uh-tee/ *n.*

**inappreciable** /in-uh-**pree**-shuh-buhl/ *adj.* imperceptible; not worth reckoning (*the difference was so slight as to be inappreciable*).

**inappropriate** /,in-uh-**proh**-pree-uht/ *adj.* not appropriate. □ **inappropriately** *adv.* **inappropriateness** *n.*

**inapt** /in-**apt**/ *adj.* **1** not apt or suitable. **2** unskilful. □ **inaptitude** *n.*

**inarticulate** /,in-ah-**tik**-yuh-luht/ *adj.* **1** unable to express oneself clearly. **2** (of speech) not articulate; indistinct. **3** dumb. **4** esp. *Anat.* not jointed. □ **inarticulately** *adv.*

**inasmuch** /,in-uhz-**much**/ *adv.* (foll. by *as*) **1** since, because. **2** to the extent that. [from *in as much*]

**inattentive** /,in-uh-**ten**-tiv/ *adj.* **1** not paying attention. **2** neglecting to show courtesy. □ **inattention** *n.* **inattentively** *adv.*

**inaudible** /in-**aw**-duh-buhl/ *adj.* unable to be heard. □ **inaudibly** *adv.*

**inaugural** /in-**aw**-gyuh-ruhl/ —*adj.* of or for an inauguration. —*n.* inaugural speech, lecture, etc. [French from Latin *auguro* take omens: related to AUGUR]

**inaugurate** /in-**aw**-gyuh-,rayt/ *v.* (**-ting**) **1** admit formally to office. **2** begin (an undertaking) or initiate the public use of (a building etc.), with a ceremony. **3** begin, introduce. □ **inauguration** /-ray-shuhn/ *n.* **inaugurator** *n.*

**inauspicious** /,in-aw-**spish**-uhs/ *adj.* **1** ill-omened, not favourable. **2** unlucky. □ **inauspiciously** *adv.* **inauspiciousness** *n.*

**in-between** *attrib. adj. colloq.* intermediate.

**inborn** /**in**-bawn/ *adj.* existing from birth; natural, innate.

**inbred** /**in**-bred, in-/ *adj.* **1** inborn. **2** produced by inbreeding.

**inbreeding** /**in**-bree-ding, in-/ *n.* breeding from closely related animals or persons. □ **inbreed** *v.* (*past* and *past part.* **-bred**).

**inbuilt** /**in**-bilt/ *adj.* built-in.

**incalculable** /in-**kal**-kyuh-luh-buhl/ *adj.* **1** too great for calculation. **2** not calculable beforehand. **3** uncertain, unpredictable. □ **incalculability** /-bil-uh-tee/ *n.* **incalculably** *adv.*

**incandesce** /ˌin-kan-**des**/ v. (**-cing**) (cause to) glow with heat.

**incandescent** /adj. **1** glowing with heat. **2** shining. **3** (of artificial light) produced by a glowing filament etc. □ **incandescence** n. [Latin *candeo* be white]

**incantation** /ˌin-kan-**tay**-shuhn/ n. magical formula; spell, charm. □ **incantational** adj. [Latin *canto* sing]

**incapable** /in-**kay**-puh-buhl/ adj. **1 a** not capable. **b** too honest, kind, etc., to do something (*incapable of hurting anyone*). **2** not capable of rational conduct (*drunk and incapable*). □ **incapability** /-bil-uh-tee/ n. **incapably** adv.

**incapacitate** /ˌin-kuh-**pas**-uh-ˌtayt/ v. (**-ting**) make incapable or unfit.

**incapacity** /ˌin-kuh-**pas**-uh-tee/ n. **1** inability; lack of power. **2** legal disqualification.

**incarcerate** /in-**kah**-suh-ˌrayt/ v. (**-ting**) imprison. □ **incarceration** /-**ray**-shuhn/ n. [medieval Latin *carcer* prison]

**incarnate** — adj. /in-**kah**-nuht/ embodied in flesh, esp. in human form (*is the devil incarnate*). — v. /in-kah-ˌnayt, -kah-nayt/ (**-ting**) **1** embody in flesh. **2** put (an idea etc.) into concrete form. **3** be the living embodiment of (a quality). [Latin *incarnor* be made flesh: related to CARNAGE]

**incarnation** /ˌin-kah-**nay**-shuhn/ n. **1 a** embodiment in (esp. human) flesh. **b** (**the Incarnation**) the embodiment of God the Son in human flesh as the Christ. **2** (often foll. by *of*) living type (of a quality etc.).

**incautious** /in-**kaw**-shuhs/ adj. heedless, rash. □ **incautiously** adv.

**incendiary** /in-**sen**-dyuh-ree/ — adj. **1** (of a bomb) designed to cause fires. **2 a** of arson. **b** guilty of arson. **3** tending to stir up strife; inflammatory (*incendiary harangue*). — n. (pl. **-ies**) **1** incendiary bomb. **2 a** arsonist. **b** agitator; troublemaker. □ **incendiarism** n. [Latin *incendo -cens-* set fire to]

**incense**¹ /**in**-sens/ n. **1** gum or spice producing a sweet smell when burned. **2** smoke of this, esp. in religious ceremonial. [Church Latin *incensum*]

**incense**² /in-**sens**/ v. (**-sing**) enrage; make angry. [Latin: related to INCENDIARY]

**incentive** /in-**sen**-tiv/ — n. **1** motive or incitement. **2** payment or concession encouraging effort in work. — attrib. adj. serving to motivate or incite (*incentive scheme*). [Latin *incentivus* that sets the tune]

**inception** /in-**sep**-shuhn/ n. beginning. [Latin *incipio -cept-* begin]

**incertitude** /in-**ser**-tuh-ˌchood, -ˌtyood/ n. uncertainty.

**incessant** /in-**ses**-uhnt/ adj. unceasing, continual, repeated. □ **incessantly** adv. [Latin *cesso* cease]

**incest** /**in**-sest/ n. sexual intercourse between persons too closely related to marry. [Latin *castus* chaste]

**incestuous** /in-**ses**-choo-uhs, -tyoo-uhs/ adj. **1** of or guilty of incest. **2** (in a non-sexual sense) having relationships restricted to a particular group or organisation (*incestuous in their business dealings*). □ **incestuously** adv.

**inch** — n. **1** linear measure of ¹/₁₂ of a foot (2.54 cm). **2** (as a unit of rainfall) 1 inch depth of water. **3** (as a unit of map-scale) so many inches representing 1 mile. **4** small amount (usu. with *neg.*: *would not yield an inch*). — v. move gradually (*inched his way*). □ **by inches** by a very small margin (*missed death by inches*). **every inch** entirely (*looked every inch a queen*). **every inch of the way** to the end (*persisted every inch of the way*). **give a person an inch and he** (or **she**) **will take a mile** make a small concession to a person and he (or she) will take utmost advantage of it to one's detriment. **inch by inch** by extremely small degrees, very gradually (*inch by inch she clawed her way to safety*). **within an inch of** almost to the point of (*came within an inch of dying*). [Old English from Latin *uncia* OUNCE]

**inchoate** /in-**koh**-ayt, **in**-/ adj. **1** just begun. **2** undeveloped; rudimentary. □ **inchoation** /-**ay**-shuhn/ n. [Latin *inchoo, incoho* begin]

---

■ **Usage** *Inchoate* is sometimes used incorrectly to mean 'chaotic' or 'incoherent'.

---

**incidence** /**in**-suh-duhns/ n. **1** (often foll. by *of*) range, scope, extent, or rate of occurrence or influence (of disease, tax, etc.). **2** falling of a line, ray, particles, etc., on a surface. [Latin *cado* fall]

**incident** — n. **1** occurrence, esp. a minor one. **2** public disturbance (*the march took place without incident*). **3** clash of armed forces (*frontier incident*). **4** distinct piece of action in a play, film, etc. — adj. **1** (often foll. by *to*) apt to occur; naturally attaching (*dangers incident to this job*). **2** (often foll. by *on*, *upon*) (of light etc.) falling. [Latin *cado* fall]

**incidental** /ˌin-suh-**den**-tuhl/ — adj. (often foll. by *to*) **1** small and relatively unimportant, minor; supplementary (*incidental expenses*; *incidental to the main story*). **2** not essential. — n. (usu. in pl.) minor detail, expense, event, etc.

**incidentally** adv. **1** by the way. **2** in an incidental way.

**incidental music** n. background music in a film, broadcast, etc.

**incinerate** /in-**sin**-uh-ˌrayt/ v. (**-ting**) burn to ashes. □ **incineration** /-**ray**-shuhn/ n. [medieval Latin *cinis ciner*- ashes]

**incinerator** n. furnace or device for incineration.

**incipient** /in-**sip**-ee-uhnt/ adj. **1** beginning. **2** in an early stage. [Latin *incipio* begin]

**incise** /in-**suyz**/ v. (**-sing**) **1** make a cut in. **2** engrave. [Latin *caedo* cut]

**incision** /in-**sizh**-uhn/ n. **1** act of cutting, esp. by a surgeon. **2** cut made in this way.

**incisive** /in-**suy**-siv/ adj. **1** mentally sharp (*incisive reasoning*). **2** clear and effective (*gave an incisive account*). **3** cutting, penetrating (*incisive wit*).

**incisor** /in-**suy**-zuh/ n. cutting-tooth, esp. at the front of the mouth.

**incite** /in-**suyt**/ v. (**-ting**) (often foll. by *to*) urge or stir up. □ **incitement** n. [Latin *cito* rouse]

**incivility** /ˌin-suh-**vil**-uh-tee/ n. (pl. **-ies**) **1** rudeness. **2** impolite act.

**inclement** /in-**klem**-uhnt/ adj. (of the weather) severe or stormy. □ **inclemency** n.

**inclination** /ˌin-kluh-**nay**-shuhn/ n. **1** disposition or propensity (*an inclination to find fault*). **2** liking, affection (*acted against his inclination*). **3** slope, slant. **4** angle between lines. **5** dip of a magnetic needle. **6** slow nod of the head. [Latin: related to INCLINE]

**incline** — v. /in-**kluyn**/ (**-ning**) **1** (usu. in *passive*) **a** dispose or influence (*am inclined to think so*; *does not incline me to agree*; *don't feel inclined*). **b** have a specified tendency (*the door is inclined to bang*). **2 a** be disposed (*I incline to think so*). **b** (often foll. by *to*, *towards*) tend. **3** (cause to) lean, usu. from the vertical; slope. **4** bend (the head, body, or oneself) forward or downward. — n. /in-**kluyn**/ slope. □ **incline one's ear** listen favourably. [Latin *clino* bend]

**include** /in-**klood**/ v. (**-ding**) **1** comprise or reckon in as part of a whole. **2** (as **including** prep.) if we include (*six, including me*). **3** put in a certain category etc. [Latin *includo -clus-* enclose, from *claudo* shut]

**inclusion** /in-**kloo**-zhuhn/ n. **1** action of including. **2** fact or condition of being included. **3** that which is included. **4** (in pl.) soft-furnishings as included in the purchase price of a house.

**inclusive** /in-**kloo**-siv/ adj. **1** (often foll. by *of*) including. **2** including the limits stated (*pages 7 to 26 inclusive*). **3** including all or much (*inclusive terms*). □ **inclusively** adv. **inclusiveness** n.

**incog** adj., adv., & n. colloq. = INCOGNITO.

**incognito** /ˌin-kog-**nee**-toh/ — predic. adj. & adv. with one's name or identity kept secret. — n. (pl. **-s**) **1** person who is incognito. **2** pretended identity. [Italian, = unknown: related to IN-¹, COGNITION]

**incoherent** /ˌin-koh-**heer**-ruhnt/ adj. **1** unintelligible (*incoherent mutterings*). **2** lacking logic or consistency; not clear (*an incoherent argument*). □ **incoherence** n. **incoherently** adv.

**incombustible** /ˌin-kuhm-**bus**-tuh-buhl/ adj. that cannot be burnt.

**income** /**in**-kum, **ing**-kum/ n. money received, esp. periodically or in a year, from one's work, investments, etc. [from IN, COME]

**-incomer** /**in**-kum-uh, **ing**-kum-uh/ comb. form earning a specified kind or level of income; income-earner (*middle-incomer*; *low-incomer*).

**income tax** n. tax levied on income.

**incoming** /**in**-kum-ing/ — adj. **1** coming in (*incoming telephone calls*). **2** succeeding another (*incoming tenant*). — n. (usu. in pl.) revenue, income.

**incommensurable** /ˌin-kuh-**men**-shuh-ruh-buhl/ adj. (often foll. by *with*) **1** not commensurable. **2** Math. having no common factor, integral or fractional. □ **incommensurability** /-**bil**-uh-tee/ n.

**incommensurate** /ˌin-kuh-**men**-shuh-ruht/ adj. **1** (often foll. by *with*, *to*) out of proportion; inadequate (*my salary is incommensurate with the long hours I work*). **2** = INCOMMENSURABLE.

**incommode** /ˌin-kuh-**mohd**/ v. (**-ding**) formal **1** inconvenience. **2** trouble, annoy.

**incommodious** adj. formal too small for comfort; inconvenient (*incommodious apartment*).

**incommunicable** /ˌin-kuh-**myoo**-ni-kuh-buhl/ adj. that cannot be communicated.

**incommunicado** /ˌin-kuh-ˌmyoo-nuh-**kah**-doh/ adj. **1** without means of communication. **2** (of a prisoner) in solitary confinement. [Spanish *incomunicado*]

**incommunicative** /ˌin-kuh-**myoo**-nuh-kuh-tiv/ adj. not communicative; taciturn.

**incomparable** /in-**kom**-puh-ruh-buhl, -pruh-buhl/ adj. without an equal; matchless. □ **incomparability** /-**bil**-uh-tee/ n. **incomparably** adv.

**incompatible** /ˌin-kuhm-**pat**-uh-buhl/ adj. **1** opposed in character; discordant (*wore incompatible colours*). **2** (often foll. by *with*) inconsistent (*your words are incompatible with your deeds*). **3** (of persons) unable to live, work, etc.

together in harmony. **4** (of medicines) not suitable for taking at the same time. **5** (of equipment, machinery, etc.) not capable of being used in combination. **6** (of an organ, tissue, blood, etc.) not suitable for transplant, grafting, transfusion, etc. because donor and recipient are not well matched. □ **incompatibility** /-bil-uh-tee/ *n*.

**incompetent** /in-**kom**-puh-tuhnt/ — *adj*. lacking the necessary skill. — *n*. incompetent person. □ **incompetence** *n*.

**incomplete** /,in-kuhm-**pleet**/ *adj*. not complete.

**incomprehensible** /in-,kom-pruh-**hen**-suh-buhl/ *adj*. that cannot be understood.

**incomprehension** /in-,kom-pruh-**hen**-shuhn/ *n*. failure to understand.

**inconceivable** /,in-kuhn-**see**-vuh-buhl/ *adj*. **1** that cannot be imagined. **2** *colloq*. most unlikely. □ **inconceivably** *adv*.

**inconclusive** /,in-kuhn-**kloo**-siv/ *adj*. (of an argument, evidence, or action) not decisive or convincing.

**incongruous** /in-**kong**-groo-uhs/ *adj*. **1** out of place; absurd. **2** (often foll. by *with*) disagreeing; out of keeping. □ **incongruity** /-**groo**-uh-tee/ *n*. (*pl*. **-ies**). **incongruously** *adv*.

**inconsequent** /in-**kon**-suh-kwuhnt/ *adj*. **1** irrelevant. **2** lacking logical sequence. **3** disconnected. □ **inconsequence** *n*.

**inconsequential** /in,kon-suh-**kwen**-shuhl/ *adj*. **1** unimportant. **2** = INCONSEQUENT. □ **inconsequentially** *adv*.

**inconsiderable** /,in-kuhn-**sid**-uh-ruh-buhl/ *adj*. **1** of small size, value, etc. **2** not worth considering. □ **inconsiderably** *adv*.

**inconsiderate** /,in-kuhn-**sid**-uh-ruht/ *adj*. (of a person or action) lacking regard for others; thoughtless. □ **inconsiderately** *adv*. **inconsiderateness** *n*.

**inconsistent** /,in-kuhn-**sis**-tuhnt/ *adj*. not consistent. □ **inconsistency** *n*. (*pl*. **-ies**). **inconsistently** *adv*.

**inconsolable** /,in-kuhn-**soh**-luh-buhl/ *adj*. (of a person, grief, etc.) that cannot be consoled. □ **inconsolably** *adv*.

**inconspicuous** /,in-kuhn-**spik**-yoo-uhs/ *adj*. not conspicuous; not easily noticed. □ **inconspicuously** *adv*. **inconspicuousness** *n*.

**inconstant** /in-**kon**-stuhnt/ *adj*. **1** fickle, changeable (*his inconstant love*). **2** variable, not fixed (*the inconstant moon*). □ **inconstancy** *n*. (*pl*. **-ies**).

**incontestable** /,in-kuhn-**tes**-tuh-buhl/ *adj*. that cannot be disputed (*incontestable rights*). □ **incontestably** *adv*.

**incontinent** /in-**kon**-tuh-nuhnt/ *adj*. **1**

unable to control the bowels or bladder. **2** lacking self-restraint (esp. in sexual matters). □ **incontinence** *n*.

**incontrovertible** /,in-kon-truh-**ver**-tuh-buhl/ *adj*. indisputable, undeniable. □ **incontrovertibly** *adv*.

**inconvenience** /,in-kuhn-**vee**-nee-uhns/ — *n*. **1** lack of ease or comfort; trouble. **2** cause or instance of this. — *v*. (**-cing**) cause inconvenience to.

**inconvenient** *adj*. causing trouble, difficulty, or discomfort; awkward. □ **inconveniently** *adv*.

**incorporate** — *v*. /in-**kaw**-puh-,rayt/ (**-ting**) **1** include as a part or ingredient (*incorporated all the latest features*). **2** (often foll. by *in*, *with*) unite (in one body). **3** admit as a member of a company etc. **4** (esp. as **incorporated** *adj*.) form into a legal corporation. — *adj*. /in-**kaw**-puh-ruht/ incorporated. □ **incorporation** /-**ray**-shuhn/ *n*. [Latin *corpus* body]

**incorporeal** /,in-kaw-**paw**-ree-uhl/ *adj*. without physical or material existence. □ **incorporeally** *adv*. **incorporeity** /-puh-**ree**-uh-tee/ *n*.

**incorrect** /,in-kuh-**rekt**/ *adj*. **1** not correct or true. **2** improper, unsuitable (*incorrect behaviour*). □ **incorrectly** *adv*.

**incorrigible** /in-**ko**-ruh-juh-buhl/ *adj*. (of a person or habit) that cannot be corrected or improved. □ **incorrigibility** /-bil-uh-tee/ *n*. **incorrigibly** *adv*.

**incorruptible** /,in-kuh-**rup**-tuh-buhl/ *adj*. **1** that cannot be corrupted, esp. by bribery. **2** that cannot decay. □ **incorruptibility** /-bil-uh-tee/ *n*. **incorruptibly** *adv*.

**increase** — *v*. /in-**krees**/ (**-sing**) make or become greater or more numerous (*increased his weight by 2 kilos*; *profits increased*). — *n*. /**in**-krees/ **1** growth, enlargement. **2** (of people, animals, or plants) growth in numbers; multiplication. **3** amount or extent of an increase. □ **on the increase** increasing. [Latin *cresco* grow]

**increasingly** /in-**kree**-sing-lee/ *adv*. more and more.

**incredible** /in-**kred**-uh-buhl/ *adj*. **1** that cannot be believed. **2** *colloq*. amazing, extremely good. □ **incredibility** /-bil-uh-tee/ *n*. **incredibly** *adv*.

**incredulous** /in-**krej**-uh-luhs, -**kred**-yuh-/ *adj*. unwilling to believe; showing disbelief. □ **incredulity** /,in-kruh-**joo**-luh-tee, -dyoo-/ *n*. **incredulously** *adv*.

**increment** /**in**-kruh-muhnt/ *n*. increase or added amount, esp. on a fixed salary scale. □ **incremental** /-**men**-tuhl/ *adj*. [Latin *cresco* grow]

**incriminate** /in-**krim**-uh-,nayt/ *v*. (**-ting**)

**1** make (a person) appear to be guilty (*the evidence incriminates him*). **2** charge with a crime. □ **incrimination** /-**nay**-shuhn/ *n.* **incriminatory** *adj.* [Latin: related to CRIME]

**incrustation** *n.* = ENCRUSTATION.

**incubate** /ing-kyoo-bayt/ *v.* (**-ting**) **1** hatch (eggs) by sitting on them or by artificial heat. **2** cause (micro-organisms) to develop. **3** develop slowly. [Latin *cubo* lie]

**incubation** /ˌin-kyoo-**bay**-shuhn/ *n.* **1** act of incubating. **2** period between infection and the appearance of the first symptoms.

**incubator** *n.* apparatus providing artificial warmth for hatching eggs, rearing premature babies, or developing micro-organisms.

**incubus** /ing-kyoo-buhs, in-/ *n.* (*pl.* **-buses** or **-bi** /-buy/ ) **1** demon formerly believed to have sexual intercourse with sleeping women (cf. SUCCUBUS). **2** nightmare. **3** person or thing that oppresses like a nightmare. [Latin: as INCUBATE]

**inculcate** /in-kul-ˌkayt/ *v.* (**-ting**) (often foll. by *upon*, *in*) urge or impress (a habit or idea) persistently. □ **inculcation** /-**kay**-shuhn/ *n.* [Latin *calco* tread]

**incumbency** /in-**kum**-buhn-see/ *n.* (*pl.* **-ies**) office or tenure of an incumbent.

**incumbent** — *adj.* **1** resting as a duty (*it is incumbent on you to do it*). **2** (often foll. by *on*) lying or pressing on. **3** currently holding office (*the incumbent president*). — *n.* holder of an office or post. [Latin *incumbo* lie upon]

**incunabulum** /ˌin-kyoo-**nab**-yoo-luhm/ *n.* (*pl.* **-la**) early printed book, esp. from before 1501. [Latin, (in *pl.*) = swaddling-clothes]

**incur** /in-**ker**/ *v.* (**-rr-**) bring on oneself (danger, blame, loss, etc.) (*incurred huge debts*). [Latin *curro* run]

**incurable** /in-**kyoo**-ruh-buhl/ — *adj.* that cannot be cured. — *n.* incurable person. □ **incurability** /-**bil**-uh-tee/ *n.* **incurably** *adv.*

**incurious** /in-**kyoo**-ree-uhs/ *adj.* lacking curiosity.

**incursion** /in-**ker**-shuhn/ *n.* invasion or attack, esp. sudden or brief. □ **incursive** *adj.* [Latin: related to INCUR]

**indebted** /in-**det**-uhd/ *adj.* (usu. foll. by *to*) owing gratitude or money. □ **indebtedness** *n.* [French *endetté*: related to DEBT]

**indecent** /in-**dee**-suhnt/ *adj.* **1** offending against decency (*indecent behaviour*). **2** unbecoming; unsuitable (*indecent haste*). □ **indecency** *n.* (*pl.* **-ies**). **indecently** *adv.*

**indecent assault** *n.* sexual attack upon a male or a female not involving rape.

**indecent exposure** *n.* exposing one's genitals in public.

**indecipherable** /ˌin-duh-**suy**-fuh-ruh-buhl/ *adj.* that cannot be deciphered.

**indecision** /ˌin-duh-**sizh**-uhn/ *n.* inability to decide; hesitation.

**indecisive** /ˌin-duh-**suy**-siv/ *adj.* **1** (of a person) not decisive; hesitating. **2** not conclusive (*an indecisive battle*). □ **indecisively** *adv.* **indecisiveness** *n.*

**indeclinable** /ˌin-duh-**kluy**-nuh-buhl/ *adj. Gram.* that cannot be declined; having no inflections.

**indecorous** /in-**dek**-uh-ruhs/ *adj.* **1** improper, undignified. **2** in bad taste. □ **indecorously** *adv.*

**indeed** /in-**deed**/ — *adv.* **1** in truth; really. **2** admittedly. — *int.* expressing irony, incredulity, etc.

**indefatigable** /ˌin-duh-**fat**-i-guh-buhl/ *adj.* unwearying, unremitting (*made indefatigable attempts*). □ **indefatigably** *adv.*

**indefeasible** /ˌin-duh-**fee**-zuh-buhl/ *adj. Law* (esp. of a claim, rights, etc.) that cannot be forfeited or annulled. □ **indefeasibly** *adv.*

**indefensible** /ˌin-duh-**fen**-suh-buhl/ *adj.* that cannot be defended or justified. □ **indefensibility** /-**bil**-uh-tee/ *n.* **indefensibly** *adv.*

**indefinable** /ˌin-duh-**fuy**-nuh-buhl/ *adj.* that cannot be defined; mysterious. □ **indefinably** *adv.*

**indefinite** /in-**def**-uh-nuht/ *adj.* **1** vague, undefined. **2** unlimited. **3** (of adjectives, adverbs, and pronouns) not determining the person etc. referred to (e.g. *some*, *someone*, *anyhow*).

**indefinite article** *n.* word (e.g. *a*, *an*, *some* in English) preceding a noun and implying 'any of several'.

**indefinitely** *adv.* **1** for an unlimited time (*was postponed indefinitely*). **2** in an indefinite manner.

**indehiscent** /ˌin-duh-**his**-uhnt/ *adj. Bot.* (of fruit) not splitting open when ripe to release seeds. □ **indehiscence** *n.*

**indelible** /in-**del**-uh-buhl/ *adj.* **1** that cannot be rubbed out or removed. **2** (of a pencil, ink, etc.) that makes indelible marks. □ **indelibly** *adv.* [Latin *deleo* efface]

**indelicate** /in-**del**-uh-kuht/ *adj.* **1** coarse, unrefined; tending to indecency. **2** tactless. □ **indelicacy** *n.* (*pl.* **-ies**). **indelicately** *adv.*

**indemnify** /in-**dem**-nuh-ˌfuy/ *v.* (**-ies**, **-ied**) **1** (often foll. by *from*, *against*) secure (a person) in respect of harm, a loss, etc. **2** (often foll. by *for*) exempt from a penalty. **3** compensate (a person) for loss, expenses, etc. □ **indemnification** /-fuh-**kay**-shuhn/ n. [Latin *indemnis* free from loss]

**indemnity** /in-**dem**-nuh-tee/ n. (pl. **-ies**) **1 a** compensation for damage. **b** sum exacted by a victor in war. **2** security against loss. **3** legal exemption from penalties incurred.

**indent** — v. /in-**dent**/ **1** make or impress marks, notches, dents, etc. in. **2** start (a line of print or writing) further from the margin than others. **3** draw up (a legal document) in duplicate. **4 a** (often foll. by *on, upon* a person, *for* a thing) make a requisition. **b** order (goods) by requisition. — n. /in-**dent**/ **1 a** order (esp. from abroad) for goods. **b** official requisition for stores. **2** indented line. **3** indentation. **4** indenture. □ **indented** adj. [Latin *dens dentis* tooth]

**indentation** /ˌin-den-**tay**-shuhn/ n. **1** act or instance of indenting or process of being indented. **2** notch.

**indention** /in-**den**-shuhn/ n. **1** indenting, esp. in printing. **2** notch.

**indenture** /in-**den**-chuh/ — n. **1** (usu. in pl.) sealed agreement or contract. **2** formal list, certificate, etc. **3** agreement binding e.g. an apprentice to service. — v. (**-ring**) bind by indentures, esp. as an apprentice. [Anglo-French: related to INDENT]

**independent** /ˌin-duh-**pen**-duhnt/ — adj. **1 a** (often foll. by *of*) not depending on authority or control. **b** self-governing. **2 a** not depending on another person for one's opinions or livelihood. **b** (of income or resources) making it unnecessary to earn one's living. **3** unwilling to be under an obligation to others. **4** not belonging to or supported by a political party. **5** not depending on something else for its validity etc. (*independent proof*). **6** (of a school) non-government. — n. person who is politically independent. □ **independence** n. **independently** adv.

**in-depth** adj. thorough (*had an in-depth discussion*).

**indescribable** /ˌin-duh-**skruy**-buh-buhl/ adj. **1** too good or bad etc. to be described. **2** that cannot be described. □ **indescribably** adv.

**indestructible** /ˌin-duh-**struk**-tuh-buhl/ adj. that cannot be destroyed. □ **indestructibility** /-bil-uh-tee/ n. **indestructibly** adv.

**indeterminable** /ˌin-duh-**ter**-muh-nuh-buhl/ adj. **1** that cannot be ascertained. **2** (of a dispute etc.) that cannot be settled. □ **indeterminably** adv.

**indeterminate** /ˌin-duh-**ter**-muh-nuht/ adj. **1** not fixed in extent, character, etc.

**2** left doubtful; vague. **3** *Math.* of no fixed value. □ **indeterminacy** n.

**indeterminate vowel** n. unstressed vowel /uh/ heard in '*a* moment *a*go'; a schwa.

**index** /in-deks/ — n. (pl. **indexes** or **indices** /in-duh-ˌseez/) **1** alphabetical list of subjects etc. with references, usu. at the end of a book. **2** = CARD INDEX. **3** measure of prices or wages compared with a previous month, year, etc. (*retail price index*). **4** *Math.* exponent of a number or the power to which it is raised. **5** pointer, esp. on an instrument, showing a position on a scale etc. **6** (usu. foll. by *of*) token, sign, indication of something (*this was the real index of his worth*). **7** *Physics* number expressing a physical property etc. in terms of a standard (*refractive index*). **8** *Computing* set of items each of which specifies one of the records of a file and contains information about its address. **9** (**Index**) *RC Ch. hist.* former list of books dangerous to faith or morals which Catholics were forbidden to read without special permission. — v. **1** provide (a book etc.) with an index. **2** enter in an index. **3** relate (wages etc.) to a price index. □ **indexation** /-**say**-shuhn/ n. (in sense 3 of v.). [Latin]

**index finger** n. forefinger.

**Indian** /in-dee-uhn/ — n. **1 a** native or national of India. **b** person of Indian descent. **2** (in full **American Indian**) **a** original inhabitant of America. **b** any of the languages of the American Indians. — adj. **1** of India or the subcontinent comprising India, Pakistan, and Bangladesh. **2** of the original peoples of America.

**Indian corn** n. maize.

**Indian file** n. = SINGLE FILE.

**Indian giver** n. *colloq.* person who gives a gift and then takes it back.

**Indian hemp** see HEMP 1.

**Indian ink** n. **1** black pigment. **2** ink made from this.

**Indian summer** n. **1** dry warm summery weather in late autumn. **2** tranquil period of life in old age.

**indiarubber** — n. rubber for erasing pencil marks etc. — adj. made of, or pertaining to, indiarubber.

**indicate** /in-duh-ˌkayt/ v. (**-ting**) (often foll. by *that*) **1** point out; make known. **2** be a sign of; show the presence of. **3** call for; require (*stronger measures are indicated*). **4** state briefly (*indicated his disapproval*). **5** give as a reading or measurement. **6** point by hand; use a vehicle's indicator (*failed to indicate*).

□**indication** /ˌin-duh-**kay**-shuhn/ *n.* [Latin *dico* make known]

**indicative** /in-**dik**-uh-tiv/ — *adj.* **1** (foll. by *of*) suggestive; serving as an indication (*fine 'sawdust' at the base of a tree is often indicative of borers*). **2** *Gram.* (of a mood) stating a fact. — *n. Gram.* **1** indicative mood. **2** verb in this mood.

**indicator** *n.* **1** flashing light on a vehicle showing the direction in which it is about to turn. **2** person or thing that indicates. **3** device indicating the condition of a machine etc. **4** recording instrument attached to an apparatus etc. **5** substance which changes colour at a given stage in a chemical reaction.

**indices** *pl.* of INDEX.

**indict** /in-**duyt**/ *v.* accuse formally by legal process. [Anglo-French: related to IN-², DICTATE]

**indictable** *adj.* (of an offence) making the doer liable to be tried by a judge and jury.

**indictment** *n.* **1 a** act of indicting; formal accusation. **b** document containing this. **2** thing that serves to condemn or censure (*poverty is an indictment of society*).

**indifference** /in-**dif**-ruhns/ *n.* **1** lack of interest or attention. **2** unimportance (*a matter of indifference*). **3** neutrality.

**indifferent** *adj.* **1** (foll. by *to*) showing indifference or lack of interest (*indifferent to our plight*). **2** neither good nor bad (*an indifferent result*). **3** of poor quality or ability (*an indifferent pianist*). □ **indifferently** *adv.*

**indigenous** /in-**dij**-uh-nuhs/ *adj.* (often foll. by *to*) native or belonging naturally to a place (opp. those coming later) (*Aborigines are indigenous to Australia; Australia's indigenous plants*). [Latin: from a root *gen-* be born]

**indigent** /in-di-juhnt/ *adj. formal* needy, poor. □ **indigence** *n.* [Latin *egeo* need]

**indigestible** /ˌin-duh-**jes**-tuh-buhl/ *adj.* **1** difficult or impossible to digest. **2** too complex to read or understand. □ **indigestibility** /-**bil**-uh-tee/ *n.*

**indigestion** /ˌin-duh-**jes**-chuhn/ *n.* **1** difficulty in digesting food. **2** pain caused by this.

**indignant** /in-**dig**-nuhnt/ *adj.* feeling or showing indignation. □ **indignantly** *adv.* [Latin *dignus* worthy]

**indignation** /ˌin-dig-**nay**-shuhn/ *n.* scornful anger at supposed unjust or unfair conduct or treatment.

**indignity** /in-**dig**-nuh-tee/ *n.* (*pl.* **-ies**) **1** humiliating treatment or quality. **2** insult.

**indigo** /**in**-di-ˌgoh/ *n.* (*pl.* **-s**) **1** colour between blue and violet in the spectrum. **2** dye of this colour. [Greek *indikon* Indian dye]

**indigofera** /ˌin-dee-**gof**-uh-ruh/ *n.* **1** any plant of the genus *Indigofera*, some species of which yield indigo dye. **2** any plant of this genus native to Australia, esp. *Indigofera australis*, a shrub with fern-like leaves and showy sprays of deep pink to purple pea-flowers. [INDIGO, Latin *fero* bear, produce]

**indirect** /ˌin-duy-**rekt**/ *adj.* **1** not going straight to the point. **2** (of a route etc.) not straight. **3 a** not directly sought (*indirect result*). **b** not primary (*indirect cause*). □ **indirectly** *adv.*

**indirect object** *n. Gram.* person or thing affected by a verbal action but not primarily acted on (e.g. *him* in *give him the book*).

**indirect speech** *n.* = REPORTED SPEECH.

**indirect tax** *n.* tax on goods and services, not on income or profits.

**indiscernible** /ˌin-duh-**ser**-nuh-buhl/ *adj.* that cannot be discerned.

**indiscreet** /ˌin-duh-**skreet**/ *adj.* **1** not discreet. **2** injudicious, unwary. □ **indiscreetly** *adv.*

**indiscretion** /ˌin-duh-**skresh**-uhn/ *n.* **1** lack of discretion; indiscreet conduct. **2** indiscreet words or action etc.

**indiscriminate** /ˌin-duh-**skrim**-uh-nuht/ *adj.* making no distinctions; done or acting at random (*indiscriminate shooting*). □ **indiscriminately** *adv.*

**indispensable** /ˌin-duh-**spen**-suh-buhl/ *adj.* **1** that cannot be dispensed with; necessary. **2** (of a law, duty, etc.) that is not to be set aside. □ **indispensability** /-bil-uh-tee/ *n.* **indispensably** *adv.*

**indisposed** /ˌin-duh-**spohzd**/ *adj.* **1** slightly unwell (*indisposed with indigestion*). **2** averse or unwilling (*indisposed to taking action*). □ **indisposition** /ˌin-dis-puh-**zish**-uhn/ *n.*

**indisputable** /ˌin-duh-**spyoo**-tuh-buhl/ *adj.* that cannot be disputed; unquestionable. □ **indisputably** *adv.*

**indissoluble** /ˌin-duh-**sol**-yuh-buhl/ *adj.* **1** that cannot be dissolved or broken up. **2** firm and lasting. □ **indissolubly** *adv.*

**indistinct** /ˌin-duh-**stingkt**/ *adj.* **1** not distinct. **2** confused, obscure. □ **indistinctly** *adv.*

**indistinguishable** /ˌin-duh-**sting**-gwish-uh-buhl/ *adj.* (often foll. by *from*) not distinguishable.

**indium** /**in**-dee-uhm/ *n.* soft silvery-white metallic element occurring in zinc ores. [Latin *indicum* INDIGO]

**individual** /ˌin-duh-**vid**-yoo-uhl/ — *adj.* **1** of, for, or characteristic of, a single person etc. **2 a** single (*individual words*).

**b** particular; not general. **3** having a distinct character. **4** designed for use by one person. — *n.* **1** single member of a class. **2** single human being. **3** *colloq.* person (*a tiresome individual*). **4** distinctive person. [medieval Latin: related to DIVIDE]

**individualise** *v.* (also **-ize**) (**-sing** or **-zing**) **1** give an individual character to. **2** (esp. as **individualised** *adj.*) personalise (*individualised notepaper*).

**individualism** *n.* **1** social theory favouring free action by individuals. **2** being independent or different. **3** self-centred feeling or conduct; egoism. □ **individualist** *n.* **individualistic** *adj.*

**individuality** /ˌin-duh-vid-yoo-**al**-uh-tee/ *n.* **1** individual character, esp. when strongly marked. **2** separate existence.

**individually** *adv.* **1** one by one. **2** personally. **3** distinctively.

**indivisible** /ˌin-duh-**viz**-uh-buhl/ *adj.* not divisible.

**indoctrinate** /in-**dok**-truh-ˌnayt/ *v.* (**-ting**) teach to accept a particular belief uncritically. □ **indoctrination** /-**nay**-shuhn/ *n.*

**Indo-European** /ˌin-doh-ˌyoo-ruh-**pee**-uhn/ — *adj.* **1** of the family of languages spoken over most of Europe and Asia as far as N. India. **2** of the hypothetical parent language of this family. — *n.* **1** Indo-European family of languages. **2** hypothetical parent language of these.

**indolent** /**in**-duh-luhnt/ *adj.* lazy; averse to exertion. □ **indolence** *n.* **indolently** *adv.* [Latin *doleo* suffer pain]

**indomitable** /in-**dom**-uh-tuh-buhl/ *adj.* **1** unconquerable. **2** unyielding. □ **indomitably** *adv.* [Latin: related to IN-¹, *domito* tame]

**indoor** *adj.* of, done, or for use in a building or under cover.

**indoors** /in-**dawz**/ *adv.* into or in a building.

**indubitable** /in-**dyoo**-buh-tuh-buhl/ *adj.* that cannot be doubted. □ **indubitably** *adv.* [Latin *dubito* doubt]

**induce** /in-**dyoos**/ *v.* (**-cing**) **1** prevail on; persuade (*induced him to sing*). **2** bring about (*smoking induces respiratory problems*). **3 a** bring on (labour) artificially. **b** bring on labour in (a mother). **c** speed up the birth of (a baby). **4** produce (a current) by induction. **5** infer; deduce. □ **inducible** *adj.* [Latin *duco duct-* lead]

**inducement** *n.* attractive offer; incentive; bribe.

**induct** /in-**dukt**/ *v.* (often foll. by *to, into*) introduce into office, formally install (into a benefice etc.). [related to INDUCE]

**inductance** *n.* property of an electric circuit generating an electromotive force by virtue of the current flowing through it.

**induction** /in-**duk**-shuhn/ *n.* **1** act of inducting or inducing. **2** act of bringing on (esp. labour) by artificial means. **3** inference of a general law from particular instances (cf. DEDUCTION). **4** (often *attrib.*) formal introduction to a new job etc. (*induction course*). **5** *Electr.* **a** production of an electric or magnetic state by the proximity (without contact) of an electrified or magnetised body. **b** production of an electric current by a change of magnetic field. **6** drawing of the fuel mixture into the cylinders of an internal-combustion engine.

**inductive** /in-**duk**-tiv/ *adj.* **1** (of reasoning etc.) based on induction. **2** of electric or magnetic induction.

**inductor** *n.* component (in an electric circuit) having inductance.

**indulge** /in-**dulj**/ *v.* (**-ging**) **1** (often foll. by *in*) take pleasure freely. **2** yield freely to (a desire etc.). **3** (also *refl.*) gratify the wishes of (*he indulges his children outrageously*; *indulged themselves on sweets till they were sick*). **4** *colloq.* take alcoholic liquor. [Latin *indulgeo* give free rein to]

**indulgence** *n.* **1** act of indulging or state of being indulgent. **2** thing indulged in. **3** *RC Ch.* remission of punishment in purgatory, still due for sins after absolution. **4** privilege granted.

**indulgent** *adj.* **1** lenient; ready to overlook faults etc. **2** indulging. □ **indulgently** *adv.*

**industrial** /in-**dus**-tree-uhl/ *adj.* **1** of, engaged in, or for use in or serving the needs of industries (*industrial reform*; *industrial workers*; *industrial alcohol*; *industrial training*). **2** (of a nation etc.) having developed industries. □ **industrially** *adv.*

**industrial action** *n.* strike or work to rule etc. undertaken by workers for better pay, conditions, safety in the workplace, etc.

**industrial estate** *n.* area of land zoned for factories etc.

**industrialise** *v.* (also **-ize**) (**-sing** or **-zing**) make (a region, nation, etc.) industrial. □ **industrialisation** /-**zay**-shuhn/ *n.*

**industrialism** *n.* social or economic system in which manufacturing industries are prevalent.

**industrialist** *n.* owner or manager in industry.

**industrial relations** *n.pl.* relations between management and workers.

**industrious** /in-**dus**-tree-uhs/ *adj.* hard-working. □ **industriously** *adv.*

**industry** /**in**-duh-stree/ *n.* (*pl.* **-ies**) **1 a** branch of production or manufacture (*mining industry*). **b** large commercial enterprise (*tourism industry*). **c** these collectively (*incentives to industry*). **2** concerted activity (*a hive of industry*). **3** diligence (*worked with great industry on the Shakespeare assignment*). [Latin *industria*]

**-ine¹** *suffix* **1** forming adjectives, meaning 'belonging to, of the nature of' (*Alpine*; *asinine*; *crystalline*). **2** forming feminine nouns (*heroine*). [Latin *-inus*]

**-ine²** *suffix* **1** forming (esp. abstract) nouns (*discipline*; *medicine*). **2** *Chem.* forming nouns denoting derived substances (*amine*; *caffeine*; *chlorine*).

**inebriate** — *v.* /in-**ee**-bree-,ayt/ (**-ting**) **1** make drunk. **2** excite. — *adj.* /in-ee-bree-uht/ drunken. — *n.* /in-ee-bree-uht/ drunkard. □ **inebriation** /-**ay**-shuhn/ *n.* **inebriety** /-**bruy**-uh-tee/ *n.* [Latin *ebrius* drunk]

**inedible** /in-**ed**-uh-buhl/ *adj.* not suitable for eating.

**ineducable** /in-**ed**-yuh-kuh-buhl/ *adj.* incapable of being educated.

**ineffable** /in-**ef**-uh-buhl/ *adj.* **1** too great for description in words (*ineffable sorrow*). **2** that must not be uttered (*ineffable name of God*). □ **ineffability** /-bil-uh-tee/ *n.* **ineffably** *adv.* [Latin *effor* speak out]

**ineffective** /,in-ee-**fek**-tiv, ,in-uh-/ *adj.* not achieving the desired effect or results. □ **ineffectively** *adv.* **ineffectiveness** *n.*

**ineffectual** /in-ee-**fek**-choo-uhl, in-uh-/ *adj.* ineffective, feeble. □ **ineffectually** *adv.* **ineffectualness** *n.*

**inefficient** /,in-uh-**fish**-uhnt/ *adj.* **1** not efficient or fully capable. **2** (of a machine etc.) wasteful. □ **inefficiency** *n.* **inefficiently** *adv.*

**inelegant** /in-**el**-uh-guhnt/ *adj.* **1** ungraceful. **2** unrefined. □ **inelegance** *n.* **inelegantly** *adv.*

**ineligible** /in-**el**-i-juh-buhl/ *adj.* not eligible or qualified. □ **ineligibility** /-bil-uh-tee/ *n.*

**ineluctable** /,in-uh-**luk**-tuh-buhl/ *adj.* inescapable, unavoidable (*an ineluctable duty*). [Latin *luctor* strive]

**inept** /in-**ept**/ *adj.* **1** unskilful (*inept workmanship*). **2** absurd, silly (*inept dress-sense*). **3** out of place (*inept choice of words in the circumstances*). □ **ineptitude** *n.* **ineptly** *adv.* [Latin: related to APT]

**inequable** /in-**ek**-wuh-buhl/ *adj.* **1** unfair. **2** not uniform.

**inequality** /,in-ee-**kwol**-uh-tee, ,in-uh-/ *n.* (*pl.* **-ies**) **1** lack of equality. **2** variability. **3** (of a surface) unevenness.

**inequitable** /in-**ek**-wuh-tuh-buhl/ *adj.* unfair, unjust.

**inequity** /in-**ek**-wuh-tee/ *n.* (*pl.* **-ies**) unfairness, injustice.

**ineradicable** /,in-ee-**rad**-uh-kuh-buhl, ,in-uh-/ *adj.* that cannot be rooted out.

**inert** /in-**ert**/ *adj.* **1** without inherent power of action, motion, or resistance. **2** not reacting chemically with other substances (*inert gas*). **3** sluggish, slow; lifeless. [Latin *iners -ert-*: related to ART]

**inertia** /in-**er**-shuh/ *n.* **1** *Physics* property of matter by which it continues in its existing state of rest or motion unless an external force is applied. **2 a** inertness, lethargy. **b** tendency to remain unchanged (*inertia of the system*). □ **inertial** *adj.* [Latin: related to INERT]

**inertia reel** *n.* reel allowing a seatbelt to unwind freely but locking on impact etc.

**inescapable** /,in-uh-**skay**-puh-buhl/ *adj.* that cannot be escaped or avoided.

**inessential** /,in-uh-**sen**-shuhl/ — *adj.* not necessary; dispensable. — *n.* inessential thing.

**inestimable** /in-**es**-tuh-muh-buhl/ *adj.* too great, precious, etc., to be estimated. □ **inestimably** *adv.*

**inevitable** /in-**ev**-uh-tuh-buhl/ — *adj.* **1** unavoidable; sure to happen. **2** *colloq.* tiresomely familiar. — *n.* (prec. by *the*) inevitable fact, event, etc. □ **inevitability** /-bil-uh-tee/ *n.* **inevitably** *adv.* [Latin *evito* avoid]

**inexact** /,in-eg-**zakt**, ,in-uhk-/ *adj.* not exact. □ **inexactitude** *n.* **inexactly** *adv.*

**inexcusable** /,in-ek-**skyoo**-zuh-buhl, ,in-uhk-/ *adj.* that cannot be excused or justified. □ **inexcusably** *adv.*

**inexhaustible** /,in-eg-**zaw**-stuh-buhl, ,in-uhg-/ *adj.* that cannot be used up, endless (*he has an inexhaustible fund of stale jokes*).

**inexorable** /in-**ek**-suh-ruh-buhl/ *adj.* **1** relentless; unstoppable (*inexorable advance by the enemy*). **2** (of a person or attribute) that cannot be persuaded by request or entreaty (*he was inexorable in his determination*). □ **inexorably** *adv.* [Latin *exoro* entreat]

**inexpedient** /,in-ek-**spee**-dee-uhnt, ,in-uhk-/ *adj.* not expedient.

**inexpensive** /,in-ek-**spen**-siv, ,in-uhk-/ *adj.* not expensive.

**inexperience** /,in-ek-**speer**-ree-uhns, ,in-uhk-/ *n.* lack of experience, knowledge, or skill. □ **inexperienced** *adj.*

**inexpert** /in-**ek**-spert/ *adj.* unskilful; lacking expertise.

**inexpiable** /in-**ek**-spee-uh-buhl/ *adj.* that cannot be expiated or appeased.

**inexplicable** /ˌin-ek-**spli**-kuh-buhl, ˌin-uhk-/ *adj.* that cannot be explained. □ **inexplicably** *adv.*

**inexpressible** /ˌin-ek-**spres**-uh-buhl, ˌin-uhk-/ *adj.* that cannot be expressed in words (*inexpressible pain*). □ **inexpressibly** *adv.*

**inextinguishable** /ˌin-ek-**sting**-gwish-uh-buhl, ˌin-uhk-/ *adj.* that cannot be extinguished or destroyed.

*in extremis* /ˌin ek-**stree**-mis/ *adj.* **1** at the point of death. **2** in great difficulties. [Latin]

**inextricable** /in-**ek**-stri-kuh-buhl, ˌin-uhk-**strik**-/ *adj.* **1** from which one cannot get free (*was in inextricable difficulties*). **2** that cannot be separated, loosened, or solved (*inextricable problem*; *inextricable knot*). □ **inextricably** *adv.*

**infallible** /in-**fal**-uh-buhl/ *adj.* **1** incapable of error. **2** unfailing; sure to succeed (*infallible method*; *infallible proof*; *infallible remedy*). **3** (of the Pope) not able to err when proclaiming, *ex cathedra*, a doctrine of faith or morals. □ **infallibility** /-**bil**-uh-tee/ *n.* **infallibly** *adv.*

**infamous** /**in**-fuh-muhs/ *adj.* notoriously bad. □ **infamously** *adv.* **infamy** /**in**-fuh-mee/ *n.* (*pl.* **-ies**).

**infancy** /**in**-fuhn-see/ *n.* **1** very early childhood. **2** very early stage in the development of an idea, undertaking, etc.

**infant** /**in**-fuhnt/ *n.* **1** child during the earliest period of its life. **2** (*esp. attrib.*) thing in an early stage of its development (*infant industries*). **3** *Law* any person under the legal age of 18. [Latin *infans* unable to speak]

**infanticide** /in-**fan**-tuh-ˌsuyd/ *n.* **1** killing of an infant, esp. soon after birth. **2** person who kills an infant.

**infantile** /**in**-fuhn-ˌtuyl/ *adj.* **1** of or like infants. **2** childish, immature. □ **infantilism** /in-**fan**-tuh-ˌliz-uhm/ *n.*

**infantile paralysis** *n.* poliomyelitis.

**infantry** /**in**-fuhn-tree/ *n.* (*pl.* **-ies**) body of foot-soldiers; foot-soldiers collectively. [Italian *infante* youth, foot-soldier]

**infantryman** *n.* soldier of an infantry regiment.

**infarct** /in-**fahkt**/ *n.* small area of dead tissue caused by an inadequate blood supply. □ **infarction** /in-**fahk**-shuhn/ *n.* [Latin *farcio farct-* stuff]

**infatuate** /in-**fach**-oo-ˌayt, -**fat**-yoo-/ *v.* (**-ting**) (usu. as **infatuated** *adj.*) **1** inspire with intense usu. transitory fondness or admiration. **2** affect with extreme folly. □ **infatuation** /-**ay**-shuhn/ *n.* [Latin: related to FATUOUS]

**infect** /in-**fekt**/ *v.* **1** affect or contaminate with a germ, virus, or disease. **2** imbue (*infected us with her enthusiasm*). **3** taint. [Latin *inficio -fect-* taint]

**infection** /in-**fek**-shuhn/ *n.* **1 a** process of infecting or being infected. **b** instance of this; disease. **2** communication of disease, esp. by air, water, etc.

**infectious** *adj.* **1** infecting. **2** (of a disease) transmissible by infection. **3** (of emotions etc.) quickly affecting or spreading to others (*her joy was infectious*). □ **infectiously** *adv.* **infectiousness** *n.*

**infelicity** /ˌin-fuh-**lis**-uh-tee/ *n.* (*pl.* **-ies**) **1** inapt expression etc. **2** unhappiness. □ **infelicitous** *adj.*

**infer** /in-**fer**/ *v.* (**-rr-**) **1** deduce or conclude. **2** imply. □ **inferable** *adj.* [Latin *fero* bring]

---

■ **Usage** The use of *infer* in sense 2 is considered incorrect by some people.

---

**inference** /**in**-fuh-ruhns/ *n.* **1** act of inferring. **2** thing inferred. **3** *colloq.* something implied. □ **inferential** /-**ren**-shuhl/ *adj.*

**inferior** /in-**feer**-ree-uh/ — *adj.* **1** (often foll. by *to*) lower in rank, quality, etc. **2** of poor quality. **3** situated below. **4** written or printed below the line. — *n.* person inferior to another, esp. in rank. [Latin, comparative of *inferus*]

**inferiority** /in-ˌfeer-ree-o-ruh-tee/ *n.* state of being inferior.

**inferiority complex** *n.* feeling of inadequacy, sometimes marked by compensating aggressive behaviour.

**infernal** /in-**fer**-nuhl/ *adj.* **1** of hell; hellish. **2** *colloq.* detestable, tiresome (*he's an infernal nuisance*). □ **infernally** *adv.* [Latin *infernus* low]

**inferno** /in-**fer**-noh/ *n.* (*pl.* **-s**) **1** raging fire. **2** scene of horror or distress. **3** hell. [Italian: related to INFERNAL]

**infertile** /in-**fer**-tuyl/ *adj.* **1** not fertile. **2** unable to have offspring. □ **infertility** /-**til**-uh-tee/ *n.*

**infest** /in-**fest**/ *v.* (esp. of vermin) overrun (a place). □ **infestation** /-**fes**-tay-shuhn/ *n.* [Latin *infestus* hostile]

**infidel** /**in**-fuh-del/ — *n.* unbeliever in esp. the supposed true religion. — *adj.* **1** of infidels. **2** unbelieving. [Latin *fides* faith]

**infidelity** /ˌin-fuh-**del**-uh-tee/ *n.* (*pl.* **-ies**) unfaithfulness, esp. adultery. [Latin: related to INFIDEL]

**infield** *n.* *Cricket* the part of the ground near the wicket.

**infighting** *n.* **1** conflict or competitiveness

between colleagues. **2** boxing within arm's length.

**infill** /in-fil/ — *n.* material used to fill a hole, gap, etc. — *v.* fill in (a cavity etc.).

**infiltrate** /in-fuhl-,trayt/ *v.* (**-ting**) **1 a** enter (a territory, political party, etc.) gradually and surreptitiously. **b** cause to do this. **2** permeate by filtration. **3** (often foll. by *into, through*) introduce (fluid) by filtration. □ **infiltration** /-**tray**-shuhn/ *n.* **infiltrator** *n.* [from IN-[2], FILTRATE]

**infinite** /in-fuh-nuht/ *adj.* **1** boundless, endless (*infinite reaches of outer space*). **2** very great or many (*his resources were infinite*). □ **infinitely** *adv.* [Latin: related to IN-[1], FINITE]

**infinitesimal** /,in-fin-uh-**tes**-uh-muhl, -**tez**-uh-muhl/ — *adj.* infinitely or extremely small. — *n.* infinitesimal amount. □ **infinitesimally** *adv.*

**infinitive** /in-**fin**-uh-tiv/ — *n.* form of a verb expressing the verbal notion without a particular subject, tense, etc. (e.g. *see* in *we came to see, let him see*). — *adj.* having this form.

**infinity** /in-**fin**-uh-tee/ *n.* (*pl.* **-ies**) **1** state of being infinite; boundlessness. **2** infinite number or extent. **3** very great distance (*gaze into infinity*). **4** *Math.* infinite quantity.

**infirm** /in-**ferm**/ *adj.* **1** physically weak, esp. through age. **2 a** (of a person, the mind, judgment, etc.) weak of will, faltering, irresolute. **b** (of a thing) not firm. **c** (of reasoning etc.) unsound.

**infirmary** *n.* (*pl.* **-ies**) **1** hospital. **2** sick-quarters in a monastery, school, etc.

**infirmity** *n.* (*pl.* **-ies**) **1** state of being infirm. **2** particular physical weakness.

**infix** /in-**fiks**/ *v.* **1** fasten or fix in. **2** impress (a fact etc. in the mind).

**in flagrante delicto** /,in fluh-,gran-tee duh-**lik**-toh/ *adv.* in the very act of committing an offence. [Latin, = in blazing crime]

**inflame** /in-**flaym**/ *v.* (**-ming**) **1** provoke to strong feeling, esp. anger. **2** cause inflammation in; make hot. **3** aggravate. **4** catch or set on fire. **5** light up with or as with flames.

**inflammable** /in-**flam**-uh-buhl/ *adj.* easily set on fire or excited. □ **inflammability** /-bil-uh-tee/ *n.*

■ **Usage** Where there is a danger of *inflammable* being understood to mean the opposite, i.e. 'not easily set on fire', *flammable* can be used to avoid confusion.

**inflammation** /,in-fluh-**may**-shuhn/ *n.* **1** act or instance of inflaming. **2** bodily condition with heat, swelling, redness, and usu. pain.

**inflammatory** /in-**flam**-uh-tuh-ree, -tree/ *adj.* **1** tending to cause anger etc. (*made an inflammatory speech*). **2** of or tending to inflammation of the body.

**inflatable** /in-**flay**-tuh-buhl/ — *adj.* that can be inflated. — *n.* inflatable object.

**inflate** /in-**flayt**/ *v.* (**-ting**) **1** distend with air or gas. **2** (usu. foll. by *with*; usu. in *passive*) puff up (with pride etc.). **3 a** cause inflation of (the currency). **b** raise (prices) artificially. **4** (as **inflated** *adj.*) (esp. of language, opinions, etc.) bombastic, overblown, exaggerated. [Latin *inflo -flat-*]

**inflation** /in-**flay**-shuhn/ *n.* **1** inflating. **2** *Econ.* **a** general increase in prices and fall in the purchasing value of money. **b** increase in the supply of money regarded as causing this. □ **inflationary** *adj.*

**inflect** /in-**flekt**/ *v.* **1** change the pitch of (the voice). **2 a** change the form of (a word) to express grammatical relation. **b** undergo such a change. **3** bend inwards, curve. □ **inflective** *adj.* [Latin *flecto flex-* bend]

**inflection** /in-**flek**-shuhn/ *n.* (also **inflexion**) **1** act or condition of inflecting or being inflected. **2 a** inflected word. **b** suffix etc. used to inflect, e.g. *-ed* in *killed*, *-en* in *oxen*, *-s* in *prayers* and *prays*. **3** modulation of the voice. □ **inflectional** *adj.* [Latin: related to INFLECT]

**inflexible** /in-**flek**-suh-buhl/ *adj.* **1** unbendable. **2** unbending; obdurate (*inflexible in his attitudes*). **3** unchangeable; inexorable (*inflexible rules*). □ **inflexibility** /-bil-uh-tee/ *n.* **inflexibly** *adv.*

**inflexion** var. of INFLECTION.

**inflict** /in-**flikt**/ *v.* (usu. foll. by *on*) **1** deal (a blow, defeat, punishment, etc.). **2** often *joc.* impose (suffering, oneself, etc.) on (*shall not inflict myself on you any longer*). □ **infliction** *n.* **inflictor** *n.* [Latin *fligo flict-* strike]

**in-flight** *attrib. adj.* occurring or provided during a flight.

**inflorescence** /,in-fluh-**res**-uhns/ *n.* **1 a** complete flower-head of a plant. **b** arrangement of this. **2 a** flowering. [Latin: related to IN-[2], FLOURISH]

**inflow** *n.* **1** a flowing in. **2** something that flows in.

**influence** /**in**-floo-uhns/ — *n.* **1** (usu. foll. by *on*) effect a person or thing has on another. **2** (usu. foll. by *over, with*) moral ascendancy or power. **3** thing or person exercising this (*is a good influence on them*). — *v.* (**-cing**) exert influence on; affect. □ **under the influence** *colloq.* drunk. [Latin *influo* flow in]

**influential** /ˌin-floo-**en**-shuhl/ adj. having great influence. □ **influentially** adv.

**influenza** /ˌin-floo-**en**-zuh/ n. virus infection causing fever, aches, and catarrh. [Italian: related to INFLUENCE]

**influx** /**in**-fluks/ n. a flowing in, esp. of people or things into a place (sudden influx of complaints). [Latin: related to FLUX]

**info** /**in**-foh/ n. colloq. information. [abbreviation]

**inform** /in-**fawm**/ v. 1 tell (informed them of their rights). 2 (usu. foll. by against, on) give incriminating information about a person to the authorities. [Latin: related to FORM]

**informal** /in-**faw**-muhl/ adj. 1 without formality (just an informal chat). 2 (of clothing etc.) everyday; not formal. 3 (of language) colloquial. 4 (of a vote) invalid. □ **vote informal** mark a ballot-paper incorrectly (or leave it blank) with the result that the vote is invalid. □ **informality** /-**mal**-uh-tee/ n. (pl. **-ies**). **informally** adv.

**informant** n. giver of information.

**information** /ˌin-fuh-**may**-shuhn/ n. 1 a something told; knowledge. b items of knowledge; news. 2 charge or complaint lodged with a court etc.

**information superhighway** n. information available via computers, esp. by means of the Internet.

**information technology** n. branch of technology concerned with the movement and storage of information, esp. using computers, telecommunications, etc.

**informative** /in-**faw**-muh-tiv/ adj. (also **informatory** /in-**faw**-muh-tuh-ree, -tree/) providing information; instructive.

**informed** adj. 1 knowing the facts; instructed (his answers show that he is badly informed). 2 educated; intelligent (informed opinion; informed listeners).

**informer** n. person who informs, esp. against others.

**infra** /**in**-fruh/ adv. below, further on (in a book etc.). [Latin, = below]

**infra-** comb. form below.

**infraction** /in-**frak**-shuhn/ n. infringement (infraction of the rules). [Latin: related to INFRINGE]

**infra dig** /ˌin-fruh **dig**/ predic. adj. colloq. beneath one's dignity. [Latin infra dignitatem]

**infra-red** /ˌin-fruh-**red**/ adj. of or using rays with a wavelength just longer than the red end of the visible spectrum.

**infrastructure** /**in**-fruh-ˌstruk-chuh/ n. 1 basic structural foundations of a society

or enterprise. 2 roads, bridges, sewers, etc., regarded as a country's economic foundation.

**infrequent** /in-**free**-kwuhnt/ adj. not frequent. □ **infrequently** adv.

**infringe** /in-**frinj**/ v. (**-ging**) 1 break or violate (a law, another's rights, etc.). 2 (usu. foll. by on) encroach; trespass (TV cameras sometimes infringe on people's privacy). □ **infringement** n. [Latin frango fract- break]

**infuriate** /in-**fyoo**-ree-ˌayt/ v. make furious; irritate greatly. □ **infuriating** adj. **infuriatingly** adv. [medieval Latin: related to FURY]

**infuse** /in-**fyooz**/ v. (**-sing**) 1 (usu. foll. by with) fill (with a quality) (anger infused with resentment). 2 steep (tea leaves etc.) in liquid to extract the content; be steeped thus. 3 (usu. foll. by into) instil (life etc.). □ **infuser** n. **infusive** adj. [Latin infundo -fus-: related to FOUND³]

**infusion** /in-**fyoo**-zhuhn/ n. 1 a act of infusing. b liquid extract obtained thus. 2 that which is infused; admixture.

**-ing¹** suffix 1 forming nouns from verbs denoting: **a** a verbal action or its result (fighting is bad). **b** material associated with a process etc. (piping; washing). **c** occupation or event (banking; wedding). 2 occasionally forming nouns from nouns (tubing; shirting). [Old English]

**-ing²** suffix 1 forming the present participle of verbs (fighting in the streets, he lost an eye), often as adjectives (charming; strapping). 2 forming adjectives from nouns (hulking) and verbs (balding). [Old English]

**ingenious** /in-**jee**-nee-uhs/ adj. 1 clever at inventing, organising, etc. 2 (of a machine, theory, etc.) cleverly contrived. □ **ingeniously** adv. [Latin ingenium cleverness]

■ **Usage** Ingenious is sometimes confused with ingenuous.

**ingénue** /ˌon-zhay-**nyoo**/ n. 1 unsophisticated young woman. 2 **a** such a part in a play. **b** actor playing such a part. [French: related to INGENUOUS]

**ingenuity** /ˌin-juh-**nyoo**-uh-tee/ n. inventiveness, cleverness.

**ingenuous** /in-**jen**-yoo-uhs/ adj. 1 innocent; artless. 2 frank. □ **ingenuously** adv. **ingenuousness** n. [Latin ingenuus free-born, frank]

■ **Usage** Ingenuous is sometimes confused with ingenious.

**ingest** /in-**jest**/ v. 1 take in (food etc.). 2

absorb (knowledge etc.). □ **ingestion** /in-**jes**-chuhn/ n. [Latin *gero* carry]

**inglorious** /in-**glaw**-ree-uhs/ adj. **1** shameful. **2** not famous; obscure.

**ingot** /**ing**-guht, -got/ n. (usu. oblong) piece of cast metal, esp. gold. [origin uncertain]

**ingrained** /in-**graynd**/, *attrib.* /**in-**/ adj. **1** deeply rooted; inveterate (*ingrained vices*). **2** (of dirt etc.) deeply embedded.

**ingrate** /**in-**grayt/ n. ungrateful person.

**ingratiate** /in-**gray**-shee-,ayt/ v.refl. (**-ting**) (usu. foll. by *with*) (usu. *pejorative*) bring oneself into favour (*ingratiated himself with his teachers*). □ **ingratiating** adj. **ingratiatingly** adv. [Latin *in gratiam* into favour]

**ingratitude** /in-**grat**-uh-,tyood/ n. lack of due gratitude.

**ingredient** /in-**gree**-dee-uhnt/ n. component part in a mixture. [Latin *ingredior* enter into]

**ingress** /**in-**gres/ n. act or right of going in; place through which one goes in. [Latin *ingressus*: related to INGREDIENT]

**in-group** n. small exclusive group or clique of people with a common interest.

**ingrowing** adj. (esp. of a toenail) growing into the flesh. □ **ingrown** adj.

**inguinal** /**ing-**gwuh-nuhl/ adj. of the groin. [Latin *inguen* groin]

**inhabit** /in-**hab**-uht/ v. (**-t-**) (of a person or animal) dwell in; occupy (a region, house, etc.). □ **inhabitable** adj. [Latin: related to HABIT]

**inhabitant** n. person etc. who inhabits a place.

**inhalant** /in-**hay**-luhnt/ n. **1** medicinal substance for inhaling. **2** (also **inhaler**) apparatus for this.

**inhale** /in-**hayl**/ v. (**-ling**) (often *absol.*) breathe in (air, gas, smoke, etc.). □ **inhalation** /-huh-**lay**-shuhn/ n. [Latin *halo* breathe]

**inhaler** n. **1** device for administering an inhalant, esp. to relieve asthma. **2** person who inhales.

**inhere** /in-**heer**/ v. (**-ring**) be inherent. [Latin *haereo haes-* stick]

**inherent** /in-**he**-ruhnt, in-**heer**-ruhnt/ adj. (often foll. by *in*) existing in something as an essential or permanent attribute. □ **inherence** n. **inherently** adv.

**inherit** /in-**he**-ruht/ v. (**-t-**) **1** receive (property, rank, title, etc.) by legal succession. **2** derive (a characteristic) from one's ancestors (*inherited his father's red hair*). **3** derive (a situation etc.) from a predecessor (*inherited their debts*). □ **inheritable** adj. **inheritor** n. [Latin *heres* heir]

**inheritance** n. **1** thing that is inherited. **2** inheriting.

**inhibit** /in-**hib**-uht/ v. (**-t-**) **1** hinder, restrain, or prevent (action or progress). **2** (as **inhibited** adj.) suffering from inhibition. **3** (usu. foll. by *from* + verbal noun) prohibit (a person etc.). □ **inhibitor** n. **inhibiter** n. **inhibitory** adj. [Latin *inhibeo -hibit-* hinder]

**inhibition** /,in-uh-**bish**-uhn, ,in-hi-**bish**-uhn/ n. **1** *Psychol.* restraint on the direct expression of an instinct. **2** emotional resistance to a thought, action, etc. (*has inhibitions about singing in public*). **3** act of inhibiting or process of being inhibited.

**inhospitable** /,in-hos-**pit**-uh-buhl/ adj. **1** not hospitable. **2** (of a region etc.) not affording shelter, favourable conditions, etc. □ **inhospitably** adv. **inhospitality** n.

**in-house** adj. & adv. within an institution, company, etc. (*an in-house project; saw an in-house video at the motel*).

**inhuman** /in-**hyoo**-muhn/ adj. **1** brutal; unfeeling; barbarous. **2** not human. □ **inhumanly** adv.

**inhumane** /,in-hyoo-**mayn**/ adj. not humane. □ **inhumanely** adv.

**inhumanity** n. (pl. **-ies**) **1** brutality; callousness; **2** inhuman or inhumane act.

**inimical** /i-**nim**-uh-kuhl/ adj. **1** hostile. **2** harmful (*smoking is inimical to health*). □ **inimically** adv. [Latin *inimicus* enemy]

**inimitable** /i-**nim**-uh-tuh-buhl/ adj. impossible to imitate. □ **inimitably** adv.

**iniquity** /i-**nik**-wuh-tee/ n. (pl. **-ies**) **1** wickedness. **2** gross injustice. □ **iniquitous** adj. [French from Latin *aequus* just]

**initial** /i-**nish**-uhl/ — adj. of or at the beginning (*initial expenses*). — n. initial letter, esp. (in pl.) those of a person's names. — v. (**-ll-**) mark or sign with one's initials. □ **initially** adv. [Latin *initium* beginning]

**initialise** /i-**nish**-uh-luyz/ v. (also **-ize**) *Computing* set the value of a variable etc. at the start of an operation.

**initialism** /i-**nish**-uh-,liz-uhm/ n. group of initial letters used as an abbreviation for a name or expression, each letter being pronounced separately (e.g. *ABC*) (cf. ACRONYM).

**initial letter** n. first letter of a word.

**initiate** — v. /i-**nish**-ee-,ayt/ (**-ting**) **1** begin; set going; originate. **2 a** admit (a person) into a society, office, etc., esp. with a ritual. **b** instruct (a person) in a subject. — n. /i-**nish**-ee-uht/ (esp. newly) initiated person. □ **initiation** /-**ay**-shuhn/ n. **initiator** n. **initiatory** adj. [Latin *initium* beginning]

**initiative** /i-**nish**-uh-tiv, i-**nish**-ee-uh-tiv/ *n.* **1** ability to initiate things; enterprise (*lacks initiative*). **2** first step (*peace initiative*). **3** (prec. by *the*) power or right to begin. □ **on one's own initiative** without being prompted by others. **take the initiative** be the first to take action. [French: related to INITIATE]

**inject** /in-**jekt**/ *v.* **1 a** (usu. foll. by *into*) drive (a solution, medicine, etc.) by or as if by a syringe. **b** (usu. foll. by *with*) fill (a cavity etc.) by injecting. **c** administer medicine etc. to (a person) by injection. **2** place (a quality, money, etc.) into something (*may I inject a note of realism into this discussion?*). □ **injection** *n.* **injector** *n.* [Latin *injicere -ject-* from *jacio* throw]

**in-joke** *n.* joke or allusion understood only by an IN-GROUP and baffling to outsiders.

**injudicious** /ˌin-joo-**dish**-uhs/ *adj.* unwise; ill-judged.

**injunction** /in-**jungk**-shuhn/ *n.* **1** authoritative order. **2** judicial order restraining a person or body from an act, or compelling redress to an injured party. [Latin: related to ENJOIN]

**injure** /in-juh/ *v.* (**-ring**) **1** do harm or damage. **2** do wrong to. [back-formation from INJURY]

**injured** *adj.* **1** harmed or hurt. **2** offended (*in an injured tone of voice*).

**injurious** /in-**joo**-ree-uhs/ *adj.* **1** hurtful. **2** (of language) insulting. **3** wrongful.

**injury** /in-juh-ree/ *n.* (*pl.* **-ies**) **1** physical harm or damage. **2** offence to feelings etc. **3** esp. *Law* wrongful action or treatment. [Latin *injuria*]

**injustice** /in-**jus**-tuhs/ *n.* **1** lack of fairness. **2** unjust act. □ **do a person an injustice** judge a person unfairly. [French from Latin: related to IN-¹]

**ink** — *n.* **1** coloured fluid or paste used for writing, printing, etc. **2** black liquid ejected by a cuttlefish etc. — *v.* **1** (usu. foll. by *in, over,* etc.) mark with ink. **2** cover (type etc.) with ink. [Greek *egkauston* purple ink used by Roman emperors]

**inked** /ingkt/ *adj. colloq.* intoxicated. [obscurely from INK]

**inkling** /**ingk**-ling/ *n.* (often foll. by *of*) slight knowledge or suspicion; hint. [origin unknown]

**inkweed** *n.* tropical American perennial herb introduced to Australia and now a weed, having purple-black fruit yielding a red juice.

**inlaid** *past* and *past part.* of INLAY.

**inland** /in-land, in-luhnd/ — *adj.* in the interior of a country. — *n.* **1** (**the Inland**) a Australian outback. **b** inhabitants of this region collectively (*all the Inland listened to the broadcast*). **2** parts of a country remote from the sea or frontiers. — *adv.* in or towards the interior of a country.

**inlander** /in-lan-duh, -luhn-duh/ *n.* one who lives in the sparsely populated interior of Australia, the Inland.

**in-law** *n.* (often in *pl.*) relative by marriage.

**inlay** — *v.* (*past* and *past part.* **inlaid** /in-**layd**/ ) **1** embed (a thing in another) so that the surfaces are even. **2** decorate (a thing with inlaid work). **3** (as **inlaid** *adj.*) (of a piece of furniture etc.) ornamented by inlaying (*an inlaid table*). — *n.* **1** inlaid work. **2** material inlaid. **3** filling shaped to fit a tooth-cavity. [from IN-², LAY¹]

**inlet** /in-luht, -let/ *n.* **1** small arm of the sea, a lake, or a river. **2** piece inserted. **3** way of entry. [from IN, LET¹]

**in loco parentis** /in ˌloh-koh puh-**ren**-tis/ *adv.* (of a teacher etc.) (acting) for or instead of a parent. [Latin]

**inmate** *n.* occupant of a hospital, prison, institution, etc. [probably from INN, MATE]

**in memoriam** /in muh-**maw**-ree-uhm/ — *prep.* in memory of (a dead person) (*in memoriam Tom Smith*). — *n.* written article or notice etc. in memory of a dead person; an obituary. [Latin]

**inmost** *adj.* most inward (*inmost region; inmost feelings*). [Old English]

**inn** *n.* small hotel providing liquor, food, accommodation, etc. for travellers (*outback inn*). [Old English: related to IN]

**innards** /in-uhdz/ *n.pl. colloq.* **1** entrails. **2** works (of an engine etc.). [special pronunciation of INWARD]

**innate** /in-**ayt**/ *adj.* inborn; natural (*innate talent*). □ **innately** *adv.* **innateness** *n.* [Latin *natus* born]

**inner** — *adj.* (usu. *attrib.*) **1** further in; inside; interior (*inner compartment*). **2** (of thoughts, feelings, etc.) deeper (*inner motives*). **3** more private, intimate, secret, etc. (*inner circle of the party*). **4** of the mind or spirit (*inner peace*). **5** hidden; not immediately obvious (*inner meaning of this book*). — *n.* Archery **1** division of the target next to the bull's-eye. **2** shot striking this. □ **innermost** *adj.* [Old English, comparative of IN]

**inner city** *n.* central area of a city, esp. regarded as having particular problems (also (with hyphen) *attrib.*: *inner-city housing*).

**innings** *n.* (*pl.* same) **1** esp. *Cricket* part of a game during which a side is batting.

**2** period during which a person can achieve something (*had a long innings in politics*). **3** person's life-span (*had a good innings and died at 94*). [obsolete *in* (verb) = go in]

**innocent** /**in**-uh-suhnt/ — *adj.* **1** free from moral wrong. **2** (usu. foll. by *of*) not guilty (of a crime etc.). **3** simple; guileless. **4** harmless (*innocent fun*). **5** not deliberate or maliciously intended (*an innocent mistake*). **6** (foll. by *of*) without, lacking (*innocent of any knowledge of law*). — *n.* innocent person, esp. a young child. □ **innocence** *n.* **innocently** *adv.* [Latin *noceo* hurt]

**innocuous** /i-**nok**-yoo-uhs/ *adj.* harmless; inoffensive. [Latin *innocuus*: related to INNOCENT]

**innovate** /**in**-uh-,vayt/ *v.* (**-ting**) bring in new methods, ideas, etc.; make changes. □ **innovation** /-**vay**-shuhn/ *n.* **innovative** *adj.* **innovator** *n.* **innovatory** *adj.* [Latin *novus* new]

**innuendo** /,in-yoo-**en**-doh/ *n.* (*pl.* **-es** or **-s**) allusive remark or hint, usu. disparaging or with a double meaning. [Latin, = by nodding at: related to IN-², *nuo* nod]

**innumerable** /i-**nyoo**-muh-ruh-buhl/ *adj.* too many to be counted. □ **innumerably** *adv.*

**innumerate** /i-**nyoo**-muh-ruht/ *adj.* having no knowledge of basic mathematics. □ **innumeracy** *n.*

**inoculate** /i-**nok**-yoo-,layt/ *v.* (**-ting**) treat (a person or animal) with vaccine or serum to promote immunity against a disease. □ **inoculation** /-**lay**-shuhn/ *n.* [Latin *oculus* eye, bud]

**inoffensive** /,in-uh-**fen**-siv/ *adj.* not objectionable; harmless.

**inoperable** /in-**op**-uh-ruh-buhl/ *adj.* **1** *Surgery* that cannot successfully be operated on (*inoperable cancer*). **2** that cannot be worked or operated; inoperative (*the machine was inoperable*).

**inoperative** /in-**op**-uh-ruh-tiv/ *adj.* not working or taking effect.

**inopportune** /in-**op**-uh-,tyoon/ *adj.* not appropriate, esp. not timely.

**inordinate** /in-**aw**-duh-nuht/ *adj.* **1** excessive (*inordinate demands*). **2** disorderly; unrestrained (*inordinate behaviour*; *inordinate rage*). □ **inordinately** *adv.* [Latin: related to ORDAIN]

**inorganic** /,in-aw-**gan**-ik/ *adj.* **1** *Chem.* (of a compound) not organic, usu. of mineral origin. **2** without organised physical structure. **3** extraneous.

**in-patient** *n.* patient who lives in hospital while under treatment.

**input** /**in**-puut/ — *n.* **1** what is put in or taken in. **2** place where energy, information, etc., enters a system (*tape-recorder with microphone input*). **3** action of putting in or feeding in. **4** contribution of information etc. (*his input on Aboriginal deaths in custody was startling*). **5** information fed into a computer. — *v.* (**inputting**; *past* and *past part.* **input** or **inputted**) (often foll. by *into*) **1** put in. **2** supply (data, programs, etc., to a computer etc.).

**inquest** /**in**-kwest, **ing**-/ *n.* **1** a *Law* inquiry by a coroner's court into the cause of a death. **b** judicial inquiry to ascertain the facts relating to an incident etc. **2** *colloq.* discussion analysing the outcome of a game, election, etc. (*footy inquest*). [Romanic: related to INQUIRE]

**inquietude** /in-**kwuy**-uh-,tyood, ing-/ *n.* uneasiness. [Latin: related to QUIET]

**inquire** /in-**kwuyuh**, ing-/ *v.* (**-ring**) **1** seek information formally; make a formal investigation. **2** = ENQUIRE. [Latin *inquaero inquisit-* seek]

**inquiry** *n.* (*pl.* **-ies**) **1** investigation, esp. an official one. **2** = ENQUIRY.

**inquisition** /,in-kwuh-**zish**-uhn, ,ing-/ *n.* **1** intensive search or investigation. **2** judicial or official inquiry. **3** (**the Inquisition**) *RC Ch. hist.* ecclesiastical tribunal for the suppression of heresy, esp. in Spain. □ **inquisitional** *adj.* [Latin: related to INQUIRE]

**inquisitive** /in-**kwiz**-uh-tiv, ing-/ *adj.* **1** unduly curious; prying. **2** seeking knowledge. □ **inquisitively** *adv.* **inquisitiveness** *n.*

**inquisitor** /in-**kwiz**-uh-tuh, ing-/ *n.* **1** official investigator. **2** *hist.* officer of the Inquisition.

**inquisitorial** /in-,kwiz-uh-**taw**-ree-uhl, ing-/ *adj.* **1** of or like an inquisitor. **2** prying. □ **inquisitorially** *adv.*

**in re** /in **ree**, **ray**/ *prep.* = RE¹. [Latin]

**INRI** *abbr.* Jesus of Nazareth, King of the Jews. [Latin *Iesus Nazarenus Rex Iudaeorum*]

**inroad** *n.* **1** (often in *pl.*) encroachment; using up of resources etc. (*made inroads on my time*). **2** hostile attack.

**insalubrious** /,in-suh-**loo**-bree-uhs/ *adj.* (of a climate or place) unhealthy.

**insane** *adj.* **1** mad. **2** *colloq.* **a** extremely foolish. **b** wonderful. □ **insanely** *adv.* **insanity** /-**san**-uh-tee/ *n.* (*pl.* **-ies**)

**insanitary** /in-**san**-uh-tuh-ree, -tree/ *adj.* not sanitary; dirty or germ-carrying.

**insatiable** /in-**say**-shuh-buhl/ *adj.* unable to be satisfied (*insatiable appetite*). □ **insatiability** /-**bil**-uh-tee/ *n.* **insatiably** *adv.*

**insatiate** /in-**say**-shee-uht/ adj. never satisfied (*insatiate greed for wealth*).

**inscribe** /in-**skruyb**/ v. (**-bing**) **1 a** (usu. foll. by *in*, *on*) write or carve (words etc.) on a surface, page, etc. **b** (usu. foll. by *with*) mark (a surface) with characters. **2** (usu. foll. by *to*) write an informal dedication in or on (a book etc.). **3** enter the name of (a person) on a list or in a book. **4** *Geom.* draw (a figure) within another so that points of it lie on the boundary of the other. [Latin *scribo* write]

**inscription** /in-**skrip**-shuhn/ n. **1** words inscribed. **2** act of inscribing. □ **inscriptional** adj. [Latin: related to INSCRIBE]

**inscrutable** /in-**skroo**-tuh-buhl/ adj. mysterious, impenetrable. □ **inscrutability** /-**bil**-uh-tee/ n. **inscrutably** adv. [Latin *scrutor* search]

**insect** /**in**-sekt/ n. **1** small invertebrate of a class characteristically having a head, thorax, abdomen, two antennae, three pairs of thoracic legs, and usu. one or two pairs of thoracic wings. **2** (loosely) any small animal such as a spider. [Latin: related to SECTION]

**insecticide** /in-**sek**-tuh-,suyd/ n. substance for killing insects.

**insectivore** /in-**sek**-tuh-,vaw/ n. **1** animal that feeds on insects. **2** plant which captures and absorbs insects. □ **insectivorous** /-**tiv**-uh-ruhs/ adj. [from INSECT, Latin *voro* devour]

**insecure** /,in-suh-**kyoor**/ adj. **1 a** unsafe; not firm. **b** (of a surface etc.) liable to give way. **2** uncertain; lacking confidence. □ **insecurity** /-**kyoo**-ruh-tee/ n.

**inseminate** /in-**sem**-uh-,nayt/ v. (**-ting**) **1** introduce semen into (a female) by natural or artificial means. **2** sow (seed etc.). □ **insemination** /-**nay**-shuhn/ n. [Latin: related to SEMEN]

**insensate** /in-**sen**-sayt/ adj. **1** without physical sensation. **2** without sensibility; unfeeling. **3** stupid. [Latin: related to SENSE]

**insensible** /in-**sen**-suh-buhl/ adj. **1 a** unconscious. **b** (of bodily extremities etc.) numb; without feeling. **2** (usu. foll. by *of*, *to*) unaware (*insensible of her needs*). **3** callous. **4** too small or gradual to be perceived. □ **insensibility** /in-,sen-suh-**bil**-uh-tee/ n. **insensibly** adv.

**insensitive** /in-**sen**-suh-tiv/ adj. (often foll. by *to*) **1** unfeeling; boorish; crass. **2** not sensitive to physical stimuli. □ **insensitively** adv. **insensitiveness** n. **insensitivity** /-**tiv**-uh-tee/ n.

**insentient** /in-**sen**-shuhnt/ adj. not sentient; inanimate.

**inseparable** /in-**sep**-uh-ruh-buhl/ adj.

(esp. of friends) unable or unwilling to be separated. □ **inseparability** /-**bil**-uh-tee/ n. **inseparably** adv.

**insert** — v. /in-**sert**/ place or put (a thing) into another (*inserted the key into the keyhole*; *inserted an ad in the newspaper*). — n. /**in**-sert/ something inserted, e.g. a loose page in a magazine, a piece of cloth in a garment, etc. [Latin *sero sert-* join]

**insertion** /in-**ser**-shuhn/ n. **1** act of inserting. **2** each appearance of an advertisement in a newspaper etc. **3** thing inserted (*lace insertion in her dress*).

**in-service** attrib. adj. (of training) intended for those actively engaged in the profession or activity concerned.

**inset** — n. /**in**-set/ **1 a** extra section inserted in a book etc.; an insert. **b** small map etc. within the border of a larger one. **2** piece let into a dress etc. — v. /in-**set**/ (**insetting**; past and past part. **inset** or **insetted**) **1** put in as an inset. **2** decorate with an inset.

**inshore** adv. & adj. at sea but close to the shore.

**inside** — n. /**in**-suyd/ **1 a** inner side. **b** inner part; interior. **2** side away from the road and nearest the kerb (*don't overtake a car on the inside*). **3** (usu. in *pl.*) *colloq.* stomach and bowels (*something wrong with my insides*). **4** *colloq.* position affording inside information (*knows someone on the inside*). — adj. /**in**-suyd/ **1** situated on or in the inside. **2** *Soccer, Hockey, etc.* nearer to the centre of the field (*inside forward*). — adv. /in-**suyd**/ **1** on, in, or to the inside (*went inside*). **2** within a more closely settled part of Australia (as opposed to the outback) (*came inside after two years hard yakka in the Northern Territory*). **3** *colloq.* in prison. — prep. /in-**suyd**/ **1** on the inner side of; within (*inside the house*). **2** in less than (*inside an hour*). □ **inside out 1 a** with the inner surface turned outwards (*wore one sock inside out*). **b** in utter confusion; topsy-turvy (*the whole house was inside out after he had searched for his wallet*). **2** thoroughly (*knew his subject inside out*).

**inside country** n. comparatively closely settled parts of Australia as opposed to the outback.

**inside information** n. information not normally accessible to outsiders.

**inside job** n. *colloq.* crime committed by a person living or working on the premises burgled etc.

**insider** /in-**suy**-duh/ n. **1** person who is within an organisation etc. **2** person privy to a secret.

**insider trading** n. Stock Exch. illegal practice of trading to one's own advantage through having access to confidential information.

**inside track** n. **1** lane (on a racecourse etc.) which is shorter because of the curve. **2** position of advantage.

**insidious** /in-**sid**-ee-uhs/ adj. **1** proceeding inconspicuously but harmfully (an insidious disease). **2** treacherous; crafty. □ **insidiously** adv. **insidiousness** n. [Latin insidiae ambush]

**insight** n. (usu. foll. by into) **1** capacity of understanding hidden truths etc., esp. of character or situations. **2** instance of this (had an insight into the difficulties urban Aborigines face).

**insignia** /in-**sig**-nee-uh/ n. (treated as sing. or pl.) badge or distinguishing mark of office etc. (wore his insignia of office). [Latin signum sign]

**insignificant** /,in-sig-**nif**-i-kuhnt/ adj. **1** unimportant (an insignificant amount; these people are insignificant). **2** meaningless. □ **insignificance** n.

**insincere** /,in-sin-**seer**/ adj. not sincere. □ **insincerely** adv. **insincerity** /-**se**-ruh-tee/ n. (pl. **-ies**)

**insinuate** /in-**sin**-yoo-,ayt/ v. (**-ting**) **1** hint obliquely, esp. unpleasantly (insinuated that she was lying). **2** (often refl.; usu. foll. by into) **a** introduce (a person etc.) into favour etc., by subtle manipulation (insinuated himself into the manager's favour). **b** introduce (a thing, oneself, etc.) deviously into a place (insinuated doubt into his mind; insinuated himself into the area reserved for important guests). □ **insinuation** /-**ay**-shuhn/ n. [Latin sinuo curve]

**insipid** /in-**sip**-uhd/ adj. **1** lacking vigour or character; dull. **2** lacking flavour; tasteless. □ **insipidity** /in-si-**pid**-uh-tee/ n. **insipidly** adv. [Latin sapio have savour]

**insist** /in-**sist**/ v. (usu. foll. by on or that; also absol.) maintain or demand assertively (insisted on my going; insisted that he was innocent). [Latin sisto stand]

**insistent** adj. **1** (often foll. by on) insisting (is insistent on taking me with him). **2** forcing itself on the attention (insistent rattle of the window frame). □ **insistence** n. **insistently** adv.

**in situ** /in **sit**-yoo/ adv. in its original place (photographed the skeleton in situ before it was removed for examination). [Latin]

**insobriety** /,in-suh-**bruy**-uh-tee/ n. intemperance, esp. in drinking.

**insofar** /,in-soh-**fah**/ adv. = in so far (see FAR).

**insole** n. fixed or removable inner sole of a boot or shoe.

**insolent** /**in**-suh-luhnt/ adj. impertinently insulting. □ **insolence** n. **insolently** adv. [Latin soleo be accustomed]

**insoluble** /in-**sol**-yoo-buhl/ adj. **1** incapable of being solved. **2** incapable of being dissolved. □ **insolubility** /-**bil**-uh-tee/ n. **insolubly** adv.

**insolvent** /in-**sol**-vuhnt/ — adj. unable to pay one's debts; bankrupt. — n. insolvent person. □ **insolvency** n.

**insomnia** /in-**som**-nee-uh/ n. sleeplessness, esp. habitual. [Latin somnus sleep]

**insomniac** /in-**som**-nee-,ak/ n. person suffering from insomnia.

**insomuch** /,in-soh-**much**/ adv. **1** (foll. by that) to such an extent. **2** (foll. by as) inasmuch. [originally in so much]

**insouciant** /in-**soo**-see-uhnt/ adj. carefree; unconcerned. □ **insouciance** n. [French souci care]

**inspect** /in-**spekt**/ v. **1** look closely at. **2** examine officially. □ **inspection** n. [Latin spicio spect- look]

**inspector** n. **1** person who inspects. **2** official employed to supervise. **3** police officer next above sergeant in rank. □ **inspectorate** n.

**inspiration** /,in-spuh-**ray**-shuhn/ n. **1 a** creative force or influence. **b** person etc. stimulating creativity etc. **c** divine influence, esp. on the writing of Scripture etc. **2** sudden brilliant idea. **3** the drawing in of breath; inhalation. □ **inspirational** adj.

**inspire** /in-**spuyuh**/ v. (**-ring**) **1** stimulate (a person) to esp. creative activity. **2 a** (usu. foll. by with) animate (a person) with a feeling. **b** create (a feeling) in a person (inspires confidence). **3** prompt; give rise to (a poem inspired by love). **4** inhale. **5** (as **inspired** adj.) characterised by inspiration (an inspired performance). □ **inspiring** adj. [Latin spiro breathe]

**inst.** abbr. = INSTANT adj. 4 (the 6th inst.).

**instability** /,in-stuh-**bil**-uh-tee/ n. **1** lack of stability. **2** unpredictability in behaviour etc.

**install** /in-**stawl**/ v. (also **instal**) (**-ll-**) **1** place (equipment etc.) in position ready for use. **2** place (a person) in an office or rank with ceremony. **3** establish (oneself, a person, etc.) in a place etc. (installed herself at the head of the table). □ **installation** /,in-stuh-**lay**-shuhn/ n. [Latin: related to STALL¹]

**instalment** n. **1** any of several usu. equal payments for something. **2** any of several parts, esp. of a broadcast or published story. [Anglo-French estaler fix]

**instance** /**in**-stuhns/ — n. **1** example or illustration of. **2** particular case (*that's not true in this instance*). — v. (**-cing**) cite as an instance (*instanced his previous record*). □ **at the instance of** at the request or suggestion of. **for instance** as an example. **in the first** (or **second** etc.) **instance** in the first (or second etc.) place; at the first (or second etc.) stage (of a proceeding). [French from Latin *instantia* contrary example]

**instant** — adj. **1** occurring immediately (*gives an instant result*). **2** (of food etc.) processed for quick preparation (*instant coffee*). **3** urgent; pressing. **4** Commerce of the current month (*the 6th instant*). — n. **1** precise moment (*come here this instant*). **2** short space of time (*was there in an instant*). [Latin *insto* be urgent]

**instantaneous** /ˌin-stuhn-**tay**-nee-uhs/ adj. occurring or done in an instant. □ **instantaneously** adv.

**instantly** adv. immediately; at once.

**instant replay** n. immediate repetition on television of part of a filmed sports event, often in slow motion.

**instead** /in-**sted**/ adv. **1** (foll. by *of*) in place or lieu of (*stayed instead of going*). **2** as an alternative (*took me instead*).

**instep** n. **1** inner arch of the foot between the toes and the ankle. **2** part of a shoe etc. over or under this. [ultimately from IN-², STEP]

**instigate** /**in**-stuh-ˌgayt/ v. (**-ting**) **1** bring about by incitement or persuasion (*who instigated the inquiry?*). **2** urge on, incite (*instigated them to practise burglary*). □ **instigation** /-**gay**-shuhn/ n. **instigator** n. [Latin *stigo* prick]

**instil** /in-**stil**/ v. (**-ll-**) (often foll. by *into*) **1** introduce (a feeling, idea, etc.) into a person's mind etc. gradually (*instilled fear into them*). **2** put (a liquid) into something in drops. □ **instillation** /-**lay**-shuhn/ n. **instilment** n. [Latin *stillo* drop]

**instinct** — n. /**in**-stingkt/ **1 a** innate pattern of behaviour, esp. in animals. **b** innate impulse. **2** unconscious skill; intuition (*an instinct for music; knew by instinct*). — predic. adj. /in-**stingkt**/ (foll. by *with*) imbued, filled (with life, beauty, etc.) (*his poetry is instinct with passion*). □ **instinctive** /in-**stingk**-tiv/ adj. **instinctively** /-**stingk**-tiv-lee/ adv. **instinctual** /-**stingk**-tyoo-uhl/ adj. [Latin *stinguo* prick]

**institute** /**in**-stuh-ˌchoot/ — n. **1** society or organisation for the promotion of science, education, etc. **2** its premises. — v. (**-ting**) **1** establish; found. **2** initiate (an inquiry etc.). [Latin *statuo* set up]

**institution** /ˌin-stuh-**choo**-shuhn/ n. **1 a** organisation or society founded for a particular purpose (*charitable institution*). **b** building used by an institution. **2** established law, practice, or custom. **3** *colloq.* (of a person etc.) familiar object (*she was quite an institution*). **4** act of instituting or being instituted.

**institutional** adj. **1** of or like an institution. **2** typical of institutions. □ **institutionally** adv.

**institutionalise** v. (also **-ize**) (**-sing** or **-zing**) **1** (as **institutionalised** adj.) (of a prisoner, a long-term patient, etc.) made apathetic and dependent after a long period in an institution. **2** place or keep (a person) in an institution. **3** make institutional.

**instruct** /in-**strukt**/ v. **1** teach (a person) a subject etc.; train. **2** (usu. foll. by *to* + infin.) direct; command. **3** (often foll. by *of* or *that* etc. + clause) inform (a person) of a fact etc. **4** Law **a** employ (a lawyer). **b** inform (*instructed my solicitor; judge instructed the jury*). □ **instructor** n. [Latin *instruo -struct-* build, teach]

**instruction** /in-**struk**-shuhn/ n. **1** (often in *pl.*) **a** order (*gave him my instructions*). **b** direction (as to how a thing works etc.) (*manual of instructions*). **2** teaching (*course of instruction*). **3** Computing description of an operation that is to be performed by a computer. □ **instructional** adj.

**instructive** /in-**struk**-tiv/ adj. tending to instruct; enlightening.

**instrument** /**in**-struh-muhnt/ n. **1** tool or implement, esp. for delicate or scientific work (*surgical instruments*). **2** (in full **musical instrument**) device for producing musical sounds (*wind instrument*). **3 a** thing used in performing an action etc. (*the meeting was an instrument in his success*). **b** person made use of (*he's merely their instrument*). **4** measuring-device, esp. in an aeroplane. **5** formal, esp. legal, document. [Latin *instrumentum*: related to INSTRUCT]

**instrumental** /ˌin-struh-**men**-tuhl/ adj. **1** serving as an instrument or means (*was instrumental in finding the money*). **2** (of music) performed on instruments. **3** of, or arising from, an instrument (*the plane crash was caused by instrumental error*).

**instrumentalist** n. performer on a musical instrument.

**instrumentality** /ˌin-struh-men-**tal**-uh-tee/ n. agency or means.

**instrumentation** /ˌin-struh-men-**tay**-shuhn/ n. **1** arrangement of music for instruments; orchestration. **2** the particular instruments used in a piece of music.

**instrument panel** n. panel, esp. in a car or aeroplane, containing the dials etc. of measuring devices.

**insubordinate** /ˌin-suh-**baw**-duh-nuht/ adj. disobedient; rebellious. □ **insubordination** /-**nay**-shuhn/ n.

**insubstantial** /ˌin-suhb-**stan**-shuhl/ adj. **1** lacking solidity or substance. **2** not real.

**insufferable** /in-**suf**-ruh-buhl/ adj. **1** intolerable (*insufferable impertinence*). **2** unbearably conceited etc. □ **insufferably** adv.

**insufficient** /ˌin-suh-**fish**-uhnt/ adj. not sufficient; inadequate. □ **insufficiency** n. **insufficiently** adv.

**insular** /**in**-syoo-luh, **in**-shoo-luh/ adj. **1 a** of or like an island. **b** separated or remote. **2** narrow-minded. □ **insularity** /-**la**-ruh-tee/ n. [Latin *insula* island]

**insulate** /**in**-syoo-ˌlayt, **in**-shoo-/ v. (**-ting**) **1** prevent the passage of electricity, heat, or sound from (a thing, room, etc.) by interposing non-conductors. **2** isolate. □ **insulation** /-**lay**-shuhn/ n. **insulator** n. [Latin *insula* island]

**insulin** /**in**-syuh-luhn, **in**-suh-, **in**-shuh-/ n. hormone regulating the amount of glucose in the blood, the lack of which causes diabetes. [Latin *insula* island]

**insult** — v. /in-**sult**/ speak to or treat with scornful abuse. — n. /**in**-sult/ **1** insulting remark or action. **2** something so worthless or contemptible as to be offensive (*the 20 cents you gave to the appeal was an insult; that excuse is an insult to my intelligence*). □ **add insult to injury** aggravate a wrong already done. □ **insulting** adj. **insultingly** adv. [Latin *insulto* leap on, assail]

**insuperable** /in-**soo**-puh-ruh-buhl, in-**syoo**-pruh-buhl/ adj. **1** (of a barrier) impossible to surmount. **2** (of a difficulty etc.) impossible to overcome. □ **insuperability** /-**bil**-uh-tee/ n. **insuperably** adv. [Latin *supero* overcome]

**insupportable** /ˌin-suh-**paw**-tuh-buhl/ adj. **1** unable to be endured. **2** unjustifiable.

**insurance** /in-**shoor**-ruhns, -**shaw**-/ n. **1** act or instance of insuring. **2** sum paid for this. **3** measure taken to provide for a possible contingency (*take an umbrella as insurance*). [French: related to ENSURE]

**insure** /in-**shoor**, -**shaw**/ v. (**-ring**) **1** (often foll. by *against*; also *absol.*) secure compensation in the event of loss or damage to (property, life, a person, etc.) by advance regular payments (*insured the house for $200,000; insured against flood damage*). **2** (usu. foll. by *against*)

provide for (a possible contingency) (*insured themselves against rain by taking umbrellas*). [var. of ENSURE]

**insured** n. (usu. prec. by *the*) person etc. covered by insurance.

**insurer** n. person or company selling insurance policies.

**insurgent** /in-**ser**-juhnt/ — adj. in active revolt. — n. rebel. □ **insurgence** n. [Latin *surgo surrect-* rise]

**insurmountable** /ˌin-suh-**mown**-tuh-buhl/ adj. unable to be surmounted or overcome (*insurmountable difficulties*).

**insurrection** /ˌin-suh-**rek**-shuhn/ n. usu. armed rising against established authority; rebellion. □ **insurrectionist** n. [Latin: related to INSURGENT]

**intact** /in-**takt**/ adj. **1** undamaged; entire. **2** untouched. □ **intactness** n. [Latin *tango tact-* touch]

**intake** /**in**-tayk/ n. **1** action of taking in. **2 a** number (of people etc.), or amount, taken in or received. **b** such people etc. (*this year's intake*). **3** place where water is taken into a pipe, or fuel or air enters an engine etc.

**intangible** /in-**tan**-juh-buhl/ — adj. **1** unable to be felt by touching. **2** unable to be grasped mentally. — n. thing that cannot be precisely assessed or defined. □ **intangibility** /-**bil**-uh-tee/ n. **intangibly** adv. [Latin: related to INTACT]

**integer** /**in**-tuh-juh/ n. whole number. [Latin, = untouched, whole]

**integral** /**in**-tuh-gruhl/ — adj. also /in-**teg**-ruhl/ **1 a** of or necessary to a whole (*the heart is an integral part of the body*). **b** forming a whole (*integral design*). **c** complete. **2** of or denoted by an integer. — n. Math. quantity of which a given function is the derivative. □ **integrally** adv. [Latin: related to INTEGER]

---

■ **Usage** The alternative pronunciation given for the adjective, stressed on the second syllable, is considered incorrect by some people.

---

**integral calculus** n. mathematics concerned with finding integrals, their properties and application, etc.

**integrate** /**in**-tuh-ˌgrayt/ v. (**-ting**) **1 a** combine (parts) into a whole. **b** complete by the addition of parts. **2** bring or come into equal membership of society, a school, etc. **3** desegregate, esp. racially (a school etc.). **4** Math. find the integral of. □ **integration** /ˌin-tuh-**gray**-shuhn/ n.

**integrated circuit** n. Electronics small chip etc. of material replacing several separate components in a conventional electronic circuit.

**integrity** /in-**teg**-ruh-tee/ *n.* **1** moral excellence; honesty. **2** wholeness; soundness. [Latin: related to INTEGER]

**integument** /in-**teg**-yoo-muhnt/ *n.* natural outer covering, as a skin, husk, rind, etc. [Latin *tego* cover]

**intellect** /**in**-tuh-ˌlekt/ *n.* **1 a** faculty of reasoning, knowing, and thinking. **b** understanding or mental powers (*his intellect is not great*). **2 a** clever or knowledgeable person (*he is quite an intellect*). **b** the intelligentsia regarded collectively (*the combined intellect of our Australian universities*). [Latin: related to INTELLIGENT]

**intellectual** /ˌin-tuh-**lek**-choo-uhl/ — *adj.* **1** of or appealing to the intellect (*intellectual games and puzzles*). **2** possessing a highly developed intellect (*an intellectual poet*). **3** requiring the intellect. — *n.* intellectual person. □ **intellectuality** /-al-uh-tee/ *n.* **intellectualise** *v.* (also **-ize**) (**-sing** or **-zing**). **intellectually** *adv.*

**intelligence** /in-**tel**-uh-juhns/ *n.* **1 a** intellect; understanding. **b** quickness of understanding. **2 a** the collecting of information, esp. of military or political value. **b** information so collected. **c** people employed in this; secret service.

**intelligence quotient** *n.* number denoting the ratio of a person's intelligence to the average.

**intelligent** *adj.* **1** having or showing intelligence, esp. of a high level. **2** clever. **3 a** (of a computerised device or machine) able to vary its behaviour in response to varying situations and requirements and past experience. **b** (esp. of a computer device) having its own processing capability; incorporating a microprocessor (opp. DUMB). □ **intelligently** *adv.* [Latin *intelligo -lect-* understand]

**intelligentsia** /ˌin-tel-uh-**jent**-see-uh/ *n.* **1** class of intellectuals regarded as possessing culture and political initiative. **2** intellectuals in general. [Russian *intelligentsiya*]

**intelligible** /in-**tel**-uh-juh-buhl/ *adj.* able to be understood. □ **intelligibility** /-**bil**-uh-tee/ *n.* **intelligibly** *adv.*

**intemperate** /in-**tem**-puh-ruht/ *adj.* **1** immoderate; violent (*intemperate language*). **2 a** given to excessive drinking of alcohol. **b** excessively indulgent in one's appetites. □ **intemperance** *n.*

**intend** /in-**tend**/ *v.* **1** have as one's purpose (*we intend to go*; *we intend going*). **2** (usu. foll. by *for, as*) design or destine (a person or a thing) (*I intend him to go*; *I intend it as a warning*). **3** mean

(*what does he intend by that?*). [Latin *tendo* stretch]

**intended** — *adj.* **1** done on purpose; intentional. **2** designed, meant (*the intended result*). — *n. colloq.* one's fiancé or fiancée.

**intense** /in-**tens**/ *adj.* (**intenser, intensest**) **1** existing in a high degree; violent; forceful; extreme (*intense joy*; *intense cold*). **2** eager; emotional (*very intense about his music*). □ **intensely** *adv.* **intenseness** *n.* [Latin *intensus* stretched]

■ *Usage* *Intense* is sometimes confused with *intensive*, and wrongly used to describe a course of study etc.

**intensifier** /in-**ten**-suh-ˌfuy-uh/ *n.* **1** thing that makes something more intense. **2** word or prefix used to give force or emphasis, e.g. *thundering* in *a thundering nuisance*.

**intensify** *v.* (**-ies, -ied**) make or become intense or more intense. □ **intensification** /-fuh-**kay**-shuhn/ *n.*

**intensity** *n.* (*pl.* **-ies**) **1** intenseness. **2** esp. *Physics* measurable amount of some quality, e.g. force, brightness, a magnetic field, etc.

**intensive** — *adj.* **1** thorough, vigorous; directed to a single point, area, or subject (*intensive study*; *intensive bombardment*). **2** of or relating to intensity. **3** serving to increase production in relation to costs (*intensive farming*). **4** (usu. in *comb.*) *Econ.* making much use of (*labour-intensive*). **5** (of an adjective, adverb, etc.) expressing intensity, e.g. *really* in *my feet are really cold*. — *n.* = INTENSIFIER. □ **intensively** *adv.* **intensiveness** *n.*

■ *Usage* See note at *intense*.

**intensive care** *n.* **1** constant monitoring etc. of a seriously ill patient. **2** part of a hospital devoted to this. **3** (*attrib.*: with hyphen: *intensive-care unit*).

**intent** /in-**tent**/ — *n.* intention; purpose (usu. without article) (*with intent to defraud*; *my intent to reach the top*). — *adj.* **1** (usu. foll. by *on*) **a** resolved, determined (*was intent on succeeding*). **b** attentively occupied (*intent on his books*). **2** (esp. of a look) earnest; eager. □ **to all intents and purposes** practically; virtually. □ **intently** *adv.* **intentness** *n.* [Latin *intentus*]

**intention** /in-**ten**-shuhn/ *n.* **1** thing intended; aim, purpose. **2** intending (*done without intention*).

**intentional** *adj.* done on purpose. □ **intentionally** *adv.*

**inter** /in-**ter**/ v. (**-rr-**) bury (a corpse etc.). [Latin *terra* earth]

**inter-** *comb. form* **1** between, among (*intercontinental*). **2** mutually, reciprocally (*interbreed*). [Latin *inter* between, among]

**interact** /,in-tuh-**rakt**/ v. act on each other. □ **interaction** n.

**interactive** *adj.* **1** reciprocally active. **2** (of a computer or other electronic device) allowing a two-way flow of information between a user and it, responding to the user's instructions as they are keyed. □ **interactively** *adv.*

*inter alia* /,in-ter **ay**-lee-uh/ *adv.* among other things. [Latin]

**interbreed** /,in-tuh-**breed**/ v. (*past and past part.* **-bred**) **1** (cause to) breed with members of a different plant or animal species etc. to produce a hybrid. **2** breed within one family etc.

**intercede** /,in-tuh-**seed**/ v. (**-ding**) (usu. foll. by *with*) intervene on behalf of another; plead. [Latin: related to CEDE]

**intercept** /,in-tuh-**sept**/ v. **1** seize, catch, or stop (a person, vehicle, message, ball, etc.) going from one place to another. **2** cut off (light, water, etc.) (*intercepted the flow; those trees intercept my view of the valley*). □ **interception** n. **interceptive** *adj.* **interceptor** n. [Latin *intercipio -cept-* from *capio* take]

**intercession** /,in-tuh-**sesh**-uhn/ n. act of interceding, often by prayer (to the Virgin Mary, saints, etc.). □ **intercessor** n. [Latin: related to INTERCEDE]

**interchange** — v. /,in-tuh-**chaynj**/ (**-ging**) **1** (of two people) exchange (things) with each other. **2** put each of (two things) in the other's place; alternate. — n. /**in**-tuh-,chaynj/ **1** (often foll. by *of*) exchange between two people etc. (*interchange of gifts*). **2** alternation (*the interchange of mallee scrubs and scrub plains*). **3** a departure and arrival point for buses etc. as part of an urban transport system. **4** a major road junction, esp. where freeways converge. **5** *Aust. Rules* player not on the field who may be substituted for an active player in the same team at any point in the game. □ **interchange bench** *Aust. Rules* bench on which the interchanges wait to enter play. [Latin]

**interchangeable** *adj.* that can be interchanged, esp. without affecting the way a thing works. □ **interchangeably** *adv.*

**inter-city** *adj.* existing or travelling between cities.

**intercom** /**in**-tuh-,kom/ n. *colloq.* **1** system of intercommunication by radio or telephone between or within offices,
ships, etc. **2** instrument used in this. [abbreviation]

**intercommunicate** /,in-tuh-kuh-**myoo**-nuh-,kayt/ v. (**-ting**) **1** communicate reciprocally. **2** (of rooms etc.) have access into each other. □ **intercommunication** /-**kay**-shuhn/ n.

**intercontinental** /,in-tuh-,kon-tuh-**nen**-tuhl/ *adj.* connecting or travelling between continents.

**intercourse** /**in**-tuh-,kaws/ n. **1** communication or dealings between individuals, nations, etc. **2** = SEXUAL INTERCOURSE. [Latin: related to COURSE]

**interdependent** /,in-tuh-duh-**pen**-duhnt/ *adj.* dependent on each other. □ **interdependence** n. **interdependency** n.

**interdict** — n. /**in**-tuh-dikt/ **1** authoritative prohibition. **2** *RC Ch.* sentence debarring a person, or esp. a place, from ecclesiastical functions and privileges. — v. /,in-tuh-**dikt**/ **1** prohibit (an action). **2** forbid the use of. **3** (usu. foll. by *from* + verbal noun) restrain (a person). **4** (usu. foll. by *to*) forbid (a thing) to a person. □ **interdiction** /-**dik**-shuhn/ n. **interdictory** /-**dik**-tuh-ree/ *adj.* [Latin *dico* say]

**interdisciplinary** /,in-tuh-**dis**-uh-pluh-nuh-ree, -pluhn-ree/ *adj.* of or between more than one branch of learning.

**interest** /**in**-truhst/ — n. **1 a** the feeling of one whose concern, curiosity, attention, etc. is fixed on something (*have a passionate interest in fishing*). **b** that quality which excites curiosity or holds the attention (*this book lacks interest*). **2** subject, hobby, etc., in which one is concerned (*his interests are knitting and playing Australian Rules*). **3** advantage or profit (*it is in my interest to go*). **4** money paid for the use of money lent. **5 a** thing in which one has a stake or concern (*business interests*). **b** financial stake (in an undertaking etc.). **c** legal concern, title, or right (in property). **6 a** party or group with a common interest (*the brewing interest*). **b** principle or cause with which this is concerned. **7** selfish pursuit of one's own welfare; self-interest. — v. **1** excite the curiosity or attention of. **2** (usu. foll. by *in*) cause (a person) to take a personal interest (*he interested me in Australian ecology*). **3** (as **interested** *adj.*) having a private interest; not impartial or disinterested (*an interested party in this dispute*). □ **declare an** (or **one's**) **interest** make known one's financial etc. interests in an undertaking before it is discussed. **with interest** with increased force etc. (*returned the blow with interest*). [Latin, = it matters]

**interesting** *adj.* causing curiosity; holding the attention. □ **interestingly** *adv.*

**interface** — *n.* /**in**-tuh-ˌfays/ **1** surface forming a boundary between two regions. **2** means or place of interaction between two systems etc.; interaction (*the interface between psychology and education*). **3** esp. *Computing* apparatus for connecting two pieces of equipment so that they can be operated jointly. — *v.* /ˌin-tuh-**fays**/ (**-cing**) (often foll. by *with*) **1** connect with (another piece of equipment etc.) by an interface. **2** interact.

■ **Usage** The use of the noun and verb in sense 2 is deplored by some people.

**interfacing** *n.* stiffish material between two layers of fabric in collars etc.

**interfere** /ˌin-tuh-**feer**/ *v.* (**-ring**) **1** (usu. foll. by *with*) **a** (of a person) meddle; obstruct a process etc. **b** (of a thing) be a hindrance; get in the way (*your activities are interfering with mine*). **2** (usu. foll. by *in*) intervene, esp. without invitation or necessity (*don't interfere in my affairs*). **3** (foll. by *with*) *euphem.* molest or assault sexually. **4** (of light or other waves) combine so as to cause interference. [Latin *ferio* strike]

**interference** *n.* **1 a** act of interfering. **b** instance of this. **2** fading or disturbance of received radio signals. **3** *Physics* combination of two or more wave motions to form a resultant wave in which the displacement is reinforced or cancelled.

**interferon** /ˌin-tuh-**feer**-ˌron/ *n.* any of various proteins inhibiting the development of a virus in a cell etc.

**interfuse** /ˌin-tuh-**fyooz**/ *v.* (**-sing**) **1 a** (usu. foll. by *with*) mix (a thing) with; intersperse. **b** blend (things). **2** (of two things) blend with each other. □ **interfusion** /-**fyoo**-*zh*uhn/ *n.* [Latin: related to FUSE¹]

**intergalactic** /ˌin-tuh-guh-**lak**-tik/ *adj.* of or situated between galaxies.

**interim** /**in**-tuh-ruhm/ — *n.* intervening time (*in the interim he had died*). — *adj.* provisional, temporary (*interim dividend*; *interim report*). [Latin, = in the interim]

**interior** /in-**teer**-ree-uh/ — *adj.* **1** inner (opp. EXTERIOR). **2** remote from the coast or frontier; inland. **3** internal; domestic (opp. FOREIGN). **4** (usu. foll. by *to*) situated further in or within. **5** existing in the mind (or soul). **6** coming from inside. — *n.* **1** interior part; the inside. **2** interior part of a region. **3** home affairs of a country (opp. FOREIGN AFFAIRS). **4** representation of the inside of a room etc. (*Dutch interior*). [Latin]

**interior decoration** *n.* (or **design**) decoration or design of the interior of a building etc. □ **interior decorator** *n.*

**interject** /ˌin-tuh-**jekt**/ *v.* **1** utter (words) abruptly or parenthetically. **2** interrupt; heckle. □ **interjector** *n.* [Latin *jacio* throw]

**interjection** /ˌin-tuh-**jek**-shuhn/ *n.* exclamation, esp. as a part of speech (e.g. *ah!*, *dear me!*).

**interlace** /ˌin-tuh-**lays**/ *v.* (**-cing**) **1** bind intricately together; interweave. **2** cross each other intricately (*fern-fronds interlacing above our heads*). □ **interlacement** *n.*

**interleave** /ˌin-tuh-**leev**/ *v.* (**-ving**) insert (usu. blank) leaves between the leaves of (a book etc.).

**interline** /ˌin-tuh-**luyn**/ *v.* (**-ning**) **1** insert words between the lines of (a document etc.). **2** put an extra layer of material between the fabric of (a garment) and its lining.

**interlink** /ˌin-tuh-**lingk**/ *v.* link or be linked together.

**interlock** /ˌin-tuh-**lok**/ — *v.* **1** engage with each other by overlapping. **2** lock or clasp within each other. — *n.* **1** machine-knitted fabric with fine stitches. **2** mechanism for preventing a set of operations from being performed in any but the prescribed sequence.

**interloper** /**in**-tuh-ˌloh-puh/ *n.* **1** intruder. **2** person who interferes in others' affairs, esp. for profit. □ **interlope** *v.* [after *landloper* vagabond, from Dutch *loopen* run]

**interlude** /**in**-tuh-ˌlood/ *n.* **1 a** pause between the acts of a play. **b** something performed during this pause (*musical interlude*). **2** contrasting event, time, etc. in the middle of something (*brief interlude of peace amidst the turmoil*). **3** piece of music played between other pieces etc. [medieval Latin *ludus* play]

**intermarry** /ˌin-tuh-**ma**-ree/ *v.* (**-ies**, **-ied**) (foll. by *with*) **1** (of races, castes, families, etc.) become connected by marriage. **2** (loosely) marry a near relation. □ **intermarriage** /ˌin-tuh-**ma**-rij/ *n.*

**intermediary** /ˌin-tuh-**mee**-dyuh-ree/ — *n.* (*pl.* **-ies**) intermediate person or thing, esp. a mediator. — *adj.* acting as mediator; intermediate.

**intermediate** /ˌin-tuh-**mee**-dee-uht/ — *adj.* coming between two things in time, place, order, character, etc. — *n.* **1** intermediate thing. **2** chemical compound formed by one reaction and then used in another. [Latin *intermedius*]

**interment** /in-**ter**-muhnt/ *n.* burial.

■ **Usage** *Interment* is sometimes confused with *internment*, which means 'confinement'.

**intermezzo** /,in-ter-**met**-soh/ *n.* (*pl.* **-mezzi** /-**met**-see/ or **-s**) **1 a** short connecting instrumental movement in a musical piece. **b** similar independent piece. **2** short light dramatic or other performance inserted between the acts of a play. [Italian]

**interminable** /in-**ter**-muh-nuh-buhl/ *adj.* **1** endless. **2** tediously long (*interminable speeches*). □ **interminably** *adv.*

**intermingle** /,in-tuh-**ming**-guhl/ *v.* (**-ling**) mix together; mingle.

**intermission** /,in-tuh-**mish**-uhn/ *n.* **1** pause or cessation. **2** interval in a cinema etc. [Latin: related to INTERMITTENT]

**intermittent** /,in-tuh-**mit**-uhnt/ *adj.* occurring at intervals; not continuous (*intermittent showers*). □ **intermittently** *adv.* [Latin *mitto miss-* let go]

**intern** — *n.* /in-**tern**/ (also **interne**)junior (esp. recently graduated) doctor living in a hospital and acting as assistant physician etc. while completing further training. — *v.* /in-**tern**/ confine; oblige (a prisoner, alien, etc.) to reside within prescribed limits. □ **internment** *n.* [French: related to INTERNAL]

■ **Usage** *Internment* is sometimes confused with *interment*, which means 'burial'.

**internal** /in-**ter**-nuhl/ *adj.* **1** of or situated in the inside or invisible part. **2** of the inside of the body (*internal injuries*). **3** of a nation's domestic affairs. **4** used or applying within an organisation. **5 a** intrinsic. **b** of the mind or soul. □ **internality** /-nal-uh-tee/ *n.* **internally** *adv.* [medieval Latin *internus* internal]

**internal-combustion engine** *n.* engine with its motive power generated by the explosion of gases or vapour with air in a cylinder.

**internalise** *v.* (also **-ize**) (**-sing** or **-zing**) **1** *Psychol.* make (attitudes, behaviour, etc.) part of one's nature by learning or unconscious assimilation. **2** suppress (an emotion etc.) (*internalised his grief*). □ **internalisation** *n.*

**international** /,in-tuh-**nash**-uh-nuhl, -**nash**-nuhl/ — *adj.* **1** existing or carried on between nations. **2** agreed on or used by all or many nations. — *n.* **1 a** contest, esp. in sport, between representatives of different countries. **b** such representative. **2** (**International**) any of four successive associations for socialist or Communist action. □ **internationality** /-nal-uh-tee/ *n.* **internationally** *adv.*

**international date-line** *n.* = DATE-LINE 1.

**internationalise** *v.* (also **-ize**) (**-sing** or **-zing**) **1** make international. **2** bring under the protection or control of two or more nations.

**internationalism** *n.* advocacy of a community of interests among nations. □ **internationalist** *n.*

**interne** var. of INTERN *n.*

**internecine** /,in-tuh-**nee**-suyn/ *adj.* mutually destructive. [Latin *internecinus* deadly]

**internee** /,in-ter-**nee**/ *n.* person interned.

**Internet** *n. propr.* international computer network linking computers from educational institutions, government agencies, industry, etc. [INTER, NETWORK]

**interpersonal** /,in-tuh-**per**-suh-nuhl/ *adj.* between persons, social (*interpersonal skills*).

**interplay** /in-tuh-,**play**/ *n.* **1** reciprocal action. **2** operation of two things on each other.

**interpolate** /in-**ter**-puh-,layt/ *v.* (**-ting**) **1 a** insert (words) in a document, book, etc., esp. to mislead. **b** make such insertions in (a book etc.). **2** interject (a remark) in a conversation. **3** estimate (values) between known ones in the same range. □ **interpolation** /-lay-shuhn/ *n.* **interpolator** *n.* [Latin *interpolo* furbish]

**interpose** /,in-tuh-**pohz**/ *v.* (**-sing**) **1** (often foll. by *between*) insert (a thing) between others. **2** say (words) as an interruption; interrupt. **3** exercise or advance (a veto or objection) so as to interfere. **4** (foll. by *between*) intervene (between parties). □ **interposition** /in-tuh-puh-**zish**-uhn/ *n.* [Latin *pono* put]

**interpret** /in-**ter**-pruht/ *v.* (**-t-**) **1** explain the meaning of (words, a dream, etc.). **2** make out or bring out the meaning of (creative work) (often by performance). **3** act as an interpreter. **4** explain or understand (behaviour etc.) in a specified manner (*interpreted his gesture as mocking*). □ **interpretation** /-tay-shuhn/ *n.* **interpretative** *adj.* **interpretive** *adj.* [Latin *interpres -pretis* explainer]

**interpreter** *n.* **1** person who interprets, esp. one who translates foreign speech orally. **2** *Computing* language processor that analyses and executes a program on a line by line basis (cf. COMPILER).

**interracial** /,in-tuh-**ray**-shuhl/ *adj.* between or affecting different races.

**interregnum** /,in-tuh-**reg**-nuhm/ *n.* (*pl.* **-s**) **1** interval when the normal government or leadership is suspended, esp.

between successive reigns or regimes. **2** interval, pause. [Latin *regnum* reign]

**interrelate** /ˌin-tuh-ruh-**layt**/ v. (**-ting**) **1** relate (two or more things) to each other. **2** (of two or more things) relate to each other. □ **interrelation** n. **interrelationship** n.

**interrogate** /in-**te**-ruh-ˌgayt/ v. (**-ting**) question (a person), esp. closely or formally. □ **interrogation** /in-ˌte-ruh-**gay**-shuhn/ n. **interrogator** n. [Latin *rogo* ask]

**interrogative** /ˌin-tuh-**rog**-uh-tiv/ — adj. of, like, or used in a question. — n. interrogative word (e.g. *what?*).

**interrogatory** /ˌin-tuh-**rog**-uh-tuh-ree, -tree/ — adj. questioning (*interrogatory tone*). — n. (pl. **-ies**) formal set of questions.

**interrupt** /ˌin-tuh-**rupt**/ — v. **1** break the continuous progress of (an action, speech, person speaking, etc.). **2** obstruct a person's view etc.). — n. *Computing* the action of interrupting the execution of a program. □ **interruption** n. [Latin: related to RUPTURE]

**interrupter** n. (also **interruptor**) **1** person or thing that interrupts. **2** device for interrupting, esp. an electric circuit.

**intersect** /ˌin-tuh-**sekt**/ v. **1** divide (a thing) by crossing it. **2** (of lines, roads, etc.) cross each other. [Latin: related to SECTION]

**intersection** /ˌin-tuh-**sek**-shuhn/ n. **1** act of intersecting. **2** place where two roads intersect. **3** point or line common to lines or planes that intersect.

**intersperse** /ˌin-tuh-**spers**/ v. (**-sing**) **1** (often foll. by *between*, *among*) scatter (*weeds interspersed among the shrubs*). **2** (foll. by *with*) vary (a thing) by scattering other things among it (*interspersed his performances with brief chats about the music*). □ **interspersion** n. [Latin: related to SPARSE]

**interstate** — adj. /**in**-tuh-ˌstayt/ existing or carried on between States, esp. those of Australia. — adv. /ˌin-tuh-**stayt**/ in, into, or from a State other than that in which one is normally resident (*owner moving interstate*).

**interstellar** /ˌin-tuh-**stel**-uh/ adj. between stars.

**interstice** /in-**ter**-stuhs/ n. (pl. **-s**) /in-**ter**-stuh-seez/ **1** intervening space. **2** chink or crevice. [Latin *interstitium* from *sisto* stand]

**interstitial** /ˌin-tuh-**stish**-uhl/ adj. of, forming, or occupying interstices. □ **interstitially** adv.

**intertwine** /ˌin-tuh-**twuyn**/ v. (**-ning**) **1** (often foll. by *with*) entwine (together). **2** become entwined. □ **intertwinement** n. **intertwiningly** adv.

**interval** /**in**-tuh-vuhl/ n. **1** intervening time or space (*interval of a month between visits*; *interval of 12 cm between plants*). **2** pause or break, esp. between the parts of a performance. **3** difference in pitch between two sounds. □ **at intervals** here and there; now and then. □ **intervallic** /ˌin-tuh-**val**-ik/ adj. [Latin *intervallum* space between ramparts]

**intervene** /ˌin-tuh-**veen**/ v. (**-ning**) **1** occur in time between events. **2** interfere; prevent or modify events. **3** be situated between things. **4** come in as an extraneous factor. [Latin *venio vent-* come]

**intervention** /ˌin-tuh-**ven**-shuhn/ n. **1** act or instance of intervening. **2** interference, esp. by one country in the internal affairs of another. **3** mediation.

**interview** /**in**-tuh-ˌvyoo/ — n. **1** oral examination of an applicant. **2** conversation with a reporter, for a broadcast or publication. **3** meeting face to face, esp. for consultation. — v. hold an interview with. □ **interviewer** n. [French *entrevue*: related to INTER-, *vue* sight]

**interviewee** /ˌin-tuh-vyoo-**ee**/ n. person being interviewed.

**interweave** /ˌin-tuh-**weev**/ v. (**-ving**; past **-wove**; past part. **-woven**) **1** weave together. **2** blend intimately (*fact interwoven with fiction*).

**intestate** /in-**tes**-tuht, in-**tes**-tayt/ — adj. not having made a valid will before death. — n. person who has died intestate. □ **intestacy** /-tuh-see/ n. [Latin: related to TESTAMENT]

**intestine** /in-**tes**-tuhn, in-**tes**-tuyn/ n. (in *sing.* or *pl.*) lower part of the alimentary canal from the end of the stomach to the anus. □ **intestinal** adj. [Latin *intus* within]

**intifada** /ˌin-tuh-**fah**-duh/ n. Arab uprising. [Arabic]

**in-thing** n. *colloq.* (usu. prec. by *the*) currently fashionable or trendy thing (*rap-dancing is the in-thing these days*).

**intimacy** /**in**-tuh-muh-see/ n. (pl. **-ies**) **1** state of being intimate. **2** intimate remark or act; sexual intercourse.

**intimate**[1] /**in**-tuh-muht/ — adj. **1** closely acquainted; familiar (*intimate friend*). **2** private and personal. **3** (usu. foll. by *with*) having sexual relations. **4** (of knowledge) detailed, thorough. **5** (of a relationship between things) close. **6** (of a place etc.) friendly (*an intimate restaurant*). — n. close friend. □ **intimately** adv. [Latin *intimus* inmost]

**intimate**[2] /**in**-tuh-ˌmayt/ v. (**-ting**) **1** (often foll. by *that*) state or make known. **2** imply, hint. □ **intimation** /-**may**-shuhn/

*n.* [Latin *intimo* announce: related to INTIMATE[1]]

**intimidate** /in-**tim**-uh-,dayt/ *v.* (**-ting**) frighten or overawe, esp. in order to subdue or influence. □ **intimidation** /-**day**-shuhn/ *n.* [medieval Latin: related to TIMID]

**into** /in-too, in-tuh/ *prep.* **1** expressing motion or direction to a point on or within (*walked into a tree; ran into the house*). **2** expressing direction of attention etc. (*will look into it*). **3** expressing a change of state (*turned into a dragon; separated into groups*). **4** after the beginning of (*five minutes into the game*). **5** *colloq.* interested in; knowledgeable about (*he's really into art*). [Old English: related to IN, TO]

**intolerable** /in-**tol**-uh-ruh-buhl/ *adj.* that cannot be endured. □ **intolerably** *adv.*

**intolerant** /in-**tol**-uh-ruhnt/ *adj.* not tolerant, esp. of others' beliefs or behaviour. □ **intolerance** *n.*

**intonation** /,in-tuh-**nay**-shuhn/ *n.* **1** modulation of the voice; accent. **2** act of intoning. **3** accuracy of musical pitch (*that singer has good intonation*). [medieval Latin: related to INTONE]

**intone** /in-**tohn**/ *v.* (**-ning**) **1** recite (prayers etc.) with prolonged sounds, esp. in a monotone. **2** utter with a particular tone. [medieval Latin: related to IN-[2]]

**in toto** /in **toh**-toh/ *adv.* completely. [Latin]

**intoxicant** /in-**tok**-suh-kuhnt/ — *adj.* intoxicating. — *n.* intoxicating substance.

**intoxicate** /in-**tok**-suh-,kayt/ *v.* (**-ting**) **1** make drunk. **2** excite or elate beyond self-control (*intoxicated by success*). □ **intoxication** /-**kay**-shuhn/ *n.* [medieval Latin: related to TOXIC]

**intra-** *prefix* on the inside, within. [Latin *intra* inside]

**intractable** /in-**trak**-tuh-buhl/ *adj.* **1** hard to control or deal with. **2** difficult, stubborn. □ **intractability** /-**bil**-uh-tee/ *n.* **intractably** *adv.*

**intramuscular** /,in-truh-**mus**-kyuh-luh/ *adj.* in or into muscle tissue (*intramuscular injection*).

**intransigent** /in-**tran**-suh-juhnt, -zuh-juhnt/ — *adj.* uncompromising, stubborn. — *n.* intransigent person. □ **intransigence** *n.* [Spanish *los intransigentes* extremists]

**intransitive** /in-**tran**-suh-tiv, -zuh-tiv/ *adj.* (of a verb) not taking a direct object, e.g. *sit* in *he sat down*.

**intrauterine** /,in-truh-**yoo**-tuh-,ruyn/ *adj.* within the womb.

**intravenous** /,in-truh-**vee**-nuhs/ *adj.* in or into a vein or veins (*intravenous injection*). □ **intravenously** *adv.*

**in-tray** *n.* tray for incoming documents, letters, etc.

**intrepid** /in-**trep**-uhd/ *adj.* fearless; very brave. □ **intrepidity** /-truh-**pid**-uh-tee/ *n.* **intrepidly** *adv.* [Latin *trepidus* alarmed]

**intricate** /in-truh-**kuht**/ *adj.* very complicated; perplexingly detailed. □ **intricacy** /-kuh-see/ *n.* (*pl.* **-ies**) **intricately** *adv.* [Latin: related to IN-[2], *tricae* tricks]

**intrigue** — *v.* (in-**treeg**/ (**-gues, -gued, -guing**) **1** (foll. by *with*) **a** carry on an underhand plot (*intrigued with them to kidnap the king*). **b** use secret influence. **2** arouse the curiosity of; fascinate (*their antics intrigued me*). — *n.* /in-treeg/ **1** underhand plot or plotting (*machiavellian intrigues*). **2** secret arrangement (*amorous intrigues*). □ **intriguing** *adj.* esp. in sense 2 of *v.* (*an intriguing novel*). **intriguingly** *adv.* [French from Italian *intrigo*]

**intrinsic** /in-**trin**-zik/ *adj.* inherent, essential (*intrinsic value*). □ **intrinsically** *adv.* [Latin *intrinsecus* inwardly]

**intro** /in-troh/ *n.* (*pl.* **-s**) *colloq.* introduction. [abbreviation]

**intro-** *comb. form* into. [Latin]

**introduce** /,in-truh-**dyoos**/ *v.* (**-cing**) **1** (foll. by *to*) make (a person or oneself) known by name to another, esp. formally. **2** announce or present to an audience. **3** bring (a custom etc.) into use. **4** bring (legislation) before parliament etc. **5** (foll. by *to*) initiate (a person) in a subject (*introduced him to fantasy fiction*). **6** insert. **7** bring in; usher in; bring forward. **8** occur just before the start of. **9** put on sale for the first time. □ **introducible** *adj.* [Latin *duco* lead]

**introduction** /,in-truh-**duk**-shuhn/ *n.* **1** introducing or being introduced. **2** formal presentation of one person to another. **3** explanatory section at the beginning of a book, a piece of music, etc. **4** introductory treatise (*An Introduction to Aboriginal Culture*). **5** thing introduced.

**introductory** /,in-truh-**duk**-tuh-ree, -tree/ *adj.* serving as an introduction; preliminary.

**introit** /in-troit/ *n.* **1** psalm or antiphon sung or said as the priest approaches the altar for the Mass. **2** any introductory psalm, anthem, etc. [Latin *introitus* entrance]

**introspection** /,in-truh-**spek**-shuhn/ *n.* examination of one's own thoughts. □ **introspective** *adj.* [Latin *specio* spectlook]

**introvert** /in-truh-,vert/ — *n.* **1** person predominantly concerned with his or her own thoughts and feelings. **2** shy thoughtful person. — *adj.* (also

**introverted**) characteristic of an intro-vert. □ **introversion** /-ver-*zh*uhn/ *n.*

**intrude** /in-**trood**/ *v.* (**-ding**) (foll. by *on, upon, into*) **1** come uninvited or un-wanted. **2** force something unwelcome on a person. [Latin *trudo trus-* thrust]

**intruder** *n.* person who intrudes, esp. a trespasser.

**intrusion** /in-**troo**-*zh*uhn/ *n.* **1** act or instance of intruding. **2** influx of molten rock between existing strata etc. □ **intrusive** /in-**troo**-siv/ *adj.*

**intrust** var. of ENTRUST.

**intuition** /,in-choo-**ish**-uhn/ *n.* immediate insight or understanding without con-scious reasoning. □ **intuit** /in-**choo**-uht/ *v.* **intuitional** *adj.* [Latin *tueor tuit-* look]

**intuitive** /in-**choo**-uh-tiv/ *adj.* of, possessing, or perceived by intuition. □ **intuitively** *adv.* **intuitiveness** *n.* [medieval Latin: related to INTUITION]

**Inuit** /**in**-yoo-uht/ *n.* (also **Innuit**) (*pl.* same or **-s**) N. American Eskimo. [Eskimo *inuit* people]

**inundate** /**in**-uhn-,dayt/ *v.* (**-ting**) (often foll. by *with*) **1** flood. **2** overwhelm (*inundated with enquiries*). □ **inundation** /-**day**-shuhn/ *n.* [Latin *unda* wave]

**inure** /i-**nyoor**/ *v.* (**-ring**) (often in *passive*; foll. by *to*) accustom (a person) to an esp. unpleasant thing (*was inured to hunger*). □ **inurement** *n.* [Anglo-French: related to IN, *eure* work, from Latin *opera*]

**invade** /in-**vayd**/ *v.* (**-ding**) (often *absol.*) **1** enter (a country etc.) under arms to control or subdue it. **2** enter, penetrate, permeate, etc. as an enemy (*invaded by locusts; smell of cooking cabbage invaded the entire house*). **3** (of a disease) attack. **4** encroach upon (a person's rights, esp. privacy). □ **invader** *n.* [Latin *vado vas-* go]

**invalid**[1] /**in**-vuh-lid, -,leed/ — *n.* person enfeebled or disabled by illness or injury. — *attrib. adj.* **1** of or for invalids (*invalid diet*). **2** sick, disabled (*cared for his invalid mother*). — *v.* (**-d-**) **1** (often foll. by *out* etc.) remove (an invalid) from active service (*invalided him out of the army*). **2** (usu. in *passive*) disable (a person) by illness (*was invalided by gout*). □ **invalid-ism** *n.* [Latin: related to IN-[1]]

**invalid**[2] /in-**val**-uhd/ *adj.* not valid, esp. having no legal force. □ **invalidity** /,in-vuh-**lid**-uh-tee/ *n.*

**invalidate** /in-**val**-uh-,dayt/ *v.* (**-ting**) make (a claim etc.) invalid. □ **invalidation** /-**day**-shuhn/ *n.*

**invaluable** /in-**val**-yuh-buhl/ *adj.* above valuation; very valuable. □ **invaluably** *adv.*

**invariable** /in-**vair**-ree-uh-buhl/ *adj.* **1** unchangeable. **2** always the same. **3** *Math.* constant. □ **invariably** *adv.*

**invasion** /in-**vay**-*zh*uhn/ *n.* act of invading or process of being invaded.

**invasive** /in-**vay**-siv, -ziv/ *adj.* **1** (of weeds, cancer cells, etc.) tending to spread. **2** (of surgery) involving large incisions etc. **3** tending to encroach.

**invective** /in-**vek**-tiv/ *n.* strong verbal attack. [Latin: related to INVEIGH]

**inveigh** /in-**vay**/ *v.* (foll. by *against*) speak or write with strong hostility (*inveighed against the rich in our society*). [Latin *invehor -vect-* assail]

**inveigle** /in-**vay**-guhl, in-**vee**-guhl/ *v.* (**-ling**) (foll. by *into*, or *to* + infin.) entice; persuade by guile (*inveigled me into going with him*). □ **inveiglement** *n.* [Anglo-French from French *aveugler* to blind]

**invent** /in-**vent**/ *v.* **1** create by thought, originate (a method, device, etc.). **2** concoct (a false story etc.). □ **inventor** *n.* [Latin *invenio -vent-* find]

**invention** /in-**ven**-shuhn/ *n.* **1** process of inventing or being invented. **2** thing invented, esp. one for which a patent is granted. **3** fictitious story. **4** inventive-ness in literature etc. (*his novel shows fine invention*).

**inventive** *adj.* **1** able or inclined to invent. **2** imaginative; creative. □ **inventively** *adv.* **inventiveness** *n.*

**inventory** /**in**-vuhn-tuh-ree, -tree/ — *n.* (*pl.* **-ies**) **1** complete list of goods in stock etc. **2** goods listed in this. — *v.* (**-ies, -ied**) **1** make an inventory of. **2** enter (goods) in an inventory. [medieval Latin: related to INVENT]

**inverse** /**in**-vers, -**vers**/ — *adj.* inverted in position, order, or relation. — *n.* **1** inverted state. **2** (often foll. by *of*) the direct opposite (*that is the inverse of the truth*). [Latin: related to INVERT]

**inverse proportion** *n.* (also **inverse ratio**) relation between two quantities such that one increases in proportion as the other decreases.

**inversion** /in-**ver**-shuhn/ *n.* **1** turning upside down or inside out. **2** reversal of a normal order, position, or relation. **3** reversal of normal word order for rhetorical effect (e.g. *come the revolution . . .*).

**invert** /in-**vert**/ *v.* **1** turn upside down or inside out. **2** reverse the position, order, or relation of. [Latin *verto vers-* turn]

**invertebrate** /in-**ver**-tuh-bruht, -,brayt/ — *adj.* (of an animal) not having a backbone. — *n.* **1** invertebrate animal. **2** *colloq.* weak-willed, spineless person.

**inverted commas** *n.pl.* = QUOTATION MARKS.

**inverted snob** *n.* person who likes, or takes pride in, what a snob might be expected to disapprove of.

**invest** /in-**vest**/ *v.* **1 a** (often foll. by *in*) apply or use (money), esp. for profit. **b** (foll. by *in*) put money for profit into (stocks etc.). **2** (often foll. by *in*) devote (time etc.) to an enterprise. **3** (foll. by *in*) *colloq.* buy (something useful) (*invested in a new car*). **4 a** (foll. by *with*) provide or credit (a person etc. with qualities) (*invested her with magical importance; invested his tone with irony*). **b** (foll. by *in*) attribute or entrust (qualities or feelings) to (a person etc.) (*distrusted the power invested in doctors*). **5** (often foll. by *with, in*) clothe with the insignia of office; install in an office. **6** cover as with a garment (*mist investing the garden with mystery*). □ **investor** *n.* [Latin *vestis* clothing]

**investigate** /in-**ves**-tuh-ˌgayt/ *v.* (**-ting**) **1** inquire into; examine. **2** make a systematic inquiry. □ **investigation** /in-ˌves-tuh-**gay**-shuhn/ *n.* **investigative** /in-**ves**-tuh-guh-tiv/ *adj.* **investigator** *n.* **investigatory** /in-**ves**-tuh-ˌgay-tuh-ree, -**ves**-tuh-guh-tree/ *adj.* [Latin *vestigo* track]

**investiture** /in-**ves**-tuh-ˌchuh/ *n.* formal investing of a person with honours or rank. [medieval Latin: related to INVEST]

**investment** *n.* **1** act of investing. **2** money invested. **3** property etc. in which money is invested. **4** the devoting of time etc. to something.

**inveterate** /in-**vet**-uh-ruht/ *adj.* **1** (of a person) confirmed in a habit etc. (*an inveterate gambler*). **2** (of a habit etc.) long-established. □ **inveteracy** *n.* [Latin *vetus* old]

**invidious** /in-**vid**-ee-uhs/ *adj.* likely to cause resentment or anger (*invidious position; invidious task*). [Latin *invidiosus*: related to ENVY]

**invigilate** /in-**vij**-uh-ˌlayt/ *v.* (**-ting**) supervise people taking an exam. □ **invigilation** /-**lay**-shuhn/ *n.* **invigilator** *n.* [Latin: related to VIGIL]

**invigorate** /in-**vig**-uh-ˌrayt/ *v.* (**-ting**) give vigour or strength to. □ **invigorating** *adj.* [medieval Latin: related to VIGOUR]

**invincible** /in-**vin**-suh-buhl/ *adj.* unconquerable (*invincible army; invincible stupidity*). □ **invincibility** /-**bil**-uh-tee/ *n.* **invincibly** *adv.* [Latin *vinco* conquer]

**inviolable** /in-**vuy**-uh-luh-buhl/ *adj.* not to be violated or dishonoured (*places of worship should be inviolable*). □ **inviolability** /-**bil**-uh-tee/ *n.* **inviolably** *adv.*

**inviolate** /in-**vuy**-uh-luht/ *adj.* **1** not violated. **2** safe (from violation or harm). □ **inviolacy** *n.*

**invisible** /in-**viz**-uh-buhl/ *adj.* **1** not visible to the eye, either characteristically or because hidden (*invisible guardian angels; the stick-insect was invisible on the twig*). **2** artfully concealed (*invisible mending*). □ **invisibility** /-**bil**-uh-tee/ *n.* **invisibly** *adv.*

**invisible exports** *n.pl.* (also **invisible imports** etc.) intangible commodities, esp. services, involving payment between countries.

**invitation** /ˌin-vuh-**tay**-shuhn/ *n.* **1** process of inviting or fact of being invited. **2** letter or card etc. used to invite.

**invite** — *v.* /in-**vuyt**/ (**-ting**) **1** (often foll. by *to*, or *to* + infin.) ask (a person) courteously to come, or to do something (*invited him to lunch; invited them to reply*). **2** make a formal courteous request for (*invited comments*). **3** tend to call forth unintentionally (*your carelessness is inviting trouble*). **4 a** attract. **b** be attractive. — *n.* /**in**-vuyt/ *colloq.* an invitation. [Latin *invito*]

**inviting** *adj.* **1** attractive. **2** tempting. □ **invitingly** *adv.*

**in vitro** /in **vee**-troh/ *adv.* (of biological processes) taking place in a test-tube or other laboratory environment. [Latin, = in glass]

**in vitro fertilisation** *n.* fertilisation of esp. a human egg by a sperm in a test-tube in order that the embryo which results might be implanted in a uterus.

**invocation** /ˌin-vuh-**kay**-shuhn/ *n.* **1** act or instance of invoking or being invoked, esp. in prayer. **2** summoning of supernatural beings, e.g. the Muses, for inspiration. **3** *Eccl.* the words 'In the name of the Father' etc. used to preface a sermon etc. □ **invocatory** /in-**vok**-uh-tree/ *adj.* [Latin: related to INVOKE]

**invoice** /**in**-vois/ — *n.* bill for usu. itemised goods or services. — *v.* (**-cing**) **1** send an invoice to. **2** make an invoice of. [earlier *invoyes* pl. of *invoy*: related to ENVOY]

**invoke** /in-**vohk**/ *v.* (**-king**) **1** call on (a deity etc.) in prayer or as a witness. **2** appeal to (the law, a person's authority, etc.). **3** summon (a spirit) by charms etc. **4** ask earnestly for (vengeance, help, etc.). [Latin *voco* call]

**involuntary** /in-**vol**-uhn-tree/ *adj.* **1** done without exercising the will; unintentional. **2** (of a muscle or movement etc.) not under the control of the will. □ **involuntarily** *adv.* **involuntariness** *n.*

**involute** /**in**-vuh-₁loot/ *adj.* **1** involved, intricate. **2** (of a shell) curled spirally. **3** (of a leaf) rolled inwards at the edges. [Latin: related to INVOLVE]

**involuted** *adj.* **1** complicated, abstruse. **2** = INVOLUTE 2.

**involution** /₁in-vuh-**loo**-shuhn/ *n.* **1** process of involving. **2** entanglement. **3** intricacy. **4** curling inwards. **5** part that curls inwards. **6** reduction in size or activity of esp. the sex organs in old age.

**involve** /in-**volv**/ *v.* (**-ving**) **1** (often foll. by *in*) cause (a person or thing) to share the experience or effect (of a situation, activity, etc.) (*involved us in the attempt to halt soil-erosion*). **2** imply, entail, make necessary (*this job involves a basic knowledge of botany*). **3** (often foll. by *in*) implicate (a person) in a charge, crime, etc. **4** include or affect in its operations (*changes in the roster won't involve us*). **5** (as **involved** *adj.*) **a** (often foll. by *in*) concerned or interested. **b** complicated in thought or form (*this novel has a highly involved plot*). **c** amorously associated (*how long have you been involved with Jim?*). □ **involvement** *n.* [Latin *volvo* roll]

**invulnerable** /in-**vul**-nuh-ruh-buhl/ *adj.* that cannot be wounded, damaged, or hurt, physically or mentally. □ **invulnerability** /-bil-uh-tee/ *n.* **invulnerably** *adv.*

**inward** /**in**-wuhd/ — *adj.* **1** directed towards the inside; going in. **2** situated within. **3** mental, spiritual. — *adv.* (also **inwards**) **1** towards the inside. **2** in the mind or soul. [Old English: related to IN, -WARD]

**inwardly** *adv.* **1** on the inside. **2** in the mind or soul. **3** (of speaking) not aloud (*murmured inwardly*).

**iodine** /**uy**-uh-₁deen, -duyn/ *n.* **1** black crystalline element forming a violet vapour. **2** solution of this as an antiseptic. [French *iode* from Greek *iōdēs* violet-like]

**ion** /**uy**-uhn/ *n.* atom or group of atoms that has lost one or more electrons (= CATION), or gained one or more electrons (= ANION). [Greek, = going]

**-ion** *suffix* (usu. as **-sion, -tion, -xion**) forming nouns denoting: **1** verbal action (*excision*). **2** instance of this (*a suggestion*). **3** resulting state or product (*vexation*; *concoction*). [Latin *-io*]

**Ionic** /uy-**on**-ik/ *adj.* of the order of Greek architecture characterised by a column with scroll-shapes on either side of the capital. [from *Ionia* in Greek Asia Minor]

**ionic** /uy-**on**-ik/ *adj.* of or using ions. □ **ionically** *adv.*

**ionise** *v.* (also **-ize**) (**-sing** or **-zing**) convert or be converted into an ion or ions. □ **ionisation** /₁uy-uh-nuy-**zay**-shuhn/ *n.*

**ioniser** *n.* (also **ionizer**) device producing ions to improve the quality of the air.

**ionosphere** /uy-**on**-uh-₁sfeer/ *n.* ionised region of the atmosphere above the stratosphere, extending to about 1,000 km above the earth's surface and able to reflect radio waves. □ **ionospheric** /-**sfe**-rik/ *adj.*

**iota** /uy-**oh**-tuh/ *n.* **1** ninth letter of the Greek alphabet (I, ι). **2** (usu. with *neg.*) a jot (*I don't give an iota for what he says*). [Greek *iōta*]

**IOU** /₁uy-oh-**yoo**/ *n.* signed document acknowledging a debt. [from *I owe you*]

**ipso facto** /₁ip-soh **fak**-toh/ *adv.* by that very fact. [Latin]

**IQ** *abbr.* intelligence quotient.

**ir-** *prefix* assim. form of IN-₁, IN-² before *r*.

**Iranian** /i-**ray**-nee-uhn/ — *adj.* **1** of Iran (formerly Persia). **2** of the group of languages including Persian. — *n.* **1** native or national of Iran. **2** person of Iranian descent.

**Iraqi** /i-**rah**-kee/ — *adj.* of Iraq. — *n.* (*pl.* **-s**) **1 a** native or national of Iraq. **b** person of Iraqi descent. **2** the form of Arabic spoken in Iraq.

**irascible** /i-**ras**-uh-buhl/ *adj.* irritable; hot-tempered. □ **irascibility** /-**bil**-uh-tee/ *n.* **irascibly** *adv.* [Latin *irascor* grow angry, from *ira* anger]

**irate** /uy-**rayt**/ *adj.* angry, enraged. □ **irately** *adv.* **irateness** *n.* [Latin *iratus* from *ira* anger]

**ire** /uyuh/ *n. literary* anger. [Latin *ira*]

**iridescent** /₁i-ruh-**des**-uhnt/ *adj.* **1** showing rainbow-like luminous colours. **2** changing colour with position. □ **iridescence** *n.*

**iridium** /i-**rid**-ee-uhm/ *n.* hard white metallic element of the platinum group.

**iris** /**uy**-ruhs/ *n.* **1** circular coloured membrane behind the cornea of the eye, with a circular opening (pupil) in the centre. **2** plant of a family with bulbs or tuberous roots, sword-shaped leaves, and showy flowers. **3** adjustable diaphragm for regulating the size of a central hole, esp. for the admission of light to a lens. [Greek *iris iridos* rainbow]

**Irish** /**uy**-rish/ — *adj.* of Ireland or its people. — *n.* **1** Celtic language of Ireland. **2** (prec. by *the*; treated as *pl.*) the people of Ireland. □ **get one's Irish up** *colloq.* become very angry. **luck of the Irish** *colloq.* extreme good fortune occurring against all the odds. [Old English]

**irk** *v.* irritate, bore, annoy (*it irks me that he doesn't reply to my letters*). [origin unknown]

**irksome** *adj.* annoying, tiresome. □ **irksomely** *adv.*

**iron** /uyuhn/ — n. **1** silver-white ductile metallic element used for tools and constructions and found in some foods, e.g. spinach. **2** this as a symbol of strength or firmness (*man of iron*). **3** tool made of iron (*branding iron*). **4** household, now electrical, implement with a flat base which is heated to smooth clothes etc. **5** golf club with an iron or steel sloping face. **6** (usu. in *pl.*) fetter (*clapped in irons*). **7** (usu. in *pl.*) stirrup. **8** (often in *pl.*) iron support for a malformed leg. — adj. **1** made of iron. **2** very robust (*he has an iron constitution*). **3** unyielding, merciless (*iron determination*). **4** made wholly or partly of sheets of corrugated iron (*lived in a fibro and iron house*). — v. **1** smooth (clothes etc.) with an iron. **2** (usu. foll. by *out*) colloq. knock down; defeat (*we well and truly ironed the visiting team; ironed out our opponents*). □ **iron out (a few wrinkles)** remove (difficulties etc.) (*we still have a few wrinkles to iron out before we submit our plan to the Board*). **rule with a rod of iron** impose stern discipline. **strike while the iron's hot** act immediately while the chance to do so still exists. □ **ironer** n. [Old English]

**Iron Age** n. period when iron replaced bronze in the making of tools and weapons.

**ironbark** n. **1** any of various eastern Australian eucalypts with a thick, hard, usu. black bark and hard, dense timber. **2** (*attrib.* passing into *adj.*) anything exceptionally hard or unyielding (*ate ironbark damper*).

**ironbark pumpkin** n. variety of pumpkin with an exceptionally hard skin.

**iron-bound** adj. **1** bound with iron. **2** rigorous; hard and fast.

**ironclad** adj. **1** clad or protected with iron. **2** impregnable; rigorous (*ironclad agreement*).

**Iron Curtain** n. hist. former notional barrier to the passage of people and information between the Soviet bloc and the West.

**ironed gang** n. (also **iron gang**) hist. detachment of convicts assigned to hard labour in fetters (see also CHAIN GANG).

**iron-fisted** adj. **1** miserly, stingy. **2** harshly severe; ruthless.

**ironic** /uy-**ron**-ik/ adj. (also **ironical**) using or displaying irony. □ **ironically** adv.

**ironing** n. clothes etc. for ironing or just ironed.

**iron in the fire** n. (usu. in *pl.*) undertaking, commitment, project, etc. (*too many irons in the fire*).

**iron lace** n. delicate-looking cast-iron decorative work orig. used in 19th-c. terrace houses.

**iron lung** n. rigid case fitted over a patient's body for administering prolonged artificial respiration.

**iron man** n. **1** winner of an Iron Man competition (an endurance event involving swimming, board-riding, beach-running, etc.) at a surf carnival etc. **2** any exceptionally strong man.

**ironstone** n. **1** any rock containing much iron. **2** (esp. in Australia) hard sandstone, siltstone, or shale rich in iron oxides and reddish to purplish in colour. **3** a kind of hard white pottery.

**ironware** n. articles made of iron, esp. domestic implements; hardware.

**iron woman** n. winner of an endurance competition at a surf carnival etc. (cf. IRON MAN)

**ironwood** n. **1** a any of several Australian trees yielding a particularly hard, heavy timber, esp. two species of wattle in northern Australia. **b** the wood of these trees. **2** any similar tree elsewhere.

**irony** /**uy**-ruh-nee/ n. (*pl.* -**ies**) **1** form of speech in which the real and intended meaning (which may be humorous, sardonic, cutting, etc.) is belied by the words used (which may at first seem innocent or guileless); at its crudest level this approximates to sarcasm (where 'charming manners!', as the tone would indicate, means just the opposite); irony is always more subtle. **2** something said with irony. **3** pretended ignorance or naivety in a discussion etc. (*Socratic irony*). **4** *Theatr.* use of language with one meaning for a privileged audience and another for those (on stage) who are being addressed (*dramatic irony*). **5** ill-timed or perverse arrival of an event or circumstance that is in itself desirable (*the irony is that when at long last his novel was accepted for publication, he was too ill to know*). [Greek *eirōneia* pretended ignorance]

**irradiate** /i-**ray**-dee-,ayt/ v. (**-ting**) **1** subject to (any form of) radiation. **2** treat food with radiation. **3** shine upon; light up, illuminate. **4** throw light on (a subject). [Latin *irradio* shine on, from *radius* ray]

**irradiation** /i-,ray-dee-**ay**-shuhn/ n. **1** process of irradiating. **2** treatment of food with a small dose of radiation (in the form of gamma rays) to arrest the development of bacteria and so extend the food's shelf-life.

**irrational** /i-**rash**-uh-nuhl/ adj. **1** illogical; unreasonable (*irrational prejudices*). **2** not endowed with reason (*animals are irrational*). **3** *Math.* not commensurate with the natural numbers. □ **irrationality** /-nal-uh-tee/ *n.* **irrationally** *adv.*

**irreconcilable** /i-rek-uhn-ˌsuy-luh-buhl/ *adj.* **1** implacably hostile (*irreconcilable foes*). **2** (of ideas etc.) incompatible. □ **irreconcilability** /-bil-uh-tee/ *n.* **irreconcilably** *adv.*

**irrecoverable** /ˌi-ruh-**kuv**-uh-ruh-buhl/ *adj.* not able to be recovered or remedied. □ **irrecoverably** *adv.*

**irredeemable** /ˌi-ruh-**dee**-muh-buhl/ *adj.* **1** not able to be redeemed. **2** hopeless. □ **irredeemably** *adv.*

**irreducible** /ˌi-ruh-**dyoo**-suh-buhl/ *adj.* **1** not able to be reduced or simplified. **2** (often foll. by *to*) that cannot be brought to a desired condition. □ **irreducibility** /-bil-uh-tee/ *n.* **irreducibly** *adv.*

**irrefutable** /i-**ref**-yuh-tuh-buhl, ˌi-ruh-**fyoo**-/ *adj.* that cannot be refuted. □ **irrefutably** *adv.*

**irregular** /i-**reg**-yuh-luh/ *adj.* **1** not regular; unsymmetrical, uneven; varying in form. **2** not occurring at regular intervals (*irregular pulse*). **3** contrary to a rule, principle, or custom; abnormal. **4** (of troops) not belonging to the regular army. **5** (of a verb, noun, etc.) not inflected according to the usual rules. **6** disorderly. □ **irregularity** /-**la**-ruh-tee/ *n.* (*pl.* **-ies**). **irregularly** *adv.*

**irrelevant** /i-**rel**-uh-vuhnt/ *adj.* (often foll. by *to*) not relevant. □ **irrelevance** *n.* **irrelevancy** *n.* (*pl.* **-ies**).

**irreligious** /ˌi-ruh-**lij**-uhs/ *adj.* **1** not religious. **2** indifferent or hostile to religion; irreverent.

**irremediable** /ˌi-ruh-**mee**-dee-uh-buhl/ *adj.* that cannot be remedied. □ **irremediably** *adv.*

**irremovable** /ˌi-ruh-**moo**-vuh-buhl/ *adj.* that cannot be removed. □ **irremovably** *adv.*

**irreparable** /i-**rep**-uh-ruh-buhl, i-**rep**-ruh-buhl/ *adj.* (of an injury, loss, etc.) that cannot be rectified or made good. □ **irreparably** *adv.*

**irreplaceable** /ˌi-ruh-**play**-suh-buhl/ *adj.* that cannot be replaced.

**irrepressible** /ˌi-ruh-**pres**-uh-buhl/ *adj.* that cannot be repressed or restrained. □ **irrepressibly** *adv.*

**irreproachable** /ˌi-ruh-**proh**-chuh-buhl/ *adj.* faultless, blameless. □ **irreproachably** *adv.*

**irresistible** /ˌi-ruh-**zis**-tuh-buhl/ *adj.* too strong, delightful, or convincing to be resisted. □ **irresistibly** *adv.*

**irresolute** /i-**rez**-uh-ˌloot/ *adj.* **1** hesit-

ant. **2** lacking in resoluteness. □ **irresolutely** *adv.* **irresoluteness** *n.* **irresolution** /-loo-shuhn/ *n.*

**irrespective** /ˌi-ruh-**spek**-tiv/ *adj.* (foll. by *of*) not taking into account; regardless of (*irrespective of your wishes, I'm going out tonight*).

**irresponsible** /ˌi-ruh-**spon**-suh-buhl/ *adj.* **1** acting or done without due sense of responsibility. **2** not responsible for one's conduct. □ **irresponsibility** /-bil-uh-tee/ *n.* **irresponsibly** *adv.*

**irretrievable** /ˌi-ruh-**tree**-vuh-buhl/ *adj.* that cannot be retrieved or restored. □ **irretrievably** *adv.*

**irreverent** /i-**rev**-uh-ruhnt, i-**rev**-ruhnt/ *adj.* lacking reverence or respect. □ **irreverence** *n.* **irreverently** *adv.*

**irreversible** /ˌi-ruh-**ver**-suh-buhl/ *adj.* not reversible or alterable (*that decision is irreversible*). □ **irreversibly** *adv.*

**irrevocable** /i-**rev**-uh-kuh-buhl/ *adj.* **1** unalterable. **2** gone beyond recall. □ **irrevocably** *adv.*

**irrigate** /**i**-ruh-ˌgayt/ *v.* (**-ting**) **1 a** water (land) by means of channels etc. **b** (of a stream etc.) supply (land) with water. **2** supply (a wound etc.) with a constant flow of liquid. □ **irrigable** *adj.* **irrigation** /-**gay**-shuhn/ *n.* **irrigator** *n.* [Latin *rigo* moisten]

**irritable** /**i**-ri-tuh-buhl/ *adj.* **1** easily annoyed. **2** (of an organ etc.) very sensitive to contact. □ **irritability** /-bil-uh-tee/ *n.* **irritably** *adv.* [Latin: related to IRRITATE]

**irritant** /**i**-ruh-tuhnt/ — *adj.* causing irritation. — *n.* irritant substance.

**irritate** /**i**-ruh-ˌtayt/ *v.* (**-ting**) **1** excite to anger; annoy. **2** stimulate discomfort in (a part of the body). **3** *Biol.* stimulate (an organ) to action. □ **irritating** *adj.* **irritation** /-**tay**-shuhn/ *n.* **irritative** *adj.* [Latin *irrito*]

**irrits** *n.pl. colloq.* (prec. by *the*) feelings of vexation, annoyance, extreme irritation (*he has the irrits*). □ **give a person the irrits** vex or annoy a person greatly (*doing his tax-return always gives me the irrits*). [abbreviation]

**irrupt** /i-**rupt**/ *v.* (foll. by *into*) enter forcibly or violently. □ **irruption** *n.* [Latin: related to RUPTURE]

**is** *3rd sing. present of* BE.

**ISBN** *abbr.* international standard book number.

**-ise**[1] /uyz/ *suffix* (also **-ize**) forming verbs, meaning: **1** make or become such (*Americanise; realise*). **2** treat in such a way (*monopolise; pasteurise*). **3 a** follow a special practice (*economise*). **b** have a specified feeling (*sympathise*). **4** affect with, provide with, or subject to (*oxidise;*

*hospitalise*). □ **-isation** /-**zay**-shuhn/ *suffix* forming nouns. [Greek *-izō*]

■ **Usage** Both forms of the suffix (*-ise* and *-ize*) have long histories of use in English. The *-ise* spelling is preferred in Australia, and is obligatory in certain cases: (*a*) where it forms part of a larger word-element, such as *-mise* (= sending) in *compromise*, and *-prise* (= taking) in *surprise*; and (*b*) in verbs corresponding to nouns with *-s-* in the stem, such as *advertise* and *televise*. The *-ize* spelling is preferred in American English and by some British publishing houses but is obligatory only in a small number of cases, e.g. *capsize*, *prize* (in the sense 'value highly'). This dictionary gives both when both are valid but prefers *-ise*: it does not matter which you prefer so long as you are consistent in your usage.

**-ise²** /uyz, eez/ *suffix* forming nouns of quality, state, or function (*exercise*; *expertise*; *franchise*; *merchandise*). [Latin *-itia* etc.]

**-ish** *suffix* forming adjectives: **1** from nouns, meaning: **a** having the qualities of (*boyish*). **b** of the nationality of (*Danish*). **2** from adjectives, meaning 'somewhat' (*thickish*). **3** *colloq.* denoting an approximate age or time of day (*fortyish*; *six-thirtyish*). [Old English]

**isinglass** /**uy**-zing-,glahs/ *n.* **1** gelatine obtained from fish, esp. sturgeon, and used in making jellies, glue, etc. **2** mica. [Dutch *huisenblas* sturgeon's bladder]

**Islam** /iz-**lahm**, -**lam**/ *n.* **1** the religion of the Muslims, proclaimed by Mohammed. **2** the Muslim world. □ **Islamic** /iz-**lam**-ik/ *adj.* [Arabic, = submission (to God)]

**island** /**uy**-luhnd/ *n.* **1** piece of land surrounded by water. **2** traffic island. **3** detached or isolated thing. [Old English *īgland*; first syllable influenced by ISLE]

**islander** *n.* **1** native or inhabitant of an island. **2** (**Islander**) **a** indigenous inhabitant of the Torres Strait Islands. **b** person indigenous to a Pacific island.

**isle** /uyl/ *n.* poet. (and in place-names) island, esp. a small one (*the Apple Isle*). [French *île* from Latin *insula*]

**islet** /**uy**-luht/ *n.* **1** small island. **2** *Anat.* structurally distinct portion of tissue. [French diminutive of ISLE]

**ism** /iz-uhm/ *n.* colloq. usu. derog. any distinctive but unspecified doctrine or practice of a kind with a name ending in *-ism* (*there are too many isms knocking around nowadays*). [from -ISM]

**-ism** *suffix* forming nouns, esp. denoting: **1** action or its result (*baptism*; *organism*). **2** system, principle, or ideological move-ment (*jingoism*; *feminism*). **3** state or quality (*heroism*; *barbarism*). **4** basis of prejudice or discrimination (*racism*; *sexism*). **5** peculiarity in language (*Americanism*). **6** pathological condition (*alcoholism*). [Greek *-ismos*]

**isn't** /iz-uhnt/ *contr.* is not.

**iso-** *comb. form* equal. [Greek *isos* equal]

**isobar** /**uy**-suh-,bah/ *n.* line on a map connecting places with the same atmospheric pressure. □ **isobaric** /-ba-rik/ *adj.* [Greek *baros* weight]

**isochronous** /uy-**sok**-ruh-nuhs/ *adj.* **1** occurring at the same time. **2** occupying equal time.

**isolate** /**uy**-suh-,layt/ *v.* (**-ting**) **1 a** place apart or alone. **b** place (a contagious or infectious patient etc.) in quarantine. **2** identify and separate for attention (*isolated the problem*). **3** separate (a substance) from a mixture. **4** insulate (electrical apparatus), esp. by a physical gap; disconnect. □ **isolation** /,uy-suh-**lay**-shuhn/ *n.* [Latin *insulatus* made into an island]

**isolationism** *n.* policy of holding aloof from the affairs of other countries or groups. □ **isolationist** *n.*

**isomer** /**uy**-suh-muh/ *n.* one of two or more compounds with the same molecular formula but a different arrangement of atoms. □ **isomeric** /-**me**-rik/ *adj.* **isomerism** /uy-**som**-uh-,riz-uhm/ *n.* [Greek ISO-, *meros* share]

**isometric** /,uy-suh-**met**-rik/ — *adj.* **1** of equal measure. **2** (of muscle action) developing tension while the muscle is prevented from contracting. — *n.* (*in pl.*) system of physical exercises in which muscles are caused to act against each other or against a fixed object. [Greek *isometria* equality of measure]

**isomorphic** /,uy-suh-**maw**-fik/ *adj.* (also **isomorphous** /-fuhs-/ ) exactly corresponding in form and relations. [from ISO-, Greek *morphē* form]

**isopogon** /,uy-suh-**poh**-guhn/ *n.* any of about 35 species of Australian shrubs with showy heads of yellow to deep pink flowers followed by the large globe-shaped fruit-cones which give most of the species the popular name 'drumsticks'.

**isosceles** /uy-**sos**-uh-,leez/ *adj.* (of a triangle) having two sides equal. [from ISO-, Greek *skelos* leg]

**isotherm** /**uy**-suh-,therm/ *n.* line on a map connecting places with the same temperature. □ **isothermal** /-**ther**-muhl/ *adj.* [from ISO-, Greek *thermē* heat]

**isotoma** /,uy-suh-**toh**-muh/ *n.* any of four species (three being small shrubby perennials and one a creeping plant) native to Australia, having masses of blue (in one case white) star-flowers.

**isotope** /uy-suh-ˌtohp/ *n.* one of two or more forms of an element differing from each other in relative atomic mass, and in nuclear but not chemical properties. □ **isotopic** /-**top**-ik/ *adj.* [from ISO-, Greek *topos* place]

**isotropic** /ˌuy-suh-**trop**-ik/ *adj.* having the same physical properties in all directions. □ **isotropy** /uy-**sot**-ruh-pee/ *n.* [from ISO-, Greek *tropos* turn]

**Israeli** /iz-**ray**-lee/ — *adj.* of the modern State of Israel. — *n.* (*pl.* **-s**) **1** native or national of Israel. **2** person of Israeli descent. [Hebrew]

**Israelite** /**iz**-ruh-ˌluyt/ *n. hist.* native of ancient Israel; Jew. [Hebrew]

**issue** /**ish**-oo, **is**-yoo/ — *n.* **1 a** act of giving out or circulating shares, notes, stamps, etc. **b** quantity of coins, copies of a newspaper, etc., circulated at one time. **c** each of a regular series of a magazine etc. (*the May issue*). **2 a** an outgoing, outflow. **b** way out, outlet, esp. the place of the emergence of a stream etc. **3** important subject of debate or litigation; point in question (*we are calling a strike on this issue*). **4** result; outcome (*what was the issue of the strike?*). **5** *Law* children, progeny (*without male issue*). — *v.* (**issues**, **issued**, **issuing**) **1** *literary* go or come out (*they issued forth*). **2 a** send forth; publish; put into circulation. **b** (foll. by *to*, *with*) supply, esp. officially or authoritatively (*issued passports to them*; *issued them with passports*). **3 a** (often foll. by *from*) be derived or result (*these disasters issued from your incompetence*). **b** (foll. by *in*) end, result (*the confrontation issued in violence*). **4** (foll. by *from*) emerge from a condition. □ **at issue** under discussion; in dispute. **join** (or **take**) **issue** (foll. by *with* a person etc., *about*, *on*, *over* a subject) disagree or argue (*I must take issue with you over your recent statements*). **make an issue of** make a fuss about; turn into a subject of contention (*there's no need to make an issue of such a minor matter*). [Latin *exitus*: related to EXIT]

**-ist** *suffix* forming personal nouns denoting: **1** adherent of a system etc. in *-ism* (*Marxist*; *fatalist*). **2** person pursuing, using, or concerned with something as an interest or profession (*balloonist*; *tobacconist*). **3** person who does something expressed by a verb in *-ise* (*plagiarist*). **4** person who subscribes to a prejudice or practises discrimination (*racist*; *sexist*). [Greek *-istēs*]

**isthmus** /**is**-muhs, **isth**-/ *n.* (*pl.* **-es**)

narrow piece of land connecting two larger bodies of land. [Greek *isthmos*]

**it** *pron.* (*poss.* **its**; *pl.* **they**) **1** animal or thing (or occasionally a child) previously named or in question (*took a stone and threw it; gave the baby its bottle*). **2** person in question (*Who is it? It is I*). **3** as the subject of an impersonal verb (*it is raining; it is winter; it is two kilometres to Ballarat*). **4** as a substitute for a deferred subject or object (*it is silly to talk like that; I take it that you agree*). **5** as a substitute for a vague object (*brazen it out; run for it*). **6** as the antecedent to a relative word or clause (*it was a kookaburra that you heard*). **7** exactly what is needed (*that's absolutely it*). **8** *colloq.* (usu. sarcastic) someone perfect (*thinks he's it and a bit*). **9 a** (in children's games) player who has to perform a required feat (*you're it*). **b** person selected for a (usu. unwelcome) task (*someone has to tell the boss what went wrong and we've all decided: you're it!*). □ **that's it** *colloq.* that is: **1** what is required. **2** the difficulty. **3** the end, enough (*that's it! — I'm leaving*). [Old English]

**Italian** /i-**tal**-yuhn, uh-/ — *n.* **1 a** native or national of Italy. **b** person of Italian descent. **2** Romance language of Italy. — *adj.* of or relating to Italy.

**italic** /i-**tal**-ik, uy-/ — *adj.* **1 a** of the sloping kind of letters now used in print esp. for emphasis and in foreign words. **b** (of handwriting) compact and pointed like early Italian handwriting. **2** (**Italic**) of ancient Italy. — *n.* **1** letter in italic type. **2** this type. [Latin *italicus*: related to ITALIAN]

**italicise** /i-**tal**-uh-ˌsuyz/ *v.* (also **-ize**) (**-sing** or **-zing**) print in italics.

**itch** — *n.* **1** irritation in the skin. **2** impatient desire (*has an itch to travel*). **3** (prec. by *the*) (in general use) scabies. — *v.* **1** feel an irritation in the skin causing a desire to scratch. **2** feel a desire to do something (*itching to tell you*). [Old English]

**itchy** *adj.* (**-ier**, **-iest**) having or causing an itch. □ **have itchy feet** *colloq.* **1** be restless. **2** have a strong urge to travel. □ **itchiness** *n.*

**itchy grub** *n.* any of many caterpillars in Australia capable of causing skin irritation.

**it'd** /**it**-uhd/ *contr. colloq.* **1** it had. **2** it would.

**-ite**[1] /uyt/ *suffix* forming nouns meaning 'a person or thing connected with': **1** in names of persons: **a** as natives of a country (*Israelite*). **b** as followers of a movement etc. (*Trotskyite*). **2** in names of things: **a** fossils (*ammonite*). **b** minerals (*graphite*). **c** explosives (*dynamite*). **d** commercial products (*vegemite*; *vulcanite*). **e** salts of acids having names in *-ous* (*nitrite*; *sulphite*). [Greek *-itēs*]

**-ite²** /uyt, it/ *suffix* **1** forming adjectives (*erudite*; *favourite*). **2** forming nouns (*appetite*). **3** forming verbs (*expedite*; *unite*). [Latin *-itus*]

**item** /**uy**-tuhm/ *n.* **1** any of a number of enumerated things (*second item on the list*). **2** separate or distinct piece of news etc. [Latin, = in like manner]

**itemise** *v.* (also **-ize**) (**-sing** or **-zing**) state item by item. □ **itemisation** /-**zay**-shuhn/ *n.*

**iterate** /**it**-uh-ˌrayt/ *v.* (**-ting**) repeat; state repeatedly. □ **iteration** /-**ray**-shuhn/ *n.* **iterative** /**it**-uh-ruh-tiv/ *adj.* [Latin *iterum* again]

**-itic** *suffix* forming adjectives and nouns corresponding to nouns in *-ite*, *-itis*, etc. (*Semitic*; *arthritic*). [Latin *-iticus*, Greek *-itikos*]

**itinerant** /uy-**tin**-uh-ruhnt/ — *adj.* travelling from place to place. — *n.* itinerant person. [Latin *iter itiner-* journey]

**itinerary** /uy-**tin**-uh-ruh-ree/ *n.* (*pl.* **-ies**) **1** detailed route. **2** record of travel. **3** guidebook.

**-ition** *suffix* forming nouns, = -ATION (*admonition*; *perdition*; *position*). [Latin *-itio -itionis*]

**-itious** *suffix* forming adjectives corresponding to nouns in *-ition* (*ambitious*; *supposititious*). [Latin *-itio* etc., -OUS]

**-itis** *suffix* forming nouns, esp.: **1** names of inflammatory diseases (*appendicitis*).

**2** *colloq.* with ref. to conditions compared to diseases (*electionitis*). [Greek]

**-itive** *suffix* forming adjectives, = -ATIVE (*positive*; *transitive*). [Latin *-itivus*]

**it'll** /it-uhl/ *contr. colloq.* it will; it shall.

**its** *poss. pron.* of it; of itself (*can see its advantages*).

**it's** *contr.* **1** it is. **2** it has.

**itself** *pron.* emphatic and refl. form of IT. □ **be itself** see ONESELF. **by itself** see *by oneself.* **in itself** viewed in its essential qualities (*not in itself a bad thing*). [Old English: related to IT, SELF]

**-ity** *suffix* forming nouns denoting: **1** quality or condition (*humility*; *purity*). **2** instance of this (*monstrosity*). [Latin *-itas*]

**IUD** *abbr.* intra-uterine (contraceptive) device.

**I've** /uyv/ *contr.* I have.

**-ive** *suffix* forming adjectives meaning 'tending to', and corresponding nouns (*suggestive*; *corrosive*; *talkative*). [Latin *-ivus*]

**IVF** *abbr.* in vitro fertilisation.

**ivory** /**uy**-vuh-ree/ *n.* (*pl.* **-ies**) **1** hard substance of the tusks of an elephant etc. **2** creamy-white colour of this. **3** (usu. in *pl.*) **a** article made of ivory. **b** *colloq.* thing made of or resembling ivory, esp. a piano key or a tooth. [Latin *ebur*]

**ivory tower** *n.* seclusion or withdrawal from the harsh realities of life (often *attrib.*: *ivory tower professors*).

**ivy** /**uy**-vee/ *n.* (*pl.* **-ies**) climbing evergreen shrub with shiny five-angled leaves. □ **ivied** *adj.* [Old English]

**-ize** var. of -ISE.

---

■ **Usage** See note at *-ise*.

# J

**J¹** /jay/ *n.* (also **j**) (*pl.* **Js** or **J's**) tenth letter of the alphabet.

**J²** *abbr.* (also **J.**) joule(s).

**jab** — *v.* (**-bb-**) **1 a** poke roughly. **b** stab. **2** (foll. by *into*) thrust (a thing) hard or abruptly. — *n.* **1** abrupt blow, thrust, or stab. **2** *colloq.* hypodermic injection. [var. of *job* = prod]

**jabber** — *v.* chatter rapidly and/or indistinctly. — *n.* chatter; meaningless gabble. [imitative]

**jabberwocky** /jab-uh-ˌwok-ee/ *n.* (*pl.* **-ies**) **1** piece of nonsensical writing or speech. **2** *colloq.* nonsense, drivel (*what you've said is a load of jabberwocky*). [title of a poem in Lewis Carroll's *Through the Looking Glass*]

**jabiru** /jab-uh-ˌroo/ *n.* (also **policeman bird**) Australia's sole stork, large, with glossy greenish-black and white plumage and red legs, occurring along the north and east coast. [Tupi]

**jacana** /juh-**kah**-nuh/ *n.* = LOTUS BIRD. [Tupi]

**jacaranda** /ˌjak-uh-**ran**-duh/ *n.* tropical American tree with trumpet-shaped blue flowers, widely cultivated in Australia. [Tupi]

**jack** — *n.* **1** device for raising heavy objects, esp. vehicles. **2** court-card with a picture of a soldier, page, etc. **3** ship's flag, esp. showing nationality. **4** device using a single-pronged plug to connect an electrical circuit. **5** small white target ball in bowls. **6** (Jack) familiar form of *John*, esp. typifying the common man, male animal, etc. (*I'm all right, Jack*). **7** (also **jacky** and **jacko**) nickname for a kookaburra. **8** device for plucking the string of a harpsichord etc., one being operated by each key. **9** *colloq.* double-headed coin. — *v.* (usu. foll. by *up*) **1** raise with or as with a jack (in sense 1). **2** *colloq.* raise (e.g. prices). **3** *colloq.* refuse to cooperate (*jacked up when I asked him to take out the garbage*). □ **every man jack** each and every person. **jack in** *colloq.* abandon (an attempt etc.). **jack of** *colloq.* fed-up with, sick and tired of (*I'm jack of all this housework*). [familiar form of the name *John*]

**jackal** /**jak**-uhl/ *n.* African or Asian wild animal of the dog family, scavenging in packs for food. [Persian]

**jackaroo** *n.* = JACKEROO.

**jackass** *n.* **1** male ass. **2** stupid person. **3** (in full laughing jackass) = KOOKABURRA.

**jackass-fish** *n.* (also **morwong**) marine food-fish, widely distributed in Australian waters, having a distinctive elongated ray of the pectoral fin.

**jackboot** *n.* **1** military boot reaching above the knee. **2** this as a militaristic or fascist symbol.

**jackdaw** *n.* black, grey-headed European bird of the crow family.

**jacked up** *adj.* *colloq.* disenchanted, fed-up (*jacked up to the eyebrows with this job*).

**jackeroo** /ˌjak-uh-**roo**/ — *n.* **1** (also **jackaroo**) *hist.* young man (usu. English and of independent means) gaining experience by working as a trainee on an Australian sheep or cattle station. **2** trainee in station management — *v.* work as a jackeroo (*he's jackerooing up north*). [origin unknown]

**jacket** /**jak**-uht/ *n.* **1 a** short coat with sleeves. **b** protective or supporting garment (*life-jacket*). **2** casing or covering round a boiler etc. **3** = DUST-JACKET. **4** skin of a potato, esp. when baked whole. **5** animal's coat. [French]

**jackhammer** *n.* pneumatic hammer or drill.

**jackie** var. of JACKY¹.

**jack-in-the-box** *n.* toy figure which springs out of a box.

**jack-jumper** *n.* = JUMPER² 1.

**jackknife** — *n.* **1** large clasp-knife. **2** dive in which the body is bent and then straightened. — *v.* (**-fing**) (of a semi-trailer) fold against itself in an accident.

**jacko** *n.* = JACK 7.

**jack of all trades** *n.* **1** multi-skilled person. **2** person who can do many different jobs but is skilled in none.

**jackpot** — *n.* large prize, esp. accumulated in a poker machine, game, lottery, etc. — *v.* (**-tt-**) (of prize-money in a lottery etc.) accumulate (if not won) (*first prize jackpotted to $1,000,000*). □ **hit the jackpot** *colloq.* **1** win a large prize. **2** have remarkable luck or success.

**jackshea** /**jak**-shay/ *n.* (also **jackshay**) tin vessel holding a quart used by bushmen for brewing tea and incorporating a smaller vessel for drinking. [origin uncertain]

**jacksonia** /ˌjak-**soh**-nee-uh/ *n.* tree-like

582

shrub of NSW and Queensland with profuse red and yellow pea-flowers in spring.

**jacky¹** *n.* = JACK 7.

**jacky²** *n. attrib.* in names of small animals.

**jacky³** *n.* = JACKY-JACKY.

**Jacky Howe** /how/ *n.* navy or black sleeveless singlet worn esp. by shearers, rural workers, etc. [John *Howe*, champion Queensland shearer (d. 1920)]

**Jacky-Jacky** /jak-ee-ˌjak-ee/ *n. colloq. offens.* **1** nickname for an Aborigine. **2** = COCONUT 2.

**jacky lizard** *n.* small, grey, mainly tree-dwelling dragon lizard of eastern Australia.

**jacky winter** *n.* small, grey-brown and white flycatcher of mainland Australia.

**Jacobean** /ˌjak-uh-**bee**-uhn/ — *adj.* **1** of the reign of James I of England. **2** (of furniture) heavy and dark in style. — *n.* Jacobean person. [Latin *Jacobus* James]

**jacquard** /jak-ahd/ *n.* **1** apparatus with perforated cards, for weaving figured fabrics. **2** (in full **jacquard loom**) loom with this. **3** fabric or article so made. [name of its inventor]

**jacuzzi** /juh-**koo**-zee/ *n.* (*pl.* **-s**) large bath with massaging underwater jets of water; spa bath. [name of its inventor and manufacturers]

**jade¹** *n.* **1** hard usu. green stone used for carving ornaments, jewellery, etc. **2** green colour of jade. [Spanish *ijada* from Latin *ilia* flanks (named as a cure for colic)]

**jade²** *n.* inferior or worn-out horse. [origin unknown]

**jaded** *adj.* tired out; surfeited.

**jaffle** /**jaf**-uhl/ *n.* sandwich with a savoury or sweet filling sealed and toasted over a fire in a jaffle-iron (or nowadays toasted in an electric jaffle-maker).

**jaffle-iron** *n. propr.* long-handled device for toasting jaffles, consisting of two saucer-shaped moulds, hinged, and locking together.

**jag¹** — *n.* sharp projection of rock etc. — *v.* (**-gg-**) **1** cut or tear unevenly. **2** make indentations in. [imitative]

**jag²** *n. colloq.* **1** drinking spree. **2** period of continuing indulgence in an activity, emotion, etc. [originally British dial., = load]

**jagged** /**jag**-uhd/ *adj.* **1** unevenly cut or torn. **2** deeply indented. □ **jaggedly** *adv.* **jaggedness** *n.*

**jaggery** /**jag**-uh-ree/ *n.* strong-flavoured dark brown sugar made from the sap of the palmyrah or coconut palm. [Sanskrit *śarkarā* sugar]

**jaguar** /**jag**-yoo-uh/ *n.* large tropical American flesh-eating spotted animal of the cat family. [Tupi]

**jail** /jayl/ (also **gaol**) — *n.* **1** prison. **2** imprisonment. — *v.* put in jail. [French *jaiole*, ultimately from Latin *cavea* cage]

**jailbird** *n.* (also **gaolbird**) prisoner or habitual criminal.

**jailbreak** *n.* (also **gaolbreak**) a prison break-out, escape from jail.

**jailer** *n.* (also **gaoler**) = WARDER.

**jake** *adj. colloq.* all right; fine. □ **she'll be jake** all will be well.

**jalopy** /juh-**lop**-ee/ *n.* (*pl.* **-ies**) *colloq.* dilapidated old vehicle. [origin unknown]

**jam¹** — *v.* (**-mm-**) **1 a** (usu. foll. by *into, together,* etc.) squeeze, cram, or wedge into a space. **b** become wedged. **2** cause (machinery etc.) to become wedged or (of machinery etc.) become wedged and unworkable. **3 a** block (a passage, road, etc.) by crowding etc. **b** (foll. by *in*) obstruct the exit of (*we were jammed in*). **4** (usu. foll. by *on*) apply (brakes etc.) forcefully or abruptly. **5** make (a radio transmission) unintelligible by interference. **6** *colloq.* (in jazz etc.) improvise with other musicians. — *n.* **1** squeeze, crush. **2** crowded mass (*traffic jam*). **3** *colloq.* predicament (*was in a real jam*). **4** stoppage (of a machine etc.) due to jamming. **5** (in full **jam session**) *colloq.* (in jazz etc.) improvised ensemble playing. [imitative]

**jam²** *n.* **1** conserve of boiled fruit and sugar. **2** *colloq.* easy or pleasant thing (*money for jam*). **3** = RASPBERRY JAM. □ **jammy** *adj.* [perhaps from JAM¹]

**jam³** *n.* affectation, pretentious display. □ **put on jam** adopt an affected way of speaking or an affected manner. □ **jammy** *adj.* (*Poms speak with a jammy accent*).

**jamb** /jam/ *n.* side post or side face of a doorway, window, or fireplace. [French *jambe* leg, from Latin]

**jamboree** /ˌjam-buh-**ree**/ *n.* **1** celebration or merrymaking; a spree. **2** large rally of Scouts. [origin unknown]

**jam-packed** *adj. colloq.* full to capacity.

**jam-tree** *n.* = RASPBERRY JAM.

**jamwood** *n.* = RASPBERRY JAM.

**jangle** /**jang**-guhl/ — *v.* (**-ling**) **1** (cause to) make a (esp. harsh) metallic sound. **2** irritate (the nerves etc.) by discord etc. — *n.* harsh metallic sound. [French]

**janitor** /**jan**-uh-tuh/ *n.* **1** doorkeeper. **2** caretaker. [Latin *janua* door]

**January** /**jan**-yoo-uh-ree/ *n.* (*pl.* **-ies**) first month of the year. [Latin *Janus*, guardian god of doors]

**Jap** *n. & adj. colloq.* often *offens.* = JAPANESE. [abbreviation]

**japan** /juh-**pan**/ — n. hard usu. black varnish, orig. from Japan. — v. (**-nn-**) **1** varnish with japan. **2** make black and glossy. [*Japan* in E. Asia]

**Japanese** /ˌjap-uh-**neez**/ — n. (pl. same) **1 a** native or national of Japan. **b** person of Japanese descent. **2** language of Japan. — adj. of Japan, its people, or its language.

**jape** — n. practical joke. — v. (**-ping**) play a joke. □ **japery** n. [origin unknown]

**japonica** /juh-**pon**-i-kuh/ n. flowering shrub with bright red flowers and round edible fruits. [Latinised name for *Japanese*]

**jar¹** n. **1** container, usu. of glass and cylindrical. **2** contents of this. [French from Arabic]

**jar²** — v. (**-rr-**) **1** (often foll. by *on*) (of sound, manner, etc.) sound discordant, grate (on the nerves etc.). **2 a** (often foll. by *against, on*) (cause to) strike (esp. part of the body) with vibration or shock (*jarred his neck*). **b** vibrate with shock etc. **3** (often foll. by *with*) be at variance or in conflict (*that blue scarf jars with your dress*). — n. **1** jarring sound or sensation. **2** physical shock or jolt. [imitative]

**jargon** /**jah**-guhn/ n. **1** words or expressions used by a particular group or profession (*medical jargon*). **2** debased or pretentious language. **3** nonsense, gibberish. [French]

**jarrah** /**ja**-ruh/ n. **1** usu. tall eucalypt of WA valued for its hard, durable, dark red wood. **2** the wood of this tree; native mahogany. [Nyungar, probably *jarrily*]

**jarrah-jerker** n. man who works in the bush getting timber etc.

**Jarrahland** n. colloq. the State of Western Australia.

**jasmine** /**jaz**-muhn/ n. **1** ornamental shrub or climber with perfumed white, pink, or yellow flowers. **2** (also **native jasmine**) any of the jasmines native to Australia, most with highly fragrant flowers. [French from Arabic from Persian]

**jasper** /**jas**-puh/ n. opaque quartz, usu. red, yellow, or brown. [French from Latin from Greek *iaspis*]

**jaundice** /**jawn**-duhs/ — n. **1** yellowing of the skin etc. caused by liver disease, bile disorder, etc. **2** disordered (esp. mental) vision. **3** envy. — v. (**-cing**) **1** affect with jaundice. **2** (esp. as **jaundiced** adj.) affect (a person) with envy, resentment, etc. [French *jaune* yellow]

**jaunt** /jawnt/ — n. short pleasure trip. — v. take a jaunt. [origin unknown]

**jaunty** /**jawn**-tee/ adj. (**-ier, -iest**) **1** cheerful and self-confident. **2** sprightly.

□ **jauntily** adv. **jauntiness** n. [French: related to GENTLE]

**Javanese** /ˌjah-vuh-**neez**/ — n. (pl. same) **1 a** native of Java. **b** person of Javanese descent. **2** language of Java. — adj. (also **Javan**) of Java, its people, or its language. [*Java* in Indonesia]

**Java sparrow** n. **1** small finch of tropical Asia popular as a cage-bird. **2** = DIAMOND FIRETAIL.

**javelin** /**jav**-uh-luhn, **jav**-luhn/ n. light spear thrown in sport or, formerly, as a weapon. [French]

**javelin fish** n. any of several marine food-fish of northern Australian waters having an enlarged anal fin resembling a javelin.

**jaw** — n. **1 a** upper or lower bony structure in vertebrates containing the teeth. **b** corresponding parts of certain invertebrates. **2 a** (in pl.) the mouth with its bones and teeth. **b** narrow mouth of a valley, channel, etc. **c** gripping parts of a tool etc. (*jaws of a vice*). **d** grip (*jaws of death*). **3** colloq. tedious talk (*hold your jaw*). — v. colloq. speak, esp. at tedious length. [French]

**jawbone** — n. lower jaw in most mammals. — v. colloq. talk or gossip at tedious length.

**jaws-of-life** n. powerful jaw-like tool used after car-crashes etc. to cut away metal etc. in order to rescue persons trapped in the wreck.

**jay** n. **1** any of several Australian birds having a loud call, such as the grey currawong and the white-winged chough. **2** noisy European bird of the crow family with vivid plumage. [Latin *gaius, gaia*, perhaps from the name *Gaius*: cf. *jackdaw, robin*]

**jaywalk** v. cross or walk on a road carelessly or dangerously. □ **jaywalker** n.

**jazz** — n. **1** rhythmic syncopated esp. improvised music of Black US origin. **2** colloq. pretentious talk or behaviour (*all that jazz*). — v. play or dance to jazz. □ **jazz up** brighten or enliven (*need to jazz up the house with some new paint*). □ **jazzer** n. [origin uncertain]

**jazzy** adj. (**-ier, -iest**) **1** of or like jazz. **2** vivid, showy.

**jealous** /**jel**-uhs/ adj. **1** resentful of rivalry in love. **2** (often foll. by *of*) envious (of a person etc.). **3** (often foll. by *of*) fiercely protective (of rights etc.). **4** (of God) intolerant of disloyalty. **5** (of inquiry, supervision, etc.) vigilant. □ **jealously** adv. [medieval Latin *zelosus*: related to ZEAL]

**jealousy** n. (pl. **-ies**) **1** jealous state or feeling. **2** instance of this. [French: related to JEALOUS]

**jeans** /jeenz/ *n.pl.* casual esp. denim trousers. [earlier *geane fustian*, = material from Genoa]

**jeep** *n. propr.* small sturdy esp. military vehicle with four-wheel drive. [originally US, from GP = *general purposes*]

**jeer** — *v.* (often foll. by *at*) scoff derisively; deride. — *n.* taunting remark. □ **jeeringly** *adv.* [origin unknown]

**jeez!** *int.* = GEEZ!

**Jehovah** /juh-**hoh**-vuh/ *n.* Hebrew name of God in the Old Testament. [Hebrew *yahveh*]

**Jehovah's Witness** *n.* member of a millenarian Christian sect rejecting the supremacy of the State and religious institutions over personal conscience, faith, etc.

**jejune** /juh-**joon**/ *adj.* 1 intellectually unsatisfying; shallow, meagre, scanty, dry. 2 puerile. 3 (of land) barren. [Latin *jejunus*]

**jejunum** /juh-**joo**-nuhm/ *n.* small intestine between the duodenum and ileum. [Latin: related to JEJUNE]

**Jekyll and Hyde** /ˌjek-uhl uhnd **huyd**/ — *n.* person having opposing good and bad qualities. — *adj.* (**Jekyll-and-Hyde**) having good and bad qualities. [names of a character in a story by R. L. Stevenson]

**jell** *v. colloq.* 1 set as jelly. 2 (of ideas etc.) take a definite form. 3 cohere. [back-formation from JELLY]

**jellify** /**jel**-uh-ˌfuy/ *v.* (**-ies, -ied**) turn into jelly; make or become like jelly. □ **jellification** /-fuh-**kay**-shuhn/ *n.*

**jelly** /**jel**-ee/ — *n.* (*pl.* **-ies**) 1 a (usu. fruit-flavoured) translucent dessert set with gelatine. b similar preparation as a jam, condiment, or sweet (*redcurrant jelly*). c similar preparation from meat, bones, etc., and gelatine (*marrowbone jelly*). 2 any similar substance. 3 *colloq.* gelignite. — *v.* (**-ies, -ied**) (cause to) set as or in a jelly; congeal. □ **jelly-like** *adj.* [French *gelée* from Latin *gelo* freeze]

**jelly blubber** *n.* = JELLYFISH 1.

**jellyfish** *n.* (*pl.* same or **-es**) 1 marine animal with a jelly-like body and stinging tentacles. 2 *colloq.* cowardly, spineless person.

**jemmy** /**jem**-ee/ — *n.* (*pl.* **-ies**) burglar's short crowbar. — *v.* force open with a jemmy. [from the name *James*]

**jeopardise** /**jep**-uh-ˌduyz/ *v.* (also **-ize**) (**-sing** or **-zing**) endanger.

**jeopardy** /**jep**-uh-dee/ *n.* danger, esp. severe. [obsolete French *iu parti* divided play]

**jerbil** var. of GERBIL.

**jerboa** /jer-**boh**-uh/ *n.* small jumping desert rodent of North Africa and Asia. [Arabic]

**Jeremiah** /ˌje-ruh-**muy**-uh/ *n.* dismal prophet, denouncer of the times. [Lamentations of *Jeremiah*, in the Old Testament]

**jerk¹** — *n.* 1 sharp sudden pull, twist, twitch, start, etc. 2 spasmodic muscular twitch. 3 (in *pl.*) *colloq.* exercises (*physical jerks*). 4 *colloq.* fool; obnoxious person. — *v.* 1 move, pull, thrust, twist, throw, etc., with a jerk (*car moved in jerks*). 2 (usu. foll. by *out*) speak in a halting way (*jerked out his reply*). [imitative]

**jerk²** *v.* cure (beef) by cutting it in long slices and drying it in the sun. [Quechua *echarqui* dried fish in strips]

**jerkin** /**jer**-kuhn/ *n.* close-fitting sleeveless jacket. [origin unknown]

**jerky** *adj.* (**-ier, -iest**) 1 moving suddenly or abruptly. 2 spasmodic. □ **jerkily** *adv.* **jerkiness** *n.*

**jerry** /**je**-ree/ *v. colloq.* (often foll. by *to*) realise; understand.

**jerry-builder** *n.* incompetent builder using cheap materials. □ **jerry-building** *n.* **jerry-built** *adj.* [origin uncertain]

**jerrycan** *n.* (also **jerrican**) rectangular can for carrying petrol or water. [from *Jerry* German]

**jersey** /**jer**-zee/ *n.* (*pl.* **-s**) 1 a knitted usu. woollen pullover. b plain-knitted (orig. woollen) fabric. 2 (**Jersey**) light brown dairy cow from Jersey. [*Jersey* in the Channel Islands]

**Jerusalem artichoke** /juh-**roo**-suh-luhm/ *n.* 1 a kind of sunflower with edible tubers. 2 this as a vegetable. [corruption of Italian *girasole* sunflower]

**jest** — *n.* 1 joke; fun. 2 a raillery, banter. b object of derision (*he is a standing jest*). — *v.* joke; fool about. □ **in jest** in fun. [Latin *gesta* exploits]

**jester** *n. hist.* professional clown at a medieval court etc.

**Jesuit** /**jez**-yoo-uht/ *n.* member of the Society of Jesus, a Roman Catholic male religious order. [Latin *Jesus*, founder of the Christian religion]

**Jesuitical** /ˌjez-yoo-**it**-uh-kuhl/ *adj.* 1 of the Jesuits. 2 often *offens.* equivocating, casuistic.

**Jesus** /**jee**-zuhs/ *int. colloq.* exclamation of surprise, dismay, etc. [name of the founder of the Christian religion]

**jet¹** — *n.* 1 stream of water, steam, gas, flame, etc., shot esp. from a small opening. 2 spout or nozzle for this purpose. 3 jet engine or jet plane. — *v.* (**-tt-**) 1 spurt out in jets. 2 *colloq.* send or travel by jet plane. [French *jeter* throw Latin *jacto*]

**jet²** *n.* (often *attrib.*) hard black lignite often carved and highly polished. [French *jaiet* from *Gagai* in Asia Minor]

**jet-about** *adj.* pertaining to, using, or including travel by air (*won a jet-about holiday*; *jet-about members of parliament*).

**jet black** *adj. & n.* (as adj. often hyphenated) deep glossy black.

**jet engine** *n.* engine using jet propulsion, esp. of an aircraft.

**jet lag** *n.* exhaustion etc. felt after a long flight across time zones.

**jet plane** *n.* plane with a jet engine.

**jet-propelled** *adj.* **1** having jet propulsion. **2** very fast.

**jet propulsion** *n.* propulsion by the backward ejection of a high-speed jet of gas etc.

**jetsam** /jet-suhm/ *n.* objects washed ashore, esp. jettisoned from a ship. [contraction of JETTISON]

**jet set** *n.* wealthy people who travel widely, esp. for pleasure. □ **jet-setter** *n.* **jet-setting** *n. & attrib. adj.*

**jettison** /jet-uh-suhn, -zuhn/ — *v.* **1 a** throw (esp. heavy material) overboard to lighten a ship etc. **b** drop (goods) from an aircraft. **2** abandon; get rid of. — *n.* jettisoning. [Anglo-French *getteson*: related to JET¹]

**jetty** /jet-ee/ *n.* (*pl.* **-ies**) **1** pier or breakwater to protect or defend a harbour, coast, etc. **2** landing-pier. [French *jetee*: related to JET¹]

**Jew** /joo/ *n.* **1** person of Hebrew descent or whose religion is Judaism. **2** *colloq. offens.* miserly person. **3** (**jew**) = JEWFISH. [Greek *ioudaios*]

■ **Usage** The stereotype conveyed in sense 2 is deeply offensive. It arose from historical associations of Jews as moneylenders in medieval England.

**jewel** /joo-uhl/ — *n.* **1 a** precious stone. **b** this used in watchmaking. **2** jewelled personal ornament. **3** precious person or thing. — *v.* (**-ll-**) (esp. as **jewelled** *adj.*) adorn or set with jewels. [French]

**jewel beetle** *n.* any of many brilliantly coloured and jewel-like Australian beetles.

**jeweller** *n.* maker of or dealer in jewels or jewellery.

**jeweller's shop** *n.* rich deposit of gold or opal.

**jewellery** /joo-uhl-ree, jool-ree/ *n.* rings, brooches, necklaces, etc., regarded collectively.

**jewfish** *n.* (also **dhufish**) **1** any of several large, edible, marine fish found only off the WA coast. **2** = MULLOWAY.

**Jewish** *adj.* **1** of Jews. **2** of Judaism. □ **Jewishness** *n.*

**jew lizard** *n.* = BEARDED DRAGON.

**Jewry** /joo-ree/ *n.* Jews collectively.

**jew's harp** *n.* small lyre-shaped musical instrument held between the teeth and struck with the finger.

**jezebel** /jez-uh-ˌbel/ *n.* shameless or immoral woman. [*Jezebel* in the Old Testament]

**jib¹** *n.* **1** triangular staysail. **2** projecting arm of a crane. [origin unknown]

**jib²** *v.* (**-bb-**) **1** (esp. of a horse) stop and refuse to go on. **2** (of a person) refuse to continue. **3** (foll. by *at*) show aversion to (a course of action etc.). □ **jibber** *n.* [origin unknown]

**jibe¹** var. of GIBE.

**jibe²** var. of GYBE.

**jiff** *n.* (also **jiffy**, *pl.* **-ies**) *colloq.* short time; moment (*in a jiffy*). [origin unknown]

**jiffy bag** /jif-ee/ *n. propr.* strong padded envelope for posting articles.

**jig¹** — *n.* **1 a** lively leaping dance. **b** music for this. **2** device that holds a piece of work and guides the tools operating on it. — *v.* (**-gg-**) **1** dance a jig. **2** (often foll. by *about*) move quickly and jerkily up and down; fidget. **3** work on or equip with a jig or jigs. □ **the jig is up** *colloq.* the game's up; one has been caught red-handed. [origin unknown]

**jig²** *v. colloq.* play truant (from school). □ **jigger** *n.*

**jigger** /jig-uh/ — *n.* **1** *colloq.* name for a tool, device, etc., the correct name for which eludes one (*I'll use this jigger to do the job*). **2** *Billiards* cue-rest. **3 a** measure of spirits etc. **b** small glass holding this. **4** *colloq.* **a** (in prisons) improvised radio receiver. **b** device for administering an illegal electric shock to a horse during a horse race. — *v. colloq.* break, ruin (*you'll jigger it if you keep fiddling*). [partly from JIG¹]

**jiggered¹** /jig-uhd/ *adj. colloq.* (as a mild substitute for a taboo word) confounded (*I'll be jiggered*). [euphemism]

**jiggered²** *past part.* of JIGGER. — *adj.* broken, ruined (*the telly's jiggered*).

**jiggery-pokery** /ˌjig-uh-ree-poh-kuh-ree/ *n. colloq.* trickery; swindling. [origin uncertain]

**jiggle** /jig-uhl/ — *v.* (**-ling**) (often foll. by *about* etc.) shake or jerk lightly; fidget. — *n.* light shake. [from JIG¹]

**jiggler** *n. colloq.* tea-bag for a tea-cup.

**jigsaw** *n.* **1 a** (in full **jigsaw puzzle**) picture on board or wood etc. cut into irregular interlocking pieces to be reassembled as a pastime. **b** problem consisting of various pieces of information. **2** mechanical fretsaw with a fine blade.

**jihad** /juh-**hahd**/ n. (also **jehad**) Muslim holy war against unbelievers. [Arabic *jihād*]

**jilleroo** /ˌjil-uh-**roo**/ — n. (also **jillaroo**) female station-hand. — v. work as a jilleroo. [jocular formation on JACKEROO]

**jilt** v. abruptly reject or abandon (esp. a lover). [origin unknown]

**jimmies** n. colloq. = JIMMY BRITTS.

**Jimmy Britts** n. colloq. state of extreme anxiety; the irrits (*the exams are giving him the Jimmy Britts*). [rhyming slang]

**jimmygrant** n. (also **jimmigrant, Jimmy Grant**) hist. an immigrant to Australia. [rhyming slang]

**Jimmy Woodser** /ˈwuud-zuh/ n. colloq. **1** person who drinks alone. **2** a drink taken on one's own. [*Jimmy Wood*, name of a character in the poem of that name by Barcroft Boake]

**Jindiworobak** /ˌjin-dee-**wo**-ruh-bak/ n. member of a literary group formed by the poet Rex Ingamells to promote Australianism in art and literature. [Wuywurung]

**jingera** /ˈjin-juh-ruh/ — n. remote and mountainous bush-covered country. — adj. of or pertaining to such terrain. [*Jingera* a town in NSW: perhaps from an Aboriginal language]

**jingle** /ˈjing-guhl/ — n. **1** mixed ringing or clinking noise. **2 a** repetition of the same sounds in words, esp. as an aid to memory or to attract attention. **b** short catchy verse or song in advertising etc. — v. (**-ling**) **1** (cause to) make a jingling sound. **2** (of writing) be full of alliteration, rhymes, etc. [imitative]

**jingoism** /ˈjing-goh-iz-uhm/ n. blustering, excessive patriotism. □ **jingoist** n.

**jingoistic** /-is-tik/ adj. [*jingo* a conjuror's word: political sense from use of *by jingo* in a song calling for aggressive Brit. military action against Russia, then applied to all excessive patriots]

**jinker** n. wheeled conveyance for moving heavy logs. [British dial. *janker* long pole on wheels used for carrying logs]

**jinnee** /jee-**nee**/ n. (also **jinn, djinn** /jin/) (pl. **jinn** or **djinn**) (in Muslim mythology) spirit in human or animal form having power over people. [Arabic]

**jinx** colloq. — n. person or thing that seems to cause bad luck. — v. (esp. as **jinxed** adj.) subject to bad luck. [perhaps variant of *jynx* wryneck (small woodpecker), charm]

**jitta** /ˈjit-uh/ n. (also **ghittoe**) **1** either of two related rainforest trees of NSW, Queensland, etc. yielding a tough flexible flammable timber easily burnt when green. **2** the wood of this used by Aborigines for a musical instrument (accompanying a special style of love-song), spears, etc. [Dyirbal and Warrgamay *jidu*]

**jitter** colloq. — n. (**the jitters**) extreme nervousness. — v. be nervous; act nervously. □ **jittery** adj. **jitteriness** n. [origin unknown]

**jitterbug** — n. **1** nervous person. **2** hist. fast popular dance. — v. (**-gg-**) hist. dance the jitterbug.

**jiu-jitsu** var. of JU-JITSU.

**jive** — n. **1** lively dance popular esp. in the 1950s. **2** music for this. — v. (**-ving**) dance to or play jive music. □ **jiver** n. [origin uncertain]

**job¹** — n. **1** piece of work to be done; task. **2** position in, or piece of, paid employment. **3** colloq. difficult task (*had a job to find it*). **4** colloq. crime, esp. a robbery. **5** state of affairs etc. (*bad job; good job*). **6** Computing item of work regarded separately. — v. (**-bb-**) **1** do jobs; do piecework. **2** deal in stocks; buy and sell (stocks or goods). **3** deal corruptly with (a matter). □ **just the job** colloq. exactly what is wanted. **make a job** (or **good job**) **of** do well. [origin unknown]

**job²** v. (**-bb-**) **1** prod. **2** colloq. punch (*jobbed him on the nose*).

**jobber** n. **1** person who jobs. **2** wholesale merchant. **3** pieceworker.

**jobbery** n. corrupt dealing.

**job-control language** n. Computing language enabling the user to determine the tasks to be undertaken by the operating system.

**jobless** — adj. unemployed. — n. (prec. by *the*) the unemployed collectively. □ **joblessness** n.

**job lot** n. mixed lot bought at auction etc.

**Job's comforter** /johbz/ n. person who intends to comfort but increases distress. [*Job* in the Old Testament]

**jobs for the boys** n.pl. colloq. appointments for members of one's own group etc.

**jobsheet** n. sheet for recording details of jobs done.

**Jock** n. colloq. Scotsman. [Scots form of the name *Jack*]

**jock** n. colloq. **1** (in pl.) = JOCKSTRAP. **2** male athlete.

**jockey** /ˈjok-ee/ — n. (pl. **-s**) **1** rider in horse races, esp. professional. **2** colloq. (in pl.) close-fitting briefs worn by men. **3** assistant to a carrier, taxi-driver, etc. — v. (**-eys, -eyed**) **1** ride a horse as a jockey. **2** trick, cheat, or outwit. **3** (foll. by *away, out, into*, etc.) manoeuvre (a person). □ **jockey for position** manoeuvre for advantage. [diminutive of JOCK]

**jockstrap** *n.* support for the male genitals, covering these but not the buttocks, and worn esp. in sport. [Brit. colloq. *jock* penis]

**jocose** /juh-**kohs**/ *adj.* playful; jocular. □ **jocosely** *adv.* **jocosity** /-**kos**-uh-tee/ *n.* (*pl.* **-ies**). [Latin *jocus* jest]

**jocular** /**jok**-yuh-luh/ *adj.* **1** fond of joking. **2** humorous. □ **jocularity** /-**la**-ruh-tee/ *n.* (*pl.* **-ies**). **jocularly** *adv.*

**jocund** /**jok**-uhnd/ *adj. literary* merry, cheerful. □ **jocundity** /juh-**kun**-duh-tee/ *n.* (*pl.* **-ies**). **jocundly** *adv.* [French from Latin *jucundus* pleasant]

**jodhpurs** /**jod**-puhz/ *n.pl.* riding breeches tight below the knee. [*Jodhpur* in India]

**joe¹** *n. colloq.* ewe (*bare-bellied joe*). [palatalised form of British dial. *yeo* ewe]

**joe²** — *n. hist.* **1** policeman, trooper, etc., esp. one charged with implementing licensing regulations on the Victorian goldfields. **2 a** cry warning of the approach of such a person. **b** term of derision or abuse. — *v.* jeer at, abuse. [probably from Charles *Joseph* La Trobe, Governor of Victoria at the time]

**Joe Blake** *n. colloq.* **1** snake. **2** (in *pl.*) the shakes. [rhyming slang]

**Joe Bloggs** *n.* (or **Blow**) *colloq.* hypothetical average man.

**joes** *n.pl. colloq.* **1** the shakes; delirium tremens. **2** fit of depression; low spirits. [abbreviation of JOE BLAKE(S)]

**joey** /**joh**-ee/ *n.* (*pl.* **-eys**) **1** young kangaroo or wallaby. **2** young possum. **3** any young creature. **4** baby or young child. □ **have a joey in the pouch** *colloq.* be pregnant. [origin unknown]

**jog** — *v.* (**-gg-**) **1** run slowly, esp. as exercise. **2** push or jerk, esp. unsteadily. **3** nudge, esp. to alert. **4** stimulate (the memory). **5** (often foll. by *on*, *along*) trudge; proceed ploddingly (*must jog on somehow*). **6** (of a horse) trot. — *n.* **1** spell of jogging; slow walk or trot. **2** push, jerk, or nudge. [probably imitative]

**jogger** *n.* person who jogs, esp. for exercise.

**joggle** /**jog**-uhl/ — *v.* (**-ling**) move in jerks. — *n.* slight shake.

**jogtrot** *n.* slow regular trot.

**john¹** /jon/ *n.* police officer. [abbreviation of *johndarme*, local pronunciation of French *gendarme*]

**john²** /jon/ *n. colloq.* toilet. [from the name *John*]

**John Bull** /jon/ *n.* England or the typical Englishman. [name of a character in an 18th-c. satire]

**John Dory** *n.* (*pl.* same or **-ies**) **1** edible and much valued marine fish of Australian waters. **2** similar fish found elsewhere. [see DORY]

**johnny** /**jon**-ee/ *n.* (*pl.* **-ies**) *colloq.* fellow; man. [diminutive of *John*]

**johnny cake** *n.* (also **charcoal tart**) small, usu. thin damper.

**johnny-come-lately** *n. colloq.* newcomer; upstart.

**joie de vivre** /ˌzhwah duh **vee**-vruh/ *n.* exuberance; high spirits. [French, = joy of living]

**join** — *v.* **1** (often foll. by *to*, *together*) put together; fasten, unite (with one or several things or people). **2** connect (points) by a line etc. **3** become a member of (a club, organisation, etc.). **4 a** take one's place with (a person, group, etc.). **b** (foll. by *in*, *for*, etc.) take part with (others) in an activity etc. (*joined them in prayer*). **5** (often foll. by *with*, *to*) come together; be united. **6** (of a river etc.) be or become connected or continuous with. — *n.* point, line, or surface at which things are joined. □ **join battle** begin fighting. **join forces** combine efforts. **join hands 1** clasp hands. **2** combine in an action etc. **join in** (also *absol.*) take part in (an activity). **join up 1** enlist for military service. **2** (often foll. by *with*) unite, connect. [Latin *jungo junct-*]

**joiner** *n.* **1** maker of finished wood fittings. **2** *colloq.* person who joins an organisation or who readily joins societies etc. □ **joinery** *n.* (in sense 1).

**joint** — *n.* **1** place at which two or more things or parts of a structure are joined; device for joining these. **2** point at which two bones fit together. **3** division of an animal carcass as meat. **4** *colloq.* restaurant, bar, etc. **5** *colloq.* marijuana cigarette. **6** *Geol.* crack in rock. — *adj.* **1** held, done by, or belonging to, two or more persons etc. (*joint account*; *joint action*). **2** sharing with another (*joint author*; *joint favourite*). — *v.* **1** connect by joint(s). **2** divide at a joint or into joints. □ **out of joint 1** (of a bone) dislocated. **2** out of order. □ **jointly** *adv.* [French: related to JOIN]

**joist** *n.* supporting beam in a floor, ceiling, etc. [French *giste* from Latin *jaceo* lie]

**jojoba** /hoh-**hoh**-buh/ *n.* plant with seeds yielding an oily extract used in cosmetics etc. [Mexican Spanish]

**joke** — *n.* **1** thing said or done to cause laughter; witticism. **2** ridiculous person or thing (*the minister's explanation was a joke*). — *v.* (**-king**) make jokes; tease (*only joking*). □ **no joke** *colloq.* serious matter. □ **jokingly** *adv.* **joky** *adj.* (also jokey). **jokily** adv. **jokiness** n. [probably Latin *jocus* jest]

**joker** n. **1** colloq. person, fellow, chap. **2** person who jokes. **3** playing-card used in some games.

**jollify** /jol-uh-ˌfuy/ v. (**-ies, -ied**) make merry. □ **jollification** /-fuh-**kay**-shuhn/ n.

**jollity** /**jol**-uh-tee/ n. (pl. **-ies**) merrymaking; festivity. [French *joliveté*: related to JOLLY]

**jolly** /**jol**-ee — adj. (**-ier, -iest**) **1** cheerful; merry. **2** festive, jovial. **3** colloq. pleasant, delightful. — adv. colloq. very. — v. (**-ies, -ied**) (usu. foll. by *along*) colloq. coax or humour in a friendly way (*jollied them along; jollied him into going*). □ **jollily** adv. **jolliness** n. [French *jolif* gay, pretty: perhaps related to YULE]

**jollytail** n. any of several small, chiefly Tasmanian, freshwater fish.

**jolt** /johlt/ — v. **1** disturb or shake (esp. in a moving vehicle) with a jerk. **2** shock; perturb. **3** move along jerkily. — n. **1** jerk. **2** surprise or shock. □ **jolty** adj. (**-ier, -iest**). [origin unknown]

**jonah** /**joh**-nuh/ n. person who seems to bring bad luck. [*Jonah* in the Old Testament]

**jonick** /**jon**-ik/ adj. colloq. fair; genuine; honest; true. [British dial. *jannock*]

**jonquil** /**jong**-kwil/ n. narcissus with small fragrant yellow or white flowers. [ultimately from Latin *juncus* rush plant]

**joonda** /**joon**-duh/ n. 'wild almond tree' of Australia, the plum-like fruit of which is poisonous but can be made edible by leaching. [Kuku-Yalanji *junda*]

**josh** colloq. — v. **1** tease, banter. **2** indulge in ridicule. — n. good-natured or teasing joke. [origin unknown]

**joss** n. Chinese idol. [ultimately from Latin *deus* god]

**joss house** n. Chinese temple.

**joss stick** n. incense-stick for burning.

**jostle** /**jos**-uhl/ — v. (**-ling**) **1** push against; elbow, esp. roughly or in a crowd. **2** (foll. by *with*) struggle roughly. — n. jostling. [from JOUST]

**jot** — v. (**-tt-**) (usu. foll. by *down*) write briefly or hastily. — n. very small amount (*not one jot*). [Greek IOTA]

**jotter** n. small pad or notebook.

**jotting** n. (usu. in pl.) something jotted down; jotted note.

**joule** /jool/ n. SI unit of work or energy. [*Joule*, name of a physicist]

**journal** /**jer**-nuhl/ n. **1** newspaper or periodical. **2** daily record of events; diary. **3** book in which transactions and accounts are entered. **4** part of a shaft or axle that rests on bearings. [Latin *diurnalis* DIURNAL]

**journalese** /ˌjer-nuh-**leez**/ n. hackneyed writing characteristic of some newspapers.

**journalism** n. profession of writing for or editing newspapers etc.

**journalist** n. person writing for or editing newspapers etc. □ **journalistic** /-**lis**-tik/ adj.

**journey** /**jer**-nee/ — n. (pl. **-s**) **1** act of going from one place to another, esp. at a long distance. **2** time taken for this (a *day's journey*). — v. (**-s, -ed**) make a journey. [French *jornee* day, day's work or travel, from Latin *diurnus* daily]

**journeyman** n. **1** qualified mechanic or artisan who works for another. **2** derog. reliable but not outstanding worker.

**journo** /**jer**-noh/ n. colloq. = JOURNALIST. [abbreviation]

**joust** /jowst/ hist. — n. combat between two knights on horseback with lances. — v. engage in a joust. □ **jouster** n. [French *jouste* from Latin *juxta* near]

**Jove** n. (in Roman mythology) Jupiter. □ **by Jove!** exclamation of surprise etc. [Latin *Jupiter Jov-*]

**jovial** /**joh**-vee-uhl/ adj. merry, convivial, hearty. □ **joviality** /-**al**-uh-tee/ n. **jovially** adv. [Latin *jovialis*: related to JOVE]

**jowl**[1] n. **1** jaw or jawbone. **2** cheek (*cheek by jowl*). [Old English]

**jowl**[2] n. **1** loose hanging skin on the throat or neck. **2** dewlap of oxen, wattle of a bird, etc. □ **jowly** adj. [Old English]

**joy** n. **1** (often foll. by *at, in*) pleasure; extreme gladness. **2** thing causing joy. **3** colloq. satisfaction, success (*got no joy*). □ **wish a person joy of** iron. be gladly rid of (what that person has to deal with). □ **joyful** adj. **joyfully** adv. **joyfulness** n. **joyless** adj. **joyous** adj. **joyously** adv. [French *joie* from Latin *gaudium*]

**joyride** colloq. — n. pleasure ride in esp. a stolen car. — v. (**-ding**; past **-rode**; past part. **-ridden**) go for a joyride. □ **joyrider** n.

**joystick** n. **1** colloq. control column of an aircraft. **2** lever controlling movement of an image on a screen used, esp. in electronic games.

**JP** abbr. Justice of the Peace.

**Jr.** abbr. Junior.

**jube** /joob/ n. = JUJUBE.

**jubilant** /**joo**-buh-luhnt/ adj. exultant, rejoicing. □ **jubilance** n. **jubilantly** adv. **jubilation** /-**lay**-shuhn/ n. [Latin *jubilo* shout]

**jubilee** /**joo**-buh-ˌlee/ n. **1** anniversary, esp. the 25th or 50th. **2** time of rejoicing. **3** *Jewish Hist.* year of emancipation and rejoicing, kept every 50 years. **4** *RC Ch.* period of remission from the penal consequences of sin, granted under certain conditions for a year, usu. every 25 years. [Hebrew, ultimately, = ram's-horn trumpet]

**Judaic** /joo-**day**-ik/ *adj.* of or characteristic of the Jews. [Greek: related to JEW]

**Judaism** /**joo**-day-ˌiz-uhm/ *n.* religion of the Jews.

**judas** /**joo**-duhs/ *n.* traitor; person who betrays a friend. [*Judas* Iscariot who betrayed Christ]

**judder** — *v.* (esp. of a mechanism) shake noisily or violently. — *n.* instance of juddering. [imitative: cf. *shudder*]

**judge** /juj/ — *n.* **1** public official appointed to hear and try legal cases. **2** person appointed to decide in a contest, dispute, etc. **3 a** person who decides a question. **b** person regarded as having judgment of a specified type (*am no judge*; *good judge of art*). — *v.* (**-ging**) **1** form an opinion or judgment (about); estimate, appraise. **2** act as a judge (of). **3 a** try (a case) at law. **b** pronounce sentence on. **4** (often foll. by *to* + infin. or *that* + clause) conclude, consider (*judged him to be stupid*; *judged that the mechanic was to blame*). [Latin *judex judic-*]

**judgment** *n.* (also **judgement**) **1** critical faculty; discernment (*error of judgment*). **2** good sense. **3** opinion or estimate (*in my judgment*). **4** sentence of a court of justice. **5** often *joc.* deserved misfortune (*it's a judgment on you for getting up late*). □ **against one's better judgment** contrary to what one really feels to be advisable. **judgment by default** see DEFAULT.

**judgmental** /juj-**men**-tuhl/ *adj.* (also **judgemental**) **1** of or by way of judgment. **2** condemning, critical. □ **judgmentally** *adv.*

**Judgment Day** *n.* (in Judaism, Christianity, and Islam) day on which mankind will be judged by God.

**judicature** /**joo**-duh-kuh-chuh, -**dik**-uh-chuh/ *n.* **1** administration of justice. **2** judge's position. **3** judges collectively. [medieval Latin *judico* judge]

**judicial** /joo-**dish**-uhl/ *adj.* **1** of, done by, or proper to a court of law. **2** having the function of judgment (*judicial assembly*). **3** of or proper to a judge. **4** impartial. □ **judicially** *adv.* [Latin *judicium* judgment]

**judiciary** /joo-**dish**-uh-ree/ *n.* (*pl.* **-ies**) judges collectively.

**judicious** /joo-**dish**-uhs/ *adj.* sensible, prudent. □ **judiciously** *adv.*

**judo** /**joo**-doh/ *n.* sport derived from jujitsu. [Japanese, = gentle way]

**jug** — *n.* **1** deep vessel for liquids, with a handle and a lip for pouring. **2** contents of this. **3** *colloq.* prison. — *v.* (**-gg-**) (usu. as **jugged** *adj.*) **1** stew or boil (hare or rabbit) in a casserole etc. **2** *colloq.* imprison. □ **jugful** *n.* (*pl.* **-s**). [origin uncertain]

**juggernaut** /**jug**-uh-ˌnawt/ *n.* **1** large heavy semi-trailer etc. **2** overwhelming force or object. **3** institution or notion to which persons blindly sacrifice themselves or others. [Hindi *Jagannath*, = lord of the world: name of a statue of Krishna in Hindu mythology, carried in procession on a huge cart under the wheels of which devotees are said to have formerly thrown themselves to be crushed]

**juggle** /**jug**-uhl/ — *v.* (**-ling**) **1 a** (often foll. by *with*) keep several objects in the air at once by throwing and catching. **b** perform such feats with (balls etc.). **2** deal with (several activities) at once. **3** misrepresent or rearrange (figures, facts, etc.) adroitly, esp. for purposes of fraud (*juggled the books*; *juggled with the accounts*). — *n.* **1** act of juggling. **2** act of fraud. [French from Latin *jocus* jest]

**juggler** *n.* **1** person who juggles. **2** impostor; a fraud. □ **jugglery** *n.*

**jugular** /**jug**-yuh-luh/ — *adj.* of the neck or throat. — *n.* = JUGULAR VEIN. [Latin *jugulum* collar-bone]

**jugular vein** *n.* any of several large veins in the neck carrying blood from the head.

**juice** /joos/ — *n.* **1** liquid part of vegetables or fruits. **2** animal fluid, esp. a secretion (*gastric juice*). **3** *colloq.* petrol; electricity. **4** essence or spirit of anything. — *v.* extract juice from (*juiced the oranges*). □ **juiceless** *adj.* [French from Latin]

**juicy** *adj.* (**-ier**, **-iest**) **1** full of juice; succulent. **2** *colloq.* interesting; racy, scandalous (*juicy titbit of gossip*). **3** *colloq.* profitable. □ **juicily** *adv.* **juiciness** *n.*

**ju-jitsu** /joo-**jit**-soo/ *n.* (also **jiu-jitsu, jujutsu**) Japanese system of unarmed combat and physical training. [Japanese *jūjutsu* gentle skill]

**jujube** /**joo**-joob/ *n.* small flavoured jellylike lozenge. [Greek *zizuphon*]

**jukebox** /**jook**-boks/ *n.* coin-operated record-playing machine. [Gullah *juke* disorderly]

**julienne** /ˌjoo-lee-**en**/ — *n.* vegetables cut into short thin strips. — *adj.* cut into thin strips. [French from name *Jules* or *Julien*]

**July** /juh-**luy**/ *n.* (*pl.* **Julys**) seventh month of the year. [Latin *Julius* Caesar]

**jumble** /jum-buhl/ — v. (-ling) (often foll. by *up*) confuse; mix up; muddle. — n. confused state or heap; muddle. □ **jumbly** adj. [probably imitative]

**jumble sale** n. sale of second-hand articles, esp. for charity.

**jumbo** /jum-boh/ n. (pl. -s) colloq. **1** (often attrib.) large animal (esp. an elephant), person, or thing (*jumbo packet*). **2** (in full **jumbo jet**) large airliner, usu. a Boeing 747, for several hundred passengers. [probably from MUMBO-JUMBO]

**jumbuck** /jum-buk/ n. a sheep. [orig. in Australian pidgin and possibly an alteration of an English word (e.g. *jump-up*)]

**jump** — v. **1** rise off the ground etc. by sudden muscular effort in the legs. **2** (often foll. by *up, from, in, out,* etc.) move suddenly or hastily (*jumped into the car; jumped up from his seat*). **3** jerk or twitch from shock or excitement etc. (*he jumped when I said 'boo!'*). **4 a** change rapidly, esp. rise or advance in status (*prices jumped*). **b** cause to do this. **5** (often foll. by *about*) change the subject etc. rapidly (*jumped from topic to topic*). **6** pass over (an obstacle etc.) by jumping. **7** skip or pass over (a passage in a book etc.) (*jump to the next chapter*). **8** cause (a horse etc.) to jump. **9** (foll. by *to, at*) reach (a conclusion) hastily (*don't jump to conclusions*). **10** (of a train) leave (the rails). **11** pass through (a red traffic-light etc.) (*jumped the lights*). **12** get on or off (a train etc.) quickly, esp. illegally or dangerously. **13** attack (a person) unexpectedly. **14** seize (a gold-mining claim etc.) in the absence of the former occupant or by resort to legal technicalities. — n. **1** act of jumping. **2** sudden jerk caused by shock or excitement. **3** abrupt rise in amount, price, value, status, etc. **4** obstacle to be jumped. **5 a** sudden transition. **b** gap in a series, logical sequence, etc. **6** descent by parachute. □ **get** (or **have**) **the jump on** colloq. get (or have) an advantage over (a person) by prompt action. **go jump in the lake!** colloq. expression of contemptuous dismissal = go away!, get lost! **jump at** accept eagerly (*jumped at the opportunity*). **jump bail** fail to appear for trial having been released on bail. **jump down a person's throat** colloq. reprimand or contradict a person fiercely. **jump the gun** colloq. start before a signal is given, or before an agreed time; be over-eager. **jump on** colloq. attack or criticise severely. **jump out of one's skin** colloq. be extremely startled. **jump the queue 1** push forward out of one's turn. **2** take unfair precedence over others. **jump ship** (of a seaman) desert. **jump to it** colloq.

act promptly. **jump up** (in Aboriginal English) come back to life. **jump up and down** colloq. make a fuss, protest vigorously, in order to get some action etc. (*you'll get no response unless you jump up and down about your rights*). **one jump ahead** one stage further on than a rival etc. **take a running jump at yourself!** colloq. expression of extreme irritation = get lost!; I have nothing more to do with you. [imitative]

**jumped-up** adj. colloq. **1** upstart; presumptuously arrogant. **2** not permanent; unreliable, dubious (*jumped-up business ventures*).

**jumper¹** n. **1** hist. smock-like outer garment, distinctive in Australia as part of the conventional attire of a gold-miner. **2** knitted pullover. **3** loose outer jacket worn by sailors. [probably *jump* short coat]

**jumper²** n. **1** (also **jack-jumper**) any of several smaller species of Australian ant capable of jumping and inflicting a painful sting. **2** person or animal that jumps. **3** person who jumps a gold-mining claim. **4** short wire used to make or break an electrical circuit.

**jumper leads** n.pl. pair of cables for conveying current from the battery of one vehicle to that of another.

**jumping-off place** n. (also **jumping-off point** etc.) place or point of starting.

**jump jet** n. vertical take-off jet aircraft.

**jump-start** — v. start (a vehicle) by pushing it or with jump-leads. — n. act of jump-starting.

**jumpsuit** n. one-piece garment for the whole body.

**jump-up** n. sudden steep rise; an escarpment.

**jumpy** adj. (-ier, -iest) **1** nervous; easily startled. **2** making sudden movements. □ **jumpiness** n.

**junction** /jungk-shuhn/ n. **1** joint; joining-point. **2** place where railway lines or roads meet. **3** act or instance of joining. [Latin: related to JOIN]

**junction box** n. box containing a junction of electric cables etc.

**juncture** /jungk-chuh/ n. **1** critical convergence of events; point of time (*at this juncture*). **2** joining-point. **3** act of joining.

**June** n. sixth month of the year. [Latin *Junius* from *Juno*, name of a goddess]

**junga** /joong-guh, jung-guh/ n. = PARAKEELIYA. [Panyjima *janga*]

**Jungian** /yuung-ee-uhn/ — adj. of the Swiss psychologist Carl Jung or his theories. — n. supporter of Jung or of his theories.

**jungle** /**jung**-guhl/ *n.* **1 a** land over-grown with tangled vegetation, esp. in the tropics. **b** an area of this. **2** wild tangled mass. **3** place of bewildering complexity, confusion, or struggle (*blackboard jungle*). □ **law of the jungle** state of ruthless competition. □ **jungled** *adj.* **jungly** *adj.* [Hindi from Sanskrit]

**jungle-fowl** *n.* (also **jungle-hen**) **1** = SCRUB FOWL. **2** East Indian wild bird of the genus *Gallus* from which the domestic fowl is supposed to have been derived.

**jungle juice** *n. colloq.* any crude alcoholic drink.

**junior** /**joo**-nyuh/ — *adj.* **1** (often foll. by *to*) inferior in age, standing, or position. **2** the younger (esp. appended to the name of a son for distinction from his father). **3** of the lower or lowest position (*junior partner*). **4** (of a school) for younger pupils. — *n.* **1** junior person. **2** person at the lowest level (in an office etc.). [Latin, comparative of *juvenis* young]

**juniper** /**joo**-nuh-puh/ *n.* evergreen shrub or tree with prickly leaves and dark purple berry-like cones used as a spice, as a medicine, and as a flavouring for gin etc. [Latin *juniperus*]

**junk**[1] — *n.* **1** discarded articles; rubbish. **2** anything regarded as of little value. **3** *colloq.* narcotic drug, esp. heroin. — *v.* discard as junk (*junked most of the things he had collected*). □ **junky** *adj.* [origin unknown]

**junk**[2] *n.* flat-bottomed sailing-vessel in the China seas. [Javanese *djong*]

**junk bond** *n.* bond bearing high interest but deemed to be a risky investment.

**junket** /**jung**-kuht/ — *n.* **1** pleasure outing. **2** usu. overseas tour for fact-finding etc. made by government officials, politicians, etc., at public expense. **3** sweetened and flavoured milk curds. **4** feast. — *v.* (**-t-**) feast, picnic. [French *jonquette* rush-basket (used for junket 3 and 4), from Latin *juncus* rush]

**junk food** *n.* food, such as sweets and crisps, with low nutritional value.

**junkie** *n.* (also **junky**) *colloq.* drug addict.

**junk mail** *n.* **1** unsolicited advertising matter sent by post. **2** such matter hand-delivered to letter-boxes.

**junk shop** *n.* second-hand or cheap antiques shop.

**junta** /**jun**-tuh, **huun**-tuh/ *n.* (usu. military) clique taking power in a *coup d'état*. [Spanish: related to JOIN]

**jural** /**joor**-ruhl, **joo**-ruhl/ *adj.* **1** of law. **2** of rights and obligations. [Latin *jus jur-* law, right]

**Jurassic** /joor-**ras**-ik, joo-/ *Geol.* — *adj.* of the second period of the Mesozoic era. — *n.* this era or system. [French from *Jura* mountains]

**juridical** /joo-**rid**-i-kuhl/ *adj.* (also **juridic**) **1** of judicial proceedings. **2** relating to the law. [Latin *jus jur-* law, *dico* say]

**jurisdiction** /ˌjoor-uhs-**dik**-shuhn, ˌjoo-ruhs-/ *n.* **1** (often foll. by *over, of*) administration of justice. **2 a** legal or other authority. **b** extent of this; territory it extends over. □ **jurisdictional** *adj.*

**jurisprudence** /ˌjoor-uhs-**proo**-duhns, ˌjoo-ruhs-/ *n.* science or philosophy of law. □ **jurisprudential** /-**den**-shuhl/ *adj.*

**jurist** /**joor**-ruhst, **joo**-ruhst/ *n.* expert in law. □ **juristic** /-ris-tik/ *adj.*

**juror** /**joor**-ruh, **joo**-ruh/ *n.* **1** member of a jury. **2** person taking an oath.

**jury** /**joor**-ree, **joo**-ree/ *n.* (*pl.* **-ies**) **1** body of usu. twelve people giving a verdict in a court of justice. **2** body of people awarding prizes in a competition.

**just** — *adj.* **1** morally right or fair. **2** (of treatment etc.) deserved (*just reward*). **3** well-grounded; justified (*just anger*). **4** right in amount etc.; proper. — *adv.* **1** exactly (*just what I need*). **2** a little time ago; very recently (*has just seen them*). **3** *colloq.* simply, merely (*just good friends*; *just doesn't make sense*). **4** barely; no more than (*just managed it*). **5** *colloq.* positively; indeed (*just splendid*; *won't I just tell him!*). **6** quite (*not just yet*). □ **just about** *colloq.* almost exactly; almost completely. **just in case** as a precaution. **just now 1** at this moment. **2** a little time ago. **just the same** see SAME. **just so 1** exactly arranged (*everything just so*). **2** it is exactly as you say. □ **justly** *adv.* **justness** *n.* [Latin *justus* from *jus* right]

**justice** /**jus**-tuhs/ *n.* **1** justness, fairness. **2** authority exercised in the maintenance of right. **3** judicial proceedings (*brought to justice*; *Court of Justice*). **4** magistrate; judge. □ **do justice to 1** treat fairly. **2** appreciate properly. **do oneself justice** perform at one's best. **with justice** reasonably. [Latin *justitia*]

**Justice of the Peace** *n.* formerly, an unpaid lay magistrate with limited judicial etc. functions; now usu. restricted to witnessing oaths, statutory declarations, etc.

**justifiable** /**jus**-tuh-ˌfuy-uh-buhl/ *adj.* able to be justified. □ **justifiably** *adv.*

**justify** /**jus**-tuh-ˌfuy/ *v.* (**-ies, -ied**) **1** show the justice or correctness of (a person, act, assertion, etc.). **2** (esp. in *passive*) cite or constitute adequate grounds for (conduct, a claim, etc.); vindicate. **3** (as **justified** *adj.*) just, right (*justified in* *assuming*). **4** *Printing* adjust (a line of type) to give even margins. □ **justification** /-fuh-**kay**-shuhn/ *n.* **justificatory** /-fuh-ˌkay-tuh-ree/ *adj.*

**jut** — *v.* (**-tt-**) (often foll. by *out, forth*) protrude, project. — *n.* projection; protruding point. [var. of JET¹]

**jute** *n.* **1 a** fibre from the bark of an E. Indian plant, used for making twine etc., and woven into sacking, mats, etc. **b** sacking etc. woven from jute fibres; GUNNY. **2** plant yielding this. [Bengali]

**juvenile** /**joo**-vuh-ˌnuyl/ — *adj.* **1 a** youthful. **b** of or for young people. **2** often *derog.* immature (*juvenile behaviour*). — *n.* **1** young person. **2** actor playing a juvenile part. [Latin *juvenis* young]

**juvenile delinquency** *n.* offences committed by people below the age of legal responsibility. □ **juvenile delinquent** *n.*

**juvenilia** /ˌjoo-vuh-**nil**-ee-uh/ *n.pl.* author's or artist's youthful works.

**juxtapose** /ˌjuk-stuh-**pohz**/ *v.* (**-sing**) **1** place (things) side by side. **2** (foll. by *to, with*) place (a thing) beside another. □ **juxtaposition** /-puh-**zish**-uhn/ *n.* **juxtapositional** /-puh-**zish**-uh-nuhl/ *adj.* [Latin *juxta* next, *pono* put]

# K

**K¹** /kay/ *n.* (also **k**) (*pl.* **Ks** or **K's**) eleventh letter of the alphabet.

**K²** *abbr.* (also **K.**) **1** kelvin(s). **2** King. **3** Köchel (catalogue of Mozart's works). **4** (also **k**) (prec. by a numeral) **a** *Computing* unit of 1,024 (i.e. 210) bytes or bits, or loosely 1,000. **b** 1,000. [sense 4 as abbreviation of KILO-]

**K³** *symb.* potassium. [Latin *Kalium*]

**k¹** *abbr.* **1** kilo-. **2** knot(s).

**k²** *n.* (*pl.* **k** or **ks** /kayz/) kilometre (cf. KM).

**kadaitcha** *n.* = KURDAITCHA.

**Kafkaesque** /ˌkaf-kuh-**esk**/ *adj.* impenetrably oppressive or nightmarish, as in the fiction of Franz Kafka.

**kaftan** var. of CAFTAN.

**kaiser** /**kuy**-zuh/ *n. hist.* emperor, esp. of Germany, Austria, or the Holy Roman Empire. [Latin CAESAR]

**kakka** /**kak**-uh/ *n.* (also **cacker**) (in WA) undersized crustacean, esp. a marine crayfish. [origin unknown]

**Kalaaku** /ku-**lah**-koo/ *n.* an Aboriginal language of southern WA at Israelite Bay and inland around the Fraser Range and Norseman.

**Kala Lagaw Ya** /kah-lah **lah**-gow yah/ *n.* an Aboriginal language of the Torres Strait islands off the far north of Queensland, still actively spoken.

**kaleidoscope** /kuh-**luy**-duh-ˌskohp/ *n.* **1** tube containing mirrors and pieces of coloured glass etc. producing changing reflected patterns when shaken. **2** constantly changing pattern, group, etc. □ **kaleidoscopic** /-**skop**-ik/ *adj.* [Greek *kalos* beautiful, *eidos* form, -SCOPE]

**kalends** var. of CALENDS.

**Kalkatungu** /ˌkal-kah-ˌtuung-oo/ *n.* an Aboriginal language spoken over a wide area of west-central Queensland: now extinct.

**kamikaze** /ˌkam-uh-**kah**-zee/ — *n. hist.* **1** explosive-laden Japanese aircraft deliberately crashed on a ship etc. during the war of 1939–45. **2** pilot of this. — *attrib. adj.* **1** of a kamikaze. **2** reckless, esp. suicidal (*goes in for kamikaze driving*). [Japanese, = divine wind]

**Kamilaroi** /**kam**-i-lu-roi/ *n.* an Aboriginal language spoken over a vast area of east-central NSW and extending into southern Queensland: no longer spoken, although some of the older people know a number of words.

**Kanaka** /kuh-**nak**-uh/ *n.* Pacific Islander, esp. (formerly) one kidnapped and made to serve as an indentured labourer in the sugar and cotton industries of Queensland. [Hawaiian, = man]

**kanga** /**kang**-guh/ *n. colloq.* **1** kangaroo. **2** = KANGA CRICKET. **3** (rhyming slang on *screw*) prison warder. **4** cash. **5** jackhammer. [abbreviation]

**kanga cricket** *n.* (also **kanga**) game of cricket with rules and equipment specially modified for young players.

**kangaroo** /ˌkang-guh-**roo**/ — *n.* (*pl.* **-s**) **1 a** any of the larger plant-eating marsupials of Australia, having short forelimbs, a large thick tail for support and balance, long feet, and powerful limbs enabling a swift bounding motion. **b** (loosely) any member of the family, including *wallaroos* and *wallabies*. **2** (with distinguishing name) any of the main types of kangaroo: *brush* (kangaroo); *bush*; *eastern grey*; *great grey*; *hill*; *Kangaroo Island*; *red*; *western grey*. **3** an Australian, esp. one representing Australia in sport. **4 a** (in *pl.*) name of the Australian international Rugby League team. **b** member of this team. — *v.* **1** hunt kangaroos. **2 a** leap like a kangaroo. **b** (of a car etc.) move forward in jerks. □ **have kangaroos in the** (or **your** etc.) **top paddock** *colloq.* be crazy or eccentric. [Guugu Yimidhirr *gangurru*]

**kangaroo apple** *n.* any of several shrubs (esp. those known as *gunyang*) of southern and eastern Australia with purple open flowers and egg-shaped fruit edible when completely ripe.

**kangaroo bar** *n.* (also **roo bar**) strong metal bar or frame mounted at the front of a vehicle to protect it in the event of a collision with a kangaroo etc., esp. at night.

**kangaroo bush** *n.* **1** = PUNTY. **2** = SANDHILL WATTLE.

**kangaroo court** *n.* illegal court, e.g. held by strikers or mutineers.

**kangaroo dance** *n.* Aboriginal ceremonial dance in which the dancers' movements represent those of a kangaroo.

**kangaroo drive** *n.* operation (usu. illegal) in which kangaroos are herded, trapped, and slaughtered.

**kangarooer** /ˌkang-guh-**roo**-uh/ *n.* **1** person who takes part in a kangaroo drive. **2** person who shoots kangaroos.

**kangaroo fence** n. fence (2.1 to 3 metres high) made to exclude esp. kangaroos from pastoral properties.

**kangaroo grass** n. tall tussocky perennial native grass widespread throughout Australia, eaten by kangaroos and useful for stock.

**kangaroo-hop** v. **1** move (like a kangaroo) in short hops or stages (*kangaroohopped his way across Australia in a jeep*). **2** (of a car etc.) = KANGAROO v. 2b.

**kangaroo hunt** n. (also **kangaroo hunting**) = KANGAROO DRIVE. □ **kangaroo hunter** n.

**kangaroo mouse** n. = HOPPING MOUSE.

**kangaroo paw** n. any plant of the genera *Anigozanthos* and *Macropidia* of WA with woolly flowers in an outstanding range of colours and shaped like the paw of a kangaroo, esp. *Anigozanthos manglesii* with red stems and vivid green flowers, the floral emblem of WA.

**kangaroo rat** n. (also **rat-kangaroo**) any of several small rabbit-sized kangaroos, including the *bettong* and the *potoroo*.

**kangaroo route** n. name for the Sydney-Singapore-London air-route, orig. as flown by Qantas.

**kangaroo shoot** n. = KANGAROO DRIVE. □ **kangaroo shooter** n.

**kangaroo-tail soup** n. soup made from the meat of the thick kangaroo tail.

**kangaroo thorn** n. wattle with stiff spines on the stems and yellow ball-flowers, found in all States and often planted as a hedge.

**kangaroo tick** n. any tick having the kangaroo or wallaby as host, the bite of one species severely affecting humans.

**kanooka** /kuh-**noo**-kuh/ n. medium-sized tree (*tristania*) of Queensland, NSW, and Victoria with yellow flowers and glossy leaves turning bright red in cold areas such as Canberra. [origin uncertain]

**kaolin** /**kay**-uh-luhn/ n. fine soft white clay used esp. for porcelain and in medicines. [Chinese *kao-ling* high hill]

**kapok** /**kay**-pok/ n. fine fibrous cotton-like substance from a tropical tree, used for padding. [Malay]

**kapok tree** n. (also **kapok**, **cotton tree**) any of several small deciduous Australian trees bearing fruit containing seeds embedded in soft, cottony fibre.

**kappa** /**kap**-uh/ n. tenth letter of the Greek alphabet (Κ, κ). [Greek]

**kaput** /ka-**puut**, kuh-/ *predic. adj. colloq.* broken, ruined. [German]

**Karadjeri** /**kah**-ru-,je-ree/ n. an Aboriginal language of northern WA.

**karaoke** /,ka-ree-**oh**-kay, -oh-kee/ n. **1** sound system with a pre-recorded soundtrack of popular music from which the vocal part has been erased so as to allow an individual to sing along with it, usu. in public at e.g. a karaoke club or bar. **2** the pastime of singing to this kind of system. [Japanese, = empty orchestra]

**karara** /kuh-**rah**-ruh/ n. (also known as **dead finish**) small tree- or shrub-sized wattle of drier Australia which forms tangled, prickly thickets. [Panyjima *kurarra*]

**karate** /kuh-**rah**-tee/ n. Japanese system of unarmed combat using the hands and feet as weapons. [Japanese, = empty hand]

**kark** v. *colloq.* (also **cark**) (often foll. by *it*) **1** die. **2** break down (*the car's finally carked it*). [probably a figurative use of *cark* to caw, from the association of the crow with carrion]

**karkalla** /kah-**kal**-uh/ n. any of several species of Australian pigface bearing edible fruit. [Gaurna *garrgala*]

**karma** /**kah**-muh/ n. *Buddhism* & *Hinduism* person's actions in previous lives, believed to decide his or her fate in future existences. [Sanskrit, = action, fate]

**karpe** /**kah**-pee/ n. parasitic Australian fig tree with glossy leaves and edible yellow fruit turning pink when ripe: the bark was used by Aborigines to make blankets. [Dyirbal *gabi*]

**karri** /**ka**-ree/ n. **1** tall eucalypt of WA with straight, silky-smooth grey trunk prized for timber. **2** the hard, heavy, red wood of this tree. [probably Nyungar]

**Kattang** /**kut**-ung/ n. an Aboriginal language of coastal eastern NSW from Port Stephens to Port Macquarie: now extinct.

**kauri** /**kow**-ree/ n. (*pl.* **-s**) coniferous New Zealand tree yielding valuable timber and resin. [Maori]

**kauri pine** n. **1** any of three tall coniferous trees of the Australian rainforest yielding a pale, light, easily worked wood. **2** the wood of this tree. [transferred use of Maori *kauri*]

**Kaurna** var. of GAURNA.

**kayak** /**kuy**-ak/ n. **1** Eskimo one-man canoe of wood and sealskins. **2** any small covered canoe. [Eskimo]

**kebab** /kuh-**bab**/ n. pieces of meat, vegetables, etc. cooked on a skewer. [Urdu from Arabic]

**kedgeree** /**kej**-uh-ree/ n. **1** Indian dish of rice, split peas, onions, eggs, etc. **2** westernised dish resembling this, usu. with fish. [Hindi]

**keel** — n. main lengthwise timber or steel structure along the base of a ship etc.

— v. **1** (often foll. by *over*) (cause to) fall down or over. **2** turn keel upwards. □ **on an even keel** steady; balanced. [Old Norse]

**keelhaul** v. **1** drag (a person) under the keel of a ship as a punishment. **2** scold or rebuke severely.

**keen**[1] adj. **1** enthusiastic, eager. **2** (foll. by *on*) enthusiastic about, fond of. **3** (of the senses) sharp. **4** intellectually acute. **5** (of a knife etc.) sharp. **6** (of a sound, light, etc.) penetrating, vivid. **7** (of a wind etc.) piercingly cold. **8** (of a pain etc.) acute. **9** (of a price) competitive. □ **keenly** adv. **keenness** n. [Old English]

**keen**[2] — n. Irish wailing funeral song. — v. (often foll. by *over, for*) wail mournfully, esp. at a funeral. [Irish *caoine* from *caoinim* wail]

**keep** — v. (*past* and *past part.* kept) **1** have continuous charge of; retain possession of. **2** (foll. by *for*) retain or reserve for (a future time) (*kept it for later*). **3** retain or remain in a specified condition, position, place, etc. (*keep cool; keep out; keep them happy; knives are kept here*). **4** (foll. by *from*) restrain, hold back (*kept him from making a fool of himself*). **5** detain (*what kept you?*). **6** observe, honour, or respect (a law, custom, commitment, secret, etc.) (*keep one's word; keep the sabbath*). **7** own and look after (animals) (*keeps bees*). **8 a** clothe, feed, maintain, etc. (a person, oneself, etc.). **b** (foll. by *in*) maintain (a person) with a supply of (*keeps us in fresh vegies*). **9** carry on; manage (a business etc.). **10** maintain (a diary, house, accounts, etc.) regularly and in proper order. **11** normally have on sale (*do you keep buttons?*). **12** guard or protect (a person or place). **13** preserve (*keep order*). **14** (foll. by verbal noun) continue; repeat habitually (*keeps telling me*). **15** continue to follow (a way or course). **16 a** (esp. of food) remain in good condition. **b** (of news etc.) not suffer from delay in telling. **17** (often foll. by *to*) remain in (one's bed, room, etc.). — n. **1** maintenance, food, etc. (*hardly earn your keep*). **2** charge or control (*is in your keep*). **3** *hist.* tower, esp. the central stronghold of a castle. □ **for keeps** *colloq.* permanently, indefinitely. **how are you keeping?** how are you? **keep at** (cause to) persist with. **keep away** (often foll. by *from*) avoid, prevent from being near. **keep back 1** remain or keep at a distance. **2** retard the progress of. **3** conceal. **4** withhold (*kept back $50*). **keep down 1** hold in subjection. **2** continue in (*keep down a job*). **3** keep low in amount. **4** stay hidden. **5** not vomit (food eaten).

**keep one's hair on** see HAIR. **keep one's hand in** see HAND. **keep in with** remain on good terms with. **keep off 1** (cause to) stay away from. **2** ward off. **3** abstain from. **4** avoid (a subject) (*let's keep off religion*). **keep on 1** continue; do continually (*kept on laughing*). **2** continue to employ. **3** (foll. by *at*) nag. **keep out 1** keep or remain outside. **2** exclude. **keep to 1** adhere to (a course, promise, etc.). **2** confine oneself to. **keep to oneself 1** avoid contact with others. **2** keep secret. **keep track of** see TRACK. **keep under** repress. **keep up 1** maintain (progress, morale, etc.). **2** keep in repair etc. **3** carry on (a correspondence etc.). **4** prevent from going to bed. **5** (often foll. by *with*) not fall behind. **keep up with the Joneses** compete socially with one's neighbours. [Old English]

**keeper** n. **1** person who looks after or is in charge of animals, people, or a thing. **2** custodian of a museum, forest, etc. **3 a** = WICKET-KEEPER. **b** = GOALKEEPER. **4 a** sleeper in a pierced ear. **b** ring that keeps another on the finger.

**keeping** n. **1** custody, charge (*in safe keeping*). **2** agreement, harmony (esp. *in* or *out of keeping* (*with*).

**keepsake** n. souvenir, esp. of a person.

**keg** n. **1** small barrel. **2** barrel of beer. [Old Norse]

**Kelly** n. **1** see NED KELLY. **2** (also **kelly**) orig. *propr.* **a** a type of axe. **b** (loosely) any axe. **3** (kelly) a crow. **4** person whose behaviour is supposed in some way to resemble that of Ned Kelly (e.g. a ticket-inspector).

**kelp** n. **1** large brown seaweed suitable for manure. **2** its calcined ashes, formerly a source of sodium, potassium, etc. [origin unknown]

**kelpie** /kel-pee/ n. Australian breed of short-haired, prick-eared dog, noted for its hardiness and ability to tend and work sheep. [from the name of a particular bitch called *Kelpie* in the early 1870s, progenitor of this breed, whose pups were known as *Kelpie's pups*; thence to *kelpies*]

**kelvin** /kel-vuhn/ n. SI unit of thermodynamic temperature. [*Kelvin* name of a physicist]

**Kelvin scale** n. scale of temperature with zero at absolute zero.

**ken** n. range of knowledge or sight (*beyond my ken*). [Old English, = make known: related to CAN[1]]

**kennedia** /kuh-ned-ee-uh, -nee-dee-uh/ n. any plant of the Australian genus of climbing and trailing perennials *Kennedia*, with trifoliate leaves and bright red, orange, purple, or black-and-yellow pea-flowers in profusion, esp. the *scarlet* *runner* or *running postman*. [John *Kennedy*, London nurseryman (d. 1842)]

**kennel** /ken-uhl/ — *n.* **1** small shelter for a dog. **2** (in *pl.*) breeding or boarding place for dogs. — *v.* (**-ll-**) put into or keep in a kennel. [French *chenil* from Latin *canis* dog]

**keno** /kee-noh/ *n.* game of chance resembling bingo or lotto. [origin unknown]

**kentia palm** /ken-tee-uh/ *n.* large shapely palm with arching leaves, native to Lord Howe Island; often grown as an indoor plant.

**Kenyan** /ken-yuhn, keen-yuhn/ — *adj.* of Kenya in E. Africa. — *n.* **1** native or national of Kenya. **2** person of Kenyan descent.

**kept** *past* and *past part.* of KEEP.

**keratin** /ke-ruh-tuhn/ *n.* fibrous protein in hair, feathers, hooves, claws, horns, etc. [Greek *keras kerat-* horn]

**kerb** *n.* stone edging to a street or raised path etc. [var. of CURB]

**kerchief** /ker-cheef, -chuhf/ *n.* **1** headscarf, neckerchief. **2** *poet.* handkerchief. [Anglo-French *courchef*: related to COVER, CHIEF]

**kerfuffle** /kuh-fuf-uhl/ *n. colloq.* fuss, commotion. [originally Scots]

**kernel** /ker-nuhl/ *n.* **1** (usu. soft) edible centre within the hard shell of a nut, fruit stone, seed, etc. **2** whole seed of a cereal. **3** essence of anything. [Old English: related to CORN[1]]

**kero** /ke-roh/ *n.* = KEROSENE; also *attrib.* (*used kero tins*).

**kerosene** /ke-ruh-seen, ke-ruh-seen/ *n.* (also **kerosine**) fuel oil for use in jet engines, boilers, etc. (also *attrib.*: *kerosene tin*). [Greek *kēros* wax]

**kerosene bush** *n.* small aromatic Australian shrub of the genus *Helichrysum*, so called because it is highly flammable.

**kerosene wood** *n.* (also **kerosene tree**) = JITTA.

**kestrel** /kes-truhl/ *n.* **1** (also **nankeen kestrel**) small Australian falcon having a characteristic hovering flight. **2** any other small hovering falcon. [origin uncertain]

**ketch** *n.* small two-masted sailing-boat. [probably from CATCH]

**ketchup** /kech-uhp/ *n.* spicy esp. tomato sauce used as a condiment. [Chinese]

**ketone** /kee-tohn/ *n.* any of a class of organic compounds including propanone (acetone). [German *Keton*, alteration of *Aketon* ACETONE]

**kettle** /ket-uhl/ *n.* **1** vessel with lid, spout, and handle, for boiling water. **2** = KETTLEDRUM. □ **a different kettle of fish** a

different matter altogether. **a fine** (or **pretty**) **kettle of fish** *iron.* an awkward state of affairs. [Old Norse]

**kettledrum** *n.* large bowl-shaped drum. □ **kettledrummer** *n.*

**key** /kee/ — *n.* (*pl.* **-s**) **1** (usu. metal) instrument for moving the bolt of a lock. **2** similar implement for operating a switch. **3** instrument for grasping screws, nuts, etc., or for winding a clock etc. **4** (often in *pl.*) finger-operated button or lever on a typewriter, piano, computer terminal, etc. (*key to success*). **6** (*attrib.*) essential (*key element*). **7a** a solution or explanation. **b** word or system for solving a cipher or code. **c** explanatory list of symbols used in a map, table, etc. **d** book etc. of solutions to mathematical problems, language exercises, etc., which have been set. **8** *Mus.* system of notes related to each other and based on a particular note (*key of C major*). **9** tone or style of thought or expression. **10** piece of wood or metal inserted between and securing others. **11** coat of wall plaster between the laths securing other coats. **12** roughness of a surface helping the adhesion of plaster etc. **13** device for making or breaking an electric circuit. — *v.* (**keys, keyed**) **1** (foll. by *in*, *on*, etc.) fasten with a pin, wedge, bolt, etc. **2 a** (often foll. by *in*, *into*) enter (data etc.) into a computer by typing on a keyboard. **b** (foll. by *into*) gain entry to a computer by keying in a specific code or command. **3** roughen (a surface) to help the adhesion of plaster etc. **4** (foll. by *to*) align or link (one thing to another). □ **keyed up** tense, nervous, excited. [Old English]

**keyboard** — *n.* **1** set of keys on a typewriter, computer, piano, etc. **2** (also **electronic keyboard**) electronic musical instrument with keys arranged as on a piano, and usu. a number of pre-programmed electronic effects such as drum rhythms etc. — *v.* enter (data etc.) into a computer by typing on its keyboard. □ **keyboarder** *n.* **keyboarding** *n.* **keyboardist** *n.*

**keycard** *n.* plastic card that enables the holder to withdraw money from an automatic teller machine.

**keyhole** *n.* hole in a door etc. for a key.

**Keynesian** /kayn-zee-uhn, keen-/ *adj.* of the economic theories of J. M. Keynes, esp. regarding State intervention in the economy.

**keynote** *n.* **1** (esp. *attrib.*) prevailing tone or idea, esp. in a speech, conference, etc. (*keynote address*). **2** *Mus.* note on which a key is based.

**keypad** n. miniature keyboard etc. for a portable electronic device, telephone, etc.

**key signature** n. Mus. any of several combinations of sharps or flats indicating the key of a composition.

**keystone** n. **1** central principle of a system, policy, etc. **2** central locking stone in an arch.

**keystroke** n. single depression of a key on a (computer etc.) keyboard, esp. as a measure of work.

**keyword** n. **1** key to a cipher etc. **2 a** word of great significance. **b** significant word used in indexing, information retrieval, etc.

**kg** abbr. kilogram(s).

**KGB** n. State security police of the former USSR. [Russian abbreviation, = committee of State security]

**khaki** /kah-kee/ — adj. dull brownish-yellow. — n. (pl. **-s**) **1** khaki fabric or uniform. **2** dull brownish-yellow colour. [Urdu, = dust-coloured]

**kHz** abbr. kilohertz.

**kibble** v. grind coarsely (kibbled wheat). [origin unknown]

**kibbutz** /kuh-**buuts**/ n. (pl. **kibbutzim** /-buut-**seem**/) communal esp. farming settlement in Israel. [Hebrew, = gathering]

**kibosh** /**kuy**-bosh/ n. (also **kybosh**) colloq. nonsense. □ **put the kibosh on** put an end to. [origin unknown]

**kick** — v. **1** strike, strike out, or propel forcibly, with the foot or hoof. **2** (often foll. by at, against) protest at; rebel against. **3** colloq. give up (a habit). **4** (often foll. by out) expel or dismiss forcibly. **5** refl. be annoyed with oneself (could have kicked himself). **6** Football score (a goal) by a kick. — n. **1** kicking action or blow. **2** colloq. **a** sharp stimulant effect, esp. of alcohol. **b** (often in pl.) thrill (did it for kicks). **3** strength, resilience (no kick left). **4** colloq. specified temporary interest (on a health-food kick). **5** recoil of a gun when fired. □ **get a kick out of** colloq. GET. **kick about** (or **around**) colloq. **1 a** drift idly from place to place. **b** be unused or unwanted. **2 a** treat roughly. **b** discuss unsystematically. **kick the bucket** colloq. die. **kick one's heels** see HEEL¹. **kick in 1** knock down (a door etc.) by kicking. **2** contribute (esp. money); pay one's share. **kick in the pants** (or **teeth**) colloq. humiliating punishment or setback. **kick off 1 a** Football start or resume a match. **b** colloq. begin. **2** remove (shoes etc.) by kicking. **kick on** maintain or gain momentum (the party is kicking on nicely). **kick over the traces** see TRACE². **kick the tin** colloq. contribute money to a cause. **kick up** (or **kick up a**

fuss, dust, etc.) colloq. create a disturbance; object. **kick a person upstairs** dispose of a person by promotion etc. [origin unknown]

**kickback** n. colloq. **1** recoil. **2** (usu. illegal) payment for help or favours, esp. in business.

**kick-off** n. Football start or resumption of a match.

**kick-start** — n. (also **kick-starter**) device to start the engine of a motor cycle etc. by the downward thrust of a pedal. — v. start (a motor cycle etc.) in this way.

**kid¹** — n. **1** young goat. **2** leather from this. **3** colloq. child. — adj. colloq. younger (kid sister). — v. (of a goat) give birth. □ **handle with kid gloves** treat carefully or with utmost tact. [Old Norse]

**kid²** v. (also refl.) (**-dd-**) colloq. deceive, trick, tease (don't kid yourself; only kidding). □ **no kidding** colloq. that is the truth. [origin uncertain]

**kidnap** v. (**-pp-**) **1** abduct (a person etc.), esp. to obtain a ransom. **2** steal (a child). □ **kidnapper** n. [from KID¹, nap = NAB]

**kidney** /**kid**-nee/ n. (pl. **-s**) **1** either of two organs in the abdominal cavity of vertebrates which remove nitrogenous wastes from the blood and excrete urine. **2** animal's kidney as food. [origin unknown]

**kidney bean** n. red-skinned dried bean.

**kidney-fat** — n. fat surrounding the kidney. — v. (in traditional Aboriginal society) remove (a person's) kidney-fat for ritual reasons.

**kidney machine** n. machine able to take over the function of a damaged kidney.

**kidney-shaped** adj. having one side concave and the other convex.

**kid-stakes** n.pl. colloq. nonsense; pretence. [probably a joc. formation on British colloq. kid humbug]

**kidult** /**kid**-ult/ — n. an adult who has the tastes, interests, etc. of a child. — adj. **1** consisting of kidults (television seems to cater for a kidult society). **2** geared to kidults (kidult programs on telly). **3** designed to appeal to all age-groups. [KID¹, ADULT]

**kill** — v. **1** (also absol.) deprive of life or vitality; cause death or the death of. **2** destroy (feelings etc.) (killed his enthusiasm). **3** refl. colloq. **a** overexert oneself (don't kill yourself trying). **b** laugh heartily. **4** colloq. overwhelm with amusement (the things he says really kill me). **5** switch off (a light, engine, etc.). **6** Computing colloq. delete. **7** colloq. cause pain or discomfort to (my feet are killing me). **8** pass (time, or a specified period) usu. while waiting (an hour to kill before the *interview*). **9** defeat (a bill in parliament). **10 a** *Tennis etc.* hit (the ball) so that it cannot be returned. **b** stop (the ball) dead. **11** make ineffective (taste, sound, pain, etc.) (*carpet killed the sound*). — *n.* **1** act of killing (esp. in hunting). **2** animal(s) killed, esp. by a hunter. **3** *colloq.* destruction or disablement of an enemy aircraft etc. □ **dressed to kill** dressed showily or alluringly. **in at the kill** present at a successful conclusion. **kill off 1** destroy completely. **2** (of an author) bring about the death of (a fictional character). **kill or cure** (usu. *attrib.*) (of a remedy etc.) drastic, extreme. **kill two birds with one stone** achieve two aims at once. **kill with kindness** spoil with overindulgence. [perhaps related to QUELL]

**killer¹** *n.* **1 a** person, animal, or thing that kills. **b** murderer. **2** *colloq.* **a** impressive, formidable, or excellent thing. **b** extremely difficult, tortuous, etc., thing (*exam-paper was a real killer*).

**killer²** *n.* an animal, esp. a bullock or sheep, selected and killed for immediate consumption.

**killer instinct** *n.* **1** innate tendency to kill. **2 a** ruthless streak. **b** (esp. in competitive sports etc.) no-holds-barred determination to win.

**killer whale** *n.* **1** voracious toothed whale with a white belly. **2** dolphin with a prominent dorsal fin.

**killing** — *n.* **1 a** causing of death. **b** instance of this. **2** *colloq.* great (esp. financial) success (*make a killing*). — *adj. colloq.* **1** very funny. **2** exhausting.

**killjoy** *n.* gloomy or censorious person, esp. at a party etc.

**kiln** *n.* furnace or oven for burning, baking, or drying, esp. for calcining lime or firing pottery etc. [Old English from Latin *culina* kitchen]

**kilo** /**kee**-loh/ *n.* (*pl.* **-s**) kilogram. [French, abbreviation]

**kilo-** *comb. form* 1,000 (esp. in metric units). [Greek *khilioi*]

**kilobyte** /**kil**-uh-,buyt/ *n.* Computing 1,024 (i.e. 2¹⁰) bytes as a measure of memory or file size etc.

**kilocalorie** /**kil**-uh-,kal-uh-ree/ *n.* = large calorie (see CALORIE).

**kilogram** /**kil**-uh-,gram/ *n.* SI unit of mass equal to 1000 grams (approx. 2.205 lb.).

**kilohertz** /**kil**-uh-,herts/ *n.* 1,000 hertz, 1,000 cycles per second.

**kilojoule** /**kil**-uh-,jool/ *n.* 1,000 joules, esp. as a measure of the energy value of foods.

**kilolitre** /**kil**-uh-,lee-tuh/ *n.* 1,000 litres (220 imperial gallons).

**kilometre** /**kil**-uh-,mee-tuh, kuh-**lom**-uh-tuh/ *n.* 1,000 metres (approx. 0.62 miles). □ **kilometric** /,kil-uh-**met**-rik/ *adj.*

**kiloton** /**kil**-uh-,ton/ *n.* (also **kilotonne**) unit of explosive power equivalent to 1,000 tons of TNT.

**kilovolt** /**kil**-uh-,volt, -,vohlt/ *n.* 1,000 volts.

**kilowatt** /**kil**-uh-,wot/ *n.* 1,000 watts.

**kilowatt-hour** *n.* electrical energy equivalent to a power consumption of 1,000 watts for one hour.

**kilt** — *n.* pleated knee-length usu. tartan skirt, traditionally worn by men of the Scottish Highlands. — *v.* **1** tuck up (the skirts) round the body. **2** (esp. as **kilted** *adj.*) gather in vertical pleats. [Scandinavian]

**kilter** /**kil**-tuh/ *n.* (also **kelter** /**kel**-/) good working order (esp. *out of kilter*). [origin unknown]

**kimono** /kuh-**moh**-noh, **kim**-uh-noh/ *n.* (*pl.* **-s**) **1** long sashed Japanese robe. **2** similar dressing gown. [Japanese]

**kin** — *n.* one's relatives or family. — *predic. adj.* related. [Old English]

**-kin** *suffix* forming diminutive nouns (*catkin*; *manikin*). [Dutch]

**kind** /kuynd/ — *n.* **1** race, species, or natural group of animals, plants, etc. (*human kind*). **2** class, type, sort, variety (*what kind of job are you after?*). **3** natural way, fashion, etc. (*true to kind*). — *adj.* (often foll. by *to*) friendly, generous, or benevolent. □ **in kind 1** in the same form, likewise (*was insulted and replied in kind*). **2** (of payment) in goods or labour, not money. **3** character, quality (*differ in degree but not in kind*). **a kind of** loosely resembling (*he's a kind of doctor*). [Old English]

■ **Usage** In sense 2 of the noun, *these kinds of* is preferred to *these kind of*.

**kinder** /**kin**-duh/ *n.* = KINDERGARTEN. [abbreviation]

**kindergarten** /**kin**-duh-,gah-tuhn/ *n.* class or school for very young children. [German, = children's garden]

**kind-hearted** *adj.* of a kind disposition. □ **kind-heartedly** *adv.* **kind-heartedness** *n.*

**kindle** /**kin**-duhl/ *v.* (**-ling**) **1** light, catch, or set on fire. **2** arouse or inspire (*kindle jealousy in a rival*; *kindle enthusiasm for the project*). **3** become aroused or animated (*her imagination kindled*). [Old Norse]

**kindling** *n.* small sticks etc. for lighting fires.

**kindly¹** /**kuynd**-lee/ *adv.* **1** in a kind manner (*spoke kindly*). **2** often *iron.* please (*kindly go away*). □ **look kindly**

**upon** regard sympathetically. **take kindly to** be pleased by; like.

**kindly²** *adj.* (**-ier, -iest**) **1** kind, kind-hearted. **2** (of a climate etc.) pleasant, mild. □ **kindlily** *adv.* **kindliness** *n.*

**kindness** *n.* **1** being kind. **2** kind act.

**kindred** /**kin**-druhd/ — *adj.* **1** related by blood or marriage. **2** allied or similar (*other kindred symptoms*). — *n.* **1** one's relations collectively. **2** blood relationship. **3** resemblance in character. [Old English, = kinship]

**kindred spirit** *n.* person like or in sympathy with oneself.

**kindy** /**kin**-dee/ *n.* (also **kindie**) *colloq.* = KINDERGARTEN.

**kinematics** /ˌkin-uh-**mat**-iks, ˌkuy-/ *n.pl.* (usu. treated as *sing.*) branch of mechanics concerned with the motion of objects without reference to cause. □ **kinematic** *adj.* [Greek *kinēma -matos* motion]

**kinetic** /kuh-**net**-ik, kuy-/ *adj.* of or due to motion. □ **kinetically** *adv.* [Greek *kineo* move]

**kinetic art** *n.* sculpture etc. designed to move.

**kinetic energy** *n.* energy of motion.

**kinetics** *n.pl.* **1** = DYNAMICS 1a. **2** (usu. treated as *sing.*) branch of physical chemistry measuring and studying the rates of chemical reactions.

**king¹** *n.* **1** (as a title usu. **King**) male sovereign, esp. a hereditary ruler. **2** pre-eminent person or thing (*oil king*). **3** (*attrib.*) large (or the largest) kind of plant, animal, etc. (*king plant*). **4** *Chess* piece which must be checkmated for a win. **5** crowned piece in draughts. **6** court-card depicting a king. □ **kingly** *adj.* **kingship** *n.* [Old English]

**king²** *n. colloq.* = KINGFISH.

**king³** = KING-HIT *v.*

**king⁴** *n. hist.* title given by colonists to the male leader of an Aboriginal community.

**King Billy** *n.* generic term for an Aboriginal leader. [probably in joc. allusion to the British king William IV]

**King Billy pine** *n.* = KING WILLIAM PINE.

**king brown (snake)** *n.* (also **mulga snake**) large brown extremely venomous snake occurring throughout northern and drier southern mainland Australia.

**kingdom** *n.* **1** territory or country ruled by a king or queen. **2** spiritual reign or sphere of God. **3** domain belonging to a person, animal, etc. **4** division of the natural world (*plant kingdom*). **5** specified mental or emotional sphere (*kingdom of the heart*). [Old English]

**king fern** *n.* either of two very large ferns, one occurring in shady forests in eastern Australia, and the other chiefly in Queensland.

**kingfish** *n.* any of several very large food-fish of Australian waters, esp. the yellow-tail and the mulloway.

**kingfisher** *n.* small bird with brightly coloured plumage, diving for fish etc.

**King George whiting** *n.* = SPOTTED WHITING.

**king-hit** *colloq.* — *n.* **1** knock-out punch or blow. **2** any sudden catastrophe etc. — *v.* **1** (also **king**) punch (a person) suddenly and hard. **2** (metaphorically) deliver a telling blow (*was king-hit by the recession*). □ **king-hitter** *n.*

**kingie** /**king**-ee/ *n. colloq.* **1** = KINGFISH. **2** = KING PRAWN.

**king parrot** *n.* any of several Australian parrots, esp. the scarlet and green parrot of eastern Australia.

**kingpin** *n.* **1** main, large, or vertical bolt, esp. as a pivot. **2** essential person or thing.

**king prawn** *n.* very large prawn (one species occurring in the waters of eastern Australia, the other in western and northern Australia) highly valued as food.

**king-size** *adj.* (also **-sized**) very large.

**king tide** *n.* a spring tide; an unusually high tide.

**King William pine** *n.* (also **King Billy pine**) conifer occurring in Tasmanian forests, the valuable softwood timber of which is straight-grained, light, and very durable.

**kink** — *n.* **1 a** twist or bend in wire etc. **b** tight wave in hair. **2** mental twist or quirk. **3** flaw, weak-spot (*a few kinks in the plan need to be ironed out*). — *v.* (cause to) form a kink. [Low German or Dutch]

**kinky** *adj.* (**-ier, -iest**) **1** *colloq.* **a** unconventional, esp. sexually. **b** (of clothing etc.) bizarre and sexually provocative. **2** having kinks. □ **kinkily** *adv.* **kinkiness** *n.*

**kinsfolk** *n.pl.* one's blood relations.

**kinship** *n.* **1** blood relationship. **2** likeness; sympathy.

**kinsman** *n.* (*fem.* **kinswoman**) **1** blood relation. **2** relation by marriage.

■ **Usage** Use of *kinsman* in sense 2 is considered incorrect by some people.

**kiosk** /**kee**-osk/ *n.* light open-fronted booth selling food, newspapers, tickets, etc. [Turkish from Persian]

**kip** *n.* small piece of wood from which coins are spun in the game of two-up. [perhaps from British dial. *kep* to catch; to throw up in the air]

**kipper¹** /**kip**-uh/ — *n.* fish, esp. a herring, split, salted, dried, and usu.

smoked. — v. cure (a herring etc.) thus. [origin uncertain]

**kipper²** — n. hist. **1** an Aboriginal boy who has been initiated into manhood. **2** the ceremony in which such initiation takes place. — v. initiate (an Aboriginal boy) into manhood. □ **kipper ground** (or **kipper ring**) the place reserved for such an initiation ceremony. [Dharuk *gibarra* an initiated boy, possibly related to *giba* stone, from the use of a stone for the ceremonial extraction of a tooth]

**kipsy** n. (also **kipsie**) (pl. **-ies**) house, home, lean-to, shelter, etc. [elaboration of British slang *kip* a lodging-house]

**kirk** n. Scot. & N.Engl. church. [Old Norse *kirkja* church]

**kirsch** /keersh, kersh/ n. brandy distilled from cherries. [German, = cherry]

**kismet** /ˈkiz-muht, kis-/ n. destiny, fate. [Turkish from Arabic]

**kiss** — v. **1** touch with the lips, esp. as a sign of love, affection, greeting, or reverence. **2** (of two people) touch each others' lips in this way. **3** lightly touch. — n. **1** touch with the lips. **2** light touch. □ **kiss the dust** submit abjectly. [Old English]

**kiss-and-ride** adj. pertaining to the practice whereby a commuter is driven in his or her car (to pick up public transport) by his or her spouse etc. (opp. a 'park-and-ride' commuter) and is picked up again in the evening.

**kiss-curl** n. small curl of hair on the forehead, nape, etc.

**kiss of death** n. apparent good luck etc. which causes ruin.

**kit** — n. **1** articles, equipment, etc., for a specific purpose (*first-aid kit*). **2** specialised clothing or uniform, esp. military. **3** set of parts needed to assemble furniture, a model, etc. — v. (**-tt-**) (often foll. by *out, up*) equip with a kit. □ **the whole kit and caboodle** see CABOODLE. [Dutch]

**kitbag** n. large usu. cylindrical bag used for a soldier's or traveller's kit.

**kitchen** /ˈkich-uhn/ n. **1** place where food is prepared and cooked. **2** (attrib.) of or belonging to the kitchen (*kitchen bench; kitchen table*). **3** kitchen fitments (*half-price kitchens*). [Latin *coquina*]

**kitchen sink** — n. sink in the kitchen. — adj. (**kitchen-sink**) (in art forms) depicting extreme realism, esp. drabness or sordidness (*kitchen-sink school of painting; kitchen-sink drama*). □ **everything but the kitchen sink** everything imaginable.

**kitchen tea** n. party given for a bride-to-be to which the (usu. female) guests bring gifts of kitchen equipment.

**kitchenware** n. cooking utensils.

**kite** n. **1** light framework with a thin covering flown on a string in the wind. **2** soaring bird of prey. [Old English]

**kitehawk** n. predominantly brown, carrion-eating bird common in Australia.

**kith** n. □ **kith and kin** friends and relations. [Old English, originally 'knowledge': related to CAN¹]

**kitsch** /kich/ n. (often attrib.) vulgar, pretentious, or worthless art, literature, décor, etc. □ **kitschy** adj. (**-ier, -iest**). [German]

**kitten** /ˈkit-uhn/ — n. young cat, ferret, etc. — v. (of a cat etc.) give birth (to). □ **have kittens** colloq. be very upset or anxious. [Anglo-French diminutive of *chat* CAT]

**kittenish** adj. playful, lively, or flirtatious.

**kitty** /ˈkit-ee/ n. (pl. **-ies**) **1** fund of money for communal use. **2** pool in some card-games. [origin unknown]

**kiwi** /ˈkee-wee/ n. (pl. **-s**) **1** flightless long-billed New Zealand bird. **2** (**Kiwi**) colloq. New Zealander. [Maori]

**kiwi fruit** n. (climbing plant bearing) a fruit having a thin brown hairy skin and green flesh (also called *Chinese gooseberry*).

**kJ** abbr. kilojoule(s).

**kl** abbr. kilolitre(s).

**klaxon** /ˈklak-suhn/ n. propr. horn or warning hooter. [name of the manufacturer]

**kleptomania** /ˌklep-tuh-ˈmay-nee-uh/ n. obsessive apparently motiveless urge to steal. □ **kleptomaniac** /-nee-ˌak/ n. & adj. [Greek *kleptēs* thief]

**klick** var. of CLICK².

**km** abbr. kilometre(s) (cf. K²). □ **km/h** kilometres per hour. **km/s** kilometres per second.

**knack** /nak/ n. **1** acquired or intuitive faculty of doing a thing adroitly. **2** habit (*a knack of offending people*). [origin unknown]

**knacker** — n. **1** buyer of useless horses etc. for slaughter, or of old houses, ships, etc. for the materials. **2** (in pl.) colloq. testicles. — v. colloq. (esp. as **knackered** adj.) **1** exhaust, wear out (*knackered after mowing the lawn*). **2** broken, not working (*this video's knackered*). **3** castrated (*has your cat been knackered yet?*). [origin unknown]

**knapsack** /ˈnap-sak/ n. soldier's or hiker's usu. canvas bag carried on the back. [German *knappen* bite, SACK¹]

**knave** n. **1** rogue, scoundrel. **2** = JACK n. 2. □ **knavery** n. (pl. **-ies**). knavish adj. [Old English, originally = boy, servant]

**knead** v. **1 a** work into a dough, paste, etc., by pummelling. **b** make (bread, pottery, etc.) thus. **2** massage (the body, muscles, etc.) as if kneading. [Old English]

**knee** — n. **1 a** (often attrib.) joint between the thigh and the lower leg in humans. **b** corresponding joint in other animals. **c** area around this. **d** lap (sat on his knee). **2** part of a garment covering the knee. — v. (**knees, kneed, kneeing**) touch or strike with the knee (kneed him in the groin). □ **bring a person to his** (or **her**) **knees** reduce a person to submission. [Old English]

**kneecap** — n. **1** convex movable bone in front of the knee. **2** protective covering for the knee. — v. (**-pp-**) colloq. (of a terrorist) shoot (a person) in the knee or leg as a punishment.

**knee-deep** adj. **1** (usu. foll. by in) **a** immersed up to the knees. **b** deeply involved. **2** so deep as to reach the knees.

**knee-high** adj. so high as to reach the knees. □ **knee-high to a grasshopper** colloq. small in height, tiny.

**knee-jerk** n. **1** sudden involuntary kick caused by a blow on the tendon just below the knee. **2** (attrib.) predictable, automatic, stereotyped (knee-jerk reaction).

**kneel** v. (past and past part. **knelt** /nelt/ or **kneeled**) fall or rest on the knees or a knee. [Old English: related to KNEE]

**knell** — n. **1** sound of a bell, esp. for a death or funeral. **2** announcement, event, etc., regarded as an ill omen. — v. **1** ring a knell. **2** proclaim by or as by a knell (knelled the death of all their hopes). [Old English]

**knelt** past and past part. of KNEEL.

**knew** past of KNOW.

**knickerbockers** /nik-uh-,bok-uhz/ n.pl. loose-fitting breeches gathered at the knee or calf. [the pseudonym of W. Irving, author of History of New York]

**knickers** n.pl. = PANTIES. [abbreviation of KNICKERBOCKERS]

**knick-knack** /nik-nak/ n. (also **nick-nack**) trinket or small dainty ornament etc. [from KNACK in the obsolete sense 'trinket']

**knife** — n. (pl. **knives**) **1** metal blade for cutting or as a weapon, with usu. one long sharp edge fixed in a handle. **2** cutting-blade in a machine. **3** (as **the knife**) surgical operation. — v. (**-fing**) **1** cut or stab with a knife. **2** betray, double-cross (esp. a friend or ally). □ **at knifepoint** threatened with a knife or an ultimatum etc. **get** (or **have got**) **one's knife into** (or **put the knife into**) treat maliciously, persecute; deliberately destroy (a person or a person's reputation). **knife in the back** n. & v. double-cross. **that one could cut with a knife** colloq. (of a person's accent, the atmosphere in a crowded room, etc.) very obvious, oppressive, etc. □ **knifelike** adj. **knifer** n. [Old English]

**knife-edge** n. **1** edge of a knife. **2** position of extreme danger or uncertainty.

**knight** /nuyt/ — n. **1** man awarded a non-hereditary title (Sir) by a sovereign. **2** hist. **a** man, usu. noble, raised to honourable military rank after service as a page and squire. **b** military follower, attendant, or lady's champion in a war or tournament. **3** Chess piece usu. shaped like a horse's head. — v. confer a knighthood on. □ **knighthood** n. **knightly** adj. poet. [Old English, originally = boy]

**knight errant** n. **1** medieval knight in search of chivalrous adventures. **2** chivalrous or quixotic man. □ **knight-errantry** n.

**knight of the road** n. **1** hist. a bushranger. **2** a swagman.

**knit** v. (**-tt-**; past and past part. **knitted** or (esp. in senses 2–4) **knit**) **1** (also absol.) **a** make (a garment etc.) by interlocking loops of esp. wool with knitting-needles or a knitting machine. **b** make (a plain stitch) in knitting (knit one, purl one). **2** momentarily wrinkle (the forehead) or (of the forehead) become momentarily wrinkled. **3** (often foll. by together) make or become close or compact. **4** (often foll. by together) (of a broken bone) become joined; heal. □ **knit up** conclude, finish, end. □ **knitter** n. [Old English]

**knitting** n. work being knitted.

**knitting needle** n. thin pointed rod used esp. in pairs for knitting by hand.

**knitwear** n. knitted garments.

**knives** pl. of KNIFE.

**knob** n. **1** rounded protuberance, esp. at the end or on the surface of a thing, e.g. the handle of a door, drawer, a radio control, etc. **2** small piece (of butter etc.). □ **with knobs on** colloq. that and more (same to you with knobs on). □ **knobby** adj. **knoblike** adj. [Low German knobbe knot, knob]

**knobbly** /nob-lee/ adj. (**-ier, -iest**) knoblike; hard and lumpy (knobbly knees). [knobble, diminutive of KNOB]

**knock** — v. **1 a** strike with an audible sharp blow. **b** (often foll. by at) strike (a door etc.) to gain admittance. **2** make (a hole etc.) by knocking. **3** (usu. foll. by in, out, off, etc.) drive (a thing, person, etc.) by striking (knocked the ball into the hole; knocked those ideas out of him;

*knocked her hand away*). **4** *colloq.* criticise (*don't knock it till you've tried it*). **5 a** (of an engine) make a thumping or rattling noise. **b** = PING *v.* 2. — *n.* **1** act or sound of knocking. **2** knocking sound in esp. an engine. □ **knock about** (or **around**) *colloq.* **1** strike repeatedly; treat roughly. **2 a** wander aimlessly or adventurously. **b** be present, esp. by chance (*the keys? — they're knocking about somewhere*). **c** (usu. foll. by *with*) be associated socially (*he knocks around with Bill*). **knock back 1** *colloq.* eat or drink, esp. quickly (*he knocked back three hamburgers in a jiff*). **2** *colloq.* refuse, rebuff (*knocked back my offers of help*). **3** thwart or impede (*the recession knocked back our chances of buying a house*). **knock down 1** strike (esp. a person) to the ground. **2** demolish. **3** (usu. foll. by *to*) (at an auction) sell (an article) to a bidder by a knock with a hammer (*knocked the Picasso down to him for five million*). **4** *colloq.* lower the price of (an article) (*knocked the price down by $100*). **5** spend (a pay-cheque etc.) freely. **knock it off!** cease (a squabble, argument, etc.) immediately! **knock off 1** strike off with a blow. **2** *colloq.* finish (work) (*knocked off at 5.30; knocked off work early*). **3** *colloq.* produce (a work of art etc.) or do (a task) rapidly (*knocked off six paintings in an hour*). **4** (often foll. by *from*) deduct (a sum) from a price etc. **5** *colloq.* steal. **6** *colloq.* kill. **knock on the head** *colloq.* put an end to (a scheme etc.). **knock out 1** make unconscious by a blow on the head. **2** defeat (a boxer) by knocking him or her down for a count of 10. **3** defeat, esp. in a knockout competition. **4** *colloq.* astonish. **5** (often *refl.*) *colloq.* exhaust (*knocked themselves out swimming*). **6** *colloq.* earn (*I hear he knocks out about $300 a week*). **knock together** assemble hastily or roughly. **knock up 1** make hastily (*I'll knock up a meal in a jiff*). **2** *Sports* score (*knocked up a handy 70 runs*). **3** practise tennis etc. before formal play begins. **4** *colloq.* exhaust (*this work has really knocked me up*). **5** waken by a knock at the door. [Old English]

**knockabout** — *attrib. adj.* **1** pertaining to an unskilled labourer on a rural property (*worked as a knockabout man*). **2** (of comedy) boisterous; slapstick. **3** (of clothes) hard-wearing. — *n.* **1** unskilled labourer on a rural property. **2** loafer; tramp.

**knock-back** *n. colloq.* a refusal, rebuff.

**knock-down** — *attrib. adj.* **1** (of a blow, misfortune, argument, etc.) overwhelming. **2** (of a price) very low. **3** (of a price at auction) reserve. **4** (of furniture etc.) easily dismantled and reassembled. — *n. colloq.* an introduction (to a person) (*can you give me a knock-down to her?*).

**knock 'em down** *adj.* (in Aboriginal English) (of rain) torrential.

**knocker** *n.* **1** hinged esp. metal instrument on a door for knocking with. **2** a carping critic (*I'm sick of all these knockers*). □ **on the knocker** *colloq.* **1** (payment made) immediately, on demand, 'on the nail' (*paid cash on the knocker*). **2** punctually (*be there on the knocker at 6*).

**knock knees** *n.pl.* abnormal curvature of the legs inwards at the knee. □ **knock-kneed** *adj.*

**knock-off** *n.* (in full **knock-off time**) time set for the day's work to finish.

**knock-on effect** *n.* secondary, indirect, or cumulative effect.

**knockout** *n.* **1** act of making unconscious by a blow. **2** (usu. *attrib.*) *Boxing* etc. such a blow. **3** competition in which the loser in each round is eliminated (also *attrib.*: *knockout round*). **4** *colloq.* outstanding or irresistible person or thing.

**knock-up** *n.* practice at tennis etc.

**knoll** /nohl, nol/ *n.* hillock, mound. [Old English]

**knot** — *n.* **1 a** intertwining of rope, string, hair, etc., with another, itself, or something else, so as to join or fasten together. **b** set method of this (*reef knot*). **c** knotted ribbon etc. as an ornament. **d** tangle in hair, knitting, etc. **2** unit of a ship's or aircraft's speed, equivalent to one nautical mile per hour. **3** (usu. foll. by *of*) cluster (*a small knot of journalists*). **4** bond, esp. of marriage. **5** hard lump of organic tissue. **6 a** hard mass in a tree-trunk where a branch grows out. **b** round cross-grained piece in timber marking this. **7** central point in a problem etc. — *v.* (**-tt-**) **1** tie in a knot. **2** entangle. **3** unite closely (*knotted together in intrigue*). □ **at a rate of knots** *colloq.* very fast. **tie in knots** *colloq.* baffle or confuse completely. [Old English]

**knot-hole** *n.* hole in timber where a knot has fallen out.

**knotty** *adj.* (**-ier, -iest**) **1** full of knots. **2** puzzling (*knotty problem*).

**know** /noh/ *v.* (*past* **knew**; *past part.* **known** /nohn/ ) **1** (often foll. by *that, how, what, etc.*) **a** have in the mind; have learnt; be able to recall (*knows a lot about cars*). **b** (also *absol.*) be aware of (a fact) (*I think he knows*). **c** have a good command of (*knew German; knows his tables*). **2** be acquainted or friendly with. **3 a** (often foll. by *to* + infin.) recognise; identify (*I knew him at once*; *knew them to be rogues*). **b** (foll. by *from*) be able to distinguish (*did not know him from Adam*). **4** be subject to (*joy knew no bounds*). **5** have personal experience of (fear etc.). **6** (as **known** *adj.*) **a** publicly acknowledged (*known fact*). **b** *Math.* (of a quantity etc.) having a value that can be stated. **7** have understanding or knowledge. □ **all one knows** 1 all one can (*did all he knew to stop it*). **2** to the utmost of one's power (*tried all she knew*). **in the know** *colloq.* knowing inside information. **know of** be aware of; heard of (*not that I know of*). **know one's own mind** be decisive, not vacillate. **know what's what** have knowledge of the world, life, etc. **you know** *colloq.* **1** implying something generally known etc. (*you know, the pub on the corner*). **2** expression used as a gap-filler in conversation. **you-know-what** (or **who**) thing or person unspecified but understood. **you never know** it is possible. □ **knowable** *adj.* [Old English]

**know-all** *n. colloq.* person who claims or seems to know everything.

**know-how** *n.* practical knowledge; natural skill.

**knowing** *adj.* **1** suggesting that one has inside information (*a knowing look*). **2** showing knowledge; shrewd.

**knowingly** *adv.* **1** consciously; intentionally (*wouldn't knowingly hurt him*). **2** in a knowing manner (*smiled knowingly*).

**knowledgable** /nol-uh-juh-buhl/ *adj.* (also **knowledgeable**) well-informed; intelligent. □ **knowledgability** /-bil-uh-tee/ *n.* **knowledgably** *adv.*

**knowledge** /nol-ij/ *n.* **1 a** (usu. foll. by *of*) awareness or familiarity gained by experience (of or with a person or thing) (*have no knowledge of that*). **b** person's range of information (*it is not within his knowledge*). **2 a** (usu. foll. by *of*) understanding of a subject etc. (*good knowledge of Greek*). **b** sum of what is known (*every branch of knowledge*). **3** = CARNAL KNOWLEDGE. □ **to my knowledge 1** so far as I know. **2** as I know for certain.

**known** *past part.* of KNOW.

**knuckle** /nuk-uhl/ — *n.* **1** bone at a finger-joint, esp. that connecting the finger to the hand. **2 a** knee- or ankle-joint of a quadruped. **b** this as a joint of meat, esp. of bacon or pork. — *v.* (**-ling**) strike, press, or rub with the knuckles. □ **go the knuckle** (or **knuckles**) *colloq.* fight; punch. **knuckle down** (often foll. by *to*) **1** apply oneself seriously (to a task etc.). **2** (also **knuckle under**) give in; submit. **rap on** (or **over**) **the knuckles** see RAP¹.

[Low German or Dutch diminutive of *knoke* bone]

**knuckleduster** *n.* metal guard worn over the knuckles in fighting, esp. in order to inflict greater damage.

**knurl** *n.* small projecting knob, ridge, etc. [Low German or Dutch]

**KO** *abbr.* knockout.

**koala** /koh-**ah**-luh/ *n.* (also often but incorrectly **koala bear**) small, slow, tree-dwelling marsupial native to eastern Australia, having a stout body, thick grey-brown fur with a pale underside, large rounded furry ears, a leathery nose, strong claws, and a vestigial tail: it feeds largely on the leaves of certain eucalypts and is the faunal emblem of Queensland. [Dharuk *gula*: the early spellings *coola* and *koolah* were replaced by *koala* probably because of scribal error]

**kobold** /**koh**-bold/ *n.* (in German mythology) **1** goblin or brownie. **2** underground spirit living in mines etc.

**koel** /koh-uhl/ *n.* (also **cooee bird**) large black cuckoo, the Indian koel, migrating to northern and eastern Australia from south-east Asia in summer, having a call supposedly indistinguishable from the human call 'cooee'. [Sanskrit *kokila*]

**kohlrabi** /kohl-**rah**-bee/ *n.* (*pl.* **-bies**) cabbage with an edible turnip-like swollen stem. [German, from Italian *cavolo rapa*]

**kookaburra** /kuu-kuh-bu-ruh/ *n.* either of two Australian kingfishers, the large, predominantly brown and white *laughing jackass* of southern and eastern Australia having a distinctive loud call resembling raucous and somewhat manic human laughter, and the *blue-winged kookaburra* of woodlands in northern Australia. [Wiradhuri *gugubarra* imitative]

**Koori¹** /kuu-ree, koor-ree/ *n.* an Aborigine. [Awabakal *gurri* 'Aboriginal person']

■ **Usage** Many Aborigines understandably dislike the use of 'Aborigine' or 'Aboriginal' since these terms have been foisted on them and can carry pejorative overtones: they prefer to use the word for 'person' from a local language. Because of the wide variety of Aboriginal languages, however, *Koori* has not gained Australia-wide acceptance, being confined to most of NSW and to Victoria. Other terms are preferred in other regions: *Murri* over most of south and central Queensland, *Bama* in north Queensland, *Nunga* in southern SA, *Yura* in SA, *Nyoongah* around Perth, *Mulba* in the Pilbara region, *Wongi* in the Kalgoorlie region, *Yammagi* in the Murchison River region,

*Yolngu* in Arnhem Land, *Anangu* in central Australia, and *Yuin* on the south coast of NSW.

**Koori²** /**kuu**-ree/ *n.* young Aboriginal woman. [probably from Panyjima *kurri* marriageable teenage girl or *kurri* spouse, sexual partner]

**kootchar** /**kuuch**-uh/ *n.* small, stingless, Australian honeybee. [Bandjalang *guja*]

**kopi** /**koh**-puy, -pee/ *n.* **1** fine powdery gypsum occurring near salt lakes in arid areas, and used in ritual Aboriginal mourning. **2** a more cohesive gypsum-rich mass, sometimes a rock, found where opal is mined. [Marawara dial. of Baagandji *gabi*]

**koradji** /kuh-**raj**-ee/ *n.* an Aborigine having recognised skills in traditional medicine and (frequently) a role in ceremonial life. [Dharuk *garraaji* doctor]

**Koran** /kaw-**rahn**, kuh-/ *n.* Islamic sacred book. [Arabic, = recitation]

**Korean** /kuh-**ree**-uhn/ — *n.* **1** native or national of N or S Korea. **2** language of Korea. — *adj.* of Korea, its people, or language.

**kosher** /**koh**-shuh, **kosh**-uh/ — *adj.* **1** (of food or a food-shop) fulfilling the requirements of Jewish law. **2** *colloq.* correct, genuine, legitimate. — *n.* kosher food or shop. [Hebrew, = proper]

**kowari** /kuh-**wah**-ree/ *n.* small yellow-brown carnivorous marsupial with a striking black brush on its tail and occurring in the gibber deserts of central Australia. [Diyari and Ngamini *kariri*]

**kowtow** /kow-**tow**/ — *n. hist.* Chinese custom of kneeling with the forehead touching the ground, esp. in submission. — *v.* **1** (usu. foll. by *to*) act obsequiously. **2** *hist.* perform the kowtow. [Chinese, = knock the head]

**Kr** *symb.* krypton.

**kremlin** /**krem**-luhn/ *n.* **1** (**the Kremlin**) **a** citadel in Moscow. **b** Russian Government housed within it. **2** citadel within a Russian town. [Russian]

**krill** *n.* tiny planktonic crustaceans. [Norwegian *kril* tiny fish]

**Kriol** /**kree**-uhl/ *n.* creole spoken by Aborigines in the north of Australia. [alteration of CREOLE]

**krummhorn** /**krum**-hawn/ *n.* (also **crumhorn**) medieval wind instrument. [German]

**krypton** /**krip**-ton/ *n.* inert gaseous element used in fluorescent lamps etc. [Greek *kruptō* hide]

**kudos** /**kyoo**-dos/ *n. colloq.* glory; renown. [Greek]

**Ku Klux Klan** /ˌkoo-kluks-**klan**/ *n.* secret, white, protestant, ultra-racist society in the southern US, often given to violence, and to persecuting and terrorising esp. blacks. [origin uncertain]

**Kuku-Yalanji** /ˌgoo-goo-**yal**-uhn-jee/ *n.* an Aboriginal language still actively spoken in the Bloomfield River region of northern Queensland.

**kultarr** /**kuul**-tah/ *n.* long-legged marsupial mouse which bounds rapidly from short forelegs to long hindlegs. [probably Yitha-yitha]

**kumarl** /**kuum**-al/ *n.* (also **goomal**) the common brushtail possum. [Nyungar *gumal*]

**kumquat** *n.* = CUMQUAT.

**kung fu** /kuung **foo**, kung/ *n.* Chinese form of karate. [Chinese]

**kunzea** /**kun**-zee-uh/ *n.* any of about 30 species of temperate Australian shrubs, all having attractive fluffy bottlebrush or ball flowers in white, yellow, pink, or red, the anthers (often tipped with gold) being the most striking feature of the flower. [G. *Kunze* German botanist]

**kurdaitcha** /kuh-**duy**-chuh/ *n.* **1** a malignant spirit of Aboriginal lore. **2 a** Aboriginal mission of vengeance (against an Aborigine). **b** ritual accompanying this. **3** (in full **kurdaitcha shoe**) shoe made of emu feathers stuck with blood so as to leave no tracks on a mission of vengeance. **4** (in full **kurdaitcha man**) person who undertakes a mission of vengeance. [perhaps from Aranda *gwerdaje*]

**Kurnai** var. of GANAY.

**kurrajong** /**ku**-ruh-ˌjong/ *n.* **1** evergreen Australian tree with glossy leaves and cream bell-flowers red on the inside, highly regarded as a fodder-tree. **2** any of several Australian plants (of this genus and others) producing (like this) a useful fibre. [Dharuk *garrajung* referring to 'fishing line', since Aborigines used kurrajong fibre for such lines, and nets, and bags]

**Kuurn Kopan Noot** /kuurn kuup-ahn nuut/ *n.* an Aboriginal language spoken over a wide area in the Portland/Warrnambool region of Victoria: now extinct.

**kW** *abbr.* kilowatt(s).

**kWh** *abbr.* kilowatt-hour(s).

**kylie** /**kuy**-lee/ *n.* boomerang (the girl's name **Kylie** is thought to be based on this word). [Nyungar *garli*]

**Kyrie** /**kee**-ree-ay, -ree-uh/ *n.* (in full **Kyrie eleison** /uh-**lay**-son/ ) short repeated invocation used in the Roman Catholic and Greek Orthodox Churches, esp. at the beginning of Mass. [Greek, = 'Lord, have mercy']

# L

**L¹** /el/ *n.* (also **l**) (*pl.* **Ls** or **L's**) **1** twelfth letter of the alphabet. **2** (as a Roman numeral) 50.

**L²** *abbr.* (also **L.**) **1** learner driver. **2** Lake.

**l** *abbr.* (also **l.**) **1** left. **2** (*pl.* **ll** or **ll.**) line. **3** litre(s).

**La** *symb.* lanthanum.

**la** var. of LAH.

**lab** *n. colloq.* laboratory. [abbreviation]

**label** /lay-buhl/ — *n.* **1** piece of paper etc. attached to an object to give information about it. **2** short classifying phrase applied to a person etc. **3** logo, title, or trademark, esp. of a fashion or recording company. **4** *Computing* **a** identifying information at the beginning of a magnetic tape. **b** identifier associated with a statement in a computer program. — *v.* (**-ll-**) **1** attach a label to. **2** (usu. foll. by *as*) assign to a category (*labelled them (as) irresponsible*). **3** replace (an atom) by an atom of a usu. radioactive isotope as a means of identification. [French]

**labial** /lay-bee-uhl/ — *adj.* **1 a** of the lips. **b** of, like, or serving as a lip. **2** (of a sound) requiring partial or complete closure of the lips. — *n.* labial sound (e.g. *p, m, v*). [Latin *labia* lips]

**labium** /lay-bee-uhm/ *n.* (*pl.* **labia**) (usu. in *pl.*) each fold of skin of the two pairs enclosing the vulva. [Latin, = lip]

**laboratory** /luh-bo-ruh-tuh-ree, -tree/ *n.* (*pl.* **-ies**) room, building, or establishment for scientific experiments, research, chemical manufacture, etc. [Latin: related to LABORIOUS]

**laborious** /luh-baw-ree-uhs/ *adj.* **1** needing hard work or toil. **2** (esp. of literary style) showing signs of toil. □ **laboriously** *adv.* [Latin: related to LABOUR]

**Labor Party** *n.* (*abbr.* **ALP**; (in full **Australian Labor Party**) major Australian political party representing the interests esp. of working people and, in its ideals, located to the left of the political spectrum.

**labour** /lay-buh/ (also **labor**) — *n.* **1** physical or mental work; exertion. **2 a** workers, esp. manual, considered as a political and economic force. **b** (**Labor**) Australian Labor Party. **3** process of childbirth. **4** a particular task. — *v.* **1** work hard; exert oneself. **2 a** elaborate needlessly (*don't labour the point*). **b** (as **laboured** *adj.*) done with great effort; not

spontaneous. **3** (often foll. by *under*) suffer under (a delusion etc.). **4** proceed with trouble or difficulty. [French from Latin *labor, -oris*]

■ **Usage** Except in the name of the political party, the *-our* spelling is generally preferred in Australia.

**Labour Day** *n.* a day (often May 1) celebrated in many countries in honour of workers; in the Australian States a public holiday on various dates; commemoration of the campaign conducted by trade unions in the 19th c. to achieve an eight-hour working day.

**labourer** *n.* person doing unskilled, usu. manual, work for wages.

**labour-intensive** *adj.* (of a form of work) needing a large work-force.

**labour-saving** *adj.* designed to reduce or eliminate work.

**Labrador** /lab-ruh-ˌdaw/ *n.* retriever of a breed with a black or golden coat. [*Labrador* in Canada]

**labyrinth** /lab-uh-rinth/ *n.* **1** complicated network of passages etc.; maze. **2** intricate or tangled arrangement. **3** the complex structure of the inner ear. □ **labyrinthine** /-rin-thuyn/ *adj.* [Latin from Greek]

**lac** *n.* resinous substance secreted as a protective covering by a SE Asian insect. [Hindustani]

**lace** — *n.* **1** fine open fabric or trimming, made by weaving thread in patterns. **2** cord etc. passed through holes or hooks for fastening shoes etc. — *v.* (**-cing**) **1** (usu. foll. by *up*) fasten or tighten with a lace or laces. **2** add spirits to (a drink). **3** (often foll. by *through*) pass (a shoelace etc.) through. [Latin *laqueus* noose]

**lace monitor** *n.* large, tree-climbing goanna of mainland Australia, dark green in colour with a lacy pattern of yellow spots.

**lacerate** /las-uh-ˌrayt/ *v.* (**-ting**) **1** mangle or tear (esp. flesh etc.). **2** cause pain to (the feelings etc.). □ **laceration** /-ray-shuhn/ *n.* [Latin *lacer* torn]

**lacewing** *n.* insect with lacy wings whose larvae feed on aphids etc.

**lachrymal** /lak-ruh-muhl/ *adj.* (also **lacrimal**) of or for tears (*lacrimal duct*). [Latin *lacrima* tear]

**lachrymose** /lak-ruh-ˌmohs/ *adj. formal* given to weeping; tearful.

**lack** — *n.* (usu. foll. by *of*) want, deficiency (*lack of talent*). — *v.* be without or deficient in (*lacks courage*). [Low German or Dutch]

**lackadaisical** /ˌlak-uh-**day**-zi-kuhl/ *adj.* unenthusiastic; listless; idle. □ **lackadaisically** *adv.* [from archaic *lackaday*]

**lackey** /**lak**-ee/ *n.* (*pl.* **-s**) **1** servile follower; toady. **2** manservant (usu. in uniform). [Catalan *alacay*]

**lacking** *adj.* absent or deficient (*money was lacking; is lacking in determination*).

**lacklustre** *adj.* **1** lacking in vitality etc. **2** dull.

**laconic** /luh-**kon**-ik/ *adj.* terse, using few words. □ **laconically** *adv.* [Greek *Lakōn* Spartan]

**lacquer** /**lak**-uh/ — *n.* **1** varnish made of shellac or a synthetic substance. **2** substance sprayed on the hair to keep it in place. — *v.* coat with lacquer. [French *lacre* LAC]

**lacrimal** *var.* of LACHRYMAL.

**lacrosse** /luh-**kros**/ *n.* game like hockey, but with the ball carried in a long-handled racquet. [French-Canadian]

**lactate¹** /lak-**tayt**/ *v.* (**-ting**) (of mammals) secrete milk. [as LACTATION]

**lactate²** /**lak**-tayt/ *n.* salt or ester of lactic acid.

**lactation** /lak-**tay**-shuhn/ *n.* **1** secretion of milk by the mammary glands. **2** the suckling of young. [Latin: related to LACTIC]

**lacteal** /**lak**-tee-uhl/ — *adj.* **1** of milk. **2** conveying chyle etc. — *n.* (in *pl.*) *Anat.* vessels which absorb fats. [Latin *lacteus*: related to LACTIC]

**lactic** /**lak**-tik/ *adj.* of milk. [Latin *lac lactis* milk]

**lactic acid** *n.* acid formed esp. in sour milk.

**lactose** /**lak**-tohs, -tohz/ *n.* sugar that occurs in milk.

**lacuna** /luh-**kyoo**-nuh/ *n.* (*pl.* **lacunae** /-nee/ or **-s**) **1** gap. **2** missing portion etc., esp. in an ancient MS etc. [Latin: related to LAKE¹]

**lacy** /**lay**-see/ *adj.* (**-ier**, **-iest**) of or resembling lace fabric.

**lad** *n.* **1** boy, youth. **2** (esp. in *pl.*) *colloq.* any male (*he's one of the lads*). [origin unknown]

**ladder** — *n.* **1** set of horizontal bars fixed between two uprights and used for climbing up or down. **2** vertical strip of unravelled stitching in a stocking etc. **3** hierarchical structure, esp. as a means of career advancement. — *v.* **1** cause a ladder in (a stocking etc.). **2** develop a ladder. [Old English]

**lade** *v.* (**-ding**; *past part.* **laden**) **1 a** load (a ship). **b** ship (goods). **2** (as **laden** *adj.*) (usu. foll. by *with*) **a** (of a vehicle, person, tree, table, etc.) heavily loaded. **b** (of the conscience, spirit, etc.) painfully burdened (*laden with sorrow*). [Old English]

**lading** *n.* **1** cargo. **2** act or process of lading.

**ladle** /**lay**-duhl/ — *n.* deep long-handled spoon used for serving liquids. — *v.* (**-ling**) (often foll. by *out*) **1** transfer (liquid) with a ladle. **2** distribute, esp. lavishly. [Old English]

**lady** /**lay**-dee/ *n.* (*pl.* **-ies**) **1 a** woman regarded as being of superior social status or as having refined manners. **b** (usu. **Our Lady**) the Virgin Mary. **c** (**Lady**) (under the British system) title of peeresses, female relatives of peers, the wives and widows of knights, etc. **2** woman (*ask that lady; cleaning lady*). **3** (in *pl.* as a form of address) female audience or the female part of an audience. **4** (**the ladies** or **ladies'**) women's public toilet. **5** (*attrib.*) female (*lady dog*). [Old English, = loaf-kneader]

**ladybird** *n.* small beetle, usu. red with black spots. [Our Lady's bird: LADY 1b]

**Lady chapel** *n.* chapel dedicated to the Virgin Mary.

**Lady Day** *n.* **1** Feast of the Annunciation, 25 March. **2** any of several other Feasts in honour of the Virgin Mary.

**ladylike** *adj.* like or befitting a lady.

**lady's finger** *n.* (also **lady finger**) **1** variety of banana of commercial importance in Australia. **2** variety of large, elongated dessert grape.

**lady's waist** *n.* small, slender, waisted beer glass.

**lag¹** — *v.* (**-gg-**) fall behind; not keep pace. — *n.* a falling behind; delay. [origin uncertain]

**lag²** — *v.* (**-gg-**) enclose in heat-insulating material. — *n.* insulating cover. [Old Norse]

**lag³** *colloq.* — *n.* **1** *hist.* convict who has been transported to a penal settlement in Australia. **2** (esp. as **old lag**) habitual offender, esp. an ex-convict. — *v.* **1 a** *hist.* transport (a convict) from Britain to a penal settlement in Australia. **b** send to prison. **2** arrest. **3** inform against. [origin unknown]

**lager** /**lah**-guh/ *n.* a kind of light effervescent beer. [German, = store]

**lagerphone** /**lah**-guh-ˌfohn/ *n.* improvised musical instrument made by loosely fixing rows of beer bottle tops to a pole which is then banged to create a jingling percussive effect.

**laggard** /lag-uhd/ n. person who lags behind.

**lagger** n. colloq. police informer, esp. a prisoner who informs against a fellow-prisoner.

**lagging** n. material used to lag a boiler etc. against loss of heat.

**lagoon** /luh-**goon**/ n. **1** expanse of fresh water, usu. shallow. **2** stretch of salt water separated from the sea by a sand-bank, reef, etc. [Latin LACUNA pool]

**lah** /lah/ n. (also **la**) Mus. sixth note of a major scale. [Latin labii, word arbitrarily taken]

**laid** past and past part. of LAY[1].

**laid-back** adj. relaxed; easygoing.

**laid up** adj. confined to bed or the house.

**lain** past part. of LIE[1].

**lair**[1] /lair/ n. **1** wild animal's resting-place. **2** person's hiding-place. [Old English]

**lair**[2] colloq. — n. **1** youth or man who dresses flashily and shows off; larrikin. **2** (as **mug lair**) person who is both stupid and vulgar. — adj. vulgarly flamboyant (a lair paint-job). — v. (often with up) **1** behave as a lair (lairing with his mates). **2** decorate, paint, etc., in bad taste (laired up his car in purple). [back-formation from LAIRY]

**lairise** /lair-ruyz/ v. = LAIR[2] v.

**lairy** /lair-ree/ adj. flashy; vulgar; socially unacceptable. [transferred use of Cockney lairy knowing, sly]

**laissez-faire** /la-say-**fair**/ n. (also **laisser-faire**) policy of non-interference. [French, = let act]

**laity** /lay-uh-tee/ n. lay people, as distinct from the clergy. [from LAY[2]]

**lake**[1] n. large body of water surrounded by land. [Latin lacus]

**lake**[2] n. **1** reddish pigment orig. made from lac. **2** pigment obtained by combining an organic colouring matter with a metallic oxide, hydroxide, or salt. [var. of LAC]

**lam** v. (**-mm-**) colloq. thrash; hit. [perhaps Scandinavian]

**lama** /lah-muh/ n. Tibetan or Mongolian Buddhist monk. [Tibetan]

**lamb** /lam/ — n. **1** young sheep. **2** its flesh as food. **3** mild, gentle, or kind person. — v. give birth to lambs. [Old English]

**lambada** /lam-bah-duh/ n. fast erotic Brazilian dance in which couples dance with their stomachs touching each other. [Portuguese, = a beating]

**lambaste** /lam-**bayst**/ v. (**-ting**) (also **lambast** /lam-**bast**/) colloq. thrash, beat. [from LAM, BASTE[1]]

**lambda** /lam-duh/ n. eleventh letter of the Greek alphabet (Λ, λ). [Greek]

**lamb down** v. **1** tend ewes at lambing time. **2** colloq. squander one's earnings on liquor.

**lambent** /lam-buhnt/ adj. **1** (of a flame or a light) playing on a surface. **2** (of the eyes, sky, wit, etc.) lightly brilliant. □ **lambency** n. [Latin lambo lick]

**lambertia** /lam-ber-shuh/ n. any of ten species of WA shrubs (genus Lambertia) with attractive flowers and often bizarre woody fruits (see HONEY FLOWER).

**lamb-marker** n. one who performs lamb-marking.

**lamb-marking** n. **1** marking of an ear of a lamb with the owner's brand. **2** completing other processes, as castrating, docking, etc., at the same time.

**lamb's fry** n. lamb's liver as food.

**lambs' tails** n. (also **lambswool**) attractive WA shrub with felt-like leaves and tail-like spikes of white, woolly flowers.

**lame** — adj. **1** disabled in the foot or leg. **2 a** (of an excuse etc.) unconvincing; feeble. **b** (of verse etc.) halting. — v. (**-ming**) make lame; disable. □ **lamely** adv. **lameness** n. [Old English]

**lamé** /lah-may/ n. fabric with gold or silver threads interwoven. [French]

**lame duck** n. **1** helpless person. **2** a firm etc. in financial difficulties.

**lament** /luh-**ment**/ — n. **1** passionate expression of grief. **2** song etc. of mourning etc. — v. (also absol.) express or feel grief for or about; regret (lamented the loss of his manly vigour). □ **lament for** (or **over**) mourn or regret. [Latin lamentor]

**lamentable** /lam-uhn-tuh-buhl/ adj. deplorable, regrettable. □ **lamentably** adv.

**lamentation** /lam-uhn-**tay**-shuhn/ n. **1** act or instance of lamenting. **2** lament.

**lamina** /lam-uh-nuh/ n. (pl. **-nae** /-nee/) thin plate or scale. □ **laminar** adj. [Latin]

**laminate** — v. /lam-uh-nayt/ (**-ting**) **1** beat or roll into thin plates. **2** overlay with metal plates, a plastic layer, etc. **3** split into layers. — n. /lam-uh-nuht/ laminated structure, esp. of layers fixed together. — adj. /lam-uh-nuht/ in the form of thin plates. □ **lamination** /-**nay**-shuhn/ n.

**laminex** /lam-uh-neks/ n. propr. hard, durable, plastic laminate used as a surfacing material for tables etc.

**lamington** /lam-ing-tuhn/ n. cube of sponge cake covered all over in chocolate icing and coated with desiccated coconut. [Baron Lamington, Governor of Queensland 1895–1901]

**lamington drive** n. organised effort (by a community group) to raise money from the sale of lamingtons.

**lamp** n. **1** device for producing a steady light, esp.: **a** an electric bulb, and usu. its holder. **b** an oil-lamp. **c** a gas-jet and mantle. **2** device producing esp. ultraviolet or infrared radiation. [Greek *lampas* torch]

**lamplighter** n. Australian cicada with three ruby-coloured spots on the head.

**lampoon** /lam-**poon**/ — n. satirical attack on a person etc. — v. satirise. □**lampoonist** n. [French *lampon*]

**lamprey** /**lam**-pree/ n. (pl. **-s**) eel-like aquatic animal with a sucker mouth. [Latin *lampreda*]

**LAN** /lan/ abbr. Computing local area network.

**lance** /lahns, lans/ — n. long spear, esp. one used by a horseman. — v. (**-cing**) **1** prick or cut open with a lancet. **2** pierce with a lance. [French from Latin]

**lance-corporal** n. lowest rank of NCO in the Army.

**lanceolate** /**lahn**-see-uh-luht, **lan**-see-/ adj. shaped like a lance-head, tapering at each end.

**lancet** /**lahn**-suht, **lan**-suht/ n. small broad two-edged surgical knife with a sharp point.

**lancet arch** n. (also **lancet light** or **window**) narrow arch or window with a pointed head.

**lancewood** n. any of several Australian trees yielding a tough, durable timber.

**land** — n. **1** solid part of the earth's surface. **2 a** expanse of country; ground, soil. **b** this in relation to its use, quality, etc., or as a basis for agriculture (*building land*). **c** any part of the earth's surface and everything annexed to it, as trees, crops, buildings, etc. **3** region, country, nation. — v. **1 a** set or go ashore. **b** (often foll. by *at*) disembark. **2** bring (an aircraft) to the ground or another surface. **3** alight on the ground etc. **4** bring (a fish) to land. **5** (also *refl.*; often foll. by *up*) colloq. bring to, reach, or find oneself in a certain situation or place (*landed up dead broke*; *landed himself in trouble*; *landed up in Wagga Wagga*). **6** colloq. **a** deal (a person etc. a blow etc.). **b** (foll. by *with*) present (a person) with (a problem, job, etc.). **7** colloq. win or obtain (a prize, job, etc.). □ **how the land lies** what is the state of affairs. **land on one's feet** attain a good position, job, etc., by luck. **on the land** in(to) a rural occupation, esp. owning or managing a rural property. □**landless** adj. [Old English]

**land claim** n. claim to ownership of land based on LAND RIGHTS.

**land council** n. body appointed to represent the interests of Aborigines in Aboriginal land.

**land crab** n. (also **land crayfish**) any of several small freshwater crayfish of eastern Australia.

**landed** adj. **1** owning land (**landed gentry**). **2** consisting of land.

**landfall** n. approach to land, esp. after a sea or air journey.

**landfill** n. **1** waste material etc. used to landscape or reclaim land. **2** process of disposing of rubbish in this way.

**landing** n. **1** platform at the top of or part way up a flight of stairs. **2** coming to land. **3** place where ships etc. land.

**landing gear** n. undercarriage of an aircraft.

**landlady** n. **1** woman who owns and lets land or premises. **2** woman who keeps a boarding-house etc.

**landlocked** adj. almost or entirely enclosed by land.

**landlord** n. **1** man who owns and lets land or premises. **2** man who keeps a boarding-house etc.

**landlubber** n. person unfamiliar with the sea.

**landmark** n. **1** conspicuous object in a district, landscape, etc. **2** prominent and critical event etc.

**land mass** n. large area of land.

**land-mine** n. explosive mine laid in or on the ground.

**land mullet** n. large mullet-like skink of eastern Australia.

**land rights** n.pl. the entitlement of indigenous people to possess their traditionally occupied territory; the acknowledgment of this.

**landscape** /**land**-skayp, **lan**-/ — n. **1** scenery as seen in a broad view. **2** (often *attrib.*) picture representing this; this genre of painting. — v. (**-ping**) improve (a piece of land) by laying out the grounds, planting, etc., so as to create a pleasing effect. [Dutch *landscap*]

**landslide** n. **1** sliding down of a mass of land from a mountain, cliff, etc. **2** overwhelming victory in an election.

**land train** n. = ROAD TRAIN.

**lane** n. **1** narrow road. **2** division of a road for a single stream of traffic (*four-lane highway*). **3** strip of track etc. for a competitor in a race. **4** path regularly followed by a ship, aircraft, etc. **5** gangway between crowds of people. **6** enclosure in a stockyard from which animals may be fed into the appropriate pen. [Old English]

**language** /**lang**-gwij, -wuhj/ *n.* **1** use of words in an agreed way as a method of human communication. **2 a** system of words of a particular community or country etc. **b** (in Aboriginal English) an Aboriginal language (*she speaks language*). **3 a** the faculty of speech. **b** style of expression; use of words, etc. (*poetic language*). **4** system of symbols and rules for writing computer programs. **5** any method of communication (*sign language*). **6** professional or specialised vocabulary. [Latin *lingua* tongue]

**languid** /**lang**-gwuhd/ *adj.* lacking vigour; idle; inert. □ **languidly** *adv.* [related to LANGUISH]

**languish** /**lang**-gwish/ *v.* lose or lack vitality. □ **languish for** droop or pine for. **languish under** suffer under (depression, confinement, etc.). [Latin *langueo*]

**languor** /**lang**-guh/ *n.* **1** lack of energy; idleness. **2** soft or tender mood or effect. **3** oppressive stillness. □ **languorous** *adj.*

**langur** /**lung**-goor/ *n.* any of various Asian long-tailed monkeys. [Hindi]

**lank** *adj.* **1** (of hair, grass, etc.) long and limp. **2** thin and tall. [Old English]

**lanky** *adj.* (**-ier**, **-iest**) ungracefully thin and long or tall. □ **lankiness** *n.*

**lanolin** /**lan**-uh-luhn/ *n.* fat found on sheep's wool and used in cosmetics etc. [Latin *lana* wool, *oleum* OIL]

**lantern** /**lan**-tuhn/ *n.* **1** lamp with a transparent case protecting a flame etc. **2** raised structure on a dome, room, etc., glazed to admit light. **3** light-chamber of a lighthouse. [Greek *lamptēr* torch]

**lanthanide** /**lan**-thuh-,nuyd/ *n.* any element of the lanthanide series. [German: related to LANTHANUM]

**lanthanide series** *n. Chem.* series of 15 metallic elements from lanthanum to lutetium in the periodic table, having similar chemical properties.

**lanthanum** /**lan**-thuh-nuhm/ *n.* metallic element, first of the lanthanide series. [Greek *lanthanō* escape notice]

**lanyard** /**lan**-yuhd, -yahd/ *n.* **1** cord worn round the neck or the shoulder, to which a knife etc. may be attached. **2** *Naut.* short rope or line used for securing, tightening, etc. **3** woven cord worn round the shoulder in some military uniforms, the colour of the cord indicating the wearer's regiment etc. [French *laniere*, assimilated to YARD[1]]

**Laotian** /,lay-**oh**-shuhn, ,lah-/ — *n.* **1** native or national of Laos in south-east Asia. **2** language of Laos. — *adj.* of or relating to Laos or its people or language.

**lap**[1] *n.* **1** front of the body from the waist to the knees of a sitting person. **2** clothing covering this. □ **in the lap of the gods** beyond human control. **in the lap of luxury** in extremely luxurious surroundings. [Old English]

**lap**[2] — *n.* **1 a** one circuit of a racetrack etc. **b** section of a journey etc. **2 a** amount of overlapping. **b** overlapping part. **3** single turn of thread etc. round a reel etc. — *v.* (**-pp-**) **1** lead or overtake (a competitor in a race) by one or more laps. **2** (often foll. by *about*, *round*) fold or wrap (a garment etc.) round. **3** (usu. foll. by *in*) enfold in wraps etc. **4** (as **lapped** *adj.*) (usu. foll. by *in*) enfolded caressingly. **5** cause to overlap. [probably from LAP[1]]

**lap**[3] — *v.* (**-pp-**) **1 a** (esp. of an animal) drink with the tongue. **b** (usu. foll. by *up*, *down*) consume (liquid) greedily. **c** (usu. foll. by *up*) consume (gossip, praise, etc.) greedily. **2** (of waves etc.) ripple; make a lapping sound against (the shore). — *n.* **1 a** act of lapping. **b** amount of liquid taken up. **2** sound of wavelets. [Old English]

**laparoscope** /**lap**-uh-ruh-,skohp/ *n.* fibre optic instrument inserted through the abdomen to view the internal organs. □ **laparoscopy** *n.* [Greek *lapara* flank, -SCOPE]

**laparotomy** /,lap-uh-**rot**-uh-mee/ *n.* surgical cutting through the abdominal wall for access to the internal organs. [Greek *lapara* flank, -TOMY]

**lapel** /luh-**pel**/ *n.* part of either side of a coat-front etc., folded back against itself. [from LAP[1]]

**lapidary** /**lap**-uh-duh-ree/ — *adj.* **1** concerned with stone or stones. **2** engraved upon stone. **3** concise, well-expressed, epigrammatic. — *n.* (*pl.* **-ies**) cutter, polisher, or engraver, of gems. [Latin *lapis lapid-* stone]

**lapis lazuli** /,lap-uhs **laz**-yoo-,lee, -,luy/ *n.* **1** blue mineral used as a gemstone. **2** bright blue pigment. **3** its colour. [related to LAPIDARY, AZURE]

**Laplander** /**lap**-,lan-duh/ *n.* native or inhabitant of Lapland; Lapp. [as LAPP]

**lap-lap** *n.* a cloth worn around the waist or loins in Papua New Guinea etc.

**lap of honour** *n.* ceremonial circuit of a racetrack etc. by a winner.

**Lapp** *n.* **1** member of a Mongol people of N. Scandinavia and NW Russia. **2** their language. [Swedish]

**lapse** — *n.* **1** slight error; slip of memory etc. **2** weak or careless decline into an inferior state. **3** (foll. by *of*) passage of time (*after the lapse of a month*). **4** termination of a right or privilege through disuse etc. — *v.* (**-sing**) **1** fail to maintain a position or standard. **2** (foll. by *into*) fall back into an inferior or previous state (*lapsed into bad habits*). **3** (of a right or privilege etc.) become invalid through disuse, failure to renew, etc. **4** (as lapsed *adj.*) that has lapsed (*a lapsed Catholic*). [Latin *lapsus* from *labor laps-* slip]

**laptop** *n.* (often *attrib.*) portable microcomputer suitable for use while travelling, in a library, etc.

**lapunyah** /luh-**pun**-yuh/ *n.* (also **yapunyah, napunyah**) any of various eucalypts occurring along watercourses in Queensland and the NT. [Gunya *yapany*]

**lapwing** /**lap**-wing/ *n.* any of various plovers with a shrill cry, including two Australian species having facial wattles: banded lapwing, masked lapwing. [Old English: related to LEAP, WINK: from its mode of flight]

**larboard** /**lah**-buhd/ *n. & adj. archaic* = PORT³. [originally *ladboard*, perhaps 'side on which cargo was taken in': related to LADE]

**larceny** /**lah**-suh-nee/ *n.* (*pl.* **-ies**) theft of personal property. □ **larcenous** *adj.* [Anglo-French from Latin *latrocinium*]

■ **Usage** Except in NSW and SA, replaced as a statutory crime by *theft*.

**lard** — *n.* pig fat used in cooking etc. — *v.* **1** insert strips of fat or bacon in (meat etc.) before cooking. **2** (foll. by *with*) garnish (talk etc.) with strange terms. [French = bacon, from Latin *lardum*]

**larder** *n.* room or large cupboard for storing food.

**Lardil** /**lahr**-dil, **ler**-dil/ *n.* an Aboriginal language spoken by the Lardil people on Mornington Island in the Gulf of Carpentaria.

**large** *adj.* **1** of relatively great size or extent. **2** of the larger kind (*large intestine*). **3** comprehensive (*large scope*). **4** pursuing an activity on a large scale (*large manufacturer*). □ **at large 1** at liberty. **2** as a body or whole (*popular with the people at large*). **3** (of a narration etc.) at full length, with all details. **4** without a specific target (*scattered insults at large*). □ **largeness** *n.* **largish** *adj.* [Latin *largus* copious]

**largely** *adv.* to a great extent (*largely my own fault*).

**largesse** /lah-*zhes*, -jes/ *n.* (also **largess**) money or gifts freely given. [Old French from Latin: related to LARGE]

**largo** /**lah**-goh/ *Mus.* — *adv. & adj.* in a slow tempo and dignified style. — *n.* (*pl.* **-s**) largo passage or movement. [Italian, = broad]

**lariat** /**la**-ree-uht/ *n.* **1** lasso. **2** tethering-rope. [Spanish *la reata*]

**lark¹** *n.* small bird with a tuneful song, esp. the skylark. [Old English]

**lark²** *colloq.* — *n.* **1** frolic; amusing incident. **2** type of activity etc. (*fed up with this digging lark*). — *v.* (foll. by *about*) play tricks. [origin uncertain]

**larrikin** /**la**-ruh-kuhn/ *n.* **1 a** *hist.* young urban rough, hooligan. **b** mischief-making youth, troublemaker. **2** person who acts with apparent disregard for social or political conventions. □ **larrikinism** *n.* [British dial. *larrikin* a mischievous or frolicsome youth]

**Larry** *n.* □ **as happy as Larry** extremely happy. [origin uncertain]

**larry-doo** *n.* = LARRY DOOLEY. [abbreviation]

**Larry Dooley** *n. colloq.* **1** a beating. **2** disturbance or fracas. □ **give** (**a person** or **thing**) **Larry Dooley** beat; treat roughly. [perhaps from British dial. *larry* disturbance or scolding, influenced by the name of *Larry Foley*, Australian boxer (d. 1917)]

**larva** /**lah**-vuh/ *n.* (*pl.* **-vae** /-vee/ ) stage of an insect's development between egg and pupa. □ **larval** *adj.* [Latin, = ghost]

**laryngeal** /la-**rin**-jee-uhl, la-ruhn-**jee**-uhl/ *adj.* of the larynx.

**laryngitis** /,la-ruhn-**juy**-tuhs/ *n.* inflammation of the larynx.

**larynx** /**la**-ringks/ *n.* (*pl.* **larynges** /luh-**rin**-jeez/ or **-xes**) hollow organ in the throat holding the vocal cords. [Latin from Greek]

**lasagne** /luh-**sahn**-yuh/ *n.* **1** pasta in the form of sheets or wide ribbons. **2** this cooked and served with minced meat, cheese, etc. [Italian pl., from Latin *lasanum* cooking-pot]

**lascivious** /luh-**siv**-ee-uhs/ *adj.* **1** lustful. **2** inciting to or arousing lust. □ **lasciviously** *adv.* [Latin]

**laser** /**lay**-zuh/ *n.* device that generates an intense beam of coherent light, or other electromagnetic radiation, in one direction. [*l*ight *a*mplification by *s*timulated *e*mission of *r*adiation]

**laser printer** *n.* high quality printer using laser technology.

**lash** — *v.* **1** make a sudden whiplike movement (*tiger lashing its tail*). **2** beat with a whip etc. **3** (often foll. by *against, down*, etc.) (of rain etc.) beat, strike. **4** criticise harshly. **5** rouse, incite. **6** (foll. by *down, together*, etc.) fasten with a cord etc. — *n.* **1** sharp blow made by a whip etc. **2** flexible end of a whip. **3** eyelash. □ **have a lash at** *colloq.* have a go at; attempt. **lash out 1** speak or hit out angrily. **2** *colloq.* spend money extravagantly. [imitative]

**lashings** *n.pl. colloq.* (foll. by *of*) plenty.

**lass** *n.* girl. [Old Norse]

**lassitude** /las-uh-,tyood/ *n.* **1** languor. **2** disinclination to exert oneself. [Latin *lassus* tired]

**lasso** /la-soo/ — *n.* (*pl.* **-s** or **-es**) rope with a noose at one end, esp. for catching cattle, brumbies, etc. — *v.* (**-es, -ed**) catch with a lasso. [Spanish *lazo*: related to LACE]

**last¹** /lahst/ — *adj.* **1** after all others; coming at or belonging to the end. **2** most recent; next before a specified time (*last Christmas*). **3** only remaining (*last chance*). **4** (prec. by *the*) least likely or suitable (*the last person I'd want*). **5** lowest in rank (*last place*). — *adv.* **1** after all others (esp. in *comb.*: *last-mentioned*). **2** on the most recent occasion (*when did you last see him?*). — *n.* **1** person or thing that is last, last-mentioned, most recent, etc. **2** (prec. by *the*) last mention or sight etc. (*shall never hear the last of it; saw the last of him*). **3** last performance of certain acts (*breathed his last*). **4** (prec. by *the*) the ending (*wait for the last*). □ **at last** (or **long last**) in the end; after much delay. **on one's last legs** see LEG. [Old English]

**last²** /lahst/ *v.* **1** remain unexhausted or alive for a specified or considerable time (*food to last a week*). **2** continue for a specified time (*match lasts an hour*). □ **last out** be strong enough or sufficient for the whole of a given period. [Old English]

**last³** /lahst/ *n.* shoemaker's model for shaping a shoe etc. □ **stick to one's last** not meddle in what one does not understand. [Old English]

**last-ditch** *attrib. adj.* (of an attempt etc.) final, desperate.

**'lastic-sides** *n.pl.* (also **elastic-sides**) *colloq.* pair of boots without laces and having a piece of elastic inset into each side: part of the traditional Australian bush costume.

**lasting** *adj.* permanent; durable.

**lastly** *adv.* finally; in the last place.

**last minute** *n.* (also **last moment**) the time just before an important event (often (with hyphen) *attrib.*: *last-minute panic*).

**last name** *n.* surname.

**last post** *n.* bugle-call at military funerals or as a signal to retire for the night.

**last rites** *n.pl.* (also **last sacraments**) the sacraments of penance, viaticum, and extreme unction administered to a person about to die.

**last straw** *n.* (prec. by *the*) slight addition to a burden that makes it finally unbearable.

**last word** *n.* (prec. by *the*) **1** final or definitive statement. **2** (often foll. by *in*) latest fashion.

**lat.** *abbr.* latitude.

**latch** — *n.* **1** bar with a catch and lever as a fastening for a gate etc. **2** spring-lock preventing a door from being opened from the outside without a key. — *v.* fasten with a latch. □ **latch on** (often foll. by *to*) *colloq.* **1** attach oneself (to). **2** understand. [Old English]

**latchet** *n.* edible marine fish of southern Australian coastal waters, having large pectoral fins and a reddish skin. [origin unknown]

**latchkey** *n.* (*pl.* **-s**) key of an outer door.

**latchkey child** *n.* (also **latchkey kid**) child who, in the absence of the parents after school etc., is forced to let himself or herself into the house, fend for himself or herself unsupervised, etc.

**late** — *adj.* **1** after the due or usual time; occurring or done after the proper time (*late for dinner; a late delivery*). **2 a** far on in the day or night or in a specified period (*a late sitting of parliament*). **b** far on in development. **3** flowering or ripening towards the end of the season. **4** no longer alive; no longer having the specified status, former (*my late husband; the late prime minister*). **5** of recent date (*the late storms*). — *adv.* **1** after the due or usual time (*arrived late*). **2** far on in time (*this happened later on*). **3** at or till a late hour. **4** at a late stage of development. **5** formerly but not now (*late of the Alice*). □ **late in the day** *colloq.* at a late stage in the proceedings. **of late** recently. □ **lateness** *n.* [Old English]

**lately** *adv.* not long ago; recently. [Old English: related to LATE]

**latent** /lay-tuhnt/ *adj.* existing but not developed or manifest; concealed, dormant. □ **latency** *n.* [Latin *lateo* be hidden]

**latent heat** *n. Physics* heat required to convert a solid into a liquid or vapour, or a liquid into a vapour, without change of temperature.

**lateral** /lat-uh-ruhl/ — *adj.* **1** of, at, towards, or from the side or sides. **2** descended from the sibling of a person in direct line. — *n.* lateral shoot or branch. □ **laterally** *adv.* [Latin *latus later-* side]

**lateral thinking** *n.* method of solving problems other than by using conventional logic.

**latex** /lay-teks/ *n.* (*pl.* **-xes**) **1** milky fluid of esp. the rubber tree. **2** synthetic product resembling this. [Latin, = liquid]

**lath** /lahth/ n. (pl. **laths** /lahths, lahthz/ ) thin flat strip of wood. [Old English]

**lathe** /layth/ n. machine for shaping wood, metal, etc., by rotating the article against cutting tools. [origin uncertain]

**lather** /lath-uh/ — n. **1** froth produced by agitating soap etc. and water. **2** frothy sweat. **3** state of agitation. — v. **1** (of soap etc.) form a lather. **2** cover with lather. [Old English]

**Latin** /lat-uhn/ — n. language of ancient Rome and its empire. — adj. **1** of or in Latin. **2** of the countries or peoples (e.g. France, Spain, etc.) using languages descended from Latin. **3** of the Roman Catholic Church (*Latin rite*). [Latin *Latium* district around Rome]

**Latin America** n. parts of Central and S. America where Spanish or Portuguese is the main language.

**latish** /lay-tish/ adj. & adv. fairly late.

**latitude** /lat-uh-,tyood/ n. **1 a** angular distance on a meridian north or south of the equator. **b** (usu. in pl.) regions or climes. **2** tolerated variety of action or opinion (*was allowed much latitude*). □ **latitudinal** /-tyoo-duh-nuhl/ adj. [Latin *latus* broad]

**latrine** /luh-treen/ n. communal toilet, esp. in a camp. [Latin *latrina*]

**latter** adj. **1 a** second-mentioned of two (opp. FORMER). **b** (prec. by *the*; usu. *absol.*) the second- or last-mentioned person or thing. **2** nearer the end (*latter part of the year*). **3** recent. **4** of the end of a period, the world, etc. [Old English, = later]

■ **Usage** The use of *latter* to mean 'last mentioned of three or more' is incorrect in standard English.

**latter-day** attrib. adj. modern, contemporary.

**latterly** adv. **1** recently. **2** in the latter part of life or a period.

**lattice** /lat-uhs/ n. **1** structure of crossed laths or bars with spaces between, used as a screen, fence, etc. **2** regular periodic arrangement of atoms, ions, or molecules. □ **latticed** adj. [French *lattis* from *latte* LATH]

**Latvian** /lat-vee-uhn/ — n. **1 a** native or national of Latvia in eastern Europe. **b** person of Latvian descent. **2** language of Latvia. — adj. of Latvia, its people, or language.

**laud** /lawd/ — v. praise or extol. — n. **1** praise; hymn of praise. **2** (in pl.) *RC Ch.* **a** second of the seven canonical hours of the breviary. **b** service for this, said or chanted after matins. [Latin *laus laud-*]

**laudable** adj. commendable. □ **laudability** /-bil-uh-tee/ n. **laudably** adv.

■ **Usage** *Laudable* is sometimes confused with *laudatory*.

**laudatory** /law-duh-tuh-ree, -tree/ adj. praising.

**laugh** /lahf/ — v. **1** make the sounds and movements usual in expressing lively amusement, scorn, etc. **2** express by laughing. **3 a** bring (a person) into a certain state by laughing (*laughed them into agreeing*). **b** pursue, drive, etc. with laughter (*laughed him off the stage*). **4** (foll. by *at*) ridicule, make fun of. **5** (**be laughing**) *colloq.* be in a fortunate or successful position. — n. **1** sound, act, or manner of laughing. **2** *colloq.* comical thing. □ **have the last laugh** be ultimately the winner. **laugh off** get rid of (embarrassment or humiliation) by joking. **laugh on the other side of one's face** change from enjoyment, amusement, etc., to displeasure, shame, etc. **laugh up one's sleeve** laugh secretly. [Old English]

**laughable** adj. ludicrous; amusing. □ **laughably** adv.

**laughing** n. laughter. □ **no laughing matter** serious matter. □ **laughingly** adv.

**laughing gas** n. nitrous oxide as an anaesthetic.

**laughing jackass** n. = KOOKABURRA.

**laughing owl** n. any of several Australian nightjars with loud laughing calls.

**laughing-sides** n.pl. colloq. = 'LASTIC-SIDES.

**laughing stock** n. person or thing open to general ridicule.

**laughter** /lahf-tuh/ n. act or sound of laughing. [Old English]

**launch**[1] /lawnch/ — v. **1** set (a vessel) afloat. **2** hurl or send forth (a weapon, rocket, etc.). **3** start or set in motion (an enterprise, person, etc.). **4** formally introduce (a new product) with publicity etc. **5** (foll. by *out*, *into*, etc.) **a** make a start on (an enterprise etc.). **b** burst into (strong language etc.). — n. act of launching. [Anglo-Norman *launcher*: related to LANCE]

**launch**[2] /lawnch/ n. **1** large motor boat. **2** warship's largest boat. [Spanish *lancha*]

**launcher** n. structure to hold a rocket during launching.

**launch pad** n. (also **launching pad**) platform with a supporting structure from which rockets are launched.

**launder** /lawn-duh/ v. **1** wash and iron (clothes etc.). **2** *colloq.* transfer (funds) to conceal their origin. [French: related to LAVE]

**laundromat** /lawn-druh-,mat/ n. establishment with coin-operated washing machines and driers for public use.

**laundry** /**lawn**-dree/ n. (pl. **-ies**) **1 a** place for washing clothes etc. **b** firm washing clothes etc. commercially. **2** clothes or linen for laundering or newly laundered.

**laureate** /**lo**-ree-uht/ adj. wreathed with laurel as a mark of honour (*England's poet laureate*). □ **laureateship** n. [related to LAUREL]

**laurel** /**lo**-ruhl/ n. **1** = BAY². **2** (in *sing.* or *pl.*) wreath of bay-leaves as an emblem of victory or poetic merit. **3** any of various plants with dark green glossy leaves. □ **look to one's laurels** beware of losing one's pre-eminence. **rest on one's laurels** see REST¹. [Latin *laurus* bay]

**lav** n. colloq. lavatory. [abbreviation]

**lava** /**lah**-vuh/ n. matter flowing from a volcano and solidifying as it cools. [Latin *lavo lavat*- wash]

**lavatorial** /ˌlav-uh-**taw**-ree-uhl/ adj. of or like lavatories; (esp. of humour) relating to excretion. [as LAVA]

**lavatory** /**lav**-uh-tuh-ree, -tree/ n. (pl. **-ies**) = TOILET. [Latin: related to LAVA]

**lave** v. (**-ving**) *literary* **1** wash, bathe. **2** (of water) wash against; flow along. [Latin *lavo* wash]

**lavender** /**lav**-uhn-duh/ n. **1 a** evergreen shrub with purple aromatic flowers. **b** its flowers and stalks dried and used to scent linen etc. **2** pale mauve colour. [Latin *lavandula*]

**lavender bug** n. Australian bug or beetle which when distressed squirts out a corrosive fluid supposedly akin to lavender in smell.

**lavender-water** n. light perfume made with distilled lavender.

**lavish** /**lav**-ish/ — adj. **1** giving or producing in large quantities; profuse. **2** generous. — v. (often foll. by *on*) bestow or spend (money, effort, praise, etc.) abundantly. □ **lavishly** adv. [French *lavasse* deluge: related to LAVE]

**law** n. **1 a** rule enacted or customary in a community and recognised as commanding or forbidding certain actions. **b** body of such rules (*law of the land*; *forbidden under Victorian law*). **2** controlling influence of laws; respect for laws (*law and order*). **3** laws collectively as a social system or subject of study (*reading law at uni*). **4** (with defining word) any of the specific branches of law (*commercial law*). **5** binding force (*her word is law*). **6** (prec. by *the*) **a** the legal profession. **b** colloq. the police. **7** (in *pl.*) jurisprudence. **8 a** the judicial remedy; litigation. **b** the lawcourts as providing this (*go to law*). **9** rule of action or procedure (e.g. in a game). **10** regularity in natural occurrences (*laws of nature*; *law of gravity*). **11**

in Aboriginal society: the body of religious belief and the social customs arising from it. □ **be a law unto oneself** do what one considers right; disregard custom. **lay down the law** be dogmatic or authoritarian. **take the law into one's own hands** redress a grievance by one's own means, esp. by force. [Old English from Old Norse, = thing laid down]

**lawful** adj. conforming with or recognised by law; not illegal. □ **lawfully** adv. **lawfulness** n.

**lawless** adj. **1 a** having no laws or law enforcement. **b** disregarding laws. **2** unbridled, uncontrolled. □ **lawlessness** n.

**lawman** n. (in Aboriginal English) spiritual leader.

**lawn¹** n. piece of closely mown grass in a garden etc. [French *launde* glade]

**lawn²** n. fine linen or cotton. [probably from *Laon* in France]

**lawn cemetery** n. public burial ground with graves marked by small plaques etc. set in lawn, rather than by headstones.

**lawrencium** /lo-**ren**-see-uhm/ n. artificially made transuranic metallic element. [*Lawrence*, name of a physicist]

**lawsuit** n. bringing of a dispute, claim, etc. before a court of law.

**lawyer** /**loi**-yuh/ n. legal practitioner, as a solicitor or a barrister.

**lawyer palm** n. (also **lawyer vine, wait-a-while**) any of several climbing palms and vines of tropical and subtropical coastal eastern Australia, having long appendages armed with recurved barbs which hook on to the skin, clothing, etc. [so called from the difficulty of getting free of the vine's clutches]

**lax** adj. **1** lacking care or precision. **2** not strict. □ **laxity** n. **laxly** adv. **laxness** n. [Latin *laxus* loose]

**laxative** /**lak**-suh-tiv/ — adj. facilitating evacuation of the bowels. — n. laxative medicine. [Latin: related to LAX]

**lay¹** — v. (*past* and *past part.* **laid**) **1** place on a surface, esp. horizontally or in the proper or specified place. **2** put or bring into the required position or state (*lay carpet*). **3** make by laying (*lay foundations*). **4** (often *absol.*) (of a hen bird) produce (an egg). **5** deal with to remove (a ghost, fears, etc.). **6** apply, place (*laid his hand on my shoulder*). **7** place or present for consideration (a case, proposal, etc.). **8** bring forward, prefer (a legal charge etc.). **9** impose (an obligation, restriction, penalty, etc.). **10** (usu. foll. by *on*) attribute or impute (blame etc.) (*laid all the blame on me*). **11** prepare or make ready (a plan or trap). **12** prepare (a table) for a meal. **13** arrange the material for (a fire). **14** put down as a wager; stake (*I'll lay you two to one*). **15** (foll. by *with*) coat or strew (a surface) — *n.* way, position, or direction in which something lies. □ **lay aside 1** put to one side. **2** cease to practise or consider. **3** save (money etc.) for future needs. **lay at the door of** impute to. **lay bare** expose, reveal. **lay down 1** put on a flat surface. **2** give up (a position of authority etc.). **3** formulate (a rule etc.). **4** store (wine) for maturing. **5** sacrifice (one's life). **lay (one's) hands on** obtain, locate (*can't lay my hands on the recipe*). **lay hands on** seize or attack. **lay hold of** seize. **lay in** provide oneself with a stock of. **lay into** *colloq.* punish or scold harshly. **lay it on thick** (or **with a trowel**) *colloq.* flatter or exaggerate grossly. **lay a person low** overthrow or humble him or her. **lay off 1** discharge (unneeded workers) temporarily; make redundant. **2** *colloq.* (usu. as a command) desist. **lay on 1** provide. **2** impose (a penalty, obligation, etc.). **3** inflict (blows). **4** spread on (paint etc.). **lay open 1** break the skin of. **2** (foll. by *to*) expose (to criticism etc.). **lay out 1** spread out, expose to view. **2** prepare (a corpse) for burial. **3** *colloq.* knock unconscious. **4** arrange (grounds etc.) according to a design. **5** expend (money, energy, etc.). **lay to rest** bury in a grave or as in a grave (*laid him to rest yesterday; it's time to lay those rumours to rest*). **lay up** store, save. **lay waste** ravage, destroy. [Old English]

■ **Usage** The intransitive use of *lay*, meaning *lie*, as in *she was laying on the floor*, is incorrect in standard English.

**lay²** *adj.* **1 a** non-clerical. **b** not ordained into the clergy. **2 a** not professionally qualified. **b** of or done by such persons. □ **lay brother** (or **sister**) person who has taken the vows of a religious order but is not ordained and does mainly ancillary (esp. manual) work. [Greek *laos* people]

**lay³** *n.* **1** short poem meant to be sung. **2** song. [French]

**lay⁴** *past* of LIE¹.

**lay-by** — *n.* (*pl.* **-bys**) **1** system of paying a deposit on an article which is then reserved by the retailer until the full price is paid, usu. in instalments. **2** article bought in this way. **3** (in WA) = REST AREA. — *v.* buy (an article) using lay-by. □ **on lay-by** (of an article) in the process of being so purchased.

**layer** — *n.* **1** thickness of matter, esp. one of several, covering a surface. **2** person or thing that lays (*bricklayer*). **3** hen that lays eggs. **4** shoot fastened down to take root while attached to the parent plant.

— *v.* **1** arrange in layers. **2** cut (hair) in layers. **3** propagate (a plant) by a layer. [LAY¹, -ER]

**layette** /lay-et/ *n.* set of clothing etc. for a newborn child. [French from Dutch]

**layman** *n.* (*fem.* **laywoman**) **1** non-ordained member of a Church. **2** person without professional or specialised knowledge.

**lay-off** *n.* temporary discharge of workers; a redundancy.

**layout** *n.* **1** way in which land, a building, printed matter, etc., is arranged or set out. **2** something arranged in a particular way; display.

**laze** — *v.* (**-zing**) **1** spend time idly. **2** (foll. by *away*) pass (time) idly. — *n.* spell of lazing. [back-formation from LAZY]

**lazy** *adj.* (**-ier, -iest**) **1** disinclined to work, doing little work. **2** of or inducing idleness. **3** (of a river etc.) slow-moving. □ **lazily** *adv.* **laziness** *n.* [perhaps from Low German]

**lb** *abbr.* (*pl.* same or **lbs**) pound (weight). [Latin *libra*]

**l.b.w.** *abbr.* leg before wicket.

**l.c.** *abbr.* **1** = LOC. CIT. **2** lower case.

**LCD** *abbr.* **1** liquid crystal display. **2** lowest (or least) common denominator.

**LCM** *abbr.* lowest (or least) common multiple.

**lea** /lee/ *n. poet.* meadow, field. [Old English]

**leach** *v.* **1** make (a liquid) percolate through some material. **2** subject (bark, ore, ash, or soil) to the action of percolating fluid. **3** (foll. by *away, out*) remove (soluble matter) or be removed in this way. [Old English]

**lead¹** /leed/ — *v.* (*past* and *past part.* **led**) **1** cause to go with one, esp. by guiding or going in front. **2 a** direct the actions or opinions of. **b** (often foll. by *to*, or *to* + infin.) guide by persuasion or example (*what led you to think that?*). **3** (also *absol.*) provide access to; bring to a certain position (*gate leads you into the paddock; road leads to Mildura*). **4** pass or go through (a life etc. of a specified kind) (*led a miserable existence*). **5 a** have the first place in. **b** (*absol.*) go first; be ahead in a race etc. **c** (*absol.*) be pre-eminent in some field. **6** be in charge of (*leads a team*). **7** (also *absol.*) play (a card) or a card of (a particular suit) as first player in a round. **8** (foll. by *to*) result in (*what does all this lead to?*). **9** (foll. by *with*) (of a newspaper or news broadcast) have as its main story (*led with the socceroos' triumph*). **10** (foll. by *through*) make (a liquid, wire, etc.) pass through a certain course. — *n.* **1 a** guidance given by going in front; example. **b** the front of a travelling mob of sheep. **2 a** leading place (*take the lead*). **b** amount by which a competitor is ahead of the others. **3** clue. **4** strap etc. for leading a dog etc. **5** conductor (usu. a wire) conveying electric current to an appliance. **6 a** chief part in a play etc. **b** person playing this. **c** (*attrib.*) chief performer or instrument of a specified type (*lead guitar*). **7** *Cards* **a** act or right of playing first. **b** card led. □ **lead by the nose** cajole into compliance. **lead off** begin. **lead on** entice dishonestly. **lead up the garden path** *colloq.* mislead. **lead up to** constitute a preparation for; direct conversation towards. [Old English]

**lead²** /led/ — *n.* **1** heavy bluish-grey soft metallic element used in building, alloys, paint, petrol, etc. **2 a** graphite. **b** thin length of this in a pencil. **3** lump of lead used in sounding water. **4** (in *pl.*) lead frames holding the glass of a stained-glass window etc. **5** blank space between lines of print. — *adj.* made of or containing lead. — *v.* **1** cover, weight, or frame with lead. **2** space (printed matter) with leads. □ **swing (the) lead** malinger, avoid one's share of work. [Old English]

**Leadbeater's cockatoo** /led-,bee-tuhz/ *n.* = MAJOR MITCHELL COCKATOO. [Benjamin *Leadbeater*, 19th-c. English natural history agent]

**Leadbeater's possum** /led-,bet-uhz, -,bee-tuhz/ *n.* rare possum restricted to mountain ash forests in Victoria and faunal emblem of that State. [John *Leadbeater*, naturalist and taxidermist at the National Museum, Melbourne (d. 1888)]

**leaden** /led-uhn/ *adj.* **1** of or like lead. **2** heavy or slow (*leaden limbs; leaden pace*). **3** lead-coloured (*leaden skies*). **4** oppressive, depressing (*suffered under his leaden rule*).

**leaden flycatcher** *n.* flycatcher of northern and eastern Australia, the male being lead-coloured and white, the female lead-coloured and red.

**leader** /lee-duh/ *n.* **1 a** person or thing that leads. **b** person followed by others. **2** principal player in a music group or of the first violins in an orchestra. **3** = EDITORIAL. **4** shoot of a plant at the apex of a stem or of the main branch. **5** bullock placed at the front in a team or pair. □ **leadership** *n.*

**lead-free** /led-,free/ *adj.* (of petrol) without added lead compounds.

**lead-in** /lee-din/ *n.* introduction, opening, etc.

**leading¹** /lee-ding/ *adj.* chief; most important.

**leading²** /led-ing/ *n. Printing* = LEAD² *n.* 5.

**leading aircraftman** *n.* rank above air-craftman in the RAAF.

**leading light** /,lee-ding/ *n.* prominent and influential person.

**leading note** *n. Mus.* seventh note of a diatonic scale.

**leading question** *n.* question prompting the answer wanted.

■ **Usage** *Leading question* does not mean a 'principal' or 'loaded' or 'searching' question.

**leaf** — *n.* (*pl.* **leaves**) **1** each of several flattened usu. green structures of a plant, growing usu. on the side of a stem. **2 a** foliage regarded collectively. **b** state of bearing leaves (*tree in leaf*). **3** single thickness of paper. **4** very thin sheet of metal, esp. gold or silver. **5** hinged part, extra section, or flap of a table etc. — *v.* **1** put forth leaves. **2** (foll. by *through*) turn over the pages of (a book etc.). □ **take a leaf out of a person's book** follow his or her example. □ **leafage** *n.* **leafy** *adj.* (**-ier, -iest**). [Old English]

**leaf-cutting bee** *n.* any of several Australian bees which cut and use pieces of leaf to construct cells for their eggs.

**leaflet** /leef-luht/ — *n.* **1** sheet of paper, pamphlet, etc., giving information. **2** young leaf. **3** *Bot.* division of a compound leaf. — *v.* (**-t-**) distribute leaflets (to) (*leafleting the electorate*).

**league¹** /leeg/ — *n.* **1** people, countries, groups, etc., combining for a particular purpose. **2** agreement to combine in this way. **3** group of sports clubs which compete for a championship. **4** class of contestants etc. — *v.* (**-gues, -gued, -guing**) (often foll. by *together*) join in a league. □ **in league** allied, conspiring. [Latin *ligo* bind]

**league²** /leeg/ *n. hist.* varying measure of distance, usu. about five kilometres. [Latin from Celtic]

**league football** *n.* **1** Australian Rules football. **2** Rugby League.

**leak** — *n.* **1 a** hole through which matter passes accidentally in or out. **b** matter passing through thus. **c** act of passing through thus. **2 a** similar escape of electrical charge. **b** charge that escapes. **3** intentional disclosure of secret information to the press etc. **4** *colloq.* act of urination. — *v.* **1 a** (of liquid, gas, etc.) pass through a leak. **b** lose or admit (liquid, gas, etc.) through a leak. **2** intentionally disclose (secret information) to the press etc. **3** (often foll. by *out*)

become known. **4** *colloq.* urinate. □ **leaky** *adj.* (**-ier, -iest**). [Low German or Dutch]
**leakage** *n.* **1** action or result of leaking. **2** that which leaks in or out.
**lean**¹ — *v.* (*past* and *past part.* **leaned** or **leant** /lent/ ) **1** (often foll. by *across, back, over,* etc.) be or place in a sloping position; incline from the perpendicular. **2** (foll. by *against, on, upon*) (cause to) rest for support against etc. (*leaned on my shoulder*). **3** (foll. by *on, upon*) rely on. **4** (foll. by *to, towards*) be inclined or partial to (*leans towards Catholicism*). — *n.* deviation from the perpendicular; inclination. □ **lean on** *colloq.* put pressure on (a person) to act in a certain way. **lean over backwards** see BACKWARDS. [Old English]
**lean**² — *adj.* **1** (of a person or animal) thin; having no superfluous fat. **2** (of meat) containing little fat. **3 a** meagre (*a lean crop*). **b** not nourishing (*lean diet*). — *n.* lean part of meat. □ **leanness** *n.* [Old English]
**leangle** /lee-**ang**-guhl/ *n.* Aboriginal fighting club with a hooked striking head. [Wemba-wemba and Wuywurung *lienggel*, related to *lia* tooth, describing the head of the club]
**leaning** *n.* tendency or partiality (*has mystical leanings*).
**lean-to** *n.* (*pl.* **-tos**) building with its roof leaning against a larger building or a wall.
**leap** — *v.* (*past* and *past part.* **leaped** or **leapt** /lept/ ) **1** jump or spring forcefully (*leapt forward; leaped the fence*). **2** (of prices etc.) increase dramatically. — *n.* forceful jump. □ **by leaps and bounds** with startlingly rapid progress. **leap at** accept eagerly, jump at. **leap in the dark** daring step or enterprise whose consequences are unpredictable. [Old English]
**leap forward** *n.* sudden, esp. sizeable, progress.
**leapfrog** — *n.* game in which players vault with parted legs over others bending down. — *v.* (**-gg-**) **1** perform such a vault (over). **2** overtake alternately.
**leap year** *n.* year with 366 days every fourth year (including 29th Feb. as the extra day).
**learn** /lern/ *v.* (*past* and *past part.* **learned** /lernt, lernd/ or **learnt**) **1** gain knowledge of or skill in. **2** commit to memory. **3** (foll. by *of*) be told about. **4** (foll. by *that, how,* etc.) become aware of. **5** receive instruction. [Old English]
**learned** /**ler**-nuhd/ *adj.* **1** having much knowledge acquired by study. **2** showing or requiring learning (*a learned work*). **3** (of a publication) academic.

**learner** *n.* **1** person who is learning a subject or skill. **2** (in full **learner driver**) person who is learning to drive but has not yet passed a driving test. **3** one not yet fully trained as a shearer.
**learning** *n.* knowledge acquired by study.
**lease** — *n.* contract by which the owner of property allows another to use it for a specified time, usu. in return for payment. — *v.* (**-sing**) grant or take on lease. □ **new lease of life** improved prospect of living, or of use after repair. [Anglo-French *lesser* let, from Latin *laxo* loosen]
**leasehold** — *n.* **1** holding of property by lease. **2** property held by lease. — *adj.* held by lease. □ **leaseholder** *n.*
**leash** — *n.* strap for holding a dog etc.; lead. — *v.* **1** put a leash on. **2** restrain. □ **straining at the leash** eager to begin. [French *lesse*: related to LEASE]
**least** — *adj.* smallest, slightest, most insignificant. — *n.* the least amount. — *adv.* in the least degree. □ **at least 1** at any rate. **2** (also **at the least**) not less than. **in the least** (or **the least**) (usu. with *neg.*) at all (*not in the least offended*). **to say the least** putting the case moderately. [Old English, superlative of LESS]
**leather** /**leth**-uh/ — *n.* material made from the skin of an animal by tanning etc. — *v.* cover with leather. [Old English]
**leatherhead** *n.* any of several Australian friar-birds having a featherless head covered with a leatherlike skin, esp. the *noisy friar-bird.*
**leatherjacket** *n.* **1** any of many marine fish, widely distributed in Australian waters, having a tough skin. **2** *hist.* thin cake made of a flour and water dough, cooked (usu. with fat) in a pan over the fire, esp. in the bush. **3** (usu. as *leather-jacket*) any of several Australian trees with a very tough bark.
**leatherwood** *n.* Tasmanian rainforest tree bearing showy, rose-like, highly scented white flowers from which a distinctive honey is produced.
**leathery** *adj.* **1** like leather. **2** tough.
**leave**¹ *v.* (**-ving**; *past* and *past part.* **left**) **1 a** go away from. **b** (often foll. by *for*) depart (*has just left for Dandenong*). **2** cause to or let remain; depart without taking (*has left his gloves*). **3** (also *absol.*) cease to reside at or belong to or work for. **4** abandon; cease to live with (one's family etc.). **5** have remaining after one's death (*leaves a wife and two children*). **6** bequeath. **7** (foll. by *to* + infin.) allow (a person or thing) to do something independently. **8** (foll. by *to*) commit to another person etc. (*leave that to me*). **9 a** abstain from consuming or dealing with.

**b** (in *passive*; often foll. by *over*) remain over. **10 a** deposit or entrust (a thing) to be attended to in one's absence (*left a message with his secretary*). **b** depute (a person) to perform a function in one's absence. **11** allow to remain or cause to be in a specified state or position (*left the door open*; *left me exhausted*). □ **leave a person cold** not impress or excite a person. **leave off 1** come to or make an end. **2** discontinue. **leave out** omit; exclude. [Old English]

**leave²** *n.* **1** (often foll. by *to* + infin.) permission. **2 a** (in full **leave of absence**) permission to be absent from duty. **b** period for which this lasts. □ **on leave** legitimately absent from duty. **take one's leave (of)** bid farewell (to). **take leave of one's senses** go mad. [Old English]

**leaved** *adj.* having a leaf or leaves, esp. (in *comb.*) of a specified kind or number (*four-leaved clover*).

**leaven** /**lev**-uhn/ — *n.* **1** substance causing dough to ferment and rise. **2** pervasive transforming influence; admixture. — *v.* **1** ferment (dough) with leaven. **2** permeate and transform; modify with a tempering element. [Latin *levo* lift]

**leaves** *pl.* of LEAF.

**Lebanese** /ˌleb-uh-**neez**/ — *adj.* of Lebanon. — *n.* (*pl.* same) **1** native or national of Lebanon. **2** person of Lebanese descent.

**lechenaultia** *n.* = LESCHENAULTIA.

**lecher** *n.* lecherous man. [French *lechier* live in debauchery]

**lecherous** *adj.* lustful, having excessive sexual desire. □ **lecherously** *adv.*

**lechery** *n.* excessive sexual desire.

**lecithin** /**les**-uh-thuhn/ *n.* a compound found in plant and animal tissue and used as an emulsifier and stabiliser in food products. [Greek *lekithos* egg yolk]

**lectern** /**lek**-tern, -tuhn/ *n.* **1** stand for holding a book in a church etc. **2** similar stand for a lecturer etc. [Latin *lectrum* from *lego lect-* read]

**lecture** /**lek**-chuh/ — *n.* **1** talk giving specified information to a class etc. **2** long serious speech, esp. as a reprimand. — *v.* (**-ring**) **1** (often foll. by *on*) deliver lecture(s). **2** talk seriously or reprovingly to. □ **lectureship** *n.* [Latin: related to LECTERN]

**lecturer** *n.* person who lectures, esp. as a teacher in higher education.

**led** *past* and *past part.* of LEAD¹.

**ledge** *n.* narrow horizontal or shelflike projection. [origin uncertain]

**ledger** *n.* main record of the accounts of a business. [Dutch]

**lee** *n.* **1** shelter given by a close object (*under the lee of*). **2** (in full **lee side**) side away from the wind. [Old English]

**leech** *n.* **1** bloodsucking worm formerly much used medically. **2** person who sponges on others. [Old English]

**leek** *n.* plant of the onion family with flat leaves forming a cylindrical bulb, used as food. [Old English]

**leer** — *v.* look slyly, lasciviously, or maliciously. — *n.* leering look. [perhaps from obsolete *leer* cheek]

**lees** /leez/ *n.pl.* **1** sediment of wine etc. **2** dregs. [French]

**leeward** /**lee**-wuhd/ *Naut.* /**loo**-uhd/ — *adj. & adv.* on or towards the side sheltered from the wind. — *n.* leeward region or side.

**leeway** *n.* **1** allowable scope of action. **2** sideways drift of a ship to leeward of the desired course.

**left¹** — *adj.* **1** on or towards the west side of the human body, or of any object, when facing north. **2** (also **Left**) *Polit.* of the Left. — *adv.* on or to the left side. — *n.* **1** left-hand part, region, or direction. **2** *Boxing* **a** left hand. **b** blow with this. **3** (often **Left**) group or section favouring socialism; socialists collectively. [Old English, originally = 'weak, worthless']

**left²** *past* and *past part.* of LEAVE¹.

**left-handed** *adj.* **1** naturally using the left hand for writing etc. **2** (of a tool etc.) for use by the left hand. **3** (of a blow) struck with the left hand. **4 a** turning to the left. **b** (of a screw) turned anticlockwise to tighten. **5** awkward, clumsy. **6 a** (of a compliment) ambiguous. **b** of doubtful sincerity. □ **left-handedly** *adv.* **left-handedness** *n.*

**left-hander** *n.* **1** left-handed person. **2** left-handed blow.

**leftist** — *n.* person who holds socialist political principles. — *adj.* having socialist political principles.

**leftover** — *n.* (usu. in *pl.*) surplus items (esp. of food). — *attrib. adj.* remaining over, surplus.

**leftward** /**lef**-twuhd/ — *adv.* (also **leftwards**) towards the left. — *adj.* going towards or facing the left.

**left wing** — *n.* **1** the more socialist section of a political party or system. **2** left side of a football etc. team on the field. — *adj.* (**left-wing**) socialist, radical. □ **left-winger** *n.*

**lefty** /**lef**-tee/ *n.* (*pl.* **-ies**) *colloq.* **1** *Polit.* often *derog.* left-winger. **2** left-handed person.

**leg** *n.* **1** each of the limbs on which a person or animal walks and stands. **2** leg of an animal or bird as food. **3** part of a garment covering a leg. **4** support of a chair, table, etc. **5** *Cricket* the half of the field (divided lengthways) in which the batsman's feet are placed. **6 a** section of a journey. **b** section of a relay race. **c** stage in a competition. □ **get one's leg in the door** see GET. **give a person a leg up 1** give support in climbing or mounting. **2** give any kind of assistance. **leg it (-gg-)** *colloq.* walk or run hard. **not have a leg to stand on** be unable to support one's argument by facts or sound reasons. **on one's last legs** near death or the end of usefulness etc. □ **legged** /legd, **leg**-uhd/ *adj.* (also in *comb.*). [Old Norse]

**legacy** /**leg**-uh-see/ *n.* (*pl.* **-ies**) **1** gift left in a will. **2** thing handed down by a predecessor. **3** result or consequence (*legacy of the recession*). [Latin *lego* bequeath]

**legal** /**lee**-guhl/ *adj.* **1** of or based on law; concerned with law. **2** appointed or required by law. **3** permitted by law. □ **legally** *adv.* [Latin *lex leg-* law]

**legal aid** *n.* government-funded assistance for legal advice or action.

**legalese** /,lee-guh-**leez**/ *n.* technical language of legal documents.

**legalise** /**lee**-guh-,luyz/ *v.* (also **-ize**) (**-sing** or **-zing**) **1** make lawful. **2** bring into harmony with the law. □ **legalisation** /-**zay**-shuhn/ *n.*

**legalistic** /,lee-guh-**lis**-tik/ *adj.* adhering excessively to a law or formula. □ **legalism** /**lee**-guh-,liz-uhm/ *n.* **legalist** /**lee**-guh-list/ *n.*

**legality** /luh-**gal**-uh-tee, lee-/ *n.* (*pl.* **-ies**) **1** lawfulness. **2** (in *pl.*) obligations imposed by law.

**legal limit** *n.* **1** the blood alcohol level which one must not exceed if in control of a motor vehicle, boat, etc. **2** maximum speed allowed for a motor vehicle in a particular area.

**legal tender** *n.* currency that cannot legally be refused in payment of a debt.

**legate** /**leg**-uht/ *n.* ambassador of the Pope. [Latin *lego legat-* depute]

**legatee** /,leg-uh-**tee**/ *n.* recipient of a legacy. [Latin *lego legat-* bequeath]

**legation** /luh-**gay**-shuhn/ *n.* **1** diplomatic minister and his or her staff. **2** this minister's official residence. [Latin: related to LEGATE]

**legato** /luh-**gah**-toh/ *Mus.* — *adv. & adj.* in a smooth flowing manner. — *n.* (*pl.* **-s**) **1** legato passage. **2** legato playing. [Italian, = bound, from Latin *ligo ligat-* bind]

**leg before** — *adj. & adv.* (in full **leg before wicket**) *Cricket* (of a batsman) out

because of stopping the ball, other than with the bat or hand, which would otherwise have hit the wicket. — *n.* such a dismissal.

**leg-bye** *n. Cricket* run scored from a ball that touches the batsman.

**legend** /**lej**-uhnd/ *n.* **1 a** a traditional story; myth. **b** these collectively. **2** *colloq.* famous or remarkable event or person. **3** inscription. **4** explanation on a map etc. of symbols used. [Latin *legenda* what is to be read]

**legendary** *adj.* **1** of, based on, or described in a legend. **2** *colloq.* remarkable.

**legerdemain** /,lej-uh-duh-**mayn**/ *n.* **1** sleight of hand. **2** trickery, sophistry. [French, = light of hand]

**legging** *n.* (usu. in *pl.*) **1** close-fitting knitted trousers for women or children. **2** stout protective outer covering for the lower leg.

**leggy** *adj.* (**-ier, -iest**) **1** long-legged. **2** long-stemmed and weak. □ **legginess** *n.*

**legible** /**lej**-uh-buhl/ *adj.* clear enough to read; readable. □ **legibility** /-**bil**-uh-tee/ *n.* **legibly** *adv.* [Latin *lego* read]

**legion** /**lee**-juhn/ — *n.* **1** division of 3,000–6,000 men in the ancient Roman army. **2** large organised body. — *predic. adj.* great in number (*his good works were legion*). [Latin *legio -onis*]

**legionary** — *adj.* of a legion or legions. — *n.* (*pl.* **-ies**) member of a legion.

**legionnaire** /,lee-juh-**nair**/ *n.* member of a legion. [French: related to LEGION]

**legionnaires' disease** *n.* form of bacterial pneumonia first identified after an outbreak at an American Legion meeting in 1976.

**legislate** /**lej**-uhs-,layt/ *v.* (**-ting**) make laws. □ **legislator** *n.* [from LEGISLATION]

**legislation** /,lej-uhs-**lay**-shuhn/ *n.* **1** lawmaking. **2** laws collectively. [Latin *lex legis* law, *latus* past part. of *fero* carry]

**legislative** /**lej**-uhs-luh-tiv/ *adj.* of or empowered to make legislation.

**Legislative Assembly** *n.* lower house of the parliaments of Victoria, NSW, and WA, and the sole house of the parliaments of Queensland, the NT and the ACT.

**Legislative Council** *n.* upper house of the parliaments of all Australian States except Queensland.

**legislature** /**lej**-uhs-,lay-chuh, -luh-chuh/ *n.* legislative body of a State, nation, etc.

**legit** /luh-**jit**/ *adj. colloq.* legitimate (in sense 2). [abbreviation]

**legitimate** /luh-**jit**-uh-muht/ — *adj.* **1** (of a child) born of parents married to each other. **2** lawful, proper, regular. **3** logically acceptable. **4** constituting or relating to serious drama as distinct from musical comedy etc. — *n. hist.* person who came to Australia as a convict, i.e. one who had a *legal* reason for coming (opp. *illegitimate* one who freely migrated to Australia). — *v.* /luh-**jit**-uh-,mayt/ = LEGITIMISE. □ **legitimacy** *n.* **legitimately** *adv.* [Latin *legitimo* legitimise, from *lex legis* law]

**legitimise** /luh-**jit**-uh-,muyz/ *v.* (also **legitimatise**) (also **-ize**) (**-sing** or **-zing**) **1** make legitimate. **2** serve as a justification for. □ **legitimisation** /-**zay**-shuhn/ *n.*

**leg-pull** *n. colloq.* hoax.

**leg-rope** — *n.* noosed rope used to secure an animal by one hind leg. — *v.* secure an animal in this way.

**legume** /**leg**-yoom, **lay**-gyoom/ *n.* **1** leguminous plant. **2** edible part of a leguminous plant. [Latin *legumen -minis* from *lego* pick, because pickable by hand]

**leguminous** /luh-**gyoo**-muh-nuhs/ *adj.* of the family of plants with seeds in pods (e.g. peas and beans).

**leg-up** *n.* help given to mount a horse etc., or to overcome an obstacle or problem; boost.

**lei** /lay/ *n.* Polynesian garland of flowers. [Hawaiian]

**Leichhardt pine** /**luy**-kaht/ *n.* northern Australian coastal tree yielding an edible fruit and a close-grained softwood. [F.W.L. *Leichhardt*, Australian naturalist and explorer, born in Prussia (d. ?1848)]

**leisure** /**lezh**-uh/ *n.* **1** free time. **2** enjoyment of free time. □ **at leisure 1** not occupied. **2** in an unhurried manner. **at one's leisure** when one has time. □ **leisured** *adj.* [Anglo-French *leisour* from Latin *licet* it is allowed]

**leisurely** /**lezh**-uh-lee/ — *adj.* unhurried, relaxed. — *adv.* without hurry. □ **leisureliness** *n.*

**leitmotif** /**luyt**-moh-,teef/ *n.* (also **leitmotiv**) recurrent theme in a musical etc. composition representing a particular person, idea, etc. [German: related to LEAD[1], MOTIVE]

**lemming** /**lem**-ing/ *n.* small Arctic rodent reputed to rush into the sea and drown during migration. [Norwegian]

**lemon** /**lem**-uhn/ *n.* **1 a** yellow oval citrus fruit with acidic juice. **b** tree bearing it. **2** pale yellow colour. **3** *colloq.* person or thing regarded as a failure. **4** (in *pl.*) *Aust. Rules* three-quarter time. □ **lemony** *adj.* [Arabic *laimūn*]

**lemonade** /,lem-uh-**nayd**/ *n.* **1** drink made from lemon juice. **2** synthetic substitute for this.

**lemon gum** *n.* (also **lemon-scented gum**) Australian tree *Eucalyptus citriodora* with smooth powdery white bark and leaves that are strongly lemon-scented.

**lemon ironwood** *n.* Queensland tree (*Backhousia citriodora*) having dense, strongly lemon-scented foliage right down to the ground, masses of white flowers, and a hard bark.

**lemur** /**lee**-muh/ *n.* tree-dwelling primate of Madagascar. [Latin *lemures* ghosts]

**lend** *v.* (*past* and *past part.* **lent**) **1** (usu. foll. by *to*) grant (to a person) the use of (a thing) on the understanding that it or its equivalent shall be returned. **2** allow the use of (money) at interest. **3** bestow or contribute (*lends a certain charm*). □ **lend an ear** listen. **lend a hand** help. **lend itself to** (of a thing) be suitable for. □ **lender** *n.* [Old English: related to LOAN]

**length** *n.* **1** measurement or extent from end to end. **2** extent in or of time. **3** distance a thing extends. **4** length of a horse, boat, etc., as a measure of the lead in a race. **5** long stretch or extent. **6** degree of thoroughness in action (*went to great lengths*). **7** piece of a certain length (*length of cloth*). **8** *Prosody* quantity of a vowel or syllable. **9** *Cricket* **a** distance from the batsman at which the ball pitches. **b** proper amount of this. **10** length of a swimming-pool as a measure of distance swum. □ **at length 1** in detail. **2** after a long time. [Old English: related to LONG[1]]

**lengthen** *v.* make or become longer.

**lengthways** *adv.* in a direction parallel with a thing's length.

**lengthwise** — *adv.* lengthways. — *adj.* lying or moving lengthways.

**lengthy** *adj.* (**-ier**, **-iest**) of unusual or tedious length. □ **lengthily** *adv.* **lengthiness** *n.*

**lenient** /**lee**-nee-uhnt/ *adj.* merciful, not severe. □ **lenience** *n.* **leniency** *n.* **leniently** *adv.* [Latin *lenis* gentle]

**lens** /lenz/ *n.* **1** piece of a transparent substance with one or (usu.) both sides curved for concentrating or dispersing light-rays esp. in optical instruments. **2** combination of lenses used in photography. **3** transparent substance behind the iris of the eye. **4** = CONTACT LENS. [Latin *lens lent-* lentil (from the similarity of shape)]

**Lent** *n. Eccl.* period of fasting and penitence from Ash Wednesday to Holy Saturday. □ **Lenten** *adj.* [Old English, = spring]

**lent** *past* and *past part.* of LEND.

**lentil** /len-tuhl/ *n.* **1** pea-like plant. **2** its seed, esp. used as food. [Latin *lens*]

**lento** /len-toh/ *Mus.* — *adj.* slow. — *adv.* slowly. [Italian]

**Leo** /lee-oh/ *n.* (*pl.* **-s**) **1** constellation and fifth sign of the zodiac (the Lion). **2** person born when the sun is in this sign. [Latin]

**leonine** /lee-uh-ˌnuyn/ *adj.* **1** like a lion. **2** of or relating to lions. [Latin: related to LEO]

**leopard** /lep-uhd/ *n.* (*fem.* **leopardess**) large African or Asian animal of the cat family with a black-spotted yellowish or all black coat, panther. [Greek *leōn* lion, *pardos* panther]

**leotard** /lee-uh-ˌtahd/ *n.* close-fitting one-piece garment worn by dancers etc. [*Léotard*, name of a trapeze artist]

**leper** /lep-uh/ *n.* **1** person with leprosy. **2** person who is shunned. [Greek *lepros* scaly]

**lepidopterous** /ˌlep-uh-**dop**-tuh-ruhs/ *adj.* of the order of insects with four scale-covered wings, including butterflies and moths. □ **lepidopterist** *n.* [Greek *lepis -idos* scale, *pteron* wing]

**leprechaun** /lep-ruh-ˌkawn/ *n.* small mischievous sprite in Irish folklore. [Irish *lu* small, *corp* body]

**leprosy** /lep-ruh-see/ *n.* disease that damages the skin and nerves. □ **leprous** *adj.* [related to LEPER]

**leptospermum** /ˌlep-toh-**sper**-muhm/ *n.* = TEA-TREE.

**lerp** /lerp/ *n.* **1** whitish, edible, very sweet, waxy secretion produced by insect larvae (of psyllids) on the leaves of certain eucalypts, esp. mallees. **2** = MANNA 3. [Wemba-wemba *lerep*]

**lesbian** /lez-bee-uhn/ — *n.* homosexual woman. — *adj.* of female homosexuality. □ **lesbianism** *n.* [*Lesbos*, name of an island in the Aegean Sea]

**leschenaultia** /ˌlesh-uh-**nol**-tee-uh/ *n.* group of mainly WA plants with vivid blue, or red, yellow, orange, etc. flowers which are extremely showy. [J.L.C.T. *Leschenault* de la Tours, French botanist (d. 1826)]

**lese-majesty** /leez **maj**-uhs-tee/ *n.* **1** treason. **2** insult to a sovereign or ruler. **3** presumptuous conduct. [French *lèse-majesté* injured sovereignty]

**lesion** /lee-*zh*uhn/ *n.* **1** damage. **2** injury. **3** morbid change in the functioning or texture of an organ etc. [Latin *laedo laes-injure*]

**less** — *adj.* **1** smaller in extent, degree, duration, number, etc. **2** of smaller quantity, not so much (*less meat*). **3** *colloq.* fewer (*less biscuits*). — *adv.* to a smaller extent, in a lower degree. — *n.* smaller amount, quantity, or number (*will take less; for less than $10*). — *prep.* minus (*made $1,000 less tax*). [Old English]

■ **Usage** The use of *less* to mean 'fewer', as in sense 3, is regarded as incorrect in standard English.

**-less** *suffix* forming adjectives and adverbs: **1** from nouns, meaning 'not having, without, free from' (*powerless*). **2** from verbs, meaning 'not accessible to, affected by, or performing the action of the verb' (*fathomless*; *ceaseless*). [Old English]

**lessee** /le-see/ *n.* (often foll. by *of*) person holding a property by lease. [French: related to LEASE]

**lessen** /les-uhn/ *v.* make or become less, diminish.

**lesser** *adj.* (usu. *attrib.*) not so great as the other(s) (*lesser evil*; *lesser mortals*).

**lesson** /les-uhn/ *n.* **1** spell of teaching. **2** (in *pl.*; foll. by *in*) systematic instruction. **3** thing learnt by a pupil. **4** experience that serves to warn or encourage (*let that be a lesson*). **5** passage from the Bible read aloud during a church service. [French *leçon* from Latin *lego lect-*]

**lessor** /le-saw, les-aw/ *n.* person who lets a property by lease. [Anglo-French: related to LEASE]

**lest** *conj. formal* **1** in order that not, for fear that (*lest he forget*). **2** that (*afraid lest we should be late*). [Old English: related to LESS]

■ **Usage** *Lest* is followed by *should* or the subjunctive (see examples above).

**Lesueur's rat-kangaroo** /luh-serz/ *n.* = BOODIE. [C.A. *Le Sueur*, French naturalist]

**let¹** — *v.* (**-tt-**; *past* and *past part.* **let**) **1 a** allow to, not prevent or forbid. **b** cause to (*let me know*). **2** (foll. by *into*) allow to enter. **3** grant the use of (rooms, land, etc.) for rent or hire. **4** allow or cause (liquid or air) to escape (*let blood*). **5** *aux.* supplying the first and third persons of the imperative in exhortations (*let us pray*), commands (*let it be done at once*; *let there be light*), assumptions, etc. (*let AB equal CD*). — *n.* act of letting a house, room, etc. □ **let alone 1** not to mention, far less or more (*hasn't got a television, let alone a video*). **2** = *let be*. **let be** not interfere with, attend to, or do. **let down 1** lower. **2** fail to support or satisfy, disappoint. **3** lengthen (a garment). **4** deflate (a tyre). **let down gently** reject or disappoint without humiliating. **let drop** (or **fall**) drop (esp. a word or hint) intentionally or by accident. **let go 1** release. **2 a** (often foll. by *of*) lose one's hold. **b** lose hold of. **c** release a shorn sheep. **let oneself go 1** act spontaneously. **2** neglect one's appearance or habits. **let in 1** allow to enter (*let the dog in*; *let in a flood of light*). **2** (foll. by *for*) involve (a person, often oneself) in loss or difficulty. **3** (foll. by *on*) allow (a person) to share a secret, privileges, etc. **let loose** release, unchain. **let off 1 a** fire (a gun). **b** explode (a bomb). **2** allow or cause (steam etc.) to escape. **3 a** not punish or compel. **b** (foll. by *with*) punish lightly. **let off steam** release pent-up energy or feeling. **let on** *colloq.* **1** reveal a secret. **2** pretend. **let out 1** release. **2** reveal (a secret etc.). **3** make (a garment) looser. **4** put out to rent or to contract. **let rip** *colloq.* **1** act without restraint. **2** speak violently. **let up** *colloq.* **1** become less intense or severe. **2** relax one's efforts. **to let** available for rent. [Old English]

**let²** — *n.* obstruction of a ball or player in tennis etc., requiring the ball to be served again. — *v.* (**-tt-**; *past* and *past part.* **letted** or **let**) *archaic* hinder, obstruct. □ **without let or hindrance** unimpeded. [Old English: related to LATE]

**-let** *suffix* forming nouns, usu. diminutive (*booklet*) or denoting articles of ornament or dress (*anklet*). [French]

**let-down** *n.* disappointment.

**lethal** /lee-thuhl/ *adj.* causing or sufficient to cause death. □ **lethally** *adv.* [Latin *letum* death]

**lethargy** /leth-uh-jee/ *n.* **1** lack of energy. **2** morbid drowsiness. □ **lethargic** /luh-thah-jik/ *adj.* **lethargically** /luh-thah-jik-lee/ *adv.* [Greek *lēthargos* forgetful]

**letter** — *n.* **1** character representing one or more of the sounds used in speech. **2** written or printed message, usu. sent in an envelope by post. **3** precise terms of a statement, the strict verbal interpretation (*letter of the law*). **4** (in *pl.*) **a** literature. **b** acquaintance with books, erudition. — *v.* inscribe letters on. □ **to the letter** with adherence to every detail. [French from Latin *littera*]

**lettered** *adj.* well-read or educated.

**letterhead** *n.* **1** printed heading on stationery. **2** stationery with this.

**letter of credit** *n.* letter from a bank authorising the bearer to draw money from another bank.

**letterpress** *n.* **1** printed words of an illustrated book. **2** printing from raised type.

**letter-stick** *n.* = MESSAGE-STICK.

**letter-winged kite** *n.* Australian bird of prey with an underwing pattern looking like a W or M.

**lettuce** /let-uhs/ *n.* plant with crisp leaves used in salads. [Latin *lactuca* from *lac lact-* milk]

**let-up** *n. colloq.* **1** reduction in intensity. **2** relaxation of effort.

**leuco-** *comb. form* white. [Greek *leukos* white]

**leucocyte** /loo-kuh-,suyt, lyoo-/ *n.* white blood cell.

**leukaemia** /loo-kee-mee-uh, lyoo-/ *n.* (also **leukemia**) malignant disease in which the bone-marrow etc. produces too many leucocytes. [Greek *leukos* white, *haima* blood]

**levee** /lev-ee/ *n.* **1** embankment against river floods. **2** natural embankment built up by a river. **3** landing-place. [French *levée* past part. of *lever* raise: related to LEVY]

**level** /lev-uhl/ — *n.* **1** horizontal line or plane. **2** height or value reached; position on a real or imaginary scale (*eye level*; *sugar level*; *danger level*). **3** social, moral, or intellectual standard. **4** plane of rank or authority (*talks at Cabinet level*). **5** instrument giving a line parallel to the plane of the horizon. **6** level surface. **7** flat tract of land. — *adj.* **1** flat and even; not bumpy. **2** horizontal. **3** (often foll. by *with*) **a** on the same horizontal plane as something else. **b** having equality with something else. **4** even, uniform, equable, or well-balanced. — *v.* (**-ll-**) **1** make level. **2** raze. **3** (also *absol.*) aim (a missile or gun). **4** (also *absol.*; foll. by *at*, *against*) direct (an accusation etc.). □ **do one's level best** *colloq.* do one's utmost. **find one's level** reach the right social, intellectual, etc., position. **level off** make or become level. **level out** make or become level. **on the level 1** honestly, without deception. **2** honest, truthful. **on a level with 1** in the same horizontal plane as. **2** equal with. [Latin diminutive of *libra* balance]

**level crossing** *n.* crossing of a railway and a road at the same level.

**level-headed** *adj.* mentally well-balanced, sensible. □ **level-headedness** *n.*

**level pegging** *n.* equality of scores, achievements, etc.

**level playing field** *n.* (esp. in international trade, commerce, etc.) equality of opportunity etc. for all participants, without (esp. government subsidised) advantages for some.

**lever** /lee-vuh/ — *n.* **1** bar resting on a pivot, used to prise. **2** bar pivoted about a fulcrum (fixed point) which can be acted upon by a force (effort) in order to move a load. **3** projecting handle moved to operate a mechanism. **4** means of exerting moral pressure. — v. **1** use a lever. **2** (often foll. by *away, out, up,* etc.) lift, move, etc. with a lever. [Latin *levo* raise]

**leverage** /lee-vuh-rij/ n. **1** action or power of a lever. **2** power to accomplish a purpose.

**leveret** /lev-uh-ruht/ n. young hare, esp. one in its first year. [Latin *lepus leporhare*]

**leviathan** /luh-**vuy**-uh-thuhn/ n. **1** *Bibl.* sea-monster. **2** very large or powerful thing. [Latin from Hebrew]

**levitate** /lev-uh-,tayt/ v. (**-ting**) **1** rise and float in the air (esp. with reference to spiritualism). **2** cause to do this. □ **levitation** /-**tay**-shuhn/ n. [Latin *levis* light, after GRAVITATE]

**levity** /lev-uh-tee/ n. lack of serious thought, frivolity. [Latin *levis* light]

**levy** /lev-ee/ — v. (**-ies, -ied**) **1** impose or collect compulsorily (payment etc.). **2** enrol (troops etc.). **3** wage (war). — n. (pl. **-ies**) **1 a** collecting of a contribution, tax, etc. **b** contribution etc. levied. **2 a** act of enrolling troops etc. **b** (in pl.) troops enrolled. [Latin *levo* raise]

**lewd** /lood, lyood/ adj. **1** lascivious. **2** obscene. [Old English, originally = lay, vulgar]

**lexical** /lek-si-kuhl/ adj. **1** of the words of a language. **2** of or as of a lexicon. [Greek *lexikos, lexikon*: see LEXICON]

**lexicography** /,lek-suh-**kog**-ruh-fee/ n. compiling of dictionaries. □ **lexicographer** n. [from LEXICON, -GRAPHY]

**lexicon** /lek-suh-kuhn/ n. **1** dictionary, esp. of Greek, Hebrew, Syriac, or Arabic. **2** vocabulary of a person, language, branch of knowledge, etc. [Greek *lexis* word]

**LF** abbr. low frequency.

**Li** symb. lithium.

**liability** /,luy-uh-**bil**-uh-tee/ n. (pl. **-ies**) **1** being liable. **2** person or thing that is a troublesome responsibility; handicap. **3** (in pl.) debts etc. for which one is liable.

**liable** /luy-uh-buhl/ predic. adj. **1** legally bound. **2** (foll. by to) subject to. **3** (foll. by to + infin.) under an obligation. **4** (foll. by to) exposed or open to (something undesirable). **5** (foll. by to + infin.) apt, likely (it is liable to rain). **6** (foll. by for) answerable. [French *lier* bind, from Latin *ligo*]

■ **Usage** Use of *liable* in sense 5, though common, is considered incorrect by some people.

**liaise** /lee-**ayz**/ v. (**-sing**) (foll. by with,

*between*) colloq. establish cooperation, act as a link. [back-formation from LIAISON]

**liaison** /lee-**ay**-zon/ n. **1** communication or cooperation. **2** illicit sexual relationship. [French *lier* bind: see LIABLE]

**liana** /lee-**ah**-nuh/ n. (also **liane** /-**ahn**/) climbing plant of tropical forests. [French]

**liar** /luy-uh/ n. person who tells a lie or lies.

**lib** n. colloq. liberation. [abbreviation]

**libation** /luy-**bay**-shuhn/ n. **1** pouring out of a drink-offering to a god. **2** such a drink-offering. **3** joc. a celebratory drink. [Latin]

**libel** /luy-buhl/ — n. **1** *Law* a published unjustified statement that is damaging to a person's reputation. **b** act of publishing this. **2** false and defamatory misrepresentation or statement. — v. (**-ll-**) **1** defame by libellous statements. **2** *Law* publish a libel against. □ **libellous** adj. [Latin *libellus* diminutive of *liber* book]

**liberal** /lib-uh-ruhl, lib-ruhl/ — adj. **1** abundant, ample. **2** giving freely, generous. **3** open-minded. **4** not strict or rigorous. **5** for the general broadening of the mind (*liberal studies*). **6 a** favouring moderate political and social reform. **b** (**Liberal**) of or characteristic of Liberals. — n. **1** person of liberal views. **2** (**Liberal**) supporter or member of a Liberal Party. □ **liberalism** n. **liberality** /lib-uh-**ral**-uh-tee/ n. **liberally** adv. [Latin *liber* free]

**liberalise** /lib-uh-ruh-,luyz/ v. (also **-ize**) (**-sing** or **-zing**) make or become more liberal or less strict. □ **liberalisation** /-zay-shuhn/ n.

**Liberal Party** n. major Australian political party supporting private enterprise (and opposed to socialism) and located to the right of the political spectrum.

**liberate** /lib-uh-,rayt/ v. (**-ting**) **1** (often foll. by from) set free. **2** free (a country etc.) from an oppressor or enemy. **3** (often as **liberated** adj.) free (a person) from rigid social conventions. **4** colloq. steal. □ **liberation** /,lib-uh-**ray**-shuhn/ n. **liberator** n. [Latin *libero liberat-* from *liber* free]

**libertine** /lib-uh-,teen, -,tuyn/ — n. licentious person, rake. — adj. licentious. [Latin, = freedman, from *liber* free]

**liberty** /lib-uh-tee/ n. (pl. **-ies**) **1** freedom from captivity etc. **2** right or power to do as one pleases. **3** (usu. in pl.) right or privilege granted by authority. □ **at liberty 1** free. **2** (foll. by to + infin.) permitted. **take liberties** (often foll. by with) **1** behave in an unduly familiar manner. **2** (foll. by *with*) deal freely or superficially with rules, facts, etc. [Latin: related to LIBERAL]

**libidinous** /luh-**bid**-uh-nuhs/ *adj.* lustful. [Latin: related to LIBIDO]

**libido** /luh-**bee**-ˌdoh/ *n.* (*pl.* **-s**) psychic drive or energy, esp. that associated with sexual desire. □ **libidinal** /luh-**bid**-uh-nuhl/ *adj.* [Latin, = lust]

**Libra** /**lee**-bruh, **lib**-ruh/ *n.* **1** constellation and seventh sign of the zodiac (the Scales). **2** person born when the sun is in this sign. [Latin, = pound weight]

**librarian** /luy-**brair**-ree-uhn/ *n.* person in charge of or assisting in a library. □ **librarianship** *n.*

**library** /**luy**-bruh-ree/ *n.* (*pl.* **-ies**) **1** collection of books. **2** room or building where these are kept. **3 a** similar collection of films, records, computer routines, etc. **b** place where these are kept. [Latin *liber* book]

**libretto** /luh-**bret**-oh/ *n.* (*pl.* **-ti** /-tee/ or **-s**) text of an opera etc. □ **librettist** *n.* [Italian, = little book]

**lice** *pl.* of LOUSE.

**licence** /**luy**-suhns/ *n.* **1** official permit to own or use something, do something, or carry on a trade. **2** permission. **3** liberty of action, esp. when excessive. **4** writer's or artist's deliberate deviation from fact, correct grammar, etc. (*poetic licence*). [Latin *licet* it is allowed]

**license** /**luy**-suhns/ *v.* (**-sing**) **1** grant a licence to. **2** authorise the use of (premises) for a certain purpose. □ **licensed** *adj.*

**licensee** /ˌluy-suhn-**see**/ *n.* holder of a licence, esp. to sell alcoholic liquor.

**licentiate** /luy-**sen**-shee-uht/ *n.* holder of a certificate of professional competence. [medieval Latin: related to LICENCE]

**licentious** /luy-**sen**-shuhs/ *adj.* sexually promiscuous. [Latin: related to LICENCE]

**lichen** /**luy**-kuhn/ *n.* plant composed of a fungus and an alga in association, growing on and colouring rocks, treetrunks, etc. [Greek *leikhēn*]

**licit** /**lis**-uht/ *adj. formal* permitted, lawful. [Latin: related to LICENCE]

**lick** — *v.* **1** pass the tongue over. **2** bring into a specified condition by licking (*licked it all up*; *licked it clean*). **3** (of a flame etc.) play lightly over. **4** *colloq.* defeat. **5** *colloq.* thrash. — *n.* **1** act of licking with the tongue. **2** *colloq.* fast pace (*at a lick*). **3** smart blow. □ **lick a person's boots** be servile. **lick into shape** make presentable or efficient. **lick one's lips** (or **chops**) look forward with relish. **lick one's wounds** be in retirement

regaining strength etc. after defeat. [Old English]

**licking** *n.* **1** *colloq.* a thrashing. **2** a defeat.

**licorice** var. of LIQUORICE.

**lid** *n.* **1** hinged or removable cover, esp. for a container. **2** = EYELID. □ **put the lid on** *colloq.* **1** be the culmination of. **2** put a stop to. □ **lidded** *adj.* (also in *comb.*) [Old English]

**lie**[1] /luy/ — *v.* (**lies**; **lying**; *past* lay; *past part.* lain) **1** be in or assume a horizontal position on a surface; be at rest on something. **2** (of a thing) rest flat on a surface (*snow lay on the ground*). **3** remain undisturbed or undiscussed etc. (*let matters lie*). **4 a** be kept, remain, or be in a specified state or place (*lie hidden*; *lie in wait*; *books lay unread*). **b** (of abstract things) exist; be in a certain position or relation (*answer lies in education*). **5 a** be situated (*the mirrnyong lies to the east*). **b** be spread out to view (*the desert lay before us*). — *n.* way, direction, or position in which a thing lies. □ **lie down** assume a lying position; have a short rest. **lie down under** accept (an insult etc.) without protest. **lie in** stay in bed late in the morning. **lie low 1** keep quiet or unseen. **2** be discreet about one's intentions. **lie with** have the responsibility of (a person) (*decision lies with you*). **take lying down** (usu. with *neg.*) accept (an insult etc.) without protest. [Old English]

■ **Usage** The transitive use of *lie*, meaning *lay*, as in *lie her on the bed*, is incorrect in standard English.

**lie**[2] /luy/ — *n.* **1** intentionally false statement (*tell a lie*). **2** something that deceives. — *v.* (**lies**, **lied**, **lying**) **1** tell a lie or lies. **2** (of a thing) be deceptive. □ **give the lie to** show the falsity of (a supposition etc.). [Old English]

**lied** /leed, leet/ *n.* (*pl.* **lieder**) German song, esp. of the Romantic period. [German]

**lie-detector** *n.* instrument supposedly determining whether a person is lying, by testing for certain physiological changes.

**liege** usu. *hist.* — *adj.* entitled to receive, or bound to give, feudal service or allegiance. — *n.* **1** (in full **liege lord**) feudal superior or sovereign. **2** (usu. in *pl.*) vassal, subject. [medieval Latin *laeticus*, probably from Germanic]

**lieu** /loo, lyoo/ *n.* □ **in lieu 1** instead. **2** (foll. by *of*) in the place of. [Latin *locus* place]

**lieutenant** /lef-**ten**-uhnt/ *n.* **1 a** army officer. **b** (usu. /luh-**ten**-uhnt/) naval officer. **2** deputy. □ **lieutenancy** *n.* (*pl.* **-ies**).

[French: related to LIEU place, TENANT holder]

**lieutenant colonel, commander, general** *n.* officers ranking next below colonel, commander, or general.

**life** *n.* (*pl.* **lives**) **1** capacity for growth, functional activity, and continual change until death. **2** living things and their activity (*insect life; is there life on Mars?*). **3 a** period during which life lasts, or the period from birth to the present time or from the present time to death (*have done it all my life; will regret it all my life*). **b** duration of a non-living thing's existence or ability to function (*battery with a life of two years*). **4 a** person's state of existence as a living individual (*sacrificed their lives*). **b** living person (*many lives were lost*). **5 a** individual's actions or fortunes; manner of existence (*start a new life*). **b** particular aspect of this (*love-life; private life*). **6** business and pleasures of the world (*in Paris you really see life*). **7 a** energy, liveliness (*full of life*). **b** animating influence (*was the life of the party*). **8** biography (*a life of Bob Hawke*). **9** *colloq.* = LIFE SENTENCE. **10** living (esp. nude) form or model (*drawn from life*). □ **for dear** (or **one's**) **life** as if or in order to escape death (*hanging on for dear life; run for your life*). **for life** for the rest of one's life. **go for your life** (as an exhortation) engage in an activity with vigour. **not on your life** *colloq.* most certainly not. [Old English]

**life and death** *adj.* vitally important; desperate.

**life assurance** *n.* = LIFE INSURANCE.

**lifebelt** *n.* buoyant belt for keeping a person afloat.

**lifeblood** *n.* **1** blood, as being necessary to life. **2** vital factor or influence.

**lifeboat** *n.* **1** special boat for rescuing those in distress at sea. **2** ship's small boat for use in emergency.

**lifebuoy** *n.* buoyant support for keeping a person afloat.

**life cycle** *n.* series of changes in the life of an organism, including reproduction.

**lifeguard** *n.* = LIFE-SAVER 1.

**life insurance** *n.* insurance for a sum to be paid after a set period or on the death of the insured person if earlier.

**life jacket** *n.* buoyant jacket for keeping a person afloat.

**lifeless** *adj.* **1** dead. **2** unconscious. **3** lacking movement or vitality. □ **lifelessly** *adv.* [Old English]

**lifelike** *adj.* closely resembling life or the person or thing represented.

**lifeline** *n.* **1** rope etc. used for life-saving.

**2** sole means of communication or transport. **3** emergency service providing help, counselling, etc.

**lifelong** *adj.* lasting a lifetime.

**lifer** *n.* *colloq.* person serving a life sentence.

**life-saver** *n.* **1** (in full **surf life-saver**) expert swimmer who supervises surfing beaches etc. esp. to rescue swimmers from drowning. **2** person or thing that is of great help; a boon.

**life sciences** *n.pl.* biology and related subjects.

**life sentence** *n.* sentence of imprisonment for an indefinite period.

**life-size** *adj.* (also **-sized**) of the same size as the person or thing represented.

**lifestyle** *n.* way of life of a person or group.

**life-support** *adj.* (of equipment) allowing a person's vital functions to continue in an adverse environment or during severe disablement.

**lifetime** *n.* **1** duration of a person's life or the usefulness of a thing (*once in a lifetime chance; lifetime of the battery*). **2** *colloq.* a very long time (*waited a lifetime*).

**lift** — *v.* **1** (often foll. by *up, off, out,* etc.) raise or remove to a higher position. **2** go up; be raised; yield to an upward force (*window will not lift*). **3** give an upward direction to (the eyes or face). **4 a** elevate to a higher plane of thought or feeling (*the news lifted their spirits*). **b** enhance, improve (*lifted their game after half-time*). **5** make louder (*lifted his voice*). **6** (of fog etc.) rise, disperse. **7** remove (a barrier or restriction). **8** transport (supplies, troops, etc.) by air. **9** move stock (esp. cattle) from one place to another. **10** *colloq.* **a** steal. **b** plagiarise (a passage of writing etc.). **11** dig up (esp. potatoes etc.). — *n.* **1** lifting or being lifted. **2** a ride in another person's vehicle (*gave them a lift*). **3 a** apparatus for raising and lowering persons or things to different floors of a building etc. **b** apparatus for carrying persons up or down a mountain etc. (*ski-lift*). **4 a** transport by air (*airlift*). **b** quantity of goods transported by air. **5** upward pressure which air exerts on an aerofoil. **6** supporting or elevating influence; feeling of elation. □ **lift a finger** (in *neg.*) make the slightest effort (*didn't lift a finger to help*). [Old Norse: related to LOFT]

**lift-off** *n.* vertical take-off of a spacecraft or rocket.

**ligament** /lig-uh-muhnt/ *n.* band of tough fibrous tissue linking bones. [Latin *ligo* bind]

**ligature** /lig-uh-chuh/ — *n.* **1** tie or bandage. **2** *Mus.* slur, tie. **3** two or more letters joined, e.g. æ. **4** bond; thing that unites. — *v.* (**-ring**) bind or connect with a ligature. [Latin *ligo ligat-* bind]

---

■ **Usage** Sense 3 of this word is sometimes confused with *digraph*, which means 'two separate letters together representing one sound', e.g. *ph*, *ea* in *ph*one, n*ea*t.

---

**light¹** /luyt/ — *n.* **1** the natural agent (electromagnetic radiation) that stimulates sight and makes things visible. **2** the medium or condition of the space in which this is present (*just enough light to see*). **3** appearance of brightness (*saw a distant light*). **4** source of light, e.g. the sun, a lamp, fire, etc. **5** (often in *pl.*) traffic-light. **6 a** flame or spark serving to ignite. **b** device producing this (*have you got a light?*). **7** aspect in which a thing is regarded (*appeared in a new light*). **8 a** mental illumination. **b** spiritual illumination by divine truth. **9** vivacity etc. in a person's face, esp. in the eyes. **10** (in *pl.*) mental powers or ability (*according to one's lights*). **11** eminent person (*leading light*). **12** bright parts of a picture etc.; highlight (*light and shade*). **13** window or opening in a wall to let light in. — *v.* (*past* **lit**; *past part.* **lit** or **lighted**) (*attrib.*) **1** set burning; begin to burn. **2** (often foll. by *up*) provide with light or lighting; make prominent by means of light. **3** show (a person) the way or surroundings with a light. **4** (usu. foll. by *up*) (of the face or eyes) brighten with animation, pleasure, etc. — *adj.* **1** well provided with light; not dark. **2** (of a colour) pale (*light blue*). □ **bring** (or **come**) **to light** reveal or be revealed. **in a good** (or **bad**) **light** giving a favourable (or unfavourable) impression. **in the light of** taking account of. **strike a light!** (exclamation of surprise etc.). **throw light on** help to explain. □ **lightish** *adj.* [Old English]

**light²** /luyt/ — *adj.* **1** not heavy. **2** relatively low in weight, amount, density, intensity, etc. (*light arms, traffic, metal, rain*). **3 a** carrying or suitable for small loads (*light aircraft*). **b** carrying only light arms, armaments, etc. (*light infantry*). **4** (of food) easy to digest (*a light lunch*). **5 a** (of entertainment, music, etc.) intended for amusement only; not profound. **b** frivolous; trivial (*a light remark*). **6** (of sleep or a sleeper) easily disturbed. **7** easily borne or done (*light duties*). **8** nimble; quick-moving (*light step; light rhythm*). **9 a** free from sorrow; cheerful (*light heart*). **b** giddy (*light in the head*).

**10** (of pastry etc.) fluffy and well-aerated during cooking. — *adv.* **1** in a light manner (*tread light; sleep light*). **2** with a minimum load (*travel light*). — *v.* (*past* and *past part.* **lit** or **lighted**) **1** (foll. by *on, upon*) come upon or find by chance. **2** *archaic* **a** alight, descend. **b** (foll. by *on*) land on (a thing etc.). — *n. colloq.* beer of light alcoholic strength. □ **light on** (often foll. by *for*) *colloq.* not well supplied with (*this place is light on for things to do*). **make light of** treat as unimportant. □ **lightish** *adj.* **lightness** *n.* [Old English]

**light bulb** *n.* = LIGHT GLOBE.

**lighten¹** *v.* **1 a** make or become lighter in weight. **b** reduce the weight or load of. **2** bring relief to (the mind etc.). **3** mitigate (a penalty).

**lighten²** *v.* **1** shed light on. **2** make or grow bright.

**lighter** *n.* device for lighting cigarettes etc.

**light-fingered** *adj.* given to stealing.

**light globe** *n.* (also **light bulb; globe**) glass globe containing an inert gas and a metal filament, providing light when an electric current is passed through it.

**light-headed** *adj.* frivolous; giddy, delirious. □ **light-headedness** *n.*

**light-hearted** *adj.* **1** cheerful. **2** (unduly) casual. □ **light-heartedly** *adv.*

**lighthouse** *n.* tower etc. containing a beacon light to warn or guide ships at sea.

**light industry** *n.* manufacture of small or light articles.

**lighting** *n.* **1** equipment in a room or street etc. for producing light. **2** arrangement or effect of lights.

**lightly** *adv.* **1** with little pressure or force (*tapped him lightly on the cheek*). **2** in a light (esp. frivolous or unserious) manner. □ **get off lightly** escape with little or no punishment. **take lightly** not be serious about (a thing).

**light meter** *n.* instrument for measuring the intensity of the light, esp. to show the correct photographic exposure.

**lightning** — *n.* flash of bright light produced by an electric discharge between clouds or between clouds and the ground. — *attrib. adj.* very quick. [from LIGHTEN²]

**lightning conductor** *n.* (also **lightning rod**) metal rod or wire fixed to an exposed part of a building or to a mast to divert lightning into the earth or sea.

**lightweight** — *adj.* **1** of below average weight. **2** of little importance or influence. — *n.* **1 a** a lightweight person, animal, or thing. **b** person of little importance or influence. **2 a** weight in certain sports between featherweight and welterweight, in amateur boxing 57–60 kg. **b** sportsman of this weight.

**lightwood** *n.* **1** (also **hickory wattle**) wattle-tree of eastern Australia yielding a usu. pale timber light in weight. **2** any tree with wood that is light (either in weight or in colour).

**light year** *n.* distance light travels in one year, 9.461 x 10¹² kilometres or nearly 6 million million miles.

**ligneous** /lig-nee-uhs/ *adj.* **1** (of a plant) woody. **2** of the nature of wood. [Latin *lignum* wood]

**lignite** /lig-nuyt/ *n.* brown coal of woody texture.

**lignum** /lig-nuhm/ *n.* any of several Australian plants which form tangled, impenetrable thickets. [alteration of *polygonum*, a word once applied to these plants and now obsolete in this sense]

**lignum vitae** /ˌlig-nuhm vee-tuy, vuy-tee/ *n.* tall rainforest tree of Queensland and NSW yielding a durable timber. [Latin, = wood of life]

**likable** var. of LIKEABLE.

**like¹** — *adj.* (**more like**, **most like**) **1 a** having some or all of the qualities of another, each other, or an original (*is very like her brother*). **b** resembling in some way, such as (*good writers like Dickens*). **c** (usu. in pairs correlatively) as one is, so will the other be (*like father, like son*). **2** characteristic of (*not like them to be late*). **3** in a suitable state or mood for (*felt like working*; *felt like a cup of tea*). **4** similar, allied (*burglary and like crimes*). — *prep.* in the manner of; to the same degree as (*drink like a fish*; *acted like an idiot*). — *adv. colloq.* **1** so to speak (*did a quick getaway, like*). **2** likely, probably (*as like as not*). — *n.* **1** counterpart; equal; similar person or thing (*shall not see its like again*). **2** (prec. by *the*) thing or things of the same kind (*will never do the like again*). □ **and the like** and similar things. **like anything** *colloq.* very much, vigorously. **the likes of** *colloq.* a person such as. **more like it** *colloq.* nearer what is required. **what is he** (or **it** etc.) **like?** what sort of person is he (or thing is it etc.)? [Old English]

**like²** — *v.* (**-king**) **1** find agreeable or enjoyable. **2 a** choose to have; prefer (*like my tea weak*). **b** wish for or be inclined to (*would like a nap*; *should like to come*). — *n.* (in *pl.*) things one likes or prefers. [Old English]

**-like** *comb. form* forming adjectives from nouns, meaning 'similar to, characteristic of' (*doglike*; *shell-like*; *tortoise-like*).

■ **Usage** In formations not generally current the hyphen should be used. It may be omitted when the first element is of one syllable, unless it ends in *-l*.

**likeable** *adj.* (also **likable**) pleasant; easy to like. □ **likeably** *adv.*

**likelihood** /luyk-lee-ˌhuud/ *n.* probability. □ **in all likelihood** very probably.

**likely** /luyk-lee/ — *adj.* (**-ier**, **-iest**) **1** probable; such as may well happen or be true. **2** to be reasonably expected (*not likely to come now*). **3** promising; apparently suitable (*a likely spot*). — *adv.* probably. □ **not likely!** *colloq.* certainly not; I refuse. [Old Norse: related to LIKE¹]

**like-minded** *adj.* having the same tastes, opinions, etc.

**liken** *v.* (foll. by *to*) point out the resemblance of (a person or thing to another). [from LIKE¹]

**likeness** *n.* **1** (usu. foll. by *between*, *to*) resemblance. **2** (foll. by *of*) semblance or guise (*in the likeness of a ghost*). **3** portrait, representation.

**likewise** *adv.* **1** also, moreover. **2** similarly (*do likewise*).

**liking** *n.* **1** what one likes; one's taste (*is it to your liking?*). **2** (foll. by *for*) regard or fondness; taste or fancy.

**lilac** /luy-luhk/ — *n.* **1** shrub with fragrant pinkish-violet or white blossoms. **2** pale pinkish-violet colour. — *adj.* of this colour. [Persian]

**liliaceous** /ˌlil-ee-ay-shuhs/ *adj.* of the lily family. [related to LILY]

**lil-lil** /lil-lil/ *n.* Aboriginal weapon used both as a missile and in close combat. [probably Wemba-wemba *liawil* (*lia* tooth + *wil* having)]

**lilliputian** /ˌlil-uh-pyoo-shuhn/ — *n.* diminutive person or thing. — *adj.* diminutive. [*Lilliput* in Swift's *Gulliver's Travels*]

**lilly-pilly** /lil-ee-ˌpil-ee/ *n.* (also **lilli-pilli**) **1** Australian rainforest tree having glossy, dark green foliage, fluffy white flowers, and pink edible fruits; widely cultivated. **2** the fruit of this tree. [origin unknown]

**lilo** /luy-loh/ *n.* (also **Li-lo**) *propr.* (*pl.* **-s**) type of inflatable mattress. [from *lie low*]

**lilt** — *n.* **1** light springing rhythm. **2** tune with this. — *v.* (esp. as **lilting** *adj.*) move or speak etc. with a lilt; have a lilt. [origin unknown]

**lily** /lil-ee/ *n.* (*pl.* **-ies**) **1** bulbous plant with usu. large trumpet-shaped flowers on a tall stem. **2** heraldic fleur-de-lis. **3** any of several Australian plants, not all liliaceous — see CHOCOLATE LILY, DARLING LILY, FLAX LILY, FRINGED LILY, GARLAND LILY,

GYMEA LILY, ROCK LILY, SWAMP LILY, TINSEL LILY, VANILLA LILY. □ **like a lily on a dust-bin** (or **garbage bin** etc.) out-of-place, incongruous. [Latin *lilium*]

**lily-livered** *adj.* cowardly.

**lily-trotter** *n.* = LOTUS BIRD.

**limb**¹ /lim/ *n.* **1** arm, leg, or wing. **2** large branch of a tree. **3** branch of a cross. □ **out on a limb** isolated. [Old English]

**limb**² /lim/ *n.* specified edge of the sun, moon, etc. [Latin *limbus* hem, border]

**limber**¹ — *adj.* **1** lithe. **2** flexible. — *v.* (usu. foll. by *up*) **1** make (oneself or a part of the body etc.) supple. **2** warm up in preparation for athletic etc. activity. [origin uncertain]

**limber**² — *n.* detachable front part of a gun-carriage. — *v.* attach a limber to. [perhaps from Latin *limo -onis* shaft]

**limbo**¹ /**lim**-boh/ *n.* (*pl.* **-s**) **1** (in some Christian beliefs) supposed abode of the souls of unbaptised infants, and of the just who died before Christ. **2** intermediate state or condition of awaiting a decision etc. [Latin *in limbo*: related to LIMB²]

**limbo**² /**lim**-boh/ *n.* (*pl.* **-s**) W. Indian dance in which the dancer bends backwards to pass under a horizontal bar which is progressively lowered. [W. Indian word, perhaps = LIMBER¹]

**lime**¹ — *n.* **1** (in full **quicklime**) white substance (calcium oxide) obtained by heating limestone. **2** (in full **slaked lime**) calcium hydroxide obtained by reacting quicklime with water, used as a fertiliser and in making mortar. — *v.* (**-ming**) treat with lime. □ **limy** *adj.* (**-ier, -iest**). [Old English]

**lime**² *n.* **1 a** fruit like a lemon but green, rounder, smaller, and more acid. **b** tree which produces this fruit. **2** (in full **lime-green**) yellowish-green colour. [French from Arabic]

**lime-juicer** *n. hist.* = LIMEY 2.

**limelight** *n.* **1** intense white light used formerly in theatres. **2** (prec. by *the*) the glare of publicity.

**limerick** /**lim**-uh-rik/ *n.* humorous five-line verse with a rhyme-scheme *aabba*. [origin uncertain]

**limestone** *n.* rock composed mainly of calcium carbonate.

**limewood** *n.* eucalypt, esp. the *ghost gum*, having a white bark yielding a chalky powder when touched.

**limey** /**luy**-mee/ *n. colloq.* **1** British person (orig. a sailor) or ship. **2** British immigrant to Australia. [from LIME², because of the former enforced consumption of lime juice against scurvy in the British Navy]

**limit** /**lim**-uht/ — *n.* **1** point, line, or level beyond which something does not or may not extend or pass. **2** (often in *pl.*) the boundary of an area. **3** greatest or smallest amount permissible (*upper limit; lower limit*). — *v.* (**-t-**) **1** set or serve as a limit to. **2** (foll. by *to*) restrict. □ **be the** (**giddy**) **limit** *colloq.* be intolerable. **within limits** with some degree of freedom. □ **limitless** *adj.* [Latin *limes limit*-boundary, frontier]

**limitation** /ˌlim-uh-**tay**-shuhn/ *n.* **1** limiting or being limited. **2** limit (of ability etc.) (often in *pl.*: *know one's limitations*). **3** limiting circumstance.

**limited** *adj.* **1** confined within limits. **2** not great in scope or talents. **3** restricted to a few examples (*limited edition*). **4** (after a company name) being a limited company.

**limited company** *n.* (also **limited liability company**) company whose owners are legally responsible only to a specified amount for its debts.

**limn** /lim/ *v. archaic* draw or paint. [French *luminer* from Latin *lumino* ILLUMINATE]

**limousine** /**lim**-uh-ˌzeen, ˌlim-uh-**zeen**/ *n.* large luxurious car. [French]

**limp**¹ — *v.* **1** walk or proceed lamely or awkwardly (*ship limped home after the explosion*). **2** (of verse) be defective. — *n.* a lame walk. [perhaps from obsolete *limphalt*: related to HALT²]

**limp**² *adj.* **1** not stiff or firm. **2** without energy or will. □ **limply** *adv.* **limpness** *n.* [perhaps from LIMP¹]

**limpet** /**lim**-puht/ *n.* **1** marine gastropod with a conical shell, sticking tightly to rocks. **2** a clinging person. [Old English]

**limpid** /**lim**-puhd/ *adj.* **1** (of water, eyes, etc.) clear, transparent. **2** (of writing) clear in style, easily understood. □ **limpidity** /-**pid**-uh-tee/ *n.* [Latin]

**linchpin** *n.* **1** pin passed through an axle-end to keep a wheel in position. **2** person or thing vital to an organisation etc. [Old English *lynis* = axle-tree]

**linctus** /**lingk**-tuhs/ *n.* syrupy medicine, esp. a soothing cough mixture. [Latin *lingo linct-* lick]

**line**¹ — *n.* **1** continuous mark made on a surface. **2** similar mark, esp. a furrow or wrinkle. **3** use of lines in art (*boldness of line*). **4 a** straight or curved continuous extent of length without breadth. **b** track of a moving point. **5** contour or outline (*admired the sculpture's clean lines*). **6 a** (on a map or graph) curve connecting all points having a specified common property. **b** (the Line) the Equator. **7 a** limit or boundary. **b** mark limiting the area of play, the starting or finishing point in a race, etc. **8 a** row of persons or things. **b** direction as indicated by them (*their line of march*). **c** queue. **9 a** row of printed or written words. **b** portion of verse written in one line. **10** (in *pl.*) **a** piece of poetry. **b** words of an actor's part. **c** specified amount of text etc. to be written out as a school punishment. **11** short letter or note (*drop me a line*). **12** length of cord, rope, etc., usu. serving a specified purpose, esp. a fishing-line or clothes-line. **13 a** wire or cable for a telephone or telegraph. **b** connection by means of this (*am trying to get a line*). **14 a** single track of a railway. **b** one branch or route of a railway system (*the Geelong line*). **15 a** regular succession of buses, ships, aircraft, etc., plying between certain places. **b** company conducting this. **16** connected series of persons following one another in time; succession (*the line of popes from St. Peter to John Paul II*). **17 a** course or manner of procedure, conduct, thought, etc. (*along these lines; don't take that line with me*). **b** policy (*the party line*). **18** direction, course, or channel (*lines of communication*). **19** department of activity; branch of business (*he's in the grocery line*). **20** type of product (*new line in hats*). **21** *colloq.* false or exaggerated account etc. (*gave me a line about missing the bus*). **22 a** connected series of military fieldworks etc. (*behind enemy lines*). **b** arrangement of soldiers or ships side by side. **23** each of the very narrow horizontal sections forming a television picture. **24** level of the base of most letters in printing and writing. — *v.* (**-ning**) **1** mark with lines. **2** cover with lines (*a face lined with pain*). **3** position or stand at intervals along (*crowds lined the route*). □ **all along the line** at every point. **bring into line** make conform. **come into line** conform. **draw the line** see DRAW. **get a line on** *colloq.* get information about. **in line for** likely to receive. **in** (or **out of**) **line with** in (or not in) accordance with. **lay** (or **put**) **it on the line** *colloq.* speak frankly. **line up 1** arrange or be arranged in a line or lines. **2** have ready (*had a job lined up*). **out of line** not in alignment; inappropriate. **read between the lines** see READ. **toe the line** see TOE. [Latin *linea* from *linum* flax]

**line²** *v.* (**-ning**) **1 a** cover the inside surface of (a garment, box, etc.) with a layer of usu. different material. **b** serve as a lining for. **2** cover as if with a lining (*shelves lined with books*). **3** *colloq.* fill, esp. plentifully (*lined his pockets*). [obsolete *line* linen used for linings]

**lineage** /lin-ee-ij/ *n.* lineal descent; ancestry. [Latin: related to LINE¹]

**lineal** /lin-ee-uhl/ *adj.* **1** in the direct line of descent or ancestry. **2** linear. □ **lineally** *adv.*

**lineament** /lin-ee-uh-muhnt/ *n.* (usu. in *pl.*) distinctive feature or characteristic, esp. of the face. [Latin: related to LINE¹]

**linear** /lin-ee-uh/ *adj.* **1** of or in lines; in lines rather than masses (*linear development*). **2** long and narrow and of uniform breadth. □ **linearity** /-a-ruh-tee/ *n.* **linearly** *adv.*

**lineation** /ˌlin-ee-ay-shuhn/ *n.* division into (or arrangement in) lines.

**line-dancing** *n.* group dancing in which the participants, arranged in a line, go through a series of set movements.

**linen** /lin-uhn/ — *n.* **1** cloth woven from flax. **2** (*collect.*) articles made or orig. made of linen, as sheets, shirts, underwear, etc. — *adj.* made of linen. [Old English: related to Latin *linum* flax]

**line-out** *n.* (in Rugby) parallel lines of opposing forwards at right angles to the touchline for the throwing in of the ball.

**line printer** *n.* machine that prints output from a computer a line at a time on continuous stationery.

**liner¹** *n.* ship or aircraft etc. carrying passengers on a regular line.

**liner²** *n.* removable lining.

**linesman** *n.* **1** umpire's or referee's assistant who decides whether a ball has fallen within the playing area or not. **2** person who repairs and maintains telephone or electrical etc. lines. **3** surf lifesaver whose duty is to handle the line being taken out to a swimmer in difficulties.

**line-up** *n.* **1** line of people for inspection. **2** arrangement of persons in a team, band, etc.

**ling** *n.* (*pl.* same) long slender marine food-fish of southern Australian waters. [probably Dutch]

**-ling¹** *suffix* **1** denoting a person or thing: **a** connected with (*hireling*). **b** having the property of being (*weakling*). **2** denoting a diminutive (*duckling*), often derogatory (*lordling*). [Old English]

**-ling²** *suffix* forming adverbs and adjectives (*darkling; grovelling*). [Old English]

**lingam** /ling-guhm/ *n.* (also **linga**) symbol or representation (in stone etc.) of the phallus, revered by Hindus esp. as a symbol of Siva (see also YONI). [Sanskrit]

**linger** /ling-guh/ *v.* **1** be reluctant to depart; stay about. **2** (foll. by *over, on,* etc.) spend extra time on; dally (*linger over dinner; lingered on the final note*). **3** (esp. of an illness) be protracted. **4** (often foll.

by *on*) be slow in dying. [Old English *lengan*: related to LONG¹]

**lingerie** /**lon**-*zh*uh-ray/ *n.* women's underwear and nightclothes. [French *linge* linen]

**lingo** /**ling**-goh/ *n.* (*pl.* **-s** or **-es**) *colloq.* **1** foreign language. **2** vocabulary of a special subject or group, esp. (in Aboriginal English) an Aboriginal language. [probably from Portuguese *lingoa* from Latin *lingua* tongue]

**lingua franca** /ˌling-gwuh **frang**-kuh/ *n.* (*pl.* **lingua francas**) **1** language used in common by speakers with different native languages. **2** system for mutual understanding. [Italian, = Frankish tongue]

**lingual** /**ling**-gwuhl/ *adj.* **1** of or formed by the tongue. **2** of speech or languages. □ **lingually** *adv.* [Latin *lingua* tongue, language]

**linguist** /**ling**-gwuhst/ *n.* person skilled in languages or linguistics.

**linguistic** /ling-**gwis**-tik/ *adj.* of language or the study of languages. □ **linguistically** *adv.*

**linguistics** *n.* the study of language and its structure.

**liniment** /**lin**-uh-muhnt/ *n.* liquid etc. for rubbing on the body to relieve muscular pain. [Latin *linio* smear]

**lining** *n.* material which lines a surface etc.

**link** — *n.* **1** one loop or ring of a chain etc. **2 a** connecting part; one in a series. **b** state or means of connection. **3** cuff-link. — *v.* **1** (foll. by *together*, *to*, *with*) connect or join (two things or one to another). **2** clasp or intertwine (hands or arms). **3** (foll. by *on*, *to*, *in to*) be joined; attach oneself to (a system, company, etc.). □ **link up** (foll. by *with*) connect or combine. [Old Norse]

**linkage** *n.* **1** act of linking or being linked. **2** link or system of links.

**links** *n.pl.* (treated as *sing.* or *pl.*) golf-course. [Old English, = rising ground]

**linnet** /**lin**-uht/ *n.* European brown-grey finch. [French *linette* from *lin* flax, because it eats flax-seed]

**lino** /**luy**-noh/ *n.* (*pl.* **-s**) linoleum. [abbreviation]

**linocut** *n.* **1** design carved in relief on a block of linoleum. **2** print made from this.

**linoleum** /luh-**noh**-lee-uhm/ *n.* canvas-backed material thickly coated with a preparation of linseed oil and powdered cork etc., esp. as a floor covering. [Latin *linum* flax, *oleum* oil]

**linotype** /**luy**-noh-ˌtuyp/ *n. Printing propr.* composing machine producing

lines of words as single strips of metal, used esp. for newspapers. [= *line o' type*]

**linseed** /**lin**-seed/ *n.* seed of flax. [Old English: related to LINE¹]

**lint** *n.* **1** linen or cotton with a raised nap on one side, used for dressing wounds. **2** fluff. [perhaps from French *linette* from *lin* flax]

**lintel** /**lin**-tuhl/ *n.* horizontal supporting piece of timber, stone, etc., across the top of a door or window. [French: related to LIMIT]

**lion** /**luy**-uhn/ *n.* **1** (*fem.* **lioness**) large tawny flesh-eating wild cat of Africa and S. Asia. **2** (**the Lion**) zodiacal sign or constellation Leo. **3** brave or celebrated person. □ **the lion's share** the largest or best part. [Latin *leo*]

**lionise** *v.* (also **-ize**) (**-sing** or **-zing**) treat as a celebrity.

**lip** — *n.* **1** either of the two fleshy parts forming the edges of the mouth-opening. **2** edge of a cup, vessel, etc., esp. the part shaped for pouring from. **3** *colloq.* impudent talk. — *v.* (**-pp-**) **1** touch with the lips; apply the lips to. **2** touch lightly. □ **lipped** *adj.* (also in *comb.*). [Old English]

**lipid** /**lip**-uhd/ *n.* any of a group of fatlike substances that are insoluble in water but soluble in organic solvents, including fatty acids, oils, waxes, and steroids. [Greek *lipos* fat]

**liposuction** /**luy**-poh-ˌsuk-shuhn/ *n.* technique in cosmetic surgery for removing excess fat from under the skin by suction.

**lippia** /**lip**-ee-uh/ *n.* spreading pink-flowered prostrate plant of northern Australia (often cultivated in the south as a lawn-substitute).

**lip-read** *v.* understand (speech) from observing a speaker's lip-movements.

**lip-service** *n.* insincere expression of support etc.

**lipstick** *n.* stick of cosmetic for colouring the lips.

**liquefy** /**lik**-wuh-ˌfuy/ *v.* (**-ies**, **-ied**) make or become liquid. □ **liquefaction** /-**fak**-shuhn/ *n.* [Latin: related to LIQUID]

**liqueur** /luh-**kyoor**/ *n.* any of several strong sweet alcoholic spirits. [French]

**liquid** /**lik**-wuhd/ — *adj.* **1** having a consistency like that of water or oil, flowing freely but of constant volume. **2** having the qualities of water in appearance. **3** (of sounds) clear and pure. **4** (of assets) easily converted into cash. — *n.* **1** liquid substance. **2** *Phonet.* sound of *l* or *r*. [Latin *liqueo* be liquid]

**liquidate** /**lik**-wuh-ˌdayt/ *v.* (**-ting**) **1** wind up the affairs of (a firm) by ascertaining liabilities and apportioning assets. **2** pay off (a debt). **3** wipe out, kill. □ **liquidator** n. [medieval Latin: related to LIQUID]

**liquidation** /ˌlik-wuh-**day**-shuhn/ n. liquidating, esp. of a firm. □ **go into liquidation** (of a firm etc.) be wound up and have its assets apportioned.

**liquid crystal** n. turbid liquid with some order in its molecular arrangement.

**liquid crystal display** n. visual display in electronic devices (e.g. clocks, calculators, etc.), in which numerals etc. change as a signal is applied to a matrix of liquid crystals.

**liquidise** /lik-wuh-ˌduyz/ v. (also **-ize**) (**-sing** or **-zing**) reduce to a liquid state. □ **liquidiser** n.

**liquidity** /luh-**kwid**-uh-tee/ n. (pl. **-ies**) **1** state of being liquid. **2** availability of liquid assets.

**liquor** /**lik**-uh/ n. **1** alcoholic (esp. distilled) drink. **2** other liquid, esp. that produced in cooking. [Latin: related to LIQUID]

**liquorice** /**lik**-uh-ruhs, **lik**-rish/ n. (also **licorice**) **1** black root extract used as a sweet and in medicine. **2** plant from which it is obtained. [Greek *glukus* sweet, *rhiza* root]

**lira** /**leer**-ruh/ n. (pl. **lire** pronunc. same or /**leer**-ray/ ) chief monetary unit of Italy and Turkey. [Latin *libra* pound]

**lisp** — n. speech defect in which s is pronounced like th in thick and z is pronounced like th in this. — v. speak or utter with a lisp. [Old English]

**lissom** /**lis**-uhm/ adj. lithe, agile. [ultimately from LITHE]

**list**[1] — n. **1** number of items, names, etc., written or printed together as a record or aid to memory. **2** (in pl.) **a** palisades enclosing an area for a tournament. **b** scene of a contest. — v. **1** make a list of. **2** enter in a list. **3** (as **listed** adj.) **a** (of securities) approved for dealings on a stock exchange. **b** (of a building) of historical importance and officially protected. □ **enter the lists** issue or accept a challenge. [Old English]

**list**[2] — v. (of a ship etc.) lean over to one side. — n. process or instance of listing. [origin unknown]

**listen** /**lis**-uhn/ v. **1 a** make an effort to hear something. **b** attentively hear a person speaking. **2** (foll. by to) **a** give attention with the ear. **b** take notice of; heed. **3** (also **listen out**) (often foll. by for) seek to hear by waiting alertly. □ **listen in 1** tap a telephonic communication. **2** use a radio receiving set. □ **listener** n. [Old English]

**listless** adj. lacking energy or enthu-

siasm. □ **listlessly** adv. **listlessness** n. [from obsolete *list* inclination]

**lit** past and past part. of LIGHT[1], LIGHT[2].

**lit.** abbr. **1** literal(ly). **2** literary. **3** literature. **4** litre. **5** little.

**litany** /**lit**-uh-nee/ n. (pl. **-ies**) **1** series of supplications to God recited by a priest etc. with set responses by the congregation. **2** colloq. tedious recital (*litany of woes*). [Greek *litaneia* prayer]

**literacy** /**lit**-uh-ruh-see/ n. ability to read and write. [Latin *littera* letter]

**literal** /**lit**-uh-ruhl, **lit**-ruhl/ adj. **1** taking words in their basic sense without metaphor or allegory. **2** corresponding exactly to the original words (*literal translation*). **3** prosaic; matter-of-fact. **4** so called without exaggeration (*literal bankruptcy*). **5** of a letter or the letters of the alphabet. □ **literally** adv. [Latin *littera* letter]

**literalism** n. insistence on a literal interpretation; adherence to the letter. □ **literalist** n.

**literary** /**lit**-uh-ruh-ree, **lit**-ruh-ree/ adj. **1** of or concerned with books or literature etc. **2** well informed about literature. **3** (of a word or idiom) used chiefly by writers; formal. □ **literariness** n. [Latin: related to LETTER]

**literate** /**lit**-uh-ruht/ — adj. able to read and write; educated. — n. literate person.

**literati** /ˌlit-uh-**rah**-tee/ n.pl. the class of learned people.

**literature** /**lit**-uh-ruh-chuh, **lit**-ruh-/ n. **1** written works, esp. those valued for form and style. **2** writings of a country or period or on a particular subject (*Australian literature; Elizabethan literature; there is a considerable literature on Australian orchids*). **3** literary production. **4** colloq. printed matter, leaflets, etc.

**-lith** suffix denoting types of stone (*megalith; monolith*).

**lithe** /luyth/ adj. flexible, supple. [Old English]

**lithic** /**lith**-ik/ adj. of, like, or made of stone. [Greek *lithikos*]

**lithium** /**lith**-ee-uhm/ n. soft silver-white metallic element. [Greek *lithion* from *lithos* stone]

**litho-** comb. form stone.

**lithograph** /**lith**-uh-ˌgrahf, **luy**-thuh-, -ˌgraf/ — n. lithographic print. — v. print by lithography. [Greek *lithos* stone]

**lithography** /li-**thog**-ruh-fee/ n. process of printing from a plate so treated that ink adheres only to the design to be printed. □ **lithographer** n. **lithographic** /ˌlith-uh-**graf**-ik/ adj. **lithographically** /ˌlith-uh-**graf**-i-kuh-lee, -i-klee/ adv.

**lithophyte** /lith-uh-,fuyt/ *n. Bot.* plant that grows on rock or stone. □ **lithophytic** /-fit-ik/ *adj.*

**lithosphere** /lith-uh-sfeer/ *n.* the earth's crust and upper mantle.

**Lithuanian** /,lith-yoo-**ay**-nee-uhn/ — *n.* **1 a** native or national of Lithuania in eastern Europe. **b** person of Lithuanian descent. **2** language of Lithuania. — *adj.* of Lithuania, its people, or language.

**litigant** /lit-uh-guhnt/ — *n.* party to a lawsuit. — *adj.* engaged in a lawsuit. [related to LITIGATE]

**litigate** /lit-uh-,gayt/ *v.* (**-ting**) **1** go to law. **2** contest (a point) at law. □ **litigation** /-**gay**-shuhn/ *n.* **litigator** *n.* [Latin *lis litlawsuit*]

**litigious** /luh-**tij**-uhs/ *adj.* **1** fond of litigation. **2** contentious. [Latin: related to LITIGATE]

**litmus** /lit-muhs/ *n.* dye from lichens, turned red by acid and blue by alkali. [Old Norse, = dye-moss]

**litmus paper** *n.* paper stained with litmus, used to test for acids or alkalis.

**litmus test** *n.* real or ultimate test.

**litotes** /luy-**toh**-teez/ *n.* (*pl.* same) ironic understatement, esp. using the negative (e.g. *I shan't be sorry for I shall be glad*). [Greek *litos* plain, meagre]

**litre** /lee-tuh/ *n.* metric unit of capacity equal to 1 cubic decimetre (1.76 pints). [Greek *litra*]

**litter** — *n.* **1 a** refuse, esp. paper, discarded in a public place. **b** odds and ends lying about. **c** leaves etc. accumulated on a forest floor. **2** young animals brought forth at one birth. **3** vehicle containing a couch and carried on men's shoulders or by animals. **4** a kind of stretcher for the sick and wounded. **5** straw etc. as bedding for animals. **6** granulated material for use as an animal's, esp. a cat's, toilet indoors. — *v.* **1** make (a place) untidy with refuse. **2** give birth to (whelps etc.). **3 a** provide (a horse etc.) with litter as bedding. **b** spread straw etc. on (a stable-floor etc.). [Latin *lectus* bed]

**litterbug** *n. colloq.* person who drops litter in the street etc.

**little** /lit-uhl/ — *adj.* (**littler**, **littlest**; **less** or **lesser**, **least**) **1** small in size, amount, degree, etc.; often used affectionately or condescendingly (*friendly little chap*; *silly little fool*). **2 a** short in stature. **b** of short distance or duration. **3** (prec. by *a*) a certain though small amount of (*give me a little butter*). **4** trivial (*questions every little thing*). **5** only a small amount (*had little sleep*). **6** operating on a small scale; humble, ordinary (*the little shop-*

keeper; *the little man*). **7** smaller or the smallest of the name (*little hand of a clock*; *little lorikeet*). **8** young or younger (*little boy*; *my little sister*). — *n.* **1** not much; only a small amount (*got little out of it*; *did what little I could*). **2** (usu. prec. by *a*) **a** a certain but no great amount (*knows a little of everything*). **b** short time or distance (*after a little*). — *adv.* (**less**, **least**) **1** to a small extent only (*little-known author*; *little more than speculation*). **2** not at all; hardly (*they little thought*). **3** (prec. by *a*) somewhat (*is a little deaf*). □ **no little** considerable (*took no little trouble over it*). **not a little** much; a great deal. [Old English]

**little by little** *adv.* by degrees; gradually.

**little house** *n.* (prec. by *the*) outdoor toilet.

**little lunch** *n.* (also **play-lunch**) light refreshment eaten during a mid-morning break at school.

**little penguin** *n.* = FAIRY PENGUIN.

**little rock wallaby** see NABARLEK.

**littley** /lit-uh-lee/ *n.* (also **littlie**) (*pl.* **-lies**) a child.

**littoral** /lit-uh-ruhl/ — *adj.* of or on the shore. — *n.* region lying along a shore. [Latin *litus litor-* shore]

**liturgy** /lit-uh-jee/ *n.* (*pl.* **-ies**) **1** prescribed form of public worship; a ritual. **2** set of formularies for this. **3** Eucharistic office of the Orthodox Church. □ **liturgical** /li-**ter**-ji-kuhl/ *adj.* **liturgically** /-**ter**-ji-kuh-lee, -klee/ *adv.* [Greek *leitourgia* public worship]

**live**[1] /liv/ *v.* (**-ving**) **1** have life; be or remain alive. **2** have one's home (*lives up the road*). **3** (foll. by *on*) subsist or feed (*lives on fruit*). **4** (foll. by *on, off*) depend for subsistence (*lives off welfare*; *lives on a pension*). **5** (foll. by *on, by*) sustain one's position (*live on their reputation*; *lives by his wits*). **6 a** spend or pass (*lived a full life*). **b** express in one's life (*lives his faith*). **7** conduct oneself, arrange one's habits, etc., in a specified way (*live quietly*). **8** (often foll. by *on*) (of a person or thing) survive; remain (*memory lived on*). **9** enjoy life to the full (*not really living*). □ **live and let live** condone others' failings so as to be similarly tolerated. **live down** cause (past guilt, a scandal, etc.) to be forgotten by blameless conduct thereafter. **live for** regard as one's life's purpose (*lives for her music*). **live in** (or **out**) reside on (or off) the premises of one's work. **live it up** *colloq.* go on a pleasure spree. **live a lie** keep up a pretence. **live together** (esp. of a couple not married to each other) share a home and have a sexual relationship. **live up to** fulfil (*couldn't live up to* *their expectations).* **live with 1** share a home with. **2** tolerate. [Old English]

**live²** /luyv/ — *adj.* **1** (*attrib.*) that is alive; living. **2** (of a broadcast, performance, etc.) heard or seen at the time of its performance or with an audience present. **3** of current interest or importance (*a live issue*). **4** glowing, burning (*live coals*). **5** (of a match, bomb, etc.) not yet kindled or exploded. **6** (of a wire etc.) charged with or carrying electricity. — *adv.* **1** in order to make a live broadcast (*we're crossing live now to the House of Representatives*). **2** as a live performance etc. (*show went out live*). [from ALIVE]

**livelihood** /luyv-lee-huud/ *n.* means of living; job, income. [Old English: related to LIFE]

**livelong** /liv-long/ *adj.* in its entire length (*the livelong day*). [from obsolete *lief*, assimilated to LIVE¹]

**lively** /luyv-lee/ *adj.* (**-ier, -iest**) **1** full of life; vigorous, energetic. **2** vivid (*lively imagination*). **3** cheerful. **4** *joc.* exciting, dangerous (*made things lively for him*). □ **liveliness** *n.* [Old English]

**liven** /luy-vuhn/ *v.* (often foll. by *up*) make or become lively, cheer up.

**liver¹** /liv-uh/ — *n.* **1** large glandular organ in the abdomen of vertebrates. **2** liver of some animals as food. — *adj.* dark reddish brown. [Old English]

**liver²** /liv-uh/ *n.* person who lives in a specified way (*a fast liver*).

**liverish** /liv-uh-rish/ *adj.* **1** suffering from a liver disorder. **2** peevish, glum.

**livery** /liv-uh-ree/ *n.* (*pl.* **-ies**) **1** distinctive uniform of a servant etc. **2** distinctive guise or marking (*birds in their winter livery*). **3** distinctive colour scheme in which a company's vehicles etc. are painted. □ **at livery** (of a horse) kept for the owner for a fixed charge. □ **liveried** *adj.* (esp. in sense 1, 2). [Anglo-French *liveré*, past part. of *livrer* DELIVER]

**lives** *pl.* of LIFE.

**livestock** *n.* (usu. treated as *pl.*) animals on a farm, kept for use or profit.

**live wire** *n.* spirited person.

**livid** /liv-uhd/ *adj.* **1** *colloq.* furious. **2** of a bluish leaden colour (*livid bruise*). [Latin]

**living** /liv-ing/ — *n.* **1** being alive (*that's what living is all about*). **2** livelihood. — *adj.* **1** contemporary; now alive. **2** (of a likeness) exact, lifelike. **3** (of a language) still in vernacular use. **4** (of rock) not detached, seeming to form part of the earth's frame. □ **within living memory** within the memory of people still alive.

**livistona** /liv-is-toh-nuh/ *n.* any of

several tall Australian palms with fan-shaped leaves, esp. the cabbage tree.

**lizard** /liz-uhd/ *n.* reptile with usu. a long body and tail, four legs, and a rough or scaly hide. □ **starve** (or **stiffen**) **the lizards!** *colloq.* (an exclamation of surprise or exasperation). [Latin *lacertus*]

**ll** *abbr.* lines.

**'ll** *v.* (usu. after pronouns) shall, will (*I'll; that'll*). [abbreviation]

**llama** /lah-muh/ *n.* S. American ruminant kept as a beast of burden and for its soft woolly fleece. [Spanish from Quechua]

**lo** /loh/ *int. archaic* look. □ **lo and behold** *joc.* formula introducing mention of a surprising fact. [Old English]

**load** — *n.* **1 a** what is carried or to be carried. **b** amount usu. or actually carried (often in *comb.*: *truck-load of bricks*). **2** unit of measure or weight of certain substances. **3** burden or commitment of work, responsibility, care, etc. **4** *colloq.* **a** (in *pl.*; often foll. by *of*) plenty, a lot (*loads of money; loads of people*). **b** (**a load of**) a quantity (*a load of nonsense*). **5** amount of power carried by an electric circuit or supplied by a generating station. — *v.* **1** a put a load on or aboard (*loaded the truck*). **b** place (a load) aboard a ship, on a vehicle, etc. (*loaded the vegies on the truck*). **2** (often foll. by *up*) (of a vehicle or person) take a load aboard (*the plane is now loading*). **3** enter a train, bus, etc. (*the fans loaded into the coach*). **4** (often foll. by *with*) burden, strain (*a table loaded with food*). **5** (also **load up**) (foll. by *with*) overburden, overwhelm (*loaded us with work; loaded me with abuse*). **6 a** put ammunition in (a gun), film in (a camera), a cassette in (a tape recorder), a program in (a computer), etc. **b** put (a film, cassette, etc.) into a device. **7** give a bias to (dice etc.) with weights. □ **get a load of** *colloq.* take note of. [Old English, = way]

**loaded** *adj.* **1** *colloq.* **a** rich. **b** drunk. **2** (of dice etc.) weighted. **3** (of a question or statement) carrying some hidden implication.

**loader** *n.* (in *comb.*) gun, machine, truck, etc., loaded in a specified way (*breech-loader; front-loader*). □ **-loading** *adj.* (in *comb.*).

**loading** *n.* **1** payment to employees in addition to an award wage or salary, in acknowledgment of special skills, or as a holiday bonus, etc. **2** freight carried by a vehicle. **3** increase in an insurance premium due to a factor increasing the risk involved.

**loaf¹** *n.* (*pl.* **loaves** /lohvz/ ) **1** unit of baked bread, usu. of a standard size or shape. **2** other food made in the shape of a loaf and cooked (*meat loaf*). **3** *colloq.* the head as the seat of common sense (*use your loaf!*). [Old English]

**loaf²** — *v.* **1** (often foll. by *about, around*) spend time idly; hang about. **2** (foll. by *away*) waste (time) idly (*loafed away the morning*). — *n.* **1** act or spell of loafing. **2** *colloq.* an undemanding job. [back-formation from LOAFER]

**loafer** *n.* **1** idle person. **2** (**Loafer**) *propr.* flat soft-soled leather shoe. [origin uncertain]

**loam** — *n.* **1** rich soil of clay, sand, and humus. **2** (in *pl.*) particles of gold found by loaming. — *v.* search for gold by washing loam. □ **loamer** *n.* **loamy** *adj.* [Old English]

**loan** — *n.* **1** thing lent, esp. a sum of money. **2** act of lending or being lent. — *v.* lend (money, works of art, etc.). □ **on loan** being lent. [Old English]

**loan shark** *n. colloq.* person who lends money at exorbitant rates of interest.

**loanword** *n.* word adopted, usu. with little modification, from a foreign language (e.g. *morale, pâté*).

**loath** /lohth/ *predic. adj.* (also **loth**) disinclined, reluctant (*loath to admit it*). [Old English]

**loathe** /loh*th*/ *v.* (**-thing**) detest, hate. □ **loathing** *n.* [Old English]

**loathsome** /loh*th*-suhm/ *adj.* arousing hatred or disgust; repulsive.

**loaves** *pl.* of LOAF¹.

**lob** — *v.* (**-bb-**) **1** hit or throw (a ball etc.) slowly or in a high arc. **2** *colloq.* (often foll. by *in(to), on to, up,* etc.) arrive without ceremony; turn up. — *n.* **1** a ball struck in a high arc. **2** stroke producing this result. [probably Low German or Dutch]

**lobar** /loh-buh/ *adj.* of a lobe, esp. of the lung (*lobar pneumonia*).

**lobate** /loh-bayt/ *adj.* having a lobe or lobes.

**lobby¹** /lob-ee/ — *n.* (*pl.* **-ies**) **1** porch, ante-room, entrance-hall, or corridor. **2 a** body of persons seeking to influence legislators on behalf of a particular interest (*anti-abortion lobby*). **b** organised rally of lobbying members of the public. **c** cause supported by such members of the public. — *v.* (**-ies, -ied**) **1** solicit the support of (an influential person). **2** (of members of the public) seek to influence (legislators, an MP, etc.). [Latin *lobia* lodge]

**lobby²** *n.* (esp. in Queensland) a yabby. □ **lobbying** fishing for yabbies. [abbreviation of LOBSTER]

**lobbyist** *n.* person who lobbies an MP etc., esp. professionally.

**lobe** *n.* **1** lower soft pendulous part of the outer ear. **2** similar part of other organs, esp. the brain, liver, and lung. □ **lobed** *adj.* [Greek *lobos* lobe, pod]

**lobelia** /luh-**bee**-lee-uh/ *n.* vigorous Australian ground-cover plant which roots at the nodes and produces bright blue flowers most of the year. [*Lobel*, botanist (d. 1616)]

**lobotomy** /luh-**bot**-uh-mee/ *n.* (*pl.* **-ies**) incision into the frontal lobe of the brain, formerly used in some cases of mental disorder. [from LOBE]

**lobster** *n.* **1** = CRAYFISH. **2** northern Atlantic marine crustacean with two pincer-like claws. **3** the flesh as food. [Latin *locusta* lobster, LOCUST]

**local** /**loh**-kuhl/ — *adj.* **1** belonging to, existing in, or peculiar to a particular place (*local history*). **2** of the neighbourhood (*local paper*). **3** of or affecting a part and not the whole (*local anaesthetic*). **4** (of a telephone call) to a nearby place and charged at a lower rate. — *n.* **1** inhabitant of a particular place. **2** (often prec. by *the*) *colloq.* local hotel. **3** local anaesthetic. □ **locally** *adv.* [Latin *locus* place]

**local area network** *n.* (*abbr.* **LAN**) *Computing* communication network linking a number of computers in the same locality, typically a building (cf. WIDE AREA NETWORK).

**local colour** *n.* touches of detail in a story etc. designed to provide a realistic background.

**locale** /loh-**kahl**/ *n.* scene or locality of an event or occurrence. [French *local*]

**local government** *n.* system of administration of a city, town, municipality, shire, etc., by the elected representatives of those who live there.

**localise** /**loh**-kuh-,luyz/ *v.* (also **-ize**) (**-sing** or **-zing**) **1** restrict or assign to a particular place. **2** invest with the characteristics of a particular place.

**locality** /loh-**kal**-uh-tee/ *n.* (*pl.* **-ies**) **1** district. **2** site or scene of a thing. **3** thing's position. [Latin: related to LOCAL]

**locate** /loh-**kayt**/ *v.* (**-ting**) **1** discover the exact place of. **2** establish in a place; situate. **3** state the locality of. [Latin: related to LOCAL]

■ **Usage** In standard English, it is not acceptable to use *locate* to mean merely 'find' as in *can't locate my key*.

**location** /loh-**kay**-shuhn/ *n.* **1** particular place or position. **2** act of locating or process of being located. **3** natural, not studio, setting for a film etc. (*filmed on location*).

**loc. cit.** *abbr.* in the passage cited. [Latin *loco citato*]

**loch** /lok, lox/ *n. Scot.* lake or narrow inlet of the sea. [Gaelic]

**loci** /**loh**-kee, **loh**-kuy, **lok**-ee/ *pl.* of LOCUS.

**lock¹** — *n.* **1** mechanism for fastening a door etc. with a bolt that requires a key of a particular shape to work it. **2** confined section of a canal or river within sluice-gates, for moving boats from one level to another. **3 a** turning of a vehicle's front wheels. **b** (in full **full lock**) maximum extent of this. **4** interlocked or jammed state. **5** wrestling-hold that keeps an opponent's limb fixed. **6** (in full **lock forward**) player in the second row of a Rugby scrum. **7** mechanism for exploding the charge of a gun. — *v.* **1 a** fasten with a lock. **b** (foll. by *up*) shut (a house etc.) thus. **c** (of a door etc.) be lockable (*does this door lock?*). **2 a** (foll. by *up, in, into*) enclose (a person or thing) by locking. **b** (foll. by *up*) *colloq.* imprison (a person). **3** (often foll. by *up, away*) store inaccessibly (*capital locked up in land*). **4** (foll. by *in*) hold fast (in sleep, an embrace, a struggle, etc.). **5** (usu. in *passive*) (of land, hills, etc.) enclose. **6** make or become rigidly fixed. **7** (cause to) jam or catch. □ **lock on to** (of a missile etc.) automatically find and then track (a target). **lock out 1** keep out by locking the door. **2** (of an employer) subject (employees) to a lockout. **under lock and key** locked up. □ **lockable** *adj.* [Old English]

**lock²** *n.* **1** portion of hair that hangs together. **2** (in *pl.*) the hair of the head (*golden locks*). **3** tuft of wool or cotton. [Old English]

**locker** *n.* (usu. lockable) cupboard or compartment, esp. each of several for public use.

**locket** /**lok**-uht/ *n.* small ornamental case for a portrait or lock of hair, worn on a chain round the neck. [French diminutive of *loc* latch, LOCK¹]

**lockjaw** *n.* form of tetanus in which the jaws become rigidly closed.

**lockout** *n.* employer's exclusion of employees from the workplace until certain terms are agreed to.

**locksmith** *n.* maker and mender of locks.

**lock, stock, and barrel** *adv.* completely.

**lock-up** — *n.* **1** house or room for the temporary detention of prisoners. **2** premises that can be locked up, esp. a small shop. — *attrib. adj.* that can be locked up (*lock-up garage*).

**locomotion** /ˌloh-kuh-**moh**-shuhn/ *n.*

motion or the power of motion from place to place. [Latin LOCUS, MOTION]

**locomotive** /ˌloh-kuh-**moh**-tiv/ — *n.* engine for pulling trains. — *adj.* of, having, or effecting locomotion.

**locum tenens** /ˌloh-kuhm **tee**-nenz, **ten**-uhnz/ *n.* (*pl.* **locum tenentes** /ˌloh-kuhm tuh-**nen**-teez/ ) (also *colloq.* **locum**) deputy acting esp. for a doctor, clergyman, etc. [Latin, = (one) holding a place]

**locus** /**loh**-kuhs, **lok**-uhs/ *n.* (*pl.* **loci** /-kee, -kuy/ ) **1** position or locality. **2** line or curve etc. formed by all the points satisfying certain conditions, or by the defined motion of a point, line, or surface. [Latin, = place]

**locust** /**loh**-kuhst/ *n.* **1 a** African or Asian grasshopper migrating in swarms and consuming all vegetation. **b** any similar grasshopper. **2** *colloq.* cicada. [Latin *locusta* locust, LOBSTER]

**locution** /luh-**kyoo**-shuhn/ *n.* **1** word, phrase, or idiom. **2** style of speech. [Latin *loquor locut-* speak]

**lode** *n.* vein of metal ore. [var. of LOAD]

**lodestar** *n.* **1** star used as a guide in navigation, esp. the pole star. **2 a** guiding principle. **b** object of pursuit. [from LODE in obsolete sense 'way, journey']

**lodestone** *n.* **1** magnetic oxide of iron. **2 a** piece of this used as a magnet. **b** thing that attracts.

**lodge** — *n.* **1** small, makeshift shelter; hut. **2** building accommodating skiers etc. during the season (*ski lodge*). **3** (**The Lodge**) official residence of the Prime Minister in Canberra. **4** *Brit.* small house at the entrance to a park or grounds of a large house, occupied by a gatekeeper etc. **5** members or meeting-place of a branch of a secret society such as the Freemasons. — *v.* (**-ging**) **1 a** reside or live, esp. as a lodger. **b** provide with temporary accommodation. **2** submit or present (a complaint etc.) for attention. **3** become fixed or caught; stick (*the bullet lodged in his brain*). **4** deposit (money etc.) for security. **5** (foll. by *in, with*) place (power etc.) in a person. [French *loge*: related to LEAF]

**lodger** *n.* person paying for accommodation in another's house.

**lodging** *n.* **1** temporary accommodation (*lodging for the night*). **2** (in *pl.*) room or rooms rented for lodging in.

**loess** /**loh**-uhs, lers/ *n.* deposit of fine wind-blown soil, esp. in the basins of large rivers. [Swiss German, = loose]

**loft** — *n.* **1** attic. **2** room over a stable. **3** gallery in a church or hall. **4** pigeon-house. **5** backward slope on the face of a golf-club. **6** lofting stroke. — *v.* **1** send (a ball etc.) high up (*batsman lofted the ball*). **2** clear (an obstacle) in this way. [Old English, = air, upper room]

**lofty** *adj.* (**-ier, -iest**) **1** (of things) of imposing height. **2** haughty, aloof (*lofty contempt*). **3** exalted, noble (*lofty ideals*). □ **loftily** *adv.* **loftiness** *n.*

**log¹** — *n.* **1** unhewn piece of a felled tree; any large rough piece of wood, esp. cut for firewood. **2** *hist.* floating device for gauging a ship's speed. **3** record of events occurring during the voyage of a ship or aircraft. **4** any systematic record of deeds, experiences, etc. **5** = LOGBOOK. **6** set of claims for an increase in wages etc., esp. as lodged by a trade union with an industrial tribunal. **7** *colloq.* a blockhead. — *v.* (**-gg-**) **1 a** enter (a ship's speed, or other transport details) in a logbook. **b** enter (data etc.) in a regular record. **2** attain (a distance, speed, etc., thus recorded) (*had logged over 600 miles*). **3** cut into logs. **4** fell trees (in a forest etc.) for timber, woodchips, etc.; fell (an area) for this reason. □ **log in** (or **on**) or **off** (or **out**) open (or close) one's online access to a computer system. **sleep like a log** sleep soundly. [origin unknown]

**log²** *n.* logarithm. [abbreviation]

**loganberry** /**loh**-guhn-buh-ree/ *n.* (*pl.* **-ies**) dark red fruit, hybrid of a blackberry and a raspberry. [*Logan*, horticulturalist (d. 1928)]

**logarithm** /**log**-uh-ˌrith-uhm/ *n.* one of a series of arithmetic exponents tabulated to simplify computation by making it possible to use addition and subtraction instead of multiplication and division. □ **logarithmic** /-**rith**-mik/ *adj.* **logarithmically** /-**rith**-mik-lee/ *adv.* [Greek *logos* reckoning, *arithmos* number]

**logbook** *n.* **1** book containing a detailed record or log. **2** record kept by truck drivers etc. of hours driven etc.

**logger** *n.* person engaged in the industry of felling (etc.) forest etc. trees for timber.

**loggerhead** /**log**-uh-ˌhed/ *n.* □ **at loggerheads** (often foll. by *with*) disagreeing or disputing. [probably British dial. from *logger* wooden block]

**loggia** /**loh**-jee-uh, **loj**-ee-uh/ *n.* open-sided gallery or arcade. [Italian, = LODGE]

**logging** *n.* felling (etc.) forest etc. trees for timber.

**logic** /**loj**-ik/ *n.* **1 a** science of reasoning, proof, inference. **b** particular system or method of reasoning. **2 a** chain of reasoning (regarded as sound or unsound). **b** use of or ability in argument. **3** inexorable force, compulsion, or consequence (*the logic of events*). **4 a** principles used in designing a computer etc. **b** circuits using

this. □ **logician** /luh-**jish**-uhn/ *n.* [related to -LOGIC]

**-logic** *comb. form* (also **-logical**) forming adjectives corresponding esp. to nouns in -*logy* (*pathological*; *zoological*). [Greek -*logikos*]

**logical** *adj.* **1** of or according to logic (*the logical conclusion*). **2** correctly reasoned. **3** defensible or explicable on the ground of consistency. **4** capable of correct reasoning. □ **logicality** /-**kal**-uh-tee/ *n.* **logically** *adv.* [Greek *logos* word, reason]

**Logie** /**loh**-gee/ *n.* any of the statuettes awarded annually since 1958 for excellence in acting etc. in an Australian television production. [John *Logie* Baird, inventor of television (d. 1946)]

**-logist** *comb. form* forming nouns meaning 'person skilled in -*logy*' (*geologist*).

**logistics** /luh-**jis**-tiks/ *n.pl.* **1** organisation of (orig. military) services and supplies. **2** organisation of any complex operation. □ **logistic** *adj.* **logistical** *adj.* **logistically** *adv.* [French *loger* lodge]

**logo** /**loh**-goh/ *n.* (*pl.* **-s**) emblem of an organisation used in its display material etc. [abbreviation of *logotype* from Greek *logos* word]

**log-runner** *n.* either of two Australian rainforest birds, esp. the chowchilla.

**-logy** *comb. form* forming nouns denoting: **1** a subject of study (*biology*). **2** speech or discourse or a characteristic of this (*trilogy*; *tautology*; *phraseology*). [Greek -*logia* from *logos* word]

**loin** *n.* **1** (in *pl.*) side and back of the body between the ribs and the hip-bones. **2** joint of meat from this part of an animal. [French *loigne* from Latin *lumbus*]

**loincloth** *n.* piece of cloth worn round the hips, so as to enclose the genitals.

**loiter** *v.* **1** stand about idly; linger. **2** go slowly with frequent stops. **3** (foll. by *away*) pass (time etc.) in loitering. □ **loiter with intent** linger in order to commit a crime. □ **loiterer** *n.* [Dutch]

**loll** *v.* **1** stand, sit, or recline in a lazy attitude. **2** hang loosely. [imitative]

**lollipop** /**lol**-ee-ˌpop/ *n.* hard sweet on a stick. [origin uncertain]

**lollipop man** *n.* (also **lollipop lady**) *colloq.* warden using a circular sign on a pole to stop traffic for children to cross the road.

**lollop** /**lol**-uhp/ *v.* (**-p-**) *colloq.* **1** flop about. **2** move in ungainly bounds. [probably from LOLL, TROLLOP]

**lolly** /**lol**-ee/ *n.* (*pl.* **-ies**) **1** any sweet, esp. boiled. **2** *colloq.* money. **3** *colloq.* the head. □ **do one's lolly** *colloq.* lose one's temper. [abbreviation of LOLLIPOP]

**lolly-pink** *n.* & *adj.* shocking pink.

**lolly water** *n. colloq.* soft drink.

**lomatia** /loh-**may**-shuh/ *n.* any of several small to medium Australian shrubs with cream flowers, attractive foliage, and usu. handsome fruits.

**London fog** /**lun**-duhn/ *n. colloq.* person who loafs on the job (i.e. who will not lift).

**lone** *attrib. adj.* **1** solitary; without companions. **2** isolated. **3** unmarried, single (*lone parent*). [from ALONE]

**lone hand** *n.* **1** hand played or player playing against the rest at cards. **2** person or action without allies.

**lonely** /**lohn**-lee/ *adj.* (**-ier, -iest**) **1** without companions (*lonely existence*). **2** sad because of this. **3** (of a place) unfrequented, isolated, uninhabited. □ **loneliness** *n.*

**loner** *n.* person or animal that prefers to be alone.

**lonesome** /**lohn**-suhm/ *adj.* **1** lonely. **2** making one feel forlorn (*a lonesome song*).

**long**[1] — *adj.* (**longer** /**long**-guh/) **1** measuring much from end to end in space or time. **2** (following a measurement) in length or duration (*2 metres long; two months long*). **3** relatively great in extent or duration (*a long meeting*). **4 a** consisting of many items (*a long list*). **b** seemingly more than the stated amount; tedious (*ten long kilometres*). **5** of elongated shape. **6** lasting or reaching far back or forward in time (*long friendship*). **7** far-reaching; acting at a distance; involving a great interval or difference. **8** (of a vowel or syllable) having the greater of the two recognised durations. **9** (of odds or a chance) reflecting a low level of probability. **10** (foll. by *on*) *colloq.* well supplied with. — *n.* long interval or period (*will not take long; won't be long*). — *adv.* (**longer** /**long**-guh/) **1** by or for a long time (*long before; long ago*). **2** (following nouns of duration) throughout a specified time (*all day long*). **3** (in *compar.*) after an implied point of time (*shall not wait any longer*). □ **as** (or **so**) **long as** provided that. **before long** soon. **in the long run** (or **term**) eventually, ultimately. **the long and the short of it 1** all that need be said. **2** the eventual outcome. **not by a long shot** (or **chalk**) by no means. □ **longish** *adj.* [Old English]

**long**[2] *v.* (foll. by *for* or *to* + infin.) have a strong wish or desire for. [Old English, = seem LONG[1] to]

**longa** /**lon**-guh/ *prep.* (in Aboriginal English) belonging to; near; about; with.

**long blow** *n.* stroke of the shears from the sheep's tail to its neck.

**long-drawn** *adj.* (also **long-drawn-out**) prolonged.

**longevity** /lon-**jev**-uh-tee/ *n. formal* long life. [Latin *longus* long, *aevum* age]

**long face** *n.* dismal expression.

**longhand** *n.* ordinary handwriting (cf. SHORTHAND).

**longing** /**long**-ing/ — *n.* intense desire. — *adj.* having or showing this. □ **longingly** *adv.*

**long in the tooth** *predic. adj. colloq.* old.

**longitude** /**long**-guh-ˌtyood/ *n.* **1** angular distance east or west from a standard meridian such as Greenwich to the meridian of any place. **2** angular distance of a celestial body, esp. along the ecliptic. [Latin *longitudo* length, from *longus* long]

**longitudinal** /ˌlong-guh-**tyoo**-duh-nuhl/ *adj.* **1** of or in length. **2** running lengthwise. **3** of longitude. □ **longitudinally** *adv.*

**long johns** *n.pl. colloq.* long underpants.

**long jump** *n.* athletic contest of jumping as far as possible along the ground in one leap.

**long paddock** *n.* public road, the grassy sides of which are used to graze stock during a drought etc.

**long-range** *adj.* **1** having a long range. **2** relating to a period of time far into the future (*long-range weather forecast*).

**long service leave** *n.* a period of paid leave granted to an employee who has served a specified period of continuous employment.

**long shot** *n.* **1** wild guess or venture. **2** bet at long odds.

**long sight** *n.* ability to see clearly only what is comparatively distant.

**long-sighted** *adj.* **1** having long sight. **2** far-sighted. □ **long-sightedness** *n.*

**long sleever** *n.* **1** tall beer glass. **2** the drink so contained.

**long-spined flathead** *n.* (also **spikey**) marine food-fish of south-eastern and western Australia, having a long, sharp spine on each side of the head.

**long-standing** *adj.* that has long existed.

**long-suffering** *adj.* bearing provocation patiently.

**long-term** *adj.* of or for a long period of time (*long-term plans*).

**long tom** *n.* **1** long trough used for washing gold-bearing material in order to separate the gold. **2** any of several Australian sea fish having long needle-like jaws.

**long wave** *n.* radio wave of frequency less than 300 kHz.

**long-winded** *adj.* (of a speech or writing) tediously lengthy.

**loo** *n. colloq.* toilet. [origin uncertain]

**loofah** /loo-fuh/ *n.* rough bath-sponge made from the dried pod of a type of gourd. [Arabic]

**look** /luuk/ — *v.* **1 a** (often foll. by *at, down, up,* etc.) use one's sight; turn one's eyes in some direction. **b** turn one's eyes on; examine (*looked me in the eyes; looked us up and down*). **2 a** make a visual or mental search (*I'll look in the morning*). **b** (foll. by *at*) consider, examine (*must look at the facts*). **3** (foll. by *for*) search for, seek, be on the watch for. **4** inquire (*when one looks deeper*). **5** have a specified appearance; seem (*look a fool; future looks bleak*). **6** (foll. by *to*) **a** consider; be concerned about (*look to the future*). **b** rely on (*look to me for support*). **7** (foll. by *into*) investigate. **8** (foll. by *what, where, whether,* etc.) ascertain or observe by sight. **9** (of a thing) face some direction. **10** indicate (emotion etc.) by one's looks. **11** (foll. by *that*) take care; make sure. **12** (foll. by *to* + infin.) aim (*am looking to finish it soon*). — *n.* **1** act of looking; gaze, glance. **2** (in *sing.* or *pl.*) appearance of a face; expression. **3** appearance of a thing (*by the look of it*). **4** style, fashion (*this year's look; the wet look*). — *int.* (also **look here!**) calling attention, expressing a protest, etc. □ **look after** attend to; take care of. **look back 1** (foll. by *on, to*) turn one's thoughts to (something past). **2** (usu. with *neg.*) cease to progress (*he's never looked back*). **look down on** (or **look down one's nose at**) regard with contempt or superiority. **look forward to** await (an expected event) eagerly or with specified feelings. **look in** make a short visit or call. **look on 1** (often foll. by *as*) regard. **2** be a spectator. **look oneself** appear well (esp. after illness etc.). **look out 1** direct one's sight or put one's head out of a window etc. **2** (often foll. by *for*) be vigilant or prepared. **3** (foll. by *on, over,* etc.) have or afford an outlook. **4** search for and produce. **5** (as *imper.*) warning of immediate danger etc. **look over** inspect. **look smart** (or **lively**) make haste. **look up 1** search for (esp. information in a book). **2** *colloq.* visit (a person). **3** improve in prospect. **look up to** respect or admire. **not like the look of** find alarming or suspicious. [Old English]

**lookalike** *n.* person or thing closely resembling another.

**looker** *n. colloq.* exceptionally attractive person of either sex.

**look-in** *n. colloq.* chance of participation or success (*never gets a look-in*).

**looking-glass** *n.* mirror.

**lookout** *n.* **1** watch or looking out (*on the lookout*). **2 a** observation-post. **b** person etc. stationed to keep watch. **3** elevated place from which a particular scenic attraction may be viewed. **4** prospect (*it's a bad lookout*). **5** *colloq.* person's own concern (*that's your lookout*).

**loom¹** *n.* apparatus for weaving. [Old English]

**loom²** *v.* **1** appear dimly, esp. as a vague and often threatening shape. **2** (of an event) be ominously close. [probably Low German or Dutch]

**loon** *n.* **1** a kind of diving bird. **2** *colloq.* crazy person (cf. LOONY). [Old Norse]

**loony** *colloq.* — *n.* (*pl.* **-ies**) lunatic. — *adj.* (**-ier, -iest**) crazy. □ **looniness** *n.* [abbreviation]

**loop** — *n.* **1 a** figure produced by a curve, or a doubled thread etc., that crosses itself. **b** thing, path, etc., forming this figure. **2** similarly shaped attachment used as a fastening. **3** ring etc. as a handle etc. **4** contraceptive coil. **5** (in full **loop-line**) railway or telegraph line that diverges from a main line and joins it again. **6** skating or aerobatic manoeuvre describing a loop. **7** complete circuit for an electric current. **8** endless band of tape or film allowing continuous repetition. **9** sequence of computer operations repeated until some condition is satisfied. — *v.* **1** form or bend into a loop. **2** fasten with a loop or loops. **3** form a loop. **4** (also **loop the loop**) fly in a circle vertically. [origin unknown]

**loophole** *n.* **1** means of evading a rule etc. without infringing it. **2** narrow vertical slit in the wall of a fort etc.

**loopy** *adj.* (**-ier, -iest**) *colloq.* **1** crazy. **2** (foll. by *about*) infatuated with.

**loose** — *adj.* **1** not tightly held, fixed, etc. (*loose handle; loose stones*). **2** free from bonds or restraint. **3** not held together (*loose papers*). **4** not compact or dense (*loose soil*). **5** inexact (*loose translation*). **6** morally lax (*loose living*). **7** (of the tongue) indiscreet. **8** (of the bowels) tending to diarrhoea. **9** (in *comb.*) loosely (*loose-fitting*). — *v.* (**-sing**) **1** free; untie or detach; release. **2** relax (*loosed my hold*). **3** discharge (a missile). □ **at a loose end** unoccupied. **on the loose 1** escaped from captivity. **2** enjoying oneself freely. □ **loosely** *adv.* **looseness** *n.* **loosish** *adj.* [Old Norse]

**loose-leaf** *adj.* (of a notebook etc.) with pages that can be removed and replaced.

**loosen** *v.* make or become loose or looser. □ **loosen a person's tongue** make a person talk freely. **loosen up 1** relax. **2** limber up.

**loot** — *n.* **1** spoil, booty. **2** *colloq.* money.

— *v.* **1** rob or steal, esp. after rioting etc. **2** plunder. □ **looter** *n.* [Hindi *lūṭ*]

**lop** *v.* (**-pp-**) **1 a** (often foll. by *off*, *away*) cut or remove (a part or parts) from a whole, esp. branches from a tree. **b** remove branches from (a tree). **2** (often foll. by *off*) remove (items) as superfluous. [Old English]

**lope** — *v.* (**-ping**) run with a long bounding stride. — *n.* long bounding stride. [Old Norse: related to LEAP]

**loppy** /lop-ee/ *n.* a rouseabout. [origin uncertain]

**lopsided** *adj.* unevenly balanced. □ **lopsidedness** *n.* [related to LOB]

**loquacious** /luh-kway-shuhs/ *adj.* talkative. □ **loquacity** /-kwas-uh-tee/ *n.* [Latin *loquor* speak]

**loquat** /loh-kwot, -kuht/ *n.* **1** small yellow egg-shaped fruit. **2** tree bearing it. [Chinese]

**lord** — *n.* **1** master or ruler. **2** *hist.* feudal superior, esp. of a manor. **3** *Brit.* person entitled to the title *Lord*. **4** (**Lord**) (often prec. by *the*) God or Christ. — *int.* (**Lord, good Lord,** etc.) expressing surprise, dismay, etc. □ **lord it over** domineer. [Old English, = bread-keeper: related to LOAF[1], WARD]

**Lord Howe Island woodhen** *n.* small brown extremely rare flightless bird native to the island. [*Lord Howe Island,* north-east of Sydney]

**lordly** *adj.* (**-ier, -iest**) **1** haughty, imperious. **2** suitable for a lord. □ **lordliness** *n.*

**Lord Mayor** *n.* title of the mayor in some large cities.

**lordship** *n.* (foll. by *over*) dominion, rule.

**Lord's Prayer** *n.* prayer taught by Jesus to his disciples, beginning 'Our Father'.

**lore** *n.* body of traditions and knowledge on a subject or held by a particular group (*bird lore*; *Aboriginal lore*). [Old English: related to LEARN]

**lorgnette** /law-nyet/ *n.* pair of eyeglasses or opera-glasses on a long handle. [French *lorgner* to squint]

**lorikeet** /lo-ruh-keet, ˌlo-ruh-**keet**/ *n.* any of several small, and usu. mainly green, nectar-feeding parrots of northern and eastern Australia. [diminutive of LORY, after *parakeet*]

**lorn** *adj. archaic* desolate, forlorn. [Old English, past part. of LOSE]

**lorry** /lo-ree/ *n.* (*pl.* **-ies**) *Brit.* = TRUCK[1]. [origin uncertain]

**lory** /law-ree/ *n.* (*pl* **-ies**) any of various brightly-coloured parrots occurring in Australasia, the Malay Archipelago, etc. [Malay]

**lose** /looz/ *v.* (**-sing**; *past* and *past part.*

lost) **1** be deprived of or cease to have, esp. by negligence. **2** be deprived of (a person) by death. **3** become unable to find, follow, or understand (*lose one's way*). **4** let or have pass from one's control or reach (*lost my chance*; *lost his composure*). **5** be defeated in (a game, lawsuit, battle, etc.). **6** get rid of (*lost our pursuers*; *lose weight*). **7** forfeit (a right to a thing). **8** spend (time, efforts, etc.) to no purpose. **9 a** suffer loss or detriment. **b** be worse off. **10** cause (a person) the loss of (*will lose you your job*). **11** (of a clock etc.) become slow; become slow by (a specified time). **12** (in *passive*) disappear, perish; be dead (*lost at sea*; *is a lost art*). □ **be lost** (or **lose oneself) in** be engrossed in. **be lost on** be wasted on, or not noticed or appreciated by. **be lost to** be no longer affected by or accessible to (*is lost to pity*; *is lost to the world*). **be lost without** be dependent on (*am lost without my diary*). **get lost** *colloq.* (usu. in *imper.*) go away. **lose face** see FACE. **lose out 1** (often foll. by *on*) *colloq.* be unsuccessful; not get a full chance or advantage (in). **2** (foll. by *to*) be beaten in competition or replaced by. [Old English]

**loser** *n.* **1** person or thing that loses, esp. a contest (*is a bad loser*). **2** *colloq.* person who regularly fails.

**loss** *n.* **1** losing or being lost. **2** thing or amount lost. **3** detriment resulting from losing. □ **at a loss** (sold etc.) for less than was paid for it. **be at a loss** be puzzled or uncertain. [probably back-formation from LOST]

**lost** *past* and *past part.* of LOSE.

**lot** *n.* **1** *colloq.* (prec. by *a* or in *pl.*) **a** a large number or amount (*a lot of people*; *lots of milk*). **b** *colloq.* much (*a lot warmer*; *smiles a lot*). **2 a** each of a set of objects used to make a chance selection. **b** this method of deciding (*chosen by lot*). **3** share or responsibility resulting from it. **4** person's destiny, fortune, or condition. **5** plot; allotment of land (*parking lot*). **6** article or set of articles for sale at an auction etc. **7** group of associated persons or things. □ **cast** (or **draw**) **lots** decide by lots. **throw in one's lot with** decide to share the fortunes of. **the** (or **the whole**) **lot** the total number or quantity. **a** (or **a whole**) **lot** *colloq.* very much (*is a whole lot better*). [Old English]

■ **Usage** In sense 1a, *a lot of* is somewhat informal, but acceptable in serious writing, whereas *lots of* is not acceptable.

**loth** var. of LOATH.

**lotion** /loh-shuhn/ *n.* medicinal or

**cosmetic liquid** preparation applied externally. [Latin *lavo lot-* wash]

**lottery** /lot-uh-ree/ n. (pl. **-ies**) **1** means of raising money by selling numbered tickets and giving prizes to the holders of numbers drawn at random. **2** thing whose success is governed by chance. [Dutch: related to LOT]

**lotto** /lot-oh/ n. game of chance like bingo, but with numbers drawn instead of called. [Italian]

**lotus** /loh-tuhs/ n. **1** legendary plant inducing luxurious languor when eaten. **2** a kind of water lily etc., esp. used symbolically in Hinduism and Buddhism. **3** either of two Australian shrubs with pink or yellow pea-flowers. [Greek *lōtos*]

**lotus bird** n. (also **jacana**; **lily-trotter**) wading bird of eastern and northern Australia, having long toes which enable it to walk on floating leaves etc.

**lotus-eater** n. person given to indolent enjoyment.

**lotus position** n. cross-legged position of meditation with the feet resting on the thighs.

**loud** — adj. **1** strongly audible, noisy. **2** clamorous, insistent (*loud complaints*). **3** (of behaviour) aggressive; coarse. **4** (of colours etc.) gaudy, obtrusive. — adv. loudly. □ **out loud** aloud; loudly (*laughed out loud*). □ **loudish** adj. **loudly** adv. **loudness** n. [Old English]

**loud hailer** n. electronic device for amplifying the voice.

**loudspeaker** n. apparatus that converts electrical signals into sound.

**lounge** — v. (**-ging**) **1** recline comfortably; loll. **2** stand or move about idly. — n. **1** place for lounging, esp.: **a** (usu. **lounge room**) sitting-room in a private house. **b** public room (e.g. in a hotel). **c** place in an airport etc. with seats for waiting passengers. **2** spell of lounging. [origin uncertain]

**lounge suit** n. man's suit for ordinary day (esp. business) wear.

**lour** /lowuh/ v. (also **lower**) **1** frown; look sullen. **2** (of the sky etc.) look dark and threatening. [origin unknown]

**louse** — n. **1** (pl. **lice**) parasitic insect. **2** (pl. **louses**) colloq. contemptible person. — v. (**-sing**) **1** delouse. **2** *Mining* pick over (waste material) looking for fragments of the mineral sought. □ **louse up** colloq. make a mess of. [Old English]

**lousy** /low-zee/ adj. (**-ier**, **-iest**) **1** colloq. very bad; disgusting; ill (*feel lousy*). **2** (often foll. by *with*) colloq. well supplied, teeming (with). **3** infested with lice. □ **lousily** adv. **lousiness** n.

**lousy jack** n. (also **apostle**) mostly grey and very noisy bird which builds its nest of mud and lives in family groups of nine or twelve in wooded parts of eastern Australia.

**lout** n. rough, crude, or ill-mannered person (usu. a man). □ **loutish** adj. [origin uncertain]

**louvre** /loo-vuh/ n. (also **louver**) each of a set of overlapping slats designed to admit air and some light and exclude rain. □ **louvred** adj. [French *lover* skylight]

**lovable** /luv-uh-buhl/ adj. (also **loveable**) inspiring love or affection.

**love** /luv/ — n. **1** deep affection or fondness. **2** sexual passion. **3** sexual relations. **4 a** beloved one; sweetheart (often as a form of address). **b** colloq. form of address regardless of affection. **5** colloq. person of whom one is fond. **6** affectionate greetings (*give him my love*). **7** (in games) no score; nil. — v. (**-ving**) **1** feel love or a deep fondness for. **2** delight in; admire; greatly cherish. **3** colloq. like very much (*loves books*). **4** (foll. by verbal noun, or *to* + infin.) be inclined, esp. as a habit; greatly enjoy (*children love dressing up*; *loves to run*). □ **fall in love** (often foll. by *with*) suddenly begin to love. **for love** for pleasure not profit. **for the love of** for the sake of. **in love** (often foll. by *with*) enamoured (of). **make love** (often foll. by *to*) have sexual intercourse (with). **not for love or money** colloq. not in any circumstances. [Old English]

**loveable** var. of LOVABLE.

**love affair** n. romantic or sexual relationship between two people.

**lovebird** n. **1** budgerigar. **2** parrot, esp. one seeming to show great affection for its mate.

**love-hate relationship** n. intense relationship involving ambivalent emotions.

**loveless** adj. unloving or unloved or both.

**lovelorn** adj. pining from unrequited love.

**lovely** adj. (**-ier**, **-iest**) **1** colloq. pleasing, delightful (*had a lovely meal*). **2** beautiful. □ **lovely and** colloq. delightfully (*lovely and warm*). □ **loveliness** n. [Old English]

**lovemaking** n. sexual play, esp. intercourse.

**lover** n. **1** person in love with another. **2** person with whom another is having sexual relations. **3** (in pl.) unmarried couple in love or having sexual relations. **4** person who likes or enjoys a specified thing (*music lover*).

**lovesick** adj. languishing with love.

**loving** — *adj.* feeling or showing love; affectionate. — *n.* affection; love (*a kind of loving*).

**low¹** /loh/ — *adj.* **1** not high or tall (*low wall*). **2 a** not elevated in position (*low altitude*). **b** (of the sun) near the horizon. **3** of or in humble rank or position (*of low birth*). **4** of small or less than normal amount, extent, or intensity (*low temperature; low in calories*). **5** small or reduced in quantity (*stocks are low*). **6** coming below the normal level (*blouse with a low neck*). **7** dejected; lacking vigour (*feeling low*). **8** (of a sound) not shrill or loud. **9** not exalted or sublime; commonplace. **10** unfavourable (*low opinion*). **11** abject, mean, vulgar (*low cunning; low slang*). **12** (of a geological period) earlier. — *n.* **1** low or the lowest level or number (*dollar reached a new low*). **2** area of low pressure. — *adv.* **1** in or to a low position or state. **2** in a low tone (*speak low*). **3** (of a sound) at or to a low pitch. □ **lowish** *adj.* **lowness** *n.* [Old Norse]

**low²** /loh/ — *n.* sound made by cattle; moo. — *v.* make this sound. [Old English]

**lowan** /loh-uhn/ *n.* = MALLEE FOWL. [Wemba-wemba *lawan*]

**low-born** *adj.* of humble birth.

**lowbrow** — *adj.* not intellectual or cultured. — *n.* lowbrow person.

**Low Church** *n.* section of the Anglican Church attaching little importance to ritual, priestly authority, and the sacraments (cf. HIGH CHURCH). □ **Low-Church** *adj.*

**low-down** — *adj.* mean, dishonourable. — *n. colloq.* (prec. by *the*; usu. foll. by *on*) relevant information.

**lower¹** — *adj.* (*compar.* of LOW¹). **1** less high in position or status. **2** situated below another part (*lower lip*). **3** (of a mammal, plant, etc.) evolved to only a slight degree. — *adv.* in or to a lower position, status, etc. □ **lowermost** *adj.*

**lower²** *v.* **1** let or haul down. **2** make or become lower (in price, pitch, elevation, etc.) (*lower your voice; lowered his eyes*). **3** degrade. **4** diminish.

**lower³** var. of LOUR.

**lower case** *n.* small letters (opp. *upper case* or *capitals*).

**lower house** *n.* **1** larger body (in a two-house legislature) directly responsible for law making (opp. *upper house*). **2 a** = HOUSE OF REPRESENTATIVES. **b** = LEGISLATIVE ASSEMBLY.

**lowest** *adj.* (*superl.* of LOW¹) least high in position or status.

**lowest common denominator** *n.* **1** *Math.* lowest common multiple of the denominators of several fractions. **2** the worst or most vulgar common feature of members of a group.

**lowest common multiple** *n. Math.* least quantity that is a multiple of two or more given quantities.

**low frequency** *n.* frequency, esp. in radio, 30 to 300 kilohertz.

**low gear** *n.* gear such that the driven end of a transmission revolves slower than the driving end.

**low-key** *adj.* lacking intensity, restrained.

**lowland** — *n.* (usu. in *pl.*) low-lying country. — *adj.* of or in lowland. □ **lowlander** *n.*

**low-level** *adj.* (of a computer language) close in form to machine code.

**lowly** *adj.* (**-ier, -iest**) humble; unpretentious. □ **lowliness** *n.*

**low-lying** *adj.* near to the ground or sea level.

**low-pitched** *adj.* **1** (of a sound) low. **2** (of a roof) having only a slight slope.

**low pressure** *n.* **1** low degree of activity or exertion. **2** atmospheric condition with the pressure below average.

**low tide** *n.* (also **low water**) time or level of the tide at its ebb.

**loyal** /loi-uhl/ *adj.* **1** (often foll. by *to*) faithful. **2** steadfast in allegiance etc. □ **loyally** *adv.* **loyalty** *n.* (*pl.* **-ies**). [Latin: related to LEGAL]

**loyalist** *n.* person who remains loyal to the legitimate sovereign etc. □ **loyalism** *n.*

**lozenge** /loz-uhnj/ *n.* **1** rhombus. **2** small sweet or medicinal tablet to be dissolved in the mouth. **3** lozenge-shaped object. [French]

**LP** *abbr.* long-playing (record).

**LPG** *abbr.* liquefied petroleum gas.

**L-plate** *n.* sign bearing the letter L, attached to a vehicle to show that it is being driven by a learner. [from PLATE]

**Lr** *symb.* lawrencium.

**LSD** *abbr.* lysergic acid diethylamide, a powerful hallucinogenic drug.

**Ltd.** *abbr.* Limited.

**Lu** *symb.* lutetium.

**lubber** *n.* clumsy fellow, lout. [origin uncertain]

**lubra** /loo-bruh/ *n. offens.* an Aboriginal woman. [perhaps from a mainland Aboriginal language]

**lubricant** /loo-bruh-kuhnt/ *n.* substance used to reduce friction.

**lubricate** /loo-bruh-ˌkayt/ *v.* (**-ting**) **1** apply oil or grease etc. to. **2** make slippery. □ **lubrication** /-kay-shuhn/ *n.* **lubricator** *n.* [Latin *lubricus* slippery]

**lubricious** /loo-brish-uhs/ *adj.*

**1** slippery, evasive. **2** lewd. □ **lubricity** n. [Latin: related to LUBRICATE]

**lucerne** /loo-**sern**/ n. a clover-like plant of the legume family, cultivated as fodder. [Provençal, = glow-worm, referring to its shiny seeds]

**lucid** /loo-suhd/ adj. **1** expressing or expressed clearly (a lucid account). **2** sane. □ **lucidity** /-**sid**-uh-tee/ n. **lucidly** adv. **lucidness** n. [Latin lux luc- light]

**Lucifer** /loo-suh-fuh/ n. **1** Satan. **2** morning star (the planet Venus). **3** (**lucifer**) obsolete a friction match. [Latin: related to LUCID, fero bring]

**luck** n. **1** good or bad fortune. **2** circumstances of life (beneficial or not) brought by this. **3** good fortune; success due to chance (in luck; out of luck). □ **bad luck!** (an exclamation of sympathy etc.). **down on one's luck** see DOWN[1]. **for luck** to bring good fortune. **good luck!** exclamation expressing hopes for success. **half your luck!** (exclamation of envy at another's good fortune etc.). **no such luck** colloq. unfortunately not. **push one's luck** (**too far**) take extreme or too many chances. **try one's luck** make a venture. [Low German or Dutch]

**luckless** adj. unlucky; ending in failure.

**lucky** adj. (**-ier, -iest**) **1** having or resulting from good luck. **2** bringing good luck (lucky charm). □ **luckily** adv.

**Lucky Country** n. (prec. by the) a (chiefly ironic) name for Australia as a land of opportunity. [title of a book by Donald Horne published in 1964]

**lucky shop** n. (in Victoria) betting shop, TAB agency.

**lucrative** /loo-kruh-tiv/ adj. profitable. □ **lucratively** adv. **lucrativeness** n. [Latin: related to LUCRE]

**lucre** /loo-kuh/ n. derog. financial gain. [Latin lucrum gain]

**Luddite** /lud-uyt/ n. **1** person opposed to industrial progress or new technology (such as computers etc.). **2** hist. member of a band of English artisans who destroyed machinery (1811–16). □ **Ludditism** n. [Ned Lud, destroyer of machinery]

**luderick** /loo-duh-rik/ n. highly esteemed brown or silvery-green marine and estuarine food-fish of eastern Australia. [Ganay luderag]

**ludicrous** /loo-duh-kruhs/ adj. absurd, ridiculous, laughable. □ **ludicrously** adv. **ludicrousness** n. [Latin ludicrum stage play]

**luff** v. (also absol.) **1** steer (a ship) nearer the wind. **2** raise or lower (a crane's jib). [French, probably from Low German]

**lug** — v. (**-gg-**) **1** drag or carry with effort. **2** pull hard. — n. **1** hard or rough pull. **2**

colloq. ear. **3** projection on an object by which it may be carried, fixed in place, etc. [probably Scandinavian]

**luggage** /lug-ij/ n. suitcases, bags, etc., for a traveller's belongings. [from LUG]

**lugger** /lug-uh/ n. small ship with four-cornered sails. [from LUGSAIL]

**lugsail** n. four-cornered sail on a yard. [probably from LUG]

**lugubrious** /luh-**goo**-bree-uhs/ adj. doleful, mournful, dismal. □ **lugubriously** adv. **lugubriousness** n. [Latin lugeo mourn]

**lukewarm** adj. **1** moderately warm; tepid. **2** unenthusiastic, indifferent. [Old English luke warm, WARM]

**lull** — v. **1** soothe or send to sleep. **2** (usu. foll. by into) deceive (a person) into undue confidence (lulled into a false sense of security). **3** allay (suspicions etc.), usu. by deception. **4** (of noise, a storm, etc.) abate or fall quiet. — n. temporary quiet period. [imitative]

**lullaby** /lul-uh-,buy/ — n. (pl. **-ies**) soothing song to send a child to sleep. — v. (**-ies, -ied**) sing to sleep. [related to LULL]

**lumbago** /lum-**bay**-goh/ n. rheumatic pain in the muscles of the lower back. [Latin lumbus loin]

**lumbar** /lum-buh/ adj. of the lower back area. [as LUMBAGO]

**lumbar puncture** n. withdrawal of spinal fluid from the lower back for diagnosis.

**lumber** /lum-buh/ — n. **1** disused and cumbersome articles. **2** partly prepared timber. — v. **1** (usu. foll. by with) leave (a person etc.) with something unwanted or unpleasant. **2** (usu. foll. by up) obstruct, fill inconveniently. **3** cut and prepare forest timber. **4** move in a slow clumsy way. **5** colloq. **a** arrest. **b** imprison. [origin uncertain]

**lumberjack** n. (US and Canada) = LOGGER.

**luminary** /loo-muh-nuh-ree/ n. (pl. **-ies**) **1** literary natural light-giving body. **2** wise or inspiring person. **3** celebrated member of a group (show-business luminaries). [Latin lumen lumin- light]

**luminescence** /,loo-muh-**nes**-uhns/ n. emission of light without heat. □ **luminescent** adj.

**luminous** /loo-muh-nuhs/ adj. **1** shedding light. **2** phosphorescent, visible in darkness (luminous paint). **3** (esp. of a writer or a writer's work) throwing light on a subject. □ **luminosity** /-**nos**-uh-tee/ n.

**lump**[1] — n. **1** compact shapeless mass. **2** tumour; swelling, bruise. **3** heavy, dull, or ungainly person. — v. **1** (usu. foll. by together etc.) treat as all alike; put together in a lump. **2** (of sauce etc.) become lumpy. □ **lump in the throat** feeling of pressure there, caused by emotion. [Scandinavian]

**lump²** v. colloq. put up with ungraciously (like it or lump it). [imitative]

**lump sum** n. large sum of money paid or received at one time (took his superannuation as a lump sum rather than as a pension).

**lumpy** adj. (-ier, -iest) full of or covered with lumps. □ **lumpily** adv. **lumpiness** n.

**lunacy** /loo-nuh-see/ n. (pl. -ies) 1 insanity. 2 mental unsoundness. 3 great folly. [Latin: related to LUNAR]

**lunar** /loo-nuh/ adj. of, like, concerned with, or determined by the moon. [Latin luna moon]

**lunar month** n. 1 period of the moon's revolution, esp. the interval between new moons (about 29½ days). 2 (in general use) four weeks.

**lunate** /loo-nayt/ adj. crescent-shaped.

**lunatic** /loo-nuh-tik/ — n. 1 insane person. 2 wildly foolish person. — adj. insane; extremely reckless or foolish. [related to LUNACY]

**lunatic asylum** n. hist. mental home or hospital.

**lunatic fringe** n. extreme or eccentric minority group.

**lunatic soup** n. colloq. alcoholic liquor of poor quality.

**lunch** — n. midday meal. — v. 1 take lunch. 2 entertain to lunch. [shortening of LUNCHEON]

**luncheon** /lun-shuhn/ n. formal lunch. [origin unknown]

**lunette** /loo-net/ n. 1 arched aperture in a dome to admit light. 2 crescent-shaped or semicircular space or alcove meant to contain a statue etc. 3 RC Ch. crescent-shaped holder for the consecrated Host in a monstrance. 4 crescent-shaped dune, formed on the lee side of a lake basin in parts of arid Australia. [French, = little moon]

**lung** n. either of the pair of respiratory organs in humans and many other vertebrates. [Old English: related to LIGHT²]

**lunge** — n. 1 sudden movement forward. 2 the basic attacking move in fencing. — v. (-ging) (usu. foll. by at, out) deliver or make a lunge. [French allonger from long LONG¹]

**lupine** /loo-puyn/ adj. of or like wolves. [Latin lupinus from lupus wolf]

**lupus** /loo-puhs/ n. autoimmune inflammatory skin disease. [Latin, = wolf]

**lurch¹** — n. stagger; sudden unsteady movement or leaning. — v. stagger; move or progress unsteadily. [originally Naut., of uncertain origin]

**lurch²** n. □ **leave in the lurch** desert (a friend etc.) in difficulties. [obsolete French lourche a kind of backgammon]

**lure** — v. (-ring) (usu. foll. by away, into) entice (a person, animal, etc.) usu. with a reward, bait, etc. — n. 1 thing used to entice. 2 (usu. foll. by of) enticing quality (of a pursuit etc.). [French from Germanic]

**lurex** /loo-reks/ n. propr. 1 type of yarn incorporating a glittering metallic thread. 2 fabric made from this.

**lurid** /loo-ruhd/ adj. 1 bright and glaring in colour. 2 sensational, shocking (lurid details). 3 ghastly, wan (lurid complexion). □ **luridly** adv. [Latin]

**Luritja** /loo-rich-u/ n. a dialect of the WESTERN DESERT LANGUAGE.

**lurk** — v. 1 linger furtively. 2 a lie in ambush. b (usu. foll. by in, under, about, etc.) hide, esp. for sinister purposes. 3 (as **lurking** adj.) dormant (a lurking suspicion). — n. colloq. 1 dodge, racket, or scheme. 2 job. [perhaps from LOUR]

**lurk-man** n. colloq. confidence man.

**luscious** /lush-uhs/ adj. 1 richly sweet in taste or smell. 2 (of style) over-rich. 3 voluptuously attractive. [perhaps related to DELICIOUS]

**lush** adj. 1 (of vegetation) luxuriant and succulent. 2 luxurious. 3 colloq. excellent. [origin uncertain]

**lust** — n. 1 strong sexual desire. 2 (usu. foll. by for, of) passionate desire for or enjoyment of (lust for power; lust of battle). 3 sensuous appetite regarded as sinful (lusts of the flesh). — v. (usu. foll. by after, for) have a strong or excessive (esp. sexual) desire. □ **lustful** adj. **lustfully** adv. [Old English]

**lustre** /lus-tuh/ n. 1 gloss, brilliance, or sheen. 2 radiance or attractiveness; splendour, glory (of achievements etc.) (his success adds lustre to our town). 3 iridescent glaze on pottery and porcelain. □ **lustrous** adj. [Latin lustro illumine]

**lusty** adj. (-ier, -iest) 1 healthy and strong. 2 vigorous, lively. □ **lustily** adv. **lustiness** n. [from LUST]

**lute** /loot/ n. guitar-like instrument with a long neck and a pear-shaped body. [Arabic]

**lutenist** /loo-tuh-nuhst/ n. (also **lutanist**) lute-player.

**lutetium** /loo-tee-shuhm/ n. silvery metallic element, the heaviest of the lanthanide series. [Lutetia, ancient name of Paris]

**Lutheran** /loo-thuh-ruhn/ — n. 1 follower of Luther. 2 member of the Lutheran Church. — adj. of Luther, or the Protestant Reformation and the doctrines associated with him. □ **Lutheranism** n. [Martin *Luther*, religious reformer (d. 1546)]

**lux** n. (pl. same) the SI unit of illumination. [Latin]

**luxuriant** /lug-**zhoo**-ree-uhnt/ adj. **1** growing profusely (of plants etc.). **2** exuberant. **3** (of style) florid, ornate. □ **luxuriance** n. **luxuriantly** adv. [Latin: related to LUXURY]

■ **Usage** *Luxuriant* is sometimes confused with *luxurious*.

**luxuriate** /lug-**zhoo**-ree-ayt/ v. (**-ting**) **1** (foll. by *in*) take self-indulgent delight in, enjoy as a luxury. **2** relax in comfort.

**luxurious** /lug-**zhoo**-ree-uhs/ adj. **1** supplied with luxuries. **2** extremely comfortable. **3** fond of luxury. □ **luxuriously** adv. [Latin: related to LUXURY]

■ **Usage** *Luxurious* is sometimes confused with *luxuriant*.

**luxury** /**luk**-shuh-ree/ n. (pl. **-ies**) **1** choice or costly surroundings, possessions, etc. **2** thing giving comfort or enjoyment but not essential. **3** (*attrib.*) comfortable and expensive (*luxury flat*). [Latin *luxus* abundance]

**-ly**[1] suffix forming adjectives, esp. from nouns, meaning: **1** having the qualities of (*princely*). **2** recurring at intervals of (*daily*). [Old English]

**-ly**[2] suffix forming adverbs from adjectives (*boldly*; *happily*). [Old English]

**lycanthrope** /**luy**-kuhn-,throhp/ n. **1** werewolf. **2** insane person who believes that he or she is a wolf (or other animal). [Greek (as LYCANTHROPY)]

**lycanthropy** /luy-**kan**-thruh-pee/ n. **1** mythical transformation of a person into a wolf (see also WEREWOLF). **2** form of madness involving the delusion of being a wolf. [Greek *lukos* wolf, *anthrōpos* man]

**lychee** /**luy**-chee/ n. **1** sweet white juicy fruit in a brown skin. **2** tree, orig. from China, bearing this. [Chinese]

**lycra** /**luy**-kruh/ n. *propr.* elastic polyurethane fabric used esp. for sportswear.

**lye** /luy/ n. **1** water made alkaline with wood ashes. **2** any alkaline solution for washing. [Old English]

**lying** *pres. part.* of LIE[1], LIE[2].

**lymph** /limf/ n. **1** colourless fluid from the tissues of the body, containing white blood cells. **2** this fluid used as a vaccine. [Latin *lympha*]

**lymphatic** /lim-**fat**-ik/ adj. **1** of, secreting, or conveying lymph. **2** (of a person) pale, flabby, or sluggish.

**lymphatic system** n. network of vessels conveying lymph.

**lymph gland** n. (also **lymph node**) small mass of tissue in the lymphatic system.

**lymphoma** /lim-**foh**-muh/ n. (pl. **-s** or **-mata**) tumour of the lymph nodes.

**lynch** /linch/ v. (of a mob) put (a person) to death without a legal trial. □ **lynching** n. [originally *US*, after *Lynch*, 18th-c. Justice of the Peace in Virginia]

**lynch law** n. procedure followed when a person is lynched.

**lynx** /lingks/ n. (pl. same or **-s**) wild cat with a short tail and spotted fur. [Greek *lugx*]

**lynx-eyed** adj. keen-sighted.

**lyre** /luyuh/ n. ancient U-shaped stringed instrument. [Greek *lura*]

**lyre-bird** n. either of two species of ground-dwelling bird of forest in southeast mainland Australia, noted for its remarkable power of mimicry, and for the long, lyre-shaped tail displayed by the male (*Albert lyre-bird*; *superb lyre-bird*).

**lyric** /**li**-rik/ — adj. **1** (of poetry) expressing the writer's emotions, usu. briefly and in stanzas. **2** (of a poet) writing in this manner. **3** meant or fit to be sung, songlike (*lyric drama*). **4** (of a voice) light in timbre (*lyric tenor*; *lyric soprano*). — n. **1** lyric poem. **2** (in *pl.*) words of a song. [Latin: related to LYRE]

**lyrical** adj. **1** = LYRIC. **2** resembling, or using language appropriate to, lyric poetry. **3** *colloq.* highly enthusiastic (*wax lyrical about*). □ **lyrically** adv.

**lyricism** /**li**-ruh-,siz-uhm/ n. quality of being lyric.

**lyricist** /**li**-ruh-suhst/ n. writer of (esp. popular) lyrics.

**lysergic acid diethylamide** /,duy-uh-**thuy**-luh-,muyd/ n. = LSD. [from hydro*lysis*, *ergot*, -IC]

**-lysis** *comb. form* forming nouns denoting disintegration or decomposition (*electrolysis*). [Greek *lusis* loosening]

**-lyte** *suffix* forming nouns denoting substances that can be decomposed (*electrolyte*). [Greek *lutos* loosened]

**-lytic** *comb. form* forming adjectives corresponding to nouns in *-lysis*. [Greek *lutikos* (as -LYSIS)]

# M

**M¹** /em/ *n.* (*pl.* **Ms** or **M's**) **1** thirteenth letter of the alphabet. **2** (as a Roman numeral) 1,000.

**M²** *abbr.* (also **M.**) **1** (of a film) classified as 'for Mature audiences only', and (on television) not to be broadcast before 8.30 p.m. **2** mega-.

**m** *abbr.* (also **m.**) **1** male. **2** masculine. **3** married. **4** mile(s). **5** metre(s). **6** million(s). **7** minute(s). **8** milli-.

**MA** *abbr.* **1** Master of Arts. **2** (of a film) classified as 'Mature Adults': restricted to persons 15 years and over, and (on television) not to be broadcast before 9 p.m.

**Mabo** /**mah**-boh/ *n.* (in full **Mabo decision**) High Court judgment of 1992 recognising continuous possession of their lands by the Torres Strait Murray Islanders. [Koiki (Eddie) *Mabo*, a principal claimant (d. 1992)]

**macabre** /muh-**kah**-buh, -bruh, -**kahbr**/ *adj.* grim, gruesome. [French]

**macadam** /muh-**kad**-uhm/ *n.* **1** successive layers of compacted broken stone as material for road-making. **2** = TARMACADAM. □ **macadamise** *v.* (also **-ize**) (**-sing** or **-zing**). [*McAdam*, name of a surveyor]

**macadamia** /,mak-uh-**day**-mee-uh/ *n.* **1** eastern Australian rainforest tree cultivated for its large edible nut. **2** this nut. [*Macadam*, Australian chemist (d. 1865)]

**macaroni** /,mak-uh-**roh**-nee/ *n.* **1** pasta in the form of tubes. **2** *colloq.* nonsense, baloney. [Italian from Greek; sense 2, rhyming slang on BALONEY]

**macaw** /muh-**kaw**/ *n.* long-tailed brightly coloured American parrot. [Portuguese *macao*]

**McCarthyism** /muh-**kah**-thee-,iz-uhm/ *n.* **1** *hist.* hunting out and sacking of Communists in the US. **2** any similar witch-hunt (although not now for Communists). [*McCarthy*, name of a senator]

**McCoy** /muh-**koi**/ *n.* □ **the real McCoy** *colloq.* the real thing; the genuine article. [origin uncertain]

**mace¹** /mays/ *n.* **1** staff of office, esp. symbol of the Speaker's authority in the House of Representatives. **2** *hist.* heavy war-club with metal head and spikes. [French from Romanic]

**mace²** *n.* dried outer covering of the nutmeg as a spice. [Latin *macir*]

**mace³** *n. propr.* (also **mace gas**) chemical spray designed to be sprayed on a person, crowd, etc., offering violence: the chemical causes extreme temporary irritation, esp. to the eyes, and thus incapacitates.

**macerate** /mas-uh-,rayt/ *v.* (**-ting**) **1** soften by soaking. **2** waste away by fasting. □ **maceration** /-**ray**-shuhn/ *n.* [Latin]

**mach** /mahk, mak/ *n.* (in full **mach number**) ratio of the speed of a body to the speed of sound in the surrounding medium. [*Mach*, name of a physicist]

**machete** /muh-**shet**-ee/ *n.* broad heavy knife, esp. of Central America. [Spanish from Latin]

**machiavellian** /,mak-ee-uh-**vel**-ee-uhn/ *adj.* elaborately cunning; scheming, unscrupulous. □ **machiavellianism** *n.* [*Machiavelli*, name of a political writer (d. 1527)]

**machination** /,mak-uh-**nay**-shuhn, ,mash-/ *n.* (usu. in *pl.*) plot, intrigue. □ **machinate** /**mak**-uh-, **mash**-uh-/ *v.* (**-ting**). [Latin: related to MACHINE]

**machine** /muh-**sheen**/ — *n.* **1** apparatus for applying mechanical power, having several interrelated parts. **2** particular machine, esp. a vehicle or an electrical or electronic apparatus, a computer, etc. **3** controlling system of an organisation etc. (*party machine*). **4** person who acts mechanically; yes-man. **5** (esp. in *comb.*) mechanical dispenser with slots for coins (*soft drink machine*). — *v.* (**-ning**) make, operate on, or finish with a machine. [Greek *mēkhanē*]

**machine code** *n.* (also **machine language**) computer language for a particular computer.

**machine-gun** — *n.* automatic gun giving continuous fire. — *v.* (**-nn-**) shoot at with a machine-gun.

**machine-independent** *adj.* (of software etc.) capable of use on any computer.

**machine-readable** *adj.* in a form that a computer can process.

**machinery** *n.* (*pl.* **-ies**) **1** machines. **2** mechanism. **3** (usu. foll. by *of*) organised system (*the machinery of government*). **4** (usu. foll. by *for*) means devised (*the machinery for decision-making*).

**machinist** *n.* **1** person who operates a machine. **2** person who makes machinery.

**machismo** /muh-**chiz**-moh, -**kiz**-/ *n.* being macho; masculine pride. [Spanish]

**macho** /**mach**-oh/ *adj.* aggressively masculine. [from MACHISMO]

**mach one** /mahk, mak/ *n.* (also **mach two** etc.) the speed (or twice etc. the speed) of sound. [as MACH]

**macintosh** var. of MACKINTOSH.

**mackerel** /**mak**-ruhl, **mak**-uh-ruhl/ *n.* (*pl.* same or **-s**) **1** silvery-greenish marine food-fish of southern Australian waters. **2** food-fish of the North Atlantic. [Anglo-French]

**mackintosh** /**mak**-uhn-, tosh/ *n.* (also **macintosh**) **1** waterproof coat or cloak. **2** cloth waterproofed with rubber. [*Macintosh*, name of its inventor]

**Macquarie perch** *n.* freshwater fish of rivers and lakes in south-eastern Australia, valued for its fine flesh. [*Macquarie* River, in central NSW]

**macramé** /muh-**krah**-mee, -may/ *n.* **1** art of knotting cord or string in patterns to make decorative articles. **2** work so made. [Arabic, = bedspread]

**macro-** *comb. form* **1** long. **2** large, large-scale. [Greek *makros* long]

**macrobiotic** /,mak-roh-buy-**ot**-ik/ — *adj.* of a diet intended to prolong life, esp. consisting of wholefoods. — *n.* (in *pl.*; treated as *sing.*) theory of such a diet. [Greek *bios* life]

**macrocosm** /**mak**-roh-,koz-uhm, **mak**-ruh-/ *n.* **1** universe. **2** the whole of a complex structure. [from MACRO-, COSMOS]

**macroeconomics** /,mak-roh-,ee-kuh-**nom**-iks, -,ek-uh-/ *n.* the study of the economy as a whole (opp. MICRO-ECONOMICS). ◻ **macroeconomic** *adj.*

**macron** /**mak**-ron/ *n.* mark (¯) over a long or stressed vowel. [Greek, neuter of *makros* long]

**macropidia** /,mak-roh-**pid**-ee-uh/ *n.* (also **black kangaroo paw**) WA kangaroo paw bearing spikes of green flowers densely covered in jet black hairs.

**macropod** /**mak**-ruh-pod/ *n.* any plant-eating marsupial such as the kangaroo and wallaby. [MACRO-, Greek *pous podos* foot]

**macroscopic** /,mak-ruh-**skop**-ik/ *adj.* **1** visible to the naked eye. **2** regarded in terms of large units.

**macrozamia** /,mak-roh-**zay**-mee-uh/ *n.* (also **wild pineapple**, **burrawang**) any of several Australian cycads with long dark green palm-like leaves and pineapple-like cones bearing seeds edible only after treatment. [MACRO-, *Zamia*, plant genus]

**mad** *adj.* (**madder**, **maddest**) **1** insane; frenzied. **2** wildly foolish (*a mad idea*). **3** (often foll. by *about, on*) *colloq.* wildly excited or infatuated (*mad about footy; she's mad about him*). **4** *colloq.* angry. **5** (of an animal) rabid. **6** *colloq.* wildly light-hearted (*had a mad time celebrating*). ◻ **like mad** *colloq.* with great energy or enthusiasm. **mad as a cut snake** (or **as a meat-axe**) *colloq.* extremely angry; crazy; eccentric. **mad as a hatter** *colloq.* crazy. **mad as a two-bob watch** *colloq.* crazy; idiotic. ◻ **madness** *n.* [Old English]

**madam** /**mad**-uhm/ *n.* polite or respectful form of address or mode of reference to a woman. [French *ma dame* my lady]

**Madame** /muh-**dahm**/ *n.* **1** (*pl.* **Mesdames** /may-**dahm**/) Mrs or madam (used of or to a French-speaking woman). **2** (**madame**) = MADAM. [French, as MADAM]

**madcap** — *adj.* wildly impulsive. — *n.* wildly impulsive person.

**mad cow disease** *n. colloq.* = BSE.

**madden** *v.* **1** make or become mad. **2** irritate. ◻ **maddening** *adj.* **maddeningly** *adv.*

**made** *past* and *past part.* of MAKE. — *adj.* **1** built or formed (*well-made*). **2** successful (*self-made man*). ◻ **have** (or **have got**) **it made** *colloq.* be sure of success. **made for** ideally suited to. **made of** consisting of. **made of money** *colloq.* very rich.

**Mademoiselle** /,mad-mwuh-**zel**/ *n.* (*pl.* **Mesdemoiselles**) /,mayd-mwuh-/ **1** Miss or madam (used of or to an unmarried French-speaking woman). **2** (**mademoiselle**) young Frenchwoman. [French *ma my, demoiselle* DAMSEL]

**made road** *n.* a formed but frequently unsealed road.

**madhouse** *n.* **1** *colloq.* scene of confused uproar. **2** *archaic* mental home or hospital.

**madly** *adv.* **1** in a mad manner. **2** *colloq.* **a** passionately. **b** extremely.

**mado** /**may**-doh/ *n.* either of two small sea fish found near wharves and inlets of eastern Australia. [perhaps from a NSW Aboriginal language]

**Madonna** /muh-**don**-uh/ *n.* **1** (prec. by *the*) the Virgin Mary. **2** (**madonna**) picture or statue of her. [Italian, = my lady]

**madrigal** /**mad**-ri-guhl/ *n.* usu. 16th-c. part-song, usu. unaccompanied, for several voices. [Italian]

**maelstrom** /**mayl**-struhm/ *n.* **1** great whirlpool. **2** state of confusion. [Dutch]

**maestro** /**muy**-stroh/ *n.* (*pl.* **maestri** /-stree/ or **-s**) **1** distinguished musician, esp. a conductor, composer, or teacher. **2** great performer in any sphere. [Italian]

**Mae West** /may west/ *n.* inflatable life-jacket. [name of a film actress]

**Mafia** /maf-ee-uh, mah-fee-/ n. **1** organised body of criminals, orig. in Sicily, now also in Italy and the US. **2** (**mafia**) group regarded as exerting an intimidating and corrupt power. [Italian dial., = bragging]

**Mafioso** /,maf-ee-**oh**-soh, ,mah-fee-/ n. (pl. **Mafiosi** /-see/) member of the Mafia. [Italian: related to MAFIA]

**mag¹** colloq. — v. prattle, talk incessantly. — n. a gossip or chat. [British dial.]

**mag²** n. colloq. = MAGAZINE 1. [abbreviation]

**magazine** /,mag-uh-**zeen**/ n. **1** illustrated periodical publication containing articles, stories, etc. **2** chamber holding cartridges to be fed automatically to the breech of a gun. **3** similar device in a slide projector etc. **4** military store for arms etc. **5** store for explosives. [Arabic makāzin plural of makzan storehouse]

**mage** /mayj/ n. **1** (now used primarily in fantasy literature) a wizard. **2** archaic wise and learned person. [Anglicised from MAGUS]

**magenta** /muh-**jen**-tuh/ — n. **1** shade of crimson. **2** aniline crimson dye. — adj. of or coloured with magenta. [Magenta in N. Italy]

**maggie** /mag-ee/ n. colloq. = MAGPIE. [abbreviation]

**maggot** /mag-uht/ n. larva, esp. of the blowfly. □ **maggoty** adj. [perhaps an alteration of maddock, from Old Norse]

**maggotty** adj. (also **maggoty**) colloq. angry; bad-tempered. [British dial.]

**magi** pl. of MAGUS.

**magic** /maj-ik/ — n. **1 a** supposed art of producing effects or of influencing or controlling events by the occult control of nature or of the spirits. **b** witchcraft. **2** conjuring tricks. **3** inexplicable or remarkable influence producing surprising results. **4** enchanting quality or phenomenon. — adj. **1** of magic. **2** producing surprising results. **3** colloq. wonderful, exciting. — v. (**-ck-**) change or create by or as if by magic. □ **like magic** very rapidly. **magic away** cause to disappear as if by magic. [Greek magikos: related to MAGUS]

**magical** adj. **1** of magic. **2** resembling, or produced as if by, magic. **3** wonderful, enchanting. □ **magically** adv.

**magician** /muh-**jish**-uhn/ n. **1** person skilled in magic. **2** conjuror.

**magisterial** /,maj-uh-**steer**-ree-uhl/ adj. **1** imperious. **2** authoritative. **3** of a magistrate. □ **magisterially** adv. [medieval Latin: related to MASTER]

**magistrate** /maj-uh-struht, -,strayt/ n. **1** civil officer administering the law. **2** official conducting a court for minor cases and preliminary hearings. [Latin: related to MASTER]

**magma** /mag-muh/ n. (pl. **-s**) molten rock under the earth's crust, from which igneous rock is formed by cooling. [Greek massō knead]

**magnanimous** /mag-**nan**-uh-muhs/ adj. nobly generous; not petty in feelings or conduct. □ **magnanimity** /,mag-nuh-**nim**-uh-tee/ n. **magnanimously** adv. [Latin magnus great, animus mind]

**magnate** /mag-nayt, -nuht/ n. wealthy and influential person, usu. in business. [Latin magnus great]

**magnesia** /mag-**nee**-zhuh, -shuh, -zee-uh/ n. **1** magnesium oxide. **2** hydrated magnesium carbonate, used as an antacid and laxative. [Magnesia in Asia Minor]

**magnesium** /mag-**nee**-zee-uhm/ n. silvery metallic element.

**magnet** /mag-nuht/ n. **1** piece of iron, steel, alloy, ore, etc., having the properties of attracting iron and of pointing approximately north and south when suspended. **2** lodestone. **3** person or thing that attracts. [Greek magnēs -ētos of Magnesia: related to MAGNESIA]

**magnetic** /mag-**net**-ik/ adj. **1 a** having the properties of a magnet. **b** produced or acting by magnetism. **2** capable of being attracted by or acquiring the properties of a magnet. **3** strongly attractive (magnetic personality). □ **magnetically** adv.

**magnetic anthill** n. wall-like nest constructed by the magnetic termite of Australia, with the long axis of the nest pointing roughly north-south.

**magnetic field** n. area of force around a magnet.

**magnetic needle** n. piece of magnetised steel used as an indicator on the dial of a compass etc.

**magnetic north** n. point indicated by the north end of a magnetic needle.

**magnetic pole** n. point near the north or south pole where a magnetic needle dips vertically.

**magnetic storm** n. disturbance of the earth's magnetic field by charged particles from the sun etc.

**magnetic tape** n. plastic strip coated with magnetic material for recording sound or pictures or for the storage of information.

**magnetic termite** n. termite of northern Australia which builds a nest like a brick wall (see MAGNETIC ANTHILL).

**magnetise** /mag-nuh-,tuyz/ v. (also **-ize**) (**-sing** or **-zing**) **1** give magnetic properties to. **2** make into a magnet. **3** attract as a magnet does. □ **magnetisable** adj. **magnetisation** /-zay-shuhn/ n.

**magnetism** /**mag**-nuh-,tiz-uhm/ n. **1 a** magnetic phenomena and their science. **b** property of producing these. **2** attraction; personal charm.

**magneto** /mag-**nee**-toh/ n. (pl. **-s**) electric generator using permanent magnets (esp. for the ignition of an internal-combustion engine). [abbreviation of *magneto-electric*]

**Magnificat** /mag-**nif**-uh-,kat, -,kaht/ n. hymn of the Virgin Mary used as a canticle at vespers. [from its opening word, = (my soul) magnifies (the Lord)]

**magnification** /,mag-nuh-fuh-**kay**-shuhn/ n. **1** magnifying or being magnified. **2** degree of this.

**magnificent** /mag-**nif**-uh-suhnt/ adj. **1** splendid, stately; sumptuously constructed or adorned. **2** colloq. fine, excellent. □ **magnificence** n. **magnificently** adv. [Latin *magnificus* from *magnus* great]

**magnify** /**mag**-nuh-,fuy/ v. (**-ies, -ied**) **1** make (a thing) appear larger than it is, as with a lens. **2** exaggerate. **3** intensify. **4** archaic glorify, extol. □ **magnifiable** adj. **magnifier** n. [Latin: related to MAGNIFICENT]

**magnitude** /**mag**-nuh-,tyood, -,chood/ n. **1** largeness. **2** size. **3** importance. **4 a** degree of brightness of a star. **b** class of stars arranged according to this (*of the third magnitude*). □ **of the first magnitude** very important. [Latin *magnus* great]

**magnolia** /mag-**noh**-lee-uh/ n. **1** tree with dark green foliage and waxy scented flowers. **2** creamy-pink colour. [*Magnol*, name of a botanist]

**magnum** /**mag**-nuhm/ n. (pl. **-s**) wine bottle twice the normal size. [Latin, neuter of *magnus* great]

**magnum opus** /,mag-nuhm **oh**-puhs/ n. great work of art, literature, etc., esp. an artist's most important work. [Latin]

**magpie** /**mag**-puy/ n. **1** black and white bird, widespread in Australia, having an extremely melodious, carolling call. **2** unrelated European and American crow with a long tail and black and white plumage. **3** an idle chatterer. **4** person who collects things indiscriminately. [from *Mag*, abbreviation of *Margaret*, obsolete *pie* magpie]

**magpie goose** n. large black and white bird with a resonant honking call found near fresh water in northern Australia.

**magpie lark** n. black and white bird, widespread in Australia, which has a loud piping call and which builds a mud nest in a tree.

**magsman** /**magz**-muhn/ n. **1** confidence trickster. **2** a talker; raconteur. [survival of British slang *magsman* swindler]

**magus** /**may**-guhs/ n. (pl. **magi** /**may**-juy/) **1** priest of ancient Persia. **2** sorcerer. **3** (**the Magi**) the 'wise men' from the East (Matt. 2:1–12). [Persian *magus*]

**mag wheel** n. colloq. magnesium alloy wheel for a car.

**maharaja** /,mah-huh-**rah**-juh/ n. (also **maharajah**) hist. title of some Indian princes. [Hindi, = great rajah]

**maharani** /,mah-huh-**rah**-nee/ n. (pl. **-s**) hist. maharaja's wife or widow. [Hindi, = great rani]

**maharishi** /,mah-huh-**rish**-ee/ n. (pl. **-s**) great Hindu sage or spiritual leader. [Hindi]

**mahatma** /muh-**hat**-muh/ n. **1** (in India etc.) revered person. **2** one of a class of persons supposed by some Buddhists to have preternatural powers. [Sanskrit, = great soul]

**mah-jong** /mah-**jong**/ n. (also **-jongg**) game played with 136 or 144 pieces called tiles. [Chinese dial. *ma-tsiang* sparrows]

**mahogany** /muh-**hog**-uh-nee/ — n. (pl. **-ies**) **1** any eucalypt, including jarrah, yielding a hard, usu. reddish-brown timber. **2** tropical tree yielding a similar wood used for furniture. **3** the wood of these trees. **4** reddish-brown colour. — adj. made of or relating to mahogany. [origin unknown]

**mahout** /muh-**howt**/ n. (in India etc.) elephant-driver. [Hindi from Sanskrit]

**maid** n. **1** female servant. **2** archaic or poet. girl, young woman. [abbreviation of MAIDEN]

**maiden** /**may**-duhn/ n. **1 a** archaic or poet. girl; young unmarried woman. **b** (attrib.) unmarried (*maiden aunt*). **2** = MAIDEN OVER. **3** (often attrib.) a horse that has never won a race. **b** race open only to such horses. **4** (attrib.) first (*maiden speech; maiden voyage*). □ **maidenhood** n. **maidenly** adj. [Old English]

**maidenhair** n. fern with hairlike black stalks and delicate fronds.

**maidenhead** n. **1** virginity. **2** hymen.

**maiden name** n. woman's surname before marriage.

**maiden over** n. over in cricket in which no runs are scored.

**mail¹** — n. **1 a** letters and parcels etc. carried by post. **b** postal system. **c** one complete delivery or collection of mail. **2** email. **3** vehicle carrying mail. **4** colloq. information, rumour (*the mail is that the government is planning a new tax*). — v. send by post or email. [French *male* wallet]

**mail²** — *n.* armour of interlinked metal rings or plates. — *v.* clothe with or as if with mail. [French *maille* from Latin *macula*]

**mailing list** *n.* list of people to whom advertising matter etc. is posted.

**mailman** *n.* person who delivers the mail; postman.

**mail order** *n.* purchase of goods by post.

**maim** *v.* cripple, disable, mutilate. [French *mahaignier*]

**main** — *adj.* **1** chief, principal. **2** exerted to the full (*by main force*). — *n.* **1** principal duct etc. for water, sewage, etc. **2** (usu. in *pl.*; prec. by *the*) **a** central distribution network for electricity, gas, water, etc. **b** domestic electricity supply as distinct from batteries. **3** *poet.* high seas (*Spanish Main*). □ **in the main** mostly. [Old English]

**mainframe** *n.* **1** central processing unit of a large computer. **2** (often *attrib.*) large computer system.

**mainland** — *n.* **1** the continent of Australia, as opposed to any of the offshore islands and esp. Tasmania. **2** any other large continuous extent of land, excluding neighbouring islands. — *adj.* of or pertaining to the Australian or other mainland (*mainland Australians*).

**mainlander** *n.* person who dwells on the Australian mainland.

**mainline** *v.* (**-ning**) *colloq.* **1** take drugs intravenously. **2** inject (drugs) intravenously. □ **mainliner** *n.*

**mainly** /**mayn**-lee/ *adv.* mostly; chiefly.

**mainspring** *n.* **1** principal spring of a watch, clock, etc. **2** chief motivating force; incentive.

**mainstay** *n.* chief support (*he is my mainstay in my trouble*).

**mainstream** *n.* (often *attrib.*) ultimately prevailing trend in opinion, fashion, etc.

**maintain** /mayn-**tayn**/ *v.* **1** cause to continue; keep up (an activity etc.). **2** support by work, expenditure, etc. **3** assert as true. **4** preserve (a house, machine, etc.) in good repair. **5** provide a living or support for (*maintains his aged parents*). [Latin *manus* hand, *teneo* hold]

**maintenance** /**mayn**-tuh-nuhns/ *n.* **1** maintaining or being maintained. **2 a** provision of the means to support life. **b** alimony. [French: related to MAINTAIN]

**maisonette** /ˌmay-zuh-**net**/ *n.* **1** semi-detached house. **2** a flat on more than one floor. [French *maisonnette* diminutive of *maison* house]

**maize** *n.* **1** cereal plant of N. America. **2** cobs or grain of this. [French or Spanish]

**majestic** /muh-**jes**-tik/ *adj.* stately and dignified; imposing. □ **majestically** *adv.*

**majesty** /**maj**-uh-stee/ *n.* (*pl.* **-ies**) **1** stateliness, dignity, or authority, esp. of bearing, language, etc. **2** (**Majesty**) (prec. by *His, Her, Your*) forms of description or address for a king or queen. [Latin *majestas*: related to MAJOR]

**major** /**may**-juh/ — *adj.* **1** relatively great in size, intensity, scope, or importance. **2** (of surgery) serious. **3** *Mus.* **a** (of a scale) having intervals of a semitone above its third and seventh notes. **b** (of an interval) greater by a semitone than a minor interval (*major third*). **c** (of a key) based on a major scale. **4** of full legal age (see Appendix 1). — *n.* **1** military rank (see Appendix 1). **2** person of full legal age. **3** university student's main subject or course. **4** *Aust. Rules* a goal, scored when the ball is kicked between the central goal-posts and earning six points. — *v.* (foll. by *in*) study or qualify in (a subject) as one's main subject (*majored in English*). [Latin, comparative of *magnus* great]

**major-general** *n.* army officer next below a lieutenant general.

**majority** /muh-jo-ruh-**tee**/ *n.* (*pl.* **-ies**) **1** (usu. foll. by *of*) greater number or part. **2 a** number of votes by which a candidate wins. **b** party etc. receiving the greater number of votes. **3** full legal age. [medieval Latin: related to MAJOR]

━━━━━━━━━━━━━━━━━━━━━━━━

■ **Usage** In sense 1, *majority* is strictly used only with countable nouns, as in *the majority of people*, and not with mass nouns, e.g. *the majority of the work*.

━━━━━━━━━━━━━━━━━━━━━━━━

**majority rule** *n.* principle that the greater number should exercise the greater power.

**Major Mitchell cockatoo** *n.* (also **Leadbeater's cockatoo**) pink and white cockatoo with a scarlet crest and central yellow band, occurring in arid and semi-arid Australia. [T.L. *Mitchell*, explorer (d. 1855)]

**makarrata** /ˌmak-uh-**rah**-tuh/ *n.* ceremonial ritual symbolising the restoration of peace between Aboriginal tribes after a dispute. [Yolngu *makarrarta*]

**make¹** — *v.* (**-king**; *past* and *past part.* **made**) **1** construct; create; form from parts or other substances. **2** cause or compel (*made me do it*). **3 a** cause to exist; bring about (*made a noise*). **b** cause to become or seem (*made him angry*; *made a fool of me*; *made him a Cardinal*). **4** compose; prepare; write (*made her will*; *made a film*). **5** constitute; amount to; be reckoned as (*2 and 2 make 4*). **6 a** undertake (*made a promise*; *make an effort*). **b** perform (an action etc.) (*made a face*;

*made a bow).* **7** gain, acquire, procure (money, a living, a profit, etc.). **8** prepare (tea, coffee, a meal, etc.). **9 a** arrange (a bed) for use. **b** arrange and light materials for (a fire). **10 a** proceed *(made towards the river).* **b** (foll. by *to* + infin.) act as if with the intention to *(he made to go).* **11** *colloq.* **a** arrive at (a place) or in time for (a train etc.). **b** manage to attend; manage to attend on (a certain day) or at (a certain time) *(couldn't make the meeting last week; can make any day except Friday).* **c** achieve a place in *(made the first eleven).* **12** establish or enact (a distinction, rule, law, etc.). **13** consider to be; estimate as *(what do you make the total?).* **14** secure the success or advancement of *(his second novel made him; it made my day).* **15** accomplish (a distance, speed, score, etc.). **16 a** become by development *(made a great leader).* **b** serve as *(makes a useful seat).* **17** (usu. foll. by *out*) represent as *(makes him out a liar).* **18** form in the mind *(make a decision).* **19** (foll. by *it* + compl.) **a** determine, establish, or choose *(let's make it Tuesday).* **b** bring to (a chosen value etc.) *(make it a dozen).* — *n.* **1** type or brand of manufacture. **2** way a thing is made. □ **make away with 1** = *make off with.* **2** = *do away with.* **make believe** pretend. **make the best of** see BEST. **make a clean breast** see BREAST. **make a clean sweep** see SWEEP. **make a day** (or **night** etc.) **of it** devote a whole day (or night etc.) to an activity. **make do 1** manage with the inadequate means available. **2** (foll. by *with*) manage with (something) as an inferior substitute. **make for 1** tend to result in *(a good conscience makes for a good night's sleep).* **2** proceed towards (a place or thing) *(made for home; made straight for the lamingtons).* **3** attack. **make good 1** compensate for, pay for *(he made good my losses).* **2** fulfil (a promise); effect (an intended action etc.). **3** achieve success *(started as a down-and-out and then made good).* **make the grade** succeed. **make it** *colloq.* **1** succeed in reaching, esp. in time. **2** succeed. **make it up 1** be reconciled. **2** remedy a deficit. **make it up to** remedy negligence, an injury, etc. to (a person). **make love** see LOVE. **make merry** see MERRY. **make money** acquire wealth. **make the most of** see MOST. **make much** (or **little**) **of** treat as important (or unimportant). **make a name for oneself** see NAME. **make no bones about** see BONE. **make nothing of 1** treat as trifling. **2** be unable to understand, use, or deal with. **make of 1** construct from. **2** conclude from or about

*(can you make anything of it?).* **make off** depart hastily. **make off with** carry away; steal. **make or break** cause the success or ruin of. **make out 1** discern or understand. **2** assert; pretend. **3** *colloq.* progress; fare. **4** write out (a cheque etc.) or fill in (a form). **make over 1** transfer the possession of. **2** refashion. **make up 1** act to overcome (a deficiency). **2** complete (an amount etc.). **3** (foll. by *for*) compensate for. **4** be reconciled. **5** put together; prepare *(made up the medicine).* **6** concoct (a story). **7** apply cosmetics (to). **8** prepare (a bed) with fresh linen. **make up one's mind** decide. **make up to** curry favour with. **make way 1** (often foll. by *for*) allow room to pass. **2** (foll. by *for*) be superseded by. **make one's way** go; prosper. **on the make** *colloq.* intent on gain. [Old English]

**make²** *v.* initiate (an Aboriginal boy) ceremonially into manhood, esp. in the phrase *make a (young) man.*

**make-believe** — *n.* pretence. — *attrib. adj.* pretended.

**maker** *n.* **1** person who makes. **2** (**Maker**) God.

**makeshift** — *adj.* temporary. — *n.* temporary substitute or device.

**make-up** *n.* **1** cosmetics, as used generally or by actors. **2** character, temperament, etc. **3** composition (of a thing).

**making** *n.* (in *pl.*) **1** earnings; profit. **2** essential qualities or ingredients *(has the makings of a pilot).* **3** *colloq.* paper and tobacco as materials for rolling a cigarette. □ **be the making of** ensure the success of. **in the making** in the course of being made or formed. [Old English: related to MAKE¹]

**mal-** *comb. form* **1 a** bad, badly *(malpractice; maltreat).* **b** faulty *(malfunction).* **2** not *(maladroit).* [French *mal* badly, from Latin *male*]

**malachite** /**mal**-uh-ˌkuyt/ *n.* green mineral used for ornament. [Greek *molokhitis*]

**maladjusted** /ˌmal-uh-**jus**-tuhd/ *adj.* (of a person) unable to adapt to or cope with the demands of a social environment. □ **maladjustment** *n.*

**maladminister** /ˌmal-uhd-**min**-uh-stuh/ *v.* manage badly or improperly. □ **maladministration** /-**stray**-shuhn/ *n.*

**maladroit** /ˌmal-uh-**droit**, **mal**-/ *adj.* clumsy; bungling. [French: related to MAL-]

**malady** /**mal**-uh-dee/ *n.* (*pl.* **-ies**) ailment, disease. [French *malade* sick]

**malaise** /muh-**layz**/ *n.* **1** general bodily discomfort or lassitude. **2** feeling of unease or demoralisation. [French: related to EASE]

**malapropism** /mal-uh-prop-,iz-uhm/ n. comical misuse of a word in mistake for one sounding similar, e.g. *alligator* for *allegory*. [Mrs *Malaprop*, name of a character in Sheridan's *The Rivals*]

**malaria** /muh-lair-ree-uh/ n. recurrent fever caused by a parasite transmitted by a mosquito bite. □ **malarial** *adj.* [Italian, = bad air]

**malarkey** /muh-lah-kee/ n. colloq. humbug; nonsense. [origin unknown]

**Malay** /muh-lay/ — n. **1** member of a people predominating in Malaysia and Indonesia. **2** their language. — *adj.* of this people or language. □ **Malayan** n. & *adj.* [Malay *maláyu*]

**malcontent** /mal-kuhn-,tent/ — n. discontented person. — *adj.* discontented. [French: related to MAL-]

**male** — *adj.* **1** of the sex that can beget offspring by fertilisation or insemination. **2** of men or male animals, plants, etc.; masculine. **3** (of plants or flowers) containing stamens but no pistil. **4** (of parts of machinery etc.) designed to enter or fill the corresponding hollow part (*male screw*). — n. male person or animal. □ **maleness** n. [Latin *masculus* from *mas* a male]

**male chauvinist** n. = CHAUVINIST 2.

**malediction** /,mal-uh-dik-shuhn/ n. **1** curse. **2** utterance of a curse. □ **maledictory** *adj.* [Latin *maledictio*: related to MAL-]

**malefactor** /mal-uh-,fak-tuh/ n. criminal; evil-doer. □ **malefaction** /-fak-shuhn/ n. [Latin *male* badly, *facio fact-* do]

**male menopause** n. colloq. crisis of potency, confidence, etc., supposed to afflict some men in middle life.

**malevolent** /muh-lev-uh-luhnt/ *adj.* wishing evil to others. □ **malevolence** n. **malevolently** *adv.* [Latin *volo* wish]

**malformation** /,mal-faw-may-shuhn/ n. faulty formation. □ **malformed** /-fawmd/ *adj.*

**malfunction** /mal-**fungk**-shuhn/ — n. failure to function normally (*a computer malfunction*). — v. fail to function normally.

**malice** /mal-uhs/ n. **1** desire to harm or cause difficulty to others; ill-will. **2** Law harmful intent. [Latin *malus* bad]

**malice aforethought** n. Law intention to commit a crime, esp. murder.

**malicious** /muh-lish-uhs/ *adj.* given to or arising from malice. □ **maliciously** *adv.*

**malign** /muh-**luyn**/ — *adj.* **1** (of a thing) injurious. **2** (of a disease) malignant. **3** malevolent. — v. speak ill of; slander. □ **malignity** /muh-**lig**-nuh-tee/ n. [Latin *malus* bad]

**malignant** /muh-**lig**-nuhnt/ *adj.* **1 a** (of a disease) very virulent or infectious. **b** (of a tumour) spreading or recurring; cancerous. **2** harmful; feeling or showing intense ill-will. □ **malignancy** n. **malignantly** *adv.* [Latin: related to MALIGN]

**malinger** /muh-**ling**-guh/ v. pretend to be ill, esp. to escape work. □ **malingerer** n. [French *malingre* sickly]

**mall** /mawl, mal/ n. **1** sheltered walk or promenade. **2** shopping precinct. [*The Mall*, street in London]

**mallard** /mal-ahd/ n. (*pl.* same) a kind of wild duck. [French]

**malleable** /mal-ee-uh-buhl/ *adj.* **1** (of metal etc.) that can be shaped by hammering. **2** easily influenced; pliable. □ **malleability** /-bil-uh-tee/ n. **malleably** *adv.* [medieval Latin: related to MALLET]

**mallee** /mal-ee/ n. **1 a** any of many eucalypts characteristically small and having several trunks or stems arising from a common base; highly ornamental examples include: bell-fruit mallee, mottlecah, Southern Cross silver mallee, square fruit mallee. **b** (also **mallee scrub**) vegetation community characterised by the presence of such trees. **2** (also **mallee country, desert, district, land**) any of the semi-arid areas of Australia (esp. in Victoria), the principal natural vegetation of which is mallee scrub. □ **dry as a mallee cow** colloq. extremely thirsty. **fit** (or **strong**) **as a mallee bull** colloq. fighting fit (or extremely strong). [probably Wemba-wemba *mali*]

**mallee fowl** n. (also **mallee hen; lowan, gnow**) mottled grey, brown, and white bird of dry, southern, inland Australia which builds its nest in large mounds.

**mallee roller** n. heavy roller, usu. a tree trunk, drawn by horses or bullocks and used to crush and flatten mallee scrub.

**mallee root** n. (also **mallee stump**) large woody rootstock of a mallee eucalypt, highly valued as firewood for the intense heat it gives.

**mallee stump** n. = MALLEE ROOT.

**mallet¹** /mal-uht/ n. **1** hammer, usu. of wood. **2** implement for striking a croquet or polo ball. [Latin *malleus* hammer]

**mallet²** n. any of several WA eucalypts with very hard flexible wood and tannin-rich bark. [Nyungar *malard*]

**malnourished** /mal-**nu**-risht/ *adj.* suffering from malnutrition. □ **malnourishment** n.

**malnutrition** /,mal-nyoo-**trish**-uhn/ n. condition resulting from the lack of foods necessary for health.

**malodorous** /mal-**oh**-duh-ruhs/ adj. evil-smelling.

**malpractice** /mal-**prak**-tuhs/ n. improper, negligent, or criminal professional conduct, esp. by a medical practitioner.

**malt** /mawlt, molt/ — n. **1** barley, or other grain, steeped, germinated, and dried, for brewing etc. **2** any liquor made from malt, as beer, malt whisky, etc. — v. convert (grain) into malt. □ **malty** adj. (**-ier, -iest**). [Old English]

**Maltese** /mawl-**teez**, mol-/ — n. (pl. same) native or language of Malta. — adj. of Malta.

**Maltese cross** n. cross with the arms broadening outwards, often indented at the ends.

**Malthusian** /mal-**thoo**-zee-uhn/ adj. of Malthus's doctrine that the population should be restricted so as to prevent an increase beyond its means of subsistence. □ **Malthusianism** n. [Malthus, name of a clergyman and economist]

**maltose** /**mawl**-tohz, **mol**-/ n. sugar made from starch by enzymes in malt, saliva, etc. [Latin mamma breast]

**maltreat** /mal-**treet**/ v. ill-treat. □ **maltreatment** n. [French: related to MAL-]

**maluka** /muh-**loo**-kuh/ n. (also **maluga**) person in charge; boss. [Djingulu marluga old man]

**Malyangaba** /**mah**-lyah-,ngah-pu/ n. an Aboriginal language spoken in a wide area in eastern SA west of Lake Frome and stretching into northern NSW: now extinct.

**mammal** /**mam**-uhl/ n. warm-blooded vertebrate of the class secreting milk to feed its young. □ **mammalian** /ma-**may**-lee-uhn/ adj. & n. [Latin mamma breast]

**mammary** /**mam**-uh-ree/ adj. of the breasts.

**mammogram** /**mam**-uh-,gram/ n. image obtained by mammography. [Latin mamma breast]

**mammography** /ma-**mog**-ruh-fee/ n. X-ray technique for screening the breasts for tumours etc.

**Mammon** /**mam**-uhn/ n. wealth regarded as a god or evil influence. [Aramaic māmōn]

**mammoth** /**mam**-uhth/ — n. large extinct elephant with a hairy coat and curved tusks. — adj. huge. [Russian]

**man** — n. (pl. **men**) **1** adult human male. **2 a** human being; person (no man is perfect; no man is an island). **b** the human race (man is mortal). **3 a** workman (the manager spoke to the men). **b** manservant, valet. **4** person showing characteristics associated with males (be

a man!). **5** (usu. in pl.) soldiers, sailors, etc., esp. non-officers. **6 a** an individual, usu. male, person (fought to the last man). **b** suitable or appropriate person; expert (he is your man; the man for the job). **7 a** husband (man and wife). **b** colloq. boyfriend, lover. **8** human being of a specified type or historical period (Renaissance man; Peking man). **9** person pursued; opponent (police caught their man). — v. (**-nn-**) **1** supply with a person or people for work or defence. **2** work, service, or defend (man the pumps). **3** fill (a post). □ **as one man** in unison. **be one's own man** be independent. **man and boy** from childhood (man and boy, I've known hardship). **separate** (or **sort out**) **the men from the boys** colloq. find those who are truly virile, competent, etc. **to a man** without exception. □ **manlike** adj. [Old English]

**mana** /**mah**-nuh/ n. **1** power; authority; prestige. **2** supernatural or magical power. [Maori]

**manacle** /**man**-uh-kuhl/ — n. (usu. in pl.) **1** fetter for the hand; handcuff. **2** any form of restraint. — v. (**-ling**) fetter with manacles. [Latin manus hand]

**manage** /**man**-ij/ v. (**-ging**) **1** organise; regulate; be in charge of. **2** succeed in achieving; contrive (managed to come; managed a smile; managed to ruin the day). **3** (often foll. by with) succeed with limited resources etc.; be able to cope. **4** succeed in controlling (cannot manage their teenage son). **5** (often prec. by can etc.) **a** cope with (can you manage by yourself?). **b** be free to attend on or at (can manage Monday). **6** use or wield (a tool, weapon, etc.). □ **manageable** adj. [Latin manus hand]

**management** n. **1** process or an instance of managing or being managed. **2 a** administration of business or public undertakings. **b** people engaged in this, esp. those controlling a workforce.

**manager** n. **1** person controlling or administering a business or part of a business. **2** person controlling the affairs, training, etc., of a person or team in sports, entertainment, etc. **3** person of a specified level of skill in household or financial affairs etc. (a good manager). □ **managerial** /,man-uh-**jeer**-ree-uhl/ adj.

**managing director** n. director with executive control or authority.

**mañana** /man-**yah**-nuh/ — adv. tomorrow (esp. to indicate procrastination). — n. indefinite future. [Spanish]

**manchester** /**man**-ches-tuh/ n. **1** household linen. **2** department of a shop

**mandala** /**man**-duh-luh/ *n.* circular figure as a religious symbol of the universe. [Sanskrit]

**mandarin** /**man**-duh-ruhn, man-duh-**rin**/ *n.* **1** (**Mandarin**) official language of China. **2** *hist.* Chinese official. **3** powerful person, esp. a top civil servant. **4** (also **mandarine** /man-duh-**reen**/) small sweet thick-skinned citrus fruit like an orange. [Hindi *mantrī*]

**mandate** /**man**-dayt/ — *n.* **1** official command or instruction. **2** authority given by electors to a government, trade union, etc. **3** authority to act for another. — *v.* (**-ting**) instruct (a delegate) how to act or vote. [Latin *mandatum*, past part. of *mando* command]

**mandatory** /**man**-duh-tuh-ree, -tree/ *adj.* **1** compulsory. **2** of or conveying a command. □ **mandatorily** *adv.* [Latin: related to MANDATE]

**mandible** /**man**-duh-buhl/ *n.* **1** jaw, esp. the lower jaw in mammals and fishes. **2** upper or lower part of a bird's beak. **3** either half of the crushing organ in the mouth-parts of an insect etc. [Latin *mando* chew]

**mandolin** /ˌman-duh-**lin**/ *n.* a kind of lute with paired metal strings plucked with a plectrum. □ **mandolinist** *n.* [French from Italian]

**mandrake** /**man**-drayk/ *n.* poisonous narcotic plant with large yellow fruit and a root once thought to resemble the human form and to shriek when uprooted. [Greek *mandragoras*]

**mandrill** /**man**-dril/ *n.* large W. African baboon. [origin uncertain]

**mane** *n.* **1** long hair on the neck of a horse, lion, etc. **2** *colloq.* person's long hair. [Old English]

**maned duck** *n.* (also **maned goose**) = WOOD DUCK.

**manège** /ma-**nayzh**/ *n.* (also **manege**) **1** riding-school. **2** movements of a trained horse. **3** horsemanship. [Italian: related to MANAGE]

**man fern** *n.* (in Tasmania) = TREE-FERN. [perhaps with reference to a supposedly male characteristic, as greater size]

**manful** *adj.* brave; resolute. □ **manfully** *adv.*

**manganese** /ˌmang-guh-ˈneez/ *n.* **1** grey brittle metallic element. **2** black mineral oxide of this used in glass-making etc. [Italian: related to MAGNESIA]

**mange** /maynj/ *n.* skin disease in hairy and woolly animals. [French *mangeue* itch, from Latin *manduco* chew]

**manger** /**mayn**-juh/ *n.* box or trough for horses or cattle to feed from. [Latin: related to MANGE]

**mangle**[1] /**mang**-guhl/ *v.* (**-ling**) **1** hack or mutilate by blows. **2** spoil (a text etc.) by gross blunders. **3** cut roughly so as to disfigure. [Anglo-French *ma(ha)ngler*: probably related to MAIM]

**mangle**[2] /**mang**-guhl/ — *n.* machine of two or more cylinders for squeezing water from and pressing wet clothes. — *v.* (**-ling**) press (clothes etc.) in a mangle. [Dutch *mangel*]

**mango** /**mang**-goh/ *n.* (*pl.* **-es** or **-s**) **1** tropical fruit with sweet yellowish flesh. **2** tree bearing this. **3** used *attrib.* as an emblem of midsummer madness (*mango season*; *mango madness*). [Tamil *mānkāy*]

**mangrove** /**mang**-grohv/ *n.* tropical tree or shrub growing in shore-mud with many tangled roots above ground. [origin unknown]

**mangrove crab** *n.* = MUD CRAB.

**mangrove jack** *n.* marine and estuarine food-fish usu. found amongst mangrove roots in northern Australia.

**mangy** /**mayn**-jee/ *adj.* (**-ier**, **-iest**) **1** having mange. **2** squalid; shabby.

**manhandle** *v.* (**-ling**) **1** handle (a person) roughly. **2** move (heavy objects) by human effort alone.

**manhole** *n.* covered opening in a pavement, sewer, etc., for workmen to gain access.

**manhood** *n.* **1** state of being a man rather than a child or woman. **2 a** manliness; courage. **b** penis. **c** a man's sexual potency. **3** men of a country etc. **4** the state of being human.

**man-hour** *n.* work done by one person in one hour.

**manhunt** *n.* organised search for a person, esp. a criminal.

**mania** /**may**-nee-uh/ *n.* **1** mental illness marked by excitement and violence. **2** (often foll. by *for*) excessive enthusiasm; obsession. [Greek *mainomai* be mad]

**-mania** *comb. form* **1** denoting a special type of mental disorder (*megalomania*). **2** denoting enthusiasm or admiration (*Beatlemania*).

**maniac** /**may**-nee-ˌak/ — *n.* **1** *colloq.* person behaving wildly (*too many maniacs on the road*). **2** *colloq.* obsessive enthusiast. **3** person suffering from mania. — *adj.* of or behaving like a maniac. □ **maniacal** /muh-**nuy**-uh-kuhl/ *adj.* **maniacally** /muh-**nuy**-uh-klee/ *adv.*

**-maniac** *comb. form* forming adjectives and nouns meaning 'affected with -mania' or 'a person affected with -mania' (*nymphomaniac*).

**manic** /man-ik/ adj. **1** of or affected by mania. **2** colloq. wildly excited; frenzied; excitable. □ **manically** adv.

**manic-depressive** — adj. relating to a mental disorder with alternating periods of elation and depression. — n. person with such a disorder. □ **manic depression** n.

**manicure** /man-uh-,kyoor/ — n. cosmetic treatment of the hands and fingernails. — v. (**-ring**) give a manicure to (the hands or a person). □ **manicurist** n. [Latin manus hand, cura care]

**manifest** /man-uh-,fest/ — adj. clear or obvious to the eye or mind. — v. **1** show (a quality or feeling) by one's acts etc. (manifested his disgust by walking away). **2** show plainly to the eye or mind. **3** be evidence of; prove. **4** refl. (of a thing) reveal itself. **5** (of a ghost) appear. — n. cargo or passenger list. □ **manifestation** /-stay-shuhn/ n. **manifestly** adv. [Latin manifestus]

**manifesto** /,man-uh-**fes**-toh/ n. (pl. **-s**) declaration of policies, esp. by a political party. [Italian: related to MANIFEST]

**manifold** /man-uh-,fohld/ — adj. **1** many and various (manifold vexations). **2** having various forms, parts, applications, etc. — n. **1** manifold thing. **2** pipe or chamber branching into several openings. [Old English: related to MANY, -FOLD]

**manikin** /man-uh-kuhn/ n. (also **mannikin**) **1** little man; dwarf. **2** anatomical model of the human body. [Dutch]

**manila** /muh-**nil**-uh/ n. **1** (in full **manila hemp**) strong fibre of a kind of tree native to the Philippines. **2** strong brown paper made from this and used for envelopes, folders, etc. [Manila in the Philippines]

**man in the street** n. ordinary average person (as distinct from an expert).

**manipulate** /muh-**nip**-yuh-,layt/ v. (**-ting**) **1** handle, esp. with skill. **2** manage (a person, situation, etc.) to one's own advantage, esp. unfairly. **3** move (part of a patient's body) by hand in order to increase flexion etc. □ **manipulable** /-luh-buhl/ adj. **manipulation** /-lay-shuhn/ n. **manipulator** n. [Latin manus hand]

**manipulative** /muh-**nip**-yuh-luh-tiv/ adj. tending to exploit a situation, person, etc., for one's own ends. □ **manipulatively** adv.

**mankind** n. **1** /,man-**kuynd**/ the human species. **2** /**man**-kuynd/ male people as distinct from female.

**manly** adj. (**-ier**, **-iest**) **1** having qualities associated with a man (e.g. strength and courage). **2** befitting a man. □ **manliness** n.

**manna** /man-uh/ n. **1** substance miraculously supplied as food to the Israelites in the wilderness (Exod. 16). **2** unexpected benefit (esp. manna from heaven). **3** white, sugary, edible substance exuded by many eucalypts. **4** = LERP. [Old English ultimately from Hebrew]

**manna gum** n. any of several eucalypts yielding manna (see MANNA 3).

**manned** adj. (of a spacecraft etc.) having a human crew.

**mannequin** /man-uh-kuhn, -kwuhn/ n. **1** fashion model. **2** window dummy. [French, = MANIKIN]

**manner** /man-uh/ n. **1** way a thing is done or happens. **2** (in pl.) **a** social behaviour (good manners). **b** polite behaviour (has no manners). **c** modes of life; social conditions. **3** outward bearing, way of speaking, etc. (had an imperious manner). **4** style (in the manner of Rembrandt). **5** kind, sort (not by any manner of means). □ **in a manner of speaking** in a way; so to speak. **to the manner born** colloq. naturally at ease in a particular situation etc. [Latin manus hand]

**mannered** adj. **1** (in comb.) having specified manners (ill-mannered). **2** esp. Art full of mannerisms (writes a mannered prose).

**mannerism** n. **1** habitual gesture or way of speaking etc; an idiosyncrasy. **2 a** stylistic trick in art etc. **b** excessive use of these. □ **mannerist** n.

**mannerly** adj. well-mannered, polite.

**mannish** adj. **1** (of a woman) masculine in appearance or manner. **2** characteristic of a man. □ **mannishly** adv.

**manoeuvre** /muh-**noo**-vuh/ — n. **1** planned and controlled movement of a vehicle or body of troops etc. **2** (in pl.) large-scale exercise of troops, ships, etc. **3** agile or skilful movement. **4** artful plan. — v. (**-ring**) **1** move (a thing, esp. a vehicle) carefully. **2** perform or cause (troops etc.) to perform manoeuvres. **3 a** (usu. foll. by into, out of, etc.) manipulate (a person, thing, etc.) by scheming or adroitness. **b** use artifice. □ **manoeuvrable** adj. **manoeuvrability** /-vruh-**bil**-uh-tee/ n. [medieval Latin manu operor work with the hand]

**man of letters** n. scholar or author.

**man of the world** see WORLD.

**man-of-war** n. (pl. **men-of-war**) warship.

**man on the land** n. person who owns or manages a rural property, esp. as representative of those engaged in rural occupations.

**manor** /man-uh/ n. **1** (also **manor house**)

chiefly *Brit.* large country house with lands. **2** *hist.* feudal lordship over lands. □ **manorial** /muh-**naw**-ree-uhl/ *adj.* [Latin *maneo* remain]

**manpower** *n.* **1** power generated by a man working. **2** number of people available for work, service, etc.

**manqué** /mong-kay/ *adj.* (placed after noun) that might have been but is not (*an actor manqué*). [French]

**mansard** /man-sahd/ *n.* roof with four sloping sides, each of which becomes steeper halfway down. [*Mansard*, name of an architect]

**manse** /mans/ *n.* ecclesiastical residence, esp. a Presbyterian minister's house. [medieval Latin: related to MANOR]

**manservant** *n.* (*pl.* **menservants**) male servant.

**-manship** /-muhn-ship/ *suffix* forming nouns denoting skill in a subject or activity (*craftsmanship; gamesmanship*).

**mansion** /man-shuhn/ *n.* large grand house. [Latin: related to MANOR]

**manslaughter** *n.* unintentional (but not accidental) culpable killing of a human being.

**mantel** /man-tuhl/ *n.* mantelpiece. [var. of MANTLE]

**mantelpiece** *n.* structure of wood, marble, etc. above and around a fireplace.

**mantilla** /man-**til**-uh/ *n.* lace scarf worn by Spanish women over the hair and shoulders. [Spanish: related to MANTLE]

**mantis** /man-tuhs/ *n.* (*pl.* same or **mantises**) (in full **praying mantis**) predatory insect that holds its forelegs like hands folded in prayer. [Greek, = prophet]

**mantissa** /man-**tis**-uh/ *n.* part of a logarithm after the decimal point. [Latin, = makeweight]

**Mantjiltjara** /**mahn**-chil-,jah-ru/ *n.* a dialect of the WESTERN DESERT LANGUAGE.

**mantle** /man-tuhl/ *n.* **1** loose sleeveless cloak. **2** a covering (*mantle of snow*). **3** fragile lacelike tube fixed round a gas-jet to give an incandescent light. **4** region between the crust and the core of the earth. — *v.* (**-ling**) clothe; conceal, envelop (*mist mantled the peak; he was mantled in gloom*). [Latin *mantellum* cloak]

**man-to-man** — *adj.* frank, candid (*a man-to-man talk between father and son*). — *adv.* candidly.

**mantra** /man-truh/ *n.* **1** Hindu or Buddhist devotional incantation. **2** Vedic hymn. [Sanskrit, = instrument of thought]

**manual** /man-yoo-uhl/ — *adj.* **1** of or done with the hands (*manual labour*). **2**

**a** worked by hand, not automatically (*manual gear-change*). **b** (of a vehicle) worked by manual gear-change. — *n.* **1** reference book. **2** organ keyboard played with the hands, not the feet. **3** *colloq.* vehicle with manual transmission. □ **manually** *adv.* [Latin *manus* hand]

**manufacture** /,man-yuh-**fak**-chuh/ — *n.* **1** making of articles, esp. in a factory etc. **2** branch of industry (*woollen manufacture*). — *v.* (**-ring**) **1** make (articles), esp. on an industrial scale. **2** invent or fabricate (evidence, a story, etc.). **3** make or produce (literature, art, etc.) in a mechanical way. □ **manufacturer** *n.* [Latin *manufactum* made by hand]

**manure** /muh-**nyoor**/ — *n.* fertiliser, esp. dung. — *v.* (**-ring**) apply manure to (land etc.). [Anglo-French *mainoverer* MANOEUVRE]

**manuscript** /man-yuh-skript/ — *n.* **1** text written by hand. **2** author's hand-written or typed text. **3** handwritten form (*produced in manuscript*). — *adj.* written by hand. [medieval Latin *manuscriptus* written by hand]

**Manx** /mangks/ — *adj.* of the Isle of Man. — *n.* **1** former Celtic language of the Isle of Man. **2** (prec. by *the*; treated as *pl.*) Manx people. [Old Norse]

**many** /men-ee/ — *adj.* (**more**; **most**) great in number; numerous (*many people*). — *n.* (as *pl.*) many people or things. □ **a good** (or **great**) **many** a large number. **many's the time** often. **many a time** many times. [Old English]

**Maori** /mow-ree/ — *n.* (*pl.* same or **-s**) **1** member of the indigenous people of New Zealand. **2** their language. **3** (also **Maori wrasse**) brightly coloured fish of southern Australia, the markings on which are supposed to resemble Maori tattoos. — *adj.* of or concerning the Maori or their language. [Maori]

**Maoriland** /mow-ree-,land/ *n. colloq.* New Zealand.

**Maoritanga** /mow-ree-,tung-uh/ *n.* **1** being Maori. **2** Maori traditions and culture. [Maori]

**map** — *n.* **1 a** flat representation of the earth's surface, or part of it. **b** diagram of a route etc. **2** similar representation of the stars, sky, moon, etc. **3** diagram showing the arrangement or components of a thing. — *v.* (**-pp-**) **1** represent on a map. **2** *Math.* associate each element of (a set) with one element of another set. □ **map out** plan in detail. **off the map** very distant. **on the map** prominent, important. **wipe off the map** obliterate. [Latin *mappa* napkin]

**maple** /**may**-puhl/ n. **1 a** Northern hemisphere tree grown for shade, ornament, wood, or sugar. **b** its wood. **2 a** (in full **Queensland maple**) unrelated Australian tree yielding an attractive, usu. pinkish, cabinet timber. **b** its wood. [Old English]

**mar** v. (-**rr**-) spoil; disfigure. [Old English]

**maraca** /muh-**rak**-uh/ n. clublike bean-filled gourd etc., shaken rhythmically in pairs in Latin American music. [Portuguese]

**maramie** /**ma**-ruh-mee/ n. freshwater Australian crayfish. [Wiradhuri, probably *marramin*]

**marara** /muh-**rah**-ruh/ n. **1** any of three large rainforest trees of Queensland and NSW: the rose marara or scrub rosewood; the brush marara or red carabeen; the rose-leaf marara. **2** the close-grained pink wood of these trees. [perhaps from a Queensland Aboriginal language]

**marathon** /**ma**-ruh-thuhn/ — n. **1** long-distance running race, usu. of 26 miles 385 yards (42.195 km). **2** long-lasting or difficult undertaking etc. — adj. of a marathon; of long distance or duration (*the delegates emerged weary after marathon talks*). [*Marathon* in Greece, scene of a decisive battle in 490 BC: a messenger supposedly ran with news of the outcome to Athens, about 40 kilometres away]

**maraud** /muh-**rawd**/ v. **1** make a plundering raid (on). **2** plunder systematically (*the Vikings marauded throughout Europe*). □ **marauder** n. [French *maraud* rogue]

**marble** /**mah**-buhl/ — n. **1** crystalline limestone capable of taking a polish, used in sculpture and architecture. **2** (often attrib.) **a** anything of marble (*marble clock*). **b** anything like marble in hardness, coldness, etc. (*her features were marble*). **3 a** small, esp. glass, ball as a toy. **b** (in pl.; treated as sing.) game using these. **4** (in pl.) colloq. one's mental faculties (*he's lost his marbles*). — v. (-**ling**) **1** (esp. as **marbled** adj.) stain or colour (paper, soap, etc.) to look like variegated marble. **2** (as **marbled** adj.) (of meat) striped with fat and lean. [Latin *marmor* from Greek]

**marblewood** n. any of several Australian trees yielding wood with an attractive mottled grain.

**marbling** n. **1** colouring or marking like marble. **2** streaks of fat in lean meat.

**marcasite** /**mah**-kuh-ˌsuyt/ n. **1** yellowish crystalline iron sulphide. **2** crystals of this used in jewellery. [Arabic *markashita*]

**March** n. third month of the year. [Latin *Martius* of Mars]

**march**¹ — v. **1** (cause to) walk in a military manner with a regular tread (*army marched past; marched him away*). **2 a** walk purposefully. **b** (often foll. by *on*) (of events etc.) continue unrelentingly (*time marches on*). **3** (foll. by *on*) advance towards (a military objective). — n. **1 a** act of marching. **b** uniform military step (*slow march*). **2** long difficult walk. **3** a procession as a protest or demonstration. **4** (usu. foll. by *of*) progress or continuity (*march of events*). **5 a** music to accompany a march. **b** similar musical piece. □ **marcher** n. [French *marcher*]

**march**² n. tract of land between two countries, esp. disputed. [French *marche* from medieval Latin *marca*]

**March fly** n. blood-sucking fly; horsefly. [from the name of the month]

**March hare** n. hare frantic and exuberant in the breeding season (*mad as a March hare*).

**marching girl** n. girl trained to march in formation.

**marching orders** n.pl. **1** order for troops to mobilise etc. **2** dismissal (*gave him his marching orders*).

**marchioness** /ˌmah-shuh-**nes**, **mah**-/ n. **1** wife or widow of a marquess. **2** woman holding the rank of marquess. [medieval Latin: related to MARCH²]

**march past** — n. marching of troops past a saluting-point at a review. — v. (of troops) carry out a march past.

**Mardi Gras** /ˌmah-dee **grah**/ n. **1 a** Shrove Tuesday in some Catholic countries. **b** merrymaking on this day. **2** carnival or fair held at any time of the year. [French, = fat Tuesday]

**mardo** /**mah**-doh/ n. yellow-footed marsupial mouse. [Nyungar *mardu*]

**mare**¹ n. female equine animal, esp. a horse. [Old English]

**mare**² /**mah**-ray/ n. (pl. **maria** /**mah**-ree-uh/ or **-s**) **1** large dark flat area on the moon, once thought to be sea. **2** similar area on Mars. [Latin, = sea]

**mare's nest** n. important discovery etc. which turns out to be illusory; a hoax.

**margarine** /ˌmah-juh-**reen**, ˌmah-guh-, **mah**-juh-ruhn/ n. butter-substitute made from vegetable oils or animal fats with milk etc. [Greek *margaron* pearl]

**margin** /**mah**-juhn/ n. **1** edge or border of a surface. **2** blank border flanking print etc. **3** amount by which a thing exceeds, falls short, etc. (*won by a narrow margin*). **4** lower limit (*his effort fell* *below the margin*). **5** increment to a basic wage, paid for an employee's particular skill. [Latin *margo -ginis*]

**marginal** *adj*. **1** of or written in a margin. **2 a** of or at the edge. **b** insignificant (*of merely marginal interest*). **3** (of a parliamentary seat etc.) held by a small majority. **4** close to the limit, esp. of profitability. **5** (of land) difficult to cultivate; unprofitable. **6** barely adequate. □ **marginally** *adv*. [medieval Latin: related to MARGIN]

**marginal cost** *n*. cost added by making one extra copy etc.

**marginalia** /ˌmah-juh-**nay**-lee-uh/ *n.pl.* marginal notes.

**marginalise** /**mah**-juh-nuh-ˌluyz/ *v.* (also **-ize**)(**-sing** or **-zing**) **1** treat (a person or group of people) as marginal and therefore unimportant. **2** push (a person or group of people) from the centre or mainstream towards the periphery of interest, power, society, etc. □ **marginalisation** /-zay-shuhn/ *n.*

**margin of error** *n.* allowance for miscalculation etc.

**margoo** /**mah**-goo/ *n.* = WITCHETTY [Western Desert language *magu*]

**Margu** /**mahr**-goo/ *n.* an Aboriginal language spoken on Croker Island and the mainland of the extreme north of the NT.

**marguerite** /ˌmah-guh-**reet**/ *n.* any of several flowers of the daisy family. [Latin *margarita* pearl]

**maria** *pl.* of MARE².

**Marian** /**mair**-ree-uhn/ *adj. RC Ch.* of or pertaining to the Virgin Mary (*Marian vespers*).

**marigold** /ma-ruh-ˌgohld/ *n.* plant with golden or bright yellow flowers. [*Mary* (probably the Virgin), *gold* (British dial.) marigold]

**marijuana** /ˌma-ruh-**wah**-nuh/ *n.* (also **marihuana**) **1** dried leaves etc. of hemp, usu. smoked in cigarettes as a drug. **2** the plant yielding these. [American Spanish]

**marimba** /muh-**rim**-buh/ *n.* **1** xylophone played by natives of Africa and Central America. **2** modern orchestral instrument derived from this. [Congo]

**marina** /muh-**ree**-nuh/ *n.* harbour for pleasure-yachts etc. [Latin: related to MARINE]

**marinade** /ˌma-ruh-**nayd**, -**nahd**/ — *n.* **1** special liquid, e.g. a mixture of wine, vinegar, oil, spices, etc., for soaking meat, fish, etc. before cooking. **2** meat, fish, etc., so soaked. — *v.* (**-ding**) soak in a marinade. [Spanish *marinar* pickle in brine: related to MARINE]

**marinate** /ma-ruh-ˌnayt/ *v.* (**-ting**) = MARINADE. □ **marination** /-nay-shuhn/ *n.* [French: related to MARINE]

**marine** /muh-**reen**/ — *adj.* **1** of, found in, or produced by the sea. **2 a** of shipping or naval matters (*marine insurance*). **b** for use at sea. — *n.* **1** soldier trained to serve on land or sea. **2** country's shipping, fleet, or navy (*merchant marine*). [Latin *mare* sea]

**mariner** /ma-ruh-nuh/ *n.* seaman.

**marionette** /ˌma-ree-uh-**net**/ *n.* puppet worked by strings. [French: related to *Mary*]

**marital** /ma-ruh-tuhl/ *adj.* of marriage or marriage relations. [Latin *maritus* husband]

**maritime** /ma-ruh-ˌtuym/ *adj.* **1** connected with the sea or seafaring (*maritime insurance*). **2** living or found near the sea. [Latin: related to MARINE]

**marjoram** /mah-juh-ruhm/ *n.* aromatic herb used in cookery. [French from medieval Latin]

**mark** — *n.* **1** spot, sign, stain, scar, etc., on a surface etc. **2** (esp. in *comb.*) **a** written or printed symbol (*question mark*). **b** number or letter denoting proficiency, conduct, etc. (*black mark*; *46 marks out of 50*). **3** (usu. foll. by *of*) sign of quality, character, feeling, etc. (*mark of respect*). **4 a** sign, seal, etc., of identification. **b** cross etc. made as a signature by an illiterate person. **5** lasting effect (*war left its mark*). **6 a** target etc. (*missed the mark*). **b** standard, norm (*his work falls below the mark*). **7** line etc. indicating a position; a marker. **8** (usu. **Mark**) (followed by a numeral) particular design, model, etc., of a car, aircraft, etc. **9** runner's starting-point in a race. **10** *Aust. Rules* **a** the catching before it reaches the ground of a ball kicked at least ten metres. **b** the spot at which a player so caught the ball, from which spot he must make his kick. **c** the kick awarded to a player who has taken such a fair catch. **d** a player skilled at taking such a fair catch (*Cazaly was a superb mark*). **e** (**high mark**) such a fair catch taken in the course of a high leap; the player who does this (*Ablett is a brilliant high mark*). **11** *Rugby* heel-mark on the ground made by a player who had caught the ball direct from a kick, knock-on, or throw-forward by an opponent. — *v.* **1 a** make a mark on. **b** mark with initials, name, etc. to identify etc. **2** correct and assess (a student's work etc.). **3** attach a price to (*marked the doll at $5*). **4** notice or observe (*marked his agitation*). **5 a** characterise (*day was marked by storms*). **b** acknowledge, celebrate (*marked the occasion with a toast*). **6** name or indicate on a map etc. (*this road isn't marked*). **7** keep close to (an opponent in sport) to hinder him or her. **8** *Aust. Rules* **a** take the ball in a fair catch. **b** (as **high marking**) leaping high in the air to take a fair catch. **9** (as **marked** *adj.*) have natural marks (*is marked with dark spots*). **10** mark the ear of (a lamb), completing at the same time other processes such as castration, docking, etc. □ **beside** (or **off** or **wide of**) **the mark 1** irrelevant. **2** not accurate. **make one's mark** attain distinction; make an impression. **one's mark** *colloq.* opponent, object, etc., of one's own size etc. (*the little one's more my mark*). **mark down 1** reduce the price of (goods etc.). **2** make a written note of. **3** reduce the examination marks of (*marked him down for poor spelling*). **mark off** separate by a boundary etc. **mark out 1** plan (a course of action etc.). **2** destine (*marked out for success*). **3** trace out (boundaries etc.). **mark time 1** march on the spot without moving forward. **2** act routinely while awaiting an opportunity to advance. **mark up 1** add a proportion to the price of (goods etc.) for profit. **2** mark or correct (text etc.). **off the mark 1** having made a start. **2** = *beside the mark*. **on the mark** ready to start. **on your mark** (or **marks**) get ready to start (esp. a race). **up to the mark** normal (esp. of health). [Old English]

**markdown** *n.* reduction in price.

**marked** *adj.* **1** having a visible mark. **2** clearly noticeable (*marked difference*). **3** (of playing-cards) marked on their backs to assist cheating. □ **markedly** /-kuhd-lee/ *adv.*

**marked man** *n.* **1** person whose conduct is watched with suspicion or hostility. **2** person singled out, esp. for attack.

**marker** *n.* **1** thing marking a position etc. **2** person or thing that marks. **3** broadtipped felt-tipped pen. **4** scorer in a game.

**market** /**mah**-kuht/ — *n.* **1** gathering of buyers and sellers of provisions, livestock, etc. **2** space for this. **3** (often foll. by *for*) demand for a commodity etc. (*no market for gazebos*). **4** place or group providing such a demand. **5** conditions etc. for buying or selling; rate of purchase and sale (*market is sluggish*). **6** (prec. by *the*) the trade in a specified commodity (*the wheat market*). **7** = STOCK MARKET. — *v.* (**-t-**) **1** offer for sale, esp. by advertising etc. **2** buy or sell goods in a market. □ **be in the market for** wish to buy. **be on the market** be offered for sale. **put on the market** offer for sale. □ **marketer** *n.* **marketing** *n.* [Latin *mercor* buy]

**marketable** *adj.* able or fit to be sold. □ **marketability** /-**bil**-uh-tee/ *n.*

**marketeer** /ˌmah-kuh-**teer**/ *n.* marketer (*black marketeer*).

**market garden** *n.* farm where vegetables and fruit are grown for sale in markets.

**market research** *n.* surveying of consumers' needs and preferences.

**market value** *n.* value if offered for sale.

**marking** *n.* (usu. in *pl.*) **1** identification mark. **2** colouring of an animal's fur etc.

**marksman** *n.* (also **markswoman**) skilled shot, esp. with a pistol or rifle. □ **marksmanship** *n.*

**mark-up** *n.* amount added to a price by the retailer for profit.

**marl** — *n.* soil of clay and lime, used as fertiliser. — *v.* apply marl to. □ **marly** *adj.* [medieval Latin *margila*]

**marlin** /**mah**-luhn/ *n.* (*pl.* same or **-s**) long-nosed marine fish. [from MARLINSPIKE]

**marlinspike** *n.* pointed iron tool used to separate strands of rope etc. [*marling* from Dutch *marlen* from *marren* bind]

**marlock** /**mah**-lok/ *n.* any of several small mallee-like eucalypts forming stands. [probably Nyungar *malag* or *malug*]

**marloo** /**mah**-loo/ *n.* WA name for the red kangaroo. [Western Desert language *marlu*]

**marmalade** /**mah**-muh-ˌlayd/ *n.* preserve of citrus fruit, usu. oranges. [Portuguese *marmelo* quince]

**marmoreal** /mah-**maw**-ree-uhl/ *adj.* of or like marble. [Latin: related to MARBLE]

**marmoset** /**mah**-muh-ˌzet/ *n.* small monkey with a long bushy tail. [French]

**marmot** /**mah**-muht/ *n.* heavy-set burrowing rodent with a short bushy tail. [Latin *mus* mouse, *mons* mountain]

**maroon¹** /muh-**rohn**, muh-**roon**/ *adj.* & *n.* brownish-crimson. [French *marron* chestnut]

**maroon²** /muh-**roon**/ *v.* **1** leave (a person) isolated, esp. on an island. **2** (of weather etc.) cause (a person) to be forcibly detained. [French *marron* wild person, from Spanish *cimarrón*]

**marque** /mahk/ *n.* make of car, as distinct from a specific model (*the Jaguar marque*). [French, = MARK]

**marquee** /mah-**kee**/ *n.* large tent for social functions etc. [French *marquise*]

**marquess** /**mah**-kwuhs/ *n.* British nobleman ranking between duke and earl. [var. of MARQUIS]

**marquetry** /**mah**-kuh-tree/ *n.* inlaid work in wood, ivory, etc. [French: related to MARQUE]

**marquis** /**mah**-kwuhs/ *n.* (*pl.* **-quises**) French nobleman ranking between duke and count. [French: related to MARCH²]

**marquise** /mah-**keez**/ n. **1** wife or widow of a marquis. **2** woman holding the rank of marquis.

**marram** /**ma**-ruhm/ n. tough shore grass that binds sand. [Old Norse, = sea-haulm]

**marri** /**ma**-ree/ n. WA eucalypt with a profusion of cream, pink, or red flowers, the red-flowered form being esp. spectacular and often cultivated. [Nyungar]

**marriage** /**ma**-rij/ n. **1** legal union of a man and a woman for cohabitation and often procreation. **2** act or ceremony marking this. **3** particular such union (*a happy marriage*). **4** intimate union, combination (*the marriage of true minds*). [French *marier* MARRY]

**marriageable** adj. free, ready, or fit for marriage. □ **marriageability** /-bil-uh-tee/ n.

**marriage celebrant** n. person empowered to perform a marriage, esp. in a non-religious ceremony.

**marriage guidance** n. counselling of people with marital problems.

**married** — adj. **1** united in marriage. **2** of marriage (*married name*; *married life*). — n. (usu. in *pl.*) married person (*young marrieds*).

**marron** /**ma**-ruhn/ n. (*pl.* usu. same) large freshwater crayfish of WA. [Nyungar *marran*]

**marrow** /**ma**-roh/ n. **1** large fleshy usu. striped gourd eaten as a vegetable. **2** soft fatty substance in the cavities of bones. **3** essential part. □ **to the marrow** right through. [Old English]

**marrowbone** n. bone containing edible marrow.

**marry** /**ma**-ree/ v. (**-ies, -ied**) **1** take, join, or give in marriage. **2 a** enter into marriage. **b** (foll. by *into*) become a member of (a family) by marriage. **3 a** unite intimately, combine. **b** pair (socks etc.). □ **marry off** find a spouse for. **marry up** link, join. [Latin *maritus* husband]

**marrying** adj. likely or inclined to marry (*he's not the marrying kind*).

**marsh** n. (often *attrib.*) low watery land. □ **marshy** adj. (**-ier, -iest**). **marshiness** n. [Old English]

**marshal** /**mah**-shuhl/ — n. **1** high-ranking officer in the armed forces. **2** officer arranging ceremonies, controlling racecourses, crowds, etc. — v. (**-ll-**) **1** arrange (soldiers, one's thoughts, etc.) in due order. **2** conduct (a person) ceremoniously. [French *mareschal*]

**marsh gas** n. methane.

**marshmallow** /mahsh-**mal**-oh, -**mel**-oh/ n. soft sticky sweet made of sugar, egg-white, gelatine, etc. [MARSH, Latin *malva*]

**marsupial** /mah-**soo**-pee-uhl, -**syoo**-/ — n. mammal giving birth to under-developed young subsequently carried in a pouch. — adj. of or like a marsupial. [Greek *marsupion* pouch]

**marsupial lion** n. large, extinct, carnivorous Australian marsupial.

**marsupial mole** n. small, blind, burrowing marsupial of arid Australia.

**marsupial mouse** n. any of many small carnivorous marsupials widespread in Australia (e.g. the DUNNART, the MULGARA) some of which are also known as bush mice and pouched mice.

**marsupial rat** n. small carnivorous marsupial of arid central Australia.

**marsupial wolf** n. = TASMANIAN TIGER.

**mart** n. **1** trade centre. **2** auction-room. **3** market. [Dutch: related to MARKET]

**marten** /**mah**-tuhn/ n. weasel-like carnivore of Canada etc. with valuable fur. [Dutch from French]

**martial** /**mah**-shuhl/ adj. **1** of or appropriate to warfare. **2** warlike; brave; fond of fighting. [Latin *martialis* of Mars]

**martial arts** n.pl. oriental fighting sports such as judo and karate.

**martial law** n. military government involving the suspension of ordinary law.

**Martian** /**mah**-shuhn/ — adj. of the planet Mars. — n. hypothetical inhabitant of Mars. [Latin]

**martin** /**mah**-tuhn/ n. **1** a kind of European swallow. **2** any swallow-like migratory bird in Australia. [probably St *Martin*, name of a 4th-c. bishop]

**martinet** /mah-tuh-**net**/ n. strict disciplinarian. [*Martinet*, name of a 17th-c. drill-master]

**martini** /mah-**tee**-nee/ n. (*pl.* **-s**) cocktail of gin and French vermouth. [*Martini* and Rossi, name of a firm selling vermouth]

**Martuthunira** /**mahr**-too-,thoo-ni-ru/ n. an Aboriginal language spoken over a large area of north-western WA.

**martyr** /**mah**-tuh/ — n. **1 a** person killed for persisting in a belief. **b** person who suffers for a cause etc. **c** person who suffers or pretends to suffer to get pity etc. **2** (foll. by *to*) *colloq.* constant sufferer from (an ailment) (*a martyr to migraine*). — v. **1** put to death as a martyr. **2** torment. □ **martyrdom** n. [Greek *martur* witness]

**marvel** /**mah**-vuhl/ — n. **1** wonderful thing. **2** (foll. by *of*) wonderful example of (a quality) (*the house was a marvel of neatness and comfort*). — v. (**-ll-**) (foll. by *at* or *that*) feel surprise or wonder. [Latin *miror* wonder at]

**marvellous** /**mah**-vuh-luhs/ *adj.* **1** astonishing. **2** excellent. **3** extremely improbable. □ **marvellously** *adv.* [French: related to MARVEL]

**Marxism** /**mahk**-siz-uhm/ *n.* political and economic theories of Marx, predicting the overthrow of capitalism and common ownership of the means of production in a classless society. □ **Marxist** *n. & adj.*

**marzipan** /**mah**-zuh-,pan/ — *n.* paste of ground almonds, sugar, etc., used in confectionery. — *v.* (**-nn-**) cover with marzipan. [German from Italian]

**mascara** /mas-**kah**-ruh/ *n.* cosmetic for darkening the eyelashes. [Italian, = mask]

**mascot** /**mas**-kot/ *n.* person, animal, or thing supposed to bring luck. [Provençal *masco* witch]

**masculine** /**mas**-kyuh-luhn/ — *adj.* **1** of men. **2** having manly qualities. **3** of or denoting the male gender. — *n.* masculine gender or word. □ **masculinity** /-**lin**-uh-tee/ *n.* [Latin: related to MALE]

**maser** /**may**-zuh/ *n.* device used to amplify or generate coherent electro-magnetic radiation in the microwave range. [*m*icrowave *a*mplification by *s*timulated *e*mission of *r*adiation]

**mash** — *n.* **1** soft or confused mixture. **2** mixture of boiled grain, bran, etc., fed to horses etc. **3** *colloq.* mashed potatoes. **4** mixture of malt and hot water used in brewing. **5** soft pulp made by crushing, mixing with water, etc. — *v.* **1** crush (potatoes etc.) to a pulp. **2** mix (malt) with hot water to form a wort. □ **masher** *n.* [Old English]

**mask** /mahsk/ — *n.* **1** covering for all or part of the face as a disguise or for protection against infection etc. **2** respirator. **3** likeness of a person's face, esp. one from a mould (*death-mask*). **4** disguise, pretence (*throw off the mask*). — *v.* **1** cover with a mask. **2** conceal. **3** protect. [Arabic *maskara* buffoon]

**masking tape** *n.* adhesive tape used in decorating to protect areas where paint is not wanted.

**masochism** /**mas**-uh-,kiz-uhm/ *n.* **1** condition in which (esp. sexual) pleasure is taken in one's own pain or humiliation. **2** *colloq.* enjoyment of what appears to be painful or tiresome. □ **masochist** *n.* **masochistic** /-**kis**-tik/ *adj.* **masochistically** /-**kis**-ti-klee/ *adv.* [von Sacher-*Masoch*, name of a novelist]

**mason** /**may**-suhn/ *n.* **1** person who builds with stone. **2** (**Mason**) Freemason. [French]

**Masonic** /muh-**son**-ik/ *adj.* of Freemasons.

**masonry** *n.* **1** stonework. **2** work of a mason.

**masque** /mahsk/ *n.* musical drama with mime, esp. in the 16th and 17th c. [var. of MASK]

**masquerade** /,mah-skuh-**rayd**/, ,mas-kuh-/ — *n.* **1** false show, pretence. **2** masked ball. — *v.* (**-ding**) (often foll. by *as*) appear falsely or in disguise. [Spanish *máscara* mask]

**mass**[1] /mas/ — *n.* **1** shapeless body of matter. **2** dense aggregation of objects (*mass of fibres*). **3** (in *sing.* or *pl.*; usu. foll. by *of*) large number or amount. **4** (usu. foll. by *of*) unbroken expanse (of colour etc.). **5** (prec. by *the*) **a** the majority. **b** (in *pl.*) ordinary people. **6** *Physics* quantity of matter a body contains. **7** (*attrib.*) on a large scale (*mass hysteria*; *mass audience*). — *v.* assemble into a mass or as one body. [Latin *massa* from Greek]

**Mass**[2] /mas, mahs/ *n.* **1** Eucharist, esp. in the Roman Catholic Church. **2** celebration of this. **3** liturgy used in this. **4** musical setting of parts of this. [Latin *missa* dismissal, from the concluding words of the rite]

**massacre** /**mas**-uh-kuh/ — *n.* **1** mass killing. **2** utter defeat or destruction. — *v.* (**-ring**) **1** kill (esp. many people) cruelly or violently. **2** *colloq.* defeat heavily. [French]

**massage** /**mas**-ah*zh*, -ahj, muh-**sahz***h*, -**sahj**/ — *n.* rubbing and kneading of the muscles and joints with the hands, to relieve stiffness, cure strains, stimulate, etc. — *v.* (**-ging**) **1** apply massage to in order to relieve or stimulate. **2** manipulate (statistics etc.) to give an acceptable result. **3** flatter (a person's ego etc.). [French]

**massage parlour** *n.* **1** establishment providing massage of various kinds. **2** *euphem.* brothel.

**masseur** /ma-**ser**/ *n.* (*fem.* **masseuse** /ma-**serz**/ ) person who gives massage for a living. [French: related to MASSAGE]

**massif** /**mas**-eef, ma-**seef**/ *n.* compact group of mountain heights. [French: related to MASSIVE]

**massive** /**mas**-iv/ *adj.* **1** large and heavy or solid. **2** (of the features, head, etc.) relatively large or solid. **3** exceptionally large or severe (*massive heart attack*). **4** substantial, impressive. □ **massively** *adv.* **massiveness** *n.* [Latin: related to MASS[1]]

**mass media** *n.pl.* = MEDIA 2.

**mass noun** *n. Gram.* noun that is not normally countable and cannot be used with the indefinite article (e.g. *bread*).

**mass production** *n.* mechanical

production of large quantities of a standardised article. □ **mass-produce** v.

**mast** /mahst/ n. **1** long upright post of timber etc. on a ship's keel to support sails. **2** post etc. for supporting a radio or television aerial. **3** flag-pole (*half-mast*). □ **before the mast** as an ordinary seaman. [Old English]

**mastectomy** /mas-**tek**-tuh-mee/ n. (pl. **-ies**) surgical removal of a breast. [Greek *mastos* breast]

**master** /**mah**-stuh/ — n. **1** person having control or ownership (*master of the house; dog obeyed his master*). **2** captain of a merchant ship. **3** male teacher. **4** person who gets the upper hand (*we shall see which of us is master*). **5 a** skilled tradesman able to teach others (often *attrib.: master carpenter*). **b** skilled practitioner (*master of innuendo*). **6** holder of a usu. post-graduate university degree (*Master of Arts*). **7** revered teacher in philosophy etc. **8** great artist. **9** *Chess etc.* player at international level. **10** original copy of a film, recording, etc., from which others can be made. **11** (**Master**) title for a boy not old enough to be called *Mr.* — *attrib. adj.* **1** commanding, superior (*master hand*). **2** main, principal (*master bedroom*). **3** controlling others (*master plan*). — v. **1** overcome, defeat. **2** gain full knowledge of or skill in. [Latin *magister*]

**masterclass** n. class given by a famous musician etc.

**masterful** adj. **1** imperious, domineering. **2** masterly. □ **masterfully** adv.

■ Usage *Masterful* is normally used of a person, whereas *masterly* is used of achievements, abilities, etc.

**master-key** n. key that opens several different locks.

**masterly** adj. very skilful.

■ Usage See note at *masterful*.

**mastermind** — n. **1** person with an outstanding intellect. **2** person directing a scheme etc. — v. plan and direct (a scheme etc.).

**Master of Ceremonies** n. **1** person introducing speakers at a banquet or entertainers in a variety show. **2** person in charge of a ceremonial or social occasion.

**masterpiece** n. **1** outstanding piece of artistry or workmanship. **2** person's best work.

**master stroke** n. skilful tactic etc.

**master switch** n. switch controlling the supply of electricity etc. to an entire system.

**mastery** n. **1** control, dominance. **2** (often foll. by *of*) comprehensive knowledge or skill.

**masthead** n. **1** top of a ship's mast, esp. as a place of observation or punishment. **2** title of a newspaper etc. at the head of the front page or editorial page.

**mastic** /**mas**-tik/ n. **1** gum or resin from the mastic tree, used in making varnish. **2** (in full **mastic tree**) evergreen tree yielding this. **3** waterproof filler and sealant. [Greek *mastikhē*]

**masticate** /**mas**-tuh-,kayt/ v. (**-ting**) grind or chew (food) with one's teeth. □ **mastication** /-**kay**-shuhn/ n. **masticatory** adj. [Latin from Greek]

**mastiff** /**mas**-tif/ n. dog of a large strong breed with drooping ears. [Latin *mansuetus* tame]

**mastitis** /mas-**tuy**-tuhs/ n. inflammation of the breast or udder. [Greek *mastos* breast]

**mastodon** /**mas**-tuh-,don/ n. (pl. same or **-s**) large extinct mammal resembling the elephant. [Greek *mastos* breast, *odous* tooth]

**mastoid** /**mas**-toid/ — adj. shaped like a breast. — n. **1** = MASTOID PROCESS. **2** (usu. in pl.) *colloq.* inflammation of the mastoid process. [Greek *mastos* breast]

**mastoid process** n. conical prominence on the temporal bone behind the ear.

**masturbate** /**mas**-tuh-,bayt/ v. (**-ting**) (usu. *absol.*) sexually arouse (oneself or another) by manual stimulation of the genitals. □ **masturbation** /-**bay**-shuhn/ n. **masturbator** n. **masturbatory** adj. [Latin]

**mat¹** — n. **1** small piece of coarse material on a floor, esp. for wiping one's shoes on. **2** piece of cork, rubber, etc., to protect a surface from a hot dish etc. placed on it. **3** padded floor covering in gymnastics, wrestling, etc. — v. (**-tt-**) (esp. as **matted** adj.) entangle or become entangled in a thick mass (*matted hair*). □ **on the mat** *colloq.* being reprimanded. [Old English]

**mat²** var. of MATT.

**matador** /**mat**-uh-,daw/ n. bullfighter whose task is to kill the bull. [Spanish from *matar* kill: related to *mate* in CHECKMATE]

**match¹** — n. **1** contest or game in which players or teams compete. **2 a** person as an equal contender (*meet one's match*). **b** person or thing exactly like or corresponding to another. **3** marriage. **4** person viewed as a marriage prospect. — v. **1** correspond (to); be like or alike; harmonise (with) (*his socks do not match; curtains match the wallpaper*). **2** equal. **3** (foll. by *against*, *with*) place in conflict or competition with. **4** find material etc.

that matches (another) (*can you match this silk?*). **5** find a person or thing suitable for another. □ **match up** (often foll. by *with*) fit to form a whole; tally. **match up to** be as good as or equal to. [Old English]

**match²** *n.* **1** short thin piece of wood etc. with a combustible tip. **2** wick or cord etc. for firing a cannon etc. [French *mesche*]

**matchless** *adj.* incomparable.

**matchmaker** *n.* person who arranges marriages or schemes to bring couples together. □ **matchmaking** *n.*

**matchwood** *n.* **1** wood suitable for matches. **2** minute splinters.

**mate** — *n.* **1 a** very close friend. **b** acquaintance or fellow-worker. **2 a** form of address, esp. to another man, implying equality and goodwill. **b** form of address implying irony or even hostility (*I'll get even with you, mate*). **3 a** each of a breeding pair, esp. of birds. **b** *colloq.* partner in marriage. **c** (in *comb.*) fellow member or joint occupant of (*team-mate; room-mate*). **4** officer on a merchant ship. **5** assistant to a skilled worker (*plumber's mate*). — *v.* (**-ting**) (often foll. by *with*) **1** (of animals or birds) come or bring together for breeding. **2 a** join or be joined in marriage. **b** associate with as a friend **3** *Mech.* fit well. [Low German]

**material** /muh-**teer**-ree-uhl/ — *n.* **1** matter from which a thing is made. **2** cloth, fabric. **3** (in *pl.*) things needed for an activity (*building materials*). **4** person or thing of a specified kind or suitable for a purpose (*officer material*). **5** (in *sing.* or *pl.*) information etc. for a book etc. (*material for a biography*). **6** (in *sing.* or *pl.*, often foll. by *of*) elements, constituent parts, or substance. — *adj.* **1** of matter; corporeal; not spiritual. **2** of bodily comfort etc. (*material well-being*). **3** (often foll. by *to*) important, significant, relevant (*at the material time; he is material to our success*). [Latin *materia* MATTER]

**materialise** *v.* (also **-ize**) (**-sing** or **-zing**) **1** become actual fact; happen. **2** *colloq.* appear or be present. **3** represent in or assume bodily form. □ **materialisation** /-**zay**-shuhn/ *n.*

**materialism** *n.* **1** greater interest in material possessions and comfort than in spiritual values. **2** *Philos.* theory that nothing exists but matter. □ **materialist** *n.* **materialistic** /-lis-tik/ *adj.* **materialistically** /-lis-ti-klee/ *adv.*

**materially** *adv.* **1** substantially, significantly. **2** in respect of matter; physically.

**materiel** /muh-,teer-ree-**el**/ *n.* means,

esp. materials and equipment in warfare. [French]

**maternal** /muh-**ter**-nuhl/ *adj.* **1** of or like a mother; motherly. **2** related through the mother (*maternal uncle*). **3** of the mother in pregnancy and childbirth. □ **maternally** *adv.* [Latin *mater* mother]

**maternity** /muh-**ter**-nuh-tee/ *n.* **1** motherhood. **2** motherliness. **3** (*attrib.*) for women during pregnancy and childbirth (*maternity ward; maternity dress*). [French from medieval Latin: related to MATERNAL]

**mateship** *n.* **1** bond between equal partners or close friends. **2** comradeship. **3** comradeship as an ideal.

**matey** — *adj.* (**-tier**, **-tiest**) sociable; familiar, friendly. — *n.* (*pl.* **-s**) *colloq.* (as a form of address) close comrade, mate. □ **mateyness** *n.*

**mathematical** /,math-uh-**mat**-i-kuhl/ *adj.* **1** of mathematics. **2** rigorously precise. □ **mathematically** *adv.*

**mathematics** /,math-uh-**mat**-iks/ *n.pl.* **1** (also treated as *sing.*) abstract science of number, quantity, and space. **2** (as *pl.*) use of this in calculation etc. □ **mathematician** /-muh-**tish**-uhn/ *n.* [Greek *manthanō* learn]

**maths** *n.* mathematics. [abbreviation]

**matilda** /muh-**til**-duh/ *n.* bushman's bundle; swag. □ **waltz matilda** carry one's swag; travel the road. [unexplained use of the name *Matilda*]

**matinée** /**mat**-uh-,nay/ *n.* (also **matinee**) afternoon performance in the theatre, cinema, etc. [French from *matin* morning: related to MATINS]

**matinée jacket** *n.* (also **matinée coat**) baby's short knitted coat.

**matins** /**mat**-uhnz/ *n.* **1** *RC Ch.* **a** first of the seven canonical hours of the breviary. **b** service for this, said or chanted at midnight or daybreak. **2** (also **mattins**) (as *sing.* or *pl.*) morning prayer, esp. in the Anglican Church. [Latin *matutinus* of the morning]

**matriarch** /**may**-tree-,ahk, **mat**-ree-/ *n.* female head of a family or tribe. □ **matriarchal** /-**ah**-kuhl/ *adj.* [Latin *mater* mother]

**matriarchy** /**may**-tree-,ah-kee, **mat**-ree-/ *n.* (*pl.* **-ies**) female-dominated system of society, with descent through the female line.

**matrices** *pl.* of MATRIX.

**matricide** /**may**-truh-,suyd, **mat**-ruh-/ *n.* **1** killing of one's mother. **2** person who does this. [Latin]

**matriculate** /muh-**trik**-yuh-,layt/ *v.* (**-ting**) be formally admitted to a university or the like. [medieval Latin: related to MATRIX]

**matriculation** /muh-trik-yuh-**lay**-shuhn/ *n.* **1** act or instance of matriculating. **2** secondary school examination to qualify for this.

**matrimony** /**mat**-ruh-muh-nee/ *n.* rite, state, or sacrament of marriage. □ **matrimonial** /-**moh**-nee-uhl/ *adj.* [Latin]

**matrix** /**may**-triks/ *n.* (*pl.* **matrices** /-truh-,seez/ *or* **-es**) **1** mould in which a thing (such as a gramophone record, printing type, etc.) is cast or shaped. **2** place etc. in which a thing is developed. **3** rock in which gems, fossils, etc., are embedded. **4** *Math.* rectangular array of elements treated as a single element. **5** *Computing* gridlike array of interconnected circuit elements. [Latin, = womb]

**matron** /**may**-truhn/ *n.* **1** woman in charge of nursing in a hospital. **2** married, esp. staid, woman. **3** woman nurse and housekeeper at a school etc. [Latin]

---

■ **Usage** In sense 1, *director of nursing* is now the official term.

---

**matronly** *adj.* like a matron, esp. portly or staid.

**matt** (also **mat**) — *adj.* not shiny or glossy; dull. — *n.* (in full **matt paint**) paint giving a dull flat finish. [French]

**matter** — *n.* **1** physical substance having mass and occupying space, as distinct from mind and spirit. **2** specified substance (*colouring matter*; *reading matter*). **3** (prec. by *the*; often foll. by *with*) (thing) amiss (*something the matter with him*). **4** content as distinct from style, form, etc. **5** (often foll. by *of, for*) situation etc. under consideration or as an occasion for (regret etc.) (*matter for concern*; *matter of discipline*). **6** pus or a similar substance discharged from the body. — *v.* (often foll. by *to*) be of importance; have significance. □ **as a matter of fact** in reality; actually. **for that matter 1** as far as that is concerned. **2** and indeed also. **a matter of** approximately; amounting to (*a matter of 40 years*). **no matter 1** (foll. by *when, how,* etc.) regardless of. **2** it is of no importance. [Latin *materia* timber, substance]

**matter of course** *n.* natural or expected thing.

**matter-of-fact** *adj.* **1** unimaginative, prosaic. **2** unemotional. □ **matter-of-factly** *adv.* **matter-of-factness** *n.*

**matting** *n.* fabric for mats.

**mattock** /**mat**-uhk/ *n.* agricultural tool like a pickaxe, with an adze and a chisel edge. [Old English]

**mattress** /**mat**-ruhs/ *n.* stuffed, or air- or water-filled cushion the size of a bed. [Arabic *almaṭraḥ*]

**maturate** /**mat**-yoo-,rayt/ *v.* (**-ting**) (of a boil etc.) come to maturation. [Latin: related to MATURE]

**maturation** /mat-yoo-**ray**-shuhn/ *n.* **1** maturing or being matured. **2** formation of pus. [French or medieval Latin: related to MATURE]

**mature** /muh-**tyoor**/ — *adj.* (**maturer, maturest**) **1 a** fully developed, adult. **b** sensible, wise. **2** ripe; seasoned. **3** (of thought etc.) careful, considered. **4** (of a bill, insurance policy, etc.) due, payable. — *v.* (**-ring**) **1** develop fully; ripen. **2** perfect (a plan etc.). **3** (of a bill, insurance policy, etc.) become due or payable. □ **maturely** *adv.* **matureness** *n.* **maturity** *n.* [Latin *maturus* timely]

**matutinal** /mat-yoo-**tuy**-nuhl, muh-**tyoo**-tuh-nuhl/ *adj.* of the morning; early. [Latin: related to MATINS]

**maudlin** /**mawd**-luhn/ *adj.* weakly or tearfully sentimental, esp. from drunkenness. [French *Madeleine*, referring to pictures of Mary Magdalen weeping]

**maul** /mawl/ — *v.* **1** tear the flesh of; claw. **2** handle roughly. **3** damage by criticism. — *n.* **1** *Rugby* loose scrum. **2** brawl. **3** heavy hammer. [Latin *malleus* hammer]

**maunder** /**mawn**-duh/ *v.* **1** talk ramblingly. **2** move or act listlessly or idly. [origin unknown]

**Maundy** /**mawn**-dee/ *n.* ceremony in which the pope, bishops, priests wash and kiss the feet of the poor on Maundy Thursday to commemorate Christ's washing of the Apostles' feet at the Last Supper. [French *mandé* from Latin *mandatum* command]

**Maundy Thursday** *n.* Thursday before Easter Sunday, commemorating the Last Supper and Christ's washing of the Apostles' feet.

**mausoleum** /maw-suh-**lee**-uhm/ *n.* magnificent tomb. [from *Mausōlos*, king of Caria, whose tomb had this name]

**mauve** /mohv/ — *adj.* pale purple. — *n.* this colour. □ **mauvish** *adj.* [Latin]

**maverick** /**mav**-uh-rik/ *n.* **1** unorthodox or independent-minded person. **2** unbranded calf or yearling. [*Maverick*, name of an owner of unbranded cattle]

**maw** *n.* **1** stomach of an animal. **2** *colloq.* stomach of a greedy person. **3** jaws or throat of a voracious animal. [Old English]

**mawkish** /**maw**-kish/ *adj.* feebly sentimental; sickly. □ **mawkishly** *adv.* **mawkishness** *n.* [obsolete *mawk* MAGGOT]

**max.** *abbr.* maximum. □ **to the max** *colloq.* to the utmost; extremely.

**maxi** /**mak**-see/ *n.* (*pl.* **-s**) *colloq.* maxi-coat, -skirt, -yacht, etc. [abbreviation]

**maxi-** *comb. form* very large or long (*maxi-skirt*; *maxi-yacht*) [abbreviation of MAXIMUM; cf. MINI-]

**maxilla** /mak-**sil**-uh/ *n.* (*pl.* **-llae** /-lee/) jaw or jawbone, esp. (in vertebrates) the upper jaw. □ **maxillary** *adj.* [Latin]

**maxim** /**mak**-suhm/ *n.* general truth or rule of conduct briefly expressed. [French or medieval Latin: related to MAXIMUM]

**maxima** *pl.* of MAXIMUM.

**maximal** /**mak**-suh-muhl/ *adj.* of or being a maximum.

**maximise** /**mak**-suh-ˌmuyz/ *v.* (also **-ize**) (**-sing** or **-zing**) make as large or great as possible. □ **maximisation** /-**zay**-shuhn/ *n.* [Latin: related to MAXIMUM]

■ **Usage** *Maximise* should not be used in standard English to mean 'to make as good as possible' or 'to make the most of'.

**maximum** /**mak**-suh-muhm/ — *n.* (*pl.* **-ma**) highest possible amount, size, etc. — *adj.* greatest in amount, size, etc. [Latin *maximus* greatest]

**May** *n.* fifth month of the year. [Latin *Maius* of the goddess Maia]

**may** *v.aux.* (*3rd sing. present* **may**; *past* **might** /muyt/) **1** expressing: **a** (often foll. by *well* for emphasis) possibility (*it may be true*; *you may well lose your way*). **b** permission (*may I come in?*). **c** a wish (*may he live to regret it*). **d** uncertainty or irony (*who may you be?*; *who are you, may I ask?*). **2** in purpose clauses and after *wish*, *fear*, etc. (*hope he may succeed*). □ **be that as it may** (or **that is as may be**) it is possible (but) (*be that as it may, I still want to go*). **may as well** = *might as well* (see MIGHT¹). [Old English]

■ **Usage** In sense 1b, both *can* and *may* are used to express permission; in more formal contexts *may* is preferred since *can* also denotes capability (*can I move?* = am I physically able to move?; *may I move?* = am I allowed to move?).

**maybe** /**may**-bee/ *adv.* perhaps. [from *it may be*]

**May Day** *n.* 1 May as an international holiday in honour of workers.

**mayday** /**may**-day/ *n.* international radio distress-signal. [representing pronunciation of French *m'aidez* help me]

**mayfly** *n.* a kind of insect living briefly in spring.

**mayfly orchid** *n.* (also **doggie**) Australian terrestrial orchid, having attractive, deep purple-brown flowers (said to resemble the English mayfly) and often forming large colonies; the epithet 'doggie' refers to the scent of the flowers (the dog-connection being variously described).

**mayhem** /**may**-hem/ *n.* destruction; havoc. [Anglo-French *mahem*: related to MAIM]

**Mayi-Kulan** /muy-yee-ˌkuu-lahn/ *n.* an Aboriginal language spoken in north-western Queensland: now extinct.

**Mayi-Kutuna** /muy-yee-ˌkuu-too-nu/ *n.* an Aboriginal language spoken in north-western Queensland to the west of the speakers of Mayi-Kulan: now extinct.

**Mayi-Yapi** /muy-yee-ˌyah-pee/ *n.* an Aboriginal language spoken in north-western Queensland in a wide region between speakers of Mayi-Kutuna and Mayi-Kulan: now extinct.

**mayonnaise** /ˌmay-uh-**nayz**/ *n.* **1** thick creamy dressing of egg-yolks, oil, vinegar, etc. **2** dish dressed with this (*egg mayonnaise*). [French]

**mayor** /mair/ *n.* head of the local council of a city or town etc. □ **mayoral** *adj.* [Latin: related to MAJOR]

**mayoralty** /**mair**-ruhl-tee/ *n.* (*pl.* **-ies**) **1** office of mayor. **2** period of this.

**mayoress** /**mair**-res/ *n.* **1** woman mayor. **2** wife or official consort of a mayor.

**maypole** *n.* decorated pole for dancing round on the first day of May (springtime in the Northern hemisphere).

**maze** *n.* **1** network of paths and hedges designed as a puzzle for those who enter it. **2** labyrinth. **3** confused network, mass, etc. [related to AMAZE]

**mazurka** /muh-**zer**-kuh/ *n.* **1** lively Polish dance in triple time. **2** music for this. [French or German from Polish]

**MB** *abbr. Computing* megabyte.

**MC** *abbr.* Master of Ceremonies.

**Md** *symb.* mendelevium.

**ME** *abbr.* myalgic encephalomyelitis, a condition with prolonged flu-like symptoms and depression.

**me¹** /mee/ *pron.* **1** *objective case of* I² (*he saw me*). **2** *colloq.* = I² (*it's me all right*; *is taller than me*). [Old English accusative and dative of I²]

**me²** /mee/ *n.* (also **mi**) *Mus.* third note of a major scale. [Latin *mira*, word arbitrarily taken]

**mead** *n.* alcoholic drink of fermented honey and water. [Old English]

**meadow** /med-oh/ n. 1 (chiefly in Northern hemisphere use) piece of grassland, esp. one used for hay. 2 low marshy ground, esp. near a river. □ **meadowy** adj. [Old English]

**meagre** /mee-guh/ adj. 1 scant in amount or quality. 2 lean, thin. [Anglo-French megre from Latin macer]

**meal**[1] n. 1 occasion when food is eaten. 2 the food eaten at a meal. [Old English]

**meal**[2] n. 1 grain or pulse ground to powder. 2 any powdery substance made by grinding (almond meal). [Old English]

**meal ticket** n. colloq. person or thing that is a source of maintenance or income (she's his meal ticket).

**mealtime** n. usual time of eating.

**mealy** adj. (-ier, -iest) 1 of, like, or containing meal. 2 (of a complexion) pale. □ **mealiness** n.

**mealy-mouthed** adj. afraid to speak plainly.

**mean**[1] v. (past and past part. **meant** /ment/) 1 have as one's purpose or intention (meant no harm by it; I didn't mean to break it). 2 design or destine for a purpose (meant to be used). 3 intend to convey or refer to (I mean Richmond in Melbourne). 4 (often foll. by that) entail, involve, portend, signify (this means war; means that he is dead). 5 (of a word) have as its equivalent in the same or another language ('nauta' means 'sailor'). 6 (foll. by to) be of specified importance to (that means a lot to me). □ **mean business** colloq. be in earnest. **mean it** not be joking or exaggerating. **mean well** have good intentions. [Old English]

**mean**[2] adj. 1 niggardly; not generous. 2 ignoble, small-minded. 3 (of capacity, understanding, etc.) inferior, poor. 4 shabby; inadequate (mean hovel). 5 a malicious, ill-tempered. b vicious or aggressive in behaviour. 6 colloq. skilful, formidable, powerful (a mean fighter). □ **no mean** a very good (no mean feat). □ **meanly** adv. **meanness** n. [Old English]

**mean**[3] — n. 1 median point (mean between modesty and pride). 2 a term midway between the first and last terms of an arithmetical etc. progression. b quotient of the sum of several quantities and their number; average. — adj. 1 (of a quantity) equally far from two extremes. 2 calculated as a mean. [Latin medianus MEDIAN]

**meander** /mee-an-duh/ — v. 1 wander at random. 2 (of a stream) wind about. — n. 1 (in pl.) sinuous windings of a river, path, etc. 2 circuitous journey. [Greek Maiandros, a winding river in ancient Phrygia]

**meanie** /mee-nee/ n. (also **meany**) (pl. -ies) colloq. niggardly or small-minded person.

**meaning** — n. 1 what is meant. 2 significance. 3 importance. — adj. expressive, significant (meaning glance). □ **meaningly** adv.

**meaningful** adj. 1 full of meaning; significant. 2 Logic able to be interpreted. □ **meaningfully** adv. **meaningfulness** n.

**meaningless** adj. having no meaning or significance. □ **meaninglessly** adv. **meaninglessness** n.

**means** n.pl. 1 (often treated as sing.) action, agent, device, or method producing a result (means of quick travel). 2 a money resources (live beyond one's means). b wealth (man of means). □ **by all means** certainly. **by means of** by the agency etc. of. **by no means** certainly not. [from MEAN[3]]

**means test** — n. inquiry into a person's income in order to determine his or her eligibility for a pension or other assistance from public funds etc. — v. (**means-test**) subject to or base on a means test.

**meant** past and past part. of MEAN[1].

**meantime** — adv. = MEANWHILE. — n. intervening period (esp. in the meantime).

■ **Usage** As an adverb, meantime is less common than meanwhile.

**meanwhile** adv. 1 in the intervening period of time. 2 at the same time.

**measles** /mee-zuhlz/ n.pl. (also treated as sing.) infectious viral disease marked by a red rash. [Low German masele or Dutch masel]

**measly** /meez-lee/ adj. (-ier, -iest) colloq. meagre, contemptible (donated a measly two dollars).

**measure** /mezh-uh/ — n. 1 size or quantity found by measuring. 2 system or unit of measuring (liquid measure; 20 measures of wheat). 3 rod, tape, vessel, etc., for measuring. 4 (often foll. by of) degree, extent, or amount (a measure of wit). 5 factor determining evaluation etc. (sales are the measure of popularity). 6 (usu. in pl.) suitable action to achieve some end (took measures to ensure a good profit). 7 legislative bill, act, etc. 8 prescribed extent or quantity. 9 poetic metre. 10 mineral stratum (coal measures). — v. (-ring) 1 ascertain the extent or quantity of (a thing) by comparison with a known standard. 2 be of a specified size (it measures two metres). 3 ascertain the size of (a person) for clothes. 4 estimate (a quality etc.) by some criterion. **5** (often foll. by *off*) mark (a line etc. of a given length). **6** (foll. by *out*) distribute in measured quantities. **7** (foll. by *with*, *against*) bring (oneself or one's strength etc.) into competition with. □ **beyond measure** excessively. **for good measure** as a finishing touch. **in some measure** partly. **measure up 1** take the measurements (of). **2** (often foll. by *to*) have the qualifications (for). □ **measurable** *adj*. [Latin *mensura* from *metior* measure]

**measured** *adj*. **1** rhythmical; regular (*measured tread*). **2** (of language) carefully considered.

**measureless** *adj*. not measurable; infinite.

**measurement** *n*. **1** act or an instance of measuring. **2** amount measured. **3** (in *pl*.) detailed dimensions.

**meat** *n*. **1** animal flesh as food. **2** (often foll. by *of*) substance; chief part. **3** edible part of fruit, nuts, eggs, shellfish, etc. **4** (in Aboriginal English) a totem; a totemic animal. □ **meat and drink** a source of great pleasure (*footy is meat and drink to him*). **meat in the sandwich** innocent victim of a conflict or clash of interests who is vulnerable to both sides. □ **meatless** *adj*. [Old English]

**meat-ant** *n*. (also **red ant, red meat-ant**) mound-building Australian ant, having a red head and purplish body, and capable of inflicting a painful bite. □ **game as a meat-ant** courageous and tenacious.

**meat pie** *n*. stewed meat in a small square or oval pastry-case for consumption by one person. □ **as Australian as meat pie** quintessentially Australian.

**meat works** *n*. = ABATTOIR.

**meaty** *adj*. (**-ier, -iest**) **1** full of meat; fleshy. **2** of or like meat. **3** substantial, full of interest, satisfying. □ **meatiness** *n*.

**Mecca** /mek-uh/ *n*. any place one aspires to visit. [*Mecca*, Muslim holy city in Arabia]

**mechanic** /muh-**kan**-ik/ *n*. person skilled in using or repairing machinery. [Latin: related to MACHINE]

**mechanical** *adj*. **1** of machines or mechanisms. **2** working or produced by machinery. **3** (of an action etc.) automatic; repetitive. **4** (of an agency, principle, etc.) belonging to mechanics. **5** of mechanics as a science. □ **mechanically** *adv*. [Latin: related to MECHANIC]

**mechanical engineer** *n*. person qualified in the design, construction, etc. of machines.

**mechanics** *n.pl*. (usu. treated as *sing*.) **1** branch of applied mathematics dealing with motion etc. **2** science of machinery.

**3** routine technical aspects of a thing (*mechanics of local government*).

**Mechanics' Institute** *n*. *hist*. nineteenth century institution in Australia providing library, lectures, etc., esp. for the working classes; also called School of Arts esp. in NSW and Queensland.

**mechanise** /mek-uh-₋nuyz/ *v*. (also **-ize**) (**-sing** or **-zing**) **1** introduce machines in (a factory etc.). **2** make mechanical. **3** equip with tanks, armoured cars, etc. □ **mechanisation** /-zay-shuhn/ *n*.

**mechanism** /mek-uh-₋niz-uhm/ *n*. **1** structure or parts of a machine. **2** system of parts working together. **3** process; method (*defence mechanism; no mechanism for complaints*). □ **mechanistic** /-nis-tik/ *adj*. [Greek: related to MACHINE]

**medal** /med-uhl/ *n*. commemorative metal disc etc., esp. awarded for military or sporting prowess. [Latin: related to METAL]

**medallion** /muh-**dal**-yuhn/ *n*. **1** large medal. **2** thing so shaped, e.g. a decorative panel etc. [Italian: related to MEDAL]

**medallist** /med-uh-luhst/ *n*. winner of a (specified) medal (*gold medallist*).

**meddle** /med-uhl/ *v*. (**-ling**) (often foll. by *with, in*) interfere in others' concerns. □ **meddler** *n*. [Latin: related to MIX]

**meddlesome** *adj*. interfering.

**media** /mee-dee-uh/ *n.pl*. **1** *pl*. of MEDIUM. **2** (usu. prec. by *the*) mass communications (esp. newspapers and broadcasting) regarded collectively.

---

■ **Usage** *Media* is commonly used with a singular verb (e.g. *the media is biased*), but this is not generally accepted (cf. DATA).

---

**mediaeval** var. of MEDIEVAL.

**medial** /mee-dee-uhl/ *adj*. = MEDIAN. □ **medially** *adv*. [Latin *medius* middle]

**median** /mee-dee-uhn/ — *adj*. situated in the middle. — *n*. **1** straight line drawn from any vertex of a triangle to the middle of the opposite side. **2** middle value of a series. [Latin: related to MEDIAL]

**mediant** /mee-dee-uhnt/ *n*. *Mus*. third note of a diatonic scale of any key. [Latin (as MEDIATE)]

**mediate** /mee-dee-₋ayt/ *v*. (**-ting**) **1** (often foll. by *between*) intervene (between disputants) to settle a quarrel etc. **2** bring about (a result) thus. □ **mediation** /-ay-shuhn/ *n*. **mediator** *n*. [Latin *medius* middle]

**medical** /med-i-kuhl/ — *adj*. of medicine in general or as distinct from surgery (*medical ward*). — *n*. *colloq*. medical examination. □ **medically** *adv*.

**medical certificate** *n.* certificate of fitness or unfitness for work etc.

**medical practitioner** *n.* physician or surgeon.

**medicament** /muh-**dik**-uh-muhnt, **med**-i-kuh-muhnt/ *n.* = MEDICINE 2.

**Medicare** /**med**-ee-,kair/ *n.* Federal system of basic health care for all Australians, introduced in 1984 by the Labor government and partly financed by a levy on taxable incomes. [from MEDICAL, CARE]

**medicate** /**med**-uh-,kayt/ *v.* (**-ting**) **1** treat medically. **2** impregnate with medicine etc. □ **medicative** /med-uh-kuh-tiv/ *adj.* [Latin *medicare medicat-*]

**medication** /,med-uh-**kay**-shuhn/ *n.* **1** = MEDICINE 2. **2** treatment using drugs.

**medicinal** /muh-**dis**-uh-nuhl/ *adj.* (of a substance) healing. □ **medicinally** *adv.*

**medicine** /**med**-suhn, **med**-uh-suhn/ *n.* **1** science or practice of the diagnosis, treatment, and prevention of disease, esp. as distinct from surgery. **2** drug etc. for the treatment or prevention of disease, esp. taken by mouth. □ **take one's medicine** submit to something disagreeable. [Latin *medicina*]

**medicine man** *n.* lay person believed to have powers of healing, esp. among Aborigines.

**medico** /**med**-ee-,koh/ *n.* (*pl.* **-s**) *colloq.* medical practitioner or student. [abbreviation]

**medieval** /,med-ee-**ee**-vuhl/ *adj.* (also **mediaeval**) **1** of the Middle Ages. **2** *colloq.* old-fashioned. [Latin *medium aevum* middle age]

**medifraud** /**med**-ee-,frawd/ *n.* **1** the practice (usu. by doctors) of making fraudulent claims against a medical insurance scheme. **2** an instance of this.

**mediocre** /,mee-dee-**oh**-kuh/ *adj.* **1** of ordinary quality, neither good nor bad. **2** second-rate. [Latin *mediocris*]

**mediocrity** /,mee-dee-**ok**-ruh-tee/ *n.* (*pl.* **-ies**) **1** being mediocre. **2** mediocre person.

**meditate** /**med**-uh-,tayt/ *v.* (**-ting**) **1** (often foll. by *on, upon*) engage in (esp. religious) contemplation. **2** plan mentally (*he meditated revenge*). □ **meditation** /-**tay**-shuhn/ *n.* **meditator** *n.* [Latin *meditor*]

**meditative** /**med**-uh-tuh-tiv, -tay-tiv/ *adj.* **1** inclined to meditate. **2** indicative of meditation, thoughtful. □ **meditatively** *adv.* **meditativeness** *n.*

**Mediterranean** /,med-uh-tuh-**ray**-nee-uhn/ *adj.* of the sea bordered by S. Europe, SW Asia, and N. Africa, or its surrounding region (*Mediterranean cookery*). [Latin *mediterraneus* inland]

**medium** /**mee**-dee-uhm/ *n.* (*pl.* **media** or **-s**) **1** middle quality, degree, etc. between extremes (*find a happy medium*). **2** means of communication (*medium of television*). **3** substance, e.g. air, through which sense-impressions are conveyed. **4** physical environment etc. of a living organism. **5** means (*the medium through which money may be raised*). **6** material or form used by an artist, composer, etc. **7** liquid (e.g. oil or gel) used for diluting paints. **8** (*pl.* **-s**) person claiming to communicate with the dead. — *adj.* **1** between two qualities, degrees, etc. **2** average (*of medium height*). [Latin *medius* middle]

**medium wave** *n.* radio wave of frequency between 300 kHz and 3 MHz.

**medley** /**med**-lee/ *n.* (*pl.* **-s**) **1** varied mixture; miscellany. **2** collection of tunes etc. played as one piece. **3 a** swimming race in which each competitor swims set distances in different strokes. **b** (in full **medley relay**) relay race between swimming teams in which each team-member swims a different stroke. [French *medlee*]

**medulla** /muh-**dul**-uh/ *n.* **1** inner part of certain organs etc., e.g. the kidney. **2** soft internal tissue of plants. □ **medullary** *adj.* [Latin]

**medulla oblongata** /,ob-long-**gah**-tuh/ *n.* lowest part of the brainstem, formed from a continuation of the spinal cord.

**medusa** /muh-**dyoo**-suh/ *n.* (*pl.* **medusae** /-see/ or **-s**) jellyfish. [Greek *Medousa*, name of a Gorgon]

**meek** *adj.* humble and submissive or gentle. □ **meekly** *adv.* **meekness** *n.* [Old Norse]

**meet¹** — *v.* (*past* and *past part.* **met**) **1** encounter (a person etc.) or (of two or more people) come together by accident or design; come face to face (with) (*met on the bridge*). **2** be present by design at the arrival of (a person, train, etc.). **3** come or seem to come together or into contact (with); join (*where the sea and the sky meet*; *jacket won't meet*). **4** make the acquaintance of (*delighted to meet you*; *all met at Mordialloc*). **5** come together for business, worship, etc. (*union met management*). **6** *a* deal with or answer (a demand, objection, etc.) (*met the proposal with hostility*). **b** satisfy or conform with (*agreed to meet the new terms*). **7** pay (a bill etc.); honour (a cheque) (*meet the cost*). **8** (often foll. by *with*) experience, encounter, or receive (*met their death*; *met with hostility*). **9** confront in battle etc. — *n.* **1** assembly for sport, esp.

athletics. **2** *colloq.* assignation, date, esp. with someone of the opposite sex. □ **make ends meet** see END. **meet the case** be adequate. **meet the eye** be visible or evident. meet a person half way compromise with. **meet up** *colloq.* (often foll. by *with*) = sense 1 of *v.* meet with **1** see sense 8 of *v.* **2** receive (a reaction) (*met with her approval*). [Old English]

**meet²** *adj. archaic* fitting, proper. [related to METE]

**meeting** *n.* **1** in senses of MEET¹. **2 a** coming together; assembly of a society, committee, etc. **b** persons assembled (*address the meeting*). **3** = RACE MEETING.

**mega** /meg-uh/ *colloq.* — *adj.* **1** excellent. **2** enormous. — *adv.* extremely.

**mega-** *comb. form* **1** large. **2** one million (10⁶) in the metric system of measurement. **3** *colloq.* extremely; very big (*mega-stupid; mega-project*). [Greek *megas* great]

**megabyte** /meg-uh-ˌbuyt/ *n. Computing* 1,048,576 (i.e. 2²⁰) bytes, or loosely 1,000,000, as a measure of data capacity or memory size.

**megahertz** /meg-uh-ˌherts/ *n.* (*pl.* same) one million hertz, esp. as a measure of radio frequency.

**megalith** /meg-uh-lith/ *n.* large stone, esp. as a prehistoric monument or part of one. □ **megalithic** /ˌmeg-uh-lith-ik/ *adj.* [Greek *lithos* stone]

**megalomania** /ˌmeg-uh-luh-may-nee-uh/ *n.* **1** mental disorder producing delusions of grandeur. **2** passion for grandiose schemes. □ **megalomaniac** *adj.* & *n.* [Greek *megas* great, MANIA]

**megalosaurus** /ˌmeg-uh-luh-saw-ruhs/ *n.* (*pl.* **-ruses**) large flesh-eating dinosaur with stout hind legs and small forelimbs. [Greek *megas* great, *sauros* lizard]

**megaphone** /meg-uh-ˌfohn/ *n.* large funnel-shaped device for amplifying the voice. [Greek *megas* great, *phōnē* sound]

**megapode** /meg-uh-ˌpohd/ *n.* bird, native to Australasia, that builds a mound of debris for the incubation of its eggs, e.g. a mallee fowl. [MEGA-, Greek *pous podos* foot]

**megastar** /meg-uh-ˌstah/ *n. colloq.* very famous entertainer etc.

**megaton** /meg-uh-ˌtun/ *n.* unit of explosive power equal to one million tons of TNT.

**meiosis** /muy-oh-suhs/ *n.* (*pl.* **meioses** /-seez/ ) **1** cell division that results in gametes with half the normal chromosome number. **2** = LITOTES. [Greek *meiōn* less]

**melaleuca** /ˌmel-uh-loo-kuh/ *n.* any plant of the large essentially Australian

genus in the Myrtaceae family, consisting of trees and shrubs with profuse white, cream, yellow, mauve, or red bottlebrush or ball flowers, many species being widely cultivated as ornamentals. [Greek *melas* black, *leukos* white, referring to the trunk and branches of some species]

**melancholia** /ˌmel-uhn-koh-lee-uh/ *n.* depression and anxiety. [Latin: related to MELANCHOLY]

**melancholy** /mel-uhn-kol-ee/ — *n.* **1** pensive sadness. **2 a** mental depression. **b** tendency to this. — *adj.* sad; saddening, depressing; expressing sadness. □ **melancholic** /-kol-ik/ *adj.* [Greek *melas* black, *kholē* bile]

**mélange** /may-lonzh/ *n.* mixture, medley. [French *mêler* mix]

**melanin** /mel-uh-nuhn/ *n.* dark pigment in the hair, skin, etc., causing tanning in sunlight. [Greek *melas* black]

**melanoma** /ˌmel-uh-noh-muh/ *n.* malignant skin tumour.

**Melba** /mel-buh/ *n.* □ **do a melba 1** return from retirement. **2** make several 'final' farewell appearances. **Melba sauce** sauce made from puréed raspberries. **Melba toast** very thin crisp toast. **peach Melba** icecream and peaches with liqueur or sauce. [Dame Nellie *Melba*, Australian operatic soprano (d. 1931)]

**Melbourne** /mel-buhn/ *n.* name of the capital city of the State of Victoria (earlier *Batmania* after John Batman; *Bearbrass, Bearport, Bearheap*, and *Bearbury*, all variations of the Wuywurung name for the area *Berrern* or *Bararing* etc.). [Lord *Melbourne*, British Prime Minister]

**Melburnian** /ˌmel-ber-nee-uhn/ — *n.* native of Melbourne. — *adj.* of or relating to Melbourne.

**meld** *v.* merge, blend. [origin uncertain]

**mêlée** /mel-ay/ *n.* (also **melee**) **1** confused fight, skirmish, or scuffle. **2** muddle. [French: related to MEDLEY]

**meliorate** /mee-lee-uh-ˌrayt/ *v.* improve (cf. AMELIORATE).

**mellifluous** /muh-lif-loo-uhs/ *adj.* (of a voice etc.) pleasing, musical, flowing. □ **mellifluously** *adv.* **mellifluousness** *n.* [Latin *mel* honey, *fluo* flow]

**mellow** /mel-oh/ — *adj.* **1** (of sound, colour, light) soft and rich, free from harshness. **2** (of character) gentle; mature. **3** genial, jovial. **4** *euphem.* partly intoxicated. **5** (of fruit) soft, sweet, and juicy. **6** (of wine) well-matured, smooth. **7** (of earth) rich, loamy. — *v.* make or become mellow. □ **mellowly** *adv.* **mellowness** *n.* [origin unknown]

**melodic** /muh-**lod**-ik/ *adj.* of melody; melodious. □ **melodically** *adv.* [Greek: related to MELODY]

**melodious** /muh-**loh**-dee-uhs/ *adj.* **1** of, producing, or having melody. **2** sweet-sounding. □ **melodiously** *adv.* **melodiousness** *n.* [French: related to MELODY]

**melodrama** /**mel**-uh-,drah-muh/ *n.* **1** sensational play etc. appealing blatantly to the emotions. **2** this type of drama. **3** language, behaviour, a situation, etc., suggestive of this. □ **melodramatic** /-druh-**mat**-ik/ *adj.* **melodramatically** /-druh-**mat**-i-klee/ *adv.* [Greek *melos* music, DRAMA]

**melody** /**mel**-uh-dee/ *n.* (*pl.* **-ies**) **1** single notes arranged to make a distinctive recognisable pattern; tune. **2** principal part in harmonised music. **3** musical arrangement of words. **4** sweet music, tunefulness. [Greek *melos* song: related to ODE]

**melon** /**mel**-uhn/ *n.* **1** sweet fleshy fruit of various climbing plants of the gourd family. **2** such a gourd. [Greek *mēlon* apple]

**melon blindness** *n.* illness of horses characterised by blindness and possibly resulting from eating paddymelon.

**melon hole** *n.* = GILGAI.

**melt** *v.* **1** become liquefied or change to liquid by the action of heat; dissolve. **2** (as **molten** *adj.*) (esp. of metals etc.) liquefied by heat (*molten lava*; *molten lead*). **3** (of food) be delicious, seeming to dissolve in the mouth. **4** soften, or (of a person, the heart, etc.) be softened, by pity, love, etc. (*a melting look*). **5** (usu. foll. by *into*) merge imperceptibly; change into (*night melted into dawn*). **6** (often foll. by *away*) (of a person) leave or disappear unobtrusively (*melted into the background*). □ **melt away** disappear by or as if by liquefaction. **melt down 1** melt (esp. metal) for reuse. **2** become liquid and lose structure. [Old English]

**meltdown** *n.* **1** melting of a structure, esp. the overheated core of a nuclear reactor. **2** disastrous event, esp. a rapid fall in share values.

**melting point** *n.* temperature at which a solid melts.

**melting pot** *n.* place where races, theories, etc. are mixed.

**member** /**mem**-buh/ *n.* **1** person etc. belonging to a society, team, group, etc. **2** (**Member**) person elected to take part in the proceedings of certain assemblies etc. (*Member of Parliament*). **3** part of a larger structure, e.g. of a group of figures or a mathematical set. **4 a** part or organ of the body, esp. a limb. **b** = PENIS. **5** used

in the title awarded to a person admitted to (usu. the lowest grade of) certain honours (*Member of the Order of Australia*). [Latin *membrum* limb]

**membership** *n.* **1** being a member. **2** number or body of members.

**membrane** /**mem**-brayn/ *n.* **1** pliable sheetlike tissue connecting or lining organs in plants and animals. **2** thin pliable sheet or skin. □ **membranous** /**mem**-bruh-nuhs/ *adj.* [Latin *membrana* skin, parchment: related to MEMBER]

**memento** /muh-**men**-toh/ *n.* (*pl.* **-es** or **-s**) souvenir of a person or event. [Latin, imperative of *memini* remember]

**memo** /**mem**-oh, **mee**-moh/ *n.* (*pl.* **-s**) memorandum. [abbreviation]

**memoir** /**mem**-wah/ *n.* **1** historical account etc. written from personal knowledge or special sources. **2** (in *pl.*) autobiography, esp. partial or dealing with specific events or people. [French *mémoire*: related to MEMORY]

**memorabilia** /,mem-uh-ruh-**bil**-ee-uh/ *n.pl.* souvenirs of memorable events, people, etc. (*Carrie Moore memorabilia*). [Latin: related to MEMORABLE]

**memorable** /**mem**-uh-ruh-buhl/ *adj.* **1** worth remembering (*a memorable event*). **2** easily remembered. □ **memorably** *adv.* [Latin *memor* mindful]

**memorandum** /,mem-uh-**ran**-duhm/ *n.* (*pl.* **-da** or **-s**) **1** note or record for future use. **2** informal written message, esp. in business, diplomacy, etc. [see MEMORABLE]

**memorial** /muh-**maw**-ree-uhl/ — *n.* object etc. established in memory of a person or event. — *attrib. adj.* commemorating (*memorial service*). [Latin: related to MEMORY]

**memorise** /**mem**-uh-,ruyz/ *v.* (also **-ize**) (**-sing** or **-zing**) commit to memory.

**memory** /**mem**-uh-ree/ *n.* (*pl.* **-ies**) **1** faculty by which things are recalled to or kept in the mind. **2 a** this in an individual (*my memory is failing*). **b** store of things remembered (*deep in my memory*). **3** recollection; remembrance, esp. of a person etc.; person or thing remembered (*memory of better times*; *her mother's memory*). **4** storage capacity of a computer etc. **5** posthumous reputation (*her memory lives on*; *of blessed memory*). **6** length of remembered time of a specific person, group, etc. (*within living memory*). **7** remembering (*deed worthy of memory*). □ **from memory** as remembered (without checking). **in memory of** to keep alive the remembrance of. [Latin *memoria* from *memor* mindful]

**men** *pl.* of MAN.

**menace** /**men**-uhs/ — n. **1** threat. **2** dangerous thing or person. **3** joc. pest, nuisance. — v. (**-cing**) threaten. □ **menacingly** adv. [Latin minax from minor threaten]

**ménage** /may-**nahzh**/ n. household. [Latin: related to MANOR]

**ménage à trois** /may,nahzh ah **trwah**/ n. (pl. **ménages à trois**) household of three, usu. a married couple and a lover. [French, = household of three]

**menagerie** /muh-**naj**-uh-ree/ n. small zoo. [French: related to MENAGE]

**menarche** /**men**-ah-kee/ n. onset of first menstruation. [Greek mēn mēnos month, arkhē beginning]

**mend** — v. **1** restore to good condition; repair. **2** regain health. **3** improve (mend matters). — n. darn or repair in material etc. □ **mend one's ways** reform oneself. **on the mend** recovering, esp. in health. [Anglo-French: related to AMEND]

**mendacious** /men-**day**-shuhs/ adj. lying, untruthful. □ **mendacity** /-**das**-uh-tee/ n. (pl. **-ies**). [Latin mendax]

**mendelevium** /,men-duh-**lee**-vee-uhm/ n. artificially made transuranic radioactive metallic element. [Mendeleev, name of a chemist]

**Mendelian** /men-**dee**-lee-uhn/ adj. of Mendel's theory of heredity by genes. [G.J. Mendel, Moravian botanist (d. 1884)]

**mendicant** /**men**-duh-kuhnt/ — adj. **1** begging. **2** (of a friar) living solely on alms. — n. **1** beggar. **2** mendicant friar. [Latin mendicus beggar]

**mending** n. **1** action of repairing. **2** things, esp. clothes, to be mended.

**menfolk** n.pl. men, esp. the men of a family.

**menhir** /**men**-heer/ n. usu. prehistoric monument of a tall upright stone. [Breton men stone, hir long]

**menial** /**mee**-nee-uhl/ — adj. (of esp. work) degrading, servile. — n. domestic servant; lackey; lowly worker (in a big firm etc.). [Anglo-French meinie retinue]

**meninges** /muh-**nin**-jeez/ n.pl. three membranes enclosing the brain and spinal cord. [Greek mēnigx membrane]

**meningitis** /,men-uhn-**juy**-tuhs/ n. (esp. viral) infection and inflammation of the meninges.

**meniscus** /muh-**nis**-kuhs/ n. (pl. **menisci** /-suy/) **1** curved upper surface of liquid in a tube. **2** lens convex on one side and concave on the other. [Greek mēniskos crescent, from mēnē moon]

**menopause** /**men**-uh-,pawz/ n. **1** ceasing of menstruation. **2** period in a woman's life (usu. 45–55) when this occurs. □ **menopausal** /-**paw**-zuhl/ adj. [Greek mēn month, PAUSE]

**menorah** /muh-**naw**-ruh/ n. seven-branched Jewish candelabrum. [Hebrew, = candlestick]

**men's business** n. an Aboriginal ritual open only to initiated males.

**menses** /**men**-seez/ n.pl. flow of menstrual blood etc. [Latin, pl. of mensis month]

**menstrual** /**men**-stroo-uhl/ adj. of menstruation. [Latin menstruus monthly]

**menstrual cycle** n. process of ovulation and menstruation.

**menstruate** /**men**-stroo-,ayt/ v. (**-ting**) undergo menstruation.

**menstruation** /,men-stroo-**ay**-shuhn/ n. process of discharging blood etc. from the uterus, usu. at monthly intervals from puberty to menopause.

**mensuration** /,men-shuh-**ray**-shuhn/ n. **1** measuring. **2** measuring of lengths, areas, and volumes. [Latin: related to MEASURE]

**-ment** suffix **1** forming nouns expressing the means or result of verbal action (abridgment; embankment). **2** forming nouns from adjectives (merriment; oddment). [Latin -mentum]

**mental** /**men**-tuhl/ adj. **1** of, in, or done by the mind. **2** caring for the mentally ill (mental hospital). **3** colloq. insane or stupid. □ **mentally** adv. [Latin mens ment-mind]

**mental age** n. degree of mental development in terms of the average age at which such development is attained.

**mental block** n. inability due to subconscious mental factors.

**mental deficiency** n. abnormally low intelligence.

**mentality** /men-**tal**-uh-tee/ n. (pl. **-ies**) mental character or disposition; kind or degree of intelligence (his mentality was only average; has a fine mentality).

**mental patient** n. sufferer from mental illness.

**menthol** /**men**-thol/ n. mint-tasting organic alcohol found in oil of peppermint etc., used as a flavouring and to relieve local pain. [Latin: related to MINT¹]

**mentholated** /**men**-thuh-,lay-tuhd/ adj. treated with or containing menthol.

**mention** /**men**-shuhn/ — v. **1** refer to briefly or by name. **2** reveal or disclose (do not mention this to anyone). **3** (usu. as **mention in dispatches**) award a minor military honour to in war. — n. **1** reference, esp. by name, to a person or thing (got a mention in 'The Geelong Advertiser'). **2** minor military or other honour. □ **don't mention it** polite reply to an apology or thanks. **not to mention** and also. [Latin *mentio*]

**mentor** /**men**-taw/ *n.* experienced and trusted adviser. [*Mentor* in Homer's *Odyssey*]

**menu** /**men**-yoo/ *n.* **1** list of dishes available in a restaurant etc., or to be served at a meal. **2** *Computing* list of options showing the commands or facilities available. [Latin: related to MINUTE²]

**mephistophelean** /ˌmef-i-stuh-**fee**-lee-uhn/ *adj.* fiendish. [*Mephistopheles*, evil spirit to whom Faust sold his soul in German legend]

**mercantile** /**mer**-kuhn-ˌtuyl/ *adj.* **1** of trade, trading. **2** commercial. [Latin: related to MERCHANT]

**Mercator projection** /mer-**kay**-tuh/ *n.* (also **Mercator's projection**) map of the world projected on to a cylinder so that all the parallels of latitude have the same length as the equator. [*Mercator*, name of a geographer]

**mercenary** /**mer**-suh-nuh-ree, -suhn-ree/ — *adj.* primarily concerned with or working for money etc. — *n.* (*pl.* **-ies**) hired soldier in foreign service. □ **mercenariness** *n.* [Latin from *merces* reward]

**mercer** *n.* dealer in textile fabrics. [Latin *merx merc-* goods]

**mercerise** /**mer**-suh-ˌruyz/ *v.* (also **-ize**) (**-sing** or **-zing**) treat (cotton) with caustic alkali to strengthen and make lustrous. [*Mercer*, name of its alleged inventor]

**merchandise** — *n.* /**mer**-chuhn-ˌduys/ goods for sale. — *v.* /-ˌduyz/ (**-sing**) **1** trade, traffic (in). **2** advertise or promote (goods, an idea, or a person). [French: related to MERCHANT]

**merchant** /**mer**-chuhnt/ *n.* **1** wholesale trader, esp. with foreign countries. **2** retail trader. **3** *colloq.* usu. *derog.* person devoted to a specified activity etc. or noted for particular behaviour (*speed merchant*; *panic merchant*). [Latin *mercor* trade (v.)]

**merchantable** *adj.* saleable, marketable.

**merchant bank** *n.* bank dealing in commercial loans and finance.

**merchantman** *n.* (*pl.* **-men**) merchant ship.

**merchant navy** *n.* nation's commercial shipping.

**merciful** /**mer**-suh-ˌfuhl/ *adj.* showing mercy. □ **mercifulness** *n.*

**mercifully** *adv.* **1** in a merciful manner. **2** fortunately (*mercifully, the sun came out*).

**merciless** /**mer**-suh-luhs/ *adj.* showing no mercy. □ **mercilessly** *adv.*

**mercurial** /mer-**kyoo**-ree-uhl/ *adj.* **1** (of a person) **a** ready-witted. **b** changeable, volatile. **2** of or containing mercury. [Latin: related to MERCURY]

**mercury** /**mer**-kyuh-ree/ *n.* **1** silvery heavy liquid metallic element used in barometers, thermometers, etc. **2** (**Mercury**) planet nearest to the sun. □ **mercuric** /-**kyoo**-rik/ *adj.* **mercurous** *adj.* [Latin *Mercurius*, Roman messenger-god]

**mercy** /**mer**-see/ — *n.* (*pl.* **-ies**) **1** compassion or forbearance towards defeated enemies or offenders or as a quality. **2** act of mercy. **3** (*attrib.*) done out of compassion (*mercy killing*). **4** thing to be thankful for (*small mercies*). — *int.* expressing surprise or fear. □ **at the mercy of 1** in the power of. **2** liable to danger or harm from. **have mercy on** (or **upon**) show mercy to. [Latin *merces* reward, pity]

**mere**¹ /meer/ *attrib. adj.* (**merest**) being solely or only what is specified (*a mere boy*; *no mere theory*). □ **merely** *adv.* [Latin *merus* unmixed]

**mere**² /meer/ *n. Brit. dial.* or *poet.* lake. [Old English, akin to Latin *mare* sea]

**meretricious** /ˌme-ruh-**trish**-uhs/ *adj.* showily but falsely attractive. [Latin *meretrix* prostitute]

**merge** *v.* (**-ging**) **1** (often foll. by *with*) **a** combine. **b** join or blend gradually. **2** (foll. by *in*) (cause to) lose character and identity in (something else). [Latin *mergo* dip]

**merger** *n.* combining, esp. of two commercial companies etc. into one.

**meridian** /muh-**rid**-ee-uhn/ *n.* **1 a** circle of constant longitude, passing through a given place and the terrestrial poles. **b** corresponding line on a map. **2** (often *attrib.*) prime; full splendour. □ **meridional** /muh-**rid**-ee-uhn-uhl/ *adj.* [Latin *meridies* midday]

**meringue** /muh-**rang**/ *n.* **1** sugar, whipped egg-whites, etc., baked crisp. **2** small cake of this, esp. filled with whipped cream. [French]

**merino** /muh-**ree**-noh/ *n.* (*pl.* **-s**) **1** (in full **merino sheep**) variety of sheep with long fine wool. **2** soft cashmere-like material, orig. of merino wool. **3** fine woollen yarn. **4** (also **pure merino**) *hist.* a free settler in Australia (opp. a convict: see LEGITIMATE *n.*). [Spanish]

**meristem** /**me**-ree-ˌstem/ *n.* plant tissue consisting of actively dividing cells forming new tissue. [Greek *meristos* divisible]

**merit** /**me**-ruht/ — *n.* **1** quality of deserving well. **2** excellence, worth. **3** (usu. in *pl.*) **a** thing that entitles one to reward or gratitude. **b** intrinsic rights and wrongs (*merits of a case*). — *v.* (**-t-**) deserve. [Latin *meritum* value, from *mereor* deserve]

**meritocracy** /ˌme-ruh-**tok**-ruh-see/ *n.* (*pl.* **-ies**) **1** government by those selected for merit. **2** group selected in this way. **3** society governed thus.

**meritorious** /ˌme-ruh-**taw**-ree-uhs/ *adj.* praiseworthy.

**mermaid** *n.* legendary creature with a woman's head and trunk and a fish's tail. [from MERE[2] 'sea', MAID]

**merman** *n.* male equivalent of a mermaid.

**merry** /**me**-ree/ *adj.* (**-ier**, **-iest**) **1 a** joyous. **b** full of laughter or gaiety. **2** *colloq.* slightly drunk. □ **make merry** be festive. □ **merrily** *adv.* **merriment** *n.* **merriness** *n.* [Old English]

**merry-go-round** *n.* **1** fairground ride with revolving model horses or cars. **2** cycle of bustling activity (*on the merry-go-round of parties, meetings, business lunches*).

**merrymaking** *n.* festivity, fun. □ **merry-maker** *n.*

**mésalliance** /may-**zal**-ee-ˌons/ *n.* marriage with a social inferior. [French]

**mesembryanthemum** /ˌmez-uhm-bree-**an**-thuh-muhm/ *n.* **1** = PIGFACE. **2** S. African fleshy-leaved plant with bright daisy-like flowers that open fully in sunlight. [Greek, = noon flower]

**mesh** — *n.* **1** network fabric or structure. **2** each of the open spaces in a net or sieve etc. **3** (in *pl.*) **a** network. **b** snare. — *v.* **1** (often foll. by *with*) (of the teeth of a wheel) be engaged. **2** be harmonious. **3** catch in a net. □ **in mesh** (of the teeth of wheels) engaged. [Dutch]

**mesmerise** /**mez**-muh-ˌruyz/ *v.* (also **-ize**) (**-sing** or **-zing**) **1** hypnotise. **2** fascinate, spellbind. □ **mesmerism** *n.* **mesmerisingly** *adv.* [*Mesmer*, name of a physician]

**meso-** *comb. form* middle, intermediate. [Greek *mesos* middle]

**mesolithic** /ˌmes-oh-**lith**-ik, ˌmee-zoh-/ *adj.* of the part of the Stone Age between the palaeolithic and neolithic periods. [Greek *lithos* stone]

**meson** /**mez**-on, **mee**-zon/ *n.* elementary particle believed to help hold nucleons together in the atomic nucleus. [from MESO-]

**mesosphere** /**mes**-oh-ˌsfeer, **mee**-zoh-/ *n.* region of the atmosphere from the top of the stratosphere to an altitude of about 80 km.

**Mesozoic** /ˌmes-oh-**zoh**-ik, ˌmee-zoh-

**zoh**-ik/ — *adj.* of the geological era marked by the development of dinosaurs, and the first mammals, birds, and flowering plants. — *n.* this era. [Greek *zōion* animal]

**mess** — *n.* **1** dirty or untidy state of things. **2** state of confusion, embarrassment, or trouble. **3** something spilt etc. **4** disagreeable concoction. **5 a** soldiers etc. dining together. **b** army dining-hall. **c** meal taken there. **6** domestic animal's excreta. **7** portion of liquid or pulpy food. **8** *colloq.* person whose life has gone awry. — *v.* **1** (often foll. by *up*) make a mess of; dirty; muddle. **2** (foll. by *with*) interfere with. **3** take one's meals as a member of a mess. □ **make a mess of** bungle. **mess about** (or **around**) **1** potter; fiddle; waste time. **2** *colloq.* make things awkward or inconvenient for (a person). **3** fool around. **4** *colloq.* (foll. by *with*) associate with as mate. [Latin *missus* course of a meal: related to MESSAGE]

**message** /**mes**-ij/ *n.* **1** communication sent by one person to another. **2** moral of a book etc. **3** (in *pl.*) shopping, or similar things to be done. □ **get the message** *colloq.* understand (a hint etc.). [Latin *mitto miss-* send]

**message-stick** *n.* piece of wood with symbolic markings which convey a message from one Aboriginal community to another and which may also indicate the bearer's standing or totem.

**messenger** /**mes**-uhn-juh/ *n.* person who carries a message.

**Messiah** /muh-**suy**-uh/ *n.* **1 a** promised deliverer of the Jews. **b** Christ regarded as this. **2** liberator of an oppressed people. [Hebrew, = anointed]

**Messianic** /ˌmes-ee-**an**-ik/ *adj.* **1** of the Messiah. **2** inspired by hope or belief in a Messiah. [French: related to MESSIAH]

**messmate** *n.* **1** person with whom one regularly takes meals, esp. in the armed forces. **2** any of several rough-barked eucalypts of south-eastern mainland Australia and Tasmania, supposedly so called because these trees associate with or are similar to stringybarks.

**Messrs** /**mes**-uhz/ *pl.* of MR. [abbreviation of *messieurs*, French plural of *monsieur* corresponding to MR]

**messy** *adj.* (**-ier**, **-iest**) **1** untidy or dirty. **2** causing or accompanied by a mess. **3** difficult to deal with; awkward (*a messy situation*). □ **messily** *adv.* **messiness** *n.*

**met** *past* and *past part.* of MEET[1].

**meta-** *comb. form* **1** denoting change of position or condition (*metabolism*). **2** denoting position: **a** behind, after, or beyond (*metaphysics*). **b** of a higher or second-order kind (*metalanguage*). [Greek *meta* with, after]

**metabolise** /muh-**tab**-uh-,luyz/ *v.* (also **-ize**) (**-sing** or **-zing**) process or be processed by metabolism.

**metabolism** /muh-**tab**-uh-,liz-uhm/ *n.* all the chemical processes in a living organism producing energy and growth. □ **metabolic** /,met-uh-**bol**-ik/ *adj.* [Greek *metabolē* change: related to META-, Greek *ballō* throw]

**metacarpus** /,met-uh-**kah**-puhs/ *n.* (*pl.* **-carpi** /-puy/ ) **1** part of the hand between the wrist and the fingers. **2** set of five bones in this. □ **metacarpal** *adj.* [related to META-, CARPUS]

**metal** /**met**-uhl/ — *n.* **1 a** any of a class of workable elements such as gold, silver, iron, or tin, usu. good conductors of heat and electricity and forming basic oxides. **b** alloy of any of these. **2** molten material for making glass. **3** = BLUE METAL. — *adj.* made of metal. — *v.* (**-ll-**) **1** make or mend (a road) with blue metal. **2** cover or fit with metal. [Greek *metallon* mine]

**metalanguage** /**met**-uh-,lang-gwij/ *n.* **1** form of language used to discuss language. **2** system of propositions about propositions.

**metallic** /muh-**tal**-ik/ *adj.* **1** of or like metal or metals (*metallic taste*). **2** sounding like struck metal. **3** shiny (*metallic blue*). □ **metallically** *adv.*

**metallic starling** *n.* bird of Queensland rainforests, having glossy black plumage with a metallic green and purple sheen.

**metalliferous** /,met-uh-**lif**-uh-ruhs/ *adj.* (of rocks) containing metal.

**metalloid** /**met**-uh-,loid/ *n.* element intermediate in properties between metals and non-metals, e.g. boron, silicon, and germanium.

**metallurgy** /**met**-uh-,ler-jee, muh-**tal**-uh-jee/ *n.* **1** science of metals and their application. **2** extraction and purification of metals. □ **metallurgic** /,met-uh-**ler**-jik/ *adj.* **metallurgical** /,met-uh-**ler**-ji-kuhl/ *adj.* **metallurgist** *n.* [Greek *metallon* METAL, *-ourgia* working]

**metalwork** *n.* **1** art of working in metal. **2** metal objects collectively. □ **metalworker** *n.*

**metamorphic** /,met-uh-**maw**-fik/ *adj.* **1** of metamorphosis. **2** (of rock) transformed naturally, e.g. by heat or pressure. □ **metamorphism** *n.* [from META-, Greek *morphē* form]

**metamorphose** /,met-uh-**maw**-fohz/ *v.* (**-sing**) (often foll. by *to, into*) change in form or nature.

**metamorphosis** /,met-uh-**maw**-fuh-suhs/ *n.* (*pl.* **-phoses** /-,seez/ ) **1** change of form (by natural or supernatural means). **2** transformation of an immature form to an adult form, e.g. of a pupa to an insect, a tadpole to a frog, etc. **3** change of character, conditions, etc. [Greek *morphē* form]

**metaphor** /**met**-uh-,faw/ *n.* **1** application of a name or description to something to which it is imaginatively but not literally applicable (see panel). **2** instance of this. □ **metaphoric** /-**fo**-rik/ *adj.* **metaphorical** /-**fo**-ri-kuhl/ *adj.* **metaphorically** /-**fo**-ri-klee/ *adv.* [Latin from Greek]

**metaphysical** *adj.* **1** of metaphysics. **2** (of esp. 17th-c. English poetry) subtle and complex in imagery.

**metaphysics** /,met-uh-**fiz**-iks/ *n.pl.* (usu. treated as *sing.*) **1** branch of philosophy dealing with the nature of existence, truth, and knowledge. **2** the philosophy of mind. [Greek, as having followed physics in Aristotle's works]

**metastasis** /me-**tas**-tuh-suhs/ *n.* (*pl.* **-stases** /-,seez/ ) transference of a bodily function, disease, etc., from one part or organ to another. [Greek, = removal]

**metatarsus** /,met-uh-**tah**-suhs/ *n.* (*pl.* **-tarsi** /-suy/ ) **1** part of the foot between the ankle and the toes. **2** set of five bones in this. □ **metatarsal** *adj.* [related to META-, TARSUS]

**metathesis** /muh-**tath**-uh-suhs/ *n.* **1** transposition of sounds or letters in a word (*Old English 'brid' became 'bird' by metathesis*). **2** an instance of this. □ **metathetic** /,met-uh-**thet**-ik/ *adj.* **metathetical** /-**thet**-i-kuhl/ *adj.* [Greek, = transposition]

**mete** *v.* (**-ting**) (usu. foll. by *out*) *literary* apportion or allot (punishment or reward). [Old English]

**meteor** /**mee**-tee-uh, -aw/ *n.* **1** small solid body from outer space that becomes incandescent when entering the earth's atmosphere. **2** streak of light from a meteor. [Greek *meteōros* lofty]

---

**Metaphor**
A metaphor is a figure of speech that goes further than a simile, either by saying that something is something else that it could not normally be called, e.g.

  *The moon was a ghostly galleon tossed upon cloudy seas.*

or by suggesting that something appears, sounds, or behaves like something else, e.g.

| | |
|---|---|
| *burning ambition* | *blindingly obvious* |
| *the long arm of the law* | *a glaring error* |

**meteoric** /ˌmee-tee-o-rik/ adj. **1** rapid; dazzling (*meteoric rise to fame*). **2** of meteors. □ **meteorically** adv.

**meteorite** /mee-tee-uh-ˌryut/ n. fallen meteor, or fragment of natural rock or metal from outer space.

**meteoroid** /mee-tee-uh-ˌroid/ n. small body that becomes visible as it passes through the earth's atmosphere as a meteor.

**meteorology** /ˌmee-tee-uh-rol-uh-jee/ n. the study of atmospheric phenomena, esp. for forecasting the weather. □ **meteorological** /-ruh-loj-i-kuhl/ adj. **meteorologist** n. [Greek *meteōrologia*: related to METEOR]

**meter** /mee-tuh/ — n. **1** instrument that measures or records, esp. gas, electricity, etc. used, distance travelled, etc. **2** = PARKING-METER. — v. measure or record by meter. [from METE]

**-meter** comb. form **1** forming nouns denoting measuring instruments (*barometer*). **2** forming nouns denoting lines of poetry with a specified number of measures (*pentameter*). [Greek *metron* measure]

**methadone** /meth-uh-ˌdohn/ n. narcotic analgesic drug used esp. as a substitute for morphine or heroin. [6-di*methyl* amino-4, 4-diphenyl-3-heptanone]

**methane** /mee-thayn, meth-ayn/ n. colourless odourless inflammable gaseous hydrocarbon, the main constituent of natural gas. [from METHYL]

**methanoic acid** /ˌmeth-uh-noh-ik/ n. = FORMIC ACID. [related to METHANE]

**methanol** /meth-uh-ˌnol/ n. colourless volatile inflammable liquid hydrocarbon, used as a solvent. [from METHANE, ALCOHOL]

**metho** n. colloq. **1** methylated spirits. **2** person addicted to drinking methylated spirits or who does so out of sheer poverty; a derelict. **3** (Metho) = METHODIST. [abbreviation]

**method** /meth-uhd/ n. **1** way of doing something; systematic procedure. **2** orderliness; regular habits. **3** scheme of classification. **4** (also **Stanislavski method**) technique of acting based on the actor's thorough emotional identification with the characters. □ **method in one's madness** sense in apparently foolish or strange behaviour. [Greek: related to META-, *hodos* way]

**methodical** /muh-thod-i-kuhl/ adj. characterised by method or order. □ **methodically** adv.

**Methodist** /meth-uh-duhst/ — n. member of a Protestant denomination originating in the 18th-c. Wesleyan evangelistic movement. — adj. of Methodists or Methodism. □ **Methodism** n.

**methodology** /ˌmeth-uh-dol-uh-jee/ n. (pl. **-ies**) **1** body of methods used in a particular activity. **2** science of method. □ **methodological** /-duh-loj-i-kuhl/ adj. **methodologically** /-duh-loj-i-klee/ adv.

**methyl** /meth-uhl, mee-thuyl/ n. univalent hydrocarbon radical $CH_3$, present in many organic compounds. [Greek *methu* wine, *hulē* wood]

**methyl alcohol** n. = METHANOL.

**methylate** /meth-uh-ˌlayt/ v. (**-ting**) **1** mix or impregnate with methanol. **2** introduce a methyl group into (a molecule or compound).

**methylated spirits** n.pl. (also **methylated spirit**) alcohol used for cleaning etc., and treated to make it unfit for drinking.

**meticulous** /muh-tik-yuh-luhs/ adj. **1** giving great attention to detail. **2** very careful and precise. □ **meticulously** adv. **meticulousness** n. [Latin *metus* fear]

**métier** /met-ee-ay/ n. **1** one's trade, profession, or field of activity. **2** one's strong point or speciality. [Latin: related to MINISTER]

**metonymy** /muh-ton-uh-mee/ n. substitution of the name of an attribute or adjunct for that of the thing meant (e.g. *Crown* for *king*, *the turf* for *horse-racing*). [Greek: related to META-, *onuma* name]

**metre¹** /mee-tuh/ n. metric unit and the base SI unit of linear measure, equal to about 39.4 inches. □ **metreage** /mee-tuh-rij/ n. [Greek *metron* measure]

**metre²** /mee-tuh/ n. **1 a** poetic rhythm, esp. as determined by the number and length of feet in a line. **b** metrical group or measure. **2** basic rhythm of music. [related to METRE¹]

**metre-kilogram-second** adj. denoting a system of measure using the metre, kilogram, and second.

**metric** /met-rik/ adj. of or based on the metre. [French: related to METRE¹]

**-metric** comb. form (also **-metrical**) forming adjectives corresponding to nouns in *-meter* and *-metry* (*thermometric*; *geometric*).

**metrical** adj. **1** of or composed in metre (*metrical psalms*). **2** of or involving measurement (*metrical geometry*). □ **metrically** adv. [Greek: related to METRE²]

**metricate** v. (**-ting**) convert to a metric system. □ **metrication** n.

**metric system** n. decimal measuring system with the metre, litre, and gram (or kilogram) as units of length, volume, and mass.

**metric ton** *n.* (also **metric tonne**) 1,000 kilograms (2205 lb).

**metro** /met-roh/ *n.* (*pl.* **-s**) underground railway system, esp. in Paris. [French shortened from *métropolitain* metropolitan]

**metronome** /met-ruh-ˌnohm/ *n.* device ticking at a selected rate to mark time for musicians. [Greek *metron* measure, *nomos* law]

**metropolis** /muh-**trop**-uh-luhs/ *n.* chief city; capital. [Greek *mētēr* mother, *polis* city]

**metropolitan** /ˌmet-ruh-**pol**-uh-tuhn/ — *adj.* of or relating to a metropolis. — *n.* **1** bishop having authority over the bishops of a province. **2** inhabitant of a metropolis.

**-metry** *comb. form* forming nouns denoting procedures and systems involving measurement (*geometry*).

**mettle** /met-uhl/ *n.* **1** quality or strength of character. **2** spirit, courage. □ **on one's mettle** keen to do one's best. □ **mettlesome** *adj.* [from METAL *n.*]

**MeV** *abbr.* mega-electronvolt(s).

**mew** /myoo/ — *n.* characteristic cry of a cat, gull, etc. — *v.* utter this sound. [imitative]

**mewl** /myool/ *v.* (also **mule**) **1** whimper. **2** mew like a cat. [imitative]

**mews** /myooz/ *n.* (treated as *sing.*) stabling round a yard etc., now used esp. for housing. [originally sing. *mew* 'cage for hawks': French from Latin *muto* change]

**Mexican** /**mek**-si-kuhn/ — *n.* **1** native or national of Mexico. **2** person of Mexican descent. **3** *colloq.* inhabitant of the State of Victoria: so called because he or she lives south of the (NSW) border. — *adj.* of Mexico or its people. [Spanish]

**Mexican wave** *n.* audience participation at a sporting event, pop concert, etc., where contiguous sections of the audience in turn stand and wave their arms in order to emulate a wave passing over the mass. [originated at the soccer World Cup finals in Mexico in 1986]

**mezzanine** /mez-uh-ˌneen, mez-uh-**neen**/ *n.* storey between two others (usu. between the ground and first floors). [Italian: related to MEDIAN]

**mezzo** /met-soh/ *Mus.* — *adv.* half, moderately. — *n.* (in full **mezzo-soprano**) (*pl.* **-s**) **1** female singing-voice between soprano and contralto. **2** singer with this voice. [Latin *medius* middle]

**mezzo forte** *adj.* & *adv.* fairly loud(ly).

**mezzo piano** *adj.* & *adv.* fairly soft(ly).

**mezzotint** /met-soh-tint/ *n.* **1** method of printing or engraving in which a plate is roughened by scraping to produce tones and halftones. **2** print so produced. [Italian: related to MEZZO, TINT]

**mf** *abbr.* mezzo forte.

**Mg** *symb.* magnesium.

**mg** *abbr.* milligram(s).

**MHA** *abbr.* Member of the House of Assembly.

**MHR** *abbr.* Member of the House of Representatives.

**MHz** *abbr.* megahertz.

**mi** var. of ME[2].

**mia-mia** /muy-uh-ˌmuy-uh, mee-uh-ˌmee-uh/ **1** = GUNYAH. **2** any temporary shelter erected by a traveller. [Nyungar *maya* or *maya-maya*]

**miaow** /mee-ow/ — *n.* characteristic cry of a cat. — *v.* make this cry. [imitative]

**miasma** /mee-az-muh, muy-/ *n.* (*pl.* **-mata** or **-s**) *archaic* infectious or noxious vapour. [Greek, = defilement]

**mica** /muy-kuh/ *n.* silicate mineral found as glittering scales in granite etc. or in crystals separable into thin transparent plates. [Latin, = crumb]

**mice** *pl.* of MOUSE.

**mick**[1] *n. colloq. offens.* **1** a Catholic. **2** an Irishman. [pet form of *Michael*]

**mick**[2] *n. abbr.* = MICKEY[1]

**mick**[3] — *n.* (in two-up) reverse side of a coin; the tail. — *v.* (in two-up) spin the coins so that they land tail uppermost. [origin uncertain]

**mickery** /mik-uh-ree/ *n.* (also **mickerie**) **1** natural soak or hollow in (often) sandy soil where water collects, on or below the surface of the ground, often several metres below. **2** excavated and formed soak, esp. in a dry river bed. [Wangganguru *migiri*]

**mickey**[1] /mik-ee/ *n.* (also **mick**, **micky**) bull calf, usu. unbranded and frequently wild. [origin uncertain]

**mickey**[2] *n.* (also **micky**) □ **chuck** (or **throw**) **a mickey** *colloq.* have a tantrum. **take the mickey** (often foll. by *out of*) *colloq.* tease, mock, ridicule. [origin uncertain]

**mickey**[3] *n.* (also **micky**) = NOISY MINER.

**Mickey Finn** *n. colloq.* drugged drink intended to make the victim unconscious. [origin uncertain]

**mickey mouse** *adj. colloq.* **1** of inferior quality; trivial; ridiculous; less than serious (*got a degree doing mickey mouse subjects*). **2** (of music, art, etc.) trite. [Walt Disney cartoon character]

**micky** var. of MICKEY.

**micro** /muy-kroh/ *n.* (*pl.* **-s**) *colloq.* = MICROCOMPUTER.

**micro-** *comb. form* **1 a** small (*microchip*). **b** on a small or local scale (*micro-economics*). **2** denoting a factor of one millionth ($10^{-6}$) (*microgram*). [Greek *mikros* small]

**microbe** /**muy**-krohb/ *n.* micro-organism (esp. a bacterium causing disease or fermentation). □ **microbial** /-**kroh**-bee-uhl/ *adj.* **microbic** /-**kroh**-bik/ *adj.* [Greek *mikros* small, *bios* life]

**microbiology** /ˌmuy-kroh-buy-**ol**-uh-jee/ *n.* the study of micro-organisms. ■ **micro-biologist** *n.*

**microchip** /**muy**-kroh-chip/ *n.* small piece of semiconductor (usu. silicon) used to carry integrated circuits.

**microcircuit** /**muy**-kroh-ˌser-kuht/ *n.* integrated circuit on a microchip.

**microclimate** /**muy**-kroh-ˌkluy-muht/ *n.* small localised climate, e.g. inside a greenhouse.

**microcomputer** /**muy**-kroh-kuhm-ˌpyoo-tuh/ *n.* small computer with a micro-processor as its central processing unit.

**microcosm** /**muy**-kruh-ˌkoz-uhm/ *n.* (often foll. by *of*) miniature representation, e.g. mankind or a community seen as a small-scale model of the universe; epitome. □ **microcosmic** /-**koz**-mik/ *adj.* [from MICRO-, COSMOS]

**microdot** /**muy**-kroh-ˌdot/ *n.* micro-photograph of a document etc. reduced to the size of a dot.

**microeconomics** /ˌmuy-kroh-ee-kuh-**nom**-iks, -ek-uh-**nom**-iks/ *n.* branch of economics dealing with individual commod-ities, producers, etc. (opp. MACROECONOMICS)

**microelectronics** /ˌmuy-kroh-ee-lek-**tron**-iks/ *n.* design, manufacture, and use of microchips and microcircuits.

**microfiche** /**muy**-kroh-ˌfeesh/ *n.* (*pl.* same or **-s**) small flat piece of film bearing microphotographs of documents etc. [from MICRO-, French *fiche* slip of paper]

**microfilm** /**muy**-kroh-film/ — *n.* length of film bearing microphotographs of docu-ments etc. — *v.* photograph on microfilm.

**micrometer** /muy-**krom**-uh-tuh/ *n.* gauge for accurate small-scale measurement.

**micron** /**muy**-kron/ *n.* one-millionth of a metre. [Greek *mikros* small]

**micro-organism** /ˌmuy-kroh-**aw**-guh-ˌniz-uhm/ *n.* microscopic organism, e.g. bacteria, protozoa, and viruses.

**microphone** /**muy**-kruh-ˌfohn/ *n.* instrument for converting sound waves into electrical energy for reconversion into sound after transmission or recording. [from MICRO-, Greek *phōnē* sound]

**microphotograph** /ˌmuy-kroh-**foh**-tuh-ˌgrahf, -ˌgraf/ *n.* photograph reduced to a very small size. [from MICRO-]

**microprocessor** /ˌmuy-kroh-**proh**-ses-uh/ *n.* integrated circuit containing all the functions of a computer's central processing unit.

**microscope** /**muy**-kruh-ˌskohp/ *n.* instrument with lenses for magnifying objects or details invisible to the naked eye. [from MICRO-, -SCOPE]

**microscopic** /ˌmuy-kruh-**skop**-ik/ *adj.* **1** visible only with a microscope. **2** extremely small. **3** of or by means of a microscope. □ **microscopically** *adv.*

**microscopy** /muy-**kros**-kuh-pee/ *n.* use of microscopes.

**microsecond** /**muy**-kroh-ˌsek-uhnd/ *n.* one-millionth of a second.

**microsurgery** /**muy**-kroh-ˌser-juh-ree/ *n.* intricate surgery using microscopes.

**microwave** /**muy**-kroh-ˌwayv/ — *n.* **1** electromagnetic wave with a wavelength in the range 0.001–0.3m. **2** (in full **microwave oven**) oven using microwaves to cook or heat food quickly. — *v.* (**-ving**) cook in a microwave oven.

**microwave proof** *adj.* (also **microwave safe**) (of dishes etc.) able to be used in a microwave oven.

**micturition** /ˌmik-chuh-**rish**-uhn/ *n.* *formal* urination. [from MUCK]

**mid¹** *attrib. adj.* (usu. in *comb.*) the middle of (*mid-air*; *mid-June*). [Old English]

**mid²** *prep. poet.* = AMID.

**midday** *n.* (often *attrib.*) middle of the day; noon. [Old English: related to MID, DAY]

**midden** /**mid**-uhn/ *n.* **1** dunghill. **2** refuse heap. **3** = MIRRNYONG. [Scandinavian: related to MUCK]

**middle** /**mid**-uhl/ — *attrib. adj.* **1** at an equal distance, time, or number from extremities; central. **2** intermediate in rank, quality, etc. **3** average (*of middle height*). **4** (of a language) of a period between the old and modern forms (*Middle English*). — *n.* **1** (often foll. by *of*) middle point, position, or part. **2** waist. — *v.* **1** place in the middle. **2** *Cricket* strike the ball squarely with the middle of the bat. □ **in the middle of 1** in the process of. **2** during. [Old English]

**middle age** *n.* period between youth and old age. □ **middle-aged** *adj.*

**Middle Ages** *n.* (prec. by *the*) period of European history from *c.* 1000 to 1453.

**middlebrow** *colloq.* — *adj.* having or appealing to non-intellectual or con-ventional tastes. — *n.* middlebrow person.

**middle C** *n.* C near the middle of the piano keyboard, (in notation) the note between the treble and bass staves.

**middle class** *n.* social class between the upper and the lower, including profes-sional and business workers. □ **middle-class** *adj.*

**middle distance** *n.* **1** (in a landscape) part between the foreground and the background. **2** *Athletics* race distance of esp. 400 or 800 metres.

**middle ear** *n.* cavity behind the eardrum.

**Middle East** *n.* (prec. by *the*) area covered by countries from Egypt to Iran inclusive. □ **Middle Eastern** *adj.*

**Middle English** *n.* English language from *c.* 1150 to 1500.

**middleman** *n.* **1** trader who handles a commodity between producer and consumer. **2** intermediary.

**middle name** *n.* **1** name between first name and surname. **2** *colloq.* person's most characteristic quality (*tact is my middle name*).

**middle-of-the-road** *adj.* **1** moderate; avoiding extremes. **2** of general appeal.

**middleweight** *n.* **1** weight in certain sports between welterweight and light heavyweight, in amateur boxing 71–5 kg. **2** sportsman of this weight.

**middling** — *adj.* moderately good. — *adv.* fairly, moderately.

**middy** *n.* **1** medium-sized measure of beer. **2** glass containing this.

**midfield** *n.* *Sports* central part of the field, away from the goals. □ **midfielder** *n.*

**midge** *n.* gnatlike insect. [Old English]

**midget** /mij-uht/ *n.* **1** extremely small person or thing. **2** (*attrib.*) very small.

**Midhaga** /mid-hah-gu/ *n.* an Aboriginal language spoken over a vast area of south-western Queensland: now extinct.

**MIDI** /mid-ee/ *n.* (also **midi**) an interface allowing electronic musical instruments, synthesisers, and computers to be interconnected and used simultaneously. [abbreviation of *m*usical *i*nstrument *d*igital *i*nterface]

**mid-life** *n.* middle age.

**mid-life crisis** *n.* crisis of self-confidence in early middle age.

**midnight** *n.* middle of the night; 12 o'clock at night. [Old English]

**midnight blue** *adj. & n.* (as adj. often hyphenated) very dark blue.

**midnight sun** *n.* sun visible at midnight during the summer in polar regions.

**mid-off** *n.* *Cricket* position of the fielder near the bowler on the off side.

**mid-on** *n.* *Cricket* position of the fielder near the bowler on the on side.

**midriff** *n.* front of the body just above the waist. [Old English, = mid-belly]

**midshipman** *n.* rank of a naval cadet training to be an officer.

**midships** *adv.* = AMIDSHIPS.

**midst** — *prep. poet.* amidst. — *n.* middle. □ **in the midst of** among; in the middle of. **in our** (or **your** or **their**) **midst** among us (or you or them). [related to MID]

**midstream** — *n.* middle of a stream etc. — *adv.* (also **in midstream**) in the middle of an action etc. (*abandoned the project midstream*).

**midsummer madness** *n.* extreme folly.

**midway** *adv.* in or towards the middle of the distance between two points.

**midwicket** *n.* *Cricket* position of a fielder on the leg side opposite the middle of the pitch.

**midwife** /mid-wuyf/ *n.* (*pl.* **-wives**) person trained to assist at childbirth. □ **midwifery** /mid-**wif**-uh-ree/ *n.* [originally = with-woman]

**mien** /meen/ *n.* *literary* person's look or bearing. [probably obsolete *demean*]

**miff** *v.* *colloq.* (usu. as **miffed** *adj.*) offend. [origin uncertain]

**migaloo** /mig-uh-loo/ *n.* a white person. [perhaps Mayi-Kutuna *migulu*]

**might**[1] /muyt/ *past* of MAY, used esp.: **1** in reported speech, expressing possibility (*said he might come*) or permission (*asked if I might leave*) (cf. MAY 1a· 1b). **2** (foll. by perfect infin.) expressing a possibility based on a condition not fulfilled (*if you'd looked you might have found it*). **3** (foll. by present infin. or perfect infin.) expressing complaint that an obligation or expectation is not or has not been fulfilled (*they might have asked*). **4** expressing a request (*you might call in at the butcher's*). **5** *colloq.* **a** = MAY 1a (*it might be true*). **b** (in tentative questions) = MAY 1b (*might I have the pleasure of this dance?*). **c** = MAY 1d (*who might you be?*). □ **might as well** expressing lukewarm acquiescence (*might as well try*).

**might**[2] /muyt/ *n.* strength, power. □ **with might and main** with all one's power. [Old English: related to MAY]

**might-have-been** *n.* *colloq.* **1** past possibility that no longer applies. **2** person of unfulfilled promise.

**mightn't** /muy-tuhnt/ *contr.* might not.

**mighty** — *adj.* (**-ier**, **-iest**) **1** powerful, strong. **2** massive, bulky. **3** *colloq.* great, considerable. — *adv. colloq.* very (*mighty difficult*). □ **mightily** *adv.* **mightiness** *n.* [Old English: related to MIGHT[2]]

**mignonette** /ˌmin-yuh-**net**/ *n.* a variety of small lettuce. [French, diminutive of *mignon* small]

**migraine** /muy-grayn, mee-/ *n.* recurrent throbbing headache that usu. affects only one side of the head, often accompanied by nausea and visual disturbance. [Greek *hēmikrania*: related to HEMI-, CRANIUM]

**migrant** /muy-gruhnt/ — *n.* **1** person who leaves his or her own country to take up permanent residence in another. **2**

animal, esp. a bird, which changes its habitation seasonally. — *adj.* migrating.

**migrate** /muy-**grayt**/ *v.* (**-ting**) **1** move from one place and settle in another, esp. abroad. **2** (of a bird or fish) change its habitation seasonally. **3** move under natural forces. □ **migration** /-**gray**-shuhn/ *n.* **migrator** *n.* **migratory** /**muy**-gruh-tuh-ree, -tree/ *adj.* [Latin *migro migrat-*]

**mikado** /muh-**kah**-doh/ *n.* (*pl.* **-s**) *hist.* emperor of Japan. [Japanese, = august door]

**mike** *n. colloq.* microphone. [abbreviation]

**mil** *n.* one-thousandth of an inch, as a unit of measure for the diameter of wire etc. [Latin *mille* thousand]

**milch** *adj.* giving milk. [Old English: related to MILK]

**mild** /muyld/ *adj.* **1** (esp. of a person) gentle and conciliatory. **2** not severe or harsh. **3** (of the weather) moderately warm. **4** (of flavour etc.) not sharp or strong. **5** tame, feeble; lacking vivacity. □ **mildish** *adj.* **mildness** *n.* [Old English]

**mildew** /**mil**-dyoo/ — *n.* **1** destructive growth of minute fungi on plants. **2** similar growth on damp paper, leather, walls, etc. — *v.* taint or be tainted with mildew. □ **mildewy** *adj.* [Old English]

**mildly** *adv.* in a mild fashion. □ **to put it mildly** as an understatement.

**mile** *n.* **1** (in the imperial system) unit of linear measure equal to 1,760 yards (approx. 1.6 kilometres). **2** (in *pl.*) *colloq.* great distance or amount (*miles better*). **3** a mile-long race. [Latin *mille* thousand]

**mileage** *n.* **1** number of miles travelled, esp. by a vehicle per unit of fuel. **2** *colloq.* profit, advantage (*there's no mileage in confessing*).

**milestone** *n.* **1** stone beside a road marking a distance in miles. **2** significant event or point in a life, history, project, etc.

**milieu** /mee-**lyer**, mee-lyer/ *n.* (*pl.* **milieux** or **-s** /-lyerz/) person's environment or social surroundings. [French]

**militant** /**mil**-uh-tuhnt/ — *adj.* **1** combative; aggressively active in support of a cause. **2** engaged in warfare. — *n.* militant person. □ **militancy** *n.* **militantly** *adv.* [Latin: related to MILITATE]

**militarise** /**mil**-uh-tuh-,ruyz/ *v.* (also **-ize**) (**-sing** or **-zing**) **1** equip with military resources. **2** make military or warlike. **3** imbue with militarism. □ **militarisation** /-,zay-shuhn/ *n.*

**militarism** /**mil**-uh-tuh-,riz-uhm/ *n.* **1** aggressively military policy etc. **2** military spirit. □ **militarist** *n.* **militaristic** /-ris-tik/ *adj.*

**military** /**mil**-uh-tuh-ree/ — *adj.* of or

characteristic of soldiers or armed forces. — *n.* (as *sing.* or *pl.*; prec. by *the*) the army. □ **militarily** *adv.* [Latin *miles milit-* soldier]

**militate** /**mil**-uh-,tayt/ *v.* (**-ting**) (usu. foll. by *against*) have force or effect (*what you say militates against our opinion*). [Latin: related to MILITARY]

------

■ *Usage* Militate is often confused with *mitigate*.

------

**militia** /muh-**lish**-uh/ *n.* military force, esp. one conscripted in an emergency. □ **militiaman** *n.* [Latin, = military service]

**milk** — *n.* **1** opaque white fluid secreted by female mammals for the nourishment of their young. **2** milk of cows, goats, or sheep as food. **3** milklike juice of the coconut etc. — *v.* **1** draw milk from (a cow etc.). **2** extract venom from a snake, spider, etc., or sap from a tree etc. **3** extract as if by milking (*milked our car of all its petrol*). **4** exploit (a person or situation) to the utmost. □ **cry over spilt milk** waste time lamenting over something which cannot be remedied. [Old English]

**milk bar** *n.* local shop selling milk, confectionery, sandwiches and, often, basic grocery items, etc. (see also MIXED BUSINESS).

**milk-bush** *n.* several Australian plants having a milky, sometimes caustic, sap.

**milker** *n.* animal (cow, goat, etc.) that yields milk esp. as specified (*this cow's a very poor milker*).

**milkmaids** *n.* any of several Australian plants, usu. of the lily family, bearing umbels of scented milky flowers.

**milkman** *n.* person who sells or delivers milk.

**milko** /**mil**-koh/ *n.* (also **milk-oh**) *colloq.* = MILKMAN.

**milk opal** *n.* variety of white or milky blue-white or green-white opal.

**milkshake** *n.* drink of whisked milk, icecream, flavouring, etc.

**milksop** *n.* weak or timid man or youth.

**milk tooth** *n.* temporary tooth in young mammals.

**milky** *adj.* (**-ier**, **-iest**) **1** of, like, or mixed with milk. **2** (of a gem or liquid) cloudy; not clear. □ **milkiness** *n.*

**milky mangrove** *n.* (also **blind-your-eye**) mangrove tree of tropical and sub-tropical Australia having an irritant milky sap.

**Milky Way** *n.* luminous band of stars encircling the heavens; the galaxy.

**mill** — *n.* **1 a** building fitted with a mechanical device for grinding cereal grains. **b** such a device. **2** device for grinding any solid to powder etc. (*pepper-mill*). **3 a** building fitted with machinery for manufacturing processes etc. (*cotton-mill*). **b** such machinery. — *v.* **1** grind (corn), produce (flour), or hull (seeds) in a mill. **2** (esp. as **milled** *adj.*) produce a ribbed edge on (a coin). **3** cut or shape (metal) with a rotating tool. **4** (often foll. by *about*, *around*) move aimlessly, esp. in a confused mass. □ **go** (or **put**) **through the mill** undergo (or cause to undergo) intensive work, pain, training, etc. [Latin *molo* grind]

**millennium** /muh-**len**-ee-uhm/ *n.* (*pl.* **-s** or **millennia**) **1** period of 1,000 years, esp. that of Christ's prophesied reign on earth (Rev. 20:1–5). **2** (esp. future) period of happiness and prosperity. □ **millennial** *adj.* [Latin *mille* thousand]

**miller** *n.* **1** proprietor or tenant of a mill, esp. a flour mill. **2** person operating a milling machine. [related to MILL]

**millesimal** /muh-**les**-uh-muhl/ — *adj.* **1** thousandth. **2** of, belonging to, or dealing with, a thousandth or thousandths. — *n.* thousandth part. [Latin *mille* thousand]

**millet** /**mil**-uht/ *n.* **1** cereal plant bearing small nutritious seeds. **2** seed of this. [Latin *milium*]

**milli-** *comb. form* thousand, esp. denoting a factor of one thousandth. [Latin *mille* thousand]

**milliard** /**mil**-yuhd, -yahd/ *n.* one thousand million. [French *mille* thousand]

■ **Usage** *Milliard* is now largely superseded by *billion*.

**millibar** /**mil**-ee-bah/ *n.* unit of atmospheric pressure equivalent to 100 pascals.

**milligram** /**mil**-uh-gram/ *n.* (also **-gramme**) one-thousandth of a gram.

**millilitre** /**mil**-uh-lee-tuh/ *n.* one-thousandth of a litre (0.002 pint).

**millimetre** /**mil**-uh-mee-tuh/ *n.* one-thousandth of a metre (0.039 in.).

**milli-milli** /**mil**-ee-mil-ee/ *n.* (also **milli**) (in Aboriginal English) a written message. [reduplication of English MAIL[1]]

**milliner** /**mil**-uh-nuh/ *n.* person who makes or sells women's hats. □ **millinery** *n.* [*Milan* in Italy]

**million** /**mil**-yuhn/ *n. & adj.* (*pl.* same or (in sense 2) **-s**) (in *sing.* prec. by *a* or *one*) **1** thousand thousand. **2** (in *pl.*) *colloq.* very large number. **3** million dollars. □ **gone a million** *colloq.* done for, finished; beyond redemption. **one in a million 1** extraordinary and highly regarded person or thing. **2** (of a possibility) utterly remote (*his chances of getting the job are one in a million*). □ **millionth** *adj. & n.* [French, probably from Italian *mille* thousand]

**millionaire** /mil-yuh-**nair**/ *n.* person who

has over a million dollars etc. [French *millionnaire*: related to MILLION]

**millipede** /**mil**-uh-peed/ *n.* (also **millepede**) small crawling invertebrate with a long segmented body with two pairs of legs on each segment. [Latin *mille* thousand, *pes ped-* foot]

**millisecond** /**mil**-ee-sek-uhnd/ *n.* one-thousandth of a second.

**millpond** *n.* pool of water retained by a dam for operating a mill-wheel. □ **like a millpond** (of water) very calm.

**millstone** *n.* **1** each of two circular stones for grinding corn. **2** heavy burden or responsibility.

**mill-wheel** *n.* wheel used to drive a water-mill.

**milt** *n.* **1** spleen in mammals. **2** sperm-filled reproductive gland or the sperm of a male fish. [Old English]

**mime** /muym/ — *n.* **1** acting without words, using only gestures. **2** performance using mime. **3** (also mime artist) mime actor. — *v.* (**-ming**) **1** (also *absol.*) convey by mime. **2** (often foll. by *to*) mouth words etc. in time with a soundtrack (*mime to a record*). □ **mimer** *n.* [Greek *mimos*]

**mimesis** /muh-**mee**-suhs, muy-/ *n.* close external resemblance of an animal to another that is distasteful or harmful to predators of the first, or of an animal to its immediate surroundings, e.g. a leaf, twig, etc. [Greek, = imitation]

**mimetic** /muh-**met**-ik/ *adj.* **1** of or practising imitation or mimicry. **2** of or exhibiting mimesis. [Greek *mimētikos* from *mimeomai* imitate]

**mimi** /**mee**-mee/ *n.* category of Aboriginal spirit people depicted in rock and bark paintings of western Arnhem Land, the figures, executed in red, characterised by their elongated and slender form. [Gunwinygu]

**mimic** /**mim**-ik/ — *v.* (**-ck-**) **1** imitate (a person, gesture, etc.) esp. to entertain or ridicule. **2** copy minutely or servilely. **3** resemble closely. — *n.* person skilled in imitation. □ **mimicry** *n.* [Greek *mimikos*: related to MIME]

**mimosa** /muh-**moh**-zuh, -suh/ *n.* **1** any shrub of the genus *Mimosa*, esp. *Mimosa pudica*, with globular flowers, and sensitive leaflets which droop when touched. **2** acacia plant with showy yellow flowers. [Latin: related to MIME]

**minaret** /min-uh-**ret**/ *n.* slender turret next to a mosque, from which the muezzin calls at hours of prayer. [French or Spanish from Turkish from Arabic]

**minatory** /**min**-uh-tuh-ree, -tree/ *adj.* *formal* threatening, menacing. [Latin *minor minat-* threaten]

**mince** — v. (**-cing**) **1** cut up or grind (esp. meat) finely. **2** (usu. as **mincing** adj.) speak or esp. walk effeminately or affectedly. — n. minced meat. □ **mince matters** (or **one's words**) (usu. with neg.) speak evasively or unduly mildly. □ **mincer** n. [Latin minutia something small]

**mincemeat** n. mixture of currants, candied peel, sugar, spices, suet, etc. □ **make mincemeat of** utterly defeat.

**mind** / muynd/ — n. **1 a** seat of consciousness, thought, volition, and feeling. **b** attention, concentration (mind keeps wandering). **2** intellect. **3** memory (can't call it to mind). **4** opinion (of the same mind). **5** way of thinking or feeling (the word 'leg' shocked the Victorian mind). **6** focused will (put one's mind to it). **7** sanity (lose one's mind). **8** person in regard to mental faculties (a great mind). — v. **1** object; be upset (do you mind if I smoke?; minded terribly when she left). **2** heed; take care (to) (mind you come on time; mind the step; mind how you go). **3** look after (mind the house). **4** apply oneself to, concern oneself with (mind my own business). **5** be obedient to (mind what your mother says). □ **be in two minds** be undecided. **blow one's mind** colloq. make one utterly enchanted, euphoric, wild with delight (this music will really blow your mind). **do you mind!** iron. expression of annoyance. **have a good** (or **half a**) **mind to** feel inclined to (I've a good mind to report you). **have** (**it**) **in mind** intend. **in one's mind's eye** in one's imagination. **mind one's Ps & Qs** be careful in one's behaviour. **mind you** used to qualify a statement (mind you, it wasn't easy). **never mind 1** let alone; not to mention. **2** used to comfort or console. **3** (also **never you mind**) used to evade a question. **out of one's mind** beside oneself with worry etc. **to my mind** in my opinion. [Old English]

**mind-blowing** adj. colloq. **1** mind-boggling; overwhelming. **2** (esp. of drugs etc.) inducing hallucinations.

**mind-boggling** adj. colloq. unbelievable, startling.

**minded** adj. **1** (in comb.) **a** inclined to think in some specified way, or with a specified interest (mathematically minded; fair-minded; car-minded). **b** having a specified kind of mind (high-minded). **2** (usu. foll. by to + infin.) disposed or inclined (I'm more than a little minded to quit teaching and become a writer).

**minder** n. **1** (often in comb.) person employed to look after a person or thing (child minder). **2** colloq. bodyguard.

**mindful** adj. (often foll. by of) taking heed or care; giving thought (to). □ **mindfully** adv.

**mindi** / **min**-duy/   n. (in Aboriginal mythology) fabulous hairy snake which can swallow an emu whole. [Wemba-wemba mirnday]

**mindic** / **min**-dik/ adj. (in Aboriginal English) ill; sick. [Nyungar mindij or mindik]

**mindless** adj. **1** lacking intelligence; brutish (mindless violence). **2** not requiring thought or skill (mindless work). **3** (usu. foll. by of) heedless of (advice etc.). □ **mindlessly** adv. **mindlessness** n.

**mind-read** v. discern the thoughts of (another person). □ **mind-reader** n.

**mine**[1] poss. pron. the one(s) of or belonging to me (it is mine; mine are over there). □ **of mine** of or belonging to me (a friend of mine). [Old English]

**mine**[2] — n. **1** excavation to extract ores, coal, precious stones, etc. **2** abundant source (of information etc.). **3** military explosive device placed in the ground or in the water. **4** subterranean gallery in which explosives are placed to blow up fortifications etc. — v. (**-ning**) **1** obtain (metal, coal, etc.) from a mine. **2** (also absol., often foll. by for) dig in (the earth etc.) for ore etc. or to tunnel. **3** lay explosive mines under or in. **4** search, delve into (books etc.) for information (mined the resources of the National Library). □ **mining** n. [French]

**minefield** n. **1** area planted with explosive mines. **2** colloq. hazardous subject or situation.

**miner**[1] n. person who works in a mine. [French: related to MINE[2]]

**miner**[2] n. any of several related Australian honeyeaters with yellow bill and legs, esp. the noisy miner and the bell miner (or bellbird). [alteration of MYNA]

**mineral** / **min**-uh-ruhl/ — n. (often attrib.) **1** any inorganic substance. **2** substance obtained by mining. — adj. **1** of or containing a mineral or minerals. **2** obtained by mining. [French or medieval Latin: related to MINE[2]]

**mineralogy** / ˌmin-uh-**ral**-uh-jee/ n. the study of minerals. □ **mineralogical** / -ruh-**loj**-i-kuhl/ adj. **mineralogist** n.

**mineral water** n. **1** natural water often containing dissolved salts. **2** artificial imitation of this.

**minestrone** / ˌmin-uh-**stroh**-nee/ n. soup containing vegetables and pasta, beans, or rice, etc. [Italian]

**minesweeper** n. ship for clearing explosive mines from the sea.

**mingle** / **ming**-guhl/ v. (**-ling**) **1** mix, blend.

**2** (often foll. by *with*) mix socially. [Old English]

**mingy** /min-jee/ *adj.* (**-ier, -iest**) *colloq.* mean, stingy. □ **mingily** *adv.* [probably from MEAN², STINGY]

**mini** /min-ee/ *n.* (*pl.* **-s**) *colloq.* miniskirt. [abbreviation]

**mini-** *comb. form* miniature; small of its kind (*minibus*).

**miniature** /min-uh-chuh/ — *adj.* **1** much smaller than normal. **2** represented on a small scale. — *n.* **1** any miniature object. **2** detailed small-scale portrait. **3** this genre. □ **in miniature** on a small scale. □ **miniaturist** *n.* (in senses 2 and 3 of *n.*). [Latin *minium* red lead]

**miniaturise** *v.* (also **-ize**) (**-sing** or **-zing**) produce in a smaller version; make small. □ **miniaturisation** /-zay-shuhn/ *n.*

**minibus** /min-ee-ˌbus/ *n.* small bus for about twelve passengers.

**minicomputer** /min-ee-kuhm-ˌpyoo-tuh/ *n.* computer of medium power.

**minim** /min-uhm/ *n.* **1** *Mus.* note equal to two crotchets or half a semibreve. **2** one-sixtieth of a fluid drachm, about a drop. [Latin *minimus* least]

**minima** *pl.* of MINIMUM.

**minimal** /min-uh-muhl/ *adj.* **1** very minute or slight. **2** being a minimum. □ **minimally** *adv.*

**minimise** /min-uh-ˌmuyz/ *v.* (also **-ize**) (**-sing** or **-zing**) **1** reduce to, or estimate at, the smallest possible amount or degree. **2** estimate or represent at less than true value or importance. □ **minimisation** /-zay-shuhn/ *n.*

**minimum** /min-uh-muhm/ — *n.* (*pl.* **minima**) least possible or attainable amount (*reduced to a minimum*). — *adj.* that is a minimum. [Latin: related to MINIM]

**minimum wage** *n.* lowest wage permitted by law or agreement.

**minion** /min-yuhn/ *n. derog.* servile subordinate. [French *mignon*]

**mini-series** /min-ee-ˌseer-reez/ *n.* (*pl.* same) short series of related television programmes.

**miniskirt** /min-ee-ˌskert/ *n.* very short skirt.

**minister** /min-uh-stuh/ — *n.* **1** (often **Minister**) head of a government department (*Minister for Defence*). **2** clergyman, esp. in the various Protestant Churches. **3** diplomat, usu. ranking below an ambassador. — *v.* (usu. foll. by *to*) help, serve, look after (a person, cause, etc.). □ **ministerial** /min-uh-steer-ee-uhl/ *adj.* [Latin, = servant]

**ministration** /ˌmin-uh-stray-shuhn/ *n.* **1** (usu. in *pl.*) help or service (*kind ministrations*). **2** ministering, esp. in religious matters. **3** (usu. foll. by *of*) supplying of help, justice, etc. □ **ministrant** /min-uh-

struhnt/ *adj. & n.* [Latin: related to MINISTER]

**ministry** /min-uh-stree/ *n.* (*pl.* **-ies**) **1 a** government department headed by a minister. **b** building for this. **2 a** (prec. by *the*) vocation, office, or profession of a religious minister. **b** period of tenure of this. **3** (prec. by *the*) body of ministers of a government or religion. **4** period of government under one prime minister. **5** ministering, ministration. [Latin: related to MINISTER]

**mink** *n.* (*pl.* same or **-s**) **1** small semi-aquatic stoatlike animal bred for its thick brown fur. **2** this fur. **3** coat of this. [Swedish]

**min-min** /min-min/ *n.* a will-o'-the-wisp. [perhaps from an Aboriginal language]

**minnerichi** /ˌmin-uh-rich-ee/ *n.* (also **minnaritchi, red mulga**) small SA wattle which typically has thin, peeling curls of reddish bark. [perhaps from a SA Aboriginal language, probably *minariji*]

**minnow** /min-oh/ *n.* small European freshwater carp. [Old English]

**minor** /muy-nuh/ — *adj.* **1** lesser or comparatively small in size or importance (*minor poet*). **2** *Mus.* **a** (of a scale) having intervals of a semitone above its second, fifth, and seventh notes. **b** (of an interval) less by a semitone than a major interval. **c** (of a key) based on a minor scale. — *n.* **1** person under full legal age. **2** *Mus.* a minor key. **3** *Aust. Rules* = a BEHIND (cf. MAJOR). **4** university student's subsidiary subject or course. [Latin, = less]

**minority** /muy-no-ruh-tee, muh-/ *n.* (*pl.* **-ies**) **1** (often foll. by *of*) smaller number or part, esp. in politics. **2** state of having less than half the votes or support (*in the minority*). **3** small group of people differing from others in race, religion, language, etc. **4** (*attrib.*) of or done by the minority (*minority interests*). **5 a** being under full legal age. **b** period of this. [French or medieval Latin: related to MINOR]

**minster** *n.* **1** large or important church. **2** church of a monastery. [Old English: related to MONASTERY]

**minstrel** /min-struhl/ *n.* **1** medieval singer or musician. **2** (usu. in *pl.*) entertainer with a blacked face singing ostensibly Black songs in a group. [related to MINISTER]

**minstrelsy** /min-struhl-see/ *n.* minstrel's art or poetry.

**mint¹** *n.* **1** aromatic herb used in cooking. **2** peppermint. **3** peppermint sweet. □ **minty** *adj.* (**-ier, -iest**). [Latin *menta* from Greek]

**mint²** — *n.* **1** (esp. Government) establishment where money is coined. **2** *colloq.* vast sum (*making a mint*). — *v.* **1** make (a coin) by stamping metal. **2** invent, coin (a word, phrase, etc.). □ **in mint condition** as new. [Latin *moneta*]

**mint bush** *n.* any shrub of the large Australian genus *Prostanthera*, many of which are cultivated as ornamentals for their strongly aromatic leaves and profusion of white, blue, or purple flowers in spring.

**mintie** /**min**-tee/ *n. propr.* (peppermint-flavoured sweet: the advertising slogan 'It's moments like these you need Minties' being now widely current as a catch-phrase) used allusively as an emblem of consolation (*there are some crises when even minties won't help*).

**minuet** /ˌmin-yoo-**et**/ — *n.* **1** slow stately dance for two in triple time. **2** music for this, often as a movement in a suite etc. — *v.* (**-t-**) dance a minuet. [French diminutive]

**minus** /**muy**-nuhs/ — *prep.* **1** with the subtraction of (*7 minus 4 equals 3*). **2** below zero (*minus 2°*). **3** *colloq.* lacking (*returned minus their dog*). — *adj.* **1** *Math.* negative. **2** *Electronics* having a negative charge. — *n.* **1** = MINUS SIGN. **2** *Math.* negative quantity. **3** *colloq.* disadvantage. [Latin, neuter of MINOR]

**minuscule** /**min**-uh-ˌskyool/ *adj.* extremely small or unimportant. [Latin diminutive: related to MINUS]

**minus sign** *n.* the symbol -, indicating subtraction or a negative value.

**minute**[1] /**min**-uht/ — *n.* **1** sixtieth part of an hour. **2** distance covered in one minute (*ten minutes from the shops*). **3 a** moment (*expecting her any minute*). **b** (prec. by *the*) *colloq.* present time (*not here at the minute*). **c** (prec. by *the*, foll. by a clause) as soon as (*the minute you get back*). **4** sixtieth part of an angular degree. **5** (in *pl.*) summary of the proceedings of a meeting. **6** official memorandum authorising or recommending a course of action. — *adj.* taking a very short time (*minute waltz*; *minute noodles*). — *v.* (**-ting**) **1** record in minutes. **2** send the minutes of a meeting to. □ **up to the minute** completely up to date. [Latin *minuo minui* lessen]

**minute**[2] /muy-**nyoot**/ *adj.* (**-est**) **1** very small. **2** petty, trifling (*can't be bothered with these minute details*). **3** accurate, detailed (*gave us a minute account*). □ **minutely** *adv.* [Latin *minutus*: related to MINUTE[1]]

**minutiae** /muy-**nyoo**-shee-uy/ *n.pl.* very small, precise, or minor details. [Latin: related to MINUTE[1]]

**minx** /mingks/ *n.* pert, sly, or playful girl. [origin unknown]

**Miocene** /**muy**-uh-ˌseen/ *Geol.* — *adj.* of the fourth epoch of the Tertiary period. — *n.* this epoch. [Greek *meiōn* less, *kainos* new]

**mips** *abbr. Computing* million instructions per second.

**miracle** /**mi**-ruh-kuhl/ *n.* **1** extraordinary event which has no natural explanation and hence is ascribed to some supernatural agency (*miracles at Lourdes*). **2** any remarkable occurrence or development (*economic miracle*). **3** (usu. foll. by *of*) remarkable specimen (*a miracle of ingenuity*). [Latin *mirus* wonderful]

**miracle play** *n.* **1** = MYSTERY PLAY. **2** medieval play dealing with the life of a saint.

**miraculous** /muh-**rak**-yuh-luhs/ *adj.* **1** constituting a miracle. **2** supernatural. **3** remarkable, surprising. □ **miraculously** *adv.* [French or medieval Latin: related to MIRACLE]

**mirage** /muh-**rahzh**/ *n.* **1** optical illusion caused by atmospheric conditions, esp. the appearance of a pool of water in a desert or on a hot road from the reflection of light. **2** any illusory thing. [Latin *miro* look at]

**mire** — *n.* **1** area of swampy ground. **2** mud, dirt. — *v.* (**-ring**) **1** plunge or sink in a mire. **2** involve in difficulties. **3** bespatter; besmirch. □ **miry** *adj.* [Old Norse]

**mirrnyong** /**mer**-nyong/ *n.* (also **mirrnyong heap**, **native oven**) mound of ashes, shells, and other debris, accumulated in a place used by Aborigines for cooking, and often of archaeological significance; a kitchen midden. [probably from a Victorian Aboriginal language]

**mirror** /**mi**-ruh/ — *n.* **1** polished surface, usu. of amalgam coated glass, reflecting an image. **2** anything reflecting or illuminating a state of affairs etc. — *v.* reflect in or as in a mirror. [Latin *miro* look at]

**mirror dory** *n.* marine food-fish of southern Australia with a brilliantly silvered and mirror-like circular body.

**mirror image** *n.* identical image or reflection with left and right reversed.

**mirth** *n.* merriment, laughter. □ **mirthful** *adj.* [Old English: related to MERRY]

**mis-**[1] *prefix* added to verbs and verbal derivatives: meaning 'amiss', 'badly', 'wrongly', 'unfavourably' (*mislead*; *misshapen*; *mistrust*). [Old English]

**mis-**[2] *prefix* occurring in some verbs, nouns, and adjectives meaning 'badly', 'wrongly', 'amiss', 'ill-', or having a negative force (*misadventure*; *mischief*). [Latin *minus*]

**misadventure** /ˌmis-uhd-**ven**-chuh/ *n.* **1** *Law* accident without crime or negligence (*death by misadventure*). **2** bad luck. **3** a misfortune.

**misalliance** /ˌmis-uh-**luy**-uhns/ n. unsuitable alliance, esp. a marriage.

**misanthrope** /**miz**-uhn-ˌthrohp/ n. (also **misanthropist** /muh-**zan**-thruh-puhst/ ) 1 person who hates mankind. 2 person who avoids human society. □ **misanthropic** /-throp-ik/ adj. **misanthropically** /-throp-i-kuh-lee,-klee/ adv. [Greek misos hatred, anthrōpos man]

**misanthropy** /muh-**zan**-thruh-pee/ n. condition or habits of a misanthrope.

**misapply** /ˌmis-uh-**pluy**/ v. (-ies, -ied) apply (esp. funds) wrongly. □ **misapplication** /misˌap-luh-**kay**-shuhn/ n.

**misapprehend** /ˌmis-ap-ruh-**hend**/ v. misunderstand (words, a person). □ **misapprehension** /-**hen**-shuhn/ n.

**misappropriate** /ˌmis-uh-**proh**-pree-ˌayt/ v. (-ting) take (another's money etc.) for one's own use; embezzle. □ **misappropriation** /-pree-**ay**-shuhn/ n.

**misbegotten** /ˌmis-buh-**got**-uhn/ adj. 1 illegitimate, bastard. 2 contemptible, disreputable.

**misbehave** /ˌmis-buh-**hayv**/ v. & refl. (-ving) behave badly. □ **misbehaviour** n.

**misc.** abbr. miscellaneous.

**miscalculate** /ˌmis-**kal**-kyuh-ˌlayt/ v. (-ting) calculate wrongly. □ **miscalculation** /-**lay**-shuhn/ n.

**miscarriage** /**mis**-ˌka-rij, mis-**ka**-rij/ n. spontaneous premature expulsion of a foetus from the womb.

**miscarriage of justice** n. failure of the judicial system to attain justice.

**miscarry** /mis-**ka**-ree/ v. (-ies, -ied) 1 (of a woman) have a miscarriage. 2 (of a plan etc.) fail.

**miscast** /mis-**kahst**/ v. (past and past part. **-cast**) allot an unsuitable part to (an actor) or unsuitable actors to (a play etc.).

**miscegenation** /mi-sej-uh-ˌnay-shuhn/ n. interbreeding of races, esp. of Whites and non-Whites. [related to MIX, GENUS]

**miscellaneous** /ˌmis-uh-**lay**-nee-uhs/ adj. 1 of mixed composition or character. 2 (foll. by a plural noun) of various kinds. □ **miscellaneously** adv. [Latin misceo mix]

**miscellany** /muh-**sel**-uh-nee/ n. (pl. -ies) 1 mixture, medley. 2 book containing various literary compositions. [Latin: related to MISCELLANEOUS]

**mischance** /mis-**chahns**, -**chans**/ n. 1 bad luck. 2 instance of this. [French: related to MIS-²]

**mischief** /**mis**-chuhf/ n. 1 troublesome, but not malicious, conduct, esp. of children (get into mischief). 2 playful malice; satire (eyes full of mischief). 3 harm, injury (do someone a mischief). □ **make mischief** create discord. [French: related to MIS-², chever happen]

**mischievous** /**mis**-chuh-vuhs/ adj. 1 (of a person) disposed to mischief. 2 (of conduct) playfully malicious. 3 harmful. □ **mischievously** adv. **mischievousness** n.

**miscible** /**mis**-uh-buhl/ adj. capable of being mixed. □ **miscibility** /-**bil**-uh-tee/ n. [medieval Latin: related to MIX]

**misconceive** /ˌmis-kuhn-**seev**/ v. (-ving) 1 (often foll. by of) have a wrong idea or conception. 2 (as **misconceived** adj.) badly planned, organised, etc. □ **misconception** /-**sep**-shuhn/ n. [from MIS-¹]

**misconduct** /mis-**kon**-dukt/ n. improper or unprofessional behaviour.

**misconstrue** /ˌmis-kuhn-**stroo**/ v. (-strues, -strued, -struing) interpret wrongly. □ **misconstruction** /-**struk**-shuhn/ n.

**miscopy** /mis-**kop**-ee/ v. (-ies, -ied) copy inaccurately.

**miscount** — v. /mis-**kownt**/ (also absol.) count inaccurately. — n. /**mis**-kownt/ inaccurate count.

**miscreant** /**mis**-kree-uhnt/ n. vile wretch, villain. [French: related to MIS-², creant believer]

**misdeal** — v. /mis-**deel**/ (also absol.) (past and past part. **-dealt** /-**delt**/ ) make a mistake in dealing (cards). — n. /**mis**-deel/ 1 mistake in dealing cards. 2 misdealt hand. [from MIS-¹]

**misdeed** /mis-**deed**/ n. evil deed, wrongdoing, crime. [Old English]

**misdemeanour** /ˌmis-duh-**mee**-nuh/ n. (also **misdemeanor**) 1 misdeed. 2 offence, less serious than a felony. [from MIS-¹]

**misdiagnose** /ˌmis-duy-uhg-ˌnohz/ v. (-sing) diagnose incorrectly. □ **misdiagnosis** /-**noh**-suhs/ n.

**misdial** /mis-**duy**-uhl/ v. (also absol.) (-ll-) dial (a telephone number etc.) incorrectly.

**misdirect** /ˌmis-duy-**rekt**, -duh-**rekt**/ v. direct wrongly. □ **misdirection** n.

**misdoing** /mis-**doo**-ing/ n. misdeed.

**mise en scène** /ˌmeez on **sen**/ n. 1 scenery and properties of a play. 2 surroundings of an event. [French]

**miser** /**muy**-zuh/ n. 1 person who hoards wealth and lives miserably. 2 avaricious person. □ **miserly** adj. [Latin, = wretched]

**miserable** /**miz**-uh-ruh-buhl/ adj. 1 wretchedly unhappy or uncomfortable. 2 contemptible. 3 causing wretchedness or discomfort (miserable weather). 4 stingy, mean (he refused to donate a cent — could anyone be more miserable?). □ **miserableness** n. **miserably** adv. [Latin: related to MISER]

**misery** /**miz**-uh-ree/ n. (pl. -ies) 1 condition or feeling of wretchedness. 2 cause of this. □ **put out of its** etc. **misery** 1 release (a person, animal, etc.) from suffering or suspense. 2 kill (an animal in pain). [Latin: related to MISER]

**misfield** — v. /mis-**feeld**/ (also absol.) (in cricket, baseball, etc.) field (the ball) badly. — n. /**mis**-feeld/ instance of this. [from MIS-¹]

**misfire** — v. /mis-**fuyuh**/ (-**ring**) **1** (of a gun, motor engine, etc.) fail to go off or start or function smoothly. **2** (of a plan etc.) fail to have the intended effect. — n. /**mis**-fuyuh/ such failure.

**misfit** — n. /**mis**-fit/ **1** person unsuited to an environment, occupation, etc. **2** garment etc. that does not fit. — v. /mis-**fit**/ (- **tt** -) fit badly (misfitting garment: misfitted to his job).

**misfortune** /mis-**faw**-choon, -chuhn/ n. **1** bad luck. **2** instance of this.

**misgive** /mis-**giv**/ v. (-**ving**; past -**gave**; past part. -**given**) (of a person's mind, heart, etc.) fill (a person) with suspicion or foreboding.

**misgiving** /mis-**giv**-ing/ n. (usu. in pl.) feeling of mistrust or apprehension.

**misgovern** /mis-**guv**-uhn/ v. govern badly. □ **misgovernment** n.

**misguided** /mis-**guy**-duhd/ adj. mistaken in thought or action. □ **misguidedly** adv. **misguidedness** n.

**mishandle** /mis-**han**-duhl/ v. (-**ling**) **1** deal with incorrectly or inefficiently. **2** handle roughly or rudely.

**mishap** /**mis**-hap/ n. unlucky accident.

**mishear** /mis-**heer**/ v. (past and past part. -**heard** /-**herd**/) hear incorrectly or imperfectly.

**mishit** — v. /mis-**hit**/ (-**tt**-; past and past part. -**hit**) hit (a ball etc.) badly. — n. /**mis**-hit/ faulty or bad hit.

**mishmash** n. confused mixture. [reduplication of MASH]

**misinform** /,mis-in-**fawm**/ v. give wrong information to, mislead. □ **misinformation** /-fuh-**may**-shuhn/ n. [from MIS-¹]

**misinterpret** /,mis-in-**ter**-pruht/ v. (-**t**-) **1** interpret wrongly. **2** draw a wrong inference from. □ **misinterpretation** /-**tay**-shuhn/ n.

**misjudge** /mis-**juj**/ v. (-**ging**) (also absol.) **1** judge wrongly. **2** have a wrong opinion of. □ **misjudgment** n. (also -**judgement**).

**miskey** /mis-**kee**/ v. (-**keys**, -**keyed**) key (data) wrongly.

**mislay** /mis-**lay**/ v. (past and past part. -**laid**) **1** accidentally put (a thing) where it cannot readily be found. **2** euphem. lose.

**mislead** /mis-**leed**/ v. (past and past part. -**led**) cause to infer what is not true; deceive. □ **misleading** adj. [Old English]

**mismanage** /mis-**man**-ij/ v. (-**ging**) manage badly or wrongly. □ **mismanagement** n. [from MIS-¹]

**mismatch** — v. /mis-**mach**/ match un-

suitably or incorrectly, esp. in marriage. — n. /**mis**-mach/ bad match.

**misnomer** /mis-**noh**-muh/ n. **1** name or term used wrongly. **2** wrong use of a name or term. [Anglo-French: related to MIS-², nommer to name]

**misogamy** /muh-**sog**-uh-mee/ n. hatred of marriage. □ **misogamist** n. [Greek misos hatred, gamos marriage]

**misogyny** /muh-**soj**-uh-nee/ n. hatred of women. □ **misogynist** n. **misogynistic** /-**nis**-tik/ adj. [Greek misos hatred, gunē woman]

**misplace** /mis-**plays**/ v. (-**cing**) **1** put in the wrong place. **2** bestow (affections, confidence, etc.) on an inappropriate object. □ **misplacement** n.

**misprint** — n. /**mis**-print/ printing error. — v. /mis-**print**/ print wrongly.

**mispronounce** /,mis-pruh-**nowns**/ v. (-**cing**) pronounce (a word etc.) wrongly. □ **mispronunciation** /-,nun-see-ay-shuhn/ n. [from MIS-¹]

**misquote** /mis-**kwoht**/ v. (-**ting**) quote inaccurately. □ **misquotation** /-**tay**-shuhn/ n.

**misread** /mis-**reed**/ v. (past and past part. -**read** /-**red**/) read or interpret wrongly.

**misrepresent** /,mis-rep-ruh-**zent**/ v. represent wrongly; give a false account or idea of. □ **misrepresentation** /-**tay**-shuhn/ n.

**misrule** /mis-**rool**/ — n. bad government; disorder. — v. (-**ling**) govern badly.

**miss¹** — v. **1** (also absol.) fail to hit, reach, find, catch, etc. (an object or goal). **2** fail to catch (a bus, train, etc.) or see (an event) or meet (a person). **3** fail to seize (an opportunity etc.) (missed my chance). **4** fail to hear or understand (missed what you said). **5 a** regret the loss or absence of (did you miss me?). **b** notice the loss or absence of (won't be missed until evening). **6** avoid (go early to miss the traffic). **7** (of an engine etc.) fail, misfire. — n. failure to hit, reach, attain, connect, etc. □ **be missing** not have (am missing a page) (see also MISSING). **give (a thing) a miss** colloq. not attend or partake of (gave the party a miss). **miss the boat** (or **bus**) lose an opportunity. **miss out 1** omit, leave out. **2 a** (usu. foll. by on) colloq. fail to get or experience (missed out on a prize). **b** fail to attend (missed out on the party). **not** (or **never**) **miss a trick** never fail to seize an opportunity, advantage, etc. [Old English]

**miss²** n. **1** (**Miss**) **a** title of an unmarried woman or girl. **b** title of a beauty queen (Miss Australia). **2** title used to address a female schoolteacher etc. **3** girl or unmarried woman. [from MISTRESS]

**missal** /mis-uhl/ n. RC Ch. **1** book containing the texts for the Mass throughout the year. **2** book of prayers. [Latin missa MASS²]

**misshapen** /mis-shay-puhn/ adj. ill-shaped, deformed, distorted. [from MIS-¹, shapen (archaic) = shaped]

**missile** /mis-uyl/ n. **1** object or weapon suitable for throwing at a target or for discharge from a machine. **2** weapon directed by remote control or automatically. [Latin mitto miss- send]

**missing** adj. **1** not in its place; lost. **2** (of a person) not yet traced or confirmed as alive but not known to be dead. **3** not present.

**missing link** n. **1** thing lacking to complete a series. **2** hypothetical intermediate type, esp. between humans and apes.

**mission** /mish-uhn/ n. **1 a** task or goal assigned to a person or group. **b** journey undertaken as part of this. **c** person's vocation. **2 a** Aboriginal settlement administered by a religious community. **b** such a settlement administered by a government agency or by Aborigines themselves. **3** military or scientific operation or expedition. **4** body of persons sent, esp. to a foreign country, to conduct negotiations or propagate a religious faith. **5** missionary post. [Latin: related to MISSILE]

**missionary** /mish-uh-nuh-ree, -uhn-ree/ — adj. of or concerned with religious missions. — n. (pl. **-ies**) person doing missionary work. [Latin: related to MISSION]

**missis** /mis-uhz/ n. (also **missus** /-suhz/) colloq. or joc. **1** form of address to a woman. **2** wife. □ **the missis** my or your wife. [from MISTRESS]

**missive** /mis-iv/ n. **1** joc. letter. **2** official letter. [Latin: related to MISSILE]

**misspell** /mis-spel/ v. (past and past part. **-spelt** or **-spelled**) spell wrongly.

**misspend** /mis-spend/ v. (past and past part. **-spent**) (esp. as **misspent** adj.) spend amiss or wastefully.

**misstate** /mis-stayt/ v. (**-ting**) state wrongly or inaccurately. □ **misstatement** n.

**missus** /mis-uhz/ n. **1** = MISSIS. **2** (in Aboriginal English) wife of a boss or manager.

**mist** — n. **1 a** water vapour near the ground in minute droplets limiting visibility. **b** condensed vapour obscuring glass etc. **2** dimness or blurring of the sight caused by tears etc. **3** cloud of particles resembling mist. — v. (usu. foll. by up, over) cover or become covered with mist or as with mist. [Old English]

**mistake** /muh-stayk/ — n. **1** incorrect idea or opinion; thing incorrectly done or thought. **2** error of judgment. — v. (**-king**; past **mistook** /-stuuk/; past part. **mistaken**) **1** misunderstand the meaning of. **2** (foll. by for) wrongly take or identify (mistook me for you). **3** choose wrongly (mistake one's vocation). □ **and** (or **make**) **no mistake** colloq. undoubtedly. **by mistake** accidentally; in error. **there is no mistaking** one is sure to recognise (a person or thing). [Old Norse: related to MIS-¹, TAKE]

**mistaken** /muh-stay-kuhn/ adj. **1** wrong in opinion or judgment. **2** based on or resulting from this (mistaken loyalty; mistaken identity). □ **mistakenly** adv.

**mister** /mis-tuh/ n. colloq. or joc. form of address to a man. [from MASTER; cf. MR]

**mistime** /mis-tuym/ v. (**-ming**) say or do at the wrong time. [related to MIS-¹]

**mistletoe** /mis-uhl-,toh/ n. **1** parasitic European plant with white berries growing on apple and other trees. **2** similar Australian plant, usu. to be seen hanging from the branches of eucalypts. [Old English]

**mistletoe bird** n. small bird of mainland Australia having a steel-blue body and scarlet and white breast, and feeding mainly on mistletoe berries.

**mistook** past of MISTAKE.

**mistral** /mis-trahl, mis-truhl/ n. cold or NW wind in S. France. [Latin: related to MASTER]

**mistreat** /mis-treet/ v. treat badly. □ **mistreatment** n.

**mistress** /mis-truhs/ n. **1** female head of a household. **2 a** woman in authority. **b** female owner of a pet. **3** female teacher. **4** woman having an illicit sexual relationship with a (usu. married) man. **5** hist. woman to whom a convict is assigned. [French maistre MASTER, -ESS]

**mistrial** /mis-truyl/ n. trial rendered invalid by some error in the proceedings.

**mistrust** /mis-trust/ — v. **1** be suspicious of. **2** feel no confidence in. — n. **1** suspicion. **2** lack of confidence. □ **mistrustful** adj. **mistrustfully** adv.

**misty** adj. (**-ier, -iest**) **1** of or covered with mist. **2** dim in outline. **3** obscure, vague (misty idea). □ **mistily** adv. **mistiness** n. [Old English: related to MIST]

**misunderstand** /,mis-un-duh-stand/ v. (past and past part. **-understood** /-stuud/) **1** understand incorrectly. **2** misinterpret the words or actions of (a person).

**misunderstanding** n. **1** failure to understand correctly. **2** slight disagreement or quarrel.

**misusage** /mis-yoo-sij/ n. **1** wrong or improper usage. **2** ill-treatment.

**misuse** — v. /mis-yooz/ (**-sing**) **1** use wrongly; apply to the wrong purpose. **2** ill-treat. — n. /mis-yoos/ wrong or improper use or application.

**Mitchell** /**mich**-uhl/ *n.* (in full **Mitchell grass**) any of the hardy tussock-forming perennial grasses of arid and semi-arid Australia, providing valuable fodder, esp. bull Mitchell and curly Mitchell. [T.L. *Mitchell*, explorer (d. 1855)]

**mite**[1] /muyt/ *n.* small arachnid, esp. of a kind found on plants, in cheese, etc. [Old English]

**mite**[2] — *n.* **1** any very small sum of money, or coin of very low value. **2** small object or person, esp. a child. **3** very small contribution (usu. all that the donor can afford). — *adv.* (usu. prec. by *a*) somewhat (*is a mite shy*). [probably the same as MITE[1]]

**mitigate** /**mit**-uh-,gayt/ *v.* (**-ting**) make less intense or severe (*your presence mitigates his grief*). □ **mitigation** /-**gay**-shuhn/ *n.* [Latin *mitis* mild]

■ Usage *Mitigate* is often confused with *militate*.

**mitigating circumstances** *n.pl. Law* circumstances permitting greater leniency.

**mitosis** /muh-**toh**-suhs, muy-/ *n. Biol.* type of cell division that results in two nuclei each having the same number and kind of chromosomes as the parent nucleus. □ **mitotic** /-**tot**-ik/ *adj.* [Greek *mitos* thread]

**mitre** /**muy**-tuh/ — *n.* **1** tall deeply cleft headdress worn by bishops and abbots, esp. as a symbol of office. **2** joint of two pieces of wood etc. at an angle of 90°, such that the line of junction bisects this angle. — *v.* (**-ring**) **1** bestow a mitre on (*mitred abbot*). **2** join (two pieces of wood) with a mitre. [Greek *mitra* turban]

**mitt** *n.* **1** (also **mitten**) glove with only two compartments, one for the thumb and the other for all four fingers. **2** glove leaving the fingers and thumb-tip exposed. **3** *colloq.* hand or fist. **4** baseball glove. [Latin: related to MOIETY]

**mix** — *v.* **1** combine or put together (two or more substances or things) so that the constituents of each are diffused among those of the other(s). **2** prepare (a compound, cocktail, etc.) by combining the ingredients. **3** combine (activities etc.) (*mix business and pleasure*). **4 a** join, be mixed, or combine, esp. readily (*oil and water will not mix*). **b** be compatible. **c** be sociable (*must learn to mix*). **5 a** (foll. by *with*) (of a person) be harmonious or sociable with; have regular dealings with. **b** (foll. by *in*) participate in. **6** combine (two or more sound signals) into one. — *n.* **1 a** mixing; mixture. **b** proportion of materials in a mixture. **2** ingredients

prepared commercially for making a cake, concrete, etc. **3** group of persons of different types (*social mix*). □ **be mixed up in** (or **with**) be involved in or with (esp. something undesirable). **mix it** *colloq.* start fighting. **mix up 1** mix thoroughly. **2** confuse (*mixed up by all these instructions*). [back-formation from MIXED]

**mix and match** — *adj.* (of items of clothing) designed to be alternated with other items of clothing (e.g. skirts, blouses, etc.). — *v.* alternate items of clothing (skirts, blouses, etc.) to achieve different effects.

**mixed** /mikst/ *adj.* **1** of diverse qualities or elements. **2** containing persons from various backgrounds etc. **3** for persons of both sexes (*mixed bathing*). [Latin *misceo mixt-* mix]

**mixed blessing** *n.* thing having advantages and disadvantages.

**mixed business** *n.* small shop, often associated with a milk bar, selling groceries and other goods.

**mixed doubles** *n.pl. Tennis* doubles game with a man and a woman on each side.

**mixed farming** *n.* farming of both crops and livestock. □ **mixed farmer** *n.*

**mixed feelings** *n.pl.* mixture of pleasure and dismay about something.

**mixed marriage** *n.* marriage between persons of different race or religion.

**mixed metaphor** *n.* combination of inconsistent metaphors (e.g. *this tower of strength will forge ahead*).

**mixed-up** *adj.* mentally or emotionally confused; socially ill-adjusted.

**mixer** *n.* **1** usu. electrical machine for mixing foods etc. **2** person who manages socially in a specified way (*a good mixer*). **3** (usu. soft) drink to be mixed with another. **4** device that receives two or more separate signals from microphones etc. and combines them in a single output.

**mixture** /**miks**-chuh/ *n.* **1** process or result of mixing. **2** combination of ingredients, qualities, characteristics, etc. (*cough mixture*; *he's a mixture of kindness and intolerance*). [Latin: related to MIXED]

**mix-up** *n.* confusion, misunderstanding.

**ml** *abbr.* **1** millilitre(s). **2** mile(s).

**MLA** *abbr.* Member of the Legislative Assembly.

**MLC** *abbr.* Member of the Legislative Council.

**mm** *abbr.* millimetre(s).

**Mn** *symb.* manganese.

**mnemonic** /nuh-**mon**-ik/ — *adj.* of or designed to aid the memory. — *n.* mnemonic word, verse, etc. □ **mnemonically** *adv.* [Greek *mnēmōn* mindful]

**Mo** *symb.* molybdenum.

**mo**[1] /moh/ *n.* (*pl.* **-s**) *colloq.* moment. [abbreviation]

**mo**[2] *n. colloq.* moustache. [abbreviation]

**moa** /moh-uh/ *n.* (*pl.* **-s**) extinct flightless New Zealand bird resembling the ostrich. [Maori]

**moan** /mohn/ — *n.* **1** long murmur expressing physical or mental suffering or pleasure. **2** low plaintive sound of wind etc. **3** *colloq.* complaint; grievance. — *v.* **1** make a moan or moans. **2** *colloq.* complain, grumble. **3** utter with moans. □ **moaner** *n.* [Old English]

**moat** /moht/ — *n.* defensive ditch round a castle, town, etc., usu. filled with water. — *v.* surround with or as with a moat. [French *mote* mound]

**mob** — *n.* **1** large disorderly crowd of people. **2** (prec. by *the*) usu. *derog.* the common people, the rabble. **3** *colloq.* gang. **4 a** number (or class) of people showing a specified characteristic, identity, etc. (*took eleven ships to bring that first mob to Oz*). **b** *colloq.* the friends one usu. associates with (*the mob's coming over this arvo*). **5** (in Aboriginal English) one's extended family, one's own particular clan or people. **6** herd or flock. **7** *colloq.* **a** (usu. in *pl.*) large quantity; considerable number (*mobs of water on the track; mobs of fish in the creek*) **b** (quasi- *adv.*) much (*it'll be mobs easier*). — *v.* (**-bb-**) crowd round in order to attack or admire. [Latin *mobile vulgus* excitable crowd]

**mobile** /moh-buyl/ — *adj.* **1** movable; able to move easily or get out and about. **2** (of the face etc.) readily changing its expression. **3** (of a library, business, etc.) accommodated in a vehicle so as to serve various places. **4** (of a person) able to change his or her social status (*suburb for the upwardly mobile*). — *n.* decoration that may be hung so as to turn freely. □ **mobility** /muh-**bil**-uh-tee, moh-/ *n.* [Latin *moveo* move]

**mobile phone** *n.* portable cellular telephone for use in a car etc.

**mobilise** /**moh**-buh-,luyz/ *v.* (also **-ize**) (**-sing** or **-zing**) **1** (esp. of troops in times of war) make or become ready for service or action. **2** make ready, muster; put into use (*mobilise your energies*). □ **mobilisation** /-**zay**-shuhn/ *n.*

**Möbius strip** /**mer**-bee-uhs/ *n. Math.* one-sided surface formed by joining the ends of a narrow rectangle after twisting one end through 180°. [*Möbius*, name of a mathematician]

**mobster** *n. colloq.* gangster.

**moccasin** /**mok**-uh-suhn/ *n.* soft flat-soled shoe orig. worn by N. American Indians. [American Indian]

**mock** — *v.* **1** (often foll. by *at*) ridicule; scoff (at); act with scorn or contempt for. **2** mimic contemptuously. **3** defy or delude contemptuously. **4** (foll. by *up*) construct (a model etc.). — *attrib. adj.* **1** sham, imitation (*mock battle; mock cream*). **2** as a trial run (*mock exam*). □ **mockingly** *adv.* [French *moquer*]

**mocker**[1] *n.* person who mocks. □ **put the mockers on** *colloq.* bring bad luck to.

**mocker**[2] *n. colloq.* clothing, dress (*wear ordinary mocker*). □ **mockered up** dressed up.

**mockery** *n.* (*pl.* **-ies**) **1** derision, ridicule. **2** counterfeit or absurdly inadequate representation. **3** ludicrously or insultingly futile action etc.

**mockingbird** *n.* bird that mimics the notes of other birds.

**mock-up** *n.* experimental model or replica of a proposed structure etc.

**mod** *colloq. adj.* modern, esp. in style of dress. [abbreviation]

**modal** /**moh**-duhl/ *adj.* **1** of mode or form, not of substance. **2** *Gram.* **a** of the mood of a verb. **b** (of an auxiliary verb, e.g. *would*) used to express the mood of another verb. **3** *Mus.* denoting a style of music using a particular mode. [Latin: related to MODE]

**mod cons** *n.pl.* modern conveniences (*house for sale with all the mod cons*).

**mode** /mohd/ *n.* **1** way in which a thing is done. **2** prevailing fashion or custom. **3** *Mus.* any of several types of scale. **4** *Computing* way of operating or using a system (*conversational mode*). [French and Latin *modus* measure]

**model** /**mod**-uhl/ — *n.* **1** representation in three dimensions of an existing person or thing or of a proposed structure, esp. on a smaller scale (often *attrib.*: *model train*). **2** simplified description of a system etc., to assist calculations and predictions. **3** figure in clay, wax, etc., to be reproduced in another material. **4** particular design or style, esp. of a car. **5 a** exemplary person or thing. **b** (*attrib.*) ideal, exemplary (*a model student*). **6** person employed to pose for an artist or photographer or to wear clothes etc. for display. **7** garment etc. by a well-known designer, or a copy of this. — *v.* (**-ll-**) **1 a** fashion or shape (a figure) in clay, wax, etc. **b** (foll. by *after*, *on*, etc.) form (a thing in imitation of). **2 a** act or pose as a model. **b** (of a person acting as a model) display (a garment). [Latin: related to MODE]

**modem** /**moh**-dem/ *n.* device which enables communication to a computer over a telephone line. [portmanteau word, *modulator + demodulator*]

**moderate**— *adj.* /**mod**-uh-ruht/ **1** avoiding extremes; temperate in conduct or expression. **2** fairly large or good. **3** (of the wind) of medium strength. **4** (of prices) fairly low. **5** average, limited (*moderate success*).— *n.* /**mod**-uh-ruht/ person who holds moderate views, esp. in politics. — *v.* /**mod**-uh-,rayt/ (**-ting**) **1** make or become less violent, intense, rigorous, etc. **2** (also *absol.*) act as moderator of or to. □ **moderately** /-ruht-lee/ *adv.* **moderateness** /-ruht-nuhs/ *n.* [Latin]

**moderation** /,mod-uh-**ray**-shuhn/ *n.* **1** moderateness. **2** moderating. □ **in moderation** in a moderate manner or degree.

**moderato** /,mod-uh-**rah**-toh/ *adj. & adv. Mus.* at a moderate pace. [Italian]

**moderator** *n.* **1** arbitrator, mediator. **2** presiding officer. **3** Presbyterian or Uniting Church minister presiding over an ecclesiastical body. **4** *Physics* substance used in a nuclear reactor to retard neutrons.

**modern** /**mod**-uhn/ — *adj.* **1** of present and recent times. **2** in current fashion; not antiquated.— *n.* **1** person living in modern times. **2** person with modern views etc. □ **modernity** /-**der**-nuh-tee/ *n.* [Latin *modo* just now]

**Modern English** *n.* English from about 1500 onwards.

**modern history** *n.* history from the end of the Middle Ages to the present day.

**modernise** *v.* (also **-ize**) (**-sing** or **-zing**) **1** make modern; adapt to modern needs or habits. **2** adopt modern ways or views. □ **modernisation** /-**zay**-shuhn/ *n.*

**modernism** *n.* modern ideas or methods, esp. the rejection of realism and traditionalism in the art and literature of the first half of the 20th century. □ **modernist** *n. & adj.*

**modest** /**mod**-uhst/ *adj.* **1** having or expressing a humble or moderate estimate of one's own merits. **2** diffident, bashful. **3** decorous in manner and conduct. **4** moderate or restrained in amount, extent, severity, etc. **5** unpretentious, not extravagant. □ **modestly** *adv.* **modesty** *n.* [French from Latin]

**modicum** /**mod**-uh-kuhm/ *n.* (foll. by *of*) small quantity. [Latin: related to MODE]

**modification** /,mod-uh-fuh-**kay**-shuhn/ *n.* **1** modifying or being modified. **2** a change made. □ **modificatory** /**mod**-uh-fuh-,kay-tree/ *adj.* [Latin: related to MODIFY]

**modifier** /**mod**-uh-,fuy-uh/ *n.* **1** person or thing that modifies. **2** *Gram.* word (esp. an adjective or noun used attributively) that qualifies the sense of another word (e.g. *good* and *family* in *a good family house*).

**modify** /**mod**-uh-,fuy/ *v.* (**-ies, -ied**) **1** make less severe or extreme (*modify one's demands*). **2** make partial changes in. **3** *Gram.* qualify or expand the sense of (a word etc.) (*the word 'slowly' modifies 'ate' in 'he ate slowly'*). [Latin: related to MODE]

**modish** /**moh**-dish/ *adj.* fashionable. □ **modishly** *adv.*

**modulate** /**mod**-yuh-,layt/ *v.* (**-ting**) **1 a** regulate or adjust. **b** moderate. **2** adjust or vary the tone or pitch of (the speaking voice). **3** alter the amplitude or frequency of (a wave) by using a wave of a lower frequency to convey a signal. **4** *Mus.* (cause to) change from one key to another. □ **modulation** /-**lay**-shuhn/ *n.* [Latin: related to MODULE]

**module** /**mod**-yool/ *n.* **1** standardised part or independent unit in construction, esp. of furniture, a building, or an electronic system. **2** independent self-contained unit of a spacecraft. **3** unit or period of training or education. □ **modular** *adj.* [Latin: related to MODULUS]

**modulus** /**mod**-yuh-luhs/ *n.* (*pl.* **moduli** /-,luy/ ) *Math.* constant factor or ratio. [Latin, = measure: related to MODE]

**modus operandi** /,mod-duhs ,op-uh-**ran**-duy, -dee/ *n.* (*pl.* **modi operandi** /,moh-dee/ ) method of working. [Latin, = way of operating]

**modus vivendi** /,moh-duhs vi-**ven**-duy, -dee/ *n.* (*pl.* **modi vivendi** /,moh-dee/ ) **1** way of living or coping. **2** arrangement between people who agree to differ. [Latin, = way of living]

**moggie** *n.* (also **moggy, mog**) *colloq.* cat. [originally a British dial. word]

**mogul** /**moh**-guhl/ *n.* **1** *colloq.* important or influential person. **2** (**Mogul**) *hist.* **a** Mongolian. **b** (often **the Great Mogul**) emperor of Delhi in the 16th–19th c. [Persian and Arabic: related to MONGOL]

**mohair** /**moh**-hair/ *n.* **1** hair of the angora goat. **2** yarn or fabric from this. [ultimately from Arabic, = choice]

**Mohammedan** /muh-**ham**-uh-duhn/ *n. & adj.* (also **Muhammadan**) = MUSLIM. [*Mohammed*, name of a prophet]

■ **Usage** The term *Mohammedan* is not used by Muslims, and is often regarded as offensive.

**moiety** /**moi**-uh-tee/ *n.* (*pl.* **-ies**) **1** half. **2** each of the two parts into which something is divided, esp. *Anthropology* one of two units into which an Aboriginal people is divided, esp. on the basis of lineal descent. [Latin *medietas* from *medius* middle]

**moist** *adj.* **1** slightly wet; damp. **2** (of the eyes) having a hint of tears. [French]

**moisten** /**moi**-suhn/ *v.* make or become moist.

**moisture** /**mois**-chuh/ *n.* water or other liquid diffused in a small quantity as vapour, or within a solid, or condensed on a surface.

**moisturise** *v.* (also **-ize**) (**-sing** or **-zing**) make less dry (esp. the skin by use of a cosmetic). □ **moisturiser** *n.*

**moke** *n. colloq.* horse; sometimes an inferior one. [origin unknown]

**molar¹** /**moh**-luh/ — *adj.* (usu. of a mammal's back teeth) serving to grind. — *n.* molar tooth. [Latin *mola* millstone]

**molar²** *adj.* of or relating to mass. acting on or by means of large masses or units. [Latin *moles* mass]

**molar³** *adj. Chem.* **1** of a mass of substance usu. per mole. **2** (of a solution) containing one mole of solute per litre of solvent. □ **molarity** *n.* [MOLE⁴ + -AR]

**molasses** /muh-**las**-uhz/ *n.pl.* (treated as *sing.*) uncrystallised syrup extracted from raw sugar. [Portuguese from Latin *mel* honey]

**mole¹** *n.* **1** small burrowing mammal with dark velvety fur and very small eyes. **2** *colloq.* spy established in a position of trust in an organisation. [Low German or Dutch]

**mole²** *n.* small permanent dark spot on the skin. [Old English]

**mole³** *n.* **1** massive structure serving as a pier, breakwater, or causeway. **2** artificial harbour. [Latin *moles* mass]

**mole⁴** *n. Chem.* the SI unit of amount of a substance equal to the quantity containing as many elementary units as there are atoms in 0.012 kg of carbon-12. [German *Mol* from *Molekül* MOLECULE]

**mole⁵** *n. colloq. derog.* girl or woman. [probably a variant of *moll* girl or woman]

**molecular** /muh-**lek**-yuh-luh/ *adj.* of, relating to, or consisting of molecules. □ **molecularity** /-la-ruh-tee/ *n.*

**molecular weight** *n.* = RELATIVE MOLECULAR MASS.

**molecule** /**mol**-uh-ˌkyool/ *n.* **1** smallest fundamental unit (usu. a group of atoms) of a chemical compound that can take part in a chemical reaction. **2** (in general use) small particle. [Latin diminutive: related to MOLE³]

**molehill** *n.* small mound thrown up by a mole in burrowing. □ **make a mountain out of a molehill** overreact to a minor difficulty.

**moleskin** *n.* kind of cotton fustian with its surface shaved before dyeing.

**moleskins** *n.pl.* trousers made of moleskin, part of the customary dress of Australian

stockmen, gold diggers, etc., from the early 19th-c. onwards.

**molest** /muh-**lest**/ *v.* **1** annoy or pester (a person). **2** attack or interfere with (a person), esp. sexually. □ **molestation** /ˌmol-es-**tay**-shuhn, ˌmoh-les-/ *n.* **molester** *n.* [Latin *molestus* troublesome]

**moll** *n. colloq.* **1** gangster's female companion. **2** prostitute. **3** girlfriend of a bikie, surfie, etc. [pet form of *Mary*]

**mollify** /**mol**-uh-ˌfuy/ *v.* (**-ies**, **-ied**) **1** appease, pacify. **2** reduce the severity of; soften. □ **mollification** /-fuh-**kay**-shuhn/ *n.* [Latin *mollis* soft]

**mollusc** /**mol**-uhsk/ *n.* invertebrate with a soft body and usu. a hard shell, e.g. snail or oyster. [Latin *molluscus* soft]

**mollycoddle** /**mol**-ee-ˌkod-uhl/ *v.* (**-ling**) coddle, pamper. [related to MOLL, CODDLE]

**molly-dook** /ˌmol-ee-**dook**/ *n. colloq.* (also **molly-dooker**) left-handed person. □ **molly-dooked** *adj.* [probably from *molly* an effeminate man, a milksop, *dook*, variant of *duke* hand]

**Molotov cocktail** /**mol**-uh-ˌtov, -ˌtof/ *n.* crude incendiary device, usu. a bottle filled with inflammable liquid. [*Molotov*, name of a Russian statesman]

**molten** /**mohl**-tuhn/ *adj.* melted, esp. made liquid by heat. [from MELT]

**molto** /**mol**-toh/ *adv. Mus.* very. [Latin *multus* much]

**moly** /**moh**-lee/ *n.* mythical herb with white flowers and black roots, endowed with powerful magic properties. [Greek *mōlu*]

**molybdenum** /muh-**lib**-duh-nuhm/ *n.* silver-white metallic element added to steel to give strength and resistance to corrosion. [Greek *molubdos* lead]

**moment** /**moh**-muhnt/ *n.* **1** very brief portion of time; an instant (*was gone in a moment*). **2** short period of time (*wait a moment*). **3** an exact point of time (*I came the moment you called*). **4** importance (*of no great moment*). **5** product of a force and the distance from its line of action to a point. □ **at the moment** now. **in a moment** very soon. **man** (or **woman** etc.) **of the moment** the one of importance at the time in question. [Latin: related to MOMENTUM]

**momentary** /**moh**-muhn-tuh-ree, -tree/ *adj.* lasting only a moment; transitory. □ **momentarily** *adv.* [Latin: related to MOMENT]

**moment of truth** *n.* time of crisis or test.

**momentous** /muh-**men**-tuhs/ *adj.* very important. □ **momentously** *adv.* **momentousness** *n.*

**momentum** /muh-**men**-tuhm/ *n.* (*pl.* **momenta**) **1** quantity of motion of a moving

body, the product of its mass and velocity.
**2** impetus gained by movement. **3** strength or continuity derived from an initial effort (*the campaign is gaining momentum*). [Latin *moveo* move]

**mon-** see MONO-.

**monad** /mon-ad, moh-nad/ *n.* **1** the number one; unit. **2** *Philos.* ultimate unit of being (e.g. a soul, an atom, a person, God). □ **monadic** /muh-**nad**-ik/ *adj.* [Greek *monas -ados* unit]

**monarch** /mon-uhk, mon-ahk/ *n.* sovereign with the title of king, queen, emperor, empress, or equivalent. □ **monarchic** /muh-**nah**-kik/ *adj.* **monarchical** /muh-**nah**-ki-kuhl/ *adj.* [Greek: related to MONO-, *arkhō* rule]

**monarchism** *n.* advocacy of monarchy. □ **monarchist** *n.* [French: related to MONARCH]

**monarchy** *n.* (*pl.* **-ies**) **1** form of government with a monarch at the head. **2** nation with this. □ **monarchical** (or **monarchial**) *adj.* [Greek: related to MONARCH]

**monastery** /mon-uh-stuh-ree, -stree/ *n.* (*pl.* **-ies**) residence of a religious community, esp. of monks living in seclusion. [Latin *monasterium* from Greek *monazō* be or live alone]

**monastic** /muh-**nas**-tik/ — *adj.* **1** of or like monasteries. **2** of or like monks or nuns or their way of life; solitary and celibate. — *n.* monk or other follower of a monastic rule. □ **monastically** *adv.* **monasticism** /-tuh-,siz-uhm/ *n.* [Greek: related to MONASTERY]

**monaych** /mon-uych/ *n.* *colloq.* police officer; the police. [Nyungar *manaj* white cockatoo]

**Monday** /mun-day/ — *n.* day of the week following Sunday. — *adv.* *colloq.* **1** on Monday. **2** (**Mondays**) on Mondays; each Monday (*Mondays he weeds the garden*). [Old English]

**Mondayitis** /,mun-day-**uy**-tuhs/ *n.* *colloq.* fictitious disease, the chief symptom of which is a marked reluctance to resume work after the weekend break. [-*itis* noun suffix indicating inflammation, disease]

**monetarism** /mun-uh-tuh-,riz-uhm/ *n.* theory or practice of controlling the supply of money as the chief method of stabilising the economy. □ **monetarist** *n.* & *adj.*

**monetary** /mun-uh-tuh-ree, -tree/ *adj.* **1** of the currency in use. **2** of or consisting of money. [Latin: related to MONEY]

**money** /mun-ee/ *n.* **1** coins and banknotes as a medium of exchange. **2** (*pl.* **-eys** or **-ies**) (in *pl.*) sums of money. **3 a** wealth. **b** wealth as power (*money talks*). **c** rich person or family (*married into money*). **d** money as a resource (*time is money*). **e** profit,

remuneration (*in it for the money*). □ **for my money** in my opinion; for my preference. **in the money** having or winning a lot of money. **put one's money where one's mouth is** back one's verbal support (for a cause etc.) with tangible evidence of that support (esp. money). **run** (or **good run**) **for one's money** see RUN. [Latin *moneta*]

**moneyed** /mun-eed/ *adj.* wealthy.

**money-grubber** *n.* *colloq.* person greedily intent on amassing money. □ **money-grubbing** *n.* & *adj.*

**moneylender** *n.* person who lends money at interest.

**moneymaker** *n.* (also **money-spinner**) thing, idea, business, etc., that produces much money. □ **moneymaking** *n.* & *adj.*

**money market** *n.* trade in short-term stocks, loans, etc.

**money-spinner** *n.* = MONEYMAKER.

**mong** /mung/ *n.* *colloq.* any dog (not necessarily of a mixed breed). [abbreviation of MONGREL]

**monger**[1] /mung-guh/ *n.* (usu. in *comb.*) **1** dealer, trader (*fishmonger*). **2** usu. *derog.* promoter, spreader (*warmonger*; *scaremonger*, *gossip-monger*). [Latin *mango* dealer]

**monger**[2] var. of MUNGA.

**Mongol** /mong-guhl/ — *adj.* **1** of the Asian people in Mongolia. **2** resembling this people. **3** (**mongol**) *offens.* suffering from Down's syndrome. — *n.* **1** Mongolian. **2** (**mongol**) *offens.* person suffering from Down's syndrome. [native name: perhaps from *mong* brave]

**Mongolian** /mong-**goh**-lee-uhn/ — *n.* **1** native or inhabitant of Mongolia. **2** language of Mongolia. — *adj.* of or relating to Mongolia or its people or language.

**mongolism** /mong-guh-,liz-uhm/ *n.* = DOWN'S SYNDROME.

■ **Usage** The term *Down's syndrome* is now preferred.

**Mongoloid** /mong-guh-,loid/ — *adj.* **1** characteristic of the Mongolians, esp. in having a broad flat yellowish face. **2** (**mongoloid**) often *offens.* having the characteristic symptoms of Down's syndrome. — *n.* Mongoloid or mongoloid person.

**mongoose** /mong-goos/ *n.* (*pl.* **-s**) small flesh-eating civet-like mammal. [Marathi *mangūs*]

**mongrel** /mung-gruhl/ — *n.* **1** dog of no definable type or breed. **2** other animal or plant resulting from the crossing of different breeds or types. **3** *colloq.* **a** *derog.* despicable person. **b** exasperating or infuriating thing (*can't get this mongrel of a car to start*). — *adj.* **1** of mixed origin, nature, or character. **2** *colloq. derog.* (intensifier expressing abuse) (*mongrel idiot us the match*). [related to MINGLE]

**monies** see MONEY 2.

**moniker** /**mon**-uh-kuh/ *n. colloq.* (also **monicker, monniker**) person's name; nickname. [origin unknown.]

**monism** /**mon**-iz-uhm/ *n.* **1** doctrine that only one ultimate principle or being exists. **2** theory denying the duality of matter and mind. □ **monist** *n.* **monistic** /muh-**nis**-tik/ *adj.* [Greek *monos* single]

**monitor** /**mon**-uh-tuh/ — *n.* **1** person or device for checking or warning. **2** school pupil with special duties. **3 a** television receiver used in a studio to select or verify the picture being broadcast. **b** = VISUAL DISPLAY UNIT. **4** person who listens to and reports on foreign broadcasts etc. **5** detector of radioactive contamination. **6** large lizard of Australia, Asia, and Africa, supposed to give warning of the approach of crocodiles. — *v.* **1** act as a monitor of. **2** maintain regular surveillance over. **3** regulate the strength of (a recorded or transmitted signal). [Latin *moneo monit-* warn]

**monk** /mungk/ *n.* member of a religious community of men living under certain vows, esp. of poverty, chastity, and obedience. □ **monkish** *adj.* [Greek *monakhos* from *monos* alone]

**monkey** /**mung**-kee/ — *n.* (*pl.* **-eys**) **1** any of various primates, including marmosets, baboons etc., esp. a small long-tailed kind. **2** mischievous person. **3** = MONKEY SHAFT. — *v.* (**-eys, -eyed**) **1** (often foll. by *with*) tamper or play mischievous tricks. **2** (foll. by *around, about*) fool around. □ **make a monkey of** humiliate by making appear ridiculous. **monkey about** (or **around**) **with** meddle, trifle with. [origin unknown]

**monkey business** *n. colloq.* mischief; trickery.

**monkey shaft** *n.* (also **monkey**) mine shaft constructed to rise vertically from a lower to a higher level.

**monkey tricks** *n.pl. colloq.* mischief.

**monkey wrench** *n.* wrench with an adjustable jaw.

**mono** /**mon**-oh/ *colloq.* — *adj.* monophonic. — *n.* monophonic reproduction (cf. STEREO). [abbreviation]

**mono-** *comb. form* (usu. **mon-** before a vowel) one, alone, single. [Greek *monos* alone]

**monochromatic** /,mon-uh-kruh-**mat**-ik/ *adj.* **1** (of light or other radiation) of a single colour or wavelength. **2** containing only one colour. □ **monochromatically** *adv.*

**monochrome** /**mon**-uh-,krohm/ — *n.*

photograph or picture done in one colour or different tones of this, or in black and white only. — *adj.* having or using only one colour or in black and white only. [from MONO-, Greek *khrōma* colour]

**monocle** /**mon**-uh-dee/ *n.* eyeglass for one eye only. □ **monocled** *adj.* [MONO-, Latin *oculus* eye]

**monocotyledon** /,mon-oh-,kot-uh-lee-duhn/ *n.* flowering plant with one cotyledon. □ **monocotyledonous** *adj.*

**monody** /**mon**-uh-dee/ *n.* (*pl.* **-ies**) **1** ode sung by a single actor in a Greek tragedy. **2** poem lamenting a person's death. **3** musical composition with only one melodic line. □ **monodist** *n.* [Greek: related to MONO-, ODE]

**monoecious** /muh-**nee**-shuhs/ *adj.* **1** *Bot.* with unisexual male and female organs on the same plant. **2** *Zool.* with both male and female organs in the same individual, hermaphrodite. [MON-, Greek *oikos* house]

**monogamy** /muh-**nog**-uh-mee/ *n.* practice or state of being married to one person at a time. □ **monogamous** *adj.* [Greek *gamos* marriage]

**monogram** /**mon**-uh-gram/ *n.* two or more letters, esp. a person's initials, interwoven as a device.

**monograph** /**mon**-uh-,grahf, -,graf/ *n.* treatise on a single subject.

**monolingual** /,mon-oh-**ling**-gwuhl/ *adj.* speaking or using only one language.

**monolith** /**mon**-uh-lith/ *n.* **1** single block of stone, esp. shaped into a pillar etc. **2** person or thing like a monolith in being massive, immovable, or solidly uniform. □ **monolithic** /-**lith**-ik/ *adj.* [Greek *lithos* stone]

**monologue** /**mon**-uh-,log/ *n.* **1 a** scene in a drama in which a person speaks alone. **b** dramatic composition for one performer. **2** long speech by one person in a conversation etc. [French from Greek *monologos* a speaking alone]

**monomania** /,mon-uh-**may**-nee-uh/ *n.* obsession of the mind by a single idea or interest. □ **monomaniac** *n. & adj.*

**monophonic** /,mon-uh-**fon**-ik/ *adj.* (of sound-reproduction) using only one channel of transmission (opp. STEREOPHONIC). [Greek *phōnē* sound]

**monopolise** /muh-**nop**-uh-,luyz/ *v.* (also **-ize**) (**-sing** or **-zing**) **1** obtain exclusive possession or control of (a trade or commodity etc.). **2** dominate or prevent others from sharing in (a conversation etc.). □ **monopolisation** /-,zay-shuhn/ *n.* **monopoliser** *n.*

**monopoly** /muh-**nop**-uh-lee/ *n.* (*pl.* **-ies**) **1 a** exclusive possession or control of the trade in a commodity or service. **b** this conferred as a privilege by a government.

**2** (foll. by *of*) exclusive possession, control, or exercise. [Greek *pōleō* sell]

**monorail** /**mon**-oh-,rayl/ *n.* railway with a single-rail track, usu. elevated with the train units suspended from it.

**monosodium glutamate** /,mon-oh-,soh-dee-uhm **gloo**-tuh-,mayt/ *n.* sodium salt of glutamic acid used to enhance the flavour of food. [Latin *gluten* glue]

**monosyllable** /**mon**-uh-,sil-uh-buhl/ *n.* word of one syllable. □ **monosyllabic** /,mon-uh-suh-**lab**-ik/ *adj.*

**monotheism** /**mon**-oh-,thee-iz-uhm/ *n.* doctrine that there is only one god. □ **monotheist** *n.* **monotheistic** /-'-tik/ *adj.*

**monotone** /**mon**-uh-,tohn/ — *n.* **1** sound or utterance continuing or repeated on one note without change of pitch. **2** sameness of style in writing. — *adj.* without change of pitch.

**monotonous** /muh-**not**-uh-nuhs/ *adj.* lacking in variety; tedious through sameness. □ **monotonously** *adv.* **monotony** *n.*

**monotreme** /**mon**-uh-,treem/ *n.* a mammal (see PLATYPUS, ECHIDNA) found only in Australia and New Guinea, which lays large yolky eggs through a common opening for urine, faeces, etc. [MONO-, Greek *trēma* hole]

**monovalent** /,mon-oh-**vay**-luhnt/ *adj.* univalent.

**monoxide** /muh-**nok**-suyd/ *n.* oxide containing one oxygen atom.

**Monsieur** /muh-**syer**/ *n.* (*pl.* **Messieurs** /me-**syer**/ ) title used of or to a French-speaking man, corresponding to Mr or sir. [French *mon* my, *sieur* lord]

**Monsignor** /mon-**see**-nyuh, -**nyaw**/ *n.* (*pl.* **-nori** /-**nyaw**-ree/ or **-s**) title of honour conferred on some Catholic priests. [Italian, = my lord]

**monsoon** /mon-**soon**/ *n.* **1** wind in S. Asia, esp. in the Indian Ocean. **2** rainy season accompanying the summer monsoon. [Arabic *mawsim*]

**monster** — *n.* **1** imaginary creature, usu. large and frightening, made up of incongruous elements. **2** inhumanly cruel or wicked person. **3** misshapen animal or plant. **4** large, usu. ugly, animal or thing. **5** (*attrib.*) huge. — *v.* attack (a person, policy, etc.); put pressure on (*the Prime Minister monstered the opposition's policy document*). [Latin *monstrum* from *moneo* warn]

**monstrance** *n.* *RC Ch.* vessel in which the consecrated Host is exposed for veneration. [Latin *monstro* show]

**monstrosity** /mon-**stros**-uh-tee/ *n.* (*pl.* **-ies**) **1** huge or outrageous thing. **2** monstrousness. **3** = MONSTER 3. [Latin: related to MONSTROUS]

**monstrous** *adj.* **1** like a monster; abnormally formed. **2** huge. **3 a** outrageously wrong or absurd. **b** atrocious. □ **monstrously** *adv.* **monstrousness** *n.* [Latin: related to MONSTER]

**montage** /mon-**tahzh**/ *n.* **1** selection, cutting, and piecing together as a consecutive whole, of separate sections of cinema or television film. **2 a** composite whole made from juxtaposed photographs etc. **b** production of this. [French: related to MOUNT¹]

**monte** /**mon**-tee/ *n.* *colloq.* a certainty (*he's regarded as a monte for the captaincy*). [transferred use of *monte*, a game of chance played with cards]

**month** /munth/ *n.* **1** (in full **calendar month**) **a** each of twelve periods into which a year is divided. **b** period of time between the same dates in successive calendar months. **2** period of 28 days or of four weeks. [Old English]

**monthly** — *adj.* done, produced, or occurring once every month. — *adv.* every month. — *n.* (*pl.* **-ies**) monthly periodical.

**month of Sundays** *n.* *colloq.* very long period.

**monument** /**mon**-yuh-muhnt/ *n.* **1** anything enduring that serves to commemorate or celebrate, esp. a structure or building. **2** stone etc. placed over a grave or in a church etc. in memory of the dead. **3** ancient building or site etc. that has been preserved. **4** lasting reminder. [Latin *moneo* remind]

**monumental** /,mon-yuh-**men**-tuhl/ *adj.* **1 a** extremely great; stupendous (*monumental effort*). **b** (of a work of art etc.) massive and permanent. **2** of or serving as a monument. □ **monumentally** *adv.*

**-mony** /-muh-nee/ *suffix* forming nouns esp. denoting an abstract state or quality (*acrimony*, *testimony*). [Latin *-monia*, *-monium*, related to -MENT]

**moo** — *n.* (*pl.* **-s**) cry of cattle. — *v.* (**moos**, **mooed**) make this sound. [imitative]

**mooch** *v.* *colloq.* **1** (usu. foll. by *about*, *around*) wander aimlessly around. **2** cadge; steal. [probably from French *muchier* skulk]

**mood¹** *n.* **1** state of mind or feeling. **2** fit of bad temper or depression. □ **in the mood** (usu. foll. by *for*, or *to* + infin.) inclined. [Old English]

**mood²** *n.* **1** *Gram.* form or set of forms of a verb indicating whether it expresses a fact, command, wish, etc. (*subjunctive mood*). **2** distinction of meaning expressed by different moods. [alteration of MODE]

**moody** *adj.* (**-ier**, **-iest**) given to changes of mood; gloomy, sullen. □ **moodily** *adv.* **moodiness** *n.* [related to MOOD¹]

**mook-mook** /**muuk**-ˌmuuk/ n. (in full **mook-mook owl**; also **muk-muk**) an owl, e.g. the 'barking owl' of all except the arid regions of Australia. [perhaps from a NT Aboriginal language *mug-mug* barking owl etc.]

**Moomba** /**moom**-buh/ n. carnival held annually in Melbourne from 1955. [Wemba-wemba, Wuywurrung, etc. *mum* anus, *ba* at, in, on; but popularly understood to mean 'Let's get together and have fun']

**moon** — n. **1 a** natural satellite of the earth, orbiting it monthly, illuminated by the sun and reflecting some light to the earth. **b** this regarded in terms of its waxing and waning in a particular month (*new moon*). **c** the moon when visible (*there is no moon tonight*). **2** satellite of any planet. **3** (prec. by *the*) *colloq.* something desirable but unattainable (*promised me the moon*). — v. wander about aimlessly or listlessly. □ **moon over** act dreamily thinking about (a loved one). **once in a blue moon** see BLUE. **over the moon** *colloq.* extremely happy. □ **moonless** *adj.* [Old English]

**moonbeam** n. ray of moonlight.

**moon-face** n. very round face.

**moonlight** — n. **1** light of the moon. **2** (*attrib.*) lit by the moon. — v. (**-lighted**) **1** *colloq.* have two paid occupations, esp. one by day and one by night. **2** (chiefly as moonlighting) muster wild cattle by moonlight.

**moonlighter** n. **1** in senses of MOONLIGHT v. **2** marine food-fish with a silver head and body with six vertical black bands, occurring near rocky reefs of southern Australia.

**moonlight flit** n. hurried departure by night, esp. to avoid paying a debt.

**moonlit** adj. lit by the moon.

**moonscape** n. **1** surface or landscape of the moon. **2** area resembling this; wasteland.

**moonshine** n. foolish or unrealistic talk or ideas.

**moonstone** n. feldspar of pearly appearance used as a gem.

**moonstruck** adj. **1** slightly mad. **2** romantically infatuated.

**moony** adj. (**-ier**, **-iest**) listless; stupidly dreamy.

**Moor** /maw/ n. member of a Muslim people of NW Africa. □ **Moorish** adj. [Greek *Mauros*]

**moor**[1] /maw/ n. *Brit.* open uncultivated upland, esp. when covered with heather. [Old English]

**moor**[2] /maw/ v. **1** attach (a boat etc.) to a fixed object. **2** attach or fix securely. □ **moorage** n. [probably Low German]

**moorhen** n. **1** small European waterfowl. **2** any of several Australian waterbirds, esp. the Tasmanian native hen, the black-tailed native hen occurring near water in inland mainland Australia, and the mallee fowl.

**mooring** n. **1** (often in *pl.*) place where a boat etc. is moored. **2** (in *pl.*) set of permanent anchors and chains.

**moose** n. (*pl.* same) N. American deer; elk. [Narragansett]

**moot** — adj. debatable, undecided (*moot point*). — v. raise (a question) for discussion. — n. *hist.* assembly. [Old English]

**mop** — n. **1** bundle of yarn or cloth or a sponge on the end of a stick, for cleaning floors etc. **2** similarly-shaped implement for various purposes. **3** thick mass of hair. **4** mopping or being mopped (*gave it a mop*). — v. (**-pp-**) **1** wipe or clean with or as with a mop. **2 a** wipe tears or sweat etc. from (one's face etc.). **b** wipe away (tears etc.). □ **mop up 1** wipe up with or as with a mop. **2** *colloq.* absorb (profits etc.). **3** dispatch; make an end of. **4 a** complete the occupation of (a district etc.) by capturing or killing enemy troops left there. **b** capture or kill (stragglers). [origin uncertain]

**mope** — v. (**-ping**) **1** be depressed or listless. **2** wander about listlessly. — n. person who mopes. □ **mopy** adj. (**-ier**, **-iest**). [origin unknown]

**mopoke** /**moh**-ˌpohk/ — n. **1** = BOOBOOK. **2** = FROGMOUTH. **3** call of the mopoke. **4** tedious or stupid person. — v. (of a mopoke) to call (*the bird mopoked all night*). [imitative of the bird's call]

**moraine** /maw-**rayn**/ n. area of debris carried down and deposited by a glacier. [French]

**moral** /**mo**-ruhl/ — adj. **1 a** concerned with goodness or badness of human character or behaviour, or with the distinction between right and wrong. **b** concerned with accepted rules and standards of human behaviour. **2 a** virtuous in general conduct. **b** capable of moral action. **3** (of rights or duties etc.) founded on moral not actual law (*she has a moral right to the property*). **4** associated with the psychological rather than the physical (*moral courage; moral support*). — n. **1** moral lesson of a fable, story, event, etc. **2** (in *pl.*) moral behaviour, e.g. in sexual conduct. **3** *colloq.* = MORAL CERTAINTY (*she's an absolute moral for the post of managing director*). □ **morally** adv. [Latin *mos mor-* custom]

**moral certainty** n. probability so great as to allow no reasonable doubt.

**morale** /muh-**rahl**/ n. confidence, determination, etc., of a person or group. [French *moral*: related to MORAL]

**moralise** /mo-ruh-ˌluyz/ v. (also **-ize**) (**-sing** or **-zing**) **1** (often foll. by *on*) indulge in moral reflection or talk. **2 a** make moral judgments. **b** point the moral; interpret morally. □ **moralisation** /-zay-shuhn/ n.

**moralist** /mo-ruh-luhst/ n. **1** person who practises or teaches morality. **2** person who follows a natural system of ethics. □ **moralistic** /-lis-tik/ adj.

**morality** /muh-ral-uh-tee/ n. (pl. **-ies**) **1** degree of conformity to moral principles. **2** right moral conduct. **3** science of morals. **4** particular system of morals (*commercial morality*). **5** = MORALITY PLAY.

**morality play** n. hist. drama (popular in the 15th and 16th centuries) with personified abstract qualities and usu. dramatising the fall and redemption of a representative Christian.

**moral law** n. the conditions to be satisfied by any right course of action.

**moral philosophy** n. branch of philosophy concerned with ethics.

**moral victory** n. defeat that has some of the satisfactory elements of victory.

**morass** /muh-ras/ n. **1** entanglement; disordered situation, esp. one impeding progress. **2** literary bog or marsh. [French *marais* related to MARSH]

**moratorium** /ˌmo-ruh-taw-ree-uhm/ n. (pl. **-s** or **-ria**) **1** (often foll. by *on*) temporary prohibition or suspension (of an activity) (*moratorium on logging native forests, pending an extensive ecological inquiry*). **2 a** legal authorisation to debtors to postpone payment. **b** period of this postponement. **3** hist. campaign of protest against US and Australian participation in the Vietnam War. [Latin *moror morat-* delay]

**moray** /mo-ray, maw-ray/ n. **1** tropical eel of northern Australia valued as a food-fish. **2** eel found in the Mediterranean and valued for food. [Greek *muraina*]

**morbid** adj. **1 a** (of the mind, ideas, etc.) unwholesome, sickly. **b** given to morbid feelings. **2** colloq. melancholy. **3** Med. of the nature of or indicative of disease. □ **morbidity** /-bid-uh-tee/ n. **morbidly** adv. [Latin *morbus* disease]

**mordant** /maw-duhnt/ — adj. **1** (of sarcasm etc.) caustic, biting. **2** pungent, smarting. **3** corrosive or cleansing. **4** serving to fix dye. — n. mordant substance (in senses 3, 4 of adj.). [Latin *mordeo* bite]

**more** /maw/ — adj. **1** existing in a greater or additional quantity or amount (*more problems than last time; bring some more water*). **2** greater in degree (*more's the pity; the more fool you*). — n. greater quantity, number, or amount (*more than three people; more to it than meets the eye*).

— adv. **1** to a greater degree or extent (*do it more carefully; people like to walk more these days*). **2** forming the comparative of adjectives and adverbs, esp. those of more than one syllable (*more absurd; more easily*). □ **more and more** to an increasing degree. **more of** to a greater extent (*more of a poet than a musician*). **more or less** approximately; effectively; nearly. **what is more** as an additional point. [Old English]

**moreover** /maw-roh-vuh/ adv. besides, in addition to what has been said.

**mores** /maw-rayz/ n.pl. customs or conventions of a community. [Latin, pl. of *mos* custom]

**Moreton Bay ash** n. (also **carbeen**) **1** large eucalypt with a pattern like tiles on its bark, occurring in Queensland and northern NSW. **2** the wood of this tree. [*Moreton Bay*, at the mouth of the Brisbane River, Queensland]

**Moreton Bay bug** n. marine crustacean of northern Australia valued for its edible tail-flesh.

**Moreton Bay chestnut** n. (also **black bean**) **1** large tree of eastern Queensland and northern NSW bearing red-and-yellow pea-flowers and heavy pods containing poisonous chestnut-like seeds. **2** the dark brown, attractively figured wood of this tree.

**Moreton Bay fig** n. (also **Moreton Bay**) massive tree to 40m with large buttresses and globular edible fruits, native to coastal NSW and Queensland, widely planted as an ornamental and shade tree.

**morganatic** /ˌmaw-guh-nat-ik/ adj. **1** (of a marriage) between a person of high rank and one of lower rank, the spouse and children having no claim to the possessions or title of the person of higher rank. **2** (of a spouse) married in this way. [Latin *matrimonium ad morganaticam* 'marriage with a morning gift', the husband's gift to the wife, on the morning after consummation of the marriage, being his only obligation in such a marriage]

**morgue** /mawg/ n. **1** mortuary. **2** (in a newspaper office) room containing files of miscellaneous information serving as a reference library. [French, originally the name of a Paris mortuary]

**moribund** /mo-ruh-ˌbund/ adj. **1** at the point of death. **2** lacking vitality. [Latin *morior* die]

**morish** var. of MOREISH.

**Mormon** /maw-muhn/ n. member of the Church of Jesus Christ of Latter-Day Saints. □ **Mormonism** n. [*Mormon*, name of the supposed author of the book on which Mormonism is founded]

**morn** *n. poet.* morning. [Old English]

**mornay** /**maw**-nay/ *n.* cheese-flavoured white sauce. [origin uncertain]

**morning** *n.* **1** early part of the day, ending at noon or lunch-time (*this morning*; *during the morning*). **2** *attrib.* taken, occurring, or appearing during the morning (*morning coffee*). □ **in the morning** *colloq.* tomorrow morning. [from MORN]

**morning after** *n. colloq.* = HANGOVER 1.

**morning-after pill** *n.* contraceptive pill taken some hours after intercourse.

**morning glory**[1] *n.* (also **convolvulus**) twining plant with trumpet-shaped flowers.

**morning glory**[2] *n.* (also **morning glory cloud**) huge dark cloud which suddenly covers the sky of a morning in the Queensland and NT Gulf Country and just as suddenly disappears.

**morning sickness** *n.* nausea felt in the morning in esp. early pregnancy.

**morning star** *n.* planet, usu. Venus, seen in the east before sunrise.

**morning tea** *n.* **1** mid-morning break. **2** refreshment taken during this break.

**moron** /**maw**-ron/ *n.* **1** *colloq.* very stupid person. **2** adult with a mental age of 8–12. □ **moronic** /muh-**ron**-ik/ *adj.* [Greek *mōros* foolish]

**morose** /muh-**rohs**/ *adj.* sullen, gloomy. □ **morosely** *adv.* **moroseness** *n.* [Latin *mos mor-* manner]

**morpheme** /**maw**-feem/ *n. Linguistics* meaningful unit of a language that cannot be further divided (e.g. *in*, *come*, *-ing*, forming *incoming*). [Greek *morphē* form]

**morphia** /**maw**-fee-uh/ *n.* (in general use) = MORPHINE.

**morphine** /**maw**-feen/ *n.* narcotic drug from opium, used to relieve pain. [Latin *Morpheus* god of sleep]

**morphology** /maw-**fol**-uh-jee/ *n.* the study of the forms of things, esp. of animals and plants and of words and their structure. □ **morphological** /ˌmaw-fuh-**loj**-i-kuhl/ *adj.* [Greek *morphē* form]

**morrel** /**mo**-ruhl, muh-**rel**/ *n.* **1** any of several eucalypts of south-western Australia, esp. the *red morrel*, with long pointed buds, which yields a strong, durable, reddish wood, and another species which yields a very strong blackish wood. **2** the wood of these trees. [Nyungar, probably *murril*]

**morrow** *n.* (usu. prec. by *the*) *literary* the following day. [related to MORN]

**morse** /maws/ — *n.* (in full **morse code**) code in which letters are represented by combinations of long and short light or sound signals. — *v.* (**-sing**) signal by morse code. [*Morse*, name of an electrician]

**morsel** /**maw**-suhl/ *n.* mouthful; small piece (esp. of food). [Latin *morsus* bite]

**mortal** — *adj.* **1** subject to death. **2** causing death; fatal. **3** (of combat) fought to the death. **4** associated with death (*mortal agony*). **5** (of an enemy) implacable. **6** (of pain, fear, an affront, etc.) intense, very serious. **7** *colloq.* long and tedious (*for two mortal hours*). **8** *colloq.* conceivable, imaginable (*every mortal thing*; *of no mortal use*). — *n.* human being. □ **mortally** *adv.* [Latin *mors mort-* death]

**mortality** /maw-**tal**-uh-tee/ *n.* (*pl.* **-ies**) **1** state of being subject to death. **2** loss of life on a large scale. **3 a** number of deaths in a given period etc. **b** (in full **mortality rate**) death rate.

**mortal sin** *n.* grave sin that deprives the soul of sanctifying grace and causes a state of spiritual death (opp. VENIAL SIN).

**mortar** /**maw**-tuh/ — *n.* **1** mixture of lime or cement, sand, and water, for bonding bricks or stones. **2** short large-bore cannon for firing shells at high angles. **3** vessel in which ingredients are pounded with a pestle. — *v.* **1** plaster or join with mortar. **2** bombard with mortar shells. [Latin *mortarium*]

**mortarboard** *n.* **1** academic cap with a stiff flat square top. **2** flat board for holding mortar.

**mortgage** /**maw**-gij/ — *n.* **1 a** conveyance of property to a creditor as security for a debt (usu. one incurred by the purchase of the property). **b** deed effecting this. **2** sum of money lent by this. — *v.* (**-ging**) convey (a property) by mortgage. □ **have a mortgage on** *colloq.* **1** be certain to win (*he has a mortgage on the marathon*). **2** have an exclusive claim to (*you haven't a mortgage on suffering*). □ **mortgageable** *adj.* [French, = dead pledge: related to GAGE]

**mortgage belt** *n.* suburb etc. in which most persons are in the process of paying off a mortgage on their home, such persons being regarded as politically volatile.

**mortgagee** /ˌmaw-guh-**jee**/ *n.* creditor in a mortgage, usu. a bank or building society.

**mortgagor** /**maw**-guh-jaw/ *n.* (also **mortgager** /-juh-/) debtor in a mortgage.

**mortice** var. of MORTISE.

**mortify** /**maw**-tuh-fuy/ *v.* (**-ies**, **-ied**) **1 a** cause (a person) to feel shamed, humiliated, or sorry. **b** wound (a person's feelings). **2** bring (the body, the flesh, the passions, etc.) into subjection by self-denial or discipline. **3** (of flesh) be affected by gangrene or necrosis. □ **mortification** /-fuh-**kay**-shuhn/ *n.* **mortifying** *adj.* [Latin *mortificare* kill, subdue, from *mors mort-* death]

**mortise** /maw-tuhs/ (also **mortice**) — n. hole in a framework designed to receive the end of another part, esp. a tenon. — v. (**-sing**) **1** join securely, esp. by mortise and tenon. **2** cut a mortise in. [French from Arabic]

**mortuary** /maw-chuh-ree/ — n. (pl. **-ies**) room or building in which dead bodies are kept until burial or cremation. — attrib. adj. of death or burial. [medieval Latin mortuus dead]

**morwong** /moh-wong, maw-wong/ n. (frequently abbreviated to **mowie**) **1** marine food-fish of southern Australia and New Zealand which has a distinctive elongated ray of the pectoral fin. **2** = JACKASS-FISH. [possibly from an Aboriginal language]

**Mosaic** /moh-zay-ik/ adj. of Moses. [French from Moses in the Old Testament]

**mosaic** /moh-zay-ik/ n. **1 a** picture or pattern produced by arranging small variously coloured pieces of glass or stone etc. **b** this as an art form. **2** diversified thing. **3** (in full **mosaic disease**) virus disease causing leaf-mottling in plants, esp. tobacco, maize, and sugar cane. **4** (attrib.) of or like a mosaic. [Greek: ultimately related to MUSE²]

**Mosaic Law** n. the laws attributed to Moses and listed in the Pentateuch.

**moselle** /moh-zel/ n. **1** light medium-dry white wine from the Moselle valley in Germany. **2** similar Australian wine.

**mosey** /moh-zee/ v. (**-eys, -eyed**) (often foll. by along) colloq. go in a leisurely manner. [origin unknown]

**mosh** v. colloq. dance to rock music in a violent manner involving colliding with others and headbanging. □ **moshing** n. [perhaps an alteration of MASH]

**mosh-pit** n. colloq. area where moshing occurs, esp. in front of the stage at a rock concert.

**Moslem** var. of MUSLIM.

**mosque** /mosk/ n. Muslim place of worship. [Arabic masgid]

**mosquito** /muh-skee-toh/ n. (pl. **-es**) biting insect, esp. one of which the female punctures the skin with a long proboscis to suck blood. [Spanish and Portuguese, diminutive of mosca fly]

**mosquito orchid** n. (also **gnat orchid**) Australian terrestrial orchid having a solitary leaf and red stem bearing up to 20 small red-purple flowers, each with a thin protruding column like a mosquito's proboscis.

**moss** n. **1** small flowerless plant growing in dense clusters in bogs, on the ground, trees, stones, etc. **2** (also **moss-jelly**) = AGAR. □ **mossy** adj. (**-ier, -iest**). [Old English]

**mossie** /moz-ee/ n. (also **mozzie**) = MOSQUITO. [abbreviation]

**most** /mohst/ — adj. **1** existing in the greatest quantity or degree. **2** the majority of (most people think so). — n. **1** greatest quantity or number (this is the most I can do). **2** the majority (most of them are missing). **3** (**the most**) colloq. the best of all (he is the most). — adv. **1** in the highest degree. **2** forming the superlative of adjectives and adverbs, esp. those of more than one syllable (most absurd; most easily). □ **at most** no more or better than (this is at most a makeshift). **at the most 1** as the greatest amount. **2** not more than. **for the most part 1** mainly. **2** usually. **make the most of** employ to the best advantage. [Old English]

**-most** suffix forming superlative adjectives and adverbs from prepositions and other words indicating relative position (foremost; uttermost). [Old English]

**mostly** adv. **1** mainly. **2** usually.

**mote** n. speck of dust. [Old English]

**motel** /moh-tel/ n. roadside hotel providing accommodation for motorists in self-contained units, with parking usu. outside each unit. [from motor hotel]

**motet** /moh-tet/ n. Mus. short religious choral work. [French]

**moth** n. **1** nocturnal insect like a butterfly but without clubbed antennae. **2** insect of this type breeding in cloth etc., on which its larva feeds. [Old English]

**mothball** n. ball of naphthalene etc. placed in stored clothes to deter moths. □ **in mothballs** stored unused for a considerable time.

**moth-eaten** adj. **1** damaged by moths. **2** time-worn.

**mother** /muth-uh/ — n. **1** female parent. **2** quality or condition etc. that gives rise to something else (necessity is the mother of invention). **3** (in full **Mother Superior**) head of a female religious community. **4** any female animal in relation to its offspring. **5** (attrib.) **a** institution etc. regarded as having maternal authority (Holy Mother Church). **b** main ship, space-craft, etc., in a convoy or mission (the mother craft). — v. **1** treat as a mother does. **2** give birth to; be the mother or origin of. □ **mother of** (as intensifier) the greatest of its kind (the mother of all battles). [Old English]

**mother board** n. circuit board in a computer into which other boards can be plugged.

**mother country** n. country in relation to its colonies (some Australians still think of Britain as the mother country).

**mother earth** n. the earth as mother of its inhabitants.

**motherhood** — n. state of being a mother. — adj. platitudinously endorsing that which everyone accepts as worthy (*the party's election platform consisted mostly of motherhood statements*).

**mother-in-law** n. (pl. **mothers-in-law**) husband's or wife's mother.

**motherland** n. one's native country.

**motherless** adj. **1** lacking a mother. **2** (in full **motherless broke**) colloq. destitute (*found himself utterly motherless and desperate*).

**motherly** adj. kind or tender like a mother. □ **motherliness** n.

**mother-of-pearl** n. smooth iridescent substance forming the inner layer of the shell of oysters etc.

**Mother's Day** n. day when mothers are honoured with presents, in Australia the second Sunday in May.

**mother tongue** n. native language.

**mothproof** — adj. (of clothes) treated so as to repel moths. — v. treat (clothes) in this way.

**motif** /moh-**teef**, moh-**tuhf**/ n. **1** theme that is repeated and developed in an artistic, musical, or literary work. **2** decorative design or pattern (*wallpaper with a Chinese motif*). [French: related to MOTIVE]

**motile** /**moh**-tuyl/ adj. Zool. & Bot. capable of motion. □ **motility** /-til-uh-tee/ n.

**motion** /**moh**-shuhn/ — n. **1** act or process of moving; changing position. **2** particular manner of moving the body in walking etc. (*a jaunty motion*). **3** gesture (*made a motion of dismissal*). **4** formal proposal put to a committee, legislature, etc. **5** application to a court for an order. **6 a** an evacuation of the bowels. **b** (in *sing.* or *pl.*) faeces. — v. (often foll. by *to* + infin.) **1** direct (a person) by a gesture (*motioned us to sit*). **2** (often foll. by *to* a person) make a gesture directing (*motioned to me to leave*). □ **go through the motions** do something perfunctorily or unofficially. **in motion** moving; not at rest. **put** (or **set**) **in motion** set going or working. □ **motionless** adj. [Latin: related to MOVE]

**motivate** /**moh**-tuh-,vayt/ v. (**-ting**) **1** supply a motive to; be the motive of. **2** cause (a person) to act in a particular way. **3** stimulate the interest of (a person in an activity). □ **motivation** /-**vay**-shuhn/ n. **motivational** /-**vay**-shuhn-nuhl/ adj.

**motive** /**moh**-tiv/ — n. **1** what induces a person to act in a particular way. **2** = MOTIF. — adj. **1** tending to initiate movement (*motive force*). **2** concerned with movement. [Latin *motivus*: related to MOVE]

**motive power** n. moving or impelling

power, esp. a source of energy used to drive machinery.

**motley** /**mot**-lee/ — adj. (**-lier**, **-liest**) **1** diversified in colour. **2** of varied character (*a motley crew*). — n. hist. jester's particoloured costume. [origin unknown]

**moto-cross** /**moh**-toh-,kros/ n. cross-country racing on motor cycles. [from MOTOR, CROSS]

**motor** /**moh**-tuh/ — n. **1** thing that imparts motion. **2** machine (esp. one using electricity or internal combustion) supplying motive power for a vehicle or other machine. **3** (*attrib.*) **a** giving, imparting, or producing motion. **b** driven by a motor (*motor mower*). **c** of or for motor vehicles. **d** Anat. relating to muscular movement or the nerves activating it (*motor nerve*). — v. go or convey in a motor vehicle. [Latin: related to MOVE]

**motorbike** n. colloq. = MOTORCYCLE.

**motor boat** n. motor-driven boat.

**motorcade** /**moh**-tuh-,kayd/ n. procession of motor vehicles. [from MOTOR, after *cavalcade*]

**motor car** n. = CAR 1.

**motorcycle** n. two-wheeled motor vehicle without pedal propulsion. □ **motorcyclist** n.

**motorise** v. (also **-ize**) (**-sing** or **-zing**) **1** equip with motor transport. **2** provide with a motor.

**motorist** n. driver of a car.

**motor scooter** see SCOOTER.

**motor vehicle** n. road vehicle powered by an internal-combustion engine.

**motser** /**mot**-suh/ n. (also **motzer**) colloq. **1** large sum of money (*Canberra cost a motser, but it's worth every cent*). **2** a certainty (*she's a motser to win the seat*). [Yiddish *matse* bread (see BREAD 3)]

**motorway** n. road for fast travel, with separate carriageways and limited access.

**mottle** v. (**-ling**) (esp. as **mottled** adj.) mark with spots or smears of colour. [back-formation from MOTLEY]

**mottlecah** /mo-tuhl-,kah/ n. spectacular small eucalypt with silvery blue leaves, salmon-red new stems, and the largest flowers of any eucalypt, crimson, 8 cm in diameter, followed by large grey fruits. [probably Nhanta]

**motto** /**mot**-oh/ n. (pl. **-es**) **1** maxim adopted as a rule of conduct. **2** phrase or sentence accompanying a coat of arms. **3** appropriate inscription. [Italian]

**mould**[1] /mohld/ — n. **1** hollow container into which a substance is poured or pressed to harden into a required shape. **2 a** vessel for shaping puddings etc. **b** pudding etc. made in this way. **3** form or shape. **4** frame or template for producing mouldings. **5** character or type (*in heroic mould*). — v. **1** make (an object) in a required shape or from certain ingredients (*moulded out of clay*). **2** give shape to. **3** influence the development of (*consultation helps to mould policies*). [Old French *modle* from Latin MODULUS]

**mould²** /mohld/ *n.* furry growth of fungi occurring esp. in moist warm conditions. [Old Norse]

**mould³** /mohld/ *n.* **1** loose earth. **2** upper soil of cultivated land, esp. when rich in organic matter. [Old English]

**moulder** *v.* **1** decay to dust. **2** (foll. by *away*) rot or crumble. **3** deteriorate. [from MOULD³]

**moulding** *n.* **1** ornamentally shaped outline of plaster etc. as an architectural feature, esp. in a cornice. **2** similar feature in woodwork etc.

**mouldy** *adj.* (**-ier, -iest**) **1** covered with mould. **2** stale; out of date. **3** *colloq.* dull, miserable. □ **mouldiness** *n.*

**moult** /mohlt/ — *v.* (also *absol.*) shed (feathers, hair, a shell etc.) in the process of renewing plumage, a coat, etc. — *n.* moulting. [Old English from Latin *muto* change]

**mound** — *n.* **1** raised mass of earth, stones, etc. **2** heap or pile; large quantity (*a mound of rubble; a mound of things to do*). **3** hillock. — *v.* heap up in a mound or mounds. [origin unknown]

**mound spring** *n.* (also **mud spring**) natural spring of artesian water, rising out of a mound of mud, in many areas of east-central Australia.

**mount¹** — *v.* **1** ascend or climb (a hill, stairs, etc.) **2 a** get up on (a horse etc.) to ride it. **b** set (a person) on horseback (*he was mounted on a thoroughbred*). **c** (as **mounted** *adj.*) serving on horseback (*mounted police*). **3** go up onto a raised surface (*mounted the dais*). **4 a** (often foll. by *up*) increase; accumulate (*prices are mounting steadily; his savings are mounting up*). **b** (of a feeling etc.) become stronger or more intense (*excitement was mounting; pressure is mounting*). **5** (esp. of a male animal) get on to (a female) to copulate. **6** (often foll. by *on*) place (an object) on an elevated support (*mounted the statue on the pedestal*). **7 a** set in or attach to a backing, setting, or other support. **b** attach (a picture etc.) to a mount or frame. **c** fix (an object for viewing) on a microscope slide. **8 a** arrange (a play, exhibition, etc.), or present for public view or display. **b** take action to initiate (a programme, campaign, etc.). **9** prepare (specimens) for preservation. **10** take, or be put in, position (as a sentry etc.) (*mounted guard*). **11** rise to a higher level of rank, power, etc. — *n.* **1** backing, setting, etc., on which a picture etc. is set for display. **2** margin surrounding a picture or

photograph. **3** horse available for riding. **4** setting for a gem etc. [Latin: related to MOUNT²]

**mount²** *n. archaic* (except before a name): mountain, hill (*Mount Kosciusko*). [Latin *mons mont-*]

**mountain** /mown-tuhn/ *n.* **1** large abrupt natural elevation of the ground. **2** large heap or pile; huge quantity (*a mountain of work*). □ **make a mountain out of a molehill** see MOLEHILL. [Latin: related to MOUNT²]

**mountain ash** *n.* **1** any of several eucalypts, esp. *E. regnans* of Victoria and Tasmania, favouring cool, moist, mountain gullies. **2** the wood of these trees.

**mountain bike** *n.* sturdy bike with many gears for riding over rough terrain.

**mountain devil** *n.* **1** small, spiny lizard *Moloch horridus* of arid Australia. **2** = HONEY FLOWER.

**mountain duck** *n.* (also **chestnut-breasted shelduck**) large duck of western and south-eastern Australia, having mostly black and brown plumage with a neck-collar of white.

**mountaineer** /ˌmown-tuh-**neer**/ — *n.* person who practises mountain-climbing. — *v.* climb mountains as a sport. □ **mountaineering** *n.*

**mountainous** *adj.* **1** having many mountains. **2** huge.

**mountain pygmy possum** *n.* small terrestrial marsupial of alpine south-eastern Australia.

**mountain range** *n.* continuous line of mountains.

**mountain sickness** *n.* sickness caused by thin air at great heights.

**mountebank** /mown-tuh-ˌbangk/ *n.* **1** swindler; charlatan. **2** *hist.* itinerant quack appealing to audiences from a platform. [Italian, = mount on bench]

**mounting** *n.* **1** = MOUNT¹ *n.* 1. **2** in senses of MOUNT¹ *v.*

**mourn** /mawn/ *v.* (often foll. by *for, over*) feel or show deep sorrow or regret for (a dead person, a lost thing, a past event, etc.). [Old English]

**mourner** *n.* person who mourns, esp. at a funeral.

**mournful** *adj.* **1** doleful, sad, sorrowing. **2** suggestive of mourning, gloomy (*mournful cypresses*). □ **mournfully** *adv.* **mournfulness** *n.*

**mourning** *n.* **1** expressing of deep sorrow for a dead person, esp. by wearing black clothes. **2** such clothes. □ **in mourning** assuming the signs of mourning, esp. in dress, after the death of a close relative.

**mouse** /mows/ — *n.* (*pl.* **mice**) **1** small rodent, esp. of a kind infesting houses. **2**

timid or shy person. **3** (*pl.* **-s**) *Computing* small hand-held device with one or more buttons controlling the cursor on a computer screen. — *v.* (**-sing**) (of a cat, owl, etc.) hunt mice. □ **mouser** *n.* [Old English]

**mouse spider** *n.* any of several large, black, burrowing spiders widespread in mainland Australia.

**mousetrap** *n.* **1** trap for catching mice. **2** (often *attrib.*) *colloq.* poor quality cheese.

**moussaka** /muu-**sah**-kuh/ *n.* (also **mousaka**) Greek dish of minced meat, eggplant, etc., with a cheese sauce. [Greek or Turkish]

**mousse** /moos/ *n.* **1 a** dessert of whipped cream, eggs, etc., usu. flavoured with fruit or chocolate. **b** meat or fish purée made with whipped cream etc. **2** foamy substance applied to the hair to enable styling. [French, = froth]

**moustache** /muh-**stahsh**/ *n.* hair left to grow on a man's upper lip. [Greek *mustax*]

**mousy** /mow-see/ *adj.* (**-ier, -iest**) **1** of or like a mouse. **2** (of a person) shy or timid. **3** mouse-coloured, a nondescript light brown.

**mouth** /mowth/ — *n.* (*pl.* **mouths** /mowthz/ ) **1 a** external opening in the head, through which most animals take in food and emit communicative sounds. **b** (in humans and some animals) cavity behind it containing the means of biting and chewing and the vocal organs. **2** opening of a container, cave, trumpet, etc. **3** place where a river enters the sea. **4** an individual as needing sustenance (*an extra mouth to feed*). **5** *colloq.* **a** meaningless or ineffectual talk. **b** impudent talk; cheek. **c** loud-mouthed person, or one who puts foot into mouth whenever it is opened. — *v.* /mowth/ (**-thing**) **1** say or speak by moving the lips but with no sound. **2** utter or speak insincerely or without understanding (*mouthing platitudes*). **3** examine the mouth of a sheep to determine its age. □ **mouth off** *colloq.* **1** speak wildly or thoughtlessly, usu. out of anger or frustration. **2** boast. **3** criticise offensively. **put words into a person's mouth** represent a person as having said something. **take the words out of a person's mouth** say what another was about to say. [Old English]

**mouthful** *n.* (*pl.* **-s**) **1** quantity of food etc. that fills the mouth. **2** small quantity. **3** *colloq.* **a** long or complicated word or phrase. **b** something important, tactless, etc., that is said.

**mouth-organ** *n.* = HARMONICA.

**mouthpiece** *n.* **1** part of a musical instrument, telephone, etc., placed next to the lips. **2** device to protect teeth, worn in the mouth by boxers and players of contact sports. **3** (often *derog.*) person who speaks for another or others.

**mouth-to-mouth** *adj.* (of resuscitation) in which a person breathes into a subject's lungs through the mouth.

**mouth-watering** *adj.* **1** (of food etc.) having a delicious smell or appearance. **2** tempting, alluring.

**movable** /**moo**-vuh-buhl/ — *adj.* (also **moveable**) **1** that can be moved. **2** variable in date from year to year (*Easter is a movable feast*). **3** *Law* (of property) of the nature of a chattel, as distinct from land or buildings. — *n.* article of furniture that may be removed from a house, as distinct from a fixture. □ **movability** /-**bil**-uh-tee/ *n.* [related to MOVE]

**move** /moov/ — *v.* (**-ving**) **1** (cause to) change position or posture. **2** put or keep in motion; rouse, stir. **3 a** take a turn in a board-game. **b** change the position of (a piece) in a board-game. **4** (often foll. by *about, away, off,* etc.) go or proceed. **5** take action, esp. promptly (*moved to reduce crime*). **6** make progress (*project is moving fast*). **7** (also *absol.*) change (one's home or place of work). **8** (foll. by *in*) be socially active in (a specified group etc.) (*moves in the best circles*). **9** affect (a person) with (usu. tender) emotion. **10** (foll. by *to*) provoke (a person to laughter etc.) (*was moved to tears*). **11** (foll. by *to,* or *to* + infin.) prompt or incline (a person to a feeling or action) (*what moved him to put his new house up for sale?*). **12** (cause to) change one's attitude (*nothing can move me on this issue*). **13 a** cause (the bowels) to be evacuated. **b** (of the bowels) be evacuated. **14** (often foll. by *that*) propose in a meeting, etc. **15** (foll. by *for*) make a formal request or application (*moved for an adjournment*). **16** (of merchandise) sell; be sold (*these items are not moving well*). — *n.* **1** act or process of moving. **2** change of house, premises, etc. **3** step taken to secure an object (*that TV advertisement campaign was a clever move*). **4 a** a changing of the position of a piece in a board-game. **b** player's turn to do this. □ **get a move on** *colloq.* hurry up. **make a move** take action. **move along** (or **on**) advance, progress, esp. to avoid crowding etc. **move away** go to live in another area. **move heaven and earth** (foll. by *to* + infin.) make extraordinary efforts. **move in 1** take up residence in a new home. **2** get into a position of readiness or proximity (for an offensive action etc.). **move in with** start to share accommodation with (an existing resident). **move out** leave one's home. **move over** (or **up**) adjust one's position to make room for another. **on the move** moving. [Latin *moveo*]

**moveable** var. of MOVABLE.

**movement** n. **1 a** act of moving or being moved. **b** instance of this (*watched his every movement*). **2** moving parts of a mechanism (esp. a clock or watch). **3 a** body of persons with a common object (*peace movement*). **b** campaign undertaken by them. **4** (in *pl.*) person's activities and whereabouts (*couldn't account for his movements on the night in question*). **5** *Mus.* principal division of a longer musical work. **6** motion of the bowels. **7** rise or fall in price(s) on the stock market. **8** progress; trend (*there is a movement towards enterprise bargaining*).

**mover** n. **1** person, animal, or thing that moves or dances, esp. in a specified way. **2** person who moves a proposition. **3** (also **prime mover**) originator.

**movie** n. film for viewing in a cinema or on video.

**moving** adj. emotionally affecting. □ **movingly** adv.

**mow** /moh/ v. (*past part.* **mowed** or **mown**) **1** (also *absol.*) cut (grass, hay, etc.) with a scythe or machine. **2** cut down the produce of (a field) or the grass etc. of (a lawn) by mowing. □ **mow down** kill or destroy randomly or in great numbers. □ **mower** n. [Old English]

**mowie** /**moh**-wee/ n. abbr. MORWONG.

**mozz** colloq. — n. (also **moz** and esp. as **put the mozz on**) a jinx, a malign influence (*his presence will put the mozz on this trip*). — v. jinx, deter (*tried to mozz him as he was about to take the kick*). [abbreviation of MOZZLE]

**mozzarella** /ˌmot-suh-**rel**-uh/ n. Italian curd cheese, orig. of buffalo milk, used in pizzas etc. [Italian]

**mozzie** n. var. of MOSSIE.

**mozzle** n. luck, fortune. [Hebrew *mazzāl* luck]

**MP** abbr. Member of Parliament.

**mp** abbr. mezzo piano.

**Mr** /**mis**-tuh/ n. (*pl.* **Messrs** /**mes**-uhz/) **1** title of a man without a higher title (*Mr Jones*). **2** title prefixed to a designation of office etc. (*Mr President; Mr Speaker*). [abbreviation of MISTER]

**Mrs** /**mis**-uhz/ n. (*pl.* same) title of a married woman without a higher title (*Mrs Jones*). [abbreviation of MISTRESS]

**MS** abbr. **1** (*pl.* **MSS**) manuscript. **2** multiple sclerosis.

**Ms** /muhz/ n. title of a (married or unmarried) woman without a higher title, used to avoid indicating marital status (in keeping with MR). [combination of MRS, MISS²]

**Msgr** abbr. Monsignor.

**MS-DOS** /ˌem-es **dos**/ abbr. propr. Computing Microsoft disk operating system.

**Mt.** abbr. (*pl.* **Mts.**) Mount.

**mu** /myoo/ n. **1** twelfth letter of the Greek alphabet (M, μ). **2** (μ, as a symbol) = MICRO- 2. [Greek]

**much** — adj. **1** existing or occurring in a great quantity (*much trouble; too much noise*). **2** (prec. by *as, how, that*, etc.) with relative sense (*I don't know how much money you want*). — n. **1** a great quantity (*much of that is true*). **2** (prec. by *as, how, that*, etc.) with relative sense (*we do not need that much*). **3** (usu. in *neg.*) noteworthy or outstanding example (*not much to look at*). — adv. **1** in a great degree (*much to my surprise; is much the same; I much regret it; much annoyed; much better; much the best*). **2** for a large part of one's time; often (*he is not here much*). □ **as much** so (*I thought as much*). **a bit much** colloq. excessive, immoderate. **make much of** see MAKE. **much as** even though (*cannot come, much as I would like to*). **much of a muchness** very nearly the same. **not much of a** colloq. a rather poor. [from *mickle* large amount]

**mucilage** /**myoo**-suh-lij/ n. **1** viscous substance obtained from plants. **2** adhesive gum. [Latin: related to MUCUS]

**muck** — n. **1** dirt or filth; anything disgusting. **2** farmyard manure. **3** colloq. a untidy state. **b** rubbish; nonsense. — v. **1** (usu. foll. by *up*) colloq. **a** bungle (a job). **b** make dirty or untidy. **2** (foll. by *out*) remove manure from. □ **make a muck of** colloq. bungle, make a mess of. **muck about** (or **around**) colloq. **1** potter or fool about. **2** (foll. by *with*) **a** fool or interfere with. **b** associate with. **muck in** (often foll. by *with*) colloq. share tasks etc. equally; share living quarters with (*can I muck in with you for a few days?*). **muck up** colloq. **1** spoil (*mucked up his chances*). **2** misbehave. [Scandinavian]

**muckrake** v. (**-king**) search out and reveal scandal. □ **muckraker** n. **muckraking** n.

**muck-up** n. colloq. a shambles, fiasco, muddle.

**mucky** adj. (**-ier, -iest**) covered with muck, dirty.

**mucous** /**myoo**-kuhs/ adj. of or covered with mucus. □ **mucosity** /-**kos**-uh-tee/ n. [Latin *mucosus*: related to MUCUS]

**mucous membrane** n. mucus-secreting tissue lining body cavities etc.

**mucus** /**myoo**-kuhs/ n. slimy substance secreted by a mucous membrane. [Latin]

**mud** n. soft wet earth. □ **as clear as mud** colloq. not at all clear. **fling** (or **sling** or **throw**) **mud** speak disparagingly or slanderously. **one's name is mud** one is in disgrace. [German]

**mud-brick** — n. brick made from baked mud. — adj. made of mud-bricks (a mud-brick house).

**mud crab** n. (also **mangrove crab**) very large swimming crab, occurring along muddy shores of estuaries in northern Australia, highly prized as food.

**muddie** n. colloq. (also **muddy**) = MUD CRAB. [abbreviation]

**muddle** — v. (-ling) (often foll. by up) **1** bring into disorder. **2** bewilder, confuse. — n. **1** disorder, mess. **2** state of confusion (got into a muddle over his tax-return). □ **muddle along** (or **on**) proceed in a haphazard way. **muddle through** succeed despite one's inefficiency. □ **muddler** n. [perhaps Dutch, related to MUD]

**muddle-headed** adj. mentally disorganised, confused.

**muddy** — adj. (-ier, -iest) **1** like mud. **2** covered in or full of mud. **3** (of liquid, colour, or sound) not clear, impure. **4** vague, confused. **5** (of the complexion) drab, not clear. — v. (-ies, -ied) make muddy. — n. colloq. = MUD CRAB. □ **muddiness** n.

**mud-eye** n. larva of a dragonfly, used by anglers as bait.

**mudflap** n. flap hanging behind the wheel of a vehicle, to prevent splashes.

**mudflat** n. stretch of muddy land uncovered at low tide.

**mudguard** n. curved strip over a bicycle wheel etc. to protect the rider from splashes.

**mudhopper** n. = MUDSKIPPER.

**mudlark** n. **1** = MAGPIE LARK. **2** horse that is able to race well on a wet and heavy track.

**mudskipper** n. (also **mudhopper**) any of several small related fish of tropical northern Australia with modified pectoral and ventral fins which enable it to move about on mudflats.

**mud-slinger** n. colloq. person given to making abusive or disparaging remarks. □ **mud-slinging** n.

**mud spring** n. = MOUND SPRING.

**muesli** /myoo-zlee/ n. breakfast food of crushed cereals, dried fruits, nuts, etc., eaten with milk. [Swiss German]

**muezzin** /moo-ez-uhn/ n. Muslim crier who proclaims the hours of prayer. [Arabic]

**muff**¹ n. covering, esp. of fur, for keeping the hands or ears warm. [Dutch mof]

**muff**² v. colloq. **1** bungle. **2** miss (a catch, ball, etc.). [origin unknown]

**muffin** /muf-uhn/ n. **1** light flat round spongy cake, eaten toasted and buttered. **2** similar round cake made from batter or dough. [origin unknown]

**muffle** v. (-ling) **1** (often foll. by up) wrap or cover for warmth. **2** cover or wrap up (a source of sound) to reduce its loudness (muffle the drums). **3** (usu. as **muffled** adj.) stifle (an utterance). [perhaps French moufle thick glove, MUFF¹]

**muffler** n. **1** wrap or scarf worn for warmth. **2** thing used to deaden sound. **3** silencer of a vehicle.

**mufti** /muf-tee/ n. civilian clothes (in mufti). □ **mufti day** day on which school students pay (a small sum usu. towards fund-raising) for the privilege of wearing casual clothes to school instead of the prescribed uniform. [Arabic]

**mug**¹ — n. **1 a** drinking-vessel, usu. cylindrical with a handle and no saucer. **b** its contents. **2** colloq. gullible person. **3** colloq. face or mouth. — adj. colloq. stupid (mug lair). — v. (-gg-) **1** attack and rob, esp. in public. **2** colloq. (often foll. by up) kiss, cuddle. □ **a mug's game** colloq. foolish or unprofitable activity. □ **mugger** n. **mugful** n. (pl. **-s**). **mugging** n. [Scandinavian]

**mug**² v. (-gg-) (usu. foll. by up) colloq. learn (a subject) by concentrated study. [origin unknown]

**mugga** /mug-uh/ n. (also **red ironbark**) medium-sized eastern Australian eucalypt with black bark, deeply furrowed and red beneath the surface, grey leaves, and abundant pink or red flowers. [Wiradhuri maga]

**muggins** /mug-uhnz/ n. (pl. same or **mugginses**) colloq. gullible person (often meaning oneself: so muggins had to pay). [perhaps from the surname]

**muggy** adj. (-ier, -iest) (of weather etc.) oppressively humid. □ **mugginess** n. [Old Norse]

**mugshot** n. colloq. photograph of a face, esp. for police records.

**Muhammadan** var. of **Mohammedan**

**muk-muk** var. of MOOK-MOOK.

**mujahidin** /moo-jah-huh-deen/ n. pl. (also **mujahedin, -deen**) guerrilla fighters in Islamic countries, esp. Muslim fundamentalists. [Persian and Arabic: related to JIHAD]

**mulatto** /myoo-lat-oh/ — n. (pl. **-s** or **-es**) person of mixed White and Black parentage. — adj. of the colour of mulattos; light brown, tawny. [Spanish mulato young mule]

**Mulba** /mul-buh/ n. an Aborigine (used in the Pilbara region of WA). [Panyjima marlba]

■ **Usage** See KOORI¹.

**mulberry** /mul-buh-ree/ n. (pl. **-ies**) **1** tree bearing edible purple or white berries, and leaves used to feed silkworms. **2** its fruit. **3** dark red or purple. [Latin morum mulberry, BERRY]

**mulch** — *n.* layer of wet straw, leaves, or compost, etc., spread around a plant to enrich or insulate the soil. — *v.* treat with mulch. [Old English, = soft]

**mulct** *v.* extract money from by fine or taxation or by fraudulent means. [Latin *mulcta* fine]

**mule** *n.* **1** offspring of a male donkey and a female horse, or (in general use) of a female donkey and a male horse (cf. HINNY). **2** stupid or obstinate person. [Latin *mulus*]

**mules** /myoolz/ *v.* (frequently as **mulesing, mulesed**) cut away the loose folds of skin in the crutch area of a sheep in order to reduce the incidence of blowfly strike and maggot infestation. [J.H.W. *Mules*, sheep-raiser (d. 1946)]

**muleteer** /,myoo-luh-**teer**/ *n.* mule-driver. [French *muletier*: related to MULE]

**mulga** /**mul**-guh/ — *n.* **1** (also **mulga bush, mulga tree, mulga wood**) any of several wattles of dry inland Australia yielding a distinctive brown and yellowish timber. **2** the wood of these trees, much used in the manufacture of Australian souvenirs. **3** (**the mulga**) the outback; remote, sparsely populated country. — *adj.* **1** of the mulga tree. **2** of the mulga. **3** characterised by the presence of mulga (*mulga country, mulga flats, mulga scrub*). **4** rustic, countrified (*mulga lifestyle*). [Kamilaroi, Yuwaalaraay, etc. *malga*]

**mulga ant** *n.* ant of inland Australia which builds a mud nest and then thatches the nest with mulga leaves.

**mulga apple** *n.* large, edible gall, soft and sweet, produced by the mulga tree.

**mulga Bill** *n.* a bush simpleton.

**mulga grass** *n.* any of several native grasses, growing in mulga country, regarded as valuable fodder.

**mulga madness** *n.* eccentricity attributed to living in the outback.

**mulga parrot** *n.* (also **mulga parakeet**) predominantly green parrot of drier mainland Australia with brilliant yellow, blue, and red markings.

**mulgara** /**mul**-guh-ruh/ *n.* small carnivorous marsupial which inhabits burrows in sandy regions of drier Australia. [probably Wangganguru *mardagura*]

**mulga snake** *n.* large, fierce, and highly venomous snake occurring throughout northern (and drier southern) mainland Australia.

**mulga wire** *n.* **1** = BUSH TELEGRAPH. **2 a** Aboriginal smoke signal as a means of long-distance communication. **b** the message so conveyed.

**mulish** *adj.* stubborn.

**mull¹** *v.* (often foll. by *over*) ponder, consider. [probably Dutch]

**mull²** *v.* warm (wine or beer) with added sugar, spices, etc. [origin unknown]

**mulla mulla** /mul-uh ,mul-uh/ *n.* = PUSSY TAIL. [probably Panyjima *mulu-mulu*]

**mullet** *n.* (*pl.* same) any of several kinds of marine fish valued as food. □ **like a stunned mullet** *colloq.* dazed, uncomprehending. [Greek *mullos*]

**mulligatawny** /,mul-uh-guh-**taw**-nee/ *n.* highly seasoned soup orig. from India. [Tamil *milaguthanni* pepper-water]

**mullion** /**mul**-yuhn/ *n.* vertical bar dividing the lights in a window. □ **mullioned** *adj.* [probably French *moinel* middle: related to MEAN³]

**mullock** /**mul**-uhk/ — *n.* **1** (also **mullock dump, mullock heap**) mining (esp. gold-mining) refuse. **2** rubbish; nonsense (*spoke a lot of mullock; made mullock of the opposition*). — *v. colloq.* perform (a task etc.) in a slovenly manner. □ **poke mullock at** *colloq.* ridicule, deride. □ **mullocky** *adj.* [Old English *myl* dust]

**mullocker** /**mul**-uh-kuh/ *n.* **1** person who clears away the refuse in a mine. **2** careless or clumsy person.

**mulloway** /**mul**-uh-way/ *n.* large food-fish occurring in marine and estuarine waters of Australia (see also BUTTERFISH, JEWFISH, KINGFISH). [Yaralde, probably *malowe*]

**mullygrub** /**mul**-ee-,grub/ *n.* a grub, esp. a witchetty grub. [origin uncertain]

**mullygrubber** *n.* (also **grubber**) *Cricket* a ball delivered so that it does not bounce after it hits the ground but rolls along instead.

**multi-** *comb. form* many. [Latin *multus* much, many]

**multi-access** /,mul-tee-**ak**-ses/ *see* TIME-SHARING.

**multicoloured** /**mul**-tee-,kul-uhd/ *adj.* of many colours.

**multicultural** /,mul-tee-**kul**-chuh-ruhl/ *adj.* of or relating to or consisting of several cultural or ethnic groups within a society (*multicultural Australia*) □ **multiculturalism** *n.*

**multifarious** /,mul-tuh-**fair**-ree-uhs/ *adj.* **1** (foll. by *pl. n.*) many and various. **2** having great variety. □ **multifariousness** *n.* [Latin *multifarius*]

**multifunction polis** *n.* high-tech, space-age city designed for a high-tech, space-age lifestyle, with the very latest in telecommunications systems etc. incorporated into it. [Greek *polis* city]

**multilateral** /,mul-tee-**lat**-uh-ruhl/ *adj.* **1 a** (of an agreement etc.) in which three or more parties participate. **b** performed by more than one party (*multilateral* *disarmament*). **2** having many sides. □ **multilaterally** *adv.*

**multilingual** /ˌmul-tee-**ling**-gwuhl/ *adj.* in, speaking, or using several languages.

**multimedia** — *attrib. adj.* using more than one medium of communication. — *n.* = HYPERMEDIA.

**multinational** /ˌmul-tee-**nash**-uh-nuhl/ — *adj.* **1** operating in several countries. **2** of several nationalities. — *n.* multinational company.

**multiple** /**mul**-tuh-puhl/ — *adj.* **1** having several parts, elements, or components. **2** many and various. — *n.* number that contains another without a remainder (*56 is a multiple of 7*). [Latin *multiplus*: related to MULTIPLEX]

**multiple sclerosis** see SCLEROSIS.

**multiplex** /**mul**-tee-ˌpleks/ *adj.* manifold; of many elements. [Latin: related to MULTI-, -*plex* -*plicis* -fold]

**multiplicand** /ˌmul-tuh-pluh-**kand**/ *n.* quantity to be multiplied by another.

**multiplication** /ˌmul-tuh-pluh-**kay**-shuhn/ *n.* **1** arithmetical process of multiplying. **2** act or instance of multiplying.

**multiplication sign** *n.* sign (×) to indicate that one quantity is to be multiplied by another.

**multiplication table** *n.* list of multiples of a particular number, usu. from 1 to 12.

**multiplicity** /ˌmul-tuh-**plis**-uh-tee/ *n.* (*pl.* -**ies**) **1** manifold variety. **2** (foll. by *of*) great number.

**multiplier** /**mul**-tuh-ˌpluy-uh/ *n.* quantity by which a given number is multiplied.

**multiply** /**mul**-tuh-ˌpluy/ *v.* (-**ies**, -**ied**) **1** (also *absol.*) obtain from (a number) another that is a specified number of times its value (*multiply 6 by 4 and you get 24*). **2** increase in number, esp. by procreation. **3** produce a large number of (instances etc.). **4 a** breed (animals). **b** propagate (plants). [Latin *multiplico*: related to MULTIPLEX]

**multiprocessing** *n. Computing* processing by a series of processors working as one.

**multiprogramming** *n. Computing* execution of two or more programs concurrently.

**multiracial** /ˌmul-tee-**ray**-shuhl/ *adj.* (of a nation, society, etc.) consisting of several races.

**multi-tasking** *n.* (also **multitasking**) *Computing* concurrent execution of a number of tasks or jobs.

**multitude** *n.* **1** (often foll. by *of*) great number. **2** large gathering of people; crowd. **3** (the multitude) the common people. [French from Latin]

**multitudinous** /ˌmul-tuh-**tyoo**-duh-nuhs/ *adj.* **1** very numerous. **2** consisting of

many individuals. [Latin: related to MULTITUDE]

**multi-user** /ˌmul-tee-**yoo**-zuh/ *attrib. adj.* (of a computer system) having a number of simultaneous users (cf. MULTI-ACCESS).

**mum**[1] *n. colloq.* = MUMMY[1].

**mum**[2] *adj. colloq.* silent (*keep mum*). □ **mum's the word** say nothing. [imitative]

**mumble** — *v.* (-**ling**) speak or utter indistinctly. — *n.* indistinct utterance or sound. [related to MUM[2]]

**mumbo-jumbo** /ˌmum-boh-**jum**-boh/ *n.* (*pl.* -**s**) **1** meaningless or ignorant ritual. **2** meaningless or unnecessarily complicated language; nonsense. [*Mumbo Jumbo*, name of a supposed African idol]

**mummer** *n.* actor in a traditional mime. [French *momeur*: cf. MUM[2]]

**mummify** /**mum**-uh-ˌfuy/ *v.* (-**ies**, -**ied**) preserve (a body) as a mummy. □ **mummification** /-fuh-**kay**-shuhn/ *n.*

**mummy**[1] /**mum**-ee/ *n.* (*pl.* -**ies**) *colloq.* mother. [imitative of a child's pronunciation]

**mummy**[2] /**mum**-ee/ *n.* (*pl.* -**ies**) body of a human being or animal embalmed for burial, esp. in ancient Egypt. [Persian *mūm* wax]

**mumps** *n.pl.* (treated as *sing.*) infectious disease with swelling of the neck and face. [archaic *mump* be sullen]

**munch** *v.* eat steadily with a marked action of the jaws. [imitative]

**munchies** *n.pl. colloq.* snacks between meals.

**mundane** /mun-**dayn**/ *adj.* **1** dull, routine. **2** of this world. □ **mundanely** *adv.* **mundanity** /-**dan**-uh-tee/ *n.* [Latin *mundus* world]

**mundarda** /ˌmun-**dah**-duh/ *n.* WA pygmy-possum which resembles a minute ball of soft, red-brown hair, generally found in the tops of grass-trees. [Nyungar, probably *mandarda*]

**mundowie** /ˌmun-**doh**-ee/ *n.* (also **mundoey**, **mundoie**) foot; footprint. [possibly Dharuk *manuwi* foot, or Awabakal *manduwang* foot]

**mung** /mung, muung/ *n.* (in full **mung bean**) leguminous Indian plant, the small seeds of which are used as food. [Hindi *mūng*]

**munga** /**mung**-guh/ *n.* (also **monger**, **munger**) *colloq.* food. [abbreviation of British slang *mungaree* food, from Italian *mangiare* to eat]

**mungite** /**mung**-guyt/ *n.* the sweet, nectar-rich flowering spike of a banksia. [Nyungar, probably *manggayit* sweet substance, banksia flower]

**municipal** /myoo-**nis**-uh-puhl, myoo-nuh-**sip**-uhl/ *adj.* of a municipality or its self-government. [Latin *municipium* free city]

**municipality** /myoo-,nuh-suh-**pal**-uh-tee/ n. (pl. **-ies**) **1** town or district having local self-government. **2** governing body of this area.

**munificent** /myoo-**nif**-uh-suhnt/ adj. (of a giver or a gift) splendidly generous. □ **munificence** n. [Latin *munus* gift: related to -FIC]

**munition** /myoo-**nish**-uhn/ — n. (usu. in pl.) military weapons, ammunition etc. — v. supply with munitions. [Latin *munitio -onis* fortification]

**munjon** /**mun**-juhn/ n. (also **munjong**) **1** an Aborigine who has had little contact with white society. **2** an Aborigine brought up in white society and unfamiliar with the traditional way of life. [Yindjibarndi *manyjangu* stranger]

**muntry** /**mun**-tree/ n. **1** (now usu. in pl. form **muntries**) regarded as either *sing.* or *pl.*) edible fruit of a prostrate *kunzea* of dry, sandy soils in western Victoria and eastern SA. **2** the plant itself. [Yaralde, probably *mandharri*]

**munyeroo** /,mun-yuh-**roo**/ n. (also **munyeru**) either of two succulent plants of the *portulaca* family, both the seeds and the leaves of which are used as food (see also PARAKEELIYA). [Diyari *manyurra*]

**mural** /**myoo**-ruhl/ — n. painting executed directly on a wall. — adj. of, on, or like a wall. [Latin *murus* wall]

**murder** — n. **1** intentional unlawful killing of a human being by another (cf. MANSLAUGHTER). **2** colloq. unpleasant, troublesome, or dangerous state of affairs (*the traffic was murder going to the footy*). — v. **1** kill (a human being) intentionally and unlawfully. **2** colloq. **a** utterly defeat (*murdered the opposition*). **b** spoil by a bad performance, mispronunciation, etc. (*murdered the soliloquy in the second act*). □ **cry** (or **scream** or **yell**) **blue murder** colloq. make an extravagant outcry. **get away with murder** colloq. do whatever one wishes and escape punishment. □ **murderer** n. **murderess** n. [Old English]

**murder bird** n. = BARKING OWL.

**murderous** adj. **1** (of a person, weapon, action, etc.) capable of, intending, or involving murder or great harm. **2** colloq. extremely arduous or unpleasant. □ **murderously** adv.

**murex** /**myoo**-reks/ n. (pl. **murices** /**myoo**-ruh-seez/ or **murexes**) gastropod mollusc yielding the purple dye famous in ancient Rome etc. and known as 'Tyrian purple'. [Latin]

**murk** n. darkness, poor visibility. [probably Scandinavian]

**murky** adj. (**-ier**, **-iest**) **1** dark, gloomy. **2** (of darkness, liquid, etc.) thick, dirty.

**3** suspiciously obscure (*murky past*). □ **murkily** adv. **murkiness** n.

**murlonga** /mer-**long**-guh/ n. (also **mymonga**) white man who sexually exploits Aboriginal women. [possibly from an Aboriginal language]

**murmur** /**mer**-muh/ — n. **1** subdued continuous sound, as made by waves, a brook, etc. **2** softly spoken or nearly inarticulate utterance. **3** subdued expression of discontent. **4** *Med.* recurring sound heard in the heart and usu. indicating abnormality. — v. **1** make a murmur. **2** utter (words) in a low voice. **3** (usu. foll. by *at*, *against*) complain in low tones, grumble. [Latin]

**murnong** /**mer**-nong/ n. (also **myrrnong**) **1** sweet, milky, edible tuber, tasting like coconut, of a temperate Australian perennial herb: these were a staple food for Aborigines in Victoria. **2** this plant, bearing a yellow, dandelion-like flower-head. [Wathawurung and Wuywurung, probably *mirnang*]

**Murphy's Law** /**mer**-feez/ n. *joc.* any of various maxims about the perverseness of things (e.g. 'if anything *can* go wrong, it *will* '). [*Murphy*, Irish surname]

**murrain** /**mu**-rayn/ n. infectious disease of cattle. [Anglo-French *moryn* from Latin *morior* die]

**Murray cod** n. large, groper-like, greenish food-fish of the Murray-Darling river system. [*Murray* River, in south-eastern Australia]

**Murray grey** n. Australian breed of grey beef-cattle.

**Murray Valley encephalitis** n. a severe form of encephalitis caused by a mosquito-borne virus. [name of the *valley* of the *Murray* River]

**Murray whaler** see WHALER 3.

**Murri** /**mu**-ree/ n. an Aborigine, esp. one from Queensland. [Kamilaroi *mari* Aboriginal person]

■ **Usage** See KOORI¹.

**murrnong** var. of MURNONG.

**Murrumbidgee whaler** see WHALER 3.

**muscat** /**mus**-kuht/ n. **1** sweet usu. fortified white wine made from musk-flavoured grapes. **2** this grape. [Provençal: related to MUSK]

**muscatel** /,mus-kuh-**tel**/ n. **1** = MUSCAT. **2** raisin from a muscat grape.

**muscle** /**mus**-uhl/ — n. **1** fibrous tissue producing movement in or maintaining the position of an animal body. **2** part of an animal body that is composed of muscles. **3** strength, power. — v. (**-ling**) (foll. by *in*, *in on*) colloq. force oneself on others; intrude by forceful means. □ **not**

**move a muscle** be completely motionless. [Latin diminutive of *mus* mouse]

**muscle-bound** *adj.* with muscles stiff and inelastic through excessive exercise.

**Muscovite** /**mus**-kuh-,vuyt/ — *n.* native or citizen of Moscow. — *adj.* of Moscow. [from *Muscovy*, principality of Moscow]

**Muscovy duck** /**mus**-kuh-vee/ *n.* crested duck with red markings on its head. [*Muscovy*, principality of Moscow]

**muscular** /**mus**-kyuh-luh/ *adj.* **1** of or affecting the muscles. **2** having well-developed muscles. **3** robust. □ **muscularity** /-la-ruh-tee/ *n.*

**muscular dystrophy** *n.* hereditary progressive wasting of the muscles.

**musculature** /**mus**-kyuh-luh-chuh/ *n.* muscular system of a body or organ.

**muse**[1] /myooz/ *v.* (**-sing**) **1** (usu. foll. by *on*, *upon*) ponder, reflect. **2** say meditatively. [French]

**muse**[2] /myooz/ *n.* **1** (in Greek and Roman mythology) any of the nine goddesses who inspire poetry, music, etc. **2** (usu. prec. by *the*) poet's inspiration. [Greek *Mousa*]

**museum** /myoo-**zee**-uhm/ *n.* building used for storing and exhibiting objects of historical, scientific, or cultural interest. [Greek: related to MUSE[2]]

**museum piece** *n.* **1** specimen of art etc. fit for a museum. **2** *derog.* old-fashioned or quaint person or object.

**mush** *n.* **1** soft pulp. **2** feeble sentimentality. **3** *colloq.* gaol food, esp. porridge. [apparently var. of MASH]

**mushie** *n. colloq.* mushroom.

**mushroom** — *n.* **1** edible fungus with a stem and domed cap. **2** pinkish-brown colour of this. **3** *colloq.* person who is deliberately kept in the dark, i.e. ignorant of the true facts etc. — *v.* **1** gather mushrooms. **2** appear or develop rapidly (*new houses mushrooming in the outer suburbs*). [French *mousseron* from Latin]

**mushroom cloud** *n.* mushroom-shaped cloud from a nuclear explosion.

**mushy** *adj.* (**-ier**, **-iest**) **1** like mush; soft. **2** feebly sentimental. □ **mushiness** *n.*

**music** /**myoo**-zik/ *n.* **1** art of combining vocal or instrumental sounds in a harmonious or expressive way. **2** sounds so produced. **3** musical composition. **4** written or printed score of this. **5** pleasant natural sound (*the music of warbling magpies in Australian gardens*). □ **music to one's ears** something one is pleased to hear. [Greek: related to MUSE[2]]

**musical** — *adj.* **1** of music. **2** (of sounds etc.) melodious, harmonious. **3** fond of, sensitive to, or skilled in music (*the musical one of the family*). **4** set to or accompanied by music.

— *n.* musical film or play. □ **musicality** /-**kal**-uh-tee/ *n.* **musically** *adv.*

**musical box** *n.* box containing a mechanism which plays a tune.

**musical chairs** *n.pl.* **1** party game in which the players compete in successive rounds for a decreasing number of chairs. **2** series of changes or political manoeuvring etc.

**music-hall** *n.* **1** variety entertainment with singing, dancing, etc. **2** theatre for this.

**musician** /myoo-**zish**-uhn/ *n.* person who plays a musical instrument, esp. professionally. □ **musicianly** *adj.* **musicianship** *n.* [French: related to MUSIC]

**musicology** /,myoo-zuh-**kol**-uh-jee/ *n.* the academic study of music. □ **musicologist** *n.* **musicological** /-kuh-**loj**-i-kuhl/ *adj.*

**music stick** *n.* = CLAP STICK.

**musk** *n.* **1** strong-smelling substance secreted by the male musk deer and used in perfumes. **2** the smell of musk. **3** tall Australian shrub (or small tree) of the *Olearia* family, with creamy daisy flowers and leaves which are silvery underneath and have a strong musky aroma. □ **musky** *adj.* (**-ier**, **-iest**). **muskiness** *n.* [Latin *muscus* from Persian, perhaps from Sanskrit *muṣka* scrotum]

**musk deer** *n.* small hornless Asian deer.

**musk duck** *n.* brown and black duck of southern Australia, the male of which has a large pendulous lobe under the bill and a strong musky odour.

**musket** *n. hist.* infantryman's (esp. smooth-bored) light gun. [Italian *moschetto* crossbow bolt]

**musketeer** /,mus-kuh-**teer**/ *n. hist.* soldier armed with a musket.

**musketry** /**mus**-kuh-tree/ *n.* **1** muskets; soldiers armed with muskets. **2** knowledge of handling small arms.

**musk lorikeet** *n.* lorikeet of south-eastern Australia, having bright green plumage with a red face-stripe and giving off a musky scent.

**musk-rose** *n.* rambling rose smelling of musk.

**muskwood** *n.* **1** rainforest tree of eastern Queensland and NSW, the timber of which has a musk-like scent. **2** the wood of this tree.

**Muslim** /**muuz**-luhm, **muz**-/ — *n.* follower of the Islamic religion. — *adj.* of the Muslims or their religion. [Arabic: related to ISLAM]

**muslin** /**muz**-luhn/ *n.* fine delicately woven cotton fabric. [Italian *Mussolo* Mosul in Iraq]

**muso** /**myoo**-zoh/ *n.* (*pl.* **-os**) *colloq.* musician, esp. a professional.

**muss** v. (often foll. by up) **1** disarrange, dishevel (she mussed up his hair). **2** spoil, ruin. [var. of MESS]

**mussel** /mus-uhl/ n. bivalve mollusc, esp. of the kind used for food. [Old English: related to MUSCLE]

**must¹** — v.aux. (present **must**; past **had to** or in indirect speech **must**) (foll. by infin., or absol.) **1 a** be obliged to (you must go to school). **b** in ironic questions (must you slam the door?). **2** be certainly (you must be her sister). **3** ought to (must see what can be done). **4** expressing insistence (must ask you to leave). **5** (foll. by not + infin.) **a** not be permitted to, be forbidden to (must not smoke). **b** ought not; need not (mustn't think he's angry; must not worry). **c** expressing insistence that something should not be done (they must not be told). — n. colloq. thing that should not be missed (if you go to Canberra, the new Parliament House is a must). □ **I must say** often iron. I cannot refrain from saying (I must say he tries hard; a fine way to behave, I must say). **must needs** see NEEDS. [Old English]

■ **Usage** In sense 1a, the negative (i.e. lack of obligation) is expressed by not have to or need not (you need not go to school); must not denotes positive forbidding, as in you must not smoke.

**must²** n. grape juice before fermentation is complete. [Old English from Latin]

**mustang** n. small wild horse of Mexico and California. [Spanish]

**mustard** /mus-tuhd/ n. **1 a** plant with slender pods and yellow flowers. **b** yellow seeds of this crushed into a paste and used as a spicy condiment. **2** brownish-yellow colour. **3** another variety with smaller black seeds used mainly in Asian recipes. □ **keen as mustard** extremely keen. [Romanic: related to MUST²]

**mustard gas** n. colourless oily liquid, whose vapour is a powerful irritant.

**muster** — v. **1** collect (orig. soldiers) for inspection, to check numbers, etc. **2** hist. assemble (convicts) for counting etc. **3** collect, gather together. **4** summon (courage etc.). **5** gather (livestock) together in one place for branding, counting, drafting, etc. — n. **1** assembly of persons for inspection. **2** hist. routine assembling of convicts for counting etc. □ **pass muster** be accepted as adequate. **tarpaulin muster** see under T. [Latin monstro show]

**musterer** n. person who musters livestock.

**mustering** n. the action of gathering together in one place (frequently widely dispersed) livestock.

**mustn't** /mus-uhnt/ contr. must not.

**musty** adj. (**-ier, -iest**) **1** mouldy, stale. **2** dull, antiquated (musty old books; musty regulations). □ **mustily** adv. **mustiness** n. [perhaps an alteration of moisty: related to MOIST]

**mutable** /myoo-tuh-buhl/ adj. literary liable to change. □ **mutability** /-bil-uh-tee/ n. [Latin muto change]

**mutagen** /myoo-tuh-juhn/ n. agent promoting genetic mutation. □ **mutagenic** /-jen-ik/ adj. **mutagenesis** /-jen-uh-suhs/ n. [from MUTATION, -GEN]

**mutant** /myoo-tuhnt/ — adj. resulting from mutation. — n. mutant organism or gene.

**mutate** /myoo-tayt/ v. (**-ting**) (cause to) undergo mutation.

**mutation** /myoo-tay-shuhn/ n. **1** process or an instance of change, alteration. **2** genetic change which, when transmitted to offspring, gives rise to heritable variations. **3** mutant. [Latin muto change]

**mute** /myoot/ — adj. **1** silent, refraining from speech or temporarily bereft of speech. **2** (of a person or animal) dumb. **3** not expressed in speech (mute protest). **4** (of a letter) not pronounced. — n. **1** dumb person. **2** device for damping the sound of a musical instrument. **3** unsounded consonant. — v. (**-ting**) **1** deaden or soften the sound of (esp. a musical instrument). **2 a** tone down, make less intense. **b** (as muted adj.) (of colours etc.) subdued. □ **mutely** adv. **muteness** n. [Latin mutus]

**mutilate** /myoo-tuh-,layt/ v. (**-ting**) **1 a** deprive (a person or animal) of a limb or organ. **b** destroy the use of (a limb or organ). **2** excise or damage part of (a book etc.). □ **mutilation** /-lay-shuhn/ n. [Latin mutilus maimed]

**mutineer** /,myoo-tuh-neer/ n. person who mutinies. [Romanic: related to MOVE]

**mutinous** /myoo-tuh-nuhs/ adj. rebellious; ready to mutiny. □ **mutinously** adv.

**mutiny** /myoo-tuh-nee/ — n. (pl. **-ies**) open revolt, esp. by soldiers or sailors against their officers. — v. (**-ies, -ied**) (often foll. by against) revolt; engage in mutiny.

**mutt** n. **1** colloq. ignorant or stupid person. **2** dog. [abbreviation of MUTTON-HEAD]

**mutter** — v. **1** (also absol.) utter (words) in a barely audible manner. **2** (often foll. by against, at) murmur or grumble (muttered at the reduction in pay). — n. **1** muttered words or sounds (heard the low mutter of their prayers). **2** muttering. [related to MUTE]

**mutton** n. flesh of sheep as food, usu. from an animal older than a lamb or hogget (see also UNDERGROUND MUTTON). [medieval Latin multo sheep]

**mutton-bird** — *n.* **1 a** brownish-black petrel breeding in south-eastern Australia, esp. on Bass Strait islands, and once indiscriminately harvested for the fat, feathers, and edible flesh. **b** any of several other birds of similar appearance or usefulness. **2** (also **mutton-bird eater**) *colloq.* a non-Aboriginal resident of (esp. northern) Tasmania. — *v.* (*chiefly as verbal n.*) catch mutton-birds as food or so as to prepare their flesh and by-products for the market (*their chief occupation is mutton-birding*).

**mutton-birder** *n.* person who catches and kills mutton-birds.

**mutton-bird gales** *n.pl.* **1** seasonal gales coinciding with the annual arrival of flocks of mutton-birds to nest on islands in Bass Strait and on the coast of Tasmania. **2** the vast flocks of incoming mutton-birds themselves.

**mutton-fish** *n.* any of several marine gastropods with edible flesh abounding in Australian waters; abalone.

**mutton-head** *n. colloq.* stupid person.

**mutual** /**myoo**-choo-uhl/ *adj.* **1** (of feelings, actions, etc.) experienced or done by each of two or more parties to or towards the other(s) (*mutual affection*). **2** *colloq.* common to two or more persons (*a mutual friend*). **3** having the same (specified) relationship to each other (*mutual well-wishers*). □ **mutuality** /-al-uh-tee/ *n.* **mutually** *adv.* [Latin *mutuus* borrowed]

■ **Usage** The use of *mutual* in sense 2, although often found, is considered incorrect by some people, for whom *common* is preferable.

**muzak** /**myoo**-zak/ *n.* **1** *propr.* system of piped background music usu. played continuously in public places. **2** (**muzak**) recorded light background music. [fanciful var. of MUSIC]

**muzzle** — *n.* **1** projecting part of an animal's face, including the nose and mouth. **2** guard, usu. of straps or wire, put over an animal's nose and mouth to stop it biting or feeding. **3** open end of a firearm. — *v.* (**-ling**) **1** put a muzzle on (an animal etc.). **2** prevent (a person etc.) from speaking, expressing an opinion, etc. (*tried to muzzle the press*). [medieval Latin *musum*]

**muzzlewood** *n.* small eucalypt of southeastern Australia, the wood of which was used to make muzzles for unweaned calves to prevent them suckling.

**my** /muy/ *poss. pron.* (*attrib.*) **1** of or belonging to me. **2** affectionate, patronising, etc. form of address (*my dear boy*). **3** in expressions of surprise (*my God!; oh my!*). **4** *colloq.* indicating a close relative

etc. of the speaker (*my Johnny's ill again*). [from MINE¹]

**myalgia** /muy-**al**-juh/ *n.* muscular pain. □ **myalgic** *adj.* [Greek *mus* muscle]

**myall¹** /muy-uhl, muy-awl/ — *n.* **1** (also **warrigal**) an Aborigine living in a traditional manner (esp. as distinct from one accustomed to, or living amongst, whites). **2** person placed in an unfamiliar environment (*Bill's a complete myall in the bush — lost himself within ten minutes*). — *adj.* **1** (of an Aborigine) living in a traditional manner. **2** (of an animal or plant) wild (*myall bullock*). [Dharuk *mayal* or *miyal* a stranger, an Aborigine from another tribe]

**myall²** /muy-uhl, muy-awl/ *n.* any of several wattles with a silvery foliage. [probably related to MYALL¹]

**mycelium** /muy-**see**-lee-uhm/ (*pl.* **-lia**) microscopic threadlike parts of a fungus. [Greek *mukēs* mushroom]

**Mycenaean** /muy-suh-**nee**-uhn/ — *adj.* of the late Bronze Age civilisation in Greece (*c.*1500–1100 BC), depicted in the Homeric poems. — *n.* person of this civilisation. [Latin *Mycenaeus*]

**mycology** /muy-**kol**-uh-jee/ *n.* **1** the study of fungi. **2** fungi of a particular region. □ **mycologist** *n.* [Greek *mukēs* mushroom]

**myna** /**muy**-nuh/ *n.* (also **mynah**, **mina**) bird (of the starling family) able to imitate the human voice, introduced to Australia from Asia and now common. [Hindi]

**myopia** /muy-**oh**-pee-uh/ *n.* **1** shortsightedness. **2** lack of imagination or insight. □ **myopic** /-**op**-ik/ *adj.* **myopically** /-**op**-i-kuh-lee, -klee/ *adv.* [Greek *muō* shut, *ōps* eye]

**myoporum** /muy-uh-**paw**-ruhm/ *n.* any of many mainly Australian trees, shrubs, and ground-covers (genus *Myoporum*), many in cultivation (see BOOBIALLA, CREEPING BOOBIALLA, SUGARWOOD).

**myriad** /**mi**-ree-uhd/ *literary* — *n.* an indefinitely great number. — *adj.* innumerable. [Greek *murioi* 10,000]

**myrnonga** var. of MURLONGA.

**myrrh** /mer/ *n.* gum resin used in perfume, medicine, incense, etc. [Latin *myrrha* from Greek]

**Myrtaceae** /mer-**tay**-see-ay/ *n.* the myrtle family, a large and varied family of plants including esp. the eucalypts, melaleucas, and leptospermums (tea-trees).

**myrtaceous** /mer-**tay**-shuhs/ *adj.* belonging to the Myrtaceae or myrtle-family.

**myrtle¹** /**mer**-tuhl/ *n.* evergreen European shrub with shiny leaves and white scented flowers. [Greek *murtos*]

**myrtle²** *n.* **1** (in full **myrtle beech**; also **Tasmanian myrtle**) tall tree of Victoria and Tasmania (not myrtaceous) with small, shiny, dark green leaves and valuable timber. **2** the wood of this tree. [transferred use of MYRTLE¹]

**myrtle³** see SWAN RIVER MYRTLE.

**myself** /muy-**self**/ *pron.* **1** *emphat. form* of I² or ME¹ (*I saw it myself*). **2** *refl. form* of ME¹ (*I was angry with myself*). **3** in my normal state of body and mind (*I am not myself today*). □ **be myself** see ONESELF. **I myself** I for my part (*I myself am doubtful*). [Old English: related to ME¹, SELF]

**mysterious** /muh-**steer**-ree-uhs/ *adj.* **1** full of or wrapped in mystery. **2** (of a person) delighting in mystery. □ **mysteriously** *adv.* [French: related to MYSTERY]

**mystery** /**mis**-tuh-ree/ *n.* (*pl.* **-ies**) **1** secret, hidden, or inexplicable matter (*his motive remains a mystery*). **2** secrecy or obscurity (*wrapped in mystery*). **3** (*attrib.*) secret, undisclosed (*mystery guest*). **4** practice of making a secret of things (*engaged in mystery and intrigue*). **5** (in full **mystery story**) fictional work dealing with a puzzling event, esp. a murder. **6 a** a religious truth divinely revealed, esp. one beyond human reason. **b** *RC Ch.* a decade of the rosary. **7** (in *pl.*) secret religious rites of the ancient Greeks, Romans, etc. [Greek *mustērion*: related to MYSTIC]

**mystery play** *n.* medieval play based on biblical events, and usu. part of a cycle of plays dramatising Christian history from Creation to Doomsday.

**mystic** /**mis**-tik/ — *n.* person who seeks by contemplation etc. to achieve unity with the Deity, or who believes in the spiritual apprehension of truths that are beyond the understanding. — *adj.* = MYSTICAL. □ **mysticism** /-ˌsiz-uhm/ *n.* [Greek *mustēs* initiated person]

**mystical** *adj.* **1** of mystics or mysticism. **2** mysterious; occult; of hidden meaning. **3** spiritually allegorical or symbolic. □ **mystically** *adv.*

**mystify** /**mis**-tuh-ˌfuy/ *v.* (**-ies**, **-ied**) **1** bewilder, confuse. **2** wrap in mystery. □ **mystification** /-fuh-**kay**-shuhn/ *n.* [French: related to MYSTIC or MYSTERY]

**mystique** /mis-**teek**/ *n.* atmosphere of mystery and veneration attending some activity, person, profession, etc. [French: related to MYSTIC]

**myth** /mith/ *n.* **1** traditional story usu. involving supernatural persons and embodying popular ideas on natural or social phenomena etc. (*the rich store of Aboriginal myth*). **2** such narratives collectively. **3** widely held but false notion. **4** fictitious person, thing, or idea. **5** allegory (*Platonic myth*). □ **mythical** *adj.* **mythically** *adv.* [Greek *muthos*]

**mythology** /mi-**thol**-uh-jee/ *n.* (*pl.* **-ies**) **1** body of myths (*Aboriginal mythology*; *Greek mythology*). **2** the study of myths. □ **mythological** /-thuh-**loj**-i-kuhl/ *adj.* **mythologise** *v.* (also **-ize**) (**-sing** or **-zing**). **mythologist** *n.* [Greek: related to MYTH]

**myxo** /**mik**-soh/ *n.* = MYXOMATOSIS. [abbreviation]

**myxomatosis** /ˌmik-suh-muh-**toh**-suhs/ *n.* infectious and usu. fatal viral disease of rabbits, introduced into Australia to exterminate these introduced creatures who were assuming plague proportions. [Greek *muxa* mucus]

# N

**N¹** /en/ *n.* (also **n**) (*pl.* **Ns** or **N's**) **1** fourteenth letter of the alphabet. **2** (usu. **n**) indefinite number. □ **to the nth degree** to the utmost.

**N²** *abbr.* (also **N.**) **1** North; Northern. **2** New. **3** newton(s).

**N³** *symb.* nitrogen.

**N-** *prefix* nuclear (*N-threat; N-ban*).

**n** *abbr.* (also **n.**) **1** name. **2** neuter. **3** noon. **4** noun.

**Na** *symb.* sodium.

**n/a** *abbr.* (also **n.a.**) **1** not applicable. **2** not available.

**nab** *v.* (**-bb-**) *colloq.* **1** arrest; catch in wrongdoing. **2** grab. [origin unknown]

**nabarlek** /**nah**-buh-lek/ *n.* **1** (also **little rock wallaby**) small wallaby of WA and Arnhem Land. **2** (this name adopted for) a uranium mine in the NT. [Gunwinygu *na-barlek*]

**nacho** /**nah**-choh, **nach**-oh/ *n.* (*pl.* **-s**) tortilla chip, usu. topped with melted cheese and chilli etc. [origin uncertain]

**nacre** /**nay**-kuh/ *n.* mother-of-pearl from any shelled mollusc. □ **nacreous** /**nay**-kree-uhs/ *adj.* [French]

**nadir** /**nay**-deer/ *n.* **1** part of the celestial sphere directly below an observer (opp. ZENITH). **2** lowest point of anything, e.g. of misfortune; time of deep despair. [Arabic, = opposite]

**naevus** /**nee**-vuhs/ *n.* (*pl.* **naevi** /-vuy/) **1** raised red birthmark. **2** = MOLE². [Latin]

**naff** — *adj.* tasteless; vulgar; ridiculous. — *v.* (foll. by *off*) go away; scram. [origin unknown]

**nag¹** *v.* (**-gg-**) **1 a** persistently criticise or scold. **b** (often foll. by *at*) find fault or urge, esp. persistently. **2** (of a pain, guilt, etc.) be persistent. [originally a British dial. word]

**nag²** *n. colloq.* horse, esp. a decrepit one. [origin unknown]

**naga** /**nah**-guh/ *n.* loin-cloth (as worn by Aborigines). [Wuna *naga* dress, covering]

**naiad** /**nuy**-ad/ *n.* water-nymph. [Latin from Greek]

**nail** — *n.* **1** small metal spike hammered in to join things together or as a peg or decoration. **2** horny covering on the upper surface of the tip of the human finger or toe. — *v.* **1** fasten with a nail or nails. **2** secure or get hold of (a person or thing) (*nailed him to a definite date*). **3** keep (a person, attention, etc.) fixed (*terror nailed him to the spot*). **4 a** expose or discover (a lie or liar). **b** catch, arrest (*the police haven't nailed him yet*). □ **nail down 1** bind (a person) to a promise etc. **2** define precisely. **3** fasten (a thing) with nails. **nail in a person's coffin** something thought to increase the risk of death. **on the nail** (esp. of payment) without delay. [Old English]

**nail-biter** *n. colloq.* highly suspenseful situation (*the match was a real nail-biter*). □ **nail-biting** *adj.*

**nail-tailed wallaby** *n.* (also **nail-tail**) any of three species of small wallaby, members of which have a horny nail-like projection at the tip of the tail.

**naive** /nuy-**eev**/ *adj.* (also **naïve**) **1** innocent; unaffected. **2** foolishly credulous. **3** (of art) produced in a sophisticated society but lacking conventional expertise. □ **naively** *adv.* **naivety** *n.* (also **naïvety**). [Latin *nativus* NATIVE]

**naked** /**nay**-kuhd/ *adj.* **1** without clothes; nude. **2** without its usual covering (*trees naked in winter*). **3** undisguised (*the naked truth*). **4** (of a light, flame, sword, etc.) unprotected or unsheathed. **5** defenceless. **6** without support, evidence, etc. (*naked assertion*). **7** (of a landscape) barren; treeless. **8** (of a room, wall, etc.) without decoration; empty; plain. □ **nakedly** *adv.* **nakedness** *n.* [Old English]

**naked eye** *n.* (prec. by *the*) unassisted vision, e.g. without a telescope etc.

**namby-pamby** /,nam-bee-**pam**-bee/ — *adj.* insipidly pretty or sentimental; weak. — *n.* (*pl.* **-ies**) namby-pamby person. [fanciful formulation on the name of the writer *Ambrose* Philips (d. 1749)]

**name** — *n.* **1** word by which an individual person, family, animal, place, or thing is spoken of etc. **2 a** usu. abusive term used of a person etc. (*called him names*). **b** word denoting an object or esp. a class of objects etc. (*what is the name of those flowers?*). **3** famous person (*many great names were there*). **4** reputation, esp. a good one (*he has a name for honesty*). — *v.* (**-ming**) **1** give a name to. **2** state the name of. **3** mention; specify; cite (*named her requirements*). **4** nominate; appoint; etc. (*was named the new chairperson*). □ **have to one's name** possess (*hasn't a cent to his name*). **in all but name** virtually.

**in name only** not in reality (*Queen in name only*). **in the name of** as representing; by virtue of (*in the name of the law*). **make a name for oneself** become famous. **name names** mention specific names, esp. in accusation (*I'm not going to name names, but ...*). □ **nameable** *adj.* [Old English]

**name-drop** *v.* mention famous people in a familiar way as if they were friends, in order to boost one's self-importance, boast, etc. □ **name-dropper** *n.* **name-dropping** *n.*

**nameless** *adj.* **1** having or showing no name. **2** unnamed (*our informant, who shall be nameless*). **3** too horrific to be named (*nameless vices*).

**namely** *adv.* that is to say; in other words.

**namesake** *n.* person or thing having the same name as another. [probably from *for the name's sake*]

**namma** var. of GNAMMA.

**nana** /nah-nuh/ *n. colloq.* idiot, fool. □ **do one's nana** lose one's temper. **off one's nana** mentally deranged. [perhaps from BANANA]

**nankeen** /nang-keen, nan-/ *n.* **1** yellowish cotton cloth. **2** yellowish buff colour. [*Nankin(g)* in China]

**nankeen kestrel** *n.* (also **sparrowhawk**) small, mainly Australian, hovering kestrel with a red-brown (supposedly nankeen) back.

**nanny** /nan-ee/ *n.* (*pl.* **-ies**) **1** child's nurse. **2** *colloq.* grandmother. **3** (in full **nanny-goat**) female goat. [related to *Nancy*, pet form of Anne]

**nannygai** /nan-ee-guy/ *n.* reddish, marine fish of southern Australia, valued as food. [probably from a NSW Aboriginal language]

**nano-** *comb. form* denoting a factor of $10^{-9}$ (*nanosecond*). [Greek *nanos* dwarf]

**nap**[1] — *v.* (**-pp-**) sleep lightly or briefly. — *n.* short sleep or doze, esp. by day. □ **catch a person napping** detect in negligence etc; catch off guard. [Old English]

**nap**[2] *n.* **1** raised pile on textiles, esp. velvet. **2** soft, downy surface, e.g. on leaves etc. **3** blankets, bedding; swag. [Low German or Dutch]

**nap**[3] — *n.* **1** form of whist in which players declare the number of tricks they expect to take. **2** racing tip claimed to be almost a certainty. — *v.* (**-pp-**) name (a horse etc.) as a probable winner. □ **go nap 1** attempt to take all five tricks in nap. **2** risk everything. [*Napoleon*]

**napalm** /nay-pahm/ — *n.* thick jellied hydrocarbon mixture used in bombs. — *v.* attack with napalm bombs. [from NAPHTHALENE, PALM[1]]

**nape** *n.* back of the neck. [origin unknown]

**naphtha** /naf-thuh/ *n.* inflammable hydrocarbon distilled from coal etc. [Latin from Greek]

**naphthalene** /naf-thuh-,leen/ *n.* white crystalline substance produced by distilling coal tar.

**napkin** /nap-kuhn/ *n.* **1** piece of linen etc. for wiping the lips, fingers, etc., at meals. **2** baby's nappy. [French *nappe* from Latin *mappa* MAP]

**nappy** /nap-ee/ *n.* (*pl.* **-ies**) piece of towelling etc. wrapped round a baby to absorb or retain urine and faeces. [from NAPKIN]

**napunyah** /nuh-pun-yuh/ *n.* var. of YAPUNYAH.

**narcissism** /nah-suh-,siz-uhm/ *n.* excessive or erotic interest in oneself. □ **narcissistic** /-sis-tik/ *adj.* [*Narkissos*, name of a beautiful youth in Greek myth who fell in love with his own reflection, pined away, and was turned into a *narcissus*]

**narcissus** /nah-sis-uhs/ *n.* (*pl.* **-cissi** /-suy/) any of several flowering bulbs, including the daffodil. [Latin from Greek]

**narcosis** /nah-koh-suhs/ *n.* **1** state of insensibility, esp. drug-induced. **2** induction of this. [Greek *narkē* numbness]

**narcotic** /nah-kot-ik/ — *adj.* **1** (of a substance, e.g. morphine) inducing drowsiness etc. **2** (of a drug) affecting the mind. — *n.* narcotic substance, drug, or influence. [Greek *narkōtikos*]

**nard** *n.* **1** plant yielding an aromatic balsam. **2** = SPIKENARD. [Latin from Greek]

**nardoo** /nah-doo/ *n.* (also **clover fern**) any of several clover-like perennial ferns of mainland Australia, occurring on or near water, the pea-sized spores of which are ground into flour and used as food. [Yandruwandha and many other Aboriginal languages]

**nardoo cake** *n.* cake made with nardoo flour and water and then baked.

**nardoo stone** *n.* set of two stones used by Aborigines for grinding nardoo spores into flour.

**Naretha parrot** /nuh-ree-thuh/ *n.* small Australian parrot with a yellow belly, red tail, and blue head, occurring on the fringes of the Nullarbor Plain. [*Naretha*, name of a railway station in southeastern WA]

**nark** *colloq.* — *n.* **1** nagging or whingeing person. **2** police informer or decoy. — *v.* **1** annoy by nagging etc. **2** act as police informer or decoy. [Romany *nāk* nose]

**Nar Nar Goon** /nah nah **goon**/ — *n.* any

small, insignificant place. — *adj.* of such a place; insignificant. [name of a small, remote town in Victoria]

**narrate** /nuh-**rayt**/ *v.* (**-ting**) **1** give a continuous story or account of. **2** provide a spoken accompaniment for (a film etc.). □ **narration** /nuh-**ray**-shuhn/ *n.* **narrator** *n.* [Latin *narro narrat-*]

**narrative** /**na**-ruh-tiv/ — *n.* **1** ordered account of connected events. **2** practice or art of narrating. — *adj.* in the form of, or concerned with, narration (*narrative verse*).

**narrow** /**na**-roh/ — *adj.* (**-er, -est**) **1 a** of small width. **b** confined or confining (*within narrow bounds*). **2** of limited scope (*in the narrowest sense*). **3** with little margin (*narrow escape*). **4** searching; precise; exact (*a narrow scrutiny*). **5** = NARROW-MINDED. — *n.* (usu. in *pl.*) narrow part of a strait, river, pass, street, etc. — *v.* become or make narrow; contract; lessen. □ **narrowly** *adv.* **narrowness** *n.* [Old English]

**narrow-leaved peppermint** *n.* eucalypt with slender, graceful foliage having a strong peppermint aroma, this being one of the species used for the commercial distillation of oil (see CINEOL).

**narrow-leaved red ironbark** *n.* medium-sized eucalypt, most widespread of the ironbarks, having hard, furrowed bark thickly covered with oozings of red gum, and long, slender leaves.

**narrow-minded** *adj.* rigid or restricted in one's views, intolerant. □ **narrow-mindedness** *n.*

**narwhal** /**nah**-wuhl/ *n.* Arctic white whale, the male of which has a long tusk. [Dutch from Danish]

**NASA** /**nas**-uh/ *abbr.* (in the US) National Aeronautics and Space Administration.

**nasal** /**nay**-zuhl/ — *adj.* **1** of the nose. **2** (of a letter or a sound) pronounced with the breath passing through the nose, e.g. *m, n, ng.* **3** (of the voice or speech) having many nasal sounds. — *n.* nasal letter or sound. □ **nasalise** *v.* (also **-ize**) (**-sing** or **-zing**). **nasally** *adv.* [Latin *nasus* nose]

**nascent** /**nas**-uhnt, **nay**-suhnt/ *adj.* **1** in the act of being born. **2** just beginning to be; not yet mature (*Australia is considered to be a nascent republic*). □ **nascency** *n.* [Latin: related to NATAL]

**nashi** /**nash**-ee/ *n.* type of apple-like Japanese pear. [Japanese]

**nasho** /**nash**-oh/ *n. colloq. hist.* **1** compulsory military training introduced in Australia under the National Service Act of 1951. **2** person who undergoes this. [abbreviation of National, + -o]

**nasturtium** /nuh-**ster**-shuhm/ *n.* trailing plant with edible leaves and bright orange, yellow, or red flowers. [Latin]

**nasty** /**nah**-stee/ *adj.* (**-ier, -iest**) **1 a** highly unpleasant (*a nasty experience; nasty weather*). **b** annoying (*my car has a nasty habit of breaking down*). **2** difficult to negotiate; dangerous (*a nasty hairpin bend; a nasty illness*). **3** (of a person or animal) ill-natured; violent; offensive (*turns nasty when he's drunk*). **4 a** disgustingly dirty, filthy. **b** extremely disagreeable (*a nasty smell*). **5** obscene. □ **nastily** *adv.* **nastiness** *n.* [origin unknown]

**natal** /**nay**-tuhl/ *adj.* of or from one's birth. [Latin *natalis* from *nascor nat-* be born]

**natch** *adv. colloq.* naturally.

**nation** /**nay**-shuhn/ *n.* **1** community of people of mainly common descent, history, language, etc. **2** community of peoples forming a sovereign State or inhabiting a territory and unified by a national language and government. [Latin: related to NATAL]

**national** /**nash**-uh-nuhl/ — *adj.* **1** of a, or the, nation as a whole. **2** characteristic of a particular nation. — *n.* **1** citizen of a specified country (*Australian nationals*). **2** fellow-countryman. □ **nationally** *adv.*

**national anthem** *n.* song adopted by a nation, intended to inspire patriotism.

**national game** *n.* **1** (also **national football**) Australian Rules football. **2** two-up.

**nationalise** /**nash**-uh-nuh-,luyz/ *v.* (also **-ize**) (**-sing** or **-zing**) take over (industries, land, etc.) from private ownership on behalf of the nation. □ **nationalisation** /-**zay**-shuhn/ *n.*

**nationalism** *n.* **1** patriotic feeling, principles, etc. **2** policy of national independence. □ **nationalist** *n.* & *adj.* **nationalistic** /-**lis**-tik/ *adj.*

**nationality** /,nash-uh-**nal**-uh-tee/ *n.* (*pl.* **-ies**) **1** status of belonging to a particular nation (*has Australian nationality*). **2** condition of being national; distinctive national qualities. **3** ethnic group forming a part of one or more political nations.

**national park** *n.* area of natural beauty protected by the Federal or a State government for the use of the public.

**National Party** *n.* Australian political party formed to represent rural interests and which, under various names, has been on the political scene since first winning federal parliamentary seats in 1918.

**national service** *n. hist.* conscripted peacetime military service.

**nationwide** *adj.* extending over the whole nation.

**native** /**nay**-tiv/ — n. **1 a** (usu. foll. by of) person born in a specified place (a native of Melbourne). **b** local inhabitant. **2** offens. member of a non-White indigenous people, e.g. the Aborigines, esp. as regarded by colonial settlers. **3** hist. white person born in Australia (opp. e.g. a person living in Australia who was born elsewhere). **4 a** animal or plant indigenous to a country. **b** animal or plant indigenous to Australia or to a particular State or region of Australia. — adj. **1** inherent; innate (spoke with the fluency native to her). **2** of one's birth (native country). **3** (usu. foll. by to) belonging to a specified place (the kangaroo is native to Australia). **4** indigenous. **5** of the indigenous people of a place (native customs of Britain). **6** (of metal etc.) found in a pure or uncombined state. **7** (of an Australian plant or animal) supposedly resembling one found elsewhere (native cherry; native bee). [Latin: related to NATAL]

**native bear** n. = KOALA.

**native bee** n. any of several small, stingless Australian bees producing honey stored in a comb, often in the hollow of a tree-trunk.

**native bread** n. large, heavy, tuber-like, underground food-storage body of an Australian fungus, roasted and eaten by Aborigines.

**native cat** n. any of several carnivorous, long-tailed, spotted Australian marsupials.

**native cherry** n. (also **ballart, cherry ballart**) small, cypress-like Australian tree bearing small, sweet, edible fruit.

**native companion** n. = BROLGA.

**native cranberry** n. (also **astroloma**) any of several Australian plants with edible fruits, esp. the prostrate Astroloma humifusum bearing a drupe with a sweet pulp.

**native cucumber** n. trailing northern Australian plant bearing a gooseberry-like fruit with a sweet pulp.

**native cumquat** n. (also **native kumquat**) tangled, often spiny Australian shrub or small tree, bearing an edible, yellow, globular fruit.

**native fig** n. small tree of drier Australia bearing edible figs.

**native fuchsia** n. any of several Australian plants bearing fuchsia-like flowers, esp. correa, epacris, and eremophila.

**native grape** n. any of several Australian woody perennial climbers of the grape family bearing edible grapes.

**native heath** see HEATH 2.

**native mahogany** n. former name for JARRAH.

**native mulberry** n. small, soft-wooded tree of Queensland, NSW, and elsewhere, bearing a white, sweet, juicy, mulberry-like fruit.

**native orange** n. any of several Australian trees and shrubs bearing sweet-smelling flowers and rounded edible fruit.

**native title** n. title to land of indigenous people, deriving from their traditions and customs.

**nativity** /nuh-**tiv**-uh-tee/ n. (pl. **-ies**) **1** (esp. **the Nativity**) **a** Christ's birth. **b** festival of Christ's birth. **2** birth. [Latin: related to NATIVE]

**NATO** /**nay**-toh/ abbr. (also **Nato**) North Atlantic Treaty Organisation.

**natter** colloq. — v. chatter idly. — n. aimless chatter; friendly chat. [imitative, originally British dial.]

**natty** /**nat**-ee/ adj. (**-ier, -iest**) colloq. trim; smart, esp. in dress. □ **nattily** adv. [cf. NEAT]

**natural** /**nach**-uh-ruhl/ — adj. **1 a** existing in or caused by nature; not artificial (natural landscape). **b** uncultivated; wild (in its natural state). **2** in the course of nature (died of natural causes). **3** not surprising; to be expected (natural for her to be upset). **4** unaffected, spontaneous (has a natural manner; friendliness is natural to her). **5** innate (has a natural talent for music; is a natural linguist). **6** not disguised or altered (as by make-up etc.). **7** lifelike (the portrait looked very natural). **8** likely or suited by its or their nature to be such (natural enemies; natural leader). **9** having a physical existence, as opposed to what is spiritual etc. (the natural world). **10** illegitimate. **11** based on the innate moral sense (natural justice). **12** Mus. (of a note) not sharpened or flattened (B natural). — n. **1** colloq. (usu. foll. by for) person or thing naturally suitable, adept, etc. (a natural for the championship). **2** Mus. **a** sign (♮) denoting a return to natural pitch. **b** natural note. □ **naturalness** n. [Latin: related to NATURE]

**natural gas** n. inflammable mainly methane gas found in the earth's crust, not manufactured.

**natural history** n. **1** the study of animals or plants. **2** aggregate of the facts concerning the flora and fauna etc. of a particular place or class (a natural history of Tasmania).

**naturalise** v. (also **-ize**) (**-sing** or **-zing**) **1** admit (a foreigner) to citizenship. **2** successfully introduce (an animal, plant, etc.) into another region. **3** adopt (a foreign word, custom, etc.). □ **naturalisation** n.

**naturalism** n. **1** theory or practice in art and literature of realistic representation of nature, character, etc. **2 a** theory of the world that excludes the supernatural or spiritual. **b** moral or religious system based on this. □ **naturalistic** adj.

**naturalist** n. **1** person who studies natural history. **2** adherent of naturalism.

**natural law** n. unchanging moral principles common to all human beings.

**naturally** adv. **1** in a natural manner. **2** (qualifying a whole sentence) as might be expected; of course.

**natural number** n. whole number greater than 0.

**natural resources** n.pl. materials or conditions occurring in nature and capable of economic exploitation.

**natural science** n. **1** the study of the natural or physical world. **2** (in pl.) sciences used for this.

**natural selection** n. Darwinian theory of the survival and propagation of organisms best adapted to their environment.

**nature** /nay-chuh/ n. **1** thing's or person's innate or essential qualities or character (not in her nature to be cruel; it is the nature of iron to rust). **2** (often **Nature**) **a** physical power causing all material phenomena (Nature is the best physician). **b** these phenomena, including plants, animals, landscape, etc. (nature gives him comfort). **3** kind or class (things of this nature). **4** = HUMAN NATURE. **5 a** specific element of human character (our animal nature). **b** person of specified character (even strong natures quail). **6** inherent impulses determining character or action. **7** heredity as influencing or determining character (opp. NURTURE). □ **by nature** innately. **in** (or **by**) **the nature of things 1** inevitable. **2** inevitably. **in** (or **of**) **the nature of** characteristically resembling or belonging to the class of (the answer was in the nature of an excuse). [Latin natura: related to NATAL]

**natured** adj. (in comb.) having a specified disposition (good-natured).

**nature reserve** n. tract of land managed so as to preserve its flora, fauna, physical features, etc.

**nature strip** n. **1** (in some Australian towns) piece of publicly-owned land (usu. lawn) between the front boundary of a property (and the footpath, if there is one) and the street. **2** median strip between two lanes of traffic, usu. grassed or planted with native shrubs etc.

**nature trail** n. signposted path through

the countryside designed to draw attention to natural phenomena.

**naturopathy** /,nach-uh-**rop**-uh-thee/ n. treatment of illness etc. without drugs, usu. involving diet, exercise, massage, etc. □ **naturopath** /nach-uh-ruh-,path/ n. **naturopathic** /-**path**-ik/ adj.

**naught** /nawt/ archaic or literary — n. nothing, nought. — adj. (usu. predic.) worthless; useless. □ **come to naught** come to nothing, fail. **set at naught** despise. [Old English: related to NO², WIGHT]

**naughty** /naw-tee/ adj. (**-ier, -iest**) **1** (esp. of children) disobedient; badly behaved. **2** colloq. joc. indecent. □ **naughtily** adv. **naughtiness** n. [from NAUGHT]

**nausea** /naw-zee-uh, -see-uh/ n. **1** inclination to vomit. **2** revulsion. [Greek naus ship]

**nauseate** /naw-zee-,ayt, -see-,ayt/ v. (**-ting**) affect with nausea. □ **nauseating** adj. **nauseatingly** adv.

**nauseous** /naw-zee-uhs, -see-uhs/ adj. **1** causing nausea. **2** inclined to vomit (feel nauseous). **3** disgusting; loathsome.

**nautical** /naw-tuh-kuhl/ adj. of sailors or navigation. [Greek nautēs sailor]

**nautical mile** n. unit of approx. 1,852 metres (2,025 yards).

**nautilus** /naw-tuh-luhs/ n. (pl. **nautiluses** or **nautili** /-,luy/) cephalopod mollusc with a spiral shell, esp. (**pearly nautilus**) one having a chambered shell with pearly inner lining. [Greek nautilos: related to NAUTICAL]

**naval** /nay-vuhl/ adj. **1** of the or a navy. **2** of ships. [Latin navis ship]

**nave** n. central part of a church, usu. from the west door to the chancel excluding the side aisles. [Latin navis ship]

**navel** /nay-vuhl/ n. depression in the centre of the belly marking the site of attachment of the umbilical cord. [Old English]

**navel orange** n. orange with a navel-like formation at the top.

**navigable** /nav-i-guh-buhl/ adj. **1** (of a river etc.) suitable for ships to pass through. **2** seaworthy. **3** steerable. □ **navigability** /-**bil**-uh-tee/ n. [Latin: related to NAVIGATE]

**navigate** /nav-uh-,gayt/ v. (**-ting**) **1** manage or direct the course of (a ship or aircraft) using maps and instruments. **2 a** sail on (a sea, river, etc.). **b** fly through (the air). **3** (in a car etc.) assist the driver by map-reading etc. **4** sail a ship; sail in a ship. □ **navigator** n. [Latin navigo navigat- from navis ship ago drive]

**navigation** /,nav-uh-**gay**-shuhn/ n. **1** act or process of navigating. **2** art or science of navigating. □ **navigational** adj.

**navvy** /nav-ee/ n. (pl. **-ies**) labourer employed in building or excavating roads etc. [abbreviation of *navigator*]

**navy** /nay-vee/ n. (pl. **-ies**) **1** (often **the Navy**) **a** whole body of a nation's ships of war, including crews, maintenance systems, etc. **b** officers and men of a navy. **2** (in full **navy blue**) dark blue colour as of naval uniforms. **3** *poet.* fleet of ships. [Romanic *navia* ship: related to NAVAL]

**nay** — adv. **1** or rather; and even; more than that (*large, nay, huge*). **2** *archaic* = NO² adv. 1. — n. **1** utterance of 'nay'. **2** (in parliament etc.) 'no' vote or voter (*the 'nays' have it*). [Old Norse, = not ever]

**Nazarene** /ˌnaz-uh-reen, naz-/ — n. **1 a** (prec. by *the*) Christ. **b** (esp. in Jewish or Muslim use) Christian. **2** native or inhabitant of Nazareth. — adj. of Nazareth. [Latin from Greek]

**Nazi** /naht-see/ — n. (pl. **-s**) **1** *hist.* member of the German National Socialist party. **2** *derog.* person holding extreme racist or authoritarian views or behaving brutally. **3** person belonging to any organisation similar to that of the Nazis. — adj. of the Nazis or Nazism. □ **Nazism** n. [representing pronunciation of *Nati-* in German *Nationalsozialist*]

**NB** *abbr.* note well. [Latin *nota bene*]

**Nb** *symb.* niobium.

**NCO** *abbr.* non-commissioned officer.

**Nd** *symb.* neodymium.

**NE** *abbr.* **1** north-east. **2** north-eastern.

**Ne** *symb.* neon.

**Neanderthal** /nee-**an**-duh-ˌthahl/ — adj. **1** of the type of human widely distributed in palaeolithic Europe, with a retreating forehead and massive brow-ridges. **2** (also **neanderthal**) primitive; archaic; hidebound (*his views are positively neanderthal*). — n. (also **neanderthal**) person whose views are hidebound, fixed on the past (*the neanderthals of the extreme right and left*). [region in Germany]

**neap** /neep/ n. (in full **neap tide**) tide at the times of the month when there is least difference between high and low water. [Old English]

**Neapolitan** /nee-uh-**pol**-uh-tuhn/ — n. native or citizen of Naples. — adj. of Naples. [Greek *Neapolis* Naples]

**near** — adv. **1** (often foll. by *to*) to or at a short distance in space or time (*dropped near to them; the time drew near*). **2** closely (*as near as one can guess*). **3** *archaic* almost, nearly (*he very near died*). — prep. **1** to or at a short distance from (in space, time, condition, or resemblance) (*stood near the back; occurs nearer the end*). **2** (in *comb.*) almost (*near-hysterical*). — adj. **1** close (to), not far (in place or time) (*my flat's very near; the man nearest you; in the near future*). **2 a** closely related (*a near relation*). **b** intimate (*a near friend*). **3** (of a part of a vehicle, animal, or road) on the left side (*the near fore leg; near side front wheel*) (opp. OFF). **4** close; narrow (*near escape*). **5** similar (to) (*is nearer the original*). — v. approach; draw near to. □ **come** (or **go**) **near** (foll. by verbal noun, or *to* + verbal noun) be on the point of, almost succeed in (*came near to falling*). **near at hand** within easy reach. **near** (or **close to**) **the knuckle** *colloq.* verging on the indecent. □ **nearish** adj. **nearness** n. [Old Norse, originally = nigher: related to NIGH]

**nearby** — adj. near in position. — adv. close; not far away.

**nearly** adv. **1** almost. **2** closely (*they are nearly related*). □ **not nearly** nothing like; far from (*not nearly enough*).

**near miss** n. **1** bomb etc. falling close to the target. **2** a narrowly avoided collision. **3** not quite successful attempt.

**nearside** n. (often *attrib.*) left side of a vehicle, animal, etc.

**near-sighted** adj. = SHORT-SIGHTED.

**near thing** n. narrow escape.

**neat** adj. **1** tidy and methodical. **2** elegantly simple in form etc. **3** (of language, style, etc.) brief, clear, and pointed (*a neat turn of phrase*). **4 a** cleverly executed (*a neat piece of work*). **b** dexterous. **5** (of esp. alcoholic liquor) undiluted. **6** *colloq.* (as a general term of approval) good, pleasing, excellent. □ **neatly** adv. **neatness** n. [French *net* from Latin *nitidus* shining]

**neaten** v. make neat.

**nebula** /**neb**-yuh-luh/ n. (pl. **nebulae** /-ˌlee/) cloud of gas and dust seen in the night sky, sometimes glowing and sometimes appearing as a dark silhouette. □ **nebular** adj. [Latin, = mist]

**nebulous** adj. **1** cloudlike. **2** indistinct, vague (*put forward a few nebulous ideas*). [Latin: related to NEBULA]

**necessarily** /ˌnes-uh-**se**-ruh-lee/ adv. as a necessary result; inevitably.

**necessary** /**nes**-uh-se-ree, nes-uhs-ree, -suh-ree/ — adj. **1** requiring to be done; requisite, essential (*it is necessary to work; lacks the necessary documents*). **2** determined, existing, or happening by natural laws etc., not by free will; inevitable (*a necessary evil*). — n. (pl. **-ies**) (usu. in *pl.*) any of the basic requirements of life. □ **the necessary** *colloq.* an action etc. needed for a purpose (*they will do the necessary*). [Latin *necesse* needful]

**necessitate** /nuh-**ses**-uh-ˌtayt/ v. (**-ting**) make necessary (esp. as a result) (*will necessitate some sacrifice*).

**necessitous** /nuh-**ses**-uh-tuhs/ adj. poor; needy.

**necessity** /nuh-**ses**-uh-tee/ n. (pl. **-ies**) **1** indispensable thing (*air-conditioning is a necessity*). **2** pressure of circumstances (*the necessity for immediate action*). **3** imperative need (*necessity is the mother of invention*). **4** want; poverty (*stole because of necessity*). **5** constraint or compulsion regarded as a natural law governing all human action. □ **of necessity** unavoidably.

**neck** — n. **1 a** part of the body connecting the head to the shoulders. **b** part of a garment round the neck. **2 a** something resembling a neck, such as the narrow part of a cavity, vessel, or object such as a bottle or violin. **b** passage, channel, pass, isthmus, etc. **3** length of a horse's head and neck as a measure of its lead in a race. **4** flesh of an animal's neck as food. — v. *colloq.* kiss and caress amorously. □ **get it in the neck** *colloq.* **1** be severely reprimanded or punished. **2** suffer a severe blow. **get under a person's neck** *colloq.* outwit, beat, or bypass him or her. **neck of the woods** *colloq.* a particular place (*what are you doing in this neck of the woods?*). **up to one's** (or **the**) **neck** *colloq.* **1** to the limit of endurance (*I've had it up to the neck with you*). **2** in deep trouble (*he's in it up to his neck with the tax people*). **3** (often foll. by *in*) very deeply involved; very busy (*I'm up to my neck in work*). [Old English]

**neck and neck** adj. & adv. (running) level in a race etc.

**neckerchief** n. square of cloth worn round the neck. [from KERCHIEF]

**neckful** n. *colloq.* too much (*I've had a neckful of these whingers*).

**necklace** /**nek**-luhs/ — n. **1** (also **necklet**) chain or string of beads, precious stones, etc., worn round the neck. **2** S.Afr. tyre soaked or filled with petrol, placed round a victim's neck, and set alight. — v. S.Afr. kill with a 'necklace'.

**necro-** *comb. form* corpse. [Greek *nekros* corpse]

**necromancy** /**nek**-ruh-ˌman-see/ n. **1** divination by supposed communication with the dead. **2** magic. □ **necromancer** n. [from NECRO-, *mantis* seer]

**necrophilia** /ˌnek-ruh-**fil**-ee-uh/ n. morbid and esp. sexual attraction to corpses. □ **necrophiliac** n.

**necrophobia** /ˌnek-ruh-**foh**-bee-uh/ n. abnormal fear of death or dead bodies.

**necropolis** /nuh-**krop**-uh-luhs/ n. ancient cemetery or burial place. [Greek: related to NECRO-, *polis* city]

**necrosis** /nuh-**kroh**-suhs/ n. death of tissue. □ **necrotic** /-**krot**-ik/ adj. [Greek *nekroō* kill]

**nectar** /**nek**-tuh/ n. **1** sugary substance produced by plants and made into honey by bees. **2** (in Greek and Roman mythology) the drink of the gods. **3** drink compared to this. □ **nectarous** adj. [Latin from Greek]

**nectarine** /**nek**-tuh-ruhn, -ˌreen/ n. smooth-skinned variety of peach. [from NECTAR]

**neddy** /**ned**-ee/ n. (pl. **-ies**) *colloq.* horse. [pet form of *Edward*]

**ned 'em** v. *colloq.* (in the game of two-up) throw two heads. [from the head of Edward VII (Ned) on the pennies traditionally used for this game]

**Ned Kelly** — n. **1** person who is unscrupulous in seeking personal gain or who resists authority. **2** *rhyming slang* belly. — *attrib. adj.* unscrupulous, esp. in seeking profit etc. (*tycoons with the Ned Kelly syndrome*). — v. **1** bushrange. **2** shoot (a bird etc.) unsportingly (*Ned Kellied the ducks while they were resting on the water*). □ **game as Ned Kelly** fearless in the face of odds. [*Ned Kelly*, Australian bushranger, hanged 1880]

**née** /nay/ adj. (also **nee**) (used in adding a married woman's maiden name after her surname) born (*Mrs Ann Hall, née Browne*). [French, feminine past part. of *naître* be born]

**need** — v. **1** stand in want of; require. **2** (foll. by *to* + infin.; *3rd sing. present neg.* or *interrog.* without *to*) be under the necessity or obligation (*needs to be done well; he need not come; need you ask?*). — n. **1 a** requirement (*my needs are few*). **b** thing wanted (*her greatest need is a car*). **2** circumstances requiring some course of action (*no need to worry; if need be*). **3** destitution; poverty. **4** crisis; emergency (*failed them in their need*). □ **have need of** require. **need not have** did not need to (but did). [Old English]

**needful** — adj. requisite; necessary. — n. (prec. by *the*) **1** what is necessary. **2** *colloq.* money or action needed for a purpose. □ **needfully** adv.

**needle** /**nee**-duhl/ — n. **1 a** very thin pointed rod of smooth steel etc. with a slit (eye) for thread at the blunt end, used in sewing. **b** larger plastic, wooden, etc., slender rod without an eye, used in knitting etc. **c** slender hooked stick used in crochet. **2** pointer on a dial. **3** any of several small thin pointed instruments, esp.: **a** surgical instrument used for stitching. **b** the end of a hypodermic syringe. **c** = STYLUS 1. **d** etching tool. **4 a** obelisk (*Cleopatra's Needle*). **b** pointed rock or peak. **5** leaf of a fir or pine tree. — *v.* (**-ling**) *colloq.* **1** goad (*needled him into taking action*). **2** irritate; make digs at; heckle; harass. □ **needle in a haystack** something almost impossible to find because it is concealed by so many other things etc. [Old English]

**needless** *adj.* **1** unnecessary. **2** uncalled for. □ **needlessly** *adv.*

**needlework** *n.* sewing or embroidery.

**needs** *adv. archaic* (usu. prec. or foll. by *must*) of necessity.

**needy** *adj.* (**-ier, -iest**) poor; destitute. □ **neediness** *n.*

**ne'er** /nair/ *adv. poet.* = NEVER. [contraction]

**ne'er-do-well** — *n.* good-for-nothing person. — *adj.* good-for-nothing.

**nefarious** /nuh-**fair**-ree-uhs/ *adj.* wicked. [Latin *nefas* sinful act]

**negate** /nuh-**gayt**/ *v.* (**-ting**) **1** nullify (*this new evidence negates their conclusion*). **2** assert or imply the non-existence of. [Latin *nego negat-* deny]

**negation** /nuh-**gay**-shuhn/ *n.* **1** absence or opposite of something actual or positive. **2** act of denying. **3** negative statement. **4** negative or unreal thing.

**negative** /**neg**-uh-tiv/ — *adj.* **1** expressing or implying denial, prohibition, or refusal (*negative answer*). **2** (of a person or attitude) lacking positive attributes; pessimistic. **3** marked by the absence of qualities (*negative reaction; negative result from the AIDS test*). **4** of the opposite nature to a thing regarded as positive (*debt is negative wealth*). **5** (of a quantity) less than zero, to be subtracted from others or from zero. **6** *Electr.* **a** of the kind of charge carried by electrons. **b** containing or producing such a charge. — *n.* **1** negative statement or word. **2** *Photog.* **a** image with black and white reversed or colours replaced by complementary ones, from which positive pictures are obtained. **b** developed film or plate bearing such an image. — *v.* (**-ving**) **1** refuse to accept or countenance; veto. **2** disprove. **3** contradict (a statement). **4** neutralise (an effect). □ **in the negative** with negative effect. □ **negatively** *adv.* **negativity** /-**tiv**-uh-tee/ *n.*

**negative gearing** *n.* plan under which the interest payments on the borrowing for an investment exceed the net revenue from that investment, the loss being set against other sources of income to reduce the borrower's tax liability.

**negativism** *n.* negative attitude; extreme scepticism.

**neglect** /nuh-**glekt**/ — *v.* **1** fail to care for or to do; be remiss about (*neglected their duty*). **2** (foll. by *to* + infin.) fail; overlook the need to (*neglected to inform them*). **3** not pay attention to; disregard (*neglected the warning signs*). — *n.* **1** lack of caring; negligence (*the house suffered from neglect*). **2 a** act of neglecting. **b** state of being neglected (*the house fell into neglect*). **3** (usu. foll. by *of*) disregard. □ **neglectful** *adj.* **neglectfully** *adv.* [Latin *neglego neglect-*]

**negligée** /**neg**-luh-**zhay**/ *n.* (also **negligee**) woman's flimsy dressing gown. [French, past part. of *négliger* NEGLECT]

**negligence** /**neg**-luh-juhns/ *n.* **1** lack of reasonable care and attention. **2** culpable carelessness. □ **negligent** *adj.* **negligently** *adv.* [Latin: related to NEGLECT]

**negligible** /**neg**-luh-juh-buhl/ *adj.* not worth considering; insignificant. □ **negligibly** *adv.* [French: related to NEGLECT]

**negotiable** /nuh-**goh**-shuh-buhl/ *adj.* **1** open to discussion. **2** able to be negotiated.

**negotiate** /nuh-**goh**-shee-,ayt/ *v.* (**-ting**) **1** (usu. foll. by *with*) confer with another or others in order to reach a compromise or an agreement. **2** arrange (an affair) or bring about (a result) by negotiating (*negotiated a settlement*). **3** find a way over, through, etc. (an obstacle, difficulty, fence, etc.). **4** convert (a cheque etc.) into money. □ **negotiation** /-shee-**ay**-shuhn, -see-**ay**-shuhn/ *n.* **negotiator** *n.* [Latin *negotium* business]

**Negress** /**nee**-gruhs/ *n.* female Negro.

■ **Usage** The term *Negress* is considered offensive; *Black* is usually preferred.

**Negro** /**nee**-groh/ — *n.* (*pl.* **-es**) **1** member of a dark-skinned race orig. native to Africa. **2** *hist.* name applied by colonists in Australia to an Aboriginal. — *adj.* **1** of Negroes. **2** (as **negro**) *Zool.* black or dark. [Latin *niger nigri* black]

■ **Usage** The term *Negro* is considered offensive; *Black* is usually preferred.

**Negroid** /**nee**-groid/ — *adj.* (of physical features etc.) characteristic of Black people. — *n.* Negro.

**neigh** /nay/ — *n.* cry of a horse. — *v.* make a neigh. [Old English]

**neighbour** /**nay**-buh/ (also **neighbor**) — *n.* **1** person living next door to or near or nearest another. **2** fellow human being (*love thy neighbour as thyself*). **3** person or thing near or next to another (*my* *neighbour at dinner).* — *v.* border on; adjoin. □ **neighbouring** *adj.* [Old English: related to NIGH, BOOR]

**neighbourhood** *n.* (also **neighborhood**) **1** district; vicinity (*Toorak is a rich neighbourhood; in our neighbourhood*). **2** people of a district (*gave a barbecue for the entire neighbourhood*). □ **in the neighbourhood of** roughly; about.

**neighbourhood watch** *n.* organised local vigilance by householders to discourage crime.

**neighbourly** *adj.* (also **neighborly**) like a good neighbour; friendly; kind. □ **neighbourliness** *n.*

**neither** /**nuy**-*th*uh, **nee**-*th*uh/ — *adj. & pron.* (foll. by sing. verb) not the one nor the other (of two things); not either (*neither of the accusations is true; neither of them knows; neither wish was granted; neither went to the fair*). — *adv.* **1** not either; not on the one hand (foll. by *nor*; introducing the first of two or more things in the negative: *neither knowing nor caring; neither the teachers nor the parents nor the children*). **2** also not (*if you do not, neither shall I*). — *conj.* archaic nor yet; nor (*I know not, neither can I guess*). □ **neither here nor there** irrelevant, of no consequence; makes no difference. [Old English: related to NO², WHETHER]

**nelia** /**nee**-lee-uh/ *n.* any of several small wattles of inland Australia. [Ngiyambaa *nhiilyi*]

**nelly** /**nel**-ee/ *n.* (also **nellie**) cheap wine. □ **nervous Nelly** timid or cautious person. **not on your nelly** *colloq.* certainly not. [perhaps from the name *Nelly*]

**nelson** /**nel**-suhn/ *n.* wrestling-hold in which one arm is passed under the opponent's arm from behind and the hand is applied to the neck (**half nelson**), or both arms and hands are applied (**full nelson**). [apparently from the name *Nelson*]

**nematode** /**nem**-uh-,tohd/ *n.* worm with a slender unsegmented cylindrical shape. [Greek *nēma* thread]

**nem. con.** with no one dissenting. [abbreviation of Latin *nemine contradicente*]

**nemesis** /**nem**-uh-suhs/ *n.* (*pl.* **nemeses** /-,seez/) **1** retributive justice. **2 a** downfall caused by this. **b** agent of such a downfall (*he was my nemesis*). [Greek, = retribution]

**neo-** *comb. form* **1** new, modern. **2** new form of (*neo-fascism; neo-Nazis*). [Greek *neos* new]

**neoclassicism** /,nee-oh-**klas**-uh-siz-uhm/ *adj.* revival of classical style or treatment in the arts. □ **neoclassical** /-**klas**-i-kuhl/ *n.*

**neodymium** /,nee-uh-**dim**-ee-uhm/ *n.* metallic element of the lanthanide series. [from NEO-, Greek *didumos* twin]

**neolithic** /,nee-uh-**lith**-ik/ *adj.* of the later part of the Stone Age. [Greek *lithos* stone]

**neologism** /nee-**ol**-uh-,jiz-uhm/ *n.* **1** new word or expression (*'hairologist' for 'barber' is a barbarous neologism*). **2** coining or use of new words. [Greek *logos* word]

**neo-mort** *n.* person who is brain-dead but whose other organs (heart, lungs, etc.) are kept artificially functioning. [Latin *mort-* dead]

**neon** /**nee**-on/ *n.* inert gaseous element giving an orange glow when electricity is passed through it, used in lights, illuminated advertisements, etc. [Greek, = new]

**neophyte** /**nee**-uh-,fuyt/ *n.* **1** new convert. **2** *RC Ch.* novice of a religious order. **3** beginner. [Greek *phuton* plant]

**Neozoic** /,nee-oh-**zoh**-ik/ *adj. Geol.* of a later period of geological history, from the end of the Mesozoic to the present. [Greek *zōion* animal]

**nepenthes** /nuh-**pen**-theez/ *n.* insectivorous pitcher plant of wet places in northern Queensland, having very large pitchers up to 20 cm in length. [Greek *nēpenthēs* soothing away sorrow]

**nephew** /**nev**-yoo, **nef**-/ *n.* son of one's brother or sister or of one's spouse's brother or sister. [Latin *nepos*]

**nephritic** /nuh-**frit**-ik/ *adj.* **1** of or in the kidneys. **2** of nephritis. [Greek *nephros* kidney]

**nephritis** /nuh-**fruy**-tuhs/ *n.* inflammation of the kidneys.

**ne plus ultra** /,nay pluus **uul**-trah/ *n.* **1** furthest attainable point. **2** acme, perfection. [Latin, = not further beyond]

**nepotism** /**nep**-uh-,tiz-uhm/ *n.* favouritism shown to relatives in giving jobs or privileges. [Italian *nepote* nephew]

**Neptune** *n.* distant planet of the solar system. [Latin *Neptunus* god of the sea]

**neptunium** /nep-**tyoo**-nee-uhm/ *n.* transuranic metallic element produced when uranium atoms absorb bombarding neutrons. [NEPTUNE]

**nerd** *n. colloq.* foolish, feeble, or uninteresting person. [origin uncertain]

**nereid** /**neer**-ree-uhd/ *n.* (*pl.* **nereides** /nuh-**ree**-uh-deez/) sea-nymph. [Latin from Greek]

**nerve** — *n.* **1 a** fibre or bundle of fibres that transmits impulses of sensation or motion between the brain or spinal cord and other parts of the body. **b** material constituting these. **2 a** coolness in danger; bravery (*climbing Mt. Arapiles requires much nerve*). **b** *colloq.* impudence (*they've got a nerve coming here uninvited*). **3** (in *pl.*) nervousness; mental or physical stress (*need to calm my nerves*). — *v.* (**-ving**) **1** (usu. *refl.*) brace (oneself) to face danger etc. (*nerved himself for the ordeal*). **2** give strength, vigour, or courage to. □ **get on a person's nerves** irritate a person. [Latin *nervus* sinew, bowstring]

**nerve cell** *n.* cell transmitting impulses in nerve tissue.

**nerve centre** *n.* **1** group of closely connected nerve cells. **2** centre of an organisation etc. from which all its activities are directed and controlled.

**nerve gas** *n.* poisonous gas affecting the nervous system.

**nerveless** *adj.* **1** lacking vigour or spirit (*a nerveless performance*). **2** confident; not nervous (*seemed quite nerveless as she climbed Mt. Arapiles*). **3** (of style) diffuse.

**nerve-racking** *adj.* causing mental strain.

**nervous** *adj.* **1** easily upset, timid, highly strung. **2** anxious. **3** affecting or acting on the nerves. **4** (foll. by *of* + verbal noun) afraid (*am nervous of meeting them*). □ **nervously** *adv.* **nervousness** *n.*

**nervous breakdown** *n.* period of mental illness, usu. resulting from severe depression or anxiety.

**nervous Nelly** see NELLY.

**nervous system** *n.* the body's network of specialised cells which transmit nerve impulses between parts of the body (cf. CENTRAL NERVOUS SYSTEM; PERIPHERAL NERVOUS SYSTEM).

**nervy** *adj.* (**-ier**, **-iest**) *colloq.* nervous; easily excited.

**nescient** /**nes**-ee-uhnt/ *adj. literary* (foll. by *of*) lacking knowledge. □ **nescience** *n.* [Latin *ne-* not, *scio* know]

**-ness** *suffix* forming nouns from adjectives, expressing: **1** state or condition, or an instance of this (*happiness*; *a kindness*). **2** something in a certain state (*wilderness*). [Old English]

**nest** — *n.* **1** structure or place where a bird lays eggs and shelters its young. **2** any creature's breeding-place or lair. **3** snug retreat or shelter. **4** (often foll. by *of*) place fostering something undesirable (*a nest of vice*). **5** brood or swarm. **6** group or set of similar objects, often of different sizes and fitting one inside the other (*nest of tables*). — *v.* **1** use or build a nest. **2** take wild birds' nests or eggs (*arrested while nesting in the bush*). **3** (of objects)

fit together or one inside another. [Old English]

**nest egg** *n.* sum of money saved for the future.

**nestle** /**nes**-uhl/ *v.* (**-ling**) **1** (often foll. by *down, in*, etc.) settle oneself comfortably. **2** press oneself against another in affection etc. **3** (foll. by *in, into*, etc.) push (a head or shoulder etc.) affectionately or snugly. **4** lie half hidden or embedded. [Old English]

**nestling** /**nes**-ling, **nest**-/ *n.* bird too young to leave its nest.

**net**[1] — *n.* **1** open-meshed fabric of cord, rope, etc. **2** piece of net used esp. to restrain, contain, or delimit, or to catch fish etc. **3** structure with a net used in various games. **4** system or procedure for catching or entrapping a person or persons. **5** = NETWORK. **6** (also **Net**) = INTERNET. — *v.* (**-tt-**) **1 a** cover, confine, or catch with a net. **b** procure as with a net. **2** hit (a ball) into the net, esp. of a goal. [Old English]

**net**[2] (also **nett**) — *adj.* **1** (esp. of money) remaining after all necessary deductions (opp. GROSS) (*net income*). **2** (of a price) not reducible. **3** (of a weight) excluding that of the packaging etc. **4** (of an effect, result, etc.) ultimate, actual. — *v.* (**-tt-**) gain or yield (a sum) as net profit. [French: related to NEAT]

**netball** *n.* team game, similar to basketball, played mostly by women.

**nether** /**neth**-uh/ *adj. archaic* = LOWER[1] (*nether lip*). [Old English]

**nether regions** *n.pl.* (also **nether world**) hell; the underworld.

**net profit** *n.* actual gain after working expenses have been paid.

**nett** var. of NET[2].

**netting** *n.* **1** netted material (*mosquito netting*; *wire netting*). **2** piece of this.

**nettle** /**net**-uhl/ — *n.* **1** plant of the genus *Urtica* with jagged leaves covered with stinging hairs. **2** plant resembling this. — *v.* (**-ling**) irritate, provoke. [Old English]

**nettle-rash** *n.* skin eruption like nettle stings (see URTICARIA; HIVES).

**network** — *n.* **1** arrangement of intersecting horizontal and vertical lines. **2** complex system of railways etc. **3** people connected by the exchange of information etc., professionally or socially. **4** system of connected electrical conductors. **5** group of broadcasting (esp. TV) stations connected for the simultaneous broadcast of a programme. **6** chain of interconnected computers. — *v.* **1** broadcast on a network. **2** establish contact with other people, groups, etc., for the interchange of ideas, information, etc.

**neural** /nyoo-ruhl/ *adj.* of a nerve or the central nervous system. [Greek *neuron* nerve]

**neuralgia** /nyoo-**ral**-juh/ *n.* intense pain along a nerve, esp. in the head or face. □ **neuralgic** *adj.*

**neurasthenia** /ˌnyoo-ruhs-**thee**-nee-uh/ *n.* general (not medical) term for lasting fatigue, listlessness, etc., associated chiefly with emotional disturbance. □ **neurasthenic** /-**then**-ik/ *adj.* & *n.*

**neuritis** /nyoo-**ruy**-tuhs/ *n.* inflammation of a nerve or nerves.

**neuro-** *comb. form* nerve or nerves. [Greek *neuron* nerve]

**neurology** /nyoo-**rol**-uh-jee/ *n.* the study of nerve systems. □ **neurological** /-ruh-**loj**-i-kuhl/ *adj.* **neurologist** *n.*

**neuron** /**nyoo**-ron/ *n.* (also **neurone** /-rohn/) nerve-cell.

**neurosis** /nyoo-**roh**-suhs/ *n.* (*pl.* **neuroses** /-seez/) irrational or disturbed behaviour pattern, associated with nervous distress.

**neurosurgery** /ˌnyoo-roh-**ser**-juh-ree/ *n.* surgery on the nervous system, esp. the brain or spinal cord. □ **neurosurgeon** *n.* **neurosurgical** *adj.*

**neurotic** /nyoo-**rot**-ik/ — *adj.* **1** caused by or relating to neurosis. **2** suffering from neurosis. **3** *colloq.* abnormally sensitive or obsessive. — *n.* neurotic person. □ **neurotically** *adv.*

**neurotransmitter** /**nyoo**-roh-tranz-ˌmit-uh/ *n.* *Biochem.* chemical substance, released from a nerve fibre, that effects the transfer of an impulse to another nerve or muscle.

**neuter** /**nyoo**-tuh/ — *adj.* **1** *Gram.* neither masculine nor feminine. **2** (of a plant) having neither pistils nor stamen. **3** (of an insect) sexually undeveloped. — *n.* **1** *Gram.* neuter gender or word. **2** a non-fertile insect, esp. a worker bee or ant. **b** castrated animal. — *v.* castrate or spay. [Latin]

**neutral** /**nyoo**-truhl/ — *adj.* **1** not supporting either of two opposing sides, impartial. **2** belonging to a neutral nation etc. (*neutral ships*). **3** indistinct, vague, indeterminate. **4** (of a gear) in which the engine is disconnected from the driven parts. **5** (of colours) not strong or positive; grey or beige. **6** *Chem.* neither acid nor alkaline. **7** *Electr.* neither positive nor negative. **8** *Biol.* sexually undeveloped; asexual. — *n.* **1** **a** neutral nation or person. **b** citizen of a neutral nation. **2** neutral gear. □ **neutrality** /-**tral**-uh-tee/ *n.* [Latin *neutralis* of neuter gender]

**neutralise** *v.* (also **-ize**) (**-sing** or **-zing**) **1** make neutral. **2** counterbalance; make ineffective by an opposite force or effect. **3** exempt or exclude (a place) from the sphere of hostilities. □ **neutralisation** /-zay-shuhn/ *n.*

**neutrino** /nyoo-**tree**-noh/ *n.* (*pl.* **-s**) elementary particle with zero electric charge and probably zero mass. [Italian, diminutive of *neutro* neutral: related to NEUTER]

**neutron** /**nyoo**-tron/ *n.* elementary particle of about the same mass as a proton but without an electric charge. [from NEUTRAL]

**neutron bomb** *n.* bomb producing neutrons and little blast, destroying life but not property.

**never¹** /**nev**-uh/ *adv.* **1 a** at no time; on no occasion; not ever. **b** *colloq.* as an emphatic negative (*I never heard you come in*). **2** not at all (*never fear*). **3** *colloq.* (expressing surprise) surely not (*you never left the door open!*). □ **well I never!** expressing great surprise. [Old English, = not ever]

**never²** *abbr.* of NEVER-NEVER 1.

**nevermore** *adv.* at no future time.

**never-never** — *n.* **1** (also **never**) the far interior of Australia; the remote outback. **2** *colloq.* hire purchase. — *adj.* of or pertaining to the remote outback of Australia (*never-never country*; *never-never land*). □ **on the never-never** *colloq.* on the hire purchase system (*bought all their furniture on the never-never*).

**nevertheless** /ˌnev-uh-thuh-**les**/ *adv.* in spite of that; notwithstanding.

**new** — *adj.* **1 a** of recent origin or arrival (*a New Australian*). **b** made, discovered, acquired, or experienced recently or now for the first time. **2** in original condition; not worn or used. **3 a** renewed; reformed (*a new life*; *the new order*). **b** reinvigorated (*felt like a new person*). **4** different from a recent previous one (*has a new job*). **5** in addition to the others already existing (*a new supermarket*). **6** (often foll. by *to*) unfamiliar or strange (*all new to me*). **7** (often foll. by *at*) (of a person) inexperienced (*I'm new at this business*). **8** (usu. prec. by *the*) often *derog.* **a** later, modern. **b** newfangled. **c** given to new or modern ideas. **d** recently affected by social change (*the new rich*). **9** (often prec. by *the*) advanced in method or theory (*the new formula*). **10** (in place-names) discovered or founded later than and named after (*New South Wales*). — *adv.* (usu. in *comb.*) newly, recently (*new-found*; *new-baked*). — *n.* a light beer, made by the bottom fermentation method and so called because it was regarded as a 'new' style when introduced (cf. OLD *n*.). ◻ **newish** *adj.* **newness** *n*. [Old English]

**New Age** — *n*. set of beliefs replacing traditional Western culture with alternative approaches to religion, medicine, the environment, etc. — *adj.* (also **new age**) of or pertaining to the New Age. ◻ **New Ageist** *n*. **New Ager** *n*.

**New Aussie** *colloq*. NEW AUSTRALIAN. [abbreviation]

**New Australian** — *n*. (also **New Aussie**) an immigrant to Australia, esp. one whose first language is not English. — *adj*. of or pertaining to New Australians.

**new broom** *n*. new employee etc. eager to make changes.

**new chum** *n*. **1** *hist*. convict newly arrived in Australia. **2 a** *hist*. newly arrived colonist to Australia (opp. OLD CHUM). **b** immigrant to Australia who has newly arrived. **3** novice; person inexperienced in a particular activity etc.

**newcomer** *n*. **1** person recently arrived. **2** beginner in some activity.

**newfangled** /nyoo-**fang**-guhld/ *adj. derog*. different from what one is used to; objectionably new. [= new taken]

**New Holland** *n. hist*. name formerly given to the Australian continent (or any part of it), sometimes including Tasmania. [Anglicisation of Latin *Nova Hollandia*, name given by Dutch navigators to part of Australia]

**New Holland honeyeater** *n*. honeyeater of southern Australia, including Tasmania, having black and white plumage with bright yellow on the wings and tail.

**newie** /**nyoo**-ee/ *n. colloq*. **1** = NEW CHUM 2 & 3. **2** anything new (*sold his car and bought a newie*).

**newly** *adv*. **1** recently. **2** afresh, anew.

**new moon** *n*. **1** moon when first seen as a crescent after conjunction with the sun. **2** time of its appearance.

**New Right** *n*. loose association of right-wing organisations and individuals advocating extreme free-market policies, reductions in government expenditure on social welfare etc., privatisation of public services, curtailment of trade unionism, etc.

**news** /nyooz/ *n.pl*. (usu. treated as *sing*.) **1** information about important or interesting recent events, esp. when published or broadcast. **2** (prec. by *the*) broadcast report of news. **3** newly received or noteworthy information. **4** (foll. by *to*) information not previously known

(to a person) (*that's news to me*). [from NEW]

**news agency** *n*. organisation that collects and distributes news items.

**newsagent** *n*. seller of or shop selling newspapers etc.

**newscast** *n*. radio or television broadcast of news reports.

**newscaster** *n*. = NEWSREADER.

**news conference** *n*. press conference.

**newsflash** *n*. single item of important news broadcast urgently and often interrupting other programmes.

**newsletter** *n*. informal printed report issued periodically to members of a club etc.

**New South Wales Christmas bush** see CHRISTMAS BUSH.

**New South Welshman** *n*. native or resident of the State of NSW.

**newspaper** *n*. **1** printed publication of loose folded sheets containing news, advertisements, correspondence, etc. **2** paper forming this (*wrapped in newspaper*).

**newspeak** /**nyoo**-,speek/ *n*. ambiguous euphemistic language used esp. in political propaganda. [an artificial official language in Orwell's *Nineteen Eighty-Four*]

**newsprint** *n*. low-quality paper on which newspapers are printed.

**newsreader** *n*. person who reads out broadcast news bulletins.

**newsreel** *n*. short cinema film of recent events.

**newsworthy** *adj*. topical; noteworthy as news.

**newsy** *adj*. (**-ier, -iest**) *colloq*. full of news.

**newt** /nyoot/ *n*. small European amphibian with a well-developed tail. [Old English *ewt*, with ◻ from *an*]

**New Testament** *n*. part of the Bible concerned with the life and teachings of Christ and his earliest followers.

**newton** /**nyoo**-tuhn/ *n*. SI unit of force that, acting on a mass of one kilogram, increases its velocity by one metre per second every second. [*Newton*, name of a scientist (d. 1727)]

**new wave** — *n*. new trend etc. which discards established ideas in the arts, fashion, religion, etc. — *adj*. of such a trend (*a new wave marriage ceremony*).

**New World** *n*. North and South America.

**new year** *n*. year just begun or about to begin; first few days of a year.

**New Year's Day** *n*. 1 January.

**New Year's Eve** *n*. 31 December.

**New Zealander** *n*. native or national of

New Zealand or a person of New Zealand descent.

**next** —*adj.* **1** (often foll. by *to*) being, positioned, or living nearest (*in the next house*; *chair next to the heater*). **2** nearest in order of time; soonest encountered (*next week*; *ask the next person you see*). — *adv.* **1** (often foll. by *to*) in the nearest place or degree (*put it next to mine*). **2** on the first or soonest occasion (*when next we meet*). — *n.* next person or thing. □ **next to** almost (*next to nothing left*). [Old English, superlative of NIGH]

**next door** *adj.* & *adv.* (as *adj.* often hyphenated) in the next house, building, or room.

**next of kin** *n.sing.* & *pl.* closest living relative(s).

**nexus** /nek-suhs/ *n.* (*pl.* same) **1** bond, link, connection. **2** connected group or series. [Latin *necto nex-* bind]

**Ngaanyatjara** /ngah-nyah-,jah-ru/ *n.* a dialect of the WESTERN DESERT LANGUAGE.

**Ngamini** /ngah-min-ee/ *n.* an Aboriginal language, spoken in the region of Goyder's Lagoon, SA: now extinct.

**Ngarigo** /ngah-rig-oh/ *n.* an Aboriginal language spoken right across from Canberra, through Cooma and the Monaro district, over the Snowy Mountains to Omeo in Victoria: the language has perished along with its speakers.

**Ngarluma** /ngahr-loo-mu/ *n.* an Aboriginal language of WA: now extinct.

**Ngiyambaa** /ngyem-pu/ *n.* an Aboriginal language spoken in the region around the Bogan, Lachlan, and Darling Rivers of NSW: now extinct, the last speakers being recorded in 1970.

**Nhangka** /nahng-ku/ *n.* an Aboriginal language of southern SA: now extinct.

**Nhanta** /nhahn-tu/ *n.* an Aboriginal language of the Geraldton region of WA: the language has perished along with its speakers.

**Ni** *symb.* nickel.

**niacin** /nuy-uh-suhn/ *n.* = NICOTINIC ACID. [shortening]

**nib** *n.* pen-point which touches the writing surface. [Low German or Dutch]

**nibble** /nib-uhl/ — *v.* (**-ling**) **1** (foll. by *at*) **a** take small bites at. **b** take cautious interest in. **2** eat in small amounts. **3** bite at gently, cautiously, or playfully. — *n.* **1** act of nibbling. **2** very small amount of food. **3** (in *pl.*) cautious expressions of interest, esp. in something offered for sale. [Low German or Dutch]

**nibblies** *n. colloq.* titbits as snacks; munchies.

**nice** *adj.* **1** pleasant, satisfactory. **2** (of a person) kind, good-natured. **3** *iron.* bad or awkward (*a nice mess you've made*). **4 a** fine or subtle (*nice distinction*). **b** requiring careful thought or attention (*nice problem*). **5** fastidious; delicately sensitive. **6** scrupulous (*were not too nice about their methods*). **7** (foll. by an *adj.*, often with *and*) satisfactory in terms of the quality described (*a nice long time*; *nice and warm*). □ **nicely** *adv.* **niceness** *n.*

**niceish** *adj.* [originally = foolish, from Latin *nescius* ignorant]

**nicety** /nuy-suh-tee/ *n.* (*pl.* **-ies**) **1** subtle distinction or detail. **2** precision. □ **to a nicety** with exactness.

**niche** /neesh, nich/ *n.* **1** shallow recess, esp. in a wall, to contain a statue etc. **2** comfortable or apt position in life or employment. **3** position from which an entrepreneur exploits a gap in the market; profitable corner of the market. [Latin *nidus* nest]

**nick** — *n.* **1** small cut or notch. **2** *colloq.* prison. **3** *colloq.* condition (*in good nick*). — *v.* **1** make a nick or nicks in. **2** *colloq.* **a** steal. **b** arrest, catch. **3** *colloq.* **a** go (somewhere) on the spur of the moment; slip (away, out, etc.), esp. for a short while (*have to nick over to the milk bar*). **b** (foll. by *off*) depart. □ **get nicked** *colloq.* 'get lost'; 'get stuffed'. **in the nick of time** only just in time. **nick off!** clear out!, scram! [origin uncertain]

**nickel** /nik-uhl/ — *n.* **1** silver-white metallic element, used esp. in magnetic alloys. **2** *colloq.* US five-cent coin. — *v.* coat with nickel. [German]

**nickel silver** *n.* white alloy of nickel, zinc, and copper.

**nickel steel** *n.* type of stainless steel with chromium and nickel.

**nickname** /nik-naym/ — *n.* familiar or humorous name given to a person or thing instead of or as well as the real name. — *v.* (**-ming**) **1** give a nickname to. **2** call by a nickname. [earlier *eke-name*, with □ from *an*: *eke* = addition, from Old English: related to EKE]

**nicotine** /nik-uh-,teen/ *n.* poisonous alkaloid present in tobacco. [French from *Nicot*, introducer of tobacco into France]

**nicotinic acid** /,nik-uh-**tin**-ik/ *n.* vitamin of the B complex.

**nictitate** /nik-tuh-,tayt/ *v.* (**-ting**) blink or wink. □ **nictitation** /-tay-shuhn/ *n.* [Latin]

**nictitating membrane** *n.* transparent third eyelid in amphibians, birds, and some other animals.

**niece** /nees/ *n.* daughter of one's brother or sister or of one's spouse's brother or sister. [Latin *neptis* granddaughter]

**nifty** /**nif**-tee/ adj. (**-ier**, **-iest**) colloq. **1** clever, adroit. **2** smart, stylish. [origin uncertain]

**niggard** /**nig**-uhd/ n. stingy person. [probably of Scandinavian origin]

**niggardly** adj. stingy. □ **niggardliness** n.

**nigger** n. **1** offens. Black or dark-skinned person. **2** = LUDERICK [Spanish NEGRO]

**niggerhead** n. **1** large (frequently blackened and rounded) block of coral deposited on a reef by a storm. **2** the small, tufted grass of mainland Australia, having blackish seed-heads.

**niggle** /**nig**-uhl/ — v. (**-ling**) **1** be over-attentive to details. **2** find fault in a petty way. **3** colloq. irritate; nag pettily. — n. **1** trifling complaint or criticism; worry or annoyance. **2** twinge of pain (a niggle in my tooth). □ **niggling** adj. **niggly** adj. [origin unknown]

**nigh** /nuy/ adv., prep., & adj. archaic near. [Old English]

**night** /nuyt/ n. **1** period of darkness between one day and the next; time from sunset to sunrise. **2** nightfall. **3** darkness of night. **4** night or evening appointed for some activity regarded in a certain way (last night of the play). [Old English]

**nightcap** n. **1** hist. cap worn in bed. **2** hot or alcoholic drink taken at bedtime.

**nightclub** n. club providing refreshment and entertainment late at night.

**nightfall** n. end of daylight.

**nightie** n. colloq. woman's or girl's loose garment worn in bed.

**nightingale** /**nuy**-ting-,gayl/ n. small reddish-brown European bird, of which the male sings melodiously, esp. at night. [Old English = night-singer]

**nightjar** n. any of various nocturnal birds including the spotted nightjar and the owlet nightjar of Australia.

**nightlife** n. entertainment available at night in a city.

**nightly** — adj. **1** happening, done, or existing in the night. **2** recurring every night. — adv. every night.

**nightmare** n. **1** frightening dream. **2** colloq. frightening or unpleasant experience or situation. **3** haunting fear. □ **nightmarish** adj. [evil spirit (incubus) once thought to lie on and suffocate sleepers: Old English mære incubus]

**night parrot** n. rare, nocturnal, ground-dwelling parrot of arid and semi-arid Australia, having predominantly green, yellow, and black plumage.

**night school** n. institution providing classes in the evening.

**nightshade** n. any of various plants with poisonous berries, esp. 'deadly night-

shade' (Atropa belladonna) of Europe (extending into Asia) from which the drug atropine is extracted. [Old English]

**nightwatchman** n. **1** person employed to keep watch at night. **2** Cricket inferior batsman sent in near the close of a day's play.

**nihilism** /**nuy**-uh-,liz-uhm/ n. **1** rejection of all religious and moral principles. **2** belief that nothing really exists. □ **nihilist** n. **nihilistic** /-lis-tik/ adj. [Latin nihil nothing]

**-nik** suffix forming nouns denoting a person associated with a specified thing or quality (beatnik). [Russian (as SPUTNIK) and Yiddish]

**Nikkei index** /**nik**-ay/ n. (also **Nikkei average**) a figure indicating the relative price of representative shares on the Tokyo Stock Exchange. [Japanese]

**nil** n. nothing; no number or amount (esp. as a score in games). [Latin]

**nimble** /**nim**-buhl/ adj. (**-bler**, **-blest**) **1** quick and light in movement or action; agile. **2** (of the mind) quick to comprehend; clever, versatile. □ **nimbly** adv. [Old English, = quick to seize]

**nimbus** /**nim**-buhs/ n. (pl. **nimbi** /-buy/ or **nimbuses**) **1** halo of a saint etc. **2** rain-cloud. [Latin, = cloud]

**nimby** /**nim**-bee/ — adj. selfishly objecting to the siting of essential but unpleasant developments (new prisons, hospitals, airports, etc.) in one's own locality, although happy to have them sited elsewhere. — n. (pl. **-ies**) person who so objects. [not in my back yard]

**nincompoop** /**ning**-kuhm-,poop/ n. foolish person. [origin unknown]

**nine** adj. & n. **1** one more than eight. **2** symbol for this (9, ix, IX). [Old English]

**nine days' wonder** n. person or thing that is briefly famous.

**ninefold** adj. & adv. **1** nine times as much or as many. **2** consisting of nine parts.

**ninepin** n. **1** (in pl.; usu. treated as sing.) game in which nine pins are bowled at. **2** pin used in this game.

**niner** n. (also **nine**) keg formerly containing nine gallons of beer, now 40.5 litres.

**nineteen** /nuyn-**teen**/ adj. & n. **1** one more than eighteen. **2** symbol for this (19, xix, XIX). □ **talk nineteen to the dozen** see DOZEN. □ **nineteenth** adj. & n. [Old English]

**ninety** /**nuyn**-tee/ adj. & n. (pl. **-ies**) **1** product of nine and ten. **2** symbol for this (90, xc, XC). **3** (in pl.) numbers from 90 to 99, esp. the years of a century or of a person's life. □ **ninetieth** adj. & n. [Old English]

**ning-nong** *n. colloq.* a fool. [British dial.]

**ninny** /**nin**-ee/ *n.* (*pl.* **-ies**) foolish person. [origin uncertain]

**ninth** /nuynth/ *adj. & n.* **1** next after eighth. **2** any of nine equal parts of a thing. □ **ninthly** *adv.*

**niobium** /nuy-**oh**-bee-uhm/ *n.* rare metallic element occurring naturally. [*Niobe* in Greek legend]

**Nip** *n. colloq. offens.* Japanese person. [abbreviation of *Nipponese* from Japanese *Nippon* Japan]

**nip¹** — *v.* (**-pp-**) **1** pinch, squeeze, or bite sharply. **2** (often foll. by *off*) remove by pinching etc. (*nip off the topmost buds*). **3** (of the cold etc.) cause pain or harm to. **4** (foll. by *in, out, down,* etc.) *colloq.* go nimbly or quickly (*nip down to the milk bar*). **5** (foll. by *over*) *colloq.* pay a short visit (to) (*nip over for a chat*). **6** *colloq.* cadge (*nipped him for a loan*) (see BITE *n. & v.*). **7** *colloq.* steal. — *n.* **1 a** pinch, sharp squeeze. **b** bite. **2** biting cold (*a nip in the air*). □ **nip and tuck** *Australian Rules* (in a game) with one team matching the other's scores throughout. **nip in the bud** suppress or destroy (esp. an idea) at an early stage. **put the nip in** (or **into**) (a person) *colloq.* cadge (from). [Low German or Dutch]

**nip²** *n.* small quantity of spirits. [from *nipperkin* small measure]

**nipper** *n.* **1** person or thing that nips. **2 a** claw of a crab etc. **b** any of several small Australian marine crustaceans commonly used as bait. **3** *colloq.* **a** young child. **b** youth employed to do odd jobs (e.g. tea-making) in a labouring gang. **4** (in *pl.*) any tool for gripping or cutting.

**nipple** /**nip**-uhl/ *n.* **1** small projection in which the mammary ducts of either sex of mammals terminate and from which in females milk is secreted for the young. **2** teat of a feeding-bottle. **3** device like a nipple in function. **4** nipple-like protuberance. [perhaps from *neb* tip]

**Nipponese** /,nip-uh-**neez**/ — *n.* (*pl.* same) Japanese person. — *adj.* Japanese. [Japanese *Nippon* Japan]

**nippy** *adj.* (**-ier, -iest**) *colloq.* **1** quick, nimble. **2** chilly, cold. [from NIP¹]

**nirvana** /ner-**vah**-nuh, neer-/ *n.* (in Buddhism) perfect bliss attained by the extinction of individuality. [Sanskrit, = extinction]

**Nissen hut** /**nis**-uhn/ *n.* tunnel-shaped hut of corrugated iron with a cement floor. [*Nissen*, name of an engineer]

**nit¹** *n.* **1** egg or young form of a louse or other parasitic insect. **2** *colloq.* stupid person. [Old English]

**nit²** *int. colloq.* used as a warning that someone is approaching. □ **keep nit** keep watch; act as guard. □ **nitkeeper** *n.* **nit-keeping** *n.* [origin unknown]

**nit-picking** *n. & adj. colloq.* fault-finding in a petty manner. □ **nit-picker** *n.*

**nitrate** — *n.* /**nuy**-trayt/ **1** any salt or ester of nitric acid. **2** potassium or sodium nitrate as a fertiliser. — *v.* /nuy-**trayt**/ (**-ting**) treat, combine, or impregnate with nitric acid. □ **nitration** /-**tray**-shuhn/ *n.* [French: related to NITRE]

**nitre** /**nuy**-tuh/ *n.* saltpetre. [Greek *nitron*]

**nitric** /**nuy**-trik/ *adj.* of or containing nitrogen.

**nitric acid** *n.* colourless corrosive poisonous liquid.

**nitride** /**nuy**-truyd/ *n.* binary compound of nitrogen. [from NITRE]

**nitrify** /**nuy**-truh-,fuy/ *v.* (**-ies, -ied**) **1** impregnate with nitrogen. **2** convert into nitrites or nitrates. □ **nitrification** /-fuh-**kay**-shuhn/ *n.* [French: related to NITRE]

**nitrite** /**nuy**-truyt/ *n.* any salt or ester of nitrous acid. [from NITRE]

**nitro** *n. colloq.* = NITROGLYCERINE. [abbreviation]

**nitro-** *comb. form* of or containing nitric acid, nitre, or nitrogen. [Greek: related to NITRE]

**nitrogen** /**nuy**-truh-juhn/ *n.* gaseous element that forms four-fifths of the atmosphere. □ **nitrogenous** /-**troj**-uh-nuhs/ *adj.* [French]

**nitrogen cycle** *n.* the interconversion of nitrogen and its compounds (usu. in the form of nitrates) in nature.

**nitrogen fixation** *n.* chemical process in which nitrogen in the atmosphere is assimilated into organic compounds in living organisms and hence into the nitrogen cycle.

**nitroglycerine** /,nuy-troh-**glis**-uh-reen, -**glis**-uh-ruhn/ *n.* explosive yellow liquid made by reacting glycerol with a mixture of concentrated sulphuric and nitric acids.

**nitrous oxide** /**nuy**-truhs/ *n.* colourless gas used as an anaesthetic. [Latin: related to NITRE]

**nitty-gritty** /,nit-ee-**grit**-ee/ *n. colloq.* realities or practical details of a matter. [origin uncertain]

**nitwit** *n. colloq.* stupid person. [perhaps from NIT, WIT]

**nix** *colloq.* — *n.* **1** nothing. **2** a denial or refusal. — *v.* cancel; reject (*the board nixed the project*). [German, colloquial variant of *nichts* nothing]

**NNE** *abbr.* north-north-east.

**NNW** *abbr.* north-north-west.

**No¹** *symb.* nobelium.

**No²** var. of NOH.

**No.** *abbr.* number. [Latin *numero*, ablative of *numerus* number]

**no¹** /noh/ *adj.* **1** not any (*there is no excuse*). **2** not a, quite other than (*is no fool*). **3** hardly any (*did it in no time*). **4** used elliptically in a notice etc., to forbid etc. the thing specified (*no parking*). □ **no way** *colloq.* **1** it is impossible. **2** I will not agree etc. **no wonder** see WONDER. [related to NONE]

**no²** /noh/ — *adv.* **1** indicating that the answer to the question is negative, the statement etc. made or course of action intended or conclusion arrived at is not correct or satisfactory, the request or command will not be complied with, or the negative statement made is correct. **2** (foll. by *compar.*) by no amount; not at all (*no better than before*). — *n.* (*pl.* **noes**) **1** utterance of the word *no*. **2** denial or refusal. **3 a** 'no' vote. **b** (in *pl.*) 'no' voters or votes (*the noes have it*). □ **no longer** not as before. **or no** or not (*pleasant or no, it is true*). [Old English]

**Noah** *n. colloq.* a shark. [abbreviation of *Noah's ark*, rhyming slang]

**nob¹** *n. colloq.* person of wealth or high social position. [origin unknown]

**nob²** *n. colloq.* two-headed coin, esp. in the game of two-up. [from KNOB]

**no-ball** *n.* Cricket unlawfully delivered ball.

**nobble** /**nob**-uhl/ *v.* (**-ling**) *colloq.* **1** try to influence (e.g. a jury or a judge), esp. unfairly. **2** tamper with (a racehorse) to prevent its winning. **3** steal. **4** seize, catch. [British dial. *knobble* beat]

**nobbler** *n. colloq.* a measure of spirits or the glass in which this is served. [from NOBBLE]

**nobby¹** *n.* irregularly shaped opal.

**nobby²** *adj.* (of a beast) lean, and therefore having protuberant bones, joints, etc. [from British dial. *knobby* lumpy]

**nobelium** /noh-**bee**-lee-uhm/ *n.* artificially produced radioactive transuranic metallic element. [from *Nobel*: see NOBEL PRIZE]

**Nobel Prize** /**noh**-bel, -**bel**/ *n.* any of six international prizes awarded annually for physics, chemistry, physiology or medicine, literature, economics, and the promotion of peace. [from *Nobel*, Swedish chemist and engineer, who endowed them]

**nobility** /noh-**bil**-uh-tee/ *n.* (*pl.* **-ies**) **1** nobleness of character, mind, birth, or rank. **2** class of nobles, highest social class.

**noble** /**noh**-buhl/ — *adj.* (**nobler**, **noblest**) **1** belonging to the aristocracy. **2** of excellent character; having lofty ideals; magnanimous. **3** of imposing appearance. — *n.* nobleman, noblewoman. □ **nobleness** *n.* **nobly** *adv.* [Latin (g)*nobilis*]

**noble gas** *n.* any of a group of gaseous elements that almost never combine with other elements.

**noblesse oblige** /noh-,bles oh-**bleezh** /*n.* privilege entails responsibility. [French]

**nobody** /**noh**-bod-ee, -buh-dee/ — *pron.* no person. — *n.* (*pl.* **-ies**) person of no importance. □ **like nobody's business** *colloq.* at a rapid rate; energetically (*went through the chores like nobody's business*).

**nock** *v.* set an arrow to the bowstring. [Dutch]

**no-claim bonus** *n.* (also **no-claims bonus**) reduction of an insurance premium after an agreed period without a claim.

**nocturnal** /nok-**ter**-nuhl/ *adj.* of or in the night; done or active by night. [Latin *nox noct-* night]

**nocturnal emission** *n.* involuntary emission of semen during sleep.

**nocturne** /**nok**-tern/ *n. Mus.* short romantic composition, usu. for piano. [French]

**nod** — *v.* (**-dd-**) **1** incline one's head slightly and briefly in assent, greeting, or command. **2** let one's head fall forward in drowsiness; be drowsy. **3** incline (one's head). **4** signify (assent etc.) by a nod. **5** (of flowers, plumes, etc.) bend downwards and sway. **6** make a mistake due to a momentary lack of alertness or attention. — *n.* nodding of the head. □ **get the nod** be chosen or approved. **give the nod to** approve; permit. **nod off** *colloq.* fall asleep. **on the nod** on credit. [origin unknown]

**nodding blue lily** *n.* (also **stypandra**) tufted perennial plant of southern and eastern Australia, having starry, bright blue flowers with golden anthers borne on slender, nodding stalks.

**nodding greenhood** *n.* Australian terrestrial orchid (a pterostylis), commonest of the greenhoods, having large, nodding, translucent, pale green flowers striped a deeper green, with crimson at the tips.

**node** *n.* **1 a** part of a plant stem from which leaves emerge. **b** knob on a root or branch. **2** *Anat.* natural swelling or bulge. **3** either of two points at which a planet's orbit intersects the plane of the ecliptic or the celestial equator. **4** point of minimum disturbance in a standing wave system. **5** point at which a curve intersects itself. **6** component in a computer network. □ **nodal** adj. [Latin *nodus* knot]

**nodule** /**nod**-yool, **noj**-ool/ n. **1** small rounded lump of anything. **2** small tumour, node, or ganglion, or a swelling on the root of a legume containing bacteria etc. □ **nodular** adj. [Latin diminutive: related to NODE]

**Noel** /noh-**el**/ n. Christmas. [Latin: related to NATAL]

**noggin** /**nog**-uhn/ n. **1** small mug. **2** small measure, usu. ¼ pint, of spirits. **3** *colloq.* head. [origin unknown]

**no go** adj. (usu. hyphenated when *attrib.*) *colloq.* impossible; hopeless; forbidden; dangerous (*tried to get him to agree, but it was clearly no go; no-go area*).

**Noh** /noh/ n. (also **No**) traditional Japanese drama. [Japanese]

**no-hoper** n. *colloq.* incompetent or ineffectual person; a failure.

**noise** /noiz/ — n. **1** sound, esp. a loud or unpleasant one. **2** series or confusion of loud sounds, esp. shouts etc. **3** extraneous signal in an electronic or communication system. **4** (in *pl.*) conventional remarks, or speechlike sounds without actual words (*made sympathetic noises*). — v. (**-sing**) (usu. in *passive*) make public; spread abroad (a person's fame or a fact, rumour, etc.). [Latin NAUSEA]

**noiseless** adj. making little or no noise. □ **noiselessly** adv.

**noisome** /**noi**-suhm/ adj. *literary* **1** harmful, noxious. **2** evil-smelling. [from ANNOY]

**noisy** adj. (**-ier, -iest**) **1** making much noise (*noisy bunch of kids*). **2** full of noise (*noisy marketplace*). □ **noisily** adv. **noisiness** n.

**noisy friar-bird** see LEATHERHEAD.

**noisy miner** n. eastern Australian honeyeater, a predominantly grey and white bird with black face-markings, and given to very noisy calls.

**noisy pitta** n. (also **anvil bird**) rainforest bird of north-eastern Queensland, having a loud, whistling call.

**noisy scrub-bird** n. rare, grounddwelling, predominantly brown bird of south-western WA, having a loud, penetrating whistle and inhabiting areas of dense, heathy vegetation.

**nomad** /**noh**-mad/ n. **1** member of a tribe roaming from place to place for hunting and gathering or for pasture. **2** any wanderer. □ **nomadic** /-**mad**-ik/ adj. [Greek *nomas nomad-* from *nemō* to pasture]

**no man's land** n. **1** space between two opposing armies. **2** any place, e.g. wilderness, that is potentially dangerous. **3**
area not assigned to any owner. **4** place, situation, etc., that is unfamiliar, uncharted (*in the no man's land between waking and sleep*).

**nom de plume** /,nom duh **ploom**/ n. (*pl.* **noms de plume** pronunc. same) writer's assumed name. [sham French, = penname]

**nomenclature** /nuh-**men**-kluh-chuh, **noh**-muhn-,klay-chuh/ n. **1** person's or community's system of names for things. **2** terminology of a science etc. **3** systematic naming. [Latin *nomen* name, *calo* call]

**nominal** /**nom**-uh-nuhl/ adj. **1** existing in name only; not real or actual (*nominal ruler*). **2** (of a sum of money, price, rent, etc.) very small. **3** of or in names. **4** of, as, or like a noun. □ **nominally** adv. [Latin *nomen* name]

**nominalism** n. doctrine that universals or general ideas are mere names. □ **nominalist** n. **nominalistic** /-lis-tik/ adj.

**nominal value** n. face value.

**nominate** /**nom**-uh-,nayt/ v. (**-ting**) **1 a** put one's name forward as standing for election. **b** propose (a candidate) for election. **2** appoint to an office. **3** name or appoint (a date or place). □ **nomination** /,nom-uh-**nay**-shuhn/ n. **nominator** n. [Latin: related to NOMINAL]

**nominative** /**nom**-uh-nuh-tiv/ *Gram.* — n. case expressing the subject of a verb. — adj. of or in this case.

**nominee** /,nom-uh-**nee**/ n. person who is nominated.

**-nomy** /nuh-mee/ *comb. form* denoting an area of knowledge or the laws governing it (*agronomy; economy*).

**non-** *prefix* giving the negative sense of words with which it is combined. [Latin *non* not]

■ **Usage** The number of words that can be formed from the prefix *non-* is unlimited; consequently, only the most current and noteworthy will be given here.

**non-Aboriginal** — adj. not Aboriginal. — n. non-Aboriginal person.

**nonagenarian** /,noh-nuh-juh-**nair**-ree-uhn, ,non-uh-/ n. person from 90 to 99 years old. [Latin *nonageni* ninety each]

**non-aggression** /,non-uh-**gresh**-uhn/ n. lack of or restraint from aggression (often *attrib.*: *non-aggression pact*).

**nonagon** /**non**-uh-guhn/ n. plane figure with nine sides and angles. [Latin *nonus* ninth, after HEXAGON]

**non-aligned** /,non-uh-**luynd**/ adj. (of a nation etc.) not aligned with a major power. □ **non-alignment** n.

**no-name** *adj.* of or pertaining to products not sold under a company's brand name (*tin of no-name asparagus tips*).

**non-belligerent** /ˌnon-buh-**lij**-uh-ruhnt/ — *adj.* not engaged in hostilities. — *n.* non-belligerent nation etc.

**non-Catholic** — *adj.* not Roman Catholic. — *n.* non-Catholic person.

**nonce** *n.* □ **for the nonce** for the time being; for the present occasion. [from *for than anes* = for the one]

**nonce-word** *n.* word coined for one occasion.

**nonchalant** /**non**-shuh-luhnt/ *adj.* calm and casual. □ **nonchalance** *n.* **nonchalantly** *adv.* [French *chaloir* be concerned]

**non-combatant** /ˌnon-**kom**-buh-tuhnt/ *n.* person not fighting in a war, esp. a civilian, army chaplain, etc.

**non-commissioned** *adj.* (of an officer, as a corporal etc.) not holding a commission.

**non-committal** /ˌnon-kuh-**mit**-uhl/ *adj.* avoiding commitment to a definite opinion or course of action.

**non compos mentis** /ˌnon kom-pos **men**-tis/ *adj.* (also **non compos**) not in one's right mind. [Latin, = not having control of one's mind]

**non-conductor** *n.* substance that does not conduct heat or electricity.

**nonconformist** /ˌnon-kuhn-**faw**-muhst/ *n.* **1** *Brit.* person who does not conform to the doctrine or discipline of an established Church, esp. (**Nonconformist**) member of a (Protestant) sect dissenting from the Church of England. **2** person who does not conform to a prevailing principle.

**nonconformity** /ˌnon-kuhn-**faw**-muh-tee/ *n.* **1** (usu. foll. by *to*) failure to conform. **2** lack of correspondence between things. **3** noncomformists as a body, or their principles.

**non-contributory** /ˌnon-kuhn-**trib**-yuh-tuh-ree, -tree/ *adj.* not involving contributions.

**nonda** /**non**-duh/ *n.* tree yielding edible, plum-like, yellow fruit and growing in groves on sand ridges in northern Queensland and the NT. [probably from a Queensland Aboriginal language]

**nondescript** /**non**-duh-skript/ — *adj.* lacking distinctive characteristics, not easily classified, neither one thing nor another. — *n.* nondescript person or thing. [related to DESCRIBE]

**none** /nun/ — *pron.* **1** (foll. by *of*) **a** not any of (*none of this concerns me; none of them have found it*). **b** not any one of (*none of them has come*). **2 a** no persons (*none but fools believe it*). **b** no person (*none but a fool believes it*). **3** (usu. with the preceding noun implied) not any (*you have money and I have none*). — *adv.* (foll. by *the* + compar., or *so, too*) by no amount; not at all (*am none the wiser*). [Old English, = not one]

■ **Usage** In sense 1b, the verb following *none* can be singular or plural according to meaning.

**nonentity** /non-**en**-tuh-tee/ *n.* (*pl.* **-ies**) **1** person or thing of no importance. **2 a** non-existence. **b** non-existent thing. [medieval Latin]

**nonetheless** /ˌnun-thuh-**les**/ *adv.* (also **none the less**) nevertheless.

**non-event** *n.* insignificant event, esp. contrary to hopes or expectations.

**non-ferrous** /non-**fe**-ruhs/ *adj.* (of a metal) other than iron or steel.

**non-fiction** *n.* literary work other than fiction (e.g. biography, a historical work, etc.).

**non-flammable** *adj.* not inflammable.

**nong** *n.* (also **ning-nong**) *colloq.* foolish or stupid person.

**non-interference** *n.* = NON-INTERVENTION.

**non-intervention** *n.* (esp. political) principle or practice of not becoming involved in others' affairs.

**non-nuclear** *adj.* **1** not involving nuclei or nuclear energy. **2** (of a nation etc.) not having nuclear weapons.

**no-no** *n. colloq.* (*pl.* **-es**) something that is to be avoided at all costs, that is completely 'not on' (*smoking in a restaurant ought to be a no-no*).

**no-nonsense** *adj. colloq.* **1** practical, businesslike. **2** strict (*had a no-nonsense attitude to child-raising*). **3** straightforward, unfussy (*wore no-nonsense clothes*).

**nonpareil** /**non**-puh-rel, ˌnon-puh-**rayl**/ — *adj.* unrivalled or unique. — *n.* such a person or thing. [French *pareil*]

**nonplus** /non-**plus**/ — *v.* (**-ss-**) completely perplex. — *n.* state of complete perplexity (*at a nonplus*). [Latin *non plus* not more]

**non-proliferation** /ˌnon-pruh-ˌlif-uh-**ray**-shuhn/ *n.* prevention of an increase in something, esp. possession of nuclear weapons.

**non-resident** /non-**rez**-uh-duhnt/ — *adj.* **1** not living on the premises (*a non-resident caretaker*). **2** (of a job) not requiring the holder to live in. — *n.* **a** person not staying at a hotel etc. □ **non-residential** /-**den**-shuhl/ *adj.*

**non-resistance** /ˌnon-ruh-**zis**-tuhns/ *n.* practice or principle of not resisting authority.

**nonsense** /**non**-suhns/ *n.* **1** (often as

*int.*) absurd or meaningless words or ideas. **2** foolish or extravagant conduct. □ **nonsensical** /-**sen**-si-kuhl/ *adj.* **nonsensically** /-**sen**-si-kuhl-lee, -klee/ *adv.*

**non sequitur** /non **sek**-wi-tuh/ *n.* conclusion that does not logically follow from the premises. [Latin, = it does not follow]

**non-starter** *n. colloq.* person or scheme that is unlikely to succeed.

**non-stick** *adj.* that does not allow things to stick to it (*non-stick frypan*).

**non-stop** — *adj.* **1** (of a train etc.) not stopping at intermediate places. **2** done without a stop or intermission. — *adv.* without stopping.

**non-U** /non-**yoo**/ *adj. colloq.* not characteristic of the upper class. [from U²]

**non-verbal** /non-**ver**-buhl/ *adj.* not involving words or speech.

**non-violence** *n.* avoidance of violence, esp. as a principle. □ **non-violent** *adj.*

**non-voting** *adj.* **1** not having or using a vote. **2** (of shares) not entitling the holder to vote.

**noodle¹** /**noo**-duhl/ *n.* strip or ring of pasta. [German]

**noodle²** /**noo**-duhl/ *n.* **1** simpleton. **2** *colloq.* head. □ **use one's noodle** *colloq.* use one's brains, think for oneself. [origin unknown]

**noodle³** *v.* search (an opal-mining dump) for opals that may have been unwittingly discarded. □ **noodler** *n.* [origin unknown]

**nook** /nuuk/ *n.* corner or recess; secluded place. [origin unknown]

**noolbenger** /**nool**-beng-guh/ *n.* Australian honey-possum which has a long snout and brush-tipped tongue. [Nyungar, probably *ngulbunggur*]

**noon** *n.* **1** twelve o'clock in the day, midday. **2** peak or brightest point. [Latin *nona (hora)* ninth (hour): originally = 3 p.m.]

**noonday** *n.* midday.

**no one** *n.* (also **no-one**) no person; nobody.

**Noongah** var. of NYOONGAH.

**noose** — *n.* **1** loop with a running knot. **2** snare, bond. — *v.* (**-sing**) catch with or enclose in a noose. [French *no(u)s* from Latin *nodus* NODE]

**nor** *conj.* **1** and not; and not either (*neither one thing nor the other; not a man nor a child was to be seen; I said I had not seen it, nor had I; can neither read nor write*). **2** and no more; neither (*I cannot go. — Nor can I.*). [contraction of obsolete *nother*: related to NO², WHETHER]

**nor'** /naw/ *n., adj., & adv.* (esp. in compour.ds) = NORTH (*nor'wester*). [abbreviation]

**Nordic** /**naw**-dik/ — *adj.* of the tall blond long-headed Germanic people of Scandinavia. — *n.* Nordic person. [French *nord* north]

**Norfolk Island** /**naw**-fuhk/ *n. hist.* used *attrib.* in allusion to the penal settlement for convicts established on the island (1788-1814 and 1825-1856). [name of an island some 1500 kilometres north-east of Sydney]

**Norfolk Island pine** *n.* tall coniferous tree of Norfolk Island, having a symmetrical, conical shape; widely planted elsewhere in Australia.

**norm** *n.* **1** standard, pattern, or type. **2** standard amount of work etc. **3** customary behaviour etc. [Latin *norma* carpenter's square]

**Norm** *n.* satirical 'norm' of the Australian male, an overweight and unfit slob who takes no exercise and spends all his leisure hours watching sport on television and drinking beer. [cartoon-character invented for the *Life, Be In It* campaign on television]

**normal** /**naw**-muhl/ — *adj.* **1** conforming to a standard; regular, usual, typical. **2** free from mental or emotional disorder. **3** *Geom.* (of a line) at right angles, perpendicular. **4** *Chem.* (of a solution) containing one gram-equivalent of solute per litre. — *n.* **1 a** normal value of a temperature etc. **b** usual state, level, etc. **2** line at right angles. □ **normalcy** *n.* **normality** /-**mal**-uh-tee/ *n.* [Latin *normalis*: related to NORM]

**normal distribution** *n.* function that represents the distribution of many random variables as a symmetrical bell-shaped graph.

**normalise** *v.* (also **-ize**) (**-sing** or **-zing**) **1** make or become normal. **2** cause to conform. □ **normalisation** /-**zay**-shuhn/ *n.*

**normally** *adv.* **1** in a normal manner. **2** usually.

**Norman** /**naw**-muhn/ — *n.* **1** native or inhabitant of medieval Normandy. **2** descendant of the people of mixed Scandinavian and Frankish origin established there in the 10th-c. **3** style of architecture found in Britain under the Normans. — *adj.* **1** of the Normans. **2** of the Norman style of architecture. [Old Norse, = North Man]

**Norman French** *n.* French as spoken by the Normans or (after 1066) in English lawcourts.

**normative** /**naw**-muh-tiv/ *adj.* of or establishing a norm. [Latin: related to NORM]

**Norn** /nawn/ *n.* any of three goddesses of destiny in Scandinavian mythology. [Old Norse]

**norne** /nawn/ n. black, highly venomous tiger snake which feeds largely on frogs and small animals. [Nyungar, probably *nurn*]

**Norse** — n. **1** Norwegian language. **2** Scandinavian language-group. — adj. of ancient Scandinavia, esp. Norway. □ **Norseman** n. [Dutch *noor(d)sch* northern]

**north** — n. **1 a** point of the horizon 90° anticlockwise from east. **b** compass point corresponding to this. **c** direction in which this lies. **2** (usu. **the North**) part of the world or a country or city lying to the north. — adj. **1** towards, at, near, or facing the north. **2** from the north (*north wind*). — adv. **1** towards, at, or near the north. **2** (foll. by *of*) further north than. □ **to the north** (often foll. by *of*) in a northerly direction. [Old English]

**North American** — adj. of North America. — n. native or inhabitant of North America, esp. a citizen of the US or Canada.

**north-east** — n. **1** point of the horizon midway between north and east. **2** direction in which this lies. — adj. of, towards, or coming from the north-east. — adv. towards, at, or near the north-east.

**northeaster** n. north-east wind.

**north-easterly** adj. & adv. = NORTH-EAST.

**north-eastern** adj. on the north-east side.

**northerly** /naw-thuh-lee/ — adj. & adv. **1** in a northern position or direction. **2** (of wind) from the north. — n. (pl. **-ies**) such a wind.

**northern** /naw-thuhn/ adj. of or in the north. □ **northernmost** adj. [Old English]

**northerner** n. native or inhabitant of the north.

**Northern hemisphere** n. the half of the earth north of the equator.

**northern lights** n.pl. aurora borealis.

**Northern Territorian** see TERRITORIAN.

**north-north-east** n. point or direction midway between north and north-east.

**north-north-west** n. point or direction midway between north and north-west.

**North Pole** n. northernmost point of the earth's axis of rotation.

**North Star** n. pole star.

**northward** /nawth-wuhd/ — adj. & adv. (also **northwards**) towards the north. — n. northward direction or region.

**north-west** — n. **1** point of the horizon midway between north and west. **2** direction in which this lies. — adj. of, towards, or coming from the north-west. — adv. towards, at, or near the north-west.

**northwester** n. north-west wind.

**north-westerly** adj. & adv. = NORTH-WEST.

**north-western** adj. on the north-west side.

**Norwegian** /naw-wee-juhn/ — n. **1 a** native or national of Norway. **b** person of Norwegian descent. **2** language of Norway. — adj. of or relating to Norway. [medieval Latin *Norvegia* from Old Norse, = northway]

**nor'wester** /naw-wes-tuh/ n. **1** north-wester. **2** inhabitant of north-western Australia.

**Nos.** pl. of No.

**nose** /nohz/ — n. **1** organ above the mouth of a human or animal, used for smelling and breathing. **2 a** sense of smell (*dogs have a good nose*). **b** ability to detect a particular thing (*a nose for scandal*). **3** odour or perfume of wine etc. **4** front end or projecting part of a thing, e.g. of a car or aircraft. — v. (**-sing**) **1** (usu. foll. by *about*, *around*, etc.) pry, eavesdrop, search, etc. **2** (often foll. by *out*) **a** perceive the smell of, discover by smell. **b** detect. **3** thrust one's nose against or into. **4** make one's way cautiously forward. □ **by a nose** by a very narrow margin. **get up a person's nose** colloq. annoy a person. **keep one's nose clean** colloq. stay out of trouble. **on the nose** colloq. **1** having an offensive smell (because rotten) (*the meat's on the nose*). **2** (of a person, behaviour, etc.) having the odour of moral corruption. **poke one's nose into** see POKE[1]. **put a person's nose out of joint** colloq. annoy; make envious. **turn up one's nose** (usu. foll. by *at*) colloq. show disdain. **under a person's nose** colloq. right before a person. **with one's nose in the air** haughtily. [Old English]

**nosebag** n. bag containing fodder, hung on a horse's head.

**nosedive** — n. **1** steep downward plunge by an aeroplane. **2** sudden plunge or drop. — v. (**-ving**) make a nosedive.

**nosegay** n. small bunch of sweet-scented flowers; posy.

**nosh** colloq. — v. eat. — n. a meal. [Yiddish]

**noshery** /nosh-uh-ree/ n. colloq. restaurant (or similar place in which a meal may be had).

**nosh-up** n. colloq. large meal; a good feed.

**nostalgia** /nos-tal-jee-uh, -juh/ n. **1** (often foll. by *for*) yearning for a past period. **2** severe homesickness. □ **nostalgic** adj. **nostalgically** adv. [Greek *nostos* a return home, -ALGIA]

**nostril** /**nos**-truhl/ n. either of the two openings in the nose. [Old English, = nose-hole]

**nostrum** /**nos**-truhm/ n. **1** quack remedy, patent medicine. **2** pet scheme, esp. for political or social reform. [Latin, = 'of our own make']

**nosy** adj. (**-ier**, **-iest**) colloq. inquisitive, prying. □ **nosily** adv. **nosiness** n.

**nosy parker** n. colloq. busybody; sticky-beak.

**not** adv. expressing negation, esp.: **1** (also **n't** joined to a preceding verb) following an auxiliary verb or be or (in a question) the subject of such a verb (I cannot say; she isn't there; am I not right?). **2** used elliptically for a negative phrase etc. (Is she coming? — I hope not; Do you want it? — Certainly not!). □ **not at all** (in polite reply to thanks) there is no need for thanks. **not half** see HALF. **not quite 1** almost. **2** noticeably not (not quite proper). [contraction of NOUGHT]

■ **Usage** The use of not with verbs other than auxiliaries or be is now archaic (I know not; fear not), except with participles and infinitives (not knowing, I cannot say; we asked them not to come).

**notable** /**noh**-tuh-buhl/ — adj. worthy of note; remarkable, eminent. — n. eminent person. □ **notability** /ˌnoh-tuh-**bil**-uh-tee/ n. **notably** adv. [Latin noto NOTE]

**notary** /**noh**-tuh-ree/ n. (pl. **-ies**) (in full **notary public**) solicitor etc. who attests or certifies deeds etc. □ **notarial** /noh-**tair**-ree-uhl/ adj. [Latin notarius secretary]

**notation** /noh-**tay**-shuhn/ n. **1** representation of numbers, quantities, the pitch and duration of musical notes, etc., by symbols. **2** any set of such symbols. [Latin: related to NOTE]

**notch** — n. **1** V-shaped indentation on an edge or surface. **2** nick made on a stick etc. in order to keep count. **3** colloq. step or degree (moved up a notch). — v. **1** make notches in. **2** (usu. foll. by up) record or score with or as with notches (notched up ten more goals after half-time; notched up a huge success with her new song). [Anglo-French]

**note** — n. **1** brief written record as an aid to memory (often in pl.: make notes). **2** observation, usu. unwritten, of experiences etc. (compare notes). **3** short or informal letter. **4** formal diplomatic communication. **5** short annotation or additional explanation in a book etc. **6 a** = BANKNOTE (ten-dollar note). **b** written promise of payment. **7 a** notice, attention (worthy of note). **b** eminence (person of note). **8 a** single musical tone of definite pitch. **b** written sign representing its pitch and duration. **c** key of a piano etc. **9** quality or tone of speaking, expressing mood or attitude etc. (note of optimism). — v. (**-ting**) **1** observe, notice; give attention to. **2** (often foll. by down) record as a thing to be remembered or observed. **3** (in passive; often foll. by for) be well known (noted for her wit). □ **hit** (or **strike**) **the right note** speak or act in exactly the right manner. [Latin nota mark (n.), noto mark (v.)]

**noteworthy** adj. worthy of attention; remarkable.

**nothing** /**nuth**-ing/ — n. **1** not anything (nothing has been done). **2** no thing (often foll. by compl.: I see nothing that I want). **3** person or thing of no importance or concern (was nothing to me). **4** non-existence; what does not exist. **5** no amount; nought. — adv. not at all, in no way (is nothing like enough; helps us nothing). □ **be** (or **have**) **nothing to do with 1** have no connection with. **2** not be involved or associated with. **for nothing 1** at no cost. **2** to no purpose. **have nothing on 1** be naked. **2** have no engagements. **nothing doing** colloq. **1** no prospect of success or agreement. **2** I refuse. **nothing** (or **nothing else**) **for it** (often foll. by but to + infin.) no alternative (nothing for it but to pay up). **nothing** (or **not much**) **in it** (or **to it**) **1** untrue or unimportant. **2** simple to do. **3** no (or little) advantage to be seen in one possibility over another. **nothing to write home about** not all that remarkable or interesting. **think nothing of it** do not apologise or feel bound to show gratitude. [Old English: related to NO[1], THING]

**nothingness** n. **1** non-existence. **2** worthlessness, triviality.

**notice** /**noh**-tuhs/ — n. **1** attention, observation (escaped my notice). **2** displayed sheet etc. bearing an announcement. **3 a** intimation or warning, esp. a formal one (give notice; a month's notice). **b** formal announcement or declaration of intention to end an agreement or leave employment at a specified time. **4** short published review of a new play, book, etc. — v. (**-cing**) (often foll. by that, how, etc.) **1** perceive, observe; take notice of (noticed that the pipe was leaking; notice the statue on the left!). **2** remark upon; speak of. □ **at short** (or **a moment's**) **notice** with little warning. **take notice** (or **no notice**) show signs (or no signs) of interest. **take notice of 1** observe. **2** act upon. [Latin notus known]

**noticeable** adj. perceptible; noteworthy. □ **noticeably** adv.

**notifiable** /**noh**-tuh-ˌfuy-uh-buhl/ *adj.*
(of a disease etc.) that must be notified to
the health authorities.

**notify** /**noh**-tuh-ˌfuy/ *v.* (**-ies**, **-ied**) **1**
(often foll. by *of* or *that*) inform or give
formal notice to (a person). **2** make
known. □ **notification** /-fuh-**kay**-shuhn/ *n.*
[Latin *notus* known]

**notion** /**noh**-shuhn/ *n.* **1 a** a concept or
idea; conception (*an absurd notion*). **b**
opinion (*has the notion that everyone is
honest*). **c** vague view or understanding
(*have no notion what you mean*). **2**
inclination or intention (*has no notion of
conforming*). [Latin *notio*: related to
NOTIFY]

**notional** *adj.* **1** hypothetical, imaginary.
**2** (of knowledge etc.) speculative; not
based on experiment etc. □ **notionally** *adv.*

**not on** *predic. adj. colloq.* not to be
countenanced or tolerated, totally unacceptable (*violence in marriage is just not
on*).

**notorious** /nuh-**taw**-ree-uhs/ *adj.* well-
known, esp. unfavourably (*a notorious
criminal; notorious for its climate*).
□ **notoriety** /-tuh-**ruy**-uh-tee/ *n.* **notoriously** *adv.* [Latin *notus* known]

**notwithstanding** /ˌnot-with-**stan**-ding/
— *prep.* in spite of; without prevention by
(*notwithstanding your objections*). — *adv.*
nevertheless; all the same. — *conj.* (usu.
foll. by *that* + clause) although. [from NOT,
WITHSTAND]

**nougat** /**noo**-gah/ *n.* sweet made from
sugar or honey, nuts, and egg white.
[French from Provençal]

**nought** /nawt/ *n.* **1** digit 0; cipher. **2** *poet.*
or *archaic* nothing. [Old English: related
to NOT, AUGHT]

**noun** *n.* a word (other than a pronoun) or
a group of words used to name or identify
any of a class of persons, places, or things
(see panel). □ **nounal** *adj.* [Latin *nomen*
name]

**nourish** /**nu**-rish/ *v.* **1** sustain with food.
**2** foster or cherish (a feeling etc.). □ **nourishing** *adj.* [Latin *nutrio* to feed]

**nourishment** *n.* sustenance, food.

**nous** /nows/ *n.* **1** *colloq.* common sense;
gumption. **2** *Philos.* mind, intellect.
[Greek]

**nouveau riche** /ˌnoo-voh **reesh**/ *n.* (*pl.*
**nouveaux riches** pronunc. same) person
who has recently acquired (usu. ostentatious) wealth. [French, = new rich]

**nouvelle cuisine** /ˌnoo-vel kwi-**zeen**/ *n.*
modern style of cookery avoiding heaviness and emphasising presentation.
[French, = new cookery]

**nova** /**noh**-vuh/ *n.* (*pl.* **novae** /-vee/ or
**-s**) star showing a sudden burst of brightness and then subsiding. [Latin, = new]

**novel**[1] /**nov**-uhl/ *n.* fictitious prose story
of book length. [Latin *novus* new]

**novel**[2] /**nov**-uhl/ *adj.* of a new kind or
nature; strange; previously unknown.
[Latin *novus* new]

**novelese** /ˌnov-uh-**leez**/ *n. derog.* style
characteristic of inferior novels.

**novelette** /ˌnov-uh-**let**/ *n.* short novel,
esp. a light romantic one.

**novelist** /**nov**-uh-luhst/ *n.* writer of
novels.

---

**Noun**

A noun is the name of a person or thing. There are four kinds:
1  common nouns (the words for articles and creatures), e.g.

| | | |
|---|---|---|
| shoe | in | The red shoe was left on the shelf. |
| box | in | The large box stood in the corner. |
| plant | in | The plant grew to two metres. |
| horse | in | A horse galloped by. |

2  proper nouns (the names of people, places, ships, institutions, and animals, which
always begin with a capital letter), e.g.

| | | |
|---|---|---|
| Kylie | HMAS Melbourne | Skippy |
| Adelaide | Railway Hotel | Australian Institute of Sport |

3  abstract nouns (the words for qualities, things we cannot see or touch, and things
which have no physical reality), e.g.

| | | |
|---|---|---|
| truth | absence | love |
| explanation | warmth | experience |

4  collective nouns (the words for groups of things), e.g.

| | | |
|---|---|---|
| committee | squad | the Cabinet |
| herd | swarm | the clergy |
| majority | team | the public |

Nouns used *attributively* (i.e. preceding the word described) are designated *attrib.* when
their function is not fully adjectival (e.g. *model* in *a model student*; *the student is very
model* is not acceptable usage).

**novella** /nuh-**vel**-uh/ *n.* (*pl.* **-s**) short novel or narrative story. [Italian: related to NOVEL[1]]

**novelty** /**nov**-uhl-tee/ *n.* (*pl.* **-ies**) **1** newness; new character. **2** new or unusual thing or occurrence. **3** small toy or trinket. **4** (*attrib.*) having novelty (*novelty toys*). [related to NOVEL[2]]

**November** /noh-**vem**-buh, nuh-/ *n.* eleventh month of the year. [Latin *novem* nine, originally the 9th month of the Roman year]

**novena** /noh-**vee**-nuh, nuh-/ *n.* RC Ch. devotion consisting of special prayers or services on nine successive days. [Latin *novem* nine]

**novice** /**nov**-uhs/ *n.* **1** probationary member of a religious order, before the taking of vows. **2** beginner; inexperienced person. [Latin *novicius*, from *novus* new]

**noviciate** /nuh-**vish**-ee-uht/ *n.* (also **novitiate**) **1** period of being a novice. **2** religious novice. **3** novices' quarters. [medieval Latin: related to NOVICE]

**now** — *adv.* **1** at the present or mentioned time. **2** immediately (*I must go now*). **3** by this time (*it was now clear that . . .*). **4** under the present circumstances (*I cannot now agree*). **5** on this further occasion (*what do you want now?*). **6** in the immediate past (*just now*). **7** (esp. in a narrative) then; next (*the police now arrived*). **8** (without reference to time, giving various tones to a sentence) surely, I insist, I wonder, etc. (*now what do you mean by that?*; *oh come now!*). — *conj.* (often foll. by *that*) as a consequence of the fact (*now that I am older*). — *n.* this time; the present (*should be there by now*). □ **for now** until a later time (*goodbye for now*). **now and again** (or **then**) from time to time; intermittently. [Old English]

**nowadays** /**now**-uh-ˌdayz/ — *adv.* at the present time or age; in these times. — *n.* the present time.

**nowhere** /**noh**-wair/ — *adv.* in or to no place. — *pron.* no place. □ **get nowhere** make no progress. **in the middle of nowhere** *colloq.* remote from urban life; in the outback. **nowhere near** not nearly. [Old English]

**no-win** *attrib. adj.* of or designating a situation in which success is impossible (opp. WIN-WIN).

**noxious** /**nok**-shuhs/ *adj.* harmful, unwholesome. [Latin *noxa* harm]

**nozzle** /**noz**-uhl/ *n.* spout on a hose etc. from which a jet issues. [diminutive of NOSE]

**Np** *symb.* neptunium.

**NSW** *abbr.* New South Wales.

**NT** *abbr.* **1** New Testament. **2** Northern Territory.

**n't** see NOT.

**nth** see N[1].

**nu** /nyoo/ *n.* thirteenth letter of the Greek alphabet (N, ν). [Greek]

**nuance** /**nyoo**-ons/ *n.* subtle shade of meaning, feeling, colour, etc. [Latin *nubes* cloud]

**nub** *n.* **1** point or gist (of a matter or story). **2** (also **nubble**) small lump, esp. of coal. □ **nubbly** *adj.* [related to KNOB]

**nubile** /**nyoo**-buyl/ *adj.* (of a woman) marriageable or sexually attractive. □ **nubility** /-**bil**-uh-tee/ *n.* [Latin *nubo* become the wife of]

**nuclear** /**nyoo**-klee-uh/ *adj.* **1** of, relating to, or constituting a nucleus. **2** using nuclear energy.

**nuclear bomb** *n.* bomb using the release of energy by nuclear fission or fusion or both.

**nuclear energy** *n.* energy obtained by nuclear fission or fusion.

**nuclear family** *n.* a couple and their child or children regarded as a basic social unit.

**nuclear fission** *n.* nuclear reaction in which a heavy nucleus splits spontaneously or on impact with another particle, with the release of energy.

**nuclear-free zone** *n.* an area (usu. the territory of a local government council in Australia) designated and signposted as such to declare that it is free of nuclear material and that the passage of nuclear material through that area is prohibited.

**nuclear fuel** *n.* source of nuclear energy.

**nuclear fusion** *n.* nuclear reaction in which atomic nuclei of low atomic number fuse to form a heavier nucleus with the release of energy.

**nuclear physics** *n.pl.* (treated as *sing.*) physics of atomic nuclei.

**nuclear power** *n.* **1** power generated by a nuclear reactor. **2** country that has nuclear weapons.

**nuclear reactor** *n.* device in which a nuclear fission chain reaction is used to produce energy.

**nuclear weapon** *n.* weapon using the release of energy by nuclear fission or fusion or both.

**nucleate** /**nyoo**-klee-ˌayt/ — *adj.* having a nucleus. — *v.* (**-ting**) form or form into a nucleus. [Latin: related to NUCLEUS]

**nucleic acid** /nyoo-**klee**-ik, -**klay**-ik/ *n.* either of two complex organic molecules (DNA and RNA), present in all living cells.

**nucleon** /**nyoo**-klee-ˌon/ *n.* proton or neutron.

**nucleus** /**nyoo**-klee-uhs/ *n.* (*pl.* **nuclei** /-lee-ˌuy/ ) **1 a** central part or thing round which others are collected. **b** kernel of an aggregate or mass. **2** initial part meant to receive additions. **3** central core of an atom. **4** large dense part of a cell, containing the genetic material. **5** discrete mass of grey matter in the central nervous system. [Latin, = kernel, diminutive of *nux nuc-* nut]

**nuddy** *n. colloq.* □ **in the nuddy** in the nude, naked.

**nude** — *adj.* naked, bare, unclothed. — *n.* **1** painting, sculpture, etc. of a nude human figure. **2** nude person. □ **in the nude** naked. □ **nudity** *n.* [Latin *nudus*]

**nudge** — *v.* (**-ging**) **1** prod gently with the elbow to attract attention. **2** push gradually. — *n.* prod; gentle push. [origin unknown]

**nudist** /**nyoo**-duhst, **noo**-/ *n.* person who advocates or practises going unclothed (esp. in a special reserve, on a declared 'nude beach', etc.) in the belief that this is beneficial to health. □ **nudism** *n.*

**nugatory** /**nyoo**-guh-tuh-ree, -tree/ *adj.* **1** futile, trifling, worthless. **2** inoperative; not valid. [Latin *nugae* jests]

**nugget** /**nug**-uht/ *n.* **1** lump of gold etc. as found in the earth. **2** lump of anything. **3** something valuable (*a little nugget of information*). **4** small, stocky animal or person. **5** an unbranded calf. [apparently from British dial. *nug* lump]

**nuggetty** /**nug**-uh-tee/ *adj.* (also **nuggety**) **1** (of gold) occurring as nuggets. **2** rich in nuggets (*discovered a nuggetty gully*). **3** (of a person) compactly built; stocky; tough.

**nuisance** /**nyoo**-suhns/ *n.* **1** person, thing, or circumstance causing trouble or annoyance. **2** anything harmful or offensive to the community or to a member of it and for which a legal remedy exists. [French, = hurt, from *nuire nuis-* injure from Latin *noceo* hurt (v.)]

**nuisance value** *n.* advantage arising from the capacity to harass or frustrate.

**nuke** /nyook/ *colloq.* — *n.* nuclear weapon. — *v.* (**-king**) **1** attack with nuclear weapons. **2** defeat or destroy as if with a nuclear weapon (*nuked the opposition*). [abbreviation]

**null** *adj.* **1** (esp. **null and void**) invalid. **2** non-existent. **3** *Computing* **a** empty; having no elements (*null list*). **b** all the elements of which are zeros (*null matrix*). **4** without character or expression. □ **nullity** *n.* [Latin *nullus* none]

**nulla** /**nul**-uh/ *n.* (also **nullah**) = NULLA-NULLA. [abbreviation]

**nulla-nulla** /**nul**-uh ˌnul-uh/ — *n.* hardwood club, used by Aborigines in fighting and hunting. — *v.* strike (a person) with a nulla-nulla. [Dharuk *ngala-ngala*]

**nullify** /**nul**-uh-ˌfuy/ *v.* (**-ies, -ied**) neutralise, invalidate, make null. □ **nullification** /-fuh-**kay**-shuhn/ *n.*

**numb** /num/ — *adj.* (often foll. by *with*) deprived of feeling or the power of motion (*numb with cold*). — *v.* **1** make numb. **2** stupefy, paralyse. □ **numbness** *n.* [obsolete *nome* past part. of *nim* take: related to NIMBLE]

**numbat** /**num**-bat/ *n.* (also **banded ant-eater**) small, termite-eating marsupial, now occurring only in south-western WA and rare, having a long, pointed snout and red to grey-brown fur with light stripes across the back and rump: faunal emblem of WA. [Nyungar *numbad*]

**number** — *n.* **1 a** arithmetical value representing a particular quantity. **b** word, symbol, or figure representing this. **c** arithmetical value showing position in a series, esp. for identification etc. (*registration number*). **2** (often foll. by *of*) total count or aggregate (*the number of accidents has decreased*). **3 a** numerical reckoning (*the laws of number*). **b** (in *pl.*) arithmetic. **4 a** (in *sing.* or *pl.*) quantity, amount (*a large number of people*; *only in small numbers*). **b** (**a number of**) several (*of*). **c** (in *pl.*) numerical preponderance (*force of numbers*). **5 a** person or thing having a place in a series, esp. a single issue of a magazine, an item in a programme, etc. **b** a song, dance, musical item, etc. **6** company, collection, group (*among our number*). **7** *Gram.* **a** classification of words by their singular or plural forms. **b** such a form. **8** *colloq.* **a** person or thing (esp. an article of merchandise, e.g. an item of clothing) regarded familiarly or affectionately (usu. qualified in some way: *an attractive little number*). **b** song (*her latest number*). — *v.* **1** include (*I number you among my friends*). **2** assign a number or numbers to. **3** have or amount to (a specified number) (*his collection numbers two hundred*; *a crowd numbering several thousand*). **4** count. □ **one's days are numbered** one does not have long to live. **have a person's number** *colloq.* understand a person's real motives, character, etc. **one's number is up** *colloq.* **1** one is doomed to die soon. **2** one is in serious trouble; one is finished. **the numbers are** (or **go**) **up** the result is known (*don't* *congratulate yourself until the numbers are up).* **without number** innumerable. [Latin *numerus*]

■ **Usage** In sense 4b, *a number of* is normally used with a plural verb: *a number of problems remain.*

**number crunching** *n. colloq.* process of making complex calculations, esp. by computer.

**numberless** *adj.* innumerable.

**number one** — *n. colloq.* oneself (*he takes good care of number one*). — *adj.* most important (*the number one priority*).

**number plate** *n.* plate on a vehicle showing its registration number.

**numbskull** *n.* stupid person. [from NUMB]

**numerable** /nyoo-muh-ruh-buhl/ *adj.* that can be counted. [Latin: related to NUMBER]

**numeracy** /nyoo-muh-ruh-see/ *n.* skill in the basic principles of mathematics (cf. LITERACY).

**numeral** /nyoo-muh-ruhl/ — *n.* word, symbol, or group of symbols denoting a number. — *adj.* of or denoting a number. [Latin: related to NUMBER]

**numerate** /nyoo-muh-ruht/ *adj.* acquainted with the basic principles of mathematics; able to do basic arithmetic etc. (cf. LITERATE). [Latin *numerus* number, after *literate*]

**numeration** /ˌnyoo-muh-ray-shuhn/ *n.* **1** method or process of numbering. **2** calculation. [Latin: related to NUMBER]

**numerator** /nyoo-muh-ˌray-tuh/ *n.* number above the line in a vulgar fraction showing how many of the parts indicated by the denominator are taken (e.g. 2 in ⅔). [Latin: related to NUMBER]

**numerical** /nyoo-me-ri-kuhl/ *adj.* of or relating to a number or numbers (*numerical superiority*). □ **numerically** *adv.* [medieval Latin: related to NUMBER]

**numerology** /ˌnyoo-muh-**rol**-uh-jee/ *n.* the study of the supposed occult significance of numbers.

**numerous** /nyoo-muh-ruhs/ *adj.* **1** many (*received numerous gifts*). **2** consisting of many (*a numerous family*). [Latin: related to NUMBER]

**numinous** /nyoo-muh-nuhs/ *adj.* **1** indicating the presence of a divinity. **2** spiritual, awe-inspiring. [Latin *numen* deity]

**numismatic** /ˌnyoo-muhz-**mat**-ik/ *adj.* of or relating to coins or medals. [Greek *nomisma* coin]

**numismatics** *n.pl.* (usu. treated as *sing.*) the study of coins or medals. □ **numismatist** /nyoo-**miz**-muh-tuhst/ *n.*

**nun** *n.* member of a religious community of women living under certain vows, esp. poverty, chastity, and obedience. [Latin *nonna*]

**nuncio** /**nun**-see-oh/ *n.* (*pl.* **-s**) papal ambassador. [Latin *nuntius* messenger]

**Nunga** /**nang**-guh/ *n.* (also **Nanga**) an Aborigine (word used by Aborigines in the southern part of SA). [Nhangka *nhanga*]

■ **Usage** See KOORI[1].

**nunnery** *n.* (*pl.* **-ies**) religious house of nuns; convent.

**nuptial** /**nup**-shuhl/ — *adj.* of marriage or weddings. — *n.* (usu. in *pl.*) wedding. [Latin *nubo nupt-* wed]

**nurse** /ners/ — *n.* **1** woman or man trained to care for the sick or infirm and assist doctors. **2** = NURSEMAID. **3** *Zool.* sexually imperfect bee, ant, etc., caring for a young brood; a worker. — *v.* (**-sing**) **1 a** work as a nurse. **b** attend to (a sick person). **c** give medical attention to (an illness or injury) (*nursed his cold*). **2** feed or be fed at the breast. **3** hold or treat carefully (*nursed her feet; nurse my suitcase for a while, will you?*). **4 a** foster; promote the development of (the arts, plants, etc.). **b** harbour or nurture (a grievance etc.) (*nursed his hatred*). **c** pay special attention to (*nursed the voters in his electorate*). [Latin: related to NOURISH]

**nursemaid** *n.* woman in charge of a child or children.

**nursery** /**ner**-suh-ree, **ners**-ree/ *n.* (*pl.* **-ies**) **1 a** a room or place equipped for young children. **b** = CRÈCHE. **2** place where plants are reared for sale. [probably Anglo-French: related to NURSE]

**nurseryman** *n.* owner of or worker in a plant nursery.

**nursery rhyme** *n.* simple traditional song or rhyme for children.

**nursery slopes** *n.pl.* gentle slopes for novice skiers.

**nursing home** *n.* hospital or home for invalids, old people, etc.

**nurture** /**ner**-chuh/ — *n.* **1** process of bringing up or training (esp. children); fostering care. **2** nourishment. **3** sociological factors as influencing or determining personality (opp. NATURE). — *v.* (**-ring**) **1** bring up; rear. **2** nourish. [French: related to NOURISH]

**nut** *n.* **1 a** fruit consisting of a hard or tough shell around an edible kernel. **b** this kernel. **2** pod containing hard seeds. **3** small usu. hexagonal flat piece of metal etc. with a threaded hole through it for screwing on the end of a bolt to secure it. **4** *colloq.* person's head. **5** *colloq.* **a** crazy or eccentric person. **b** enthusiast; fanatic (*he's a real nut for model planes*). **6** small lump (of coal etc.). **7** (in *pl.*) *coarse colloq.* testicles. □ **do one's nut** *colloq.* be extremely angry. **a hard nut to crack 1** extremely difficult person to persuade, deal with, etc. **2** extremely difficult problem, situation, etc. **nut out** plan, figure out (*we need to nut out the details*). **off one's nut** *colloq.* crazy. [Old English]

**nutcase** *n. colloq.* crazy person.

**nutmeg** *n.* **1 a** hard aromatic seed used as a spice and in medicine. **b** south-east Asian tree bearing this. **2 a** either of two Australian trees, related to the Asian nutmeg, occurring in Queensland and the NT. **b** the spicy fruit of these trees. [French *nois* nut, *mugue* MUSK]

**nutrient** /**nyoo**-tree-uhnt/ — *n.* substance that provides essential nourishment. — *adj.* serving as or providing nourishment. [Latin *nutrio* nourish]

**nutriment** /**nyoo**-truh-muhnt/ *n.* **1** nourishing food. **2** intellectual or artistic etc. nourishment.

**nutrition** /nyoo-**trish**-uhn/ *n.* **1** process of providing or receiving nourishing substances. **2** food, nourishment. **3** the study of nutrients and nutrition. □ **nutritional** *adj.* **nutritionist** *n.*

**nutritious** /nyoo-**trish**-uhs/ *adj.* efficient as food.

**nutritive** /**nyoo**-truh-tiv/ *adj.* **1** of nutrition. **2** nutritious.

**nuts** *colloq.* — *predic. adj.* crazy, mad; eccentric. — *int.* an expression of contempt or derision (*nuts to you!*). □ **be nuts about** (or **on** or **over**) be very fond of (*he's nuts about her*). [pl. of NUT]

**nuts and bolts** *n.pl. colloq.* practical details.

**nutshell** *n.* hard exterior covering of a nut. □ **in a nutshell** in a few words.

**nutter** *n. colloq.* crazy or eccentric person.

**nut tree** *n.* any of several Australian nut-bearing trees, esp. NUTWOOD and QUANDONG.

**nutty** *adj.* (**-ier**, **-iest**) **1 a** full of nuts. **b** tasting like nuts. **2** *colloq.* crazy. □ **nutty**

**as a fruitcake** *colloq.* completely crazy or thoroughly eccentric. □ **nuttiness** *n.*

**nutwood** *n.* small, willow-like tree (of the NT and parts of WA) bearing fruit with an edible kernel.

**nuytsia** /noit-see-uh/ *n.* (also **Western Australian Christmas tree**) parasitic tree with a profuse and spectacular display of brilliant golden flowers in summer.

**nuzzle** /**nuz**-uhl/ *v.* (**-ling**) **1** prod or rub gently with the nose. **2** (foll. by *into*, *against*, *up to*) press the nose gently. **3** (also *refl.*) nestle; lie snug. [from NOSE]

**NW** *abbr.* **1** north-west. **2** north-western.

**Nyangumarda** /**nyahng**-oo-mahr-du/ *n.* an Aboriginal language spoken to the north of Port Hedland in WA.

**Nyawaygi** /nyah-wuy-gee/ *n.* an Aboriginal language spoken to the south of Ingham in northern Queensland.

**nylon** /**nuy**-lon/ *n.* **1** tough light elastic synthetic fibre. **2** nylon fabric. **3** (in *pl.*) stockings of nylon. [invented word]

**nymph** /nimf/ *n.* **1** mythological semidivine spirit regarded as a maiden and associated with an aspect of nature, esp. rivers and woods. **2** *poet.* beautiful young woman. **3** immature form of some insects. [Greek *numphē* nymph, bride]

**nympho** /**nim**-foh/ *n.* (*pl.* **-s**) *colloq.* nymphomaniac. [abbreviation]

**nymphomania** /ˌnim-fuh-**may**-nee-uh/ *n.* excessive sexual desire in a woman. □ **nymphomaniac** *n.* & *adj.* [from NYMPH, -MANIA]

**Nyoongah** /**nyuung**-u, **nyoong**-u/ *n.* (also **Noongah**) an Aborigine (word used by Aborigines in the south-west of WA). [Nyungar *nyungar*]

■ **Usage** See KOORI[1].

**Nyungar** /**nyuung**-uh/ *n.* an Aboriginal language spoken over a large extent of south-western WA, including present-day Perth, Albany, and Esperance: now extinct (except for a few words remembered by some older people).

**NZ** *abbr.* New Zealand.

# O

**O¹** /oh/ n. (also **o**) (pl. **Os** or **O's**) **1** fifteenth letter of the alphabet. **2** (**0**) nought, zero.

**O²** abbr. (also **O.**) Old.

**O³** symb. oxygen.

**O⁴** /oh/ int. **1** var. of OH. **2** prefixed to a name in the vocative (*O God*). [natural exclamation]

**O'** /oh/ prefix of Irish family names (*O'Connor*). [Irish ó, ua, descendant]

**o'** /uh/ prep. of, on (esp. in phrases: *o'clock*; *will-o'-the-wisp*). [abbreviation]

**-o** suffix colloq. added to: **1** shortened forms, as *garbo* garb(age collector), *journo* journ(alist), *arvo* af(ternoon). **2** one-syllable forms, as *milko* milkman, *smoko* a smoke, *goodo*, *weirdo*. **3** (esp. as a mark of familiarity) personal names, as *Johnno*, *Tommo*. [perhaps from OH]

■ **Usage** The habit of using this suffix leads to the ongoing formation of nonce-words, e.g. *euco* eucalypt, *houso* house-work, *cemo* cemetery. Only those forms which are settled have been entered into this dictionary.

**-o-** suffix the terminal vowel of comb. forms (*chemico-*; *spectro-*). [originally Greek]

■ **Usage** This suffix is often elided before a vowel, as in *neuralgia*.

**oaf** n. (pl. **-s**) **1** awkward lout. **2** stupid person. □ **oafish** adj. **oafishly** adv. **oafishness** n. [Old Norse: related to ELF]

**oak** n. **1 a** acorn-bearing European tree with lobed leaves. **b** its durable wood. **2** (*attrib.*) of oak. **3 a** any of many Australian trees thought to resemble the European oak, usu. in the appearance of the timber, esp. the casuarina or she-oak. **b** the wood of these trees. □ **oaken** adj. [Old English]

**OAM** abbr. Medal of the Order of Australia.

**oar** /aw/ n. **1** pole with a blade used to propel a boat by leverage against the water. **2** rower. □ **put one's oar in** interfere. [Old English]

**oasis** /oh-**ay**-suhs/ n. (pl. **oases** /-seez/) **1** fertile place in a desert. **2** area or period of calm in the midst of turbulence. [Latin from Greek]

**oast** /ohst/ n. kiln for drying hops. [Old English]

**oast-house** n. building containing an oast.

**oat** n. **1 a** hardy cereal plant grown as food. **b** (in pl.) grain yielded by this. **2** oat plant or a variety of it. □ **oaten** adj. [Old English]

**oat grass** n. any of several Australian grasses used as fodder, esp. tall oat grass.

**oath** /ohth/ n. (pl. **-s** /ohthz/) **1** solemn declaration naming God etc. as witness. **2** statement or promise contained in an oath (*oath of allegiance*). **3** profane or blasphemous utterance, curse. □ **my oath!** emphatic exclamation of agreement. **on** (or **under**) **oath** having sworn a solemn oath. [Old English]

**oatmeal** n. **1** meal ground from oats and used esp. in porridge. **2** greyish-fawn colour flecked with brown.

**ob-** prefix (also **oc-** before c, **of-** before f, **op-** before p) esp. in words of Latin origin, meaning: **1** exposure. **2** meeting or facing. **3** direction. **4** resistance. **5** hindrance or concealment. **6** finality or completeness. [Latin ob towards, against, in the way of]

**obbligato** /,ob-luh-**gah**-toh/ n. (pl. **-s**) Mus. accompaniment forming an integral part of a composition. [Italian, = obligatory]

**obdurate** /**ob**-dyoo-ruht/ adj. **1** stubborn. **2** hardened against persuasion or influence. □ **obduracy** n. **obdurateness** n. [Latin duro harden]

**obedient** /oh-**bee**-dee-uhnt, uh-/ adj. **1** obeying or ready to obey. **2** submissive to another's will. □ **obedience** n. **obediently** adv. [Latin: related to OBEY]

**obeisance** /oh-**bay**-suhns/ n. **1** bow, curtsy, or other respectful gesture. **2** homage, submission. □ **obeisant** adj. [French: related to OBEY]

**obelisk** /**ob**-uh-lisk/ n. tapering usu. four-sided stone pillar as a monument or landmark. [Greek diminutive: related to OBELUS]

**obelus** /**ob**-uh-luhs/ n. (pl. **obeli** /-,luy/) dagger-shaped reference mark (†). [Greek, = pointed pillar, SPIT²]

**obese** /oh-**bees**/ adj. very fat. □ **obesity** n. [Latin edo eat]

**obey** /oh-**bay**/ v. **1 a** carry out the command of (*you will obey me*). **b** carry out (a command) (*obey orders*). **2** do what one is told to do. **3** be actuated by (a force or impulse). [Latin obedio from audio hear]

735

**obfuscate** /ob-fuhs-ˌkayt/ v. (**-ting**) **1** obscure or confuse (a mind, topic, etc.). **2** stupefy, bewilder. □ **obfuscation** /-**kay**-shuhn/ n. **obfuscatory** /**kay**-tuh-ree, -tree/ adj. [Latin *fuscus* dark]

**obituary** /uh-**bich**-uh-ree/ n. (pl. **-ies**) **1** notice of a death or deaths. **2** account of the life of a deceased person. **3** (*attrib.*) of or serving as an obituary. [Latin *obitus* death]

**object** — n. /**ob**-jekt/ **1** material thing that can be seen or touched. **2** person or thing to which action or feeling is directed (*object of attention*; *love-object*). **3** thing sought or aimed at. **4** *Gram.* noun or its equivalent governed by an active transitive verb or by a preposition (see panel). **5** *Philos.* thing external to the thinking mind or subject. — v. /uhb-**jekt**/ (often foll. by *to*, *against*) **1** express opposition, disapproval, or reluctance. **2** protest. □ **no object** not forming an important or restricting factor (*money no object*). □ **objector** /uhb-**jek**-tuh/ n. [Latin *jacio ject-* throw]

**objectify** /uhb-**jek**-tuh-ˌfuy/ v. (**-ies**, **-ied**) present as an object; express in concrete form.

**objection** /uhb-**jek**-shuhn/ n. **1** expression or feeling of opposition or disapproval. **2** act of objecting. **3** adverse reason or statement. [Latin: related to OBJECT]

**objectionable** adj. **1** unpleasant, offensive. **2** open to objection. □ **objectionably** adv.

**objective** /uhb-**jek**-tiv/ — adj. **1** external to the mind; actually existing. **2** dealing with outward things or exhibiting facts uncoloured by feelings or opinions; not subjective. **3** *Gram.* (of a case or word) in the form appropriate to the object. — n. **1** something sought or aimed at. **2** *Gram.* objective case. □ **objectively** adv. **objectivity** /ˌob-jek-**tiv**-uh-tee/ n. [medieval Latin: related to OBJECT]

**object lesson** n. striking practical example of some principle.

**objet d'art** /ˌob-zhay **dah**/ n. (pl. **objets d'art** pronunc. same) small decorative object. [French, = object of art]

**oblate** /**ob**-layt/ adj. *Geom.* (of a spheroid) flattened at the poles. [Latin: related to OFFER]

**oblation** /oh-**blay**-shuhn/ n. thing offered to a divine being. [Latin: related to OFFER]

**obligate** /**ob**-luh-ˌgayt/ v. (**-ting**) bind (a person) legally or morally (*was obligated to attend*). [Latin: related to OBLIGE]

**obligation** /ˌob-luh-**gay**-shuhn/ n. **1** constraining power of a law, duty, contract, etc. **2** duty, task. **3** binding agreement. **4** indebtedness for a service or benefit (*be under an obligation*). □ **day of obligation** *Eccl.* day on which attendance at Mass is compulsory under the Commandments of the Church. [Latin: related to OBLIGE]

**obligatory** /uh-**blig**-uh-tuh-ree, -tree/ adj. **1** binding. **2** compulsory. □ **obligatorily** adv. [Latin: related to OBLIGE]

**oblige** /uh-**bluyj**/ v. (**-ging**) **1** constrain, compel. **2** be binding on. **3** do (a person) a small favour, help. **4** (as **obliged** adj.) indebted, grateful (*am obliged to you for your help*). **5** (foll. by *with*) make a contribution of a specified kind (*she obliged with a song*). □ **much obliged** thank you. [Latin *obligo* bind]

**obliging** adj. accommodating, helpful. □ **obligingly** adv.

---

## Object

There are two types of object:

1  A direct object is the person or thing directly affected by the verb and can usually be found by asking the question 'whom or what?' after the verb, e.g.
    *the electors chose* Mr Smith.
    *Charles wrote* a letter.

2  An indirect object is usually a person or thing receiving something from the subject of the verb, e.g.
    *He gave* me *the pen.*
    (*me* is the indirect object, and *the pen* is the direct object.)
    *I sent* my bank *a letter.*
    (*my bank* is the indirect object, and *a letter* is the direct object.)
    The indirect object can usually be rewritten with the preposition *to*: *he gave the pen to me*; *I sent a letter to my bank.*
    Sentences containing an indirect object usually contain a direct object as well, but not always, e.g.
    *Pay* me.

'Object' on its own usually means a direct object.

**oblique** /uh-**bleek**/ — *adj.* **1** slanting; at an angle. **2** not going straight to the point; indirect (*made an oblique reference to the scandal*). **3** *Gram.* (of a case) other than nominative or vocative. — *n.* oblique stroke (/). □ **obliquely** *adv.* **obliqueness** *n.* **obliquity** /uh-**blik**-wuh-tee/ *n.* [French from Latin]

**obliterate** /uh-**blit**-uh-,rayt/ *v.* (**-ting**) blot out, destroy, leave no clear traces of. □ **obliteration** /-**ray**-shuhn/ *n.* [Latin *oblitero* erase, from *litera* letter]

**oblivion** /uh-**bliv**-ee-uhn/ *n.* state of having or being forgotten. [Latin *obliviscor* forget]

**oblivious** /uh-**bliv**-ee-uhs/ *adj.* **1** (often foll. by *of*) forgetful, unmindful (*oblivious of his youthful follies*). **2** (foll. by *of*, *to*) unaware or unconscious (*oblivious of our plight*). □ **obliviously** *adv.* **obliviousness** *n.*

**oblong** /**ob**-long/ — *adj.* rectangular with adjacent sides unequal. — *n.* oblong figure or object. [Latin *oblongus* longish]

**obloquy** /**ob**-luh-kwee/ *n.* **1** state of being generally ill spoken of. **2** abuse, detraction. [Latin *obloquium* contradiction, from *loquor* speak]

**obnoxious** /uhb-**nok**-shuhs, ob-/ *adj.* offensive, objectionable. □ **obnoxiously** *adv.* **obnoxiousness** *n.* [Latin *noxa* injury]

**oboe** /**oh**-boh/ *n.* woodwind double-reed instrument with a piercing plaintive tone. □ **oboist** /**oh**-boh-uhst/ *n.* [French *hautbois* from *haut* high, *bois* wood]

**obscene** /uhb-**seen**, ob-/ *adj.* **1** offensively indecent. **2** highly offensive (*an obscene accumulation of wealth*). □ **obscenely** *adv.* **obscenity** /uhb-**sen**-uh-tee/ *n.* (pl. **-ies**). [Latin *obsc(a)enus* abominable]

**obscurantism** /,ob-skyuh-**ran**-tiz-uhm/ *n.* opposition to knowledge and enlightenment. □ **obscurantist** *n.* & *adj.* [Latin *obscurus* dark]

**obscure** /uhb-**skyoo**-uh, -**skyoor**/ — *adj.* **1** not clearly expressed or easily understood. **2** unexplained. **3** dark, dim. **4** indistinct. **5** hidden; unnoticed. **6** (of a person) undistinguished, hardly known. — *v.* (**-ring**) **1** make obscure or unintelligible. **2** conceal. □ **obscurity** *n.* [French from Latin]

**obsequies** /**ob**-suh-kweez/ *n.pl.* funeral rites. [Latin *obsequiae*]

**obsequious** /uhb-**see**-kwee-uhs/ *adj.* servile, fawning. □ **obsequiously** *adv.* **obsequiousness** *n.* [Latin *obsequor* comply with]

**observance** /uhb-**zer**-vuhns/ *n.* **1** keeping or performing of a law, duty, custom, etc. **2** rite or ceremony.

**observant** *adj.* **1** acute in taking notice. **2** attentive in esp. religious observance. □ **observantly** *adv.*

**observation** /,ob-zuh-**vay**-shuhn/ *n.* **1** act or instance of observing or being observed (*police had him under observation*). **2** power of perception. **3** remark, comment. **4** accurate watching and noting of phenomena etc., esp. in the process of scientific study. □ **observational** *adj.*

**observatory** /uhb-**zer**-vuh-tuh-ree, -tree/ *n.* (pl. **-ies**) building equipped for astronomical or other observation.

**observe** /uhb-**zerv**, ob-/ *v.* (**-ving**) **1** perceive, become aware of. **2** watch carefully. **3 a** follow or keep (rules etc.). **b** celebrate (an anniversary etc.) or perform duly (a rite etc.). **4** make a remark (*observed that grammar was going to the dogs*). **5** take note of scientifically. □ **observable** *adj.* **observably** *adv.* [Latin *servo* watch, keep]

**observer** *n.* **1** person who observes. **2** interested spectator. **3** person who attends a conference, meeting, etc., to note the proceedings but does not participate.

**obsess** /uhb-**ses**, ob-/ *v.* (often in *passive*) fill the mind of (a person) continually; totally preoccupy (*obsessed by fears of death*). □ **obsessive** *adj.* & *n.* **obsessively** *adv.* **obsessiveness** *n.* [Latin *obsideo obsess-* besiege]

**obsession** /uhb-**sesh**-uhn, ob-/ *n.* **1** act of obsessing or state of being obsessed. **2** persistent idea dominating a person's mind and affecting his or her behaviour. □ **obsessional** *adj.* **obsessionally** *adv.*

**obsidian** /uhb-**sid**-ee-uhn/ *n.* dark glassy rock formed from lava. [Latin from *Obsius*, discoverer of a similar stone]

**obsolescent** /,ob-suh-**les**-uhnt/ *adj.* **1** (of a word) becoming obsolete. **2** (of equipment etc.) going out of use or date. □ **obsolescence** *n.* [Latin *soleo* be accustomed]

**obsolete** /**ob**-suh-,leet/ *adj.* **1** (of a word) no longer in use. **2** (of equipment etc.) discarded; antiquated. **3** *Biol.* less developed than formerly or than in a cognate species; rudimentary.

**obstacle** /**ob**-stuh-kuhl/ *n.* person or thing that obstructs progress. [Latin *obsto* stand in the way]

**obstetrician** /,ob-stuh-**trish**-uhn/ *n.* specialist in obstetrics.

**obstetrics** /uhb-**stet**-riks, ob-/ *n.pl.* (treated as *sing.*) branch of medicine and surgery dealing with childbirth. □ **obstetric** *adj.* [Latin *obstetrix* midwife, from *obsto* be present]

**obstinate** /**ob**-stuh-nuht/ *adj.* **1** stubborn, intractable. **2** firmly continuing in one's action or opinion despite advice. **3** inflexible, unyielding (*obstinate opposition to the plan*). **4** persistent, not yielding to treatment etc. (*an obstinate cough*). □ **obstinacy** *n.* **obstinately** *adv.* [Latin *obstino* persist]

**obstreperous** /uhb-**strep**-uh-ruhs, ob-/ *adj.* **1** turbulent, unruly. **2** noisy. □ **obstreperously** *adv.* **obstreperousness** *n.* [Latin *obstrepo* shout at]

**obstruct** /uhb-**strukt**/ *v.* **1** block up; make hard or impossible to pass along or through. **2** get in the way of, impede (*those trees obstruct the view*). **3** prevent or retard the progress of. [Latin *obstruo obstruct-* block up]

**obstruction** /uhb-**struk**-shuhn/ *n.* **1** act or instance of blocking; state of being blocked. **2** thing that obstructs, blockage. **3** *Sport* act of unlawfully obstructing another player. **4** *Med.* blockage in a bodily passage, esp. in an intestine.

**obstructive** *adj.* causing or intended to cause an obstruction. □ **obstructively** *adv.* **obstructiveness** *n.*

**obtain** /uhb-**tayn**/ *v.* **1** acquire, secure; have granted to one, get. **2** be prevalent or established; prevail (*conditions obtaining in the convict stations*). □ **obtainable** *adj.* [Latin *teneo* hold]

**obtrude** /uhb-**trood**, ob-/ *v.* (**-ding**) **1** be or become obtrusive. **2** (often foll. by *on*, *upon*) thrust (oneself, one's opinions, etc.) importunately forward (*obtruded on our privacy*; *tried to obtrude his views upon others*). □ **obtrusion** *n.* [Latin *obtrudo* thrust against]

**obtrusive** /uhb-**troo**-siv, ob-/ *adj.* **1** unpleasantly noticeable. **2** obtruding oneself. □ **obtrusively** *adv.* **obtrusiveness** *n.*

**obtuse** /uhb-**tyoos**, ob-/ *adj.* **1** dull-witted. **2** (of an angle) between 90° and 180°. **3** of blunt form; not sharp-pointed or sharp-edged. □ **obtuseness** *n.* [Latin *obtundo obtus-* beat against, blunt]

**obverse** /**ob**-vers/ — *n.* **1** counterpart; opposite of a fact or truth. **2** side of a coin or medal etc. bearing the head or principal design (opp. REVERSE). **3** front, proper, or top side of a thing. — *adj.* answering as the counterpart to something else. [Latin *obverto obvers-* turn towards]

**obviate** /**ob**-vee-,ayt/ *v.* (**-ting**) get round or do away with (a need, inconvenience, etc.). [Latin *obvio* prevent]

**obvious** /**ob**-vee-uhs/ *adj.* easily seen, recognised, or understood. □ **obviously**

*adv.* **obviousness** *n.* [Latin *ob viam* in the way]

**oc-** see OB-.

**occasion** /uh-**kay**-zhuhn/ — *n.* **1** a special event or happening (*dressed for the occasion*). **b** time of this (*on the occasion of their marriage*). **2** reason, need (*there is no occasion to be angry*). **3** suitable time for doing something; opportunity. **4** immediate but subordinate cause (*the assassination was the occasion of the war*). — *v.* **1** be the cause of; bring about, esp. incidentally (*his remarks occasioned some surprise*). **2** cause (a person or thing) to do something. □ **on occasion** now and then; when the need arises. **rise to the occasion** see RISE. [Latin *occido occas-* go down]

**occasional** *adj.* **1** happening irregularly and infrequently (*gets occasional cramps*). **2 a** made or meant for, or acting on, a special occasion. **b** for use as required (*an occasional table*). □ **occasionally** *adv.*

**Occident** /**ok**-suh-duhnt/ *n. poet.* or *rhet.* **1** (prec. by *the*) West. **2** western Europe. **3** Europe and America as distinct from the Orient. [Latin *occidens -entis* setting, sunset, west]

**occidental** /,ok-suh-**den**-tuhl/ — *adj.* **1** of the Occident. **2** western. — *n.* native of the Occident.

**occiput** /**ok**-si-,put/ *n.* back of the head. □ **occipital** /-**sip**-uh-tuhl/ *adj.* [Latin *caput* head]

**occlude** /uh-**klood**/ *v.* (**-ding**) **1** stop up or close (pores, a passage, etc.). **2** *Chem.* absorb and retain (gases). **3** (as **occluded** *adj.*) *Meteorol.* (of a frontal system) formed when a cold front overtakes a warm front, raising warm air from ground level. □ **occlusion** *n.* [Latin *occludo occlus-* close up]

**occult** /o-**kult**, uh-**kult**/ *adj.* **1** involving the supernatural; mystical; magical. **2** extremely secret; esoteric. **3** beyond the range of ordinary knowledge; mysterious (*the occult 'sciences' such as astrology*). □ **the occult** occult phenomena generally. [Latin *occulo occult-* hide]

**occupant** /**ok**-yuh-puhnt/ *n.* person who occupies, lives in, or is in, a place etc. (*occupants of the flat*; *both occupants of the car were unhurt*). □ **occupancy** *n.* (*pl.* **-ies**). [Latin: related to OCCUPY]

**occupation** /,ok-yuh-**pay**-shuhn/ *n.* **1** person's employment or profession. **2** pastime. **3** act of occupying or state of being occupied. **4** taking or holding of a country etc. by force.

**occupational** *adj.* **1** of or connected with one's occupation. **2** (of a disease, hazard, etc.) connected with one's occupation.

**occupational health** *n.* (also **occupational health and safety**) programmes designed to maintain and improve the health and safety of workers in their place of work.

**occupational therapy** *n.* programme of mental or physical activity to assist recovery from disease or injury.

**occupy** /**ok**-yuh-,puy/ *v.* (**-ies, -ied**) **1** live in; be the tenant of. **2** take up or fill (space, time, or a place). **3** hold (a position or office). **4** take military possession of. **5** place oneself in (a building etc.) forcibly or without authority as a protest. **6** keep busy or engaged. □ **occupier** *n.* [Latin *occupo* seize]

**occur** /uh-**ker**/ *v.* (**-rr-**) **1** come into being as an event or process. **2** exist or be encountered in some place or conditions (*kangaroo paws occur naturally only in Western Australia*). **3** (foll. by *to*) come into the mind of, esp. as an unexpected or casual thought (*it occurred to me that you were right*). [Latin *occurro* befall]

**occurrence** /uh-**ku**-ruhns/ *n.* **1** act or instance of occurring. **2** incident or event.

**ocean** /**oh**-shuhn/ *n.* **1** large expanse of sea, esp. each of the main areas called the Atlantic, Pacific, Indian, Arctic, and Antarctic Oceans. **2** (often in *pl.*) *colloq.* very large expanse or quantity (*we have oceans of time*). □ **oceanic** /,oh-shee-**an**-ik, ,oh-see-/ *adj.* [Greek *ōkeanos*]

**oceanography** /,oh-shuh-**nog**-ruh-fee/ *n.* the study of the oceans. □ **oceanographer** *n.*

**ocelot** /**os**-uh-,lot/ *n.* leopard-like cat of S. and Central America. [French from Nahuatl]

**ochre** /**oh**-kuh/ *n.* **1** earth used as yellow, brown, or red pigment. **2** pale brownish-yellow colour. □ **ochreous** /**oh**-kree-uhs/ *adj.* [Greek *ōkhra*]

**ock** *n.* = OCKER *n.* [abbreviation]

**-ock** *suffix* forming nouns, orig. with diminutive sense (*hillock; bullock*).

**ocker** — *n.* rough, boorish, aggressively Australian male. — *adj.* characterised by a discernible vulgarity, boorishness, crassness, etc. (*ocker attitude to women*). — *v.* behave as an ocker (*Aussies ockering it up when abroad*). □ **ockerisation** *n.* **ockerised** *adj.* [a nickname, esp. for a person named *Oscar*, used as a nickname for a character devised and played by Ron Frazer in a television series 'The Mavis Bramston Show' (1965–68), and hence applied generically]

**ockerdom** *n.* ockers collectively; their social impact.

**ockerism** *n.* behaviour characteristic of an ocker.

**o'clock** /uh-**klok**/ *adv.* of the clock (used to specify the hour) (*6 o'clock*).

**octa-** *comb. form* (also **oct-** before a vowel) eight. [Greek *octo*, Greek *oktō* eight]

**octagon** /**ok**-tuh-guhn, -gon/ *n.* plane figure with eight sides and angles. □ **octagonal** /-**tag**-uh-nuhl/ *adj.* [Greek: related to OCTA-, *-gōnos* -angled]

**octahedron** /,ok-tuh-**hee**-druhn, -**hed**-ruhn/ *n.* (*pl.* **-s**) solid figure contained by eight (esp. triangular) plane faces. □ **octahedral** *adj.* [Greek]

**octane** /**ok**-tayn/ *n.* colourless inflammable hydrocarbon occurring in petrol. [from OCTA-]

**octave** /**ok**-tuhv/ *n.* **1** *Mus.* **a** interval between (and including) two notes, one having twice or half the frequency of vibration of the other. **b** eight notes occupying this interval. **c** each of the two notes at the extremes of this interval. **2** group of or stanza of eight-lines, OCTET. [Latin *octavus* eighth]

**octavo** /ok-**tay**-voh, ok-**tah**-voh/ *n.* (*pl.* **-s**) **1** size of a book or page given by folding a sheet of standard size three times to form eight leaves. **2** book or sheet of this size (abbr.: 8ᵛᵒ). [Latin: related to OCTAVE]

**octet** /ok-**tet**/ *n.* (also **octette**) **1 a** musical composition for eight performers. **b** the performers. **2** group of eight. **3** first eight lines of a sonnet. [Italian or German: related to OCTA-]

**octo-** *comb. form* eight. [see OCTA-]

**October** /ok-**toh**-buh/ *n.* tenth month of the year. [Latin *octo* eight, originally the 8th month of the Roman year]

**octogenarian** /,ok-toh-juh-**nair**-ree-uhn/ — *n.* person from 80 to 89 years old. — *adj.* of this age. [Latin *octogeni* 80 each]

**octopus** /**ok**-tuh-puhs, -puus/ *n.* (*pl.* **-puses**) sea mollusc with eight suckered tentacles, a soft saclike body, and strong beaklike jaws. [Greek: related to OCTO-, *pous* foot]

**ocular** /**ok**-yuh-luh/ — *adj.* of or connected with the eyes or sight; visual. — *n.* eyepiece of an optical instrument. [Latin *oculus* eye]

**oculist** /**ok**-yuh-luhst/ *n.* specialist in the medical treatment of eye disorders or defects.

**OD** /oh-**dee**/ *colloq.* — *n.* overdose of a drug. — *v.* (**OD's, OD'd, OD'ing**) take an overdose. [abbreviation]

**odd** *adj.* **1** strange, remarkable, eccentric. **2** casual, occasional (*odd jobs; odd moments; earned the odd dollar*). **3** not normally considered; unconnected (*in some odd corner; picks up odd bargains*).

**4** additional to a round number stated (*earned fifty odd dollars*; *had ten dollars and some odd change*). **5 a** (of numbers) not integrally divisible by two, e.g. 1, 3, 5. **b** bearing such a number (*no parking on odd dates*). **6 a** left over when the rest have been distributed or divided into pairs (*odd sock*). **b** (of a pair) mismatched (*was wearing odd socks*). **7** detached from a set or series (*a few odd volumes*). **8** (appended to a number, sum, weight, etc.) somewhat more than (*forty odd*; *forty-odd people*). **9** by which a round number, given sum, etc., is exceeded (*we have 102 — do you want the odd 2?*). □ **oddly** *adv.* **oddness** *n.* [Old Norse *oddi* angle, point, third or odd number]

**oddball** *n.* (also **oddbod**) *colloq.* eccentric person.

**oddbod** *n.* = ODDBALL.

**oddity** /od-uh-tee/ *n.* (*pl.* **-ies**) **1** strange person, thing, or occurrence. **2** peculiar trait. **3** strangeness.

**odd man out** *n.* **1** person left over after everyone else has been paired or selected into a group etc. **2** person or thing differing from the others in a group in some respect; misfit.

**oddment** *n.* **1** odd article; something left over. **2** (in *pl.*) miscellaneous articles.

**odds** *n.pl.* **1** ratio between the amounts staked by the parties to a bet, based on the expected probability either way. **2** balance of probability or advantage (*the odds are that it will rain*; *the odds are in your favour*). **3** equalising allowance given to a weaker competitor. □ **at odds** (often foll. by *with*) in conflict or at variance. **make no odds** make no difference. **over the odds** above the normal price etc. [apparently from ODD]

**odds and ends** *n.pl.* miscellaneous articles or remnants.

**odds and sods** *n.pl. colloq.* **1** random, motley collection of people or things. **2** = ODDS AND ENDS.

**odds-on** — *n.* state when success is more likely than failure. — *adj.* (of a chance) better than even; likely.

**ode** *n.* lyric poem of exalted style and tone. [Greek *ōidē* song]

**odious** /oh-dee-uhs/ *adj.* hateful, repulsive. □ **odiously** *adv.* **odiousness** *n.* [related to ODIUM]

**odium** /oh-dee-uhm/ *n.* widespread dislike or disapproval incurred by a person or associated with an action. [Latin, = hatred]

**odometer** /oh-dom-uh-tuh/ *n.* instrument for measuring the distance travelled by a wheeled vehicle. [Greek *hodos* way]

**odoriferous** /,oh-duh-**rif**-uh-ruhs/ *adj.* diffusing a (usu. agreeable) odour. [Latin: related to ODOUR]

**odour** /oh-duh/ *n.* (also **odor**) **1** property of a substance that has an effect on the nasal sense of smell. **2** smell or fragrance. **3** lasting quality attaching to a person or thing (*an odour of intolerance*; *died in the odour of sanctity*). **4** regard, repute (*in bad odour*). □ **odorous** *adj.* **odourless** *adj.* (in sense 1). [Latin *odor*]

**odyssey** /od-uh-see/ *n.* (*pl.* **-s**) series of wanderings; long adventurous journey. [title of the Homeric epic poem on the adventures of Odysseus]

**OECD** *abbr.* Organisation for Economic Cooperation and Development.

**OED** *abbr.* Oxford English Dictionary.

**oedema** /uh-dee-muh/ *n.* (also **edema**) accumulation of excess fluid in body tissues, causing swelling. □ **oedematose** *adj.* **oedematous** *adj.* [Greek *oideō* swell]

**Oedipus complex** /ee-duh-puhs/ *n.* child's, esp. a boy's, subconscious sexual desire for the parent of the opposite sex and wish to exclude the parent of the same sex. □ **Oedipal** *adj.* [Greek *Oidipous*, who unknowingly married his mother]

**o'er** /oh-uh/ *adv. & prep. poet.* = OVER. [contraction]

**oesophagus** /uh-sof-uh-guhs/ *n.* (also **esophagus**) (*pl.* **-gi** /-,guy, -,juy/ or **-guses**) passage from the mouth to the stomach; gullet. □ **oesophageal** /,uh-sof-uh-**jee**-uhl/ *adj.* [Greek]

**oestrogen** /ees-truh-juhn, es-/ *n.* (also **estrogen**) **1** sex hormone developing and maintaining female characteristics of the body. **2** this produced artificially for use in medicine. [Greek *oistros* frenzy, -GEN]

**oestrus** /ees-truhs, es-/ *n.* (also **estrus**, **oestrum**) recurring period of sexual receptivity in many female mammals. □ **oestrous** *adj.* [Greek *oistros* frenzy]

**œuvre** /er-vruh/ *n.* works of a creative artist regarded collectively. [French, = work, from Latin *opera*]

**of** /ov, uhv/ *prep.* expressing: **1** origin or cause (*paintings of Dobell*; *died of cancer*). **2** material or substance (*house of cards*; *built of bricks*). **3** belonging or connection (*thing of the past*; *articles of clothing*; *head of the business*). **4** identity or close relation (*city of Rome*; *a pound of apples*; *a fool of a man*). **5** removal or separation (*north of the city*; *got rid of them*; *robbed us of $1000*). **6** reference or direction (*beware of the dog*; *suspected of lying*; *very good of you*; *short of money*). **7** objective relation (*love of music*; *in search of peace*). **8** partition, classification, or inclusion (*no more of that*; *part of the* story; *this sort of book*). **9** description, quality, or condition (*the hour of prayer*; *person of tact*; *girl of ten*; *on the point of leaving*). □ **be of** possess, give rise to (*is of great interest*). **of an evening** (or **morning** etc.) *colloq.* **1** on most evenings (or mornings etc.). **2** at some time in the evenings (or mornings etc.). **of late** recently. **of old** formerly. [Old English]

**of-** see OB-.

**off** — *adv.* **1** away; at or to a distance (*drove off*; *3 kilometres off*). **2** out of position; not on, or touching, or attached; loose, separate, gone (*has come off*; *take your coat off*). **3** so as to be rid of (*sleep it off*). **4** so as to break continuity or continuance; discontinued, stopped (*turn off the radio*; *take a day off*; *the game is off*). **5** not available on a menu etc. (*barramundi is off*). **6** to the end; entirely; so as to be clear (*clear off*; *finish off*; *pay off*). **7** situated as regards money, supplies, etc. (*well off*; *badly off for vegetables*). **8** off stage (*noises off*). **9** (of food etc.) beginning to decay. — *prep.* **1 a** from; away, down, or up from (*fell off the chair*; *took something off the price*). **b** not on (*off the pitch*). **2 a** temporarily relieved of or abstaining from (*off duty*). **b** temporarily not attracted by (*off his food*). **c** not achieving (*off form*). **d** not up to (usual) standard (*off his game today*). **3** using as a source or means of support (*live off the land*). **4** leading from; not far from (*a street off Bennelong Avenue*). **5** at a short distance to sea from (*sank off Cape York Peninsula*). — *adj.* **1** far, further (*the off side of the wall*). **2** (of a part of a vehicle, animal, or road) right (*the off front wheel*). **3** *Cricket* designating the half of the field (as divided lengthways through the pitch) to which the striker's feet are pointed. **4** *colloq.* **a** annoying; unfair; in bad taste (*that's really off*). **b** somewhat unwell (*feeling a bit off*). **5** (of the period) not spent at work (*off days*; *off hours*). **6** worse than usual, bad (*it's been an off year for the tourist industry*). — *n.* **1** the off side in cricket. **2** start of a race. □ **off and on** intermittently; now and then. **off the cuff** see CUFF¹. [var. of OF]

---

■ **Usage** The use of *off of* for the preposition *off* (sense 1a), e.g. *picked it up off of the floor*, is non-standard and should be avoided.

---

**offal** /**of**-uhl/ *n.* **1** less valuable edible parts of a carcass, esp. the heart, liver, brain, etc. **2** inedible parts of a carcass. **3** refuse; scraps. [Dutch *afval*: related to OFF, FALL]

**offbeat** — *adj.* **1** not coinciding with the beat. **2** eccentric, unconventional. — *n.* any of the unaccented beats in a bar.

**off-centre** *adj. & adv.* not quite centrally placed.

**off chance** *n.* (often prec. by *the*) remote possibility.

**off colour** *predic. adj.* **1** unwell. **2** somewhat indecent.

**offcourse** /of-**kaws**/ *adj.* (of betting etc.) taking place away from a racecourse (opp. ONCOURSE).

**offcut** *n.* remnant of timber, paper, etc., after cutting.

**off day** *n. colloq.* day when one is not at one's best.

**offence** /uh-**fens**/ *n.* **1** illegal act; crime. **2** sin; wrongdoing. **3** upsetting of feelings; insult; umbrage (*give offence*; *take offence*). **4** act of attacking or taking the offensive; aggressive action. [related to OFFEND]

**offend** /uh-**fend**/ *v.* **1** cause offence to or resentment in; upset. **2** displease, anger. **3** (often foll. by *against*) do wrong; transgress; sin. □ **offender** *n.* **offending** *adj.* [Latin *offendo offens-* strike against, displease]

**offensive** /uh-**fen**-siv/ — *adj.* **1** causing offence; insulting (*offensive language*). **2** disgusting (*offensive smell*). **3 a** aggressive, attacking. **b** (of a weapon) for attacking. — *n.* **1** aggressive action, attitude (*take the offensive*). **2** military campaign (*the UN offensive against Iraq*). **3** aggressive or forceful action in pursuit of a cause (*a big peace offensive*). □ **offensively** *adv.* **offensiveness** *n.*

**offer** — *v.* **1** present for acceptance, refusal, or consideration (*offered me a lift*; *offer one's services*; *no apology was offered*). **2** (foll. by *to* + infin.) express readiness or show intention (*offered to take the children*). **3** provide; give an opportunity for. **4** make available for sale. **5** present to the attention (*each day offers new opportunities*). **6** present (a sacrifice etc.) to a deity. **7** present itself; occur (*as opportunity offers*). **8** attempt (violence, resistance, etc.). — *n.* **1** expression of readiness to do or give if desired, or to buy or sell (for a certain amount). **2** amount offered. **3** proposal (esp. of marriage). **4** a bid. □ **on offer** for sale at a certain (esp. reduced) price. [Latin *offero oblat-*]

**offering** *n.* **1** contribution or gift, esp. of money. **2** thing offered as a religious sacrifice etc.

**offertory** /**of**-uh-tuh-ree, -tree/ *n.* (*pl.* **-ies**) **1** (in the Mass) offering of the bread and wine to God by the priest before the consecration. **2 a** the offering, esp. of money, by the people during a religious service. **b** what has been so offered. [Church Latin: related to OFFER]

**offhand** — *adj.* curt or casual in manner. — *adv.* without preparation or thought (*can't say offhand*). □ **offhanded** *adj.* **offhandedly** *adv.* **offhandedness** *n.*

**office** /of-uhs/ *n.* **1** room or building used as a place of business, esp. for clerical or administrative work. **2** room or area for a particular business (*post office*). **3** local centre of a large business (*our Brisbane office*). **4** position with duties attached to it. **5** tenure of an official position (*hold office*). **6** (**Office**) quarters, staff, or collective authority of a Government department etc. (*Taxation Office*). **7** duty, task, function. **8** (usu. in *pl.*) piece of kindness; service (esp. *through the good offices of*). **9 a** *Eccl.* (in full **divine office**) daily recital by all in major orders of the prayers, psalms, readings from Scripture, etc., in the breviary. **b** (often in *pl.*) religious service or ceremony. [Latin *officium* from *opus* work, *facio (-fic-)* do]

**officer** /of-uh-suh/ *n.* **1** person holding a position of authority or trust, esp. one with a commission in the army, navy, air force, etc. **2** policeman or policewoman. **3** holder of a post in a society (e.g. the president or secretary). **4** holder of an office in the public service etc. (usu. with a qualifying word: *housing officer*; *probation officer*). **5** (**Officer**) member of the grade below Companion in the Order of Australia.

**official** /uh-**fish**-uhl/ — *adj.* **1** of an office or its tenure. **2** characteristic of officials and bureaucracy. **3** properly authorised. — *n.* person holding office or engaged in official duties. □ **officialdom** *n.* **officially** *adv.*

**officialese** /uh-,fish-uh-**leez**/ *n. derog.* language characteristic of official documents.

**officiate** /uh-**fish**-ee-ayt/ *v.* (**-ting**) **1** act in an official capacity. **2** conduct a religious service. □ **officiation** /-ay-shuhn/ *n.* **officiator** *n.*

**officious** /uh-**fish**-uhs/ *adj.* **1** exerting authority aggressively; domineering. **2** intrusive in correcting, offering help, etc. □ **officiously** *adv.* **officiousness** *n.*

**offing** *n.* more distant part of the sea in view. □ **in the offing** not far away; likely to appear or happen soon. [probably from OFF]

**off-key** *adj. & adv.* **1** out of tune. **2** not quite appropriate.

**off-line** *Computing* — *adj.* not on-line. — *adv.* with a delay between the

production of data and its processing; not under direct computer control.

**offload** *v.* **1** get rid of (esp. something unpleasant) by passing it to someone else. **2** = UNLOAD (senses 1, 2).

**off-peak** *adj.* used or for use at times other than those of greatest demand.

**off-putting** /of-**puut**-ing/ *adj.* disconcerting; repellent.

**off-season** *n.* time of the year when business etc. is slack.

**offset** — *n.* /of-set/ **1** side-shoot from a plant serving for propagation. **2** compensation; consideration or amount diminishing or neutralising the effect of a contrary one. **3** sloping ledge in a wall etc. **4** (often *attrib.*) method of printing in which ink is transferred from a plate or stone to a rubber surface and from there to paper etc. — *v.* /of-set, of-**set**/ (**-setting**; *past* and *past part.* **-set**) **1** counterbalance, compensate (*this win offsets all my losses*). **2** print by the offset process.

**offshoot** *n.* **1** side-shoot or branch. **2** derivative.

**offshore** *adj.* **1** at sea some distance from the shore. **2** (of the wind) blowing seawards. **3** (of a business) based in a foreign country in order to minimise taxation etc.

**offside** — *adj.* **1** (of a player in a field game) in a position (usu. ahead of the ball) that is not allowed if it affects play. **2** (of a bullock team) of or pertaining to the right-hand side (opp. the near or left-hand side). **3 a** (foll. by *with*) incurring hostility or opposition from (*found himself offside with most of the committee*). **b** opposed, hostile (*don't get her offside – we need her support*). — *n.* right side of a vehicle, animal, etc. — *v.* act as an offsider.

**offsider** *n.* **1** partner; assistant (orig. a bullock-driver's assistant). **2** friend, mate.

**offspring** *n.* (*pl.* same) **1** person's child, children, or descendants. **2** animal's young or descendants. **3** result. [Old English: see OFF, SPRING]

**off-stage** *adj. & adv.* not on the stage; not visible to the audience.

**oft** *adv. archaic* often. [Old English]

**often** /of-uhn, of-tuhn/ *adv.* (**oftener, oftenest**) **1 a** frequently; many times. **b** at short intervals. **2** in many instances.

**ogee** /oh-jee/ *n.* S-shaped line or moulding. [apparently from OGIVE]

**ogive** /oh-juyv/ *n.* **1** pointed arch. **2** diagonal rib of a vault. [French]

**ogle** /oh-guhl/ — *v.* (**-ling**) look amorously or lecherously (at). — *n.* amorous or lecherous look. [probably Low German or Dutch]

**ogre** /**oh**-guh/ n. (fem. **ogress** /-gruhs/) **1** man-eating giant in folklore. **2** terrifying person. □ **ogreish** /**oh**-guh-rish/ adj. (also **ogrish**). [French]

**oh** /oh/ int. (also **O**) expressing surprise, pain, entreaty, etc. □ **oh** (or **o**) **for** I wish I had. **oh well** expressing resignation. [var. of O⁴]

**ohm** /ohm/ n. SI unit of electrical resistance. [*Ohm*, name of a physicist]

**-oid** suffix forming adjectives and nouns, denoting form or resemblance (*asteroid*; *rhomboid*; *thyroid*). [Greek *eidos* form]

**oil** — n. **1** any of various viscous, usu. inflammable liquids insoluble in water (*cooking oil*; *drill for oil*). **2** (in comb.) using oil as fuel (*oil-heater*). **3 a** (usu. in pl.) = OIL-PAINT. **b** picture painted in oil-paints. **4** (prec. by *the*) information, news (*what's the oil on . . .?*). **5** (prec. by *the* + *dinkum* or *good* or *straight*) reliable information (*gave us the dinkum oil on the crisis*). — v. **1** apply oil to; lubricate. **2** impregnate or treat with oil (*oiled silk*). **3 a** (foll. by *up*) colloq. give information or news to (*oiled him up on the latest developments*). **b** flatter. [Latin *oleum* olive oil]

**oilcloth** n. fabric, esp. canvas, water-proofed with oil or another substance.

**oil-colour** var. of OIL-PAINT.

**oilfield** n. area yielding mineral oil.

**oil-paint** n. (also **oil-colour**) paint made by mixing powdered pigment in oil. □ **oil-painting** n.

**oil rig** n. structure with equipment for drilling an oil well.

**oilskin** n. **1** cloth waterproofed with oil. **2 a** garment of this. **b** (in pl.) suit of this.

**oil slick** n. patch of oil, esp. on the sea.

**oil well** n. well from which mineral oil is drawn.

**oily** adj. (**-ier**, **-iest**) **1** of or like oil. **2** covered or soaked with oil. **3** (of a manner etc.) fawning, unctuous, ingratiating. □ **live off the smell of an oily rag** colloq. barely subsist; survive on next to nothing. □ **oiliness** n.

**ointment** /**oint**-muhnt/ n. smooth greasy healing or cosmetic preparation for the skin. [Latin *unguo* anoint]

**OK** /oh-**kay**/ (also **okay**) colloq. — adj. (often as int.) all right; satisfactory. — adv. well, satisfactorily. — n. (pl. **OKs**) approval, sanction. — v. (**OK's**, **OK'd**, **OK'ing**) approve, sanction. [originally US: probably abbreviation of *orl* (or *oll*) *korrect*, jocular form of 'all correct']

**okay** var. of OK.

**okra** /**ok**-ruh/ n. tall, orig. African plant

with long ridged seed-pods used for food. [West African native name]

**-ol** suffix in the names of alcohols or analogous compounds. [from ALCOHOL and Latin *oleum* oil]

**old** /ohld/ — adj. (**older**, **oldest**) **1 a** advanced in age; far on in the natural period of existence. **b** not young or near its beginning. **2** made long ago. **3** long in use. **4** worn, dilapidated, or shabby from the passage of time. **5** having the characteristics of age (*child has an old face*). **6** practised, inveterate (*old offender*). **7** belonging to the past; lingering on; former (*old times*; *old memories*; *our old house*). **8** dating from far back; long established or known; ancient, primeval (*an old family*; *old friends*; *old as the hills*). **9** (appended to a period of time) of age (*is four years old*; *four-year-old boy*; *a four-year-old*). **10** (of a language) as used in former or earliest times (*Old English*). **11** colloq. as a term of affection or casual reference (*good old Charlie*; *old thing*). — n. an ale, so called because made by top fermentation in the traditional manner (cf. NEW n.). □ **oldish** adj. **oldness** n. [Old English]

**old age** n. later part of normal life.

**old-age pension** n. means-tested pension paid by the government to people above a certain age. □ **old-age pensioner** n.

**old boy** n. former male pupil of a school.

**old chum** n. hist. immigrant with experience of life in Australia, esp. in the outback (opp. NEW CHUM 2 a).

**Old Dart** n. (Australian term for) Britain, esp. England. [British dial. pronunciation of *dirt*]

**olden** attrib. adj. archaic old; of old.

**old-fashioned** adj. showing or favouring the tastes of former times.

**old girl** n. former female pupil of a school.

**old guard** n. original, past, or conservative members of a group.

**old hand** n. **1** person who has had long experience of an activity, occupation, or place. **2** hist. convict with long experience of life in an Australian penal colony (opp. one newly arrived); an ex-convict. **3** hist. immigrant with some experience of life in Australia (opp. one newly arrived) (cf. OLD CHUM).

**old hat** adj. colloq. out of fashion, no longer 'in' (*Westerns are old hat*).

**oldie** n. colloq. **1** old person or thing. **2** (in pl.) parents (*he doesn't get on with his oldies*).

**old maid** n. **1** offens. elderly unmarried woman. **2** derog. prim and fussy person of either sex.

**old man** n. colloq. **1** (in full **old man kangaroo**) a fully grown male kangaroo. **2** attrib. of exceptional size, or duration, or intensity, etc. (old man crocodile; old man drought).

**old man saltbush** n. either of two shrubs of arid Australia, having grey-green foliage, used as fodder.

**old man's beard** n. Australian clematis, a vigorous climber with silvery young foliage, perfumed starry white flowers, and silvery beard-like hairs around the fruits.

**old master** n. **1** great artist of former times, esp. of the 13th–17th c. in Europe. **2** painting by such a painter.

**Old Norse** n. **1** Germanic language from which the Scandinavian languages are derived. **2** language of Norway and its colonies until the 14th c.

**old people** n.pl. **1** Aborigines who live in the traditional manner. **2** elderly Aborigines regarded by their descendants as repositories of traditional knowledge.

**old school tie** n. excessive loyalty to traditional values and to former pupils of one's own, esp. private, school.

**old stager** n. experienced person, an old hand.

**Old Testament** n. part of the Bible containing the scriptures of the Hebrews.

**old-time** attrib. adj. belonging to former times (old-time dancing).

**old wife** n. edible Australian fish, silvery with black stripes and supposedly venomous dorsal fins, purportedly so called because it grunts like an old wife when caught.

**old wives' tale** n. foolish or unscientific tradition or belief.

**old woman** n. colloq. **1** one's wife or mother. **2** fussy or timid man.

**Old World** n. Europe, Asia, and Africa.

**oleaginous** /ˌoh-lee-**aj**-uh-nuhs/ adj. **1** like or producing oil. **2 a** oily. **b** obsequious, ingratiating. [Latin: related to OIL]

**oleander** /ˌoh-lee-**an**-duh, ol-ee-/ n. poisonous evergreen flowering Mediterranean shrub. [Latin]

**olearia** /oh-lee-**air**-ree-uh, ol-ee-/ n. (also **daisy bush**) any of a large genus of shrubs, about 80 of the 100 or so species of which are endemic to Australia, having daisy flowers in white, blue, pink, or mauve.

**olefin** /**oh**-luh-fuhn/ n. (also **olefine**) Chem. = ALKENE. [French oléfiant oil-forming]

**oleo-** comb. form oil. [Latin oleum oil]

**olfaction** /ol-**fak**-shuhn/ n. act or capacity of smelling; the sense of smell. [Latin olfactus a smell]

**olfactory** /ol-**fak**-tuh-ree/ adj. of the sense of smell (olfactory nerves). [Latin oleo smell, facio make]

**oligarch** /**ol**-uh-ˌgahk/ n. member of an oligarchy. [Greek oligoi few]

**oligarchy** /**ol**-uh-ˌgah-kee/ n. (pl. **-ies**) **1** government, or nation governed, by a small group of people. **2** members of such a government. □ **oligarchic** /-**gah**-kik/ adj. **oligarchical** /-**gah**-ki-kuhl/ adj.

**oligo-** comb. form few, slight. [Greek oligos small, oligoi few]

**Oligocene** /**ol**-uh-guh-ˌseen/ — adj. of the third geological epoch of the Tertiary period. — n. this epoch. [OLIGO- Greek kainos new]

**oligotrophic** /ˌol-uh-goh-**trof**-ik, -**troh**-fik/ adj. (of a lake etc.) relatively poor in plant nutrients. [OLIGO-, Greek trophē nourishment]

**olive** /**ol**-uhv, ol-iv/ — n. **1** small oval hard-stoned fruit, green when unripe and bluish-black when ripe. **2** tree bearing this. **3** its wood. **4** olive green. — adj. **1** olive-green. **2** (of the complexion) yellowish-brown. [Latin oliva from Greek]

**olive branch** n. gesture of reconciliation or peace.

**olive green** adj. & n. (as adj. often hyphenated) dull yellowish green.

**olivine** /**ol**-uh-ˌveen/ n. mineral (usu. olive-green) composed of magnesium-iron silicate.

**Olympiad** /uh-**lim**-pee-ˌad/ n. **1 a** period of four years between Olympic Games, used by the ancient Greeks in dating events. **b** four-yearly celebration of the ancient Olympic Games. **2** celebration of the modern Olympic Games. **3** regular international contest in chess etc. [Greek Olumpias Olumpiad-: related to OLYMPIC]

**Olympian** /uh-**lim**-pee-uhn/ — adj. **1 a** of Mt. Olympus in Greece, traditionally the home of the Greek gods. **b** celestial, godlike. **2** (of manners etc.) magnificent, condescending, superior. **3** = OLYMPIC. — n. **1** any of the twelve Greek gods dwelling on Olympus. **2** person of great attainments or of superhuman detachment and calm. **3** competitor in the Olympic games. [from Mt. Olympus in Greece, or as OLYMPIC]

**Olympic** /uh-**lim**-pik/ — adj. of the Olympic games. — n.pl. (**the Olympics**) Olympic games. [Greek from Olympia in S. Greece]

**Olympic Games** n.pl. **1** ancient Greek

athletic, literary, and musical festival held in the plain of Olympia every four years. **2** modern international revival of the sports side of this.

**-oma** *suffix* forming nouns denoting tumours and other abnormal growths (*carcinoma*). [Greek]

**ombudsman** /**om**-buhdz-muhn/ *n.* (*pl.* **-men**) official appointed by a government to investigate complaints against public authorities. [Swedish, = legal representative]

**omega** /**oh**-muh-guh, oh-**mee**-guh/ *n.* **1** last (24th) letter of the Greek alphabet (Ω, ω). **2** last of a series; final development. [Greek *ō mega* = great O]

**omelette** /**om**-luht/ *n.* beaten eggs fried and often folded round a savoury filling. [French]

**omen** /**oh**-muhn/ — *n.* **1** event or object portending good or evil. **2** prophetic significance (*of good omen*). — *v.* (usu. in *passive*) portend. [Latin]

**omicron** /oh-**muy**-kruhn, **om**-ee-kron/ *n.* fifteenth letter of the Greek alphabet (O, o). [Greek *o mikron* = small o]

**ominous** /**om**-uh-nuhs/ *adj.* **1** threatening. **2** of evil omen; inauspicious. □ **ominously** *adv.* [Latin: related to OMEN]

**omission** /oh-**mish**-uhn, uh-/ *n.* **1** act or instance of omitting or being omitted. **2** something that has been omitted or overlooked.

**omit** /oh-**mit**, uh-/ *v.* (**-tt-**) **1** leave out; not insert or include. **2** leave undone. **3** (foll. by verbal noun or *to* + infin.) fail or neglect (*omitted saying anything*; *omitted to say*). [Latin *omitto omiss-*]

**omni-** *comb. form* **1** all; of all things. **2** in all ways or places. [Latin *omnis* all]

**omnibus** /**om**-nee-buhs, -bus/ — *n.* **1** *formal* bus. **2** volume containing several literary works previously published separately. — *adj.* **1** serving several purposes at once. **2** comprising several items. [Latin, = for all]

**omnipotent** /om-**nip**-uh-tuhnt/ *adj.* having great or absolute power. □ **omnipotence** *n.* [Latin: related to POTENT]

**omnipresent** /,om-nee-**prez**-uhnt/ *adj.* present everywhere at the same time. □ **omnipresence** *n.* [Latin: related to PRESENT[1]]

**omniscient** /om-**nis**-ee-uhnt/ *adj.* knowing everything or much. □ **omniscience** *n.* [Latin *scio* know]

**omnivorous** /om-**niv**-uh-ruhs/ *adj.* **1** feeding on both plant and animal material. **2** reading, observing, etc., everything that comes one's way. □ **omnivore** /**om**-nee-,vaw/ *n.* **omnivorousness** *n.* [Latin *voro* devour]

**on** — *prep.* **1** (so as to be) supported by, attached to, covering, or enclosing (*sat on a chair*; *stuck on the wall*; *rings on her fingers*; *leaned on his elbow*). **2** carried with; about the person of (*have you a pen on you?*). **3** (of time) exactly at; during (*on 29 May*; *on the hour*; *on schedule*; *closed on Tuesday*). **4** immediately after or before (*I saw them on my return*). **5** as a result (*on further examination, I found this*). **6** (so as to be) having membership etc. of or residence at or in (*is on the board of directors*; *lives on the continent*). **7** supported, succoured, or fuelled by (*lives on a grant*; *lives on sandwiches*; *runs on diesel*). **8** close to; just by (*house on the sea*; *lives on the main road*). **9** in the direction of; against. **10** so as to threaten; touching or striking (*advanced on Rome*; *pulled a knife on me*; *a punch on the nose*). **11** having as an axis or pivot (*turned on his heels*). **12** having as a basis or motive (*works on a ratchet*; *arrested on suspicion*). **13** having as a standard, confirmation, or guarantee (*had it on good authority*; *did it on purpose*; *I promise on my word*). **14** concerning or about (*writes on frogs*). **15** using or engaged with (*is on the pill*; *here on business*). **16** so as to affect (*walked out on her*). **17** at the expense of (*the drinks are on me*; *the joke is on him*). **18** added to (*disaster on disaster*; *ten cents on a glass of beer*). **19** in a specified manner or state (*on the cheap*; *on the run*). **20** denoting place where (*on the diggings*). — *adv.* **1** (so as to be) covering or in contact (*put your boots on*). **2** in the appropriate direction; towards something (*look on*). **3** further forward; in an advanced position or state (*time is getting on*). **4** with continued movement or action (*play on*). **5** in operation or activity (*light is on*; *chase was on*). **6** due to take place as planned (*is the party still on?*). **7** *colloq.* **a** willing to participate or approve, make a bet, etc. (*you're on*). **b** practicable or acceptable (*that's just not on*). **8** being shown or performed (*a good film on tonight*). **9** on stage. **10** on duty. **11** forward (*head on*). — *adj.* *Cricket* designating the part of the field on the striker's side and in front of the wicket. — *n.* *Cricket* the on side. □ **be on about** *colloq.* discuss, esp. tediously (*what are they on about?*). **be on at** *colloq.* nag or grumble at. **be on to** *colloq.* realise the significance or intentions of (*was on to him from the start*). **have oneself on** see HAVE. **not on** see under N. **on and off** intermittently; now and then. **on and on** continually; at tedious length. **on for young and old** (of an argument, fight, party, etc.) lacking restraint, with everyone drawn in, participating. **on the weekend** (or **on weekends**) at or during the weekend (or weekends). **on with** *colloq.* amorously involved with. **on time** punctual, punctually. **on to** to a position on. [Old English]

**onanism** /**oh**-nuh-, niz-uhm/ *n. literary* **1** masturbation. **2** = COITUS INTERRUPTUS. [*Onan*, biblical person]

**once** /wuns/ — *adv.* **1** on one occasion only (*have read it once*). **2** at some point or period in the past (*could once touch my toes*). **3** ever or at all (*if you once forget it*). **4** multiplied by one; by one degree (*a cousin once removed*). — *conj.* as soon as (*once they have gone we can relax*). — *n.* one time or occasion (*just the once*). □ **all at once 1** suddenly. **2** all together. **at once 1** immediately. **2** simultaneously. **for once** on this (or that) occasion, even if at no other. **once again** (or **more**) another time. **once and for all** (or **once for all**) in a final manner, esp. after much hesitation. **once** (or **every once**) **in a while** from time to time. **once or twice** a few times. **once upon a time** at some unspecified time in the past. [originally genitive of ONE]

**once-over** *n. colloq.* **1** rapid inspection. **2** a beating up.

**oncer** /**wun**-suh/ *n. colloq.* **1** thing that occurs only once. **2** person elected as a member of parliament (esp. in a marginal seat), who is considered unlikely to hold the seat for more than one term.

**oncogene** /**ong**-kuh-, jeen/ *n.* gene which can transform a cell into a cancer cell. [Greek *ogkos* mass]

**oncology** /ong-**kol**-uh-jee/ *n.* the study of tumours. [Greek *ogkos* mass]

**oncoming** *adj.* approaching from the front.

**oncourse** *adj.* (of betting etc.) taking place at a racecourse (opp. OFFCOURSE).

**one** /wun/ — *adj.* **1** single and integral in number (*one tree*). **2** (with a noun implied) a single person or thing of the kind expressed or implied (*one of the best; a nasty one*). **3** particular but undefined, esp. as contrasted with another (*that is one view; one night last week*). **4** only such (*the one man who can do it*). **5** forming a unity (*one and undivided*). **6** identical; the same (*of one opinion*). **7** (in Aboriginal English) the indefinite article. — *n.* **1 a** lowest cardinal number. **b** thing numbered with it. **2** unity; a unit (*one is half of two; came in ones and twos*). **3** single thing, person, or example (often referring to a noun previously expressed or implied: *the big dog and the small one*).

**4** *colloq.* drink (*a quick one; have one on me*). **5** story or joke (*the one about the parrot*). **6** (in *pl.*) a call in two-up indicating that the coins have fallen unmatched. — *pron.* **1** person of a specified kind (*loved ones; like one possessed*). **2** any person, as representing people in general (*one is bound to lose in the end*). **3** I, me. □ **all one** (often foll. by *to*) a matter of indifference (*all one to me*). **at one** in agreement. **for one** being one, even if the only one (*I for one don't believe it*). **in one** in one's very first attempt (*got it in one; guessed it in one*). **one and all** everyone. **one by one** singly, successively. **one day 1** on an unspecified day. **2** at some unspecified future date. **one for the bitumen** (also **one for the road**) *colloq.* a last drink before leaving. **one or two** *colloq.* a few. [Old English]

───────────────

■ **Usage** The use of the pronoun *one* to mean 'I' or 'me' (e.g. *one would like to help*) is often regarded as an affectation.

───────────────

**one another** *pron.* each the other or others (as a formula of reciprocity: *love one another*).

**one-armed bandit** *n. colloq.* poker machine. [from the single lever to be pulled on (older) poker machines]

**one day of the year** *n.* (usu. prec. by *the*) Anzac Day.

**one-eyed** *adj.* strongly biased towards (a thing or a person) (*she's a one-eyed supporter of Labor*).

**one flag** *n.* (also **one flag only**) *Aust. Rules* signal for a behind.

**one-horse** *attrib. adj.* **1** using a single horse. **2** *colloq.* small, poorly equipped (*a one-horse town*).

**one-horse race** *n.* contest in which one competitor is far superior to all the others.

**one-liner** *n.* short joke or remark in a play, comedy routine, etc.

**oneness** *n.* **1** singleness. **2** uniqueness. **3** agreement. **4** sameness.

**one-night stand** *n.* **1** single performance of a play etc. in a place. **2** *colloq.* sexual liaison lasting only one night.

**one-off** — *attrib. adj.* made or done as the only one; not repeated. — *n.* one-off occurrence, achievement, etc.

**one-pub** *adj.* (of a town etc.) small, uninteresting, one-horse.

**onerous** /**oh**-nuh-ruhs/ *adj.* burdensome. □ **onerousness** *n.* [Latin: related to ONUS]

**oneself** *pron.* reflexive and emphatic form of *one* (*kill oneself; do it oneself*). □ **be oneself** act in one's normal unconstrained manner.

**one-sided** *adj.* **1** unfair, partial. **2** unequal (*the bout was a one-sided contest*). **3** having, or occurring on, one side only. **4** larger or more developed on one side. □ **one-sidedly** *adv.* **one-sidedness** *n.*

**one-sided bottlebrush** see CALOTHAMNUS.

**one-teacher school** *n.* small school in an isolated area in which one teacher teaches all grades.

**one-time** *attrib. adj.* former.

**one-to-one** *adj. & adv.* **1** involving or between only two people. **2** with one member of one group corresponding to one of another.

**one-track mind** *n.* mind preoccupied with one subject.

**one-upmanship** *n.* art of maintaining a psychological advantage over others.

**ongoing** *adj.* **1** continuing. **2** in progress.

**onion** /**un**-yuhn/ *n.* **1** vegetable with an edible bulb of a pungent smell and flavour. **2** *colloq.* the head (*use your onion*). □ **do one's onion** *colloq.* lose one's temper, fly into a rage. **know one's onions** be fully knowledgeable or experienced. **off one's onion** *colloq.* mad. □ **oniony** *adj.* [Latin *unio -onis*]

**onka** /**ong**-kuh/ *n.* (in full **onkaparinga** /,ong-kuh-puh-**ring**-guh/ ) *rhyming slang* a finger. [*Onkaparinga* propr. for a blanket]

**onkus** /**ong**-kuhs/ *adj. colloq.* **1** disagreeable; distasteful. **2** not functioning properly, out of order. [origin unknown]

**on-line** *Computing* — *adj.* directly connected, so that a computer immediately receives an input from or sends an output to a peripheral process etc.; carried out while so connected or under direct computer control. — *adv.* with the processing of data carried out simultaneously with its production; while connected to a computer; under direct computer control.

**onlooker** *n.* spectator. □ **onlooking** *adj.*

**only** /**ohn**-lee/ — *adv.* **1** solely, merely, exclusively; and no one or nothing more besides (*needed six only; is only a child*). **2** no longer ago than (*saw them only yesterday*). **3** not until (*arrives on only on Tuesday*). **4** with no better result than (*hurried home only to find her gone*). — *attrib. adj.* **1** existing alone of its or their kind (*their only son*). **2** best or alone worth considering (*the only place to eat*). — *conj. colloq.* except that; but (*I would go, only I feel ill*). [Old English: related to ONE]

■ **Usage** In informal English *only* is usually placed between the subject and verb regardless of what it refers to (e.g. *I only want to talk to you*); in more formal English it is often placed more exactly, esp. to avoid ambiguity (e.g. *I want to talk only to you*). In speech, intonation usually serves to clarify the sense.

**only too** *adv.* extremely (*is only too willing*).

**o.n.o.** *abbr.* or nearest offer.

**onomatopoeia** /,on-uh-,mat-uh-**pee**-uh/ *n.* formation of a word from a sound associated with what is named (e.g. *cuckoo, sizzle*). □ **onomatopoeic** *adj.* [Greek *onoma* name, *poieō* make]

**onrush** *n.* onward rush.

**onset** *n.* **1** attack. **2** beginning, esp. an energetic or determined one.

**onshore** *adj.* **1** on the shore. **2** (of the wind) blowing landwards from the sea.

**onside** *adj.* **1** (of a player in a field game) not offside. **2** cooperative, agreeing (*we need him to be onside with us on this*).

**onslaught** /**on**-slawt/ *n.* fierce attack. [Dutch: related to ON, *slag* blow]

**onto** *prep.* = *on to.*

■ **Usage** The form *onto* is still not fully accepted in the way that *into* is, although it is in wide use. It is however useful in distinguishing sense as between *we drove on to the beach* (i.e. in that direction) and *we drove onto the beach* (i.e. in contact with it).

**ontology** /on-**tol**-uh-jee/ *n.* branch of metaphysics dealing with the nature of being. □ **ontological** /-tuh-**loj**-i-kuhl/ *adj.* **ontologically** /-tuh-**loj**-i-kuh-lee, -klee/ *adv.* **ontologist** *n.* [Greek *ont-* being]

**onus** /**oh**-nuhs/ *n.* (*pl.* **onuses**) burden, duty, responsibility. [Latin]

**onward** /**on**-wuhd/ — *adv.* (also **onwards**) **1** forward, advancing. **2** into the future (*from 1993 onwards*). — *adj.* forward, advancing.

**onya!** /**on**-yuh/ *int. colloq.* = *good on you!* (see GOOD) (*onya, Bill! — that's a beaut!*). [abbreviation]

**onyx** /**on**-iks/ *n.* semiprecious variety of agate with coloured layers. [Greek *onux*]

**oodles** /**oo**-duhlz/ *n.pl. colloq.* very great amount. [origin unknown]

**Oodnagalahbi** /,ood-nuh-guh-**lah**-bee/ *n.* (also **Oodnagalabie**) an imaginary place, utterly remote and backward. [from *Oodna(datta)* name of a town in South Australia, GALAH, *- bi* (see also BULLAMAKANKA; WOOP WOOP)]

**oolite** /**oh**-uh-,luyt/ *n.* granular limestone. □ **oolitic** /-**lit**-ik/ *adj.* [Greek *ōion* egg]

**oomph** /uumf/ *n. colloq.* **1** energy, enthusiasm. **2** attractiveness, esp. sex appeal. [origin uncertain]

**oont** /uunt/ *n.* a camel. [Hindi *ūṇṭ*]

**oops** /uups, oops/ *int. colloq.* on making an obvious mistake. [natural exclamation]

**ooroo** var. of HOOROO.

**ooze¹** — *v.* (**-zing**) **1** trickle or leak slowly out. **2** (of a substance) exude fluid. **3** (often foll. by *with*) exudêe (a feeling) freely (*oozed (with) charm*). — *n.* sluggish flow. □ **oozy** *adj.* **oozily** *adv.* **ooziness** *n.* [Old English]

**ooze²** *n.* **1** wet mud; slime, esp. at the bottom of a lake etc. **2** bog or marsh. □ **oozy** *adj.* [Old English]

**op** *n. colloq.* operation. [abbreviation]

**op.** *abbr.* opus.

**op-** see OB-.

**opacity** /oh-**pas**-uh-tee/ *n.* **1** opaqueness. **2** obscurity of meaning. **3** dullness of understanding. [Latin: related to OPAQUE]

**opal** /**oh**-puhl/ *n.* semiprecious stone usu. of a milky or bluish colour and sometimes showing changing colours. [Latin]

**opal dirt** *n.* the type of earth in which opal occurs.

**opalescent** /ˌoh-puh-**les**-uhnt/ *adj.* iridescent. □ **opalescence** *n.*

**opaline** /**oh**-puh-ˌluyn/ *adj.* opal-like, opalescent.

**opaque** /oh-**payk**/ *adj.* (**opaquer**, **opaquest**) **1** not transmitting light. **2** impenetrable to sight. **3** unintelligible. **4** unintelligent, stupid. □ **opaquely** *adv.* **opaqueness** *n.* [Latin *opacus* shaded]

**op. cit.** *abbr.* in the work already quoted. [Latin *opere citato*]

**OPEC** /**oh**-pek/ *abbr.* Organisation of Petroleum Exporting Countries.

**open** /**oh**-puhn/ — *adj.* **1** not closed, locked, or blocked up; allowing access. **2** unenclosed, unconfined, unobstructed (*open forest*; *the open road*; *open views*). **3 a** uncovered, bare, exposed (*open drain*; *open wound*). **b** *Sport* (of a goal etc.) unprotected, undefended. **4** undisguised, public, manifest (*open scandal*; *open hostilities*). **5** expanded, unfolded, or spread out (*had the map open on the table*). **6** (of a fabric) not close; with gaps (*an open weave*). **7 a** frank and communicative. **b** open-minded. **8 a** accessible to visitors or customers; ready for business. **b** (of a meeting) admitting all, not restricted to members etc. **9** (of a race, competition, scholarship, etc.) unrestricted as to who may compete. **10** (of a government) conducted in an informative manner receptive to enquiry, criticism, etc., from the public. **11** (foll. by *to*) **a** willing to receive (*is open to offers*). **b** (of a choice, offer, or opportunity) available (*three courses open to us*). **c** vulnerable to, allowing of (*open to abuse*; *open to doubt*). **12 a** (of the mouth) with lips apart, esp. in surprise etc. **b** (of the eyes or ears) eagerly attentive. **13** *Mus.* (of a string) allowed to vibrate along its whole length. **14** (of a vowel) produced with a relatively wide opening of the mouth. **15** (of a return ticket) not restricted as to the day of travel. — *v.* **1** make or become open or more open (*opened the door*; *opened the box*; *the door slowly opened*). **2** remove the fastening etc. of (a container) to get access to the contents (*opened the envelope*). **3** (foll. by *into*, *on to*, etc.) (of a door, room, etc.) give access as specified (*opened on to a patio*). **4 a** start, establish, or set going (a business, activity, etc.) (*opened a new shop*; *opened fire*). **b** start (*conference opens today*). **5** (often foll. by *with*) start; begin speaking, writing, etc. (*show opens with a song*; *he opened with a joke*). **6** ceremonially declare (a building etc.) in use. **7** spread out or unfold (a map, newspaper, etc.). **8** reveal or communicate (one's feelings, intentions, etc.). **9** make (one's mind, heart, etc.) more sympathetic or enlightened. — *n.* **1** (prec. by *the*) **a** open space, country, or air. **b** public notice; general attention (esp. *into the open*). **2** open championship or competition etc. □ **open a person's eyes** enlighten a person. **open out 1** unfold. **2** develop, expand. **3** become communicative. **open up 1** unlock (premises). **2** make accessible. **3** reveal; bring to notice. **4** accelerate. **5** begin shooting or sounding. □ **openness** *n.* [Old English]

**open air** *n.* outdoors. □ **open-air** *attrib. adj.*

**open-and-shut** *adj.* straightforward.

**open book** *n.* **1** person whose motives, feelings, etc. are transparent, easily read. **2** anything which is easily understood.

**open-cut** *adj.* (of a mine or mining) with removal of the surface layers and working from above, not from shafts.

**open day** *n.* **1** day when the public may visit a place normally closed to them. **2** day when a university etc. puts itself, its courses, etc., on display for prospective students.

**open-door** *attrib. adj.* open, accessible.

**open-ended** *adj.* having no predetermined limit.

**opener** *n.* **1** device for opening tins,

bottles, etc. **2** *colloq.* first item on a programme etc. **3** *Cricket* opening batsman.

**open go** n. = OPEN SLATHER.

**open-handed** adj. generous.

**open-hearted** adj. frank and kindly.

**open-heart surgery** n. surgery with the heart exposed and the blood made to bypass it.

**open house** n. hospitality for all visitors.

**opening** — n. **1** aperture or gap. **2** opportunity; vacancy (for a job). **3** beginning; initial part. — *attrib. adj.* initial, first (*opening remarks*).

**open letter** n. letter of protest etc. addressed to an individual and published in a newspaper etc.

**openly** adv. **1** frankly. **2** publicly.

**open-minded** adj. accessible to new ideas; unprejudiced.

**open-mouthed** adj. aghast with surprise.

**open prison** n. prison with few restraints on prisoners' movements.

**open question** n. matter on which different views are legitimate.

**open sea** n. expanse of sea away from land.

**open secret** n. supposed secret known to many.

**open slather** n. (also **open go**) *colloq.* **1** freedom to operate without impediment, a free rein. **2** a free-for-all. [British dial. *slather* to squander]

**open verdict** n. verdict affirming that a crime has been committed but not specifying the criminal or (in case of violent death) the cause.

**opera¹** / *op-uh-ruh*/ n. **1 a** drama set to music for singers and instrumentalists. **b** this as a genre. **2** opera-house. [Latin, = labour, work]

**opera²** pl. of OPUS.

**operable** / *op-uh-ruh-buhl*/ adj. **1** that can be operated. **2** suitable for treatment by surgical operation. [Latin: related to OPERATE]

**opera house** n. **1** theatre for operas. **2** (in full **the Opera House**) the Sydney Opera House.

**operate** / *op-uh-,rayt*/ v. (**-ting**) **1** work, control (*operated the machinery*). **2** be in action; function (*the machine is operating well*). **3** produce an effect (*the tax operates to our disadvantage*). **4 a** perform a surgical operation. **b** conduct a military etc. action. **c** be active in business etc. **5** bring about. [Latin *operor* work: related to OPUS]

**operatic** / ,op-uh-*rat*-ik/ adj. **1** of or like an opera or opera singer (*an operatic voice*). **2** in opera (*an operatic soprano*). □ **operatically** adv.

**operating system** n. controlling software on a computer.

**operating theatre** n. room for surgical operations.

**operation** / ,op-uh-*ray*-shuhn/ n. **1** action, scope, or method of working or operating. **2** active process (*the operation of breathing*). **3** piece of work, esp. one in a series (*begin operations*). **4** act of surgery on a patient. **5** military manoeuvre. **6** financial transaction. **7** state of being active or functioning (*in operation*). **8** subjection of a number etc. to a process affecting its value or form, e.g. multiplication. [Latin: related to OPERATE]

**operational** adj. **1** of or engaged in or used for operations. **2** able or ready to function. □ **operationally** adv.

**operative** / *op-uh-ruh-tiv*/ — adj. **1** in operation; having effect. **2** having the main relevance (*'may' is the operative word*). **3** of or by surgery. — n. worker, esp. a skilled one. [Latin: related to OPERATE]

**operator** n. **1** person operating a machine etc., esp. connecting lines in a telephone exchange. **2** person engaging in business. **3** *colloq.* person acting in a specified way (*smooth operator*). **4** symbol or function denoting an operation in mathematics, computing, etc.

**operculum** / uh-*per*-kyuh-luhm, oh-*per*-/ n. (pl. **-cula**) **1** fish's gill-cover. **2** any of various other parts covering or closing an aperture in an animal or plant. [Latin *operio* cover (v.)]

**ophidian** / oh-*fid*-ee-uhn/ — n. member of a suborder of reptiles including snakes. — adj. **1** of this order. **2** snakelike. [Greek *ophis* snake]

**ophthalmia** / of-*thal*-mee-uh/ n. inflammation of the eye. [Greek *ophthalmos* eye]

**ophthalmic** / of-*thal*-mik/ adj. of or relating to the eye and its diseases.

**ophthalmology** / ,of-thal-*mol*-uh-jee/ n. study of the eye and its diseases. □ **ophthalmologist** n.

**ophthalmoscope** / of-*thal*-muh-,skohp/ n. instrument for examining the eye.

**-opia** comb. form denoting a visual disorder (*myopia*). [Greek *ōps* eye]

**opiate** / *oh*-pee-uht/ — adj. **1** containing opium. **2** narcotic, soporific. — n. **1** drug containing opium, usu. to ease pain or induce sleep. **2** soothing influence. [Latin: related to OPIUM]

**opine** / oh-*puyn*/ v. (**-ning**) (often foll. by *that*) *literary* hold or express as an opinion. [Latin *opinor* believe]

**opinion** /uh-**pin**-yuhn/ n. **1** unproven belief. **2** view held as probable. **3** what one thinks about something. **4** piece of professional advice (*a second opinion*). **5** estimation (*low opinion of*). □ **public opinion** see under P. [Latin: related to OPINE]

**opinionated** /uh-**pin**-yuh-,nay-tuhd/ adj. dogmatic in one's opinions.

**opinion poll** n. assessment of public opinion by questioning a representative sample.

**opium** /**oh**-pee-uhm/ n. drug made from the juice of a certain poppy, used esp. as an analgesic and narcotic. [Latin from Greek *opion*]

**opossum** /uh-**pos**-uhm/ n. **1** tree-living American marsupial. **2** = POSSUM. [Virginian Indian]

■ **Usage** In Australia and New Zealand, *opossum* has now been replaced by *possum*.

**opp.** abbr. opposite.

**opponent** /uh-**poh**-nuhnt/ n. person who opposes. [Latin *oppono opposit-* set against]

**opportune** /**op**-uh-,tyoon/ adj. **1** well-chosen or especially favourable (*opportune moment*). **2** (of an action or event) well-timed. [Latin *opportunus* (of the wind) driving towards the PORT[1]]

**opportunism** /,op-uh-**tyoo**-niz-uhm, op-uh-choo-/ n. adaptation of one's policy or judgment to circumstances or opportunity, esp. regardless of principle. □ **opportunist** n. **opportunistic** /-**nis**-tik/ adj. **opportunistically** /-**nis**-ti-kuh-lee, -klee/ adv.

**opportunity** /,op-uh-**tyoo**-nuh-tee/ n. (pl. **-ies**) favourable chance or opening offered by circumstances.

**opportunity shop** n. shop (run by a charitable organisation) in which donated second-hand goods, esp. clothes, are sold.

**opposable** /uh-**poh**-zuh-buhl/ adj. Zool. (of the thumb in primates) capable of facing and touching the other digits on the same hand.

**oppose** /uh-**pohz**/ v. (**-sing**) **1** set oneself against; resist; argue or compete against. **2** (foll. by *to*) place in opposition or contrast. □ **as opposed to** in contrast with. □ **opposer** n. [Latin: related to OPPONENT]

**opposite** /**op**-uh-suht/ — adj. **1** facing, on the other side (*opposite page; the house opposite*). **2** (often foll. by *to*, *from*) contrary; diametrically different (*opposite opinion*). — n. opposite thing, person, or term. — adv. facing, on the other side

(*lives opposite*). — prep. **1** facing (*sat opposite me*). **2** in a complementary role to (another actor etc.) (*she played opposite Laurence Olivier*).

**opposite number** n. person holding an equivalent position in another group etc.

**opposite sex** n. (prec. by *the*) either sex in relation to the other.

**opposition** /,op-uh-**zish**-uhn/ n. **1** resistance, antagonism. **2** being hostile or in conflict or disagreement. **3** contrast, antithesis. **4 a** group or party of opponents or competitors. **b** (**the Opposition**) chief parliamentary party opposed to that in office. **5** act of placing opposite. **6 a** diametrically opposite position. **b** *Astron.* the position of two celestial bodies when their longitude differs by 180°, as seen from the earth. [Latin: related to POSITION]

**oppress** /uh-**pres**/ v. **1** keep in subservience. **2** govern or treat cruelly. **3** weigh down (with cares or unhappiness). □ **oppression** n. **oppressor** n. [Latin: related to PRESS[1]]

**oppressive** adj. **1** oppressing; harsh or cruel. **2** (of weather) close and sultry. □ **oppressively** adv. **oppressiveness** n.

**opprobrious** /uh-**proh**-bree-uhs/ adj. (of language) very scornful; abusive.

**opprobrium** /uh-**proh**-bree-uhm/ n. **1** disgrace. **2** cause of this. [Latin, = infamy, reproach]

**oppugn** /uh-**pyoon**/ v. controvert, call in question. [Latin *oppugno* fight against]

**op shop** n. (also **opp shop**) = OPPORTUNITY SHOP. [abbreviation]

**opt** v. (usu. foll. by *for*) make a choice, decide. □ **opt out** (often foll. by *of*) choose not to participate (in). [Latin *opto* choose, wish]

**optic** /**op**-tik/ adj. of the eye or sight (*optic nerve*). [Greek *optos* seen]

**optical** adj. **1** of sight; visual. **2** of or according to optics. **3** aiding sight. □ **optically** adv.

**optical disc** see DISC.

**optical fibre** n. thin glass fibre through which light can be transmitted to carry signals.

**optical illusion** n. **1** image which deceives the eye. **2** mental misapprehension caused by this.

**optician** /op-**tish**-uhn/ n. **1** maker, seller, or prescriber of spectacles and contact lenses etc. **2** person trained in the detection and correction of poor eyesight. [medieval Latin: related to OPTIC]

**optics** n.pl. (treated as *sing.*) science of light and vision.

**optimal** /**op**-tuh-muhl/ adj. best or most

favourable (*achieved the optimal result*). [Latin *optimus* best]

**optimise** /op-tuh-muyz/ *v.* (also **-ize**) (**-sing** or **-zing**) make the best or most effective use of. □ **optimisation** /-zay-shuhn/ *n.*

**optimism** /op-tuh-,miz-uhm/ *n.* **1** inclination to hopefulness and confidence (opp. PESSIMISM). **2** *Philos.* belief that this world is as good as it could be or that good must ultimately prevail over evil. □ **optimist** *n.* **optimistic** /-mis-tik/ *adj.* **optimistically** /-mis-ti-kuh-lee, -klee/ *adv.* [Latin *optimus* best]

**optimum** /op-tuh-muhm/ — *n.* (*pl.* **optima**, **-mums**) **1** most favourable conditions (for growth etc.). **2** best practical solution. — *adj.* = OPTIMAL. [Latin, neuter of *optimus* best]

**option** /op-shuhn/ *n.* **1 a** act or instance of choosing; a choice. **b** thing that is or may be chosen. **2** liberty to choose. **3** right to buy or sell at a specified price within a set time. □ **keep** (or **leave**) **one's options open** not commit oneself. [Latin: related to OPT]

**optional** *adj.* not obligatory. □ **optionally** *adv.*

**opulent** /op-yuh-luhnt/ *adj.* **1** wealthy. **2** luxurious (*opulent surroundings*). **3** abundant. □ **opulence** *n.* [Latin *opes* wealth]

**opus** /oh-puhs, op-uhs/ *n.* (*pl.* **opuses** or **opera** /op-uh-ruh/) **1** musical composition numbered as one of a composer's works (*Beethoven, opus 15*). **2** any artistic work (cf. MAGNUM OPUS). [Latin, = work]

**or¹** *conj.* **1** introducing an alternative (*white or black*; *take it or leave it*; *either come in or go out*; *whether or not*). **2** introducing an alternative name (*the lapwing or peewit*). **3** introducing an afterthought (*came in laughing – or was it crying?*). **4** = *or else* 1 (*run or you'll be late*). □ **or else** 1 otherwise (*run, or else you will be late*). **2** *colloq.* expressing a warning or threat (*be good or else*). [Old English]

**or²** *n.* Heraldry gold. [Latin *aurum* gold]

**-or** *suffix* forming nouns denoting esp. an agent (*actor*; *escalator*) or condition (*error*; *horror*). [Latin]

**oracle** /o-ruh-kuhl/ *n.* **1 a** place at which divine advice or prophecy was sought in classical antiquity. **b** the usu. ambiguous response given at an oracle. **c** prophet or prophetess at an oracle. **2** person or thing regarded as a source of wisdom etc. □ **oracular** /uh-rak-yuh-luh/ *adj.* [Latin *oraculum* from *oro* speak]

**oracy** /o-ruh-see, aw-/ *n.* ability to express oneself fluently in speech. [Latin *os*, *oris* mouth, after LITERACY]

**oral** /o-ruhl, aw-/ — *adj.* **1** by word of mouth; spoken; not written (*oral examination*). **2** done or taken by the mouth (*oral contraceptive*). **3** of the mouth. — *n. colloq.* spoken examination. □ **orally** *adv.* [Latin *os oris* mouth]

**orange** /o-rinj/ — *n.* **1 a** roundish reddish-yellow juicy citrus fruit. **b** tree bearing this. **2** its colour. — *adj.* orange-coloured. [Arabic *nāranj*]

**orange-bellied parrot** *n.* rare, chiefly coastal parrot of south-eastern Australia, having grass-green plumage above and a brilliant orange undersurface.

**orange blossom** *n.* flowers of the orange tree, traditionally worn by brides.

**orange horseshoe bat** *n.* tropical northern Australian bat with bright orange fur.

**orang-utan** /uh-,rang-uh-tan, uh-rang-uh-,tan/ *n.* (also **orang-outang**) large reddish-haired long-armed anthropoid ape of Borneo and Sumatra. [Malay, = wild man]

**oration** /o-ray-shuhn, uh-/ *n.* a formal or ceremonial speech. [Latin *oratio* discourse, prayer, from *oro* speak, pray]

**orator** /o-ruh-tuh/ *n.* **1** person making a formal speech. **2** eloquent public speaker. [Latin: related to ORATION]

**oratorio** /,o-ruh-taw-ree-oh/ *n.* (*pl.* **-s**) semi-dramatic work for orchestra and voices esp. on a sacred theme, performed without costume, scenery, or action. [Church Latin]

**oratory** /o-ruh-tuh-ree, -tree/ *n.* (*pl.* **-ies**) **1** art of or skill in public speaking. **2** small private chapel. □ **oratorical** /-to-ri-kuhl/ *adj.* [French and Latin *oro orat-* speak, pray]

**orb** — *n.* **1** globe surmounted by a cross as part of coronation regalia. **2** sphere, globe. **3** *poet.* celestial body. **4** *poet.* eye. — *v.* **1** enclose in (an orb); encircle. **2** form or gather into an orb. [Latin *orbis* ring]

**orbicular** /aw-bik-yuh-luh/ *adj. formal* circular or spherical. [Latin *orbiculus* diminutive of *orbis* ring]

**orbit** /aw-buht/ — *n.* **1 a** curved course of a planet, satellite, etc. **b** one complete passage around an orbited body. **2** person's range or sphere of action. **3 a** eye socket. **b** area around the eye of a bird or insect. **4** path of an electron round an atomic nucleus. — *v.* (**-t-**) **1** (of a satellite etc.) go round in orbit. **2** move in orbit round. **3** put into orbit. □ **orbital** *adj.* **orbiter** *n.* [Latin *orbitus* circular]

**orc** *n.* fierce goblin; monster; ogre. [origin uncertain]

**orca** /aw-kuh/ n. **1** any of various cetaceans, esp. the killer whale. **2** any other large sea-animal or monster. [Latin]

**orchard** /aw-chuhd/ n. piece of enclosed land with fruit-trees. [Latin *hortus garden*, YARD²]

**orchardist** n. commercial fruit-grower.

**orchestra** /aw-ki-struh/ n. **1** large group of instrumentalists combining strings, woodwinds, brass, and percussion. **2** (in full **orchestra pit**) part of a theatre etc. where the orchestra plays, usu. in front of the stage and on a lower level. □ **orchestral** /-kes-truhl/ adj. [Greek, = area for the chorus in drama]

**orchestrate** /aw-kuh-strayt/ v. (**-ting**) **1** arrange or compose for orchestral performance. **2** arrange or build up (elements of a situation etc.) to achieve maximum effect. □ **orchestration** /-stray-shuhn/ n.

**orchid** /aw-kuhd/ n. **1** any of various plants bearing flowers in fantastic shapes and brilliant colours, usu. having one petal larger than the others and variously spurred, lobed, pouched, etc. **2** flower of any of these plants. [Greek *orkhis*, originally = testicle]

**orchitis** /aw-kuy-tuhs/ n. inflammation of the testicles. [Greek *orkhis* testicle]

**ordain** /aw-dayn/ v. **1** confer the sacrament of holy orders on; appoint to the priesthood or the ministry. **2 a** decree, order (*ordained that he should resign*). **b** (of God, fate, etc.) destine (*has ordained us to die*). [Latin *ordino*: related to ORDER]

**ordeal** /aw-deel/ n. **1** painful or horrific experience; severe trial. **2** *hist.* test of an accused person by subjection to severe pain, with survival taken as divine proof of innocence. [Old English]

**order** — n. **1 a** condition in which every part, unit, etc., is in its right place; tidiness. **b** specified sequence, succession, etc. (*alphabetical order; the order of events*). **2** authoritative command, direction, instruction, etc. **3** state of peaceful harmony under a constituted authority (*order was restored; law and order*). **4 a** direction to supply or pay something. **b** goods etc. to be supplied. **5** a social class; its members (*the lower orders*). **6** kind; sort (*talents of a high order*). **7** constitution or nature of the world, society, etc. (*the moral order; the order of things*). **8** *Biol.* taxonomic rank below a class and above a family. **9** (**Order**) community of monks, friars, priests, or nuns, bound by a common rule of life (*Franciscan Order*). **10 a** any of the grades of the Christian ministry. **b** (in *pl.*) status of a member of

the clergy (*women now being admitted to Anglican orders*). **11** any of the five classical styles of architecture (*Doric order*). **12** company of persons distinguished by a particular honour (*Order of Australia*). **13** *Eccl.* the stated form of divine service (*the order of confirmation*). **14** system of rules or procedure (at meetings etc.) (*point of order*). **15** *Mil.* a style of dress and equipment (*review order*). **16** any of the nine grades of angelic beings. — v. **1** command; bid; prescribe. **2** command or direct (a person) to a specified destination (*ordered them home*). **3** direct a waiter, tradesman, etc., to supply (*ordered dinner; ordered a new suit*). **4** (often as **ordered** adj.) put in order; regulate (*an ordered life*). **5** (of God, fate, etc.) ordain (*fate ordered it otherwise*). □ **in** (or **out of**) **order 1** in the correct (or incorrect) sequence or position. **2** fit (or not fit) for use. **3** according (or not according) to the rules at a meeting etc. **in order that** with the intention; so that. **in order to** with the purpose of doing; with a view to. **major orders** *Eccl.* the higher grades of ordination: bishop, priest, deacon, subdeacon. **minor orders** grades of ordination below subdeacon. **of** (or **in**) **the order of** approximately. **on order** ordered but not yet received. **order about** command officiously. **to order** as specified by the customer. [Latin *ordo ordin-* row, series, command]

**orderly** — adj. **1** methodically arranged or inclined, tidy. **2** well-behaved. — n. (pl. **-ies**) **1** male cleaner in a hospital. **2** soldier who carries orders for an officer etc. □ **orderliness** n.

**orderly room** n. room in a barracks used for company business.

**ordinal** /aw-duh-nuhl/ n. (in full **ordinal number**) number defining position in a series, e.g. 'first', 'second', 'third', etc. (cf. CARDINAL NUMBER). [Latin: related to ORDER]

**ordinance** /aw-duh-nuhns/ n. an authoritative order; a decree. [Latin: related to ORDAIN]

**ordinand** /aw-duh-nuhnd/ n. candidate for ordination, esp. to the degree of priesthood. [Latin: related to ORDAIN]

**ordinary** /aw-duh-nuh-ree, aw-duhn-ree/ — adj. **1** normal, usual. **2** commonplace, unexceptional. — n. (pl. **-ies**) *RC Ch.* parts of the Mass (opp. PROPER) that do not vary from day to day. □ **in the ordinary way** in normal circumstances. **out of the ordinary** unusual. □ **ordinarily** adv. **ordinariness** n. [Latin: related to ORDER]

**ordinate** /aw-duh-nuht/ n. Math. co-ordinate measured usu. vertically. [Latin: related to ORDAIN]

**ordination** /,aw-duh-**nay**-shuhn/ n. act of conferring of holy orders.

**ordnance** /awd-nuhns/ n. **1** artillery; military supplies. **2** government service dealing with these. [contraction of ORDINANCE]

**Ordovician** /,aw-doh-**vish**-ee-uhn/ — adj. of the second period in the Palaeozoic era. — n. this period. [Latin Ordovices, an ancient British tribe in N. Wales]

**ordure** /aw-dyor/ n. dung. [Latin horridus: related to HORRID]

**ore** /aw/ n. solid rock or mineral from which metal or other valuable minerals may be extracted. [Old English]

**oregano** /,o-ruh-**gah**-noh/ n. dried wild marjoram as seasoning. [Spanish]

**organ** /aw-guhn/ n. **1 a** musical instrument having pipes supplied with air from bellows and operated by keyboards and pedals. **b** instrument producing similar sounds electronically. **c** harmonium. **2 a** part of an animal or plant body serving a particular function (vocal organs; digestive organs). **b** esp. joc. penis. **3** medium of communication, esp. a newspaper representing a party or interest. [Greek organon tool]

**organ bird** n. either of two Australian birds having an extremely melodious song: the pied butcherbird and the magpie.

**organdie** /aw-guhn-dee/ n. fine translucent muslin, usu. stiffened. [French]

**organ-grinder** n. **1** player of a barrel-organ. **2** (in full **organ-grinder lizard**) any of many Australian lizards having a characteristic waving movement of a forelimb as if turning the handle of a barrel-organ.

**organic** /aw-**gan**-ik/ adj. **1** of or affecting a bodily organ or organs. **2** (of a plant or animal) having organs or an organised physical structure. **3** produced without the use of artificial fertilisers, pesticides, etc. (organic vegetables; organic gardening). **4** (of a chemical compound etc.) containing carbon. **5 a** structural, inherent. **b** constitutional. **6** organised or systematic (an organic whole). □ **organically** adv. [Greek: related to ORGAN]

**organic chemistry** n. chemistry of carbon compounds.

**organisation** /,aw-guh-nuy-**zay**-shuhn/ n. (also **-ization**) **1** act or instance of organising; state of being organised. **2** organised body, esp. a business, charity, etc. **3** systematic arrangement; tidiness. □ **organisational** adj.

**organise** /aw-guh-,nuyz/ v. (also **-ize**) (**-sing** or **-zing**) **1 a** give an orderly structure to, systematise (must organise my notes). **b** make arrangements for (a person or oneself) (helped to organise his affairs). **2 a** initiate, arrange for (organised a working-party). **b** provide; take responsibility for (who will organise the sandwiches?). **3** (often absol.) **a** enlist (a person or group) in a trade union, political party, etc. **b** form (a trade union etc.) (organised the workers). **4** (esp. as **organised** adj.) make organic; make into living tissue. □ **organiser** n. [Latin: related to ORGAN]

**organism** /aw-guh-,niz-uhm/ n. **1** living being with interdependent parts sharing the life processes. **2** individual plant or animal. **3** system made up of interdependent parts compared to a living being. [French: related to ORGANISE]

**organist** /aw-guh-nuhst/ n. organ-player.

**organo-** comb. form **1** esp. Biol. organ. **2** Chem. organic. [Greek]

**organza** /aw-gan-zuh/ n. thin stiff transparent silk or synthetic dress fabric. [origin uncertain]

**orgasm** /aw-gaz-uhm/ — n. climax of sexual excitement esp. in the genital organs, esp. in sexual intercourse. — v. have a sexual orgasm. □ **orgasmic** /-gaz-mik/ adj. [Greek, = excitement]

**orgy** /aw-jee/ n. (pl. **-ies**) **1** a wild drunken festivity with indiscriminate sexual activity. **2** uncontrolled, wild activity of any kind (an orgy of spending). □ **orgiastic** /,aw-jee-as-tik/ adj. [Greek orgia pl.]

**oriel** /aw-ree-uhl, o-/ n. (in full **oriel window**) projecting window of an upper storey. [French]

**orient** — n. /aw-ree-uhnt, o-/ (**the Orient**) countries east of the Mediterranean, esp. E. Asia. — v. /aw-ree-,ent, o-/ **1 a** place or determine the position of with the aid of a compass; find the bearings of. **b** (often foll. by towards) direct. **2** place (a building etc.) to face east. **3** turn eastward or in a specified direction. □ **orient oneself** determine how one stands in relation to one's surroundings. [Latin oriens -entis rising, sunrise, east]

**oriental** /,aw-ree-**en**-tuhl, ,o-/ (often **Oriental**) — adj. of the East, esp. E. Asia; of the Orient. — n. native of the Orient.

**orientate** /o-ree-en-,tayt, aw-/ v. (**-ting**) = ORIENT v. [apparently from ORIENT]

**orientation** /,o-ree-en-**tay**-shuhn, ,aw-/ n. **1** act or instance of orienting or state of being oriented. **2 a** relative position. **b** person's attitude or adjustment in relation to circumstances. **3** introduction to a subject or situation; briefing. □ **orientational** *adj.*

**orienteering** /ˌaw-ree-en-**teer**-ring, ˌo-/ *n.* competitive sport in which runners cross open country with a map, compass, etc. [Swedish]

**orifice** /**o**-ruh-fuhs/ *n.* an opening, esp. the mouth of a cavity, a bodily aperture, etc. [Latin *os or-* mouth, *facio* make]

**origami** /ˌo-ruh-**gah**-mee/ *n.* art of folding paper into decorative shapes, figures of birds, etc. [Japanese]

**origin** /**o**-ruh-juhn/ *n.* **1** starting-point; source (*'kangaroo' is a word of Aboriginal origin*). **2** (often in *pl.*) ancestry, parentage. **3** *Math.* point from which coordinates are measured. [Latin *origo origin-* from *orior* rise]

**original** /uh-**rij**-uh-nuhl/ — *adj.* **1** existing from the beginning; earliest; innate. **2** *hist.* Aboriginal. **3** inventive; creative; not derivative or imitative (*has an original mind*). **4** not copied or translated; by the artist etc. himself (*in the original Greek; has an original Rembrandt*). — *n.* **1** original model, pattern, picture, etc., from which another is copied or translated (*kept the copy and destroyed the original*). **2** eccentric or unusual person. □ **originally** *adv.*

**originality** /uh-ˌrij-uh-**nal**-uh-tee/ *n.* (*pl.* **-ies**) **1** power of creating or thinking creatively. **2** newness or freshness (*this vase has originality*).

**original sin** *n.* innate human sinfulness held to be a result of the Fall of Adam and Eve.

**originate** /uh-**rij**-uh-ˌnayt/ *v.* (**-ting**) **1** cause to begin; initiate. **2** have as an origin; begin. □ **origination** /-**nay**-shuhn/ *n.* **originator** *n.*

**oriole** /**aw**-ree-ohl/ *n.* any bird of the genus *Oriolus*, many of which have striking plumage, esp. the yellow oriole of Australia. [Latin *aurum* gold]

**ormolu** /**aw**-muh-ˌloo/ *n.* **1** (often *attrib.*) gilded bronze or gold-coloured alloy. **2** articles made of or decorated with these. [French *or moulu* powdered gold]

**ornament** — *n.* /**aw**-nuh-muhnt/ **1 a** thing used to adorn or decorate. **b** quality or person bringing honour or distinction (*she's an ornament to the legal profession*). **2** decoration, esp. on a building (*tower rich in ornament*). **3** embellishments and decorations made to a melody. — *v.* /**aw**-nuh-ˌment/ adorn; beautify. □ **ornamental** /ˌaw-nuh-**men**-tuhl/ *adj.* **ornamentation** /-men-**tay**-shuhn/ *n.* [Latin *orno ornat-* adorn]

**ornate** /aw-**nayt**/ *adj.* **1** elaborately adorned; highly decorated. **2** (of literary style) convoluted; flowery. □ **ornately** *adv.* **ornateness** *n.* [Latin: related to ORNAMENT]

**ornitho-** *comb. form* bird. [Greek, from *ornis ornithos* bird]

**ornithology** /ˌaw-nuh-**thol**-uh-jee/ *n.* the scientific study of birds. □ **ornithological** /-thuh-**loj**-i-kuhl/ *adj.* **ornithologist** *n.* [Greek *ornithologos* treating of birds (as ORNITHO-, -LOGY)]

**ornithorhynchus** /ˌaw-nuh-thuh-**ring**-kuhs/ *n.* = PLATYPUS. [ORNITHO-, Greek *rhugkhos* bill]

**orotund** /**o**-ruh-ˌtund/ *adj.* **1** (of the voice) full, round; imposing. **2** (of writing, style, etc.) pompous; pretentious. [Latin *ore rotundo* with rounded mouth]

**orphan** /**aw**-fuhn/ — *n.* child whose parents are dead. — *v.* bereave (a child) of its parents (*children orphaned by war*). [Latin from Greek, = bereaved]

**orphanage** *n.* home for orphans.

**orris** /**o**-ruhs/ *n.* **1** a kind of iris. **2** = ORRISROOT. [alteration of IRIS]

**orrisroot** *n.* fragrant iris root used in perfumery etc.

**Orstralia** /aw-**stray**-lee-uh/ *n.* (also **Orstralier**) representation for satiric effect of an exaggerated, esp. British, pronunciation of 'Australia' (*the Queen of Australia calls it 'Orstralia'*).

**ort** *n. colloq.* backside; anus. [origin unknown]

**ortho-** *comb. form* **1** straight. **2** right, correct. [Greek *orthos* straight]

**orthodontics** /ˌaw-thuh-**don**-tiks/ *n.pl.* (treated as *sing.*) (also **orthodontia**) correction of irregularities in the teeth and jaws. □ **orthodontic** *adj.* **orthodontist** *n.* [Greek *odous odont-* tooth]

**orthodox** /**aw**-thuh-ˌdoks/ *adj.* **1** holding usual or accepted opinions, esp. on religion, morals, etc. **2** generally approved; conventional (*orthodox medicine*). **3** (also **Orthodox**) (of Judaism) strictly traditional. □ **orthodoxy** *n.* [Greek *doxa* opinion]

**Orthodox Church** *n.* Eastern Church with the Patriarch of Constantinople as its head, and including the national Churches of Russia, Romania, Greece, etc.

**orthography** /aw-**thog**-ruh-fee/ *n.* (*pl.* **-ies**) **1** spelling (esp. with reference to its correctness). **2** the study or science of spelling. □ **orthographic** /-**graf**-ik/ *adj.* [Greek *orthographia*]

**orthopaedics** /ˌaw-thuh-**pee**-diks/ *n.pl.* (treated as *sing.*) (also **-pedics**) branch of medicine dealing with the correction of diseased, deformed, or injured bones or muscles. □ **orthopaedic** *adj.* **orthopaedist** *n.* [Greek *pais paid-* child]

**-ory** *suffix* **1** forming nouns denoting a place (*dormitory*; *refectory*). **2** forming adjectives and nouns relating to or involving a verbal action (*accessory*; *compulsory*). [Latin *-orius, -orium*]

**OS** *abbr.* **1** outsize. **2** *Computing* operating system.

**Os** *symb.* osmium.

**Oscar** /**os**-kuh/ *n.* any of the statuettes awarded by the US Academy of Motion Picture Arts and Sciences for excellence in film acting, directing, etc. [man's name]

**oscillate** /**os**-uh-ˌlayt/ *v.* (**-ting**) **1** (cause to) swing to and fro. **2** vacillate; vary between extremes. **3** (of an electric current) undergo high-frequency alternations. □ **oscillation** /-**lay**-shuhn/ *n.* **oscillator** *n.* [Latin *oscillo oscillat-* swing]

**oscillo-** *comb. form* oscillation, esp. of an electric current.

**oscilloscope** /o-**sil**-uh-ˌskohp/ *n.* device for viewing oscillations by a display on the screen of a cathode-ray tube.

**-ose¹** *suffix* forming adjectives denoting possession of a quality (*grandiose*; *verbose*). [Latin *-osus*]

**-ose²** *suffix Chem.* forming names of carbohydrates (*cellulose*; *sucrose*). [after GLUCOSE]

**osier** /**oh**-zee-uh/ *n.* **1** willow used in basketwork. **2** shoot of this. [French]

**-osis** *suffix* denoting a process or condition (*apotheosis*; *metamorphosis*), esp. a pathological state (*neurosis*; *thrombosis*). [Latin or Greek]

**-osity** *suffix* forming nouns from adjectives in *-ose* and *-ous* (*verbosity*; *curiosity*). [Latin *-ositas*]

**osmium** /**oz**-mee-uhm/ *n.* heavy hard bluish-white metallic element. [Greek *osmē* smell]

**osmosis** /oz-**moh**-suhs/ *n.* **1** passage of a solvent through a semi-permeable partition into another solution. **2** process by which something is acquired by absorption. □ **osmotic** /-**mot**-ik/ *adj.* [Greek *ōsmos* push]

**osprey** /**os**-pray, -pree/ *n.* (*pl.* **-s**) large bird of prey feeding on fish. [Latin *ossifraga* from *os* bone, *frango* break]

**osseous** /**os**-ee-uhs/ *adj.* **1** of bone. **2** bony. [Latin *os oss-* bone]

**ossicle** /**os**-i-kuhl/ *n.* small bone or piece of bonelike substance. [Latin diminutive: related to OSSEOUS]

**ossify** /**os**-uh-ˌfuy/ *v.* (**-ies, -ied**) **1** turn into bone; harden. **2** make or become

rigid, callous, or unprogressive. □ **ossification** /-fuh-**kay**-shuhn/ *n.* [Latin: related to OSSEOUS]

**ostensible** /os-**ten**-suh-buhl/ *adj.* concealing the real; professed (*his ostensible function was that of interpreter*). □ **ostensibly** *adv.* [Latin *ostendo ostens-* show]

**ostentation** /ˌos-ten-**tay**-shuhn/ *n.* **1** pretentious display of wealth etc. **2** showing off. □ **ostentatious** *adj.* **ostentatiously** *adv.*

**osteo-** *comb. form* bone. [Greek *osteon*]

**osteoarthritis** /ˌos-tee-oh-ah-**thruy**-tuhs/ *n.* degenerative disease of joint cartilage. □ **osteoarthritic** /-**thrit**-ik/ *adj.*

**osteopathy** /ˌos-tee-**op**-uh-thee/ *n.* treatment of disease through the manipulation of bones. □ **osteopath** /**os**-tee-uh-ˌpath/ *n.*

**osteoporosis** /ˌos-tee-oh-puh-**roh**-suhs/ *n.* condition of brittle bones caused esp. by hormonal changes or deficiency of calcium or vitamin D.

**ostler** /**os**-luh/ *n. hist.* stableman at an inn. [related to HOSTEL]

**ostracise** /**os**-truh-ˌsuyz/ *v.* (also **-ize**) (**-sing** or **-zing**) exclude from society; refuse to associate with. □ **ostracism** /-ˌsiz-uhm/ *n.* [Greek *ostrakon* potsherd, on which a vote was recorded in ancient Athens to expel a powerful or unpopular citizen]

**ostrich** /**os**-trich/ *n.* **1** large African swift-running flightless bird. **2** person who refuses to acknowledge an awkward truth. [Latin *avis* bird, *struthio* (from Greek) ostrich]

**other** /**uth**-uh/ — *adj.* **1** not the same as one or some already mentioned or implied; separate in identity or distinct in kind (*other people*; *use other means*; *I assure you, my reason is quite other*). **2 a** further; additional (*a few other examples*). **b** second of two (*open your other eye*). **3** (prec. by *the*) only remaining. (*must be in the other pocket*; *where are the other two?*). **4** (foll. by *than*) apart from; excepting (*any person other than you*). — *n.* or *pron.* other person or thing (*some others have come*; *give me one other*; *one or other of us will be there*; *where are the others?*). — *adv.* (usu. followed by *than*) otherwise (*cannot react other than angrily*). □ **other than 1** except (*never speaks to me other than to insult me*; *has no friends other than me*). **2** differently; not (*cannot do other than laugh*; *never appears other than happy*). [Old English]

**other day** *n.* (also **other night** etc.) (prec. by *the*) a few days (or nights) ago.

**othersider** *n.* = TOTHERSIDER.

**otherwise** — *adv.* **1** or else; in different circumstances (*hurry, otherwise we'll be late*). **2** in other respects (*is otherwise very suitable*). **3** in a different way (*could not have acted otherwise*). **4** as an alternative (*otherwise known as Jack*). — *predic. adj.* different (*the matter is quite otherwise*). [Old English: related to WISE²]

**other-worldly** *adj.* **1** of another world. **2** dreamily distracted from mundane life.

**otic** /**oh**-tik/ *adj.* of or relating to the ear. [Greek *ous ōt-* ear]

**-otic** *suffix* **1** forming adjectives and nouns corresponding to nouns in *-osis*, meaning 'affected with or producing or resembling a condition in *-osis*' or 'a person affected with this' (*narcotic; hypnotic; neurotic*). **2** forming adjectives or nouns meaning 'resembling' (*demotic; quixotic*). □ **-otically** *suffix* forming adverbs. [Greek *-otikos* adj. suffix]

**otiose** /**oh**-tee-ohs, -ohz/ *adj.* serving no practical purpose; not required. [Latin *otium* leisure]

**otitis** /oh-**tuy**-tuhs/ *n.* inflammation of the ear.

**otter** /**ot**-uh/ *n.* aquatic fish-eating mammal with webbed feet and thick brown fur. [Old English]

**Ottoman** /**ot**-uh-muhn/ — *adj.* **1** of the dynasty of Osman (or Othman) I or the empire ruled by his descendants. **2** Turkish. — *n.* (*pl.* **-s**) **1** Turk of the Ottoman period. **2** (**ottoman**) upholstered seat without back or arms, sometimes a box with a padded top. [French from Arabic]

**ouch** /owch/ *int.* expressing sharp or sudden pain. [imitative]

**ought** /awt/ *v.aux.* (as present and past, the only form now in use) **1** expressing duty or rightness (*we ought to be thankful; it ought to have been done long ago*). **2** advisability (*you ought to see a dentist*). **3** probability (*it ought to rain soon*). □ **ought not** negative form of *ought* (*he ought not to have stolen it*). [Old English, past of OWE]

**oughtn't** /**aw**-tuhnt/ *contr.* ought not.

**ouija** /**wee**-juh, **wee**-jee/ *n.* (in full **ouija board**) *propr.* board marked with letters or signs and used with a movable pointer to try to obtain messages at a seance. [French *oui*, German *ja*, yes]

**ounce** *n.* **1** (in imperial system) unit of weight, ⅟₁₆ lb. or approx. 28 g. **2** = FLUID OUNCE. **3** very small quantity (*hasn't an ounce of sense*). [Latin *uncia* twelfth part of a pound or a foot]

**our** *poss. pron.* **1** of or belonging to us (*our own business*). **2** of or belonging to all people (*our common heritage*). [Old English]

**Our Lady** *n.* Virgin Mary.

**Our Lord** *n.* Christ.

**ours** *poss. pron.* the one or ones belonging to or associated with us (*it is ours; ours are best; a friend of ours*).

**ourselves** *pron.* **1 a** *emphat.* form of WE or US (*we did it ourselves*). **b** *refl.* form of US (*we are pleased with ourselves*). **2** in our normal state of body or mind (*not quite ourselves today*). □ **be ourselves** see ONESELF. **by ourselves** see *by oneself*.

**-ous** *suffix* **1** forming adjectives meaning 'abounding in, characterised by, of the nature of' (*envious; glorious; mountainous; poisonous*). **2** *Chem.* denoting a state of lower valence than *-ic* (*ferrous; sulphurous*). □ **-ously** *suffix* forming adverbs. **-ousness** *suffix* forming nouns. [Anglo-French *-ous*, from Latin *osus*]

**oust** *v.* drive out or expel, esp. by seizing the place of (*ousted him from his job*). [Latin *obsto* oppose]

**out¹** — *adv.* **1** away from or not in or at a place etc. (*keep him out; get out; tide is out*). **2** indicating: **a** dispersal away from a centre etc. (*hire out; share out*). **b** coming or bringing into the open (*call out; send out; stand out*). **c** need for attentiveness (*watch out; listen out*). **3** not in one's house, office, etc. (*tell them I'm out*). **4** to or at an end; completely (*tired out; die out; fight it out; my luck was out; typed it out*). **5** (of a fire, candle, etc.) not burning. **6** in error (*was 3% out*). **7** *colloq.* unconscious (*is out cold*). **8** (of a limb etc.) dislocated (*put his arm out*). **9** (of a political party etc.) not in office. **10** (of a jury) considering its verdict. **11** (of workers) on strike. **12** (of a secret) revealed. **13** (of a flower) open. **14** (of a book, record, etc.) published, on sale. **15** (of a star) visible after dark. **16** no longer in fashion (*turn-ups are out*). **17** (of a batsman etc.) no longer taking part as such, having been caught, stumped, etc. **18** not worth considering (*that idea is out*). **19** (prec. by *superl.*) *colloq.* known to exist (*the best game out*). **20** (of a mark etc.) removed (*washed the stain out*). **21** (of the tide) at the lowest point. **22** (in a radio conversation etc.) transmission ends (*over and out*). — *prep.* out of (*looked out the window*). — *n.* **1** way of escape; an excuse (*has an out for every contingency*). **2** see *ins and outs* (at IN). — *v.* **1** come or go out; emerge (*murder will out*). **2** suspend from a team (*he was outed for two matches*). **3** *int.* a peremptory dismissal (*out!*). **4** publicly reveal (a person) to be homosexual (*he was outed* *by some sections of the gay press.* □ **out and away** by far (*he is out and away the best Australian bat*). **out for** intent on, determined to get. **out of 1** from within (*came out of the house*). **2** not within (*I was never out of Oodnadatta*). **3** from among (*nine people out of ten*). **4** beyond the range of (*out of reach*). **5** so as to be without, lacking (*was swindled out of his money; out of sugar*). **6** from (*get money out of him*). **7** because of (*asked out of curiosity*). **8** by the use of (material) (*what did you make it out of?*). **9** at a specified distance from (*a kilometre out of Kalgoorlie*). **out of bounds** see BOUND². **out of date** see DATE¹. **out of order** see ORDER. **out of pocket** see POCKET. **out of the question** see QUESTION. **out of sorts** see SORT. **out of this world** see WORLD. **out of the way** see WAY. **out to** determined to. [Old English]

■ **Usage** The use of *out* as a preposition, e.g. *he walked out the room*, is non-standard: *out of* should be used.

**out²** *colloq.* particle (used to form compound verbs and compound adjectives) indicating the utmost degree of a specified behaviour, emotion, etc., e.g. 'veg out' (intensified form of the verb to VEG); 'stressed out' (intensified form of *stressed*) (see also -OUT).

**out-** *prefix* in senses: **1** so as to surpass or exceed (*outdo; outnumber*). **2** external, separate (*outhouse; outdoors*). **3** out of; away from; outward (*outgrowth*).

**-out** *suffix colloq.* in compound nouns formed from compound verbs ending in 'out' (see OUT²) and indicating the utmost degree of a specified behaviour, emotion, etc. (*wipe-out, wimp-out*).

**out and out** — *adj.* thorough; utter (*an out and out bludger*). — *adv.* thoroughly; utterly.

**outback** — *n.* (also **Outback**) (prec. by *the*) remote and usu. uninhabited or sparsely inhabited inland areas, esp. of Australia. — *adv.* out, in, or to areas remote from a major centre of population (*they live outback*). — *adj.* of or relating to remote parts of the country. □ **great (Australian) outback** the outback, esp. as romanticised in some Australian literature etc.

**outbacker** *n.* non-Aboriginal person dwelling in the outback.

**outbackery** *n.* the cultivation of attitudes and values supposedly characteristic of those who live in the outback.

**outbalance** /owt-**bal**-uhns/ *v.* (-**cing**) outweigh.

**outbid** /owt-**bid**/ *v.* (-**bidding**; *past* and *past part.* -**bid**) bid higher than.

**outboard motor** *n.* portable engine attached to the outside of a boat.

**outbreak** *n.* sudden eruption of anger, war, disease, fire, etc.

**outbuilding** *n.* shed, barn, etc., detached from a main building.

**outburst** *n.* **1** verbal explosion of anger etc. **2** bursting out (*outburst of steam*).

**out bush** *adv.* into or in an area of back country or outback country (*prospecting out bush in the far north*).

**outcast** — *n.* person rejected by family or society. — *adj.* rejected; homeless.

**outclass** /owt-**klahs**/ *v.* surpass in quality.

**outcome** *n.* result.

**outcrop** *n.* **1 a** emergence of a stratum, vein, or rock, at the surface. **b** stratum etc. emerging. **2** noticeable manifestation (*sudden outcrop of strikes*).

**outcry** *n.* (*pl.* -**ies**) **1** an uproar. **2** strong public protest.

**outdated** /owt-**day**-tuhd/ *adj.* out of date; obsolete.

**outdistance** /owt-**dis**-tuhns/ *v.* (-**cing**) leave (a competitor) behind completely.

**outdo** /owt-**doo**/ *v.* (-**doing**; *3rd sing. present* -**does**; *past* -**did**; *past part.* -**done**) exceed, excel, surpass.

**outdoor** /owt-**daw**/ *attrib. adj.* **1** done, existing, or used out of doors. **2** fond of the open air (*an outdoor type*).

**outdoors** /owt-**dawz**/ — *adv.* in or into the open air. — *n.* the open air. □ **the great outdoors** nature, esp. as in the bush.

**outer** — *adj.* **1** outside; external (*pierced the outer layer*). **2** farther from the centre or the inside. — *n.* **1** uncovered area for non-members at a racecourse or sports ground. **2** (in the game of two-up) periphery of the ring. □ **on the outer** excluded from the group; rejected. □ **outermost** *adj.*

**outer space** *n.* universe beyond the earth's atmosphere.

**outface** /owt-**fays**/ *v.* (-**cing**) disconcert by staring or by a display of confidence.

**outfall** *n.* outlet of a river, drain, etc.

**outfield** *n.* outer part of a cricket or baseball pitch. □ **outfielder** *n.*

**outfit** — *n.* **1** set of clothes worn or designed to be worn together (*her new outfit*). **2** equipment etc. for a specific purpose. **3** *colloq.* group of people regarded as an organisation. — *v.* (-**tt-**) provide with an outfit, esp. of clothes.

**outflank** /owt-**flangk**/ *v.* **1** extend beyond the flank of (an enemy). **2** outmanoeuvre, outwit.

**outflow** n. **1** outward flow. **2** amount that flows out.

**outfox** /owt-**foks**/ v. outwit.

**outgoing** — adj. **1** friendly. **2** retiring from office. **3** going out or away (*outgoing aircraft*). — n. (in pl.) expenditure.

**outgrow** /owt-**groh**/ v. (*past* **-grew**; *past part.* **-grown**) **1** grow too big for. **2** leave behind (a childish habit etc.). **3** grow faster or taller than.

**outgrowth** n. **1** something that grows out. **2** offshoot. **3** natural product or development.

**outhouse** n. **1** small building adjoining or apart from a house. **2** outdoor toilet.

**outing** n. pleasure trip, excursion.

**outlandish** /owt-**lan**-dish/ adj. bizarre, strange; remote, foreign. □ **outlandishly** adv. **outlandishness** n. [Old English, from *outland* foreign country]

**outlast** /owt-**lahst**/ v. last longer than.

**outlaw** — n. **1** fugitive from the law. **2** *hist.* person deprived of the protection of the law. **3** intractable horse. — v. **1** declare (a person) an outlaw. **2** make illegal; proscribe.

**outlay** — n. /**owt**-lay/ expenditure. — v. /owt-**lay**/ spend.

**outlet** n. **1** means of exit or escape. **2** means of expressing feelings (*find an outlet for your tension*). **3 a** market for goods. **b** shop (*retail outlet*).

**outline** — n. **1** rough draft. **2** summary. **3** sketch consisting of only contour lines. **4** (in *sing.* or *pl.*) **a** lines enclosing or indicating an object (*outline of a shape under the blankets*). **b** contour. **c** external boundary. **5** (in *pl.*) main features or principles (*outlines of a plan*). — v. (**-ning**) **1** draw or describe in outline. **2** mark the outline of.

**outlive** /owt-**liv**/ v. (**-ving**) **1** live longer than (a person). **2** live beyond (a period or date). **3** live through (an experience).

**outlook** n. **1** prospect for the future (*the outlook is bleak*). **2** mental attitude (*narrow in their outlook*). **3** what is seen on looking out; view.

**outlying** adj. far from a centre; remote.

**outmanoeuvre** /,owt-muh-**noo**-vuh/ v. (**-ring**) secure an advantage over by skilful manoeuvring.

**outmoded** /owt-**moh**-duhd/ adj. **1** outdated. **2** out of fashion.

**outnumber** /owt-**num**-buh/ v. exceed in number.

**out of doors** adj. & adv. in or into the open air.

**outpace** /owt-**pays**/ v. (**-cing**) **1** go faster than. **2** outdo in a contest.

**outpatient** n. non-resident hospital patient.

**outpost** n. **1** detachment posted at a distance from an army. **2** distant branch or settlement (*this little island is one of the outposts of Australia*).

**outpouring** n. **1** (often in *pl.*) copious expression of emotion. **2** what pours out.

**output** — n. **1 a** amount produced (by a machine, worker, writer, etc.). **b** the act of so producing. **2** electrical power etc. delivered by an apparatus. **3** printout, files, etc., produced by a computer process. **4** place where energy, information, etc., leaves a system. — v. (**-tt-**; *past* and *past part.* **-put** or **-putted**) (of a computer) supply (results etc.).

**outrage** — n. **1** extreme violation of others' rights, sentiments, etc. **2** gross offence or indignity. **3** fierce resentment. — v. (**-ging**) **1** subject to outrage. **2** commit an outrage against. **3** shock and anger. [French *outrer* exceed, from Latin *ultra* beyond]

**outrageous** /owt-**ray**-juhs/ adj. **1** immoderate. **2** shocking. **3** grossly cruel. **4** immoral, offensive. □ **outrageously** adv.

**outrank** /owt-**rangk**/ v. be superior in rank to.

**outride** v. (*past* **-rode**; *past part.* **-ridden**) **1** ride better, faster, or further than. **2** (of a ship) come safely through (a storm etc.).

**outrider** n. guard or motor cyclist riding ahead of or flanking a car, a procession, etc.

**outrigger** n. **1** spar or framework projecting over the side of a ship, racing boat, or canoe, to give stability. **2** boat fitted with this.

**outright** — adv. **1** altogether, entirely (*proved outright*). **2** not gradually (*bought it outright*). **3** without reservation, openly (*denied the charge outright*). — adj. **1** downright, complete (*resentment turned to outright rage*). **2** undisputed (*outright winner*).

**outrun** /owt-**run**/ v. (**-nn-**; *past* **-ran**; *past part.* **-run**) **1** run faster or farther than. **2** go beyond (a point or limit).

**outsell** /owt-**sel**/ v. (*past* and *past part.* **-sold**) **1** sell more than. **2** be sold in greater quantities than.

**outset** n. □ **at** (or **from**) **the outset** from the beginning.

**outshine** /owt-**shuyn**/ v. (**-ning**; *past* and *past part.* **-shone**) **1** shine brighter than. **2** surpass in excellence etc.

**outside** — n. /owt-**suyd**, **owt**-suyd/ **1** external side or surface; outer parts (*painted blue on the outside*). **2** external appearance; outward aspect. **3** position on the outer side (*gate opens from the outside*). **4 a** all that is beyond, without. **b** (also **Outside**) (prec. by *the*) area remote from a major population centre; the Australian outback. — *adj.* /**owt**-suyd/ **1 a** of, on, or nearer the outside; outer. **b** not in the main building (*outside toilet*). **2** not belonging to a particular group or organisation (*outside help*). **3** (of a chance etc.) remote; very unlikely. **4** (of an estimate etc.) the greatest or highest possible (*the outside price*). **5** (of a player in football etc.) positioned nearest to the edge of the field (*outside left*). **6** (of fishing) offshore. — *adv.* /owt-**suyd**/ **1** on or to the outside. **2** in or to the open air. **3** not within, enclosed, or included. **4** *colloq.* not in prison. **5** (of fishing) out to sea. — *prep.* /owt-**suyd**/ **1** not in; to or at the exterior of (*meet me outside the post office*). **2** external to, not included in, beyond the limits of (*outside the law*). □ **at the outside** (of an estimate etc.) at the most. **from the outside** from an objective or impartial standpoint (*viewed from the outside the problem seems simple*).

**outside interest** *n.* hobby etc. not connected with one's work.

**outsider** /owt-**suy**-duh/ *n.* **1** non-member of some group, organisation, profession, etc. **2** competitor, racehorse, etc., thought to have little chance.

**outsize** — *adj.* unusually large. — *n.* unusually large person or thing, esp. a garment.

**outskirts** *n.pl.* outer area of a town etc.

**outsmart** /owt-**smaht**/ *v.* outwit, be cleverer than.

**outspoken** /owt-**spoh**-kuhn/ *adj.* saying openly what one thinks; frank. □ **outspokenly** *adv.* **outspokenness** *n.*

**outspread** /owt-**spred**/ — *adj.* spread out; expanded. — *v.* spread out; expand.

**outstanding** /owt-**stan**-ding/ *adj.* **1** conspicuous because of excellence. **2 a** (of a debt) not yet settled. **b** still to be dealt with (*work outstanding*). □ **outstandingly** *adv.*

**outstation** *n.* **1** (on a grazing property) subordinate station at some distance from the main establishment. **2** autonomous Aboriginal community at some distance from the centre on which it depends for services and supplies.

**outstation movement** *n.* campaign among Aboriginal people to move out of mission stations, government reserves, towns, etc., and establish autonomous communities in remote areas, esp. on traditional tribal lands.

**outstay** /owt-**stay**/ *v.* stay longer than (one's welcome etc.).

**outstretched** /owt-**strecht**/ *adj.* stretched out.

**outstrip** /owt-**strip**/ *v.* (**-pp-**) **1** go faster than. **2** surpass, esp. competitively.

**out-take** *n.* film or tape sequence rejected in editing.

**out to it** *predic. adj. colloq.* **1** asleep. **2** unconscious. **3** utterly exhausted.

**outvote** /owt-**voht**/ *v.* (**-ting**) defeat by a majority of votes.

**outward** /owt-**wuhd**/ — *adj.* **1** situated on or directed towards the outside. **2** going out (*on the outward voyage*). **3** bodily, external, apparent (*in all outward respects*). — *adv.* (also **outwards**) in an outward direction; towards the outside. □ **outwardly** *adv.* [Old English: related to OUT-, -WARD]

**outweigh** /owt-**way**/ *v.* exceed in weight, value, importance, or influence (*his good qualities outweigh his vices*).

**outwit** /owt-**wit**/ *v.* (**-tt-**) be too clever for; overcome by greater ingenuity.

**outworker** *n.* person who works away from an employer's premises.

**outworn** /owt-**wawn**/ *adj.* worn out, obsolete, out of date (*outworn beliefs*).

**ouzo** /**oo**-zoh/ *n.* (*pl.* **-s**) Greek aniseed-flavoured spirit. [Greek]

**ova** *pl.* of OVUM.

**oval** /**oh**-vuhl/ — *adj.* **1** egg-shaped, ellipsoidal. **2** having the outline of an egg, elliptical. — *n.* **1** egg-shaped or elliptical closed curve. **2** thing with an oval outline. **3** sports ground (not necessarily oval in shape). [Latin: related to OVUM]

**ovary** /**oh**-vuh-ree/ *n.* (*pl.* **-ies**) **1** each of the female reproductive organs in which ova are produced. **2** hollow base of the carpel of a flower. □ **ovarian** /oh-**vair**-ree-uhn/ *adj.* [Latin: related to OVUM]

**ovation** /oh-**vay**-shuhn/ *n.* enthusiastic reception, esp. applause. [Latin *ovo ovat-exult*]

**oven** /**uv**-uhn/ *n.* enclosed compartment for heating or cooking food etc. [Old English]

**ovenproof** *adj.* suitable for use in an oven; heat-resistant.

**ovenware** *n.* dishes for cooking food in the oven.

**over** — *adv.* expressing movement, position, or state, above or beyond something stated or implied: **1** outward and downward from a brink or from any erect position (*knocked me over*). **2** so as to cover or touch a whole surface (*paint it over*). **3** so as to produce a fold or reverse position (*bend it over*; *turn it over*). **4 a** across a street or other space (*cross over*; *came over from New Zealand*). **b** for a visit etc. (*invited them over*). **5** with transference or change from one hand, part, etc., to another (*went over to the enemy*; *swapped them over*). **6** with motion above something; so as to pass across something (*climb over*; *fly over*; *boil over*). **7** from beginning to end with repetition or detailed consideration (*think it over*; *did it six times over*). **8** in excess; in addition, besides (*left over*). **9** for or until a later time (*hold it over*). **10** at an end; settled; completely finished (*crisis is over*; *it's over between us*; *get it over with*). **11** (in full **over to you**) (as *int.*) (in radio conversations etc.) it is your turn to speak. **12** umpire's call to change ends in cricket. — *prep.* **1** above, in, or to a position higher than (*canopy over the bed*). **2** out and down from; down from the edge of (*fell over the cliff*). **3** so as to cover (*hat over his eyes*). **4** above and across; so as to clear, on or to the other side of (*flew over the South Pole*; *bridge over the Murrumbidgee*; *look over the wall*). **5** concerning; while occupied with (*laughed over it*; *fell asleep over a book*). **6 a** in superiority of; superior to; in charge of (*victory over them*; *reigned over two kingdoms*). **b** in preference to (*chose exile over execution*). **7 a** throughout (*travelled over most of Australia*). **b** so as to deal with completely (*went over the plans*). **8 a** for or through the duration of (*stay over Monday night*; *over the years*). **b** during the course of (*did it over the weekend*). **9** beyond; more than (*bids of over $50*; *is he over 18?*). **10** transmitted by (*heard it over the radio*). **11** in comparison with (*gained 20% over last year*). **12** recovered from (*am over my cold*; *got over it in time*). — *n.* **1** sequence of six balls in cricket bowled from one end of the pitch. **2** play resulting from this. — *adj.* (see also OVER-) **1** upper, outer. **2** superior. **3** extra. □ **over again** once again, again from the beginning. **over against** in contrast with. **over all** taken as a whole. **over and above** in addition to; not to mention. **over and over** repeatedly. **over one's head** see HEAD. **over the fence 1** excessive in the circumstances (*his behaviour was a bit over the fence*). **2** unreasonable; unfair (*their demands are really over the fence*). **over the hill** see HILL. **over the moon** see MOON. **over the way** (in a street etc.) facing or opposite. [Old English]

**over-** *prefix* added to verbs, nouns, adjectives, and adverbs, meaning: **1** excessively (*overheat*; *overdue*). **2** upper, outer (*overcoat*; *overdrive*). **3** = OVER in various senses (*overhang*; *overshadow*). **4** completely (*overawe*; *overjoyed*).

**over-abundance** /ˌoh-vuh-ruh-**bun**-duhns/ *n.* excessive quantity. □ **over-abundant** *adj.*

**overact** /ˌoh-ver-**akt**/ *v.* act (a role) in an exaggerated manner.

**overall** — *attrib. adj.* /**oh**-ver-ˌawl/ **1** from end to end (*overall length*). **2** total, inclusive of all (*overall cost*). **3** taking everything into account, general (*overall improvement*). — *adv.* /oh-ver-**awl**/ **1** including everything (*cost $50 overall*). **2** on the whole, generally (*did well overall*). — *n.* /**oh**-ver-ˌawl/ **1** protective outer garment. **2** (in *pl.*) protective outer trousers or suit.

**overarm** *adj. & adv.* with the hand above the shoulder (*bowl overarm*).

**overawe** /ˌoh-ver-**aw**/ *v.* (**-wing**) overcome with awe.

**overbalance** /ˌoh-vuh-**bal**-uhns/ *v.* (**-cing**) **1** lose balance and fall. **2** cause to do this.

**overbear** /ˌoh-vuh-**bair**/ *v.* (*past* **-bore**; *past part.* **-borne**) **1** (as **overbearing** *adj.*) **a** domineering, bullying. **b** overpowering. **2** bear down by weight, force, or emotion. **3** repress by power or authority.

**overbid** — *v.* /ˌoh-vuh-**bid**/ (**-dd-**; *past* and *past part.* **-bid**) make a higher bid than. — *n.* /**oh**-vuh-bid/ bid that is higher than another, or higher than is justified.

**overblown** /ˌoh-vuh-**blohn**/ *adj.* **1** inflated or pretentious (*overblown style of writing*). **2** (of a flower) past its prime.

**overboard** *adv.* from a ship into the water (*fall overboard*). □ **go overboard** *colloq.* **1** be highly enthusiastic. **2** behave immoderately.

**overbore** *past* of OVERBEAR.

**overborne** *past part.* of OVERBEAR.

**overburden** /ˌoh-vuh-**ber**-duhn/ *v.* burden (a person, feelings, etc.) to excess.

**overcame** *past* of OVERCOME.

**overcast** /**oh**-vuh-ˌkahst/ *adj.* **1** (of the sky) covered with cloud. **2** (in sewing) edged with stitching to prevent fraying.

**overcharge** — *v.* /ˌoh-vuh-**chahj**/ (**-ging**) **1** charge too high a price to (a person). **2** put too much charge into (a battery, gun, etc.). **3** put excessive detail into (a description, picture, etc.). — *n.* /**oh**-vuh-/ excessive charge (of money, explosive, etc.).

**overcoat** *n.* warm outdoor coat.

**overcome** /ˌoh-vuh-**kum**/ *v.* (**-ming**; *past* **-came**; *past part.* **-come**) **1** prevail over, master, be victorious. **2** (usu. as **overcome** *adj.*) **a** make faint (*overcome by smoke*). **b** (usu. foll. by *with*, *by*) make weak or helpless (*overcome with grief*).

**overcompensate** /ˌoh-vuh-**kom**-puhn-ˌsayt/ v. (**-ting**) **1** (usu. foll. by *for*) compensate excessively. **2** strive for power etc. in an exaggerated way, esp. to make allowance or amends for a real or fancied grievance, defect, handicap, etc.

**overconfident** /ˌoh-vuh-**kon**-fuh-duhnt/ adj. excessively confident.

**overdo** /ˌoh-vuh-**doo**/ v. (**-doing**; *3rd sing. present* **-does**; *past* **-did**; *past part.* **-done**) **1** carry to excess, go too far. **2** (esp. as **overdone** adj.) overcook. □ **overdo it** (or **things**) colloq. exhaust oneself.

**overdose** — n. excessive dose of a drug etc. — v. give or take an overdose.

**overdraft** n. **1** overdrawing of a bank account. **2** amount by which an account is overdrawn.

**overdraw** /ˌoh-vuh-**draw**/ v. (*past* **-drew**; *past part.* **-drawn**) **1** draw more from a bank account than the amount credited to it. **2** (as **overdrawn** adj.) having overdrawn one's account. **3** exaggerate in describing or depicting.

**overdress** /ˌoh-vuh-**dres**/ v. dress with too much display or formality.

**overdrive** — n. **1** mechanism in a vehicle providing a gear above top gear for economy at high speeds. **2** state of high activity (*now that it's election time, the politicians are going into overdrive*). — v. **1** overwork or drive to exhaustion. **2** drive (cattle) too hard.

**overdue** /ˌoh-vuh-**dyoo**/ adj. past the due time for payment, arrival, return, etc.

**overestimate** — v. /ˌoh-ver-**es**-tuh-ˌmayt/ (**-ting**) form too high an estimate of (a person, ability, cost, etc.). — n. /ˌoh-ver-**es**-tuh-muht/ too high an estimate. □ **overestimation** /-**may**-shuhn/ n.

**overexpose** /ˌoh-ver-ek-**spohz**/ v. (**-sing**) **1** expose too much to the public. **2** expose (film) too long. □ **overexposure** n.

**overfish** /ˌoh-vuh-**fish**/ v. deplete (a stream etc.) by too much fishing.

**overflow** — v. /ˌoh-vuh-**floh**/ **1** flow over (the brim, limits, etc.). **2 a** (of a receptacle etc.) be so full that the contents overflow. **b** (of contents) overflow a container. **3** (of a crowd etc.) extend beyond the limits of (a room etc.). **4** flood (a surface or area). **5** (of kindness, a harvest, etc.) be very abundant. — n. /**oh**-vuh-ˌfloh/ **1** what overflows or is superfluous. **2** outlet for excess water etc.

**overfond** /ˌoh-vuh-**fond**/ adj. (often foll. by *of*) having too great an affection or liking for (*overfond of chocolate*; *overfond parent*).

**overgraze** v. allow stock to graze land so

extensively that it is seriously damaged, with consequent erosion etc.

**overgrown** /ˌoh-vuh-**grohn**/ adj. **1** grown too big. **2** (of a garden etc.) wild; covered with weeds etc. □ **overgrowth** n.

**overhang** — v. /ˌoh-vuh-**hang**/ (*past and past part.* **-hung**) project or hang over. — n. /**oh**-vuh-ˌhang/ **1** an overhanging. **2 a** overhanging part of a structure or rock formation. **b** amount by which this projects.

**overhaul** — v. /ˌoh-vuh-**hawl**/ **1** thoroughly examine the condition of and repair if necessary. **2** overtake. — n. /**oh**-vuh-ˌhawl/ thorough examination, with repairs if necessary.

**overhead** — adv. /ˌoh-vuh-**hed**/ **1** above head height. **2** in the sky. — adj. /**oh**-vuh-ˌhed/ placed overhead. — n. /**oh**-vuh-ˌhed/ (in pl.) routine administrative and maintenance expenses of a business.

**overhead projector** n. projector for producing an enlarged image of a transparency.

**overhear** /ˌoh-vuh-**heer**/ v. (*past and past part.* **-heard**) (also *absol.*) hear unintentionally or as an eavesdropper.

**overheat** /ˌoh-vuh-**heet**/ v. **1** make or become too hot. **2** cause inflation (in) by placing excessive pressure on resources at a time of expanding demand. **3** (as **overheated** adj.) overexcited.

**overindulge** /ˌoh-vuh-rin-**dulj**/ v. (**-ging**) indulge to excess. □ **overindulgence** n. **overindulgent** adj.

**overjoyed** /ˌoh-vuh-**joid**/ adj. filled with great joy.

**overkill** n. **1** amount by which destruction or the capacity for destruction exceeds what is necessary for victory etc. **2 a** more energy, resources, etc., used than is required to achieve an aim (*running the election ads every hour on TV was sheer overkill*). **b** excess; excessive behaviour.

**overland** /**oh**-vuh-ˌland, -**land**/ — adj. & adv. by land or across the land (*an overland journey*; *travelling overland from Melbourne to Perth*). — v. drive (large mobs of stock) overland, esp. for a very great distance.

**overlander** n. drover who drives large mobs of stock over a very great distance, e.g. into the NT from the south.

**overland fish** n. (also **overland trout**) a lizard or snake, esp. when used for human consumption.

**overlanding** n. the driving of stock over very large distances.

**overlap** — v. /ˌoh-vuh-**lap**/ (**-pp-**) **1** (cause to) partly cover and extend beyond (*don't overlap them*). **2** (of two things) be placed so that one overlaps the other (*overlapping tiles*). **3** partly coincide (*where psychology and philosophy overlap*). — *n.* /**oh**-vuh-ˌlap/ **1** instance of overlapping. **2** overlapping part or amount.

**overlay** — *v.* /ˌoh-vuh-**lay**/ (*past* and *past part.* -**laid**) **1** lay one thing over another. **2** (foll. by *with*) cover (a thing) with (a coating etc.). — *n.* /**oh**-vuh-ˌlay/ thing laid over another.

**overleaf** /ˌoh-vuh-**leef**/ *adv.* on the other side of the leaf (page) of a book (*see overleaf for the diagram*).

**overload** — *v.* /ˌoh-vuh-**lohd**/ **1** load excessively (with baggage, work, etc.). **2** put too great a demand on (an electrical circuit etc.). — *n.* /**oh**-vuh-ˌlohd/ excessive quantity or demand.

**overlook** /ˌoh-vuh-**luuk**/ *v.* **1** fail to notice. **2** ignore, condone (an offence etc.). **3** have a view of from above; be higher than. **4** supervise.

**overly** *adv.* excessively; too (*not overly risky*).

**overnight** — *adv.* /ˌoh-vuh-**nuyt**/ **1** for a night (*stayed overnight*). **2** during the night. **3** instantly, suddenly (*the situation changed overnight*). — *adj.* /**oh**-vuh-/ **1** done or for use etc. overnight (*an overnight bag*). **2** instant (*overnight success*).

**overpass** *n.* road that passes over another by means of a bridge.

**overplay** /ˌoh-vuh-**play**/ *v.* give undue importance to; overemphasise. □ **overplay one's hand** act on an unduly optimistic estimation of one's chances.

**overpower** /ˌoh-vuh-**powuh**/ *v.* **1** subdue, conquer. **2** (esp. as **overpowering** *adj.*) be too intense or overwhelming for (*overpowering smell*). □ **overpoweringly** *adv.*

**overrate** /ˌoh-vuh-**rayt**/ *v.* (-**ting**) **1** assess or value too highly. **2** (as **overrated** *adj.*) not as good as it is said to be.

**overreach** /ˌoh-vuh-**reech**/ *v.* outwit, cheat. □ **overreach oneself** fail by attempting too much.

**overreact** /ˌoh-vuh-ree-**akt**/ *v.* respond more forcibly than is justified. □ **overreaction** *n.*

**override** — *v.* /ˌoh-vuh-**ruyd**/ (-**ding**; *past* -**rode**; *past part.* -**ridden**) **1** (often as **overriding** /**oh**-vuh-/ *adj.*) have priority over (*overriding consideration*). **2 a** intervene and make ineffective. **b** interrupt the action of (an automatic device), esp. to take manual control. — *n.* /**oh**-vuh-ˌruyd/ **1** suspension of an automatic function. **2** device for this.

**overrule** /ˌoh-vuh-**rool**/ *v.* (-**ling**) **1** set aside (a decision etc.) by superior authority. **2** reject a proposal of (a person) in this way.

**overrun** — *v.* /ˌoh-vuh-**run**/ (-**nn**-; *past* -**ran**; *past part.* -**run**) **1** (of vermin, weeds, etc.) swarm or spread over. **2** conquer (a territory) by force. **3** (usu. *absol.*) exceed (an allotted time). — *n.* /**oh**-vuh-/ **1** instance of overrunning (in sense 3). **2** amount of this.

**overseas** — *adv.* /ˌoh-vuh-**seez**/ across the sea; abroad (*was sent overseas for training*). — *attrib. adj.* /**oh**-vuh-**seez**/ **1** of places across the sea; foreign. **2** of or connected with movement or transport over the sea (*overseas postage rates*).

**oversee** /ˌoh-vuh-**see**/ *v.* (-**sees**; *past* -**saw**; *past part.* -**seen**) officially supervise (workers etc.); superintend.

**overseer** *n.* **1** person who supervises others, esp. workers. **2** *hist.* convict who supervises the work of a party of convicts. **3** person who manages a rural property.

**over-sensitive** /ˌoh-vuh-**sen**-suh-tiv/ *adj.* excessively sensitive; easily hurt or quick to react. □ **over-sensitiveness** *n.* **over-sensitivity** /-tiv-uh-tee/ *n.*

**overservicing** *n.* the practice by some doctors of providing more medical services than their patients require in order that greater claims may be made by these doctors on the government medical fund. □ **overservice** *v.*

**oversexed** /ˌoh-vuh-**sekst**/ *adj.* having unusually strong sexual desires.

**overshadow** /ˌoh-vuh-**shad**-oh/ *v.* **1** appear much more prominent or important than (*men's sports always overshadow women's in the Australian media*). **2** cast into the shade; shelter from the sun.

**overshoot** /ˌoh-vuh-**shoot**/ *v.* (*past* and *past part.* -**shot**) **1** pass or send beyond (a target or limit). **2** fly beyond or taxi too far along (the runway) when landing or taking off. □ **overshoot the mark** go beyond what is intended or proper.

**oversight** *n.* **1** failure to do or notice something. **2** inadvertent mistake. **3** supervision.

**oversimplify** /ˌoh-vuh-**sim**-pluh-ˌfuy/ *v.* (-**ies**, -**ied**) (also *absol.*) distort (a problem etc.) by stating it in too simple terms. □ **oversimplification** /-fuh-**kay**-shuhn/ *n.*

**overstate** /ˌoh-vuh-**stayt**/ *v.* (-**ting**) **1** state too strongly. **2** exaggerate. □ **overstatement** *n.*

**overstay** /ˌoh-vuh-**stay**/ *v.* stay longer than (one's welcome etc.).

**oversteer** — *n.* /**oh**-vuh-steer/ tendency of a vehicle to turn more sharply than was intended. — *v.* /ˌoh-vuh-**steer**/ (of a vehicle) exhibit oversteer.

**overstep** /ˌoh-vuh-**step**/ *v.* (-**pp**-) pass beyond (a permitted or acceptable limit).

□ **overstep the mark** violate conventional behaviour etc.

**overstock** /,oh-vuh-**stok**/ v. stock excessively.

**overstretch** /,oh-vuh-**strech**/ v. **1** stretch too much. **2** (esp. as **overstretched** /**oh**-vuh-/ adj.) make excessive demands on (resources, a person, etc.).

**overstrung** adj. **1** /,oh-vuh-**strung**/ (of a person, nerves, etc.) too highly strung. **2** /**oh**-vuh-,**strung**/ (of a piano) with strings in sets crossing each other obliquely.

**oversubscribe** /,oh-vuh-suhb-**skruyb**/ v. (**-bing**) (usu. as **oversubscribed** /**oh**-vuh-/ adj.) subscribe for more than the amount available of (shares, tickets, places, etc.).

**overt** /oh-**vert**/ adj. done openly; unconcealed. □ **overtly** adv. [French, past part. of ouvrir open]

**overtake** /,oh-vuh-**tayk**/ v. (**-king**; past **-took**; past part. **-taken**) **1** (also absol.) catch up with and pass while travelling in the same direction. **2** (of misfortune etc.) come suddenly upon.

**overtax** /,oh-vuh-**taks**/ v. **1** make excessive demands on (don't overtax your strength). **2** tax too heavily.

**over there** adv. on the other side of the world; in Europe.

**over-the-top** adj. colloq. excessive.

**overthrow** — v. /,oh-vuh-**throh**/ (past **-threw**; past part. **-thrown**) **1** remove forcibly from power. **2** put an end to (an institution etc.). **3** conquer, overcome. — n. /**oh**-vuh-,**throh**/ **1** defeat, downfall. **2 a** Cricket a fielder's return of the ball, not stopped near the wicket and so allowing further runs. **b** such a run.

**overtime** — n. **1** time worked in addition to regular hours. **2** payment for this. — adv. in addition to regular hours.

**overtone** n. **1** Mus. any of the tones above the lowest in a harmonic series. **2** subtle extra quality or implication (sinister overtones).

**overture** /**oh**-vuh-,**tyoor**/ n. **1** orchestral piece opening an opera etc. **2** composition in this style. **3** (usu. in pl.) **a** opening of negotiations. **b** formal proposal or offer (esp. make overtures to). [French: related to OVERT]

**overturn** /,oh-vuh-**tern**/ v. **1** (cause to) fall down or over. **2** reverse; overthrow (Cabinet overturned the Minister's ruling).

**overuse** — v. /,oh-vuh-**yooz**/ (**-sing**) use too much. — n. /,oh-vuh-**yoos**/ excessive use.

**overview** n. general survey.

**overweening** /,oh-vuh-**wee**-ning/ adj. arrogant, presumptuous, conceited.

**overweight** — adj. /,oh-vuh-**wayt**/ above an allowed or suitable weight. — n. /**oh**-vuh-,**wayt**/ excess weight; preponderance.

**overwhelm** /,oh-vuh-**welm**/ v. **1** overpower with emotion or a burden (overwhelmed by grief). **2** overcome by force of numbers. **3** bury or drown beneath a huge mass.

**overwhelming** adj. **1** too great to resist or overcome (an overwhelming desire to laugh). **2** by a great number (the overwhelming majority). □ **overwhelmingly** adv.

**overwork** — v. /,oh-vuh-**werk**/ **1** (cause to) work too hard. **2** weary or exhaust with too much work. **3** (esp. as **overworked** adj.) make excessive use of (an overworked phrase). **4** (as **overworked** adj.) = OVERWROUGHT 2. — n. /**oh**-vuh-/ excessive work.

**overwrought** /,oh-vuh-**rawt**/ adj. **1** overexcited, nervous, distraught. **2** overdone; too elaborate.

**ovi-** comb. form egg, ovum. [from OVUM]

**oviduct** /**oh**-vee-,**dukt**/ n. tube through which an ovum passes from the ovary.

**oviform** /**oh**-vee-,**fawm**/ adj. egg-shaped.

**ovine** /**oh**-vuyn/ adj. of or like sheep. [Latin ovis sheep]

**oviparous** /oh-**vip**-uh-ruhs/ adj. producing young from eggs hatching after leaving the body (cf. VIVIPAROUS). [from OVUM, Latin -parus bearing]

**ovoid** /**oh**-void/ adj. (of a solid) egg-shaped. [related to OVUM]

**ovulate** /**ov**-yuh-,layt/ v. (**-ting**) produce ova or ovules, or discharge them from the ovary. □ **ovulation** /-**lay**-shuhn/ n. [related to OVUM]

**ovule** /**ov**-yool/ n. structure that contains the germ cell in a female plant. [related to OVUM]

**ovum** /**oh**-vuhm/ n. (pl. **ova**) female egg cell from which young develop after fertilisation. [Latin, = egg]

**ow** int. expressing sudden pain. [natural exclamation]

**owe** /oh/ v. (**-wing**) **1 a** be under obligation (to a person etc.) to pay or repay (money, gratitude, etc.) (I owe you fifty dollars). **b** (usu. foll. by for) be in debt (I still owe for my car). **2** have a duty to render (owe allegiance). **3** (usu. foll. by to) be indebted to a person or thing for (we owe our success to the weather). [Old English]

**owing** /**oh**-ing/ predic. adj. **1** owed; yet to be paid (the balance owing). **2** (foll. by to) **a** caused by (the cancellation was owing to ill health). **b** (as prep.) because of (the train is delayed owing to the floods).

■ **Usage** The use of *owing to* as a preposition meaning 'because of' is entirely acceptable (e.g. *couldn't come owing to the bushfires*), unlike the use of *due to* in such constructions.

**owl** /owl/ *n.* **1** nocturnal bird of prey with large eyes and a hooked beak. **2** solemn or wise-looking person. □ **owlish** *adj.* [Old English]

**owlet** *n.* small or young owl.

**owlet nightjar** *n.* small nocturnal bird widespread in Australia, having grey or brown plumage with barred wing and tail feathers.

**own** /ohn/ — *adj.* (prec. by possessive) **1 a** belonging to oneself or itself; not another's (*saw it with my own eyes*). **b** individual, peculiar, particular (*has its own charm*). **2** used to emphasise identity rather than possession (*cooks his own meals*). **3** (*absol.*) a private property (*is it your own?*). **b** kindred (*among my own*). — *v.* **1 a** have as property; possess. **b** (in Aboriginal English) have a spiritual responsibility (for a place). **2 a** confess; admit as valid, true, etc. (*own their faults*; *owns he did not know*). **b** (foll. by *to*) confess to (*owned to a prejudice against Asians*). **3** acknowledge paternity, authorship, or possession of (*I own him as my son*). □ **come into one's own 1** receive one's due. **2** achieve recognition. **get one's own back** get revenge. **hold one's own** maintain one's position. **of one's own** belonging to oneself. **on one's own 1** alone, independent. **2** independently, without help. **own up** (often foll. by *to*) confess frankly. □ **-owned** *adj.* (in *comb.*). [Old English]

**owner** *n.* **1** person who owns something. **2** = TRADITIONAL OWNER. □ **ownership** *n.*

**ox** *n.* (*pl.* **oxen**) **1** large usu. horned ruminant used for draught, milk, and meat. **2** castrated male of a domesticated species of cattle. [Old English]

■ **Usage** The term *ox* is little used in Australia, *bullock* being preferred, except in facetious special combinations such as *ox conductor* and *ox persuader*.

**oxalic acid** /ok-**sal**-ik/ *n.* very poisonous and sour acid found in sorrel and rhubarb leaves. [Greek *oxalis* wood sorrel]

**oxalis** /ok-**sah**-luhs/ *n.* clover-like exotic plant, one species of which has been declared a noxious weed in South Australia, Tasmania, and Victoria. [Greek, from *oxus* sour]

**ox conductor** *n. colloq. facetious* bullock-driver, drover.

**oxen** *pl.* of OX.

**oxidation** /,ok-suh-**day**-shuhn/ *n.* process of oxidising. [French: related to OXIDE]

**oxide** /**ok**-suyd/ *n.* binary compound of oxygen. [French: related to OXYGEN]

**oxidise** /**ok**-suh-,duyz/ *v.* (also **-ize**) (**-sing** or **-zing**) **1** combine with oxygen. **2** make or become rusty. **3** coat (metal) with oxide. □ **oxidation** /-**zay**-shuhn/ *n.*

**ox persuader** *n. colloq. facetious* **1** bullock whip (see PERSUADER). **2** bullock-driver.

**oxyacetylene** /,ok-see-uh-**set**-uh-,leen/ *adj.* of or using a mixture of oxygen and acetylene, esp. in cutting or welding metals.

**oxygen** /**ok**-suh-juhn/ *n.* tasteless odourless gaseous element essential to plant and animal life. [Greek *oxus* acid, -GEN (because it was thought to be present in all acids)]

**oxygenate** /**ok**-suh-juh-,nayt, ok-**sij**-uh-/ *v.* (**-ting**) supply, treat, or mix with oxygen; oxidise.

**oxymoron** /,ok-see-**maw**-ron/ *n.* figure of speech in which apparently contradictory terms appear in conjunction (e.g. *faith unfaithful kept him falsely true*). [Greek, = pointedly foolish, from *oxus* sharp, *mōros* dull]

**oyster** — *n.* **1** bivalve mollusc, esp. an edible kind, sometimes producing a pearl. **2** *colloq.* uncommunicative or secretive person. **3** symbol of all one desires (*the world is my oyster*). — *adj.* **1** *colloq.* (abbr. of *oyster-like*) unforthcoming; secretive (*he was questioned closely, but remained oyster*). **2** oyster white. [Greek *ostreon*]

**Oyster Bay pine** *n.* pyramidal conifer of south-eastern Australia. [*Oyster Bay*, on the east coast of Tasmania]

**oystercatcher** *n.* **1** wading orange-billed sea-bird which feeds on shellfish. **2** either of two Australian oystercatchers: pied oystercatcher, sooty oystercatcher.

**oyster white** *adj. & n.* (as adj. often hyphenated) greyish white.

**Oz** *colloq.* — *n.* **1** Australia. **2** an Australian. — *adj.* (also **oz**) Australian. [abbreviation]

**ozone** /**oh**-zohn/ *n.* **1** *Chem.* unstable form of oxygen with three atoms in a molecule, having a pungent odour. **2** *colloq.* **a** invigorating air at the seaside etc. **b** exhilarating influence. [Greek *ozō* smell (v.)]

**ozone-friendly** *adj.* not containing chemicals destructive to the ozone layer.

**ozone layer** *n.* layer of ozone in the stratosphere that absorbs most of the sun's ultraviolet radiation.

**Ozzie** var. of AUSSIE.

# P

**P¹** /pee/ *n.* (also **p**) (*pl.* **Ps** or **P's**) sixteenth letter of the alphabet.

**P²** *abbr.* (on road signs) parking.

**P³** *symb.* phosphorus.

**p** *abbr.* (also **p.**) **1** page. **2** piano (softly).

**PA** *abbr.* public address (system).

**Pa** *symb.* protactinium.

**pa** /pah/ *n. colloq.* father. [abbreviation of PAPA]

**p.a.** *abbr.* per annum.

**pabulum** /**pab**-yuh-luhm/ *n.* food, esp. for the mind. [Latin]

**pace** — *n.* **1 a** single step in walking or running. **b** distance covered in this. **2** speed in walking or running (*kept up a brisk pace*). **3** rate of movement or progression (*criticised the pace of the reforms*). **4** way of walking or running; gait (*ambling pace*). **5** speed or tempo in a theatrical or musical performance (*played with great pace*). — *v.* (**-cing**) **1 a** walk slowly and evenly (*pace up and down*). **b** (of a horse) amble. **2** traverse by pacing. **3** set the pace for (a rider, runner, etc.). **4** (foll. by *out*) measure by pacing. □ **keep pace** (often foll. by *with*) advance at an equal rate (to). **put a person** etc. **through his** (or **her**) **paces** test a person's qualities in action etc. **set the pace** determine the speed; lead. [French *pas* from Latin *passus*]

**pace bowler** *n. Cricket* fast bowler.

**pacemaker** *n.* **1** competitor who sets the pace in a race. **2** natural or artificial device for stimulating the heart muscle.

**paceman** *n.* = PACE BOWLER.

**pace-setter** *n.* **1** leader. **2** = PACEMAKER 1.

**pachyderm** /**pak**-ee-,derm/ *n.* thick-skinned mammal, esp. an elephant or rhinoceros. □ **pachydermatous** /-der-muh-tuhs/ *adj.* [Greek *pakhus* thick, *derma* skin]

**pacific** /puh-**sif**-ik/ — *adj.* **1 a** peaceful; tranquil. **b** tending to bring about a state of peace (*pacific endeavours*). **2** (**Pacific**) of or adjoining the Pacific. — *n.* (**the Pacific**) ocean between America to the east and Asia to the west. [Latin *pax pacis* peace]

**pacifier** /**pas**-uh-,fuy-uh/ *n.* **1** person or thing that pacifies. **2** baby's dummy.

**pacifism** /**pas**-uh-,fiz-uhm/ *n.* belief that war and violence are morally unjustifiable and that all disputes can be settled by peaceful means. □ **pacifist** *n. & adj.*

**pacify** /**pas**-uh-,fuy/ *v.* (**-ies, -ied**) **1** appease (a person, anger, etc.). **2** bring (a country etc.) to a state of peace. □ **pacification** /,pas-uh-fuh-**kay**-shuhn/ *n.* **pacificatory** /puh-**sif**-i-kuh-tree, ,pas-uh-fuh-**kay**-tuh-ree/ *adj.*

**pack¹** — *n.* **1 a** collection of things wrapped up or tied together for carrying. **b** = BACKPACK. **2** set of packaged items. **3** usu. *derog.* lot or set (*pack of lies*; *pack of thieves*). **4** set of playing-cards. **5** group of hounds, wild animals, etc. **6** organised group of Cub Scouts or Brownies. **7 a** *Aust. Rules* group of players contesting the ball. **b** *Rugby* team's forwards. **8** = PACK ICE. — *v.* **1** (often foll. by *up*) **a** fill (a suitcase, bag, etc.) with clothes etc. **b** put (things) in a bag or suitcase, esp. for travelling. **2** (often foll. by *in, into*) crowd or cram (*packed a lot into a few hours*; *packed in like sardines*). **3** (esp. in *passive*; often foll. by *with*) fill (*restaurant was packed*; *fans packed the stadium*; *packed with information*). **4** cover (a thing) with packaging. **5** be suitable for packing. **6** *colloq.* **a** carry (a gun etc.). **b** be capable of delivering (a forceful punch). **7** (of animals or Rugby forwards) form a pack. □ **go to the pack** *colloq.* collapse, go to pieces. **pack in** *colloq.* stop, give up (*packed in his job*). **pack it** (or **pack death** or **pack** some other specified object) *colloq.* lose one's nerve; be terrified (*was packing it at the thought of speaking in public*). **pack it in 1** *colloq.* (also **pack the game in**) end or stop it. **2** break down; cease functioning (*the car's packed it in*). **pack off** send (a person) away, esp. summarily. **pack a punch** see PUNCH. **pack them in** fill a theatre etc. with a capacity audience. **pack up** *colloq.* **1** stop functioning; break down. **2** retire from an activity, contest, etc. **send packing** *colloq.* dismiss summarily. [Low German or Dutch]

**pack²** *v.* select (a jury etc.) or fill (a meeting) so as to secure a decision in one's favour. [probably from PACT]

**package** /**pak**-ij/ — *n.* **1 a** bundle of things packed. **b** parcel, box, etc., in which things are packed. **2** (in full **package deal**) set of proposals or items offered or agreed to as a whole. **3** *Computing* piece of software suitable for various applications or a wide range of users. — *v.* (**-ging**) make up into or enclose in a package. □ **packager** *n.*

**package holiday** n. (also **package tour**) holiday (or tour) with travel, hotels, etc. at an inclusive price.

**packaging** n. **1** wrapping or container for goods. **2** process of packing goods.

**packed lunch** n. lunch of sandwiches etc. prepared and packed to be eaten away from home.

**packed out** adj. full, crowded.

**packer** n. person or thing that packs, esp. a dealer who prepares and packs food.

**packet** /**pak**-uht/ n. **1 a** small package of something (packet of cornflakes). **b** container for this. **2** colloq. large sum of money won, lost, or spent.

**packhorse** n. horse for carrying loads.

**pack ice** n. crowded floating ice in the sea.

**packing** n. **1** material used to pack esp. fragile articles. **2** material used to seal a join etc.

**pact** n. agreement; treaty. [Latin pactum]

**pad¹** — n. **1** thick piece of soft material used to protect, fill out hollows, hold or absorb liquid, etc. **2** sheets of blank paper fastened together at one edge, for writing or drawing on. **3** fleshy underpart of an animal's foot or of a human finger. **4** guard for the leg and ankle in sports. **5** flat surface for helicopter take-off or rocket-launching. **6** colloq. lodgings, flat, etc. **7** floating leaf of a water lily. — v. (**-dd-**) **1** provide with a pad or padding; stuff. **2** (foll. by out) lengthen or fill out (a book etc.) with unnecessary material. □ **pad down** colloq. sleep; spend a night or nights (can I pad down with you tonight?). [probably Low German or Dutch]

**pad²** — v. (**-dd-**) **1** walk with a soft dull steady step. **2** travel, or tramp along (a road etc.), on foot. — n. **1** sound of soft steady steps. **2** track or trail made by animals (followed the kangaroo pads). [Low German pad PATH]

**padded cell** n. room with padded walls in a psychiatric hospital.

**padding** n. **1** soft material used to pad or stuff. **2** unnecessary material used to lengthen or fill out (a book etc.).

**paddle¹** /**pad**-uhl/ — n. **1** short broad-bladed oar used without a rowlock. **2** paddle-shaped instrument. **3** fin, flipper. **4** board on a paddle-wheel or mill-wheel. **5** action or spell of paddling. — v. (**-ling**) **1** move on water or propel a boat by paddles. **2** row gently. □ **paddle one's own canoe** be independent; do one's own thing. □ **paddler** n. [origin unknown]

**paddle²** /**pad**-uhl/ — v. (**-ling**) walk barefoot, or dabble the feet or hands, in shallow water. — n. act of paddling. □ **paddler** n. [probably Low German or Dutch]

**paddle boat** n. (also **paddle steamer**) boat (or steamer) propelled by a paddle wheel.

**paddle wheel** n. wheel for propelling a ship, with boards round the circumference.

**paddock** /**pad**-uhk/ — n. **1** piece of land (usu. of considerable size) fenced, defined by natural boundaries, or otherwise considered distinct, usu. a section of a rural property. **2** Brit. small field, esp. for keeping horses in. **3 a** turf enclosure, for spectators at a racecourse, adjacent to the saddling paddock. **b** = SADDLING PADDOCK. **4** a playing field. — v. **1** confine (livestock) in a paddock. **2** fence or enclose an area to turn it into a paddock. [parrock, var. of PARK]

**Paddy** /**pad**-ee/ n. (pl. **-ies**) colloq. often offens. Irishman. [Irish Padraig Patrick]

**paddy¹** /**pad**-ee/ n. (pl. **-ies**) (in full **paddy-field**) field where rice is grown. **2** rice before threshing or in the husk. [Malay pādī]

**paddy²** /**pad**-ee/ n. (pl. **-ies**) colloq. rage; fit of temper. [from PADDY]

**paddymelon¹** /**pad**-ee- mel-uhn/ n. (also **pademelon**) **1** any of several small, compact-bodied wallabies inhabiting dense vegetation in moist forests of eastern Australia. **2** (occasionally) any of several other, usu. small, macropods. [Dharuk badimaliyan, altered by folk etymology to paddymelon]

**paddymelon²** n. (also **pademelon**) any of several cucurbits, esp. the trailing or climbing annual African plant natural-ised in inland Australia, bearing a bristly, melon-like fruit, and widely regarded as a weed. [probably from an erroneous association with PADDYMELON¹]

**Paddy's market** n. any of various markets; a FLEA MARKET.

**paddy-wagon** n. secure van used by police for transporting prisoners. [probably paddy policeman]

**pademelon** var. of PADDYMELON.

**padlock** /**pad**-lok/ — n. detachable lock hanging by a pivoted hook on the object fastened. — v. secure with a padlock. [origin unknown]

**padre** /**pah**-dray/ n. **1** minister or priest. **2** chaplain in the army etc. [Italian, Spanish, and Portuguese, = father, priest]

**paean** /**pee**-uhn/ n. (also **pean**) song of praise or triumph. [Latin from Greek]

**paederast** var. of PEDERAST.

**paederasty** var. of PEDERASTY.

**paediatrics** /ˌpee-dee-**at**-riks/ *n.pl.* (treated as *sing.*) (also **pediatrics**) branch of medicine dealing with children and their diseases. □ **paediatric** *adj.*

**paediatrician** /-uh-**trish**-uhn/ *n.* [from PAEDO-, Greek *iatros* physician]

**paedo-** *comb. form* (also **pedo-**) child. [Greek *pais paid-* child]

**paedophile** /**pee**-duh-ˌfuyl, **ped**-uh-/ *n.* (also **pedophile**) person who displays paedophilia.

**paedophilia** /ˌpee-duh-**fil**-ee-uh, ˌped-uh-/ *n.* (also **pedophilia**) sexual attraction felt towards children.

**paella** /puy-**el**-uh/ *n.* Spanish dish of rice, saffron, chicken, seafood, etc., cooked and served in a large shallow pan. [Latin PATELLA]

**pagan** /**pay**-guhn/ — *n.* non-religious person, pantheist, or heathen, esp. in pre-Christian times. — *adj.* **1 a** of pagans. **b** irreligious. **2** pantheistic. □ **paganism** *n.* [Latin *paganus* from *pagus* country district]

**page**[1] — *n.* **1 a** leaf of a book, periodical, etc. **b** each side of this. **c** what is written or printed on this. **2** episode that might fill a page in written history; memorable event. — *v.* (**-ging**) paginate. [Latin *pagina*]

**page**[2] — *n.* **1** uniformed boy or man employed to run errands, attend to a door, etc. (*hotel page*). **2** boy as a personal attendant of a bride etc. — *v.* (**-ging**) **1** (in hotels, airports, etc.) summon by esp. making an announcement. **2** summon by pager. [French]

**pageant** /**paj**-uhnt/ *n.* **1** brilliant spectacle, esp. an elaborate parade. **2** spectacular procession or play illustrating historical events. **3** tableau etc. on a fixed stage or moving vehicle. [origin unknown]

**pageantry** *n.* (esp. on State occasions) spectacular show; pomp.

**page-boy** *n.* **1** = PAGE[2] *n.* 2. **2** woman's hairstyle with the hair bobbed and rolled under.

**pager** *n.* bleeping radio device, calling its wearer to the telephone etc.

**paginate** /**paj**-uh-ˌnayt/ *v.* (**-ting**) assign numbers to the pages of (a book etc.). □ **pagination** /-**nay**-shuhn/ *n.* [Latin: related to PAGE[1]]

**pagoda** /puh-**goh**-duh/ *n.* **1** Hindu or Buddhist temple etc., esp. a many-tiered tower, in India and E. Asia. **2** ornamental imitation of this. [Portuguese]

**paid** *past* and *past part.* of PAY.

**paid-up** *adj.* having paid one's subscription to a trade-union, club, etc., or having done what is required to be considered a full member of a particular group (*paid-up feminist*).

**pail** *n.* **1** bucket. **2** amount contained in this. □ **pailful** *n.* (*pl.* **-s**) [Old English]

**pain** — *n.* **1** any unpleasant bodily sensation produced by illness, accident, etc. **2** mental suffering. **3** (in *pl.*) careful effort; trouble taken (*got nothing for my pains*). **4** (also **pain in the neck** etc.) *colloq.* troublesome person or thing; nuisance. — *v.* **1** cause pain to. **2** (as **pained** *adj.*) expressing pain (*pained expression*). □ **be at** (or **take**) **pains** take great care. **in pain** suffering pain. **on** (or **under**) **pain of** with (death etc.) as the penalty. [Latin *poena* penalty]

**painful** *adj.* **1** causing bodily or mental pain. **2** (esp. of part of the body) suffering pain. **3** causing trouble or difficulty; laborious (*painful climb*). □ **painfully** *adv.*

**painkiller** *n.* drug for alleviating pain. □ **painkilling** *adj.*

**painless** *adj.* not causing pain. □ **painlessly** *adv.*

**painstaking** /**paynz**-ˌtay-king/ *adj.* careful, industrious, thorough. □ **painstakingly** *adv.*

**paint** — *n.* **1** pigment, esp. in liquid form, for colouring a surface. **2** this as a dried film or coating (*paint peeled off*). **3** cosmetic make-up, esp. rouge or nail varnish. — *v.* **1 a** cover (a wall, object, etc.) with paint. **b** apply paint of a specified colour to (*paint the door green*). **2** depict (an object, scene, etc.) in paint; produce (a picture) thus. **3** describe vividly (*painted a gloomy picture*). **4** *joc.* or *archaic* **a** apply make-up to (the face, skin, etc.). **b** apply (e.g. a medicinal liquid) to the skin etc.). □ **paint out** efface with paint. **paint the town red** *colloq.* enjoy oneself flamboyantly. [Latin *pingo pict-*]

**painter**[1] *n.* **1** person who covers surfaces (of buildings etc.) with paint. **2** person who paints pictures; artist.

**painter**[2] *n.* rope attached to the bow of a boat for tying it to a quay etc. [origin unknown]

**painterly** *adj.* **1** characteristic of a painter or paintings; artistic. **2** (of a painting) lacking clearly defined outlines.

**painting** *n.* **1** process or art of using paint. **2** painted picture.

**paintwork** *n.* painted, esp. wooden, surface or area in a building etc.

**paint-up** — *n.* (in Aboriginal English) decoration of the body for ceremonial purposes. — *v.* (**paint up**) decorate the body with a paint-up.

**pair** — n. **1** set of two people or things used together or regarded as a unit (*pair of gloves*). **2** article (e.g. scissors, trousers, or pyjamas) consisting of two joined or corresponding parts not used separately. **3 a** engaged or married couple. **b** mated couple of animals. **4** member of a pair in relation to the other (*cannot find its pair*). **5** two playing-cards of the same denomination. **6** *Parl.* either or both of two MPs etc. on opposite sides agreeing not to vote on certain occasions. — v. **1** (often foll. by *off*) arrange or be arranged in couples. **2 a** join or be joined in marriage. **b** (of animals) mate. **3** *Parl.* form a pair. [Latin *paria*: related to PAR]

**paisley** /**payz**-lee/ n. (pl. **-s**) (often *attrib.*) **1** pattern of curved feather-shaped figures. **2** soft woollen shawl etc. having this pattern. [*Paisley* in Scotland]

**Pajamal** /**buy**-chah-mahlh/ n. an Aboriginal language spoken in the regions west of Darwin.

**pakapoo** /,pak-uh-**poo**/ n. Chinese gambling game played with slips of paper marked with columns of Chinese characters. □ **like** (etc.) **a pakapoo ticket** difficult to decipher or make sense of (*some doctors' prescriptions are like a pakapoo ticket*). [Chinese *pai ko p'iao* white pigeon ticket]

**pakeha** /**pah**-kuh-hah, -kee-hah/ n. NZ a white person as opposed to a Maori. [Maori]

**Pakistani** /,pak-uh-**stah**-nee, ,pah-kuh-/ — n. (pl. **-s**) **1** native or national of Pakistan. **2** person of Pakistani descent. — adj. of Pakistan.

**pal** — n. colloq. friend, mate, comrade. — v. (**-ll-**) (usu. foll. by *up*) associate; form a friendship. [Romany, = brother, mate]

**palace** /**pal**-uhs/ n. **1** official residence of a sovereign, president, archbishop, or bishop. **2** splendid or spacious building. [Latin *palatium*]

**palace revolution** n. (also **palace coup**) (usu. non-violent) overthrow of a sovereign, government, etc., by a bureaucracy.

**palaeo-** *comb. form* (also **paleo-**) ancient; prehistoric. [Greek *palaios*]

**Palaeocene** /**pal**-ee-uh-,seen, **pay**-lee-uh-/ *Geol.* — adj. of the earliest epoch of the Tertiary period. — n. this epoch or system. [from PALAEO-, Greek *kainos* new]

**palaeography** /,pal-ee-**og**-ruh-fee, ,pay-lee-/ n. the study of ancient writing and documents. □ **palaeographer** n. [French: related to PALAEO-]

**palaeolithic** /,pal-ee-oh-**lith**-ik, ,pay-lee-oh-/ adj. of the early part of the Stone Age. [Greek *lithos* stone]

**palaeontology** /,pal-ee-on-**tol**-uh-jee, ,pay-lee-/ n. the study of life in the geological past. □ **palaeontologist** n. [Greek *ōn, ont-* being]

**Palaeozoic** /,pal-ee-oh-**zoh**-ik, ,pay-lee-oh-/ — adj. of an era of geological time marked by the appearance of plants and animals, esp. invertebrates. — n. this era. [Greek *zōion* animal]

**palais** /**pal**-ay/ n. colloq. public dancehall. [French, = hall]

**palanquin** /,pal-uhn-**keen**/ n. (also **palankeen**) (in India and some other Asian countries) covered litter for one. [Portuguese]

**palatable** /**pal**-uh-tuh-buhl/ adj. **1** pleasant to taste. **2** (of an idea etc.) acceptable, satisfactory.

**palatal** /**pal**-uh-tuhl/ — adj. **1** of the palate. **2** (of a sound) made by placing the tongue against the hard palate (e.g. *y* in *yes*). — n. a palatal sound.

**palate** /**pal**-uht/ n. **1** structure closing the upper part of the mouth cavity in vertebrates. **2** sense of taste. **3** mental taste; liking. [Latin *palatum*]

**palatial** /puh-**lay**-shuhl/ adj. (of a building) like a palace; spacious and splendid. □ **palatially** adv. [Latin: related to PALACE]

**palaver** /puh-**lah**-vuh/ — n. **1** tedious fuss and bother. **2** profuse or idle talk. **3** cajolery. **4** an affair or business. — v. **1** talk lengthily, esp. to little purpose. **2** flatter; wheedle. [Latin: related to PARABLE]

**pale**[1] — adj. **1** (of a person or complexion) of a whitish or ashen appearance. **2** (of a colour) faint; not dark or deep (*pale blue*). **3** of faint lustre; dim. — v. (**-ling**) **1** grow or make pale. **2** (often foll. by *before*, *beside*) seem feeble in comparison (with) (*her beauty paled beside that of her companion*). □ **palely** adv. **paleness** n. [Latin *pallidus*]

**pale**[2] n. **1** pointed piece of wood for fencing etc.; stake. **2** boundary; outer limits. □ **beyond the pale** outside the bounds of acceptable behaviour. [Latin *palus*]

**paleface** n. name supposedly used by N. American Indians for the White man.

**paleo-** *comb. form* var. of PALAEO-.

**Palestinian** /,pal-uh-**stin**-ee-uhn/ — adj. of Palestine. — n. **1** native of Palestine. **2** Arab, or a descendant of one, born or living in the area formerly called Palestine.

**palette** /**pal**-uht/ n. **1** artist's thin board or slab for laying and mixing colours on. **2** range of colours used by an artist. [French from Latin *pala* spade]

**palette knife** n. **1** thin flexible steel blade with a handle for mixing colours or applying or removing paint. **2** blunt round-ended flexible kitchen knife.

**palimony** /pal-uh-muh-nee/ n. colloq. allowance paid by either partner of a separated unmarried couple to the other. [from PAL, ALIMONY]

**palimpsest** /pal-uhmp-ˌsest/ n. **1** writing-material or manuscript on which the original writing has been effaced for re-use. **2** monumental brass turned and re-engraved on the reverse side. [Greek palin again, psēstos rubbed]

**palindrome** /pal-uhn-ˌdrohm/ n. word or phrase reading the same backwards as forwards (e.g. nurses run). □ **palindromic** /-drom-ik/ adj. [Greek palindromos running back: related to PALIMPSEST, drom- run]

**paling** n. **1** fence of pales. **2** a pale.

**palisade** /ˌpal-uh-sayd/ — n. **1** fence of pales or iron railings. **2** strong pointed wooden stake used in a close row for defence. — v. (**-ding**) enclose or provide with a palisade. [French: related to PALE²]

**pall¹** /pawl/ n. **1** cloth spread over a coffin etc. **2** shoulder-band with pendants, worn as an ecclesiastical vestment and sign of authority. **3** dark covering (pall of darkness). [Latin pallium cloak]

**pall²** /pawl/ v. (often foll. by on) become uninteresting (to) (his jokes soon palled on us). [from APPAL]

**palladium** /puh-lay-dee-uhm/ n. rare white metallic element used as a catalyst and in jewellery. [Pallas, name of an asteroid]

**pallbearer** n. person helping to carry or escort a coffin at a funeral.

**pallet¹** /pal-uht/ n. **1** straw mattress. **2** mean or makeshift bed. [Latin palea straw]

**pallet²** /pal-uht/ n. portable platform for transporting and storing loads. [French: related to PALETTE]

**palliasse** /pal-ee-ˌas/ n. straw mattress. [Latin: related to PALLET¹]

**palliate** /pal-ee-ˌayt/ v. (**-ting**) **1** alleviate (disease) without curing it. **2** excuse, extenuate. □ **palliative** /pal-ee-uh-tiv/ n. & adj. [Latin pallio cloak: related to PALL¹]

**pallid** /pal-uhd/ adj. pale, esp. from illness. [Latin: related to PALE¹]

**pallid cuckoo** n. Australian cuckoo with a melodious five-note call.

**pallor** /pal-uh/ n. paleness. [Latin palleo be pale]

**pally** adj. (**-ier, -iest**) colloq. friendly.

**palm¹** /pahm/ n. **1** (usu. tropical) tree-like plant with no branches and a mass of large leaves, usu. fan-shaped, at the top. **2** leaf of this as a symbol of victory. [Latin palma]

**palm²** /pahm/ — n. **1** inner surface of the hand between the wrist and fingers. **2** part of a glove that covers this. — v. conceal (a card, coin, etc.) in the hand while conjuring. □ **palm off 1** (often foll. by on) impose fraudulently (on a person) (palmed my old car off on him). **2** (often foll. by with) cause (a person) to accept unwillingly or unknowingly (palmed him off with my old car). □ **palmar** adj. [Latin palma]

**palmate** /pal-mayt, -muht/ adj. **1** shaped like an open hand. **2** having lobes etc. like spread fingers. [Latin palmatus: related to PALM²]

**palmistry** /pah-muh-stree/ n. fortune-telling from lines etc. on the palm of the hand. □ **palmist** n.

**Palm Sunday** n. Sunday before Easter, celebrating Christ's entry into Jerusalem.

**palmy** /pah-mee/ adj. (**-ier, -iest**) **1** of, like, or abounding in palms. **2** triumphant, flourishing (palmy days).

**palomino** /ˌpal-uh-mee-noh/ n. (pl. **-s**) golden or cream-coloured horse with light-coloured mane and tail. [Latin palumba dove]

**palpable** /pal-puh-buhl/ adj. **1** able to be touched or felt (palpable lump in the breast). **2** readily perceived (a palpable lie). □ **palpability** n. **palpably** adv. [Latin palpo caress]

**palpate** /pal-payt/ v. (**-ting**) examine (esp. medically) by touch. □ **palpation** /-pay-shuhn/ n.

**palpitate** /pal-puh-ˌtayt/ v. (**-ting**) **1** pulsate, throb, tremble. **2** (of the heart) beat faster due to exertion, agitation, or disease. [Latin palpito frequentative of palpo touch gently]

**palpitation** /ˌpal-puh-tay-shuhn/ n. **1** throbbing, trembling. **2** (often in pl.) increased rate of heartbeat due to exertion, agitation, or disease.

**palsy** /pawl-zee/ — n. (pl. **-ies**) paralysis, esp. with involuntary tremors. — v. (**-ies, -ied**) affect with palsy. [French: related to PARALYSIS]

**paltry** /pawl-tree/ adj. (**-ier, -iest**) worthless, contemptible, trifling (donated a paltry fifty cents). □ **paltriness** n. [from palt rubbish]

**pampas** /pam-puhs/ n.pl. large treeless plains in S. America. [Spanish from Quechua]

**pamper** v. overindulge (a person, taste, etc.); spoil (a person) with luxury. [obsolete pamp cram]

**pamphlet** /pam-fluht/ — n. small usu. unbound booklet or leaflet containing information etc. — v. (**-t-**) distribute pamphlets to (*pamphleted the area for Labor*). [*Pamphilus*, name of a medieval poem]

**pamphleteer** /ˌpam-fluh-**teer**/ *n.* writer of (esp. political) pamphlets.

**pan**[1] — *n.* **1 a** broad usu. metal vessel used for cooking etc. **b** contents of this. **2** panlike vessel in which substances are heated etc. **3** similar shallow container, e.g. the bowl of a pair of scales. **4** bedpan. **5** hollow in the ground (*salt-pan*). — *v.* (**-nn-**) **1** colloq. criticise severely (*the film was panned by the critics*). **2 a** (foll. by *off*, *out*) wash (gold-bearing gravel) in a pan. **b** search for gold thus. □ **pan out 1** (of an action etc.) turn out; work out well or in a specified way. **2** (of gravel) yield gold. □ **panful** *n.* (*pl.* **-s**). **panlike** *adj.* [Old English]

**pan**[2] — *v.* (**-nn-**) **1** swing (a film camera) horizontally to give a panoramic effect or to follow a moving object. **2** (of a camera) be moved thus. — *n.* panning movement. [from PANORAMA]

**pan-** *comb. form* **1** all; the whole of. **2** relating to the whole of a continent, racial group, religion, etc. (*pan-American*). [Greek *pan*, neuter of *pas pantos* all]

**panacea** /ˌpan-uh-**see**-uh/ *n.* universal remedy. [Greek: related to PAN-, *akos* remedy]

**panache** /puh-**nash**/ *n.* assertive flamboyance; confidence of style or manner. [French; = plume]

**panama** /ˈpan-uh-ˌmah/ *n.* straw hat with a brim and indented crown. [*Panama* in Central America]

**pancake** — *n.* **1** thin flat cake of fried batter usu. rolled up with a filling. **2** flat cake of make-up etc. — *v.* (of an aircraft) make a pancake landing.

**pancake landing** *n.* colloq. emergency aircraft landing with the undercarriage still retracted.

**pancetta** /ˌpan-**chet**-uh/ *n.* Italian tissue-thin bacon, often spicy hot.

**panchromatic** /ˌpan-kroh-**mat**-ik/ *adj.* (of a film etc.) sensitive to all visible colours of the spectrum.

**pancreas** /ˈpang-kree-uhs/ *n.* gland near the stomach supplying digestive fluid and secreting insulin. □ **pancreatic** /-ˈat-ik/ *adj.* [Greek *kreas* flesh]

**panda** /ˈpan-duh/ *n.* **1** (also **giant panda**) large bearlike black and white mammal native to China and Tibet. **2** (also **red panda**) reddish-brown Himalayan racoon-like mammal. [Nepali]

**pandanny** /ˌpan-**dan**-ee/ *n.* (also **pandani, pandanni, pandanus palm**) palm-like shrub or tree of the heath family, endemic to Tasmania, having pink or white flowers in sprays. [so called from its resemblance to the unrelated PANDANUS]

**pandanus** /ˌpan-**dan**-uhs, -**day**-nuhs/ *n.* **1 a** screw pine of Queensland and NSW, having spined leaves and large fruits resembling a pineapple. **b** any other related Australian plant with thorny leaves. **2** screw pine of esp. Malaysia. [Malay *pandan*]

**pandemic** /ˌpan-**dem**-ik/ *adj.* (of a disease etc.) widespread; universal. [Greek *dēmos* people]

**pandemonium** /ˌpan-duh-**moh**-nee-uhm/ *n.* **1** uproar; utter confusion. **2** scene of this. [place in hell in Milton's *Paradise Lost*: related to PAN-, DEMON]

**pander** /ˈpan-duh/ — *v.* (foll. by *to*) gratify or indulge (a person or weakness etc.) (*pandered to his vanity*). — *n.* procurer; pimp. [*Pandare*, name of a character in the story of Troilus and Cressida]

**pandit** var. of PUNDIT 1.

**Pandora's box** /pan-**daw**-ruhz/ *n.* process that once begun will generate many unmanageable problems. [in Greek mythology: a box, given by Jupiter to Pandora (the first mortal woman), from which many ills were released on mankind]

**pandorea** /ˌpan-duh-**ree**-uh/ *n.* either of two climbers: **1** from Queensland and NSW, having large trumpet-flowers, rosy pink with a maroon centre. **2** = WONGA-WONGA VINE. [Latin, = like Pandora]

**pane** *n.* single sheet of glass in a window or door. [Latin *pannus* a cloth]

**panegyric** /ˌpan-uh-**ji**-rik/ *n.* eulogy; speech or essay of praise. [Greek *agora* assembly]

**panel** /ˈpan-uhl/ — *n.* **1** distinct, usu. rectangular, section of a surface (e.g. of a wall, door, or vehicle). **2** control panel (see CONTROL *n.* 5). **3** = INSTRUMENT PANEL. **4** strip of material in a garment. **5** team in a broadcast game, discussion, etc. **6 a** list of available jurors. **b** jury. — *v.* (**-ll-**) fit, cover, or decorate with panels. [Latin diminutive of *pannus*: related to PANE]

**panel beater** *n.* person who beats out the metal panels of vehicles.

**panelling** *n.* **1** panelled work. **2** wood for making panels.

**panellist** *n.* member of a panel.

**panel van** *n.* motor vehicle similar in size and shape to a station wagon, having two doors, a single row of seats in front, a flat tray in the rear, and usu. with closed sides.

**pang** n. (often in pl.) sudden sharp pain or painful emotion (pangs of hunger; pang of grief). [obsolete pronge]

**panic** /pan-ik/ — n. **1** sudden uncontrollable fear. **2** infectious apprehension or fright, esp. in commercial dealings. — adj. characterised or caused by panic (panic buying). — v. (**-ck-**) (often foll. by into) affect or be affected with panic (was panicked into buying). □ **panicky** adj. [Greek Pan, rural god]

**panic button** n. colloq. imaginary button needing to be pressed in an emergency etc. which gives rise to panic. □ **hit the panic button** it's time to react or panic because this is an emergency.

**panicle** /pan-i-kuhl/ n. loose branching cluster of stalked flowers with the youngest flowers at the top. □ **panicled** /pan-i-kuhld/ adj. [Latin paniculum diminutive of panus thread]

**panic merchant** n. colloq. person prone to panic for the slightest of reasons or for no reason at all.

**panic stations** n.pl. colloq. state of emergency.

**panic-stricken** adj. (also **panic-struck**) affected with panic.

**pannier** /pan-ee-uh/ n. basket, bag, or box, esp. one of a pair carried on either side of a bicycle, motor cycle, beast of burden, etc. [Latin panis bread]

**pannikin** /pan-uh-kuhn/ n. **1** small metal drinking vessel. **2** contents of this.

**pannikin boss** n. person who has only a small degree of authority but who often acts as if he or she had complete power.

**panoply** /pan-uh-plee/ n. (pl. **-ies**) **1** complete or splendid array. **2** complete suit of armour. [Greek hopla arms]

**panorama** /,pan-uh-**rah**-muh/ n. **1** unbroken view of a surrounding region. **2** complete survey of a subject, series of events, etc. **3** picture or photograph containing a wide view. **4** continuous passing scene. □ **panoramic** /-**ram**-ik/ adj. [Greek horama view]

**pan pipes** n.pl. musical instrument made of a series of short graduated pipes fixed together. [from Pan, Greek rural god]

**pansy** /pan-zee/ n. (pl. **-ies**) **1** cultivated plant with flowers of various rich colours. **2** colloq. offens. **a** effeminate man. **b** male homosexual. [French pensée thought, pansy]

**pant** — v. **1** breathe with short quick breaths. **2** (often foll. by out) utter breathlessly. **3** (usu. foll. by for) yearn, crave (panting for revenge). **4** (of the heart etc.) throb violently. — n. **1** panting breath. **2** throb. □ **pantingly** adv. [Greek: related to FANTASY]

**pantheism** /pan-thee-,iz-uhm/ n. **1** belief that God is identifiable with the forces of nature and with natural substances. **2** worship that admits or tolerates all gods. □ **pantheist** n. **pantheistic** /-is-tik/ adj. [Greek theos god]

**pantheon** /pan-thee-uhn/ n. **1** building in which illustrious dead are buried or have memorials. **2** the deities of a people collectively. **3** temple dedicated to all the gods. [Greek theion divine]

**panther** n. **1** leopard, esp. with black fur. **2** US puma. [Greek panthēr]

**panties** /pan-teez/ n.pl. colloq. short-legged or legless underpants worn by women and girls. [diminutive of PANTS]

**pantihose** /pan-tee-,hohz/ n. (also **pantyhose**) (usu. treated as pl.) women's tights, usu. made of the fine material of which stockings are made.

**pantograph** /pan-tuh-,grahf, -,graf/ n. **1** instrument with jointed rods for copying a plan or drawing etc. on a different scale. **2** jointed framework conveying a current to an electric vehicle from overhead wires. [from PAN-, -GRAPH]

**pantomime** /pan-tuh-,muym/ n. **1** Christmas theatrical entertainment based on a fairy tale. **2** gestures and facial expression conveying meaning, esp. in drama and dance. **3** colloq. absurd or outrageous piece of behaviour. [Greek: related to PAN-, MIME]

**pantry** /pan-tree/ n. (pl. **-ies**) **1** small room or cupboard in which crockery, cutlery, table linen, etc., are kept. **2** larder. [Latin panis bread]

**pants** n.pl. **1** underpants or knickers. **2** trousers or slacks. □ **bore** (or **scare** etc.) **the pants off** colloq. bore, scare, etc., greatly. **with one's pants down** colloq. in an embarrassingly unprepared state. [abbreviation of pantaloons, French from Italian, baggy trousers]

**Panyjima** /pun-ju-mu/ n. Aboriginal language once spoken over a large area of the north-west of WA: only a few dozen speakers are now left.

**pap** n. **1** soft or semi-liquid food for infants or invalids. **2** light or trivial reading matter. [Low German or Dutch]

**papa** /puh-pah/ n. archaic father (esp. as a child's word). [Greek papas]

**papacy** /pay-puh-see/ n. (pl. **-ies**) **1** pope's office or tenure. **2** papal system. [medieval Latin papatia: related to POPE]

**papal** /pay-puhl/ adj. of a pope or the papacy. [medieval Latin: related to POPE]

**paparazzo** /ˌpap-uh-**raht**-soh/ *n.* (*pl.* **-zzi** /-**raht**-see/) freelance photographer who pursues celebrities to photograph them. [Italian]

**papaw** var. of PAWPAW.

**papaya** var. of PAWPAW. [earlier form of PAWPAW]

**paper** — *n.* **1** material made in thin sheets from the pulp of wood etc., used for writing, drawing, or printing on, or as wrapping material etc. **2** (*attrib.*) **a** made of or using paper. **b** flimsy like paper. **3** = NEWSPAPER. **4 a** printed document. **b** (in *pl.*) identification etc. documents. **c** (in *pl.*) documents of a specified kind (*divorce papers*). **5** *Commerce* **a** negotiable documents, e.g. bills of exchange. **b** (*attrib.*) not actual; theoretical (*paper profits*). **6 a** set of printed questions in an examination. **b** written answers to these. **7** = WALLPAPER. **8** essay or dissertation, esp. one read to a learned society. **9** piece of paper, esp. as a wrapper etc. — *v.* **1** decorate (a wall etc.) with wallpaper. **2** (foll. by *over*) **a** cover (a hole or blemish) with paper. **b** disguise or try to hide (a fault etc.). □ **on paper 1** in writing. **2 a** in the planning stage; in theory (*sounds good on paper, but I can't see it working*). **b** from written or printed evidence. [Latin PAPYRUS]

**paperback** *n.* (often *attrib.*) book bound in paper or card, not boards.

**paper bag** *n.* □ **unable to fight one's way out of a paper bag** *colloq.* weak, ineffectual.

**paperbark** *n.* **1** any of several Australian trees of the genus *Melaleuca* (of the family *Myrtaceae*) having a papery, often peeling, bark. **2** the bark of these trees.

**paper clip** *n.* clip of bent wire or plastic for fastening papers together.

**paper daisy** *n.* any of several Australian plants bearing a daisy flower-head with stiff, papery, petal-like bracts (see HELICHRYSUM, HELIPTERUM).

**paper money** *n.* banknotes.

**paper tiger** *n.* apparently threatening, but ineffectual, person or thing.

**paperweight** *n.* small heavy object for keeping loose papers in place.

**paperwork** *n.* routine clerical or administrative work.

**papery** *adj.* like paper in thinness or texture.

**papier mâché** /ˌpay-puh **mash**-ay/ *n.* paper pulp moulded into boxes, trays, etc. [French, = chewed paper]

**papilla** /puh-**pil**-uh/ *n.* (*pl.* **papillae** /-ee/) small nipple-like protuberance in or on the body, as that at the base of a hair, feather, etc. □ **papillary** *adj.* [Latin]

**papist** /**pay**-puhst/ *n. offens.* (often *attrib.*) Roman Catholic. [related to POPE]

**papoose** /puh-**poos**/ *n.* N. American Indian young child. [Algonquian]

**pappadam** /**pup**-uh-dum/ *n.* thin, crisp, fried lentil wafer eaten with rice and curry. [Tamil]

**paprika** /puh-**pree**-kuh, **pap**-ri-kuh/ *n.* **1** red pepper. **2** condiment made from this. [Magyar]

**pap smear** *n.* (also **cervical smear**) smear taken from the cervix or vagina and used in the pap test for cancer.

**pap test** *n.* cervical smear test to detect pre-cancerous cell changes. [*Papanicolaou*, name of a US scientist]

**papyrus** /puh-**puy**-ruhs/ *n.* (*pl.* **papyri** /-ruy/) **1** aquatic plant of N. Africa. **2 a** writing-material made in ancient Egypt from the pithy stem of this. **b** text written on this. [Latin from Greek]

**par** *n.* **1** average or normal amount, degree, condition, etc. (*feel below par*). **2** equality; equal status or footing (*on a par with*). **3** *Golf* number of strokes a first-class player should normally require for a hole or course. **4** face value of stocks and shares etc. (*at par*). **5** (in full **par of exchange**) recognised value of one country's currency in terms of another's. □ **par for the course** *colloq.* what is normal or to be expected. [Latin, = equal]

**par-** var. of PARA-[1] before a vowel or *h* (*parody*).

**para** /**pa**-ruh/ *n. colloq.* paragraph. [abbreviation]

**para-[1]** *prefix* (also **par-**) **1** beside (*paramilitary*). **2** beyond (*paranormal*). [Greek]

**para-[2]** *comb. form* protect, ward off (*parachute*; *parasol*). [Latin *paro* defend]

**parable** /**pa**-ruh-buhl/ *n.* **1** story used to illustrate a moral or spiritual lesson. **2** allegory. [Greek *parabolē* comparison]

**parabola** /puh-**rab**-uh-luh/ *n.* open plane curve formed by the intersection of a cone with a plane parallel to its side. □ **parabolic** /ˌpa-ruh-**bol**-ik/ *adj.* [Greek *parabolē* placing side by side: related to PARABLE]

**paracetamol** /ˌpa-ruh-**see**-tuh-ˌmol/ *n.* **1** drug used to relieve pain and reduce fever. **2** tablet of this. [from *para*-acetyl-aminophenol]

**parachute** /**pa**-ruh-ˌshoot/ — *n.* rectangular or umbrella-shaped apparatus allowing a slow and safe descent esp. from an aircraft, or used to retard forward motion etc. (often *attrib.*: *parachute troops*). — *v.* (**-ting**) convey or descend by parachute. □ **parachutist** *n.* [French: related to PARA-[2], CHUTE[1]]

**parade** /puh-**rayd**/ — n. **1** public procession. **2** ceremonial muster of troops for inspection. **3** ostentatious display (*made a parade of their wealth*). **4** public square, promenade; sometimes the name of a street. — v. (**-ding**) **1** march ceremonially. **2** assemble for parade. **3** display ostentatiously. **4** march through (streets etc.) in procession. □ **on parade 1** taking part in a parade. **2** on display. [Latin *paro* prepare]

**parade ground** n. place for the muster and drilling of troops.

**paradigm** /**pa**-ruh-,duym/ n. example or pattern, esp. a set of noun or verb inflections. □ **paradigmatic** /-dig-**mat**-ik/ adj. [Latin from Greek]

**paradise** /**pa**-ruh-,duys/ n. **1** (in some religions) heaven. **2** place or state of complete happiness. **3** (in full **earthly paradise**) abode of Adam and Eve; garden of Eden. □ **paradisaical** /-duh-**say**-uh-kuhl/ adj. **paradisal** /**pa**-ruh-,duy-suhl/ adj. **paradisiacal** /-duh-**suy**-uh-kuhl/ adj. **paradisical** /-**dis**-i-kuhl/ adj. [Greek *paradeisos*]

**paradise parrot** n. predominantly brown, red, and turquoise parrot of central eastern Australia, now possibly extinct.

**paradox** /**pa**-ruh-,doks/ n. **1 a** seemingly absurd or contradictory though often true statement. **b** self-contradictory or absurd statement. **2** person or thing having contradictory qualities etc. **3** paradoxical quality. □ **paradoxical** /,pa-ruh-**dok**-si-kuhl/ adj. **paradoxically** /-**dok**-si-kuh-lee, -klee/ adv. [Greek: related to PARA-[1], *doxa* opinion]

**paraffin** /**pa**-ruh-fuhn/ n. **1** inflammable waxy or oily hydrocarbon distilled from petroleum or shale, used in liquid form (also **paraffin oil**) esp. as a fuel. **2** *Chem.* = ALKANE. [Latin, = having little affinity]

**paraffin wax** n. paraffin in its solid form.

**paragon** /**pa**-ruh-guhn/ n. **1 a** model of excellence. **b** supremely excellent person or thing. **2** (foll. by *of*) model (of virtue etc.). [Greek *parakonē* whetstone]

**paragraph** /**pa**-ruh-,grahf, -,graf/ — n. **1** distinct section of a piece of writing, beginning on a new often indented line. **2** symbol (usu. ¶) used to mark a new paragraph, or as a reference mark. **3** short item in a newspaper. — v. arrange (a piece of writing) in paragraphs. [Greek: related to PARA-[1], -GRAPH]

**parakeeliya** /,pa-ruh-**keel**-yuh/ n. (also **parakeelya, junga**) any of several herbs of arid, inland Australia, having thick, succulent, edible leaves, seeds which may be ground into a paste and eaten,

and purplish-mauve flowers (see also MUNYEROO). [Guyani, probably *barrgilya*]

**parakeet** /**pa**-ruh-,keet/ n. small usu. long-tailed parrot. [French: related to PARROT]

**parallax** /**pa**-ruh-,laks/ n. **1** apparent difference in the position or direction of an object caused when the observer's position is changed. **2** angular amount of this. [Greek, = change]

**parallel** /**pa**-ruh-,lel/ — adj. **1 a** (of lines or planes) continuously side by side and equidistant. **b** (foll. by *to, with*) (of a line or plane) having this relation (to or with another). **2** (of circumstances etc.) precisely similar, analogous, or corresponding. **3 a** (of processes etc.) occurring or performed simultaneously. **b** *Computing* involving the simultaneous performance of operations. — n. **1** person or thing precisely analogous to another. **2** comparison (*drew a parallel between the two situations*). **3** (in full **parallel of latitude**) **a** each of the imaginary parallel circles of constant latitude on the earth's surface. **b** corresponding line on a map (*49th parallel*). **4** *Printing* two parallel lines ( ǁ ) as a reference mark. — v. (**-l-**) **1** be parallel, or correspond, to. **2** represent as similar; compare. **3** cite as a parallel instance. □ **in parallel** (of electric circuits) arranged so as to join at common points at each end. □ **parallelism** n. [Greek, = alongside one another]

■ **Usage** Exceptionally for a verb ending in *l*, 'parallel' does not double the final *l* in forming the past tense etc. (*paralleled, parallels, paralleling*).

**parallel bars** n.pl. pair of parallel rails on posts for gymnastics.

**parallelepiped** /,pa-ruh-lel-uh-**puy**-ped, ,pa-ruh-luh-**lep**-uh-ped/ n. solid body of which each face is a parallelogram. [Greek: related to PARALLEL, *epipedon* plane surface]

**parallelogram** /,pa-ruh-**lel**-uh-,gram/ n. four-sided plane rectilinear figure with opposite sides parallel.

**paralyse** /**pa**-ruh-,luyz/ v. (**-sing**) **1** affect (the body) with paralysis. **2** render powerless; cripple (*nation paralysed by strikes*). [Greek: related to PARA-[1], *luō* loosen]

**paralysis** /puh-**ral**-uh-suhs/ n. **1** impairment or loss of esp. the motor function of the nerves, causing immobility. **2** powerlessness.

**paralytic** /,pa-ruh-**lit**-ik/ — adj. **1** affected by paralysis. **2** *colloq.* very drunk. — n. person affected by paralysis.

**paramedic** /ˌpa-ruh-**med**-ik/ n. paramedical worker.

**paramedical** adj. (of services etc.) supplementing and assisting medical work.

**parameter** /puh-**ram**-uh-tuh/ n. **1** Math. quantity constant in the case considered but varying in different cases. **2 a** (esp. measurable or quantifiable) characteristic or feature. **b** (loosely) limit or boundary, esp. of a subject for discussion. □ **parametric** /ˌpa-ruh-**met**-rik/ adj. [Greek PARA-¹, -METER]

**paramilitary** /ˌpa-ruh-**mil**-uh-tuh-ree/ adj. (of forces) organised similarly to military forces.

**paramount** /**pa**-ruh-ˌmownt/ adj. **1** supreme; most important. **2** in supreme authority. [Anglo-French par by, amont above: see AMOUNT]

**paramour** /**pa**-ruh-ˌmaw/ n. archaic or derog. illicit lover, esp. of a married person. [French par amour by love]

**paranoia** /ˌpa-ruh-**noi**-uh/ n. **1** mental disorder with delusions of persecution and self-importance. **2** abnormal suspicion and mistrust. □ **paranoiac** adj. & n. **paranoiacally** adv. **paranoic** /-**noh**-ik, -**noi**-ik/ adj. **paranoically** adv. **paranoid** /**pa**-ruh-ˌnoid/ adj. & n. [Greek: related to NOUS]

**paranormal** /ˌpa-ruh-**naw**-muhl/ adj. beyond the scope of normal scientific investigation or explanation.

**parapet** /**pa**-ruh-puht/ n. **1** low wall at the edge of a roof, balcony, bridge, etc. **2** defence of earth or stone to conceal and protect troops. [French or Italian: related to PARA-², petto breast]

**paraphernalia** /ˌpa-ruh-fuh-**nay**-lee-uh/ n.pl. (also treated as sing.) miscellaneous belongings, equipment, accessories, etc. [Greek: related to PARA-¹, phernē dower]

**paraphrase** /**pa**-ruh-ˌfrayz/ — n. expression of a passage in other words. — v. (-sing) express the meaning of (a passage) thus. □ **paraphrastic** /-**fras**-tik/ adj. [Greek: related to PARA-¹]

**paraplegia** /ˌpa-ruh-**plee**-juh/ n. paralysis below the waist. □ **paraplegic** adj. & n. [Greek: related to PARA-¹, plēssō strike]

**parapsychology** /ˌpa-ruh-suy-**kol**-uh-jee/ n. the study of mental phenomena outside the sphere of ordinary psychology (hypnosis, telepathy, etc.).

**parasite** /**pa**-ruh-ˌsuyt/ n. **1** organism living in or on another and feeding on it. **2** person exploiting another or others. □ **parasitic** /-**sit**-ik/ adj. **parasitically** /-**sit**-i-kuh-lee, -klee/ adv. **parasitism** n. [Greek: related to PARA-¹, sitos food]

**parasol** /**pa**-ruh-ˌsol/ n. light umbrella giving shade from the sun. [Italian: related to PARA-², sole sun]

**paratrooper** /**pa**-ruh-ˌtroo-puh/ n. member of a body of paratroops.

**paratroops** /**pa**-ruh-ˌtroops/ n.pl. parachute troops. [contraction]

**par avion** /ˌpahr **av**-ee-on/ adv. by airmail. [French, = by aeroplane]

**parboil** /**pah**-boil/ v. boil until partly cooked. [Latin par- = PER-, confused with PART]

**parcel** /**pah**-suhl/ — n. **1** goods etc. wrapped up in a package for posting or carrying. **2** piece of land. **3 a** quantity dealt with in one commercial transaction. **b** quantity of a mineral, esp. as prepared for sale (sold a parcel to the opal dealer). — v. (-ll-) **1** (foll. by up) wrap as a parcel. **2** (foll. by out) divide into portions. [Latin: related to PARTICLE]

**parcel post** — n. branch of the postal service dealing with parcels. — adj. colloq. (esp. of a station hand) inexperienced, just arrived and new to the job.

**parch** v. make or become hot and dry (parched by the summer heat). [origin unknown]

**parched** /pahcht/ adj. extremely thirsty.

**parchment** /**pahch**-muhnt/ n. **1 a** skin, esp. of sheep or goat, prepared for writing or painting on. **b** manuscript written on this. **2** high-grade paper resembling parchment. [Latin Pergamum, now Bergama in Turkey]

**pardalote** /**pah**-duh-loht/ n. any of several small, colourful, spotted, finch-like birds of all Australian States, esp. the DIAMOND BIRD. [Greek, = spotted like a (leo)pard]

**pardon** /**pah**-duhn/ — n. **1** forgiveness for an offence, error, etc. **2** (in full **free pardon**) remission of the legal consequences of a crime or conviction. — v. **1** forgive or excuse; make (esp. courteous) allowances for. **2** release from the legal consequences of an offence, error, etc. — int. (also **pardon me** or **I beg your pardon**) **1** formula of apology or disagreement. **2** request to repeat something said. □ **no beg-pardons** without concern for the niceties (barged in, no beg-pardons). □ **pardonable** adj. [Latin perdono: related to PER-, dono give]

**pare** /pair/ v. (-ring) **1 a** trim or shave (esp. fruit or vegetables) by cutting away the surface or edge. **b** (often foll. by off, away) cut off (the surface or edge). **2** (often foll. by away, down) diminish little by little (inflation is paring away our savings). [Latin paro prepare]

**parent** /**pair**-ruhnt/ — n. **1** person who has or adopts a child; father or mother. **2** animal or plant from which others are derived. **3** (often *attrib.*) source, origin, etc. (*parent company*). — v. (also *absol.*) be the parent of; take good care of one's child(ren). □**parental** /puh-**ren**-tuhl/ *adj.* **parenthood** n. [Latin *pario* bring forth]

**parentage** n. lineage; descent from or through parents.

**parent company** n. company of which others are subsidiaries.

**parenthesis** /puh-**ren**-thuh-suhs/ n. (pl. **parentheses** /-ˌseez/) **1 a** explanatory or qualifying word, clause, or sentence, inserted into a sentence etc., and usu. marked off by brackets, dashes, or commas. **b** (in *pl.*) round brackets ( ) used for this. **2** interlude or interval. □**parenthetic** /ˌpa-ruhn-**thet**-ik/ *adj.* **parenthetically** /-**thet**-i-kuh-lee, -klee/ *adv.* [Greek: related to PARA-¹, EN-, THESIS]

**parenting** n. (skill of) bringing up children.

**par excellence** /ˌpah **ek**-suh-luhns/ *adv.* being the supreme example of its kind (*the short story par excellence*). [French]

**parfait** /**pah**-fay/ n. **1** rich iced pudding of whipped cream, eggs, etc. **2** layers of ice-cream, meringue, etc., served in a tall glass. [French *parfait* PERFECT]

**pariah** /puh-**ruy**-uh/ n. **1** social outcast. **2** *hist.* member of a low caste or of no caste in S. India. [Tamil *paraiyar*]

**parietal** /puh-**ruy**-uh-tuhl/ *adj.* of the wall of the body or any of its cavities. [Latin *paries* wall]

**parietal bone** n. either of a pair of bones in the skull.

**paring** n. strip or piece cut off.

**parish** /**pa**-rish/ n. **1** area having its own church and clergyman. **2** inhabitants of a parish. [Latin *parochia* from Greek *oikos* dwelling]

**parishioner** /puh-**rish**-uh-nuh/ n. inhabitant of a parish. [obsolete *parishen*: related to PARISH]

**parity** /**pa**-ruh-tee/ n. **1** equality, equal status or pay. **2** parallelism or analogy (*parity of reasoning*). **3** equivalence of one currency with another; being at par. [Latin *paritas*: related to PAR]

**park** — n. **1 a** large public garden in a city or town, for recreation. **b** similar area set aside for various sports (*Kardinia Park*; *Harold Park*). **2 a** large area of land kept in its natural state for the public benefit (NATIONAL PARK). **b** large enclosed area where wild animals are kept in captivity (*wildlife park*). **3** area for parking vehicles etc. (*car park*). — v. (also *absol.*) leave (a vehicle) temporarily in a car-park, by the side of the road, etc. □**park oneself** *colloq.* sit down. [French from Germanic]

**parka** /**pah**-kuh/ n. **1** warm padded, usu. hooded, jacket. **2** hooded skin jacket worn by Eskimos. [Aleutian]

**park-and-ride** *adj.* pertaining to the practice whereby a commuter drives a car to a bus or train station, parks the car for the day, and takes that public transport (cf. KISS-AND-RIDE).

**parkers** n.pl. *colloq.* = PARKING LIGHTS.

**parking lights** n.pl. small lights for a motor vehicle for use when it is parked after dark.

**parking meter** n. coin-operated meter allocating a length of time for which a vehicle may be parked in a street etc.

**parking-ticket** n. notice of a penalty imposed for parking illegally.

**Parkinson's disease** /**pah**-kuhn-suhnz/ n. (also **Parkinsonism**) progressive disease of the nervous system with tremor, muscular rigidity, and emaciation. [*Parkinson*, name of a surgeon (d. 1824)]

**Parkinson's law** n. notion that work expands to fill the time available for it. [*Parkinson*, name of the writer (d. 1993) who expounded the theory]

**parkland** n. open grassland with trees etc.

**parlance** /**pah**-luhns/ n. vocabulary or idiom of a particular subject, group, etc. (*medical parlance*). [French from *parler* speak]

**parley** /**pah**-lee/ — n. (pl. **-s**) conference of disputants, esp. to discuss peace terms etc. — v. (**-leys**, **-leyed**) (often foll. by *with*) hold a parley. [French: related to PARLANCE]

**parliament** /**pah**-luh-muhnt/ n. **1** the legislature of a country. **2 a** (also **the Parliament**) the national legislature of Australia, consisting of the Queen (usu. represented by the Governor-General), the House of Representatives, and the Senate. **b** the legislature of an Australian State. **c** the members of any of these legislatures for a particular period, esp. between elections. [French: related to PARLANCE]

**parliamentarian** /ˌpah-luh-muhn-**tair**-ree-uhn/ n. member of a parliament, esp. an expert in its procedures.

**parliamentary** /ˌpah-luh-**men**-tuh-ree, -tree/ *adj.* **1** of a parliament. **2** enacted or established by a parliament. **3** (of language, behaviour, etc.) admissible in a parliament; polite.

**parlour** /**pah**-luh/ *n*. (also **parlor**) **1** *archaic* sitting-room in a private house. **2** a room in a hotel, convent, etc., in which residents may relax, receive guests, etc. **3** shop providing specified goods or services (*beauty parlour*; *ice-cream parlour*). [Anglo-French: related to PARLEY]

**parlous** /**pah**-luhs/ *adj*. *archaic* or *joc*. dangerous or difficult. □ **parlously** *adv*. [from PERILOUS]

**parma wallaby** *n*. greyish-brown wallaby of NSW (and introduced to Kawau Island, New Zealand) having a white throat and white cheek-stripe. [Dharawal, probably *bama*]

**parmesan** /**pah**-muh-zan, -zuhn/ *n*. hard dry cheese made orig. at Parma in Italy and usu. used grated. [Italian *parmegiano* of Parma]

**parochial** /puh-**roh**-kee-uhl/ *adj*. **1** of a parish. **2** (of affairs, views, etc.) merely local, narrow, or restricted in scope. □ **parochialism** *n*. **parochially** *adv*. [Latin: related to PARISH]

**parody** /**pa**-ruh-dee/ — *n*. (*pl*. **-ies**) **1** humorous exaggerated imitation of an author, literary work, style, etc. **2** feeble imitation; travesty. — *v*. (**-ies**, **-ied**) **1** compose a parody of. **2** mimic humorously. □ **parodist** *n*. [Latin or Greek: related to PARA-[1], ODE]

**parole** /puh-**rohl**/ — *n*. **1** temporary or permanent release of a prisoner before the expiry of a sentence, on the promise of good behaviour. **2** such a promise. — *v*. (**-ling**) put (a prisoner) on parole. [French: = word: related to PARLANCE]

**parotid** /puh-**rot**-uhd/ — *adj*. situated near the ear. — *n*. (in full **parotid gland**) salivary gland in front of the ear. [Greek: related to PARA-[1], *ous ōt*- ear]

**paroxysm** /**pa**-ruhk-, siz-uhm/ *n*. **1** (often foll. by *of*) sudden attack or outburst (of rage, coughing, etc.). **2** fit of disease. □ **paroxysmal** /-**siz**-muhl/ *adj*. [Greek *oxus* sharp]

**parquet** /**pah**-kay, -kee/ — *n*. flooring of wooden blocks arranged in a pattern. — *v*. (**-eted** /-ayd/; **-eting** /-ay-ing/) floor (a room) thus. [French, diminutive of *parc* PARK]

**parquetry** /**pah**-kuh-tree/ *n*. use of wooden blocks to make floors or inlay for furniture.

**parricide** /**pa**-ruh-, suyd/ *n*. **1** murder of a near relative, esp. of a parent. **2** person who commits parricide. □ **parricidal** /-suy-duhl/ *adj*. [Latin *parricida*]

**parrot** /**pa**-ruht/ — *n*. **1** any of various birds (e.g. the Australian cockatoo) with a short hooked bill, often vivid plumage,

and the ability to mimic the human voice. **2** person who mechanically repeats another's words or actions. — *v*. (**-t-**) repeat mechanically, by rote. [French, diminutive of *Pierre* Peter]

**parrot-fashion** *adv*. (learning or repeating) mechanically, by rote.

**parrot fish** *n*. any (usu. brightly coloured) fish of Australian coastal waters having fused teeth resembling a parrot's beak.

**parry** /**pa**-ree/ — *v*. (**-ies**, **-ied**) **1** avert or ward off (a weapon or attack), esp. with a countermove. **2** deal skilfully with (an awkward question etc.). — *n*. (*pl*. **-ies**) act of parrying. [Italian *parare* ward off]

**parse** /pahz/ *v*. (**-sing**) **1** describe (a word in context) grammatically, stating its inflection, relation to the sentence, etc. **2** resolve (a sentence) into its component parts and describe them grammatically. [perhaps from French *pars* parts: related to PART]

**parsec** /**pah**-sek/ *n*. unit of stellar distance, equal to about 3.25 light-years. [from PARALLAX, SECOND[2]]

**Parsee** /pah-**see**/ *n*. descendant of the Persians who fled to India from Muslim persecution in the 7th–8th c.; Zoroastrian. □ **Parseeism** *n*. [Persian, = Persian]

**parsimony** /**pah**-suh-muh-nee/ *n*. carefulness in the use of money etc.; stinginess. □ **parsimonious** /-**moh**-nee-uhs/ *adj*. [Latin *parco pars*- spare]

**parsley** /**pahs**-lee/ *n*. herb with crinkly aromatic leaves, used to season and garnish food. [Greek *petra* rock, *selinon* parsley]

**parsnip** /**pahs**-nip/ *n*. **1** plant with a pale yellow tapering root. **2** this root eaten as a vegetable. [Latin *pastinaca*]

**parson** /**pah**-suhn/ *n*. any (esp. Protestant) clergyman or minister. [Latin: related to PERSON]

**parsonage** *n*. church house provided for a parson.

**parson's bands** *n*. Australian terrestrial orchid of the eastern States, having two white sepals sticking out in front like a parson's (neck)bands.

**parson's nose** *n*. fatty flesh at the rump of a cooked fowl.

**part** — *n*. **1** some but not all of a thing or group of things. **2** essential member, constituent, or component (*part of the family*; *spare parts*). **3 a** portion of a human or animal body. **b** (in *pl*.) = PRIVATE PARTS. **4** division of a book, broadcast serial, etc., esp. issued or broadcast at one time. **5** each of several equal portions of a whole (*3 parts sugar to 2 parts flour*).

**6 a** allotted share. **b** person's share in an action etc. (*had no part in it*). **c** duty (*not my part to interfere*). **7 a** character assigned to, or words spoken by, an actor on stage. **b** melody etc. assigned to a particular voice or instrument. **c** printed or written copy of an actor's or musician's part. **8** each of the sides in an agreement or dispute. **9** (in *pl.*) region or district (*am not from these parts*). **10** (in *pl.*) abilities (*man of many parts*). — *v.* **1** divide or separate into parts (*the crowd parted to let them through*). **2 a** leave one another's company (*parted the best of friends*). **b** (foll. by *from*) say goodbye to. **3** cause to separate (*they were fighting so fiercely it was difficult to part them*). **4** (foll. by *with*) give up; hand over (*parted with all his money*). **5** separate (hair of the head) to make a parting. — *adv.* **1** in part; partly (*part iron and part wood*). **2** (of an Aborigine) partly descended from another race. □ **for the most part** see MOST. **for one's part** as far as one is concerned. **in part** (or **parts**) partly. **on the part of** made or done by (*no objection on the part of Australia*; *no objection on my part*). **part and parcel** (usu. foll. by *of*) an essential part. **part company** see COMPANY. **part up 1** pay (what is owed) (esp. grudgingly) (*if he doesn't part up we'll have the law on him*). **2** pay; contribute. **play a part 1** be significant or contributory. **2** act deceitfully. **3** perform a theatrical role. **take in good part** not be offended by. **take part** (often foll. by *in*) assist or have a share (in). **take the part of** support; side with. [Latin *pars part*-]

**partake** /pah-**tayk**/ *v.* (-**king**; *past* **partook**; *past part.* **partaken**) **1** (foll. by *of*, *in*) take a share or part. **2** (foll. by *of*) eat or drink some or *colloq.* all (of a thing). [back-formation from *partaker* = *part-taker*]

**parthenogenesis** /ˌpah-thuh-noh-**jen**-uh-suhs/ *n.* reproduction without fertilisation, esp. in invertebrates and lower plants. [Greek *parthenos* virgin]

**Parthian shot** /**pah**-thee-uhn/ *n.* remark or glance etc. on leaving. [*Parthia*, ancient kingdom in W. Asia: from the custom of a retreating Parthian horseman firing a shot at the enemy]

**partial** /**pah**-shuhl/ *adj.* **1** not complete; forming only part (*partial success*). **2** biased. **3** (foll. by *to*) having a liking for (*she's partial to hot curries*). □ **partiality** /ˌpah-shee-**al**-uh-tee/ *n.* **partially** *adv.* **partialness** *n.* [Latin: related to PART]

**participant** /pah-**tis**-uh-puhnt/ *n.* participator.

**participate** /pah-**tis**-uh-ˌpayt/ *v.* (-**ting**) (often foll. by *in*) take part or a share (in).

□ **participation** /-pay-shuhn/ *n.* **participator** *n.* **participatory** *adj.* [Latin *particeps* - *cip*- taking PART]

**participle** /**pah**-tuh-suh-puhl/ *n.* word formed from a verb (e.g. *going*, *gone*, *being*, *been*) and used in compound verb-forms (e.g. *is going*, *has been*) or as an adjective (e.g. *working woman*, *burnt toast*). □ **participial** /-**sip**-ee-uhl/ *adj.* [Latin: related to PARTICIPATE]

**particle** /**pah**-tuh-kuhl/ *n.* **1** minute portion of matter. **2** smallest possible amount (*not a particle of sense*). **3 a** minor part of speech, esp. a short indeclinable one. **b** common prefix or suffix such as *in*, -*ness*. [Latin *particula* diminutive of *pars* PART]

**particoloured** /**pah**-tee-ˌkul-uhd/ *adj.* of more than one colour. [related to PART, COLOUR]

**particular** /puh-**tik**-yuh-luh/ — *adj.* **1** relating to or considered as one thing or person as distinct from others; individual (*in this particular case*). **2** more than is usual; special (*took particular care*). **3** scrupulously exact; fastidious. **4** detailed (*full and particular account*). — *n.* **1** detail; item (*attended to every particular*). **2** (in *pl.*) information; detailed account (*give me all the particulars*). □ **in particular** especially, specifically. [Latin: related to PARTICLE]

**particularise** /puh-**tik**-yuh-luh-ˌruyz/ *v.* (also -**ize**) (-**sing** or -**zing**) (also *absol.*) **1** name specially or one by one. **2** specify (items). □ **particularisation** /-zay-shuhn/ *n.*

**particularity** /puh-ˌtik-yuh-**la**-ruh-tee/ *n.* **1** quality of being individual or particular. **2** fullness or minuteness of detail.

**particularly** /puh-**tik**-yuh-luh-lee/ *adv.* **1** especially, very (*examined me with particularly great care*). **2** specifically (*particularly asked for you*). **3** in a particular or fastidious manner.

**parting** *n.* **1** leave-taking or departure (often *attrib.*: *parting words*). **2** dividing line of combed hair. **3** a division; act of separating.

**parting shot** *n.* = PARTHIAN SHOT.

**partisan** /ˌpah-tuh-**zan**, **pah**-tuh-zuhn/ — *n.* **1** strong, esp. unreasoning, supporter of a party, cause, etc. **2** guerrilla in wartime. — *adj.* **1** of partisans. **2** biased. □ **partisanship** *n.* [Italian: related to PART]

**partition** /pah-**tish**-uhn/ — *n.* **1** structure dividing a space, esp. a light interior wall. **2** division into parts, esp. *Polit.* of a country. — *v.* **1** divide into parts. **2** (foll. by *off*) separate (part of a room etc.) with a partition. [Latin *partior partit*- divide]

**partitive** /pah-tuh-tiv/ — *adj.* (of a word, form, etc.) denoting part of a collective group or quantity. — *n.* partitive word (e.g. *some, any*) or form. [French or medieval Latin: related to PARTITION]

**partly** *adv.* **1** with respect to a part or parts. **2** to some extent.

**partner** /paht-nuh/ — *n.* **1** person who shares or takes part with another or others, esp. in a business. **2** companion in dancing. **3** player (esp. one of two) on the same side in a game. **4** either member of a married or unmarried couple. — *v.* be the partner of (*will you partner me?*). [alteration of *parcener* joint heir]

**partnership** *n.* **1** state of being a partner or partners. **2** joint business. **3** pair or group of partners.

**part of speech** *n.* each of the classes to which words are assigned (in English: noun, pronoun, adjective, adverb, verb, preposition, conjunction, and interjection).

**partook** *past* of PARTAKE.

**partridge** /pah-trij/ *n.* (*pl.* same or **-s**) game-bird, esp. European or Asian. [Greek *perdix*]

**partridge pigeon** *n.* bird of tropical woodlands in WA and the NT, having dark brown plumage spotted on the breast and a white face with red around the eyes.

**part-song** *n.* song with three or more voice-parts, often unaccompanied.

**part-time** — *adj.* (esp. of a job) occupying less than the normal working week etc. — *adv.* (also **part time**) as a part-time activity (*works part time*). □ **part-timer** *n.*

**parturient** /pah-choo-ree-uhnt, pah-**choor**-/ *adj. formal* about to give birth. [Latin *pario part-* bring forth]

**parturition** /ˌpah-chuh-rish-uhn, -tyoo-/ *n. formal* the act of giving birth.

**party** /pah-tee/ — *n.* (*pl.* **-ies**) **1** social gathering, usu. of invited guests. **2** people engaged in an activity or travelling together (*search party*). **3** political group putting forward candidates in elections and usu. organised on a national basis (*Labor Party*). **4** each side in an agreement or dispute. **5** (foll. by *to*) *Law* accessory (to an action). **6** *colloq.* person. **7** (*attrib.*) **a** of or relating to a political party etc. (*party politics*). **b** of or for a celebration etc. (*party pies; party clothes*). — *v.* (**-ies, -ied**) attend a party; celebrate. [Romanic: related to PART]

**party hack** *n.* person who has dutifully served a political party for a long time, esp. as a dogsbody, a drudge.

**party line** *n.* **1** policy adopted by a political party etc. **2** shared telephone line.

**parvenu** /pah-vuh-ˌnoo, -ˌnyoo/ *n.* (*pl.* **-s**; *fem.* **parvenue**) (often *attrib.*) newly rich social climber; upstart. [Latin: related to PER-, *venio* come]

**pas** /pah/ *n.* (*pl.* same) step in esp. in ballet. [French, = step]

**pascal** *n.* **1** /pas-kuhl/ SI unit of pressure. **2** (**Pascal** /pas-**kahl**, pas-kuhl/) *Computing* programming language used esp. in education. [*Pascal,* name of a scientist (d. 1662); sense 2 so named because he built a calculating machine]

**paschal** /pas-kuhl, pahs-/ *adj.* **1** of the Jewish Passover. **2** of Easter. [Hebrew *pesah*]

**pas de deux** /ˌpah duh **der**/ *n.* dance for two in ballet. [French, = step for two]

**pash** *colloq.* — *n.* **1** infatuation (*has a pash on the boy next door*). **2** a kiss and cuddle. — *v.* to kiss and cuddle. [abbreviation of PASSION]

**paspalum** /ˌpas-**pay**-luhm/ *n.* robust pasture grass native to southern America, now naturalised and widespread in non-arid regions of Australia. [Greek *paspalos* a kind of millet]

**pass**¹ /pahs/ — *v.* **1** (often foll. by *along, by, down, on,* etc.) move onward, esp. past something (*saw the procession passing*). **2 a** go past; leave on one side or behind. **b** overtake, esp. in a vehicle. **c** go across (a frontier etc.). **3** (cause to) be transferred from one person or place to another (*title passes to his son; pass the butter*). **4** surpass; exceed (*passes all understanding*). **5** get through. **6 a** go unremarked or uncensored (*let the matter pass*). **b** (foll. by *as, for*) be accepted or known as (*he passes for a saint, but...*). **7** move; cause to go (*passed her hand over her face*). **8 a** be successful or adequate, esp. in an examination (*I've passed*). **b** be successful in (an examination) (*I've passed English and Maths*). **c** (of an examiner) judge (a candidate) to be satisfactory. **9 a** (of a bill) be approved by (Parliament etc.). **b** cause or allow (a bill) to proceed. **c** (of a bill or proposal) be approved. **10** occur, elapse; happen (*time passes slowly; heard what passed*). **11** (cause to) circulate; be current (*was passing forged cheques*). **12** spend (time or a period) (*passed the afternoon reading*). **13** (also *absol.*) (in field games) send (the ball) to a team-mate. **14 a** forgo one's turn or chance in a game etc. **b** leave a quiz question etc. unanswered. **15** (foll. by *to, into, from*) change (from one form or state to another). **16** come to an end (*the pain will pass*). **17** discharge (esp. faeces or urine) from the body. **18** (foll. by *on*, *upon*) utter (legal sentence, criticism) upon; adjudicate (*passed judgment on the accused*). — *n.* **1** act or instance of passing. **2 a** success in an examination. **b** university degree without honours. **3 a** permit, esp. for admission, leave, etc. **b** ticket or permit giving free entry, access, travel, etc. **4** (in field games) transference of the ball to a team-mate. **5** desperate position (*come to a fine pass*). □ **in passing** in the course of conversation etc. **make a pass at** *colloq.* make sexual advances to. **pass away 1** *euphem.* die. **2** cease to exist. **pass the buck** see BUCK. **pass by 1** go past. **2** disregard, omit. **pass muster** see MUSTER. **pass off 1** (of feelings etc.) disappear gradually. **2** (of proceedings) be carried through (in a specified way). **3** (foll. by *as*) misrepresent or disguise (a person or thing) as something else. **4** evade or lightly dismiss (an awkward remark etc.). **pass on 1** proceed. **2** *euphem.* die. **3** transmit to the next person in a series. **pass out 1** become unconscious. **2** complete military etc. training. **pass over 1** omit, ignore, or disregard. **2** ignore the claims of (a person) to promotion etc. **3** *euphem.* die. **pass round 1** distribute. **2** give to one person after another. **pass the time of day** see TIME. **pass up** *colloq.* refuse or neglect (an opportunity etc.). **pass water** urinate. [Latin *passus* PACE]

**pass²** /pahs/ *n.* narrow way through mountains. [var. of PACE]

**passable** *adj.* **1** barely satisfactory; adequate (*passable skill as a typist*). **2** (of a road, pass, etc.) that can be traversed. □ **passably** *adv.*

**passage** /pas-ij/ *n.* **1** process or means of passing; transit (*the passage of time*). **2** = PASSAGEWAY. **3** liberty or right to pass through. **4** journey by sea or air (*booked a passage to Rome*). **5** transition from one state to another. **6** short extract from a book, piece of music, etc. **7** passing of a bill etc. into law. **8** duct etc. in the body. [French: related to PASS¹]

**passageway** *n.* narrow path or way; corridor.

**passbook** *n.* book issued to an account-holder recording deposits and withdrawals.

**passé** /pah-say, pah-say/ *adj.* **1** old-fashioned. **2** past its prime. [French]

**passenger** /pas-uhn-juh/ *n.* **1** (often *attrib.*) traveller in or on a vehicle (other than the driver, pilot, crew, etc.) (*passenger seat*). **2** *colloq.* idle member of

a team, crew, etc. [French *passager*: related to PASSAGE]

**passer-by** *n.* (*pl.* **passers-by**) person who goes past, esp. by chance.

**passerine** /pas-uh-,reen/ — *n.* perching bird such as the sparrow and most land birds. — *adj.* of passerines. [Latin *passer* sparrow]

**passim** /pas-im/ *adv.* throughout; at several points in a book, article, etc. [Latin]

**passing** — *adj.* **1** in senses of PASS *v.* **2** transient, fleeting (*a passing glance*). **3** cursory, incidental (*a passing reference*). — *n.* **1** in senses of PASS *v.* **2** *euphem.* death of a person (*mourned his passing*).

**passion** /pash-uhn/ *n.* **1** strong emotion. **2** outburst of anger (*flew into a passion*). **3** intense sexual love. **4 a** strong enthusiasm (*passion for footy*). **b** object arousing this (*footy is her passion*). **5** (**the Passion**) **a** suffering of Christ during his last days. **b** Gospel account of this. **c** musical setting of this. □ **passionless** *adj.* [Latin *patior pass-* suffer]

**passionate** /pash-uh-nuht/ *adj.* dominated, displaying, or caused by strong emotion. □ **passionately** *adv.*

**passion flower** *n.* **1** climbing plant with a flower supposedly suggestive of the instruments of the Crucifixion. **2** very showy creeper of this family native to Australia (*Passiflora cinnabarina*), bearing complex red flowers.

**passionfruit** *n.* edible fruit of some species of passion flower.

**passive** /pas-iv/ *adj.* **1** acted upon, not acting. **2** showing no interest or initiative; submissive. **3** *Chem.* not active; inert. **4** *Gram.* indicating that the subject undergoes the action of the verb (e.g. in *they were seen*). □ **passively** *adv.* **passivity** /-siv-uh-tee/ *n.* [Latin: related to PASSION]

**passive resistance** *n.* non-violent refusal to cooperate.

**passive smoking** *n.* involuntary inhalation, esp. by a non-smoker, of others' cigarette etc. smoke. □ **passive smoker** *n.*

**Passover** /pahs-,oh-vuh/ *n.* Jewish spring festival commemorating the Exodus of the Israelites from slavery in Egypt and their entry into the Promised Land. [from PASS¹, OVER]

**passport** *n.* **1** official document certifying the holder's identity and citizenship, and authorising travel abroad. **2** (foll. by *to*) thing that ensures admission or attainment (*passport to success*). [French *passeport*: related to PASS¹, PORT¹]

**password** *n.* prearranged selected word or phrase securing recognition, admission, etc.

**past** /pahst/ — *adj.* **1** gone by in time (*in past years; the time is past*). **2** recently gone by (*the past month*). **3** of a former time (*past president*). **4** *Gram.* expressing a past action or state. — *n.* **1** (prec. by *the*) **a** past time. **b** past events (*cannot undo the past*). **2** person's past life, esp. if discreditable (*man with a past*). **3** past tense or form. — *prep.* **1** beyond in time or place (*past two o'clock; lives just past the pub*). **2** beyond the range, duration, or compass of (*this is past belief; pain past endurance*). — *adv.* so as to pass by (*ran past*). □ **not put it past** believe it possible of (a person). **past it** *colloq.* old and useless. [from PASS¹]

**pasta** /pas-tuh, pah-stuh/ *n.* dried flour paste in various shapes (e.g. lasagne or spaghetti). [Italian: related to PASTE]

**paste** /payst/ — *n.* **1** any moist fairly stiff mixture, esp. of powder and liquid. **2** dough of flour with fat, water, etc. **3** adhesive of flour, water, etc., used for sticking paper etc. **4** food rendered to a smooth, moist mixture for use as a spread or in cooking etc. (*anchovy paste; tomato paste*). **5** hard glasslike composition used for imitation gems. **6** mixture of clay, water, etc., used in making ceramic ware, porcelain. — *v.* (**-ting**) **1** fasten or coat with paste. **2** *colloq.* beat or thrash. □ **pasting** *n.* (esp. in sense 2 of *v.*). [Latin *pasta* lozenge, from Greek]

**pasteboard** *n.* **1** stiff material made by pasting together sheets of paper. **2** (*attrib.*) flimsy, unsubstantial.

**pastel** /pas-tuhl/ *n.* **1** (often *attrib.*) light shade of a colour (*pastel blue*). **2** crayon of powdered pigments bound with a gum solution. **3** drawing in pastel. [French *pastel*, or Italian *pastello* diminutive of PASTA]

**pastern** /pas-tuhn/ *n.* part of a horse's foot between fetlock and hoof. [French from Latin]

**pasteurise** /pahs-chuh-ˌruyz/ *v.* (also **-ize**) (**-sing** or **-zing**) partially sterilise (milk etc.) by heating. □ **pasteurisation** /-ˌzay-shuhn/ *n.* [*Pasteur*, name of a chemist]

**pastiche** /pas-teesh/ *n.* **1** picture or musical composition made up from or imitating various sources. **2** literary or other work composed in the style of a well-known author etc. [Latin *pasta* PASTE]

**pastille** /pas-tuhl, pas-teel/ *n.* small sweet or lozenge. [French from Latin]

**pastime** /pahs-tuym/ *n.* recreation, hobby. [from PASS¹, TIME]

**past master** *n.* person who is especially adept or expert in an activity, subject, etc.

**pastor** /pahs-tuh/ *n.* **1** minister, esp. of a Protestant church. **2** person exercising spiritual guidance. [Latin *pasco past-* feed]

**pastoral** /pahs-tuh-ruhl/ — *adj.* **1** of shepherds, flocks, or herds. **2 a** of, pertaining to, or engaged in, stock-raising as distinct from crop-raising. **b** (of land) used for, or suitable to be used for, stock-raising. **3** (of a poem, picture, etc.) portraying (esp. romanticised) country life. **4** of a pastor. — *n.* **1** pastoral poem, play, picture, etc. **2** letter from a pastor (esp. a bishop) to the clergy or people. [Latin *pastoralis*: related to PASTOR]

**pastoral company** *n.* commercial enterprise engaged in large-scale stock-raising.

**pastoral district** *n.* area in which the principal industry is stock-raising.

**pastorale** /ˌpas-tuh-rahl, rah-lee/ *n.* (*pl.* **-s** or **-li** /-lee/) musical work with a rustic theme or atmosphere. [Italian: related to PASTORAL]

**pastoralist** *n.* owner of a substantial stock-raising establishment or of a number of such establishments (see also GRAZIER).

**pastoral lease** *n.* **1** agreement under which an area of land is held on condition that it is used for stock-raising. **2** the land so held.

**pastoral property** *n.* (also **pastoral run**) stock-raising establishment.

**pastrami** /pas-trah-mee/ *n.* seasoned smoked beef. [Yiddish]

**pastry** /pays-tree/ *n.* (*pl.* **-ies**) **1** dough of flour, fat, and water used as a base and covering for pies etc. **2 a** food made wholly or partly of this. **b** piece of this food. [from PASTE]

**pastry-cook** *n.* cook who specialises in pastry.

**pasturage** /pahs-chuh-rij/ *n.* **1** land for pasture. **2** pasturing of cattle etc.

**pasture** /pahs-chuh/ — *n.* **1** grassland suitable for grazing. **2** herbage for animals. — *v.* (**-ring**) **1** put (animals) to pasture. **2** (of animals) graze. [Latin: related to PASTOR]

**pasty¹** /pahs-tee, pas-tee/ *n.* (*pl.* **-ies**) pastry shaped around esp. a meat and vegetable filling. [Latin: related to PASTE]

**pasty²** /pays-tee/ *adj.* (**-ier, -iest**) **1** of or like or covered with paste. **2** unhealthily pale (*pasty-faced*). □ **pastiness** *n.*

**Pat.** *abbr.* Patent.

**pat¹** — v. (**-tt-**) **1** strike gently with a flat palm, esp. in affection, sympathy, etc. **2** flatten or mould by patting. **3** strike gently with the hand or a flat surface. — n. **1** light stroke or tap, esp. with the hand in affection etc. **2** sound made by this. **3** small mass (esp. of butter) formed by patting. □ **pat on the back** gesture of approval, encouragement, or congratulation. **pat a person on the back** congratulate etc. a person. [probably imitative]

**pat²** — adj. **1** prepared or known thoroughly. **2** apposite or opportune, esp. glibly so (a pat answer). — adv. **1** in a pat manner. **2** appositely. □ **have off pat** know or have memorised perfectly. [related to PAT¹]

**pat³** n. = COW-PAT.

**pat⁴** n. □ **on one's pat** colloq. on one's own (spends weekends in the bush on his pat). [Pat Malone, rhyming slang for own]

**patch** — n. **1** piece of material or metal etc. used to mend a hole or as reinforcement. **2 a** shield protecting an injured eye. **b** dressing etc. put over a wound. **c** self-adhesive piece of material impregnated with a drug (e.g. nicotine) for absorption through the skin. **3** large or irregular distinguishable area on a surface. **4** colloq. period of a specified, esp. unpleasant, kind (hit a bad patch financially). **5** stretch of land, road, etc. **6** a number of plants growing in one place (cabbage patch). **7** scrap, remnant. — v. **1** (often foll. by up) repair with a patch or patches. **2** (of material) serve as a patch to. **3** (often foll. by up) put together, repair, etc., esp. hastily. **4** (foll. by up) settle (a quarrel etc.), esp. hastily or temporarily. □ **not a patch on** colloq. greatly inferior to. [perhaps French, var. of PIECE]

**patch test** n. test for allergy by applying patches of allergenic substances to the skin.

**patchwork** n. **1** (often. attrib.) stitching together of small pieces of variegated cloth to form a pattern (patchwork quilt). **2** thing composed of fragments etc.

**patchy** adj. (**-ier**, **-iest**) **1** uneven in quality. **2** having or existing in patches. □ **patchily** adv. **patchiness** n.

**pate** /payt/ n. archaic or colloq. head. [origin unknown]

**pâté** /pat-ay, pah-tay/ n. paste of mashed and spiced liver, meat, or fish etc. [French, = PASTY¹]

**pâté de foie gras** /duh fwah grah/ n. fatted goose liver pâté. [French]

**patella** /puh-tel-uh/ n. (pl. **patellae** /-ee/) kneecap. □ **patellar** adj. [Latin, =

pan, diminutive of patina: related to PATEN]

**paten** /pat-uhn/ n. shallow dish on which the consecrated Host, or the bread, is placed during the Mass, a eucharistic service, etc. [Latin patina]

**patent** /pay-tuhnt/ — n. **1** government document conferring a right or title, esp. the sole right to make, use, or sell a specified invention. **2** invention or process so protected. — adj. **1** obvious, plain (a patent lie). **2** conferred or protected by patent. **3 a** proprietary. **b** to which one has a proprietary claim. — v. obtain a patent for (an invention). □ **patently** /pay-tuhnt-lee/ adv. (in sense 1 of adj.). [Latin pateo lie open]

**patent leather** n. leather with a highly glossy, varnished surface.

**patent medicine** n. proprietary medicine made under a patent and available without prescription.

**paterfamilias** /pay-tuh-fuh-mil-ee-uhs/ n. male head of a family or household. [Latin, = father of the family]

**paternal** /puh-ter-nuhl/ adj. **1** of, like, or appropriate to a father; fatherly. **2** related through the father (paternal uncle). **3** (of a government etc.) limiting freedom and responsibility by well-meant regulations. □ **paternally** adv. [Latin]

**paternalism** n. often derog. policy of governing or behaving in a paternal way. □ **paternalistic** /-lis-tik/ adj.

**paternity** /puh-ter-nuh-tee/ n. **1** fatherhood. **2** one's paternal origin.

**paternity suit** n. lawsuit held to determine if a certain man is the father of a certain child.

**paternoster** /pat-uh-nos-tuh/ n. **1** the Lord's Prayer, esp. in Latin. **2** rosary bead which indicates that this prayer be said. [Latin pater noster our father]

**patersonia** /pat-uh-soh-nee-uh/ n. any of twenty or so species of Australian iris, one with yellow flowers, the others violet-hued, all showy and often in cultivation. [W. Paterson, botanist]

**Paterson's curse** n. (also **Patterson's curse**, **Riverina bluebell**, **Salvation Jane**) European herb with bluish-purple flowers naturalised in Australia and growing rampantly; variously regarded as a noxious weed, useful drought fodder, or valuable honey-plant. [probably R.E. Patterson, grazier (d. 1918)]

**path** /pahth/ n. (pl. **paths** /pahthz/) **1** way or track made for or by walking. **2** line along which a person or thing moves (flight path). **3** course of action. [Old English]

**-path** *comb. form* forming nouns denoting: **1** a practitioner of curative treatment (*homeopath*; *osteopath*). **2** a person who suffers from a disease (*psychopath*). [back-formation from -PATHY]

**pathetic** /puh-**thet**-ik/ *adj.* **1** arousing pity, sadness, or contempt. **2** *colloq.* miserably inadequate. □ **pathetically** *adv.* [Greek *pathos* from *paskhō* suffer]

**pathetic fallacy** *n.* attribution of human emotions to inanimate things, esp. in literature.

**pathfinder** *n.* explorer; pioneer.

**patho-** *comb. form* disease. [Greek *pathos* suffering: see PATHETIC]

**pathogen** /**path**-uh-juhn/ *n.* agent causing disease. □ **pathogenic** /-**jen**-ik/ *adj.* [from PATHO-, -GEN]

**pathological** /,path-uh-**loj**-i-kuhl/ *adj.* **1** of pathology. **2** of or caused by physical or mental disorder (*pathological fear of spiders*). □ **pathologically** *adv.*

**pathology** /puh-**thol**-uh-jee/ *n.* the study or symptoms of disease. □ **pathologist** *n.* [from PATHO-, -LOGY]

**pathos** /**pay**-thos/ *n.* evocation of pity or sadness in speech, writing, events, etc. [Greek: related to PATHETIC]

**pathway** *n.* path or its course.

**-pathy** *comb. form* forming nouns denoting: **1** curative treatment (*allopathy*; *homoeopathy*). **2** feeling (*telepathy*; *sympathy*). [Greek *patheia* suffering]

**patience** /**pay**-shuhns/ *n.* **1** calm endurance of delay, hardship, provocation, pain, etc. **2** perseverance or forbearance. **3** solo card-game. [Latin: related to PASSION]

**patient** — *adj.* having or showing patience. — *n.* person receiving or seeking medical or surgical treatment. □ **patiently** *adv.*

**patina** /**pat**-uh-nuh, puh-**tee**-nuh/ *n.* (*pl.* **-s**) **1** film, usu. green, formed on old bronze. **2** similar film on other surfaces. **3** gloss produced by age on woodwork. [Latin: related to PATEN]

**patio** /**pat**-ee-oh/ *n.* (*pl.* **-s**) paved usu. roofless area adjoining a house and used for outdoor living, entertaining, etc. [Spanish]

**patisserie** /puh-**tis**-uh-ree/ *n.* **1** shop where pastries are made and sold. **2** pastries collectively. [Latin: related to PASTE]

**Pat Malone** /muh-**lohn**/ *n.* □ **on one's Pat Malone** *colloq.* on one's own; alone. [rhyming slang]

**patois** /**pat**-wah/ *n.* (*pl.* same /-wahz/) regional dialect, differing from the literary language. [French]

**patriarch** /**pay**-tree-,ahk, **pat**-ree-/ *n.* **1** male head of a family or tribe. **2** (often in *pl.*) any of those regarded as fathers of the human race, esp. the sons of Jacob, or Abraham, Isaac, and Jacob, and their forefathers. **3** *Eccl.* **a** chief bishop in an Orthodox Church (*Patriarch of Antioch*; *Ecumenical Patriarch*). **b** *RC Ch.* the Pope (*Patriarch of Rome*); also any bishop ranking immediately below the Pope (*Patriarch of Venice*). **c** head of a Uniate Church. **4** venerable old man. □ **patriarchal** /-**ah**-kuhl/ *adj.* [Greek *patria* family, *arkhēs* ruler]

**patriarchate** /**pay**-tree-,ah-kuht, **pat**-ree-/ *n.* **1** office, see, or residence of a Church patriarch. **2** rank of a tribal patriarch.

**patriarchy** /**pay**-tree-,ah-kee, **pat**-ree-/ *n.* (*pl.* **-ies**) male-dominated social system, with descent through the male line.

**patrician** /puh-**trish**-uhn/ — *n. hist.* member of the nobility in ancient Rome — *adj.* **1** aristocratic. **2** *hist.* of the ancient Roman nobility. [Latin *patricius*]

**patricide** /**pat**-ruh-,suyd/ *n.* = PARRICIDE (esp. with reference to the killing of one's father). □ **patricidal** /-**suy**-duhl/ *adj.* [Latin, alteration of *parricida*]

**patrimony** /**pat**-ruh-muh-nee/ *n.* (*pl.* **-ies**) **1** property inherited from one's father or ancestor. **2** heritage. □ **patrimonial** /-**moh**-nee-uhl/ *adj.* [Latin]

**patriot** /**pay**-tree-uht, **pat**-ree-/ *n.* person devoted to and ready to support his or her country. □ **patriotic** /-**ot**-ik/ *adj.* **patriotically** /-**ot**-i-klee/ *adv.* **patriotism** *n.* [Greek *patris* fatherland]

**patristic** /puh-**tris**-tik/ *adj.* of the early Christian writers or their work. [Latin related to PATER]

**patrol** /puh-**trohl**/ — *n.* **1** act of walking or travelling around an area, esp. regularly, for security or supervision. **2** guards, police, etc., sent out on patrol. **3** **a** troops sent out to reconnoitre. **b** such reconnaissance. — *v.* (**-ll-**) **1** carry out a patrol of. **2** act as a patrol. [German *Patrolle* from French]

**patron** /**pay**-truhn/ *n.* (*fem.* **patroness**) **1** person financially supporting a person, cause, etc. **2** customer of a shop etc. [Latin *patronus*]

**patronage** /**pat**-ruh-nij/ *n.* **1** patron's or customer's support. **2** control of appointments to office, privileges, etc. **3** patronising or condescending manner.

**patronise** /**pat**-ruh-,nuyz/ *v.* (also **-ize**) (**-sing** or **-zing**) **1** treat condescendingly. **2** be a patron or customer of. □ **patronising** *adj.* **patronisingly** *adv.*

**patron saint** *n.* saint regarded as protecting a person, place, activity, etc.

**patronymic** /ˌpat-ruh-**nim**-ik/ *n.* name derived from the name of a father or ancestor, e.g. *Johnson, O'Brien, Ivanovich*. [Greek *patēr* father, *onoma* name]

**patter¹** — *n.* sound of quick light steps or taps. — *v.* make this sound (*rain pattering on the window-panes*). [from PAT¹]

**patter²** — *n.* **1** rapid speech used by a comedian or introduced into a song. **2** salesman's persuasive talk. — *v.* talk or say glibly or mechanically. [originally *pater*, = PATERNOSTER]

**pattern** /**pat**-uhn/ — *n.* **1** repeated decorative design (on wallpaper, cloth, etc.). **2** regular or logical form, order, etc. (*behaviour pattern; pattern of one's daily life*). **3** model, design, or instructions for making something (*knitting pattern*). **4** excellent example, model (*pattern of elegance*). **5** wooden or metal shape from which a mould is made for a casting. **6** random combination of shapes or colours. — *v.* **1** (usu. foll. by *after, on*) model (a thing) on a design etc. **2** decorate with a pattern. [from PATRON]

**patty** /**pat**-ee/ *n.* (*pl.* **-ies**) little pie or pasty; small flattened cake of meat etc., usu. grilled or fried. [French *pâté*, after PASTY¹]

**paucity** /**paw**-suh-tee/ *n.* smallness of number or quantity. [Latin *paucus* few]

**paunch** /pawnch/ *n.* belly, stomach, esp. when protruding. □ **paunchy** *adj.* (**-ier, -iest**). [Anglo-French *pa(u)nche* from Latin *pantices* bowels]

**pauper** /**paw**-puh/ *n.* poor person. □ **pauperism** *n.* [Latin, = poor]

**pause** /pawz/ — *n.* **1** temporary stop or silence. **2** *Mus.* mark (⌢) over a note or rest that is to be lengthened. — *v.* (**-sing**) make a pause; wait. □ **give pause to** cause to hesitate. [Greek *pauō paus-* stop]

**pav** *n.* = PAVLOVA. [abbreviation]

**pave** *v.* (**-ving**) **1** cover (a street, floor, etc.) with a durable surface. **2** cover or strew (a floor etc.) with anything (*paved with flowers*). □ **pave the way** (usu. foll. by *for*) make preparations. □ **paving** *n.* [Latin *pavio* ram (v.)]

**pavement** *n.* paved path for pedestrians beside a road. [Latin *pavimentum*: related to PAVE]

**pavement artist** *n.* artist who draws in chalk on a pavement for tips.

**pavilion** /puh-**vil**-yuhn/ *n.* **1** decorative shelter in a park. **2** large tent at a show, fair, etc. **3** building at a cricket or other sports ground used for changing etc. [Latin *papilio* butterfly]

**pavlova** /pav-**loh**-vuh/ *n.* Australian dessert: a large, soft-centred meringue cake topped with whipped cream and fruit, traditionally passionfruit. [Anna *Pavlova*, Russian ballerina (d. 1931)]

**Pavlovian** /pav-**loh**-vee-uhn/ *adj.* **1** reacting predictably to a stimulus. **2** of such a stimulus or response. [*Pavlov*, Russian physiologist (d. 1936)]

**paw** — *n.* **1** foot of an animal having claws or nails. **2** *colloq.* person's hand. — *v.* **1** strike or scrape with a paw or foot (*pawed the ground*). **2** *colloq.* fondle awkwardly or indecently. [French *poue* from Germanic]

**pawn¹** *n.* **1** *Chess* piece of the smallest size and value. **2** person used by others for their own purposes. [French *poun* from Latin *pedo -onis* foot-soldier]

**pawn²** — *v.* **1** deposit (a thing) with a pawnbroker as security for money lent. **2** pledge or wager (one's life, honour, etc.). — *n.* object left in pawn. □ **in pawn** held as security. [French *pan* from Germanic]

**pawnbroker** *n.* person who lends money at interest on the security of personal property.

**pawnshop** *n.* pawnbroker's shop.

**pawpaw** /**paw**-paw/ *n.* (also **papaw** /puh-**paw**, pa-paw/) **1** elongated melon-shaped fruit with orange flesh. **2** tropical tree bearing this. [Spanish and Portuguese *papaya*]

**pay** — *v.* (*past* and *past part.* **paid**) **1** (also *absol.*) give (a person etc.) what is due for services done, goods received, debts incurred, etc. (*paid him in full; I assure you I have paid*). **2 a** give (a usu. specified amount) for work done, a debt, etc. (*they pay $10 an hour*). **b** (foll. by *to*) hand over the amount of (a debt, wages, etc.) to (*paid the money to the assistant*). **3 a** give, bestow, or express (attention, a compliment, etc.) (*paid them no heed*). **b** make (a visit) (*paid a call on their uncle*). **4** (also *absol.*) (of a business, attitude, etc.) be profitable or advantageous to (a person etc.) (*courtesy pays; his business pays him well*). **5** reward or punish (*shall pay you for that*). **6** acknowledge the validity of a remark, repartee, etc.; acknowledge that one has been outwitted (*I'll pay that*). **7** (usu. as **paid** *adj.*) recompense (work, time, etc.) (*paid holiday*). **8** (usu. foll. by *out, away*) let out (a rope) by slackening it. — *n.* wages. □ **in the pay of** employed by. **pay back 1** repay. **2** punish or have revenge on. **pay for 1** hand over the money for. **2** bear the cost of. **3** suffer or be punished for (a fault etc.). **pay in** pay (money) into a bank etc. account. **pay it** (or **one's**) **way** cover costs; not be indebted. **pay one's last respects** attend a funeral to show respect. **pay off 1** dismiss (workers) with a final payment. **2** *colloq.* yield good results; succeed (*that venture paid off in the end*). **3** pay (a debt) in full. **pay through the nose** *colloq.* pay much more than a fair price. **pay up** pay the full amount (of). **put paid to** *colloq.* **1** deal effectively with (a person). **2** terminate (hopes etc.). □ **payee** /pay-ee/ *n.* [Latin *paco* appease: related to PEACE]

**payable** *adj.* that must or may be paid; due (*payable in April*).

**pay-as-you-earn** *n.* deduction of income tax from wages at source.

**payback** *n.* **1** reward, return. **2** (act of) revenge or retaliation.

**pay claim** *n.* (esp. a trade union's) demand for a pay increase.

**PAYE** *abbr.* pay-as-you-earn.

**payload** *n.* **1** part of an aircraft's load yielding revenue. **2** explosive warhead carried by a rocket etc. **3** equipment etc. carried by a spacecraft to monitor operations, conduct experiments, etc. **4** goods carried by a road vehicle.

**paymaster** *n.* **1** official who pays troops, workmen, etc. **2** usu. *derog.* person, organisation, etc., to whom another owes loyalty because of payment given.

**payment** *n.* **1** an act or instance of paying. **2** amount paid. **3** reward, recompense.

**pay-off** *n. colloq.* **1** payment. **2** climax. **3** final reckoning.

**payola** /pay-oh-luh/ *n.* esp. *US colloq.* bribe offered for unofficial promotion of a product etc. in the media.

**pay phone** *n.* coin-box or phonecard telephone.

**payroll** *n.* list of employees receiving regular pay.

**pay television** *n.* = CABLE TELEVISION.

**Pb** *symb.* lead. [Latin *plumbum*]

**PC** *abbr.* personal computer.

**p.c.** *abbr.* **1** per cent. **2** postcard.

**PCB** *abbr.* **1** polychlorinated biphenyl, any of several toxic aromatic compounds formed as waste in industrial processes. **2** *Computing* printed circuit board.

**Pd** *symb.* palladium.

**pd.** *abbr.* paid.

**PE** *abbr.* physical education.

**pea** *n.* **1 a** hardy climbing plant with edible seeds growing in pods. **b** its seed. **2** similar plant (*sweet pea*; *chick-pea*). **3** = DARLING PEA. **4** *colloq.* **a** (in horse racing) a favourite; a likely winner. **b** person expected to win a job etc. over other applicants (*she's the pea for the post of managing director*). [from PEASE taken as a plural]

**peabrain** *n. colloq.* stupid or dim-witted person. □ **peabrained** *adj.*

**pea-bush** *n.* (also **Sesbania pea**) any of several shrubs of the genus *Sesbania* widespread in northern Australia.

**peace** *n.* **1 a** quiet; tranquillity (*needs peace to work*). **b** mental calm; serenity (*peace of mind*). **2 a** (often *attrib.*) freedom from or the cessation of war (*peace talks*). **b** (as **Peace**) treaty of peace between nations etc. at war. **3** freedom from civil disorder. □ **at peace 1** in a state of friendliness. **2** serene. **3** *euphem.* dead. **hold one's peace** keep silent. **keep the peace** prevent, or refrain from, strife. **make one's peace** (often foll. by *with*) re-establish friendly relations. [Latin *pax pac-*]

**peaceable** *adj.* **1** disposed to peace. **2** peaceful; tranquil. [Latin *placibilis* pleasing: related to PLEASE]

**peaceful** *adj.* **1** characterised by peace; tranquil. **2** not infringing peace (*peaceful coexistence*). □ **peacefully** *adv.* **peacefulness** *n.*

**peaceful dove** *n.* predominantly grey to brown dove with black bars, found in eastern and northern mainland Australia.

**peacekeeper** *n.* **1** person who keeps or maintains peace. **2** member of a peacekeeping organisation or force.

**peacekeeping** *n.* (also *attrib.*) active maintenance of a truce between nations or communities, esp. by international military forces.

**peacemaker** *n.* person who brings about peace. □ **peacemaking** *n.* & *adj.*

**peacenik** *n.* committed pacifist, esp. one who joins demonstrations etc. [-NIK]

**peace-offering** *n.* propitiatory or conciliatory gift.

**peacetime** *n.* period when a country is not at war.

**peach**[1] *n.* **1 a** round juicy stone-fruit with downy yellow or pink skin. **b** tree bearing this. **2** yellowish-pink colour. **3** *colloq.* person or thing of superlative quality. □ **peachy** *adj.* (**-ier, -iest**). [Latin *persica* Persian (apple)]

**peach**[2] *v.* (usu. foll. by *against*, *on*) *colloq.* turn informer; inform. [from obsolete *appeach*: related to IMPEACH]

**peach Melba** see MELBA.

**peacock** — *n.* (*pl.* same or **-s**) **1** male peafowl, native to India, with brilliant plumage and an erectile fanlike tail with eyelike markings. **2** vain or ostentatious person. — *v.* (of a person) strut like a peacock, displaying oneself. [from Latin *pavo* peacock, COCK]

**peacock blue** *adj. & n.* (as adj. often hyphenated) lustrous greenish blue of a peacock's neck.

**pea-eater** *n.* **1** an animal poisoned by eating Darling pea. **2** *colloq.* idiot; brainless person (as brainless as an animal which eats Darling pea).

**peafowl** *n.* peacock, peahen.

**pea green** *adj. & n.* (as adj. often hyphenated) bright green.

**peahen** *n.* female peafowl.

**peak¹** — *n.* **1** projecting usu. pointed part, esp.: **a** the pointed top of a mountain. **b** a mountain with a peak. **c** a stiff brim at the front of a cap. **2 a** highest point of a curve (*on the peak of the wave*). **b** time of greatest success, fitness, etc. (*at the peak of her career*). **c** highest point on a graph etc. **3** *attrib.* maximum, busiest (*peak viewing*; *peak hours*). — *v.* reach its highest value, quality, etc. (*output peaked in September*). □ **peaked** *adj.* [related to PICK²]

**peak²** *v.* **1** waste away. **2** (as **peaked** *adj.*) sharp-featured; pinched. [origin unknown]

**peak hour** *n.* time of the most intense traffic etc. □ **peak-hour** *adj.*

**peak load** *n.* maximum of electric power demand etc.

**peal** — *n.* **1 a** loud ringing of a bell or bells, esp. a series of changes. **b** set of bells. **2** loud repeated sound, esp. of thunder, laughter, etc. — *v.* **1** (cause to) sound in a peal. **2** utter sonorously. [from APPEAL]

**peanut** *n.* **1** plant of the pea family bearing pods underground that contain seeds used for food and oil. **2** seed of this. **3** (in *pl.*) *colloq.* paltry amount, esp. of money (*if the rich bosses had their way, we'd be working for peanuts*). **4** *colloq.* **a** insignificant, worthless person. **b** short person.

**pear** /pair/ *n.* **1** yellowish or greenish fleshy fruit, tapering towards the stalk. **2** tree bearing this. (See also WOODY PEAR). [Latin *pirum*]

**pearl** /perl/ — *n.* **1 a** (often *attrib.*) rounded usu. white or bluish-grey lustrous solid formed within the shell of certain oysters, highly prized as a gem. **b** imitation of this. **c** (in *pl.*) necklace of pearls. **d** = MOTHER-OF-PEARL. **2** precious thing; finest example. **3** thing like a pearl, e.g. a dewdrop or tear. — *v.* **1** *poet.* form or sprinkle with pearly drops. **2** reduce (barley etc.) to small rounded grains. **3** fish for pearls. — *adj.* **1** of the colour of pearl. **2** (of a light globe) translucent. [Italian *perla*, from Latin *perna* leg]

**pearl barley** *n.* barley ground to small rounded grains.

**pearler¹** *n.* **1** person who dives or fishes for pearls. **2** boat used in pearl fishing.

**pearler²** var. of PURLER.

**pearl perch** *n.* greenish to silvery-grey marine food-fish of reefs off the Queensland coast.

**pearly** *adj.* (**-ier, -iest**) like, containing, or adorned with pearls; lustrous.

**pearly nautilus** see NAUTILUS.

**peasant** /pez-uhnt/ *n.* **1** (in some rural agricultural countries) small farmer, agricultural worker. **2** *derog.* lout; boor. □ **peasantry** *n.* (*pl.* **-ies**). [Anglo-French *paisant* from *païs* country]

**pease** /peez/ *n.pl. archaic* peas. [Latin *pisa*]

**pea-shooter** *n.* small tube for blowing dried peas through as a toy.

**pea-souper** *n. colloq.* thick yellowish fog.

**pea-struck** *adj.* (of an animal) poisoned by eating Darling pea.

**peat** *n.* partly carbonised vegetable matter used in horticulture etc. □ **peaty** *adj.* [perhaps Celtic: related to PIECE]

**peatmoss** *n.* any of various mosses, of the genus *Sphagnum*, which form peat as they decay: much used in horticulture for potting mixes etc.

**pebble** /peb-uhl/ *n.* small stone worn smooth esp. by the action of water. □ **pebbly** *adj.* [Old English]

**pecan** /pee-kuhn, pee-**kan**/ *n.* **1** pinkish-brown smooth nut with an edible kernel. **2** type of hickory producing this. [Algonquian]

**peccadillo** /pek-uh-**dil**-oh/ *n.* (*pl.* **-es** or **-s**) trifling offence; venial sin. [Spanish *pecadillo*, from Latin *pecco* sin (v.)]

**peck¹** — *v.* **1** strike or bite with a beak. **2** kiss hastily or perfunctorily. **3 a** make (a hole) by pecking. **b** (foll. by *out, off*) remove or pluck out by pecking. **4** (also *absol.*) *colloq.* eat listlessly; nibble at. **5** (as **pecked** *adj.*) (of Aboriginal rock engravings) characterised by pecked strokes or marks. — *n.* **1** stroke, mark, or bite made by a beak. **2** hasty or perfunctory kiss. □ **peck at 1** eat (food) listlessly; nibble. **2** carp at; nag. **3** strike repeatedly with a beak. [probably Low German]

**peck²** *n.* (in the imperial system) a measure of capacity for dry goods, equal to 2 gallons or 8 quarts. □ **a peck of** large number or amount of (troubles etc.). [Anglo-French]

**pecker** *n.* **1** that which pecks; beak. **2** *colloq.* courage; spirit. □ **keep one's pecker up** *colloq.* remain cheerful.

**pecking order** n. social hierarchy, orig. as observed among hens (*rigid pecking order in this department*).

**peckish** adj. colloq. hungry.

**pectin** /**pek**-tuhn/ n. soluble gelatinous carbohydrate found in ripe fruits etc. and used as a setting agent in jams and jellies. □ **pectic** adj. [Greek *pēgnumi* make solid]

**pectoral** /**pek**-tuh-ruhl/ — adj. of or worn on the breast or chest (*pectoral fin*; *pectoral muscle*; *a bishop's pectoral cross*). — n. pectoral muscle or fin. [Latin *pectus* -*tor*- chest]

**peculate** /**pek**-yuh-,layt/ v. (**-ting**) embezzle (money). □ **peculation** /-**lay**-shuhn/ n. **peculator** n. [Latin: related to PECULIAR]

**peculiar** /puh-**kyoo**-lee-uh, -lyuh/ adj. 1 strange; odd; unusual (*peculiar flavour*; *he's a bit peculiar*). 2 a (usu. foll. by *to*) belonging exclusively (*peculiar to the early 19th century*). b belonging to the individual (*in their own peculiar way*). 3 particular; special (*point of peculiar interest*). [Latin *peculium* private property, from *pecu* cattle]

**peculiarity** /puh-,kyoo-lee-a-ruh-tee/ n. (pl. **-ies**) 1 idiosyncrasy; oddity. 2 a characteristic or habit (*meanness is his peculiarity*). 3 state of being peculiar.

**peculiarly** /puh-**kyoo**-lyuh-lee/ adv. 1 more than usually, especially (*peculiarly annoying*). 2 oddly.

**pecuniary** /puh-**kyoo**-nyuh-ree/ adj. 1 of or concerning money (*pecuniary aid*). 2 (of an offence) entailing a money penalty. [Latin *pecunia* money, from *pecu* cattle]

**pedagogue** /**ped**-uh-,gog/ n. archaic or derog. schoolmaster; teacher. □ **pedagogic** /-**goj**-ik/ adj. **pedagogical** /-**goj**-i-kuhl/ adj. [Greek *pais paid*- child, *agō* lead]

**pedagogy** /**ped**-uh-,goj-ee/ n. science of teaching.

**pedal** — n. /**ped**-uhl/ lever or key operated by foot, esp. in a vehicle, on a bicycle, or on some musical instruments (e.g. the organ). — v. /**ped**-uhl/ (**-ll-**) 1 operate the pedals of a bicycle, organ, etc. 2 propel (a bicycle etc.) with the pedals. — adj. /**pee**-duhl/ of the foot or feet. [Latin *pes ped*- foot]

**pedant** /**ped**-uhnt/ n. derog. person who insists on adherence to formal rules or literal meaning, or who is obsessed by theory to the exclusion of practical application. □ **pedantic** /puh-**dan**-tik/ adj. **pedantically** /puh-**dan**-ti-kuh-lee, -klee/ adv. **pedantry** n. [French from Italian]

**peddle** /**ped**-uhl/ v. (**-ling**) 1 a sell (goods) as a pedlar. b advocate or promote (ideas, a way of life, etc.) (*peddle lies*). 2 sell (drugs) illegally. 3 engage in selling, esp. as a pedlar. [back-formation from PEDLAR]

**peddler** n. person who sells drugs illegally.

**pederast** /**ped**-uh-,rast/ n. (also **paederast**) man who engages in pederasty.

**pederasty** /**ped**-uh-,ras-tee/ n. (also **paederasty**) anal intercourse between a man and a boy. [Greek *pais paid*- boy, *erastēs* lover]

**pedestal** /**ped**-uhs-tuhl/ n. 1 base supporting a column or pillar. 2 stone etc. base of a statue etc. □ **put on a pedestal** admire disproportionately, idolise. [Italian *piedestallo*, = foot of stall]

**pedestrian** /puh-**des**-tree-uhn/ — n. (often *attrib.*) person who is walking, esp. in a town. — adj. prosaic; dull; uninspired (*his poetry is pedestrian*). [Latin: related to PEDAL]

**pedestrian crossing** n. part of a road where crossing pedestrians have right of way.

**pedestrianise** v. (also **-ize**) (**-sing** or **-zing**) close (a street etc.) to vehicular traffic, esp. in busy shopping areas, and reserve for pedestrian use only.

**pediatrics** var. of PAEDIATRICS.

**pedicure** /**ped**-uh-,kyoor/ n. 1 care or treatment of the feet, esp. the toenails. 2 person practising this for a living. [Latin *pes ped*- foot, *cura* care]

**pedigree** /**ped**-uh-,gree/ n. 1 (often *attrib.*) recorded line of descent (esp. a distinguished one) of a person or pure-bred animal. 2 genealogical table. 3 derivation of a word. 4 colloq. 'life history' of a person, thing, idea, etc. □ **pedigreed** adj. [*pedegru* from French *pie de grue* (unrecorded) crane's foot, a mark denoting succession in pedigrees]

**pediment** /**ped**-uh-muhnt/ n. triangular part crowning the front of a building, esp. over a portico. [from *periment*, perhaps a corruption of PYRAMID]

**pedlar** /**ped**-luh/ n. 1 travelling seller of small items. 2 (usu. foll. by *of*) retailer (of gossip etc.). [alteration of *pedder* from *ped* pannier]

**pedo-** var. of PAEDO-.

**pedometer** /puh-**dom**-uh-tuh/ n. instrument for estimating distance walked by recording the number of steps taken. [Latin *pes ped*- foot: related to -METER]

**pedophile** var. of PAEDOPHILE.

**pedophilia** var. of PAEDOPHILIA.

**peduncle** /puh-**dung**-kuhl/ n. 1 stalk of a flower, fruit, or cluster, esp. a main stalk bearing a solitary flower or subordinate stalks. **2** a stalklike projection in an animal body. □ **peduncular** /-kyuh-luh/ adj. [related to PEDOMETER, -UNCLE]

**pee** colloq. — v. (**pees, peed**) urinate. — n. **1** act of urinating. **2** urine. [from PISS]

**peek** — v. (usu. foll. by in, out, at) peep slyly, glance. — n. quick or sly look. [origin unknown]

**peel** — v. **1** a strip the skin, rind, wrapping, etc. from. **b** (usu. foll. by off) strip (skin, peel, wrapping, etc.). **2** a (of a tree, an animal's or person's body, a painted surface, etc.) become bare of bark, skin, paint, etc. **b** (often foll. by off) (of skin, paint, etc.) flake off. **3** (often foll. by off) colloq. (of a person) strip ready for exercise etc. — n. outer covering of a fruit, vegetable, etc.; rind. □ **keep one's eyes peeled** see EYE. **peel off** veer away and detach oneself from a group of marchers, a formation of aircraft, etc. **2** colloq. strip off one's clothes. [Old English from Latin pilo strip of hair]

**peeling** n. (usu. in pl.) stripped-off piece of peel.

**peen** n. wedge-shaped or thin or curved end of a hammer-head. [Latin pinna point]

**peep**[1] — v. **1** (usu. foll. by at, in, out, into) look through a narrow opening; look furtively. **2** (usu. foll. by out) come slowly into view; emerge (the sun peeping over the eastern hills). — n. **1** furtive or peering glance. **2** first appearance (peep of day). [origin unknown]

**peep**[2] — v. make a shrill feeble sound as of young birds, mice, etc.; cheep; chirp; squeak. — n. **1** such a sound. **2** slight sound, utterance, or complaint (not a peep out of them). [imitative]

**peep-hole** n. small hole for peeping through.

**peeping Tom** n. a furtive voyeur.

**peep-show** n. small exhibition of pictures etc. viewed through a lens or hole set into a box etc.

**peer**[1] v. **1** (usu. foll. by into, at, etc.) look closely at or with difficulty (peered into the fog). **2** appear; peep out. [origin unknown]

**peer**[2] n. **1** person who is equal in ability, standing, rank, or value; a contemporary (tried by a jury of his peers). **2** (fem. **peeress**) nobleman. [Latin par equal]

**peerage** n. **1** peers as a class. **2** rank of peer.

**peer group** n. group of people of the same age, status, social background, etc.

**peerless** adj. unequalled; superb.

**peeve** colloq. — v. (**-ving**) (usu. as **peeved** adj.) irritate, annoy. — n. cause or state

of irritation. [back-formation from PEEVISH]

**peevish** adj. irritable. □ **peevishly** adv. [origin unknown]

**peewee** /pee-wee/ n. (also **peewit**) = MAGPIE LARK. [imitative]

**peewit** /pee-wit/ n. (also **peewee**) = MAGPIE LARK. [imitative]

**peg** — n. **1** pin or bolt of wood, metal, etc., for holding things together, hanging garments on, holding up a tent, stopping a hole (in a cask etc.), etc. **2** each of the pins used to tighten or loosen the strings of a violin etc. **3** pin for marking position. **4** clothes-peg. **5** occasion or pretext (peg to hang an argument on). **6** drink, esp. of spirits. — v. (**-gg-**) **1** (usu. foll. by down, in, out, to) fix (a thing) with a peg. **2** stabilise (prices, wages, etc.). **3** (usu. foll. by out) mark with pegs (pegged out his claim). □ **off the peg** = off the hook (see HOOK). **peg away** (often foll. by at) work consistently. **peg it** (or a thing specified) **on a person** hang the blame (or a thing specified) on a person (tried to peg it on me; pegged the theft on the boy next door). **peg out** colloq. die. **square peg in a round hole** a misfit. **take a person down a peg (or two)** humble a person. [probably Low German or Dutch]

**peggy** n. colloq. unskilled worker responsible for tea-making etc. [transferred use of peggy a ship's mess-steward]

**peg-leg** n. colloq. **1** artificial leg. **2** person with this. **3** disease of cattle attributed to phosphorus deficiency.

**pejorative** /puh-jo-ruh-tiv/ — adj. derogatory. — n. derogatory word. □ **pejoration** n. [Latin pejor worse]

**Pekingese** /pee-kuh-neez/ n. (also **Pekinese**) (pl. same) lap-dog of a short-legged breed with long hair and a snub nose. [from Peking (Beijing) in China]

**pekoe** /pee-koh/ n. superior grade of black tea from Ceylon etc. [Chinese dial. pek-ho white down, leaves being picked young with down on them]

**pelargonium** /pel-uh-goh-nee-uhm/ n. **1** plant with red, pink, or white flowers and, often, fragrant leaves; often erroneously called 'geranium'. **2** any of the Australian members of this family, esp. Pelargonium rodneyanum, Australia's most beautiful pelargonium, with striking magenta flowers. [Greek pelargos stork]

**pelf** n. derog. or joc. money; wealth. [French: related to PILFER]

**pelican** /pel-uh-kuhn/ n. large water-bird with a large bill and a pouch in its throat for storing fish. [Greek pelekan]

**pellagra** /puh-**lag**-ruh, -**lay**-gruh/ *n.* disease with cracking of the skin and often ending in insanity. [Italian *pelle* skin]

**pellet** /**pel**-uht/ *n.* **1** small compressed ball of paper, bread, etc. **2** pill. **3** piece of small shot. [French *pelote* from Latin *pila* ball]

**pellicle** /**pel**-i-kuhl/ *n.* thin skin, membrane, or film. [Latin diminutive of *pellis* skin]

**pell-mell** /pel-**mel**/ *adv.* **1** headlong, recklessly. **2** in disorder or confusion. [French *pêle-mêle*]

**pellucid** /puh-**loo**-sid/ *adj.* **1** transparent. **2** (of style, speech, etc.) clear. [Latin *pellucidus* (as PER-, *luco* shine)]

**pelmet** /**pel**-muht/ *n.* narrow border of cloth, wood, etc. fitted esp. above a window to conceal the curtain rail. [probably French]

**peloton** /**pel**-uh-ton/ *n.* the main field or group of cyclists in a race. [related to PELLET]

**pelt**[1] — *v.* **1 a** (usu. foll. by *with*) strike repeatedly with thrown objects (*pelted him with rotten eggs*). **b** assail (a person etc.) with insults, abuse, etc. **2** (usu. foll. by *down*) (of rain etc.) fall quickly and torrentially. **3** run fast (*they pelted down the street*). — *n.* act or instance of pelting. □ **at full pelt** as fast as possible. [origin unknown]

**pelt**[2] *n.* undressed skin, usu. of a fur-bearing mammal. [French, ultimately from Latin *pellis* skin]

**Pelvic Inflammatory Disease** *n.* (also **PID**) inflammation of the female genital tract, esp. the fallopian tubes.

**pelvis** /**pel**-vuhs/ *n.* basin-shaped cavity in most vertebrates, formed from the hip-bone with the sacrum and other vertebrae. □ **pelvic** *adj.* [Latin, = basin]

**pen**[1] — *n.* **1** instrument for writing etc. with ink. **2** (**the pen**) occupation of writing. — *v.* (**-nn-**) write. [Latin *penna* feather]

**pen**[2] — *n.* **1 a** small enclosure for cows, sheep, poultry, etc. **b** a division in a shearing shed. **c** a job as a shearer. **2** any place of confinement. — *v.* (**-nn-**) (often foll. by *in*, *up*) enclose or shut up, esp. in a pen. [Old English]

**pen**[3] *n.* female swan. [origin unknown]

**pen**[4] *n. colloq.* prison. [abbreviation of PENITENTIARY]

**penal** /**pee**-nuhl/ *adj.* **1** of or concerning punishment or its infliction (*penal laws*; *penal colony*). **2** (of an offence) punishable, esp. by law. **3** extremely severe, punishing (*penal taxation*). □ **penally** *adv.* [Latin *poena* PAIN]

**penal colony** *n.* (also **convict colony**) *hist.* an Australian Colony regarded primarily as a place of penal servitude for convicts from Britain.

**penalise** /**pee**-nuh-,luyz/ *v.* (**-ize**) (**-sing** or **-zing**) **1** subject (a person) to a penalty or disadvantage. **2** make or declare (an action) penal.

**penal settlement** *n.* (also **convict settlement**) *hist.* any of several places in Australia where convicts from Britain were confined.

**penal station** *n. hist.* = PENAL SETTLEMENT.

**penalty** /**pen**-uhl-tee/ *n.* (*pl.* **-ies**) **1** punishment for breaking a law, rule, or contract. **2** disadvantage, loss, etc., esp. as a result of one's own actions (*paid the penalty for his carelessness*). **3** *Sport* (also *attrib.*) disadvantage imposed for a breach of the rules etc. (*penalty kick*). [medieval Latin: related to PENAL]

**penalty rate** *n.* increased rate of pay for overtime or in recognition of abnormal conditions.

**penance** /**pen**-uhns/ *n.* **1 a** (in the Roman Catholic and Orthodox Church) sacrament including confession of and absolution for sins. **b** penalty imposed, esp. by a priest, for a sin. **2** act of self-punishment as reparation for guilt. □ **do penance** perform a penance. [related to PENITENT]

**pence** *pl.* of PENNY.

**penchant** /pon-**shon**, pen-shuhnt/ *n.* (followed by *for*) inclination or liking (*has a penchant for sword-and-sorcery films*). [French]

**pencil** /**pen**-suhl/ — *n.* **1** instrument for writing or drawing, usu. a thin rod of graphite etc. enclosed in a wooden cylinder or metal case. **2** (*attrib.*) resembling a pencil in shape (*pencil pine*). — *v.* (**-ll-**) **1** write, draw, or mark with a pencil. **2** (usu. foll. by *in*) write, note, or arrange provisionally (*have pencilled in the 29th for our meeting*). [Latin *penicillum* paintbrush]

**pencil cedar** *n.* **1** any of several Australian trees (of various families) yielding a useful timber. **2** the wood of these trees.

**pencil pine** *n.* narrow, tapering, coniferous tree of wet sites in Tasmania with tiny leaves close-pressed to the stem.

**penda** /**pen**-duh/ *n.* **1** any of several trees (family Myrtaceae) of south-eastern Queensland valued for their very hard, brown wood. **2** the wood of these trees. [probably from Gabi-gabi]

**pendant** /**pen**-duhnt/ *n.* **1** hanging jewel

**pendent** /pen-duhnt/ adj. formal **1 a** hanging. **b** overhanging. **2** undecided, pending. □ **pendency** n.

**pending** — predic. adj. **1** awaiting decision or settlement, undecided. **2** about to come into existence (patent pending). — prep. **1** during (pending further inquiries). **2** until (bailed pending trial). [after French: see PENDANT]

**pendulous** /pen-dyoo-luhs/ adj. hanging down; drooping and swinging. [Latin pendulus from pendeo hang]

**pendulum** /pen-dyoo-luhm/ n. (pl. -s) weight suspended so as to swing freely, esp. a rod with a weighted end regulating a clock. [Latin neuter adjective: related to PENDULOUS]

**penetrate** /pen-uh-,trayt/ v. (-ting) **1 a** find access into or through, esp. forcibly. **b** (usu. foll. by with) imbue with; permeate. **2** see into, find out, or discern (a person's mind, the truth, etc.). **3** see through (darkness, fog, etc.) (could not penetrate the gloom). **4** be absorbed by the mind (my hint did not penetrate). **5** (as **penetrating** adj.) **a** having or suggesting sensitivity or insight (a penetrating remark). **b** (of a voice etc.) easily heard through or above other sounds; piercing. □ **penetrable** /-truh-buhl/ adj. **penetrability** /-truh-bil-uh-tee/ n. **penetration** /-tray-shuhn/ n. **penetrative** /-truh-tiv/ adj. [Latin]

**penfriend** n. friend communicated with by letter only.

**penguin** /peng-gwuhn/ n. flightless black and white sea bird of the Southern hemisphere, with wings developed into flippers for swimming underwater. [origin unknown]

**Penguin Award** n. any of the annual awards for excellence made by the Television Society of Australia.

**penicillin** /,pen-uh-sil-uhn/ n. antibiotic, produced naturally by mould or synthetically. [Latin penicillum: related to PENCIL]

**penile** /pee-nuyl/ adj. of or concerning the penis. [Latin]

**peninsula** /puh-nin-shuh-luh, -syoo-luh/ n. piece of land almost surrounded by water or projecting far into a sea etc. □ **peninsular** adj. [Latin paene almost, insula island]

**penis** /pee-nuhs/ n. male organ of copulation and (in mammals) urination. [Latin, = tail]

**penitent** /pen-uh-tuhnt/ — adj. repentant. — n. **1** repentant sinner. **2** person doing penance under the direction of a confessor. □ **penitence** n. **penitently** adv. [Latin paeniteo repent]

**penitential** /,pen-uh-ten-shuhl/ adj. of penitence or penance.

**penitentiary** /,pen-uh-ten-shuh-ree/ — n. (pl. -ies) US federal or State prison. — adj. **1** of penance. **2** of reformatory treatment. [Latin: related to PENITENT]

**penknife** n. small folding knife (originally for sharpening quills into pens).

**pen-name** n. literary pseudonym.

**pennant** /pen-uhnt/ n. **1** tapering flag, esp. that flown at the masthead of a vessel in commission. **2** = PENNON. **3** flag as symbol of success in sports, of a championship, etc. [blend of PENDANT and PENNON]

**penniless** /pen-ee-luhs/ adj. having no money; destitute.

**pennon** /pen-uhn/ n. **1** long narrow flag, triangular or swallow-tailed. **2** long pointed streamer on a ship. [Latin penna feather]

**penny** /pen-ee/ n. (pl. for separate coins **-ies**, for a sum of money **pence** /pens/) **1** British coin and monetary unit equal to one-hundredth of a pound. **2** hist. Australian (and British) bronze coin and monetary unit equal to one-two-hundred-and-fortieth of a pound. □ **bad penny** undesirable person or thing continually returning when unwanted. **in for a penny, in for a pound** exhortation to total commitment to an undertaking. **pennies from heaven** unexpected benefits. **the penny drops** colloq. one understands at last. **a penny for your thoughts** request to a person lost in thought to confide in the speaker. **penny wise and pound foolish** mean in small expenditures but wasteful of large amounts. **a pretty penny** a large sum of money. **two a penny** easily obtained and so almost worthless. [Old English]

**penny-farthing** n. early type of bicycle with a large front and small rear wheel.

**penny-pinching** — n. meanness, stinginess. — adj. mean. □ **penny-pincher** n.

**pennyworth** n. as much as can be bought for a penny.

**penology** /pee-nol-uh-jee/ n. the study of the punishment of crime and prison management. □ **penologist** n. [Latin poena penalty]

**pen pal** n. colloq. = PENFRIEND.

**pen-pushing** n. colloq. derog. clerical work. □ **pen-pusher** n.

**pension** /pen-shuhn/ — n. **1** regular payment made by a government to people above a specified age, to widows, or to the disabled. **2** regular payment from a fund etc. to which the recipient has contributed (usu. with an employer) as an investment during his or her working life in order to realise a return upon retirement. — v. grant a pension to. □ **pension off 1** dismiss with a pension. **2** cease to employ or use. [Latin *pendo pens-* pay]

**pensionable** adj. **1** entitled to a pension. **2** (of a service, job, etc.) entitling an employee to a pension.

**pensioner** n. recipient of a pension, esp. the retirement pension. [French: related to PENSION]

**pensive** /pen-siv/ adj. deep in thought. □ **pensively** adv. [French *penser* think]

**pent** adj. (often foll. by *in*, *up*) closely confined; shut in (*pent-up feelings*). [from PEN²]

**penta-** comb. form five. [Greek *pente* five]

**pentacle** /pen-tuh-kuhl/ n. figure used as a symbol, esp. in magic, e.g. a pentagram. [medieval Latin *pentaculum*: related to PENTA-]

**pentagon** /pen-tuh-guhn, -gon/ n. **1** plane figure with five sides and angles. **2** (**the Pentagon**) **a** pentagonal Washington headquarters of the US forces. **b** leaders of the US forces. □ **pentagonal** /-tag-uh-nuhl/ adj. [Greek *pentagōnon*: related to PENTA-]

**pentagram** /pen-tuh-,gram/ n. (also **pentangle**) five-pointed star. [Greek: see PENTA-, -GRAM]

**pentameter** /pen-tam-uh-tuh/ n. line of verse with five metrical feet. [Greek: see PENTA-, -METER]

**pentangle** n. = PENTAGRAM.

**Pentateuch** /pen-tuh-,tyook/ n. first five books of the Old Testament. [Greek *teukhos* book]

**pentathlon** /pen-tath-luhn/ n. athletic event comprising five different events for each competitor. □ **pentathlete** /-tath-leet/ n. [Greek: see PENTA-, *athlon* contest]

**pentatonic** /,pen-tuh-ton-ik/ adj. Mus. consisting of five notes (*pentatonic scale*).

**Pentecost** /pen-tuh-,kost/ n. **1** Whit Sunday. **2** Jewish harvest festival, on the fiftieth day after the second day of Passover. [Greek *pentēkostē* fiftieth (day)]

**pentecostal** /,pen-tuh-kos-tuhl/ adj. of or designating Christian sects which emphasise divine gifts such as miraculous healing of the sick, are usu. fundamentalist in outlook, and the members of which express religious fervour by clapping, shouting, glossolalia, etc.

**penthouse** /pent-hows/ n. (esp. luxurious) flat on the roof or top floor of a tall building. [Latin: related to APPEND]

**penultimate** /puh-nul-tuh-muht/ adj. & n. last but one. [Latin *paenultimus* from *paene* almost, *ultimus* last]

**penumbra** /puh-num-bruh/ n. (pl. **-brae** /-bree/ or **-s**) **1** partly shaded region around the shadow of an opaque body, esp. that around the shadow of the moon or earth in an eclipse. **2** partial shadow. □ **penumbral** adj. [Latin *paene* almost, UMBRA]

**penurious** /puh-nyoo-ree-uhs/ adj. **1** poor. **2** stingy; grudging. **3** scanty. [medieval Latin: related to PENURY]

**penury** /pen-yuh-ree/ n. (pl. **-ies**) **1** destitution; poverty. **2** lack; scarcity. [Latin]

**people** /pee-puhl/ — n.pl. (except in sense 2). **1** persons in general or of a specified kind (*people don't like rudeness*; *famous people*). **2** persons composing a community, tribe, race, nation, etc. (*a warlike people*; *peoples of the Commonwealth*). **3** (**the people**) **a** the mass of people in a country etc. not having special rank or authority. **b** these as an electorate (*the people will reject it*). **4** parents or other relatives (*my people disapprove*). **5** **a** subjects, armed followers, etc. **b** congregation of a parish priest etc. — v. (**-ling**) (usu. foll. by *with*) **1** fill with people, animals, etc.; populate. **2** (esp. as **peopled** adj.) inhabit. [Latin *populus*]

**people meter** n. device which, when connected to a television, records people's viewing patterns and preferences, this information being used to revise etc. the ratings of television shows and channels.

**pep** colloq. — n. vigour; spirit. — v. (**-pp-**) (usu. foll. by *up*) fill with vigour. [abbreviation of PEPPER]

**pepino** /puh-pee-noh/ n. **1** spiny plant grown for its fruit. **2** the elongated fruit of this plant, which is yellow with purple streaks and tastes like a melon. [Spanish, = cucumber]

**pepper** — n. **1** hot aromatic condiment from the dried berries of certain plants. **2** anything hot or pungent. **3 a** capsicum plant. **b** its fruit, used esp. as a vegetable or salad ingredient. **4** = CAYENNE. **5** any shrub of the Australian genus *Tasmannia*, having hot-tasting fruits and leaves, esp. the *mountain pepper*, having red stems, creamy flowers, and black fruits which have been used as a peppery seasoning (see also PEPPER TREE 1). — v.

**1** sprinkle or treat with or as if with pepper. **2** pelt with missiles. [Sanskrit *pippalī*]

**pepper-and-salt** *adj.* with small patches of dark and light colour intermingled.

**peppercorn** *n.* **1** dried pepper berry. **2** (in full **peppercorn rent**) nominal rent. **3** = PEPPER TREE 2.

**peppercorn tree** *n.* = PEPPER TREE 2.

**pepperina** /ˌpep-uh-**ree**-nuh/ *n.* (also **pepperina tree**) = PEPPER TREE 2.

**pepper-mill** *n.* device for grinding pepper by hand.

**peppermint** *n.* **1 a** mint plant grown for its strong-flavoured oil. **b** this oil. **2** sweet flavoured with peppermint. **3 a** any of many small to large eucalypts of south-eastern Australia, the leaves of which yield aromatic, peppermint-like essential oils, the trunk often having a fine, fibrous bark. **b** the wood of these trees. **4** any of several other Australian plants, esp. the tree or shrub *agonis* (family Myrtaceae) of WA, having peppermint-scented foliage.

**pepperoni** /ˌpep-uh-**roh**-nee/ *n.* beef and pork sausage seasoned with pepper. [Italian *peperone* chilli]

**pepper tree** *n.* **1** (also **pepper bush, pepper shrub**) any of several small Australian trees of the genus *Tasmannia* having pungent and hot-tasting fruit and seeds. **2** (also **peppercorn, peppercorn tree, pepperina**) the introduced South American tree *Schinus molle*, bearing a small, red, aromatic fruit, and widely planted as an ornamental and shade tree, esp. near homesteads in inland Australia.

**peppery** *adj.* **1** of, like, or containing pepper. **2** hot-tempered. **3** pungent.

**pep pill** *n.* pill containing a stimulant drug.

**pepsin** /**pep**-suhn/ *n.* enzyme contained in the gastric juice. [Greek *pepsis* digestion]

**pep talk** *n.* (usu. short) talk intended to enthuse, encourage, etc.

**peptic** /**pep**-tik/ *adj.* concerning or promoting digestion. [Greek *peptikos* able to digest]

**peptic ulcer** *n.* ulcer in the stomach or duodenum.

**peptide** /**pep**-tuyd/ *n. Biochem.* compound consisting of two or more amino acids bonded in sequence. [Greek *peptos* cooked]

**per** *prep.* **1** for each (*two sweets per child*; *five kilometres per hour*). **2** by means of; by; through (*per post*). **3** (in full **as per**) in accordance with (*as per instructions*). □ **as per usual** *colloq.* as usual. [Latin]

**per-** *prefix* **1** through; all over (*pervade*). **2** completely; very (*perturb*). **3** to

destruction; to the bad (*perdition*; *pervert*). [Latin *per-*: related to PER]

**perambulate** /puh-**ram**-byuh-ˌlayt/ *v.* (**-ting**) **1** walk through, over, or about (streets, the country, etc.). **2** walk from place to place. □ **perambulation** /-**lay**-shuhn/ *n.* [Latin *perambulo*: related to AMBLE]

**perambulator** *n. formal* = PRAM.

**per annum** /per **an**-uhm/ *adv.* for each year. [Latin]

**per capita** /puh **kap**-uh-tuh/ *adv. & adj.* (also **per caput** /**kap**-uut/) for each person. [Latin, = by heads]

**perceive** /puh-**seev**/ *v.* (**-ving**) **1** apprehend, esp. through the sight; observe. **2** (usu. foll. by *that, how,* etc.) apprehend with the mind; understand; see or regard. □ **perceivable** *adj.* [Latin *percipio -cept-* seize, understand]

**per cent** /puh **sent**/ — *adv.* in every hundred. — *n.* **1** percentage. **2** one part in every hundred (*half a per cent*). [Latin *per centum* by the hundred]

**percentage** — *n.* **1** rate or proportion per cent. **2** proportion. **3** *colloq.* personal benefit or advantage (*there's no percentage in pursuing the matter*). — *adj.* (in tennis, football, etc.) pertaining to a style of play which avoids risk-taking and concentrates on achieving a higher percentage of orthodox strokes etc. than the opposing player or team.

**percentile** /puh-**sen**-tuyl/ *n. Statistics* **1** each of 99 points at which a range of data is divided to make 100 groups of equal size. **2** each of these groups.

**perceptible** /puh-**sep**-tuh-buhl/ *adj.* capable of being perceived by the senses or intellect. □ **perceptibility** /-**bil**-uh-tee/ *n.* **perceptibly** *adv.* [Latin: related to PERCEIVE]

**perception** /puh-**sep**-shuhn/ *n.* **1 a** act or faculty of perceiving. **b** an instance of this. **2** (often foll. by *of*) **a** intuitive recognition of a truth, aesthetic quality, etc. **b** an instance of this (*a sudden perception of the true position*). □ **perceptual** /puh-**sep**-choo-uhl/ *adj.*

**perceptive** /puh-**sep**-tiv/ *adj.* **1** sensitive; discerning (*a perceptive remark*). **2** capable of perceiving. □ **perceptively** *adv.* **perceptiveness** *n.* **perceptivity** /ˌper-sep-**tiv**-uh-tee/ *n.*

**perch¹** — *n.* **1** bar, branch, etc., used by a bird to rest on. **2** high place for a person or thing to rest on. **3** measure of length in the imperial system, esp. for land, of 5½ yards. — *v.* (usu. foll. by *on*) settle or rest on or as on a perch etc. (*the bird perched on the branch*; *a town perched on a hill*). [Latin *pertica* pole]

**perch²** n. (*pl.* same or **-es**) **1** edible European spiny-finned freshwater fish. **2** any of many similar freshwater or marine food-fish found in Australia. [Latin *perca* from Greek]

**perchance** /puh-**chahns**, -**chans**/ adv. archaic or poet. **1** by chance. **2** maybe. [Anglo-French *par* by]

**percipient** /puh-**sip**-ee-uhnt/ — adj. **1** able to perceive; conscious. **2** discerning; observant. — n. person who perceives, esp. something outside the range of the senses. □ **percipience** n. [Latin: related to PERCEIVE]

**percolate** /**per**-kuh-,layt/ v. (**-ting**) **1** (often foll. by *through*) **a** (of liquid etc.) filter or ooze gradually (esp. through a porous surface). **b** (of news, an idea, etc.) permeate gradually (*the news percolated through the town that* ...). **2** prepare (coffee) in a percolator. **3** strain (a liquid, powder, etc.) through a fine mesh etc. □ **percolation** /-**lay**-shuhn/ n. [Latin *colum* strainer]

**percolator** n. machine making coffee by circulating boiling water through ground beans.

**percussion** /puh-**kush**-uhn/ n. **1 a** (often *attrib.*) playing of music by striking instruments with sticks etc. (*percussion instrument*). **b** such instruments collectively. **2** gentle tapping of the body in medical diagnosis. **3** forcible striking of one esp. solid body against another. □ **percussionist** n. **percussive** adj. [Latin *percutio -cuss-* strike]

**percussion cap** n. small amount of explosive powder contained in metal or paper and exploded by striking.

**perdition** /puh-**dish**-uhn/ n. eternal death; damnation. [Latin *perdo -dit-* destroy]

**peremptory** /puh-**remp**-tuh-ree/ adj. **1** (of a statement or command) admitting no denial or refusal. **2** (of a person, a person's manner, etc.) imperious; dictatorial. □ **peremptorily** adv. **peremptoriness** n. [Latin *peremptorius* deadly, decisive]

**perennial** /puh-**ren**-ee-uhl/ — adj. **1** lasting through a year or several years. **2** (of a plant) lasting several years (opp. ANNUAL). **3** lasting a long time or for ever. — n. perennial plant. □ **perennially** adv. [Latin *perennis* from *annus* year]

**perentie** /puh-**ren**-tee/ n. giant monitor lizard, the largest of the Australian lizards (often 2 m long), of rocky country in arid central and western Australia. [Diyari *pirrinthi*]

**perestroika** /,pe-ruh-**stroi**-kuh/ n. (in the former USSR) reform of the economic and political system. [Russian, = restructuring]

**perfect** /**per**-fuhkt/ — adj. **1** complete; not deficient. **2** faultless (*a perfect diamond*). **3** very enjoyable, excellent (*perfect evening*). **4** exact, precise (*perfect circle*). **5** entire, unqualified (*perfect stranger*). **6** Gram. (of a tense) denoting a completed action or event (e.g. *he has gone*). — v. /puh-**fekt**/ **1** make perfect; improve. **2** carry through; complete. — n. Gram. the perfect tense. □ **perfectible** /puh-**fek**-tuh-buhl/ adj. **perfectibility** /puh-,fek-tuh-**bil**-uh-tee/ n. [Latin *perficere -fect-* complete (v.)]

**perfection** /puh-**fek**-shuhn/ n. **1** making, becoming, or being perfect. **2** faultlessness. **3** perfect person, thing, or example. □ **to perfection** exactly; completely. [Latin: related to PERFECT]

**perfectionism** n. uncompromising pursuit of excellence. □ **perfectionist** n. & adj.

**perfectly** adv. **1** completely; absolutely (*I understand you perfectly*). **2** quite, completely (*is perfectly capable of doing it*). **3** in a perfect way.

**perfect pitch** n. = ABSOLUTE PITCH.

**perfidy** /**per**-fuh-dee/ n. breach of faith; treachery. □ **perfidious** /-**fid**-ee-uhs/ adj. [Latin *perfidia* from *fides* faith]

**perforate** /**per**-fuh-,rayt/ v. (**-ting**) **1** make a hole or holes through; pierce. **2** make a row of small holes in (paper etc.) so that a part may be torn off easily. **3** make an opening into; pass into; penetrate. □ **perforated** adj. **perforation** /-**ray**-shuhn/ n. [Latin *perforo* pierce through]

**perforce** /puh-**faws**/ adv. archaic unavoidably; necessarily. [French *par force* by FORCE]

**perform** /puh-**fawm**/ v. **1** (also *absol.*) carry into effect; do. **2** go through; execute (a function, play, piece of music, etc.) (*performed Bach on the organ*). **3** act in a play; play music, sing, etc.; execute tricks (*likes performing*). **4** function (*how is the new computer performing?*). **5** colloq. display anger or bad temper. □ **performer** n. [Anglo-French: related to PER-, FURNISH]

**performance** /puh-**faw**-muhns/ n. **1** (usu. foll. by *of*) **a** act, process, or manner of performing or functioning. **b** execution (of a duty etc.). **2** performing of a play, music, etc.; instance of this. **3** person's achievement under test conditions etc. (*put up a good performance*). **4** colloq. fuss; emotional scene (*made such a performance about leaving*).

**performing arts** *n.pl.* drama, music, dance, etc.

**perfume** /**per**-fyoom/ — *n.* **1** sweet smell. **2** fluid containing the essence of flowers etc.; scent. — *v.* also /puh-**fyoom**/ (**-ming**) impart a sweet scent to. [Italian *parfumare* smoke through]

**perfumer** /puh-**fyoo**-muh/ *n.* maker or seller of perfumes. □ **perfumery** *n.* (*pl.* **-ies**).

**perfunctory** /puh-**fungk**-tuh-ree/ *adj.* done merely out of duty; superficial, careless. □ **perfunctorily** *adv.* **perfunctoriness** *n.* [Latin: related to FUNCTION]

**pergola** /puh-**goh**-luh, **per**-guh-luh/ *n.* **1** horizontal wooden framework with vertical supports, attached to a house and usu. with climbing plants trained over it, used for recreation. **2** arbour or covered walk formed of growing plants trained over trellis-work. [Italian]

**perhaps** /puh-**haps**/ *adv.* it may be; possibly.

**peri-** *prefix* round, about. [Greek]

**perianth** /**pe**-ree-,anth/ *n.* outer part of a flower. [Greek *anthos* flower]

**pericardium** /,pe-ree-**kah**-dee-uhm/ *n.* (*pl.* **-dia**) membranous sac enclosing the heart. [Greek *kardia* heart]

**perigee** /**pe**-ruh-,jee/ *n.* point of a planet's or comet's orbit where it is nearest the earth (opp. APOGEE). [Greek *perigeion*]

**perihelion** /,pe-ree-**hee**-lee-uhn/ *n.* (*pl.* **-lia**) point of a planet's or comet's orbit where it is nearest the sun's centre. [related to PERI-, Greek *hēlios* sun]

**peril** /**pe**-ruhl/ *n.* serious and immediate danger. □ **perilous** *adj.* **perilously** *adv.* [Latin *peric(u)lum*]

**perimeter** /puh-**rim**-uh-tuh/ *n.* **1 a** circumference or outline of a closed figure. **b** length of this. **2** outer boundary of an enclosed area. □ **perimetric** /,pe-ree-**met**-rik/ *adj.* [Greek: related to -METER]

**perineum** /,pe-ruh-**nee**-uhm/ *n.* (*pl.* **-nea**) region of the body between the anus and the scrotum or vulva. □ **perineal** *adj.* [Latin from Greek]

**period** /**peer**-ree-uhd/ — *n.* **1** length or portion of time. **2** distinct portion of history, a person's life, etc. **3** time forming part of a geological era. **4** interval between recurrences of an astronomical or other phenomenon. **5** time allowed for a lesson in school. **6** occurrence of menstruation (often *attrib.*: *period pains*). **7** complete sentence, esp. one consisting of several clauses. **8 a** = FULL STOP. **b** *colloq.* used at the end of a statement to indicate finality (*I'm not going, period*). — *adj.*

characteristic of some past period (*period furniture*). [Greek *hodos* way]

**periodic** /,peer-ree-**od**-ik/ *adj.* appearing or occurring at intervals. □ **periodicity** /-ree-uh-**dis**-uh-tee/ *n.*

**periodical** — *n.* newspaper, magazine, etc., issued at regular intervals. — *adj.* periodic. □ **periodically** *adv.*

**periodic table** *n.* arrangement of elements in order of increasing atomic number and in which elements of similar chemical properties appear at regular intervals.

**periodontics** /,pe-ree-oh-**don**-tiks/ *n.pl.* (treated as *sing.*) branch of dentistry concerned with the structures surrounding and supporting the teeth. [Greek *odous odont-* tooth]

**peripatetic** /,pe-ree-puh-**tet**-ik/ — *adj.* going from place to place; itinerant. — *n.* peripatetic person. [Greek *pateō* walk]

**peripheral** /puh-**rif**-uh-ruhl/ — *adj.* **1** of minor importance; marginal. **2** of the periphery; on the fringe. **3** near the surface of the body. — *n.* any input, output, or storage device that can be controlled by a computer's central processing unit, e.g. a floppy disk or printer.

**peripheral nervous system** *n.* nervous system outside the brain and spinal cord.

**periphery** /puh-**rif**-uh-ree/ *n.* (*pl.* **-ies**) **1** boundary of an area or surface. **2** outer or surrounding region (*on the periphery of Canberra*). [Greek *pherō* bear]

**periphrasis** /puh-**rif**-ruh-suhs/ *n.* (*pl.* **-phrases** /-,seez/) **1** roundabout way of speaking; circumlocution. **2** roundabout phrase. □ **periphrastic** /,pe-ruh-**fras**-tik/ *adj.* [Greek: related to PHRASE]

**periscope** /**pe**-ruh-,skohp/ *n.* apparatus with a tube and mirrors or prisms, by which an observer in a trench, submerged submarine, or at the back of a crowd etc., can see things otherwise out of sight. □ **periscopic** /-**skop**-ik/ *adj.* [PERI-, -SCOPE]

**perish** /**pe**-rish/ — *v.* **1** be destroyed; suffer death or ruin. **2 a** (esp. of rubber) lose its normal qualities; deteriorate, rot. **b** cause to rot or deteriorate. **3** suffer from cold, hunger, etc. **4** suffer (extreme) heat. — *n.* period of extreme privation, esp. as caused by lack of water (*suffered badly during the perish*). □ **do a perish** *colloq.* **1** suffer a period of extreme privation; be without sustenance (esp. water). **2** die (of thirst). **3** suffer hardship or privation of any kind, not always of an extreme nature (*doing a perish for a tinny*). [Latin *pereo* pass away]

**perishable** — *adj.* liable to perish; subject to decay. — *n.* thing, esp. a foodstuff, subject to rapid decay.

**perisher** *n. colloq.* **1** a freezing cold day. **2** annoying child.

**peristalsis** /,pe-ruh-**stal**-suhs/ *n.* involuntary muscular wavelike movement by which the contents of the digestive tract are propelled along it. □ **peristaltic** *adj.* [Greek *peristellō* wrap around]

**peritoneum** /,pe-ruh-tuh-**nee**-uhm/ *n.* (*pl.* **-s** or **-nea**) membrane lining the cavity of the abdomen. □ **peritoneal** *adj.* [Greek *peritonos* stretched around]

**peritonitis** /,pe-ruh-tuh-**nuy**-tuhs/ *n.* inflammatory disease of the peritoneum.

**perjure** /**per**-juh/ *v.refl.* (**-ring**) *Law* **1** wilfully tell a lie when on oath. **2** (as **perjured** *adj.*) guilty of or involving perjury. □ **perjurer** *n.* [French from Latin *juro* swear]

**perjury** *n.* (*pl.* **-ies**) *Law* act of wilfully telling a lie when on oath.

**perk¹** *v.* □ **perk up 1** recover confidence, courage, life, health, or zest. **2** restore confidence, courage, or liveliness in. **3** smarten up. **4** raise (one's head etc.) briskly. [origin unknown]

**perk²** *n. colloq.* perquisite. [abbreviation]

**perky** *adj.* (**-ier, -iest**) lively; cheerful. □ **perkily** *adv.* **perkiness** *n.*

**perlite** /**per**-luyt/ *n.* (also **pearlite**) glassy type of vermiculite used for insulation etc. [French *perle* pearl]

**perm** — *n.* permanent wave. — *v.* give a permanent wave to. [abbreviation]

**permafrost** /**per**-muh-,frost/ *n.* subsoil which remains frozen all year, as in polar regions. [from PERMANENT, FROST]

**permanent** /**per**-muh-nuhnt/ *adj.* lasting, or intended to last or function, indefinitely (*permanent creek*; *permanent water*) (opp. TEMPORARY). □ **permanence** *n.* **permanency** *n.* **permanently** *adv.* [Latin *permaneo* remain to the end]

**permanent head** *n.* senior executive officer of a public service department; the Secretary of such a department.

**permanent wave** *n.* long-lasting artificial wave in the hair.

**permeable** /**per**-mee-uh-buhl/ *adj.* capable of being permeated. □ **permeability** /,per-mee-uh-**bil**-uh-tee/ *n.* [related to PERMEATE]

**permeate** /**per**-mee-,ayt/ *v.* (**-ting**) **1** penetrate throughout; pervade; saturate. **2** (usu. foll. by *through*, *among*, etc.) diffuse itself. □ **permeation** /-ay-shuhn/ *n.* [Latin *permeo* pass through]

**Permian** /**per**-mee-uhn/ — *adj.* of the last period of the Palaeozoic era. — *n.* this period. [*Perm* in Russia]

**permissible** /puh-**mis**-uh-buhl/ *adj.* allowable. □ **permissibility** /-bil-uh-tee/ *n.* [French or medieval Latin: related to PERMIT]

**permission** /puh-**mish**-uhn/ *n.* (often foll. by *to* + infin.) consent; authorisation. [Latin *permissio*: related to PERMIT]

**permissive** /puh-**mis**-iv/ *adj.* **1** tolerant or liberal, esp. in sexual matters (*the permissive society*). **2** giving permission. □ **permissiveness** *n.* [French or medieval Latin: related to PERMIT]

**permit** — *v.* /puh-**mit**/ (**-tt-**) **1** give permission or consent to; authorise (*permit me to say*). **2 a** allow; give an opportunity to (*permit the traffic to flow again*). **b** give an opportunity (*circumstances permitting*). **3** (foll. by *of*) admit; allow for. — *n.* /**per**-muht/ **1 a** document giving permission to act. **b** document etc. which allows entry. **2** *formal* permission. [Latin *permitto -miss-* allow]

**permutation** /,per-myuh-**tay**-shuhn/ *n.* **1** one of the possible ordered arrangements or groupings of a set of things. **2** combination or selection of a specified number of things from a larger group. [Latin *permuto* change thoroughly]

**pernicious** /puh-**nish**-uhs/ *adj.* **1** very harmful or destructive; deadly. **2** wicked, evil. [Latin *pernicies* ruin]

**pernicious anaemia** *n.* defective formation of red blood cells through lack of vitamin B.

**pernickety** /puh-**nik**-uh-tee/ *adj. colloq.* fastidious; over-precise. [origin unknown]

**peroration** /,pe-ruh-**ray**-shuhn/ *n.* concluding part of a speech, forcefully summing up what has been said. [Latin *oro* speak]

**peroxide** /puh-**rok**-suyd/ — *n.* **1 a** = HYDROGEN PEROXIDE. **b** (often *attrib.*) solution of hydrogen peroxide used esp. to bleach the hair. **2** compound of oxygen with another element containing the greatest possible proportion of oxygen. — *v.* (**-ding**) bleach (the hair) with peroxide. [from PER-, OXIDE]

**perpendicular** /,per-puhn-**dik**-yuh-luh/ — *adj.* **1 a** (usu. foll. by *to*) at right angles (to a given line, plane, or surface). **b** at right angles to the plane of the horizon. **2** upright, vertical. **3** (of a slope etc.) very steep. **4** (**Perpendicular**) *Archit.* of the third stage of English Gothic (15th–16th c.) with vertical tracery in large windows. — *n.* **1** perpendicular line. **2** (prec. by *the*) perpendicular line or direction (*is out of the perpendicular*).

□ **perpendicularity** /-la-ruh-tee/ *n.* [Latin *perpendiculum* plumb-line]

**perpetrate** /per-puh-‚trayt/ *v.* (**-ting**) commit (a crime, blunder, or anything outrageous). □ **perpetration** /-tray-shuhn/ *n.* **perpetrator** *n.* [Latin *perpetro* perform]

**perpetual** /puh-**pech**-oo-uhl, -pet-yoo-uhl/ *adj.* **1** lasting for ever or indefinitely. **2** continuous, uninterrupted. **3** *colloq.* frequent (*perpetual interruptions*). □ **perpetually** *adv.* [Latin *perpetuus* continuous]

**perpetual motion** *n.* motion of a hypothetical machine which once set in motion would run for ever unless subject to an external force or to wear.

**perpetuate** /puh-**pech**-oo-‚ayt, -pet-yoo-/ *v.* (**-ting**) **1** make perpetual. **2** preserve from oblivion. □ **perpetuation** /-ay-shuhn/ *n.* **perpetuator** *n.* [Latin *perpetuo*]

**perpetuity** /‚per-puh-**choo**-uh-tee, -tyoo-/ *n.* (*pl.* **-ies**) **1** state or quality of being perpetual. **2** perpetual annuity. **3** perpetual possession or position. □ **in perpetuity** for ever. [Latin: related to PERPETUAL]

**perplex** /puh-**pleks**/ *v.* **1** puzzle, bewilder, or disconcert. **2** complicate or confuse (a matter). □ **perplexedly** /-uhd-lee/ *adv.* **perplexing** *adj.* [Latin *perplexus* involved]

**perplexity** /puh-**plek**-suh-tee/ *n.* (*pl.* **-ies**) **1** bewilderment; state of being perplexed. **2** thing that perplexes.

**perquisite** /per-kwuh-zuht/ *n.* **1** (also **perk**) an incidental benefit attached to one's employment etc. **2** extra profit or allowance additional to a main income etc. **3** customary extra right or privilege. [Latin *perquiro -quisit-* search diligently for]

■ **Usage** *Perquisite* is sometimes confused with *prerequisite*, which means 'thing required as a precondition'.

**per se** /per say/ *adv.* by or in itself; intrinsically. [Latin]

**persecute** /**per**-suh-‚kyoot/ *v.* (**-ting**) **1** subject (a person etc.) to hostility or ill-treatment, esp. on grounds of political or religious belief. **2** harass, worry. □ **persecution** /‚per-suh-**kyoo**-shuhn/ *n.* **persecutor** *n.* [Latin *persequor -secut-* pursue]

**persevere** /‚per-suh-**veer**/ *v.* (**-ring**) (often foll. by *in*, *with*) continue steadfastly or determinedly; persist. □ **perseverance** *n.* [Latin: related to SEVERE]

**Persian** /**per**-*zh*uhn/ — *n.* **1** native or inhabitant of ancient or modern Persia (now Iran); person of Persian descent. **2** language of ancient Persia or modern Iran. **3** (in full **Persian cat**) cat of a breed with long silky hair. — *adj.* of or relating to Persia or its people or language.

■ **Usage** The preferred terms for the language (see sense 2 of the noun) are *Iranian* and *Farsi* respectively.

**persiflage** /**per**-suh-‚flah*zh*/ *n.* light raillery, banter. [French]

**persimmon** /per-**sim**-uhn/ *n.* **1** tropical evergreen tree. **2** its edible tomato-like fruit. [Algonquian]

**persist** /puh-**sist**/ *v.* **1** (often foll. by *in*) continue firmly or obstinately (in an opinion or action) esp. despite obstacles, remonstrance, etc. **2** (of a phenomenon, institution, custom, etc.) continue in existence; survive. □ **persistence** *n.* **persistent** *adj.* **persistently** *adv.* [Latin *sisto* stand]

**person** /**per**-suhn/ *n.* **1** individual human being. **2** living body of a human being including clothing (*found on my person*). **3** *Gram.* any of three classes of personal pronouns, verb-forms, etc.: the person speaking (**first person**); the person spoken to (**second person**); the person spoken of (**third person**). **4** (in *comb.*) used to replace *-man* in occupations etc. open to either sex (*salesperson*). **5** (in Christianity) God as Father, Son, or Holy Ghost (*three persons in one God*). □ **in person** physically present. [Latin: related to PERSONA]

**persona** /per-**soh**-nuh/ *n.* (*pl.* **-nae** /-nee/) **1** aspect of the personality as shown to or perceived by others (opp. ANIMA). **2** an author's assumed character in his or her writing. [Latin, = actor's mask]

**personable** /**per**-suh-nuh-buhl/ *adj.* pleasing in appearance and behaviour.

**personage** *n.* **1** person, esp. of rank or importance. **2** character in a play etc.

**persona grata** /puh-‚soh-nuh **grah**-tuh/ *n.* (*pl.* **personae gratae** /-nee, -tee/) person acceptable to certain others.

**personal** /**per**-suh-nuhl/ *adj.* **1** one's own; individual; private (*my own personal reasons*). **2** done or made in person (*will give it my personal attention*). **3** directed to or concerning an individual (*personal letter*). **4** referring (esp. in a hostile way) to an individual's private life or concerns (*personal remarks*; *no need to be personal*). **5** of the body and clothing (*personal hygiene*). **6** existing as a person, not as an abstraction (*a personal God*). **7** *Gram.* of or denoting one of the three persons (*personal pronoun*).

**personal column** *n.* part of a newspaper devoted to private advertisements and personal messages.

**personal computer** *n.* small general-purpose computer designed for use by one person at a time.

**personal identification number** *n.* = PIN.

**personalise** *v.* (also **-ize**) (**-sing** or **-zing**) **1** make personal, esp. by marking with one's name etc. **2** personify.

**personality** /ˌper-suh-**nal**-uh-tee/ *n.* (*pl.* **-ies**) **1 a** a person's distinctive character or qualities (*has a strong personality*). **b** socially attractive qualities (*was clever but had no personality*). **2** famous person (*TV personality*). **3** person who stands out from others by virtue of his or her character (*is a real personality*). **4** personal existence or identity; condition of being a person.

**personally** *adv.* **1** in person (*see to it personally*). **2** for one's own part (*speaking personally*). **3** in a personal manner (*took the criticism personally*).

**personal pronoun** *n.* pronoun indicating grammatical person and replacing the subject, object, etc., of a clause etc., e.g. *I*, *we*, *you*, *them*, *us*.

**personal property** *n. Law* all one's property except land and interests in land other than a lease.

**persona non grata** /puh-ˌsoh-nuh non **grah**-tuh/ *n.* (*pl.* **personae non gratae** /-nee, -tee/) person not acceptable.

**personate** /**per**-suh-ˌnayt/ *v.* (**-ting**) **1** play the part of (a character in a drama etc.). **2** pretend to be (another person), esp. for fraudulent purposes. □ **personation** /-**nay**-shuhn/ *n.* **personator** *n.*

**personify** /puh-**son**-uh-ˌfuy/ *v.* (**-ies**, **-ied**) **1** represent (an abstraction or thing) as having human characteristics (as in *the pav was simply asking to be eaten*). **2** symbolise (a quality etc.) by a figure in human form. **3** (usu. as **personified** *adj.*) be a typical example of; embody (*she personifies youthful arrogance*; *he was niceness personified*). □ **personification** /puh-ˌson-uh-fuh-**kay**-shuhn/ *n.*

**personnel** /ˌper-suh-**nel**/ *n.* staff of an organisation, the armed forces, a public service, etc. [French, = personal]

**personnel department** *n.* part of an organisation concerned with the appointment, training, and welfare of employees.

**person with AIDS** *n.* (also **PWA**) person who has AIDS or ARC.

■ **Usage** This is the preferred term and should displace terms such as 'Aids victim' which many find offensive.

**Persoonia** /puh-**soh**-nee-uh/ *n.* genus of plants (related to banksias) endemic to Australia (see GEEBUNG). [C.H. *Persoon*, name of a botanist]

**perspective** /puh-**spek**-tiv/ — *n.* **1 a** art of drawing solid objects on a two-dimensional surface so as to give the right impression of relative positions, size, etc. **b** picture so drawn. **2** apparent relation between visible objects as to position, distance, etc. **3** mental view of the relative importance of things (*one must have the right perspective*). **4** view, esp. stretching into the distance. — *adj.* of or in perspective. □ **in** (or **out of**) **perspective 1** drawn or viewed according (or not according) to the rules of perspective. **2** correctly (or incorrectly) regarded in terms of relative importance (*you must keep things in perspective*). [Latin *perspicio -spect-* look at]

**perspex** /**per**-speks/ *n. propr.* tough light transparent thermoplastic. [related to PERSPECTIVE]

**perspicacious** /ˌper-spuh-**kay**-shuhs/ *adj.* having mental penetration or discernment. □ **perspicacity** /-**kas**-uh-tee/ *n.* [Latin *perspicax*: related to PERSPECTIVE]

■ **Usage** *Perspicacious* is sometimes confused with *perspicuous*.

**perspicuous** /puh-**spik**-yoo-uhs/ *adj.* **1** easily understood; clearly expressed. **2** expressing things clearly. □ **perspicuity** /-**kyoo**-uh-tee/ *n.* [Latin: related to PERSPECTIVE]

■ **Usage** *Perspicuous* is sometimes confused with *perspicacious*.

**perspiration** /ˌper-spuh-**ray**-shuhn/ *n.* **1** sweat. **2** sweating. [French: related to PERSPIRE]

**perspire** /puh-**spuyuh**/ *v.* (**-ring**) sweat. [Latin *spiro* breathe]

**persuade** /puh-**swayd**/ *v.* (**-ding**) **1** (often foll. by *of* or *that*) cause (another person or oneself) to believe. **2** (often foll. by *to* + infin.) induce (*persuaded us to join them*; *persuaded them at last*). □ **persuadable** *adj.* **persuasible** *adj.* [Latin *persuadeo -suas-* induce]

**persuader** *n.* **1** person who persuades. **2** *colloq.* bullock-driver's or jockey's whip.

**persuasion** /puh-**sway**-zhuhn/ *n.* **1** persuading (*yielded to persuasion*). **2** persuasiveness (*use all your persuasion*). **3** belief or conviction (*my private persuasion*). **4** religious belief, or the group or sect holding it (*of a different persuasion*). **5** *colloq. joc.* any group or party (*the male persuasion*). [Latin: related to PERSUADE]

**persuasive** /puh-**sway**-siv/ *adj.* good at persuading. □ **persuasively** *adv.* **persuasiveness** *n.* [French or medieval Latin: related to PERSUADE]

**pert** *adj.* **1** saucy, impudent. **2** jaunty. □ **pertly** *adv.* **pertness** *n.* [Latin *apertus* open]

**pertain** /puh-**tayn**/ *v.* **1** (foll. by *to*) **a** relate or have reference to (*words pertaining to law*). **b** belong to as a part, appendage, or accessory. **2** (usu. foll. by *to*) be appropriate to. [Latin *pertineo* belong to]

**Perth** *n.* name of the capital city of the State of WA. [named in honour of George Murray, Britain's Secretary of State for War and the Colonies, who was born in *Perthshire*, Scotland]

**pertinacious** /,per-tuh-**nay**-shuhs/ *adj.* stubborn; persistent; obstinate (in a course of action etc.). □ **pertinacity** /-**nas**-uh-tee/ *n.* [Latin *pertinax*: related to PERTAIN]

**pertinent** /**per**-tuh-nuhnt/ *adj.* (often foll. by *to*) relevant (*what are the pertinent facts?*). □ **pertinence** *n.* **pertinency** *n.* [Latin: related to PERTAIN]

**perturb** /puh-**terb**/ *v.* **1** disturb mentally; agitate. **2** throw into confusion or disorder. □ **perturbation** /,per-tuh-**bay**-shuhn/ *n.* [French from Latin]

**peruse** /puh-**rooz**/ *v.* (**-sing**) **1** read or study carefully. **2** *joc.* read or look at desultorily. □ **perusal** *n.* [originally = 'use up']

**perv** var. of PERVE.

**pervade** /puh-**vayd**/ *v.* (**-ding**) **1** spread throughout, permeate (*the scent of the brown boronia pervaded the entire garden*). **2** be rife among or through. □ **pervasion** *n.* **pervasive** *adj.* [Latin *pervado* penetrate]

**perve** (also **perv**) *colloq.* — *n.* **1** a sexual pervert. **2 a** one who observes another (or others) with erotic or sexual interest. **b** the act of so observing. — *v.* (frequently with *on*) **1** observe (an other or others) with erotic or sexual interest. **2** observe anything with interest, fascination, etc. (*tourists perving on our fairy penguins*).

**perverse** /puh-**vers**/ *adj.* **1** deliberately or stubbornly departing from what is reasonable or required. **2** persistent in error. **3** wayward; intractable. **4** perverted; wicked. **5** (of a verdict etc.) against the weight of evidence or the judge's direction. □ **perversely** *adv.* **perversity** *n.* (*pl.* **-ies**). [Latin: related to PERVERT]

**perversion** /puh-**ver**-zhuhn/ *n.* **1** act of perverting or state of being perverted. **2** perverted form of an act or thing. **3 a** preference for a form of sexual activity which is not the norm. **b** such an activity. [Latin: related to PERVERT]

**pervert** — *v.* /puh-**vert**/ **1** turn (a person or thing) aside from what is deemed to be its proper use or nature. **2** misapply or misconstrue (words etc.). **3** lead astray (a person, a person's mind, etc.) from what is deemed to be right opinion or conduct or (esp. religious) beliefs. **4** (as **perverted** *adj.*) showing perversion. — *n.* /**per**-vert/ **1** perverted person. **2** person showing sexual perversion. [Latin *verto vers-* turn]

**pervious** /**per**-vee-uhs/ *adj.* **1** permeable. **2** (usu. foll. by *to*) **a** affording passage. **b** accessible (to reason etc.). [Latin *via* road]

**peso** /**pay**-soh/ *n.* (*pl.* **-s**) chief monetary unit of several Latin American countries and of the Philippines. [Spanish]

**pessary** /**pes**-uh-ree/ *n.* (*pl.* **-ies**) **1** device worn in the vagina to support the uterus or as a contraceptive. **2** vaginal suppository. [Latin from Greek]

**pessimism** /**pes**-uh-,miz-uhm/ *n.* **1** tendency to be gloomy or expect the worst. **2** *Philos.* belief that this world is as bad as it could be or that all things tend to evil (opp. OPTIMISM). □ **pessimist** *n.* **pessimistic** /-**mis**-tik/ *adj.* **pessimistically** /-**mis**-ti-kuh-lee, -klee/ *adv.* [Latin *pessimus* worst]

**pest** *n.* **1** troublesome or annoying person or thing; a nuisance. **2** destructive animal, esp. one which attacks food sources. [Latin *pestis* plague]

**pester** *v.* trouble or annoy, esp. with frequent or persistent requests. [probably French *empestrer* encumber: influenced by PEST]

**pesticide** /**pes**-tuh-,suyd/ *n.* substance for destroying pests, esp. insects.

**pestiferous** /pes-**tif**-uh-ruhs/ *adj.* **1** noxious; pestilent. **2** harmful; pernicious; bearing moral contagion. [Latin: related to PEST]

**pestilence** /**pes**-tuh-luhns/ *n.* fatal epidemic disease, esp. bubonic plague. [Latin *pestis* plague]

**pestilent** *adj.* **1** deadly. **2** harmful or morally destructive. **3** *colloq.* troublesome, annoying.

**pestilential** /,pes-tuh-**len**-shuhl/ *adj.* **1** of or relating to pestilence. **2** dangerous; troublesome; pestilent.

**pestle** /**pes**-uhl/ *n.* club-shaped instrument for pounding substances in a mortar. [Latin *pistillum* from *pinso* pound]

**pet¹** — n. **1** domestic or tamed animal kept for pleasure or companionship. **2** a darling, a favourite (often as a term of endearment). — attrib. adj. **1** kept as a pet (pet lamb). **2** of or for pet animals (pet food). **3** often joc. favourite or particular (pet hate). **4** expressing fondness or familiarity (pet name). — v. (**-tt-**) **1** fondle erotically. **2** treat as a pet; stroke, pat. [origin unknown]

**pet²** n. fit of ill-humour (esp. be in a pet). [origin unknown]

**petal** /pet-uhl/ n. each of the parts of the corolla of a flower. □ **petalled** adj. **petal-like** adj. [Greek petalon leaf]

**petard** /puh-**tahd**/ n. hist. small bomb used to blast down a door etc. □ **hoist with one's own petard** see HOIST. [French]

**peter¹** /pee-tuh/ v. (foll. by out) (orig. of a vein of ore etc.) diminish, come to an end. [origin unknown]

**peter²** n. colloq. a prison cell; a prison. [transferred use of British slang peter a box or safe]

**peter³** n. colloq. cash register, till. □ **tickle the peter** steal, embezzle (esp. by ringing up false amounts). [British slang peter a box or safe]

**Peter Pan** n. person who retains youthful features or is immature. [unageing boy, hero of J. M. Barrie's play (1904)]

**Peter's pence** n.pl. RC Ch. **1** hist. annual tax of one penny, formerly paid to the Papal See. **2** (since 1860) annual voluntary contribution by Catholics all over the world to the pope. [the apostle St. Peter, as first pope]

**pethidine** /peth-uh-,deen/ n. synthetic soluble analgesic, chemically similar to morphine, used esp. in childbirth. [perhaps from the chemical piperidine]

**petiole** /pet-ee-,ohl/ n. slender stalk joining a leaf to a stem. [French from Latin]

**petit bourgeois** /,pet-ee boor-zhwah, boo-/ n. (pl. **petits bourgeois** pronunc. same) member of the lower middle classes. [French]

**petite** /puh-**teet**/ adj. (of a woman) of small and dainty build. [French, = little]

**petition** /puh-**tish**-uhn/ — n. **1** supplication, request. **2** formal written request, esp. one signed by many people, appealing to an authority. **3** Law application to a court for a writ etc. — v. **1** make or address a petition to (petition your MP). **2** (often foll. by for, to) appeal earnestly or humbly. [Latin peto petit-ask]

**petit mal** /,pet-ee **mal**/ n. mild form of epilepsy with only momentary loss of consciousness (cf. GRAND MAL). [French, = little sickness]

**petrel** /pet-ruhl/ n. sea bird, usu. flying far from land. [origin unknown]

**Petri dish** /pee-tree, pet-ree/ n. shallow covered dish used for the culture of bacteria etc. [Petri, name of a bacteriologist]

**petrify** /**pet**-ruh-,fuy/ v. (**-ies, -ied**) **1** paralyse with fear, astonishment, etc. **2** change (organic matter) into a stony substance. **3** become like stone. □ **petrifaction** /,pet-ruh-**fak**-shuhn/ n. [Latin petra rock, from Greek]

**petro-** comb. form **1** rock. **2** petroleum. [Greek petros stone or petra rock]

**petrochemical** /,pet-roh-**kem**-i-kuhl/ n. substance industrially obtained from petroleum or natural gas.

**petrodollar** /**pet**-roh-,dol-uh/ n. notional unit of currency earned by a petroleum-exporting country.

**petrol** /pet-ruhl/ n. **1** refined petroleum used as a fuel in motor vehicles, aircraft, etc. **2** (attrib.) concerned with the supply of petrol (petrol pump). [Latin: related to PETROLEUM]

**petroleum** /puh-**troh**-lee-uhm/ n. hydrocarbon oil found in the upper strata of the earth, refined for use as fuel etc. [Latin petra rock, oleum oil]

**petroleum jelly** n. translucent solid mixture of hydrocarbons used as a lubricant, ointment, etc.

**petrolhead** n. colloq. person who is a motor car (or motor car racing) fanatic.

**petrology** /puh-**trol**-uh-jee/ scientific study of the origin, structure, etc., of rocks. □ **petrologist** n.

**Petrophile** /puh-**trof**-uh-lee/ n. see CONESTICKS. [Greek, = rock-loving]

**petticoat** /pet-ee-,koht/ n. **1** woman's or girl's undergarment hanging from the waist or shoulders. **2** (attrib.) often derog. feminine; associated with women. [petty coat]

**pettifog** /pet-ee-,fog/ v. (**-gg-**) **1** practise legal trickery. **2** quibble or wrangle about trivial points. □ **pettifogger** n. **pettifoggery** n. [origin unknown]

**pettish** adj. peevish, petulant; easily put out. □ **pettishly** adv. **pettishness** n. [from PET²]

**petty** adj. (**-ier, -iest**) **1** unimportant; trivial (petty complaints). **2** small-minded, mean, contemptible (petty revenges). **3** minor, inferior, on a small scale (petty princes). **4** Law (of a crime) of lesser importance (petty sessions). □ **pettily** adv. **pettiness** n. [French petit small]

**petty cash** *n.* money from or for small items of receipt or expenditure.

**petty officer** *n.* naval NCO.

**petulant** /**pech**-uh-luhnt, **pet**-yoo-/ *adj.* peevishly impatient or irritable. □ **petulance** *n.* **petulantly** *adv.* [Latin *peto* seek]

**petunia** /puh-**choo**-nyuh, -**tyoo**-/ *n.* cultivated plant (native to tropical America) with white, purple, red, etc., funnel-shaped flowers. [French *petun* tobacco]

**pew** /pyoo/ *n.* **1** (in a church) long bench with a back; enclosed compartment. **2** *colloq.* seat (esp. *take a pew*). [Latin PODIUM]

**pewter** /**pyoo**-tuh/ *n.* **1** grey alloy of tin, antimony, and copper, etc. **2** utensils made of this. [French *peutre*]

**peyote** /pay-**oh**-tee/ *n.* **1** Mexican cactus. **2** hallucinogenic drug prepared from this. [American Spanish from Nahuatl]

**pH** /pee-**aych**/ *n.* measure of the acidity or alkalinity (e.g. of soil) tested in a solution, on a scale from 1 (extreme acidity) to 14 (extreme alkalinity), most plants preferring a soil close to neutral (pH 7), while Australian natives generally prefer a pH of 5.5 to 7. [German *Potenz* power, *H* (symbol for hydrogen)]

**phagocyte** /**fag**-uh-ˌsuyt/ *n.* leucocyte capable of engulfing and absorbing foreign matter, esp. bacteria in the body. [Greek *phag-* eat, *kutos* cell]

**phaius** /**fuy**-uhs/ *n.* any of three Australian orchids, esp. *Phaius tancarvilliae*, having the largest flowers of any Australian orchid in brown, white, and purple.

**phalanger** /fuh-**lan**-juh/ *n.* any of various Australian tree-dwelling marsupials, including cuscuses and possums, having thick woolly fur and, frequently, prehensile tails. [Greek *phalaggion* spider's web, from the webbed toes of its hind feet]

**phalanx** /**fal**-angks/ *n.* (*pl.* **phalanxes** or **phalanges** /fuh-**lan**-jeez/) **1** *Gk Antiq.* line of battle, esp. a body of infantry drawn up in close order. **2** set of people etc. forming a compact mass, or banded for a common purpose. [Latin from Greek]

**phallic** /**fal**-ik/ *adj.* **1** of, relating to, or resembling a phallus. **2** denoting the stage of male sexual development characterised by preoccupation with the penis.

**phallocentric** /ˌfal-oh-**sen**-trik/ *adj.* centred on the phallus, esp. as a symbol of male superiority or dominance.

**phallus** /**fal**-uhs/ *n.* (*pl.* **phalli** /-uy/ or **phalluses**) **1** (esp. erect) penis. **2** image of

this as a symbol of natural generative power. [Latin from Greek]

**phantasm** /**fan**-ˌtaz-uhm/ *n.* **1** illusion, phantom. **2** (usu. foll. by *of*) an illusory likeness. □ **phantasmal** /-**taz**-muhl/ *adj.* [Latin: related to PHANTOM]

**phantasmagoria** /ˌfan-taz-muh-**gaw**-ree-uh/ *n.* shifting series of real or imaginary figures as seen in a dream. □ **phantasmagoric** /-**go**-rik/ *adj.* **phantasmagorical** *adj.* [probably from French *fantasmagorie*: related to PHANTASM]

**phantom** /**fan**-tuhm/ — *n.* **1** ghost, apparition, spectre. **2** a form without substance or reality; a mental illusion. — *attrib. adj.* illusory. [Greek *phantasma*]

**phantom limb** *n.* continuing sensation of the presence of a limb which has been amputated.

**phantom pregnancy** *n.* symptoms of pregnancy in a person not actually pregnant.

**Pharaoh** /**fair**-roh/ *n.* **1** ruler of ancient Egypt. **2** title of this ruler. [Old English from Church Latin *Pharao*, ultimately from Egyptian]

**Pharisee** /**fa**-ruh-ˌsee/ *n.* **1** member of an ancient Jewish sect, distinguished by strict observance of the traditional and written law. **2** (**pharisee**) self-righteous person; hypocrite. □ **pharisaic** /ˌfa-ruh-**say**-ik/ *adj.* **pharisaical** *adj.* **pharisaism** /**fa**-ruh-say-ˌiz-uhm/ *n.* [Hebrew *pārûš*]

**pharmaceutical** /ˌfah-muh-**syoo**-ti-kuhl/ *adj.* **1** of or engaged in pharmacy. **2** of the use or sale of medicinal drugs. [Latin from Greek *pharmakon* drug]

**pharmaceutics** *n.pl.* (usu. treated as *sing.*) = PHARMACY 1.

**pharmacist** /**fah**-muh-suhst/ *n.* person qualified to prepare and dispense drugs, chemist.

**pharmacology** /ˌfah-muh-**kol**-uh-jee/ *n.* the study of the action of drugs on the body. □ **pharmacological** /-kuh-**loj**-i-kuhl/ *adj.* **pharmacologist** *n.*

**pharmacopoeia** /ˌfah-muh-kuh-**pee**-uh/ *n.* **1** book, esp. one officially published, containing a list of drugs with directions for use. **2** stock of drugs. [Greek *pharmakopoios* drug-maker]

**pharmacy** /**fah**-muh-see/ *n.* (*pl.* **-ies**) **1** preparation and (esp. medicinal) dispensing of drugs. **2** chemist's shop.

**pharynx** /**fa**-ringks/ *n.* (*pl.* **pharynges** /fuh-**rin**-jeez/ or **-xes**) cavity, with enclosing muscles and mucous membrane, behind the nose and mouth, and connecting them to the oesophagus. □ **pharyngeal** /ˌfa-rin-**jee**-uhl/ *adj.* **pharyngitis** /-**juy**-tuhs/ *n.* [Latin from Greek]

**phascogale** /**fas**-kuh-gayl, ,fas-kuh-**gah**-lee/ n. either of two species of largely tree-dwelling Australian carnivorous marsupials: the tuan or the wambenger. [Greek *phaskōlos* pouch, *galē* weasel]

**phase** /fayz/ — n. **1** distinct stage in a process of change or development. **2** each of the aspects of the moon or a planet, according to the amount of its illumination. **3** *Physics* stage in a periodically recurring sequence, esp. the wave-form of alternating electric currents or light. **4** a difficult or unhappy period, esp. in adolescence. — v. (**-sing**) carry out (a programme etc.) in phases or stages. □ **in phase** having the same phase at the same time; happening together. **out of phase** not in phase. **phase in** (or **out**) bring gradually into (or out of) use. [Greek *phasis* appearance]

**phatic** /**fat**-ik/ adj. (of speech, an utterance, etc.) used to convey general sociability rather than to communicate a specific meaning, e.g. 'lovely day!'; 'how are you?'. [Greek *phatos* spoken]

**Ph.D.** abbr. Doctor of Philosophy. [Latin *philosophiae doctor*]

**pheasant** /**fez**-uhnt/ n. long-tailed game-bird, originally from Asia, now increasingly farmed in Australia. [Greek *Phasianos* of Phasis, name of a river associated with the bird]

**pheasant coucal** /**koo**-kuhl/ n. (also **coucal, swamp pheasant**) very large, long-tailed, nest-building cuckoo of northern and eastern Australia, having the back and wings variegated with red, yellow, brown, and black. [probably related to CUCKOO]

**phenobarbitone** /,fee-noh-**bah**-buh-,tohn/ n. narcotic and sedative barbiturate drug used esp. to treat epilepsy. [from PHENOL, BARBITURATE]

**phenol** /**fee**-nol/ n. **1** hydroxyl derivative of benzene. **2** any hydroxyl derivative of an aromatic hydrocarbon. [French]

**phenomenal** /fuh-**nom**-uh-nuhl/ adj. **1** extraordinary, remarkable. **2** of the nature of a phenomenon. □ **phenomenally** adv.

**phenomenalism** /fuh-**nom**-uh-nuh-,liz-uhm/ n. *Philos.* **1** doctrine that human knowledge is confined to the appearances presented to the senses. **2** doctrine that appearances are the foundation of all knowledge.

**phenomenon** /fuh-**nom**-uh-nuhn/ n. (pl. **-mena**) **1** fact or occurrence that appears or is perceived, esp. one of which the cause is in question. **2** remarkable person or thing. [Greek *phainō* show]

■ **Usage** The plural form of this word, *phenomena*, is often used mistakenly for the singular. This should be avoided.

**pheromone** /**fe**-ruh-,mohn/ n. substance secreted and released by an animal for detection and response by another usu. of the same species. [Greek *pherō* convey, HORMONE]

**phew** /fyoo/ int. expression of relief, astonishment, weariness, etc. [imitative]

**phi** /fuy/ n. twenty-first letter of the Greek alphabet (Φ, φ). [Greek]

**phial** /**fuy**-uhl/ n. small glass bottle, esp. for liquid medicine. [Greek *phialē* broad flat dish]

**phil-** var. of PHILO-.

**-phil** var. of -PHILE.

**philander** /fuh-**lan**-duh/ v. flirt or have casual love-affairs. □ **philanderer** n. [Greek *philandros* fond of men, from PHIL-, *anēr andr-* male person]

**philanthropy** /fuh-**lan**-thruh-pee/ n. **1** love of mankind. **2** practical benevolence, esp. charity on a large scale. □ **philanthropic** /,fil-uhn-**throp**-ik/ adj. **philanthropist** n. [PHIL-, Greek *anthrōpos* human being]

**philately** /fuh-**lat**-uh-lee/ n. the study and collecting of postage stamps. □ **philatelist** n. [Greek *atelēs* tax-free]

**-phile** comb. form (also **-phil**) forming nouns and adjectives denoting fondness for what is specified (*bibliophile*). [Greek *philos* loving]

**philharmonic** /,fil-ah-**mon**-ik, fil-uh-/ adj. fond of music (usu. in the names of orchestras etc.). [Italian: related to HARMONIC]

**-philia** comb. form **1** denoting (esp. abnormal) fondness or love for what is specified (*necrophilia*). **2** denoting undue inclination (*haemophilia*). □ **-philiac** comb. form forming nouns and adjectives. [Greek, from *philos* loving]

**philippic** /fuh-**lip**-ik/ n. bitter verbal attack. [Greek *philippikos* the name of the orator Demosthenes' speeches against *Philip* II of Macedon]

**Philistine** /**fil**-uh-,stuyn/ — n. **1** member of a people of ancient Palestine. **2** (usu. **philistine**) person who is hostile or indifferent to culture, or one whose tastes, interests, etc., are commonplace, or material, or 'ocker'. — adj. (usu. **philistine**) hostile or indifferent to culture, commonplace, 'ocker'. □ **philistinism** /-stuh-niz-uhm/ n. [Hebrew *pelišti*]

**Phillips screw** /**fil**-uhps/ n. *propr.* screw with a cross-shaped slot in the head, turned with a Phillips screwdriver. [name of the US manufacturer]

**Phillips screwdriver** *n.* screwdriver with a cross-shaped point for driving a Phillips screw.

**philo-** *comb. form* (also **phil-** before a vowel or *h*) denoting a liking for what is specified (*philosophy*). [Greek *philos* loving, fond of]

**philodendron** /ˌfil-uh-**den**-druhn/ *n.* (*pl.* **-s** or **-dra**) tropical evergreen climber cultivated as a house-plant. [PHILO-, Greek *dendron* tree]

**philology** /fuh-**lol**-uh-jee/ *n.* the study of language, esp. in its historical and comparative aspects. □ **philological** /ˌfil-uh-**loj**-i-kuhl/ *adj.* **philologist** *n.* [French from Latin from Greek: related to PHILO-, -LOGY]

**philosopher** /fuh-**los**-uh-fuh/ *n.* **1** expert in or student of philosophy. **2** person who lives by a philosophy. **3** person who shows philosophic calmness in trying circumstances. [PHILO-, Greek *sophos* wise]

**philosophers' stone** *n.* (also **philosopher's stone**) supreme object of alchemy, a substance supposed to change other metals into gold or silver.

**philosophical** /ˌfil-uh-**sof**-i-kuhl/ *adj.* (also **philosophic**) **1** of or according to philosophy. **2** skilled in or devoted to philosophy. **3** wise, serene; calm in adversity (*philosophical acceptance of what must be*). □ **philosophically** *adv.*

**philosophise** /fuh-**los**-uh-ˌfuyz/ *v.* (also **-ize**) (**-sing** or **-zing**) **1** reason like a philosopher. **2** speculate; theorise; moralise. □ **philosophiser** *n.*

**philosophy** /fuh-**los**-uh-fee/ *n.* (*pl.* **-ies**) **1** use of reason and argument in seeking truth and knowledge of reality, esp. knowledge of the causes and nature of things and of the principles governing existence. **2 a** particular system or set of beliefs reached by this. **b** personal rule of life. **3** advanced learning in general (*she is a doctor of philosophy, has a Ph.D*). [PHILO-, Greek *sophia* wisdom]

**philtre** /**fil**-tuh/ *n.* love-potion, a drink supposed to excite sexual love in the drinker. [Greek *phileō* to love]

**phimosis** /fuy-**moh**-suhs/ *n.* constriction of the foreskin, making it difficult to draw back. [Greek, = muzzling]

**phlebitis** /ˌfluh-**buy**-tuhs/ *n.* inflammation of a vein. □ **phlebitic** /-**bit**-ik/ *adj.* [Greek *phleps phleb-* vein]

**phlegm** /flem/ *n.* **1** thick viscous substance secreted by the mucous membranes of the respiratory passages, discharged by coughing. **2** *hist.* phlegm regarded as one of the four bodily humours. [Greek *phlegma*]

**phlegmatic** /fleg-**mat**-ik/ *adj.* **1** calm, unexcitable, unemotional. **2** apathetic. □ **phlegmatically** *adv.*

**phloem** /**floh**-em/ *n.* tissue conducting sap in plants. [Greek *phloos* bark]

**phlox** /floks/ *n.* (*pl.* same or **-es**) North American plant with scented clusters of esp. white, blue, or red flowers. [Greek *phlox*, name of a plant (literally 'flame')]

**-phobe** *comb. form* forming nouns denoting a person with a specified fear or hatred (*xenophobe*; *homophobe*). [Greek *phobos* fear]

**phobia** /**foh**-bee-uh/ *n.* abnormal or morbid fear or aversion. □ **phobic** *adj.* & *n.* [-PHOBIA, used as a separate word]

**-phobia** *comb. form* forming nouns denoting a specified fear or hatred (*agoraphobia*; *homophobia*). □ **-phobic** *comb. form* forming adjectives. [Latin from Greek *phobos* fear]

**phoenix** /**fee**-niks/ *n.* mythical bird, the only one of its kind, that burnt itself on a pyre and rose from the ashes to live again. [Greek *phoinix*]

**phone** *n.* & *v.* (**-ning**) = TELEPHONE. [abbreviation]

**-phone** *comb. form* forming nouns and adjectives meaning an instrument using or connected with sound (*telephone*; *xylophone*; *lagerphone*). [Greek *phōnē* voice, sound]

**phone book** *n.* telephone directory.

**phonecard** *n.* card containing prepaid units for use with a cardphone.

**phone-in** *n.* broadcast programme during which listeners or viewers telephone the studio and participate.

**phoneme** /**foh**-neem/ *n.* unit of sound in a specified language that distinguishes one word from another (e.g. *p*, *b*, *d*, *t* as in pad, pat, bad, bat, in English). □ **phonemic** /-**nee**-mik/ *adj.* [Greek *phōneō* speak]

**phonetic** /fuh-**net**-ik/ *adj.* **1** representing vocal sounds. **2** (of spelling etc.) corresponding to pronunciation. □ **phonetically** *adv.* [Greek: related to PHONEME]

**phonetics** *n.pl.* (usu. treated as *sing.*) **1** vocal sounds and their classification. **2** the study of these. □ **phonetician** /ˌfoh-nuh-**tish**-uhn/ *n.*

**phoney** /**foh**-nee/ (also **phony**) *colloq.* — *adj.* (**-ier**, **-iest**) **1** sham; counterfeit. **2** fictitious. — *n.* (*pl.* **-eys** or **-ies**) phoney person or thing. □ **phoniness** *n.* [origin unknown]

**phonic** /**fo**-nik, **foh**-nik/ — *adj.* of sound; of vocal sounds. — *n.* (in *pl.*) method of teaching reading based on sounds. [Greek *phōnē* voice]

**phono-** *comb. form* sound. [Greek *phōnē* voice, sound]

**phonology** /fuh-**nol**-uh-jee/ *n.* the study of sounds in language or a particular language; a language's sound system. □ **phonological** /ˌfoh-nuh-**loj**-i-kuhl/ *adj.*

**phony** var. of PHONEY.

**phosphate** /**fos**-fayt/ *n.* salt or ester of phosphoric acid, esp. used as a fertiliser. [French: related to PHOSPHORUS]

**phosphor** /**fos**-fuh/ *n.* synthetic fluorescent or phosphorescent substance. [Latin PHOSPHORUS]

**phosphorescence** /ˌfos-fuh-**res**-uhns/ *n.* **1** radiation similar to fluorescence but detectable after excitation ceases. **2** emission of light without combustion or perceptible heat. □ **phosphoresce** *v.* (**-cing**). **phosphorescent** *adj.*

**phosphorus** /**fos**-fuh-ruhs/ *n. Chem.* non-metallic element existing in allotropic forms, esp. as a poisonous whitish waxy substance burning slowly at ordinary temperatures and so luminous in the dark, and a reddish form used in matches, fertilisers, etc. □ **phosphoric** /-**fo**-rik/ *adj.* **phosphorous** *adj.* [Greek *phōs* light, *-phoros* -bringing]

**photo** /**foh**-toh/ *n.* (*pl.* **-s**) = PHOTOGRAPH *n.* [abbreviation]

**photo-** *comb. form* denoting: **1** light (*photosensitive*). **2** photography. [Greek *phōs phōt-* light]

**photochemistry** /ˌfoh-toh-**kem**-uhs-tree/ *n.* the study of the chemical effects of light.

**photocopier** /**foh**-toh-ˌkop-ee-uh/ *n.* machine for producing photocopies.

**photocopy** — *n.* (*pl.* **-ies**) photographic copy of printed or written material. — *v.* (**-ies, -ied**) make a photocopy of.

**photoelectric** /ˌfoh-toh-ee-**lek**-trik, ˌfoh-toh-/ *adj.* marked by or using emissions of electrons from substances exposed to light. □ **photoelectricity** /-tris-uh-tee/ *n.*

**photoelectric cell** *n.* device using the effect of light to generate current.

**photo finish** *n.* close finish of a race or contest, where the winner is distinguishable only on a photograph taken at the finishing line.

**photogenic** /ˌfoh-toh-**jen**-ik, -jee-nik/ *adj.* **1** (esp. of a person) looking attractive in photographs. **2** *Biol.* producing or emitting light.

**photograph** /**foh**-tuh-ˌgrahf, -ˌgraf/ — *n.* picture formed by means of the chemical action of light or other radiation on sensitive film. — *v.* (also *absol.*) take a photograph of (a person etc.). □ **photo-**

**grapher** /fuh-**tog**-ruh-fuh/ *n.* **photographically** /-**graf**-i-kuh-lee, -klee/ *adv.*

**photographic** /ˌfoh-tuh-**graf**-ik/ *adj.* **1** of or pertaining to photography. **2** retaining all detail (*a photographic memory*). **3** mechanical, merely imitative, lacking individuality and artistic expression (*his art is merely photographic, not painterly*).

**photography** /fuh-**tog**-ruh-fee/ *n.* the taking and processing of photographs.

**photogravure** /ˌfoh-toh-gruh-**vyoor**/ *n.* **1** image produced from a photographic negative transferred to a metal plate and etched in. **2** this process. [French *gravure* engraving]

**photojournalism** /ˌfoh-toh-**jer**-nuh-ˌliz-uhm/ *n.* the relating of news by photographs, esp. in magazines etc. □ **photojournalist** *n.*

**photolithography** /ˌfoh-toh-li-**thog**-ruh-fee/ *n.* lithography using plates made photographically.

**photometer** /foh-**tom**-uh-tuh/ *n.* instrument for measuring light. □ **photometric** /ˌfoh-toh-**met**-rik/ *adj.* **photometry** /-**tom**-uh-tree/ *n.*

**photon** /**foh**-ton/ *n.* quantum of electromagnetic radiation energy, proportional to the frequency of radiation. [after ELECTRON]

**photosensitive** /ˌfoh-toh-**sen**-suh-tiv/ *adj.* reacting to light.

**photostat** /**foh**-toh-ˌstat/ — *n. propr.* **1** type of photocopier. **2** copy made by it. — *v.* (**-tt-**) make a photostat of.

**photosynthesis** /ˌfoh-toh-**sin**-thuh-suhs/ *n.* process in which the energy of sunlight is used by organisms, esp. green plants, to synthesise carbohydrates from carbon dioxide and water. □ **photosynthesise** *v.* (also **-ize**) (**-sing** or **-zing**). **photosynthetic** /-**thet**-ik/ *adj.*

**phototropism** /fuh-**tot**-ruh-ˌpiz-uhm/ *n.* tendency of a plant etc. to bend or turn towards or away from a source of light. □ **phototropic** /ˌfoh-toh-**trop**-ik/ *adj.* [PHOTO-, TROPISM]

**phrasal** /**fray**-zuhl/ *adj.* consisting of a phrase. □ **phrasal verb** idiomatic phrase consisting of a verb and an adverb (e.g. *break down*) or a verb and a preposition (e.g. *see to*).

**phrase** /frayz/ — *n.* **1** group of words forming a conceptual unit, but not a sentence (see panel). **2** idiomatic or short pithy expression. **3** mode of expression (*an elegant turn of phrase*). **4** *Mus.* group of notes forming a distinct unit within a melody. — *v.* (**-sing**) **1** express in words (*phrased the reply badly*). **2** *Mus.* divide (music) into phrases, esp. in performance. [Greek *phrasis* from *phrazō* tell]

**phraseology** /ˌfray-zee-**ol**-uh-jee/ *n.* (*pl.* **-ies**) **1** choice or arrangement of words. **2** mode of expression. □ **phraseological** /-zee-uh-**loj**-i-kuhl/ *adj.*

**phrenetic** var. of FRENETIC.

**phrenology** /fruh-**nol**-uh-jee/ *n. hist.* the study of the shape and size of the cranium as a supposed indication of character and mental faculties. □**phrenological** /fren-uh-**loj**-i-kuhl/ *adj.* **phrenologist** *n.* [Greek *phrēn* mind]

**phut** /fut/ *n.* dull abrupt sound as of impact or an explosion. □ **go phut** *colloq.* (esp. of a plan) collapse, break down. [perhaps from Hindi *phaṭnā* to burst]

**phyla** /**fuy**-luh/ *n.* = LIPPIA.

**phylactery** /fuh-**lak**-tuh-ree/ *n.* (*pl.* **-ies**) small leather box containing Hebrew texts, worn by Jewish men at prayer. [Greek *phulassō* guard]

**phyllode** /**fil**-ohd/ *n.* flattened leaf-stalk resembling, and functioning as, a true leaf, as in many Australian wattles. [Greek *phullōdes* leaflike, from *phullon* leaf]

**phylum** /**fuy**-luhm/ *n.* (*pl.* **phyla**) *Biol.* taxonomic rank below a kingdom, comprising a class or classes and subordinate taxa. [Greek *phulon* race]

**physic** /**fiz**-ik/ *n. esp. archaic* **1** medicine. **2** art of healing. **3** medical profession. [Greek *phusikē* of nature]

**physical** /**fiz**-i-kuhl/ — *adj.* **1** of the body (*physical exercise; physical education*). **2** of matter; material (*both mental and physical force*). **3 a** of, or according to, the laws of nature (*a physical impossibility*). **b** of physics (*physical science*). — *n.* (in full **physical examination**) medical examination. □ **physically** *adv.*

**physical chemistry** *n.* application of physics to the study of chemical behaviour.

**physical geography** *n.* branch of geography dealing with natural features.

**physical jerks** *n.pl. colloq.* physical exercises.

**physical science** *n.* sciences used in the study of inanimate natural objects.

**physician** /fuh-**zish**-uhn/ *n.* **1** doctor, esp. a specialist in medical diagnosis and treatment. **2** healer, healing agent (*rest is the best physician*).

**physicist** /**fiz**-uh-sist/ *n.* person skilled in physics.

**physics** /**fiz**-iks/ *n.pl.* (treated as *sing.*) branch of science dealing with the properties and interactions of matter and energy. [Latin *physica* (pl.) from Greek: related to PHYSIC]

**physio** /**fiz**-ee-oh/ *n. colloq.* **1** physiotherapy. **2** physiotherapist. [abbreviation]

**physio-** *comb. form* nature; what is natural. [Greek *phusis* nature]

**physiognomy** /ˌfiz-ee-**on**-uh-mee/ *n.* (*pl.* **-ies**) **1 a** the form of a person's features, expression, body, etc. **b** supposed art of judging character from facial characteristics etc. **2** external features of a landscape etc. [Greek: related to PHYSIC, GNOMON]

**physiology** /ˌfiz-ee-**ol**-uh-jee/ *n.* **1** science of the functions of living organisms and their parts. **2** these functions. □ **physiological** /ˌfiz-ee-uh-**loj**-i-kuhl/ *adj.* **physiologist** *n.* [Latin: related to PHYSIC, -LOGY]

**physiotherapy** /ˌfiz-ee-oh-**the**-ruh-pee/ *n.* treatment of disease, injury, deformity, etc., by physical methods including massage, heat treatment, remedial exercise, etc. □**physiotherapist** *n.* [related to PHYSIC, THERAPY]

**physique** /fuh-**zeek**/ *n.* bodily structure and development of a person (*has an undernourished physique*). [French: related to PHYSIC]

**pi** /puy/ *n.* **1** sixteenth letter of the Greek alphabet (Π, π). **2** (as π) the symbol of the ratio of the circumference of a circle to its diameter (approx. 3.14). [Greek]

**pia mater** /ˌpuy-uh **may**-tuh, ˌpee-uh **mah**-tuh/ *n.* delicate innermost membrane enveloping the brain and spinal cord. [Latin, = tender mother]

---

## Phrase

A phrase is a group of words that has meaning but (unlike a clause or sentence) does not have the complete structure of subject, verb (and object). It can be:

**1** a noun phrase, functioning as a noun, e.g.
    *I went to see* my friend Tom.
    The only ones they have *are too small*.
**2** an adjective phrase, functioning as an adjective, e.g.
    *I was* very pleased indeed.
    This one is better than mine.
**3** an adverb phrase, functioning as an adverb, e.g.
    *They drove off* in their car.
    *I was there* ten days ago.

**pianissimo** /ˌpee-uh-**nis**-uh-ˌmoh/ *Mus.* — *adj.* very soft. — *adv.* very softly. — *n.* (*pl.* **-s** or **-mi** /-mee/) very soft playing or passage. [Italian, superlative of PIANO²]

**pianist** /**pee**-uh-nuhst/ *n.* piano-player.

**piano¹** /pee-**an**-oh/ *n.* (*pl.* **-s**) keyboard instrument with metal strings struck by hammers when keys on a keyboard are pressed. [Italian, abbreviation of PIANOFORTE]

**piano²** /**pyah**-noh/ *Mus.* — *adj.* soft. — *adv.* softly. — *n.* (*pl.* **-s** or **-ni** /-nee/) soft playing or passage. [Latin *planus* flat, (of sound) soft]

**piano accordion** *n.* accordion with a small keyboard like that of a piano.

**pianoforte** /ˌpee-an-oh-**faw**-tee/ *n.* *formal* or *archaic* = PIANO¹. [Italian, earlier *piano e forte* soft and loud]

**pianola** /ˌpee-uh-**noh**-luh/ *n. propr.* a kind of automatic piano. [diminutive]

**piazza** /pee-**at**-suh, -**aht**-suh/ *n.* public square or market-place. [Italian: related to PLACE]

**pica** /**puy**-kuh/ *n.* **1** a unit of type-size. **2** a size of letters in typewriting. [Latin]

**picaresque** /ˌpik-uh-**resk**/ *adj.* (of a style of fiction) dealing with the episodic adventures of a rogue etc. who is the hero. [Spanish *pícaro* rogue]

■ **Usage** *Picaresque* is sometimes used to mean 'transitory' or 'roaming', but this is considered incorrect in standard English.

**picayune** /ˌpik-uh-**yoon**/ *US colloq.* — *n.* insignificant person or thing. — *adj.* mean; contemptible; petty. [French *picaillon*]

**piccabeen** /**pik**-uh-been/ *n.* (also **bangalow**) palm of Queensland and NSW to 13m high with long pinnate leaves, lilac flowers, and red fruits: the green heart of the palm was eaten by Aborigines and the expanded leaf-base used as a water-carrier. [Yagara *bigi* for the palm and the leaf-base water-carrier; the *-been* may have been added from English]

**piccaninny** /ˌpik-uh-**nin**-ee/ *n.* (*pl.* **-ies**) often *offens.* **1** an Aboriginal child. **2** Black child. [West Indian Negro from Spanish *pequeño* or Portuguese *pequeno* little]

**piccaninny dawn** *n.* (also **piccaninny daylight**) the approach of dawn, infant dawn; first light.

**piccaninny twilight** *n.* the last glow of the setting sun.

**piccolo** /**pik**-uh-ˌloh/ *n.* (*pl.* **-s**) small flute sounding an octave higher than the ordinary one. [Italian, = small]

**pick¹** — *v.* **1** (also *absol.*) choose carefully from available alternatives (*picked the pink one*; *picked a team*; *picked the right moment*). **2** detach or pluck (a flower, fruit, etc.) from a stem, tree, etc. **3 a** probe with the finger, an instrument, etc., to remove unwanted matter (*picked his teeth*; *picked his pimples*). **b** clear (a bone, carcass, etc.) of scraps of meat etc. **4** (also *absol.*) (of a person) eat (food, a meal, etc.) in small bits; nibble without appetite. **5 a** select (a route or path) carefully over difficult terrain by foot. **b** place (one's steps etc.) carefully. **6** *colloq.* victimise, pick on (*three drunken louts picked me outside the pub*). — *n.* **1** act or instance of picking. **2 a** selection, choice. **b** right to select (*had first pick of the prizes*). **3** (usu. foll. by *of*) best (*the pick of the bunch*). **4 a** = GREEN PICK. **b** PICKING. □ **pick and choose** select fastidiously. **pick at 1** eat (food) without interest. **2** find fault with (*picking at me all the time*). **pick a person's brains** extract ideas, information, etc., from a person for one's own use. **pick holes in** find fault with (an idea etc.). **pick a lock** open a lock with an instrument other than the proper key, esp. with criminal intent. **pick off 1** pluck (leaves etc.) off. **2** shoot (people etc.) one by one without haste. **pick on 1** find fault with; nag at. **2 a** select. **b** single (a person) out (for an unpleasant chore etc.). **pick out 1** take from a larger number (*picked him out from the others*). **2** distinguish from surrounding objects or at a distance; identify (*can just pick out the church spire*). **3** play (a tune) by ear on the piano etc. **4** (often foll. by *in*, *with*) accentuate (decoration, a painting, etc.) with a contrasting colour (*picked out the handles in red*). **pick over** select the best from. **pick a person's pockets** steal from a person's pockets. **pick a quarrel** start an argument or a fight deliberately. **pick to pieces** = *take to pieces* (see PIECE). **pick up 1** grasp and raise (from the ground etc.). **2 a** acquire by chance or without effort (*picked up a cold*). **b** learn effortlessly (*picked up French in a fortnight*). **3** stop for and take along with one, esp. in a vehicle (*pick me up at the corner*). **4** become acquainted with (a person) casually, esp. for sexual purposes. **5** (of one's health, the weather, share prices, etc.) recover, improve, etc. **6** (of an engine etc.) recover speed. **7** (of the police etc.) arrest. **8** detect by scrutiny or with a telescope, radio, etc. (*picked up most of the mistakes*; *picked up a distress signal*). **9** accept the responsibility of paying (a bill etc.) (*I'll pick up the tab*). **10** resume, take up anew (*picked up where we left off*). **11** (*refl.*) raise (oneself) after a fall etc. **12** *Shearing* gather up (a shorn fleece), preparatory to placing it on a table for skirting, classing, etc. □ **picker** *n.* [from PIKE¹]

**pick²** — *n.* **1** long-handled tool with a usu. curved iron bar pointed at one or both ends, used for breaking up hard ground etc. **2** *colloq.* plectrum. **3** any instrument for picking, e.g. a toothpick. — *v.* **1** break the surface of (the ground etc.) with or as if with a pick. **2** make (holes etc.) in this way. [from PIKE¹]

**pickaxe** /pik-aks/ — *n.* = PICK² 1. — *v.* **1** break (the ground etc.) with a pickaxe (*pickaxed the top paddock*). **2** work with a pickaxe (*spent half the day pickaxing*). [French: related to PIKE¹]

**picker** *n.* **1** person or thing that picks (*pickers wanted in the orchard*). **2** = PICKER-UP.

**picker-up** *n.* *Shearing* shed-hand who gathers up the shorn fleeces.

**picket** /pik-uht/ — *n.* **1** one or more persons stationed outside a place of work to persuade others not to enter during a strike etc. **2** pointed stake driven into the ground to form a fence, to tether a horse, etc. **3** (also **picquet**, **piquet**) **a** small body of troops sent out to watch for the enemy. **b** group of sentries. — *v.* (**-t-**) **1 a** station or act as a picket. **b** beset or guard (a factory, workers, etc.) with a picket or pickets. **2** secure (a place) with stakes. **3** tether (an animal). □ **picketer** *n.* [French *piquer* prick]

**picket line** *n.* boundary established by workers on strike, esp. at the entrance to the place of work, which others are asked not to cross.

**picking** *n.* (also **pick**) sparse pasture.

**pickings** *n.pl.* **1** profits or gains acquired easily or dishonestly. **2** leftovers.

**pickle** /pik-uhl/ — *n.* **1 a** (often in *pl.*) food, esp. vegetables, preserved in brine, vinegar, mustard, etc. **b** the liquid used for this. **2** *colloq.* plight (*in a pickle*). — *v.* (**-ling**) **1** preserve in or treat with pickle. **2** (as **pickled** *adj.*) *colloq.* drunk. [Low German or Dutch *pekel*]

**pick-me-up** *n.* **1** tonic for the nerves etc. **2** a good experience that cheers.

**pickpocket** *n.* person who steals from people's pockets.

**pick-up** *n.* **1** *colloq.* person met casually, esp. for sexual purposes. **2** (also **pick-up truck**) small open motor truck. **3** part of a record-player carrying the stylus. **4** device on an electric guitar etc. that converts string vibrations into electrical signals. **5 a** act of picking up. **b** person or

thing picked up. **6 a** act of engaging casual employees. **b** time and place where this is done (*hanging about at the pick-up, hoping for a job*).

**picky** *adj.* (**-ier**, **-iest**) *colloq.* excessively fastidious.

**picnic** /pik-nik/ — *n.* **1** outing including a packed meal eaten outdoors. **2** any meal eaten out of doors. **3 a** (usu. with *neg.*) *colloq.* something agreeable or easily accomplished etc. (*the exam was a picnic; it was no picnic organising the meeting*). **b** awkward or disorganised occasion or experience (*it was a real picnic in the trenches; I'm in for a picnic if I don't get home in time*). — *v.* (**-ck-**) take part in a picnic. [French *pique-nique*]

**picnic races** *n.pl.* (also **picnic race meeting**) day of horse racing, usu. in a rural district, the primary purpose of which is to be an informal social occasion.

**Pict** *n.* member of an ancient people of N. Britain. □ **Pictish** *adj.* [Latin]

**pictograph** /pik-tuh-grahf, -graf/ *n.* (also **pictogram** /pik-tuh-gram/) **1** pictorial symbol for a word or phrase. **2** pictorial representation of statistics etc. □ **pictographic** /-graf-ik/ *adj.* [Latin *pingo pict-* paint]

**pictorial** /pik-taw-ree-uhl/ — *adj.* **1** of or expressed in a picture or pictures. **2** illustrated. — *n.* periodical with pictures as the main feature. □ **pictorially** *adv.* [Latin *pictor* painter: related to PICTURE]

**picture** /pik-chuh/ — *n.* **1 a** (often *attrib.*) painting, drawing, photograph, etc., esp. as a work of art. **b** portrait, esp. a photograph, of a person. **c** beautiful object (*your garden's a picture*). **2 a** total mental or visual impression produced; scene (*the picture looks bleak*). **b** written or spoken description (*drew a vivid picture of moral decay*). **3 a** a film. **b** (**the pictures**) cinema; cinema performance. **4** image on a television screen (*can't get a clear picture*). **5 a** esp. *iron.* person or thing exemplifying something (*he was the picture of innocence*). **b** person or thing resembling another closely (*she's the picture of her aunt*). — *v.* (**-ring**) **1** (also *refl.*; often foll. by *to*) imagine (*pictured it to herself*). **2** represent in a picture. **3** describe graphically (*pictured for us the reception we would get*). □ **get the picture** *colloq.* grasp the drift of information etc. **in the picture** *colloq.* fully informed. [Latin *pingo pict-* paint]

**picturesque** /pik-chuh-resk/ *adj.* **1** beautiful or striking to look at. **2** (of language etc.) strikingly graphic. [Italian *pittoresco*, assimilated to PICTURE]

**picture window** n. large window of one pane of glass.

**piddle** /pid-uhl/ v. (**-ling**) **1** colloq. urinate. **2** (as **piddling** adj.) colloq. trivial; trifling. **3** (foll. by about, around) work or act in a trifling way (stop piddling around and get the job done). [sense 1 possibly from PISS conflated with PUDDLE; sense 3 perhaps from PEDDLE]

**piddly** adj. colloq. trivial; trifling.

**pidgin** /pij-uhn/ n. simplified language containing vocabulary from two or more languages, used between people not having a common language. □ **Australian pidgin** a pidgin used in colonial Australia, in which English is combined with one or more Aboriginal languages. [corruption of business]

**pidgin English** n. pidgin in which the chief language is English, used orig. between Chinese and Europeans.

**pie** /puy/ n. **1** baked dish of meat, fish, fruit, etc., usu. with a top and base of pastry. **2** thing resembling a pie (mud pie). □ **easy as pie** very easy. **have a finger in every pie** be involved in many (usu. profitable) activities. [origin uncertain]

**piebald** /puy-bawld/ — adj. (esp. of a horse) having irregular patches of two colours, esp. black and white. — n. piebald animal. [from (MAG)PIE, BALD]

**piece** /pees/ — n. **1 a** (often foll. by of) distinct portion forming part of or broken off from a larger object; a bit (a piece of string). **b** each of the parts of which a set or category is composed (five-piece band; piece of furniture). **c** each of the parts into which something is broken (pick up the pieces; tore it to pieces). **d** a limited quantity of something (a piece of land; a piece of wood). **2** coin (50-cent piece). **3** (usu. short) literary or musical composition; picture; play. **4** item or instance (piece of news; piece of impudence). **5 a** object used to make moves in a board-game. **b** chessman (strictly, other than a pawn). **6** definite quantity in which a thing is sold (sold by the piece). **7** (in pl.) Shearing oddments of wool detached from the skirtings of a fleece. **8** colloq. offens. a woman. — v. (**-cing**) **1** (usu. foll. by together) form into a whole; put together; join (finally pieced his story together). **2** (usu. foll. by out) **a** eke out. **b** form (a theory etc.) by combining parts etc. □ **go to pieces** collapse emotionally. **have** (or **take**) **a piece out of** (a person) rebuke severely, take to task. **in** (or **all in**) **one piece 1** unbroken. **2** unharmed. **nasty piece of work** obnoxious person. **of a piece** (often foll. by with) uniform, consistent. **a piece of cake** see CAKE. **a**

**piece of one's mind** sharp rebuke or lecture. **say one's piece** give one's opinion or make a prepared statement. **take to pieces 1** break up or dismantle. **2** criticise harshly. [Anglo-French, probably from Celtic]

**pièce de résistance** /,pyes duh ray-**zis**-tons/ n. (pl. **pièces de résistance** pronunc. same) most important or remarkable item, esp. a dish at a meal. [French]

**piecemeal** — adv. piece by piece; gradually. — adj. gradual; unsystematic. [from PIECE, MEAL[1]]

**piece-picker** n. Shearing person who gathers up and sorts the pieces of wool.

**piecework** n. work paid for according to the amount produced.

**pie chart** n. circle divided into sectors to represent relative quantities.

**pied** /puyd/ adj. **1** particoloured. **2** (as applied to Australian birds) black and white. [from (MAG)PIE]

**pied butcherbird** n. (also **organ bird**) black and white bird of mainland Australia with an extremely beautiful song.

**pied currawong** n. (also **crow-shrike** or **bell magpie**) one of the three species of currawong, a black and white bird of eastern Australia with a ringing, bell-like call.

**pied goose** n. = MAGPIE GOOSE.

**pie-dish beetle** n. any of many beetles of drier Australia, flat in shape with a pie-dish like flange.

**pie-eater** n. colloq. **1** person of little account. **2** an Australian. [from the ubiquitous Australian meat-pie]

**pie-eyed** adj. colloq. drunk.

**pie in the sky** n. unrealistic prospect of future happiness.

**pie-melon** n. (also **wild melon**) any of several plants with a melon-like fruit used for pies, making jam, etc.

**pie night** n. (in full **beer and pie night**) social occasion in many Australian sports clubs etc.

**pier** /peer/ n. **1 a** structure built out into the sea, a lake, etc., as a promenade and landing-stage. **b** breakwater. **2 a** support of an arch or of the span of a bridge; pillar. **b** solid masonry between windows etc. [Latin pera]

**pierce** v. (**-cing**) **1 a** (of a sharp instrument etc.) penetrate (the needle pierced his flesh). **b** (often foll. by with) make a hole in or through with a sharp-pointed instrument (pierced the leather with the awl). **c** make (a hole etc.) (pierced a hole in her belt; had his ears pierced). **d** (of cold, grief, etc.) affect keenly or sharply (*grief pierced his heart*). **e** (of a light, glance, sound, etc.) penetrate keenly or sharply (*the searchlight pierced the night; her look pierced him to the quick*). **2** (as **piercing** *adj.*) (of a glance, intuition, sound, light, pain, cold, etc.) keen, sharp, or unpleasantly penetrating. **3** (often foll. by *through, into*) force a way through or into (something), penetrate (*pierced their way through the jungle*). [French *percer* from Latin *pertundo* bore through]

**pierrot** /**peer**-roh/ *n.* (*fem.* **pierrette** /peer-**ret**/) white-faced entertainer with a loose white clown's costume, in French pantomime etc. [French, diminutive of *Pierre* Peter]

**pietà** /,pee-uh-**tah**, pee-ay-tuh/ *n.* representation of the Virgin Mary holding the dead body of Christ on her lap. [Italian, = PIETY]

**pietism** /**puy**-uh-,tiz-uhm/ *n.* **1** pious sentiment. **2** exaggerated or affected piety. [German: related to PIETY]

**piety** /**puy**-uh-tee/ *n.* (*pl.* **-ies**) **1** quality of being pious. **2** pious act. [Latin: related to PIOUS]

**piffle** /**pif**-uhl/ *colloq.* — *n.* nonsense; empty speech. — *v.* (**-ling**) talk or act feebly; trifle. [imitative]

**piffling** *adj. colloq.* trivial; worthless.

**pig** — *n.* **1** omnivorous, hoofed, bristly, broad-snouted mammal, esp. a domesticated kind. **2** its flesh as food. **3** *colloq.* **a** greedy, dirty, or unpleasant person. **b** unpleasant, awkward, or difficult thing, task, etc. (*a pig of a job*). **4** oblong mass of metal (esp. iron or lead) from a smelting-furnace. **5** *colloq. offens.* member of a police force. **6** *colloq. Rugby Union* a forward. **7** (in the possessive, as an abbr. of *pig's bum, pig's eye*, etc.) *colloq.* a derisive retort (*pigs!; pigs to you!*). — *v.* (**-gg-**) *colloq.* eat (food) greedily. □ **bleed like a pig** (or **like a stuck pig**) bleed copiously. **buy a pig in a poke** acquire something without previous sight or knowledge of it. **home on the pig's back** *colloq.* assured of success. **make a pig of oneself** overeat. **pig it** *colloq.* live in a disorderly or filthy fashion. **pig out** (often foll. by *on*) *colloq.* eat gluttonously. **ride** (or **fly**) **on the pig's back** *colloq.* be extremely successful or fortunate. [Old English]

**pig-dog** *n.* dog bred to hunt the wild pig.

**pigeon** /**pij**-uhn/ *n.* **1** bird of the dove family, often domesticated and bred and trained to race, carry messages, etc. **2** any of various Australian birds including bronzewings (flock bronzewing, crested pigeon, etc.) and fruit-pigeons (purple-crowned pigeon, wompoo pigeon), with many of the smaller species being called 'doves' (peaceful dove, bar-shouldered dove). **3** person who is easily duped or swindled. [Latin *pipio -onis*]

**pigeon-hole** — *n.* each of a set of compartments in a cabinet etc. for papers, letters, etc. — *v.* **1** assign to a pre-conceived category. **2** deposit in a pigeon-hole. **3** put aside for future consideration.

**pigeon-toed** *adj.* having the toes turned inwards.

**pigface** *n.* any of several succulent, prostrate, perennial plants of coastal and dry inland Australia, having extremely showy daisy-flowers in various colours; so called because the ripe fruit bears resemblance to a pig's head.

**pig fish** *n.* any of several marine fish of northern and eastern Australia, having an elongated 'snout'.

**pig-footed bandicoot** *n.* bandicoot, probably now extinct, of drier southern and central Australia, having only two well-developed toes on the fore foot.

**piggery** *n.* (*pl.* **-ies**) **1** pig farm. **2** = PIGSTY.

**piggish** *adj.* greedy; dirty; mean.

**piggy** — *n.* (*pl.* **-ies**) *colloq.* little pig. — *adj.* (**-ier, -iest**) **1** like a pig. **2** (of features etc.) like those of a pig (*little piggy eyes*).

**piggyback** — *n.* ride on the back and shoulders of another person. — *adv.* on the back and shoulders of another person. — *adj.* (of an article etc.) attached to another article. — *v.* attach an article to another (*it's unsafe to piggyback plugs*). [origin unknown]

**pig-headed** *adj.* obstinate. □ **pig-headedness** *n.*

**pig-iron** *n.* crude iron from a smelting-furnace.

**pig Island** — *n.* (also **pig Islands**) *colloq.* New Zealand. — *adj.* (**pig-Island**) of or pertaining to New Zealand. □ **pig Islander** *n.* [allusion to the wild pigs introduced by Captain James Cook]

**piglet** /**pig**-luht/ *n.* young pig.

**pigment** /**pig**-muhnt/ — *n.* **1** colouring-matter used as paint or dye. **2** natural colouring-matter of animal or plant tissue, e.g. chlorophyll, haemoglobin. — *v.* colour with or as if with pigment. □ **pigmentary** *adj.* [Latin *pingo* paint]

**pigmentation** /,pig-muhn-**tay**-shuhn/ *n.* **1** natural colouring of plants, animals, etc. **2** excessive colouring of tissue by the deposition of pigment.

**pigmy** var. of PYGMY.

**pig-root** *v.* (of a horse or other animal) kick upwards with the hind legs while the forelegs are firmly planted and the head held down. □ **pig-rooter** *n.*

**pig's ear** *n. colloq.* beer. [rhyming slang]

**pigskin** *n.* **1** hide of a pig. **2** leather made from this.

**pigsty** *n.* (*pl.* **-ies**) **1** pen for pigs. **2** filthy house, room, etc.

**pigswill** *n.* kitchen refuse and scraps fed to pigs.

**pigtail** *n.* plait of hair hanging from the back of the head.

**pigweed** *n.* (also **munyeroo**) spreading, prostrate plant (a portulaca) of Australia, having thick, edible, succulent stems and leaves, and often regarded as a weed of cultivation.

**pike¹** *n.* (*pl.* same or **-s**) **1** large voracious freshwater fish of the Northern hemisphere with a long narrow snout. **2** any of several voracious Australian marine fish, having an elongated head and sharp teeth. **3** *hist.* weapon with a pointed metal head on a long wooden shaft. [Old English *pic* point, prick]

**pike²** *v.* (- **king**) *colloq.* **1** (foll. by *on*) let (a person) down (*piked on me after all his promises*). **2** (foll. by *out*) go back on (one's word, a deal, an arrangement, etc.) (*piked out at the last minute; piked out on our bargain*).

**pike³** *n.* jackknife position in diving or gymnastics. □ **with pike** *colloq.* with greater difficulty involving added depth (as in a dive with pike) (*Did you get your degree? — Yes, mate, with pike!*). [origin unknown]

**pikelet** /**puyk**-luht/ *n.* (also **drop scone**) small, thickish pancake eaten buttered. [Welsh (*bara*) *pyglyd* pitchy (bread)]

**piker** *n.* **1** cautious, timid, or mean and miserly person. **2** *colloq.* person who lets others down or who welshes on an agreement, promise, etc. **3** person who does not pull his or her weight; a shirker. **4** bullock living in the wild.

**pikestaff** *n.* wooden shaft of a pike. □ **plain as a pikestaff** quite plain or obvious.

**pilaf** /pee-**laf**/ *n.* (also **pilaff, pilau** /-**low**/) Middle Eastern or Indian dish of rice boiled with meat, vegetables, spices, etc. [Turkish]

**pilaster** /puh-**las**-tuh/ *n.* rectangular column projecting slightly from a wall. □ **pilastered** *adj.* [Latin *pila* pillar]

**pilchard** /**pil**-chuhd/ *n.* **1** small marine fish of the herring family found in the Atlantic and the Mediterranean. **2** related marine food-fish abounding in southern Australian waters. [origin unknown]

**pile¹** — *n.* **1** heap of things laid upon one another. **2** large imposing building. **3** *colloq.* **a** large quantity. **b** large amount of money. **4** a series of plates of dissimilar metals laid one on another alternately to produce an electric current. **b** = NUCLEAR REACTOR. — *v.* (-**ling**) **1 a** (often foll. by *up*, *on*) heap up. **b** (foll. by *with*) load (*piled the ute with all his junk*). **2** (usu. foll. by *in*, *into*, *on*, *out of*, etc.) crowd hurriedly or tightly (*all piled into the car; piled out of the restaurant*). □ **pile it on** *colloq.* exaggerate. **pile up 1** accumulate; heap up. **2** *colloq.* cause (a vehicle etc.) to crash. [Latin *pila*]

**pile²** *n.* **1** heavy beam driven vertically into the ground to support a bridge, the foundations of a house, etc. **2** pointed stake or post. [Latin *pilum* javelin]

**pile³** *n.* soft projecting surface on a carpet, velvet, etc. [Latin *pilus* hair]

**pileanthus** /,puy-lee-**an**-thuhs, ,pee-/ *n.* = COPPER CUPS. [Greek, = cap flower, alluding to the buds]

**piledriver** *n.* machine for driving piles into the ground.

**piles** *n.pl. colloq.* haemorrhoids. [Latin *pila* ball]

**pile-up** *n. colloq.* multiple crash of road vehicles.

**pilfer** /**pil**-fuh/ *v.* (also *absol.*) steal (objects), esp. in small quantities. □ **pilferage** *n.* **pilferer** *n.* [French *pelfre*]

**pilgrim** /**pil**-gruhm/ *n.* **1** person who journeys to a sacred place for religious reasons. **2** traveller. [Latin]

**pilgrimage** *n.* **1** pilgrim's journey. **2** any journey taken for sentimental reasons.

**pill** *n.* **1 a** ball or a flat disc of solid medicine for swallowing whole. **b** (usu. prec. by *the*) *colloq.* contraceptive pill. **2** an unpleasant or painful necessity; a humiliation (*bitter pill; must swallow the pill*). **3** *colloq.* obnoxious or painfully boring person. □ **sugar the pill** make an unpleasant necessity easier to bear. [Latin *pila* ball]

**pillage** /**pil**-ij/ — *v.* (-**ging**) (also *absol.*) plunder, sack. — *n.* pillaging, esp. in war. [French *piller* plunder]

**pillar** /**pil**-uh/ *n.* **1** slender vertical structure of stone etc. used as a support for a roof etc. or for ornament. **2** person regarded as a mainstay (*pillar of the faith*). **3** upright mass of air, water, rock, etc. (*pillar of salt*). □ **from pillar to post** (rushing, driven, etc.) from one place to another. [Latin *pila* pillar]

**pillbox** *n.* **1** shallow cylindrical box for holding pills. **2** hat of a similar shape. **3** *Mil.* small partly underground enclosed concrete fort.

**pillion** /**pil**-yuhn/ *n.* seating for a passenger behind a motor cyclist. □ **ride pillion** travel seated behind a motor cyclist. [Gaelic *pillean* small cushion]

**pillory** /**pil**-uh-ree/ — *n.* (*pl.* **-ies**) *hist.*

wooden framework with holes for the head and hands, imprisoning a person and allowing him or her to be publicly assaulted or ridiculed. — v. (-ies, -ied) 1 expose to ridicule or public contempt (*was pilloried in the press*). 2 *hist.* put in the pillory. [French]

**pillow** /**pil**-oh/ — n. 1 soft support for the head, esp. in bed. 2 pillow-shaped block or support. — v. rest on or as if on a pillow (*pillowed his head on her breast*). [Latin *pulvinus* cushion]

**pilot** /**puy**-luht/ — n. 1 person who operates the controls of an aircraft. 2 person qualified to take charge of a ship entering or leaving harbour. 3 (usu. *attrib.*) experimental undertaking or test esp. in advance of a larger one (*pilot scheme*). 4 guide. — v. (-t-) 1 act as a pilot of. 2 conduct or initiate as a pilot (*piloted the new scheme*). [Greek *pēdon* oar]

**pilot bird** n. reddish-brown, chiefly terrestrial bird of south-eastern mainland Australia, having a penetrating whistle: once thought to pilot its frequent companion, the lyrebird.

**pilot light** n. 1 small gas burner kept alight to light another. 2 electric indicator light or control light.

**pimelea** /puh-**mee**-lyuh, puy-/ n. (also **rice-flower**) any shrub of the mainly Australian genus *Pimelea*, the ones usu. cultivated having terminal heads of flowers surrounded by prominent bracts, their colours ranging from white to deep pink (see also QUALUP BELL). [Greek *pimelē* fat, alluding to the plant's oily seeds]

**pimento** /puh-**men**-toh/ n. (pl. **-s**) 1 tree native to Jamaica. 2 berries of this, usu. crushed for culinary use; allspice. 3 = PIMIENTO. [Latin: related to PIGMENT]

**pimiento** /ˌpim-ee-**en**-toh, pim-**yen**-toh/ n. (pl. **-s**) red capsicum, orig. from Spain, with a sweet flavour. [see PIMENTO]

**pimp** — n. 1 man who lives off the earnings of a prostitute or a brothel. 2 informer, tale-teller, sneak. — v. act as a pimp. [origin unknown]

**pimple** /**pim**-puhl/ n. 1 small hard inflamed spot on the skin; pustule. 2 anything resembling a pimple, esp. in relative size. □ **pimply** adj. [Old English]

**PIN** /pin/ abbr. (also **PIN number**) personal identification number as issued by a bank etc. to validate electronic transactions with a cashcard in an automatic teller machine.

**pin** — n. 1 a small thin pointed piece of metal with a round or flattened head used (esp. in sewing) for holding things in place, attaching one thing to another,

etc. **b** any of several types of pin (*drawing-pin*; *safety-pin*; etc.). **c** small brooch (*diamond pin*). 2 peg of wood or metal for various purposes. 3 (in idioms) something of small value (*not worth a pin*). 4 (in *pl.*) *colloq.* legs. — v. (**-nn-**) 1 a (often foll. by *to*, *up*, *together*) fasten with a pin or pins. **b** transfix with a pin, lance, etc. 2 (usu. foll. by *on*) put (blame, responsibility, etc.) on (a person etc.) (*pinned the blame on his friend*). 3 (often foll. by *against*, *on*, etc.) seize and hold fast (*pinned him against the wall*). □ **on pins** in an agitated state of suspense. **pin down** 1 (often foll. by *to*) bind (a person etc.) to a promise, arrangement, etc. 2 force (a person) to declare his or her intentions. 3 restrict the actions of (an enemy etc.). 4 specify (a thing) precisely (*couldn't pin down his unease*). 5 hold (a person etc.) down by force. **pin one's faith** (or **hopes** etc.) **on** rely implicitly on. [Latin *pinna* point etc.]

**pinafore** /**pin**-uh-ˌfaw/ n. 1 apron, esp. with a bib. 2 (in full **pinafore dress**) collarless sleeveless dress worn over a blouse or jumper. [from PIN, AFORE-]

**pinball** n. game in which small metal balls are shot across a board to strike pins.

**pince-nez** /**pans**-nay/ n. (*pl.* same) pair of eyeglasses with a nose-clip instead of earpieces. [French, = pinch-nose]

**pincer movement** n. movement by two wings of an army converging to surround an enemy.

**pincers** /**pin**-suhz/ n.pl. 1 (also **pair of pincers**) gripping-tool resembling scissors but with blunt jaws. 2 front claws of lobsters and some other crustaceans. [related to PINCH]

**pinch** — v. 1 a squeeze tightly, esp. between finger and thumb. **b** (often *absol.*) (of a shoe etc.) constrict painfully. 2 (of cold, hunger, etc.) affect painfully (*she was pinched with cold*). 3 *colloq.* a steal. **b** arrest. 4 (as **pinched** *adj.*) (of the features) drawn, as with cold, hunger, worry, etc. 5 a be niggardly (*the recession has forced us to pinch and scrape*). **b** (usu. in passive) cramp, restrict (*pinched for space*; *am pinched for time*). 6 (usu. foll. by *out*, *back*, *down*) remove (leaves, buds, etc.) to encourage bushy growth. — n. 1 act or instance of pinching. 2 amount that can be taken up with fingers and thumb (*pinch of pepper*). 3 the stress or pain caused by poverty, cold, hunger, etc. 4 steep or difficult section of a road (*my car stalled on the pinch*). □ **at** (or **in**) **a pinch** in an emergency. **with a pinch of salt** see SALT. [French *pincer*]

**pinchbeck** — *n.* goldlike alloy of copper and zinc used in cheap jewellery etc. — *adj.* counterfeit, sham. [*Pinchbeck*, name of a watchmaker]

**pincushion** *n.* **1** small pad for holding pins. **2** (in full **blue pincushion** or **Austral pincushion**) small shrub of temperate Australia (*Brunonia australis*) producing many heads of cornflower-blue flowers. **3** (in full **pincushion hakea**) shrub or small tree of WA producing abundant pincushion-like red flower heads with protruding white styles resembling pins stuck in.

**pindan** /pin-dan/ *n.* **1** (also **pindan country**) arid, sandy country characteristic of stretches of northern WA. **2** (also **pindan scrub**) the low, scrubby vegetation occurring in such country. **3** any of several plants typifying such vegetation, esp. a small wattle. [Bardi *bindan* the bush]

**pine**[1] *n.* **1** evergreen coniferous tree with needle-shaped leaves growing in clusters. **2** any of several, usu. large, coniferous trees native to Australia, as the Huon pine. **3** the soft timber of these trees, often used to make furniture. **4** (*attrib.*) made of pine. **5** = CYPRESS PINE. **6** = PINEAPPLE. [Latin *pinus*]

**pine**[2] *v.* (**-ning**) **1** (often foll. by *away*) decline or waste away from grief etc. **2** (usu. foll. by *for*, *after*, or *to* + infin.) long eagerly; yearn. [Old English]

**pineal** /pin-ee-uhl, puy-nee-/ *adj.* shaped like a pine cone. [Latin *pinea*: related to PINE[1]]

**pineal gland** *n.* (also **pineal body**) conical gland in the brain, secreting a hormone-like substance.

**pineapple** /puyn-ap-uhl/ *n.* **1** large juicy tropical fruit with yellow flesh and tough segmented skin. **2** plant bearing this. □ **the rough** (or **wrong**) **end of the pineapple** *colloq.* a raw deal; rough or hostile treatment. [from PINE[1], APPLE]

**pine cone** *n.* fruit of the pine.

**pine nut** *n.* edible seed of various pines.

**ping** — *n.* **1** single short high ringing sound. **2** high-pitched explosive sound emitted by the faulty engine of a motor vehicle. — *v.* **1** (cause to) make a ping. **2** (of a vehicle engine) emit a series of high-pitched explosive sounds caused by faulty combustion. [imitative]

**ping-pong** *n.* = TABLE TENNIS. [imitative]

**pinhead** *n.* **1** head of a pin. **2** very small thing or spot. **3** *colloq.* stupid person.

**pinion**[1] /pin-yuhn/ — *n.* **1** outer part of a bird's wing. **2** *poet.* wing; flight-feather. — *v.* **1** cut off the pinion of (a wing or bird) to prevent flight. **2 a** bind the arms of (a

person). **b** (often foll. by *to*) bind (the arms, a person, etc.) fast to a thing (*pinioned him to the tree*). [Latin *pinna*]

**pinion**[2] /pin-yuhn/ *n.* **1** small cog-wheel engaging with a larger one. **2** cogged spindle engaging with a wheel. [Latin *pinea* pine-cone: related to PINE[1]]

**pink**[1] — *n.* **1** pale red colour. **2** cultivated plant of the genus *Dianthus* (related to the carnation) with fragrant flowers. **3** (prec. by *the*) the most perfect condition, the peak (*the pink of health*). **4** person with mildly socialist tendencies (*the closet pinks in the Liberal Party*). — *adj.* **1** of a pale red colour. **2** tending to mild socialism. □ **in the pink** *colloq.* in very good health. □ **pinkish** *adj.* **pinkness** *n.* **pinky** *adj.* [origin unknown]

**pink**[2] *v.* **1** pierce slightly (with a sword etc.) (*pinked him with the scissors*). **2** cut a scalloped or zigzag edge on. **3** (often foll. by *out*) ornament (leather etc.) with perforations. **4** *Shearing* shear a sheep so closely that the skin shows. [perhaps from Low German or Dutch]

**pink bells** *n.* = PINK-EYE[2].

**pink cockatoo** *n.* = MAJOR MITCHELL COCKATOO.

**pink-eared duck** *n.* (also **zebra duck, widgeon**) nomadic duck of various parts of Australia, having a pink patch behind the eye, white underparts with brown bars, and a shovel-shaped bill.

**pink elephants** *n. pl. colloq.* hallucination, purportedly caused by alcoholism.

**pink-eye**[1] *n.* **1** contagious fever in horses. **2** contagious ophthalmia in humans and some livestock.

**pink-eye**[2] *n.* (also **pink bells**) any of many small shrubs (tetrathecas) of southern Australia, having bell-like, purplish-pink to red flowers with a dark centre or eye.

**pink-eye**[3] *n.* (also **pink-hi**) **1** = WALKABOUT 2. **2** (in extended use) a holiday; a festivity (*the picnic races promise to be a good pink-eye*). [Yindjibarndi, possibly *binggayi* holiday or *binigayi* go]

**pink-eye**[4] *n. colloq.* **1** = PINKY 2. **2** a drinking bout.

**pink fingers** *n.* Australian terrestrial orchid, a caladenia, having often musk-scented pale to deep pink flowers with four segments pointing downwards like fingers.

**pinkie** var. of PINKY.

**pinking shears** *n.pl.* dressmaker's serrated shears for cutting a zigzag edge.

**pinko** /ping-koh/ *adj. colloq.* drunk.

**pinky** *n.* (also **pinkie**) **1** = BILBY. **2** *colloq.* cheap or home-made (fortified) wine.

[sense 1 from Gaurna *binggu*; sense 2: origin unknown]

**pinnace** /pin-uhs/ *n.* ship's small boat. [French]

**pinnacle** /pin-uh-kuhl/ *n.* **1** culmination or climax (of endeavour, success, etc.). **2** natural peak. **3** small ornamental turret crowning a buttress, roof, etc. [Latin *pinna* PIN]

**pinnate** /pin-ayt/ *adj.* (of a compound leaf) having leaflets on either side of the leaf-stalk. [Latin *pinnatus* feathered: related to PINNACLE]

**pinpoint** — *n.* **1** point of a pin. **2** something very small or sharp. **3** (*attrib.*) precise, accurate. — *v.* locate with precision (*pinpointed the target*).

**pinprick** *n.* **1** tiny puncture made with or as with a pin. **2** a trifling irritation.

**pins and needles** *n.pl.* tingling sensation in a limb recovering from numbness.

**pint** /puynt/ *n.* (in the imperial system) measure of capacity for liquids etc., ⅛ gal. (0.568 litre). [French]

**pint-sized** *adj. colloq.* very small.

**Pintupi** /pin-tu-pee/ *n.* dialect of the Aboriginal language called the Western Desert language, spoken over about one and a quarter million square kilometres of arid country, mostly in WA.

**pin-up** *n.* **1** photograph of a popular or sexually attractive person, hung on the wall. **2** person in such a photograph.

**pion** /puy-uhn/ *n.* (also **pi meson**) subatomic particle having a mass many times greater than that of an electron. [from PI]

**pioneer** /puy-uh-neer/ — *n.* **1** initiator of a new enterprise; investigator of a subject etc. (*pioneer in AIDS research*). **2** (also *attrib.*) explorer or settler; colonist; esp. one of the first or early settlers in an Australian district (*pioneer settlers*; *pioneers in the Buninyong settlement*; *pioneer bushman*). — *v.* **1** initiate (an enterprise etc.) for others to follow. **2** act or prepare the way as a pioneer. **3** go before, lead (another or others). [French *pionnier*: related to PAWN¹]

**piosphere** /puy-uh-sfeer/ *n.* (also *attrib.*) an ecological system defined as the area around a watering point, in an arid zone, in which the grazing animals interact (*piosphere effect*). [Greek *pinein* to drink, combining *-o-*, SPHERE]

**pious** /puy-uhs/ *adj.* **1** devout; religious. **2** hypocritically virtuous; sanctimonious. **3** dutiful. □ **piously** *adv.* **piousness** *n.* [Latin]

**pip¹** — *n.* seed of an apple, pear, orange, grape, etc. — *v.* (**-pp-**) remove the pips from (fruit etc.). □ **pipless** *adj.* [abbreviation of PIPPIN]

**pip²** *n.* short high-pitched sound, usu. electronically produced, esp. as a time signal. [imitative]

**pip³** *v.* (**-pp-**) *colloq.* (also **pip at the post**) defeat narrowly or at the last moment. [origin unknown]

**pip⁴** *n.* **1** any of the spots on a playing-card, dice, or domino. **2** star (1–3 according to rank) on the shoulder of an army officer's uniform. **3** diamond-shaped segment on the surface of a pineapple. [origin unknown]

**pip⁵** *n.* **1** disease of poultry etc. **2** *colloq.* fit of disgust or bad temper. □ **give a person the pip** *colloq.* irritate; thoroughly annoy him or her. [Low German or Dutch]

**pipe** — *n.* **1** tube of metal, plastic, etc., used to convey water, gas, etc. **2** narrow tube with a bowl at one end containing tobacco for smoking. **3** *Mus.* **a** wind instrument of a single tube. **b** any of the tubes by which sound is produced in an organ. **c** (in *pl.*) = bagpipes. **d** set of pipes joined together, e.g. pan-pipes. **4** tubular organ, vessel, etc. in an animal's body. **5** high note or song, esp. of a bird. **6 a** boatswain's whistle. **b** sounding of this. — *v.* (**-ping**) **1 a** convey (oil, water, gas, etc.) by pipes. **b** provide with pipes. **2** play (a tune etc.) on a pipe or pipes. **3** (esp. as **piped** *adj.*) transmit (recorded music etc.) by wire or cable. **4** (usu. foll. by *up*, *on*, *to*, etc.) *Naut.* **a** summon (a crew). **b** signal the arrival of (an officer etc.) on board. **5** utter in a shrill voice. **6 a** decorate or trim (a dress etc.) with piping. **b** arrange (icing, cream, etc.) in decorative lines or twists on a cake etc.; ornament (a cake etc.) with piping. **7** lead or bring (a person etc.) by the sound of a pipe or pipes. □ **pipe down** *colloq.* be quiet or less insistent. **pipe up** begin to play, sing, speak, etc. □ **pipeful** *n.* (*pl.* **-s**). [Latin *pipo* chirp]

**pipeclay** *n.* fine white clay which forms a paste when mixed with water and is used as ritual body-paint by Aborigines.

**pipe dream** *n.* unattainable or fanciful hope or scheme. [originally as experienced when smoking an opium pipe]

**pipeline** *n.* **1** long, usu. underground, pipe for conveying esp. oil. **2** channel supplying goods, information, etc. □ **in the pipeline** being dealt with or prepared; under discussion, on the way.

**piper** *n.* person who plays a pipe, esp. the bagpipes.

**pipette** /pi-pet/ *n. Chem.* slender tube for transferring or measuring small quantities of liquids. [French diminutive: related to PIPE]

**pipi** *n.* (also **ugari**) edible marine bivalve of southern Australian coasts, often used as a bait. [Maori]

**piping** *n.* **1** pipelike fold or cord for edging or decorating clothing, upholstery, etc. **2** ornamental lines of icing, cream, potato, etc., on a cake or other dish. **3** lengths of pipe, system of pipes. **4** act of a person or thing that pipes. □ **piping hot** (of food, water, etc.) very hot.

**piping crow** *n.* = MAGPIE.

**piping shrike** *n.* = MAGPIE, faunal emblem of South Australia.

**pipit** /pip-uht/ *n.* small bird resembling a lark, having brownish plumage streaked with a lighter colour, and found Australia-wide. [imitative]

**pippin** /pip-uhn/ *n.* **1** apple grown from seed. **2** variety of eating apple. [French]

**pipsqueak** *n. colloq.* insignificant or contemptible person or thing. [imitative]

**piquant** /pee-kuhnt/ *adj.* **1** agreeably pungent, sharp, or appetising. **2** pleasantly stimulating to the mind. □ **piquancy** *n.* [French *piquer* prick]

**pique** /peek/ — *v.* (**piques, piqued, piquing**) **1** wound the pride of, irritate. **2** arouse (curiosity, interest, etc.). — *n.* resentment; hurt pride (*in a fit of pique*). [French: related to PIQUANT]

**piracy** /puy-ruh-see/ *n.* (*pl.* **-ies**) **1** robbery of ships at sea. **2** similar practice elsewhere, esp. hijacking. **3** infringement of copyright etc. [related to PIRATE]

**piranha** /puh-rah-nuh/ *n.* voracious S. American freshwater fish. [Portuguese]

**pirate** /puy-ruht/ — *n.* **1 a** seafaring robber attacking ships. **b** ship used by pirates. **2** (often *attrib.*) person who infringes another's copyright or business rights or who broadcasts without official authorisation (*pirate radio station*). — *v.* (**-ting**) **1** appropriate or reproduce (the work or ideas etc. of another) without permission, or trade (goods) without permission. **2** plunder. □ **piratical** /-rat-i-kuhl/ *adj.* [Latin *pirata* from Greek]

**pirouette** /ˌpi-roo-et/ — *n.* dancer's spin on one foot or the point of the toe. — *v.* (**-tting**) perform a pirouette. [French, = spinning-top]

**pirri** /pi-ree/ *n.* (also **pirrie**) Aboriginal leaf-shaped engraving tool made of stone or quartz. [Arabana *birri* fingernail, extended to anything pointed]

**piscatorial** /ˌpis-kuh-taw-ree-uhl/ *adj.* of fishermen or fishing. □ **piscatorially** *adv.* [Latin *piscator* angler, from *piscis* fish]

**Pisces** /puy-seez/ *n.* (*pl.* same) **1** constellation and twelfth sign of the zodiac (the Fish or Fishes). **2** person born when the sun is in this sign. [Latin, pl. of *piscis* fish]

**piscina** /puh-see-nuh, -suy-nuh/ *n.* (*pl.* **-nae** /-nee/ or **-s**) **1** stone basin near the altar in a church for draining water used in rinsing the chalice etc. in the Mass. **2** fish-pond. [Latin, from *piscis* fish]

**piscine** /pis-een/ *adj.* of or concerning fish.

**pisonia** /puh-zoh-nee-uh/ *n.* either of two trees occurring in Australia, esp. the 'birdlime tree' of rainforests in Queensland and NSW, having shiny leaves and very sticky fruits, cultivated as an indoor plant and used for bonsai. [Willem *Piso*, 17th-c. Dutch physician]

**piss** *colloq.* — *v.* **1** urinate. **2** wet with urine (*pissed the bed*). **3** (as **pissed** *adj.*) drunk. — *adv.* (as an intensifier) extremely (*piss-awful; piss-weak*). — *n.* **1** urine. **2** act of urinating. **3** alcoholic drink, esp. beer. □ **piss off 1** go away. **2** (often as **pissed off** *adj.*) annoy; depress. **take the piss out of a person 1** ridicule. **2** humble, puncture the pretensions of. [French, imitative]

**pissant** /pis-ant/ *n. colloq.* □ **game as a pissant** brave; foolhardy. [British dial. *piss-ant* worthless individual]

**pisspot** *n. colloq.* drunkard; alcoholic.

**piss-up** *n. colloq.* beer-drinking spree.

**pistachio** /puhs-tah-shee-oh/ *n.* (*pl.* **-s**) **1** edible pale green nut. **2** tree yielding this. [Persian *pistah*]

**piste** /peest/ *n.* ski-run of compacted snow. [French, = racetrack]

**pistil** /pis-tuhl/ *n.* female organs of a flower, comprising the stigma, style, and ovary. □ **pistillate** *adj.* [Latin: related to PESTLE]

**pistol** /pis-tuhl/ *n.* small handgun. [Czech *pišt'al*]

**piston** /pis-tuhn/ *n.* **1** sliding cylinder fitting closely in a tube in which it moves up and down, used in an internal-combustion engine to impart motion, or in a pump to receive motion. **2** sliding valve in a trumpet etc. [Italian: related to PESTLE]

**pit¹** — *n.* **1 a** deep hole in the ground, usu. large. **b** hole made in digging for industrial purposes (*gravel pit*). **c** coalmine. **d** covered hole as a trap for animals. **2 a** an indentation of the skin left after acne etc. **b** a hollow in a plant or animal body or on any surface (*pit of the stomach; armpit*). **3 a** = *orchestra pit* (see ORCHESTRA 2). **b** usu. *hist.* seating at the back of the stalls. **4** (**the pits**) *colloq.* worst imaginable place, situation, person, etc. **5 a** area at the side of a track where racing cars are serviced and refuelled. **b**

sunken area in a workshop floor for access to a car's underside. — v. (**-tt-**) **1** (usu. foll. by *against*) set (one's wits, strength, etc.) in competition (*pitted her strength against mine*). **2** (usu. as **pitted** *adj.*) make pits, scars, craters, etc. in (*face pitted by acne*). **3** put into a pit. [Old English from Latin *puteus* well]

**pit²** — n. stone of a fruit, as of a cherry etc. — v. (**-tt-**) (usu. as **pitted** *adj.*) remove stones (from fruit). [origin uncertain]

**pita** var. of PITTA².

**pit-a-pat** /pit-uh-ˌpat/ (also **pitter-patter**) — *adv.* **1** with a sound like quick light steps. **2** falteringly (*heart went pit-a-pat*). — n. such a sound. [imitative]

**pit bull terrier** n. small American dog noted for ferocity.

**pitch¹** — v. **1** erect and fix (a tent, camp, etc.). **2** throw. **3** fix in a definite position. **4** express in a particular style or at a particular level (*pitched his argument at the most basic level*). **5** (often foll. by *against*, *into*, etc.) fall heavily, esp. headlong. **6** (of a ship etc.) plunge backwards and forwards in a lengthwise direction (cf. ROLL *v.* 7). **7** *Mus.* set at a particular pitch. **8** *Cricket* **a** cause (a bowled ball) to strike the ground at a specified point etc. **b** (of a ball) strike the ground thus. **9** tell (a tale etc.) (*pitched some yarn about. . .*). — n. **1 a** area of play in a field-game. **b** *Cricket* area between the creases. **2** height, degree, intensity, etc. (*excitement had reached such a pitch*). **3** degree of slope, esp. of a roof. **4** *Mus.* quality of a sound governed by the rate of vibrations producing it; highness or lowness of a note. **5** act of throwing. **6** pitching motion of a ship etc. **7** *colloq.* salesman's persuasive talk; spiel. **8** distance between successive points, lines, etc. (e.g. character spacing on a typewriter). □ **pitch in** *colloq.* **1** set to (eat, work, etc.) vigorously. **2** contribute (money etc.) for a cause (*pitched in to help the bushfire victims*). **3** join in, participate. **pitch into** *colloq.* **1** attack forcibly. **2** assail (food, work, etc.) vigorously. [origin uncertain]

**pitch²** — n. **1** dark resinous substance from the distillation of tar or turpentine, used for making ships watertight etc. **2** any of various bituminous substances including asphalt. — v. coat with pitch. □ **pitchy** *adj.* (**-ier, -iest**). [Latin *pix picis*]

**pitch-black** *adj.* (also **pitch-dark**) very or completely dark.

**pitchblende** /pich-blend/ n. uranium oxide occurring in pitchlike masses and yielding radium. [German: related to PITCH²]

**pitched battle** n. **1** vigorous argument etc. **2** planned battle between sides in prepared positions and on chosen ground.

**pitched roof** n. sloping roof.

**pitcher¹** n. large jug with a lip and a handle. [related to BEAKER]

**pitcher²** n. player who delivers the ball in baseball.

**pitcher plant** n. **1** any of several usu. insectivorous plants having leaves modified as pitchers in which to trap insects. **2** (also **Albany pitcher plant**) WA insectivorous perennial herb with light green leaves, large pitchers, and green flowers; now on the endangered species list.

**pitchfork** — n. long-handled two-pronged fork for pitching hay etc. — v. **1** throw with or as if with a pitchfork. **2** (usu. foll. by *into*) thrust (a person) forcibly into a position, office, etc.

**pitchi** /pich-ee/ n. = COOLAMON. [Western Desert language (and neighbouring languages) *bidi*]

**piteous** /pit-ee-uhs/ *adj.* deserving or arousing pity; wretched. □ **piteously** *adv.* **piteousness** n. [Romanic: related to PITY]

**pitfall** n. **1** unsuspected danger or drawback. **2** covered pit for trapping animals.

**pith** n. **1** spongy white tissue lining the rind of an orange etc. **2** essential part (*the pith of her argument*). **3** spongy tissue in the stems and branches of plants. **4** strength; vigour; energy. [Old English]

**pithead** n. **1** top of a mineshaft. **2** area surrounding this.

**pith helmet** n. protective sun-helmet made of dried pith from plants.

**pithy** /pith-ee/ *adj.* (**-ier, -iest**) **1** (of style, speech, etc.) terse and forcible. **2** of, like, or containing much pith. □ **pithily** *adv.* **pithiness** n.

**pitiable** /pit-ee-uh-buhl/ *adj.* deserving or arousing pity or contempt. □ **pitiably** *adv.* [French: related to PITY]

**pitiful** /pit-uh-ˌfuhl/ *adj.* **1** causing pity. **2** contemptible (*pitiful attempt at an excuse*). □ **pitifully** *adv.*

**pitiless** /pit-ee-luhs/ *adj.* showing no pity (*pitiless heat*). □ **pitilessly** *adv.*

**Pitjantjatjara** /pich-uhn-ˌja-ru, pich-uhn-ju-ˌja-ru/ — n. **1** a member of an Aboriginal people of northern SA; this people. **2** the language of this people, a dialect of the Western Desert language. — *adj.* of this people or their language.

**piton** /pee-ton/ n. peg driven into rock or a crack to support a climber or rope. [French]

**pitta¹** /pit-uh/ n. any of various passerine birds of Australia, India, etc., often with vivid colouring. [Telugu *pitta* anything small, a pet]

**pitta²** /pit-uh/ n. (also **pita**) flat hollow unleavened bread which can be split and filled. [modern Greek, = a kind of cake]

**pittance** /pit-uhns/ n. **1** very small allowance, remuneration, etc. (*paid her a pittance*). **2** small number or amount. [Romanic: related to PITY]

**Pitta-pitta** /pit-uh-,pit-uh/ n. Aboriginal language spoken in the Boulia district of central Queensland.

**pitter-patter** var. of PIT-A-PAT.

**pittosporum** /puh-tos-puh-ruhm/ n. large genus of trees and shrubs, nine or so species of which are native to Australia, having usu. cream to yellow fragrant flowers and orange fruit. [Greek *pitta* PITCH², *sporos* seed]

**Pitt Street farmer** n. (also **Collins Street cocky**) usu. *derog.* person whose interests are in the city but who buys rural property, farms, etc., often as a tax write-off. [*Pitt Street, Collins Street* principal business streets in Sydney and Melbourne respectively]

**pituitary** /puh-tyoo-uh-tuh-ree, -tree/ n. (*pl.* **-ies**) (also **pituitary gland**) small ductless gland at the base of the brain secreting hormones essential for growth etc. [Latin *pituita* phlegm]

**pituri** /pich-uh-ree/ n. shrub widespread in arid, sandy, central Australia, the leaves being traditionally chewed by Aborigines for their powerful narcotic effect, as well as being crushed and placed in waterholes to stun food-animals, esp. emus. [Yandruwandha *bijirri*]

**piturine** n. alkaloid extracted from pituri.

**pity** /pit-ee/ — n. **1** sorrow and compassion for another's suffering. **2** cause for regret (*what a pity!*). — v. (**-ies, -ied**) feel (often contemptuous) pity for (*they are to be pitied; I pity you if you think that*). □ **take pity on** help out of pity for. □**pitying** adj. **pityingly** adv. [Latin: related to PIETY]

**pivot** /piv-uht/ — n. **1** shaft or pin on which something turns or oscillates. **2** crucial or essential person, point, etc. — v. (**-t-**) **1** turn on or as on a pivot. **2** provide with a pivot. □ **pivotal** adj. [French]

**pixel** /pik-suhl/ n. any of the minute areas of illumination of which an image on a display screen is composed. [abbreviation of *picture element*]

**pixie** /pik-see/ n. (also **pixy**) (*pl.* **-ies**) fairy-like being. [origin unknown]

**pizazz** /puh-zaz/ n. (also **pizzazz**) *colloq.* verve, energy, liveliness, sparkle.

**pizza** /peet-suh/ n. Italian dish of a layer of dough baked with a topping of tomatoes, cheese, etc. [Italian, = pie]

**pizzeria** /,peet-suh-ree-uh/ n. pizza restaurant.

**pizzicato** /,pit-see-kah-toh/ *Mus.* — *adv.* plucking the strings of a violin etc. with the finger. — *adj.* (of a note, passage, etc.) performed pizzicato. — n. (*pl.* **-s** or **-ti** /-tee/ ) note, passage, etc., played pizzicato. [Italian]

**pizzle** n. penis of an animal, esp. of a bull or ram. [Low German *pesel*]

**pl.** *abbr.* **1** plural. **2** (usu. **Pl.**) place.

**placable** /plak-uh-buhl/ adj. easily placated; mild; forgiving. □ **placability** /-bil-uh-tee/ n. [Latin *placo* appease]

**placard** /plak-ahd/ — n. large notice for public display. — v. **1** set up placards on (a wall etc.). **2** advertise by placards. [French from Dutch *placken* glue (v.)]

**placate** /pluh-kayt/ v. (**-ting**) pacify; conciliate. □ **placatory** /pluh-kay-tuh-ree/ adj. [Latin *placo* appease]

**place** — n. **1 a** particular portion of space. **b** portion of space occupied by a person or thing (*it has changed its place*). **c** proper or natural position (*he is out of his place*). **2** city, town, village, etc. (*was born in this place*). **3** residence, home (*come round to my place*). **4** group of houses in a town etc., esp. a square. **5** rank or status (*they know their place*). **6** space, esp. a seat, for a person (*two places in the coach*). **7** building or area for a specific purpose (*place of work*). **8** point reached in a book etc. (*lost my place*). **9** particular spot on a surface, esp. of the skin (*sore place*). **10 a** employment or office (*lost his place at the Ministry*). **b** duties or entitlements of office etc. (*not my place to criticise*). **11** position as a member of a team, student in a college, etc. **12** any of usu. the first three positions in a race, esp. other than the winner (*backed it for a place*). **13** position of a digit in a series indicated in decimal or similar notation (*calculated to 50 decimal places*). — v. (**-cing**) **1** put in a particular or proper place or state or order; arrange. **2** identify, classify, or remember correctly (*cannot place him*). **3** assign to a particular place, class, or rank; locate. **4** find employment or a living etc. for (*placed him in the public service*). **b** consign to a person's care etc. (*placed him with his aunt*). **5** assign rank, importance, or worth, to (*place him among the best teachers*). **6** make or state (an order or bet etc.). **7** (often foll. by *in, on*, etc.) have (confidence etc.) (*I place my* *trust in you*). **8** state the position of (any of usu. the first three runners) in a race. **9** (as **placed** *adj.*) among usu. the first three in a race. □ **all over the place** in disorder; chaotic. **give place to 1** make room for. **2** yield precedence to. **3** be succeeded by. **go places** *colloq.* be successful. **in place** in the right position; suitable. **in place of** in exchange for; instead of. **in places** at only some places or parts. **out of place 1** in the wrong position. **2** unsuitable. **put a person in his** (or **her**) **place** deflate a person. **take place** occur. **take the place of** be substituted for; replace. □ **placement** *n.* [Latin *platea* broad way]

**placebo** /pluh-see-boh/ *n.* (*pl.* **-s**) **1** medicine prescribed for psychological reasons but having no physiological effects. **2** dummy pill etc. used in a controlled trial. [Latin, = I shall be acceptable]

**placenta** /pluh-sen-tuh/ *n.* (*pl.* **-tae** /-tee/ or **-s**) flattened circular organ in the uterus of pregnant mammals nourishing the foetus through the umbilical cord and expelled after birth. □ **placental** *adj.* [Greek, = flat cake]

**placid** /plas-uhd/ *adj.* **1** calm; not easily excited or irritated. **2** tranquil, serene. □ **placidity** /pluh-sid-uh-tee/ *n.* **placidly** *adv.* **placidness** *n.* [Latin *placeo* please]

**plagiarise** /play-juh-,ruyz/ *v.* (also **-ize**) (**-sing** or **-zing**) **1** (also *absol.*) take and pass off (another's thoughts, writings, etc.) as one's own. **2** pass off the thoughts etc. of (another person) as one's own. □ **plagiarism** *n.* **plagiarist** *n.* **plagiariser** *n.* [Latin *plagiarius* kidnapper]

**plague** /playg/ — *n.* **1** a deadly contagious or infectious disease spreading rapidly over a wide area. **2** (foll. by *of*) an unusual infestation of a pest etc. **3** great trouble or affliction. **4** *colloq.* nuisance. — *v.* (**plagues, plagued, plaguing**) **1** *colloq.* pester, annoy. **2** afflict, hinder (*plagued by back pain*). **3** affect with plague. [Latin *plaga* stroke, infection]

**plaice** /plays/ *n.* (*pl.* same) European marine flat-fish used as food. [Latin *platessa*]

**plaid** /plad/ *n.* (often *attrib.*) chequered or tartan, esp. woollen, twilled cloth (*plaid skirt*). [Gaelic]

**plain** — *adj.* **1** clear, evident. **2** readily understood, simple (*in plain words*). **3** (of food, decoration, etc.) simple. **4** not beautiful or distinguished-looking. **5** outspoken; straightforward. **6** unsophisticated; not luxurious (*a plain man; plain living*). — *adv.* **1** clearly. **2** simply. — *n.* **1 a** level tract of treeless

country. **b** tract of land, often undulating and usu. lightly treed, suitable for use as pasture. **2** basic knitting stitch. □ **plainly** *adv.* **plainness** *n.* [Latin *planus*]

**plainchant** *n.* (also **Gregorian chant**; **plainsong**) unaccompanied liturgical music (for High Mass etc.) chanted in unison in medieval modes and in free rhythm corresponding to the accentuation of the words (usu. in monasteries etc.).

**plain clothes** *n.pl.* ordinary clothes, not uniform (*plain-clothes police*).

**plain dealing** *n.* candour; straightforwardness.

**plain sailing** *n.* uncomplicated situation or course of action free from difficulties etc.

**plainsong** *n.* = PLAINCHANT.

**plain-spoken** *adj.* frank.

**plaint** *n.* **1** *Law* accusation; charge. **2** *literary* complaint, lamentation. [French *plainte* from Latin *plango* lament]

**plaintiff** /playn-tuhf/ *n.* person who brings a case against another into court (opp. DEFENDANT). [French *plaintif*: related to PLAINTIVE]

**plaintive** /playn-tiv/ *adj.* expressing sorrow; mournful-sounding. □ **plaintively** *adv.* [French: related to PLAINT]

**plain turkey** *n.* (also **plains turkey**) **1** large, nomadic, often solitary game bird of mainland Australia. **2** (nickname for a) SWAGGIE.

**plain wanderer** *n.* (also **plains wanderer**) terrestrial bird of south-eastern mainland Australia, having mottled brown plumage with a black and white spotted collar in the female.

**plait** /plat/ — *n.* length of hair, straw, etc., in three or more interlaced strands. — *v.* **1** weave (hair etc.) into a plait. **2** make by interlacing strands (*plaited belt*). [French *pleit* from Latin *plico* fold]

**plan** — *n.* **1 a** method or procedure for doing something; design, scheme (*plan of campaign*). **b** intention (*my plan was to distract them*). **2** drawing etc. of a building or structure, made by projection on to a horizontal plane. **3** map of a town or district. **4** scheme of an arrangement (*seating plan*). — *v.* (**-nn-**) **1** arrange (a procedure etc.) beforehand; form a plan; intend (*planned to catch the last train*). **2** make a plan of or design for. **3** (as **planned** *adj.*) in accordance with a plan (*planned parenthood*). **4** make plans. □ **plan on** (often foll. by *pres. part.*) *colloq.* aim at; intend. □ **planning** *n.* [French]

**plane**¹ — *n.* **1** flat surface such that a straight line joining any two points on it lies wholly in it. **2** level surface. **3** *colloq.*

= AEROPLANE. **4** flat surface producing lift by the action of air or water over and under it (usu. in *comb.*: *hydroplane*). **5** (often foll. by *of*) level of attainment, knowledge, etc. — *adj.* **1** (of a surface etc.) perfectly level. **2** (of an angle, figure, etc.) lying in a plane. — *v.* (**-ning**) glide. [Latin *planus* PLAIN]

**plane²** — *n.* tool for smoothing a usu. wooden surface by paring shavings from it. — *v.* (**-ning**) **1** smooth with a plane. **2** (often foll. by *away*, *down*) pare with a plane. [Latin: related to PLANE¹]

**plane³** *n.* tall tree with maple-like leaves and bark which peels in uneven patches. [Greek *platanos*]

**planet** /**plan**-uht/ *n.* celestial body orbiting round a star; the earth. □ **off this planet** *colloq.* unbelievably wonderful. □ **planetary** *adj.* [Greek, = wanderer]

**planetarium** /ˌplan-uh-**tair**-ree-uhm/ *n.* (*pl.* **-s** or **-ria**) **1** domed building in which images of stars, planets, constellations, etc., are projected. **2** device for such projection.

**plangent** /**plan**-juhnt/ *adj. literary* **1** loud and reverberating. **2** plaintive. [Latin: related to PLAINT]

**plank** — *n.* **1** long flat piece of timber. **2** item in a political or other programme (cf. PLATFORM). — *v.* **1** provide, cover, or floor, with planks. **2** (usu. foll. by *down*). **a** put down or deposit (a thing or person) roughly or violently. **b** pay (money) on the spot (*planked down $5*). □ **walk the plank** *hist.* be made to walk blindfold along a plank over the side of a ship to one's death in the sea. [Latin *planca*]

**planking** *n.* planks as flooring etc.

**plankton** /**plangk**-tuhn/ *n.* chiefly microscopic organisms drifting in the sea or fresh water. [Greek, = wandering]

**planner** *n.* **1** person who plans new towns etc. **2** person who makes plans. **3** list, table, etc., with information helpful in planning.

**planning permission** *n.* formal permission for building etc., esp. from a local council.

**plant** /plahnt, plant/ — *n.* **1 a** organism usu. containing chlorophyll enabling it to live wholly on inorganic substances, and lacking the power of voluntary movement. **b** small organism of this kind, as distinguished from a shrub or tree. **2 a** machinery, fixtures, etc., used in industry. **b** factory. **3** the working animals, equipment, vehicles, personnel, employed by a drover, stockman, etc., on the move. **4** *colloq.* someone or something deliberately placed so as to incriminate another. — *v.* **1** place (seeds, plants, etc.)

in soil for growing. **2** (often foll. by *in*, *on*, etc.) put or fix in position. **3 a** *refl.* conceal oneself. **b** station (a person etc.), esp. as a spy. **4** *refl.* take up a position (*planted myself by the entrance*). **5** cause (an idea etc.) to be established, esp. in another person's mind (*planted a doubt in his mind*). **6** deliver (a blow, kiss, etc.) with a deliberate aim. **7 a** hide (articles, cattle, etc.) esp. if stolen. **b** *colloq.* place (something incriminating) for later discovery. □ **plant one's foot** (also **plant it**) *colloq.* accelerate (a car) quickly. **plant out** transfer from a pot or frame to the open ground; set out (seedlings) at intervals. □ **plantlike** *adj.* [Latin *planta*]

**plantain** /**plahn**-tuhn, **plan**-tuhn/ *n.* **1** variety of banana plant. **2** starchy fruit of this containing less sugar than the dessert varieties and chiefly used in cooking. [Spanish]

**plantation** /plan-**tay**-shuhn, plahn-/ *n.* **1** estate on which cotton, tobacco, etc., is cultivated. **2** area planted with trees etc. [Latin: related to PLANT]

**planter** *n.* **1** manager or owner of a plantation. **2** machine for planting seeds etc **3** container for house-plants.

**plaque** /plahk, plak/ *n.* **1** commemorative tablet, esp. fixed to a building. **2** deposit on teeth where bacteria proliferate. [Dutch *plak* tablet: related to PLACARD]

**plash** — *n.* **1** a splash; a plunge. **2** puddle. — *v.* **1** splash. **2** strike the surface of (water). □ **plashy** *adj.* [Old English]

**plasma** /**plaz**-muh/ *n.* (also **plasm** /**plaz**-uhm/ ) **1 a** colourless fluid part of blood, lymph, or milk, in which corpuscles or fat-globules are suspended. **b** this taken from blood for transfusions. **2** = PROTOPLASM. **3** gas of positive ions and free electrons in about equal numbers. □ **plasmatic** /-**mat**-ik/ *adj.* **plasmic** *adj.* [Greek *plassō* shape (v.)]

**plaster** /**plah**-stuh/ — *n.* **1** soft mixture of lime, sand, and water etc., applied to walls, ceilings, etc., to dry into a smooth hard surface. **2** = STICKING-PLASTER. **3** = PLASTER OF PARIS. — *v.* **1** cover (a wall etc.) with plaster. **2** coat, daub, cover thickly (*plastered the bread with vegemite*; *plastered the wall with posters*). **3** stick or apply (a thing) thickly like plaster (*plastered glue all over it*). **4** (often foll. by *down*) smooth (esp. hair) with water etc. **5** (as **plastered** *adj.*) *colloq.* drunk. **6** apply a medical plaster or a plaster cast to. **7** *colloq.* **a** hit repeatedly, thrash. **b** bomb or shell heavily. □ **plasterer** *n.* [Greek *emplastron*]

**plasterboard** n. two boards with a filling of plaster for partitions, walls, etc.

**plaster cast** n. **1** bandage stiffened with plaster of Paris and applied to a broken limb etc. **2** statue or mould made of plaster.

**plaster of Paris** n. fine white gypsum plaster for plaster casts etc.

**plastic** /**plas**-tik/ — n. **1** synthetic resinous substance that can be given any shape. **2** (in full **plastic money**) *colloq.* credit card(s). — *adj.* **1** made of plastic. **2** capable of being moulded; pliant, supple (*a plastic mind*). **3** (of people) artificial in manner, false, etc. (*the socialite set, full of plastic people*). **4** giving form to clay, wax, etc. □ **plasticise** /-ˌsuyz/ v. (also **-ize**) (**-sing** or **-zing**). **plasticiser** /-ˌsuy-zuh/ n. (also **-izer**). **plasticity** /-tis-uh-tee/ n. **plasticky** adj. [Greek: related to PLASMA]

**plastic arts** n.pl. arts involving modelling or the representation of solid objects.

**plasticine** /**plas**-tuh-ˌseen/ n. propr. pliant material used for modelling.

**plastic surgery** n. reconstruction or repair of damaged or unsightly skin, muscle, etc., esp. by the transfer of tissue. □ **plastic surgeon** n.

**plate** — n. **1 a** shallow usu. circular vessel from which food is eaten or served. **b** contents of this (*ate a plate of sandwiches*). **2** similar vessel used for a collection in church etc. **3** contribution of cakes, sandwiches, etc., brought by invitees to a party, social gathering, etc. **4** (*collect.*) **a** utensils of silver, gold, or other metal. **b** objects of plated metal. **5** piece of metal with a name or inscription for affixing to a door etc. **6** illustration on special paper in a book. **7** thin sheet of metal, glass, etc., coated with a sensitive film for photography. **8** flat thin usu. rigid sheet of metal etc., often as part of a mechanism. **9 a** smooth piece of metal etc. for engraving. **b** impression from this. **10 a** silver or gold cup as a prize for a horse race etc. **b** race with this as a prize. **11 a** thin piece of plastic material, moulded to the shape of the mouth, on which artificial teeth or an orthodontic appliance are mounted. **b** *colloq.* denture or orthodontic appliance. **12** each of several rigid sheets of rock thought to form the earth's outer crust. **13** thin flat organic structure or formation. — v. (**-ting**) **1** apply a thin coat esp. of silver, gold, or tin, to (another metal). **2** cover (esp. a ship) with plates of metal, for protection. □ **on a plate** *colloq.* available with little trouble to the recipient. **on one's plate** *colloq.* for one to deal with.

□ **plateful** n. (pl. **-s**). [Latin *platta* from *plattus* flat]

**plateau** /**plat**-oh/ — n. (pl. **-x** or **-s** /-ohz/) **1** area of fairly level high ground. **2** state of little variation after an increase. — v. (**plateauing**, **plateaus**, **plateaued**) (often foll. by *out*) reach a level or static state after an increase. [French: related to PLATE]

**plate glass** n. thick fine-quality glass for shop windows etc.

**platelet** /**playt**-luht/ n. small colourless disc of protoplasm found in blood and involved in clotting.

**platen** /**plat**-uhn/ n. **1** plate in a printing-press which presses the paper against the type. **2** cylindrical roller in a typewriter etc. against which the paper is held. [French *platine*: related to PLATE]

**plate tectonics** n.pl. (usu. treated as *sing.*) the study of the earth's surface based on the concept of moving 'plates' (see PLATE 12) forming its structure.

**platform** /**plat**-fawm/ n. **1** raised level surface, esp. one from which a speaker addresses an audience or one alongside the line at a railway station. **2** floor area at the entrance to a bus etc. **3** thick sole of a shoe. **4** declared policy of a political party. [French: related to PLATE, FORM]

**platinum** /**plat**-uh-nuhm/ n. *Chem.* white heavy precious metallic element that does not tarnish. [earlier *platina* from Spanish, diminutive from *plata* silver]

**platinum blonde** (also **platinum blond**) — *adj.* silvery-blond. — n. person with such hair.

**platitude** /**plat**-uh-ˌtyood/ n. trite or commonplace remark, esp. one solemnly delivered. □ **platitudinise** /-tyood-in-ˌnuyz/ v. (also **-ize**) **platitudinous** /-tyood-uh-nuhs/ adj. [French: related to PLATE]

**Platonic** /pluh-**ton**-ik/ adj. **1** of Plato or his ideas. **2** (**platonic**) (of love or friendship) not sexual. [Greek *Platōn* (5th–4th c. BC), name of a Greek philosopher]

**platoon** /pluh-**toon**/ n. **1** subdivision of a military company. **2** group of persons acting together. [French *peloton* diminutive of *pelote* PELLET]

**platter** n. large flat dish or plate, esp. for serving food. □ **on a platter** = *on a plate* (see PLATE). [Anglo-French *plater*: related to PLATE]

**platylobium** /ˌplat-uh-**loh**-bee-uhm/ n. any of four eastern Australian shrubs bearing a profusion of bi-coloured (yellow and red) pea-flowers. [Greek, = broad pod]

**platypus** /plat-uh-puus/ *n.* (also **duck-billed platypus**) (*pl.* **-puses**) amphibious, burrowing, egg-laying mammal of freshwater lakes and watercourses of eastern Australia, having thick brown fur, a ducklike bill with leathery skin, webbed feet, and a broad, flat tail: in summer the male carries venom in a hollow spur on each hind leg. [Greek, = flat foot]

■ **Usage** The plural of *platypus* is *platypuses* and not *platypi*. The *-pus* element is from Greek *pous* 'foot', the plural of which is *podes* (cf. ANTIPODES). In scientific and conservationist contexts the word sometimes appears with zero inflection in the plural: *there are six platypus in this section of the river.*

**platypus frog** *n.* = GASTRIC BROODING FROG.

**plaudit** /plaw-duht/ *n.* (usu. in *pl.*) **1** round of applause. **2** expression of approval. [Latin *plaudite*, imperative of *plaudo plaus-* clap]

**plausible** /plaw-zuh-buhl/ *adj.* **1** (of an argument, statement, etc.) reasonable or probable. **2** (of a person) persuasive but deceptive. □ **plausibility** /-bil-uh-tee/ *n.* **plausibly** *adv.* [Latin: related to PLAUDIT]

**play** — *v.* **1** (often foll. by *with*) occupy or amuse oneself pleasantly. **2** (foll. by *with*) act light-heartedly or flippantly with (a person's feelings etc.). **3 a** perform on or be able to perform on (a musical instrument). **b** perform (a piece of music etc.). **c** cause (a record, record-player, etc.) to produce sounds. **4 a** (foll. by *in*) perform a role in (a drama etc.). **b** perform (a drama or role) on stage etc. **c** give a dramatic performance at (a particular theatre or place). **5** act in real life the part of (*play truant*; *play the fool*). **6** (foll. by *on*) perform (a trick or joke etc.) on (a person). **7** gamble, gamble on. **8 a** take part in (a game or recreation). **b** compete with (another player or team) in a game. **c** occupy (a specified position) in a team for a game. **d** (foll. by *in, on, at,* etc.) assign (a player) to a position. **9** move (a piece) or display (a playing-card) in one's turn in a game. **10** (also *absol.*) strike (a ball etc.) or execute (a stroke) in a game. **11** move about in a lively manner; flit, dart. **12** (often foll. by *on*) **a** touch gently. **b** emit light, water, etc. (*fountains gently playing*; *played the hose on the burning shed*). **13** allow (a fish) to exhaust itself pulling against a line. **14** (often foll. by *at*) **a** engage half-heartedly (in an activity). **b** pretend to be. **15** act as specified (*play fair*). — *n.* **1** recreation, amusement, esp. as the spontaneous activity of children. **2 a** playing of a game. **b** action or manner of

this. **3** dramatic piece for the stage etc. **4** activity or operation (*the play of fancy*). **5 a** freedom of movement. **b** space or scope for this. **6** brisk, light, or fitful movement. **7** gambling. □ **in play** in jest, not seriously. **in** (or **out of**) **play** *Sport* (of the ball etc.) in (or not in) a position to be played according to the rules. **make a play for** *colloq.* make a conspicuous attempt to acquire. **make play with** use ostentatiously. **play about** (or **around**) behave irresponsibly. **play along** pretend to cooperate. **play around** (esp. of a married person) flirt; make love promiscuously; be unfaithful. **play back** play (sounds recently recorded). **play ball** *colloq.* cooperate. **play by ear 1** perform (music) without having seen it written down. **2** (also **play it by ear**) *colloq.* proceed step by step according to results. **play one's cards right** (or **well**) *colloq.* make good use of opportunities; act shrewdly. **play down** minimise the importance of. **played out** exhausted of energy or usefulness. **play fast and loose** act unreliably; ignore one's obligations. **play the field** see FIELD. **play for time** seek to gain time by delaying. **play the game 1** abide by a given set of rules etc. (*if you don't play the game the boss's way, you'll be sacked*). **2** behave honourably, justly. **play havoc** (or **hell**) *colloq.* cause great confusion or difficulty to; disrupt. **play into a person's hands** act so as unwittingly to give a person an advantage. **play it cool** *colloq.* be relaxed or apparently indifferent. **play the market** speculate in stocks etc. **play off** (usu. foll. by *against*) **1** oppose (one person against another), esp. for one's own advantage. **2** play an extra match to decide a draw or tie. **play on 1** continue to play. **2** take advantage of (a person's feelings etc.). **play safe** (or **for safety**) avoid risks. **play up 1** behave mischievously. **2** annoy in this way. **3** cause trouble; be irritating (*my piles are playing up again*). **play up to** flatter, esp. to win favour. **play with fire** take foolish risks. [Old English]

**play-act** *v.* **1** act in a play. **2** pretend; behave insincerely. □ **play-acting** *n.*

**play-back** *n.* playing back of a sound recording or a video recording.

**playboy** *n.* wealthy pleasure-seeking man.

**player** *n.* **1** participant in a game. **2** person playing a musical instrument. **3** actor.

**playful** *adj.* **1** fond of or inclined to play. **2** done in fun. □ **playfully** *adv.* **playfulness** *n.*

**playing card** *n.* one of a set of usu. 52 oblong cards, divided into four suits and used in games.

**playlet** n. short play.

**play-lunch** n. (also **little lunch**) **1** snack taken by children to school to eat during the pre-lunch mid-morning break. **2** the break itself.

**play-off** n. match played to decide a draw or tie.

**play on** v. Aust. Rules keep the ball in play without stopping to take a kick after a mark or penalty.

**play on words** n. pun.

**plaything** n. **1** toy or other thing to play with. **2** person used merely as an object of amusement or pleasure.

**playwright** n. person who writes plays.

**plaza** /**plah**-zuh/ n. open square in a city or town.

**plea** n. **1** appeal, entreaty. **2** Law formal statement by or on behalf of a defendant. **3** excuse. [Latin placitum decree: related to PLEASE]

**plea-bargaining** n. esp. US practice whereby a defendant pleads guilty to a reduced charge in exchange for the prosecution's cooperation in securing a more lenient sentence or an agreement to drop other charges. □ **plea-bargain** v.

**plead** v. **1** (foll. by with) make an earnest appeal to. **2** (of an advocate) address a lawcourt. **3** maintain (a cause) in a lawcourt. **4** (foll. by guilty or not guilty) declare oneself to be guilty or not guilty of a charge. **5** allege as an excuse (pleaded forgetfulness). **6** (often as **pleading** adj.) make an appeal or entreaty (in a pleading voice). [Anglo-French pleder: related to PLEA]

**pleasant** /**plez**-uhnt/ adj. (**-er**, **-est**) pleasing to the mind, feelings, or senses. □ **pleasantly** adv. [French: related to PLEASE]

**pleasantry** n. (pl. **-ies**) **1** amusing or polite remark. **2** humorous manner of speech. **3** jocularity.

**please** /pleez/ v. (**-sing**) **1** be agreeable to; make glad; give pleasure. **2** (in passive) **a** (foll. by to + infin.) be glad or willing to (am pleased to help). **b** (often foll. by about, at, with) derive pleasure or satisfaction (from). **3** (with it as subject) be the inclination or wish of (it did not please him to attend). **4** think fit (take as many as you please). **5** (short for may it please you) used in polite requests (come in, please). □ **if you please** if you are willing, esp. iron. (then, if you please, we had to pay). **please oneself** do as one likes. □ **pleased** adj. **pleasing** adj. [French plaisir from Latin placeo]

**pleasurable** /**plezh**-uh-ruh-buhl/ adj. causing pleasure. □ **pleasurably** adv.

**pleasure** /**plezh**-uh/ — n. **1** feeling of satisfaction or joy. **2** enjoyment. **3** source of pleasure or gratification. **4** one's will or desire (what is your pleasure?). **5** sensual gratification (a life of pleasure). **6** (attrib.) done or used for pleasure. — v. give pleasure to. [French: related to PLEASE]

**pleat** — n. fold or crease, esp. a flattened fold in cloth doubled upon itself. — v. make a pleat or pleats in. [from PLAIT]

**pleb** n. colloq. usu. derog. = PLEBEIAN n. 2. [abbreviation of PLEBEIAN]

**plebeian** /pluh-**bee**-uhn/ — n. **1** commoner, esp. in ancient Rome. **2** working-class person, esp. an uncultured one. — adj. **1** of the common people. **2** uncultured, coarse. [Latin plebs plebis common people]

**plebiscite** /**pleb**-uh-suht, -,suyt/ n. referendum. [Latin plebiscitum: related to PLEBEIAN]

**plectranthus** /,plek-**tran**-thuhs/ n. vigorous Australian ground-cover with strongly aromatic velvety grey leaves and blue flowers in spikes. [Greek, = spur flower]

**plectrum** /**plek**-truhm/ n. (pl. **-s** or **-tra**) **1** thin flat piece of plastic etc. for plucking the strings of a guitar etc. **2** corresponding mechanical part of a harpsichord etc. [Greek plēssō strike]

**pledge** — n. **1** solemn promise. **2** thing given as security against a debt etc. **3** thing put in pawn. **4** thing given as a token of love, favour, etc., or of something to come. **5** drinking of a person's health, toast. **6** vow of temperance. — v. (**-ging**) **1 a** deposit as security. **b** pawn. **2** promise solemnly by the pledge of (one's honour, word, etc.). **3** bind by a solemn promise. **4** drink to the health of. □ **pledge one's troth** see TROTH. [French plege]

**Pleistocene** /**play**-stuh-,seen/ Geol. — adj. of the first epoch of the Quaternary period. — n. this epoch. [Greek pleistos most, kainos new]

**plenary** /**plee**-nuh-ree/ adj. **1** (of an assembly) to be attended by all members. **2** entire, unqualified (a plenary indulgence). [Latin plenus full]

**plenipotentiary** /,plen-uh-puh-**ten**-shuh-ree/ — n. (pl. **-ies**) person (esp. a diplomat) invested with full authority to act. — adj. having this power. [Latin: related to PLENARY, POTENT]

**plenitude** /**plen**-uh-,tyood/ n. literary **1** fullness, completeness. **2** abundance. [Latin: related to PLENARY]

**plenteous** /**plen**-tee-uhs/ adj. literary plentiful. [French plentivous: related to PLENTY]

**plentiful** /**plen**-tuh-ˌfuhl/ *adj.* abundant, copious. □ **plentifully** *adv.*

**plenty** /**plen**-tee/ *n.* (often foll. by *of*) abundance, sufficient quantity or number (*we have plenty*; *plenty of time*; *a time of plenty*). [Latin *plenitas*: related to PLENARY]

**plenum** /**plee**-nuhm/ *n.* full assembly of people or a committee etc. [Latin, neuter of *plenus* full]

**pleonasm** /**plee**-uh-ˌnaz-uhm/ *n.* use of more words than are needed (e.g. *see with one's eyes*). □ **pleonastic** /-**nas**-tik/ *adj.* **pleonastically** *adv.* [Greek *pleonazō* be superfluous]

**plethora** /**pleth**-uh-ruh/ *n.* over-abundance. [Greek, = fullness]

**pleura** /**ploo**-ruh/ *n.* (*pl.* **-rae** /-ree/) membrane enveloping the lungs. □ **pleural** *adj.* [Greek *pleura* rib]

**pleurisy** /**ploo**-ruh-see/ *n.* inflammation of the pleura. □ **pleuritic** /-**rit**-ik/ *adj.* [Greek: related to PLEURA]

**plexus** /**plek**-suhs/ *n.* (*pl.* same or **plexuses**) *Anat.* network of nerves or vessels (*solar plexus*). [Latin *plecto plex-* plait]

**pliable** /**pluy**-uh-buhl/ *adj.* **1** bending easily; supple. **2** yielding, compliant. □ **pliability** /-**bil**-uh-tee/ *n.* [French: related to PLY[1]]

**pliant** /**pluy**-uhnt/ *adj.* = PLIABLE 1. □ **pliancy** *n.*

**pliers** /**pluy**-uhz/ *n.pl.* pincers with parallel flat surfaces for holding small objects, bending wire, etc. [from British dial. *ply* bend: related to PLIABLE]

**plight[1]** /pluyt/ *n.* unfortunate condition or state. [Anglo-French *plit* PLAIT]

**plight[2]** /pluyt/ *v. archaic* **1** pledge. **2** (foll. by *to*) engage (oneself) in marriage. □ **plight one's troth** see TROTH. [Old English]

**Plimsoll line** /**plim**-suhl/ *n.* (also **Plimsoll mark**) marking on a ship's side showing the limit of legal submersion under various conditions. [*Plimsoll*, name of a politician]

**plinth** *n.* **1** lower square slab at the base of a column. **2** base supporting a vase or statue etc. [Greek, = tile]

**Pliocene** /**pluy**-uh-ˌseen/ *Geol.* — *adj.* of the last epoch of the Tertiary period. — *n.* this epoch. [Greek *pleiōn* more, *kainos* new]

**plod** — *v.* (**-dd-**) **1** walk doggedly or laboriously; trudge. — *n.* **1** spell of plodding. **2** work-sheet recording details of an employee's day's work; the work itself. □ **plodder** *n.* [probably imitative]

**plonk[1]** — *v.* (often foll. by *down*) set down hurriedly or clumsily or heavily (*plonk it over there*; *plonked it down on the table*). — *adv. colloq.* exactly (*hit him plonk on the nose*). — *n.* heavy thud. [imitative]

**plonk[2]** *n. colloq.* cheap or inferior wine. [probably altered form of French *blanc* in *vin blanc* white wine]

**plop** — *n.* sound as of a smooth object dropping into water without a splash. — *v.* (**-pp-**) fall or drop with a plop. — *adv.* with a plop. [imitative]

**plosive** /**ploh**-siv/ *Phonet.* — *adj.* pronounced with a sudden release of breath. — *n.* sound resulting from this (the sounds *p*, *b*, *t*, *d*, *k*, and *g*). [from EXPLOSIVE]

**plot** — *n.* **1** defined and usu. small piece of land. **2** interrelationship of the main events in a play, novel, film, etc. **3** conspiracy or secret plan. — *v.* (**-tt-**) **1** make a plan or map of. **2** (also *absol.*) plan or contrive secretly (a crime etc.). **3** mark on a chart or diagram. **4** make (a curve etc.) by marking out a number of points. **5** provide (a play, novel, film, etc.) with a plot. □ **plotter** *n.* [Old English and French *complot*]

**plough** /plow/ — *n.* **1** implement for cutting furrows in the soil and turning it up. **2** implement resembling this (*snowplough*). **3** (**the Plough**) the Great Bear (see BEAR[2]) or its seven bright stars. — *v.* **1** (also *absol.*) turn up (the earth) with a plough. **2** (foll. by *out*, *up*, etc.) turn or extract with a plough. **3** furrow or scratch (a surface) as with a plough. **4** produce (a furrow or line) thus. **5** (foll. by *through*) advance laboriously, esp. through work, a book, etc. **6** (foll. by *through*, *into*) move violently like a plough; get into or consume with vigour or laboriously (*ploughed through the paperwork*; *ploughed into the pâté*). □ **plough back 1** plough (grass etc.) into the soil to enrich it. **2** reinvest (profits) in the business producing them. [Old English]

**ploughman** *n.* person who uses a plough.

**ploughshare** *n.* cutting blade of a plough.

**plover** /**pluv**-uh/ *n.* plump-breasted, often migratory, wading bird (*grey plover*; *mongolian sand-plover*; etc.): those with facial wattles are called lapwings, and smaller forms are called dotterels. [Latin *pluvia* rain]

**ploy** *n.* cunning manoeuvre to gain advantage. [origin unknown]

**pluck** — *v.* **1** pick or pull out or away. **2** strip (a bird) of feathers. **3** pull at, twitch. **4** (foll. by *at*) tug or snatch at. **5** sound (the string of a musical instrument) with a finger or plectrum. **6** plunder; rob; swindle. — *n.* **1** courage, spirit. **2** act of plucking; a twitch. **3** animal's heart, liver, and lungs as food. □ **pluck up** summon up (one's courage etc.). [Old English]

**plucky** *adj.* (**-ier**, **-iest**) brave, spirited. □ **pluckily** *adv.* **pluckiness** *n.*

**plug** — *n.* **1** piece of solid material fitting tightly into a hole, used to fill a gap or cavity or act as a wedge or stopper. **2** device of metal pins in an insulated casing, fitting into holes in a socket for making an electrical connection. **3** = SPARK-PLUG. **4** *colloq.* piece of free publicity for an idea, product, etc. **5** cake of compressed tobacco. — *v.* (**-gg-**) **1** (often foll. by *up*) stop (a hole etc.) with a plug. **2** *colloq.* shoot or hit (a person etc.). **3** *colloq.* seek to popularise (an idea, product, etc.) by constant recommendation. **4** *colloq.* (foll. by *on*, *away* (*at*)) work steadily (at). □ **plug in** connect electrically by inserting a plug into a socket. **pull the plug on** (a person, scheme, etc.) *colloq.* ruin; make ineffective. [Low German or Dutch]

**plughole** *n.* **1** hole, esp. in a sink or bath, which can be closed by a plug. **2** electric socket. □ **gone down the plughole** (or **down the gurgler**) *colloq.* (of money, efforts, etc.) irretrievably lost; gone to waste.

**plum** *n.* **1 a** small sweet oval fleshy fruit with a flattish pointed stone. **b** tree bearing this. **2** any of several Australian trees or shrubs bearing edible plum-like fruit (see BLACK PLUM, BURDEKIN PLUM, and DAVIDSON PLUM). **3** reddish-purple colour. **4** raisin used in cooking. **5** *colloq.* something prized (often *attrib.*: *plum job*). □ **have a plum in one's mouth** have an affected (esp. 'pommy') pronunciation. [Latin: related to PRUNE[1]]

**plumage** /ˈploo-mij/ *n.* bird's feathers. [French: related to PLUME]

**plumb** /plum/ — *n.* lead ball, esp. attached to the end of a line for finding the depth of water or testing whether a wall etc. is vertical. — *adv.* **1** exactly (*plumb in the centre*). **2** vertically. **3** *colloq.* quite, utterly (*plumb stupid*). — *adj.* vertical. — *v.* **1 a** measure the depth of (water) with a plumb. **b** determine a depth. **2** test (an upright surface) to determine the vertical. **3** reach or experience (an extreme feeling) (*plumb the depths of fear*). **4** learn in detail the facts about (a matter). □ **out of plumb** not vertical. [Latin *plumbum* lead]

**plumber** *n.* person who fits and repairs the apparatus of a water-supply, drainage, etc., in a building. [Latin *plumbarius* from *plumbum* lead]

**plumbing** *n.* **1** system or apparatus of water-supply, drainage, etc., in a building. **2** work of a plumber.

**plumb line** *n.* line with a plumb attached for finding the depth of (water) or testing whether a wall etc. is vertical.

**plume** /ploom/ — *n.* **1** feather, esp. a large one used for ornament. **2** ornament of feathers etc. worn on a helmet or hat or in the hair. **3** something resembling this (*plume of smoke*). — *v.* (**-ming**) **1** decorate or provide with a plume or plumes. **2** *refl.* (foll. by *on*, *upon*) pride (oneself on esp. something trivial). **3** (of a bird) preen (itself or its feathers). **4** (as **plumed** *adj.*) used as a distinguishing epithet in the names of some Australian birds (*plumed egret*). [Latin *pluma*]

**plume grass** *n.* any of several Australian perennial grasses having a plume-like flower-head.

**plummet** /ˈplum-uht/ — *n.* **1** plumb, plumb-line. **2** sounding-line. **3** weight attached to a fishing-line to keep the float upright. — *v.* (**-t-**) fall or plunge rapidly. [French: related to PLUMB]

**plummy** *adj.* (**-ier**, **-iest**) *colloq.* (of a voice) sounding affectedly rich in tone or English ('pommy') in pronunciation.

**plump**[1] — *adj.* full or rounded in shape; fleshy. — *v.* (often foll. by *up*, *out*) make or become plump (*plumped up the cushion*). □ **plumpness** *n.* [Low German or Dutch *plomp* blunt]

**plump**[2] — *v.* **1** (foll. by *for*) decide on, choose. **2** (often foll. by *down*) drop or fall abruptly. — *n.* abrupt or heavy fall. — *adv.* *colloq.* with a plump. [Low German or Dutch *plompen*, imitative]

**plum pine** *n.* (also **she pine**) rainforest conifer of NSW and Queensland, having a small seed at the head of a short, egg-shaped, edible receptacle similar in appearance to a bluish-black plum.

**plumy** /ˈploo-mee/ *adj.* (**-ier**, **-iest**) **1** plumelike, feathery. **2** adorned with plumes.

**plunder** /ˈplun-duh/ — *v.* **1** rob or steal, esp. in wartime; loot. **2** exploit (another person's or common property) for one's own profit. — *n.* **1** activity of plundering. **2** property so acquired. [German *plündern*]

**plunge** — *v.* (**-ging**) **1** (usu. foll. by *in*, *into*) **a** thrust forcefully or abruptly (*plunged the knife into his heart*). **b** dive. **c** (cause to) enter a condition or embark on a course impetuously (*they plunged into marriage*; *the room was plunged into darkness*). **2** immerse completely. **3 a** move suddenly and dramatically downward. **b** (foll. by *down*, *into*, etc.) move with a rush (*plunged down the stairs*). **c** diminish rapidly (*share prices have plunged*). **4** (of a ship) pitch. — *n.* **1** plunging action or movement; dive. **2** (also **betting plunge**) sudden placing of many bets on a horse etc. □ **take the plunge** *colloq.* commit oneself to a (usu. risky) course of action. [Romanic: related to PLUMB]

**plunger** *n.* **1** part of a mechanism that works with a plunging or thrusting movement. **2** rubber cup on a handle for clearing blocked pipes by a plunging and sucking action. **3** cafetière

**pluperfect** /ploo-**per**-fekt/ *Gram.* — *adj.* (of a tense) denoting an action completed prior to some past point of time as: *he had gone by then*. — *n.* pluperfect tense. [Latin *plus quam perfectum* more than perfect]

**plural** /**ploo**-ruhl/ — *adj.* **1** more than one in number. **2** *Gram.* (of a word or form) denoting more than one. — *n. Gram.* **1** plural word or form. **2** plural number. □ **pluralise** *v.* [Latin: related to PLUS]

**pluralism** *n.* **1** form of society embracing many minority groups and cultural traditions; multiculturalism. **2** *Philos.* system that recognises more than one ultimate principle (cf. MONISM). □ **pluralist** *n.* **pluralistic** /-**lis**-tik/ *adj.*

**plurality** /ploo-**ral**-uh-tee/ *n.* (*pl.* **-ies**) **1** state of being plural. **2** large or the greater number.

**plus** — *prep.* **1** with the addition of (symbol +). **2** (of temperature) above zero (*plus 2 °*). — *adj.* **1** (after a number) at least (*fifteen plus*). **2** (after a grade etc.) rather better than (*B+*). **3** *Math.* positive. **4** having a positive electrical charge. — *n.* **1** the symbol +. **2** additional or positive quantity. **3** advantage, bonus (*experience is a definite plus*). — *conj. colloq.* also; and furthermore. [Latin, = more]

■ **Usage** The use of *plus* as a conjunction, as in *they arrived late, plus they wanted a meal*, is considered incorrect by some people.

**plus-fours** *n.pl.* men's long wide knickerbockers, worn esp. by golfers. [the length was increased by 4 inches to create an overhang]

**plush** — *n.* cloth of silk or cotton etc., with a long soft nap. — *adj.* **1** made of plush. **2** *colloq.* = PLUSHY. □ **plushly** *adv.* **plushness** *n.* [Latin: related to PILE³]

**plushy** *adj.* (**-ier**, **-iest**) *colloq.* stylish, luxurious. □ **plushiness** *n.*

**Pluto** /**ploo**-toh/ *n.* outermost known planet of the solar system. [Greek *Ploutōn* god of the underworld]

**plutocracy** /ploo-**tok**-ruh-see/ *n.* (*pl.* **-ies**) **1 a** government by the wealthy. **b** nation so governed. **2** wealthy élite; ruling class. □ **plutocratic** /,ploo-tuh-**krat**-ik/ *adj.* [Greek *ploutos* wealth]

**plutocrat** /**ploo**-tuh-,krat/ *n.* **1** member of a plutocracy. **2** wealthy person.

**plutonic** /ploo-**ton**-ik/ *adj.* formed as igneous rock by solidification below the surface of the earth. [Latin *Pluto*, god of the underworld]

**plutonium** /ploo-**toh**-nee-uhm/ *n.* radioactive metallic element used in some nuclear reactors and weapons. [*Pluto*, name of a planet]

**pluvial** /**ploo**-vee-uhl/ *adj.* **1** of rain; rainy. **2** *Geol.* caused by rain. [Latin *pluvia* rain]

**ply**¹ /pluy/ *n.* (*pl.* **-ies**) **1** thickness or layer of cloth or wood etc. (*three-ply*). **2** strand of yarn or rope etc. [French *pli*: related to PLAIT]

**ply**² /pluy/ *v.* (**-ies**, **-ied**) **1** use or wield (a tool, weapon, etc.). **2** work steadily at (*ply one's trade*). **3** (foll. by *with*) **a** supply (a person) continuously (with food, drink, etc.). **b** approach repeatedly (with questions, etc.). **4 a** (often foll. by *between*) (of a vehicle etc.) travel regularly to and fro. **b** work (a route) thus. **5** (of a taxi-driver etc.) attend regularly for custom (*ply for trade*). [from APPLY]

**plywood** *n.* strong thin board made by gluing layers of wood with the direction of the grain alternating.

**PM** *abbr.* **1** prime minister. **2** postmortem.

**Pm** *symb.* promethium.

**p.m.** *abbr.* after noon. [Latin *post meridiem*]

**PMS** *abbr.* premenstrual syndrome.

**PMT** *abbr.* premenstrual tension.

**pneumatic** /nyoo-**mat**-ik/ *adj.* **1** filled with air or wind (*pneumatic tyre*). **2** operated by compressed air (*pneumatic drill*). □ **pneumatically** *adv.* [Greek *pneuma* wind]

**pneumonia** /nyoo-**moh**-nyuh/ *n.* inflammation of one or both lungs. [Greek *pneumōn* lung]

**PO** *abbr.* Post Office.

**Po** *symb.* polonium.

**po** /poh/ *n.* (*pl.* **-s**) *colloq.* chamber-pot. [from POT¹]

**POA** *abbr.* price on application.

**poach**¹ *v.* **1** cook (an egg) without its shell in or over boiling water. **2** cook (fish etc.) by simmering in a small amount of liquid. □ **poacher** n. [French *pochier*: related to POKE²]

**poach²** v. **1** (also *absol.*) catch (game or fish) illegally. **2** (often foll. by *on*) trespass or encroach on (another's property, ideas, etc.). **3** appropriate (another's ideas, staff, etc.). □ **poacher** n. [earlier *poche*: related to POACH¹]

**poached egg daisy** n. (also **poached eggs, ham-and-egg daisy**) Australian annual of drier areas, having large, very showy flowers with papery white bracts surrounding a large, egg-yolk yellow centre.

**pobblebonk** /pob-uhl-ˌbongk/ n. either of two Australian frogs having a loud, single-note call. [origin uncertain]

**pock** n. (also **pock-mark**) **1** small pus-filled spot on the skin, esp. caused by chickenpox or smallpox. **2** mark or scar left by this. □ **pock-marked** adj. [Old English]

**pocket** /pok-uht/ — n. **1** small bag sewn into or on clothing, for carrying small articles. **2** pouchlike compartment in a suitcase, car door, etc. **3** one's financial resources (*that's beyond my pocket*). **4** isolated group or area (*pockets of resistance*). **5** cavity in the earth containing ore, esp. gold. **6** *Aust. Rules* a side position, as back-pocket, forward-pocket. **7** pouch at the corner or on the side of a billiard- or snooker-table into which balls are driven. **8** = AIR POCKET. **9** (*attrib.*) **a** small enough or intended for carrying in a pocket (*pocket knife*). **b** smaller than the usual size (*pocket dictionary*). — v. (**-t-**) **1** put into one's pocket. **2** appropriate, esp. dishonestly. **3** confine as in a pocket. **4** submit to (an injury or affront) (*pocketed the insults*). **5** conceal or suppress (one's feelings) (*pocketed his anger*). **6** *Billiards etc.* drive (a ball) into a pocket. □ **in pocket** having gained in a transaction. **in a person's pocket 1** under a person's control. **2** close to or intimate with a person. **line one's pockets** make money, profits, esp. by dishonest means. **out of pocket** having lost in a transaction. **piss in a person's pocket** see PISS. [Anglo-French diminutive: related to POKE²]

**pocketbook** n. **1** notebook. **2** folding case for papers or money carried in a pocket.

**pocket bread** n. = PITTA².

**pocketful** n. (pl. **-s**) as much as a pocket will hold.

**pocket knife** n. = PENKNIFE.

**pocket money** n. money for minor expenses, esp. given to children.

**pod¹** — n. long seed-vessel, esp. of a pea or bean. — v. (**-dd-**) **1** bear or form pods.

**2** remove (peas etc.) from pods. [origin unknown]

**pod²** n. small herd of marine mammals, esp. whales, dolphins, or seals. [origin unknown]

**poddy** — n. **1** calf old enough to wean and fatten; unbranded calf. **2** calf (less frequently a lamb or foal) which is being hand-fed. — adj. hand-fed. — v. feed (a young animal) by hand [British dial. *poddy* fat]

**poddy-dodge** v. steal unbranded cattle. □ **poddy-dodger** n.

**poddy mullet** n. any of several food-fish, esp. the young of the sea mullet of southern Australia. [probably an alteration of Yagara *budinba* or *bunba*]

**poddy-rear** v. = PODDY v.

**podgy** /poj-ee/ adj. (**-ier, -iest**) **1** short and fat. **2** plump, fleshy. □ **podginess** n. [*podge* short fat person]

**podium** /poh-dee-uhm/ n. (pl. **-s** or **podia**) rostrum. [Greek *podion* diminutive of *pous* pod- foot]

**poem** /poh-uhm/ n. **1** metrical composition, usu. concerned with feeling or imaginative description. **2** elevated composition in verse or prose. **3** something with poetic qualities (*a poem in stone*). [Greek *poieō* make]

**poesy** /poh-uh-zee/ n. archaic poetry. [French, ultimately as POEM]

**poet** /poh-uht/ n. **1** writer of poems. **2** highly imaginative or expressive person. [Greek *poiētēs* maker: related to POEM]

**poetaster** /ˌpoh-uh-**tas**-tuh/ n. paltry inferior poet. [from POET, Latin *-aster* derogatory suffix]

**poetic** /poh-et-ik/ adj. (also **poetical**) **1 a** of or like poetry or poets. **b** written in verse. **2** elevated or sublime in expression. □ **poetically** adv.

**poetic justice** n. very appropriate punishment or reward.

**poetic licence** n. writer's or artist's transgression of established rules for effect.

**poetry** /poh-uh-tree/ n. **1** art or work of a poet. **2** poems collectively. **3** poetic or tenderly pleasing quality. **4** anything compared to poetry (*his movements in dance are poetry in motion*). [medieval Latin: related to POET]

**po-faced** adj. **1** solemn-faced, humourless. **2** smug. [perhaps from PO, influenced by *poker-faced*]

**pogo** /poh-goh/ n. (pl. **-s**) (also **pogo stick**) stiltlike toy with a spring, used for jumping about on. [origin uncertain]

**pogrom** /pog-ruhm, -rom/ n. organised massacre (orig. of Jews in Russia). [Russian]

**pohutukawa** /poh-ˌhoo-tuh-**kah**-wuh/ n. (also **New Zealand Christmas tree**) evergreen tree from New Zealand with brilliant crimson flowers, often cultivated in Australia. [Maori]

**poignant** /**poi**-nyuhnt/ adj. **1** painfully sharp to the emotions or senses; deeply moving. **2** arousing sympathy. **3** sharp or pungent in taste or smell. **4** pleasantly piquant. □ **poignance** n. **poignancy** n. **poignantly** adv. [Latin: related to POINT]

**poinsettia** /poin-**set**-ee-uh/ n. plant with large scarlet bracts surrounding small yellow flowers. [*Poinsett*, name of a diplomat]

**point** — n. **1** sharp or tapered end of a tool, weapon, pencil, etc. **2** tip or extreme end. **3** that which in geometry has position but not magnitude. **4** particular place or position (*Perth and points east*; *point of contact*). **5** precise or critical moment (*when it came to the point, he refused*). **6** very small mark on a surface. **7** dot or other punctuation mark. **8** = DECIMAL POINT. **9** stage or degree in progress or increase (*abrupt to the point of rudeness*). **10** temperature at which a change of state occurs (*freezing-point*). **11** single item or particular (*explained it point by point*). **12 a** unit of scoring in games or of various value etc. **b** *Aust. Rules* = BEHIND n. **c** an advantage or success in e.g. an argument or discussion (*the point goes to her*). **d** unit (of varying value) in quoting the price of stocks etc. **13** significant or essential thing; what is intended or under discussion (*the point of my question*; *get to the point*). **14 a** sense, purpose; advantage, value (*saw no point in staying*). **b** (usu. prec. by *the*) salient feature of a story, joke, remark, etc. (*don't see the point*). **15** distinctive feature or characteristic (*tact is not his strong point*). **16 a** each of 32 directions marked at equal distances round a compass. **b** corresponding direction towards the horizon. **17** (usu. in *pl.*) pair of movable tapering rails that allow a train to pass from one line to another. **18** (usu. in *pl.*) electrical contact in the distributor of a vehicle. **19** *Cricket* **a** a fielder on the off side near the batsman. **b** this position. **20** tip of the toe in ballet. **21** promontory. **22** (usu. in *pl.*) extremities of a dog, horse, etc. **23** *Printing* unit of measurement for type bodies (*print it in 12 point*). **24** *hist.* a unit measuring rainfall. — v. **1** (usu. foll. by *to, at*) **a** direct or aim (a finger, weapon, etc.). **b** direct attention in a certain direction (*pointed to the house across the road*). **2** (foll. by *at, towards*) aim or be directed to (*telescope pointed at*

*the stars*; *the church was built pointing towards the east*). **3** (foll. by *to*) indicate; be evidence of (*it all points to murder*). **4** give force to (words or actions) (*pointed his remarks by referring to the latest statistics*). □ **at** (or **on**) **the point of** on the verge of (*at the point of death*). **beside the point** irrelevant. **in point** relevant (*the case in point*). **in point of fact** see FACT. **make a point of** insist on (doing etc.); treat or regard as essential; call particular attention to (an action). **point out** indicate; draw attention to. **point up** emphasise. **to the point** relevant; relevantly. **up to a point** to some extent but not completely. [Latin *pungo punct-prick*]

**point-blank** — adj. **1 a** (of a shot) aimed or fired at very close range. **b** (of a range) very close. **2** (of a remark etc.) blunt, direct. — adv. **1** at very close range. **2** directly, bluntly (*refused point-blank*).

**pointed** adj. **1** sharpened or tapering to a point. **2** (of a remark etc.) having point; penetrating; cutting. **3** emphasised; made evident. □ **pointedly** adv.

**pointer** n. **1** thing that points, e.g. the index hand of a gauge. **2** rod for pointing to features on a chart etc. **3** *colloq.* hint; indication (*gave us some pointers on how to do it*).

**pointillism** /**pwan**-tuh-ˌliz-uhm, **poin**-/ n. technique of impressionist painting using tiny dots of pure colour which become blended in the viewer's eye. □ **pointillist** n. & adj. [French *pointiller* mark with dots]

**pointing** n. **1** (in Aboriginal ritual practice) the ceremony of pointing the bone at a person whose death is willed. **2** cement filling the joints of brickwork.

**pointless** adj. lacking purpose or meaning; ineffective, fruitless. □ **pointlessly** adv. **pointlessness** n.

**point of honour** n. thing of great importance to one's reputation or conscience.

**point of no return** n. point in a journey or enterprise at which it becomes essential or more practical to continue to the end.

**point of order** n. query in a debate etc. as to whether correct procedure is being followed.

**point of view** n. **1** position from which a thing is viewed. **2** way of considering a matter.

**point the bone** v. **1** (in Aboriginal ritual practice) point a bone at a person whose death is willed. **2** (in extended use) jinx (*someone must have pointed the bone at me, seeing that I didn't get the job*).

**poise** /poiz/ — n. **1** composure, self-possession. **2** equilibrium; a stable state. **3** carriage (of the head etc.). — v. (**-sing**) **1** balance; hold suspended or supported. **2** be balanced or suspended. [Latin *pendo pens-* weigh]

**poised** adj. **1 a** composed, self-assured. **b** carrying oneself gracefully or with dignity. **2** (often foll. by *for*, or *to* + infin.) ready for action.

**poison** /poi-zuhn/ — n. **1** substance that when introduced into or absorbed by a living organism causes death or injury, esp. one that kills by rapid action even in a small quantity. **2** *colloq.* harmful influence etc. (*their gossip is pure poison*). **3** (also **poison plant**) any of several plants poisonous to stock, esp. the poison peas of (mainly) WA. — v. **1** administer poison to. **2** kill, injure, or infect with poison. **3 a** treat (a weapon) with poison. **b** infect (air, water, etc.) with poison (*rivers poisoned by factory effluents*). **4** corrupt or pervert (a person or mind). **5** spoil or destroy (a person's pleasure etc.). — adj. (in Aboriginal English) characterising a party in an avoidance relationship (*poison uncle*). □ **poisoner** n. **poisonous** adj. [Latin: related to POTION]

**poison pea** n. any of several (mainly WA) plants having striking pea-flowers in yellow and red, all red, or orange and red, seen in garden cultivation: considered a menace in the wild because their foliage is poisonous to stock.

**poison pen letter** n. malicious anonymous letter.

**poke¹** — v. (**-king**) **1 a** thrust or push with the hand, a stick, etc. **b** (foll. by *out, up,* etc.) be thrust forward, protrude (*the bone was poking out of his flesh*). **2** (foll. by *at* etc.) make thrusts (*poked at the snake to see if it were dead*). **3** thrust the end of a finger etc. against (*poked him in the ribs*). **4** (foll. by *in*) produce (a hole etc. in a thing) by poking. **5** thrust forward, esp. obtrusively (*poked his way into the crowd*). **6** stir (a fire) with a poker. **7 a** (often foll. by *about, around*) potter. **b** (foll. by *about, into*) pry; search (*stop poking into my affairs*). **8** (foll. by *up*) confine (esp. oneself) in a poky place (*am poked up in this tiny flat*). — n. **1** act of poking. **2** a thrust or nudge. □ **poke fun at** ridicule. **poke one's nose into** *colloq.* pry or intrude into. [German or Dutch]

**poke²** n. *Brit. dial.* bag, sack. □ **buy a pig in a poke** see PIG. [French dial.]

**poker¹** n. metal rod for stirring a fire.

**poker²** n. card-game in which bluff is used as players bet on the value of their hands. [origin unknown]

**poker-face** n. impassive countenance as assumed by a poker-player. □ **poker-faced** adj.

**poker machine** n. coin-operated gaming machine which pays according to the combination of symbols appearing on the edges of the wheels spun by the operation of a lever or, increasingly nowadays, by pressing a button.

**pokie** n. (also **pokey**) (usu. in *pl.* prec. by *the*) *colloq.* = POKER MACHINE (*am off to play the pokies*). [abbreviation]

**poky** /poh-kee/ adj. (**-ier, -iest**) (of a room etc.) small and cramped. □ **pokiness** n. [from POKE¹]

**polar** /poh-luh/ adj. **1** of or near a pole of the earth or of the celestial sphere. **2** having magnetic or electric polarity. **3** directly opposite in character or tendency (*he's the polar opposite of his brother*). [Latin: related to POLE²]

**polar bear** n. large white bear living in the Arctic regions.

**polar circle** n. each of the circles parallel to the equator at 23° 27′ from either pole.

**polarise** /poh-luh-ruyz/ v. (also **-ize**) (**-sing** or **-zing**) **1** restrict the vibrations of (light-waves etc.) to one direction. **2** give magnetic or electric polarity to. **3** divide into two opposing groups (*the electorate was polarised on the issue of the proposed tax*). □ **polarisation** /-zay-shuhn/ n.

**polarity** /poh-la-ruh-tee/ n. (pl. **-ies**) **1** tendency of a magnet etc. to point with its extremities to the magnetic poles of the earth or of a body to lie with its axis in a particular direction. **2** state of having two poles with contrary qualities. **3** state of having two opposite tendencies, opinions, etc. **4** electrical condition of a body (positive or negative). **5** attraction towards an object.

**polaroid** /poh-luh-royd/ n. *propr.* **1** material in thin sheets polarising light passing through it. **2** camera with internal processing that produces a print rapidly after each exposure. **3** (in *pl.*) sunglasses with polaroid lenses.

**Pole** n. **1** native or national of Poland. **2** person of Polish descent. [German from Polish]

**pole¹** — n. **1** long slender rounded piece of wood, metal, etc., esp. with the end placed in the ground as a support etc. **2** = PERCH¹ **3**. **3** wooden shaft fitted to the front of a vehicle and attached to the yokes or collars of draught animals. — v. **1** push off or propel (a punt, boat, etc.) with a pole. **2** = POLE-FISH. □ **up the pole** *colloq.* **1** crazy. **2** in difficulty. **3** totally wrong. [Latin *palus* stake]

**pole²** n. **1** (in full **north pole, south pole**) a each of the two points in the celestial sphere about which the stars appear to revolve. **b** each of the ends of the axis of rotation of the earth (*North Pole; South Pole*). **2** each of the two opposite points on the surface of a magnet at which magnetic forces are strongest. **3** each of two terminals (positive and negative) of an electric cell or battery etc. **4** each of two opposed principles. □ **be poles apart** differ greatly, esp. in nature or opinion. [Greek, = axis]

■ **Usage** The spelling is *North Pole* and *South Pole* when used as geographical designations.

**poleaxe** /pohl-aks/ — n. **1** hist. = BATTLEAXE 1. **2** butcher's axe. — v. (**-xing**) **1** hit or kill with a poleaxe. **2** (esp. as **poleaxed** adj.) colloq. dumbfound, overwhelm. [Low German or Dutch: related to POLL, AXE]

**polecat** /pohl-kat/ n. small European brownish-black fetid mammal of the weasel family. [origin unknown]

**pole-fish** v. (also **pole**) fish (esp. for tuna), using a pole, a short line, and a barbless lure. □ **pole-fishing** n.

**polemic** /puh-lem-ik/ — n. **1** forceful oral or written controversy or argument; an attack on some belief, opinion, etc. **2** (in pl.) art or practice of controversial discussion. — adj. (also **polemical**) involving dispute; controversial. □ **polemicist** /-uh-suhst/ n. [Greek polemos war]

**pole position** n. **1** most favourable position at the start of a motor race. **2** any favourable starting position (*has the pole position in the race for promotion*).

**poler** n. **1** each of the pair of bullocks attached to the pole of a vehicle (and leaving most of the pulling to the others in the front). **2** shirker, sponger, person who does not pull his or her weight. **3** person who hoists tuna fish on board with a pole.

**pole star** n. **1** star in the Little Bear constellation, near the North Pole in the sky. **2** thing serving as a guide.

**pole-vault** — n. vault, or sport of vaulting, over a high bar with the aid of a pole held in the hands. — v. perform this. □ **pole-vaulter** n.

**poley** /poh-lee/ — adj. hornless, dehorned. — n. **1** dehorned or hornless bullock or cow. **2** type of saddle which does not have knee-pads. [British dial. poll hornless cow or ox]

**police** /puh-lees/ — n. (as pl.) **1** (usu. prec. by the) the civil force responsible for maintaining public order. **2** its members.

**3** force with similar functions (*military police*). — v. (**-cing**) **1** keep (a place or people) in order by means of police or a similar body. **2** provide with police. **3** keep in order, administer, control (*problem of policing the new law*). [Latin: related to POLICY¹]

**police dog** n. dog, esp. a German shepherd, used in police work.

**police force** n. body of police of a country, district, or town.

**policeman** n. (fem. **policewoman**) member of a police force.

**policeman bird** n. = JABIRU.

**policeman fly** n. any of many small Australian wasps which swoop down on flies and capture them as food for the wasp larvae.

**police officer** n. member of a police force.

**police State** n. totalitarian State controlled by political police.

**police station** n. office of a local police force.

**policy¹** /pol-uh-see/ n. (pl. **-ies**) **1** course or principle of action adopted or proposed by a government, political party, business, individual, etc. **2** prudent conduct; practical sense; sagacity. [Latin politia POLITY]

■ **Usage** See note at *polity*.

**policy²** /pol-uh-see/ n. (pl. **-ies**) **1** contract of insurance. **2** document containing this. [French police, ultimately from Greek apodeixis proof]

**policyholder** n. person or body holding an insurance policy.

**polio** /poh-lee-oh/ n. = POLIOMYELITIS. [abbreviation]

**poliomyelitis** /poh-lee-oh-, muy-uh-luy-tuhs/ n. infectious viral disease of the grey matter of the central nervous system with temporary or permanent paralysis. [Greek polios grey, muelos marrow]

**Polish** /poh-lish/ — adj. **1** of Poland. **2** of the Poles or their language. — n. language of Poland.

**polish** /pol-ish/ — v. (often foll. by up) **1** make or become smooth or glossy by rubbing. **2** (esp. as **polished** adj.) refine or improve; add the finishing touches to (*help me to polish this short story; a polished performance*). — n. **1** substance used for polishing. **2** smoothness or glossiness produced by friction. **3** act or instance of polishing. **4** refinement, elegance, of manner, conduct, etc. □ **polish off** finish (esp. food) quickly (*polished off the meal; polished off his political opponents*). **polish up** (often foll. by on) revise or improve (a skill etc.) (*need to polish up on my French*). [Latin *polio polit-*]

**polite** /puh-**luyt**/ *adj.* (**politer**, **politest**) **1** having good manners; courteous. **2** cultivated, refined. □ **politely** *adv.* **politeness** *n.* [Latin *politus*: related to POLISH]

**politic** /**pol**-uh-tik/ — *adj.* **1** (of an action) judicious, expedient. **2** (of a person) prudent, sagacious. **3** political (now only in *body politic*). — *v.* (**-ck-**) engage in politics (*the Prime Minister is away politicking in the outback*). [Greek: related to POLITY]

**political** /puh-**lit**-i-kuhl/ *adj.* **1 a** of or concerning a nation or its government, or public affairs generally. **b** of or relating to or engaged in politics. **2** taking or belonging to a side in politics. **3** concerned with seeking power, status, etc., rather than matters of principle (*a political decision*). □ **politically** *adv.* [Latin: related to POLITIC]

**political asylum** *n.* State protection given to a political refugee from another country.

**political correctness** *n.* avoidance of forms of expression or action that exclude, marginalise, or denigrate women, ethnic or cultural minorities, etc. □ **politically correct** (also **politically incorrect**) exhibiting (or failing to exhibit) political correctness.

**political economy** *n.* the study of the economic aspects of government.

**political prisoner** *n.* person imprisoned for political reasons.

**political science** *n.* the study of political activity and systems of government.

**politician** /ˌpol-uh-**tish**-uhn/ *n.* person involved in politics, esp. professionally as an MP.

**politicise** /puh-**lit**-uh-ˌsuyz/ *v.* (also **-ize**) (**-sing** or **-zing**) **1 a** give a political character to. **b** make politically aware. **2** engage in or talk politics. □ **politicisation** /-**zay**-shuhn/ *n.*

**politics** /**pol**-uh-tiks/ *n.pl.* **1** (treated as *sing.* or *pl.*) **a** art and science of government. **b** public life and affairs as involving authority and government. **2** (usu. treated as *pl.*) political principles or practice (*what are his politics?*). **3** activities concerned with seeking power, status, etc.

**polity** /**pol**-uh-tee/ *n.* (*pl.* **-ies**) **1** a form or process of civil government. **2** an organised society; a State as a political entity. [Greek *politēs* citizen from *polis* city]

■ **Usage** This word is sometimes confused with *policy*.

**polka** /**pol**-kuh/ — *n.* **1** lively dance of Bohemian origin. **2** music for this. — *v.* (**-kas**, **-kaed** /-kuhd/ or **-ka'd**, **-kaing** /-kuh-ing/) dance the polka. [Czech *pålka*]

**polka dot** *n.* round dot as one of many forming a regular pattern on a textile fabric etc.

**poll** /pohl/ — *n.* **1 a** (often in *pl.*) voting or the counting of votes at an election (*go to the polls*). **b** result of voting or number of votes recorded. **2** = OPINION POLL. **3** a human head. — *v.* **1 a** take the vote or votes of. **b** receive (so many votes). **c** give (a vote). **2** record the opinion of (a person or group) in an opinion poll. **3** cut off the top of (a tree or plant), esp. make a pollard of. **4** (esp. as **polled** *adj.*) cut the horns off (cattle). [perhaps from Low German or Dutch]

**pollard** /**pol**-uhd/ — *n.* **1** animal that has lost or cast its horns; ox, sheep, or goat of a hornless breed. **2** tree whose branches have been cut back to encourage the dense growth of young branches. — *v.* make (a tree) a pollard. [from POLL]

**pollen** /**pol**-uhn/ *n.* fine dustlike grains discharged from the male part of a flower, each containing the fertilising element. [Latin]

**pollen count** *n.* index of the amount of pollen in the air, published as a warning to hay fever sufferers.

**pollie** var. of POLLY.

**pollinate** /**pol**-uh-ˌnayt/ *v.* (**-ting**) (also *absol.*) convey pollen to or sprinkle (a stigma) with pollen. □ **pollination** /-**nay**-shuhn/ *n.* **pollinator** *n.*

**polling** *n.* registering or casting of votes.

**polling booth** *n.* compartment in which a voter stands to mark the ballot-paper.

**polling station** *n.* building, often a school, used for voting at an election.

**pollster** *n.* person who organises an opinion poll.

**pollute** /puh-**loot**/ *v.* (**-ting**) **1** contaminate or defile (the environment). **2** make foul or impure. **3** destroy the purity or sanctity of. □ **pollutant** *adj.* & *n.* **polluter** *n.* **pollution** *n.* [Latin *polluo -lut-*]

**polly** *n.* (also **pollie**) *colloq.* a politician. [abbreviation]

**polo** /**poh**-loh/ *n.* game like hockey played on horseback with a long-handled mallet. [Balti, = ball]

**polonaise** /ˌpol-uh-**nayz**/ *n.* **1** slow dance of Polish origin. **2** music for this. [French: related to POLE]

**polo neck** n. **1** high round turned-over collar. **2** garment with this.

**polonium** /puh-**loh**-nee-uhm/ n. radio-active metallic element, occurring naturally in uranium ores. [medieval Latin *Polonia* Poland]

**polony** /puh-**loh**-nee/ n. bland sausage usu. sliced and eaten cold. [alteration of *Bologna*]

**poltergeist** /**pol**-tuh-,guyst/ n. noisy mischievous ghost, esp. one causing physical damage. [German]

**poltroon** /pol-**troon**/ n. spiritless coward. □ **poltroonery** n. [Italian *poltro* sluggard]

**Polwarth** /**pol**-wuhth/ n. **1** breed of Australian sheep. **2** a sheep of this breed. [*Polwarth* district in south-western Victoria]

**poly-** comb. form **1** many (*polygamy*). **2** polymerised (*polyunsaturated*; *poly-ester*). [Greek *polus* many]

**polyandry** /**pol**-ee-,an-dree/ n. polygamy in which a woman has more than one husband. □ **polyandrous** /-an-druhs/ adj. [Greek *anēr andr-* male]

**polyanthus** /,pol-ee-**an**-thuhs/ n. (pl. **-thuses**) flowering plant cultivated from hybridised primulas. [Greek *anthos* flower]

**polychromatic** /,pol-ee-kroh-**mat**-ik/ adj. **1** many-coloured. **2** (of radiation) con-taining more than one wavelength. □ **polychromatism** /-kroh-muh-,tiz-uhm/ n.

**polychrome** /**pol**-ee-,krohm/ — adj. in many colours. — n. polychrome work of art. [Greek: related to POLY-, CHROME]

**polyester** /,pol-ee-**es**-tuh/ n. synthetic fibre or resin.

**polygamy** /puh-**lig**-uh-mee/ n. practice of having more than one wife or (less usu.) husband at once. □ **polygamist** n. **polygamous** adj. [Greek *gamos* marriage]

**polyglot** /**pol**-ee-,glot/ — adj. **1** of many languages. **2** (of a person) speaking or writing several languages. **3** (of a book) with the text translated into several languages. — n. **1** a polyglot person. **2** a polyglot book, esp. a bible. [Greek *glōtta* tongue]

**polygon** /**pol**-ee-guhn, -,gon/ n. figure with many (usu. five or more) sides and angles. □ **polygonal** /puh-**lig**-uh-nuhl/ adj. [Greek *-gōnos* angled]

**polygraph** /**pol**-ee-,grahf, -,graf/ n. ma-chine for reading physiological charac-teristics (e.g. pulse-rate); lie-detector.

**polygyny** /puh-**lij**-uh-nee/ n. polygamy in which a man has more than one wife. □ **polygynous** /puh-**lij**-uh-nuhs/ adj. [Greek *gunē* woman]

**polyhedron** /,pol-ee-**hee**-druhn, -**hed**-ruhn/ n. (pl. **-dra**) solid figure with many (usu. more than six) faces. □ **polyhedral** adj. [Greek *hedra* base]

**polymath** /**pol**-ee-,math/ n. person of great or varied learning. [Greek *manthanō math-* learn]

**polymer** /**pol**-uh-muh/ n. compound of one or more large molecules formed from repeated units of smaller molecules. □ **polymeric** /-**me**-rik/ adj. **polymerise** v. (also **-ize**) (**-sing** or **-zing**). **polymerisation** /-**zay**-shuhn/ n. [Greek *polumeros* having many parts]

**polymorphous** /,pol-ee-**maw**-fuhs/ adj. (also **polymorphic**) passing through various forms in successive stages of development.

**Polynesian** /,pol-uh-**nee**-zhuhn/ — adj. of or relating to Polynesia, a group of Pacific islands including New Zealand, Hawaii, Samoa, etc. — **1 a** native of Poly-nesia. **b** person of Polynesian descent. **2** family of languages including Maori, Hawaiian, and Samoan. [POLY-, Greek *nēsos* island]

**polynomial** /,pol-ee-**noh**-mee-uhl/ — n. expression of more than two algebraic terms. — adj. of or being a polynomial. [from POLY-, BINOMIAL]

**polyp** /**pol**-uhp/ n. **1** simple organism with a tube-shaped body. **2** small usu. benign growth on a mucous membrane. [Greek *pous* foot]

**polyphony** /puh-**lif**-uh-nee/ n. (pl. **-ies**) *Mus.* contrapuntal music. □ **polyphonic** /,pol-ee-**fon**-ik/ adj. [Greek *phōnē* sound]

**polypropene** /,pol-ee-**proh**-peen/ n. = POLYPROPYLENE.

**polypropylene** /,pol-ee-**proh**-puh-,leen/ n. any polymer of propylene, including thermoplastic materials used for films, fibres, or moulding materials.

**polysaccharide** /,pol-ee-**sak**-uh-,ruyd/ n. any of a group of complex carbo-hydrates, e.g. starch. [see SACCHARIN]

**polystyrene** /,pol-ee-**stuy**-reen/ n. a polymer of styrene, a kind of hard plastic, often foamed for packaging. [*styrene* from Greek *sturax* a resin]

**polysyllabic** /,pol-ee-suh-**lab**-ik/ adj. **1** having many syllables. **2** using words of many syllables. [medieval Latin from Greek]

**polysyllable** /**pol**-ee-,sil-uh-buhl/ n. polysyllabic word.

**polytheism** /**pol**-ee-thee-,iz-uhm/ n. belief in or worship of more than one god. □ **polytheist** n. **polytheistic** /-is-tik/ adj. [Greek *theos* god]

**polythene** /**pol**-uh-,theen/ n. a tough light plastic. [POLYMER, ETHYLENE]

**polyunsaturated** /ˌpol-ee-un-**sach**-uh-ˌray-tuhd/ adj. (of fat) containing several double or triple bonds in each molecule and therefore capable of combining with hydrogen and not associated with accumulation of cholesterol.

**polyurethane** /ˌpol-ee-**yoo**-ruh-ˌthayn/ n. synthetic resin or plastic used esp. in paints or foam. [related to UREA, ETHANE]

**polyvinyl chloride** /ˌpol-ee-**vuy**-nuhl/ n. a vinyl plastic used for electrical insulation or as a fabric etc.; PVC.

**pom** n. colloq. = POMMY. □ **the poms** the British, esp. the English. [abbreviation]

**pomander** /puh-**man**-duh/ n. 1 ball of mixed aromatic substances. 2 container for this. [Anglo-French from medieval Latin]

**pomegranate** /**pom**-uh-ˌgran-uht, **pom**-ee-/ n. 1 tropical fruit with a tough rind, reddish pulp, and many seeds. 2 tree bearing this. 3 (also **pommygranate**, **pommygrant**) hist. British immigrant to Australia (now replaced by POM and POMMY). [French pome grenate from Romanic; = many-seeded apple]

**pomelo** /**pom**-uh-ˌloh/ n. (pl. **-s**) citrus fruit resembling a grapefruit. [origin unknown]

**pommel** /**pum**-uhl, **pom**-/ — n. 1 knob, esp. at the end of a sword-hilt. 2 upward projecting front of a saddle. — v. (**-ll-**) = PUMMEL. [Latin pomum apple]

**pommified** adj. derog. 1 (of an Australian) affecting an English manner, esp. in speech. 2 characterised or influenced by an English model (pommified behaviour). [POMMY]

**pommy** /**pom**-ee/ (also **pommie**) — n. (pl. **-ies**) colloq. 1 British (esp. English) person, esp. a recent immigrant to Australia. 2 inhabitant of the British Isles (esp. of England). — adj. of or pertaining to a pommy; British; English. [probably an abbreviation of POMEGRANATE rhyming slang for immigrant]

**Pommyland** n. colloq. Britain, esp. England.

**pomp** n. 1 splendid display; splendour. 2 specious glory, vainglory. [Latin from Greek pompē]

**pompom** n. (also **pompon**) 1 ornamental tuft or bobble, made of wool etc., used as a decoration on hats etc. 2 dahlia or chrysanthemum with small, highly-clustered petals. [French]

**pompous** /**pom**-puhs/ n. 1 self-important, affectedly grand or solemn (pompous behaviour). 2 (of language) pretentious; unduly grand in style; pommified. □ **pomposity** /pom-**pos**-uh-tee/ n. (pl. **-ies**). **pompously** adv. **pompousness** n. [Latin: related to POMP]

**ponce** /pons/ colloq. — n. 1 man who lives off a prostitute's earnings; pimp. 2 offens. homosexual or effeminate man. — v. (**-cing**) act as a ponce. □ **ponce about** move about effeminately or ineffectually. □ **poncy** adj. [origin unknown]

**poncho** /**pon**-choh/ n. (pl. **-s**) cloak of a usu. blanket-like piece of cloth with a slit in the middle for the head. [South American Spanish]

**pond** n. small body of still water formed naturally or artificially. [var. of POUND³]

**ponder** v. 1 think over; consider. 2 muse, be deep in thought. [Latin pondero weigh]

**ponderable** adj. literary having appreciable weight or significance. [Latin: related to PONDER]

**ponderous** /**pon**-duh-ruhs/ adj. 1 slow and awkward, esp. because of great weight. 2 (of style etc.) laborious; dull. □ **ponderously** adv. **ponderousness** n. [Latin pondus -der- weight]

**pong** colloq. — v. stink. — n. an offensive smell. □ **pongy** adj. (**-ier**, **-iest**). [origin unknown]

**poniard** /**pon**-yuhd, -yahd/ n. dagger. [French poignard from Latin pugnus fist]

**pontiff** /**pon**-tif/ n. (in full **supreme** or **sovereign pontiff**) the Pope. [Latin pontifex -fic- priest]

**pontifical** /pon-**tif**-uh-kuhl/ adj. papal. □ **Pontifical Mass** high Mass celebrated by a bishop, cardinal, etc. □ **pontifically** adv.

**pontificate** — v. /pon-**tif**-uh-ˌkayt/ (**-ting**) 1 be pompously dogmatic. 2 officiate as bishop, esp. at Mass. — n. /pon-**tif**-uh-kuht/ 1 office of a Pope or bishop. 2 period of this.

**pontoon¹** /pon-**toon**/ n. card-game in which players try to acquire cards with a face value totalling 21. [probably a corruption of French vingt-et-un twenty-one]

**pontoon²** /pon-**toon**/ n. 1 flat-bottomed boat. 2 each of several boats etc. used to support a temporary bridge. [Latin ponto -onis punt]

**pony** /**poh**-nee/ n. (pl. **-ies**) 1 horse of any small breed. 2 a small glass for beer. b the beer in this. [perhaps from French poulenet foal]

**ponytail** n. hair drawn back, tied, and hanging down behind the head.

**poo** colloq. — n. faeces. — v. (**pooed**, **pooing**) 1 defecate. 2 soil with faeces (the baby has pooed its nappy). □ **in the poo** in deep trouble.

**pooch** n. colloq. a dog. [origin unknown]

**poodle** /**poo**-duhl/ *n.* dog of a breed with a curly coat that is usually clipped. [German *Pudel*]

**poof** /puuf/ *n.*, *adj.*, & *v.* = POOFTER.

**poofter** /**puuf**-tuh/ *colloq. offens.* — *n.* **1** a male homosexual. **2** man whose manner or behaviour does not conform with that conventionally regarded as masculine. **3** general term of abuse for any man. — *adj.* pertaining to a poofter. — *v.* behave in a poofter manner. □ **poofterish** *adj.* [extension of POOF: perhaps from *puff* braggart]

**poofter basher** *n.* male who victimises homosexuals, usu. operating as one of a gang, and usu. inflicting grave physical violence on the victims. □ **poofter bashing** *n.*

**pooh** /poo/ — *int.* expressing impatience, contempt, or disgust at a bad smell. — *n.* = POO. □ **in the pooh** *colloq.* in deep trouble. [imitative]

**pooh-pooh** /poo-boo/ *v.* express contempt for, ridicule. [reduplication of POOH]

**pool**[1] *n.* **1** small body of still water. **2** small shallow body of any liquid (*lay in a pool of blood*). **3** swimming-pool. **4** deep place in a river. [Old English]

**pool**[2] — *n.* **1 a** common supply of persons, vehicles, commodities, etc., for sharing by a group of people (*a typing pool*). **b** group of persons sharing duties etc. **2** common fund, e.g. of profits of separate firms or of players' stakes in gambling. **3** arrangement between competing parties to fix prices and share business. **4 a** game on a billiard-table with usu. 16 balls. **b** game on a billiard-table in which each player has a ball of a different colour with which he or she tries to pocket the others in fixed order, the winner taking all of the stakes. — *v.* **1** put into a common fund (*pooled their resources*). **2** share in common. **3** *colloq.* **a** involve (a person) in a scheme etc. often by deception. **b** implicate (a person). **c** inform on (a person). [French *poule*]

**pools** *n.pl.* (prec. by *the*) = FOOTBALL POOLS.

**poon**[1] /poon/ *v.* (foll. by *up*) dress to impress, usu. with sexual success in view. □ **pooned up** *adj.* [origin unknown]

**poon**[2] /poon/ *n. colloq.* simpleton or fool. [origin unknown]

**poonce** /puuns/ *colloq. offens.* — *n.* **1** a man who is not, or is thought not to be, macho or aggressively masculine (*in some circles, if you're not an ocker you must be a poonce*). **2** a homosexual male. **3** (a general term of abuse for) any man. — *v.* (**pooncing**, **poonced**) (often foll. by *around*) act or behave like a poonce.

□ **pooncy** *adj.* [variation of PONCE, perhaps influenced by POON *v.*]

**poop**[1] /poop/ *n.* stern of a ship; the aftermost and highest deck. [Latin *puppis*]

**poop**[2] /poop/ *v.* (esp. as **pooped** *adj.*) *colloq.* exhaust; tire out. [origin unknown]

**poor** — *adj.* **1** without enough money to live comfortably. **2** (foll. by *in*) deficient in (a possession or quality) (*poor in judgment*). **3 a** scanty, inadequate (*a poor crop*). **b** less good than is usual or expected (*poor visibility*; *is a poor driver*). **c** paltry; inferior (*came a poor third*). **4** deserving pity or sympathy; unfortunate (*you poor thing*). **5** (often *iron.* or *joc.*) humble; insignificant (*in my poor opinion*). — *n.* (prec. by *the*) poor people as a group. □ **poor excuse for** bad example of (*given his neglect of his children, he's a poor excuse for a father*). **poor man's** inferior or cheaper substitute for (*lumpfish roe is poor man's caviar*). [Latin *pauper*]

**poorly** — *adv.* in a poor manner, badly. — *predic. adj.* unwell.

**pop**[1] — *n.* **1** sudden sharp explosive sound as of a cork when drawn. **2** *colloq.* individual item (*bought these ducks at a dollar a pop*). **3** *colloq.* effervescent non-alcoholic drink. — *v.* (**-pp-**) **1** (cause to) make a pop. **2** (foll. by *in, out, up, on,* etc.) go, move, come, or put unexpectedly or abruptly (*pop out to the shop*; *pop in for a quick visit*; *pop it on the bed*). **3** *colloq.* (cause to) burst with a popping sound. — *adv.* with the sound of a pop (*go pop*). □ **pop off** *colloq.* die. **pop the question** *colloq.* propose marriage. [imitative]

**pop**[2] *n. colloq.* **1** (in full **pop music**) highly successful commercial music, esp. since the 1950s. **2** (*attrib.*) of or relating to pop music (*pop concert*). **3** pop record or song (*top of the pops*). [abbreviation of POPULAR]

**pop.** *abbr.* population.

**pop art** *n.* art based on modern popular culture and the mass media.

**popcorn** *n.* Indian corn which bursts open when heated.

**pop culture** *n.* commercial culture based on popular taste.

**pope** *n.* (as title **Pope**) head of the Roman Catholic Church (*the Pope*; *Pope John XXIII*; *we have a new pope*). [Greek *papas* patriarch]

**pop-eyed** *adj. colloq.* **1** having bulging eyes. **2** wide-eyed (with surprise etc.).

**popinjay** /**pop**-uhn-,jay/ *n.* fop, conceited person. [Arabic *babagha* parrot]

**popish** /**poh**-pish/ *adj. derog.* Roman Catholic.

**poplar** /**pop**-luh/ *n.* tall slender tree with a straight trunk and often tremulous leaves. [Latin *populus*]

**poplar gum** *n.* partly deciduous eucalypt of northern Australia, having a white, smooth bark, broad, pale green new foliage, and creamy flowers.

**poplin** /**pop**-luhn/ *n.* plain-woven fabric usu. of cotton, with a corded surface. [French from Italian *papalina* PAPAL, from the papal town Avignon where it was made]

**popper** *n. propr.* individual serve of fruit juice etc. in a small plastic box with plastic drinking-straw attached, the straw being meant to be popped through a small circular membrane on top of the box.

**poppet** /**pop**-uht/ *n. colloq.* term of endearment for a small child. [Latin *pup(p)a* doll]

**popping crease** *n. Cricket* line in front of and parallel to the wicket, within which the batsman stands. [from POP¹]

**poppy** /**pop**-ee/ *n.* (*pl.* **-ies**) **1** plant with showy esp. scarlet flowers and a milky sap. **2** artificial poppy worn on Remembrance Day. [Latin *papaver*]

**poppycock** *n. colloq.* nonsense. [Dutch *pappekak*]

**Poppy Day** *n.* = REMEMBRANCE DAY.

**populace** /**pop**-yuh-luhs/ *n.* the common people. [Italian: related to POPULAR]

**popular** /**pop**-yuh-luh/ *adj.* **1** liked or admired by many people or by a specified group (*a popular hero*; *a teacher popular with his students*). **2 a** of or for the general public (*popular meetings*). **b** prevalent among the general public (*popular fallacies*). **3** (sometimes *derog.*) adapted to the understanding, taste, or means of the people (*popular science*; *the popular press*). □ **popularity** /-la-ruh-tee/ *n.* **popularly** *adv.* [Anglo-Latin *populus* PEOPLE]

**popular front** *n.* party or coalition combining left-wing or progressive groups.

**popularise** *v.* (also **-ize**) (**-sing** or **-zing**) **1** make popular. **2** present (a difficult subject) in a readily understandable form. □ **popularisation** /-zay-shuhn/ *n.* **populariser** *n.*

**populate** /**pop**-yuh-layt/ *v.* (**-ting**) **1** inhabit, form the population of (a town, country, etc.). **2** supply with inhabitants (*a densely populated district*). [medieval Latin: related to PEOPLE]

**population** /ˌpop-yuh-**lay**-shuhn/ *n.* **1 a** inhabitants of a place, country, etc., referred to collectively. **b** any specified group within this (*the Greek population of Melbourne*). **2** total number of these or any group of living things (*a population of two million*; *the total penguin population*). **3** act or process of supplying with inhabitants (*pressing ahead with the population of forest areas*).

**population explosion** *n.* sudden large increase of population.

**populist** /**pop**-yuh-luhst/ — *n.* politician claiming to represent the ordinary people. — *adj.* concerned with the ordinary people. [Latin *populus* people]

**populous** /**pop**-yuh-luhs/ *adj.* thickly inhabited.

**pop-up** *adj.* involving parts that pop up automatically (*pop-up toaster*; *pop-up book*).

**porcelain** /**paw**-suh-luhn/ *n.* **1** hard fine translucent ceramic with a transparent glaze. **2** objects made of this. [Italian diminutive of *porca* sow]

**porch** *n.* covered entrance to a building. [Latin *porticus*]

**porcine** /**paw**-suyn/ *adj.* of or like pigs. [Latin: related to PORK]

**porcupine** /**paw**-kyuh-ˌpuyn/ *n.* **1** rodent (of Europe etc.) with a body and tail covered with erectile spines. **2** = ECHIDNA. **3** = PORCUPINE GRASS. **4** (*attrib.*) denoting any of various animals or other organisms with spines. □ **porcupinish** *adj.* **porcupiny** *adj.* [Provençal: related to PORK, SPINE]

**porcupine grass** *n.* (also **porcupine**) = SPINIFEX.

**pore¹** *n.* minute opening in a surface through which fluids etc. may pass. [Greek *poros*]

**pore²** *v.* (**-ring**) (foll. by *over*) **1** be absorbed in studying (a book etc.). **2** meditate on; think intently about (*pored over the problem for several hours*). [origin unknown]

**pork** *n.* flesh (esp. unsalted) of a pig, used as food. [Latin *porcus* pig]

**pork barrel** — *n.* government funds allocated so as to derive political benefit. — *v.* (**-ll-**) (of a government) allocate funds to (a particular region, electorate, etc.) in the hope of obtaining votes. □ **pork-barrelling** *n.*

**porky** *adj.* (**-ier**, **-iest**) **1** *colloq.* fat. **2** of or like pork. **3** a lie. [sense 3 from *pork pie* rhyming slang for *lie*]

**porn** *colloq.* — *n.* pornographic books, videos, etc.; pornography. — *attrib. adj.* pornographic. [abbreviation]

**pornography** /paw-**nog**-ruh-fee/ *n.* **1** explicit representation of sexual activity in literature, films, etc., intended to stimulate erotic feelings. **2** literature etc.

containing this. □ **pornographer** n. **pornographic** /-nuh-**graf**-ik/ adj. [Greek *pornē* prostitute]

**porous** /**paw**-ruhs/ adj. **1** full of pores. **2** letting through air, water, etc. □ **porosity** /paw-**ros**-uh-tee/ n. **porousness** n. [Latin: related to PORE[1]]

**porphyry** /**paw**-fuh-ree/ n. (pl. **-ies**) hard rock composed of crystals of white or red feldspar in a red matrix. □ **porphyritic** /-**rit**-ik/ adj. [Greek: related to PURPLE]

**porpoise** /**paw**-puhs/ n. sea mammal of the whale family, with a blunt rounded snout. [Latin *porcus* pig, *piscis* fish]

**porridge** /**po**-rij/ n. dish of oatmeal or cereal boiled in water or milk. [alteration of POTTAGE]

**port**[1] n. **1** harbour. **2** place of refuge. **3** town possessing a harbour. [Latin *portus*]

**port**[2] n. a kind of sweet, dark red (occasionally brown or white), fortified wine. [*Oporto* in Portugal]

**port**[3] — n. left-hand side of a ship or aircraft looking forward (cf. STARBOARD). — adj. on or concerning the port side. — v. (also *absol.*) turn (the helm) to port. [probably originally the side turned to PORT[1]]

**port**[4] n. **1 a** opening in the side of a ship for entrance, loading, etc. **b** porthole. **2** aperture for the passage of steam, water, etc. **3** socket or aperture in an electronic circuit, esp. in a computer network, where connections can be made with peripheral equipment. [Latin *porta* gate]

**port**[5] n. colloq. (esp. Queensland) **1 a** suitcase, travelling bag; school satchel. **b** (in pl.) baggage. **2** shopping bag, sugar bag, etc. [abbreviation of PORTMANTEAU]

**portable** /**paw**-tuh-buhl/ — adj. **1** easily movable, convenient for carrying (*portable TV; portable computer*). **2** (of a right, opinion, etc.) capable of being transferred or adapted in altered circumstances (*portable superannuation*). **3** = MACHINE-INDEPENDENT. — n. portable version of an item, e.g. a television. □ **portability** /,paw-tuh-**bil**-uh-tee/ n. [Latin *porto* carry]

**portal** /**paw**-tuhl/ n. doorway or gate etc., esp. an elaborate one. [Latin: related to PORT[4]]

**portcullis** /pawt-**kul**-uhs/ n. strong heavy grating lowered to block a gateway in a fortress etc. [French, = sliding door]

**portend** /paw-**tend**/ v. **1** foreshadow as an omen. **2** give warning of. [Latin *portendo*: related to PRO-[1], TEND[1]]

**portent** /**paw**-tent, -tuhnt/ n. **1** omen, significant sign of something to come. **2** prodigy; marvellous thing. [Latin *portentum*: related to PORTEND]

**portentous** /paw-**ten**-tuhs/ adj. **1** like or being a portent. **2** pompously solemn.

**porter**[1] n. person employed to carry luggage etc. [Latin *porto* carry]

**porter**[2] n. gatekeeper or doorman, esp. of a large building. [Latin: related to PORT[4]]

**portfolio** /pawt-**foh**-lee-oh/ n. (pl. **-s**) **1 a** folder for loose sheets of paper, drawings, etc. **b** samples of an artist's work. **2** range of investments held by a person, company, etc. **3** office or post of a minister (sense 1). [Italian *portafogli* sheet-carrier]

**porthole** n. aperture (esp. glazed) in a ship's side for letting in light.

**portico** /**paw**-tuh-,koh/ n. (pl. **-es** or **-s**) colonnade; roof supported by columns at regular intervals, usu. attached as a porch to a building. [Latin *porticus* porch]

**portion** /**paw**-shuhn/ — n. **1** part or share. **2** amount of food allotted to one person. **3** specified or limited quantity. **4** one's destiny or lot (*our portion in life*). **5** dowry. — v. **1** divide (a thing) into portions. **2** (foll. by *out*) distribute. [Latin *portio*]

**Port Jackson fig** n. shrub to large tree (depending on where planted) native to eastern NSW, having shiny leaves rusty on the underside and 1cm diameter fruits; often cultivated as an indoor plant. [*Port Jackson*, the port of Sydney]

**Port Jackson pine** n. tall, attractive, cypress pine tree of southern Australia, growing in a slender column and having an extremely formal appearance.

**Port Jackson shark** n. small, harmless, primitive shark of southern Australia which feeds on shellfish.

**Portland cement** /**pawt**-luhnd/ n. cement manufactured from chalk and clay. [Isle of *Portland* in England]

**Port Lincoln parrot** n. (also **twenty-eight**) parrot of central and western Australia, a predominantly green bird with a black head, and yellow collar and belly. [*Port Lincoln*, a town in SA]

**portly** /**pawt**-lee/ adj. (**-ier**, **-iest**) corpulent; stout. [Latin *porto* carry]

**portmanteau** /pawt-**man**-toh/ n. (pl. **-s** or **-x** /-tohz/) trunk for clothes etc., opening into two equal parts. [Latin *porto* carry: related to MANTLE]

**portmanteau word** n. word combining the sounds and meanings of two others, e.g. *motel* (motor + hotel), *brunch* (breakfast + lunch).

**portrait** /**paw**-truht/ n. **1** drawing, painting, photograph, etc., of a person or animal, esp. of the face. **2** graphic description in words. **3** person etc. strongly resembling another (*is the portrait of his father*). □ **portraitist** n. [French: related to PORTRAY]

**portraiture** /paw-truh-chuh/ n. **1** the art of making portraits. **2** description in words. **3** portrait.

**portray** /paw-tray/ v. **1** make a likeness of. **2** describe graphically in words. □ **portrayal** n. **portrayer** n. [French *portraire -trait* depict]

**Portuguese** /,paw-chuh-**geez**/ — n. (pl. same) **1 a** native or national of Portugal. **b** person of Portuguese descent. **2** language of Portugal. — adj. of Portugal, its people, or language. [medieval Latin]

**Portuguese man-of-war** n. (pl. **men-**) (also **bluebottle**) dangerous jellyfish with a large crest and poisonous sting.

**portulaca** /,paw-chuh-**lak**-uh/ n. any of several plants of the genus of the same name, having thick, succulent leaves and brightly coloured flowers (see MUNYEROO). [Latin]

**pose** /pohz/ — v. (**-sing**) **1** assume a certain attitude of the body, esp. when being photographed or painted. **2** (foll. by *as*) pretend to be (another person etc.) (*posing as a celebrity*). **3** behave affectedly to impress others. **4** put forward or present (a question etc.) (*the power failure posed a grave problem for the surgeons*). **5** place (an artist's model etc.) in a certain attitude. — n. **1** attitude of body or mind. **2** affectation, pretence (*his generosity is a mere pose*). [Latin *pauso* PAUSE, confused with Latin *pono* PLACE]

**poser** /poh-zuh/ n. **1** poseur. **2** colloq. puzzling question or problem.

**poseur** /poh-**zer**/ n. person who behaves affectedly. [French *poser* POSE]

**posh** colloq. — adj. **1** smart; stylish; luxurious and expensive. **2** superior, supposedly upper-class (*spoke with a posh accent*). — adv. in a supposedly upper-class way (*talk posh*). □ **posh up** smarten up. □ **poshly** adv. **poshness** n. [perhaps from British *posh* a dandy; the phrase *p(ort) o(ut), s(tarboard) h(ome)*, referring to the more comfortable accommodation on ships between the UK and India, is a later association and not the true origin of *posh*]

**posit** /poz-uht/ v. (**-t-**) assume as a fact, postulate. [Latin: related to POSITION]

**position** /puh-**zish**-uhn/ — n. **1** place occupied by a person or thing. **2** way in which a person, or a thing or its parts are placed or arranged (*sitting in an uncomfortable position*). **3** proper place (*in position*). **4** advantage (*jockeying for*

*position*). **5** attitude; view on a question (*changed their position on nuclear disarmament*). **6** person's situation in relation to others (*puts one in an awkward position*). **7** rank, status; social standing. **8** paid employment (*a position in the public service*). **9** place where troops etc. are posted for strategical purposes (*their position was stormed*). — v. place in position. □ **in a position to** able to. □ **positional** adj. [Latin *pono posit-* place]

**positive** /poz-uh-tiv/ — adj. **1** explicit; definite, unquestionable (*positive proof*). **2** (of a person) convinced, confident, or overconfident in an opinion (*I'm positive I wasn't there*). **3 a** absolute; not relative. **b** Gram. (of an adjective or adverb) expressing a simple quality without comparison (cf. COMPARATIVE; SUPERLATIVE). **4** colloq. downright; complete (*it was a positive miracle*). **5** constructive (*positive thinking*). **6** marked by the presence and not absence of qualities or Med. symptoms (*positive reaction to the plan; the test for AIDS was positive*). **7** esp. Philos. dealing only with matters of fact; practical. **8** tending in a direction naturally or arbitrarily taken as that of increase or progress (*clockwise rotation is positive*). **9** greater than zero (*positive and negative integers*). **10** Electr. of, containing, or producing the kind of electrical charge produced by rubbing glass with silk; lacking electrons. **11** (of a photographic image) showing lights and shades or colours unreversed (opp. NEGATIVE). — n. positive adjective, photograph, quantity, etc. □ **positively** adv. **positiveness** n. [Latin: related to POSITION]

**positive discrimination** n. practice of actively discriminating in favour of groups considered to be underprivileged or disadvantaged.

**positivism** n. philosophical system recognising only facts and observable phenomena. □ **positivist** n. & adj.

**positron** /poz-uh-,tron/ n. Physics elementary particle with the same mass as, but opposite (positive) charge to, an electron. [*posi*tron elec*tron*]

**posse** /pos-ee/ n. **1** strong force or company. **2** body of law-enforcers. [Latin, = be able]

**possess** /puh-**zes**/ v. **1** hold as property; own. **2** have (a faculty, quality, etc.) (*they possess a special value for us*). **3** occupy or dominate the mind of (*possessed by the devil; possessed by fear*). □ **be possessed of** own, have. **what possessed you?** an expression of incredulity. □ **possessor** n. [Latin *possideo possess-*]

**possession** /puh-**zesh**-uhn/ *n.* **1** act or state of possessing or being possessed. **2** thing possessed. **3** act or state of actual holding or occupancy. **4** *Law* power or control similar to ownership but which may exist separately from it (*prosecuted for possession of drugs*). **5** (in *pl.*) property, wealth, subject territory, etc. **6** *Football etc.* control of the ball by a player.

**possessive** /puh-**zes**-iv/ — *adj.* **1** wanting to retain what one has, reluctant to share. **2** jealous and domineering. **3** *Gram.* indicating possession. — *n.* (in full **possessive case**) *Gram.* case of nouns and pronouns expressing possession. □ **possessiveness** *n.*

**possibility** /ˌpos-uh-**bil**-uh-tee/ *n.* (*pl.* **-ies**) **1** state or fact of being possible. **2** thing that may exist or happen. **3** (usu. in *pl.*) capability of being used; potential (*this project has possibilities*). [Latin *posse* be able]

**possible** /**pos**-uh-buhl/ — *adj.* **1** capable of existing, happening, being done, etc. (*come as early as possible; did as much as possible*). **2** that is likely to happen etc. (*few thought their victory possible*). **3** acceptable; potential (*a possible way of doing it*). — *n.* **1** possible candidate, member of a team, etc. (*he's a possible*). **2** (prec. by *the*) whatever is likely, manageable, etc.

**possibly** *adv.* **1** perhaps. **2** in accordance with possibility (*cannot possibly go*).

**possie** /**poz**-ee/ *n.* (also **possy**) *colloq.* position of supposed advantage to the occupant (*secured a good possie along the route of the procession; has a possy in the bank with little work and decent pay*).

**possum** /**pos**-uhm/ *n.* **1** any of many chiefly herbivorous, long-tailed, tree-dwelling, mainly Australian marsupials, some of which are gliding animals (*brush-tailed possum; flying possum; honey possum; Leadbetter's possum; mountain pygmy possum; pygmy possum; ringtail possum*). **2 a** mildly derogatory term for a person. **b** affectionate mode of address. □ **play possum 1** pretend to be asleep or unconscious when threatened etc. **2** feign ignorance. **stir the possum** excite interest or controversy; liven things up. [abbreviation of OPOSSUM]

**possum banksia** *n.* small WA banksia with toothed leaves and very large, woolly, browny-grey flowers which remain woolly even after they die and resemble possums on the bush.

**post**[1] /pohst/ — *n.* **1** long stout piece of timber or metal set upright in the ground etc. to support something, mark a

position or boundary, etc. **2** pole etc. marking the start or finish of a race. — *v.* **1** (often foll. by *up*) attach (a notice etc.) in a prominent place (*post no bills*). **2** announce or advertise by poster or list. [Latin *postis*]

**post**[2] /pohst/ — *n.* **1** official conveyance of parcels, letters, etc. (*send it by post*). **2** single collection or delivery of these; the letters etc. dispatched (*has the post arrived?*). **3** place where letters etc. are collected, dealt with: postbox, post office (*take it to the post*). — *v.* **1** put (a letter etc.) in the post. **2** (esp. as **posted** *adj.*) (often foll. by *up*) supply with information (*keep me posted*). **3 a** enter (an item) in a ledger. **b** (often foll. by *up*) complete (a ledger) in this way. [Latin: related to POSITION]

**post**[3] /pohst/ — *n.* **1** place where a soldier is stationed or which he or she patrols. **2** place of duty. **3 a** position taken up by a body of soldiers. **b** force occupying this. **c** fort. **4** job, paid employment. — *v.* **1** place or station (soldiers, an employee, etc.). **2** appoint to a post or command. [French: related to POST[2]]

**post**[4] *n.* (in some Australian universities) supplementary examination, chiefly for candidates who missed the first through illness.

**post-** *prefix* after, behind. [Latin *post* (adv. and prep.)]

**postage** *n.* charge for sending a letter etc. by post, usu. prepaid by means of a stamp.

**postal** *adj.* of or by post. [French: related to POST[2]]

**postal note** *n.* = POSTAL ORDER.

**postal order** *n.* (also **postal note**) money order issued by the Post Office, payable to a specified person.

**post-and-rail fence** *n.* (also **post-and-rail fencing**) wooden fence consisting of two or more horizontal rails morticed into upright posts.

**post-and-rail tea** *n. colloq.* **1** strong, roughly made bush tea in which particles of stalk etc. float on the surface. **2** any tea of inferior quality.

**postbox** *n.* public box for posting mail.

**postcard** *n.* card for sending by post without an envelope.

**postcode** *n.* group of figures in a postal address to assist sorting.

**post-coital** /pohst-**koh**-uh-tuhl/ *adj. formal* occurring after sexual intercourse.

**post-date** /pohst-**dayt**/ *v.* (**-ting**) **1** give a date later than the actual one to (a document etc.). **2** follow in time.

**poster** *n.* **1** placard in a public place. **2** large printed picture. **3** one who puts up posters, billposter. **4** *Aust. Rules* kick for goal which hits one of the goal posts and hence scores only a point.

**poste restante** /ˌpohst res-**tahnt**/ *n.* department in a post office where letters are kept till called for. [French]

**posterior** /pos-**teer**-ree-uh/ — *adj.* **1** later; coming after in series, order, or time. **2** at the back. — *n.* buttocks. [Latin, comparative of *posterus*: related to POST-]

**posterity** /pos-**te**-ruh-tee/ *n.* **1** succeeding generations. **2** person's descendants. [Latin: related to POSTERIOR]

**postern** /**pos**-tuhn, **poh**-stuhn/ *n.* back door; side way or entrance. [Latin: related to POSTERIOR]

**postgraduate** — *n.* person engaged in a course of study after taking a first degree. — *adj.* of or concerning postgraduates.

**post-haste** *adv.* with great speed.

**posthumous** /**pos**-chuh-muhs, -tyoo-/ *adj.* **1** occurring after death. **2** (of a book etc.) published after the author's death. **3** (of a child) born after the death of its father. □ **posthumously** *adv.* [Latin *postumus* last]

**postie** /**poh**-stee/ *n. colloq.* postman or postwoman.

**postilion** /pos-**til**-yuhn/ *n.* (also **postillion**) person riding on the near horse of a team drawing a coach when there is no coachman. [Italian: related to POST²]

**post-Impressionism** /ˌpohst-im-**presh**-uh-ˌniz-uhm/ *n.* artistic aims and methods developed as a reaction against Impressionism and intending to express the individual artist's conception of the objects represented rather than the ordinary observer's view. □ **post-Impressionist** *n. & adj.*

**post-industrial** *adj.* of a society or economy which no longer relies on heavy industry.

**postman** *n.* (*fem.* **postwoman**) person employed to deliver and collect letters etc.

**postmark** — *n.* official mark on a letter, giving the place, date, etc., and cancelling the stamp. — *v.* mark (an envelope etc.) with this.

**postmaster** *n.* (*fem.* **postmistress**) official in charge of a post office.

**postmodern** *adj.* (in the arts etc.) of the movement reacting against modernism, esp. by drawing attention to former conventions. □ **postmodernism** *n.* **postmodernist** *n. & adj.*

**post-mortem** /pohst-**maw**-tuhm/ — *n.* **1** examination made after death, esp. to determine its cause. **2** *colloq.* discussion analysing the course and result of a game, election, etc. — *adv. & adj.* after death. [Latin]

**post-natal** /pohst-**nay**-tuhl/ *adj.* of the period after childbirth.

**Post Office** *n.* **1** government department responsible for postal services. **2** (**post office**) room or building where postal business is carried on.

**postpone** /pohst-**pohn**, pohs-**pohn**/ *v.* (**-ning**) cause or arrange (an event etc.) to take place at a later time. □ **postponement** *n.* [Latin *pono* place]

**postprandial** /pohst-**pran**-dee-uhl/ *adj.* *formal* or *joc.* after dinner or lunch. [Latin *prandium* a meal]

**postscript** /**pohst**-skript, **poh**-skript/ *n.* **1** additional paragraph or remark, usu. at the end of a letter after the signature and introduced by 'PS'. **2** any additional information, action, etc. **3** (**Postscript**) *propr. Computing* programming language used esp. in word processing and desk top publishing to control page layout.

**post-structuralism** *n.* a movement in literature, psychology, linguistics, etc., modifying the principles of structuralism and questioning the concepts of form and representation.

**post-traumatic stress disorder** *n.* *Psychol.* nervous disorder occurring after an event which has caused severe emotional and/or physical stress and producing such symptoms as depression, withdrawal, and the tendency to relive the event which caused the initial stress: associated e.g. with survivors of a massacre in a shopping mall, etc., and esp. with many Vietnam veterans.

**postulant** /**pos**-chuh-luhnt, **pos**-tyoo-/ *n.* candidate, esp. for admission to a religious order. □ **postulancy** *n.* [Latin: related to POSTULATE]

**postulate** — *v.* /**pos**-chuh-ˌlayt, **pos**-tyoo-/ (**-ting**) **1** (often foll. by *that*) assume as a necessary condition, esp. as a basis for reasoning; take for granted. **2** claim. — *n.* /**pos**-chuh-luht, **pos**-tyoo-luht/ **1** thing postulated. **2** prerequisite or condition. □ **postulation** /ˌpos-chuh-**lay**-shuhn, ˌpos-tyoo-/ *n.* [Latin *postulo* claim]

**postulator** /**pos**-chuh-ˌlay-tuh, **pos**-tyoo-/ *n. RC Ch.* person who presents and argues the case for a dead person's canonisation or beatification (opp. DEVIL'S ADVOCATE).

**posture** /**pos**-chuh/ — *n.* **1 a** relative position of parts, esp. of the body (*a reclining posture*). **b** carriage, bearing (*improved by good posture*). **2** mental or spiritual attitude. **3** condition or state (of affairs etc.) (*a more diplomatic posture*). — *v.* (**-ring**) **1** assume a mental or physical attitude, esp. for effect (*inclined to strut and posture*). **2** pose (a person). □ **postural** *adj.* [Latin: related to POSIT]

**posy** /**poh**-zee/ *n.* (*pl.* **-ies**) small bunch of flowers. [alteration of POESY]

**pot¹** — *n.* **1** rounded ceramic, metal, or glass vessel for holding liquids or solids or for cooking in. **2** flowerpot, teapot, etc. **3** contents of a pot (*there's no jam — Bruce ate the whole pot*). **4** total amount bet in a game etc. **5** (usu. in *pl.*) *colloq.* large sum (*pots of money*). **6** = POT-SHOT. **7** = POT-BELLY. **8** = CHAMBER-POT. **9 a** medium-to-large glass for beer. **b** the beer it contains. — *v.* (**-tt-**) **1** place in a pot. **2** plant in a pot of potting mix. **3** pocket (a ball) in billiards etc. **4** abridge or epitomise (*in a potted version; potted wisdom*). **5** shoot at, hit, or kill (an animal) with a pot-shot. **6** seize or secure (*potted the trophy*). **7** make pots (as a potter). □ **go to pot** *colloq.* deteriorate; be ruined. □ **potful** *n.* (*pl.* **-s**). [Old English from Latin]

**pot²** *n. colloq.* marijuana. [Mexican Spanish *potiguaya*]

**potable** /**poh**-tuh-buhl/ *adj.* drinkable. [Latin *poto* drink]

**potage** /po-**tahzh**/ *n.* thick soup. [French: related to POT¹]

**potash** /**pot**-ash/ *n.* an alkaline potassium compound. [Dutch: related to POT¹, ASH¹]

**potassium** /puh-**tas**-ee-uhm/ *n.* soft silver-white metallic element. [from POTASH]

**potation** /poh-**tay**-shuhn/ *n.* **1** a drink. **2** drinking. [Latin: related to POTION]

**potato** /puh-**tay**-toh/ *n.* (*pl.* **-es**) **1** starchy plant tuber used for food. **2** plant bearing this. [Spanish *patata* from Taino *batata*]

**potato cake** *n.* = POTATO SCALLOP.

**potato chip** *n.* = CHIP *n.* 3.

**potato crisp** *n.* = CRISP *n.* 1

**potato orchid** *n.* saprophytic terrestrial orchid of southern and eastern Australia, having large, thick rhizomes and bell-shaped, cinnamon-brown flowers.

**potato peeler** *n.* small implement with double, swivelling blades, used for peeling potatoes etc.

**potato scallop** /**skol**-uhp/ *n.* (also **potato cake**) slice of potato (or flattened pounded potato) battered and fried.

**pot belly** *n.* **1** protruding stomach. **2** person with this.

**potboiler** *n.* piece of art, writing, etc., done merely to earn money.

**pot-bound** *adj* (of a plant) with roots filling its container, leaving no room to expand.

**potch** *n.* **1** an opal that has little or no play of colour and is of no value. **2** opal-bearing material found in association with precious opal. [origin unknown]

**potent** /**poh**-tuhnt/ *adj.* **1** powerful; strong. **2** (of a reason) cogent; forceful. **3** (of a male) capable of sexual erection or orgasm. □ **potency** *n.* [Latin *potens* *-ent-*: related to POSSE]

**potentate** /**poh**-tuhn-tayt/ *n.* monarch or ruler. [Latin: related to POTENT]

**potential** /puh-**ten**-shuhl/ — *adj.* capable of coming into being or action; latent. — *n.* **1** capacity for use or development (*achieved its highest potential*). **2** usable resources. **3** *Physics* quantity determining the energy of mass in a gravitational field or of charge in an electric field. □ **potentiality** /-shee-**al**-uh-tee/ *n.* **potentially** *adv.* [Latin: related to POTENT]

**potential difference** *n.* difference of electric potential between two points.

**pother** /**poth**-uh/ *n. literary* noise, commotion, fuss. [origin unknown]

**pothole** *n.* **1** deep hole or underground cave system in rock. **2** hole in a road surface. □ **potholer** *n.* **potholing** *n.*

**potion** /**poh**-shuhn/ *n.* dose of a liquid medicine, drug, poison, etc. [Latin *poto* drink]

**pot luck** *n.* whatever is available. □ **take pot luck 1** share a meal (of whatever happens to be already cooked or available). **2** take whatever is to be had.

**potoroo** /ˌpot-uh-**roo**/ *n.* (also **rat-kangaroo**) small, long-nosed, nocturnal macropod inhabiting areas of dense ground vegetation of south-eastern (and formerly south-western) Australia. [probably from Dharuk *badaru*]

**pot plant** *n.* plant grown in a container.

**pot-pourri** /poh-**poor**-ree, ˌpot-, poh-puh-**ree**/ *n.* (*pl.* **-s**) **1** scented mixture of dried petals and spices. **2** musical or literary medley. [French, = rotten pot]

**potsherd** /**pot**-ˌsherd/ *n.* esp. *Archaeol.* broken piece of ceramic material. [POT¹, SHARD]

**pot-shot** *n.* **1** random shot from a gun. **2** a gibe (esp. oral) (*MPs taking pot-shots at one another across the floor*). **3** an attempt (*I'll have a pot-shot at the lottery*).

**pottage** /**pot**-ij/ *n. archaic* soup, stew. [French: related to POT¹]

**potter¹** *v.* **1** (often foll. by *about, around*) work or occupy oneself in a desultory but enjoyable manner (*likes pottering* *around in his garden).* **2** go slowly, dawdle, loiter *(pottered along to the pub).* [British dial. *pote* push]

**potter²** *n.* maker of ceramic vessels. [Old English: related to POT¹]

**pottery** *n.* (*pl.* **-ies**) **1** vessels etc. made of fired clay. **2** potter's work. **3** potter's workshop. [French: related to POTTER²]

**potting mix** *n.* specially formulated mixture of materials in which to grow, esp., pot plants.

**potty¹** *adj.* (**-ier, -iest**) *colloq.* foolish, crazy. □ **pottiness** *n.* [origin unknown]

**potty²** *n.* (*pl.* **-ies**) *colloq.* chamber-pot, esp. for a child.

**pouch** — *n.* **1** small bag or detachable outside pocket. **2** baggy area of skin under the eyes etc. **3 a** pocket-like receptacle in which marsupials carry their young. **b** similar structure in various animals, e.g. in the cheeks of rodents. — *v.* put or make into a pouch. [French: related to POKE²]

**pouched mouse** *n.* any of several small, carnivorous, Australian marsupials, esp. the dunnart and the phascogale.

**pouffe** /puuf, poof/ *n.* large firm cushion used as a low seat or footstool. [French]

**poulterer** /**pohl**-tuh-ruh/ *n.* dealer in poultry and usu. game.

**poultice** /**pohl**-tuhs/ — *n.* **1** soft medicated usu. heated mass applied to the body and kept in place with muslin etc., to relieve soreness and inflammation. **2** *colloq.* **a** large sum of money. **b** a mortgage. — *v.* (**-cing**) apply a poultice to. [Latin *puls* pottage]

**poultry** /**pohl**-tree/ *n.* domestic fowls (ducks, geese, turkeys, chickens, etc.), esp. as a source of food. [French]

**pounce** — *v.* (**-cing**) **1** spring or swoop, esp. as in capturing prey. **2** (often foll. by *on, upon*) **a** make a sudden attack. **b** seize eagerly upon a remark etc. *(pounced on what I said).* — *n.* act of pouncing. [origin unknown]

**pound¹** *n.* **1** unit of weight in the imperial system equal to 16 oz. avoirdupois (0.4536 kg), 12 oz. troy (0.3732 kg). **2** (in full **pound sterling**) (*pl.* same or **-s**) chief monetary unit of the UK etc. [Latin *pondo*]

**pound²** *v.* **1 a** crush or beat with repeated blows. **b** thump or pummel, esp. with the fists *(pounded the door as if to break it down).* **c** grind to a powder or pulp. **2** (foll. by *at, on*) deliver heavy blows or gunfire *(pounded on the door; ships pounding at the coast).* **3** (foll. by *along* etc.) make one's way heavily or clumsily. **4** (of the heart) beat heavily. □ **pound out** produce with or as with heavy blows *(pounding*

*out Waltzing Matilda on the piano).* [Old English]

**pound³** — *n.* **1** enclosure where stray animals or officially removed vehicles are kept until claimed. **2** a natural basin surrounded by high, rocky terrain *(Wilpena pound).* — *v.* enclose (cattle etc.) in a pound. [Old English]

**pounder** *n.* (usu. in *comb.*) **1** thing or person weighing a specified number of pounds *(a five-pounder).* **2** gun firing a shell of a specified number of pounds.

**pour** /paw/ *v.* **1** (usu. foll. by *down, out, over,* etc.) flow or cause to flow esp. downwards in a stream or shower. **2** dispense (a drink) by pouring. **3** rain heavily. **4** (usu. foll. by *in, out,* etc.) come or go in profusion or rapid succession *(the crowd poured out; letters poured in).* **5** discharge or send freely. **6** (often foll. by *out*) utter at length or in a rush *(poured out their story).* [origin unknown]

**pout** — *v.* **1** push the lips forward as a sign of displeasure or sulking. **2** (of the lips) be pushed forward. — *n.* this action. [origin unknown]

**pouter** *n.* **1** person who pouts. **2** kind of pigeon that is able to inflate its crop.

**poverty** /**pov**-uh-tee/ *n.* **1** state of being poor; want of the necessities of life. **2** (often foll. by *of, in*) scarcity or lack *(poverty of invention in his novel).* **3** inferiority, poorness *(the poverty of sandy soils).* [Latin *pauper*]

**poverty bush** *n.* any of many shrubs of drier Australia (esp. the emu bush) growing in poor soil.

**poverty line** *n.* minimum income needed for the necessities of life.

**poverty-stricken** *adj.* very poor.

**poverty trap** *n.* situation in which an increase of income incurs a loss of government benefits, making real improvement impossible.

**POW** *abbr.* prisoner of war.

**powder** — *n.* **1** mass of fine dry particles. **2** medicine or cosmetic in this form. **3** = GUNPOWDER. — *v.* **1** apply powder to. **2** (esp. as **powdered** *adj.*) reduce to a fine powder *(powdered milk).* □ **powder one's nose** *euphem.* (of a female) go to the toilet. □ **powdery** *adj.* [Latin *pulvis -ver-* dust]

**powder room** *n. euphem.* women's toilet in a public building.

**power** — *n.* **1** ability to do or act. **2** particular faculty of body or mind *(lost the power of speech).* **3 a** influence, authority. **b** political ascendancy, control *(the party in power).* **4** authorisation; delegated authority *(power of attorney; police powers).* **5** (often foll. by *over*) personal ascendancy. **6** influential person, body, or thing. **7** nation having international influence. **8** vigour, energy. **9** active property or function (*has a high heating power*). **10** *colloq.* large number or amount (*did me a power of good*). **11** capacity for exerting mechanical force or doing work (*horsepower*). **12** mechanical or electrical energy as distinct from manual labour (often *attrib.*: *power tools*; *power steering*). **13** a electricity supply. **b** particular source or form of energy (*hydroelectric power*). **14** *Physics* rate of energy output. **15** product obtained when a number is multiplied by itself a certain number of times (*2 to the power of 3 = 8*). **16** magnifying capacity of a lens. **17** a deity. — *v.* **1** supply with mechanical or electrical energy. **2** (foll. by *up*, *down*) increase or decrease the power supplied to (a device); switch on or off. □ **the powers that be** those in authority. [Latin *posse* be able]

**power dressing** *n.* wearing of clothes calculated to proclaim one's power, esp. in contexts in which one's power would not otherwise be given due weight (*many businesswomen find it an advantage to go in for power dressing*).

**powerful** *adj.* **1** having much power, potency, strength, etc. **2** politically or socially influential. □ **powerfully** *adv.* **powerfulness** *n.*

**powerful owl** *n.* large owl of eastern Australia, having predominantly brown and cream plumage and a deep, resonant, two-note hoot.

**powerhouse** *n.* **1** = POWER STATION. **2** person or thing of great energy.

**powerless** *adj.* **1** without power. **2** wholly unable. □ **powerlessness** *n.*

**power of attorney** *n.* authority to act for another person in legal and financial matters.

**power point** *n.* socket in a wall etc. for connecting an electrical device to the mains.

**power station** *n.* building where electrical power is generated for distribution.

**power steering** *n.* hydraulic etc. mechanism for aiding steering in a motor vehicle.

**powwow** — *n.* meeting for discussion (orig. among N. American Indians). — *v.* hold a powwow. [Algonquian]

**pox** *n.* **1** any virus disease producing a rash of pimples that become pus-filled and leave pock-marks on healing. **2** *colloq.* = SYPHILIS or any other venereal disease. [alteration of *pocks* pl. of POCK]

**pp** *abbr.* pianissimo.

**pp.** *abbr.* pages.

**P-plate** *n.* sign bearing the letter P (for 'provisional') which by law must be attached to the front and rear of a motor vehicle to indicate that the driver has a provisional licence.

**p.p.m.** *abbr.* parts per million.

**PPS** *abbr.* additional postscript. [from *post-postscript*]

**PR** *abbr.* **1** public relations. **2** proportional representation.

**Pr** *symb.* praseodymium.

**practicable** /prak-ti-kuh-buhl/ *adj.* **1** that can be done or used. **2** possible in practice. □ **practicability** /-bil-uh-tee/ *n.* [French: related to PRACTICAL]

**practical** /prak-ti-kuhl/ — *adj.* **1** of or concerned with practice rather than theory (*practical difficulties*). **2** suited to use; functional (*practical shoes*). **3** (of a person) good at making, organising, or mending things. **4** sensible, realistic. **5** that is such in effect, virtual (*in practical control*). — *n.* practical examination or lesson. □ **practicality** /-kal-uh-tee/ *n.* (*pl.* **-ies**). [Greek *praktikos* from *prassō* do]

**practical joke** *n.* humorous trick played on a person.

**practically** *adv.* **1** virtually, almost (*practically nothing*). **2** in a practical way.

**practice** /prak-tuhs/ — *n.* **1** habitual action or performance (*makes a practice of saving*). **2** a habit or custom (*has been my regular practice*). **3** a repeated activity undertaken in order to improve a skill. **b** session of this. **4** action as opposed to theory. **5** the work, business, or place of business, of a doctor, lawyer, etc. (*has a practice in the local shopping centre*). **6** procedure, esp. of a specified kind (*bad practice*). — *adj.* done as a trial, or to improve skill, etc. (*a practice run*). □ **in practice 1** when actually applied; in reality. **2** skilful from recent practice. **out of practice** lacking a former skill from lack of practice. [from PRACTISE]

**practician** /ˌprak-**tish**-uhn/ *n.* a worker; a practitioner.

**practise** /prak-tuhs/ *v.* (**-sing**) **1** perform habitually; carry out in action. **2** do repeatedly as an exercise to improve a skill; exercise oneself in or on (an activity requiring skill). **3** (as **practised** *adj.*) experienced, expert; skilful through much practice (*with a practised hand*; *a practised liar*). **4** a (also *absol.*) be engaged in (a profession, religion, etc.). **b** (as **practising** *adj.*) currently active or engaged in (a profession, activity, etc.) (*a practising Catholic*; *a practising lawyer*). [Latin: related to PRACTICAL]

**practitioner** /prak-**tish**-uh-nuh/ *n.*

person practising a profession, esp. medicine.

**prad** *n. colloq.* a horse. [by metathesis from Dutch *paard*]

**pragmatic** /prag-**mat**-ik/ *adj.* dealing with matters from a practical point of view. □ **pragmatically** *adv.* [Greek *pragma -mat-* deed]

**pragmatism** /**prag**-muh-,tiz-uhm/ *n.* **1** pragmatic attitude or procedure. **2** philosophy that evaluates assertions solely by their practical consequences and bearing on human interests. □ **pragmatist** *n.* [Greek *pragma*: related to PRAGMATIC]

**prairie** /**prair**-ree/ *n.* large area of treeless grassland, esp. in N. America. [Latin *pratum* meadow]

**praise** /prayz/ — *v.* (**-sing**) **1** express warm approval or admiration of. **2** glorify (God) in words. — *n.* act or instance of praising; commendation. □ **sing the praises of** commend (a person or thing) highly. [French *preisier* from Latin *pretium* price]

**praiseworthy** *adj.* worthy of praise.

**pram** *n.* four-wheeled conveyance for a baby, pushed by a person on foot. [abbreviation of PERAMBULATOR]

**prance** /prahns, prans/ — *v.* (**-cing**) **1** (of a horse) raise the forelegs and spring from the hind legs. **2** walk or behave in an elated or arrogant manner. — *n.* act of prancing; a prancing movement. [origin unknown]

**prang** *colloq.* — *v.* **1** crash (esp. a car). **2** damage (a car etc.) by impact. **3** have a crash. — *n.* act or instance of pranging. [imitative]

**prank** *n.* practical joke; piece of mischief. [origin unknown]

**prankster** *n.* practical joker.

**praseodymium** /,pray-zee-uh-**dim**-ee-uhm/ *n.* soft silvery metallic element of the lanthanide series. [Greek *prasios* green]

**prat** *n. colloq.* bum, buttocks. [origin unknown]

**prate** — *v.* (**-ting**) **1** chatter; talk too much. **2** talk foolishly or irrelevantly. **3** tell or say in a prating manner. — *n.* prating; idle talk. [Low German or Dutch]

**pratincole** /**prat**-ing-,kohl, **pray**-ting-/ *n.* (in full **Australian pratincole**) small, long-legged, browny-red bird of open plains in northern and central Australia etc. which runs with great speed along the ground and has a swallow-like flight. [modern Latin *pratincola* from Latin *pratum* meadow, *incola* inhabitant]

**prattle** /**prat**-uhl/ — *v.* (**-ling**) chatter in a childish or inconsequential way. — *n.* childish or inconsequential chatter. [Low German *pratelen*: related to PRATE]

**prawn** — *n.* **1** any of several, often large, marine crustaceans, several species of which are prized as food. **2** *colloq.* a fool. — *v.* fish for prawns. □ **come the raw prawn** (often foll. by *with*) *colloq.* attempt to deceive (a person); misrepresent a situation (*don't come the raw prawn with me, mate!*). [origin unknown]

**prawnie** *n. colloq.* a prawn fisherman.

**praxis** /**prak**-suhs/ *n.* **1** accepted practice or custom. **2** the practising of an art or skill. [Greek, = doing]

**pray** *v.* (often foll. by *for* or *to* + infin. or *that* + clause) **1** say prayers; make devout supplication. **2 a** entreat (a person). **b** ask earnestly (*prayed to be released*). **3** (as *imper.*) *archaic* please (*pray tell me*). [Latin *precor*]

**prayer¹** /prair/ *n.* **1 a** request or thanksgiving to God or an object of worship. **b** formula used in praying (*the Lord's prayer*). **c** act of praying (*he's at prayer*). **d** religious service consisting largely of prayers (*morning prayer*). **2 a** entreaty to a person. **b** thing entreated or prayed for. [Latin: related to PRECARIOUS]

**prayer²** /**pray**-uh/ *n.* person who prays.

**praying mantis** see MANTIS.

**pre-** *prefix* before (in time, place, order, degree, or importance). [Latin *prae* before]

**preach** /preech/ *v.* **1** (also *absol.*) deliver (a sermon); proclaim or expound (the gospel etc.). **2** give moral advice in an obtrusive way (*don't you dare preach at me, you of all people!*). **3** advocate or inculcate (a quality or practice etc.). □ **preacher** *n.* [Latin *praedico* proclaim]

**preachify** /**pree**-chuh-fuy/ *v. colloq.* preach or moralise tediously.

**preachy** *adj. colloq. derog.* inclined to preach or moralise.

**preamble** /pree-**am**-buhl, **pree**-/ *n.* **1** preliminary statement. **2** introductory part of a statute or deed etc. [Latin: related to AMBLE]

**preamp** /**pree**-amp/ *n.* = PREAMPLIFIER. [abbreviation]

**preamplifier** /pree-**am**-pluh-,fuy-uh/ *n.* electronic device that amplifies a weak signal (e.g. from a microphone or pickup) and transmits it to a main amplifier.

**pre-arrange** /,pree-uh-**raynj**/ *v.* (**-ging**) arrange beforehand. □ **pre-arrangement** *n.*

**Precambrian** /pree-**kam**-bree-uhn/ *Geol.* — *adj.* of the earliest geological era. — *n.* this era.

**precarious** /pruh-**kair**-ree-uhs/ *adj.* **1** uncertain; dependent on chance (*makes a precarious living*). **2** insecure, perilous (*in precarious health*). □ **precariously** *adv.* **precariousness** *n.* [Latin *precarius*: related to PRAY]

**pre-cast** /pree-**kahst**/ *adj.* (of concrete) cast in its final shape before positioning.

**precaution** /pruh-**kaw**-shuhn/ *n.* action taken beforehand to avoid risk or ensure a good result. □ **precautionary** *adj.* [Latin: related to CAUTION]

**precede** /pree-**seed**/ *v.* (**-ding**) **1** come or go before in time, order, importance, etc. **2** (foll. by *by*) cause to be preceded (*you must precede punishment by stern warnings*). □ **preceding** *adj.* [Latin: related to CEDE]

**precedence** /**pres**-uh-duhns, pree-**see**-duhns/ *n.* **1** priority in time, order, importance, etc. **2** right of preceding others. □ **take precedence** (often foll. by *over, of*) have priority (over).

**precedent** — *n.* /**pree**-suh-duhnt, **pres**-uh-/ previous case etc. taken as a guide for subsequent cases or as a justification. — *adj.* /pree-**see**-duhnt, **pres**-uh-/ preceding in time, order, importance, etc. [French: related to PRECEDE]

**precentor** /pruh-**sen**-tuh/ *n.* person who leads the singing or (in a synagogue) the prayers of a congregation. [Latin *praecentor* from *cano* sing]

**precept** /**pree**-sept/ *n.* a command; a rule of conduct; a moral instruction. [Latin *praeceptum* maxim, order]

**preceptor** /pruh-**sep**-tuh/ *n.* teacher, instructor. □ **preceptorial** /,pree-sep-**taw**-ree-uhl/ *adj.* [Latin: related to PRECEPT]

**precession** /pree-**sesh**-uhn/ *n.* slow movement of the axis of a spinning body around another axis. [Latin: related to PRECEDE]

**precinct** /**pree**-singkt/ *n.* **1** enclosed or specially defined area around a place or building etc. **2** designated area in a town, esp. where traffic is excluded. **3** (in *pl.*) environs. [Latin *praecingo -cinct-* encircle]

**preciosity** /,pres-ee-**os**-uh-tee/ *n.* affected refinement in art or language, esp. in the choice of words. [related to PRECIOUS]

**precious** /**presh**-uhs/ — *adj.* **1** of great value or worth. **2** beloved; much prized (*precious memories*). **3** affectedly refined. **4** *colloq.* often *iron.* a considerable (*a precious lot of good*). **b** expressing contempt or disdain (*keep your precious flowers!*). — *adv. colloq.* extremely, very (*had precious little left*). □ **preciousness** *n.* [Latin *pretium* price]

**precious metals** *n.pl.* gold, silver, and platinum.

**precipice** /**pres**-uh-puhs/ *n.* **1** vertical or steep face of a rock, cliff, mountain, etc. **2** dangerous situation. [Latin *praeceps -cipit-* headlong]

**precipitant** /pruh-**sip**-uh-tuhnt/ — *adj.* = PRECIPITATE *adj.* — *n. Chem.* substance that causes another substance to precipitate. □ **precipitance** *n.* **precipitancy** *n.* [as PRECIPITATE]

**precipitate** — *v.* (**-ting**) /pruh-**sip**-uh-,tayt/ **1** hasten the occurrence of; cause to occur prematurely (*drink precipitated his decline*). **2** (foll. by *into*) send rapidly into a certain state or condition (*was precipitated into war*). **3** throw down headlong. **4** *Chem.* cause (a substance) to be deposited in solid form from a solution. **5** *Physics* condense (vapour) into drops and so deposit it. — *adj.* /pruh-**sip**-uh-tuht/ **1** headlong; violently hurried (*precipitate departure*). **2** (of a person or act) hasty, rash; inconsiderate. — *n.* /pruh-**sip**-uh-tuht/ **1** *Chem.* substance precipitated from a solution. **2** *Physics* moisture condensed from vapour, e.g. rain, dew. □ **precipitately** *adv.* **precipitateness** *n.* [Latin *praeceps, praecipitis* headlong]

**precipitation** /pruh-,sip-uh-**tay**-shuhn/ *n.* **1** act of precipitating or process of being precipitated. **2** rash haste. **3 a** rain or snow etc. falling to the ground. **b** quantity of this.

**precipitous** /pruh-**sip**-uh-tuhs/ *adj.* **1 a** of or like a precipice. **b** dangerously steep. **2** = PRECIPITATE *adj.*

**précis** /**pray**-see/ — *n.* (*pl.* same /-seez/) summary or abstract, esp. of a text or speech. — *v.* (**-cises** /-seez/; **-cised** /-seed/; **-cising** /-see-ing/) make a précis of. [French]

**precise** /pruh-**suys**/ *adj.* **1 a** accurately expressed. **b** definite, exact. **2** punctilious; scrupulous in being exact. **3** identical, exact (*at that precise moment . . .*). □ **preciseness** *n.* [Latin *praecido praecis-* cut short]

**precisely** *adv.* **1** in a precise manner; exactly. **2** (as a reply) quite so, as you say.

**precision** /pruh-**sizh**-uhn/ *n.* **1** accuracy. **2** degree of refinement in measurement etc. **3** (*attrib.*) marked by or adapted for precision (*precision instruments*).

**preclude** /pree-**klood**/ *v.* (**-ding**) **1** (foll. by *from*) prevent, exclude (*precluded from taking part*). **2** make impossible; remove (*so as to preclude all doubt*). [Latin *praecludo*: related to CLOSE[1]]

**precocious** /pruh-**koh**-shuhs/ *adj.* **1** often *derog.* (of esp. a child) prematurely developed in some (mental, physical, etc.) respect. **2** (of an action etc.) indicating such development. **3** (of a plant) flowering or fruiting earlier than usual. □ **precociously** adv. **precociousness** n. **precocity** /-**kos**-uh-tee/ n. [Latin praecox -cocis early ripe]

**precognition** /,pree-kog-**nish**-uhn/ n. supposed foreknowledge, esp. of a supernatural kind. □ **precognitive** /-**kog**-nuh-tiv/ adj.

**preconceive** /,pree-kuhn-**seev**/ v. (-ving) form (an idea or opinion etc.) beforehand.

**preconception** /,pree-kuhn-**sep**-shuhn/ n. preconceived idea, prejudice.

**precondition** /,pree-kuhn-**dish**-uhn/ n. condition that must be fulfilled in advance.

**precursor** /pree-**ker**-suh/ n. **1 a** person or thing that went before; forerunner. **b** person who precedes in office etc.; predecessor. **2** harbinger. **3** substance from which another is formed by decay or chemical reaction etc. □ **precursory** adj. **precursive** adj. [Latin praecurro -curs- run before]

**pre-date** /pree-**dayt**/ v. (-ting) precede in time.

**predator** /**pred**-uh-tuh/ n. predatory animal. [Latin]

**predatory** adj. **1** (of an animal) preying naturally upon others. **2** (of a person, a nation, etc.) plundering or exploiting others.

**predecease** /,pree-duh-**sees**/ v. (-sing) die earlier than (another person).

**predecessor** /**pree**-duh-,ses-uh/ n. **1** former holder of an office or position with respect to a later holder. **2** ancestor. **3** thing to which another has succeeded (the new plan will share the fate of its predecessor). [Latin decessor: related to DECEASE]

**predestination** /pree-,des-tuh-**nay**-shuhn/ n. belief or doctrine that everything has been preordained by God, including who is to be saved and who is damned.

**predestine** /pree-**des**-tuhn/ v. (-ning) **1** determine beforehand. **2** ordain in advance by divine will or as if by fate. [French or Church Latin: related to PRE-]

**predetermine** /,pree-duh-**ter**-muhn/ v. (-ning) **1** decree beforehand. **2** predestine. □ **predetermination** n.

**predicable** /**pred**-i-kuh-buhl/ adj. that may be predicated or affirmed. [medieval Latin: related to PREDICATE]

**predicament** /pruh-**dik**-uh-muhnt/ n. difficult, unpleasant, or embarrassing situation. [Latin: related to PREDICATE]

**predicate** — v. /**pred**-i-,kayt/ **1** (also absol.) assert (something) about the subject of a proposition. **2** (foll. by on) found or base (a statement etc.) on. — n. /**pred**-uh-kuht/ Gram. & Logic what is said about the subject of a sentence or proposition etc. (e.g. went home in John went home). □ **predication** /-**kay**-shuhn/ n. [Latin praedico -dicat- declare]

**predicative** /pruh-**dik**-uh-tiv/ adj. **1** Gram. (of an adjective or noun) forming or contained in the predicate, as old in the dog is old (but not in the old dog) (opp. ATTRIBUTIVE). **2** that predicates. [Latin: related to PREDICATE]

**predict** /pruh-**dikt**/ v. (often foll. by that) foretell, prophesy. □ **predictor** n. [Latin praedico -dict- foretell]

**predictable** adj. that can be predicted or is to be expected. □ **predictability** /-**bil**-uh-tee/ n. **predictably** adv.

**prediction** /pruh-**dik**-shuhn/ n. **1** the art of predicting or the process of being predicted. **2** thing predicted.

**predilection** /,pree-duh-**lek**-shuhn/ n. (often foll. by for) preference or special liking. [Latin praediligo, praedilect- prefer]

**predispose** /,pree-duhs-**pohz**/ v. (-sing) **1** influence favourably in advance. **2** (foll. by to, or to + infin.) render liable or inclined beforehand. □ **predisposition** /-dis-puh-**zish**-uhn/ n.

**predominant** /pruh-**dom**-uh-nuhnt/ adj. **1** predominating. **2** being the strongest or main element. □ **predominance** n. **predominantly** adv.

**predominate** /pruh-**dom**-uh-,nayt/ v. (-ting) **1** (foll. by over) have or exert control. **2** be superior. **3** be the strongest or main element (a garden in which Australian natives predominate).

**pre-echo** /pree-**ek**-oh/ n. (pl. -es) **1** faint copy heard just before an actual sound in a recording, caused by the accidental transfer of signals. **2** foreshadowing.

**pre-eminent** /pree-**em**-uh-nuhnt/ adj. **1** excelling others. **2** outstanding. □ **pre-eminence** n. **pre-eminently** adv.

**pre-empt** /pree-**empt**/ v. **1 a** forestall (pre-empted my main argument; pre-empted the attack by disabling the enemy). **b** appropriate in advance. **2** obtain by pre-emption. □ **pre-emptor** n. **pre-emptory** adj. [back-formation from PRE-EMPTION]

■ **Usage** Pre-empt is sometimes used to mean prevent, but this is considered incorrect in standard English.

**pre-emption** /pree-**emp**-shuhn/ n. purchase or taking by one person or party before the opportunity is offered to others. [medieval Latin *emo empt-* buy]

**pre-emptive** /pree-**emp**-tiv/ adj. **1** pre-empting. **2** (of military action) intended to prevent attack by disabling the enemy (*pre-emptive strike*).

**preen** v. **1** (of a bird) tidy (the feathers or itself) with its beak. **2** (of a person) smarten or admire (oneself, one's hair, clothes, etc.). **3** (often foll. by *on*) congratulate or pride (oneself). [origin unknown]

**prefab** /**pree**-fab/ n. colloq. prefabricated building. [abbreviation]

**prefabricate** /pree-**fab**-ruh-,kayt/ v. (**-ting**) **1** manufacture sections of (a building etc.) prior to their assembly on site. **2 a** produce in an artificially standardised way (*prefabricated romance novels by the dozen*). **b** concoct beforehand (*prefabricated his excuse*).

**preface** /**pref**-uhs/ — n. **1** introduction to a book stating its subject, scope, etc. **2** preliminary part of a speech. **3** Eccl. introduction to the central part of the Mass, a eucharistic service, etc. — v. (**-cing**) **1** (foll. by *with*) introduce or begin (a speech or event) (*prefaced his remarks with a warning*). **2** provide (a book etc.) with a preface. **3** (of an event etc.) lead up to (another). □ **prefatory** /**pref**-uh-tuh-ree, -tree/ adj. [Latin *praefatio*]

**prefect** /**pree**-fekt/ n. **1** chief administrative officer of a district, esp. in France. **2** senior pupil in a school, helping to maintain order. [Latin *praeficio -fect-* set in authority over]

**prefecture** /**pree**-fek-chuh/ n. **1** district under the government of a prefect. **2** prefect's office or tenure. [Latin: related to PREFECT]

**prefer** /pruh-**fer**/ v. (**-rr-**) **1** (often foll. by *to*, or *to* + infin.) like better (*prefers coffee to tea*). **2** submit (information, an accusation, etc.) for consideration. **3** promote or advance (a person). [Latin *praefero -lat-*]

**preferable** /**pref**-uh-ruh-buhl/ adj. to be preferred; more desirable. □ **preferably** adv.

**preference** /**pref**-uh-ruhns/ n. **1** act or instance of preferring or being preferred. **2** thing preferred. **3** favouring of one person etc. before others. **4** (in a system of preferential voting) numerical ranking given to a candidate on a ballot paper. **5** prior right, esp. to the payment of debts. □ **first preference** the first choice, as expressed by a voter on a ballot paper. **in**

**preference to** as a thing preferred over (another).

**preference shares** n.pl. (also **preference stock** n.sing.) shares or stock whose entitlement to dividend takes precedence over that of ordinary shares.

**preferential** /,pref-uh-**ren**-shuhl/ adj. **1** of or involving preference (*preferential treatment*). **2** giving or receiving a favour. □ **preferentially** adv.

**preferential voting** n. system of voting in which the voter marks candidates in order of preference.

**preferment** /pruh-**fer**-muhnt/ n. formal promotion to a higher office.

**prefigure** /pree-**fig**-uh/ v. formal (**-ring**) **1** represent beforehand by a figure or type (*Abel prefigured Christ*). **2** imagine beforehand. □ **prefiguration** n. **prefigurative** adj.

**prefix** /**pree**-fiks/ — n. **1** verbal element placed at the beginning of a word to qualify its meaning (e.g. *ex-*, *non-*, *un-*, as in *exterminate*, *nonconformist*, *unstable*). **2** title before a name (e.g. *Mr*). — v. (often foll. by *to*) **1** add as an introduction. **2** join (a word or element) as a prefix.

**pregnant** /**preg**-nuhnt/ adj. **1** (of a woman or female animal) having a child or young developing in the uterus. **2** full of meaning; significant; suggestive (*a pregnant pause*). **3** (foll. by *with*) plentifully provided (*situation pregnant with danger*). □ **pregnancy** n. (pl. **-ies**). [Latin *praegnans*]

**prehensile** /pree-**hen**-suyl/ adj. Zool. (of a tail or limb) capable of grasping. [Latin *prehendo -hens-* grasp]

**prehistoric** /,pree-his-**to**-rik/ adj. **1** of the period before written records. **2** colloq. utterly out of date. □ **prehistory** /-**his**-tuh-ree, -tree/ n.

**prejudge** /pree-**juj**/ v. (**-ging**) **1** form a premature judgment on (a person, issue, etc.). **2** pass judgment on (a person) before a trial or proper inquiry is held or before all the facts are known.

**prejudice** /**prej**-uh-duhs/ — n. **1 a** preconceived opinion. **b** (foll. by *against*, *in favour of*) bias, partiality. **2** harm that results or may result from some action or judgment (*to the prejudice of*). — v. (**-cing**) **1** impair the validity or force of (a right, claim, statement, etc.). **2** (esp. as **prejudiced** adj.) cause (a person) to have a prejudice. □ **without prejudice** (often foll. by *to*) without detriment (to an existing right or claim). [Latin: related to JUDGE]

**prejudicial** /,prej-uh-**dish**-uhl/ adj. (often foll. by *to*) causing prejudice; detrimental.

**prelacy** /**prel**-uh-see/ n. (pl. **-ies**) **1** church government by prelates. **2** (prec. by *the*) prelates collectively. **3** office or rank of prelate. [Anglo-French from medieval Latin: related to PRELATE]

**prelate** /**prel**-uht/ n. high ecclesiastical dignitary, e.g. a cardinal, an archbishop, etc. [Latin: related to PREFER]

**prelim** /**pree**-lim/ n. *colloq.* any event which precedes a main one (e.g. an examination, a sports match, etc.). [abbreviation]

**preliminary** /pruh-**lim**-uh-nuh-ree/ — adj. introductory, preparatory. — n. (pl. **-ies**) (usu. in pl.) **1** preliminary action or arrangement (*dispense with the preliminaries*). **2** preliminary trial or contest. — adv. (foll. by *to*) preparatory to; in advance of (*a match played preliminary to the main game*). [Latin *limen* threshold]

**preliterate** adj. of or relating to a society or culture that has not developed the use of writing.

**pre-loved** adj. *colloq.* second-hand, pre-owned.

**prelude** /**prel**-yood/ — n. (often foll. by *to*) **1** action, event, or situation serving as an introduction. **2** introductory part of a poem etc. **3** *Mus.* **a** introductory piece to a fugue, suite, etc. **b** short piece of a similar type, esp. for the piano. — v. (**-ding**) **1** serve as a prelude to. **2** introduce with a prelude. [Latin *ludo lusplay*]

**premarital** /pree-**ma**-ruh-tuhl/ adj. existing or (esp. of sexual relations) occurring before marriage.

**premature** /**prem**-uh-chuh, -**choor**/ adj. **1 a** occurring or done before the usual or proper time (*a premature decision*). **b** too hasty (*we must not be premature*). **2** (of a baby) born (esp. three or more weeks) before the end of gestation. □ **prematurely** adv. [Latin: related to PRE-, MATURE]

**pre-med** /pree-**med**/ n. *colloq.* = PRE-MEDICATION. [abbreviation]

**pre-medication** /pree-med-uh-**kay**-shuhn/ n. medication to prepare (a patient) for an operation etc.

**premeditate** /pree-**med**-uh-tayt/ v. (**-ting**) think out or plan beforehand (*premeditated murder*). □ **premeditation** /-**tay**-shuhn/ n. [Latin: related to MEDITATE]

**premenstrual** /pree-**men**-stroo-uhl/ adj. of the time shortly before each menstruation (*premenstrual tension*).

**premenstrual syndrome** n. syndrome experienced by some women prior to

menstruation and characterised by any of several symptoms such as tension, headaches, irritability, etc.

**premier** /**prem**-ee-uh, **prem**-yuh/ — n. **1** (**Premier**) chief minister of a State government in Australia. **2** (in pl.) sporting team which wins a premiership. — adj. **1** first in importance, order, or time. **2** of earliest creation (*New South Wales is the premier State*). [French, = first]

**premiere** /**prem**-ee-,air/ (also **première**) — n. first performance or showing of a play or film. — v. (**-ring**) give a premiere of. [French feminine: related to PREMIER]

**premiership** n. **1** the office of a Premier. **2** organised competition among sporting clubs. **3** the winning of this. □ **minor premiership** the position of a team leading the points table before the finals series begins.

**premise** /**prem**-uhs/ n. **1** *Logic* (also **premiss**) previous statement from which another is inferred. **2** (in pl.) house or other building with its grounds, outbuildings, etc. [Latin *praemissa* set in front]

**premiss** /**prem**-is/ n. *Logic* = PREMISE (sense 1).

**premium** /**pree**-mee-uhm/ n. **1** amount to be paid for a contract of insurance. **2 a** sum added to interest, wages, price, etc.; a bonus. **b** sum added to ordinary charges. **3** reward or prize. **4** (*attrib.*) (of a commodity) of the best quality and therefore more expensive (*premium mince*). □ **at a premium 1** highly valued; above the usual or nominal price. **2** scarce and in demand. [Latin *praemium* reward]

**premonition** /,prem-uh-**nish**-uhn, ,pree-muh-/ n. forewarning of something about to happen; presentiment. □ **premonitory** /pree-**mon**-uh-tuh-ree, -tree/ adj. [Latin *moneo monit-* warn]

**prenatal** /pree-**nay**-tuhl/ adj. of the period before childbirth.

**prenuptial** /pree-**nup**-shuhl/ adj. existing or occurring before marriage.

**prenuptial contract** n. *Law* contract between two persons intending to marry each other, setting out the terms and conditions of their marriage, esp. as to property and financial matters.

**preoccupy** /pree-**ok**-yuh-,puy/ v. (**-ies**, **-ied**) **1** (of a thought etc.) dominate the mind of (a person) to the exclusion of all else. **2** (as **preoccupied** adj.) otherwise engrossed; mentally distracted. □ **preoccupation** /pree-,ok-yuh-**pay**-shuhn/ n. [Latin *praeoccupo* seize beforehand]

**preordain** /ˌpree-aw-**dayn**/ v. ordain or determine beforehand.

**prep** — n. colloq. **1** preparation. **2** homework. — adj. preparatory (prep school). [abbreviation of PREPARATION]

**preparation** /ˌprep-uh-**ray**-shuhn/ n. **1** act or instance of preparing or the process of being prepared. **2** (often in pl.) something done to make ready. **3** specially prepared substance, esp. a food or medicine. **4** = PREP (sense 2).

**preparatory** /pruh-**pa**-ruh-tuh-ree, -tree/ — adj. (often foll. by to) serving to prepare; introductory. — adv. (often foll. by to) in a preparatory manner (was packing preparatory to departure).

**preparatory school** n. private primary school.

**prepare** /pruh-**pair**/ v. (-**ring**) **1** make or get ready for use, consideration, etc. **2** make ready or assemble (a meal etc.). **3 a** make (a person or oneself) ready or disposed in some way (prepared them for a shock). **b** get ready (prepare to jump). □ **be prepared** (often foll. by for, or to + infin.) be disposed or willing to. [Latin paro make ready]

**preparedness** /pruh-**pair**-ruhd-nuhs/ n. state of readiness.

**preponderate** /pruh-**pon**-duh-ˌrayt/ v. (-**ting**) (often foll. by over) **1** be greater in influence, quantity, or number; predominate. **2** be of greater importance. □ **preponderance** n. **preponderant** adj. [Latin pondus -der- weight]

**preposition** /ˌprep-uh-**zish**-uhn/ n. Gram. word governing (and usu. preceding) a noun or pronoun and expressing a relation to another word (see panel). □ **prepositional** adj. [Latin praepono -posit- place before]

**prepossess** /ˌpree-puh-**zes**/ v. **1** (usu. in passive) (of an idea, feeling, etc.) take possession of (a person). **2 a** prejudice (usu. favourably and spontaneously). **b** (as **prepossessing** adj.) attractive, appealing. □ **prepossession** n. /-zesh-uhn/ n.

**preposterous** /pruh-**pos**-tuh-ruhs/ adj. **1** utterly absurd; outrageous. **2** contrary to nature, reason, or sense. □ **preposterously** adv. [Latin, = topsy-turvy]

**prepuce** /**pree**-pyoos/ n. **1** = FORESKIN. **2** fold of skin surrounding the clitoris. [Latin praeputium]

**prerequisite** /pree-**rek**-wuh-zuht/ — adj. required as a precondition. — n. prerequisite thing.

■ **Usage** Prerequisite is sometimes confused with perquisite which means 'an extra profit, allowance, or right'.

**prerogative** /pruh-**rog**-uh-tiv/ n. right or privilege exclusive to an individual or office. [Latin praerogo ask first]

**Pres.** abbr. President.

**presage** /**pres**-ij/ — n. **1** omen, portent. **2** presentiment, foreboding. — v. (also /pruh-**sayj**/) (-**ging**) **1** portend, foreshadow. **2** give warning of (an event etc.) by natural means. **3** (of a person) predict or have a presentiment of. [Latin praesagium]

**Presbo** /**prez**-boh/ colloq. — n. a Presbyterian. — adj. Presbyterian. [abbreviation]

**presbyopia** /ˌprez-bee-**oh**-pee-uh/ n. long-sightedness caused by loss of elasticity of the eye lens, occurring esp. in middle and old age. □ **presbyopic** /-**op**-ik/ adj. [Greek presbus old man, ōps eye]

**presbyter** /**prez**-buh-tuh/ n. (in some churches) an elder. [Church Latin from Greek, = elder]

**Presbyterian** /ˌprez-buh-**teer**-ree-uhn, **pres**-puh-/ — adj. (of a church) governed by elders all of equal rank. — n. member

---

## Preposition

A preposition is used in front of a noun or pronoun to form a phrase. It often describes the position of something, e.g. under the chair, or the time at which something happens, e.g. in the evening.

Prepositions in common use are:

| | | | |
|---|---|---|---|
| about | behind | into | through |
| above | beside | like | till |
| across | between | near | to |
| after | by | of | towards |
| against | down | off | under |
| along | during | on | underneath |
| among | except | outside | until |
| around | for | over | up |
| as | from | past | upon |
| at | in | round | with |
| before | inside | since | without |

of a Presbyterian Church. □ **Presbyterianism** n.

**presbytery** /**prez**-buh-tuh-ree, **pres**-puh-/ n. (pl. **-ies**) **1** eastern part of a chancel; the sanctuary. **2** body of presbyters. **3** house of a Roman Catholic priest.

**preschool** /**pree**-skool/ — adj. of the time before a child is old enough to go to school. — n. = KINDERGARTEN.

**prescient** /**pres**-ee-uhnt/ adj. having foreknowledge or foresight. □ **prescience** n. [Latin praescio know before]

**prescribe** /pruh-**skruyb**/ v. (**-bing**) **1 a** advise the use of (a medicine etc.), esp. by an authorised prescription. **b** recommend, esp. as a benefit (prescribed a change of scenery). **2** lay down or impose authoritatively. [Latin praescribo -script-]

■ **Usage** Prescribe is sometimes confused with proscribe.

**prescript** /**pree**-skript/ n. ordinance, law, command. [Latin: related to PRESCRIBE]

**prescription** /pruh-**skrip**-shuhn/ n. **1** act or an instance of prescribing. **2 a** doctor's (usu. written) instruction for the supply and use of a medicine. **b** medicine prescribed.

**prescriptive** /pruh-**skrip**-tiv/ adj. **1** prescribing, laying down rules. **2** arising from custom.

**preselection** n. the choice of a candidate for a forthcoming election by (local) members of a political party.

**presence** /**prez**-uhns/ n. **1** state or condition of being present. **2** place where a person is (admitted to their presence). **3** person's appearance or bearing, esp. when imposing (has an august presence). **4** person or spirit that is present (aware of a presence in the room). [Latin: related to PRESENT[1]]

**presence of mind** n. calmness and quick-wittedness in sudden difficulty etc.

**present[1]** /**prez**-uhnt/ — adj. **1** (usu. predic.) being in the place in question (was present at the trial). **2 a** now existing, occurring, or being such (the present Prime Minister). **b** now being considered etc. (in the present case). **3** Gram. expressing an action etc. now going on or habitually performed (present participle). — n. (prec. by the) **1** the time now passing (no time like the present). **2** Gram. present tense. □ **at present** now. **by these presents** Law by this document. **for the present** just now; for the time being. [Latin praesens -ent-]

**present[2]** /pruh-**zent**/ v. **1** introduce, offer, or exhibit for attention or consideration. **2 a** (with a thing as object, foll. by to) offer or give as a gift (to a person). **b** (with a person as object, foll. by with) make available to; cause to have (that presents us with a problem). **3 a** (of a company, producer, etc.) put (a piece of entertainment) before the public. **b** (of a performer, compère, etc.) introduce. **4** introduce (a person) formally (may I present my fiancée?). **5 a** (of a circumstance) reveal (some quality etc.) (this presents some difficulty). **b** exhibit (an appearance etc.) (presented a rough exterior). **6** (of an idea etc.) offer or suggest itself. **7** deliver (a cheque, bill, etc.) for acceptance or payment. **8 a** (usu. foll. by at) aim (a weapon). **b** hold out (a weapon) in position for aiming. □ **present arms** hold a rifle etc. vertically in front of the body as a salute. □ **presenter** n. (in sense 3b). [Latin praesento: related to PRESENT[1]]

**present[3]** /**prez**-uhnt/ n. thing given, gift. [French: related to PRESENT[1]]

**presentable** /pruh-**zen**-tuh-buhl/ adj. of good appearance; fit to be presented to other people. □ **presentability** /-bil-uh-tee/ n. **presentably** adv.

**presentation** /,prez-uhn-**tay**-shuhn/ n. **1 a** act or instance of presenting or the process of being presented. **b** thing presented. **2** manner or quality of presenting. **3** demonstration or display of materials, information, etc.; lecture. **4** exhibition or theatrical performance.

**present-day** attrib. adj. of this time; modern.

**presentiment** /pruh-**zen**-tuh-muhnt, -**sen**-/ n. vague expectation; foreboding (esp. of misfortune).

**presently** adv. **1** soon; after a short time. **2** at the present time; now.

**preservative** /pruh-**zer**-vuh-tiv/ — n. substance for preserving perishable foodstuffs, wood, etc. — adj. tending to preserve.

**preserve** /pruh-**zerv**/ — v. (**-ving**) **1 a** keep safe or free from decay etc. **b** keep alive (a name, memory, etc.). **2** maintain (a thing) in its existing state. **3** retain (a quality or condition). **4** treat (food) to prevent decomposition or fermentation. **5** prepare (fruit) by boiling it with sugar, for long-term storage. — n. (in sing. or pl.) **1** preserved fruit; jam. **2** thing, place, etc., that is preserved. **3** sphere of activity regarded as a person's own. □ **preservation** /,prez-uh-**vay**-shuhn/ n. [Latin servo keep]

**pre-set** /**pree**-set/ v. (**-tt**-; past and past part. **-set**) **1** set or fix (a device) in advance of its operation. **2** settle or decide beforehand.

**preside** /pruh-**zuyd**/ v. (**-ding**) **1** (often foll. by *at*, *over*) be chairperson or president of a meeting etc. **2** exercise control or authority. [Latin *sedeo* sit]

**presidency** /**prez**-uh-duhn-see/ n. (pl. **-ies**) **1** office of president. **2** period of this.

**president** /**prez**-uh-duhnt/ n. **1** head of a republican nation. **2** head of a society or council etc. **3** person in charge of a meeting. □ **presidential** /-**den**-shuhl/ adj.

**press**[1] — v. **1** apply steady force to (a thing in contact) (*pressed the two surfaces together*). **2 a** compress or apply pressure to a thing to flatten, shape, or smooth it (*had the curtains pressed*). **b** squeeze (a fruit etc.) to extract its juice. **3** (foll. by *out of*, *from*, etc.) squeeze (juice etc.). **4** embrace or caress by squeezing (*pressed my hand*). **5** (foll. by *on*, *against*, etc.) exert pressure. **6** be urgent; demand immediate action (*time presses*). **7** (foll. by *for*) make an insistent demand. **8** (foll. by *up*, *round*, etc.) crowd. **9** (foll. by *on*, *forward*, etc.) hasten insistently. **10** (often in *passive*) (of an enemy etc.) bear heavily on (*our troops were heavily pressed*). **11** (often foll. by *for*, or *to* + infin.) urge or entreat (*pressed me to stay*; *pressed me for an answer*). **12** (foll. by *on*, *upon*) **a** put forward or urge (an opinion, claim, or course of action). **b** insist on the acceptance of (an offer, a gift, etc.). **13** insist on (*did not press the point*). **14** manufacture (a gramophone record, car part, etc.) by using pressure to shape and extract from a sheet of material. — n. **1** act or instance of pressing (*give it a slight press*). **2** device for compressing, flattening, shaping, extracting juice, etc. (*trouser press*; *wine press*). **3** = PRINTING-PRESS. **4** (prec. by *the*) **a** art or practice of printing. **b** newspapers, journalists, etc. generally or collectively (*read it in the press*; *pursued by the press*). **5** notice or publicity in newspapers etc. (*got a good press*). **6** (**Press**) printing or publishing company (*Oxford University Press of Australia*). **7 a** crowding. **b** crowd (of people etc.). **8** the pressure of affairs. □ **be pressed for** have barely enough (time etc.). **go to press** go to be printed. [Latin *premo press-* press]

**press**[2] v. **1** *hist.* force to serve in the army or navy. **2** bring into use as a makeshift (*was pressed into service*). [obsolete *prest* from French, = loan]

**press agent** n. person employed to obtain advertising and press publicity.

**press conference** n. interview given to a number of journalists.

**press gallery** n. **1** gallery for reporters, esp. in a legislative assembly. **2** the reporters authorised to attend such a gallery.

**press-gang** — n. **1** *hist.* body of men employed to press men into army or navy service. **2** any group using coercive methods. — v. force into service.

**pressie** /**prez**-ee/ n. = PREZZIE.

**pressing** — adj. **1** urgent (*pressing business*). **2 a** urging strongly (*pressing invitation*). **b** persistent, importunate (*since you are so pressing . . .*). — n. **1** thing made by pressing, e.g. a gramophone record. **2** series of these made at one time. **3** act or instance of pressing a thing, esp. a gramophone record, grapes, etc. (*all at one pressing*). □ **pressingly** adv.

**press release** n. statement issued to newspapers.

**press stud** n. small fastening device (esp. for clothing) engaged by pressing its two halves together.

**press-up** n. = PUSH-UP.

**pressure** /**presh**-uh/ — n. **1 a** exertion of continuous force on or against a body by another in contact with it. **b** the force exerted. **c** amount of this (expressed by the force on a unit area) (*atmospheric pressure*). **2** urgency (*work under pressure*). **3** affliction or difficulty (*under financial pressure*). **4** constraining influence (*put pressure on us*). — v. (**-ring**) (often foll. by *into*) apply (esp. moral) pressure to; coerce; persuade. [Latin: related to PRESS[1]]

**pressure cooker** n. airtight pan for cooking quickly under steam pressure. □ **pressure cook** v.

**pressure group** n. group (representing an industry etc.) applying esp. political pressure to serve its own interests by trying to influence public policy-making (*pressure group of the logging industry*).

**pressure point** n. point where an artery can be pressed against a bone to inhibit bleeding.

**pressure suit** n. inflatable suit which maintains body pressure and supplies air, worn by those flying in high altitudes, or in outer space.

**pressurise** v. (also **-ize**) (**-sing** or **-zing**) **1** (esp. as **pressurised** adj.) maintain normal atmospheric pressure in (an aircraft cabin etc.) at a high altitude. **2** raise to a high pressure. **3** pressure (a person). □ **pressurisation** /-**zay**-shuhn/ n.

**pressurised-water reactor** n. nuclear reactor with water at high pressure as the coolant.

**prestidigitator** /ˌpres-tuh-**dij**-uh-ˌtay-tuh/ *n. formal* conjuror. □ **prestidigitation** /-**tay**-shuhn/ *n.* [French: related to PRESTO, DIGIT]

**prestige** /pres-**teezh**/ *n.* **1** respect or reputation derived from achievements, power, associations, etc. **2** (*attrib.*) having or conferring prestige (*has a prestige job*). □ **prestigious** /pres-**tij**-uhs/ *adj.* [Latin *praestigiae* juggler's tricks]

**presto** /**pres**-toh/ — *adv.* **1** *Mus.* in quick tempo. **2** quickly (*do it presto!*). — *adj.* **1** *Mus.* in quick tempo (*the presto passages*). **2** quick. — *int.* = HEY PRESTO! — *n.* (*pl.* -**s**) *Mus.* presto passage or movement. [Latin *praestus* quick]

**prestressed** /pree-**strest**/ *adj.* (of concrete) strengthened by stretched wires within it.

**presumably** /pruh-**zyoo**-muh-blee/ *adv.* as may reasonably be presumed.

**presume** /pruh-**zyoom**/ *v.* (-**ming**) **1** (often foll. by *that*) suppose to be true; take for granted. **2** (often foll. by *to* + *infin.*) **a** take the liberty, be impudent enough (*presumed to question their authority*). **b** dare, venture (*may I presume to ask?*). **3** be presumptuous. **4** (foll. by *on*, *upon*) take advantage of or make unscrupulous use of (a person's good nature etc.). [Latin *praesumo*]

**presumption** /pruh-**zump**-shuhn/ *n.* **1** arrogance, presumptuous behaviour. **2 a** presuming a thing to be true. **b** thing that is or may be presumed to be true. **3** ground for presuming (*a strong presumption against their guilt*). **4** *Law* an inference from known facts. [Latin: related to PRESUME]

**presumptive** /pruh-**zump**-tiv/ *adj.* giving grounds for presumption (*presumptive evidence*).

**presumptuous** /pruh-**zump**-choo-uhs/ *adj.* unduly or overbearingly confident. □ **presumptuously** *adv.* **presumptuousness** *n.*

**presuppose** /ˌpree-suh-**pohz**/ *v.* (-**sing**) **1** assume beforehand. **2** imply. □ **presupposition** /pree-ˌsup-uh-**zish**-uhn/ *n.*

**pre-tax** /**pree**-taks/ *adj.* (of income or profits) before deduction of taxes.

**pretence** /pruh-**tens**/ *n.* **1** pretending, make-believe. **2 a** pretext, excuse (*on the slightest pretence*). **b** false show of intentions or motives (*under the pretence of friendship*). **3** (foll. by *to*) a claim, esp. a false one (*has no pretence to any great talent*). **4** display; ostentation (*stripped of all pretence*). [Anglo-Latin: related to PRETEND]

**pretend** /pruh-**tend**/ — *v.* **1** claim or assert falsely so as to deceive (*pretend knowledge; pretended to be rich*). **2** imagine to oneself in play (*pretended it was night*). **3 a** profess, esp. falsely or extravagantly (*does not pretend to be a scholar*). **b** (as **pretended** *adj.*) falsely claim to be such (*a pretended friend*). **4** (foll. by *to*) **a** lay claim to (a right or title etc.). **b** profess to have (a quality etc.). — *adj. colloq.* pretended; in pretence (*pretend money*). [Latin *praetendo*: related to TEND¹]

**pretender** *n.* person who claims a throne, title, etc.

**pretension** /pruh-**ten**-shuhn/ *n.* **1** (often foll. by *to*) **a** assertion of a claim. **b** justifiable claim (*has some pretensions to be included*). **2** pretentiousness. [medieval Latin: related to PRETEND]

**pretentious** /pruh-**ten**-shuhs/ *adj.* **1** making an excessive claim to great merit or importance. **2** ostentatious. □ **pretentiously** *adv.* **pretentiousness** *n.*

**preterite** /**pret**-uh-ruht/ *Gram.* — *adj.* expressing a past action or state. — *n.* preterite tense or form. [Latin *praeteritum* past]

**preternatural** /ˌpree-tuh-**nach**-uh-ruhl/ *adj.* outside the ordinary course of nature; supernatural. [Latin *praeter* beyond]

**pretext** /**pree**-tekst/ *n.* ostensible or alleged reason; excuse offered. [Latin *praetextus*: related to TEXT]

**prettify** /**prit**-uh-ˌfuy/ *v.* (-**ies**, -**ied**) make pretty, esp. in an affected way.

**pretty** /**prit**-ee/ — *adj.* (-**ier**, -**iest**) **1** attractive in a delicate way without being truly beautiful (*pretty girl; pretty tune*). **2** fine or good of its kind (*has a pretty wit*). **3** *iron.* considerable, fine (*cost a pretty penny; a pretty mess you've made of things*). — *adv.* **1** fairly, moderately (*that's pretty good in the circumstances*). **2** very (*raining pretty hard*). — *v.* (-**ies**, -**ied**) (often foll. by *up*) make pretty. □ **pretty much** (or **nearly** or **well**) *colloq.* almost; very nearly. **sitting pretty** see SIT. □ **prettily** *adv.* **prettiness** *n.* [Old English]

**pretty face** *n.* (in full **pretty-face wallaby**) = WHIPTAIL WALLABY.

**pretty-pretty** *adj. colloq.* too pretty.

**pretzel** /**pret**-suhl/ *n.* crisp stick- or knot-shaped salted biscuit. [German]

**prevail** /pruh-**vayl**/ *v.* **1** (often foll. by *against*, *over*) be victorious or gain mastery. **2** be the more usual or predominant (*wattles and gums prevail in the Australian landscape*). **3** exist or occur in general use or experience; be current (*republican views now prevail in Australia*). **4** (foll. by *on*, *upon*) persuade. [Latin *praevaleo*: related to AVAIL]

**prevalent** /**prev**-uh-luhnt/ *adj.* **1** generally existing or occurring. **2** predominant. ◻**prevalence** *n.* [related to PREVAIL]

**prevaricate** /pruh-**va**-ruh-ˌkayt/ *v.* (**-ting**) **1** speak or act evasively or misleadingly. **2** quibble, equivocate. ◻**prevarication** /-**kay**-shuhn/ *n.* **prevaricator** *n.* [Latin, = walk crookedly]

■ **Usage** *Prevaricate* is often confused with *procrastinate*, which means 'to defer or put off action'.

**prevent** /pruh-**vent**/ *v.* (often foll. by *from* + verbal noun) stop from happening or doing something; hinder; make impossible (*the weather prevented me from going*). ◻**preventable** *adj.* (also **preventible**). **prevention** *n.* [Latin *praevenio -vent-* hinder]

■ **Usage** The use of *prevent* without 'from' as in *prevented me going* is informal. An acceptable alternative is *prevented my going*.

**preventative** /pruh-**ven**-tuh-tiv/ *adj. & n.* = PREVENTIVE.

**preventive** /pruh-**ven**-tiv/ — *adj.* serving to prevent, esp. disease (*preventive medicine; took preventive action*). — *n.* preventive agent, measure, drug, etc.

**preview** /**pree**-vyoo/ — *n.* showing of a film, play, exhibition, etc., before it is seen by the general public. — *v.* see or show in advance.

**previous** /**pree**-vee-uhs/ — *adj.* **1** (often foll. by *to*) coming before in time or order. **2** *colloq.* hasty, premature. — *adv.* (foll. by *to*) before (*had phoned previous to arriving*). ◻ **previously** *adv.* [Latin *praevius* from *via* way]

**prey** /pray/ — *n.* **1** animal that is hunted or killed by another for food. **2** (often foll. by *to*) person or thing that is influenced by or vulnerable to (something undesirable) (*became a prey to morbid fears*). — *v.* (foll. by *on, upon*) **1** seek or take as prey. **2** make a victim of. **3** (of a disease, emotion, etc.) exert a harmful influence (*it preyed on his mind*). [Latin *praeda*]

**prezzie** *n.* (also **pressie**) *colloq.* a present, a gift (*Chrissie prezzies*). [abbreviation]

**priapic** /ˌpruy-**ap**-ik/ *adj.* phallic. [Greek *Priapos* god of procreation]

**price** — *n.* **1 a** amount of money (or its equivalent) for which a thing is bought or sold. **b** value or worth (*beyond price*). **2** what is or must be given, done, sacrificed, etc., to obtain or achieve something (*peace at any price*). **3** odds in betting (*starting price*). — *v.* (**-cing**) **1** fix or find the price of (a thing for sale). **2** estimate the value of. ◻ **above** (or **beyond** or **without**) **price** so valuable that no price can be stated. **at a price** at a high cost. **price oneself out of the market** lose to one's competitors by charging more than customers are willing to pay. **what price . . . ?** *colloq.* **1** what is the chance of . . . ? (*what price your finishing the course?*). **2** *iron.* the much boasted . . . proves disappointing (*what price your friendship now?*). [Latin *pretium*]

**price control** *n.* establishment by a government of a maximum price for specified goods and services. ◻ **price-control** *adj.*

**price-cutting** *n.* lowering of prices, usu. in a price war.

**price-fixing** *n.* maintaining of prices at a certain level by agreement between competing sellers.

**priceless** *adj.* **1** invaluable; beyond price. **2** *colloq.* very amusing or absurd.

**price tag** *n.* **1** label on an item showing its price. **2** cost of an undertaking.

**price war** *n.* period of fierce competition among traders cutting prices.

**pricey** *adj.* (**-cier, -ciest**) *colloq.* expensive.

**prick** — *v.* **1** pierce slightly; make a small hole in. **2** (foll. by *off, out*) mark (esp. a pattern) with small holes or dots. **3** trouble mentally (*my conscience pricked me*). **4** tingle (*my skin's pricking all over*). **5** (foll. by *out*) plant (seedlings etc.) in small holes pricked in the soil. — *n.* **1** act of pricking. **2** small hole or mark made by pricking. **3** pain caused as by pricking. **4** mental pain (*pricks of remorse*). **5** *coarse colloq.* **a** penis. **b** *derog.* contemptible person. ◻ **prick up one's ears 1** (of a dog etc.) make the ears erect when alert. **2** (of a person) become suddenly attentive. [Old English]

**prickle** /**prik**-uhl/ — *n.* **1** small thorn. **2** hard-pointed spine of an echidna etc. **3** prickling sensation. — *v.* (**-ling**) affect or be affected with a sensation of multiple pricking. [Old English]

**prickly** *adj.* (**-ier, -iest**) **1** (esp. in the names of plants and animals) having prickles. **2** (of a person) ready to take offence. **3** tingling. ◻**prickliness** *n.*

**prickly acacia** *n.* (also **prickly wattle**) any of several wattles having prickles (e.g. *Acacia armata* of all States).

**prickly heat** *n.* itchy inflammation of the skin, causing a tingling sensation and common in hot countries.

**prickly jack** *n.* = DOUBLEGEE.

**prickly moses** *n.* any of several wattles with prickles, esp. *Acacia verticillata* of eastern Australia and *A. pulchella* of WA.

**prickly pear** n. **1** cactus native to arid America (but widespread as a pest in Australia) with barbed bristles and large pear-shaped prickly fruit. **2** its fruit.

**prickly poison** n. WA shrub with attractive pea-flowers and leaves extremely poisonous to stock (see POISON PEA).

**prickly wattle** n. = PRICKLY ACACIA.

**pride** — n. **1 a** elation or satisfaction at one's achievements, qualities, possessions, etc. **b** object of this feeling (*her garden is her pride*). **2** high or overbearing opinion of one's worth or importance; arrogance; haughtiness. **3** proper sense of what befits one's position; self-respect. **4** group of lions. **5** best condition, prime (*in the pride of young manhood*). — v.refl. (**-ding**) (foll. by *on*, *upon*) be proud of (*prided himself on his skill in embroidery*). □ **take pride** (or **a pride**) **in 1** be proud of. **2** maintain in good condition or appearance. [Old English: related to PROUD]

**pride of place** n. most important or prominent position.

**prie-dieu** /pree-**dyer**/ n. (pl. **prie-dieux** pronunc. same) kneeling-desk for prayer. [French, = pray God]

**priest** n. **1 a** ordained minister of the Roman Catholic or Orthodox Church empowered to offer sacrifice, administer the sacraments, etc. (ranking above a deacon and below a bishop). **b** ordained minister in some other Christian churches. **2** (*fem.* **priestess**) official minister of a non-Christian religion. □ **priestly** adj. [Latin PRESBYTER]

**priesthood** n. (usu. prec. by *the*) **1** the office or position of priest. **2** priests in general.

**prig** n. self-righteous or moralistic person. □ **priggish** adj. **priggishness** n. [origin unknown]

**prim** adj. (**primmer**, **primmest**) stiffly formal and precise; prudish. □ **primly** adv. **primness** n. [French: related to PRIME¹]

**prima ballerina** /ˌpree-muh ˌbal-uh-ree-nuh/ n. chief female dancer in a ballet. [Italian]

**primacy** /**pruy**-muh-see/ n. (pl. **-ies**) **1** pre-eminence. **2** office of a primate. [Latin: related to PRIMATE]

**prima donna** /ˌpree-muh **don**-uh, ˌprim-uh/ n. (pl. **prima donnas**) **1** chief female singer in an opera. **2** temperamentally self-important person (*he's such a prima donna*). □ **prima donna-ish** adj. [Italian]

**prima facie** /ˌpruy-muh **fay**-see/ — adv. at first sight. — adj. (of evidence) based on the first impression. [Latin]

**primal** /**pruy**-muhl/ adj. **1** primitive,

primeval. **2** chief, fundamental. [Latin: related to PRIME¹]

**primary** /**pruy**-muh-ree/ — adj. **1 a** of the first importance; chief (*that is our primary concern*). **b** fundamental, basic. **2** earliest, original; first in a series. **3** of the first rank in a series; not derived (*the primary meaning of a word*). **4** designating any of the colours red, green, and blue, or (for pigments) red, blue, and yellow, of which all other colours are mixtures. **5** (of education) for children from the age of approximately 5 to 11. **6** (**Primary**) *Geol.* of the lowest series of strata. **7** *Biol.* of the first stage of development. — n. (pl. **-ies**) **1** thing that is primary. **2** = PRIMARY FEATHER. **3** (in full **primary vote**) = *first preference* (see PREFERENCE). □ **primarily** /**pruy**-muh-ruh-lee, -**mair**-ruh-lee/ adv. [Latin: related to PRIME¹]

**primary feather** n. large flight-feather of a bird's wing.

**primary industry** n. agriculture, sheep and cattle raising, fishing, forestry, etc., as distinct from manufacturing industry.

**primary producer** n. person who is engaged in primary industry.

**primary school** n. school for children between the ages of approximately 5 and 11.

**primary source** n. literary text, historical document, etc., on which a thesis, essay, etc., is based (opp. SECONDARY SOURCE) (*Shakespeare's 'Macbeth' is the primary source in this thesis and the secondary sources include E.F.C. Ludowyk's 'Understanding Shakespeare'*).

**primate** /**pruy**-mayt/ n. **1** member of the highest order of mammals, including apes, monkeys, and man. **2** (/**pruy**-muht/) the chief bishop of a country; archbishop. [Latin *primas -at-* chief]

**prime¹** — adj. **1** chief, most important (*prime agent*; *prime motive*). **2** first-rate, excellent (*prime beef*). **3** primary, fundamental. **4** *Math.* **a** (of a number etc.) divisible only by itself and unity (e.g. 2, 3, 5, 7, 11). **b** (of numbers) having no common factor but unity. — n. **1** state of the highest perfection (*prime of life*). **2** (prec. by *the*; foll. by *of*) the best part. [Latin *primus* first]

**prime²** v. (**-ming**) **1** prepare (a thing) for use or action. **2** prepare (a gun) for firing or (an explosive) for detonation. **3** pour (liquid) into a pump to enable it to work. **4** prepare (wood etc.) for painting by applying a substance that prevents paint from being absorbed. **5** equip (a person) with information etc. **6** ply (a person) with food or drink in preparation for something. [origin unknown]

**primed** *adj. colloq.* drunk.

**prime minister** *n.* (in some political systems) head of an elected government; principal minister.

**prime mover** *n.* **1** initial natural or mechanical source of motive power. **2 a** author of a fruitful idea. **b** person who is the main organiser of, or motive force behind, a project etc. **3** powerful motor of a semi-trailer.

**primer**[1] /**pruy**-muh/ *n.* **1** substance used to prime wood etc. **2** cap, cylinder, etc., used to ignite the powder of a cartridge etc.

**primer**[2] /**pruy**-muh, **prim**-uh/ *n.* **1** elementary textbook for teaching children to read. **2** book which introduces, or provides basic instruction in, a subject (*a primer of Latin grammar*). [Latin: related to PRIME[1]]

**prime time** *n.* period of the day when television viewing is at its peak.

**primeval** /pruy-**mee**-vuhl/ *adj.* **1** of the first age of the world. **2** ancient, primitive. □ **primevally** *adv.* [Latin: related to PRIME[1], *aevum* age]

■ **Usage** The spelling *primaeval* is still occasionally encountered: *primeval* is preferred.

**primitive** /**prim**-uh-tiv/ — *adj.* **1** at an early stage of civilisation (*primitive man*). **2** undeveloped, crude, simple (*primitive methods*). **3** original, primary. **4** *Biol.* appearing in the earliest or a very early stage of growth or evolution. — *n.* **1** untutored painter with a direct naïve style. **2** picture by such a painter. □ **primitively** *adv.* **primitiveness** *n.* [Latin: related to PRIME[1]]

**primogenitor** /,pruy-moh-**jen**-uh-tuh/ *n.* **1** earliest ancestor of a people etc. **2** an ancestor. [variant of *progenitor*, after PRIMOGENITURE]

**primogeniture** /,pruy-moh-**jen**-uh-chuh/ *n.* **1** fact of being the first-born child. **2** (in full **right of primogeniture**) right of succession belonging to the first-born. [medieval Latin: related to PRIME[1], Latin *genitura* birth]

**primordial** /pruy-**maw**-dee-uhl/ *adj.* **1** existing at or from the beginning, primeval. **2** original, fundamental. [Latin: related to PRIME[1], *ordior* begin]

**primp** *v.* **1** make (the hair, clothes, etc.) tidy. **2** *refl.* make (oneself) smart. [var. of PRIM]

**primrose** /**prim**-rohz/ *n.* **1 a** European wild plant bearing pale yellow spring flowers. **b** its flower. **2** pale yellow colour. □ **primrose path** the pursuit of pleasure, esp. with disastrous consequences. [French and medieval Latin, = first rose]

**primula** /**prim**-yuh-luh/ *n.* cultivated plant bearing primrose-like flowers in a wide variety of colours. [Latin diminutive: related to PRIME[1]]

**primus** /**pruy**-muhs/ *n. propr.* portable cooking stove burning vaporised oil, gas, etc. [Latin, = first]

**prince** *n.* (as a title usu. **Prince**) **1** male member of a royal family other than the reigning king. **2** ruler of a small nation. **3** nobleman in some countries. **4** (often foll. by *of*) chief or greatest (*the prince of pop singers*). [Latin *princeps -cip-*]

**princeling** /**prins**-ling/ *n.* young or petty prince.

**princely** *adj.* (**-ier**, **-iest**) **1** of or worthy of a prince. **2** sumptuous, generous, splendid.

**Prince of Wales** *n.* (title conferred on) the eldest son and heir apparent of the British monarch.

**princess** /**prin**-ses/ *n.* (as a title usu. **Princess**) **1** wife of a prince. **2** female member of a royal family other than a queen. [French: related to PRINCE]

**Princess parrot** *n.* delicately pastel-coloured parrot of arid inland central and western Australia. [from *Princess Alexandra*, wife of the British king Edward VII]

**principal** /**prin**-suh-puhl/ — *adj.* **1** (usu. *attrib.*) first in rank or importance; chief. **2** main, leading (*principal cause of my success*). — *n.* **1** chief person. **2** head of some schools. **3** leading performer in a concert, play, etc. **4** capital sum as distinct from interest or income. **5** person for whom another is agent etc. **6** person for whom another is surety. **7** person directly responsible for a crime (cf. ACCESSORY). **8** leading player in each section of an orchestra. □ **principally** *adv.* [Latin: related to PRINCE]

**principality** /,prin-suh-**pal**-uh-tee/ *n.* (*pl.* **-ies**) nation ruled by or government of a prince.

**principle** /**prin**-suh-puhl/ *n.* **1** fundamental truth or law as the basis of reasoning or action (*arguing from first principles*). **2 a** personal code of conduct (*person of high principle*). **b** (in *pl.*) personal rules of conduct (*has no principles*). **3** general law in physics etc. (*the uncertainty principle*). **4** law of nature forming the basis for the construction or working of a machine etc. **5** fundamental source; primary element (*held water to be the first principle of all things*). □ **in**

**principle** as regards fundamentals but not necessarily in detail. **on principle** on the basis of a moral attitude (*I refuse on principle*). [Latin *principium* source]

**principled** *adj.* based on or having (esp. praiseworthy) principles of behaviour.

**prink** *v.* **1 a** (usu. *refl.*; often foll. by *up*) smarten (oneself) up. **b** dress oneself up. **2** (of a bird) preen. [origin unknown]

**print** — *v.* **1** produce or cause (a book, picture, etc.) to be produced by applying inked type, blocks, or plates, to paper, etc. **2** express or publish in print (*they are going to print my fantasy trilogy*). **3 a** (often foll. by *on*, *in*) impress or stamp (a mark on a surface). **b** (often foll. by *with*) impress or stamp (a soft surface, e.g. wax, with a seal, die, etc.). **4** (often *absol.*) write (letters) without joining them up (*this form requires us to print our answers*). **5** (often foll. by *off*, *out*) produce (a photograph) from a negative. **6** (usu. foll. by *out*) (of a computer etc.) produce output in printed form. **7** mark (a textile fabric) with a coloured design. **8** (foll. by *on*) impress (an idea, scene, etc., on the mind or memory) (*these events are printed on my mind*). — *n.* **1** indentation or mark on a surface left by the pressure of a thing in contact with it (*footprint*; *fingerprint*). **2 a** printed lettering or writing (*large print*). **b** words in printed form. **c** printed publication, esp. a newspaper. **3** picture or design printed from a block or plate (*a fine Hans Heysen print*). **4** photograph produced on paper from a negative. **5** printed cotton fabric. □ **in print 1** (of a book etc.) available from the publisher. **2** in printed form. **out of print** no longer available from the publisher. [Latin *premo*: related to PRESS¹]

**printed circuit** *n.* electric circuit with thin strips of conductor printed on a flat insulating sheet.

**printer** *n.* **1** person who prints books etc. **2** owner of a printing business. **3** device that prints, esp. as part of a computer system.

**printhead** *n.* *Computing* the component in a printer (see PRINTER 3) that assembles and prints the characters on the paper.

**printing** *n.* **1** production of printed books etc. **2** copies of a book printed at one time. **3** printed letters or writing imitating them.

**printing press** *n.* machine for printing from types or plates etc.

**print journalism** *n.* journalism intended for the print media rather than for television or radio. □ **print journalist** *n.*

**print media** *n.* newspapers, journals, magazines (opp. ELECTRONIC MEDIA).

**printout** *n.* computer output in printed form.

**prion** /**pruy**-on/ *n.* any of several bluey-grey and white migratory sea-birds with a serrated bill, which feed on plankton while skimming the surface of the sea in southern Australian waters. [Greek *priōn* a saw]

**prior** /**pruy**-uh/ — *adj.* **1** earlier. **2** (often foll. by *to*) coming before in time, order, or importance. — *adv.* (foll. by *to*) before (*left prior to his arrival*). — *n.* **1** superior of certain monasteries of friars (e.g. the Dominicans). **2** (in an abbey) deputy of an abbot. [Latin, = earlier, elder]

**prioress** *n.* a nun holding an office equivalent to that of a prior.

**priority** /pruy-o-ruh-tee/ *n.* (*pl.* **-ies**) **1** fact or condition of being earlier or antecedent. **2** thing that is regarded as more important than others. **3** high(est) place among various things to be done (*gave priority to*). **4** right to do something before other people. **5** right to proceed ahead of other traffic. **6** (state of) being more important. □ **prioritise** *v.* (also **-ize**). (**-sing** or **-zing**). [medieval Latin: related to PRIOR]

**priory** /**pruy**-uh-ree/ *n.* (*pl.* **-ies**) monastery governed by a prior or nunnery governed by a prioress. [Anglo-French and medieval Latin: related to PRIOR]

**prise** /pruyz/ *v.* (also **prize**) (**-sing** or **-zing**) force open or out by leverage (*prised up the lid*; *prised the crate open*). [French: related to PRIZE²]

**prism** /**priz**-uhm/ *n.* **1** solid figure whose two ends are equal parallel rectilinear figures, and whose sides are parallelo-grams. **2** transparent body in this form, usu. triangular with refracting surfaces at an acute angle with each other, which separates white light into a spectrum of colours. [Greek *prisma -mat-* thing sawn]

**prismatic** /priz-**mat**-ik/ *adj.* **1** of, like, or using a prism. **2** (of colours) distributed (as if) by a transparent prism. [Greek: related to PRISM]

**prison** /**priz**-uhn/ — *n.* **1** place of captivity, esp. a building to which persons are committed while awaiting trial or for punishment; gaol. **2** custody, confinement. **3** any place in which a person feels imprisoned or confined (*home's a prison to many women*). — *v.* *poet.* (**prisoned**, **prisoning**) imprison. [Latin *prehendo* seize]

**prisoner** /**priz**-nuh, **priz**-uh-nuh/ *n.* **1** person kept in prison. **2** (in full **prisoner at the bar**) person in custody on a criminal charge and on trial. **3** person or thing confined by illness, another's grasp, etc.

◻ **take prisoner** seize and hold as a prisoner. [Anglo-French: related to PRISON]

**prisoner of conscience** see CONSCIENCE.

**prisoner of war** *n.* person captured in war and held by the enemy.

**prissy** /**pris**-ee/ *adj.* (**-ier**, **-iest**) prim, prudish. ◻ **prissily** *adv.* **prissiness** *n.* [perhaps from PRIM, SISSY]

**pristine** /**pris**-teen/ *adj.* **1** in its original condition; unspoilt. **2** spotless; fresh as if new. **3** ancient, primitive. [Latin *pristinus* former]

■ **Usage** The use of *pristine* in sense 2 is considered incorrect by some people.

**privacy** /**pruy**-vuh-see, **priv**-uh-/ *n.* **1 a** state of being private and undisturbed. **b** person's right to this. **2** freedom from intrusion or public attention. **3** avoidance of publicity.

**private** /**pruy**-vuht/ — *adj.* **1** belonging to an individual, one's own, personal (*private property*). **2** confidential, not to be disclosed to others (*private talks*). **3** kept or removed from public knowledge or observation. **4** not open to the public (*a private road*). **5** (of a place) secluded; affording privacy. **6** (of a person) not holding public office or an official position. **7** (of education or medical treatment) conducted outside the publicly funded system, at the individual's expense. — *n.* **1** private soldier. **2** (in *pl.*) *colloq.* genitals. ◻ **in private** privately. ◻ **privately** *adv.* [Latin *privo privat-* deprive]

**private bill** *n.* parliamentary bill based on a petition from, and affecting, an individual or corporation only.

**private company** *n.* company with restricted membership and no public share issue.

**private enterprise** *n.* businesses not under government control.

**privateer** /ˌpruy-vuh-**teer**/ *n.* **1** privately owned and officered warship holding a government commission. **2** its commander.

**private eye** *n.* *colloq.* private investigator.

**private hotel** *n.* (unlicensed) hotel not obliged to take all comers.

**private investigator** *n.* detective engaged privately, outside an official police force.

**private means** *n.pl.* income from investments etc., apart from earned income.

**private member** *n.* MP not holding government office.

**private member's bill** *n.* bill introduced by a private member, not part of government legislation.

**private parts** *n.pl. euphem.* male or female genitals.

**private practice** *n.* medical practice that is not part of the public health service. ◻ **private practitioner** *n.*

**private school** *n.* (also **independent school**) fee-charging school not supported mainly by government-funding (cf. PUBLIC SCHOOL sense 1).

**private sector** *n.* the part of the economy free of direct government control.

**private soldier** *n.* ordinary soldier other than the officers.

**privation** /pruy-**vay**-shuhn/ *n.* lack of the comforts or necessities of life. [Latin: related to PRIVATE]

**privatise** /**pruy**-vuh-ˌtuyz/ *v.* (also **-ize**) (**-sing** or **-zing**) transfer (a business etc.) from government to private ownership. ◻ **privatisation** /-**zay**-shuhn/ *n.*

**privative** /**priv**-uh-tiv/ *adj.* consisting in or marked by loss or absence. [Latin: related to PRIVATE]

**privet** /**priv**-uht/ *n.* bushy evergreen European shrub used for hedges and now a serious pest in the Australian bush. [origin unknown]

**privilege** /**priv**-uh-lij/ — *n.* **1 a** right, advantage, or immunity, belonging to a person, class, or office. **b** (in full **parliamentary privilege**) special right of members of parliament to speak freely in parliament without the risk of prosecution they might incur if they said the same things outside. **2** *Law* the right of a lawyer, priest or minister of religion, doctor, etc., to refuse to disclose communications made by a client, penitent, patient, etc., in the course of a professional relationship. **3** special benefit or honour (*a privilege to meet you*). — *v.* (**-ging**) **1** invest with a privilege. **2** (foll. by *to* + infin.) allow (a person) as a privilege (to do something). **3** (often foll. by *from*) exempt (a person from a liability etc.). ◻ **privileged** *adj.* [Latin: related to PRIVY, *lex leg-* law]

**privy** /**priv**-ee/ — *adj.* **1** (foll. by *to*) sharing in the secret of (a person's plans etc.) (*too many were privy to his plot for it to succeed*). **2** *archaic* hidden, secret. — *n.* (*pl.* **-ies**) toilet, esp. an outside one. [French *privé* private place]

**prize**[1] — *n.* **1** something that can be won in a competition, lottery, etc. **2** reward given as a symbol of victory or superiority. **3** something striven for or worth striving for. **4** (*attrib.*) **a** to which a prize is awarded (*prize poem*). **b** excellent of its kind. **c** outstanding (*a prize idiot*). — *v.* (**-zing**) value highly (*a much prized possession*). [French: related to PRAISE]

**prize²** *n.* ship or property captured in naval warfare. [French *prise* from Latin *prehendo* seize]

**prize³** var. of PRISE.

**prizefight** *n.* boxing match fought for a prize of money. □ **prizefighter** *n.*

**prize-giving** *n.* awarding of prizes, esp. formally at a school etc.

**pro¹** /proh/ *n.* **1** (*pl.* **-s**) *colloq.* a professional. **2** prostitute. [abbreviation]

**pro²** /proh/ — *adj.* (of an argument or reason) for; in favour. — *n.* (*pl.* **-s**) **1** person who votes etc. in favour of something. **2** reason or argument for or in favour. — *prep.* in favour of. □ **pros and cons** reasons or considerations for and against a proposition etc. [Latin, = for, on behalf of]

**pro-¹** *prefix* **1** favouring or supporting (opp. ANTI-) (*pro-abortion*). **2** acting as a substitute or deputy for (*pro-vice-chancellor*). **3** forwards (*produce*). **4** forwards and downwards (*prostrate*). **5** onwards (*progress*). **6** in front of (*protect*). [Latin *pro* in front (of)]

**pro-²** *prefix* before in time, place, order, etc. (*problem*; *proboscis*; *prophet*). [Greek *pro* before]

**proactive** /proh-ak-tiv/ *adj.* (of a person, policy, etc.) taking the initiative. [from PRO-², after REACTIVE]

**probability** /,prob-uh-bil-uh-tee/ *n.* (*pl.* **-ies**) **1** state or condition of being probable. **2** likelihood of something happening. **3** probable or most probable event (*the probability is that Australia will win the Ashes*). **4** *Math.* extent to which an event is likely to occur, measured by the ratio of the favourable cases to the total number of possible cases. □ **in all probability** most probably.

**probable** /prob-uh-buhl/ — *adj.* (often foll. by *that*) that may be expected to happen or prove true; likely (*the probable explanation*; *it is probable that they forgot*). — *n.* probable candidate, member of a team, etc. □ **probably** *adv.* [Latin: related to PROVE]

**probate** /proh-bayt/ *n.* **1** official proving of a will. **2** verified copy of a will with a certificate as handed to executors. [Latin *probo* PROVE]

**probation** /pruh-bay-shuhn/ *n.* **1** *Law* system of supervising and monitoring the behaviour of (esp. young) offenders, as an alternative to prison. **2** period of testing the character or abilities of esp. a new employee. □ **on probation** undergoing probation. □ **probationary** *adj.* [Latin: related to PROVE]

**probationer** *n.* person on probation.

**probation officer** *n.* official supervising offenders on probation.

**probe** — *n.* **1** a penetrating investigation. **2** small device, esp. an electrode, for measuring, testing, etc. **3** blunt-ended surgical instrument for exploring a wound etc. **4** (in full **space probe**) unmanned exploratory spacecraft transmitting information about its environment. — *v.* (**-bing**) **1** examine or enquire into closely. **2** explore with or as with a probe. **3** penetrate with a sharp instrument. [Latin *proba*: related to PROVE]

**probity** /proh-buh-tee/ *n.* uprightness, honesty. [Latin *probus* good]

**problem** /prob-luhm/ *n.* **1** doubtful or difficult matter requiring a solution. **2** something hard to understand or accomplish or deal with. **3** (*attrib.*) causing problems (*problem child*). **4** puzzle or question for solution; exercise. [Greek *problēma -mat-*]

**problematic** /,prob-luh-mat-ik/ *adj.* (also **problematical**) attended by difficulty; doubtful or questionable. □ **problematically** *adv.* [Greek: related to PROBLEM]

**proboscis** /pruh-bos-kuhs, -boh-suhs/ *n.* (*pl.* **-sces** /seez/, **-scides** /suh-deez/, **-scises**) **1** long flexible trunk or snout of some mammals, e.g. an elephant or tapir. **2** elongated mouth parts of some insects. [Greek *boskō* feed]

**procedure** /pruh-see-juh/ *n.* **1** way of acting or advancing, esp. in business or legal action. **2** way of performing a task (*his normal procedure was to begin by setting out his tools*). **3** series of actions conducted in a certain order or manner. □ **procedural** *adj.* [French: related to PROCEED]

**proceed** /pruh-seed, proh-/ *v.* **1** (often foll. by *to*) go forward or on further; make one's way. **2** (often foll. by *with*, or *to* + infin.) continue with an activity; go on to do something (*proceeded with their work*; *proceeded to tell the whole story*). **3** (of an action) be carried on or continued (*the case will now proceed*). **4** adopt a course of action (*how shall we proceed?*). **5** go on to say. **6** (foll. by *against*) start a lawsuit against (a person). **7** (often foll. by *from*) originate (*shouts proceeded from the bedroom*). [Latin *cedo cess-* go]

**proceeding** *n.* **1** action or piece of conduct (*high-handed proceeding*). **2** (in *pl.*) (in full **legal proceedings**) lawsuit. **3** (in *pl.*) published report of discussions or a conference.

**proceeds** /**proh**-seedz/ n.pl. profits from sale etc. [pl. of obsolete *proceed* (n.) from PROCEED]

**process**[1] /**proh**-ses/ — n. **1** course of action or proceeding, esp. a series of stages in manufacture, computing, etc. (*the process of making quandong jam*). **2** progress or course (*in process of construction*). **3** natural or involuntary course or change (*process of growing old*). **4** action at law; summons or writ. **5** natural projection of a bone, stem, etc. — v. **1** deal with by a particular process (*processing bauxite for aluminium*; *began to process the applicants*). **2** (as **processed** adj.) treat (food, esp. to prevent decay) (*processed cheese*). **3** *Computing* operate on (data) by means of a program. [Latin: related to PROCEED]

**process**[2] /pruh-**ses**/ v. walk in procession (*processed to the altar*). [back-formation from PROCESSION]

**procession** /pruh-**sesh**-uhn/ n. **1** people (or vehicles etc.) advancing in orderly succession, esp. in the course of a religious or academic etc. ceremony, or at a demonstration or festivity. **2** movement of such a group (*go in procession*). [Latin: related to PROCEED]

**processional** — adj. **1** of processions. **2** used, carried, or sung in processions. — n. *Eccl.* **1** processional hymn. **2** office-book containing processional hymns.

**procession caterpillar** n. Australian caterpillar, having slender hairs which can cause severe skin irritation: so called because they appear in large numbers, moving in a long single file.

**processor** /**proh**-ses-uh/ n. machine that processes things, esp.: **1** = CENTRAL PROCESSOR. **2** = FOOD PROCESSOR.

**proclaim** /pruh-**klaym**/ v. **1** (often foll. by *that*) announce or declare publicly or officially. **2** declare (a person) to be (king, a traitor, etc.). **3** reveal as being (*your accent proclaims you an Australian*). □ **proclamation** /,prok-luh-**may**-shuhn/ n. [Latin: related to CLAIM]

**proclivity** /pruh-**kliv**-uh-tee/ n. (pl. **-ies**) tendency, inclination (*has a proclivity to swearing*). [Latin *clivus* slope]

**procrastinate** /proh-**kras**-tuh-,nayt/ v. (**-ting**) defer action; delay, put off (*the longer you procrastinate, the harder it will be to heal the rift*). □ **procrastination** /-**nay**-shuhn/ n. **procrastinator** n. [Latin *cras* tomorrow]

■ *Usage* Procrastinate is often confused with *prevaricate* which means 'to be evasive, quibble'.

**procreate** /**proh**-kree-,ayt/ v. (**-ting**)

(often *absol.*) beget (offspring) by the natural process of sexual intercourse (opp. in vitro fertilisation etc.). □ **procreation** /-**ay**-shuhn/ n. **procreative** adj. **procreator** n. [Latin: related to CREATE]

**procrustean** /proh-**krus**-tee-uhn/ adj. seeking to enforce uniformity ruthlessly or violently. [Greek *Prokroustēs*, name of a robber who fitted his victims to a standard-size bed by stretching them (if they were too short) or cutting bits off them (if they were too tall)]

**proctor** /**prok**-tuh/ n. disciplinary officer (usu. one of two) at certain universities. □ **proctorial** /-**taw**-ree-uhl/ adj. **proctorship** n. [from Latin *procurator* agent]

**procumbent** /proh-**kum**-buhnt/ adj. lying on the face; prostrate. [Latin *procumbo* fall forwards]

**procure** /pruh-**kyoor**/ v. (**-ring**) **1** obtain, esp. by care or effort; acquire (*managed to procure a copy*). **2** bring about (*procured their dismissal*). **3** bring about (an abortion by artificial means). **4** (also *absol.*) obtain (women) for prostitution. □ **procurable** adj. **procurement** n. [Latin *curo* look after]

**procurer** n. (fem. **procuress**) person who obtains women for prostitution. [from Latin *procurator* agent]

**prod**[1] — v. (**-dd-**) **1** poke with a finger, stick, etc. (*prodded the snake to see if it were dead*). **2** stimulate to action (*he kept prodding her to fix the fuse*). **3** (foll. by *at*) make a prodding motion. — n. **1** a poke or a thrust. **2** stimulus to action. **3** any pointed instrument, as a goad. [origin unknown]

**prod**[2] (also **proddie**, **proddy**) colloq. — n. a Protestant. — adj. Protestant. [corruption and abbreviation of *Protestant*]

**prodigal** /**prod**-i-guhl/ — adj. **1** recklessly wasteful. **2** (foll. by *of*) lavish, overgenerous (*he is prodigal of good advice*). — n. **1** prodigal person. **2** (in full **prodigal son**) repentant wastrel, returned wanderer, etc. (Luke 15:11–32). □ **prodigality** /-**gal**-uh-tee/ n. [Latin *prodigus* lavish]

**prodigious** /pruh-**dij**-uhs/ adj. **1** marvellous or amazing. **2** enormous. **3** abnormal. [Latin: related to PRODIGY]

**prodigy** /**prod**-uh-jee/ n. (pl. **-ies**) **1** exceptionally gifted or able person, esp. a precocious child. **2** marvellous thing, esp. one out of the ordinary course of nature. **3** (foll. by *of*) wonderful example (of a quality) (*he is a prodigy of strength*). [Latin *prodigium* portent]

**produce** — v. /pruh-**dyoos**/ (**-cing**) **1** manufacture or prepare (goods etc.). **2** bring forward for consideration, inspection, or use (*will produce evidence*). **3** bear, yield, or bring into existence (offspring, fruit, a harvest, etc.). **4** cause or bring about (a reaction, sensation, etc.) (*produced some surprise when he played the violin with his feet*). **5** *Geom.* extend or continue (a line). **6** supervise the production of (a play, film, broadcast, record, etc.). — *n.* /**prod**-yoos/ **1 a** what is produced, esp. agricultural products collectively (*dairy produce*). **b** amount of this (*the total produce of his toil*). **2** (often foll. by *of*) result (of labour, efforts, etc.). □ **producible** /pruh-**dyoo**-suh-buhl/ *adj.* [Latin *duco duct-* lead]

**producer** /pruh-**dyoo**-suh/ *n.* **1** person who produces goods or commodities. **2** person who supervises the production of a play, film, broadcast, etc.

**product** /**prod**-ukt/ *n.* **1** thing or substance produced by natural processes or by manufacture. **2** result (*product of their labours*). **3** quantity obtained by multiplying quantities together. [Latin: related to PRODUCE]

**production** /pruh-**duk**-shuhn/ *n.* **1** act or instance of producing or the process of being produced, esp. in large quantities (*go into production*). **2** total yield (*production from the vineyard has never been higher*). **3** thing produced, esp. a film, play, book, etc. [Latin: related to PRODUCE]

**production line** *n.* systematised sequence of operations involved in producing a commodity.

**productive** /pruh-**duk**-tiv/ *adj.* **1** of or engaged in the production of goods. **2** producing much (*productive writer*). **3** producing commodities of exchangeable value (*productive labour*). **4** (foll. by *of*) producing or giving rise to (*productive of great annoyance*). □ **productively** *adv.* **productiveness** *n.* [Latin: related to PRODUCE]

**productivity** /,prod-uk-**tiv**-uh-tee/ *n.* **1** the capacity to produce. **2** quality or state of being productive. **3** amount produced by an industry, workforce, etc.

**productivity bargaining** *n.* process of negotiating a deal between unions and employers whereby wage increases are granted in exchange for work practices which result in increased productivity.

**proem** /**proh**-em/ *n.* preface etc. to a book or speech; a beginning or prelude. [Latin from Greek]

**Prof.** *abbr.* Professor.

**profane** /pruh-**fayn**-/ — *adj.* **1 a** irreverent, blasphemous. **b** (of language) vulgar, coarse; shocking in the circumstances. **2** not sacred or biblical; secular. — *v.* (**-ning**) **1** treat (esp. a sacred thing) irreverently or with disrespect. **2** violate or debase (what is entitled to respect). □ **profanation** /,prof-uh-**nay**-shuhn/ *n.* [Latin *fanum* temple]

**profanity** /pruh-**fan**-uh-tee/ *n.* (*pl.* **-ies**) **1** profane act or language; blasphemy. **2** a swear-word.

**profess** /pruh-**fes**/ *v.* **1** claim openly to have (a quality or feeling) (*professed outrage at the invasion*). **2** (often foll. by *to* + infin.) pretend (*professed to be unaware*). **3** declare (*professed ignorance*). **4** affirm one's faith in or allegiance to. **5** take the vows of a religious order at the end of the novitiate. **6** have as one's profession or business. [Latin *profiteor -fess-* declare]

**professed** *adj.* **1** self-acknowledged (*professed Christian*). **2** alleged, ostensible. **3** (of a monk, friar, nun, etc.) having taken the vows of a religious order. **4** claiming to be duly qualified. □ **professedly** *adv.*

**profession** /pruh-**fesh**-uhn/ *n.* **1** vocation or calling, esp. learned or scientific (*a doctor by profession*). **2** people in a profession (*belongs to the medical profession*). **3** declaration or avowal (*his professions of undying love*). **4** declaration of belief in a religion (*made profession of Buddhism*). **5** the taking of vows in a religious order; the ceremony at which this is done. □ **the oldest profession** *joc.* prostitution.

**professional** — *adj.* **1** of, belonging to, or connected with a profession. **2 a** skilful, competent, as befits a professional. **b** worthy of a professional (*professional conduct*). **3** engaged in a specified activity as one's main paid occupation (opp. AMATEUR) (*professional boxer*). **4** *derog.* engaged in a specified activity, esp. fanatically (*professional agitator*). — *n.* professional person, esp. one in some branch of advanced learning. □ **professionally** *adv.*

**professionalism** *n.* qualities associated with a profession or professionals, esp. competence, skill, etc.

**professor** /pruh-**fes**-uh/ *n.* (often as a title) highest-ranking academic teaching in a university department; holder of a university chair. □ **professorial** /,prof-uh-**saw**-ree-uhl/ *adj.* **professorship** *n.*

**proffer** — *v.* offer (a gift, services, etc.). — *n. literary* an offer. [French: related to PRO-¹, OFFER]

**proficient** /pruh-**fish**-uhnt/ *adj.* (often foll. by *in, at*) adept, expert. □ **proficiency** *n.* **proficiently** *adv.* [Latin *proficio -fect-* advance]

**profile** /**proh**-fuyl/ — *n.* **1 a** outline, esp. of a human face, as seen from one side. **b** drawing or other representation of this. **2** short biographical or character sketch. **3** *Statistics* representation by a graph or chart of information (esp. on certain characteristics) recorded in a quantified form. **4** vertical cross-section of a structure. — *v.* (**-ling**) represent or describe by a profile. □ **keep a low profile** remain inconspicuous. [Italian *profilare* draw in outline]

**profit** /**prof**-uht/ — *n.* **1** advantage or benefit. **2** financial gain; excess of returns over outlay. — *v.* (**-t-**) **1** (also *absol.*) be beneficial to. **2** obtain advantage or benefit (*profited by the experience*). □ **at a profit** with financial gain. [Latin *profectus*: related to PROFICIENT]

**profitable** *adj.* **1** yielding profit. **2** beneficial. □ **profitability** *n.* **profitably** *adv.*

**profiteer** /ˌprof-uh-**teer**/ — *v.* make or seek excessive profits, esp. illegally or on the black market. — *n.* person who profiteers.

**profit margin** *n.* profit after the deduction of costs.

**profit-sharing** *n.* sharing of profits, esp. between employer and employees.

**profligate** /**prof**-luh-guht/ — *adj.* **1** recklessly extravagant. **2** licentious, dissolute. — *n.* profligate person. □ **profligacy** *n.* **profligately** *adv.* [Latin *profligo* ruin]

**pro forma** /proh **faw**-muh/ — *adv.* & *adj.* as or being a matter of form. — *n.* (in full **pro forma invoice**) invoice sent in advance of goods supplied. [Latin]

**profound** /pruh-**fownd**/ *adj.* (**-er, -est**) **1** having or demanding great knowledge, study, or insight (*profound treatise*; *profound doctrines*). **2** intense, unqualified, thorough (*a profound sleep*; *profound indifference*). **3** deep (*profound crevasses*). **4** (of a sigh) deep-drawn. □ **profoundly** *adv.* **profoundness** *n.* **profundity** /pruh-**fun**-duh-tee/ *n.* (*pl.* **-ies**). [Latin *profundus*]

**profuse** /pruh-**fyoos**/ *adj.* **1** (often foll. by *in, of*) lavish; extravagant. **2** exuberantly plentiful; copious (*profuse variety*; *profuse bleeding*). □ **profusely** *adv.* **profusion** /pruh-**fyoo**-zhuhn/ *n.* [Latin *fundo fus-* pour]

**progenitor** /proh-**jen**-uh-tuh, pruh-/ *n.* **1** ancestor. **2** predecessor; originator. [Latin *progigno -genit-* beget]

**progeny** /**proj**-uh-nee/ *n.* **1** offspring; descendant(s). **2** outcome, issue. [Latin: related to PROGENITOR]

**progesterone** /proh-**jes**-tuh-ˌrohn, pruh-/ *n.* steroid hormone which stimulates the preparation of the uterus for pregnancy and maintains the uterus in the event of fertilisation. [German: related to PRO-[1], GESTATION]

**prognosis** /prog-**noh**-suhs/ *n.* (*pl.* **-noses** /-seez/) forecast, esp. of the course of a disease. [Greek *gignōskō* know]

**prognostic** /prog-**nos**-tik/ — *n.* **1** (often foll. by *of*) advance indication, esp. of the course of a disease. **2** prediction, forecast. — *adj.* (often foll. by *of*) foretelling, predictive (*prognostic of a good result*). [Latin: related to PROGNOSIS]

**prognosticate** /prog-**nos**-tuh-ˌkayt/ *v.* (**-ting**) **1** (often foll. by *that*) foretell, foresee, prophesy. **2** (of a thing) betoken, indicate (future events etc.). □ **prognostication** /-kay-shuhn/ *n.* **prognosticator** *n.* [medieval Latin: related to PROGNOSTIC]

**program** see PROGRAMME.

**programme** /**proh**-gram/ — *n.* (also **program**) **1** list of events, performers, etc., at a public function, concert, etc. **2** radio or television broadcast. **3** plan of events (*programme is dinner and an early night*). **4** course or series of studies, lectures, etc. **5** (always **program**) series of coded instructions which controls the operation of a computer etc. — *v.* (**-mm-**) **1** make a programme or definite plan of. **2** (always **program**) express (a problem) or instruct (a computer) by means of a program. □ **programmable** *adj.* **programmatic** /-gruh-**mat**-ik/ *adj.* **programmer** *n.* (in sense 5 of *n.*). [Greek *graphō*, *gegrammai* write]

---

■ **Usage** While either spelling of this word is acceptable in general, the spelling *program* must be used in senses to do with computing.

---

**programming** *n.* *Computing* technical activities involved in the production of a program.

**programming language** *n.* *Computing* any of numerous artificial languages with rigid syntax and semantics used for writing computer programs.

**progress** — *n.* /**proh**-gres/ **1** forward or onward movement towards a destination. **2** advance or development towards completion, betterment, etc.; improvement (*made little progress*). — *v.* /pruh-**gres**/ **1** move or be moved forward or onward; continue. **2** advance, develop, or improve (*science progresses*). □ **in progress** developing; going on. [Latin *progredior -gress-* go forward]

**Progress Association** *n.* association of residents, usu. in a suburb or small town, concerned primarily with the improvement of local amenities.

**progression** /pruh-**gresh**-uhn/ n. **1** act or instance of progressing. **2** succession; series. **3** *Math.* **a** = ARITHMETIC PROGRESSION. **b** = GEOMETRIC PROGRESSION. [Latin: related to PROGRESS]

**progressive** /pruh-**gres**-iv/ — adj. **1** moving forward (*progressive motion*). **2** proceeding step by step; cumulative (*progressive drug use*). **3 a** favouring rapid political or social reform. **b** modern; efficient (*a progressive company*). **4** (of disease, violence, etc.) increasing in severity or extent. **5** (of taxation) at rates increasing with the sum taxed. **6** (of a card-game, dance, etc.) with periodic changes of partners. **7** *Gram.* (of a tense) expressing action in progress, e.g. *am writing, was writing*. — n. advocate of progressive political etc. policies. □ **progressively** adv. [French or medieval Latin: related to PROGRESS]

**prohibit** /pruh-**hib**-uht/ v. (**-t-**) (often foll. by *from* + verbal noun) **1** formally forbid, esp. by authority. **2** prevent (*his accident prohibits him from playing footy ever again*). □ **prohibitor** n. **prohibitory** adj. [Latin *prohibeo -hibit-*]

**prohibition** /,proh-uh-**bish**-uhn/ n. **1** act or instance of forbidding or a state of being forbidden. **2** *Law* an edict or order that forbids.

**prohibitive** /proh-**hib**-uh-tiv/ adj. **1** prohibiting. **2** (of prices, taxes, etc.) so high as to prevent purchase, use, etc. (*prohibitive price*). □ **prohibitively** adv.

**project** — n. /**proj**-ekt, **proh**-jekt/ **1** plan; scheme. **2** a planned undertaking. **3** extensive essay, piece of research, etc., by a student. — v. /pruh-**jekt**/ **1** protrude; jut out. **2** throw; cast; impel. **3** extrapolate (results etc.) to a future time; forecast (*I project that we shall produce two million next year*). **4** plan or contrive (a scheme etc.). **5** cause (light, shadow, images, etc.) to fall on a surface, screen, etc. **6** cause (a sound, esp. the voice) to be heard at a distance. **7** (often *refl.* or *absol.*) express or promote forcefully or effectively (*he projects complete confidence*). **8** make a projection of (the earth, sky, etc.). **9 a** (also *absol.*) attribute (an emotion etc.) to an external object or person, esp. unconsciously. **b** (*refl.*) imagine (oneself) having another's feelings, being in the future, etc. □ **projective** adj. [Latin *projicio -ject-* throw forth]

**projectile** /pruh-**jek**-tuyl/ — n. **1** missile, esp. fired by a rocket. **2** bullet, shell, etc. — adj. **1** capable of being projected by force, esp. from a gun. **2** projecting or impelling.

**projection** /pruh-**jek**-shuhn/ n. **1** act or instance of projecting or the process of being projected. **2** thing that projects or obtrudes. **3** presentation of an image etc. on a surface or screen. **4** forecast or estimate (*projection of next year's profits*). **5 a** a mental image viewed as an objective reality. **b** unconscious transfer of feelings etc. to external objects or persons. **6** representation on a plane surface of any part of the surface of the earth or a celestial sphere (*Mercator projection*). □ **projectionist** n. (in sense 3).

**projector** /pruh-**jek**-tuh/ n. apparatus for projecting slides or film on to a screen.

**prolactin** /proh-**lak**-tuhn/ n. hormone that stimulates milk production after childbirth. [from PRO-[1], LACTATION]

**prolapse** /**proh**-laps/ — n. (also **prolapsus** /-**lap**-suhs/ ) **1** forward or downward displacement of a part or organ. **2** prolapsed womb, rectum, etc. — v. (**-sing**) undergo prolapse. [Latin: related to LAPSE]

**prolegomenon** /,proh-luh-**gom**-uh-nuhn/ n. (pl. **-mena**) (usu. in pl.) preface to a book etc., esp. when critical or discursive. [Greek *legō* say]

**proletarian** /,proh-luh-**tair**-ree-uhn/ — adj. of the proletariat. — n. member of the proletariat. [Latin *proles* offspring]

**proletariat** /,proh-luh-**tair**-ree-uht/ n. **1** wage-earners collectively, esp. those without capital and dependent on selling their labour. **2** esp. *derog.* lowest, esp. uneducated, group in society. [French: related to PROLETARIAN]

**pro-life** adj. opposed to legal abortion.

**pro-life movement** n. movement which, on moral grounds, seeks the banning of legal abortions, whatever the circumstances (or in most circumstances) (see also RIGHT-TO-LIFE).

**pro-lifer** n. *colloq.* member or supporter (esp. a militant one) of the pro-life movement (see also RIGHT-TO-LIFER).

**proliferate** /pruh-**lif**-uh-,rayt/ v. (**-ting**) **1** reproduce; produce (cells etc.) rapidly. **2** increase rapidly in numbers; grow by multiplication. □ **proliferation** /-**ray**-shuhn/ n. **proliferative** /-ruh-tiv/ adj. [Latin *proles* offspring]

**proliferous** /pruh-**lif**-uh-ruhs/ adj. **1** (of a plant) producing many leaf or flower buds; growing luxuriantly. **2** spreading by proliferation.

**prolific** /pruh-**lif**-ik/ adj. **1** producing many offspring or much output (*rabbits are prolific breeders*; *a prolific writer*). **2** (often foll. by *of*) abundantly productive (*prolific of good ideas*). **3** (often foll. by *in*) abounding, copious (*prolific in Australian fauna and flora*). □ **prolifically** *adv.* [medieval Latin: related to PROLIFERATE]

**prolix** /**proh**-liks/ *adj.* **1** (of speech, writing, etc.) lengthy; tedious. **2** (of a person) speaking or writing at great or tedious length (*prolix politicians*). □ **prolixity** /-**lik**-suh-tee/ *n.* [Latin]

**prologue** /**proh**-log/ *n.* **1 a** preliminary speech, poem, etc., esp. of a play (cf. EPILOGUE). **b** the actor speaking the prologue. **2** (usu. foll. by *to*) introductory event. [Greek *logos* word]

**prolong** /pruh-**long**/ *v.* **1** extend (an action, condition, etc.) in time or space (*prolonged his 'brief remarks' for an hour; prolonged the line*). **2** (as **prolonged** *adj.*) lengthy, esp. tediously so (*a prolonged discussion*). □ **prolongation** /,proh-long-**gay**-shuhn/ *n.* [Latin *longus* long]

**prom** *n. colloq.* = PROM CONCERT. [abbreviation]

**prom concert** *n.* (in full **promenade concert**) concert at which the audience, or part of it, can stand, sit on the floor, or move about.

**promenade** /,prom-uh-**nahd**, -**nayd**/ — *n.* **1** (also **esplanade**) paved public walk, esp. along the sea front. **2** walk, ride, or drive, taken esp. for display or pleasure. — *v.* (**-ding**) **1** make a promenade (through). **2** lead (a person etc.) about, esp. for display. [French]

**Promethean** /pruh-**mee**-thee-uhn/ *adj.* daring or inventive. [*Prometheus*, a mortal punished by the Greek gods for stealing fire from the gods and giving it to a fire-less human race]

**promethium** /pruh-**mee**-thee-uhm/ *n.* radioactive metallic element of the lanthanide series, found in nuclear waste. [*Prometheus*: see PROMETHEAN]

**prominence** /**prom**-uh-nuhns/ *n.* **1** the state of being prominent. **2** prominent thing, esp. a jutting outcrop, mountain, etc. [Latin: related to PROMINENT]

**prominent** /**prom**-uh-nuhnt/ *adj.* **1** jutting out, projecting. **2** conspicuous. **3** distinguished, important. [Latin *promineo* project]

**promiscuous** /pruh-**mis**-kyoo-uhs/ *adj.* **1** having frequent, esp. casual, sexual relationships. **2** mixed and indiscriminate; without order (*a promiscuous jumble of books for sale*). **3** *colloq.* carelessly irregular; casual. □ **promiscuity** /prom-uhs-**kyoo**-uh-tee/ *n.* **promiscuously** *adv.* **promiscuousness** *n.* [Latin *misceo* mix]

**promise** /**prom**-uhs/ — *n.* **1** assurance that one will or will not undertake a certain action etc. (*gave a promise of help*). **2** sign of future achievements, good results, etc. (*writer of great promise*). **3** hope, expectation (*the promise of snow*). — *v.* (**-sing**) **1** (usu. foll. by *to* + infin., or *that* + clause; also *absol.*) make a promise (*I promise you a fair hearing; promise not to be late; promised that he would come; I promise*). **2** (often foll. by *to* + infin.) seem likely (to) (*promises to be a good book; is promising to rain*). **3** *colloq.* assure (*I promise you, it will not be easy*). **4** *archaic* (except in Aboriginal traditional society) betroth (*she is promised to another*). □ **promise well** (or **ill** etc.) hold out good (or bad etc.) prospects. □ **promiser** *n.* **promisor** *n.* (*esp. Law*). [Latin *promissum* from *mitto miss-* send]

**promised land** *n.* (prec. by *the*) **1** *Bibl.* Canaan (Gen. 12:7 etc.). **2** any desired place, esp. heaven.

**promising** *adj.* likely to turn out well; hopeful, full of promise (*promising start*). □ **promisingly** *adv.*

**promissory** /**prom**-uh-suh-ree/ *adj.* conveying or implying a promise. [medieval Latin: related to PROMISE]

**promissory note** *n.* signed document containing a written promise to pay a stated sum.

**promo** /**proh**-moh/ *n.* (*pl.* **-s**) *colloq.* **1** (often *attrib.*) publicity, advertising (*promo for the new show; made a promo video*). **2** promotional video, trailer, etc. [abbreviation]

**promontory** /**prom**-uhn-tuh-ree, -tree/ *n.* (*pl.* **-ies**) point of high land jutting out into the sea etc.; headland. [Latin]

**promote** /pruh-**moht**/ *v.* (**-ting**) **1** (often foll. by *to*) raise (a person) to a higher office, rank, etc. (*was promoted to captain*). **2** help forward; encourage (a cause, process, etc.) (*promoted the right of women to abortion on demand; promoting the cause of Mother Mary McKillop to sainthood*). **3** publicise and sell (a product) (*promoting the new purple toothpaste*). **4** finance or organise (*promoted the new show*). □ **promotion** /-**moh**-shuhn/ *n.* **promotional** /-**moh**-shuh-nuhl/ *adj.* [Latin *promoveo -mot-*]

**promoter** *n.* person who promotes, esp. a sporting event, theatrical production, etc. [medieval Latin: related to PROMOTE]

**prompt** — *adj.* **1** acting, made, or done with alacrity; ready (*prompt reply*). **2** (of a payment) made forthwith. — *adv.* punctually (*at six o'clock prompt*). — *v.* **1** (usu. foll. by *to*, or *to* + infin.) incite; urge (*prompted them to action*). **2 a** (*also absol.*) supply a forgotten word etc. to (an actor etc.). **b** assist (a hesitating speaker) with a suggestion. **3** give rise to; inspire (feeling, thought, action, etc.) (*their plight prompted pity*). — *n.* **1 a** act of prompting. **b** thing said to prompt an actor etc. **c** = PROMPTER. **2** *Computing* sign on a computer screen to show that the system is waiting for input. □ **promptitude** *n.* **promptly** *adv.* **promptness** *n.* [Latin]

**prompter** *n.* (also **prompt**) person seated out of sight of the audience who prompts the actors.

**prompt side** *n.* side of the stage where the prompter sits, usu. to the actor's left.

**promulgate** /prom-uhl-gayt/ *v.* (**-ting**) **1** make known to the public; disseminate; promote (a cause etc.). **2** proclaim (a decree, news, etc.). □ **promulgation** /-gay-shuhn/ *n.* **promulgator** *n.* [Latin]

**prone** *adj.* **1 a** lying face downwards (cf. SUPINE). **b** lying flat, prostrate. **c** having the front part downwards, esp. the palm of the hand. **2** (usu. foll. by *to*, or *to* + infin.) disposed or liable, esp. to a bad action, condition, etc. (*prone to pick his nose*). **3** (usu. in *comb.*) more than usually likely to suffer (*accident-prone*). □ **proneness** /prohn-nuhs/ *n.* [Latin]

**prong** — *n.* each of two or more projecting pointed parts at the end of a fork, antler, etc.; tine. — *v.* pierce or stab with a prong. [origin unknown]

**pronominal** /proh-nom-uh-nuhl/ *adj.* of, concerning, or being, a pronoun. [Latin: related to PRONOUN]

**pronoun** /proh-nown/ *n.* word used instead of and to indicate a noun already mentioned or known, esp. to avoid repetition (see panel). [from PRO-¹, NOUN]

**pronounce** /pruh-nowns/ *v.* (**-cing**) **1** (also *absol.*) utter or speak (words, sounds, etc.) in a certain, or esp. in the approved, way (*Australians pronounce English quite differently from other speakers of the language*). **2** utter or proclaim (a judgment, sentence, etc.) officially, formally, or solemnly (*I pronounce you man and wife*). **3** state as one's opinion (*pronounced the beef excellent*). **4** (usu. foll. by *on*, *for*, *against*, *in favour of*) pass judgment (*pronounced for the defendant*). □ **pronounceable** *adj.*

**pronouncement** *n.* [Latin *nuntio* announce]

**pronounced** *adj.* **1** strongly marked; noticeable (*pronounced limp*). **2** forthright, decided (*has pronounced views on Aboriginal land rights*).

**pronto** /pron-toh/ *adv. colloq.* promptly, quickly. [Latin: related to PROMPT]

**pronunciation** /pruh-nun-see-ay-shuhn/ *n.* **1** pronouncing of a word, esp. with reference to a standard (*classifying Australian pronunciation*). **2** act or instance of pronouncing. **3** a person's way of pronouncing words etc. [Latin: related to PRONOUNCE]

**proof** — *n.* **1** facts, evidence, reasoning, etc., establishing or helping to establish a fact (*no proof that he was there*). **2** demonstration or act of proving (*not capable of proof*). **3** test, trial (*put them to the proof*). **4** standard of strength of distilled alcohol (i.e. liquors). **5** *Printing* trial impression taken from type or film, used for making corrections before final printing. **6** step by step resolution of a mathematical or philosophical problem. **7** photographic print made for selection etc. — *adj.* **1** (often in *comb.*) impervious to penetration, ill effects, etc., esp. by a specified agent (*proof against corruption*; *childproof*). **2** being of proof alcoholic strength. — *v.* **1** make (something) proof, esp. make (fabric) waterproof. **2** make a proof of (a printed work). [Latin *proba*: related to PROVE]

**proofread** *v.* (*past* and *past part.* **-read** /-red/) read and correct (esp. a printer's proofs). □ **proofreader** *n.*

**prop¹** — *n.* **1** rigid, esp. separate, support. **2** person who supplies support, comfort, etc. **3** horse's action of propping. **4** *Rugby* a forward at either end of the front row of a scrum. — *v.* (**-pp-**) **1** (often foll. by *against*, *up*, etc.) support with or as if with a prop (*propped him against the wall*; *propped it up with a brick*; *the textile industry needs to be propped up by the government*). **2 a** (of a horse) come to a dead stop, with the forelegs rigid, when moving at speed. **b** (of a person) stay, stop,

---

**Pronoun**

A pronoun is used as a substitute for a noun or a noun phrase, e.g.

He *was* upstairs.     Did *you* see that?
Anything *can* happen now.     It *is* important that *you* come.

Using a pronoun often avoids repetition, e.g.

I found Jim—*he* was outside.
(instead of I found Jim—*Jim* was outside.)
Where are your keys?—I've got *them*.
(instead of Where are your keys?—I've got *my keys*.)

remain (*I'll prop here for a bit*). [Low German or Dutch]

**prop²** *n. Theatr. colloq.* **1** = PROPERTY 4. **2** (in *pl.*) person in charge of theatrical properties. [abbreviation]

**prop³** *n. colloq.* aircraft propeller. [abbreviation]

**prop⁴** *abbr.* proprietor.

**propaganda** /ˌprop-uh-**gan**-duh/ *n.* **1** organised propagation of a doctrine, religion, cause, etc., by use of publicity, selected information, etc. **2** usu. *derog.* ideas etc. so propagated (*neo-Nazi propaganda*; *vicious anti-Semitic propaganda*). □ **propagandise** *v.* (also **-ize**) **propagandist** *n. & adj.* [from the Latin title *Sacra Congregatio de Propaganda Fide* Sacred Congregation for Propagation of the Faith, a committee of cardinals responsible for foreign missions.]

**propagate** /**prop**-uh-ˌgayt/ *v.* (**-ting**) **1 a** breed specimens of (a plant, animal, etc.) from the parent stock. **b** (*refl.* or *absol.*) (of a plant, animal, etc.) reproduce itself. **2** disseminate, spread (a belief, theory, ideas, etc.). **3** hand down (a quality etc.) from one generation to another. **4** extend the operation of; transmit (a vibration, earthquake, etc.). □ **propagation** /-**gay**-shuhn/ *n.* **propagative** *adj.* [Latin *propago*]

**propagator** *n.* **1** person or thing that propagates. **2** small box that can be heated, used for germinating seeds or raising seedlings.

**propane** /**proh**-payn/ *n.* gaseous hydrocarbon used as bottled fuel. [*propionic acid*: related to PRO-², Greek *piōn* fat]

**propel** /pruh-**pel**/ *v.* (**-ll-**) drive or push forward; urge on. [Latin *pello puls-* drive]

**propellant** /pruh-**pel**-uhnt/ *n.* **1** thing that propels. **2** explosive that fires bullets etc. from a firearm. **3** substance used as a reagent in a rocket engine etc. to provide thrust. **4** compressed gas in an aerosol used to thrust the contents out in the form of a spray.

**propeller** *n.* revolving shaft with blades, esp. for propelling a ship or aircraft.

**propene** /**proh**-peen/ *n. Chem.* = PROPYLENE. [from PROPANE, ALKENE]

**propensity** /pruh-**pen**-suh-tee/ *n.* (*pl.* **-ies**) inclination, tendency (*has a propensity for wandering*). [Latin *propensus* inclined]

**proper** /**prop**-uh/ — *adj.* **1 a** accurate, correct (*gave him the proper amount*). **b** fit, suitable, right (*at the proper time*). **2** decent; respectable, esp. excessively so (*not quite proper*). **3** (usu. foll. by *to*) belonging or relating (*respect proper to them*). **4** (usu. placed after the noun) strictly so called; genuine (*this is the crypt, not the cathedral proper*). **5** *colloq.* thorough; complete (*a proper fool you made me look!*). — *n.* that part of the Mass etc. which varies from day to day (opp. ORDINARY *n.*). [Latin *proprius* one's own]

**proper fraction** *n.* fraction less than unity, with the numerator less than the denominator.

**properly** *adv.* **1** fittingly, suitably (*do it properly*). **2** accurately, correctly (*properly speaking*). **3** rightly (*he very properly refused her*). **4** with decency; respectably (*behave properly*). **5** *colloq.* thoroughly (*properly ashamed of himself*).

**proper noun** *n.* capitalised name for an individual person, place, animal, country, title, etc., e.g. 'Kylie', 'Kosciusko'.

**propertied** /**prop**-uh-teed/ *adj.* having property, esp. land.

**property** /**prop**-uh-tee/ *n.* (*pl.* **-ies**) **1** thing(s) owned; possession, esp. a house, land, etc. (*has money in property*). **2** rural landholding used for stock-raising or crop-growing; station. **3** attribute, quality, or characteristic (*has the property of dissolving grease*). **4** movable object used on a theatre stage or in a film etc. □ **common property** thing known by most people (*the secret affairs of the royals have now become common property*). [Latin *proprietas*: related to PROPER]

**prophecy** /**prof**-uh-see/ *n.* (*pl.* **-ies**) **1 a** prophetic utterance, esp. biblical. **b** prediction of future events. **2** faculty, practice, etc., of prophesying (*gift of prophecy*). [Greek: related to PROPHET]

**prophesy** /**prof**-uh-ˌsuy/ *v.* (**-ies, -ied**) **1** (usu. foll. by *that*, *who*, etc.) foretell (an event etc.). **2** speak as a prophet; foretell the future. [French *profecier*: related to PROPHECY]

**prophet** /**prof**-uht/ *n.* (*fem.* **prophetess**) **1** teacher or interpreter of the supposed will of God. **2 a** person who foretells events. **b** spokesman; advocate (*prophet of the new order*). **3** (**the Prophet**) Mohammed. [Greek *prophētēs* spokesman]

**prophetic** /pruh-**fet**-ik/ *adj.* **1** (often foll. by *of*) containing a prediction; predicting. **2** of or concerning a prophet. □ **prophetically** *adv.* [Latin: related to PROPHET]

**prophylactic** /ˌprof-uh-**lak**-tik/ — *adj.* tending to prevent disease etc. — *n.* **1** preventive medicine or action. **2** condom. [Greek, = keeping guard before]

**prophylaxis** /ˌprof-uh-**lak**-suhs/ *n.*

preventive treatment against disease. [from PRO-², Greek *phulaxis* guarding]

**propinquity** /pruh-**ping**-kwuh-tee/ *n.* **1** nearness in position; proximity. **2** close kinship. **3** similarity. [Latin *prope* near]

**propitiate** /pruh-**pish**-ee-,ayt/ *v.* (**-ting**) appease (an offended person etc.). □**propitiable** *adj.* **propitiation** /pruh-,pish-ee-**ay**-shuhn/ *n.* **propitiator** *n.* **propitiatory** /pruh-**pish**-ee-uh-tuh-ree, -tree/ *adj.* [Latin: related to PROPITIOUS]

**propitious** /pruh-**pish**-uhs/ *adj.* **1** (of an omen etc.) favourable, auspicious. **2** (often foll. by *for, to*) (of the weather, an occasion, etc.) suitable, advantageous. **3** well-disposed (*the conditions were propitious*). [Latin *propitius*]

**proponent** /pruh-**poh**-nuhnt/ *n.* person advocating a motion, theory, or proposal (cf. OPPONENT). [Latin: related to PROPOSE]

**proportion** /pruh-**paw**-shuhn/ — *n.* **1 a** comparative part or share (*large proportion of the profits*). **b** comparative ratio (*proportion of births to deaths*). **2** correct or pleasing relation of things or parts of a thing (*has fine proportions*; *exaggerated out of all proportion*). **3** (in *pl.*) dimensions; size (*termites' nest of huge proportions*). **4** *Math.* equality of ratios between two pairs of quantities, e.g. 3:5 and 9:15. — *v.* (usu. foll. by *to*) make proportionate (*you must proportion the punishment to the crime*). [Latin: related to PORTION]

**proportional** *adj.* in due proportion; comparable (*resentment proportional to his injuries*). □**proportionally** *adv.*

**proportional representation** *n.* electoral system in which parties gain seats in proportion to the number of votes cast for them.

**proportionate** /pruh-**paw**-shuh-nuht/ *adj.* = PROPORTIONAL. □ **proportionately** *adv.*

**proposal** /pruh-**poh**-zuhl/ *n.* **1 a** act or instance of proposing something. **b** course of action etc. so proposed (*the proposal was never put into effect*). **2** offer of marriage.

**propose** /pruh-**pohz**/ *v.* (**-sing**) **1** (also *absol.*) put forward for consideration or as a plan; suggest. **2** (usu. foll. by *to* + infin., or verbal noun) intend; purpose (*I propose to open a café*). **3** (usu. foll. by *to*) offer oneself in marriage. **4** nominate (a person) as a member of a society, for an office, etc. □ **propose a toast** (or **somebody's health**) ask people to drink to someone's health. □ **proposer** *n.* [Latin *pono posit-* place]

**proposition** /,prop-uh-**zish**-uhn/ — *n.* **1** statement, assertion. **2** scheme pro-

posed, proposal. **3** *Logic* statement subject to proof or disproof. **4** *colloq.* problem, opponent, prospect, etc., that is to be dealt with (*he's a difficult proposition*). **5** *Math.* formal statement of a theorem or problem, often including the demonstration. **6 a** likely commercial etc. enterprise etc. **b** person regarded similarly. **7** proposal or request for sexual intercourse. — *v.* make a (esp. sexual) proposal to (*he propositioned her*). [Latin: related to PROPOSE]

**propound** /pruh-**pownd**/ *v.* offer for consideration; propose. [earlier *propo(u)ne* from Latin: related to PROPOSE]

**proppy** *adj.* (of a horse) disposed to be restive when ridden; inclined to prop. [PROP¹ sense 2a of verb]

**proprietary** /pruh-**pruy**-uh-tuh-ree, -tree/ *adj.* **1 a** of or holding property (*proprietary classes*). **b** of a proprietor (*proprietary rights*). **2** held in private ownership. [Latin *proprietarius*: related to PROPERTY]

**proprietary company** *n.* = PRIVATE COMPANY.

**proprietary medicine** *n.* drug, medicine, etc., produced by a company, usu. under a patent.

**proprietary name** *n.* (also **proprietary term**) name of a product etc. registered by its owner as a trade mark and not usable by another without permission.

**proprietor** /pruh-**pruy**-uh-tuh/ *n.* (*fem.* **proprietress**) **1** holder of property. **2** owner of a business etc. □ **proprietorial** /-**taw**-ree-uhl/ *adj.* [related to PROPRIETARY]

**propriety** /pruh-**pruy**-uh-tee/ *n.* (*pl.* **-ies**) **1** fitness; rightness (*I doubt the propriety of refusing him*). **2** correctness of behaviour or morals (*highest standards of propriety*). **3** (in *pl.*) details or rules of correct conduct (*must observe the proprieties*). [French: related to PROPERTY]

**propulsion** /pruh-**pul**-shuhn/ *n.* **1** act or instance of driving or pushing forward. **2** an impelling influence. □ **propulsive** /-**pul**-siv/ *adj.* [related to PROPEL]

**propylene** /**proh**-puh-,leen/ *n.* gaseous hydrocarbon used in the manufacture of chemicals. [from *propyl*, a univalent radical of propane]

**pro rata** /proh **rah**-tuh, **ray**-tuh/ — *adj.* proportional. — *adv.* proportionally. [Latin]

**prorogue** /pruh-**rohg**/ *v.* (**-gues, -gued, -guing**) **1** discontinue the meetings of (a parliament etc.) without dissolving it. **2** (of a parliament etc.) be prorogued. □ **prorogation** /proh-ruh-**gay**-shuhn/ *n.* [Latin *prorogo* extend]

**prosaic** /proh-**zay**-ik, pruh-/ *adj.* **1** like prose, lacking poetic beauty. **2** unromantic; dull; commonplace (*took a prosaic view of life*). □ **prosaically** *adv.* [Latin: related to PROSE]

**proscenium** /pruh-**see**-nee-uhm/ *n.* (*pl.* **-s** or **-nia**) **1** part of the stage in front of the curtain and the enclosing arch. **2** the stage of an ancient theatre. [Greek: related to SCENE]

**prosciutto** /pruh-**shoo**-toh/ *n.* Italian cured ham. [Italian]

**proscribe** /pruh-**skruyb**/ *v.* (**-bing**) **1** forbid, esp. by law. **2** reject or denounce (a practice etc.). **3** outlaw (a person); banish, exile (*he was proscribed from the club*). □ **proscription** /-**skrip**-shuhn/ *n.* **proscriptive** /-**skrip**-tiv/ *adj.* [Latin, = publish in writing]

■ **Usage** *Proscribe* is sometimes confused with *prescribe*.

**prose** /prohz/ — *n.* **1** ordinary written or spoken language (opp. POETRY, VERSE). **2** dull or matter-of-fact quality (*the prose of daily life*). — *v.* (**-sing**) talk tediously (*prosing on about his private life*). [Latin *prosa oratio* straightforward discourse]

**prosecute** /**pros**-uh-ˌkyoot/ *v.* (**-ting**) **1** (also *absol.*) institute legal proceedings against (a person), or with reference to (a claim, crime, etc.) (*decided not to prosecute*). **2** follow up, pursue (an inquiry, studies, etc.). **3** *formal* carry on (a trade, pursuit, etc.). □ **prosecutor** *n.* [Latin *prosequor -secut-* pursue]

**prosecution** /ˌpros-uh-**kyoo**-shuhn/ *n.* **1 a** institution and continuation of (esp. criminal) legal proceedings. **b** prosecuting party in a court case. **2** act or instance of prosecuting or being prosecuted (*lost his legs in the prosecution of his hobby*).

**proselyte** /**pros**-uh-ˌluyt/ *n.* person converted, esp. recently, from one opinion, creed, party, etc., to another. □ **proselytism** /-luh-ˌtiz-uhm/ *n.* [Latin *proselytus* from Greek]

**proselytise** /**pros**-uh-luh-ˌtuyz/ *v.* (also **-ize**) (**-sing** or **-zing**) (also *absol.*) convert or seek to convert from one belief etc. to another.

**prosody** /**pros**-uh-dee, **proz**-/ *n.* **1** theory and practice of versification; the laws of metre. **2** the study of speech-rhythms. □ **prosodic** /pruh-**sod**-ik, -**zod**-ik/ *adj.* **prosodist** *n.* [Greek *pros* to: related to ODE]

**prospect** — *n.* /**pros**-pekt/ **1 a** (often in *pl.*) expectation, esp. of success in a career etc. (*job with no prospects*). **b** something one expects (*don't relish the prospect of meeting him*). **2** extensive view of landscape etc. (*striking prospect*). **3** mental picture or survey of a subject etc. (*had a prospect of the difficulties ahead*). **4** possible or probable customer, subscriber, etc. (*a likely prospect*). — *v.* /**pros**-pekt, pruh-**spekt**/ (usu. foll. by *for*) explore, search (esp. a region) for gold etc. □ **prospector** /**pros**-pek-tuh, pruh-**spek**-tuh/ *n.* [Latin: related to PROSPECTUS]

**prospective** /pruh-**spek**-tiv/ *adj.* some day to be; expected; future (*prospective bridegroom*). [Latin: related to PROSPECTUS]

**prospectus** /pruh-**spek**-tuhs/ *n.* (*pl.* **-tuses**) printed document advertising or describing a school, commercial enterprise, forthcoming book, etc. [Latin, = prospect, from *prospicio -spect-* look forward]

**prosper** *v.* **1** be successful, thrive. **2** make successful (*Heaven prosper him!*). [Latin *prospero*]

**prosperity** /pros-**pe**-ruh-tee/ *n.* prosperous state; wealth; success.

**prosperous** /**pros**-puh-ruhs/ *adj.* **1** successful; rich. **2** flourishing; thriving (*a prosperous business*). **3** auspicious (*a prosperous wind*). □ **prosperously** *adv.* [French from Latin]

**prostanthera** /ˌpros-**tan**-thuh-ruh/ *n.* = MINT BUSH.

**prostate** /**pros**-tayt/ *n.* (in full **prostate gland**) gland round the neck of the bladder in male mammals, releasing a fluid forming part of the semen. □ **prostatic** /-**tat**-ik/ *adj.* [Greek *prostatēs* one who stands before]

**prosthesis** /pros-**thee**-suhs/ *n.* (*pl.* **-theses** /-seez/) **1** an artificial part supplied to remedy a deficiency, e.g. a false breast, leg, tooth, etc. **2** branch of surgery dealing with prostheses. □ **prosthetic** /-**thet**-ik/ *adj.* [Greek, = placing in addition]

**prostitute** /**pros**-tuh-ˌtyoot/ — *n.* **1** woman or girl who engages in sexual activity for payment. **2** (usu. **male prostitute**) man or boy who engages in sexual activity, esp. with homosexual men, for payment. — *v.* (**-ting**) **1** (esp. *refl.*) make a prostitute of (esp. oneself). **2 a** misuse (one's talents, skills, name, etc.) for money etc. **b** offer (oneself, one's honour, etc.) for unworthy ends, esp. for money. □ **prostitution** /-**tyoo**-shuhn/ *n.* [Latin *prostituo -tut-* offer for sale]

**prostrate** — *adj.* /**pros**-trayt/ **1 a** lying face downwards, esp. in submission. **b** lying horizontally. **2** overcome, esp. by grief, exhaustion, etc. (*prostrate with self-pity*). **3** (of a plant) growing (usu. flat) along the ground. — *v.* /pros-**trayt**/

**(-ting) 1** throw (esp. a person) flat on the ground. **2** *refl.* throw (oneself) down in submission etc. **3** overcome; make physically weak (*prostrated by the heat*). □ **prostration** /pros-**tray**-shuhn/ *n.* [Latin *prosterno -strat-* throw in front]

**prosy** /**proh**-zee/ *adj.* (**-ier, -iest**) tedious, commonplace, dull (*prosy talk*). □ **prosily** *adv.* **prosiness** *n.*

**protactinium** /,proh-tak-**tin**-ee-uhm/ *n.* radioactive metallic element. [German: related to ACTINIUM]

**protagonist** /proh-**tag**-uh-nuhst/ *n.* **1** chief person in a drama, story, etc. **2** leading person in a contest etc.; principal performer. **3** (usu. foll. by *of, for*) advocate or champion of a cause etc. (*protagonist of women's rights*). [Greek: related to PROTO-, *agōnistēs* actor]

■ **Usage** The use of *protagonist* in sense 3 is considered incorrect by some people.

**protean** /**proh**-tee-uhn, -**tee**-uhn/ *adj.* variable, taking many forms; versatile. [*Proteus*, Greek sea-god who took various shapes]

**protect** /pruh-**tekt**/ *v.* **1** (often foll. by *from, against*) keep (a person, thing, etc.) safe; defend, guard. **2** shield (home industry) from competition by imposing import duties etc. on foreign goods. [Latin *tego tect-* cover]

**protection** /pruh-**tek**-shuhn/ *n.* **1 a** act or instance of protecting or state of being protected; defence. **b** thing, person, or animal that protects (*bought a dog as protection*). **2** (also **protectionism**) theory or practice of protecting home industries by imposing import duties on foreign goods etc. **3** *colloq.* **a** immunity from violence etc. obtained by payment to gangsters etc. **b** (in full **protection money**) money so paid, esp. on a regular basis.

**protectionism** *n.* economic system of PROTECTION (sense 2). □ **protectionist** *n.*

**protective** /pruh-**tek**-tiv/ *adj.* protecting; intended or tending to protect. □ **protectively** *adv.* **protectiveness** *n.*

**protective custody** *n.* detention of a person for his or her own protection.

**protector** *n.* (*fem.* **protectress**) **1** person or device that protects (*chest-protector*). **2** (**Protector**) *hist.* an official responsible for the Aboriginal population of a particular district. □ **protectorship** *n.*

**protectorate** /pruh-**tek**-tuh-ruht/ *n.* **1 a** nation that is controlled and protected by another. **b** this relation. **2** (**Protectorate**) *hist.* the office of a Protector of Aborigines.

**protégé** /**prot**-uh-,zhay, **proh**-tuh-/ (*fem.* **protégée** pronunc. same) person

under the protection, patronage, tutelage, etc., of another. [French: related to PROTECT]

**protein** /**proh**-teen/ *n.* any of a group of organic compounds composed of one or more chains of amino acids and forming an essential part of all living organisms. [Greek *prōtos* first]

**pro tem** /proh **tem**/ *adj.* & *adv. colloq.* = PRO TEMPORE. [abbreviation]

**pro tempore** /proh **tem**-puh-ray, -,puh-ree/ *adj.* & *adv.* for the time being. [Latin]

**Proterozoic** /,proh-tuh-roh-**zoh**-ik/ *Geol.* — *adj.* of the later part of the Pre-cambrian era. — *n.* this time. [Greek *proteros* former, *zōē* life]

**protest** — *n.* /**proh**-test/ **1** statement or act of dissent or disapproval. **2** (often *attrib.*) a usu. public demonstration of objection to government etc. policy (*marched in protest*; *a protest march*). **3** *Law* written declaration that a bill has been presented and payment or acceptance refused. — *v.* /pruh-**test**/ **1** (usu. foll. by *against, at, about*, etc.) make a protest. **2** affirm (one's innocence etc.) solemnly. **3** *Law* write or obtain a protest in regard to (a bill). □ **under protest** unwillingly. □ **protester** *n.* [Latin *protestor* declare formally]

**Protestant** /**prot**-uhs-tuhnt/ — *n.* member or follower of any of the Christian groups separating from the Roman Catholic Church at the Reformation, or any group subsequently splitting from or descending from these. — *adj.* of the Protestants or their forms of religion etc. □ **Protestantism** *n.* [related to PROTEST]

**protestation** /,prot-uh-**stay**-shuhn/ *n.* **1** strong affirmation. **2** protest. [Latin: related to PROTEST]

**protium** /**proh**-tee-uhm/ *n.* ordinary isotope of hydrogen. [Latin: related to PROTO-]

**proto-** *comb. form* **1** original, primitive (*proto-Aboriginal*; *proto-Germanic*). **2** first, original (*protomartyr*). [Greek *prōtos*]

**protocol** /,proh-tuh-**kol**/ — *n.* **1** official, esp. diplomatic, formality and etiquette, esp. as observed on State occasions etc. **2** original draft of esp. the terms of a treaty. **3** formal statement of a transaction. — *v.* (**-ll-**) draw up or record in a protocol. [Greek *kolla* glue]

**protomartyr** /,proh-toh-**mah**-tuh/ *n.* the first martyr in any cause.

**proton** /**proh**-ton/ *n.* elementary particle with a positive electric charge equal to that of an electron, and occurring in all atomic nuclei. [Greek *prōtos* first]

**protoplasm** /**proh**-tuh-ˌplaz-uhm/ *n.* material comprising the living part of a cell, consisting of a nucleus in membrane-enclosed cytoplasm. □ **protoplasmic** /-**plaz**-mik/ *adj.* [Greek: related to PROTO-, PLASMA]

**prototype** /**proh**-tuh-ˌtuyp/ *n.* **1** the original or model from which copies, imitations, improved forms, representations, etc., are made. **2** trial model or preliminary version of a vehicle, machine, etc. □ **prototypic** /-**tip**-ik/ *adj.* **prototypical** /-**tip**-i-kuhl/ *adj.* [Greek: related to PROTO-]

**protozoan** /ˌproh-tuh-**zoh**-uhn/ — *n.* (also **protozoon** /-**zoh**-on/) (*pl.* **protozoa** /-**zoh**-uh/ or **-s**) unicellular microscopic organism, e.g. amoebae and ciliates. — *adj.* (also **protozoic** /-**zoh**-ik/) of this group. [from PROTO-, Greek *zōion* animal]

**protract** /pruh-**trakt**/ *v.* (often as **protracted** *adj.*) prolong or lengthen in time. □ **protraction** *n.* [Latin *traho tract*-draw]

**protractor** *n.* instrument for measuring angles, usu. in the form of a graduated semicircle.

**protrude** /pruh-**trood**/ *v.* (**-ding**) (cause to) thrust forward; stick out; project. □ **protrusion** *n.* **protrusive** *adj.* [Latin *trudo trus*- thrust]

**protuberant** /pruh-**tyoo**-buh-ruhnt/ *adj.* bulging out; prominent. □ **protuberance** *n.* [Latin: related to TUBER]

**proud** *adj.* **1** feeling greatly honoured or pleased (*proud to know him*). **2 a** (often foll. by *of*) haughty, arrogant (*too proud to speak to us*). **b** (often in *comb.*) having a proper pride; satisfied (*house-proud*; *proud of a job well done*). **3** (of an occasion, action, etc.) justly arousing or showing pride (*a proud day for Australia*; *proud smile*). **4** (of a thing) imposing, splendid (*a proud monument*). □ **do proud** treat with lavish generosity or honour (*did us proud*). □ **proudly** *adv.* [French *prud* valiant]

**prove** /proov/ *v.* (**-ving**; *past part.* **proved** or **proven** /**proo**-vuhn/) **1** (often foll. by *that*) demonstrate the truth of by evidence or argument. **2 a** (usu. foll. by *to* + infin.) be found (*it proved to be untrue*). **b** emerge as (*will prove the winner*). **3** test the accuracy of (a calculation). **4** establish the validity of (a will). **5** (of dough) rise in bread-making. □ **prove oneself** show one's abilities, courage, etc. □ **provable** *adj.* [Latin *probo probat*- test, approve]

■ **Usage** In Australian English it is not standard to use *proven* as the past

participle (e.g. *his worth has been proven*). It is, however, common in certain expressions, such as *of proven ability*.

**provedore** /**prov**-uh-daw/ *n.* (also **providore, provedor**) supplier of provisions to a ship, a canteen, etc. [Italian]

**provenance** /**prov**-uh-nuhns/ *n.* **1** place of origin or history, esp. of a work of art. **2** origin (*what is the provenance of the word 'kangaroo'?*). [French *provenir* from Latin]

**provender** /**prov**-uhn-duh/ *n.* **1** animal fodder. **2** *joc.* food for human beings. [Latin]

**proverb** /**prov**-erb/ *n.* short pithy saying in general use, held to embody a general truth. [Latin *proverbium* from *verbum* word]

**proverbial** /pruh-**ver**-bee-uhl/ *adj.* **1** (esp. of a characteristic) well known; notorious (*his honesty is proverbial*). **2** of or referred to in a proverb (*the proverbial ill wind*). □ **proverbially** *adv.* [Latin: related to PROVERB]

**provide** /pruh-**vuyd**/ *v.* (**-ding**) **1** supply, furnish (*provided me with food*; *provided food for me*). **2 a** (usu. foll. by *for*, *against*) make due preparation (*provided for any eventuality*; *provided against invasion*). **b** (usu. foll. by *for*) take care of a person etc. with money, food, etc. (*provides for a large family*). **3** (usu. foll. by *that*) stipulate in a will, statute, etc. □ **provider** *n.* [Latin *provideo -vis-* foresee]

**provided** *conj.* (often foll. by *that*) on the condition or understanding (that) (*I shall come, provided (that) the rest of your family agree*).

**providence** /**prov**-uh-duhns/ *n.* **1** protective care of God or nature. **2** (**Providence**) God in this aspect. **3** timely preparation; foresight; thrift. [Latin: related to PROVIDE]

**provident** *adj.* having or showing foresight; thrifty. [Latin: related to PROVIDE]

**providential** /ˌprov-uh-**den**-shuhl/ *adj.* **1** of or by divine foresight or interposition. **2** opportune, lucky. □ **providentially** *adv.*

**providing** *conj.* = PROVIDED.

**province** /**prov**-uhns/ *n.* **1** principal administrative division of a country etc. **2** (**the provinces**) country outside a capital city, esp. regarded as uncultured or unsophisticated. **3** sphere of action; business (*outside my province*). **4** branch of learning etc. (*in the province of aesthetics*). [Latin *provincia*]

**provincial** /pruh-**vin**-shuhl/ — *adj.* **1** of a province or provinces. **2** unsophisticated or uncultured. — *n.* **1** inhabitant of a province or the provinces. **2** unsophisticated or uncultured person. □ **provincialism** *n.*

**provision** /pruh-**vizh**-uhn/ — *n.* **1 a** act or instance of providing (*provision of preschools*). **b** preparation, esp. for the future (*made provision for their old age*). **2** (in *pl.*) food, drink, etc., esp. for an expedition. **3** legal or formal stipulation or proviso. — *v.* supply with provisions. [Latin: related to PROVIDE]

**provisional** *adj.* providing for immediate needs only; temporary (*a provisional agreement*). □ **provisionally** *adv.*

**provisional licence** *n.* initial licence to drive a motor vehicle, requiring (for a specified period, e.g. three years) the display of P-plates on any vehicle driven, and imposing certain restrictions (e.g. in Victoria the driver must be alcohol-free whenever driving).

**provisional tax** *n.* an advance payment anticipating tax on income not taxed at source.

**proviso** /pruh-**vuy**-zoh/ *n.* (*pl.* **-s**) **1** stipulation. **2** clause containing this in a legal document etc. □ **provisory** *adj.* [Latin, = it being provided]

**provocation** /ˌprov-uh-**kay**-shuhn/ *n.* **1** act or instance of provoking or state of being provoked (*did it under severe provocation*). **2** cause of annoyance.

**provocative** /pruh-**vok**-uh-tiv/ *adj.* **1** (usu. foll. by *of*) tending to provoke, esp. anger or sexual desire. **2** intentionally annoying or controversial. □ **provocatively** *adv.* **provocativeness** *n.*

**provoke** /pruh-**vohk**/ *v.* (**-king**) **1 a** (often foll. by *to*, or *to* + infin.) rouse or incite (*provoked him to fury*). **b** (as **provoking** *adj.*) exasperating; irritating. **2** call forth; instigate; cause (indignation, an inquiry, some process, etc.). **3** (usu. foll. by *into* + verbal noun) irritate or stimulate (a person) (*provoked him into retaliating*). **4** tempt; allure. [Latin *provoco* call forth]

**provost** /**prov**-uhst/ *n.* **1** head of certain schools, colleges, etc. **2** head of a chapter etc. of certain religious foundations. [Latin *propositus* from *pono* place]

**prow** /prow/ *n.* **1** fore-part or bow of a ship. **2** pointed or projecting front part. [French *proue* from Greek *prōira*]

**prowess** /**prow**-es, prow-**es**/ *n.* **1** skill, expertise. **2** valour, gallantry. [French: related to PROUD]

**prowl** — *v.* (often foll. by *about*, *around*) roam (a place) esp. stealthily or restlessly or in search of prey, plunder, etc. — *n.* act or instance of prowling. □ **on the prowl** moving about secretively or rapaciously,

esp. in search of sexual contact etc. □ **prowler** *n.* [origin unknown]

**prox.** *abbr.* proximo.

**proximate** /**prok**-suh-muht/ *adj.* **1** nearest or next before or after (in place, order, time, causation, thought process, etc.). **2** approximate. [Latin *proximus* nearest]

**proximity** /prok-**sim**-uh-tee/ *n.* nearness in space, time, etc. (*in close proximity*). [Latin: related to PROXIMATE]

**proximo** /**prok**-suh-ˌmoh/ *adj. Commerce* of next month (*the third proximo*) (cf. ULTIMO). [Latin, = in the next (*mense month*)]

**proxy** /**prok**-see/ *n.* (*pl.* **-ies**) (also *attrib.*) **1** authorisation given to a substitute or deputy (*proxy vote*; *married by proxy*). **2** person authorised to act thus. **3 a** written authorisation for esp. proxy voting. **b** proxy vote. [obsolete *procuracy* procuration]

**prude** /prood/ *n.* excessively (often affectedly) squeamish or sexually modest person. □ **prudery** *n.* **prudish** *adj.* **prudishly** *adv.* **prudishness** *n.* [French: related to PROUD]

**prudent** /**proo**-duhnt/ *adj.* (of a person or conduct) careful to avoid undesired circumstances; cautious; politic. □ **prudence** *n.* **prudently** *adv.* [Latin *prudens* *-ent-*: related to PROVIDENT]

**prudential** /proo-**den**-shuhl/ *adj.* of or showing prudence. □ **prudentially** *adv.*

**prune**¹ /proon/ *n.* dried plum. [Latin *prunum* from Greek]

**prune**² /proon/ *v.* (**-ning**) **1 a** (often foll. by *down*) trim (a bush etc.) by cutting away dead or overgrown branches etc. **b** (usu. foll. by *off*, *away*) lop (branches etc.) thus. **2** reduce (costs etc.) (*prune expenses*). **3 a** (often foll. by *of*) clear or remove superfluities from. **b** remove (superfluities). [French *prooignier* from Romanic: related to ROUND]

**prunus** /**proo**-nuhs/ *n.* shrub or tree of the plum family, esp. purple-leaved varieties grown as garden ornamentals.

**prurient** /**proo**-ree-uhnt/ *adj.* having or encouraging unhealthy sexual curiosity. □ **prurience** *n.* **pruriently** *adv.* [Latin *prurio* itch]

**Prussian** /**prush**-uhn/ — *adj.* of Prussia, or esp. its rigidly militaristic tradition. — *n.* native of Prussia. [*Prussia*, former German state]

**Prussian blue** *n. & adj.* (as *adj.* often hyphenated) deep blue (pigment).

**prussic acid** /**prus**-ik/ *n.* hydrocyanic acid. [French]

**pry** /pruy/ *v.* (**pries**, **pried**) **1** (often foll. by *into*) inquire impertinently (into a person's private affairs etc.), snoop. **2** (usu. foll. by *into*, *about*, etc.) look or peer inquisitively. □ **prying** *adj.* [origin unknown]

**PS** *abbr.* postscript.

**psalm** /sahm/ *n.* **1** sacred song or hymn. **2** (also **Psalm**) sacred song from the Book of Psalms. **3** (**the Psalms**) or (**the book of Psalms**) Old Testament book containing the Psalms. [Latin *psalmus* from Greek]

**psalmist** *n.* composer of a psalm.

**psalmody** /sahm-uh-dee, sah-muh-/ *n.* practice or art of singing psalms, hymns, etc., esp. in public worship. [Greek: related to PSALM]

**Psalter** /sawl-tuh, sol-/ *n.* **1** the Book of Psalms. **2** (**psalter**) version or copy of this for liturgical use. [Old English and French from Greek *psaltērion* stringed instrument]

**psaltery** /sawl-tuh-ree, sol-/ *n.* (*pl.* **-ies**) ancient and medieval instrument like a dulcimer but played by plucking the strings. [Latin: related to PSALTER]

**psephology** /se-fol-uh-jee/ *n.* the statistical study of elections, voting, etc. □ **psephologist** *n.* [Greek *psēphos* pebble, vote]

**pseudo** /syoo-doh/ *colloq.* — *adj.* (esp. intellectually) pretentious; not genuine. — *n.* such a person; poseur. [from PSEUDO-]

**pseudo-** *comb. form* (also **pseud-** before a vowel) **1** false; not genuine (*pseudo-intellectual*). **2** resembling or imitating (often in technical applications) (*pseudo-acid*). [Greek *pseudēs* false]

**pseudonym** /syoo-duh-nim/ *n.* fictitious name, esp. of an author. [Greek: related to PSEUDO-, *onoma* name]

**pseudonymous** /syoo-**don**-uh-muhs/ *adj.* writing or written under a false name. □ **pseudonymity** /-duh-**nim**-uh-tee/ *n.* **pseudonymously** *adv.*

**psi** /psuy/ *n.* twenty-third letter of the Greek alphabet (Ψ, ψ). [Greek]

**psittacosis** /,sit-uh-**koh**-suhs/ *n.* contagious viral disease of esp. parrots, transmissible to human beings. [Greek *psittakos* parrot]

**psoriasis** /suh-**ruy**-uh-suhs/ *n.* skin disease marked by red scaly patches. [Greek *psōra* itch]

**psych** /suyk/ *v. colloq.* **1** (usu. foll. by *up*; often *refl.*) prepare (oneself or another) psychologically for an ordeal etc. **2** (often foll. by *out*) intimidate or frighten (a person), esp. for one's own advantage. **3** (usu. foll. by *out*) analyse (a person's motivation etc.) for one's own advantage (*can't psych him out*). **4** (foll. by *out*) go under the influence of some drug, esp.

marijuana. □ **psyched out** *adj.* **psyched up** *adj.* [abbreviation]

**psyche** /suy-kee/ *n.* the soul, spirit, or mind. [Latin from Greek]

**psychedelic** /,suy-kuh-**del**-ik/ *adj.* **1 a** expanding the mind's awareness etc., esp. with hallucinogenic drugs. **b** hallucinatory; bizarre. **c** (of a drug) producing hallucinations. **2** *colloq.* **a** producing a hallucinatory effect; vivid in colour or design etc. **b** (of colours, patterns, etc.) bright, bold, and often abstract. □ **psychedelically** *adv.* [Greek *psukhē* mind, *dēlos* clear]

**psychiatry** /suy-**kuy**-uh-tree, suh-/ *n.* the study and treatment of mental disease. □ **psychiatric** /,suy-kee-**at**-rik/. **psychiatrist** *n.* [from PSYCHO-, Greek *iatros* physician]

**psychic** /suy-kik/ — *adj.* **1 a** (of a person) considered to have occult powers such as telepathy, clairvoyance, etc. **b** (of a faculty, phenomenon, etc.) inexplicable by natural laws. **2** of the soul or mind. — *n.* person considered to have psychic powers; medium. [Greek *psukhē* soul, mind]

**psychical** *adj.* **1** concerning psychic phenomena or faculties (*psychical research*). **2** of the soul or mind. □ **psychically** *adv.*

**psycho** /suy-koh/ *colloq.* — *n.* (*pl.* **-s**) **1** psychopath. **2** insane or eccentric person; weirdo. — *adj.* **1** psychopathic. **2** highly eccentric. [abbreviation]

**psycho-** *comb. form* of the mind or psychology. [Greek: related to PSYCHIC]

**psychoanalysis** /,suy-koh-uh-**nal**-uh-suhs/ *n.* treatment of mental disorders by bringing repressed fears and conflicts into the conscious mind over a long course of interviews. □ **psychoanalyse** /-**an**-uh-,luyz/ *v.* (**-sing**). **psychoanalyst** /-**an**-uh-luhst/ *n.* **psychoanalytic** /-,an-uh-**lit**-ik/ *adj.* **psychoanalytical** /-,an-uh-**lit**-i-kuhl/ *adj.*

**psychokinesis** /,suy-koh-kuh-**nee**-suhs/ *n.* movement of objects supposedly by telepathy or mental effort alone.

**psychological** /,suy-kuh-**loj**-i-kuhl/ *adj.* **1** of, relating to, or arising in the mind. **2** of, or relating to, psychology. **3** *colloq.* (of an ailment etc.) arising from the mind, imaginary (*his backache is purely psychological*). □ **psychologically** *adv.*

**psychological block** *n.* mental inability or inhibition caused by emotional factors.

**psychological moment** *n.* best time for achieving a particular effect or purpose.

**psychological warfare** *n.* campaign directed at reducing enemy morale.

**psychology** /suy-**kol**-uh-jee/ n. (pl. **-ies**) **1** the scientific study of the human mind and its functions, esp. those affecting behaviour in a given context. **2** treatise on or theory of this. **3 a** mental characteristics etc. of a person or group. **b** mental aspects of an activity, situation, etc. (*psychology of crime*). □ **psychologise** v. (also **-ize**). **psychologist** n.

**psychopath** /**suy**-kuh-,path/ n. **1** person suffering from chronic mental derangement, esp. with abnormal or violent social behaviour. **2** colloq. mentally or emotionally unstable person. □ **psychopathic** /-**path**-ik/ adj.

**psychopathology** /,suy-koh-puh-**thol**-uh-jee/ n. **1** the scientific study of mental disorders. **2** mentally or behaviourally disordered state. □ **psychopathological** /-,path-uh-**loj**-i-kuhl/ adj.

**psychopathy** /suy-**kop**-uh-thee/ n. psychopathic or psychologically abnormal behaviour.

**psychosexual** /,suy-koh-**sek**-shoo-uhl/ adj. of or involving the psychological aspects of the sexual impulse. □ **psychosexually** adv.

**psychosis** /suy-koh-suhs/ n. (pl. **-choses** /-seez/ ) severe mental derangement, esp. when resulting in delusions and loss of contact with external reality. [Greek: related to PSYCHE]

**psychosomatic** /,suy-koh-suh-**mat**-ik/ adj. **1** (of a bodily disorder) mental, not physical, in origin. **2** of the mind and body together.

**psychotherapy** /,suy-koh-**the**-ruh-pee/ n. treatment of mental disorder by psychological means. □ **psychotherapeutic** /-**pyoo**-tik/ adj. **psychotherapist** n.

**psychotic** /suy-**kot**-ik/ — adj. of or suffering from a psychosis. — n. psychotic person.

**PT** abbr. physical training.

**Pt** symb. platinum.

**pt.** abbr. **1** part. **2** pint. **3** point. **4** Naut. port.

**pteridophyte** /te-ruh-duh-,fuyt/ n. flowerless plant, e.g. ferns, club-mosses, etc. [Greek pteris fern]

**pterodactyl** /,te-ruh-**dak**-tuhl/ n. large extinct flying birdlike reptile with a long slender head and neck. [Greek pteron wing, DACTYL]

**pterostylis** /,te-roh-**stuy**-luhs/ n. any of several Australian terrestrial orchids bearing deeply hooded flowers and often forming colonies (see GREENHOOD). [Greek]

**ptilotus** /tuh-**loh**-tuhs/ n. = PUSSY TAIL. [Greek ptilon feather]

**PTO** abbr. please turn over.

**Ptolemaic** /,tol-uh-**may**-ik/ adj. hist. of Ptolemy or his theories. [Greek Ptolemaios, 2nd-c. astronomer]

**Ptolemaic system** n. theory that the earth is the stationary centre of the universe.

**ptomaine** /tuh-**mayn**, toh-/ n. any of various esp. toxic amine compounds in putrefying animal and vegetable matter. [Greek ptōma corpse]

**Pty.** abbr. proprietary.

**Pu** symb. plutonium.

**pub** n. colloq. hotel. [abbreviation of public house]

**pub crawl** n. colloq. drinking tour of several hotels in the one outing.

**puberty** /**pyoo**-buh-tee/ n. period of sexual maturation during which a person first becomes capable of reproducing offspring. □ **pubertal** adj. [Latin puber adult]

**pubes¹** /**pyoo**-beez/ n. (pl. same) **1** lower part of the abdomen at the front of the pelvis, covered with hair at puberty. **2** the hair, scanty at first, which appears in this region at puberty. [Latin]

**pubes²** pl. of PUBIS.

**pubescence** /pyoo-**bes**-uhns/ n. **1** the time when puberty begins. **2** soft, fine hair or down on plants, or on animals, esp. insects. □ **pubescent** adj. [Latin: related to PUBES¹]

**pubic** /**pyoo**-bik/ adj. of the pubes or pubis (*pubic hair*).

**pubis** /**pyoo**-buhs/ n. (pl. **pubes** /-beez/ ) either of a pair of bones forming the two sides of the pelvis. [Latin os pubis bone of the PUBES]

**public** /**pub**-lik/ — adj. **1** of or concerning the people as a whole (*public holiday*). **2** open to or shared by all (*public library*). **3** done or existing openly (*public apology*). **4** (of a service, funds, etc.) provided by or concerning government (*public money; public expenditure*). **5** of or involved in the affairs, esp. the government or entertainment, of the community (*distinguished public career; public figures*). — n. **1** (as sing. or pl.) the community, or members of it, in general. **2** specified section of the community (*reading public; my public*). **3** colloq. pupil of a public school (*the majority of students are publics*). □ **go public 1** become a public company. **2** reveal one's plans etc. **in public** openly, publicly. □ **publicly** adv. [Latin]

**public address system** n. set of loudspeakers, microphones, amplifiers, etc., used in addressing large audiences.

**publican** /**pub**-li-kuhn/ n. keeper of a hotel. [Latin: related to PUBLIC]

**publication** /ˌpub-luh-**kay**-shuhn/ n. **1 a** preparation and issuing of a book, newspaper, etc., to the public. **b** book etc. so issued. **2** act or instance of making something publicly known. [Latin: related to PUBLIC]

**public company** n. company that sells shares on the open market.

**public convenience** n. public toilet.

**public enemy** n. notorious wanted criminal.

**public figure** n. famous person.

**public health** n. provision of adequate sanitation, drainage, etc., by government.

**public housing** n. government-owned housing made available, usu. at a low rent, to those on a low income.

**publicise** /**pub**-luh-ˌsuyz/ v. (also **-ize**) (**-sing** or **-zing**) advertise; make publicly known.

**publicist** /**pub**-luh-suhst/ n. **1** publicity agent or public relations officer. **2** writer or expert in current public affairs.

**publicity** /pub-**lis**-uh-tee/ n. **1** public exposure; notoriety. **2 a** professional exploitation of a product, company, person, etc., by advertising etc. **b** material used for this. [French: related to PUBLIC]

**public lending right** n. right of authors to payment when their books etc. are lent by public libraries.

**public opinion** n. views generally prevalent among the general public.

**public ownership** n. ownership by the nation, a State, etc., of the means of production, distribution, or exchange.

**public relations** n.pl. (usu. treated as *sing.*) professional promotion of a favourable public image, esp. by a company, famous person, etc.

**public school** n. (also *attrib.*) **1** school established and maintained at public expense as part of a system of public (and usu. free) education (cf. PRIVATE SCHOOL). **2** (occasionally, imitating the British system) a private school.

**public sector** n. that part of an economy, industry, etc., that is controlled by the government (opp. PRIVATE SECTOR).

**public servant** n. **1** *hist.* a convict assigned to public labour. **2** a member of the public service.

**public service** n. the permanent professional branches of (State or Commonwealth) administration, excluding military and judicial branches and elected politicians.

**public spirit** n. willingness to engage in community action. □ **public-spirited** *adj.*

**public utility** n. organisation supplying water, gas, transport, etc. to the community.

**public works** n.pl. building operations etc. done by or for a government on behalf of the community.

**publish** /**pub**-lish/ v. **1** (also *absol.*) prepare and issue (a book, newspaper, etc.) for public sale. **2** make generally known. **3** announce formally. □ **publishable** *adj.* [Latin: related to PUBLIC]

**publisher** n. person or (esp.) company that publishes books etc. for sale.

**puce** /pyoos/ adj. & n. dark red or purple-brown. [Latin *pulex* flea]

**puck¹** n. rubber disc used as a ball in ice hockey. [origin unknown]

**puck²** n. mischievous or evil sprite. □ **puckish** *adj.* **puckishly** *adv.* **puckishness** n. [Old English]

**pucker** — v. (often foll. by *up*) gather or cause to gather into wrinkles, folds, or bulges (*this seam is puckered up*). — n. such a wrinkle, bulge, fold, etc. [origin unknown]

**pudding** /**puud**-ing/ n. **1 a** any of various sweet cooked dishes (*plum pudding*). **b** sweet course of a meal; dessert. **c** any of various sausages stuffed with oatmeal, spices, blood, etc. (*black pudding*). **2** *colloq.* plump, stupid, or lazy person. □ **puddingy** *adj.* [Latin *botellus* sausage]

**puddle** /**pud**-uhl/ — n. **1** small pool, esp. of rainwater, on a road etc. **2** clay and sand worked with water used as a watertight covering for embankments etc. — v. (**-ling**) **1** knead (clay and sand) into puddle. **2** stir (molten iron) to produce wrought iron by expelling carbon. **3** work (clayey gold-bearing or opal-bearing material) with water in a tub so as to separate out (the gold or opal). □ **puddler** n. **puddling** n. **puddly** *adj.* [Old English]

**pudendum** /pyoo-**den**-duhm/ n. (*pl.* **pudenda**) (usu. in *pl.*) genitals, esp. of a woman. [Latin = that of which one should be ashamed]

**pudgy** /**puj**-ee/ adj. (**-ier**, **-iest**) *colloq.* (esp. of a person) plump, podgy. □ **pudginess** n. [cf. PODGY]

**puerile** /**pyoor**-ruyl/ adj. childish, immature (*puerile practical joke*). □ **puerility** /-**ril**-uh-tee/ n. (*pl.* **-ies**). [Latin *puer* boy]

**puerperal** /pyoo-**er**-puh-ruhl/ adj. of or caused by childbirth. [Latin *puer* boy, *pario* bear]

**puerperal fever** n. fever following childbirth and caused by uterine infection.

**puff** — n. **1 a** short quick blast of breath

or wind. **b** the sound of this or a similar sound. **c** small quantity of vapour, smoke, etc., emitted in one blast (*puff of smoke*). **2** light pastry cake containing jam, cream, etc. **3** gathered material in a dress etc. (*puff sleeve*). **4** extravagantly enthusiastic review, advertisement, etc., esp. in a newspaper. — *v.* **1** emit a puff of air or breath; blow with short blasts. **2** (usu. foll. by *away*, *out*, etc.) (of a person smoking, a steam-engine, etc.) emit or move with puffs (*puffing away at his cigar*; *train puffed out of the station*). **3** (usu. in *passive*; often foll. by *out*) *colloq.* put out of breath; exhaust (*am completely puffed*). **4** breathe hard; pant. **5** utter pantingly ('*No more,*' *he puffed*). **6** (usu. foll. by *up*, *out*) inflate; swell (*his eye was puffed up*). **7** (usu. foll. by *out*, *up*, *away*) blow or emit (dust, smoke, etc.) with a puff. **8** smoke (a pipe etc.) in puffs. **9** (usu. as **puffed up** *adj.*) make proud or boastful (*puffed up with conceit*). **10** advertise or promote with exaggerated or false praise. □ **puff up** = sense 9 of *v.* [imitative]

**puffball** *n.* ball-shaped fungus emitting clouds of spores.

**puffin** /**puf**-uhn/ *n.* N. Atlantic and N. Pacific sea bird with a large head and brightly coloured triangular bill. [origin unknown]

**puff pastry** *n.* leaved pastry made light and flaky by rolling and folding the dough many times.

**puffy** *adj.* (**-ier**, **-iest**) (esp. of the face) swollen, puffed out. □ **puffily** *adv.* **puffiness** *n.*

**puftaloon** /ˌpuf-tuh-**loon**/ *n.* small fried cake, usu. spread with jam, sugar, or honey. [origin unknown]

**pug** *n.* (in full **pug-dog**) dog of a dwarf breed with a broad flat nose and wrinkled face. [origin unknown]

**pugilist** /**pyoo**-juh-luhst/ *n.* (esp. professional) boxer. □ **pugilism** *n.* **pugilistic** /-**lis**-tik/ *adj.* [Latin *pugil* boxer]

**pugnacious** /pug-**nay**-shuhs/ *adj.* quarrelsome; disposed to fight. □ **pugnaciously** *adv.* **pugnacity** /-**nas**-uh-tee/ *n.* [Latin *pugnax* -*acis* from *pugno* fight]

**pug-nose** *n.* short squat or snub nose. □ **pug-nosed** *adj.*

**puissant** /**pyoo**-i-suhnt, **pwee**-suhnt/ *adj. literary* or *archaic* powerful; mighty. [Romanic: related to POTENT]

**puke** /pyook/ *v. & n.* (**-king**) *colloq.* vomit. [imitative]

**pukka** /**puk**-uh/ *adj. Anglo-Ind. colloq.* **1** genuine. **2** of good quality; reliable (*a pukka job*). [Hindi]

**pukumani pole** /ˌpoo-kuh-mah-**nee**/ *n.* decorated mortuary pole of the Tiwi people of Bathurst and Melville Islands. [probably from Tiwi]

**pulchritude** /**pul**-kruh-ˌtyood, **puul**-/ *n. literary* beauty. □ **pulchritudinous** /-ˌtyoo-duh-nuhs/ *adj.* [Latin *pulcher* beautiful]

**pule** /pyool/ *v.* (**-ling**) *literary* cry querulously or weakly; whimper. [imitative]

**pull** /puul/ — *v.* **1** exert force upon (a thing, person, etc.) to move it to oneself or the origin of the force (*pulled it nearer*; *stop pulling my hair*). **2** exert a pulling force (*engine will not pull*). **3** extract (a cork or tooth) by pulling. **4** damage (a muscle etc.) by abnormal strain. **5** (foll. by *on*) bring out (a weapon) for use against (a person) (*pulled a gun on me*). **6 a** check the speed of (a horse), esp. to lose a race. **b** (of a horse) strain against the bit. **7** draw (liquor) from a barrel etc. **8** (foll. by *at*) tear or pluck at. **9** (often foll. by *on*, *at*) inhale or drink deeply; draw or suck (on a pipe etc.). **10** (often foll. by *up*) remove (a plant) by the root. **11 a** *Cricket* strike (the ball) to the leg side. **b** *Golf* strike (the ball) widely to the left. **12** *colloq.* achieve or accomplish (esp. something shady or illicit) (*what are you trying to pull?*). — *n.* **1** act of pulling. **2** force exerted by this. **3** influence; advantage (*he has a lot of pull with the politicians*). **4** an attraction or attention-getter (*the Australian Ballet was a big pull overseas*). **5** deep draught of liquor. **6** prolonged effort, e.g. in going up a hill (*a long hard pull*). **7** *Cricket & Golf* a pulling stroke. **8** a suck at a cigarette etc. (*took a pull and nearly choked to death*). □ **pull about 1** treat roughly. **2** pull from side to side. **pull apart** (or **to pieces**) = *take to pieces* (see PIECE). **pull back** retreat or cause to retreat. **pull down** demolish (esp. a building). **pull a face** distort the features, grimace. **pull a fast one** see FAST¹. **pull one's finger** (or **the digit**) **out** *colloq.* stop slacking and get on with it. **pull one's head in** *colloq.* mind one's own business. **pull in 1** (of a bus, train, etc.) arrive to take passengers. **2** (of a vehicle) move to the side of or off the road. **3** arrive (at a destination) (*the train pulled in at Spencer Street Station*). **4** *colloq.* earn or acquire (*what does he pull in each week?*). **5** *colloq.* arrest (*was pulled in for trapping Australian parrots*). **6** draw crowds (*the new show is pulling them in by the thousands*). **pull a person's leg** deceive playfully. **pull off 1** remove by pulling. **2** succeed in achieving or winning (*I doubt if he can pull off this venture*). **pull oneself together** recover control of oneself. **pull the other one** *colloq.* expressing disbelief (with ref. to *pull a person's leg).* **pull out 1** take out by pulling. **2** depart. **3** withdraw from an undertaking. **4** (of a bus, train, etc.) leave a station, stop, etc. **5** (of a vehicle) move out from the side of the road, or to overtake. **pull over** (of a vehicle) pull in to the side of the road and stop (*pull over, driver!*). **pull one's punches** avoid using one's full force. **pull the plug on** put an end to (by withdrawing resources etc.). **pull rank** take unfair advantage of one's seniority. **pull round** (or **through**) (cause to) recover from an illness. **pull strings** gain an advantage by using people in a position of influence. **pull the strings** be the real activator of what another does. **pull together** work in harmony. **pull up 1** stop (or cause to stop) moving. **2** pull out of the ground. **3** reprimand. **4** check oneself. **pull one's weight** (often *refl.*) do one's fair share of work. [Old English]

**pull-back** *n.* a withdrawal (of troops etc.).

**pullet** /puul-uht/ *n.* young hen, esp. one less than one year old. [Latin *pullus*]

**pulley** /puul-ee/ *n.* (pl. **-s**) **1** grooved wheel or wheels for a cord etc. to pass over, set in a block and used for changing the direction of a force. **2** wheel or drum fixed on a shaft and turned by a belt, used esp. to increase speed or power. [French *polie*: related to POLE²]

**pull-out** *n.* removable section of a magazine etc.

**pullover** *n.* knitted garment put on over the head and covering the top half of the body.

**pullulate** /pul-yuh-layt/ *v.* (**-ting**) **1** (of a seed, shoot, etc.) bud, sprout. **2** swarm, teem; breed prolifically. **3** develop; spring up. **4** (foll. by *with*) abound. □ **pullulation** /-lay-shuhn/ *n.* [Latin *pullulo* sprout]

**pulmonary** /pul-muh-nuh-ree, puul-/ *adj.* of or relating to the lungs. [Latin *pulmo -onis* lung]

**pulp** — *n.* **1** soft fleshy part of fruit etc. **a** any soft thick wet mass. **b** such a mass, esp. from rags, wood, etc., used in paper-making. **3** (often *attrib.*) cheap fiction etc., orig. printed on rough paper. — *v.* reduce to or become pulp. □ **pulpy** *adj.* **pulpiness** *n.* [Latin]

**pulpit** /puul-puht/ *n.* raised enclosed platform in a church etc. from which the priest or minister delivers a sermon. [Latin *pulpitum* platform]

**pulpwood** *n.* timber suitable for making paper-pulp.

**pulsar** /pul-sah/ *n.* cosmic source of regular rapid pulses of radiation, e.g. a rotating neutron star. [from *puls*ating st*ar*, after *quasar*]

**pulsate** /pul-sayt/ *v.* (**-ting**) **1** expand and contract rhythmically; throb. **2** vibrate, quiver, thrill. □ **pulsation** *n.* **pulsator** *n.* **pulsatory** *adj.* [Latin: related to PULSE¹]

**pulse¹** — *n.* **1 a** rhythmical throbbing of the arteries as blood is propelled through them, esp. in the wrists, temples, etc. **b** each beat of the arteries or heart. **2** throb or thrill of life or emotion. **3** general feeling or opinion. **4** single vibration of sound, electric current, light, etc., esp. as a signal. **5** rhythmical beat, esp. of music. — *v.* (**-sing**) pulsate. [Latin *pello puls-* drive, beat]

**pulse²** *n.* (as *sing.* or *pl.*) **1** edible seeds of various leguminous plants, e.g. chick-peas, lentils, beans, etc. **2** plant producing these. [Latin *puls*]

**Pultenaea** /puul-tuh-nay-yuh/ *n.* (also **bacon-and-eggs**) Australian genus of shrubs with about 100 species, all showy, with handsome foliage and prolific yellow or yellow-and-red pea-flowers. [R. *Pulteney*, English botanist]

**pulverise** /pul-vuh-ruyz/ *v.* (also **-ize**) (**-sing** or **-zing**) **1** reduce or crumble to fine particles or dust. **2** *colloq.* demolish, defeat utterly. □ **pulverisation** /-zay-shuhn/ *n.* [Latin *pulvis -ver-* dust]

**puma** /pyoo-muh/ *n.* wild American greyish-brown animal of the cat family. [Spanish from Quechua]

**pumice** /pum-uhs/ *n.* (in full **pumice stone**) **1** light porous volcanic rock used in cleaning or polishing. **2** piece of this used for removing hard skin etc. [Latin *pumex pumic-*]

**pummel** /pum-uhl/ *v.* (**-ll-**) strike repeatedly, esp. with the fists. [from POMMEL]

**pump¹** — *n.* **1** machine or device for raising or moving liquids, compressing gases, inflating tyres, etc. **2** act of pumping; stroke of a pump. — *v.* **1** (often foll. by *in, out, into, up,* etc.) raise or remove (liquid, gas, etc.) with a pump. **2** (often foll. by *up*) fill (a tyre etc.) with air. **3** remove (water etc.) with a pump. **4** work a pump. **5** (often foll. by *out*) (cause to) move, pour forth, etc., as if by pumping. **6** persistently question (a person) to obtain information. **7 a** move vigorously up and down. **b** shake (a person's hand) effusively. □ **pump iron** *colloq.* exercise with weights. **the sets are pumping** *Surfing* the waves are very good. [origin uncertain]

**pump²** *n.* light shoe for dancing etc. [origin unknown]

**pumpernickel** /pum-puh-nik-uhl/ *n.* German wholemeal rye bread. [German]

**pumpkin** /pump-kuhn/ *n.* **1** any of many

varieties of large or small, usu. rounded yellow or orange fruit, cooked as a vegetable etc. or made into a pie etc. (see GRAMMA). **2** large-leaved tendrilled plant bearing this. [Greek *pepōn* melon]

**pumpkin beetle** *n.* Australian insect that is a serious pest on pumpkins and similar plants.

**pun** — *n.* humorous use of a word or words with two or more meanings; play on words of the same sound and different meanings (*Christ used a pun when he said to Peter, whose name means 'Rock', 'thou art Peter and upon this Rock I will build my Church'*). — *v.* (**-nn-**) (foll. by *on*; also *absol.*) make a pun or puns with (words). [origin unknown]

**punch¹** — *v.* **1** strike, esp. with a closed fist. **2 a** pierce a hole in (metal, paper, etc.) with or as with a punch. **b** pierce (a hole) thus. — *n.* **1** blow with a fist. **2** the ability to deliver this (*has a mean punch*). **3** *colloq.* **a** vigour, momentum; effective force (*his speech lacked punch*). **b** (of an aerated drink or an alcoholic one) fizz; potency (*lemonade has lost its punch*; *cocktail lacks punch*). **4** tool, machine, or device for punching holes or impressing a design in leather, metal etc. □ **pack a punch 1** (of a person) have the ability to deliver a telling blow with the fist. **2** (of an alcoholic drink) be extremely potent. **3** have great force or impact, esp. adversarial (*the editorial packed quite a punch*). □ **puncher** *n.* [var. of *pounce* emboss]

**punch²** *n.* drink of wine or spirits mixed with water, fruit juices, spices, etc., and served chilled or hot. [origin unknown]

**punch³** *n.* (**Punch**) grotesque hump-backed puppet in *Punch and Judy* shows. □ **as pleased as Punch** extremely pleased. [abbreviation of *Punchinello*, name of the chief character in an Italian puppet-show]

**punch-drunk** *adj.* stupefied from or as if from a series of heavy blows.

**punchline** *n.* words giving the point of a joke or story.

**punch-up** *n. colloq.* fist-fight; brawl.

**punctilio** /pungk-**til**-ee-oh/ *n.* (*pl.* **-s**) **1** delicate point of ceremony or honour. **2** etiquette of such points. **3** petty formality. [Italian and Spanish: related to POINT]

**punctilious** /pungk-**til**-ee-uhs/ *adj.* **1** attentive to formality or etiquette. **2** precise in behaviour. □ **punctiliously** *adv.* **punctiliousness** *n.* [Italian: related to PUNCTILIO]

**punctual** /**pungk**-choo-uhl/ *adj.* keeping to the appointed time; prompt.

□ **punctuality** /-al-uh-tee/ *n.* **punctually** *adv.* [medieval Latin: related to POINT]

**punctuate** /**pungk**-choo-,ayt/ *v.* (**-ting**) **1** insert punctuation marks in. **2** interrupt at intervals (*punctuated his tale with heavy sighs*). [medieval Latin: related to PUNCTUAL]

**punctuation** /,pungk-choo-**ay**-shuhn/ *n.* **1** system of marks used to punctuate a written passage. **2** use of, or skill in using, these.

**punctuation mark** *n.* any of the marks (e.g. full stop and comma) used in writing to separate sentences etc. and clarify meaning.

**puncture** /**pungk**-chuh/ — *n.* **1** a prick or pricking, esp. the accidental piercing of a pneumatic tyre. **2** hole made in this way. — *v.* (**-ring**) **1** make or undergo a puncture (in) (*needle punctured his skin*). **2** prick, pierce, or deflate (pomposity etc.) (*their laughter punctured his ego*). **3** *colloq.* exhaust, tire out (*after an hour of it I was punctured*). [Latin *punctura*: related to POINT]

**pundit** /**pun**-duht/ *n.* **1** (also **pandit**) a Hindu learned in Sanskrit, and in the philosophy, theology, etc. of India. **2** often *iron.* an expert. □ **punditry** *n.* [Hindustani from Sanskrit]

**pungent** /**pun**-juhnt/ *adj.* **1** sharp or strong in taste or smell, esp. producing a smarting or pricking sensation. **2** (of remarks) penetrating, biting, caustic (*pungent satire*). **3** mentally stimulating (*a pungent sermon*). □ **pungency** *n.* [Latin: related to POINT]

**punish** /**pun**-ish/ *v.* **1** inflict retribution on (an offender) or for (an offence). **2** *colloq.* inflict severe blows on (an opponent). **3** tax, abuse, or treat severely or improperly. **4** make heavy demands on; deplete (*these new carpets will punish my bank balance*). □ **punishable** *adj.* **punishing** *adj.* [Latin *punio*]

**punishment** *n.* **1** act or instance of punishing or the condition of being punished. **2** loss or suffering inflicted in this. **3** *colloq.* severe treatment or suffering.

**punitive** /**pyoo**-nuh-tiv/ *adj.* **1** inflicting or intended to inflict punishment. **2** (of taxation etc.) extremely severe. **3** *Law* (of damages etc.) = VINDICTIVE. [French or medieval Latin: related to PUNISH]

**punk** — *n.* **1 a** (in full **punk rock**) anti-establishment and deliberately outrageous style of rock music. **b** (in full **punk rocker**) devotee of this. **2 a** young hooligan or petty criminal; lout. **b** *colloq.* worthless person or thing (often as a general term of abuse). — *adj. colloq.*

worthless; rotten; of very poor quality. [origin unknown]

**punkari** /pungk-uh-ree/ n. the white-eyed duck of all Australian States, the mature male having predominantly brown plumage and a white eye. [Yaralde, probably *banggari*]

**punnet** /**pun**-uht/ n. small light basket or container for small fruit such as strawberries, or for seedlings. [origin unknown]

**punster** n. person who makes puns, esp. habitually.

**punt**[1] v. **1** bet on a horse etc. **2** speculate in shares etc. □ **take** (or **have**) **a punt 1** wager, place a bet. **2** try, have a go at (anything). [French *ponter*]

**punt**[2] — v. **1** *Aust. Rules* kick the ball, after it has dropped from the hands and before it reaches the ground. **2** make a similar kick in soccer, Rugby, etc. — n. (in full **punt kick**) such a kick. [origin unknown]

**punt**[3] — n. square-ended flat-bottomed boat propelled by a long pole. — v. **1** propel (a punt) with a pole. **2** travel or convey in a punt. □ **punter** n. [Low German or Dutch]

**punter** n. *colloq.* person who gambles or lays a bet.

**punty** n. (also **punty bush**) any Australian shrub of the genus *Cassia*, having delicate pinnate leaves and brilliant yellow flowers, esp. *C. nemophila* of all mainland States. [Western Desert language *bundi*]

**puny** /**pyoo**-nee/ adj. (**-ier**, **-iest**) **1** undersized. **2** weak, feeble; petty (*puny attempt at humour*). [French *puisné* born afterwards]

**pup** — n. **1** young animal, esp. a dog or seal. **2** unpleasant or arrogant young man or boy. — v. (**-pp-**) (also *absol.*) (of a bitch etc.) bring forth (young). □ **be sold a pup** be cheated. **in pup** (of a bitch etc.) pregnant. [from PUPPY]

**pupa** /**pyoo**-puh/ n. (pl. **pupae** /-pee/) insect in the stage between larva and imago. □ **pupal** adj. [Latin, = doll]

**pupate** /pyoo-**payt**/ v. become a pupa. □ **pupation** n.

**pupil**[1] /**pyoo**-puhl/ n. person taught by another, esp. a schoolchild or student. [Latin *pupillus*, *-illa* diminutives of *pupus* boy, *pupa* girl]

**pupil**[2] n. dark circular opening in the centre of the iris of the eye, varying in size to regulate the passage of light to the retina. [related to PUPIL[1]]

**puppet** /**pup**-uht/ — n. **1** small figure representing a human being or animal and moved esp. by strings as entertainment. **2** person controlled by another. — *attrib. adj.* controlled or manipulated by external agencies (*puppet government*). □ **puppetry** n. [var. of POPPET]

**puppet State** n. country that is nominally independent but actually under the control of another power.

**puppy** /**pup**-ee/ n. (pl. **-ies**) **1** young dog. **2** conceited or arrogant young man. [French: related to POPPET]

**puppy fat** n. temporary fatness of a child or adolescent.

**puppy love** n. (also **calf-love**) romantic adolescent love.

**purblind** /**per**-bluynd/ adj. **1** partly blind; dim-sighted. **2** obtuse, dim-witted. □ **purblindness** n. [from *pur(e)* (= 'utterly') *blind*]

**purchase** /**per**-chuhs/ — v. (**-sing**) **1** buy. **2** (often foll. by *with*) obtain or achieve at some cost. — n. **1** act or instance of buying. **2** something bought. **3 a** firm hold to prevent slipping; leverage. **b** device or tackle for moving heavy objects. □ **purchaser** n. [Anglo-French: related to PRO-[1], CHASE[1]]

**purdah** /**per**-duh/ n. *Ind.* screening of women from strangers by a veil or curtain in some Muslim and Hindu societies. [Urdu]

**pure** /pyoor, **pyoo**-uh/ adj. **1** unmixed, unadulterated (*pure white*; *pure gold*). **2** of unmixed origin or descent (*pure-blooded*). **3** chaste. **4** not morally corrupt. **5** guiltless. **6** sincere. **7** mere, simple, nothing but, sheer (*pure accident*; *it was pure malice*). **8** (of a sound) perfectly in tune. **9** (of a subject of study) abstract or theoretical, not applied (*pure science*). □ **pureness** n. [Latin *purus*]

**purée** /**pyoo**-ray, **pyoor**-ray/ — n. smooth pulp of vegetables or fruit etc. — v. (**-ées**, **-éed**) make a purée of. [French]

**purely** adv. **1** in a pure manner. **2** merely, solely, exclusively.

**pure merino** see MERINO (sense 4).

**purgation** /per-**gay**-shuhn/ n. **1** purification. **2** purging of the bowels. **3** spiritual cleansing, esp. of a soul in purgatory. [Latin: related to PURGE]

**purgative** /**per**-guh-tiv/ — adj. **1** serving to purify. **2** strongly laxative. — n. **1** purgative thing. **2** laxative.

**purgatory** /**per**-guh-tuh-ree, -tree/ n. (pl. **-ies**) **1** *RC Ch.* place or state of expiation of venial sins after death to fit the soul to enter heaven. **2** place or state of temporary suffering or expiation. □ **purgatorial** /-**taw**-ree-uhl/ adj. [medieval Latin: related to PURGE]

**purge** — *v.* (**-ging**) **1** (often foll. by *of, from*) make physically or spiritually clean. **2** remove by cleansing. **3** rid (an organisation, party, etc.) of unacceptable members. **4 a** empty (the bowels). **b** empty the bowels of (a person). **5** *Law* atone for (an offence, esp. contempt of court). — *n.* **1** act or instance of purging (in senses of the verb). **2** purgative. [Latin *purgo* purify]

**purify** /**pyoo**-ruh-, fuy, **pyoor**-/ *v.* (**-ies, -ied**) **1** clear of extraneous elements; make pure. **2** (often foll. by *of, from*) make ceremonially pure or clean. □ **purification** /-fuh-**kay**-shuhn/ *n.* **purificatory** /-fuh-**kay**-tuh-ree/ *adj.* **purifier** *n.*

**Purim** /**puu**-rim, poo-**reem**/ *n.* Jewish festival commemorating the defeat of Haman's plot to massacre the Jews. [Hebrew]

**purist** /**pyoo**-ruhst, **pyoor**-rist/ *n.* advocate of scrupulous purity, esp. in language or art. □ **purism** *n.* **puristic** /-**ris**-tik/ *adj.*

**puritan** /**pyoo**-ruh-tuhn, **pyoor**-/ — *n.* **1** (**Puritan**) *hist.* member of a group of English Protestants who regarded the Reformation of the English Church under Elizabeth I as incomplete and sought to simplify and regulate forms of worship. **2** purist member of any party. **3** person practising or affecting extreme strictness in religion or morals. — *adj.* **1** (**Puritan**) *hist.* of the Puritans. **2** scrupulous and austere in religion or morals. □ **puritanism** *n.* [Latin: related to PURE]

**puritanical** /,pyoo-ruh-**tan**-i-kuhl, ,pyoor-/ *adj.* (often *derog.*) practising or affecting strict religious or moral behaviour. □ **puritanically** *adv.*

**purity** /**pyoo**-ruh-tee, **pyoor**-/ *n.* **1** pureness, cleanness. **2** freedom from physical or moral pollution.

**purl**[1] — *n.* **1** knitting stitch made by putting the needle through the front of the previous stitch and passing the yarn round the back of the needle. **2** cord or twisted gold or silver wire for bordering. **3** chain of minute loops in a lace edging. — *v.* (also *absol.*) knit with a purl stitch. [origin unknown]

**purl**[2] — *v.* (of a brook etc.) flow with a swirling motion and a babbling sound. — *n.* this motion or sound. [imitative]

**purler** *n.* (also **pearler**) *colloq.* **1** headlong fall. **2** something surpassingly good or otherwise remarkable (of its kind) (*played a pearler of an innings; the prime minister's speech was a purler*). [*purl* overturn]

**purlieu** /**per**-lyoo/ *n.* (*pl.* **-s**) **1** person's bounds, limits, or usual haunts. **2** (in *pl.*) outskirts, outlying region. [Anglo-French *puralé* from *aller* go]

**purloin** /per-**loin**/ *v. formal* or *joc.* steal, pilfer. [Anglo-French *purloigner* from *loign* far]

**purple** /**per**-puhl/ — *n.* **1** colour between red and blue. **2** (in full **Tyrian purple**) crimson dye obtained from some molluscs. **3** purple robe, esp. of an emperor or senior magistrate. **4** office or rank of a cardinal or bishop, with reference to the scarlet or purple official dress. **5** (prec. by *the*) position of rank, authority, or privilege. — *adj.* of a purple colour. — *v.* (**-ling**) make or become purple. □ **purplish** *adj.* [Greek *porphura*, a shellfish yielding dye]

**purple apple-berry** see APPLE DUMPLING.

**purple coral pea** *n.* = HARDENBERGIA.

**purple passage** *n.* ornate or elaborate literary passage.

**purple patch** *n.* **1** run of luck or success. **2** = PURPLE PASSAGE.

**purport** — *v.* /per-**pawt**/ **1** profess; be intended to seem (*purports to be Gough Whitlam's autograph*). **2** (often foll. by *that*) (of a document or speech) have as its meaning; state. — *n.* /**per**-pawt/ **1** ostensible meaning of something. **2** sense or tenor (of a document or statement). □ **purportedly** /per-**paw**-tuhd-lee/ *adv.* [Latin: related to PRO-[1], *porto* carry]

**purpose** /**per**-puhs/ — *n.* **1** object to be attained; thing intended. **2** intention to act. **3** resolution, determination (*was full of purpose*). — *v.* (**-sing**) have as one's purpose; design, intend (*this is what he purposes*). □ **on purpose** intentionally. **to no purpose** with no result or effect. **to the purpose 1** relevant. **2** useful. [Latin *propono* PROPOSE]

**purposeful** *adj.* **1** having or indicating purpose. **2** intentional. **3** resolute. □ **purposefully** *adv.* **purposefulness** *n.*

**purposeless** *adj.* having no aim or plan.

**purposely** *adv.* on purpose.

**purposive** /**per**-puh-siv/ *adj.* **1** having, serving, or done with a purpose. **2** purposeful; resolute.

**purr** /per/ — *v.* **1** (of a cat) make a low vibratory sound expressing contentment. **2** (of machinery etc.) run smoothly and quietly. **3** (of a person) express pleasure; utter purringly. — *n.* purring sound. [imitative]

**purse** — *n.* **1** small bag or pouch for carrying money, personal items, etc. **2** money, funds. **3** sum as a present or prize in a contest. — *v.* (**-sing**) **1** (often foll. by *up*) pucker or contract (the lips etc.)

(*pursed his lips primly*). **2** become wrinkled. □ **hold the purse strings** have control of expenditure. [Greek, = leather bag]

**purser** *n.* officer on a ship who keeps the accounts, esp. the head steward in a passenger vessel.

**pursuance** /puh-**syoo**-uhns/ *n.* (foll. by *of*) carrying out or observance (of a plan, idea, etc.).

**pursuant** *adv.* (foll. by *to*) in accordance with (*pursuant to your instructions*). [French: related to PURSUE]

**pursue** /puh-**syoo**/ *v.* (**-sues, -sued, -suing**) **1** follow with intent to overtake, capture, or do harm to; go in pursuit. **2** continue or proceed along (a route or course of action). **3** follow or engage in (study or other activity) (*pursuing his studies in Rome*). **4** proceed according to (a plan etc.). **5** seek after, aim at (*pursues wealth*). **6** continue to investigate or discuss (a topic) (*pursuing their inquiries*). **7** importune (a person) persistently. **8** (of misfortune etc.) persistently assail (*ill-luck has pursued me since childhood*). □ **pursuer** *n.* [Latin *sequor* follow]

**pursuit** /puh-**syoot**/ *n.* **1** act or instance of pursuing. **2** occupation or activity pursued (*pursuit of pleasure*; *her pursuit is dentistry*). □ **in pursuit** of pursuing. [French: related to SUIT]

**purulent** /**pyoo**-ruh-luhnt, **pyoor**-/ *adj.* of, containing, or discharging pus (*a purulent abscess*). □ **purulence** *n.* [Latin: related to PUS]

**purvey** /puh-**vay**/ *v.* provide or supply (food etc.) as one's business. □ **purveyor** *n.* [Latin: related to PROVIDE]

**purview** /**per**-vyoo/ *n.* **1** scope or range of a document, scheme, etc. **2** range of physical or mental vision (*photographed everything in his purview*). [Anglo-French past part.: related to PURVEY]

**pus** *n.* thick yellowish or greenish liquid produced from infected tissue. [Latin *pus puris*]

**push** /puush/ — *v.* **1** exert a force on (a thing) to move it or cause it to move away from oneself or from the origin of the force. **2** exert such a force (*do not push against the door*). **3 a** thrust forward or upward. **b** (cause to) project (*pushes out new roots*). **4** move forward or make (one's) way by force or persistence (*he pushed through the crowd*). **5** exert oneself, esp. to surpass others (*pushing herself to increase her speed*). **6** (often foll. by *to, into,* or *to* + infin.) urge, impel, or press (a person) hard; harass (*pushing me to join their church*). **7** (often foll. by *for*) pursue or demand (a claim etc.) persistently (*pushing for a wage increase*; *pushed hard for reform*). **8** promote, e.g. by advertising (*pushing the latest in lipsticks*). **9** *colloq.* sell (a drug) illegally (*arrested for pushing marijuana*). — *n.* **1** act or instance of pushing; a shove, thrust. **2** the force exerted in this. **3** a vigorous effort. **4** military attack in force. **5** enterprise, ambition (*I admire her push*). **6** use of influence to advance a person (*used some push to get the job*). **7** group of people having a common interest or background (*the old-boy network or private school push*). □ **be pushed for** *colloq.* have very little of (esp. time). **give** (or **get**) **the push** *colloq.* **1** dismiss, sack; dismissed, sacked. **2** reject or be rejected (*she gave him the push*; *got the push from his girlfriend*). **push about** = *push around*. **push along** *colloq.* depart, leave. **push around** *colloq.* bully. **push it** *colloq.* **1** work harder or faster, esp. to meet a deadline (*we'll be pushing it to get this job done on time*). **2** importune or press (a person) too far (*watch it! — you're pushing it*). **push one's luck 1** take undue risks. **2** act presumptuously. **push off 1** push with an oar etc. to get a boat out into a river etc. **2** (often in *imper.*) *colloq.* go away. **push on** *colloq.* continue (esp. in spite of difficulty) (*just have to push on with it*). **push through** get (a scheme, proposal, etc.) completed or accepted quickly. [Latin: related to PULSATE]

**push-bike** *n.* bicycle.

**push-button** *n.* **1** button to be pushed, esp. to operate an electrical device. **2** (*attrib.*) operated thus.

**pusher** *n.* **1** *colloq.* seller of illegal drugs. **2** (also **stroller**) collapsible chair on wheels for very small children.

**pushing** *adj.* **1** pushy. **2** *colloq.* having nearly reached (a specified age) (*he must be pushing ninety*). □ **pushing up daisies** *colloq.* dead and buried.

**pushover** *n. colloq.* **1** something easily done. **2** person easily persuaded, defeated, swindled, etc.

**push polling** *n.* political election campaign tactic which makes damaging allegations about a candidate (usu. by telephone) under the guise of market research etc.

**push-start** — *n.* starting of a vehicle by pushing it to turn the engine. — *v.* start (a vehicle) in this way.

**push-up** *n.* (also **press-up**) exercise in which the prone body is raised from the ground by placing the hands on the floor and straightening the arms.

**pushy** *adj.* (**-ier, -iest**) *colloq.* **1** excessively or annoyingly self-assertive. **2** selfishly determined to succeed. □ **pushily** adv. **pushiness** n.

**pusillanimous** /ˌpyoo-suh-**lan**-uh-muhs/ adj. cowardly, timid. □ **pusillanimity** /-luh-**nim**-uh-tee/ n. [Church Latin pusillanimis from pusillus very small, animus mind]

**puss** /puus/ n. colloq. cat (esp. as a form of address). [Low German or Dutch]

**pussy** /puus-ee/ n. (pl. **-ies**) (also **pussy cat**) colloq. cat.

**pussyfoot** v. colloq. **1** move stealthily like a cat. **2** equivocate; stall (stop pussyfooting around and say what you mean!).

**pussy tail** n. (also **ptilotus, mulla mulla**) any of many Australian shrubs of the genus Ptilotus having a soft, fluffy flowerhead.

**pustulate** /pus-chuh-ˌlayt/ v. (**-ting**) form into pustules. [Latin: related to PUSTULE]

**pustule** /pus-tyool/ n. pimple containing pus. □ **pustular** adj. **pustulous** adj. [Latin pustula]

**put** /puut/ — v. (**-tt-**; past and past part. **put**) **1** move to or cause to be in a specified place or position (put it in your pocket; put the children to bed). **2** bring into a specified condition or state (puts me in great difficulty; the crash has put the car out of action). **3** (often foll. by on, to) impose, enforce, assign, or apply (put a tax on beer; where do you put the blame?; put a stop to it; put a veto on it). **4** place (a person) or (refl.) imagine (oneself) in a specified position (put them at their ease; put yourself in my shoes). **5** (foll. by for) substitute (one thing) for (another) (the words 'raised to the purple' are sometimes put for the words 'promoted to bishop'). **6** express in a specified way (to put it mildly). **7** (foll. by at) estimate (an amount etc.) at so much (put the cost at $50). **8** (foll. by into) express or translate in (words, or another language) (put these Aboriginal songs into English). **9** (foll. by into) invest (money in an asset, e.g. land). **10** (foll. by on) stake (money) on (a horse etc.). **11** (foll. by to) apply or devote to a use or purpose (put it to good use). **12** (foll. by to) submit for attention (put it to a vote; let me put it to you another way). **13** (foll. by to) subject (a person) to (death, suffering, etc.) (put him to torture). **14** throw (esp. a shot or weight) as a sport. **15** (foll. by back, off, out to sea, etc.) (of a ship etc.) proceed in a specified direction. — n. throw of the shot etc. □ **put about 1** spread (information, a rumour, etc.) (put the rumour about that . . .). **2** Naut. turn round; put (a ship) on the opposite tack. **put across 1** communicate (an idea etc.)

effectively (can really put the subject across to his students). **2** (often in **put it** (or **one**) **across**) achieve by deceit (tried to put one across on me). **put away 1** restore (a thing) to its usual or former place. **2** (also **put aside; put by**) lay (money etc.) aside for future use. **3** imprison or commit to a home etc. **4** consume (food and drink), esp. in large quantities. **5** = put down 7. **put back 1** = put away 1, 2 change (a meeting etc.) to a later date or time. **3** move back the hands of (a clock or watch). **put a bold** etc. **face on it** see FACE. **put the boot in** see BOOT[1]. **put by** = put away 2. **put down 1** suppress by force. **2** colloq. snub, humiliate. **3** record or enter in writing. **4** enter the name of (a person) on a list. **5** (foll. by as, for) account or reckon (he put me down for a fool because of you). **6** (foll. by to) attribute (put it down to bad planning). **7** put (an old or sick animal) to death. **8** pay (a specified sum) as a deposit. **9** put (a baby) to bed. **10** land (an aircraft). **11** stop to let (passengers) get off. **put an end to** see END. **put the fangs** (or **hooks** or **nips** or **screws**) **into** (a person) colloq. **1** pressure (a person) for a loan. **2** browbeat or intimidate. **put one's foot down** see FOOT. **put one's foot in it** see FOOT. **put forward 1** suggest or propose. **2** advance the time shown on (a clock or watch). **put the hard word on** (a person) colloq. **1** pressure (a person) for sex. **2** = put the fangs into. **put in 1 a** enter or submit (a claim etc.). **b** (foll. by for) submit a claim for (a specified thing). **2** (foll. by for) be a candidate for (an appointment, election, etc.). **3** do, get through (put in a good day's work). **4** interpose (a remark, blow, etc.). **5** colloq. inform on; frame (he was put in by his favourite son). **6** contribute money (who will put in for a farewell gift for her?). **put the mockers** (or **mozz**) **on a person** see MOCKER[1]; MOZZ. **put off 1 a** postpone. **b** postpone an engagement with (a person). **2** (often foll. by with) evade (a person) with an excuse etc. **3** hinder, dissuade (put me off from applying for the job). **4** offend, disconcert (I was put off by his ocker antics). **put on 1** clothe oneself with. **2** cause (a light etc.) to function. **3** cause (transport) to be available. **4** stage (a play, show, etc.). **5** advance the hands of (a clock or watch). **6 a** pretend to (an emotion) (he's only putting on that show of grief). **b** assume, take on (a character or appearance). **c** (**put it on**) exaggerate one's feelings etc. (the hypocrite's only putting it on). **7** increase one's weight by (a specified amount). **8** (foll. by to) make aware of or put in touch with (put us on *to their new accountant*). **9** cause a person to be connected with another on the telephone (*I insist on speaking to the headmaster — put him on!*). **put on weight** increase one's weight. **put out 1 a** (often as **put out** *adj.*) disconcert or annoy. **b** (often *refl.*) inconvenience (*don't put yourself out*). **2** extinguish (a fire or light). **put over** = *put across* 1. **put paid to** see PAY. **put a sock in it** see SOCK¹. **put through 1** carry out or complete. **2** (often foll. by *to*) connect by telephone. **put to flight** see FLIGHT². **put under** make unconscious by anaesthetic etc. **put up 1** build, erect. **2** raise (a price etc.). **3** take or provide with accommodation (*put me up for the night*). **4** engage in (a defensive fight, struggle, etc.). **5** present (a proposal). **6** present oneself, or propose, for election. **7** provide (money) as a backer. **8** display (a notice). **9** offer for sale or competition. **put upon** (usu. in *passive*) *colloq.* take advantage of (a person) unfairly or excessively. **put up or shut up** either back up, prove, etc., what you say, or quit arguing. **put a person up to** (usu. foll. by verbal noun) instigate a person to (*put them up to stealing*). **put up with** endure, tolerate. **put the wind up** see WIND¹. **put a person wise** see WISE¹. **put words into a person's mouth** see MOUTH. [Old English]

**putative** /**pyoo**-tuh-tiv/ *adj.* formal reputed, supposed (*his putative father*). [Latin *puto* think]

**put-down** *n. colloq.* snub.

**put-on** *n. colloq.* deception or hoax.

**putrefy** /**pyoo**-truh-,fuy/ *v.* (**-ies, -ied**) **1** become or make putrid; go bad. **2** fester, suppurate. **3** become morally corrupt. □ **putrefaction** /-fak-shuhn/ *n.* **putrefactive** /-**fak**-tiv/ *adj.* [Latin *puter putris* rotten]

**putrescent** /pyoo-**tres**-uhnt/ *adj.* rotting. □ **putrescence** *n.* [Latin: related to PUTRID]

**putrid** /**pyoo**-truhd/ *adj.* **1** decomposed, rotten. **2** foul, noxious. **3** corrupt. □ **putridity** /-**trid**-uh-tee/ *n.* [Latin *putreo* rot (v.)]

**putsch** /puuch/ *n.* attempt at political revolution; violent uprising. [Swiss German]

**putt** /put/ — *v.* (**-tt-**) strike (a golf ball) gently on a putting-green. — *n.* putting stroke. [from PUT]

**putter** *n.* golf club for putting.

**putting green** *n.* (in golf) smooth area of grass round a hole.

**putto** /**puut**-oh/ *n.* (*pl.* **putti** /-tee/) representation of a naked boy (esp. a cherub or a cupid) in (esp. Renaissance) art. [Italian, = boy, from Latin *putus*]

**putty** /**put**-ee/ — *n.* cement of whiting and linseed oil, used for fixing panes of glass, filling holes, etc. — *v.* (**-ies, -ied**) cover, fix, join, or fill with putty. □ **putty in someone's hands** (of a person) easily influenced or made conformable to someone's manipulation (*he is putty in my hands*). **up to putty** *colloq.* worthless (*these cheap secateurs are up to putty*). [French *potée*: related to POT¹]

**put-up job** *n. colloq.* fraudulent scheme.

**puzzle** /**puz**-uhl/ — *n.* **1** difficult or confusing problem. **2** problem or toy designed to test knowledge or ingenuity. **3** person or situation etc. that is difficult to work out, confusing (*she's a puzzle even to her friends*). — *v.* (**-ling**) **1** confound or disconcert mentally. **2** (usu. foll. by *over* etc.) be perplexed (about). **3** (usu. as **puzzling** *adj.*) require much mental effort (*puzzling situation*). **4** (foll. by *out*) solve or understand by hard thought. □ **puzzlement** *n.* [origin unknown]

**puzzler** *n.* difficult question or problem.

**PVC** *abbr.* polyvinyl chloride.

**PWA** *abbr.* = PERSON WITH AIDS.

**pyaemia** /puy-**ee**-mee-uh/ *n.* (also **pyemia**) blood-poisoning caused by pus-forming bacteria in the bloodstream. [Greek *puon* pus, *haima* blood]

**pycnantha** /pik-**nan**-thuh/ *n.* = GOLDEN WATTLE. [Greek *pyknos* dense, *anthos* flower, referring to the dense flowering of the plant]

**pygmy** /**pig**-mee/ *n.* (also **pigmy**) (*pl.* **-ies**) (often *attrib.*) **1** member of a dwarf people of esp. equatorial Africa. **2** very small person, animal, or thing. **3** insignificant person. **4** (*attrib.*) **a** of or relating to pygmies. **b** (of a person, animal, etc.) dwarf. [Latin from Greek]

**pygmy goose** *n.* either of two short-billed waterbirds, like a goose in miniature, occurring on deep lagoons in northern and eastern Australia.

**pygmy possum** *n.* any of several small (mouse-sized) mainly nocturnal marsupials of northern, eastern, and southern Australia.

**pyjama cricket** *n.* cricket as played under the rules governing one-day international matches. [from the multi-coloured uniforms worn by the teams, as opposed to the all-white uniforms of traditional cricket]

**pyjamas** /puh-**jah**-muhz/ *n.pl.* **1** suit of loose trousers and jacket for sleeping in. **2** loose trousers worn by both sexes in some Asian countries. **3** (**pyjama**) (*attrib.*) of either part of a pair of pyjamas (*pyjama jacket*). [Urdu, = leg-clothing]

**pylon** /**puy**-lon/ *n.* tall structure, esp. as

**pyorrhoea** /ˌpuy-uh-**ree**-uh/ *n.* (also **pyorrhea**) **1** gum disease causing loosening of the teeth. **2** discharge of pus. [Greek *puon* pus, *rheō* flow]

**pyramid** /**pi**-ruh-mid/ *n.* **1** monumental, esp. stone, structure, with a square base and sloping triangular sides meeting at an apex, esp. an ancient Egyptian royal tomb. **2** solid of this shape with esp. a square or triangular base. **3** pyramid-shaped thing or pile of things. □ **pyramidal** /-**ram**-i-duhl/ *adj.* [Greek *puramis -mid-*]

**pyramid selling** *n.* system of selling goods in which agency rights are sold to an increasing number of distributors at successively lower levels, with only those at the very bottom actually selling any goods.

**pyre** /**puyuh**/ *n.* heap of combustible material, esp. for burning a corpse. [Greek: related to PYRO-]

**pyrethrin** /puy-**ree**-thruhn/ *n.* any of several active constituents of pyrethrum flowers used in the manufacture of insecticides.

**pyrethrum** /puy-**ree**-thruhm/ *n.* **1** an aromatic chrysanthemum. **2** an insecticide made from its dried flowers. [Latin from Greek]

**pyrex** /**puy**-reks/ *n. propr.* hard heat-resistant glass, used esp. for ovenware. [invented word]

**pyrexia** /puy-**rek**-see-uh/ *n. Med.* = FEVER. [Greek *purexis*]

**pyrites** /puy-**ruy**-teez/ *n.* (in full **iron pyrites**) lustrous yellow mineral that is a sulphide of iron. [Greek: related to PYRE]

**pyro-** *comb. form* **1** denoting fire. **2** denoting a mineral etc. changed under the action of heat, or fiery in colour. [Greek *pur* fire]

**pyromania** /ˌpuy-roh-**may**-nee-uh, ˌpuy-ruh-/ *n.* obsessive desire to start fires. □ **pyromaniac** *n. & adj.*

**pyrotechnics** /ˌpuy-roh-**tek**-niks/ *n.pl.* **1** art of making fireworks. **2** display of fireworks. **3** any brilliant display. □ **pyrotechnic** *adj.*

**pyrrhic** /**pi**-rik/ *adj.* (of a victory) won at too great a cost. [*Pyrrhus* of Epirus, who defeated the Romans in 279 BC, but suffered heavy losses]

**Pythagoras' theorem** /puy-**thag**-uh-ruhs/ *n.* theorem that the square on the hypotenuse of a right-angled triangle is equal to the sum of the squares on the other two sides. [*Pythagoras* (6th c. BC), name of a Greek philosopher]

**python** /**puy**-thuhn/ *n.* large tropical non-venomous snake which kills its prey by constriction. [Greek *Puthōn*, name of a snake-like monster killed by the god Apollo]

**pyx** /piks/ *n.* **1** *Eccl.* vessel in which the consecrated Host is kept within the tabernacle. **2** small, flat, circular box in which the Host is carried to a sick person for communion. [Greek *puxis* BOX[1]]

# Q

**Q** /kyoo/ n. (also **q**) (pl. **Qs** or **Q's**) seventeenth letter of the alphabet.

**Qantas** /**kwon**-tuhs/ n. Australia's international airline. [abbreviation of *Queensland and Northern Territory Aerial Services*]

**QC** abbr. Queen's Counsel.

**QED** abbr. which was to be proved. [Latin *quod erat demonstrandum*]

**Q fever** n. often acute febrile disease, first identified and described in Australia, caused by a parasitic micro-organism of the type that causes typhus etc. [Q = query; many wrongly believe that Q = Queensland]

**Qld.** abbr. Queensland.

**qr.** abbr. quarter(s).

**q.t.** n. colloq. quiet. □ **on the q.t.** on the quiet, surreptitiously. [abbreviation]

**qua** /kwah, kway/ conj. in the capacity of. [Latin, = in the way in which]

**quack¹** — n. harsh sound made by ducks. — v. utter this sound. [imitative]

**quack²** n. **1** unqualified practitioner, esp. of medicine; charlatan (often attrib.: *quack cure*). **2** colloq. any doctor. □ **quackery** n. [abbreviation of *quacksalver* from Dutch: probably related to QUACK¹, SALVE]

**quad¹** /kwod/ n. colloq. quadrangle. [abbreviation]

**quad²** /kwod/ n. colloq. quadruplet. [abbreviation]

**quad³** /kwod/ colloq. — n. quadraphonics. — adj. quadraphonic. [abbreviation]

**quadrangle** /**kwod**-,rang-guhl/ n. **1** four-sided plane figure, esp. a square or rectangle. **2** four-sided court, orig. in colleges. □ **quadrangular** /-**rang**-gyuh-luh/ adj. [Latin: related to QUADRI-, ANGLE¹]

**quadrant** /**kwod**-ruhnt/ n. **1** quarter of a circle's circumference. **2** quarter of a circle enclosed by two radii at right angles. **3** quarter of a sphere etc. **4** any of four parts of a plane divided by two lines at right angles. **5 a** graduated quarter-circular strip of metal etc. **b** instrument graduated (esp. through an arc of 90°) for measuring angles. [Latin *quadrans -ant*]

**quadraphonic** /,kwod-ruh-**fon**-ik/ adj. (also **quadrophonic**) (of sound reproduction) using four transmission channels. □ **quadraphonically** adv. **quadraphonics** n.pl. [from QUADRI-, STEREOPHONIC]

**quadrate** — adj. /**kwod**-ruht/ esp. Anat. & Zool. square or rectangular. — n. /**kwod**-ruht, -rayt/ rectangular object. — v. /kwod-**rayt**/ (**-ting**) make square. [Latin *quadro* make square]

**quadratic** /kwod-**rat**-ik/ Math. — adj. involving the square (and no higher power) of an unknown quantity or variable (*quadratic equation*). — n. quadratic equation.

**quadrella** /,kwod-**rel**-uh/ n. form of betting on horse races etc. in which the better must select the winners of four specified races. [QUADRI-, after QUINELLA]

**quadri-** comb. form four. [Latin *quattuor* four]

**quadriceps** /**kwod**-ruh-,seps/ n. four-headed muscle at the front of the thigh. [from QUADRI-, BICEPS]

**quadrilateral** /,kwod-ruh-**lat**-uh-ruhl/ — adj. having four sides. — n. four-sided figure.

**quadrille** /kwuh-**dril**/ n. **1** a kind of square dance. **2** music for this. [French]

**quadriplegia** /,kwod-ruh-**plee**-juh/ n. paralysis of all four limbs. □ **quadriplegic** adj. & n. [from QUADRI-, Greek *plēgē* a blow]

**quadruped** /**kwod**-ruh-,ped/ n. four-footed animal, esp. a mammal. [Latin: related to QUADRI-, *pes ped-* foot]

**quadruple** /**kwo**-droo-puhl/ — adj. **1** fourfold; having four parts. **2** (of time in music) having four beats in a bar. — n. fourfold number or amount. — v. (**-ling**) multiply by four. [Latin: related to QUADRI-]

**quadruplet** /kwo-**droo**-pluht/ n. each of four children born at one birth.

**quadruplicate** — adj. /kwo-**droo**-pluh-kuht/ **1** fourfold. **2** of which four copies are made. — v. /kwo-**droo**-pluh-,kayt/ (**-ting**) multiply by four.

**quaff** /kwof/ — v. literary **1** drink deeply. **2** drain (a cup etc.) in long draughts. — n. act of quaffing. □ **quaffable** adj. [perhaps imitative]

**quagmire** /**kwog**-,muy-uh, **kwag**-/ n. **1** muddy or boggy area. **2** hazardous situation (*bogged down in a quagmire of red-tape*). [from *quag* bog, MIRE]

**quail¹** n. (pl. same or **-s**) **1** European small game-bird related to the partridge (and now farmed in Australia). **2** any of several ground-dwelling Australian birds similar in appearance to the European

878

quail (*brown quail*; *king quail*; *stubble quail*). **3** = BUTTON QUAIL. [French *quaille*]

**quail²** v. flinch; show fear. [origin unknown]

**quail thrush** n. any of several small, predominantly chestnut-coloured, ground-dwelling Australian birds, which, when disturbed, produce a quail-like whirring sound with their wings (*chestnut-breasted quail thrush*; *Nullarbor quail thrush*; *spotted quail thrush*).

**quaint** adj. attractively odd or old-fashioned. □ **quaintly** adv. **quaintness** n. [French *cointe* from Latin *cognosco* ascertain]

**quake** — v. (**-king**) shake, tremble. — n. earthquake. [Old English]

**Quaker** n. member of the Society of Friends, a Christian sect devoted to pacifist principles and eschewing formal doctrine, sacraments and ordained ministers. □ **Quakerism** n.

**Quaky Isles** n. colloq. New Zealand. [allusion to earthquakes in New Zealand]

**qualification** /ˌkwol-uh-fuh-**kay**-shuhn/ n. **1** accomplishment fitting a person for a position or purpose. **2** thing that modifies or limits (*statement had many qualifications*). **3** act or instance of qualifying or being qualified. □ **qualificatory** /**kwol**-uh-fuh-ˌkay-tuh-ree, -tree/ adj. [French or medieval Latin: related to QUALIFY]

**qualify** /**kwol**-uh-ˌfuy/ v. (**-ies, -ied**) **1** (often as **qualified** adj.) make competent or fit for a position or purpose. **2** make legally entitled. **3** (usu. foll. by *for*) (of a person) satisfy conditions or requirements (*qualify for a loan*). **4** modify or limit (a statement etc.) (*qualified approval*). **5** Gram. (of a word) attribute a quality to esp. a noun (*in 'the red car' the adjective 'red' qualifies the noun 'car'*). **6** moderate, mitigate; make less severe (*qualified her earlier condemnation of his behaviour*). **7** (foll. by *as*) be describable as, count as (*a grunt hardly qualifies as conversation*). □ **qualifier** n. [Latin *qualis* such as, of what kind]

**qualitative** /**kwol**-uh-tuh-tiv, -ˌtay-tiv/ adj. of quality as opposed to quantity. □ **qualitatively** adv. [Latin: related to QUALITY]

**quality** /**kwol**-uh-tee/ n. (pl. **-ies**) **1** degree of excellence. **2 a** general excellence (*has quality*). **b** (*attrib.*) of high quality (*a quality product*). **3** attribute, faculty (*has many good qualities*). **4** relative nature or character (*is made in three qualities*). **5** timbre of a voice or sound. **6** archaic high social standing (*people of quality*). [Latin *qualis* such as, of what kind]

**quality control** n. maintaining of standards in products or services by testing samples.

**qualm** /kwahm/ n. **1** misgiving; uneasy doubt (*I have some qualms about the wisdom of buying this house*). **2** scruple of conscience (*had no qualms about pilfering small amounts from the till*). **3** momentary faint or sick feeling. [origin uncertain]

**Qualup bell** /**kway**-luhp/ n. a WA pimelea, a small shrub bearing bracts streaked with crimson or purple. [*Qualup*, place in south-western WA]

**quamby** /**kwom**-bee/ — v. hist. lie down (esp. for the night etc.); stop; die. — n. camp; temporary shelter. [probably Wuywurung *guwambi* a sleeping place]

**quandary** /**kwon**-duh-ree, -dree/ n. (pl. **-ies**) **1** perplexed state. **2** practical dilemma. [origin uncertain]

**quandong** /**kwon**-dong/ n. **1** shrub or small tree of dry country in southern Australia bearing a globular, usu. bright red edible fruit with a wrinkled stone that contains an edible kernel. **2** large rainforest tree of eastern Queensland and eastern NSW bearing a globular blue edible fruit with a deeply wrinkled stone, and yielding a useful timber. **3** colloq. **a** person who exploits, or imposes upon, another. **b** a country bumpkin. [Wiradhuri *guwandhaang*]

**quango** /**kwang**-goh/ n. (pl. **-s**) semi-public body with financial support from and senior appointments made by the government. [abbreviation of *qua*si (or *qua*si-*a*utonomous) *n*on-*g*overnment(al) *o*rganisation]

**quanta** pl. of QUANTUM.

**quantify** /**kwon**-tuh-ˌfuy/ v. (**-ies, -ied**) **1** determine the quantity of. **2** express as a quantity. □ **quantifiable** adj. **quantification** /ˌkwon-tuh-fuh-**kay**-shuhn/ n. [medieval Latin: related to QUANTITY]

**quantitative** /**kwon**-tuh-tuh-tiv, -ˌtay-tiv/ adj. **1** of quantity as opposed to quality. **2** measured or measurable by quantity.

**quantity** /**kwon**-tuh-tee/ n. (pl. **-ies**) **1** property of things that is measurable. **2** size, extent, weight, amount, or number. **3** specified or considerable portion, number, or amount (*buys in quantity*; *small quantity of food*). **4** (in *pl.*) large amounts or numbers; an abundance. **5** length or shortness of vowel sounds or syllables. **6** Math. value, component, etc., that may be expressed in numbers. [Latin *quantus* how much]

**quantity surveyor** n. person who measures and prices building work.

**quantum** /**kwon**-tuhm/ *n.* (*pl.* **quanta**) **1** *Physics* discrete amount of energy proportional in magnitude to the frequency of radiation it represents. **2** a required or allowed amount (*he's had his quantum of narrow escapes*). [Latin *quantus* how much]

**quantum jump** *n.* (also **quantum leap**) **1** sudden large increase or advance. **2** *Physics* abrupt transition in an atom or molecule from one quantum state to another.

**quantum mechanics** *n.pl.* (usu. treated as *sing.*) (also **quantum theory**) *Physics* theory assuming that energy exists in discrete units.

**quarantine** /**kwo**-ruhn-‚teen/ — *n.* **1** isolation imposed on persons, animals, or plants to prevent infection or contagion and the introduction to a country of plant diseases or pests. **2** period of this. — *v.* (**-ning**) put in quarantine. [Italian *quaranta* forty]

**quark** /kwahk/ *n. Physics* component of elementary particles. [word used by Joyce in *Finnegans Wake* (1939)]

**quarrel** /**kwo**-ruhl/ — *n.* **1** severe or angry dispute or contention. **2** break in friendly relations. **3** cause of complaint (*have no quarrel with him*). — *v.* (**-ll-**) **1** (often foll. by *with*) find fault. **2** dispute; break off friendly relations. [Latin *querela* from *queror* complain]

**quarrelsome** *adj.* given to quarrelling.

**quarrion** /**kwo**-ree-uhn/ *n.* (also **quarrian**, **quarry hen**) name for the cockatiel, the crested, predominantly grey parrot widespread in mainland Australia. [Wiradhuri *guwarraying*]

**quarry¹** /**kwo**-ree/ — *n.* (*pl.* **-ies**) place from which stone etc. may be extracted. — *v.* (**-ies**, **-ied**) extract (stone) from a quarry. [Latin *quadrum* square]

**quarry²** /**kwo**-ree/ *n.* (*pl.* **-ies**) **1** intended victim or prey. **2** object of pursuit. [Latin *cor* heart]

**quarry hen** *n.* = QUARRION.

**quarry tile** *n.* unglazed floor-tile.

**quart** /kwawt/ *n.* **1** imperial liquid measure equal to a quarter of a gallon; two pints (0.946 litre). **2** = QUART-POT. [Latin *quartus* fourth]

**quarter** /**kwaw**-tuh/ — *n.* **1** each of four equal parts into which a thing is divided. **2** period of three months. **3** point of time 15 minutes before or after any hour. **4 a** 25 US or Canadian cents. **b** coin for this. **5** part of a town, esp. as occupied by a particular class (*residential quarter*). **6 a** point of the compass. **b** region at this. **7** direction, district, or source of supply (*help from any quarter*). **8** (in *pl.*) **a** lodgings. **b** accommodation of troops etc. **9 a** one fourth of a lunar month. **b** moon's position between the first and second (*first quarter*) or third and fourth (*last quarter*) of these. **10 a** each of the four parts into which a carcass is divided. **b** (in *pl.*) = HINDQUARTERS. **11** mercy towards an enemy etc. on condition of surrender. **12** each of four divisions on a shield. **13** (in Australian Rules, netball, etc.) each of the four equal periods into which a match is divided. — *v.* **1** divide into quarters. **2** *hist.* divide (the body of an executed person) in this way. **3 a** put (troops etc.) into quarters. **b** provide with lodgings. [Latin *quartarius*: related to QUART]

**quarterdeck** *n.* part of a ship's upper deck near the stern, usu. reserved for officers.

**quarter-final** *n.* match or round preceding the semifinal.

**quarter horse** *n.* small stocky horse noted for agility and speed over short distances (orig. usu. a quarter of a mile).

**quarter-hour** *n.* **1** period of 15 minutes. **2** = QUARTER *n.* 3.

**quarterly** — *adj.* produced or occurring once every quarter of a year. — *adv.* once every quarter of a year. — *n.* (*pl.* **-ies**) quarterly journal.

**quartermaster** *n.* **1** regimental officer in charge of quartering, rations, etc. **2** naval petty officer in charge of steering, signals, etc.

**quartet** /kwaw-**tet**/ *n.* **1** *Mus.* **a** composition for four performers. **b** the performers. **2** any group of four. [Latin *quartus*]

**quarto** /**kwaw**-toh/ *n.* (*pl.* **-s**) **1** size of a book or page given by folding a sheet of standard size twice to form four leaves. **2** book or sheet of this size. [Latin: related to QUART]

**quart-pot** *n.* (also **quart**) tin vessel (orig. of a quart capacity) used for boiling water etc., esp. out bush.

**quartz** /kwawts/ *n.* silica in various mineral forms. [German from Slavonic]

**quartz clock** *n.* (also **quartz watch**) clock or watch operated by vibrations of an electrically driven quartz crystal.

**quasar** /**kway**-zah/ *n. Astron.* starlike object with a large red shift. [from *quasi-stellar*]

**quash** /kwosh/ *v.* **1** annul; reject as invalid, esp. by a legal procedure (*the judge quashed the conviction for burglary*). **2** suppress, crush (*the rebellion was quashed*). [French *quasser* from Latin]

**quasi-** /**kway**-zuy, **kwah**-zee/ *comb. form* **1** seemingly, not really (*quasi-*

*scientific).* **2** almost (*quasi-independent*). [Latin *quasi* as if]

**quaternary** /kwuh-**ter**-nuh-ree/ — *adj.* **1** having four parts. **2** (**Quaternary**) *Geol.* of the most recent period in the Cenozoic era. — *n.* (**Quaternary**) *Geol.* this period. [Latin *quaterni* four each]

**quatrain** /**kwot**-rayn/ *n.* four-line stanza. [French *quatre* four]

**quatrefoil** /**kat**-ruh-,foil/ *n.* four-pointed or -leafed figure, esp. as an architectural ornament. [Anglo-French *quatre* four: related to FOIL[2]]

**quattrocento** /,kwat-roh-**chen**-toh, ,kwot-roh-/ *n.* 15th-c. Italian art. [Italian, = 400, used for the years 1400–99]

**quaver** /**kway**-vuh/ — *v.* **1** (esp. of a voice or sound) vibrate, shake, tremble. **2** sing or say with a quavering voice. — *n.* **1** *Mus.* note half as long as a crotchet. **2** trill in singing. **3** tremble in speech. □ **quavery** *adj.* [probably imitative]

**quay** /kee/ *n.* artificial landing-place for loading and unloading ships. [French]

**queasy** /**kwee**-zee/ *adj.* (**-ier**, **-iest**) **1 a** (of a person) nauseous. **b** (of the stomach) easily upset, weak of digestion. **2** (of the conscience etc.) uneasy. □ **queasily** *adv.* **queasiness** *n.* [origin uncertain]

**queen** *n.* **1** (as a title usu. **Queen**) female sovereign. **2** (in full **queen consort**) king's wife. **3** woman, country, or thing pre-eminent of its kind (*queen of crime-writers*; *beauty queen*). **4** fertile female among ants, bees, etc. **5** most powerful piece in chess. **6** court-card depicting a queen. **7** *colloq. offens.* male homosexual. □ **queenly** *adj.* (**-ier**, **-iest**). **queenliness** *n.* [Old English]

**Queen-Anne** *n.* (often *attrib.*) style of English architecture, furniture, etc., in the early 18th c. [British Queen, reigned 1702–14]

**queen bee** *n.* **1** fertile female bee. **2** woman who behaves as if she is the most important person in a group.

**queenfish** *n.* any of several marine fish, esp. those valued as game in northern and southern Australia.

**Queensberry Rules** /**kweenz**-buh-ree/ *n.pl.* standard rules, esp. of boxing. [from the name Marquis of *Queensberry*]

**Queen's Counsel** *n.* appointment bestowed on a barrister by an Attorney-General in recognition of excellence as an advocate etc.

**Queen's English** *n.* (prec. by *the*) English language correctly written or spoken.

**Queensland blue** *n.* variety of pumpkin having a deep blue-grey skin, cultivated in Queensland and elsewhere.

**Queensland blue (heeler)** *n.* = BLUE HEELER.

**Queensland bottle tree** *n.* = BOTTLE TREE 1.

**Queensland cane toad** *n.* = CANE TOAD.

**Queenslander** *n.* person who is native to, or resident in, Queensland.

**Queensland groper** *n.* = GROPER[1].

**Queensland heeler** *n.* = BLUE HEELER.

**Queensland maple** *n.* (also **silkwood**) **1** rainforest tree of north-eastern Queensland yielding a valuable timber much used in furniture making. **2** its wood.

**Queensland nut** *n.* = MACADAMIA.

**Queensland trumpeter** *n.* = JAVELIN FISH.

**Queensland walnut** *n.* **1** tall rainforest tree of north-eastern Queensland yielding a valuable timber much used in furniture making. **2** its wood.

**queer** — *adj.* **1** strange, odd, eccentric. **2** shady, suspect, of questionable character. **3** slightly ill; faint. **4** *colloq. offens.* (esp. of a man) homosexual. — *n. colloq. offens.* a homosexual. — *v. colloq.* spoil, put out of order. □ **in Queer Street** *colloq.* in difficulty, in debt. **queer a person's pitch** *colloq.* spoil a person's chances. [origin uncertain]

**quell** *v.* **1** crush or put down (a rebellion etc.). **2** suppress (fear, anger, etc.). [Old English]

**quench** *v.* **1** satisfy (thirst) by drinking. **2** extinguish (a fire or light). **3** cool, esp. with water. **4** esp. *Metallurgy* cool (a hot substance) in cold water etc. **5** stifle or suppress (desire etc.). [Old English]

**querulous** /**kwe**-ruh-luhs/ *adj.* complaining, peevish. □ **querulously** *adv.* [Latin *queror* complain]

**query** /**kweer**-ree/ — *n.* (*pl.* **-ies**) **1** question. **2** question mark or the word *query* as a mark of interrogation. — *v.* (**-ies**, **-ied**) **1** (often foll. by *whether*, *if*, etc. + clause) ask or inquire. **2** call in question (*queried the appointment of a male to the post*). **3** dispute the accuracy of. [Latin *quaere* imperative of *quaero* inquire]

**quest** — *n.* **1** a search or act of seeking. **2** thing sought, esp. by a medieval knight and in modern fantasy literature. — *v.* (often foll. by *for*) go about in search of something (esp. in modern fantasy literature). [Latin *quaero quaesit-* seek]

**question** /**kwes**-chuhn/ — *n.* **1** sentence worded or expressed so as to seek information or an answer. **2 a** doubt or dispute about a matter (*no question that he is dead*). **b** raising of such doubt etc. **3** matter to be discussed or decided. **4** problem requiring a solution. — *v.* **1** ask questions of; interrogate; subject (a person) to examination. **2** throw doubt upon;

raise objections to. □ **be just a question of time** be certain to happen sooner or later. **be a question of** be at issue, be a problem (*it's a question of money*). **beyond (all) question** undoubtedly. **call in** (or **into**) **question** express doubts about. **in question** that is being discussed or referred to (*the person in question*). **out of the question** not worth discussing; impossible. □ **questioner** *n.* **questioning** *adj. & n.* **questioningly** *adv.* [Latin: related to QUEST]

**questionable** *adj.* doubtful as regards truth, quality, honesty, wisdom, etc.

**question mark** *n.* **1** punctuation mark (?) indicating a question (see panel). **2** a doubt as to validity etc. (*there's a question mark about this whole project*).

**questionnaire** /ˌkwes-chuh-**nair**, ˌkes-/ *n.* formulated series of questions, esp. for statistical analysis. [French: related to QUESTION]

**question time** *n.* period in Parliament when MPs may question ministers.

**queue** /kyoo/ — *n.* line or sequence of persons, computer programs, vehicles, etc., waiting their turn to be attended to or to proceed. — *v.* (**queues**, **queued**, **queuing** or **queueing**) (often foll. by *up*) form or join a queue. [Latin *cauda* tail]

**queue-jump** *v.* push forward out of turn in a queue.

**quibble** /**kwib**-uhl/ — *n.* **1** petty objection; trivial point of criticism. **2** argument relying on evasion, equivocation, etc. — *v.* (**-ling**) use quibbles. □ **quibbling** *adj.* [origin uncertain]

**quiche** /keesh/ *n.* savoury flan. [French]

**quick** — *adj.* **1** taking only a short time (*quick worker*). **2** arriving after a short time, prompt (*quick results*). **3** with only a short interval (*in quick succession*). **4** lively, eager, alert (*a quick intelligence; a quick ear*). **5** (of a temper) easily roused. **6** *archaic* alive (*the quick and the dead*). — *adv.* (also as *int.*) quickly. — *n.* **1** soft sensitive flesh, esp. below the nails. **2** seat of emotion (*cut to the quick*). □ **quickly** *adv.* [Old English]

**quicken** *v.* **1** make or become quicker; accelerate. **2** give life or vigour to; rouse. **3 a** (of a woman) reach a stage in pregnancy when movements of the foetus can

be felt. **b** (of a foetus) begin to show signs of life.

**quick-fire** *attrib. adj.* rapid; in rapid succession.

**quick-freeze** *v.* freeze (food) rapidly so as to preserve its natural qualities.

**quickie** *n. colloq.* **1** thing done or made quickly. **2** *Cricket* a quick bowler.

**quicklime** *n.* = LIME¹.

**quicksand** *n.* (often in *pl.*) **1** area of loose wet sand that sucks in anything placed on it. **2** treacherous situation etc.

**quicksilver** *n.* mercury.

**quick smart** *adv.* very quickly.

**quickstep** *n.* fast foxtrot.

**quick-tempered** *adj.* easily angered.

**quick-witted** *adj.* quick to grasp a situation, make repartee, etc. □ **quick-wittedness** *n.*

**quid** *n.* (*pl.* same) *colloq.* (formerly) one Australian pound. □ **make a quick quid** earn or gain money, often by dubious means. **make a quid** earn money. **not for quids** under no circumstances. **(not) the full quid** (not) in full possession of one's mental faculties. **quids in** in a position of profit. [probably from Latin *quid* what]

**quiddity** /**kwid**-uh-tee/ *n.* (*pl.* **-ies**) **1** *Philos.* essence of a thing. **2** quibble; trivial objection. [Latin *quidditas* from *quid* what]

**quid pro quo** /ˌkwid proh **kwoh**/ *n.* (*pl.* **quid pro quos**) something in return for another; return made (esp. for a gift, favour, etc.). [Latin, = something for something]

**quiescent** /kwee-**es**-uhnt/ *adj.* inert, dormant. □ **quiescence** *n.* [related to QUIET]

**quiet** /**kwuy**-uht/ — *adj.* **1** with little or no sound or motion. **2** of gentle or peaceful disposition (*a fairly quiet person*). **3** (of colour, a piece of clothing, etc.) unobtrusive; not showy. **4** not overt; disguised (*quiet resentment*). **5** undisturbed, uninterrupted; free or far from vigorous action (*a quiet time for prayer*). **6** informal (*quiet wedding*). **7** enjoyed in quiet (*a quiet cuppa*). **8** not anxious or remorseful. **9** not busy (*it is very quiet at work*). **10** peaceful (*all quiet on the frontier*). — *n.* **1** silence; stillness. **2** undisturbed state; tranquillity. — *v.* (often foll.

---

**Question mark ?**

This is used instead of a full stop at the end of a sentence to show that it is a question, e.g.

*Have you seen the film yet?*

*You didn't lose my purse, did you?*

It is **not** used at the end of a reported question, e.g.

*I asked you whether you'd seen the film yet.*

by *down*) make or become quiet or calm. □ **be quiet** (esp. in *imper.*) cease talking etc. **just quietly** confidentially; just between you and me. **keep quiet** (often foll. by *about*) say nothing. **on the quiet** secretly. □ **quietly** *adv.* **quietness** *n.* [Latin *quiesco* become calm]

**quieten** *v.* (often foll. by *down*) = QUIET *v.*

**quietism** *n.* passive contemplative attitude towards life, esp. as a form of mysticism. □ **quietist** *n.* & *adj.* [Italian: related to QUIET]

**quietude** /kwuy-uh-,tyood/ *n.* state of quiet.

**quietus** /kwuy-ee-tuhs/ *n.* release from life; death, final riddance (*will get its quietus*). [medieval Latin: related to QUIET]

**quill** *n.* **1** (in full **quill-feather**) large feather in a wing or tail. **2** hollow stem of this. **3** (in full **quill pen**) pen made of a quill. **4** (usu. in *pl.*) spine of an echidna or porcupine. [probably Low German *quiele*]

**quilt**[1] — *n.* coverlet, esp. of quilted material. — *v.* line a coverlet or garment with padding enclosed between layers of cloth by lines of stitching. □ **quilter** *n.* **quilting** *n.* [Latin *culcita* cushion]

**quilt**[2] *v. colloq.* beat soundly; give a thrashing to (*quilted him good and proper*). □ **quilting** *n.* [British dial.]

**quin** *n. colloq.* a quintuplet. [abbreviation]

**quince** *n.* **1** acid pear-shaped fruit used in jams etc. **2** tree bearing this. □ **get on a person's quince** *colloq.* irritate or exasperate him or her beyond measure. [originally a plural, from French *cooin*, from *Cydonia* in Crete]

**quincentenary** /,kwin-sen-tee-nuh-ree/ — *n.* (*pl.* **-ies**) 500th anniversary; celebration of this. — *adj.* of this anniversary. [Latin *quinque* five]

**quincunx** /kwin-kungks/ *n.* five objects, esp. trees, at the corners and centre of a square or rectangle. [Latin, = five-twelfths]

**quinella** *n.* form of betting in horse racing etc. in which the gambler must select the first two place-getters in a race, not necessarily in the correct order. [American Spanish *quiniela*]

**quinine** /kwin-een, kwuh-neen/ *n.* bitter drug obtained from cinchona bark, used as a tonic and to reduce fever. [Spanish *quina* cinchona bark, from Quechua *kina* bark]

**quinine tree** *n.* **1** any of several Australian bushes or small trees bearing bitter (a quality formerly attributed to the presence of quinine) orange fruits. **2** (also **quinine bush**) medium-sized Australian tree having an intensely bitter bark (formerly thought to contain quinine) and a profusion of golden flowers followed by thin, elongated fruits.

**Quinkan** /kwing-kuhn/ *n.* (also **Quinkin**) category of spirit people depicted in rock paintings of northern Queensland. [Kuku-Yalanji *guwin-gan* ghost, spirit]

**quinquereme** /kwing-kwuh-,reem/ *n.* ancient Roman galley with five files of oarsmen on each side. [Latin *quinque* five, *remus* oar]

**quintessence** /kwin-tes-uhns/ *n.* **1** (usu. foll. by *of*) purest and most perfect form, manifestation, or embodiment of a quality etc. **2** highly refined extract. □ **quintessential** /,kwin-tuh-sen-shuhl/ *adj.* **quintessentially** /,kwin-tuh-sen-shuh-lee/ *adv.* [Latin *quinta essentia* fifth substance (underlying the four elements)]

**quintet** /kwin-tet/ *n.* **1** *Mus.* **a** composition for five performers. **b** the performers. **2** any group of five. [Latin *quintus*]

**quintuple** /kwin-tyoo-puhl/ — *adj.* fivefold; having five parts. — *n.* fivefold number or amount. — *v.* (**-ling**) multiply by five. [Latin *quintus* fifth]

**quintuplet** /kwin-tup-luht/ *n.* each of five children born at one birth.

**quip** — *n.* clever saying; epigram. — *v.* (**-pp-**) make quips. [perhaps from Latin *quippe* forsooth]

**quire** *n.* 25 (formerly 24) sheets of paper. [Latin: related to QUATERNARY]

**quirk** *n.* **1** peculiar feature, peculiarity. **2** trick of fate. □ **quirky** *adj.* (**-ier, -iest**). [origin unknown]

**quisling** /kwiz-ling/ *n.* collaborator, traitor. [*Quisling*, name of a Norwegian officer and collaborator with the Nazis]

**quit** — *v.* (**-tting**; *past* and *past part.* **quitted** or **quit**) **1** (also *absol.*) give up, let go, abandon (a task etc.). **2 a** cease, stop (doing something) (*quit grumbling*). **b** give up (a job); resign. **3** leave or depart from. — *predic. adj.* (foll. by *of*) rid (*glad to be quit of the problem*). [Latin: related to QUIET]

**quitch** *n.* (in full **quitch-grass**) = COUCH[2]. [Old English]

**quite** *adv.* **1** completely, entirely, wholly. **2** to some extent, rather (*quite charming*). **3** (often foll. by *so*) said to indicate agreement. □ **quite a** (or **some**) remarkable or outstanding (thing). **quite a few** a fairly large number of. **quite something** *colloq.* remarkable thing or person. [var. of QUIT]

**quits** *predic. adj.* on even terms by retaliation or repayment. □ **call it quits 1** acknowledge that things are now even; agree to stop quarrelling. **2** cease work for a time. [probably related to QUIT]

**quitter** *n.* **1** person who gives up easily. **2** shirker.

**quiver**[1] /**kwiv**-uh/ — *v.* tremble or vibrate with a slight rapid motion. — *n.* quivering motion or sound. [obsolete *quiver* nimble]

**quiver**[2] /**kwiv**-uh/ *n.* case for arrows. [Anglo-French from Germanic]

**quixotic** /kwik-**sot**-ik/ *adj.* extravagantly and romantically chivalrous; pursuing lofty or unattainable ideals. □ **quixotically** *adv.* [Don *Quixote*, in Cervantes' romance]

**quiz** — *n.* (*pl.* **quizzes**) **1** test of knowledge, esp. as an entertainment or schoolroom test. **2** interrogation, examination. — *v.* (**-zz-**) examine by questioning. [origin unknown]

**quizzical** /**kwiz**-i-kuhl/ *adj.* expressing or done with mild or amused perplexity. □ **quizzically** *adv.*

**quoin** /koin/ *n.* **1** external angle of a building. **2** cornerstone. **3** wedge used in printing and gunnery. [var. of COIN]

**quoit** /koit/ *n.* **1** ring thrown to encircle an iron peg. **2** (in *pl.*) game using these. [origin unknown]

**quokka** /**kwok**-uh/ *n.* small short-tailed wallaby of south-western WA, including Rottnest and Bald Islands, having long, greyish-brown fur. [Nyungar, probably *gwaga*]

**quoll** /kwol/ *n.* = NATIVE CAT. [Guugu Yimidhirr *dhigul*]

**quondam** /**kwon**-dam/ *attrib. adj.* that once was, sometime, former. [Latin *adv.*, = formerly]

**quorum** /**kwaw**-ruhm/ *n.* minimum number of members that must be present to constitute a valid meeting. [Latin, = of whom]

**quota** /**kwoh**-tuh/ *n.* **1** share to be contributed to, or received from, a total. **2** quantity of natural products, goods, etc. which, under official controls, may be harvested, manufactured, exported, imported, etc. **3 a** yearly number of immigrants allowed to enter a country. **b** number of students allowed to enrol for a course etc. [Latin *quotus* from *quot* how many]

**quotable** /**kwoh**-tuh-buhl/ *adj.* worth quoting.

**quotation** /kwoh-**tay**-shuhn/ *n.* **1** passage or remark quoted. **2** act or an instance of quoting or being quoted. **3** contractor's estimate. [medieval Latin: related to QUOTE]

**quotation marks** *n.pl.* inverted commas (' ' or " ") used at the beginning and end of a quotation etc. (see panel).

**quote** — *v.* (**-ting**) **1** cite or appeal to (an author, book, etc.) in confirmation of

---

**Quotation marks ' ' " "**

Also called inverted commas, these are used:

**1** round a direct quotation (closing quotation marks come after any punctuation which is part of the quotation), e.g.

> He said, 'That is nonsense.'
> 'That', he said, 'is nonsense.'
> 'That, however,' he said, 'is nonsense.'
> Did he say, 'That is nonsense'?
> He asked, 'Is that nonsense?'

**2** round a quoted word or phrase, e.g.

> What does 'integrated circuit' mean?

**3** round a word or phrase to which the writer wishes to draw attention, e.g.

> Joan Sutherland was known as 'La Stupenda'.
> He said he had enough 'bread' to buy a car.

**4** round the title of a book, song, poem, magazine article, television programme, etc. (but not a book of the Bible), e.g.

> 'Cloudstreet' by Tim Winton

In printing, word processing, etc., it is more usual to use italics for titles of novels, plays, long poems, etc.

**5** as double quotation marks round a quotation within a quotation, e.g.

> He asked, 'Do you know what "integrated circuit" means?'

In handwriting, double quotation marks are usual.

There is legitimate variety of opinion as to how quotation marks should be used. For example, some people prefer the use of double quotation marks (in which case, at point 5, the quotation within a quotation would be in single quotation marks: "Do you know what 'integrated circuit' means?").

some view. **2 a** repeat a statement by (another person) (*don't quote me*). **b** copy out a passage from. **c** (foll. by *from*) cite (an author, book, etc.). **3** (foll. by *as*) cite (an author etc.) as proof, evidence, etc. **4 a** enclose (words) in quotation marks. **b** (as *int.*) verbal formula indicating opening quotation marks (*he said, quote, 'I shall stay'*). **5** (often foll. by *at*, also *absol.*) state the price of a commodity, bet, etc. (*quoted at 100 to 1*). — *n. colloq.* **1** passage quoted. **2** price quoted. **3** (usu. in *pl.*) quotation marks. [Latin *quoto* mark with numbers]

**quoth** /kwohth/ *v.* (only in 1st and 3rd person) *archaic* said. [Old English]

**quotidian** /kwo-**tid**-ee-uhn/ *adj.* **1** occurring or recurring daily. **2** commonplace, trivial. [Latin *cotidie* daily]

**quotient** /**kwoh**-shuhnt/ *n.* result of a division sum. [Latin *quotiens -ent-* how many times]

**q.v.** *abbr.* which see (in references). [Latin *quod vide*]

**qwerty** /**kwer**-tee/ *attrib. adj.* denoting the standard keyboard on English-language typewriters, word processors, etc., with *q, w, e, r, t,* and *y* as the first keys on the top row of letters.

# R

**R¹** /ah/ n. (also **r**) (pl. **Rs** or **R's**) eighteenth letter of the alphabet.

**R²** abbr. (also **R.**) **1** River. **2** (of a film) not suitable for persons under eighteen.

**r.** abbr. (also **r**) **1** right. **2** radius.

**Ra** symb. radium.

**rabbet** /**rab**-uht/ — n. step-shaped channel cut along the edge or face of a length of wood etc., usu. to receive the edge or tongue of another piece. — v. (**-t-**) **1** join or fix with a rabbet. **2** make a rabbet in. [French rab(b)at: related to REBATE¹]

**rabbi** /**rab**-uy/ n. (pl. **-s**) **1** Jewish scholar or teacher, esp. of the law. **2** Jewish religious leader. □ **rabbinical** /ruh-**bin**-i-kuhl/ adj. [Hebrew, = my master]

**rabbit** /**rab**-uht/ — n. burrowing plant-eating mammal of the hare family. — v. (**-t-**) **1** hunt rabbits. **2** (often foll. by on, away) colloq. talk pointlessly; chatter. **3** Aust. Rules duck down in the path of an opposing player, so causing him to trip or fall. [origin uncertain]

**rabbit calicivirus disease** see CALICIVIRUS.

**rabbit-eared bandicoot** n. = BILBY.

**rabbit-ears** n.pl. Australian terrestrial orchid of coastal heaths and the inland, having scented cream to yellow flowers and two prominent appendages like the ears of a rabbit at the centre of the flower.

**rabbiter** /**rab**-uh-tuh/ n. person who kills rabbits professionally.

**rabbit-oh** /**rab**-uh-toh/ n. person who sells rabbits as food; rabbiter.

**rabbit punch** n. short chop with the edge of the hand to the nape of the neck.

**rabbit-rat** n. **1** either of two rodents of northern Australia, having long ears and a long, brushy tail. **2 a** = BILBY. **b** = STICK-NEST RAT.

**rabble** /**rab**-uhl/ n. **1** disorderly crowd, mob. **2** contemptible or inferior set of people. **3** (prec. by the) offens. the lowest stratum of society (as viewed from higher up the social scale). [origin uncertain]

**rabble-rouser** n. person who stirs up the rabble or a crowd, esp. to agitate for social change.

**Rabelaisian** /,rab-uh-**lay**-zee-uhn, -zhuhn/ adj. **1** of or like the French satirist Rabelais or his writings. **2** marked by exuberant imagination and coarse humour.

**rabid** /**rab**-uhd/ adj. **1** affected with rabies, mad. **2** violent, fanatical (rabid rabble-rouser; rabid right-to-lifer). □ **rabidity** /ruh-**bid**-uh-tee/ n. [Latin rabio rave]

**rabies** /**ray**-beez/ n. contagious viral disease of esp. dogs, transmissible through saliva to humans etc. and causing madness; hydrophobia. [Latin: related to RABID]

**raccoon** /ruh-**koon**/ n. (also **racoon**) (pl. same or **-s**) N. American mammal with a bushy tail and sharp snout. [Algonquian]

**race¹** — n. **1** contest of speed between runners, horses, vehicles, ships, etc. **2** (in pl.) series of these for horses, dogs, etc., at a fixed time on a regular course. **3** contest between persons to be first to achieve something. **4 a** strong current in the sea or a river. **b** channel or bed (of a stream), esp. an artificial channel leading water to or from a point where its energy is utilised. **5** narrow, fenced passageway through which stock pass, singly, for branding, dipping, etc. — v. (**-cing**) **1** take part in a race. **2** have a race with. **3** try to surpass in speed. **4** (foll. by with) compete in speed with. **5** cause to race (raced her horse in the Melbourne Cup). **6 a** go at full or excessive speed (pulse raced violently). **b** cause to do this (raced the bill through the Senate). **7** (usu. as **racing** adj.) follow or take part in horse racing (a racing man). □ **not in the race** colloq. having no chance. **race off with** colloq. steal. [Old Norse]

**race²** n. **1** each of the major divisions of humankind, each having distinct physical characteristics. **2** fact or concept of division into races (discrimination based on race). **3** genus, species, breed, or variety of animals or plants. **4** group of persons, animals, or plants connected by common descent. **5** any great division of living creatures (the human race). [Italian razza]

**racecourse** n. ground for horse racing.

**racegoer** n. person who frequents horse races.

**racehorse** n. horse bred or kept for racing.

**racehorse goanna** n. any of several swift-moving goannas of central and northern Australia.

**raceme** /ruh-**seem**/ n. flower cluster with separate flowers attached by short stalks at equal distances along the stem. [Latin racemus grape-bunch]

**race meeting** n. sequence of horse races at one place.

**race relations** n.pl. relations between members of different races in the same country.

**race riot** n. outbreak of violence due to racial antagonism.

**racetrack** n. **1** = RACECOURSE. **2** track for motor racing.

**racial** /ray-shuhl/ adj. **1** of or concerning race. **2** on the grounds of or connected with difference in race. □ **racially** adv.

**racism** n. **1** belief in the superiority of a particular race; prejudice based on this. **2** antagonism towards other races. □ **racist** n. & adj.

**rack**[1] — n. **1** framework, usu. with rails, bars, etc., for holding things. **2** cogged or toothed bar or rail engaging with a wheel or pinion etc. **3** hist. instrument of torture stretching the victim's joints. — v. **1** (of disease, pain, etc.) inflict suffering on; torment (racked by fever; racked by doubt). **2** hist. torture (a person) on the rack. **3** place in or on a rack. **4** shake violently. **5** injure by straining. □ **on the rack** suffering acute mental or physical pain. **rack one's brains** make a great mental effort. [Low German or Dutch]

**rack**[2] n. destruction (esp. rack and ruin). [from WRACK]

**rack**[3] v. colloq. (foll. by off) leave, go (racked off when they saw the police). □ **rack off!** get lost! [origin uncertain]

**racket**[1] /rak-uht/ n. **1** disturbance, uproar, din. **2** colloq. **a** scheme for obtaining money etc. by dishonest means. **b** dodge; sly game. **3** colloq. activity; line of business (starting up a new racket; what's your racket?). [perhaps imitative]

**racket**[2] var. of RACQUET.

**racketeer** /rak-uh-teer/ n. person who operates a dishonest business. □ **racketeering** n.

**raconteur** /rak-on-ter/ n. teller of anecdotes. [French: related to RECOUNT]

**racoon** var. of RACCOON.

**racquet** /rak-uht/ n. (also **racket**) **1** bat with a round or oval frame strung with catgut, nylon, etc., used in tennis, squash, etc. **2** (in pl.) game like squash, played in a court of four plain walls. [French raquette from Arabic rahat palm of the hand]

**racy** /ray-see/ adj. (-ier, -iest) **1** lively and vigorous in style. **2** risqué. **3** of distinctive quality (a racy wine). □ **raciness** n. [from RACE[2]]

**rad**[1] n. unit of absorbed dose of ionising radiation. [from radiation absorbed dose]

**rad**[2] adj. colloq. radical; excellent (her ideas are really rad; a really rad party). [abbreviation]

**radar** /ray-dah/ n. **1** system for detecting the direction, range, or presence of objects, by sending out pulses of high frequency electromagnetic waves which they reflect. **2** apparatus for this. [from radio detection and ranging]

**radar detector** n. device (now usu. illegal) in a motor vehicle for detecting a radar trap ahead.

**radar trap** n. device using radar to detect speeding vehicles.

**raddle** /rad-uhl/ — n. red ochre. — v. (-ling) **1** colour with raddle or too much rouge. **2** (as **raddled** adj.) worn out. **3** mark (an imperfectly shorn sheep) with a red dye. [related to RUDDY]

**radial** /ray-dee-uhl/ — adj. **1** of or in rays. **2 a** arranged like rays or radii. **b** having spokes or radiating lines. **c** acting or moving along lines diverging from a centre. **3** (in full **radial-ply**) (of a tyre) having fabric layers arranged radially and the tread strengthened. — n. radial-ply tyre. □ **radially** adv. [medieval Latin: related to RADIUS]

**radian** /ray-dee-uhn/ n. SI unit of angle, equal to an angle at the centre of a circle the arc of which is equal in length to the radius (1 radian is approx. 57°).

**radiant** /ray-dee-uhnt/ — adj. **1** emitting rays of light. **2** (of eyes or looks) beaming with joy, hope, or love. **3** (of beauty) splendid or dazzling. **4** (of light) issuing in rays. — n. point or object from which light or heat radiates. □ **radiance** n. **radiantly** adv.

**radiant heat** n. heat transmitted by radiation.

**radiata pine** /ray-dee-ah-tuh/ n. Californian conifer cultivated in plantations in Australia for its softwood timber.

**radiate** — v. /ray-dee-ayt/ (-ting) **1 a** emit rays of light, heat, etc. **b** (of light or heat) be emitted in rays. **2** emit (light, heat, etc.) from a centre. **3** transmit or demonstrate (joy, love, etc.) (radiates happiness). **4** diverge or spread from a centre. — adj. /ray-dee-uht/ having divergent rays or parts radially arranged.

**radiation** /ray-dee-ay-shuhn/ n. **1** act or instance of radiating; process of being radiated. **2** Physics **a** emission of energy as electromagnetic waves or as moving particles. **b** energy transmitted in this way, esp. invisibly. **3** (in full **radiation therapy**) treatment of cancer etc. using radiation, e.g. X-rays or ultraviolet light.

**radiation sickness** n. sickness caused by exposure to radiation, such as gamma rays.

**radiator** /**ray**-dee-,ay-tuh/ n. **1** usu. portable electrical appliance for warming a room by radiating heat from red-hot bars. **2** device for heating a room etc., consisting of a metal case through which hot water or steam circulates. **3** engine-cooling device in a motor vehicle or aircraft.

**radical** /**rad**-i-kuhl/ — adj. **1** fundamental (a radical error). **2** far-reaching; thorough (radical change). **3** advocating thorough reform; holding extreme political views; revolutionary. **4** forming the basis; primary. **5** of the root of a number or quantity. **6** (of surgery etc.) seeking to ensure the removal of all diseased tissue. **7** of the roots of words. **8** Bot. of the root. — n. **1** person holding radical views or belonging to a radical party. **2** Chem. **a** = FREE RADICAL. **b** atom or a group of these normally forming part of a compound and remaining unaltered during the compound's ordinary chemical changes. **3** root of a word. **4** Math. quantity forming or expressed as the root of another. □ **radicalism** n. **radically** adv. [Latin: related to RADIX]

**radicle** /**rad**-i-kuhl/ n. part of a plant embryo that develops into the primary root; rootlet. [Latin: related to RADIX]

**radii** pl. of RADIUS.

**radio** /**ray**-dee-oh/ — n. (pl. **-s**) **1** (often attrib.) **a** transmission and reception of sound messages etc. by electromagnetic waves of radio-frequency. **b** apparatus for receiving, broadcasting, or transmitting radio signals. **2 a** sound broadcasting (prefers the radio). **b** broadcasting station or channel (Radio National). — v. (**-es, -ed**) **1 a** send (a message) by radio. **b** send a message to (a person) by radio. **2** communicate or broadcast by radio. [short for radio-telegraphy etc.]

**radio-** comb. form **1** denoting radio or broadcasting. **2** connected with radioactivity. **3** connected with rays or radiation.

**radioactive** /,ray-dee-oh-**ak**-tiv/ adj. of or exhibiting radioactivity.

**radioactivity** /,ray-dee-oh-ak-**tiv**-uh-tee/ n. spontaneous disintegration of atomic nuclei, with the emission of usu. penetrating radiation or particles.

**radiocarbon** /,ray-dee-oh-**kah**-buhn/ n. radioactive isotope of carbon.

**radiocarbon dating** n. = CARBON DATING.

**radio-controlled** adj. controlled from a distance by radio.

**radio frequency** n. (pl. **-ies**) frequency band of telecommunication, ranging from $10^4$ to $10^{11}$ or $10^{12}$ Hz.

**radiogram** /**ray**-dee-oh-,gram/ n. **1** combined radio and record-player. **2** picture obtained by X-rays etc. **3** telegram sent by radio.

**radiograph** /**ray**-dee-oh-,grahf, -,graf/ — n. **1** instrument recording the intensity of radiation. **2** = RADIOGRAM 2. — v. obtain a picture of by X-ray, gamma ray, etc. □ **radiographer** /-**og**-ruh-fuh/ n. **radiography** /-**og**-ruh-fee/ n.

**radioisotope** /,ray-dee-oh-**uy**-suh-,tohp/ n. radioactive isotope.

**radiology** /,ray-dee-**ol**-uh-jee/ n. the study of X-rays and other high-energy radiation, esp. as used in medicine. □ **radiologist** n.

**radiophonic** /,ray-dee-oh-**fon**-ik/ adj. of or relating to electronically produced sound, esp. music.

**radioscopy** /,ray-dee-**os**-kuh-pee/ n. examination by X-rays etc. of objects opaque to light.

**radio-telegraphy** /,ray-dee-oh-tuh-**leg**-ruh-fee/ n. telegraphy using radio.

**radio-telephony** /,ray-dee-oh-tuh-**lef**-uh-nee/ n. telephony using radio. □ **radio-telephone** /-**tel**-uh-,fohn/ n.

**radio telescope** n. directional aerial system for collecting and analysing radiation in the radio-frequency range from stars etc.

**radiotherapy** /,ray-dee-oh-**the**-ruh-pee/ n. treatment of disease by X-rays or other forms of radiation.

**radish** /**rad**-ish/ n. **1** plant with a fleshy pungent root. **2** this root, eaten esp. raw. [Latin RADIX]

**radium** /**ray**-dee-uhm/ n. radioactive metallic element orig. obtained from pitchblende etc., used esp. in radiotherapy.

**radius** /**ray**-dee-uhs/ n. (pl. **radii** /-dee-,uy/ or **radiuses**) **1 a** straight line from the centre to the circumference of a circle or sphere. **b** length of this. **2** distance from a centre (within a radius of 20 kilometres). **3 a** thicker and shorter of the two bones in the human forearm. **b** corresponding bone in a vertebrate's foreleg or a bird's wing. [Latin]

**radix** /**ray**-diks/ n. (pl. **radices** /-duh-,seez/) Math. number or symbol used as the basis of a numeration scale (e.g. ten in the decimal system). [Latin, = root]

**radon** /**ray**-don/ n. gaseous radioactive inert element arising from the disintegration of radium.

**Rafferty's rules** /**raf**-uh-teez/ n.pl. no rules at all (i.e. anything goes). [joc. use of Irish surname Rafferty with punning allusion to British dial. raffety irregular; or perhaps British dial. corruption of refractory]

**raffia** /raf-ee-uh/ n. **1** palm-tree native to Madagascar. **2** fibre from its leaves, used for weaving and for tying plants etc. [Malagasy]

**raffish** /raf-ish/ adj. disreputable, rakish. [raff rubbish]

**raffle** /raf-uhl/ — n. fund-raising lottery with prizes. — v. (-ling) (often foll. by off) sell by means of a raffle. [French raf(f)le, a dice-game]

**raft¹** /rahft/ n. **1** flat floating structure of timber or other materials for conveying persons or things. **2** slab of reinforced concrete as foundation of building. [Old Norse]

**raft²** n. large collection (presented a raft of proposals to the board). [raff rubbish, perhaps of Scandinavian origin]

**rafter** /rahf-tuh/ n. each of the sloping beams forming the framework of a roof. [Old English]

**rag¹** n. **1** torn, frayed, or worn piece of woven material. **2** (in pl.) old or worn clothes. **3** (collect.) scraps of cloth used as material for paper, stuffing, etc. **4** often derog. newspaper. □ **in rags 1** much torn. **2** in worn clothes. **rags to riches** poverty to affluence. [probably a back-formation from RAGGED]

**rag²** — n. **1** prank, esp. one performed by students. **2** a rowdy celebration. **b** noisy disorderly scene. — v. (-gg-) **1** tease; play rough jokes on. **2** engage in rough play; be noisy and riotous. [origin unknown]

**ragamuffin** /rag-uh-ˌmuf-uhn/ n. child in ragged dirty clothes. [probably from RAG¹]

**rag-and-bone man** n. itinerant dealer in old clothes, furniture, etc.

**ragbag** n. **1** bag for scraps of fabric etc. **2** miscellaneous collection.

**rag doll** n. stuffed cloth doll.

**rage** — n. **1** fierce or violent anger. **2** fit of this (flew into a rage). **3** violent action of a natural force (the rage of the cyclone). **4** colloq. lively, usu. frenetic social occasion (the office party was a rage). — v. (-ging) **1** be full of anger. **2** (often foll. by at, against) speak furiously or madly. **3** (of wind, battle, etc.) be violent; be at its height. **4** colloq. enjoy oneself with no holds barred; party on with total abandon (we raged till dawn). □ **all the rage** very popular, fashionable. [Latin RABIES]

**rager** /ray-juh/ n. colloq. person who enjoys himself or herself at a party etc. with total abandon.

**ragged** /rag-uhd/ adj. **1** torn; frayed. **2** in ragged clothes. **3** with a broken or jagged outline or surface. **4** faulty, imperfect; lacking finish, smoothness, or uniformity (ragged rhymes). [Old Norse]

**raging** — n. colloq. enjoying oneself with total abandon at a party etc. — adj. extreme; very painful (raging thirst; raging headache).

**raglan** /rag-luhn/ — adj. (of a sleeve) running up to the neck of a garment. — n. (often attrib.) overcoat without shoulder seams, the sleeves running up to the neck. [Lord Raglan]

**ragout** /ra-goo/ n. meat stewed with vegetables and highly seasoned. [French]

**ragtag** n. (in full **ragtag and bobtail**) derog. rabble or common people. [from RAG¹]

**ragtime** n. form of highly syncopated early jazz, esp. for the piano.

**rag trade** n. colloq. the clothing business.

**raid** — n. **1** rapid surprise attack, esp.: **a** in warfare. **b** in order to commit a crime, steal, or do harm. **2** surprise attack by police etc. to arrest suspected persons or seize illicit goods. — v. **1** make a raid on. **2** make a foray for food etc. (raided the fridge). □ **raider** n. [Scots form of ROAD]

**rail¹** — n. **1** level or sloping bar or series of bars: **a** used to hang things on. **b** as the top of banisters. **c** forming part of a fence or barrier as protection. **2** steel bar or continuous line of bars laid on the ground, usu. as a railway. **3** (often attrib.) railway (travel by rail; rail fares). — v. **1** furnish with a rail or rails. **2** (usu. foll. by in, off) enclose with rails (a small space was railed off). □ **off the rails** disorganised; out of order; deranged. [French reille from Latin regula RULE]

**rail²** v. (often foll. by at, against) complain or protest strongly; rant. [French railler]

**rail³** n. wading bird, including the Australian buff-banded rail etc., often inhabiting marshes. [French]

**railing** n. (usu. in pl.) fence or barrier made of rails.

**raillery** /ray-luh-ree/ n. good-humoured ridicule. [French raillerie: related to RAIL²]

**railroad** — n. esp. US = RAILWAY. — v. (often foll. by into, through, etc.) coerce; rush (railroaded into agreeing; railroaded through the Cabinet).

**railway** n. **1** track or set of tracks of steel rails upon which trains run. **2** such a system worked by a government instrumentality etc. **3** organisation and personnel required for its working.

**raiment** /ray-muhnt/ n. archaic clothing. [arrayment: related to ARRAY]

**rain** — n. **1 a** condensed atmospheric moisture falling in drops. **b** fall of such drops. **2** (in pl.) **a** (prec. by the) rainy season. **b** rainfalls. **3 a** falling liquid or solid particles or objects (rain of petals from the trees above). **b** rainlike descent of these. **4** large or overwhelming quantity (*a rain of bullets*). — *v.* **1** (prec. by *it* as subject) rain falls. **2 a** fall like rain (*tears rained down his cheeks*). **b** (prec. by *it* as subject) send in large quantities. **3** send down like rain; bestow in great quantities (*rained blows upon him*). **4** (of the sky, clouds, etc.) send down rain. □ (**come**) **rain or** (**come**) **shine** whatever happens. **rain cats and dogs** rain very heavily. **right as rain** fine; perfectly okay. [Old English]

**rain bird** *n.* bird whose call is said to foretell rain, as the Australian channel-billed cuckoo and grey currawong.

**rainbow** /**rayn**-boh/ — *n.* arch of colours formed in the sky by reflection, refraction, and dispersion of the sun's rays in falling rain or in spray or mist. — *adj.* many-coloured. [Old English: related to RAIN, BOW[1]]

**rainbow bird** *n.* (also **rainbow bee-eater**) migratory bee-eater of mainland Australia and islands to the north, having blue, green, and orange plumage.

**rainbow lorikeet** *n.* Australian bird with blue head, green wings, and orange or red breast.

**Rainbow Serpent** *n.* (also **Rainbow Snake, Rainbow Spirit**) widely venerated Spirit of Aboriginal sacred lore, esp. associated with the fashioning of the earth in the Dreamtime.

**rainbow trout** *n.* large trout, orig. of the Pacific coast of N. America, introduced into rivers in Australia.

**rain check** *n.* **1** esp. *US* ticket given for later use when an outdoor event is interrupted or postponed by rain. **2** voucher, issued by a shop, promising that marked-down goods advertised in a sale catalogue etc., but which are temporarily out of stock, will be made available later to the voucher-holder at the marked-down price. □ **take a rain check on** reserve the right not to take up (an offer) until convenient.

**raincoat** *n.* waterproof or water-resistant coat.

**raindrop** *n.* single drop of rain.

**rainfall** *n.* **1** fall of rain. **2** quantity of rain falling within a given area in a given time.

**rainforest** *n.* luxuriant tropical forest with heavy rainfall.

**rainmaker** *n.* highly esteemed Aborigine (usu. a man) who is skilled in performing the ceremonies to bring down rain.

**rainmaking** *n.* rituals and ceremonies used by Aboriginal rainmakers to bring down rain when needed.

**rainproof** *adj.* impervious to rain.

**rainwater** *n.* water collected from fallen rain.

**rainy** *adj.* (**-ier**, **-iest**) (of weather, a climate, day, etc.) in or on which rain is falling or much rain usually falls. [Old English: related to RAIN]

**rainy day** *n.* time of special need in the future (*saving for a rainy day*).

**raise** /rayz/ — *v.* (**-sing**) **1** put or take into a higher position. **2** (often foll. by *up*) cause to rise or stand up or be vertical. **3** increase the amount, value, or strength of (*raised the price*). **4** (often foll. by *up*) construct or build up. **5** levy, collect, or bring together (*raise money*). **6** cause to be heard or considered (*raise an objection*). **7** set going or bring into being (*raise hopes*). **8** bring up, educate (*raised ten children*). **9** breed, grow (*raised a crop of tasty tomatoes*). **10** promote to a higher rank. **11** (foll. by *to*) multiply a quantity to a power. **12** cause (bread) to rise. **13** *Cards* bet more than (another player). **14** end (a siege etc.). **15** remove (a barrier, an embargo, etc.). **16** cause (a ghost etc.) to appear. **17** establish contact by radio or telephone (*raised him on the line*). **18** rouse from death. — *n.* **1** *Cards* increase in a stake or bid. **2** increase in salary. □ **raise Cain** *colloq.* = *raise the roof.* **raise one's eyebrows** see EYEBROW. **raise a laugh** cause others to laugh. **raise the roof** be very angry; cause an uproar. [Old Norse]

**raisin** /**ray**-zuhn/ *n.* dried grape. [Latin: related to RACEME]

**raison d'être** /,ray-zon **det**-ruh/ *n.* (*pl.* **raisons d'être** pronunc. same) purpose or reason that accounts for, justifies, or originally caused a thing's existence. [French]

**raj** /rahj/ *n.* (prec. by *the*) *hist.* British sovereignty in India. [Hindi]

**rajah** /**rah**-juh/ *n.* (also **raja**) *hist.* Indian king or prince. [Hindi from Sanskrit]

**rajah shieldrake** /**sheel**-drayk/ *n.* = BURDEKIN DUCK.

**rake**[1] — *n.* **1** implement consisting of a pole with a toothed crossbar at the end for drawing together fallen leaves, mown grass, etc., or smoothing loose soil or gravel. **2** similar implement used (e.g.) to draw in money at a gaming-table. — *v.* (**-king**) **1** collect or gather with or as with a rake. **2** make tidy or smooth with a rake. **3** use a rake. **4** search thoroughly, ransack (*raked the house from top to bottom*). **5** direct gunfire along (a line) from end to end (*ships raked the coastline with shells*). □ **rake in** *colloq.* amass (profits etc.). **rake up 1** revive the (unwelcome) memory of. **2** *colloq.* find, collect (*can you rake up enough money?*).

**3** reveal, expose (*the press raking up scandals about the British royals*). [Old English]

**rake²** *n.* dissolute man of fashion. [*rakehell*: related to RAKE¹, HELL]

**rake³** — *v.* (**-king**) **1** set or be set at a sloping angle. **2** (of a mast or funnel) incline from the perpendicular towards the stern. — *n.* **1** raking position or build. **2** amount by which a thing rakes. [origin unknown]

**rake-off** *n. colloq.* commission or share (esp. in illicit profits).

**rakish** *adj.* **1** dashing; jaunty. **2** dissolute. □ **rakishly** *adv.* [from RAKE²]

**rallentando** /ˌral-uhn-tan-doh/ *Mus.* — *adv. & adj.* with a gradual decrease of speed. — *n.* (*pl.* **-s** or **-di** /-dee/ ) passage to be performed in this way. [Italian]

**rally¹** /ral-ee/ — *v.* (**-ies, -ied**) **1** (often foll. by *round, to*) bring or come together as support or for action (*rallied round their leader*; *rallied to the cause*). **2** bring or come together again after a rout or dispersion (*troops rallied after the enemy onslaught*). **3** recover after illness etc., revive. **4** revive (courage etc.). **5** (of share-prices etc.) increase after a fall. — *n.* (*pl.* **-ies**) **1** rallying or being rallied. **2** mass meeting of supporters or persons with a common interest. **3** competition for motor vehicles, mainly over public roads. **4** (in tennis etc.) extended exchange of strokes. [French *rallier*: related to RE-, ALLY]

**rally²** /ral-ee/ *v.* (**-ies, -ied**) ridicule good-humouredly. [French *railler*: related to RAIL²]

**rallycross** *n.* motor racing over roads and cross-country.

**ralph** *colloq.* — *v.* vomit. — *n.* an act of vomiting. [imitative]

**RAM** *abbr. Computing* random-access memory.

**ram** — *n.* **1** uncastrated male sheep. **2** (**the Ram**) zodiacal sign or constellation Aries. **3** *hist.* = BATTERING-RAM. **4** falling weight of a pile-driving machine. **5** hydraulically operated water pump. — *v.* (**-mm-**) **1** force or squeeze into place by pressure. **2** (usu. foll. by *down, in*, etc.) beat down or drive in by heavy blows. **3** (of a ship, vehicle, etc.) strike violently, crash against. **4** (foll. by *against, into*) dash or violently impel. □ **ram home** stress forcefully (an argument, lesson, etc.). [Old English]

**Ramadan** /ram-uh-ˌdan, rum-uh-ˌdahn/ *n.* ninth month of the Muslim year, with strict fasting from sunrise to sunset. [Arabic]

**ramble** /ram-buhl/ — *v.* (**-ling**) **1** walk for pleasure. **2** talk or write incoherently. — *n.* walk taken for pleasure. [Dutch *rammelen*]

**rambler** *n.* **1** person who rambles. **2** straggling or spreading rose.

**rambling** *adj.* **1** wandering. **2** disconnected, incoherent (*a rambling argument*). **3** (of a house, street, etc.) irregularly arranged. **4** (of a plant) straggling, climbing.

**rambutan** /ram-boo-tahn/ *n.* **1** red plum-sized prickly fruit. **2** E. Indian tree bearing this. [Malay]

**ramekin** /ram-uh-kuhn/ *n.* **1** small dish for baking and serving an individual portion of food. **2** food served in this. [French *ramequin*]

**ramification** /ˌram-uh-fuh-kay-shuhn/ *n.* (usu. in *pl.*) **1** consequence. **2** subdivision of a complex structure or process, comparable to a tree's branches. [French: related to RAMIFY]

**ramify** /ram-uh-ˌfuy/ *v.* (**-ies, -ied**) (cause to) form branches, subdivisions, or off-shoots; branch out. [Latin *ramus* branch]

**ramp** — *n.* **1** slope, esp. joining two levels of ground, floor, etc. **2** movable stairs for entering or leaving an aircraft. **3** transverse ridge in a road making vehicles slow down; speed hump. **4** cattle-grid. — *v.* **1** furnish or build with a ramp. **2 a** *archaic* (of an animal) assume a threatening posture by rearing up on its hindlegs. **b** (often foll. by *about*) storm, rage. [French *ramper* crawl]

**rampage** — *v.* /ram-payj/ (**-ging**) **1** (often foll. by *about*) rush wildly or violently about. **2** rage, storm. — *n.* /ram-puhj/ wild or violent behaviour. □ **on the rampage** rampaging. [perhaps from RAMP]

**rampant** /ram-puhnt/ *adj.* **1** unchecked, flourishing excessively (*rampant violence*). **2** rank, luxuriant (*rampant growth of weeds*). **3** (placed after the noun) *Heraldry* (of an animal) standing on its left hind foot with its forepaws in the air (*lion rampant*). **4 a** violent (*rampant wild boars*). **b** fanatical (*rampant right-wingers*). □ **rampancy** *n.* [French: related to RAMP]

**rampart** /ram-paht/ *n.* **1 a** defensive wall with a broad top and usu. a stone parapet. **b** walkway on top of this. **2** defence, protection. [French *remparer* fortify]

**ramrod** *n.* **1** rod for ramming down the charge of a muzzle-loading firearm. **2 a** thing that is very straight or rigid. **b** excessively rigid, formal, or unbending person.

**ramshackle** /ram-,shak-uhl/ adj. tumbledown, rickety. [related to RANSACK]

**ran** past of RUN.

**ranch** /ranch, rahnch/ — n. cattle-breeding establishment, esp. in the US and Canada. □ **rancher** n. [Spanish *rancho* group of persons eating together]

**rancid** /ran-suhd/ adj. smelling or tasting like rank stale fat. □ **rancidity** /-**sid**-uh-tee/ n. [Latin *rancidus* stinking]

**rancour** /rang-kuh/ n. (also **rancor**) inveterate bitterness, malignant hate. □ **rancorous** adj. [Latin *rancor*: related to RANCID]

**rand** n. chief monetary unit of South Africa. [the *Rand*, goldfield district near Johannesburg]

**R & D** abbr. research and development.

**random** /ran-duhm/ adj. made, done, etc., without method or conscious choice. □ **at random** without a particular aim. □ **randomise** v. (also **-ize**) (**-sing** or **-zing**). **randomisation** /-zay-shuhn/ n. **randomly** adv. **randomness** n. [French *randon* from *randir* gallop]

**random-access memory** n. Computing memory or file having all parts directly accessible, so that it need not be read sequentially.

**random breath-test** n. measurement of the amount of alcohol in the breath of a motorist chosen randomly from a line of traffic.

**randy** /ran-dee/ adj. (**-ier**, **-iest**) eager for sexual gratification, lustful. □ **randily** adv. **randiness** n. [perhaps related to RANT]

**ranee** var. of RANI.

**rang** past of RING².

**range** /raynj/ — n. **1 a** region between limits of variation, esp. scope of effective operation (*voice of astonishing range; the whole range of politics*). **b** such limits. **2** area relevant to something (*comes within the range of politics*). **3 a** distance attainable by a gun or projectile (*has a range of 500 metres*). **b** distance between a gun or projectile and its objective (*are at a range of 50 metres*). **4** row, series, etc., esp. of mountains (*Great Dividing Range*). **5** area with targets for shooting. **6** electric or gas stove. **7** area over which a thing is distributed. **8** distance that can be covered by a vehicle without refuelling. **9** distance between a camera and the subject to be photographed. **10** esp. *US* large area of open land for grazing (*home, home on the range*). — v. (**-ging**) **1 a** lie spread out; extend (*her knowledge ranged from astrology to zoology*). **b** be found over a specified district (esp. of a plant or animal) (*the noisy friar-bird ranges from South Australia to Queensland*). **c** vary

between limits (*ages ranged from ten to twenty*). **2** (usu. in *passive* or *refl.*) line up, arrange (*contestants were ranged in ascending order of height; ranged themselves with the majority*). **3** rove, wander. **4** traverse in all directions (*bushwalkers ranged the forest*). [French: related to RANK¹]

**rangefinder** n. instrument for estimating the distance of an object to be shot at or photographed.

**ranger** n. **1** keeper of a national park etc. **2** (**Ranger**) senior Guide. **3** hist. = BUSH-RANGER.

**rangy** /rayn-jee/ adj. (**-ier**, **-iest**) tall and slim.

**rani** /rah-nee/ n. (also **ranee**) (pl. **-s**) hist. rajah's wife or widow. [Hindi]

**rank¹** — n. **1 a** position in a hierarchy, grade of advancement. **b** distinct social class; grade of dignity or achievement (*people of all ranks; in the top social rank of performers*). **c** high social position. **d** place in a scale. **2** row or line. **3** single line of soldiers drawn up abreast. **4** place where taxis await customers. **5** order, array. — v. **1** have a rank or place. **2** classify, give a certain grade to (*rank them on a scale of 1 to 10*). **3** arrange (esp. soldiers) in rank. **4** have value as specified (*courtesy ranks highly with him*). □ **break ranks** fail to remain in line. **close ranks** maintain solidarity. **pull rank** see PULL. **the ranks** common soldiers. [French *ranc*]

**rank²** adj. **1** luxuriant, coarse; choked with or apt to produce weeds or excessive foliage. **2** foul-smelling. **b** loathsome, corrupt. **3** flagrant, virulent, gross, complete (*rank outsider*). [Old English]

**rank and file** n. (usu. treated as *pl.*) ordinary members of an organisation.

**rankle** /rang-kuhl/ v. (**-ling**) (of envy, disappointment, etc., or their cause) cause persistent annoyance or resentment. [French *(d)rancler* fester, from medieval Latin *dra(cu)nculus* little serpent]

**ransack** /ran-sak/ v. **1** pillage or plunder (a house, country, etc.). **2** thoroughly search. [Old Norse *rannsaka* from *rann* house, *-saka* seek]

**ransom** /ran-suhm/ — n. **1** money demanded or paid for the release of a prisoner. **2** liberation of a prisoner in return for this. — v. **1** buy the freedom or restoration of; redeem. **2** = hold to ransom (see HOLD¹). **3** release for a ransom. [Latin: related to REDEMPTION]

**rant** — v. speak loudly, bombastically, violently, or theatrically. — n. piece of ranting. □ **rant and rave** express anger noisily and forcefully. [Dutch]

**ranunculus** /ruh-**nung**-kyuh-luhs/ n. (pl. **-luses** or **-li** /-luy/) plant of the genus including buttercups. [Latin, diminutive of *rana* frog]

**rap**[1] — n. **1** smart slight blow. **2** knock, sharp tapping sound. **3** *colloq.* **a** blame, punishment. **b** criminal charge (*got a life-sentence on a murder rap*). **4 a** rhythmic monologue, often in rhyming sentences, recited to music. **b** (in full **rap music**) style of rock music with words recited. **c** (in full **rap dancing**) energetic dancing associated with this. — v. (**-pp-**) **1** strike smartly. **2** knock; make a sharp tapping sound. **3** criticise adversely. **4** perform rap music; talk, sing, or dance in the style of rap. **5** (also **rap on**) *colloq.* talk, chat. □ **rap on** (or **over**) **the knuckles 1** severe reprimand. **2** reprimand severely. **take the rap** suffer the consequences. □ **rapper** n. [probably imitative]

**rap**[2] n. small amount, the least bit (*don't care a rap*). [Irish *ropaire* counterfeit coin]

**rap**[3] *colloq.* — n. praise, commendation (*coach gave him a rap after his good game*). — v. praise. [British dial.]

**rapacious** /ruh-**pay**-shuhs/ adj. grasping, extortionate, predatory. □ **rapacity** /ruh-**pas**-uh-tee/ n. [Latin *rapax*: related to RAPE[1]]

**rape**[1] — n. **1 a** act of forcing a woman or girl to have sexual intercourse against her will. **b** forcible sodomy. **2** (often foll. by *of*) **a** violent assault or plunder, forcible interference. **b** destruction, structive exploitation (*the rape of our rainforests*). — v. (**-ping**) commit rape on (in all senses of the noun). [Latin *rapio* seize]

**rape**[2] n. plant grown as fodder, and for its seed from which oil is extracted. [Latin *rapum, rapa* turnip]

**rapid** /**rap**-uhd/ — adj. (**-er, -est**) **1** quick, swift. **2** acting or completed in a short time. **3** (of a slope) descending steeply. — n. (usu. in *pl.*) steep descent in a river-bed, with a swift current. □ **rapidity** /ruh-**pid**-uh-tee/ n. **rapidly** adv. **rapidness** n. [Latin: related to RAPE[1]]

**rapid eye-movement** n. type of jerky movement of the eyes during dreaming.

**rapier** /**ray**-pee-uh/ n. **1** light slender sword for thrusting. **2** (*attrib.*) sharp (*rapier wit*). [French *rapière*]

**rapine** /**ra**-peen, -puyn/ n. *rhet.* plundering. [Latin: related to RAPE[1]]

**rapist** /**ray**-puhst/ n. person who commits rape.

**rapport** /ra-**paw**/ n. harmonious and understanding relationship between people; feeling of being in harmony with something) (*established a rapport with his neighbours; Aborigines have a strong rapport with the land*). [Latin *porto* carry]

**rapprochement** /ruh-**prosh**-mon, -muhnt/ n. resumption of harmonious relations, esp. between nations. [French: related to APPROACH]

**rapscallion** /rap-**skal**-yuhn/ n. *archaic* or *joc.* rascal. [perhaps from RASCAL]

**rapt** adj. **1** fully absorbed or intent, enraptured (*listened with rapt attention*). **2** carried away with feeling or lofty thought. [Latin *raptus*: related to RAPE[1]]

**raptor** n. bird of prey. [Latin *raptor* robber: related to RAPE[1]]

**raptorial** /rap-**taw**-ree-uhl/ adj. (of an animal, esp. a bird) predatory.

**rapture** /**rap**-chuh/ n. **1** ecstatic delight. **2** (in *pl.*) great pleasure or enthusiasm or the expression of it. □ **go into** (or **be in**) **raptures** be enthusiastic; talk enthusiastically. □ **rapturous** adj. [French or medieval Latin: related to RAPE[1]]

**rare**[1] adj. (**rarer, rarest**) **1** seldom done, found, or occurring; uncommon, unusual. **2** exceptionally good (*had a rare time*). **3** of less than the usual density (*rare atmosphere on the mountain top*). □ **rareness** n. [Latin *rarus*]

**rare**[2] adj. (**rarer, rarest**) (of meat) cooked so that the inside is still red and juicy; underdone. [Old English]

**rare earth** n. lanthanide element.

**rarefy** /**rair**-uh-,fuy/ v. (**-ies, -ied**) **1** make or become less dense or solid. **2** purify or refine (a person's nature etc.). **3** (as **rarefied**) highly intellectual (*the rarefied atmosphere of the university*). □ **rarefaction** /-**fak**-shuhn/ n. [French or medieval Latin: related to RARE[1]]

**rarely** adv. seldom, not often.

**raring** /**rair**-ring/ adj. *colloq.* enthusiastic, eager (*raring to go*). [participle of *rare*, British dial. var. of ROAR or REAR[2]]

**rarity** /**rair**-ruh-tee/ n. (pl. **-ies**) **1** rareness. **2** uncommon thing (*courtesy is a rarity these days*). [Latin: related to RARE[1]]

**rascal** /**rah**-skuhl, **ras**-kuhl/ n. dishonest or mischievous person, esp. a child. □ **rascally** adj. [French *rascaille* rabble]

**rase** var. of RAZE.

**rash**[1] adj. reckless, impetuous, hasty. □ **rashly** adv. **rashness** n. [probably Old English]

**rash**[2] n. **1** eruption of the skin in spots or patches. **2** (usu. foll. by *of*) sudden widespread phenomenon (*rash of strikes*). [origin uncertain]

**rasher** n. thin slice of bacon or ham. [origin unknown]

**rasp** /rahsp, rasp/ — n. **1** coarse kind of file having separate teeth. **2** grating noise or utterance (*spoke with a rasp*). — v. **1 a** scrape with a rasp. **b** scrape roughly. **c** (foll. by *off*, *away*) remove by scraping. **2 a** make a grating sound. **b** say gratingly (*'Shut your mouth!' he rasped*). **3** grate upon (a person or feelings) (*his whistling rasped my nerves*). [French *raspe(r)*]

**raspberry** /**rahz**-buh-ree/ n. (pl. **-ies**) **1 a** red blackberry-like fruit. **b** bramble bearing this. **2** colloq. sound made by blowing through the lips, expressing derision or disapproval. [origin unknown]

**raspberry jam** n. WA wattle yielding a durable timber having a fragrance said to be like raspberry jam.

**Rastafarian** /ˌrah-stuh-**fair**-ree-uhn/ — n. member of a Jamaican sect, often having dreadlocks and regarding Haile Selassie of Ethiopia as God. — adj. of this sect. [*Ras Tafari*, title of former Emperor Haile Selassie]

**rat** — n. **1 a** rodent like a large mouse. **b** similar rodent (*swamp rat*). **c** (in comb.) designating various Australian rat-like animals (*rock rat*). **2** turncoat, deserter (from the tradition that rats desert a sinking ship). **3** colloq. unpleasant or treacherous person. **4** (in pl.) colloq. exclamation of annoyance etc. — v. (**-tt-**) **1** hunt or kill rats. **2** (usu. foll. by *on*) colloq. **a** inform (on). **b** desert, betray. **c** renege on an agreement. **3** colloq. rob (a person); steal (money etc.). [Old English]

**ratable** var. of RATEABLE.

**ratatouille** /ˌra-tuh-**too**-ee/ n. dish of stewed onions, zucchinis, tomatoes, egg-plant, and peppers. [French dial.]

**ratbag** n. colloq. **1** obnoxious person. **2** trouble-maker. **3** eccentric or unconventional person. **4** (also attrib.) person who is rigid or extreme in (esp. left-wing) political views etc. (*lunatic-left ratbag*; *ratbag fringe of the Labor Party*). ◻ **ratbaggery** n.

**ratchet** /**rach**-uht/ n. **1** set of teeth on the edge of a bar or wheel with a catch ensuring motion in one direction only. **2** (in full **ratchet-wheel**) wheel with a rim so toothed. [French *rochet* lance-head]

**rate¹** — n. **1** numerical proportion between two sets of things (e.g. kilometres and hours) (*moving at a rate of 100 kilometres per hour*) or as the basis of calculating an amount or value (*rate of interest*). **2** fixed or appropriate charge, cost, or value; measure of this (*postal rates*; *the rate for the job*). **3** pace of movement, work, or change (*working at*

a steady rate; prices increasing at a great rate). **4** (in comb.) class or rank (*first-rate*). **5** (in pl.) tax on land and buildings levied by local governments, the money gained being used for local services. — v. (**-ting**) **1 a** estimate the worth or value of (*I do not rate him very highly*). **b** assign a value to. **2** consider, regard as (*I rate him among my mates*). **3** (foll. by *as*) rank or be considered (*that rates as his worst performance*). **4 a** subject to the payment of a local rate. **b** value for the purpose of assessing rates. **5** be worthy of, deserve (*that rates a commendation*). ◻ **at any rate** in any case, whatever happens. **at this rate** if this example is typical; if things continue as now. [Latin *rata*: related to RATIO]

**rate²** v. (**-ting**) scold angrily (*rated him severely*). [origin unknown]

**rateable** adj. (also **ratable**) liable to rates.

**rateable value** n. value at which a business etc. is assessed for rates.

**ratepayer** n. person liable to pay rates.

**rather** /**rah**-thuh/ adv. **1** by preference (*would rather not go*). **2** (foll. by *than*) in preference to (*bought a boat rather than a car*). **3** (usu. foll. by *than*) more truly; as a more likely alternative (*is stupid rather than dishonest*). **4** more precisely (*a book, or rather, a pamphlet*). **5** slightly, to some extent; somewhat (*became rather drunk*; *that painting is rather good*). **6** on the contrary; instead (*he won't help with the housework — rather, he sits in front of the telly all day*). **7** /rah-**ther**/ mainly BRIT. (as an emphatic response) assuredly (*Did you like it? – Rather!*). ◻ **had rather** would rather. [Old English comparative of *rathe* early]

**ratify** /**rat**-uh-ˌfuy/ v. (**-ies**, **-ied**) confirm or accept (an agreement made in one's name) by formal consent, signature, etc. ◻ **ratification** /-fuh-**kay**-shuhn/ n. [medieval Latin: related to RATE¹]

**rating** n. **1** placing in a rank or class. **2** estimated standing of a person as regards credit etc. **3 a** relative popularity of a broadcast programme as determined by the estimated size of the audience. **b** (in pl.) (often attrib.) pertaining to the calculation of the rating of broadcast programmes (*we should see some good programmes now — it's ratings week*).

**ratio** /**ray**-shee-oh/ n. (pl. **-s**) quantitative relation between two similar magnitudes expressed as the number of times one contains the other (*in the ratio of three to two*). [Latin *reor rat-* reckon]

**ratiocinate** /ˌrat-ee-**oh**-suh-ˌnayt, ˌrash-ee-/ v. (**-ting**) literary think logically; reason, esp. using syllogisms. ◻ **rati-**

**ocination** /-**nay**-shuhn/ n. **ratiocinative** /-**sin**-uh-tiv/ adj. [Latin: related to RATIO]

**ration** /**rash**-uhn/ — n. **1** official allowance of food, clothing, etc., in a time of shortage. **2** (usu. in pl.) fixed daily allowance of food, esp. in the armed forces or on a station. — v. **1** limit (persons or provisions) to a fixed ration. **2** (usu. foll. by out) share out (food etc.) in fixed quantities. [Latin: related to RATIO]

**rational** /**rash**-uh-nuhl/ adj. **1** of or based on reason (rational faculty of the mind; a rational decision). **2** sensible; sane (you're not being rational; the patient was rational at all times). **3** endowed with reason (human beings are rational creatures). **4** rejecting what is unreasonable or cannot be tested by reason in religion or custom. **5** (of a quantity or ratio) expressible as a ratio of whole numbers. □ **rationality** /-**nal**-uh-tee/ n. **rationally** adv. [Latin: related to RATIO]

**rationale** /,rash-uh-**nahl**/ n. fundamental reason, logical basis. [neuter of Latin rationalis: related to RATIONAL]

**rationalise** v. (also **-ize**) (**-sing** or **-zing**) **1** (often foll. by away) offer or adopt a rational but specious explanation of (one's behaviour or attitude). **2** make logical and consistent. **3** make (a business etc.) more efficient by reorganising it to reduce or eliminate waste. □ **rationalisation** /-**zay**-shuhn/ n.

**rationalism** /**rash**-uh-nuh-,liz-uhm/ n. **1** practice of treating reason as the basis of belief and knowledge. **2** belief in reason rather than religion as a guiding principle in life. □ **rationalist** n. & adj. **rationalistic** /-**lis**-tik/ adj.

**rat-kangaroo** n. = KANGAROO RAT.

**rat race** n. colloq. **1** fiercely competitive struggle for position, power, etc. **2** hectic pace of life in a large city etc.

**rattan** /ruh-**tan**/ n. **1** climbing palm with long thin jointed pliable stems, used for furniture etc. **2** piece of rattan stem used as a walking-stick etc. [Malay]

**rattle** /**rat**-uhl/ — v. (**-ling**) **1 a** give out a rapid succession of short sharp hard sounds. **b** cause to do this. **c** cause such sounds by shaking something. **2** (often foll. by along) **a** move with a rattling noise. **b** move or travel briskly. **3 a** (usu. foll. by off) say or recite rapidly (rattled off the speech). **b** (usu. foll. by on) talk in a lively thoughtless way (rattled on about this, that, and the other). **4** colloq. disconcert, alarm (the question rattled him). — n. **1** rattling sound. **2** device or plaything made to rattle. □ **rattly** adj. [probably Low German or Dutch]

**rattlesnake** n. poisonous American snake with a rattling structure of horny rings on its tail.

**rattling** — adj. **1** that rattles. **2** brisk, vigorous (rattling pace). — adv. colloq. remarkably (rattling good story).

**ratty** adj. (**-ier**, **-iest**) **1** relating to or infested with rats. **2** colloq. irritable, bad-tempered. **3** colloq. mad; eccentric. □ **rattily** adv. **rattiness** n.

**raucous** /**raw**-kuhs/ adj. harsh-sounding, loud and hoarse. □ **raucously** adv. **raucousness** n. [Latin]

**raunchy** /**rawn**-chee/ adj. (**-ier**, **-iest**) colloq. coarse, earthy; sexually boisterous; randy. □ **raunchily** adv. **raunchiness** n. [origin unknown]

**ravage** /**rav**-ij/ — v. (**-ging**) devastate, plunder. — n. **1** devastation. **2** (usu. in pl.; foll. by of) destructive effect (ravages of time). [French alteration from ravine rush of water]

**rave** — v. (**-ving**) **1** talk wildly or furiously in or as in delirium. **2** (usu. foll. by about, over) speak with rapturous admiration; go into raptures. **3** colloq. enjoy oneself freely (esp. rave it up). — n. **1** act or instance of raving. **2** (usu. attrib.) colloq. highly enthusiastic review. **3** (also **rave party**) all-night party with loud rock music attended by large numbers of young people. □ **rave on** colloq. talk tediously and at length (what's he raving on about?). [probably French dial. raver]

**ravel** /**rav**-uhl/ v. (**-ll-**) **1** entangle or become entangled. **2** fray out. **3** (often foll. by out) disentangle, unravel, separate into threads. [probably Dutch ravelen]

**raven** /**ray**-vuhn/ — n. **1** large glossy blue-black crow with a hoarse cry, found in many parts of the world. **2** any of three Australian birds of the crow family: Australian raven, forest raven, little raven. — adj. glossy black. [Old English]

**ravening** /**rav**-uh-ning/ adj. hungrily seeking prey; voracious. [French raviner from Latin: related to RAPINE]

**ravenous** /**rav**-uh-nuhs/ adj. **1** very hungry. **2** voracious. **3** rapacious. □ **ravenously** adv. [obsolete raven plunder, from French raviner ravage]

**ravine** /ruh-**veen**/ n. deep narrow gorge. [Latin: related to RAPINE]

**raving** — n. (usu. in pl.) wild or delirious talk. — adj. & adv. colloq. as an intensifier (a raving beauty; raving mad).

**ravioli** /,rav-ee-**oh**-lee/ n. small pasta envelopes containing minced meat etc. [Italian]

**ravish** /**rav**-ish/ v. **1** archaic rape (a woman). **2** enrapture. □ **ravishment** n. [Latin: related to RAPE[1]]

**ravishing** adj. lovely, beautiful. □ **ravishingly** adv.

**raw** adj. **1** uncooked. **2** in the natural state; not processed or manufactured (*raw sewage*). **3** inexperienced, untrained (*raw recruit*). **4 a** stripped of skin; with the flesh exposed, unhealed. **b** sensitive to the touch from being so exposed. **5** (of the atmosphere, day, etc.) cold and damp. **6** crude in artistic quality; lacking finish. □ **come the raw prawn** see PRAWN. **in the raw 1** in its natural state without mitigation (*life in the raw*). **2** naked. **touch on the raw** upset (a person) on a sensitive matter. [Old English]

**raw deal** n. harsh or unfair treatment.

**rawhide** n. **1** untanned hide. **2** rope or whip of this.

**raw material** n. material from which manufactured goods are made.

**ray¹** n. **1** single line or narrow beam of light from a small or distant source. **2** straight line in which radiation travels to a given point. **3** (in pl.) radiation of a specified type (*X-rays*). **4** trace or beginning of an enlightening or cheering influence (*ray of hope*). **5** any of a set of radiating lines, parts, or things. **6** marginal floret of a composite flower, e.g. a daisy. [Latin RADIUS]

**ray²** n. large edible marine fish with a flat body and a long slender tail. [Latin *raia*]

**ray³** n. (also **re**) *Mus.* second note of a major scale. [Latin *resonare*, word arbitrarily taken]

**rayon** /**ray**-on/ n. textile fibre or fabric made from cellulose. [from RAY¹]

**raze** v. (also **rase**) (**-zing** or **-sing**) completely destroy; tear down (esp. *raze to the ground*). [Latin *rado ras-* scrape]

**razoo** /rah-**zoo**/ n. (also **brass razoo**) non-existent coin of trivial value (used in negative contexts only). □ **not have a brass razoo** *colloq.* have no money at all. **not worth a brass razoo** worth nothing. [origin unknown]

**razor** /**ray**-zuh/ n. instrument with a sharp blade used in cutting hair, esp. shaving. [French *rasor*: related to RAZE]

**razorback** n. narrow, steep-sided ridge of land.

**razor blade** n. flat piece of metal with a sharp edge, used in a safety razor.

**razor edge** n. (also **razor's edge**) **1** keen edge. **2** sharp mountain-ridge. **3** critical situation. **4** sharp line of division.

**razor-gang** n. *colloq.* parliamentary committee established to examine ways of reducing government expenditure.

**razor-grinder** n. = RESTLESS FLYCATCHER.

**razzamatazz** /ˌraz-uh-muh-**taz**/ n. (also

**razzmatazz**) *colloq.* glamorous excitement, bustle. [probably an alteration of RAZZLE-DAZZLE]

**razzle-dazzle** /**raz**-uhl-ˌdaz-uhl/ n. (also **razzle**) *colloq.* **1 a** excitement; bustle. **b** spree. **2** extravagant publicity. [reduplication of DAZZLE]

**Rb** symb. rubidium.

**RC** abbr. Roman Catholic.

**Rd.** abbr. Road.

**Re** symb. rhenium.

**re¹** /ree, ray/ prep. **1** in the matter of (as the first word in a heading, esp. of a legal document). **2** about; concerning (in letters). [Latin, ablative of *res* thing]

**re²** var. of RAY³.

**re-** prefix **1** attachable to almost any verb or its derivative, meaning: **a** once more; afresh, anew (*readjust*; *renumber*). **b** back; with return to a previous state (*reassemble*; *refreeze*). **2** (also **red-** before a vowel, as in *redolent*) in verbs and verbal derivatives denoting: **a** in return; mutually (*react*). **b** opposition (*resist*). **c** behind or after (*relic*; *remain*). **d** retirement or secrecy (*recluse*). **e** off, away, down (*recede*; *relegate*; *repress*). **f** frequentative or intensive force (*redouble*; *resplendent*). **g** negative force (*recant*; *reveal*). [Latin]

■ **Usage** In sense 1, a hyphen is normally used when the word begins with *e* (*re-enact*), or to distinguish the compound from a more familiar one-word form (*re-form* = form again).

**reach** — v. **1** (often foll. by *out*) stretch out, extend. **2** (often foll. by *for*) stretch out the hand etc.; make a stretch or effort (*reached out for the glass*). **3** get as far as (*hoping to reach Hobart by noon*; *will the cord reach the socket?*). **4** get to or attain (*the temperature reached 38°*). **5** succeed in achieving (*have reached an agreement*). **6** make contact with the hand etc., or by telephone etc. (*could not be reached*). **7** hand, pass (*reach me that book*). **8** take with an outstretched hand. **9** succeed in influencing or in having the required effect (*could not manage to reach their audience*). **10** *Naut.* sail with the wind abeam or abaft the beam. — n. **1** extent to which a hand etc. can be reached out, influence exerted, motion carried out, or mental powers used. **2** act of reaching out. **3** continuous extent, esp. of river between two bends or of canal between locks. **4** *Naut.* distance traversed in reaching. □ **reachable** adj. [Old English]

**react** /ree-**akt**/ v. **1** (often foll. by *to*) respond to a stimulus; change or behave differently due to some influence (*reacted badly to the news*). **2** (often foll. by *against*) respond with repulsion to; tend in a reverse or contrary direction. **3** (foll. by *with*) (of a substance or particle) be the cause of chemical activity or interaction with another (*nitrous oxide reacts with the metal*). **4** (foll. by *with*) cause (a substance) to react with another.

**reactant** /ree-**ak**-tuhnt/ *n. Chem.* substance that takes part in, and undergoes, change during a reaction.

**reaction** /ree-**ak**-shuhn/ *n.* **1** act or instance of reacting; responsive or reciprocal action. **2 a** responsive feeling (*what was her reaction to the tragedy?*). **b** immediate or first impression (*what was your reaction to 'Blue Poles'?*). **3** bad physical response to a drug etc. **4** occurrence of a condition after a period of its opposite (*the permissiveness of the 1960s was a reaction to decades of conservatism*). **5** tendency to oppose change or reform, esp. in politics. **6** interaction of substances undergoing chemical change.

**reactionary** — *adj.* tending to oppose (esp. political) change or reform; conservative. — *n.* (*pl.* **-ies**) reactionary person.

**reactive** /ree-**ak**-tiv/ *adj.* **1** showing reaction. **2** reacting rather than taking the initiative. **3** susceptible to chemical reaction.

**reactor** *n.* **1** person or thing that reacts. **2** = NUCLEAR REACTOR.

**read** /reed/ — *v.* (*past* and *past part.* **read** /red/) **1** (also *absol.*) reproduce mentally or (often foll. by *aloud, out, off,* etc.) vocally the written or printed words of (a book, author, etc.). **2** convert or be able to convert into the intended words or meaning (written or other symbols or the things expressed in this way) (*can't read music; can read Egyptian hieroglyphics*). **3** understand by observing; interpret (*read me like a book; read his silence as consent; read my mind; reads tea-leaves*). **4** find (a thing) stated in print etc. (*read that you were leaving*). **5** (often foll. by *into*) assume as intended or deducible (*read too much into it*). **6** bring into a specified state by reading (*read myself to sleep*). **7 a** (of a recording instrument) show (a specified figure etc.) (*thermometer reads 30°*). **b** interpret (a recording instrument) (*read the meter*). **8** convey meaning when read; have a certain wording (*it reads persuasively; reads from left to right*). **9** sound or affect a hearer or reader when read (*the book reads like a parody*). **10** study by reading (esp. a subject at university). **11** (as **read** /red/ *adj.*) versed in a subject (esp. literature)

by reading (*well-read person*). **12** (of a computer) copy or transfer (data). **13** hear and understand (over a radio) (*are you reading me?*). **14** replace (a word etc.) with the correct one(s) (*for 'this' read 'these'*). — *n.* **1** spell of reading. **2** *colloq.* book etc. as regards readability (*is a good read*). □ **read between the lines** look for or find hidden meaning. **read up** (often foll. by *on*) make a special study of (a subject). **take as read** treat (a thing) as if it has been agreed. **you wouldn't read about it** *colloq.* exclamation used to express disbelief (*every horse I backed came last — you wouldn't read about it!*). [Old English]

**readable** *adj.* **1** able to be read. **2** interesting to read. □ **readability** *n.*

**readdress** /,ree-uh-**dres**/ *v.* **1** change the address of (an item for posting). **2** address (a problem etc.) anew. **3** speak to anew.

**reader** *n.* **1** person who reads. **2** book intended to give reading practice, esp. in a foreign language. **3** device for producing an image that can be read from microfilm etc. **4** (**Reader**) university lecturer of the highest grade below professor. **5** publisher's employee who reports on submitted manuscripts. **6** printer's proof-corrector.

**readership** *n.* **1** readers of a newspaper etc. **2** (also **Readership**) position of Reader.

**readily** /**red**-uh-lee/ *adv.* **1** without showing reluctance, willingly (*went readily to his aid*). **2** without difficulty (*the allusion should be readily understood*).

**readiness** *n.* **1** ready or prepared state. **2** willingness. **3** facility; promptness in argument or action.

**reading** *n.* **1 a** act of reading (*reading of the will*). **b** matter to be read (*made exciting reading*). **2** (in *comb.*) used for reading (*reading-lamp; reading-room*). **3** literary knowledge (*person of wide reading*). **4** entertainment at which a play, poems, etc., are read. **5** figure etc. shown by a recording instrument. **6** interpretation or view taken (*what is your reading of the facts?*). **7** interpretation made (of drama, music, etc.) (*fine reading of the role of Hamlet*). **8** each of the successive occasions on which a bill must be presented to a legislature for acceptance. [Old English: related to READ]

**ready** /**red**-ee/ — *adj.* (**-ier, -iest**) (usu. *predic.*) **1** with preparations complete (*dinner is ready*). **2** in a fit state (*are you ready to go?*). **3** willing, inclined, or resolved (*no-one I'm more ready to trust; he is always ready to complain*). **4** within reach; easily secured (*ready source of income*). **5** fit for immediate use (*your car is now ready*). **6** immediate, unqualified (*found ready acceptance*). **7** prompt (*is always ready with excuses*). **8** (foll. by *to* + infin.) about to (*ready to burst*). — *adv.* (usu. in *comb.*) beforehand; so as not to require doing when the time comes for use etc. (*is ready packed*; *ready-mixed concrete*). — *v.* (**-ies, -ied**) make ready, prepare. □ **at the ready** ready for action. **make ready** prepare. [Old English]

**ready-made** *adj.* (also **ready-to-wear**) (esp. of clothes) made in a standard size, not to measure.

**ready money** *n.* money available for immediate use.

**ready reckoner** *n.* book or table listing standard numerical calculations as used esp. in commerce.

**reafforest** /,ree-uh-**fo**-ruhst/ *v.* = RE-FOREST. □ **reafforestation** /-**stay**-shuhn/ *n.*

**reagent** /ree-**ay**-juhnt/ *n. Chem.* substance used to cause a reaction, esp. to detect another substance.

**real** — *adj.* **1** actually existing or occurring. **2 a** genuine (*real pearls*). **b** rightly so called (*her real name is Smith*). **c** not artificial or merely apparent (*the real cause of his fear*). **3** *Law* consisting of immovable property such as land or houses (*real estate*). **4** appraised by purchasing power (*real value*). **5** *Math.* (of a quantity) having no imaginary part (see IMAGINARY 2). — *adv. colloq.* really, very (*real hard work*). □ **for real** *colloq.* definite; genuine (*are you for real?*); seriously, in earnest (*this time he's playing for real*). **get real** see GET. **the real thing** (of an object or emotion) genuine, not inferior. [Anglo-French and Latin *realis* from *res* thing]

**real estate** *n.* land and other immovable property (houses etc.).

**realign** /,ree-uh-**luyn**/ *v.* **1** align again. **2** regroup in politics etc. □ **realignment** *n.*

**realise** *v.* (also **-ize**) (**-sing** or **-zing**) **1** (often foll. by *that*) be fully aware of; conceive as real. **2** understand clearly (*she now realised his treachery*). **3** present as real (*the story was powerfully realised on stage*). **4** convert into actuality (*realised a childhood dream*). **5 a** convert into money. **b** acquire (profit). **c** be sold for (a specified price). □ **realisable** *adj.* **realisation** *n.*

**realism** *n.* **1** practice of regarding things in their true nature and dealing with them as they are. **2** fidelity to nature in representation; the showing of life etc. as it is. **3** *Philos.* doctrine that abstract

concepts have an objective existence. □ **realist** *n.*

**realistic** /ree-uh-**lis**-tik/ *adj.* **1** regarding things as they are; following a policy of realism. **2** based on facts rather than ideals. □ **realistically** *adv.*

**reality** /ree-**al**-uh-tee/ *n.* (*pl.* **-ies**) **1** what is real or existent or underlies appearances. **2** (foll. by *of*) the real nature of. **3** real existence; state of being real. **4** resemblance to an original (*the wax model of the Prime Minister was impressive in its reality*). □ **in reality** in fact. [medieval Latin or French: related to REAL]

**real life** *n.* **1** life lived by actual people. **2** (*attrib.*) (**real-life**) actual, not fictional (*her real-life husband*).

**really** /**reer**-lee/ *adv.* **1** in reality. **2** very (*really useful*). **3** indeed, I assure you. **4** expression of mild protest or surprise (*They're musicians. — Really?*).

**realm** /relm/ *n.* **1** *formal* kingdom. **2** sphere, domain (*the realm of myth*). [Latin REGIMEN]

**real McCoy** see McCOY.

**real time** *n.* **1** actual time during which a process occurs. **2** (*attrib.*) (**real-time**) *Computing* (of a system) in which the response time is negligible, e.g. in an airline booking system.

**realty** /**ree**-uhl-tee/ *n.* real estate.

**ream** *n.* **1** twenty quires of paper. **2** (in *pl.*) large quantity of writing (*wrote reams for the assignment*). [Arabic, = bundle]

**reap** *v.* **1** cut or gather (a crop, esp. grain) as a harvest. **2** harvest the crop of (a field etc.). **3** receive as the consequence of one's own or others' actions (*reaped the rewards of her hard work*). [Old English]

**reaper** *n.* **1** person who reaps. **2** reaping machine. **3** (**the Reaper** or **grim Reaper**) death personified.

**reapply** /,ree-uh-**pluy**/ *v.* (**-ies, -ied**) apply again, esp. submit a further application (for a position etc.). □ **reapplication** /,ree-ap-luh-**kay**-shuhn/ *n.*

**reappoint** /,ree-uh-**point**/ *v.* appoint to a position previously held. □ **reappointment** *n.*

**reappraise** /,ree-uh-**prayz**/ *v.* (**-sing**) appraise or assess again or differently. □ **reappraisal** *n.*

**rear¹** — *n.* **1** back part of anything. **2** space behind, or position at the back of, anything. **3** *colloq.* buttocks. — *adj.* at the back. □ **bring up the rear** come last. [probably from REARWARD or REARGUARD]

**rear²** *v.* **1 a** bring up and educate (children). **b** breed and care for (animals). **c** cultivate (crops). **2** (of a horse etc.) raise itself on its hind legs. **3 a** set upright (*help us rear the mast*). **b** build. **c** hold upwards (*reared his head*). **4** extend to a great height (*mountains reared in the distance*). [Old English]

**rear admiral** *n.* naval officer ranking below vice admiral.

**rearguard** *n.* body of troops detached to protect the rear, esp. in retreats. [French *rereguarde*]

**rearguard action** *n.* **1** engagement undertaken by a rearguard. **2** defensive stand or struggle, esp. when losing.

**rearm** /ree-**ahm**/ *v.* (also *absol.*) arm again, esp. with improved weapons. □ **rearmament** *n.*

**rearmost** *adj.* furthest back.

**rearrange** /ree-uh-**raynj**/ *v.* (**-ging**) arrange again in a different way. □ **rearrangement** *n.*

**rearward** /**reer**-wuhd/ — *n.* (esp. in prepositional phrases) rear (*to the rearward of*; *in the rearward*). — *adj.* to the rear. — *adv.* (also **rearwards**) towards the rear. [Anglo-French *rerewarde* = REARGUARD]

**reason** /**ree**-zuhn/ — *n.* **1** motive, cause, or justification (*has good reasons for doing this*). **2** fact adduced or serving as this (*I can give you my reasons*). **3** intellectual faculty by which conclusions are drawn from premises. **4** sanity (*lost his reason*). **5** sense; sensible conduct; what is right, practical, or practicable; moderation. — *v.* **1** form or try to reach conclusions by connected thought. **2** (foll. by *with*) use argument with (a person) by way of persuasion. **3** (foll. by *that*) conclude or assert in argument. **4** (foll. by *into*, *out of*) persuade or move by argument (*she reasoned him out of his fears*). **5** (foll. by *out*) think out (consequences etc.). **6** (often as **reasoned** *adj.*) express in logical or argumentative form. □ **by reason of** owing to. **in** (or **within**) **reason** within the bounds of moderation. **it stands to reason** it is evident or logical. **with reason** justifiably. [Latin *ratio*]

**reasonable** *adj.* **1** having sound judgment; moderate; ready to listen to reason. **2** not absurd. **3 a** not greatly less or more than might be expected. **b** inexpensive; not extortionate (*a reasonable price*). **c** tolerable (*reasonable weather*). □ **reasonableness** *n.* **reasonably** *adv.*

**reassert** /ree-uh-**sert**/ *v.* assert again, esp. with renewed emphasis. □ **reassertion** *n.*

**reassess** /ree-uh-**ses**/ *v.* assess again or differently. □ **reassessment** *n.*

**reassure** /ree-uh-**shaw**/ *v.* (**-ring**) **1** restore confidence to; dispel the apprehensions of. **2** confirm in an opinion or

impression. □ **reassurance** *n.* **reassuring** *adj.*

**rebate**¹ /**ree**-bayt/ — *n.* **1** partial refund. **2** deduction from a sum to be paid; discount. — *v.* pay back as a rebate. □ **rebatable** *adj.* [French *rabattre*: related to RE-, ABATE]

**rebate**² /**ree**-bayt/ — *n.* step-shaped channel cut along the edge or face of a length of wood etc., usu. to receive the edge or tongue of another piece. — *v.* (**-t-**) **1** join or fix with a rebate. **2** make a rebate in. [French *rab(b)at*: related to REBATE¹]

**rebel** — *n.* /**reb**-uhl/ **1** person who fights against, resists, or refuses allegiance to, the established government. **2** person or thing that resists authority or control. — *attrib. adj.* /**reb**-uhl/ **1** rebellious. **2** of rebels. **3** in rebellion. — *v.* /ruh-**bel**/ (**-ll-**) (usu. foll. by *against*) **1** act as a rebel; revolt. **2** feel or display repugnance (*my stomach rebelled against eating a live witchetty grub*). [Latin: related to RE-, *bellum* war]

**rebellion** /ruh-**bel**-yuhn/ *n.* open resistance to authority, esp. organised armed resistance to an established government. [Latin: related to REBEL]

**rebellious** /ruh-**bel**-yuhs/ *adj.* **1** tending to rebel. **2** in rebellion. **3** defying lawful authority. **4** (of a thing) unmanageable, refractory (*couldn't do anything with his hair, it was so rebellious*). □ **rebelliously** *adv.* **rebelliousness** *n.*

**rebind** /ree-**buynd**/ *v.* (*past* and *past part.* **rebound**) bind (esp. a book) again or differently.

**rebirth** /ree-**berth**, ree-/ *n.* **1** new incarnation. **2** spiritual enlightenment. **3** revival (*rebirth of learning*). □ **reborn** /ree-**bawn**/ *adj.*

**reboot** /ree-**boot**/ *v.* (often *absol.*) Computing boot up (a system) again.

**rebound** — *v.* /ruh-**bownd**/ **1** spring back after impact. **2** (foll. by *upon*) (of an action) have an adverse effect upon (the doer). — *n.* /**ree**-bownd/ act of rebounding; recoil, reaction. □ **on the rebound** while still recovering from an emotional shock, esp. rejection by a lover. [French *rebonder*: related to BOUND¹]

**rebuff** /ruh-**buf**/ — *n.* **1** rejection of one who makes advances, proffers help, shows interest, makes a request, etc. **2** snub. — *v.* give a rebuff to. [French from Italian]

**rebuild** /ree-**bild**/ *v.* (*past* and *past part.* **rebuilt**) build again or differently.

**rebuke** /ruh-**byook**/ — *v.* (**-king**) express sharp disapproval of (a person) for a fault; censure. — *n.* rebuking or being rebuked. [Anglo-French]

**rebus** /**ree**-buhs/ n. (pl. **rebuses**) representation of a word (esp. a name) by pictures etc. suggesting its parts (*a picture of a man with his chains falling off while he stands next to a cloak may well be a rebus for Fremantle; the letters IOU are a rebus for 'I owe you'*). [Latin *rebus*, ablative pl. of *res* thing]

**rebut** /ruh-**but**/ v. (**-tt-**) refute or disprove (evidence or a charge). □ **rebuttal** n. [Anglo-French *rebuter*: related to BUTT¹]

**recalcitrant** /ruh-**kal**-suh-truhnt/ adj. **1** obstinately disobedient. **2** objecting to restraint. □ **recalcitrance** n. [Latin *recalcitro* kick out, from *calx* heel]

**recall** /ruh-**kawl**/ — v. **1** summon to return. **2** recollect, remember (*I don't recall her name*). **3** bring back to memory; serve as a reminder of (*it recalls to me the days of my youth*). **4** revoke or annul (an action or decision). **5** (of a manufacturer) withdraw from sale or take back an article etc. found to be defective. — n. also /**ree**-kawl/ **1** summons to come back. **2** act of remembering. **3** ability to remember (*has good recall*). **4** possibility of recalling, esp. in the sense of revoking (*beyond recall*).

**recant** /ruh-**kant**/ v. (also *absol.*) withdraw and renounce (a former belief or statement) as erroneous or heretical. □ **recantation** /ˌree-kan-**tay**-shuhn/ n. [Latin: related to CHANT]

**recap¹** /**ree**-kap/ *colloq.* — v. (**-pp-**) recapitulate. — n. recapitulation. [abbreviation]

**recap²** — v. /ree-**kap**/ partially replace the worn tread of (a tyre). — n. /**ree**-kap/ such a tyre.

**recapitulate** /ˌree-kuh-**pich**-uh-ˌlayt/ v. (**-ting**) **1** go briefly through again; summarise. **2** go over the main points or headings of. [Latin: related to CAPITAL]

**recapitulation** /ˌree-kuh-ˌpich-uh-**lay**-shuhn/ n. **1** act of recapitulating. **2** *Mus.* part of a movement in which themes are restated. [Latin: related to RECAPITULATE]

**recapture** /ree-**kap**-chuh/ — v. (**-ring**) **1** capture again; recover by capture. **2** re-experience (a past emotion etc.). — n. act of recapturing.

**recast** /ree-**kahst**/ — v. (*past* and *past part.* **recast**) **1** cast again (a play, net, votes, etc.). **2** put into a new form; improve the arrangement of. — n. **1** act or instance of recasting. **2** new form etc. of a thing after recasting.

**recede** /ruh-**seed**/ v. (**-ding**) **1** go or shrink back or further off. **2** be left at an increasing distance by an observer's motion. **3** slope backwards (*a receding chin*). **4** decline in force or value. **5** (of a

man's hair) cease to grow at the front, sides, etc. [Latin *recedere -cess-*: related to CEDE]

**receipt** /ruh-**seet**/ — n. **1** act or instance of receiving or being received (*will pay on receipt of the goods*). **2** written acknowledgment of payment received. **3** (usu. in pl.) amount of money etc. received (*the receipts from the concert were good*). — v. place a written or printed receipt on (a bill). □ **in receipt of** having received. [Anglo-French *receite*: related to RECEIVE]

**receive** /ruh-**seev**/ v. (**-ving**) **1** take or accept (a thing offered, sent, or given). **2** acquire; be provided with (*received bad news*). **3** have conferred or inflicted on one (*received many honours; received a blow to the head*). **4** react to (news, a play, etc.) in a particular way. **5 a** stand the force or weight of (*his shield received the full impetus of the blow*). **b** bear up against; encounter with opposition (*the Bill received much hostile criticism*). **6** consent to hear (a confession or oath) or consider (a petition). **7** (also *absol.*) accept (stolen goods knowingly). **8** admit; provide accommodation for (*Canberra receives many visitors in spring*). **9** (of a receptacle) be able to hold. **10** greet or welcome, esp. in a specified manner (*received them with chilly courtesy*). **11** greet or entertain as a guest etc. **12** admit to membership (*were received into the Roman Catholic Church*). **13** convert (broadcast signals) into sound or pictures. **14** (often as **received** adj.) give credit to; accept as authoritative or true (*a received opinion*). **15** *Tennis* be the player to whom the server serves (the ball). □ **be at** (or **on**) **the receiving end** *colloq.* bear the brunt of something unpleasant. [Latin *recipio -cept-* get back again]

**received pronunciation** n. the form of educated spoken English used in southern England.

**receiver** n. **1** person or thing that receives. **2** part of a machine or instrument that receives something (esp. the part of a telephone that contains the earpiece). **3** person appointed usu. by a court to administer the property of a bankrupt person or company, or property under litigation. **4** radio or television receiving apparatus. **5** person who receives stolen goods.

**receivership** n. **1** office of receiver. **2** state of being dealt with by a receiver (esp. *in receivership*).

**recent** /**ree**-suhnt/ — adj. **1** not long past; that happened, began to exist, or existed, lately. **2** not long established;

lately begun; modern. **3 (Recent)** *Geol.* of the most recent epoch of the Quaternary period. — *n.* (**Recent**) *Geol.* this epoch. □ **recently** *adv.* [Latin *recens -ent-*]

**receptacle** /ruh-**sep**-tuh-kuhl/ *n.* **1** containing vessel, place, or space. **2** *Bot.* enlarged and modified area of the stem apex which bears the flower. [Latin: related to RECEIVE]

**reception** /ruh-**sep**-shuhn/ *n.* **1** act or instance of receiving or the process of being received. **2** way in which a person or thing is received (*cool reception*). **3** social occasion for receiving guests, esp. after a wedding. **4** place where guests or clients etc. report on arrival at a hotel, office, etc. **5 a** receiving of broadcast signals. **b** quality of this. [Latin: related to RECEIVE]

**receptionist** *n.* person employed to receive guests, clients, etc.

**reception room** *n.* room for receiving guests, clients, etc.

**receptive** /ruh-**sep**-tiv/ *adj.* able or quick to receive impressions or ideas. □ **receptively** *adv.* **receptiveness** *n.* **receptivity** /,ree-sep-**tiv**-uh-tee/ *n.* [French or medieval Latin: related to RECEIVE]

**recess** /ruh-**ses**, **ree**-ses/ — *n.* **1** space set back in a wall. **2** (often in *pl.*) remote or secret place. **3** temporary cessation from work, esp. of a parliament. **4** midmorning or midafternoon break between school classes. — *v.* **1** make a recess in. **2** place in a recess. [Latin *recessus*: related to RECEDE]

**recession** /ruh-**sesh**-uhn/ *n.* **1** temporary decline in economic activity or prosperity. **2** receding or withdrawal from a place or point. [Latin: related to RECESS]

**recessional** — *adj.* sung while the clergy and choir withdraw after a service. — *n.* recessional hymn.

**recessive** /ruh-**ses**-iv/ *adj.* **1** tending to recede. **2** (of an inherited characteristic) appearing in offspring only when not masked by a dominant characteristic inherited from one parent.

**recharge** — *v.* /ree-**chahj**/ (**-ging**) charge (a battery etc.) again or be recharged. — *n.* /**ree**-chahj/ act or instance of recharging or being recharged. □ **rechargeable** /ree-**chah**-juh-buhl/ *adj.*

**recherché** /ruh-**shair**-shay/ *adj.* **1** carefully sought out; rare or exotic. **2** farfetched. [French]

**rechristen** /ree-**kris**-uhn/ *v.* **1** christen again. **2** give a new name to.

**recidivist** /ruh-**sid**-uh-vuhst/ *n.* person who relapses into crime. □ **recidivism** *n.*

[Latin *recidivus* falling back: related to RECEDE]

**recipe** /**res**-uh-pee/ *n.* **1** statement of the ingredients and procedure required for preparing a cooked dish. **2** (foll. by *for*) certain means to (an outcome) (*recipe for disaster*). [2nd sing. imperative of Latin *recipio* RECEIVE]

**recipient** /ruh-**sip**-ee-uhnt/ *n.* person who receives something. [Italian or Latin: related to RECEIVE]

**reciprocal** /ruh-**sip**-ruh-kuhl/ — *adj.* **1** in return (*a reciprocal greeting*). **2** mutual (*their feelings are reciprocal*). **3** *Gram.* (of a pronoun) expressing mutual relation (as in *each other*). — *n. Math.* expression or function so related to another that their product is unity (½ *is the reciprocal of* 2). □ **reciprocally** *adv.* [Latin *reciprocus* moving to and fro]

**reciprocate** /ruh-**sip**-ruh-,kayt/ *v.* (**-ting**) **1** requite (affection etc.). **2** (foll. by *with*) give in return (*reciprocated with an invitation to lunch*). **3** give and receive mutually; interchange. **4** (of a part of a machine) move backwards and forwards. □ **reciprocation** /-**kay**-shuhn/ *n.*

**reciprocity** /,res-uh-**pros**-uh-tee/ *n.* **1** condition of being reciprocal. **2** mutual action. **3** give and take, esp. the interchange of privileges between countries and organisations.

**recital** /ruh-**suy**-tuhl/ *n.* **1** act or instance of reciting or being recited. **2** concert of classical music given by a soloist or small group. **3** (foll. by *of*) detailed account of (connected things or facts); narrative.

**recitation** /,res-uh-**tay**-shuhn/ *n.* **1** act or instance of reciting. **2** thing recited.

**recitative** /,res-uh-tuh-**teev**/ *n.* musical declamation in the narrative and dialogue parts of opera and oratorio. [Italian *recitativo*: related to RECITE]

**recite** /ruh-**suyt**/ *v.* (**-ting**) **1** repeat aloud or declaim (a poem or passage) from memory. **2** give a recitation. **3** enumerate. [Latin *recito* read out]

**reckless** /**rek**-luhs/ *adj.* disregarding the consequences or danger etc.; rash. □ **recklessly** *adv.* **recklessness** *n.* [Old English *reck* concern oneself]

**reckon** /**rek**-uhn/ *v.* **1** (often foll. by *that*) be of the considered opinion; think. **2** consider or regard (*reckoned to be the best*). **3** count or compute by calculation. **4** (foll. by *in*) count in or include in computation. **5** make calculations; add up an account or sum. **6** (foll. by *on*) rely on, count on, or base plans on. **7** (foll. by *with* or *without*) take (or fail to take) into account. [Old English]

**reckoning** n. **1** act or instance of counting or calculating. **2** consideration or opinion (*on his reckoning, Australia should have won the test*). **3** settlement of an account.

**reclaim** /ree-**klaym**/ v. **1** seek the return of (one's property, rights, etc.). **2** bring (land) under cultivation, esp. from being under water. **3** win back or away from vice, error, or a waste condition. □ **reclaimable** adj. **reclamation** /,rek-luh-**may**-shuhn/ n. [Latin *reclamare* cry out against]

**reclassify** /ree-**klas**-uh-,fuy/ v. (**-ies**, **-ied**) classify again or differently. □ **reclassification** /-fuh-**kay**-shuhn/ n.

**recline** /ruh-**kluyn**/ v. (**-ning**) assume or be in a horizontal or relaxed leaning position. [Latin *reclino*]

**recluse** /ruh-**kloos**/ n. person given to or living in seclusion or isolation; hermit. □ **reclusive** adj. [Latin *recludo* -*clus*- shut away]

**recognisance** /ruh-**kog**-nuh-zuhns/ n. (also **recognizance**) **1** bond by which a person undertakes before a court or magistrate to observe some condition, e.g. to appear when summoned. **2** sum pledged as surety for this. [French: related to RE-]

**recognise** /**rek**-uhg-,nuyz/ v. (also **-ize**) (**-sing** or **-zing**) **1** identify as already known. **2** realise or discover the nature of. **3** (foll. by *that*) realise or admit. **4** acknowledge the existence, validity, character, or claims of. **5** show appreciation of; reward (*the award recognises her talents*). **6** (foll. by *as*, *for*) treat. □ **recognisable** adj. [Latin *recognosco*]

**recognition** /,rek-uhg-**nish**-uhn/ n. act or instance of recognising or being recognised. [Latin: related to RECOGNISE]

**recoil** /ruh-**koil**/ — v. **1** suddenly move or spring back in fear, horror, or disgust. **2** shrink mentally in this way. **3** rebound after an impact. **4** (foll. by *on*, *upon*) have an adverse reactive effect on (the originator). **5** (of a gun) be driven backwards by its discharge. — n. also /**ree**-koil/ act or sensation of recoiling. [French *reculer* from Latin *culus* buttocks]

**recollect** /,rek-uh-**lekt**/ v. **1** remember. **2** succeed in remembering; call to mind. [Latin *recolligo*: related to COLLECT[1]]

**recollection** /,rek-uh-**lek**-shuhn/ n. **1** act or power of recollecting. **2** thing recollected. **3 a** person's memory. **b** time over which memory extends (*happened within my recollection*). [French or medieval Latin: related to RECOLLECT]

**recommence** /,ree-kuh-**mens**/ v. (**-cing**) begin again. □ **recommencement** n.

**recommend** /,rek-uh-**mend**/ v. **1** suggest as fit for some purpose or use. **2** advise as a course of action etc. **3** (of qualities, conduct, etc.) make acceptable or desirable (*the new tax has nothing to recommend it*). **4** (foll. by *to*) commend or entrust (to a person or a person's care). □ **recommendation** /-**day**-shuhn/ n. [medieval Latin: related to RE-]

**recompense** /**rek**-uhm-,pens/ — v. (**-sing**) **1** make amends to (a person) or for (a loss etc.). **2** requite; reward or punish (a person or action). — n. **1** reward, requital. **2** retribution; satisfaction given for an injury. [Latin: related to COMPENSATE]

**reconcile** /**rek**-uhn-,suyl/ v. (**-ling**) **1** make friendly again after an estrangement. **2** (usu. in *refl.* or *passive*; foll. by *to*) make acquiescent or contentedly submissive to (something disagreeable) (*we must reconcile ourselves to growing old*). **3** settle (a quarrel etc.). **4 a** harmonise, make compatible. **b** show the compatibility of by argument or in practice (*I cannot reconcile your views with the facts*). □ **reconcilable** adj. **reconciliation** /-,sil-ee-ay-shuhn/ n. [Latin: related to CONCILIATE]

**recondite** /**rek**-uhn-,duyt, ruh-**kon**-/ adj. **1** (of a subject or knowledge) abstruse, out of the way, little known. **2** (of an author or style) dealing in abstruse knowledge or allusions, obscure. [Latin *recondo* -*dit*- put away]

**recondition** /,ree-kuhn-**dish**-uhn/ v. overhaul, renovate, make usable again.

**reconnaissance** /ruh-**kon**-uh-suhns/ n. **1** survey of a region, esp. to locate an enemy or ascertain strategic features. **2** preliminary survey. [French: related to RECONNOITRE]

**reconnoitre** /,rek-uh-**noi**-tuh/ v. (**-ring**) make a reconnaissance (of). [French: related to RECOGNISE]

**reconsider** /,ree-kuhn-**sid**-uh/ v. consider again, esp. for a possible change of decision. □ **reconsideration** /-**ray**-shuhn/ n.

**reconstitute** /ree-**kon**-stuh-,tyoot/ v. (**-ting**) **1** reconstruct. **2** reorganise. **3** restore the previous constitution of (dried food etc.) by adding water. □ **reconstitution** /-**tyoo**-shuhn/ n.

**reconstruct** /,ree-kuhn-**strukt**/ v. **1** build again. **2 a** form an impression of (past events) by assembling the evidence for them. **b** re-enact (a crime). **3** reorganise. □ **reconstruction** n.

**reconvene** /,ree-kuhn-**veen**/ v. (**-ning**) convene again, esp. after a pause in proceedings.

**record** — n. /**rek**-awd/ **1 a** piece of evidence or information constituting an (esp. official) account of something that has occurred, been said, etc. **b** document etc. preserving this. **2** state of being set down or preserved in writing etc. **3** disc or other device carrying recorded sound, esp. for reproduction by record-player, stereo, etc. **4** official report of the proceedings and judgment in a court of justice. **5 a** facts known about a person's past (*has a fine record of service*). **b** list of a person's previous criminal convictions. **6** (often *attrib.*) best performance (esp. in sport) or most remarkable event of its kind on record (*record month for rain*). **7** object serving as a memorial; portrait. — v. /ruh-**kawd**/ **1** set down in writing or some other permanent form for later reference. **2** convert (sound, a broadcast, etc.) into permanent form for later reproduction. **3** register (a vote, protest, etc.). □ **for the record** as an official statement etc. **go on record** state one's opinion openly, so that it is recorded. **have a record** have a recorded criminal conviction or convictions. **off the record** unofficially, confidentially. **on record** officially recorded; publicly known. **put** (or **set**) **the record straight** correct a misapprehension. [Latin *cor cordis* heart]

**recorder** /ruh-**kaw**-duh/ n. **1** apparatus for recording, esp. a video or tape recorder. **2** wooden or plastic wind instrument with holes covered by the fingers. **3** keeper of records.

**recording** n. **1** process by which audio or video signals are recorded for later reproduction. **2** material or a programme recorded.

**recordist** n. person who records sound.

**record-player** n. apparatus for reproducing sound from gramophone records.

**recount** /ruh-**kownt**/ v. **1** narrate. **2** tell in detail. [Anglo-French *reconter*: related to RE-, COUNT¹]

**re-count** — v. /ree-**kownt**/ count again. — n. /**ree**-kownt/ act or instance of re-counting, esp. of votes in an election.

**recoup** /ruh-**koop**/ v. **1** recover or regain (a loss). **2** compensate or reimburse for a loss. □ **recoupment** n. [French *recouper* cut back]

**recourse** /ruh-**kaws**/ n. **1** resort to a possible source of help. **2** person or thing resorted to. □ **have recourse to** turn to (a person or thing) for help. [Latin: related to COURSE]

**recover** /ruh-**kuv**-uh/ v. **1** regain possession, use, or control of. **2** return to health, consciousness, or to a normal state or position (*I have recovered from my illness*; *the country has never recovered from the war*). **3** obtain or secure by legal process. **4** retrieve or make up for (a loss, setback, etc.). **5** *refl.* regain composure, consciousness, or control of one's limbs. **6** retrieve (reusable substances) from waste. □ **recoverable** adj. [Latin: related to RECUPERATE]

**re-cover** /ree-**kuv**-uh/ v. **1** cover again. **2** provide (a chair etc.) with a new cover.

**recovery** n. (*pl.* **-ies**) act or instance of recovering or the process of being recovered. [Anglo-French *recoverie*: related to RECOVER]

**recreant** /**rek**-ree-uhnt/ *literary* — adj. craven, cowardly. — n. coward. [medieval Latin: related to CREED]

**recreate** /ˌree-kree-**ayt**/ v. (**-ting**) create over again, reproduce. □ **re-creation** n.

**recreation** /ˌrek-ree-**ay**-shuhn/ n. **1** process or means of refreshing or entertaining oneself. **2** pleasurable activity. □ **recreational** adj. [Latin: related to CREATE]

**recriminate** /ruh-**krim**-uh-ˌnayt/ v. (**-ting**) make mutual or counter accusations. □ **recrimination** /-**nay**-shuhn/ n. **recriminatory** /-nuh-tree/ adj. [medieval Latin: related to CRIME]

**recross** /ree-**kros**/ v. cross again.

**recrudesce** /ˌree-kroo-**des**/ v. (**-cing**) *formal* (of a disease or difficulty etc.) break out again. □ **recrudescence** n. **recrudescent** adj. [Latin: related to CRUDE]

**recruit** /ruh-**kroot**/ — n. **1** newly enlisted serviceman or servicewoman. **2** new member of a society etc. **3** beginner. — v. **1** enlist (a person) as a recruit. **2** form (an army etc.) by enlisting recruits. **3** get or seek recruits. □ **recruitment** n. [French dial. *recrute*: related to CREW¹]

**rectal** /**rek**-tuhl/ adj. of or by means of the rectum.

**rectangle** /**rek**-ˌtang-guhl/ n. plane figure with four straight sides and four right angles, esp. other than a square. □ **rectangular** /rek-**tang**-gyuh-luh/ adj. [French or medieval Latin]

**rectify** /**rek**-tuh-ˌfuy/ v. (**-ies**, **-ied**) **1** adjust or make right. **2** purify or refine, esp. by repeated distillation. **3** convert (alternating current) to direct current. □ **rectifiable** adj. **rectification** /-fuh-**kay**-shuhn/ n. **rectifier** n. [Latin *rectus* straight, right]

**rectilinear** /ˌrek-tuh-**lin**-ee-uh/ adj. **1** bounded or characterised by straight lines. **2** in or forming a straight line. [Latin: related to RECTIFY]

**rectitude** /**rek**-tuh-ˌtyood/ n. **1** moral uprightness, righteousness. **2** correctness. [Latin *rectus* right]

**recto** /**rek**-toh/ n. (pl. **-s**) **1** right-hand page of an open book. **2** front of a printed leaf (opp. VERSO). [Latin, = on the right]

**rector** /**rek**-tuh/ n. **1** (in the Anglican Church) clergyman in charge of a parish. **2** RC Ch. priest in charge of a church or religious institution. **3** head of some universities and colleges. □ **rectorship** n. [Latin rego rect- rule]

**rectory** n. (pl. **-ies**) rector's house. [French or medieval Latin: related to RECTOR]

**rectum** /**rek**-tuhm/ n. (pl. **-s**) final section of the large intestine, terminating at the anus. [Latin, = straight]

**recumbent** /ruh-**kum**-buhnt/ adj. lying down; reclining. [Latin cumbo lie]

**recuperate** /ree-**koo**-puh-,rayt, ruh-/ v. (**-ting**) **1** recover from illness, exhaustion, loss, etc. **2** regain (health, a loss, etc.). □ **recuperation** /-**ray**-shuhn/ n. **recuperative** /-ruh-tiv/ adj. [Latin recupero]

**recur** /ree-**ker**, ruh-/ v. (**-rr-**) **1** occur again; be repeated. **2** (foll. by to) go back in thought or speech. **3** (as **recurring** adj.) (of a decimal fraction) with the same figure(s) repeated indefinitely (1.66 recurring). [Latin curro run]

**recurrent** /ree-**ku**-ruhnt, ruh-/ adj. recurring; happening repeatedly. □ **recurrence** n.

**recusant** /**rek**-yuh-zuhnt/ — n. person who refuses submission to an authority or compliance with a regulation. — adj. of or being a recusant. □ **recusancy** n. [Latin recuso refuse]

**recycle** /ree-**suy**-kuhl/ v. (**-ling**) convert (waste) to reusable material. □ **recyclable** adj.

**red** — adj. (**redder, reddest**) **1** of the colour ranging from that of blood to deep pink or orange. **2** flushed in the face with shame, anger, etc. **3** (of the eyes) bloodshot or red-rimmed. **4** (of the hair) reddish-brown, tawny. **5** having to do with bloodshed, burning, violence, or revolution. **6** colloq. communist or socialist. — n. **1** red colour or pigment. **2** red clothes or material (dressed in red). **3** red ball in snooker. **4** red wine. **5** colloq. communist or socialist. □ **in the red** in debt or deficit. □ **reddish** adj. **redness** n. [Old English]

**red-and-green kangaroo paw** see KANGAROO PAW.

**red ant** n. = MEAT-ANT.

**red ash** n. **1** any of several Australian trees yielding a reddish timber. **2** the wood of these trees.

**red-back** n. (in full **redbacked spider**) small black spider, the female having a pea-sized body with a red abdominal band and an extremely toxic bite.

**red bean** n. **1** any of several Australian trees yielding a deep red timber. **2** the wood of these trees.

**red-bellied black snake** n. highly venomous and dangerous eastern Australian snake, having a red belly, black scales, and a tendency to rear and puff up its neck in the manner of its relative the cobra.

**red-blooded** adj. virile, vigorous.

**red bloodwood** n. **1** eucalypt of southeastern mainland Australia yielding a durable red timber. **2** its wood.

**red box** n. **1** any of several eucalypts yielding a red timber. **2** the wood of these trees.

**red bream** /brim/ n. young snapper.

**redbreast** n. colloq. = ROBIN REDBREAST.

**red card** n. Soccer card shown by the referee to a player being sent off the field.

**red carpet** n. privileged treatment of an eminent visitor.

**red cedar** n. **1** large deciduous Australian rainforest tree, valued for its deep red timber, and now rare because of extensive, indiscriminate logging. **2** its wood.

**red cell** n. (also **red corpuscle**) erythrocyte.

**red centre** n. (prec. by the) (also **the Red Centre**) central Australia (so called because of the reddish colour of iron oxide in the soil and rocks).

**Red Crescent** n. equivalent of the Red Cross in Muslim countries.

**Red Cross** n. international organisation bringing relief to victims of war or disaster.

**redcurrant** n. **1** small red edible berry. **2** shrub bearing this.

**redden** v. **1** make or become red. **2** blush.

**redecorate** /ree-**dek**-uh-,rayt/ v. (**-ting**) decorate (a room etc.) again or differently. □ **redecoration** /-**ray**-shuhn/ n.

**redeem** /ruh-**deem**/ v. **1** recover by expenditure of effort or by a stipulated payment. **2** make a single payment to cancel (a loan etc.). **3** convert (tokens or bonds etc.) into goods or cash. **4** (of Christ) deliver from sin and damnation. **5** make up for; be a compensating factor in (has one redeeming feature). **6** (foll. by from) save from (a defect). **7** refl. save (oneself) from blame. **8** purchase the freedom of (a person). **9** save (a person's life) by ransom. **10** save or rescue or reclaim. **11** fulfil (a promise). □ **redeemable** adj. [Latin emo buy]

**redeemer** n. **1** person who redeems. **2** (**the Redeemer**) Christ.

**redefine** /ree-duh-**fuyn**/ v. (**-ning**) define again or differently. □ **redefinition** /-def-uh-**nish**-uhn/ n.

**red emperor** *n.* red and white marine fish of northern Australia.

**redemption** /ruh-**demp**-shuhn/ *n.* **1** act or instance of redeeming or the process of being redeemed. **2** thing that redeems. **3** mankind's deliverance from sin and damnation. [Latin: related to REDEEM]

**redeploy** /,ree-duh-**ploi**/ *v.* send (troops, workers, etc.) to a new place or task. □ **redeployment** *n.*

**redevelop** /,ree-duh-**vel**-uhp/ *v.* replan or rebuild (esp. an urban area). □ **redevelopment** *n.*

**redfin** *n.* European freshwater food-fish, naturalised in streams etc. of southern Australia, having orange to bright red fins.

**redfish** *n.* any of several Australian fish, esp. the nannygai.

**red flag** *n.* **1** symbol of socialist revolution. **2** warning of danger.

**red-flowering gum** *n.* see FLOWERING GUM.

**red gum** *n.* **1** any of many Australian eucalypts yielding a ruby red timber, esp. the widespread river red gum. **2** the wood of these trees.

**red hand** *n.* impression of a human hand made with red ochre on rock, a frequent motif in Aboriginal painting.

**red-handed** *adv.* in the act of committing a crime, doing wrong, etc.

**red hat** *n.* **1** cardinal's hat. **2** symbol of a cardinal's office (*was elevated to the red hat*).

**red heart** *n.* **1** (prec. by *the*) (also **the Red Heart**) = RED CENTRE. **2 a** Queensland rainforest tree yielding a hard, durable timber. **b** its wood. **3 a** eucalypt of south-western WA with creamy flowers. **b** its wood.

**red herring** *n.* misleading clue; distraction.

**red-hot** *adj.* **1** heated until red. **2** *colloq.* highly exciting. **3** *colloq.* (of news) fresh; completely new. **4** intensely excited. **5** (of prices) extremely low (*red-hot specials*). **6** (of anger) violent, quick to flare up (*red-hot temper*). **7** *colloq.* (of a person) performing at the peak of ability (*that bowler was really red-hot today*).

**red-hot favourite** *n.* (of a horse, athlete, team, etc.) highly favoured to win (a race etc.).

**rediffusion** /,ree-duh-**fyoo**-*zh*uhn/ *n.* relaying of broadcast programmes, esp. by cable from a central receiver.

**redirect** /,ree-duy-**rekt**, -duh-**rekt**/ *v.* **1** direct again; send in a different direction. **2** readdress (a letter etc.).

**red ironbark** *n.* **1** any of several iron-

barks (eucalypts) having bark which is red under the surface, and yielding a durable red timber, esp. MUGGA. **2** the wood of these trees.

**redistribute** /,ree-duh-**strib**-yoot/ *v.* (**-ting**) **1** distribute again or differently. **2** change electoral boundaries in order to even out the number of voters in all the electorates. □ **redistribution** /,ree-dis-truh-**byoo**-shuhn/ *n.*

**red kangaroo** *n.* (also, in WA, **marloo**) large kangaroo widely distributed in drier inland Australia, having red to blue-grey fur above and white below.

**red lead** *n.* red form of lead oxide used as a pigment.

**red-letter day** *n.* day that is pleasantly noteworthy or memorable (orig. a festival marked in red on the calendar).

**red light** *n.* **1** signal to stop on a road, railway, etc. **2** warning.

**red-light camera** *n.* device to photograph the numberplate of a car which fails to stop at a red light.

**red meat** *n.* meat that is red when raw (e.g. beef or lamb).

**red meat-ant** *n.* = MEAT ANT.

**red mulga** *n.* = MINNERICHI.

**redneck** *n.* often *derog.* **1** *US* politically conservative working-class White in the southern US. **2** any analogous conservative elsewhere. □ **rednecked** *adj.*

**red ned** *n.* *colloq.* red wine of inferior quality.

**redo** /ree-**doo**/ *v.* (**redoing**; *3rd sing. present* **redoes**; *past* **redid**; *past part.* **redone**) **1** do again. **2** redecorate.

**redolent** /**red**-uh-luhnt/ *adj.* **1** (foll. by *of*) strongly reminiscent, suggestive, or smelling (*Australian homesteads redolent of the past; a massage-oil redolent of wattle and boronia*). **2** fragrant. □ **redolence** *n.* [Latin *oleo* smell]

**redouble** /ree-**dub**-uhl/ — *v.* (**-ling**) **1** make or grow greater or more intense or numerous. **2** *Bridge* double again a bid already doubled by an opponent. — *n.* *Bridge* redoubling of a bid.

**redoubtable** /ruh-**dow**-tuh-buhl/ *adj.* formidable.

**redound** /ree-**downd**, ruh-/ *v.* **1** (foll. by *to*) make a great contribution to (one's credit or advantage etc.). **2** (foll. by *upon*, *on*) come back or recoil upon. [Latin *unda* wave]

**red pepper** *n.* **1** cayenne pepper. **2** ripe red fruit of the capsicum plant.

**redraft** /ree-**drahft**/ *v.* draft (a text) again, usu. differently.

**red rag** *n.* something that excites a person's rage.

**red-ragger** n. colloq. a communist; socialist. [alludes to the red flag as a symbol of revolution]

**redraw** /ree-**draw**/ v. (past **redrew**; past part. **redrawn**) draw again or differently.

**redress** /ruh-**dres**/ — v. **1** remedy or rectify (a wrong or grievance etc.). **2** readjust, set straight again. — n. **1** reparation for a wrong. **2** (foll. by of) redressing (a grievance etc.). □ **redress the balance** restore equality. [French: related to DRESS]

**red river gum** n. = RED GUM.

**red shift** n. displacement of the spectrum to longer wavelengths in the light coming from receding galaxies etc.

**red steer** n. colloq. a destructive fire, esp. a bushfire.

**red stringybark** n. **1** any of several eucalypts of south-eastern mainland Australia yielding durable timber darker in colour than that of the white stringybark. **2** the wood of these trees.

**red tape** n. excessive bureaucracy or formality, esp. in public business.

**reduce** /ruh-**dyoos**/ v. (**-cing**) **1** make or become smaller or less. **2** (foll. by to) bring by force or necessity (to some undesirable state or action) (reduced them to tears; reduced to begging). **3** convert to another (esp. simpler) form (reduced it to a powder). **4** convert (a fraction) to the form with the lowest terms. **5** (foll. by to) bring, simplify, or adapt by classification or analysis (the dispute may be reduced to three issues). **6** make lower in status or rank. **7** lower the price of. **8** lessen one's weight or size. **9** weaken (is in a very reduced state). **10** subdue, bring back to obedience. **11** Chem. **a** (cause to) combine with hydrogen. **b** (cause to) undergo addition of electrons. □ **reducible** adj. [Latin duco bring]

**reduced circumstances** n.pl. poverty after relative prosperity.

**reductio ad absurdum** /ruh-,duk-tee-oh ad ab-**zer**-duhm/ n. proof of the falsity of a premise by showing that its logical consequence is absurd. [Latin, = reduction to the absurd]

**reduction** /ruh-**duk**-shuhn/ n. **1** act or instance of reducing or the process of being reduced. **2** amount by which prices etc. are reduced. **3** smaller copy of a picture etc. □ **reductive** adj.

**redundant** /ruh-**dun**-duhnt/ adj. **1** superfluous. **2** that can be omitted without any loss of significance. **3** (of a person) no longer needed at work and therefore unemployed. □ **redundancy** n. (pl. **-ies**). [Latin: related to REDOUND]

**reduplicate** /ruh-**dyoo**-pluh-,kayt/ v. (**-ting**) **1** make double. **2** repeat. **3** repeat (a letter or syllable or word) exactly or with a slight change (e.g. hurly-burly, see-saw). □ **reduplication** /-**kay**-shuhn/ n.

**re-echo** /ree-**ek**-oh/ v. (**-es, -ed**) echo repeatedly; resound.

**reed** n. **1 a** water or marsh plant with a firm stem. **b** tall straight stalk of this. **2 a** strip of cane etc. vibrating to produce the sound in some wind instruments. **b** (esp. in pl.) such an instrument. [Old English]

**re-educate** /ree-**ej**-uh-,kayt/ v. (**-ting**) educate again, esp. to change a person's views. □ **re-education** /-**kay**-shuhn/ n.

**reed warbler** n. widespread, predominantly brown Australian bird of reedy wetlands, having a highly melodious voice.

**reedy** adj. (**-ier, -iest**) **1** full of reeds. **2** like a reed. **3** (of a voice) like a reed instrument in tone. □ **reediness** n.

**reef**[1] n. **1** ridge of rock or coral etc. at or near the surface of the sea. **2 a** lode of ore. **b** bedrock surrounding this. [Old Norse rif]

**reef**[2] — n. each of several strips across a sail, for taking it in or rolling it up to reduce its surface area in a high wind. — v. take in a reef or reefs of (a sail). [Dutch from Old Norse]

**reefer** n. colloq. marijuana cigarette. [from REEF[2]]

**reefer jacket** n. **1** thick double-breasted jacket. **2** sportscoat usually with gold or silver buttons. [from REEF[2]]

**reef knot** n. symmetrical double knot. [from REEF[2]]

**reek** — v. (often foll. by of) **1** smell strongly and unpleasantly. **2** have unpleasant or suspicious associations (reeks of corruption). — n. **1** foul or stale smell. **2** vapour, visible exhalation. [Old English]

**reel** — n. **1** cylindrical device on which thread, silk, yarn, paper, film, wire, etc., are wound. **2** quantity of thread etc. wound on a reel. **3** device for winding and unwinding a line as required, esp. in fishing and surf-lifesaving. **4** revolving part in various machines. **5 a** lively folk or Scottish dance. **b** music for this. — v. **1** wind (thread, fishing-line, etc.) on a reel. **2** (foll. by in, up) draw (fish etc.) in or up with a reel. **3** stand, walk, or run unsteadily. **4** be shaken mentally or physically. **5** rock from side to side, or swing violently. □ **reel off** say, recite, or write very rapidly and without apparent effort. [Old English]

**re-elect** /,ree-uh-**lekt**/ v. elect again, esp. to a further term of office. □ **re-election** /-uh-**lek**-shuhn/ n.

**reelman** *n.* member of a surf-lifesaving team who controls the reel.

**re-embark** /ˌree-em-**bahk**/ *v.* go or put on board ship again.

**re-emerge** /ˌree-uh-**merj**/ *v.* (**-ging**) emerge again; come back out. □ **re-emergence** *n.*

**re-emphasise** /ree-em-fuh-ˌsuyz/ *v.* (also **-ize**) (**-sing** or **-zing**) place renewed emphasis on.

**re-enact** /ree-uh-**nakt**/ *v.* act out (a past event). □ re-enactment *n.*

**re-enter** /ree-en-tuh/ *v.* enter again; go back in.

**re-entrant** /ree-en-truhnt/ *adj.* (of an angle) pointing inwards, reflex.

**re-entry** /ree-en-tree/ *n.* (*pl.* **-ies**) act of entering again, esp. (of a spacecraft, missile, etc.) re-entering the earth's atmosphere.

**re-equip** /ˌree-uh-**kwip**/ *v.* (**-pp-**) provide or be provided with new equipment.

**reeve¹** *n. Brit. hist.* **1** chief magistrate of a town or district. **2** official supervising a landowner's estate. [Old English]

**reeve²** *v.* (past **rove** or **reeved**) *Naut.* **1** (usu. foll. by *through*) thread (a rope or rod etc.) through a ring or other aperture. **2** fasten (a rope or block) in this way. [probably Dutch *reven*]

**re-examine** /ˌree-uhg-**zam**-uhn/ *v.* (**-ning**) examine again or further. □ **re-examination** /**-nay**-shuhn/ *n.*

**ref** *n. colloq.* referee in sports. [abbreviation]

**reface** /ree-**fays**/ *v.* (**-cing**) put a new facing on (a building).

**refashion** /ree-**fash**-uhn/ *v.* fashion again or differently.

**refectory** /ruh-**fek**-tuh-ree, -tree/ *n.* (*pl.* **-ies**) dining-room, esp. in a monastery or college. [Latin *reficio* renew]

**refer** /ruh-**fer**/ *v.* (**-rr-**) (usu. foll. by *to*) **1** make an appeal or have recourse to (some authority or source of information) (*referred to his notes*). **2** send on or direct (a person, or a question for decision) (*referred him to her previous answer*; *the matter was referred to arbitration*). **3** (of a person speaking) make an allusion or direct the hearer's or reader's attention (*did not refer to our problems*). **4** (of a statement etc.) be relevant; relate (*these figures refer to last year*). **5** send (a person) to a medical specialist etc. **6** (foll. by *back to*) **a** return (a document etc.) to its sender for clarification. **b** send (a proposal etc.) back to (a lower body, court, etc.). □ **referable** /ruh-**fer**-ruh-buhl/ *adj.* [Latin *refero relat-* carry back]

**referee** /ˌref-uh-**ree**/ — *n.* **1** umpire, esp. in soccer or boxing. **2** person referred to for a decision in a dispute etc. **3** person willing to testify to the character of an applicant for employment etc. — *v.* (**-rees**, **-reed**) act as referee (for).

**reference** /**ref**-uh-ruhns, **ref**-ruhns/ *n.* **1** referring of a matter for decision or settlement or consideration to some authority. **2** scope given to this authority. **3** (foll. by *to*) **a** relation, respect, or correspondence (*success seems to have little reference to merit*). **b** allusion. **c** direction to a book etc. (or a passage in it) where information may be found. **d** book or passage so cited. **4** act of looking up a passage etc., or referring to a book or person for information. **5 a** written testimonial supporting an applicant for employment etc. **b** person giving this. □ **terms of reference** points referred to an individual or body of persons for decision or report; the scope of an inquiry etc. **with** (or **in**) **reference to** regarding; as regards; about. □ **referential** /-ren-shuhl/ *adj.*

**reference book** *n.* book intended to be consulted for occasional information rather than to be read continuously.

**referendum** /ˌref-uh-**ren**-duhm/ *n.* (*pl.* **-s** or **-da**) vote on an important political or social question open to all the electors of a country, municipality, etc. [Latin: related to REFER]

**referent** *n.* idea or thing that a word etc. symbolises. [Latin]

**referral** /ruh-**fer**-ruhl/ *n.* referring of a person to a medical specialist etc.

**referred pain** *n.* pain felt in a part of the body other than its actual source.

**reffo** /**ref**-oh/ *n. hist. colloq.* refugee from Europe; any migrant to Australia other than from Britain. [abbreviation: REF(UGEE) + -o]

**refill** — *v.* /ree-**fil**/ fill again. — *n.* /**ree**-fil/ **1** thing that refills, esp. another drink. **2** act of refilling. □ **refillable** /-**fil**-uh-buhl/ *adj.*

**refine** /ruh-**fuyn**/ *v.* (**-ning**) **1** free from impurities or defects. **2** make or become more polished, elegant, or cultured.

**refined** *adj.* **1** polished, elegant, cultured. **2** freed from impurities (*refined sugar*).

**refinement** *n.* **1** act of refining or the process of being refined. **2** fineness of feeling or taste. **3** polish or elegance in behaviour or manner. **4** added development or improvement (*car with several refinements*). **5** subtle reasoning; fine distinction.

**refiner** *n.* person or firm whose business is to refine crude oil, metal, sugar, etc.

**refinery** *n.* (*pl.* **-ies**) place where oil, sugar, etc. is refined.

**refit** — v. /ree-**fit**/ (**-tt-**) (esp. of a ship) make or become serviceable again by repairs, renewals, etc. — n. /**ree**-fit/ refitting.

**reflate** /ree-**flayt**/ v. (**-ting**) cause reflation of (a currency or economy etc.). [from RE-, after *inflate*, *deflate*]

**reflation** /ree-**flay**-shuhn/ n. inflation of a financial system to restore its previous condition after deflation. □ **reflationary** adj. [from RE-, after *inflation*, *deflation*]

**reflect** /ruh-**flekt**/ v. **1** (of a surface or body) throw back (heat, light, sound, etc.). **2** (of a mirror) show an image of; reproduce to the eye or mind. **3** correspond in appearance or effect (*their behaviour reflects their upbringing*). **4 a** (of an action, result, etc.) show or bring (credit, discredit, etc.). **b** (*absol.*; usu. foll. by *on*, *upon*) bring discredit on (*your behaviour will reflect on the entire team*). **5 a** (often foll. by *on*, *upon*) meditate on; think about. **b** (foll. by *that*, *how*, etc.) consider; remind oneself. [Latin *flecto flex-* bend]

**reflection** /ruh-**flek**-shuhn/ n. (also **reflexion**) **1** act or instance of reflecting or the process of being reflected. **2 a** reflected light, heat, or colour. **b** reflected image. **3** reconsideration (*on reflection*). **4** (often foll. by *on*) discredit or thing bringing discredit (*that remark's a reflection on my morals*). **5** (often foll. by *on*, *upon*) **a** idea arising in the mind (*paralysed by morbid reflections on death*). **b** comment (*offered some reflections on Shakespeare*).

**reflective** adj. **1** (of a surface etc.) reflecting. **2** (of mental faculties) concerned in reflection or thought. **3** (of a person or mood etc.) thoughtful; given to meditation. □ **reflectively** adv. **reflectiveness** n.

**reflector** n. **1** piece of glass or metal etc. for reflecting light in a required direction, e.g. a red one on the back of a motor vehicle or bicycle. **2 a** telescope etc. using a mirror to produce images. **b** the mirror itself.

**reflex** /**ree**-fleks/ — adj. **1 a** (of an action) independent of the will, as an automatic response to the stimulation of a nerve (e.g. a sneeze). **b** (of an action or response) mechanical and unthinking. **2** (of an angle) exceeding 180°. — n. **1** reflex action. **2** sign or secondary manifestation (*law is a reflex of public opinion*). **3** reflected light or image. [Latin: related to REFLECT]

**reflexion** var. of REFLECTION.

**reflexive** /ruh-**flek**-siv/ *Gram.* — adj. **1** (of a word or form, esp. of a pronoun)

referring back to the subject of a sentence (e.g. *myself*). **2** (of a verb) having a reflexive pronoun as its object (as in *to wash oneself*). — n. reflexive word or form, esp. a pronoun (e.g. *myself*).

**reflexology** /ˌree-flek-**sol**-uh-jee/ n. massage through points on the feet, hands, and head, to relieve tension and treat illness. □ **reflexologist** n.

**refloat** /ree-**floht**/ v. set (a stranded ship) afloat again.

**refocus** /ree-**foh**-kuhs/ v. (**-s-** or **-ss-**) focus again or anew.

**reforest** /ree-fo-ruhst/ v. replant (former forest land) with trees. □ **reforestation** /-**stay**-shuhn/ n.

**reform** /ruh-**fawm**/ — v. **1** make or become better by the removal of faults and errors. **2** abolish or cure (an abuse or malpractice). — n. **1** removal of faults or abuses, esp. moral, political, or social. **2** improvement made or suggested. □ **reformative** adj.

**reformation** /ˌref-uh-**may**-shuhn/ n. **1** act of reforming or process of being reformed, esp. a radical change in political, religious, or social affairs. **2** (**the Reformation**) *hist.* 16th-c. movement for the reform of the Roman Catholic Church ending in the establishment of the Reformed or Protestant Churches.

**reformatory** /ruh-**faw**-muh-tuh-ree, -tree/ — n. (pl. **-ies**) **1** *hist.* institution for the reform of young offenders. **2** = REFORM SCHOOL. — adj. producing reform.

**reformer** n. person who advocates or brings about (esp. political or social) reform.

**reformism** /ruh-**faw**-miz-uhm/ n. policy of reform rather than abolition or revolution. □ **reformist** n. & adj.

**reform school** n. institution for the reform of young offenders.

**refract** /ree-**frakt**, ruh-/ v. (of water, air, glass, etc.) deflect (a ray of light etc.) at a certain angle when it enters obliquely from another medium. □ **refraction** n.

**refractive** adj. [Latin *refringo -fract-* break open]

**refractor** n. **1** refracting medium or lens. **2** telescope using a lens to produce an image.

**refractory** /ruh-**frak**-tuh-ree/ adj. **1** stubborn, unmanageable, rebellious. **2** (of a wound, disease, etc.) not yielding to treatment. **3** (of a substance) hard to fuse or work. [Latin: related to REFRACT]

**refrain¹** /ruh-**frayn**/ v. (foll. by *from*) avoid doing (an action) (*refrain from smoking*). [Latin *frenum* bridle]

**refrain²** /ruh-**frayn**/ n. **1** recurring phrase or lines, esp. at the ends of

**stanzas. 2** music accompanying this. [Latin: related to REFRACT]

**refrangible** /ree-**fran**-juh-buhl, ruh-/ *adj.* that can be refracted. [Latin: related to REFRACT]

**refresh** /ruh-**fresh**/ *v.* **1 a** give new spirit or vigour to. **b** (esp. *refl.*) revive with food, rest, etc. (*refreshed myself with a short sleep*). **2** revive (the memory), esp. by consulting the source of one's information. □ **refreshing** *adj.* **refreshingly** *adv.* [French: related to FRESH]

**refresher** *n.* **1** something that refreshes, esp. a drink. **2** *Law* extra fee payable to counsel in a prolonged case.

**refresher course** *n.* course reviewing or updating previous studies.

**refreshment** *n.* **1** act of refreshing or the process of being refreshed. **2** (usu. in *pl.*) food or drink, esp. when not regarded as constituting a meal.

**refrigerant** /ree-**frij**-uh-ruhnt, ruh-/ — *n.* substance used for refrigeration. — *adj.* cooling. [Latin: related to REFRIGERATE]

**refrigerate** /ree-**frij**-uh-,rayt, ruh-/ *v.* (**-ting**) **1** make or become cool or cold. **2** subject (food etc.) to cold in order to freeze or preserve it. □ **refrigeration** /-**ray**-shuhn/ *n.* [Latin *refrigero* from *frigus* cold]

**refrigerator** *n.* cabinet or room in which food etc. is kept cold.

**refuel** /ree-**fyool**/ *v.* (**-ll-**) replenish a fuel supply; supply with more fuel.

**refuge** /**ref**-yooj/ *n.* **1** shelter from pursuit, danger, or trouble. **2** person or place etc. offering this. [Latin *refugium* from *fugio* flee]

**refugee** /,ref-yoo-**jee**/ *n.* person taking refuge, esp. in a foreign country from war, persecution, or natural disaster. [French *réfugié*: related to REFUGE]

**refulgent** /ruh-**ful**-juhnt/ *adj. literary* shining, gloriously bright. □ **refulgence** *n.* [Latin *refulgeo* shine brightly]

**refund** — *v.* /ruh-**fund**/ (also *absol.*) **1** pay back (money or expenses). **2** reimburse (a person). — *n.* /**ree**-fund/ **1** act of refunding. **2** sum refunded. □ **refundable** /ruh-**fun**-duh-buhl/ *adj.* [Latin *fundo* pour]

**refurbish** /ree-**fer**-bish/ *v.* **1** brighten up. **2** restore and redecorate. □ **refurbishment** *n.*

**refurnish** /ree-**fer**-nish/ *v.* furnish again or differently.

**refusal** /ruh-**fyoo**-zuhl/ *n.* **1** act or instance of refusing or state of being refused. **2** (in full **first refusal**) right or privilege of deciding to take or leave a thing before it is offered to others.

**refuse¹** /ruh-**fyooz**/ *v.* (**-sing**) **1** withhold

acceptance of or consent to (*refuse an offer*). **2** (often foll. by *to* + infin.) indicate unwillingness or inability (*I refuse to go*; *car refuses to start*; *I refuse!*). **3** (often with double object) not grant (a request) made by (a person) (*refused me a day off*). **4** (also *absol.*) (of a horse) be unwilling to jump (a fence etc.). [French *refuser*]

**refuse²** /**ref**-yoos/ *n.* items rejected as worthless; waste. [French: related to REFUSE¹]

**refusenik** /ruh-**fyooz**-nik/ *n.* Jew in the former Soviet Union who was refused permission to emigrate to Israel.

**refute** /ruh-**fyoot**/ *v.* (**-ting**) **1** prove the falsity or error of (a statement etc. or the person advancing it). **2** rebut by argument. **3** deny or contradict (without argument) (*I absolutely refute your accusations*). □ **refutation** /,ref-yoo-**tay**-shuhn/ *n.* [Latin *refuto*]

■ **Usage** The use of *refute* in sense 3 is considered incorrect by some people. It is often confused in this sense with *repudiate*.

**regain** /ruh-**gayn**/ *v.* **1** obtain possession, use, or control of (a thing) again after losing it (*regain consciousness*). **2** reach again (*regained the shore*).

**regal** /**ree**-guhl/ *adj.* **1** of or by a monarch or monarchs. **2** fit for a monarch; magnificent. □ **regality** /ruh-**gal**-uh-tee/ *n.* **regally** *adv.* [Latin *rex reg-* king]

**regale** /ruh-**gayl**/ *v.* (**-ling**) **1** entertain lavishly with feasting. **2** (foll. by *with*) entertain with (talk etc.). [French *régaler*: related to GALLANT]

**regalia** /ruh-**gay**-lyuh/ *n.pl.* **1** insignia of royalty used at coronations. **2** insignia of an order or of civic dignity. [medieval Latin: related to REGAL]

**regard** /ruh-**gahd**/ — *v.* **1** gaze on steadily (usu. in a specified way) (*regarded them suspiciously*). **2** heed; take into account. **3** look upon or think of in a specified way (*regard it as an insult*). — *n.* **1** gaze; steady or significant look. **2** (foll. by *to*, *for*) attention or care (*has no regard for the fate of the hostages*). **3** (foll. by *for*) esteem; kindly feeling; respectful opinion (*has regard for his elders*). **4** respect; point attended to (*in this regard*). **5** (in *pl.*) expression of friendliness in a letter etc.; compliments. □ **as regards** about, concerning; in respect of. **in** (or **with**) **regard to** as concerns; in respect of. [French *regard(er)*: related to GUARD]

**regardful** *adj.* (foll. by *of*) mindful of.

**regarding** *prep.* about, concerning; in respect of.

**regardless** — adj. (foll. by of) without regard or consideration for. — adv. nonetheless (there were hazards, but they carried on regardless).

**regatta** /ruh-**gat**-uh/ n. event consisting of rowing or yacht races. [Italian]

**regency** /**ree**-juhn-see/ n. (pl. **-ies**) **1** office of regent. **2** commission acting as regent. **3** period of office of a regent. **4 a** (**Regency**) (in Britain) period (1811 to 1820) when George (later George IV) was Prince Regent. **b** style of furniture etc. of this period. [medieval Latin regentia: related to REGENT]

**regenerate** — v. /ree-**jen**-uh-,rayt, ruh-/ (**-ting**) **1** bring or come into renewed existence; generate again. **2** improve the moral condition of. **3** impart new, more vigorous, or spiritually higher life or nature to. **4** Biol. regrow or cause (new tissue) to regrow. — adj. /ree-**jen**-uh-ruht/ spiritually born again, reformed. □ **regeneration** /-**ray**-shuhn/ n. **regenerative** /-ruh-tiv/ adj.

**regent** /**ree**-juhnt/ — n. person appointed to administer a country because the monarch is a minor or is absent or incapacitated. — adj. **1** (after the noun) acting as regent (Prince Regent). **2** (attrib.) used in the names of some Australian birds (regent bird; regent honeyeater; regent parrot). [Latin rego rule]

**regent bird** n. (also **regent bowerbird**) bowerbird of dense rainforests in near-coastal Queensland and NSW, the male having brilliant golden-yellow and black plumage. [named after the Prince Regent: see REGENCY 4 a]

**reggae** /**reg**-ay/ n. W. Indian style of music with a strongly accented subsidiary beat. [origin unknown]

**reggo** /**rej**-oh/ var. of REGO.

**regicide** /**rej**-uh-,suyd/ n. **1** person who kills or helps to kill a king. **2** killing of a king. [Latin rex reg- king, -CIDE]

**regime** /ray-**zheem**/ n. (also **régime**) **1 a** method or system of government. **b** (usu. derog.) a particular government. **2** prevailing order or system of things. **3** regimen. [French: related to REGIMEN]

**regimen** /**rej**-uh-muhn/ n. prescribed course of exercise, way of life, and diet. [Latin rego rule]

**regiment** — n. /**rej**-uh-muhnt/ **1 a** permanent unit of an army, usu. commanded by a colonel and divided into several companies, troops, or batteries. **b** operational unit of artillery etc. **2** (usu. foll. by of) large or formidable array or number. — v. /**rej**-uh-,ment/ **1** organise (esp. oppressively) in groups or according to a system (tried to regiment the senior students, but met with little success). **2** form into a regiment or regiments. □ **regimental** /,rej-uh-**men**-tuhl/ adj. **regimentation** /-**tay**-shuhn/ n. [Latin: related to REGIMEN]

**Regina** /ruh-**juy**-nuh/ n. (after the name) reigning queen (Elizabeth Regina). [Latin, = queen]

**region** /**ree**-juhn/ n. **1** geographical area or division, having definable boundaries or characteristics (region between Canberra and the coast; mountainous region). **2** administrative area of a country. **3** part of the body (lumbar region). **4** sphere or realm (region of metaphysics). □ **in the region of** approximately. □ **regional** adj. **regionally** adv. [Latin rego rule]

**register** /**rej**-uh-stuh/ — n. **1** official list, e.g. of births, marriages, and deaths, of shipping, of professionally qualified persons, or of qualified voters in an electorate. **2** book in which items are recorded for reference. **3** device recording speed, force, etc. **4 a** range of a voice or instrument. **b** part of this range (lower register). **5** adjustable plate for widening or narrowing an opening and regulating a draught, esp. in a fire-grate. **6 a** set of organ pipes. **b** sliding device controlling this. **7** = CASH REGISTER. **8** form of a language (colloquial, literary, etc.) used in particular circumstances. **9** Computing a memory location having specific properties and quick access time. — v. **1** set down (a name, fact, complaint, etc.) formally; record in writing. **2 a** enter or cause to be entered in a particular register (register a birth). **b** pay an annual fee on a motor vehicle. **3** commit (a letter etc.) to registered post. **4** (of an instrument) record automatically; indicate. **5 a** express (an emotion) facially or by gesture (registered surprise). **b** (of an emotion) show in a person's face or gestures. **6** make an impression on a person's mind (he's still in shock — the death of his wife hasn't registered yet). [Latin regero -gest- transcribe, record]

**registered nurse** n. nurse with a certificate of competence.

**registered post** n. postal procedure with special precautions for safety and for compensation in case of loss.

**registrar** /**rej**-uhs-trah/ n. **1** official responsible for keeping a register. **2** chief administrator in a university, college, etc. **3** hospital doctor training as a specialist. [medieval Latin: related to REGISTER]

**registration** /,rej-uhs-**tray**-shuhn/ n. **1** act or instance of registering or the process of being registered. **2** annual fee payable by the owner of a motor vehicle. [French or medieval Latin: related to REGISTER]

**registration number** n. combination of letters and numbers identifying a vehicle etc.

**registration plate** n. vehicle number plate.

**registry** /**rej**-uh-stree/ n. (pl. **-ies**) place where registers or records are kept. [medieval Latin: related to REGISTER]

**registry office** n. office where civil marriages are conducted and births, marriages, and deaths are recorded.

**rego** /**rej**-oh/ n. (also **reggo**) (also attrib.) colloq. motor vehicle registration. [abbreviation: REG(ISTRATION) + -O]

**regress** — v. /ruh-**gres**/ **1** move backwards; return to a former, esp. worse, state. **2** Psychol. (cause to) return mentally to a former stage of life. — n. /**ree**-gres/ act of regressing. □ **regression** /ree-**gresh**-uhn, ruh-/ n. **regressive** /ree-**gres**-iv, ruh-/ adj. [Latin regredior -gress-go back]

**regret** /ruh-**gret**/ — v. (**-tt-**) **1** feel or express sorrow, repentance, or distress over (an action or loss etc.). **2** acknowledge with sorrow or remorse (regret to say). — n. feeling of sorrow, repentance, etc., over an action or loss etc. □ **give** (or **send**) **one's regrets** formally decline an invitation. [French regretter]

**regretful** adj. feeling or showing regret. □ **regretfully** adv.

**regrettable** adj. (of events or conduct) undesirable, unwelcome; deserving censure. □ **regrettably** adv.

**regroup** /ree-**groop**/ v. **1** form into new groups; arrange again differently. **2** reorganise (people, troops, etc.) after a setback etc.; prepare for a fresh start or attack.

**regrow** /ree-**groh**/ v. grow again, esp. after an interval. □ **regrowth** n.

**regular** /**reg**-yuh-luh/ — adj. **1 a** acting, done, or recurring uniformly or calculably in time or manner (keeps regular hours; regular heartbeat). **b** habitual, constant, orderly (regular time for going to bed; the planet revolves in its regular orbit). **2** conforming to a rule or principle; systematic (regular diet). **3** harmonious, symmetrical (his regular features make him attractive). **4** conforming to a standard of behaviour or procedure (a regular life; regular court sessions). **5** properly constituted or qualified; pursuing an occupation as one's main pursuit (regular soldier). **6** Gram. (of a noun, verb, etc.) following the normal type of inflection. **7**

colloq. thorough, absolute (a regular hero). **8** (before or after the noun) bound by religious rule; belonging to a religious or monastic order (canon regular). **9** (of a person) defecating or menstruating at predictable times. — n. **1** regular soldier. **2** colloq. regular customer, visitor, etc. (most pubs have their regulars). □ **regularise** v. (also **-ize**) (**-sing** or **-zing**). **regularity** /-la-ruh-tee/ n. **regularly** adv. [Latin regula rule]

**regulate** /**reg**-yuh-ˌlayt/ v. (**-ting**) **1** control by rule. **2** subject to restrictions. **3** adapt to requirements (regulate the temperature control). **4** alter the speed of (a machine or clock) so that it works accurately. □ **regulator** n. **regulatory** /-luh-tree/ adj. [Latin: related to REGULAR]

**regulation** /ˌreg-yuh-**lay**-shuhn/ n. **1** act or instance of regulating or the process of being regulated. **2** prescribed rule. **3** (attrib.) **a** in accordance with regulations; of the correct type etc. (must wear the regulation uniform). **b** colloq. usual (had his regulation tinnie before tea).

**regurgitate** /ree-**ger**-juh-ˌtayt, ruh-/ v. (**-ting**) **1** bring (swallowed food) up again to the mouth. **2** reproduce, rehash (information etc.). □ **regurgitation** /-**tay**-shuhn/ n. [Latin gurges -git- whirlpool]

**rehabilitate** /ˌree-huh-**bil**-uh-ˌtayt/ v. (**-ting**) **1** restore to effectiveness or normal life by training etc., esp. after imprisonment or illness. **2** restore to former privileges or reputation or a proper condition. □ **rehabilitation** /-**tay**-shuhn/ n. [medieval Latin: related to RE-, ABILITY]

**rehash** — v. /ree-**hash**/ put (old material) into a new form without significant change or improvement. — n. /**ree**-hash/ **1** material rehashed. **2** act or instance of rehashing.

**rehear** /ree-**heer**/ v. (past and past part. **reheard** /ree-**herd**/ ) hear (esp. a judicial case) again.

**rehearsal** /ruh-**her**-suhl/ n. **1** trial performance or practice of a play, music, etc. **2** process of rehearsing.

**rehearse** /ruh-**hers**/ v. (**-sing**) **1** practise (a play, music, etc.) for later public performance. **2** hold a rehearsal. **3** train (a person) by rehearsal. **4** recite or say over (rehearsed in his mind the excuses he'd prepared). [Anglo-French: related to HEARSE]

**rehouse** /ree-**howz**/ v. (**-sing**) house elsewhere.

**Reich** /ruyk/ n. the former German State, esp. the Third Reich. [German, = empire]

**reign** /rayn/ — v. **1** be king or queen. **2** prevail (*confusion reigns*). **3** (as **reigning** *attrib. adj.*) (of a winner, champion, etc.) currently holding the title etc. — n. **1** sovereignty, rule. **2** period during which a sovereign rules. **3** controlling or dominating effect of a person or thing (*a reign of terror*). [Latin *regnum*]

**reimburse** /ˌree-im-**bers**/ v. (**-sing**) **1** repay (a person who has expended money). **2** repay (a person's expenses). □ **reimbursement** n.

**reimpose** /ˌree-im-**pohz**/ v. (**-sing**) impose again, esp. after a lapse.

**rein** /rayn/ — n. (in *sing.* or *pl.*) **1** long narrow strap with each end attached to the bit, used to guide or check a horse etc. **2** means of control (*has no rein on his lust*). — v. **1** check or manage with reins. **2** (foll. by *up*, *back*) pull up or back with reins. **3** (foll. by *in*) hold in as with reins. **4** govern, restrain, control. □ **give free rein to** allow freedom of action or expression. **keep a tight rein on** allow little freedom to; control rigidly (*government is keeping a tight rein on fiscal policy*). [French *rene* from Latin *retinēre* RETAIN]

**reincarnation** /ˌree-in-kah-**nay**-shuhn/ n. rebirth of a soul in a new body. □ **reincarnate** /-**kah**-nayt/ v. (**-ting**). **reincarnate** /-**kah**-nuht/ adj.

**reindeer** /**rayn**-deer/ n. (*pl.* same or **-s**) subarctic deer with large antlers. [Old Norse]

**reinforce** /ˌree-in-**faws**/ v. (**-cing**) strengthen or support, esp. with additional personnel or material or by an increase of numbers or quantity or size etc. [French *renforcer*]

**reinforced concrete** n. concrete with metal bars or wire etc. embedded to increase its strength.

**reinforcement** n. **1** reinforcing or being reinforced. **2** thing that reinforces. **3** (in *pl.*) reinforcing personnel or equipment etc.

**reinstate** /ˌree-in-**stayt**/ v. (**-ting**) **1** replace in a former position. **2** restore (a person etc.) to former privileges. □ **reinstatement** n.

**reinterpret** /ˌree-in-**ter**-pruht/ v. (**-t-**) interpret again or differently. □ **reinterpretation** /-**tay**-shuhn/ n.

**reintroduce** /ˌree-in-truh-**dyoos**/ v. (**-cing**) introduce again. □ **reintroduction** /-**duk**-shuhn/ n.

**reinvest** /ˌree-in-**vest**/ v. invest again (esp. proceeds or interest). □ **reinvestment** n.

**reissue** /ree-**ish**-oo, -**is**-yoo/ — v. (**-ues**, **-ued**, **-uing**) issue again or in a different form. — n. new issue, esp. of a previously published book.

**reiterate** /ree-**it**-uh-ˌrayt/ v. (**-ting**) say or do again or repeatedly. □ **reiteration** /-**ray**-shuhn/ n.

**reject** — v. /ruh-**jekt**/ **1** put aside or send back as not to be used, done, or complied with etc. **2** refuse to accept or believe in. **3** rebuff or withhold affection from (a person). **4** show an immune response to (a transplant) so that it fails. — n. /**ree**-jekt/ thing or person rejected as unfit or below standard. □ **rejection** /ruh-**jek**-shuhn/ n. [Latin *rejicio -ject-* throw back]

**rejig** /ree-**jig**/ v. (**-gg-**) **1** re-equip (a factory etc.) for a new kind of work. **2** rearrange.

**rejoice** /ruh-**jois**/ v. (**-cing**) **1** feel great joy. **2** be glad. **3** (foll. by *in*, *at*) take delight. [French *rejoir*: related to JOY]

**rejoin**¹ /ree-**join**/ v. **1** join together again; reunite. **2** join (a companion etc.) again.

**rejoin**² /ruh-**join**/ v. **1** say in answer, retort. **2** reply to a charge or pleading in a lawsuit. [French *rejoindre*: related to JOIN]

**rejoinder** /ruh-**join**-duh/ n. what is said in reply; retort. [Anglo-French: related to REJOIN²]

**rejuvenate** /ree-**joo**-vuh-ˌnayt, ruh-/ v. (**-ting**) make (as if) young again. □ **rejuvenation** /-**nay**-shuhn/ n. [Latin *juvenis* young]

**rekindle** /ree-**kin**-duhl/ v. (**-ling**) kindle again (*the sight rekindled old emotions*).

**-rel** *suffix* with diminutive or derogatory force (*cockerel*; *scoundrel*).

**relapse** /ruh-**laps**/ — v. (**-sing**) (usu. foll. by *into*) fall back or sink again (esp. into a worse state after improvement). — n. also /**ree**-laps/ act or instance of relapsing, esp. a deterioration in a patient's condition after partial recovery. [Latin *labor laps-* siip]

**relate** /ruh-**layt**/ v. (**-ting**) **1** narrate or recount. **2** (usu. foll. by *to*, *with*) connect (two things) in thought or meaning; associate. **3** (foll. by *to*) have reference to. **4** (foll. by *to*) feel connected or sympathetic to (*related to her in her grief*). [Latin: related to REFER]

**related** *adj.* connected, esp. by blood or marriage.

**relation** /ruh-**lay**-shuhn/ n. **1 a** the way in which one person or thing is related or connected to another. **b** connection, correspondence, contrast, or feeling prevailing between persons or things (*bears no relation to the facts*; *enjoyed good relations for many years*; *foreign relations*). **2** a relative. **3** (in *pl.*) (foll. by *with*) dealings (with others). **4** = RELATIONSHIP.

**5 a** narration (*his relation of the events*). **b** narrative. □ **in relation to** as regards. [Latin: related to REFER]

**relationship** *n.* **1** state or instance of being related. **2 a** connection or association (*good working relationship*). **b** *colloq.* emotional (esp. sexual) association between two people.

**relative** /**rel**-uh-tiv/ — *adj.* **1** considered in relation to something else (*relative velocity*). **2** (foll. by *to*) proportioned to (something else) (*growth is relative to input*). **3** implying comparison or contextual relation (*'heat' is a relative word*). **4** comparative (*their relative merits*). **5** having mutual relations; corresponding in some way; related to each other. **6** (foll. by *to*) having reference or relating to (*the facts relative to the issue*). **7** *Gram.* **a** (of a word, esp. a pronoun) referring to an expressed or implied antecedent and attaching a subordinate clause to it, e.g. *which, who*. **b** (of a clause) attached to an antecedent by a relative word. — *n.* **1** person connected by blood or marriage. **2** *Gram.* relative word, esp. a pronoun. □ **relatively** *adv.* [Latin: related to REFER]

**relative atomic mass** *n.* the ratio of the average mass of one atom of an element to one-twelfth of the mass of an atom of carbon-12.

**relative density** *n.* the ratio between the mass of a substance and that of the same volume of a substance used as a standard (usu. water or air).

**relative molecular mass** *n.* the ratio of the average mass of one molecule of an element or compound to one-twelfth of the mass of an atom of carbon-12.

**relativity** /,rel-uh-**tiv**-uh-tee/ *n.* **1** fact or state of being relative. **2** *Physics* **a** (**special theory of relativity**) theory based on the principle that all motion is relative and that light has a constant velocity. **b** (**general theory of relativity**) theory extending this to gravitation and accelerated motion. **3** relative differences in wages between occupational groups (*the union movement is concerned to maintain relativities*).

**relax** /ruh-**laks**/ *v.* **1** make or become less stiff, rigid, or tense. **2** make or become less formal or strict (*rules were relaxed*). **3** reduce or abate (one's attention, efforts, etc.). **4** cease work or effort. **5** (as **relaxed** *adj.*) at ease; unperturbed. [Latin *relaxo*: related to LAX]

**relaxation** /,ree-lak-**say**-shuhn/ *n.* **1** act of relaxing or state of being relaxed. **2** recreation.

**relay** /**ree**-lay/ — *n.* **1** fresh set of people etc. substituted for tired ones. **2** supply of material similarly used. **3** = RELAY RACE. **4** device activating an electric circuit etc. in response to changes affecting itself. **5 a** device to receive, reinforce, and transmit a message, broadcast, etc. **b** relayed message or transmission. — *v.* also /ruh-**lay**/ receive (a message, broadcast, etc.) and transmit it to others. [French *relai* from Latin *laxo*: see LAX]

**relay race** *n.* race between teams of which each member in turn covers part of the distance.

**release** /ruh-**lees**/ — *v.* (**-sing**) **1** (often foll. by *from*) set free; liberate, unfasten. **2** allow to move from a fixed position. **3 a** make (information, a recording, etc.) publicly available. **b** issue (a film etc.) for general exhibition. — *n.* **1** liberation from a restriction, duty, or difficulty. **2** handle or catch that releases part of a mechanism. **3** news item etc. made available for publication (*press release*). **4 a** film or record etc. that is released. **b** act or instance of releasing or the process of being released in this way. [French *relesser* from Latin *relaxo* RELAX]

**relegate** /**rel**-uh-,gayt/ *v.* (**-ting**) **1** consign or dismiss to an inferior position. **2** transfer (a sports team) to a lower division of a league etc. **3** banish. □ **relegation** /-**gay**-shuhn/ *n.* [Latin *relego* send away]

**relent** /ruh-**lent**/ *v.* relax severity, abandon a harsh intention, yield to compassion. [medieval Latin *lentus* flexible]

**relentless** *adj.* unrelenting, oppressively constant (*relentless effort; the pressure was relentless*). □ **relentlessly** *adv.*

**relevant** /**rel**-uh-vuhnt/ *adj.* (often foll. by *to*) bearing on or having reference to the matter in hand. □ **relevance** *n.* [Latin *relevo*: related to RELIEVE]

**reliable** /ruh-**luy**-uh-buhl/ *adj.* of consistently good character or quality; dependable. □ **reliability** /-bil-uh-tee/ *n.* **reliably** *adv.*

**reliance** /ruh-**luy**-uhns/ *n.* (foll. by *in, on*) trust, confidence. □ **reliant** *adj.*

**relic** /**rel**-ik/ *n.* **1** object that is interesting because of its age or association. **2** part of a saint's body or belongings kept as an object of reverence. **3** surviving custom or belief etc. from a past age. **4** memento or souvenir. **5** (in *pl.*) what has survived destruction or wasting or use. [Latin *reliquiae* remains: related to RELINQUISH]

**relict** /**rel**-ikt/ *n.* **1** geological or other object surviving in its primitive form. **2** animal or plant known to have existed in the same form in previous geological ages. [French *relicte*: related to RELIC]

**relief** /ruh-**leef**/ n. **1 a** alleviation of or deliverance from pain, distress, anxiety, etc. **b** feeling accompanying such deliverance. **2** feature etc. that diversifies monotony or relaxes tension. **3** assistance (esp. financial, or in the form of food, clothing, etc.) given to those in special need or difficulty (*rent relief; famine relief*). **4 a** replacing of a person or persons on duty by another or others. **b** person or persons replacing others in this way. **5 a** method of moulding, carving, or stamping, in which the design stands out from the surface. **b** piece of sculpture etc. in relief. **c** representation of relief given by an arrangement of line, colour, or shading. **6** vividness, distinctness (*brings the facts out in sharp relief*). [French and Italian: related to RELIEVE]

**relief map** n. map indicating hills and valleys by shading etc. rather than by contour lines alone.

**relieve** /ruh-**leev**/ v. (**-ving**) **1** bring or give relief to. **2** mitigate the tedium or monotony of. **3** release (a person) from a duty by acting as or providing a substitute. **4** (foll. by *of*) take (esp. a burden or duty) away from (a person). □ **relieve one's feelings** use strong language or vigorous behaviour when annoyed. **relieve oneself** urinate or defecate. **relieve a person of something** steal from him or her (*relieved him of his wallet*). □ **relieved** adj. [Latin *relevo* raise again, alleviate]

**religion** /ruh-**lij**-uhn/ n. **1** belief in a superhuman controlling power, esp. in a personal God or gods entitled to obedience and worship. **2** expression of this in worship. **3** particular system of faith and worship. **4** thing that one is devoted to (*cricket is her religion*). [Latin *religio* bond]

**religiosity** /ruh-ˌlij-ee-**os**-uh-tee/ n. (usu. *derog.*) state of being obtrusively religious or too religious. [Latin: related to RELIGIOUS]

**religious** /ruh-**lij**-uhs/ — adj. **1** devoted to religion; pious, devout. **2** of or concerned with religion. **3** of or belonging to a monastic order. **4** scrupulous, conscientious (*a religious attention to detail*). — n. (pl. same) person bound by monastic vows. □ **religiously** adv. [Latin *religiosus*: related to RELIGION]

**relinquish** /ruh-**ling**-kwish/ v. **1** surrender or resign (a right or possession). **2** give up or cease from (a habit, plan, belief, etc.). **3** relax hold of (an object held). □ **relinquishment** n. [Latin *relinquo -lict-* leave behind]

**reliquary** /**rel**-i-kwuh-ree/ n. (pl. **-ies**) esp. *Relig.* receptacle for a relic or relics. [French *reliquaire*: related to RELIC]

**relish** /**rel**-ish/ — n. **1** (often foll. by *for*) great liking or enjoyment. **2 a** appetising flavour. **b** attractive quality (*fishing loses its relish in winter*). **3** condiment eaten with plainer food to add flavour. — v. **1** get pleasure out of; enjoy greatly. **2** anticipate with pleasure. [French *reles* remainder: related to RELEASE]

**relive** /ree-**liv**/ v. (**-ving**) live (an experience etc.) over again, esp. in the imagination.

**rellie** /**rel**-ee/ n. (also **relo**) *colloq.* (often in *pl.*) relative (*all the rellies will be here for Christmas*).

**relo** /**rel**-oh/ n. = RELLIE.

**relocate** /ˌree-loh-**kayt**/ v. (**-ting**) **1** move (a person or thing) to a new place. **2** move to a new place (esp. to live or work). □ **relocation** /-**kay**-shuhn/ n.

**reluctant** /ruh-**luk**-tuhnt/ adj. (often foll. by *to* + infin.) unwilling or disinclined. □ **reluctance** n. **reluctantly** adv. [Latin *luctor* struggle]

**rely** /ruh-**luy**/ v. (**-ies, -ied**) (foll. by *on, upon*) **1** depend on with confidence or assurance (*am relying on your judgment*). **2** be dependent on (*he relies on her for everything*). [Latin *religo* bind closely]

**REM** abbr. n. & adj. = RAPID EYE-MOVEMENT (*is in the REM stage of sleep*).

**remade** past and past part. of REMAKE.

**remain** /ruh-**mayn**/ v. **1** be left over after others or other parts have been removed, used, or dealt with. **2** be in the same place or condition during further time; stay (*it should remain hot; remained at home*). **3** (foll. by compl.) continue to be (*remained calm; remains Prime Minister*). [Latin *remaneo*]

**remainder** — n. **1** residue. **2** remaining persons or things. **3** number left after division or subtraction. **4** (usu. in *pl.*) copies of a book left unsold when demand has almost ceased. — v. dispose of (a remainder of books) at a reduced price (*his novel has been remaindered*). [Anglo-French: related to REMAIN]

**remains** n.pl. **1** what remains after other parts have been removed or used etc. **2** relics of antiquity, esp. of buildings (*Roman remains in Italy*). **3** dead body.

**remake** — v. /ree-**mayk**/ (**-king**; past and past part. **remade**) make again or differently. — n. /**ree**-mayk/ thing that has been remade, esp. a cinema film.

**remand** /ruh-**mahnd, -mand**/ — v. return (a prisoner) to custody, esp. to allow further inquiry. — n. recommittal to custody. □ **on remand** in custody pending trial. [Latin *remando*]

**remand centre** *n.* institution to which accused persons are remanded.

**remark** /ruh-**mahk**/ — *v.* **1** (often foll. by *that*) **a** say by way of comment. **b** *archaic* take notice of; regard with attention (*remarked the abundance of dead roos on the road*). **2** (usu. foll. by *on, upon*) make a comment. — *n.* **1** written or spoken comment; anything said. **2 a** noticing (*worthy of remark*). **b** commenting (*let it pass without remark*). [French *remarquer*: related to MARK]

**remarkable** *adj.* worth notice; exceptional; striking. □ **remarkably** *adv.* [French *remarquable*: related to REMARK]

**remarry** /ree-**ma**-ree/ *v.* (**-ies, -ied**) marry again. □ **remarriage** *n.*

**remedial** /ruh-**mee**-dee-uhl/ *adj.* **1** affording or intended as a remedy. **2** (of teaching etc.) for slow or disadvantaged pupils. [Latin: related to REMEDY]

**remedy** /**rem**-uh-dee/ *n.* (*pl.* **-ies**) (often foll. by *for, against*) **1** medicine or treatment (for a disease etc.). **2** means of counteracting or removing anything undesirable (*there are no quick remedies for massive unemployment*). **3** redress; legal or other reparation. — *v.* (**-ies, -ied**) **1** cure, heal. **2** rectify; make good. □ **remediable** /ruh-**mee**-dee-uh-buhl/ *adj.* [Latin *remedium* from *medeor* heal]

**remember** /ruh-**mem**-buh/ *v.* **1** (often foll. by *to* + infin. or *that* + clause) keep in the memory; not forget (*remember to lock the door; remember that I'm your friend*). **2** (also *absol.*) bring back into one's thoughts (*she suddenly remembered his name*). **3** think of or acknowledge (a person), esp. in making a gift etc. **4** (foll. by *to*) convey greetings from (one person) to (another) (*remember me to John*). [Latin: related to MEMORY]

**remembrance** /ruh-**mem**-bruhns/ *n.* **1** act of remembering or the process of being remembered. **2** a memory or recollection. **3** keepsake, souvenir. **4** (in *pl.*) greetings conveyed through a third person. [French: related to REMEMBER]

**Remembrance Day** *n.* **1** *hist.* Armistice Day (11 November 1918). **2** 11 November, when those killed in the wars of 1914–18 and 1939–45 and in later conflicts are remembered.

**remind** /ruh-**muynd**/ *v.* (usu. foll. by *of* or *to* + infin. or *that* + clause) cause (a person) to remember or think of (*reminds me of her father; reminded them of the time*).

**reminder** *n.* **1** thing that reminds, esp. a repeat letter or bill. **2** (often foll. by *of*) memento.

**reminisce** /ˌrem-uh-**nis**/ *v.* (**-cing**) indulge in reminiscence.

**reminiscence** /ˌrem-uh-**nis**-uhns/ *n.* **1** act of remembering things past. **2** (in *pl.*) collection in literary form of incidents and experiences remembered. [Latin *reminiscor* remember]

**reminiscent** *adj.* **1** (foll. by *of*) reminding or suggestive of. **2** concerned with reminiscence.

**remiss** /ruh-**mis**/ *adj.* careless of duty; lax, negligent. [Latin: related to REMIT]

**remission** /ruh-**mish**-uhn/ *n.* **1** reduction of a prison sentence on account of good behaviour. **2** remitting of a debt or penalty etc. **3** diminution of force, effect, or degree (esp. of disease or pain). **4** (often foll. by *of*) forgiveness (of sins etc.). [Latin: related to REMIT]

**remit** *v.* /ruh-**mit**/ (**-tt-**) **1** cancel or refrain from exacting or inflicting (a debt, punishment, etc.). **2** abate or slacken; cease partly or entirely (*nothing will remit his rage; your pain will remit in time*). **3** send (money etc.) in payment. **4** (foll. by *to*) refer (a matter for decision etc.) to some authority (*I'll remit your complaint to the manager*). **5** pardon (sins etc.). [Latin *remitto -miss-*]

**remittance** *n.* **1** money sent, esp. by post. **2** the sending of money.

**remittance man** *n. hist.* British immigrant to Australia financially supported by his family overseas (usu. with the implication that the family was prepared to pay to keep him away from Britain).

**remittent** *adj.* (of a fever or disease) abating at intervals.

**remix** — *v.* /ree-**miks**/ **1** mix again. **2** (of a recording) alter the relative sound levels of the various performers etc. — *n.* /**ree**-miks/ remixed recording.

**remnant** /**rem**-nuhnt/ *n.* **1** small remaining quantity. **2** piece of cloth etc. left when the greater part has been used or sold. [French: related to REMAIN]

**remodel** /ree-**mod**-uhl/ *v.* (**-ll-**) **1** model again or differently. **2** reconstruct.

**remonstrate** /**rem**-uhn-ˌstrayt/ *v.* (**-ting**) (foll. by *with*) make a protest; argue forcibly. □ **remonstrance** /ruh-**mon**-struhns/ *n.* **remonstration** /-**stray**-shuhn/ *n.* [medieval Latin *monstro* show]

**remorse** /ruh-**maws**/ *n.* **1** deep regret for a wrong committed. **2** compunction; compassion, mercy (*without remorse*). [medieval Latin *mordeo mors-* bite]

**remorseful** *adj.* filled with repentance. □ **remorsefully** *adv.*

**remorseless** *adj.* without compassion. □ **remorselessly** *adv.*

**remote** /ruh-**moht**/ adj. (**remoter, remotest**) 1 far away, far apart, distant (*remote from civilisation*). 2 isolated; secluded (*a remote country town*). 3 distantly related (*remote ancestor*). 4 slight, faint (*a remote hope*; *not the remotest chance*). 5 aloof; not friendly. 6 (foll. by *from*) widely different; separate by nature (*ideas remote from the subject*). □ **remotely** adv. **remoteness** □ [Latin *remotus*: related to REMOVE]

**remote control** n. 1 control of an apparatus from a distance by means of signals transmitted from a radio or electronic device. 2 such a device.

**removal** /ruh-**moo**-vuhl/ n. 1 act or instance of removing or the process of being removed. 2 transfer of furniture etc. on moving house.

**removalist** n. (often in pl.) person or firm whose work is the transferring of furniture etc. for those moving house.

**remove** /ruh-**moov**/ — v. (**-ving**) 1 take off or away from the place occupied (*remove the lid carefully*). 2 a convey to another place; change the situation of. b get rid of; dismiss (*will remove all doubts*; *removed from the office of Prime Minister*). c (as **removed** adj.) (of Aboriginal children) forcibly taken from their parents. 3 cause to be no longer present or available; take away (*privileges were removed*). 4 (in passive; foll. by *from*) distant or remote in condition (*country is not far removed from anarchy*). 5 (as **removed** adj.) (esp. of cousins) separated by a specified number of steps of descent (*a first cousin twice removed = a grandchild of a first cousin*). — n. 1 degree of remoteness; distance. 2 stage in a gradation; degree (*several removes from what I expected*). □ **removable** adj. [Latin *removeo -mot-*]

**remunerate** /ruh-**myoo**-nuh-,rayt/ v. (**-ting**) 1 reward; pay for services rendered. 2 serve as or provide recompense for (work etc.) or to (a person). □ **remuneration** /-**ray**-shuhn/ n. **remunerative** /-ruh-tiv/ adj. [Latin *munus -ner-* gift]

**Renaissance** /ruh-**nay**-suhns, -sons/ n. 1 revival of art and literature in the 14th–16th c. 2 period of this. 3 (often attrib.) style of art, architecture, etc. developed by it. 4 (**renaissance**) any similar revival. [French *naissance* birth]

**renal** /**ree**-nuhl/ adj. of the kidneys. [Latin *renes* kidneys]

**rename** /ree-**naym**/ v. (**-ming**) name again; give a new name to.

**renascent** /ruh-**nas**-uhnt/ adj. springing up anew; being reborn. □ **renascence** n. [Latin *renasci* be born again]

**rend** v. (past and past part. **rent**) tear or wrench forcibly. [Old English]

**render** v. 1 cause to be or become (*rendered us helpless*). 2 give or pay (money, service, etc.), esp. in return for or as a thing due (*render thanks*). 3 (often foll. by *to*) a give (assistance) (*rendered aid to the injured driver*). b show (obedience etc.). c do (a service etc.). 4 submit; send in; present (an account, reason, etc.). 5 a represent or portray (*rendered his likeness faithfully*). b act (a role). c *Mus.* perform; execute. 6 translate (*rendered the poem into French*). 7 (often foll. by *down*) melt down (fat etc.). 8 cover (stone or brick) with a coat of plaster. □ **rendering** n. (esp. in senses 5, 6, and 8). [Latin *reddo* give back]

**rendezvous** /**ron**-day-,voo/ — n. (pl. same /-,vooz/) 1 agreed or regular meeting-place. 2 meeting by arrangement. 3 place appointed for assembling troops, ships, etc. — v. (**rendezvouses** /-,vooz/) meet at a rendezvous. [French, = present yourselves]

**rendition** /ren-**dish**-uhn/ n. interpretation or rendering of a dramatic role, piece of music, etc. [French: related to RENDER]

**renegade** /**ren**-uh-,gayd/ n. person who deserts a party or principles. [medieval Latin: related to RENEGE]

**renege** /ree-**neg**, ruh-, -**nig**/ v. (**-ging**) 1 (often foll. by *on*) go back on (one's word etc.). 2 *Cards* fail to follow suit when able to do so. [Latin *nego* deny]

**renegotiate** /,ree-nuh-**goh**-shee-,ayt/ v. (**-ting**) (also absol.) negotiate again or on different terms. □ **renegotiation** /-**ay**-shuhn/ n.

**renew** /ruh-**nyoo**/ v. 1 revive; make new again; restore to the original state. 2 reinforce; resupply; replace. 3 repeat or re-establish, resume after an interruption (*renewed our acquaintance*). 4 (also absol.) grant or be granted continuation of (a licence, subscription, lease, etc.). 5 recover (strength etc.). □ **renewable** adj. **renewal** n.

**rennet** /**ren**-uht/ n. 1 curdled milk found in the stomach of an unweaned calf. 2 preparation made from the stomach-membrane of a calf or from certain fungi, used in making cheese. [probably Old English: related to RUN]

**renounce** /ruh-**nowns**/ v. (**-cing**) 1 consent formally to abandon (a claim, right, etc.). 2 repudiate; refuse to recognise any longer (*renounced their father's authority*). 3 decline further association or disclaim relationship with *(renounced his former friends).* [Latin *nuntio* announce]

**renovate** /**ren**-uh-,vayt/ v. (**-ting**) restore to good condition; repair. □ **renovation** /-**vay**-shuhn/ n. **renovator** n. [Latin *novus* new]

**renown** /ruh-**nown**/ n. fame, high distinction. [French *renomer* make famous]

**renowned** adj. famous, celebrated.

**rent**[1] — n. **1** tenant's periodical payment to an owner for the use of land or premises. **2** payment for the use of equipment etc. — v. **1** (often foll. by *from*) take, occupy, or use at a rent. **2** (often foll. by *out*) let or hire (a thing) for rent. **3** (foll. by *at*) be let at a specified rate. [French *rente*: related to RENDER]

**rent**[2] n. **1** large tear in a garment etc. **2** opening in clouds etc. *(the rent in the rainclouds showed glimpses of blue).* [from REND]

**rent**[3] past and past part. of REND.

**rental** /**ren**-tuhl/ n. **1** amount paid or received as rent. **2** act of renting. [Anglo-French or Anglo-Latin: related to RENT[1]]

**renumber** /ree-**num**-buh/ v. change the number or numbers given or allocated to.

**renunciation** /ruh-,nun-see-**ay**-shuhn/ n. **1** act or instance of renouncing or giving up. **2** self-denial.

**reorder** /ree-**aw**-duh/ — v. **1** order again. **2** put into a new order. — n. renewed or repeated order for goods.

**reorganise** /ree-**aw**-guh-,nuyz/ v. (also **-ize**) (**-sing** or **-zing**) organise differently. □ **reorganisation** /-**zay**-shuhn/ n.

**reorient** /ree-**aw**-ree-,ent, -o-ree-,ent/ v. **1** give a new direction or outlook to (ideas, a person, etc.). **2** help (a person) find his or her bearings again. **3** (refl., often foll. by *to*) adjust oneself to or come to terms with something.

**reorientate** /ree-**aw**-ree-uhn-,tayt, -o-ree-uhn-/ v. (**-ting**) = REORIENT. □ **reorientation** /-**tay**-shuhn/ n.

**rep**[1] n. colloq. representative, esp. a commercial traveller or the elected representative of a group of employees *(union rep; shearers' rep).* [abbreviation]

**rep**[2] n. colloq. **1** repertory. **2** repertory theatre or company. [abbreviation]

**repackage** /ree-**pak**-ij/ v. (**-ging**) **1** package again or differently. **2** present in a new form *(he needs to be repackaged if he's ever to be elected).*

**repaid** past and past part. of REPAY.

**repaint** — v. /ree-**paynt**/ **1** paint again or differently. **2** restore the paint or colouring of. — n. /**ree**-paynt/ act of repainting.

**repair**[1] /ruh-**pair**/ — v. **1** restore to good condition after damage or wear. **2** set right or make amends for (loss, wrong, error, etc.). — n. **1** act or instance of restoring to sound condition *(in need of repair; closed during repair).* **2** result of this *(the repair hardly shows).* **3** good or relative condition for working or using *(in bad repair).* □ **repairable** adj. **repairer** n. [Latin *paro* make ready]

**repair**[2] /ruh-**pair**/ v. (foll. by *to*) resort; have recourse; go *(repaired to a monastery).* [Latin: related to REPATRIATE]

**reparable** /**rep**-uh-ruh-buhl/ adj. (of a loss etc.) that can be made good. [Latin: related to REPAIR[1]]

**reparation** /,rep-uh-**ray**-shuhn/ n. **1** act or instance of making amends. **2** (esp. in pl.) compensation for war damages paid by a defeated country.

**repartee** /,rep-ah-**tee**/ n. **1** practice or skill of making witty retorts. **2** conversation characterised by such retorts. [French *repartie* from *repartir* reply promptly: related to PART]

**repast** /ruh-**pahst**/ n. formal meal. [Latin *repasco -past-* feed]

**repatriate** — v. /ree-**pat**-ree-,ayt/ (**-ting**) return (a person) to his or her native land. — n. /ree-**pat**-ree-uht/ repatriated person. [Latin *repatrio* go back home, from *patria* native land]

**repatriation** n. **1** act or instance of returning to one's native land. **2** rehabilitation of former service personnel, including the provision of pensions, loans, medical care, etc.

**repay** /ree-**pay**/ v. (past and past part. **repaid**) **1** pay back (money). **2** make repayment to (a person). **3** make return for; requite (a service, action, etc.) *(must repay their kindness; the book repays close study).* □ **repayable** adj. **repayment** n.

**repeal** /ruh-**peel**/ — v. revoke or annul (a law etc.). — n. act or instance of repealing. [French: related to APPEAL]

**repeat** /ruh-**peet**/ — v. **1** say or do over again. **2** recite, rehearse, or report (something learnt or heard) *(repeated a poem).* **3** recur; appear again *(a repeating pattern).* **4** (of food) (often foll. by *on*) be tasted after being swallowed due to belching *(garlic tends to repeat on me).* — n. **1 a** act or instance of repeating. **b** thing repeated (often *attrib.*: *repeat prescription*). **2** repeated broadcast of a television or radio programme. **3** *Mus.* **a** passage intended to be repeated. **b** mark indicating this. □ **repeat itself** recur in the same form. **repeat oneself** say or do the same thing over again. □ **repeatable** adj. **repeatedly** adv. [Latin *peto* seek]

**repeater** *n.* **1** person or thing that repeats. **2** firearm which fires several shots without reloading. **3** watch or clock which repeats its last strike when required. **4** device for the re-transmission of an electrical message.

**repechage** /rep-uh-ˌchahj/ *n.* (in rowing etc.) extra contest in which the runners-up in the elimination heats compete for a place in the final. [French *repêcher* fish out, rescue]

**repel** /ruh-pel/ *v.* (**-ll-**) **1** drive back; ward off (*repel an attacker; this spray repels insects*). **2** refuse to accept (*repelled offers of help*). **3** be repulsive or distasteful to. **4** resist mixing with or admitting (*oil and water repel each other; surface repels moisture*). **5** (of a magnetic pole) push away from itself (*like poles repel*). [Latin *repello -puls-*]

**repellent** — *adj.* **1** repelling, arousing distaste. **2** not penetrable by a specified substance (*the fabric is water-repellent*). — *n.* substance that repels something (*insect repellent*).

**repent** /ruh-pent/ *v.* **1** (often foll. by *of*) feel deep sorrow about one's actions etc. **2** (also *absol.*) wish one had not done; resolve not to continue (a wrongdoing etc.). ◻ **repentance** *n.* **repentant** *adj.* [Latin *paeniteo*]

**repercussion** /ˌree-puh-kush-uhn/ *n.* **1** (often foll. by *of*) indirect effect or reaction following an event or act (*consider the repercussions of this move*). **2** recoil after impact. **3** echo. [Latin: related to RE-]

**repertoire** /rep-uh-ˌtwah/ *n.* **1** stock of works that a performer etc. knows or is prepared to perform. **2** stock of techniques etc. (*repertoire of excuses*). [Latin: related to REPERTORY]

**repertory** /rep-uh-tuh-ree, -tree/ *n.* (*pl.* **-ies**) **1** performance of various plays for short periods by one company. **2** repertory theatres collectively. **3** store or collection, esp. of information, instances, etc. **4** = REPERTOIRE. [Latin *reperio* find]

**repertory company** *n.* theatrical company that performs plays from a repertoire.

**repetition** /ˌrep-uh-tish-uhn/ *n.* **1** an act or instance of repeating or being repeated. **2** thing repeated.

**repetition strain injury** *n.* (also **repetitive strain injury**) damage to tendons etc. caused by work which involves repetitive muscular movements over long periods of time.

**repetitious** *adj.* characterised by (esp. tedious or unnecessary) repetition.

**repetitive** /ruh-pet-uh-tiv/ *adj.* repetitious. ◻ **repetitively** *adv.*

**rephrase** /ree-frayz/ *v.* (**-sing**) express differently.

**repine** /ruh-puyn/ *v.* (**-ning**) (often foll. by *at, against*) fret; be discontented. [from PINE², after *repent*]

**replace** /ruh-plays/ *v.* (**-cing**) **1** put back in place (*please replace books on shelves*). **2** take the place of; succeed; be substituted for (*personal computers have largely replaced typewriters; replaced him as leader*). **3** find or provide a substitute for. **4** (often foll. by *with, by*) fill up the place of (*replaced her old car with a new one*).

**replacement** *n.* **1** act or instance of replacing or being replaced. **2** person or thing that replaces another.

**replant** /ree-plahnt, -plant/ *v.* **1** transfer (a plant etc.). **2** plant (ground) again.

**replay** — *v.* /ree-play/ play (a match, recording, etc.) again. — *n.* /ree-play/ replaying of a match, recorded incident in a game, etc.

**replenish** /ree-plen-ish, ruh-/ *v.* (often foll. by *with*) fill up again (*replenish your glasses*). **2** renew (a supply etc.). ◻ **replenishment** *n.* [French *plenir* from *plein* full]

**replete** /ruh-pleet/ *adj.* (often foll. by *with*) **1** well-fed, gorged (*replete with Christmas pudding*). **2** filled or well-supplied. ◻ **repletion** *n.* [Latin *pleo* fill]

**replica** /rep-li-kuh/ *n.* **1** exact copy, esp. a duplicate of a work, made by the original artist. **2** copy or model, esp. on a smaller scale. [Italian *replicare* REPLY]

**replicate** *v.* make a replica of; reproduce; repeat. ◻ **replication** *n.*

**reply** /ruh-pluy/ — *v.* (**-ies, -ied**) **1** (often foll. by *to*) make an answer, respond in word or action. **2** say in answer. — *n.* (*pl.* **-ies**) **1** act of replying (*what did they say in reply?*). **2** what is replied; response. [Latin *replico* fold back]

**report** /ruh-pawt/ — *v.* **1 a** bring back or give an account of. **b** state as fact or news, narrate or describe or repeat, esp. as an eyewitness or hearer etc. (*reported that she saw the plane crash*). **c** relate as spoken by another (*reported what the Aborigines had said*). **2** make an official or formal statement about (*committee reported its findings*). **3** (often foll. by *to*) bring (an offender or offence) to the attention of the authorities (*reported him to the police*). **4** (often foll. by *to*) present oneself to a person as having returned or arrived. **5** (also *absol.*) take down word for word, summarise, or write a description of for publication. **6** make or send in a report. **7** (foll. by *to*) be responsible to (a superior etc.) (*reports* *directly to the general manager*). **8** act as a reporter. — *n.* **1** account given or opinion formally expressed after investigation or consideration (*report of the Royal Commission*). **2** description, summary, or reproduction of a scene, speech, law case, etc., esp. for newspaper publication or broadcast. **3** common talk; rumour (*report has it that . . .*). **4** way a person or thing is spoken of (*hear a good report of you*). **5** periodical statement on (esp. a school pupil's) work, conduct, etc. **6** sound of a gunshot etc. □ **report sick** inform one's employer that one is unable to attend work because of illness. □ **reportedly** *adv.* [Latin *porto* bring]

**reportage** /ˌre-paw-**tahzh**, ruh-**paw**-tij/ *n.* **1** reporting of news for the media. **2** typical style of this. **3** factual journalistic material in a book etc. [from REPORT, after French]

**reported speech** *n.* speaker's words with the person, tense, etc. adapted, e.g. *he said that he would go* (cf. DIRECT SPEECH).

**reporter** *n.* person employed to report news etc. for the media.

**repose**[1] /ruh-**pohz**/ — *n.* **1** cessation of activity, excitement, or toil. **2** sleep. **3** peaceful or quiescent state; tranquillity. — *v.* (**-sing**) **1** (also *refl.*) lie down in rest. **2** (often foll. by *in, on*) lie, be lying or laid, esp. in sleep or death. [Latin: related to PAUSE]

**repose**[2] /ruh-**pohz**/ *v.* (**-sing**) (foll. by *in*) place (trust etc.) in. [from RE-, POSE]

**reposeful** *adj.* showing or inducing repose. □ **reposefully** *adv.* [from REPOSE[1]]

**reposition** /ˌree-puh-**zish**-uhn/ *v.* **1** move or place in a different position. **2** alter one's position.

**repository** /ruh-**poz**-uh-tree/ *n.* (*pl.* **-ies**) **1** place where things are stored or may be found, esp. a warehouse or museum. **2** receptacle. **3** (often foll. by *of*) a book, person, etc. regarded as a store of information etc. **b** recipient of secrets etc. [Latin: related to REPOSE[2]]

**repossess** /ˌree-puh-**zes**/ *v.* regain possession of (esp. goods on which payment is in arrears). □ **repossession** *n.*

**repot** /ree-**pot**/ *v.* (**-tt-**) move (a plant) to another, esp. larger, pot.

**reprehend** /ˌrep-ruh-**hend**/ *v. formal* rebuke; find fault with. [Latin *prehendo* seize]

**reprehensible** /ˌrep-ruh-**hen**-suh-buhl/ *adj.* deserving rebuke; blameworthy.

**represent**[1] /ˌrep-ruh-**zent**/ *v.* **1** stand for or correspond to (*the chairperson's statement does not represent our views*). **2** (often in *passive*) be a specimen of;

exemplify (*all types of people were represented in the audience*). **3** embody; symbolise (*numbers are represented by letters*). **4** place a likeness of before the mind or senses. **5** (often foll. by *as, to be*) describe or depict as; declare (*represented them as martyrs; not what you represent it to be*). **6** (foll. by *that*) allege. **7** show, or play the part of, on stage. **8** be a substitute or deputy for; be entitled to act or speak for (*she is representing the Prime Minister*). **9** be elected as a member of a legislature etc. by (*represents a rural electorate*). [Latin: related to PRESENT[2]]

**re-present**[2] /ˌree-pruh-**zent**/ *v.* submit (a cheque etc.) again for payment.

**representation** /ˌrep-ruh-zen-**tay**-shuhn/ *n.* **1** act or an instance of representing or being represented. **2** thing that represents another. **3** (esp. in *pl.*) statement made of allegations or opinions (*the welfare lobby made representations to the government*).

**representational** *adj.* Art depicting a subject as it appears to the eye.

**representative** /ˌrep-ruh-**zen**-tuh-tiv/ — *adj.* **1** typical of a class or category (*he's truly representative of the Australian ocker*). **2** containing typical specimens of all or many classes (*representative sample*). **3 a** consisting of members elected to a government to represent various constituencies of the people. **b** based on representation by these (*representative government*). **4** (foll. by *of*) serving as a portrayal or symbol of (*representative of their attitude to work*). — *n.* **1** (foll. by *of*) sample, specimen, or typical embodiment of. **2 a** agent of a person or society. **b** elected agent of a trade union. **c** commercial traveller. **3** delegate; substitute. **4** elected member in a representative assembly. [French or medieval Latin: related to REPRESENT[1]]

**repress** /ruh-**pres**/ *v.* **1 a** check; restrain; keep under; quell (*tried to repress his anger*). **b** suppress; prevent from sounding, rioting, or bursting out (*repressed the rebellion*). **2** *Psychol.* actively exclude (an unwelcome thought) from conscious awareness. **3** (usu. as **repressed** *adj.*) subject (a person) to the suppression of his or her thoughts or impulses (*many gays feel repressed*). □ **repression** *n.* **repressive** *adj.* [Latin: related to PRESS[1]]

**reprieve** /ruh-**preev**/ — *v.* (**-ving**) **1** remit or postpone the execution of (a condemned person). **2** give respite to. — *n.* **1 a** act or instance of reprieving or being reprieved. **b** warrant for this. **2** respite (*brief reprieve from the demands* *of work*). [*repry* from French *reprendre -pris* take back]

**reprimand** /**rep**-ruh-,mahnd, -,mand/ — *n.* (esp. official) rebuke. — *v.* administer this to. [Latin: related to REPRESS]

**reprint** — *v.* /ree-**print**/ print again. — *n.* /**ree**-print/ **1** reprinting of a book etc. **2** book etc. reprinted. **3** quantity reprinted.

**reprisal** /ruh-**pruy**-zuhl/ *n.* act of retaliation. [medieval Latin: related to REPREHEND]

**reprise** /ruh-**preez**/ *n.* **1** repeated passage in music. **2** repeated item in a musical programme. [French: related to REPRIEVE]

**reproach** /ruh-**prohch**/ — *v.* express disapproval to (a person or oneself) for a fault. — *n.* **1** rebuke or censure (*heaped reproaches on them*). **2** (often foll. by *to*) thing that brings disgrace or discredit (*their behaviour is a reproach to us all*). **3** state of disgrace or discredit. □ **above** (or **beyond**) **reproach** perfect, blameless. [French *reprochier*]

**reproachful** *adj.* full of or expressing reproach. □ **reproachfully** *adv.*

**reprobate** /**rep**-ruh-,bayt/ — *adj.* immoral; bad. — *v.* express or feel disapproval of; censure. — *n.* unprincipled or immoral person. □ **reprobation** *n.* [Latin: related to PROVE]

**reproduce** /,ree-pruh-**dyoos**/ *v.* (**-cing**) **1** produce a copy or representation of. **2** cause to be seen or heard etc. again (*tried to reproduce the sound exactly*). **3** produce further members of the same species by natural means. **4** *refl.* produce offspring. □ **reproducible** *adj.*

**reproduction** /,ree-pruh-**duk**-shuhn/ *n.* **1** act or instance of reproducing or the process of being reproduced, esp. the production of further members of the same species. **2** copy of a work of art. **3** (*attrib.*) (of furniture etc.) imitating an earlier style. **4** quality of reproduced sound. □ **reproductive** *adj.*

**reprogram** /ree-**proh**-gram/ *v.* (also **reprogramme**) (**-mm-**) program (esp. a computer) again or differently. □ **reprogramable** *adj.* (also **reprogrammable**).

■ **Usage** See note at **programme**.

**reproof** /ruh-**proof**/ *n. formal* **1** blame (*glance of reproof*). **2** rebuke (*he wilted under her reproof*). [French *reprove*: related to REPROVE]

**reprove** /ruh-**proov**/ *v.* (**-ving**) rebuke (a person, conduct, etc.). [Latin: related to REPROBATE]

**Reps.** *n.* (prec. by *the*) *colloq.* = HOUSE OF REPRESENTATIVES. [abbreviation]

**reptile** /**rep**-tuyl/ *n.* **1** cold-blooded scaly animal of a class including snakes, lizards, crocodiles, turtles, tortoises, etc. **2** mean, grovelling, or repulsive person. □ **reptilian** /-**til**-ee-uhn/ *adj. & n.* [Latin *repo rept-* creep]

**republic** /ruh-**pub**-lik/ *n.* nation in which supreme power is held by the people or their elected representatives or by an elected or nominated president, not by a monarch etc. [Latin *res* concern: related to PUBLIC]

**republican** — *adj.* **1** of or constituted as a republic. **2** characteristic of a republic. **3** advocating or supporting republican government (*the growing republican movement in Australia*). — *n.* person advocating or supporting republican government. □ **republicanism** *n.*

**republish** /ree-**pub**-lish/ *v.* publish again or in a new edition etc. □ **republication** /-li-kay-shuhn/ *n.*

**repudiate** /ruh-**pyoo**-dee-,ayt/ *v.* (**-ting**) **1 a** disown, disavow, reject (*repudiated by his family*; *repudiated his religion*). **b** deny (*repudiated the accusation*). **2** refuse to recognise or obey (authority or a treaty). **3** refuse to discharge (an obligation or debt). □ **repudiation** /-ay-shuhn/ *n.* [Latin *repudium* divorce]

■ **Usage** See note at **refute**.

**repugnance** /ruh-**pug**-nuhns/ *n.* antipathy; aversion. [Latin *pugno* fight]

**repugnant** *adj.* **1** extremely distasteful, disgusting (*racism is utterly repugnant*). **2** contradictory (*a vacuum is repugnant to nature*).

**repulse** /ruh-**puls**/ — *v.* (**-sing**) **1** drive back by force of arms. **2 a** rebuff (friendly advances or their maker). **b** refuse (a request or offer, or its maker). — *n.* **1** act or instance of repulsing or being repulsed. **2** rebuff. [Latin: related to REPEL]

**repulsion** /ruh-**pul**-shuhn/ *n.* **1** aversion, disgust (*felt nothing but repulsion towards the rednecked racists in our society*). **2** *Physics* tendency of bodies to repel each other.

**repulsive** /ruh-**pul**-siv/ *adj.* causing aversion or loathing; disgusting. □ **repulsively** *adv.* [French *répulsif* or REPULSE]

**reputable** /**rep**-yuh-tuh-buhl/ *adj.* of good repute; respectable. [French or medieval Latin: related to REPUTE]

**reputation** /,rep-yuh-**tay**-shuhn/ *n.* **1** what is generally said or believed about a person's or thing's character (*reputation for honesty*; *reputation of being a* *crook*). **2** state of being well thought of; respectability (*have my reputation to think of*). **3** (foll. by *of*, *for*, + pres. part.) credit or discredit (*has a reputation for being generous*; *has the reputation of being a hard marker*). [Latin: related to REPUTE]

**repute** /ruh-**pyoot**/ — *n*. reputation (*known by repute*). — *v*. (as **reputed** *adj*.) **1** be generally considered (*is reputed to be the best*). **2** passing as, but probably not (*his reputed father*). □ **reputedly** *adv*. [Latin *puto* think]

**request** /ruh-**kwest**/ — *n*. **1** act of asking for something (*came at his request*). **2** thing asked for. **3** state of being sought after; demand (*in great request*). — *v*. **1** ask to be given, allowed, or favoured with (*request a hearing*; *requests your presence*). **2** (foll. by *to* + infin.) ask (a person) to do something (*requested him to answer*). **3** (foll. by *that*) ask (*that*) □ **by** (or **on**) **request** in response to an expressed wish. [Latin: related to REQUIRE]

**requiem** /**rek**-wee-,uhm/ *n*. **1** (**Requiem**) (also *attrib*.) *RC Ch*. Mass for the repose of the souls of the dead. **2** music for this. [Latin, = rest]

**requiescat** /,rek-wee-**es**-kat/ *n*. (in full **requiescat in pace**) /in **pah**-chay/ ) wish or prayer, esp. in obituaries, on tombstones, etc., that a dead person's soul may rest in peace. [Latin, = may he (or she) rest in peace]

**require** /ruh-**kwuyuh**/ *v*. (**-ring**) **1** need; depend on for success or fulfilment (*the work requires patience*). **2** lay down as an imperative (*required by law*). **3** command; instruct (a person etc.) (*we required the police to use no provocation*). **4** order; insist on (an action or measure). □ **requirement** *n*. [Latin *requiro -quisit-* seek]

**requisite** /**rek**-wuh-zuht/ — *adj*. required by circumstances; necessary to success etc. (*has all the requisite skills*). — *n*. (often foll. by *for*) thing needed (for some purpose) (*has none of the requisites for the job*). [Latin: related to REQUIRE]

**requisition** /,rek-wuh-**zish**-uhn/ — *n*. **1** official order laying claim to the use of property or materials. **2** formal written demand that some duty should be performed. **3** being called or put into service. — *v*. (esp. of the military or a public authority) demand the use or supply of, esp. by requisition order. [Latin: related to REQUIRE]

**requite** /ruh-**kwuyt**/ *v*. (**-ting**) **1** make return for (a service). **2** reward or avenge (a favour or injury). **3** (often foll. by *for*)

make return to (a person) (*requited her for her generosity to him*). **4** repay with good or evil (*requite like for like*; *requite hate with love*). □ **requital** *n*. [from RE-, QUITE = QUIT]

**reread** /ree-**reed**/ *v*. (*past* and *past part*. **reread** /-**red**/ ) read again.

**reredos** /**reer**-dos/ *n*. ornamental screen covering the wall at the back of an altar. [Anglo-French: related to ARREARS, *dos* back]

**re-release** /,ree-ruh-**lees**/ — *v*. (**-sing**) release (a record, film, etc.) again. — *n*. re-released record, film, etc.

**re-route** /ree-**root**/ *v*. (**-teing**) send or carry by a different route.

**rerun** — *v*. /ree-**run**/ (**-nn-**; *past* **reran**; *past part*. **rerun**) **1** run (a race, film, computer program, etc.) again. **2** repeat (a course of action). — *n*. /**ree**-run/ **1** act of rerunning. **2** film etc. shown again. **3** repetition (of events) (*this match is nothing but a rerun of last week's*).

**resale** /ree-**sayl**, ree-**sayl**/ — *n*. sale of a thing previously bought. — *attrib. adj*. pertaining to the sale of something previously bought (*resale value*; *resale prospects*).

**reschedule** /ree-**shed**-yool, ree-**ske**-jool/ *v*. (**-ling**) alter the schedule of; replan.

**rescind** /ruh-**sind**/ *v*. abrogate, revoke, cancel. □ **rescission** /-**sizh**-uhn/ *n*. [Latin *rescindo -sciss-* cut off]

**rescue** /**res**-kyoo/ — *v*. (**-ues, -ued, -uing**) (often foll. by *from*) save or set free from danger or harm. — *n*. act or instance of rescuing or being rescued. □ **rescuer** *n*. [Romanic: related to RE-, EX-[1], QUASH]

**research** /ruh-**serch**, **ree**-serch/ — *n*. (often *attrib*.) systematic investigation and study of materials, sources, etc., in order to establish facts and reach conclusions. — *v*. do research into or for. □ **researcher** *n*. [French: related to SEARCH]

■ **Usage** The second pronunciation, with the stress on the first syllable, is considered incorrect by some people.

**research and development** *n*. work directed towards the innovation, introduction, and improvement of products and processes.

**resemblance** /ruh-**zem**-bluhns/ *n*. likeness or similarity. [Anglo-French: related to RESEMBLE]

**resemble** /ruh-**zem**-buhl/ *v*. (**-ling**) be like; have a similarity to, or the same appearance as. [French *sembler* seem]

**resent** /ruh-**zent**/ *v*. feel indignation at; be aggrieved by (a circumstance, action, or person). [Latin *sentio* feel]

**resentful** *adj.* feeling resentment. □ **resentfully** *adv.*

**resentment** *n.* indignant or bitter feelings. [Italian or French: related to RESENT]

**reservation** /ˌrez-uh-**vay**-shuhn/ *n.* **1** act or instance of reserving or being reserved. **2** thing booked, e.g. a room in a hotel. **3** spoken or unspoken limitation or exception to an agreement etc. (*had reservations about the plan*). **4** area of land reserved for occupation by American Indians etc. [Latin: related to RESERVE]

**reserve** /ruh-**zerv**/ — *v.* (**-ving**) **1** put aside, keep back for a later occasion or special use (*reserved the best bottles for Christmas*). **2** order to be specially retained or allocated for a particular person or at a particular time (*reserved a seat in the grandstand*). **3** retain or secure (*reserve the right to*). **4** postpone delivery (of judgment etc.) (*reserved my comments until the end*). — *n.* **1** thing reserved for future use; extra amount (*great reserve of strength; huge energy reserves*). **2** limitation or exception attached to something (*I recommend her without reserve*). **3** self-restraint; reticence; lack of cordiality. **4** company's profit added to capital. **5** (in *sing.* or *pl.*) assets kept readily available. **6** (in *sing.* or *pl.*) **a** troops withheld from action to reinforce or protect others. **b** forces in addition to the regular army etc., but available in an emergency. **7** member of the military reserve. **8** extra player chosen as a possible substitute in a team. **9** (in *pl.*) sporting club's second-grade team. **10 a** land set aside for recreational use, as a public park, etc. **b** land set aside for the exclusive use of Aborigines (*Arnhem Land Reserve*). **c** land set aside for the protection of flora and fauna (*nature reserve; wildlife reserve*). □ **in reserve** unused and available if required. **reserve grade** (in sport) second-grade. **reserve judgment** postpone giving one's opinion. [Latin *servo* keep]

**reserve bank** *n.* country's central bank, responsible for the administration of the monetary policy of that country.

**reserved** *adj.* **1** reticent; slow to reveal emotion or opinions; uncommunicative. **2** set apart, destined for a particular use.

**reserve price** *n.* lowest acceptable price stipulated for an item sold at auction.

**reservoir** /**rez**-uh-ˌvwah/ *n.* **1** large natural or artificial lake as a source of water supply. **2** receptacle for fluid. **3** supply of information etc. [French: related to RESERVE]

**reset** /ree-**set**/ *v.* (**-tt-**; *past* and *past part.* **reset**) set (a bone, gems, a clock etc.) again or differently.

**resettle** /ree-**se**-tuhl/ *v.* (**-ling**) **1** settle again (*let the dust resettle*). **2** move or be moved elsewhere to live. □ **resettlement** *n.*

**reshape** /ree-**shayp**/ *v.* (**-ping**) shape or form again or differently.

**reshuffle** /ree-**shuf**-uhl/ — *v.* (**-ling**) **1** shuffle (cards) again. **2** change the posts of (government ministers etc.). — *n.* act of reshuffling.

**reside** /ruh-**zuyd**/ *v.* (**-ding**) **1** have one's home, dwell permanently. **2** (foll. by *in*) (of power, a right, etc.) be vested in (*power resides in the military in that country*). **3** (foll. by *in*) (of a quality) be present or inherent in (*the potential for good resides in all human beings*). [Latin *sedeo* sit]

**residence** /**rez**-uh-duhns/ *n.* **1** process of residing or being resident. **2 a** place where a person resides. **b** house, esp. one of pretension. □ **in residence** living or working at a specified place, esp. for the performance of specialist duties, and usu. for a specified time (*artist in residence; writer in residence*).

**resident** — *n.* **1** (often foll. by *of*) **a** permanent inhabitant. **b** non-migratory species of bird. **2** guest in a hotel etc. staying overnight. — *adj.* **1** residing; in residence. **2** having quarters at one's workplace etc. (*resident caretaker*). **3** located in; inherent (*powers of feeling are resident in the nerves*). **4** (of birds etc.) non-migratory.

**residential** /ˌrez-uh-**den**-shuhl/ *adj.* **1** suitable for or occupied by dwellings (*residential area*). **2** used as a residence (*residential hotel*). **3** based on or connected with residence (*residential qualification for voting*).

**residual** /ruh-**zid**-yoo-uhl/ — *adj.* left as a residue or residuum. — *n.* residual quantity.

**residuary** /ruh-**zid**-yoo-uh-ree/ *adj.* **1** of the residue of an estate (*residuary bequest*). **2** residual.

**residue** /**rez**-uh-ˌdyoo/ *n.* **1** what is left over or remains; remainder. **2** what remains of an estate after the payment of charges, debts, and bequests. [Latin *residuum*: related to RESIDUUM]

**residuum** /ruh-**zid**-yoo-uhm/ *n.* (*pl.* **-dua**) **1** substance left after combustion or evaporation. **2** residue. [Latin: related to RESIDE]

**resign** /ruh-**zuyn**/ *v.* **1** (often foll. by *from*) give up office, one's employment, etc. **2** relinquish, surrender (a right, task, etc.). **3** *refl.* (usu. foll. by *to*) reconcile (oneself etc.) to the inevitable (*have* *resigned myself to the separation).* [Latin *signo* sign]

**resignation** /ˌrez-ig-**nay**-shuhn/ *n.* **1** act or instance of resigning, esp. from one's job or office. **2** letter etc. conveying this. **3** reluctant acceptance of the inevitable. [medieval Latin: related to RESIGN]

**resigned** *adj.* **1** (often foll. by *to*) having resigned oneself; submissive, acquiescent. **2** indicative of this (*resigned expression*). □ **resignedly** /-nuhd-lee/ *adv.*

**resile** /ruh-**zuyl**/ *v.* **1** show resilience. **2** (usu. foll. by *from*) withdraw from a course of action etc. [Latin]

**resilient** /ruh-**zil**-ee-uhnt/ *adj.* **1** resuming its original shape after compression etc. **2** readily recovering from a shock, illness, etc.; buoyant. □ **resilience** *n.* [Latin: related to SALIENT]

**resin** /**rez**-uhn/ — *n.* **1** adhesive substance secreted by some plants and trees. **2** (in full **synthetic resin**) organic compound made by polymerisation etc. and used in plastics. — *v.* (**-n-**) rub or treat with resin. □ **resinous** *adj.* [Latin]

**resist** /ruh-**zist**/ — *v.* **1** withstand the action or effect of (*untreated iron cannot resist the process of rusting*). **2** stop the course or progress of (*my body seems to be resisting the advance of the disease*). **3** abstain from (pleasure, temptation, etc.) (*I managed to resist his advances*). **4** strive against; try to impede; refuse to comply with (*resist arrest*). **5** offer opposition; refuse to comply. — *n.* protective coating of a resistant substance. □ **resistible** *adj.* [Latin *sisto* stop]

**resistance** *n.* **1** act or instance of resisting; refusal to comply. **2** power of resisting (*good resistance to wear and tear*). **3** ability to withstand disease. **4** impeding or stopping effect exerted by one thing on another. **5** *Physics* property of hindering the conduction of electricity, heat, etc. **6** resistor. **7** secret organisation resisting a régime, esp. in an occupied country. □ **resistant** *adj.* [Latin: related to RESIST]

**resistor** *n.* device having resistance to the passage of an electric current.

**resit** *v.* /ree-**sit**/ (**-tt-**; *past* and *past part.* **resat**) sit (an examination) again after failing.

**resolute** /**rez**-uh-ˌloot/ *adj.* determined, decided, firm of purpose. □ **resolutely** *adv.* [Latin: related to RESOLVE]

**resolution** /ˌrez-uh-**loo**-shuhn/ *n.* **1** resolute temper or character. **2** thing resolved on; intention (*New Year's resolution*). **3** a formal expression of opinion or intention by a legislative body or public meeting. **b** formulation of this

(*meeting passed a resolution*). **4** (usu. foll. by *of*) act or instance of solving of a doubt, problem, or question. **5** separation into components. **6** (foll. by *into*) conversion into another form. **7** *Mus.* causing discord to pass into concord. **8 a** smallest interval measurable by a scientific instrument. **b** resolving power.

**resolve** /ruh-**zolv**/ — *v.* (**-ving**) **1** make up one's mind; decide firmly (*resolved to leave*). **2** cause (a person) to do this (*events resolved him to leave*). **3** solve, explain, or settle (a doubt, argument, etc.). **4** (foll. by *that*) (of an assembly or meeting) pass a resolution by vote. **5** (often foll. by *into*) (cause to) separate into constituent parts; analyse. **6** (foll. by *into*) reduce by mental analysis into. **7** *Mus.* convert or be converted into concord. — *n.* firm mental decision or intention; determination. [Latin: related to SOLVE]

**resolved** *adj.* resolute, determined.

**resonant** /**rez**-uh-nuhnt/ *adj.* **1** (of sound) echoing; resounding; continuing to sound; reinforced or prolonged by reflection or vibration. **2** (of a body, room, etc.) tending to reinforce or prolong sounds, esp. by vibration. **3** (often foll. by *with*) (of a place) resounding. □ **resonance** *n.* [Latin: related to RESOUND]

**resonate** /**rez**-uh-ˌnayt/ *v.* (**-ting**) produce or show resonance; resound. □ **resonator** *n.* [Latin: related to RESONANT]

**resort** /ruh-**zawt**/ — *n.* **1** place frequented esp. for holidays or for a specified purpose or quality (*seaside resort; health resort*). **2 a** thing to which one has recourse; expedient, measure. **b** (foll. by *to*) recourse to; use of (*without resort to violence*). — *v.* **1** (foll. by *to*) turn to as an expedient (*resorted to force*). **2** (foll. by *to*) go often or in large numbers to (*many resort to the beaches in summer*). □ **in the** (or **as a**) **last resort** when all else has failed. [French *sortir* go out]

**resound** /ruh-**zownd**/ *v.* **1** (often foll. by *with*) (of a place) ring or echo (*the whole hall resounded with laughter*). **2** (of a voice, instrument, sound, etc.) produce echoes; go on sounding; fill a place with sound. **3 a** (of a reputation etc.) be much talked of (*even Woop Woop resounded with his praise*). **b** (foll. by *through*) produce a sensation (*the scandal resounded through Victoria*). **4** (of a place) re-echo (a sound). [Latin: related to SOUND[1]]

**resounding** *adj.* **1** ringing, echoing. **2** notable, emphatic (*a resounding success*).

**resource** /ruh-**saws**, ree-**zaws**/ — *n.* **1** expedient or device (*escape was their only resource*). **2** (often in *pl.*) means available;

stock or supply that can be drawn on; asset. **3** (in *pl.*) country's collective wealth. **4** skill in devising expedients (*person of great resource*). **5** (in *pl.*) one's inner strength, ingenuity, etc. — *v.* (**-cing**) provide with resources. □ **resourceful** *adj.* (in sense 4). **resourcefully** *adv.* **resourcefulness** *n.* [French: related to SOURCE]

**respect** /ruh-**spekt**/ — *n.* **1** deferential esteem felt or shown towards a person or quality. **2** (foll. by *of, for*) heed or regard. **3** aspect, detail, etc. (*correct in all respects*). **4** reference, relation (*with respect to*). **5** (in *pl.*) polite messages or attentions (*give her my respects*). — *v.* **1** regard with deference or esteem (*you should respect your teachers*). **2 a** avoid interfering with or harming (*the need to respect Aboriginal sacred sites*). **b** treat with consideration (*respect his need to be alone*). **c** refrain from offending (a person, feelings, etc.). □ **in respect of** (or **with respect to**) as concerns. □ **respecter** *n.* [Latin *respicio -spect-* look back at]

**respectable** *adj.* **1** of acceptable social standing; decent and proper in appearance or behaviour. **2** fairly competent (*a respectable try*). **3** reasonably good in condition, appearance, number, size, etc. (*wear some respectable clothes for a change*; *there was a respectable crowd last night*). □ **respectability** /ruh-,spek-tuh-**bil**-uh-tee/ *n.* **respectably** *adv.*

**respectful** *adj.* showing deference. □ **respectfully** *adv.*

**respecting** *prep.* with regard to; concerning.

**respective** *adj.* of or relating to each of several individually (*go to your respective seats*). [French or medieval Latin: related to RESPECT]

**respectively** *adv.* for each separately or in turn, and in the order mentioned (*she and I gave $20 and $10 respectively*).

**respell** /ree-**spel**/ *v.* (*past and past part.* **respelt** or **respelled**) spell again or differently, esp. phonetically.

**respiration** /,res-puh-**ray**-shuhn/ *n.* **1 a** act or instance of breathing. **b** single breath in or out. **2** *Biol.* (in living organisms) the absorption of oxygen and the release of energy and carbon dioxide. [Latin *spiro* breathe]

**respirator** /**res**-puh-,ray-tuh/ *n.* **1** apparatus worn over the face to warm, filter, or purify inhaled air. **2** apparatus for maintaining artificial respiration.

**respire** /ruh-**spuyuh**/ *v.* (**-ring**) **1** (also *absol.*) breathe (air etc.); inhale and exhale. **2** (of a plant) carry out

respiration. □ **respiratory** /ruh-**spi**-ruh-tree, **res**-puh-,ray-tree, **res**-pruh-tree/ *adj.*

**respite** /**res**-puht, **res**-puyt/ — *n.* **1** interval of rest or relief (*brief respite from work*; *drug gave some respite from the pain*). **2** delay permitted before the discharge of an obligation or the suffering of a penalty. — *v.* grant respite to. [Latin: related to RESPECT]

**resplendent** /ruh-**splen**-duhnt/ *adj.* brilliant, dazzlingly or gloriously bright. □ **resplendence** *n.* [Latin *resplendeo* shine]

**respond** /ruh-**spond**/ *v.* **1** answer, reply. **2** act or behave in a corresponding manner (*the public responded well to the hunger-appeal*). **3** (usu. foll. by *to*) show sensitiveness to by behaviour or change (*does not respond to kindness*). **4** (of a congregation) make set answers to a priest etc. [Latin *respondeo -spons-*]

**respondent** — *n.* defendant, esp. in an appeal case. — *adj.* in the position of defendant.

**response** /ruh-**spons**/ *n.* **1** answer given in a word or act; reply. **2** feeling, movement, or change caused by a stimulus or influence. **3** (often in *pl.*) any part of the liturgy said or sung in answer to the priest. □ **response time** time between the performance of an action by a user and a response from a computer etc. [Latin: related to RESPOND]

**responsibility** /ruh-,spon-suh-**bil**-uh-tee/ *n.* (*pl.* **-ies**) **1 a** (often foll. by *for, of*) state or fact of being responsible (*he refuses all responsibility for it*). **b** authority; managerial freedom (*job with more responsibility*). **2** person or thing for which one is responsible; duty, commitment (*the food is my responsibility*). **3** capacity for rational conduct (*diminished responsibility*).

**responsible** /ruh-**spon**-suh-buhl/ *adj.* **1** (often foll. by *to, for*) liable to be called to account (to a person or for a thing). **2** morally accountable for one's actions; capable of rational conduct. **3** of good credit, position, or repute; respectable; evidently trustworthy. **4** (often foll. by *for*) being the primary cause (*faulty brakes were responsible for the crash*). **5** involving responsibility (*a responsible job*). □ **responsibly** *adv.*

**responsive** /ruh-**spon**-siv/ *adj.* **1** (often foll. by *to*) responding readily (to some influence). **2** sympathetic. **3 a** answering (*responsive call of the magpie*). **b** by way of answer. □ **responsiveness** *n.*

**respray** — *v.* /ree-**spray**/ spray again (esp. a vehicle with paint). — *n.* /**ree**-spray/ act or instance of respraying.

**rest¹** — v. **1** cease from exertion, action, etc. **2** be still or asleep, esp. to refresh oneself or recover strength. **3** give relief or repose to; allow to rest (*a chair to rest my weary bones*). **4** (foll. by *on, upon, against*) lie on; be supported by. **5** (foll. by *on, upon*) depend or be based on (*the case rests on slim evidence*). **6** (foll. by *on, upon*) (of a look) alight or be steadily directed on. **7** (foll. by *on, upon*) place for support or foundation on. **8** (of a problem or subject) be left without further investigation or discussion (*let the matter rest*). **9 a** lie in or remain with a person, as something to be determined or accomplished (*sorting out this mess rests entirely with you; the responsibility rests entirely in you*). **b** (foll. by *with*) repose in or justly be ascribed to (a person) (*the blame rests with you*). **10 a** lie in death. **b** (foll. by *in*) lie buried in (a churchyard etc.). **11** (as **rested** *adj.*) refreshed by resting. — n. **1** repose or sleep. **2** cessation of exertion, activity, etc. **3** period of resting (*take a 5-minute rest*). **4** freedom from or cessation of exertion, worry, activity, etc. (*give the subject a rest*). **5** support for holding or steadying something. **6** *Mus.* **a** interval of silence. **b** sign denoting this. □ **at rest** not moving; not agitated or troubled; dead. **rest one's case** conclude one's argument etc. **rest on one's laurels** not seek further success. **rest on one's oars** relax one's efforts. **set at rest** settle or relieve (a question, a person's mind, etc.). [Old English]

**rest²** — n. (prec. by *the*) the remaining part or parts; the others; the remainder of some quantity or number. — v. **1** remain in a specified state (*rest assured*). **2** (foll. by *with*) be left in the hands or charge of (*the final arrangements rest with you*). □ **for the rest** as regards anything else. [French *rester* remain]

**rest area** n. area off a highway where a motorist can stop for a time, these areas being sometimes provided with tables, toilet facilities, gas barbecues, etc.

**restate** /ree-stayt/ v. (**-ting**) express again or differently, esp. for emphasis. □ **restatement** n.

**restaurant** /res-tuh-ront/ n. public premises where meals may be bought and eaten. [French from *restaurer* RESTORE]

**restaurateur** /res-tuh-ruh-ter/ n. (also **restauranteur**) restaurant-keeper.

**restful** adj. giving rest or a feeling of rest; quiet, undisturbed. □ **restfully** adv. **restfulness** n.

**rest home** n. place where old or convalescent people are cared for.

**restitution** /res-tuh-tyoo-shuhn/ n. **1** act or instance of restoring of a thing to its proper owner. **2** reparation for an injury (esp. *make restitution*). [Latin]

**restive** /res-tiv/ adj. **1** fidgety; restless. **2** (of a horse) jibbing; refractory. **3** (of a person) resisting control. □ **restively** adv. **restiveness** n. [French: related to REST²]

**restless** adj. **1** without rest or sleep. **2** uneasy; agitated. **3** constantly in motion, fidgeting, etc. □ **restlessly** adv. **restlessness** n. [Old English: related to REST¹]

**restless flycatcher** n. (also **razor-grinder, scissors-grinder**) black and white busy bird of mainland Australia, having harsh notes which are often compared with the grinding of a razor or scissors.

**restoration** /res-tuh-ray-shuhn/ n. **1** act or instance of restoring or being restored. **2 a** act or process of bringing something back to its original condition. **b** act or process of carrying out alterations and repairs to restore a building etc. to something like its original form. **3** model or representation of the supposed original form of an extinct animal, ruined building, etc. **4** (**Restoration**) *hist.* **a** (prec. by *the*) re-establishment of the British monarchy in 1660. **b** (often *attrib.*) literary period following this (*Restoration comedy*).

**restorative** /ruh-sto-ruh-tiv/ — adj. tending to restore health or strength. — n. restorative medicine, food, etc.

**restore** /ruh-staw/ v. (**-ring**) **1** bring back to the original state by rebuilding, repairing, repainting, etc. **2** bring back to health etc. **3** give back to the original owner etc. **4** reinstate. **5** replace; put back; bring back to a former condition (*restored the missing word in the manuscript; restored to consciousness; restored order*). **6** make a representation of the supposed original state of (a ruin, extinct animal, etc.). □ **restorer** n. [Latin *restauro*]

**restrain** /ruh-strayn/ v. **1** (often *refl.*, usu. foll. by *from*) check or hold in; keep in check, under control, or within bounds. **2** repress, keep down. **3** confine, imprison. [Latin *restringo -strict-*]

**restraining order** n. court order placing certain restrictions on a person (e.g. that a husband must not attempt to make contact with his wife during a separation).

**restraint** n. **1** act or instance of restraining or being restrained. **2** restraining agency or influence. **3** moderation; self-control. **4** reserve of manner. **5** confinement, state of limited freedom.

**restrict** /ruh-**strikt**/ v. **1** confine, limit (*speakers are restricted to 5 minutes each*; *his movements were severely restricted after the operation*). **2** (often as **restricted** *adj.*) withhold from general circulation or disclosure (*restricted publication*; *restricted films may not be viewed by persons under 18*; *restricted area*). □ **restriction** n. [Latin: related to RESTRAIN]

**restrictive** /ruh-**strik**-tiv/ *adj.* restricting. [French or medieval Latin: related to RESTRICT]

**restrictive practice** n. agreement that limits competition or output in industry.

**rest room** n. public toilet.

**restructure** /ree-**struk**-chuh/ v. (**-ring**) give a new structure to; rebuild; rearrange.

**result** /ruh-**zult**/ — n. **1** consequence, issue, or outcome of something. **2** satisfactory outcome (*gets results*). **3** end product of calculation. **4** (in *pl.*) list of scores or winners etc. in examinations or sporting events. — v. **1** (often foll. by *from*) arise as the actual, or follow as a logical, consequence (*your fatigue results from too many sleepless nights*). **2** (often foll. by *in*) have a specified end or outcome (*resulted in a large profit*). [Latin *resulto* spring back]

**resultant** — *adj.* resulting, esp. as the total outcome of more or less opposed forces. — n. *Math.* force etc. equivalent to two or more acting in different directions at the same point.

**resume** /ruh-**zyoom**/ v. (**-ming**) **1** begin again or continue after an interruption. **2** begin to speak, work, or use again; recommence. **3** get back; take back; reoccupy (*resume one's seat*). **4** (of a public authority) take back (land) into public ownership. [Latin *sumo sumpt-* take]

**résumé** /**rez**-yuh-,may/ n. (also **resumé**) summary. [French: related to RESUME]

**resumption** /ruh-**zump**-shuhn/ n. act or instance of resuming (*resumption of trade negotiations*). □ **resumptive** *adj.* [Latin: related to RESUME]

**resurface** /ree-**ser**-fuhs/ v. (**-cing**) **1** lay a new surface on (a road etc.). **2** return to the surface. **3** turn up again.

**resurgent** /ruh-**ser**-juhnt/ *adj.* rising or arising again (*resurgent republicanism in Australia*). □ **resurgence** n. [Latin *resurgo -surrect-* rise again]

**resurrect** /,rez-uh-**rekt**/ v. **1** revive the practice, use, or memory of (*resurrect old grievances*). **2** raise or rise from the dead. [back-formation from RESURRECTION]

**resurrection** /,rez-uh-**rek**-shuhn/ n. **1** rising from the dead. **2 a** (**Resurrection**) Christ's rising from the dead. **b** rising of the dead at the Last Judgment. **3** revival after disuse, inactivity, or decay. [Latin: related to RESURGENT]

**resuscitate** /ruh-**sus**-uh-,tayt/ v. (**-ting**) **1** revive from unconsciousness or apparent death. **2** revive, restore. □ **resuscitation** /-**tay**-shuhn/ n. [Latin *suscito* raise]

**retail** /**ree**-tayl/ — n. sale of goods in small quantities to the public, and usu. not for resale (opp. WHOLESALE). — *adj.* & *adv.* by retail; at a retail price. — v. **1** sell (goods) by retail. **2** (often foll. by *at, of*) (of goods) be sold in this way (esp. for a specified price) (*retails at $9.95*). **3** also /ree-**tayl**/ recount; relate details of (*retailed all the latest gossip he had heard*). □ **retailer** n. [French *taillier* cut: related to TALLY]

**retail price index** n. index of the variation in prices of retail goods.

**retain** /ruh-**tayn**/ v. **1 a** keep possession of; not lose; continue to have. **b** not abolish, discard, or alter. **2** keep in one's memory. **3** keep in place; hold fixed. **4** secure the services of (a person, esp. a barrister) with a preliminary payment. [Latin *retineo -tent-*]

**retainer** n. **1** fee for securing a person's services. **2** faithful servant (esp. *old retainer*). **3** person or thing that retains.

**retaining wall** n. wall supporting and confining a mass of earth or water.

**retake** — v. /ree-**tayk**/ (**-king**; *past* **retook**; *past part.* **retaken**) **1** take (a photograph, exam, etc.) again. **2** recapture. — n. /**ree**-tayk/ **1** act of filming a scene or recording music etc. again. **2** film or recording obtained in this way. **3** act of taking an exam etc. again.

**retaliate** /ruh-**tal**-ee-,ayt/ v. (**-ting**) repay an injury, insult, etc., in kind; attack in return. □ **retaliation** /-**ay**-shuhn/ n. **retaliatory** /-**tal**-yuh-tree/ *adj.* [Latin *talis* such]

**retard** /ruh-**tahd**/ v. **1** make slow or late. **2** delay the progress, development, or accomplishment of. □ **retardant** *adj.* & n. **retardation** /,ree-tah-**day**-shuhn/ n. [Latin *tardus* slow]

**retarded** *adj.* backward in mental or physical development.

**retch** — v. make a motion of vomiting, esp. involuntarily and without effect. — n. such a motion or the sound of it. [Old English]

**retell** /ree-**tel**/ v. (*past* and *past part.* **retold**) tell again or differently.

**retention** /ruh-**ten**-shuhn/ n. **1** act or instance of retaining or being retained. **2** ability to retain (in the mind) things experienced or learned; memory. **3** condition of retaining bodily fluid (esp. urine) normally evacuated. [Latin: related to RETAIN]

**retentive** /ruh-**ten**-tiv/ *adj.* **1** tending to retain. **2** (of memory etc.) not forgetful. [French or medieval Latin: related to RETAIN]

**rethink** — *v.* /ree-**thingk**/ (*past* and *past part.* **rethought**) consider again, esp. with a view to making changes. — *n.* /**ree**-thingk/ reassessment; rethinking.

**reticence** /**ret**-uh-suhns/ *n.* **1** avoidance of saying all one knows or feels, or more than is necessary. **2** disposition to silence; taciturnity. □ **reticent** *adj.* [Latin *reticeo* keep silent]

**reticulate** — *v.* /ruh-**tik**-yuh-,layt/ (**-ting**) divide or be divided in fact or appearance into a network. — *adj.* /ruh-**tik**-yuh-luht/ reticulated. □ **reticulation** /-**lay**-shuhn/ *n.* [Latin *reticulum* diminutive of *rete* net]

**retina** /**ret**-uh-nuh/ *n.* (*pl.* **-s** or **-nae** /-,nee/ ) layer at the back of the eyeball sensitive to light. □ **retinal** *adj.* [Latin *rete* net]

**retinue** /**ret**-uh-,nyoo/ *n.* body of attendants accompanying an important person. [French: related to RETAIN]

**retire** /ruh-**tuyuh**/ *v.* (**-ring**) **1 a** leave office or employment, esp. because of age. **b** cause (a person) to retire from work. **2** withdraw, go away, retreat. **3** seek seclusion or shelter. **4** go to bed. **5** withdraw (troops). **6** *Cricket* (of a batsman) voluntarily end or be compelled to suspend one's innings (*retired hurt*). □ **retire into oneself** become uncommunicative or unsociable. [French *tirer* draw]

**retired** *adj.* **1** having retired from employment. **2** withdrawn from society or observation; secluded (*lived a retired life in the Blue Mountains*).

**retirement** *n.* **1 a** act or instance of retiring. **b** period of one's life as a retired person. **2** seclusion.

**retirement village** *n.* complex of usu. self-contained and separate dwellings in which retired people live.

**retiring** *adj.* shy; fond of seclusion.

**retold** *past* and *past part.* of RETELL.

**retort**[1] /ruh-**tawt**/ — *n.* incisive, witty, or angry reply. — *v.* **1 a** say by way of a retort. **b** make a retort. **2** repay (an insult or attack) in kind. [Latin *retorqueo -tort-* twist]

**retort**[2] /ruh-**tawt**/ — *n.* **1** vessel with a long neck turned downwards, used in distilling liquids. **2** vessel for heating coal to generate gas. — *v.* purify (mercury) by heating in a retort. [medieval Latin: related to RETORT[1]]

**retouch** /ree-**tuch**/ *v.* improve (a picture, photograph, etc.) by minor alterations.

**retrace** /ree-**trays**/ *v.* (**-cing**) **1** go back over (one's steps etc.). **2** trace back to a source or beginning. **3** recall the course of (a thing) in one's memory.

**retract** /ruh-**trakt**/ *v.* **1** withdraw (a statement or undertaking). **2** draw or be drawn back or in (*the tortoise retracted its head*). □ **retractable** *adj.* **retraction** *n.* [Latin *retraho -tract-* draw back]

**retractile** /ruh-**trak**-tuyl/ *adj.* capable of being retracted.

**retrain** /ree-**trayn**/ *v.* train again or further, esp. for new work.

**retread** — *v.* /ree-**tred**/ **1** (*past* **retrod**; *past part.* **retrodden**) tread (a path etc.) again. **2** (*past*, *past part.* **retreaded**) put a fresh tread on (a tyre). — *n.* /**ree**-tred/ **1** retreaded tyre. **2** *colloq.* **a** retired person who is re-engaged. **b** person (esp. a politician) who regains office, position, etc., after a forced absence (*the new Cabinet is full of retreads*).

**retreat** /ruh-**treet**/ — *v.* **1** (esp. of military forces) go back, retire; relinquish a position. **2** recede. — *n.* **1 a** act of retreating. **b** *Mil.* signal for this. **2** withdrawal into privacy or security. **3** place of shelter or seclusion. **4** short period of seclusion (in a monastery etc.) for prayer and meditation. **5** *Mil.* bugle-call at sunset. [Latin: related to RETRACT]

**retrench** /ruh-**trench**/ *v.* **1** sack an employee (or employees) in order to reduce costs, because of a downturn in profits etc. **2** cut down expenses; introduce economies. **3** reduce the amount of (costs). □ **retrenchment** *n.* [French: related to TRENCH]

**retrial** /,ree-**truy**-uhl, ree-,**truy**-uhl/ *n.* second or further (judicial) trial.

**retribution** /,ret-ruh-**byoo**-shuhn/ *n.* requital, usu. for evil done; vengeance. □ **retributive** /ruh-**trib**-yuh-tiv/ *adj.* [Latin: related to TRIBUTE]

**retrieve** /ruh-**treev**/ — *v.* (**-ving**) **1 a** regain possession of. **b** recover by investigation or effort of memory. **2** obtain (information stored in a computer etc.). **3** (of a dog) find and bring back (killed game, a thrown stick, etc.). **4** (foll. by *from*) rescue (esp. from a bad state). **5** restore to a flourishing state; revive. **6** repair or set right (a loss or error etc.) (*managed to retrieve the situation*). — *n.* possibility of recovery (*beyond retrieve*). □ **retrievable** *adj.* **retrieval** *n.* [French *trouver* find]

**retriever** *n.* dog of a breed used for retrieving game.

**retro-** *ret*-roh/ *colloq.* — *adj.* reviving or harking back to the past. — *n.* retro fashion or style.

**retro-** *comb. form* **1** denoting action back or in return. **2** *Anat. & Med.* denoting location behind. [Latin]

**retroactive** /ret-roh-**ak**-tiv/ *adj.* (esp. of legislation) effective from a past date.

**retrograde** /**ret**-ruh-grayd/ — *adj.* **1** directed backwards. **2** reverting, esp. to an inferior state (*it would be a retrograde step to bring back capital punishment*). **3** reversed (*retrograde order*). — *v.* **1** move backwards; recede. **2** decline, revert. [Latin *retrogradior -gress-* move backwards]

**retrogress** /re-truh-**gres**/ *v.* **1** move backwards. **2** deteriorate. □ **retrogression** /re-truh-**gresh**-uhn/ *n.* **retrogressive** *adj.*

**retrorocket** /**ret**-roh-rok-uht/ *n.* auxiliary rocket for slowing down a spacecraft etc.

**retrospect** /**ret**-ruh-spekt/ *n.* survey of a past time or events. □ **in retrospect** when looking back. [from RETRO-, PROSPECT]

**retrospection** /re-truh-**spek**-shuhn/ *n.* looking back into the past.

**retrospective** /re-truh-**spek**-tiv/ — *adj.* **1** looking back on or dealing with the past. **2** (of a law etc.) applying to the past as well as the future. — *n.* exhibition, recital, etc. showing an artist's development over his or her lifetime. □ **retrospectively** *adv.*

**retroussé** /ruh-**troo**-say/ *adj.* (of the nose) turned up at the tip. [French]

**retroverted** /**ret**-roh-ver-tuhd, ret-ruh-/ *adj.* (esp. of the womb) inclined backwards. [Latin: related to RETRO-, *verto* turn]

**retrovirus** /**ret**-roh-vuy-ruhs/ *n.* any of a group of RNA viruses (including the Aids viruses or HIV) which form DNA during the replication of their RNA, and so transfer genetic material into the DNA of host cells. [from the initial letters of *reverse transcriptase* + VIRUS]

**retry** /ree-**truy**/ *v.* (-ies, -ied) try (a defendant or lawsuit) a second or further time.

**retsina** /ret-**see**-nuh/ *n.* Greek white wine flavoured with resin. [modern Greek]

**retune** /ree-**tyoon**/ *v.* (-ning) **1** tune (a musical instrument) again or differently. **2** tune (a radio etc.) to a different frequency. **3** tune (an engine) again to make it run more efficiently.

**return** /ruh-**tern**/ — *v.* **1** come or go back.

**2** bring, put, or send back (*returned the lawnmower*). **3** pay back or reciprocate; give in response (*did not return the compliment*). **4** yield (a profit). **5** say in reply; retort (*to the charge that he was a fool, he wittily returned, 'I am not!'*). **6** (in cricket or tennis etc.) hit or send (the ball) back. **7** state, mention, or describe officially, esp. in answer to a writ or formal demand. **8** (of an electorate) elect as an MP, government, etc. — *n.* **1** act or instance of coming or going back. **2 a** act or instance of giving, sending, putting, or paying back. **b** thing given or sent back. **3** (in full **return ticket**) ticket for a journey to a place and back to the starting-point. **4** (in *sing.* or *pl.*) **a** proceeds or profit of an undertaking. **b** acquisition of these. **5** formal statement compiled or submitted by order (*income-tax return*). **6** (in full **return match** or **game**) second match etc. between the same opponents. **7 a** person's election as an MP etc. **b** returning officer's announcement of this. **8** recurrence (of a certain time or thing) (*many happy returns of the day*). **9** (*attrib.*) relating to a return (*return visit*). □ **by return (of post)** by the next available post in the return direction. **in return** as an exchange or reciprocal action. □ **returnable** *adj.* [Romanic: related to TURN]

**returned soldier** *n.* soldier who has returned home from war.

**returning officer** *n.* official conducting an election in an electorate and announcing the results.

**reunify** /ree-**yoo**-nuh-fuy/ *v.* (-ies, -ied) restore (esp. separated territories) to a political unity. □ **reunification** /-fuh-**kay**-shuhn/ *n.*

**reunion** /ree-**yoon**-yuhn/ *n.* **1** act or instance of reuniting or the condition of being reunited. **2** social gathering, esp. of people formerly associated.

**reunite** /ree-yoo-**nuyt**/ *v.* (-ting) (cause to) come together again.

**reuse** — *v.* /ree-**yooz**/ (-sing) use again. — *n.* /ree-**yoos**/ second or further use. □ **reusable** /-**yoo**-zuh-buhl/ *adj.*

**Rev.** *abbr.* Reverend.

**rev** *colloq.* — *n.* (in *pl.*) number of revolutions of an engine per minute. — *v.* (-vv-) **1** (of an engine) revolve; turn over. **2 a** (also *absol.*; often foll. by *up*) cause (an engine) to run quickly. **b** (foll. by *up*) inject life, vim, vigour, etc. (into a person, a flagging party, etc.). [abbreviation of REVOLUTION]

**revalue** /ree-**val**-yoo/ *v.* (-ues, -ued, -uing) **1** give a higher value to a currency (*the Australian dollar has been revalued by 5% in the past year*) (opp. DEVALUE). **2**

give a different, esp. higher, value to (assets, a literary work, etc.). □ **revaluation** /-ay-shuhn/.

**revamp** — v. /ree-vamp/ **1** renovate, revise, improve (*management practices need to be revamped*). **2** (often as **revamped** adj.) patch up (*driving along in a revamped old Holden*). — n. /ree-vamp/ act or instance of revamping. [RE-, VAMP¹]

**Revd** abbr. (also **Rev.**) Reverend.

**reveal** /ruh-veel/ v. **1** display or show; allow to appear. **2** (often as **revealing** adj.) disclose, divulge, betray (*reveal a secret; a revealing remark*). **3** (in refl. or passive) come to sight or knowledge (*revealed himself as the prince; the destruction was revealed in the morning light*). [Latin *velum* veil]

**reveille** /ruh-val-ee/ n. military waking-signal. [French *réveillez* wake up]

**revel** /rev-uhl/ — v. (**-ll-**) **1** have a good time; be extravagantly festive. **2** (foll. by in) take keen delight in. — n. (in sing. or pl.) act or instance of revelling. □ **reveller** n. **revelry** n. (pl. **-ies**). [Latin: related to REBEL]

**revelation** /rev-uh-lay-shuhn/ n. **1 a** revealing, esp. the supposed disclosure of knowledge to man by a divine or supernatural agency. **b** knowledge disclosed in this way. **2** striking disclosure (*the book contains startling revelations about his private life*). **3** (**Revelation** or colloq. **Revelations**) (in full **the Revelation of St John the Divine**) last book of the New Testament.

**revenge** /ruh-venj/ — n. **1** retaliation for an offence or injury. **2** act of retaliation. **3** desire for this; vindictive feeling (*consumed by revenge*). **4** (in games) win after an earlier defeat. — v. (**-ging**) **1** (in refl. or passive; often foll. by on, upon) inflict retaliation for (an offence) (*revenged herself on her enemies*). **2** take revenge for (an offence). **3** avenge (a person). [Latin: related to VINDICATE]

**revengeful** adj. eager for revenge. □ **revengefully** adv.

**revenue** /rev-uh-nyoo/ n. **1** (also pl.) income, esp. a substantial one. **2** nation's annual income from which public expenses are met. [French *revenu* from Latin *revenio* return]

**reverberate** /ruh-ver-buh-rayt/ v. (**-ting**) **1** (of sound etc.) be returned, echoed, or reflected repeatedly (*the chanting reverberated through the cathedral*). **2** return (a sound etc.) in this way (*the hills reverberated the cry*). **3** (of an event etc.) produce a continuing effect,

shock, etc. (*news of the disaster reverberated through Australia*). □ **reverberant** adj. **reverberation** /-ray-shuhn/ n. **reverberative** /-ruh-tiv/ adj. [Latin *verbero* beat]

**revere** /ruh-veer/ v. (**-ring**) hold in deep and usu. affectionate or religious respect. [Latin *vereor* fear]

**reverence** /rev-uh-ruhns/ — n. **1** act of revering or state of being revered. **2** capacity for revering (*lacks reverence*). — v. (**-cing**) regard or treat with reverence. [Latin: related to REVERE]

**reverend** /rev-ruhnd/ adj. (esp. as the title of a clergyman) deserving reverence. [Latin *reverendus*: related to REVERE]

**Reverend Mother** n. Mother Superior of a convent.

**reverent** /rev-uh-ruhnt/ adj. feeling or showing reverence. □ **reverently** adv. [Latin: related to REVERE]

**reverential** /rev-uh-ren-shuhl/ n. of the nature of, due to, or characterised by reverence. □ **reverentially** adv. [medieval Latin: related to REVERENCE]

**reverie** /rev-uh-ree/ n. **1** fit of abstracted musing, day-dream. **2** Mus. instrumental piece suggesting a dreamy or musing mood. [French]

**revers** /ruh-veer/ n. (pl. same /ruh-veerz/) **1** turned-back edge of a garment revealing the undersurface. **2** material on this surface. [French: related to REVERSE]

**reverse** /ruh-vers/ — v. (**-sing**) **1** turn the other way round or up or inside out. **2** change to the opposite character or effect (*government reversed its immigration policy*). **3** (cause to) travel backwards. **4** make (an engine etc.) work in a contrary direction. **5** revoke or annul (a decree, act, legal judgment, etc.). — adj. **1** backwards or upside down. **2** opposite or contrary in character or order (*reverse gear; line up in reverse order*). — n. **1** opposite or contrary (*the reverse is the case*). **2** contrary of the usual manner (*printed in reverse*). **3** piece of misfortune; disaster; defeat (*suffered a reverse*). **4** reverse gear or motion. **5** reverse side. **6** side of a coin etc. bearing the secondary design (*the reverse side of a coin is usually called 'tails'*). **7** verso of a printed leaf. □ **reverse arms** hold a rifle with the butt upwards. **reverse the charges** have the recipient of a telephone call pay for it. □ **reversal** n. **reversible** adj. [Latin *verto vers-* turn]

**reversion** /ruh-ver-zhuhn/ n. **1** return to a previous state, habit, etc. **2** Biol. return to ancestral type. [Latin: related to REVERSE]

**revert** /ruh-**vert**/ v. (foll. by *to*) return to a former state, practice, opinion, etc.

**revhead** n. *colloq.* person with a passionate interest in cars. [REV, -HEAD²]

**review** /ruh-**vyoo**/ — n. **1** general survey or assessment of a subject or thing. **2** survey of the past (*reviewed his life's achievements*). **3** revision or reconsideration (*is under review*). **4** display and formal inspection of troops etc. **5** published criticism of a book, play, etc. **6** periodical with critical articles on current events, the arts, etc. — v. **1** survey or look back on. **2** reconsider or revise (*the government will review the deportation order*). **3** hold a review of (troops etc.). **4** write a review of (a book, play, etc.). □ **reviewer** n. [French *revoir*: related to VIEW]

**revile** /ruh-**vuyl**/ v. (**-ling**) abuse verbally. [French: related to VILE]

**revise** /ruh-**vuyz**/ v. (**-sing**) **1** examine or re-examine and improve or amend (esp. written or printed matter). **2** consider and alter (an opinion etc.). **3** (also *absol.*) go over (work learnt or done) again, esp. for an examination (*I'm going to revise tonight*; *revising her Bahasa Indonesia*). □ **revisory** adj. [Latin *reviso* from *video vis-* see]

**revision** /ruh-**vizh**-uhn/ n. **1** act or instance of revising or process of being revised. **2** revised edition or form. [Latin: related to REVISE]

**revisionism** n. often *derog.* revision or modification of an orthodoxy, esp. of Marxism. □ **revisionist** n. & adj.

**revitalise** /ree-**vuy**-tuh-,luyz/ v. (also **-ize**) (**-sing** or **-zing**) imbue with new life and vitality.

**revival** /ruh-**vuy**-vuhl/ n. **1** act or instance of reviving or process of being revived. **2** new production of an old play etc. **3** revived use of an old practice, style, etc. (*revival of paganism*; *Gothic revival*). **4 a** reawakening of religious fervour. **b** campaign or series of evangelical meetings to promote this.

**revivalism** n. promotion of a revival, esp. of religious fervour. □ **revivalist** n. & adj.

**revive** /ruh-**vuyv**/ v. (**-ving**) **1** come or bring back to consciousness, life, or strength (*the music revived old memories*; *the doctor managed to revive him*). **2** come or bring back to existence, or to use or notice etc. (*few would want to revive the theory that the earth is flat*; *revived old rumours*). [Latin *vivo* live]

**revivify** /ree-**viv**-uh-,fuy/ v. (**-ies**, **-ied**) restore to animation, vigour, or life. □ **revivification** /-fuh-**kay**-shuhn/ n. [Latin: related to VIVIFY]

**revoke** /ree-**vohk**, ruh-/ v. (**-king**) **1** rescind, withdraw, or cancel (a decree, promise, etc.). **2** *Cards* = RENEGE. □ **revocable** /rev-uh-kuh-buhl/ adj. **revocation** /,rev-uh-**kay**-shuhn/ n. [Latin *voco* call]

**revolt** /ruh-**volt**/ — v. **1** rise in rebellion. **2 a** affect with strong disgust (*was revolted by the thought of it*). **b** (often foll. by *at*, *against*) feel strong disgust (*revolted against giving children the strap*). — n. **1** act of rebelling. **2** state of insurrection (*in revolt*). **3** sense of disgust (*my stomach rose in revolt at the thought of eating tripe*). **4** mood of protest or defiance (*there was revolt in the air at the student meeting*). [Italian: related to REVOLVE]

**revolting** adj. disgusting, horrible. □ **revoltingly** adv.

**revolution** /,rev-uh-**loo**-shuhn/ n. **1** forcible overthrow of a government or social order. **2** any fundamental change or reversal of conditions. **3** act or instance of revolving. **4 a** single completion of an orbit or rotation. **b** time taken for this. **5** cyclic recurrence (*the revolution of the planets*). [Latin: related to REVOLVE]

**revolutionary** — adj. **1** involving great and often violent change (*Darwin's revolutionary theory of evolution*). **2** of or causing political revolution. — n. (pl. **-ies**) instigator or supporter of political revolution.

**revolutionise** v. (also **-ize**) (**-sing** or **-zing**) change fundamentally.

**revolve** /ruh-**volv**/ v. (**-ving**) **1** (cause to) turn round, esp. on an axis; rotate. **2** move in a circular orbit. **3** ponder (a problem etc.) in the mind (*had been revolving the idea in his mind for some time*). **4** (foll. by *around*) have as its chief concern; be centred upon (*his life revolves around his job*). [Latin *revolvo -volut-*]

**revolver** n. pistol with revolving chambers enabling several shots to be fired without reloading.

**revue** /ruh-**vyoo**/ n. entertainment of short usu. satirical sketches and songs. [French: related to REVIEW]

**revulsion** /ruh-**vul**-shuhn/ n. **1** abhorrence; intense disgust. **2** sudden violent change of feeling (*his emotions underwent a revulsion from anger to pity*). [Latin *vello vuls-* pull]

**reward** /ruh-**wawd**/ — n. **1 a** return or recompense for service or merit. **b** requital for good or evil (*the reward of the wicked, they say, is hell*). **2** sum offered for the detection of a criminal, restoration of lost property, etc. — v. give a reward to (a person) or for (a service etc.). [Anglo-French *reward(er)* REGARD]

**rewarding** *adj.* (of an activity etc.) worthwhile; satisfying.

**rewind** /ree-**wuynd**/ *v.* (*past* and *past part.* **rewound**) wind (a film or tape etc.) back.

**rewire** /ree-**wuyuh**/ *v.* (**-ring**) provide with new electrical wiring.

**reword** /ree-**werd**/ *v.* express in different words.

**rework** /ree-**werk**/ *v.* revise; refashion; remake. □ **reworking** *n.*

**rewrite** — *v.* /ree-**ruyt**/ (**-ting**; *past* **rewrote**; *past part.* **rewritten**) write again or differently. — *n.* /**ree**-ruyt/ **1** re-writing (*this essay needs a rewrite*). **2** thing rewritten. □ **rewritable** *adj.*

**Rex** *n.* (after the name) reigning king (*George Rex*). [Latin]

**Rf** *symb.* rutherfordium.

**Rh** *symb.* rhodium.

**rhapsodise** /**rap**-suh-,duyz/ *v.* (also **-ize**) (**-sing** or **-zing**) talk or write rhapsodies.

**rhapsody** /**rap**-suh-dee/ *n.* (*pl.* **-ies**) **1** enthusiastic or extravagant speech or composition. **2** piece of music in one movement, often based on national, folk, or popular melodies. □ **rhapsodic** /rap-**sod**-ik/ *adj.* [Greek *rhaptō* stitch: related to ODE]

**rhenium** /**ree**-nee-uhm/ *n.* rare metallic element occurring naturally in molyb-denum ores. [Latin *Rhenus* Rhine]

**rheostat** /**ree**-uh-,stat/ *n.* instrument used to control an electric current by varying the resistance. [Greek *rheos* stream]

**rhesus** /**ree**-suhs/ *n.* (in full **rhesus mon-key**) small N. Indian monkey. [*Rhesus*, mythical king of Thrace]

**rhesus factor** *n.* (also **Rh factor**) antigen occurring in the red blood cells of most humans and some other primates (as in the rhesus monkey in which it was first observed).

**rhesus-negative** *adj.* lacking the rhesus factor.

**rhesus-positive** *adj.* having the rhesus factor.

**rhetoric** /**ret**-uh-rik/ *n.* **1** art of effective or persuasive speaking or writing. **2** lan-guage designed to persuade or impress (esp. seen as overblown and meaning-less). [Greek *rhētōr* orator]

**rhetorical** /ruh-**to**-ri-kuhl/ *adj.* **1** ex-pressed artificially or extravagantly. **2** of the nature or art of rhetoric. □ **rhetorically** *adv.* [Greek: related to RHETORIC]

**rhetorical question** *n.* question used for effect but not seeking an answer (e.g. *who cares?* for *nobody cares*).

**rheumatic** /roo-**mat**-ik/ — *adj.* of, suffering from, producing, or produced by rheumatism. — *n.* person suffering from rheumatism. □ **rheumatically** *adv.* **rheum-aticky** *adj. colloq.* [Greek *rheuma* stream]

**rheumatic fever** *n.* fever with inflam-mation and pain in the joints.

**rheumatism** /**roo**-muh-,tiz-uhm/ *n.* disease marked by inflammation and pain in the joints, muscles, or fibrous tissue, esp. rheumatoid arthritis.

**rheumatoid** /**roo**-muh-,toid/ *adj.* having the character of rheumatism.

**rheumatoid arthritis** *n.* chronic pro-gressive disease causing inflammation and stiffening of the joints.

**rhinestone** *n.* imitation diamond. [river *Rhine* in Germany]

**rhino** /**ruy**-noh/ *n.* (*pl.* same or **-s**) *colloq.* rhinoceros. [abbreviation]

**rhinoceros** /ruy-**nos**-uh-ruhs/ *n.* (*pl.* same or **-roses**) large thick-skinned mammal of Africa and S. Asia, with one or two horns on its nose. [Greek *rhis rhin-*nose, *keras* horn]

**rhinoceros beetle** *n.* black Australian scarab beetle having a horned head resembling that of a rhinoceros.

**rhizome** /**ruy**-zohm/ *n.* underground rootlike stem bearing both roots and shoots. [Greek *rhizoma*]

**rho** /roh/ *n.* seventeenth letter of the Greek alphabet (P, ρ). [Greek]

**rhodium** /**roh**-dee-uhm/ *n.* hard white metallic element used in making alloys and plating jewellery. [Greek *rhodon* rose]

**rhododendron** /,roh-duh-**den**-druhn/ *n.* (*pl.* **-s** or **-dra**) evergreen shrub with large clusters of trumpet-shaped flowers, native to S. Asia, but widely cultivated elsewhere (cf. AZALEA). [Greek *rhodon* rose, *dendron* tree]

**Rhododendron lochae** /**lok**-ee/ *n.* Aus-tralia's sole rhododendron, a low shrub with dark green leaves and red trumpet-flowers of a spectacular brilliance. [named after Lady *Loch*, wife of the Governor of Victoria 1884–89]

**rhomboid** /**rom**-boid/ — *adj.* (also **rhomboidal** /-**boi**-duhl/ ) like a rhombus. — *n.* quadrilateral of which only the opposite sides and angles are equal. [Greek: related to RHOMBUS]

**rhombus** /**rom**-buhs/ *n.* (*pl.* **-buses** or **-bi** /-buy/ ) *Geom.* parallelogram with oblique angles and equal sides. [Greek *rhombos*]

**rhubarb** /**roo**-bahb/ *n.* **1 a** plant with long fleshy dark red leaf-stalks cooked as a dessert. **b** these stalks. **2 a** *colloq.*

indistinct conversation or hubbub, from the stage convention of repeatedly using the word 'rhubarb' by actors playing a crowd. **b** *colloq.* nonsense; worthless stuff (*gave us a heap of rhubarb about why they were late*). **c** *colloq.* heated dispute; commotion (*husband and wife had a right royal rhubarb last night*). [Greek *rha* rhubarb, *barbaros* foreign]

**rhyme** /ruym/ — *n.* **1** identity of sound between words or their endings, esp. in verse. **2** (in *sing.* or *pl.*) verse or a poem having rhymes. **3** use of rhyme. **4** word providing a rhyme. — *v.* (**-ming**) **1 a** (of words or lines) produce a rhyme. **b** (foll. by *with*) act as or treat (a word) as a rhyme (with another). **2** make or write rhymes. **3** put or make (a story etc.) into rhyme. □ **rhyme or reason** sense, logic. [Latin: related to RHYTHM]

**rhymester** *n.* writer of (esp. simple) rhymes.

**rhyming slang** *n.* slang that replaces words by rhyming words or phrases, e.g. *shark* by *Noah's Ark*, often with the rhyming word omitted (as in SEPTIC).

**rhythm** /rith-uhm/ *n.* **1 a** periodical accent and the duration of notes in music, esp. as beats in a bar. **b** type of structure formed by this (*samba rhythm*). **2** measured regular flow of verse or prose determined by the length of and stress on syllables. **3** *Physiol.* pattern of successive strong and weak movements (*rhythm of the heart*). **4** regularly recurring sequence of events. □ **rhythmic** *adj.* **rhythmical** *adj.* **rhythmically** *adv.* [Greek *rhuthmos*]

**rhythm and blues** *n.* popular music with blues themes and a strong rhythm.

**rhythm method** *n.* abstention from sexual intercourse near the time of ovulation, as a method of birth control.

**rib** — *n.* **1** each of the curved bones joined to the spine in pairs and protecting the chest. **2** joint of meat from this part of an animal. **3** supporting ridge, timber, rod, etc., across a surface or through a structure. **4** *Knitting* combination of plain and purl stitches producing a ribbed design. **5** vein of a leaf or on an insect's wing. — *v.* (**-bb-**) **1** provide with ribs; act as the ribs of. **2** *colloq.* make fun of; tease. **3** mark with ridges. [Old English]

**ribald** /rib-uhld, ruy-bawld/ *adj.* coarsely or disrespectfully humorous; obscene. [French *riber* be licentious]

**ribaldry** *n.* ribald talk or behaviour.

**ribbed** *adj.* having ribs or riblike markings.

**ribbing** *n.* **1** ribs or a riblike structure. **2** *colloq.* the act or an instance of teasing.

**ribbon** /rib-uhn/ *n.* **1 a** narrow strip or band of fabric, used esp. for trimming or decoration. **b** material in this form. **2** ribbon worn to indicate some honour or membership of a sports team etc. **3** long narrow strip of anything (*typewriter ribbon*). **4** (in *pl.*) ragged strips (*torn to ribbons*). [French *riban*]

**ribbon fern** *n.* epiphytic rainforest fern of Queensland and NSW, having extremely long, hanging, glossy, ribbon-like fronds.

**ribbon gum** *n.* any of several Australian eucalypts having bark which tends to hang from the trunk in ribbons as it is shed.

**ribcage** *n.* wall of bones formed by the ribs round the chest.

**riboflavin** /ruy-boh-**flay**-vuhn/ *n.* (also **riboflavine** /-veen/ ) vitamin of the B complex, found in liver, milk, and eggs. [*ribose* sugar, Latin *flavus* yellow]

**ribonucleic acid** /ruy-boh-nyoo-**klay**-ik/ *n.* nucleic acid in living cells, involved in protein synthesis. [*ribose* sugar]

**rib-tickler** *n.* something amusing; joke.

**rice** *n.* **1** swamp grass cultivated in esp. Asian marshes. **2** grains of this, used as food. [French *ris* ultimately from Greek *oruza*]

**rice flower** *n.* = PIMELEA.

**rice-paper** *n.* edible paper made from the pith of an oriental tree and used for painting and in cookery.

**rich** *adj.* **1** having much wealth. **2** splendid, costly, elaborate. **3** valuable (*rich offerings*). **4** copious, abundant, ample (*rich harvest; rich supply of ideas*). **5** (often foll. by *in*, *with*) (of soil or a region etc.) fertile; abundant in resources etc. (*rich in nutrients*). **6** (of food or diet) containing much fat or spice etc. **7** (of the mixture in an internal-combustion engine) containing a high proportion of fuel. **8** (of colour, sound, or smell) mellow and deep, strong and full (*rich purple*; *rich voice; rich aroma*). **9 a** (of an incident or assertion etc.) highly amusing or ludicrous; preposterous. **b** (of humour) earthy; indecent. □ **richness** *n.* [Old English and French]

**Richard** /rich-uhd/ *n.* *colloq.* (also **richard**) □ **have had the Richard** be finished; be irreparably damaged. [abbreviation of *Richard the Third*, rhyming slang for 'turd']

**richea** /rich-ee-uh/ *n.* shrub or tree, chiefly of Tasmania (esp. PANDANNY) with pink or white flowers in terminal spikes, and with highly ornamental, often

**riches** *n.pl.* abundant means; valuable possessions. [French *richeise*: related to RICH]

**richly** *adv.* **1** in a rich way (*richly ornamented*). **2** fully, thoroughly (*richly deserves success*).

**Richter scale** /rik-tuh/ *n.* scale of 0 to 10 for representing the strength of an earthquake. [*Richter*, name of a seismologist]

**rick¹** *n.* stack of hay etc. [Old English]

**rick²** — *n.* slight sprain or strain (of the neck, back, etc.). — *v.* sprain or strain slightly. [Low German *wricken*]

**rickets** /rik-uhts/ *n.* (treated as *sing.* or *pl.*) disease of children with softening of the bones, caused by a deficiency of vitamin D. [origin uncertain]

**rickety** /rik-uh-tee/ *adj.* **1 a** insecure or shaky in construction (*rickety stairs*). **b** feeble (*a bit rickety after the operation*). **2** suffering from rickets. □ **ricketiness** *n.*

**rickshaw** /rik-shaw/ *n.* (also **ricksha** /-shuh/) light two-wheeled hooded vehicle drawn by one or more persons. [abbreviation of *jinrickshaw* from Japanese]

**ricochet** /rik-uh-,shay/ — *n.* **1** rebounding of esp. a shell or bullet off a surface. **2** hit made after this. — *v.* (**-cheted** /-,shayd/ **-cheting** /-,shay-ing/ or **-chetted** /-,shet-uhd/ **-chetting** /-,shet-ing/) (of a projectile) make a ricochet. [French]

**ricotta** /ruh-kot-uh/ *n.* soft Italian cheese. [Latin: related to RE-, *coquo* cook]

**rid** *v.* (**-dd-**; *past* and *past part.* **rid**) (foll. by *of*) free (a person or place) of something unwanted. □ **be** (or **get**) **rid of** be freed or relieved of; dispose of. [Old Norse]

**riddance** /rid-uhns/ *n.* getting rid of something. □ **good riddance** expression of relief at getting rid of something.

**ridden** — *past part.* of RIDE. — *adj.* full of or dominated by (*rat-ridden cellars*; *guilt-ridden*).

**riddle¹** /rid-uhl/ — *n.* **1** verbal puzzle or test, often with a trick answer. **2** puzzling fact, thing, or person. — *v.* (**-ling**) speak in riddles. [Old English: related to READ]

**riddle²** /rid-uhl/ — *v.* (**-ling**) (usu. foll. by *with*) **1** make many holes in, esp. with gunshot. **2** (in *passive*) fill; permeate (*riddled with errors*). **3** pass through a riddle. — *n.* coarse sieve. [Old English]

**ride** — *v.* (**-ding**; *past* **rode**; *past part.* **ridden** /rid-uhn/) **1** (often foll. by *on, in*) travel or be carried on (a bicycle etc.) or in (a vehicle); be conveyed (*rode her bike*; *rode on her bike*; *rode the tram*). **2** (often foll. by *on*; also *absol.*) be carried by (a horse etc.). **3** be carried or supported by (*ship rides the waves*). **4 a** traverse or take part in on horseback etc. (*ride 50 kilometres*; *rode a good race*). **b** traverse (a station boundary) in order to inspect or maintain. **5 a** lie at anchor; float buoyantly. **b** (of the moon) seem to float. **6** yield to (a blow) so as to reduce its impact (*he rode the punch*). **7** give a ride to; cause to ride (*rode me home*). **8** (of a rider) cause (a horse etc.) to move forward (*rode their horses at the fence*). **9 a** torment; harass (*rides him out of spite*). **b** domineer; impose (authority, rules, restrictions, etc.) on (*you are riding him too hard*). **10** (as **ridden** *adj.*) (foll. by *by*, *with*, or in *comb.*) be dominated by; be infested with (*ridden with guilt*; *rat-ridden cellar*). — *n.* **1** journey or spell of riding in a vehicle, or on a horse, bicycle, person's back, etc. **2** specified kind of ride (*bumpy ride*). **3** amusement for riding on at a fairground etc. **ride for fun**; as an observer only (*I'm in it only for the ride*). **let a thing ride** leave it undisturbed; allow it to take its natural course. **ride again** reappear as strong etc. as ever (*Elvis Presley rides again*). **ride the clutch** (of the driver of a car etc.) keep one's foot too long on the clutch pedal, depressing it slightly and risking damage. **ride high** be elated or successful. **ride on** depend on (*everything rides on her agreement with the deal*). **ride out** come safely through (a storm, danger, etc.). **ride roughshod over** see ROUGHSHOD. **ride up** (of a garment) work upwards out of its proper position. **take for a ride** *colloq.* hoax or deceive. [Old English]

**rider** *n.* **1** person who rides (esp. a horse). **2** additional remark following a statement, verdict, etc. □ **riderless** *adj.*

**ridge¹** — *n.* **1** line of the junction of two surfaces sloping upwards towards each other (*ridge of a roof*). **2** long narrow hilltop, mountain range, or watershed. **3** top part or crest of anything, esp. when long and narrow (*ridge of the spine*; *riding the ridge of the wave*). **4** any narrow elevation across a surface. **5** elongated region of high barometric pressure. **6** raised strip of esp. ploughed land. — *v.* (**-ging**) mark with ridges. □ **ridgy** *adj.* [Old English]

**ridge²** *adj.* (also **ridgy-didge**) *colloq.* all right, genuine, dinkum (*this is gospel, mate, absolutely ridge*). [Brit. cant *ridge* gold coin]

**ridge pole** *n.* horizontal roof pole of a long tent.

**ridicule** /**rid**-uh-ˌkyool/ — *n.* derision, mockery. — *v.* (**-ling**) make fun of; mock; laugh at. [Latin *rideo* laugh]

**ridiculous** /ruh-**dik**-yuh-luhs/ *adj.* **1** deserving or inviting ridicule (*wore a ridiculous hat*). **2** unreasonable; absurd (*his excuses were ridiculous*). □ **ridiculously** *adv.* **ridiculousness** *n.*

**riding¹** /**ruy**-ding/ *n.* sport or pastime of travelling on horseback.

**riding²** /**ruy**-ding/ *n.* electoral division of a shire. [Old English from Old Norse, = third part]

**riesling** /**rees**-ling, **reez**-ling/ *n.* **1** a kind of grape. **2** white wine made from this. [German]

**rife** *predic. adj.* **1** of common occurrence; widespread. **2** (foll. by *with*) abounding in (*rife with wildlife*). [Old English, probably from Old Norse]

**riff** *n.* short repeated phrase in jazz etc. [abbreviation of RIFFLE]

**riffle** /**rif**-uhl/ — *v.* (**-ling**) **1** (often foll. by *through*) leaf quickly through (pages). **2 a** turn (pages) in quick succession. **b** shuffle (playing-cards), esp. by flexing and combining the two halves of a pack. — *n.* act of riffling. [perhaps var. of RUFFLE]

**riff-raff** /**rif**-raf/ *n.* (often prec. by *the*) rabble; disreputable people. [French *rif et raf*]

**rifle¹** /**ruy**-fuhl/ *n.* gun with a long grooved barrel, esp. one fired from the shoulder. [French]

**rifle²** /**ruy**-fuhl/ *v.* (**-ling**) (often foll. by *through*) **1** search and rob (*burglar rifled the house*). **2** search messily for something mislaid etc. (*rifled through all the cupboards*). [French]

**rifle-bird** *n.* any of three Australian birds of paradise, the male having velvety black plumage with metallic patches. [possibly from colour resemblance to the uniform of the Rifle Brigade, or from its call sounding like a rifle-shot]

**rifle fish** *n.* northern Australian fish, so called because it ejects a jet of water from its mouth to shoot down insects etc.

**rifle range** *n.* place for rifle-practice.

**rifle-shot** *n.* **1** shot fired with a rifle. **2** distance coverable by this.

**rifling** *n.* arrangement of grooves on the inside of a gun's barrel.

**rift** *n.* **1** crack, split; break (in cloud etc.). **2** disagreement; breach. **3** cleft in earth or rock. [Scandinavian: related to RIVEN]

**rift valley** *n.* steep-sided valley formed by subsidence between nearly parallel faults.

**rig¹** — *v.* (**-gg-**) **1** provide (a ship) with

sails, rigging, etc. **2** (often foll. by *out, up*) fit with clothes or other equipment. **3** (foll. by *up*) set up hastily or as a makeshift. **4** assemble and adjust the parts of (an aircraft). — *n.* **1** arrangement of a ship's masts, sails, etc. **2** equipment for a special purpose, e.g. a radio transmitter. **3** = OIL RIG. **4** large truck; semi-trailer. **5** *colloq.* style of dress; uniform (*in full rig*). □ **rigged out** dressed, esp. in one's best (or flashily) (*rigged out in his working gear; rigged out for the opera*). □ **rigout** *n.* (also in *comb.*). [perhaps from Scandinavian]

**rig²** *v.* (**-gg-**) manage or fix (a result etc.) fraudulently (*rigged the election*). □ **rig the market** cause an artificial rise or fall in prices. [origin unknown]

**rigger** *n.* **1** worker on an oil rig. **2** person who rigs or who arranges rigging.

**rigging** *n.* ship's spars, ropes, etc.

**right** /ruyt/ — *adj.* **1** (of conduct etc.) just, morally or socially correct (*it is only right that I tell you; do the right thing*). **2** true, correct (*which is the right way?*). **3** suitable or preferable (*right person for the job*). **4** sound or normal; healthy; satisfactory (*engine doesn't sound right*). **5** on or towards the east side of the human body, or of any object etc., when facing north. **6** (of a side of fabric etc.) meant for display or use (*turn it right side up*). **7** *colloq.* real; complete (*made a right mess of it*). **8** (also **Right**) *Polit.* of the Right. **9** *colloq.* **a** in good shape; all right (*Want another chop? — No, I'm right thanks mate*). **b** (as **are you right?** or **you right?**) (in shopping) are you being served?; may I help you? — *n.* **1** that which is correct or just; fair treatment (often in *pl.*: *rights and wrongs of the case*). **2** justification or fair claim (*has no right to speak*). **3** legal or moral entitlement; authority to act (*Aboriginal land rights; right of reply*). **4** right-hand part, region, or direction. **5** *Boxing* **a** right hand. **b** blow with this. **6** (often **Right**) **a** conservative political group or section (originally the more conservative section of a European legislature, seated on the president's right). **b** conservatives collectively. **7** side of a stage to the right of a person facing the audience. — *v.* **1** (often *refl.*) restore to a proper, straight, or vertical position. **2** correct or avenge (mistakes, wrongs, etc.); set in order; make reparation. — *adv.* **1** straight (*go right on*). **2** *colloq.* immediately (*do it right now*). **3 a** (foll. by *to, round, through,* etc.) all the way (*sank right to the bottom; ran right round the block*). **b** (foll. by *off, out,* etc.) completely (*came right off its* hinges; *am right out of vegemite*). **4** exactly, quite (*right in the middle*). **5** justly, properly, correctly, truly, satisfactorily (*not holding it right; if I remember right*). **6** on or to the right side. — *int. colloq.* expressing agreement or assent. □ **be right behind (a person)** give total support to; be in full agreement with. **by right** (or **rights**) if right were done. **do right by** act dutifully towards (a person). **in one's own right** through one's own position or effort etc. **in the right** having justice or truth on one's side. **in one's right mind** sane. **of** (or **as of**) **right** having legal or moral etc. entitlement. **on the right side of** (a person etc.). **1** in the favour of (a person etc.). **2** somewhat less than a specified age). **put** (or **set**) **right 1** restore to order, health, etc. **2** correct the mistaken impression etc. of (a person). **put** (or **set**) **to rights** make correct or well ordered. **right about** (or **about-turn** or **about-face**) **1** a right turn continued to face the rear. **2** reversal of policy (*the opposition did an about-turn on its tax-policy*). **3** a hasty retreat. **right away** (or **off**) immediately. **right oh!** (or **ho!**) = RIGHTO. **right on!** *colloq.* expression of strong approval or encouragement. **right you are!** *colloq.* exclamation of assent. **she'll be right** *colloq.* that will be all right; all will be well (*she'll be right, mate, someone's sure to turn up soon*). **she's right** *colloq.* all is under control; all is in order (*Do you need a hand? — No, she's right, mate, thanks!*) **too right** *colloq.* expression of agreement. □ **rightness** *n.* [Old English]

**right angle** *n.* angle of 90°.

**right arm** *n.* one's most reliable helper.

**righten** *v.* make right or correct.

**righteous** /**ruy**-chuhs/ *adj.* (of a person or conduct) morally right; virtuous, law-abiding. □ **righteously** *adv.* **righteousness** *n.* [Old English]

**rightful** *adj.* **1 a** (of a person) legitimately entitled to (a position etc.) (*rightful heir*). **b** (of status or property etc.) that one is entitled to. **2** (of an action etc.) equitable, fair. □ **rightfully** *adv.* [Old English]

**right hand** *n.* = RIGHT-HAND MAN.

**right-hand** *attrib. adj.* **1** on or towards the right side of a person or thing. **2** done with the right hand.

**right-handed** *adj.* **1** naturally using the right hand for writing etc. (*right-handed batsman*). **2** (of a tool etc.) for use by the right hand. **3** (of a blow) struck with the right hand. **4** turning to the right. □ **right-handedly** *adv.* **right-handedness** *n.*

**right-hander** *n.* **1** right-handed person. **2** right-handed blow.

**right-hand man** *n.* indispensable or chief assistant.

**rightism** *n.* political conservatism. □ **rightist** *n. & adj.*

**rightly** *adv.* justly, properly, correctly, justifiably.

**right-minded** *adj.* (also **right-thinking**) having sound views and principles.

**righto** /**ruy**-toh, ruy-**toh**/ *int.* (also **rightio, righty-o** /**ruy**-tee-oh/ ) *colloq.* expressing agreement or assent.

**right of way** *n.* **1** right established by usage to pass over another's ground. **2** path subject to such a right. **3** right of a vehicle to precedence.

**Right Reverend** *n.* bishop's title.

**right-to-life** *adj.* of or pertaining to a movement opposing legal abortion.

**right-to-lifer** *n.* person who opposes abortion absolutely or would allow it only in the most extreme circumstances.

**right turn** *n.* turn of 90 degrees to the right.

**right wing** — *n.* more conservative or reactionary section of a political party or system. — *adj.* conservative or reactionary. □ **right-winger** *n.*

**rigid** /**rij**-uhd/ *adj.* **1** not flexible; unbendable (*rigid frame*). **2** (of a person, conduct, etc.) inflexible, unbending, harsh (*rigid disciplinarian*). □ **rigidity** /ruh-**jid**-uh-tee/ *n.* **rigidly** *adv.* **rigidness** *n.* [Latin *rigidus* from *rigeo* be stiff]

**rigmarole** /**rig**-muh-rohl/ *n.* **1** lengthy and complicated procedure (*all the rigmarole involved in opening a bank account these days*). **2** rambling or meaningless talk or tale (*went on with a long rigmarole about losing his hat*). [originally *ragman roll* catalogue]

**rigor** /**rig**-uh/ *n.* feeling of cold with shivering and a rise in temperature, preceding a fever etc. [Latin *rigeo* be stiff]

**rigor mortis** /ˌrig-uh **maw**-tuhs/ *n.* stiffening of the body after death.

**rigorous** /**rig**-uh-ruhs/ *adj.* **1** firm; strict, severe. **2** strictly exact or accurate. □ **rigorously** *adv.* **rigorousness** *n.* [related to RIGOUR]

**rigour** /**rig**-uh/ *n.* (also **rigor**) **1 a** severity, strictness, harshness. **b** (in *pl.*) harsh measures or conditions. **2** logical exactitude (*argued with convincing rigour*). **3** strict enforcement of rules etc. (*utmost rigour of the law*). **4** austerity of life. [Latin: related to RIGOR]

**rig-out** *n. colloq.* outfit of clothes.

**rile** *v.* (-**ling**) *colloq.* anger, irritate. [French from Latin]

**rill** *n.* small stream. [probably Low German or Dutch]

**rim** *n.* **1** edge or border, esp. of something circular. **2** outer edge of a wheel, holding the tyre. **3** part of spectacle frames around the lens. □ **rimless** *adj.* **rimmed** *adj.* (also in *comb.*). [Old English]

**rime** — *n.* **1** frost. **2** hoar-frost. — *v.* (**-ming**) cover with rime. [Old English]

**rind** /ruynd/ *n.* tough outer layer or covering of fruit and vegetables, cheese, bacon, etc. [Old English]

**ring¹** — *n.* **1** circular band, usu. of metal, worn on a finger. **2** circular band of any material. **3** rim of a cylindrical or circular object, or a line or band round it. **4** mark etc. resembling a ring (*rings round his eyes; smoke rings*). **5** ring in the cross-section of a tree, produced by one year's growth. **6 a** enclosure for a circus performance, boxing, betting at races, a two-up game, showing of cattle, etc. **b** (prec. by *the*) bookmakers collectively. **7 a** people or things in a circle. **b** such an arrangement. **8** traders, spies, politicians, etc., combined illicitly for profit etc. (*information about a drug ring*). **9** circular or spiral course. **10 a** thin disc of particles etc. round a planet. **b** halo round the moon. — *v.* **1** (often foll. by *round, about, in*) make or draw a circle round; encircle. **2** = RINGBARK 1. **3** beat (one's fellow shearers) by shearing the most sheep in a given period (*ring the shed*). **4 a** (of livestock) keep moving restlessly in a mass. **b** turn (a mob, esp. of cattle) back on itself. **c** work with cattle as a drover. □ **run** (or **make**) **rings round** *colloq.* outclass or outwit (another person). [Old English]

**ring²** — *v.* (*past* **rang**; *past part.* **rung**) **1** (often foll. by *out* etc.) give a clear resonant or vibrating sound of or as of a bell (*a shot rang out; ringing laughter; telephone rang*). **2** make (esp. a bell) ring. **3** (also *absol.*; often foll. by *up*) call by telephone (*will ring you*). **4** (usu. foll. by *with, to*) (of a place) resound with a sound, fame, etc. (*theatre rang with applause*). **5** (of the ears) be filled with a sensation of ringing. **6** sound (a peal etc.) on a bell or bells (*rang the doorbell*). **7** (foll. by *in, out*) usher in or out with bell-ringing (*rang out the Old Year*). **8** convey a specified impression (*words rang true*). — *n.* **1** ringing sound or tone. **2** act or sound of ringing a bell. **3** *colloq.* telephone call (*give me a ring*). **4** specified feeling or quality conveyed by words etc. (*had a melancholy ring; a ring of confidence*). □ **ring back** make a return telephone call to. **ring a bell** *colloq.* begin to revive a memory. **ring down** (or **up**) **the curtain 1** cause the curtain to be lowered or raised. **2** (foll. by *on*) mark the end or the beginning of (an enterprise etc.). **ring in** report or make contact by telephone. **ring off** end a telephone call. **ring round** telephone several people. **ring up 1** call by telephone. **2** record (an amount etc.) on a cash register. [Old English]

**ringbark** *v.* (also **ring**) kill (a tree) by cutting a ring of bark from around the trunk.

**ring-binder** *n.* loose-leaf binder with ring-shaped clasps.

**ringer¹** *n.* bell-ringer. □ **be a ringer** (or **dead ringer**) **for** *colloq.* resemble (a person) exactly.

**ringer²** *n.* **1** shearer with the highest tally of sheep shorn in a given period. **2** stockman, esp. as employed in droving. **3** person who excels (at an activity etc.). [senses 1 & 3 from British dial. *ringer* anything superlatively good; sense 2 from RING¹ *v.* 4]

**ring finger** *n.* third finger, esp. of the left hand, on which a wedding ring is usu. worn.

**ringie** /ring-ee/ *n. colloq.* = RING-KEEPER.

**ring-in** — *v.* **1** substitute fraudulently (a horse) for another in a race. **2** (in two-up) substitute (a double-headed or double-tailed coin) for a genuine coin. — *n.* **1 a** fraudulent substitution, esp. of one horse for another in a race. **b** a horse etc. so substituted. **2** person or thing that is not of a kind with others in a group or set.

**ring-keeper** *n.* (also **ringie**) person in charge of a two-up game.

**ringleader** *n.* leading instigator of a crime, mischief, etc.

**ringlet** /ring-luht/ *n.* curly lock of esp. long hair. □ **ringleted** *adj.*

**ringmaster** *n.* person directing a circus performance.

**ringneck** *n.* (also **ringneck parrot** or **ringnecked parrot**) any of several predominantly green Australian parrots having a narrow yellow collar on the plumage of the neck.

**ring-pull** *attrib. adj.* (of a tin) having a ring for pulling to break its seal.

**ring road** *n.* bypass encircling a town or city.

**ringside** *n.* area immediately beside a boxing or circus ring etc. (often *attrib.*: *ringside view*).

**ringtail** *n.* (also **ringtail possum** or **ring-tailed possum**) any of several Australian possums with a long prehensile tail which curls into a ring at the end.

**ringworm** *n.* fungal skin infection causing circular inflamed patches, esp. on the scalp.

**rink** *n.* **1** area of ice for skating or curling etc. **2** enclosed area for roller-skating. **3** building containing either of these. **4** strip of bowling-green. **5** team in bowls or curling. [apparently from French *renc* RANK[1]]

**rinse** — *v.* (**-sing**) (often foll. by *through*, *out*) **1** wash or treat with clean water etc. **2** wash lightly. **3** put (clothes etc.) through clean water after washing. **4** (foll. by *out*, *away*) clear (impurities) by rinsing. — *n.* **1** act or instance of rinsing (*give it a rinse*). **2** temporary hair tint (*blue rinse*). [French *rincer*]

**riot** /**ruy**-uht/ — *n.* **1 a** violent disturbance by a crowd of people. **b** (*attrib.*) involved in suppressing riots (*riot police*). **2** loud uncontrolled revelry. **3** (foll. by *of*) lavish display or sensation (*riot of colour and sound*). **4** *colloq.* very amusing thing or person. — *v.* make or engage in a riot. □ **read the Riot Act** act firmly to suppress insubordination; give stern warning (*read his unruly children the riot act*) (from the name of a former act partly read out to disperse rioters). **run riot 1** throw off all restraint. **2** (of plants) grow or spread uncontrolled. □ **rioter** *n.* **riotous** *adj.* [French]

**RIP** *abbr.* may he, she, or they rest in peace. [Latin *requiesca(n)t in pace*]

**rip**[1] — *v.* (**-pp-**) **1** tear or cut (a thing) quickly or forcibly away or apart (*ripped out the lining*). **2 a** make (a hole etc.) by ripping. **b** make a long tear or cut in. **3** come violently apart; split (*his trousers ripped when he bent*). **4** rush along. — *n.* **1** long tear or cut. **2** act of ripping. □ **let it rip!** *colloq.* exclamation signalling that something (e.g. a car-engine) should be started. **let rip** *colloq.* **1** express emotion, esp. anger, without restraint. **2** speak violently or obscenely. **rip into** *colloq.* **1** attack (a person) verbally. **2** engage in (a task, activity, etc.) with energy and speed (*ripped into the housework*; *ripped into the chocolates*). **rip off** *colloq.* **1** swindle. **2** steal. **wouldn't it rip you!** *colloq.* exclamation of dismay, exasperation, or disgust. [origin unknown]

**rip**[2] *n.* stretch of rough water caused by meeting currents. [origin uncertain]

**ripcord** *n.* cord for releasing a parachute from its pack.

**ripe** *adj.* **1** (of grain, fruit, cheese, etc.) ready to be reaped, picked, or eaten. **2** mature, fully developed (*ripe in judgment*). **3** (of a person's age) advanced. **4** (often foll. by *for*) fit or ready (*when time is ripe*; *ripe for development*). □ **ripeness** *n.* [Old English]

**ripen** *v.* make or become ripe.

**rip-off** *n. colloq.* **1** swindle or fraud. **2** financial exploitation; exorbitant charge or price. **3** (*attrib.*) financially exploitative; swindling, cheating (*a rip-off merchant*).

**riposte** /ruh-**post**/ — *n.* **1** quick retort. **2** quick return thrust in fencing. — *v.* (**-ting**) deliver a riposte. [Italian: related to RESPOND]

**ripper** /**rip**-uh/ *colloq.* — *n.* something (or someone) exciting admiration, enthusiasm, etc. (*the party was a ripper*; *had a ripper of a day*; *he's a real ripper*). — *attrib. adj.* excellent, admirable, great (*a ripper day for the beach*; *a ripper bloke*). □ **you little ripper!** exclamation of enthusiastic admiration for a person or thing. [British slang and dial. *ripper* something especially good]

**ripple** /**rip**-uhl/ — *n.* **1** ruffling of the water's surface, small wave or waves. **2** gentle lively sound, e.g. of laughter or applause. **3** slight variation in the strength of a current etc. **4** ice-cream with veins of syrup (*raspberry ripple*). — *v.* (**-ling**) **1** (cause to) form or flow in ripples. **2** show or sound like ripples. □ **ripply** *adj.* [origin unknown]

**rip-roaring** *adj.* **1** wildly noisy or boisterous (*got a rip-roaring welcome*). **2** excellent, first-rate (*a rip-roaring performance*).

**rise** /ruyz/ — *v.* (**-sing**; *past* **rose** /rohz/; *past part.* **risen** /**riz**-uhn/) **1** move from a lower position to a higher one; come or go up. **2** grow, project, expand, or incline upwards; become higher. **3** (of the sun, moon, or stars) appear or be visible above the horizon. **4 a** get up from lying, sitting, or kneeling. **b** get out of bed. **c** recover a standing or vertical position; become erect (*rose to his full height*). **5** (of a meeting, parliament, etc.) adjourn. **6** reach a higher position, level, amount, intensity, etc. (*river rose two metres*; *wind is rising*; *his voice rose*). **7** make progress socially etc. (*rose from the ranks*). **8 a** come to the surface of liquid (*bubbles rose from the bottom*). **b** (of a person) react to provocation (*rise to the bait*). **9** come to life again. **10** (of dough) swell by the action of yeast etc. **11** (often foll. by *up*) rebel (*rise up against them*). **12** originate (*river rises in the mountains*). **13** (of wind) start to blow. **14** (of a person's spirits) become cheerful. — *n.* **1** act or manner or amount of rising. **2** upward slope, hill, or movement (*house stood on a rise*). **3 a** increase in amount, extent, sound, pitch, etc. (*rise in unemployment*). **b** increase in salary. **4** increase in status or power; upward progress. **5** vertical height of a step, arch, incline, etc. □ **get** (or **take**) **a rise out of** *colloq.* provoke a reaction from (a person), esp. by teasing. **give rise to** cause. **on the rise** on the increase. **rise above** be superior to (petty feelings, difficulties, etc.). **rise to the occasion** produce the necessary will, energy, ability, etc., in unusually demanding circumstances. [Old English]

**risible** /**riz**-uh-buhl/ *adj.* laughable, ludicrous. [Latin *rideo ris-* laugh]

**rising** — *adj.* **1** advancing to maturity or high standing (*rising young lawyer*). **2** approaching a specified age (*rising five*). **3** (of ground) sloping upwards. — *n.* revolt or insurrection.

**rising damp** *n.* moisture absorbed from the ground from a wall.

**risk** — *n.* **1** chance or possibility of danger, loss, injury, etc. (*health risk*; *risk of fire*). **2** person or thing causing a risk or regarded in relation to risk (*is a poor risk*). — *v.* **1** expose to risk. **2** accept the chance of (*risk getting wet*). **3** venture on (with possible danger) (*you should not risk the climb in this weather*). □ **at risk** exposed to danger. **at one's** (**own**) **risk** accepting responsibility, agreeing to make no claims. **at the risk of** with the possibility of (an adverse consequence). **no risk!** *colloq.* exclamation of assurance or assent. **put at risk** expose to danger. **run a** (or **the**) **risk** (often foll. by *of*) expose oneself to danger or loss etc. **take a risk** (or **risks**) chance the possibility of danger etc. □ **risky** *adj.* (**-ier, -iest**). **riskily** *adv.* **riskiness** *n.* [French *risque(r)* from Italian]

**risotto** /ruh-**zot**-oh/ *n.* (*pl.* **-s**) Italian savoury rice dish cooked in stock. [Italian]

**risqué** /**ris**-kay, -**kay**/ *adj.* (of a story etc.) slightly indecent. [French: related to RISK]

**rissole** /**ris**-ohl/ *n.* compressed mixture of minced meat and spices, mixed with or coated in breadcrumbs and fried. [French]

**rit.** *abbr. Mus.* ritardando.

**ritardando** /rit-uh-**dan**-doh/ *adv.* & *n.* (*pl.* **-s** or **-di** /-dee/) *Mus.* = RALLENTANDO. [Italian]

**rite** /ruyt/ *n.* **1** religious or solemn observance, act, or procedure (*burial rites*). **2** body of customary observances characteristic of a Church etc. (*the Roman rite*). [Latin *ritus*]

**rite of passage** *n.* (often in *pl.* **rites of passage**) event marking a significant change or stage in life, e.g. marriage.

**ritual** /**rich**-oo-uhl/ — *n.* **1 a** prescribed order of a religious or other rite,

ceremony, etc. **b** solemn or colourful pageantry etc. **2** procedure regularly followed (*a visit to the park was one of his daily rituals*). — *adj.* of or done as a ritual or rite (*ritual murder*). □ **ritually** *adv.* [Latin: related to RITE]

**ritzy** /**rit**-see/ *adj.* (**-ier, -iest**) *colloq.* high-class, luxurious, showily smart. [from *Ritz*, name of luxury hotels]

**rival** /**ruy**-vuhl/ — *n.* (often *attrib.*) **1** person etc. competing with another (*beat all his rivals*; *rival firm*). **2** person or thing that equals another in quality (*he has no rival*). — *v.* (**-ll-**) be, seem, or claim to be the rival of or comparable to. [Latin *rivus* stream]

**rivalry** *n.* (*pl.* **-ies**) the state or an instance of being rivals; competition.

**riven** /**riv**-uhn/ *adj. literary* split, torn. [past part. of *rive* from Old Norse]

**river** /**riv**-uh/ *n.* **1** copious natural stream of water flowing to the sea or a lake etc. **2** copious flow (*rivers of blood*). □ **sell down the river** *colloq.* betray or let down. [Latin *ripa* bank]

**Riverina bluebell** /,riv-uh-**ree**-nuh/ *n.* = PATERSON'S CURSE.

**river oak** *n.* any of several casuarinas which grow near watercourses, esp. the usu. large tree *Casuarina cunninghamiana.*

**river red gum** *n.* (also **river gum**) any of several eucalypts which grow near watercourses, esp. *Eucalyptus camaldulensis.*

**river rose** *n.* (also **dog rose**) shrub of NSW, Tasmania, and Victoria, having a profusion of rose-like pink flowers almost all the year round.

**rivet** /**riv**-uht/ — *n.* nail or bolt for joining metal plates etc., with the headless end beaten out when in place. — *v.* (**-t-**) **1 a** join or fasten with rivets. **b** beat out or press down the end of (a nail or bolt). **c** fix, make immovable. **2 a** (foll. by *on, upon*) direct intently (one's eyes or attention etc.). **b** (esp. as **riveting** *adj.*) engross (a person or the attention) (*a riveting performance*). [French *river* fasten]

**riviera** /,riv-ee-**air**-ruh/ *n.* coastal subtropical region, esp. that of SE France and NW Italy. [Italian, = sea-shore]

**rivulet** /**riv**-yuh-luht/ *n.* small stream. [Latin *rivus* stream]

**Rn** *symb.* radon.

**RNA** *abbr.* ribonucleic acid.

**roach**[1] *n.* (*pl.* same or **-es**) small European freshwater fish of the carp family, introduced into Australian rivers. [French]

**roach**[2] *n.* cockroach.

**road** *n.* **1** way with a prepared surface, for

vehicles, pedestrians, etc. **2** one's way or route (*our road takes us via Dandenong*). □ **get out of the** (or **my** etc.) **road** *colloq.* stop obstructing a person. **in the** (or **one's**) **road** *colloq.* forming an obstruction. **one for the road** *colloq.* final (esp. alcoholic) drink before departure. **on the road** travelling, esp. as a firm's representative, drover, itinerant performer, or swagman. **the road to** way of getting to or achieving (*road to Tantanoola*; *road to ruin*). [Old English: related to RIDE]

**roadblock** *n.* barrier set up on a road in order to stop and examine traffic.

**road gang** *n. hist.* detachment of convicts detailed to work at road construction.

**road hog** *n. colloq.* reckless or inconsiderate road-user.

**road-holding** *n.* (often *attrib.*) stability of a moving vehicle.

**roadhouse** *n.* petrol station which also provides food etc. on a major road.

**roadie** *n. colloq.* assistant of a touring band etc., erecting and maintaining equipment.

**road plant** *n.* equipment etc. for road repairs.

**road sense** *n.* capacity for safe behaviour in traffic etc.

**roadshow** *n.* **1 a** performance given by a touring company, esp. a group of pop musicians. **b** company giving such performances. **2** television or radio series broadcasting each programme from a different venue.

**roadside** *n.* (often *attrib.*) strip of land beside a road.

**roadster** *n.* open car without rear seats.

**road test** — *n.* test of a vehicle's performance. — *v.* (**road-test**) test (a vehicle) on the road.

**road toll** *n.* the number of people killed in motor vehicle accidents.

**road train** *n.* group of several long trailers (usu. carrying cattle) pulled along the road by a prime-mover.

**roadworks** *n.pl.* construction, repair, etc., of roads.

**roadworthy** — *adj.* fit to be used on the road. — *n.* **1** (in full **roadworthy certificate**) official certificate indicating that a motor vehicle has passed a roadworthiness test (*my car has got its roadworthy*). **2** (in full **roadworthy test**) official test of a motor vehicle's roadworthiness (*I've got to take my car in for its roadworthy*). □ **roadworthiness** *n.*

**roam** — *v.* **1** ramble, wander. **2** travel unsystematically over, through, or about. — *n.* act of roaming; ramble. □ **roamer** *n.* [origin unknown]

**roan** — *adj.* (of esp. a horse) having a coat thickly interspersed with hairs of another colour, esp. reddish-brown mixed with white or grey. — *n.* roan animal. [French]

**roar** — *n.* **1 a** loud deep hoarse sound, as made by a lion. **b** similar sound as made by a person in pain or rage or excitement. **c** loud sound of thunder, an engine, a fire, waves, etc. **2** loud laugh. — *v.* **1** (often foll. by *out*) utter loudly or make a roar, roaring laugh, etc. **2** travel in a vehicle at high speed, esp. with the engine roaring. □ **roar a person up** *colloq.* reprimand; berate. □ **roarer** *n.* [Old English]

**roaring drunk** *predic. adj.* very drunk and noisy.

**roaring forties** *n.pl.* stormy ocean tracts between lat. 40° and 50° S.

**roaring success** *n.* great success.

**roaring trade** *n.* (also **roaring business**) very brisk trade or business.

**roast** — *v.* **1 a** cook (food, esp. meat) or (of food) be cooked in an oven or by open heat (*roast chestnuts*). **b** heat (coffee beans) before grinding. **2** *refl.* expose (oneself etc.) to fire or heat. **3** criticise severely, denounce. — *attrib. adj.* roasted (*roast beef*). — *n.* **1 a** roast meat. **b** dish of this. **c** piece of meat for roasting. **2** process of roasting. [French *rost(ir)* from Germanic]

**roasting** — *adj.* very hot. — *n.* severe criticism or denunciation.

**rob** *v.* (**-bb-**) (often foll. by *of*) **1** (also *absol.*) take unlawfully from, esp. by force or threat (*robbed the safe*; *robbed her of her jewels*). **2** deprive of what is due or normal (*robbed of sleep*). □ **robber** *n.* [French *rob(b)er* from Germanic]

**robbery** *n.* (*pl.* **-ies**) **1** act of robbing. **2** *colloq.* excessive charge or cost.

**robbery under arms** *n. hist.* the committing of armed robbery by one who has escaped into, or lives in, the Australian bush; bushranging.

**robe**¹ — *n.* **1** long loose outer garment. **2** (often in *pl.*) this worn as an indication of rank, office, profession, etc. — *v.* (**-bing**) clothe in a robe; dress. [French]

**robe**² *n.* = WARDROBE.

**robin** /*rob-uhn*/ *n.* **1** = ROBIN REDBREAST 1 & 2. **2** any of many small, active, Australian etc. birds, some having a brightly coloured breast (*pink-breasted robin*; *scarlet robin*; *yellow robin*). [pet form of *Robert*]

**robin redbreast** *n.* **1** small European bird with a red breast. **2** any of various red-breasted Australian robins, esp. the scarlet robin. **3** the melaleuca (*M. lateritia*), a shrub having linear leaves and bright orange-red bottlebrush-flowers in profusion in spring.

**robot** /**roh**-bot/ n. **1** machine resembling or functioning like a human. **2** machine automatically completing a mechanical process. **3** person who acts mechanically. □ **robotic** /-bot-ik/ adj. **robotise** v. (also **-ize**) (**-sing** or **-zing**). [Czech (in Karel Čapek's play R.U.R., 1920) derived from robota forced labour]

**robotics** /roh-**bot**-iks/ n.pl. (usu. treated as sing.) art, science, or study of robot design and operation.

**robust** /roh-**bust**, **roh**-/ adj. (**-er**, **-est**) **1** strong and sturdy, esp. in physique or construction. **2** (of exercise, discipline, etc.) vigorous, requiring strength. **3** (of mental attitude, argument, etc.) straightforward, vigorous. **4** (of a statement, reply, etc.) bold, firm, unyielding. □ **robustly** adv. **robustness** n. [Latin robur strength]

**roc** n. gigantic bird of Arabian legend. [Spanish from Arabic]

**rock**[1] n. **1 a** hard material of the earth's crust, often exposed on the surface. **b** similar material on other planets. **2** Geol. any natural material, hard or soft (e.g. clay), consisting of one or more minerals. **3 a** projecting rock forming a hill, cliff, reef, etc. **b** (**the Rock**) ULURU. **c** (**the Rocks**) rocky area of Sydney, west of Sydney Cove, famed for its historic buildings and historical associations. **4** large detached stone. **5** stone of any size. **6** firm and dependable support or protection (she was a rock of strength during the crisis). **7** hard sweet usu. in the form of a peppermint-flavoured stick. **8** colloq. precious stone, esp. a diamond. **9** used as a distinguishing epithet in the names of Australian fauna and flora (rock flathead; rock ringtail; rock warbler; rock whiting; rock fern). □ **between a rock and a hard place** in a no-win situation. **on the rocks** colloq. **1** (of a marriage etc.) broken down. **2** (of a drink) served neat with ice-cubes. [French roque, roche]

**rock**[2] — v. **1** move gently to and fro; set, maintain, or be in, such motion. **2** (cause to) sway; shake, oscillate, reel. **3** distress, perturb (rocked by the news). — n. **1** rocking movement. **2** spell of this (gave the baby a rock in the cradle). **3 a** = ROCK AND ROLL. **b** rock and roll-influenced popular music. □ **rock the boat** colloq. disturb a stable situation. [Old English]

**rock and roll** n. (also **rock 'n' roll**) popular dance-music originating in the 1950s with a heavy beat and often a blues element.

**rock art** n. Aboriginal rock painting.

**rock-bottom** — adj. (of prices etc.) the very lowest. — n. very lowest level.

**rock-chopper** n. colloq. offens. a Roman Catholic. [from rock-chopper navvy; influenced by the initials R.C.]

**rock cod** n. any of several Australian marine food-fish inhabiting reefs and rocky waters.

**rock-crystal** n. transparent colourless quartz, usu. in hexagonal prisms.

**rocker** n. **1** curved bar etc. on which something can rock. **2** rocking-chair. **3** devotee of rock music. □ **off one's rocker** colloq. crazy.

**rockery** n. (pl. **-ies**) construction of stones with soil between them for growing rock-plants on.

**rocket**[1] /**rok**-uht/ — n. **1** cylindrical firework or signal etc. propelled to a great height after ignition. **2** engine operating on the same principle, providing thrust but not dependent on air intake. **3** rocket-propelled missile, spacecraft, etc. **4** colloq. severe reprimand. — v. (**-t-**) **1 a** move rapidly upwards or away. **b** increase rapidly (prices rocketed). **2** bombard with rockets. [French roquette from Italian]

**rocket**[2] n. plant whose leaves are used as salad vegetable. [French roquette from Italian]

**rocketry** n. science or practice of rocket propulsion.

**rock-face** n. vertical surface of natural rock.

**rock fern** n. small fern, widely distributed throughout Australia and elsewhere, and poisonous to stock.

**rock garden** n. = ROCKERY.

**rock-hole** n. (also **rock water-hole**) = GNAMMA.

**rock-hopper** n. person who fishes from coastal rocks. □ **rock-hop** v. **rock-hopping** n.

**rocking chair** n. chair mounted on rockers or springs for gently rocking in.

**rocking horse** n. toy horse on rockers or springs.

**rock lily** n. = ROCK ORCHID.

**rock lobster** n. any of several Australian marine crayfish, some of which are fished commercially.

**rock melon** n. melon with fragrant orange-coloured flesh; cantaloupe.

**rock orchid** n. either of two forms of Dendrobium speciosum: **1** epiphytic Australian orchid of rainforest areas with large, leathery leaves and sprays of creamy white flowers, often used as a rockery plant etc. **2** lithophytic Australian orchid of rocky sandstone areas with creamy yellow flowers.

**rock oyster** *n.* any of several Australian oysters occurring on the rocky substrata of estuaries and bays.

**rock painting** *n.* traditional, usu. ancient, Aboriginal painting on the wall of a cave, rock shelter, etc.

**rock plant** *n.* plant growing on or among rocks (or, in the garden, planted in a rockery).

**rock poison** *n.* one of the Australian poison peas, an attractive shrub having long sprays of bright yellow-orange pea-flowers.

**rock python** *n.* any of several Australian non-venomous constricting snakes, including Australia's largest python, the Amethystine.

**rock salt** *n.* common salt as a solid mineral.

**rock shelter** *n.* Aboriginal cave dwelling.

**rock wallaby** *n.* any of several small wallabies with long bushy tails, inhabiting rocky ranges and rock-strewn outcrops of mainland Australia, including the brush-tailed rock wallaby and the yellow-footed rock wallaby.

**rocky¹** *adj.* (**-ier, -iest**) of, like, or full of rock or rocks. □ **rockiness** *n.*

**rocky²** *adj.* (**-ier, -iest**) *colloq.* unsteady, tottering, unstable (*a rocky relationship*). □ **rockiness** *n.*

**rococo** /ruh-**koh**-koh/ — *adj.* **1** of a late baroque style of 18th-c. decoration. **2** (of literature, music, architecture, etc.) highly ornate. — *n.* this style. [French]

**rod** *n.* **1** slender straight cylindrical bar or stick. **2 a** cane for flogging. **b** (prec. by *the*) use of this. **3** = FISHING-ROD. **4** *hist.* (as a measure) perch or square perch (see PERCH¹). □ **make a rod for one's own back** make trouble for oneself. [Old English]

**rode** *past of* RIDE.

**rodent** /**roh**-duhnt/ *n.* mammal with strong incisors and no canine teeth, e.g. the rat, mouse, squirrel, beaver, and porcupine. [Latin *rodo* gnaw]

**rodeo** /**roh**-dee-oh, roh-**day**-oh/ *n.* (*pl.* **-s**) exhibition of cowboy-like skills in handling animals. [Spanish]

**rodomontade** /ˌrod-uh-mon-**tayd**/ *n.* boastful talk or behaviour. [French from Italian]

**roe¹** /roh/ *n.* **1** (also **hard roe**) mass of eggs in a female fish's ovary. **2** (also **soft roe**) sperm of a male fish. [Low German or Dutch]

**roe²** /roh/ *n.* (*pl.* same or **-s**) (also **roe-deer**) small kind of deer. [Old English]

**roentgen** /**ront**-yuhn/ *n.* (also **röntgen**) unit of ionising radiation. [*Röntgen*, name of a physicist]

**rogaine** /**roh**-gayn/ *n.* a rogaining event.

**rogaining** /roh-**gay**-ning/ *n.* a sport similar to orienteering, held over a greater time and distance. □ **rogainer** *n.* [origin uncertain]

**roger** /**roj**-uh/ *int.* **1** your message has been received and understood (used in radio communication etc.). **2** *colloq.* I agree. [from the name, code for *R*]

**rogue** /rohg/ *n.* **1** dishonest or unprincipled person. **2** *joc.* mischievous person, esp. a child. **3** (usu. *attrib.*) wild fierce animal driven away or living apart from others (*rogue elephant*). **4** (often *attrib.*) **a** inexplicably aberrant result or phenomenon. **b** inferior or defective specimen among many acceptable ones. [origin unknown]

**roguery** /**roh**-guh-ree/ *n.* (*pl.* **-ies**) conduct or action characteristic of rogues.

**roguish** *adj.* **1** playfully mischievous. **2** characteristic of rogues. □ **roguishly** *adv.* **roguishness** *n.*

**role** *n.* (also **rôle**) **1** actor's part in a play, film, etc. **2** person's or thing's function (*the role of the computer in the modern office*). [French: related to ROLL]

**role model** *n.* person on whom others model themselves.

**role-playing** *n.* (also **role-play**) acting of characters or situations as an aid in psychotherapy, language-teaching, etc. □ **role-play** *v.*

**role-playing game** *n.* game in which players take on the roles of imaginary characters who take part in adventures in a (usu. fantasy) setting.

**roll** /rohl/ — *v.* **1** (cause to) move or go in some direction by turning on an axis (*ball rolled under the table*; *rolled the barrel into the cellar*). **2 a** make cylindrical or spherical by revolving between two surfaces or over on itself (*rolled a newspaper*). **b** make thus (*rolled a cigarette*). **c** gather into a mass or shape (*rolled the dough into a ball*; *rolled himself into a ball*). **3** (often foll. by *along, by,* etc.) (cause to) move, advance, or be conveyed on or (of time etc.) as if on wheels (*bus rolled past*; *rolled the tea trolley*; *years rolled by*; *rolled by in his car*). **4** flatten or form by passing a roller etc. over or by passing between rollers (*roll the lawn*; *roll pastry*). **5** rotate (*his eyes rolled*; *he rolled his eyes*). **6 a** wallow (*dog rolled in the dust*). **b** (of a horse etc.) lie on its back and kick about. **7 a** (of a moving ship, aircraft or vehicle) sway to and fro sideways. **b** (of a person) walk unsteadily (*rolled out of the pub*). **8 a** undulate (*hills rolled into the distance*; *rolling mist*). **b** carry or propel with undulations (*river rolls its waters to the sea*). **9** (cause to) start functioning or moving (*cameras rolled*). **10** sound or utter with vibrations or a trill (*thunder rolled; rolls his* rs). **11** throw (dice). **12** *colloq.* **a** overturn (a car etc.) while in motion. **b** (of a car etc. in motion) overturn. **13** *colloq.* **a** soundly defeat (*thought he would win the election, but he got rolled; Cabinet rolled his proposal*). **b** rob (esp. a helpless victim) (*got rolled in the park at night*). — *n.* **1** rolling motion or gait; undulation (*roll of the hills*). **2 a** spell of rolling (*roll in the mud*). **b** gymnastic exercise in which the body rolls in a forward or backward circle. **3** rhythmic rumbling sound of thunder, a drum, etc. **4** complete revolution of an aircraft about its longitudinal axis. **5** anything forming a cylinder by being turned over on itself without folding (*roll of carpet; sausage roll*). **6 a** small portion of bread individually baked. **b** this with a specified filling (*ham roll*). **7** thing cylindrical in shape (*rolls of fat*). **8 a** official list or register (*electoral roll*). **b** total numbers on this. **9** money, esp. as several notes rolled together. □ **be on a roll** *colloq.* experience a bout of success or progress. **be rolling in** *colloq.* have plenty of (esp. money). **rolled into one** combined in one person or thing. **roll in** arrive in great numbers or quantity (*donations rolled in*). **roll on** *v.* **1** put on or apply by rolling. **2** (in *imper.*) *colloq.* come quickly (*roll on this arvo or tonight!*). **roll one's swag** (**or bluey**) pack (one's belongings, swag, etc.) preparatory to departure. **roll up 1** *colloq.* arrive; appear on the scene. **2** make into or form a roll. **start** (or **set**) **the ball rolling** initiate an activity; begin. [Latin *rotulus* diminutive]

**roll-call** *n.* process of calling out a list of names to establish who is present.

**rolled gold** *n.* thin coating of gold applied to a base metal by rolling.

**rolled oats** *n.pl.* husked and crushed oats.

**roller** *n.* **1 a** hard revolving cylinder for smoothing, spreading, crushing, stamping, hanging a towel on, etc., used alone or in a machine. **b** cylinder for diminishing friction when moving a heavy object. **2** small cylinder on which hair is rolled for setting. **3** long swelling wave.

**rollerblade** *n.* (also **in-line skate**) rollerskate with the four wheels on one track.

**roller-coaster** *n.* **1** big dipper at an amusement park etc. **2** (*attrib.*) (of emotions etc.) uncontrollable, unstable.

**roller skate** — *n.* metal frame with four small wheels on two tracks, fitted to

shoes for riding on a hard surface. — *v.* (**-ting**) move on roller-skates. □ **roller-skater** *n.*

**rollicking** /ˈrol-i-king/ *adj.* jovial, exuberant. [origin unknown]

**rolling mill** *n.* machine or factory for rolling metal into shape.

**rolling pin** *n.* cylinder for rolling out pastry, dough, etc.

**rolling stock** *n.* locomotives, carriages, etc. used on a railway.

**rolling stone** *n.* unsettled rootless person.

**rolling strike** *n.* industrial action (against an employer or within an industry) that takes place in different places in succession or is engaged in by consecutive groups, each for a limited period.

**rollmop** *n.* rolled uncooked pickled herring fillet. [German *Rollmops*]

**roll-neck** *adj.* (of a garment) having a high loosely turned-over neck.

**roll of honour** *n.* list of those honoured, esp. the dead in war.

**roll-on** — *attrib. adj.* (of deodorant etc.) applied by means of a rotating ball in the neck of the container. — *n.* light elastic corset.

**roll-on roll-off** *adj.* (of a ship, etc.) in which vehicles are driven directly on and off.

**roll over** — *v.* invest a lump-sum superannuation payout in a government-approved investment fund, thus deferring the payment of lump-sum tax. — *n.* (**roll-over**) act or instance of this. — *adj.* (**roll-over**) pertaining to this.

**roll-up** *n.* number of persons attending a meeting etc. (*did you get a good roll-up?*).

**roly-poly** /ˌroh-lee-ˈpoh-lee/ — *n.* (*pl.* -**ies**) **1** (also **roly-poly pudding**) pudding made of a rolled strip of suet pastry covered with jam etc. and boiled or baked. **2** any of several plants, usu. of arid and semi-arid Australia, which break off at ground level and roll along in the wind. — *adj.* podgy, plump. [probably ROLL]

**ROM** *n. Computing* read-only memory. [abbreviation]

**rom.** *abbr.* roman (type).

**Roman** /ˈroh-muhn/ — *adj.* **1** of ancient Rome, its territory, people, etc. **2** of medieval or modern Rome. **3** = ROMAN CATHOLIC. **4** (**roman**) (of type) plain and upright, used in ordinary print. **5** (of the alphabet etc.) based on the ancient Roman system with letters A–Z. — *n.* **1** citizen or soldier of the ancient Roman Republic or Empire. **2** citizen of modern Rome. **3** (**roman**) roman type. [Latin]

**Roman Catholic** — *adj.* of the largest section of the Christian Church acknowledging the Pope as its head. — *n.* member of this Church. □ **Roman Catholicism** *n.*

**romance** /roh-**mans**, ruh-/ — *n.* also /**roh**-mans/ **1** idealised, poetic, or unworldly atmosphere or tendency. **2 a** love affair. **b** mutual attraction in this. **c** sentimental or idealised love. **3 a** literary genre concerning romantic love, stirring action, etc. **b** work of this genre. **4** medieval, esp. verse, tale of chivalry, common in the Romance languages. **5 a** exaggeration; picturesque falsehood. **b** instance of this. **6** (**Romance**) (often *attrib.*) languages descended from Latin. — *v.* (**-cing**) **1** exaggerate or distort the truth, esp. fantastically. **2** court, woo. [Romanic]

■ **Usage** The alternative pronunciation given for the noun, with the stress on the first syllable, is considered incorrect by some people.

**Roman Empire** *n. hist.* that established by Augustus in 27 BC and divided by Theodosius in AD 395.

**Romanesque** /,roh-muh-**nesk**/ — *n.* style of European architecture *c.* 900–1200, with massive vaulting and round arches. — *adj.* of this style.

**Romanian** /roh-**may**-nee-uhn, ruh-/ — *n.* **1 a** native or national of Romania. **b** person of Romanian descent. **2** language of Romania. — *adj.* of Romania, its people, or language.

**Roman nose** *n.* aquiline high-bridged nose.

**Roman numeral** *n.* any of the Roman letters representing numbers: I = 1, V = 5, X = 10, L = 50, C = 100, D = 500, M = 1000.

**romantic** /roh-**man**-tik, ruh-/ — *adj.* **1** of, characterised by, or suggestive of an idealised, sentimental, or fantastic view of reality; remote from experience (*romantic picture*; *romantic setting*). **2** inclined towards or suggestive of romance in love (*romantic evening*; *romantic words*). **3** (of a person) imaginative, visionary, idealistic. **4 a** (of style in art, music, etc.) concerned more with feeling and emotion than with form and aesthetic qualities. **b** (also **Romantic**) of the 18th–19th-c. romantic movement or style in the European arts. **5** (of a project etc.) unpractical, fantastic. — *n.* romantic person. □ **romantically** *adv.* [French: related to ROMANCE]

**romanticise** *v.* (also **-ize**) (**-sing** or **-zing**) **1** make romantic; exaggerate (*roman-* *ticised account*). **2** indulge in romantic thoughts or actions.

**romanticism** *n.* (also **Romanticism**) adherence to a romantic style in art, music, etc.

**Romany** /**rom**-uh-nee, **roh**-muh-/ — *n.* (*pl.* **-ies**) **1** Gypsy. **2** language of the Gypsies. — *adj.* of Gypsies or the Romany language. [Romany *Rom* gypsy]

**Romeo** /**roh**-mee-oh/ *n.* (*pl.* **-s**) passionate male lover or seducer. [name of a character in Shakespeare]

**romp** — *v.* **1** play roughly and energetically. **2** (foll. by *along, past,* etc.) *colloq.* proceed without effort. — *n.* spell of romping. □ **romp in** (or **home**) *colloq.* win easily. [perhaps from RAMP]

**rompers** *n.pl.* (also **romper suit**) young child's one-piece garment covering the legs and trunk.

**rondeau** /**ron**-doh/ *n.* (*pl.* **rondeaux** pronunc. same or /-ohz/ ) poem of ten or thirteen lines with only two rhymes throughout and with the opening words used twice as a refrain. [French]

**rondo** /**ron**-doh/ *n.* (*pl.* **-s**) musical form with a recurring leading theme. [French RONDEAU]

**roo** /roo/ — *n.* (also **'roo**) kangaroo. — *attrib. adj.* pertaining to a kangaroo (*roo dog*; *roo shooter*; *roo-shooting*).

**roo bar** *n.* = KANGAROO BAR.

**rood** *n.* **1 a** the cross on which Christ was crucified. **b** a crucifix, esp. a large one in a church. **2** *hist.* quarter of an acre. [Old English]

**roof** — *n.* (*pl.* **-s**) **1 a** upper covering of a building. **b** top of a covered vehicle. **c** top inner surface of an oven, refrigerator, etc. **2** overhead rock in a cave or mine etc. — *v.* **1** (often foll. by *in, over*) cover with or as with a roof. **2** be the roof of. □ **go through the roof** *colloq.* (of prices etc.) rise dramatically. **hit** (or **go through** or **raise**) **the roof** *colloq.* become very angry. □ **roofer** *n.* **roofing** *n.* [Old English]

**roof of the mouth** *n.* palate.

**roof-rack** *n.* framework for luggage on top of a vehicle.

**rooftop** *n.* **1** outer surface of a roof. **2** (in *pl.*) tops of houses etc. □ **shout it from the rooftops** make a thing embarrassingly public.

**rook¹** /ruuk/ — *n.* European black bird of the crow family nesting in colonies. — *v.* **1** *colloq.* charge (a customer) extortionately. **2** win money at cards etc., esp. by swindling. [Old English]

**rook²** /ruuk/ *n.* chess piece with a battlement-shaped top. [French from Arabic]

**rookery** n. (pl. **-ies**) colony of rooks, penguins, or seals.

**rookie** /**ruuk**-ee/ n. colloq. new recruit. [corruption]

**room** /room/ — n. **1** space for, or occupied by, something; capacity (takes up too much room; room for improvement). **2 a** part of a building enclosed by walls, floor, and ceiling. **b** (in pl.) apartments or lodgings. **c** people in a room (room fell silent). **3** (foll. by for, or to + infin.) opportunity or scope (room for man-oeuvre; room to improve things). — v. **1** lodge, board. **2** share a room (I roomed with Jill at college). [Old English]

**room-mate** n. person sharing a room.

**room service** n. provision of food etc. in a hotel bedroom.

**roomy** adj. (**-ier, -iest**) having much room, spacious. □ **roominess** n.

**roost** — n. branch or perch for a bird, esp. to sleep. — v. settle for rest or sleep. □ **come home to roost** (of a scheme etc.) recoil unfavourably. **rule the roost** see RULE. [Old English hrōst]

**rooster** n. male of the domestic fowl.

**root**[1] — n. **1 a** part of a plant normally below the ground, conveying nourishment from the soil. **b** (in pl.) branches or fibres of this. **2 a** plant with an edible root. **b** such a root. **3** (in pl.) emotional attachment or family ties to a place or community. **4** embedded part of a hair, tooth, nail, etc. **5** (often attrib.) basic cause, source, nature, or origin (root of all evil; roots in the distant past; root cause; the root of things). **6** Math. **a** number that when multiplied by itself a usu. specified number of times gives a specified number or quantity (cube root of eight is two). **b** square root. **c** value of an unknown quantity satisfying a given equation. **7** Philology core of a word, without prefixes, suffixes, etc. **8** coarse colloq. act of sexual intercourse. — v. **1** (cause to) take root; grow roots (root them firmly). **2** (esp. as **rooted** adj.) fix firmly; establish (rooted objection to; reaction rooted in fear). **3** (foll. by out, up) **a** drag or dig up by the roots. **b** eradicate; exterminate (root out all team members who are not pulling their weight; root out heresy). **4 a** colloq. (esp. as **rooted**) adj.) ruin; exhaust; frustrate (the telly's rooted; felt rooted after all that heavy work; his schemes were rooted). **b** coarse colloq. have sexual intercourse (with). □ **put down roots** become settled or established (in a locality etc.). **root and branch** thorough(ly), radical(ly). **root out** find and get rid of. **strike** (or **take**) **root 1** begin to grow and draw nourishment from the soil. **2**

become established. **wouldn't it root you!** colloq. exclamation of dismay, disgust, etc. □ **rooter** n. **rootless** adj. [Old English]

**root**[2] v. **1** (also absol.) (often foll. by up) turn up (the ground) with the snout, beak, etc., in search of food. **2 a** (foll. by around, in, etc.) rummage. **b** (foll. by out or up) find or extract by rummaging. **3** (foll. by for) = barrack for (see BARRACK[2]). [Old English and Old Norse]

**rootstock** n. **1** rhizome. **2** plant into which a graft is inserted. **3** primary form from which offshoots have arisen.

**rope** — n. **1 a** stout cord made by twisting together strands of hemp, wire, etc. **b** piece of this. **2** (foll. by of) quantity of onions, pearls, etc., strung together. **3** (prec. by the) **a** halter for hanging a person. **b** execution by hanging. — v. (**-ping**) **1** fasten, secure, or catch with rope. **2** (usu. foll. by off, in) enclose with rope. **3** Mountaineering connect with or attach to a rope. □ **give a person enough** (or **plenty of**) **rope to hang himself** (or **herself**) give a person enough freedom to bring about his or her own downfall. **know** (or **learn** or **show**) **the ropes** know (or learn or show) how to do a thing properly. **on the ropes 1** Boxing forced against the ropes by an opponent's attack. **2** near defeat. **rope in** persuade to take part. **rope into** persuade to take part in (roped into washing up). [Old English]

**ropeable** /**roh**-puh-buhl/ adj. (also **ropable**) requiring to be restrained; furious; bad-tempered.

**rope ladder** n. two ropes with cross-pieces, used as a ladder.

**rorqual** /**raw**-kwuhl/ n. whale with a dorsal fin. [French from Norwegian]

**Rorschach test** /**raw**-shahk/ n. personality test based on the subject's interpretation of a standard set of ink-blots. [Rorschach, name of a psychiatrist]

**rort** /rawt/ — n. **1** act of fraud or sharp practice (knows all about tax rorts). **2** colloq. a wild party; escapade. — v. **1** (often as verbal noun) engage in sharp practice (an expert at rorting the system). **2** manipulate (a ballot, records, etc.) fraudulently; rig (a splinter group tried to rort the union election). □ **rorter** n. [back-formation from **rorty** boisterous; of dubious propriety]

**rosaceous** /roh-**zay**-shuhs/ adj. of a large plant family including the rose. [Latin: related to ROSE[1]]

**rosary** /**roh**-zuh-ree/ n. (pl. **-ies**) RC Ch. **1** repeated sequence of prayers, to be said while meditating on the annunciation, birth, suffering, death, resurrection, etc., of Christ. **2** string of beads for keeping count in this. [Latin *rosarium* rose-garden]

**rose¹** /rohz/ — *n.* **1** prickly bush or shrub bearing usu. fragrant red, pink, yellow, or white flowers. **2** this flower. **3** flowering plant resembling this (*desert rose*; *native rose*). **4 a** pinkish-red colour. **b** (usu. in *pl.*) rosy complexion (*roses in her cheeks*). **5** sprinkling-nozzle of a watering-can etc. **6** (in *pl.*) used to express luck, ease, success, etc. (*roses all the way*; *everything's roses*). — *adj.* = ROSE-COLOURED 1. [Latin *rosa*]

**rose²** *past* of RISE.

**rosé** /roh-zay/ *n.* light pink wine. [French]

**rosebowl** *n.* bowl for cut roses, esp. as a prize in a competition.

**rose-breasted cockatoo** *n.* = GALAH.

**rose-coloured** *adj.* **1** pinkish-red. **2** optimistic, cheerful (*wears rose-coloured glasses*).

**rose-hip** *n.* = HIP².

**rosella¹** /roh-zel-uh/ *n.* **1** any of several brightly coloured, long-tailed, Australian parrots, with white, yellow, or red cheek-patches (*crimson rosella*; *eastern rosella*; *yellow rosella*; etc.). **2** sheep which is losing its wool (and said to resemble a rosella parrot which has lost some of its feathers) and is therefore easy to shear. [corruption of *Rose Hill* (the original name for Parramatta, NSW) where the bird was first found]

**rosella²** *n.* **1** (also **native hibiscus**) tall shrub or small tree of NSW, Queensland, and the NT, having large pinky red (sometimes yellow) flowers and edible young growth and buds, used as a food-plant and as an attractive ornamental. **2** the fruit of this, often used for jam. [transferred use of *rosella* European red sorrel plant]

**rosemary** /rohz-muh-ree/ *n.* evergreen fragrant shrub used as a herb. [*rosmarine* from Latin *ros* dew: related to MARINE]

**rose of the west** *n.* small eucalypt of WA with silvery-blue rounded leaves, large ridged buds, and extremely large cardinal-red flowers powdered with bright gold, carried on the shrub for most of the year.

**rosette** /roh-zet/ *n.* **1** rose-shaped ornament of ribbon etc., esp. as a supporter's badge or as a prize in a competition. **2** rose-shaped carving. [French diminutive: related to ROSE¹]

**rose water** *n.* perfume made from roses.

**rose window** *n.* circular window with roselike tracery.

**rosewood** *n.* **1** any of several Australian trees or shrubs having a fragrant (often reddish) timber, esp. the tall rainforest tree *Dysoxylum fraserianum* of NSW and Queensland (see also BOONAREE). **2** the wood of these trees, esp. used in making furniture.

**rosin** /roz-uhn/ — *n.* resin, esp. in solid form. — *v.* (**-n-**) rub (esp. a violin bow etc.) with rosin. [alteration of RESIN]

**rosiner** /roz-uh-nuh/ *n.* (also **roziner**) a measure (esp. a generous one) of spirits. [*rosin* alcoholic drink]

**Ross River virus** *n.* **1** mosquito-borne virus causing a non-fatal disease characterised by a rash, and joint and muscle pain. **2** (also **Ross River fever**) this disease. [*Ross River*, near Townsville]

**roster** /ros-tuh/ — *n.* list or plan of turns of duty etc. — *v.* place on a roster. [Dutch *rooster*, literally 'gridiron']

**rostrum** /ros-truhm/ *n.* (*pl.* **rostra** or **-s**) platform for public speaking, an orchestral conductor, etc. [Latin]

**rosy** /roh-zee/ *adj.* (**-ier**, **-iest**) **1** pink or red. **2** optimistic, hopeful (*rosy future*). □ **rosily** *adv.* **rosiness** *n.*

**rot** — *v.* (**-tt-**) **1** (of animal or vegetable matter) lose its original form by the chemical action of bacteria, fungi, etc.; decay. **2** gradually perish or waste away (*left to rot in prison*). **3** cause to rot, make rotten. — *n.* **1** rotting; decay. **2** *colloq.* nonsense (*talks rot*). **3** decline in standards etc. (*rot set in*). — *int.* expressing incredulity or ridicule. [Old English]

**rotary** /roh-tuh-ree/ — *adj.* acting by rotation (*rotary drill*). — *n.* (*pl.* **-ies**) rotary machine. [medieval Latin]

**rotary hoe** — *n.* machine with many rotating spikes for breaking up soil prior to planting a lawn etc. — *v.* break up the ground with a rotary hoe.

**rotary-hoist** *n.* = CLOTHES-HOIST.

**rotate** /roh-tayt/ *v.* (**-ting**) **1** move round an axis or centre, revolve. **2** take or arrange (esp. crops) in rotation. **3** act or take place in rotation (*chairmanship will rotate*). □ **rotatable** *adj.* **rotatory** /roh-tuh-tuh-ree, -tay-tuh-ree/ *adj.* [Latin *rota* wheel]

**rotation** /roh-tay-shuhn/ *n.* **1** act or instance of rotating or being rotated. **2** regular succession (*each member will act as chair by rotation*). **3** the growing of different crops in regular order to avoid exhausting the soil. □ **rotational** *adj.*

**rote** *n.* (usu. prec. by *by*; also *attrib.*) mechanical or habitual repetition (in order to memorise) (*rote learning*). [origin unknown]

**rotisserie** /roh-**tis**-uh-ree/ n. 1 restaurant etc. where meat is roasted or barbecued. 2 rotating spit for roasting or barbecuing meat. [French: related to ROAST]

**rotor** /**roh**-tuh/ n. 1 rotary part of a machine. 2 rotary aerofoil on a helicopter, providing lift. [related to ROTATE]

**rotten** /**rot**-uhn/ adj. (**-er**, **-est**) 1 rotting or rotted; fragile from age or use (*rotten meat; rotten timber*). 2 morally or politically corrupt. 3 *colloq.* a disagreeable, unpleasant, bad (*had a rotten time*). b (of a plan etc.) worthless; ill-advised (*rotten idea*). c ill (*feel rotten*). d very drunk. □ **rottenly** adv. **rottenness** n. [Old Norse: related to ROT]

**rotter** n. *colloq.* nasty or contemptible person. [from ROT]

**Rottweiler** /**rot**-wuy-luh/ n. black-and-tan dog noted for ferocity. [*Rottweil* in Germany]

**rotund** /roh-**tund**/ adj. 1 plump, podgy. 2 (of voice, literary style, etc.) sonorous, grandiloquent. □ **rotundity** n. [Latin *rotundus*]

**rotunda** /roh-**tun**-duh/ n. circular building, hall, or room, esp. domed. [Italian *rotonda*: related to ROTUND]

**rouble** /**roo**-buhl/ n. (also **ruble**) chief monetary unit of Russia and some other former republics of the USSR. [French from Russian]

**rouge** /roozh/ — n. 1 red cosmetic for colouring the cheeks. 2 powdered ferric oxide etc. as a polishing agent esp. for metal. — v. (**-ging**) colour with or apply rouge. [Latin *rubeus* red]

**rough** /ruf/ — adj. 1 uneven or bumpy, not smooth, level, or polished. 2 a shaggy, hairy. b (of cloth) coarse in texture. 3 boisterous, coarse; violent, not mild, quiet, or gentle (*rough fellow; rough play; rough part of town; rough sea*). 4 (of wine etc.) sharp or harsh in taste. 5 harsh, insensitive (*rough words; rough treatment*). 6 a unpleasant, severe, demanding (*had a rough time*). b unfortunate; undeserved (*had rough luck*). c (often foll. by *on*) hard or unfair (towards). 7 lacking finish, comfort, etc. (*rough lodgings*). 8 a incomplete, rudimentary, approximate (*rough attempt; rough sketch; rough estimate*). b (of chance) not very good (*only a rough chance of winning*). — adv. in a rough manner (*play rough*). — n. 1 (usu. prec. by *the*) hardship (*take the rough with the smooth*). 2 rough ground, esp. on a golf-course (*ball went into the rough*). 3 violent person (*bunch of roughs*). 4 unfinished or natural state (*have written it in rough — will polish it later*). — v. 1 (foll. by *up*) ruffle (feathers, hair, etc.), esp. by rubbing. 2 (foll. by *out, in*) shape, plan, or sketch roughly. □ **a bit rough** *colloq.* 1 unfair, unreasonable (*that decision by the umpire was a bit rough*). 2 lacking taste; unseemly (*that joke was a bit rough in the circumstances*). **rough as bags** (or **guts**) *colloq.* very rough; uncouth. **rough it** *colloq.* do without basic comforts. **rough up** *colloq.* attack violently. □ **roughish** adj. **roughness** n. [Old English]

**roughage** n. coarse fibrous material in food, stimulating intestinal action.

**rough-and-ready** adj. crude but effective; not over-particular.

**rough-and-tumble** — adj. irregular, scrambling, disorderly. — n. disorderly fight; scuffle.

**roughcast** — n. (often *attrib.*) plaster of lime and gravel, used on outside walls. — adj. (of a plan etc.) roughly formed, preliminary. — v. (*past* and *past part.* **-cast**) 1 coat with roughcast. 2 prepare in outline.

**rough diamond** n. 1 uncut diamond. 2 rough-mannered but honest person.

**roughen** v. make or become rough.

**rough-handle** v. treat or handle roughly.

**rough-hewn** adj. uncouth, unrefined.

**roughie** /**ruf**-ee/ n. *colloq.* 1 (in horse racing etc.) a a rank outsider. b an outsider with some chance of winning (*my roughie for the Melbourne Cup is Fred's Boy*). 2 unfair or unreasonable act; a 'swiftie'.

**rough justice** n. 1 treatment that is approximately fair. 2 unjust treatment.

**roughly** adv. 1 in a rough manner. 2 approximately (*roughly 20 people*). □ **roughly speaking** approximately.

**rough passage** n. 1 crossing over rough sea. 2 difficult time or experience (*he's going through a rough passage after the divorce*).

**roughshod** adj. (of a horse) having shoes with nail-heads projecting to prevent slipping. □ **ride roughshod over** treat inconsiderately or arrogantly.

**rough spin** n. = ROUGH TROT.

**rough trot** n. period of difficulty or misfortune (*she's had a rough trot recently*).

**rough-up** n. fight, brawl.

**roughy** /**ruf**-ee/ n. 1 = TOMMY ROUGH. 2 small, reef-dwelling, Australian food-fish.

**roulade** /roo-**lahd**/ n. 1 rolled piece of meat, sponge, etc. with a filling. 2 quick succession of notes, usu. sung to one syllable. [French *rouler* roll]

**roulette** /roo-let/ n. gambling game in which a ball is dropped on to a revolving numbered wheel. [French, = little wheel]

**round** — adj. **1** shaped like a circle, sphere, or cylinder; convex; circular, curved, not angular. **2** entire, continuous, complete (*round dozen*). **3 a** candid, outspoken (*a round assertion of her independence*). **b** harsh; unstinting (*received nothing but round abuse for her pains*). **4** (usu. *attrib.*) (of a number) expressed for brevity as a complete number (*$297.32, or in round figures $300*). **5 a** (of a voice, sound, etc.) not harsh; sonorous. **b** (of style etc.) flowing. **6** *Phonet.* (of a vowel) pronounced with rounded lips. **7** (of a character in a literary work) well developed; not stereotyped. — n. **1** round object or form. **2 a** revolving motion or course (*yearly round*). **b** recurring series of activities, meetings, etc. (*continuous round of pleasure; round of talks*). **3** a fixed route for deliveries (*milk round*). **b** route etc. for supervision or inspection (*watchman's round; doctor's rounds*). **4** drink etc. for each member of a group. **5 a** one bullet, shell, etc. **b** act of firing this. **6** sandwich made from two slices of bread. **7** joint of beef from the haunch. **8** set, series, or sequence of actions in turn, esp.: **a** one spell of play or activity in a game, boxing match, etc. **b** one stage in a competition. **9** *Golf* playing of all the holes in a course once. **10** song for unaccompanied voices overlapping at intervals. **11** rung of a ladder. **12** (foll. by *of*) circumference or extent of (*in all the round of Nature*). **13** separate or distinct outburst (of applause, jeering, etc.). — adv. **1** with circular motion (*wheels go round*). **2** with return to the starting-point or an earlier state (*summer soon comes round*). **3** with change to an opposite position, opinion, etc. (*turned round to look; soon won them round*). **4 a** to, at, or affecting a circumference, area, group, etc. (*tea was handed round; may I look round?*). **b** so as to form a ring or mass (*the crowd gathered round*). **5** in every direction within a radius (*spread destruction round*). **6** circuitously (*go the long way round*). **7** to a person's house, a convenient place, etc. (*ask him round; will be round soon; brought the car round*). **8** measuring (a specified distance) in girth (*the pipe is 20 centimetres round*). — prep. **1 a** so as to encircle or enclose (*a blanket round him*). **b** (of measurement) encircling (*85 centimetres round the waist*). **2** at or to points on the circumference of (*sat round the table*). **3** with successive visits to (*hawks them round the pubs*). **4** within a radius of (*towns round Adelaide*). **5** having as an axis or central point (*planned a book round the War*). **6 a** so as to pass in a curved course (*go round the corner*). **b** having so passed (*be round the corner*). **c** in the resulting position (*find them round the corner*). — v. **1** give or take a round shape. **2** pass round (a corner, cape, etc.). **3** (usu. foll. by *up, down*) express (a number) approximately, for brevity. □ **all year round** throughout the year. **bring a person round 1** revive from a state of unconsciousness. **2** persuade him or her to one's own point of view. **go the round** (or **rounds**) (of news etc.) be passed on from person to person. **in the round 1** with all features shown; all things considered. **2** with the audience on at least three sides of the stage. **3** (of sculpture) with all sides shown. **round about 1** all round; on all sides (of). **2** approximately (*round about $50*). **round and round** several times round. **round the bend** see BEND. **round off** (or **out**) **1** bring to a complete or well-ordered state. **2** smooth out; blunt the corners or angles of. **round on** attack unexpectedly, esp. verbally. **round out 1** provide with more details. **2** complete, finish. **round the twist** see TWIST. **round up 1 a** gather (scattered) livestock together by riding round a paddock etc.; muster. **b** collect or bring together. **2** = sense 3 of *v.* □ **roundish** adj. **roundness** n. [Latin: related to ROTUND]

**roundabout** — n. **1** road junction at which traffic circulates in one direction round a central island. **2 a** large revolving device for children to ride on in a playground. **b** = MERRY-GO-ROUND 1. — adj. circuitous. — adv. approximately (*at roundabout 6 o'clock*).

**rounder** n. **1** (in *pl.*; treated as *sing.*) ball game in which players hit the ball and run through a round of bases. **2** complete run as a unit of scoring in rounders.

**roundly** adv. bluntly, severely (*told them roundly; was roundly criticised*).

**round robin** n. **1** petition, esp. with signatures in a circle to conceal the order of writing. **2** tournament in which each competitor plays every other.

**round-shouldered** adj. with shoulders bent forward and a rounded back.

**roundsman** n. journalist covering a specific subject (*political roundsman*).

**round table** n. assembly for discussion, esp. at a conference or in a situation where those who are not normally equals meet as equals (often *attrib.*: *round-table talks*). [in allusion to the Round Table at which King Arthur and his knights sat so that none should have precedence]

**round trip** *n.* trip to one or more places and back again.

**round-up** *n.* **1** systematic rounding up (of scattered livestock, persons, etc.). **2** summary or résumé.

**rouse**[1] /rowz/ *v.* (**-sing**) **1** (cause to) wake. **2** (often foll. by *up*, often *refl.*) stir up, make or become active or excited (*was roused to protest*). **3** anger (*terrible when roused*). **4** evoke (feelings). [origin unknown]

**rouse**[2] /rows/ *v.* **1** scold (*Mum really rouses if I come home late for tea*). **2** (foll. by *at* or *on*) berate, tongue-lash (*roused at him; I was well and truly roused on*). [Scottish dial. *roust* roar, bellow]

**rouseabout** /row-suh-,bowt/ — *n.* **1** unskilled labourer or odd-jobber on a farm, in a shearing shed, etc. **2** any unskilled worker or odd-jobber. — *v.* work as a rouseabout. [British dial., = a rough, bustling person]

**rousing** /row-zing/ *adj.* exciting, stirring (*rousing song*).

**roust** /rowst/ *v.* (usu. foll. by *on* or *at*) scold, 'go crook at' (*rousted on them; rousted at me for tracking dirt onto her carpet*). □ **rousting** *n.* [Scottish dial., = roar, bellow]

**roustabout** /row-stuh-,bowt/ *n.* = ROUSEABOUT. [*roust* roust out, rouse]

**rout** /rowt/ — *n.* **1** disorderly retreat of defeated troops (*put them to rout*). **2** an overthrow, a defeat. — *v.* put to flight, defeat. [French: related to ROUTE]

**route** /root/ — *n.* way or course taken (esp. regularly) from one place to another. — *v.* (**-teing**) send, forward, or direct by a particular route. [French *route* road, from Latin *rupta* (*via*)]

**routine** /roo-**teen**/ — *n.* **1** regular course or procedure, unvarying performance of certain acts. **2** set sequence in a dance, comedy act, etc. **3** *Computing* see SUBROUTINE. — *adj.* **1** performed as part of a routine (*routine duties*). **2** of a customary or standard kind. □ **routinely** *adv.* [French: related to ROUTE]

**roux** /roo/ *n.* (*pl.* same) mixture of fat and flour used in sauces etc. [French]

**rove**[1] *v.* (**-ving**) **1** wander without settling; roam, ramble. **2** (of eyes) look about. **3** act as a rover (sense 2). [probably Scandinavian]

**rove**[2] *past* of REEVE[2].

**rover** *n.* **1** wanderer. **2** *Aust. Rules* one of three players making up the ruck, usu. small, fast, and adept at securing possession of the ball.

**row**[1] /roh/ *n.* **1** line of persons or things.

**2** line of seats across a theatre etc. □ **in a row 1** forming a row. **2** *colloq.* in succession (*two days in a row*). [Old English]

**row**[2] /roh/ — *v.* **1** (often *absol.*) propel (a boat) with oars. **2** convey (a passenger) thus. — *n.* **1** spell of rowing. **2** trip in a rowing-boat. □ **rower** *n.* [Old English]

**row**[3] /row/ — *n.* **1** loud noise or commotion. **2** fierce quarrel or dispute. **3** state of being reprimanded (*you'll get into a row over this*). — *v.* make or engage in a row. [origin unknown]

**rowdy** /row-dee/ *adj.* (**-ier, -iest**) noisy and disorderly. — *n.* (*pl.* **-ies**) rowdy person. □ **rowdily** *adv.* **rowdiness** *n.* **rowdyism** *n.* [origin unknown]

**rowel** /row-uhl/ *n.* spiked revolving disc at the end of a spur. [Latin *rotella*]

**rowlock** /rol-uhk, rul-uhk/ *n.* device on a boat's side for holding an oar in place. [*oarlock* from Old English: related to OAR, LOCK[1]]

**royal** /roi-uhl/ — *adj.* **1** of, suited to, or worthy of a king or queen. **2** in the service, under the patronage, etc., of a king or queen. **3** of the family of a king or queen. **4** majestic, splendid. **5** exceptional, first-rate (*had a royal time*). — *n.* *colloq.* member of a (esp. British) royal family (*antics of the younger royals*). □ **royally** *adv.* [Latin: related to REGAL]

**royal blue** *adj.* & *n.* (as adj. often hyphenated) deep vivid blue.

**royal bluebell** *n.* (also **Austral bluebell, wahlenbergia**) small perennial herb *Wahlenbergia gloriosa* of higher altitudes in south-eastern mainland Australia, having large royal blue flowers held erect: floral emblem of the Australian Capital Territory.

**Royal Commission** *n.* **1** commission of inquiry appointed by the representative of the Crown at the request of the Government. **2** committee so appointed.

**royal flush** *n.* straight poker flush headed by an ace.

**royal icing** *n.* hard white icing for cakes.

**royalist** *n.* supporter of monarchy (also *attrib.*: *has royalist sympathies*). □ **royalism** *n.*

**royal jelly** *n.* substance secreted by worker bees and fed by them to future queen bees.

**royalty** *n.* (*pl.* **-ies**) **1** royal office, dignity, or power; being royal. **2** royal persons. **3** percentage of profit from a book, public performance, patent, etc., paid to the author etc. **4** payment made by a producer of minerals etc. to the owner of the site at which the minerals etc. are mined. [French: related to ROYAL]

**royal 'we'** n. use of 'we' instead of 'I' by a single person.

**RPI** abbr. retail price index.

**r.p.m.** abbr. revolutions per minute.

**RSI** abbr. REPETITION STRAIN INJURY.

**RSL** abbr. organisation to provide assistance to returned Australian servicemen and servicewomen and their families. [Returned Services League]

**RSPCA** abbr. Royal Society for the Prevention of Cruelty to Animals.

**RSVP** abbr. (in an invitation etc.) please answer. [French *répondez s'il vous plaît*]

**Rt. Revd.** abbr. (also **Rt. Rev.**) Right Reverend.

**Ru** symb. ruthenium.

**rub** — v. (**-bb-**) **1** move something, esp. one's hand, with firm pressure over the surface of. **2** (usu. foll. by *against, in, on, over*) apply (one's hand etc.) in this way. **3** clean, polish, chafe, or make dry, sore, or bare by rubbing. **4** (foll. by *in, into, through, over*) apply (polish, ointment, etc.) by rubbing. **5** (often foll. by *together, against, on*) move with contact or friction or slide (objects) against each other. **6** (of cloth, skin, etc.) become frayed, worn, sore, or bare with friction. — n. **1** act or spell of rubbing (*give it a rub*). **2** impediment or difficulty (*there's the rub*). □ **rub down 1** dry, smooth, or clean by rubbing. **2** massage (an athlete etc.) after strenuous exercise. **rub it in** (or **rub a person's nose in it**) emphasise or repeat an embarrassing fact etc. **rub off 1** (usu. foll. by *on*) be transferred by contact, transmitted (*his attitudes have rubbed off on me*). **2** remove by rubbing. **rub out 1** erase with a rubber. **2** colloq. (of a sportsperson) suspend (*he was rubbed out for three weeks for kicking in danger*). **rub shoulders** (or **elbows**) **with** associate with. **rub up 1** polish. **2** brush up (a subject or one's memory). **rub up the wrong way** irritate. [Low German]

**rubato** /roo-bah-toh/ n. *Mus.* (pl. **-s** or **-ti** /-tee/ ) temporary disregarding of strict tempo. [Italian, = robbed]

**rubber**[1] n. **1** tough elastic substance made from the latex of plants or synthetically. **2** piece of this or a similar substance for erasing esp. pencil marks. **3** colloq. condom. □ **rubberiness** n. [from RUB]

**rubber**[2] n. match of esp. three successive games between the same sides or persons at whist, bridge, tennis, etc. [origin unknown]

**rubber band** n. loop of rubber for holding papers etc. together.

**rubber duckie** n. colloq. inflated rubber boat with motor, used in surf rescue work etc.

**rubberise** v. (also **-ize**) (**-sing** or **-zing**) treat or coat with rubber.

**rubber plant** n. **1** evergreen tropical plant often cultivated as a house-plant. **2** (also **rubber tree**) tropical tree yielding latex.

**rubber stamp** — n. **1** device for inking and imprinting on a surface. **2 a** person who mechanically copies or endorses others' actions. **b** indication of such endorsement. — v. (**rubber-stamp**) approve automatically.

**rubbery** adj. **1** like rubber. **2** (of figures, financial statements, etc.) unreliable; to be regarded with some suspicion.

**rubbing** n. impression or copy made by rubbing.

**rubbish** /rub-ish/ — n. **1** waste material; refuse, litter. **2** worthless material; trash. **3** (often as *int.*) nonsense. — v. colloq. denigrate; disparage (*rubbished every effort he made*). — adj. (in Aboriginal English) inferior, worthless (*rubbish language*). □ **rubbishy** adj. [Anglo-French *rubbous*]

**rubbity** /rub-uh-tee/ n. (in full **rubbity-dub**) colloq. pub. [rhyming slang]

**rubble** /rub-uhl/ n. rough fragments of stone, brick, etc., esp. from a demolished building. [French *robe* spoils]

**rub-down** n. **1** an instance of rubbing down. **2** a massage.

**rubella** /roo-bel-uh/ n. a contagious viral disease which resembles a mild form of measles but can foetal malformation if caught by a woman early in pregnancy. [Latin *rubellus* reddish]

**Rubicon** /roo-buh-ˌkon/ n. boundary; point from which there is no going back. [*Rubicon*, river on ancient frontier of Italy]

**rubicund** /roo-buh-ˌkund/ adj. (of a face, complexion, etc.) ruddy, high-coloured. [Latin *rubeo* be red]

**rubidium** /roo-bid-ee-uhm/ n. soft silvery metallic element. [Latin *rubidus* red]

**rubric** /roo-brik/ n. **1** heading or passage in red or special lettering. **2** explanatory words. **3** established custom or rule. **4** direction for the conduct of divine service in a liturgical book. **5** (often in *pl.*) instructions to candidates on an examination paper. [Latin *ruber* red]

**ruby** /roo-bee/ — n. (pl. **-ies**) **1** rare precious stone varying in colour from deep crimson to pale rose. **2** deep red colour. — adj. of this colour. [Latin *rubeus* red]

**ruby wedding** *n.* fortieth wedding anniversary.

**ruck** — *n.* **1** (*prec. by the*) main body of competitors (in a race) not likely to overtake the leaders. **2** crowd or mass of undistinguished people or things. **3** *Aust. Rules* **a** group of three players (two followers and a rover) who do not have fixed positions but follow the play. **b** = RUCKMAN. **4** *Rugby* loose scrum. **5** a crease or wrinkle. — *v. Aust. Rules* (of the two followers) play as one of the ruck. [apparently Scandinavian]

**ruckman** *n.* = FOLLOWER 3.

**ruck-rover** *n. Aust. Rules* tall and agile ruckman chosen for his ability to combine the roles of follower and rover.

**rucksack** /ruk-sak/ *n.* bag carried on the back, esp. by hikers. [German]

**ruckus** /ruk-uhs/ *n. colloq.* row, commotion. [perhaps from RUCTION or RUMPUS]

**ruction** /ruk-shuhn/ *n.* **1** disturbance or tumult. **2** (in *pl.*) row, heated arguments. [origin unknown]

**rudder** *n.* flat piece hinged vertically to the stern of a ship or on the tailplane of an aircraft etc., for steering. □ **rudderless** *adj.* [Old English]

**ruddy** /rud-ee/ *adj.* (**-ier, -iest**) **1** (of a person, complexion, etc.) freshly or healthily red. **2** reddish. **3** *colloq.* bloody, damnable. □ **ruddily** *adv.* **ruddiness** *n.* [Old English]

**rude** *adj.* **1** impolite or offensive (*a rude remark*). **2** roughly made or done (*the Aborigines often put together a rude shelter to protect them from the rain*). **3** primitive or uneducated (*rude simplicity*). **4** abrupt, sudden, startling (*rude awakening*). **5** *colloq.* indecent, lewd (*rude joke*). □ **rudely** *adv.* **rudeness** *n.* [Latin *rudis*]

**rudiment** /roo-duh-muhnt/ *n.* **1** (in *pl.*) elements or first principles of a subject (*rudiments of Latin*). **2** (in *pl.*) imperfect beginning of something undeveloped or yet to develop (*rudiments of a good idea*). **3** vestigial or undeveloped part or organ. □ **rudimentary** /roo-duh-**men**-tuh-ree, -tree/ *adj.* [Latin: related to RUDE]

**rue**¹ *v.* (**rues, rued, rueing** or **ruing**) repent of; wish to be undone or non-existent (esp. *rue the day*). [Old English]

**rue**² *n.* evergreen European shrub with bitter strong-scented leaves. [Greek *rhutē*]

**rueful** *adj.* genuinely or humorously sorrowful. □ **ruefully** *adv.* **ruefulness** *n.* [from RUE¹]

**ruff** *n.* **1** projecting starched frill worn round the neck, esp. in the 16th c. **2** projecting or coloured ring of feathers or hair round a bird's or animal's neck. **3** (*fem.* **reeve** /reev/ ) wading bird with a ruff. [perhaps = ROUGH]

**ruffian** /ruf-ee-uhn/ *n.* violent lawless person. [Italian *ruffiano*]

**ruffle** /ruf-uhl/ — *v.* (**-ling**) **1 a** disturb the smoothness or tranquillity of. **b** undergo this. **2** gather (lace etc.) into a ruffle. **3** (often foll. by *up*) (of a bird) erect (its feathers) in anger, display, etc. — *n.* frill of lace etc., esp. round the wrist or neck. [origin unknown]

**rufous** /roo-fuhs/ *adj.* (esp. as a distinguishing epithet in the names of birds and animals) reddish-brown (*rufous fantail*; *rufous owl*; *rufous rat-kangaroo*; *rufous treecreeper*). [Latin *rufus*]

**rug** *n.* **1** thick floor covering, usu. smaller than a carpet. **2** thick woollen coverlet or wrap. □ **pull the rug from under** deprive of support; weaken, unsettle. **rug up** wear extra clothes as protection against the cold. [probably Scandinavian]

**Rugby** /rug-bee/ *n.* (in full **Rugby football**) team game played with an oval ball that may be kicked or carried. [*Rugby school* (in England), where it was first played]

**Rugby League** *n.* partly professional Rugby with teams of 13.

**Rugby Union** *n.* amateur Rugby with teams of 15.

**rugged** /rug-uhd/ *adj.* **1** (esp. of ground) rough, uneven. **2** (of features) wrinkled, furrowed, irregular. **3 a** unpolished; lacking refinement (*rugged grandeur*). **b** involving hardship (*a rugged life*). **4** (esp. of a machine) robust, hardy. □ **ruggedly** *adv.* **ruggedness** *n.* [probably Scandinavian]

**rugger** /rug-uh/ *n. colloq.* Rugby.

**ruin** /roo-uhn/ — *n.* **1** destroyed, wrecked, or spoiled state. **2** downfall or elimination (*ruin of my hopes*). **3** complete loss of one's property or position (*bring to ruin*). **4** (in *sing.* or *pl.*) remains of a building etc. that has suffered ruin. **5** cause of ruin (*will be the ruin of us*; *drink was his ruin*). — *v.* **1 a** bring to ruin (*extravagance has ruined me*). **b** spoil, damage (*rain ruined the picnic*). **2** (esp. as **ruined** *adj.*) reduce to ruins. □ **in ruins** completely wrecked (*hopes were in ruins*). [Latin *ruo* fall]

**ruination** /roo-uh-**nay**-shuhn/ *n.* **1** act of bringing to ruin. **2** act of ruining or state of being ruined.

**ruinous** *adj.* **1** bringing ruin, disastrous (*ruinous expense*). **2** in ruins; dilapidated. □ **ruinously** *adv.*

**rule** — *n.* **1** compulsory principle governing action (*rules of the road*). **2** prevailing custom or standard; normal state of things (*punctuality is the rule in this house*). **3** government or dominion (*under foreign rule*). **4** graduated straight measure; ruler. **5** code of discipline of a religious order (*Dominican Rule*). **6** order made by a judge or court with reference to a particular case only. **7** *Printing* thin line or dash. **8** (**Rules**) *colloq.* = AUSTRALIAN RULES. **9** (usu. **Rules** or **Old Rule**) (in Aboriginal English) the body of religious belief and social custom. — *v.* (**-ling**) **1** dominate; keep under control (*she rules him with an iron fist*). **2** (often foll. by *over*) have sovereign control of (*rules over a vast kingdom*). **3** be the prevailing custom or usual condition (*cheerful chaos rules in our house*). **4** govern (*Labor rules in most States*). **5** hold sway (*footy rules in the Australian sporting scene*). **6** (often foll. by *that*) pronounce authoritatively (*the High Court ruled that freedom of speech is paramount*). **7 a** make parallel lines across (paper). **b** make (a straight line) with a ruler etc. □ **as a rule** usually. **go through the rules** (in Aboriginal English) (of a boy) be initiated. **rule out** exclude; pronounce irrelevant or ineligible. **rule the roost** be in control. [Latin *regula*]

**rule of thumb** *n.* rule based on experience or practice rather than theory.

**ruler** *n.* **1** person exercising government or dominion. **2** straight usu. graduated strip of wood, metal, or plastic used to draw or measure.

**ruling** *n.* authoritative pronouncement.

**rum**[1] *n.* spirit distilled from sugar-cane or molasses. [origin unknown]

**rum**[2] *adj.* (**rummer, rummest**) *colloq.* odd, strange, queer. [origin unknown]

**Rumanian** var. of ROMANIAN.

**rumba** /**rum**-buh/ *n.* **1** Latin American ballroom dance orig. from Cuba. **2** music for this. [American Spanish]

**rumble** /**rum**-buhl/ — *v.* (**-ling**) **1** make a continuous deep resonant sound as of distant thunder. **2** (foll. by *along, by, past,* etc.) (esp. of a vehicle) move with a rumbling noise. — *n.* **1** rumbling sound. **2** *colloq.* fight; argument. [probably Dutch *rommelen*]

**rumbustious** /rum-**bus**-chuhs/ *adj.* *colloq.* boisterous, noisy, uproarious. [probably var. of *robustious* from ROBUST]

**ruminant** /**roo**-muh-nuhnt/ — *n.* animal that chews the cud. — *adj.* **1** of ruminants. **2** meditative. [related to RUMINATE]

**ruminate** /**roo**-muh-nayt/ *v.* (**-ting**) **1** meditate, ponder. **2** chew the cud. □ **ru-**

mination /-**nay**-shuhn/ *n.* **ruminative** /-nuh-tiv/ *adj.* [Latin *rumen* throat]

**rummage** /**rum**-ij/ — *v.* (**-ging**) **1** search, esp. unsystematically. **2** (foll. by *out, up*) find among other things. — *n.* instance of rummaging. [French *arrumage* from *arrumer* stow cargo]

**rummy** /**rum**-ee/ *n.* card-game, played usu. with two packs, in which the players try to form sets and sequences of cards. [origin unknown]

**rumour** /**roo**-muh/ (also **rumor**) — *n.* (often foll. by *of* or *that*) general talk, assertion, or hearsay of doubtful accuracy (*heard a rumour that you are leaving*). — *v.* (usu. in *passive*) report by way of rumour (*it is rumoured that you are leaving*). [Latin *rumor* noise]

**rump** *n.* hind part of a mammal or bird, esp. the buttocks. [probably Scandinavian]

**rumple** /**rum**-puhl/ *v.* (**-ling**) crease, ruffle. [Dutch *rompelen*]

**rumpus** /**rum**-puhs/ *n.* *colloq.* disturbance, brawl, row, or uproar. [origin unknown]

**rumpus room** *n.* room in a house for recreation, which does not need to be kept tidy.

**run** — *v.* (**-nn-**; *past* **ran**; *past part.* **run**) **1** go with quick steps, never having both or all feet on the ground at once. **2** flee, abscond. **3** go or travel hurriedly or briefly (*I'll just run down to the shops*). **4 a** advance by or as by rolling or on wheels, or smoothly or easily. **b** (cause to) be in action or operation or go in a specified way (*left the engine running; ran the car into a tree; ran the computer program*). **5** be current or operative (*lease runs for 99 years*). **6** travel on its route (*train is running late*). **7** (of a play etc.) be staged or presented (*now running at the Sydney Opera House*). **8** extend; have a course, order, or tendency (*road runs by the coast; prices are running high*). **9 a** (often *absol.*) compete in (a race). **b** finish a race in a specified position (*ran third*). **10** (often foll. by *for*) seek election (*ran for president*). **11** flow (with) or be wet; drip (with) (*walls running with condensation*). **12 a** cause (water etc.) to flow (*run water into the barrel*). **b** fill (a bath) thus (*run the bath for me*). **13** spread rapidly (*ink ran over the table*). **14** traverse (a course, race, or distance). **15** perform (an errand). **16** publish (an article etc.) in a newspaper etc. (*ran the story about the royals*). **17** direct or manage (a business etc.). **18** own and use (a vehicle) regularly. **19** transport in a private vehicle (*ran me to the station*). **20** enter (a horse etc.) for a race. **21** smuggle (guns etc.). **22** chase or hunt. **23** allow (an account) to accumulate before paying. **24** (of a dyed colour) spread from the dyed parts. **25 a** (of a thought, the eye, the memory, etc.) pass quickly (*ideas ran through my mind; his eyes ran over the obituaries*). **b** pass (one's eye) quickly (*ran my eye down the page*). **26** (of stockings etc.) ladder. **27** (of esp. the eyes or nose) exude liquid. **28** provide pasture (for sheep, cattle, etc.); raise (livestock) (*runs a few thousand sheep on her property*). **29** round up (wild cattle, horses, etc.) (*spent a few weeks running brumbies*). **30** (in Aboriginal English) live, usu. in the bush, in the traditional way (*he was running in the bush*). **31** (in Aboriginal English) (of an idea, belief, ceremony, etc.) prevail (the *law runs right down to the Alice*). — *n.* **1** act or spell of running. **2** short excursion. **3** distance travelled (*the run to Bourke was 600 kilometres*). **4** general tendency (*scored a goal against the run of play*). **5** regular route. **6** continuous stretch, spell, or course (*run of bad luck*). **7** (often foll. by *on*) high general demand (for a commodity, currency, etc.) (*run on the dollar*). **8** quantity produced at one time (*print run*). **9** average type or class (*general run of customers*). **10** point scored in cricket or baseball. **11** (foll. by *of*) free use of or access to (*run of the house*). **12** a bird's or other animal's regular track (*lyrebird's run*). **b** enclosure for fowls etc. **13 a** tract (usu. extensive) of land used as pasture. **b** extensive tract of land used for the raising of stock and containing the requisite improvements such as dwellings, yards, etc. **14** (in Aboriginal English) = COUNTRY (sense 6). **15 a** *Shearing* uninterrupted period worked during a day; period of employment as a shearer. **b** period of any employment (*brickies wanted — long run*). **16** ladder in stockings etc. **17** *Mus.* rapid scale passage. **18** (in full **the runs**) *colloq.* diarrhoea. □ **on the run 1** escaping; running away. **2** hurrying about from place to place. **run about 1** bustle, hurry. **2** (esp. of children) play freely. **run across 1** happen to meet or find. **2** (foll. by *to*) make a brief journey or a flying visit (to a place). **run after 1** pursue at a run. **2** pursue, esp. sexually. **run all over** *colloq.* have a walkover victory; defeat easily (*our Australian eleven ran all over the poms*). **run along** *colloq.* depart. **run around 1** take from place to place by car etc. **2** (often foll. by *with*) *colloq.* **a** associate with; keep company with. **b** engage in esp. promiscuous sexual rela-

tions. **run away** (often foll. by *from*) **1** flee, abscond. **2** mentally evade (a problem etc.). **run away with 1** carry off. **2** win easily. **3 a** deprive of self-control, carry away (*his emotions ran away with him*). **b** accept (a notion etc.) hastily (*he's run away with the idea that he's God's gift to women*). **4** (of a horse) bolt with (a rider etc.). **5** leave home to have a relationship with (esp. another person's husband or wife). **run down 1** knock down. **2** reduce the strength or numbers of (resources). **3** (of an unwound clock etc.) stop. **4** discover after a search (*ran him down at last in Woolloomooloo*). **5** *colloq.* disparage. **run dry 1** cease to flow. **2** = *run out* 1. **run for it** seek safety by fleeing. **run** (or **good run**) **for one's money 1** vigorous or close competition. **2** some return for outlay or effort. **run the gauntlet** see GAUNTLET². **run high** (of feelings) be strong. **run hot** *colloq.* **1** perform exceptionally well, be in excellent form (*the team's running hot at present*). **2** be very busy (*the phones have been running hot all day*). **run in 1** run (an engine or vehicle) carefully when new. **2** *colloq.* arrest. **3** pursue and confine (cattle or sheep). **run in the family** (of a trait) be common in a family. **run into 1** collide with (*the car ran into a post; the ship ran into rocks*). **2** encounter (*ran into an old friend; the project has run into problems*). **3** reach as many as (a usu. high figure) (*the cost will run into millions of dollars*). **run into the ground** *colloq.* bring (a person) to exhaustion etc. **run low** (or **short**) become depleted, have too little (*we're running low on ideas; ran short of milk*). **run off 1** flee. **2** produce (copies etc.) on a machine. **3** decide (a race etc.) after heats or a tie. **4** (cause to) flow away. **5** write or recite fluently (*ran off all 750 stanzas from memory and without pausing for breath*). **run off with** = *run away with* 5. **run on 1** continue in operation. **2** speak volubly or incessantly. **3** continue on the same line (of print etc.) as the preceding matter. **4** (of written characters) be joined together, ligatured. **run out 1** come to an end. **2** (foll. by *of*) exhaust one's stock of. **3** put down the wicket of (a running batsman). **4** come out of a contest in a specified position etc. (*ran out easy winners*). **run out on** *colloq.* desert (a person). **run over 1** (of a vehicle etc.) **a** pass over (*we ran over a snake but didn't kill it*). **b** knock down or crush. **2** overflow. **3** study or repeat quickly. **4** (foll. by *to*) go quickly, or by a brief journey, or for a flying visit (*run over to the milk bar; ran over to Tassie*). **run over time** exceed a set time-limit (*his speech ran over time* by *at least 20 minutes*). **run ragged** exhaust (a person). **run rings round** see RING¹. **run riot** see RIOT. **run a** (or **the**) **risk** see RISK. **run the show** *colloq.* dominate in an undertaking etc. **run a temperature** be feverish. **run through 1** examine or rehearse briefly (*the actor ran through her lines*). **2** peruse (*ran through the accounts with an eagle eye*). **3** deal successively with (*run through the applicants in turn*). **4** spend money rapidly or recklessly. **5** pervade (*fear ran through the entire camp*). **6** persist (in the mind) (*the tune ran through her mind all day*). **7** pierce with a sword etc. **run to 1** have the money, resources, or ability for. **2** reach (an amount or number). **3** (of a person) show a tendency to (*runs to fat*). **run to earth** see EARTH. **run to seed** see SEED. **run up 1** accumulate (a debt etc.). **2** build or make hurriedly. **3** raise (a flag). **run up against** meet with (a difficulty etc.). [Old English]

**runabout** *n.* small car, boat, or aircraft.

**run-around** *n. colloq.* deceit or evasion. □ **give a person the run-around** put off or lead astray (a person) with evasions or deceits.

**runaway** *n.* **1** fugitive. **2** bolting animal; vehicle out of control. **3** (*attrib.*) that is running away or out of control (*runaway slave; runaway inflation*).

**rundown** — *n.* **1** reduction in numbers. **2** detailed analysis. — *adj.* (**run-down**) **1** decayed, dilapidated. **2** exhausted (from overwork, illness, etc.).

**rune** *n.* **1** letter of the earliest Germanic alphabet. **2** similar mark of mysterious or magic significance. □ **runic** *adj.* [Old Norse]

**rung¹** *n.* **1** step of a ladder. **2** strengthening crosspiece in a chair etc. [Old English]

**rung²** *past part.* of RING².

**run-in** *n. colloq.* quarrel.

**runnel** /**run**-uhl/ *n.* **1** brook. **2** gutter. [Old English]

**runner** *n.* **1** person, horse, etc. that runs, esp. in a race. **2** creeping rooting plant-stem. **3** rod, groove, roller, or blade on which a thing, e.g. a sledge, slides. **4** sliding ring on a rod etc. **5 a** messenger. **b** *Sport* messenger who conveys the coach's instructions to players on the field. **6** (in full **runner bean**) twining bean plant with long flat green edible seed pods. **7** long narrow ornamental cloth or rug. **8** (in *pl.*) running shoes, sneakers.

**runner-up** *n.* (*pl.* **runners-up** or **runner-ups**) competitor or team taking second place.

**running** — *n.* **1** action of runners in a race etc. **2** way a race etc. proceeds. — *adj.* **1** continuous (*running battle*). **2** consecutive (*three days running*). **3** done with a run (*running jump*). □ **in** (or **out of**) **the running** (of a competitor) having a good (or poor) chance of success. **make** (or **take up**) **the running** take the lead; set the pace.

**running commentary** *n.* ongoing verbal description of esp. a sporting event.

**running postman** see KENNEDIA.

**running repairs** *n.pl.* minor or temporary repairs etc.

**running sore** *n.* suppurating sore; festering situation etc.

**runny** *adj.* (**-ier, -iest**) **1** tending to run or flow. **2** excessively fluid.

**run-off** *n.* **1** additional election, race, etc., after a tie. **2** amount of rainfall that is carried off an area by streams or rivers.

**run-of-the-mill** *adj.* ordinary, undistinguished.

**run-out** *n.* dismissal of a batsman by being run out.

**runt** *n.* **1** smallest pig etc. in a litter. **2** weakling; undersized person. [origin unknown]

**run-through** *n.* **1** rehearsal. **2** brief survey.

**run-up** *n.* (often foll. by *to*) preparatory period (*run-up to the elections*).

**runway** *n.* specially prepared surface for aircraft taking off and landing.

**rupee** /roo-**pee**/ *n.* chief monetary unit of India, Pakistan, etc. [Hindustani]

**rupiah** /roo-pee-uh/ *n.* chief monetary unit of Indonesia. [related to RUPEE]

**rupture** /**rup**-chuh/ — *n.* **1** act or instance of breaking; a breach. **2** breach in a relationship; disagreement and parting. **3** abdominal hernia. — *v.* (**-ring**) **1** burst (a cell or membrane etc.). **2** sever (a connection). **3** affect with or suffer a hernia. [Latin *rumpo rupt-* break]

**rural** /**roo**-ruhl/ *adj.* in, of, or suggesting the country; pastoral or agricultural (opp. URBAN) (*rural seclusion; rural electorate; rural property; rural school*). [Latin *rus rur-* the country]

**ruse** /rooz/ *n.* stratagem or trick. [French]

**rush¹** — *v.* **1** go, move, flow, or act precipitately or with great speed. **2** move or transport with great haste (*was rushed to hospital*). **3** (foll. by *at*) **a** move suddenly towards. **b** begin or attack impetuously. **c** (of cattle etc.) stampede. **4** perform or deal with hurriedly (*don't rush your dinner; the bill was rushed through parliament*). **5** force or induce (a person) to act hastily (*don't try to rush me!*). **6** attack or capture by sudden assault. **7** *hist.* occupy (a place) by a rush of goldminers. — *n.* **1 a** act or instance of rushing; violent or speedy advance or attack. **b** sudden flow, flood. **2** period of great activity. **3** (*attrib.*) done with great haste or speed (*a rush job*). **4** sudden migration of large numbers (esp. to a newly discovered goldfield). **5** (foll. by *on*, *for*) sudden strong demand for a commodity. **6** (in *pl.*) *colloq.* first uncut prints of a film. [French *ruser*: related to RUSE]

**rush²** *n.* **1** marsh plant with slender tapering pith-filled stems, used for making chair-bottoms, baskets, etc. **2** stem of this. □ **rushy** *adj.* [Old English]

**rush hour** *n.* time(s) each day when traffic is heaviest.

**rush-oh** *int. hist.* exclamatory call, announcing the discovery of a new goldfield.

**rusk** *n.* slice of bread rebaked as a light biscuit, esp. as baby food. [Spanish or Portuguese *rosca* twist]

**russet** /**rus**-uht/ — *adj.* reddish-brown. — *n.* russet colour. [Latin *russus*]

**Russian** /**rush**-uhn/ — *n.* **1 a** native or national of Russia. **b** person of Russian descent. **2** language of Russia. — *adj.* **1** of Russia or its people. **2** of or in Russian.

**Russian roulette** *n.* **1** firing of a revolver, with one chamber loaded, at one's head, after spinning the chamber. **2** any potentially dangerous enterprise.

**Russo-** *comb. form* Russian; Russian and.

**rust** — *n.* **1** reddish corrosive coating formed on iron, steel, etc. by oxidation, esp. when wet. **2** fungal plant-disease with rust-coloured spots. **3** impaired state due to disuse or inactivity (*his skills have gone to rust*). **4** reddish-brown. — *v.* **1** affect or be affected with rust. **2** become impaired through disuse. [Old English]

**rust belt** *n.* declining industrial area.

**rustbucket** *n. colloq.* motor vehicle greatly affected by rust or otherwise dilapidated.

**rustic** /**rus**-tik/ — *adj.* **1** of or like country people or country life. **2** unsophisticaed. **3** of rude or rough workmanship. **4** made of untrimmed branches or rough timber (*rustic fence of tea-tree stakes*). — *n.* country person, esp.

a simple or unsophisticated one. □ **rusticity** /-**tis**-uh-tee/ *n.* [Latin *rus* the country]

**rusticate** /**rus**-tuh-,kayt/ *v.* (**-ting**) retire to or live in the country. □ **rustication** /-**kay**-shuhn/ *n.*

**rustle** /**rus**-uhl/ — *v.* (**-ling**) **1** (cause to) make a gentle sound as of dry blown leaves. **2** (also *absol.*) steal (cattle or horses). — *n.* rustling sound. □ **rustle up** *colloq.* produce at short notice. □ **rustler** *n.* (esp. in sense 2 of *v.*). [imitative]

**rustproof** — *adj.* not susceptible to corrosion by rust. — *v.* make rustproof.

**rusty** *adj.* (**-ier, -iest**) **1** rusted or affected by rust. **2** stiff with age or disuse. **3** (of knowledge etc.) impaired, esp. by neglect (*my French is rusty*). **4** rust-coloured. **5** (of black clothes) discoloured by age. □ **rustiness** *n.*

**rut¹** — *n.* **1** deep track made by the passage of wheels. **2** established (esp. tedious) practice or routine (*in a rut*). — *v.* (**-tt-**) mark with ruts. [probably French: related to ROUTE]

**rut²** — *n.* periodic sexual excitement of a male deer etc. — *v.* (**-tt-**) be affected with rut. [Latin *rugio* roar]

**ruthenium** /roo-**thee**-nee-uhm/ *n.* rare hard white metallic element from platinum ores. [medieval Latin *Ruthenia* Russia]

**rutherfordium** /,ruth-uh-**faw**-dee-uhm/ *n.* artificial metallic element. [*Rutherford*, name of a physicist]

**Rutherglen bug** /**ruth**-uh-glen/ *n.* small bug which causes damage to cultivated food-plants. [*Rutherglen* town in Victoria]

**ruthless** /**rooth**-luhs/ *adj.* having no pity or compassion. □ **ruthlessly** *adv.* **ruthlessness** *n.* [*ruth* pity, from RUE¹]

**rutile** /**roo**-tuyl/ *n.* mineral form of titanium dioxide. [Latin *rutilus* reddish]

**-ry** *suffix* = -ERY (*infantry*; *rivalry*).

**rye** /ruy/ *n.* **1 a** cereal plant. **b** grain of this used for bread and fodder. **2** (in full **rye whisky**) whisky distilled from fermented rye. [Old English]

**ryegrass** *n.* forage or coarse lawn grass. [alteration of *ray-grass*]

# S

**S¹** /es/ *n.* (also **s**) (*pl.* **Ss** or **S's**) **1** nineteenth letter of the alphabet. **2** S-shaped thing (*S-bend*).

**S²** *abbr.* (also **S.**) **1** Saint. **2** South, Southern.

**S³** *symb.* sulphur.

**s.** *abbr.* **1** second(s). **2** *hist.* shilling(s).

**-s'** *suffix* denoting the possessive case of plural nouns and sometimes of singular nouns ending in s (*the boys' shoes; Charles' book*). [Old English inflection]

**'s** *abbr.* **1** is; has (*he's here; she's got it; John's gone*). **2** us (*let's*).

**-'s** *suffix* denoting the possessive case of singular nouns and of plural nouns not ending in -s (*John's book; book's cover; children's shoes*).

**SA** *abbr.* **1** South Australia. **2** South Australian.

**sabbath** /sab-uhth/ *n.* religious day of rest kept by most Christians on Sunday, Jews on Saturday, and Muslims on Friday. [Hebrew, = rest]

**sabbatical** /suh-**bat**-i-kuhl/ — *adj.* **1** of or appropriate to the sabbath. **2** (of leave) granted at intervals to a university teacher for study or travel. — *n.* period of sabbatical leave. [Greek: related to SABBATH]

**sable** /say-buhl/ — *n.* (*pl.* same or **-s**) **1** small brown-furred mammal of N. Europe and N. Asia. **2** its skin or fur. — *adj.* **1** (usu. placed after noun) *Heraldry* black. **2** esp. *poet.* gloomy. [Slavonic]

**sabot** /sab-oh/ *n.* **1** shoe carved from wood. **2** wooden-soled shoe. [French]

**sabotage** /sab-uh-ˌtahzh/ — *n.* deliberate damage to productive capacity, esp. as a political act. — *v.* (**-ging**) **1** commit sabotage on. **2** destroy, spoil (*sabotaged my plans*). [French: related to SABOT]

**saboteur** /ˌsab-uh-**ter**/ *n.* person who commits sabotage. [French]

**sabre** /say-buh/ *n.* **1** curved cavalry sword. **2** light tapering fencing-sword. [French from German *Sabel*]

**sabre-rattling** *n.* display or threat of military force.

**sabre-toothed** *adj.* designating any of various extinct mammals having long, sabre-shaped upper canine teeth.

**sac** *n.* membranous bag in an animal or plant. [Latin: related to SACK¹]

**saccharin** /sak-uh-ruhn/ *n.* a highly sweet substitute for sugar. [medieval Latin *saccharum* sugar]

**saccharine** /sak-uh-ˌreen, -ruhn/ *adj.* sickly sentimental or sweet (*a novel of saccharine romance*).

**sacerdotal** /ˌsak-uh-**doh**-tuhl, ˌsas-uh-/ *adj.* of priests or priestly office. [Latin *sacerdos -dot-* priest]

**sachet** /sash-ay/ *n.* **1** small bag or packet containing shampoo etc. **2** small scented bag for perfuming drawers etc. [French diminutive: related to SAC]

**sack¹** — *n.* **1 a** large strong bag for storage or conveyance. **b** quantity contained in a sack. **2** (prec. by *the*) *colloq.* dismissal from employment. **3** (prec. by *the*) *colloq.* bed. — *v.* **1** put into a sack or sacks. **2** *colloq.* dismiss from employment. □ **hit the sack** go to bed. **sad sack** *colloq.* habitually gloomy or miserable person; completely inept person. [Latin *saccus*]

**sack²** — *v.* plunder and destroy (a captured town etc.). — *n.* such sacking. [French *mettre à sac* put in a sack]

**sackbut** /sak-but/ *n.* early form of trombone. [French]

**sackcloth** *n.* **1** coarse fabric of flax or hemp used for sacks. **2** clothing for penance or mourning (esp. *sackcloth and ashes*).

**sacking** *n.* material for making sacks; sackcloth.

**sacral** /say-kruhl/ *adj.* **1** *Anat.* of the sacrum. **2** of or for sacred rites. [Latin *sacrum* sacred]

**sacrament** /sak-ruh-muhnt/ *n.* **1** Christian ceremony which is an outward and visible sign of God's gift of an inward and spiritual grace, namely the seven rites of baptism, confirmation, the Eucharist, penance (confession and absolution), extreme unction, ordination (to the priesthood), and matrimony, as practised by the Roman Catholic and Orthodox Churches, but restricted by most Protestants to baptism and the Eucharist. **2** (also **Blessed or Holy Sacrament**) (prec. by *the*) the Eucharist; the consecrated Host. **3** sacred thing. □ **sacramental** /ˌsak-ruh-**men**-tuhl/ *adj.* [Latin: related to SACRED]

**sacred** /say-kruhd/ *adj.* **1 a** (often foll. by *to*) dedicated to a god. **b** connected with religion (opp. SECULAR) (*sacred music*). **2 a** safeguarded or required esp. by tradition; inviolable (*sacred duty to defend the country*). **b** reverently dedicated (*sacred to the memory of the fallen in all wars*). [Latin *sacer* holy]

**Sacred College** n. the Cardinals of the Roman Catholic Church.

**sacred cow** n. colloq. traditionally hallowed idea or institution held to be above criticism.

**sacred kingfisher** n. predominantly blue, green, and buff kingfisher of Australia and elsewhere.

**sacred site** n. place venerated by Aborigines because of its spiritual significance to them.

**sacrifice** /sak-ruh-,fuys/ — n. **1 a** voluntary relinquishing of something more important or worthy (gave their lives in sacrifice for their country). **b** thing so relinquished. **c** the loss entailed. **2 a** slaughter of an animal or person or surrender of a possession, as an offering to a deity. **b** animal, person, or thing so offered. **3** Theol. **a** Christ's offering of himself in the Crucifixion for the redemption of the human species. **b** the Mass as re-presentation of Christ's sacrifice on the Cross. — v. (**-cing**) **1** give up (a thing) as a sacrifice. **2** (foll. by to) devote or give over to (sacrificed her every moment to the poor in India). **3** (also absol.) offer or kill as a sacrifice. □ **sacrificial** /-fish-uhl/ adj. [Latin: related to SACRED]

**sacrilege** /sak-ruh-lij/ n. violation of what is regarded as sacred. □ **sacrilegious** /-lij-uhs/ adj. [Latin: related to SACRED, lego take]

**sacristan** /sak-ruh-stuhn/ n. person in charge of a sacristy and church contents. [medieval Latin: related to SACRED]

**sacristy** /sak-ruh-stee/ n. (pl. **-ies**) room in a church where vestments, sacred vessels, etc., are kept. [medieval Latin: related to SACRED]

**sacrosanct** /sak-roh-,sangkt/ adj. most sacred; inviolable. □ **sacrosanctity** /-sangk-tuh-tee/ n. [Latin: related to SACRED, SAINT]

**sacrum** /say-kruhm/ n. (pl. **sacra** or **-s**) triangular bone between the two hip-bones. [Latin os sacrum sacred bone]

**sad** adj. (**sadder**, **saddest**) **1** unhappy; feeling sorrow. **2** causing sorrow (a sad story). **3** regrettable (made a sad miscalculation). **4** shameful, deplorable (is in a sad state). □ **sadden** v. **sadly** adv. **sadness** n. [Old English]

**saddle** /sad-uhl/ — n. **1** seat of leather etc. strapped on a horse etc. for riding. **2** bicycle etc. seat. **3** joint of meat consisting of the two loins. **4** ridge rising to a summit at each end. — v. (**-ling**) **1** put a saddle on (a horse etc.). **2** (foll. by with) burden (a person) with a task etc. □ **in the saddle 1** mounted. **2** in office or control. [Old English]

**saddleback** n. **1** roof of a tower with two opposite gables. **2** hill with a concave upper outline. **3** saddle-like markings on the back of a bird or animal. □ **saddle-backed** adj.

**saddlebag** n. **1** each of a pair of bags laid across the back of a horse etc. **2** bag attached to a bicycle saddle etc.

**saddler** n. maker of or dealer in saddles etc.

**saddlery** /sad-luh-ree/ n. (pl. **-ies**) saddler's goods, trade, or premises.

**saddling paddock** n. (also **saddling enclosure**) enclosure in which horses are saddled before a race.

**sadism** /say-diz-uhm, sad-iz-uhm/ n. **1** colloq. enjoyment of cruelty to others. **2** condition in which sexual pleasure is taken in this (cf. MASOCHISM). □ **sadist** n. **sadistic** /suh-**dis**-tik/ adj. **sadistically** adv. [de Sade, name of an author]

**sado-masochism** /,say-doh-**mas**-uh-,kiz-uhm, ,sad-oh-/ n. sadism and masochism in one person. □ **sado-masochist** n. **sado-masochistic** /-kis-tik/ adj.

**s.a.e.** abbr. stamped addressed envelope.

**safari** /suh-**fah**-ree/ n. (pl. **-s**) expedition, esp. in Africa, to observe or hunt animals (go on safari). [Swahili from Arabic safara to travel]

**safe** — adj. **1** free of danger or injury. **2** secure, not risky (in a safe place). **3** reliable, certain (missed a safe catch; a safe method). **4** prevented from escaping or doing harm (have got him safe behind bars). **5** (also **safe and sound**) uninjured; with no harm done. **6** cautious, unenterprising (a safe performance of the piano concerto). — n. strong lockable cabinet etc. for valuables. □ **on the safe side** with a margin for error. □ **safely** adv. [French sauf from Latin salvus]

**safe bet** n. wager that is sure to succeed; a certainty.

**safe conduct** n. **1** immunity given from arrest or harm. **2** document securing this.

**safeguard** — n. proviso, circumstance, etc., that tends to protect, or to prevent something undesirable. — v. guard or protect (rights etc.).

**safe period** n. time during the month when conception is least likely.

**safe seat** n. seat in a parliament etc. that is usu. won with a large margin by a particular political party.

**safe sex** — n. sexual activity in which precautions (esp. the use of a condom) are taken against Aids and other sexually transmitted diseases (cf. UNSAFE SEX). — attrib. adj. (**safe-sex**) of or pertaining to safe sex (the safe-sex campaign).

**safety** n. the condition of being safe; freedom from danger or risks.

**safety belt** n. **1** = SEATBELT. **2** belt or strap worn to prevent injury.

**safety catch** n. device preventing a gun-trigger or machinery from being operated accidentally.

**safety curtain** n. fireproof curtain between a stage and auditorium.

**safety fuse** n. **1** protective fuse (see FUSE¹). **2** fuse containing a slow-burning composition for firing detonators from a distance.

**Safety House** — adj. of or pertaining to a scheme which provides that certain houses occupied by adults can be entered by children who are being sexually or otherwise harassed in the street. — n. a house so designated.

**safety match** n. match igniting only on a specially prepared surface.

**safety net** n. net placed to catch an acrobat etc. in case of a fall.

**safety pin** n. pin with a guarded point.

**safety ramp** n. road for a vehicle to turn into if unable to negotiate a bend, descent, etc.

**safety razor** n. razor with a guard to prevent cutting the skin.

**safety valve** n. **1** (in a steam boiler) automatic valve relieving excess pressure. **2** means of venting excitement etc. harmlessly.

**safflower** n. thistle-like European plant yielding a red dye and an edible oil.

**saffron** /saf-ruhn/ — n. **1** deep yellow food colouring and flavouring made from dried crocus stigmas. **2** colour of this. — adj. deep yellow. [French from Arabic]

**saffron thistle** n. introduced Mediterranean annual, now naturalised, and proclaimed a noxious weed, in all Australian States.

**sag** — v. (**-gg-**) **1** sink or subside, esp. unevenly. **2** have a downward bulge or curve in the middle. **3 a** (of a part of the body) droop (*shoulders sagged*). **b** (of a garment) hang unevenly. **4** fall in price. — n. state or extent of sagging. □ **saggy** adj. [Low German or Dutch]

**saga** /**sah**-guh/ n. **1** long heroic story, esp. medieval Icelandic or Norwegian. **2** series of connected novels concerning a family's history etc. **3** long involved story. [Old Norse: related to SAW³]

**sagacious** /suh-**gay**-shuhs/ adj. showing insight or good judgment. □ **sagacity** /suh-**gas**-uh-tee/ n. [Latin *sagax -acis*]

**sage¹** n. culinary herb with dull greyish-green leaves. [French from Latin]

**sage²** — n. often iron. wise man. — adj. wise, judicious, experienced. □ **sagely** adv. [French from Latin *sapio* be wise]

**Sagittarius** /saj-uh-**tair**-ree-uhs/ n. (pl. **-es**) **1** constellation and ninth sign of the zodiac (the Archer). **2** person born when the sun is in this sign. □ **Sagittarian** adj. & n. [Latin, = archer]

**sago** /**say**-goh/ n. (pl. **-s**) **1** a starch used in puddings etc. **2** (in full **sago palm**) any of several tropical palms and cycads yielding this. [Malay]

**sago grass** n. tall Australian grass grown as stock forage.

**sahib** /sahb, **sah**-hib/ n. hist. (in India) form of address, often placed after the name, to any European man. [Arabic, = lord]

**said** past and past part. of SAY.

**sail** — n. **1** piece of material extended on rigging to catch the wind and propel a boat or ship. **2** ship's sails collectively. **3** voyage or excursion in a sailing-boat. **4** ship, esp. as discerned from its sails. **5** wind-catching apparatus of a windmill. — v. **1** travel on water by the use of sails or engine-power. **2** begin a voyage (*sails at nine*). **3 a** navigate (a ship etc.). **b** travel on (a sea). **4** set (a toy boat) afloat. **5** glide or move smoothly or in a stately manner (*she sailed onto the stage*). **6** (often foll. by *through*) colloq. succeed easily (*sailed through the exams*). □ **sail close to the wind 1** sail as nearly against the wind as possible. **2** come close to indecency or dishonesty. **sail into** colloq. attack physically or verbally. **under sail** with sails set. [Old English]

**sailboard** n. board with a mast and sail, used in windsurfing. □ **sailboarder** n. **sailboarding** n.

**sailcloth** n. **1** material used for sails. **2** canvas-like material used for clothing etc.

**sailor** n. **1** member of a ship's crew, esp. one below the rank of officer. **2** person considered with regard to seasickness (*a good sailor*). [originally *sailer*: see -ER¹]

**sailplane** n. glider designed for sustained flight.

**saint** /saynt/ /suhnt/ — n. (abbr. **St** or **S**; pl. **Sts** or **SS**) **1** holy or (in some Churches) formally canonised person regarded as worthy of special veneration. **2** very virtuous person. — v. (as **sainted** adj.) saintly. □ **sainthood** n. **saintlike** adj. [Latin *sanctus* holy]

**St Andrew's Cross spider** n. Australian spider (the female having an abdomen banded in gold and red) which aligns its legs in pairs along the cross-shaped (x) centre piece of its web.

**St Bernard** /**ber**-nuhd/ n. (in full **St Bernard dog**) very large dog of a breed orig. kept in the Alps to rescue travellers.

**saintly** adj. (**-ier**, **-iest**) very holy or virtuous. □ **saintliness** n.

**St Vitus's dance** /**vuy**-tuhs-uhz/ n. disease producing involuntary convulsive movements of the body, esp. in children.

**sake¹** n. □ **for Christ's** (or **God's** or **goodness'** or **Heaven's** or **Pete's** etc.) **sake** expression of impatience, supplication, anger, etc. **for the sake of** (or **for one's sake**) out of consideration for; in the interest of; because of; in order to please, honour, get, or keep (*for my own sake as well as yours*; *for the sake of uniformity*). [Old English]

**sake²** / **sah**-kee/ n. Japanese rice wine. [Japanese]

**salaam** /suh-**lahm**/ — n. **1** the oriental greeting 'Peace!' (in India etc.). **2** a low bow with the right palm on the forehead. **3** (in pl.) respectful compliments. — v. make a salaam (to). [Arabic]

**salacious** /suh-**lay**-shuhs/ adj. **1** (of writings, pictures, talk, etc.) tending to cause sexual desire; indecently erotic. **2** lecherous. □ **salaciousness** n. **salacity** /suh-**las**-uh-tee/ n. [Latin *salax -acis*: related to SALIENT]

**salad** /**sal**-uhd/ n. cold mixture of usu. raw vegetables, often with a dressing. [French *salade* from Latin *sal* salt]

**salad days** n. period of youthful inexperience.

**salad-dressing** n. = DRESSING 2a.

**salamander** /**sal**-uh-,man-duh/ n. **1** tailed newtlike amphibian once thought able to endure fire. **2** similar mythical creature. [Greek *salamandra*]

**salami** /suh-**lah**-mee/ n. (pl. **-s**) highly-seasoned orig. Italian sausage. [Italian]

**salary** /**sal**-uh-ree/ — n. (pl. **-ies**) fixed regular wages, esp. for white-collar work. — v. (**-ies**, **-ied**) (usu. as **salaried** adj.) pay a salary to. [Latin *salarium* money for buying salt]

**sale** n. **1** exchange of a commodity for money etc.; act or instance of selling. **2** amount sold (*sales were enormous*). **3** offering of goods at temporarily reduced prices. **4 a** event at which goods are sold. **b** public auction. □ **on** (or **for**) **sale** offered for purchase. [Old English]

**saleable** adj. fit or likely to be sold. □ **saleability** n.

**salesman** n. man employed to sell goods.

**salesmanship** n. skill in selling.

**salesperson** n. salesman or saleswoman.

**sales talk** n. persuasive talk promoting goods or an idea etc.

**sales tax** n. tax levied on the retail price of goods.

**saleswoman** n. woman employed to sell goods.

**saleyard** n. **1** enclosure in which livestock is sold. **2** (also **saleyards**) set of such enclosures.

**salicylic acid** /,sal-uh-**sil**-ik/ n. chemical used as a fungicide and in aspirin and dyes. □ **salicylate** /suh-**lis**-uh-,layt/ n. [Latin *salix* willow]

**salient** /**say**-lee-uhnt/ adj. **1 a** jutting out; prominent; conspicuous (*salient feature of the landscape*). **b** main; most pertinent (*the salient point of his argument*). **2** (of an angle, esp. in fortification) pointing outwards. [Latin *salio* leap]

**salination** /,sal-uh-**nay**-shuhn/ n. (also **salinisation** /,sal-uh-nuy-**zay**-shuhn/) increase in the salt content of soil (caused by bad land management, poor irrigation methods, etc.), resulting in progressive infertility (see SCALDED EARTH).

**saline** /**say**-luyn/ — adj. **1** containing salt or salts. **2** tasting of salt. **3** of chemical salts. **4** of the nature of a salt. — n. saline solution. □ **salinity** /suh-**lin**-uh-tee/ n. [Latin *sal* salt]

**saliva** /suh-**luy**-vuh/ n. colourless liquid secreted into the mouth by glands. □ **salivary** adj. [Latin]

**salivate** /**sal**-uh-,vayt/ v. (**-ting**) secrete saliva, esp. in excess or in greedy anticipation. □ **salivation** /,sal-uh-**vay**-shuhn/ n. [Latin *salivare*: related to SALIVA]

**sallee** var. of SALLY².

**sallow¹** /**sal**-oh/ adj. (**-er**, **-est**) (esp. of the skin) yellowish. □ **sallowish** adj. **sallowness** n. [Old English]

**sallow²** /**sal**-oh/ n. low-growing willow. □ **sallowy** adj. [Old English]

**sally¹** /**sal**-ee/ (pl. **-ies**) — n. **1** sudden military charge; sortie. **2** an excursion. **3** a witticism; a lively remark esp. by way of attack upon a person or thing or of a diversion in argument. — v. (**-ies**, **-ied**) **1** (usu. foll. by *out*, *forth*) set out on a walk, journey, etc. **2** (usu. foll. by *out*) make a military sally. [French *saillie* from Latin *salio* leap]

**sally²** n. (also **sallee**) any of several eucalypts and wattles resembling the willow. [British dial. *sally* variant of SALLOW²]

**sally wattle** n. any of several wattles, esp. *Acacia longifolia*, having narrow, elongated phyllodes.

**salmon** /**sam**-uhn/ — n. (pl. usu. same or **-s**) **1** large expensive edible fish of the Northern hemisphere, having orange-pink flesh; now introduced into Australia. **2** any of several marine and freshwater food-fish abundant in southern Australian waters. — adj. salmon-pink. [Latin *salmo*]

**salmonella** /,sal-muh-**nel**-uh/ n. (pl. **-llae** /-lee/) **1** bacterium causing food poisoning. **2** such food poisoning. [*Salmon*, name of a veterinary surgeon]

**salmon gum** n. WA eucalypt having a silky-smooth salmon-pink trunk.

**salmon pink** adj. & n. (as adj. often hyphenated) orange-pink colour of salmon flesh.

**salmon trout** n. **1** large silver-coloured trout. **2** the young of some Australian salmon, having brown trout-like markings on the upper surface.

**salon** /sal-on/ n. **1** room or establishment of a hairdresser, beautician, etc. **2** hist. meeting of eminent people in the home of a lady of fashion. [French: related to SALOON]

**saloon** /suh-loon/ n. **1 a** large room or hall on a ship, in a hotel, etc. **b** public room for a specified purpose (billiard-saloon). **2** (in full saloon car) (usu. four-seater) car with the body closed off from the luggage area. **3** (in full saloon bar) more comfortable bar in a hotel. [French salon]

**salsa** /sal-suh/ n. **1** a kind of dance music of Cuban origin, with jazz and rock elements. **2** (esp. in Latin American cooking) spicy sauce served with meat or as a dip. [Spanish: related to SAUCE]

**salt** /sawlt, solt/ — n. **1** (also common salt) sodium chloride, esp. mined or evaporated from sea water, and used for seasoning or preserving food. **2** chemical compound formed from the reaction of an acid with a base. **3** piquancy; wit (her remarks added salt to the conversation). **4** (in sing. or pl.) **a** substance resembling salt in taste, form, etc. (bath salts). **b** (esp. in pl.) substance used as a laxative. **5** (also old salt) experienced sailor. — adj. containing, tasting of, or preserved with salt. — v. cure, preserve, or season with salt or brine. □ **rub salt into the wound** make a person's state of misfortune even worse; add insult to injury. **salt away** (or **down**) colloq. put (money etc.) by. **the salt of the earth** most admirable or honest person or people (Matt. 5:13). **take with a pinch** (or **grain**) **of salt** regard sceptically. **worth one's salt** efficient, capable. [Old English]

**saltbush** n. any of various shrubs or herbs typically dominating tracts of saline and alkaline land in drier Australia (see BERRY SALTBUSH; BLADDER SALTBUSH; OLD MAN SALTBUSH).

**salt cellar** n. container for salt at table. [earlier salt saler from French salier salt-box]

**saltie** n. colloq. = SALT-WATER CROCODILE.

**salt pan** n. **1** dried-up salt lake. **2** vessel, or depression near the sea, used for getting salt by evaporation.

**saltpetre** /solt-pee-tuh, sawlt-/ n. white crystalline salty substance used in preserving meat and in gunpowder. [Latin sal petrae, = salt of rock]

**salt-water** adj. of or living in the sea.

**salt-water crocodile** n. large crocodile of coastal and near-coastal north and north-eastern Australia, inhabiting estuarine, sea, and fresh water.

**salty** adj. (-ier, -iest) **1** tasting of or containing salt. **2** (of wit etc.) piquant. □ **saltiness** n.

**salubrious** /suh-loo-bree-uhs/ adj. health-giving; healthy. □ **salubrity** n. [Latin salus health]

**salutary** /sal-yuh-tuh-ree, -tree/ adj. having a good effect (learned a salutary lesson from that experience). [Latin: related to SALUTE]

**salutation** /sal-yuh-tay-shuhn/ n. formal sign or expression of greeting.

**salute** /suh-loot/ — n. **1** gesture of respect, homage, greeting etc. **2** Mil. & Naut. prescribed gesture or use of weapons or flags as a sign of respect etc. **3** ceremonial discharge of a gun or guns. **4** = GREAT AUSTRALIAN SALUTE. — v. (-ting) **1 a** make a salute to. **b** (often foll. by to) perform a salute. **2** greet. [Latin salus -ut- health]

**salvage** /sal-vij/ — n. **1** rescue of property from the sea, a fire, etc. **2** property etc. so saved. **3 a** saving and use of waste materials. **b** materials salvaged. — v. (-ging) **1** save from a wreck etc. **2** retrieve or preserve (something favourable) in adverse circumstances (salvaged her pride). □ **salvageable** adj. [Latin: related to SALVE[1]]

**salvation** /sal-vay-shuhn/ n. **1** act of saving or being saved. **2** Theol. deliverance from sin and damnation. **3** person or thing that saves (was the salvation of ...). [Latin: related to SAVE[1]]

**Salvation Army** n. worldwide evangelical Christian quasi-military organisation helping the poor.

**salvation Jane** n. = PATERSON'S CURSE.

**salve** — n. **1** a healing ointment. **2** (often foll. by for) thing that soothes or consoles (wounded feelings, an uneasy conscience, etc.). — v. (-ving) soothe. [Old English]

**salver** n. tray, esp. silver, for drinks, letters, etc. [Spanish salva assaying of food]

**Salvo** /sal-voh/ n. (pl. -es or -s) colloq. **1** member of the Salvation Army. **2** (in pl.) the Salvation Army. [abbreviation: Salv(ation Army), -o]

**salvo[1]** /sal-voh/ n. (pl. -es or -s) **1** simultaneous discharge of guns etc. **2** round of applause. [Italian salva]

**salvo[2]** n. (pl. -s) saving clause; reservation (gave her consent, with the salvo that ...). [Latin, ablative of salvus safe]

**sal volatile** /sal vuh-lat-uh-lee/ n. solution of ammonium carbonate used as smelling-salts. [Latin, = volatile salt]

**Samaritan** /suh-**ma**-ruh-tuhn/ n. (in full **good Samaritan**) charitable or helpful person (Luke 10:33 etc.). [originally = inhabitant of ancient Samaria]

**samarium** /suh-**mair**-ree-uhm/ n. metallic element of the lanthanide series. [ultimately from *Samarski*, name of an official]

**samba** /**sam**-buh/ — n. **1** ballroom dance of Brazilian origin. **2** music for this. — v. (**-bas, -baed** or **-ba'd** /-buhd/, **-baing** /-buh-ing/) dance the samba. [Portuguese]

**sambal** /**sam**-bahl/ n. (in Malaysian and Indonesian cuisines) condiment used as an accompaniment to rice and curry etc. and in cooking. [Malay]

**sambo** /**sam**-boh/ n. colloq. sandwich. [abbreviation]

**sambol** /**sam**-bawl/ n. (in Sri Lankan, South Indian, etc., cuisines) any of a variety of relishes eaten with rice and curry.

**same** — adj. **1** (often prec. by *the*) identical; not different (*on the same bus*). **2** unvarying (*same old story*). **3** (usu. prec. by *this, these, that, those*) just mentioned (*this same man later died*). — pron. (prec. by *the*) **1** the same person or thing (*the others asked for the same*). **2** Law or archaic the person or thing just mentioned (*detected the youth breaking in and apprehended the same*). — adv. (usu. prec. by *the*) similarly; in the same way (*feel the same*). □ **all the same 1** nevertheless. **2** immaterial; of no consequence (*it's all the same to me*). **at the same time 1** simultaneously. **2** notwithstanding. **be all (or just) the same to** make no difference to. **just the same 1** exactly in the same manner. **2** nevertheless. **same here** colloq. the same applies to me. □ **sameness** n. [Old Norse]

**samosa** /suh-**moh**-suh/ n. fried triangular pastry containing spiced vegetables or meat. [Hindustani]

**samovar** /**sam**-uh-,vah/ n. Russian tea-urn. [Russian]

**sampan** /**sam**-pan/ n. small boat used in China etc. [Chinese]

**sample** /**sahm**-puhl, **sam**-puhl/ — n. **1** small representative part or quantity. **2** specimen. **3** illustrative or typical example. — v. (**-ling**) **1** take or give samples of. **2** try the qualities of. **3** experience briefly. [Anglo-French: related to EXAMPLE]

**sample bag** n. = SHOW BAG.

**sampler**[1] n. **1** piece of embroidery using various stitches as a specimen of proficiency. **2** compact disc providing samples of the output of an orchestra, pop group, etc. [French: related to EXEMPLAR]

**sampler**[2] n. **1** person or thing that samples. **2** machine used in sampling.

**sampling** n. (in electronic music) technique or process of taking a piece of digitally encoded sound and re-using it, often in a modified form, as part of a composition or recording.

**Samson fish** n. any of several Australian marine fish noted for their strength, esp. in game-fishing contexts. [*Samson*, person of great strength in the Old Testament]

**samurai** /**sam**-uu-,ruy, -yuh-,ruy/ n. (pl. same) hist. member of a Japanese military caste. [Japanese]

**sanatorium** /,san-uh-**taw**-ree-uhm/ n. (pl. **-s** or **-ria**) residential clinic esp. for convalescents and the chronically sick. [Latin *sano* heal]

**sanctify** /**sangk**-tuh-,fuy/ v. (**-ies, -ied**) **1** consecrate; treat as holy. **2** free from sin. **3** justify; sanction (*a custom sanctified by tradition*). □ **sanctification** /-fuh-**kay**-shuhn/ n. [Latin *sanctus* holy]

**sanctimonious** /,sangk-tuh-**moh**-nee-uhs/ adj. ostentatiously pious (*sanctimonious hypocrite*). □ **sanctimoniously** adv. **sanctimoniousness** n. **sanctimony** /**sangk**-tuh-muh-nee/ n. [Latin *sanctimonia* sanctity]

**sanction** /**sangk**-shuhn/ — n. **1** approval by custom or tradition; explicit permission. **2** confirmation of a law etc. **3** penalty for disobeying a law or rule, or a reward for obeying it. **4** Ethics moral force encouraging obedience to any rule of conduct. **5** (esp. in pl.) (esp. economic) action by a country against another to abide by an international agreement etc. (*trade sanctions*). — v. **1** authorise or agree to (an action etc.). **2** ratify; make (a law etc.) binding. [Latin *sancio sanct-* make sacred]

**sanctity** /**sangk**-tuh-tee/ n. **1** holiness, sacredness. **2** inviolability (*the sanctity of marriage*). [Latin *sanctus* holy]

**sanctuary** /**sangk**-choor-ree, -chuh-ree/ n. (pl. **-ies**) **1** holy place. **2 a** holiest part of a temple etc. **b** chancel. **3** place where birds, wild animals, etc., are bred and protected. **4** place of refuge.

**sanctum** /**sangk**-tuhm/ n. (pl. **-s**) **1** holy place. **2** person's private room, study, etc.

**sand** — n. **1** fine loose grains resulting from the erosion of esp. siliceous rocks and forming the seashore, deserts, etc. **2** (in pl.) **a** grains of sand. **b** expanse of sand. **c** sandbank. — v. smooth with sandpaper or sand. [Old English]

**sandal** /**san**-duhl/ n. shoe with an open-work upper or no upper, usu. fastened by straps. [Latin from Greek]

**sandal tree** n. tree yielding sandalwood.

**sandalwood** n. **1** scented wood of a sandal-tree. **2** perfume from this.

**sandbag** — n. bag filled with sand, used for temporary defences etc. — v. (-gg-) defend or hit with sandbag(s).

**sandbank** n. (also **sandbar**) sand forming a shallow place in the sea or a river.

**sandblast** — v. roughen, treat, or clean with a jet of sand driven by compressed air or steam. — n. this jet. □ **sandblaster** n.

**sand dune** n. (also **sandhill**) = DUNE.

**sander** n. power tool for sanding.

**sanderling** n. small migrant sandpiper (from Siberia) of Australian sandy coastal regions.

**sand-fly** n. any of various small blood-sucking flies found among and near sand, and often transmitting diseases to humans.

**sand goanna** n. = BUNGARRA.

**Sandgroper** n. colloq. a Western Australian.

**sandie** n. (also **blue swimmer**) colloq. edible Queensland sand crab.

**sandman** n. imaginary person causing tiredness in children towards bedtime.

**sand mullet** n. (also **tallegalane**) small marine and estuarine food-fish of southern Australia, excluding Tasmania.

**sandpaper** — n. paper with an abrasive coating for smoothing or polishing. — v. rub with this.

**sandpiper** n. any of many wading birds, generally migrants from the Northern hemisphere, frequenting wet sandy areas (curlew sandpiper; sharp-tailed sandpiper; etc.).

**sand-plover** n. either of two plovers migrant to coastal Australia (large sand-plover; Mongolian sand-plover).

**sandshoe** n. canvas shoe with rubber sole used primarily for sport (formerly, for wearing on the sand).

**sandstone** n. sedimentary rock of compressed sand.

**sandstorm** n. storm with clouds of sand raised by the wind.

**sandwich** /san-wij, -wich/ — n. two or more slices of bread with a filling. — v. 1 put (a thing, statement, etc.) between two of another character. 2 squeeze in between others (sat sandwiched in the middle). □ **be the meat in the sandwich** be the innocent victim in the middle of a conflict between two opposing parties, neither of whom the victim wishes to side with or against (when parents divorce the child is often the meat in the sandwich). [from the Earl of Sandwich]

**sandworm** n. any of various worms which live in sandy shores.

**sandy** adj. (-ier, -iest) 1 having much sand. 2 a (of hair) yellowish-red. b sand-coloured. □ **sandiness** n.

**sandy blight** n. (also **sand blight**) acute conjunctivitis, usu. contagious, characterised by granular follicles on the inner surface of the eyelids, and common in arid Australia (see TRACHOMA).

**sane** adj. 1 of sound mind; not mad. 2 (of views etc.) moderate, sensible. □ **sanely** adv. **saneness** n. [Latin sanus healthy]

**sang** past of SING.

**sanger** /sang-uh/ n. (also **sango** /sang-oh/) colloq. a sandwich. [abbreviation]

**sang-froid** /sahng-frwah/ n. calmness in danger or difficulty. [French, = cold blood]

**sanguinary** /sang-gwuh-nuh-ree/ adj. 1 bloody. 2 bloodthirsty. [Latin sanguis -guin- blood]

**sanguine** /sang-gwuhn/ adj. 1 optimistic, confident. 2 (of the complexion) florid, ruddy.

**sanitary**[1] /san-uh-tuh-ree, -tree/ adj. 1 (of conditions etc.) affecting health. 2 hygienic. □ **sanitariness** n. [Latin sanitas: related to SANE]

**sanitary**[2] n. (in full **sanitary cart**); also **dunny cart**) vehicle used to collect excrement from houses in unsewered areas.

**sanitary pad** n. (also **sanitary napkin**) absorbent pad used during menstruation.

**sanitation** /san-uh-tay-shuhn/ n. 1 sanitary conditions. 2 maintenance etc. of these. 3 disposal of sewage and refuse etc.

**sanitise** /san-uh-tuyz/ v. (also **-ize**) (-sing or -zing) 1 make sanitary; disinfect. 2 colloq. censor (information etc.) to make it more acceptable.

**sanity** /san-uh-tee/ n. 1 being sane. 2 moderation; tendency to avoid extreme views. 3 sound judgment. [Latin sanitas: related to SANE]

**sank** past of SINK.

**Sanskrit** /san-skrit/ — n. ancient and sacred language of the Hindus in India. — adj. of or in this language. [Sanskrit, = composed]

**sans serif** /san-se-ruhf/ n. (also **sanserif**) form of type without serifs. [apparently from sans without, SERIF]

**Santa Claus** /san-tuh klawz/ n. person said to bring children presents on Christmas Eve. [Dutch, = St Nicholas]

**sap**[1] — n. 1 vital juice circulating in plants. 2 vigour, vitality. 3 colloq. foolish or weak person. — v. (-pp-) 1 drain or dry (wood) of sap. 2 exhaust the vigour of; weaken. [Old English]

**sap**[2] — n. tunnel or trench dug to get nearer to the enemy. — v. (-pp-) 1 dig saps. 2 undermine. [French sappe or Italian zappa spade]

**sapient** /say-pee-uhnt/ adj. literary 1 wise. 2 aping wisdom. □ **sapience** n. [Latin sapio be wise]

**sapling** *n.* young tree. [from SAP¹]

**sapper** *n.* **1** person who digs saps. **2** soldier of the Royal Australian Engineers.

**Sapphic** /**saf**-ik/ *adj.* **1** of Sappho or her poetry. **2** lesbian. [Greek *Sappho*, poet of Lesbos]

**sapphire** /**saf**-uyuh/ — *n.* **1** transparent blue precious stone. **2** its bright blue colour. — *adj.* (also **sapphire blue**) bright blue. [Greek *sappheiros* lapis lazuli]

**sappy** *adj.* (**-ier, -iest**) **1** full of sap. **2** young and vigorous. **3** *colloq.* silly (*sappy sort of thing to do*).

**saprogenic** /ˌsap-ruh-**jen**-ik/ *adj.* caused or produced by putrefaction. [Greek *sapros* rotten]

**saprophyte** /**sap**-ruh-ˌfuyt/ *n.* plant or micro-organism living on dead or decayed organic matter. □ **saprophytic** /-**fit**-ik/ *adj.* [Greek *sapros* rotten, *phuō* grow]

**saraband** /**sa**-ruh-ˌband/ *n.* **1** slow stately Spanish dance. **2** music for this. [Spanish *zarabanda*]

**Saracen** /**sa**-ruh-suhn/ *n. hist.* Arab or Muslim at the time of the Crusades. [Greek *sarakénos*]

**sarcasm** /**sah**-ˌkaz-uhm/ *n.* ironically scornful language. □ **sarcastic** /sah-**kas**-tik/ *adj.* **sarcastically** *adv.* [Greek *sarkazō* speak bitterly]

**sarcoma** /sah-**koh**-muh/ *n.* (*pl.* **-s** or **-mata**) malignant tumour of connective tissue etc. [Greek *sarx sark*- flesh]

**sarcophagus** /sah-**kof**-uh-guhs/ *n.* (*pl.* **-phagi** /-ˌguy/) stone coffin. [Greek, = flesh-consumer]

**sardine** /sah-**deen**/ *n.* (*pl.* same or **-s**) young pilchard etc. sold in closely packed tins. □ **like sardines** crowded close together (as sardines in a tin). [French from Latin]

**sardonic** /sah-**don**-ik/ *adj.* bitterly mocking or cynical. □ **sardonically** *adv.* [Greek *sardonios* Sardinian]

**sardonyx** /**sah**-duh-niks/ *n.* onyx in which white layers alternate with yellow or orange ones. [Greek *sardonux*]

**sarge** *n. colloq.* sergeant. [abbreviation]

**sari** /**sah**-ree/ *n.* (*pl.* **-s**) length of cloth draped round the body, traditionally worn by women of the Indian subcontinent. [Hindi]

**Sarich engine** /**sa**-rich/ *n. propr.* orbital engine. [T.R. *Sarich* Australian inventor]

**sarong** /suh-**rong**/ *n.* **1** Malay and Javanese garment of a long strip of cloth tucked round the waist or under the armpits. **2** ankle-length tube of cloth worn tucked around the waist by men in Sri Lanka and other Asian countries. [Malay]

**sarsaparilla** /ˌsah-suh-puh-**ril**-uh, ˌsah-spuh-/ *n.* **1** preparation of the dried roots of various plants, esp. smilax, used to flavour some drinks and medicines and formerly as a tonic. **2** plant yielding this. **3** (also **false sarsaparilla**) = HARDENBERGIA. **4** (also **native sarsaparilla**) climber of Queensland and NSW, having strongly flavoured leaves formerly used in the bush etc. as a substitute for tea. [Spanish]

**sarsen** /**sah**-suhn/ *n.* sandstone boulder carried by ice during a glacial period. [from SARACEN]

**sartorial** /sah-**taw**-ree-uhl/ *adj.* of or relating to clothes, esp. fashionable, elegant, well-tailored (*the sartorial splendour of his Italian suit*). □ **sartorially** *adv.* [Latin *sartor* tailor]

**sarvo** /**sah**-voh/ *adv. colloq.* this afternoon. [contraction of THIS + ARVO]

**sash**¹ *n.* strip or loop of cloth etc. worn over one shoulder or round the waist. [Arabic, = muslin]

**sash**² *n.* frame holding the glass in a sash-window. [from CHASSIS]

**sashimi** /sa-**shee**-mee/ *n.* Japanese dish of slices of raw fish served with grated horseradish and soy sauce. [Japanese]

**sash-window** *n.* window sliding up and down in grooves.

**sassafras** /**sas**-uh-ˌfras/ *n.* **1** small N. American tree with aromatic bark. **2** medicinal preparation from its leaves or bark. **3** any of several Australian trees having pungently aromatic bark and spicily fragrant leaves. [Spanish or Portuguese]

**sat** *past and past part.* of SIT.

**Satan** /**say**-tuhn/ *n.* the Devil; Lucifer. [Hebrew, = enemy]

**satanic** /suh-**tan**-ik/ *adj.* of or like Satan; hellish; evil. □ **satanically** *adv.*

**Satanism** /**say**-tuh-ˌniz-uhm/ *n.* **1** worship of Satan. **2** pursuit of evil. □ **Satanist** *n. & adj.*

**satay** /**sat**-ay, suh-**tay**/ *n.* Indonesian and Malaysian dish consisting of small pieces of meat grilled on a skewer and usu. served with a spiced sauce. [Malayan *satai sate*, Indonesian *sate*]

**satay sauce** *n.* spicy sauce containing peanuts, chilli, etc.

**satchel** /**sach**-uhl/ *n.* small shoulder-bag for carrying school-books etc. [Latin: related to SACK¹]

**sate** /sayt/ *v.* (**-ting**) *formal* **1** gratify (desire or a desirous person) to the full. **2** cloy, surfeit, weary with overabundance (*sated with pleasure*). [probably British dial. *sade* satisfy]

**satellite** /**sat**-uh-ˌluyt/ — *n.* **1** celestial or artificial body orbiting the earth or another planet. **2** (in full **satellite State**) small country controlled by another. — *attrib.*

*adj.* transmitted by satellite (*satellite television*). [Latin *satelles -lit-* attendant]

**satellite dish** *n.* dish-shaped aerial for receiving satellite television.

**satellite town** *n.* small town economically or otherwise dependent on a nearby city.

**satiate** /say-shee-,ayt/ *v.* (**-ting**) = SATE. □ **satiable** /-shuh-buhl/ *adj.* **satiation** /-shee-ay-shuhn/ *n.* [Latin *satis* enough]

**satiety** /suh-**tuy**-uh-tee/ *n. formal* being sated. [Latin: related to SATIATE]

**satin** /sat-uhn/ — *n.* silk etc. fabric glossy on one side. — *adj.* smooth as satin. □ **satiny** *adj.* [Arabic *zaitūnī*]

**satin bowerbird** *n.* bowerbird of eastern Australia, the mature male having glossy black plumage shot through with a rich blue satiny sheen.

**satin flycatcher** *n.* bird of eastern Australia, the mature male having glossy bluish-black upperparts and chest, and a white belly.

**satin oak** *n.* tall rainforest tree of northern Queensland bearing masses of bright red flowers, spectacular in bloom.

**satinwood** *n.* **1** (in full **Ceylon satinwood**) tree native to Sri Lanka (Ceylon) yielding a golden satiny timber with a beautiful grain. **2** any of several eastern Australian trees (unrelated to *Ceylon satinwood*) yielding a glossy, usu. yellowish timber.

**satire** /sat-uyuh/ *n.* **1** ridicule, irony, etc., used to expose folly or vice etc. **2** work using this. □ **satirical** /suh-**ti**-ri-kuhl/ *adj.* **satirically** /suh-**ti**-ri-klee/ *adv.* [Latin *satira* medley]

**satirise** /sat-uh-,ruyz/ *v.* (also **-ize**) (**-sing** or **-zing**) attack or describe with satire.

**satirist** /sat-uh-ruhst/ *n.* **1** writer of satires. **2** satirical person.

**satisfaction** /,sat-uhs-**fak**-shuhn/ *n.* **1** act or instance of satisfying or the state of being satisfied (*derived great satisfaction*). **2** thing that satisfies (*is a great satisfaction to me*). **3** (foll. by *for*) atonement; compensation (*demanded satisfaction*).

**satisfactory** /,sat-uhs-**fak**-tuh-ree, -tree/ *adj.* adequate; giving satisfaction. □ **satisfactorily** *adv.*

**satisfy** /sat-uhs-,fuy/ *v.* (**-ies**, **-ied**) **1 a** meet the expectations or desires of. **b** be adequate. **2** put an end to (an appetite or want) by supplying what was required (*satisfied his curiosity by feeding him full details*). **3** rid (a person) of such an appetite or want (*satisfied the children with a pre-lunch snack*). **4** pay (a debt or creditor). **5** adequately fulfil or comply with (conditions etc.) (*satisfied all the legal requirements*). **6** (often foll. by *of*,

*that*) convince, esp. with proof etc. (*satisfied the court of his innocence*; *satisfied the others that he was right*). □ **satisfy oneself** (often foll. by *that*) become certain. [Latin *satisfacio*]

**saturate** /sach-uh-,rayt/ *v.* (**-ting**) **1** fill with moisture. **2** (often foll. by *with*) fill to capacity. **3** cause (a substance etc.) to absorb, hold, etc., as much as possible of another substance etc. **4** supply (a market) beyond demand. **5** (as **saturated** *adj.*) (of fat molecules) containing the greatest number of hydrogen atoms. **6** (foll. by *with*, *in*) imbue with or steep in (learning, tradition, etc.). **7** overwhelm (enemy defences etc.) by concentrated bombing. [Latin *satur* full]

**saturation** /,sach-uh-**ray**-shuhn/ *n.* **1** act or instance of saturating or the state of being saturated. **2** (*attrib.*) to the maximum (*saturation bombing*; *saturation coverage of the Olympics*).

**saturation point** *n.* stage beyond which no more can be absorbed or accepted.

**Saturday** /sat-uh-,day/ — *n.* day of the week following Friday. — *adv.* *colloq.* **1** on Saturday. **2** (**Saturdays**) on Saturdays; each Saturday. [Latin: related to SATURN]

**saturnalia** /,sat-uh-**nay**-lee-uh/ *n.* (*pl.* same or **-s**) **1** (usu. **Saturnalia**) *Rom. Hist.* festival of Saturn in December, the predecessor of Christmas. **2** (as *sing.* or *pl.*) scene of wild revelry; orgy. □ **saturnalian** *adj.* [Latin, pl. from *Saturnus* Roman god]

**saturnine** /sat-uh-,nuyn/ *adj.* of gloomy temperament or appearance. [the planet *Saturn*, supposedly giving those born under its sign the qualities of coldness and gloominess]

**satyr** /sat-uh, **say**-tuh/ *n.* **1** (in Greek and Roman mythology) woodland god with some horselike or goatlike features. **2** lecherous man. [Greek *saturos*]

**sauce** /saws/ — *n.* **1** liquid or semi-liquid accompaniment to a dish (*mint sauce*; *tomato sauce*). **2** something adding piquancy or excitement. **3** *colloq.* impudence, impertinence, cheek. — *v.* (**-cing**) **1** give piquancy or excitement to. **2** *colloq.* be impudent to; cheek. [Latin *salsus* salted]

**saucepan** *n.* cooking pan, usu. round with a lid and a projecting handle, used for boiling etc. on top of a stove.

**saucer** *n.* **1 a** shallow circular dish for standing a cup on. **b** similar dish used to stand a plant pot etc. on. **2** thing of this shape (*flying saucer*). □ **saucerful** *n.* (*pl.* **-s**). [French *saussier*]

**saucy** *adj.* (**-ier**, **-iest**) **1** impudent, cheeky. **2** *colloq.* smart-looking (*a saucy hat*). □ **saucily** *adv.* **sauciness** *n.*

**sauerkraut** /**sowuh**-ˌkrowt/ n. German dish of pickled cabbage. [German]

**sauna** /**saw**-nuh/ n. 1 Finnish-style steam bath. 2 building or room with this. [Finnish]

**saunter** /**sawn**-tuh/ — v. walk slowly; stroll. — n. leisurely walk. [origin unknown]

**saurian** /**saw**-ree-uhn/ — adj. of or like a lizard. — n. a lizard. [Greek *saura* lizard]

**sausage** /**sos**-ij/ n. 1 a seasoned minced meat etc. in a cylindrical edible skin. b piece of this. 2 a sausage-shaped object. b colloq. penis. □ **not a sausage** colloq. nothing at all. [French *saussiche*]

**sausage roll** n. seasoned minced meat in a pastry roll.

**sausage sizzle** n. fund-raising or social event for clubs, groups of employees, etc., at which barbecued sausages etc. are sold or provided.

**sauté** /**soh**-tay/ — attrib. adj. (esp. of potatoes) fried quickly in a little fat. — n. food so cooked. — v. (**sautéd** or **sautéed**) cook in this way. [French *sauter* jump]

**sauterne** /soh-**tern**, suh-/ n. (also **sauternes**) sweet white wine orig. from Sauternes in the Bordeaux region of France. [*Sauternes* in France]

**sav** n. colloq. saveloy.

**savage** /**sav**-ij/ — adj. 1 fierce; cruel (*savage attack*). 2 wild; primitive (*savage animal; savage terrain*). 3 colloq. angry; bad-tempered (*in a savage mood*). — n. 1 a offens. member of a primitive tribe. b hist. (in 19th-c. white use) an Aborigine. 2 cruel or barbarous person. — v. (**-ging**) 1 attack and maul. 2 attack verbally (*the Prime Minister savaged the Opposition in parliament*). □ **savagely** adv. **savagery** n. (pl. **-ies**). [French from Latin *silva* a wood]

**savannah** /suh-**van**-uh/ n. (also **savanna**) grassy plain in tropical and subtropical regions. [Spanish]

**savant** /**sav**-uhnt, sa-**vont**/ n. learned person. [French]

**save¹** — v. (**-ving**) 1 (often foll. by *from*) rescue or keep from danger, harm, etc. (*surf lifesavers save many from drowning*). 2 (often foll. by *up*) keep (esp. money) for future use (*saved up for a new bicycle*). 3 a (often *refl.*) relieve (another or oneself) from spending (money, time, trouble, etc.); prevent exposure to (annoyance etc.) (*saved myself $50 by shopping around; a word processor saves time*). b obviate the need for (*soaking saves scrubbing*). 4 preserve from damnation; convert. 5 a avoid losing (a game, match, etc.). b prevent (a goal etc.) from being scored. — n. Soccer etc. prevention of a goal etc.

□ **saved by the bell** rescued at the very last moment. □ **savable** adj. (also **saveable**). [Latin *salvo* from *salvus* safe]

**save²** archaic or poet. — prep. except; but. — conj. (often foll. by *for*) except; but. [Latin *salvo, salva*, ablative sing. of *salvus* safe]

**saveloy** /**sav**-uh-ˌloi/ n. seasoned red pork sausage, dried and smoked, and sold ready to eat. [Italian *cervellata*]

**saver** n. 1 person who saves esp. money. 2 (often in *comb.*) thing that saves (time etc.). 3 *Racing colloq.* hedging bet; bet laid to insure against loss on another (more risky) bet.

**saving** — adj. 1 that delivers, rescues, or preserves from peril etc. 2 (often in *comb.*) making economical use of (*labour-saving*). — n. 1 anything that is saved. 2 an economy (*a saving in expenses*). 3 (usu. in *pl.*) money saved. 4 act of preserving or rescuing. — prep. 1 except (*I'll have all saving the red one*). 2 without offence to (*saving your presence*).

**saving grace** n. redeeming quality.

**savings bank** n. bank paying interest on deposits from individual members of the public, dealing in housing loans, etc. (cf. TRADING BANK).

**saviour** /**say**-vyuh/ n. (also **savior**) 1 person who saves from danger etc. 2 (**Saviour**) (prec. by *the*, *our*) Christ. [Latin: related to SAVE¹]

**savoir faire** /ˌsav-wah **fair**/ n. ability to behave appropriately; tact. [French]

**savour** /**say**-vuh/ — n. 1 characteristic taste, flavour, smell, etc. (*unforgettable savour of kangaroo-tail soup*). 2 hint of a different quality etc. in something (*has just a savour of thyme; savour of the sea in all her novels*). 3 attractiveness; interest (*found that writing had suddenly lost its savour*). — v. 1 appreciate and enjoy (food, an experience, etc.). 2 (foll. by *of*) a suggest by taste, smell, etc. (*savours of mushrooms*). b imply or suggest (a specified quality) (*savours of impertinence*). [Latin *sapor*]

**savoury** /**say**-vuh-ree/ — adj. 1 having an appetising taste or smell. 2 (of food) salty or piquant, not sweet. 3 pleasant; acceptable. — n. (pl. **-ies**) 1 bite-sized salty or spicy snack; canapé. 2 savoury dish served as an appetiser or at the end of a dinner. □ **savouriness** n.

**savoy** /suh-**voi**/ n. cabbage with wrinkled leaves. [*Savoy* in SE France]

**savvy** /**sav**-ee/ colloq. — v. (**-ies, -ied**) know. — n. knowingness; understanding. [Pidgin alteration of Spanish *sabe usted* you know]

**saw¹** — n. **1** hand tool with a toothed blade used to cut esp. wood with a to-and-fro movement. **2** power tool with a toothed rotating disk or moving band, for cutting. — v. (past part. **sawn** or **sawed**) **1** cut (wood etc.) or make (boards etc.) with a saw. **2** use a saw. **3 a** move with a sawing motion (sawing away on his violin). **b** divide (the air etc.) with gesticulations. [Old English]

**saw²** past of SEE¹.

**saw³** n. proverb; maxim. [Old English: related to SAY]

**sawdust** n. powdery wood particles produced in sawing.

**sawfish** n. (pl. same or **-es**) large tropical marine fish with a toothed flat snout.

**sawn** past part. of SAW¹.

**sawn-off** adj. (of a shotgun) with part of the barrel sawn off.

**saw shark** n. shark of southern Australian waters and elsewhere, having a long flattened snout and saw-like teeth.

**sawtooth** adj. (also **sawtoothed**) serrated.

**sawyer** n. person who saws timber, esp. for a living.

**sax** n. colloq. saxophone. [abbreviation]

**Saxon** /**sak**-suhn/ — n. **1** hist. **a** member of the Germanic people that conquered parts of England in 5th–6th c. **b** (usu. **Old Saxon**) language of the Saxons. **2** = ANGLO-SAXON. — adj. **1** hist. of the Saxons. **2** = ANGLO-SAXON. [Latin Saxo -onis]

**saxophone** /**sak**-suh-,fohn/ n. metal woodwind reed instrument used esp. in jazz. □ **saxophonist** /-**sof**-uh-nuhst, -suh-,foh-nuhst/ n. [Sax, name of the maker]

**say** — v. (3rd sing. present **says** /sez/; past and past part. **said** /sed/ ) **1** (often foll. by that) **a** utter (specified words); remark. **b** express (say what you feel). **2** (often foll. by that) **a** state; promise or prophesy (says that there will be war). **b** have specified wording; indicate (says here that he was murdered; clock says ten to six). **3** (in passive; usu. foll. by to + infin.) be asserted (is said to be 93 years old). **4** (foll. by to + infin.) colloq. tell a person to do something (he said to hurry). **5** convey (information) (spoke, but said little). **6** offer as an argument or excuse (much to be said in favour of it). **7** (often absol.) give an opinion or decision as to (hard to say). **8** take as an example or as near enough (paid, say, $20). **9** recite or repeat (prayers, Mass, tables, a lesson, etc.). **10** convey (inner meaning etc.) (what is the poem saying?). **11** (**the said**) Law or joc. the previously mentioned (the said witness then said . . .). — n. **1** opportunity to express a view (let him have his say). **2** share in a decision (had no say in it). □ **have the last say 1** (be given the opportunity to) make the final comment in a debate etc. **2** be the ultimate authority (the Prime Minister has the last say on all policy). **I'll say** colloq. yes indeed. **I say!** exclamation of surprise etc. or drawing attention. **say when!** colloq. indicate when enough drink has been poured or enough food has been served. **that is to say** in other words, more explicitly. **you can say that again!** (or **you said it!**) colloq. I agree emphatically. **you don't say so!** colloq. expression of amazement or disbelief. [Old English]

**saying** n. maxim, proverb, etc. □ **go without saying** be too obvious to need mention.

**say-so** n. colloq. **1** power of decision; authority (she has the say-so in this house). **2** mere assertion (his say-so is not enough).

**Sb** symb. antimony. [Latin stibium]

**SBS** abbr. Special Broadcasting Service.

**Sc** symb. scandium.

**sc.** abbr. **1** scilicet. **2** scene (Act V, sc. 2).

**s.c.** abbr. small capitals.

**scab** — n. **1** crust over a healing cut, sore, etc. **2** (often attrib.) derog. person who refuses to join a strike, who tries to break a strike by working, or who refuses to join a union. **3** skin disease, esp. in animals. **4** fungous plant disease. **5** colloq. dislikeable or contemptible person. — v. (**-bb-**) **1** derog. act as a scab (sense 2). **2** form a scab, heal over. [Old Norse: cf. SHABBY]

**scabbard** /**skab**-uhd/ n. sheath of a sword etc. [Anglo-French]

**scabby** adj. **1** having scabs (on the skin). **2** non-union. **3** colloq. despicable; contemptible.

**scabies** /**skay**-beez/ n. contagious skin disease causing severe itching. [Latin]

**scabrous** /**skay**-bruhs/ adj. **1** rough; bearing short stiff hairs, scales, etc.; scaly. **2** indecent, salacious (scabrous gossip). [Latin]

**scads** /skadz/ n.pl. colloq. a large amount; lots (she has scads of money; scads of places we can go to for a holiday). [origin unknown]

**scaffold** /**skaf**-ohld, -uhld/ n. **1** hist. platform for the execution of criminals. **2** = SCAFFOLDING. [Romanic: related to EX-¹, CATAFALQUE]

**scaffolding** n. **1 a** temporary structure of poles, planks, etc., for building work. **b** materials for this. **2** any temporary framework.

**scalar** /**skay**-luh/ Math. & Physics — adj. (of a quantity) having only magnitude, not direction. — n. scalar quantity. [Latin: related to SCALE³]

**scald** /skawld, skold/ — v. **1** burn (the skin etc.) with hot liquid or steam. **2** heat (esp. milk) to near boiling-point. **3** (usu. foll. by *out*) clean with boiling water. — n. burn etc. caused by scalding. [Latin *excaldo* from *calidus* hot]

**scalded earth** n. (also **scalded land**, **country**, etc.) land that is now bare of vegetation because of soil erosion or salination.

**scale¹** — n. **1** each of the thin horny plates protecting the skin of fish and reptiles. **2** something resembling this. **3** white deposit formed in a kettle etc. by the action of heat on, esp., hard water. **4** tartar formed on teeth. **5** = SCALE INSECT. — v. (**-ling**) **1** remove scale(s) from. **2** form or come off in scales. □ **scaly** adj. (**-ier**, **-iest**). [French *escale*]

**scale²** n. **1 a** (often in *pl.*) weighing machine. **b** (also **scale-pan**) each of the dishes on a simple balance. **2** (**the Scales**) zodiacal sign or constellation Libra. □ **tip** (or **turn**) **the scales 1** be the decisive factor. **2** (usu. foll. by *at*) weigh. [Old Norse *skál* bowl]

**scale³** — n. **1** graded classification system (*high on the social scale; the earthquake measured 7 on the Richter scale*). **2 a** (often *attrib.*) ratio of reduction or enlargement in a map, model, picture, etc. (*on a scale of one centimetre to the kilometre; a scale model*). **b** relative dimensions or degree (*generosity on a grand scale*). **3** *Mus.* set of notes at fixed intervals, arranged in order of pitch. **4 a** set of marks on a line used in measuring etc. **b** rule determining the distances between these. **c** rod etc. on which these are marked. **5** *Math.* ratio between units in a numerical system (*decimal scale*). — v. (**-ling**) **1 a** climb (a wall, height, etc.). **b** climb the social scale, heights of ambition, etc.). **2** represent proportionally; reduce to a common scale. □ **in scale** in proportion. **scale down** (or **up**) make or become smaller (or larger) in proportion. **to scale** uniformly in proportion. [Latin *scala* ladder]

**scale⁴** v. *colloq.* **1** avoid paying what is due, esp. a fare. **2** defraud, cheat. □ **scaler** n. [origin unknown]

**scale insect** n. any of various sap-sucking insect pests which cling to plants and secrete a shield-like scale as covering. [origin unknown]

**scalene** /skay-leen/ adj. (esp. of a triangle) having unequal sides. [Greek *skalēnos* unequal]

**scallop** /skol-uhp/ — n. **1** edible mollusc with two fan-shaped ridged shells. **2** (in full **scallop shell**) single shell of a scallop, often used for cooking or serving food in. **3** (in *pl.*) ornamental edging of semi-circular curves. **4** = POTATO SCALLOP. — v. (**-p-**) ornament with scallops. □ **scalloping** n. (in sense 3 of n.). [French ESCALOPE]

**scallywag** /skal-ee-,wag/ n. (used esp. of a child) scamp, rascal. [origin unknown]

**scaloppine** /,skal-up-**pee**-nee/ n. Italian dish consisting of escalopes of meat (esp. veal) sautéed or fried. [Italian]

**scalp** — n. **1** skin on the head, with the hair etc. attached. **2 a** this part of an animal, taken in order to obtain a bounty. **b** *hist.* scalp of an enemy cut off as a trophy by an American Indian. — v. **1 a** take the scalp of a hunted animal. **b** *hist.* take the scalp of (an enemy). **2 a** resell (shares etc.) at a high or quick profit. **b** buy tickets for a pop-concert, sporting event, etc., in order to sell them later at a highly inflated price. □ **scalper** n. [probably Scandinavian]

**scalpel** /skal-puhl/ n. surgeon's small sharp knife. [Latin *scalpo* scratch]

**scam** n. *colloq.* **1** trick, fraud. **2** illegal business racket. [origin unknown]

**scamp** n. *colloq.* rascal; rogue. [probably Dutch]

**scamper** — v. **1** run and skip; move hurriedly. **2** (usu. foll. by *through*) perform (a task etc.) in a hurried and skimpy manner (*scampered through her homework; scampered through the book; do it thoroughly – don't scamper*). — n. act of scampering. [perhaps from SCAMP]

**scampi** /**skam**-pee/ n.pl. large prawns. [Italian]

**scan** — v. (**-nn-**) **1** look at intently or quickly (*scanned the horizon; rapidly scanned the headlines*). **2** (of a verse etc.) be metrically correct (*this line doesn't scan*). **3 a** examine (a surface etc.) to detect radioactivity etc. **b** traverse (a particular region) with a radar etc. beam. **4** resolve (a picture) into its elements of light and shade for esp. television transmission. **5** analyse the metrical structure of (verse). **6** obtain an image of (part of the body) using a scanner. **7** read a bar-code on packaging etc. **8** (of a document scanner) read a document or a picture in order to reproduce it in computer-readable form etc. — n. **1** scanning. **2** image obtained by scanning. [Latin *scando* climb, scan]

**scandal** /skan-duhl/ n. **1** cause of public outrage. **2** outrage etc. so caused. **3** malicious gossip. □ **scandalous** adj. **scandalously** adv. [Greek *skandalon*, = snare]

**scandalise** v. (also **-ize**) (**-sing** or **-zing**) offend morally; shock.

**scandalmonger** n. person who habitually spreads scandal.

**Scandinavian** /,skan-duh-**nay**-vee-uhn/

— *n*. **1 a** native or inhabitant of Scandinavia (Denmark, Norway, Sweden, and Iceland). **b** person of Scandinavian descent. **2** family of languages of Scandinavia. — *adj*. of Scandinavia. [Latin]

**scandium** /**skan**-dee-uhm/ *n*. metallic element occurring naturally in lanthanide ores. [Latin *Scandia* Scandinavia]

**scanner** *n*. **1** device for scanning or systematically examining all the parts of something. **2** machine for measuring radiation, ultrasound reflections, etc., from the body as a diagnostic aid. **3** (in full **document scanner** or **optical scanner**) machine for reproducing a document etc. in computer-readable form etc.

**scansion** /**skan**-shuhn/ *n*. metrical scanning of verse. [Latin: related to SCAN]

**scant** *adj*. barely sufficient; deficient (*scant regard for truth; scant of breath*). [Old Norse]

**scanty** *adj*. (**-ier, -iest**) **1** of small extent or amount. **2** barely sufficient. □ **scantily** *adv*. **scantiness** *n*.

**-scape** /skayp/ *comb. form* forming nouns denoting a view or a representation of a view (*moonscape; seascape*).

**scapegoat** /**skayp**-goht/ *n*. person blamed for others' shortcomings (with ref. to the goat in Lev. 16, sent into the wilderness after the Jewish chief priest had symbolically laid the sins of the people upon it). [obsolete *scape* escape]

**scapula** /**skap**-yuh-luh/ *n*. (*pl*. **-lae** /-,lee/ or **-s**) shoulder-blade. [Latin]

**scapular** /**skap**-yuh-luh/ — *adj*. of the shoulder or shoulder-blade. — *n*. **1** monastic outer garment consisting of two long strips of cloth hanging down the breast and back and joined across the shoulders. **2** miniature version of this worn under their clothing by lay persons affiliated to a monastic order.

**scar¹** — *n*. **1** usu. permanent mark on the skin from a wound etc. **2** emotional damage from grief etc. **3** sign of damage (*the table bore many scars*). **4** mark left on a plant by the loss of a leaf etc. — *v*. (**-rr-**) **1** (esp. as **scarred** *adj*.) mark with a scar or scars (*scarred for life*). **2** form a scar. [French *eschar(r)e*]

**scar²** *n*. steep craggy outcrop of a mountain or cliff. [Old Norse, = reef]

**scarab** /**ska**-ruhb/ *n*. **1 a** sacred dung-beetle of ancient Egypt. **b** a kind of beetle. **2** ancient Egyptian gem cut in the form of a beetle. [Latin *scarabaeus* from Greek]

**scarce** /skairs/ — *adj*. **1** (usu. *predic*.) (esp. of food, money, etc.) in short supply. **2** rare. — *adv*. *archaic* or *literary* scarcely. □ **make oneself scarce** *colloq*. keep out of the way; surreptitiously disappear. **scarce**

**as hen's teeth** *colloq*. extremely rare. [French *scars* Latin *excerpto* EXCERPT]

**scarcely** *adv*. **1** hardly, only just (*had scarcely arrived*). **2** surely not (*can scarcely have said so*). **3** esp. *iron*. not (*scarcely expected to be insulted*).

**scarcity** *n*. (*pl*. **-ies**) (often foll. by *of*) lack or shortage, esp. of food.

**scare** /skair/ — *v*. (**-ring**) **1** frighten, esp. suddenly. **2** (as **scared** *adj*.) (usu. foll. by *of*, or to + infin.) frightened; terrified. **3** (usu. foll. by *away, off, up*, etc.) drive away by frightening. **4** become scared (*they don't scare easily*). — *n*. **1** sudden attack of fright (*gave me a scare*). **2** widespread alarm caused by the rumour of invasion, epidemic, etc. (*a malaria scare*). □ **scare the living daylights out of** *colloq*. scare almost to death. [Old Norse]

**scarecrow** *n*. **1** human figure dressed in old clothes and set up in a field to scare birds away. **2** *colloq*. badly dressed, grotesque-looking, or very thin person.

**scaremonger** *n*. person who spreads alarming rumours. □ **scaremongering** *n*.

**scarf¹** *n*. (*pl*. **scarves** /skahvz/ or **-s**) piece of material worn esp. round the neck or over the head, for warmth or ornament. [French *escarpe*]

**scarf²** — *v*. join the ends of (timber etc.) by bevelling or notching them to fit and then bolting them etc. — *n*. (*pl*. **-s**) joint made by scarfing. [probably French *escarf*]

**scarifier** /**ska**-ruh-fuy-uh, **skair**-/ *n*. **1** machine with prongs for loosening soil without turning it. **2** similar machine for removing thatch etc. from a lawn. [SCARIFY¹]

**scarify¹** /**ska**-ruh-,fuy, **skair**-/ *v*. (**-ies, -ied**) **1 a** make slight incisions in. **b** cut off skin from. **2** hurt by severe criticism etc. **3** loosen (soil) with a machine. □ **scarification** /-fuh-**kay**-shuhn/ *n*. [Greek *skariphos* stylus]

**scarify²** /**skair**-ruh-,fuy/ *v*. (**-ies, -ied**) *colloq*. scare.

**scarlet** /**skah**-luht/ — *adj*. **1** of brilliant red tinged with orange. **2** used as a distinguishing epithet in the names of Australian fauna and flora (*scarlet-breasted parrot; scarlet honeyeater; scarlet robin; scarlet running postman; etc.*). — *n*. **1** scarlet colour or pigment. **2** scarlet clothes or material (*dressed in scarlet*). [French *escarlate*]

**scarlet fever** *n*. infectious bacterial fever with a scarlet rash.

**scarlet running postman** *n*. (also **scarlet runner**) prostrate native plant (*Kennedia prostrata*) having a profusion of scarlet flowers with gold bosses (see KENNEDIA).

**scarp** — n. **1** steep slope. **2** inner side of a ditch in a fortification. — v. make perpendicular or steep. [Italian *scarpa*]

**scarper** v. *colloq.* run away, escape. □ **do a scarper** leave quickly. [probably Italian *scappare* escape]

**scarves** pl. of SCARF[1].

**scary** /skair-ree/ adj. (-ier, -iest) frightening.

**scat**[1] v. (-tt-) (usu. in *imper.*) *colloq.* depart quickly. [perhaps an abbreviation of SCATTER]

**scat**[2] — n. wordless jazz singing using sounds imitating instruments. — v. (-tt-) sing scat. [probably imitative]

**scathing** /skay-thing/ adj. witheringly scornful. □ **scathingly** adv. [Old Norse]

**scatology** /ska-tol-uh-jee/ n. excessive interest in excrement or obscenity. □ **scatological** /-tuh-loj-i-kuhl/ adj. [Greek *skōr skat-* dung]

**scatter** — v. **1 a** throw about; strew. **b** cover by scattering (*scattered the path with gravel*). **2 a** (cause to) move in flight etc.; disperse. **b** disperse or cause (hopes, clouds, etc.) to disperse (*the crowd scattered when the rain came*). **3** (as **scattered** adj.) wide apart or sporadic (*scattered settlements*). **4** *Physics* deflect or diffuse (light, particles, etc.). — n. **1** act or an instance of scattering. **2** small amount scattered. **3** extent of distribution (of esp. shot). [probably var. of SHATTER]

**scatterbrain** n. person given to silly or disorganised thought. □ **scatterbrained** adj.

**scatty** /skat-ee/ adj. (-ier, -iest) *colloq.* scatterbrained. □ **scattily** adv. **scattiness** n.

**scavenge** /skav-uhnj/ v. (-ging) (usu. foll. by *for*; also *absol.*) search for and collect (discarded items) from garbage bins, rubbish heaps, tips, etc. (*seagulls scavenging the tip for food*). [back-formation from SCAVENGER]

**scavenger** n. **1** person who scavenges. **2** animal feeding on carrion, refuse, etc. [Anglo-French *scawager*: related to SHOW]

**scenario** /si-nah-ree-oh, -nair-ree-oh/ n. (pl. -s) **1** outline of the plot of a play, film, etc. **2** postulated sequence of future events. [Italian]

■ **Usage** *Scenario* should not be used to mean 'situation', as in *it was an unpleasant scenario*.

**scene** /seen/ n. **1** place in which events, real or fictional, occur (*the scene was set in the outback; the scene of the disaster*). **2 a** incident, real or fictional (*distressing scenes occurred*). **b** description or representation of an incident etc. (*scenes of life in the bush*). **3** public display of emotion, temper, etc. (*made a scene in the*

*restaurant*). **4 a** continuous portion of a play in a fixed setting; subdivision of an act. **b** similar section of a film, book, etc. **5 a** piece of scenery used in a play. **b** these collectively. **6** landscape or view (*a desolate scene*). **7** *colloq.* **a** area of interest (*not my scene*). **b** milieu (*well-known on the jazz scene*). □ **behind the scenes 1** offstage. **2** secret; secretly. **set the scene** describe the location of events. [Greek *skēnē* tent, stage]

**scenery** n. **1** natural features of a landscape, esp. when picturesque. **2** painted backcloths, props, etc., used as the background in a play etc. [Italian: related to SCENARIO]

**scenic** adj. **1 a** picturesque (*the scenic road to Lorne*). **b** of natural scenery (*flatness is the main scenic feature*). **2** of or on the stage. □ **scenically** adv.

**scent** /sent/ — n. **1** distinctive, esp. pleasant, smell. **2** = PERFUME 2. **3 a** perceptible smell left by an animal. **b** clues etc. leading to a discovery (*lost the scent in Surfers Paradise*). **c** power of detecting esp. smells (*some dogs have little scent*). — v. **1 a** discern by scent. **b** sense (*scented danger*). **2** (esp. as **scented** adj.) make fragrant (*scented soap*). □ **put** (or **throw**) **off the scent** deceive by false clues etc. **scent out** discover by smelling or searching. [French *sentir* perceive]

**sceptic** /skep-tik/ n. **1** person inclined to doubt accepted opinions; a cynic. **2** person who doubts the truth of religions. **3** philosopher who questions the possibility of knowledge. □ **scepticism** /-tuh-siz-uhm/ n. [Greek *skeptomai* observe]

**sceptical** adj. inclined to doubt accepted opinions; critical; incredulous. □ **sceptically** adv.

**sceptre** /sep-tuh/ n. staff as a symbol of sovereignty. [Greek *skēptō* lean on]

**schedule** /shed-yool, sked-, -jool/ — n. **1 a** list of intended events, times, etc. **b** plan of work (*not on my schedule for this week*). **2** list of rates or prices. **3** tabulated list. — v. (-ling) **1** include in a schedule. **2** make a schedule of. □ **according to** (or **on**) **schedule** as planned; on time. [Latin *schedula* slip of paper]

**scheduled fee** n. government approved fee for a medical service (esp. with regard to the payment of medical benefits) (*most doctors charge above the scheduled fee*).

**schema** /skee-muh/ n. (pl. **schemata** or -s) synopsis, outline, or diagram. [Greek *skhēma -at-* form, figure]

**schematic** /skuh-mat-ik, skee-/ — adj. of or as a scheme or schema; diagrammatic. — n. diagram, esp. of an electronic circuit. □ **schematically** adv.

**schematise** /skee-muh-ˌtuyz/ v. (also **-ize**) (**-sing** or **-zing**) put in schematic form; arrange.

**scheme** /skeem/ — n. **1** systematic plan or arrangement (*colour scheme*). **2** artful plot. — v. (**-ming**) plan, esp. secretly or deceitfully. □ **scheming** adj. [Greek: related to SCHEMA]

**scherzo** /skairt-ˌsoh/ n. (pl. **-s**) Mus. vigorous, often playful, piece, esp. as part of a larger work. [Italian, = jest]

**schism** /siz-uhm, shiz-, skiz-/ n. division of a group (esp. religious) into sects etc., usu. over doctrine. □ **schismatic** /-mat-ik/ adj. & n. [Greek skhizō to split]

**schist** /shist/ n. layered crystalline rock. [Greek skhizō to split]

**schizo** /skit-soh/ colloq. — adj. schizophrenic. — n. (pl. **-s**) schizophrenic person. [abbreviation]

**schizoid** /skit-soid/ — adj. tending to schizophrenia but usu. without delusions. — n. schizoid person.

**schizophrenia** /ˌskit-suh-free-nee-uh/ n. mental disease marked by a breakdown in the relation between thoughts, feelings, and actions, and often with delusions and retreat from social life. □ **schizophrenic** /-fren-ik, -free-nik/ adj. & n. [Greek skhizō split, phrēn mind]

**schmaltz** /shmawlts, shmalts/ n. colloq. sentimentality, esp. in music, drama, etc. □ **schmaltzy** adj. [Yiddish]

**schmuck** /shmuk/ n. colloq. foolish or contemptible person. [Yiddish, = penis]

**schnapper** var. of SNAPPER.

**schnapps** /shnaps/ n. any of various spirits drunk in N. Europe. [German]

**schnitzel** /shnit-suhl/ n. escalope of veal. [German]

**schnook** /shnuuk/ n. colloq. foolish or contemptible person. [Yiddish]

**scholar** /skol-uh/ n. **1** learned person, academic. **2** holder of a scholarship. **3** person of specified academic ability (*poor scholar*). □ **scholarly** adj. [Latin: related to SCHOOL¹]

**scholarship** n. **1 a** academic achievement, esp. of a high level. **b** standards of a good scholar (*shows great scholarship*). **2** financial award for a student etc., given for scholarly achievement and to enable him or her to continue study.

**scholastic** /skuh-las-tik/ adj. **1** of universities, schools, education, etc.; academic. **2** hist. of scholasticism. [Greek: related to SCHOOL¹]

**scholasticism** /skuh-las-tuh-ˌsiz-uhm/ n. hist. medieval Western Church philosophy based on the Church Fathers and Aristotle.

**school¹** /skool/ — n. **1 a** institution for educating or giving instruction, esp. for children. **b** (attrib.) of or for use in school (*school books*). **2 a** school buildings, pupils, staff, etc. **b** time of teaching; the teaching itself (*no school today*). **3** university department or faculty. **4 a** group of similar artists etc., esp. followers of an artist etc. (*the Heidelberg school in Australia*). **b** group of like-minded people (*belongs to the old school*). **5** group of drinkers, gamblers, etc. (*two-up school*). **6** colloq. instructive circumstances etc. (*school of hard knocks*). — v. **1** send to school; educate; train. **2** (as **schooled** adj.) (foll. by in) educated or trained (*schooled in humility*). [Greek skholē]

**school²** /skool/ n. (often foll. by of) shoal of fish, whales, etc. [Low German or Dutch]

**schoolhouse** n. school building, esp. in a rural or outback region.

**schoolie** n. colloq. **1 a** schoolteacher. **b** student. **2 a** a school prawn. **b** a school shark. [abbreviation]

**schoolies' week** n. colloq. (in Queensland) period of post-exam celebrations for year 12 students.

**schooling** n. education, esp. at school.

**school leaver** n. person finishing secondary school (esp. considered as joining the job market).

**School of Arts** n. hist. (esp. in NSW and Queensland) = MECHANICS' INSTITUTE.

**School of the Air** n. government educational programme using a two-way radio system to enable children in the outback to participate in a 'classroom' learning situation with a teacher or teachers.

**school prawn** n. small prawn occurring in large shoals.

**school shark** n. medium-sized shark of southern and eastern Australian waters occurring in schools and commercially fished, its flesh being sold as flake etc. (SEE FLAKE).

**school sores** n.pl. colloq. = IMPETIGO.

**schooner** /skoo-nuh/ n. **1** fore-and-aft rigged ship with two or more masts. **2 a** large beer-glass. **b** the beer contained in it. [origin uncertain]

**schwa** /shwah/ n. Phonet. **1** indistinct unstressed vowel sound as in another. **2** symbol /ə/ (or in this dictionary /uh/ ) representing this. [German from Hebrew]

**sciatic** /suy-at-ik/ adj. **1** of the hip. **2** of the sciatic nerve. **3** suffering from or liable to sciatica. [Greek iskhion hip]

**sciatica** /suy-at-i-kuh/ n. neuralgia of the hip and leg. [Latin: related to SCIATIC]

**sciatic nerve** n. largest nerve, running from pelvis to thigh.

**science** /**suy**-uhns/ n. **1** branch of knowledge involving systematised observation and experiment, and esp. concerned with the material and functions of the physical universe. **2 a** knowledge so gained, or on a specific subject. **b** pursuit or principles of this. **3** colloq. skilful technique (the science of boxing). [Latin scio know]

**science fiction** n. fiction with a scientific theme, esp. concerned with the future, space, other worlds, etc. (cf. FANTASY).

**scientific** /ˌsuh-uhn-**tif**-ik/ adj. **1 a** following the systematic methods of science. **b** systematic, accurate. **2** of, used in, or engaged in science (scientific discoveries; scientific terminology). □ **scientifically** adv.

**scientism** /**suy**-uhn-ˌtiz-uhm/ n. derog. **1** excessive belief in, or application of, scientific method. **2** uncritical belief in science as an absolute authority or as a panacea for all human ills.

**scientist** /**suy**-uhn-tuhst/ n. student or expert in science.

**Scientology** /ˌsuy-uhn-**tol**-uh-jee/ n. propr. system of religious philosophy based on self-improvement and graded courses of study and training. □ **Scientologist** n. & adj. [Latin scientia knowledge]

**sci-fi** /**suy**-fuy, suy-**fuy**/ n. (often attrib.) colloq. science fiction. [abbreviation]

**scilicet** /**suy**-luh-ˌset, **sil**-uh-set/ adv. that is to say (used esp. in explanation of an ambiguity). [Latin]

**scimitar** /**sim**-uh-tuh/ n. curved oriental sword. [French and Italian]

**scintilla** /sin-**til**-uh/ n. trace (not a scintilla of evidence). [Latin, = spark]

**scintillate** /**sin**-tuh-ˌlayt/ v. (**-ting**) **1** (esp. as **scintillating** adj.) talk cleverly; be brilliant. **2** sparkle; twinkle. □ **scintillation** /ˌsin-tuh-**lay**-shuhn/ n. [Latin: related to SCINTILLA]

**scion** /**suy**-uhn/ n. **1** shoot of a plant etc., esp. one cut for grafting or planting. **2** descendant; younger member of (esp. a noble) family. [French]

**scissors** /**siz**-uhz/ n.pl. (also **pair of scissors** sing.) hand-held cutting instrument with two pivoted blades opening and closing. [Latin caedo cut: related to CHISEL]

**scissors-grinder** n. = RESTLESS FLYCATCHER.

**sclerosis** /skluh-**roh**-suhs/ n. **1** abnormal hardening of body tissue. **2** (in full **multiple** or **disseminated sclerosis**) serious progressive disease of the nervous system. □ **sclerotic** /skluh-**rot**-ik/ adj. [Greek sklēros hard]

**scoff¹** — v. (usu. foll. by at) speak scornfully; mock. — n. mocking words; taunt. [perhaps from Scandinavian]

**scoff²** colloq. v. eat greedily. □ **scoff-out** a lavish or appetising meal. [Afrikaans schoff from Dutch]

**scold** /skohld/ — v. **1** rebuke (esp. a child). **2** find fault noisily. — n. archaic nagging woman. □ **scolding** n. [probably Old Norse]

**sconce** n. **1** wall-bracket for a candlestick or light-fitting. **2** colloq. the head. [Latin (ab)sconsa covered (light)]

**scone** /skon/ n. **1** small cake of flour, fat, and milk, baked quickly. **2** colloq. the head. □ **do one's scone** colloq. become angry. **off one's scone** colloq. crazy; insane. [origin uncertain]

**scoop** — n. **1** spoon-shaped object, esp.: **a** a short-handled deep shovel for loose materials such as sugar, grain, etc. **b** a large long-handled ladle for liquids. **c** the excavating part of a digging machine etc. **d** an instrument for serving ice-cream etc. **2** quantity taken up by a scoop. **3** scooping movement. **4** exclusive news item. **5** large profit made quickly. — v. **1** (usu. foll. by out) hollow out (as if) with a scoop. **2** (usu. foll. by up) lift (as if) with a scoop. **3** forestall (a rival newspaper etc.) with a scoop. **4** secure (a large profit etc.), esp. suddenly. [Low German or Dutch]

**scoot** v. (esp. in imper.) colloq. run or dart away, esp. hastily. □ **on** (or **upon**) **the scoot** colloq. engaged in a drinking bout or spree. [origin unknown]

**scooter** n. **1** child's toy with a footboard on two wheels and a long steering-handle. **2** (in full **motor scooter**) low-powered motor cycle with a shieldlike protective front.

**scope** n. **1** range or opportunity (beyond the scope of our research). **2** extent of mental ability, outlook, etc. (intellect limited in its scope). [Greek, = target]

**-scope** comb. form forming nouns denoting: **1** device looked at or through (telescope). **2** instrument for observing or showing (oscilloscope). □ **-scopic** /**skop**-ik/ comb. form forming adjectives. [Greek skopeō look at]

**-scopy** comb. form indicating viewing or observation, usu. with an instrument ending in -scope (microscopy).

**scorbutic** /skaw-**byoo**-tik/ adj. of, like, or affected with scurvy. [Latin scorbutus scurvy]

**scorch** — v. **1** burn or discolour the surface of with dry heat. **2** become so discoloured etc. **3** (as **scorching** adj.) colloq. **a** (of the weather) very hot. **b** (of criticism etc.) stringent; harsh. **4** colloq. (of a motorist) travel at an excessive speed. — n. **1** mark made by scorching. **2** colloq. a spell of fast driving (went for a *scorch and got nabbed by the cops).* [origin unknown]

**scorched earth policy** n. policy of burning crops etc., and removing and destroying anything that might be of use to an invading enemy.

**scorcher** n. *colloq.* very hot day.

**score** — n. **1 a** number of points, goals, runs, etc., made by or awarded to a player or side in some games. **b** respective numbers of points etc. at the end of a game (*score was five–nil*). **c** act of gaining esp. a goal. **2** (*pl.* same or **-s**) twenty or a set of twenty. **3** (in *pl.*) a great many (*scores of people*). **4** reason or motive (*rejected on that score*). **5** *Mus.* **a** copy of a composition showing all the vocal and instrumental parts arranged one below the other. **b** music for a film or play, esp. for a musical. **6** notch, line, etc. cut or scratched into a surface. **7** record of money owing. **8** state of affairs; the present situation (*asked what the score was*). **9** mark or level gained in a test or examination. — v. (**-ring**) **1 a** win or gain (a goal, points, success, etc.). **b** count for (points in a game etc.) (*a boundary scores six*). **2 a** make a score in a game (*failed to score*). **b** keep score in a game. **3** mark or carve with notches, incisions etc. (*scored his name on the desk*). **4** have an advantage (*that is where he scores*). **5** *Mus.* (often foll. by *for*) orchestrate or arrange (a piece of music). **6** *colloq.* **a** obtain drugs illegally. **b** make a sexual conquest. □ **keep score** (or **the score**) register scores as they are made. **know the score** *colloq.* be aware of the essential facts. **on that score** so far as that is concerned. **score off** (or **score points off**) *colloq.* humiliate, esp. verbally in repartee etc. **score out** draw a line through (words etc.); delete. □ **scorer** n. [Old Norse: related to SHEAR]

**scoria** /skaw-ree-uh/ n. (*pl.* **scoriae** /-ree‚ee/) **1** cellular lava, or fragments of it. **2** slag or dross of metals. □ **scoriaceous** /-ay-shuhs/ adj. [Greek *skōria* refuse]

**scorn** — n. disdain, contempt, derision. — v. **1** hold in contempt. **2** reject or refuse to do as unworthy. [French *escarnir*]

**scornful** adj. (often foll. by *of*) contemptuous. □ **scornfully** adv.

**Scorpio** /skaw-pee-oh/ n. (*pl.* **-s**) **1** constellation and eighth sign of the zodiac (the Scorpion). **2** person born when the sun is in this sign. [Greek *skorpios* scorpion]

**scorpion** /skaw-pee-uhn/ n. **1** arachnid with pincers and a jointed stinging tail. **2** (**the Scorpion**) zodiacal sign or constellation Scorpio.

**Scot** n. **1** native of Scotland. **2** person of Scottish descent. [Latin *Scottus*]

**Scotch** — adj. (also **Scottish** or **Scots**) of Scotland or its inhabitants. — n. **1** (also **Scottish** or **Scots**) (prec. by *the*; treated as *pl.*) people of Scotland. **2** language of Scotland. **3** (**Scotch**) Scotch whisky. [from *Scottish*]

■ **Usage** *Scots* or *Scottish* is preferred to *Scotch* in Scotland, except in some compound nouns, e.g. *Scotch whisky.*

**scotch** v. **1** put an end to; frustrate (*scotched the rumour*). **2** *archaic* wound without killing. [origin unknown]

**Scotch whisky** n. whisky distilled in Scotland.

**scot-free** adv. unharmed, unpunished. [obsolete *scot* tax]

**scotty** /skot-ee/ adj. *colloq.* irritable, bad-tempered. [alteration of *Scot*]

**scoundrel** /skown-druhl/ n. unscrupulous villain; rogue. [origin unknown]

**scour¹** — v. **1 a** cleanse by rubbing. **b** (usu. foll. by *away*, *off*, etc.) clear (rust, stains, etc.) by rubbing etc. **2** clear out (a pipe, channel, etc.) by flushing through. **3** remove grease, dirt, etc. from (wool etc.) by washing. — n. act or instance of scouring or state of being scoured. □ **scourer** n. [French *escurer*]

**scour²** v. search thoroughly, esp. by scanning (*scoured the streets for him; scoured the newspaper*). [origin unknown]

**scoured** n. scoured wool. [abbreviation]

**scourge** /skerj/ — n. **1** person or thing seen as causing suffering, esp. on a large scale (*the scourge of famine*). **2** whip. — v. (**-ging**) **1** whip. **2** punish, oppress. [Latin *corrigia* whip]

**scout¹** — n. **1** soldier etc. sent ahead to get esp. military intelligence. **2** search for this. **3** = TALENT-SCOUT. **4** (also **Scout**) member of the Scout Association, an (orig. boys') association intended to develop character (see GUIDE sense 8). **5** fellow; person (*she's a good scout*). **6** ship or aircraft for reconnoitring. — v. **1** (often foll. by *for*) go about searching for information etc. **2** (foll. by *around*) make a search (*scouted around to see if he could find any tracks*). **3** (often foll. by *out*) explore to get information about (territory etc.) (*I'll scout out the lie of the land*). □ **scouting** n. [French *escoute(r)* from Latin *ausculto* listen]

**scout²** v. reject (an idea etc.) with scorn. [Scandinavian]

**scowl** — n. severe frowning or sullen expression. — v. make a scowl. [Scandinavian]

**scrabble** /skrab-uhl/ — v. (**-ling**) (often foll. by *about*, *at*) scratch or grope to find or collect or hold on to something. — *n.* act of scrabbling. [Dutch]

**scrag** — *n.* **1** (also **scrag-end**) inferior end of a neck of mutton. **2** skinny person or animal. — *v.* (**-gg-**) *colloq.* **1** strangle, hang. **2** seize roughly by the neck. **3** handle roughly, beat up. [origin uncertain]

**scraggy** *adj.* (**-ier**, **-iest**) thin and bony. □ **scragginess** *n.*

**scram** *v.* (**-mm-**) (esp. in *imper.*) *colloq.* leave quickly, go away. [perhaps from SCRAMBLE]

**scramble** /skram-buhl/ — *v.* (**-ling**) **1** clamber, crawl, climb, etc., esp. hurriedly or anxiously. **2** (foll. by *for*, *at*) struggle with competitors (for a thing or share). **3** mix together indiscriminately. **4** cook (eggs) by stirring them in a pan over heat. **5** change the speech frequency of (a broadcast transmission or telephone conversation) so as to make it unintelligible without a decoding device. **6** (of fighter aircraft or pilots) take off quickly in an emergency or for action. **7** *colloq.* roundly defeat (*the poms were well and truly scrambled by the Aussies in pyjama cricket*). — *n.* **1** act of scrambling. **2** difficult climb or walk. **3** (foll. by *for*) eager struggle or competition. **4** motorcycle race over rough ground. **5** emergency take-off by fighter aircraft. [imitative]

**scrambler** *n.* device for scrambling telephone conversations.

**scrap¹** — *n.* **1** small detached piece; fragment. **2** rubbish or waste material. **3** discarded metal for reprocessing (often *attrib.*: *scrap metal*). **4** (with *neg.*) smallest piece or amount (*not a scrap left*). **5** (in *pl.*) **a** odds and ends. **b** bits of uneaten food. — *v.* (**-pp-**) discard as useless. [Old Norse: related to SCRAPE]

**scrap²** *colloq.* — *n.* fight or rough quarrel. — *v.* (**-pp-**) have a scrap. [perhaps from SCRAPE]

**scrapbook** *n.* blank book for sticking cuttings, drawings, etc., in.

**scrape** — *v.* (**-ping**) **1 a** move a hard or sharp edge across (a surface), esp. to make smooth, remove paint or dirt, etc. **b** apply (a hard or sharp edge) in this way. **2** (foll. by *away*, *off*, etc.) remove by scraping. **3 a** rub (a surface) harshly against another. **b** scratch or damage by scraping. **4** make (a hollow) by scraping. **5 a** draw or move with a scraping sound. **b** make such a sound. **c** produce such a sound from. **6** (often foll. by *along*, *by*, *through*, etc.) move almost touching surrounding features, obstacles etc. (*scraped through the gap*). **7** narrowly achieve (a living, an examination pass, etc.). **8** (often foll. by *by*, *through*) **a** barely manage. **b** pass an examination

etc. with difficulty. **9** (foll. by *together*, *up*) bring, provide, or amass with difficulty (*scraped together a few bob*; *scraped up a meal*). **10** be economical. **11** draw back a foot in making a clumsy bow. **12** completely clear (a plate) of food. — *n.* **1** act or sound of scraping. **2** scraped place; graze. **3** *colloq.* predicament caused by rashness etc. **4** *colloq.* a fight; quarrel. □ **scrape the** (**bottom of the**) **barrel** *colloq.* **1** be reduced to a limited choice etc. **2** vilify in a scurrilous way (*he scraped the bottom of the barrel when he said that about my wife*). [Old Norse]

**scraper** *n.* device for scraping, esp. paint etc. from a surface.

**scrap heap** *n.* **1** pile of scrap. **2** state of being discarded as useless.

**scrapie** /skray-pee/ *n.* viral disease of sheep, characterised by lack of coordination.

**scraping** *n.* (esp. in *pl.*) fragment produced by scraping.

**scrappy** *adj.* (**-ier**, **-iest**) **1** consisting of scraps. **2** incomplete; carelessly arranged or put together. **3** *colloq.* aggressive; quarrelsome.

**scrapyard** *n.* place where (esp. metal) scrap is collected for reuse.

**scratch** — *v.* **1** score, mark, or wound superficially, esp. with a sharp object. **2** (also *absol.*) scrape, esp. with the nails to relieve itching. **3** make or form by scratching (*scratched a hole in the ground*). **4** (foll. by *together*, *up*, etc.) = SCRAPE 9 (*scratched up a meal*). **5** (foll. by *out*, *off*, *through*) strike (out) (writing etc.). **6** (also *absol.*) withdraw (a competitor, oneself, etc.) from a race or competition. **7** (often foll. by *about*, *around*, etc.) **a** search the ground etc. in search. **b** search haphazardly (*scratching about for evidence*). — *n.* **1** mark or wound made by scratching. **2** sound of scratching. **3** spell of scratching oneself (*had a good scratch*). **4** *colloq.* superficial wound. **5** line from which competitors in a race (esp. those not receiving a handicap) start. — *attrib. adj.* **1** collected or done by chance. **2** collected or made from whatever is available; heterogeneous (*scratch meal*; *scratch team*). **3** with no handicap given (*scratch race*). □ **from scratch 1** from the beginning. **2** without help. **scratch along** *colloq.* make a living with difficulty. **scratch my back and I'll scratch yours 1** do me a favour and I will return it. **2** used in reference to mutual aid or flattery. **scratch one's head** be perplexed. **scratch the surface** deal with a matter only superficially. **up to scratch** up to the required standard. [origin uncertain]

**scratchie** *n.* (also **scratchy**) *colloq.* **1** instant lottery ticket requiring the surface to be scratched off to reveal symbols etc. which indicate if a prize has been won. **2** a safety match.

**scratch-ticket** *n.* = SCRATCHIE (sense 1).

**scratchy** — *adj.* (**-ier, -iest**) **1** tending to make scratches or a scratching noise. **2** causing itching. **3** (of a drawing etc.) untidy, careless. **4** *colloq.* **a** ill-tempered; peevish. **b** out of practice (*my piano-playing is a bit scratchy, but I'll try*). — *n. colloq.* = SCRATCHIE (senses 1 & 2). □ **scratchily** *adv.* **scratchiness** *n.*

**scrawl** — *v.* **1** write or make (marks) in a hurried untidy way. **2** (foll. by *out*) cross out by scrawling over. — *n.* **1** hurried untidy manner of writing. **2** example of this. □ **scrawly** *adj.* [origin uncertain]

**scrawny** *adj.* (**-ier, -iest**) lean, scraggy. [British dial.]

**scream** — *n.* **1** loud high-pitched cry of fear, pain, etc. **2** similar sound or cry. **3** *colloq.* hilarious occurrence or person. — *v.* **1** emit a scream. **2** speak or sing (words etc.) in a screaming tone. **3** make or move with a screaming sound. **4** laugh uncontrollably. **5** be blatantly obvious, esp. of colours. □ **scream blue murder** *colloq.* make a great outcry. **scream** (**out**) **for** be in desperate need of (*the house is screaming out for a lick of paint*). [Old English]

**screamer** *n.* **1** person or thing that screams. **2** (in full **two-pot screamer**) *colloq.* person who has a very low tolerance of alcohol. **3** *colloq.* person or thing that is spectacularly funny. **4** *colloq.* outstanding specimen of anything (*hit a screamer to the boundary; the party was a screamer*). **5** *Aust. Rules* spectacular overhead mark.

**screaming-woman bird** *n.* = BARKING OWL.

**scree** *n.* (in *sing.* or *pl.*) **1** small loose stones. **2** mountain slope covered with these. [Old Norse, = landslip]

**screech** — *n.* harsh piercing scream. — *v.* utter with or make a screech. □ **screechy** *adj.* (**-ier, -iest**) [Old English (imitative)]

**screech-owl** *n.* owl that screeches, esp. a barn-owl.

**screed** *n.* **1** long usu. tiresome piece of writing or speech. **2** layer of cement etc. applied to level a surface. [probably from SHRED]

**screen** — *n.* **1** fixed or movable upright partition for separating, concealing, or protecting from heat etc. **2** thing used to conceal or shelter, esp. from observation. **3 a** concealing stratagem. **b** protection thus given (*under the screen of night*). **4 a** blank surface on which a photographic image is projected. **b** (prec. by *the*) the cinema industry; films collectively. **5** surface of a cathode-ray tube etc., esp. of a television, VDU, etc., on which images appear. **6** = SIGHT-SCREEN. **7** = WINDSCREEN. **8** frame with fine netting to keep out insects etc. **9** large sieve or riddle, esp. for sorting grain, coal, gravel, etc., into sizes. **10** system of checking for disease, an ability, attribute, etc. — *v.* **1** (often foll. by *from*) **a** shelter; hide. **b** protect from detection, censure, etc. **2** (foll. by *off*) conceal behind a screen. **3** show (a film, television programme, etc.). **4** prevent from causing, or protect from, electrical interference. **5 a** test or check (a person or group) for a disease. **b** check on (a person, esp. when applying for a job etc.) for desired as well as undesirable qualities. **6** sieve. [French]

**screen door** *n.* door fitted with a flyscreen.

**screenplay** *n.* film script.

**screen printing** *n.* printing process with ink forced through a prepared sheet of fine material.

**screen test** *n.* audition for a part in a film.

**screenwriter** *n.* person who writes for the cinema.

**screw** /skrooo/ — *n.* **1** thin cylinder or cone with a spiral ridge or thread running round the outside (**male screw**) or the inside (**female screw**). **2** (in full **wood-screw**) metal male screw with a slotted head and a sharp point. **3** (in full **screw-bolt**) blunt metal male screw on which a nut is threaded to bolt things together. **4** straight screw used to exert pressure. **5** (in *sing.* or *pl.*) instrument of torture acting in this way. **6** (in full **screw propeller**) propeller with twisted blades acting like a screw on the water or air. **7** one turn of a screw. **8** (in billiards etc.) an oblique curling motion of the ball. **9** *colloq.* prison warder. **10** *coarse colloq.* **a** act of sexual intercourse. **b** partner in this. **11** *colloq.* wages, living (*earning a good screw*). **12** *colloq.* a miser. — *v.* **1** fasten or tighten with a screw or screws. **2** turn (a screw). **3** twist or turn round like a screw. **4** (of a ball etc.) swerve. **5** (foll. by *out of*) extort (consent, money, etc.) from. **6** (also *absol.*) *coarse colloq.* have sexual intercourse with. **7** swindle. □ **have one's head screwed on the right way** *colloq.* have common sense. **have a screw loose** *colloq.* be slightly crazy. **put the screws on** *colloq.* pressurise, intimidate. **screw up 1** contract or contort (one's face etc.). **2** contract and crush (a piece of paper etc.) into a tight mass. **3** summon up (one's courage etc.). **4** *colloq.* **a** bungle or mismanage. **b** spoil (an event, opportunity, etc.). **c** upset, disturb mentally. [French *escroue*]

**screwball** n. colloq. crazy or eccentric person.

**screwdriver** n. 1 tool with a tip that fits into the head of a screw to turn it. 2 cocktail of vodka and orange juice.

**screwed** adj. colloq. 1 twisted. 2 drunk.

**screwed-up** adj. colloq. 1 ruined; bungled. 2 (of a person) muddled; neurotic.

**screw pine** n. = PANDANUS.

**screw top** n. (also (with hyphen) attrib.) screwed-on cap or lid.

**screw-up** n. colloq. bungle, mess.

**screwy** adj. (-ier, -iest) colloq. 1 crazy or eccentric. 2 absurd. □ **screwiness** n.

**scribble** /skrib-uhl/ — v. (-ling) 1 write or draw carelessly or hurriedly. 2 joc. be an author or writer. — n. 1 scrawl. 2 hasty note etc. [Latin scribillo diminutive: related to SCRIBE]

**scribbly gum** n. any of several smooth-barked eucalypts having characteristic scribbles on the bark made by the burrowing larvae of the scribbly gum moth.

**scribe** — n. 1 ancient or medieval copyist of manuscripts. 2 ancient Jewish record-keeper or professional theologian and jurist. 3 pointed instrument for making marks on wood etc. — v. (-bing) mark with a scribe. □ **scribal** adj. [Latin scriba from scribo write]

**scrim** n. open-weave fabric for lining or upholstery etc. [origin unknown]

**scrimmage** /skrim-ij/ — n. tussle; brawl. — v. (-ging) engage in this. [from SKIRMISH]

**scrimp** v. use sparingly; skimp (scrimped what little food she had so that all her children could eat; scrimped on the bare necessities of life). [origin unknown]

**scrip** n. 1 provisional certificate of money subscribed, entitling the holder to dividends. 2 (collect.) such certificates. 3 extra share or shares instead of a dividend. 4 colloq. a doctor's prescription. [abbreviation of subscription receipt; in sense 4, of prescription]

**script** — n. 1 text of a play, film, etc. 2 handwriting; written characters. 3 type imitating handwriting. 4 alphabet or system of writing (the Greek script). 5 examinee's written answers. 6 a doctor's prescription. — v. write a script for (a film etc.). [Latin scriptum from scribo write]

**scripture** /skrip-chuh/ n. 1 sacred writings. 2 (**Scripture** or **the Scriptures**) the Bible. □ **scriptural** adj. [Latin: related to SCRIPT]

**scrivener** /skriv-uh-nuh/ n. hist. 1 copyist or drafter of documents. 2 notary. [French escrivein]

**scrofula** /skrof-yuh-luh/ n. disease with glandular swellings, probably a form of tuberculosis. □ **scrofulous** adj. [Latin scrofa a sow]

**scroll** /skrohl/ — n. 1 roll of parchment or paper, esp. written on. 2 book in the ancient roll form. 3 ornamental design imitating a roll of parchment. — v. (often foll. by down, up) move (a display on a computer screen) to view earlier or later material. [originally (sc)rowle ROLL]

**scrolled** adj. having a scroll design.

**scrooge** /skrooj/ n. miser. [name of a character in Dickens]

**scrotum** /skroh-tuhm/ n. (pl. **scrota** or **-s**) pouch of skin containing the testicles. □ **scrotal** adj. [Latin]

**scrounge** v. (-ging) colloq. 1 sponge on, or live at the expense of others. 2 obtain by cadging. □ **on the scrounge** scrounging.

**scrounge around** (or **about**) for hunt or rummage for (something). □ **scrounger** n. [British dial. scrunge steal]

**scrub**[1] — v. (-bb-) 1 clean by rubbing, esp. with a hard brush and water. 2 (often foll. by up) (of a surgeon etc.) clean and disinfect the hands and arms before operating. 3 colloq. scrap or cancel. 4 use water to remove impurities from (gases etc.). — n. scrubbing or being scrubbed. [Low German or Dutch]

**scrub**[2] — n. 1 a generally low and apparently stunted forms of vegetation, often thick, and frequently growing in poor soil. b land covered with this. 2 (prec. by the) country areas in general (opp. the city). — adj. (usu. attrib.) 1 a of a small or dwarf variety (scrub pine). b (of livestock) of inferior breed or physique (scrub horses). 2 as a distinguishing epithet in the names of Australian flora and fauna (scrub bloodwood; scrub box; scrub ironwood; scrub oak; scrub wattle; scrub kangaroo; scrub robin; scrub wallaby; scrub wren). [from SHRUB]

**scrub-bash** v. 1 = SCRUB-DASH. 2 make a track through the scrub; travel cross-country.

**scrubber** n. 1 colloq. derog. promiscuous woman. 2 (of cattle) beast which has been bred in, or has strayed and established itself in, the scrub. 3 colloq. person of rough or unkempt appearance. 4 apparatus for purifying gases etc.

**scrub block** n. scrub-covered rural landholding.

**scrubby** adj. 1 covered with scrub. 2 consisting of or in the form of scrub.

**scrub-cutter** n. person employed to cut scrub, either to clear land or to provide fodder. □ **scrub-cutting** n.

**scrub-dash** v. ride at speed through thick scrub, esp. in pursuit of wild or straying cattle.

**scrub-fire** n. bushfire which burns mainly scrub and undergrowth.

**scrub fowl** n. (also **scrub hen, jungle fowl**) grey-brown bird of northern coastal Australia which nests in a huge mound (up to 12m across and up to 5m high) made of soil and leaves.

**scrub itch** n. skin irritation caused by the parasitic larvae of mites, affecting humans in northern tropical Australia.

**scrub plain** n. expanse of relatively flat country covered in scrub vegetation and small mallees.

**scrub roller** n. = MALLEE ROLLER.

**scrub tick** n. any of several burrowing ticks that attack humans and animals and can cause paralysis and death in dogs etc.

**scrub turkey** n. = BRUSH TURKEY.

**scruff**[1] — n. back of the neck (esp. *scruff of the neck*). — v. seize and hold (a calf) for branding, castrating, etc., without the use of rope. [perhaps from Old Norse *skoft* hair]

**scruff**[2] n. *colloq.* scruffy person. [origin uncertain]

**scruffy** adj. (**-ier, -iest**) *colloq.* shabby, slovenly, untidy. □ **scruffily** adv. **scruffiness** n. [*scruff* = SCURF]

**scrum** n. *Rugby* massed forwards on each side pushing to gain possession of the ball thrown on the ground between them; scrummage. [abbreviation of *scrummage*]

**scrum-half** n. *Rugby* half-back who puts the ball into the scrum.

**scrummage** n. *Rugby* = SCRUM. [related to SCRIMMAGE]

**scrumptious** /skrump-shuhs/ adj. *colloq.* **1** delicious. **2** delightful. [origin unknown]

**scrumpy** /skrum-pee/ n. *colloq.* rough cider. [British dial. *scrump* small apple]

**scrunch** — v. **1** (usu. foll. by *up*) crumple. **2** crunch. — n. crunching sound. [var. of CRUNCH]

**scruple** /skroo-puhl/ — n. **1** (often in *pl.*) moral concern. **2** doubt caused by this. — v. (**-ling**) (foll. by *to* + infin.; usu. with *neg.*) hesitate because of scruples (*did not scruple to steal from the till*). [Latin]

**scrupulous** /skroo-pyuh-luhs/ adj. **1** conscientious, thorough. **2** careful to avoid doing wrong. **3** punctilious; over-attentive to details. □ **scrupulosity** /-los-uh-tee/ n. **scrupulously** adv. **scrupulousness** n. [Latin: related to SCRUPLE]

**scrutineer** /skroo-tuh-neer/ n. political candidate's personal representative who scrutinises ballot-papers and the electoral process.

**scrutinise** /skroo-tuh-,nuyz/ v. (also **-ize**) (**-sing** or **-zing**) subject to scrutiny.

**scrutiny** /skroo-tuh-nee/ n. (pl. **-ies**) **1** critical gaze. **2** close investigation. [Latin *scrutinium* from *scrutor* examine]

**scuba** /skoo-buh/ n. (pl. **-s**) aqualung. [acronym of *self-contained underwater breathing apparatus*]

**scuba-diving** n. swimming underwater using a scuba. □ **scuba-dive** v. **scuba-diver** n.

**scud** — v. (**-dd-**) **1** move straight and fast; skim along (*scudding clouds*). **2** *Naut.* run before the wind. — n. **1** spell of scudding. **2** scudding motion. **3 a** vapoury driving clouds. **b** driving shower. **c** wind-blown spray. [perhaps an alteration of SCUT]

**scuff** — v. **1** graze or brush against. **2** mark (shoes, furniture, etc.) in this way. **3** shuffle or drag the feet. — n. mark of scuffing. [imitative]

**scuffle** /skuf-uhl/ — n. confused struggle or fight at close quarters. — v. (**-ling**) engage in a scuffle. [probably Scandinavian: related to SHOVE]

**scull** — n. **1** either of a pair of small oars. **2** single oar over the stern of a boat to propel it, usu. by a side-to-side motion. **3** (in *pl.*) sculling race. — v. **1** (often *absol.*) propel (a boat) with sculls. **2** (also **skol**) *colloq.* **a** drink (a glass etc. of alcoholic liquor) in a single draught. **b** finish one's drink quickly (*scull your drink and let's go*). [origin unknown]

**scullery** /skul-uh-ree/ n. (pl. **-ies**) chiefly *Brit.* back kitchen; room for washing dishes etc. [Anglo-French *squillerie*]

**scullion** /skul-yuhn/ n. *archaic* **1** cook's boy. **2** person who washes dishes etc. [origin unknown]

**sculpt** v. sculpture. [shortening of SCULPTOR]

**sculptor** n. artist who sculptures. [Latin: related to SCULPTURE]

**sculpture** /skulp-chuh/ — n. **1** art of making three-dimensional or relief forms, by chiselling, carving, modelling, casting, etc. **2** work of sculpture. — v. (**-ring**) **1** represent in or adorn with sculpture. **2** practise sculpture. □ **sculptural** adj. [Latin *sculpo sculpt-* carve]

**scum** — n. **1** layer of dirt, froth, etc., at the top of liquid. **2** *derog.* worst part, person, or group (*scum of the earth*). — v. (**-mm-**) **1** remove scum from. **2** form a scum (on). □ **scummy** adj. (**-ier, -iest**). [Low German or Dutch]

**scumbag** n. *coarse colloq.* contemptible person.

**scunge** n. *colloq.* **1** dirt; scum; mess. **2** dirty or disagreeable person. **3** person who is tight with money or who habitually cadges. □ **scungy** adj. (**-gier, -giest**) (in all senses of noun). [perhaps related to *scrounge*]

**scungies** /**skun**-jeez/ *n.pl.* (taken as *sing.*) *colloq.* stretch sports briefs worn under board-shorts, netball skirt, etc. [origin unknown]

**scupper¹** *n.* hole in a ship's side to drain water from the deck. [French *escopir* to spit]

**scupper²** *v. colloq.* **1** sink (a ship or its crew). **2** defeat or ruin (a plan etc.). [origin unknown]

**scurf** *n.* **1** dandruff. **2** any scaly matter on a surface. □ **scurfy** *adj.* [Old English]

**scurrilous** /**sku**-ruh-luhs/ *adj.* grossly or indecently abusive. □ **scurrility** /-**ril**-uh-tee/ *n.* (*pl.* **-ies**). **scurrilously** *adv.* **scurrilousness** *n.* [Latin *scurra* buffoon]

**scurry** /**sku**-ree/ — *v.* (**-ies**, **-ied**) run or move hurriedly, esp. with short quick steps; scamper. — *n.* (*pl.* **-ies**) **1** act or sound of scurrying. **2** flurry of rain or snow. [abbreviation of *hurry-scurry* reduplication of HURRY]

**scurvy** /**sker**-vee/ — *n.* disease caused by a deficiency of vitamin C. — *adj.* (**-ier**, **-iest**) paltry, contemptible. □ **scurvily** *adv.* [from SCURF]

**scut** *n.* short tail, esp. of a hare, rabbit, or deer. [origin unknown]

**scutter** *v. & n. colloq.* scurry. [perhaps an alteration of SCUTTLE²]

**scuttle¹** /**skut**-uhl/ *n.* = COAL-SCUTTLE. [Old Norse from Latin *scutella* dish]

**scuttle²** /**skut**-uhl/ — *v.* (**-ling**) scurry; flee from danger etc. — *n.* hurried gait; precipitate flight. [perhaps related to British dial. *scuddle* frequentative of SCUD]

**scuttle³** /**skut**-uhl/ — *n.* hole with a lid in a ship's deck or side. — *v.* let water into (a ship) to sink it. [Spanish *escotilla* hatchway]

**Scylla and Charybdis** /ˌsil-uh and kuh-**rib**-dis/ *n.pl.* two dangers or extremes such that one can be avoided only by approaching the other. [names of a monster and a whirlpool in Greek mythology]

**scythe** /suyth/ — *n.* mowing and reaping implement with a long handle and curved blade swung over the ground. — *v.* (**-thing**) cut with a scythe. [Old English]

**SE** *abbr.* **1** south-east. **2** south-eastern.

**Se** *symb.* selenium.

**sea** *n.* **1** expanse of salt water that covers most of the earth's surface. **2** any part of this. **3** named tract of this partly or wholly enclosed or bounded by land (*Tasman Sea*). **4** large inland lake (*Sea of Galilee*). **5** waves of the sea; their motion or state (*choppy sea*). **6** (foll. by *of*) vast quantity or expanse (*sea of troubles*; *sea of faces*). **7** (*attrib.*) living or used in, on, or near the sea (often prefixed to the name of a marine animal, plant, etc., having a superficial resemblance to what it is named after) (*sea horse*). **8** used attrib. in the names of some Australian fish (*sea garfish* (cf. BEAKIE); *sea mullet* (cf. PODDY MULLET); *sea perch*). □ **at sea 1** in a ship on the sea. **2** (also **all at sea**) perplexed, confused. **by sea** in a ship or ships. **go to sea** become a sailor. **on the sea 1** = *at sea* 1. **2** on the coast. [Old English]

**sea anemone** *n.* marine animal with tube-shaped body and petal-like tentacles.

**seabed** *n.* ocean floor.

**seaboard** *n.* **1** seashore or coastline. **2** coastal region.

**seaborne** *adj.* transported by sea.

**sea change** *n.* notable or unexpected transformation.

**sea cow** *n.* **1** herbivorous mammal which lives in the sea, e.g. the dugong. **2** walrus.

**sea dog** *n.* old sailor.

**sea eagle** see WHITE-BREASTED SEA EAGLE.

**seafarer** *n.* **1** sailor. **2** traveller by sea. □ **seafaring** *adj. & n.*

**seafood** *n.* (often *attrib.*) edible sea fish or shellfish (*seafood restaurant*).

**seagoing** *adj.* (of ships) fit for crossing the sea.

**sea green** *adj. & n.* (as adj. often hyphenated) bluish-green.

**seagull** *n.* any of various gulls which live near the sea, esp. the *silver gull* which is also common at rubbish tips, cricket grounds, airports, etc.

**sea horse** *n.* **1** small upright fish with a head like a horse's. **2** mythical creature with a horse's head and fish's tail.

**seal¹** — *n.* **1** piece of stamped wax, lead, paper, etc., attached to a document or to a receptacle, envelope, etc., to guarantee authenticity or security. **2** engraved piece of metal etc. for stamping a design on a seal. **3** substance or device used to close a gap etc. **4** anything regarded as a confirmation or guarantee (*seal of approval*). — *v.* **1** close securely or hermetically. **2** stamp, fasten, or fix with a seal. **3** certify as correct with a seal or stamp. **4** (often foll. by *up*) confine securely. **5** settle or decide (*their fate is sealed*). **6** (foll. by *off*) prevent entry to or exit from (an area). **7 a** apply a non-porous coating to (a surface) to make it impervious. **b** surface (a road) with tar, bitumen, etc. □ **set one's seal to** (or **on**) authorise or confirm. [Latin *sigillum*]

**seal²** — *n.* fish-eating amphibious marine mammal with flippers. — *v.* hunt for seals. [Old English]

**sealant** *n.* material for sealing, esp. to make airtight or watertight.

**sea legs** *n.pl.* ability to keep one's balance and avoid seasickness at sea.

**sea level** *n.* mean level of the sea's surface, used in reckoning the height of hills etc. and as a barometric standard.

**sealing wax** *n.* mixture softened by heating and used to make seals.

**sea lion** *n.* **1** any of several large, eared seals of the Pacific region. **2** large, eared seal of coastal areas and esp. islands from WA to SA, the male having a white mane of hair on its nape.

**seal leopard** *n.* (also **leopard seal**) large seal of Antarctic regions, having spotted fur and feeding on penguins.

**seam** — *n.* **1** line where two edges join, esp. of cloth or boards. **2** fissure between parallel edges. **3** wrinkle. **4** stratum of coal etc. — *v.* **1** join with a seam. **2** (esp. as **seamed** *adj.*) mark or score with a seam. □ **seamless** *adj.* [Old English]

**seaman** *n.* **1** person whose work is at sea. **2** sailor, esp. one below the rank of officer.

**seamanship** *n.* skill in managing a ship or boat.

**seam bowler** *n.* *Cricket* bowler who makes the ball deviate by bouncing it off its seam.

**seamer** *n.* = SEAM BOWLER.

**sea mile** *n.* = NAUTICAL MILE.

**seamstress** /**sem**-struhs, **seem**-/ *n.* (also **sempstress**) woman who sews, esp. for a living. [Old English: related to SEAM]

**seamy** *adj.* (**-ier, -iest**) **1** disreputable or sordid (esp. *the seamy side*). **2** marked with or showing seams. □ **seaminess** *n.*

**seance** /**say**-ons/ *n.* meeting at which a spiritualist attempts to make contact with the dead. [French]

**seaplane** *n.* aircraft designed to take off from and land on water.

**seaport** *n.* town with a harbour.

**sear** /seer/ *v.* **1 a** scorch esp. with a hot iron; cauterise; brand. **b** (as **searing** *adj.*) scorching, burning (*searing pain*). **2** cause anguish to (*seared his heart with grief*). **3** brown (meat) quickly at a high temperature to retain its juices in cooking. [Old English]

**search** /serch/ — *v.* **1** (also *absol.*) look through or go over thoroughly to find something. **2** examine or feel over (a person) to find anything concealed. **3 a** probe or penetrate into. **b** examine or question (one's mind, conscience, etc.) thoroughly. **4** (foll. by *for*) look thoroughly in order to find. **5** (as **searching** *adj.*) (of an examination) thorough; keenly questioning (*searching gaze*). **6** (foll. by

*out*) look for; seek out. — *n.* **1** act of searching. **2** investigation. □ **in search of** trying to find. **search me!** *colloq.* I do not know. □ **searcher** *n.* **searchingly** *adv.* [Anglo-French *cerchier*]

**searchlight** *n.* **1** powerful outdoor electric light with a concentrated beam that can be turned in any direction. **2** light or beam from this.

**search-party** *n.* group of people conducting an organised search.

**search warrant** *n.* official authorisation to enter and search a building.

**seascape** *n.* picture or view of the sea.

**Sea Scout** *n.* member of the maritime branch of the Scout Association.

**seashell** *n.* shell of a salt-water mollusc.

**seasick** *adj.* nauseous from the motion of a ship at sea. □ **seasickness** *n.*

**season** /**see**-zuhn/ — *n.* **1 a** each of the climatic divisions of the year (spring, summer, autumn, winter). **b** time of the year characterised by climatic features (*the wet season*). **2** proper or suitable time (*season to be jolly, fa-la-la*). **3** time when something is plentiful, active, etc. (*wild-flower season in WA; duck season*). **4** time of year regularly devoted to an activity (*footy season*). **5** indefinite period (*season of ups and downs in the housing market*). — *v.* **1** flavour (food) with salt, herbs, spices, etc. **2** enhance with wit etc. **3** temper or moderate (*an angry young man who cannot season his impatience with the world*). **4** (esp. as **seasoned** *adj.*) make or become suitable by exposure to the weather or experience (*seasoned wood; seasoned campaigner*). □ **in season 1** (of food) plentiful and good. **2** (of an animal) on heat. [Latin *satio* sowing]

**seasonable** *adj.* **1** suitable or usual to the season (*seasonable weather*). **2** opportune (*his intervention came at the most seasonable moment*). **3** apt; meeting the needs of the occasion (*a seasonable response*).

---

■ **Usage** *Seasonable* is sometimes confused with *seasonal*.

---

**seasonal** *adj.* of, depending on, or varying with the season (*seasonal work; accommodation charges are seasonal*). □ **seasonally** *adv.* [Latin *satio -onis*]

**seasoning** *n.* salt, herbs, spices, etc. added to food to enhance its flavour.

**season ticket** *n.* ticket entitling the holder to unlimited travel, access, etc., in a given period.

**seat** — *n.* **1** thing made or used for sitting on. **2 a** buttocks. **b** part of a garment covering them. **3** part of a chair etc. on which the buttocks rest. **4** place for one person in a theatre, vehicle, etc. **5 a** right to occupy a seat, esp. as an elected member of parliament. **b** such a member's electorate (*the seat of Wills*). **6** supporting part of a machine etc.; base (*the valve fits its seat so badly that it allows steam to escape*). **7** site or location of some thing specified (*the university is a seat of learning; the seat of the emotions*). **8** manner of sitting on a horse etc. (*has a good seat*). — *v.* **1** cause to sit (*seated them as they arrived*). **2** provide sitting accommodation for (*bus seats 50*). **3** (as **seated** adj.) sitting. **4** put or fit in position (*seat the valve securely*). □**be seated** sit down. **take a seat** sit down. [Old Norse: related to SIT]

**seatbelt** *n.* belt securing car or aircraft passengers.

**-seater** *comb. form* having a specified number of seats.

**seating** *n.* **1** seats collectively. **2** sitting accommodation.

**sea urchin** *n.* small marine animal with a spiny shell.

**sea-urchin hakea** *n.* tall WA hakea bearing globular red flowers studded with cream-white spikes, each flower resembling the sea creature.

**sea wall** *n.* wall built to stop flooding or erosion by the sea.

**seaward** /see-wuhd/ — *adv.* (also **sea-wards**) towards the sea. — *adj.* going or facing towards the sea.

**seaweed** *n.* plant growing in the sea or on rocks in or near the sea.

**seaworthy** *adj.* fit to put to sea. □ **sea-worthiness** *n.*

**sebaceous** /suh-**bay**-shuhs/ *adj.* fatty; secreting oily matter. [Latin *sebum* tallow]

**sec**[1] *abbr.* secant.

**sec**[2] *n. colloq.* (in phrases) second, moment (*wait a sec*). [abbreviation]

**sec.** *abbr.* second(s).

**secant** /**see**-kuhnt, **sek**-uhnt/ *n. Math.* **1** ratio of the hypotenuse to the shorter side adjacent to an acute angle (in a right-angled triangle). **2** line cutting a curve at one or more points. [French]

**secateurs** /ˌsek-uh-**terz**, **sek**-uh-tuhz/ *n.pl.* pruning clippers used with one hand. [French]

**secede** /suh-**seed**/ *v.* (**-ding**) withdraw formally from a political federation or religious body. [Latin *secedo -cess-*]

**secession** /suh-**sesh**-uhn/ *n.* act of seceding. □ **secessionist** *n. & adj.* [Latin: related to SECEDE]

**seclude** /suh-**klood**/ *v.* (**-ding**) (also *refl.*) **1** keep (a person or place) apart from others. **2** (esp. as **secluded** adj.) screen from view. [Latin *secludo -clus-*]

**seclusion** /suh-**kloo**-*zh*uhn/ *n.* secluded state or place (*needed seclusion for his work; the outback was his seclusion*).

**second**[1] /**sek**-uhnd/ — *adj.* **1** next after first. **2** additional (*ate a second cake*). **3** subordinate; inferior. **4** *Mus.* performing a lower or subordinate part (*second violins*). **5** such as to be comparable to (*a second Joan Sutherland*). **6** alternate (*every second week*). — *n.* **1** runner-up. **2** person or thing besides the first or previously mentioned one (*the policeman was then joined by a second*). **3** second gear (*put it into second*). **4** (in *pl.*) inferior goods. **5** (in *pl.*) *colloq.* second helping or course. **6** assistant to a duellist, boxer, etc. **7** *Mus.* **a** interval or chord spanning two consecutive notes. **b** note separated from another by this interval. **8** (*pl.*) reserve or second-grade team in sporting clubs. — *v.* **1** support; back up. **2** formally support (a nomination, resolution, or its proposer). □ **at second hand** indirectly. □ **seconder** *n.* (esp. in sense 2 of *v.*). [Latin *secundus* from *sequor* follow]

**second**[2] /**sek**-uhnd/ *n.* **1** sixtieth of a minute of time or of an angle. **2** *colloq.* very short time (*wait a second*). [medieval Latin *secunda* (*minuta*) secondary (minute)]

**second**[3] /suh-**kond**/ *v.* transfer (a person) temporarily to another department etc. □ **secondment** *n.* [French *en second* in the second rank]

**secondary** /**sek**-uhn-duh-ree, -dree/ — *adj.* **1** coming after or next below what is primary (*secondary stress; of secondary importance*). **2** derived from or supplementing what is primary (*secondary source; secondary colour*). **3** (of education, a school, etc.) following primary. **4** *Elect.* **a** (of a cell or battery) having a reversible chemical reaction and therefore able to store energy. **b** denoting a device using electromagnetic induction, esp. a transformer. — *n.* (*pl.* **-ies**) secondary thing. □ **secondarily** *adv.* [Latin: related to SECOND[1]]

**secondary boycott** *n.* an attempt to influence the outcome of an industrial dispute through action against an employer not directly involved in the dispute.

**secondary colour** *n.* result of mixing two primary colours (*mixing the primary colours blue and yellow produces the secondary colour green*).

**secondary industry** *n.* industry which produces manufactured goods (opp. PRIMARY INDUSTRY).

**secondary school** *n.* school providing education after primary school and before university etc.

**secondary source** *n.* critical book,

journal article, etc., used as supporting evidence in the discussion of a PRIMARY SOURCE (*Shakespeare's 'Macbeth' is the primary source in this thesis, and the secondary sources include E.F.C. Ludowyk's 'Understanding Shakespeare'*).

**second-best** *adj. & n.* next after best. □ **come off second-best** be defeated in a fight, argument, etc.

**second chamber** *n.* upper house of a parliament.

**second class** — *n.* second-best group, category, or accommodation. — *adj.* (**second-class**) **1** of or belonging to the second class (*second-class compartment on the train*). **2** inferior, or treated as inferior, in quality, status, etc. (*second-class citizens*). — *adv.* (**second-class**) by second class (in a train etc.) (*travelled second-class*).

**second cousin** *n.* son or daughter of one's parent's cousin.

**second cut** *n.* **1** blow made to remove poorly-cut fleece. **2** piece of inferior wool resulting from this. □ **second-cutter** *n.*

**second-degree** *adj.* denoting burns that cause blistering but not permanent scars.

**second fiddle** SEE FIDDLE.

**Second Fleet** *n. hist.* fleet of convict-carrying ships from Britain reaching Sydney in September 1791 (see FIRST FLEET).

**Second Fleeter** *n. hist.* British convict arriving in Sydney on the Second Fleet (see FIRST FLEETER).

**second-generation** *adj.* denoting the offspring of a first generation, esp. of immigrants to Australia, but also of machines etc. (*a second-generation computer*).

**second-guess** *v. colloq.* **1** anticipate by guesswork. **2** criticise with hindsight.

**second-hand** — *adj.* **1 a** having had a previous owner; not new. **b** (*attrib.*) (of a shop etc.) where such goods can be bought. **2** (of information etc.) indirect, not from one's own observation etc. — *adv.* **1** on a second-hand basis (*always buys cars second-hand*). **2** indirectly (*heard the news second-hand*).

**second lieutenant** *n.* army officer next below lieutenant.

**secondly** *adv.* **1** furthermore. **2** as a second item.

**second nature** *n.* acquired tendency that has become instinctive.

**second person** SEE PERSON.

**second-rate** *adj.* mediocre; inferior.

**second sight** *n.* clairvoyance.

**second string** *n.* alternative course of action, means of livelihood, etc., invoked if the main one is unsuccessful.

**second thoughts** *n.pl.* revised opinion or resolution.

**second wind** *n.* **1** recovery of normal breathing during exercise after initial breathlessness. **2** renewed energy to continue.

**secrecy** /see-kruh-see/ *n.* state of being secret; habit or faculty of keeping secrets (*done in secrecy*).

**secret** /see-kruht/ — *adj.* **1** kept or meant to be kept private, unknown, or hidden. **2** acting or operating secretly. **3** fond of secrecy. — *n.* **1** thing kept or meant to be kept secret. **2** mystery (*secrets of the universe*). **3** effective but not generally known method (*what's their secret?; the secret of success*). □ **in secret** secretly. □ **secretly** *adv.* [Latin *secerno secret-* separate]

**secret agent** *n.* spy.

**secretariat** /ˌsek-ruh-**tair**-ree-uht/ *n.* **1** administrative office or department, esp. a government one. **2** its members or premises. [medieval Latin: related to SECRETARY]

**secretary** /**sek**-ruh-tuh-ree, **sek**-ruh-tree/ *n.* (*pl.* **-ies**) **1** employee who assists with correspondence, records, making appointments, etc. **2** official of a society etc. who keeps minutes, writes letters, etc. **3** head of a public service department. □ **secretarial** /-**tair**-ree-uhl/ *adj.* **secretaryship** *n.* [Latin *secretarius*: related to SECRET]

**secret ballot** *n.* ballot in which votes are cast in secret.

**secrete** /suh-**kreet**/ *v.* (**-ting**) **1** (of a cell, organ, etc.) produce by secretion. **2** conceal (*secreted the roll of exposed film in his briefs*). □ **secretory** *adj.* [from SECRET]

**secretion** /suh-**kree**-shuhn/ *n.* **1 a** process by which substances are produced and discharged from a cell for a function in the organism or for excretion. **b** the secreted substance. **2** act or an instance of concealing (*the secretion of stolen goods*). [Latin: related to SECRET]

**secretive** /**see**-kruh-tiv/ *adj.* inclined to make or keep secrets; uncommunicative. □ **secretively** *adv.* **secretiveness** *n.*

**secret police** *n.* police force operating secretly for political ends.

**secret service** *n.* government department concerned with espionage.

**secret society** *n.* society whose members are sworn to secrecy about it.

**sect** *n.* **1** group sharing (usu. unorthodox) religious, political, or philosophical doctrines. **2** (esp. exclusive) religious denomination. [Latin *sequor* follow]

**sectarian** /sek-**tair**-ree-uhn/ — *adj.* **1** of or concerning a sect. **2** bigoted or narrow-minded in following the doctrines of one's sect. — *n.* **1** member of a sect. **2** a bigot. □ **sectarianism** *n.* [medieval Latin *sectarius* adherent]

**section** /**sek**-shuhn/ — *n.* **1** part cut off or separated from something. **2** each of the parts into which a thing is divided or divisible or out of which a structure can be fitted together. **3** distinct group or subdivision of a larger body of people (*poorer section of the community*; *the wind section of an orchestra*). **4** subdivision of a book, document, statute, etc. **5** act of cutting or separating surgically (*caesarian section*). **6 a** cutting of a solid by a plane. **b** resulting figure or area. **7** representation of the internal structure of something as if cut across along a vertical or horizontal plane. **8** fare stage on a bus or tram. — *v.* arrange in or divide into sections. [Latin *seco sect-* cut]

**sectional** /**sek**-shuh-nuhl/ *adj.* **1 a** of a social group (*sectional interests*). **b** partisan (*the Aussie team can rely on sectional support whenever it plays in Australia*). **2** made in sections. **3** local rather than general. □ **sectionally** *adv.*

**sector** /**sek**-tuh/ *n.* **1** distinct part of an enterprise, society, the economy, etc. **2** military subdivision of an area. **3** plane figure enclosed by two radii of a circle, ellipse, etc., and the arc between them. **4** *Computing* subdivision of a track on a magnetic disk. □ **sectoral** *adj.* [Latin: related to SECTION]

**secular** /**sek**-yuh-luh/ — *adj.* **1** concerned with the affairs of this world; not spiritual or concerned with religion (*secular state*; *secular music*). **2** (of education) not concerned with religion or religious belief; excluding religious instruction. **3** (of priests) not monastic. — *n.* priest who does not belong to a monastic or other religious Order. □ **secularise** *v.* (also **-ize**) (**-sing** or **-zing**). **secularisation** /-zay-shuhn/ *n.* [Latin *saeculum* an age]

**secularism** /**sek**-yuh-luh-,riz-uhm/ *n.* **1** the attitude or belief that religions or religious doctrines should have no place or say in the conduct of a public education system and in the civil affairs and policies of a nation. **2** *Philos.* doctrine that religion, religious dogmas, etc., have no place in the formulation of a system of ethics.

**secure** /**suh-kyoor**/ — *adj.* **1** untroubled by danger or fear. **2** safe. **3 a** reliable; certain not to fail (*the plan is secure*). **b** stable (*the structure seems secure enough*). **c** fixed or fastened so as not to give way etc. (*made the door secure*). **4** (foll. by *of*) certain to achieve (*secure of victory*). — *v.* (**-ring**) **1** make secure or

safe. **2** fasten or close securely. **3** succeed in obtaining (*secured good seats for the opera*). **4** guarantee (a loan) against loss (*a loan secured by property*). □ **securely** *adv.* [Latin *se* without, *cura* care]

**security** *n.* (*pl.* **-ies**) **1** secure condition or feeling. **2** thing that guards or guarantees. **3 a** safety against espionage, theft, etc. **b** organisation for ensuring this. **4** thing deposited as a guarantee of an undertaking or loan, to be forfeited in case of default. **5** (often in *pl.*) document as evidence of a loan, certificate of stock, bonds, etc.

**security risk** *n.* person or thing that threatens security.

**sedan** /**suh-dan**/ *n.* **1** (in full **sedan chair**) *hist.* enclosed chair for one, carried on poles by two men. **2** enclosed car with four or more seats. [origin uncertain]

**sedate** /**suh-dayt**/ — *adj.* tranquil and dignified; serious. — *v.* (**-ting**) put under sedation. □ **sedately** *adv.* **sedateness** *n.* [Latin *sedo sedat-* settle, calm]

**sedation** /**suh-day-shuhn**/ *n.* act of calming, esp. by sedatives. [Latin: related to SEDATE]

**sedative** /**sed-uh-tiv**/ — *n.* calming drug or influence. — *adj.* calming, soothing. [medieval Latin: related to SEDATE]

**sedentary** /**sed-uhn-tuh-ree, -tree**/ *adj.* **1** sitting (*a sedentary posture*). **2** (of work etc.) done while sitting. **3** (of a person) disinclined to exercise. **4** (of animals) not migratory. [Latin *sedeo* sit]

**sedge** *n.* waterside or marsh plant resembling coarse grass. □ **sedgy** *adj.* [Old English]

**sediment** /**sed-uh-muhnt**/ *n.* **1** matter that settles to the bottom of a liquid; dregs. **2** matter deposited on the land by water or wind, and which may in time become consolidated into rock. □ **sedimentary** /-men-tuh-ree, -tree/ *adj.* **sedimentation** /-tay-shuhn/ *n.* [Latin *sedeo* sit]

**sedition** /**suh-dish-uhn**/ *n.* conduct or speech inciting to rebellion. □ **seditious** *adj.* [Latin *seditio*]

**seduce** /**suh-dyoos**/ *v.* (**-cing**) **1 a** tempt or entice into sexual activity. **b** tempt or entice into wrongdoing. **2** coax or lead astray; tempt (*seduced by the aroma of freshly ground coffee*). □ **seducer** *n.* [Latin *se-* away, *duco duct-* lead]

**seduction** /**suh-duk-shuhn**/ *n.* **1** act or instance of seducing or the process of being seduced. **2** thing that tempts or attracts.

**seductive** /**suh-duk-tiv**/ *adj.* tending to seduce; alluring, enticing. □ **seductively** *adv.* **seductiveness** *n.*

**seductress** /**suh-duk-truhs**/ *n.* female

seducer. [obsolete *seductor* male seducer: related to SEDUCE]

**sedulous** /ˈsej-uh-luhs, ˈsed-yuh-luhs/ *adj.* **1** persevering, diligent. **2** (of an action etc.) deliberately and consciously continued; painstaking (*sedulous attempt to seduce him*). □ **sedulity** /suh-**dyoo**-luh-tee/ *n.* **sedulously** *adv.* [Latin *sedulus* zealous]

**see¹** *v.* (*past* **saw**; *past part.* **seen**) **1** perceive with the eyes. **2** have or use this power. **3** discern mentally; understand (*I see what you mean; couldn't see the joke*). **4** watch (a film, game, etc.). **5** ascertain, learn (*will see if he's here*). **6** imagine, foresee (*see trouble ahead*). **7** look at for information (*see page 15*). **8** meet and recognise (*I saw your mother in town*). **9 a** meet socially or on business; visit or be visited by (*is too ill to see anyone; must see a doctor*). **b** meet regularly as a boyfriend or girlfriend. **10** reflect, wait for clarification (*we shall have to see*). **11** experience (*I never thought to see it*). **12** find attractive (*can't think what she sees in him*). **13** escort, conduct (*saw them home*). **14** witness (an event etc.) (*see the New Year in*). **15** (usu. foll. by *to* or *that* + clause) make provision for; ensure (*shall see to your request immediately; see that he gets home safely; see that it is done*). **16 a** (in poker etc.) equal (a bet). **b** equal the bet of (a player). □ **let me see** an appeal for time to think before speaking etc. **see about 1** attend to. **2** consider. **see the back of** *colloq.* be rid of. **see eye to eye** see EYE. **see fit** see FIT¹. **see the light 1** realise one's mistakes etc. **2** undergo religious conversion. **see off** be present at the departure of (a person). **see out 1** accompany out of a building etc. **2** finish (a project etc.) completely. **3** survive (a period etc.). **4** last longer than; survive. **see red** *colloq.* become enraged. **see stars** *colloq.* see lights as a result of a blow on the head. **see things** *colloq.* have hallucinations. **see through** detect the truth or true nature of. **see a person through** support (emotionally, financially, etc.) a person during a difficult time or an important undertaking (*his parents are seeing him through university*). **see a thing through** persist with until it is completed. **see to it** (foll. by *that*) ensure. **we shall see 1** let us await the outcome. **2** a formula for declining to act at once. **you see 1** you understand. **2** you will see when I explain. [Old English]

**see²** *n.* **1** area under the authority of a bishop or archbishop. **2** his office or jurisdiction. [Latin *sedes* seat]

**seed** — *n.* **1 a** flowering plant's unit of reproduction (esp. in the form of grain)

capable of developing into another such plant. **b** seeds collectively, esp. for sowing. **2** semen. **3** prime cause, beginning, germ (*a seed of doubt*). **4** *archaic* offspring, descendants (*Abraham and all his seed*). **5** (in tennis etc.) seeded player. — *v.* **1 a** place seeds in. **b** sprinkle (as) with seed. **2** sow seeds. **3** produce or drop seed. **4** remove seeds from (fruit etc.). **5** place a crystal etc. in (a cloud) to produce rain. **6** *Sport* **a** so position (a strong competitor in a knockout competition) that he or she will not meet other strong competitors in early rounds. **b** arrange (the order of play) in this way. □ **go** (or **run**) **to seed 1** cease flowering as seed develops. **2** become degenerate, unkempt, etc. □ **seedless** *adj.* [Old English]

**seedbed** *n.* **1** bed prepared for sowing. **2** place of development (*a seedbed of rebellion*).

**seedling** *n.* young plant raised from seed rather than from a cutting etc.

**seedy** *adj.* (**-ier, -iest**) **1** shabby, unkempt; disreputable. **2** *colloq.* unwell. **3** full of or going to seed. □ **seediness** *n.*

**seeing** *conj.* (usu. foll. by *that*) considering that, inasmuch as, because.

**seek** *v.* (*past* and *past part.* **sought** /sawt/) **1** (often foll. by *for, after*) search or inquire. **2 a** try or want to find or get or reach (*sought the shore; sought a fortune-teller; sought my hand*). **b** request (*sought help*). **3** endeavour (*seek to please*). □ **seek out** search for and find. **2** single out as a friend etc. □ **seeker** *n.* [Old English]

**seem** *v.* (often foll. by *to* + infin.) appear or feel (*seems ridiculous*). □ **I** etc. **can't seem to** I etc. appear unable to (*can't seem to manage it*). **it seems** (or **would seem**) (often foll. by *that*) it appears to be the case. [Old Norse]

**seeming** *adj.* apparent but perhaps doubtful (*his seeming interest*). □ **seemingly** *adv.*

**seemly** *adj.* (**-ier, -iest**) in good taste; decorous. □ **seemliness** *n.* [Old Norse: related to SEEM]

**seen** *past part.* of SEE¹.

**See of Rome** *n.* the papacy, the Holy See.

**seep** *v.* ooze out; percolate. [Old English]

**seepage** *n.* **1** act of seeping. **2** quantity that seeps out.

**seer** /ˈsee-uh/ *n.* **1** person who sees. **2** prophet; visionary.

**seersucker** /ˈseer-suk-uh/ *n.* linen, cotton, etc. fabric with a puckered surface. [Persian]

**see-saw** /ˈsee-saw/ — *n.* **1 a** long plank balanced on a central support, for children to sit on at each end and move up and down alternately. **b** this game. **2** up-and-down or to-and-fro motion. **3** close contest with alternating advantage. — *v.* **1** play on a see-saw. **2** move up and down. **3** vacillate in policy, emotion, etc. — *adj. & adv.* with up-and-down or backward-and-forward motion. [reduplication of SAW[1]]

**seethe** /seeth/ *v.* (**-thing**) **1** boil, bubble over. **2** be very angry, resentful, agitated, etc. (*I was seething inwardly*; *seething with discontent*). [Old English]

**segment** /**seg**-muhnt/ — *n.* **1** each part into which a thing is or can be divided. **2** part of a circle or sphere etc. cut off by an intersecting line or plane. **3** *Zool.* each of the longitudinal sections of the body of certain animals (e.g. worms). — *v.* usu. /seg-**ment**/ divide into segments. □ **segmental** /-**men**-tuhl/ *adj.* **segmentation** /-**tay**-shuhn/ *n.* [Latin *seco* cut]

**segregate** /**seg**-ruh-gayt/ *v.* (**-ting**) **1** put apart from the rest; isolate. **2** enforce racial segregation on (persons) or in (a community etc.). [Latin *grex greg-* flock]

**segregation** /,seg-ruh-**gay**-shuhn/ *n.* **1** enforced separation of ethnic groups in a community etc. **2** act or instance of segregating or state of being segregated. □ **segregationist** *n. & adj.*

**seine** /sayn/ — *n.* fishing-net with floats at the top and weights at the bottom edge. — *v.* (**-ning**) fish or catch with a seine. [Old English *segne*]

**seismic** /**suyz**-mik/ *adj.* of earthquakes. [Greek *seismos* earthquake]

**seismogram** /**suyz**-muh-,gram/ *n.* record given by a seismograph.

**seismograph** /**suyz**-muh-,grahf, -,graf/ *n.* instrument that records the force, direction, etc., of earthquakes. □ **seismographic** /-**graf**-ik/ *adj.*

**seismology** /suyz-**mol**-uh-jee/ *n.* the study of earthquakes. □ **seismological** /-muh-**loj**-i-kuhl/ *adj.* **seismologist** *n.*

**seize** /seez/ *v.* (**-zing**) **1** (often foll. by *on, upon*) take hold of forcibly or suddenly. **2** take possession of forcibly or by legal power (*seized the fortress*; *police seized a haul of drugs*). **3** affect suddenly (*panic seized us*). **4** (often foll. by *on, upon*) take advantage of (an opportunity etc.). **5** (often foll. by *on, upon*) comprehend quickly or clearly (*seized the point immediately*; *seized on her innuendo*). **6** (often foll. by *up*) **a** (of a moving part in a machine) become stuck or jammed (*the engine's seized*). **b** (foll. by *up*) (of part of the body etc.) become stiff. [French *saisir*]

**seizure** /**see**-zhuh/ *n.* **1** act or instance of seizing or state of being seized. **2** sudden attack, esp. of epilepsy or apoplexy.

**seldom** /**sel**-duhm/ *adv.* rarely, not often. [Old English]

**select** /suh-**lekt**/ — *v.* **1** choose, esp. with

care. **2** = FREE-SELECT. — *adj.* **1** chosen for excellence or suitability. **2** (of a society etc.) exclusive. [Latin *seligo -lect-*]

**select committee** *n.* small parliamentary committee conducting a special inquiry.

**selection** /suh-**lek**-shuhn/ *n.* **1** act or instance of selecting or state of being selected. **2** selected person or thing. **3** things from which a choice may be made. **4** *Biol.* process in which environmental and genetic influences determine which types of organism thrive better than others, regarded as a factor in evolution. **5 a** = FREE-SELECTION. **b** small or medium-sized rural property.

**selective** *adj.* **1 a** of or using selection. **b** choosing carefully, picking only the best. **2** able to select. **3** (of memory etc.) selecting what is convenient. □ **selectively** *adv.* **selectivity** /suh-lek-**tiv**-uh-tee/ *n.*

**selector** *n.* **1** person who selects, esp. a team. **2** device in a vehicle, machinery, etc., that selects the required gear etc. **3 a** = FREE-SELECTOR. **b** farmer who owns a small to medium-sized property.

**selenium** /suh-**lee**-nee-uhm/ *n.* non-metallic element occurring naturally in various metallic sulphide ores. [Greek *selēnē* moon]

**self** *n.* (*pl.* **selves**) **1** individuality, personality, or essence (*showed his true self*; *is her old self again*). **2** object of introspection or reflexive action (*consciousness of self*). **3 a** one's own interests or pleasure (*cares for nothing but self*). **b** concentration on these. **4** *Commerce* or *colloq.* myself, yourself, etc. (*cheque drawn to self*). □ **one's better self** one's finer impulses. [Old English]

**self-** *comb. form* expressing reflexive action: **1** of or by oneself or itself (*self-respect*; *self-locking*). **2** on, in, for, or of oneself or itself (*self-absorbed*).

**self-abasement** *n.* self-humiliation; cringing.

**self-absorption** *n.* preoccupation with oneself. □ **self-absorbed** *adj.*

**self-abuse** *n. archaic* masturbation.

**self-addressed** *adj.* (of an envelope) bearing one's own address for a reply.

**self-adhesive** *adj.* = SELF-STICKING.

**self-advancement** *n.* advancement of oneself.

**self-aggrandisement** *n.* process of enriching oneself or making oneself powerful. □ **self-aggrandising** *adj.*

**self-analysis** *n.* analysis of oneself, one's motives, character, etc.

**self-appointed** *adj.* designated so by oneself, not by others (*self-appointed critic*).

**self-assembly** *adj.* assembled by the buyer from a kit.

**self-assertive** *adj.* confident or aggressive in promoting oneself, one's rights, etc. □ **self-assertion** *n.*

**self-assured** *n.* self-confident. □ **self-assurance** *n.*

**self-aware** *adj.* conscious of one's character, feelings, motives, etc. □ **self-awareness** *n.*

**self-catering** *adj.* (of a holiday, accommodation etc.) with cooking facilities provided, but no food.

**self-censorship** *n.* censoring of oneself.

**self-centred** *adj.* preoccupied with oneself; selfish. □ **self-centredly** *adv.* **self-centredness** *n.*

**self-cleaning** *adj.* (esp. of an oven) cleaning itself when heated.

**self-conceit** *n.* high or exaggerated opinion of oneself.

**self-confessed** *adj.* openly admitting (or inadvertently revealing) oneself to be (*a self-confessed liar*).

**self-confident** *adj.* having confidence in oneself. □ **self-confidence** *n.* **self-confidently** *adv.*

**self-congratulatory** *adj.* = SELF-SATISFIED. □ **self-congratulation** *n.*

**self-conscious** *adj.* nervous, shy, or embarrassed. □ **self-consciously** *adv.* **self-consciousness** *n.*

**self-consistent** *adj.* (of parts of the same whole etc.) consistent; not conflicting. □ **self-consistency** *n.*

**self-contained** *adj.* **1** (of a person) **a** reserved or restrained in behaviour. **b** independent. **2** (of accommodation) complete in itself, having no shared entrance or facilities.

**self-control** *n.* power of controlling one's behaviour, emotions, etc. □ **self-controlled** *adj.*

**self-critical** *adj.* critical of oneself, one's abilities, etc. □ **self-criticism** *n.*

**self-deception** *n.* deceiving of oneself, esp. about one's motives or feelings. □ **self-deceit** *n.*

**self-defeating** *adj.* (of an action etc.) doomed to failure because of internal inconsistencies; achieving the opposite of what is intended.

**self-defence** *n.* physical or verbal defence of one's body, property, rights, reputation, etc.

**self-delusion** *n.* act of deluding oneself.

**self-denial** *n.* denial of one's desires, asceticism, esp. so as to discipline oneself, or do penance, etc. □ **self-denying** *adj.*

**self-deprecation** *n.* act of disparaging or belittling oneself. □ **self-deprecating** *adj.*

**self-destruct** — *v.* (of a spacecraft, bomb, etc.) explode or disintegrate automatically, esp. when pre-set to do so. — *attrib. adj.* enabling a thing to self-destruct (*self-destruct device*).

**self-destruction** *n.* **1** the process or an act of destroying itself or oneself or one's chances, happiness, etc. **2** act of self-destructing. □ **self-destructive** *adj.*

**self-determination** *n.* **1** nation's right to determine its own government etc. **2** ability to act with free will.

**self-discipline** *n.* **1** ability to apply oneself. **2** self-control. □ **self-disciplined** *adj.*

**self-discovery** *n.* process of acquiring insight into oneself, one's character, desires, etc.

**self-doubt** *n.* lack of confidence in oneself.

**self-educated** *adj.* educated by one's own reading etc., without formal instruction. □ **self-education** *n.*

**self-effacing** /self-uh-**fays**-ing/ *adj.* retiring; modest; timid. □ **self-effacement** *n.*

**self-employed** *adj.* working as a freelance or for one's own business etc.; not employed by an employer. □ **self-employment** *n.*

**self-esteem** /self-uh-**steem**/ *n.* good opinion of oneself; contentment with oneself, one's personality, etc. (*suffers from low self-esteem*).

**self-evident** *adj.* obvious; without the need of proof or further explanation. □ **self-evidence** *n.* **self-evidently** *adv.*

**self-examination** *n.* **1** the study of one's own conduct, motives, etc. **2** examining of one's body for signs of illness (*self-examination revealed a lump in her breast*).

**self-explanatory** *adj.* easily understood, not needing explanation.

**self-expression** *n.* expression of one's feelings, thoughts, etc., esp. in writing, painting, music, dancing, etc.

**self-fertilisation** *n.* fertilisation of plants by their own pollen, not from others (opp. CROSS-FERTILISATION). □ **self-fertile** *adj.* **self-fertilising** *adj.*

**self-financing** *adj.* (of an institution or undertaking) that pays for itself without subsidy.

**self-flattery** *n.* high, esp. exaggerated, opinion of oneself; conceit. □ **self-flattering** *adj.*

**self-fulfilling** *adj.* (of a prophecy, forecast, etc.) bound to come true as a result of actions brought about by its being made.

**self-fulfilment** *n.* fulfilment of one's hopes, ambitions, etc.

**self-governing** *adj.* governing itself or oneself. □ **self-government** *n.*

**self-hatred** *n.* (also **self-hate**) very low opinion or hatred of oneself, esp. of one's actual self when contrasted with one's imagined or idealised self.

**self-help** *n.* (often *attrib.*) use of one's own abilities, resources, etc., to solve one's problems etc. (*formed a self-help group*).

**self-image** *n.* one's conception of oneself, esp. in relation to others.

**self-important** *adj.* conceited; pompous. □ **self-importance** *n.*

**self-imposed** *adj.* (of a task etc.) imposed on and by oneself, not externally (*self-imposed exile*).

**self-improvement** *n.* improvement of oneself or one's life etc. by one's own efforts.

**self-induced** *adj.* induced by oneself or itself.

**self-indulgent** *adj.* **1** indulging in one's own pleasure, feelings, etc. **2** (of a work of art etc.) lacking economy and control. □ **self-indulgence** *n.*

**self-inflicted** *adj.* (of a wound, damage, etc.) inflicted by and on oneself.

**self-interest** *n.* one's personal interest or advantage (esp. when associated with disregard for others). □ **self-interested** *adj.*

**selfish** *adj.* concerned chiefly with one's own interests or pleasure; actuated by or appealing to self-interest. □ **selfishly** *adv.* **selfishness** *n.*

**self-justification** *n.* the justification or excusing of oneself, one's actions, etc.

**self-knowledge** *n.* understanding of oneself, one's motives, etc.

**selfless** *adj.* disregarding oneself or one's own interests; unselfish. □ **selflessly** *adv.* **selflessness** *n.*

**self-love** *n.* **1** selfishness; self-indulgence. **2** *Philos.* regard for one's own well-being and happiness.

**self-made** *adj.* **1** successful or rich by one's own effort. **2** made by oneself.

**self-opinionated** *adj.* stubbornly adhering to one's opinions.

**self-perpetuating** *adj.* perpetuating itself without external agency.

**self-pity** *n.* extreme sorrow for one's own troubles etc.; feeling sorry for oneself. □ **self-pitying** *adj.*

**self-pollination** *n.* pollination of a flower by pollen from the same plant (opp. CROSS-POLLINATION). □ **self-pollinate** *v.* **self-pollinating** *adj.*

**self-portrait** *n.* portrait or description of oneself by oneself.

**self-possessed** *adj.* habitually exercising self-control; calm and composed. □ **self-possession** *n.*

**self-preservation** *n.* **1** keeping oneself safe. **2** this as a basic instinct of human beings and animals.

**self-proclaimed** *adj.* proclaimed by oneself or itself to be such (*a self-proclaimed messiah*).

**self-propelled** *adj.* (of a vehicle etc.) propelled by its own power. □ **self-propelling** *adj.*

**self-publishing** *n.* publishing one's own work at one's own expense (without the aid of a commercial publisher) (cf. VANITY PUBLISHING).

**self-raising** *adj.* (of flour) containing a raising agent such as baking powder.

**self-realisation** *n.* **1** development of one's abilities etc. **2** this as an ethical principle.

**self-regard** *n.* **1** proper regard for oneself. **2 a** selfishness. **b** conceit.

**self-regulating** *adj.* regulating oneself or itself without intervention. □ **self-regulation** *n.* **self-regulatory** *adj.*

**self-reliance** *n.* reliance on one's own resources etc.; independence. □ **self-reliant** *adj.*

**self-reproach** *n.* reproach or blame directed at oneself.

**self-respect** *n.* respect for oneself, a feeling that one is behaving with honour, dignity, etc. □ **self-respecting** *adj.*

**self-restraint** *n.* self-control.

**self-righteous** *adj.* smugly sure of one's rightness, virtue, etc.; pharisaic (*self-righteous moralisers*; *a self-righteous little wowser*). □ **self-righteously** *adv.* **self-righteousness** *n.*

**self-rule** *n.* self-government.

**self-sacrifice** *n.* selflessness; negation of one's own interests, wishes, etc., in favour of those of others. □ **self-sacrificing** *adj.*

**selfsame** *adj.* (prec. by *the*) the very same, identical.

**self-satisfied** *adj.* excessively and unjustifiably complacent about oneself; self-righteous. □ **self-satisfaction** *n.* **self-satisfiedly** *adv.*

**self-sealing** *adj.* **1** (of a tyre etc.) automatically able to seal small punctures. **2** (of an envelope) = SELF-STICKING.

**self-seed** *v.* (of a plant) propagate itself by sowing its own seed. □ **self-seeder** *n.*

**self-seeking** *adj. & n.* selfish.

**self-serve** — *adj.* = SELF-SERVICE. — *n.* = SELF-SERVICE.

**self-service** (also **self-serve**) — *adj.* (often *attrib.*) (of a garage, shop, restaurant, etc.) with customers serving themselves and paying at a checkout etc. — *n. colloq.* self-service garage, shop, restaurant, etc.

**self-serving** *adj.* pandering to one's own interests (*self-serving politician*).

**self-sown** *adj.* grown from seed scattered naturally.

**self-starter** *n.* **1** electrical appliance for starting an engine. **2** ambitious person with initiative.

**self-sticking** *adj.* (also **self-stick**) (of an envelope, label, etc.) adhesive, esp. without wetting.

**self-styled** *adj.* called so by oneself; would be; pretended (*a self-styled artist*).

**self-sufficient** *adj.* **1 a** needing nothing; independent. **b** (of a person, nation, etc.) able to supply one's needs for a commodity, esp. food, from one's own resources. **2** content with one's own opinion; arrogant. □ **self-sufficiency** *n.*

**self-supporting** *adj.* **1** financially self-sufficient. **2** staying up or standing without external aid.

**self-taught** *adj.* educated or trained by oneself, not externally.

**self-willed** *adj.* obstinately pursuing one's own wishes.

**self-worth** *n.* = SELF-ESTEEM.

**sell** — *v.* (*past* and *past part.* **sold** /sohld/) **1** exchange or be exchanged for money (*these sell well*). **2** keep a stock of for sale or be a dealer in (*do you sell eggs?*; *she sells insurance*). **3** (foll. by *at, for*) have a specified price (*sells at $5*). **4** (also *refl.*) betray or prostitute for money etc. (*sell one's country*; *sell one's honour*). **5** (also *refl.*) advertise or publicise (a product, oneself, etc.). **6 a** cause to be sold (*the author's name alone will sell many copies*). **b** cause to be accepted (*the government will never sell this idea to the public*). **7** *colloq.* make (a person) enthusiastic about (an idea etc.) (*sold him on the benefits of planting Australian natives*). **8** *colloq.* disappoint by not keeping an engagement etc., by failing in some way, or by trickery (*sold again!*). — *n. colloq.* **1** manner of selling (*soft sell*). **2** deception; disappointment (*what a sell!*). □ **sell down the river** see RIVER. **sell off** sell at reduced prices. **sell out 1** (also *absol.*) sell (all one's stock, shares, etc.). **2** betray; be treacherous or disloyal. **sell short** disparage, underestimate. **sell up** sell one's business, house, etc. **sold on** *colloq.* enthusiastic about (*is now sold on growing Australian natives*). [Old English]

**sell-by date** *n.* latest recommended date of sale.

**seller** *n.* **1** person who sells. **2** thing that sells well or badly (*this product just isn't a seller*).

**seller's market** *n.* (also **sellers' market**) trading conditions favourable to the seller.

**selling-point** *n.* advantageous feature.

**sellotape** /sel-uh-tayp/ — *n. propr.* adhesive usu. transparent tape. — *v.* (**-ping**) fix with sellotape. [from CELLULOSE]

**sell-out** *n.* **1** commercial success, esp. the selling of all tickets for a show. **2** betrayal.

**selvage** /sel-vij/ *n.* (also **selvedge**) fabric edging woven to prevent cloth from fraying. [from SELF, EDGE]

**selves** *pl.* of SELF.

**semantic** /suh-man-tik/ *adj.* relating to meaning in language; relating to the connotations of words. □ **semantically** *adv.* [Greek *sēmainō* to mean]

**semantics** *n.pl.* (usu. treated as *sing.*) branch of linguistics concerned with meaning.

**semaphore** /sem-uh-faw/ — *n.* **1** system of sending messages by holding the arms or two flags in certain positions according to an alphabetic code. **2** railway signalling apparatus consisting of a post with a movable arm or arms etc. — *v.* (**-ring**) signal or send by semaphore. [Greek *sēma* sign, *pherō* bear]

**semaphore crab** *n.* burrowing crab of eastern Australia which moves its claws in the manner of semaphoring.

**semblance** /sem-bluhns/ *n.* (foll. by *of*) appearance; show (*a semblance of anger*). [French *sembler* resemble]

**semen** /see-muhn/ *n.* reproductive fluid of males, containing spermatozoa in suspension, and ejaculated by the penis; sperm. [Latin *semen semin-* seed]

**semester** /suh-mes-tuh/ *n.* half-year course or term in universities, schools, etc. [Latin *semestris* from *sex* six, *mensis* month]

**semi** /sem-ee/ *n.* (*pl.* **-s**) *colloq.* **1** semi-detached house. **2** semi-trailer. **3** semi-final. [abbreviation]

---

**Semicolon ;**

This is used:

1 between clauses that are too short or too closely related to be made into separate sentences; such clauses are not usually connected by a conjunction, e.g.

*To err is human; to forgive, divine.*
*You could wait for him here; on the other hand I could wait in your place; this would save you valuable time.*

2 between items in a list which themselves contain commas, if it is necessary to avoid confusion, e.g.

*The party consisted of three teachers, who had already climbed with the leader; seven pupils; and two parents.*

**semi-** *prefix* **1** half (*semicircle*). **2** partly; in some degree or particular (*semi-official*; *semi-detached*). [Latin]

**semibreve** /**sem**-ee-ˌbreev/ *n. Mus.* note equal to four crotchets.

**semicircle** /**sem**-ee-ˌser-kuhl/ *n.* half of a circle or of its circumference. □ **semicircular** /ˌsem-ee-**ser**-kyuh-luh/ *adj.*

**semicolon** /ˌsem-ee-**koh**-luhn/ *n.* punctuation mark (;) of intermediate value between a comma and full stop (see panel).

**semiconductor** /ˌsem-ee-kuhn-**duk**-tuh/ *n.* substance that in certain conditions has electrical conductivity intermediate between insulators and metals and is used in integrated circuits, transistors, diodes, etc.

**semiconductor memory** *n.* (also **solid-state memory**) memory device used in digital equipment, esp. computers.

**semi-conscious** /ˌsem-ee-**kon**-shuhs/ *adj.* partly or imperfectly conscious.

**semi-detached** /ˌsem-ee-duh-**tacht**/ — *adj.* (of a house) joined to one other on one side only. — *n.* such a house.

**semi-final** /ˌsem-ee-**fuy**-nuhl/ *n.* match or round between any two of the last four competitors or teams in a competition. □ **semi-finalist** *n.*

**semillon** /**sem**-ee-yon/ *n.* **1** variety of white grape. **2** white table wine made from this.

**seminal** /**sem**-uh-nuhl/ *adj.* **1** of seed, semen, or reproduction; germinal. **2** (of ideas etc.) forming a basis for future development. **3** (of books etc.) highly original and influential. [Latin: related to SEMEN]

**seminar** /**sem**-uh-ˌnah/ *n.* **1** small discussion class at a university etc. **2** short intensive course of study (*one-day public seminar on personal finances*). **3** conference of specialists. [German: related to SEMINARY]

**seminary** /**sem**-uh-nuh-ree/ *n.* (*pl.* **-ies**) training-college for Catholic priests or rabbis etc. □ **seminarist** *n.* [Latin: related to SEMEN]

**semiotics** /ˌsem-ee-**ot**-iks/ *n.* the study of signs and symbols and their use, esp. in language. □ **semiotic** *adj.* [Greek *sēmeiōtikos* of signs]

**semi-permeable** /ˌsem-ee-**per**-mee-uh-buhl/ *adj.* (of a membrane etc.) allowing small molecules to pass through.

**semi-precious** /ˌsem-ee-**presh**-uhs/ *adj.* (of a gem, e.g. a garnet) less valuable than a precious stone (e.g. a diamond).

**semi-professional** /ˌsem-ee-pruh-**fesh**-uh-nuhl/ — *adj.* **1** (of a footballer, musician, etc.) paid for an activity but not relying on it for a living. **2** of semi-professionals. — *n.* semi-professional person.

**semiquaver** /**sem**-ee-ˌkway-vuh/ *n. Mus.* note equal to half a quaver.

**semi-skilled** /ˌsem-ee-**skild**/ *adj.* (of work or a worker) needing or having some training, but less than for a skilled worker.

**Semite** /**see**-muyt, **sem**-uyt/ *n.* member of the peoples said to be descended from Shem (Gen. 10), including esp. the Jews and Arabs. [Greek *Sēm* Shem]

**Semitic** /suh-**mit**-ik/ *adj.* **1** of the Semites, esp. the Jews. **2** of languages of the family including Hebrew and Arabic.

**semitone** /**sem**-ee-ˌtohn/ *n.* half a tone, the smallest interval used in classical European music.

**semitrailer** /ˌsem-ee-**tray**-luh/ *n.* articulated vehicle consisting of a prime-mover and a long trailer, the trailer having wheels at the back but supported at the front by the towing vehicle.

**semitropical** /ˌsem-ee-**trop**-i-kuhl/ *adj.* = SUBTROPICAL.

**semivowel** /**sem**-ee-ˌvow-uhl/ *n.* **1** sound intermediate between a vowel and a consonant (e.g. *w*, *y*). **2** letter representing this.

**semolina** /ˌsem-uh-**lee**-nuh/ *n.* **1** hard grains left after the milling of flour, used in milk puddings etc. **2** pudding of this. [Italian *semolino*]

**sempstress** var. of SEAMSTRESS.

**senate** /**sen**-uht/ *n.* **1** upper house of the Australian Federal Parliament. **2** legislative body, esp. the upper and smaller assembly in some countries. **3** governing body of a university. **4** ancient Roman State council. [Latin *senatus* from *senex* old man]

**senator** /**sen**-uh-tuh/ *n.* member of a senate. □ **senatorial** /ˌ-**taw**-ree-uhl/ *adj.* [Latin: related to SENATE]

**send** *v.* (*past* and *past part.* **sent**) **1 a** order or cause to go or be conveyed (*sent the parcel by air mail*). **b** dismiss with or without force (*sent him away*; *sent them packing*). **c** propel (*sent a bullet into its body*; *sent him flying*). **d** cause to become (*sent me mad*; *sent into raptures*). **2** send a message etc. (*he sent to warn me*). **3** (of God, etc.) grant, bestow, or inflict; bring about; cause to be (*send rain*; *sent a judgment on them*). **4** *colloq.* put into ecstasy, excite (*her trumpet-playing really sends me*). □ **send away for** order (goods) by post. **send down 1** expel from a university. **2** send to prison. **send for 1** summon. **2** order by post. **send her down, Hughie** see HUGHIE. **send in 1** cause to go in. **2** submit (an entry etc.) for a competition etc. **send off 1** dispatch (a letter, parcel, etc.). **2** attend the departure of (a person) as a sign of respect etc. **3** *Sport* (of a referee) order (a player) to leave the field. **send off for** = *send away for*. **send on** transmit further or in advance of oneself. **send a person packing** dismiss vigorously. **send up 1** cause to go up. **2** transmit to a higher authority. **3** *colloq.* ridicule by mimicking. **send word** send information. □ **sender** *n*. [Old English]

**send-off** *n*. party etc. at the departure of a person, start of a project, etc.

**send-up** *n. colloq.* satire, parody.

**senescent** /suh-**nes**-uhnt/ *adj.* growing old. □ **senesce** *v.* **senescence** *n.* [Latin *senex* old]

**seneschal** /**sen**-uh-shuhl/ *n.* steward of a medieval great house. [French, = old servant]

**senile** /**see**-nuyl, **sen**-uyl/ *adj.* **1** of or characteristic of old age (*senile dementia*). **2** mentally or physically infirm because of old age. □ **senility** /suh-**nil**-uh-tee/ *n.* [Latin: related to SENESCENT]

**senile dementia** *n.* illness of old people with loss of memory and control of bodily functions etc.

**senior** /**see**-nyuh/ — *adj.* **1** (often foll. by *to*) more or most advanced in age, standing, or position. **2** (placed after a person's name) senior to a relative of the same name. — *n.* **1** senior person. **2** one's elder or superior. □ **seniority** /,see-nee-o-ruh-tee/ *n.* [Latin comparative of *senex* old]

**senior citizen** *n.* elderly person.

**senior cits** /sits/ *n.pl. colloq.* **1** elderly people collectively. **2** (*attrib.*) (also **senior cit**) pertaining to elderly people (*senior cits bingo evening*; *senior cit outing*).

**senna** /**sen**-uh/ *n.* **1** cassia. **2** laxative from the dried pod of this. [Arabic]

**señor** /sen-**yaw**/ *n.* (*pl.* **señores** /-rez/) title used of or to a Spanish-speaking man. [Spanish from Latin senior SENIOR]

**señora** /sen-**yaw**-ruh/ *n.* title used of or to a Spanish-speaking married woman.

**señorita** /,sen-yuh-**ree**-tuh/ *n.* title used of or to a young or unmarried Spanish-speaking woman.

**sensation** /sen-**say**-shuhn/ *n.* **1** the consciousness of perceiving or seeming to perceive some state or condition of one's body or its parts or senses or of one's mind or its emotions; an instance of such consciousness (*lost all sensation in my left arm*; *had a sensation of being watched*; *a sensation of pride*; *in search of a new sensation*). **2 a** intense interest, shock, etc. felt among a large group (*the news caused a sensation*). **b** person, event, etc., causing this. [medieval Latin: related to SENSE]

**sensational** *adj.* **1** causing or intended to

cause great public excitement etc. **2** dazzling; wonderful (*you look sensational*). □ **sensationally** *adv.*

**sensationalise** *v.* (also **-ize**) (**-sing** or **-zing**) portray events etc. (esp. in newspaper reporting) as being more lurid, salacious, etc., than they really are.

**sensationalism** *n.* **1** use of or interest in the sensational. **2** the process of sensationalising. □ **sensationalist** *n. & adj.*

**sense** — *n.* **1 a** any of the five bodily faculties transmitting sensation (sight, hearing, touch, taste, smell). **b** sensitiveness of all or any of these (*good sense of smell*). **2** ability to perceive or feel (*stones have no sense*). **3** (foll. by *of*) consciousness; awareness (*sense of guilt*; *sense of one's own importance*). **4** quick or accurate appreciation, understanding, or instinct (*sense of humour*; *road sense*; *the moral sense*). **5** practical wisdom, common sense (*has plenty of sense*; *what is the sense of talking like that?*). **6 a** meaning of a word etc. (*the sense of the word is crystal clear*; *I mean that in the literal sense*). **b** intelligibility or coherence (*can't make sense of this passage*). **7** prevailing opinion among a number of people (*sense of the meeting*). **8** (in *pl.*) sanity, ability to think (*bring him to his senses, if you can*). — *v.* (**-sing**) **1** perceive by a sense or senses (*the kangaroos sensed our presence and hopped away*). **2** be vaguely aware of (*sensed that something was amiss*). **3** realise (*you must travel for days before you can really sense the vast emptiness of the outback*). **4** (of a machine etc.) detect (*sensed a trace of smoke and beeped its alarm*). □ **come to one's senses 1** regain consciousness. **2** regain common sense. **in a** (or **one**) **sense** if the statement etc. is understood in a particular way. **make sense** be intelligible or practicable. **make sense of** show or find the meaning of. **take leave of one's senses** go mad. [Latin *sensus* from *sentio* sens- feel]

**senseless** *adj.* **1** pointless; foolish. **2** unconscious. □ **senselessly** *adv.* **senselessness** *n.*

**sense-organ** *n.* bodily organ conveying external stimuli to the sensory system.

**sensibility** /,sen-suh-**bil**-uh-tee/ *n.* (*pl.* **-ies**) **1** capacity to feel (*lost all sensibility in his toes*). **2 a** sensitiveness, openness to emotional impressions, etc. (*he has more sensibility to fine sounds than to my feelings*). **b** exceptional degree of this. **3** (in *pl.*) tendency to feel offended etc. (*ruffled his sensibilities*).

---

■ **Usage** *Sensibility* should not be used to mean 'possession of good sense'.

**sensible** /**sen**-suh-buhl/ *adj.* **1** having or showing wisdom or common sense (*a sensible compromise*). **2 a** perceptible by the senses (*sensible phenomena*). **b** great enough to be perceived (*a sensible difference*). **3** (of clothing etc.) practical. **4** (foll. by *of*) aware (*was sensible of his peril*). □ **sensibly** *adv.*

**sensitise** /**sen**-suh-**tuyz**/ *v.* (also **-ize**)(**-sing** or **-zing**) make sensitive. □ **sensitisation** /-tuy-**zay**-shuhn/ *n.*

**sensitive** /**sen**-suh-tiv/ *adj.* **1** (often foll. by *to*) acutely susceptible to external stimuli or mental impressions; having sensibility (*highly sensitive part of the body*; *the sight of starving African children shocked his sensitive nature*). **2** easily offended or hurt. **3** (often foll. by *to*) (of an instrument etc.) responsive to or recording slight changes. **4** (of photographic materials) responding (esp. rapidly) to light. **5** (of a topic etc.) requiring tactful treatment or secrecy. □ **sensitively** *adv.* **sensitiveness** *n.* **sensitivity** /ˌsen-suh-**tiv**-uh-tee/ *n.*

**sensitive plant** *n.* plant whose leaves curve downwards and leaflets fold together when touched, esp. *Neptunia gracilis* of mainland Australia (and the naturalised *Mimosa pudica*).

**sensor** *n.* device for detecting or measuring a physical property. [from SENSORY]

**sensory** *adj.* of sensation or the senses. [Latin *sentio sens-* feel]

**sensual** /**sen**-shoo-uhl/ *adj.* **1 a** of physical, esp. sexual, pleasure. **b** enjoying or giving this, voluptuous. **2** showing sensuality (*sensual lips*). □ **sensualism** *n.* **sensually** *adv.* [Latin: related to SENSE]

■ **Usage** *Sensual* is sometimes confused with *sensuous*, which does not have the sexual overtones of *sensual*.

**sensuality** /ˌsen-shoo-**al**-uh-tee/ *n.* (esp. sexual) gratification of the senses.

**sensuous** /**sen**-shoo-uhs/ *adj.* of or affecting the senses, esp. aesthetically rather than

sensually (*the sensuous colours and forms of this painting*; *the sensuous quality of Keats's poetry*). □ **sensuously** *adv.* **sensuousness** *n.* [Latin: related to SENSE]

■ **Usage** See note at *sensual*.

**sent** *past* and *past part.* of SEND.

**sentence** /**sen**-tuhns/ — *n.* **1** statement, question, exclamation, or command containing or implying a subject and predicate (see panel). **2 a** decision of a lawcourt, esp. the punishment allotted to a convicted criminal. **b** declaration of this. — *v.* (**-cing**) **1** declare the sentence of (a convicted criminal etc.). **2** (foll. by *to*) declare (such a person) to be condemned to (a punishment) (*sentenced to three years in gaol*). [Latin *sententia* from *sentio* consider]

**sententious** /sen-**ten**-shuhs/ *adj.* **1** pompously moralising. **2** affectedly formal in style. **3** aphoristic; using maxims. □ **sententiousness** *n.* [Latin: related to SENTENCE]

**sentient** /**sen**-tee-uhnt, **sen**-shuhnt/ *adj.* capable of perception and feeling. □ **sentience** *n.* **sentiency** *n.* **sentiently** *adv.* [Latin *sentio* feel]

**sentiment** /**sen**-tuh-muhnt/ *n.* **1** mental feeling (*the sentiment of pity*). **2** (often in *pl.*) what one feels, opinion (*public sentiment on this matter is divided*). **3** opinion or feeling, as distinct from its expression (*the sentiment is good, though the words are injudicious*). **4** view or tendency based on or coloured with emotion (*moved by noble sentiments*). **5** such views collectively, esp. as an influence (*sentiment unchecked by reason is a bad guide*). **6** tendency to be swayed by feeling rather than reason (*bought it out of sentiment*). **7 a** mawkish tenderness (*oozing with sentiment*). **b** display of this.

**sentimental** /ˌsen-tuh-**men**-tuhl/ *adj.* **1** of or showing sentiment (*a sentimental reunion*). **2** showing or affected by emotion

---

**Sentence**

A sentence is the basic unit of language in use and expresses a complete thought. There are three types of sentence, each starting with a capital letter, and each normally ending with a full stop, a question mark, or an exclamation mark:

      Statement:     *You're happy.*
      Question:      *Is it raining?*
      Exclamation:  *I wouldn't have believed it!*

A sentence, especially a statement, often has no punctuation at the end in a public notice, a newspaper headline, or a legal document, e.g.

      *Government cuts public spending*

A sentence normally contains a subject and a verb, but may not, e.g.

      *What a mess!  Where?  In the sink.*

rather than reason (*she was the sentimental choice for the position, although her rival was better qualified*). **3** appealing to sentiment. □ **sentimentalise** *v.* (also **-ize**) **(-sing** or **-zing**). **sentimentalism** *n.* **sentimentalist** *n.* **sentimentality** /-tal-uh-tee/ *n.* **sentimentally** *adv.*

**sentimental value** *n.* value given to a thing because of its associations.

**sentinel** /sen-tuh-nuhl/ *n.* sentry or lookout. [French from Italian]

**sentry** /sen-tree/ *n.* (*pl.* **-ies**) soldier etc. stationed to keep guard. [perhaps from obsolete *centrinel*, var. of SENTINEL]

**sepal** /see-puhl, sep-uhl/ *n.* division or leaf of a calyx. [perhaps from SEPARATE, PETAL]

**separable** /sep-uh-ruh-buhl/ *adj.* able to be separated. □ **separability** /-bil-uh-tee/ *n.* [Latin: related to SEPARATE]

**separate** — *adj.* /sep-uh-ruht, sep-ruht/ (often foll. by *from*) forming a unit by itself, existing apart; disconnected, distinct, or individual (*living in separate rooms; the two questions are essentially separate*). — *n.* /sep-uh-ruht, sep-ruht/ (in *pl.*) trousers, skirts, etc. that are not parts of suits. — *v.* /sep-uh-,rayt/ (**-ting**) **1** make separate, sever (*separated the Siamese twins through delicate surgery*). **2** prevent union or contact of (*need to pull down the barriers that separate Aboriginal and non-Aboriginal Australians*). **3** go different ways (*kissed sadly and separated*). **4** (esp. as **separated** *adj.*) cease to live together as a married or de facto couple. **5** (foll. by *from*) secede (*some Queenslanders wanted their State to separate from Australia*). **6 a** divide or sort (milk, ore, light, etc.) into consistent parts or sizes. **b** (often foll. by *out*) extract or remove (an ingredient etc.) (*separated out the blemished fruit*). □ **separately** *adv.* **separateness** *n.* [Latin *separo* (v.)]

**separation** /,sep-uh-ray-shuhn/ *n.* **1** act or instance of separating or state of being separated. **2** usu. mutual arrangement by which a couple remain married but live apart. [Latin: related to SEPARATE]

**separatist** /sep-uh-ruh-tuhst/ *n.* person who favours separation, esp. political or ecclesiastical independence. □ **separatism** *n.*

**separator** /sep-uh-,ray-tuh/ *n.* machine for separating, e.g. cream from milk.

**sepia** /see-pee-uh/ *n.* **1** dark reddish-brown colour or paint. **2** brown tint used in photography. [Greek, = cuttlefish]

**seppo** /sep-oh/ *colloq.* — *n.* an American. — *adj.* American. [abbreviation of SEPTIC TANK 2]

**sepsis** /sep-suhs/ *n.* septic condition. [Greek: related to SEPTIC]

**September** /sep-tem-buh/ *n.* ninth month of the year. [Latin *septem* seven, originally the 7th month of the Roman year]

**septennial** /sep-ten-ee-uhl/ *adj.* **1** lasting for seven years. **2** recurring every seven years.

**septet** /sep-tet/ *n.* **1** *Mus.* **a** composition for seven performers. **b** the performers. **2** any group of seven. [Latin *septem* seven]

**septic**[1] /sep-tik/ *adj.* contaminated with bacteria from a festering sore etc., putrefying. [Greek *sēpō* rot]

**septic**[2] *n.* **1** septic tank. **2** (also **seppo**) *colloq.* an American (see SEPTIC TANK 2).

**septicaemia** /,sep-tuh-see-mee-uh/ *n.* (also **septicemia**) blood-poisoning. □ **septicaemic** *adj.* [from SEPTIC[1], Greek *haima* blood]

**septic tank** *n.* **1** tank in which sewage is disintegrated through bacterial activity. **2** *rhyming slang* 'Yank', an American.

**septuagenarian** /,sep-choo-uh-juh-nair-ree-uhn/ *n.* person from 70 to 79 years old. [Latin from *septuaginta* seventy]

**septum** /sep-tuhm/ *n.* (*pl.* **septa**) partition such as that between the nostrils or the chambers of a poppy-fruit or of a shell. [Latin *s(a)eptum* from *saepio* enclose]

**septuple** /sep-tyoo-puhl/ — *adj.* **1** sevenfold, having seven parts. **2** being seven times as many or as much. — *n.* sevenfold number or amount. [Latin *septem* seven]

**sepulchral** /suh-pul-kruhl/ *adj.* **1** of a tomb or interment. **2** funereal, gloomy. [Latin: related to SEPULCHRE]

**sepulchre** /sep-uhl-kuh/ — *n.* tomb esp. cut in rock or built of stone or brick. — *v.* (**-ring**) **1** place in a sepulchre. **2** serve as a sepulchre for. [Latin *sepelio* bury]

**sequel** /see-kwuhl/ *n.* **1** what follows (esp. as a result). **2** novel, film, etc., that continues the story of an earlier one. [Latin *sequor* follow]

**sequence** /see-kwuhns/ *n.* **1** succession. **2** order of succession (*give the facts in historical sequence*). **3** set of things belonging next to one another; unbroken series (*a sonnet sequence*). **4** part of a film dealing with one scene or topic. **5** *Mus.* repetition of a phrase or melody at a higher or lower pitch. **6** *Eccl.* hymn said or sung after the Gradual or Alleluia that precedes the Gospel (*that great sequence from the Mass for the Dead, the 'Dies irae'*). □ **sequent** *adj.* [Latin: related to SEQUEL]

**sequencer** *n.* programmable electronic device for storing sequences of musical notes, chords, etc., and transmitting them when required to an electronic musical instrument. □ **sequencing** *n.*

**sequential** /suh-**kwen**-shuhl, see-/ *adj.* forming a sequence or consequence. □ **sequentially** *adv.* [from SEQUENCE]

**sequential file** *n. Computing* set of data which must be read in the same order as it is written.

**sequester** /suh-**kwes**-tuh, see-/ *v.* **1** (esp. as **sequestered** *adj.*) seclude, isolate. **2** = SEQUESTRATE. [Latin *sequester* trustee]

**sequestrate** /suh-**kwes**-trayt, see-/ *v.* (**-ting**) **1** confiscate. **2** *Law* take temporary possession of (a debtor's estate etc.). □ **sequestration** /,see-kwuhs-**tray**-shuhn/ *n.* **sequestrator** /,see-kwuhs-,tray-tuh/ *n.* [Latin: related to SEQUESTER]

**sequin** /see-kwuhn/ *n.* circular spangle, esp. sewn on to clothing. □ **sequinned** *adj.* (also **sequined**). [Italian *zecchino* a gold coin]

**seraglio** /se-**rah**-lee-oh/ *n.* (*pl.* **-s**) harem. [Italian *serraglio* from Turkish]

**seraph** /se-ruhf/ *n.* (*pl.* **-im** or **-s**) angelic being of the highest order of the celestial hierarchy. □ **seraphic** /suh-**raf**-ik/ *adj.* [Hebrew]

**Serb** — *n.* **1** native of Serbia. **2** person of Serbian descent. — *adj.* = SERBIAN. [Serbian *Srb*]

**Serbian** /ser-bee-uhn/ — *n.* **1** dialect of the Serbs. **2** = SERB. — *adj.* of Serbia.

**Serbo-Croat** /,ser-boh-**kroh**-at/ (also **Serbo-Croatian** /kroh-**ay**-shuhn/ ) — *n.* language combining Serbian and Croatian. — *adj.* of this language.

**sere**[1] /seer/ *n.* sequence of animal or plant communities in an ecological system. [Latin *sero* join in a SERIES]

**sere**[2] *adj.* (also **sear**) *literary* (esp. of a plant etc.) withered, dried up. [Old English]

**serenade** /,se-ruh-**nayd**/ — *n.* **1** piece of music performed at night, esp. beneath a lover's window. **2** orchestral suite for a small ensemble. — *v.* (**-ding**) perform a serenade to. □ **serenader** *n.* [Italian: related to SERENE]

**serendipity** /,se-ruhn-**dip**-uh-tee/ *n.* faculty of making happy and unexpected discoveries by accident. □ **serendipitous** *adj.* [coined by Horace Walpole (1754) from *Serendip* former name of Sri Lanka (Ceylon)]

**serene** /suh-**reen**/ *adj.* (**-ner, -nest**) **1** (of the weather, sky, etc.) clear and calm. **2** (of the sea) unruffled, calm. **3** (of a person, a mood, etc.) tranquil, unperturbed. □ **serenely** *adv.* **sereneness** *n.* **serenity** /suh-**ren**-uh-tee/ *n.* [Latin]

**serf** *n.* **1** *hist.* labourer who was not allowed to leave the land on which he worked. **2** oppressed person, drudge. □ **serfdom** *n.* [Latin *servus* slave]

**serge** *n.* durable twilled worsted etc. fabric. [French *sarge, serge*]

**sergeant** /**sah**-juhnt/ *n.* **1** military officer in the Army or Air Force ranking above corporal. **2** police officer below inspector. [French *sergent* from Latin *serviens -ent*- servant]

**sergeant baker** *n.* crimson, purple, and white marine food-fish of all Australian States. [origin unknown]

**sergeant major** *n.* (in full **regimental sergeant major**) warrant officer assisting the adjutant of a regiment or battalion.

**serial** /**seer**-ee-uhl/ — *n.* (also *attrib.*) story etc. published, broadcast, or shown in regular instalments. — *adj.* **1** of, in, or forming a series (*a serial killer*). **2** *Mus.* using transformations of a fixed series of notes (see SERIES 5). □ **serially** *adv.* [from SERIES]

**serialise** *v.* (also **-ize**) (**-sing** or **-zing**) publish or produce in instalments. □ **serialisation** /-**zay**-shuhn/ *n.*

**serial killer** *n.* person who murders continually with no apparent motive.

**serial number** *n.* number identifying an item in a series.

**series** /**seer**-reez/ *n.* (*pl.* same) **1** number of similar or related things, events, etc.; succession, row, or set. **2** set of related but individual programmes. **3** *Philately* set of stamps, coins, etc., of different denominations but issued at one time, in one reign, etc. **4** set of related geological strata. **5** arrangement of the twelve notes of the chromatic scale as a basis for serial music. **6** set of electrical circuits or components arranged so that the same current passes through each successively. □ **in series** in ordered succession. [Latin *sero* join]

**serif** /se-ruhf/ *n.* slight projection at the extremities of a printed letter (as in T contrasted with T) (cf. SANSERIF). [origin uncertain]

**serio-comic** /,seer-ree-oh-**kom**-ik/ *adj.* combining the serious and the comic.

**serious** /seer-ree-uhs/ *adj.* **1** thoughtful, earnest (*serious young man*). **2** important, demanding consideration (*serious issue*). **3** not negligible; dangerous, frightening (*serious injury*). **4** sincere, in earnest, not frivolous (*are you serious?*). **5** (of music, literature, etc.) intellectual in content or appeal; not popular. □ **seriously** *adv.* **seriousness** *n.* [Latin *seriosus*]

**serjeant-at-arms** *n.* (*pl.* **serjeants-at-arms**) official of a parliament, court, etc., with ceremonial duties. [var. of SERGEANT]

**sermon** /ser-muhn/ *n.* **1** spoken or written discourse on religion or morals etc., esp. delivered in church. **2** piece of admonition

**sermonise** *v.* (also **-ize**) (**-sing** or **-zing**) moralise (to).

**serous** /seer-ruhs/ *adj.* **1** of or like serum; watery. **2** (of a gland or membrane) having a serous secretion. □ **serosity** /-ros-uh-tee/ *n.* [related to SERUM]

**serpent** /ser-puhnt/ *n.* **1** snake, esp. large. **2** sly or treacherous person. [Latin *serpo* creep]

**serpentine** /ser-puhn-,tuyn/ — *adj.* **1** of or like a serpent. **2** coiling, meandering. **3** cunning, treacherous. — *n.* soft usu. dark green rock, sometimes mottled.

**serrated** /suh-ray-tuhd/ *adj.* with a saw-like edge. □ **serration** *n.* [Latin *serra* saw]

**serried** /se-reed/ *adj.* (of ranks of soldiers etc.) close together. [French *serrer* to close]

**serum** /seer-ruhm/ *n.* (*pl.* **sera** or **-s**) **1** liquid that separates from a clot when blood coagulates, esp. used for inoculation. **2** watery fluid in animal bodies. [Latin, = whey]

**servant** /ser-vuhnt/ *n.* **1** person employed to do domestic duties, esp. in a wealthy household. **2** devoted follower or helper. **3** *hist.* (in full **assigned servant**) convict assigned to be the servant of a private person in Australia. [French: related to SERVE]

**servant of the crown** *n. hist.* euphemism for CONVICT, whether in private or official custody in Australia.

**serve** — *v.* (**-ving**) **1** do a service for (a person, community, etc.). **2** be a servant to. **3** carry out duties (*served on six committees*). **4** (foll. by *in*) be employed in (esp. the armed forces) (*served in the navy*). **5 a** be useful to or serviceable for (*serves his purpose*). **b** meet requirements; perform a function (*sofa serving as a bed*). **c** (foll. by *to* + infin.) avail, suffice (*his attempt served only to postpone the inevitable; it serves to show the folly of such action*). **6** go through a due period of (apprenticeship, office, a prison sentence, etc.). **7** present (food) to eat. **8** (in full **serve at table**) act as a waiter. **9 a** attend to (a customer etc.). **b** (foll. by *with*) supply with (goods). **10** distribute (*served the rations out*). **11** treat (a person) in a specified way (*has served me shamefully*). **12 a** (often foll. by *on*) deliver (a writ etc.) (*served a summons on him*). **b** (foll. by *with*) deliver a writ etc. to. (*served him with a summons*). **13** (also *absol.*) (in tennis etc.) deliver (a ball etc.) to begin or resume play. **14** (of an animal) copulate with (a female). — *n.* **1** = SERVICE *n.*15a, b. **2** *colloq.* severe reprimand, rebuke, adverse criticism (*got a serve from his wife for not doing the dishes*). □ **give a person a serve** see GIVE. **it will serve** it will be adequate; it will do. **serve a person right** be a person's deserved punishment etc. **serve up** *derog.* offer (*served up the same old excuses*). [Latin *servio*]

**server** *n.* **1 a** person who serves. **b** utensil for serving food. **2** (in full **altar server**) celebrant's assistant at Mass etc.

**servery** *n.* (*pl.* **-ies**) room or counter from which meals etc. are served.

**service** /ser-vuhs/ — *n.* **1 a** act of helping or doing work for another or for a community etc. (often in *pl.*: *the services of a lawyer*). **b** the work done in this way. **2** work done by a machine etc. (*has given good service*). **3** assistance or benefit given (*my guide-dog gives me invaluable service, since I am blind*). **4** provision or supplying of a public need, e.g. transport, or (often in *pl.*) of water, gas, electricity, etc. **5** employment as a servant. **6** state or period of employment (*resigned after 15 years' service*). **7** public or Crown department or organisation (*public service*). **8** (in *pl.*) the armed forces. **9** (*attrib.*) of the kind issued to the armed forces (*service revolver*). **10 a** ceremony of worship. **b** form of liturgy for this. **11 a** provision for the maintenance of a machine etc. **b** routine maintenance of a vehicle etc. **12** assistance given to customers. **13 a** serving of food, drinks, etc. **b** quality of this. **14** set of dishes, plates, etc., for serving meals (*dinner service*). **15 a** act of serving in tennis etc. **b** person's turn to serve. **c** (in full **service game**) game in which a specified player serves. — *v.* (**-cing**) **1** maintain or repair (a car, machine, etc.). **2** supply with a service. **3** pay interest etc. on (a debt). □ **at a person's service** ready to serve a person. **be of service** be helpful or useful. **in service 1** employed as a servant. **2** in use. **out of service** not available for use, not working. [Latin *servitium* from *servus* slave]

**serviceable** *adj.* **1** useful or usable; able to render service. **2** durable but plain. □ **serviceability** /-bil-uh-tee/ *n.*

**service industry** *n.* industry providing services, not goods.

**serviceman** *n.* **1** man in the armed forces. **2** man providing service or maintenance.

**service road** *n.* road serving houses, shops, etc., lying back from the main road.

**service station** *n.* = GARAGE *n.* 2.

**servicewoman** *n.* woman in the armed forces.

**serviette** /ˌser-vee-et/ n. = NAPKIN (sense 1). [French: related to SERVE]

**servile** /ser-vuyl/ adj. **1** of or like a slave. **2** fawning; subservient. □ **servility** /-vil-uh-tee/ n. [Latin *servus* slave]

**serving** n. quantity of food for one person.

**servitude** /ser-vuh-ˌtyood/ n. **1** slavery, subjection. **2** hist. (also **penal servitude**) compulsory labour to which a convict (later, a prisoner) in Australia was sentenced. [Latin *servus* slave]

**servo** /ser-voh/ n. (pl. **-s**) **1** (in full **servo-mechanism**) powered mechanism producing motion at a higher level of energy than the input level. **2** (in comb.) involving this (*servo-assisted*). [Latin *servus* slave]

**sesame** /ses-uh-mee/ n. **1** E. Indian plant with seeds used as food and yielding an edible oil. **2** its seeds. □ **open sesame** magic phrase for opening a locked door or gaining access (*lacked an open sesame to the exclusive celebrations, so he gate-crashed*). [Greek]

**Sesbania pea** /sez-bay-nee-uh/ n. = PEA-BUSH.

**sesqui-** /ses-kwee/ comb. form denoting 1½ (*sesquicentennial*). [Latin]

**sessile** /ses-uyl/ adj. **1** (of a flower, leaf, eye, etc.) attached directly by its base without a stalk or peduncle. **2** fixed in one position; immobile. [Latin: related to SESSION]

**session** /sesh-uhn/ n. **1 a** period devoted to an activity (*recording session*). **b** colloq. period spent drinking; GROG-ON. **2** assembly of a parliament, court, etc. **3** single meeting for this. **4** period during which these are regularly held. **5** division (usu. into two) of the academic year. □ **in session** assembled for business; not on vacation. □ **sessional** adj. [Latin *sedeo sess-* sit]

**sestet** /ses-tet/ n. **1** last six lines of a sonnet. **2** sextet. [Italian *sesto* sixth]

**set¹** v. (**-tt-**; past and past part. **set**) **1** put, lay, or stand in a certain position etc. (*set it on the table*; *set it upright*). **2** apply (one thing) to (another) (*set pen to paper*). **3 a** fix ready or in position (*set the mouse-trap*; *set the mast*). **b** dispose suitably for use, action, or display (*set the sails*; *set the exhibits in place*). **4 a** adjust (a clock or watch) to show the right time. **b** adjust (an alarm clock) to sound at the required time. **5 a** fix, arrange, or mount (*large, square windows set in stone*; *set the false teeth in place on the plate*). **b** insert (a jewel) in a ring etc. **6** make (a device) ready to operate. **7** lay (a table) for a meal. **8** style (the hair) while damp. **9** (foll. by *with*) ornament (a surface, esp. a precious item) (*gold brooch set with gems*). **10** make or bring into a specified

state; cause to be (*set things in motion*; *set it on fire*). **11** (of jelly, cement, etc.) harden or solidify. **12** (of the sun, moon, etc.) move towards or below the earth's horizon. **13** show (a story etc.) as happening in a certain time or place (*set the film in pre-First-Fleet Australia*). **14 a** (foll. by *to* + infin.) cause (a person or oneself) to do a specified thing (*set them to work*). **b** (foll. by pres. part.) start (a person or thing) doing something (*set the ball rolling*). **15** give as work to be done or a matter to be dealt with (*set them an essay*). **16** exhibit as a model etc. (*set an example*). **17** initiate; lead (*set the fashion*; *set the pace*). **18** establish (a record etc.). **19** determine or decide (*the itinerary is set*; *set a date for the wedding*). **20** appoint or establish (*set them in authority*). **21 a** put parts of (a broken or dislocated bone, limb, etc.) together for healing. **b** deal with (a fracture etc.) in this way. **22** (in full **set to music**) provide (words etc.) with music for singing. **23 a** compose (type etc.). **b** compose the type etc. for (a book etc.). **24** (of a tide, current, etc.) have a certain motion or direction. **25** (of a face) assume a hard expression. **26 a** cause (a hen) to sit on eggs. **b** place (eggs) for a hen to sit on. **27** (of eyes etc.) become motionless (*her eyes were set on the distant hills*; *had a set look*). **28** feel or show a certain tendency (*opinion is setting against it*). **29 a** (of blossom) form into fruit. **b** (of fruit) develop from blossom. **c** (of a tree) develop fruit. **30** (of a dancer) take a position facing one's partner. **31** (of a hunting dog) take a rigid attitude indicating the presence of game. **32 a** prescribe (a book etc.) for study. **b** formulate (an examination paper). **33** (in passive or in the phrase **to get set**) arrange (a wager), esp. in a two-up game (*get set at 10 to 1*; *all set and away she goes!*). □ **set about 1** begin or take steps towards. **2** colloq. attack. **set against 1** consider or reckon as a balance or compensation for. **2** cause to oppose. **set apart** separate, reserve, differentiate. **set aside 1** put to one side. **2** keep for future use. **3** disregard or reject. **set back 1** place further back in place or time. **2** impede or reverse the progress of. **3** colloq. cost (a person) a specified amount. **set the centre** (in two-up) ensure that the sum wagered by the spinner is covered by the players. **set down 1** record in writing. **2** allow to alight from a vehicle. **3** (foll. by *to*) attribute to (*they set the losses down to his incompetence*). **4** (foll. by *as*) explain or describe to oneself as (*set it down as a sheer coincidence*). **set eyes on** see EYE. **set foot on** (or **in**) enter or go to (a place etc.). **set forth 1** begin a journey. **2** expound. **set in 1** (of weather etc.) begin, become established. **2** insert (esp. a sleeve in a garment). **set off 1** begin a journey. **2** detonate (a bomb etc.). **3** initiate, stimulate. **4** cause (a person) to start laughing, talking, etc. **5** adorn; enhance. **6** (foll. by *against*) use as a compensating item. **set on** (or **upon**) **1** attack violently. **2** cause or urge to attack. **set a person straight** convey the true facts of a matter to a person. **set oneself up as** pretend or claim to be. **set out 1** begin a journey. **2** (foll. by *to* + infin.) intend. **3** demonstrate, arrange, or exhibit. **4** mark out. **5** declare. **set sail** hoist the sails, begin a voyage. **set to** begin vigorously, esp. fighting, arguing, or eating. **set up 1** place in position or view. **2** start (a business etc.). **3** establish in some capacity. **4** supply the needs of. **5** begin making (a loud sound) (*set up an outcry about . . .*). **6** cause (a condition or situation). **7** prepare (a task etc. for another). **8** establish (a record). **9** *colloq.* frame or cause (a person) to look foolish; cheat. [Old English]

**set²** *n.* **1** group of linked or similar things or persons. **2** *Surfing* series of waves followed by a lull. **3** section of society consorting together or having similar interests (*jet set; jazz set*). **4** collection of objects for a specified purpose (*cricket set; teaset*). **5** radio or television receiver. **6** (in tennis etc.) group of games counting as a unit towards winning a match. **7** *Math.* collection of things sharing a property. **8** habitual posture or conformation; the way the head etc. is carried or a dress etc. flows. **9** way in which a machine, device, etc., is set or adjusted. **10** setting, stage furniture, etc., for a play or film etc. **11** styling of the hair while damp. **12** *colloq.* grudge. □ **have** (or **take**) **a set on** (or **against**) **a person** *colloq.* have a grudge against him or her. [senses 1–7 from French *sette*; senses 8–12 from SET¹]

**set³** *adj.* **1** prescribed or determined in advance (*a set menu*). **b** fixed, unchanging (*set in his ways*). **2** (of a phrase or speech etc.) having invariable or predetermined wording; not extempore. **3** prepared for action. **4** (foll. by *on, upon*) determined to get or achieve etc. **5** (of a book etc.) prescribed for a course, an examination, etc. □ **get set** arrange a bet (esp. in a two-up game). **set to** likely to; about to (*interest rates are set to rise*). [past part. of SET¹]

**setback** *n.* reversal or arrest of progress; relapse.

**set piece** *n.* formal or elaborate arrangement, esp. in art or literature.

**set square** *n.* right-angled triangular plate for drawing lines, esp. at 90°, 45°, 60°, or 30°.

**settee** / se-tee, suh-**tee** / *n.* = SOFA. [origin uncertain]

**setter** *n.* dog of a long-haired breed trained to stand rigid when scenting game.

**set theory** *n.* the study or use of sets in mathematics.

**setting** *n.* **1** position or manner in which a thing is set. **2** immediate surroundings of a house etc. **3** period, place, etc., of a story, drama, etc. **4** frame etc. for a jewel. **5** music to which words are set. **6** cutlery etc. for one person at a table. **7** level at which a machine is set to operate (*on a high setting*).

**settle** / se-t-uhl / *v.* (**-ling**) **1** (often foll. by *down, in*) establish or become established in an abode or lifestyle. **2** (often foll. by *down*) **a** regain calm after disturbance; come to rest. **b** put (children) to bed. **c** adopt a regular or secure style of life (*settled down after his marriage*). **d** (foll. by *to*) apply oneself (*settled down to work*). **3** (cause to) sit, alight, or come down to stay for some time (*settled her on the sofa; the bird settled; settled in our neighbourhood for a year*). **4** make or become composed, certain, quiet, or fixed. **5** determine, decide, or agree upon (*shall we settle a date?*). **6 a** resolve (a dispute, matter, etc.). **b** deal with (a matter) finally (*settle an estate*). **7** agree to terminate (a lawsuit). **8 a** (foll. by *for*) accept or agree to (esp. a less desirable alternative) (*settled for a small, private celebration*). **b** (foll. by *on*) decide on (*settled on the green one*). **9** (also *absol.*) pay (a debt, account, etc.). **10** (as **settled** *adj.*) established; not likely to change for some time (*settled weather*). **11** calm (nerves, the stomach, etc.). **12 a** colonise. **b** establish colonists in. **c** *hist.* establish oneself, esp. as a farmer, on land not previously occupied by non-Aboriginal inhabitants. **13** subside; fall to the bottom or on to a surface (*foundations have settled; wait till the sediment settles; the dust will settle*). □ **settle up** (also *absol.*) pay (an account, debt, etc.). **settle with 1** pay (a creditor). **2** get revenge on. [Old English: related to SIT]

**settlement** *n.* **1** act or instance of settling or process of being settled. **2 a** place occupied by settlers. **b** small community, esp. in outback areas etc. **c** (often *attrib.*) an Aboriginal community. **d** *hist.* the British community established in Australia in 1788 and as subsequently enlarged; the

Aboriginal lands so occupied. **e** *hist.* the act by the British of settling in Australia (see SETTLE 12 c). **3 a** political or financial etc. agreement. **b** arrangement ending a dispute. **4 a** terms on which property is given to a person. **b** deed stating these. **c** amount or property given.

**settler** *n.* **1** person who goes to settle in a new country or place. **2 a** *hist.* British person who settled in Australia; a (small) farmer (see SETTLE 12 c). **b** (as **old settler**) (also *attrib.*) one of the earliest British colonists in Australia or in a particular district (of Australia) (*descended from the old settlers; comes from an old settler family*).

**settler's clock** *n.* = KOOKABURRA.

**set-to** *n.* (*pl.* **-tos**) *colloq.* fight, argument.

**set-up** *n.* **1** arrangement or organisation. **2** manner, structure, or position of this. **3** instance of setting a person up (see *set up* 9).

**seven** /**sev**-uhn/ *adj. & n.* **1** one more than six. **2** symbol for this (7, vii, VII). **3** seven o'clock. □ **chuck** (or **throw**) **a seven** *colloq.* **1** die; faint. **2** lose one's temper. **3** vomit. [Old English]

**sevener** /**sev**-uh-nuh/ *n. hist.* convict sentenced to seven years of penal servitude in Australia (opp. LIFER).

**sevenfold** *adj. & adv.* **1** seven times as much or as many. **2** consisting of seven parts.

**seven seas** *n.* (prec. by *the*) the oceans of the world.

**seventeen** /ˌsev-uhn-**teen**/ *adj. & n.* **1** one more than sixteen. **2** symbol for this (17, xvii, XVII). □ **seventeenth** *adj. & n.* [Old English]

**seventh** *adj. & n.* **1** next after sixth. **2** one of seven equal parts of a thing. □ **seventhly** *adv.*

**Seventh-Day Adventist** *n.* member of a Protestant sect observing the sabbath on Saturday.

**seventh heaven** *n.* state of intense joy.

**seventy** /**sev**-uhn-tee/ *adj. & n.* (*pl.* **-ies**) **1** seven times ten. **2** symbol for this (70, lxx, LXX). **3** (in *pl.*) numbers from 70 to 79, esp. the years of a century or of a person's life. □ **seventieth** *adj. & n.* [Old English]

**sever** /**sev**-uh/ *v.* **1** divide, break, or make separate, esp. by cutting (*severed an artery*). **2** break off or away; separate (*severed our friendship*). **3** end the employment contract (of a person). [Anglo-French *severer* from Latin *separo*]

**several** /**sev**-ruhl/ — *adj. & pron.* more than two but not many; a few. — *adj. formal* separate or respective (*went their several ways*). □ **severally** *adv.* [Latin *separ* distinct]

**severance** *n.* **1** act of severing. **2** severed state.

**severance pay** *n.* payment made to an employee on termination of a contract.

**severe** /suh-**veer**/ *adj.* **1** rigorous and harsh (*severe critic*). **2** serious (*severe shortage*). **3** forceful (*severe storm*). **4** extreme (*severe winter*). **5** exacting (*severe competition*). **6** plain in style (*wore a severe dress*). □ **severely** *adv.* **severity** /-**ve**-ruh-tee/ *n.* [Latin *severus*]

**sew** /soh/ *v.* (*past part.* **sewn** or **sewed**) **1** fasten, join, etc., with a needle and thread or a sewing machine. **2** make (a garment etc.) by such means. □ **sew up 1** join or enclose by sewing. **2** (esp. in *passive*) *colloq.* satisfactorily arrange or finish; gain control of; be more than likely to win (*the plans are sewn up; Essendon have got the game sewn up with that goal*). [Old English]

**sewage** /**soo**-ij/ *n.* waste matter conveyed in sewers. [from SEWER]

**sewage farm** *n.* (also **sewage works**) place where sewage is treated.

**sewer** /**soo**-uh/ *n.* conduit, usu. underground, for carrying off drainage water and sewage. [Anglo-French *sever* (e): related to EX-¹, *aqua* water]

**sewerage** /**soor**-rij/ *n.* system of, or drainage by, sewers.

**sewing** /**soh**-ing/ *n.* material or work to be sewn.

**sewn** *past part.* of SEW.

**sex** — *n.* **1** each of the main groups (male and female) into which living things are categorised on the basis of their reproductive functions (*what sex is your dog?*). **2** sexual instincts, desires, etc., or their manifestation. **3** sexual intercourse. **4** (*attrib.*) of or relating to sex or sexual differences (*sex education; sex antagonism; the sex urge*). — *v.* **1** determine the sex of. **2** (as **sexed** *adj.*) having a specified sexual appetite (*highly sexed*). [Latin *sexus*]

**sexagenarian** /ˌsek-suh-juh-**nair**-ree-uhn/ *n.* person from 60 to 69 years old. [Latin from *sexaginta* sixty]

**sex appeal** *n.* sexual attractiveness.

**sex change** *n.* apparent change of sex by hormone treatment and surgery.

**sexism** *n.* prejudice or discrimination, esp. against women, on the grounds of sex. □ **sexist** *adj. & n.*

**sexless** *adj.* **1** neither male nor female. **2** lacking sexual desire or attractiveness.

**sex maniac** *n. colloq.* person obsessed with sex.

**sex object** *n.* person regarded not as a person but solely as an object of sexual gratification.

**sex offender** *n.* person who commits a sexual crime.

**sex symbol** *n.* person widely noted for sex appeal.

**sextant** /**seks**-tuhnt/ *n.* instrument with a graduated arc of 60°, used in navigation and surveying for measuring the angular distance of objects by means of mirrors. [Latin *sextans -tantis* sixth part]

**sextet** /seks-**tet**/ *n.* **1** *Mus.* a composition for six performers. **b** the performers. **2** any group of six. [alteration of SESTET after Latin *sex* six]

**sexton** /**seks**-tuhn/ *n.* person who looks after a church and churchyard, often acting as bell-ringer and gravedigger. [French *segerstein* from Latin *sacristanus*]

**sextuple** /**seks**-, tyoo-puhl/ — *adj.* **1** sixfold. **2** having six parts. **3** being six times as many or as much. — *n.* sixfold number or amount. [medieval Latin from Latin *sex* six]

**sextuplet** /seks-**tup**-luht, -**tyoo**-pluht/ *n.* each of six children born at one birth.

**sexual** /**sek**-shoo-uhl/ *adj.* of sex, the sexes, or relations between them. □ **sexually** *adv.*

**sexual harassment** *n.* subjection of a person to unwelcome sexual advances, actions, words, etc., esp. in the workplace.

**sexual intercourse** *n.* method of reproduction involving insertion of the penis into the vagina, usu. followed by ejaculation.

**sexuality** /sek-shoo-**al**-uh-tee, seks-yoo-/ *n.* **1** the fact of belonging to one of the sexes; one's sexual orientation or preference. **2** sexual feelings, desires, etc.

**sexually transmitted disease** *n.* any disease which is transmitted by sexual contact, e.g. AIDS, syphilis, gonorrhoea, etc.

**sex worker** *n.* person who offers sex etc. for payment; prostitute.

**sexy** *adj.* (**-ier, -iest**) **1** sexually attractive, stimulating, or aroused. **2** *colloq.* (of a project etc.) exciting, trendy. □ **sexily** *adv.* **sexiness** *n.*

**SF** *abbr.* science fiction.

**sf** *abbr.* sforzando.

**sforzando** /sfaw-**tsan**-doh/ — *adj. & adv. Mus.* with sudden emphasis. — *n.* (*pl.* **-s** or **-di** /-dee/ ) **1** suddenly emphasised note or group of notes. **2** increase in emphasis and loudness. [Italian]

**Sgt.** *abbr.* Sergeant.

**sh** *int.* = HUSH.

**shabby** /**shab**-ee/ *adj.* (**-ier, -iest**) **1** faded and worn, dingy, dilapidated. **2** contemptible (*a shabby trick*). □ **shabbily** *adv.* **shabbiness** *n.* [related to SCAB]

**shack** — *n.* roughly built hut or cabin; small holiday house. — *v.* (foll. by *up*) *colloq.* cohabit, esp. as lovers. [perhaps from Mexican *jacal* wooden hut]

**shackle** /**shak**-uhl/ — *n.* **1** metal loop or link, closed by a bolt, used to connect chains etc. **2** fetter for the ankle or wrist. **3** (usu. in *pl.*) restraint, impediment (*grumbled about the shackles of marriage*). — *v.* (**-ling**) fetter, impede, restrain. [Old English]

**shade** — *n.* **1** comparative darkness (and usu. coolness) given by shelter from direct light and heat. **2** area so sheltered. **3** darker part of a picture etc. **4** colour, esp. as darker or lighter than one similar. **5** comparative obscurity. **6** slight amount (*a shade better*). **7** lampshade. **8** screen against the light. **9** slightly different variety (*all shades of opinion*). **10** *literary* ghost. **11** (in *pl.*; foll. by *of*) reminder of, suggesting (esp. something undesirable) (*shades of Hitler!*). — *v.* (**-ding**) **1** screen from light. **2** cover, moderate, or exclude the light of. **3** darken, esp. with parallel lines to show modelling etc. **4** (often foll. by *away, off, into*) pass or change gradually. [Old English]

**shadecloth** *n.* network fabric, usu. made of plastic, used in shadehouses etc., esp. to provide tender plants with (differing degrees of) protection from the summer sun.

**shadehouse** *n.* structure, usu. roofed and sided with shadecloth, in which sensitive plants may be shaded from the summer sun.

**shading** *n.* light and shade shown on a map or drawing by parallel lines etc.

**shadow** /**shad**-oh/ — *n.* **1** shade; patch of shade. **2** dark shape projected by a body intercepting rays of light. **3** inseparable attendant or companion; bosom friend, constant mate. **4** person secretly following another to spy etc. **5** slightest trace (*not a shadow of doubt*). **6** weak or insubstantial remnant (*a shadow of his former self*). **7** (*attrib.*) denoting members of an opposition party holding posts parallel to those of the government (*shadow cabinet*). **8** shaded part of a picture. **9 a** gloom, sadness, unease, etc. (*the episode cast a shadow over their friendship*). **b** ongoing threat (*their marriage was under a shadow*; *living in the shadow of war*). — *v.* **1** cast a shadow over. **2** secretly follow and watch. [Old English: related to SHADE]

**shadow-boxing** *n.* boxing with an imaginary opponent as training.

**shadowy** *adj.* **1** like or having a shadow. **2** vague, indistinct.

**shady** /**shay**-dee/ *adj.* (**-ier, -iest**) **1** giving shade. **2** situated in shade. **3** disreputable; of doubtful honesty. □ **shadily** *adv.* **shadiness** *n.*

**shaft** /shahft/ — n. **1** narrow usu. vertical space, for access to a mine, or (in a building) for a lift, ventilation, etc. **2** (foll. by of) **a** a ray (of light). **b** bolt (of lightning). **3** stem or handle of a tool etc. **4** long narrow part supporting, connecting, or driving thicker part(s) etc. **5 a** archaic arrow, spear. **b** its long slender stem. **6** hurtful or provocative remark (shaft of malice; shafts of wit). **7** each of the pair of poles between which a horse is harnessed to a vehicle. **8** central stem of a feather. **9** column, esp. between the base and capital. **10** Mech. large axle or revolving bar transferring force by belts or cogs. **11** colloq. harsh or unfair treatment (gave him the shaft). — v. colloq. treat harshly or unfairly (was shafted by his best friend). [Old English]

**shag¹** n. **1** coarse kind of cut tobacco. **2 a** rough mass of hair etc. **b** (attrib.) (of a carpet) with a long rough pile **3** cormorant. □ **shag on a rock** emblem of isolation, deprivation, etc. (living all alone like a shag on a rock). [Old English]

**shag²** v. (-gg-) coarse colloq. **1** have sexual intercourse with. **2** (usu. in passive; often foll. by out) exhaust, tire out. [origin unknown]

**shaggy** adj. (-ier, -iest) **1** hairy, rough-haired. **2** unkempt. □ **shagginess** n.

**shaggy-dog story** n. long rambling joke, amusing only by its pointlessness.

**shagreen** /shuh-**green**/ n. **1** a kind of untanned granulated leather. **2** sharkskin. [var. of CHAGRIN]

**shagwagon** n. (also **shaggin' wagon**) colloq. panel van fitted out for sleeping in, as a convenient place in which to engage in sex etc.

**shah** n. hist. former monarch of Iran. [Persian]

**shake** — v. (-king; past **shook** /shuuk/; past part. **shaken**) **1 a** move forcefully or quickly up and down or to and fro. **b** (cause to) move in this way to dislodge something adhering to or discharge something contained (the dog shook and we were drenched; shook the crumbs off the tablecloth; shook the bottle to get the sauce out). **2** (cause to) tremble or vibrate (he shook with fear). **3** agitate, shock, or upset the composure of (was shaken by the news). **4** weaken or impair in courage, effectiveness, etc. (shook his confidence). **5** (of a voice, note, etc.) tremble; trill (a voice shaking with emotion). **6** gesture with (one's fist, a stick, etc.). **7** shake hands (they shook on the deal). **8** colloq. steal (something); rob (someone). — n. **1** act or instance of shaking or process of being shaken. **2** jerk or shock. **3** (in pl.;

prec. by the) colloq. fit of trembling (has got the shakes). **4** Mus. trill. **5** = MILKSHAKE. **6** colloq. very short period of time (be with you in half a shake). □ **be shook on** (or **after**) colloq. be enamoured of; be well-disposed towards. **no great shakes** colloq. mediocre, poor. **shake down 1** settle or cause to fall by shaking. **2** settle down; become adjusted to new conditions. **3** sleep in an improvised bed. **shake hands** (often foll. by with) clasp hands as a greeting, farewell, in congratulation, as confirmation of a deal, etc. **shake one's head** turn one's head from side to side in refusal, denial, disapproval, or concern. **shake off** get rid of or evade (a person or thing). **shake out 1** empty by shaking. **2** open (a sail, flag, etc.) by shaking. **shake up 1** mix by shaking. **2** restore to shape by shaking. **3** disturb or make uncomfortable; rouse from apathy, conventionality, etc. [Old English]

**shake-a-leg** n. style of traditional Aboriginal dancing.

**shakedown merchant** n. colloq. = CONFIDENCE MAN.

**shaker** n. **1** person or thing that shakes. **2** container for shaking together the ingredients of cocktails etc. **3** machine in which auriferous gravel, sand, etc., is agitated to separate out alluvial gold without the need of water.

**shaker dryblower** n. machine which combines the properties of a SHAKER (sense 3) and a DRYBLOWER.

**Shakespearean** /shayk-**speer**-ree-uhn/ adj. (also **Shakespearian**) of Shakespeare.

**shake-up** n. upheaval or drastic reorganisation.

**shaky** adj. (-ier, -iest) **1** unsteady; trembling. **2** unsound, infirm. **3** unreliable. □ **shakily** adv. **shakiness** n.

**Shaky Isles** n. (also **Shakey Isles**) colloq. New Zealand (from the frequency there of earthquakes).

**shale** n. soft rock of consolidated mud or clay that splits easily. □ **shaly** adj. [German: related to SCALE²]

**shall** /shal/ v.aux. (3rd sing. present **shall**; archaic 2nd sing. present **shalt**; past **should** /shuud/) (foll. by infin. without to, or absol.; present and past only in use) **1** (in the 1st person singular and plural) expressing the simple future tense (I shall return soon) or (with shall stressed in speech) emphatic intention (I shall have a party). **2** (in the 2nd and 3rd persons singular and plural) expressing a strong assertion, command, or duty, rather than the simple future (cf. WILL¹) (you shall go to the party; thou shalt not steal; you shall obey). **3** (in 2nd-person questions) expressing an enquiry, esp. to avoid the form of a request (cf. WILL¹) (*shall you go to Oodnadatta?*). □ **shall I?** (or **we**) do you want me (or us) to? (*shall I go?*; *shall we dance?*). [Old English]

■ **Usage** The distinction between the use of *shall* in the 1st person (expressing the simple future) and *shall* in the 2nd and 3rd persons (expressing determination etc.) remains valid, but in common (esp. *colloq.* usage) *shall* is used to express determination in all persons, and *will* is used in all persons to express the simple future, with an increasing tendency for the emphatic use of *will* to replace *shall*.

**shallot** /shuh-**lot**/ *n.* **1** onion-like plant with a cluster of small bulbs. **2** any long-necked onion with a small bulb. [French]

**shallow** /**shal**-oh/ — *adj.* **1** of little depth. **2** superficial, trivial (*a shallow remark*). — *n.* (often in *pl.*) shallow place. □ **shallowness** *n.* [Old English]

**shalom** /shuh-**lom**/ *n.* & *int.* Jewish salutation at meeting or parting. [Hebrew]

**shalt** *archaic* 2nd person sing. of SHALL.

**sham** — *v.* (**-mm-**) **1** feign, pretend (*is only shamming*). **2** pretend to be; simulate (*is shamming sleep*). — *n.* **1** imposture, pretence. **2** bogus or false person or thing. — *adj.* pretended, counterfeit. [origin unknown]

**shaman** /**shah**-muhn, **shay**-/ *n.* witch-doctor or priest claiming to communicate with gods etc. □ **shamanism** *n.* [Russian]

**shamble** /**sham**-buhl/ — *v.* (**-ling**) walk or run awkwardly, dragging the feet. — *n.* shambling gait. [perhaps related to SHAMBLES]

**shambles** *n.pl.* (usu. treated as *sing.*) **1** *colloq.* mess, muddle. **2** butcher's slaughterhouse. **3** scene of carnage. [pl. of *shamble* table for selling meat]

**shambolic** /sham-**bol**-ik/ *adj. colloq.* chaotic, unorganised. [from SHAMBLES after *symbolic*]

**shame** — *n.* **1** distress or humiliation caused by consciousness of one's guilt, dishonour, or folly. **2** capacity for feeling this (*has no sense of shame*). **3** state of disgrace or discredit. **4 a** person or thing that brings disgrace etc. **b** thing that is wrong or regrettable (*it's a shame you didn't get an invitation*). — *v.* (**-ming**) **1** bring shame on; make ashamed; put to shame. **2** (foll. by *into*, *out of*) force by shame (*shamed into confessing*). — *adj.* (in Aboriginal English) self-conscious, embarrassed. □ **put to shame** humiliate by being greatly superior. [Old English]

**shamefaced** *adj.* **1** showing shame. **2** bashful, shy. □ **shamefacedly** *adv.*

**shameful** *adj.* disgraceful, scandalous. □ **shamefully** *adv.* **shamefulness** *n.*

**shame job** *n.* (in Aboriginal English) an act occasioning embarrassment.

**shameless** *adj.* **1** having or showing no shame. **2** impudent. □ **shamelessly** *adv.*

**shammy** /**sham**-ee/ *n.* (*pl.* **-ies**) (in full **shammy leather**) *colloq.* = CHAMOIS 2. [representing corrupted pronunciation]

**shampoo** /sham-**poo**/ — *n.* **1** liquid for washing the hair. **2** similar substance for washing cars, carpets, etc. — *v.* (**-poos**, **-pooed**) wash with shampoo. [Hindustani]

**shamrock** /**sham**-rok/ *n.* clover-like plant with trifoliate leaves, used as an emblem of Ireland. [Irish]

**shandy** /**shan**-dee/ *n.* (*pl.* **-ies**) beer with lemonade or ginger beer. [origin unknown]

**shanghai** /shang-**huy**/ — *v.* (**-hais**, **-haied**, **-haiing**) **1** *colloq.* trick or force someone into doing something. **2** force (a person) into serving as a sailor by using drugs or other trickery. **3** shoot with a catapult. **4** *colloq.* steal. — *n.* (*pl.* **shanghais**) a (child's) catapult, ging. [*Shanghai* in China]

**shank** *n.* **1 a** leg. **b** lower part of the leg. **c** shin-bone. **2** shaft or stem, esp. the part of a tool etc. joining the handle to the working end. [Old English]

**shanks's pony** *n.* (also **shanks's mare**) one's own legs as transport.

**shan't** /shahnt/ *contr.* shall not.

**shantung** /shan-**tung**/ *n.* soft undressed Chinese silk. [*Shantung*, Chinese province]

**shanty¹** /**shan**-tee/ *n.* (*pl.* **-ies**) **1** hut or cabin. **2** crudely built shack. **3 a** (in full **grog shanty**) *hist.* roughly constructed unlicensed public house, esp. on a goldfield. **b** small tavern, usu. in a rural area. [origin unknown]

**shanty²** /**shan**-tee/ *n.* (*pl.* **-ies**) (in full **sea shanty**) sailors' work song. [probably French *chanter* to CHANT]

**shanty town** *n.* area with makeshift housing.

**shape** — *n.* **1** effect produced by a thing's outline. **2** external form or appearance. **3** specific form or guise (*in the shape of an excuse*). **4** definite or proper arrangement (*must get our ideas into shape*). **5 a** condition, as qualified in some way (*in good shape*; *in poor shape*). **b** (when unqualified) good condition (*back in shape*). **6** person or thing seen in outline or indistinctly (*a shape emerged from the mist*). **7** mould or pattern. **8** piece of material, paper, etc., made or cut in a particular form. — *v.* (**-ping**) **1** give a

certain shape or form to; fashion, create.
**2** influence (one's life, course, etc.) (*the events that shaped his life*). **3** (foll. by *to*) adapt or make conform (*shaped his policies to accord with public opinion*). □ **in any shape or form** in any form at all (*don't like jazz in any shape or form*). **lick** (or **knock**) **into shape** make presentable or efficient. **shape up** show promise; make good progress; perform better (*is shaping up well*; *shape up or get out!*). **take shape** take on a definite form. [Old English]

**shapeless** *adj.* lacking definite or attractive shape. □ **shapelessness** *n.*

**shapely** *adj.* (**-ier, -iest**) pleasing in appearance, elegant, well-proportioned. □ **shapeliness** *n.*

**shard** *n.* broken piece of pottery or glass etc. [Old English]

**share** — *n.* **1** portion of a whole allotted to or taken from a person. **2 a** part contributed by an individual to an enterprise or commitment. **b** part received by an individual from this (*got a large share of the credit*). **3** each of the equal parts into which a company's capital is divided, entitling its owner to a proportion of the profits. — *v.* (**-ring**) **1** (also *absol.*) have or use with another or others; get, have, or give a share of (*we shared a room*; *refused to share*; *shared his food*). **2** (foll. by *in*) participate. **3** (often foll. by *out*) divide and distribute (*let's share the last cake*). **4** have in common (*shared the same beliefs*). [Old English: related to SHEAR]

**share-farmer** *n.* one of two or more people contributing part of resources required to produce crop etc., and receiving proportional share of the profits. □ **share-farm** *n.* **share-farming** *n.*

**shareholder** *n.* owner of shares in a company.

**shark**[1] *n.* large voracious marine fish with a prominent dorsal fin. [origin unknown]

**shark**[2] — *n. colloq.* swindler, profiteer. — *v.* **1** *colloq.* obtain by swindling; steal. **2** *Aust. Rules* interrupt (steal) a ball being passed between two opponents, esp. at ball-ups or throw-ins. [origin unknown]

**shark bait** *n.* person who swims alone or well out from the shore.

**shark meshing** *n.* the netting of sharks off coastal beaches patronised by swimmers.

**shark patrol** *n.* patrol of surfing beaches by boat or aircraft to warn swimmers of the presence of sharks.

**sharkskin** *n.* smooth slightly shiny fabric.

**shark spotter** *n.* person who watches for sharks at surf beaches etc. □ **shark spotting** *n.*

**sharp** — *adj.* **1** having an edge or point able to cut or pierce. **2** tapering to a point or edge. **3** abrupt, steep, angular (*a sharp fall*; *a sharp turn*). **4** well-defined, clean-cut (*sharp features*; *a good sharp picture on telly*). **5 a** severe or intense (*a sharp pain*). **b** (of weather etc.) cuttingly cold (*a sharp wind*). **c** (of food etc.) pungent, acid. **6** (of a voice etc.) shrill and piercing. **7** (of words or temper etc.) harsh (*a sharp tongue*). **8** acute; quick to understand (*the sharpest girl in the class*). **9** artful, unscrupulous (*sharp practices*). **10** vigorous or brisk (*a sharp walk before breakfast*). **11** *Mus.* above the normal pitch; a semitone higher than a specified pitch (*C sharp*). — *n.* **1** *Mus.* **a** note a semitone above natural pitch. **b** sign (♯) indicating this. **2** *colloq.* swindler, cheat. — *adv.* **1** punctually (*at nine o'clock sharp*). **2** suddenly (*pulled up sharp*). **3** at a sharp angle. **4** *Mus.* above true pitch (*sings sharp*). □ **as sharp as a bowling ball** *colloq.* stupid. **as sharp as a tack** *colloq.* intelligent; quick-witted. □ **sharply** *adv.* **sharpness** *n.* [Old English]

**sharpen** *v.* make or become sharp. □ **sharpener** *n.*

**sharp practice** *n.* dishonest or dubious dealings.

**sharpshooter** *n.* skilled marksman.

**sharp-witted** *adj.* keenly perceptive or intelligent.

**shashlik** / shash-lik / *n.* (also **shaslik**) eastern European and Asian kebab of mutton and garnishings, usu. served on a skewer. [Russian from Turkish]

**shat** *past* and *past. part.* of SHIT.

**shatter** *v.* **1** break suddenly in pieces. **2** severely damage or destroy. **3** (esp. in *passive*) greatly upset or discompose. [origin unknown]

**shatterwood** *n.* rainforest tree of Queensland and NSW, having aromatic foliage, showy white flowers, and timber which tends to shatter easily.

**shave** — *v.* (**-ving**; *past part.* **shaved** or (as *adj.*) **shaven**) **1** remove (bristles or hair) with a razor. **2** (also *absol.*) remove bristles or hair with a razor from (a person, face, leg, etc.). **3** reduce by a small amount. **4** pare (wood etc.) to shape it. **5** miss or pass narrowly. — *n.* **1** act of shaving or process of being shaved. **2** narrow miss or escape (*a close shave*). **3** tool for shaving wood etc. [Old English]

**shaver** *n.* **1** thing that shaves. **2** electric razor. **3** *colloq.* young lad.

**shaving** *n.* thin strip cut off wood etc.

**shawl** *n.* large usu. rectangular piece of fabric worn over the shoulders or head, or wrapped round a baby. [Urdu from Persian *shāl*]

**she** /shee/ — *pron.* (*obj.* **her**; *poss.* **her**; *pl.* **they**) **1** the woman, girl, female animal, ship, or country, etc., previously named or in question. **2** (in Australia) applied to things to which the female sex is not conventionally attributed, = it; the state of affairs; etc. ('*Bet you five to one.*' — '*She's on!*'; *she's starting to get a bit chilly*; *she'll be right*; *she's a beaut ditch — best I ever dug*) (cf. APPLES; RIGHT; SWEET). **3** (*attrib.*) used in the names of some Australian trees, apparently indicative of the perceived inferiority of the timber (*she-oak*; *she pine*). — *n.* **1** female; woman. **2** (in *comb.*) female (*she-goat*). [Old English]

**s/he** *pron.* written representation of 'he or she' used to indicate either sex.

**sheaf** — *n.* (*pl.* **sheaves**) bundle of things laid lengthways together and usu. tied, esp. reaped corn or a collection of papers. — *v.* make into sheaves. [Old English]

**sheaf tossing** *n.* sport (esp. at country shows) of tossing a sheaf or bag of straw, usu. with a pitchfork, as high as possible.

**shear** — *v.* (*past* **sheared** or (esp. in shearers' use) **shore**; *past part.* **shorn** or **sheared**) **1** (also *absol.*) clip the wool off (a sheep etc.). **2** remove or take off by cutting. **3** cut with scissors or shears etc. **4** be employed as a shearer (*he shore from one end of Australia to the other*). **5** (foll. by *of*) **a** strip bare. **b** deprive. **6** (often foll. by *off*) distort, be distorted, or break, from structural strain. — *n.* **1** Mech. & Geol. strain produced by pressure in the structure of a substance when its layers are laterally shifted in relation to each other. **2** (in *pl.*) (also **pair of shears** *sing.*) large scissor-shaped clipping or cutting instrument. □ **off (the) shears** (of sheep) newly shorn. □ **shearing** *n.* (also *attrib.*) [Old English]

**shearer** *n.* itinerant worker hired seasonally to shear sheep.

**shearing shed** *n.* building in which sheep are shorn and fleeces processed and packed.

**shearwater** *n.* any of various long-winged seabirds, usu. flying near to the surface of the water, many of which migrate to Australian waters, often breeding on coastal islands (*wedge-tailed shearwater*; *fleshy-footed shearwater*).

**sheath** *n.* (*pl.* **-s** /sheethz, sheeths/) **1** close-fitting cover, esp. for the blade of a knife or sword. **2** condom. **3** enclosing case, covering, or tissue. **4** woman's close-fitting dress. [Old English]

**sheathe** /sheeth/ *v.* (**-thing**) **1** put into a sheath. **2** encase; protect with a sheath.

**sheath knife** *n.* dagger-like knife carried in a sheath.

**sheaves** *pl.* of SHEAF.

**shebang** /shuh-**bang**/ *n. colloq.*, matter or affair (*I'm fed up with the whole shebang*). [origin unknown]

**shed¹** *n.* **1** one-storeyed structure for storage or shelter, or as a workshop. **2** = SHEARING SHED. **3** (also *attrib.*) gang of shearers working in a particular shed (*the shed went on strike*; *topped the shed tally and was declared the ringer*). [from SHADE]

**shed²** *v.* (**-dd-**; *past* and *past part.* **shed**) **1** let, or cause to, fall off (*trees shed their leaves*). **2** take off (clothes). **3** reduce (an electrical power load) by disconnection etc. **4** cause to fall or flow (*shed blood*; *shed tears*). **5** disperse, diffuse, radiate (*shed light*). **6** get rid of (*the company is shedding 200 jobs*; *shed your inhibitions*). □ **shed light on** help to explain. [Old English]

**she'd** /sheed/ *contr.* **1** she had. **2** she would.

**shed-hand** *n.* unskilled worker in a shearing shed.

**sheen** *n.* **1** gloss or lustre. **2** brightness. □ **sheeny** *adj.* [Old English, = beautiful]

**sheep** *n.* (*pl.* same) **1** mammal with a thick woolly coat, esp. kept for its wool or meat. **2** timid, silly, or easily led person. □ **on** (or **off**) **the sheep's back** used in allusion to wool as the source of the nation's prosperity (*politicians often claimed that Australia lives off the sheep's back*). **separate the sheep from the goats** divide into superior and inferior groups (cf. Matt. 25: 33). [Old English]

**sheep-bush** *n.* = WILGA.

**sheep-dip** *n.* preparation or place for cleansing sheep of vermin etc. by dipping.

**sheepdog** *n.* **1** dog trained to guard and herd sheep. **2** dog of a breed suitable for this.

**sheepish** *adj.* embarrassed or shy; ashamed. □ **sheepishly** *adv.*

**sheep-run** *n.* tract (often extensive) of land used for grazing sheep.

**sheep-sick** *adj.* (of land) degraded as a result of over-grazing sheep.

**sheepskin** *n.* **1** garment or rug of sheep's skin with the wool on. **2** leather from sheep's skin used in bookbinding etc.

**sheep station** *n.* extensive establishment for the raising of sheep.

**sheer¹** — *adj.* **1** mere, complete (*sheer luck*). **2** (of a cliff etc.) perpendicular. **3** (of a textile) very thin, diaphanous. — *adv.* directly, perpendicularly. [Old English]

**sheer²** v. **1** esp. *Naut.* swerve or change course. **2** (foll. by *away*, *off*) turn away, esp. from a person or topic one dislikes or fears. [origin unknown]

**sheet¹** — n. **1** large rectangle of cotton etc. used esp. in pairs as inner bedclothes. **2** broad usu. thin flat piece of paper, metal, etc. **3** wide expanse of water, ice, flame, falling rain, etc. **4** page of unseparated postage stamps. — v. **1** provide or cover with sheets. **2** form into sheets. **3** (of rain etc.) fall in sheets. [Old English]

**sheet²** n. rope or chain attached to the lower corner of a sail to hold or control it. [Old English: related to SHEET¹]

**sheet anchor** n. **1** emergency reserve anchor. **2** person or thing depended on in the last resort.

**sheet lightning** n. lightning-flash with its brightness diffused by reflection.

**sheet metal** n. metal rolled or hammered etc. into thin sheets.

**sheet music** n. music published in sheets, not bound.

**sheikh** /shayk, sheek/ n. **1** chief or head of an Arab tribe, family, or village. **2** Muslim leader. □ **sheikhdom** n. [Arabic]

**sheila** /shee-luh/ n. *colloq.* usu. *offens.* girl, young woman; girlfriend. [origin uncertain]

**shekel** /shek-uhl/ n. **1** *hist.* silver coin and unit of weight in ancient Israel etc. **2** the unit of money in modern Israel. **3** (in *pl.*) *colloq.* money; riches. [Hebrew]

**shelduck** /shel-duk/ n. (*pl.* same or **-s**; *masc.* **sheldrake**, *pl.* same or **-s**) any of various bright-plumaged wild ducks, including the *Australian shelduck.* [probably from British dial. *sheld* pied, DUCK¹]

**shelf¹** n. (*pl.* **shelves**) **1 a** wooden etc. board projecting from a wall, or as part of a unit, used to store things. **b** contents of such a shelf (*a shelf of books*). **2 a** projecting horizontal ledge in a cliff face etc. **b** reef or sandbank. □ **on the shelf 1** (of a woman) *offens.* regarded as too old to hope for marriage. **2** (esp. of a retired person) put aside as if no longer useful. [Low German]

**shelf²** *colloq.* — n. informer. — v. inform upon.

**shelf-life** n. time for which a stored item remains usable.

**shelf-mark** n. code on a library book showing where it is kept.

**shell** — n. **1 a** hard outer case of many molluscs, the tortoise, etc. **b** hard but fragile case of an egg. **c** hard outer case of a nut-kernel, seed, etc. **2 a** explosive projectile for use in a big gun etc. **b** hollow container for fireworks, cartridges, etc. **c** cartridge. **3** shell-like thing, esp.: **a** a light racing-boat. **b** the metal framework of a vehicle etc. **c** the walls of an unfinished or gutted building, ship, etc. **4** mere semblance or outer form without substance (*a mere shell of his former self*). **5** group of electrons with almost equal energy to an atom. — v. **1** remove the shell or pod from. **2** bombard with shells. □ **come out of one's shell** become less shy and more sociable. **shell out** (also *absol.*) *colloq.* pay (money). □ **shell-less** adj. **shell-like** adj. [Old English]

**she'll** /sheel/ *contr.* she will; she shall.

**shellac** /shuh-**lak**/ — n. resin used for making varnish. — v. (**-ck-**) varnish with shellac. [from SHELL, LAC]

**shellfish** n. (*pl.* same) **1** aquatic mollusc with a shell. **2** crustacean.

**shell-shock** n. nervous breakdown caused by warfare. □ **shell-shocked** adj.

**shelter** — n. **1** protection from danger, bad weather, etc. **2** place giving shelter or refuge. — v. **1** act or serve as a shelter to; protect; conceal; defend (*sheltered them from the storm*; *had a sheltered upbringing*). **2** find refuge; take cover (*sheltered under a tree*; *sheltered themselves behind a wall*). [origin unknown]

**sheltered workshop** n. building etc. designed to provide work for people with disabilities.

**shelter-shed** n. roofed structure, usu. partly enclosed, affording protection (in school playgrounds etc.) from inclement weather, and providing a place for eating lunch etc.

**shelve** v. (**-ving**) **1** put aside, esp. temporarily. **2** put (books etc.) on a shelf. **3** fit with shelves. **4** (of ground etc.) slope. □ **shelving** n.

**shelves** *pl.* of SHELF.

**shemozzle** /shuh-**moz**-uhl/ n. *colloq.* **1** brawl or commotion. **2** muddle. [Yiddish]

**shenanigan** /shuh-**nan**-uh-guhn/ n. (esp. in *pl.*) *colloq.* mischievous or questionable behaviour, carryings-on. [origin unknown]

**she-oak** n. **1** any of various Australian trees or shrubs of the casuarina family. **2** the wood of these trees, the grain of which resembles that of English oak, although the wood itself is considered inferior. [SHE (sense 3 *attrib.*), OAK]

**shepherd** /**shep**-uhd/ — n. **1** (*fem.* **shepherdess**) person employed to tend sheep. **2** member of the clergy etc. in charge of a congregation. **3** *hist.* miner who holds a claim (in an Australian goldfield) but does not work it, waiting instead to see if neighbouring claims yield gold. — v. **1 a**

tend (sheep etc.). **b** guide (followers etc.).
**2** marshal or drive (a crowd etc.) like
sheep. **3 a** *hist.* effect token occupation (by,
e.g., digging small pits) of a goldmining
claim in order to comply with the
regulations governing possession, but
put off hard work on it until neighbouring
claims prove to be rich. **b** guard or keep
under close surveillance. **4** *Aust. Rules*
guard a team-mate in possession of the
ball by blocking opponents etc. [Old
English: related to SHEEP, HERD]

**shepherd's clock** *n.* = KOOKABURRA.

**shepherd's pie** *n.* dish of minced meat
topped with mashed potato.

**she pine** *n.* = PLUM PINE. [SHE (sense 3
*attrib.*), PINE[1]]

**sherbet** /**sher**-buht/ *n.* **1** flavoured sweet
effervescent powder or drink. **2** *colloq.*
alcoholic liquor, esp. beer. [Turkish and
Persian from Arabic]

**sheriff** /**she**-ruhf/ *n.* **1** officer of the Supreme
Court who enforces judgments and the
execution of writs, and attends to other
administrative matters. **2** *US* elected
chief law-enforcing officer in a county.
[Old English: related to SHIRE, REEVE[1]]

**Sherpa** *n.* (*pl.* same or **-s**) member of a
Himalayan people living on the borders
of Nepal and Tibet. [native name]

**sherry** /**she**-ree/ *n.* (*pl.* **-ies**) **1** fortified
wine orig. from S. Spain. **2** glass of this.
[*Xeres* in Andalusia]

**she's** /sheez/ *contr.* **1** she is. **2** she has.

**Shetland pony** /**shet**-luhnd/ *n.* pony of
a small hardy rough-coated breed.
[*Shetland Islands*, NNE of Scotland]

**shew** *archaic* var. of SHOW.

**shiatsu** /shee-**at**-soo/ *n.* Japanese therapy
in which pressure is applied, chiefly with
fingers and hands, to specific points on
the body. [Japanese, = finger pressure]

**shibboleth** /**shib**-uh-leth/ *n.* **1** custom,
mode of dress, etc., which distinguishes
a particular class or set of people. **2** catchword or formula adopted by a party or
sect by which their followers may be
discerned, or those not their followers
may be excluded. **3** long-standing doctrine
held to be true by a party or sect (*the
extreme left of the Labor Party must abandon
some of its precious shibboleths*). [Hebrew,
= ear of corn; used as a test of nationality
because of the difficulty foreigners found
in pronouncing the word (Judg. 12:6)]

**shicer** /**shuy**-suh/ *n.* **1** unproductive
claim, mine, or goldfield. **2** *colloq.* cheat,
swindler. [British slang *shicer* a worthless person]

**shickered** /**shik**-uhd/ *adj.* (also **shicker**)
*colloq.* drunk. □ **on the shicker** drunk.
[Yiddish from Hebrew]

**shied** *past* & *past part.* of SHY[2].

**shield** — *n.* **1 a** piece of armour held in
front of the body for protection when
fighting. **b** person or thing giving protection. **2** shield-shaped trophy. **3** protective
plate or screen in machinery etc. **4** shield-
like part of an animal, esp. a shell. **5** large
rigid area of the earth's crust, usu. of
Precambrian rock, unaffected by later
displacements of the crust. — *v.* protect
or screen. [Old English]

**shield cricket** *n.* cricket competition involving teams from the six Australian
States.

**shield-fern** *n.* (also **mother shield-fern**)
common Australian fern having large
fronds, and producing small new fern-
plants at the extremities of mature fronds.

**shier** *compar.* of SHY[1].

**shiest** *superl.* of SHY[1].

**shift** — *v.* **1** (cause to) change or move
from one position to another (*shifted the
fridge*; *wind shifted to the east*; *public
opinion has shifted towards Australia
becoming a Republic*). **2** remove, esp.
with effort (*washing won't shift those
stains*). **3** *colloq.* hurry (*we'll have to shift*).
**4** change (gear) in a vehicle. — *n.* **1** act or
instance of shifting. **2 a** relay of workers.
**b** time for which they work. **3** woman's
straight unwaisted dress or petticoat. **4**
*Physics* displacement of a spectral line. **5**
key on a keyboard used to switch between lower and upper case etc. **6 a** gear
lever in a vehicle. **b** mechanism for this.
□ **make shift** manage; get along somehow.
**shift one's ground** take up a new position
in an argument etc. [Old English]

**shifting spanner** *n.* (also **shifter**) an
adjustable spanner.

**shiftless** *adj.* lacking resourcefulness;
lazy.

**shifty** *adj.* *colloq.* (**-ier, -iest**) evasive;
deceitful. □ **shiftily** *adv.* **shiftiness** *n.*

**Shiite** /**shee**-uyt/ — *n.* adherent of the
branch of Islam rejecting the first three
Sunni caliphs. — *adj.* of this branch.
[Arabic *Shiah*, = party]

**shilling** /**shil**-ing/ *n.* *hist.* former coin and
monetary unit of Australia, Britain, etc.,
worth one-twentieth of a pound. [Old
English]

**shilly-shally** /**shil**-ee shal-ee/ *v.* (**-ies, -ied**)
be undecided; vacillate. [from *shall I?*]

**shimmer** — *v.* shine tremulously or faintly.
— *n.* tremulous or faint light. [Old English]

**shin** — *n.* **1** front of the leg below the
knee. **2** cut of beef from this part. — *v.*
(**-nn-**) (usu. foll. by *up*, *down*) climb
quickly by clinging with the arms and
legs. [Old English]

**shin bone** *n.* = TIBIA.

**shindig** /shin-dig/ *n. colloq.* **1** lively noisy party. **2** = SHINDY 1. [probably from SHINDY]

**shindy** /shin-dee/ *n. (pl. -ies) colloq.* **1** brawl, disturbance, or noise. **2** = SHINDIG 1. [perhaps an alteration of *shinty* type of hockey]

**shine** — *v.* (**-ning;** *past* and *past part.* **shone** /shon/ or **shined**) **1** emit or reflect light; be bright; glow (*the lamp was shining; his face shone with gratitude*). **2** (of the sun, a star, etc.) be visible. **3** cause (a lamp etc.) to shine (*shined a light in my face*). **4** (*past* and *past part.* **shined**) polish. **5** be brilliant; excel (*she shines at maths; is a shining example*). — *n.* **1** light; brightness. **2** high polish; lustre. □ **take the shine out of 1** spoil the brilliance or newness of. **2** mar the pleasure of (*his gloom took the shine out of the party for her*). **3** throw into the shade by surpassing (*she took the shine out of his hard-won credit pass by getting a distinction in the same subject*). **take a shine to** *colloq.* take a fancy to. □ **shiny** (**ier, -iest**) *adj.* [Old English]

**shiner** *n. colloq.* black eye.

**shingle¹** /shing-guhl/ *n.* small smooth pebbles, esp. on the sea-shore. □ **shingly** *adj.* [origin uncertain]

**shingle²** /shing-guhl/ — *n.* rectangular wooden tile used on roofs etc. — *v.* (**-ling**) roof with shingles. □ **a shingle short** *colloq.* mentally deficient; stupid, dull. [Latin *scindula*]

**shingleback** *n.* = BOBTAIL.

**shingles** /shing-guhlz/ *n.pl.* (usu. treated as *sing.*) acute painful viral inflammation of the nerve ganglia, with a rash often encircling the body. [Latin *cingulum* girdle]

**shining** *adj.* used as a distinguishing epithet in the names of Australian flora and fauna (*shining gum; shining fly-catcher; shining starling*).

**Shinto** /shin-toh/ *n.* Japanese religion with the worship of ancestors and nature-spirits. □ **Shintoism** *n.* **Shintoist** *n.* [Chinese, = way of the gods]

**shiny** *n.* = SHINY BUM.

**shiny bum** *n. colloq.* an office worker; administrator; public servant.

**ship** — *n.* **1** large seagoing vessel. **2** spaceship. — *v.* (**-pp-**) **1** put, take, or send away in a ship. **2 a** take in (water) over a ship's side etc. **b** lay (oars) at the bottom of a boat. **c** fix (a rudder, lifeboat, etc.) in place. **3** deliver (goods) to an agent for forwarding. □ **ship off** send away. **when a person's ship comes home** (or **in**) when a person's fortune is made. [Old English]

**-ship** *suffix* forming nouns denoting: **1** quality or condition (*friendship; hardship*). **2** status, office, etc. (*authorship*). **3** tenure of office (*chairmanship*). **4** specific skill (*workmanship*). **5** collective members of a group (*readership*). [Old English]

**shipboard** *attrib. adj.* used or occurring on board a ship.

**shipmate** *n.* fellow member of a ship's crew.

**shipment** *n.* **1** amount of goods shipped. **2** act or an instance of shipping goods etc.

**shipping** *n.* **1 a** transport of goods etc. **b** cost of this (*shipping is extra*). **2** ships, esp. a navy.

**shipshape** *adv. & predic. adj.* trim, neat, tidy.

**shipwreck** — *n.* **1 a** destruction of a ship by a storm, foundering, etc. **b** ship so destroyed. **2** (often foll. by *of*) ruin of hopes, dreams, etc. — *v.* **1** inflict shipwreck on (a ship, a person's hopes, etc.). **2** suffer shipwreck.

**shipwright** *n.* **1** shipbuilder. **2** ship's carpenter.

**shipyard** *n.* place where ships are built, repaired, etc.

**shiralee** /shi-ruh-lee, shi-/ *n.* a swag. [origin unknown]

**shire** *n.* **1** (also *attrib.*) rural administrative district, with its own local council, in some Australian States (*Corio Shire; shire engineer*). **2** Brit. county. [Old English]

**shirk** *v.* (also *absol.*) avoid (duty, work, etc.). □ **shirker** *n.* [German *Schurke* scoundrel]

**shirr** *v.* elasticated gathered threads in a garment etc. forming smocking. — *v.* gather (material) with parallel threads. □ **shirring** *n.* [origin unknown]

**shirt** *n.* upper-body garment of cotton etc., usu. front-opening. □ **keep one's shirt on** *colloq.* keep one's temper. **put one's shirt on** *colloq.* bet all one has on. □ **shirting** *n.* **shirtless** *adj.* [Old English]

**shirt-front** — *n.* (also *attrib.*) *Aust. Rules* fierce tackle usu. delivered by the shoulder to the chest of an opponent. — *v.* deliver such a tackle.

**shirtsleeve** *n.* (usu. in *pl.*) sleeve of a shirt. □ **in shirtsleeves** without one's jacket on.

**shirt-tail** *n.* curved part of a shirt below the waist.

**shirty** *adj.* (**-ier, -iest**) *colloq.* angry; annoyed. □ **shirtily** *adv.* **shirtiness** *n.*

**shish kebab** /shish kuh-bab/ *n.* pieces of meat and vegetables grilled on skewers. [Turkish: related to KEBAB]

**shit** *coarse colloq.* — *n.* **1** faeces. **2** act of defecating. **3** contemptible person. **4** nonsense. **5** (in *pl.*, prec. by *the*) **a** diarrhoea.

**b** state of extreme anger or annoyance. — *int.* exclamation of anger etc. — *v.* (**-tt-**; *past* and *past part.* **shitted, shat** or **shit**) defecate or cause the defecation of (faeces etc.). [Old English]

**shithouse** *coarse colloq.* — *n.* toilet. — *adj.* bad; awful.

**shitty** *colloq.* — *adj.* (**-ier, -iest**) **1** bad-tempered. **2** disgusting, contemptible. **3** bad, awful. — *n.* fit of bad temper.

**shiver**[1] /shiv-uh/ — *v.* tremble with cold, fear, etc. — *n.* **1** momentary shivering movement. **2** (in *pl.*, prec. by *the*) attack of shivering. □ **shivery** *adj.* [origin uncertain]

**shiver**[2] /shiv-uh/ — *n.* (esp. in *pl.*) small fragment or splinter; sliver. — *v.* break into shivers. [related to British dial. *shive* slice]

**shivoo** /shuh-voo/ *n. colloq.* party or celebration; a revel. [corruption of French *chez vous*, = at your place]

**shoal**[1] — *n.* multitude, esp. of fish swimming together. — *v.* (of fish) form shoals. [Dutch: cf. SCHOOL[2]]

**shoal**[2] — *n.* **1 a** area of shallow water. **b** submerged sandbank visible at low water. **2** (esp. in *pl.*) hidden danger. — *v.* (of water) get shallower. [Old English]

**shock**[1] — *n.* **1** violent collision, impact, tremor, etc. **2** sudden and disturbing effect on the emotions etc. (*the news came as a great shock*). **3** acute prostration following an accident, a serious wound, pain, etc. **4** = ELECTRIC SHOCK. **5** disturbance in the stability of an organisation etc. — *v.* **1 a** horrify; outrage. **b** (*absol.*) cause shock. **2** affect with an electric or pathological shock. **3** experience shock (*I don't shock easily*). [French *choc, choquer*]

**shock**[2] *n.* unkempt or shaggy mass of hair. [origin unknown]

**shock absorber** *n.* device on a vehicle etc. for absorbing shocks, vibrations, etc.

**shocker** *n. colloq.* **1** shocking person or thing. **2** extremely bad or disappointing person or thing (*his performance was a shocker; had a shocker of a day*).

**shocking** *adj.* **1** causing shock; scandalous. **2** *colloq.* very bad. □ **shockingly** *adv.*

**shocking pink** *adj.* & *n.* (as adj. often hyphenated) vibrant shade of pink.

**shockproof** *adj.* resistant to the effects of (esp. physical) shock.

**shock therapy** *n.* (also **shock treatment**) treatment of depressive patients by electric shock etc.

**shock troops** *n.pl.* troops specially trained for assault.

**shock wave** *n.* **1** moving region of high air pressure caused by an explosion or by a supersonic body. **2** wave of emotional shock (*the news sent shock waves throughout the region*).

**shod** *past* and *past part.* of SHOE.

**shoddy** /shod-ee/ *adj.* (**-ier, -iest**) **1** poorly made. **2** base, mean (*got shoddy treatment from the authorities*). □ **shoddily** *adv.* **shoddiness** *n.* [origin unknown]

**shoe** /shoo/ — *n.* **1** protective foot-covering of leather etc., esp. one not reaching above the ankle. **2** protective metal rim for a horse's hoof. **3** thing like a shoe in shape or use. — *v.* (**shoes, shoeing;** *past* and *past part.* **shod**) **1** fit (esp. a horse etc.) with a shoe or shoes. **2** (as **shod** *adj.*) (in *comb.*) having shoes etc. of a specified kind (*roughshod*). □ **be in a person's shoes** be in his or her situation, difficulty, etc. [Old English]

**shoehorn** *n.* curved implement for easing the heel into a shoe.

**shoelace** *n.* cord for lacing up shoes.

**shoestring** *n.* **1** shoelace. **2** *colloq.* small esp. inadequate amount of money.

**shone** *past* and *past part.* of SHINE.

**shonky** /shong-kee/ (also **shonkie**) *colloq.* — *adj.* (**-ier, -iest**) **1** unreliable; unsound; dishonest (*the budget figures are shonky; a shonky used-car salesman*). **2** out of sorts, unwell (*feeling a bit shonky today*). — *n.* person who engages in sharp practice. [origin unknown]

**shoo** /shoo/ — *int.* exclamation used to frighten away animals etc. — *v.* (**shoos, shooed**) **1** utter the word 'shoo!'. **2** (usu. foll. by *away*) drive away by shooing. [imitative]

**shook** /shuuk/ *past* of SHAKE. — *predic. adj. colloq.* **1** (foll. by *up*) emotionally or physically disturbed; greatly upset (*am all shook up*). **2** (foll. by *on*) keen on; enthusiastic about (*Aussies are not too shook on the pommy climate*).

**shoot** — *v.* (*past* and *past part.* **shot**) **1 a** (also *absol.*) cause (a weapon) to fire. **b** kill or wound with a bullet, arrow, etc. **2** send out, discharge, etc., esp. swiftly (*shot a glance at her neighbours*). **3** (often foll. by *out, along, forth,* etc.) come or go swiftly or vigorously. **4 a** (of a plant etc.) put forth buds etc. **b** (of a bud etc.) appear. **5** hunt game etc. with a gun. **6** film or photograph. **7** (also *absol.*) *Football* etc. **a** score (a goal). **b** take a shot at (the goal). **8 a** (of a boat) sweep swiftly down or under (a bridge, rapids, etc.). **b** *Surfing* ride (a wave). **9** (usu. foll. by *through, up,* etc.) (of a pain) seem to stab. **10** (often foll. by *up*; also *absol.*) *colloq.* inject (a drug). — *n.* **1** act or instance of shooting. **2 a** young branch or sucker. **b** new growth of a plant. **3** hunting party, expedition, etc. **4** *Surfing* **a** breaking wave which carries a surfer towards the beach. **b** act of riding such a wave. **5** = CHUTE[1]. — *int. colloq.* invitation to ask questions etc.; fire away! □ **shoot down 1** kill by shooting. **2** (also **shoot down in flames**) **a** cause (an aircraft etc.) to crash by shooting. **b** overwhelm (a person) in argument; destroy (an argument or theory). **shoot one's bolt** *colloq.* **1** do all that is in one's power and have nothing left. **2** (of a man) ejaculate, esp. prematurely. **shoot oneself in the foot** cause oneself an injury; bring about one's downfall or subject oneself to ridicule by foolish or unnecessary action etc. (*the government seems determined to shoot itself in the foot*). **shoot one's mouth off** *colloq.* talk too much or indiscreetly. **shoot off** *colloq.* depart quickly. **shoot through** *colloq.* leave quickly; escape, abscond; disappear (*shot through and left all the bills unpaid*). **shoot up 1** grow rapidly. **2** rise suddenly. **3** terrorise (a district) by indiscriminate shooting. □ **shooter** *n.* **shooting** *n.* [Old English]

**shooting star** *n.* small rapidly moving meteor.

**shoot-out** *n. colloq.* decisive gun battle.

**shop** — *n.* **1** place for the retail sale of goods or services. **2** act of going shopping (*went for a shop at the hyperdome*). **3** place for manufacture or repair (*engineering-shop*). **4** one's profession etc. as a subject of conversation (*talk shop*). — *v.* (**-pp-**) go to a shop or shops to buy goods. □ **set up shop** establish oneself in business etc. **shop around 1** look for the best bargain. **2** make wide-ranging enquiries. □ **shopper** *n.* [French *eschoppe*]

**shop floor** *n.* **1** production area in a factory etc. **2** workers as distinct from management.

**shoplift** *v.* steal goods while appearing to shop. □ **shoplifter** *n.*

**shopping** *n.* (often *attrib.*) purchase of goods etc. **2** goods purchased.

**shop-soiled** *adj.* soiled or faded by display in a shop.

**shop steward** *n.* elected representative of workers in a factory etc.

**shore**[1] *n.* **1** land adjoining the sea, a lake, etc. **2** (usu. in *pl.*) country (*foreign shores*). □ **on shore** ashore. [Low German or Dutch]

**shore**[2] — *n.* prop or beam set against a ship, wall, etc., as a support. — *v.* (**-ring**) (often foll. by *up*) support (as if) with a shore or shores; hold up. [Low German or Dutch]

**shore**[3] (esp. in sheep-shearing contexts) *past* of SHEAR.

**shoreline** *n.* line where shore and water meet.

**shorn** *past part.* of SHEAR.

**short** — *adj.* **1 a** measuring little from head to foot, top to bottom, or end to end; not long. **b** not long in duration. **c** seeming short (*a few short years of happiness*). **2 a** (usu. foll. by *of, on*) deficient; scanty (*short of spoons*; *short of money*; *short on sense*). **b** *colloq.* lacking in money (*I'm a bit short at the moment*). **c** not far-reaching; acting or being near at hand (*short range*). **3 a** concise; brief (*the Shorter Oxford Dictionary*). **b** curt; uncivil (*was short with him*). **4** (of the memory) unable to remember distant events. **5** (of a vowel or syllable) **a** having the lesser of the two recognised durations (*the first vowel in 'kangaroo' is short and the third is long*). **b** unstressed (*the second vowel in 'kangaroo' is short*). **6** (of pastry) easily crumbled. **7** (of stocks etc.) sold or selling when the amount is not in hand, with reliance on getting the deficit at a lower price in time for delivery. **8** (of odds or a chance) nearly even. — *adv.* **1** before the natural or expected time or place; abruptly (*cut short the celebrations*; *pulled up short*). **2** rudely (*spoke to him short and sharp*). — *n.* **1** short circuit. **2** short film. — *v.* short-circuit. □ **be caught** (or **taken**) **short 1** be put at a disadvantage. **2** *colloq.* urgently need to use the lavatory. **be short for** be an abbreviation for. **come short of** = *fall short of.* **for short** as a short name (*Tom for short*). **get** (or **have**) **by the short hairs** (or **by the short and curlies**) *colloq.* have (a person) at one's mercy or at a complete disadvantage. **in short** briefly. **make short work of** finish expeditiously. **short of 1** see sense 2a of *adj.* **2** less than (*nothing short of a miracle*). **3** distant from (*two miles short of home*). **4** without going so far as (*did everything short of resigning*). **short of a sheet of bark** *colloq.* mentally deficient; stupid, dull. **short on** *colloq.* see sense 2a of *adj.* □ **shortish** *adj.* **shortness** *n.* [Old English]

**shortage** *n.* (often foll. by *of*) deficiency; amount lacking.

**short back and sides** *n.* short simple haircut.

**shortbread** *n.* rich biscuit of butter, flour, and sugar.

**shortcake** *n.* **1** = SHORTBREAD. **2** cake of short pastry filled with fruit and cream.

**short-change** *v.* cheat, esp. by giving insufficient change.

**short circuit** — *n.* electric circuit through small resistance, esp. instead of the resistance of a normal circuit. — *v.* (**short-circuit**) **1** cause a short circuit (in). **2 a** shorten or avoid (a journey, work, etc.) by taking a more direct route etc. **b** disrupt, cause a breakdown in (a person's plans, a project, etc.).

**shortcoming** *n.* deficiency; defect.

**shortcrust** *n.* (in full **shortcrust pastry**) a type of crumbly pastry.

**short cut** *n.* **1** route shorter than the usual one. **2** quick method.

**shorten** *v.* become or make shorter or short.

**shortening** *n.* fat etc. for pastry.

**shortfall** *n.* deficit.

**shorthand** *n.* **1** (often *attrib.*) system of rapid writing using special symbols. **2** abbreviated or symbolic mode of expression.

**short-handed** *adj.* understaffed.

**shorthorn** *n.* animal of a breed of cattle with short horns.

**short leg** *n. Cricket* **1** fielding position near the batsman on the leg side. **2** fielder in this position.

**short list** — *n.* list of selected candidates from which a final choice is made. — *v.* (**short-list**) put on a short list.

**short-lived** *adj.* ephemeral; not long-lasting.

**shortly** *adv.* **1** (often foll. by *before, after*) soon. **2** in a few words; curtly. [Old English]

**short-range** *adj.* **1** having a short range. **2** relating to the immediate future.

**shorts** *n.pl.* trousers reaching to the knees or higher.

**short shrift** *n.* curt or dismissive treatment. [Old English *shrift* confession: related to SHRIVE]

**short sight** *n.* inability to focus on distant objects.

**short-sighted** *adj.* **1** having short sight. **2** lacking imagination or foresight. □ **short-sightedly** *adv.* **short-sightedness** *n.*

**short story** *n.* story with a fully developed theme but much shorter than a novel.

**short temper** *n.* temper easily lost. □ **short-tempered** *adj.*

**short-term** *adj.* of or for a short period of time.

**short wave** *n.* radio wave of frequency greater than 3 MHz.

**short-winded** *adj.* easily becoming breathless.

**shot**[1] *n.* **1** firing of a gun, cannon, etc. (*heard a shot*). **2** attempt to hit by shooting or throwing etc. **3 a** single non-explosive missile for a gun etc. **b** (*pl.* same or **-s**) small lead pellet used in quantity in a single charge. **c** (as *pl.*) these collectively. **4 a** photograph. **b** continuous film sequence. **5 a** stroke or a kick in a ball game. **b** *colloq.* attempt, guess (*had a shot at it*). **6** *colloq.* person of specified shooting skill (*a good shot*). **7** ball thrown by a shot-putter. **8** launch of a space rocket (*moonshot*). **9** range

etc. to or at which a thing will carry or act (*out of earshot*). **10** *colloq.* **a** drink of esp. spirits. **b** injection of a vaccine, drug, etc. **11** remark or crack aimed at a person (*took a parting shot at him*). □ **call the shots** see CALL. **have a shot at** *colloq.* **1** criticise; attempt to provoke or 'get at' (a person). **2** make an attempt at (something). **like a shot** *colloq.* without hesitation; willingly. **that's the shot** *colloq.* (as an expression of approval) that's the best course of action. [Old English]

**shot**[2] *past* and *past part.* of SHOOT. — *adj.* **1** (of coloured material) woven so as to show different colours at different angles. **2** *colloq.* **a** exhausted. **b** drunk. □ **shot through** (usu. foll. by *with*) permeated or suffused.

**shotgun** *n.* gun for firing small shot at short range.

**shotgun wedding** *n. colloq.* wedding enforced because of the bride's pregnancy.

**shot in the arm** *n. colloq.* stimulus or encouragement.

**shot in the dark** *n.* mere guess.

**shot-put** *n.* athletic contest in which a shot is thrown. □ **shot-putter** *n.*

**should** /shuud/ *v.aux.* (*3rd sing.* **should**) *past* of SHALL, used esp.: **1** in reported speech (*I said I should be home soon*). **2 a** to express obligation or likelihood (*I should tell you*; *you should have read it*; *they should have arrived by now*). **b** to express a tentative suggestion (*I should like to add*). **3 a** expressing the conditional mood in the 1st person (*I should have been killed if I had gone*). **b** forming a conditional clause (*if you should see him*).

**shoulder** /shohl-duh/ — *n.* **1** part of the body at which the arm, foreleg, or wing is attached. **2** either of the two projections below the neck. **3** upper foreleg of an animal as meat. **4** (often in *pl.*) shoulder regarded as supportive, encouraging, etc. (*a shoulder to cry on*; *has broad shoulders*). **5** strip of land next to a road. **6** the part of a garment covering the shoulder. **7** part of anything resembling a shoulder in form or function (*shoulder of a mountain*). — *v.* **1 a** push with the shoulder. **b** make one's way thus (*shouldered his way through the crowd*). **2** take on (a burden, responsibility, etc.). □ **put one's shoulder to the wheel** make a great effort. **shoulder arms** hold a rifle with the barrel against the shoulder and the butt in the hand. **shoulder to shoulder 1** side by side. **2** with united effort. [Old English]

**shoulder blade** *n.* either of the large flat bones of the upper back.

**shouldn't** /shuud-uhnt/ *contr.* should not.

**shouse** /shows/ *n.* (also **shoush** /showsh/) *colloq.* toilet, lavatory. [abbreviated form of *shit-house*]

**shout** — *v.* **1** speak or cry loudly. **2** say or express loudly. **3 a** buy a round of drinks for an assembled company (*shouted them all a beer; I'm shouting*). **b** buy a drink for a person (*I'll shout you a beer*). **c** buy or give as a treat etc. (*shouted all the kids an icecream*). — *n.* **1** loud cry of joy etc., or calling attention. **2 a** the purchase of a round of drinks for an assembled company (or for a person) (*stood us all a shout*). **b** the round of drinks itself (*got ourselves outside four or five shouts this arvo*). **c** one's turn to buy a round of drinks etc. (*your shout I think*). □ **shout down** reduce to silence by shouting. [perhaps related to SHOOT]

**shove** /shuv/ — *v.* (**-ving**) **1** (also *absol.*) push vigorously. **2** *colloq.* put casually (*shoved it in a drawer*). — *n.* act of shoving. □ **shove off 1** start from the shore in a boat. **2** *colloq.* depart. [Old English]

**shovel** /shuv-uhl/ — *n.* **1** spadelike tool with raised sides, for shifting earth etc. **2** (part of) a machine with a similar form or function. — *v.* (**-ll-**) **1** move with or as if with a shovel. **2** *colloq.* move in large quantities or roughly (*shovelled peas into his mouth*). □ **shovelful** *n.* (*pl.* **-s**). [Old English]

**shoveller** /shuv-uh-luh/ *n.* (also **shoveler**, **Australasian shoveller**) duck of southwestern and eastern Australia with a shovel-like beak.

**shovel-nosed lobster** *n.* any of several Australian marine crustaceans, valued as food, having a flattened appearance and shovel-shaped ends of the main feelers, including the MORETON BAY BUG and the BALMAIN BUG.

**show** /shoh/ — *v.* (*past part.* **shown** or **showed**) **1** be, allow, or cause to be, visible; manifest (*buds are beginning to show*; *white shows the dirt*). **2** (often foll. by *to*) offer for scrutiny etc. (*show your tickets please*). **3 a** indicate (one's feelings) (*showed his anger*). **b** accord, grant (favour, mercy, etc.). **4** (of feelings etc.) be manifest (*his dislike shows*). **5 a** demonstrate; explain; point out; prove (*showed it to be false*; *showed his competence*; *show me what you intend*). **b** (usu. foll. by *how to* + infin.) instruct by example (*showed him how to knit*). **6** (*refl.*) exhibit oneself (as being) (*showed herself to be fair*). **7** exhibit in a show. **8** (often foll. by *in, out, up, round*, etc.) conduct or lead (*showed them to their rooms*). **9** *colloq.* = show up 3 (*he didn't show*). — *n.* **1** act or instance of showing; state of being shown. **2** spectacle, display,

exhibition, etc. (*a fine show of wattle blossom*). **3 a** collection of things etc. shown for public entertainment or a competition (*flower show*). **b** annual exhibition of livestock, produce, etc., with entertainments etc., in a city or town. **c** any public entertainment or performance (*the opera in the park was a spectacular show*). **4 a** outward appearance or display (*made a show of agreeing*). **b** empty appearance; mere display (*did it for show*). **5 a** *colloq.* undertaking, business, etc. (*sold the whole show; who's running this show?*). **b** a mine (*the Aborigines have agreed to the new show on their land*). **6** *Med.* discharge of blood etc. at the onset of childbirth. **7** *colloq.* opportunity of acting, defending oneself, etc.; chance (*gave him a fair show; made a good show of it; hasn't got a show of winning*). □ **give the show** (or **the whole show**) **away** demonstrate inadequacies or (esp. inadvertently) reveal the truth. **good** (or **bad** or **poor**) **show!** *colloq.* that was well (or badly) done. **on show** being exhibited. **show one's hand** disclose one's plans. **show off 1** display to advantage. **2** *colloq.* act pretentiously. **show up 1** make or be conspicuous or clearly visible. **2** expose or humiliate. **3** *colloq.* appear; arrive. [Old English]

**show bag** *n.* (also **sample bag**) bag of goods, esp. trade or company samples, available at annual shows etc.

**showbiz** *n. colloq.* = SHOW BUSINESS.

**show business** *n.* the theatrical profession.

**showcase** — *n.* **1** glass case for exhibiting goods etc. **2** event etc. designed to exhibit someone or something to advantage. — *v.* (**-sing**) display in or as if in a showcase.

**showdown** *n.* final test or confrontation.

**shower** — *n.* **1** brief fall of rain, snow, etc. **2 a** brisk flurry of arrows, bullets, etc. **b** dust storm (*Darling shower; Wimmera shower*). **c** sudden copious arrival of gifts, honours, etc. **3 a** cubicle, bath, etc., in which one stands under a spray of water. **b** apparatus etc. used for this. **c** act of bathing in a shower. **4** (in full **shower party** or **shower tea**) party for giving (a 'shower' of) presents to a prospective bride etc. **5** group of particles initiated by a cosmic-ray particle in the earth's atmosphere. — *v.* **1** discharge (water, missiles, etc.) in a shower. **2** take a shower. **3** (usu. foll. by *on, upon*) lavishly bestow (gifts etc.). **4** descend in a shower (*it showered on and off all day*). □ **I** (**he, they,** etc.) **didn't come down in the last shower** *colloq.* an indication that one is not without experience, is not a fool. □ **showery** *adj.* [Old English]

**showing** n. **1** display, performance. **2** quality of performance (*made a poor showing*). **3** presentation of a case; evidence (*on present showing it must be true*).

**showjumping** n. sport of riding horses competitively over a course of fences etc. □ **showjumper** n.

**showman** n. **1** proprietor or manager of a circus etc. **2** skilled performer. **3** person skilled in publicity, esp. self-advertisement. □ **showmanship** n.

**shown** *past part.* of SHOW.

**show-off** n. *colloq.* person who acts pretentiously, who displays his or her wealth, knowledge, etc., in an irritating manner.

**showpiece** n. **1** item presented for display. **2** outstanding specimen.

**show pony** n. *colloq.* person who gives more attention to appearances than to performance (*he's the show pony of the political arena*).

**showroom** n. room used to display goods for sale.

**show-stopper** n. *colloq.* act in a show receiving prolonged applause.

**show trial** n. judicial trial designed to frighten or impress the public.

**showy** adj. (**-ier**, **-iest**) **1** brilliant; gaudy, esp. vulgarly so. **2** striking (*a grevillea with very showy flowers*). □ **showily** adv. **showiness** n.

**shrank** *past* of SHRINK.

**shrapnel** /**shrap**-nuhl/ n. **1** fragments of an exploded bomb etc. **2** shell containing pieces of metal etc., timed to burst short of impact. [*Shrapnel*, name of the inventor of the shell]

**shred** — n. **1** scrap or fragment. **2** least amount (*not a shred of evidence*). — v. (**-dd-**) tear or cut into shreds. [Old English]

**shredder** n. machine (esp. in an office) designed to reduce (esp. confidential) documents to unreadable shreds.

**shrew** /shroo/ n. **1** small mouselike long-nosed mammal of Europe etc. **2** bad-tempered or scolding woman. □ **shrewish** adj. (in sense 2). [Old English]

**shrewd** /shrood/ adj. astute; clever and judicious (*a shrewd observer*; *made a shrewd guess*). □ **shrewdly** adv. **shrewdness** n. [perhaps from obsolete *shrew* to curse, from SHREW]

**shrewdie** /**shroo**-dee/ n. (also **shrewdy**) *colloq.* shrewd or cunning person.

**shriek** — n. shrill scream or sound. — v. make or utter in a shriek. [Old Norse]

**shrift** see SHORT SHRIFT.

**shrike** n. **1** bird of Africa, Europe, etc., with a strong hooked and toothed bill. **2** = SHRIKE-THRUSH. **3** = SHRIKE-TIT. **4** = CUCKOO-SHRIKE. [Old English]

**shrike-thrush** n. any of several usu. grey or brown birds of all Australian States, having a melodious song (*little* (or *rufous*) *shrike-thrush*; Bower's *shrike-thrush*; grey *shrike-thrush*; sandstone *shrike-thrush*; etc.).

**shrike-tit** n. (also **crested shrike-tit**) bird of eastern, south-western, and northern mainland Australia, having a yellow breast, black and white striped crested head, and hooked bill.

**shrill** — adj. **1** piercing and high-pitched in sound. **2** *derog.* sharp, unrestrained. — v. utter with or make a shrill sound. □ **shrillness** n. **shrilly** adv. [origin uncertain]

**shrimp** — n. **1** (pl. same or **-s**) small edible crustacean, turning pink when boiled; prawn. **2** *colloq.* very small person. — v. try to catch shrimps. [origin uncertain]

**shrine** n. **1** esp. *RC Ch.* **a** chapel, church, altar, place, etc., sacred to a saint, holy person, relic, etc. (*Shrine of the Virgin Mary at Lourdes*). **b** tomb of a saint, or casket containing sacred relics; reliquary. **2** place hallowed by some memory or association (*Shrine of Remembrance*). [Latin *scrinium* bookcase]

**shrink** — v. (past **shrank**; past part. **shrunk** or (esp. as adj.) **shrunken**) **1** make or become smaller, esp. from moisture, heat, or cold; contract (*the shirt shrank when washed*; *profits are shrinking*). **2** (usu. foll. by *from*) recoil; flinch (*shrank from his touch*). — n. **1** act of shrinking. **2** *colloq.* psychiatrist. □ **shrinkable** adj. **shrinkage** n. [Old English]

**shrink-wrap** v. enclose (an article) in film that shrinks tightly on to it.

**shrive** v. (**-ving**; past **shrove**; past part. **shriven**) *RC Ch. archaic* **1** (of a priest) hear the confession of, assign penance to, and absolve (a penitent). **2** (*refl.*) submit oneself to a priest for confession etc. [Old English *scrifan* impose as penance]

**shrivel** /**shriv**-uhl/ v. (**-ll-**) contract into a wrinkled or dried-up state. [perhaps from Old Norse]

**shroud** — n. **1** wrapping for a corpse. **2** thing that conceals (*wrapped in a shroud of mystery*). **3** (in pl.) ropes supporting a mast. — v. **1** clothe (a body) for burial. **2** cover or conceal. [Old English, = garment]

**shrove** *past* of SHRIVE.

**Shrovetide** n. Shrove Tuesday and the two days preceding it. [from SHROVE + TIDE sense 2]

**Shrove Tuesday** n. day before Ash Wednesday.

**shrub** n. any woody plant smaller than a tree and with branches usu. near the ground. □ **shrubby** adj. [Old English]

**shrubbery** *n.* (*pl.* **-ies**) area planted with shrubs.

**shrug** — *v.* (**-gg-**) (often *absol.*) slightly and momentarily raise (the shoulders) to express indifference, doubt, etc. — *n.* act of shrugging. □ **shrug off** dismiss as unimportant. [origin unknown]

**shrunk** (also **shrunken**) *past part.* of SHRINK.

**shudder** — *v.* **1** shiver, esp. convulsively, from fear, cold, etc. **2** feel strong repugnance, fear, etc. (*shudder at the thought*). **3** (of a machine) vibrate. — *n.* **1** act of shuddering. **2** (in *pl.*; prec. by *the*) *colloq.* state of shuddering. [Low German or Dutch]

**shuffle** /shuf-uhl/ — *v.* (**-ling**) **1** (also *absol.*) drag the feet in walking etc. **2** (also *absol.*) rearrange or intermingle (esp. cards or papers). **3** keep shifting one's position. — *n.* **1** act of shuffling; shuffling walk or movement. **2** change of relative positions. □ **shuffle off 1** remove, get rid of. **2** *colloq.* die. [Low German]

**shufti** /shuuf-tee/ *n.* (*pl.* **-s**) *colloq.* look, glimpse. [Arabic *šaffa* try to see]

**shun** *v.* (**-nn-**) avoid; keep clear of. [Old English]

**shunt** — *v.* **1** move (a train) between sidings etc.; (of a train) be shunted. **2** move or turn aside (*shunted him from pillar to post*). **3** divert (a decision etc.) onto another person etc. — *n.* **1** act or instance of shunting or being shunted. **2** *Electr.* conductor joining two points of a circuit, through which current may be diverted. **3** *Surgery* alternative path for the circulation of the blood. **4** *colloq.* collision of vehicles, esp. one behind another. □ **get the shunt** *colloq.* be dismissed from a job etc. [perhaps from SHUN]

**shush** /shuush/ — *int.* hush! — *v.* **1** quieten (a person or people) by saying 'shush'. **2** fall silent. [imitative]

**shut** *v.* (**-tt-**; *past* and *past part.* **shut**) **1 a** move (a door, window, lid, etc.) into position to block an opening. **b** close or seal a room, box, eye, etc.) by moving a door etc. **2** become or be capable of being closed or sealed (*the door shut with a bang; the lid shuts automatically*). **3** become or make closed for trade (*shop shuts at six*). **4** fold or contract (a book, telescope, etc.). **5** (usu. foll. by *in*, *out*) keep in or out of a room etc. **6** (usu. foll. by *in*) catch (a finger, dress, etc.) by shutting something on it (*shut his finger in the door*). **7** bar access to (*this entrance is shut*). □ **shut down 1** stop (a factory etc.) from operating. **2** (of a factory etc.) stop operating. **shut one's eyes** (or **ears** or **heart**) **to** pretend not, or refuse, to see (or hear or feel sympathy for) or think about. **shut in** confine; (of hills, houses, etc.) encircle; prevent access etc. to or escape from (*were shut in by the sea on three sides*). **shut off 1** stop the flow of (water, gas, etc.). **2** separate from society etc. **shut out 1** exclude (a person, light, etc.) from a place. **2** screen from view. **3** prevent (a possibility etc.) **4** block from the mind. **shut up 1** close all doors and windows of. **2** imprison. **3** put (a thing) away in a box etc. **4** (esp. in *imper.*) *colloq.* stop talking. **5** *colloq.* reduce to silence by rebuke etc. (*that should shut them up*). **shut up shop** close a business, shop, etc., temporarily or permanently. [Old English]

**shutdown** *n.* closure of a factory etc.

**shut-eye** *n.* *colloq.* sleep.

**shutter** — *n.* **1** movable hinged cover for a window. **2** device that exposes the film in a camera. — *v.* provide with shutters.

**shuttle** /shut-uhl/ — *n.* **1 a** (in a loom) instrument pulling the weft-thread between the warp-threads. **b** (in a sewing machine) bobbin carrying the lower thread. **2** train, bus, etc., used in a shuttle service. **3** = SPACE SHUTTLE. — *v.* (**-ling**) (cause to) move to and fro like a shuttle. [Old English: related to SHOOT]

**shuttlecock** *n.* cork with a ring of feathers, or a similar plastic device, struck to and fro in badminton.

**shuttle diplomacy** *n.* negotiations at an international level conducted by a mediator travelling between disputing parties.

**shuttle service** *n.* transport service operating to and fro over a short route.

**shy**[1] /shuy/ — *adj.* (**shyer**, **shyest** or **shier**, **shiest**) **1 a** timid and nervous in company; self-conscious. **b** (of animals etc.) easily startled. **2** (in *comb.*) disliking or fearing (*work-shy*). **3** (often foll. by *of*, *on*) *colloq.* having lost; short of (*shy of three dollars*). — *v.* (**shies**, **shied**) **1** (usu. foll. by *at*) (esp. of a horse) turn suddenly aside in fright. **2** (usu. foll. by *away from*, *at*) avoid involvement in. — *n.* sudden startled movement. □ **shyly** *adv.* **shyness** *n.* [Old English]

**shy**[2] — *v.* (**shies**, **shied**) (also *absol.*) fling, throw. — *n.* (*pl.* **shies**) fling, throw. [origin unknown]

**Shylock** /shuy-lok/ *n.* hard-hearted money-lender. [name of a character in Shakespeare]

**shyster** /shuy-stuh/ *n.* *colloq.* unscrupulous or unprofessional person. [origin uncertain]

**SI** *abbr.* the international system of units of measurement. [French *Système International*]

**Si** *symb.* silicon.

**si** /see/ *n.* = TE. [French from Italian]

**Siamese** /ˌsuy-uh-**meez**/ — n. (pl. same) **1** native or language of Siam (now Thailand) in Asia. **2** (in full **Siamese cat**) cat of a cream-coloured short-haired breed with dark markings and blue eyes. — adj. of Siam, its people, or language.

**Siamese twins** n.pl. twins joined at some part of the body.

**sibilant** /sib-uh-luhnt/ — adj. **1** sounded with a hiss. **2** hissing. — n. sibilant letter or sound, as s, sh. □ **sibilance** n. **sibilancy** n. [Latin]

**sibling** n. each of two or more children having one or both parents in common. [Old English, = akin]

**sibyl** /sib-uhl/ n. pagan prophetess. [Greek sibulla]

**sibylline** /sib-uh-ˌluyn/ adj. **1** of or from a sibyl. **2** oracular; prophetic. [Latin: related to SIBYL]

**sic**[1] /sik/ adv. (usu. in brackets) used, spelt, etc., as written (confirming, or emphasising the quoted or copied words). [Latin, = so]

**sic**[2] var. of SICK[2].

**sick**[1] — adj. **1** unwell, ill. **2** vomiting or likely to vomit. **3** (often foll. by of) colloq. **a** disgusted; surfeited (sick of chocolates). **b** angry, esp. because of surfeit (sick of being teased). **4** colloq. (of a joke etc.) cruel, morbid, perverted, offensive. **5 a** mentally disordered (that comes from a sick mind). **b** emotionally disturbed (sick at heart). **c** (esp. in comb.) pining (lovesick). **6** (in comb.) relating to sickness (sickbed; sick-leave; sick-pay). — n. colloq. vomit. — v. (usu. foll. by up) colloq. vomit. □ **sick as a dog** colloq. extremely unwell. **take** (or **fall**) **sick** colloq. be taken ill. [Old English]

**sick**[2] v. (also **sic**) (usu. in imper.) (usu. to a dog) set upon; attack. [British dial.]

**sickbay** n. room, cabin, etc. for those who are sick.

**sicken** v. **1** affect with disgust etc. **2 a** (often foll. by for) show symptoms of illness (sickening for flu). **b** (often foll. by at, or to + infin.) feel nausea or disgust (was sickened at the sight). **3** (as **sickening** adj.) **a** disgusting. **b** colloq. very annoying. □ **sickeningly** adv.

**sickie** n. colloq. a day's sick-leave, esp. as taken without sufficient medical reason. [sick (-leave), -y[2]]

**sickle** /sik-uhl/ n. short-handled tool with a semicircular blade, used for reaping etc. [Old English]

**sickle-cell** n. sickle-shaped blood cell, esp. as found in a type of severe hereditary anaemia.

**sickly** adj. (**-ier, -iest**) **1 a** weak; apt to be ill. **b** (of a person's complexion, appearance, etc.) languid, faint, or pale. **2** causing ill health (sickly climate). **3** (of a novel etc.) sentimental or mawkish. **4** of or inducing nausea. [related to SICK[1]]

**sickness** n. **1** being ill; disease. **2** vomiting or a tendency to vomit.

**sickness country** n. (also **sickness site**) (in Aboriginal belief) area of spiritual significance where mythological beings may cause illness, esp. to those disturbing or profaning the area.

**side** — n. **1 a** each of the surfaces bounding an object (a cube has six sides). **b** vertical inner or outer surface (the side of a house; a mountainside). **c** such a surface as distinct from the top or bottom, front or back (at the side of the house). **2 a** right or left part of a person or animal, esp. of the torso. **b** left or right half or a specified part of a thing. **c** (often in comb.) position next to a person or thing (seaside; stood at my side). **d** specified direction relating to a person or thing (the north side of; from all sides). **3 a** either surface of a thing regarded as having two surfaces. **b** writing filling one side of a sheet of paper (write three sides). **4** aspect of a question, character, etc. (look on the bright side). **5 a** each of two competing groups in war, politics, games, etc. **b** cause etc. regarded as being in conflict with another. **6 a** part or region near the edge and remote from the centre (at the side of the room). **b** (attrib.) subordinate, peripheral, or detached part (side-road; side-table). **c** (in two-up) the body of players as distinct from the spinner and the ring-keeper. **7** each of the bounding lines of a plane rectilinear figure (a hexagon has six sides). **8** position nearer or farther than, or right or left of, a given dividing line (on the other side of the road). **9** line of descent through one parent. **10** (in full **side spin**) spin given to a billiard-ball etc. by hitting it on one side. — v. (**-ding**) (usu. foll. by with) take part or be on the same side (sided with her as usual). □ **let the side down** embarrass or fail one's colleagues. **on one side 1** not in the main or central position. **2** aside (took her on one side to explain). **on the . . . side** somewhat (their prices are on the high side). **on the side 1** as a sideline. **2** illicitly. **side by side** standing close together, esp. for mutual support. **take sides** support one or other cause etc. [Old English]

**side-bet** n. **1** bet between opponents, esp. in card games, over and above the ordinary stakes. **2** (in two-up) bet between players rather than with the spinner.

**sideboard** n. **1** table or esp. a flat-topped cupboard for dishes, table linen, etc. **2** (in full **sideboard shed**) shearing shed in which the shearing is done along the two long sides rather than in the centre.

**sideboards** n.pl. colloq. hair grown by a man down the sides of his face.

**sideburns** n.pl. = SIDEBOARDS. [earlier burnsides, after General Burnside (d. 1881)]

**sidecar** n. passenger compartment attached to the side of a motor cycle.

**sided** adj. **1** having sides. **2** (in comb.) having a specified number or type of sides.

**side-effect** n. secondary (usu. undesirable) effect (of a medical drug, an event, etc.).

**sidekick** n. colloq. friend, associate; henchman.

**sidelight** n. **1** light from the side. **2** small light at the side of the front of a vehicle. **3** Naut. light on the side of a moving ship. **4** incidental information.

**sideline** n. **1** work etc. done in addition to one's main activity. **2** (usu. in pl.) **a** line bounding the side of a hockey-pitch etc. **b** space next to these where spectators etc. sit. □ **on the sidelines** not directly concerned.

**sidelong** — adj. (esp. of a glance) inclining to one side; oblique. — adv. obliquely.

**sidereal** /suy-**deer**-ree-uhl/ adj. of the constellations or fixed stars. [Latin sidus sider- star]

**side-saddle** — n. saddle for a woman riding with both legs on the same side of the horse. — adv. riding in this position.

**sideshow** n. **1** small show or stall in an exhibition, fair, etc. **2** minor incident or issue.

**side-splitting** adj. causing violent laughter.

**sidestep** — n. step to the side. — v. (-pp-) **1** avoid by stepping sideways. **2** evade (sidestepped the main issue).

**sidestroke** n. swimming stroke in which the swimmer lies sideways, paddles with the arms, and makes a scissors-like kick with the legs.

**sideswipe** — n. **1** glancing blow on or from the side. **2** incidental criticism etc. — v. hit (as if) with a side-swipe.

**sidetrack** v. divert or diverge from the main course or issue.

**sideways** — adv. **1** to or from a side. **2** with one side facing forward. — adj. to or from a side.

**siding** n. **1** short track at the side of a railway line, used for shunting. **2** slope or declivity.

**sidle** /suy-duhl/ v. (-ling) (usu. foll. by along,

up) walk timidly or furtively. [shortening of SIDELONG]

**SIDS** abbr. sudden infant death syndrome; cot death.

**siege** n. **1** surrounding and blockading of a town, castle, etc. **2** similar operation by police etc. to force an armed person out of a building. □ **lay siege to** conduct the siege of. **raise the siege of** abandon, or cause the abandonment of, an attempted siege of. [French sege seat]

**siemens** /**see**-muhnz/ n. SI unit of conductance, equal to one reciprocal ohm. [von Siemens, name of an engineer]

**sienna** /see-**en**-uh/ n. **1** a kind of earth containing iron and used as a pigment. **2** its colour of yellowish-brown (**raw sienna**) or reddish-brown (**burnt sienna**). [Siena in Tuscany]

**sierra** /see-**e**-ruh, -**air**-ruh/ n. long jagged mountain chain, esp. in Spain or Spanish America. [Spanish from Latin serra saw]

**siesta** /see-**es**-tuh/ n. afternoon sleep or rest, esp. in hot countries. [Spanish from Latin sexta (hora) sixth hour]

**sieve** /siv/ — n. perforated or meshed utensil for separating solids or coarse material from liquids or fine particles, or for pulping. — v. (-ving) put through a sieve; sift. [Old English]

**sift** v. **1** put through a sieve. **2** (usu. foll. by from, out) separate (finer or coarser parts) from material. **3** sprinkle (esp. sugar) from a perforated container. **4** examine (evidence, facts, etc.). **5** (of snow, light, etc.) fall as if from a sieve. [Old English]

**sigh** /suy/ — v. **1** emit an audible breath in sadness, weariness, relief, etc. **2** (foll. by for) yearn for. **3** express with sighs. **4** (of the wind etc.) make a sighing sound. — n. **1** act or instance of sighing. **2** sound made in sighing (a sigh of relief). [Old English]

**sight** /suyt/ — n. **1 a** faculty of seeing. **b** act or instance of seeing or the state of being seen. **2** thing seen. **3** way of looking at or considering a thing (in my sight he can do no wrong). **4** range of vision (out of sight). **5** (usu. in pl.) noteworthy features of a town etc. **6 a** device on a gun, telescope, etc. for assisting aim or observation. **b** aim or observation so gained. **7** colloq. unsightly person or thing (looked a sight). **8** colloq. great deal (a sight too clever). — v. **1** get sight of, observe the presence of (they sighted land). **2** aim (a gun etc.) with a sight. □ **at first sight** on first glimpse or impression. **at** (or **on**) **sight** as soon as a person or a thing has been seen. **catch** (or **lose**) **sight of** begin (or cease) to see or be aware of. **in sight 1** visible. **2** near at hand. **lower** (or **raise**) **one's sights** become less (or more) ambitious. **set one's sights on** aim at. [Old English: related to SEE[1]]

**sighted** adj. **1** not blind. **2** (in comb.) having specified vision (long-sighted).

**sight for sore eyes** n. colloq. welcome person or thing.

**sightless** adj. blind.

**sight-read** v. read (music) at sight.

**sight-screen** n. Cricket large usu. white screen placed near the boundary in line with the wicket to help the batsman see the ball.

**sightseer** n. person visiting the sights of a place. □ **sightseeing** n.

**sight unseen** adv. without previous inspection.

**sigma** /sig-muh/ n. eighteenth letter of the Greek alphabet (Σ, σ, or, when final, ς). [Latin from Greek]

**sign** /suyn/ — n. **1** thing indicating a quality, state, future event, etc. (violence is a sign of weakness). **2** mark, symbol, etc. (marked the jar with a sign; the cross is a sign of Christ). **3** gesture or action conveying an order etc. (gave him a sign to leave; conversed by signs). **4** signboard; signpost. **5** each of the twelve divisions of the zodiac. — v. **1 a** (also absol.) write (one's name) on a document etc. as authorisation. **b** sign (a document) as authorisation. **2** communicate by gesture (signed to me to come). **3** engage or be engaged by signing a contract etc. (see also *sign on*, *sign up*). □ **sign away** relinquish (property etc.) by signing. **sign in 1** sign a register on arrival. **2** get (a person) admitted by signing a register. **sign off** end work, broadcasting, etc. **sign on 1** agree to a contract etc. **2** employ (a person) by signing a register. **sign out** sign a register on departing. **sign up 1** engage (a person). **2** enlist in the armed forces. **3** enrol (signed up for evening classes). [Latin signum]

**signal**[1] /sig-nuhl/ — n. **1 a** sign (usu. prearranged) conveying information etc. (waved as a signal to begin). **b** message made up of such signs. **2** immediate cause of action etc. (the prince's murder was the signal for widespread riots). **3 a** electrical impulse or impulses or radio waves transmitted as a signal. **b** sequence of these. **4** device on a railway giving instructions or warnings to train-drivers etc. — v. (**-ll-**) **1** make signals. **2 a** (often foll. by to + infin.) make signals to; direct. **b** transmit or express by signal; announce (signalled her agreement). □ **signaller** n. [Latin: signum sign]

**signal**[2] /sig-nuhl/ attrib. adj. remarkable, noteworthy (a signal achievement).

□ **signally** adv. [French signalé: related to SIGNAL[1]]

**signalman** n. **1** railway signal operator. **2** a private soldier in the Royal Australian Corps of Signals.

**signatory** /sig-nuh-tuh-ree, -tree/ — n. (pl. **-ies**) party that has signed an agreement, esp. a treaty. — adj. having signed such an agreement etc. [Latin: related to SIGN]

**signature** /sig-nuh-chuh/ n. **1 a** a person's name, initials, etc., used in signing. **b** act of signing. **2** Mus. **a** = KEY SIGNATURE. **b** = TIME SIGNATURE. [medieval Latin: related to SIGNATORY]

**signet** /sig-nuht/ n. small seal used instead of or with a signature as authentication. [French or medieval Latin: related to SIGN]

**signet-ring** n. ring with a seal set in it.

**significance** /sig-**nif**-uh-kuhns/ n. **1** importance. **2** concealed or real meaning (what is the significance of her statement?). **3** being significant. **4** Statistics extent to which a result deviates from a hypothesis such that the difference is due to more than errors in sampling. [Latin: related to SIGNIFY]

**significant** adj. **1** having a meaning; indicative. **2** noteworthy; important. □ **significantly** adv. [Latin: related to SIGNIFY]

**significant figure** n. Math. digit conveying information about a number containing it, and not a zero used simply to fill vacant space at the beginning and end.

**signification** /ˌsig-nuh-fuh-**kay**-shuhn/ n. **1** act of signifying. **2** (usu. foll. by of) exact meaning or sense, esp. of a word or phrase.

**signify** /sig-nuh-ˌfuy/ v. (**-ies, -ied**) **1** be a sign or indication of. **2** mean; symbolise. **3** communicate; make known (signified their agreement). **4** be of importance; matter (signifies little). [Latin: related to SIGN]

**sign language** n. system of communication by gestures, used esp. by the deaf.

**signor** /see-**nyaw**/ n. (pl. **-nori** /-**nyaw**-ree/) title used of or to an Italian-speaking man. [Latin senior SENIOR]

**signora** /see-**nyaw**-ruh/ n. title used of or to an Italian-speaking married woman.

**signorina** /ˌsee-nyuh-**ree**-nuh/ n. title used of or to an Italian-speaking unmarried woman.

**signpost** — n. **1** post on a road etc. indicating direction etc. **2** indication, guide. — v. provide with a signpost or signposts.

**signwriter** n. person who paints signboards etc.

**Sikh** /seek/ n. member of an Indian monotheistic sect. [Hindi, = disciple]

**silage** /suy-lij/ n. **1** green fodder stored in a silo. **2** storage in a silo. [related to SILO]

**silence** /suy-luhns/ — n. **1** absence of sound. **2** abstinence from speech or noise. **3** avoidance of mentioning a thing, betraying a secret, etc. — v. (-cing) make silent, esp. by force or superior argument. □ **in silence** without speech or other sound. [Latin: related to SILENT]

**silencer** n. device for reducing the noise of a vehicle's exhaust, a gun, etc.

**silent** adj. **1** not speaking; not making or accompanied by any sound. **2** (of a letter) written but not pronounced, e.g *b* in *doubt*. **3** saying or recording nothing on some subject (*the records are silent on the incident*). □ **silently** adv. [Latin *sileo* silent]

**silent cop** n. colloq. small raised dome marking the centre of a traffic intersection etc.

**silent majority** n. the mass of allegedly moderate people who rarely express an opinion.

**silent partner** n. partner not sharing in the actual work of a firm.

**silhouette** /ˌsil-oo-et, ˌsil-uh-wet/ — n. **1** picture showing the outline only, usu. in black on white or cut from paper. **2** dark shadow or outline against a lighter background. — v. (-ting) represent or (usu. in passive) show in silhouette. [*Silhouette*, name of a French author and politician]

**silica** /sil-i-kuh/ n. silicon dioxide, occurring as quartz etc. and as a main constituent of sandstone and other rocks. □ **siliceous** /si-lish-uhs/ adj. [Latin *silex -lic-* flint]

**silica gel** n. hydrated silica in a hard granular form used as a drying agent.

**silicate** /sil-uh-ˌkayt/ n. compound of a metal with silicon and oxygen.

**silicon** /sil-uh-kuhn/ n. Chem. non-metallic element occurring widely in silica and silicates.

**silicon chip** n. silicon microchip.

**silicone** /sil-uh-ˌkohn/ n. any organic compound of silicon, with high resistance to cold, heat, water, etc.

**silicosis** /ˌsil-uh-koh-suhs/ n. lung fibrosis caused by inhaling dust containing silica.

**silk** n. **1** fine soft lustrous fibre produced by silkworms. **2** (often *attrib.*) thread or cloth from this. **3** (in *pl.*) cloth or garments of silk, esp. as worn by a jockey. **4** Queen's Counsel, as having the right to wear a silk gown. **5** fine soft thread (*embroidery silk*). □ **take silk** become a Queen's Counsel. [Old English *sioloc*]

**silken** adj. **1** made of silk. **2** soft or lustrous.

**silk-screen printing** n. = SCREEN PRINTING.

**silkworm** n. caterpillar that spins a cocoon of silk.

**silky** adj. (-ier, -iest) **1** soft and smooth like silk. **2** suave. □ **silkily** adv. **silkiness** n.

**silky heads** n. tussocky perennial grass, esp. of inland Australia.

**silky oak** n. **1** any of various usu. rainforest trees of northern and eastern Australia yielding an oak-like timber of silky texture, esp. the tall, commonly cultivated *Grevillea robusta*, having feathery foliage and masses of golden orange flowers. **2** the wood of these trees.

**sill** n. slab of stone, wood, or metal, at the foot of a window or doorway. [Old English]

**silly** /sil-ee/ — adj. (-ier, -iest) **1** foolish, imprudent. **2 a** weak-minded. **b** (in Aboriginal English) (esp. of a drunken person) mad, crazy. **3** *Cricket* (of a fielder or position) very close to the batsman (*silly mid-off*). — n. (pl. -ies) colloq. foolish person. □ **sillily** adv. **silliness** n. [Old English, = happy]

**silo** /suy-loh/ n. (pl. -s) **1** pit or tower for storing grain, cement, etc. **2** pit or air-tight barn etc. in which green crops are kept for fodder. **3** underground storage chamber for a guided missile. [Spanish from Latin]

**silt** — n. sediment in a channel, harbour, etc. — v. (often foll. by *up*) choke or be choked with silt. [perhaps Scandinavian]

**Silurian** /suy-lyoor-ree-uhn/ Geol. — adj. of the third period of the Palaeozoic era. — n. this period. [*Silures*, people of ancient Wales]

**silvan** var. of SYLVAN.

**silver** — n. **1** greyish-white lustrous precious metallic element. **2** colour of this. **3** silver or cupro-nickel coins. **4** household cutlery. **5** = SILVER MEDAL. — adj. **1** of or coloured like silver. **2** used as a distinguishing epithet in the names of: **a** Australian fish (*silver belly*; *silver biddy*; *silver bream*; *silver dory*; *silver fish*; etc.); **b** Australian birds (*silver-eye*; *silver gull*). **c** Australian flora, indicating wood-colour (*silver ash*) or foliage colour (*silver banksia*; *silver grass*; *silver-leaf box*; *silver wattle*). — v. **1** coat or plate with silver. **2** provide (a mirror-glass) with a backing of tin amalgam etc. **3** make silvery. **4** turn grey or white. [Old English]

**silver beet** n. kind of beet with edible broad white leaf-stalks and green blades.

**silver birch** n. common birch of Europe etc., with silver-coloured bark.

**silver-eye** n. small bird of south-western, southern, and eastern Australia, having yellow-green plumage, with usu. a grey breast, and a conspicuous white eye-ring.

**silverfish** n. (pl. same or **-es**) small silvery wingless insect, thoroughly destructive of books, paper, etc.

**silver jubilee** n. 25th anniversary.

**silver lining** n. consolation or hope in misfortune.

**silver medal** n. medal of silver, usu. awarded as second prize.

**silvern** /**sil**-vuhn/ adj. poet. silver. [Old English]

**silver perch** n. (also **grunter**) Australian freshwater food and game-fish that makes a grunting noise when caught.

**silver plate** n. vessels, cutlery, etc., plated with silver. □ **silver-plated** adj.

**silver screen** n. (usu. prec. by the) cinema films collectively.

**silverside** n. upper side of a round of beef, often corned.

**silversmith** n. worker in silver.

**silvertail** — adj. socially prominent; having social aspirations; privileged. — n. person who is socially prominent or who displays social aspirations; privileged person. □ **silvertailed** adj. [originally with reference to the wearing of dress uniforms]

**silver tongue** n. eloquence.

**silverware** n. articles of or plated with silver.

**silver wattle** n. any of several wattles having a silvery foliage.

**silver wedding** n. 25th anniversary of a wedding.

**silvery** adj. **1** like silver in colour or appearance. **2** having a clear gentle ringing sound.

**simian** /**sim**-ee-uhn/ — adj. **1** of the anthropoid apes. **2** like an ape or monkey. — n. ape or monkey. [Latin simia ape]

**similar** /**sim**-uh-luh/ adj. **1** like, alike. **2** (often foll. by to) having a resemblance. **3** Geom. shaped alike. □ **similarity** /-la-ruh-

tee/ n. (pl. **-ies**). **similarly** adv. [Latin similis like]

**simile** /**sim**-uh-lee/ n. **1** esp. poetical comparison of one thing with another using the words 'like' or 'as' (see panel). **2** use of this. [Latin, neuter of similis like]

**similitude** /suh-**mil**-uh-ˌtyood/ n. **1** guise, appearance. **2** comparison; expression of a comparison. [Latin: related to SIMILE]

**simmer** — v. **1** bubble or boil gently. **2** be in a state of suppressed anger or excitement. — n. simmering condition. □ **simmer down** become less agitated. [perhaps imitative]

**simony** /**suy**-muh-nee, **sim**-uh-/ n. buying or selling of ecclesiastical privileges. [from Simon Magus (Acts 8:18)]

**simper** — v. **1** smile in a silly or affected way. **2** express by or with simpering. — n. such a smile. [origin unknown]

**simple** /**sim**-puhl/ adj. (**simpler**, **simplest**) **1** understood or done easily and without difficulty (a simple explanation; a simple task). **2** not complicated or elaborate; plain (led a simple life). **3** not compound or complex (a simple sentence; a simple organism). **4** absolute, unqualified, straightforward (the simple truth). **5** foolish; gullible, feeble-minded. **6** of low rank; insignificant; humble (simple people). □ **simpleness** n. [Latin simplus]

**simple fracture** n. fracture of the bone only without a wound.

**simple interest** n. interest payable on a capital sum only (opp. COMPOUND INTEREST).

**simple-minded** adj. foolish; feeble-minded. □ **simple-mindedness** n.

**simple sentence** n. sentence with only one clause.

**simpleton** n. gullible or halfwitted person.

**simplicity** /sim-**plis**-uh-tee/ n. fact or condition of being simple.

**simplify** /**sim**-pluh-ˌfuy/ v. (**-ies**, **-ied**) make simple; make easy or easier to do or understand. □ **simplification** /-fuh-**kay**-shuhn/ n.

---

### Simile

A simile is a figure of speech involving the comparison of one thing with another of a different kind, using as or like, e.g.

The water was as clear as glass.
Cherry blossom lay like driven snow upon the lawn.

Everyday language is rich in similes:

| | | |
|---|---|---|
| with as: | as mad as a cut snake | as poor as a church mouse |
| | as strong as an ox | as fit as a mallee bull |
| with like: | spread like wildfire | run like the wind |
| | sell like hot cakes | like a bull in a china shop |

**simplistic** /sim-**plis**-tik/ *adj.* excessively or affectedly simple; too simple for accuracy etc. □ **simplistically** *adv.*

**simply** *adv.* **1** in a simple manner. **2** absolutely (*simply astonishing*). **3** merely (*was simply trying to please*).

**simulate** /**sim**-yuh-,layt/ *v.* (**-ting**) **1** pretend to be, have, or feel (*was good at simulating a passion he did not feel*). **2** imitate or counterfeit (*simulated pearls*). **3** reproduce the conditions of (a situation etc.), e.g. for training. **4** produce a computer model of (a process). □ **simulation** /-**lay**-shuhn/ *n.* **simulator** *n.* [Latin: related to SIMILAR]

**simulcast** /**sim**-uhl-kahst/ — *v.* broadcast (a programme) simultaneously on radio and television or on two or more channels. — *n.* a programme broadcast in this way. [SIMUL(TANEOUS)(BROAD)CAST]

**simultaneous** /,sim-uhl-**tay**-nee-uhs/ *adj.* (often foll. by *with*) occurring or operating at the same time. □ **simultaneity** /-**nay**-uh-tee/ *n.* **simultaneously** *adv.* [Latin *simul* at the same time]

**simultaneous equations** *n.pl. Math.* equations involving two or more unknowns that are to have the same values in each equation.

**sin¹** — *n.* **1 a** breaking of divine or moral law, esp. deliberately. **b** such an act. **2** offence against good taste or propriety etc. — *v.* (**-nn-**) **1** commit a sin. **2** (foll. by *against*) offend. □ **sinner** *n.* [Old English]

**sin²** /suyn/ *abbr.* sine.

**sin-bin** *colloq.* — *n.* **1** (in ice-hockey, rugby league, etc.) place where a player sent off the field for an infringement of the rules spends a specified period of time. **2** = SHAGWAGON. — *v.* penalise (a player) by sending to the sin-bin (*sin-binned him for ten minutes*).

**since** — *prep.* throughout or during the period after (*has been here since June*; *happened since yesterday*). — *conj.* **1** during or in the time after (*what have you done since we met?*). **2** because (*since you're drunk I'll do the driving*). — *adv.* **1** from that time or event until now (*has not seen him since*). **2** ago (*many years since*). [Old English, = after that]

**sincere** /sin-**seer**, suhn-/ *adj.* (**sincerer**, **sincerest**) **1** free from pretence or deceit. **2** genuine, honest, frank. □ **sincerity** /-**se**-ruh-tee/ *n.* [Latin]

**sincerely** *adv.* in a sincere manner. □ **yours sincerely** formula for ending an informal letter.

**sine** /suyn/ *n. Math.* ratio of the side opposite a given angle (in a right-angled triangle) to the hypotenuse. [Latin SINUS]

**sinecure** /**suy**-nuh-,kyoor, **sin**-uh-/ *n.* profitable or prestigious position requiring little or no work. [Latin *sine cura* without care]

**sine die** /,suy-nee **duy**-ee, ,see-nay **dee**-ay/ *adv. formal* indefinitely (*postponed sine die*). [Latin]

**sine qua non** /,see-nay kwah **nohn**, ,suy-nee-, -**non**/ *n.* indispensable condition or qualification. [Latin, = without which not]

**sinew** /**sin**-yoo/ *n.* **1** tough fibrous tissue uniting muscle to bone; a tendon. **2** (in *pl.*) muscles; bodily strength. **3** (in *pl.*) strength or framework of a thing. □ **sinewy** *adj.* [Old English]

**sinful** *adj.* committing or involving sin. □ **sinfully** *adv.* **sinfulness** *n.*

**sing** — *v.* (*past* **sang**; *past part.* **sung**) **1 a** utter musical sounds, esp. words with a set tune. **b** (of birds) produce musical sounds. **2** utter or produce by singing. **3** (of the wind, a kettle, etc.) hum, buzz, or whistle. **4** (of the ears) hear a humming sound. **5** *colloq.* turn informer. **6** (foll. by *of*) *literary* celebrate in verse. **7** (of an Aborigine) **a** impart supernatural powers to (an object) by incantation (*sang the spear*; *singing the sea-cow*). **b** bring a (frequently malign) supernatural influence to bear on (a person or thing) by incantation (*sang the white man*). **8** bring to a specified state by singing (*sang the child to sleep*). — *n.* act or spell of singing. □ **sing out** *colloq.* shout; call out. **sing the cattle** (of stockmen) soothe cattle by 'singing'. **sing the praises of** praise enthusiastically. □ **singer** *n.* [Old English]

**singe** /sinj/ — *v.* (**-geing**) **1** burn superficially; scorch. **2** burn off the tips of (hair). — *n.* superficial burn. [Old English]

**single** /**sing**-guhl/ — *adj.* **1** one only, not double or multiple. **2** united or undivided (*a single nation*). **3** for or done by one person etc. (*a single bed*). **4** one by itself (*a single tree*). **5** regarded separately (*every single thing*). **6** not married. **7** (with *neg.* or *interrog.*) even one (*not a single car*). **8** (of a flower) having only one circle of petals (opp. *double*). — *n.* **1** single thing, esp. a single room in a hotel. **2** (in full **single ticket**) ticket valid for an outward journey only. **3** pop record with one item on each side. **4** *Cricket* hit for one run. **5** (usu. in *pl.*) game with one player on each side (*tennis singles*). **6** (in *pl.*) unmarried people. — *v.* (foll. by *out*) choose for special attention etc. □ **singly** *adv.* [Latin *singulus*]

**single combat** *n.* duel.

**single file** — *n.* line of people one behind another. — *adv.* one behind the other.

**single-handed** *adv.* without help. □ **single-handedly** *adv.*

**single-minded** *adj.* having or intent on only one aim. □ **single-mindedly** *adv.* **single-mindedness** *n.*

**single parent** *n.* person bringing up a child or children alone.

**singlet** /**sing**-gluht/ *n.* sleeveless vest worn under or instead of a shirt. [after *doublet*]

**singleton** /**sing**-guhl-tuhn/ *n.* **1** one card only of a suit in a player's hand. **2** single person or thing. [after *simpleton*]

**sing-song** — *n.* informal singing party. — *adj.* (of voice, intonation, speaking, etc.) monotonously rising and falling. [from SING, SONG]

**singular** /**sing**-gyuh-luh/ — *adj.* **1 a** unique; outstanding; extraordinary. **b** eccentric or strange (*a singular character*; *a most singular occurrence*). **2** *Gram.* (of a word or form) denoting a single person or thing. — *n. Gram.* **1** singular word or form. **2** the singular number. □ **singularity** /ˌsing-gyuh-**la**-ruh-tee/ *n.* **singularly** *adv.* [Latin: related to SINGLE]

**Sinhalese** /ˌsing-huh-**leez**, ˌsing-huh-**leez**/ — *n.* (also **Sinhala** /**sing**-huh-luh/ ) (*pl.* same) **1** member of an Indo-Aryan people now forming the majority of the population of Sri Lanka. **2** the Indo-European language of this people. — *adj.* of this people or their language. [Sanskrit]

**sinister** /**sin**-uh-stuh/ *adj.* **1** evil or villainous in appearance or manner. **2** wicked, criminal (*a sinister motive*). **3** ominous (*a sinister sound*). **4** *Heraldry* of or on the left-hand side of a shield etc. (i.e. to the observer's right). [Latin, = left]

**sink** — *v.* (*past* **sank** or **sunk**; *past part.* **sunk** or as *adj.* **sunken**) **1** fall or come slowly downwards. **2** disappear below the horizon. **3 a** go or penetrate below the surface esp. of a liquid. **b** (of a ship) go to the bottom of the sea etc. **4** settle comfortably (*sank into the chair*). **5 a** (gradually) lose strength or value or quality etc., decline (*my heart sank*; *house prices are sinking*). **b** (of the voice) descend in pitch or volume. **c** (of a sick person) approach death. **6** cause or allow to sink or penetrate (*the dog sank its teeth into my thigh*). **7** cause (a plan, person, etc.) to fail. **8** dig (a well) or bore (a shaft). **9** subside into a different state (*sank into sleep*; *famous in his time but now sunk into oblivion*). **10 a** invest (money) (*sank all he had into the business*). **b** lose (money) by investment. **11 a** knock (a ball) into a pocket or hole in billiards, golf, etc. **b** achieve this by (a stroke). **12** overlook or forget (*sank their differences*).

**13** *colloq.* consume (an alcoholic drink) (*sank a few tinnies*). — *n.* **1** plumbed-in basin, esp. in a kitchen. **2** place where foul liquid collects. **3** place of vice. □ **sink in 1** penetrate or permeate. **2** become understood. [Old English]

**sinker** *n.* weight used to sink a fishing-line or sounding-line.

**sinking fund** *n.* money set aside gradually for the eventual repayment of a debt.

**sink or swim** — *adj.* do or die (*a sink or swim effort to recoup his losses*). — *v.* make a last desperate attempt to succeed, the alternative being disaster. — *adv.* even at the risk of complete failure (*I'm determined to try, sink or swim*).

**Sinn Fein** /shin **fayn**/ *n.* political wing of the Irish Republican Army. [Irish, = we ourselves]

**Sino-** /**suy**-noh/ *comb. form* Chinese; Chinese and (*Sino-Russian relations*). [Greek *Sinai* the Chinese]

**sinology** /suy-**nol**-uh-jee, si-/ *n.* the study of the Chinese language, Chinese history, etc. □ **sinologist** *n.*

**sinuous** /**sin**-yoo-uhs/ *adj.* **1** with many curves; undulating. **2** roundabout, devious. **3** lithe; slinky (*a sinuous dress*). □ **sinuosity** /ˌsin-yoo-**os**-uh-tee/ *n.* [Latin: related to SINUS]

**sinus** /**suy**-nuhs/ *n.* cavity of bone or tissue, esp. in the skull connecting with the nostrils. [Latin, = bosom, recess]

**sinusitis** /ˌsuy-nuh-**suy**-tuhs/ *n.* inflammation of a sinus.

**-sion** see -ION.

**sip** — *v.* (**-pp-**) drink in small amounts or by spoonfuls. — *n.* **1** small mouthful of liquid. **2** act of taking this. [perhaps var. of SUP¹]

**siphon** /**suy**-fuhn/ — *n.* **1** tube shaped like an inverted V or U with unequal legs, used to convey liquid from a container to a lower level by atmospheric pressure. **2** bottle from which aerated water is forced by the pressure of gas. — *v.* (often foll. by *off*) **1** (cause to) flow through a siphon. **2** divert or set aside (funds etc.). [Greek, = pipe]

**sir** *n.* **1** polite form of address or reference to a man. **2** (**Sir**) title prefixed to the forename of a knight or baronet. [from SIRE]

**sire** — *n.* **1** male parent of an animal, esp. a stallion. **2** *archaic* form of address to a king. — *v.* (**-ring**) (esp. of an animal) beget. [French from Latin *senior* SENIOR]

**siren** /**suy**-ruhn/ *n.* **1 a** device for making a loud wailing or warning sound. **b** this sound. **2** (in Greek mythology) woman or winged creature whose singing lured unwary sailors on to rocks. **3** (often *attrib.*) temptress; seductress. [Greek *Seirēn*]

**sirloin** /ser-loin/ *n.* upper and choicer part of a loin of beef. [French: related to sur-[1], LOIN]

**sis** *n. colloq.* sissy. [abbreviation]

**sisal** /suy-suhl/ *n.* **1** fibre made from a Mexican plant and used for ropes etc. **2** this plant. [*Sisal*, the port of Yucatan]

**sissy** /sis-ee/ (also **cissy**) *colloq.* — *n.* (pl. **-ies**) effeminate or cowardly person. — *adj.* (**-ier, -iest**) effeminate; cowardly. [related to SISTER]

**sister** *n.* **1 a** woman or girl in relation to her siblings. **b** (in Aboriginal English) female relative of the same generation as the speaker; (loosely) a female Aborigine. **2** female fellow member of a trade union, feminist group, profession, etc. **3** senior female nurse. **4** member of a female religious order. **5** (often *attrib.*) of the same type, design, or origin etc. (*sister ship*). □ **sisterly** *adj.* [Old English]

**sisterhood** *n.* **1** relationship between or as between sisters. **2** society of esp. religious or charitable women. **3** community of feeling between sisters.

**sister-in-law** *n.* (*pl.* **sisters-in-law**) **1** sister of one's wife or husband. **2** wife of one's brother.

**Sistine** /sis-teen/ *adj.* of any of the Popes called Sixtus, esp. Sixtus IV.

**Sisyphean** /sis-uh-fee-uhn/ *adj.* (of toil) endless and fruitless like that of Sisyphus (who endlessly pushed a stone uphill in Hades). [Latin from Greek]

**sit** *v.* (**-tt-**; *past* and *past part.* **sat**) **1** support the body by resting the buttocks on the ground or on a seat etc. **2** cause to sit; place in a sitting position. **3 a** (of a bird) perch or warm the eggs in its nest. **b** (of an animal) rest with the hind legs bent and the buttocks on the ground. **4 a** (of a committee etc.) be in session. **b** (of an individual) be entitled to hold some office or position (*sat as a magistrate*). **5** (usu. foll. by *for*) pose (for a portrait). **6** (foll. by *for*) be a member of parliament for (an electorate). **7** (often foll. by *for*) take (an examination) (*sat History this morning; sitting for Physics tomorrow*). **8** be in a more or less inactive position or condition (*left sitting in Alice Springs; parcel sitting on the doorstep*). **9** (of clothes etc.) fit or hang in a certain way. **10** act as a babysitter. □ **be sitting pretty** be comfortably or advantageously placed. **sit at a person's feet** be a person's pupil. **sit back 1** relax one's efforts. **2** be inactive or passive (*just sat back and ignored our requests*). **sit down 1** sit after standing. **2** cause to sit. **3** (in Aboriginal English) be

(in a place); settle (somewhere) permanently. **sit in 1** occupy a place as a protest. **2** (foll. by *for*) take the place of. **3** (foll. by *on*) be present as a guest or observer at (a meeting etc.). **sit in judgment** be censorious or self-righteous. **sit on 1** be a member of (a committee etc.). **2** hold a session or inquiry concerning. **3** *colloq.* delay action about (*the government has been sitting on the report for a year*). **4** *colloq.* repress, rebuke, or snub (*felt rather sat on*). **sit on the fence** remain neutral or undecided. **sit out 1** take no part in (a dance etc.). **2** stay till the end of (esp. an ordeal). **3** sit outdoors. **sit tight** *colloq.* **1** remain firmly in one's place. **2** not yield. **sit up 1** rise from lying to sitting. **2** sit firmly upright. **3** go to bed late. **4** *colloq.* become interested or aroused etc. (*that will make him sit up!*). **sit well on** suit or fit. [Old English]

**sitar** /si-tah, si-tah, see-tah/ *n.* long-necked Indian lute. [Hindi]

**sitcom** *n. colloq.* situation comedy. [abbreviation]

**sit-down** — *attrib. adj.* **1** (of a meal) eaten sitting at a table. **2** (of a protest etc.) with demonstrators occupying their workplace or sitting down on the ground in a public place. — *n.* **1** spell of sitting. **2** sit-down protest etc. **3** (in Aboriginal English) a rest; a stay.

**site** — *n.* **1** ground chosen or used for a town or building. **2** place where some activity is or has been conducted (*Aboriginal sacred site; launching site*). — *v.* (**-ting**) locate, place. [Latin *situs*]

**sit-in** *n.* protest involving sitting in.

**sittella** /suh-tel-uh/ *n.* (also **sitella**) small tree-living bird of mainland Australia (*black-capped sittella; orange-winged sittella; white-headed sittella*). [Latin, = nuthatch (bird which climbs up and down tree-trunks)]

**sitter** *n.* **1** person who sits, esp. for a portrait. **2** babysitter (see BABYSIT). **3** *colloq.* easy catch or shot.

**sitting** — *n.* **1** continuous period spent engaged in an activity (*finished the book in one sitting*). **2** time during which an assembly is engaged in business. **3** session in which a meal is served. — *adj.* **1** having sat down. **2** (of an animal or bird) still. **3** (of a member of parliament etc.) current.

**sitting duck** *n.* (also **sitting target**) *colloq.* easy target; vulnerable person or thing.

**situate** /sich-oo-ayt, sit-yoo-/ *v.* (**-ting**) (usu. in *passive*) **1** put in a certain position or circumstances (*situated at the top of the hill; how are you situated at the moment?*). **2** establish or indicate the place of; put in a context. [Latin *situo*: related to SITE]

**situation** /ˌsich-oo-**ay**-shuhn, sit-yoo-/ *n.* **1** place and its surroundings. **2** circumstances; position; state of affairs. **3** *formal* paid job. □ **situational** *adj.*

**situation comedy** *n.* broadcast comedy based on characters dealing with awkward domestic situations.

**sit-up** *n.* physical exercise of sitting up from a supine position without using the arms or hands.

**six** *adj. & n.* **1** one more than five. **2** symbol for this (6, vi, VI). **3** *Cricket* hit scoring six runs by clearing the boundary without first touching the ground. **4** six o'clock. □ **at sixes and sevens** in confusion or disagreement. **hit** (or **knock**) **for six** *colloq.* utterly surprise or overcome. [Old English]

**sixer** *n. Cricket* hit for six runs. □ **go for a sixer** *colloq.* suffer a fall or setback.

**sixfold** *adj. & adv.* **1** six times as much or as many. **2** consisting of six parts.

**six-pack** *n.* pack of six cans, stubbies, etc., of beer, etc.

**sixpence** /**siks**-puhns/ *n. hist.* **1** sum of six pennies. **2** coin worth this.

**six-shooter** *n.* (also **six-gun**) revolver with six chambers.

**sixteen** /siks-**teen**, **siks-**/ *adj. & n.* **1** one more than fifteen. **2** symbol for this (16, xvi, XVI). □ **sixteenth** *adj. & n.* [Old English]

**sixth** *adj. & n.* **1** next after fifth. **2** any of six equal parts of a thing. □ **sixthly** *adv.*

**sixth sense** *n.* supposed intuitive or extrasensory faculty.

**sixty** /**siks**-tee/ *adj. & n.* (*pl.* **-ies**) **1** six times ten. **2** symbol for this (60, lx, LX). **3** (in *pl.*) numbers from 60 to 69, esp. the years of a century or of a person's life. □ **sixtieth** *adj. & n.* [Old English]

**sizable** var. of SIZEABLE.

**size¹** — *n.* **1** relative dimensions, magnitude. **2** each of the classes into which similar things are divided according to size. — *v.* (**-zing**) sort in sizes or according to size. □ **the size of it** *colloq.* the truth of the matter (*that's about the size of it*). **size up** *colloq.* form a judgment of. □ **sized** *adj.* (also in *comb.*). [French *sise*]

**size²** — *n.* sticky solution used in glazing paper, stiffening textiles, etc. — *v.* (**-zing**) treat with size. [perhaps = SIZE¹]

**sizeable** *adj.* (also **sizable**) large or fairly large.

**sizzle** /**siz**-uhl/ — *v.* (**-ling**) **1** sputter or hiss, esp. in frying. **2** *colloq.* be very hot or excited etc. — *n.* **1** sizzling sound. **2**

= SAUSAGE SIZZLE. □ **sizzling** *adj. & adv.* [imitative]

**ska** /skah/ *n.* a kind of fast orig. Jamaican pop music. [origin unknown]

**skate¹** — *n.* **1** boot with a blade attached for gliding on ice; this blade. **2** = ROLLER-SKATE. — *v.* (**-ting**) **1 a** move on skates. **b** perform (a specified figure) on skates. **2** (foll. by *over*) refer fleetingly to, disregard. □ **skate on thin ice** *colloq.* behave rashly, risk danger. □ **skater** *n.* [Dutch *schaats* from French]

**skate²** *n.* (*pl.* same or **-s**) large flat marine fish used as food. [Old Norse]

**skateboard** — *n.* short narrow board on two pairs of trucks, for riding on while standing. — *v.* ride on a skateboard. □ **skateboarder** *n.* **skateboarding** *n.*

**sked** *colloq.* — *n.* schedule — *v.* (**-dd-**) to schedule. [abbreviation]

**skedaddle** /skuh-**dad**-uhl/ *v.* (**-ling**) *colloq.* run away, depart quickly. [origin unknown]

**skeeter** /**skee**-tuh/ *n. colloq.* mosquito. [abbreviation]

**skeg** *n.* **1** fin underneath the rear of a surfboard. **2** *colloq.* surfie; person who is addicted to riding a surfboard. [Old Norse, = beard]

**skeghead** *n. colloq.* = SKEG 2.

**skein** /skayn/ *n.* **1** loosely-coiled bundle of yarn or thread. **2** flock of wild geese etc. in flight. [French *escaigne*]

**skeleton** /**skel**-uh-tuhn/ *n.* **1 a** hard framework of bones, woody fibre, etc., supporting the body of an animal or plant (*human skeleton*; *skeleton of a leaf*). **b** the dried bones of a human being or other animal fastened together in the same relative positions as in life. **2** supporting framework or structure of a thing (*skeleton of a ship*). **3** very thin person or animal. **4** useless or dead remnant (*only a seeming skeleton of the forest remained after the bushfire*). **5** outline sketch, epitome (*this is the skeleton of my next novel*). **6** (*attrib.*) having only the essential or minimum number of persons, parts, etc. (*skeleton staff*). □ **skeletal** *adj.* [Greek *skellō* dry up]

**skeleton in the cupboard** *n.* discreditable or embarrassing secret.

**skeleton key** *n.* key designed to fit many locks.

**skeleton weed** *n.* perennial herb of central Asia, now naturalised in Australia and generally regarded as a weed, esp. of wheat and other cereals.

**skerrick** /**ske**-rik/ *n.* (usu. with *neg.*) *colloq.* the smallest bit (*not a skerrick left*). [origin uncertain]

**sketch** — n. **1** rough or unfinished drawing or painting. **2** rough draft or general outline. **3** short usu. humorous play. **4** short descriptive essay etc. — v. **1** make or give a sketch of. **2** draw sketches. **3** (often foll. by *in*, *out*) outline briefly. [Greek *skhēdios* extempore]

**sketch map** n. roughly drawn map with few details.

**sketchy** adj. (**-ier**, **-iest**) **1** giving only a rough outline, like a sketch. **2** *colloq.* unsubstantial or imperfect, esp. through haste. □ **sketchily** adv. **sketchiness** n.

**skew** — adj. oblique, slanting, set askew. — n. slant. — v. **1** make skew. **2** distort (*his account is somewhat skewed*). **3** move obliquely. □ **on the skew** askew. [French: related to ESCHEW]

**skewbald** /skyoo-bawld/ — adj. (esp. of a horse) with irregular patches of white and another colour. — n. skewbald animal. [origin uncertain]

**skewer** /skyoo-uh/ — n. long pin designed for holding meat together while cooking. — v. fasten together or pierce (as) with a skewer. [origin uncertain]

**skew-whiff** adj. & adv. colloq. askew.

**ski** /skee/ — n. (pl. **-s**) **1** each of a pair of long narrow pieces of wood, metal, etc., fastened under the feet for travelling over snow. **2** similar device under a vehicle or aircraft. — v. (**skis**, **ski'd** or **skied** /skeed/; **skiing**) travel on skis. □ **skier** n. [Norwegian from Old Norse]

**skid** — v. (**-dd-**) **1** (of a vehicle etc.) slide on slippery ground, esp. sideways or obliquely. **2** cause (a vehicle) to skid. — n. **1** act of skidding. **2** runner beneath an aircraft for use when landing. □ **on the skids** colloq. about to be discarded or defeated. **put the skids under** colloq. hasten the downfall or failure of. [origin unknown]

**skidlid** n. colloq. crash-helmet worn by motorcyclists etc.

**skid row** n. part of a town frequented by vagrants etc.

**skiff** n. light rowing- or sculling-boat. [French *esquif*: related to SHIP]

**ski jump** n. steep slope levelling off before a sharp drop to allow a skier to leap through the air. □ **ski jumping** n.

**skilful** adj. (often foll. by *at*, *in*) having or showing skill. □ **skilfully** adv.

**ski-lift** n. device for carrying skiers up a slope, usu. a cable with hanging seats.

**skill** n. (often foll. by *in*) ability to do something well; technique, expertise. [Old Norse, = difference]

**skilled** adj. **1** (often foll. by *in*) skilful. **2** (of work or a worker) requiring or having skill or special training.

**skillet** /skil-uht/ n. frying-pan. [French]

**skillion** /skil-yuhn/ n. (also **skilling**) lean-to attached to a dwelling and providing additional accommodation (esp. as a kitchen). [British dial.]

**skillion roof** n. sloping roof characteristic of a lean-to building.

**skim** — v. (**-mm-**) **1 a** take a floating layer from the surface of (a liquid). **b** take (cream etc.) from the surface of a liquid. **2 a** barely touch (a surface) in passing over. **b** (often followed by *over*) deal with or treat (a matter) superficially. **3** (often foll. by *over*, *along*) go or glide lightly. **4** (often followed by *through*) read or look over cursorily. — n. skimming. [French: related to SCUM]

**skim milk** n. (also **skimmed milk**) milk from which the cream has been removed.

**skimp** v. **1** (often foll. by *on*) economise; use a meagre or insufficient amount of, stint. **2** (often foll. by *in*) supply (a person etc.) meagrely with food etc. **3** do hastily or carelessly. [cf. SCRIMP]

**skimpy** — adj. (**-ier**, **-iest**) **1** meagre; insufficient. **2** greatly concerned to economise; stingy. — n. colloq. (in WA) scantily clad barmaid. □ **skimpiness** n.

**skin** — n. **1** flexible covering of a human or other animal body. **2 a** skin of a flayed animal with or without the hair etc. **b** material prepared from skins. **3** complexion of the skin (*has an attractive dark skin*). **4** outer layer or covering, esp. of a fruit, sausage, etc. **5** film like skin on a liquid etc. **6** container for liquid, made of an animal's skin. **7** unit into which an Aboriginal people is divided, usu. on the basis of lineal descent; moiety; each skin being associated with a totemic bird, animal, or insect. **8** prize in a game of skins golf. — v. (**-nn-**) **1** remove the skin from. **2** graze (part of the body). **3** colloq. swindle. □ **be skin and bone** be very thin. **by (or with) the skin of one's teeth** by a very narrow margin. **get under a person's skin** colloq. interest or annoy a person intensely. **have a thick (or thin) skin** be insensitive (or sensitive). **no skin off one's nose** colloq. of no consequence to one. **skin a person alive** colloq. punish severely (*I'll skin him alive if he's not home by 10*). □ **skinless** adj. [Old Norse]

**skin cancer** n. a cancer occurring on the skin, caused by overexposure of unprotected skin to sunlight.

**skin-deep** adj. superficial.

**skin-diver** n. underwater swimmer without a diving-suit, usu. with aqualung and flippers. □ **skin-diving** n.

**skinflint** n. miser.

**skinful** n. colloq. enough alcohol to make one drunk. □ **have had a skinful** colloq. **1** be drunk. **2** be weary of; be fed up with (*I've had a skinful of those kids today*).

**skin graft** n. **1** surgical transplanting of skin. **2** skin transferred in this way.

**skinhead** n. youth with a shaven head, esp. one of an aggressive gang.

**skink** n. any small lizard of the family Scincidae, including numerous Australian species usu. ranging in size from about 30 to 70 mm, but including the large *land mullet* and *blue-tongue* (about 300 mm).

**skinner** /skin-uh/ n. colloq. **1** racehorse that wins at very long odds. **2** a betting coup. [British slang *skinner* one who strips another of money]

**skinny** — adj. (**-ier**, **-iest**) thin or emaciated. — n. (also **skinnyfish**) any of several food-fish of northern Australia and elsewhere, having a notably compressed body. □ **skinniness** n.

**skinny-dip** colloq. — v. swim in the nude. — n. act or instance of skinny-dipping.

**skins golf** n. form of golf in which prize-money is awarded to the winner of each hole: if a hole is not won outright, the prize-money jackpots to the next hole, and so on.

**skint** adj. colloq. having no money left. [= skinned]

**skin-tight** adj. (of a garment) very close-fitting.

**skip**[1] — v. (**-pp-**) **1 a** move along lightly, esp. with alternate hops. **b** jump lightly, esp. over a skipping-rope. **c** gambol, caper, frisk. **2** (often foll. by *from*, *off*, *to*) move quickly from one point, subject, etc., to another. **3** (also *absol.*) omit parts of (a text, subject, etc.). **4** colloq. miss intentionally, not attend (*skipped the Geography class*). **5** colloq. leave hurriedly. — n. skipping movement or action. □ **skip it** colloq. abandon a topic etc. [probably Scandinavian]

**skip**[2] n. **1** large container for building refuse etc. **2** container for transporting or raising materials in mining etc. [Old Norse]

**skip**[3] n. joc. an Australian of British descent. [*Skippy*, name of a kangaroo in an Australian TV series for children]

**skipper** — n. **1** captain of a ship or aircraft. **2** captain of a sporting team. — v. be captain of. [Low German or Dutch *schipper*]

**skipping rope** n. length of rope turned over the head and under the feet while jumping it as a game or exercise.

**skippy** n. (in WA and Tasmania) silvery marine food-fish of southern Australia.

**skirmish** /sker-mish/ — n. **1** minor battle. **2** short argument or contest of wit etc. — v. engage in a skirmish. [French from Germanic]

**skirt** — n. **1** woman's garment hanging from the waist. **2** the part of a coat etc. hanging below the waist. **3** hanging part at the base of a hovercraft. **4** (in *sing.* or *pl.*) edge, border, extreme part. **5** (in full **skirt of beef** etc.) cut of meat from the flank. — v. (often foll. by *around*) **1** go (or lie) along or round the edge of (*the street skirts the beach*; *skirting the city will save us time*). **2** avoid dealing with (an issue etc.) (*skirted the question of who was responsible*). **3** trim the skirtings from (a fleece). [Old Norse: related to SHIRT]

**skirting-board** n. narrow board etc. along the bottom of a room-wall.

**skirtings** n.pl. trimmings or inferior parts of a fleece.

**skirting table** n. table at which the skirtings are removed.

**ski run** n. slope prepared for skiing.

**skit** n. light, usu. short, piece of satire or burlesque. [perhaps from Old Norse: related to SHOOT]

**skite** /skyut/ colloq. — v. boast, brag. — n. **1** braggart, boaster. **2** boasting. □ **skiter** n. [British dial., = person regarded with contempt]

**skittish** adj. **1** lively, playful. **2** (of a horse etc.) nervous, inclined to shy. [perhaps related to SKIT]

**skittle** /skit-uhl/ — n. **1** pin used in skittles. **2** (in *pl.*; usu. treated as *sing.*) game of trying to bowl down usu. nine wooden pins. — v. knock over, in the manner of skittles; defeat (*skittled the Opposition in debate*). [origin unknown]

**skivvy** /skiv-ee/ n. thin, high-necked, long-sleeved garment. [origin unknown]

**skol** /skol, skohl/ — n. used as a toast in drinking. — v. (also **scull**) colloq. **1** drink (a glass etc. of alcoholic liquor) in a single draught. **2** finish one's drink quickly (*skol your drink and let's go*). [Old Norse]

**skua** /skyoo-uh/ n. any of several large predatory sea birds which pursue other birds and make them disgorge the fish they have caught, including some migrants from Antarctica to southern Australian coastal waters in winter (*southern skua*; *south polar skua*). [Old Norse]

**skulduggery** /skul-**dug**-uh-ree/ n. trickery; unscrupulous behaviour. [origin unknown]

**skulk** v. **1** move stealthily; lurk, hide. **2** shirk duty. [Scandinavian]

**skull** n. **1** bony case of the brain of a vertebrate. **2** bony skeleton of the head. **3** head as the seat of intelligence (use your skull!). [origin unknown]

**skull and crossbones** n.pl. representation of a skull with two crossed thigh-bones as an emblem of piracy or death.

**skullcap** n. round, peakless, close-fitting cap covering the crown of the head only, and worn by popes, bishops, etc.

**skunk** n. (pl. same or **-s**) **1** black and white striped, cat-sized, flesh-eating, N. American mammal emitting a powerful stench from its anal glands when attacked. **2** colloq. contemptible person. [American Indian]

**sky** /skuy/ — n. (pl. **skies**) (in sing. or pl.) **1** atmosphere and outer space as seen from the earth. **2** weather or climate evidenced by this (stormy skies). — v. (**skies, skied**) Cricket etc. hit (a ball) high. □ **the sky's the limit** there is practically no limit. **to the skies** without reserve (praise to the skies). [Old Norse; = cloud]

**skydiving** n. sport of performing acrobatic manoeuvres under free fall before opening a parachute. □ **skydiver** n.

**sky-high** adv. & adj. very high.

**skyjack** v. colloq. hijack (an aircraft).

**skylark** — n. lark of Eurasia and N. Africa that sings while soaring. — v. play tricks, frolic.

**skylight** n. window in a roof.

**skyline** n. outline of hills, buildings, etc., against the sky; the visible horizon.

**skyrocket** — n. = ROCKET 1. — v. (esp. of prices) rise very rapidly.

**skyscraper** n. very tall building.

**skyward** /skuy-wuhd/ — adv. (also **skywards**) towards the sky. — adj. moving skyward.

**slab** n. **1** flat thick esp. rectangular piece of solid material, esp. stone. **2** (also attrib.) thick, rough-hewn plank of wood used for building purposes, esp. in the bush (slab hut; slab fence). **3** large flat piece of chocolate, bread, etc. **4** colloq. carton of 24 cans of beer. **5** mortuary table. [origin unknown]

**slack** — adj. **1** (of rope etc.) not taut. **2** (of a stream etc.) inactive or sluggish. **3** (of trade or business or a market) with little happening. **4** negligent, remiss. **5** (of tide etc.) neither ebbing nor flowing. — n. **1** slack part of a rope (haul in the slack). **2** slack period in trade etc. **3** (in pl.) informal trousers. — v. **1** slacken. **2** loosen (rope etc.). **3** be remiss in; shirk; neglect (slacking his responsibilities). **4**

colloq. take a rest, be lazy (he's slacking as usual). □ **slack off 1** loosen. **2** reduce one's level of activity; reduce speed. □ **slackness** n. [Old English]

**slacken** v. make or become slack. □ **slacken off** = slack off (see SLACK).

**slacker** n. shirker.

**slag**[1] — n. **1** refuse left after smelting etc. **2** volcanic scoria. — v. (**-gg-**) **1** form slag. **2** (often foll. by off) colloq. criticise, insult, slander. □ **slaggy** adj. [Low German]

**slag**[2] v. & n. colloq. spit. [Scottish dialect]

**slag heap** n. hill of refuse from a coalmine, steelworks, etc.

**slain** past part. of SLAY.

**slake** v. (**-king**) **1** assuage or satisfy (thirst, a desire, etc.). **2** temper (quicklime) by combination with water. [Old English: related to SLACK]

**slalom** /slay-luhm, slah-luhm/ n. **1** ski-race down a zigzag obstacle course. **2** obstacle race in canoes etc. [Norwegian]

**slam**[1] — v. (**-mm-**) **1** shut forcefully and loudly. **2** put down loudly. **3** put or move suddenly (slam the brakes on; car slammed to a halt). **4** colloq. criticise severely. **5** colloq. hit. — n. sound or action of slamming. [probably Scandinavian]

**slam**[2] n. Cards winning of every trick in a game. [origin uncertain]

**slam dunk** — n. (also **slamdunk**) Basketball a point-scoring play in which a player jumps and thrusts the ball forcefully down through the basket. — v. perform this play.

**slander** — n. **1** malicious, false, and damaging utterance about a person. **2** uttering of this. — v. utter slander about. □ **slanderous** adj. [French esclandre: related to SCANDAL]

**slang** — n. very informal words, phrases, or meanings, not regarded as standard and often used by a specific profession, class, etc. — v. use insulting language (to). □ **slangy** adj. [origin unknown]

**slanging match** n. prolonged exchange of insults.

**slanguage** n. (also **slangwidge** or **Australian slanguage**) distinctively Australian expression, esp. of the more colourful variety; Australian colloquial speech. [SLANG, (LANG)UAGE]

**slant** /slahnt, slant/ — v. **1** slope; lie or (cause to) go obliquely. **2** (often as **slanted** adj.) present (information) in a biased or particular way. — n. **1** slope; oblique position. **2** point of view, esp. a biased one. — adj. sloping, oblique. □ **on a** (or **the**) **slant** aslant. [Scandinavian]

**slanter** /slahn-tuh, slan-tuh/ (also **slinter**) colloq. — n. trick; fraudulent stratagem.

— *adj.* crooked, dishonest. [Dutch *slenter* knavery, trick]

**slantwise** *adv.* aslant.

**slap** — *v.* (**-pp-**) **1** strike with the palm or a flat object, or so as to make a similar noise. **2** lay forcefully (*slapped it down*). **3** put hastily or carelessly (*slap paint on*). **4** (often foll. by *down*) *colloq.* reprimand or snub. — *n.* **1** blow with the palm or a flat object. **2** slapping sound. — *adv.* suddenly, fully, directly (*ran slap into him*). [Low German, imitative]

**slap bang** *adv. colloq.* **1** violently, headlong. **2** precisely; exactly (*slap-bang in the middle*).

**slapdash** — *adj.* hasty and careless. — *adv.* in a slapdash manner.

**slap in the face** *n.* rebuff or affront.

**slap on the back** *n.* congratulations.

**slapstick** *n.* boisterous knockabout comedy.

**slap-up** *attrib. adj. colloq.* excellent, lavish (*a slap-up meal*).

**slash** — *v.* **1** cut or gash with a knife etc. **2** (often foll. by *at*) deliver or aim cutting blows. **3** reduce (prices etc.) drastically. — *n.* **1** slashing cut or stroke. **2** *Printing* oblique stroke; solidus. [origin unknown]

**slat** *n.* thin narrow piece of wood, plastic, or metal, esp. as in a fence or venetian blind. [French *esclat* splinter]

**slate** — *n.* **1** (esp. bluish-grey) metamorphic rock easily split into flat smooth plates. **2** piece of this as a tile or *hist.* for writing on. **3** bluish-grey colour of slate. — *v.* (**-ting**) **1** roof with slates. **2** *colloq.* criticise severely (*his latest book was slated by the critics*). — *adj.* of slate or the colour of slate. □ **on the slate** on (in usu. informal) credit. **wipe the slate clean** forgive (or cancel the record of) past offences. □ **slating** *n.* **slaty** *adj.* [French *esclate*, feminine of *esclat*: related to SLAT]

**slater** /**slay**-tuh/ *n.* wood-louse or similar crustacean, usu. grey or brown and oval-shaped.

**slather** /**slath**-uh/ *v.* spread thickly (*slathered his toast with peanut butter*). □ **open slather 1** unrestricted scope for action (*gave him open slather as manager*). **2** a fight, argument, etc., which is a free-for-all, 'on for young and old'. [origin uncertain]

**slattern** /**slat**-uhn/ *n.* slovenly woman. □ **slatternly** *adj.* [origin uncertain]

**slaughter** /**slaw**-tuh/ — *v.* **1** kill (animals) for food or skins or because of disease. **2** kill (people) ruthlessly or on a great scale. **3** *colloq.* defeat utterly. — *n.* act of slaughtering. □ **slaughterer** *n.* [Old Norse: related to SLAY]

**slaughterhouse** *n.* = ABATTOIR.

**Slav** /slahv/ — *n.* member of a group of peoples in central and eastern Europe speaking Slavonic languages. — *adj.* of the Slavs. [Latin *Sclavus*, ethnic name]

**slave** — *n.* **1** person who is owned by and has to serve another. **2** drudge, hard worker. **3** (foll. by *of, to*) obsessive devotee (*slave of fashion*). **4** machine, or part of one, directly controlled by another. — *v.* (**-ving**) (often foll. by *at, over*) work very hard. [French *esclave* from Latin *Sclavus* SLAV (captive)]

**slave-driver** *n.* **1** overseer of slaves. **2** demanding boss.

**slave labour** *n.* forced labour.

**slaver** /**slav**-uh/ — *v.* **1** dribble. **2** (foll. by *over*) drool over. — *n.* **1** dribbling saliva. **2 a** fulsome flattery. **b** drivel, nonsense. [Low German or Dutch]

**slavery** /**slay**-vuh-ree/ *n.* **1** condition of a slave. **2** drudgery. **3** practice of having slaves.

**Slavic** /**slah**-vik, **slav**-ik/ *adj. & n.* = SLAVONIC.

**slavish** *adj.* **1** like slaves. **2** showing no attempt at originality or development (*a slavish imitator of the style of Patrick White*). **3** abject, servile, base. □ **slavishly** *adv.*

**Slavonic** /sluh-**von**-ik/ — *adj.* **1** of the group of languages including Russian, Polish, and Czech. **2** of the Slavs. — *n.* Slavonic language-group. [related to SLAV]

**slay** *v.* (*past* **slew** /sloo/; *past part.* **slain**) **1** *literary* = KILL 1. **2** = KILL 4. □ **slayer** *n.* [Old English]

**sleaze** *colloq.* — *n.* **1** sleaziness. **2** person of low moral standards. — *v.* live, behave, etc., in a sleazy fashion. [back-formation from SLEAZY]

**sleazy** *adj.* (**-ier**, **-iest**) squalid; tawdry; slummy. □ **sleazily** *adv.* **sleaziness** *n.* [origin unknown]

**sled** — *n.* = SLEDGE¹. — *v.* (**-dd-**) ride on a sledge. [Low German]

**sledge¹** — *n.* vehicle on runners for use on snow. — *v.* (**-ging**) travel or convey by sledge. [Dutch *sleedse*]

**sledge²** *v. colloq.* **1** *Cricket* (of a fielder) attempt to break the concentration of (a person batting) by offering abuse, needling, etc. **2** act in this way in other contexts. □ **sledging** *n.* [origin unknown]

**sledgehammer** /**slej**-ham-uh/ *n.* **1** large heavy long-handled hammer used to break stone etc. **2** (*attrib.*) heavy or powerful (*a sledgehammer blow to the jaw*). [Old English *slecg*: related to SLAY]

**sleek** — *adj.* **1** (of hair, an animal's fur, skin, etc.) smooth and glossy. **2** looking well-fed and comfortable. **3** ingratiating; slick, smooth in speech, behaviour, etc. **4** (of a thing) smooth and polished etc. (*the sleek lines of the car*). — *v.* make sleek. □ **sleekly** *adv.* **sleekness** *n.* **sleeky** *adj.* [var. of SLICK]

**sleep** — *n.* **1** natural recurring condition of suspended consciousness, with the eyes closed and the muscles relaxed. **2** period of sleep (*had a sleep*). **3** state like sleep; rest, quiet, death. — *v.* (*past* and *past part.* **slept**) **1 a** be in a state of sleep. **b** (foll. by *at, in,* etc.) spend the night. **3** provide beds etc. for (*house sleeps six*). **4** (foll. by *with, together*) have sexual intercourse, esp. in bed. **5** (foll. by *on*) put off (a decision) until the next day. **6** (foll. by *through*) fail to be woken by (*slept through the earthquake*). **7** be inactive or dead. **8** (foll. by *off*) remedy by sleeping (*slept off his hangover*). □ **get to sleep** manage to fall asleep. **go to sleep 1** begin to sleep. **2** (of a limb) become numb. **put to sleep 1** anaesthetise. **2** put down (an animal). **sleep in** sleep later than usual in the morning. [Old English]

**sleeper** *n.* **1** person or animal that sleeps. **2** horizontal beam supporting a railway track. **3 a** sleeping-car. **b** berth in this. **4** ring or stud worn in a pierced ear to keep the hole open. **5** thing (or person) that is suddenly successful after being undistinguished.

**sleeping bag** *n.* padded bag to sleep in when camping etc.

**sleeping car** *n.* (also **sleeping carriage**) railway coach with berths.

**sleeping partner** *n.* partner not sharing in the actual work of a firm.

**sleeping sickness** *n.* tropical disease causing extreme lethargy.

**sleepless** *adj.* **1** lacking sleep (*sleepless night*). **2** unable to sleep. **3** continually active; tireless (*sleepless pursuit of the facts*). □ **sleeplessness** *n.*

**sleep-out** *n.* verandah or porch (often glassed-in or partitioned off) or outbuilding providing sleeping accommodation.

**sleepwalk** *v.* walk about while asleep. □ **sleepwalker** *n.*

**sleepy** *adj.* (**-ier, -iest**) **1** drowsy. **2** quiet, inactive (*sleepy town*). □ **sleepily** *adv.* **sleepiness** *n.*

**sleepy lizard** *n.* (also **boggi**) any of several Australian lizards noted for their sluggish habits, including the BOBTAIL and the BLUE-TONGUE.

**sleet** — *n.* **1** snow and rain falling together. **2** hail or snow melting as it falls. — *v.* (prec. by *it* as subject) sleet falls (*it is sleeting*). □ **sleety** *adj.* [Old English]

**sleeve** *n.* **1** part of a garment that encloses an arm. **2** cover of a gramophone record. **3** tube enclosing a rod etc. □ **up one's sleeve** in reserve. □ **sleeved** *adj.* (also in *comb.*). **sleeveless** *adj.* [Old English]

**sleigh** /slay/ — *n.* sledge, esp. for riding on. — *v.* travel on a sleigh. [Dutch *slee*: related to SLEDGE]

**sleight** /slyt/ *n.* dexterity; cunning. □ **sleight of hand** dexterity, esp. in conjuring. [Old Norse: related to SLY]

**slender** *adj.* (**-er, -est**) **1 a** of small girth or breadth (*a slender pillar*). **b** gracefully thin (*a slender waist*). **2** relatively small, scanty, inadequate (*slender resources*). [origin unknown]

**slept** *past* and *past part.* of SLEEP.

**sleuth** /slooth/ — *n.* detective. — *v.* **1** investigate crime etc. **2** poke and pry (*sleuthing into my private life*). [Old Norse]

**slew¹** /sloo/ (also **slue**) — *v.* (often foll. by *round*) turn or swing forcibly to a new position. — *n.* such a turn. [origin unknown]

**slew²** *past* of SLAY.

**slewed** /slood/ *adj. colloq.* drunk. □ **get** (or **be**) **slewed** become lost, esp. in the bush. [SLEW¹]

**slice** /slys/ — *n.* **1** thin flat piece or wedge of esp. food cut off or out. **2** sweet cake-like biscuit, usu. of two or more layers, and cut into pieces for serving. **3** share; part (*slice of the profits*). **4** long-handled kitchen utensil with a broad flat perforated blade. **5** *Sport* stroke that sends the ball obliquely. — *v.* (**-cing**) **1** (often foll. by *up*) cut into slices. **2** (foll. by *off*) cut off. **3** (foll. by *into, through*) cut (as) with a knife. **4** strike (a ball) with a slice. [French *esclice* from Germanic]

**slick** — *adj.* **1 a** skilful or efficient (*a slick performance*). **b** superficially or pretentiously smooth and dexterous; glib (*a slick salesman*). **2 a** sleek, smooth (*slick appearance; slick hair*). **b** slippery. — *n.* **1** large patch of oil etc., esp. on the sea. **2** *Motor Racing* a smooth tyre. — *v. colloq.* **1** (usu. foll. by *back, down*) flatten (one's hair etc.). **2** (usu. foll. by *up*) make sleek or smart. □ **slickly** *adv.* **slickness** *n.* [Old English]

**slide** — *v.* (*past* and *past part.* **slid**) **1** move along a smooth surface with continuous contact on the same part of the thing moving. **2** move quietly or smoothly; glide. **3** glide over ice without skates. **4** (foll. by *over*) barely touch upon (a delicate subject etc.) (*I shall slide over your, shall we say, sleeping around*). **5** (often foll. by *into*) move quietly or unobtrusively (*slid his hand into mine*). — *n.* **1** act of sliding. **2** rapid decline.

**3** inclined plane down which children, goods, etc., slide. **4** track made by or for sliding, esp. on ice. **5** part of a machine or instrument that slides. **6 a** mounted transparency viewed with a projector. **b** piece of glass holding an object for a microscope. □ **let things slide** be negligent; allow deterioration. [Old English]

**slide rule** *n.* ruler with a sliding central strip, graduated logarithmically for making rapid calculations.

**sliding scale** *n.* scale of fees, taxes, wages, etc., that varies according to some other factor.

**slight** /sluyt/ — *adj.* **1 a** small; insignificant. **b** inadequate (*based on slight evidence*). **2** slender, frail-looking. **3** (in *superl.*) any whatever (*if there were the slightest chance*). — *v.* treat disrespectfully; ignore. — *n.* marked piece of neglect; failure to show due respect. □ **slightly** *adv.* **slightness** *n.* [Old Norse]

**slim** — *adj.* (**slimmer, slimmest**) **1** not fat, slender. **2** small, insufficient (*slim chance*). — *v.* (**-mm-**) (often foll. by *down*) **1** become slimmer by dieting, exercise, etc. **2** make smaller (*slimmed it down to 40 pages*). □ **slimmer** *n.* **slimming** *n.* & *adj.* **slimmish** *adj.* [Low German or Dutch]

**slime** *n.* thick slippery mud or sticky substance produced by an animal or plant. [Old English]

**slimy** /sluy-mee/ *adj.* (**-ier, -iest**) **1** like, covered with, or full of slime. **2** *colloq.* disgustingly obsequious. □ **sliminess** *n.*

**sling**[1] — *n.* **1** strap etc. used to support or raise a thing. **2** bandage supporting an injured arm from the neck. **3** strap etc. for firing a stone etc. by hand. **4** *colloq.* a tip or bribe (*must have been given a massive sling*). — *v.* (*past* and *past part.* **slung**) **1** *colloq.* throw. **2** suspend with a sling. **3** *colloq.* pay a tip or bribe (*sling him $10 and she'll be apples*). □ **sling one's hook** *colloq.* go away. **sling off at** ridicule; disparage; mock; be scathingly critical of (*I wasn't slinging off at your religion*). [Old Norse or Low German or Dutch]

**sling**[2] *n.* sweetened drink of spirits (esp. gin) and water. [origin unknown]

**sling the billy** see BILLY[1].

**slink** *v.* (*past* and *past part.* **slunk**) (often foll. by *off, away, by*) move in a stealthy or guilty manner. [Old English]

**slinky** *adj.* (**-ier, -iest**) (of a garment) close-fitting and sinuous.

**slinter** var. of SLANTER.

**slip**[1] — *v.* (**-pp-**) **1** slide unintentionally or momentarily; lose one's footing or balance. **2 a** go or move with a sliding motion. **b** (of prices etc.) fall. **3** escape or

fall from being slippery or not being held properly. **4** (often foll. by *in, out, away*) go unobserved or quietly. **5 a** make a careless or slight error. **b** fall below standard. **6** place or slide stealthily or casually (*slipped him a coin*). **7** release from restraint or connection (*slipped the key off the ring*). **8** move (a stitch) to the other needle without knitting it. **9 a** (foll. by *on, off*) pull (a garment) easily or hastily on or off. **b** (foll. by *into*) wear (*think I'll slip into something more comfortable*). **10** escape from; evade (*dog slipped its collar; slipped my mind*). — *n.* **1** act or instance of slipping. **2** careless or slight error. **3 a** pillowcase. **b** petticoat. **4** (in *sing.* or *pl.*) = SLIPWAY. **5** *Cricket* a fielder stationed for balls glancing off the bat to the off side. **b** (in *sing.* or *pl.*) this position. □ **give a person the slip** escape from; evade. **let slip 1** utter inadvertently. **2** miss (an opportunity). **3** release, esp. from a leash. **slip into a person 1** give a physical beating to. **2** verbally attack. **slip up** *colloq.* make a mistake. □ **slippage** *n.* [probably from Low German *slippen*]

**slip**[2] *n.* **1** small piece of paper, esp. for writing on. **2** piece cut from a plant for grafting or planting. □ **slip of a** small and slim (*slip of a girl*). [Low German or Dutch]

**slip-knot** *n.* **1** knot that can be undone by a pull. **2** running knot.

**slip of the tongue** *n.* (also **slip of the pen**) small spoken (or written) mistake.

**slipped disc** *n.* displaced disc between vertebrae causing lumbar pain.

**slipper** *n.* light loose soft indoor shoe.

**slippery** — *adj.* **1** difficult to grasp, stand on, etc., because smooth or wet. **2** unreliable, unscrupulous (*a slippery customer*). — *n.* (also **blackfish**) dark-coloured freshwater food-fish of south-eastern Australia (so called because of the heavy coating of slime on its skin). □ **slipperiness** *n.* [Old English]

**slippery dip** *n.* slide in a children's playground.

**slip-rail** *n.* **1** a fence-rail, forming one of a set which can be slipped out so as to leave an opening. **2** the opening so formed.

**slipshod** *adj.* careless, slovenly.

**slipstream** *n.* current of air or water driven back by a revolving propeller or a moving vehicle.

**slip-up** *n.* *colloq.* mistake.

**slipway** *n.* ramp for building ships or landing boats.

**slit** — *n.* **1** straight narrow incision or opening. — *v.* (**-tt-**; *past* and *past part.* **slit**) **1** make a slit in. **2** cut into strips. [Old English]

**slither** /**slith**-uh/ — v. **1** slide unsteadily; go with an irregular slipping motion (as on an icy surface). **2** move with a sinuous motion (*the snake slithered across the floor*). — n. act of slithering. □ **slithery** adj. [var. of *slidder*: related to SLIDE]

**sliver** /**sliv**-uh/ — n. long thin piece cut or split off. — v. **1** break off as a sliver. **2** break or form into slivers. [Old English]

**slob** n. colloq. derog. lazy, untidy, or fat person. [Irish *slab* mud]

**slobber** — v. **1** slaver. **2** (foll. by *over*) drool over. — n. slaver. □ **slobbery** adj. [Dutch]

**slog** — v. (**-gg-**) **1** hit hard and usu. wildly. **2** work or walk doggedly. — n. **1** hard random hit. **2 a** hard steady work or walk. **b** spell of this. [origin unknown]

**slogan** /**sloh**-guhn/ n. **1** catchy phrase used in advertising etc. **2** motto of a political party etc. [Gaelic, = war cry]

**sloop** n. small one-masted fore-and-aft-rigged vessel. [Dutch *sloep*]

**slop** — v. (**-pp-**) **1** (often foll. by *over*) spill over the edge of a vessel. **2** wet (the floor etc.) by slopping. — n. **1** liquid spilled or splashed. **2** (in *pl.*) dirty waste water or other waste liquids etc. from a kitchen. **3** (in *sing.* or *pl.*) unappetising weak liquid food. **4** (in *pl.*) colloq. beer; alcoholic liquor generally. □ **on the slops** colloq. drinking alcohol (esp. beer) excessively. **slop about** move about in a slovenly manner. [Old English]

**slope** — n. **1** inclined position, direction, or state. **2** piece of rising or falling ground. **3** difference in level between the two ends or sides of a thing. **4** place for skiing on a mountain etc. — v. (**-ping**) **1** have or take a slope; slant. **2** cause to slope. □ **slope off** colloq. go away, esp. to evade work etc. [*aslope* crosswise]

**sloper** n. colloq. person who slopes off without paying debts. [British dial. *sloper* trickster, defrauder]

**sloppy** adj. (**-ier**, **-iest**) **1 a** (of the ground) wet with rain, full of puddles **b** (of food etc.) watery and disagreeable. **2** careless, untidy (*sloppy work-practices*). **3** foolishly sentimental; maudlin. **4** (of a garment) ill-fitting or untidy; badly made. □ **sloppily** adv. **sloppiness** n.

**sloppy joe** n. loose, (deliberately) overlarge jumper.

**slosh** — v. **1** (often foll. by *about*) splash or flounder about, move with a splashing sound (through watery or muddy terrain etc.). **2** colloq. hit, esp. heavily (*sloshed him one*). **3** colloq. **a** pour (liquid) clumsily. **b** pour liquid on. — n. **1** slush. **2** act or sound of splashing. **3** colloq. heavy blow. [var. of SLUSH]

**sloshed** predic. adj. colloq. drunk.

**slot** — n. **1** slit in a machine etc. for a thing, esp. a coin, to be inserted. **2** slit, groove, etc., for a thing. **3** allotted place in a schedule, esp. in broadcasting. **4** colloq. prison-cell; gaol. — v. (**-tt-**) **1** (often foll. by *in*, *into*) place or be placed (as if) into a slot. **2** provide with slots. [French *esclot* hollow of breast]

**sloth** /slohth/ n. **1** laziness, indolence. **2** slow-moving S. American mammal that hangs upside down in trees. [from SLOW]

**slothful** adj. lazy. □ **slothfully** adv.

**slot machine** n. machine worked by the insertion of a coin, esp. selling small items or providing amusement.

**slouch** — v. stand, move, or sit, in a drooping fashion. — n. **1** slouching posture or movement. **2** colloq. incompetent or slovenly worker, performer, etc. (*he's no slouch when it comes to digging in at the table*). [origin unknown]

**slouch hat** n. **1** hat with a wide flexible brim. **2 a** hat with the left brim turned up, worn by an Australian soldier. **b** this as an emblem of Australian patriotism, courage, etc.

**slough**[1] /slow/ n. **1** swamp; muddy place. **2** state of depression, helplessness, etc. [Old English]

**slough**[2] /sluf/ — n. part that an animal casts or moults, esp. a snake's cast skin. — v. (often foll. by *off*) cast or drop off as a slough. [origin unknown]

**Slough of Despond** /slow/ n. state of hopeless depression.

**Slovak** /**sloh**-vak, -vahk/ — n. **1** native or national of the Slovak Republic in what was formerly Czechoslovakia. **2** language of the Slovak Republic. — adj. of the Slovaks or their language. [native name]

**sloven** /**sluv**-uhn/ n. untidy or careless person. [origin uncertain]

**slovenly** — adj. careless and untidy; unmethodical. — adv. in a slovenly manner. □ **slovenliness** n.

**slow** /sloh/ — adj. **1 a** taking a relatively long time to do a thing (also foll. by *of*: *slow of speech*). **b** acting, moving, or done without speed, not quick. **2** not conducive to speed (*slow route*; *slow racetrack*). **3** (of a clock etc.) showing a time earlier than is correct. **4** (of a person) not understanding or learning readily. **5** dull, tedious. **6** slack, sluggish (*business is slow*). **7** (of a fire or oven) giving little heat. **8** Photog. (of a film) needing long exposure. **9** reluctant; not hasty (*slow to anger*). — adv. slowly (also in comb.: *slow-moving traffic*). — v. (usu. foll. by *down*, *up*) **1** reduce one's speed or the speed of (a vehicle etc.). **2** reduce one's pace of life. □ **slowish** *adj.* **slowly** *adv.* **slowness** *n.* [Old English]

**slowcoach** *n. colloq.* slow person.

**slow motion** *n.* **1** speed of a film at which actions etc. appear much slower than usual. **2** simulation of this in real action.

**slow-worm** *n.* **1** any of the small, worm-like, burrowing snakes of mainland Australia. **2** any of many legless lizards of mainland Australia. [Old English *slow* uncertain]

**sludge** *n.* **1** thick greasy mud or sediment. **2** sewage. □ **sludgy** *adj.* [cf. SLUSH]

**slue** var. of SLEW¹.

**slug¹** /slug/ *n.* **1** small shell-less mollusc often destroying plants. **2 a** bullet, esp. of irregular shape. **b** missile for an airgun. **3** *Printing* **a** metal bar used in spacing. **b** line of type in linotype printing. **4** mouthful of drink (esp. spirits). **5** roundish lump of metal, esp. a nugget of gold found on or just below the surface. [Scandinavian]

**slug²** — *v.* (**-gg-**) **1** hit hard. **2** charge an exorbitant price; impose an exorbitant tax. — *n.* **1** hard blow. **2** exorbitant price or tax. □ **slug it out** fight it out. [origin unknown]

**sluggard** /slug-uhd/ *n.* lazy person. [related to SLUG¹]

**sluggish** *adj.* inert; slow-moving. □ **sluggishly** *adv.* **sluggishness** *n.*

**sluice** /sloos/ — *n.* **1** (also **sluice-gate**, **sluice-valve**) sliding gate or other contrivance for regulating the volume or flow of water. **2** water so regulated. **3** (**sluiceway**) artificial water-channel, esp. for washing ore. **4** place for rinsing. **5** act of rinsing. — *v.* (**-cing**) **1** provide or wash with a sluice or sluices. **2** rinse, esp. with running water. **3** (foll. by *out*, *away*) wash out or away with a flow of water. **4** (of water) rush out (as if) from a sluice. [French *escluse*]

**slum** *n.* **1** house unfit for human habitation. **2** (often in *pl.*) overcrowded and squalid district in a city. □ **slum it** *colloq.* put up with conditions less comfortable than usual (*slumming it in the sleep-out*). □ **slummy** *adj.* [originally cant]

**slumber** — *v.* **1** sleep, esp. in a specified manner (*slumbered peacefully*). **2** be idle or inactive (*the government slumbers while unemployment grows*). **3** be quiet, peaceful (*a slumbering outback township*). — *n.* sleep, esp. of a specified kind (*fell into a fitful slumber*). [Old English]

**slump** — *n.* **1** sudden severe or prolonged fall in the prices of commodities etc. **2** sharp decline in trade or business. — *v.* **1** undergo a slump. **2** sit or fall heavily or limply (*slumped into a chair*). [imitative]

**slung** *past* and *past part.* of SLING¹.

**slunk** *past* and *past part.* of SLINK.

**slur** — *v.* (**-rr-**) **1** pronounce indistinctly with sounds running into one another. **2** *Mus.* perform (notes) legato. **3** make insinuations against (a person or a person's character). **4** (usu. foll. by *over*) pass over (a fact, fault, etc.) lightly. — *n.* **1** imputation of wrongdoing (*a slur on my reputation*). **2** act or instance of slurring in pronunciation etc. **3** *Mus.* curved line joining notes to be slurred. [origin unknown]

**slurp** *colloq.* — *v.* eat or esp. drink noisily. — *n.* sound of this. [Dutch]

**slurry** /slu-ree/ *n.* thin semi-liquid cement, mud, manure, etc. [related to British dial. *slur* thin mud]

**slush** *n.* **1** thawing muddy snow. **2** silly sentimentality. [origin unknown]

**slush fund** *n.* reserve fund, esp. for political bribery.

**slushy** — *adj.* (**-ier, -iest**) **1** like slush. **2** mawkishly sentimental. — *n.* (also **slusher**) assistant to a cook, esp. in a shearing gang.

**slut** *n. derog.* slovenly or promiscuous woman. □ **sluttish** *adj.* [origin unknown]

**sly** /sly/ *adj.* (**slyer, slyest**) **1** cunning, crafty, wily. **2** secretive. **3** knowing; insinuating. **4** illicit, illegal (esp. of the retailing of alcoholic liquor – see SLY GROGGER). □ **on the sly** secretly. □ **slyly** *adv.* **slyness** *n.* [Old Norse: related to SLAY]

**sly grog** *n. colloq.* **1** alcoholic liquor sold by an unlicensed vendor. **2** = SLY GROG SHOP.

**sly grogger** *n. colloq.* person who sells alcoholic liquor without a licence. □ **sly grogging** *n.*

**sly grog shop** *n.* **1** (also **sly grog**) place where sly grog is sold. **2** (also **sly grog shanty**, **sly grog tent**) *hist.* venue for the sale of sly grog, esp. on the Australian goldfields.

**Sm** *symb.* samarium.

**smack¹** — *n.* **1** sharp slap or blow. **2** hard hit at cricket etc. **3** loud kiss. **4** loud sharp sound. — *v.* **1** slap. **2** part (one's lips) noisily in anticipation of food. **3** move, hit, etc., with a smack. — *adv. colloq.* **1** with a smack. **2** suddenly; directly; violently (*landed smack on my head*). **3** exactly (*smack in the centre*). □ **a smack in the eye** (or **face**) *colloq.* rebuff; setback. [imitative]

**smack²** (foll. by *of*) — *v.* **1** have a flavour of; taste of (*smacks of garlic*). **2** suggest (*smacks of nepotism*). — *n.* **1** flavour. **2** (in a person's character etc.) barely discernible quality (*just a smack of snobbishness*). **3** (in food etc) a very small amount (*add a smack of chilli*). [Old English]

**smack³** n. single-masted sailing-boat. [Low German or Dutch]

**smack⁴** n. colloq. heroin or other hard drug. [probably alteration of Yiddish *schmeck* sniff]

**smacker** n. colloq. **1** loud kiss. **2** $1 (formerly £1) (*can you hit me with ten smackers*).

**small** /smawl/ — adj. **1** not large or big. **2** not great in importance, amount, number, power, etc. **3** not much; little (*paid small attention*). **4** insignificant (*from small beginnings*). **5** of small particles (*small shot*). **6** on a small scale (*small farmer*). **7** mean; ungenerous (*a small, spiteful nature*). **8** young (*small child*). — n. slenderest part of a thing (esp. *small of the back*). — adv. into small pieces (*chop it small*). □ **feel** (or **look**) **small** be humiliated or ashamed. □ **smallish** adj. **smallness** n. [Old English]

**small arms** n.pl. portable firearms.

**small beer** n. trifling thing.

**small change** n. coins, not notes.

**small fry** n. unimportant people; children.

**smallgoods** n.pl. cooked meats and meat products (often *attrib.*: *smallgoods shop*).

**small hours** n.pl. period soon after midnight.

**small-minded** adj. petty; narrow in outlook.

**smallpox** n. hist. acute contagious disease with fever and pustules, usu. leaving scars.

**small print** n. unfavourable clauses etc. in a contract, usu. printed small.

**small-scaled snake** n. extremely venomous large snake of eastern central Australia, having the most potent snake-venom in the world.

**small screen** n. television (opp. CINEMA).

**small talk** n. light social conversation.

**small-time** adj. colloq. unimportant, petty.

**small-town** adj. relating to or characteristic of a small town; unsophisticated; provincial.

**smarmy** adj. (**-ier, -iest**) colloq. ingratiating; flattering; obsequious. □ **smarmily** adv. **smarminess** n. [British dial.]

**smart** — adj. **1** well-groomed, neat. **2** brightly coloured, newly painted, etc. **3** stylish, fashionable (*in all the smart restaurants*). **4** clever, ingenious, quick-witted. **5** quick, brisk (*smart walk to the shops*). **6** painfully severe; sharp, vigorous. — v. **1** feel or give pain. **2** (of an insult, grievance, etc) rankle. — n. sharp pain; stinging sensation. — adv. smartly. □ **smartish** adj. & adv. **smartly** adv. **smartness** n. [Old English]

**smart alec** n. (also **smart aleck**) colloq. conceited know-all.

**smarten** v. (usu. foll. by *up*) make or become smart.

**smart money** n. money invested or gambled by people with expert knowledge.

**smash** — v. **1** (often foll. by *up*) **a** break into pieces; shatter. **b** bring or come to sudden destruction, defeat, or disaster. **2** (foll. by *into, through*) move with great force. **3** (foll. by *in*) break with a crushing blow (*smashed in the window*). **4** hit (a ball etc.) with great force, esp. downwards. — n. **1** act or instance of smashing; collision. **2** sound of this. **3** stroke in tennis, squash, etc., in which the ball is hit downwards with great force. **4** (in full **smash hit**) very successful play, song, performer, etc. — adv. with a smash (*fell smash to the floor*). [imitative]

**smash-and-grab** n. robbery in which a shop-window is smashed and goods seized.

**smashed** adj. colloq. affected by alcohol or other drugs.

**smasher** n. colloq. beautiful or pleasing person or thing.

**smashing** adj. colloq. excellent, wonderful.

**smash-up** n. violent collision.

**smattering** n. slight superficial knowledge of a language etc. [origin unknown]

**smear** — v. **1** daub or mark with grease etc. **2** smudge. **3** defame the character of; slander. — n. **1** act or instance of smearing. **2** Med. **a** material smeared on a microscopic slide etc. for examination. **b** specimen of this. □ **smeary** adj. [Old English]

**smear test** n. = CERVICAL SMEAR.

**smegma** /smeg-muh/ n. sebaceous secretion which collects esp. under the foreskin of the penis. [Greek, = soap]

**smell** — n. **1** faculty of perceiving odours. **2** quality in substances that is perceived by this (*smell of brown boronia; some flowers have no smell*). **3** unpleasant odour. **4** act of inhaling to ascertain smell. — v. (*past* and *past part.* **smelt** or **smelled**) **1** perceive or examine by smell. **2** emit an odour; stink. **3** seem by smell to be (*smells sour*). **4** (foll. by *of*) **a** emit the odour of (*smells of fish*). **b** be suggestive of (*smells of dishonesty*). **5** perceive; detect (*smell a bargain*). **6** have or use a sense of smell. □ **smell a rat** suspect trickery etc. **smell out** detect by smell or investigation. [Old English]

**smelling salts** n.pl. sharp-smelling substances sniffed to relieve faintness etc.

**smelly** adj. (**-ier, -iest**) having a strong or unpleasant smell. □ **smelliness** n.

**smelt¹** v. **1** extract metal from (ore) by

melting. **2** extract (metal) in this way. □ **smelter** n. [Low German or Dutch *smelten*]

**smelt²** *past* and *past part.* of SMELL.

**smelt³** n. (pl. same or **-s**) **1** small edible green and silver European fish. **2** any of several small marine and freshwater food-fish of south-eastern Australia. [Old English]

**smidgen** /smij-uhn/ n. (also **smidgin**) *colloq.* small bit or amount (*hasn't a smidgen of sense*). [perhaps from *smitch* in the same sense]

**smile** — v. (**-ling**) **1** have or assume a happy, kind, or amused expression, with the corners of the mouth turned up. **2** express by smiling (*smiled a welcome*). **3** give (a smile) of a specified kind (*smiled a sardonic smile*). **4** (foll. by *on, upon*) favour (*fortune smiled on me*). — n. **1** act or instance of smiling. **2** smiling expression or aspect. [perhaps from Scandinavian]

**smirch** — v. mark, soil, or smear (a thing, a person's reputation, etc.). — n. **1** spot or stain. **2** blot (on one's character etc.). [origin unknown]

**smirk** — n. conceited or silly smile. — v. give a smirk. [Old English]

**smite** v. (**-ting**; *past* **smote**; *past part.* **smitten** /smit-uhn/) **1** *archaic* or *literary* **a** hit. **b** chastise; defeat. **2** (in *passive*) affect strongly; seize (*smitten with regret*; *smitten by her beauty*). [Old English]

**smith** n. **1** blacksmith. **2** (esp. in *comb.*) worker in metal (*goldsmith*). **3** (esp. in *comb.*) craftsman (*wordsmith*). [Old English]

**smithereens** /ˌsmith-uh-**reenz**/ n.pl. small fragments. [British dial. *smithers*]

**smithy** /smith-ee/ n. (pl. **-ies**) blacksmith's workshop, forge. [related to SMITH]

**smitten** *past part.* of SMITE.

**smock** — n. **1** loose shirtlike garment often ornamented with smocking. **2** loose overall. — v. adorn with smocking. [Old English]

**smocking** n. ornamental effect on cloth made by gathering it tightly with stitches.

**smog** n. smoke-laden fog. □ **smoggy** adj. (**-ier, -iest**). [portmanteau word]

**smoke** — n. **1** visible vapour from a burning substance. **2** act of smoking tobacco. **3** *colloq.* cigarette or cigar. **4** (**the Smoke** or **the big Smoke**) *colloq.* large city, e.g. Sydney. — v. (**-king**) **1 a** inhale and exhale the smoke of (a cigarette etc.). **b** do this habitually (*we don't smoke*). **2** emit smoke or visible vapour. **3** darken or preserve with smoke (*smoked salmon*). □ **go up in smoke** *colloq.* come to nothing. **in smoke** *colloq.* in hiding. **smoke out 1**

drive out by means of smoke. **2** drive out of hiding etc. **3** (in Aboriginal English) ritually cleanse (a person or place) of unwelcome spirits, esp. after death, by the use of smoke. [Old English]

**smokebush** n. any of about 50 shrubs or trees of mostly south-western WA, having wispy, woolly, grey-blue and white flowers held well above the long leaves, so that at a distance they seem to be clouds of smoke.

**smoke-free** adj. **1** free from smoke. **2** where smoking is not permitted.

**smokeless** adj. producing little or no smoke; free from smoke.

**smoker** n. **1** parrot with smoky yellow plumage and long dark tail. **2** person who habitually smokes.

**smokescreen** n. **1** cloud of smoke concealing (esp. military) operations. **2** ruse for disguising one's activities.

**smokestack** n. **1** chimney or funnel of a locomotive or steamer. **2** tall chimney.

**smoko** /smoh-koh/ n. (also **smoke-o**, **smoke-oh**) *colloq.* teabreak; brief rest from work (orig. time to have a cigarette etc.).

**smoky** adj. (**-ier, -iest**) **1** emitting, filled with, or obscured by, smoke. **2** stained with or coloured like smoke. **3** having the flavour of smoked food. □ **smokiness** n.

**smooch** *colloq.* — n. period of kissing and caressing. — v. engage in a smooch. □ **smoochy** adj. [imitative]

**smoodge** /smooj/ (also **smooge**) *colloq.* — v. **1** behave amorously. **2** behave in a fawning or ingratiating manner. — n. **1** display of amorous affection. **2** act or instance of ingratiation. [probably a variant of British dial. *smudge* kiss, slide up to, beg in a sneaking way]

**smoodger** /smoo-juh/ n. *colloq.* flatterer; sycophant.

**smooth** /smooth/ — adj. **1** having an even surface; free from projections, dents, and roughness (*smooth, highly polished table-top*). **2** not wrinkled, hairy, etc. (*smooth complexion*; *a smooth body*). **3** (of liquids) of even consistency; without lumps. **4** having an easy flow or correct rhythm (*smooth breathing*). **5** that can be traversed without check (*said that the road to Hell is smooth and short*). **6** (of the sea etc.) calm, flat. **7** (of a journey etc.) easy. **8** not harsh in sound or taste. **9** suave, conciliatory; slick (*a smooth operator*). **10** not jerky (*a smooth ride*). — v. **1** (often foll. by *out, down*) make or become smooth. **2** (often foll. by *out, down, over, away*) reduce or get rid of (differences, faults, difficulties, etc.) in fact or appearance. — n. **1** smoothing touch or stroke (*gave his hair a smooth*). **2** the easy part of life (*take the rough with the smooth*). — *adv.* smoothly. □ **smoothly** *adv.* **smoothness** *n.* [Old English]

**smoothie** /**smooth**-ee/ *n.* **1** *colloq.*, often *derog.* charming but perhaps insincere person. **2** smooth thick drink consisting of fresh fruit puréed with milk, ice cream, etc.

**smooth-tongued** *adj.* insincerely flattering.

**smorgasbord** /**smaw**-guhs-,bawd/ *n.* **1** a buffet meal with a variety of dishes to choose from. **2** a wide variety or choice in general (*given this smorgasbord of options being put to them, the public is bound to be confused*). [Swedish]

**smote** *past* of SMITE.

**smother** /**smu**th-uh/ *v.* **1** suffocate, stifle. **2** (foll. by *in, with*) overwhelm or cover with (kisses, gifts, kindness, etc.). **3** extinguish (a fire) by covering it. **4 a** die of suffocation. **b** have difficulty breathing. **5** (often foll. by *up*) suppress or conceal. [Old English]

**smoulder** /**smohl**-duh/ — *v.* **1** burn slowly without flame or internally. **2** (of emotions) be fierce but suppressed. **3** (of a person) show silent or barely suppressed emotion. — *n.* smouldering. [origin unknown]

**smudge** — *n.* blurred or smeared line, mark, blot, etc. — *v.* (**-ging**) **1** make a smudge on or of. **2** become smeared or blurred. □ **smudgy** *adj.* [origin unknown]

**smug** *adj.* (**smugger, smuggest**) self-satisfied. □ **smugly** *adv.* **smugness** *n.* [Low German *smuk* pretty]

**smuggle** /**smug**-uhl/ *v.* (**-ling**) **1** (also *absol.*) import or export illegally, esp. without paying duties. **2** (foll. by *in, out*) convey secretly. □ **smuggler** *n.* **smuggling** *n.* [Low German]

**smut** — *n.* **1** small flake of soot etc. **2** spot or smudge made by this. **3** obscene talk, pictures, or stories. **4** fungous disease of cereals. — *v.* (**-tt-**) mark with smuts. □ **smutty** *adj.* (**-ier, -iest**) [origin unknown]

**Sn** *symb.* tin.

**snack** *n.* **1** light, casual, or hurried meal. **2** small amount of food eaten between meals. **3** *colloq.* something which is easy to accomplish, a 'pushover'. [Dutch]

**snack bar** *n.* place where snacks are sold.

**snaffle** /**snaf**-uhl/ — *n.* (in full **snaffle-bit**) simple bridle-bit without a curb. — *v.* (**-ling**) *colloq.* **1** steal. **2** seize. **3** (often foll. by *up*) acquire quickly (*the early customers snaffled up the bargains*). [Low German or Dutch perhaps from *snavel* beak]

**snag**[1] — *n.* **1** unexpected obstacle or drawback (*negotiations have hit a snag*). **2** jagged projection, esp. a submerged tree or branch. **3** tear in material etc. — *v.* (**-gg-**) catch or tear on a snag. [probably Scandinavian]

**snag**[2] *n. colloq.* sausage. [origin unknown]

**snagger** *n. colloq.* slow, inexpert, or inept shearer.

**snail** *n.* slow-moving gastropod mollusc with a spiral shell. [Old English]

**snail mail** *n.* airmail or surface mail (as distinct from electronic mail).

**snail's pace** *n.* very slow movement.

**snake** — *n.* **1** long limbless venomous or non-venomous reptile. **2** (also **snake in the grass**) traitor; secret enemy. — *v.* (**-king**) move or twist like a snake (*road snaking through the hills*). [Old English]

**snake-charmer** *n.* person appearing to make snakes move by music etc.

**snake flower** *n.* traditional epithet for any deep purple or blackish purple Australian flower.

**Snake Gully** *n.* imaginary place (in Australia), perceived as remote and backward.

**snake lizard** *n.* any of various small Australian lizards and skinks having reduced or absent limbs and so often mistaken for snakes.

**snake orchid** *n.* = GOLDEN MOTHS.

**snakeskin** — *n.* skin of a snake. — *adj.* made of snakeskin.

**snakewood** *n.* traditional epithet for any Australian tree having twisted branches, as the wattle *Acacia grasbyi* of WA.

**snaky** *adj.* **1** of or like a snake. **2** winding, sinuous. **3** cunning, treacherous. **4** *colloq.* angry; irritable (*became very snaky indeed when questioned*).

**snap** — *v.* (**-pp-**) **1** break suddenly or with a cracking sound. **2** (cause to) emit a sudden sharp crack. **3** open or close with a snapping sound. **4 a** (often foll. by *at*) speak irritably or spitefully (to a person). **b** say irritably or spitefully. **5** (often foll. by *at*) make a sudden audible bite. **6** move quickly (*snap into action*). **7** photograph. — *n.* **1** act or sound of snapping. **2** crisp biscuit (*brandy snap*). **3** snapshot. **4** (in full **cold snap**) sudden brief spell of cold weather. **5** card-game in which players call 'snap' when two similar cards are exposed. **6** vigour, liveliness (*has plenty of snap in him*). **7** *colloq.* easy task (*it was a real snap*). **8** *Aust.* Rules a quickly taken kick at goal. — *adv.* with a snap (*heard it go snap*). — *adj.* done without forethought (*snap decision*). □ **snap out of** *colloq.* get rid of (a mood etc.) by a sudden effort. **snap a person's head off**

*colloq.* address a person angrily or rudely.
**snap up** accept (an offer, a bargain, etc.)
quickly or eagerly. [Low German or
Dutch *snappen* seize]

**snapdragon** *n.* plant with a two-lipped
flower shaped like a dragon's mouth.

**snapper** *n.* (also **schnapper**) any of several
usu. pinkish-coloured Australian marine
fish valued as food.

**snappish** *adj.* **1** curt; ill-tempered; sharp.
**2** (of a dog etc.) inclined to bite or snap.

**snappy** *adj.* (**-ier, -iest**) *colloq.* **1** brisk,
lively. **2** neat and elegant (*snappy dresser*).
**3** snappish. □ **make it snappy** be quick.
□ **snappily** *adv.*

**snappy gum** *n.* any of several eucalypts
yielding a brittle timber, e.g. the SCRIBBLY
GUM.

**snapshot** *n.* casual or informal photograph.

**snare** /snair/ — *n.* **1** trap, esp. with a
noose, for birds or animals. **2** trap, trick,
or temptation. **3** (in *sing.* or *pl.*) twisted
strings of gut, hide, or wire, stretched
across the lower head of a side-drum to
produce a rattle. **4** (in full **snare drum**)
drum fitted with snares. — *v.* (**-ring**) catch
in a snare; trap. [Old Norse]

**snarl**[1] — *v.* **1** growl with bared teeth. **2**
speak, say, or express angrily. — *n.* act or
sound of snarling. [*snar* from Low
German]

**snarl**[2] — *v.* (often foll. by *up*) twist;
entangle; hamper the movement of (traffic etc.). — *n.* knot, tangle. [from SNARE]

**snarl-up** *n. colloq.* traffic jam; muddle.

**snatch** — *v.* **1** (often foll. by *away, from,
up*) seize or remove quickly, eagerly, or
unexpectedly. **2 a** steal (a handbag etc.)
by grabbing. **b** *colloq.* kidnap. **3** secure
with difficulty (*snatched an hour's sleep*).
**4** (foll. by *at*) **a** try to seize. **b** take (an offer
etc.) eagerly. **5** (foll. by *from*) rescue
narrowly (*snatched from the jaws of
death*). — *n.* **1** act of snatching. **2** fragment of a song or talk etc. **3** (in weight-
lifting) rapid raising of a weight from the
floor to above the head. **4** short spell of
activity etc. □ **in** (or **by**) **snatches** in fits
and starts. **snatch it** (or **one's bit** or **one's
rent** or **one's time**) *colloq.* resign; take the
wages due and leave one's job. [related to
SNACK]

**snazzy** *adj.* (**-ier, -iest**) *colloq.* smart,
stylish, showy. □ **snazzily** *adv.* **snazziness**
*n.* [origin unknown]

**sneak** — *v.* **1** (foll. by *in, out, past, away,*
etc.) go or convey furtively. **2** *colloq.* steal
unobserved. **3** *colloq.* tell tales; turn informer. **4** (as **sneaking** *adj.*) **a** furtive
(*sneaking affection*). **b** persistent and

puzzling (*sneaking feeling*). — *n.* **1** mean-
spirited underhand person. **2** *colloq.* tell-
tale; informer. — *adj.* acting or done
without warning; secret (*a sneak attack*).
□ **sneaky** *adj.* (**-ier, -iest**). [origin
uncertain]

**sneaker** *n. colloq.* soft-soled canvas shoe.

**sneer** — *n.* contemptuous smile or remark.
— *v.* **1** (often foll. by *at*) smile or speak
derisively, esp. covertly or ironically. **2**
say with a sneer. □ **sneering** *adj.*
**sneeringly** *adv.* [origin unknown]

**sneeze** — *n.* sudden loud involuntary
expulsion of air from the nose and mouth
caused by irritation of the nostrils. — *v.*
(**-zing**) make a sneeze. □ **not to be sneezed
at** *colloq.* worth having or considering.
[Old English]

**sneezewood** *n.* any of several aromatic
Australian herbs which cause sneezing,
esp. when the leaves are crushed.

**snib** — *v.* (**-bb-**) bolt, fasten, or lock (a door
etc.). — *n.* lock, catch, or fastening, for a
door or window. [origin unknown]

**snick** — *v.* **1** make a small notch or incision in. **2** *Cricket* deflect (the ball)
slightly with the bat. — *n.* **1** small notch
or cut. **2** *Cricket* slight deflection of the
ball. [*snickersnee* long knife, ultimately
from Dutch]

**snicker** *n. & v.* = SNIGGER. [imitative]

**snide** /snyd/ *adj.* sneering; slyly derogatory (*made some snide remarks about
her boyfriend*). [origin unknown]

**sniff** — *v.* **1** inhale air audibly through the
nose. **2** (often foll. by *up*) draw (a scent,
drug, liquid, or air) in through the nose.
**3** smell the scent of by sniffing. **4** (often
foll. by *at*) show contempt for (*sniffed at
the offer*). — *n.* **1** act or sound of sniffing.
**2** amount of air etc. sniffed up. □ **sniff out**
= *smell out.* [imitative]

**sniffer** *n.* person who sniffs, esp. a drug
etc. (often in *comb.*: *glue-sniffer*).

**sniffer dog** *n.* dog trained to sniff out
drugs or explosives.

**sniffle** /snif-uhl/ — *v.* (**-ling**) sniff slightly
or repeatedly. — *n.* **1** act or sound of
sniffling. **2** (in *sing.* or *pl.*) cold in the head
causing sniffling. [imitative: cf. SNIVEL]

**snifter** *colloq.* — *n.* small alcoholic drink.
— *adj.* excellent. [Brit. dial. *snift* sniff]

**snig** *v.* (**-gg-**) haul (a log) with ropes or
chains. [British dial.]

**snigger** — *n.* half-suppressed laugh. — *v.*
utter this. [var. of SNICKER]

**snig track** *n.* (also **snigging track**) track
along which timber is hauled. [SNIG]

**snip** — *v.* (**-pp-**) (also *absol.*) cut with
scissors etc., esp. in small quick strokes.
— *n.* **1** act of snipping. **2** piece snipped off.

**3** *colloq.* a bargain; a certainty; something very easy to do. [Low German or Dutch *snippen*]

**snipe** — *n.* (*pl.* same or **-s**) wading bird with a long straight bill, some species of which migrate from Asia and Russia to northern and eastern Australia in spring. — *v.* (**-ping**) **1** fire shots from hiding, usu. at long range. **2** (often foll. by *at*) make a sly critical attack. □ **sniper** *n.* (in sense 1 of *v.*). [probably Scandinavian]

**snipe-shooting** *n.* (also **dispersing the natives**) *hist.* (in white usage) killing Aborigines.

**snippet** /snip-uht/ *n.* **1** small piece cut off. **2** (usu. in *pl.*) **a** scrap of information etc. **b** short extract from a book etc.

**snitch** *colloq.* — *v.* **1** steal. **2** (often foll. by *on*) inform on a person. — *n.* informer. [origin unknown]

**snitchy** *adj. colloq.* bad-tempered.

**snivel** /sniv-uhl/ — *v.* (**-ll-**) **1** cry or complain in a miserable or whining way. **2** run at the nose; sniffle. — *n.* act or instance of snivelling. [Old English]

**snob** *n.* **1** person who despises those inferior in social position, wealth, intellect, taste, etc. (*intellectual snob*). **2** = COBBLER 4. □ **snobbery** *n.* **snobbish** *adj.* **snobby** *adj.* (**-ier, -iest**). [origin unknown]

**snog** *colloq.* — *v.* (**-gg-**) engage in kissing and caressing. — *n.* period of this. [origin unknown]

**snood** *n.* ornamental hairnet, worn usu. at the back of the head. [Old English]

**snook** /snuuk/ *n.* **1** *colloq.* contemptuous gesture with the thumb to the nose and the fingers spread. **2** = BARRACUDA. □ **cock a snook** (often foll. by *at*) **1** make this contemptuous gesture. **2** register one's contempt. [origin unknown]

**snooker** *n.* **1** game played on an oblong cloth-covered table with a cue-ball, 15 red, and 6 coloured balls. **2** position in this game in which a direct shot would lose points. — *v.* **1** (also *refl.*) subject (oneself or an opponent) to a snooker. **2** (esp. as **snookered** *adj.*) *colloq.* thwart, defeat. [origin unknown]

**snoop** — *v.* **1** pry into another's affairs. **2** (often foll. by *about, around*) investigate transgressions of rules, the law, etc. — *n.* act of snooping. □ **snooper** *n.* **snoopy** *adj.* [Dutch]

**snooty** *adj.* (**-ier, -iest**) *colloq.* supercilious; conceited; snobbish. □ **snootily** *adv.* [origin unknown]

**snooze** — *n.* short sleep, nap. — *v.* (**-zing**) take a snooze. [origin unknown]

**snore** /snaw/ — *n.* snorting or grunting sound of breathing during sleep. — *v.* (**-ring**) make this sound. [imitative]

**snorkel** /snaw-kuhl/ — *n.* **1** breathing-tube for an underwater swimmer. **2** device for supplying air to a submerged submarine. — *v.* (**-ll-**) use a snorkel. [German *Schnorchel*]

**snort** — *n.* **1** explosive sound made esp. by horses by the sudden forcing of breath through the nose. **2** similar human sound showing contempt, incredulity, etc. **3** *colloq.* small drink of liquor. — *v.* **1** make a snort. **2** express or utter with a snort. **3** *colloq.* inhale (cocaine). [imitative]

**snorter** *n. colloq.* **1** something very impressive or difficult. **2** something vigorous or violent (*real snorter of a gale*).

**snot** *n. colloq.* nasal mucus. [probably Low German or Dutch: related to SNOUT]

**snotty** *adj.* (**-ier, -iest**) *colloq.* **1** running or covered with nasal mucus. **2** snooty, contemptible. □ **snottily** *adv.* **snottiness** *n.*

**snottygobble** *n.* any of several (chiefly WA) trees or shrubs yielding an edible fruit. [British dial., = fruit of the yew-tree]

**snout** *n.* **1** projecting nose and mouth of an animal. **2** *derog.* person's nose. **3** pointed front of a thing; nozzle. □ **have a snout on** (or **against**) *colloq.* be ill-disposed towards; have an aversion to. [Low German or Dutch]

**snow** /snoh/ — *n.* **1** frozen atmospheric vapour falling to earth in light white flakes. **2** fall or layer of this. **3** thing resembling snow in whiteness or texture etc. **4** flickering white spots on a television screen caused by interference or a weak signal. **5** *colloq.* cocaine. — *v.* **1** (prec. by *it* as subject) snow falls (*it is snowing; if it snows*). **2** (foll. by *in, over, up*, etc.) confine or block with snow. □ **be snowed under** be overwhelmed, esp. with work. □ **snowy** *adj.* (**-ier, -iest**) [Old English]

**snowball** — *n.* ball of compressed snow for throwing in play. — *v.* **1** throw or pelt with snowballs. **2** increase rapidly.

**snow chain** *n.* (usu. in *pl.*) chain placed around the driving wheel of a motor vehicle to aid traction on icy roads etc.

**snow daisy** *n.* alpine perennial of NSW and Victoria having large, snow-white daisy flowers.

**snowfall** *n.* **1** fall of snow. **2** amount of this.

**snowflake** *n.* each of the flakes in which snow falls.

**snow gum** *n.* any of several eucalypts of south-eastern Australia occurring both above and below the snowline, and having a smooth, usu. whitish trunk.

**snow-in-summer** *n.* any of several plants with such abundant masses of white flowers that the tree seems covered with snow, esp. *Melaleuca linariifolia.*

**snow job** n. colloq. attempt to cover up, or distract (a person's attention) from, the truth or unwelcome facts etc.

**snowline** n. level above which snow never melts entirely.

**snow pea** n. = SUGAR PEA.

**snowshoe** n. racquet-shaped attachment to a boot for walking on snow without sinking in.

**snowstorm** n. heavy fall of snow, esp. with a high wind.

**snow white** adj. & n. (as adj. often hyphenated) pure white.

**snub** — v. (-bb-) rebuff or humiliate with sharp words or coldness. — n. act of snubbing. — adj. short and blunt in shape. [Old Norse = chide]

**snub nose** n. short turned-up nose. □ **snub-nosed** adj.

**snuff¹** — n. charred part of a candle-wick. — v. trim the snuff from (a candle). □ **snuff it** colloq. die. **snuff out 1** extinguish (a candle flame). **2** put an end to (hopes etc.). [origin unknown]

**snuff²** — n. powdered tobacco or medicine taken by sniffing. — v. take snuff. [Dutch]

**snuffer** n. device for snuffing or extinguishing a candle.

**snuffle** /snuf-uhl/ — v. (-ling) **1** make sniffing sounds. **2** speak or say nasally or whiningly. **3** breathe noisily, esp. with a blocked nose. — n. snuffling sound or tone. □ **snuffly** adj. [Low German or Dutch snuffelen]

**snug** adj. (**snugger, snuggest**) **1** cosy, comfortable, sheltered. **2** (of a garment) close-fitting. **3** (of an income etc.) allowing comfort. □ **snugly** adv. [probably Low German or Dutch]

**snuggery** n. (pl. **-ies**) snug place, den.

**snuggle** /snug-uhl/ v. (-ling) settle or draw into a warm comfortable position.

**so¹** /soh/ — adv. **1** to such an extent (stop complaining so; so small as to be invisible; not so late as I expected; they were so pleased that they gave us a bonus). **2** in this or that way; in the manner, position, or state described or implied (place your feet so; am not cold but may become so). **3** also (he went and so did I). **4** indeed, actually (you said it was good, and so it is). **5** very (I am so glad). **6** (with verbs of saying or thinking etc.) thus, this, that (I think so; so he said). — conj. (often foll. by that) **1** consequently (was ill, so he couldn't come). **2** in order that (come early so that you may see my garden). **3** and then; as the next step (so then I gave up; and so to bed). **4 a** (introducing a question) then; after that (so what did you do?). **b** (absol.)

= so what? □ **and so on** (or **forth**) **1** and others of the same kind. **2** and in other similar ways. **or so** approximately (50 or so). **so as to** in order to. **so be it** expression of acceptance or resignation. **so long!** colloq. goodbye. **so much 1** a certain amount (of). **2** nothing but (so much nonsense). **so much for** that is all that need be done or said about (a thing). **so so** adj. & adv. colloq. only moderately good or well. **so to speak** expression of reserve or apology for an exaggeration etc.; in a manner of speaking. **so what?** colloq. why should that be considered significant? [Old English]

**so²** var. of SOH.

**-so** comb. form = -SOEVER.

**soak** — v. **1** make or become thoroughly wet through saturation. **2** (of rain etc.) drench. **3** (foll. by in, up) absorb (liquid, knowledge, etc.). **4** refl. (often foll. by in) steep (oneself) in a subject etc. **5** (foll. by in, into, through) (of liquid) go or penetrate by saturation. **6** colloq. extort money from (soak the rich). — n. **1** act of soaking; prolonged spell in a bath. **2** colloq. hard drinker. **3** a hollow in (often sandy) soil where water collects, on or below the surface of the ground; a waterhole. [Old English]

**soaking** adj. (in full **soaking wet**) wet through.

**so-and-so** /soh-uhn-,soh/ n. (pl. **-so's**) **1** particular but unspecified person or thing. **2** colloq. objectionable person.

**soap** — n. **1** cleansing agent yielding lather when rubbed in water. **2** colloq. = SOAP OPERA. — v. apply soap to. □ **not to know a person from a bar of soap** not to have the slightest acquaintance with. [Old English]

**soapbox** n. makeshift stand for a speaker in the street etc.

**soapie** /soh-pee/ n. **1** a young fish, esp. a jewfish. **2** colloq. = SOAP OPERA.

**soap opera** n. broadcast drama serial with domestic themes (orig. sponsored in the US by soap manufacturers).

**soapstone** n. steatite.

**soap tree** n. rainforest tree of Queensland and NSW having edible red fleshy fruit and leaves which may be used as a substitute for soap.

**soapy** adj. (**-ier, -iest**) **1** of or like soap. **2** containing or smeared with soap. **3** unctuous, flattering. □ **soapily** adv. **soapiness** n.

**soar** v. **1** fly or rise high. **2** reach a high level or standard. **3** fly without flapping the wings or using power. [French essorer]

**sob** — v. (-bb-) **1** inhale convulsively, usu. with weeping. **2** utter with sobs. — n. act or sound of sobbing. [imitative]

**sober** /**soh**-buh/ — adj. (**soberer**, **soberest**) **1** not drunk. **2** not given to drink. **3** moderate, tranquil, sedate, serious (*led a sober life*). **4** not exaggerated (*the sober truth*). **5** (of a colour etc.) quiet; inconspicuous. — v. (often foll. by *down*, *up*) make or become more sober. □ **soberly** adv. [French from Latin]

**sobriety** /suh-**bruy**-uh-tee/ n. the state of being sober. [Latin: related to SOBER]

**sobriquet** /**soh**-bruh-,kay/ n. (also **soubriquet** /**soo**-/) nickname. [French]

**sob story** n. colloq. story or explanation appealing for sympathy.

**so-called** adj. commonly called, often incorrectly.

**soccer** /**sok**-uh/ n. form of football played by sides of 11 in which players (except the goalkeepers) must not touch the ball with their hands or arms (except at throwins). [alteration of *Association Football*]

**Socceroo** /sok-uh-**roo**/ n. **1** (in pl.) the Australian international soccer team. **2** member of this team. [portmanteau word: SOCCER, KANGAROO]

**sociable** /**soh**-shuh-buhl/ adj. liking company, gregarious; friendly. □ **sociability** /-bil-uh-tee/ n. **sociably** adv. [Latin *socius* companion]

**social** /**soh**-shuhl/ — adj. **1** of society or its organisation, esp. of the relations of people or classes of people. **2** living in organised communities (*man is a social animal*). **3** needing companionship; gregarious. — n. social gathering, esp. of a club, school, etc. □ **socially** adv. [Latin: related to SOCIABLE]

**social climber** n. person anxious to gain a higher social status.

**social democracy** n. political system favouring a mixed economy and democratic social change. □ **social democrat** n.

**socialise** /**soh**-shuh-,luyz/ v. (also -**ize**) (-**sing** or -**zing**) **1** mix socially. **2** make social. **3** organise on socialistic principles. □ **socialisation** /-**zay**-shuhn/ n.

**socialism** n. **1** political and economic theory of social organisation which advocates that the community as a whole should own and control the means of production, distribution, and exchange. **2** social system based on this. □ **socialist** n. & adj. **socialistic** adj. [French: related to SOCIAL]

**socialite** /**soh**-shuh-,luyt/ n. person moving in fashionable society.

**social science** n. the study of society and social relationships. □ **social scientist** n.

**social security** n. government assistance to those lacking in economic security

and welfare, e.g. the aged and the unemployed.

**social welfare** n. services provided by the government for disadvantaged groups, esp. education, health, and housing.

**social work** n. professional or voluntary work with disadvantaged groups. □ **social worker** n.

**society** /suh-**suy**-uh-tee/ n. (pl. -**ies**) **1** organised and interdependent community. **2** system and organisation of this. **3** socially advantaged members of a community (*society would not approve*; *one needs to be well off to be in society*). **4** mixing with others; companionship, company (*avoids society*; *avoids the society of such people*). **5** club, association (*music society*; *building society*). □ **societal** adj. [Latin *societas*]

**socio-** comb. form of society or sociology (and) (*socio-economic*). [Latin: related to SOCIAL]

**socio-economic** adj. relating to or concerned with the interaction of social and economic matters.

**sociology** /,soh-see-**ol**-uh-jee/ n. **1** the study of the development, structure, and functioning, of human society. **2** the study of social problems. □ **sociological** /-uh-**loj**-i-kuhl/ adj. **sociologist** n. [French: related to SOCIAL]

**sock**[1] n. knitted covering for the foot and lower leg. □ **pull one's socks up** colloq. make an effort to improve. **put a sock in it** colloq. be quiet. [Old English *socc* from Greek *sukkhos* slipper]

**sock**[2] colloq. — v. hit hard. — n. hard blow. □ **sock it to** attack or address (a person or people) vigorously. [origin unknown]

**socket** /**sok**-uht/ n. **1** natural or artificial hollow for something to fit into or stand firm or revolve in (*eye socket*). **2** device for receiving an electric plug, lightbulb, etc. [Anglo-French]

**Socratic** /suh-**krat**-ik/ adj. of Socrates or his philosophy.

**Socratic irony** see IRONY.

**sod**[1] n. **1** turf, piece of turf. **2** surface of the ground. **3** damper, esp. one that has not risen. [Low German or Dutch]

**sod**[2] n. colloq. **1** unpleasant or awkward person or thing. **2** fellow (*lucky sod*). [abbreviation of SODOMITE]

**soda** /**soh**-duh/ n. **1** compound of sodium in common use, e.g. caustic soda. **2** (in full **soda water**) effervescent water used esp. with spirits etc. as a drink. **3** sweet effervescent drink. **4** colloq. **a** easy victim. **b** simple task, a pushover. [perhaps from Latin *sodanum* from Arabic]

**sodden** /**sod**-uhn/ adj. **1** saturated; soaked through. **2** (of bread etc.) heavy and moist. **3** stupid or dull etc. with drunkenness. [archaic past part. of SEETHE]

**sodium** /soh-dee-uhm/ n. soft silver-white metallic element. [from SODA]

**sodium bicarbonate** n. white crystalline compound used in baking-powder etc.

**sodium chloride** n. common salt.

**sodium hydroxide** n. strongly alkaline compound used in soap etc.; caustic soda.

**sodium nitrate** n. white powdery compound used in fertilisers etc.

**sodomite** /sod-uh-muyt/ n. person who practises sodomy. [Greek: related to SODOMY]

**sodomy** /sod-uh-mee/ n. = BUGGERY. □ **sodomise** v. (also **-ize**) (**-sing** or **-zing**). [Latin from *Sodom*: Gen. 18,19]

**soever** /soh-ev-uh/ adv. literary of any kind; to any extent (*how great soever it may be*).

**-soever** comb. form of any kind; to any extent (*whatsoever*; *howsoever*).

**sofa** /soh-fuh/ n. long upholstered seat with a back and arms. [Arabic *shuffa*]

**sofa bed** n. sofa that can be converted into a bed.

**soft** — adj. **1** (of a substance, material, etc.) not hard; easily cut or dented; malleable. **2** (of cloth etc.) smooth; fine; not rough. **3** (of wind etc.) mild, gentle. **4** (of water) low in mineral salts and lathering easily. **5** (of light or colour etc.) not brilliant or glaring. **6** (of sound) gentle, not loud. **7** (of a consonant) sibilant (as *c* in *ice*, *s* in *pleasure*). **8** (of an outline etc.) vague, blurred. **9** (of an action or manner etc.) gentle, conciliatory. **10** (of the heart, feelings, etc.) compassionate, sympathetic. **11** feeble, half-witted, silly, sentimental (*a bit soft in the head*). **12** colloq. (of a job etc.) easy, cushy. **13** (of drugs) not highly addictive (opp. HARD sense 8 b) (*marijuana is said to be a soft drug*). **14** (also **soft-core**) (of pornography) not highly obscene. **15** (of currency) likely to fall in value; not readily exchangeable into other currencies. **16** Polit. moderate (*Labor's soft left*). — adv. softly. □ **be soft on** colloq. **1** be lenient towards. **2** be infatuated with. **have a soft spot for** be fond of. □ **softish** adj. **softly** adv. **softness** n. [Old English]

**softball** n. form of baseball using a softer and larger ball.

**soft-centred** adj. **1** (of a sweet) having a soft centre. **2** soft-hearted; sentimental.

**soft drink** n. non-alcoholic drink.

**soften** /sof-uhn/ v. **1** make or become soft or softer. **2** (often foll. by *up*) **a** make weaker by preliminary attack. **b** make (a person) more receptive to persuasion. □ **softener** n.

**soft fruit** n. small stoneless fruit (a strawberry or currant).

**soft furnishings** n.pl. curtains, rugs, etc.

**soft-hearted** adj. tender, compassionate. □ **soft-heartedness** n.

**softie** n. (also **softy**) (pl. **-ies**) colloq. weak, silly, or soft-hearted person.

**softly-softly** adj. (also **softly, softly**) (of strategy) cautious and cunning.

**soft option** n. easier alternative.

**soft palate** n. rear part of the palate.

**soft pedal** — n. piano pedal that softens the tone. — v. (**soft-pedal**) (**-ll-**) refrain from emphasising; be restrained (*will need to soft-pedal this proposal*).

**soft roe** see ROE¹.

**soft sell** n. restrained or subtle salesmanship.

**soft soap** — n. colloq. persuasive flattery. — v. (**soft-soap**) colloq. persuade with flattery.

**soft-spoken** adj. having a gentle voice.

**soft touch** n. colloq. gullible person, esp. over money.

**software** n. programs for a computer (opp. HARDWARE 3).

**softwood** n. easily sawn wood of pine trees etc.

**softy** var. of SOFTIE.

**soggy** /sog-ee/ adj. (**-ier**, **-iest**) sodden, saturated; too moist (*soggy bread*; *soggy soil*). □ **sogginess** n. [British dial. *sog* marsh]

**soh** /soh/ n. (also **so**) Mus. fifth note of a major scale. [Latin *solve*, word arbitrarily taken]

**soil¹** n. **1** upper layer of earth in which plants grow. **2** ground belonging to a nation; territory (*on Australian soil*). [Latin *solium* seat, *solum* ground]

**soil²** — v. **1** make dirty; smear or stain (*soiled linen*). **2** defile; discredit (*would not soil my hands with it*; *reputation soiled by the scandal*). — n. **1** dirty mark. **2** filth; refuse; sewage. [French *soill(i)er*]

**soirée** /swah-ray, -ray/ n. evening party, usu. for conversation or music. [French]

**soixante-neuf** /swah-zon nerf/ n. coarse colloq. mutual oral stimulation of the genitals. [French, = sixty-nine]

**sojourn** /soh-jern, so-, su-/ — n. temporary stay. — v. stay temporarily. [French *sojorner*]

**solace** /sol-uhs/ — n. comfort in sadness, disappointment, or tedium. — v. (**-cing**) give solace to. [Latin *solatium*]

**solar** /soh-luh/ adj. **1** of or reckoned by the sun (*solar eclipse*; *solar time*). **2** using the energy of the sun (*solar energy*; *solar power*). [Latin *sol* sun]

**solar battery** n. (also **solar cell**) device converting solar radiation into electricity.

**solar day** n. interval between meridian transits of the sun.

**solarium** /suh-**lair**-ree-uhm/ n. (pl. **-ria**) room with sun-lamps or a glass roof etc. [Latin: related to SOLAR]

**solar panel** n. panel that absorbs the sun's rays as an energy source.

**solar plexus** n. complex of nerves at the pit of the stomach.

**solar system** n. the sun and the celestial bodies whose motion it governs.

**solar year** n. time taken for the earth to travel once round the sun.

**sold** past and past part. of SELL. — adj. (foll. by on) colloq. enthusiastic about.

**solder** /**sohl**-duh, **sol**-/ — n. fusible alloy used to join metals or wires etc. — v. join with solder. [Latin: related to SOLID]

**soldering iron** n. heated tool for melting and applying solder.

**soldier** /**sohl**-juh/ — n. **1** member of an army. **2** private or NCO in an army (opp. OFFICER). — v. serve as a soldier. □ **soldier on** colloq. persevere doggedly. □ **soldierly** adj. [French soulde, originally = soldier's pay]

**soldier ant** n. wingless ant or termite with a large head and jaws for fighting in defence of its colony, esp. the BULLDOG ANT.

**soldier bird** n. = NOISY MINER.

**soldier crab** n. small crab occurring in large numbers on sandy tidal flats, so called because of the way they move across the sand in large groups resembling formations of troops.

**soldier of fortune** n. mercenary.

**soldier-settlement** n. scheme by which Australian ex-service personnel were given land grants, usu. of previously uncultivated land.

**sole**[1] — n. **1** undersurface of the foot. **2** part of a shoe, sock, etc., under the foot, esp. other than the heel. — v. (**-ling**) provide (a shoe etc.) with a sole. □ **-soled** adj. (in comb.). [Latin solea sandal]

**sole**[2] n. (pl. same or **-s**) any of various flatfish (including those occurring in Australian waters) used as food. [Latin solea sandal, which the shape of the fish resembles]

**sole**[3] adj. one and only; single, exclusive (the sole reason; has the sole right). [French from Latin solus]

**solecism** /**sol**-uh-,siz-uhm/ n. **1** mistake of grammar or idiom e.g.: they done their homework; its a bad day; for sale: fresh ladies finger's. **2** offence against good manners or etiquette. □ **solecistic** /-**sis**-tik/ adj. [Greek soloikos speaking incorrectly]

**solely** /**soh**-lee/ adv. **1** alone (solely responsible). **2** only (did it solely out of duty).

**solemn** /**sol**-uhm/ adj. **1** serious and dignified (a solemn occasion). **2** formal (a solemn oath). **3** awe-inspiring (a solemn monument). **4** (of a person) serious or cheerless in manner. **5** grave, sober (solemn promise). □ **solemnly** adv. **solemness** n. [Latin solemnis]

**solemnise** /**sol**-uhm-,nuyz/ v. (also **-ize**) (**-sing** or **-zing**) **1** duly perform (esp. a marriage ceremony). **2** make solemn. □ **solemnisation** /-**zay**-shuhn/ n.

**solemnity** /suh-**lem**-nuh-tee/ n. (pl. **-ies**) **1** being solemn. **2** rite, ceremony.

**solenoid** /**soh**-luh-,noid, **so**-/ n. cylindrical coil of wire acting as a magnet when carrying electric current. [French from Greek sōlēn tube]

**sole parent** n. = SINGLE PARENT.

**sol-fa** /**sol**-fah/ n. system of syllables representing musical notes. [sol var. of SOH, FA]

**solicit** /suh-**lis**-uht/ v. (**-t-**) **1** seek (esp. business) repeatedly or earnestly. **2** (also absol.) accost as a prostitute. □ **solicitation** /-**tay**-shuhn/ n. [Latin sollicitus anxious]

**solicitor** n. lawyer qualified to advise clients, represent them in the lower courts, and instruct barristers. [French: related to SOLICIT]

**Solicitor-General** n. (pl. **Solicitors-General**) **1** principal legal adviser and counsel to the Australian government. **2** (in some other countries) law officer below the Attorney-General.

**solicitous** adj. **1** showing interest, concern, or anxiety (most solicitous of our welfare). **2** (foll. by to + infin.) eager, anxious. □ **solicitously** adv. **solicitude** n. [Latin: related to SOLICIT]

**solid** /**sol**-uhd/ — adj. (**-der**, **-dest**) **1** firm and stable in shape; not liquid or fluid (on solid ground; water becomes solid at 0° C). **2** of such material throughout, not hollow (a solid sphere). **3** of the same substance throughout (solid silver). **4** sturdily built; not flimsy or slender (solid garden furniture). **5 a** three-dimensional. **b** of solids (solid geometry). **6 a** sound, reliable (solid arguments). **b** dependable (solid friend). **7** sound but unexciting (solid piece of work). **8** financially sound. **9** uninterrupted (four solid hours). **10** unanimous, undivided (support has remained pretty solid so far). **11** (of printing) without spaces between the lines etc. **12** colloq. severe; unreasonable (they'll be solid on him for that mistake; got detention for a week — a bit solid, I reckon). — n. **1** solid substance or body.

**2** (in *pl.*) solid food. **3** *Geom.* three-dimensional body or magnitude. — *adv.* solidly (*jammed solid*). □ **solidly** *adv.* **solidness** *n.* [Latin *solidus*]

**solidarity** /ˌsol-uh-**da**-ruh-tee/ *n.* **1** unity, esp. political or in an industrial dispute. **2** mutual dependence. [French: related to SOLID]

**solidify** /suh-**lid**-uh-ˌfuy/ *v.* (**-ies, -ied**) make or become solid. □ **solidification** /-fuh-**kay**-shuhn/ *n.*

**solidity** /suh-**lid**-uh-tee/ *n.* being solid; firmness.

**solid-state** *adj.* using the electronic properties of solids (e.g. a semiconductor) to replace those of valves.

**solidus** /**sol**-uh-duhs/ *n.* (*pl.* **solidi** /-ˌduy/) oblique stroke (/) used in writing fractions, to denote alternatives (*and*/*or*), etc. [Latin: related to SOLID]

**solifluction** /ˌsol-uh-**fluk**-shuhn/ *n.* gradual movement of wet soil etc. down a slope.

**soliloquy** /suh-**lil**-uh-kwee/ *n.* (*pl.* **-quies**) **1** talking without or regardless of hearers, esp. in a play. **2** this part of a play. □ **soliloquise** *v.* (also **-ize**) (**-sing** or **-zing**) **soliloquist** *n.* [Latin *solus* alone, *loquor* speak]

**solipsism** /**sol**-ip-ˌsiz-uhm/ *n.* philosophical theory that the self is all that exists or can be known. □ **solipsist** *n.* [Latin *solus* alone, *ipse* self]

**solitaire** /ˌsol-uh-**tair**/ *n.* **1** jewel set by itself. **2** ring etc. with this. **3** game for one player in which pegs etc. are removed from a board by jumping others over them. **4** *US* = PATIENCE 3. [French: see SOLITARY]

**solitary** /**sol**-uh-tuh-ree, -tree/ — *adj.* **1** living or being alone; not gregarious; lonely. **2** (of a place) secluded or unfrequented. **3** single, sole (*a solitary instance*). — *n.* (*pl.* **-ies**) **1** recluse. **2** *colloq.* = SOLITARY CONFINEMENT. □ **solitariness** *n.* [Latin *solitarius* from *solus* alone]

**solitary confinement** *n.* isolation of a prisoner in a separate cell.

**solitude** /**sol**-uh-ˌtyood/ *n.* **1** the state of being solitary. **2** lonely place. [Latin *solitudo*: related to SOLITARY]

**solo** /**soh**-loh/ — *n.* (*pl.* **-s**) **1** (*pl.* **-s** or **soli** /-lee/) **a** a musical piece or passage, or a dance, performed by one person. **b** (*attrib.*) performed or performing as a solo (*solo passage*; *solo violin*). **2** thing done by one person, esp. an unaccompanied flight. **3** (in full **solo whist**) type of whist in which one player may oppose the others. — *v.* (**-es, -ed**) perform a solo. — *adv.* unaccompanied, alone (*flew solo for the first time*). [Italian from Latin: related to SOLE³]

**soloist** /**soh**-loh-uhst/ *n.* performer of a solo, esp. in music.

**solstice** /**sol**-stuhs/ *n.* either of the times when the sun is furthest from the equator, about 22 December (*summer solstice*) and about 21 June (*winter solstice*) in the Southern hemisphere. [Latin *solstitium* 'the sun standing still']

**soluble** /**sol**-yuh-buhl/ *adj.* **1** that can be dissolved, esp. in water. **2** (of a problem) solvable. □ **solubility** /-**bil**-uh-tee/ *n.* [Latin *solvo solut-* release]

**solute** /**sol**-yoot/ *n.* dissolved substance.

**solution** /suh-**loo**-shuhn/ *n.* **1** act of solving or means of solving a problem. **2 a** conversion of a solid or gas into a liquid by mixture with a liquid. **b** state resulting from this (*held in solution*). **3** act of dissolving or state of being dissolved.

**solve** *v.* (**-ving**) answer, remove, or effectively deal with (a problem). □ **solvable** *adj.*

**solvent** — *adj.* **1** able to pay one's debts; not in debt. **2** able to dissolve or form a solution with something. — *n.* liquid etc. that can dissolve substances or form a solution with something. □ **solvency** *n.* (in senses of *adj.*).

**somatic** /soh-**mat**-ik/ *adj.* of the body, not of the mind. □ **somatically** *adv.* [Greek *sōma -mat-* body]

**sombre** /**som**-buh/ *adj.* **1** dark, gloomy (*a sombre sky*). **2** dismal; forbidding (*a sombre prospect*). □ **sombrely** *adv.* **sombreness** *n.* [Latin *sub ombra* under shade]

**sombrero** /som-**brair**-roh/ *n.* (*pl.* **-s**) broad-brimmed hat worn esp. in Latin America. [Spanish: related to SOMBRE]

**some** /sum/ — *adj.* **1** unspecified amount or number of (*some water*; *some apples*; *some of them*). **2** unknown or unspecified (*some day*; *some fool broke it*). **3** approximately (*some ten days*). **4** considerable (*went to some trouble*; *at some cost*). **5** (usu. stressed) **a** at least a modicum of (*have some consideration*). **b** such up to a point (*that is some help*). **c** *colloq.* remarkable (*that was some party!*). — *pron.* some people or things, some number or amount (*I have some already*). — *adv. colloq.* to some extent (*do it some more*). [Old English]

**-some¹** *suffix* forming adjectives meaning: **1** producing (*fearsome*). **2** characterised by being (*gladsome*). **3** apt to (*tiresome*; *meddlesome*). **4** suitable for (*cuddlesome*). [Old English]

**-some²** *suffix* forming nouns from numerals, meaning 'a group of' (*foursome*). [Old English]

**somebody** — *pron.* some person. — *n.* (*pl.* **-ies**) important person (*thinks he's really somebody now*).

**someday** *adv.* at some time in the future.

**somehow** *adv.* **1** for some reason or other (*somehow I don't trust him*). **2** in some way; by some means (*he somehow dropped behind*).

**someone** *n. & pron.* = SOMEBODY.

**somersault** / **sum**-uh-solt, -ˌsawlt/ — *n.* **1** acrobatic leap or roll with the body turning through a circle. **2** complete about-turn (*the government has done a somersault on immigration policy*). — *v.* perform a somersault. [French *sobre* above, *saut* jump]

**something** *n. & pron.* **1** unspecified or unknown thing (*something has happened*). **2** unexpressed or intangible quantity, quality, or extent (*something strange about it*). **3** *colloq.* notable person or thing (*the party was quite something*). □ **or something** or some unspecified alternative (*must have run away or something*). **something else** *colloq.* an exceptional or remarkable person or thing. **something like 1** approximately (*left something like a million dollars*). **2** somewhat like (*shaped something like a saucer*). **something of** to some extent (*something of an expert*). [Old English: related to SOME, THING]

**sometime** — *adv.* **1** at some time. **2** formerly. — *attrib. adj.* former (*the sometime mayor*).

**sometimes** *adv.* occasionally.

**somewhat** *adv.* to some extent (*his behaviour was somewhat strange; answered somewhat hastily*).

**somewhere** — *adv.* in or to or at some place or point (*somewhere in that drawer; they went somewhere with the kids; she must be somewhere around 30*). — *pron.* some unspecified place (*most people now somewhere they can call their own*). □ **get somewhere** *colloq.* achieve success.

**somnambulism** / som-**nam**-byuh-ˌliz-uhm/ *n.* sleepwalking. □ **somnambulant** *adj.* **somnambulist** *n.* [Latin *somnus* sleep, *ambulo* walk]

**somnolent** / **som**-nuh-luhnt/ *adj.* **1** sleepy, drowsy. **2** inducing drowsiness (*a most somnolent sermon; the soft sounds of the stream had a somnolent effect*). □ **somnolence** *n.* [Latin *somnus* sleep]

**son** / sun/ *n.* **1** boy or man in relation to his parent(s). **2** male descendant. **3** (foll. by *of*) male member of a family, etc. **4** male descendant or inheritor of a quality etc. (*sons of the soil*). **5** form of address, esp. to a boy. **6** (**the Son**) (in Christian belief) the second person of the Trinity.

□ **I'll be a son of a gun!** expression of surprise. **son of a gun** jocular or affectionate form of address. [Old English]

**sonar** / **soh**-nuh/ *n.* **1** system for the underwater detection of objects by reflected sound. **2** apparatus for this. [*sound navigation and ranging*]

**sonata** / suh-**nah**-tuh/ *n.* composition for one or two instruments, usu. in three or four movements. [Italian, = sounded]

**sonatina** /ˌson-uh-**tee**-nuh/ *n.* simple or short sonata. [Italian, diminutive of SONATA]

**son et lumière** /ˌson ay **loo**-mee-air/ *n.* entertainment by night at a historic building etc., using lighting effects and recorded sound to give a dramatic narrative of its history. [French, = sound and light]

**song** *n.* **1** words set to music or meant to be sung. **2** singing or vocal music (*burst into song*). **3** musical composition suggestive of a song. **4** cry of some birds. **5** short poem, usu. in rhymed stanzas. □ **for a song** *colloq.* very cheaply. [Old English: related to SING]

**song and dance** *n. colloq.* fuss, commotion.

**song cycle** *n.* set of linked songs.

**song-lark** *n.* **1** the brown song-lark, melodious bird widespread throughout Australia. **2** the rufous song-lark, a brown bird with a red rump and melodious voice, widespread throughout Australia.

**songman** *n.* an Aborigine who memorises and performs sacred and other traditional songs of a community.

**songster** *n.* (*fem.* **songstress**) **1** singer. **2** songbird. **3** poet.

**sonic** / **son**-ik/ *adj.* of or using sound or sound waves. [Latin *sonus* sound]

**sonic bang** *n.* (also **sonic boom**) noise made when an aircraft passes the speed of sound.

**sonic barrier** *n.* = SOUND BARRIER.

**son-in-law** *n.* (*pl.* **sons-in-law**) daughter's husband.

**sonky** / **song**-kee/ *adj. colloq.* foolish; gawky. [British dial.]

**sonnet** / **son**-uht/ *n.* poem of 14 lines with a fixed rhyme scheme and, in English, usu. ten syllables per line. [French *sonnet* or Italian *sonetto*]

**sonny** / **sun**-ee/ *n. colloq.* familiar form of address to a young boy.

**sonorous** / **son**-uh-ruhs/ *adj.* **1** having a loud, full, or deep sound; resonant. **2** (of language, style, etc.) imposing, grand. □ **sonority** /suh-**no**-ruh-tee/ *n.* [Latin]

**sook** / suuk/ *n. colloq.* **1** timid, bashful person; crybaby. **2** timid racehorse. **3** hand-reared calf. □ **sooky** *adj.* [British dial. *suck* call-word for a calf]

**sool** /sool/ v. *colloq.* **1** (of a dog) attack or worry (an animal). **2** (frequently as *imper.*) incite or goad a dog to attack. **3** (often foll. by *on*) urge, excite to go after (*sooled his dog on the feral pig; who sooled the priest on me?*).

**soon** *adv.* **1** in a short time (*shall soon know*). **2** relatively early (*must you go so soon?*). **3** readily or willingly (*would sooner go; would as soon stay*). **4** early; quickly (*how soon will you be ready?*). □ **as** (or **so**) **soon as** at the moment that; not later than; as early as (*came as soon as I could*). **no sooner . . . than** at the very moment that (*no sooner had we arrived than the rain stopped*). **sooner or later** at some future time; eventually. □ **soonish** *adv.* [Old English]

**sooner** *n. colloq.* an idler; shirker (*a 'sooner' is one who would sooner rest than work*).

**soot** /suut/ *n.* black powdery deposit from smoke. [Old English]

**sooth** /sooth/ *n. archaic* truth. [Old English]

**soothe** /sooth/ v. (**-thing**) **1** calm (a person, feelings, etc.). **2** soften or mitigate (pain etc.). [Old English]

**soothsayer** /sooth-,say-uh/ *n.* seer, prophet.

**sooty** /suut-ee/ *adj.* (**-ier, -iest**) **1** covered with soot. **2** black or brownish-black. **3** used as a distinguishing epithet in the names of some Australian birds (*sooty owl; sooty oystercatcher*).

**sop** — *n.* **1** thing given or done to pacify or bribe. **2** piece of bread etc. dipped in gravy etc. **3** *colloq.* coward; weak or stupid person. — v. (**-pp-**) **1** (as **sopping** *adj.*) drenched (*came home sopping; sopping wet clothes*). **2** (foll. by *up*) soak or mop up. [Old English]

**sophism** /sof-iz-uhm/ *n.* false argument, esp. one intended to deceive. [Greek *sophos* wise]

**sophist** /sof-uhst/ *n.* one who reasons with clever but fallacious arguments. □ **sophistic** /so-**fis**-tik/ *adj.* [Greek: related to SOPHISM]

**sophisticate** — v. /suh-**fis**-tuh-kayt/ make sophisticated. — *n.* /suh-**fis**-tuh-kuht/ sophisticated person. [medieval Latin: related to SOPHISM]

**sophisticated** /suh-**fis**-tuh-,kay-tuhd/ *adj.* **1** (of a person) worldly-wise; cultured; elegant; discriminating in taste and judgment. **2** (of a thing, idea, etc.) highly developed and complex. □ **sophistication** /-**kay**-shuhn/ *n.*

**sophistry** /sof-uhs-tree/ *n.* (*pl.* **-ies**) **1** use of sophisms. **2** a sophism.

**soporific** /,sop-uh-**rif**-ik/ — *adj.* inducing sleep. — *n.* soporific drug or influence. □ **soporifically** *adv.* [Latin *sopor* sleep]

**sopping** see SOP.

**soppy** *adj.* (**-ier, -iest**) **1** soaked with water. **2** *colloq.* mawkishly sentimental; silly; infatuated (*a soppy romantic novel; is soppy about him*). □ **soppily** *adv.* **soppiness** *n.* [from SOP]

**soprano** /suh-**prah**-noh/ *n.* (*pl.* **-s**) **1 a** highest singing-voice. **b** female or boy singer with this voice. **2** instrument of a high or the highest pitch in its family. [Italian *sopra* above]

**sorbet** /saw-bay, -buht/ *n.* **1** iced dessert made with fruit, liqueurs, etc. **2** frozen dessert made with fruit-juice, egg whites, etc. [Arabic *sharba* to drink]

**sorcerer** /saw-suh-ruh/ *n.* **1** (*fem.* **sorceress**) magician, wizard. **2** = KORADJI. □ **sorcery** *n.* (*pl.* **-ies**). [French *sourcier*: related to SORT]

**sordid** /saw-duhd/ *adj.* **1** dirty, squalid (*sordid hovels*). **2** ignoble, mercenary (*acted from the most sordid of motives*). □ **sordidly** *adv.* **sordidness** *n.* [Latin *sordidus*]

**sore** — *adj.* **1** (of a part of the body) painful. **2** (of a person) **a** suffering physical pain (*still feeling a bit sore*). **b** suffering (or causing to suffer) mental or emotional pain (*sore at heart; my deepest sympathies on your sore loss*). **3** (often foll. by *about, at*) aggrieved, vexed; angry (*sore about losing the job*). **4** *archaic* grievous or severe (*in sore need*). — *n.* **1** inflamed place on the skin or flesh. **2** source of distress or annoyance. — *adv. archaic* grievously, severely (*was sore distressed*). □ **soreness** *n.* [Old English]

**sore loser** *n.* bad loser, unsporting in defeat.

**sorely** *adv.* extremely (*sorely tempted; sorely vexed*).

**sore point** *n.* subject causing distress or annoyance.

**sorghum** /saw-guhm/ *n.* tropical cereal grass. [Italian *sorgo*]

**sorrel¹** /so-ruhl/ *n.* sour-leaved herb. [Germanic: related to SOUR]

**sorrel²** /so-ruhl/ — *adj.* of a light reddish-brown colour. — *n.* **1** this colour. **2** sorrel animal, esp. a horse. [French]

**sorrow** /so-roh/ — *n.* **1** mental distress caused by loss or disappointment etc. **2** cause of sorrow (*the loss was a great sorrow to her*). — v. feel sorrow, mourn. [Old English]

**sorrowful** *adj.* **1** feeling or showing sorrow. **2** distressing, lamentable. □ **sorrowfully** *adv.*

**sorry** /so-ree/ — adj. (**-ier, -iest**) **1** pained, regretful, penitent (sorry about the mess). **2** (foll. by for) feeling pity or sympathy for. **3** (attrib.) wretched (a sorry sight). **4** (in Aboriginal English) of or relating to mourning (sorry business; sorry camp; sorry cut). — int. expression of apology. □ **sorry for oneself** dejected. [Old English: related to SORE]

**sorry business** n. (in Aboriginal English) mortuary rites.

**sorry camp** n. (in Aboriginal English) a mourning camp.

**sorry cut** n. (in Aboriginal English) incision signifying ritual mourning.

**sort** — n. **1** group of similar things etc.; class or kind (this sort of person; these sorts of events; what sorts of books sell best? arrange them by sorts). **2** (foll. by of) roughly of the kind specified (is some sort of doctor). **3** colloq. **a** person of a specified kind (a good sort). **b** female, esp. one who is young and attractive; girl-friend. — v. (often foll. by out, over) arrange systematically or according to type, class, etc.; put in order. □ **of a sort** (or **of sorts**) colloq. barely deserving the name (a holiday of sorts). **out of sorts** slightly unwell; in low spirits. **sort of** colloq. as it were; to some extent. **sort out 1** separate into sorts. **2** select from a varied group. **3** disentangle or put into order. **4** resolve (a problem or difficulty). **5** colloq. deal with or reprimand; set straight (need to sort him out). [Latin sors sort- lot]

**sortie** /saw-tee/ — n. **1** sally, esp. from a besieged garrison. **2** operational military flight. — v. (**-ties, -tied, -tieing**) make a sortie. [French]

**SOS** /,es-oh-es/ n. (pl. **SOSs**) **1** international code-signal of extreme distress. **2** urgent appeal for help. [letters easily recognised in Morse]

**sostenuto** /sos-tuh-**noo**-toh/ Mus. — adv. & adj. in a sustained or prolonged manner. — n. (pl. **-s**) passage to be played in this way. [Italian]

**sot** n. habitual drunkard. □ **sottish** adj. [Old English]

**sotto voce** /,sot-oh **voh**-chee, -chay/ adv. in an undertone or aside. [Italian]

**sou** /soo/ n. **1** colloq. very small sum of money (haven't a sou). **2** hist. former French coin of low value. [French from Latin: related to SOLID]

**soubrette** /soo-**bret**/ n. **1** pert maid-servant etc. in a comedy. **2** actress taking this part. [French]

**soubriquet** var. of SOBRIQUET.

**soufflé** /soo-flay/ n. light spongy sweet or savoury dish usu. made with stiffly beaten egg whites and gelatine. [French, = blown]

**sough** /sow/ — v. moan or whisper like the wind in trees etc. — n. this sound. [Old English]

**sought** past and past part. of SEEK.

**sought-after** adj. generally desired; much in demand.

**soul** /sohl/ n. **1** spiritual or immaterial part of a person, often regarded as immortal. **2** moral, emotional, or intellectual nature of a person. **3** personification or pattern (the very soul of discretion). **4** an individual (not a soul in sight). **5** person regarded with familiarity or pity etc. (the poor soul; a good soul). **6** person regarded as an animating or essential part (life and soul of the party). **7** energy or intensity, esp. in a work of art. **8** Black American culture or music etc. □ **upon my soul** exclamation of surprise. [Old English]

**soul-destroying** adj. (of an activity etc.) tedious, monotonous.

**soulful** adj. having, expressing, or evoking deep feeling. □ **soulfully** adv.

**soulless** adj. **1** having no soul. **2** lacking sensitivity or noble qualities. **3** undistinguished or uninteresting.

**soul mate** n. person ideally suited to another.

**soul music** n. Black American music with rhythm and blues, gospel, and rock elements.

**soul-searching** n. examination of one's emotions or motives.

**sound¹** — n. **1** sensation caused in the ear by the vibration of the surrounding air or other medium. **2** vibrations causing this sensation. **3** what is or may be heard (the sound of thunder; the sound of his voice). **4** idea or impression conveyed by words (don't like the sound of that). **5** mere words (all sound and fury). — v. **1** (cause to) emit sound (sounded the trumpets; the trumpets sounded). **2** utter, pronounce (sound a warning note). **3** convey an impression when heard (he sounds worried). **4** give an audible signal for (an alarm etc.). **5** test by noting the sound produced (the doctor sounds a patient's lungs with a stethoscope). □ **sound off 1** talk loudly or express one's opinions forcefully or angrily. **2** exaggerate, boast (sounding off about his new car). □ **soundless** adj. [Latin sonus]

**sound²** — adj. **1** healthy; not diseased, injured, or rotten. **2** (of an opinion, policy, etc.) correct, well-founded. **3** financially secure (a sound investment). **4** undisturbed (sound sleeper). **5** thorough (sound thrashing). — adv. soundly (sound *asleep*). □ **sound as a bell** perfectly sound and healthy; in fine condition. □ **soundly** *adv.* **soundness** *n.* [Old English]

**sound³** *v.* **1** test the depth or quality of the bottom of (the sea or a river etc.). **2** (often foll. by *out*) inquire (esp. discreetly) into the opinions or feelings of (a person). **3** (of a whale or fish) dive to the bottom. □ **sounding** *n.* [French *sonder* from Latin *sub unda* under the wave]

**sound⁴** *n.* narrow passage (of water) connecting two seas, a sea and a lake, or the mainland and an island. [Old English, = swimming]

**sound barrier** *n.* high resistance of air to objects moving at speeds near that of sound.

**soundbox** *n.* the hollow body of a stringed musical instrument, providing resonance.

**sound centre** *n.* set of equipment comprising radio, compact disc player, video, etc.

**sound effect** *n.* sound other than speech or music made artificially for a film, broadcast, stage play, etc.

**sounding-board** *n.* **1** thin sheet of wood over which the strings of a piano etc. pass to increase the sound produced. **2 a** person etc. used as a trial audience to test opinion. **b** means of causing opinions etc. to be more widely known (*used his students as a sounding-board*). **3** canopy directing sound towards an audience.

**sound mixer** *n.* **1** person who combines sounds from various sources (for a film, radio broadcast, etc.). **2** equipment for mixing sound.

**soundproof** — *adj.* impervious to sound. — *v.* make soundproof.

**sound system** *n.* equipment for sound reproduction.

**soundtrack** *n.* **1** the sound element of a film or video. **2** recording of this made available separately.

**sound wave** *n.* wave of compression and rarefaction, by which sound is transmitted in the air etc.

**soup** /soop/ — *n.* liquid food made by boiling meat, fish, or vegetables. — *v.* (usu. foll. by *up*) *colloq.* **1** increase the power of (an engine). **2** enliven (*a souped-up version of the original*). □ **in the soup** *colloq.* in difficulties. [French]

**soupçon** /soop-song, -son/ *n.* small quantity; trace. [French: related to SUSPICION]

**soup kitchen** *n.* place dispensing soup etc. to the disadvantaged etc.

**soupy** *adj.* (**-ier, -iest**) **1** like soup. **2** sentimental.

**sour** — *adj.* **1** acid in taste or smell, esp. because unripe or fermented (*a sour apple*; *sour milk*). **2** morose; bitter (*in a sour mood*; *the experience left him very sour*). **3** (of a thing) unpleasant; distasteful (*a sour duty to perform*). **4** (of the soil) deficient in lime; excessively acid. — *v.* make or become sour. □ **go** (or **turn**) **sour 1** turn out badly (*the job went sour on him*). **2** lose one's keenness (*went sour on the idea*). □ **sourly** *adv.* **sourness** *n.* [Old English]

**source** /saws/ *n.* **1** place from which a river or stream issues. **2** place, person, or thing from which something originates (*source of all our troubles*). **3** person or document etc. providing information. □ **at source** at the point of origin or issue. [French: related to SURGE]

**sour grapes** *n.pl.* resentful disparagement of something one covets.

**sourpuss** *n.* *colloq.* sour-tempered person.

**soursob** *n.* (also **soursobs, soursops**) any of several perennial herbs of the genus *Oxalis*, esp. the S. African species *O. pes-caprae* which is naturalised in all Australian States and declared a noxious weed in some. [British dial.]

**souse** /sows/ — *v.* (**-sing**) **1** immerse in pickle or other liquid. **2** (as **soused** *adj.*) *colloq.* drunk. **3** (usu. foll. by *in*) soak (a thing) in liquid. — *n.* **1** pickle made with salt. **2** a plunge or a drench in liquid. [French *sous*]

**soutane** /soo-**tahn**, -**tan**/ *n.* cassock worn by a Roman Catholic priest. [French from Italian *sotto* under]

**south** — *n.* **1** point of the horizon 90° clockwise from east. **2** compass point corresponding to this. **3** direction in which this lies. **4** (usu. **the South**) part of the world, a country, or a town, to the south. — *adj.* **1** towards, at, near, or facing the south. **2** from the south (*south wind*). — *adv.* **1** towards, at, or near the south. **2** (foll. by *of*) further south than. □ **to the south** (often foll. by *of*) in a southerly direction. [Old English]

**South African** — *adj.* of the republic of South Africa. — *n.* **1** native or national of South Africa. **2** person of South African descent.

**South American** — *adj.* of South America. — *n.* native or national of a South American country.

**South Australian** — *adj.* of or relating to the State of South Australia. — *n.* native or resident of South Australia.

**southbound** *adj.* travelling or leading southwards.

**south-east** — *n.* **1** point of the horizon midway between south and east. **2** direction in which this lies. — *adj.* of, towards, or coming from the south-east. — *adv.* towards, at, or near the south-east.

**southeaster** /sowth-**ee**-stuh/ *n.* south-east wind.

**south-easterly** *adj. & adv.* = SOUTH-EAST.

**south-eastern** *adj.* on the south-east side.

**southerly** /*suth*-uh-lee/ — *adj. & adv.* **1** in a southern position or direction. **2** (of a wind) from the south. — *n.* (*pl.* **-ies**) such a wind.

**southerly buster** *n.* sudden strong cool wind from the south, affecting the south-eastern coast of Australia; cool change.

**southern** /*suth*-uhn/ *adj.* **1** of or in the south. **2** used as a distinguishing epithet in the names of Australian fauna and flora (*southern bluefin; southern blue gum*). □ **southernmost** *adj.*

**Southern Cross** *n.* **1** southern constellation in the shape of a cross, and represented on the flags of Australia and New Zealand. **2** = EUREKA FLAG. **3** WA perennial with heartshaped toothed leaves and attractive flowers which, with their bracts, form a perfect white cross. □ **land of the Southern Cross** Australia.

**southerner** *n.* **1** native or inhabitant of the south. **2** often derisive epithet used by Queenslanders and Northern Territorians to designate a person normally resident in a southern State.

**Southern hemisphere** *n.* the half of the earth south of the equator.

**southern lights** *n.pl.* aurora australis.

**southpaw** *colloq.* — *n.* left-handed person, esp. in boxing. — *adj.* left-handed.

**south pole** see POLE².

**South Sea** *n.* (also **Seas**) southern Pacific Ocean.

**south-south-east** *n.* point or direction midway between south and south-east.

**south-south-west** *n.* point or direction midway between south and south-west.

**southward** /**sowth**-wuhd/ — *adj. & adv.* (also **southwards**) towards the south. — *n.* southward direction or region.

**south-west** — *n.* **1** point of the horizon midway between south and west. **2** direction in which this lies. — *adj.* of, towards, or coming from the south-west. — *adv.* towards, at, or near the south-west.

**southwester** /sowth-**wes**-tuh/ *n.* south-west wind.

**south-westerly** *adj. & adv.* = SOUTH-WEST.

**south-western** *adj.* on the south-west side.

**souvenir** /ˌsoo-vuh-**neer**/ — *n.* memento

of an occasion, place, etc. — *v. colloq.* steal (usu. a small item) to use as a souvenir (*souvenired an ashtray from the motel*). [French]

**souvlaki** /soo-**vlah**-kee/ *n.* Greek dish of pieces of meat (esp. lamb) grilled on a skewer. [modern Greek]

**sou'wester** /sow-**wes**-tuh/ *n.* **1** waterproof hat with a broad flap covering the neck. **2** south-west wind. [from SOUTHWESTER]

**sovereign** /**sov**-ruhn/ — *n.* **1** supreme ruler, esp. a monarch. **2** *hist.* British gold coin nominally worth £1. — *adj.* **1** supreme (*sovereign power*). **2** self-governing (*sovereign State*). **3** royal. **4** excellent; effective (*sovereign remedy*). **5** unmitigated (*sovereign contempt*). [French *so(u)verain*: -*g*- by association with *reign*]

**sovereignty** *n.* (*pl.* **-ies**) **1** supremacy. **2 a** self-government. **b** self-governing State.

**soviet** /**soh**-vee-uht, **sov**-ee-uht/ — *n.* **1** elected local, district, or national council. **2** *hist.* revolutionary council of workers, peasants, etc., in Russia before 1917. — *adj.* (usu. **Soviet**) of or concerning the former Soviet Union. [Russian]

**sow¹** /soh/ *v.* (*past* **sowed**; *past part.* **sown** or **sowed**) **1** (also *absol.*) **a** scatter (seed) on or in the earth. **b** (often foll. by *with*) plant with seed. **2** initiate (*sow hatred*). □ **sow the seed** (or **the seeds**) **of** first give rise to; implant (an idea etc.). **sow one's wild oats** indulge in youthful excess or promiscuity. [Old English]

**sow²** /sow/ *n.* adult female pig. [Old English]

**soy** *n.* **1** (in full **soy sauce**) sauce from fermented soya beans. **2** (in full **soybean**) = SOYA 1. [Japanese]

**soya** /**soi**-yuh/ *n.* **1** (in full **soya bean**) **a** leguminous plant yielding edible oil and flour and used to replace animal protein. **b** seed of this. **2** (in full **soya sauce**) = SOY 1. [Malay: related to SOY]

**soy milk** *n.* beverage of soaked and ground soya beans with water, often used as a milk substitute.

**sozzled** /**soz**-uhld/ *adj. colloq.* very drunk. [British dial. *sozzle* mix sloppily (imitative)]

**SP** *abbr. Racing* starting price; the final odds of a horse or greyhound at the start of a race.

**spa** /spah/ *n.* **1** curative mineral spring. **2** resort with this. **3 a** (also **spa bath**) = JACUZZI. **b** (also **spa pool**) usu. outdoor pool, usu. attached to a swimming pool, with massaging underwater jets of water. [*Spa* in Belgium]

**space** — *n.* **1 a** continuous expanse in which things exist and move. **b** amount of this taken by a thing or available (*bed takes up too much space*; *space for three more books*). **2** interval between points or objects (*1 metre space between each pair of trees*). **3** empty area (*make a space*). **4 a** outdoor urban recreation area (*open space*). **b** large unoccupied region (*wide open spaces*). **5** = OUTER SPACE. **6** interval of time (*in the space of an hour*). **7** amount of paper used in writing, available for advertising, etc. (*no space left for the footnote*). **8 a** blank between printed, typed, or written words, etc. **b** piece of metal providing this. **9** freedom to think, be oneself, etc. (*need my own space*). **10** *Mus.* each of the blanks between the lines of a staff. — *v.* (**-cing**) **1** set or arrange at intervals. **2** put spaces between. **3** (as **spaced** *adj.*) (often foll. by *out*) *colloq.* **a** euphoric, esp. from taking drugs. **b** acting strangely, as if from taking drugs. □ **space out** spread out (more) widely. □ **spacer** *n.* [Latin *spatium*]

**space age** — *n.* era of space travel. — *attrib. adj.* (**space-age**) very modern (*space-age technology*).

**spacecraft** *n.* vehicle for travelling in outer space.

**spaceman** *n.* (*fem.* **spacewoman**) astronaut.

**space-saving** *adj.* occupying little space or helping to save space.

**spaceship** *n.* spacecraft.

**space shuttle** *n.* spacecraft for repeated use, esp. between the earth and a space station.

**space station** *n.* artificial satellite as a base for operations in outer space.

**spacesuit** *n.* sealed pressurised suit for an astronaut in outer space.

**space-time** *n.* (also **space-time continuum**) fusion of the concepts of space and time, esp. as a four-dimensional continuum.

**spacious** /spay-shuhs/ *adj.* having ample space; roomy. □ **spaciously** *adv.* **spaciousness** *n.* [Latin: related to SPACE]

**spade¹** — *n.* long-handled digging tool with a broad sharp-edged metal blade. — *v.* dig over (ground) with a spade. □ **call a spade a spade** speak bluntly. □ **spadeful** *n.* (*pl.* **-s**). [Old English]

**spade²** *n.* **1** playing-card of a suit denoted by black inverted heart-shaped figures with short stalks. **2** (in *pl.*) this suit. [Italian *spada* sword: related to SPADE¹]

**spadework** *n.* hard preparatory work.

**spaghetti** /spuh-**get**-ee/ *n.* pasta in long thin strands. [Italian]

**spaghetti western** *n.* cowboy film made cheaply in Italy.

**span¹** — *n.* **1** full extent from end to end (*the span of a bridge*; *the whole span of history*). **2** each part of a bridge between supports. **3** maximum lateral extent of an aeroplane or its wing, or a bird's wing, etc. **4 a** maximum distance between the tips of the thumb and little finger. **b** this as a measure of 9 in. (23 cm). — *v.* (**-nn-**) **1** stretch from side to side of; extend across. **2** bridge (a river etc.). [Old English]

**span²** see SPICK AND SPAN.

**spandrel** /**span**-druhl/ *n.* space between the curve of an arch and the surrounding rectangular moulding, or between the curves of adjoining arches and the moulding above. [origin uncertain]

**spangle** /**spang**-guhl/ — *n.* small piece of glittering material, esp. one of many used to ornament a dress etc.; sequin. — *v.* (**-ling**) (esp. as **spangled** *adj.*) cover with or as with spangles (*star-spangled*). [obsolete *spang* from Dutch]

**spangled drongo** /**drong**-goh/ *n.* bird of northern and eastern Australia, having glossy black plumage with iridescent blue-green spangles or spots.

**Spaniard** /**span**-yuhd/ *n.* **1** native or national of Spain. **2** person of Spanish descent. [French *Espaigne* Spain]

**spaniel** /**span**-yuhl/ *n.* dog of a breed with a long silky coat and drooping ears. [French *espaigneul* Spanish (dog)]

**Spanish** /**span**-ish/ — *adj.* of Spain, its people, or language. — *n.* **1** the language of Spain and Spanish America. **2** (**the Spanish**) (*pl.*) the people of Spain. [*Spain* in Europe]

**Spanish Main** *n. hist.* NE coast of S. America and adjoining parts of the Caribbean Sea.

**spank** — *v.* slap, esp. on the buttocks, as punishment. — *n.* slap, esp. on the buttocks. [imitative]

**spanking** — *adj.* **1** brisk (*at a spanking pace*). **2** *colloq.* striking; excellent. — *adv. colloq.* very (*spanking new*). — *n.* slapping on the buttocks.

**spanner** *n.* tool for turning a nut on a bolt etc. [German]

**spanner in the works** *n. colloq.* drawback or impediment.

**spar¹** *n.* **1** stout pole, esp. as a ship's mast etc. **2** main longitudinal beam of an aeroplane wing. [Old Norse *sperra* or French *esparre*]

**spar²** — *v.* (**-rr-**) **1** make the motions of boxing without heavy blows. **2** engage in argument, but not with great seriousness (*they are always sparring*). — *n.* **1** sparring motion. **2** boxing match. [Old English]

**spar³** *n.* easily split crystalline mineral. [Low German]

**spare** — adj. **1 a** not required for normal or immediate use; extra (spare cash; spare time). **b** for emergency or occasional use (spare room). **2** lean; thin. **3** frugal (spare diet). **4** not wanted or used by others (spare seat in the front row). — n. = SPARE PART. — v. (**-ring**) **1** afford to give, do without; dispense with (spared me ten minutes; cannot spare him just now). **2 a** refrain from killing, hurting, etc. (spared his feelings). **b** abstain from inflicting (spare me this task). **3** be frugal or grudging of (no expense spared). □ **not spare oneself** exert one's utmost efforts. **spare a person's life** not kill him or her. **to spare** left over; additional (an hour to spare). □ **sparely** adv. **spareness** n. [Old English]

**spare part** n. (also **spare**) duplicate part, esp. as a replacement.

**spare rib** n. closely trimmed ribs of esp. pork. [Low German ribbesper, associated with SPARE]

**spare tyre** n. **1** extra tyre carried for emergencies. **2** colloq. roll of fat round the waist.

**sparing** adj. **1** frugal; economical (be more sparing with your advice; be sparing with the chilli). **2** restrained, not lavish (she was rather sparing in her praise of our efforts). □ **sparingly** adv.

**spark** — n. **1** fiery particle thrown from a fire, alight in ashes, or produced by a flint, match, etc. **2** (often foll. by of) small amount (spark of interest; not a spark of life). **3 a** flash of light between electric conductors etc. **b** this serving to ignite the explosive mixture in an internal-combustion engine. **4 a** flash of wit etc.; liveliness. **b** (also **bright spark**) witty or lively person. — v. **1** emit a spark or sparks. **2** (often foll. by off) stir into activity; initiate (sparked off a heated debate). [Old English]

**sparkle** / spah-kuhl/ — v. (**-ling**) **1 a** emit or seem to emit sparks; glitter, glisten (his eyes sparkled). **b** be witty; scintillate (sparkling repartee). **2** (of wine etc.) effervesce. — n. **1** glitter (the sparkle of her diamonds). **2** lively quality (the song lacks sparkle).

**sparkler** n. hand-held sparkling firework.

**spark plug** n. device for making a spark in an internal-combustion engine.

**sparring partner** n. **1** boxer employed to spar with another as training. **2** person with whom one enjoys arguing.

**sparrow** / spa-roh/ n. (also **house-sparrow**) small brownish-grey introduced bird, extremely common in eastern Australia, but not yet in WA. [Old English]

**sparrowhawk** n. **1** = COLLARED SPARROW-HAWK. **2** = NANKEEN KESTREL.

**sparse** adj. thinly dispersed or scattered; not dense (sparse population; sparse grey hair). □ **sparsely** adv. **sparseness** n. **sparsity** n. [Latin spargo spars- scatter]

**Spartan** / spah-tuhn/ — adj. **1** of Sparta in ancient Greece. **2** (**spartan**) austere, rigorous, sternly frugal (a spartan lifestyle). — n. citizen of Sparta. [Latin]

**spasm** / spaz-uhm/ n. **1** sudden involuntary muscular contraction. **2** convulsive movement or emotion etc. (spasm of coughing; a spasm of grief). **3** (usu. foll. by of) colloq. brief spell of an activity (does his gardening in spasms). [Greek spasma from spaō pull]

**spasmodic** / spaz-**mod**-ik/ adj. **1** of, caused by, or subject to a spasm or spasms (spasmodic asthma). **2** occurring or done by fits and starts (spasmodic efforts). □ **spasmodically** adv. [Greek: related to SPASM]

**spastic** / **spas**-tik/ — adj. **1** = SPASMODIC (sense 1), esp. of cerebral palsy. **2** colloq. offens. drunk. — n. **1** person who is spastic, esp. suffering from cerebral palsy. **2** colloq. offens. **a** stupid or incompetent person. **b** a drunk. [Greek: related to SPASM]

**spat¹** past and past part. of SPIT¹.

**spat²** n. (usu. in pl.) hist. short gaiter covering a shoe. [abbreviation of spatter-dash: related to SPATTER]

**spat³** colloq. — n. petty or brief quarrel. — v. (**-tt-**) quarrel pettily. [probably imitative]

**spat⁴** — n. spawn of shellfish, esp. the oyster. — v. (of an oyster etc.) spawn; shed (spawn). [Anglo-French, of unknown origin]

**spatchcock** n. extremely small chicken (or very small game-bird) split open and grilled.

**spate** n. **1** river-flood (river in spate). **2 a** unexpected occurrence of similar events (spate of car thefts). **b** large or excessive amount (spate of enquiries). [origin unknown]

**spathe** / spayth/ n. large bract(s) enveloping a flower-cluster. [Greek spathē broad blade]

**spatial** / **spay**-shuhl/ adj. of or concerning space. □ **spatially** adv. [Latin: related to SPACE]

**spätlese** / shpet-**lay**-zuh/ n. very sweet white wine made from late-picked grapes.

**spatter** — v. **1 a** (often foll. by with) splash (a person etc.) (spattered him with mud). **b** scatter or splash (liquid, mud, etc.) here and there. **2** (of rain etc.) fall here and there (the window shattered *and bits of glass spattered everywhere).* — *n.* **1** splash (*a spatter of mud*). **2** quick pattering sound. □ **spattering** *n.* [imitative]

**spatula** / **spach**-uh-luh/ *n.* broad-bladed flexible implement used for spreading, stirring, mixing paints, etc. [Latin diminutive: related to SPATHE]

**spawn** — *v.* **1 a** (of a fish, frog, etc.) produce (eggs). **b** be produced as eggs or young. **2 a** *derog.* (of people) produce offspring (esp. in large numbers). **b** produce or generate in large numbers (*spawned a spate of trashy novels*). — *n.* **1** eggs of fish, frogs, etc. **2** *derog.* human offspring. **3** mycelium of mushrooms or other fungi. □ **spawner** *n.* [Anglo-French *espaundre*: related to EXPAND]

**spay** *v.* sterilise (a female animal) by removing the ovaries. [Anglo-French: related to *épée* sword]

**speak** *v.* (*past* **spoke**; *past part.* **spoken**) **1** utter words in an ordinary (not singing) voice. **2** utter (words, the truth, etc.) (*she speaks sense*). **3 a** converse; talk (*spoke to her earlier; had to speak to the children about rudeness*). **b** (foll. by *of, about*) mention in writing etc. (*speaks of it in his novel*). **c** (foll. by *for*) act as spokesman for (*speaks for the Aborigines; speaks for our generation*). **d** (foll. by *for*) recommend (*I can speak for her expertise*). **4** (foll. by *to*) speak with reference to; support in words (*spoke to the resolution*). **5** make a speech. **6** use or be able to use (a specified language) (*can speak Dyirbal well enough to be understood*). **7 a** convey an idea (*actions speak louder than words; her look spoke volumes*). **b** (usu. foll. by *to*) communicate feeling etc.; affect, touch (*the ruined abbeys of England speak of glories past*). **8** (of a gun, musical instrument, etc.) sound out. □ **generally** (or **strictly** etc.) **speaking** in the general (or strict etc.) sense. **not** (or **nothing**) **to speak of** not (or nothing) worth mentioning. **on speaking terms** friendly enough to converse. **speak for itself** be sufficient evidence. **speaking acquaintance** person one knows slightly. **speak out** (often followed by *against*) give one's opinion courageously. **speak up 1** speak loudly or freely; speak louder. **2** (followed by *for*) defend. **speak volumes** be very significant. **speak with** (or **in**) **tongues** see GLOSSOLALIA. [Old English]

**-speak** *comb. form* jargon (*Newspeak; computer speak*).

**speaker** *n.* **1** person who speaks, esp. in public. **2** person who speaks a specified language (esp. in *comb.: a French-speaker*). **3** (**Speaker**) presiding officer in a legislative assembly, as the House of Representatives. **4** = LOUDSPEAKER.

**speaking** — *n.* act or instance of uttering words etc. — *adj.* **1** (of a portrait) lifelike; true to its subject (*a speaking likeness*). **2** (in *comb.*) speaking or capable of speaking a specified foreign language (*French-speaking*). **3** with a reference, or from a point of view, specified (*roughly speaking; professionally speaking*).

**spear** — *n.* **1 a** thrusting or throwing weapon with a long shaft and a pointed usu. steel tip. **b** formidable, lance-like, Aboriginal weapon, made of wood and usu. headed with razor-sharp shaped quartz etc., often impelled by means of a WOOMERA. **2 a** tip and stem of asparagus, broccoli, etc. **b** blade of grass etc. — *v.* **1** pierce or strike with or as with a spear (*speared an olive*). **2** dismiss from employment; fire. □ **get the spear** be dismissed from employment etc. [Old English]

**spear grass** *n.* any of many Australian grasses bearing a seed with a spear-like husk, capable of working its way into the soil, clothing, flesh, etc., and often injurious to stock.

**speargun** *n.* gun used to propel a spear in underwater fishing.

**spearhead** — *n.* **1** point of a spear. **2** person or group leading an attack etc. — *v.* act as the spearhead of (an attack etc.).

**spearmint** *n.* common garden mint, used in cookery and to flavour chewing-gum etc.

**spear-thrower** *n.* = WOOMERA.

**spearwood** *n.* any of several Australian plants furnishing wood traditionally used by Aborigines for making spears, esp. YARRAN.

**spec**[1] *colloq.* — *n.* speculation. — *adj.* speculative; without a firm order or contract (*spec-builder; spec-house*). □ **on spec** as a gamble; on the off chance. [abbreviation]

**spec**[2] *n. colloq.* detailed working description; specification. [abbreviation of SPECIFICATION]

**special** / **spesh**-uhl/ — *adj.* **1 a** exceptional; out of the ordinary (*a special occasion; took special pains*). **b** peculiar; specific (*the word has a special sense; lacks the special qualifications required*). **2** for a particular purpose (*a special assignment*). **3** in which a person specialises (*statistics is her special field*). **4** for children with special needs (*special school*). — *n.* **1** special person or thing, e.g. a special train, edition of a newspaper, dish on a menu, etc. **2** item purchased at a reduced price. **3** *hist.* = GENTLEMAN CONVICT. □ **on special** (of goods etc.) available at a reduced price. □ **specially** *adv.* **specialness** *n.* [Latin: related to SPECIES]

**special effects** *n.pl.* illusions created by props, camera-work, etc.

**specialise** /spesh-uh-,luyz/ *v.* (also **-ize**) (**-sing** or **-zing**) **1** (often foll. by *in*) **a** be or become a specialist. **b** devote oneself to an interest, skill, etc. (*specialises in insulting people*). **2** (esp. in *passive*) adapt for a particular purpose (*specialised organs*). **3** (as **specialised** *adj.*) of a specialist (*specialised work*). □ **specialisation** /-zay-shuhn/ *n.* [French: related to SPECIAL]

**specialist** *n.* **1** person trained in a particular branch of a profession, esp. medicine. **2** person who specially studies a subject or area.

**speciality** /,spesh-ee-**al**-uh-tee/ *n.* (*pl.* **-ies**) **1** special pursuit, subject, product, activity, etc. **2** special feature or skill.

**special pleading** *n.* biased reasoning.

**specialty** /spesh-uhl-tee/ *n.* (*pl.* **-ies**) = SPECIALITY. □ **specialty of the house** a dish claimed by a restaurant to be unique (in recipe, method of preparation, etc.), characterising that establishment and setting it apart from rivals.

**specie** /spee-shee/ *n.* coin as opposed to paper money. [related to SPECIES]

**species** /spee-sheez, -seez/ *n.* (*pl.* same) **1** class of things having some common characteristics. **2** group of animals or plants within a genus, differing only slightly from others and capable of interbreeding. **3** kind, sort. **4** *Eccl.* the visible form of the consecrated bread and wine, the substance of either being the body and blood of Christ. [Latin *specio* look]

**specific** /spuh-**sif**-ik/ — *adj.* **1** clearly defined (*a specific purpose*). **2** relating to a particular subject; peculiar (*a style specific to . . .*). **3** of or concerning a species (*the specific name for a plant*). **4** exact, giving full details (*was specific about his wishes*). — *n.* specific aspect or factor (*discussed specifics; from the general to the specific*). □ **specifically** *adv.* **specificity** /,spes-uh-**fis**-uh-tee/ *n.* [Latin: related to SPECIES]

**specification** /,spes-uh-fuh-**kay**-shuhn/ *n.* **1** act or instance of specifying or the state of being specified. **2** (esp. in *pl.*) detail of the design and materials etc. of work done or to be done. [medieval Latin: related to SPECIFY]

**specific gravity** *n.* = RELATIVE DENSITY.

**specific heat capacity** *n.* heat required to raise the temperature of the unit mass of a given substance by a given amount (usu. one degree).

**specify** /spes-uh-,fuy/ *v.* (**-ies**, **-ied**) **1** (also *absol.*) name or mention expressly or as a condition (*specified the type he needed*; *specified that he must be paid at once*). **2** include in specifications (*a French window was not specified*). [Latin: related to SPECIFIC]

**specimen** /spes-uh-muhn/ *n.* **1** individual or sample taken as an example of a class or whole, esp. in experiments etc. (*specimen of your handwriting*; *specimens of copper ore*). **2** sample of urine for testing. [Latin *specio* look]

**specious** /spee-shuhs/ *adj.* **1** plausible but wrong (*specious argument*). **2** misleadingly attractive in appearance. [Latin: related to SPECIES]

**speck** — *n.* **1** small spot or stain. **2** a particle (*speck of dirt*). **b** particle of gold. **3** anything very small (by comparison, through the effect of distance, etc.). **4** *derog.* Tasmania. — *v.* **1** (esp. as **specked** *adj.*) **a** marked with specks. **b** (of gold etc.) found on the surface. **2 a** search for surface gold, opal, etc. (*specking in Coober Pedy*). **b** search (the ground) for gold or opal (*specked the entire Steiglitz area*). **c** discover (particles of gold etc.) (*specked some small nuggets*). [Old English]

**specker** *n.* one who searches for surface deposits of gold, opal, etc.

**speckle** /spek-uhl/ — *n.* small spot or mark, esp. one of many, on the skin, a bird's egg, etc. — *v.* (**-ling**) (esp. as **speckled** *adj.*) mark with speckles. [Dutch *spekkel*]

**specs** *n.pl. colloq.* spectacles. [abbreviation]

**spectacle** /spek-tuh-kuhl/ *n.* **1** striking, impressive, or ridiculous sight (*a charming spectacle; disgusting spectacle*). **2** large public show, ceremony, etc. □ **make a spectacle of oneself** make oneself an object of ridicule. [Latin *specio spect-* look]

**spectacled** *adj.* **1** wearing spectacles. **2** (of an animal) having facial markings resembling spectacles (*spectacled flycatcher; spectacled hare-wallaby*).

**spectacles** *n.pl.* pair of lenses in a frame resting on the nose and ears, used to correct defective eyesight.

**spectacular** /spek-**tak**-yuh-luh/ — *adj.* **1** striking, impressive, lavish. **2** strikingly large or obvious (*spectacular increase in output*). — *n.* event intended to be spectacular, esp. a film or play. □ **spectacularly** *adv.*

**spectator** *n.* person who watches a show, game, incident, etc. □ **spectate** *v.* (**-ting**) *colloq.* [Latin: related to SPECTACLE]

**spectator sport** *n.* sport attracting many spectators.

**spectra** *pl.* of SPECTRUM.

**spectral** /spek-truhl/ *adj.* **1 a** of or relating to spectres. **b** ghostly. **2** of or concerning spectra or the spectrum (*spectral analysis*). □ **spectrally** *adv.*

**spectre** /spek-tuh/ *n.* **1** ghost. **2** haunting presentiment or preoccupation (*spectre of war*). [Latin *spectrum* from *specio* look]

**spectrometer** /spek-**trom**-uh-tuh/ *n.* instrument for measuring observed spectra.

**spectroscope** /spek-truh-,skohp/ *n.* instrument for recording spectra for examination. □ **spectroscopic** /-skop-ik/ *adj.* **spectroscopy** /-tros-kuh-pee/ *n.*

**spectrum** /spek-truhm/ *n.* (*pl.* **-tra**) **1** band of colours as seen in a rainbow etc., arranged in a progressive series according to their wavelength. **2** entire or wide range of a subject, emotion, etc. (*their views reflected the wide range of the Australian political spectrum*). **3** distribution of electromagnetic radiation in which the parts are arranged according to wavelength. [Latin *specio* look]

**speculate** /spek-yuh-,layt/ *v.* (**-ting**) **1** (usu. foll. by *on, upon, about*) theorise, conjecture (*speculated on the prospects of Australia becoming a Republic*). **2** deal in a commodity or asset in the hope of profiting from fluctuating prices. □ **speculation** /,spek-yuh-**lay**-shuhn/ *n.* **speculative** /spek-yuh-luh-tiv/ *adj.* **speculator** *n.* [Latin *specula* watch-tower, from *specio* look]

**sped** *past* and *past part.* of SPEED.

**speech** *n.* **1** faculty or act of speaking. **2** formal public address. **3** manner of speaking (*a man of blunt speech*). **4** language of a nation, group, etc. (*varieties of Australian speech*; *the speech of the Wathawurrung Aborigines in the Geelong region*). [Old English: related to SPEAK]

**speechify** /spee-chuh-,fuy/ *v.* (**-ies, -ied**) *joc.* or *derog.* make esp. boring or long speeches.

**speechless** *adj.* temporarily silent because of emotion etc. (*speechless with rage*).

**speech recognition** *n. Computing* interpretation by a computer of spoken material.

**speed** — *n.* **1** rapidity of movement. **2** rate of progress or motion over a distance in time. **3** *Photog.* **a** sensitivity of film to light. **b** light-gathering power of a lens. **c** duration of an exposure. **4** *colloq.* amphetamine drug. — *v.* (*past* and *past part.* **sped**) **1** go quickly (*sped down the street*). **2** (*past* and *past part.* **speeded**) travel at an illegal or dangerous speed. □ **at speed** moving quickly. **speed up** move or work faster. □ **speeder** *n.* [Old English]

**speed limit** *n.* maximum permitted speed on a road.

**speedo** /spee-doh/ *n.* (*pl.* **-s**) *colloq.* = SPEEDOMETER. [abbreviation]

**speedometer** /spee-**dom**-uh-tuh/ *n.* in-

strument on a vehicle indicating its speed.

**speedos** *n.pl. propr.* brief, usu. nylon man's or woman's swimming costume.

**speedway** *n.* **1** arena for motor-cycle racing. **2** road or track for fast traffic.

**speedwell** *n.* any Australian shrub of the genus *Parahebe* (synonymous with *Veronica*), esp. *P. perfoliata* having blue-green leaves which surround the stem and sprays of bright blue flowers. [from SPEED, WELL[1]]

**speedy** *adj.* (**-ier, -iest**) **1** rapid. **2** done without delay; prompt. □ **speedily** *adv.* **speediness** *n.*

**Speewah** /spee-wah/ *n.* (also **Speewa**) *colloq.* **1** imaginary station or place used as a setting for tall stories of the outback. **2** such a story.

**speleology** /,spee-lee-**ol**-uh-jee/ *n.* the study of caves. [Greek *spēlaion* cave]

**spell**[1] *v.* (*past* and *past part.* **spelt** or **spelled**) **1** (also *absol.*) write or name correctly the letters of (a word etc.). **2 a** (of letters) form (a word etc.). **b** result in (*these rains spell ruin for the crop*). □ **spell out 1** make out (words etc.) letter by letter. **2** explain in detail. □ **speller** *n.* [French *espeller* related to SPELL[2]]

**spell**[2] *n.* **1** words used as a magical charm or incantation etc. **2** effect of these. **3** fascination exercised by a person, activity, etc. [Old English]

**spell**[3] — *n.* **1** short or fairly short period (*a cold spell*; *sit down for a spell*). **2** period or turn of some activity or work (*took a spell at digging*). **3** period of rest from work, training, etc.; holiday. — *v.* **1** rest. **2** relieve or take the place of (a person) in work etc. so that he or she may have a break. **3** cause (an animal etc.) to rest; allow land to lie fallow. [Old English, = substitute]

**spellbind** /spel-buynd/ *v.* (*past* and *past part.* **spellbound**) **1** (esp. as **spellbinding** *adj.*) hold the attention as if with a spell; entrance. **2** (as **spellbound** *adj.*) entranced, fascinated. □ **spellbinder** *n.*

**spell checker** *n. Computing* (also **spelling checker**) facility for checking any word or all of the words of a computer document against a specified dictionary or dictionaries.

**spelling** *n.* **1** way a word is spelt. **2** ability to spell (*his spelling is atrocious*).

**spelt** *past* and *past part.* of SPELL[1].

**spencer** *n.* woman's usu. woollen sleeved-singlet worn for extra warmth. [origin uncertain]

**spend** *v.* (*past* and *past part.* **spent**) **1** pay out (money). **2 a** use or consume (time or energy). **b** use up; exhaust; wear out (*spent all his ammunition*; *his anger was soon* *spent*; *spent herself campaigning for justice*. **3** (as **spent** *adj.*) having lost its original force or strength; exhausted (*the storm is spent*). □ **spending money** money for usu. small personal items; pocket money. **spend a penny** *colloq.* urinate or defecate. □ **spender** *n.* [Latin: related to EXPEND]

**spendthrift** — *n.* extravagant person. — *adj.* extravagant.

**sperm** *n.* (*pl.* same or **-s**) **1** = SPERMATOZOON. **2** semen. [Greek *sperma -mat-*]

**spermaceti** /ˌsper-muh-**set**-ee/ *n.* white waxy substance from the sperm whale, used for ointments etc. [medieval Latin, = whale sperm]

**spermatozoon** /ˌsper-muh-toh-**zoh**-on/ *n.* (*pl.* **-zoa**) mature motile sex cell in semen. [from SPERM, Greek *zōion* animal]

**sperm bank** *n.* store of semen for artificial insemination.

**sperm count** *n.* number of spermatozoa in one ejaculation or a measured amount of semen.

**spermicide** /sper-muh-ˌsuyd/ *n.* substance able to kill spermatozoa. □ **spermicidal** /-ˌsuy-duhl/ *adj.*

**sperm whale** *n.* large whale yielding spermaceti.

**spew** *v.* (also **spue**) **1** (often foll. by *up*) vomit. **2** (often foll. by *out*) (cause to) gush out. **3** *colloq.* become extremely angry (*is spewing because he can't go on the trip*). [Old English]

**sphagnum** /**sfag**-nuhm/ *n.* (*pl.* **-na**) (in full **sphagnum moss**) any of various mosses of the genus *Sphagnum* growing in bogs and peat, widely used in horticulture (see PEATMOSS). [Greek *sphagnos*]

---

■ **Usage** The pronunciation /**spag**-nuhm/ is sometimes heard: it is non-standard.

---

**sphere** /sfeer/ *n.* **1** solid figure with every point on its surface equidistant from its centre; its surface. **2** ball, globe. **3 a** any celestial body. **b** globe representing the earth. **4 a** field of action, influence, or existence (*have done wonders within their own sphere*). **b** a (usu. specified) stratum of society (*moves in quite another sphere*). **5** *hist.* each of the revolving shells in which celestial bodies were thought to be set. [Greek *sphaira* ball]

**spherical** /**sfe**-ruh-kuhl/ *adj.* **1** shaped like a sphere. **2** of spheres. □ **spherically** *adv.*

**spheroid** /**sfeer**-royd/ *n.* spherelike but not perfectly spherical body. □ **spheroidal** /sfeer-**roi**-duhl/ *adj.*

**sphincter** /**sfingk**-tuh/ *n.* ring of muscle surrounding and closing an opening in the body, esp. the anus (*anal sphincter*). [Greek *sphiggō* bind tight]

**sphinx** /sfingks/ *n.* **1** (**Sphinx**) (in Greek mythology) winged monster with a woman's head and a lion's body, whose riddle Oedipus guessed. **2** *Antiq.* **a** ancient Egyptian stone figure with a lion's body and a human or animal head. **b** (**the Sphinx**) huge sphinx near the Pyramids at Giza. **3** enigmatic or inscrutable person. [Greek]

**sphygmomanometer** /ˌsfig-moh-muh-**nom**-uh-tuh/ *n.* instrument used by doctors etc. for measuring a person's blood pressure. [Greek *sphugmos* pulse]

**spic** var. of SPICK.

**spice** — *n.* **1** aromatic or pungent vegetable substance used to flavour food, e.g. cinnamon, cloves, pepper, etc. **2 a** piquant quality (*his circumstances added spice to his tale*). **b** (foll. by *of*) slight flavour or suggestion (*a spice of malice*). — *v.* (**-cing**) **1** flavour with spice. **2** (foll. by *with*) enhance (*a book spiced with humour*). [French *espice*]

**spick** *n.* (also **spic, spik**) *colloq. offens.* person of European, esp. Latin, descent. [SPEAK as allegedly used in 'no spika da English']

**spick and span** *adj.* **1** neat and clean. **2** smart and new. [earlier *span and span new*, fresh and new like a shaved chip]

**spicy** *adj.* (**-ier, -iest**) **1 a** of, flavoured with, or fragrant with spice. **b** hot to the taste. **2** piquant; sensational, improper (*a spicy story*). □ **spiciness** *n.*

**spider** /**spuy**-duh/ — *n.* **1** eight-legged arthropod of which many species spin webs esp. to capture insects as food. **2** any object comparable to a spider, esp. as having numerous or prominent legs, radiating spokes, etc. **3** a soft drink to which ice-cream has been added. — *v.* **1** move in a scuttling manner suggestive of a spider. **2** (also as **spidering**) *adj.* ) be spiderlike in form, manner, or movement (*streets spidering in all directions*). [Old English: related to SPIN]

**spider flower** *n.* any of several species of grevillea having spidery flowers.

**spider orchid** *n.* **1** any of several terrestrial Australian orchids of the genus *Caladenia*, having long, narrowed sepals and petals. **2** (in full **tree spider orchid**) Australian DENDROBIUM, having many racemes of attractive spidery yellow-green flowers bordered in red.

**spidery** *adj.* elongated and thin (*spidery handwriting*).

**spiel** /speel, shpeel/ *colloq.* — *n.* glib speech or story; sales pitch. — *v.* **1** speak glibly; hold forth. **2** reel off (a sales pitch etc.) [German, = game]

**spieler** /**spee**-luh, **shpee**-luh/ *n. colloq.*
**1** person who spiels. **2** person who engages
in sharp practice; a swindler. [from SPIEL]

**spigot** /**spig**-uht/ *n.* **1** small peg or plug,
esp. in a cask. **2** device for controlling the
flow of liquid in a tap. [related to SPIKE²]

**spik** var. of SPICK.

**spike**¹ — *n.* **1 a** sharp point. **b** pointed piece
of metal, esp. the top of an iron railing. **2**
**a** any of several metal points in the sole
of a running-shoe to prevent slipping. **b**
(in *pl.*) spiked running-shoes. **3** pointed
metal rod standing on a base and used for
filing rejected news items, bills, etc. **4**
large nail. **5** forceful attacking hit over
net in volleyball. — *v.* (**-king**) **1** put spikes
on or into. **2** fix (bills etc.) on a spike. **3** *colloq.*
**a** lace (a drink) with alcohol etc. **b** contaminate with something added. **4** *colloq.*
reject (a newspaper story). **5** *Volleyball*
hit ball forcefully over net with overarm
action. □ **spike a person's guns** spoil his or
her plans. [Low German or Dutch:
related to SPOKE¹]

**spike**² *n.* cluster of flower-heads on a long
stem (*my cymbidiums are in spike*).
[Latin *spica*]

**spikenard** /**spuyk**-nahd/ *n.* **1** tall sweet-
smelling Indian plant. **2** *hist.* perfumed
ointment formerly made from this. [medi-
eval Latin *spica nardi*]

**spikey** /**spuyk**-kee/ *n.* = LONG-SPINED FLATHEAD.

**spiky** *adj.* (**-ier, -iest**) **1** like a spike; having
or sticking up in spikes. **2** *colloq.* touchy,
irritable. □ **spikily** *adv.* **spikiness** *n.*

**spill**¹ — *v.* (*past* and *past part.* **spilt** or
**spilled**) **1** fall or run or cause (liquid, powder, etc.) to fall or run out of a container,
esp. accidentally. **2 a** throw (a person etc.)
from a vehicle, saddle, etc. **b** (foll. by *into,
out* etc.) (esp. of a crowd) tumble or fall
quickly from a place etc. (*the fans spilled
into the street*). **3** *colloq.* disclose (information etc.). **4** shed (blood). — *n.* **1** act or
instance of spilling or being spilt. **2** tumble,
esp. from a horse, bicycle, etc. (*had a
nasty spill*). **3** the vacating of all or several
posts of a parliamentary party, esp. after
one important change of office. □ **spill the
beans** *colloq.* divulge information etc.,
esp. indiscreetly. **spill over** overflow.
□ **spillage** *n.* **spiller** *n.* [Old English]

**spill**² *n.* thin strip of wood or paper etc. for
lighting a fire, pipe, etc. [Low German or
Dutch]

**spin** — *v.* (**-nn-**; *past* and *past part.* **spun**)
**1** (cause to) turn or whirl round quickly.
**2** (also *absol.*) **a** draw out and twist (wool,
cotton, etc.) into threads. **b** make (yarn)
in this way. **3** (of a spider, silkworm, etc.)
make (a web, cocoon, etc.) by extruding a
fine viscous thread. **4** (esp. of the head)

be dizzy through excitement etc. **5** tell or
write (a story etc.) (*spun a wonderful
fantasy*). **6** impart spin to (a ball). **7** *can
spun adj.*) made into threads (*spun glass;
spun gold*). **8 a** toss (a coin). **b** toss (the coins)
in a game of two-up. — *n.* **1** spinning
motion; whirl. **2** rotating dive of an aircraft. **3** secondary twisting motion, e.g. of
a ball in flight. **4** *colloq.* brief, often fast, drive,
esp. in a car. **5** (in two-up) the act of tossing the coins. **6** *colloq.* (with qualifying
word) a (good, bad, fair, rough, etc.) run
of luck. □ **in a (flat) spin** *colloq.* in a state of
hectic confusion, busyness, etc. **spin out**
**1** prolong (*spin out an explanation; spinning out the agony*). **2** (usu. foll. by *at*)
*colloq.* **a** abuse or attack (someone) orally.
**b** panic badly, freak out; cause (a person)
to panic or freak out. **spin a yarn 1** tell a story.
**2** fabricate a story, explanation, excuse,
etc. [Old English]

**spina bifida** /ˌspuy-nuh-**bif**-uh-duh/ *n.*
congenital spinal defect in which part of
the spinal cord protrudes. [Latin, = cleft
spine]

**spinach** /**spin**-ij, -ich/ *n.* green vegetable
with edible leaves. [French *espinache*]

**spinal** /**spuy**-nuhl/ *adj.* of or relating to
the spine. [Latin: related to SPINE]

**spinal column** *n.* spine.

**spinal cord** *n.* cylindrical nervous structure within the spine.

**spin bowler** *n. Cricket* bowler who imparts
spin to a ball.

**spindle** /**spin**-duhl/ *n.* **1** slender rod or
bar, often tapered, for twisting and winding
thread. **2** pin or axis that revolves or on
which something revolves. **3** *Biol.* spindle-
shaped mass of microtubules formed when
a cell divides. **4** turned piece of wood used
as a banister, chair leg, etc. [Old English:
related to SPIN]

**spindly** *adj.* (**-ier, -iest**) long or tall and
thin; thin and weak.

**spin-drier** *n.* (also **spin-dryer**) machine
for drying clothes by spinning them in a
rapidly revolving drum. □ **spin-dry** *v.*

**spindrift** /**spin**-drift/ *n.* spray on the
surface of the sea. [Scots var. of *spoondrift*
from obsolete *spoon* scud]

**spine** *n.* **1** vertebrae extending from the
skull to the coccyx; backbone. **2** needle-like
outgrowth of an animal or plant. **3** part of
a book enclosing the page-fastening and
usu. facing outwards on a shelf. **4** sharp
ridge or projection, esp. of a mountain
range or slope. [Latin *spina*]

**spine-bash** *v. & n. colloq.* rest; sleep; loaf.
□ **spine-basher** *n.*

**spinebill** *n.* either of two small honeyeaters having a long, spine-like bill,
of south-western Australia (*western*

*spinebill*) and of eastern Australia (*eastern spinebill*).

**spine-chiller** *n.* frightening and usu. exciting story, film, etc. □ **spine-chilling** *adj.*

**spinel** /spuh-**nel**/ *n.* any of a group of hard crystalline minerals of various colours, consisting chiefly of oxides of magnesium and aluminium. [French *spinelle*]

**spineless** *adj.* **1** having no spine; invertebrate. **2** (of a person) lacking resolve, feeble, weak-willed, cowardly.

**spinel ruby** *n.* deep red variety of spinel used as a gem.

**spinet** /spin-uht, spuh-**net**/ *n. hist.* small harpsichord with oblique strings. [Italian *spinetta*]

**spinifex** /spin-uh-,feks/ *n.* (also **porcupine, porcupine grass**) any of many tussocky, often spiny, perennial grasses of arid and semi-arid Australia, or of coastal sand dunes. [Latin, = spine-maker]

**spinifex country** *n.* (also **spinifex plain**) vast areas associated with spinifex.

**spinifex parrot** *n.* **1** = NIGHT PARROT. **2** = PRINCESS PARROT.

**spinifex snake** *n.* **1** exceedingly venomous green snake of spinifex country. **2** harmless legless lizard occurring in spinifex country.

**spinnaker** /spin-uh-kuh/ *n.* large triangular sail opposite the mainsail of a racing-yacht. [*Sphinx*, name of the yacht first using it]

**spinner** *n.* **1** person or thing that spins. **2** *Cricket* **a** a spin bowler. **b** a spun ball. **3** the player who tosses the coins in two-up. **4** revolving bait or lure. **5** = SPINNERET. □ **come in spinner** (in two-up) the call which signals to the spinner that all bets have been placed and that it is time to toss the coins.

**spinneret** /spin-uh-,ret/ *n.* spinning-organ in a spider, silkworm, etc.

**spinning gum** *n.* (also **spinning-wheel gum**) small eucalypt of NSW, Victoria, and Tasmania, having silvery circular juvenile leaves which completely surround the stem, and which, when dead, spin around the stem in the slightest breeze.

**spinning wheel** *n.* household device for spinning yarn or thread, with a spindle driven by a wheel with a crank or treadle.

**spin-off** *n.* incidental result or benefit, esp. as a side-benefit from technology.

**spinster** *n. formal* any unmarried woman. □ **spinsterish** *adj.* [originally = woman who spins]

**spiny** /spuy-nee/ *adj.* (**-ier, -iest**) **1 a** having many spines; prickly. **b** used as a distinguishing epithet in the names of

Australian fauna and flora (*spiny-cheeked honeyeater; spiny emex*). **2** perplexing, troublesome, thorny (*a spiny problem*).

**spiny anteater** *n.* = ECHIDNA.

**spiracle** /spuy-ruh-kuhl, spi-/ *n.* external respiratory opening in insects, whales, and some fish.

**spiral** /spuy-ruhl/ — *adj.* **1** winding about a centre in an enlarging or decreasing continuous circular motion, either on a flat plane or rising in a cone; coiled. **2** winding continuously along or as if along a cylinder, as does the thread of a screw. — *n.* **1** spiral curve or thing (*spiral of smoke*). **2** progressive rise or fall of prices, wages, etc., each responding to an upward or downward stimulus provided by the other (*wage-price spiral*). — *v.* (**-ll-**) **1** move in a spiral course, esp. upwards or downwards. **2** (of prices, wages, etc.) rise or fall continuously. □ **spirally** *adv.* [Greek *speira* coil]

**spiral staircase** *n.* circular staircase round a central axis.

**spirant** /spuy-ruhnt/ — *adj.* (of a consonant) uttered with a continuous expulsion of breath. — *n.* such a consonant. [Latin *spiro* breathe]

**spire** *n.* **1** tapering cone- or pyramid-shaped structure, esp. on a church tower. **2** any tapering thing, e.g. the spike of a flower. [Old English]

**spirit** /spi-ruht/ — *n.* **1 a** vital animating essence of a person or animal (*broken in spirit*). **b** the intelligent non-physical part of a person (*I'll be present in spirit*). **c** the soul. **2 a** rational or intelligent being without a material body. **b** ghost. **3 a** person's character (*an unbending spirit*). **b** attitude (*took it in the wrong spirit*). **c** type of person (*is a free spirit; a kindred spirit*). **d** prevailing tendency (*spirit of the age*). **4 a** (usu. in *pl.*) strong distilled liquor, e.g. whisky or gin. **b** distilled volatile liquid (*wood spirit*). **c** purified alcohol (*methylated spirits*). **5 a** courage, vivacity (*played with spirit*). **b** (in *pl.*) state of mind, mood (*in high spirits; his spirits were dashed*). **6** essential as opposed to formal meaning (*the spirit of the law*). — *v.* (**-t-**) (usu. foll. by *away, off,* etc.) convey rapidly or mysteriously. □ **in spirit** inwardly. [Latin *spiritus*]

**spirited** *adj.* **1** lively; courageous (*a spirited translation; a spirited attack*). **2** (in *comb.*) in a specified mood (*high-spirited*). □ **spiritedly** *adv.*

**spirit gum** *n.* quick-drying gum for attaching false hair.

**spiritless** *adj.* lacking vigour.

**spirit level** *n.* device with a glass tube nearly filled with alcohol, used to test horizontality by the position of an air-bubble.

**spiritual** /spi-ruh-choo-uhl, -chuhl/ — *adj.* **1** of or concerning the spirit as opposed to matter (*spiritual relationship; spiritual home*). **2** religious, divine, inspired (*the spiritual life*). **3** refined, sensitive. — *n.* (also **Negro spiritual**) religious song orig. of American Blacks. □ **spirituality** /-al-uh-tee/ *n.* **spiritually** *adv.*

**spiritualism** *n.* **1** belief in, and supposed practice of, communication with the dead, esp. through mediums. **2** belief that the spirit exists as distinct from matter, or that spirit is the only reality (cf. MATERIALISM). □ **spiritualist** *n.* **spiritualistic** *adj.*

**spirituous** /spi-ruh-choo-uhs/ *adj.* **1** very alcoholic. **2** distilled as well as fermented.

**spit¹** — *v.* (**-tt-**; *past* and *past part.* **spat** or **spit**) **1 a** (also *absol.*) eject saliva from the mouth. **b** do this in contempt or anger (*spat on him*). **2** eject (blood, food, etc.) from the mouth (*spat the oyster out*). **3** utter vehemently (*'Damn you!' he spat*). **4** (of a fire, pan, etc.) throw out sparks, hot fat, etc. **5** (of rain) fall lightly (*it's only spitting*). **6** (of a cat) make a spitting or hissing noise in hostility. — *n.* **1** spittle. **2** act or instance of spitting. **3** foamy liquid secretion of some insects used to protect their young. □ **spit chips** *colloq.* be extremely angry or frustrated. **spit the dummy** *colloq.* **1** be very angry. **2** give up (contesting, participating, etc.) prematurely (*when he realised he couldn't win, he spat the dummy, gave the race away*). **spit it out** *colloq.* say it quickly and concisely. **the spit** (or **dead spit** or **very spit**) **of** the exact double of. [Old English]

**spit²** — *n.* **1** rod for skewering meat for roasting on a fire etc. **2** point of land projecting into the sea. — *v.* (**-tt-**) **1** thrust a spit through (meat etc.). **2** pierce or transfix with a sword etc. [Old English]

**spit and polish** *n.* **1** esp. military cleaning and polishing. **2** exaggerated or obsessive neatness, smartness, etc.

**spite** — *n.* **1** ill will, malice. **2** a grudge. — *v.* (**-ting**) hurt, harm, or frustrate (a person) through spite (*does it to spite me*). □ **in spite of** notwithstanding. **in spite of oneself** though one would rather have done otherwise (*in spite of himself he could not help admiring his enemy*). [French: related to DESPITE]

**spiteful** *adj.* malicious. □ **spitefully** *adv.*

**spitfire** *n.* **1** person of fiery temper. **2** large dark larva of an Australian sawfly, often as one of a huge cluster esp. on eucalypts, and prone to spit forth a sticky greenish fluid when disturbed.

**spit-roast** — *v.* roast on a spit. — *n.* **1** meat roasted in this way. **2** occasion on which a spit-roasting occurs (*invited to a spit-roast*).

**spitting distance** *n. colloq.* very short distance.

**spitting image** *n.* (foll. by *of*) *colloq.* double of (a person).

**spittle** /spit-uhl/ *n.* **1** saliva. **2** = SPIT¹ *n.* 3. [related to SPIT¹]

**spittoon** /spi-toon/ *n.* vessel to spit into.

**splash** — *v.* **1** spatter or cause (liquid) to spatter in drops. **2** wet with spattered liquid etc. (*the passing car splashed them with mud*). **3 a** (usu. foll. by *across*, *along*, *about*, etc.) move while spattering liquid etc. (*splashed about in the bath*). **b** jump or fall into water etc. with a splash. **4** display (news) prominently (*splashed across the front page*). **5** (usu. foll. by *out*) spend (money) ostentatiously. — *n.* **1 a** act or instance of splashing. **b** the resulting noise (*heard a splash*). **2** quantity of liquid, mud, etc., splashed. **3** mark etc. made by splashing. **4** prominent news feature, sensation, etc. (*the separation of the Prince and Princess of Wales was quite a splash*). **5** patch of colour. □ **make a splash** attract attention. □ **splashy** *adj.* (**-ier**, **-iest**). [imitative]

**splashdown** *n.* landing of a spacecraft on the sea. □ **splash down** *v.*

**splat** *colloq.* — *n.* dull splattering or wetly slapping sound (*his brains hit the wall with a splat*). — *adv.* with a splat. — *v.* (**-tt-**) fall or hit with a splat. [abbreviation of SPLATTER]

**splatter** — *v.* splash esp. with a continuous noisy action; spatter. — *n.* noisy splashing sound. [imitative]

**splay** — *v.* **1** spread apart. **2** (of an opening) have its sides diverging. **3** construct (an opening) with divergent sides. — *n.* surface at an oblique angle to another. — *adj.* splayed. [from DISPLAY]

**splayd** *n. propr.* fork with a spoon-shaped bowl and the cutting-edge of a knife, a three-in-one table utensil.

**spleen** *n.* **1** abdominal organ regulating the quality of the blood. **2** moroseness, irritability (from the earlier belief that the spleen was the seat of such feelings) (*vented their spleen; a fit of spleen*). [Greek *splēn*]

**splendid** /splen-duhd/ *adj.* **1** magnificent, sumptuous (*a splendid achievement; a splendid mansion*). **2** impressive, glorious, dignified (*splendid isolation*). **3** excellent; fine (*a splendid chance*). □ **splendidly** *adv.* [Latin: related to SPLENDOUR]

**splendour** /splen-duh/ n. (also **splendor**) dazzling brightness; magnificence. [Latin *splendeo* shine]

**splenetic** /spluh-**net**-ik/ adj. bad-tempered; peevish. □ **splenetically** adv. [Latin: related to SPLEEN]

**splenic** /**splen**-ik, **splee**-nik/ adj. of or in the spleen. [Latin from Greek: related to SPLEEN]

**splice** — v. (**-cing**) **1** join (ropes) by interweaving strands. **2** join (pieces of wood or tape etc.) by overlapping. — n. join made by splicing. [probably Dutch *splissen*]

**splint** — n. strip of rigid material bound to a broken limb while it sets. — v. secure with a splint. [Low German or Dutch]

**splinter** — n. small sharp fragment of wood, stone, glass, etc., broken off from a larger body. — v. break into splinters; shatter. □ **splintery** adj. [Dutch: related to SPLINT]

**splinter group** n. group (esp. political) that has broken away from a larger one.

**split** — v. (**-tt-**; past and past part. **split**) **1 a** break, or cause to break, into parts, esp. with the grain or into halves; break forcibly (*the ground split open; split these logs*). **b** (often foll. by *up*) divide into parts, esp. equal shares (*they split the money; split up into groups; let's split a bottle of wine*). **2** (often foll. by *off, away*) remove or be removed by breaking or dividing (*split away from the main group*). **3 a** (usu. foll. by *on, over,* etc.) divide into disagreeing or hostile parties (*they split on the question of picketing*). **b** (foll. by *with*) quarrel or cease association with (*he split with the local branch of the party*). **4** cause the fission of (an atom). **5** colloq. leave, esp. suddenly (*I've got to split*). **6** (usu. foll. by *on*) colloq. inform, betray (*split on them to the police*). **7 a** (as **splitting** adj.) (of a headache) severe. **b** (of the head) suffer from a severe headache, noise, etc. — n. **1** act or instance of splitting or the state of being split. **2** a fissure, crack, cleft, etc. **3** disagreement; schism. **4** (in pl.) feat of leaping in the air or sitting down with the legs at right angles to the body in front and behind or on either side. **5** colloq. a share (*here's your split of our winnings*). **6** dish of split bananas etc. with ice-cream. **7 a** half a glass of liquor. **b** drink composed of half alcoholic liquor and half soft-drink. □ **split the difference** take the average of two proposed amounts. **split hairs** make insignificant distinctions; quibble. **split one's sides** laugh uncontrollably. **split up** separate, end a relationship. [Dutch]

**split infinitive** n. infinitive with an adverb etc. inserted between *to* and the verb, e.g. *seems to really like it*.

■ **Usage** Some people oppose the use of the split infinitive under any circumstances, while others approve of it in cases where it avoids stylistic awkwardness. Occasionally a split infinitive neatly avoids ambiguity, e.g. the difference in meaning between *he failed to entirely understand the issue* and **1** *he entirely failed to understand the issue*, and **2** *he failed to understand the issue entirely*.

**split-level** adj. (of a building) having a room or rooms a fraction of a storey higher than other parts.

**split pea** n. pea dried and split in half for cooking.

**split personality** n. alteration or dissociation of personality occurring in some mental illnesses, e.g. a person seeming to have two or more alternating personalities.

**split-screen** n. screen, usu. associated with a computer, on which two or more separate images are displayed.

**split second** — n. very brief moment of time. — attrib. adj. (**split-second**) **1** very rapid. **2** (of timing) very accurate.

**split stuff** n. timber sawn into lengths and then split.

**splodge** colloq. — n. daub, blot, or smear. — v. (**-ging**) make a splodge on. □ **splodgy** adj. [alteration of SPLOTCH]

**splosh** colloq. — v. move with a splashing sound. — n. **1** splashing sound. **2** splash of water etc. **3** colloq. money. [imitative]

**splotch** n. & v. = SPLODGE. □ **splotchy** adj. [origin uncertain]

**splurge** colloq. — n. **1** sudden extravagance. **2** ostentatious display or effort. — v. (**-ging**) (usu. foll. by *on*) spend large sums of money or make a great effort (*splurged on new furniture*). [probably imitative]

**splutter** — v. **1 a** speak, say, or express in a hurried, vehement, or choking manner. **b** emit sparks, hot oil, etc., with spitting sounds. **2** speak or utter (words, threats, etc.) rapidly or incoherently. — n. spluttering speech or sound. [SPUTTER by association with *splash*]

**spoil** — v. (past and past part. **spoilt** or **spoiled**) **1 a** make or become useless or unsatisfactory (*the new paint-work was spoiled by the rain*). **b** reduce the enjoyment etc. of (*the news spoiled his dinner*). **2** make (esp. a child) unpleasant by over-indulgence. **3** (of food) go bad. **4** render (a ballot-paper) invalid by improper marking. **5** archaic or literary (foll. by *of*)

**plunder** or **deprive** by force etc. (*spoiled him of all he possessed*). — *n.* (usu. in *pl.*) **1** plunder, stolen goods (*the spoils of war*). **2** profit or advantage from success or position (*enjoyed the spoils and perks of high office*). □ **be spoiling for** aggressively seek (a fight etc.). [Latin *spolio*]

**spoilage** *n.* **1** paper spoilt in printing. **2** spoiling of food etc. by decay.

**spoilsport** *n.* person who spoils others' enjoyment.

**spoilt** *past* and *past part.* of SPOIL.

**spoke**[1] *n.* each of the rods running from the hub to the rim of a wheel. □ **put a spoke in a person's wheel** thwart or hinder a person. □ **spoked** *adj.* [Old English]

**spoke**[2] *past* of SPEAK.

**spoken** *past part.* of SPEAK. — *adj.* (in *comb.*) speaking in a specified way (*plain-spoken; well-spoken*). □ **spoken for** claimed (*this seat is spoken for*).

**spokesman** *n.* (*fem.* **spokeswoman**) **1** person who speaks on behalf of others, esp. in the course of public relations. **2** person deputed to express the views of a group etc. [from SPOKE[2]]

**spokesperson** *n.* (*pl.* **-s** or **-people**) spokesman or spokeswoman.

**spoliation** /ˌspoh-lee-ay-shuhn/ *n.* plundering, pillage. [Latin: related to SPOIL]

**spondee** /spon-dee/ *n.* metrical foot consisting of two long (or stressed) syllables. □ **spondaic** /spon-day-ik/ *adj.* [Greek *spondē* libation, with which songs in this metre were associated]

**sponge** /spunj/ — *n.* **1** sea animal with a porous body wall and a rigid internal skeleton. **2** this skeleton or a piece of porous rubber etc. used in bathing, cleaning, etc. **3** thing like a sponge in consistency etc., esp. a sponge cake. **4 a** act of sponging. **b** person who sponges. **5** *colloq.* a heavy drinker. — *v.* (**-ging**) **1** wipe or cleanse with a sponge. **2** (often foll. by *out, away*, etc.) wipe off or efface (as) with a sponge. **3** (often foll. by *up*) absorb (as) with a sponge. **4 a** (often foll. by *on, off*) live as a parasite; be meanly dependent upon (another person) (*sponges shamelessly on his relatives*). **b** obtain (a drink, a cigarette, etc.) by cadging. □ **throw in the sponge** see THROW. □ **spongiform** *adj.* (esp. in senses 1, 2 of the *n.*). [Latin *spongia*]

**sponge bag** *n.* waterproof bag for toilet articles.

**sponge cake** *n.* (also **sponge pudding**) light spongy cake or pudding.

**sponger** *n.* (also **sponge**) parasitic person.

**sponge rubber** *n.* porous rubber.

**spongy** *adj.* (**-ier**, **-iest**) like a sponge, porous, elastic, absorbent. □ **sponginess** *n.*

**sponsor** /spon-suh/ — *n.* **1** person who pledges money to a charity etc. in return for another person fulfilling a sporting etc. challenge. **2 a** patron of an artistic or sporting activity etc. **b** company etc. promoting a broadcast in return for advertising time. **3** person who introduces legislation. **4** godparent at a baptism or (esp. *RC Ch.*) person who presents a candidate for baptism. — *v.* be a sponsor for. □ **sponsorial** /spon-saw-ree-uhl/ *adj.* **sponsorship** *n.* [Latin *spondeo* sponspledge]

**spontaneous** /spon-tay-nee-uhs/ *adj.* **1** acting, done, or occurring without external cause. **2** voluntary, without external incitement (*made a spontaneous offer of his services*). **3** instinctive, automatic, natural. **4** (of style or manner) gracefully natural. **5** growing naturally without cultivation. □ **spontaneity** /ˌspon-tuh-nee-uh-tee, -nay-uh-tee/ *n.* **spontaneously** *adv.* [Latin *sponte* of one's own accord]

**spontaneous combustion** *n.* ignition of a substance from heat generated within itself, usu. by rapid oxidation.

**spontaneous generation** *n.* supposed production of living from non-living matter; abiogenesis.

**spoof**[1] /spoof/ *n.* & *v. colloq.* **1** parody. **2** hoax, swindle. □ **spoofer** *n.* [invented word]

**spoof**[2] /spuuf/ *n. coarse colloq.* semen. [origin unknown]

**spook** /spook/ — *n. colloq.* **1** ghost. **2** spy, esp. in the secret service. — *v.* **1** frighten, unnerve. **2** take fright; become alarmed. □ **spooked** *adj.* [Low German or Dutch]

**spooky** /spoo-kee/ *adj.* (**-ier**, **-iest**) *colloq.* ghostly, eerie. □ **spookily** *adv.* **spookiness** *n.*

**spool** /spool/ — *n.* **1** reel for winding magnetic tape, photographic film, yarn, etc. on. **2** revolving cylinder of an angler's reel. — *v.* wind on a spool. [French *espole* or Germanic *spole*]

**spoon** /spoon/ — *n.* **1 a** utensil with a bowl and a handle for lifting food to the mouth, stirring, etc. **b** spoonful, esp. of sugar. **2** spoon-shaped thing, esp. (in full **spoon-bait**) a revolving metal fish-lure. — *v.* **1** (often foll. by *up, out*) take (liquid etc.) with a spoon. **2** hit (a ball) feebly upwards. **3** *colloq.* behave in an amorous way, esp. foolishly or with silly sentimentality. □ **born with a silver spoon in one's mouth** born in affluence and privilege. □ **spoonful** *n.* (*pl.* **-s**). [Old English]

**spoonbill** *n.* long-legged white wading bird with a broad flat-tipped bill, including two Australian birds: the royal spoonbill (with a black bill) and the yellow-billed spoonbill.

**spoonerism** /spoo-nuh-,riz-uhm/ n. (usu. accidental) transposition of the initial letters etc. of two or more words, e.g. *you have hissed my mystery lectures*. [Spooner, name of a scholar reputed to have made such errors in speaking]

**spoonfeed** v. (*past* and *past part.* **-fed**) **1** feed with a spoon. **2** give such extensive help etc. to (a person) that he or she need make no effort.

**spoor** n. animal's track or scent. [Dutch]

**sporadic** /spuh-**rad**-ik/ adj. occurring only here and there or occasionally, separate, scattered (*sporadic fighting*; *sporadic dust-storms*). □ **sporadically** adv. [Greek *sporas -ad-* scattered]

**sporangium** /spuh-**ran**-jee-uhm/ n. (pl. **sporangia** /-jee-uh/) *Bot.* receptacle in which spores are found. [Greek *spora* SPORE, *aggeion* vessel]

**spore** n. **1** specialised reproductive cell of many plants and micro-organisms. **2** these collectively. [Greek *spora* seed]

**sporran** /spo-ruhn/ n. pouch worn in front of the kilt. [Gaelic *sporan*]

**sport** — n. **1 a** game or competitive activity, usu. played outdoors and involving physical exertion, e.g. cricket, football, racing. **b** these collectively. **2** (in *pl.*) meeting for competing in sports, esp. athletics (*school sports*). **3 a** amusement, fun. **b** jest, play (*I said it in sport*). **c** shooting or fishing as a pastime. **4** *colloq.* **a** fair or generous person (*she's a real sport*). **b** person with a specified attitude to games, rules, etc. (*a bad sport at tennis*). **c** familiar form of address, esp. between males (*what's yours, sport?*). **5** animal or plant deviating from the normal type (*my blue rose is a unique sport*). **6** victim, butt (*was the sport of Fortune*; *made him the sport of all their jests*). — v. **1** amuse oneself, play about. **2** wear or exhibit, esp. ostentatiously (*sported opal buttons on his shirt*). **3** *Biol.* become or produce a sport. □ **be a sport 1** abide by the rules; play fair. **2** be generous in agreeing to a request or plea (*come on, be a sport and give me a hand*). **a good** (or **bad**) **sport** person who displays good (or bad) sportsmanship. **a good sport** *colloq.* **1** a fine person. **2** a friendly, agreeable, sociable person. **have good sport** be successful in shooting or fishing. **in sport** jestingly. **make sport of** ridicule. [from DISPORT]

**sporting** adj. **1** interested in sport (*a sporting type*). **2** generous, fair (*a sporting offer*). **3** concerned in sport (*sporting dog*; *the sporting news*). □ **a sporting chance** some possibility of success. □ **sportingly** adv.

**sportive** adj. playful. □ **sportively** adv. **sportiveness** n.

**sports car** n. low-built fast car.

**sportscast** n. sporting broadcast or telecast.

**sports coat** n. (also **sports jacket**) man's informal jacket.

**sportsground** n. area reserved for organised sport, usu. with accommodation for spectators and facilities for players.

**sportsman** n. (*fem.* **sportswoman**) **1** person who takes part in much sport, esp. professionally. **2** person who displays those qualities valued in those who play sport, such as abiding by the rules and playing fair, abiding by the umpire's (or referee's etc.) decision, etc. □ **sportsman-like** adj. **sportsmanship** n.

**sportswear** n. clothes for sports or informal wear.

**sporty** adj. (**-ier**, **-iest**) *colloq.* **1** fond of sport. **2** loud and vulgar, rakish, showy. □ **sportily** adv. **sportiness** n.

**spot** — n. **1** small roundish area or mark differing in colour, texture, etc., from the surface it is on. **2** pimple or blemish. **3** moral blemish or stain (*not a spot on his reputation*). **4** particular place, locality (*spot where many Aborigines were massacred by whites*). **5** particular part of one's body or aspect of one's character (*yes, that's the spot*; *has a blind spot about racism*). **6** one's esp. regular position in an organisation, programme, etc. (*has a regular spot in ABC TV's gardening show*). **7** slot for advertising on radio or television. **8 a** *colloq.* small quantity (*spot of trouble*). **b** drop (*spot of rain*). **c** *colloq.* drink of alcoholic liquor (not necessarily small). **9** = SPOTLIGHT. **10** (usu. *attrib.*) money paid or goods delivered immediately after a sale (*spot cash*). **11** *colloq.* $100. — v. (**-tt-**) **1** *colloq.* pick out, recognise, catch sight of (*spotted the winner in every race*; *spotted her in the crowd*). **2** watch for and take note of (talent etc.). **3** mark or become marked with spots. **4** make spots, rain slightly. **5** stain or blemish (one's or a person's reputation etc.). **6** (of a bushfire) break out in patches ahead of the main fire (*must prevent the bushfire from spotting*). □ **hit the spot** *colloq.* (esp. of food and drink) be exactly what is required. **in a spot** (or **in a tight etc. spot**) *colloq.* in difficulty. **on the spot 1** at the scene of an event. **2** *colloq.* in a position demanding response or action (*the questions put him on the spot*). **3** without delay. **4** without moving forwards or backwards (*running on the spot*). **5** (of a person) wide awake, equal to the situation, in good form at a game etc. **soft spot** feeling of special affection (see also SOFT). [perhaps from Low German or Dutch]

**spot check** n. sudden or random check.

**spotless** adj. absolutely clean or pure. □ **spotlessly** adv.

**spotlight** — n. **1** beam of light directed on a small area. **2** lamp projecting this. **3** full publicity. — v. (past and past part. **-lighted** or **-lit**) **1** direct a spotlight on. **2** draw attention to.

**spot on** colloq. — adj. **1** precise; on target. **2** excellent (being just what was wanted). — adv. precisely; exactly. — int. **1** that is exactly right! **2** that is just what was required!; excellent!

**spotted** adj. **1** marked or decorated with spots. **2** used as a distinguishing epithet in the names of Australian fauna and flora (spotted bower-bird; spotted firetail; spotted harrier; spotted nightjar; spotted pardalote; spotted quail-thrush; spotted emu-bush).

**spotted gum** n. any of several eucalypts having a smooth, colourfully mottled trunk.

**spotted whiting** n. (also **King George whiting**) carnivorous marine fish of southern Australia, highly valued as food.

**spotter** n. **1** (often in comb.) person who spots people or things (talent-spotter). **2** (in full **spotter plane**) aircraft used to locate bushfires, sharks, etc.

**spotty** adj. (**-ier, -iest**) **1** marked with spots. **2** patchy, irregular. □ **spottiness** n.

**spouse** /spows, spowz/ n. husband or wife. [Latin sponsus sponsa betrothed]

**spout** — n. **1** projecting tube or lip used for pouring from a teapot, kettle, jug, etc., or on a fountain, roof-gutter, etc. **2** = SPOUTING (sense 1). **3** jet or column of liquid etc. — v. **1** discharge or issue forcibly in a jet. **2** (often foll. by off) utter or speak at length or boastfully or angrily. □ **up the spout** colloq. **1** useless, ruined, broken down. **2** pregnant. [Dutch]

**spouting** n. (also **spout**) **1** downpipe for carrying rainwater from a roof. **2** such pipes collectively.

**sprain** — v. wrench (an ankle, wrist, etc.), causing pain or swelling. — n. such a wrench. [origin unknown]

**sprang** past of SPRING.

**sprat** n. small edible marine fish (often used dried in Asian cooking). [Old English]

**sprawl** — v. **1 a** sit, lie, or fall, with limbs flung out untidily. **b** spread (one's limbs) thus. **2** (of handwriting, a plant, a town, etc.) be irregular or straggling. — n. **1** sprawling movement, position, or mass. **2** straggling urban expansion (urban sprawl). [Old English]

**spray**[1] — n. **1** water etc. flying in small drops. **2** liquid sprayed with an aerosol etc. **3** device for this. **4** quantity of small particles, e.g. bullets, flying through the air. — v. **1** (also absol.) throw (liquid) as spray. **2** (also absol.) sprinkle (an object) thus, esp. (a plant) with insecticide. **3** direct a spray of bullets at (sprayed the enemy position with rapid fire). □ **sprayer** n. [origin uncertain]

**spray**[2] n. **1** sprig of flowers or leaves, or a small branch; decoratively arranged bunch of flowers. **2** ornament in a similar form (a spray of diamonds). [Old English]

**spray-gun** n. device for spraying paint etc.

**spread** /spred/ — v. (past and past part. **spread**) **1** (often foll. by out) **a** open, extend, or unfold (spread the charts out on the table). **b** cause to cover a surface or larger area (spread butter on bread). **c** display to the eye or mind (the view was spread out before us). **2** (often foll. by out) have a wide, specified, or increasing extent (on every side spread a vast desert). **3** become or make more widely known, felt, etc. (rumours are spreading). **4 a** cover (spread the wall with paint). **b** lay (a table). — n. **1** act or instance of spreading. **2** capability or extent of expanding (has a large spread). **3** diffusion (spread of learning). **4** breadth, compass (arches of equal spread). **5** increased girth (middle-aged spread). **6** difference between two rates, prices, etc. **7** colloq. elaborate meal. **8** paste for spreading on bread etc. (get out the bread and spreads). **9** bedspread. **10** printed matter spread across more than one column. **11** (also **good spread**) wide publicity. □ **spread it on thick** colloq. **1** dispense (flattery, advice, etc.) with a heavy hand. **2** boast, exaggerate. **spread oneself** be lavish or discursive. **spread one's wings** develop one's powers fully. [Old English]

**spread eagle** — n. figure of an eagle with legs and wings extended as an emblem. — v. (**spreadeagle**) **1** (usu. as **spread-eagled** adj.) place (a person) with arms and legs spread out. **2** defeat utterly.

**spreadsheet** n. computer program for the manipulation and flexible retrieval of tabulated data.

**spree** n. colloq. **1** lively extravagant outing (shopping spree). **2** bout of fun or drinking etc. [origin unknown]

**sprig** — n. **1** small branch or shoot. **2** ornament resembling this, esp. on fabric. **3** usu. derog. a youth or young man (a sprig of the British nobility playing at being a jackeroo). — v. (**-gg-**) ornament with sprigs (sprigged muslin). [Low German sprick]

**sprightly** /**spruyt**-lee/ adj. (**-ier, -iest**) vivacious, lively, brisk. □ **sprightliness** n. [from **spright**, var. of SPRITE]

**spring** — v. (past **sprang**; past part. **sprung**) **1** rise rapidly or suddenly, leap, jump. **2** move rapidly by or as by the action of a spring (the branch sprang back). **3** (usu. foll. by from) originate (from ancestors, a source, etc.) (springs from a family dating back to the Second Fleet; their actions spring from a false belief). **4** (usu. foll. by up) come into being; act or appear suddenly or unexpectedly (new houses springing up; a breeze sprang up; spring to mind). **5 a** (often foll. by on) present (a thing or circumstance etc.) suddenly or unexpectedly (sprang it on me). **b** colloq. discover or come upon (something or someone, usu. a concealed object or someone engaged in an illicit activity) (the police sprang a marijuana plantation in the forest; got sprung smoking behind the shelter shed and was sent to the headmaster). **6** colloq. contrive the escape of (a person from prison etc.). **7** cause to act suddenly, esp. by means of a spring (spring a trap). **8** (usu. as **sprung** adj.) provide (a mattress etc.) with springs. **9 a** become warped or split. **b** split, crack (wood or a wooden implement). — n. **1** jump, leap. **2** recoil. **3** elasticity (mattress with plenty of spring). **4** elastic device, usu. of coiled metal, used esp. to drive clockwork or for cushioning in furniture or vehicles. **5 a** (often attrib.) the first season of the year (September to November), in which new vegetation begins to appear. **b** (often foll. by of) early stage of life etc. **6** place where water, oil, etc., wells up from the earth; basin or flow so formed. **7** motive for or origin of an action, custom, etc. (the springs of human action). □ **spring a leak** develop a leak. **spring one on a person** colloq. surprise a person. **spring up** come into being, appear. □ **springlike** adj. [Old English]

**spring balance** n. balance that measures weight by the tension of a spring.

**springboard** n. **1** flexible board for leaping or diving from. **2** source of impetus. **3** platform inserted in the side of a tree, on which a timber-cutter stands to chop at some height from the ground.

**springbok** /**spring**-bok/ n. (pl. same or **-s**) S. African gazelle. [Afrikaans]

**spring chicken** n. **1** young fowl for eating. **2** (usu. with neg.) youthful person (she's no spring chicken).

**spring-clean** — n. (also **spring-cleaning**) thorough cleaning of a house, esp. in spring. — v. clean (a house) thus.

**spring onion** n. form of onion with a very small bulb, usu. eaten raw.

**spring roll** n. Chinese fried pancake filled with vegetables.

**spring tide** n. tide just after the new and the full moon when there is the greatest difference between high and low water.

**springtime** n. **1** season of spring. **2** period likened to this (in the springtime of his life).

**springy** adj. (**-ier, -iest**) springing back quickly when squeezed, bent, or stretched; elastic. □ **springiness** n.

**sprinkle** /**spring**-kuhl/ — v. (**-ling**) **1** scatter in small drops or particles. **2** (often foll. by with) subject (the ground or an object) to sprinkling with liquid etc. **3** (of liquid etc.) fall on in this way. **4** distribute in small amounts. — n. **1** action or act of sprinkling. **2** (usu. foll. by of) quantity sprinkled; a sprinkling. **3** light shower. [origin uncertain]

**sprinkler** n. device for sprinkling a lawn or extinguishing fires.

**sprinkling** n. small sparse number or amount.

**sprint** — v. **1** run a short distance at full speed. **2** run (a specified distance) thus. — n. **1** such a run. **2** short burst in cycling, swimming, etc. □ **sprinter** n. [Old Norse]

**sprit** n. small diagonal spar from the mast to the upper outer corner of a sail. [Old English]

**sprite** n. elf, fairy. [sprit, contraction of SPIRIT]

**sprocket** /**sprok**-uht/ n. each of several teeth on a wheel engaging with links of a chain. [origin unknown]

**sprout** — v. **1** put forth (shoots, hair, etc.). **2** begin to grow; spring up. — n. **1** shoot of a plant. **2** beansprout. **3** = BRUSSELS SPROUT. [Old English]

**spruce**[1] /sproos/ — adj. neatly dressed etc.; smart. — v. (**-cing**) (usu. foll. by up) make or become smart. □ **sprucely** adv. **spruceness** n. [perhaps from SPRUCE[2]]

**spruce**[2] /sproos/ n. **1** conifer with dense conical foliage. **2** its wood. [obsolete Pruce Prussia]

**spruik** /sprook/ v. hold forth in public; deliver a harangue, esp. to advertise a show etc. □ **spruiker** n. **spruiking** n. [origin unknown]

**sprung** see SPRING.

**spry** /spruy/ adj. (**spryer, spryest**) lively, nimble. □ **spryly** adv. [origin unknown]

**spud** — n. **1** colloq. potato. **2** small narrow spade for weeding. — v. (**-dd-**) (foll. by up, out) remove with a spud. [origin unknown]

**spumante** /spyoo-**man**-tee, spuh-/ n.

Italian sparkling white wine. [Italian, = sparkling]

**spume** /spyoom/ *n. & v.* (**-ming**) froth, foam. □ **spumy** *adj.* (**-ier, -iest**). [Latin *spuma*]

**spun** *past* and *past part.* of SPIN.

**spunk** *n.* **1** *colloq.* courage, mettle, spirit. **2** *coarse colloq.* semen. **3** *colloq.* sexually attractive person. [origin unknown]

**spunky** *colloq.* — *adj.* (**-ier, -iest**) **1** brave, spirited. **2** highly attractive sexually. — *n.* = SPUNK 3.

**spur** — *n.* **1** small spike or spiked wheel worn on a rider's heel for urging on a horse. **2** stimulus, incentive. **3** spur-shaped thing, esp.: **a** a projection from a mountain or mountain range. **b** a branch road or railway. **c** a hard projection on a rooster's leg. **d** slender hollow projection from part of a flower. **e** short fruit-bearing shoot. — *v.* (**-rr-**) **1** prick (a horse) with spurs. **2** incite or stimulate. □ **on the spur of the moment** on impulse. [Old English]

**spurious** /spyoo-ree-uhs/ *adj.* not genuine; fake. [Latin]

**spurn** *v.* reject with disdain or contempt. [Old English]

**spurt** — *v.* **1** (cause to) gush out in a jet or stream. **2** make a sudden effort. — *n.* **1** sudden gushing out, jet. **2** short burst of speed, growth, etc. [origin unknown]

**spur-winged plover** *n.* (also **masked lapwing**) wading bird of eastern and southern Australia, having olive-brown and white plumage, yellow facial wattles, a white claw-like projection on the shoulder of each wing, and a loud call said to be like a dingo's howl.

**sputnik** /**spuut**-nik, **sput**-/ *n.* Russian artificial satellite orbiting the earth. [Russian]

**sputter** — *v.* **1** emit spitting sounds, esp. when being heated. **2** speak or utter (words, threats, etc.) rapidly or incoherently. — *n.* sputtering sound, esp. sputtering speech. [Dutch (imitative)]

**sputum** /**spyoo**-tuhm/ *n.* (*pl.* **sputa**) **1** saliva. **2** expectorated matter, used esp. in diagnosis. [Latin]

**spy** /spuy/ — *n.* (*pl.* **spies**) **1** person who secretly collects and reports information for a government, company, etc. **2** person watching others secretly. — *v.* (**spies, spied**) **1** discern, see. **2** (often foll. by *on*) act as a spy. **3** (often foll. by *into*) pry. □ **spy out** explore or discover, esp. secretly. [French *espie, espier*]

**sq.** *abbr.* square.

**squab** /skwob/ *n.* young (esp. unfledged) pigeon or other bird. [perhaps from Scandinavian]

**squabble** /**skwob**-uhl/ — *n.* petty or noisy quarrel. — *v.* (**-ling**) engage in this. [probably imitative]

**squad** /skwod/ *n.* **1** small group sharing a task etc., esp. of soldiers or policemen (*drug squad*). **2** *Sport* team. [French *escouade*]

**squadron** /**skwod**-ruhn/ *n.* **1** basic tactical and administrative unit of an Air Force. **2** detachment of warships employed on a particular duty. **3** organised group etc., esp. a cavalry division of two companies. [Italian *squadrone*: related to SQUAD]

**squadron leader** *n.* commander of a RAAF squadron, next below wing commander.

**squalid** /**skwol**-uhd/ *adj.* **1** filthy, dirty (*squalid living conditions*). **2** morally repulsive or degraded. [Latin]

**squall** /skwawl/ — *n.* **1** sudden or violent wind, esp. with rain, snow, or sleet. **2** discordant cry; scream (esp. of a baby). — *v.* **1** utter a squall; scream. **2** utter with a squall. □ **squally** *adj.* [probably alteration of SQUEAL after BAWL]

**squalor** /**skwol**-uh/ *n.* filthy or squalid state. [Latin]

**squander** /**skwon**-duh/ *v.* spend (money, time, etc.) wastefully. [origin unknown]

**square** /skwair/ — *n.* **1** rectangle with four equal sides. **2** object of (approximately) this shape. **3 a** open (usu. four-sided) area surrounded by buildings. **b** area within a barracks etc. for drill. **4** product of a number multiplied by itself (*16 is the square of 4*). **5** L- or T-shaped instrument for obtaining or testing right angles. **6** *colloq.* conventional or old-fashioned person. **7** (formerly) unit of 100 sq. ft. as a measure of flooring etc. — *adj.* **1** square-shaped. **2** having or in the form of a right angle (*square corner*). **3** angular, not round (*has a square jaw*). **4** designating a unit of measure equal to the area of a square whose side is one of the unit specified (*square metre*). **5** (often foll. by *with*) level, parallel. **6** (usu. foll. by *to*) at right angles. **7** sturdy, squat (*a man of square frame*). **8** arranged; settled (*get things square*). **9** (also **all square**) **a** with no money owed. **b** (of scores) equal. **10** fair and honest (*his dealings are not always quite square*). **11** direct (*met with a square refusal*). **12** *colloq.* conventional or old-fashioned. — *adv.* **1** squarely (*a hat set square upon his head*). **2** exactly; directly (*hit me square between the eyes*). **3** fairly, honestly (*play square*). — *v.* (**-ring**) **1** make square. **2** multiply (a number) by itself. **3** (usu. foll. by *to, with*) adjust; make or be suitable or consistent; reconcile (*the evidence does not square with your conclusion*). **4** mark out in squares. **5** settle or pay (a bill etc.). **6** place (one's shoulders etc.) squarely facing forwards. **7** *colloq.*

bribe (a person) (*tried to square the official*). **8** (also *absol.*) make the scores of (a match etc.) equal. □ **back to square one** *colloq.* back to the starting-point with no progress made. **on the square** *colloq.* **1** honest, fair. **2** abstaining from alcohol. **out of square** not at right angles. **silly as a square wheel** *colloq.* extremely silly; quite crazy. **square the circle 1** construct a square equal in area to a given circle. **2** do what is impossible. **square off 1** (often foll. by *with*) *colloq.* placate or conciliate (a person). **2** pay (a person) back; get revenge. **square peg in a round hole** see PEG. **square up** settle an account etc. **square up to 1** move threateningly towards (a person). **2** face and tackle (a difficulty etc.) resolutely. □ **squarely** *adv.* **squareness** *n.* **squarish** *adj.* [French *esquare*, Latin *quadra*]

**square brackets** *n.pl.* brackets of the form [ ].

**square dance** *n.* dance with usu. four couples facing inwards from four sides.

**square deal** *n.* fair bargain or treatment.

**square-eyed** *adj. colloq.* affected by, or given to, excessive viewing of television.

**square leg** *n.* fielding position in cricket at some distance on the batsman's leg side and nearly opposite the stumps.

**square meal** *n.* substantial meal.

**square-rigged** *adj.* with the principal sails at right angles to the length of the ship.

**square root** *n.* number that multiplied by itself gives a specified number.

**squash**[1] /skwosh/ — *v.* **1** crush or squeeze, esp. flat or into pulp. **2** (often foll. by *into*) pack tight, or make one's way by squeezing. **3** silence (a person) with a crushing retort etc. **4 a** suppress (a proposal, allegation, etc.). **b** quash (a rebellion etc.). — *n.* **1** crowd; crowded state. **2** drink made of crushed fruit (*lemon squash*). **3** (in full **squash racquets**) game played with racquets and a small ball in a closed court. □ **squashy** *adj.* (**-ier, -iest**). [French *esquasser*: related to EX-[1], QUASH]

**squash**[2] /skwosh/ *n.* (*pl.* same or **-es**) **1** trailing annual plant having pumpkin-like fruits. **2** fruit of this cooked and eaten as a vegetable. [Narragansett]

**squat** /skwot/ — *v.* (**-tt-**) **1** sit on one's heels or on the ground with the knees drawn up. **2** *colloq.* sit down. **3** *hist.* occupy a tract of Crown land in order to graze cattle or sheep. **4** occupy a building as a squatter. — *adj.* (**squatter, squattest**) short and thick, dumpy. — *n.* **1** squatting posture. **2** place occupied by squatters. □ **squatting** *n.* [French *esquatir* flatten]

**squatter** *n.* **1** person who inhabits unoc-cupied premises without permission. **2** *hist.* person who occupies a tract of Crown land in order to graze livestock, having title by licence or lease. **3** *hist.* person, esp. an ex-convict, who occupies Crown land without legal title. **4** sheep-farmer, esp. on a large scale; such a person as being of an elevated socio-economic status; (also *attrib.*). **5** = SQUATTER PIGEON.

**squatter pigeon** *n.* ground-dwelling brown bronzewing of Queensland and NSW.

**squatter's chair** *n.* (also **squatter's delight**) outdoor reclining chair consisting of a wooden frame from which a length of canvas is suspended and having a leg rest.

**squattocracy** /skwo-**tok**-ruh-see/ *n.* wealthy farmers as an interest group or as a socio-economic group.

**squaw** *n.* N. American Indian woman or wife. [Narragansett]

**squawk** — *n.* **1** loud harsh cry, esp. of a bird. **2** *colloq.* complaint. — *v.* **1** utter a squawk. **2** *colloq.* complain. [imitative]

**squeak** — *n.* **1** short high-pitched cry or sound. **2** (also **narrow squeak**) narrow escape. — *v.* **1** make a squeak. **2** utter (words) shrilly. **3** (foll. by *by, through*) *colloq.* pass narrowly. **4** *colloq.* turn informer. [imitative: related to SQUEAL, SHRIEK]

**squeaker** *n.* name applied to the bettong, to various birds with a squeaky call (esp. the grey currawong), and to various cicadas.

**squeaky** *adj.* (**-ier, -iest**) making a squeaking sound. □ **squeakily** *adv.* **squeakiness** *n.*

**squeaky clean** *adj.* (usu. hyphenated when *attrib.*) *colloq.* **1** completely clean. **2** above criticism.

**squeal** — *n.* prolonged shrill sound or cry. — *v.* **1** make, or utter with, a squeal. **2** *colloq.* turn informer. **3** *colloq.* protest vociferously. [imitative]

**squeamish** /skwee-mish/ *adj.* **1 a** easily nauseated. **b** slightly sick. **2** easily shocked; prudish. □ **squeamishly** *adv.* **squeamishness** *n.* [Anglo-French *escoymos*]

**squeegee** /skwee-jee/ *n.* rubber-edged implement on a handle, for cleaning windows etc. [*squeegee*, alteration of SQUEEZE]

**squeeze** — *v.* (**-zing**) **1** (often foll. by *out*) **a** exert pressure on, esp. to extract moisture etc. **b** extract (moisture) by squeezing. **c** force out as if by squeezing (*small shops are being squeezed out of business by supermarkets*). **2** reduce in size or alter in shape by squeezing. **3** force or push into or through a small or narrow space. **4 a** harass or pressure (a person). **b** (usu. foll. by *out of*) obtain by extortion, entreaty, etc. **5** press (a person's hand) in sympathy etc. — *n.* **1** instance of squeezing or state of being squeezed. **2** close embrace. **3** crowd, crowded state. **4** small quantity produced by squeezing (*just a squeeze of lemon*). **5** restriction on borrowing, investment, etc., in a financial crisis. **6** (also **tight squeeze**) *colloq.* difficult situation. □ **put the squeeze on** *colloq.* coerce or pressure. [origin unknown]

**squelch** — *v.* **1 a** make a sucking sound as of treading in thick mud. **b** move with a squelching sound. **2 a** disconcert, silence (*squelched him with a look*). **b** stamp on; crush flat; put an end to (*squelched a snail underfoot; squelched her hopes*). — *n.* act or sound of squelching. □ **squelchy** *adj.* [imitative]

**squib** — *n.* **1** small hissing firework that finally explodes. **2** satirical essay. **3 a** horse lacking stamina. **b** spineless person; coward. **4** = DAMP SQUIB. — *v.* **1** (often with *it* as object) evade (a difficulty or responsibility); shirk through fear or cowardice (*he squibbed the challenge; should have taken tough action but he squibbed it*). **2 a** fail to act; back down; give in (*when the going got tough, he squibbed*). **b** (foll. by *on*) betray or let down (*squibbed on his mates*). [perhaps imitative]

**squid** *n.* (*pl.* same or **-s**) ten-armed marine cephalopod used as food. [origin unknown]

**squidgy** /skwij-ee/ *adj.* (**-ier, -iest**) *colloq.* squashy, soggy. [imitative]

**squiffy** /skwif-ee/ *adj.* (**-ier, -iest**) *colloq.* slightly drunk. [origin unknown]

**squiggle** /skwig-uhl/ *n.* short curly line, esp. in handwriting. □ **squiggly** *adj.* [imitative]

**squillion** /skwil-yuhn/ *n. colloq.* **1** large number of millions. **2** (in *pl.*) large amount of money. [alteration of *million* etc.]

**squint** — *v.* **1** have eyes that do not move together but look in different directions. **2** (often foll. by *at*) look obliquely or with half-closed eyes. — *n.* **1** condition causing squinting. **2** stealthy or sidelong glance. **3** *colloq.* glance, look (*take a squint at this*). [obsolete *asquint*, perhaps from Dutch *schuinte* slant]

**squire** — *n.* **1** (in Britain) country gentleman, esp. the chief landowner of a district. **2** *hist.* knight's attendant. — *v.* (**-ring**) (of a man) attend or escort (a woman). [related to ESQUIRE]

**squirm** — *v.* **1** wriggle, writhe. **2** show or feel embarrassment. — *n.* squirming movement. [imitative]

**squirrel** /skwi-ruhl/ — *n.* **1** bushy-tailed usu. tree-living rodent of Europe, Asia, etc. **2** person who hoards small objects etc. — *v.*

(**-ll-**) **1** (often foll. by *away*) hoard. **2** (often foll. by *around*) bustle about. [Greek *skiouros*, from *skia* shade, *oura* tail]

**squirrel glider** *n.* gliding possum of eastern mainland Australia.

**squirt** — *v.* **1** eject (liquid etc.) in a jet. **2** be ejected in this way. **3** splash with a squirted substance. — *n.* **1 a** jet of water etc. **b** small quantity squirted. **2** syringe. **3** *colloq.* **a** insignificant but self-assertive person. **b** short person. [imitative]

**squish** *colloq.* — *n.* slight squelching sound. — *v.* move with a squish. □ **squishy** *adj.* (**-ier, -iest**). [imitative]

**squizz** /skwiz/ *colloq.* — *n.* a look; an inspection (*take a squizz at this!; he's gone to have a squizz at the workmen*). — *v.* look (at); inspect.

**Sr** *symb.* strontium.

**SS** *abbr.* **1** steamship. **2** *hist.* Nazi special police force. [sense 2 from German *Schutz-Staffel*]

**SSE** *abbr.* south-south-east.

**SSW** *abbr.* south-south-west.

**St** *abbr.* Saint.

**St.** *abbr.* Street.

**stab** — *v.* (**-bb-**) **1** pierce or wound with a knife etc. **2** (often foll. by *at*) aim a blow with such a weapon. **3** cause a sensation like being stabbed (*stabbing pain*). **4** hurt or distress (a person, feelings, conscience, etc.). — *n.* **1** act of stabbing. **2** wound from this. **3** *colloq.* attempt; a try (*go on — have a stab at it*). [origin unknown]

**stabilise** /stay-buh-luyz/ *v.* (also **-ize**) (**-sing** or **-zing**) make or become stable. □ **stabilisation** /-zay-shuhn/ *n.*

**stabiliser** *n.* (also **-izer**) **1** device used to keep esp. a ship, aircraft, or (in *pl.*) child's bicycle stable. **2** food additive for preserving texture.

**stability** /stuh-bil-uh-tee/ *n.* quality or state of being stable. [Latin: related to STABLE¹]

**stab in the back** — *n.* treacherous or slanderous attack. — *v.* betray.

**stab in the dark** *n.* a guess; a gamble.

**stab kick** *n.* (also **stab pass**) *Aust. Rules* fast, low kick to a team-mate.

**stable¹** /stay-buhl/ *adj.* (**-bler, -blest**) **1** firmly fixed or established; not easily adjusted, destroyed, or altered (*a stable structure; stable government*). **2** (of a person) not easily upset or disturbed. □ **stably** *adv.* [Latin *stabilis* from *sto* stand]

**stable²** — *n.* **1** building for keeping horses. **2** establishment for training racehorses. **3** racehorses from one stable. **4** persons, products, etc., having a common origin or affiliation. **5** such an origin or affiliation (*all these magazines come from the same stable*). — *v.* (**-ling**) put or keep in a stable. [as STABLE¹]

**stabling** n. accommodation for horses.

**staccato** /stuh-**kah**-toh/ esp. Mus. — adv. & adj. with each sound or note sharply detached or separated from the others. — n. (pl. **-s**) staccato passage or delivery. [Italian]

**stack** — n. **1** (esp. orderly) pile or heap. **2** colloq. large quantity (a stack of work; stacks of money). **3 a** = CHIMNEY-STACK. **b** = SMOKESTACK. **c** tall factory chimney. **4** stacked group of aircraft. **5** part of a library where books are compactly stored, esp. one to which the public does not have direct access. **6** column of rock detached (by the agency of water and weather) from a cliff, and rising precipitously out of the sea. — v. **1** pile in a stack or stacks. **2 a** arrange (cards) secretly for cheating. **b** manipulate (circumstances etc.) to suit one. **c** manipulate the proceedings of a meeting by ensuring the attendance of many of one's supporters. **3** cause (aircraft) to fly round the same point at different levels while waiting to land. **4** colloq. crash (a motor vehicle). □ **blow one's stack** explode in rage. **stack it on** colloq. exaggerate (one's feelings etc.). **stack on** colloq. turn on; produce (stacked on a bonzer party for her 21st). **stack on an act** colloq. carry out a pretence. **stack on a blue** (or **a turn**) colloq. make a great fuss; create a disturbance; become furious and show it. **stacks on the mill** colloq. situation (in Australian Rules, Rugby, children's games, etc.) where several players are piled up promiscuously, chaotically, one on top of the other (with the ball at the very bottom of the pile). [Old Norse]

**stadium** /**stay**-dee-uhm/ n. (pl. **-s**) athletic or sportsground with tiered seats for spectators. [Greek stadion]

**staff** /stahf/ — n. **1 a** stick or pole for use in walking or as a weapon. **b** stick or rod as a sign of office etc. **c** person or thing that supports. **2 a** people employed in a business etc. **b** those in authority in a school etc. **c** body of officers assisting an officer in high command (general staff). **3** (pl. **-s** or **staves**) Mus. set of usu. five parallel lines on or between which notes are placed to indicate their pitch. — v. provide (an institution etc.) with staff. [Old English]

**staff sergeant** n. senior sergeant of a non-infantry company.

**stag** — n. **1** adult male deer. **2** beast castrated after maturity when the sexual organs have fully grown; an inferior bullock. — adj. of or for males only (stag-party; stag-turn). □ **go stag** (of a man) attend a mixed party etc. unaccompanied by a woman. [Old English]

**stage** — n. **1** point or period in a process or development (reached a critical stage; is in the larval stage). **2 a** raised platform, esp. for performing plays etc. on. **b** (prec. by the) theatrical profession, drama. **c** scene of action (bit player on the stage of politics). **3 a** regular stopping-place on a route. **b** distance between two stopping-places. **4** Astronaut. section of a rocket with a separate engine jettisoned when its propellant is exhausted. — v. (**-ging**) **1** present (a play etc.) on stage. **2** arrange, organise (staged a demonstration). □ **hold the stage** dominate a conversation etc. □ **staging** n. [French estage, ultimately from Latin sto stand]

**stagecoach** n. hist. large closed horse-drawn coach running on a regular route by stages.

**stage direction** n. instruction in a play as to actors' movements, sound effects, etc.

**stage fright** n. performer's fear of an audience.

**stagehand** n. person moving stage scenery etc.

**stage-manage** v. **1** be the stage manager of. **2** arrange and control for effect.

**stage manager** n. person responsible for lighting and mechanical arrangements etc. on stage.

**stage whisper** n. **1** an aside. **2** loud whisper meant to be overheard.

**stagflation** /stag-**flay**-shuhn/ n. Econ. state of inflation without a corresponding increase of demand and employment. [blend of stagnation, inflation]

**stagger** — v. **1** (cause to) walk unsteadily or totter (was staggered by the blow). **2** shock, confuse (they were staggered at the suggestion). **3** arrange (events, hours of work, etc.) so that they do not coincide. **4** arrange (objects) so that they are not in line. — n. **1** tottering movement. **2** (in pl.) disease, esp. of horses and cattle, causing staggering. [Old Norse]

**staggering** adj. astonishing; bewildering. □ **staggeringly** adv.

**staggering bob** n. colloq. **1** newly born calf. **2** veal.

**stagger-weed** n. European annual herb, naturalised in temperate Australia, and noxious to stock.

**staghorn** n. extremely large epiphytic fern of NSW, Queensland, and elsewhere, having long, pendulous, much-divided leaves resembling the horns of a stag.

**stagnant** /**stag**-nuhnt/ adj. **1** (of liquid) motionless, having no current, and often unwholesome. **2** (of life, action, business, etc.) dull, sluggish. □ **stagnancy** n. [Latin stagnum pool]

**stagnate** /stag-**nayt**, **stag**-/ v. (**-ting**) be or become stagnant. □ **stagnation** n.

**stag-party** n. (also **stag-night**) all-male celebration held esp. for a man about to marry.

**stag-turn** n. stag-party or other all-male event.

**stagy** /**stay**-jee/ adj. (**-ier**, **-iest**) theatrical, artificial, exaggerated.

**staid** adj. of quiet and steady character; sedate. [= stayed, past part. of STAY¹]

**stain** — v. **1** discolour or be discoloured by the action of liquid sinking in. **2** spoil, damage (a reputation, character, etc.). **3** colour (wood, glass, etc.) with a penetrating substance. **4** impregnate (a specimen) with a colouring agent for microscopic examination. — n. **1** discoloration; spot, mark. **2** damage to a reputation etc. **3** substance used in staining. [earlier *distain* from French *desteindre*]

**stained glass** n. coloured glass in a leaded window etc.

**stainless steel** n. chrome steel resisting rust or tarnish.

**stair** n. **1** each of a set of fixed steps. **2** (usu. in pl.) set of these. [Old English]

**staircase** n. flight of stairs and the supporting structure.

**stairway** n. = STAIRCASE.

**stairwell** n. shaft in which a staircase is built.

**stake¹** — n. **1** stout sharpened stick driven into the ground as a support, boundary mark, etc. **2** hist. a post to which a condemned person was tied to be burnt alive. **b** (prec. by the) such death as a punishment. — v. (**-king**) **1** secure or support with a stake or stakes (*staked the plants*). **2** (foll. by off, out) mark off (an area) with stakes. **3** establish (a claim). □ **pull (up) stakes** depart; go to live elsewhere. **stake out** colloq. place under surveillance. [Old English]

**stake²** — n. **1** sum of money etc. wagered on an event. **2** (often foll. by in) interest or concern, esp. financial (*we've all got a stake in the success of this project*). **3** (in pl.) **a** prize-money, esp. in a horse race. **b** such a race. **4** (in pl.) (with defining word) particular business or way of life in which success is attained through competition (*beauty stakes; fashion stakes*). — v. wager. □ **at stake** risked, to be won or lost (*her life is at stake*). [Old English]

**stalactite** /**stal**-uhk-ˌtuyt/ n. icicle-like deposit of calcium carbonate hanging from the roof of a cave etc. [Greek *stalaktos* dripping]

**stalagmite** /**stal**-uhg-ˌmuyt/ n. icicle-like deposit of calcium carbonate rising from the floor of a cave etc. [Greek *stalagma* a drop]

**stale** — adj. **1 a** not fresh (*the bread is a bit stale*). **b** musty, insipid, or otherwise the worse for age or use. **2** trite, unoriginal (*stale joke*). **3** having one's ability to perform spoilt by too much practice. — v. (**-ling**) make or become stale. □ **staleness** n. [Anglo-French *estaler* halt]

**stalemate** — n. **1** Chess position counting as a draw, in which a player cannot move except into check. **2** deadlock or drawn contest (*negotiations have reached a stalemate*). — v. (**-ting**) **1** Chess bring (a player) to a stalemate. **2** bring to deadlock or standstill. [obsolete *stale*: related to STALE, (CHECK)MATE]

**Stalinism** /**stah**-luh-ˌniz-uhm/ n. rigid centralised authoritarian form of socialism associated with Stalin. □ **Stalinist** n. & adj. [*Stalin*, name of a Russian statesman]

**stalk¹** /stawk/ n. **1** main stem of a herbaceous plant. **2** slender attachment or support of a leaf, flower, fruit, etc. **3** any similar slender support, e.g. the stem of a wine-glass. [diminutive of (now British dial.) *stale* rung]

**stalk²** /stawk/ — v. **1** pursue (game or an enemy) stealthily. **2** stride, walk in a haughty manner. **3** formal or rhet. move silently or threateningly through (a place) (*fear stalked the land*). — n. **1** stalking of game. **2** haughty gait. [Old English: related to STEAL]

**stalker** n. **1** person who stalks game etc. **2** person who stalks people, e.g. one who obsessively pesters a public figure, a former lover, etc.

**stalking-horse** n. **1** horse concealing a hunter. **2** pretext concealing one's real intentions or actions.

**stall¹** /stawl/ — n. **1** booth or table in a market etc. displaying goods for sale. **2** compartment for one animal in a stable. **3** (usu. in pl.) each of the seats on the ground floor of a theatre. **4** compartment for one horse at the start of a race. **5 a** stalling of an engine or aircraft. **b** condition resulting from this. — v. **1** (of a vehicle or its engine) stop because of an overload on the engine or an inadequate supply of fuel to it. **2** (of an aircraft or its pilot) lose control because the speed is too low. **3** cause to stall. [Old English]

**stall²** /stawl/ v. **1** play for time when being questioned etc. **2** delay, obstruct. [*stall* 'decoy': probably related to STALL¹]

**stallion** /**stal**-yuhn/ n. uncastrated adult male horse. [French *estalon*]

**stalwart** /**stawl**-wuht/ — adj. **1** strong, sturdy. **2** courageous, resolute, reliable (*stalwart supporters of the Geelong footy team*). — n. stalwart person, esp. a loyal comrade. [Old English, = place, WORTH]

**stamen** /**stay**-muhn/ *n.* organ producing pollen in a flower. [Latin, = warp, thread]

**stamina** /**stam**-uh-nuh/ *n.* physical or mental endurance. [Latin, pl. of STAMEN]

**stammer** — *v.* **1** speak haltingly, esp. with pauses or rapid repetitions of the same syllable, often because of a speech impairment. **2** (often foll. by *out*) utter (words) in this way. — *n.* **1** tendency to stammer. **2** instance of stammering. [Old English]

**stamp** — *v.* **1 a** bring down (one's foot) heavily, esp. on the ground. **b** (often foll. by *on*) crush or flatten in this way. **c** walk heavily (*stamped round the room in a rage*). **2 a** impress (a design, mark, etc.) on a surface. **b** impress (a surface) with a pattern etc. **3** affix a postage or other stamp to. **4** assign a specific character to; mark out (*that performance stamps her as the likely winner*). — *n.* **1** instrument for stamping. **2 a** mark or design made by this. **b** impression of an official mark required to be made on deeds, bills of exchange, etc., as evidence of the validity of the document etc. or of payment of tax. **3** small adhesive piece of paper indicating that payment has been made, esp. a postage stamp. **4** mark or label etc. on a commodity as evidence of quality etc. **5** act or sound of stamping the foot. **6** characteristic mark or quality (*bears the stamp of genius; this music has the stamp of Bach*). □ **stamp on 1** impress (an idea etc.) on (the memory etc.). **2** suppress. **stamp out 1** produce by cutting out with a die etc. **2** put an end to, destroy (*stamped out the fire; the need to stamp out racism in Australia*). [Old English]

**stamp-duty** *n.* duty imposed on certain legal documents.

**stampede** /stam-**peed**/ — *n.* **1** sudden rush of a herd of frightened animals. **2** rush of people under a sudden common impulse. — *v.* (**-ding**) (cause to) take part in a stampede. [Spanish *estampida* crash, uproar]

**stamping ground** *n. colloq.* favourite haunt.

**stance** /stahns, stans/ *n.* **1** standpoint; attitude of mind (*has taken a hostile stance towards the proposal*). **2** attitude or position of the body, esp. when hitting a ball, preparing to box, etc. [Italian *stanza* standing]

**stanch** var. of STANCH[2].

**stanchion** /**stahn**-shuhn, **stan**-chuhn/ — *n.* post or pillar; upright support; vertical strut. — *v.* supply with a stanchion. [Anglo-French]

**stand** — *v.* (*past* and *past part.* **stood** /stuud/) **1** have, take, or maintain an upright position, esp. on the feet or a base. **2** be situated (*here once stood a village*). **3** be of a specified height (*stands 175 cm tall*). **4** be in a specified condition (*stands accused; it stands as follows; the thermometer stands at 36°*). **5** set in an upright or specified position (*stood it against the wall*). **6 a** move to and remain in a specified position (*stand aside*). **b** take a specified attitude (*stand aloof*). **7** maintain a position; avoid falling, moving, or being moved (*stood for hours arguing; this house will stand for another century*). **8** assume a stationary position; cease to move. **9** remain valid or unaltered (*the former conditions must stand*). **10** *Naut.* hold a specified course. **11** endure, tolerate (*can't stand the pain; how can you stand him?*). **12** provide at one's own expense (*stood him a drink*). **13** (often foll. by *for*) be a candidate (for office etc.) (*stood for parliament*). **14** act in a specified capacity (*stood proxy*). **15** undergo (trial). — *n.* **1** cessation from progress, stoppage (*was brought to a stand*). **2 a** *Mil.* halt made to repel an attack. **b** resistance to attack or compulsion (esp. *make a stand*). **c** *Cricket* prolonged period at the wicket by two batsmen. **3** position taken up; attitude (*took his stand near the door; his stand on this issue is ultra conservative*). **4** rack, set of shelves, etc. for storage. **5** openfronted stall or structure for a trader, exhibitor, etc. **6** standing-place for vehicles (*taxi-stand*). **7 a** raised structure to sit or stand on. **b** witness-box (*take the stand*). **8** each halt made for a performance on a tour (*a one-night stand*). **9** group of growing plants (*stand of trees*). □ **as it stands 1** in its present condition. **2** in the present circumstances. **stand by 1** stand nearby; look on without interfering. **2** uphold, support (a person). **3** adhere to (a promise etc.). **4** be ready for action, news, etc. **stand a chance** see CHANCE. **stand corrected** accept correction. **stand down 1** withdraw from a position or candidacy. **2** terminate (a person's) employment, esp. as a result of the effects of a strike. **stand for 1** represent, signify, imply. **2** *colloq.* endure, tolerate. **stand one's ground** not yield. **stand in** (usu. foll. by *for*) deputise. **stand in good stead** see STEAD. **stand off 1** move or keep away. **2** temporarily dismiss, lay-off (an employee). **stand on** insist on, observe scrupulously. **stand on one's own feet** (or **two feet**) be self-reliant or independent. **stand out 1** be prominent or outstanding. **2** (usu. foll. by *against, for*) persist in opposition or support. **3** (foll. by any of various similes) be conspicuous (*stand out like a sore thumb*). **stand over 1** stand close to (a person) to watch, control, intimidate, etc. **2** intimidate or threaten; extort money (from someone). **stand to 1** *Mil.* stand ready for an attack. **2** abide by.

**3** be likely or certain to. **stand to reason** be obvious. **stand up 1 a** rise to one's feet. **b** come to, remain in, or place in a standing position. **2** (of an argument etc.) be valid. **3** *colloq.* fail to keep an appointment with (*stood me up*). **stand up for** support, side with. **stand up to 1** face (an opponent) courageously. **2** be resistant to (wear, use, etc.). **take one's stand on** base one's argument etc. on, rely on. [Old English]

**standard** /stan-duhd/ — *n.* **1** object, quality, or measure serving as a basis, example, or principle to which others conform or should conform or by which others are judged. **2 a** level of excellence etc. required or specified (*not up to standard*; *has very poor moral standards*). **b** average quality (*of a low standard*). **3** ordinary procedure, or quality, or design (of a product), without added or novel features. **4** distinctive flag (of a king, army, etc.). **5 a** upright support. **b** upright pipe. **6** shrub grafted on an upright stem and trained in tree form (*standard rose*). **7** tune or song of established popularity. — *adj.* **1** serving or used as a standard (*standard size*). **2** of a normal or prescribed quality, type, or size (*standard uniform*; *standard light-fitting*). **3** of recognised and permanent value; authoritative (*standard book on jazz*). **4** (of language) conforming to established educated usage. [Anglo-French: related to EXTEND, and in senses 5 and 6 of *n.* influenced by STAND]

**standard-bearer** *n.* **1** soldier who carries a standard. **2** prominent leader in a cause.

**standard deviation** *n. Statistics* quantity calculated to indicate the extent of deviation for a group as a whole.

**standardise** *v.* (also **-ize**) (**-sing** or **-zing**) cause to conform to a standard. □ **standardisation** *n.*

**standard lamp** *n.* lamp on a tall upright with a base.

**standard of living** *n.* degree of material comfort of a person or group.

**standard time** *n.* uniform time for places in approximately the same longitude, established in a country or region by law or custom.

**standby** *n.* (*pl.* **-bys**) **1** (often *attrib.*) person or thing ready if needed in an emergency etc. **2** readiness for duty (*on stand-by*). **3** (of air travel) not booked in advance but allocated on the basis of earliest availability.

**stand-in** *n.* deputy or substitute.

**standing** — *n.* **1** esteem or repute, esp. high; status. **2** duration (*of long standing*). — *adj.* **1** that stands; upright. **2** established, permanent (*a standing rule*; *a

*standing army*). **3** (of a jump, start, etc.) performed with no run-up. **4** (of water) stagnant.

**standing committee** *n.* committee (of a parliament, a university, etc.) which is appointed to deal with a particular issue or area of responsibility, and which is permanent during the existence of the appointing body.

**standing joke** *n.* object of permanent ridicule.

**standing orders** *n.pl.* rules governing procedure in a parliament, council, etc.

**standing ovation** *n.* prolonged applause from an audience which has risen to its feet.

**standing wave** *n. Physics* vibration of a system in which some particular points remain fixed while others between them vibrate with the maximum amplitude.

**stand-off** *n.* deadlock or stalemate in negotiations etc.

**standoffish** /stand-of-ish/ *adj.* cold or distant in manner.

**standover** *n.* (also **standover merchant**) person who engages in intimidatory tactics.

**standpoint** *n.* point of view.

**standstill** *n.* stoppage; inability to proceed.

**stand-up** *attrib. adj.* **1** (of a meal) eaten standing. **2** (of a fight) violent and thorough. **3** (of a collar) not turned down. **4** (of a comedian) telling jokes to an audience.

**Stanislavski method** see METHOD (sense 4).

**stank** *past* of STINK.

**stannic** /stan-ik/ *adj. Chem.* of or relating to tetravalent tin. [Latin *stannum* tin]

**stannous** /stan-uhs/ *adj. Chem.* of or relating to bivalent tin.

**stanza** /stan-zuh/ *n.* basic structural unit in a poem or verse consisting of a recurring group of lines (often four lines and usu. not more than twelve) which may or may not rhyme. □ **stanzaic** *adj.* [Italian]

**staphylococcus** /staf-uh-luh-kok-uhs/ *n.* (*pl.* **-cocci** /-kok-kuy/) bacterium occurring in grapelike clusters, and sometimes causing pus formation usu. in the skin and mucous membranes. □ **staphylococcal** *adj.* [Greek *staphylē* bunch of grapes, *kokkos* berry]

**staple¹** /stay-puhl/ — *n.* U-shaped metal bar or piece of wire with pointed ends for driving into and holding papers together, for holding an electrical wire in place, etc. — *v.* (**-ling**) fasten or provide with a staple. □ **stapler** *n.* [Old English]

**staple²** /stay-puhl/ — *n.* **1** principal or important article of commerce (*staples of Australian industry*). **2** chief element or main component (e.g. of a diet). **3** fibre of cotton or wool etc. with regard to its quality (*cotton of fine staple*). — *attrib. adj.* **1** main or principal (*staple commodities*). **2** important as a product or export. [French *estaple* market]

**star** /stah/ — *n.* **1** celestial body appearing as a luminous point in the night sky. **2** large naturally luminous gaseous body such as the sun. **3 a** celestial body regarded as influencing fortunes etc. (*born under a lucky star*). **b** (in *pl.*) = HOROSCOPE. **4** thing like a star in shape or appearance. **5** figure or object with radiating points esp. as a decoration or mark of rank or showing a category of excellence (*a five-star motel*). **6 a** famous or brilliant person; principal performer (*star of the show*). **b** (*attrib.*) outstanding (*star pupil*). — *v.* (**-rr-**) **1** appear or present as principal performer(s) (*has starred in many films*). **2** (esp. as **starred** *adj.*) **a** mark, set, or adorn with a star or stars. **b** put an asterisk or star beside (a name, a list, an item in a list or agenda, etc.) to indicate special importance (*does anyone want to star any of these items?*). □ **see stars** imagine one sees starry flashes, e.g. after hitting, or being hit on, one's head; suffer sudden sharp pain. □ **stardom** *n.* [Old English]

**starboard** /stah-buhd/ *n.* right-hand side of a ship or aircraft looking forward (opp. PORT³). [Old English, = *steer board*]

**starch** — *n.* **1** polysaccharide obtained chiefly from cereals and potatoes. **2** preparation of this for stiffening fabric. **3** stiffness of manner; formality. — *v.* stiffen (clothing) with starch. [Old English: related to STARK]

**starchy** *adj.* (**-ier, -iest**) **1 a** of or like starch. **b** containing much starch. **2** prim, formal. □ **starchily** *adv.* **starchiness** *n.*

**stare** /stair/ — *v.* (**-ring**) **1** (usu. foll. by *at*) look fixedly, esp. in curiosity, surprise, horror, etc. **2** reduce (a person) to a specified condition by staring (*stared me into silence*). — *n.* staring gaze. □ **stare a person in the face** be evident or imminent. [Old English]

**starfish** *n.* (*pl.* same or **-es**) echinoderm with five or more radiating arms.

**starfruit** *n.* the fruit (which is star-shaped in cross section) of a SE Asian tree.

**stargazer** *n.* colloq. **1** usu. derog. or joc. astronomer or astrologer. **2** romantic optimist; daydreamer.

**stark** — *adj.* **1** sharply evident (*in stark contrast*). **2** desolate, bare (*a stark landscape*). **3** absolute (*stark madness*). — *adv.* completely, wholly (*stark naked*). □ **starkly** *adv.* **starkness** *n.* [Old English]

**starkers** /stah-kuhz/ *predic. adj. colloq.* **1** stark naked. **2** mad, insane.

**starlet** /stah-luht/ *n.* promising young performer, esp. a film actress.

**starlight** *n.* light of the stars.

**starling** /stah-ling/ *n.* **1** gregarious bird with blackish speckled lustrous plumage, introduced into, and now common in, (eastern) Australia. **2** = METALLIC STARLING. [Old English]

**Star of David** *n.* two interlaced equilateral triangles used as a Jewish and Israeli symbol.

**starry** *adj.* (**-ier, -iest**) **1** full of stars. **2** like a star.

**starry-eyed** *adj. colloq.* **1** enthusiastic but impractical. **2** euphoric.

**star-studded** *adj.* **1** covered with stars. **2** featuring many famous performers.

**start** — *v.* **1** begin. **2** set in motion or action (*started a fire*). **3** set oneself in motion or action ('*Wait!*' *he shouted, and started after her*). **4** begin a journey etc. **5** (often foll. by *up*) (cause to) begin operating (*started the engine; the car wouldn't start*). **6 a** cause or enable (a person) to make a beginning (*started me in business*). **b** (foll. by pres. part.) cause (a person) to begin (*started me coughing*). **c** colloq. complain or warn (*don't you start*). **7** (often foll. by *up*) establish (*started up a new boys' club*). **8** give a signal to (competitors) to start in a race. **9** (often foll. by *up, from*, etc.) make a sudden movement from surprise, pain, etc. (*started at the sound of my voice*). **10** spring out, up, etc. (*started up from the chair*). **11 a** (of timbers etc.) spring out; give way. **b** cause (timbers etc.) to do this. **12** (foll. by *out, to*, etc.) (of a thing) move or appear suddenly (*tears started to his eyes*). **13** (foll. by *from*) (of eyes, usu. with exaggeration) burst forward (from their sockets) in fear, surprise, etc. — *n.* **1** beginning of an event, journey, etc. **2** place from which a race etc. begins. **3** advantage given at the beginning of a race etc. (*a 15-second start*). **4** advantageous initial position in life, business, etc. **5** sudden movement of surprise, pain, etc. **6** intermittent or spasmodic effort or movement (esp. *in* or *by fits and starts*). □ **for a start** colloq. as a beginning. **start off** begin; begin to move. **start out** begin a journey. **start up** arise; occur. [Old English]

**starter** *n.* **1** device for starting a vehicle engine etc. **2** (also in *pl.*) first course of a meal. **3** person giving the signal for the start of a race. **4** horse or competitor starting in a race. □ **for starters** to start with.

**starting block** *n.* shaped block for a runner's feet at the start of a race.

**starting price** n. odds ruling at the start of a horse race.

**startle** /stah-tuhl/ v. (-ling) shock or surprise. [Old English]

**starve** v. (-ving) 1 (cause to) die of hunger or suffer from malnourishment. 2 colloq. feel very hungry (I'm starving). 3 (foll. by for) feel a strong craving for (sympathy, amusement, knowledge, etc.). 4 (foll. by of) deprive of (starved of affection). 5 compel by starving (starved into surrender). □ **starve the bardies!** (or **crows!** or **lizards!** or **roan bullock!** etc.) colloq. exclamation of exasperation, astonishment, etc. (more often to be met with now in caricatures of Australian speech than in Australian speech itself). □ **starvation** /-vay-shuhn/ n. [Old English, = die]

**stash** colloq. — v. (often foll. by away) 1 conceal; put in a safe place. 2 hoard. — n. 1 hiding-place. 2 thing hidden. [origin unknown]

**stasis** /stay-suhs/ n. (pl. **stases** /-seez/) 1 inactivity, stagnation. 2 state of equilibrium. 3 stoppage of circulation. [Greek]

**state** — n. 1 existing condition or position of a person or thing (in a precarious state of health; in a bad state of repair). 2 colloq. **a** excited or agitated mental condition (esp. in a state). **b** untidy condition (what a state this room is in!). 3 (usu. **State**) political community under one government (the State of Israel) or forming part of a federal republic (States of the USA) or forming part of a federal union (the States of the Commonwealth of Australia). 4 (usu. **State**) (attrib.) **a** of, for, or concerned with the State. **b** reserved for or done on occasions of ceremony (State visit). 5 (usu. **State**) civil government (Church and State). 6 pomp, rank, dignity (as befits their state). — v. (-ting) 1 express in speech or writing. 2 fix, specify (at stated intervals). 3 Mus. play (a theme etc.), esp. for the first time. □ **in state** with all due ceremony. **lie in state** be laid in a public place of honour before burial. **state of play** (or **affairs** or **things**) present circumstances; current situation. [partly from ESTATE, partly from Latin STATUS]

**State aid** n. financial assistance from the government of an Australian State, esp. as given to private schools.

**stateless** adj. having no nationality or citizenship.

**stately** adj. (-ier, -iest) dignified; imposing. □ **stateliness** n.

**statement** n. 1 act or instance of stating or being stated; expression in words. 2 thing stated; declaration (that statement is unfounded). 3 formal account of facts, esp. to the police or in a court of law. 4 record of transactions in a bank account etc. 5 notification of the amount due to a tradesman etc.

**state of emergency** n. condition of danger or disaster in a country, with normal constitutional procedures suspended. [medieval Latin: related to EMERGE]

**state of the art** — n. current stage of esp. technological development. — attrib. adj. (usu. **state-of-the-art**) absolutely up-to-date (state-of-the-art weaponry).

**State rights** n.pl. administrative and legislative responsibilities reserved to an Australian State.

**stateroom** n. 1 state apartment. 2 large private cabin in a passenger ship.

**state school** n. school largely managed and funded by the public authorities.

**statesman** n. (fem. **stateswoman**) distinguished and extremely capable politician or diplomat. □ **statesmanlike** adj. **statesmanship** n.

**static** /stat-ik/ — adj. 1 stationary; not acting or changing. 2 Physics concerned with bodies at rest or forces in equilibrium. — n. 1 static electricity. 2 atmospherics. □ **statically** adv. [Greek statikos from sta- stand]

**static electricity** n. electricity not flowing as a current, e.g. as caused by friction.

**statics** n.pl. (usu. treated as sing.) 1 science of bodies at rest or of forces in equilibrium. 2 = STATIC.

**station** /stay-shuhn/ — n. 1 **a** regular stopping-place on a railway line. **b** buildings of this. **c** (in comb.) centre where vehicles of a specified type depart and arrive (coach station). 2 place to stand in, esp. a position assigned to a person on duty or in games. 3 centre for a particular service or activity (police station; polling station). 4 **a** establishment involved in broadcasting. **b** = CHANNEL (sense 3). 5 **a** military or naval base. **b** inhabitants of this. 6 position in life; rank, status. 7 **a** hist. outpost of colonial government in Australia, esp. as established for the employment of convict labour on public works (convict station; penal station). **b** hist. tract of land occupied by Aborigines; a reserve for Aborigines, esp. as established by a religious mission or a government agency. **c** tract of grazing land, usu. having a discernible centre of occupation. **d** = HOME STATION. **e** extensive sheep or cattle raising establishment. **f** (attrib. in sense **e**) (station boss; station hand). — v. 1 assign a station to. 2 put in position. [Latin statio from sto stat- stand]

**stationary** adj. 1 not moving (hit a stationary car). 2 not meant to be moved; not portable. 3 unchanging in magnitude, quality, efficiency, etc. (*stationary temperature*). [Latin: related to STATION]

**stationer** *n.* dealer in stationery.

**stationery** *n.* writing-materials, office supplies, etc.

**station hand** *n.* worker on a large sheep or cattle raising establishment.

**stationmaster** *n.* official in charge of a railway station.

**station of the cross** *n. RC Ch.* each of a series of fourteen paintings or sculptures, distributed around the interior of a church and representing the events in Christ's Passion, before which prayers are said, esp. in Lent.

**station wagon** *n.* car with passenger area extended, with space for luggage behind the back seat (which can be lowered to make extra luggage space), and with a rear door.

**statistic** /stuh-**tis**-tik/ *n.* statistical fact or item. [German: related to STATE]

**statistical** *adj.* of statistics. □ **statistically** *adv.*

**statistics** *n.pl.* **1** (usu. treated as *sing.*) science of collecting and analysing significant numerical data. **2** such analysed data. □ **statistician** /ˌstat-uh-**stish**-uhn/ *n.*

**statue** /**sta**-choo, -tyoo/ *n.* sculptured, carved, cast, or moulded figure of a person or animal, esp. life-size or larger. [Latin *statua*]

**statuesque** /ˌsta-choo-**esk**, -tyoo-/ *adj.* like, or having the dignity or beauty of, a statue.

**stature** /**sta**-chuh/ *n.* **1** height of a (esp. human) body. **2** degree of eminence, social standing, etc. (*recruit someone of her stature*). [Latin *statura*]

**status** /**stay**-tuhs, **stat**-uhs/ *n.* **1** rank, social position, relative importance. **2** superior social etc. position. **3** position of affairs (*let me know if the status changes*). [Latin: related to STATURE]

**status quo** /ˌstay-tuhs **kwoh**/ *n.* existing state of affairs. [Latin]

**status symbol** *n.* a possession etc. intended to indicate the owner's superiority.

**statute** /**sta**-choot, **stat**-yoot/ *n.* **1** written law passed by a legislative body. **2** rule of a corporation, founder, etc., intended to be permanent. [Latin *statutum* from *statuo* set up]

**statutory** *adj.* required or enacted by statute. □ **statutorily** *adv.*

**statutory declaration** *n.* written and signed declaration witnessed by a justice of the peace etc., stating e.g. that an item has been lost or damaged, a document has been read, etc.

**staunch¹** /stawnch/ *adj.* **1** trustworthy; loyal. **2** (of a ship, joint, etc.) strong,

watertight, airtight, etc. □ **staunchly** *adv.* [French *estanche*]

**staunch²** /stahnch, stawnch/ *v.* (also **stanch**) **1** restrain the flow of (esp. blood). **2** restrain the flow from (esp. a wound). [French *estancher*]

**stave** — *n.* **1** each of the curved slats forming the sides of a cask, pail, etc. **2** = STAFF *n.* 3. **3** stanza or verse. — *v.* (**-ving**; *past* and *past part.* **stove** or **staved**) (usu. foll. by *in*) break a hole in, damage, crush by forcing inwards. □ **stave off** avert or defer (danger etc.). [from STAFF]

**stay¹** — *v.* **1** continue in the same place or condition; not depart or change. **2** (often foll. by *at*, *in*, *with*) reside temporarily (*stayed with them for Christmas*). **3** *archaic* or *literary* **a** stop or check (progress, the inroads of a disease, etc.). **b** (esp. in *imper.*) pause (*Stay! You forget one thing . . .*). **4** postpone (judgment etc.). **5** assuage (hunger etc.), esp. temporarily. **6 a** show endurance (*to win the Melbourne Cup you need a horse that can stay*). **b** show endurance to the end of (a long race etc.) (*stayed the course*). — *n.* **1** act or period of staying. **2** suspension or postponement of a sentence, judgment, etc. **3** prop, support (*he's my strength and stay*). **4** (in *pl.*) *hist.* (esp. boned) corset. □ **stay the course** endure to the end. **stay in** remain indoors. **stay put** *colloq.* remain where it is placed or where one is. **stay up** not go to bed (until late). [Anglo-French from Latin *sto* stand: sense 3 of *n.* from French, formed as STAY²]

**stay²** *n.* **1** *Naut.* rope or guy supporting a mast, flagstaff, etc. **2** supporting cable on an aircraft etc. [Old English from Germanic]

**stayer** *n.* person or animal with great endurance.

**staying power** *n.* endurance.

**STD** *abbr.* **1** subscriber trunk dialling. **2** sexually transmitted disease.

**stead** /sted/ *n.* □ **in a person's or thing's stead** as a substitute; in a person's or thing's place. **stand a person in good stead** be advantageous or useful to him or her. [Old English, = place]

**steadfast** /**sted**-fahst, **sted**-fuhst/ *adj.* constant, firm, unwavering. □ **steadfastly** *adv.* **steadfastness** *n.* [Old English: related to STEAD]

**steady** /**sted**-ee/ — *adj.* (**-ier**, **-iest**) **1** firmly fixed or supported; unwavering. **2** uniform and regular (*steady pace*; *steady increase*). **3 a** constant (*steady in his affection for her*). **b** persistent (*steady attacks on him in the press*). **4** (of a person) serious and dependable. **5** regular, established (*steady girlfriend*). **6** accurately directed; not faltering (*a steady* hand; *a steady eye*). — v. (**-ies, -ied**) make or become steady (*steady the boat; steadied with an effort*). — adv. steadily (*hold it steady*). — n. (pl. **-ies**) *colloq.* regular boyfriend or girlfriend. □ **go steady** (often foll. by *with*) *colloq.* have as a regular boyfriend or girlfriend. **steady on!** be careful! □ **steadily** adv. **steadiness** n. [from STEAD]

**steady state** n. unvarying condition, esp. in a physical process, e.g. of the universe having no beginning and no end.

**steak** /stayk/ n. **1** thick slice of meat (esp. beef) or fish, usu. grilled or fried. **2** beef cut for stewing or braising. [Old Norse]

**steal** — v. (*past* **stole**; *past part.* **stolen**) **1** (also *absol.*) **a** take (another's property etc.) illegally (*stole the car*). **b** take (property etc.) without right or permission, esp. in secret (*stole her ideas*). **2** obtain surreptitiously or by surprise (*stole a quick nap while the boss was busy; stole a kiss*). **3** gain insidiously or artfully (*stole the lead from their business rivals by using slick advertising*). **4** (foll. by *in, out, away, up,* etc.) move, esp. silently or stealthily (*stole out of the room*). — n. *colloq.* easy task or good bargain. □ **steal a march on** get an advantage over by surreptitious means; anticipate. **steal the show** outshine other performers, esp. unexpectedly. **steal a person's thunder** take away the attention due to someone else by using his or her words, ideas, etc. [Old English]

**stealth** /stelth/ n. secrecy; secret procedure. [Old English: related to STEAL]

**stealthy** adj. (**-ier, -iest**) done or moving with stealth; furtive. □ **stealthily** adv. **stealthiness** n.

**steam** — n. **1 a** gas into which water is changed by boiling. **b** condensed vapour formed from this. **2 a** power obtained from steam. **b** *colloq.* power or energy (*he ran out of steam and came last*). — v. **1 a** cook (food) in steam. **b** treat with steam. **2** give off steam. **3 a** move under steam power. **b** (foll. by *ahead, away,* etc.) *colloq.* proceed or travel fast or with vigour. **4** (usu. foll. by *up*) **a** cover or become covered with condensed steam. **b** (as **steamed up** *adj.*) *colloq.* angry or excited. — *attrib. adj.* **1** powered etc. by steam (*steam engine; steam hammer*). **2** emitting steam (*steam iron*). □ **let off steam** see LET. **run out of steam** lose one's impetus or energy. [Old English]

**steamer** n. **1** steam-driven ship. **2** vessel for steaming food in.

**steamroller** — n. **1** heavy slow-moving vehicle with a roller, used in road-making. **2** a crushing power or force. — v. (also **steamroll**) **1** crush or break down (opposi-

tion etc.) as with a steamroller; ride roughshod over. **2** (foll. by *through*) force (a measure etc.) through a legislature etc. by overriding or crushing opposition. **3** (foll. by *into*) force (a person) into a course of action, a situation, etc.

**steamy** adj. (**-ier, -iest**) **1** like or full of steam. **2** *colloq.* erotic; salacious. □ **steamily** adv. **steaminess** n.

**steatite** /stee-tuyt/ n. impure form of talc, esp. soapstone. [Greek *stear steat-* tallow]

**steed** n. *archaic* or *poet.* horse. [Old English]

**steel** — n. **1** strong malleable alloy of iron and carbon, used esp. for making tools, weapons, etc. **2** strength, firmness (*nerves of steel*). **3** steel rod for sharpening knives. — *adj.* of or like steel. — v. (also *refl.*) harden or make resolute (*steeled myself for a shock*). [Old English]

**steel wool** n. abrasive substance consisting of a mass of fine steel shavings.

**steelworks** n.pl. (usu. treated as *sing.*) factory producing steel. □ **steelworker** n.

**steely** adj. (**-ier, -iest**) **1** of, or as hard as, steel. **2** severe; resolute; cold; ruthless (*steely composure; steely-eyed glance*). □ **steeliness** n.

**steep**[1] — *adj.* **1** sloping sharply (*steep hill; steep stairs*). **2** (of a rise or fall) rapid (*steep drop in prices*). **3** (*predic.*) *colloq.* **a** (of a price, demand, etc.) exorbitant; unreasonable (esp. *a bit steep*). **b** (of a story etc.) exaggerated; incredible. — n. steep slope; precipice. □ **steepen** v. **steepish** *adj.* **steeply** adv. **steepness** n. [Old English]

**steep**[2] — v. soak or bathe in liquid. — n. **1** act or process of steeping. **2** liquid for steeping. □ **steep in 1** pervade or imbue with (*steeped in misery*). **2** make deeply acquainted with (a subject etc.) (*steeped in Australian literature*). [Old English]

**steeple** /stee-puhl/ n. tall tower, esp. with a spire, above the roof of a church. [Old English: related to STEEP[1]]

**steeplechase** — n. **1** horse race with ditches, hedges, etc., to jump. **2** foot-race with similar obstacles, either cross-country or on an athletics track. — v. take part in a steeplechase. □ **steeplechaser** n. **steeplechasing** n.

**steeplejack** n. repairer of tall chimneys, steeples, etc.

**steer**[1] v. **1** (also *absol.*) guide (a vehicle, ship, etc.) with a wheel or rudder etc. **2** direct or guide (one's course, other people, a conversation, etc.) in a specified direction. □ **steer clear of** avoid. □ **steering** n. [Old English]

**steer**[2] n. = BULLOCK. [Old English]

**steerage** n. **1** act of steering. **2** *archaic* cheapest part of a ship's accommodation.

**steering committee** n. committee deciding the order of business, the course of operations, etc.

**stegosaurus** /ˌsteg-uh-**saw**-ruhs/ n. (pl. **-ruses**) plant-eating dinosaur with a double row of bony plates along the spine. [Greek *stegē* covering, *sauros* lizard]

**stela** /**stee**-luh/ n. (pl. **stelae** /-lee/ ) (also **stele**) *Archaeol.* upright slab or pillar usu. inscribed and sculpted, esp. as a gravestone. [Latin and Greek]

**stele** /**stee**-lee, steel/ n. **1** *Bot.* axial cylinder of vascular tissue in the stem and roots of most plants. **2** *Archaeol.* = STELA. [Latin *stela* Greek]

**stellar** /**stel**-uh/ adj. of a star or stars. [Latin *stella* star]

**stem**[1] — n. **1** main body or stalk of a plant. **2** stalk supporting a fruit, flower, or leaf. **3** stem-shaped part, as: **a** the slender part of a wineglass. **b** the tube of a tobacco-pipe. **c** a vertical stroke in a letter or musical note. **4** *Gram.* root or main part of a noun, verb, etc., to which inflections are added. **5** main upright timber at the bow of a ship (*from stem to stern*). — v. (**-mm-**) (foll. by *from*) spring or originate from. [Old English]

**stem**[2] v. (**-mm-**) check or stop (*stem the flow*). [Old Norse]

**stench** n. foul smell. [Old English: related to STINK]

**stencil** /**sten**-suhl/ — n. **1** (in full **stencil-plate**) thin sheet of plastic, metal, card, etc., in which a pattern is cut, placed on a surface and printed or inked over etc. to reproduce the pattern. **2** pattern so produced. — v. (**-ll-**) **1** (often foll. by *on*) produce (a pattern) with a stencil. **2** mark (a surface) in this way. [French *estanceler* sparkle, from Latin *scintilla* spark]

**stenographer** /stuh-**nog**-ruh-fuh/ n. person who is skilled in using shorthand. [Greek *stenos* narrow]

**stentorian** /sten-**taw**-ree-uhn/ adj. loud and powerful (*he has a stentorian voice*). [*Stentor*, name of a herald in Homer's *Iliad*]

**step** — n. **1 a** complete movement of one leg in walking or running. **b** distance so covered. **2** unit of movement in dancing. **3** measure taken, esp. one of several in a course of action (*took steps to prevent it*). **4** surface on which a foot is placed on ascending or descending a stair, stepladder, etc. **5** short distance (*lives only a step from my door*). **6** sound or mark made by a foot in walking etc. (*heard a step on the stairs*). **7** manner of walking etc. as seen or heard (*know him by his step*). **8** degree in the scale of promotion or precedence etc. **9 a** stepping in unison or to music (esp. *in or out of step*). **b** state

of conforming (*refuses to keep step with the team*). **10** (in pl.) (also **pair of steps**) = STEPLADDER. — v. (**-pp-**) **1** lift and set down one's foot or alternate feet in walking. **2** come or go in a specified direction by stepping (*stepped forward*). **3** make progress in a specified way (*stepped into a new job*). **4** (foll. by *off, out*) measure (distance) by stepping. □ **in step 1** (of marching, dancing, etc.) in unison. **2** *colloq.* in harmony or agreement (*in step with the times*). **mind** (or **watch**) **one's step** be careful. **out of step 1** (of marching, dancing, etc.) not in unison. **2** *colloq.* not in harmony or agreement (*out of step with the times*). **step along** move (more) quickly. **step by step** gradually; cautiously. **step down** resign. **step in 1** enter. **2** intervene. **step on it** *colloq.* accelerate; hurry up. **step out 1** leave a room, building, etc., esp. temporarily. **2** be active socially. **3** take large steps. **step out of line** behave inappropriately or disobediently. **step up** increase, intensify. [Old English]

**step-** *comb. form* denoting a relationship like the one specified but resulting from a parent's later marriage (*stepchild*; *step-daughter*; *stepmother*; *step-parent* etc.). [Old English, = orphaned]

**stepladder** n. short folding ladder with flat steps.

**steppe** n. level grassy unforested plain. [Russian]

**stepping-stone** n. **1** large stone in a stream etc. helping one to cross. **2** means of progress.

**-ster** *suffix* denoting a person engaged in or associated with a particular activity or quality (*gangster*; *youngster*). [Old English]

**stereo** /**ste**-ree-oh, **steer**-ee-oh/ — n. (pl. **-s**) **1 a** = STEREOGRAM. **b** stereophonic sound reproduction (see STEREOPHONIC). **2** = STEREOSCOPE. — adj. **1** = STEREOPHONIC. **2** = STEREOSCOPIC (see STEREOSCOPE). [abbreviation]

**stereo-** *comb. form* solid; having three dimensions. [Greek *stereos* solid]

**stereogram** /**ste**-ree-oh-ˌgram, -**steer**-/ n. stereophonic record-player.

**stereophonic** /ˌste-ree-oh-**fon**-ik, ˌsteer-/ adj. using two or more channels, giving the effect of naturally distributed sound.

**stereoscope** /**ste**-ree-uh-ˌskohp, **steer**-/ n. device for producing a three-dimensional effect by viewing two slightly different photographs together. □ **stereoscopic** /-**skop**-ik/ adj.

**stereotype** /**ste**-ree-oh-ˌtuyp, **steer**-/ — n. **1 a** a person or thing seeming to conform to an unjustifiably fixed, usu. standardised, widely accepted mental picture or type. **b** such a type, idea, or attitude (*the common stereotype of the young Australian male as a bronzed, well-muscled surfie*). **2** printing-plate cast from a mould of composed type. — *v.* (**-ping**) **1** (esp. as **stereotyped** *adj.*) cause to conform to a type; standardise. **2 a** print from a stereotype. **b** make a stereotype of. □ **stereotypical** /-tip-i-kuhl/ *adj.* **stereotypically** *adv.* [French: related to STEREO-]

**sterile** /ste-ruyl/ *adj.* **1** unable to produce a crop, fruit, or young; barren. **2** unproductive (*sterile discussion*). **3** free from living micro-organisms etc. (*sterile needle*). □ **sterility** /stuh-ril-uh-tee/ *n.* [Latin]

**sterilise** /ste-ruh-ˌluyz/ *v.* (also **-ize**) (**-sing** or **-zing**) **1** make sterile. **2** deprive of reproductive powers. □ **sterilisation** /-zay-shuhn/ *n.*

**sterling** /ster-ling/ — *adj.* **1** of or in British money (*pound sterling*). **2** (of a coin or precious metal) genuine; of standard value or purity. **3** (of a person or qualities etc.) of solid worth; genuine, reliable (*sterling work*). **4** *hist.* of or pertaining to non-convict, British-born residents of Australia (*the currency lads despised the new-chum sterling class*). — *n.* **1** British money. **2** *hist.* non-convict, British-born resident of Australia (opp. CURRENCY). [Old English, = penny]

**sterling silver** *n.* silver of 92½% purity.

**stern¹** *adj.* severe, grim; authoritarian (*a stern expression; stern treatment*). □ **sternly** *adv.* **sternness** *n.* [Old English]

**stern²** *n.* rear part, esp. of a ship or boat. [Old Norse: related to STEER¹]

**sternum** /ster-nuhm/ *n.* (*pl.* **-s** or **sterna**) breastbone. [Greek *sternon* chest]

**steroid** /ste-roid, steer-/ *n.* **1** any of a group of organic compounds including many hormones, alkaloids, and vitamins. **2** this used (often illegally) as a performance-enhancing drug by athletes etc. [from STEROL]

**sterol** /ste-rol/ *n.* naturally occurring steroid alcohol. [from CHOLESTEROL, etc.]

**stertorous** /ster-tuh-ruhs/ *adj.* (of breathing etc.) laboured and noisy. [Latin *sterto* snore]

**stet** *v.* (**-tt-**) (usu. written on a proof-sheet etc.) ignore or cancel (the alteration); let the original stand. [Latin, = let it stand]

**stethoscope** /steth-uh-ˌskohp/ *n.* instrument used in listening to the heart, lungs, etc. [Greek *stēthos* breast]

**stetson** /stet-suhn/ *n.* American cowboy hat with a very wide brim and high crown. [*Stetson*, name of a hat-maker]

**stevedore** /stee-vuh-ˌdaw/ *n.* person

employed in loading and unloading ships. [Spanish *estivador*]

**stew** — *v.* **1** cook by long simmering in a closed vessel. **2** (often foll. by *over*) fret, be anxious. **3** *colloq.* swelter. **4** (as **stewed** *adj.*) *colloq.* drunk. — *n.* **1** dish of stewed meat etc. **2** *colloq.* agitated or angry state. □ **stew in one's own juice** suffer the consequences of one's actions. [French *estuver*]

**steward** /styoo-uhd/ — *n.* **1** passengers' attendant on a ship or aircraft. **2** official supervising a meeting, show, race meeting, etc. **3** person responsible for supplies of food etc. for a club etc. — *v.* act as a steward (of). □ **stewardship** *n.* [Old English, = house-warden]

**stewardess** /ˌstyoo-uh-des, styoo-uh-duhs/ *n.* female steward, esp. on a ship or aircraft.

**stick¹** *n.* **1 a** short slender length of wood broken or cut from a tree. **b** this as a support or weapon. **2** thin rod of wood etc. for a particular purpose (*walking-stick*). **3** implement used to propel the ball in hockey or polo etc. **4** gear lever. **5** conductor's baton. **6** sticklike piece of celery, dynamite, etc. **7** (often prec. by *the*) punishment, esp. by beating. **8** *colloq.* adverse criticism (*can't take a bit of stick*). **9** *colloq.* piece of wood as part of a house or furniture (*doesn't own a stick of furniture*). **10** *colloq.* person (as specified) (*not a bad old stick*). **11** (in *pl.* prec. by *the*) **a** remote rural areas; the Australian outback. **b** *Aust. Rules* goalposts. □ **cop some stick** *colloq.* receive much adverse criticism. [Old English]

**stick²** *v.* (*past* and *past part.* **stuck**) **1** (foll. by *in, into, through*) insert or thrust (a thing or its point) (*stuck a finger in my eye; stick a pin through it*). **2** stab (*stuck him with a stiletto*). **3** (foll. by *in, into, on*, etc.) **a** fix or be fixed on a pointed thing (*stick the meat on the skewers; their severed heads were stuck upon stakes*). **b** fix or be fixed by, or as by, a pointed end (*stuck on the horns of a dilemma*). **4** thrust, put forward, protrude (one's head, hand, etc.) in, into, over, out, etc. (*his foot was stuck in the hole; stuck her head out of the window and yelled*). **5** fix or be fixed by, or as by, adhesive etc. (*stick a label on it; chewing gum stuck to his shoe*). **6** make a continued impression; endure (*the scene stuck in my memory; the name stuck*). **7** lose or be deprived of movement or action through adhesion, jamming, etc. (*the car is stuck in the mud; the words stuck in her throat; the drawer is stuck; the food stuck in his gullet*). **8** *colloq.* **a** put in a specified position or place (*stick them down any-*

*where*). **b** remain in a place (*stuck indoors*). **9** *colloq.* (of an accusation etc.) be convincing or regarded as valid (*could not make the charges stick*). **10** *colloq.* endure, tolerate (*couldn't stick it any longer*). **11** (foll. by *at*) *colloq.* persevere with (*you'll succeed if you stick at it*). **12** *hist.* (of an armed Australian bushranger) (foll. by *up*) stop by force and rob (a person or persons) on the road; rob (a building, coach, etc.) under threat of violence (see also BAIL²) (*a bushranger stuck up the gold escort*). □ **be stuck for** be at a loss for or in need of. **be stuck on** *colloq.* be infatuated with. **be stuck with** *colloq.* be unable to get rid of. **get stuck into** *colloq.* **1** lay into; make a physical assault on (someone). **2** make a verbal assault on (someone); vehemently scold or criticise. **3** attack (a task, a meal, etc.) with gusto. **stick around** *colloq.* linger; remain. **stick at nothing** be absolutely ruthless. **stick by** (or **with**) stay loyal or close to. **stick in one's throat** be against one's principles. **stick it** *coarse colloq.* expression of contemptuous rejection. **stick it out** *colloq.* endure a burden etc. to the end. **stick one's neck out** be rashly bold. **stick out 1** (cause to) protrude. **2** (foll. by any of various similes etc.) be conspicuous (*sticks out like a sore thumb*; *sticks out like udders on a bull*). **stick out for** persist in demanding. **stick to 1** remain fixed on or to. **2** remain loyal to. **3** keep to (a subject etc.). **stick together** *colloq.* remain united or mutually loyal. **stick to one's guns** see GUN. **stick up 1** be or make erect or protruding upwards. **2** fasten to an upright surface. **3** *colloq.* rob or threaten with a gun. **stick up for** support or defend. **stick up to** be assertive in the face of; offer resistance to. [Old English]

**sticker** *n.* **1** adhesive label. **2** persistent person.

**sticking plaster** *n.* adhesive plaster for wounds etc.

**stick insect** *n.* insect with a twiglike body.

**stick-in-the-mud** *n. colloq.* unprogressive or old-fashioned person.

**stickler** *n.* (foll. by *for*) person who insists on something (*stickler for accuracy*). [obsolete *stickle* be umpire]

**stick-nest rat** *n.* Australian rodent (esp. on Franklin Island, SA) which builds a dwelling of sticks containing a soft nest or burrow.

**stick-up** *n. colloq.* robbery using a gun.

**sticky** — *adj.* (**-ier**, **-iest**) **1** tending or intended to stick or adhere. **2** (of weather) humid. **3** *colloq.* difficult, awkward (*a sticky situation*). **4** unpleasant, painful (*came to a sticky end*). — *n.* = STICKYBEAK. □ **stickily** *adv.* **stickiness** *n.*

**stickybeak** *colloq.* — *n.* (also **sticky**) **1** inquisitive or prying person; person who sticks his or her nose (beak) into others' affairs. **2** an inquisitive look (*having a stickybeak*). — *v.* pry, snoop (*stickybeaks all the time*). □ **stickybeaking** *n.*

**sticky tape** *n.* adhesive tape.

**sticky wattle** *n.* Australian wattle-shrub, *Acacia howittii*, having small, sticky leaves and scented flowers, cultivated as an ornamental.

**sticky wicket** *n.* **1** *Cricket* pitch that has been affected by rain and is difficult for the batsman. **2** *colloq.* difficult circumstances.

**stiff** — *adj.* **1** rigid; inflexible. **2** hard to bend, move, or turn, etc. **3** hard to cope with; needing strength or effort (*stiff test*; *stiff climb*). **4** severe, strong, excessive, etc. (*stiff breeze*; *stiff penalty*; *stiff prices*). **5** formal, constrained; lacking spontaneity (*his manner was stiff*). **6** (of a muscle, limb, or person, etc.) aching owing to exertion, injury, etc. **7** (of esp. an alcoholic drink) strong. **8** (foll. by *with*) *colloq.* abounding in (*roads stiff with cops during the traffic-blitz*). **9** *colloq.* **a** bad, hard (*stiff luck*). **b** unlucky (*a bit stiff, us getting wiped out by the Windies!*). — *adv. colloq.* utterly, extremely (*bored stiff*; *worried stiff*). — *n. colloq.* **1** corpse. **2** (penile) erection. □ **stiff cheese!** (or **stiff cheddar!**) *colloq.* bad luck! (used either to express sympathy, concern, etc., or to express a decided lack of sympathy, to snub, rebuff). □ **stiffish** *adj.* **stiffly** *adv.* **stiffness** *n.* [Old English]

**stiffen** *v.* make or become stiff. □ **stiffening** *n.*

**stiff-necked** *adj.* obstinate; haughty.

**stiff upper lip** *n.* appearance of being calm in adversity.

**stifle** /stuy-fuhl/ *v.* (**-ling**) **1** suppress (*stifled a yawn*). **2** feel or make unable to breathe easily; suffocate (*feeling quite stifled by this heat*). **3** kill by suffocating. □ **stifling** *adj.* & *adv.* [origin uncertain]

**stigma** /stig-muh/ *n.* (*pl.* **-s** or, esp. in sense 4, **stigmata** /-muh-tuh, -**mah**-tuh/ ) **1** mark or sign of shame or disgrace. **2** part of the pistil that receives the pollen in pollination. **3** visible sign or characteristic of a disease. **4** (in *pl.*) (in Christian belief) wounds corresponding to those on Christ's body after the Crucifixion, imposed on the bodies of some saintly persons (*the stigmata of Father Pio*). [Greek *stigma* -*mat*- brand, dot]

**stigmatic** /stig-**mat**-ik/ *n. Eccl.* person bearing stigmata.

**stigmatise** /**stig**-muh- tuyz/ *v.* (also **-ize**) (**-sing** or **-zing**) (often foll. by *as*) brand as unworthy or disgraceful. [Greek *stigmatizō*: related to STIGMA]

**stile** *n.* arrangement of steps allowing people but not animals to climb over a fence or wall. [Old English]

**stiletto** /stuh-**let**-oh/ *n.* (*pl.* **-s**) **1** short dagger. **2** (in full **stiletto heel**) **a** long tapering heel of a shoe. **b** shoe with such a heel. **3** pointed instrument for making eyelets etc. [Italian diminutive: related to STYLE]

**still¹** — *adj.* **1** not or hardly moving. **2** with little or no sound; calm and tranquil. **3** (of a drink) not effervescing. — *n.* **1** deep silence (*still of the night*). **2** static photograph (as opposed to a motion picture), esp. a single shot from a cinema film. — *adv.* **1** without moving (*sit still*). **2** even now or at a particular time (*is he still here?*). **3** nevertheless. **4** (with *compar.*) even, yet, increasingly (*still greater efforts*). — *v.* make or become still; quieten. □ **stillness** *n.* [Old English]

**still²** *n.* apparatus for distilling spirits etc. [obsolete *still* (v.) = DISTIL]

**stillbirth** *n.* birth of a dead child.

**stillborn** *adj.* **1** born dead. **2** (of an idea, plan, etc.) abortive; not able to succeed.

**still life** *n.* (*pl.* **lifes**) painting or drawing of inanimate objects, e.g. fruit or flowers.

**stilt** *n.* **1** either of a pair of poles with foot supports for walking at a distance above the ground. **2** each of a set of piles or posts supporting a building etc. **3** long-legged wading bird with a very thin bill, including the black-winged stilt of Australia and elsewhere, and the Australian pied banded stilt, esp. associated with salt lakes. [Low German or Dutch]

**stilted** *adj.* **1** (of literary style etc.) stiff and unnatural; bombastic. **2** standing on stilts.

**stimulant** /stim-yuh-luhnt/ — *adj.* stimulating, esp. bodily or mental activity. — *n.* **1** stimulant substance, esp. a drug or an alcoholic drink. **2** stimulating influence. [Latin: related to STIMULATE]

**stimulate** /stim-yuh-layt/ *v.* (**-ting**) **1** act as a stimulus to. **2** animate, excite, arouse. □ **stimulation** /-lay-shuhn/ *n.* **stimulative** /-luh-tiv/ *adj.* **stimulator** *n.* [Latin: related to STIMULUS]

**stimulus** /stim-yuh-luhs/ *n.* (*pl.* **-li** /-luy/) thing that rouses to activity. [Latin, = goad]

**sting** — *n.* **1** sharp wounding organ of an insect, snake, nettle, etc. **2 a** act of inflicting a wound with this. **b** the wound itself or the pain caused by it. **3** painful quality or effect (*the sting of hunger*). **4** pungency, vigour, sharpness (*spoke with a sting in her voice*). **5** *colloq.* swindle.

— *v.* (*past* and *past part.* **stung**) **1 a** wound or pierce with a sting. **b** be able to sting. **2** feel or give a tingling physical or sharp mental pain (*stung by his cruel words*). **3** (foll. by *into*) incite, esp. painfully (*stung into replying*). **4** *colloq.* swindle, charge exorbitantly. **5** *colloq.* cadge from (a person) (*stung me for $20*). □ **sting in the tail** unexpected final pain or difficulty. [Old English]

**stingaree** /sting-uh-ree, sting-uh-**ree**/ *n.* = STINGRAY.

**stinger** *n.* **1** stinging animal or thing. **2** = STING *n.* 1. **3** = STINGING TREE. **4** = BOX JELLYFISH. **5** a sharp, stinging blow.

**stinging nettle** *n.* nettle with stinging hairs.

**stinging tree** *n.* = GYMPIE.

**stingray** *n.* broad flat-fish with a venomous spine at the base of its tail.

**stingy** /stin-jee/ *adj.* (**-ier**, **-iest**) *colloq.* niggardly, mean. □ **stingily** *adv.* **stinginess** *n.* [perhaps from STING]

**stink** — *v.* (*past* **stank** or **stunk**; *past part.* **stunk**) **1** emit a strong offensive smell. **2** (often foll. by *out*) fill (a place) with a stink. **3** (foll. by *out* etc.) drive (a person) out etc. by a stink. **4** *colloq.* be or seem very unpleasant. — *n.* **1** strong or offensive smell. **2** *colloq.* row or fuss (*the affair caused quite a stink*). [Old English]

**stinkbird** *n.* either of two Australian songbirds which have a strong scent-trail: the striated fieldwren and the rufous fieldwren.

**stinker** *n.* *colloq.* **1** objectionable person or thing. **2** difficult task. **3** unpleasantly hot day.

**stinkfish** *n.* any of several Australian marine fish having a disagreeable odour and taste, some of which are poisonous.

**stinking** — *adj.* **1** that stinks. **2** *colloq.* very objectionable. — *adv.* *colloq.* extremely and usu. objectionably (*stinking rich*).

**stinking Roger** *n.* strongly, rankly aromatic American herb, naturalised in eastern Australia.

**stinkwood** *n.* any of several trees or shrubs esp. of south-eastern Australia, the leaves of which smell unpleasant when crushed, and the wood of which emits a highly offensive odour when burned.

**stint** — *v.* **1** supply (food or aid etc.) meanly or grudgingly. **2** (often *refl.*) supply (a person etc.) in this way. — *n.* **1** limitation of supply or effort (*without stint*). **2** allotted amount of work (*do one's stint*). **3** any of various small sandpipers, migrants to Australia from the Northern hemisphere during spring to early autumn (*red-necked stint; little stint; long-toed stint*). [Old English]

**stipe** /stuyp/ *n. colloq.* = STIPENDIARY STEWARD. [abbreviation]

**stipend** /**stuy**-pend/ *n.* fixed regular allowance or salary. [Latin *stipendium*]

**stipendiary** /stuy-**pen**-duh-ree/ — *adj.* receiving a stipend. — *n.* (*pl.* **-ies**) person receiving a stipend. [Latin: related to STIPEND]

**stipendiary magistrate** *n.* paid professional magistrate.

**stipendiary steward** *n.* paid official who controls the running of horseraces etc., esp. the enforcement of rules.

**stipple** /**stip**-uhl/ — *v.* (**-ling**) **1** draw or paint or engrave etc. with dots instead of lines. **2** roughen the surface of (paint, cement, etc.). — *n.* **1** stippling. **2** effect of stippling. [Dutch]

**stipulate** /**stip**-yuh-layt/ *v.* (**-ting**) demand or specify as part of a bargain or agreement. □ **stipulation** /-**lay**-shuhn/ *n.* [Latin *stipulari*]

**stir¹** — *v.* (**-rr-**) **1** move a spoon etc. round and round in (a liquid etc.), esp. to mix ingredients. **2 a** cause to move, esp. slightly (*a breeze stirred the lake*). **b** be or begin to be in motion (*not a creature was stirring*). **3 a** *refl.* rouse (oneself), esp. from a lethargic state. **b** rise from sleep (*is he stirring yet?*). **c** (foll. by *out of* or *from*) leave (*hasn't stirred out of the house all day*). **4** arouse, inspire, or excite (the emotions, a person, etc.) (*was stirred to anger*). **5** *colloq.* **a** cause trouble for its own sake. **b** provoke (a person) into exhibiting exasperation etc. — *n.* **1** act of stirring. **2** commotion, excitement. □ **not stir a finger** make no effort to help. **stir in** add (an ingredient) by stirring. **stir the possum** see POSSUM. **stir up 1** mix thoroughly by stirring. **2** stimulate, excite. **3** incite (trouble etc.). □ **stirrer** *n.* [Old English]

**stir²** *n. colloq.* prison. [origin unknown]

**stir-fry** — *v.* fry rapidly while stirring. — *n.* stir-fried dish.

**stirrer** *n. colloq.* person who provokes (another) to exasperation; trouble-maker; agitator.

**stirrup** /**sti**-ruhp/ *n.* metal loop supporting a horse-rider's foot. [Old English, = climbing-rope]

**stirry** /**ster**-ree/ *adj.* (of a bullock etc.) bad-tempered; restive.

**stitch** — *n.* **1 a** (in sewing, knitting, or crocheting) single pass of a needle, or the resulting thread or loop etc. **b** particular method of sewing etc. **2** (usu. in *pl.*) *Surgery* each of the loops of material used in sewing up a wound. **3** least bit of clothing

(*hadn't a stitch on*). **4** sharp pain in the side induced by running etc. — *v.* sew; make stitches (in). □ **in stitches** *colloq.* laughing uncontrollably. **stitch up 1** join or mend by sewing. **2** mend or resolve (a quarrel etc.). [Old English: related to STICK²]

**stitch in time** *n.* timely remedy.

**stoat** *n.* mammal of the weasel family of Europe etc., with brown fur turning mainly white in the winter. [origin unknown]

**stobie pole** /**stoh**-bee/ *n.* (in SA) pole of steel and concrete carrying electricity lines. [J.C. *Stobie* Australian engineer (d. 1953)]

**stock** — *n.* **1** store of goods etc. ready for sale or distribution etc. **2** supply or quantity of anything for use (*lay in winter stocks of fuel; a great stock of information*). **3** equipment or raw material for manufacture or trade etc. (*rolling-stock*). **4** farm animals or equipment. **5 a** capital of a business. **b** shares in this. **6** reputation or popularity (*his stock is rising*). **7** line of ancestry (*comes of convict stock*). **8** liquid basis for soup etc. made by stewing bones, vegetables, etc. **9** fragrant-flowered cruciferous cultivated plant. **10** plant into which a graft is inserted. **11** plant etc. from which cuttings etc. are taken. **12** (in *pl.*) *hist.* timber frame with holes for the feet in which offenders were locked as a public punishment. **13** base, support, or handle for an implement or machine. **14** butt of a rifle etc. **15** (in *pl.*) supports for a ship during building or repair. — *attrib. adj.* **1** kept in stock and so regularly available (*stock sizes*). **2** hackneyed, conventional (*a stock answer*). — *v.* **1** have (goods) in stock. **2** provide (a shop or a farm etc.) with goods, livestock, etc. **3** fill with items needed (*shelves well-stocked with books*). □ **in** (or **out of**) **stock** available (or not available) immediately for sale etc. **stock up** (often foll. by *with*) provide with or get stocks or supplies (of). **take stock 1** make an inventory of one's stock. **2** (often foll. by *of*) review (a situation etc.). [Old English]

**stockade** /sto-**kayd**/ — *n.* **1** line or enclosure of upright stakes. **2** *hist.* structure in which convict gangs in Australia, working in outlying districts, were accommodated. — *v.* (**-ding**) fortify with a stockade. [Spanish *estacada*]

**stock agent** *n.* person who deals in the buying and selling of livestock.

**stock and station** *attrib. adj.* relating to firms or their employees dealing in farm land, products, and supplies (*stock and station agent*).

**stockbroker** *n.* person dealing in stocks

and shares for a commission. □ **stock-broking** n.

**stock car** n. specially strengthened car for use in racing in which deliberate collisions occur.

**stock exchange** n. **1** place for dealing in stocks and shares. **2** dealers working there.

**stock horse** n. horse trained to work with cattle etc.

**stocking** n. **1** long knitted covering for the leg and foot, of nylon, wool, silk, etc. **2** differently-coloured lower leg of a horse etc. [from STOCK]

**stock-in-trade** n. **1** requisite(s) of a trade or profession. **2** characteristic or essential product; characteristic behaviour, actions, etc.

**stockman** n. person employed to tend livestock, esp. cattle.

**stockman-cut** n. (also attrib.) narrow-legged style of trousers.

**stockman's hat** n. broad-brimmed felt hat.

**stock market** n. **1** = STOCK EXCHANGE. **2** transactions on this.

**stockpile** — n. accumulated stock of goods etc. held in reserve. — v. (-**ling**) accumulate a stockpile of.

**stock saddle** n. heavy saddle made for a stock horse.

**stock-still** adj. motionless.

**stocktaking** n. **1** making an inventory of stock. **2** review of one's position etc.

**stocktaking sale** n. sale of goods at reduced prices preparatory to, or as a consequence of, a stocktaking.

**stockwhip** n. long whip used in the handling of cattle.

**stocky** adj. (-**ier**, -**iest**) short and sturdy. □ **stockily** adv. **stockiness** n.

**stockyard** n. enclosure for the sorting or temporary keeping of cattle.

**stodge** /stoj/ n. colloq. heavy fattening food. [imitative, after *stuff* and *podge*]

**stodgy** adj. (-**ier**, -**iest**) **1** (of food) heavy and indigestible. **2** dull and uninteresting (*the wedding was a stodgy affair*). **3** (of a literary style etc.) turgid and dull. □ **stodgily** adv. **stodginess** n.

**Stoic** /**stoh**-ik/ — n. **1** member of the ancient Greek school of philosophy which sought virtue as the greatest good and taught control of one's feelings and passions. **2** (**stoic**) stoical person. — adj. **1** of or like the Stoics. **2** (**stoic**) = STOICAL. [Greek *stoa* portico]

**stoical** adj. having or showing great self-control in adversity. □ **stoically** adv.

**Stoicism** /**stoh**-uh-ˌsiz-uhm/ n. **1** philosophy of the Stoics. **2** (**stoicism**) stoical attitude.

**stoke** v. (-**king**) **1** (often foll. by *up*) feed and tend (a fire or furnace etc.). **2** (often foll. by *up*) colloq. fill oneself with food. **3** (as **stoked** adj.) colloq. **a** affected by alcohol or drugs. **b** (often foll. by *on*) thrilled; excited; elated by (*is really stoked on surfing*). [back-formation from STOKER]

**stokehold** n. compartment in a steamship containing its boilers and furnace.

**stoker** n. person who tends a furnace, esp. on a steamship. [Dutch]

**stole**[1] n. **1** woman's garment like a long wide scarf, worn over the shoulders. **2** strip of silk etc. worn similarly as a vestment by a priest. [Greek *stolē* equipment, clothing]

**stole**[2] past of STEAL.

**stolen** past part. of STEAL.

**stolid** /**stol**-uhd/ adj. not easily excited or moved; impassive, unemotional. □ **stolidity** /sto-**lid**-uh-tee/ n. **stolidly** adv. [Latin]

**stoma** /**stoh**-muh/ n. (pl. -**s** or **stomata**) **1** minute pore in the epidermis of a leaf. **2** a Zool. small mouthlike opening in some lower animals. **b** Surgery small mouthlike artificial orifice made in the stomach. [Greek *stoma* mouth]

**stomach** /**stum**-uhk/ — n. **1 a** internal organ in which digestion occurs. **b** any of several such organs in animals. **2** lower front of the body. **3** (usu. foll. by *for*) **a** appetite (for food). **b** inclination (*had no stomach for the fight*). — v. **1** find palatable. **2** endure (usu. with neg.: *cannot stomach it*). [Greek *stoma* mouth]

**stomp** — v. tread or stamp heavily. — n. lively jazz dance with heavy stamping. [var. of STAMP]

**stone** — n. **1 a** solid non-metallic mineral matter; rock. **b** small piece of this. **2** (often in comb.) piece of stone of a definite shape or for a particular purpose (*tombstone*). **3** a thing resembling stone, e.g. the hard case of the kernel in some fruits. **b** (often in pl.) hard morbid concretion in the body (*gallstones*). **4** (pl. same) unit of weight in the imperial system equal to 14 lb. **5** precious stone. **6** (attrib.) made of stone. — v. (-**ning**) **1** pelt with stones. **2** remove the stones from (fruit). — adv. (in comb.) completely (*stone-cold; stone-dead; stone-deaf*). □ **cast** (or **throw**) **stones** speak ill of a person. **leave no stone unturned** try all possible means. **stone the crows!** exclamation of surprise, disgust, etc. **stone motherless last** colloq. (of a competitor in a race etc.) finishing last, esp. by a long distance. **a stone's throw** a short distance. [Old English]

**Stone Age** n. prehistoric period when weapons and tools were made of stone.

**stone-broke** adj. (also **stony-broke**) colloq. entirely without money.

**stone-cold sober** *predic. adj.* completely sober.

**stone-country** *n.* = GIBBER PLAIN.

**stoned** *adj. colloq.* drunk or drugged.

**stonefish** *n.* any of several highly venomous fish of northern Australia and elsewhere in the tropics, having dorsal fins capable of inflicting a painful and potentially fatal sting, and resembling a lump of weathered rock.

**stone-fruit** *n.* fruit with flesh enclosing a stone.

**stonemason** *n.* person who cuts, prepares, and builds with stone.

**stonewall** *v.* obstruct (a discussion or investigation) with evasive answers etc.

**stoneware** *n.* ceramic ware which is impermeable and partly vitrified but opaque.

**stonewashed** *adj.* (esp. of denim) washed with abrasives to give a worn or faded look.

**stonkered** *adj. colloq.* **1** utterly exhausted. **2** utterly confounded or defeated (*this one has got me stonkered*). **3** very drunk. [origin unknown]

**stony** *adj.* (**-ier, -iest**) **1** full of stones. **2 a** hard, rigid. **b** unfeeling, hardened (*a stony heart*). **c** rigid; uncompromising (*a stony stare*). □ **stonily** *adv.* **stoniness** *n.*

**stood** *past* and *past part.* of STAND.

**stooge** *colloq.* — *n.* **1** butt or foil, esp. for a comedian. **2 a** assistant or subordinate, esp. for routine or unpleasant work. **b** unquestioningly loyal or obsequious subordinate; lackey. **c** person used as an instrument by or for someone behind the scenes. — *v.* (**-ging**) (foll. by *for*) act as a stooge for. [origin unknown]

**stool** *n.* **1** single seat usu. without a back or arms. **2** = FOOTSTOOL. **3** (usu. in *pl.*) = FAECES. [Old English]

**stool-pigeon** *n.* **1** person acting as a decoy (orig. a decoy of a pigeon fixed to a stool). **2** informer, esp. for the police.

**stoop** — *v.* **1** lower the body, sometimes bending the knee; bend down. **2** stand or walk with the shoulders habitually bent forward. **3** (foll. by *to* + infin.) condescend (*would never stoop to speak to those he considered his inferiors*). **4** (foll. by *to*) descend or lower oneself to (some conduct) (*necessity has made her stoop to shoplifting*). — *n.* stooping posture. [Old English]

**stop** — *v.* (**-pp-**) **1 a** put an end to the progress, motion, or operation of (*stop the car!*). **b** effectively hinder or prevent (*stopped them playing so loudly*). **c** discontinue (*stop playing; stopped my visits*). **2** come to an end (*supplies suddenly stopped*). **3** cease from motion, speaking, or action (*the car stopped; he stopped in the middle of a sentence*). **4** cause to cease action; defeat (*their plot must be stopped at any cost*). **5** remain; stay for a short time. **6 a** (often foll. by *up*) block or close up (a hole, leak, etc.). **b** obstruct the external orifice (of a bodily organ) (*stopped his ears with his fingers*). **7** not permit or supply as usual (*stop their wages*). **8** (in full **stop payment of** or **on**) instruct a bank to withhold payment on (a cheque). **9** press (a violin etc. string) to obtain the required pitch. — *n.* **1** act or instance of stopping or state of being stopped. **2** designated stopping-place for a bus or train etc. **3** = FULL STOP. **4** device for stopping motion at a particular point. **5** change of pitch effected by stopping a string. **6 a** (in an organ) row of pipes of one character. **b** knob etc. operating these. **7** (of sound) = PLOSIVE. □ **pull out all the stops** make extreme effort. **put a stop to** cause to end. **stop at nothing** be ruthless. **stop by** call at, visit (a place). **stop off** (or **over**) break one's journey. [Old English]

**stopcock** *n.* externally operated valve regulating the flow through a pipe etc.

**stopgap** *n.* (often *attrib.*) temporary substitute (*a stopgap measure*).

**stop-go** *n.* alternate stopping and restarting, esp. of the economy.

**stopover** *n.* break in a journey, esp. overnight.

**stoppage** *n.* **1** interruption of work owing to a strike etc. **2** condition of being blocked or stopped.

**stopper** — *n.* plug for closing a bottle etc. — *v.* close with this.

**stop press** *n.* (often *attrib.*) late news inserted in a newspaper after printing has begun.

**stopwatch** *n.* watch that can be stopped and started, used to time races etc.

**stopwork meeting** *n.* meeting (to consider working conditions, possible strike action, etc.) that employees must stop working to attend.

**storage** /staw-rij/ *n.* **1 a** storing of goods etc. **b** method of or space for storing. **2** cost of storing. **3** storing of data in a computer etc.

**store** — *n.* **1** quantity of something kept available for use (*a store of wine; a store of wit*). **2** (in *pl.*) **a** articles gathered for a particular purpose (*naval stores*). **b** supply of, or place for keeping, these. **3 a** = DEPARTMENT STORE. **b** = GENERAL STORE. **c** (often in *pl.*) shop selling basic necessities. **4** warehouse for keeping furniture etc. temporarily. **5** device in a computer for keeping retrievable data. — *v.* (**-ring**) **1** (often foll. by *up, away*) accumulate for future use. **2** put (furniture etc.) in a store. **3** stock or provide with something useful (*a mind stored with encyclopaedic facts*). **4** enter or retain (data) for retrieval. □ **in store 1** kept in readiness. **2** coming in the future. **3** (foll. by *for*) destined or intended. **set store by** consider important. [French *estore(r)* from Latin *instauro* renew]

**storehouse** *n.* storage place.

**storekeeper** *n.* shopkeeper, esp. the proprietor of a general store.

**storeman** *n.* person responsible for stored goods.

**storey** /staw-ree/ *n.* (*pl.* **-s**) any of the parts into which a building is divided horizontally; the whole of the rooms etc. housing a continuous floor (*a house of three storeys*). □ **-storeyed** *adj.* (in comb.). [Anglo-Latin: related to HISTORY, perhaps originally meaning a tier of painted windows]

**storied** /staw-reed/ *adj. literary* celebrated in or associated with stories or legends.

**stork** *n.* **1** long-legged usu. white wading bird of Europe etc. **2** = JABIRU. [Old English]

**storm** — *n.* **1** violent atmospheric disturbance with strong winds and usu. thunder, rain, or dust, etc. **2** violent political etc. disturbance. **3** (foll. by *of*) a violent shower of missiles or blows. **b** outbreak of applause, hisses, etc. **4** a direct assault by troops on a fortified place. **b** capture by such an assault. — *v.* **1** (of wind, rain, etc.) rage; be violent (*it stormed all night*). **2** attack or capture by storm. **3** (usu. foll. by *in, out of*, etc.) move violently or angrily (*stormed out*). **4** (often foll. by *at, away*) talk violently, rage, bluster. □ **take by storm 1** capture by direct assault. **2** rapidly captivate (a person, an audience, etc.). [Old English]

**storm bird** *n.* any of several Australian birds, the movements or cries of which are supposed to presage a storm, esp. the channel-billed cuckoo.

**storm cloud** *n.* **1** heavy rain-cloud. **2** threatening situation.

**storm in a teacup** *n.* great excitement over a trivial matter.

**storm petrel** *n.* **1** small black and white N. Atlantic petrel. **2** any of various small migratory seabirds, often seen in Australian waters, brownish-grey in colour, and some having white on their underparts.

**storm trooper** *n.* member of the storm troops.

**storm troops** *n.pl.* **1** troops specially trained for assault. **2** *hist.* Nazi political militia.

**stormy** *adj.* (**-ier, -iest**) **1** of or affected by storms. **2** (of a wind etc.) violent. **3** full of angry feeling or outbursts (*stormy meeting*). □ **stormily** *adv.* **storminess** *n.*

**story** /staw-ree/ *n.* (*pl.* **-ies**) **1 a** account of imaginary or past events; tale, anecdote. **b** (in Aboriginal English) account of the sacred events associated with a dreaming site. **2** history of a person or institution etc. (*my story is a strange one*). **3** (in full **storyline**) narrative or plot of a novel, play, etc. **4** facts or experiences worthy of narration. **5** item of news etc. in a television broadcast etc. **6** *colloq.* **a** fib or lie. **b** explanation (*so what's your story this time?*). [Anglo-French *estorie* from Latin: related to HISTORY]

**stoup** /stoop/ *n.* basin for holy-water in a church. [Old Norse]

**stoush** /stowsh/ *colloq.* — *n.* brawl; fight. — *v.* hit; fight with. □ **the Big Stoush** *hist.* the 1914-18 war. [origin unknown]

**stout** — *adj.* **1** rather fat, corpulent, bulky. **2** thick or strong (*a stout weapon*). **3** brave, resolute (*put up some stout resistance*). — *n.* strong dark beer brewed with roasted malt or barley. □ **stoutly** *adv.* **stoutness** *n.* [Anglo-French from Germanic]

**stove**[1] *n.* closed apparatus burning fuel or using electricity for heating or cooking. [Low German or Dutch]

**stove**[2] *past* and *past part.* of STAVE *v.*

**stow** /stoh/ *v.* pack (goods, cargo, etc.) tidily and compactly. □ **stow away 1** place (a thing) out of the way. **2** be a stowaway on a ship etc. [from BESTOW]

**stowaway** *n.* person who hides on a ship or aircraft etc. to travel free.

**strabismus** /struh-biz-muhs/ *n. Med.* squinting, squint. [Greek *strabos* squinting]

**straddle** /strad-uhl/ — *v.* (**-ling**) **1 a** sit or stand across (a thing) with the legs spread. **b** be situated on both sides of (*the town straddles the border*). **2** part (one's legs) widely. — *n.* act or instance of straddling. □ **straddler** *n.* [from STRIDE]

**strafe** /strahf, strayf/ *v.* (**-fing**) bombard; attack with gunfire. [German, = punish]

**straggle** /strag-uhl/ — *v.* (**-ling**) **1** wander or stray from a proper road, one's companions, etc.; rove without fixed direction. **2** be dispersed or sporadic (*the town straggles along the bank of the river*). **3** trail behind in a race etc. **4** (of a plant, beard, etc.) grow long and untidy. — *n.* body or group of straggling or scattered persons or things. □ **straggler** *n.* **straggly** *adj.* (**-ier, -iest**). [origin uncertain]

**straight** /strayt/ — *adj.* **1** extending uniformly in the same direction; not bent or curved (*straight line; a straight back;*

*straight hair*). **2** successive, uninterrupted (*three straight wins*). **3** ordered; level; tidy (*is the picture straight?*; *put things straight*). **4** honest, candid (*a straight answer*). **5** (of thinking etc.) logical. **6** (of theatre, music, etc.) serious, classical, not popular or comic. **7** (of a drink) undiluted. **8** *colloq.* **a** (of a person etc.) conventional, respectable. **b** heterosexual. **9** (of an aim, look, blow, or course) going direct to the mark. **10** (of a person's legs) not bandy or knock-kneed; (of a person's back) upright, not bowed or bent. **11** *Cricket* (of the bat) held so as not to incline to either side. **12** designating a bet which backs (a horse etc.) to win (cf. PLACE *n.* 12 or EACH WAY). — *n.* **1** straight part, esp. the concluding stretch of a race-track. **2** straight condition. **3** sequence of five cards in poker. **4** *colloq.* a conventional person; a heterosexual. — *adv.* **1** in a straight line; directly; without deviation or hesitation (*came straight from Queanbeyan*; *I told them straight*). **2** in the right direction (*shoot straight*). **3** correctly (*can't see straight*). **4** immediately (*come straight over*). □ **get** (*something*) **straight** make something clear. **go straight** (of a criminal) become honest. **play a straight bat** act in a straightforward and honest way. **put a person straight** put him or her right, esp. by way of explanation. **straight away** immediately. **straight off** *colloq.* without hesitation. □ **straightish** *adj.* **straightness** *n.* [originally a past part. of STRETCH]

**straightaway** /**strayt**-uh-,way/ *adv.* = straight away.

**straighten** /**stray**-tuhn/ *v.* **1** (often foll. by *out*) make or become straight. **2** (foll. by *up*) stand erect after bending. □ **straighten oneself out** get one's life etc. in order. **straighten a person out** = *put a person straight* (see STRAIGHT).

**straight face** *n.* intentionally expressionless face. □ **straight-faced** *adj.*

**straightforward** /strayt-**faw**-wuhd/ *adj.* **1** honest or frank. **2** (of a task etc.) simple.

**straight man** *n.* comedian's stooge.

**strain¹** — *v.* **1** stretch tightly; make or become taut or tense. **2** injure by overuse or excessive demands (*strain a muscle*; *strained their loyalty*). **3** exercise (oneself, one's senses, a thing, etc.) intensely; press to extremes (*strain one's ears*; *strains our resources*). **4** strive intensively (*straining after perfection*). **5** (foll. by *at*) tug, pull. **6** distort from the true intention or meaning (*you are straining the meaning of loyalty*). **7 a** clear (a liquid) of solid matter by passing it through a sieve etc. **b** (foll. by *out*) filter (solids) out from a liquid. — *n.* **1 a**

act or instance of straining. **b** force exerted in this. **2** injury caused by straining a muscle etc. **3** severe mental or physical demand or exertion (*suffering from strain*). **4** stretch of fencing wire between two strainers. **5** snatch of music or poetry. **6** tone or tendency in speech or writing (*more in the same strain*). **7** *Physics* **a** condition of a body subjected to stress; molecular displacement. **b** a quantity measuring this. [French *estrei(g)n-* from Latin *stringo*]

**strain²** *n.* **1** breed or stock of animals, plants, etc. **2** tendency; characteristic (*a strain of aggression in her*). [Old English, = begetting]

**strained** *adj.* **1** (of behaviour or manner) constrained, artificial. **2** (of a relationship) mutually distrustful or tense.

**strainer** *n.* **1** device for straining liquids etc. **2 a** device for keeping wire etc. taut. **b** (also **strainer post**) strong post against which the wires of a fence are tightened.

**strait** *n.* **1** (in *sing.* or *pl.*) narrow channel connecting two large bodies of water. **2** (usu. in *pl.*) difficulty or distress (*in dire straits*). [French *estreit* from Latin *strictus* narrow]

**straitened** /**stray**-tuhnd/ *adj.* of or marked by poverty (*in straitened circumstances*).

**straitjacket** — *n.* **1** strong garment with long sleeves for confining a violent prisoner etc. **2** restrictive measures. — *v.* (**-t-**) **1** restrain with a strait-jacket. **2** severely restrict.

**strait-laced** *adj.* puritanical.

**strand¹** — *v.* **1** run aground. **2** (as **stranded** *adj.*) in difficulties, esp. without money or transport. — *n.* foreshore; beach. [Old English]

**strand²** *n.* **1** each of the twisted threads or wires making a rope or cable etc. **2** single thread or strip of fibre. **3** lock of hair. **4** string (of pearls etc.). **5** element; component (*when I consider the next strand in your argument . . .*). [origin unknown]

**strange** /straynj/ *adj.* **1** unusual, peculiar, surprising, eccentric. **2** (often foll. by *to*) unfamiliar, foreign. **3** (foll. by *to*) unaccustomed. **4** not at ease (*felt strange in such company*). □ **strangely** *adv.* **strangeness** *n.* [French *estrange* from Latin *extraneus*]

**stranger** *n.* **1** person new to a particular place or company. **2** (often foll. by *to*) person one does not know. **3** (foll. by *to*) person unaccustomed to (*no stranger to controversy*).

**strangle** /**strang**-guhl/ *v.* (**-ling**) **1** squeeze the windpipe or neck of, esp. so as to kill. **2** hamper or suppress (a movement, impulse, cry, etc.). □ **strangler** *n.* [Latin *strangulo*]

**stranglehold** n. **1** throttling hold in wrestling. **2** deadly grip. **3** complete and exclusive control.

**strangulate** /strang-gyuh-,layt/ v. (**-ting**) compress (a vein, intestine, etc.), preventing circulation. [Latin: related to STRANGLE]

**strangulation** /,strang-gyuh-**lay**-shuhn/ n. **1** act of strangling or state of being strangled. **2** act of strangulating.

**strap** — n. **1** strip of leather etc., often with a buckle, for holding things together etc. **2** narrow strip of fabric worn over the shoulders as part of a garment. **3** loop for grasping to steady oneself in a moving vehicle. **4** (**the strap**) punishment by beating with a leather strap. — v. (**-pp-**) **1** (often foll. by *down*, *up*, etc.) secure or bind with a strap. **2** beat with a strap. **3** (esp. as **strapped** adj.) colloq. subjected to a shortage (*strapped for cash*). □ **strapless** adj. [British dial., = STROP]

**straphanger** n. colloq. **1** standing passenger in a bus, train, etc. **2** a hanger-on. □ **straphang** v.

**strapping** adj. large and sturdy.

**strasbourg** /straz-berg/ n. (also **stras** /straz/) **1** spiced sausage. **2** = DEVON or FRITZ. [*Strasbourg* in France]

**strata** pl. of STRATUM.

■ **Usage** It is incorrect to use *strata* as the singular noun instead of *stratum*.

**stratagem** /strat-uh-juhm/ n. **1** cunning plan or scheme, esp. for deceiving an enemy. **2** trickery. [Greek *stratēgos* a general]

**strata title** n. registered ownership of a certain amount of space (rather than ground area) in a multi-storey building, complex of home-units, etc.

**strategic** /struh-**tee**-jik/ adj. **1** of or promoting strategy. **2** (of materials) essential in war. **3** (of bombing or weapons) done or for use as a longer-term military objective. □ **strategically** adv.

**strategy** /strat-uh-jee/ n. (pl. **-ies**) **1** long-term plan or policy (*economic strategy*). **2 a** art of war. **b** art of moving troops, ships, aircraft, etc. into favourable positions. **c** an instance of this or a plan formed according to it. □ **strategist** n.

**stratify** /strat-uh-,fuy/ v. (**-ies**, **-ied**) (esp. as **stratified** adj.) arrange in strata or grades etc. □ **stratification** /-fuh-**kay**-shuhn/ n. [French: related to STRATUM]

**stratigraphy** /struh-**tig**-ruh-fee/ n. Geol. & Archaeol. **1** relative position of strata. **2** the study of this as a means of historical interpretation. □ **stratigraphic** /,strat-uh-**graf**-ik/ adj. [from STRATUM]

**stratosphere** /strat-uh-,sfeer/ n. layer of atmosphere above the troposphere, extending to about 50 km from the earth's surface. □ **stratospheric** /-sfe-rik/ adj. [from STRATUM]

**stratum** /strah-tuhm, stray-/ n. (pl. **strata**) **1** layer or set of layers of any deposited substance, esp. of rock. **2** atmospheric layer. **3** Biol. layer of tissue etc. **4 a** social grade etc. (*the various strata of society*). **b** Statistics each of the groups into which a population is divided in stratified sampling. [Latin *sterno* strew]

**straw** n. **1** dry cut stalks of grain as fodder or material for bedding, packing, etc. **2** single stalk of straw. **3** thin tube for sucking drink through. **4** insignificant thing (*not worth a straw*). **5** pale yellow colour. □ **clutch at straws** try any remedy in desperation. [Old English]

**strawberry** /straw-buh-ree/ n. (pl. **-ies**) **1** pulpy red fruit with a seed-studded surface. **2** plant with runners and white flowers bearing this. **3** deep pinkish-red colour. [Old English: related to STRAW, for unknown reason]

**strawberry mark** n. reddish birthmark.

**strawflower** n. = HELICHRYSUM.

**straw vote** n. (also **straw poll**) unofficial ballot as a test of opinion.

**stray** — v. **1** wander from the right place or from one's companions; go astray; digress. **2** deviate morally or mentally. — n. strayed person, animal, or thing. — adj. **1** strayed, lost. **2** isolated, occasional (*hit by a stray bullet; a stray customer or two*). **3** Physics wasted or unwanted (*eliminate stray magnetic fields*). [Anglo-French *strey*: related to ASTRAY]

**streak** — n. **1** long thin usu. irregular line or band, esp. of colour. **2** strain in a person's character (*has a streak of mischief in him*). **3** spell or series (*winning streak*). **4** colloq. tall, thin person. — v. **1** mark with streaks. **2** move very rapidly. **3** colloq. run naked in public as a stunt, for a wager, etc. □ **streaker** n. [Old English, = pen-stroke]

**streaky** adj. (**-ier**, **-iest**) **1** full of streaks. **2** (of bacon) with streaks of fat.

**stream** — n. **1** flowing body of water, esp. a small river. **2** flow of a fluid or of a mass of people. **3** current or flow (of air etc.); beam (of light). **4** continuous flow (*a stream of abuse; stream of complaints*). **5** current or direction in which things are moving or tending (*against the stream*). **6** group of schoolchildren of similar ability taught together. — v. **1** move as a stream. **2** run with liquid (*my eyes were streaming*). **3** be blown in the wind (*streaming banners*). **4** emit a stream of (blood etc.). **5** arrange (schoolchildren) in streams. □ **on stream** in operation or production. [Old English]

**streamer** n. **1** long narrow strip of ribbon or paper. **2** long narrow flag.

**streamline** v. (**-ning**) **1** give (a vehicle etc.) the form which presents the least resistance to motion. **2** make simple or more efficient.

**stream of consciousness** n. **1** *Psychol.* person's thoughts and conscious reactions to events, perceived as a continuous flow. **2** literary style depicting events in such a flow in the mind of a character.

**street** — n. **1 a** public road in a city or town. **b** this with the houses etc. on each side. **2** people who live or work in a particular street. — v. *colloq.* outdistance (other competitors). □ **by a street** (esp. of a sporting victory) by a wide margin. **on the streets** living by prostitution. **streets ahead** (often foll. by *of*) *colloq.* much superior (to). **up** (or **right up**) **one's street** *colloq.* what one likes, knows about, etc. [Old English]

**street kid** n. homeless young person in an urban area.

**streetwalker** n. prostitute seeking customers in the street.

**streetwise** adj. (of street kids etc.) knowing how to survive modern urban life; knowing how to survive on the streets.

**strength** n. **1** state of being strong (physically, mentally, morally, etc.); degree or manner of this. **2 a** person or thing giving strength (*she is my strength*). **b** positive attribute (*patience is your great strength*). **3 a** number of people present or available. **b** full number (*below strength*). □ **from strength to strength** with ever-increasing success. **in strength** in large numbers. **on the strength of** on the basis of. **the strength of** the point or meaning of; the truth about (*what's the strength of this rumour I hear about you?*). **that's about the strength of it** that is what it amounts to. [Old English: related to STRONG]

**strengthen** /streng-thuhn, strengkthuhn/ v. make or become stronger.

**strenuous** /stren-yoo-uhs/ adj. **1** requiring or using great effort. **2** energetic. □ **strenuously** adv. [Latin]

**streptococcus** /ˌstrep-tuh-**kok**-uhs/ n. (pl. **-cocci** /-**kok**-uy/ ) bacterium of a type occurring in chains, and often causing infectious diseases. □ **streptococcal** adj. [Greek *streptos* twisted, *kokkos* berry]

**streptomycin** /ˌstrep-tuh-**muy**-suhn/ n. antibiotic effective against many disease-producing bacteria. [Greek *streptos* twisted, *mukēs* fungus]

**stress** — n. **1 a** pressure or tension exerted on a material object. **b** quantity measuring this. **2 a** physical or mental strain. **b** distress caused by this. **3 a** emphasis (*the stress was on the need for success*). **b** emphasis on a syllable or word. — v. **1** emphasise. **2** subject to mechanical or physical or mental stress. □ **lay stress on** emphasise. **stressed out** *colloq.* suffering greatly from stress, anxiety, etc. [shortening of DISTRESS]

**stressful** adj. causing stress.

**stretch** — v. **1** draw, be drawn, or be able to be drawn out into greater length or size. **2** make or become taut. **3** place or lie at full length or spread out (*with a canopy stretched over the two of them*). **4** (also *absol.*) **a** extend (a limb etc.). **b** thrust out one's limbs and tighten one's muscles after being relaxed. **5** lengthen or widen, esp. by force (*I'll have to stretch these shoes; this jumper has become stretched*). **6** have a specified length or extension; extend (*the property stretches for miles*). **7** strain or exert extremely; exaggerate (*stretch a friendship; stretch the truth*). — n. **1** continuous extent, expanse, or period (*stretch of open road; stretch of time*). **2** act or instance of stretching or the state of being stretched. **3** (*attrib.*) elastic (*stretch fabric*). **4** *colloq.* period of imprisonment etc. **5** straight side of a racetrack, esp. leading to the winning post. □ **at full stretch** to capacity; as fully or as hard as possible. **at a stretch** in one period. **stretch one's legs** exercise oneself by walking. **stretch out 1** extend (a limb etc.). **2** last; prolong. **stretch a point** agree to something not normally allowed. □ **stretchy** adj. (**-ier**, **-iest**) [Old English]

**stretcher** — n. **1** two poles with canvas etc. between, for carrying a person in a lying position. **2** (collapsible) bed usu. made of canvas etc. on a frame. **3** brick etc. laid along the face of a wall. — v. remove (a person, esp. an injured player from the field) on a stretcher.

**strew** /stroo/ v. (*past part.* **strewn** or **strewed**) **1** scatter or spread about over a surface. **2** (usu. foll. by *with*) spread (a surface) with scattered things. [Old English: related to STRAW]

**stria** /struy-uh/ n. (pl. **striae** /-ee/ ) slight ridge or furrow. [Latin]

**striate** — adj. /struy-uht/ (also **striated** /struy-**ay**-tuhd/ ) **1** marked with striae. **2** (as **striated**) (as a distinguishing epithet in the names of birds etc.) marked with ridges, stripes, etc.; streaked. — v. /struy-ayt/ (**-ting**) mark with slight ridges. □ **striation** /struy-ay-shuhn/ n.

**striated pardalote** n. small bird of all Australian States, having a single spot on the wing and a black crown sometimes streaked ('striated') with white (see PARDALOTE).

**stricken** /strik-uhn/ adj. overcome with

illness or misfortune etc. [archaic past part. of STRIKE]

**strict** *adj.* **1** precisely limited or defined; without exception or deviation (*a strict interpretation of the law*; *strict diet*; *lives in strict seclusion*). **2** requiring complete obedience or exact performance (*a strict teacher*; *gave strict orders*). **3** complete, total (*I mention this in strictest confidence*). □ **strictly speaking** applying words or rules in their strict sense. □ **strictly** *adv.* **strictness** *n.* [Latin *stringo strict-* draw tight]

**stricture** /strik-chuh/ *n.* **1** (usu. in *pl.*; often foll. by *on, upon*) critical or censorious remark. **2** *Med.* morbid narrowing of a canal or duct in the body. [Latin: related to STRICT]

**stride** — *v.* (**-ding**; *past* **strode**; *past part.* **stridden** /strid-uhn/ ) **1** walk with long firm steps. **2** cross with one step. **3** bestride. — *n.* **1 a** single long step. **b** length of this. **2** gait as determined by the length of stride. **3** (usu. in *pl.*) progress (*great strides*). **4** steady progress (*get into one's stride*). **5** (in *pl.*) *colloq.* trousers. □ **take in one's stride** manage easily. [Old English]

**strident** /struy-duhnt/ *adj.* loud and harsh. □ **stridency** *n.* **stridently** *adv.* [Latin *strido* creak]

**strife** *n.* **1** conflict; struggle. **2** *colloq.* trouble of any kind; difficulty. □ **in strife** *colloq.* in trouble. [French *estrif*: related to STRIVE]

**strike** — *v.* (**-king**; *past* **struck**; *past part.* **struck** or **stricken**) **1** deliver (a blow) or inflict a blow on; hit. **2** come or bring sharply into contact with (*ship struck a rock*). **3** propel or divert with a blow. **4** (cause to) penetrate (*struck terror into him*). **5** ignite (a match) or produce (sparks etc.) by friction. **6** make (a coin) by stamping. **7** produce (a musical note) by striking. **8 a** (also *absol.*) (of a clock) indicate (the time) with a chime etc. **b** (of time) be so indicated. **9 a** attack suddenly (*was struck (or stricken) with terror*). **b** (of a disease) afflict (*stricken with asthma*). **10** cause to become suddenly (*struck dumb*). **11** reach or achieve (*strike a balance*). **12** agree on (a bargain). **13** assume (an attitude) suddenly and dramatically (*struck a pose*). **14 a** come across (*struck the right path at last*). **b** discover or find (oil, gold, etc.) by drilling, digging, etc. **15** occur to or appear to (*strikes me as silly*). **16** (of employees) engage in a strike. **17** lower or take down (a flag, sail, etc.). **18** take a specified direction (*struck east*). **19** (of a snake) wound with its fangs. **20 a** insert (the cutting of a plant) in soil etc. to take root. **b** (also *absol.*) (of a plant or cutting etc.) put forth (roots). — *n.* **1** act or instance of

striking. **2 a** organised refusal to work until a grievance is remedied. **b** similar refusal to participate. **3** sudden find or success (*a lucky strike*). **4** attack, esp. from the air. **5** act of knocking down all the pins with the first ball in tenpin bowling. □ **on strike** taking part in an industrial etc. strike. **strike home 1** deal an effective blow. **2** have the intended effect (*my words struck home*). **strike it rich** *colloq.* find a source of abundance or success. **strike a light!** *colloq.* expression of surprise, disgust, etc. **strike me lucky** (or **blue** or **dead** or **fat** or **pink** or **roan** etc.) *colloq.* a mild oath. **strike off 1** remove with a stroke. **2** delete (a name etc.) from a list, esp. a professional register. **strike out 1** hit out. **2** act vigorously. **3** delete (an item or name etc.). **4** set off (*struck out eastwards*). **strike up 1** start (an acquaintance, conversation, etc.), esp. casually. **2** (also *absol.*) begin playing (a tune etc.). **struck on** *colloq.* infatuated with. □ **striker** *n.* [Old English, = go, stroke]

**strikebreaker** *n.* person working or employed in place of strikers.

**strike pay** *n.* allowance paid to strikers by their union.

**striker** *n.* **1** employee on strike. **2** *Soccer* attacking player positioned forward.

**striking** *adj.* impressive; attracting attention. □ **strikingly** *adv.*

**Strine** — *n.* comic transliteration of Australian pronunciation characterised by excessive elision etc., e.g. *Emma Chisit* = 'How much is it?', *Gloria Some* = 'glorious home'. — *adj.* Australian (*the Strine language*). [= *Australian* in Strine]

**string** — *n.* **1** twine or narrow cord. **2** piece of this or of similar material used for tying or holding together, pulling, forming the head of a racquet, etc. **3** length of catgut or wire etc. on a musical instrument, producing a note by vibration. **4 a** (in *pl.*) stringed instruments in an orchestra etc. **b** (*attrib.*) of stringed instruments (*string quartet*). **5** (in *pl.*) condition or complication (*no strings attached*). **6** set of things strung together; series or line (*string of pearls*; *string of oaths*). **7** tough side of a bean-pod etc. — *v.* (*past and past part.* **strung**) **1** fit (a racquet, violin, archer's bow, etc.) with a string or strings, or (a violin etc. bow) with horsehairs etc. **2** tie with string. **3** thread on a string. **4** arrange in or as a string (*strung the clothes on the line*). **5** furnish, equip, or adorn with something suspended (*hall strung with streamers*). **6** remove the strings from (a bean). □ **on a string** under one's control. **pull strings** see PULL. **string along** *colloq.* **1** deceive, esp. by appearing to comply with (a person). **2** (often foll. by *with*) keep company (with). **string out** extend; prolong. **string up 1** hang up on strings etc. **2** kill by hanging. **3** (usu. as **strung up** *adj.*) make tense. [Old English]

**string-course** *n.* raised horizontal band of bricks etc. on a building.

**stringed** *adj.* (of musical instruments) having strings.

**stringent** /strin-juhnt/ *adj.* (of rules etc.) strict, precise; leaving no loophole for discretion. □ **stringency** *n.* **stringently** *adv.* [Latin: related to STRICT]

**stringer** *n.* **1** longitudinal structural member in a framework, esp. of a ship or aircraft. **2** a horizontal timber connecting uprights in a framework, supporting a floor, etc.

**stringy** *adj.* (-**ier**, -**iest**) like string, fibrous. □ **stringiness** *n.*

**stringybark** *n.* **1** any of many eucalypts chiefly of south-eastern mainland Australia, having thick, rough, long-fibred bark. **2** bark or wood of these trees. **3** (*attrib.*) of or pertaining to stringybarks (*stringybark forest*; *stringybark cockatoo*).

**stringybark cockatoo** *n.* farmer of small means.

**strip¹** — *v.* (-**pp**-) **1** (often foll. by *of*) remove the clothes or covering from (a person or thing) (*stripped him*; *stripped the wrapping from the parcel*; *stripped the orange of its peel*). **2** (often foll. by *off*) undress oneself (*he stripped and jumped into bed*). **3** (often foll. by *of*) deprive (a person or thing) of property or titles. **4** leave bare of accessories or fittings (*stripped the room of all its contents*). **5 a** deprive (a plant etc.) of its foliage or fruit (*storm stripped the trees*; *locusts stripped the crops*). **b** remove seed or grain from a crop. **6** (often foll. by *down*) remove the accessory fittings of or take apart (a machine etc.). **7** damage the thread of (a screw) or the teeth of (a gearwheel). **8** remove (paint) or remove paint from (a surface) with solvent. **9** (often foll. by *from*) pull (a covering etc.) off (*stripped the masks from their faces*). — *n.* **1** act of stripping, esp. of undressing in striptease. **2** identifying outfit worn by the members of a sports team while playing. [Old English]

**strip²** *n.* long narrow piece (*strip of land*). □ **tear a strip off a person** *colloq.* rebuke a person severely. [Low German *strippe* strap]

**strip cartoon** *n.* = COMIC STRIP.

**stripe** *n.* **1** long narrow band or strip differing in colour or texture from the surface on either side of it. **2** *Mil.* chevron etc. denoting military rank. [perhaps from Low German or Dutch]

**striped** *adj.* marked with stripes.

**stripey** *n.* (*pl.* **stripeys** or **stripies**) any of several (usu. horizontally) striped Australian marine food-fish.

**strip light** *n.* tubular fluorescent lamp.

**stripling** *n.* youth who has not yet fully emerged into manhood. [from STRIP²]

**stripper** *n.* **1** person or thing that strips something. **2** device or solvent for removing paint etc. **3** machine used to harvest grain. **4** striptease performer.

**strip-search** — *n.* search involving the removal of all a person's clothes. — *v.* search in this way.

**striptease** /strip-teez/ *n.* entertainment in which the performer slowly and erotically undresses.

**stripy** *adj.* (-**ier**, -**iest**) striped.

**strive** *v.* (-**ving**; *past* **strove**; *past part.* **striven** /striv-uhn/) **1** try hard (*strive to succeed*). **2** (often foll. by *with*, *against*) struggle (*striving against poverty*). [French *estriver*]

**strobe** *n. colloq.* stroboscope. [abbreviation]

**strobe lighting** *n.* electric light that flashes on and off rapidly and automatically, used at discos, pop-concerts, etc.

**stroboscope** /stroh-buh-,skohp/ *n.* **1** *Physics* instrument for determining speeds of rotation etc. by shining a bright light at intervals so that a rotating object appears stationary. **2** lamp made to flash intermittently, esp. for this purpose. □ **stroboscopic** /-skop-ik/ *adj.* [Greek *strobos* whirling]

**strode** *past* of STRIDE.

**stroganoff** /strog-uh-nof/ *n.* a dish of strips of beef cooked in a sauce containing sour cream. [P. *Stroganoff*, Russian diplomat (d. 1817)]

**stroke** — *n.* **1** act or instance of striking; blow, hit (*with a single stroke*; *a stroke of lightning*). **2** sudden disabling attack caused esp. by thrombosis; apoplexy. **3 a** action or movement, esp. as one of a series (*cut through the log with the third stroke of his axe*). **b** slightest such action (*has not done a stroke of work*). **4** single complete motion of a wing, oar, etc. **5** (in rowing) the mode or action of moving the oar (*row a fast stroke*). **6** whole motion of a piston in either direction. **7** specified mode of swimming (*butterfly stroke*). **8** *Golf* action of hitting a ball with a club, as a unit of scoring. **9** method of striking with the bat etc. in games etc. (*played some unorthodox strokes*). **10** specially successful or skilful effort (*a stroke of diplomacy*). **11** mark made by a single movement of a pen, paintbrush, etc. **12** detail contributing to the general effect in a description (*she laid bare his character in a few sure strokes*). **13** sound of a striking clock. **14** (in full **stroke oar**) oar or oarsman nearest

the stern, setting the time of the stroke.
**15** act or spell of stroking. — v. (**-king**) **1**
pass one's hand gently along the surface
of (hair, fur, a person's body, etc.). **2** act as
the stroke of (a boat or crew). □ **at a stroke**
by a single action. **on the stroke (of)** punctually (at). **stroke of genius** original or
strikingly successful idea. [Old English:
related to STRIKE]

**stroll** /strohl/ — v. walk in a leisurely way.
— n. short leisurely walk. [probably from
German *Strolch* vagabond]

**strong** — adj. (**stronger** /strong-guh'/) **1**
able to resist; not easily damaged, overcome, or disturbed (*strong material*; *strong
faith*; *strong character*). **2** healthy. **3** capable
of exerting great force or of doing much;
muscular, powerful. **4** forceful in effect
(*strong wind*). **5** firmly held (*strong
suspicion*). **6** (of an argument etc.) convincing. **7** powerfully affecting the senses
or emotions (*strong light*; *strong acting by
John Gielgud*). **8** formidable (*strong candidate*). **9** (of a solution or drink etc.) not
very diluted. **10** (of language) **a** indicative of
angry or excited feeling. **b** vulgar; coarse.
**11** powerful in taste or smell. **12** of a
specified number (*200 strong*). **13** *Gram.*
(of a verb) forming inflections by a change
of vowel within the stem (e.g. *swim*, *swam*).
— adv. strongly. □ **come on strong** behave
aggressively. **going strong** *colloq.* continuing vigorously; in good health etc. **strong
of** *colloq.* point or meaning of; the truth
about (*what's the strong of these empty
glasses?* — *let's have another*; *we'll never
get the strong of why they split*). □ **strongish**
adj. **strongly** adv. [Old English]

**strong-arm** *attrib. adj.* using force (*strong-
arm tactics*).

**strongfish** n. = TILLYWURTI.

**stronghold** n. **1** fortified place. **2** secure
refuge. **3** centre of support for a cause etc.

**strong-minded** adj. determined.

**strong point** n. thing at which one excels.

**strongroom** n. room, esp. in a bank, for
keeping valuables safe from fire and
theft.

**strontium** /stron-tee-uhm/ n. soft silver-
white metallic element. [*Strontian* in
Scotland]

**strontium-90** n. radioactive isotope of
strontium found in nuclear fallout and
concentrated in bones and teeth when
ingested.

**strop** — n. device, esp. a strip of leather,
for sharpening razors. — v. (**-pp-**) sharpen
on a strop. [Low German or Dutch]

**stroppy** /strop-ee/ adj. (**-ier**, **-iest**) *colloq.*
bad-tempered; awkward to deal with.
[origin uncertain]

**strove** *past* of STRIVE.

**struck** *past* and *past part.* of STRIKE.

**structural** /struk-chuh-ruhl/ adj. of a
structure. □ **structurally** adv.

**structuralism** n. theory that societies,
languages, works of literature, etc., can
be understood only by analysis of their
structure (rather than their function).
□ **structuralist** n. & adj.

**structure** /struk-chuh/ — n. **1** a constructed unit, esp. a building. **b** way in
which a building etc. is constructed (*has
a flimsy structure*). **2** set of interconnecting
parts of any complex thing; framework
(*the structure of a sentence*; *new wages
structure*). — v. (**-ring**) give structure to;
organise. [Latin *struo struct-* build]

**structured programming** n. *Computing*
method of dividing a computer program
into small, separately testable, units.

**strudel** /stroo-duhl/ n. thin leaved pastry
rolled round a sweet filling and baked.
[German]

**struggle** /strug-uhl/ — v. (**-ling**) **1** violently
try to get free of restraint. **2** (often foll. by
*for*, or *to* + infin.) try hard under difficulties (*struggled for power*; *struggled to
win*). **3** (foll. by *with*, *against*) contend; fight.
**4** (foll. by *along*, *on*, etc.) progress with
difficulty. **5** (esp. as **struggling** adj.) have
difficulty in gaining recognition or a
living (*struggling artist*). — n. **1** act or
spell of struggling. **2** hard or confused
contest. **3** determined effort under difficulties. [origin uncertain]

**strum** — v. (**-mm-**) **1** (often foll. by *on*; also
*absol.*) play (chords) on (a guitar, piano,
etc.), esp. carelessly or unskilfully or as a
very basic accompaniment. **2** play (a tune
etc.) in this way. — n. sound or spell of
strumming. [imitative: cf. THRUM]

**strumpet** /strum-puht/ n. *archaic* or
*rhet.* prostitute. [origin unknown]

**strung** *past* and *past part.* of STRING.

**strut** — n. **1** bar in a framework, designed
to resist compression. **2** strutting gait. — v.
(**-tt-**) **1** walk stiffly and pompously. **2** brace
with struts. [Old English]

**strychnine** /strik-neen, -nuhn/ n. highly
poisonous alkaloid used in small doses as
a stimulant. [Greek *strukhnos* nightshade]

**stub** — n. **1** remnant of a pencil or cigarette etc. **2** counterfoil of a cheque or receipt
etc. **3** stump (of a tree, tooth, etc.). — v.
(**-bb-**) **1** strike (one's toe) against something. **2** (usu. foll. by *out*) extinguish (a
cigarette) by pressure. [Old English]

**stubble** /stub-uhl/ n. **1** stalks of cereal
crops etc. left in the ground after the
harvest. **2** short stiff hair or bristles, as
on the face of a man who has not recently
shaved. □ **stubbled** adj. **stubbly** adj.
[Latin *stupula* straw]

**stubble quail** n. bird of chiefly southern mainland Australia, having predominantly grey-brown plumage with pale and dark streaks, usu. found in stubble etc., and sought as a game-bird.

**stubborn** /stub-uhn/ adj. obstinate, inflexible. □ **stubbornly** adv. **stubbornness** n. [origin unknown]

**stubby** — adj. (**-ier, -est**) short and thick; squat. — n. (pl. **-ies**) **1** (also **stubbie**) small (375 ml) squat bottle of beer. **2** (**stubbies**) propr. pair of brief shorts for men. □ **a stubby short of a six-pack** colloq. slightly crazy; mentally dull; stupid.

**stubby cooler** n. (also **stubby holder**) casing made of insulating material in which a stubby is held while the contents are being drunk.

**stucco** /stuk-oh/ — n. (pl. **-es**) plaster or cement for coating walls or moulding into decorations. — v. (**-es, -ed**) coat with stucco. [Italian]

**stuck** past and past part. of STICK². □ **get stuck into a person** (or **something**) see GET.

**stuck-up** adj. conceited, snobbish. [STICK²]

**stud**¹ — n. **1** large-headed projecting nail, boss, or knob, esp. for ornament. **2** double button, esp. for use with two buttonholes in a shirt-front. **3** post (in the frame of a building) to which laths are nailed. — v. (**-dd-**) **1** set with or as with studs. **2** (as **studded** adj.) (foll. by **with**) thickly set or strewn (studded with diamonds). [Old English]

**stud**² n. **1** a number of horses kept for breeding etc. **b** (in full **stud-farm**) place where these are kept. **2** (in full **stud-horse**) stallion. **3** colloq. good-looking young man, esp. one noted for sexual prowess. **4** (in full **stud poker**) form of poker with betting after the dealing of cards face up. □ **at stud** (of a stallion) hired out for breeding. [Old English]

**student** /styoo-duhnt/ n. **1** person who is studying, esp. at a place of higher or further education. **2** (attrib.) studying in order to become (student nurse). □ **studentship** n. [Latin: related to STUDY]

**studied** adj. deliberate, affected, carefully and intentionally contrived (studied politeness).

**studio** /styoo-dee-oh/ n. (pl. **-s**) **1** workroom of a painter, photographer, etc. **2** place for making films, recordings, or broadcast programmes. [Italian]

**studious** /styoo-dee-uhs/ adj. **1** assiduous in study. **2** painstaking (with studious care). □ **studiously** adv. [Latin: related to STUDY]

**study** /stud-ee/ — n. (pl. **-ies**) **1** acquisition of knowledge, esp. from books. **2** (in pl.) pursuit of academic knowledge (con-

tinued his studies abroad). **3** private room used for reading, writing, etc. **4** piece of work, esp. a drawing, done for practice or as an experiment (charcoal study of a male torso). **5** portrayal in literature etc. of behaviour or character etc. (Shakespeare's character Hamlet is a study in procrastination). **6** musical composition designed to develop a player's skill. **7** thing worth observing (his face was a study). **8** thing that is or deserves to be investigated (completed a study of Australian skinks). — v. (**-ies, -ied**) **1** make a study of; investigate (a subject) (study law). **2** (often foll. by for) apply oneself to study (studying for the exam). **3** scrutinise closely (a visible object) (studied their faces). **4** learn (the words of one's role etc.). [Latin studium]

**stuff** — n. **1** material; fabric. **2** substance; collection of things not needing to be specified; material, matter (what sort of stuff are these pillows filled with?; get your stuff off the kitchen table; lot of stuff on the news). **3** particular knowledge or activity (know one's stuff). **4** what a person is made of: capabilities or inward character (he hasn't the right stuff in him to control 200 men). **5** valueless matter; trash, nonsense (surely you're not going to keep all that stuff?). **6** (as characterised by preceding epithet) material, matter, business, actions, talk, etc. (the play was full of feminist stuff; cut out the rough stuff!; you can write better stuff than that; what he said was pretty strong stuff). — v. **1** pack (a receptacle) tightly (stuff a cushion with feathers; his head is stuffed with obnoxious racist notions). **2** (foll. by in, into) force or cram (a thing) (stuffed his underwear into the pocket of the holdall). **3** fill out the skin of (an animal etc.) with material to restore the original shape. **4** fill (food, esp. poultry) with a mixture, esp. before cooking. **5** (also refl.) fill with food; eat greedily. **6** push, esp. hastily or clumsily (stuffed the book behind the cushion when he heard her footsteps). **7** (usu. in passive; foll. by up) block up (the nose etc.). **8** colloq. (expressing contempt) dispose of (you can stuff the job). **9** (as **stuffed** adj.) colloq. ruined; exhausted. □ **get stuffed** colloq. exclamation of dismissal, contempt, etc. **not give a stuff** colloq. not care at all. **stuff and nonsense** exclamation of incredulity or ridicule. **stuff it** colloq. coarse expression of contempt, rejection, defiance, etc. **stuff up** colloq. ruin; bungle. **that's the stuff** colloq. that is just what is required. [French estoffe]

**stuffed shirt** n. colloq. pompous person.

**stuffing** n. **1** padding for cushions etc. **2** mixture used to stuff poultry etc., esp.

before cooking. □ **knock** (or **beat** or **take**) **the stuffing out of** *colloq.* make feeble or weak; defeat; vanquish.

**stuff-up** *n. colloq.* a bungled action; a ruined event etc.; a mess.

**stuffy** *adj.* (**-ier, -iest**) **1** (of a room etc.) lacking fresh air. **2** prim, straitlaced; formal, pompous; boring, conventional. **3** (of the nose etc.) stuffed up. □ **stuffily** *adv.* **stuffiness** *n.*

**stultify** /**stul**-tuh-ˌfuy/ *v.* (**-ies, -ied**) make ineffective or useless, esp. by routine. □ **stultification** /-fuh-**kay**-shuhn/ *n.* [Latin *stultus* foolish]

**stumble** /**stum**-buhl/ — *v.* (**-ling**) **1** involuntarily lurch forward or almost fall. **2** (often foll. by *along*) walk with repeated stumbles. **3** make a mistake or repeated mistakes in speaking etc. **4** (foll. by *on, upon, across*) find by chance. — *n.* act of stumbling. [related to STAMMER]

**stumbling block** *n.* obstacle.

**stumer** /**styoo**-muh, **stoo**-/ *n. colloq.* worthless cheque. □ **come a stumer** lose one's money. [origin unknown]

**stumered** *adj. colloq.* without any money; 'stone broke'.

**stump** — *n.* **1** part of a cut or fallen tree still in the ground. **2** similar part (e.g. of a leg, arm, pencil, branch, etc.) cut off or worn down. **3** *Cricket* **a** each of the three uprights of a wicket. **b** (in *pl.*) end of the day's play. **c** (in *pl.*) *joc.* legs. **5** (esp. in Queensland) one of the piles supporting a dwelling. — *v.* **1** (of a question etc.) be too hard for; baffle. **2** (as **stumped** *adj.*) at a loss, baffled. **3** *Cricket* put (a batsman) out by touching the stumps with the ball while he or she is out of the crease. **4** walk stiffly or noisily. □ **beyond** (or **back of**) **the black stump** see BLACK STUMP. [Low German or Dutch]

**stump-grub** *v.* remove the stumps of felled trees (from a paddock etc.) by manual or mechanical means (*spent days stump-grubbing the paddock*). □ **stump-grubbing** *n.*

**stump-jump plough** *n.* plough specially designed for use on land which has not been cleared of stumps.

**stumpy** — *adj.* (**-ier, -iest**) short and thick. — *n.* = STUMPY TAIL. □ **stumpiness** *n.*

**stumpy tail** *n.* (also **stump-tailed lizard (skink), stumpy, stumpy-tailed lizard**) = BOBTAIL.

**stun** *v.* (**-nn-**) **1** knock senseless; stupefy. **2** bewilder, shock, amaze. **3** (of a sound) deafen temporarily. □ **like a stunned mullet** see MULLET. [French: related to ASTONISH]

**stung** *past* and *past part.* of STING. □ **stung up** (also **stung**) *colloq.* drunk.

**stunk** *past* and *past part.* of STINK.

**stunner** *n. colloq.* stunning person or thing.

**stunning** *adj. colloq.* extremely attractive or impressive. □ **stunningly** *adv.*

**stunt**[1] *v.* retard the growth or development of. [obsolete *stunt* foolish, short]

**stunt**[2] *n.* **1** something unusual done for publicity. **2** trick or daring feat. [origin unknown]

**stunt man** *n.* man employed to perform dangerous stunts in place of an actor.

**stupefy** /**styoo**-puh-ˌfuy/ *v.* (**-ies, -ied**) **1** make stupid or insensible (*stupefied with beer*). **2** astonish, amaze. □ **stupefaction** /-fak-shuhn/ *n.* [French from Latin *stupeo* be amazed]

**stupendous** /styoo-**pen**-duhs/ *adj.* amazing or prodigious, esp. in size or degree (*a stupendous achievement*). □ **stupendously** *adv.* [Latin: related to STUPEFY]

**stupid** /**styoo**-puhd/ *adj.* (**stupider, stupidest**) **1** unintelligent, foolish (*a stupid fellow*). **2** typical of stupid persons (*stupid mistake*). **3** uninteresting, boring (*this is a stupid film*). **4** in a stupor. □ **stupidity** /-**pid**-uh-tee/ *n.* (*pl.* **-ies**). **stupidly** *adv.* [Latin: related to STUPEFY]

**stupor** /**styoo**-puh/ *n.* dazed, torpid, or helplessly amazed state. [Latin: related to STUPEFY]

**sturdy** /**ster**-dee/ *adj.* (**-ier, -iest**) **1** robust; strongly built. **2** vigorous (*sturdy resistance*). □ **sturdily** *adv.* **sturdiness** *n.* [French *esturdi*]

**sturgeon** /**ster**-juhn/ *n.* (*pl.* same or **-s**) large sharklike fish (of the Northern hemisphere) yielding caviare. [Anglo-French from Germanic]

**Sturt's desert pea** *n.* (also **clianthus**) trailing plant of sandy soils in arid parts of all States except Victoria and Tasmania, bearing masses of extremely large brilliant red pea-flowers with a shiny black boss: the floral emblem of South Australia. [Charles *Sturt*, Australian explorer (d. 1869)]

**Sturt's desert rose** *n.* shrub of arid central Australia bearing large, bluish-mauve, hibiscus-like flowers with a dark red basal splotch: the floral emblem of the Northern Territory.

**stutter** — *v.* **1** stammer, esp. by involuntary repetition of the initial consonants of words. **2** (often foll. by *out*) utter (words) in this way. — *n.* act or habit of stuttering. [British dial. *stut*]

**sty**[1] /stuy/ *n.* (*pl.* **sties**) = PIGSTY. [Old English]

**sty**[2] /stuy/ *n.* (also **stye**) (*pl.* **sties** or **styes**) inflamed swelling on the edge of an eyelid. [Old English]

**Stygian** /**stij**-ee-uhn/ *adj. literary* dark, gloomy. [literally = of the *Styx*, a river round Hades in Greek mythology]

**style** /stuyl/ — n. **1** kind or sort, esp. in regard to appearance and form (*elegant style of house*). **2** manner of writing, speaking, performing, living, etc. **3** distinctive manner of a person, artistic school, or period, esp. in relation to painting, architecture, furniture, etc. **4** superior quality or manner (*do it in style*). **5** fashion in dress etc. **6** *Bot.* narrow extension of the ovary supporting the stigma. — v. (**-ling**) **1** design or make etc. in a particular (esp. fashionable) style. **2** designate in a specified way. [Latin *stilus*]

**stylidium** /ˌstuy-**lid**-ee-uhm/ n. = TRIGGER PLANT.

**stylised** /**stuy**-luyzd/ adj. (also **-ized**) painted, drawn, etc. in a conventional non-realistic style.

**stylish** adj. fashionable; elegant. □ **stylishly** adv. **stylishness** n.

**stylist** /**stuy**-luhst/ n. **1 a** designer of fashionable styles etc. **b** hairdresser. **2** stylish writer or performer.

**stylistic** /stuy-**lis**-tik/ adj. of or concerning esp. literary style. □ **stylistically** adv.

**stylus** /**stuy**-luhs/ n. (pl. **-luses**) **1** sharp needle following a groove in a gramophone record and transmitting the recorded sound for reproduction. **2** pointed writing tool. [Latin: related to STYLE]

**stymie** /**stuy**-mee/ (also **stimy**) — n. (pl. **-ies**) **1** *Golf* situation where an opponent's ball lies between one's ball and the hole. **2** difficult situation. — v. (**-mies, -mied, -mying** or **-mieing**) **1** obstruct; thwart. **2** *Golf* block with a stymie. [origin unknown]

**stypandra** /ˌstuy-**pan**-druh/ n. SEE NODDING BLUE LILY. [Greek *stūpe* tow, coarse part of flax, *anēr andros* man]

**styptic** /**stip**-tik/ — adj. checking bleeding. — n. styptic substance. [Greek *stuphō* contract]

**styrene** /**styr**-reen/ n. liquid hydrocarbon easily polymerised and used in making plastics etc. [Greek *sturax* a resin]

**suasion** /**sway**-zhuhn/ n. formal persuasion (*moral suasion*). [Latin *suadeo suas-* urge]

**suave** /swahv/ adj. smooth; polite; sophisticated. □ **suavely** adv. **suavity** /**swah**-vuh-tee/ n. [Latin *suavis*]

**sub** colloq. n. **1** submarine. **2** subscription. **3** substitute. **4** sub-editor. [abbreviation]

**sub-** prefix **1** at, to, or from a lower position (*subordinate; submerge; subtract*). **2** secondary or inferior position (*subclass; subtotal*). **3** nearly; more or less (*subarctic*). [Latin]

**subaltern** /**sub**-uhl-tuhn/ n. officer below the rank of captain, esp. a second lieutenant. [Latin: related to ALTERNATE]

**sub-artesian** /ˌsub-ah-**tee**-zhuhn/ adj. (of bore water) rising but not to the surface.

**subatomic** /ˌsub-uh-**tom**-ik/ adj. occurring in, or smaller than, an atom.

**subby** /**sub**-ee/ n. (also **subbie**) colloq. subcontractor. [abbreviation]

**subcommittee** n. committee formed from a main committee for a special purpose.

**subconscious** /sub-**kon**-shuhs/ — adj. of the part of the mind which is not fully conscious but influences actions etc. — n. this part of the mind. □ **subconsciously** adv.

**subcontinent** /**sub**-ˌkon-tuh-nuhnt/ n. **1** large land mass, smaller than a continent. **2** large geographically or politically independent part of a continent.

**subcontract** — v. /ˌsub-kuhn-**trakt**/ **1** employ another contractor to do (work) as part of a larger project. **2** make or carry out a subcontract. — n. /sub-**kon**-trakt/ secondary contract, esp. to supply materials. □ **subcontractor** /-**trak**-tuh/ n.

**subculture** /**sub**-ˌkul-chuh/ n. distinct cultural group within a larger culture, often having beliefs or interests at variance with those of the larger culture.

**subcutaneous** /ˌsub-kyoo-**tay**-nee-uhs/ adj. under the skin.

**subdivide** /**sub**-duh-ˌvuyd, -**vuyd**/ v. (**-ding**) divide again after a first division. □ **subdivision** /**sub**-duh-ˌvizh-uhn/ n.

**subdominant** /sub-**dom**-uh-nuhnt/ n. *Mus.* fourth note of the diatonic scale in any key.

**subdue** /suhb-**dyoo**/ v. (**-dues, -dued, -duing**) **1** conquer, subjugate, or tame (an enemy, nature, one's emotions, etc.). **2** (as **subdued** adj.) softened; lacking in intensity; toned down (*subdued lighting; in a subdued mood*). [Latin *subduco*]

**sub-editor** /sub-**ed**-uh-tuh/ n. **1** assistant editor. **2** person who edits material for printing. □ **sub-edit** v. (**-t-**).

**subfamily** n. *Biol.* taxonomic category below a family.

**subgroup** /**sub**-groop/ n. subset of a group.

**subheading** /**sub**-ˌhed-ing/ n. subordinate heading or title.

**subhuman** /sub-**hyoo**-muhn/ adj. (of behaviour, intelligence, etc.) less than human.

**subincise** /ˌsub-in-**suyz**/ v. (in Aboriginal ritual) slit the underside of the penis to make a permanent opening into the urethra. □ **subincision** /ˌsub-in-**sizh**-uhn/ n.

**subject** — n. /**sub**-jekt/ **1 a** matter, theme, etc. to be discussed, described, represented, etc. **b** (foll. by *for*) person, circumstance, etc., giving rise to a specified feeling, action, etc. (*subject for congratulation*). **2** field of study (*Australian Literature is his best subject*). **3** *Logic & Gram.* noun or its equivalent about which a sentence is predicated and with which the verb agrees (see panel). **4** person owing allegiance to and under the protection of a national government; member of a specified nation (*Australian subjects*). **5** *Philos.* **a** thinking or feeling entity; the conscious mind esp. as opposed to anything external to it. **b** central substance of a thing as opposed to its attributes. **6** *Mus.* theme; leading phrase or motif. **7** person of specified tendencies (*a hysterical subject*). — *adj.* /**sub**-jekt/ **1** (foll. by *to*) conditional upon (*this arrangement is subject to your approval*). **2** (foll. by *to*) liable or exposed to (*subject to infection*). **3** (often foll. by *to*) owing obedience to a government etc.; in subjection. — *adv.* /**sub**-jekt/ (foll. by *to*) conditionally upon (*subject to your consent, I shall go*). — *v.* /suhb-**jekt**/ **1** (foll. by *to*) make liable; expose (*subjected us to hours of waiting*). **2** (usu. foll. by *to*) subdue (a person, nation, etc.) to one's sway etc. □ **subjection** /suhb-**jek**-shuhn/ *n.* [Latin *subjectus* placed under]

**subjective** /suhb-**jek**-tiv/ *adj.* **1** (of art, written history, an opinion, etc.) not impartial or literal; personal (opp. OBJECTIVE). **2** esp. *Philos.* of the individual consciousness or perception; imaginary, partial, or distorted. **3** *Gram.* of the subject. □ **subjectively** *adv.* **subjectivity** /,sub-jek-**tiv**-uh-tee/ *n.* [Latin: related to SUBJECT]

**subjoin** /sub-**join**/ *v.* add (an illustration, anecdote, etc.) at the end. [Latin *subjungo -junct-*]

***sub judice*** /sub joo-duh-see, suub **yoo**-di-,kay/ *adj. Law* under judicial consideration and therefore prohibited from public discussion elsewhere. [Latin]

**subjugate** /sub-juh-,gayt/ *v.* (**-ting**) bring into subjection; vanquish. □ **subjugation** /-**gay**-shuhn/ *n.* **subjugator** *n.* [Latin *jugum* yoke]

**subjunctive** /suhb-**jungk**-tiv/ *Gram.* — *adj.* (of a mood) expressing what is imagined, wished, or possible (e.g. *if I*

were you; *be that as it may*). — *n.* this mood or form. [Latin: related to SUBJOIN]

**sub-lease** — *n.* /**sub**-lees/ lease granted by a tenant to a subtenant. — *v.* /sub-**lees**/ (**-sing**) lease to a subtenant.

**sub-let** — *n.* /**sub**-let/ = SUB-LEASE *n.* — *v.* /sub-**let**/ (**-tt**-; *past* and *past part.* **-let**) = SUB-LEASE *v.*

**sub-lieutenant** /,sub-luh-**ten**-uhnt/ *n.* naval officer ranking next below lieutenant.

**sublimate** — *v.* /**sub**-luh-,mayt/ (**-ting**) **1** divert (esp. sexual energy) into socially more acceptable activity. **2** *Chem.* convert (a substance) from the solid state directly to vapour by heat, and usu. allow it to solidify again. — *n.* /**sub**-luh-muht/ *Chem.* sublimated substance. □ **sublimation** /-**may**-shuhn/ *n.* [Latin: related to SUBLIME]

**sublime** /suh-**bluym**/ — *adj.* (**sublimer, sublimest**) **1** of the most exalted or noble kind; awe-inspiring (*sublime music; sublime genius*). **2 a** arrogantly unruffled (*sublime indifference*). **b** (*iron.*) lofty (*has a sublime sense of his own importance*). — *v.* = SUBLIMATE *v.* 2. □ **sublimely** *adv.* **sublimity** /-**blim**-uh-tee/ *n.* [Latin *sublimis*]

**subliminal** /suh-**blim**-uh-nuhl/ *adj. Psychol.* (of a stimulus etc.) below the threshold of sensation or consciousness. □ **subliminally** *adv.* [Latin *limen -min-* threshold]

**submarine** /,sub-muh-**reen**, **sub**-/ — *n.* vessel, esp. an armed warship, capable of operating under water. — *attrib. adj.* existing, occurring, done, or used under the sea. □ **submariner** /-**ma**-ruh-nuh/ *n.*

**submediant** /sub-**mee**-dee-uhnt/ *n. Mus.* the sixth note of the diatonic scale of any key.

**submerge** /suhb-**merj**/ *v.* (**-ging**) **1** place, go, or dive under water. **2** inundate with work, problems, etc. □ **submergence** *n.* **submersion** /-**mer**-shuhn/ *n.* [Latin *mergo mers-* dip]

**submission** /suhb-**mish**-uhn/ *n.* **1 a** act or instance of submitting or state of being submitted. **b** thing submitted. **2** obedience; submissiveness. [Latin *submissio*: related to SUBMIT]

---

### Subject

The subject of a sentence is the person or thing that carries out the action of the verb and can be found by asking the question 'who or what?' before the verb, e.g.

*The full forward kicked a winning goal.*

*Hundreds of books are now available on CD-ROM.*

In a passive construction, the subject of the sentence is in fact the person or thing to which the action of the verb is done, e.g.

*I was hit by a ball.*

*Has the programme been broadcast yet?*

**submissive** /suhb-**mis**-iv/ *adj.* humble, obedient. □ **submissively** *adv.* **submissiveness** *n.*

**submit** /suhb-**mit**/ *v.* (**-tt-**) **1** (usu. foll. by *to*) **a** cease resistance; yield. **b** *refl.* surrender (oneself) to the control of another etc. **2** present for consideration or decision (*submitted her thesis*). **3** (usu. foll. by *to*) subject (a person or thing) to an operation, process, treatment, etc. (*submitted it to the flames*). **4** esp. *Law* urge or represent esp. deferentially (*that, I submit, is a misrepresentation*). [Latin *mitto miss-* send]

**subnormal** /sub-**naw**-muhl/ *adj.* below or less than normal, esp. in intelligence.

**subordinate** — *adj.* /suh-**baw**-duh-nuht/ (usu. foll. by *to*) of inferior importance or rank; secondary, subservient. — *n.* /suh-**baw**-duh-nuht/ person working under another's control or orders. — *v.* /suh-**baw**-duh-,nayt/ (**-ting**) (usu. foll. by *to*) make or treat as subordinate. □ **subordination** /-**nay**-shuhn/ *n.* [Latin: related to ORDAIN]

**subordinate clause** *n.* clause serving as an adjective, adverb, or noun in a main sentence.

**suborn** /suh-**bawn**/ *v.* induce by bribery etc. to commit perjury etc. [Latin *orno* equip]

**sub-plot** *n.* secondary plot in a play etc.

**subpoena** /suh-**pee**-nuh/ — *n.* writ ordering a person to attend a lawcourt. — *v.* (*past* and *past part.* **-naed**) serve a subpoena on. [Latin, = under penalty]

**sub rosa** /,sub roh-zuh/ *adj. & adv.* in secrecy or confidence. [Latin, = under the rose]

**subroutine** *n.* *Computing* routine designed to perform a frequently used operation within a program.

**subscribe** /suhb-**skruyb**/ *v.* (**-bing**) **1** (usu. foll. by *to, for*) **a** pay (a specified sum), esp. regularly, for membership of an organisation, receipt of a publication, etc. **b** contribute money to a fund, for a cause, etc. **2** (usu. foll. by *to*) agree with an opinion etc. (*I cannot subscribe to such a racist view*). □ **subscribe to** arrange to receive (a periodical etc.) regularly. [Latin *scribo script-* write]

**subscriber** *n.* **1** person who subscribes. **2** person hiring a telephone line.

**subscriber trunk dialling** *n.* automatic connection of trunk calls by dialling.

**subscript** /sub-**skript**/ — *adj.* written or printed below the line. — *n.* subscript number or symbol (e.g. 2 as in $H_2O$).

**subscription** /suhb-**skrip**-shuhn/ *n.* **1 a** act or instance of subscribing. **b** money subscribed. **2** membership fee, esp. paid regularly.

**subsection** *n.* division of a section.

**subsequent** /**sub**-suh-kwuhnt/ *adj.* (sometimes foll. by *to*) following a specified event etc. in time, esp. as a consequence (*subsequent events have proved me right; a public outcry subsequent to her sacking*). □ **subsequently** *adv.* [Latin *sequor* follow]

**subservient** /suhb-**ser**-vee-uhnt/ *adj.* **1** cringing; servile. **2** (usu. foll. by *to*) subordinate. □ **subservience** *n.* [Latin *subservio*]

**subset** *n.* *Math.* set of which all the elements are contained in another set.

**subshrub** *n.* low-growing or small shrub.

**subside** /suhb-**suyd**/ *v.* (**-ding**) **1** become tranquil; abate (*excitement subsided*). **2** (of water etc.) sink. **3** (of the ground) cave in; sink. □ **subsidence** /suhb-**suy**-duhns, **sub**-suh-duhns/ *n.* [Latin *subsido*]

**subsidiary** /suhb-**sij**-uh-ree/ — *adj.* **1** supplementary; auxiliary. **2** (of a company) controlled by another. — *n.* (*pl.* **-ies**) subsidiary thing, person, or company. [Latin: related to SUBSIDY]

**subsidise** /**sub**-suh-,duyz/ *v.* (also **-ize**) (**-sing** or **-zing**) **1** pay a subsidy to. **2** partially pay for by subsidy.

**subsidy** /**sub**-suh-dee/ *n.* (*pl.* **-ies**) **1** money granted esp. by a government to keep down the price of commodities etc. **2** any monetary grant. [Latin *subsidium* help]

**subsist** /suhb-**sist**/ *v.* **1** (often foll. by *on*) keep oneself alive; be kept alive. **2** remain in being; exist. [Latin *subsisto*]

**subsistence** /suhb-**sis**-tuhns/ *n.* **1** state or instance of subsisting. **2 a** means of support; livelihood. **b** (often *attrib.*) minimal level of existence or income.

**subsistence farming** *n.* farming which supports the farmer's household but produces no surplus for sale.

**subsistence level** *n.* a standard of living providing only the barest necessities of life.

**subsoil** /**sub**-soil/ *n.* soil immediately under the surface soil.

**subsonic** /sub-**son**-ik/ *adj.* of speeds less than that of sound.

**substance** /**sub**-stuhns/ *n.* **1 a** essential material, esp. solid, forming a thing (*the substance was transparent*). **b** particular kind of material having uniform properties (*this substance is salt*). **2 a** reality; solidity (*ghosts have no substance*). **b** seriousness or steadiness of character (*there is no substance in him*). **3** content or essence as opposed to form etc. (*substance of his remarks*). **4** wealth and possessions (*woman of substance*). **5** *Philos.* the essential nature of a thing, that which makes it what it is (as opposed to its *accidents* such as colour, shape, external appearances, etc.). □ **in substance** generally; essentially. [Latin *substantia*]

**substandard** /sub-**stan**-duhd/ *adj.* of less than the required or normal quality or size.

**substantial** /suhb-**stan**-shuhl/ *adj.* **1 a** of real importance or value (*a substantial contribution*). **b** large in size or amount (*awarded her substantial damages*). **2** solid; sturdy (*a man of substantial build*; *a substantial house*). **3** commercially successful; wealthy (*a substantial businessman*). **4** essential; largely true (*the substantial truth*). **5** real; existing. □ **substantially** *adv.* [Latin: related to SUBSTANCE]

**substantiate** /suhb-**stan**-shee-,ayt/ *v.* (**-ting**) prove the truth of (a charge, claim, etc.). □ **substantiation** /-ay-shuhn/ *n.*

**substantive** /sub-stuhn-tiv, sub-**stan**-tiv/ — *adj.* **1** genuine, actual, real. **2** not slight; substantial. — *n. Gram.* = NOUN. □ **substantively** *adv.*

**substitute** /sub-stuh-,tyoot/ — *n.* (also *attrib.*) person or thing acting or used in place of another. — *v.* (**-ting**) (often foll. by *for*) (cause to) act as a substitute. □ **substitution** /-tyoo-shuhn/ *n.* [Latin *substituo -tut-*]

**substratum** /sub-,strah-tuhm, -,stray-tuhm/ *n.* (*pl.* **-ta**) underlying layer or substance.

**subsume** /suhb-**syoom**/ *v.* (**-ming**) (usu. foll. by *under*) include (an instance, idea, category, etc.) in a rule, class, etc. (*many differing Aboriginal dialects are subsumed under the one name 'The Western Desert Language'*). □ **subsumable** *adj.* **subsumption** *n.* [Latin *sumo* take]

**subtenant** /sub-,ten-uhnt/ *n.* person renting a room etc. from its tenant. □ **subtenancy** *n.* (*pl.* **-ies**).

**subtend** /sub-**tend**/ *v.* (of a line) be opposite (an angle or arc). [Latin: related to TEND[1]]

**subterfuge** /sub-tuh-,fyooj/ *n.* **1 a** an attempt to avoid blame or defeat esp. by lying or deceit. **b** a statement etc. used for such a purpose. **2** this as a practice or policy. [Latin]

**subterranean** /,sub-tuh-**ray**-nee-uhn/ *adj.* **1** underground. **2** secret, concealed. [Latin *terra* land]

**subtext** *n.* underlying theme.

**subtitle** /sub-,tuy-tuhl/ — *n.* **1** secondary or additional title of a book etc. **2** caption on a film etc., esp. translating dialogue. — *v.* (**-ling**) provide with a subtitle or subtitles.

**subtle** /sut-uhl/ *adj.* (**subtler, subtlest**) **1** elusive, mysterious; hard to grasp (*subtle charm*; *a subtle distinction*). **2** (of scent,

colour, etc.) faint, delicate (*a subtle perfume*). **3 a** capable of making fine distinctions; perceptive (*subtle intellect*). **b** ingenious (*subtle device*). □ **subtlety** *n.* (*pl.* **-ies**). **subtly** *adv.* [Latin *subtilis*]

**subtotal** *n.* total of one part of a group of figures to be added.

**subtract** /suhb-**trakt**/ *v.* (often foll. by *from*) deduct (a number etc.) from another. □ **subtraction** /-**trak**-shuhn/ *n.* [Latin *subtraho* draw away]

**subtropics** /sub-**trop**-iks/ *n.pl.* regions adjacent to the tropics. □ **subtropical** *adj.*

**suburb** /**sub**-erb/ *n.* (outlying) esp. residential, district of a city. [Latin *urbs* city]

**suburban** /suh-**ber**-buhn/ *adj.* **1** of or characteristic of suburbs. **2** *derog.* provincial in outlook; uncultured. □ **suburbanite** *n.*

**suburbia** /suh-**ber**-bee-uh/ *n.* often *derog.* suburbs, their inhabitants, and their way of life.

**subversive** /suhb-**ver**-siv/ — *adj.* seeking to subvert (esp. a government). — *n.* subversive person. □ **subversion** *n.* **subversively** *adv.* **subversiveness** *n.* [medieval Latin *subversivus*: related to SUBVERT]

**subvert** /suhb-**vert**/ *v.* overthrow or weaken (government, religion, morality, etc.). [Latin *verto vers-* turn]

**subway** /**sub**-way/ *n.* pedestrian tunnel beneath a road etc.

**suc-** *prefix* assim. form of SUB- before *c*.

**succeed** /suhk-**seed**/ *v.* **1 a** (often foll. by *in*) accomplish one's purpose; have success; prosper. **b** (of a plan etc.) be successful. **2** follow; come next after (*night succeeded day*). **3** (often foll. by *to*) come into an inheritance, office, title, or property (*succeeded to the throne*). **4** take the place of (*she succeeded him as manager*). [Latin *succedo -cess-* come after]

**success** /suhk-**ses**/ *n.* **1** accomplishment of an aim; favourable outcome. **2** attainment of wealth, fame, or position. **3** successful thing or person. [Latin: related to SUCCEED]

**successful** *adj.* having success; prosperous. □ **successfully** *adv.*

**succession** /suhk-**sesh**-uhn/ *n.* **1 a** process of following in order; succeeding. **b** series of things or people one after another. **2 a** right of succeeding to the throne, an office, inheritance, etc. **b** act or process of so succeeding. **c** those having such a right. **3** *Biol.* order of development of a species or community. □ **in succession** one after another.

**successive** /suhk-**ses**-iv/ *adj.* following one after another; consecutive. □ **successively** *adv.*

**successor** /suhk-**ses**-uh/ *n.* (often foll. by *to*) person or thing that succeeds another.

**succinct** /suhk-**singkt**/ *adj.* brief; concise. □ **succinctly** *adv.* **succinctness** *n.* [Latin *cingo cinct-* gird]

**succour** /**suk**-uh/ (also **succor**) — *n.* aid, esp. in time of need. — *v.* assist or aid (esp. a person in danger or distress). [Latin *succurro* run to help]

**succubus** /**suk**-yuh-buhs/ *n.* (*pl.* **-buses** or **-bi** /-buy/ ) female demon formerly believed to have sexual intercourse with sleeping men (cf. INCUBUS). [Latin, = prostitute]

**succulent** /**suk**-yuh-luhnt/ — *adj.* **1** juicy; palatable. **2** *Bot.* (of a plant, its leaves, or stems) thick and fleshy. — *n.* *Bot.* succulent plant. □ **succulence** *n.* [Latin *succus* juice]

**succumb** /suh-**kum**/ *v.* (usu. foll. by *to*) **1** surrender; be overcome (*succumbed to temptation*). **2** die (from) (*succumbed to his injuries*). [Latin *cumbo* lie]

**such** — *adj.* **1** (often foll. by *as*) of the kind or degree in question or under consideration (*such people; people such as these*). **2** so great or extreme (*not such a fool as that*). **3** of a more than normal kind or degree (*such an enjoyable evening*). **4** of the kind or degree already indicated, or implied by the context (*there are no such things; such is life*). — *pron.* such a person or persons; such a thing or things (*such will inherit the kingdom of heaven*; *such was not my intention*; *brought sandwiches and such*). □ **as such** as being what has been indicated or named; in itself (*there is no theatre as such*). **such as 1** a kind that; like (*a person such as we all admire*). **2** for example (*insects, such as moths and bees*). [Old English, = so like]

**such-and-such** — *attrib. adj.* of a particular kind but not needing to be specified. — *n.* such a person or thing.

**suck** — *v.* **1** draw (a liquid, air, etc.) into the mouth by suction. **2** (also *absol.*) draw fluid from (a thing) in this way (*sucking her breast; sucked the orange dry; the infant is sucking*). **3** extract or draw (moisture, sustenance, goodness, etc.) from or out of a thing (*plants suck goodness from the soil*). **4** roll the tongue round (a sweet, a thumb, etc.). **5** make a sucking action or sound (*sucking at his pipe*). **6** (usu. foll. by *down, in, into*) engulf or drown or draw in with (or as with) a sucking movement (*sucked into the whirlpool; got sucked into the fray*). **7** *colloq.* be contemptible or disgusting (*homework sucks; sucking sucks*). **8** = *suck up* 1 (*sucking the boss for all he's worth*). — *n.* **1** act or

period of sucking. **2** (in *pl.*; esp. as *int.*) *colloq.* **a** expression of disappointment. **b** expression of derision or amusement at another's discomfiture (*sucks to you!*). **3** = SOAK *n.* 3. □ **suck dry 1** exhaust the contents of by sucking. **2** exhaust (a person's sympathy, resources, etc.) as if by sucking. **suck in 1** absorb. **2** *colloq.* involve (a person) esp. against his or her will (*sucked him in to keep guard while they robbed the house*). **3** *colloq.* deceive (*don't be sucked in by his padre-like manner*). **suck up 1** (often foll. by *to*) *colloq.* behave obsequiously (*sucking up to the boss for all he's worth*). **2** absorb. [Old English]

**sucker** /**suk**-uh/ *n.* **1** person or thing that sucks. **2** *colloq.* **a** gullible person. **b** (foll. by *for*) person susceptible to (*a sucker for punishment*). **3 a** rubber cup etc. adhering by suction. **b** organ enabling an organism to cling to a surface by suction. **4 a** shoot springing from a root or stem below ground. **b** adventitious growth (esp. of eucalypts) from a branch or trunk that has been severed or bruised.

**sucker-bash** *colloq.* — *v.* cut down suckers or new growth on newly cleared land. — *n.* act or instance of sucker-bashing. □ **sucker-basher** *n.*

**suckhole** *colloq.* — *n.* a sycophant. — *v.* toady, crawl to.

**suckle** /**suk**-uhl/ *v.* (**-ling**) **1** feed (young) from the breast or udder. **2** feed by sucking the breast etc.

**suckling** *n.* unweaned child or animal.

**sucrose** /**soo**-krohz/ *n.* sugar from sugar cane, sugar beet, etc. [French *sucre* SUGAR]

**suction** /**suk**-shuhn/ *n.* **1** act or instance of sucking. **2 a** production of a partial vacuum by the removal of air etc. so that liquid etc. is forced in or adhesion is procured. **b** force so produced (*suction keeps the lid on*). [Latin *sugo suct-* suck]

**Sudanese** /soo-duh-**neez**/ — *adj.* of Sudan. — *n.* (*pl.* same) **1** native, national, or inhabitant of Sudan. **2** person of Sudanese descent. [*Sudan* in NE Africa]

**sudden** /**sud**-uhn/ *adj.* done or occurring unexpectedly or abruptly. □ **all of a sudden** suddenly. □ **suddenly** *adv.* **suddenness** *n.* [Latin *subitaneus*]

**sudden death** *n. colloq.* decision in a tied game etc. dependent on one move, card, etc.

**sudden infant death syndrome** *n.* = COT DEATH.

**sudorific** /syoo-duh-**rif**-ik/ — *adj.* causing sweating. — *n.* sudorific drug. [Latin *sudor* sweat]

**suds** *n.pl.* froth of soap and water. □ **sudsy** *adj.* [Low German *sudde* or Dutch *sudse* marsh, bog]

**sue** /soo/ v. (**sues, sued, suing**) **1** (also *absol.*) begin a law suit against. **2** (often foll. by *to, for*) make entreaty to a person for a favour. [Anglo-French *suer* from Latin *sequor* follow]

**suede** /swayd/ n. (often *attrib.*) **1** leather with the flesh side rubbed to a nap. **2** cloth imitating it. [French, = Sweden]

**suet** /soo-uht/ n. hard white fat on the kidneys or loins of oxen, sheep, etc. □ **suety** *adj.* [Anglo-French *seu*, from Latin *sebum*]

**suf-** *prefix* assim. form of SUB- before *f*.

**suffer** /suf-uh-/ v. **1** undergo pain, grief, damage, etc. **2** undergo, experience, or be subjected to (pain, loss, grief, defeat, change, etc.). **3** tolerate (*does not suffer fools gladly*). **4** (usu. foll. by *to* + infin.) *archaic* allow. □ **sufferer** n. [Latin *suffero*]

**sufferance** n. tacit consent. □ **on sufferance** tolerated but not encouraged. [Latin: related to SUFFER]

**suffice** /suh-**fuys**/ v. (**-cing**) **1** (often foll. by *for*, or *to* + infin.) be adequate. **2** satisfy. □ **suffice to say** I shall say only this. [Latin *sufficio*]

**sufficiency** /suh-**fish**-uhn-see/ n. (*pl.* **-ies**) (often foll. by *of*) adequate amount.

**sufficient** *adj.* sufficing, adequate. □ **sufficiently** *adv.*

**suffix** /suf-iks/ — n. letter(s) added at the end of a word to form a derivative (e.g. *-ation, -fy, -ing, -itis*). — v. append, esp. as a suffix. [Latin *figo fix-* fasten]

**suffocate** /suf-uh-,kayt/ v. (**-ting**) **1** choke or kill by stopping breathing, esp. by pressure, fumes, etc. **2** (often foll. by *by, with*) produce a choking or breathlessness in. **3** be or feel suffocated or breathless. □ **suffocating** *adj.* **suffocation** /-**kay**-shuhn/ n. [Latin *suffoco* from *fauces* throat]

**suffrage** /suf-rij/ n. right of voting in political elections. [Latin *suffragium*]

**suffragette** /,suf-ruh-**jet**/ n. *hist.* woman seeking suffrage through organised protest.

**suffuse** /suh-**fyooz**/ v. (**-sing**) overspread as with a fluid, a colour, a gleam of light (*a blush suffused his cheeks*). □ **suffusion** /-**fyoo**-zhuhn/ n. [Latin *suffundo* pour over]

**sug-** *prefix* assim. form of SUB- before *g*.

**sugar** /**shuug**-uh/ — n. **1** sweet crystalline substance esp. from sugar cane and sugar beet, used in cookery etc.; sucrose. **2** *Chem.* soluble usu. sweet crystalline carbohydrate, e.g. glucose. — v. **1** sweeten or coat with sugar. **2** make (one's words, meaning, etc.) more pleasant or welcome. [French *sukere*, from Arabic *sukkar*]

**sugar ant** n. any of several related stingless Australian ants, esp. one with an orange thorax and legs and black head.

**sugar bag** n. **1** (in Aboriginal English) **a** honey of the wild Australian stingless bee; its honeycomb or hive. **b** bee of any kind; the honey of such a bee. **c** = HONEY-ANT. **2** bag of fine sacking, orig. made for containing sugar, and used subsequently for a variety of purposes (e.g. as a shopping-bag, a small matilda, etc.).

**sugar beet** n. beet yielding sugar.

**sugar cane** n. tropical grass yielding sugar.

**sugar cocky** n. (also **cane cocky**) proprietor of a sugar cane farm.

**sugar daddy** n. *colloq.* elderly man who lavishes gifts on, or maintains, a young person in return for sexual favours.

**sugar glider** n. gliding possum of northern and eastern Australia including Tasmania, feeding on nectar, insects, etc.

**sugar gum** n. any of several eucalypts, esp. *E. cladocalyx* of southern SA, widely planted as a windbreak.

**sugar pea** n. (also **sugar pod, snow pea**) variety of pea, used esp. in Asian cooking, eaten whole including the pod.

**sugar soap** n. alkaline compound for cleaning or removing paint.

**sugarwood** n. **1** myoporum of eastern Australia, having a rough bark which often exudes a sugary substance, and providing an extremely sweet-smelling, sandalwood-like timber. **2** the wood of this tree.

**sugary** *adj.* **1** containing or like sugar. **2** excessively sweet or esp. sentimental. □ **sugariness** n.

**suggest** /suh-**jest**/ v. **1** (often foll. by *that*) propose (a theory, plan, etc.). **2 a** evoke (an idea etc.) (*the poem suggests peace*). **b** hint at (*his behaviour suggests guilt*). □ **suggest itself** (of an idea etc.) come into the mind. [Latin *suggero -gest-*]

**suggestible** *adj.* **1** open to suggestion; easily swayed. **2** capable of being suggested. □ **suggestibility** /-**bil**-uh-tee/ n.

**suggestion** /suh-**jes**-chuhn/ n. **1** act or instance of suggesting or state of being suggested. **2** theory, plan, etc., suggested. **3** slight trace, hint (*a suggestion of garlic*). **4** *Psychol.* insinuation of a belief etc. into the mind. [Latin: related to SUGGEST]

**suggestive** /suh-**jes**-tiv/ *adj.* **1** (usu. foll. by *of*) hinting (at). **2** (of a remark, joke, etc.) indecent. □ **suggestively** *adv.*

**suicidal** /,soo-uh-**suy**-duhl/ *adj.* **1** inclined to commit suicide. **2** of or concerning suicide. **3** self-destructive; rash. □ **suicidally** *adv.*

**suicide** /soo-uh-,suyd/ — n. **1 a** intentional killing of oneself. **b** person who commits suicide. **2** self-destructive action or course (*political suicide*). — v. commit suicide. [Latin *sui* of oneself, -CIDE]

**sui generis** /ˌsoo-uy **jen**-uh-ris, ˌsoo-ee, ˌsyoo-uy/ *adj.* of its own kind; unique. [Latin]

**suit** /soot/ — *n.* **1** set of matching clothes, usu. a jacket and trousers or skirt. **2** (esp. in *comb.*) clothes for a special purpose (*swimsuit*). **3** any of the four sets (spades, hearts, diamonds, clubs) making up a pack of cards. **4** lawsuit. **5 a** petition, esp. to a person in authority. **b** *archaic* courting a woman (*paid suit to her*). — *v.* **1** go well with (a person's appearance etc.). **2** (also *absol.*) meet the demands or requirements of; satisfy; agree with (*does not suit all tastes; that date will suit*). **3** make fitting; accommodate; adapt (*suited his style to his audience*). **4** (as **suited** *adj.*) appropriate; well-fitted (*not suited to be a nurse*). □ **follow suit** see FOLLOW. **suit oneself** do as one chooses. [Anglo-French *siute*]

**suitable** *adj.* (usu. foll. by *to, for*) well-fitted; appropriate. □ **suitability** /-bil-uh-tee/ *n.* **suitably** *adv.*

**suitcase** *n.* case for carrying clothes etc., with a handle and a flat hinged lid.

**suite** /sweet/ *n.* **1** set of things belonging together, esp. **a** a set of rooms in a hotel etc. **b** a sofa and armchairs etc. of the same design. **2** *Mus.* set of instrumental pieces performed as a unit. [French: related to SUIT]

**suitor** /soo-tuh/ *n.* **1** man wooing a woman. **2** plaintiff or petitioner in a lawsuit. [Anglo-French from Latin]

**sulfur** etc. var. of SULPHUR etc.

**sulk** — *v.* be sulky. — *n.* **1** (also in *pl.*, prec. by *the*) period of sullen resentful silence. **2** person who sulks. □ **sulker** *n.* [perhaps a back-formation from SULKY]

**sulky** — *adj.* (**-ier, -iest**) **1** sullen or silent, esp. from resentment or bad temper. **2** (in Aboriginal English) angry, threatening. — *n.* (*pl.* **sulkies**) light two-wheeled horse-drawn vehicle for one, esp. used in trotting-races. □ **sulkily** *adv.* **sulkiness** *n.* [perhaps from obsolete *sulke* hard to dispose of]

**sullen** /**sul**-uhn/ *adj.* **1** passively resentful, sulky, morose. **2** dismal, melancholy (*a sullen sky*). □ **sullenly** *adv.* **sullenness** *n.* [Anglo-French *sol* SOLE³]

**sully** /**sul**-ee/ *v.* (**-ies, -ied**) disgrace or tarnish (a reputation etc.). [French *souiller*: related to SOIL²]

**sulpha** /**sul**-fuh/ *n.* any of various sulphonamides (often *attrib.*: *sulpha drug*). [abbreviation]

**sulphate** /**sul**-fayt/ *n.* salt or ester of sulphuric acid. [Latin SULPHUR]

**sulphide** /**sul**-fuyd/ *n.* binary compound of sulphur.

**sulphite** /**sul**-fuyt/ *n.* salt or ester of sulphurous acid. [French: related to SULPHATE]

**sulphonamide** /sul-**fon**-uh-ˌmuyd/ *n.* any of a class of antibiotic drugs containing sulphur. [German *Sulfon* (related to SULPHUR)]

**sulphur** /**sul**-fuh/ *n.* **1** (also **sulfur**) pale yellow non-metallic element burning with a blue flame and a suffocating smell. **2** pale greenish-yellow colour. [Anglo-French from Latin]

**sulphur-crested cockatoo** *n.* = WHITE COCKATOO.

**sulphur dioxide** *n.* colourless pungent gas formed by burning sulphur in air and dissolving in water.

**sulphureous** /sul-**fyoo**-ree-uhs/ *adj.* of or like sulphur.

**sulphuric** /sul-**fyoo**-rik/ *adj. Chem.* containing sulphur with a valency of six.

**sulphuric acid** *n.* dense oily highly corrosive acid.

**sulphurous** /**sul**-fuh-ruhs/ *adj.* **1** of or like sulphur. **2** *Chem.* containing sulphur with a valency of four.

**sulphurous acid** *n.* unstable weak acid used as a reducing and bleaching acid.

**sultan** /**sul**-tuhn/ *n.* Muslim sovereign. □ **sultanate** *n.* [Arabic]

**sultana** /sul-**tah**-nuh, suhl-/ *n.* **1 a** seedless raisin. **b** small pale yellow grape producing this. **2** sultan's mother, wife, concubine, or daughter. [Italian]

**sultry** /**sul**-tree/ *adj.* (**-ier, -iest**) **1** (of weather etc.) hot and humid. **2** (of a person etc.) passionate, sensual. □ **sultrily** *adv.* **sultriness** *n.* [obsolete *sulter* (v.): related to SWELTER]

**sum** — *n.* **1** total resulting from addition. **2** amount of money (*a large sum*). **3 a** arithmetical problem. **b** (esp. *pl.*) *colloq.* arithmetic work, esp. elementary. — *v.* (**-mm-**) find the sum of. □ **in sum** in brief. **sum up 1** (esp. of a judge) give a summing-up. **2** form or express an opinion of (a person, situation, etc.). **3** summarise. [Latin *summa*]

**summarise** /**sum**-uh-ˌruyz/ *v.* (also **-ize**) (**-sing** or **-zing**) make or be a summary of.

**summary** /**sum**-uh-ree/ — *n.* (*pl.* **-ies**) brief account or abridgment. — *adj.* **1** without details or formalities; brief. **2** without the customary legal formalities (*summary justice*). □ **summarily** *adv.* [Latin: related to SUM]

**summation** /suh-**may**-shuhn/ *n.* **1** finding of a total. **2** a summing-up.

**summer** /**sum**-uh/ *n.* **1** (often *attrib.*) warmest season of the year. **2** (often foll. by *of*) mature stage of life etc. □ **summery** *adj.* [Old English]

**summer house** n. light building in a garden etc. for sitting in in fine weather.

**summer pudding** n. pudding of soft fruit pressed in a bread case.

**summer school** n. course of summer lectures etc. held esp. at a university.

**summer solstice** n. solstice about 22 December.

**summing-up** n. **1** judge's review of evidence given to a jury. **2** recapitulation of the main points of an argument etc.

**summit** /sum-uht/ n. **1** highest point, top. **2** highest degree of power, ambition, etc. **3** (in full **summit meeting, talks,** etc.) **a** conference of heads of government. **b** conference of national leaders, organisations, etc. called upon to discuss and make recommendations about issues of national importance (*tax summit*; *youth unemployment summit*). [Latin *summus* highest]

**summon** /sum-uhn/ v. **1** order to come or appear, esp. in a lawcourt. **2** (usu. foll. by *to* + infin.) call upon (*summoned her to assist*). **3** call together (*summoned the members to attend*). **4** (often foll. by *up*) gather (courage, spirits, resources, etc.). [Latin *summoneo*]

**summons** — n. (pl. **summonses**) authoritative call to attend or do something, esp. to appear in court. — v. esp. *Law* serve with a summons.

**sumo** /soo-moh/ n. Japanese wrestling in which a wrestler is defeated by touching the ground with any part of the body except the soles of the feet or by moving outside the ring. [Japanese]

**sump** n. **1** casing holding the oil in an internal-combustion engine. **2** pit, well, hole, etc. in which superfluous liquid collects. [Low German or Dutch]

**sumptuous** /sump-choo-uhs/ adj. rich, lavish, costly. □ **sumptuously** adv. **sumptuousness** n. [Latin]

**sun** — n. **1 a** the star round which the earth orbits and from which it receives light and warmth. **b** this light or warmth. **2** any star. — v. (**-nn-**) **1** refl. bask in the sun. **2** expose to the sun. □ **under the sun** anywhere in the world. □ **sunless** adj. [Old English]

**sunbake** — v. sunbathe. — n. (period of) basking in the sun.

**sunbathe** v. (**-thing**) bask in the sun, esp. to tan the body. □ **sunbather** n.

**sunbeam** n. ray of sunlight.

**sunbird** n. any of various small birds with brilliant and variegated plumage found in tropical and sub-tropical regions of Africa, Asia, and Australia (*yellow-bellied sunbird*).

**sunblock** n. cream protecting the skin from the sun's harmful ultraviolet rays.

**sunburn** — n. inflammation of the skin from exposure to the sun. — v. suffer from sunburn. □ **sunburnt** adj. (also **sunburned**).

**suncream** n. = SUNBLOCK.

**sundae** /sun-day/ n. ice-cream with fruit, nuts, syrup, etc. [perhaps from SUNDAY]

**Sunday** /sun-day/ — n. first day of the week, a Christian holiday and day of worship (see also BIG SUNDAY). — adv. colloq. on Sunday. [Old English]

**Sunday business** n. (in Aboriginal English) religious matters (see also BUSINESS 5; BUSINESS GROUND).

**sunder** v. archaic or literary separate. [Old English]

**sundew** n. genus (about 70 species in Australia) of small, insect-consuming plants having extremely sticky hairs on the leaves, each hair tipped with a globule of nectar which gleams jewel-like in the sun and attracts insects.

**sundial** n. instrument showing the time by the shadow of a pointer in sunlight.

**sundown** n. sunset.

**sundowner** n. an itinerant, ostensibly seeking work, who times his arrival (at a station etc.) to coincide with the end of the day's work and the provision of food and bed; loafer, sponger.

**sundown way** n. (in Aboriginal English) the west.

**sundry** /sun-dree/ — adj. various; several. — n. (pl. **-ies**) **1** (in pl.) items or oddments not mentioned individually. **2** *Cricket* an extra; run scored otherwise than off the bat. [Old English: related to SUNDER]

**sunfish** n. (pl. same or **-es**) any of various almost spherical fish of Australian waters and elsewhere.

**sunflower** n. tall plant with large golden-rayed flowers grown for its seeds which yield an edible oil.

**sung** past part. of SING.

**sunglasses** n.pl. glasses tinted to protect the eyes from sunlight or glare.

**sunk** past and past part. of SINK.

**sunken** adj. **1** at a lower level; submerged. **2** (of the cheeks etc.) hollow, depressed. [past part. of SINK]

**sunlamp** n. lamp giving ultraviolet rays for therapy, to tan, etc.

**sunlight** n. light from the sun.

**sunlit** adj. illuminated by sunlight.

**Sunni** /sun-ee/ — n. (pl. same or **-s**) **1** one of the two main branches of Islam, accepting law based not only on the Koran, but on Muhammad's words and acts. **2** adherent of this branch. — adj. (also **Sunnite**) of or relating to Sunni. [Arabic *Sunna* = way, rule]

**sunnies** *n.pl. colloq.* a pair of sun-glasses.

**sunny** *adj.* (**-ier, -iest**) **1** bright with or warmed by sunlight. **2** cheery, bright. □ **sunnily** *adv.* **sunniness** *n.*

**sun orchid** *n.* any of several species of Australian terrestrial orchid with highly colourful flowers (see THELYMITRA).

**sunrise** *n.* **1** sun's rising. **2** time of this.

**sunrise industry** *n.* any newly established industry, esp. in electronics, telecommunications, etc., regarded as signalling prosperity.

**sunrise way** *n.* (in Aboriginal English) the east.

**sunroof** *n.* panel in a car's roof that can be opened.

**sunscreen** *n.* = SUNBLOCK.

**sunset** *n.* **1** sun's setting. **2** time of this.

**sunshade** *n.* parasol; awning.

**sunshine** *n.* **1 a** light of the sun. **b** area lit by the sun. **2** cheerfulness.

**Sunshine State** *n.* Queensland.

**sunshine wattle** *n.* dense wattle of NSW, Victoria, and Tasmania, having deep yellow flowers which 'light up' the gloom of winter.

**sunspot** *n.* dark patch on the sun's surface.

**sunstroke** *n.* acute prostration from excessive exposure to the sun.

**suntan** *n.* brownish skin colour caused by exposure to the sun. □ **suntanned** *adj.*

**sup**[1] *v.* (**-pp-**) take by sips or spoonfuls. [Old English]

**sup**[2] *v.* (**-pp-**) *archaic* take supper. [French]

**sup-** *prefix* assim. form of SUB- before *p*.

**super** /soo-puh/ — *adj.* (also as *int.*) *colloq.* excellent; splendid. — *n. colloq.* **1** superintendent. **2** supernumerary. **3** superphosphate. **4** superannuation. **5 a** petrol of a high-octane grade. **b** leaded petrol (opp. *unleaded petrol*). [shortening of words beginning *super-*]

**super-** *comb. form* forming nouns, adjectives, and verbs, meaning: **1** above, beyond, or over (*superstructure*; *supernormal*). **2** to an extreme degree (*superabundant*). **3** extra good or large of its kind (*supertanker*). **4** of a higher kind (*superintendent*). [Latin]

**superabundant** /,soo-puh-ruh-**bun**-duhnt/ *adj.* abounding beyond what is normal or right. □ **superabundance** *n.* [Latin: related to SUPER-, ABOUND]

**superannuate** /,soo-puh-**ran**-yoo-,ayt/ *v.* (**-ting**) **1** pension (a person) off. **2** dismiss or discard as too old. **3** (as **superannuated** *adj.*) too old for work or use. [Latin *annus* year]

**superannuation** /,soo-puh-,ran-yoo-**ay**-shuhn/ *n.* **1** pension paid on retirement to a worker who has contributed to a superannuation scheme. **2** payment towards this by an employed person.

**superb** /soo-**perb**, suh-/ *adj.* **1** excellent. **2** magnificent. □ **superbly** *adv.* [Latin, = proud]

**superb blue wren** *n.* (also **superb fairy wren**) small bird of south-eastern Australia, the breeding male having light blue and dark blue plumage.

**superb lyre-bird** *n.* greyish-brown lyrebird of south-eastern Australia, the male having a magnificent lyre-shaped taildisplay, dark on the outside and silvery on the inside, and a superb song, including uncanny mimicry of forest sounds, the songs and calls of other birds, etc.

**superb parrot** *n.* magnificent bright green parrot with a golden face and vermilion throat, inhabiting inland south-eastern Australia.

**supercargo** /soo-puh-,kah-goh/ *n.* (*pl.* **-es**) officer in a merchant ship managing sales etc. of cargo. [Spanish *sobrecargo*]

**supercharge** /soo-puh-,chahj/ *v.* (**-ging**) **1** (usu. foll. by *with*) charge (the atmosphere etc.) with energy, emotion, etc. **2** use a supercharger on.

**supercharger** *n.* device supplying air or fuel to an internal-combustion engine at above atmospheric pressure to increase efficiency.

**supercilious** /,soo-puh-**sil**-ee-uhs/ *adj.* contemptuous; haughty. □ **superciliously** *adv.* **superciliousness** *n.* [Latin *supercilium* eyebrow]

**supercomputer** *n.* powerful computer capable of dealing with complex problems.

**superconductivity** /,soo-puh-,kon-duk-tiv-uh-tee/ *n. Physics* property of certain metals, at temperatures near absolute zero, of having no electrical resistance, so that once a current is started it flows without a voltage to keep it going. □ **superconducting** /-kuhn-**duk**-ting/ *adj.*

**superconductor** *n. Physics* substance having superconductivity.

**superego** /,soo-puhr-**ee**-goh/ *n.* (*pl.* **-s**) *Psychol.* part of the mind that acts as a conscience and responds to social rules.

**superficial** /,soo-puh-**fish**-uhl/ *adj.* **1** of or on the surface; lacking depth (*superficial knowledge*; *superficial wound*). **2** swift or cursory (*superficial examination*). **3** apparent but not real (*superficial resemblance*). **4** (esp. of a person) shallow. □ **superficiality** /-ee-al-uh-tee/ *n.* **superficially** *adv.* [Latin: related to FACE]

**superfine** /soo-puh-,fuyn/ *adj. Commerce* of extra quality (*superfine wool*). [Latin: related to FINE[1]]

**superfluity** /,soo-puh-**floo**-uh-tee/ *n.* (*pl.*

**-ies) 1** state of being superfluous. **2** superfluous amount or thing. [Latin *fluo* to flow]

**superfluous** /soo-**per**-floo-uhs/ *adj.* more than is needed or wanted; unnecessary. [Latin *fluo* to flow]

**superhuman** /ˌsoo-puh-**hyoo**-muhn/ *adj.* exceeding normal human capability.

**superimpose** /ˌsoo-puh-rim-**pohz**/ *v.* (**-sing**) (usu. foll. by *on*) lay (a thing) on something else. □ **superimposition** /-puh-**zish**-uhn/ *n.*

**superintend** /ˌsoo-puh-rin-**tend**/ *v.* supervise, direct. □ **superintendence** *n.*

**superintendent** /ˌsoo-puh-rin-**ten**-duhnt/ *n.* **1** police officer above the rank of chief inspector. **2** a person who superintends. **b** director of an institution etc.

**superior** /soo-**peer**-ree-uh, suh-/ *— adj.* **1** in a higher position; of higher rank. **2 a** high-quality (*superior leather*). **b** supercilious (*had a superior air*). **3** (often foll. by *to*) better or greater in some respect (*superior to its rivals in speed*). **4** written or printed above the line. *— n.* **1** person superior to another in rank, character, etc. (*envies his superiors*; *is his superior in courage*). **2** head of a monastery, convent, etc. (*Mother Superior*). □ **superiority** /soo-ˌpeer-ree-o-ruh-tee, suh-/ *n.* [Latin comparative of *superus* above]

**superlative** /soo-**per**-luh-tiv/ *— adj.* **1** of the highest quality or degree; excellent (*superlative wisdom*). **2** *Gram.* (of an adjective or adverb) expressing the highest degree of a quality (e.g. *bravest*, *most fiercely*). *— n.* **1** *Gram.* superlative form of an adjective or adverb. **2** (in *pl.*) high praise; exaggerated language. [French from Latin]

**superman** /**soo**-puh-ˌman/ *n.* **1** *colloq.* man of exceptional strength or ability. **2** esp. *Philos.* ideal superior person of the future (esp. as envisaged by the German philosopher Nietzsche).

**supermarket** /**soo**-puh-ˌmah-kuht/ *n.* large self-service store selling food, household goods, etc.

**supernatural** /ˌsoo-puh-**nach**-uh-ruhl/ *— adj.* not attributable to, or explicable by, the laws of nature; magical; mystical. *— n.* (prec. by *the*) supernatural forces, effects, etc. □ **supernaturally** *adv.*

**supernova** /ˌsoo-puh-**noh**-vuh/ *n.* (*pl.* **-vae** /-vee/ or **-s**) star increasing suddenly in brightness.

**supernumerary** /ˌsoo-puh-**nyoo**-muh-ruh-ree/ *— adj.* **1** in excess of the normal number; extra. **2** engaged for extra work. **3** (of an actor) appearing on stage but not speaking. *— n.* (*pl.* **-ies**) supernumerary person or thing. [Latin: related to NUMBER]

**superphosphate** /ˌsoo-puh-**fos**-fayt/ *n.* fertiliser made from phosphate rock.

**superpower** *n.* extremely powerful nation.

**superscript** /**soo**-puh-skript/ *— adj.* written or printed above the line (e.g. 2 in *snuff²*). *— n.* superscript number or symbol. [Latin *scribo* write]

**supersede** /ˌsoo-puh-**seed**/ *v.* (**-ding**) **1** take the place of. **2** replace with another person or thing. □ **supersession** /-**sesh**-uhn/ *n.* [Latin *supersedeo*]

**supersonic** /ˌsoo-puh-**son**-ik/ *adj.* of or having a speed greater than that of sound. □ **supersonically** *adv.*

**superstar** *n.* extremely famous or renowned actor, musician, etc.

**superstition** /ˌsoo-puh-**stish**-uhn/ *n.* **1** belief in the supernatural; irrational fear of the unknown. **2** practice, belief, or religion based on this. **3** widely held but unjustified idea of the effects or nature of a thing (*the superstition that you should not open an umbrella inside the house*). □ **superstitious** *adj.* **superstitiously** *adv.* [Latin]

**superstructure** /**soo**-puh-ˌstruk-chuh/ *n.* **1** the part of a building above its foundations. **2** structure built on top of another.

**supervene** /ˌsoo-puh-**veen**/ *v.* (**-ning**) *formal* occur as an interruption or change. □ **supervention** /-**ven**-shuhn/ *n.* [Latin *supervenio*]

**supervise** /**soo**-puh-ˌvuyz/ *v.* (**-sing**) superintend, oversee. □ **supervision** /-**vizh**-uhn/ *n.* **supervisor** *n.* **supervisory** *adj.* [Latin *supervideo -vis-*]

**supine** /**soo**-puyn/ *adj.* **1** lying face upwards. **2** inert, indolent. [Latin]

**supper** *n.* **1** late evening snack. **2** light evening meal taken as part of or following a social event. [French *souper*]

**supplant** /suh-**plahnt**, -**plant**/ *v.* take the place of. [Latin *supplanto* trip up]

**supple** /**sup**-uhl/ *adj.* (**suppler**, **supplest**) flexible, pliant. □ **suppleness** *n.* [Latin *supplex*]

**supplejack** *n.* any of several Australian plants having tough, flexible stems, esp. *Flagellaria indica* of rainforests in Queensland, NSW, and the NT, a tree which, unable to support itself, grows along the ground until it encounters a 'host', whereupon it grows upwards with very great vigour.

**supplement** *— n.* /**sup**-luh-muhnt/ **1** thing or part added to improve or provide further information. **2** separate section, esp. a colour magazine, of a newspaper etc. *— v.* /**sup**-luh-muhnt, -ˌment/ provide a supplement for. □ **supplemental**

/-men-tuhl/ *adj.* **supplementary** /ˌsup-luh-**men**-tuh-ree, -tree/ *adj.* **supplementation** /-**tay**-shuhn/ *n.* [Latin *suppleo* supply]

**suppliant** /**sup**-lee-uhnt/ — *adj.* supplicating. — *n.* supplicating person. [Latin: related to SUPPLICATE]

**supplicate** /**sup**-luh-ˌkayt/ *v.* (**-ting**) *literary* **1** petition humbly to (a person) or for (a thing). **2** (foll. by *to, for*) make a petition. □ **supplicant** *adj. & n.* **supplication** /-**kay**-shuhn/ *n.* **supplicatory** *adj.* [Latin *supplico*]

**supply** /suh-**pluy**/ — *v.* (**-ies, -ied**) **1** provide (a thing needed). **2** (often foll. by *with*) provide (a person etc. with a thing). **3** meet or make up for (a deficiency or need etc.). — *n.* (*pl.* **-ies**) **1** act or instance of providing what is needed. **2** stock, store, amount, etc., of something provided or obtainable. **3** (in *pl.*) provisions and equipment for an army, expedition, etc. **4** grant of money by parliament for the costs of government (*the opposition threatened to block supply in the Senate*). □ **in short supply** scarce. **supply and demand** *Econ.* quantities available and required, as factors regulating price. □ **supplier** *n.* [Latin *suppleo* fill up]

**supply-side** *attrib. adj. Econ.* denoting a policy of low taxation etc. to encourage production and investment.

**support** /suh-**pawt**/ — *v.* **1** carry all or part of the weight of; keep from falling, sinking, or failing. **2** provide for (a family etc.). **3** strengthen, encourage. **4** bear out; tend to substantiate (a statement, charge, theory, etc.). **5** give help or approval to (a person, team, sport, etc.); further (a cause etc.). **6** speak in favour of (a resolution etc.). **7** (also *absol.*) take a secondary part to (a principal actor etc.); perform a secondary act to (the main act) at a pop concert etc. — *n.* **1** act or instance of supporting or process of being supported. **2** person or thing that supports. **3** secondary act at a pop concert etc. □ **in support of** so as to support. [Latin *porto* carry]

**supporter** *n.* person or thing that supports, esp. a person supporting a team or sport.

**supportive** *adj.* providing (esp. emotional) support or encouragement. □ **supportively** *adv.* **supportiveness** *n.*

**suppose** /suh-**pohz**/ *v.* (**-sing**) (often foll. by *that*) **1** assume; be inclined to think (*what do you suppose he meant?*). **2** take as a possibility or hypothesis (*let us suppose you are right*). **3** (in *imper.*) as a formula of proposal (*suppose we try again*). **4** (of a theory or result etc.) require as a condition (*that supposes we're on time*). **5** (in *imper.* or *pres. part.*) forming a question in the circumstances that; if

(*suppose he won't let you?*; *supposing we stay?*). **6** (as **supposed** *adj.*) presumed (*his supposed brother*). **7** (in *passive*; foll. by *to* + *infin.*) **a** be expected or required (*was supposed to write to you*). **b** (with *neg.*) ought not; not be allowed to (*you are not supposed to go in there*). □ **I suppose so** expression of hesitant agreement. [French: related to POSE]

**supposedly** /suh-**pohz**-uhd-lee/ *adv.* allegedly; as is generally believed.

**supposition** /ˌsup-uh-**zish**-uhn/ *n.* **1** thing supposed. **2** act or instance of supposing. □ **suppositional** *adj.*

**suppositious** /ˌsup-uh-**zish**-uhs/ *adj.* hypothetical.

**supposititious** /suh-ˌpoz-i-**tish**-uhs/ *adj.* spurious. [Latin *pono posit-* place]

**suppository** /suh-**poz**-uh-tuh-ree, -tree/ *n.* (*pl.* **-ies**) medical preparation melting in the rectum or vagina. [Latin *suppositorius* placed underneath]

**suppress** /suh-**pres**/ *v.* **1** put an end to, esp. forcibly (*suppressed the rebellion*). **2** prevent (information, feelings, a reaction, etc.) from being seen, heard, or known (*tried to suppress the report*; *suppressed a yawn*). **3** *Psychol.* keep out of one's consciousness. □ **suppressible** *adj.* **suppression** *n.* **suppressor** *n.* [Latin: related to PRESS¹]

**suppurate** /**sup**-yuh-ˌrayt/ *v.* (**-ting**) **1** form pus. **2** fester. □ **suppuration** /-**ray**-shuhn/ *n.* [Latin: related to PUS]

**supra** /**soo**-pruh, **syoo**-/ *adv.* above or earlier (in a book etc.). [Latin]

**supremacy** /soo-**prem**-uh-see/ *n.* (*pl.* **-ies**) **1** state of being supreme. **2** highest authority.

**supreme** /soo-**preem**, suh-/ *adj.* **1** highest in authority or rank. **2** greatest; most important. **3** (of a penalty or sacrifice etc.) involving death. □ **supremely** *adv.* [Latin]

**Supreme Court** *n.* highest judicial court in an Australian State.

**supremo** /soo-**pree**-moh/ *n.* (*pl.* **-s**) person in overall charge. [Spanish, = SUPREME]

**sur-¹** *prefix* = SUPER- (*surcharge*; *surrealism*). [French]

**sur-²** *prefix* assim. form of SUB- before *r*.

**surcharge** — *n.* /**ser**-chahj/ additional charge or payment. — *v.* /**ser**-chahj, ser-**chahj**/ (**-ging**) exact a surcharge from. [French: related to SUR-¹]

**surd** *n.* a mathematical quantity (esp. a root) that cannot be expressed in finite terms of whole numbers or quantities; an irrational number. [Latin, = deaf]

**sure** /shaw/ — *adj.* **1** (often foll. by *of* or *that*) convinced. **2** having adequate reason for a belief or assertion. **3** (foll. by *of*) confident in anticipation or knowledge of. **4** reliable or unfailing (*there is one sure way to find out*). **5** (foll. by *to* + infin.) certain (*she is sure to be there*). **6** undoubtedly true or truthful. — *adv. colloq.* certainly. □ **be sure** (in *imper.* or *infin.*; foll. by *that* + clause or *to* + infin.) take care to; not fail to. **for sure** *colloq.* certainly. **make sure** make or become certain; ensure. **sure enough** *colloq.* in fact; certainly. **sure thing 1** a certainty; secure prospect. **2** *colloq.* certainly. **to be sure** admittedly; indeed, certainly. □ **sureness** *n.* [French from Latin *securus*]

**sure-fire** *attrib. adj. colloq.* certain to succeed.

**surely** *adv.* **1** with certainty or safety (*slowly but surely*). **2** as an appeal to likelihood or reason (*surely that can't be right*).

**surety** /**shaw**-ruh-tee/ *n.* (*pl.* **-ies**) **1** money given as a guarantee of performance etc. **2** (esp. in phr. **stand surety for**) person who takes responsibility for another's debt, obligation, etc. [French from Latin]

**surf** — *n.* **1 a** swell of the sea breaking on the shore or reefs. **b** the foam caused by this. **2** the surf as a place of recreation. **3** a swim in the surf, esp. with the intention of riding waves; the riding of a wave. — *v.* **1** swim in the surf. **2 a** ride waves on a board. **b** = BODY SURF. **3** surf at (a specified place) (*have you surfed North Narrabeen yet?*). **4** ride the electronic waves (of the Internet). □ **surf the Internet** spend time exploring various locations on the Internet. □ **surfer** *n.* **surfing** *n.* [origin unknown]

**surface** /**ser**-fuhs/ — *n.* **1 a** the outside of a thing. **b** area of this. **2** any of the limits of a solid. **3** top of a liquid or of the ground etc. **4** outward aspect of anything; what is apparent on a casual view or consideration (*presents a large surface to view; all is quiet on the surface, but . . .*). **5** *Geom.* set of points with length and breadth but no thickness. **6** (*attrib.*) **a** of or on the surface (*surface area*). **b** superficial (*surface politeness*). — *v.* (**-cing**) **1** give the required surface to (a road, paper, etc.). **2** rise or bring to the surface. **3** become visible or known. **4** *colloq.* **a** wake up; get up. **b** arrive (at a place); finally appear. □ **come to the surface** become perceptible. [French: related to SUR-¹]

**surface mail** *n.* mail carried by land or sea.

**surface tension** *n.* tension of the surface-film of a liquid, tending to minimise its surface area.

**surf beach** *n.* beach from which people surf.

**surfboard** *n.* long narrow board used in surfing. □ **surfboarding** *n.*

**surfboat** *n.* oared boat designed for rescue work etc. in the surf.

**surf carnival** *n.* competitive display of the skills of a surf life-saver.

**surf club** *n.* = SURF LIFE-SAVING CLUB.

**surfeit** /**ser**-fuht/ — *n.* **1** an excess, esp. in eating or drinking. **2** feeling of fullness or disgust resulting from this. — *v.* (**-t-**) **1** overfeed. **2** (foll. by *with*) (cause to) be wearied through excess. [French: related to SUR-¹, FEAT]

**surfie** /**ser**-fee/ *colloq.* — *n.* (also **surfy**) **1** surfer, esp. one dedicated to surfboard-riding. **2** *derog.* person (usu. with bleached hair etc.) who frequents surf beaches, esp. in a gang, and does little or no actual surfing. — *adj.* of or pertaining to a surfie (*surfie chicks*).

**surfing** *n.* sport of riding the surf on a board or as a body surfer.

**surf life-saver** *n.* member of a surf life-saving club.

**surf life-saving club** *n.* **1** voluntary organisation formed to safeguard lives in the surf. **2** premises of such an organisation.

**surf ski** *n.* long narrow board propelled with a paddle by the rider.

**surge** — *n.* **1** sudden rush. **2** heavy forward or upward motion. **3** sudden increase in price, activity, etc. **4** sudden increase in voltage of an electric current. **5** swell of the sea. — *v.* (**-ging**) **1** move suddenly and powerfully forwards. **2** (of an electric current etc.) increase suddenly. **3** (of the sea etc.) swell. [Latin *surgo* rise]

**surgeon** /**ser**-juhn/ *n.* medical practitioner qualified in surgery.

**surgery** /**ser**-juh-ree/ *n.* (*pl.* **-ies**) **1 a** treatment of bodily injuries or disorders by incision or manipulation etc. as opposed to drugs. **b** the branch of medicine concerned with this. **c** operation performed by a surgeon. **2** place where or time when a doctor, dentist, etc., treats patients. [Latin *chirurgia*, from Greek *kheir* hand, *ergō* work]

**surgical** /**ser**-ji-kuhl/ *adj.* **1** of or relating to or done by surgeons or surgery. **2 a** used in surgery. **b** worn to correct a deformity etc. **3** (esp. of military action) swift and precise. □ **surgically** *adv.*

**surly** /**ser**-lee/ *adj.* (**-ier, -iest**) bad-tempered; unfriendly. □ **surliness** *n.* [obsolete *sirly* haughty: related to SIR]

**surmise** /suh-**muyz**/ — *n.* conjecture or suspicion about the existence or truth of something (*a very early surmise was that the sun moves and the earth is fixed*). — *v.* (**-sing**) (often foll. by *that*) infer doubtfully; guess; suppose (*I surmise, from what you say, that they are having an affair*). [Latin *supermitto -miss-* accuse]

**surmount** /suh-**mownt**/ *v.* **1** overcome or get over (a difficulty or obstacle). **2** (usu. in *passive*) cap or crown; rest on the top of (*peaks surmounted by snow*). □ **surmountable** *adj.* [French: related to SUR-¹]

**surname** /**ser**-naym/ *n.* family name, usu. inherited or acquired by marriage. [obsolete *surnoun* from Anglo-French: related to SUR-¹]

**surpass** /suh-**pahs**/ *v.* **1** be greater or better than, outdo. **2** (as **surpassing** *adj.*) pre-eminent. [French: related to SUR-¹]

**surplice** /**ser**-pluhs/ *n.* loose white vestment worn by clergy and choristers. [Anglo-French *surplis*]

**surplus** /**ser**-pluhs/ — *n.* **1** amount left over. **2** excess of revenue over expenditure (opp. DEFICIT). — *adj.* exceeding what is needed or used. [Anglo-French]

**surprise** /suh-**pruyz**/ — *n.* **1** unexpected or astonishing thing. **2** emotion caused by this. **3** act of catching or process of being caught unawares. **4** (*attrib.*) unexpected; made or done etc. without warning (*a surprise party*). — *v.* (**-sing**) **1** affect with surprise; turn out contrary to the expectations of (*your answer surprised me*; *I surprised her by arriving early*). **2** (usu. in *passive*; foll. by *at*) shock, scandalise (*I am surprised at you*). **3** capture or attack by surprise. **4** come upon (a person) unawares (*surprised him in the act*). **5** (foll. by *into*) startle (a person) into an action etc. (*surprised him into consenting*). □ **take by surprise** affect with surprise, esp. by an unexpected encounter or statement. □ **surprising** *adj.* **surprisingly** *adv.* [French]

**surreal** /suh-**ree**-uhl/ *adj.* unreal; dreamlike; bizarre. [back-formation from SURREALISM]

**surrealism** *n.* 20th-c. movement in art and literature, attempting to express the subconscious mind by dream imagery, bizarre juxtapositions, etc. □ **surrealist** *n.* & *adj.* **surrealistic** /-**lis**-tik/ *adj.* **surrealistically** /-**lis**-ti-kuh-lee, -klee/ *adv.* [French: related to SUR-¹, REAL]

**surrender** /suh-**ren**-duh/ — *v.* **1** hand over; relinquish, esp. on compulsion or demand. **2** submit, esp. to an enemy. **3** *refl.* (foll. by *to*) yield to a habit, emotion, influence, etc. (*surrendered himself to despair*). **4** give up rights under (a life-insurance policy) in return for a smaller sum received immediately. **5** abandon (hope etc.). — *n.* act or instance of surrendering. [Anglo-French: related to SUR-¹]

**surreptitious** /ˌsu-ruhp-**tish**-uhs/ *adj.*

done by stealth; clandestine. □ **surreptitiously** *adv.* [Latin *surripio* seize secretly]

**surrogate** /**su**-ruh-guht/ *n.* substitute, esp. for a person in a specific role or office. □ **surrogacy** *n.* [Latin *rogo* ask]

**surrogate mother** *n.* woman who bears a child on behalf of another woman, usu. by artificial insemination of her own egg by the other woman's partner.

**surround** /suh-**rownd**/ — *v.* come or be all round; encircle, enclose (*they surrounded me completely*; *the house is surrounded by wattles and gums*). — *n.* **1** border or edging, esp. an area of floor between the walls and carpet of a room. **2** surrounding area or substance. [Latin: related to SUR-¹, *unda* wave]

**surroundings** *n.pl.* objects or conditions around or affecting a person or thing; environment.

**surtax** /**ser**-taks/ *n.* additional tax, esp. on high incomes. [French: related to SUR-¹]

**surtitle** /**ser**-ˌtuy-tuhl/ *n.* (esp. in opera) each of a sequence of captions projected onto a screen above the stage, translating the text being sung.

**surveillance** /ser-**vay**-luhns/ *n.* close observation undertaken by the police etc. [French: related to SUR-¹, *veiller* watch]

**survey** — *v.* /suh-**vay**/ **1** view or consider as a whole. **2** examine the condition of (a building etc.). **3** determine the boundaries, extent, ownership, etc. of (a district, an area of land, etc.). — *n.* /**ser**-vay/ **1** general view or consideration. **2 a** act of surveying property. **b** result or findings of this, esp. in a written report. **3** investigation of public opinion etc. **4** map or plan made by surveying. [Latin: related to SUPER-, *video* see]

**surveyor** /suh-**vay**-uh/ *n.* person who surveys land and buildings, esp. for a living.

**survival** /suh-**vuy**-vuhl/ *n.* **1** process or instance of surviving. **2** person, thing, or practice that has remained from a former time.

**survive** /suh-**vuyv**/ *v.* (**-ving**) **1** continue to live or exist. **2** live or exist longer than (*she survived her husband by a year*). **3** remain alive after or continue to exist in spite of (a danger, accident, etc.). □ **survivor** *n.* [Anglo-French *survivre* from Latin *supervivo*]

**sus** var. of SUSS.

**sus-** *prefix* assim. form of SUB- before *c, p, t.*

**susceptibility** /suh-ˌsep-tuh-**bil**-uh-tee/ *n.* (*pl.* **-ies**) **1** state of being susceptible. **2** (in *pl.*) person's sensitive feelings (*she wounded his susceptibilities*).

**susceptible** /suh-**sep**-tuh-buhl/ *adj.* **1** impressionable, sensitive, emotional. **2**

**sushi** /**soo**-shee/ n. Japanese dish of balls of cold rice topped with raw fish etc. [Japanese]

**suspect** — v. /suh-**spekt**/ **1** imagine something evil, wrong, or undesirable (in a person or thing) on slight or no evidence (*I suspect him of being involved in my wife's death; the café looks spotless, but I suspect the cleanliness of whoever is doing the cooking*). **2** have an impression of the existence or presence of (*suspect poisoning*). **3** imagine or fancy something about (a person or thing) with slight or no proof (*I suspect him of being gay — it's just a feeling I have*). **4** imagine or fancy (something) to be possible or likely (*I suspect the world is going to end next week*). **5** doubt the genuineness or truth of (*I suspect his motives*). — n. /**sus**-pekt/ suspected person. — adj. /**sus**-pekt/ subject to or deserving suspicion (*his behaviour is highly suspect*). [Latin *suspicio -spect-*]

**suspend** /suh-**spend**/ v. **1** hang up. **2** keep inoperative or undecided for a time (*suspended judgment*). **3** debar temporarily from a function, office, etc. (*suspended him for 3 weeks for kicking in danger*). **4** (as **suspended** adj.) (of particles or a body in a fluid) floating between the top and bottom. [Latin *suspendo -pens-*]

**suspended animation** n. temporary deathlike condition (*some yogis can put themselves into a state of suspended animation; don't ask me now — my brain's in suspended animation*).

**suspended sentence** n. judicial sentence left unenforced subject to good behaviour during a specified period.

**suspender** n. attachment to hold up a stocking or sock by its top.

**suspense** /suh-**spens**/ n. **1** state of extremely anxious uncertainty or expectation (*unbearable suspense while waiting for the verdict*). **2** (*attrib.*) inducing suspense (*one of the best suspense novels I have read*). □ **suspenseful** adj. [French, = delay]

**suspension** /suh-**spen**-shuhn/ n. **1** act of suspending or condition of being suspended. **2** springs etc. supporting a vehicle on its axles. **3** substance consisting of particles suspended in a medium.

**suspension bridge** n. bridge with a roadway or walkway suspended from cables supported by towers.

**suspicion** /suh-**spish**-uhn/ n. **1** unconfirmed belief; distrust (*I have a suspicion that he did it; I view that claim with*

suspicion). **2** act or instance of suspecting or state of being suspected. **3** (foll. by *of*) slight trace of (*a suspicion of garlic in this sauce*). □ **above suspicion** too obviously good etc. to be suspected. **under suspicion** suspected. [Latin: related to SUSPECT]

**suspicious** /suh-**spish**-uhs/ adj. **1** prone to or feeling suspicion (*a suspicious glance*). **2** causing suspicion (*a suspicious lack of surprise*). □ **suspiciously** adv.

**suss¹** (also **sus**) colloq. — adj. **1** suspicious (*a bit suss the way he's lurking around; says she feels suss about what I get up to when she's not around*). **2** suspect (*I think the milk's a bit sus, way past its use-by date*). — v. (-**ss**-) **1** suspect of crime (*sussed him of the thefts*). **2** (usu. foll. by *out*) investigate, inspect (*need to suss out the local restaurants*). **3** work out; realise (*sussed that I am gay*). — n. **1** a suspect. **2** suspicion; suspicious behaviour (*stopped and questioned us on suss*). □ **on suss** on suspicion (of having committed a crime). [abbreviation]

**suss²** n. (also **susso**) hist. any of several forms of unemployment relief provided during the Depression. [abbreviation of SUSTENANCE]

**sustain** /suh-**stayn**/ v. **1** support, bear the weight of, esp. for a long period. **2** give strength to; encourage, support (*their kindness sustained him*). **3** (of food) nourish. **4** endure, stand; bear up against (*this wattle can sustain long periods of dryness*). **5** suffer (defeat or injury etc.) (*sustained a heavy blow to the head; sustained severe losses during the drought*). **6** (of a court etc.) uphold or decide in favour of (an objection etc.). **7** substantiate or corroborate (a statement or charge). **8** maintain or keep (a sound, conversation, effort, etc.) going continuously. □ **sustainable** adj. [Latin *sustineo* keep up]

**sustenance** /**sus**-tuh-nuhns/ n. **1** nourishment, food. **2** means of support; livelihood. [Anglo-French: related to SUSTAIN]

**suttee** /su-**tee**, **sut**-ee/ n. esp. hist. **1** Hindu custom of a widow's suicide on her husband's funeral pyre. **2** widow undergoing this. [Sanskrit *satī* faithful wife]

**suture** /**soo**-chuh/ — n. **1** stitching of the edges of a wound or incision. **2** thread or wire used for this. — v. (-**ring**) stitch (a wound or incision). [Latin *suo sut-* sew]

**sux** var. of SUCK v. 7 (*I saw 'sex sux' written on a wall*).

**suzerain** /**soo**-zuh-rayn/ n. **1** hist. feudal overlord. **2** archaic sovereign or State partially controlling another State that is internally autonomous. □ **suzerainty** n. [French]

**svelte** /svelt/ *adj.* slender, lissom, graceful. [French from Italian]

**SW** *abbr.* **1** south-west. **2** south-western.

**swab** /swob/ — *n.* **1 a** absorbent pad used in surgery. **b** specimen of a secretion taken for examination. **2** mop etc. for cleaning or mopping up. — *v.* (**-bb-**) **1** clean with a swab. **2** (foll. by *up*) absorb (moisture) with a swab. **3** mop clean (a ship's deck). **4** take a specimen of saliva etc. from a racehorse etc. to test for the presence of illegal substances. [Dutch]

**swaddle** /swod-uhl/ *v.* (**-ling**) wrap (esp. a baby) tightly. [from SWATHE]

**swaddling-clothes** *n.pl.* narrow bandages formerly used to wrap and restrain a baby.

**swag** — *n.* **1 a** collection of possessions and daily necessaries carried by a person travelling, usu. on foot, in the bush; esp. the blanket-wrapped roll carried, usu. on the back or across the shoulders, by an itinerant worker; a MATILDA; BLUEY. **b** a bed-roll. **2** *colloq.* booty of burglars etc. **3** *colloq.* a large number (*Australian swimmers came home with a swag of medals*). — *v.* (also **swag it**) carry one's swag; travel as a swagman. □ **swagged** *adj.* [probably Scandinavian]

**swagger** — *v.* walk or behave arrogantly. — *n.* **1** swaggering gait or manner. **2** (esp. New Zealand) a swagman. [from SWAG]

**swaggie** /swag-ee/ *n.* a swagman. [SWAG *n.* 1, -Y²]

**swagman** /swag-muhn/ *n.* (also **swagger**, **swaggie**) **1** person who carries a swag, esp. an itinerant. **2** tramp.

**Swahili** /swah-**hee**-lee/ *n.* (*pl.* same) **1** member of a Bantu people of Zanzibar and adjacent coasts. **2** their language. [Arabic]

**swain** *n.* **1** *archaic* country youth. **2** *poet.* young lover or suitor. [Old Norse, = lad]

**swainsona** /ˌswayn-**soh**-nuh/ *n.* (also **swainsonia** /-**soh**-nee-uh/ ) any plant of a group of herbaceous perennials or annuals, chiefly of drier Australia, having pinnate leaves and colourful pea-flowers ranging in colour from white through pink, red, blue, purple, and violet (see also DARLING PEA). [Isaac *Swainson*, English naturalist (d. 1812)]

**swallow¹** /swol-oh/ — *v.* **1** cause or allow (food etc.) to pass down the throat. **2** perform the muscular movement required to do this. **3 a** accept meekly; put up with (an affront etc.). **b** accept credulously (an unlikely assertion, story, etc.). **4** repress (a feeling etc.) (*swallow one's pride*). **5** articulate (words etc.) indistinctly. **6** (often foll. by *up*) engulf or absorb; exhaust.

— *n.* **1** act of swallowing. **2** amount swallowed in one action. [Old English]

**swallow²** /swol-oh/ *n.* migratory swift-flying bird with a forked tail. [Old English]

**swallow-dive** *n. & v.* dive with the arms outspread until close to the water.

**swallow-tail** *n.* **1** deeply forked tail. **2** butterfly etc. with this.

**swam** *past* of SWIM.

**swami** /swah-mee/ *n.* (*pl.* **-s**) Hindu religious teacher. [Hindi *svami*]

**swamp** /swomp/ — *n.* **1** (area of) waterlogged ground. **2** used in the names of Australian fauna and flora having a swampy or periodically flooded habitat (*swamp pheasant*; *swamp rat*; *swamp wallaby*; *swamp box*; *swamp grass*; *swamp gum*; *swamp stringybark*). — *v.* **1** overwhelm, flood, or soak with water. **2** overwhelm or make invisible etc. with an excess or large amount of something (*am swamped with paper work*). **3 a** travel as a swamper. **b** work as an assistant to a bullock driver or other carrier. □ **swampy** *adj.* (**-ier**, **-iest**). [origin uncertain]

**swamp cypress** *n.* WA conifer, formal, compact, and regularly pyramidal in shape, with dense, vivid green foliage all the way to the ground.

**swamper** *n.* person who travels on foot but whose baggage is carried on a wagon.

**swamphen** *n.* (also **purple swamphen**) bird with bright blue (or purple) and black plumage and a red bill, inhabiting wetlands in south-western and eastern Australia.

**swamp lily** *n.* large Australian plant of the lily family, having long leaves and fragrant white flowers, and occurring in swampy land of coastal Queensland and NSW.

**swan** /swon/ — *n.* **1** large usu. white water-bird with a long flexible neck. **2** the black swan, Australia's only representative of this group of birds, a jet-black bird with a red bill, a faunal emblem of WA. — *v.* (**-nn-**) (usu. foll. by *about*, *off*, etc.) *colloq.* move or go aimlessly, casually, or with a superior air. [Old English]

**swank** *colloq.* — *n.* ostentation, swagger. — *v.* show off. [origin uncertain]

**swanky** *adj.* (**-ier**, **-iest**) *colloq.* marked by swank; ostentatiously smart or showy; stylish, posh (*went to a swanky restaurant*).

**Swan River daisy** see BRACHYCOME.

**Swan River myrtle** *n.* (also **myrtle**) WA shrub of the myrtle family bearing masses of deep rose-red flowers. [*Swan River* in WA on which Perth stands]

**swansong** *n.* person's last work or act before death or retirement etc.

**swap** /swop/ (also **swop**) — v. (**-pp-**) exchange or barter. — n. **1** act of swapping. **2** thing for swapping or thing swapped. [originally = 'hit', imitative]

**sward** /swawd/ n. literary expanse of short grass; turf. [Old English, = skin]

**swarm¹** /swawm/ — n. **1** cluster of bees leaving the hive with the queen to establish a new colony. **2** large cluster of insects, birds, or people. **3** (in pl.; foll. by of) great numbers. — v. **1** move in or form a swarm. **2** (foll. by with) (of a place) be overrun, crowded, or infested with (swarming with tourists). [Old English]

**swarm²** /swawm/ v. (foll. by up) climb (a rope or tree etc.) by clinging with the hands and knees etc. [origin unknown]

**swarthy** /swaw-thee/ adj. (**-ier, -iest**) dark, dark-complexioned. [obsolete swarty from swart black, from Old English]

**swashbuckler** /swosh-,buk-luh/ n. swaggering adventurer. □ **swashbuckling** adj. & n. [swash strike noisily, BUCKLER]

**swastika** /swos-ti-kuh/ n. **1** ancient symbol formed by an equal-armed cross with each arm continued at a right angle. **2** this with clockwise continuations as the symbol of Nazi Germany. [Sanskrit]

**swat** /swot/ — v. (**-tt-**) **1** crush (a fly etc.) with a sharp blow. **2** hit hard and abruptly. — n. swatting blow. [British dial. var. of SQUAT]

**swatch** /swoch/ n. **1** sample, esp. of cloth. **2** collection of samples. [origin unknown]

**Swatch** /swoch/ n. decorative watch patterned with bright colours, worn as a fashion accessory. [Swiss watch]

**swath** /swawth/ n. (also **swathe** /swayth/) (pl. **-s** /swawths, swawthz, swaythz/) **1** ridge of cut grass or wheat etc. **2** space left clear by a mower etc. **3** broad strip. □ **cut a (wide) swathe** **1** clear a passage through (a crowd etc.). **2** be effective in destruction. [Old English]

**swathe** /swayth/ — v. (**-thing**) bind or wrap in bandages or garments etc. — n. bandage or wrapping. [Old English]

**sway** — v. **1** (cause to) lean or move unsteadily from side to side (wind swaying the trees; he swayed and fell in a faint). **2** (of opinions etc.) fluctuate, waver (his sympathies swayed from Labor to Liberal and back again). **3** (of a person) tend or incline in opinion, sympathy, etc. (he began to sway towards Catholicism). **4** cause (a person, a person's opinions, etc.) to veer in a particular direction (tried to sway the meeting to his point of view). **5** deflect or dissuade (swayed him from his determination to abandon his marriage). **6** dominate (swayed by greed for wealth). — n. **1** rule, influence, or government (hold sway). **2** swaying motion. [origin uncertain]

**swear** /swair/ — v. (past **swore**; past part. **sworn**) **1 a** (often foll. by to + infin. or that + clause) state or promise solemnly or on oath. **b** (cause to) take (an oath) (swore them to secrecy). **2** colloq. insist (swore he was fit). **3** (often foll. by at) use profane or obscene language. **4** (foll. by by) **a** appeal to as a witness in taking an oath (swear by Almighty God). **b** colloq. have great confidence in (swears by yoga). **5** (foll. by to; usu. in neg.) say certainly (could not swear to it). — n. spell of swearing. □ **swear blind** (or **black and blue**) colloq. affirm emphatically. **swear in** induct into office etc. with an oath. [Old English]

**swear word** n. profane or indecent word.

**sweat** /swet/ — n. **1** moisture exuded through the pores, esp. from heat or nervousness. **2** state or period of sweating. **3** colloq. state of anxiety (in a sweat). **4** colloq. **a** drudgery, effort. **b** laborious task. **5** condensed moisture on a surface. — v. (past and past part. **sweated**) **1** exude sweat. **2** be terrified or suffer. **3** (of a wall etc.) exhibit surface moisture. **4** (cause to) drudge or toil. **5** emit (blood, gum, etc.) like sweat. **6** make (a horse, athlete, etc.) sweat by exercise. **7** (as **sweated** adj.) (of goods, labour, etc.) produced by or subjected to exploitation. □ **no sweat** colloq. no bother, no trouble. **sweat blood** colloq. **1** work strenuously. **2** be very anxious. **sweat it out** colloq. **1** endure a difficult experience to the end. **2** await anxiously or with unease. **sweat on** colloq. anxiously await (an event or person) (sweating on his arrival). □ **sweaty** adj. (**-ier, -iest**). [Old English]

**sweatband** n. band fitted inside a hat or worn round a wrist etc. to absorb sweat.

**sweater** n. jumper or pullover.

**sweating pen** n. holding pen in which sheep, sweating from being mustered etc., are confined till they dry out, whence they are moved to the holding pen in the shearing shed.

**sweatshirt** n. sleeved cotton sweater.

**sweatshop** n. factory where sweated labour is used.

**Swede** n. **1 a** native or national of Sweden. **b** person of Swedish descent. **2** (**swede**) large yellow-fleshed turnip orig. from Sweden. [Low German or Dutch]

**Swedish** — adj. of Sweden, its people, or language. — n. language of Sweden.

**sweep¹** — v. (past and past part. **swept**) **1** clean or clear (a room or area etc.) with or as with a broom (swept the floor; swept the table clean of crumbs with his hand).

**2** (often foll. by *up*) clean a room etc. in this way. **3** (often foll. by *up*) collect or remove (dirt etc.) by sweeping. **4** (foll. by *aside, away*, etc.) **a** push with or as with a broom (*swept away the broken glass; swept him aside*). **b** dismiss abruptly (*their objections were swept aside*). **5** (foll. by *along, down*, etc.) carry or drive along with force (*swept along by the panicked crowd*). **6** (foll. by *off, away*, etc.) remove or clear forcefully (*swept off into slavery; swept away by the current*). **7** traverse swiftly or lightly (*the wind swept the hillside*). **8** impart a sweeping motion to (*swept his hand across his face*). **9 a** swiftly cover or affect (*the new fashion swept the country*). **b** *Polit.* win government by an overwhelming margin (*Labor swept into office*). **10 a** glide swiftly; speed along. **b** go majestically (*the motorcade swept past*). **11** (of landscape etc.) be rolling or spacious; have continuous extent. — *n.* **1** act or motion or an instance of sweeping. **2** curve in the road, sweeping line of a hill, etc. **3** range or scope (*beyond the sweep of the human mind*). **4** = CHIMNEY-SWEEP. **5** sortie by aircraft. **6** *colloq.* = SWEEPSTAKE. **7** *Electronics* movement of a beam across the screen of a cathode-ray tube. □ **make a clean sweep of 1** completely abolish or expel. **2** win all the prizes etc. in (a competition etc.). **sweep away 1** abolish swiftly. **2** (usu. in *passive*) powerfully affect, esp. emotionally. **sweep the board 1** win all the money at stake. **2** win all possible prizes etc. **sweep under the carpet** see CARPET. [Old English]

**sweep²** *n.* (*pl.* **sweep** or **sweeps**) any of several marine food-fish of south-eastern Australia.

**sweeper** *n.* **1** person who cleans by sweeping. **2** manual device for sweeping carpets etc. **3** person employed to sweep up wool in a shearing shed. **4** steerer of a surfboat.

**sweeping** — *adj.* **1** wide in range or effect (*sweeping changes*). **2** generalised, arbitrary (*sweeping statement*). — *n.* (in *pl.*) dirt etc. collected by sweeping.

**sweepstake** *n.* **1** form of gambling on horse-races etc. in which all stakes are pooled and paid to the winners. **2** race with betting of this kind. **3** (usu. as **sweep**) version of this (esp. in association with the Melbourne Cup) in which the participants are allotted horses by chance.

**sweet** — *adj.* **1** having the pleasant taste characteristic of sugar. **2** smelling pleasant like roses or perfume etc.; fragrant. **3** (of sound etc.) melodious or harmonious. **4** fresh; not salt, sour, bitter, etc. **5** amiable, pleasant (*he has a sweet nature*). **6** *colloq.* pretty, charming. **7** (foll. by *on*) *colloq.* fond of; in love with. **8** *colloq.* good; all right; advantageously situated. — *n.* **1** small shaped piece of sweet substance, usu. made with sugar or chocolate. **2** sweet dish or course of a meal. □ **cop it sweet** see COP. **she's sweet** *colloq.* all is well. □ **sweetish** *adj.* **sweetly** *adv.* [Old English]

**sweetbread** *n.* pancreas or thymus of an animal, esp. as food.

**sweet bursaria** see BURSARIA.

**sweeten** *v.* **1** make or become sweet or sweeter. **2** make agreeable or less painful. □ **sweetening** *n.*

**sweetener** *n.* **1** substance used to sweeten food or drink. **2** *colloq.* bribe or inducement.

**sweetheart** *n.* **1** lover or darling. **2** term of endearment.

**sweetheart deal** *n.* agreement arranged privately between trade unions and employers, giving workers benefits etc. beyond what is set down in an industrial award.

**sweetlip** *n.* (also **sweetlips**) any of many thick-lipped food-fish mainly of Australian tropical waters.

**sweetlip emperor** *n.* fish of Queensland coral reefs.

**sweetness** *n.* quality of being sweet; fragrance. □ **sweetness and light** (esp. uncharacteristic) mildness and reason.

**sweet pea** *n.* climbing plant with fragrant flowers.

**sweet potato** *n.* **1** tropical climbing plant with sweet tuberous roots used for food. **2** root of this.

**sweet talk** *colloq.* — *n.* flattery, blandishment. — *v.* (**sweet-talk**) flatter in order to persuade.

**sweet tooth** *n.* liking for sweet-tasting things.

**sweet william** *n.* **1** cultivated dianthus with clusters of vivid fragrant flowers. **2 a** = GUMMY² *n.* 1 (so called because of its smell). **b** its flesh as food.

**swell** — *v.* (*past part.* **swollen** /**swohluhn**/ or **swelled**) **1** grow (or cause to grow): **a** bigger (*the seed swelled; the crowd swelled in numbers*). **b** louder (*the music swelled*). **c** more intense (*the pressure for reform continued to swell*). **2** (often foll. by *up*) rise or raise up from the surrounding surface (*the blow caused his eye to swell*). **3** (foll. by *out*) bulge (*the sails swelled out*). **4 a** (of a body of water, as a river or the tide) rise (or be made to rise) above the ordinary level (*the river is swelling fast; the torrential rains have swollen the streams*). **b** rise in waves (*braved the swelling seas*). **5** (of the heart etc.) feel full of joy, pride, relief, etc. (*his heart swelled*).

**6** (foll. by *with*) be hardly able to restrain (pride etc.) (*her heart swelled with joy*). — *n.* **1** act or the state of swelling. **2** heaving of the sea with unbreaking waves. **3 a** crescendo. **b** mechanism in an organ etc. for producing a crescendo or diminuendo. **4** *colloq.* person of social distinction or of dashing or fashionable appearance. **5** protuberance. — *adj. colloq.* **1** fine, excellent. **2** smart, fashionable. [Old English]

**swelled head** *n.* (also **swollen head**) *colloq.* conceit.

**swelling** *n.* abnormal bodily protuberance.

**swelter** — *v.* be uncomfortably hot. — *n.* sweltering condition. [Old English]

**swept** *past* and *past part.* of SWEEP.

**swerve** — *v.* (**-ving**) (cause to) change direction, esp. abruptly. — *n.* swerving movement. [Old English, = scour]

**swift** — *adj.* **1** quick, rapid. **2** prompt (*a swift response; was swift to act*). — *n.* swift-flying bird with long wings and black plumage with white markings, migrant to Australia from spring to early autumn. □ **swiftly** *adv.* **swiftness** *n.* [Old English]

**swiftie** *n. colloq.* piece of sharp practice; act of deception; trick. □ **pull a swiftie** perform a piece of sharp practice etc.

**swig** — *v.* (**-gg-**) *colloq.* drink in large draughts. — *n.* swallow of drink, esp. large. [origin unknown]

**swill** — *v.* **1** (often foll. by *out*) rinse or flush. **2** drink greedily. — *n.* **1** act of rinsing. **2** mainly liquid refuse as pig-food. [Old English]

**swim** — *v.* (**-mm-**; *past* **swam**; *past part.* **swum**) **1** propel the body through water with limbs, fins, or tail. **2** traverse (a stretch of water or distance) by swimming. **3** perform (a particular stroke) by swimming. **4** float on a liquid (*bubbles swimming on the surface*). **5** appear to undulate, reel, or whirl (*everything began to swim before my eyes*). **6** feel dizzy (*my head swam*). **7** (foll. by *in*, *with*) be flooded (*ate a floater swimming in gravy; the room was swimming in blood*). — *n.* period or act of swimming. □ **in the swim** *colloq.* involved in or aware of what is going on. □ **swimmer** *n.* [Old English]

**swimmers** *n.pl.* swimming costume.

**swimming-costume** *n.* garment worn for swimming; swimmers.

**swimmingly** *adv. colloq.* smoothly, without impediment.

**swimming-pool** *n.* artificial pool for swimming.

**swimming togs** see TOGS.

**swimsuit** *n.* swimming-costume, esp. one-piece for women and girls.

**swimwear** *n.* clothing for swimming in.

**swindle** /swin-duhl/ — *v.* (**-ling**) (often foll. by *out of*) **1** cheat of money etc. **2** cheat a person of (money etc.) (*swindled $200 out of him*). — *n.* **1** act of swindling. **2** fraudulent person or thing. □ **swindler** *n.* [back-formation from *swindler* from German]

**swine** *n.* (*pl.* same) **1** pig. **2** *colloq.* (*pl.* same or **-s**) **a** contemptible person. **b** unpleasant or difficult thing. □ **swinish** *adj.* [Old English]

**swing** — *v.* (*past* and *past part.* **swung**) **1 a** move or cause to move with a to-and-fro or curving motion, as of an object attached at one end and hanging free at the other; sway (*lantern swinging in the breeze; he swung the axe; the car swung round the corner*). **b** hang so as to be free to swing (*swung the gate on strong hinges*). **2 a** move to and fro, or in either direction upon a fixed centre or axis, e.g. upon a hinge; oscillate (*the door swung open; the pendulum swings tick tock*). **b** revolve (*swung the bullroarer round and round above his head*). **3** move by gripping something and leaping etc. (*swung from tree to tree*). **4** walk with a swinging gait (*swung out of the room*). **5** (foll. by *round*) move to face the opposite direction. **6** change one's opinion or mood (*swung from gloom to glee in the space of a minute*). **7** (foll. by *at*) attempt to hit. **8** (also **swing it**) play (music) with a swing rhythm. **9** *colloq.* **a** (of a person, a party, etc.) be lively etc. **b** (of a person) be up to date, with it. **c** (of a person) be promiscuous. **10** have a decisive influence on (voting etc.) (*his new grab-bag of promises should swing many voters his way*). **11** *colloq.* achieve, manage (*we should be able to swing this deal*). **12** *colloq.* be executed by hanging. **13** move or be moved on a swing (*I can swing higher than you; swing me*). — *n.* **1** act, motion, or extent of swinging. **2** swinging or smooth gait, rhythm, or action. **3 a** seat slung by ropes etc. for swinging on or in. **b** period of swinging on this. **4 a** jazz or dance music with an easy flowing rhythm. **b** rhythmic feeling or drive of this. **5** discernible change, esp. in public opinion, votes or points scored, etc. □ **swing the banjo** see BANJO. **swing the billy** see BILLY¹. **swing both ways** enjoy homosexual and heterosexual sexual relations. [Old English]

**swing-bridge** *n.* bridge that can be swung aside to let ships pass.

**swingeing** /swin-jing/ *adj.* **1** (of a blow) forcible. **2** huge or far-reaching (*swingeing economies*). [archaic *swinge* strike hard, from Old English]

**swinger** *n*. **1** person who swings. **2** *colloq.* person who is sexually promiscuous.

**swinging vote** *n*. collective votes of swinging voters which can have a decisive effect at an election.

**swinging voter** *n*. voter who is not committed to a particular political party.

**swipe** *colloq.* — *v*. (**-ping**) **1** (often foll. by *at*) hit hard and recklessly. **2** steal. — *n*. **1** reckless hard hit or attempted hit. **2** electronic device for reading information from a card (e.g. a credit card) when the card is passed through a slot. [perhaps var. of SWEEP]

**swirl** — *v*. move, flow, or carry along with a whirling motion. — *n*. **1** swirling motion. **2** twist or curl, esp. as part of a pattern or design. □ **swirly** *adj*. [perhaps from Low German or Dutch]

**swish** — *v*. **1** swing (a scythe, stick, etc.) audibly through the air, grass, etc. **2** move with or make a swishing sound. **3** (foll. by *off*) cut (the tops of plants etc.) in this way (*swished off the weeds with his switch*). — *n*. swishing action or sound. — *adj*. *colloq.* smart, fashionable. [imitative]

**Swiss** — *adj*. of Switzerland or its people. — *n*. (*pl.* same) **1** native or national of Switzerland. **2** person of Swiss descent. [French *Suisse*]

**switch** — *n*. **1** device for completing and breaking an electric circuit. **2 a** transfer, change-over, or deviation. **b** exchange. **3** flexible shoot cut from a tree. **4** light tapering rod or cane. — *v*. **1** (foll. by *on*, *off*) turn (an electrical device) on or off. **2** change or transfer (*I need to switch my job; switched to a better area*). **3** reverse the position of; exchange (*switched chairs*). **4** whip or flick with a switch. □ **switch off** *colloq.* cease to pay attention. [Low German]

**switchback** *n*. **1** ride at a fair etc., with extremely steep ascents and descents. **2** (often *attrib.*) such a railway or road.

**switchboard** *n*. apparatus for making connections between electric circuits, esp. in telephony.

**switched-on** *adj. colloq.* **1** up to date; aware of what is going on. **2** excited; under the influence of drugs.

**swivel** /swiv-uhl/ — *n*. coupling between two parts enabling one to revolve without turning the other. — *v*. (**-ll-**) turn on or as on a swivel. [Old English]

**swizz** *n*. (also **swiz**) *colloq.* **1** something unfair or disappointing. **2** swindle. [origin unknown]

**swizzle** /swiz-uhl/ *n*. **1** *colloq.* frothy mixed alcoholic drink esp. of rum or gin and bitters. **2** *colloq.* = SWIZZ. [origin unknown]

**swizzle-stick** *n*. stick used for frothing or flattening drinks.

**swollen** *past part.* of SWELL.

**swoon** — *n*. loss of consciousness; a faint. — *v*. **1** lose consciousness; faint. **2** be so enraptured that one is close to fainting (*swooning over the latest pop star*). [Old English]

**swoop** — *v*. **1** (often foll. by *down*) descend rapidly like a bird of prey. **2** (often foll. by *on*) make a sudden attack. — *n*. swooping movement or action. [Old English]

**swoosh** /swuush/ — *n*. noise of a sudden rush of air, liquid, etc. — *v*. move with this noise. [imitative]

**sword** /sawd/ *n*. **1** weapon with a long blade and hilt with a handguard. **2** (prec. by *the*) **a** war. **b** military power. □ **put to the sword** kill. [Old English]

**swordfish** *n*. (*pl.* same or **-es**) large marine fish with swordlike upper jaw.

**sword-grass** *n*. (also **cutting grass**) any of several Australian plants having long serrated or sharp-edged leaves capable of inflicting lacerations.

**sword of Damocles** /dam-uh-,kleez/ *n*. an imminent danger. [from *Damokles*, who had a sword hung by a hair over his head]

**swordsman** *n*. person of (usu. specified) skill with a sword (*good swordsman*). □ **swordsmanship** *n*.

**swore** *past* of SWEAR.

**sworn** *past part.* of SWEAR. — *attrib. adj.* bound by, or as by, an oath (*sworn friends*; *sworn enemies*).

**swot** *colloq.* — *v*. (**-tt-**) **1** study hard. **2** (usu. foll. by *up*, *up on*) study (a subject) hard or hurriedly. — *n*. usu. *derog.* person who swots. [British dial. var. of SWEAT]

**swum** *past part.* of SWIM.

**swung** *past* and *past part.* of SWING.

**swy** *n*. **1** *hist.* Australian two-shilling coin. **2** = TWO-UP. [German *zwei* two]

**sybarite** /sib-uh-,ruyt/ *n*. self-indulgent or voluptuous person. □ **sybaritic** /-rit-ik/ *adj*. [*Sybaris*, ancient city in S. Italy, noted for luxury]

**sycamore** /sik-uh-,maw/ *n*. **1** (in Europe) large maple or its wood. **2** (in US) plane-tree or its wood. **3** (in Egypt etc.) a kind of fig-tree. [Greek *sukomoros*]

**sycophant** /sik-uh-,fuhnt, -,fant/ *n*. flatterer; toady. □ **sycophancy** *n*. **sycophantic** /-fan-tik/ *adj*. [Greek *sukophantēs*]

**Sydney** /sid-nee/ *n*. name of the capital city of the State of NSW (Aboriginal name for the area *Warrane*). □ **Sydney or the bush** **1** all or nothing. **2** used allusively with reference to the extremes of urban and rural life. [after Viscount *Sydney*, British Home Secretary, who initiated the plan for a convict settlement at Botany Bay]

**Sydney blue gum** n. tall, smooth-barked eucalypt of eastern NSW and Queensland.

**Sydney rock oyster** n. (also **Sydney oyster**) oyster of rocky substrata of bays and estuaries from southern Queensland to eastern Victoria, highly valued for eating; also cultivated commercially.

**Sydney-side** — n. the city of Sydney and its environs (orig. NSW as being on the other side of a natural barrier) (*I come from Sydney-side*). — adj. of or pertaining to Sydney and its environs (*Sydney-side con artists*).

**Sydney-sider** n. **1** person native to or resident in the city of Sydney. **2** person native to or resident in NSW.

**Sydney silky** n. = AUSTRALIAN TERRIER.

**syl-** prefix assim. form of SYN- before l.

**syllabic** /suh-**lab**-ik/ adj. **1** of or in syllables. **2** Prosody based on the number of syllables. □ **syllabically** adv.

**syllable** /**sil**-uh-buhl/ n. **1** unit of pronunciation uttered without interruption, forming the whole or part of a word and usu. having one vowel sound often with consonant(s) before or after (see panel). **2** character(s) representing a syllable. **3** the least amount of speech or writing (*did not utter a syllable*). □ **in words of one syllable** plainly, bluntly. [Greek *sullabē*]

**syllabus** /**sil**-uh-buhs/ n. (pl. **-buses** or **-bi** /-,buy/ ) programme or outline of a course of study, teaching, etc. [misreading of Greek *sittuba* label]

**syllepsis** /suh-**lep**-suhs/ n. (pl. **syllepses** /-seez/ ) figure of speech in which a word is applied to two others in different senses (e.g. *caught the train and a cold*) or to two others of which it grammatically suits one only (e.g. *neither they nor he knows it is working*) (cf. ZEUGMA). [Greek: related to SYLLABLE]

**syllogism** /**sil**-uh-,jiz-uhm/ n. form of reasoning consisting of two propositions (premises) from which a conclusion may be validly or invalidly drawn: e.g. *all Aussies are human beings* (major premise); *John is an Aussie* (minor premise); *therefore John is a human being* (valid conclusion); *all Aussies are human*

beings; *John is a human being; therefore John is an Aussie* (invalid conclusion); *all Aussies are ockers; Johnno's an Aussie; therefore Johnno's an ocker* (valid in form if the major premise were true). □ **syllogistic** /-**jis**-tik/ adj. [Greek *logos* reason]

**sylph** /silf/ n. **1** elemental spirit of the air. **2** slender graceful woman or girl. □ **sylphlike** adj. [Latin]

**sylvan** /**sil**-vuhn/ adj. (also **silvan**) **1 a** of the woods. **b** having woods. **2** rural. [Latin *silva* a wood]

**sym-** prefix assim. form of SYN- before b, m, p.

**symbiosis** /,sim-bee-**oh**-suhs, ,sim-buy-/ n. (pl. **-bioses** /-seez/ ) **1** interaction between two different organisms living in close physical association, usu. to the advantage of both. **2** mutually advantageous association between persons. □ **symbiotic** /-**ot**-ik/ adj. [Greek, = living together]

**symbol** /**sim**-buhl/ n. **1** thing regarded as typifying or representing something (*white is a symbol of purity*). **2** mark, sign, etc. representing an object, idea, function, or process, e.g. the letters standing for the various chemical elements or the characters in musical notation. □ **symbolic** /sim-**bol**-ik/ adj. **symbolically** /-**bol**-i-kuh-lee, -klee/ adv. [Greek *sumbolon*]

**symbolic logic** n. use of symbols to denote propositions etc. in order to assist reasoning.

**symbolise** v. (also **-ize**) (**-sing** or **-zing**) **1** be a symbol of. **2** represent by symbols. [French: related to SYMBOL]

**symbolism** n. **1 a** use of symbols. **b** symbols collectively. **2** artistic and poetic movement or style using symbols to express ideas, emotions, etc. □ **symbolist** n.

**symmetry** /**sim**-uh-tree/ n. (pl. **-ies**) **1 a** correct proportion of parts; balance, harmony. **b** beauty resulting from this. **2 a** structure allowing an object to be divided into parts of an equal shape and size. **b** possession of such a structure. **3** repetition of exactly similar parts facing each other or a centre. □ **symmetrical** /suh-**met**-ri-kuhl/ adj. **symmetrically** /-**met**-ri-kuh-lee, -klee/ adv. [Greek *summetria*]

---

**Syllable**

A syllable is the smallest unit of speech that can normally occur alone, such as a, at, ta, or tat. A word can be made up of one or more syllables.

    cat, fought, and twinge each have one syllable;
    rating, deny, and collapse each have two syllables;
    excitement, superman, and telephoned each have three syllables;
    Victorian and complicated each have four syllables;
    examination and uncontrollable each have five syllables.

**sympathetic** /ˌsim-puh-**thet**-ik/ *adj.* **1** of or expressing sympathy. **2** pleasant, likeable. **3** (foll. by *to*) inclined to favour (a proposal etc.) (*was most sympathetic to the idea*). **4** (of a pain etc.) caused by a pain or injury to someone else or in another part of the body (*he began to feel sympathetic labour pains*). □ **sympathetically** *adv.*

**sympathetic magic** *n.* type of magic that seeks to achieve an effect by performing an associated action or using an associated thing.

**sympathise** /**sim**-puh-ˌthuyz/ *v.* (also **-ize**) (**-sing** or **-zing**) (often foll. by *with*) **1** feel or express sympathy. **2** agree with a sentiment or opinion. □ **sympathiser** *n.*

**sympathy** /**sim**-puh-thee/ *n.* (*pl.* **-ies**) **1 a** sharing of another's feelings. **b** capacity for this. **2 a** (often foll. by *with*) sharing or tendency to share (with a person etc.) in an emotion, sensation, or condition. **b** (in *sing.* or *pl.*) compassion or commiseration. **3** (often foll. by *for*) favourable attitude; approval. **4** (in *sing.* or *pl.*; often foll. by *with*) agreement (with a person etc.) in opinion or desire. □ **in sympathy** (often foll. by *with*) having, showing, or resulting from sympathy. [Greek, = fellow-feeling]

**sympathy strike** *n.* strike by workers in support of the action of strikers in another union, industry, etc.

**symph** /simf/ *n. colloq.* symphony orchestra (*the Melbourne symph*). [abbreviation]

**symphony** /**sim**-fuh-nee/ *n.* (*pl.* **-ies**) **1** large-scale composition for full orchestra in several movements. **2** instrumental interlude in a large-scale vocal work. **3** = SYMPHONY ORCHESTRA. □ **symphonic** /sim-**fon**-ik/ *adj.* [from SYN-, Greek *phōnē* sound]

**symphony orchestra** *n.* large orchestra suitable for playing symphonies etc.

**symposium** /sim-**poh**-zee-uhm/ *n.* (*pl.* **-sia**) conference, or collection of essays, on a particular subject. [Greek *sumpotēs* fellow-drinker]

**symptom** /**simp**-tuhm/ *n.* **1** physical or mental sign of disease. **2** sign of the existence of something (*crime is often a symptom of social inequality*). □ **symptomatic** /ˌsimp-tuh-**mat**-ik/ *adj.* [Greek *piptō* fall]

**syn.** *abbr.* synonymous (with).

**syn-** *prefix* with, together, alike. [Greek *sun* with]

**synagogue** /**sin**-uh-ˌgog/ *n.* **1** building for Jewish religious observance and instruction. **2** Jewish congregation. [Greek, = assembly]

**synapse** /**suy**-naps, **sin**-/ *n. Anat.* junction of two nerve-cells. [Greek *haptō* join]

**sync** /singk/ (also **synch**) *colloq.* — *n.* synchronisation. — *v.* synchronise. □ **in** (or **out of**) **sync** (often foll. by *with*) according or agreeing well (or badly). [abbreviation]

**synchromesh** /**sing**-kroh-ˌmesh/ *n.* (often *attrib.*) system of gear-changing, esp. in vehicles, in which the gearwheels revolve at the same speed during engagement by means of a set of friction clutches, thereby easing the change. [abbreviation of *synchronised mesh*]

**synchronic** /sing-**kron**-ik/ *adj.* concerned with a subject as it exists at one point in time (opp. DIACHRONIC). □ **synchronically** *adv.* [from SYN-, Greek *khronos* time]

**synchronise** /**sing**-kruh-ˌnuyz/ *v.* (also **-ize**) (**-sing** or **-zing**) **1** (often foll. by *with*) make or be synchronous (with). **2** make the sound and picture of (a film etc.) coincide. **3** cause (clocks etc.) to show the same time. □ **synchronisation** /-ˌzay-shuhn/ *n.*

■ **Usage** *Synchronise* should not be used to mean 'coordinate' or 'combine'.

**synchronised swimming** *n.* form of swimming in which participants make ballet-like co-ordinated leg and arm movements in time to music.

**synchronous** /**sing**-kruh-nuhs/ *adj.* (often foll. by *with*) existing or occurring at the same time.

**syncopate** /**sing**-kuh-ˌpayt/ *v.* (**-ting**) **1** displace the beats or accents in (music) so that strong beats become weak and vice versa. **2** *Gram.* shorten (a word) by dropping interior sounds or letters, as *pacifist* for 'pacificist', *idolatry* for 'idololatry', etc. □ **syncopation** /-**pay**-shuhn/ *n.* [Latin: related to SYNCOPE]

**syncope** /**sing**-kuh-pee/ *n.* **1** *Gram.* syncopation. **2** fainting through a fall in blood pressure. [Greek *sunkopē* cutting off]

**syncretise** /**sing**-kruh-ˌtuyz/ *v.* (also **-ize**) (**-sing** or **-zing**) attempt, esp. inconsistently, to unify or reconcile differing schools of thought. □ **syncretic** /-**kret**-ik/ *adj.* **syncretism** *n.* [Greek]

**syndicate** — *n.* /**sin**-di-kuht/ **1** combination of individuals or businesses to promote a common interest. **2** agency supplying material simultaneously to a number of newspapers etc. **3** group of people who combine to gamble, organise crime, etc. — *v.* /**sin**-duh-ˌkayt/ (**-ting**) **1** form into a syndicate. **2** publish (material) through a syndicate. □ **syndication** /-**kay**-shuhn/

*n.* [Latin: related to Greek *sundikos*, = advocate]

**syndrome** /sin-drohm/ *n.* **1** group of concurrent symptoms of a disease. **2** characteristic combination of opinions, emotions, behaviour, etc. [Greek *sundromē* running together]

**synecdoche** /si-**nek**-duh-kee/ *n.* figure of speech in which a part is made to represent the whole or vice versa (e.g. *new faces at the club*; *Australia beat England by six wickets*). [Greek, = taking together]

**synod** /sin-uhd/ *n.* **1** Church council of delegated clergy and sometimes laity. **2** any meeting for debate. □ **synodal** /sin-uh-duhl/ *adj.* **synodical** /suh-**nod**-i-kuhl/ *adj.* [Greek, = meeting]

**synonym** /sin-uh-nim/ *n.* word or phrase that means the same as another (see panel). [Greek *onoma* name]

**synonymous** /suh-**non**-uh-muhs/ *adj.* (often foll. by *with*) **1** having the same meaning. **2** suggestive of; associated with (*his name is synonymous with terror*).

**synopsis** /suh-**nop**-suhs/ *n.* (*pl.* **synopses** /-seez/) summary or outline. [Greek *opsis* view]

**synoptic** /suh-**nop**-tik/ *adj.* of or giving a synopsis. [Greek: related to SYNOPSIS]

**Synoptic Gospels** *n.pl.* Gospels of Matthew, Mark, and Luke, describing events from a similar point of view.

**synovia** /suy-**noh**-vee-uh, suh-/ *n. Physiol.* viscous fluid lubricating joints etc. □ **synovial** *adj.* [medieval Latin]

**syntax** /sin-taks/ *n.* **1** grammatical arrangement of words, showing their connection and relation. **2** rules or analysis of this. □ **syntactic** /sin-tak-tik/ *adj.* **syntactically** /-**tak**-ti-kuh-lee, -klee/ *adv.* [Greek, = arrangement]

**synthesis** /sin-thuh-suhs/ *n.* (*pl.* **-theses** /-,seez/) **1 a** combining of separate elements, esp. ideas, into a connected whole, esp. a theory or system. **b** result of this. **2** *Chem.* artificial production of compounds from their constituents as

distinct from extraction from plants etc. [Greek, = placing together]

**synthesise** /sin-thuh-,suyz/ *v.* (also **-ize**) (**-sing** or **-zing**) make a synthesis of.

**synthesiser** *n.* (also **-izer**) electronic usu. keyboard instrument producing a wide variety of sounds.

**synthetic** /sin-**thet**-ik/ — *adj.* **1** made by chemical synthesis, esp. to imitate a natural product (*synthetic rubber*). **2** (of emotions etc.) affected, insincere. — *n.* synthetic substance. □ **synthetically** *adv.*

**syphilis** /sif-uh-luhs/ *n.* contagious venereal disease progressing from infection of the genitals via the skin and mucous membrane to the bones, muscles, and brain. □ **syphilitic** /-**lit**-ik/ *adj.* [*Syphilus*, name of a character in a poem of 1530, the supposed first sufferer from the disease]

**Syriac** /si-ree-,ak/ — *n.* language of ancient Syria, western Aramaic. — *adj.* of or in Syriac.

**Syrian** /si-ree-uhn/ — *n.* **1** native or national of Syria. **2** person of Syrian descent. — *adj.* of Syria.

**syringe** /suh-**rinj**, si-rinj/ — *n.* device for sucking in and ejecting liquid in a fine stream. — *v.* (**-ging**) sluice or spray (the ear, a plant, etc.) with a syringe. [Greek *surigx* pipe]

**syrup** /si-ruhp/ *n.* **1 a** sweet sauce of sugar dissolved in boiling water. **b** similar fluid of a specified flavour as a drink, medicine, etc. (*rose-hip syrup*). **2** condensed sugar-cane juice; molasses, treacle. **3** excessive sweetness of manner or style. □ **syrupy** *adj.* [Arabic *sharab*]

**system** /sis-tuhm/ *n.* **1** complex whole; set of connected things or parts; organised body of material or immaterial things (*solar system*; *railway system*; *different systems of philosophy*). **2 a** set of organs in the body with a common structure or function (*the digestive system*). **b** human or animal body as a whole. **3** method; scheme of action, procedure, or classification (*must work out a system to clear*

---

**Synonym**

A synonym is a word that has the same meaning as, or a similar meaning to, another word:

   *cheerful, happy, merry*, and *jolly*

are synonyms that are quite close to each other in meaning, as are

   *lazy, indolent*, and *slothful*

In contrast, the following words all mean 'a person who works with another', but their meanings vary considerably:

| | | |
|---|---|---|
| *colleague* | *conspirator* | *ally* |
| *collaborator* | *accomplice* | *partner* |

*up this mess*; *the Dewey system of library classification*). **4** orderliness. **5 a** body of theory or practice relating to a particular form of government, religion, etc. **b** (prec. by *the*) prevailing political or social order, esp. regarded as oppressive. **6** method of choosing one's procedure in gambling etc. **7** *Computing* group of related hardware units or programs or both, esp. when dedicated to a single application. □ **get a thing out of one's system** *colloq.* get rid of a preoccupation or anxiety. [Greek *sustēma -mat-*]

**systematic** /ˌsis-tuh-**mat**-ik/ *adj.* **1** methodical; according to a system. **2** regular, deliberate (*a systematic liar*). □ **systematically** *adv.*

**systematise** /**sis**-tuh-muh-ˌtuyz/ *v.* (also **-ize**) (**-sing** or **-zing**) make systematic. □ **systematisation** /-**zay**-shuhn/ *n.*

**systemic** /sis-**tem**-ik, sis-**tee**-mik/ *adj.* **1** *Physiol.* of the whole body. **2** (of an insecticide etc.) entering the plant via the roots or shoots and freely transported within its tissues. □ **systemically** *adv.*

**systems analysis** *n.* analysis of a complex process etc. in order to improve its efficiency, esp. by using a computer.

**systems programmer** *n.* person who specialises in low-level software and machine-support tasks.

**systole** /**sis**-tuh-lee/ *n. Physiol.* contraction of the heart, when blood is pumped into the arteries (cf. DIASTOLE). □ **systolic** /sis-**tol**-ik/ *adj.* [Greek *sustellō* contract]

# T

**T¹** /tee/ *n.* (also **t**)(*pl.* **Ts** or **T's**) **1** twentieth letter of the alphabet. **2** T-shaped thing (esp. *attrib.*: *T-joint*). □ **to a T** exactly; to a nicety.

**T²** *symb.* tritium.

**t.** *abbr.* **1** ton(s). **2** tonne(s).

**Ta** *symb.* tantalum.

**ta** /tah/ *int. colloq.* thank you. [infantile form]

**TAB** /tee-ay-bee, tab/ *n.* **1** acronym of *T*otalisator *A*gency *B*oard, the government agency which controls off-course betting. **2** branch of this body (*the local TAB*). **3** (*attrib.*) of or related to TAB betting (*TAB dividend*).

**tab¹** — *n.* **1** small flap or strip of material attached for grasping, fastening, or hanging up, or for identification. **2** *colloq.* bill (*picked up the tab*). — *v.* (**-bb-**) provide with a tab or tabs. □ **have a person tabbed** have him or her identified or summed up. **keep tabs** (or **a tab**) **on** *colloq.* **1** keep account of. **2** have under observation or in check. [probably British dial.]

**tab²** *n.* = TABULATOR 2. [abbreviation]

**tabard** /**tab**-uhd/ *n.* **1** herald's official coat emblazoned with royal arms. **2** *hist.* knight's short emblazoned garment worn over armour. [French]

**tabasco** /tuh-**bas**-koh/ *n.* **1** pungent pepper. **2** (**Tabasco**) *propr.* sauce made from this. [*Tabasco* in Mexico]

**tabby** /**tab**-ee/ *n.* (*pl.* **-ies**) **1** grey or brownish cat with dark stripes. **2** a kind of watered silk. [French from Arabic]

**tabernacle** /**tab**-uh-,nak-uhl/ *n.* **1** *hist.* tent used as a sanctuary for the Ark of the Covenant by the Israelites during the Exodus. **2** niche or receptacle over the main altar, having a lockable door concealed by a veil, used for reserving the consecrated Host(s). **3** place of worship in nonconformist creeds. [Latin: related to TAVERN]

**table** /**tay**-buhl/ — *n.* **1** flat surface on a leg or legs, used for eating, working at, etc. **2 a** food provided in a household (*keeps a good table*). **b** group seated for dinner etc. **3 a** set of facts or figures in columns etc. (*table of contents*). **b** matter contained in this. **c** = MULTIPLICATION TABLE. — *v.* (**-ling**) bring forward for discussion etc. at a meeting. □ **on the table** offered for discussion. **turn the tables** (often foll. by *on*) reverse circumstances to one's advantage (against). **under the table** *colloq.* **1** very drunk. **2** = *under the counter* (see COUNTER¹). [Latin *tabula* board]

**tableau** /**tab**-loh/ *n.* (*pl.* **-x** /-lohz/ ) **1** picturesque presentation. **2** group of silent motionless people representing a scene on stage. [French, = picture, diminutive of TABLE]

**tableland** *n.* elevated plateau.

**tablespoon** *n.* **1** large spoon for serving food and as a measurement in cooking. **2** amount (4 teaspoons or 20ml) held by this. □ **tablespoonful** *n.* (*pl.* **-s**).

**tablet** /**tab**-luht/ *n.* **1** small solid dose of a medicine etc. **2** bar of soap etc. **3** flat slab of esp. stone, usu. inscribed. [Latin diminutive: related to TABLE]

**table tennis** *n.* indoor ball game played with small bats on a table divided by a net.

**tableware** *n.* dishes, plates, etc., for meals.

**tabloid** /**tab**-loid/ *n.* small-sized, often popular or sensational, newspaper. [from TABLET]

**taboo** /tuh-**boo**/ (also **tabu**) — *n.* (*pl.* **-s**) **1** ritual isolation of a person or thing as sacred or accursed. **2** prohibition imposed by social custom. — *adj.* avoided or prohibited, esp. by social custom (*taboo words*). — *v.* (**-oos**, **-ooed** or **-us**, **-ued**) **1** put under taboo. **2** exclude or prohibit, esp. socially. [Tongan]

**tabor** /**tay**-buh/ *n. hist.* small drum, esp. used to accompany a pipe. [French]

**tabouli** /tuh-**boo**-lee/ *n.* Syrian and Lebanese salad made with bulgur, parsley, onion, etc. [Arabic]

**tabu** var. of TABOO.

**tabular** /**tab**-yuh-luh/ *adj.* of or arranged in tables or lists. [Latin: related to TABLE]

**tabulate** /**tab**-yuh-,layt/ *v.* (**-ting**) arrange (figures or facts) in tabular form. □ **tabulation** /-**lay**-shuhn/ *n.*

**tabulator** *n.* **1** person or thing that tabulates. **2** (also **tab**) device on a typewriter etc. for advancing to a sequence of set positions in tabular work.

**tacho** /**tak**-oh/ *n.* (*pl.* **-s**) *colloq.* = TACHOMETER. [abbreviation]

**tachograph** /**tak**-uh-,grahf, -,graf/ *n.* device in a vehicle recording speed and travel time. [Greek *takhos* speed]

**tachometer** /ta-**kom**-uh-tuh/ n. instrument measuring velocity or rate of rotation of a shaft (esp. in a vehicle).

**tacit** /**tas**-uht/ adj. understood or implied without being stated (*tacit consent*). □ **tacitly** adv. [Latin *taceo* be silent]

**taciturn** /**tas**-uh-ˌtern/ adj. saying little; uncommunicative. □ **taciturnity** /-**ter**-nuh-tee/ n. [Latin: related to TACIT]

**tack¹** — n. **1** small sharp broad-headed nail. **2** long stitch for joining fabrics etc. lightly or temporarily together. **3** (in sailing) direction, or temporary change of direction, esp. taking advantage of a side wind (*starboard tack*). **4** course of action or policy (*change tack*). — v. **1** (often foll. by *down* etc.) fasten with tacks. **2** stitch lightly together. **3** (foll. by *to, on, on to*) add or append. **4 a** change a ship's course by turning its head to the wind. **b** make a series of such tacks. [probably related to French *tache* clasp, nail]

**tack²** n. saddle, bridle, etc., of a horse. [from TACKLE]

**tackle** /**tak**-uhl/ — n. **1** equipment for a task or sport (*fishing tackle*). **2** mechanism, esp. of ropes, pulley-blocks, hooks, etc., for lifting weights, managing sails, etc. **3** windlass with its ropes and hooks. **4** act of tackling in football etc. — v. (**-ling**) **1** try to deal with (a problem or difficulty). **2** grapple with (an opponent). **3** confront (a person) in discussion or argument. **4** intercept or stop (a player running with the ball). □ **tackler** n. [Low German]

**tacky¹** adj. (**-ier, -iest**) slightly sticky (*the paint is still tacky*). □ **tackiness** n. [from TACK¹]

**tacky²** adj. (**-ier, -iest**) colloq. **1** in poor taste, cheap. **2** tatty, shabby. □ **tackiness** n. [origin unknown]

**taco** /**tah**-koh, **tak**-oh/ n. (pl. **-s**) Mexican dish of meat etc. in a folded tortilla. [Mexican Spanish]

**tact** n. **1** skill in dealing with others, esp. in delicate situations. **2** intuitive perception of the right thing to do or say. [Latin *tango tact-* touch]

**tactful** adj. having or showing tact. □ **tactfully** adv.

**tactic** /**tak**-tik/ n. **1** tactical manoeuvre. **2** = TACTICS. [Greek from *tasso* arrange]

**tactical** adj. **1** of tactics (*tactical retreat*). **2** (of bombing etc.) done in direct support of military or naval operations. **3** adroitly planning or adroitly planned. □ **tactically** adv.

**tactics** n.pl. **1** (also treated as *sing.*) disposition of armed forces, esp. in warfare. **2** short-term procedure adopted in carrying out a scheme or achieving an end. □ **tactician** /tak-**tish**-uhn/ n.

**tactile** /**tak**-tuyl/ adj. **1** of the sense of touch. **2** perceived by touch; tangible. □ **tactility** /-**til**-uh-tee/ n. [Latin: related to TACT]

**tactless** adj. having or showing no tact. □ **tactlessly** adv.

**tad** n. colloq. small amount. □ **a tad** a little; slightly (*feeling a tad off-colour*). [origin uncertain; perhaps a shortening of TADPOLE]

**taddie** /**tad**-ee/ n. colloq. tadpole.

**tadpole** n. larva, esp. of a frog, toad, etc. [related to TOAD, POLL]

**TAFE** /tayf/ n. **1** acronym of *Technical and Further Education*, a system of tertiary education offering courses mainly in technical and vocational subjects. **2** institution offering such courses. **3** (*attrib.*) of or relating to TAFE (*am doing a TAFE course*).

**taffeta** /**taf**-uh-tuh/ n. fine lustrous silk or silklike fabric. [French or medieval Latin from Persian]

**tag¹** — n. **1** label, esp. on an object to show its address, price, etc. **2** metal etc. point on a shoelace etc. **3** loop or flap for handling or hanging a thing. **4** loose or ragged end. **5** label or popular designation (*the tag 'feminist' is often loosely applied*). **6** personal signature (a nickname etc.) of a graffiti artist. **7** *Computing* character or set of characters appended to an item of data in order to identify it. — v. (**-gg-**) **1** provide with a tag or tags. **2** (often foll. by *on, on to*) join or attach. **3** colloq. follow closely. **4** *Computing* label (an item of data) for later retrieval etc. □ **tag along** (often foll. by *with*) go along, accompany passively. [origin unknown]

**tag²** — n. children's chasing game. — v. (**-gg-**) touch in a game of tag. [origin unknown]

**tagliatelle** /ˌtal-yuh-**tel**-ee/ n. narrow ribbon-shaped pasta. [Italian]

**tahina** /tah-**hee**-nuh/ n. (also **tahini**) Middle Eastern paste or sauce made from sesame seeds. [Arabic, = grind, pulverise]

**t'ai chi** /tuy **chee**/ n. (in full **t'ai chi chu'an** /ˌtuy chee **chwahn**/ ) Chinese martial art and system of callisthenics with slow controlled movements. [Chinese, = great ultimate boxing]

**tail** — n. **1 a** hindmost part of an animal, esp. extending beyond the body. **b** person's buttocks. **2 a** thing like a tail, esp. an extension at the rear. **b** rear end of anything, e.g. of a procession. **3** rear part of an aeroplane, vehicle, or rocket. **4** luminous trail following a comet. **5 a** inferior, weaker, or last part of anything, esp. in a sequence. **b** *Cricket* end of the batting order, with the weakest batsmen. **6** part of a shirt or coat below the waist at the back. **7** (in *pl.*) **a** tailcoat. **b** evening dress including this. **8** (in *pl.*) reverse of a coin as a choice when tossing. **9** *colloq.* person following or shadowing another. — *v.* **1** remove the stalks of (fruit). **2** (often foll. by *after*) *colloq.* follow closely. **3** dock the tail (of a lamb etc.). **4** follow, herd, and tend (livestock). □ **on a person's tail** closely following a person. **tail off** (or **away**) gradually decrease or diminish; end inconclusively. **tail them** (in two-up) toss the coins so that they fall tails uppermost. **turn tail** see TURN. **with one's tail between one's legs** dejected, humiliated. **with one's tail up** in good spirits; cheerful. □ **tailless** *adj.* [Old English]

**tailcoat** *n.* man's coat with a long divided flap at the back, worn as part of formal dress.

**tail-end** *n.* hindmost, lowest, or last part.

**tailgate** — *n.* **1** hinged or removable flap at the rear of a truck etc. **2** rear door of a station wagon or hatchback. — *v.* drive dangerously close to the vehicle in front.

**tail light** *n.* rear light on a vehicle etc.

**tailor** /tay-luh/ — *n.* **1** maker of clothes, esp. men's outer garments to measure. **2** (also **taylor**) marine food-fish of Australian waters, a voracious feeder. — *v.* **1** make (clothes) as a tailor. **2** make or adapt for a special purpose. **3** work as or be a tailor. [Anglo-French *taillour*]

**tailor-bird** *n.* Australian golden-headed warbler, a bird which stitches leaves etc. together with spiderwebs to form its nest.

**tailored** *adj.* **1** (of clothing) well or closely fitted. **2** = TAILOR-MADE.

**tailor-made** *adj.* **1** made to order by a tailor. **2** made or suited for a particular purpose.

**tailplane** *n.* horizontal aerofoil at the tail of an aircraft.

**tailspin** *n.* **1** spin by an aircraft with the tail spiralling. **2** state of chaos or panic.

**tail wind** *n.* wind blowing in the direction of travel.

**taint** — *n.* **1** spot or trace of decay, infection, corruption, some bad quality, etc. **2** corrupt condition or infection. — *v.* **1** affect with a taint; become tainted. **2** (foll. by *with*) affect slightly (*tainted with remorse*). [Latin: related to TINGE]

**taipan** /tuy-pan/ *n.* long-fanged brownish snake of northern Australia (and New Guinea), the longest (2–4m) and perhaps deadliest of Australian venomous snakes. [Wik-Mungkan *dhayban*]

**take** — *v.* (**-king**; *past* **took** /tuuk/; *past part.* **taken**) **1** lay hold of; get into one's hands. **2** acquire, capture, earn, or win. **3** get by purchase, hire, or formal agreement (*take lodgings; took a taxi*). **4** (in a recipe) use. **5** regularly buy (a newspaper etc.). **6** obtain after qualifying (*take a degree*). **7** occupy (*take a chair*). **8** make use of (*take the next turning on the left; take the bus*). **9** consume (food or medicine). **10 a** be effective (*inoculation did not take*). **b** (of a plant, seed, cutting, etc.) begin to grow. **11** require or use up (*will only take a minute*). **12** cause to come or go with one; convey (*take the book home; bus will take you*). **13** remove; steal (*someone has taken my pen*). **14** catch or be infected with (fire or fever etc.). **15 a** experience, seek, or be affected by (*take fright; take pleasure*). **b** exert (*take no notice*). **16** find out and note (*took his address; took her temperature*). **17** understand; assume (*I take your point; I took you to mean yes*). **18** treat, deal with, or regard in a specified way (*took it badly; took the corner too fast*). **19** (foll. by *for*) regard as being (*do you take me for an idiot?*). **20 a** accept, receive (*take the offer; take a call; takes boarders*). **b** hold (*takes 3 litres*). **c** submit to; tolerate (*take a joke; takes no nonsense*). **21** wear (*takes size 10*). **22** choose or assume (*took a job; took the initiative; took holy orders*). **23** derive (*takes its name from the inventor*). **24** (foll. by *from*) subtract (*take 3 from 9*). **25** perform or effect (*take notes; take an oath; take a look*). **26** occupy or engage oneself in (*take a rest*). **27** conduct (*took prayers*). **28** teach, be taught, or be examined in (a subject). **29 a** make (a photograph). **b** photograph (a person etc.). **30** (in *imper.*) use as an example (*take Napoleon*). **31** *Gram.* have or require as part of a construction (*this verb takes an object*). **32** (in *passive*; foll. by *by, with*) be attracted or charmed by (*is very taken with him*). — *n.* **1** amount taken or caught at a time etc. **2** scene or film sequence photographed continuously at one time. **3** *colloq.* a swindle. □ **be taken ill** become ill, esp. suddenly. **have what it takes** *colloq.* have the necessary qualities etc. for success. **on the take** *colloq.* taking bribes; receiving money etc. by illicit means. **take aback** startle; disconcert. **take after** resemble (a parent etc.). **take apart 1** dismantle. **2** *colloq.* beat or defeat. **3** *colloq.* criticise severely. **take away 1** remove or carry elsewhere. **2** subtract. **take back 1** retract (a statement). **2** convey to an original position; return (unsatisfactory etc. purchases). **3** carry in thought to a past time (*this takes me back to my childhood*). **4** accept (a person) back into one's affections, into employment, etc. **take the cake** *colloq.* be the most remarkable (*his effrontery takes the cake*). **take down 1** write down (spoken words). **2** remove or dismantle. **3** lower (a garment worn below the waist). **4** *colloq.* humiliate; rebuke (*took him down a peg or two*). **5** *colloq.* cheat; trick; swindle. **take for granted** see GRANT. **take heart** be encouraged. **take in 1** receive as a lodger etc. **2** undertake (work) at home. **3** make (a garment etc.) smaller. **4** understand; observe (*did you take that in?*). **5** cheat. **6** include. **7** *colloq.* visit (a place) on the way to another (*took in the You Yangs*). **8** absorb into the body. **9** *colloq.* take into custody; arrest. **take in hand 1** undertake; start doing or dealing with. **2** undertake to control or reform (a person). **take it 1** (often foll. by *that*) assume. **2** *colloq.* endure in a specified way (*took it badly; just can't take it any more*). **take it into one's head** see HEAD. **take it on one** (or **oneself**) (foll. by *to* + infin.) venture or presume. **take it or leave it** (esp. in *imper.*) accept it or not. **take it out of 1** exhaust the strength of. **2** have revenge on. **take it out on** relieve one's frustration by treating aggressively. **take off 1 a** remove (clothing) from the body. **b** remove or lead away. **c** withdraw (transport, a show, etc.). **2** deduct (part of an amount). **3** depart, esp. hastily. **4** mimic humorously. **5** begin a jump. **6** become airborne. **7** (of a scheme, enterprise, etc.) become successful. **8** have (a period) away from work. **9** (of prices etc.) rise steeply or suddenly. **take oneself off** go away. **take on 1** undertake (work etc.). **2** engage (an employee). **3** be willing or ready to meet (an opponent in sport, argument, etc., esp. a stronger one). **4** acquire (new meaning etc.). **take out 1** remove; extract. **2 a** escort on an outing (*took the kids out to the pictures*). **b** be emotionally involved with (*is he taking anyone out at the moment?*). **3** get (a licence, summons, etc.) issued. **take a person out of himself** or **herself** make a person forget his or her worries. **take over 1** succeed to the management or ownership of. **2** take control. **take shape** assume a distinct form; develop. **take one's time** not hurry. **take to 1** begin or fall into the habit of (*took to smoking*). **2** have recourse to. **3** adapt oneself to. **4** form a liking for. **5** *colloq.* attack. **take up 1** become interested or engaged in (a pursuit). **2**

adopt as a protégé. **3** occupy (time or space). **4** begin (residence etc.). **5** resume after an interruption. **6** (often foll. by *on*) interrupt or question (a speaker) (on a point). **7** accept (an offer etc.). **8** shorten (a garment). **9** lift up. **10** absorb. **11** pursue (a matter etc.) further, esp. with those in authority. **12** *hist.* acquire (land) from the Crown as owner or as tenant (*took up a selection*). **take a person up on** accept (a person's offer etc.). **take up with** begin to associate with. [Old English from Old Norse]

**take-all** *n.* disease of wheat and other cereals caused by a fungus producing root-rot.

**take-away** — *attrib. adj.* (of food) bought cooked for eating elsewhere. — *n.* **1** this food. **2** establishment selling this.

**take-home pay** *n.* employee's pay after the deduction of tax etc.

**take-off** *n.* **1** act of becoming airborne. **2** act of mimicking.

**take-over** *n.* assumption of control (esp. of a business); buying-out.

**taker** *n.* **1** person who takes a bet, accepts an offer, etc. **2** potential buyer (*I think we have a taker for the house*).

**taking** — *adj.* attractive, captivating. — *n.* (in *pl.*) amount of money taken at a show, in a shop, etc.

**talc** *n.* **1** talcum powder. **2** magnesium silicate formed as soft flat plates, used as a lubricator etc. [Arabic from Persian *talk*]

**talcum** /tal-kuhm/ *n.* **1** = TALC 2. **2** (in full **talcum powder**) powdered talc for toilet use, usu. perfumed. [medieval Latin: see TALC]

**tale** *n.* **1** (usu. fictitious) narrative or story. **2** allegation, often malicious or in breach of confidence. [Old English]

**talent** /tal-uhnt/ *n.* **1** special aptitude or faculty (*talent for music*). **2** high mental ability. **3 a** person or persons of talent. **b** *colloq.* attractive members of the opposite sex (*plenty of local talent*). **4** ancient esp. Greek weight and unit of currency. □ **talented** *adj.* [Greek *talanton*]

**talent scout** *n.* (also **talent spotter**) person seeking new talent, esp. in sport or entertainment.

**talisman** /tal-uhz-muhn/ *n.* (*pl.* **-s**) ring, stone, etc., thought to have magic powers, esp. to bring good luck. □ **talismanic** /-man-ik/ *adj.* [French and Spanish from Greek]

**talk** /tawk/ — *v.* **1** (often foll. by *to, with*) converse or communicate verbally. **2** have the power of speech. **3** (often foll. by *about*) **a** discuss; express; utter (*talked cricket; talking nonsense*). **b** (in *imper.*)

*colloq.* as an emphatic statement (*talk about expense!*). **4** use (a language) in speech (*talking Spanish*). **5** (foll. by *at*) address pompously. **6** (usu. foll. by *into*, *out of*) bring into a specified condition etc. by talking (*talked himself hoarse; did you talk them into it?*). **7** reveal (esp. secret) information; betray secrets. **8** gossip (*people will talk*). **9** have influence (*money talks*). — *n.* **1** conversation, talking. **2** particular mode of speech (*baby-talk*). **3** informal address or lecture. **4 a** rumour or gossip (*talk of a merger*). **b** theme of such rumour or gossip (*the talk was all babies*). **5** empty promises; boasting. **6** (often in *pl.*) discussions or negotiations. □ **now you're talking** *colloq.* I like what you say, suggest, etc. **talk back** reply defiantly. **talk big** *colloq.* talk boastfully. **talk down 1** reduce or diminish by talking; denigrate or belittle. **2** *Econ.* depress the economy generally, the value of (a currency), or the price of (a commodity) by making tactical public statements (*he was accused of talking down the Australian dollar*) (cf. *talk up*). **talk down to** speak patronisingly or condescendingly to. **talk a person down 1** silence by loudness or persistence. **2** bring (a pilot or aircraft) to landing by radio. **talk a person into** persuade (a person) by talking. **talk nineteen to the dozen** see DOZEN. **talk of 1** discuss or mention. **2** (often foll. by verbal noun) express some intention of (*talked of moving to the Gold Coast*). **talk of the town** what is being talked or gossiped about generally. **talk out** discuss in order to reach a solution etc. (*we need to talk this matter out*). **talk a person out of** dissuade a person from (something) by talking. **talk a person over** (or **round**) gain agreement by talking. **talk over** discuss at length. **talk over a person's head** use language, knowledge, etc., which the addressee cannot understand. **talk shop** talk about one's occupation etc. **talk till the cows come home** talk at length (*you can talk till the cows come home, but I won't change my mind*). **talk to** rebuke, scold. **talk turkey** see TURKEY. **talk up 1** discuss favourably; praise or advocate. **2** *Econ.* raise the economy generally, the value of (a currency), or the price of (a commodity) by making tactical public statements (cf. *talk down*). **you can't** (or **can**) **talk!** *colloq.* reproof that the person addressed is just as culpable etc. in the matter at issue. □ **talker** *n.* [from TALE or TELL]

**talkative** /taw-kuh-tiv/ *adj.* fond of or given to talking.

**talkback** *n.* (often *attrib.*) **1** system of two-way communication by loudspeaker. **2** broadcast programme in which the listeners telephone the presenter and participate.

**talkfest** /tawk-fest/ *n.* lengthy discussion, conference, etc., at which much is said but little is achieved (cf. GABFEST).

**talkie** *n. colloq.* (esp. early) film with a soundtrack.

**talking** — *adj.* **1** that talks, or is able to talk (*talking parrot*). **2** expressive (*talking eyes*). — *n.* in senses of TALK *v.* □ **talking of** while we are discussing.

**talking book** *n.* recorded reading of a book, esp. for the blind.

**talking point** *n.* topic for discussion.

**talking-to** *n. colloq.* reproof, reprimand.

**talk show** *n.* interview programme on radio or television.

**tall** /tawl/ — *adj.* **1** of more than average height. **2** of a specified height (*about 175cm tall*). **3** higher than the surrounding objects (*tall building*). **4** exaggerated, extravagant; hard to believe (*a tall story*). — *adv.* as if tall; proudly (*sit tall*). □ **tallish** *adj.* **tallness** *n.* [Old English, = swift]

**tallboy** *n.* tall chest of drawers.

**tallegalane** /tuh-leg-uh-layn/ *n.* (also **sand mullet**) small marine and estuarine food-fish of southern Australia. [possibly from an Aboriginal language]

**tall oat grass** *n.* tall Australian grass having purple stems and oaten heads of seed, valued as fodder.

**tall order** *n.* unreasonable demand.

**tallow** /tal-oh/ *n.* hard (esp. animal) fat melted down to make candles, soap, etc. □ **tallowy** *adj.* [Low German]

**tallow-wood** *n.* **1** tall eucalypt of Queensland and NSW, having a persistently furrowed red-brown bark. **2** the greasy, extremely durable wood of this tree.

**tall poppy** *n.* person who is conspicuously successful and whose distinction frequently attracts envious notice or hostility.

**tall-poppy syndrome** *n.* habit of denigrating or 'cutting down' those who are successful, high-achievers, etc.

**tall ship** *n.* sailing-ship with a high mast.

**tally** /tal-ee/ — *n.* (*pl.* **-ies**) **1** reckoning of a debt or score. **2** total score or amount. **3** mark registering the number of objects delivered or received. **4** *hist.* **a** piece of notched wood for keeping account. **b** account kept thus. **5** the number of sheep shorn by an individual shearer in a specified period. — *v.* (**-ies, -ied**) **1** (often foll. by *with*) agree or correspond (*your account doesn't tally with mine*). **2** record or reckon by tally; enumerate. [Latin *talea* rod]

**tally-room** n. centre at which votes are counted or posted in an election.

**tally-walka** /tal-ee-waw-kuh/ n. (also **tally-walker**) branch of a river which separates from and then rejoins the main river further on; anabranch. [Baagandji *daliwalga*]

**Talmud** /tal-muud, -muhd/ n. body of Jewish civil and ceremonial law and legend. □ **Talmudic** /-muud-ik/ adj. **Talmudist** n. [Hebrew, = instruction]

**talon** /tal-uhn/ n. claw, esp. of a bird of prey. [Latin *talus* ankle]

**talus** /tay-luhs/ n. (pl. **tali** /-luy/) anklebone supporting the tibia. [Latin, = ankle]

**tamar** var. of TAMMAR.

**tamarillo** /,tam-uh-**ril**-oh/ n. (also **tree tomato**) egg-shaped acidic red fruit of a South American shrub. [arbitrary marketing name]

**tamarind** /tam-uh-rind/ n. 1 tropical evergreen tree. 2 fruit of this containing an acid pulp used in food (curries etc.) and in drinks. [Arabic, = Indian date]

**tambour** /tam-boor, tam-baw/ n. 1 drum. 2 circular frame holding fabric taut for embroidery. [French: related to TABOR]

**tambourine** /,tam-buh-**reen**/ n. small shallow drum with jingling discs in its rim, shaken or banged as an accompaniment. [French, diminutive of TAMBOUR]

**tame** — adj. 1 (of an animal) domesticated; not wild or shy. 2 insipid; dull (*tame entertainment*). 3 (of a person) amenable. — v. (**-ming**) 1 make tame; domesticate. 2 subdue, curb; humble; break the spirit of. □ **tameable** adj. **tamely** adv. **tameness** n. **tamer** n. (also in comb.). [Old English]

**Tamil** /tam-uhl/ — n. 1 member of a Dravidian people indigenous to South India and Sri Lanka. 2 language of this people. — adj. of this people or language. [native name *Tamil*, related to Sanskrit *Dravida* a province of South India]

**tammar** /tam-uh/ n. (also **tamar** or **tammar wallaby**) greyish-brown wallaby of southern Australia. [Nyungar *damar*]

**tamp** v. ram down hard or tightly. [*tampion* stopper for gun-muzzle, from French *tampon*]

**tamper** v. (foll. by *with*) 1 meddle with or change illicitly. 2 exert a secret or corrupt influence upon; bribe. [var. of TEMPER]

**tampon** /tam-pon/ n. plug of soft material used esp. to absorb menstrual blood. [French: related to TAMP]

**tan¹** — n. 1 = SUNTAN. 2 yellowish-brown colour. 3 bark (of wattle trees etc.)

bruised and used to tan hides. — adj. yellowish-brown. — v. (**-nn-**) 1 make or become brown by exposure to sunlight. 2 convert (raw hide) into leather. 3 colloq. beat, thrash. [medieval Latin *tanno*, perhaps from Celtic]

**tan²** abbr. tangent.

**tanbark** /tan-bahk/ n. bark (which had been used in the tanning process) broken up into chips and used as a mulch in gardens etc.

**tandem** /tan-duhm/ — n. 1 bicycle with two or more seats one behind another. 2 group of two people etc. with one behind or following the other. — adv. with two or more horses harnessed one behind another (*drive tandem*). □ **in tandem** 1 one behind another. 2 alongside each other; together. [Latin, = at length]

**tandoor** /tan-door/ n. clay oven used in some Indian cooking. [Hindustani]

**tandoori** /tan-**door**-ree/ n. food spiced and cooked over charcoal in a tandoor (often *attrib.*: *tandoori chicken*). [Hindustani]

**tang** n. 1 strong taste or flavour or smell. 2 characteristic quality (*the tang of gumlogs burning*). 3 slight hint or trace of some quality (*after decades in Australia his speech has still a pommy tang*). 4 projection on the blade of esp. a knife, by which it is held firm in the handle. [Old Norse *tange* point]

**tangent** /tan-juhnt/ n. 1 (often *attrib.*) straight line, curve, or surface that meets a curve at a point, but does not intersect it. 2 ratio of two sides (other than the hypotenuse) opposite and adjacent to an acute angle in a right-angled triangle. □ **at a tangent** diverging from a previous course or from what is relevant or central (*go off at a tangent*). [Latin *tango tact-* touch]

**tangential** /tan-**jen**-shuhl/ adj. 1 of or along a tangent. 2 at a tangent; divergent (*a collection of mixed and tangential information*). 3 that merely touches a subject or matter; peripheral (*the issue you raise is quite tangential to the purpose of this meeting*). □ **tangentially** adv.

**tangerine** /,tan-juh-**reen**/ n. 1 small sweet thin-skinned citrus fruit like an orange; mandarin. 2 deep orange-yellow colour. [*Tangier* in Morocco]

**tangible** /tan-juh-buhl/ adj. 1 perceptible by touch. 2 definite; clearly intelligible; not elusive (*tangible proof*). □ **tangibility** /-**bil**-uh-tee/ n. **tangibleness** n. **tangibly** adv. [Latin: related to TANGENT]

**tangle** /tang-guhl/ — v. (**-ling**) 1 intertwine (threads or hairs etc.) or become entwined in a confused mass;

entangle. **2** (foll. by *with*) become involved (esp. in conflict or argument) with (*don't tangle with me*). **3** complicate (*tangled affair*). — *n.* **1** confused mass of intertwined threads etc. **2** confused state. [origin uncertain]

**tanglefoot** *n.* **1** deciduous shrub or small tree having wiry, tangled branches, and occurring in the mountains of Tasmania. **2** any of several other Australian plants of similar habit.

**tangly** *adj.* (**-ier, -iest**) tangled.

**tango** /tang-goh/ — *n.* (*pl.* **-s**) **1** slow S. American ballroom dance. **2** music for this. — *v.* (**-goes, -goed**) dance the tango. [American Spanish]

**tangy** /tang-ee/ *adj.* (**-ier, -iest**) having a strong usu. acid tang.

**tank** — *n.* **1** large container, usu. for liquid or gas. **2** reservoir; dam. **3** heavy armoured fighting vehicle moving on continuous tracks. — *v.* (usu. foll. by *up*) fill the tank of (a vehicle etc.) with fuel. □ **tankful** *n.* (*pl.* **-s**). [originally Indian, = pond, from Gujarati]

**tankard** /tang-kuhd/ *n.* **1** tall beer mug with a handle. **2** contents of or amount held by this (*drank a tankard of beer*). [probably Dutch *tankaert*]

**tanked** *predic. adj.* (also **tanked up**) *colloq.* drunk.

**tanker** *n.* ship, aircraft, or road vehicle, for carrying liquids, esp. oil, in bulk.

**tank-stand** *n.* structure that supports a tank in which water is stored.

**tanner** *n.* person who tans hides.

**tannery** *n.* (*pl.* **-ies**) place where hides are tanned.

**tannic** /tan-ik/ *adj.* of tan (sense 3). [French *tannique*: related to TANNIN]

**tannic acid** *n.* natural yellowish organic compound used as a mordant and astringent.

**tannin** /tan-uhn/ *n.* **1** any of various organic compounds found in wattle-tree barks etc., used in leather production. **2** **a** a compound, deriving from grape skins, seeds, stalks, and from oak barrels, which gives certain red wines a desirable astringency. **b** compound in the leaves which gives (esp. strong or overbrewed) tea an astringent quality. [French *tanin*: related to TAN[1]]

**tanning** *n. colloq.* a beating, thrashing.

**tantalise** /tan-tuh-luyz/ *v.* (also **-ize**) (**-sing** or **-zing**) **1** torment or tease by the sight or promise of the unobtainable. **2** raise and then dash the hopes of. □ **tantalisation** /-zay-shuhn/ *n.* [*Tantalus*, mythical king punished in Hades with sight of water and fruit which drew back when he tried to reach them]

**tantalum** /tan-tuh-luhm/ *n.* rare hard white metallic element. □ **tantalic** *adj.* [related to TANTALISE]

**tantamount** /tan-tuh-,mownt/ *predic. adj.* (foll. by *to*) equivalent to (*what you say is tantamount to blackmail*). [Italian *tanto montare* amount to so much]

**Tantanoola tiger** /tan-tuh-,noo-luh/ *n.* fabulous animal, first reported at Tantanoola, SA, in 1889, and 'sighted' thereafter in Victoria as well.

**tantra** /tan-truh/ *n.* any of a class of Hindu or Buddhist mystical and devotional writings. □ **tantric** *adj.* **tantrism** *n.* [Sanskrit, = doctrine]

**tantrum** /tan-truhm/ *n.* (esp. child's) outburst of bad temper or petulance. [origin unknown]

**Taoism** /tow-iz-uhm/ *n.* Chinese religious and philosophical system whose central concept and goal is the Tao, the code of behaviour in harmony with the natural order. □ **Taoist** *n.* & *adj.* [Chinese *dao* right way]

**tap[1]** — *n.* **1** device by which a flow of liquid or gas from a pipe or vessel can be controlled. **2** tapping of a telephone etc. — *v.* (**-pp-**) **1 a** provide (a cask) with a tap. **b** let out (liquid) by means of, or as if by means of, a tap. **2** draw sap from (a tree) by cutting into it. **3** obtain information or supplies from. **4** extract or obtain; discover and exploit (*mineral wealth waiting to be tapped*; *tap skills of young people*). **5** connect a listening device to (a telephone etc.). □ **on tap 1** ready to be drawn off by tap. **2** *colloq.* freely available. [Old English]

**tap[2]** — *v.* (**-pp-**) **1** (foll. by *at, on*) strike a gentle but audible blow. **2** (often foll. by *against, on,* etc.) strike or cause (a thing) to strike lightly (*tapped me on the shoulder*; *tapped a stick against the window*). **3** (often foll. by *out*) make by a tap or taps (*tapped out the rhythm*). — *n.* **1 a** light blow; rap. **b** sound of this (*heard a tap at the door*). **2** *colloq.* (in a negative context) slightest amount (*hasn't done a tap of work*). **3** metal attachment on a tap-dancer's shoe. [imitative]

**tap-dance** — *n.* rhythmic dance performed with shoes with metal taps. — *v.* perform a tap-dance. □ **tap-dancer** *n.* **tap-dancing** *n.*

**tape** — *n.* **1** narrow strip of woven material for tying up, fastening, etc. **2** this across the finishing line of a race. **3** (in full **adhesive tape**) strip of adhesive plastic etc. for fastening, masking, insulating, etc. **4 a** = MAGNETIC TAPE. **b** tape recording, reel, or cassette. **5** = TAPE-MEASURE. — *v.* (**-ping**) **1 a** fasten or join etc.

with tape. **b** apply tape to. **2** (foll. by *off*) seal or mark off an area or thing with tape. **3** record on magnetic tape. **4** measure with tape. □ **have** (or **get**) **a person** (or **thing**) **taped** *colloq.* understand (him, it, etc.) fully. [Old English]

**tape deck** *n.* machine for using audio-tape (separate from the amplifier, speakers, etc.).

**tape-measure** *n.* strip of marked tape or flexible metal for measuring.

**taper** /*tay*-puh/ — *n.* **1** wick coated with wax etc. for conveying a flame. **2** slender candle. **3** gradual diminution in width or thickness in an elongated object; gradual decrease of action, power, capacity, etc. — *v.* (often foll. by *off*) **1** diminish or reduce in thickness towards one end. **2** make or become gradually less (*interest in the monarchy has tapered off*). [Old English]

**tape recorder** *n.* apparatus for recording and replaying sounds on magnetic tape. □ **tape-record** *v.* **tape recording** *n.*

**tapestry** /*tap*-uh-stree/ *n.* (*pl.* **-ies**) **1 a** thick fabric in which coloured weft threads are woven to form pictures or designs. **b** (usu. wool) embroidery imitating this. **c** piece of this. **2** events or circumstances etc. seen as interwoven etc. (*life's rich tapestry*). □ **tapestried** *adj.* [*tapissery* from French *tapis* carpet]

**tapeworm** *n.* parasitic intestinal flatworm with a segmented body.

**tapioca** /ˌtap-ee-*oh*-kuh/ *n.* starchy substance in hard white grains, obtained from cassava and used for puddings etc. [Tupi-Guarani]

**tapir** /*tay*-puh/ *n.* nocturnal Central and S. American or Malaysian hoofed mammal with a short flexible snout. [Tupi]

**tappet** /*tap*-uht/ *n.* lever or projecting part in machinery giving intermittent motion. [from TAP²]

**tap root** *n.* tapering main root growing vertically downwards.

**tar¹** — *n.* **1** dark thick inflammable liquid distilled from wood or coal etc., used as a preservative of wood and iron, in making roads, as an antiseptic, etc. **2** similar substance formed in the combustion of tobacco etc. — *v.* (**-rr-**) cover with tar. □ **tar and feather** smear with tar and then cover with feathers as a punishment. **tarred with the same brush** having the same faults. [Old English]

**tar²** *n. colloq.* sailor. [from TARPAULIN]

**taramasalata** /ˌta-ruh-ma-suh-*lah*-tuh/ *n.* (also **taramosalata**) pâté made from roe with olive oil, seasoning, etc. [Greek *taramas* roe, *salata* SALAD]

**tarantella** /ˌta-ruhn-*tel*-uh/ *n.* **1** whirling S. Italian dance. **2** music for this. [Italian from *Taranto* in Italy (because the dance was once thought to be a cure for a tarantula bite)]

**tarantula** /tuh-*ran*-chuh-luh/ *n.* **1** = HUNTSMAN². **2** large hairy tropical spider. **3** large black S. European spider. [medieval Latin: related to TARANTELLA]

**tar-boy** *n.* shearers' worker employed chiefly to apply a disinfectant, orig. tar, to a wound accidentally inflicted on a sheep.

**tardy** /*tah*-dee/ *adj.* (**-ier**, **-iest**) **1** slow to act, come, or happen. **2** delaying or delayed. □ **tardily** *adv.* **tardiness** *n.* [Latin *tardus* slow]

**tare¹** /tair/ *n.* (in *pl.*) *Bibl.* an injurious cornfield weed (Matt. 13:24-30). [origin unknown]

**tare²** /tair/ *n.* **1** allowance made for the weight of packing or wrapping around goods. **2** weight of a vehicle without fuel or load. [Arabic *tarha*]

**target** /*tah*-guht/ — *n.* **1** mark fired or aimed at, esp. a round object marked with concentric circles. **2 a** person or thing aimed or fired at etc. (*an easy target*). **b** persons or social group aimed at by advertisers for marketing etc. **3** objective or result aimed at (*export target*). **4** butt for criticism, abuse, etc. — *v.* (**-t-**) **1** identify or single out as a target. **2** aim or direct (*missiles targeted on major cities*; *should target our efforts where most needed*). [French *targe* shield]

**tariff** /*ta*-ruhf/ *n.* **1** table of fixed charges (*hotel tariff*). **2 a** duty on a particular class of exports or esp. imports. **b** list of duties or customs due. [Arabic, = notification]

**tarmac** /*tah*-mak/ — *n. propr.* **1** = TARMACADAM. **2** runway etc. made of this. — *v.* (**-ck-**) apply tarmacadam to. [abbreviation]

**tarmacadam** /ˌtah-muh-*kad*-uhm/ *n.* stone, gravel, etc., bound with bitumen, used in paving roads etc. [from TAR¹, MACADAM]

**tarn** *n.* small mountain lake. [Old Norse]

**tarnish** /*tah*-nish/ — *v.* **1** (of metal etc.) (cause to) lose lustre. **2** impair (one's reputation etc.). — *n.* **1** loss of lustre, esp. as a film on a metal's surface. **2** blemish, stain. [French *ternir* from *terne* dark]

**taro** /*ta*-roh, *tah*-roh/ *n.* (*pl.* **-s**) tropical plant with tuberous roots used as food. [Polynesian]

**tarot** /*ta*-roh/ *n.* (often *attrib.*) **1** (in *sing.* or *pl.*) **a** pack of mainly picture cards used in fortune-telling. **b** any game played with a similar pack of 78 cards. **2** any card from a tarot pack. [French]

**tarp** *n. colloq.* tarpaulin. [abbreviation]

**tarpaulin** /tah-**paw**-luhn/ *n.* **1** heavy-duty cloth waterproofed esp. with tar. **2** sheet or covering of this. [from TAR¹, PALL¹]

**tarpaulin muster** *n.* collecting of a pool of money, to be used either to buy drinks etc. for the contributors or to provide assistance to some other person or cause (*held a tarpaulin muster for the bushfire victims*).

**tarragon** /**ta**-ruh-guhn/ *n.* bushy herb with aniseed flavour used in salads, stuffings, vinegar, etc. [medieval Latin from Greek]

**tarry¹** /**tah**-ree/ *adj.* (**-ier, -iest**) of, like, or smeared with tar.

**tarry²** /**ta**-ree/ *v.* (**-ies, -ied**) *archaic* linger, stay, wait. [origin unknown]

**tarsal** /**tah**-suhl/ — *adj.* of the ankle-bones. — *n.* tarsal bone. [from TARSUS]

**tarsus** /**tah**-suhs/ *n.* (*pl.* **tarsi** /-suy/ ) group of bones of the ankle and upper foot. [Greek]

**tart¹** *n.* **1** open pastry case containing jam etc. **2** pie with a fruit or other sweet filling. □ **tartlet** *n.* [French *tarte*]

**tart²** *n. colloq.* **1** prostitute; promis-cuous woman. **2** *colloq. offens.* girl or woman. — *v.* (foll. by *up*) *colloq.* (usu. *refl.*) smarten or dress up, esp. gaudily (*tarting himself up for the social; tarted up his car with purple paint and silver cushions*). [probably abbreviation of SWEETHEART]

**tart³** *adj.* **1** sharp or acid in taste. **2** (of a remark etc.) cutting, bitter. □ **tartly** *adv.* **tartness** *n.* [Old English]

**tartan** /**tah**-tuhn/ *n.* **1** pattern of col-oured stripes crossing at right angles, esp. denoting a Scottish Highland clan. **2** woollen cloth woven in this pattern (often *attrib.*: *tartan scarf*). [origin un-certain]

**Tartar** /**tah**-tuh/ — *n.* **1 a** member of a group of Central Asian peoples including Mongols and Turks. **b** Turkic language of these peoples. **2** (**tartar**) harsh or for-midable person. — *adj.* **1** of Tartars. **2** of Central Asia east of the Caspian Sea. [French or medieval Latin]

**tartar** /**tah**-tuh/ *n.* **1** hard deposit that forms on the teeth. **2** deposit that forms a hard crust in wine. [medieval Latin from Greek]

**tartare sauce** /tah-**tair**/ *n.* (also **sauce tartare, tartar sauce** /**tah**-tuh/ ) sauce of mayonnaise and chopped gherkins, capers, etc. [from TARTAR]

**tartaric** /tah-**ta**-rik/ *adj.* of or from tartar.

**tartaric acid** *n.* natural acid found esp. in unripe grapes, used in baking powders etc.

**tartrazine** /**tah**-truh-,zeen/ *n.* brilliant yellow dye from tartaric acid, used to colour food etc.

**tar tree** *n.* tree of northern Australia and elsewhere which exudes a tar-like sap.

**tarwhine** /**tah**-wuyn/ *n.* marine food-fish of Queensland, NSW, and WA, silvery-grey with gold flecks along its body. [probably Dharuk *darrawayin*]

**task** /tahsk/ — *n.* piece of work to be done. — *v.* make great demands on (a person's powers etc.). □ **take to task** rebuke, scold. [medieval Latin *tasca*, probably = *taxa* TAX]

**task force** *n.* armed force or other group organised for a specific operation or task.

**taskmaster** *n.* person who makes others work hard.

**Tasmanian** /taz-**may**-nee-uhn/ — *adj.* of or pertaining to the island or State of Tasmania. — *n.* **1** person native to or resident in Tasmania. **2 a** member of an Aboriginal people of Tasmania. **b** a descendant thereof. [A.J. *Tasman* Dutch navigator (d. 1659)]

**Tasmanian blackwood** *n.* = BLACKWOOD, esp. the wood of this tree.

**Tasmanian blue gum** *n.* medium euc-alypt (*Eucalyptus globulus*) of southern Victoria and Tasmania, having grey-blue juvenile foliage and dark green adult foliage: the floral emblem of Tasmania.

**Tasmanian devil** *n.* carnivorous marsupial, coloured black with white markings, mainly carrion-eating and of fierce appearance, and occurring only in Tasmania.

**Tasmanian native hen** *n.* plump brown bird occurring in fields near water throughout most of Tasmania.

**Tasmanian scallop** *n.* variety of scallop found in Tasmanian waters.

**Tasmanian tiger** *n.* (also **marsupial wolf, thylacine, tiger**) carnivorous marsupial having sandy brown fur with dark brown stripes across the back and rump; now probably extinct.

**Tasmanian trumpeter** *n.* fish of south-eastern, primarily Tasmanian, waters, highly valued as a food-fish (see TRUMPETER).

**Tasmanian waratah** *n.* a telopea en-demic to Tasmania bearing bright red flower-heads (less spectacular than the NSW waratah); a rare and beautiful form with yellow flowers also occurs.

**Tasmanoid** /**taz**-muh-noid/ *adj.* of, allied to, or resembling the ethnological type of the Aborigines of Tasmania (cf. AUSTRALOID).

**tassel** /tas-uhl/ n. 1 tuft of loosely hanging threads or cords etc. as decoration. 2 tassel-like flower-head of some plants, esp. maize. □ **tasselled** adj. [French tas(s)el clasp]

**tassel fern** n. epiphytic plant of Queensland (a survival from the Carboniferous period and related to the true ferns), having long bright green tassels on the ends of hanging stems; often cultivated as a basket plant.

**Tassie** /taz-ee/ — n. 1 Tasmania. 2 a Tasmanian. — adj. Tasmanian. [abbreviation]

**taste** /tayst/ — n. 1 a sensation caused in the mouth by contact with a soluble substance (dislikes the taste of cabbage). b faculty of perceiving this (bitter to the taste). 2 small sample of food or drink. 3 slight experience (taste of success). 4 (often foll. by for) liking or predilection (expensive tastes; a taste for chocolate). 5 aesthetic discernment in art, clothes, conduct, etc. (dresses in poor taste). — v. (-ting) 1 sample the flavour of (food etc.) by taking it into the mouth. 2 (also absol.) perceive the flavour of (could taste the lemon; cannot taste with a cold). 3 (esp. with neg.) eat or drink a small portion of (had not tasted food for days). 4 experience (never tasted failure). 5 (often foll. by of) have a specified flavour (tastes of onions). □ **to taste** in the amount needed for a pleasing result (add salt to taste). **to one's taste** pleasing, suitable. [French from Romanic]

**taste bud** n. cell or nerve-ending on the surface of the tongue by which things are tasted.

**tasteful** adj. having, or done in, good taste. □ **tastefully** adv. **tastefulness** n.

**tasteless** adj. 1 lacking flavour. 2 having, or done in, bad taste. □ **tastelessly** adv. **tastelessness** n.

**tasty** adj. (-ier, -iest) pleasing in flavour; appetising. □ **tastily** adv. **tastiness** n.

**Taswegian** /taz-wee-juhn/ joc. or derog. — n. person native to or resident in Tasmania. — adj. Tasmanian. [Tas (manian), -wegian as in Norwegian, etc., pointing to the supposed 'foreignness' of Tasmania and Tasmanians]

**tat** see TIT².

**tatter** n. (usu. in pl.) rag; irregularly torn cloth or paper etc. □ **in tatters** 1 torn in many places. 2 (of a negotiation, plan, argument, etc.) destroyed, ruined. [Old Norse]

**tattered** adj. in tatters.

**tatting** /tat-ing/ n. 1 a kind of knotted lace made by hand with a small shuttle and used for trimming etc. 2 process of making this. [origin unknown]

**tattle** /tat-uhl/ — v. (-ling) prattle, chatter, gossip. — n. gossip; idle talk. [Flemish tatelen, imitative]

**tattler** n. any of various sandpipers with a vociferous cry, some of which migrate to Australia from the Northern hemisphere in spring to autumn (wandering tattler; grey-tailed tattler). [TATTLE, -ER¹]

**tattoo¹** /ta-too/ n. 1 evening drum or bugle signal recalling soldiers to quarters. 2 elaboration of this with music, marching, etc., as an entertainment. 3 rhythmic tapping or drumming. [earlier tap-too from Dutch taptoe, literally 'close the tap' (of the cask)]

**tattoo²** /ta-too/ — v. (-oos, -ooed) 1 mark (skin) indelibly by puncturing it and inserting pigment. 2 make (a design) in this way. — n. such a design. □ **tattooer** n. **tattooist** n. [Polynesian]

**Tatts** /tats/ n. 1 (formerly) a large-scale lottery. 2 = TATTSLOTTO. [abbreviation of Tattersall's Sweep, name of a lottery established in 1881 by George Adams, licensee of Tattersall's Hotel, Sydney; the lottery was later based in Melbourne]

**Tattslotto** n. prop. large-scale lottery in which the main prize-winner must select the 6 drawn numbers (out of a total of 45 numbers). [TATTS, LOTTO]

**tatty** /tat-ee/ adj. (-ier, -iest) colloq. 1 (of clothes, decoration, etc.) shabby. 2 tawdry, cheap (some tatty old curtains). 3 (of a place, building, etc.) badly cared for; dirty, run down (a tatty restaurant). □ **tattily** adv. **tattiness** n. [originally Scots, = shaggy, apparently related to TATTER]

**tau** /tow, taw/ n. nineteenth letter of the Greek alphabet (T, τ). [Greek]

**taught** past and past part. of TEACH.

**taunt** /tawnt/ — n. insult; provocation. — v. insult; provoke contemptuously. [French tant pour tant tit for tat, smart rejoinder]

**Taurus** /taw-ruhs/ n. (pl. -es) 1 constellation and second sign of the zodiac (the Bull). 2 person born when the sun is in this sign. □ **Taurean** adj. & n. [Latin, = bull]

**taut** /tawt/ adj. 1 (of a rope etc.) tight; not slack. 2 (of nerves etc.) tense. 3 (of a ship etc.) in good condition. □ **tauten** v. **tautly** adv. **tautness** n. [perhaps = TOUGH]

**tautology** /taw-tol-uh-jee/ n. (pl. -ies) 1 repetition using different words, esp. as a fault of style (e.g. arrived one after the other in succession). 2 statement which is so obviously true that it does not need stating (*they are either coming or they aren't*). □ **tautological** /-tuh-**loj**-i-kuhl/ *adj.* **tautologous** /-**tol**-uh-guhs/ *adj.* [Greek *tauto* the same]

**tavern** /**tav**-uhn/ *n.* place where alcoholic liquor is sold to be drunk on the premises and which does not provide accommodation. [Latin *taberna*]

**taverna** /tuh-**ver**-nuh/ *n.* Greek restaurant. [modern Greek: related to TAVERN]

**taw** /taw/ *n.* **1** large marble. **2** (usu. in *pl.*) game of marbles. **3** line from which players throw their marbles. □ **back to taws** *colloq.* back to the beginning. [origin unknown]

**tawdry** /**taw**-dree/ *adj.* (**-ier, -iest**) showy but worthless; gaudy. □ **tawdrily** *adv.* **tawdriness** *n.* [*tawdry lace* from *St Audrey's lace*]

**tawny** /**taw**-nee/ *adj.* (**-ier, -iest**) orange-brown or yellow-brown. [Anglo-French *tauné*: related to TAN[1]]

**tawny frogmouth** *n.* mottled grey to brown nocturnal Australian bird having a low, soft call often mistaken for that of the mopoke.

**tax** — *n.* **1** money compulsorily levied by the government on individuals, property, businesses, goods, etc. **2** (usu. foll. by *on*, *upon*) strain, heavy demand, or burdensome obligation (*a tax on our strength*). — *v.* **1** impose a tax on. **2** deduct tax from (income etc.). **3** make heavy demands on (*taxes my patience*). **4** (often foll. by *with*) confront (a person) with a fault etc; call to account. □ **taxable** *adj.* [Latin *taxo* censure, compute]

**taxa** *pl.* of TAXON.

**taxation** /tak-**say**-shuhn/ *n.* imposition or payment of tax. [Latin: related to TAX]

**tax avoidance** *n.* minimising payment of tax by financial manoeuvring.

**tax-deductible** *adj.* (of expenditure) legally deductible from income before tax assessment.

**tax evasion** *n.* illegal non-payment or underpayment of tax.

**tax haven** *n.* country etc. where taxes are low.

**taxi** /**tak**-see/ — *n.* (*pl.* **-s**) (in full **taxicab**) car licensed to ply for hire and usu. fitted with an automatic fare-indicator. — *v.* (**-xis, -xied, -xiing** or **-xying**) **1** (of an aircraft or pilot) drive on the ground before take-off or after landing. **2** go or convey in a taxi. [abbreviation of *taxi cab*: related to TAX]

**taxidermy** /**tak**-suh-,der-mee/ *n.* art of preparing, stuffing, and mounting the skins of animals with lifelike effect. □ **taxidermist** *n.* [Greek *taxis* arrangement, *derma* skin]

**taxi rank** *n.* place where taxis wait to be hired.

**taxman** *n. colloq.* inspector or collector of taxes.

**taxon** /**tak**-suhn/ *n.* (*pl.* **taxa**) any taxonomic group. [back-formation from TAXONOMY]

**taxonomy** /tak-**son**-uh-mee/ *n.* classification of living and extinct organisms. □ **taxonomic** /-suh-**nom**-ik/ *adj.* **taxonomical** /-suh-**nom**-i-kuhl/ *adj.* **taxonomically** /-suh-**nom**-i-klee/ *adv.* **taxonomist** *n.* [Greek *taxis* arrangement, *-nomia* distribution]

**taxpayer** *n.* person who pays taxes.

**tax return** *n.* declaration of income for taxation purposes.

**TB** *abbr.* **1** tubercle bacillus. **2** tuberculosis.

**Tb** *symb.* terbium.

**T-bone** /**tee**-bohn/ *n.* T-shaped bone, esp. in steak from the thin end of a loin.

**tbsp.** *abbr.* tablespoonful.

**Tc** *symb.* technetium.

**tchuringa** var. of CHURINGA.

**Te** *symb.* tellurium.

**te** /tee/ *n.* (also **ti**) seventh note of a major scale. [earlier *si*: French from Italian]

**tea** *n.* **1 a** (in full **tea plant**) evergreen shrub of the camellia family, widely cultivated in Sri Lanka (Ceylon), China, etc. **b** its dried leaves. **2** drink made by infusing tea-leaves in boiling water. **3** infusion of other leaves etc. (*camomile tea; beef tea*). **4 a** morning tea. **b** afternoon tea. **5** main meal of the day eaten in the evening. [probably Dutch *tee* from Chinese]

**tea bag** *n.* small perforated bag of tea for infusion in a pot or cup.

**teach** *v.* (*past* and *past part.* **taught** /tawt/) **1 a** give systematic information, instruction, or training to (a person) or about (a subject or skill) (*taught me to swim*). **b** (*absol.*) practise this professionally. **c** communicate, instruct in (*suffering taught me patience*). **2** advocate as a moral etc. principle (*taught forgiveness*). **3** (foll. by *to* + infin.) **a** instruct (a person) by example or punishment (*that will teach you not to disobey*). **b** *colloq.* discourage (a person) from (*that will teach you to laugh*). □ **teachable** *adj.* [Old English]

**teacher** *n.* person who teaches, esp. in a school.

**tea chest** *n.* **1** light metal-lined plywood box for transporting tea. **2** this or a similar box used for storing or transporting goods.

**teaching** n. **1** profession of a teacher. **2** (often in pl.) what is taught; doctrine (teachings of the Buddha).

**teacup** n. **1** cup from which tea is drunk. **2** amount held by this. □ **storm in a teacup** fuss over a trivial matter. □ **teacupful** n. (pl. **-s**).

**teak** n. **1** a hard durable timber. **2** large Sri Lankan, Indian, or SE Asian deciduous tree yielding this. **3** any of several Australian trees yielding a durable timber resembling teak, esp. CROW'S ASH. [Portuguese from Malayalam]

**teal** n. (pl. same) small freshwater duck (Australian grey teal; chestnut teal). [origin unknown]

**tea leaf** n. **1** dried leaf of tea. **2** (esp. in pl.) these as dregs.

**team** — n. **1** set of players forming one side in a game. **2** two or more people working together. **3** set of draught animals. — v. **1** (usu. foll. by up) join in a team or in common action (teamed up with them). **2** (foll. by with) match or coordinate (clothes). [Old English]

**team-mate** n. fellow-member of a team.

**team spirit** n. willingness to act for the communal good.

**teamster** n. driver of a team of animals.

**teamwork** n. combined action; co-operation.

**teapot** n. pot with a handle, spout, and lid, for brewing and then pouring tea.

**tear**¹ /tair/ — v. (past **tore**; past part. **torn**) **1** (often foll. by up) pull apart or to pieces with some force (tore up the letter). **2 a** make a hole or rent in this way; undergo this (have torn my coat; curtain tore). **b** make (a hole or rent). **3** (foll. by away, off, at, etc.) pull violently or with some force (tore off the cover; tore down the notice). **4** violently disrupt or divide (country torn by war; torn by conflicting emotions). **5** colloq. go or leave hurriedly (tore across the road; I've got to tear). — n. **1** hole etc. caused by tearing. **2** torn part of cloth etc. □ **be torn between** have difficulty in choosing between. **tear apart 1** search (a place) exhaustively. **2** criticise forcefully. **3** destroy; divide utterly; distress greatly. **tear one's hair out** colloq. behave with extreme desperation or anger. **tear into** colloq. **1** severely reprimand. **2** start (an activity) vigorously. **tear off** colloq. leave in a hurry. **tear oneself away** leave reluctantly. **tear strips off** colloq. reprimand severely. **tear to shreds** (or **pieces**) colloq. refute or criticise thoroughly. [Old English]

**tear**² /teer/ n. **1** drop of clear salty liquid secreted by glands from the eye, and shed esp. in grief. **2** tearlike thing; drop. □ **in tears** crying. [Old English]

**tearaway** /tair-ruh-way/ n. unruly young person.

**teardrop** n. single tear.

**tear duct** n. drain for carrying tears to or from the eye.

**tearful** adj. **1** crying or inclined to cry. **2** sad (tearful event). □ **tearfully** adv.

**tear gas** n. gas causing severe irritation to the eyes.

**tearing hurry** /tair-ring/ n. colloq. great hurry.

**tear-jerker** n. colloq. sentimental story, film, etc.

**TEAS** /tees/ n. acronym of Tertiary Education Assistance Scheme.

**tease** /teez/ — v. (**-sing**) (also absol.) **1 a** make fun of playfully, unkindly, or annoyingly; irritate. **b** allure, esp. sexually, while withholding satisfaction. **2** pick (wool etc.) into separate fibres. **3** comb (the hair) towards the scalp to impart fullness. — n. **1** colloq. person fond of teasing. **2** act of teasing (only a tease). □ **tease out** separate by disentangling. [Old English]

**teaser** n. **1** person who teases. **2** colloq. hard question or task.

**teaspoon** n. **1** small spoon for stirring tea. **2** amount held by this as a measure in cooking (5ml). □ **teaspoonful** n. (pl. **-s**).

**teat** n. **1** mammary nipple, esp. of an animal. **2** rubber nipple for sucking from a bottle. [French from Germanic]

**tea towel** n. towel for drying washed crockery etc.

**tea-tree** n. **1** (also **leptospermum**) any of about 40 species (as well as numerous cultivars) of the genus Leptospermum widespread throughout Australia, having white, pink, or red flowers and highly aromatic foliage, the common name deriving from the fact that early settlers used the leaves of some species as a tea-substitute. **2** (attrib.) consisting of thin straight stakes (branches) of these trees (used for fencing) (tea-tree fence).

**tea-tree oil** n. volatile essential oil distilled from the leaves of some species of MELALEUCA.

**tech** n. colloq. technical college or school. [abbreviation]

**technetium** /tek-nee-shuhm/ n. artificially produced radioactive metallic element. [Greek tekhnētos artificial]

**technic** /tek-nik/ n. **1** (usu. in pl.) **a** technology. **b** technical terms, details, methods, etc. **2** technique. [Greek tekhnē art]

**echnical** *adj.* **1** of the mechanical arts and applied sciences (*technical college*). **2** of a particular subject or craft etc. or its techniques (*technical terms*). **3** (of a book or discourse etc.) using technical language; specialised. **4** due to mechanical failure (*technical hitch*). **5** strictly or legally interpreted (*lost on a technical point*). □ **technically** *adv.*

**technicality** /ˌtek-nuh-**kal**-uh-tee/ *n.* (*pl.* **-ies**) **1** being technical. **2** technical expression. **3** technical point or detail (*acquitted on a technicality*).

**technical knockout** *n.* ruling by the referee that a boxer has lost because he is not fit to continue.

**technician** /tek-**nish**-uhn/ *n.* **1** person doing practical or maintenance work in a laboratory etc. **2** person skilled in artistic etc. technique. **3** expert in practical science.

**Technicolor** /**tek**-nuh-ˌkul-uh/ *n.* (often *attrib.*) **1** *propr.* process of colour cinematography. **2** (**technicolour** or **-color**) *colloq.* **a** vivid colour. **b** artificial brilliance.

**technicolour yawn** *n.* *colloq.* act or instance of vomiting.

**technique** /tek-**neek**/ *n.* **1** mechanical skill in art. **2** skilful manipulation of a situation, people, etc. **3** manner of artistic execution in music, painting, etc. [French: related to TECHNIC]

**technocracy** /tek-**nok**-ruh-see/ *n.* (*pl.* **-ies**) **1** rule or control of society or industry by technical experts. **2** instance or application of this. **3** those who exercise such rule or control. [Greek *tekhnē* art]

**technocrat** /**tek**-nuh-ˌkrat/ *n.* exponent or advocate of technocracy. □ **technocratic** /-**krat**-ik/ *adj.*

**technology** /tek-**nol**-uh-jee/ *n.* (*pl.* **-ies**) **1** knowledge or use of the mechanical arts and applied sciences (*lacked the technology*). **2** these subjects collectively. □ **technological** /ˌtek-nuh-**loj**-i-kuhl/ *adj.* **technologically** /-nuh-**loj**-i-klee/ *adv.* **technologist** *n.* [Greek *tekhnologia* systematic treatment, from *tekhnē* art]

**tectonic** /tek-**ton**-ik/ *adj.* **1** of building or construction. **2** of the deformation and subsequent structural changes of the earth's crust (see PLATE TECTONICS). [Greek *tektōn* craftsman]

**tectonics** *n.pl.* (usu. treated as *sing.*) study of the earth's large-scale structural features (see PLATE TECTONICS).

**teddy** /**ted**-ee/ *n.* (*pl.* **-ies**) (in full **teddy bear**) soft toy bear. [*Teddy*, pet form of *Theodore* Roosevelt]

**tedious** /**tee**-dee-uhs/ *adj.* tiresomely long; wearisome. □ **tediously** *adv.* **tediousness** *n.* [Latin: related to TEDIUM]

**tedium** /**tee**-dee-uhm/ *n.* state of being tedious; boredom. [Latin *taedium* from *taedet* it bores]

**tee¹** *n.* = T¹. [phonetic spelling]

**tee²** /tee/ — *n.* **1 a** cleared space from which the golf ball is struck at the start of play for each hole. **b** small wooden or plastic support for a golf ball used then. **2** mark aimed at in bowls, quoits, etc. — *v.* (**tees**, **teed**) (often foll. by *up*) place (a ball) on a golf tee. □ **tee off 1** play a ball from a tee. **2** *colloq.* start, begin. **tee up** *colloq.* make ready; arrange (*have you teed up the barbie yet?*). [origin unknown]

**teem¹** *v.* **1** be abundant (*yabbies teem in this dam*). **2** (foll. by *with*) be full of or swarming with (*the river's teeming with fish; teeming with ideas*). [Old English, = give birth to]

**teem²** *v.* (often foll. by *down*) (of water etc.) flow copiously; pour (*teeming with rain*). [Old Norse]

**teen** *attrib. adj.* = TEENAGE. [abbreviation]

**-teen** *suffix* forming numerals from 13 to 19. [Old English]

**teenage** *attrib. adj.* of or characteristic of teenagers (*having typical teenage problems*). □ **teenaged** *adj.*

**teenager** *n.* person from 13 to 19 years of age.

**teens** /teenz/ *n.pl.* years of one's age from 13 to 19 (*in his teens*).

**teensy** /**teen**-zee/ *adj.* (**-ier**, **-iest**) *colloq.* = TEENY.

**teeny** /**tee**-nee/ *adj.* (**-ier**, **-iest**) *colloq.* tiny. [var. of TINY]

**teeny-bopper** *n.* *colloq.* young teenager who follows the latest fashions.

**teeny-weeny** *adj.* (also **teensy-weensy**) very tiny.

**teepee** var. of TEPEE.

**teeshirt** var. of T-SHIRT.

**teeter** *v.* totter; move unsteadily. [British dial. *titter*]

**teeth** *pl.* of TOOTH.

**teethe** /teeth/ *v.* (**-thing**) grow or cut teeth, esp. milk teeth.

**teething ring** *n.* ring for an infant to bite on while teething.

**teething troubles** *n.pl.* initial difficulties in an enterprise etc.

**teetotal** /tee-**toh**-tuhl/ *adj.* of or advocating total abstinence from alcohol. □ **teetotalism** *n.* **teetotaller** *n.* [reduplication of TOTAL]

**teflon** /**tef**-lon/ *n.* *propr.* non-stick coating for kitchen utensils. [from *tetra-*, *fluor-*, *-on*]

**tektite** /**tek**-tuyt/ *n. Geol.* small roundish glassy body of unknown origin occurring in various parts of the earth (in Australia called an AUSTRALITE). [Greek, = molten]

**tele-** *comb. form* **1** at or to a distance (*telekinesis, telescope*). **2** television (*telecast*). **3** by telephone (*telesales*). [Greek *tēle* far off]

**telecast** — *n.* television broadcast. — *v.* transmit by television. □ **telecaster** *n.*

**telecommunication** /,tel-uh-kuh-,myoo-nuh-**kay**-shuhn/ *n.* **1** communication over a distance by circuits using cable, fibre optics, satellites, radio, etc. **2** (usu. in *pl.*) technology of this.

**teleconference** /,tel-ee-**kon**-fuh-ruhns/ *n.* conference with participants in different locations linked by telecommunication devices. □ **teleconferencing** *n.*

**telegenic** /,tel-ee-**jen**-ik/ *adj.* having an appearance or manner that looks pleasing on television. [portmanteau word: TELE(VISION), (PHOTO)GENIC]

**telegram** /**tel**-uh-,gram/ *n.* message sent by telegraph.

**telegraph** /**tel**-uh-,grahf, -,graf/ — *n.* (often *attrib.*) device or system for transmitting messages or signals to a distance, esp. by making and breaking an electrical connection (*telegraph wire*). — *v.* **1** (often followed by *to*) send a message by telegraph to. **2** send or communicate by telegraph (*telegraphed my concern*). **3** give advance indication of (*telegraphed his punch*). □ **telegraphic** /-**graf**-ik/ *adj.* **telegraphically** *adv.* **telegraphist** /tuh-**leg**-ruh-fuhst/ *n.* **telegraphy** /tuh-**leg**-ruh-fee/ *n.*

**telekinesis** /,tel-ee-kuh-**nee**-suhs/ *n.* supposed paranormal force moving objects at a distance. □ **telekinetic** /-**net**-ik/ *adj.* [Greek *kineō* move]

**telemarketing** /**tel**-ee-,mah-kuh-ting/ *n.* marketing of goods etc. by unsolicited telephone calls.

**teleology** /,tee-lee-**ol**-uh-jee, ,tel-/ *n.* (*pl.* -ies) *Philos.* **1** explanation of phenomena by the purpose they serve rather than by postulated causes. **2** *Theol.* doctrine of design and purpose in the material world. □ **teleological** /-lee-uh-**loj**-i-kuhl/ *adj.* [Greek *telos* end]

**telepath** /**tel**-uh-,path/ *n.* telepathic person.

**telepathy** /tuh-**lep**-uh-thee/ *n.* supposed paranormal communication of thoughts. □ **telepathic** /,tel-uh-**path**-ik/ *adj.* **telepathically** /,tel-uh-**path**-i-klee/ *adv.*

**telephone** /**tel**-uh-,fohn/ — *n.* **1** apparatus for transmitting sound (esp. speech) to a distance, esp. by using optical or electrical signals. **2** handset etc. used in this. **3** system of communication using a network of telephones. — *v.* (**-ning**) **1** speak to or send (a message) by telephone. **2** make a telephone call. □ **on the telephone** having or using a telephone. **over the telephone** using the telephone. □ **telephonic** /-**fon**-ik/ *adj.* **telephonically** /-**fon**-i-klee/ *adv.*

**telephonist** /tuh-**lef**-uh-nuhst/ *n.* operator in a telephone exchange or at a switchboard.

**telephony** /tuh-**lef**-uh-nee/ *n.* transmission of sound by telephone.

**telephoto** /,tel-uh-**foh**-toh/ *n.* (*pl.* -s) (in full **telephoto lens**) lens used in telephotography.

**telephotography** /,tel-uh-fuh-**tog**-ruh-fee/ *n.* photographing of distant objects with a system of lenses giving a large image. □ **telephotographic** /,tel-uh-,foh-tuh-**graf**-ik/ *adj.*

**teleprinter** /**tel**-ee-,prin-tuh/ *n.* device for transmitting telegraph messages as they are keyed, and for printing messages received.

**telescope** /**tel**-uh-,skohp/ — *n.* **1** optical instrument using lenses or mirrors to magnify distant objects. **2** = RADIO TELESCOPE. — *v.* (**-ping**) **1** press or drive (sections of a tube, colliding vehicles, etc.) together so that one slides into another. **2** close or be capable of closing in this way. **3** compress so as to occupy less space or time.

**telescopic** /,tel-uh-**skop**-ik/ *adj.* **1** of or made with a telescope (*telescopic observations*). **2** (esp. of a lens) able to focus on and magnify distant objects. **3** consisting of sections that telescope. □ **telescopically** *adv.*

**telescopic sight** *n.* telescope on a rifle etc. used for sighting.

**telethon** /**tel**-uh-,thon/ *n.* exceptionally long television programme, esp. to raise money for charity. [TELE-, -THON]

**televangelist** /,tel-ee-**van**-juh-luhst/ *n.* Protestant evangelical preacher who uses television to promote his or her doctrines and solicit funds. □ **televangelism** *n.*

**televise** /**tel**-uh-,vuyz/ *v.* (**-sing**) broadcast on television.

**television** /**tel**-uh-,vizh-uhn/ *n.* **1** system for reproducing on a screen visual images transmitted (usu. with sound) by radio signals or cable. **2** (in full **television set**) device with a screen for receiving these signals. **3** television broadcasting. □ **televisual** *adj.*

**telex** /**tel**-eks/ — n. **1** international system of telegraphy by teleprinters using the public telecommunications network. **2** message sent or received by telex. — v. send, or communicate with, by telex. [from TEL(EPRINTER), EX(CHANGE)]

**tell** v. (past and past part. **told** /tohld/) **1** relate in speech or writing (tell me a story). **2** make known; express in words (tell me your name). **3** reveal or signify to (a person) (your face tells me everything). **4** utter (tell lies). **5 a** (often foll. by of, about) divulge information etc.; reveal a secret, the truth etc. (told her about Tallygaroopna; book tells you how to cook; promise you won't tell; time will tell). **b** (foll. by on) colloq. inform against. **6** (foll. by to + infin.) direct; order (tell them to wait). **7** assure (it's true, I tell you). **8** decide, determine, distinguish (tell one from the other). **9** (often foll. by on) produce a noticeable effect or influence (strain told on them; evidence tells against you). □ **tell apart** distinguish between (could not tell them apart). **tell me** (or **us**) **another!** colloq. expression of incredulity. **tell off** colloq. scold. **tell tales** report a discreditable fact about another person. **tell the time** read the time from a clock or watch. **there is no telling** it is impossible to know (there's no telling what may happen). **you're telling me!** colloq. I agree wholeheartedly. [Old English: related to TALE]

**teller** n. **1** person working at the counter of a bank etc. **2** person who counts votes. **3** person who tells esp. stories (teller of tales).

**telling** adj. having a marked effect; striking; impressive. □ **tellingly** adv.

**telling-off** n. (pl. **tellings-off**) colloq. scolding.

**tell-tale** n. **1** person who reveals secrets about another. **2** (attrib.) that reveals or betrays (tell-tale smile).

**tellurium** /te-**lyoor**-ree-uhm/ n. rare lustrous silver-white element used in semiconductors. □ **telluric** adj. [Latin tellus -ur- earth]

**telly** /**tel**-ee/ n. (pl. **-ies**) colloq. **1** television. **2** television set. [abbreviation]

**telopea** /tuh-**loh**-pee-uh/ n. shrub or tree of the Australian genus of the same name, confined to NSW, Victoria, and Tasmania (see WARATAH). [Greek, = seen from afar (alluding to the conspicuous flower-heads of the four species of this genus)]

**temerity** /tuh-**me**-ruh-tee/ n. rashness; audacity. [Latin temere rashly]

**temp** colloq. — n. temporary employee, esp. a secretary. — v. work as a temp. [abbreviation]

**temper** — n. **1** mental disposition, mood (placid temper). **2** irritation or anger (fit of temper). **3** tendency to lose one's temper (have a temper). **4** composure, calmness (lose one's temper). **5** hardness or elasticity of metal. — v. **1** bring (metal or clay) to a proper hardness or consistency. **2** (foll. by with) moderate, mitigate (temper justice with mercy). **3** tune or modulate (a piano, harpsichord, etc.) so as to distance intervals correctly. **4** (in Asian cooking) season (cooked rice etc.) with fried onions and spices etc. □ **in a bad** (or **out of**) **temper** irritable, angry. **in a good temper** amicable, happy. [Latin tempero mingle]

**tempera** /**tem**-puh-ruh/ n. **1** method of painting using an emulsion, e.g. of pigment with egg yolk and water, esp. on canvas. **2** this emulsion. [Italian]

**temperament** /**tem**-pruh-muhnt/ n. **1** person's or animal's nature and character (nervous temperament; an artistic temperament). **2** adjustment of intervals in tuning a piano etc. so as to fit the scale for use in all keys. [Latin: related to TEMPER]

**temperamental** /ˌtem-pruh-**men**-tuhl/ adj. **1** of temperament. **2 a** (of a person) unreliable; moody. **b** colloq. (of esp. a machine) unreliable, unpredictable. □ **temperamentally** adv.

**temperance** /**tem**-puh-ruhns, -pruhns/ n. **1** moderation or self-restraint, esp. in eating and drinking. **2** abstinence, esp. total, from alcohol. [Latin: related to TEMPER]

**temperate** /**tem**-puh-ruht, -pruht/ adj. **1** avoiding excess, self-controlled as regards indulging one's appetites or desires; abstemious. **2** not extreme, violent, or strongly partisan; moderate. **3** (of qualities, things, etc.) moderate, not excessive; modest (a man of temperate means). **4** (of a region or climate) mild. [Latin: related to TEMPER]

**temperate zone** n. belt of earth between the frigid and the torrid zones.

**temperature** /**tem**-pruh-chuh/ n. **1** measured or perceived degree of heat or cold of a thing, region, etc. **2** Med. degree of internal heat of the body (normally about 37° C). **3** body temperature above the normal (have a temperature). **4** degree of excitement in a discussion etc. [Latin: related to TEMPER]

**tempest** /**tem**-puhst/ n. **1** violent storm. **2** violent agitation or tumult. [Latin tempus time]

**tempestuous** /tem-**pes**-choo-uhs/ *adj.*
**1** stormy. **2** (of a person, emotion, etc.)
turbulent, violent, passionate. □ **tem-
pestuously** *adv.*

**tempi** *pl.* of TEMPO.

**template** /**tem**-pluht, -playt/ *n.* **1** piece
of thin board or metal plate etc., used as
a pattern in cutting or drilling etc. **2**
timber or plate used to distribute the
weight in a wall or under a beam etc.
[originally *templet*, diminutive of *temple*,
device in a loom to keep the cloth
stretched]

**temple**¹ /**tem**-puhl/ *n.* **1** building for the
worship, or seen as the dwelling-place, of
a god or gods etc. **2** person or place
believed to be occupied or dwelt in by a
god or gods (*the body is the temple of the
Holy Ghost*). [Latin *templum*]

**temple**² /**tem**-puhl/ *n.* flat part of either
side of the head between the forehead
and the ear. [French from Latin]

**tempo** /**tem**-poh/ *n.* (*pl.* **-s** or **-pi** /-pee/)
**1** speed at which music is or should be
played. **2** speed or pace (*the tempo of the
war is quickening*). [Latin *tempus -por-
time*]

**temporal** /**tem**-puh-ruhl, -pruhl/ *adj.* **1**
worldly as opposed to spiritual; of this
life; secular. **2** of time. **3** *Gram.* denoting
time or tense (*temporal conjunction*). **4** of
the temples of the head (*temporal artery*).
[Latin *tempus -por-* time]

**temporary** /**tem**-puh-ruh-ree, -pruh-ree/
— *adj.* lasting or meant to last only for a
limited time (*temporary buildings*). — *n.*
(*pl.* **-ies**) person employed temporarily.
□ **temporarily** *adv.* **temporariness** *n.*

**temporise** /**tem**-puh-,ruyz/ *v.* (also **-ize**)
(**-sing** or **-zing**) **1** avoid committing
oneself so as to gain time; procrastinate.
**2** comply temporarily with the requirements of a situation; adopt a time-
serving policy.

**tempt** *v.* **1** entice or incite (a person) to do
what is wrong or forbidden (*tempted him
to steal it*). **2** allure, attract (*I'm tempted
by this job-offer*). **3** risk provoking (esp.
an abstract force or power) (*would be
tempting fate to try it*). □ **be tempted to** be
strongly disposed to. □ **tempter** *n.* **temptress** *n.* [Latin *tempto, tento* try, test]

**temptation** /tem-**tay**-shuhn/ *n.* **1** act or
instance of tempting or state of being
tempted; incitement, esp. to wrongdoing.
**2** attractive thing or course of action. **3**
*archaic* putting to the test.

**tempting** *adj.* attractive, inviting.
□ **temptingly** *adv.*

**tempura** /tem-**poo**-ruh/ *n.* Japanese
dish of fish, shellfish, etc., fried in batter.
[Japanese]

**ten** *adj. & n.* **1** one more than nine. **2**
symbol for this (10, x, X). **3** ten o'clock. **4**
*colloq.* thing or person of the best quality
(on a scale of 1 to 10). □ **ten to one** very
probably. [Old English]

**tenable** /**ten**-uh-buhl/ *adj.* **1** maintain-
able or defensible against attack or
objection (*tenable position*). **2** (foll. by *for*,
*by*) (of an office etc.) that can be held for
(a specified period) or by (a specified class
of person). □ **tenability** /-**bil**-uh-tee/ *n.*
[French *tenir* hold]

**tenacious** /tuh-**nay**-shuhs/ *adj.* **1** (often
foll. by *of*) keeping a firm hold of property,
principles, life, etc.; not easily relinquishing (*tenacious of his principles*;
*tenacious fight for life*). **2** persistent,
resolute (*a tenacious onslaught*; *has a
tenacious character*; *ivy with its spreading, tenacious roots*). **3** (of memory)
retentive. **4** holding fast (*a tenacious
grip*). □ **tenaciously** *adv.* **tenacity** /tuh-
**nas**-uh-tee/ *n.* [Latin *tenax -acis* from
*teneo* hold]

**tenancy** /**ten**-uhn-see/ *n.* (*pl.* **-ies**) **1**
status of or possession as a tenant; lease.
**2** duration of this.

**tenant** /**ten**-uhnt/ — *n.* **1** person who
rents land or property from a landlord. **2**
(often foll. by *of*) occupant of a place. — *v.*
occupy as a tenant (*my garden has been
tenanted by magpies and skinks*). □ **tenanted** *adj.* [French: related to TENABLE]

**Ten Commandments** *n.pl.* (prec. by *the*)
rules of conduct given by God to Moses
(Exod. 20:1–17).

**tend**¹ *v.* **1** (often foll. by *to*) be apt or
inclined (*tends to lose his temper*; *tends to
fat*). **2** be moving; hold a course (*tends in
our direction*; *tends to the same conclusion*). **3** (foll. by *to* + infin.) serve;
conduce (*harsh repression tended only to
inflame the rebellion*). [Latin *tendo tens-*
or *tent-* stretch]

**tend**² *v.* take care of, look after (an invalid,
an animal, a machine, a fire, etc.). [from
ATTEND]

**tendency** /**ten**-duhn-see/ *n.* (*pl.* **-ies**)
(often foll. by *to*, *towards*) leaning or
inclination. [medieval Latin: related to
TEND¹]

**tendentious** /ten-**den**-shuhs/ *adj.*
*derog.* calculated to promote a particular
cause or viewpoint; biased; controversial.
□ **tendentiously** *adv.* **tendentiousness** *n.*

**tender**¹ *adj.* (**tenderer**, **tenderest**) **1** easily
cut or chewed, not tough (*tender steak*). **2**
susceptible to pain or grief; vulnerable;
compassionate (*tender heart*). **3** sensitive; fragile; delicate (*tender skin*; *tender
reputation*). **4** loving, affectionate (*tender
parents*). **5** requiring tact (*tender subject*).

**6** (of age) early, immature (*of tender years*). □ **tenderly** *adv.* **tenderness** *n.* [Latin *tener*]

**tender²** — *v.* **1** offer, present (one's services, apologies, resignation, money as payment, etc.). **2** (often foll. by *for*) offer a tender. — *n.* offer, esp. in writing, to execute work or supply goods at a stated price. □ **put out to tender** seek competitive tenders for (work etc.). □ **tenderer** *n.* [French: related to TEND¹]

**tender³** *n.* **1** person who looks after people or things. **2** supply ship attending a larger one etc. **3** truck coupled to a steam locomotive to carry fuel and water. [from TEND¹]

**tenderfoot** *n.* (*pl* **-s** or **-feet**) newcomer, novice.

**tender-hearted** /ˌten-duh-**hah**-tuhd/ *adj.* easily moved; compassionate. □ **tender-heartedness** *n.*

**tenderise** /ten-duh-ˌruyz/ *v.* (also **-ize**) (**-sing** or **-zing**) make (esp. meat) tender by beating, marinating, etc. □ **tenderiser** *n.*

**tender mercies** *n.pl.* *iron.* harsh treatment.

**tender muster** *n.* round-up of all the cattle in a particular district (comprising several cattle stations) at which owners lay claim to their strayed cattle.

**tender spot** *n.* subject on which a person is touchy.

**tendinitis** /ˌten-duh-**nuy**-tuhs/ *n.* inflammation of a tendon.

**tendon** /ten-duhn/ *n.* cord of strong connective tissue attaching a muscle to a bone etc. [Latin *tendo* stretch]

**tendril** /ten-druhl/ *n.* slender leafless shoot by which some climbing plants cling. [probably from French *tendrillon*]

**tenebrous** /ten-uh-bruhs/ *adj. literary* dark, gloomy. [Latin *tenebrosus*]

**tenement** /ten-uh-muhnt/ *n.* **1** room or flat within a house or block of flats. **2** house or block so divided. [Latin *teneo* hold]

**tenet** /ten-uht/ *n.* doctrine, principle, dogma. [Latin, = he holds]

**tenfold** *adj. & adv.* **1** ten times as much or as many. **2** consisting of ten parts.

**tennis** /ten-uhs/ *n.* game in which two or four players strike a ball with racquets over a net stretched across a court. [probably French *tenez* take! (as a server's call)]

**tennis elbow** *n.* sprain caused by overuse of forearm muscles.

**teno** /ten-oh/ *n.* (frequently *attrib.*) *colloq.* = TENOSYNOVITIS (*several teno cases in the courts*).

**tenon** /ten-uhn/ *n.* wooden projection made for insertion into a cavity, esp. a mortise, in another piece. [Latin: related to TENOR]

**tenor** /ten-uh/ *n.* **1 a** male singing-voice between baritone and alto or countertenor, the highest of the ordinary adult male range. **b** singer with this voice. **2** (often *attrib.*) instrument with a similar range (*tenor recorder*). **3** (usu. foll. by *of*) general purport or drift of a document or speech. **4** (usu. foll. by *of*) prevailing course, esp. of a person's life or habits. [Latin *teneo* hold]

**tenor clef** *n. Mus.* clef placing middle C on the second highest line of the staff.

**tenosynovitis** /ˌten-oh-ˌsuy-nuh-**vuy**-tuhs/ *n.* (also **repetition strain injury**) injury of esp. a wrist tendon resulting from repetitive strain. [Greek *tenōn* tendon, SYNOVIA]

**tenpin bowling** *n.* game in which ten pins or skittles are bowled at in a special alley.

**tense¹** — *adj.* **1** stretched tight, strained (*is the wire tense enough?; my nerves are tense*). **2** causing tenseness (*tense moment*). — *v.* (**-sing**) make or become tense. □ **tense up** become tense. □ **tensely** *adv.* **tenseness** *n.* [Latin *tensus*: related to TEND¹]

**tense²** *n. Gram.* **1** form of a verb indicating the time (also the continuance or completeness) of the action etc. (*present tense; future tense*). **2** set of such forms for the various persons and numbers. [Latin *tempus* time]

**tensile** /ten-suyl/ *adj.* **1** of or relating to tension. **2** capable of being stretched. □ **tensility** /ten-**sil**-uh-tee/ *n.* [medieval Latin: related to TENSE¹]

**tensile strength** *n.* resistance to breaking under tension.

**tension** /ten-shuhn/ *n.* **1** act or instance of stretching or state of being stretched; tenseness. **2** mental strain or excitement. **3** strained (political, social, etc.) state or relationship. **4** *Mech.* stress by which a bar, rod, etc., is pulled when it is part of a system in equilibrium or motion. **5** degree of tightness of stitches in knitting and machine sewing. **6** voltage (*high tension; low tension*). □ **tensional** *adj.* [Latin: related to TEND¹]

**tent** *n.* **1** portable canvas etc. shelter or dwelling supported by poles and cords attached to pegs driven into the ground. **2** tentlike enclosure, e.g. supplying oxygen to a patient. □ **born in a tent** *colloq.* apt to leave doors open. **were you born in a tent?** *colloq.* why did you leave the door open? [Latin: related to TEND¹]

**tentacle** /ten-tuh-kuhl/ n. **1** long slender flexible appendage of an (esp. invertebrate) animal, used for feeling, grasping, or moving. **2** channel for gathering information, exercising influence, etc. □ **tentacled** adj. [Latin: related to TEMPT]

**tentative** /ten-tuh-tiv/ adj. **1** experimental. **2** hesitant, not definite (tentative suggestion). □ **tentatively** adv. **tentativeness** n. [medieval Latin: related to TEMPT]

**tenter** n. machine for stretching cloth to dry in shape. [medieval Latin tentorium: related to TEND¹]

**tenterhook** n. hook to which cloth is fastened on a tenter. □ **on tenterhooks** in a state of suspense or agitation due to uncertainty.

**tenth** adj. & n. **1** next after ninth. **2** any of ten equal parts of a thing. □ **tenthly** adv.

**tenuous** /ten-yoo-uhs/ adj. **1** slight; insubstantial; weak; vague (tenuous connection; tenuous claim to fame; a tenuous grasp of reality). **2** (of a distinction etc.) oversubtle (made a tenuous distinction between abject poverty and destitution). **3** thin, slender, small (watched the spider weave its tenuous thread). □ **tenuity** /tuh-nyoo-uh-tee/ n. **tenuously** adv. [Latin tenuis thin]

**tenure** /ten-yuh/ n. **1** condition, or form of right or title, under which (esp. real) property is held. **2** (often foll. by of) **a** holding or possession of an office or property. **b** period of this (during his tenure of office). **3** guaranteed permanent employment, esp. as a teacher, lecturer, or public servant. □ **tenured** adj. [Latin teneo hold]

**tepee** /tee-pee/ n. (also **teepee**) N. American Indian's conical tent. [Dakota]

**tepid** /tep-uhd/ adj. **1** lukewarm (the water is tepid). **2** unenthusiastic (received some tepid applause). □ **tepidity** /tuh-pid-uh-tee/ n. **tepidly** adv. [Latin]

**tequila** /tuh-kee-luh/ n. Mexican liquor made from an agave. [Tequila in Mexico]

**teraglin** /tuh-rag-luhn/ n. (also **trag**) marine fish of NSW and elsewhere, valued as a food-fish. [possibly from an Aboriginal language]

**terbium** /ter-bee-uhm/ n. silvery metallic element of the lanthanide series. [Ytterby in Sweden]

**tercentenary** /ter-sen-tee-nuh-ree, -ten-uh-ree/ n. (pl. **-ies**) **1** three-hundredth anniversary. **2** celebration of this. [Latin ter three times]

**teredo** /tuh-ree-doh/ n. (pl. **-s**) bivalve mollusc that bores into submerged timbers of ships etc. [Latin from Greek]

**tergiversate** /ter-juh-,ver-sayt, ter-jiv-uh-,sayt/ v. (**-ting**) **1** change one's party or principles; apostatise. **2** make conflicting or evasive statements. □ **tergiversation** /-say-shuhn/ n. **tergiversator** n. [Latin tergum back, verto turn]

**teriyaki** /te-ree-yah-kee/ n. Japanese dish of grilled marinated meat or fish. [Japanese teri gloss, lustre, yaki grill]

**term** — n. **1** word for a definite concept, esp. specialised (technical term). **2** (in pl.) language used; mode of expression (in no uncertain terms). **3** (in pl.) relation, footing (on good terms). **4** (in pl.) **a** conditions or stipulations (accepts your terms). **b** charge or price (reasonable terms; her terms are $200 a lesson). **5 a** limited, usu. specified, period (term of five years; in the short term). **b** period of weeks during which instruction is given in a school etc. **6** Logic word or words that may be the subject or predicate of a proposition. **7** Math. **a** each of the quantities in a ratio or series. **b** part of an algebraic expression. **8** completion of a normal length of pregnancy. **9** Aust. Rules = QUARTER 13. — v. call, name (was termed a bigot). □ **come to terms with 1** reconcile oneself to (a difficulty etc.). **2** conclude an agreement with. **in terms of** in the language peculiar to; referring to. **terms of reference** see REFERENCE. □ **termly** adj. & adv. [Latin TERMINUS]

**termagant** /ter-muh-guhnt/ n. overbearing or brawling woman; virago. [French Tervagan from Italian]

**terminable** /ter-muh-nuh-buhl/ adj. able to be terminated.

**terminal** /ter-muh-nuhl/ — adj. **1 a** (of a condition or disease) fatal. **b** (of a patient) in the last stage of a fatal disease. **2** of or forming a limit or terminus (terminal station). **3 a** Zool. etc. ending a series (terminal joints). **b** Bot. borne at the end of a stem etc. (terminal heads of flowers). — n. **1** terminating thing; extremity. **2** terminus for trains or long-distance buses. **3** = AIR TERMINAL. **4** point of connection for closing an electric circuit. **5** apparatus for the transmission of messages to and from a computer, communications system, etc. □ **terminally** adv. [Latin: related to TERMINUS]

**terminal velocity** n. Physics velocity of a falling body such that the resistance of the air etc. prevents further increase of speed under gravity.

**terminate** /ter-muh-,nayt/ v. (**-ting**) **1** bring or come to an end. **2** (foll. by in) (of a word) end in (a specified letter etc.). **3** end (a pregnancy) before term by artificial means.

**termination** /ˌter-muh-**nay**-shuhn/ *n.* **1** act or instance of terminating or state of being terminated. **2** induced abortion. **3** ending or result of a specified kind (*a happy termination*).

**termini** *pl.* of TERMINUS.

**terminology** /ˌter-muh-**nol**-uh-jee/ *n.* (*pl.* **-ies**) **1** system of specialised terms. **2** science of the use of terms. □ **terminological** /ˌter-muh-nuh-**loj**-i-kuhl/ *adj.* [German: related to TERMINUS]

**terminus** /**ter**-muh-nuhs/ *n.* (*pl.* **-ni** /-ˌnuy/ or **-nuses**) **1** station at the end of a railway or bus route. **2** point at the end of a pipeline etc. **3** final point, goal. [Latin, = end, limit, boundary]

**termite** /**ter**-muyt/ *n.* small antlike social insect destructive to timber. [Latin *termes -mitis*]

**terms of reference** see REFERENCE.

**tern** *n.* marine gull-like bird, usu. coloured grey and white with a black cap, and with a long forked tail (*gull-billed tern*; *whiskered tern*). [Scandinavian]

**ternary** /**ter**-nuh-ree/ *adj.* composed of three parts. [Latin *terni* three each]

**terrace** /**te**-ruhs/ — *n.* **1** flat area made on a slope for cultivation. **2** level paved area next to a house. **3** row of houses built in one block of uniform style. **4** = TERRACE HOUSE. **5** tiered standing accommodation for spectators at a sportsground. **6** *Geol.* raised beach, or a similar formation beside a river etc. — *v.* (**-cing**) form into or provide with a terrace or terraces. [Latin *terra* earth]

**terrace house** *n.* house in a terrace.

**terracotta** /ˌte-ruh-**kot**-uh/ *n.* **1** unglazed usu. brownish-red earthenware used chiefly as an ornamental building material, for pots, etc. **2** its colour. [Italian, = baked earth]

**terra firma** /ˌte-ruh **fer**-muh/ *n.* dry land, firm ground. [Latin]

**terrain** /tuh-**rayn**/ *n.* tract of land, esp. in geographical or military contexts. [Latin]

**terra incognita** /ˌte-ruh in-kog-**nee**-tuh/ *n.* unexplored region. [Latin, = unknown land]

**terra nullius** /ˌte-ruh **nul**-ee-uhs/ *n.* **1** 'land belonging to no-one', hence, in international law, land which could be occupied for the first time by another country and so brought under that country's ownership. **2** fiction that, prior to white settlement, Australia belonged to no-one (in spite of more than 40,000 years of Aboriginal occupation) and hence could be legally taken over, a fiction effectively quashed by the Mabo

decision of the High Court of Australia in 1992 (see MABO). [Latin]

**terrapin** /**te**-ruh-pin/ *n.* N. American edible freshwater turtle. [Algonquian]

**terrarium** /tuh-**rair**-ree-uhm/ *n.* (*pl.* **-s** or **-ria**) **1** place for keeping small land animals such as lizards, snakes, etc. **2** sealed transparent globe etc. containing growing plants. [Latin *terra* earth, after *aquarium*]

**terrazzo** /tuh-**rat**-soh, -**raht**-soh/ *n.* (*pl.* **-s**) flooring material of stone chips set in concrete and given a smooth surface. [Italian, = terrace]

**terrestrial** /tuh-**res**-tree-uhl/ *adj.* **1** of or on the earth; earthly. **2 a** of or on dry land. **b** *Zool.* living on or in the ground (opp. AQUATIC, ARBOREAL, AERIAL). **c** *Bot.* growing in the soil (opp. epiphytic — see EPIPHYTE, AQUATIC). [Latin *terrestris*]

**terrible** /**te**-ruh-buhl/ *adj.* **1** *colloq.* very great or bad (*terrible bore*). **2** *colloq.* very incompetent (*terrible at maths*). **3** causing or likely to cause terror; dreadful, formidable. [Latin *terreo* frighten]

**terribly** *adv.* **1** *colloq.* very, extremely (*terribly nice*). **2** in a terrible manner.

**terrier** /**te**-ree-uh/ *n.* small dog of various breeds (originally used for digging out foxes etc.), e.g. AUSTRALIAN TERRIER. [French *chien terrier* dog that chases to earth]

**terrific** /tuh-**rif**-ik/ *adj.* **1** *colloq.* **a** huge; intense (*terrific noise*). **b** excellent (*did a terrific job*). **2** causing terror. □ **terrifically** *adv.* [Latin: related to TERRIBLE]

**terrify** /**te**-ruh-ˌfuy/ *v.* (**-ies**, **-ied**) fill with terror (*terrified of dogs*). □ **terrifying** *adj.* **terrifyingly** *adv.*

**terrine** /tuh-**reen**/ *n.* **1** pâté or similar food. **2** earthenware vessel, esp. for pâté. [Latin *terra* earth]

**territorial** /ˌte-ruh-**taw**-ree-uhl/ *adj.* **1** of territory or a district (*territorial possessions*; *territorial right*). **2** tending to defend one's territory (*the magpie is a very territorial bird*). □ **territorially** *adv.* [Latin: related to TERRITORY]

**territorial waters** *n.pl.* area of sea under the jurisdiction of a country, esp. within a stated distance of the shore.

**Territorian** *n.* person native to or resident in the NT.

**territory** /**te**-ruh-tuh-ree, -tree/ *n.* (*pl.* **-ies**) **1** extent of the land under the jurisdiction of a ruler, country, etc. **2** (**Territory**) organised division of a country, esp. one not yet admitted to the full rights of a State (*Australian Capital Territory*). **3** sphere of action etc.; province (*sorry I can't help you — defence matters aren't in* *my territory*). **4** (**the Territory**) the Northern Territory. **5** animal's or human's defended space or area. **6** area defended by a team or player in a game. **7** large tract of land. [Latin *terra* land]

**Territory rig** *n.* = DARWIN RIG.

**terror** /te-ruh/ *n.* **1** extreme fear. **2 a** terrifying person or thing. **b** *colloq.* formidable or troublesome person or thing, esp. a child. **3** organised intimidation; terrorism. [Latin *terreo* frighten]

**terrorise** /te-ruh-,ruyz/ *v.* (also **-ize**) (**-sing** or **-zing**) **1** fill with terror. **2** use terrorism against. □ **terrorisation** /-zay-shuhn/ *n.*

**terrorist** *n.* (often *attrib.*) person using esp. organised violence against a government etc. □ **terrorism** *n.* [French: related to TERROR]

**terror-stricken** *adj.* (also **terror-struck**) affected with terror.

**terry** /te-ree/ *n.* (often *attrib.*) looped pile fabric used esp. for towels and nappies (*terry towelling*). [origin unknown]

**terse** *adj.* (**terser**, **tersest**) **1** (of language, a speech, etc.) brief, concise, to the point. **2** curt, abrupt (*gave a terse reply*). □ **tersely** *adv.* **terseness** *n.* [Latin *tergo ters-* wipe]

**tertiary** /ter-shuh-ree/ — *adj.* **1** third in order or rank etc. **2** (**Tertiary**) of the first period in the Cenozoic era with evidence of the development of mammals and flowering plants. — *n.* (**Tertiary**) Tertiary period. [Latin *tertius* third]

**tertiary education** *n.* education, in a university etc., that follows secondary education.

**tervalent** /ter-vay-luhnt/ *adj.* having a valency of three. [from TERCENTENARY, VALENCE[1]]

**terylene** /te-ruh-,leen/ *n. propr.* synthetic textile fibre of polyester. [from *terephthalic* acid, ETHYLENE]

**TESL** /tee-suhl/ *abbr.* teaching of English as a second language.

**tesla** /tes-luh/ *n.* SI unit of magnetic flux density. [*Tesla*, name of a scientist]

**tessellated** /tes-uh-,lay-tuhd/ *adj.* **1** of or resembling a mosaic. **2** regularly chequered. [Latin *tessella*]

**tessellation** /,tes-uh-**lay**-shuhn/ *n.* close arrangement of polygons, esp. in a repeated pattern.

**tessitura** /,tes-uh-**tyoor**-ruh/ *n.* range of a singing voice or vocal part. [Italian, = TEXTURE]

**test[1]** — *n.* **1** critical examination or trial of a person's or thing's qualities. **2** means, procedure, or standard for so doing. **3** minor examination, esp. in school (*spelling test*). **4** *colloq.* test match. **5** *Chem.* action or process of examining a substance in order to determine its identity or that of one of its constituents, usu. by means of a reagent. — *v.* **1** put to the test. **2** try or tax severely. **3** examine by means of a reagent. □ **put to the test** cause to undergo a test. **test out** put to a practical test (*tested out his theory*). □ **testable** *adj.* [Latin *testu(m)* = *testa*: related to TEST[2]]

**test[2]** *n.* shell of some invertebrates. [Latin *testa* pot, tile, shell]

**testa** /tes-tuh/ *n.* (*pl.* **testae** /-tee/) *Bot.* the (usu. hard) outer coat or covering of a seed. [Latin: related to TEST[2]]

**testaceous** /tes-**tay**-shuhs/ *adj.* having a hard continuous shell.

**testament** /tes-tuh-muhnt/ *n.* **1** will (esp. *last will and testament*). **2** (usu. foll. by *to*) evidence, proof (*is testament to his loyalty*). **3** *Bibl.* **a** covenant, dispensation. **b** (**Testament**) division of the Bible (see OLD TESTAMENT, NEW TESTAMENT). □ **testamentary** *adj.* [Latin *testamentum* will: related to TESTATE]

**testate** /tes-tayt/ — *adj.* having left a valid will at death. — *n.* testate person. □ **testacy** *n.* (*pl.* **-ies**). [Latin *testor* testify, from *testis* witness]

**testator** /tes-**tay**-tuh/ *n.* (*fem.* **testatrix** /tes-**tay**-triks/ ) (esp. deceased) person who has made a will. [Latin: related to TESTATE]

**test case** *n. Law* case setting a precedent for other similar cases.

**test drive** *n.* drive taken to judge the performance of a vehicle. □ **test-drive** *v.*

**testes** *pl.* of TESTIS.

**testicle** /tes-ti-kuhl/ *n.* male organ that produces spermatozoa etc., esp. one of a pair in the scrotum in man and most mammals. [Latin, = little witness, diminutive of *testis* witness]

**testify** /tes-tuh-,fuy/ *v.* (**-ies**, **-ied**) **1** (often foll. by *to*) (of a person or thing) bear witness; be evidence of (*testified to the facts*). **2** *Law* give evidence. **3** affirm or declare (*testified that she had been present*). [Latin *testificor* from *testis* witness]

**testimonial** /,tes-tuh-**moh**-nee-uhl/ *n.* **1** certificate of character, conduct, or qualifications. **2** gift etc. presented to a person (esp. in public) as a mark of esteem etc. (also *attrib.*: *cricketer's testimonial year*; *testimonial dinner*). [French: related to TESTIMONY]

**testimony** /tes-tuh-muh-nee/ *n.* (*pl.* **-ies**) **1** witness's statement under oath etc. **2** declaration or statement of fact. **3**

something which serves as evidence, demonstration, proof, etc. (*the success of this enterprise is testimony to her grit*). [Latin *testimonium* from *testis* witness]

**testis** /*tes*-tuhs/ *n.* (*pl.* **testes** /-teez/) *Anat.* & *Zool.* testicle. [Latin, = witness (cf. TESTICLE)]

**test match** *n.* international cricket, Rugby, etc., match, usu. between two countries in a series.

**testosterone** /tes-*tos*-tuh-ˌrohn/ *n.* male sex hormone formed in the testicles. [from TESTIS, STEROL]

**test paper** *n. Chem.* paper impregnated with a substance changing colour under known conditions.

**test tube** *n.* thin glass tube closed at one end, used for chemical tests etc.

**test-tube baby** *n. colloq.* baby conceived by in vitro fertilisation.

**testy** *adj.* (**-ier**, **-iest**) irritable, touchy. □ **testily** *adv.* **testiness** *n.* [French *teste* head: related to TEST²]

**tetanus** /*tet*-uh-nuhs/ *n.* bacterial disease affecting the nervous system and causing painful spasm of the voluntary muscles. [Greek *teinō* stretch]

**tetchy** /*tech*-ee/ *adj.* (also **techy**) (**-ier**, **-iest**) peevish, irritable. □ **tetchily** *adv.* **tetchiness** *n.* [*teche* blemish, fault]

**tête-à-tête** /ˌtay-tah-*tayt*, ˌtet-ah-*tet*/ — *n.* (often *attrib.*) private conversation between two persons. — *adv.* privately without a third person (*dined tête-à-tête*). [French, literally 'head-to-head']

**tether** /*te*-thuh/ — *n.* rope etc. confining a grazing animal. — *v.* tie with a tether. □ **at the end of one's tether** at the limit of one's patience, resources, etc. [Old Norse]

**tetra-** *comb. form* four. [Greek *tettares* four]

**tetrad** /*tet*-rad/ *n.* group of four. [Greek: related to TETRA-]

**tetragon** /*tet*-ruh-ˌgon/ *n.* plane figure with four angles and sides. □ **tetragonal** /te-*trag*-uh-nuhl/ *adj.* [Greek *-gōnos* -angled]

**tetrahedron** /ˌtet-ruh-*hee*-druhn, -*hed*-ruhn/ *n.* (*pl.* **-dra** or **-s**) four-sided solid; triangular pyramid. □ **tetrahedral** *adj.* [Greek *hedra* base]

**tetralogy** /te-*tral*-uh-jee/ *n.* (*pl.* **-ies**) group of four related literary, dramatic, or operatic works.

**tetrameter** /te-*tram*-uh-tuh/ *n. Prosody* verse of four measures.

**tetratheca** /ˌtet-ruh-*thee*-kuh/ *n.* (also **black-eyed Susan**) any of several small Australian shrubs having pendulous, bell-like, pink, mauve, or purple flowers with a black spot or eye in the centre of the bell. [Greek *tetra-* four, *thēkē* case or

chest (referring to the four chambers of the anther)]

**Teuton** /*tyoo*-tuhn/ *n.* member of a Teutonic nation, esp. a German. [Latin *Teutones*, ancient tribe of N. Europe]

**Teutonic** /tyoo-*ton*-ik/ *adj.* **1** of the Germanic peoples or languages. **2** German. [Latin: related to TEUTON]

**text** *n.* **1** main body of a book as distinct from notes etc. **2** original book or document, esp. as distinct from a paraphrase or a commentary. **3** passage from Scripture, esp. as the subject of a sermon. **4** subject, theme. **5** book prescribed for study. **6** data in textual form, esp. as stored, processed, or displayed in a word processor etc. [Latin *texo text-* weave]

**textbook** — *n.* book for use in studying, esp. a standard account of a subject. — *attrib. adj.* **1** exemplary, accurate. **2** instructively typical (*the batsman made a textbook stroke for four*).

**text editor** *n. Computing* program allowing the user to enter and edit text.

**textile** /*teks*-tuyl/ — *n.* **1** (often in *pl.*) fabric, cloth, or fibrous material, esp. woven. **2** fibre, yarn. — *adj.* **1** of weaving or cloth (*textile industry*). **2** woven (*textile fabrics*). [Latin: related to TEXT]

**text processing** *n. Computing* manipulation of text, esp. transforming it from one format to another.

**textual** /*teks*-choo-uhl/ *adj.* of, in, or concerning a text (*textual errors*; *textual commentary*). □ **textually** *adv.*

**texture** /*teks*-chuh/ — *n.* **1** feel or appearance of a surface or substance. **2** arrangement of threads etc. in textile fabric. — *v.* (**-ring**) (usu. as **textured** *adj.*) **1** provide with a texture. **2** (of vegetable protein) provide with a texture resembling meat. □ **textural** *adj.* [Latin: related to TEXT]

**Th** *symb.* thorium.

**-th** *suffix* (also **-eth**) forming ordinal and fractional numbers from *four* onwards (*fourth*; *thirtieth*). [Old English]

**Thai** /tuy/ — *n.* (*pl.* same or **-s**) **1 a** native or national of Thailand. **b** person of Thai descent. **2** language of Thailand. — *adj.* of Thailand. [Thai, = free]

**thalidomide** /thuh-*lid*-uh-ˌmuyd/ *n.* sedative drug found in 1961 to cause foetal malformation when taken early in pregnancy. [from ph*thali*mido*glutari*-mide]

**thallium** /*thal*-ee-uhm/ *n.* rare soft white metallic element. [as THALLUS, from the green line in its spectrum]

**thallus** /*thal*-uhs/ *n.* (*pl.* **thalli** /-uy/) plant-body not differentiated into root, stem, and leaves, e.g. fungus or lichen. [Greek *thallos* green shoot]

**than** /than, thuhn/ *conj.* introducing a comparison (*plays better than he did before*; *more vegies than meat in these pies*; *cost more than $100*; *you are older than he*). [Old English, originally = THEN]

■ **Usage** With reference to the last example, it is also legitimate to say *you are older than him*, with *than* treated as a preposition, esp. in less formal contexts.

**thanatology** /,than-uh-**tol**-uh-jee/ *n.* study of death and dying and their associated phenomena and practices. [Greek *thanatos* death, -LOGY]

**thane** *n. Brit. Hist.* **1** man who held land from an English king or other superior by military service. **2** man who held land from a Scottish king and ranked with an earl's son; chief of a clan. [Old English]

**thank** — *v.* **1** express gratitude to (*thanked him for the present*). **2** hold responsible (*you can thank yourself for that*). — *n.* (in *pl.*) **1** gratitude (*expressed her heartfelt thanks*). **2** expression of gratitude (*gave thanks to heaven*). **3** (as a formula) thank you (*thanks for your help*). □ **thank goodness** (or **God** or **heavens** etc.) *colloq.* expression of relief etc. **thanks to** as the (good or bad) result of (*thanks to my foresight*; *thanks to your obstinacy*). **thank you** polite formula acknowledging a gift or service or an offer accepted or refused. [Old English]

**thankful** *adj.* **1** grateful, pleased. **2** (of words or acts) expressive of thanks.

**thankfully** *adv.* **1** in a thankful manner. **2** let us be thankful (that) (*thankfully, it didn't rain*).

■ **Usage** The use of *thankfully* in sense 2 is common but considered incorrect by some people.

**thankless** *adj.* **1** not expressing or feeling gratitude. **2** (of a task etc.) giving no pleasure or profit; unappreciated.

**thanksgiving** *n.* expression of gratitude, esp. to God.

**that** /that/ — *demons. pron.* (*pl.* **those** /thohz/ ) **1** person or thing indicated, named, or understood (*I heard that*; *who is that in the garden?*). **2** contrasted with *this* (*this is much better than that*). **3** action, behaviour, or circumstances, just observed or mentioned (*don't do that again*). **4** (esp. in relative constructions) the one, the person, etc., described or specified in some way (*those who have cars can take the luggage*; *a table like that described above*). **5** /thuht/ (*pl.* **that**) used instead of *which* or *whom* to introduce a defining clause, esp. one essential to identification (*the book that you sent me*; *there is nothing here that matters*). — *demons. adj.* (*pl.* **those** /thohz/ ) **1** designating the person or thing indicated, named, understood, etc. (cf. sense 1 of *pron.*) (*look at that koala*; *things were easier in those days*). **2** contrasted with *this* (cf. sense 2 of *pron.*) (*this bag is heavier than that one.*). **3** expressing strong feeling (*shall not easily forget that day*). — *adv.* **1** to such a degree; so (*have done that much*). **2** *colloq.* very (*not that good*). — *conj.* /thuht/ introducing a subordinate clause indicating: **1** statement or hypothesis (*they say that he is better*). **2** purpose (*we eat that we may live*). **3** result (*am so sleepy that I cannot work*). **4** reason or cause (*it's just that I lack the time*). **5 a** wish (*Oh, that summer were here!*). □ **all that** very (*not all that good*). **at that** see AT. **like that 1** of that kind (*is fond of books like that*). **2** in that manner, as you are doing, as he has been doing, etc. (*wish they would not talk like that*). **3** *colloq.* without effort (*had the job done just like that*). **4** of that character (*he wouldn't accept any payment—he's like that*). **that is** (or **that is to say**) formula introducing or following an explanation of a preceding word or words. **that's** *colloq.* **you are** (by virtue of present or future obedience etc.) (*that's a good boy*). **that's that** formula indicating conclusion or completion. [Old English]

■ **Usage** In sense 5 of the pronoun, *that* usually specifies or identifies something referred to, whereas *who* or *which* need not: compare *the book that you sent me is lost* with *the book, which I gave you, is lost*. *That* is often omitted in senses 1 and 3 of the conjunction: *they say he is ill*.

**thatch** — *n.* **1** roof-covering of straw, reeds, etc. **2** a matted layer of plant debris etc. in a lawn. **3** *colloq.* hair of the head. — *v.* (also *absol.*) cover (a roof or a building) with thatch. □ **thatcher** *n.* [Old English]

**thaw** — *v.* **1** (often foll. by *out*) pass from a frozen into a liquid or unfrozen state. **2** (usu. prec. by *it* as subject) (of the weather) become warm enough to melt ice etc. (*it's beginning to thaw*). **3** become warm enough to lose numbness etc. **4** become or make less cold or stiff in manner; become or make genial. **5** (often foll. by *out*) cause to thaw. — *n.* **1** act or instance of thawing. **2** warmth of weather that thaws. **3** *Polit.* lessening of hostility, tension, etc., (between nations etc.). [Old English]

**Thawa** /**tah**-wu/ *n.* Aboriginal language once spoken in south-eastern NSW (a few fragments of the language being recorded in 1844): the language and its speakers are now extinct.

**the** before a vowel /*thee*/, before a consonant /*thuh*/, when stressed /*thee*/ — *adj.* (called the definite article) **1** denoting person(s) or thing(s) already mentioned, under discussion, implied, or familiar (*gave the man a wave*). **2 a** describing as unique (*the Murrumbidgee*). **b** used with the names of some towns (esp. in northern Australia), often with omission of a secondary element of the name, as *the Alice, the Isa, the Tennant* (for Alice Springs, Mount Isa, Tennant Creek). **3 a** (foll. by defining adj.) which is, who are, etc. (*John-Paul the Second*). **b** (foll. by adj. used *absol.*) denoting a class described (*from the sublime to the ridiculous*). **4** best known or best entitled to the name (with the stressed: *this* is the *book on the subject; do you mean* the *Whitlam?*). **5** indicating a following defining clause or phrase (*the book that you borrowed*). **6 a** indicating that a singular noun represents a species, class, etc. (*the cat is a mammal; has the novel a future?*). **b** used with a noun which figuratively represents an occupation etc. (*went on the stage; too fond of the bottle*). **c** (foll. by the name of a unit) a, per (*10 cents in the dollar*). **d** designating a disease, affliction, etc. (*the measles; the blues; the sulks*). **7** (foll. by a unit of time) the present, the current (*man of the moment; book of the month*). — *adv.* (preceding comparatives) in or by that (or such a) degree; on that account (*the more the merrier; the more he has the more he wants*). [Old English]

**theatre** /**theer**-tuh/ *n.* **1** building or outdoor area for dramatic performances. **2** writing and production of plays. **3** room or hall for lectures etc. with seats in tiers. **4** cinema. **5** operating theatre. **6** scene or field of action (*the theatre of war*). [Greek *theatron*]

**theatrical** /thee-**at**-ruh-kuhl/ — *adj.* **1** of or for the theatre or acting. **2** (of a manner or person etc.) calculated for effect; showy (*a theatrical gesture*). — *n.* (in *pl.*) dramatic performances (*amateur theatricals*). □ **theatricality** /-**kal**-uh-tee/ *n.* **theatrically** *adv.*

**thee** *objective case of* THOU[1].

**theft** *n.* act or instance of stealing. [Old English: related to THIEF]

**their** /*thair*/ *poss. pron.* (attrib.) **1** of or belonging to them. **2** as a third person sing. indefinite, meaning 'his or her' (*has anyone lost their keys?*) [Old Norse]

■ **Usage** The use of *their* in sense 2, though common, is considered incorrect by some people.

**theirs** /*thairz*/ *poss. pron.* the one or ones of or belonging to them (*it is theirs; theirs are over here*). □ **of theirs** of or belonging to them (*a friend of theirs*).

**theism** /**thee**-iz-uhm/ *n.* belief in gods or a god, esp. a god supernaturally revealed (opp. ATHEISM). □ **theist** *n.* **theistic** /-**is**-tik/ *adj.* [Greek *theos* god]

**Thelymitra** /,thel-ee-**mit**-ruh/ *n.* genus of (mainly Australian) terrestrial orchids with about 50 species in Australia, each species having a solitary leaf and large, highly colourful flowers (often blue, a colour rare among orchids) in a terminal raceme, most species being known as 'sun orchids' because the flowers open only in the sun. [Greek *thelys* woman, *mitra* cap or hood (referring to the hooded column)]

**them** /*thuhm*/ or, when stressed /*them*/ — *pron.* **1** *objective case* of THEY. **2** *colloq.* they (*it's them again*). — *demons. adj. colloq.* those (*them next-door moggies are after the maggies again*). [Old Norse]

■ **Usage** The use of *them* as a demonstrative adjective is not acceptable in standard English.

**theme** *n.* **1** subject or topic of a talk, book, etc. **2** *Mus.* prominent melody in a composition. □ **thematic** /thee-**mat**-ik/ *adj.* **thematically** /thee-**mat**-i-klee/ *adv.* [Greek *thema* -*mat*-]

**theme park** *n.* amusement park organised round a unifying idea.

**themselves** /thuhm-**selvz**/ *pron.* **1** *emphat. form* of THEY or THEM. **2** *refl. form* of THEM. □ **be themselves** act in their normal, unconstrained manner (*are quite themselves again*).

**then** /*then*/ — *adv.* **1** at that time (*was then too busy; the then existing laws*). **2 a** next; after that (*then she told me to come in*). **b** and also (*then, there are the children to consider*). **c** after all (*it is a problem, but then that is what we are here for*). **3 a** in that case; therefore (*then you should have said so*). **b** if what you say is true (*but then why did you take it?*). **c** (implying grudging or impatient concession) if you must have it so (*all right then, have it your own way*). **d** used parenthetically to resume a narrative etc. (*the policeman, then, knocked on the* door). — *attrib. adj.* such at the time in question (*the then Premier*). — *n.* that time (*until then*). □ **then and there** immediately and on the spot. [Old English]

**thence** /thens/ *adv.* (also **from thence**) *archaic* or *literary* **1** from that place (*we're cycling to Geelong, and thence to Ballarat*). **2** from that time, thenceforth (*became a monk and thence was lost to us*). **3** for that reason (*it would thence follow that* . . .). [Old English]

■ **Usage** The formulation *from thence*, as in *travelled to Rome and from thence to Venice*, is considered incorrect by some people as the sense 'from' is already present in 'thence'.

**thenceforth** /thens-**fawth**/ *adv.* (also **thenceforward** /thens-**faw**-wuhd/ ) *archaic* or *literary* from that time onward.

**theo-** *comb. form* God or god(s). [Greek *theos* god]

**theocracy** /thee-**ok**-ruh-see/ *n.* (*pl.* **-ies**) form of government by God or a god directly or through a priestly order etc. □ **theocratic** /thee-uh-**krat**-ik/ *adj.*

**theodolite** /thee-**od**-uh-,luyt/ *n.* surveying-instrument for measuring horizontal and vertical angles with a rotating telescope. [origin unknown]

**theologian** /thee-uh-**loh**-juhn/ *n.* expert in theology. [French: related to THEOLOGY]

**theology** /thee-**ol**-uh-jee/ *n.* (*pl.* **-ies**) the study or a system of theistic (esp. Christian) religion. □ **theological** /thee-uh-**loj**-i-kuhl/ *adj.* **theologically** /thee-uh-**loj**-i-klee/ *adv.* [Greek: related to THEO-]

**theorem** /**theer**-ruhm/ *n. esp. Math.* **1** general proposition that is not self-evident but is proved by reasoning. **2** rule in algebra etc., esp. one expressed by symbols or formulae. [Greek *theōreō* look at]

**theoretical** /theer-**ret**-i-kuhl/ *adj.* **1** concerned with knowledge but not with its practical application. **2** based on theory rather than experience. □ **theoretically** *adv.*

**theoretician** /,theer-ruh-**tish**-uhn/ *n.* person concerned with the theoretical aspects of a subject.

**theorise** /**theer**-ruyz/ *v.* (also **-ize**) (**-sing** or **-zing**) evolve or indulge in theories.

**theorist** /**theer**-ruhst/ *n.* holder or inventor of a theory.

**theory** /**theer**-ree/ *n.* (*pl.* **-ies**) **1** supposition or system of ideas explaining something, esp. one based on general principles independent of the particular things to be explained (*atomic theory; theory of evolution*). **2** speculative (esp.

fanciful) view (*one of my pet theories*). **3** abstract knowledge or speculative thought (*all very well in theory*). **4** exposition of the principles of a science etc. (*the theory of music*). **5** collection of propositions to illustrate the principles of a mathematical subject (*probability theory*). [Greek: related to THEOREM]

**theosophy** /thee-**os**-uh-fee/ *n.* (*pl.* **-ies**) any of various philosophies professing to achieve knowledge of God by spiritual ecstasy, direct intuition, or special individual relations, esp. a modern movement following Hindu and Buddhist teachings and seeking universal brotherhood. □ **theosophical** /thee-uh-**sof**-i-kuhl/ *adj.* **theosophist** *n.* [Greek *theosophos* wise concerning God]

**therapeutic** /,the-ruh-**pyoo**-tik/ *adj.* **1** of, for, or contributing to the cure of disease. **2** soothing, conducive to well-being (*finds walking therapeutic*). □ **therapeutically** *adv.* [Greek *therapeuō* wait on, cure]

**therapeutics** *n.pl.* (usu. treated as *sing.*) branch of medicine concerned with cures and remedies.

**therapy** /**the**-ruh-pee/ *n.* (*pl.* **-ies**) **1** treatment of physical or mental disorders, other than by surgery. **2** particular type of such treatment. □ **therapist** *n.* [Greek *therapeia* healing]

**there** /thair/ — *adv.* **1** in, at, or to that place or position (*lived there for a year; goes there daily*). **2** at that point (in speech, performance, writing, etc.) (*there she stopped*). **3** in that respect (*I agree with you there*). **4** used for emphasis in calling attention (*you there!*). **5** used unemphatically (esp. with the verb *to be*) to introduce a sentence or clause in which, for the sake of emphasis or preparing the hearer, the verb comes before its subject (*there comes a time when* . . .; *believes that there is no God; there being no moon; there is a house on the corner*). — *n.* that place (*lives near there*). — *int.* **1** expressing confirmation, triumph, dismay, etc. (*there! what did I tell you?*). **2** used to soothe a child etc. (*there, there, never mind*). □ **all there** see ALL. **have been there before** *colloq.* know all about it. **so there** *colloq.* that is my final decision etc. (*whether you like it or not*). **there and then** var. **there it is 1** that is the trouble. **2** nothing can be done about it. **there you are** (or **go**) *colloq.* **1** this is what you wanted etc. **2** expressing confirmation, triumph, resignation, etc. [Old English]

**thereabouts** *adv.* (also **thereabout**) **1** near that place. **2** near that number, quantity, etc.

**thereafter** *adv. formal* after that.

**thereby** *adv.* by that means, as a result of that. □ **thereby hangs a tale** much could be said about that.

**therefore** /*th*air-faw/ *adv.* for that reason; accordingly, consequently.

**therein** *adv. formal* **1** in that place etc. **2** in that respect.

**thereof** *adv. formal* of that or it.

**thereto** *adv. formal* **1** to that or it. **2** in addition.

**thereupon** *adv.* **1** in consequence of that. **2** immediately after that.

**therewith** *adv. formal* **1** with that. **2** soon after that.

**therm** *n.* unit of heat equivalent to 100,000 British thermal units (1.055 x $10^8$ joules). [Greek *thermē* heat]

**thermal** /**ther**-muhl/ — *adj.* **1** of, for, or producing heat. **2** promoting the retention of heat (*thermal underwear*). — *n.* rising current of warm air (used by gliders, birds, etc., to gain height). □ **thermally** *adv.* [French: related to THERM]

**thermal unit** *n.* unit for measuring heat.

**thermionic** /ˌther-mee-**on**-ik/ *adj.* of electrons emitted from a very hot substance. [from THERMO-, ION]

**thermionic valve** *n.* device giving a flow of thermionic electrons in one direction, used esp. in the rectification of a current and in radio reception.

**thermo-** *comb. form* heat. [Greek]

**thermocouple** /**ther**-moh-ˌkup-uhl/ *n.* pair of different metals in contact at a point, generating a thermoelectric voltage that can serve as a measure of temperature at this point relative to their other parts.

**thermodynamics** /ˌther-moh-duy-**nam**-iks/ *n.pl.* (usu. treated as *sing.*) science of the relations between heat and other forms of energy. □ **thermodynamic** *adj.*

**thermoelectric** /ˌther-moh-ee-**lek**-trik, ˌther-moh-uh-/ *adj.* producing electricity by a difference of temperatures.

**thermometer** /thuh-**mom**-uh-tuh/ *n.* instrument for measuring temperature, esp. a graduated glass tube containing mercury or alcohol. [French: related to THERMO-, -METER]

**thermonuclear** /ˌther-moh-**nyoo**-klee-uh/ *adj.* **1** relating to nuclear reactions that occur only at very high temperatures. **2** (of weapons) using thermonuclear reactions.

**thermoplastic** /ˌther-moh-**plas**-tik/ — *adj.* that becomes plastic on heating and hardens on cooling. — *n.* thermoplastic substance.

**thermos** /**ther**-muhs/ *n.* (in full **thermos flask**) *propr.* vacuum flask. [Greek: related to THERMO-]

**thermosetting** /ˌther-moh-**set**-ing/ *adj.* (of plastics) setting permanently when heated.

**thermosphere** /**ther**-muh-ˌsfeer/ *n.* region of the atmosphere beyond the mesosphere.

**thermostat** /**ther**-muh-ˌstat/ *n.* device that automatically regulates or responds to temperature. □ **thermostatic** /-**stat**-ik/ *adj.* **thermostatically** /-**stat**-i-klee/ *adv.* [from THERMO-, Greek *statos* standing]

**thesaurus** /thuh-**saw**-ruhs/ *n.* (*pl.* **-ri** /-ruy/ or **-ruses**) **1** book that lists words in groups of synonyms and related concepts. **2** *Computing* list of similes, definitions, etc., used with a word processing system. [Greek: related to TREASURE]

**these** *pl.* of THIS.

**thesis** /**thee**-suhs/ *n.* (*pl.* **theses** /-seez/) **1** proposition to be maintained or proved. **2** detailed discourse on a subject, esp. as submitted in fulfilment or partial fulfilment of the requirements of a degree or diploma. [Greek, = putting]

**thespian** /**thes**-pee-uhn/ — *adj.* of drama. — *n.* actor or actress. [Greek *Thespis*, name of a Greek tragedian]

**theta** /**thee**-tuh/ *n.* eighth letter of the Greek alphabet (Θ, θ). [Greek]

**they** /thay/ *pron.* (*obj.* **them**; *poss.* **their**, **theirs**) **1** *pl.* of HE, SHE, IT. **2** people in general (*so they say*). **3** those in authority (*they have raised taxes*). **4** third person *sing.* indefinite pronoun meaning 'he or she' (*anyone can come if they want to*). [Old Norse]

■ **Usage** The use of *they* in sense 4, though common, is considered incorrect by some people.

**they'd** /thayd/ *contr.* **1** they had. **2** they would.

**they'll** /thayl/ *contr.* **1** they will. **2** they shall.

**they're** /thair, **th**ay-uh/ *contr.* they are.

**they've** /thayv/ *contr.* they have.

**thiamine** /**thuy**-uh-meen/ *n.* (also **thiamin**) B vitamin found in unrefined cereals, beans, and liver, a deficiency of which causes beriberi. [Greek *theion* sulphur, *amin* from VITAMIN]

**thick** — *adj.* **1 a** of great or specified extent between opposite surfaces (*a thick wall*). **b** of large diameter (*a thick rope*). **2** (of a line etc.) broad; not fine. **3**

arranged closely; crowded together; dense. **4** (usu. foll. by *with*) densely covered or filled (*air thick with smoke*). **5 a** firm in consistency; containing much solid matter (*a thick paste*; *thick soup*). **b** made of thick material (*a thick coat*). **6 a** muddy, cloudy; impenetrable by sight (*thick darkness*). **b** (of one's head) suffering from a hangover, headache, etc. **7** *colloq.* stupid. **8 a** (of a voice) indistinct. **b** (of an accent) very marked (*his foreign accent was quite thick*). **9** *colloq.* intimate, very friendly (esp. *thick as thieves*). — *n.* thick part of anything. — *adv.* thickly (*snow was falling thick*; *blows rained down thick and fast*). □ **a bit thick** *colloq.* unreasonable or intolerable. **in the thick of** at the busiest part of. **thick as a brick** (or **as a log of wood** or **as two short planks**) *colloq.* extremely dimwitted; stupid. **thick with** *colloq.* full of; abounding in (*the place was thick with tourists*). **through thick and thin** under all conditions; in spite of all difficulties. □ **thickish** *adj.* **thickly** *adv.* [Old English]

**thick ear** *n.* an ear swollen or numbed by a sharp blow (esp. in *give* (*a person*) *a thick ear*).

**thicken** *v.* **1** make or become thick or thicker. **2** become more complicated (*plot thickens*). □ **thickener** *n.*

**thickening** *n.* **1** process of becoming thick or thicker. **2** substance used to thicken liquid. **3** thickened part.

**thicket** /thik-uht/ *n.* tangle of shrubs or trees. [Old English: related to THICK]

**thickhead** *n.* **1** *colloq.* stupid person. **2** = WHISTLER. □ **thickheaded** *adj.*

**thickness** *n.* **1** state of being thick. **2** extent of this. **3** layer of material of a certain thickness (*use three thicknesses*).

**thickset** *adj.* **1** heavily or solidly built. **2** set or growing close together.

**thick-skinned** *adj.* not sensitive to criticism.

**thick-skulled** *adj.* (also **thick-witted**) *colloq.* stupid, dull; slow to learn.

**thief** *n.* (*pl.* **thieves** /theevz/) person who steals, esp. secretly. [Old English]

**thieve** *v.* (**-ving**) **1** be a thief. **2** steal (a thing). [Old English: related to THIEF]

**thievery** *n.* stealing.

**thievish** *adj.* given to stealing.

**thigh** /thuy/ *n.* **1** part of the human leg between the hip and the knee. **2** corresponding part in other animals. [Old English]

**thigh bone** *n.* = FEMUR.

**thimble** *n.* metal or plastic cap worn to protect the finger and push the needle in sewing. [Old English: related to THUMB]

**thimbleful** *n.* (*pl.* **-s**) small quantity, esp. of drink.

**thin** — *adj.* (**thinner, thinnest**) **1** having opposite surfaces close together; of small thickness or diameter. **2** (of a line) narrow or fine. **3** made of thin material (*thin dress*). **4** lean; not plump. **5** not dense or copious (*thin hair*). **6** of slight consistency (*a thin paste*). **7** weak; lacking an important ingredient (*thin blood*; *a thin voice*). **8** (of an excuse etc.) flimsy or transparent. — *adv.* thinly (*cut the bread very thin*). — *v.* (**-nn-**) **1** (often foll. by *down*) make or become thin or thinner. **2** (often foll. by *out*) make or become less dense or crowded or numerous. □ **thin edge of the wedge** see WEDGE. **thin on the ground** few in number. □ **thinly** *adv.* **thinness** *n.* **thinnish** *adj.* [Old English]

**thin air** *n.* state of invisibility or nonexistence (*vanished into thin air*).

**thine** /thuyn/ *poss. pron. archaic* **1** (*predic.* or *absol.*) of or belonging to thee. **2** (*attrib.* before a vowel) = THY. [Old English]

**thing** *n.* **1** entity, idea, action, etc., that exists or may be thought about or perceived. **2** inanimate material object (*take that thing away*). **3** unspecified item (*a few things to buy*). **4** act, idea, or utterance (*silly thing to do*). **5** event (*unfortunate thing to happen*). **6** quality (*patience is a useful thing*). **7** person regarded with pity, contempt, or affection (*poor thing!*). **8** specimen or type (*latest thing in hats*). **9** *colloq.* one's special interest or concern (*not my thing*). **10** *colloq.* something remarkable (*there's a thing!*). **11** (prec. by *the*) *colloq.* **a** what is proper or fashionable (*just the thing*). **c** what is to be considered (*the thing is, shall we go or not?*). **d** what is important (*the thing about them is their reliability*). **12** (in *pl.*) personal belongings or clothing (*where are my things?*). **13** (in *pl.*) equipment (*painting things*). **14** (in *pl.*) affairs in general (*not in the nature of things*). **15** (in *pl.*) circumstances, conditions (*things look good*). **16** (in *pl.* with a following adjective) all that is so describable (*things Greek*). □ **do one's own thing** *colloq.* pursue one's own interests or inclinations. **have a thing about** *colloq.* be obsessed or prejudiced about; have a fear about. **just the thing** precisely what is required. **make a** (**big**) **thing of** *colloq.* cause a fuss about. **not get a thing out of 1** fail to gain benefit or enjoyment from. **2** fail to elicit information from. **on** (**to**) **a**

**good thing** *colloq.* **1** engaged in a profitable enterprise etc. **2** have reliable information about the likely winner of a horse race etc. **one** (or **just one**) **of those things** *colloq.* something unavoidable or to be accepted. [Old English]

**thingie** /**thing**-ee/ *adj. colloq.* oversensitive; tense; emotional.

**thingummyjig** /**thing**-uh-mee-ˌjig/ *n.* (also **thingumabob** /-muh-ˌbob/, **thingummybob** /-mee-ˌbob/, **thingummy** /**thing**-uh-mee/ (*pl.* **-ies**) *colloq.* person or thing whose name one has forgotten or does not know.

**thingy** /**thing**-ee/ *n.* (*pl.* **-ies**) (also **thingo** /**thing**-oh/ ) = THINGUMMYJIG.

**think** — *v.* (*past* and *past part.* **thought** /thawt/ ) **1** be of the opinion (*think that they will come*). **2** judge or consider (*is thought to be a fraud*). **3** exercise the mind (*let me think for a moment*). **4** (foll. by *of* or *about*) **a** consider; be or become aware of (*I think of you constantly*). **b** form or entertain the idea of; imagine (*I couldn't think of such a thing*). **5** have a half-formed intention (*I think I'll stay*). **6** form a conception of (*cannot think how you do it*). **7** recognise the presence or existence of (*thought no harm in it*). — *n. colloq.* act of thinking (*have a think*). □ **think again** revise one's plans or opinions. **think aloud** utter one's thoughts as soon as they occur. **think better of** change one's mind about (an intention) after reconsideration. **think big** be ambitious. **think fit** see FIT¹. **think for oneself** have an independent mind or attitude. **think little** (or **nothing**) **of** consider to be insignificant. **think much** (or **a lot** or **highly**) **of** have a high opinion of. **think out** **1** consider carefully. **2** produce (an idea etc.) by thinking. **think over** reflect upon in order to reach a decision. **think through** reflect fully upon (a problem etc.). **think twice** use careful consideration, avoid hasty action, etc. **think up** *colloq.* devise. [Old English]

**thinker** *n.* **1** person who thinks, esp. in a specified way (*an original thinker*). **2** person with a skilled or powerful mind.

**thinking** — *attrib. adj.* using thought or rational judgment. — *n.* opinion or judgment. □ **put on one's thinking cap** *colloq.* meditate on a problem.

**think-tank** *n. colloq.* body of experts providing advice and ideas on national, commercial, etc., problems.

**thinner** /**thin**-uh/ *n.* solvent used to dilute paint etc.

**thin-skinned** *adj.* sensitive to criticism.

**third** *adj. & n.* **1** next after second. **2** each of three equal parts of a thing. **3** *Mus.* **a** an interval or chord spanning three consecutive notes in the diatonic scale (e.g. C to E). **b** note separated from another by this interval. □ **thirdly** *adv.* [Old English: related to THREE]

**third degree** — *n.* long and severe questioning, esp. by police to obtain information or a confession. — *adj.* (**third-degree**) denoting burns of the most severe kind, affecting lower layers of tissue.

**third man** *n. Cricket* fielder positioned near the boundary behind the slips.

**third party** — *n.* **1** another party besides the two principals. **2** bystander etc. — *adj.* (**third-party**) (of insurance) covering damage or injury suffered by a person other than the insured.

**third person** *n.* **1** = THIRD PARTY. **2** *Gram.* see PERSON.

**third-rate** *adj.* inferior; very poor.

**Third World** *n.* (usu. prec. by *the*) developing countries of Asia, Africa, and Latin America.

**thirst** — *n.* **1** need to drink; discomfort caused by this. **2** desire, craving (*thirst for power*; *thirst for knowledge*). — *v.* (often foll. by *for* or *after*) **1** feel thirst. **2** have a strong desire. [Old English]

**thirsty** *adj.* (**-ier, -iest**) **1** feeling thirst. **2** (of land, a season, etc.) dry or parched. **3** (often foll. by *for* or *after*) eager. **4** *colloq.* causing thirst (*thirsty work*). □ **thirstily** *adv.* **thirstiness** *n.* [Old English: related to THIRST]

**thirteen** /ther-**teen**/ *adj. & n.* **1** one more than twelve. **2** symbol for this (13, xiii, XIII). □ **thirteenth** *adj. & n.* [Old English: related to THREE]

**thirty** /**ther**-tee/ *adj. & n.* (*pl.* **-ies**) **1** three times ten. **2** symbol for this (30, xxx, XXX). **3** (in *pl.*) numbers from 30 to 39, esp. the years of a century or of a person's life. □ **thirtieth** *adj. & n.* [Old English: related to THREE]

**this** /this/ — *demons. pron.* (*pl.* **these** /theez/ ) **1** person or thing close at hand or indicated or already named or understood (*can you see this?*; *this is my cousin*). **2** (contrasted with *that*) the person or thing nearer to hand and more immediately in mind (*this is heavier than that*). — *demons. adj.* (*pl.* **these** /theez/ ) **1** designating the person or thing close at hand etc. (cf. senses 1, 2 of *pron.*). **2** (of time) the present or current (*am busy all this week*). **3** *colloq.* (in narrative) designating a person or thing previously unmentioned (*then up came this policeman*). — *adv.* to the degree or extent indicated (*knew him when he was this high*). □ **this and that** *colloq.* various

**thistle** /this-uhl/ *n.* prickly plant, usu. with globular heads of purple flowers. [Old English]

**thistledown** *n.* light down containing thistle-seeds and blown about in the wind.

**thither** /thi-thuh/ *adv. archaic* or *formal* to or towards that place. [Old English]

**tho'** (also **tho**) var. of THOUGH.

**-thon** var. of -ATHON.

**thong** *n.* **1** narrow strip of hide or leather. **2** flat-soled sandal held on the foot by a bifurcated thong passing between the first and second toes. [Old English]

**thorax** /thaw-raks/ *n.* (*pl.* **-races** /-ruh-,seez/ or **-raxes**) *Anat.* & *Zool.* part of the trunk between the neck and the abdomen. □ **thoracic** /thaw-ras-ik/ *adj.* [Latin from Greek]

**thorium** /thaw-ree-uhm/ *n. Chem.* radioactive metallic element. [*Thor*, name of the Scandinavian god of thunder]

**thorn** *n.* **1** sharp-pointed projection on a plant. **2** thorn-bearing shrub or tree. □ **thorn in one's flesh** (or **side**) constant nuisance. □ **thornless** *adj.* [Old English]

**thornback** *n.* marine fish of southern Australia, having thorn-like spines on the dorsal surface.

**thornbill** *n.* any of various small, plump Australian birds, often with a freckled forehead (*yellow thornbill*; *chestnut-rumped thornbill*; *Tasmanian thornbill*). [transferred use of the name of an American hummingbird]

**thorny** *adj.* (**-ier**, **-iest**) **1** having many thorns. **2** problematic, causing disagreement. □ **thornily** *adv.* **thorniness** *n.* [Old English: related to THORN]

**thorny devil** *n.* = MOUNTAIN DEVIL. [from the thorn-like spines which cover the lizard]

**thorough** /thu-ruh/ *adj.* **1** complete and unqualified; not superficial (*needs a thorough overhaul*). **2** acting or done with great care and completeness (*the report is most thorough*). **3** absolute (*thorough nuisance*). □ **thoroughly** *adv.* **thoroughness** *n.* [related to THROUGH]

**thoroughbred** — *adj.* of pure breed. — *n.* thoroughbred animal, esp. a horse.

**thoroughfare** *n.* road or path open at both ends, esp. for traffic.

**thoroughgoing** *attrib. adj.* thorough; complete.

**those** *pl.* of THAT.

**thou¹** /thow/ *pron.* (*obj.* **thee** /thee/; *oss.* **thy** or **thine**; *pl.* **ye** or **you**) *archaic* second person singular pronoun. [Old English]

■ **Usage** *Thou* has now been replaced by *you* except in some formal, liturgical, dialect, and poetic uses.

**thou²** /thow/ *n.* (*pl.* same or **-s**) *colloq.* **1** thousand. **2** one thousandth. [abbreviation]

**though** /thoh/ (also **tho'**) — *conj.* **1** despite the fact that; in spite of being (*though it was early we left*; *though annoyed, I agreed*). **2** (introducing a possibility) even if (*ask him though he may refuse*). **3** and yet; nevertheless (*she read on, though she stopped short of completing the book*). **4** in spite of being (*ready though unwilling*). — *adv. colloq.* however; all the same (*I wish you had told me, though*). [Old English]

**thought¹** /thawt/ *n.* **1** process or power of thinking; faculty of reason. **2** way of thinking associated with a particular time, group, etc. (*medieval thought*). **3** sober reflection or consideration (*I gave it much thought*). **4** idea or piece of reasoning produced by thinking (*many good thoughts came out of the discussion*). **5** (foll. by *of* + verbal noun or *to* + infin.) partly formed intention (*had no thought to go*). **6** (usu. in *pl.*) what one is thinking; one's opinion (*have you any thoughts on this?*; *my one thought was to get away*). **7** expectation (*I had no thought of meeting him there*). □ **in thought** meditating. [Old English: related to THINK]

**thought²** *past* and *past part.* of THINK.

**thoughtful** *adj.* **1** engaged in or given to meditation. **2** (of a book, writer, etc.) giving signs of serious thought. **3** (often foll. by *of*) (of a person or conduct) considerate. □ **thoughtfully** *adv.* **thoughtfulness** *n.*

**thoughtless** *adj.* **1** careless of consequences or of others' feelings. **2** due to lack of thought. □ **thoughtlessly** *adv.* **thoughtlessness** *n.*

**thousand** /thow-zuhnd/ *adj.* & *n.* (*pl.* **thousands** or (in sense 1) **thousand**) (in *sing.* prec. by *a* or *one*) **1** ten hundred. **2** symbol for this (1,000, m, M). **3** (in *sing.* or *pl.*) *colloq.* large number. □ **thousandfold** *adj.* & *adv.* **thousandth** *adj.* & *n.* [Old English]

**thrall** /thrawl/ *n. literary* **1** (often foll. by *of*, *to*) slave (of a person, or of a power or influence). **2** slavery (*in thrall*). □ **thraldom** *n.* [Old English from Old Norse]

**thrash** — *v.* **1** beat or whip severely. **2** defeat thoroughly. **3** (foll. by *about*, *around*) move or fling (esp. the limbs) about violently. **4** = THRESH 1. — *n.* (in full **thrash metal**) style of rock music which includes elements of heavy metal combined with punk rock. □ **thrash out** discuss to a conclusion. [Old English]

**thread** /thred/ — *n.* **1 a** spun-out cotton, silk, or glass, etc.; yarn. **b** length of this. **2** thin cord of twisted yarns used esp. in sewing and weaving. **3** continuous aspect of a thing (*the thread of life; thread of his argument*). **4** spiral ridge of a screw. — *v.* **1** pass a thread through (a needle). **2** put (beads) on a thread. **3** insert (a strip of material, e.g. film or magnetic tape) into equipment. **4** make (one's way) carefully through a crowded place, over a difficult route, etc. □ **hang by a thread** be in a precarious state, position, etc. **lose the thread** cease to follow the sense of what is being said. **pick up** (or **take up**) **the threads** continue (with) after an interruption or separation. [Old English: related to THROW]

**threadbare** *adj.* **1** (of cloth) with the nap worn away and the thread visible. **2** (of a person) wearing such clothes. **3** poor, meagre (*a threadbare existence*). **4 a** hackneyed; stale (*threadbare justifications for logging virgin forests*). **b** feeble or insubstantial (*a threadbare excuse*).

**threadworm** *n.* parasitic threadlike worm.

**threat** /thret/ *n.* **1** declaration of an intention to punish or hurt if an order etc. is not obeyed. **2** indication of something undesirable coming (*threat of war*). **3** person or thing as a likely cause of harm etc. [Old English]

**threaten** *v.* **1** make a threat or threats against. **2** be a sign of (something undesirable) (*these continuing skirmishes threaten an all-out war*). **3** (foll. by *to* + infin.) announce one's intention to do an undesirable thing (*threatened to resign*). **4** (also *absol.*) warn of the infliction of (harm etc.) (*these clouds threaten a storm*). **5** (as **threatened** *adj.*) (of a species etc.) likely to become extinct. [Old English]

**three** *adj.* & *n.* **1** one more than two. **2** symbol for this (3, iii, III). [Old English]

**three-cornered** *adj.* **1** triangular. **2** (of a contest etc.) involving three parties.

**three-cornered jack** *n.* = DOUBLEGEE.

**three-D** — *adj.* (also **3-D**) three-dimensional. — *n.* (also **3-D**) three-dimensional realisation or state (*saw it in 3-D*).

**three-dimensional** *adj.* having or appearing to have length, breadth, and depth.

**threefold** *adj.* & *adv.* **1** three times as much or as many. **2** consisting of three parts.

**three-quarter** *n.* (also **three-quarter back**) *Rugby* any of three or four players just behind the half-backs.

**three-quarters** *n.pl.* three parts out of four.

**three-ring circus 1** circus with three rings for simultaneous performances. **2** extravagant display. **3** chaotic mess.

**three Rs** *n.pl.* (prec. by *the*) reading, writing, and arithmetic.

**threesome** *n.* **1** group of three persons. **2** something in which three persons take part. **3** a game etc. for three, esp. in golf.

**three-way** *adj.* involving three directions or participants.

**threnody** /**thren**-uh-dee/ *n.* (*pl.* **-ies**) song of lamentation or mourning. [Greek]

**thresh** *v.* **1** beat out or separate grain from (cereal plants etc.). **2** = THRASH *v.* 3. □ **thresher** *n.* [Old English]

**thresher shark** *n.* shark of Australian waters having a very long upper lobe to its tail which it uses to lash fish into groups for ease in feeding.

**threshold** /**thresh**-hohld/ *n.* **1** strip of wood or stone forming the bottom of a doorway and crossed in entering a house etc. **2** point of entry or beginning (*on the threshold of discovering a cure for AIDS*). **3** limit below which a stimulus causes no reaction (*pain threshold*). [Old English: related to THRASH in the sense 'tread']

**threw** *past* of THROW.

**thrice** *adv. archaic* or *literary* **1** three times. **2** (esp. in *comb.*) highly (*thrice-blessed*). [related to THREE]

**thrift** *n.* frugality; careful use of money etc. [Old Norse: related to THRIVE]

**thrifty** *adj.* (**-ier**, **-iest**) economical, frugal. □ **thriftily** *adv.* **thriftiness** *n.*

**thrill** — *n.* **1** wave or nervous tremor of emotion or sensation (*a thrill of joy*). **2** throb, pulsation (*visible thrill in the taut string when plucked*). **3** thrilling experience or incident (*abseiling is a thrill*). — *attrib. adj.* (of a crime) committed solely for the thrill of carrying it out (*a wave of thrill killings in America*). — *v.* **1** (cause to) feel a thrill (*thrilled to the touch; a voice that thrilled millions*). **2** quiver or throb with or as with emotion (*the harp strings thrilled, quivered with the vibration*). **3** (foll. by *through, over, along*) (of an emotion etc.) pass with a thrill through etc. (*fear thrilled through my veins*). **4** (foll. by *to*) be greatly stirred or excited by (*millions have thrilled to Joan Sutherland's voice*). **5** (as **thrilled**

*adj.*) *colloq.* extremely pleased or delighted (*was thrilled to bits to see him again*). [Old English, = pierce: related to THROUGH]

**thriller** *n.* exciting or sensational story, film, or play, esp. about crime or espionage.

**thrips** *n.* (*pl.* same) small sap-sucking insect harmful to plants. [Greek, = woodworm]

**thrive** *v.* (**-ving**; *past* **throve** or **thrived**; *past part.* **thriven** /thriv-uhn/ or **thrived**) **1** prosper, flourish. **2** grow rich. **3** (of a child, animal, or plant) grow vigorously. [Old Norse]

**thro'** var. of THROUGH.

**throat** *n.* **1 a** windpipe or gullet. **b** front part of the neck containing this. **2** *literary* narrow passage, entrance, or exit. □ **be at each other's throats** *colloq.* quarrel violently. **cut one's own throat** harm oneself or one's interests. **have** (or **have got**) **the game** (or **it**) **by the throat** *colloq.* have complete control of a situation. **ram** (or **thrust**) **down a person's throat** force (a thing) on a person's attention. □ **-throated** *adj.* (in *comb.*). [Old English]

**throaty** *adj.* (**-ier**, **-iest**) (of a voice) hoarsely resonant. □ **throatily** *adv.* **throatiness** *n.*

**throb** — *v.* (**-bb-**) **1** pulsate, esp. with more than the usual force or rapidity. **2** vibrate with a persistent rhythm or with emotion. — *n.* **1** throbbing. **2** palpitation or (esp. violent) pulsation. [imitative]

**throe** /throh/ *n.* (usu. in *pl.*) violent pang, esp. of childbirth or death. □ **in the throes of** struggling with the task of. [Old English, alteration of original *throwe*, perhaps by association with *woe*]

**thrombosis** /throm-**boh**-suhs/ *n.* (*pl.* **-boses** /-seez/ ) coagulation of the blood in a blood-vessel or organ. [Greek, = curdling]

**throne** — *n.* **1** chair of State for a sovereign or bishop etc. **2** sovereign power (*came to the throne*). — *v.* (**-ning**) enthrone. [Greek *thronos*]

**throng** — *n.* (often foll. by *of*) crowd, esp. of people. — *v.* **1** come in great numbers (*crowds thronged to the stadium*). **2** flock into or crowd round; fill with or as with a crowd (*crowds thronged the streets*). [Old English]

**throttle** — *n.* **1 a** valve controlling the flow of fuel or steam etc. in an engine. **b** (in full **throttle-lever**) lever or pedal operating this valve. **2** throat, gullet, or windpipe. — *v.* (**-ling**) **1** choke or strangle. **2** prevent the utterance etc. of. **3** control (an engine or steam etc.) with a throttle. [perhaps from THROAT]

**through** /throo/ (also **thro'**) — *prep.* **1 a** from end to end or side to side of. **b** going in one side or end and out the other side of. **2** between or among (*swam through the waves; walked through the tall grass*). **3** from beginning to end of (*read through the letter; went through many difficulties*). **4** because of; by the agency, means, or fault of (*lost it through carelessness*). **5** past (traffic lights) (*went through the red light*). **6** throughout; in or to all parts of (a region, or a body) (*toured through Australia; disease spread through his body*). **7** *US* up to and including (*Monday through Friday*). — *adv.* **1** through a thing; from side to side, end to end, or beginning to end (*went through to the garden; would not let us through*). **2** throughout; thoroughly (*wet through*). **3** so as to be connected by telephone (*will put you through*). **4** having completed (esp. successfully) (*are through their exams*). — *attrib. adj.* **1** (of a journey, route, etc.) done without a change of line or vehicle etc. or with one ticket. **2** (of traffic) going through a place to its destination. **3** (of a road) open at both ends. □ **be through** *colloq.* **1** (often foll. by *with*) have finished (*am through with this book*). **2** (often foll. by *with*) cease to have dealings (*am through with him at last*). **3** have no further prospects (*is through as a politician*). **go through** see GO. **through and through** thoroughly, completely. [Old English]

**throughout** /throo-**owt**/ — *prep.* right through; from end to end of. — *adv.* in every part or respect.

**throughput** *n.* amount of material put through a process, esp. in manufacturing or computing.

**throve** *past* of THRIVE.

**throw** /throh/ — *v.* (*past* **threw** /throo/; *past part.* **thrown**) **1** propel with force through the air. **2** force violently into, or compel to be in, a specified position or state (*thrown on the rocks; threw themselves down; thrown out of work*). **3** turn or move (part of the body) quickly or suddenly (*threw an arm out*). **4** project or cast (light, a shadow, a spell, a voice (as in ventriloquism), etc.). **5 a** bring to the ground in wrestling. **b** (of a horse) unseat (its rider). **c** cast (an animal) to the ground, preparatory to branding etc. **6** *colloq.* disconcert (*the question threw me*). **7** (foll. by *on*, *off*, etc.) put (clothes etc.) hastily on or off etc. **8 a** cause (dice) to fall on a table etc. **b** obtain (a specified number) by throwing dice. **9** cause to pass or extend suddenly to another state or position (*threw a bridge across the* *river*). **10** operate (a switch or lever). **11** form on a potter's wheel. **12** have (a fit or tantrum etc.). **13** give (a party). **14** lose (a contest, race, etc.) intentionally, esp. for a bribe. **15** *Cricket* bowl (a ball) with an illegitimate sudden straightening of the arm. — *n.* **1** act of throwing or being thrown. **2** distance a thing is or may be thrown (*a record throw with the discus*). **3** (*prec. by a*) *colloq.* each; per item (*sold at $10 a throw*). □ **throw away 1** discard as useless or unwanted. **2** waste or fail to make use of (an opportunity etc.). **throw back 1** revert to ancestral character. **2** (usu. in *passive*; foll. by *on*) compel to rely on (*was thrown back on his own resources*). **throw one's hat in the ring** see HAT. **throw in 1** interpose (a word or remark). **2** include at no extra cost. **3** throw (a football) from the edge of the pitch where it has gone out of play. **throw in the towel** (or **sponge**) admit defeat; lose hope; give up. **throw it in** *colloq.* **1** give up; accept defeat (*this job's the pits — think I'll throw it in; I'm throwing it in — you lot are too smart for me*). **2** cease working, call a halt (*I'm throwing it in for a while*). **throw off 1** discard; contrive to get rid of. **2** write or utter in an offhand manner. **3** confuse, disconcert (*don't be thrown off by his comments*). **throw off at** *colloq.* ridicule or criticise. **throw oneself at** seek blatantly as a sexual partner. **throw oneself into** engage vigorously in. **throw oneself on** (or **upon**) rely completely on. **throw open** (often foll. by *to*) **1** cause to be suddenly or widely open. **2** make accessible. **throw out 1** put out forcibly or suddenly. **2** discard as unwanted. **3** reject (a proposal). **throw over** desert, abandon. **throw a seven** see SEVEN. **throw together 1** assemble hastily. **2** bring into casual contact. **throw up 1** abandon. **2** resign from. **3** *colloq.* vomit. **4** erect hastily. **5** bring to notice (*the enquiry threw up some interesting facts*). **throw a wobbly** (or **wobbler**) *colloq.* have a fit of annoyance, temper, or panic. [Old English, = twist]

**throwaway** *attrib. adj.* **1** meant to be thrown away after (one) use. **2** spoken in a deliberately casual way (*a throw-away remark*). **3** disposed to throwing things away (*throw-away society*).

**throwback** *n.* **1** reversion to ancestral character. **2** instance of this.

**throw-in** *n.* throwing in of a football during play.

**throwing stick** *n.* **1** = WOOMERA. **2** = BOOMERANG. **3** straight stick of wood used as a missile.

**thrum** — *v.* (**-mm-**) **1** play (a stringed instrument) monotonously or unskil- fully. **2** (often foll. by *on*) drum idly. — *n.* **1** such playing. **2** resulting sound. [imitative]

**thrush**[1] *n.* **1** any of various songbirds, esp. the song thrush (introduced into Australia from Europe). **2** any of several Australian birds having a melodious song, including the SHRIKE-THRUSH and GROUND THRUSH. [Old English]

**thrush**[2] *n.* **1** fungous disease, esp. of children, affecting the mouth and throat. **2** similar disease of the vagina. [origin unknown]

**thrust** — *v.* (*past* and *past part.* **thrust**) **1** push with a sudden impulse or with force (*thrust the letter into my pocket; was thrust into the limelight*). **2** (foll. by *on*) impose (a thing) forcibly; enforce acceptance of (a thing) (*had it thrust on me*). **3** (foll. by *at*, *through*) pierce, stab; lunge suddenly. **4** make (one's way) forcibly. **5** (as **thrusting** *adj.*) aggressive, ambitious. — *n.* **1** sudden or forcible push or lunge. **2** propulsive force produced by a jet or rocket engine. **3** strong attempt to penetrate an enemy's line or territory. **4** hostile remark aimed at a person. **5** an attack with the point of a weapon. **6** (often foll. by *of*) chief theme or gist of remarks etc. [Old Norse]

**thud** — *n.* low dull sound as of a blow on a non-resonant surface. — *v.* (**-dd-**) make or fall with a thud. □ **come a thud** *colloq.* be disappointed; be embarrassed by failing to fulfil an expectation. [probably Old English]

**thug** *n.* **1** violent ruffian. **2** (**Thug**) *hist.* member of a religious organisation of robbers and assassins in India. □ **thuggery** *n.* **thuggish** *adj.* [Hindi]

**thulium** /thyoo-lee-uhm/ *n.* metallic element of the lanthanide series. [Latin *Thule* region in the remote north]

**thumb** /thum/ — *n.* **1** short thick finger on the human hand, set apart from the other four. **2** part of a glove etc. for a thumb. — *v.* **1** wear or soil (pages etc.) with a thumb. **2** turn over pages with or as with a thumb (*thumbed through the directory*). **3** request or get (a lift) by signalling with a raised thumb. **4** use the thumb in a gesture. □ **be all thumbs** be clumsy with one's hands. **thumb one's nose** = *cock a snook* (see SNOOK). **thumbs down** indication of rejection. **thumbs up** indication of satisfaction or approval. **under a person's thumb** completely dominated by a person. [Old English]

**thumb index** *n.* set of lettered grooves cut down the side of a book for easy reference.

**thumbnail** *n.* **1** nail of a thumb. **2** (*attrib.*) concise (*thumbnail sketch*).

**thumbscrew** *n.* instrument of torture for crushing the thumbs.

**thump** — *v.* **1** beat or strike heavily, esp. with the fist. **2** throb strongly (*my heart was thumping*). **3** (foll. by *at, on*, etc.) knock loudly. **4** tread heavily. **5** pound (the keys of a piano) heavily, unmusically, or (as a child would) meaninglessly. — *n.* **1** heavy blow. **2** dull sound of this. [imitative]

**thumping** *adj. colloq.* (esp. as an intensifier) huge (*a thumping lie; a thumping majority*).

**thunder** /thun-duh/ — *n.* **1** loud noise caused by lightning and due to the expansion of rapidly heated air. **2** resounding loud deep noise (*thunders of applause*). **3** strong censure or denunciation. — *v.* **1** (prec. by *it* as subject) thunder sounds (*it is thundering; if it thunders*). **2** make or proceed with a noise like thunder (*the traffic thundered past*). **3** utter (threats, compliments, etc.) loudly (*thundered his disgust at our behaviour*). **4** (foll. by *against* etc.) make violent threats, a speech, a sermon, etc., against (*thundered against immorality from the pulpit*). □ **steal a person's thunder** see STEAL. □ **thundery** *adj.* [Old English]

**thunderbird** *n.* either of two Australian birds, the golden whistler or the rufous whistler, whose call is popularly regarded as presaging a thunderstorm.

**thunderbolt** *n.* **1** flash of lightning with a simultaneous crash of thunder. **2** unexpected occurrence or announcement. **3** supposed bolt or shaft as a destructive agent, esp. as an attribute of a god.

**thunderclap** *n.* **1** crash of thunder. **2** something startling or unexpected.

**thundercloud** *n.* cumulus cloud charged with electricity and producing thunder and lightning.

**thundering** *adj. colloq.* (esp. as an intensifier) huge (*a thundering nuisance; a thundering great bruise*).

**thunderous** *adj.* **1** like thunder. **2** very loud.

**thunderstorm** *n.* storm with thunder and lightning and usu. heavy rain or hail.

**thunderstruck** *predic. adj.* amazed.

**thurible** /thyoo-ruh-buhl/ *n.* censer. [Latin *thus thur-* incense]

**thurifer** /thyoo-ruh-fuh/ *n.* acolyte who carries the censer at Mass etc.

**Thursday** /therz-day/ — *n.* day of the week following Wednesday. — *adv. colloq.* **1** on Thursday. **2** (**Thursdays**) on Thursdays; each Thursday. [Old English]

**thus** /thus/ *adv. formal* **1 a** in this way. **b** as indicated. **2 a** accordingly. **b** as a result or inference. **3** to this extent; so (*thus far; thus much*). [Old English]

**thwack** — *v.* hit with a heavy blow. — *n.* heavy blow. [imitative]

**thwart** /thwawt/ — *v.* frustrate or foil (a person, plan, etc.). — *n.* rower's seat. [Old Norse, = across]

**thy** /thuy/ *poss. pron.* (*attrib.*) (also **thine** *predic.* or before a vowel) *archaic* of or belonging to thee. [from THINE]

■ **Usage** *Thy* has now been replaced by *your* except in some formal, liturgical, dialect, and poetic uses.

**thylacine** /thuy-luh-seen/ *n.* = TASMANIAN TIGER. [Greek *thulakos* pouch]

**thyme** /tuym/ *n.* any of several herbs with aromatic leaves. [Greek *thumon*]

**thymus** /thuy-muhs/ *n.* (*pl.* **thymi** /-muy/ ) lymphoid organ situated in the neck of vertebrates. [Greek]

**thyroid** /thuy-roid/ *n.* (in full **thyroid gland**) **1** large ductless gland in the neck of vertebrates, secreting a hormone which regulates growth and development. **2** extract prepared from the thyroid gland of animals and used in treating goitre etc. [Greek *thureos* oblong shield]

**thyroid cartilage** *n.* large cartilage of the larynx, forming the Adam's apple.

**thyself** *pron. archaic* emphat. & refl. form of THOU[1], THEE.

**Ti** *symb.* titanium.

**ti** var. of TE.

**tiara** /tee-ah-ruh/ *n.* **1** jewelled ornamental band worn on the front of a woman's hair. **2** (in full **papal tiara**) triple-crowned diadem worn by a pope. □ **tiaraed** *adj.* [Latin from Greek]

**tibia** /tib-ee-uh/ *n.* (*pl.* **tibiae** /tib-ee-ee/ ) *Anat.* inner of two bones extending from the knee to the ankle. □ **tibial** *adj.* [Latin]

**tic** *n.* (in full **nervous tic**) occasional involuntary contraction of the muscles, esp. of the face. [French from Italian]

**tich** var. of TITCHY.

**tick**[1] — *n.* **1** slight recurring click, esp. that of a watch or clock. **2** *colloq.* moment. **3** mark (✔) to denote correctness, check items in a list, etc. — *v.* **1 a** (of a clock etc.) make ticks. **b** (often foll. by *away*) (of time) pass. **2 a** mark with a tick. **b** (often foll. by *off*) mark (an item) with a tick in checking. **3** (of a mechanism) work, function (*take it apart to see how it ticks*). □ **tick off** *colloq.* reprimand. **tick over 1** (of an engine etc.) idle. **2** (of a person, project, etc.) be functioning at a basic level. **what**

makes **a person tick** *colloq.* person's motivation. [probably imitative]

**tick²** *n.* **1** parasitic arachnid on the skin of dogs, cattle, etc. **2** parasitic insect on sheep and birds etc. [Old English]

**tick³** *n. colloq.* credit (*buy goods on tick*). [apparently an abbreviation of TICKET in *on the ticket*]

**tick⁴** *n.* case or cover containing feathers, down, etc., forming a mattress or pillow. [Greek *thēkē* case]

**ticker** *n. colloq.* **1** heart. **2** watch.

**ticker tape** *n.* **1** paper strip from a tape machine. **2** this or similar material thrown from windows etc. to greet a celebrity.

**ticket** /tik-uht/ — *n.* **1 a** written or printed piece of paper or card entitling the holder to enter a place, participate in an event, travel by public transport, etc. **b** document certifying that the bearer is a member of a trade union (*no ticket, no start*). **2** *hist.* = TICKET-OF-LEAVE. **3** notification of a traffic offence etc. (*parking ticket*). **4** price etc. label. **5** list of candidates put forward by one group, esp. a political party. **6** (prec. by *the*) *colloq.* what is correct or needed (*that's the ticket!*). — *v.* (**-t-**) attach a ticket to. □ **have tickets on oneself** *colloq.* be conceited. [obsolete French *étiquet*]

**ticket-of-leave** *n. hist.* (also *attrib.*) permit entitling a convict in Australia to live and work as a private individual within a stipulated area until the expiration or remission of sentence. □ **ticket-of-leaver** *n.*

**ticking** *n.* stout usu. striped material used to cover mattresses etc. [from TICK⁴]

**tickle** /tik-uhl/ — *v.* (**-ling**) **1 a** touch or stroke (a person) lightly in some sensitive spot so as to excite the nerves, titillate, and usu. produce laughter and spasmodic movement. **b** feel this sensation (*my foot tickles; my nose is tickling*). **2** excite agreeably; amuse (*was tickled by his antics*). — *n.* **1** act of tickling. **2** tickling sensation. □ **tickled pink** (or **to death**) *colloq.* extremely amused or pleased. **tickle the peter** see PETER³. □ **tickly** *adj.* [probably frequentative of TICK¹]

**ticklish** *adj.* **1** sensitive to tickling. **2** (of a matter or person to be dealt with) difficult; requiring careful handling.

**tidal** /tuy-duhl/ *adj.* relating to, like, or affected by, tides. □ **tidally** *adv.*

**tidal wave** *n.* **1** exceptionally large ocean wave, esp. one caused by an underwater earthquake. **2** widespread manifestation of feeling etc.

**tiddler** *n. colloq.* **1** small fish, esp. a minnow. **2** unusually small thing (esp. a child). [perhaps related to TIDDLY² and *tittlebat*, a childish form of *stickleback* small spiny-backed fish of the Northern hemisphere.]

**tiddly¹** *adj.* (**-ier, -iest**) *colloq.* slightly drunk. [origin unknown]

**tiddly²** *adj.* (**-ier, -iest**) *colloq.* little.

**tiddly-wink** /tid-lee-wingk/ *n.* **1** counter flicked with another into a cup etc. **2** (in *pl.*) this game. [perhaps related to TIDDLY¹]

**tide** *n.* **1 a** periodic rise and fall of the sea due to the attraction of the moon and sun. **b** water as affected by this. **2** time or season (usu. in *comb.*: *Eastertide*). **3** marked trend of opinion, fortune, or events. □ **the tide is out** *colloq.* my glass etc. is not full; my glass etc. needs refilling. **tide over** (**-ding**) provide (a person) with what is needed during a difficult period etc. [Old English, = TIME]

**tidings** /tuy-dingz/ *n.* (as *sing.* or *pl.*) *archaic* or *joc.* news. [Old English, probably from Old Norse]

**tidy** — *adj.* (**-ier, -iest**) **1** neat, orderly. **2** (of a person) methodical. **3** *colloq.* considerable (*a tidy sum*). — *n.* (*pl.* **-ies**) receptacle for holding small objects, waste scraps of food, etc. (*kitchen tidy*). — *v.* (**-ies, -ied**) (also *absol.*; often foll. by *up*) put in good order; make (oneself, a room, etc.) tidy. □ **tidily** *adv.* **tidiness** *n.* [originally = timely etc., from TIDE]

**tie** /tuy/ — *v.* (**tying**) **1** attach or fasten with string or cord etc. **2 a** form (a string, ribbon, shoelace, necktie, etc.) into a knot or bow. **b** form (a knot or bow) in this way. **3** (often foll. by *down*) restrict (a person) in some way (*is tied to his job; is tied to the house*). **4** (often foll. by *with*) achieve the same score or place as another competitor (*tied with her for first place*). **5** *Mus.* unite (written notes) by a tie. — *n.* **1** cord or wire etc. used for fastening. **2** strip of material worn round the collar and tied in a knot at the front with the ends hanging down. **3** thing that unites or restricts persons (*family ties; children are a real tie; ties of friendship*). **4** draw, dead heat, or equality of score among competitors. **5** match between any pair from a group of competing players or teams in an elimination competition (*Davis Cup tie*). **6** *Mus.* curved line above or below two notes of the same pitch indicating that they are to be played without a break between them. □ **fit to be tied** *colloq.* very angry. **tie in** (foll. by *with*) bring into or have a close association or agreement. **tie in knots** see

KNOT. **tie up 1** fasten or bind securely with cord etc. **2** invest or reserve (capital etc.) so that it is not immediately available for use. **3** (often foll. by *with*) = *tie in*. **4** (usu. in *passive*) fully occupy (a person) (*I'm tied up all this week*). **5** bring to a satisfactory conclusion (*tie up all the loose ends*). [Old English]

**tie-break** *n.* (also **tie-breaker**) means of deciding a winner from competitors who have tied.

**tie-dye** *n.* method of producing dyed patterns by tying string etc. to keep the dye away from parts of the fabric.

**tie-in** *n.* connection or association.

**tie-pin** *n.* ornamental pin for holding a tie in place.

**tier** /teer/ *n.* **1** row, rank, or unit of a structure, as one of several placed one above another (*tiers of seats*). **2** (often in *pl.*) (in Tasmania and SA) forested mountain range, esp. one of a series. □ **tiered** *adj.* [French *tire* from *tirer* draw, elongate]

**tie-up** *n.* connection or association.

**tie-wire** *n.* piece of wire etc. used to fasten two objects, or two parts of an object, together.

**tiff** *n.* slight or petty quarrel. [origin unknown]

**tiffin** /tif-uhn/ *n.* (in India, Sri Lanka, etc.) a light meal, as lunch, afternoon tea. [apparently from *tiffing* sipping]

**tiger** /tuy-guh/ *n.* **1** large Asian animal of the cat family, with a yellow-brown coat with black stripes. **2** = TASMANIAN TIGER. **3** fierce, energetic, or formidable person. □ **a tiger for punishment** *colloq.* person who works extremely hard or relentlessly (at a task etc.). [Greek *tigris*]

**tiger-cat** *n.* **1** any moderate-sized feline resembling the tiger, e.g. the ocelot. **2** large, carnivorous marsupial of eastern Australia, having brown fur with white spots on the body and tail.

**tiger country** *n.* remote and inaccessible parts of Australia.

**tiger flathead** *n.* marine food-fish, predominantly brown with darker bands or blotches, of southern NSW, eastern Victoria, and eastern Tasmania, an important commercial species.

**tiger prawn** *n.* large prawn of esp. northern Australia, having dark vertical stripes.

**tiger snake** *n.* either of two highly venomous Australian snakes, usu. with distinctive bands of lighter and darker colouring.

**tight** /tuyt/ — *adj.* **1** closely held, drawn, fastened, fitting, etc. (*tight hold*; *tight skirt*). **2** too closely fitting (*these shoes are a bit tight*). **3** impermeable, impervious, esp. (in *comb.*) to a specified thing (*watertight*). **4** tense; stretched (*a tight bowstring*). **5** *colloq.* drunk. **6** *colloq.* stingy. **7** (of money or materials) not easily obtainable. **8 a** (of precautions, a programme, a budget, discipline, etc.) stringent, demanding. **b** presenting difficulties (*tight situation*). **9** produced by or requiring great exertion or pressure (*tight squeeze*). **10** (of a contest etc.) close; evenly matched. **11** (of a group or formation) having the individual members positioned close together. **12** *Sport* (esp. *Cricket*) that allows the opposition little chance to score (*tight bowling*; *tight fielding*). **13** (of a turn or curve etc.) having a short radius. — *adv.* tightly (*hold tight!*). □ **tightly** *adv.* **tightness** *n.* [Old Norse]

**tight corner** *n.* (also **tight place** or **spot**) difficult situation.

**tighten** *v.* make or become tighter.

**tight-fisted** *adj.* stingy.

**tight-lipped** *adj.* with or as with the lips compressed to restrain emotion or speech; determinedly reticent.

**tightrope** *n.* rope stretched tightly high above the ground, on which acrobats perform. □ **walk a tightrope** be in a precarious or difficult situation.

**tights** *n.pl.* **1** thin close-fitting wool or nylon etc. garment covering the legs, feet, and the lower part of the torso, worn by women and girls. **2** similar garment worn by a (male or female) dancer, acrobat, etc.

**tigress** /tuy-gruhs/ *n.* female tiger.

**tike** var. of TYKE.

**tiki** /tee-kee/ *n.* (*pl.* **-s**) large wooden or small ornamental greenstone image representing a human figure. [Maori]

**tilde** /til-duh/ *n.* mark (~) put over a letter, e.g. over a Spanish *n* when pronounced *ny* (as in *señor*). [Latin: related to TITLE]

**tile** — *n.* **1** thin slab of concrete or baked clay etc. used for roofing or paving etc. **2** similar slab of glazed pottery, cork, linoleum, etc., for covering a wall, floor, etc. **3** thin flat piece used in a game (esp. in mah-jong). — *v.* (**-ling**) cover with tiles. □ **on the tiles** *colloq.* having a spree. □ **tiler** *n.* [Latin *tegula*]

**tiling** *n.* **1** process of fixing tiles. **2** area of tiles.

**till¹** — *prep.* **1** up to or as late as (*wait till six o'clock*). **2** up to the time of (*faithful till death*). — *conj.* **1** up to the time when (*wait till I return*). **2** so long that (*laughed till I cried*). [Old Norse: related to TILL³]

■ **Usage** In all senses, *till* can be replaced by *until* which is more formal in style, and which is more usual when beginning a sentence.

**till²** *n.* drawer for money in a shop or bank etc., esp. with a device recording the amount of each purchase. [origin unknown]

**till³** *v.* cultivate (land). □ **tiller** *n.* [Old English, = strive for]

**till⁴** *n.* stiff clay containing boulders, sand, etc., deposited by melting glaciers and ice-sheets. [origin unknown]

**tillage** /til-ij/ *n.* **1** preparation of land for growing crops. **2** tilled land.

**tiller** *n.* bar fitted to a boat's rudder to turn it in steering. [Anglo-French *telier* weaver's beam]

**tilly** *n. colloq.* = UTE. [abbreviation of UTILITY]

**tillywurti** /til-ee-wer-tee/ *n.* (also **butterfish**, **dusky morwong**, **strongfish**, **tilliwurty**) greyish, marine food-fish of southern Australia. [probably from a SA Aboriginal language]

**tilt** — *v.* **1** (cause to) assume a sloping position; heel over. **2** (foll. by *at*) strike, thrust, or run at, with a weapon. **3** (foll. by *with*) engage in a contest. — *n.* **1** act or instance of tilting. **2** sloping position. **3** (of medieval knights etc.) charging with a lance against an opponent or at a mark. **4** attack, esp. with argument or satire (*have a tilt at*). □ **full** (or **at full**) **tilt 1** at full speed. **2** with full force. **tilt at windmills** see WINDMILL. [Old English, = unsteady]

**tilth** *n.* **1** tillage, cultivation. **2** condition of tilled soil. [Old English: related to TILL³]

**timber** *n.* **1** wood prepared for building, carpentry, etc. **2** piece of wood or beam, esp. as the rib of a vessel. **3** large standing trees suitable for timber. **4** (esp. as *int.*) warning cry that a tree is about to fall. [Old English, = building]

**timbered** *adj.* **1** made wholly or partly of timber. **2** (of country) wooded.

**timber-getter** *n.* person employed in felling trees for their wood. □ **timber-getting** *n.*

**timberline** *n.* line or level above which no trees grow.

**timbre** /tam-buh/ *n.* distinctive character of a musical sound or voice apart from its pitch and volume. [Greek: related to TYMPANUM]

**Timbuktu** /tim-buk-too/ *n.* any distant or remote place. [*Timbuktu* in W. Africa]

**time** — *n.* **1** indefinite continued progress of existence, events, etc., in the past,

present, and future, regarded as a whole. **2** progress of this as affecting persons or things (*stood the test of time*). **3** portion of time belonging to particular events or circumstances (*the time of the Plague*; *prehistoric times*). **4** allotted or available portion of time (*had no time to eat*). **5** point of time, esp. in hours and minutes (*the time is 7.30*). **6** (prec. by *a*) indefinite period (*waited for a time*). **7** time or an amount of time as reckoned by a conventional standard (*eight o'clock New York time*; *the time allowed is one hour*). **8 a** occasion (*last time I saw you*). **b** event or occasion qualified in some way (*had a good time last night*). **9** moment etc. suitable for a purpose etc. (*the time to act*). **10** (in *pl.*) expressing multiplication (*five times six is thirty*). **11** lifetime (*will last my time*). **12** (in *sing.* or *pl.*) conditions of life or of a period (*hard times*). **13** *colloq.* prison sentence (*is doing time*). **14** apprenticeship (*served his time*). **15** period of gestation. **16** date or expected date of childbirth or death (*is nearing her time*; *my time is drawing near*). **17** measured time spent in work (*put them on part time*). **18 a** any of several rhythmic patterns of music (*in waltz time*). **b** duration of a note as indicated by a crotchet, minim, etc. **19** (in *comb.*, with various senses of the noun: *time-basis*, *time bomb*, *time-honoured*, *time-waster*, etc.). **20** point or fixed part (of a day, year, etc.) (*Christmas time*, *dinner-time*, *holiday-time*, *winter-time*). — *v.* (**-ming**) **1** choose the time for (*the concert is timed to begin at nine*). **2** do at a chosen, correct, or most advantageous time (*timed his entrance to the party with perfection*; *the release-date of this new car is well timed*; *their visit was not timed to afford me any great joy*). **3 a** arrange the time of arrival of (*the Prime Minister is timed to arrive at 9.50 a.m.*). **b** regulate the duration or interval of; set times for (*trains are timed to arrive every hour on the hour*). **4** ascertain the time taken by (a process or activity, or a person doing it). □ **about time** (usu. *iron.*) **1** approximately the right time; long past the right time (*about time you showed up!*). **2** (foll. by *too*) this should have happened much earlier; this is long overdue (*Well, I've done it. — About time too!*). **against time** with utmost speed, so as to finish by a specified time. **ahead of time** earlier than expected. **ahead of one's time** having ideas too enlightened or advanced to be accepted by one's contemporaries. **all the time 1** during the whole of the time referred to (often despite some contrary expectation etc.). **2** constantly. **at one time 1** in a known but unspecified past period. **2** simultaneously. **at the same time 1** simultaneously. **2** nevertheless. **at times** intermittently. **behind the times** decidedly old-fashioned. **do time** *colloq.* serve a prison sentence. **for the time being** until some other arrangement is made. **half the time** *colloq.* as often as not (*half the time he doesn't know if he's coming or going!*). **have no time for 1** be unable or unwilling to spend time on. **2** dislike. **have a time of it** undergo trouble or difficulty. **high time** = *about time.* **in no time (flat) 1** very soon. **2** very quickly (*I'll get it done in no time flat*). **in time 1** not late, punctual. **2** eventually. **3** in accordance with a given rhythm. **keep time** move or sing etc. in time. **kill time** occupy oneself desultorily to pass the time, esp. while waiting (for something in particular). **pass the time of day** *colloq.* exchange a greeting or casual remarks. **take time off** take (a period of) leave. **take time out** make time available (to do something needing to be done) (*you must take time out to play with your kids*). **time after time 1** on many occasions. **2** in many instances. **time and (or time and time) again** on many occasions. **the time of one's life** period of exceptional enjoyment. **time out of mind** a longer time than anyone can remember. **time was** there was a time. [Old English]

**time and a half** *n.* one and a half times the normal rate of payment.

**time-and-motion** *adj.* (usu. *attrib.*) measuring the efficiency of industrial and other operations.

**time bomb** *n.* bomb designed to explode at a pre-set time.

**time capsule** *n.* box etc. containing objects typical of the present time, buried for future discovery.

**time exposure** *n.* exposure of photographic film for longer than the slowest normal shutter setting.

**time-honoured** *adj.* esteemed by tradition or through custom.

**timekeeper** *n.* **1** person who records time, esp. in a game. **2** watch or clock as regards accuracy (*a good timekeeper*). □ **timekeeping** *n.*

**time lag** *n.* interval of time between a cause and effect.

**timeless** *adj.* not affected by the passage of time. □ **timelessly** *adv.* **timelessness** *n.*

**time limit** *n.* limit of time within which a task must be done.

**timely** *adj.* (**-ier, -iest**) opportune; coming at the right time. □ **timeliness** *n.*

**time on** *n. Aust. Rules* time added to the normal playing time of each quarter to compensate for interruptions to play.

**time payment** *n.* = HIRE PURCHASE.

**timepiece** *n.* clock or watch.

**timer** *n.* person or device that measures or records time taken.

**time-server** *n. derog.* person who changes his or her view to suit the prevailing circumstances, fashion, etc. □ **time-serving** *adj.*

**timeshare** *n.* share in a property under a time-sharing scheme.

**time-sharing** *n.* **1** use of a holiday home at contractually agreed different times by several joint owners. **2** operation of a computer system by several users so that each user appears to have exclusive use at the same time.

**time signature** *n. Mus.* indication of tempo following a clef.

**timetable** — *n.* list of times at which events are scheduled to take place, esp. the arrival and departure of transport or a sequence of lessons. — *v.* (**-ling**) include in or arrange to a timetable; schedule.

**time zone** *n.* range of longitudes where a common standard time is used.

**timid** *adj.* (**timider, timidest**) easily frightened; apprehensive. □ **timidity** /tuh-**mid**-uh-tee/ *n.* **timidly** *adv.* [Latin *timeo* fear]

**timing** *n.* **1** way an action or process is timed or regulated, esp. in relation to others (*that actor has a superb sense of timing; the batsman had lost his timing*). **2** regulation of the opening and closing of valves in an internal-combustion engine.

**timorous** /**tim**-uh-ruhs/ *adj.* **1** timid; easily alarmed. **2** frightened. □ **timorously** *adv.* [medieval Latin: related to TIMID]

**Timor pony** *n.* small stocky Australian horse of a breed introduced from Timor. [*Timor*, island off the north-western coast of Australia]

**timothy** /**tim**-uh-thee/ *n. colloq.* a brothel. [origin unknown]

**timpani** /**tim**-puh-nee/ *n.pl.* (also **tympani**) kettledrums. □ **timpanist** *n.* [Italian, pl. of *timpano* = TYMPANUM]

**tin** — *n.* **1** silvery-white metallic element, used esp. in alloys and in making tin plate. **2 a** container made of tin or tinned iron, esp. airtight for preserving food. **b** contents of this. **3** = TIN PLATE. — *v.* (**-nn-**) **1** seal (food) in a tin for preservation. **2** cover or coat with tin. [Old English]

**tin arse** *n. colloq.* an exceptionally lucky person. □ **tin-arsed** *adj.* [from figurative use of *tin* cash, money]

**tin can** n. tin container, esp. an empty one.

**tincture** /**tingk**-chuh/ — n. (often foll. by of) **1** slight flavour or trace. **2** tinge (of a colour). **3** medicinal solution (of a drug) in alcohol (tincture of quinine). — v. (-ring) **1** colour slightly; tinge, flavour. **2** (often foll. by with) affect slightly (with a quality). [Latin: related to TINGE]

**tinder** n. dry substance that readily catches fire from a spark. □ **tindery** adj. [Old English]

**tinderbox** n. hist. box containing tinder, flint, and steel, formerly used for kindling fires.

**tine** n. prong, tooth, or point of a fork, comb, antler, etc. [Old English]

**tinea** /**tin**-ee-uh/ n. any of several fungal diseases of the skin, e.g. athlete's foot. [Latin, = moth, worm]

**tinfoil** n. foil made of tin, aluminium, or tin alloy, used for wrapping food.

**ting** — n. tinkling sound as of a bell. — v. (cause to) emit this sound. [imitative]

**tinge** /tinj/ — v. (-ging) (often foll. by with; also in passive) **1** colour slightly. **2** affect slightly (spoke in a voice tinged with sadness). — n. **1** tendency towards or trace of some colour. **2** slight admixture of a feeling or quality (felt a tinge of regret). [Latin tingo tinct- dye]

**tingle** /**ting**-guhl/ — v. (-ling) **1** feel a slight prickling, stinging, or throbbing sensation. **2** cause this (the reply tingled in my ears). — n. tingling sensation. □ **tingly** adj. [probably from TINKLE]

**tin god** n. **1** object of unjustified veneration. **2** self-important person.

**tinker** — n. **1** itinerant mender of kettles and pans etc. **2** colloq. mischievous person or animal. **3** spell of tinkering. — v. **1** (foll. by at, with) work in an amateurish or desultory way, esp. to adjust or mend machinery (stop tinkering with the clock). **2** work as a tinker. [origin unknown]

**tinkle** /**ting**-kuhl/ — v. (-ling) (cause to) make a succession of short light ringing sounds. — n. **1** tinkling sound. **2** colloq. telephone call. □ **tinkly** adj. [imitative]

**tin lid** n. colloq. kid, child. [rhyming slang]

**tinnie** var. of TINNY n.

**tinnitus** /tuh-**nuy**-tuhs/ n. Med. condition with ringing in the ears. [Latin tinnio tinnit- ring, tinkle]

**tinny** — n. (also **tinnie**) (pl. **-ies**) colloq. **1** can of beer. **2** contents of such a can (drank two tinnies). — adj. (**-ier**, **-iest**) **1** of or like tin. **2** flimsy, insubstantial. **3** (of sound) thin and metallic. **4** colloq. lucky (how tinny can you get?).

**tin plate** n. sheet iron or sheet steel coated with tin.

**tinpot** attrib. adj. cheap, inferior.

**tinsel** /**tin**-suhl/ n. **1** glittering metallic strips, threads, etc., used as decoration. **2** superficial brilliance or splendour. **3** (attrib.) gaudy, flashy. □ **tinselled** adj. **tinselly** adj. [Latin scintilla spark]

**tinsel lily** n. (also **blue tinsel-lily**) spectacular shrub of WA, western Victoria, and eastern SA, having needle-like leaves and numerous vivid blue to blue-purple star-flowers having a highly metallic gloss.

**tinsnips** n. clippers for cutting sheet metal.

**tint** — n. **1** variety of a colour, esp. made by adding white. **2** tendency towards or admixture of a different colour (red with a blue tint). **3** faint kind of hair dye; the application of this (having a tint). — v. **1** apply a tint to; colour. **2 a** apply a polyester film to glass etc. (in order to screen out glare etc.). **b** colour (in order to shade light etc.) (tinted glass; tinted spectacles). [related to TINGE]

**tin-tack** n. iron tack. □ **get down to tin-tacks** deal with the central issues, get down to the core (of a matter).

**T-intersection** n. (also **T-junction**) junction where one road or pipe etc. meets another but does not cross it, forming the shape of a T.

**tintinnabulation** /,tin-tuh-,nab-yuh-**lay**-shuhn/ n. ringing or tinkling of bells. [Latin tintinnabulum bell]

**tiny** /**tuy**-nee/ adj. (**-ier**, **-iest**) very small or slight. □ **tinily** adv. **tininess** n. [origin unknown]

**-tion** see -ION.

**tip¹** — n. **1** extremity or end, esp. of a small or tapering thing (tips of the fingers). **2** summit, apex, highest extremity (tip of the iceberg). **3** small piece or part attached to the end of a thing. **4** leaf-tip of tea. — v. (**-pp-**) provide with a tip. □ **on the tip of one's tongue** about to be said or remembered. **tip of the iceberg** small evident part of something much larger. [Old Norse]

**tip²** — v. (**-pp-**) **1** (often foll. by over, up) **a** lean or slant. **b** cause to do this. **2** (foll. by into etc.) **a** overturn or cause to overbalance (was tipped into the pond). **b** discharge the contents of (a container etc.) in this way. **3 a** strike or touch lightly (just tipped the ball with the bat and was caught in the slips). **b** tilt slightly (tipped his hat). — n. **1 a** slight push or tilt. **b** light stroke. **2** place where material (esp. refuse) is tipped. □ **tip the scales** see SCALE². [origin uncertain]

**tip³** — v. (**-pp-**) **1** make a small present of money to, esp. for a service given. **2** name as the likely winner of a race or contest etc. **3** colloq. guess (*the kids haven't yet tipped that it's me in the Santa suit*). — n. **1** small money present, esp. for a service given. **2** piece of private or special information, esp. regarding betting or investment. **3** small or casual piece of advice. □ **tip off** give (a person) a hint or piece of special information or warning. **tip a person the wink** give a person private information. [origin uncertain]

**tip-off** n. hint or warning etc. given secretly or anonymously or in confidence.

**tipper** n. = TIP-TRUCK.

**tipple** /**tip**-uhl/ v. (**-ling**) **1** drink intoxicating liquor habitually. **2** drink (liquor) repeatedly in small amounts. □ **tippler** n. [origin unknown]

**tipster** n. person who gives tips, esp. about betting at horse races.

**tipsy** /**tip**-see/ adj. (**-ier, -iest**) slightly drunk. □ **tipsily** adv. **tipsiness** n. [from TIP²]

**tiptoe** — n. the tips of the toes. — v. (**-toes, -toed, -toeing**) walk on tiptoe, or very stealthily. — adv. (also **on tiptoe**) with the heels off the ground. □ **on tiptoe 1** on the tips of one's toes. **2** eagerly expectant, anxious (*am on tiptoe for the results*). **3** stealthy; furtive.

**tip-top** colloq. — adj. highest in excellence. — n. highest point of excellence. — adv. most excellently.

**tip-truck** n. road haulage vehicle that tips at the back to discharge its load.

**tirade** /tuy-**rayd**/ n. long vehement denunciation or declamation. [French from Italian]

**tire** v. (**-ring**) **1** make or grow weary. **2** exhaust the patience or interest of; bore. **3** (in *passive*; foll. by *of*) have had enough of; be fed up with. [Old English]

**tired** adj. **1** weary; ready for sleep. **2** (of an idea etc.) hackneyed (*tired old excuses*). □ **make a person tired** colloq. get on the nerves of; irritate him or her. □ **tiredly** adv. **tiredness** n.

**tireless** adj. not tiring easily, energetic. □ **tirelessly** adv. **tirelessness** n.

**tiresome** adj. **1** wearisome, tedious. **2** annoying (*don't be tiresome!*). □ **tiresomely** adv. **tiresomeness** n.

**tiro** var. of TYRO.

**'tis** /tiz/ archaic it is. [contraction]

**tissue** /**tish**-oo, **tis**-yoo/ n. **1** any of the coherent collections of specialised cells of which animals or plants are made (*muscular tissue*). **2** = TISSUE-PAPER. **3** disposable piece of thin soft absorbent paper for wiping, drying, etc. **4** fine woven esp. gauzy fabric. **5** (foll. by *of*) connected series (*tissue of lies*). **6** (also **tisher**) colloq. (chiefly in Tasmania) cigarette paper for a roll-your-own. [French *tissu* woven cloth]

**tissue paper** n. thin soft paper for wrapping etc.

**tit¹** n. any of various small birds. [probably from Scandinavian]

**tit²** n. □ **tit for tat** blow for blow; retaliation. [= earlier *tip* in *tip for tap*: see TIP²]

**tit³** n. **1** coarse colloq. woman's breast. **2** colloq. nipple. [Old English]

**Titan** /**tuy**-tuhn/ n. **1** (often **titan**) person of very great strength, intellect, or importance. **2** (in Greek mythology) member of a race of giants, the offspring of Heaven and Earth. [Greek]

**titanic** /tuy-**tan**-ik/ adj. gigantic, colossal. □ **titanically** adv. [Greek: related to TITAN]

**titanium** /tuy-**tay**-nee-uhm/ n. grey metallic element. [Greek: related to TITAN]

**titbit** n. **1** dainty morsel. **2** piquant item of news etc. [perhaps from British dial. *tid* tender]

**titchy** n. (also **tich**) colloq. **1** small person. **2** small amount. [*Tich* name of a comedian (d. 1928)]

**tithe** /tuyth/ — n. **1** one-tenth of the annual produce of land or labour, formerly taken as a tax for the Church. **2** tenth part. — v. (**-thing**) **1** subject to tithes. **2** pay tithes. [Old English, = tenth]

**titian** /**tish**-uhn, **tee**-shuhn/ adj. (of hair) bright auburn. [*Titian*, name of an Italian painter (d. 1576)]

**titillate** /**tit**-uh-,layt/ v. (**-ting**) **1** excite, esp. sexually. **2** tickle. □ **titillation** /-**lay**-shuhn/ n. [Latin]

**titivate** /**tit**-uh-,vayt/ v. (**-ting**) (often *refl.*) colloq. smarten up; put the finishing touches to. □ **titivation** /-**vay**-shuhn/ n. [earlier *tidivate*, perhaps from TIDY after *cultivate*]

**title** /**tuy**-tuhl/ — n. **1** name of a book, work of art, etc. **2** heading of a chapter, document, etc. **3** book, magazine, etc., in terms of its title (*brought out two new titles*). **4** (usu. in *pl.*) caption or credit in a film etc. **5** name indicating a person's status (e.g. *professor, cardinal*) or used as a form of address or reference (e.g. *Your Eminence, Mr, Your Honour*). **6** championship in sport (*lost the title*). **7** *Law* **a** right to ownership of property with or without possession. **b** facts constituting this. **c** (foll. by *to*) just or recognised claim. — v. give a title to. □ **titled** adj. [Latin *titulus*]

**title deed** *n.* legal instrument as evidence of a right, esp. to property.

**title-page** *n.* page at the beginning of a book giving the title, author, etc.

**title role** *n.* part in a play etc. that gives it its name, e.g. Othello (*Sutherland singing the title role in 'Lucia di Lammermoor'*).

**titrate** /tuy-trayt/ *v.* (**-ting**) *Chem.* ascertain the amount of a constituent in (a solution) by reaction with a known concentration of reagent. □ **titration** /-tray-shuhn/ *n.* [French *titre* title]

**ti-tree** erroneous var. of TEA-TREE.

**titter** — *v.* laugh in a furtive or restrained way; giggle. — *n.* furtive or restrained laugh. [imitative]

**tittle** /tit-uhl/ *n.* **1** small written or printed stroke or dot. **2** particle; whit (*not one jot or tittle*). [Latin: related to TITLE]

**tittle-tattle** — *n.* petty gossip. — *v.* (**-ling**) gossip, chatter. [reduplication of TATTLE]

**titular** /tich-uh-luh, tit-yuh-luh/ *adj.* **1** of or relating to a title (*the book's titular hero*). **2** existing, or being, in name or title only (*titular ruler*). [French: related to TITLE]

**Tiwi** /tee-wee/ *n.* Aboriginal language spoken on Melville and Bathurst Islands.

**tizz** /tiz/ *n.* (also **tizzy**) (*pl.* **-ies**) *colloq.* state of nervous agitation (*in a tizz*). [origin unknown]

**tizzy** /tiz-ee/ — *adj.* gaudy, showy, in bad taste. — *v.* (usu. foll. by *up*; often as **tizzied up** *adj.*) (try to) improve the appearance of, esp. in a gaudy or showy manner (*all tizzied up for the party*; *is tizzying up his car*).

**tjilpi** /tyil-pee/ *n.* an old man. [Western Desert language]

**tjukurpa** /tyoo-koor-pu/ *n.* = DREAMING. [Western Desert language *tjukurpa*, *tjukurrpa*]

**T-junction** *n.* = T-INTERSECTION.

**tjuringa** var. of CHURINGA.

**Tl** *symb.* thallium.

**TLC** *abbr. colloq.* tender loving care.

**Tm** *symb.* thulium.

**tmesis** /tmee-suhs/ *n.* (*pl.* **tmeses** /-seez/ *Gram.* the separation of parts of a compound word by an intervening word or words (esp. in Australian colloq. speech with 'bloody' as the intervener) (*kanga-bloody-roos at the billa-bloody-bong*). [Greek, = cutting]

**TNT** *abbr.* trinitrotoluene, a high explosive formed from toluene.

**to** /tuh/ *emphat.* /too/ — *prep.* **1** introducing a noun expressing: **a** what is reached, approached, or touched (*fell to the ground*; *went to Wee Waa*; *five minutes to six*). **b** what is aimed at: often introducing the indirect object of a verb (*throw it to me*; *explained it to them*). **c** as far as; up to (*went on to the end*; *am staying from Monday to Friday*). **d** to the extent of (*were all drunk to a man*; *starved to death*). **e** expressing what is followed (*according to instructions*; *made to order*). **f** what is considered or affected (*am used to that*; *that is nothing to me*). **g** what is caused or produced (*turn to stone*). **h** what is compared (*nothing to what it once was*; *equal to the occasion*; *won by three goals to two*). **i** what is increased (*add it to mine*). **j** what is involved or composed as specified (*there is nothing to it*; *more to him than meets the eye*). **2** introducing the infinitive: **a** as a verbal noun (*to get there is the priority*). **b** expressing purpose, consequence, or cause (*we eat to live*; *left him to starve*; *I'm sorry to hear that*). **c** as a substitute for *to* + infinitive (*wanted to come but was unable to*). — *adv.* **1** in the normal or required position or condition (*come to*; *heave to*). **2** (of a door) in a nearly closed position. □ **to and fro 1** backwards and forwards. **2** repeatedly between the same points. [Old English]

**toa** /toh-uh/ *n.* Aboriginal direction marker made of gypsum, wood, and feathers, and used to indicate precisely where a departing group had gone to. [Diyari *dhuwa*]

**toad** *n.* **1** froglike amphibian breeding in water but living chiefly on land. **2** repulsive person. [Old English]

**toadfish** *n.* any of many self-inflating, usu. poisonous and spiny, Australian marine and estuarine fish.

**toadstool** *n.* fungus, often poisonous, with a round top and slender stalk.

**toady** — *n.* (*pl.* **-ies**) **1** sycophant. **2** = TOADFISH. — *v.* (foll. by *to*) (**-ies**, **-ied**) behave servilely to; fawn upon. □ **toadyism** *n.* [contraction of *toad-eater*, a charlatan's attendant who ate toads (regarded as poisonous)]

**to and from** *n.* (*pl.* **-s**) *colloq.* a pom. [rhyming slang]

**toast** — *n.* **1** sliced bread browned on both sides by radiant heat. **2 a** person or thing in whose honour a company is requested to drink. **b** call to drink (usu. including a speech of congratulations etc.) or an instance of drinking in this way. **c** celebrated person of the moment (*toast of the town*). — *v.* **1** brown by radiant heat. **2** warm (one's feet, oneself, etc.) at a fire etc. **3** drink to the health or in honour of (a person or thing). [French *toster* roast]

**toaster** *n.* electrical device for making toast.

**toastmaster** *n.* (*fem.* **toastmistress**) person responsible for announcing toasts at a public occasion.

**tobacco** /tuh-**bak**-oh/ *n.* (*pl.* **-s**) **1** plant of American origin with narcotic leaves used for smoking, chewing, or snuff. **2** its leaves, esp. as prepared for smoking. [Spanish *tabaco*, of American Indian origin]

**tobacconist** /tuh-**bak**-uh-nuhst/ *n.* dealer in tobacco, cigarettes, etc.

**toboggan** /tuh-**bog**-uhn/ — *n.* long light narrow sledge for sliding downhill over snow or ice. — *v.* ride on a toboggan. □ **tobogganer** *n.* **tobogganing** *n.* **tobogganist** *n.* [Canadian French from Algonquian]

**toby jug** /**toh**-bee/ *n.* jug or mug in the form of a stout man wearing a three-cornered hat. [familiar form of the name *Tobias*]

**toccata** /tuh-**kah**-tuh/ *n.* musical composition for a keyboard instrument, designed to exhibit the performer's touch and technique. [Italian, = touched]

**tocsin** /**tok**-suhn/ *n.* alarm bell or signal. [Provençal *tocasenh*]

**today** /tuh-**day**/ — *adv.* **1** on this present day. **2** nowadays. — *n.* **1** this present day. **2** modern times. [Old English]

**toddle** /**tod**-uhl/ — *v.* (**-ling**) **1** walk with short unsteady steps like a small child. **2** *colloq.* **a** walk, stroll. **b** (usu. foll. by *off* or *along*) depart. — *n.* act or instance of toddling. [origin unknown]

**toddler** *n.* child who is just learning to walk.

**toddy** /**tod**-ee/ *n.* (*pl.* **-ies**) **1** drink of spirits with hot water and sugar etc. **2** sap of some kinds of palm (palmyra, coconut, etc.) drunk fresh (**sweet toddy**), or fermented, or distilled to make arrack. [Hindustani *tār* palm]

**to-do** /tuh-**doo**/ *n.* (*pl.* **-s**) commotion or fuss.

**toe** — *n.* **1** any of the five terminal projections of the foot. **2** corresponding part of an animal. **3** part of a shoe etc. that covers the toes. **4** lower end or tip of an implement etc. **5** *colloq.* strength; speed (*Aussie fast bowlers have enough toe to keep pommie batsmen on their toes*). — *v.* (**toes**, **toed**, **toeing**) touch or reach with the toes. □ **on one's toes** alert. **toe the line** conform, esp. unwillingly under pressure. [Old English]

**toehold** *n.* **1** small foothold. **2** small beginning or advantage.

**toenail** *n.* nail of each toe.

**toe-rag** /**toh**-rag/ *n.* (also **toe-ragger**) *colloq.* term of contempt for a person. [formerly = tramp, vagrant, from the rag wrapped around the foot in place of a sock]

**toey** /**toh**-ee/ *adj. colloq.* **1** restless, eager to go. **2** touchy, bad-tempered.

**toff** *n. colloq. derog.* person of wealth and social prestige. □ **toffy** *adj.* [perhaps from *tuft*, = titled undergraduate]

**toffee** /**tof**-ee/ *n.* **1** firm or hard sweet made by boiling sugar, butter, etc. **2** this substance. [origin unknown]

**toffee-nosed** *adj. colloq. derog.* snobbish, superior. [pun on *toffy*]

**tofu** /**toh**-foo/ *n.* curd of mashed soya beans. [Japanese]

**tog** *colloq.* — *n.* (in *pl.*) **1** (when unqualified) swimming costume (*get your togs and let's head for the beach*). **2** (when qualified) clothes (*footy togs*; *shearing togs*). — *v.* (**-gg-**) (foll. by *out*, *up*) dress. [apparently originally cant: ultimately related to Latin TOGA]

**toga** /**toh**-guh/ *n. hist.* ancient Roman citizen's loose flowing outer garment. □ **togaed** *adj.* (also **toga'd**). [Latin]

**together** /tuh-**geth**-uh/ — *adv.* **1** in company or conjunction (*walking together*; *were at school together*). **2** simultaneously (*both shouted together*). **3** one with another (*talking together*). **4** into conjunction; so as to unite (*tied them together*; *put two and two together*). **5** into company or companionship (*came together in friendship*). **6** uninterruptedly (*he could talk for three hours together*). — *adj. colloq.* well-organised; self-assured; emotionally stable (*he's really together since he stopped drinking*). □ **get it (all) together** see GET. **get oneself (yourself** etc.**) together** calm down, get a grip on oneself (*yourself* etc.); be rational. **together with** as well as. [Old English: related to TO, GATHER]

**togetherness** *n.* **1** being together. **2** feeling of comfort from this.

**toggle** /**tog**-uhl/ *n.* **1** fastener for a garment consisting of a crosspiece which passes through a hole or loop. **2** pin or other crosspiece put through the eye of a rope, a link of a chain, etc., to keep it in place. **3** *Computing* switch action that is operated the same way but with opposite effect on successive occasions. [origin unknown]

**togs** see TOG.

**toil** — *v.* **1** work laboriously or incessantly. **2** make slow painful progress (*toiled up the hill*). — *n.* intensive labour; drudgery. [Anglo-French *toil(er)* dispute]

**toiler** n. hard worker; battler.

**toilet** /**toi**-luht/ n. **1** large receptacle for urine and faeces, usu. with running water and a flush mechanism as a means of disposal. **2** room or compartment containing one or more of these. **3** process of washing oneself, dressing, etc. (*at one's toilet*). [French *toilette* diminutive of *toile* cloth]

**toiletry** /**toi**-luh-tree/ n. (*pl.* **-ies**) (usu. in *pl.*) article or cosmetic used in washing, dressing, etc.

**toilet-training** n. training of a young child to use the toilet. □ **toilet-train** v.

**toils** /toilz/ n.pl. net, snare; power that acts as does a snare or net (*I'm caught in his toils*). [*toil* from French: related to TOILET]

**toilsome** /**toil**-suhm/ adj. involving toil; laborious.

**toing and froing** /**too**-ing uhn **froh**-ing/ n. going to and fro; repeatedly changing one's mind, decision, etc., vacillating. [from TO, FRO]

**token** /**toh**-kuhn/ n. **1** thing serving as a symbol, reminder, or mark (*as a token of affection*; *in token of my esteem*). **2** voucher exchangeable for goods (often of a specified kind), given as a gift. **3** thing equivalent to something else, esp. a metal disc etc. used instead of money in coin-operated machines etc. **4** (*attrib.*) **a** perfunctory (*token effort*). **b** conducted briefly to demonstrate strength of feeling (*token strike*). **c** serving to acknowledge a principle only (*token payment*). **d** chosen by tokenism to represent a group (*token woman on the committee*). □ **by this** (or **the same**) **token 1** similarly. **2** moreover. [Old English]

**tokenism** n. **1** granting of minimum concessions, esp. to minority groups. **2** making of only a token effort.

**told** past and past part. of TELL.

**tolerable** /**tol**-uh-ruh-buhl/ adj. **1** endurable. **2** fairly good; mediocre. □ **tolerably** adv. [Latin: related to TOLERATE]

**tolerance** /**tol**-uh-ruhns/ n. **1** willingness or ability to tolerate; disposition to be patient with or indulgent to the opinions or practices of others; freedom from bigotry or undue severity in judging the conduct of others; forbearance. **2** allowable variation in any measurable property. **3** ability to tolerate the effects of a drug etc. after use or continued use.

**tolerant** adj. **1** disposed to tolerate others or their acts or opinions; displaying tolerance. **2** (foll. by *of*) enduring or patient.

**tolerate** /**tol**-uh-,rayt/ v. (**-ting**) **1** display tolerance; allow the existence or occurrence of without authoritative interference. **2** endure (suffering etc.). **3** find or treat as endurable. **4** be able to take or undergo (drugs, treatment, etc.) without adverse effects. [Latin *tolero*]

**toleration** /,tol-uh-**ray**-shuhn/ n. process or practice of tolerating or being tolerated, esp. the allowing of religious differences without discrimination. [Latin: related to TOLERATE]

**toll¹** /tohl/ n. **1** charge to use a bridge, road, etc. **2** cost or damage caused by a disaster etc. □ **take its toll** be accompanied by loss, injury, etc. [Old English, ultimately from Greek *telos* tax]

**toll²** /tohl/ — v. **1 a** (of a bell) sound with slow uniform strokes. **b** ring (a bell) in this way. **c** (of a bell) announce or mark (a death etc.) in this way. **2** strike (the hour). — n. **1** act of tolling. **2** stroke of a bell. [(now British dial.) *toll* entice, pull, from an Old English root]

**toll-bridge** n. bridge at which a toll is charged.

**toll-free** adj. & adv. (esp. of a telephone call) without charge (*toll-free number*; *call toll-free*).

**toll gate** n. gate preventing passage until a toll is paid.

**tollroad** n. road maintained by the tolls collected on it.

**toluene** /**tol**-yoo-,een/ n. colourless aromatic liquid hydrocarbon derivative of benzene, used in the manufacture of explosives etc. [*Tolu* in Colombia]

**tom** n. (in full **tom-cat**) male cat. [abbreviation of the name *Thomas*]

**tomahawk** /**tom**-uh-,hawk/ — n. **1** N. American Indian war-axe. **2** hatchet. — v. **1** strike, cut, or kill with a tomahawk. **2** shear (a sheep) roughly. [Renape]

**tomato** /tuh-**mah**-toh/ n. (*pl.* **-es**) **1** glossy red or yellow pulpy edible fruit. **2** plant bearing this. [ultimately from Mexican *tomatl*]

**tomb** /toom/ n. **1** burial-vault. **2** grave. **3** sepulchral monument. [Greek *tumbos*]

**tombola** /tom-**boh**-luh/ n. lottery with tickets drawn from a drum for immediate prizes. [French or Italian]

**tomboy** n. energetic girl who enjoys activities traditionally or stereotypically associated with boys. □ **tomboyish** adj. [from TOM]

**tombstone** n. memorial stone over a grave, usu. with an epitaph.

**Tom Collins** n. a gossip; a rumour-monger. [mythical 19th-c Australian character]

**Tom, Dick, and Harry** n. (also **Tom, Dick, or Harry**) (usu. prec. by *any* or *every*) person taken at random (*any Tom, Dick, or Harry can walk in*).

**tome** *n.* heavy book or volume. [Greek *temnō* cut]

**tomfoolery** /tom-**foo**-luh-ree/ *n.* foolish behaviour.

**tommy-gun** *n.* sub-machine-gun. [*Thompson*, name of its co-inventor (d. 1940)]

**tommyrot** *n. colloq.* nonsense. [from TOM]

**tommy rough** *n.* (also **herring**, **roughy**, **tommy ruff**) marine fish of Australian waters, highly valued as food. [*Tommy* diminutive of 'Thomas', *ruff* a fish with rough scales]

**tomography** /tuh-**mog**-ruh-fee/ *n.* method of radiography displaying details in a selected plane within the body. [Greek *tomē* a cutting]

**tomorrow** /tuh-**mo**-roh/ — *adv.* **1** on the day after today. **2** at some future time. — *n.* **1** the day after today. **2** the near future. [from TO, MORROW]

**tomtit** *n.* any of several small Australian birds, esp. a thornbill.

**tom-tom** /**tom**-tom/ *n.* **1** primitive drum beaten with the hands. **2** tall drum used in jazz bands etc. [Hindi *tamtam*, imitative]

**-tomy** /tuh-mee/ *comb. form* forming nouns denoting cutting, esp. in surgery (*lobotomy*; *appendectomy*). [Greek, = cutting]

**ton** /tun/ *n.* **1** (in full **long ton**) unit of weight in the imperial system equal to 2,240 lb. (1016.05 kg). **2** (in full **short ton**) unit of weight, esp. in the US, equal to 2,000 lb. (907.19 kg). **3** = METRIC TON or TONNE. **4** (in full **displacement ton**) unit of measurement in the imperial system of a ship's weight or volume. **5** (usu. in *pl.*) *colloq.* large number or amount (*tons of people*; *tons of things to see to*). **6** *colloq.* **a** speed of 100 km/h. **b** $100. **c** score of a 100. □ **hit the ton** *colloq.* **1** score 100 runs in cricket. **2** reach a speed of 100 km/h in a car or on a motorcycle. **weigh a ton** *colloq.* be very heavy. [originally the same word as TUN]

**tonal** /**toh**-nuhl/ *adj.* of or relating to tone or tonality. □ **tonally** *adv.* [medieval Latin: related to TONE]

**tonality** /toh-**nal**-uh-tee/ *n.* (*pl.* **-ies**) **1** *Mus.* **a** relationship between the tones of a musical scale. **b** observance of a single tonic key as the basis of a composition. **2** colour scheme of a picture.

**tone** — *n.* **1** musical or vocal sound, esp. with reference to its pitch, quality, and strength (*rich tone*). **2** (often in *pl.*) modulation of the voice expressing a particular feeling or mood (*a cheerful tone*; *aggressive tone*). **3 a** manner of expression in writing or speaking. **b** (in literary criticism) author's attitude to his or her subject matter or audience; distinctive mood created by this. **4** *Mus.* **a** musical sound, esp. of a definite pitch and character. **b** interval of a major second, e.g. C–D. **5 a** general effect of colour or of light and shade in a picture. **b** tint or shade of a colour. **6** prevailing character of the morals, sentiments, etc., in a group (*the tone of the gathering was somewhat raunchy*; *the tone of the meeting was positive*; *they are lowering the tone of our club*). **7** proper firmness of the body (*good muscle tone*). — *v.* (**-ning**) **1** give the desired tone to. **2** modify the tone of. **3** (often foll. by *to*) attune. **4** (foll. by *with* or *in with*) (esp. of colour) be in harmony with (*does not tone in with the wallpaper*). □ **tone down 1** make or become softer in tone. **2** make (a statement etc.) less harsh or emphatic. **tone up** make or become stronger in tone (*exercise tones up the body*). □ **toneless** *adj.* **tonelessly** *adv.* **toner** *n.* [Greek *tonos* from *teinō* stretch]

**tone-deaf** *adj.* unable to perceive differences of musical pitch accurately.

**tongs** *n.pl.* implement with two arms for grasping coal, sugar, etc. [Old English]

**tongue** /tung/ — *n.* **1** fleshy muscular organ in the mouth used in tasting, licking, and swallowing, and (in man) for speech. **2** tongue of an ox etc. as food. **3** faculty of or tendency in speech (*a sharp tongue*). **4** particular language (*the German tongue*). **5** thing like a tongue in shape or position, esp.: **a** a long low promontory. **b** a strip of leather etc. under the laces in a shoe. **c** the clapper of a bell. **d** the pin of a buckle. **e** a projecting strip on a board etc. fitting into the groove of another. — *v.* (**-guing**) **1** use the tongue to articulate (notes) in playing a wind instrument. **2** touch, lick, etc., with the tongue. □ **find** (or **lose**) **one's tongue** be able (or unable) to express oneself after a shock etc. **hold one's tongue** see HOLD¹. **mind one's tongue** be careful in what one says. **on the tip of one's tongue** on the verge of being remembered. **speak with tongues** see GLOSSOLALIA. **with one's tongue in one's cheek** insincerely or ironically. [Old English]

**tongue-and-groove** — *n.* (often *attrib.*) planking etc. with a projecting strip down one side and a groove down the other. — *v.* **1** panel with tongue-and-groove. **2** (as **tongued and grooved** *adj.*) having a tongue-and-groove joint.

**tongue-in-cheek** — *adj.* ironic. — *adv.* insincerely or ironically.

**tongue-lashing** *n.* severe scolding or reprimand.

**tongue-tied** *adj.* **1** too shy or embarrassed to speak. **2** having a speech impediment due to a malformation of the tongue.

**tongue-twister** *n.* **1** sequence of words difficult to pronounce quickly and correctly esp. at speed, e.g. *she'll chew, chew, chew, till her jaws drop off.* **2** *colloq.* any word perceived to be difficult or too long, a 'jaw breaker'.

**tonic** /ton-ik/ — *n.* **1** invigorating medicine. **2** anything serving to invigorate. **3** = TONIC WATER. **4** *Mus.* first degree of a scale, forming the keynote of a piece. — *adj.* **1** invigorating. **2** *Mus.* denoting the first degree of a scale. **3 a** producing tension, esp. of the muscles. **b** restoring normal tone to organs. [Greek: related to TONE]

**tonic sol-fa** *n. Mus.* system of notation used esp. in teaching singing.

**tonic water** *n.* carbonated water flavoured with quinine.

**tonight** /tuh-nuyt/ — *adv.* on the present or approaching evening or night. — *n.* the evening or night of the present day. [Old English]

**tonk** *n. colloq.* **1** male who in speech or manner appears to set himself above his fellows. **2** a fool. [origin unknown]

**tonnage** /tun-ij/ *n.* **1** ship's internal cubic capacity or freight-carrying capacity. **2** charge per ton on freight or cargo. [related to TON]

**tonne** /ton, tun/ *n.* (also **metric ton** or **metric tonne**) 1,000 kilograms. [French: related to TON]

■ **Usage** When the metric system was introduced into Australia, the preferred pronunciation for *tonne* was /ton/ to distinguish it from the imperial *ton*, but both /ton/ and /tun/ are now acceptable.

**tonsil** /ton-suhl/ *n.* either of two small organs, one on each side of the root of the tongue. [Latin]

**tonsillectomy** /,ton-suh-lek-tuh-mee/ *n.* (*pl.* **-ies**) surgical removal of the tonsils.

**tonsillitis** /,ton-suh-luy-tuhs/ *n.* inflammation of the tonsils.

**tonsure** /ton-shuh/ — *n.* **1** shaving of the crown of the head or the entire head, esp. of a person entering the priesthood or a monastic order. **2** bare patch made in this way. — *v.* (**-ring**) give a tonsure to. [Latin *tondeo tons-* shave]

**too** *adv.* **1** to a greater extent than is desirable, permissible, or possible for a specified or understood purpose (*too large to fit; too hard*). **2** *colloq.* very (*not too sure*). **3** in addition (*I'm coming too*). **4** moreover (*food was bad, and expensive too*). □ **none too** rather less than (*feeling none too good*). **too bad** see BAD. **too much** intolerable. **too much for 1** more than a match for. **2** beyond what is endurable by. **too right** see RIGHT. [stressed form of TO]

**too-hard basket** *n.* imaginary basket into which one 'puts' matters, problems, etc., which are too difficult to deal with at the moment.

**took** *past* of TAKE.

**tool** — *n.* **1** implement used to carry out mechanical functions by hand or by machine. **2** thing used in an occupation or pursuit (*tools of one's trade*). **3** person merely used by another. **4** *coarse colloq.* penis. — *v.* **1** dress (stone) with a chisel. **2** impress a design on (leather). **3** (foll. by *along, around*, etc.) *colloq.* drive or ride, esp. in a casual or leisurely manner. [Old English]

**toolache** /too-lay-chee/ *n.* large wallaby, formerly of south-eastern SA and adjacent Victoria, much exploited for its attractive fur and now probably extinct. [Yaralde, probably *dulaj*]

**toolmaker** *n.* person who makes precision tools. □ **toolmaking** *n.*

**toopong** var. of TUPONG.

**too right** see RIGHT.

**tooroo** /too-roo/ *int.* = GOODBYE. [var. of *toodle-oo* goodbye]

**toot**[1] /toot/ — *n.* short sharp sound as made by the horn of a car, a trumpet, etc. — *v.* **1** sound (a car horn, a trumpet etc.) with a short sharp sound (*he's tooting the horn, hurry!*). **2** give out such a sound (*stop tooting, I'm coming*). [probably imitative]

**toot**[2] /tuut/ *n. colloq.* TOILET 1, 2. [origin unknown]

**tooth** *n.* (*pl.* **teeth**) **1** each of a set of hard bony enamel-coated structures in the jaws of most vertebrates, used for biting and chewing. **2** toothlike part or projection, e.g. the cog of a gearwheel, the point of a saw or comb, etc. **3** (often foll. by *for*) taste; appetite. **4** (in *pl.*) force, effectiveness (*these penalties give this law teeth*). □ **armed to the teeth** completely and elaborately armed. **fight tooth and nail** fight very fiercely. **get one's teeth into** devote oneself seriously to. **in the teeth of 1** in spite of (opposition or difficulty etc.). **2** contrary to (instructions etc.). **3** directly against (the wind etc.). **scarce** (or **rare**) **as hen's teeth** see SCARCE.

set a person's teeth on edge see EDGE.
□ **toothed** *adj.* (also in *comb.*). [Old English]

**toothache** *n.* pain in a tooth or teeth.

**tooth-billed cat bird** *n.* bowerbird of rainforest in north-eastern Queensland, having a double notch at the tip of its bill, used for collecting leaves for the bower, and a wailing cat-like call.

**toothcomb** *n.* = FINE-TOOTH COMB.

**toothless** *adj.* **1** lacking teeth. **2** lacking the means of compulsion or enforcement; ineffectual.

**toothpick** *n.* small sharp stick for removing food lodged between the teeth.

**toothy** *adj.* (**-ier, -iest**) having large, numerous, or prominent teeth.

**tootle** *v.* (**-ling**) **1** toot (on a trumpet etc.) gently or repeatedly. **2** (usu. foll. by *along, around*, etc.) *colloq.* move casually.

**top¹** — *n.* **1** highest point or part. **2 a** highest rank or place (*at the top of the class*). **b** person occupying this. **c** upper end or head (*top of the table*). **3** upper surface or part of a thing. **4** (prec. by *the*) (also **Top**) northern Australia. **5** stopper of a bottle, lid of a jar, etc. **6** garment for the upper part of the body. **7** utmost degree; height (*at the top of his voice*). **8** (in *pl.*) *colloq.* person or thing of the best quality (*she's tops at cricket*). **9** (esp. in *pl.*) leaves etc. of a plant grown esp. for its root (*turnip-tops*). **10** *Naut.* platform round the head of the lower mast. **11** = TOP GEAR (*climbed the hill in top*). — *attrib. adj.* **1** highest in position (*top shelf*). **2 a** highest in degree (*at top speed*). **b** highest in importance (*a top job*). **c** greatest in amount (*paid top prices for the paintings; top dollar*). **d** *colloq.* excellent, first-rate (*he's a top bloke*). — *v.* (**-pp-**) **1** provide with a top, cap, covering, etc. (*cake topped with icing*). **2** be higher or better than; surpass; be at the top of (*topped the list*). **3** reach the top of (*a hill* etc.). **4** remove the top of (a plant, fruit, etc.), esp. to improve growth, prepare for cooking, etc. **5** *Golf* hit (a ball) above the centre. □ **have little** (or **nothing** or **not much**) **up top** *colloq.* be lacking in intelligence; be stupid. **off the top of one's head** see HEAD. **on top** in a superior position; above. **on top of 1** fully in command of. **2** in close proximity to. **3** in addition to. **on top of the world** *colloq.* exuberant. **over the top 1** over the parapet of a trench (and into battle). **2** beyond what is normally acceptable (*that joke was over the top*). **top off** (or **up**) put an end or the finishing touch to. **top up 1** complete (an amount or number). **2** fill up (a partly full container). **3** top up

something for (a person) (*may I top you up with sherry?*). **up top** (also **Up Top**) **1** northern Australia. **2** in northern Australia. □ **topmost** *adj.* [Old English]

**top²** *n.* toy spinning on a point when set in motion. [Old English]

**topaz** /**toh**-paz/ *n.* transparent mineral, usu. yellow, used as a gem. [Greek *topazos*]

**top brass** *n. colloq.* persons in authority or of high (esp. military) rank.

**top dog** *n. colloq.* victor; master.

**top dollar** *n. colloq.* highest price (*paid top dollar for the horse*).

**top dress** *v.* apply fertiliser, loam, etc., on the top of (earth) instead of ploughing it in. □ **top dressing** *n.*

**top end** *n.* (also **Top End**) northern part of the NT (also *attrib.*) (*Darwin is in the Top End; the top end team*).

**top ender** *n.* (also **Top Ender**) person native to or resident in the northern part of the NT.

**top-flight** *adj.* of the highest rank of achievement.

**top gear** *n.* **1** highest gear. **2** fast pace; full speed (*the reforms are proceeding in top gear*).

**top hat** *n.* tall silk hat.

**top-heavy** *adj.* disproportionately heavy at the top.

**topiary** /**toh**-pee-uh-ree/ — *adj.* concerned with or formed by clipping shrubs, trees, etc., into ornamental shapes. — *n.* topiary art. [Greek *topos* place]

**topic** /**top**-ik/ *n.* subject of a discourse, conversation, or argument. [Greek *topos* place, commonplace]

**topical** *adj.* dealing with the news, current affairs, etc. □ **topicality** /-**kal**-uh-tee/ *n.* **topically** *adv.*

**topknot** *n.* **1** tuft, crest, etc. (of hair or feathers) growing on the head. **2** hair worn in a knot on top of the head.

**topknot pigeon** *n.* grey pigeon with a black banded tail and distinctive rusty-red crest, inhabiting rainforest in eastern Australia.

**topless** *adj.* **1** without a top. **2 a** (of clothes) having no upper part. **b** (esp. of a woman) bare-breasted. **c** (of a place) where women go topless; employing bare-breasted women (*topless bar*).

**top-level** *adj.* of the highest level of importance, prestige, etc.

**topmast** *n.* mast next above the lower mast.

**top-notch** *adj. colloq.* first-rate.

**topography** /tu-**pog**-ruh-fee/ *n.* **1** detailed description, representation on a map, etc., of the natural and artificial

**features** of a town, district, etc. **2** such features. □ **topographer** n. **topographical** /-**graf**-i-kuhl/ adj. [Greek topos place]

**topology** /tuh-**pol**-uh-jee/ n. the study of geometrical properties and spatial relations unaffected by the continuous change of shape or size of figures. □ **topological** /,top-uh-**loj**-i-kuhl/ adj. [Greek topos place]

**topping** n. thing that tops another thing, esp. sauce on a dessert etc.

**topple** v. (-**ling**) **1** (often foll. by over, down) (cause to) fall as if top-heavy. **2** overthrow (the government was toppled in a coup). [from TOP¹]

**topside** n. outer side of a round of beef.

**topsoil** n. top layer of soil.

**topspin** n. spinning motion imparted to a ball in tennis etc. by hitting it forward and upward. □ **topspinner** n.

**topsy-turvy** /,top-see-**ter**-vee/ adv. & adj. **1** upside down. **2** in utter confusion. [from TOP¹, obsolete terve overturn]

**top-up** n. addition; something that serves to top up.

**tor** n. hill or rocky peak. [Old English]

**torch** — n. **1** portable battery-powered electric lamp. **2** thing lit for illumination. **3** source of heat, illumination, or enlightenment (bore aloft the torch of freedom). **4** blowlamp. — v. purposely set fire to. □ **carry a torch for** suffer from unrequited love for. [Latin: related to TORT]

**torch song** n. popular song of unrequited love.

**tore** past of TEAR¹.

**toreador** /to-ree-uh-,daw/ n. bullfighter. [Latin taurus]

**torment** — n. /**taw**-ment/ **1** severe physical or mental suffering. **2** cause of this. — v. /taw-**ment**/ **1** subject to torment. **2** tease or worry excessively (enjoyed tormenting the teacher). □ **tormentor** /-**men**-tuh/ n. [Latin tormentum: related to TORT]

**torn** past part. of TEAR¹.

**tornado** /taw-**nay**-doh/ n. (pl. -es) **1** violent storm of small extent with whirling winds, often accompanied by a funnel-shaped cloud. **2** outburst or volley of cheers, hisses, missiles, etc. [Spanish tronada thunderstorm]

**torpedo** /taw-**pee**-doh/ — n. (pl. -es) **1** cigar-shaped self-propelled underwater missile that explodes on impact with a ship. **2** similar device dropped from an aircraft. — v. (-es, -ed) **1** destroy or attack with a torpedo. **2** destroy or damage (a policy, institution, plan, etc.) as if with a torpedo (torpedoed the project

with just a few words). [Latin, = electric ray: related to TORPOR]

**torpid** /**taw**-puhd/ adj. **1** sluggish, inactive, apathetic. **2** numb. **3** (of a hibernating animal) dormant. □ **torpidity** /-**pid**-uh-tee/ n. [Latin: related to TORPOR]

**torpor** /**taw**-puh/ n. torpid condition. [Latin torpeo be sluggish]

**torque** /tawk/ n. **1** Mech. twisting or rotating force, esp. in a machine. **2** (also **torc**) hist. necklace of twisted metal, esp. of the ancient Gauls and Britons. [Latin: related to TORT]

**torr** /taw/ n. (pl. same) unit of pressure equal to 133.32 pascals (¹⁄₇₆₀ of one atmosphere). [Torricelli, name of a physicist]

**Torrens system** /**to**-ruhnz/ n. (also **Torrens title**) system of land ownership in which title to land derives from the registration of documents by a public official. [R. Torrens first Premier of SA (d. 1884)]

**torrent** /**to**-ruhnt/ n. **1** rushing stream of liquid. **2** (in pl.) great downpour of rain. **3** (usu. foll. by of) violent or copious flow (torrent of abuse). □ **torrential** /tuh-**ren**-shuhl/ adj. [French from Latin]

**torrid** /**to**-ruhd/ adj. **1 a** (of the weather) very hot and dry. **b** (of land etc.) parched by such weather. **2** (of language and emotions) emotionally charged; passionate, intense. [Latin torreo tost- parch]

**torrid zone** n. the part of the earth between the Tropics of Cancer and Capricorn.

**torsion** /**taw**-shuhn/ n. twisting, esp. of one end of a body while the other is held fixed. □ **torsional** adj. [Latin: related to TORT]

**torso** /**taw**-soh/ n. (pl. **-s**) trunk of the human body. [Latin thyrsus rod]

**tort** n. Law breach of duty (other than under contract) leading to liability for damages. □ **tortious** /**taw**-shuhs/ adj. [Latin torqueo tort- twist]

**tortellini** /,taw-tuh-**lee**-nee/ n.pl. small squares of pasta stuffed with meat, cheese, etc., rolled and shaped into rings; an Italian dish of these and a sauce. [Italian]

**tortilla** /taw-**tee**-yuh/ n. thin flat orig. Mexican maize cake eaten hot with or without a filling. [Spanish diminutive of torta cake]

**tortoise** /**taw**-tuhs/ n. slow-moving land or freshwater reptile with a horny domed shell. [medieval Latin tortuca]

**tortoiseshell** /**taw**-tuhs-,shel/ — n. yellowish-brown mottled or clouded outer shell of some turtles. — adj. having the colouring or appearance of tortoiseshell.

**tortuous** /**taw**-choo-uhs/ *adj.* **1** full of twists and turns (*followed a tortuous route*). **2** devious; circuitous (*has a tortuous mind; a tortuous argument*). □ **tortuously** *adv.* [Latin: related to TORT]

■ **Usage** *Tortuous* should not be confused with *torturous* which means 'involving torture, excruciating'.

**torture** /**taw**-chuh/ — *n.* **1** infliction of severe bodily pain, esp. as a punishment or means of persuasion. **2** severe physical or mental suffering. — *v.* (**-ring**) **1** subject to torture (*tortured by guilt*). **2** force out of a natural position or state (*tea-trees tortured by storms to shapes like serpents interlaced*). **3** twist, deform, pervert (words, language, meaning, etc.) (*he tortures scripture to justify his doctrines; this word might be tortured to bear that meaning*). □ **torturer** *n.* **torturous** *adj.* [Latin *tortura* twisting: related to TORT]

**Tory** /**taw**-ree/ *n.* (*pl.* **-ies**) **1** *Brit. colloq.* member of the Conservative Party. **2** *Brit. hist.* member of the party that gave rise to the Conservative party. **3** *colloq. derog.* member or supporter of the political right in Australia; an extreme conservative. [originally = Irish outlaw]

**tosh** *n. colloq.* rubbish, nonsense. [origin unknown]

**toss** — *v.* **1** throw up (a ball etc.), esp. with the hand. **2** roll about, throw, or be thrown, restlessly or from side to side (*the ship tossed in the heavy seas; was tossing and turning all night*). **3** (usu. foll. by *to, away, aside, out,* etc.) throw (a thing) lightly or carelessly (*tossed the letter away*). **4 a** throw (a coin) into the air to decide a choice etc. by the side on which it lands. **b** (also *absol.*; often foll. by *for*) settle a question or dispute with (a person) in this way. **5** (of a horse etc.) throw (a rider) off its back. **6** coat (food) with dressing etc. by shaking it. — *n.* **1** act of tossing (a coin, the head, etc.). **2** fall, esp. from a horse. □ **argue the toss** see ARGUE. **toss one's head** throw it back esp. in anger, impatience, etc. **toss it in** *colloq.* finish; give up; die. **toss off 1** drink off at a draught. **2** dispatch (work) rapidly or without effort (*tossed off three essays in a single afternoon*). **toss up** toss a coin to decide a choice etc. [origin unknown]

**toss-up** *n.* **1** a doubtful matter; an even chance (*it's a toss-up as to which party will win the election*). **2** tossing of a coin.

**tot¹** *n.* **1** small child. **2** dram of liquor. [originally British dial.]

**tot²** *v.* (**-tt-**) **1** (usu. foll. by *up*) add (figures etc.). **2** (foll. by *up*) (of items) mount up. □ **tot up** to amount to. [abbreviation of TOTAL or of Latin *totum* the whole]

**total** /**toh**-tuhl/ — *adj.* **1** complete, comprising the whole (*total number of votes*). **2** absolute, unqualified (*in total ignorance*). — *n.* total number or amount. — *v.* (**-ll-**) **1 a** amount in number to. **b** find the total of. **2** (foll. by *to, up to*) amount to. [medieval Latin *totus* entire]

**totalisator** /**toh**-tuh-luy-,zay-tuh/ *n.* (also *attrib.*) (also **totalizator**) **1** device automatically registering the number and amount of bets staked on a race, with a view to dividing the total amount among those backing the winner(s). **2** system of betting based on this.

**totalitarian** /toh-,tal-uh-**tair**-ree-uhn/ *adj.* of a one-party dictatorial form of government requiring complete subservience to the State. □ **totalitarianism** *n.*

**totality** /toh-**tal**-uh-tee/ *n.* **1** complete amount. **2** entirety.

**totally** *adv.* completely.

**tote¹** *n.* (also *attrib.*) *colloq.* totalisator (*tote pay-out*). [abbreviation]

**tote²** *v.* (**-ting**) *colloq.* carry, convey (*toting a gun; toting his friend around from place to place*). [originally US, probably of British dial. origin]

**totem** /**toh**-tuhm/ *n.* **1 a** natural object, esp. an animal, adopted esp. by N. American Indians as an emblem of a clan or individual. **b** image of this. **2** (in Aboriginal culture) a natural object similarly adopted. □ **totemic** /-**tem**-ik/ *adj.* [Algonquian]

**totem pole** *n.* pole on which totems of N. American Indians are carved or hung.

**t'other** /**tuth**-uh/ *adj. & pron.* the other. [*thet other* 'that other']

**tothersider** /,tuth-uh-**suy**-duh/ *n.* person from the 'other side': (in WA) person from an eastern State; (in Tasmania) person from the mainland. [variant of OTHERSIDER based on T'OTHER]

**totter** — *v.* **1** stand or walk unsteadily or feebly. **2 a** (of a building etc.) shake as if about to collapse. **b** (of a system of government etc.) be about to fall. — *n.* unsteady or shaky movement or gait. □ **tottery** *adj.* [Dutch]

**toucan** /**too**-kan/ *n.* tropical American fruit-eating bird with an immense beak. [Tupi]

**touch** /**tuch**/ — *v.* **1** come into or be in physical contact with (a thing, each other, etc.) at one or more points. **2** (often foll. by *with*) bring the hand etc. into contact with (*touched her arm*). **3 a** (of two things etc.) be in or come into contact with each other (*the balls were touching*). **b** bring (two things) into mutual contact (*they touched hands*). **4** rouse tender or painful feelings in (*was touched by his appeal*). **5** strike lightly (*just touched the wall with my back bumper*). **6** (usu. with *neg.*) **a** disturb, harm, or affect (*don't touch my things; soap won't touch this dirt*). **b** have any dealings with (*won't touch door-to-door selling*). **c** consume, use (*I don't touch alcohol*). **7** concern (*it touches you closely*). **8 a** reach as far as, esp. momentarily (*the temperature touched 40°C*). **b** (usu. with *neg.*) approach in excellence etc. (*can't touch him for style*). **9** modify (*pity touched with fear*). **10** (as **touched** *adj.*) *colloq.* slightly mad. **11** (usu. foll. by *for*) *colloq.* ask for and get money etc. from (a person) (*touched him for $20*). — *n.* **1** act or instance of touching (*felt a touch on my arm*). **2 a** faculty of perception through physical contact, esp. with the fingers (*sense of touch*). **b** qualities of an object etc. as perceived in this way (*the soft touch of silk*). **3 a** small amount; slight trace (*just a touch of salt; a touch of irony*). **b** mild attack (of illness) (*a touch of flu*). **c** (prec. by *a*) slightly (*a touch too salty*). **4 a** musician's manner of playing keys or strings (*he has a delicate touch*). **b** response of the keys or strings (*this piano has a heavy touch*). **c** style of workmanship, writing, etc. (*has a deft touch with characterisation*). **5** distinguishing manner or detail (*a professional touch*). **6** special skill (*have lost my touch*). **7** (esp. in *pl.*) light stroke with a pencil etc. **8** *colloq.* **a** act of getting money etc. from a person by asking (*avoid him — he's on his way for another touch*). **b** = SOFT TOUCH; EASY TOUCH. **9** *Rugby* etc. part of the field outside the side limits. **10** (also **touch football**) ball game based on Rugby, played by teams of seven. □ **in touch** (often foll. by *with*) **1** in communication. **2** up to date, esp. regarding news etc. (*keeps in touch with events*). **3** aware, conscious, empathetic (*not in touch with his own deeper feelings*). **lose touch** (often foll. by *with*) **1** cease to be informed. **2** cease to be in contact. **lose one's touch** not show one's customary skill. **out of touch** (often foll. by *with*) **1** not in correspondence. **2** not up to date. **3** lacking in awareness (*out of touch with community feeling*). **touch at** (of a ship) call at (a port etc.). **touch bottom 1** reach the bottom of water with one's feet. **2** be at the lowest or worst point. **touch down** (of an aircraft) make contact with the ground in landing. **touch off 1** explode by touching with a match

etc. **2** initiate (a process) suddenly (*touched off a run on the Aussie dollar*). **touch on** (or **upon**) **1** refer to or mention briefly or casually. **2** verge on. **touch the sides** (usu. with *neg.*) *colloq.* satisfy (thirst) (*I'm so thirsty, that drink didn't even touch the sides*). **touch up** give finishing touches to or retouch. **touch wood** touch something wooden with the hand to avert ill luck. [French *tochier*]

**touch-and-go** *adj.* critical, risky.

**touchdown** *n.* **1** act of touching down by an aircraft. **2** *Rugby* act or instance of touching the ground with the ball behind the opponent's goal in order to score a try.

**touché** /too-shay/ *int.* **1** acknowledgment of a justified accusation or retort. **2** acknowledgment of a hit by a fencing-opponent. [French, = *touched*]

**touching** — *adj.* moving; pathetic. — *prep. literary* concerning (*touching your request . . .*). □ **touchingly** *adv.*

**touchline** *n.* (in various sports) either of the lines marking the side boundaries of the pitch.

**touch screen** *n.* computer display which can detect pressure from a finger etc.

**touchstone** *n.* **1** dark schist or jasper used for testing alloys by marking it with them. **2** standard or criterion.

**touch-type** *v.* type without looking at the keys. □ **touch-typist** *n.*

**touchy** *adj.* (**-ier**, **-iest**) **1** apt to take offence; over-sensitive. **2** apt to cause offence (*this is a touchy issue*). □ **touchily** *adv.* **touchiness** *n.*

**tough** /tuf/ — *adj.* **1** hard to break, cut, tear, or chew. **2** (of a person) able to endure hardship; hardy. **3** unyielding, stubborn, difficult (*it was a tough job; a tough customer*). **4** *colloq.* **a** acting sternly; hard (*get tough with*). **b** (of circumstances, luck, etc.) severe, hard, unjust. **5** *colloq.* criminal or violent (*tough guys*). — *adv. colloq.* in an uncompromising, aggressive, or unyielding manner (*play it tough, you guys; act tough*). — *n.* tough person, esp. a ruffian. □ **tough!** (or **tough luck!**) *colloq.* hard luck! (esp. as an expression of (sometimes ironic) commiseration. **tough it** (or **tough it out**) *colloq.* endure or withstand difficult circumstances. □ **toughen** *v.* **toughness** *n.* [Old English]

**toughie** /tuf-ee/ *n. colloq.* tough person or problem.

**toupee** /too-pay/ *n.* hairpiece to cover a bald spot. [French]

**tour** /toor/ — *n.* **1 a** holiday journey or excursion including stops at various places. **b** a walk round; inspection (*made* *a tour of the garden*). **2** spell of duty on military or diplomatic service. **3** series of performances, matches, etc., at different places. — *v.* **1** (usu. foll. by *through*) make a tour. **2** make a tour of (a country etc.). □ **on tour** (esp. of a team, theatre company, etc.) touring. [Latin: related to TURN]

**tourang** var. of TAWARANG.

**tour de force** /ˌtoor duh **faws**/ *n.* (*pl.* **tours de force**) outstanding feat or performance. [French]

**tourism** *n.* commercial organisation and operation of holidays.

**tourist** *n.* **1** holiday-maker, esp. abroad (often *attrib.*: *tourist season*). **2** member of a touring sports team.

**tourist class** *n.* lowest class of passenger accommodation in a ship, aircraft, etc.

**touristy** *adj.* usu. *derog.* appealing to or visited by many tourists.

**tourmaline** /ˈtoor-muh-leen/ *n.* mineral of various colours used as a gemstone. [French from Sinhalese *toramalli*]

**tournament** /ˈtaw-nuh-muhnt/ *n.* **1** large contest of many rounds (*chess tournament*). **2** *hist.* pageant in which jousting between knights (with blunted weapons etc.) took place. [French: related to TOURNEY]

**tournedos** /ˈtoor-nuh-ˌdoh/ *n.* (*pl.* same /-ˌdohz/ ) small round thick cut from a fillet of beef. [French]

**tourney** /ˈtoor-nee, ˈtaw-/ — *n.* (*pl.* **-s**) tournament. — *v.* (**-eys, -eyed**) take part in a tournament. [French: related to TURN]

**tourniquet** /ˈtoor-nuh-ˌkay, ˈtaw-/ *n.* device for stopping the flow of blood through an artery by constriction. [French]

**tousle** /ˈtow-zuhl/ *v.* (**-ling**) make (esp. the hair) untidy (*she tousled his hair*). [British dial. *touse*]

**tout** /towt/ — *v.* **1** (usu. foll. by *for*) solicit custom persistently; pester customers (*touting for business*). **2 a** (foll. by *for*) solicit for (support, votes, etc.) (*touting for votes in marginal seats*). **b** try to sell (*touting vacuum cleaners door-to-door*). **c** proclaim the advantages of (a place, thing, etc.) for commercial reasons (*ads touting New South Wales as a tourist paradise*). **d** recommend, push (the candidacy etc. of) a person (*is busy touting his mate as next captain*). **3** spy out the movements and condition of racehorses in training. **4** (as **touted** *past part.*) (usu. with qualifying *adv.*) vaunted, extolled (*the much touted new drug offensive*). — *n.* person who touts. [Old English, = peep]

**tow¹** /toh/ — *v.* pull (a boat, vehicle, etc.) along by a rope etc. — *n.* act or instance of towing or state of being towed. □ **have in** (or **on**) **tow 1** be towing. **2** be accompanied by and often in charge of (a person). **on** (or **under**) **tow** being towed. [Old English]

**tow²** *n.* coarse part of flax or hemp prepared for spinning. [Low German *touw*]

**toward** — *prep.* /tuh-**wawd**/ = TOWARDS. — *adj.* /ˈtoh-uhd/ *archaic* about to take place; in process (*I've come to see what is toward*).

**towards** /tuh-**wawdz**, twawdz, tawdz/ *prep.* **1** in the direction of (*set out towards town*). **2** as regards; in relation to (*attitude towards death*). **3** as a contribution to; for (*put it towards her holiday*). **4** near (*towards the end of our journey*). [Old English, = future: related to TO, -WARD]

**tow bar** *n.* bar for towing esp. a trailer or caravan.

**towel** /towl/ — *n.* absorbent cloth or paper etc. used for drying after washing. — *v.* (**-ll-**) **1** (often *refl.*) wipe or dry with a towel (*towelled himself and the kids*). **2** (also foll. by *up*) *colloq.* thrash or beat (a person) (*my serve was working beaut and I towelled him up in straight sets*). □ **throw in the towel** see THROW. [French *toail(l)e* from Germanic]

**towelling** /ˈtow-ling/ *n.* **1** thick soft absorbent cloth, used esp. for towels. **2** *colloq.* a thrashing.

**tower** — *n.* **1** tall structure, often part of a church, castle, etc. **2** fortress etc. with a tower. **3** tall structure housing machinery etc. (*cooling tower*; *control tower*). — *v.* **1** (usu. foll. by *above, up*) reach or be high or above; be superior. **2** (as **towering** *adj.*) **a** high, lofty (*towering intellect*). **b** violent (*towering rage*). [Greek *turris*]

**towerang** var. of TAWARANG.

**tower of strength** *n.* person who gives strong emotional support.

**tow-headed** /toh/ *adj.* having very light or unkempt hair.

**town** *n.* **1 a** densely populated built-up defined area, larger than a township (esp. one that has not been created a city), and having local government. **b** any densely populated area, esp. as opposed to the country. **c** any small cluster of dwellings and other buildings recognised as a distinct place, even if remote and rural. **2** central business or shopping area serving, and contrasted with, the surrounding suburbs. □ **go to town** see GO. **go to town on** see GO. **on the town** *colloq.*

enjoying night-life in a town. [Old English]

**town camp** n. Aboriginal camp within or near a town.

**town clerk** n. official responsible for the administration of a local government area.

**town hall** n. headquarters of local government, with public meeting rooms etc.

**town house** n. **1** town residence, esp. of a person with a house in the country. **2** terrace house or house in a planned group in a town, usu. of a stylish modern type, and usu. with strata title.

**townie** /tow-nee/ n. (also **townee**) colloq. usu. derog. town-dweller as distinct from a country-dweller.

**town planning** n. planning of the construction and growth of towns. □ **town planner** n.

**township** n. small Australian town.

**towri** /tow-ree/ n. = COUNTRY 6. [Kamilaroi dhawuray]

**tow-truck** n. truck specially designed to tow broken-down or accident-damaged motor vehicles.

**toxaemia** /tok-see-mee-uh/ n. (also **toxemia**) **1** blood-poisoning. **2** increased blood pressure in pregnancy. [related to TOXIC, Greek haima blood]

**toxic** /tok-sik/ adj. **1** of or relating to poison (toxic symptoms). **2** poisonous (toxic gas; some potting-mixes have proved toxic to some people). **3** caused by poison (toxic anaemia). □ **toxicity** /-sis-uh-tee/ n. [Greek toxikon poison for arrows]

**toxicology** /ˌtok-suh-**kol**-uh-jee/ n. the study of poisons. □ **toxicological** /-kuh-loj-i-kuhl/ adj. **toxicologist** n.

**toxic shock syndrome** n. potentially fatal blood-poisoning disease caused by bacteria in the vagina, and often associated with the use of tampons.

**toxin** /tok-suhn/ n. poison produced by a living organism.

**toy** — n. **1 a** plaything, esp. for a child. **b** (often attrib.) model or miniature replica of a thing, esp. as a plaything (toy gun). **2** thing regarded as providing amusement, esp. for an adult (my husband's driving the family crazy with his latest toy, a camcorder). **3** (usu. attrib.) diminutive breed of dog etc. — v. (usu. foll. by with) **1** trifle, amuse oneself, flirt (toyed with the idea of a trip to Antarctica; he toyed quite callously with her emotions). **2 a** move a thing idly (toyed with his earring). **b** nibble at food etc. unenthusiastically (toyed with his broccoli). [origin unknown]

**toyboy** n. colloq. person's much younger boyfriend.

**trac** n. (also attrib.) colloq. a refractory prisoner (I was put in with the tracs; trac section of the prison). [abbreviation of INTRACTABLE]

**trace**[1] — v. (**-cing**) **1 a** observe, discover, or find vestiges or signs of by investigation (traced the missing boy to King's Cross and then lost the trail). **b** (often foll. by along, through, to, etc.) follow or mark the track or position of (traced his footprints along the beach). **c** (often foll. by back) follow to its origins (can trace her family back to the First Fleet; the leak has been traced back to you). **2** copy (a drawing etc.) by drawing over its lines on superimposed translucent paper. **3** (often foll. by out) mark out, delineate, sketch, or write, esp. painstakingly (traced out his vision for the future). **4** make one's way along (a path etc.). — n. **1 a** indication of something having existed; vestige (hardly a trace remains of the Aboriginal languages of Tasmania). **b** very small quantity (found a trace of blood in my urine). **2** track or footprint (dingo traces everywhere). **3** track registered by a self-recording instrument etc. □ **traceable** adj. **tracing** n. [Latin traho draw]

**trace**[2] n. each of the two side-straps, chains, or ropes, by which a horse draws a vehicle. □ **kick over the traces** become insubordinate or reckless. [French trais, pl. of TRAIT]

**trace element** n. chemical element required only in minute amounts by living organisms for normal growth.

**tracer** n. **1** bullet etc. that is visible in flight because of flames etc. emitted. **2** artificial radioactive isotope which can be followed through the body by the radiation it produces.

**tracery** n. (pl. **-ies**) **1** ornamental stone openwork, esp. in the upper part of a Gothic window. **2** fine decorative pattern.

**trachea** /truh-**keer**/ n. (pl. **-cheae** /-kee-ee/) windpipe. [Latin from Greek]

**tracheotomy** /ˌtrak-ee-ot-uh-mee/ n. (pl. **-ies**) incision of the trachea to relieve an obstruction.

**trachoma** /ˌtruh-**koh**-muh/ n. contagious disease of the eye with inflamed granulation on the inner surface of the lids, leading eventually to blindness. [Greek, from trakhus rough]

**track**[1] — n. **1 a** mark(s) left by a person, animal, vehicle, etc. (in pl.) such marks, esp. footprints. **2 a** rough path, esp. one beaten by use. **b** route followed by a drover. **3** the Stuart Highway between Darwin and Alice Springs. **4** continuous railway line. **5 a** racecourse; circuit.

**b** prepared course for runners etc. **6 a** groove on a gramophone record. **b** section (of a record, CD, or magnetic tape) containing one song etc. **c** *Computing* path followed by a head over the surface of a magnetic or optical recording medium. **7** line of travel (*track of the comet*). **8** band round the wheels of a tank, tractor, etc. **9 a** line of thought or action (*this track proved fruitless*). **b** course or progress of an event, action, etc. (*an effective vaccine for AIDS is a long way down the track*). **10** metal or plastic strip designed to carry the sliding fittings from which a curtain is hung. — *v.* **1** follow the track of (an animal, person, spacecraft, etc.). **2** trace (a course, development, etc.) by vestiges (*tracking the evolution of Australian marsupials*). **3** (often foll. by *back*, *in*, etc.) (of a film or television camera) move in relation to the subject being filmed. **4** deposit (dirt etc.) with one's feet (*you're tracking mud all over my brand new carpet*). □ **in one's tracks** *colloq.* where one stands, instantly (*stopped him in his tracks*). **keep** (or **lose**) **track of** follow (or fail to follow) the course of. **make tracks** *colloq.* depart. **make tracks for** *colloq.* go in pursuit of or towards. **off the beaten track** isolated; unfamiliar. **off the track** away from the subject. **on the track** = *on the wallaby track* (see WALLABY TRACK). **on the wrong side of the tracks** *colloq.* in an inferior or socially disadvantaged part of town. **on the wrong** (or **right**) **track** following the wrong (or right) line of inquiry. **track down** reach or capture by tracking. **track square with** *colloq.* keep company with (a girl) with marriage or a permanent relationship in mind. **track with** *colloq.* **1** keep company with (a member of the opposite sex). **2** associate with, be mates with (see also TRACK MATE). □ **tracker** *n.* [French *trac*]

**track²** *v.* **1** tow (a boat) by rope etc. from a bank. **2** pull after one by means of a rope (*a small boy tracking a wheeled toy along the road*). [probably from Dutch *trekken* to draw]

**tracker dog** *n.* police dog tracking by scent.

**track events** *n.pl.* running-races as opposed to FIELD EVENTS (e.g. jumping, discus, etc.).

**track mate** *n.* travelling companion.

**track record** *n.* **1** person's past performance. **2** best performance on a particular track.

**track shoe** *n.* runner's spiked shoe.

**track suit** *n.* loose warm garment worn for exercising etc.

**tract¹** *n.* **1** stretch or extent of territory, esp. large. **2** bodily organ or system (*digestive tract*). [Latin *traho tract-* pull]

**tract²** *n.* short treatise, often in pamphlet form; pamphlet, esp. propagandist, on a religious subject, etc. [apparently Latin *tractatus* from *tracto* handle]

**tractable** /**trak**-tuh-buhl/ *adj.* **1** (of a person) easily handled; manageable. **2** (of material etc.) pliant, malleable. □ **tractability** /-**bil**-uh-tee/ *n.* [Latin *tracto* handle]

**traction** /**trak**-shuhn/ *n.* **1** act of hauling or pulling a thing over a surface. **2** sustained therapeutic pulling on a limb etc. with pulleys, weights, etc. **3** grip of a tyre on a road, a wheel on a rail, etc. [French or medieval Latin: related to TRACT¹]

**tractor** /**trak**-tuh/ *n.* vehicle used for pulling farm machinery etc. [related to TRACTION]

**trad** *colloq.* — *n.* traditional jazz. — *adj.* traditional. [abbreviation]

**trade** — *n.* **1 a** buying and selling. **b** this between nations etc. **c** business conducted for profit (esp. as distinct from a profession. **d** business of a specified nature or time (*Christmas trade*; *tourist trade*). **2** skilled craft practised professionally (*trade of a plumber*). **3** (usu. prec. by *the*) people engaged in a specific trade (*the trade will never agree*; *trade enquiries only*). **4** a swap. — *v.* (**-ding**) **1** (often foll. by *in*, *with*) engage in trade; buy and sell. **2 a** exchange in commerce. **b** exchange (insults, blows, etc.). **c** swap. **3** (usu. foll. by *with*, *for*) have a transaction with a person for a thing. □ **trade in** (often foll. by *for*) exchange (esp. a used car) in part payment for another. **trade off** exchange, esp. as a compromise. **trade on** take advantage of (*he's trading on my good nature*). □ **tradable** *adj.* **tradeable** *adj.* **trading** *n.* [Low German, = track: related to TREAD]

**trade-in** *n.* thing given in part exchange for another (also *attrib.*: *trade-in price*).

**trade mark** *n.* (also **trademark**) **1** device or name secured by law or custom as representing a company, product, etc. **2** distinctive characteristic, way of doing things, etc., of a person (*bluntness is his trade mark*).

**trade name** *n.* **1** name by which a thing is called in a trade. **2** name given to a product. **3** name under which a business trades.

**trade-off** *n.* balance, compromise.

**trade price** *n.* wholesale price charged to the retailer.

**trader** *n.* **1** person engaged in trade. **2** ship used in trade.

**trade secret** *n.* **1** secret device or technique used esp. in a trade. **2** *joc.* any secret.

**tradesman** *n.* (*fem.* **tradeswoman**) person engaged in trade.

**trade union** *n.* organised association of workers in a trade, profession, etc., formed to protect and further their rights and interests. □ **trade-unionism** *n.* **trade-unionist** *n.*

■ **Usage** The esp. British alternative singular *trades union* and plural *trades unions* are not common in Australian usage. The preferred plural is *trade unions*.

**trade wind** *n.* wind blowing continually towards the equator and deflected westward.

**trading bank** *n.* bank that handles a range of business transactions, issues cheques in its own name, etc. (cf. SAVINGS BANK).

**trading post** *n.* store etc. in a remote or unsettled region.

**tradition** /truh-**dish**-uhn/ *n.* **1 a** custom, opinion, or belief handed down to posterity, esp. orally or by practice. **b** this process of handing down. **c** esp. *joc.* established practice or custom (*it's a tradition to blame the government*). **2** artistic, literary, etc. principles based on experience and practice; any one of these (*stage tradition*). [Latin *trado -dit-* hand on, betray]

**traditional** *adj.* **1** of, based on, or obtained by tradition. **2** (of Aboriginal society, now chiefly that of central and northern Australia) characterised by social practices and religious beliefs that prevailed before European settlement. **3** (of jazz) in the style of the early 20th c. □ **traditionally** *adv.*

**traditionalism** *n.* respect or support for tradition. □ **traditionalist** *n.* & *adj.*

**traditional owner** *n.* an Aborigine who is a member of a local descent group having certain rights in a tract of land.

**traduce** /truh-**dyoos**/ *v.* (**-cing**) speak ill of; misrepresent. □ **traducement** *n.* **traducer** *n.* [Latin, = disgrace]

**traffic** /**traf**-ik/ — *n.* **1** vehicles moving on a public highway or in the air or at sea. **2** (usu. foll. by *in*) trade, esp. illegal (*drugs traffic*). **3** coming and going of people or goods by road, rail, air, sea, etc. **4** dealings between people etc. (*had no traffic with them*). **5** messages etc. transmitted through a communications system; volume of this. — *v.* (**-ck-**) **1** (usu. foll. by *in*) deal in something, esp. illegally. **2** deal in; barter. □ **trafficker** *n.* [French from Italian]

**traffic jam** *n.* traffic at a standstill because of an accident etc.

**traffic light** *n.* (also **traffic lights** *n.pl.*) signal controlling road traffic by coloured lights.

**trag** *n.* (*pl.* same or **-s**) = TERAGLIN. [abbreviation]

**tragedian** /truh-jee-dee-uhn/ *n.* **1** writer of tragedies. **2** (*fem.* **tragedienne** /truh-,jee-dee-**en**/ ) actor in tragedy. [French: related to TRAGEDY]

**tragedy** /**traj**-uh-dee/ *n.* (*pl.* **-ies**) **1** serious accident, disaster, etc.; sad event. **2 a** play dealing with tragic events and ending unhappily, esp. with the downfall of the protagonist. **b** such plays as a genre. [Greek *tragōidia*]

**tragic** /**traj**-ik/ *adj.* **1** disastrous; greatly distressing; very sad. **2** of tragedy. □ **tragically** *adv.*

**tragicomedy** /,traj-ee-**kom**-uh-dee/ *n.* (*pl.* **-ies**) play or situation with a mixture of comedy and tragedy. □ **tragicomic** *adj.*

**trail** — *n.* **1** track left behind by a moving thing, person, etc. (*left a trail of wreckage; a snail's silvery trail*). **2** beaten path, esp. through a wild region. **3** long line of people or things following behind something. **4** part dragging behind a thing or person (*a trail of smoke*). — *v.* **1** draw or be drawn along behind, esp. on the ground. **2** (often foll. by *behind*) walk wearily; lag. **3** follow the trail of; pursue. **4** be losing in a contest (*trailing by three points*). **5** (usu. foll. by *away*, *off*) peter out; tail off. **6 a** (of a plant etc.) grow or hang over a wall, along the ground, etc. **b** (of a garment etc.) hang loosely. **7** (often *refl.*) drag (oneself, one's limbs, etc.) along wearily etc. [French or Low German]

**trail-bike** *n.* light motor cycle designed for use in rough terrain.

**trailblazer** *n.* **1** person who marks a new track through wild country. **2** pioneer; innovator. □ **trailblazing** *n.*

**trailer** *n.* **1** set of brief extracts from a film etc., used to advertise it in advance. **2** vehicle towed by another, esp. the large rear section of a semi-trailer, or the small open cart, attached to a car, and used for transporting goods, garden rubbish, etc.

**train** — *v.* **1 a** (often foll. by *to* + infin.) teach (a person, animal, oneself, etc.) a specified skill, esp. by practice. **b** undergo this process (*trained as a teacher*). **2** bring or come to physical fitness by exercise, diet, etc.; undergo physical exercise, esp. for a specific purpose. **3** (often foll. by *along, up*) guide the growth of (a plant). **4** (usu. as **trained** *adj.*) make (the mind, eye, etc.) discerning through practice etc. **5** (often foll. by *on*) point or aim (a gun, camera, etc.) at an object etc. — *n.* **1** series of railway carriages etc. drawn by an engine. **2** thing dragged along behind or forming the back part of a dress, robe, etc. (*wore a dress with a long train; the train of the peacock*). **3** succession or series of people, things, events, consequences, etc. (*long train of camels; train of thought; the earthquake brought starvation and disease in its train*). **4** body of followers; retinue (*a train of admirers*). □ **in train** properly arranged or directed. □ **trainee** /-**nee**/ *n.* **training** *n.* [Latin *traho* draw]

**trainer** *n.* **1** person who trains horses, athletes, footballers, etc. **2** aircraft or simulator used to train pilots. **3** soft running shoe.

**traipse** *colloq.* — *v.* (**-sing**) tramp or trudge wearily. — *n.* tedious journey on foot. [origin unknown]

**trait** /tray, trayt/ *n.* distinguishing feature or characteristic. [Latin *tractus*: related to TRACT[1]]

**traitor** /**tray**-tuh/ *n.* (*fem.* **traitress**)(often foll. by *to*) person who is treacherous or disloyal, esp. to his or her country. □ **traitorous** *adj.* [Latin *traditor*: related to TRADITION]

**trajectory** /truh-**jek**-tuh-ree/ *n.* (*pl.* **-ies**) path of an object moving under given forces. [Latin *traicio -ject-* throw across]

**tram** *n.* electrically-powered passenger road vehicle running on rails. □ **be on the wrong tram** *colloq.* be pursuing an unproductive course (*the government seems to be on the wrong tram economically*). [Low German and Dutch *trame* beam]

**tramline** *n.* **1** (usu. in *pl.*) rails for a tram. **2** route of a tram.

**trammel** /**tram**-uhl/ — *n.* **1** (usu. in *pl.*) impediment; hindrance (*trammels of domesticity*). **2** triple drag-net for fishing. — *v.* (**-ll-**) confine or hamper with, or as with, trammels. [medieval Latin *tremaculum*]

**trammie** /**tram**-ee/ *n. colloq.* driver or conductor of a tram. [TRAM, -Y[2]]

**tramp** — *v.* **1 a** walk heavily and firmly. **b** go on foot, esp. a distance. **2 a** cross on foot, esp. wearily or reluctantly. **b** cover (a distance) in this way (*tramped forty kilometres*). **3** (often foll. by *down*) tread on; trample; stamp on. **4** *colloq.* dismiss (a person) from employment (*the recession has resulted in many hundreds being tramped*). — *n.* **1** itinerant vagrant or beggar. **2** sound of a person, or esp.

people, walking, marching, etc. **3** long walk. **4** *colloq. derog.* promiscuous person (used esp. of a woman). [Germanic]

**trample** /**tram**-puhl/ — *v.* (**-ling**) **1** tread under foot. **2** press down or crush in this way. — *n.* sound or act of trampling (*heard the trample of feet*). □ **trample on 1** tread heavily on. **2** treat roughly or with contempt (*trampled on the people's wishes*). [from TRAMP]

**trampoline** /**tram**-puh-,leen, ,tram-puh-**leen**/ — *n.* strong fabric sheet connected by springs to a horizontal frame, used for gymnastic jumping. — *v.* (**-ning**) use a trampoline. [Italian *trampolino*]

**trance** /trahns, trans/ *n.* **1 a** sleeplike state without response to stimuli. **b** hypnotic or cataleptic state. **2** such a state as entered into by a medium. **3** rapture, ecstasy. [Latin *transeo* pass over]

**tranny** /**tran**-ee/ *n.* (*pl.* **-ies**) (also **trannie**) *colloq.* transistor radio. [abbreviation]

**tranquil** /**trang**-kwuhl/ *adj.* calm, serene, undisturbed. □ **tranquillity** /-**kwil**-uh-tee/ *n.* **tranquilly** *adv.* [Latin]

**tranquillise** *v.* (also **-ize**) (**-sing** or **-zing**) make tranquil, esp. by a drug etc.

**tranquilliser** *n.* (also **-izer**) drug used to diminish anxiety.

**trans-** *prefix* **1** across, beyond (*transcontinental; transgress*). **2** on or to the other side of (*trans-Tasman*). **3** through (*translucent*). **4** into another state or place (*transform; transcribe*). **5** surpassing, transcending (*transfiguration*). [Latin]

**transact** /tran-**zakt**/ *v.* perform or carry through (business). [Latin: related to ACT]

**transaction** /tran-**zak**-shuhn/ *n.* **1 a** piece of esp. commercial business done. **b** transacting of business etc. **2** (in *pl.*) published reports of discussions, papers read, etc., at the meetings of a learned society.

**transceiver** /tran-**see**-vuh/ *n.* combined radio transmitter and receiver.

**transcend** /tran-**send**/ *v.* **1** be beyond the range or grasp of (human experience, reason, belief, etc.). **2** excel; surpass. [Latin *scando* climb]

**transcendent** *adj.* **1** excelling, surpassing (*transcendent merit*). **2** transcending human experience. **3** (esp. of God) existing apart from, not subject to the limitations of, the material universe (opp. IMMANENT). □ **transcendence** *n.* **transcendency** *n.*

**transcendental** /,tran-sen-**den**-tuhl/ *adj.* **1** = TRANSCENDENT. **2** *Philos.* a priori, not based on experience; intuitively accepted; innate in the mind. **3** visionary, abstract. **4** *Math.* (of a function) not capable of being produced by the algebraical operations of addition, multiplication, and involution, or the inverse operations. □ **transcendentally** *adv.*

**transcendentalism** *n.* transcendental philosophy. □ **transcendentalist** *n.*

**transcendental meditation** *n.* method of detaching oneself from problems, anxiety, etc., by silent meditation and repetition of a mantra.

**transcontinental** /tranz-,kon-tuh-**nen**-tuhl/ *adj.* extending across a continent.

**transcribe** /tran-**skruyb**/ *v.* (**-bing**) **1** make a copy of, esp. in writing. **2** write out (shorthand, notes, etc.) in full. **3** arrange (music) for a different instrument etc. □ **transcriber** *n.* **transcription** /-**skrip**-shuhn/ *n.* [Latin *transcribo -script-*]

**transcript** /**tran**-skript/ *n.* written or recorded copy.

**transducer** /tranz-**dyoo**-suh/ *n.* any device for converting a non-electrical signal into an electrical one, e.g. pressure into voltage. [Latin: related to DUCT]

**transept** /**tran**-sept/ *n.* **1** that part of a cross-shaped church which is at right angles to the nave. **2** either arm of this. [Latin: related to SEPTUM]

**transexual** var. of TRANSSEXUAL.

**transfer** — *v.* /trans-**fer**/ (**-rr-**) **1** (often foll. by *to*) **a** convey, remove, or hand over (a thing etc.). **b** make over the possession of (property, a ticket, rights, etc.) to a person. **2** change or move to another group, club, department, etc. **3** change from one station, route, etc., to another on a journey. **4** convey (a design) from one surface to another. **5** change (meaning) by extension or metaphor. — *n.* /**trans**-fer/ **1** act or instance of transferring or being transferred. **2 a** design etc. conveyed or to be conveyed from one surface to another. **b** small, usu. coloured, picture or design on paper, which is transferred to another surface. **3** document effecting conveyance of property, a right, etc. □ **transferable** /trans-**fer**-ruh-buhl/ *adj.* [Latin *fero lat-* bear]

**transference** /trans-**fuh**-ruhns/ *n.* **1** act or instance of transferring or state of being transferred. **2** *Psychol.* redirection of childhood emotions to a new object, esp. to a psychoanalyst.

**transfer fee** *n.* fee paid for the transfer of esp. a professional footballer.

**transfiguration** /trans-,fig-uh-**ray**-shuhn/ *n.* **1** change of form or appearance. **2 a** Christ's appearance in radiant glory to three of his disciples (Matt. 17:2, Mark 9:2–3). **b** (**Transfiguration**) festival of Christ's transfiguration, 6 August. [Latin: related to TRANSFIGURE]

**transfigure** /trans-**fig**-uh/ *v.* (**-ring**) change in form or appearance, esp. so as to elevate or idealise. [Latin]

**transfix** /trans-**fiks**/ *v.* **1** paralyse with horror or astonishment. **2** pierce with a sharp implement or weapon. [Latin: related to FIX]

**transform** /trans-**fawm**/ *v.* **1** make a thorough or dramatic change in the form, appearance, character, etc., of. **2** change the voltage etc. of (an alternating current). □ **transformation** /,trans-fuh-**may**-shuhn/ *n.* [Latin]

**transformer** *n.* apparatus for reducing or increasing the voltage of an alternating current.

**transfuse** /trans-**fyooz**/ *v.* (**-sing**) **1 a** transfer (blood) from one person or animal to another. **b** inject (liquid) into a blood-vessel to replace lost fluid. **2** permeate (*the river is transfused with blue-green algae; a deep blush transfused his cheeks*). □ **transfusion** *n.* [Latin: related to FOUND[3]]

**transgress** /tranz-**gres**/ *v.* (also *absol.*) go beyond the bounds or limits set by (a commandment, law, etc.); violate, sin. □ **transgression** *n.* **transgressor** *n.* [Latin *transgredior -gress-*]

**transient** /**tran**-zee-uhnt/ — *adj.* of short duration; passing; impermanent (*life is transient; of transient interest*). — *n.* temporary visitor, worker, etc. □ **transience** *n.* [Latin: related to TRANCE]

**transistor** /tran-**zis**-tuh/ *n.* **1** semiconductor device with three connections, capable of amplification in addition to rectification. **2** (in full **transistor radio**) portable radio with transistors. [from TRANSFER, RESISTOR]

**transit** /**tran**-zuht/ *n.* **1** act or process of going, conveying, or being conveyed, esp. over a distance. **2** passage or route (*the overland transit*). **3** apparent passage of a celestial body across the meridian of a place, or across the sun or a planet. □ **in transit** while going or being conveyed. [Latin: related to TRANCE]

**transit camp** *n.* camp for the temporary accommodation of soldiers, refugees, etc.

**transition** /tran-**zish**-uhn/ *n.* **1** passing or change from one place, state, condition, etc., to another (*age of transition*). **2** *Mus.* momentary modulation. **3** *Physics* change in an atomic nucleus or orbital electron with emission or absorption of radiation. □ **transitional** *adj.* **transitionally** *adv.* [Latin: related to TRANSIT]

**transitive** /**tran**-zuh-tiv/ *adj.* (of a verb) taking a direct object (whether expressed or implied), e.g. *saw* in *saw the donkey*, *saw that she was ill.* [Latin: related to TRANSIT]

**transit lounge** *n.* lounge at an airport for (usu. international) passengers waiting between flights.

**transitory** /**tran**-zuh-tuh-ree, -tree/ *adj.* not permanent; brief, transient. □ **transitorily** *adv.* **transitoriness** *n.* [Latin: related to TRANSIT]

**translate** /tranz-**layt**/ *v.* (**-ting**) **1** (also *absol.*) (often foll. by *into*) express the sense of (a word, text, etc.) in another language. **2** be translatable, bear translation (*does not translate well*). **3** express (an idea etc.) in another, esp. simpler, form (*I'll translate that into words even the thickest of you will understand*). **4** interpret (*translated his silence as dissent*). **5** move or change, esp. from one person, place, or condition, to another (*was translated by joy*). **6** *Mech.* **a** cause (a body) to move so that all its parts travel in the same direction. **b** impart motion without rotation to. □ **translatable** *adj.* **translation** *n.* **translator** *n.* [Latin: related to TRANSFER]

**transliterate** /tranz-**lit**-uh-, rayt/ *v.* (**-ting**) represent (a word etc.) in the closest corresponding letters of a different script. □ **transliteration** /-**ray**-shuhn/ *n.* [Latin *littera* letter]

**translucent** /tranz-**loo**-suhnt/ *adj.* allowing light to pass through; semitransparent. □ **translucence** *n.* **translucency** *n.* [Latin *luceo* shine]

**transmigrate** /,tranz-muy-**grayt**/ *v.* (**-ting**) **1** (of the soul) pass into a different body. **2** migrate. □ **transmigration** /-**gray**-shuhn/ *n.* [Latin]

**transmission** /tranz-**mish**-uhn/ *n.* **1** act or instance of transmitting or state of being transmitted. **2** broadcasting of a radio or television programme. **3** mechanism transmitting power from the engine to the axle in a vehicle.

**transmit** /tranz-**mit**/ *v.* (**-tt-**) **1 a** pass or hand on; transfer (*transmitted the message*; *how diseases are transmitted*). **b** communicate (ideas, emotions, etc.). **2 a** allow (heat, light, sound, electricity, etc.) to pass through. **b** be a medium for (ideas, emotions, etc.) (*his message transmits hope*). **3** broadcast (a radio or television programme). □ **transmissible** *adj.* **transmittable** *adj.* [Latin *mitto miss-* send]

**transmitter** *n.* **1** person or thing that transmits. **2** equipment used to transmit radio or other electronic signals.

**transmogrify** /tranz-**mog**-ruh-,fuy/ *v.* (**-ies, -ied**) *joc.* transform, esp. in a magical or surprising manner (*the prince, to his great annoyance, was transmogrified into an ordinary human being*). □ **transmogrification** /-fuh-**kay**-shuhn/ *n.* [origin unknown]

**transmute** /tranz-**myoot**/ *v.* (**-ting**) **1** change the form, nature, or substance of. **2** *hist.* change (base metals) into gold. □ **transmutation** /,tranz-myoo-**tay**-shuhn/ *n.* [Latin *muto* change]

**transnational** /,tranz-**nash**-uh-nuhl/ *adj.* extending beyond national boundaries.

**transoceanic** /tranz-,oh-shee-**an**-ik/ *adj.* **1** beyond the ocean. **2** crossing the ocean.

**transom** /**tran**-suhm/ *n.* horizontal bar of wood or stone across a window or the top of a door. [French *traversin*: related to TRAVERSE]

**transom window** *n.* window above a transom; fanlight.

**transparency** /trans-**pair**-ruhn-see/ *n.* (*pl.* **-ies**) **1** condition of being transparent. **2** picture, esp. a positive transparent photograph, to be viewed by light passing through it. [medieval Latin: related to TRANSPARENT]

**transparent** /trans-**pair**-ruhnt/ *adj.* **1** allowing light to pass through so that bodies can be distinctly seen. **2 a** (of a disguise, pretext, etc.) easily seen through. **b** (of a motive, quality, etc.) easily discerned; evident; obvious. **3** (of a person etc.) easily understood; frank. □ **transparently** *adv.* [Latin *pareo* appear]

**transpire** /tran-**spuyuh**/ *v.* (**-ring**) **1** (usu. prec. by *it* as subject) (of a secret or fact) come to be known; turn out; prove to be the case (*it transpired he knew nothing about it*). **2** occur; happen (*we shall see what transpires*). **3** emit (vapour or moisture), or be emitted, through the skin, lungs, or leaves; perspire. □ **transpiration** /-spuh-**ray**-shuhn/ *n.* (in sense 3). [Latin *spiro* breathe]

■ **Usage** Use of *transpire* in sense 2 is considered incorrect by some people.

**transplant** — *v.* /trans-**plahnt**, -**plant**/ **1** plant in another place (*transplanted the daffodils*). **2 a** convey or remove from one place to another. **b** bring (people etc.) from one country to settle in another. **3** transfer (living tissue or an organ) to another part of the body or to another body. — *n.* /**trans**-plahnt, -plant/ **1 a** transplanting of an organ or tissue. **b** such an organ etc. **2** thing, esp. a plant, transplanted. □ **transplantation** /-**tay**-shuhn/ *n.* [Latin]

**ransponder** /tran-**spon**-duh/ n. device for receiving a radio signal and automatically transmitting a different signal. [from TRANSMIT, RESPOND]

**ransport** — v. /trans-**pawt**/ **1** take or carry (a person, goods, etc.) to another place. **2** hist. deport (a person sentenced in the British Isles) to a penal colony in Australia. **3** (as **transported** adj.) (usu. foll. by with) affected with strong emotion. — n. /**trans**-pawt/ **1 a** system of conveying people, goods, etc., from place to place. **b** means of this (our transport has arrived). **2** ship, aircraft, etc., used to carry soldiers, stores, etc. **3** (esp. in pl.) vehement emotion (transports of joy). **4** hist. person sentenced in the British Isles to a term of servitude in a penal colony in Australia. □ **transportable** /trans-**paw**-tuh-buhl/ adj. [Latin porto carry]

**ransportation** /ˌtrans-paw-**tay**-shuhn/ n. **1** act of conveying or process of being conveyed. **2 a** system of conveying. **b** means of this. **3** hist. deportation to a penal colony in Australia of a person sentenced in the British Isles.

**ranspose** /trans-**pohz**/ v. (**-sing**) **1 a** cause (two or more things) to change places. **b** change the position of (a thing) in a series. **2** change the order or position of (words or a word) in a sentence. **3** put (music) into a different key. **4** Algebra transfer (a term) with a changed sign to the other side of an equation. □ **transposition** /ˌtrans-puh-**zish**-uhn/ n. [French: related to POSE]

**ransputer** /tranz-**pyoo**-tuh/ n. high-performance microprocessor designed to work with others of its type in parallel processing operations. [from TRANSISTOR, COMPUTER]

**ranssexual** /tranz-**sek**-shoo-uhl/ (also **transexual**) — adj. having the physical characteristics of one sex and an overwhelming psychological identification with the other. — n. **1** transsexual person. **2** person whose sex has been changed by surgery.

**ransubstantiation** /ˌtran-suhb-ˌstan-shee-**ay**-shuhn/ n. Theol. conversion of the substance of the Eucharistic elements, bread and wine, wholly into the body and blood of Christ, only the appearance and taste (the accidents) of bread and wine still remaining. [medieval Latin: related to TRANS-, SUBSTANCE]

**ransuranic** /ˌtranz-yoo-**ran**-ik/ adj. (of a chemical element) having a higher atomic number than uranium.

**ransverse** /**tranz**-vers/ adj. situated, arranged, or acting in a crosswise direction. □ **transversely** adv. [Latin transverto -vers- turn across]

**transvestite** /tranz-**ves**-tuyt/ n. person who wears the clothes of the opposite sex, esp. as a sexual stimulus. □ **transvestism** n. [Latin vestio clothe]

**trap**[1] — n. **1 a** enclosure or device, often baited, for catching animals, usu. by affording a way in but not a way out. **b** device with bait for killing vermin, esp. a mousetrap. **2** trick betraying a person into speech or an act (is this question a trap?). **3** arrangement to catch an unsuspecting person, esp. a speeding motorist. **4** device for hurling an object, e.g. a clay pigeon, into the air to be shot at. **5 a** curve in a downpipe etc. that fills with liquid and forms a seal against the return of gases. **b** device for preventing the passage of steam etc. **6** two-wheeled carriage (pony and trap). **7** = TRAPDOOR. **8** Golf bunker. **9** (traps) colloq. percussion instruments, esp. in a jazz band. **10** colloq. mouth (esp. shut one's trap). **11** (usu. in pl.) colloq. police officer. — v. (**-pp-**) **1** catch (an animal) in a trap. **2** catch or catch out (a person) by means of a trick etc. **3** stop and retain in or as in a trap. **4** provide (a place) with traps. □ **go round the traps 1** inspect a series of traps (on a farm etc.) to see what has been caught. **2** make a tour of inspection in general; visit one's regular haunts, esp. to elicit information. **3** colloq. (as **been around the traps**) possessed of the necessary information; be experienced in the ways of the world. [Old English]

**trap**[2] n. (in full **trap-rock**) dark-coloured igneous rock. [Swedish]

**trapdoor** n. door in a floor, ceiling, or roof.

**trapdoor spider** n. any of many large burrowing spiders of Australia (and elsewhere) which dig a nest in the shape of a tube, concealing the entrance at the top with a hinged flap which opens and shuts as does a trapdoor.

**trapeze** /truh-**peez**/ n. **1** crossbar suspended by ropes as a swing for acrobatics etc. **2** similar device which enables a person to lean safely out of a small sailing boat. [Latin: related to TRAPEZIUM]

**trapezium** /truh-**pee**-zee-uhm/ n. (pl. **-zia** /-zee-uh/ or **-s**) quadrilateral with only one pair of sides parallel. [Greek trapezion]

**trapezoid** /**trap**-uh-ˌzoid/ n. quadrilateral with no two sides parallel. [Greek: related to TRAPEZIUM]

**trapper** n. person who traps wild animals, esp. for their fur.

**trappings** n.pl. **1** ornamental accessories, esp. as an indication of status (the *trappings of office*). **2** harness of a horse, esp. when ornamental. [*trap* from French *drap* cloth]

**Trappist** — *n.* monk of an order, founded at La Trappe in Normandy in 1664, noted for the extreme austerity of its rule which includes the vow of perpetual silence. — *adj.* of this order. [*La Trappe*]

**trash** *n.* **1** worthless or waste stuff; rubbish. **2** worthless person or persons, etc. □ **trashy** *adj.* (**-ier**, **-iest**). [origin unknown]

**trattoria** /trat-uh-ree-uh/ *n.* Italian restaurant. [Italian]

**trauma** /traw-muh/ *n.* (*pl.* **traumata** /-muh-tuh/ or **-s**) **1** profound emotional shock following a stressful event. **2** physical wound or injury. **3** physical shock syndrome following this, characterised by a drop in body temperature, mental confusion, etc. □ **traumatise** *v.* (also **-ize**) (**-sing** or **-zing**). [Greek, = wound]

**traumatic** /traw-**mat**-ik/ *adj.* **1** of or causing trauma. **2** *colloq.* distressing; emotionally disturbing (*traumatic experience*). □ **traumatically** *adv.* [Greek: related to TRAUMA]

**travail** /**trav**-ayl/ *literary* — *n.* **1** painful or laborious effort. **2** pangs of childbirth. — *v.* make a painful effort, esp. in childbirth. [French *travaillier*]

**travel** /**trav**-uhl/ — *v.* (**-ll-**) **1** go from one place to another; make a journey, esp. a long one or abroad. **2** a journey along or through (a country). **b** cover (a distance) in travelling. **3** *colloq.* withstand a long journey (*wines that do not travel*). **4** go from place to place as a salesman. **5** move or proceed as specified (*light travels faster than sound*). **6** *colloq.* move quickly. **7** pass, esp. in a deliberate manner, from point to point (*her eye travelled over the scene*). **8** (of a machine or part) move or operate in a specified way. — *n.* **1 a** travelling, esp. in foreign countries. **b** (often in *pl.*) spell of this. **2** range, rate, or mode of motion of a part in machinery. □ **traveller** *n.* [originally = TRAVAIL]

**travelled** *adj.* experienced in travelling (also in *comb.*: *much-travelled*).

**traveller's cheque** *n.* cheque for a fixed amount that may be cashed on signature abroad.

**traveller's joy** *n.* = OLD MAN'S BEARD.

**traveller's tale** *n.* incredible and probably untrue story.

**travelling salesman** *n.* = COMMERCIAL TRAVELLER.

**travelogue** /**trav**-uh-ˌlog/ *n.* film or illustrated lecture about travel. [from TRAVEL, after *monologue*]

**travel-sick** *adj.* suffering from nausea caused by motion in travelling. □ **travel-sickness** *n.*

**traverse** — *v.* /**trav**-uhs, truh-**vers**/ (**-sing**) **1** travel or lie across (*traversed the country*; *pit traversed by a beam*). **2** consider or discuss the whole extent of (a subject) (*tried to traverse the entire topic in half an hour*). — *n.* /**trav**-ers/ **1** sideways movement. **2** act of traversing. **3** thing, esp. part of a structure, that crosses another. □ **traversal** *n.* [French related to TRANSVERSE]

**travesty** /**trav**-uh-stee/ — *n.* (*pl.* **-ies**) grotesque misrepresentation or imitation (*travesty of justice*). — *v.* (**-ies**, **-ied**) make or be a travesty of. [French *travestir* disguise, from Italian]

**trawl** — *v.* **1** fish with a trawl. **2 a** catch by trawling. **b** (often foll. by *through*) search thoroughly (*trawled her memory for their names*). — *n.* **1** act of trawling. **2** (in full **trawl-net**) large wide-mouthed fishing-net dragged by a boat along the sea bottom. [probably Dutch *traghel* drag-net]

**trawler** *n.* **1** boat used for trawling. **2** person who trawls.

**tray** *n.* **1** flat board, usu. with a raised rim, for carrying dishes etc. **2** shallow lidless box for papers or small articles, sometimes forming a drawer in a cabinet etc. **3** flat open part of a truck on which goods are carried. [Old English]

**treacherous** /**trech**-uh-ruhs/ *adj.* **1** guilty of or involving treachery. **2** (of the weather, ice, the memory, etc.) not to be relied on; likely to fail or give way. □ **treacherously** *adv.* [French from *trichier* cheat: related to TRICK]

**treachery** /**trech**-uh-ree/ *n.* (*pl.* **-ies**) **1** violation of faith or trust; betrayal. **2** an instance of this.

**treacle** /**tree**-kuhl/ *n.* **1** syrup produced in refining sugar. **2 a** molasses. **b** golden syrup. **3** cloying sentimentality or flattery (*I can't listen to this treacle any more*). □ **treacly** *adj.* [French from Latin *theriaca* antidote against a snake-bite, from Greek *thērion* wild animal]

**tread** /tred/ — *v.* (*past* **trod**; *past part.* **trodden** or **trod**) **1** (often foll. by *on*) set down one's foot; walk, step. **2 a** walk on. **b** (often foll. by *down*) press or crush with the feet. **3** perform (steps etc.) by walking. **4** (often foll. by *in, into*) press down into the ground with the feet (*trod dirt into the carpet*). — *n.* **1** manner or sound of walking (*recognised the heavy tread*). **2** top surface of a step or stair. **3** thick moulded part of a vehicle tyre for gripping the road. **4 a** part of a wheel that touches the ground or rail. **b** part of a rail that the wheels touch. **5** part of the sole of a shoe that rests on the ground. □ **tread the boards** be an actor. **tread on air** feel elated. **tread on a person's toes** offend a person; encroach on a person's privileges etc. **tread water** maintain an upright position in water by moving the feet and hands. [Old English]

**treadle** /tred-uhl/ n. lever worked by the foot and imparting motion to a machine. [Old English: related to TREAD]

**treadmill** n. **1** device for producing motion by the weight of persons or animals stepping on steps attached to a revolving upright wheel. **2** monotonous routine work.

**treason** /tree-zuhn/ n. violation by a subject of allegiance to his or her country, e.g. by giving military information to the enemy at a time of war. [Latin: related to TRADITION]

■ **Usage** The term *high treason*, originally distinguished from *petty treason*, now means the same as *treason*.

**treasonable** adj. involving or guilty of treason.

**treasure** /trezh-uh/ — n. **1 a** precious metals or gems. **b** hoard of these. **c** accumulated wealth. **2** thing valued for its rarity, workmanship, associations, etc. (*art treasures*). **3** *colloq.* much loved or highly valued person. — v. (**-ring**) **1** value highly. **2** (often foll. by *up*) store up as valuable. [Greek *thēsauros*]

**treasurer** n. **1** person in charge of the funds of a society etc. **2** (**Treasurer**) minister responsible for the Treasury.

**treasure trove** n. **1** treasure of unknown ownership found hidden. **2** any collection or source of valuable things etc. (*the old Aborigine was a treasure trove of information about his near-extinct language*).

**treasury** n. (pl. **-ies**) **1** place or building where treasure is stored. **2** funds or revenue of a nation, institution, etc. **3** (**Treasury**) **a** department managing the public revenue of a nation. **b** offices and officers of this.

**treat** — v. **1** act or behave towards or deal with (a person or thing) in a certain way (*treated me kindly*; *treat it as a joke*). **2** apply a process to (*treat it with acid*). **3** apply medical care or attention to. **4** present or deal with (a subject) in literature or art. **5** (often foll. by *to*) provide with food, drink, or entertainment at one's own expense (*treated us to dinner*). **6** (often foll. by *with*) negotiate terms (with a person). **7** (often foll. by *of*) give a spoken or written exposition. — n. **1** event or circumstance (esp. when unexpected or unusual) that gives great pleasure. **2** meal, entertainment, etc., designed to do this. **3** (prec. by *a*) extremely good or well (*they looked a treat*; *has come on a treat*). □ **treatable** adj. [Latin *tracto* handle]

**treatise** /tree-tuhs/ n. a written work dealing formally and systematically with a subject. [Anglo-French: related to TREAT]

**treatment** n. **1** process or manner of behaving towards or dealing with a person or thing. **2** medical care or attention. **3** manner of treating a subject in literature or art. **4** (prec. by *the*) *colloq.* the customary way of dealing with a person, situation, etc. (*got the full treatment*).

**treaty** /tree-tee/ n. (pl. **-ies**) **1** formal agreement between nations, concerning cessation of hostilities, trade, human rights, etc. **2** agreement between individuals or parties. [Latin: related to TREAT]

**treble** /treb-uhl/ — adj. **1 a** threefold. **b** triple. **c** three times as much or many (*treble the amount*). **2 a** (of a voice) of the highest pitch. **b** (of an instrument) usu. of the highest pitch. — n. **1** treble quantity or thing. **2 a** *Mus.* = SOPRANO (esp. a boy's voice or part, or an instrument). **b** high-pitched voice. **3** high-frequency output of a radio, record-player, etc. **4** form of betting (on horse races etc.) which requires picking the winners of three designated races. — v. (**-ling**) make or become three times as much or many; increase threefold; multiply by three. □ **trebly** adv. [Latin: related to TRIPLE]

**treble clef** n. clef placing the G above middle C on the second lowest line of the staff.

**tree** — n. **1 a** perennial plant with a woody self-supporting main stem or trunk and usu. unbranched for some distance above the ground. **b** any similar plant having a tall, erect, usu. single stem, e.g. a palm tree. **c** shrub having a tree-like shape or form (*tree dahlia*; *tree tomato*). **2 a** diagram having a structure of branching connected lines. **b** = FAMILY TREE. — v. (**trees**; **treed**) force to take refuge in a tree (*I was treed by a dog for several hours*). □ **grow on trees** (usu. with *neg.*) be plentiful (*happiness doesn't grow on trees*). □ **treeless** adj. **tree-like** adj. **treey** /tree-ee/ adj. [Old English]

**treecreeper** n. any of many small birds of Australia (and elsewhere), creeping up tree-trunks and feeding on insects in tree-bark.

**tree duck** see WHISTLING DUCK.

**tree fern** n. (also **man fern**) any of many Australian ferns having a tall woody trunk and a canopy of arching green fronds often several metres in length.

**tree-kangaroo** n. (also **tree-climbing kangaroo**) any of various wallaby-like macropods inhabiting jungle areas of north-eastern Queensland and New Guinea, and adapted to living and foraging in trees.

**tree line** n. = TIMBERLINE.

**tree-rat** n. tree-dwelling rodent of northern Australia.

**tree ring** n. ring, in a cross-section of a tree, from one year's growth.

**tree tomato** n. = TAMARILLO.

**trefoil** /tref-oil/ n. **1** leguminous plant with leaves of three leaflets, esp. clover. **2** three-lobed ornamentation, esp. in tracery windows. [Anglo-French: related to TRI-, FOIL²]

**trek** — v. (**-kk-**) **1** travel or make one's way arduously. **2** make a long journey by foot. — n. long or arduous journey or walk. □ **trekker** n. [Dutch, = draw]

**trellis** /trel-uhs/ n. (in full **trellis-work**) lattice of light wooden or metal bars, esp. as a support for climbing plants. [French *trelis*]

**tremble** /trem-buhl/ — v. (**-ling**) **1** shake involuntarily from emotion, weakness, etc. **2** be in a state of extreme apprehension. **3** quiver (*leaves trembled in the breeze*). — n. **1** trembling; quiver (*tremble in his voice*). **2** disease or condition marked by trembling. [medieval Latin: related to TREMULOUS]

**trembly** adj. (**-ier, -iest**) *colloq.* inclined to tremble; agitated.

**tremendous** /truh-**men**-duhs/ adj. **1** *colloq.* remarkable, considerable, excellent (*tremendous surge in popularity*; *tremendous party last night*). **2** awe-inspiring, overpowering (*tremendous cataclysm of nature*). □ **tremendously** adv. [Latin *tremendus* to be trembled at: related to TREMOR]

**tremolo** /trem-uh-loh/ n. *Mus.* **1** tremulous effect in playing stringed and keyboard instruments or singing, esp. by rapid reiteration of a note. **2** device in an organ producing a tremulous effect. [Italian: related to TREMULOUS]

**tremor** /trem-uh/ n. **1** shaking, quivering. **2** thrill (*of fear, exultation, etc.*). **3** (in full **earth tremor**) slight earthquake. [Latin *tremo* tremble]

**tremulous** /trem-yuh-luhs/ adj. trembling or quivering (*in a tremulous voice*).

□ **tremulously** adv. [Latin *tremulus*: related to TREMOR]

**trench** — n. **1** long narrow usu. deep ditch. **2** *Mil.* **a** this dug by troops as a shelter from enemy fire. **b** (in *pl.*) defensive system of these. — v. dig a trench or trenches in (the ground). [French *trenche, -ier* cut]

**trenchant** /tren-chuhnt/ adj. (of style or language etc.) incisive, terse, vigorous. □ **trenchancy** n. **trenchantly** adv. [French: related to TRENCH]

**trench coat** n. **1** soldier's lined or padded waterproof coat. **2** loose belted raincoat.

**trencher** n. **1** *hist.* wooden or earthenware platter for serving food. **2** stiff square academic cap. [Anglo-French: related to TRENCH]

**trend** — n. general direction and tendency (esp. of events, fashion, or opinion). — v. **1** bend or turn away in a specified direction. **2** have a general tendency. [Old English]

**trendoid** /tren-doid/ *colloq. derog.* — n. person who is ultra-trendy in dress, life-style, etc. — adj. ultra-trendy. [TRENDY, -OID]

**trendsetter** n. person who leads the way in fashion etc.

**trendy** *colloq.*; often *derog.* — adj. (**-ier, -iest**) fashionable, 'with it'. — n. (*pl.* **-ies**) person who is fashionable, 'with it', as regards clothes, life-style, etc. □ **trendily** adv. **trendiness** n.

**trepan** /truh-**pan**/ n. cylindrical saw formerly used by surgeons for removing part of the skull. [Greek *trupanon* auger]

**trepidation** /trep-uh-**day**-shuhn/ n. fear, anxiety. [Latin *trepidus* flurried]

**trespass** /tres-puhs/ — v. **1** (usu. foll. by *on, upon*) make an unlawful or unauthorised intrusion (esp. on land or property). **2** (foll. by *on*) make unjustifiable claims on; encroach on (*trespass on your hospitality*). — n. **1** *Law* act of trespassing. **2** *archaic* sin, offence. □ **trespasser** n. [medieval Latin: related to TRANS-, PASS¹]

**tress** n. **1** long lock of human (esp. female) hair. **2** (in *pl.*) woman's or girl's head of hair. [French]

**trestle** /tres-uhl/ n. **1** supporting structure for a table etc., consisting of two frames fixed at an angle or hinged, or of a bar with two divergent pairs of legs. **2** (in full **trestle-table**) table of a board or boards on trestles etc. **3** (in full **trestle-work**) open braced framework to support a bridge etc. [Latin *transtrum* crossbeam]

**trevally** /truh-**val**-ee/ n. (*pl.* same or **-ies**) any of several Australian marine fish, many of which are fished commercially.

[possibly an alteration of *cavally* horse-mackerel]

**trey** /tray/ *n.* (in full **trey-bit**) *hist.* Australian threepenny coin. [ultimately from Latin *tres* three]

**tri-** *comb. form* three or three times. [Latin and Greek]

**triad** /truy-ad/ *n.* **1** group of three connected persons or things (esp. notes in a chord). **2** (also **Triad**) Chinese secret society, usu. criminal. □ **triadic** /-ad-ik/ *adj.* [Latin from Greek]

**triage** /tree-ahj/ *n.* **1** act of sorting according to quality. **2** assignment of degrees of urgency to decide the order of treatment of wounds, illnesses, etc. [French]

**trial** /truyl/ *n.* **1** judicial examination and determination of issues between parties by a judge with or without a jury. **2 a** process or mode of testing qualities. **b** experimental treatment. **c** test (*will give you a trial*). **3** trying thing or experience or person, esp. hardship or trouble (*trials of old age*; *he's such a trial*). **4** match or competition held to select players for a team. **5** (often in *pl.*) contest involving performance by horses, dogs, motor cycles, etc. □ **on trial 1** being tried in a court of law. **2** being tested; to be chosen or retained only if suitable. [Anglo-French: related to TRY]

**trial and error** *n.* repeated (usu. unsystematic) attempts continued until successful.

**trial run** *n.* preliminary operational test.

**triangle** /truy-ang-guhl/ *n.* **1** plane figure with three sides and angles. **2** any three things not in a straight line, with imaginary lines joining them. **3** implement of this shape. **4** musical instrument consisting of a steel rod bent into a triangle, struck with a small steel rod. **5** *hist.* tripod to which a convict in Australia (later any prisoner) was tied before being flogged. **6** a relationship of three people, esp. one involving sexual rivalry. □ **triangular** /truy-ang-gyuh-luh/ *adj.* [Latin: related to TRI-]

**triangulate** /truy-ang-gyuh-layt/ *v.* (**-ting**) measure and map out (an area) by dividing it into triangles. □ **triangulation** /-lay-shuhn/ *n.*

**triantelope** /truy-an-tuh-lohp/ *n.* = HUNTSMAN[2]. [corruption of TARANTULA sense 3]

**Triassic** /truy-as-ik/ *Geol.* — *adj.* of the earliest period of the Mesozoic era. — *n.* this period. [related to TRIAD]

**triathlon** /truy-ath-lon/ *n.* athletic contest of three events (swimming, cycling,

running) for all competitors. [from TRI- after DECATHLON]

**tribal** /truy-buhl/ *adj.* of, relating to, or characteristic of, a tribe or tribes, esp., in Australia, a traditional Aboriginal community.

**tribe** *n.* **1 a** group of families or communities, linked by social, religious, or blood ties, and usu. having a common culture and dialect and a recognised leader. **b** name applied, orig. by colonists in Australia, to a traditional Aboriginal community. **2** any similar natural or political division. **3** usu. *derog.* or *joc.* set or number of persons, esp. of one profession etc. or family (*the whole tribe is gathering at our place this Christmas*). **4** *Biol.* group of plants or animals usu. ranking between genus and the subfamily. □ **tribalism** *n.* [Latin *tribus*]

**tribesman** *n.* (*fem.* **-woman**) member of a tribe.

**tribology** /truy-bol-uh-jee/ *n.* the study of friction, wear, lubrication, and the design of bearings. [Greek *tribō* rub]

**tribulation** /trib-yuh-lay-shuhn/ *n.* great affliction or oppression. [Latin *tribulum* threshing-sledge]

**tribunal** /truy-byoo-nuhl/ *n.* **1** board appointed to adjudicate in some matter. **2** court of justice. [Latin: related to TRIBUNE]

**tribune[1]** /trib-yoon/ *n.* **1** protector of the rights of the people; popular leader. **2** (in full **tribune of the people**) official in ancient Rome chosen by the people to protect their interests. [Latin *tribunus*: related to TRIBE]

**tribune[2]** /trib-yoon/ *n.* **1 a** bishop's throne in a basilica. **b** apse containing this. **2** dais, rostrum. [medieval Latin *tribuna*: related to TRIBUNAL]

**tributary** /trib-yuh-tuh-ree, -tree/ — *n.* (*pl.* **-ies**) **1** river or stream flowing into a larger river or lake. **2** *hist.* person or nation paying or subject to tribute. — *adj.* **1** (of a river etc.) that is a tributary. **2** *hist.* **a** paying tribute. **b** serving as tribute. [Latin: related to TRIBUTE]

**tribute** /trib-yoot/ *n.* **1** thing said or done or given as a mark of respect or affection etc. (*paid tribute to their achievement*; *floral tributes*). **2** (foll. by *to*) indication of (some praiseworthy quality) (*their success is a tribute to their perseverance*). **3** *hist.* **a** periodic payment by one nation or ruler to another, esp. as a sign of dependence. **b** obligation to pay this. [Latin *tributum* neuter past part. of *tribuo* -*ut*- assign, originally divide between tribes]

**trice** n. □ **in a trice** in an instant. [*trice* haul up, from Low German and Dutch]

**triceps** /**truy**-seps/ n. muscle (esp. in the upper arm) with three points of attachment. [Latin *caput* head]

**triceratops** /ˌtruy-**se**-ruh-ˌtops/ n. dinosaur with three sharp horns on the forehead and a wavy-edged collar round the neck. [Greek, = three-horned face]

**trichinosis** /ˌtrik-uh-**noh**-suhs/ n. disease caused by hairlike worms usu. ingested in meat. [Greek *thrix trikh*- hair]

**trichromatic** /ˌtruy-kruh-**mat**-ik/ adj. **1** having or using three colours. **2** (of vision) having the normal three colour-sensations, i.e. red, green, and purple.

**trick** — n. **1** action or scheme undertaken to deceive or outwit. **2** illusion (*trick of the light*). **3** special technique; knack (*he has the trick of making perfect pastry*). **4 a** feat of skill or dexterity (*juggling six eggs is quite a trick*; *magic tricks*). **b** unusual action (e.g. begging) learned by an animal. **5** foolish or discreditable act; practical joke (*a mean trick to play*). **6** peculiar or characteristic habit or mannerism (*has a trick of repeating himself*). **7 a** cards played in one round of a card-game. **b** point gained in this. **8** (attrib.) done to deceive or mystify (*trick photography*; *trick question*). **9** colloq. prostitute's client; casual sexual partner. — v. **1** deceive by a trick; outwit. **2** (often foll. by *out of*) swindle (*tricked out of his savings*). **3** (foll. by *into*) cause to do something by trickery (*tricked into marriage*; *tricked me into agreeing*). **4** foil, baffle; take by surprise. □ **can't** (or **not be able to**) **take a trick** be consistently unsuccessful or unlucky. **do the trick** colloq. achieve the required result. **how's tricks?** colloq. how are you? **not miss a trick** see MISS. **trick or treat** children's custom of calling at houses at Hallowe'en with the threat of pranks if they are not given a small gift. **trick out** (or **up**) dress or deck out. [French]

**trickery** n. deception, use of tricks.

**trickle** /**trik**-uhl/ — v. (**-ling**) **1** (cause to) flow in drops or a small stream. **2** come or go slowly or gradually (*information trickles out*). — n. trickling flow (*trickle of water*; *trickle of enquiries*). [probably imitative]

**trickster** n. deceiver, rogue.

**tricksy** adj. (**-ier**, **-iest**) full of tricks; playful.

**tricky** adj. (**-ier**, **-iest**) **1** requiring care and adroitness (*tricky job*). **2** crafty, deceitful. □ **trickily** adv. **trickiness** n.

**tricolour** /**truy**-ˌkul-uh, **trik**-uh-luh/ n. (also **tricolor**) flag of three bands of different colours, esp. the French or Irish national flags. [French: related to TRI-]

**tricycle** /**truy**-si-kuhl/ n. three-wheeled pedal-driven vehicle similar to a bicycle.

**trident** /**truy**-duhnt/ n. three-pronged spear. [Latin *dens dent*- tooth]

**Tridentine** /truy-**den**-tuyn/ adj. of the Council of Trent, held at Trento in Italy 1545–63, esp. as the basis of Roman Catholic orthodoxy. [medieval Latin *Tridentum* Trento]

**tried** past and past part. of TRY.

**triennial** /truy-**en**-ee-uhl/ adj. lasting, or recurring every, three years. [Latin *annus* year]

**trier** /**truy**-uh/ n. person or animal that perseveres.

**trifecta** /truy-**fek**-tuh/ n. form of betting in which the first three places in a race must be predicted in the correct order. [TRI-, (*per*)*fecta* form of betting in which the gambler must pick first and second]

**trifle** /**truy**-fuhl/ — n. **1** thing of slight value or importance. **2 a** small amount, esp. of money (*was sold for a trifle*). **b** (prec. by *a*) somewhat (*a trifle annoyed*). **3** dessert of sponge cake with custard, jelly, fruit, cream, etc. — v. (**-ling**) **1** talk or act frivolously. **2** (foll. by *with*) treat or deal with frivolously; flirt heartlessly with. **3** (follow. by *away*) waste (time, energies, money, etc.) frivolously. [originally *trufle* from French = *truf(f)e* deceit]

**trifling** adj. **1** unimportant, petty. **2** frivolous.

**triforium** /truy-**faw**-ree-uhm/ n. (pl. **-ria**) gallery or arcade above the arches of the nave, choir, and transepts of a church. [Anglo-Latin]

**trig** n. colloq. trigonometry. [abbreviation]

**trigger** — n. **1** movable device for releasing a spring or catch and so setting off a mechanism (esp. that of a gun). **2** event, occurrence, etc., that sets off a chain reaction. — v. (often foll. by *off*) set (an action or process) in motion; precipitate. □ **quick on the trigger** quick to respond. **trigger-happy** apt to shoot on the slightest provocation. [*tricker* from Dutch *trekker* from *trekken* pull]

**trigger plant** n. (also **trigger flower**, **stylidium**) any of numerous Australian plants in the genus *Stylidium*, the flowers (white to deep rose-red) having a unique device for pollination: an insect landing on a flower triggers a hammer which springs down and hits the insect on the back, dusting it with pollen, the hammer automatically resetting itself after a while.

**trigonometry** /ˌtrig-uh-**nom**-uh-tree/ *n.* branch of mathematics dealing with the relations of the sides and angles of triangles and with the relevant functions of any angles. □ **trigonometric** /-nuh-**met**-rik/ *adj.* **trigonometrical** /-nuh-**met**-ri-kuhl/ *adj.* [Greek *trigōnon* triangle]

**trike** *n. colloq.* tricycle. [abbreviation]

**trilateral** /truy-**lat**-uh-ruhl/ *adj.* **1** of, on, or with three sides. **2** involving three parties. [Latin: related to TRI-]

**trilingual** /truy-**ling**-gwuhl/ *adj.* **1** able to speak three languages. **2** spoken or written in three languages.

**trill** — *n.* **1** quavering sound, esp. a rapid alternation of two consecutive notes being sung or played on an instrument. **2** similar sound made by a bird; a warble. **3** pronunciation of *r* with vibration of the tongue. — *v.* **1** produce a trill. **2** warble (a song) or pronounce (*r* etc.) with a trill. [Italian]

**triller** *n.* either of two Australian birds with a distinctive trilling call (*varied triller*; *white-winged triller*).

**trillion** /**tril**-yuhn/ *n.* (*pl.* same) **1** a million million ($10^{12}$). **2** (now less often) a million million million ($10^{18}$). □ **trillionth** *adj. & n.* [French or Italian: related to TRI-, MILLION, after *billion*]

**trilobite** /**truy**-luh-ˌbuyt/ *n.* a kind of fossil marine arthropod of Palæozoic times, characterised by a three-lobed body. [from TRI-, Greek *lobos* lobe]

**trilogy** /**tril**-uh-jee/ *n.* (*pl.* **-ies**) group of three related novels, plays, operas, etc.

**trim** — *v.* (**-mm-**) **1 a** make neat or of the required size or form, esp. by cutting away irregular or unwanted parts (*trim the joint of fat*; *will you trim my hair?*). **b** set in good order (*trim the garden beds*). **2** (foll. by *off*, *away*) cut off (unwanted parts) (*trimmed away the spent flowers*). **3** ornament, decorate (*trim a Christmas tree*). **4** adjust the balance of (a ship or aircraft) by arranging its cargo etc. **5** arrange (sails) to suit the wind. **6 a** associate oneself with currently prevailing views, esp. to advance oneself (*he trims to every popular notion*). **b** hold a middle course in politics or opinion. **7** reduce the size, amount, or number of; eliminate (wasteful expenditure etc.) (*need to trim the budget*). — *n.* **1** state of readiness or fitness (*in perfect trim*). **2** ornament or decorative material. **3** trimming of a person's hair. — *adj.* (**trimmer**, **trimmest**) **1** neat or spruce. **2** in good order; well arranged or equipped. □ **trim one's sails** (**to the wind**) adapt oneself to

circumstances. [Old English, = make firm]

**trimaran** /**truy**-muh-ˌran/ *n.* vessel like a catamaran, with a central hull and a float on each side. [from CATAMARAN]

**trimeter** /**trim**-uh-tuh/ *n. Prosody* line of verse of three measures. [Greek: see TRI-, -METER]

**trimmer** *n. colloq.* striking or outstanding person or thing.

**trimming** *n.* **1** ornamentation or decoration, esp. for clothing. **2** (in *pl.*) usual accompaniments, esp. of the main course of a meal.

**Trinitarian** /ˌtrin-uh-**tair**-ree-uhn/ — *n.* believer in the Trinity. — *adj.* of this belief. □ **Trinitarianism** *n.*

**trinitrotoluene** /truy-ˌnuy-truh-**tol**-yoo-ˌeen/ *n.* (also **trinitrotoluol** /-**tol**-yoo-ˌol/) = TNT.

**trinity** /**trin**-uh-tee/ *n.* (*pl.* **-ies**) **1** state of being three. **2** group of three. **3** (**the Trinity** or **Holy Trinity**) *Theol.* the three persons of the Christian Godhead (Father, Son, and Holy Spirit), each being God, although there is only one God not three. [Latin *trinitas* from *trinus* threefold]

**Trinity Sunday** *n.* Sunday next after Whit Sunday.

**trinket** /**tring**-kuht/ *n.* trifling ornament, esp. a piece of jewellery. □ **trinketry** *n.* [origin unknown]

**trinomial** /truy-**noh**-mee-uhl/ — *adj.* consisting of three terms. — *n.* scientific name or algebraic expression consisting of three terms. [TRI- after BINOMIAL]

**trio** /**tree**-oh/ *n.* (*pl.* **-s**) **1** group of three. **2** *Mus.* **a** composition for three performers. **b** the performers. [French and Italian from Latin]

**trip** — *v.* (**-pp-**) **1 a** (often foll. by *up*) stumble or cause to stumble, esp. by catching or entangling the feet. **b** (foll. by *up*) make or cause to make a slip or blunder. **2 a** move with quick light steps. **b** (of a rhythm etc.) run lightly. **3** make an excursion to a place. **4 a** operate (a mechanism) suddenly by knocking aside a catch etc. **b** automatically cut out. **5** *colloq.* have a hallucinatory experience caused by a drug. — *n.* **1** journey or excursion, esp. for pleasure. **2 a** stumble or blunder. **b** act of tripping or state of being tripped up. **3** nimble step. **4** *colloq.* drug-induced hallucinatory experience. **5** device for tripping a mechanism etc. [Dutch *trippen* skip, hop]

**tripartite** /truy-**pah**-tuyt/ *adj.* **1** consisting of three parts. **2** shared by or involving three parties. [Latin *partior* divide]

**tripe** n. **1** first or second stomach of a ruminant, esp. an ox, as food. **2** colloq. nonsense, rubbish. □ **beat the tripe out of** colloq. thrash or defeat thoroughly. [French]

**triple** /**trip**-uhl/ — adj. **1** consisting of three usu. equal parts or things; threefold. **2** involving three parties. **3** three times as much or many. — n. **1** threefold number or amount. **2** set of three. — v. (**-ling**) multiply by three. □ **triply** adv. [Latin triplus from Greek]

**triple antigen** /**an**-tuh-juhn/ n. vaccine administered, usu. in infancy, as protection against diphtheria, whooping cough, and tetanus.

**triple crown** n. official tiara of the pope.

**triple jump** n. athletic contest comprising a hop, step, and jump.

**triplet** /**trip**-luht/ n. **1** each of three children or animals born at one birth. **2** set of three things, esp. three equal notes played in the time of two of the same value, or three lines of verse rhyming together.

**triple time** n. Mus. three beats to the bar, as in a waltz.

**triplicate** — adj. /**trip**-luh-kuht/ **1** existing in three examples or copies. **2** having three corresponding parts. **3** tripled. — n. /**trip**-luh-kuht/ each of a set of three copies or corresponding parts. — v. /**trip**-luh-ˌkayt/ (**-ting**) **1** make in three copies. **2** multiply by three. □ **in triplicate** in three copies. □ **triplication** /-**kay**-shuhn/ n. [Latin tri-, plico fold (v.)]

**tripod** /**truy**-pod/ n. **1** three-legged stand for a camera etc. **2** stool, table, or utensil resting on three feet or legs. [Greek, = three-footed]

**triptych** /**trip**-tik/ n. picture or relief carving on three panels, usu. hinged together at the sides. [after DIPTYCH]

**tripwire** n. wire stretched close to the ground to trip up an intruder or to operate an alarm or other device when disturbed.

**trireme** /**truy**-reem/ n. ancient Greek warship, with three files of oarsmen on each side. [Latin remus oar]

**trisect** /truy-**sekt**/ v. divide into three (usu. equal) parts. □ **trisection** n. [Latin seco sect- cut]

**trite** adj. (of a phrase, observation, etc.) hackneyed; worn out by constant repetition. □ **tritely** adv. **triteness** n. [Latin tero trit- rub]

**tritium** /**trit**-ee-uhm/ n. radioactive isotope of hydrogen with a mass about three times that of ordinary hydrogen. [Greek tritos third]

**triumph** /**truy**-uhmf, -umf/ — n. **1 a** state of victory or success (returned in triumph). **b** a great success or achievement. **2** supreme example (a triumph of engineering). **3** joy at success; exultation (triumph in her face). **4** processional entry of a victorious general into ancient Rome. — v. **1** (often foll. by over) gain a victory; be successful. **2** (of an ancient Roman general) ride in triumph. **3** (often foll. by over) rejoice; exult. □ **triumphal** /truy-**um**-fuhl/ adj. [French from Latin]

■ Usage Triumphal, meaning 'of or used in celebrating a triumph' as in triumphal arch should not be confused with triumphant meaning 'victorious' or 'exultant'.

**triumphant** /truy-**um**-fuhnt/ adj. **1** victorious, successful. **2** exultant. □ **triumphantly** adv.

■ Usage See note at triumph.

**triumvirate** /truy-**um**-vuh-ruht/ n. ruling group of three men, esp. in ancient Rome. [Latin tres three, vir man]

**triune** /**truy**-yoon/ adj. three in one, esp. with ref. to the Trinity. [TRI-, Latin unus one]

**trivalent** /truy-**vay**-luhnt/ adj. Chem. having a valency of three. □ **trivalency** n.

**trivia** /**triv**-ee-uh/ n.pl. trifles or trivialities.

**trivial** /**triv**-ee-uhl/ adj. **1** of small value or importance; trifling. **2** (of a person etc.) concerned only with trivial things. □ **triviality** /-al-uh-tee/ n. (pl. **-ies**). **trivially** adv. [Latin trivialis commonplace, from trivium three-way street corner]

**trivialise** v. (also **-ize**) (**-sing** or **-zing**) make or treat as trivial; minimise. □ **trivialisation** /-**zay**-shuhn/ n.

**trochee** /**troh**-kee/ n. Prosody metrical foot consisting of one long followed by one short syllable (– ˘). □ **trochaic** /truh-**kay**-ik/ adj. [Greek, = running]

**trod** past and past part. of TREAD.

**trodden** past part. of TREAD.

**troglodyte** /**trog**-luh-ˌduyt/ n. **1** cave-dweller. **2** colloq. derog. **a** wilfully obscurantist or old-fashioned person. **b** boorish or obnoxious person. [Greek trōglē hole]

**troika** /**troi**-kuh/ n. **1 a** Russian vehicle with a team of three horses abreast. **b** this team. **2** group of three people, esp. as an administrative council. [Russian]

**Trojan** /**troh**-juhn/ — adj. of ancient Troy in Asia Minor. — n. **1** native or inhabitant of Troy. **2** (**trojan**) person who works, fights, etc., courageously. [Latin Troia Troy]

**Trojan Horse** *n.* **1** hollow wooden horse inside which the Greeks entered Troy. **2 a** person or device planted to bring about an enemy's downfall. **b** computer program, performing some useful function, which simultaneously breaches the security of any computer that it is used on, causing damage to data, etc.

**troll**¹ *n.* (in Scandinavian folklore) fabulous being, esp. a giant or dwarf dwelling in a cave. [Old Norse]

**troll**² *v.* fish by drawing bait along in the water. [perhaps related to French *troller* to quest]

**trolley** /trol-ee/ *n.* (*pl.* **-s**) **1** table, stand, or basket on wheels or castors for serving food, transporting luggage etc., gathering purchases in a supermarket, etc. **2** low truck running on rails. [British dial., perhaps from TROLL²]

**trollop** /trol-uhp/ *n.* disreputable girl or woman. [perhaps related to archaic *trull* prostitute]

**trombone** /trom-**bohn**/ *n.* brass wind instrument with a sliding tube. □ **trombonist** *n.* [French or Italian *tromba* TRUMPET]

***trompe-l'œil*** /tromp-**ler**-ee/ *n.* (often *attrib.*) painting etc. designed to give an illusion of reality. [French, literally 'deceives the eye']

**-tron** *suffix Physics* forming nouns denoting: **1** elementary particle (*positron*). **2** particle accelerator. [from ELECTRON]

**troop** — *n.* **1** assembled company; assemblage of people or animals. **2** (in *pl.*) soldiers, armed forces. **3** cavalry unit under a captain. **4** unit of artillery or armoured vehicles. **5** grouping of three or more Scout patrols. — *v.* **1** (foll. by *in*, *out*, *off*, etc.) come together or move in large numbers. **2** carry or parade (a COLOUR *n.* 8b or flag) in a ceremonial manner before assembled troops. [French *troupe*]

**trooper** *n.* **1** private soldier in a cavalry or armoured unit. **2** *hist.* mounted police officer in Australia, esp. on the goldfields. **3** = TROUPER. □ **swear like a trooper** swear excessively or forcefully.

**trophic** /**troh**-fik/ *adj.* of or concerned with nutrition (*trophic nerves*). [Greek]

**trophy** /**troh**-fee/ *n.* (*pl.* **-ies**) **1** cup etc. as a prize in a contest. **2** memento or souvenir of success in hunting, war, etc. [Greek *tropaion*]

**tropic** /**trop**-ik/ — *n.* **1** parallel of latitude 23°27′ north (**tropic of Cancer**) or south (**tropic of Capricorn**) of the Equator. **2** each of two corresponding circles on the celestial sphere where the sun appears to turn when at its greatest declination. **3** (**the tropics** or **the Tropics**) region

between the tropics of Cancer and Capricorn. — *adj.* = TROPICAL. [Greek *tropē* turn]

**tropical** *adj.* **1** of or typical of the tropics. **2** very hot; luxuriant.

**tropism** /**troh**-piz-uhm/ *n. Biol.* turning of all or part of an organism in a particular direction in response to an external stimulus. [Greek, = a turning]

**troposphere** /**trop**-uh-ˌsfeer, **troh**-puh-/ *n.* layer of atmosphere extending about 6–10 km upwards from the earth's surface. [Greek *tropos* turn]

**troppo** /**trop**-oh/ *adj. colloq.* mentally disturbed, allegedly as a result of spending too much time in the tropics; mad, crazy. □ **go troppo** *colloq.* become so disturbed. [TROP(IC), -O]

**trot** — *v.* (**-tt-**) **1** (of a person) run at a moderate pace, esp. with short strides. **2** (of a horse) proceed at a steady pace faster than a walk, lifting each diagonal pair of legs alternately. **3** *colloq.* walk, go. **4** cause (a horse or person) to trot. **5** traverse (a distance) at a trot. — *n.* **1** action or exercise of trotting (*proceed at a trot*; *went for a trot*). **2** (in *pl.*) programme of harness-racing. **3** (**the trots**) *colloq.* diarrhoea. **4** uninterrupted sequence, esp. in a game of chance; run of good or bad luck. □ **on the trot** *colloq.* **1** in succession (*six days on the trot*). **2** continually busy (*kept me on the trot*). **trot out** *colloq.* introduce (an opinion etc.) tediously or repeatedly. [French]

**troth** /trohth/ *n. archaic* **1** faith, loyalty. **2** truth. □ **pledge** (or **plight**) **one's troth** pledge one's word, esp. in marriage or betrothal. [Old English: related to TRUTH]

**Trotskyism** /**trot**-skee-ˌiz-uhm/ *n.* political principles of L. Trotsky (d. 1940), esp. as urging worldwide socialist revolution. □ **Trotskyist** *n.* **Trotskyite** *n.*

**trotter** *n.* **1** (usu. in *pl.*) animal's foot as food. **2** horse bred or trained for trotting.

**trotting** *n.* (also **harness-racing**) form of horse racing in which a horse pulls a two-wheeled vehicle (a sulky) while trotting.

**troubadour** /**troo**-buh-ˌdaw/ *n.* **1** singer or poet. **2** French medieval lyric poet singing of courtly love. [Provençal *trobar* find, compose]

**trouble** /**trub**-uhl/ — *n.* **1** difficulty or distress; vexation, affliction (*had trouble with my car*). **2 a** inconvenience; unpleasant exertion; bother (*went to a lot of trouble*). **b** cause of this (*she was no trouble*). **3** perceived failing (*the trouble with me is that I can't say no*). **4** dysfunction (*kidney trouble*; *engine trouble*). **5 a** disturbance; unrest (*crowd trouble*; *don't want any trouble*). **b** disagreement;

strife (*is having trouble at home*). — *v.* (**-ling**) **1** cause distress or anxiety to; disturb. **2** be disturbed or worried (*don't trouble about it*). **3** afflict; cause pain etc. to (*am troubled with arthritis*). **4** (often *refl.*) subject or be subjected to inconvenience or unpleasant exertion (*sorry to trouble you; don't trouble yourself*). □ **ask** (or **look**) **for trouble** invite trouble by one's actions, behaviour, etc.; be rash or indiscreet. **in trouble** involved in a matter likely to bring censure or punishment. [Latin: related to TURBID]

**troublemaker** *n.* person habitually causing trouble. □ **troublemaking** *n.*

**troubleshooter** *n.* **1** mediator in a dispute. **2** person who traces and corrects faults in machinery or in an organisation etc. □ **troubleshooting** *n.*

**troublesome** *adj.* causing trouble, annoying.

**trough** /trof/ *n.* **1** long narrow open receptacle for water, animal feed, etc. **2** channel or hollow like this. **3** elongated region of low barometric pressure. [Old English]

**trounce** *v.* (**-cing**) **1** defeat heavily. **2** beat, thrash. **3** punish severely. [origin unknown]

**troupe** /troop/ *n.* company or band of actors etc. [French, = TROOP]

**trouper** *n.* **1** member of a theatrical troupe. **2** staunch colleague.

**trousers** /trow-zuhz/ *n.pl.* **1** two-legged outer garment reaching from the waist usu. to the ankles. **2** (**trouser**) (*attrib.*) designating part of this (*trouser leg*). [in pl. after *drawers*: Irish and Gaelic *triubhas* trews]

**trousseau** /troo-soh/ *n.* (*pl.* **-s** or **-x** /-sohz/) bride's collection of clothes etc. [French: related to TRUSS]

**trout** *n.* (*pl.* same or **-s**) **1** any of various mainly Northern hemisphere freshwater fish, famed as food, some of which have been introduced into Australian waters. **2** any of several Australian food-fish unrelated to the Northern hemisphere trout (e.g. the *salmon trout*). [Latin *tructa*]

**trowel** /trowl/ — *n.* **1** small flat-bladed tool for spreading mortar etc. **2** scoop for lifting small plants or earth. — *v.* (**-ll-**) apply or spread (mortar etc.) with a trowel. [Latin *trulla*]

**troy** *n.* (in full **troy weight**) imperial system of weights used for precious metals and gems, with a pound of 12 ounces or 5,760 grains; 1 oz. troy = 31.1035 g. [probably *Troyes* in France]

**truant** /troo-uhnt/ — *n.* **1** child who stays away from school. **2** person who

avoids work etc. — *adj.* (of a person, conduct, thoughts, etc.) shirking, idle, wandering. — *v.* (also **play truant**) be a truant. □ **truancy** *n.* [French, probably from Celtic]

**truce** /troos/ *n.* temporary agreement to cease hostilities. [originally *trewes* pl.: Old English, = covenant: related to TRUE]

**truck¹** — *n.* **1** large powerful motor vehicle for transporting goods etc. **2** open railway wagon for freight. — *v.* convey in or on a truck. □ **fall off the back of a truck** see FALL. **keep on trucking** *colloq.* (phrase of encouragement) persevere. [perhaps from TRUCKLE]

**truck²** *n.* dealings. □ **have no truck with** avoid dealing with. [French *troquer*]

**truckie** /truk-ee/ *n. colloq.* driver of a truck. [*truck* (*driver*), -Y²]

**truckle** /truk-uhl/ — *n.* (in full **truckle-bed**) low bed on wheels, stored under a larger bed. — *v.* (**-ling**) (foll. by *to*) submit obsequiously (*he would not truckle to threats*). [Latin *trochlea* pulley]

**truculent** /truk-yuh-luhnt/ *adj.* aggressively defiant. □ **truculence** *n.* **truculently** *adv.* [Latin *trux truc-* fierce]

**trudge** — *v.* (**-ging**) **1** go on foot, esp. laboriously. **2** traverse (a distance) in this way. — *n.* trudging walk. [origin unknown]

**true** /troo/ — *adj.* (**truer, truest**) **1** in accordance with fact or reality (*a true story*). **2** genuine; rightly or strictly so called (*a true friend*; *true heir to the throne*). **3** (often foll. by *to*) loyal, faithful (*true to one's word*; *true to me through thick and thin*). **4** (foll. by *to*) accurately conforming to (a type or standard) (*true to form*). **5** correctly positioned or balanced; upright, level. **6** exact, accurate (*a true copy*). — *adv.* **1** *archaic* truly (*tell me true*). **2** accurately (*aim true*). **3** without variation (*breed true*). □ **come true** actually happen. [Old English]

**true-blue** *adj.* **1 a** extremely loyal. **b** extremely orthodox or conservative. **2** genuine (*a true-blue Aussie*).

**true north** *n.* north according to the earth's axis, not magnetic north.

**truffle** /truf-uhl/ *n.* **1** edible rich-flavoured underground fungus. **2** sweet made of a chocolate mixture covered with cocoa etc. [probably Dutch from French]

**trugo** /troo-goh/ *n.* game in which a disc is struck towards a goal with a mallet. [TRUE, GO]

**truism** /troo-iz-uhm/ *n.* statement too hackneyed to be worth making, e.g. 'Nothing lasts for ever'.

**truly** /**troo**-lee/ *adv.* **1** sincerely (*am truly grateful*). **2** really, indeed (*truly, I do not know*). **3** loyally (*served them truly*). **4** accurately (*is not truly depicted*). **5** properly (*well and truly*). [Old English: related to TRUE]

**trump**[1] — *n.* **1 a** playing-card of a suit temporarily ranking above the others. **b** (in *pl.*) this suit (*hearts are trumps*). **2** *colloq.* **a** generous or loyal person. **b** person in authority. — *v.* **1** defeat (a card or its player) with a trump. **2** *colloq.* outdo. □ **come** (or **turn**) **up trumps** *colloq.* **1** turn out better than expected. **2** be greatly successful or helpful. **trump up** fabricate or invent (an accusation etc.) (*trumped-up charge*). [corruption of TRIUMPH in the same (now obsolete) sense]

**trump**[2] *n. archaic* trumpet-blast. [French *trompe*]

**trump card** *n.* **1** card belonging to, or turned up to determine, a trump suit. **2** *colloq.* valuable resource, esp. kept in reserve.

**trumpery** /**trum**-puh-ree/ — *n.* (*pl.* **-ies**) **1** worthless finery. **2** worthless thing; rubbish. — *adj.* showy but worthless; trashy; shallow. [French *tromperie* deceit]

**trumpet** /**trum**-puht/ — *n.* **1** brass instrument with a flared bell and bright penetrating tone. **2** trumpet-shaped thing (*ear-trumpet*). **3** sound of or like a trumpet. — *v.* (**-t-**) **1 a** blow a trumpet. **b** (of an enraged elephant etc.) make a trumpet-like cry. **2** proclaim loudly. [French diminutive: related to TRUMP[2]]

**trumpeter** *n.* **1** person who plays or sounds a trumpet. **2** (also **stripey, Tasmanian trumpeter**) any of several food-fish of south-eastern Australian waters, reputed to make a grunting or trumpeting sound when taken out of the water.

**trumpeter whiting** *n.* any of several food-fish of the whiting family, inhabiting northern, eastern, and western waters of Australia.

**truncate** /trung-**kayt**/ *v.* (**-ting**) cut the top or the end from; shorten. □ **truncation** /-**kay**-shuhn/ *n.* [Latin: related to TRUNK]

**truncheon** /**trun**-shuhn/ *n.* short club carried by a police officer. [French *tronchon* stump: related to TRUNK]

**trundle** /**trun**-duhl/ *v.* (**-ling**) roll or move, esp. heavily or noisily, esp. on, or as on, wheels. [var. of obsolete or British dial. *trendle*: related to TREND]

**trunk** *n.* **1** main stem of a tree. **2** body without the limbs and head. **3** large box with a hinged lid for luggage, storage, etc. **4** elephant's elongated prehensile nose. **5** (in *pl.*) men's close-fitting shorts worn for swimming etc. [Latin *truncus* cut short]

**trunk line** *n.* main line of a railway, telephone system, etc.

**truss** — *n.* **1** framework supporting a roof, bridge, etc. **2** surgical appliance worn to support a hernia. **3** bundle of hay or straw. **4** compact terminal cluster of flowers or fruit. — *v.* **1** tie up (a fowl) for cooking. **2** (often foll. by *up*) tie (a person) up with the arms to the sides. **3** support (a roof or bridge etc.) with a truss or trusses. [French]

**trust** — *n.* **1** firm belief in the reliability, truth, or strength etc., of a person or thing. **2** confident expectation. **3** obligation or responsibility (for a thing or person committed to one's care) (*have fulfilled my trust*). **4** commercial credit (*obtained goods on trust*). **5** *Law* **a** arrangement whereby a person or group manages property on another's behalf. **b** property so held. **c** body of trustees. **6** association of companies for reducing competition etc. — *v.* **1** place trust in; believe in; rely on the character or behaviour of. **2** (foll. by *with*) allow (a person) to have or use (a thing) from confidence in its careful use (*trusted her with my car*). **3** (often foll. by *that*) have faith, confidence, or hope, that a thing will take place (*I trust you will come*). **4** (foll. by *to*) consign (a thing) to (a person) with trust. **5** (foll. by *in*) place reliance in (*we trust in you*). **6** (foll. by *to*) place (esp. undue) reliance on (*trust to luck*). □ **in trust** (of property) managed by one or more persons on behalf of another. **take on trust** accept (an assertion etc.) without evidence or investigation. [Old Norse]

**trustee** /trus-**tee**/ *n.* person or member of a board managing property in trust with a legal obligation to administer it solely for the purposes specified. □ **trusteeship** *n.*

**trustful** *adj.* full of trust or confidence. □ **trustfully** *adv.*

**trusting** *adj.* having trust; trustful. □ **trustingly** *adv.*

**trustworthy** *adj.* deserving of trust; reliable. □ **trustworthiness** *n.*

**trusty** *adj.* (**-ier, -iest**) *archaic* or *joc.* trustworthy (*a trusty steed*).

**truth** /trooth/ *n.* (*pl.* **truths** /troothz, trooths/ ) **1** quality or state of being true or truthful (*doubted the truth of the statement*). **2 a** what is true (*tell us the whole truth; the truth is that I forgot*). **b** what is accepted as true (*one of the fundamental truths*). □ **in truth** *literary* truly, really. [Old English: related to TRUE]

**truthful** *adj.* **1** habitually speaking the truth. **2** (of a story etc.) true. □ **truthfully** *adv.* **truthfulness** *n.*

**try** /truy/ — *v.* (**-ies, -ied**) **1** make an effort with a view to success (often foll. by *to* + infin.; *colloq.* foll. by *and* + infin.: *tried to be on time*; *try and be early*). **2** make an effort to achieve (*tried my best*). **3** test the quality or qualities of (a person or thing) (*his trustworthiness has not yet been tried*; *the consumer association tries several products each year under strict scientific conditions*; *try a bit of my curry and tell me what you think*). **4** make severe demands on (a person, quality, etc.) (*tries them to the limit*; *tries my patience*). **5** examine the effectiveness of for a purpose (*try cold water*; *have you tried kicking it?*). **6** ascertain the state of fastening of (a door, window, etc.). **7 a** investigate and decide (a case or issue) judicially. **b** (often foll. by *for*) subject (a person) to trial (*tried for murder*). **8** make an experiment in order to find out (*let us try which takes longest*). **9** (foll. by *for*) apply or compete for; seek to reach or attain (*try for a gold medal*). — *n.* (*pl.* **-ies**) **1** an effort to accomplish something (*at least give it a try*). **2** *Rugby* touching-down of the ball behind the opposing goal-line, scoring points and entitling the scoring side to a kick at the goal. □ **try one's hand** test how skilful one is, esp. at the first attempt. **try it on** *colloq.* **1** test another's patience. **2** try to get away with an unreasonable request etc. **try on** put on (clothes etc.) to see if they fit etc. **try out** put to the test, test thoroughly. [originally = separate, distinguish, from French *trier* sift]

**trying** *adj.* annoying, vexatious; hard to endure.

**try-on** *n. colloq.* **1** act of trying it on or trying on (clothes etc.). **2** attempt to deceive.

**tryst** /trist/ *n. archaic* meeting, esp. of lovers. [French]

**tsar** /zah/ *n.* (also **czar**) (*fem.* **tsarina** /zah-**ree**-nuh/ ) *hist.* title of the former emperors of Russia. □ **tsarist** *n.* (usu. *attrib.*). [Latin *Caesar*]

**tsetse** /**tset**-see, **tet**-see/ *n.* African fly feeding on blood and transmitting esp. sleeping-sickness. [Tswana]

**T-shirt** /**tee**-shert/ *n.* short-sleeved casual top having the form of a T when spread out.

**tsk-tsk!** (an alveolar click formed by suction; also, *joc.*, /tisk-tisk/ ) (also **tsk!**) — *int.* a sound expressing commiseration; an exclamation of disapproval or irritation (*'I'm henpecked.' — 'Tsk-tsk!' said his mate sympathetically*). — *v.* make this sound or utter this exclamation; say disapprovingly (*he tsk-ed his displeasure*; *don't you tsk-tsk at me in that tone of voice!*) (see also TUT-TUT).

**tsp** *abbr.* (*pl.* **tsps.**) teaspoonful.

**T-square** /**tee**-skwair/ *n.* T-shaped instrument for drawing right angles.

**tsunami** /tsoo-**nah**-mee/ *n.* (*pl.* **-s**) long high sea wave caused by underwater earthquakes etc. [Japanese]

**tuan** /**tyoo**-uhn/ *n.* **1** = PHASCOGALE. **2** = FLYING POSSUM. [Wathawurung *duwan* small gliding possum]

**tuart** /**tyoo**-aht, -uht/ *n.* **1** medium to large eucalypt of coastal south-western WA, the flowers of which, rich in nectar, produce a much-valued honey. **2** the strong, hard, yellowish wood of this tree. □ **tuart honey** honey produced by bees from the nectar of the tuart. [Nyungar, probably *duward*]

**tub** — *n.* **1** open flat-bottomed usu. round vessel. **2** tub-shaped (usu. plastic) carton. **3** *colloq.* bath. **4** *colloq.* clumsy slow boat. — *v.* (**-bb-**) plant, bathe, or wash in a tub. [probably Low German or Dutch]

**tuba** /**tyoo**-buh/ *n.* (*pl.* **-s**) low-pitched brass wind instrument. [Latin, = trumpet]

**tubby** /**tub**-ee/ *adj.* (**-ier, -iest**) short and fat. □ **tubbiness** *n.*

**tube** /tyoob/ — *n.* **1** long hollow rigid or flexible cylinder esp. for holding or carrying air, liquids, etc. **2** soft metal or plastic cylinder sealed at one end and holding a semi-liquid substance (*tube of toothpaste*). **3** hollow cylindrical organ in the body (*bronchial tubes*; *Fallopian tubes*). **4** (often prec. by *the*) *Brit. colloq.* underground railway (*went by tube*). **5 a** cathode-ray tube, esp. in a television set. **b** (prec. by *the*) *colloq.* television. **6** *Surfing* hollow curve of a breaking wave. **7** inflatable part of a pneumatic tyre. **8** *colloq.* can of beer. — *v.* (**-bing**) **1** equip with tubes. **2** enclose in a tube. [Latin]

**tuber** /**tyoo**-buh/ *n.* **1** thick rounded part of a stem or rhizome, usu. found underground and covered with modified buds, e.g. in a potato. **2** similar root of a terrestrial orchid etc. [Latin, = hump, swelling]

**tubercle** /**tyoo**-buh-kuhl/ *n.* small rounded swelling on the body or in an organ, esp. as characteristic of tuberculosis. □ **tubercular** /tuh-**ber**-kyuh-luh/ *adj.* **tuberculous** /tuh-**ber**-kyuh-luhs/ *adj.* [Latin *tuberculum*, diminutive of TUBER]

**tuberculosis** /tuh-ˌber-kyuh-**loh**-suhs/ *n.* infectious bacterial disease marked by tubercles, esp. in the lungs.

**tuberose** /**tyoo**-buh-ˌrohz/ *n.* plant with scented white funnel-like flowers.

**tuberous** /**tyoo**-buh-ruhs/ *adj.* having tubers; of or like a tuber.

**tubing** *n.* length of tube or quantity of tubes.

**tubular** /**tyoo**-byuh-luh/ *adj.* **1** tube-shaped. **2** having or consisting of tubes. **3** (of furniture etc.) having a tubular framework.

**tubular bells** *n.pl.* orchestral instrument of vertically suspended brass tubes struck with a hammer.

**tubule** /**tyoo**-byool/ *n.* small tube in a plant or animal body. [Latin *tubulus*, diminutive: related to TUBE]

**tuck** — *v.* **1** (often foll. by *in*, *up*) **a** draw, fold, or turn the outer or end parts of (cloth or clothes etc.) close together so as to be held; push in the edge of (a thing) so as to confine it (*tucked his shirt into his trousers*). **b** push in the edges of bedclothes around (a person) (*came to tuck me in*). **2** draw together into a small space (*tucked its head under its wing*). **3** stow (a thing) away in a specified place or way (*tucked it in a corner*; *tucked it out of sight*). **4** make a stitched fold in (cloth etc.). — *n.* flattened usu. stitched fold in cloth etc. □ **tuck in** *colloq.* eat heartily. **tuck into** (or **tuck it away**) *colloq.* eat (food) heartily (*tucked into their dinner*; *could really tuck it away*). [Low German or Dutch]

**tucker**[1] — *n.* **1** food. **2** the means of subsistence. — *v.* **1** eat food, take a meal (*he was tuckering away as if there was no tomorrow*). **2** supply (a person) with food (*tuckered us for the trip*). □ **make tucker** earn enough for the bare means of subsistence (*with the few opals I find I just make tucker*). [British dial.]

**tucker**[2] *v.* (esp. in *passive*; often foll. by *out*) *colloq.* tire, exhaust (*I'm tuckered out after all that hard yakka*). [US, = tire]

**tucker bag** *n.* provision bag, esp. as carried by a swagman etc.

**tucker box** *n.* box for the storing or conveyance of provisions, esp. as used by a swagman etc.

**tuckeroo** /tuk-uh-**roo**/ *n.* small to medium tree of northern and eastern Australia, cultivated as an ornamental. [probably Yagara *dagaru*]

**tucker track** *n.* route followed by itinerant rural workers (and other travellers), judged by the generosity with which provisions are supplied along the way (cf. WALLABY TRACK) (*she's a good tucker track, that*).

**tuck-in** *n. colloq.* large meal.

**tuck shop** *n.* canteen, esp. in a school, selling snacks, lunches, drinks, etc.

**-tude** *suffix* forming abstract nouns (*altitude*; *solitude*). [Latin *-tudo*]

**Tudor** /**tyoo**-duh/ *adj.* **1** of the royal family of England 1485–1603 or this period. **2** of the architectural style of this period. [Owen *Tudor*, name of the grandfather of Henry VII]

**Tuesday** /**tyooz**-day/ — *n.* day of the week following Monday. — *adv. colloq.* **1** on Tuesday. **2** (**Tuesdays**) on Tuesdays; each Tuesday. [Old English]

**tufa** /**tyoo**-fuh/ *n.* **1** porous limestone rock formed round mineral springs. **2** = TUFF. [Italian: related to TUFF]

**tuff** *n.* rock formed from volcanic ash. [Latin *tofus*]

**tuffet** /**tuf**-uht/ *n.* clump of grass; small mound. [var. of TUFT]

**tuft** *n.* bunch or collection of threads, grass, feathers, hair, etc., held or growing together at the base. □ **tufted** *adj.* **tufty** *adj.* [probably French *tofe*]

**tug** — *v.* (**-gg-**) **1** (often foll. by *at*) pull hard or violently; jerk; drag with effort. **2** tow (a ship etc.) by a tugboat. — *n.* **1** hard, violent, or jerky pull. **2** sudden strong emotional feeling (*felt a tug as I watched them go*). **3** small powerful boat for towing ships. [related to TOW[1]]

**tugboat** *n.* = TUG in 3.

**tug of war** *n.* **1** trial of strength between two sides pulling opposite ways on a rope. **2** decisive or severe contest.

**tuition** /tyoo-**ish**-uhn/ *n.* **1** teaching, esp. if paid for. **2** fee for this. [Latin *tueor tuit-* look after]

**tula** /**too**-luh/ *n.* (also **tuhla**, **tula adze**) Aboriginal tool, having a curved wooden handle and sharp stone chisel-edge, used for wood-working. [Arabana *dhurla* small cutting-tool made of stone]

**tulip** /**tyoo**-luhp/ *n.* **1** bulbous spring-flowering plant with showy cup-shaped flowers. **2** its flower. [Turkish *tul(i)band* TURBAN (from its shape), from Persian]

**tulip oak** *n.* = BOOYONG.

**tulipwood** *n.* (also **tulip**) **1** medium rainforest tree of NSW and Queensland, having perfumed flowers and colourful red and yellow fruit; often cultivated as an ornamental. **2** the beautifully figured wood of this tree, highly prized for cabinet making etc.

**tulle** /tyool/ *n.* soft fine silk etc. net for veils and dresses. [*Tulle* in France]

**tumble** /**tum**-buhl/ — *v.* (**-ling**) **1** fall or cause to fall suddenly, clumsily, or headlong (*tumbled down the stairs*; *the tower tumbled down*). **2** fall rapidly in amount etc. (*prices tumbled*). **3** (often foll. by *about*, *around*) roll or toss to and fro. **4** move or rush in a headlong or blundering manner (*the children tumbled out of the car*). **5** (often foll. by to) *colloq.* grasp the meaning behind an idea, circumstance, etc. (*he quickly tumbled to our plan*). **6** overturn; fling or push roughly or carelessly (*tumbled the mulberries onto my lap*). **7** perform acrobatic feats, esp. somersaults. **8** rumple or disarrange (*bedclothes sadly tumbled after the pillow-fight*). — *n.* **1** sudden or headlong fall. **2** somersault or other acrobatic feat. **3** untidy or confused state. [Low German *tummeln*]

**tumbledown** *adj.* falling or fallen into ruin; dilapidated.

**tumble-dryer** *n.* (also **tumble-drier**) machine for drying washing in a heated rotating drum. □ **tumble-dry** *v.*

**tumbler** *n.* **1** drinking-glass with no handle or foot. **2** acrobat.

**tumbleweed** *n.* plant that forms a globular bush which breaks off in late summer and is tumbled about by the wind.

**tumbril** /**tum**-bruhl/ *n.* (also **tumbrel**) *hist.* open cart in which condemned persons were taken to the guillotine in the French Revolution. [French *tomber* fall]

**tumescent** /tyoo-**mes**-uhnt/ *adj.* **1** becoming tumid; swelling. **2** swelling as a response to sexual stimulation. □ **tumescence** *n.* [Latin: related to TUMOUR]

**tumid** /**tyoo**-muhd/ *adj.* **1** (of parts of the body etc.) swollen, inflated. **2** (of style etc.) inflated, bombastic. □ **tumidity** /-**mid**-uh-tee/ *n.*

**tummy** /**tum**-ee/ *n.* (*pl.* **-ies**) *colloq.* stomach. [a childish pronunciation]

**tumour** /**tyoo**-muh/ *n.* (also **tumor**) a swelling, esp. from an abnormal growth of tissue. □ **tumorous** *adj.* [Latin *tumeo* swell]

**tumult** /**tyoo**-mult/ *n.* **1** uproar or din, esp. of a disorderly crowd. **2** angry demonstration by a mob; riot. **3** conflict of emotions in the mind. [Latin: related to TUMOUR]

**tumultuous** /tyoo-**mul**-choo-uhs/ *adj.* noisy; turbulent; violent.

**tun** *n.* **1** large beer or wine cask. **2** brewer's fermenting-vat. [Old English]

**tuna** /**tyoo**-nuh/ *n.* (*pl.* same or **-s**) any of various large edible marine fish of tropical and warm waters (including a number of Australian varieties), having a round body and pointed snout. [American Spanish]

**tundra** /**tun**-druh/ *n.* vast level treeless Arctic region with underlying permafrost. [Lappish]

**tune** /tyoon/ — *n.* melody. — *v.* (**-ning**) **1** put (a musical instrument) in tune. **2 a** adjust (a radio etc.) to the frequency of a signal. **b** (foll. by *in*) adjust a radio receiver to the required signal. **3** adjust (an engine etc.) to run efficiently. □ **call the tune** see CALL. **change one's tune** see CHANGE. **in** (or **out of**) **tune 1** having (or not having) the correct pitch or intonation (*sings in tune*). **2** (usu. foll. by *with*) harmonising (or clashing) with one's company, surroundings, etc. **to the tune of** *colloq.* to the considerable sum of. **tuned in** (often foll. by *to*) *colloq.* acquainted; in rapport; up to date. **tune up 1** bring one's instrument to the proper pitch. **2** bring to the most efficient condition. □ **tunable** *adj.* (also **tuneable**). [var. of TONE]

**tuneful** *adj.* melodious, musical (*a tuneful whistling*). □ **tunefully** *adv.*

**tuneless** *adj.* unmelodious, unmusical (*a tuneless whistling*). □ **tunelessly** *adv.*

**tuner** *n.* **1** person who tunes musical instruments, esp. pianos. **2 a** part of a radio or television receiver for tuning. **b** radio receiver as a separate unit in a hi-fi system. **3** electronic device for tuning a guitar etc.

**tune-up** *n.* act or instance of adjusting (an engine etc.) to run smoothly and efficiently.

**tungoo** /**tung**-goo, **tung**-goh/ *n.* (also **tungo**) central Australian name for the BOODIE. [Western Desert language *junggu*]

**tungsten** /**tung**-stuhn/ *n.* dense metallic element with a very high melting-point. [Swedish, = heavy stone]

**tunic** /**tyoo**-nik/ *n.* **1** close-fitting short coat of police or military etc. uniform. **2** loose often sleeveless garment reaching to the knees. [Latin]

**tuning fork** *n.* two-pronged steel fork giving a particular note when struck, used in tuning musical instruments.

**tunnel** /**tun**-uhl/ — *n.* **1** underground passage dug through a hill or under a road, river, etc., esp. for a railway or road. **2** underground passage dug by an animal. — *v.* (**-ll-**) **1** (foll. by *through*, *into*, etc.) make a tunnel through. **2** make (one's way) by tunnelling. [French diminutive of *tonne* TUN]

**tunnel vision** *n.* **1** vision which is poor or lost outside the centre of the normal field of vision. **2** *colloq.* inability to grasp a situation's wider implications.

**tup** — *n.* ram. — *v.* (**-pp-**) (of a ram) copulate with (a ewe). [origin unknown]

**tupong** /*too*-pong/ *n.* (also **toopong**) small, chiefly marine food-fish of south-eastern Australia (also known as **congolli**). [Kuurn Kopan Noot *dubong*]

**tuppence** /*tup*-uhns/ *n.* = TWOPENCE. [phonetic spelling]

**turban** /*ter*-buhn/ *n.* **1** man's headdress of fabric wound round a cap or the head, worn esp. by Muslims and Sikhs. **2** woman's hat resembling this. □ **turbaned** *adj.* [Persian: cf. TULIP]

**turbid** /*ter*-buhd/ *adj.* **1** (of a liquid or colour) muddy, thick; not clear. **2** (of style etc.) confused, disordered. □ **turbidity** /-*bid*-uh-tee/ *n.* [Latin *turba* crowd]

■ **Usage** *Turbid* is sometimes confused with *turgid* which means 'swollen, inflated; pompous'.

**turbine** /*ter*-buyn/ *n.* rotary motor driven by a flow of water, steam, gas, wind, etc. [Latin *turbo* -*in*- spinning-top, whirlwind]

**turbo** /*ter*-boh/ *n.* (*pl.* **-s**) = TURBOCHARGER.

**turbo-** *comb. form* turbine.

**turbocharger** *n.* supercharger driven by a turbine powered by the engine's exhaust gases.

**turbojet** *n.* **1** jet engine in which the jet also operates a turbine-driven air-compressor. **2** aircraft powered by this.

**turboprop** *n.* **1** jet engine in which a turbine is used as in a turbojet and also to drive a propeller. **2** aircraft powered by this. [from PROP³]

**turbulent** /*ter*-byuh-luhnt/ *adj.* **1** (of persons, their actions, etc.) causing disturbance or commotion; unruly. **2** (of the mind, emotions, social or political affairs, etc.) violently disturbed or agitated. **3 a** (of a flow of air etc.) varying irregularly. **b** (of a flow of water) agitated. **c** (of the weather, the sea, etc.) stormy, tempestuous. □ **turbulence** *n.* **turbulently** *adv.* [Latin *turba* crowd]

**turd** *n. coarse colloq.* **1** lump of excrement. **2** contemptible person. [Old English]

**tureen** /tyoo-*reen*, tuh-/ *n.* deep covered dish for soup. [from TERRINE]

**turf** — *n.* (*pl.* **-s** or **turves**) **1 a** layer of grass etc. with earth and matted roots as the surface of grassland. **b** piece of this cut

from the ground. **2** slab of peat for fuel. **3** (prec. by *the*) **a** horse racing generally. **b** general term for racecourses. — *v.* **1** cover (ground) with turf. **2** (foll. by *out*) *colloq.* expel or eject (a person or thing). □ **turfy** *adj.* [Old English]

**turgid** /*ter*-juhd/ *adj.* **1** swollen, inflated; distended (*turgid belly*). **2** (of language) pompous, bombastic. □ **turgidity** /-*jid*-uh-tee/ *n.* [Latin *turgeo* swell]

■ **Usage** *Turgid* is sometimes confused with *turbid* which means 'muddy, not clear; confused'.

**Turk** *n.* **1 a** native or national of Turkey. **b** person of Turkish descent. **2** member of a Central Asian people from whom the Ottomans derived, speaking a Turkic language. **3** *offens.* ferocious or wild person. [origin unknown]

**turkey** /*ter*-kee/ *n.* (*pl.* **-s**) **1 a** large orig. American bird bred for food. **b** its flesh as food. **2 a** = BRUSH TURKEY. **b** = PLAIN TURKEY. **1**. **3** *colloq.* stupid or inept person. □ **head over turkey** head over heels. **talk turkey** *colloq.* talk frankly; get down to business. [originally of the guinea-fowl, imported from *Turkey*]

**turkey bush** *n.* **1** (also **purple-stemmed turkey bush**) tea-tree of Cape York, Queensland, having gnarled and twisted limbs and smooth bark (constantly peeling off to reveal purple and pink tints beneath) and white flowers. **2** (also **Ellangowan poison-bush**, **emu bush**) any of many shrubs of the mainland Australian genus *Eremophila*, the leaves of some species being poisonous to stock and the berries of others being eaten by emus. [*turkey bush* common name for any low, branching bush or tree on which brush turkeys may roost]

**turkey-bush scrub** *n.* a name applied to vast areas of Cape York, Queensland, covered by turkey bushes.

**turkey lolly** *n.* sugar syrup spun into thread-like brittle strands (often mistakenly called *fairy floss*): a confection originating in India.

**turkey nest** *n.* (in full **turkey nest dam**; also **turkey nest tank**) reservoir built in flat country where there is no natural run-off, having high earthen walls and so resembling the mound of the brush turkey.

**Turki** /*ter*-kee/ — *adj.* of a group of languages and peoples including Turkish. — *n.* this group. □ **Turkic** *adj.* [Persian: related to TURK]

**Turkish** — *adj.* of Turkey, the Turks, or their language. — *n.* this language.

**Turkish bath** n. **1** hot-air or steam bath followed by washing, massage, etc. **2** (in *sing.* or *pl.*) building for this.

**Turkish carpet** n. wool carpet with a thick pile and traditional bold design.

**Turkish delight** n. sweet of lumps of flavoured gelatine coated in powdered sugar.

**turmeric** /ter-muh-rik/ n. **1** E. Indian plant of the ginger family. **2** its aromatic powdered rhizome used as a spice in Sri Lankan and Indian curries, rice dishes, etc., or for yellow dye. [perhaps from French *terre mérite*]

**turmoil** /ter-moil/ n. **1** violent confusion; agitation. **2** din and bustle. [origin unknown]

**turn** /tern/ — v. **1** move around a point or axis; give or receive a rotary motion (*turned the wheel*; *the wheel turns*). **2** change in position so that a different side, end, or part becomes outermost or uppermost etc.; invert or reverse (*turned inside out*; *turned it upside down*). **3 a** give a new direction to (*turn your face this way*). **b** take a new direction (*turn left here*). **4** aim in a certain way (*turned the hose on them*). **5** (foll. by *into*) change in nature, form, or condition to (*turned into a frog*; *turned the book into a play*). **6** (foll. by *to*) **a** set about (*turned to doing the ironing*). **b** have recourse to (*turned to drink*; *turned to me for help*). **c** go on to consider next (*let us now turn to your report*). **7** become (*turned nasty*). **8 a** (foll. by *against*) make or become hostile to (*has turned her against us*). **b** (foll. by *on*, *upon*) become hostile to; attack (*suddenly turned on them*). **9** (of hair or leaves) change colour. **10** (of milk) become sour. **11** (of the stomach) be nauseated. **12** cause (milk) to become sour or (the stomach) to be nauseated. **13** (of the head) become giddy. **14** translate (*turn it into French*). **15** move to the other side of; go round (*turned the corner*). **16** pass the age or time of (*he has turned 40*; *it has turned 4 o'clock*). **17** (foll. by *on*) depend on; be determined by (*it all turns on how he casts his vote*). **18** send or put; cause to go (*was turned loose*; *turned the water out into a basin*). **19** perform (a somersault etc.). **20** make (a profit). **21** divert (a bullet). **22** shape (an object) on a lathe. **23** give an (esp. elegant) form to (*turn a compliment*). **24** (of the tide) change direction. **25** change one's religion (esp. of an Anglican etc. becoming a Roman Catholic) (*some Anglican priests are thinking of turning*). **26** colloq. earn (*turned a dollar or two during the vac. washing cars*). — n. **1** act or process or

instance of turning; rotary motion. **2** changed or a change of direction or tendency (*took a sudden turn to the left*). **3** point at which a turning or change occurs. **4** turning of a road. **5** change of direction of the tide. **6** change in the course of events (*a turn for the worse*). **7** tendency or disposition; facility of forming (*is of a mechanical turn of mind*; *has a neat turn of phrase*). **8** opportunity or obligation etc. that comes successively to each of several persons etc. (*my turn to pay*). **9** short walk or ride (*took a turn in the park*). **10** short performance, variety act. **11** service of a specified kind (*did me a good turn*). **12** purpose (*it served my turn well enough*). **13** colloq. momentary nervous shock (*gave me a turn*). **14** colloq. short illness, esp. one involving giddiness etc. (*she had a bit of a turn last week*). **15** colloq. display of anger, peevishness, etc.; a fuss etc. **16** Mus. ornament consisting of the principal note with those above and below it. **17** colloq. a party. □ **at every turn** continually. **by turns** in rotation; alternately. **in turn** in succession. **in one's turn** when one's turn comes. **not know which way** (or **where**) **to turn** be at a loss, unsure how to act, etc. **out of turn 1** when it is not one's turn. **2** inappropriately (*did I speak out of turn?*). **stack on a turn** colloq. make an inordinate fuss. **take turns** (or **take it in turns**) act alternately. **to a turn** (esp. cooked) perfectly. **turn about** move so as to face into a new direction. **turn and turn about** alternately. **turn away 1** turn to face in another direction. **2** reject. **3** send away. **turn down 1** reject (a proposal etc.). **2** reduce the volume or strength of (sound, heat, etc.) by turning a knob etc. **3** fold down (*turned down the bed*). **turn one's hand to** see HAND. **turn a person's head** see HEAD. **turn in 1** hand in or return. **2** achieve or register (a performance, score, etc.). **3** colloq. go to bed for the night. **4** incline inwards. **5** hand over (a suspect etc.) to the authorities. **6** colloq. abandon (a plan etc.). **turn it on** colloq. provide (drinks, a party, etc.). **turn it up!** colloq. fair go!; you must be joking! **turn off 1** stop the flow or operation of (water, electricity, etc.) by a tap, switch, etc. **b** operate (a tap, switch, etc.) to achieve this. **2** enter a side-road. **3** colloq. cause to lose interest. **turn on 1 a** start the flow or operation of (water, electricity, etc.) by means of a tap, switch, etc. **b** operate (a tap, switch, etc.) to achieve this. **2** colloq. excite; stimulate, esp. sexually (*turned him on*). **3** = *turn it on*. **turn on one's heel** see HEEL[1]. **turn out 1** expel. **2** extinguish (an electric light etc.). **3** dress or equip (*well turned out*). **4** produce (goods etc.). **5** empty or clean out (a room etc.). **6** empty (a pocket). **7** *colloq.* assemble; attend a meeting etc. **8** (often foll. by *to* + infin. or *that* + clause) prove to be the case; result (*turned out to be true*; *see how things turn out*). turn over **1** reverse the position of (*turn over the page*). **2 a** cause (an engine) to run. **b** (of an engine) start running. **3** consider; ponder. **4** (foll. by *to*) **a** transfer the care or conduct of (a person or thing) to (a person) (*shall turn it all over to my deputy*). **b** = *turn in* 5. **5** do business to the gross value of (*turns over $5000 a week*). **turn over a new leaf** reform one's conduct. **turn round 1** turn so as to face in a new direction. **2 a** unload and reload (a ship etc.). **b** receive, process, and send out again; cause to progress through a system. **3** adopt new opinions or policy. **turn the tables** see TABLE. **turn tail** turn one's back; run away. **turn to** set about one's work. **turn turtle** see TURTLE. **turn up 1** increase the volume or strength of by turning a knob etc. **2** discover or reveal. **3** be found, esp. by chance. **4** happen or present itself; (of a person) arrive (*people turned up late*). **5** shorten (a garment) by raising its hem. **6** fold over or upwards. [Old English *tyrnan*, from Greek *tornos* lathe]

**turnabout** *n.* **1** act of turning about. **2** abrupt change of policy etc.

**turncoat** *n.* person who changes sides in a conflict, dispute, etc.

**turner** *n.* person who works with a lathe.

**turning point** *n.* point at which a decisive change occurs.

**turnip** /ter-nuhp/ *n.* **1** plant with a whitish globular root. **2** its root as a vegetable. □ **turnipy** *adj.* [British dial. *neep* (Old English from Latin *napu*)]

**turnkey** *n.* (*pl.* **-s**) *archaic* warder.

**turn-off** *n.* **1** turning off a main road. **2** *colloq.* something that repels or causes a loss of interest.

**turn-on** *n. colloq.* person or thing that causes (esp. sexual) excitement.

**turnout** *n.* **1** number of people attending a meeting, voting at an election, etc. **2** set or display of equipment, clothes, etc.

**turnover** *n.* **1** act or instance of turning over. **2** gross amount of money taken in a business. **3** rate at which goods are sold and replaced in a shop. **4** rate at which people enter and leave employment etc. **5** small pie made by folding pastry over a filling.

**turnpike** *n. hist.* **1** toll-gate. **2** road on which a toll was charged.

**turn-round** *n.* **1 a** unloading and reloading between trips. **b** receiving, processing, and sending out again; progress through a system. **2** reversal of an opinion or tendency.

**turnstile** *n.* gate with revolving arms allowing people through singly.

**turntable** *n.* **1** circular revolving plate on which records are played. **2** circular revolving platform for turning a railway locomotive.

**turn-up** *n.* **1** turned up end of a trouser leg. **2** *colloq.* unexpected happening. □ **a turn-up for the books** *colloq.* unexpected turn of fortune; a surprise.

**turpentine** /ter-puhn-,tuyn/ *n.* **1** an oleo-resin from any of various (esp. coniferous) trees, used in various commercial preparations. **2 a** tall tree of NSW and Queensland (family Myrtaceae) having a thick, fibrous bark, fluffy creamy flowers, woody fruit, and a resin in its timber which acts as a preservative. **b** the reddish timber of this tree, valued for its durability even in sea-water. **3** = TURPENTINE BUSH. [Latin]

**turpentine bush** *n.* (also **turpentine**) any of several very resinous or aromatic Australian shrubs.

**turpitude** /ter-puh-,tyood/ *n. formal* depravity, wickedness. [Latin *turpis* disgraceful]

**turps** *n. colloq.* **1** oil of turpentine. **2** any alcoholic liquor. □ **on the turps** drinking alcoholic liquor to excess. [abbreviation]

**turquoise** /ter-kwoiz/ — *n.* **1** semiprecious stone, usu. opaque and greenish- or sky-blue. **2** greenish-blue colour. — *adj.* of this colour. [French, = Turkish]

**turret** /tu-ruht/ *n.* **1** small tower, esp. decorating a building. **2** low, flat, usu. revolving, armoured tower for a gun and gunners in a ship, aircraft, fort, or tank. **3** rotating holder for tools in a lathe etc. □ **turreted** *adj.* [French diminutive: related to TOWER]

**turrum** /tu-ruhm/ *n.* any of several large marine fish of northern Australia valued as game fish. [possibly from an Aboriginal language]

**turtle** *n.* **1** any of various marine or freshwater reptiles encased in a horny shell and having flippers or webbed toes used in swimming. **2** its flesh, used for soup. □ **turn turtle** capsize. [alteration of earlier *tortue*: related to TORTOISE]

**turtle-dove** /ter-tuhl-,duv/ *n.* wild dove of Europe, Asia, etc. (two species of which, the *spotted turtle-dove* and the *laughing turtle-dove*, have been introduced into Australia), noted for its soft cooing and affection for its mate. [Latin *turtur*]

**turtleneck** *n.* high close-fitting neck on a knitted garment.

**Tuscan** /**tus**-kuhn/ — n. **1** inhabitant of Tuscany. **2** form of Italian spoken in Tuscany; standard Italian. — adj. of Tuscany or the Tuscans. [Latin]

**tusk** n. long pointed tooth, esp. protruding from a closed mouth, as in the elephant, walrus, etc. □ **tusked** adj. [Old English]

**tussle** /tus-uhl/ — n. struggle, scuffle. — v. (**-ling**) engage in a tussle. [originally Scots and Northern English, perhaps diminutive of touse: related to TOUSLE]

**tussock** /**tus**-uhk/ n. clump of grass etc. □ **tussocky** adj. [perhaps from British dial. tusk tuft]

**tussock grass** n. **1** any of several Australian tussock-forming plants, usu. perennial grasses. **2** introduced South American grass (serrated tussock), naturalised as a weed of pasture in much of south-eastern Australia.

**tut** var. of TUT-TUT.

**tute** /tyoot/ n. colloq. tutorial. [abbreviation]

**tutelage** /**tyoo**-tuh-lij/ n. **1** guardianship. **2** state or duration of being under this. **3** tuition. [Latin tutela: related to TUTOR]

**tutelary** /**tyoo**-tuh-luh-ree/ adj. **1 a** serving as guardian. **b** of a guardian (tutelary authority). **2** giving protection (tutelary saint). [Latin: related to TUTELAGE]

**tutor** /**tyoo**-tuh/ — n. **1** private teacher. **2** university teacher supervising the studies of assigned undergraduates, usu. in small groups. — v. **1** act as tutor to. **2** work as a tutor. □ **tutorship** n. [Latin tueor tut- watch]

**tutorial** /tyoo-**taw**-ree-uhl/ — adj. of a tutor or tuition. — n. period of undergraduate tuition individually or in a small group. [Latin tutorius: related to TUTOR]

**tutti** /**tuut**-ee/ Mus. — adj. & adv. with all voices or instruments together. — n. (pl. **-s**) a passage to be performed in this way. [Italian, pl. of tutto all]

**tut-tut** /tut-**tut**/ (also **tut**) — int. expressing disapproval or impatience. — n. such an exclamation. — v. (**-tt-**) exclaim this; say disapprovingly (do something constructive instead of sitting there tutting; his enthusiasm was tut-tutted by the elderly members) (see also TSK-TSK!). □ **tut-tutting** n. & adj. [imitative of a click of the tongue]

**tutu** /**too**-too/ n. ballet dancer's short skirt of stiffened frills. [French]

**tuxedo** /tuk-**see**-doh/ n. (pl. **-s** or **-es**) dinner-jacket. [Tuxedo Park in US]

**TV** abbr. television.

**twaddle** /**twod**-uhl/ — n. silly writing or talk; nonsense. — v. indulge in this (twaddling on about how he'd run the country). [earlier twattle, alteration of TATTLE]

**twain** adj. & n. archaic two. [Old English, masculine form of TWO]

**twang** — n. **1** sound made by a plucked string or released bowstring. **2** nasal quality of a voice. — v. emit or cause to emit this sound. □ **twangy** adj. [imitative]

**'twas** /twoz, twuhz/ archaic it was. [contraction]

**tweak** — v. **1** pinch and twist sharply; jerk. **2** make fine adjustments to (a mechanism). **3** Cricket (esp. of a left-arm leg-spinner) impart spin (to the ball). — n. act of tweaking. □ **tweaker** n. [probably British dial. twick, TWITCH]

**twee** adj. (**tweer** /twee-uh/, **tweest** /twee-uhst/) derog. affectedly dainty or quaint. [a childish pronunciation of SWEET]

**tweed** n. **1** rough-surfaced woollen cloth, usu. of mixed flecked colours. **2** (in pl.) **a** clothes made of tweed. **b** colloq. trousers. [alteration of tweel (Scots var. of TWILL)]

**'tween** prep. archaic = BETWEEN. [abbreviation]

**tweet** — n. chirp of a small bird. — v. make this noise. [imitative]

**tweeter** n. loudspeaker for high frequencies.

**tweezers** /**twee**-zuhz/ n.pl. small pair of pincers for taking up small objects, plucking out hairs, etc. [originally tweezes pl. of obsolete tweeze, a case for small instruments]

**twelfth** adj. & n. **1** next after eleventh. **2** each of twelve equal parts of a thing. [Old English: related to TWELVE]

**Twelfth Night** n. 5 January, eve of Epiphany.

**twelve** adj. & n. **1** one more than eleven. **2** symbol for this (12, xii, XII). **3** twelve o'clock. **4** (**the Twelve**) the apostles. [Old English]

**twelve apostles** see LOUSY JACK.

**twelvefold** adj. & adv. **1** twelve times as much or as many. **2** consisting of twelve parts.

**twenty** /**twen**-tee/ adj. & n. (pl. **-ies**) **1** product of two and ten. **2** symbol for this (20, xx, XX). **3** (in pl.) numbers from 20 to 29, esp. the years of a century or of a person's life. □ **twentieth** adj. & n. [Old English]

**twenty-eight** n. (also **Port Lincoln parrot**) parrot of south-western WA with predominantly green plumage, black head, red bar on forehead, and yellow collar; its call resembles the word 'twenty-eight' in sound.

**twenty-twenty vision** *n.* (also **20/20 vision**) **1** vision of normal acuity. **2** *colloq.* good eyesight.

**'twere** /twer/ *archaic* it were. [contraction]

**twerp** *n.* (also **twirp**) *colloq.* stupid or objectionable person. [origin unknown]

**twice** *adv.* **1** two times; on two occasions. **2** in double degree or quantity (*twice as good*). [Old English: related to TWO]

**twiddle** — *v.* (**-ling**) twirl, adjust, or play randomly or idly. — *n.* act of twiddling. □ **twiddle one's thumbs 1** make them rotate round each other. **2** have nothing to do. □ **twiddly** *adj.* [probably imitative]

**twig**[1] *n.* very small thin branch of a tree or shrub. □ **twiggy** *adj.* [Old English]

**twig**[2] *v.* (**-gg-**) *colloq.* understand; realise (*he hasn't yet twigged what is going on*). [origin unknown]

**twilight** /twuy-luyt/ — *n.* **1** light from the sky when the sun is below the horizon, esp. in the evening. **2** period of this. **3** faint light. **4** period of decline or destruction. — *attrib. adj.* of or relating to or resembling twilight (*twilight hour*; *twilight years*). [from TWO, LIGHT[1]]

**twilight zone** *n.* undefined or intermediate zone or area.

**twilit** /twuy-lit/ *adj.* dimly illuminated by twilight.

**twill** *n.* fabric so woven as to have a surface of diagonal parallel ridges. □ **twilled** *adj.* [Old English, = two-thread]

**'twill** *archaic* it will. [contraction]

**twin** — *n.* **1** each of a closely related or associated pair, esp. of children or animals born at a birth. **2** exact counterpart of a person or thing. **3** (**the Twins**) zodiacal sign or constellation Gemini. — *adj.* forming, or being one of, such a pair (*twin brothers*). — *v.* (**-nn-**) **1 a** join intimately together. **b** (foll. by *with*) pair. **2** bear twins. □ **twinning** *n.* [Old English: related to TWO]

**twin bed** *n.* each of a pair of single beds.

**twine** — *n.* **1** strong coarse string of twisted strands of fibre. **2** coil, twist. — *v.* (**-ning**) **1** form (a string etc.) by twisting strands. **2** weave (a garland etc.). **3** (often foll. by *with*) garland (a brow etc.). **4** (often foll. by *round*, *about*) coil or wind. **5** *refl.* (of a plant) grow in this way. [Old English]

**twinge** /twinj/ *n.* sharp momentary local pain or pang. [Old English]

**twinkle** /twing-kuhl/ — *v.* (**-ling**) **1** (of a star or light etc.) shine with rapidly intermittent gleams. **2** (of the eyes)

sparkle. **3** (of the feet) move lightly and rapidly. — *n.* **1** sparkle or gleam of the eyes. **2** twinkling light. **3** light rapid movement. □ **in a twinkle** (or **a twinkling** or **the twinkling of an eye**) in an instant. □ **twinkly** *adj.* [Old English]

**twinset** *n.* woman's matching cardigan and jumper. □ **twin-set and pearls** *colloq.* (of a woman) conservative in dress and attitudes.

**twirl** — *v.* spin, swing, or twist quickly and lightly round. — *n.* **1** twirling motion. **2** flourish made with a pen. [origin uncertain]

**twist** — *v.* **1 a** change the form of by rotating one end and not the other or the two ends in opposite directions. **b** undergo such a change; take a twisted position (*twisted round in his seat*). **c** wrench or pull out of shape with a twisting action (*twisted my ankle*). **2 a** wind (strands etc.) about each other. **b** form (a rope etc.) in this way. **3 a** give a spiral form to. **b** take a spiral form. **4** (foll. by *off*) break off by twisting. **5** distort or misrepresent the meaning of (words). **6 a** take a winding course. **b** make (one's way) in a winding manner. **7** turn so as to face another way. **8** (as **twisted** *adj.*) *derog.* (of a person or mind) neurotic; perverted. **9** dance the twist. — *n.* **1** act or instance of twisting. **2** twisted state. **3** thing formed by twisting. **4** point at which a thing twists or bends. **5** usu. *derog.* peculiar tendency of mind or character etc. **6** unexpected development of events, esp. in a story etc. (*a surprising twist at the end*). **7** (prec. by *the*) popular 1960s dance with a twisting movement of the hips. □ **round the twist** *colloq.* crazy. **twist a person's arm** *colloq.* coerce, esp. using moral pressure. **twist round one's finger** see FINGER. □ **twisty** *adj.* (**-ier**, **-iest**). [related to TWIN, TWINE]

**twit**[1] *n.* *colloq.* foolish person. [originally British dial., perhaps from TWIT[2]]

**twit**[2] *v.* (**-tt-**) reproach or taunt, usu. good-humouredly (*twitted him about his mismatched socks*). [Old English]

**twitch** — *v.* **1** (of features, muscles, etc.) move or contract spasmodically. **2** pull sharply at (*twitched aside the curtain*). — *n.* **1** sudden involuntary contraction or movement. **2** sudden pull or jerk. **3** *colloq.* state of nervousness. □ **twitchy** *adj.* (**-ier**, **-iest**) (in sense 3 of *n.*). [probably Old English]

**twitcher** *n.* *colloq.* bird-watcher seeking sightings of rare birds.

**twitter** — *v.* **1** (esp. of a bird) emit a succession of light tremulous sounds. **2** utter or express in this way. — *n.* **1** act of twittering. **2** *colloq.* tremulously excited state. □ **twittery** *adj.* [imitative]

**'twixt** *prep. archaic* = BETWIXT. [contraction]

**two** /too/ *adj. & n.* **1** one more than one. **2** symbol for this (2, ii, II). **3** two o'clock. **4** (*adj.*) (in Aboriginal English) both. □ **in two** in or into two pieces. **put two and two together** infer from known facts. [Old English]

**two-bob** *colloq.* — *n.* (formerly) sum of two shillings. — *adj.* cheap; of little consequence. □ **have two-bob each way** arrange one's affairs so that one cannot lose; hedge one's bets. **mad as a two-bob watch** see MAD. **not the full two-bob** mentally deficient; eccentric.

**two-dimensional** *adj.* **1** having or appearing to have length and breadth but no depth. **2** lacking substance; superficial.

**two-edged** *adj.* double-edged.

**two-faced** *adj.* insincere; deceitful.

**twofold** *adj. & adv.* **1** twice as much or as many. **2** consisting of two parts.

**two-handed** *adj.* **1** having, using, or requiring the use of two hands. **2** (of a card-game) for two players.

**twopence** /tup-uhns/ *n.* (also **tuppence**) **1** *hist.* sum of two pence. **2** (esp. with *neg.*) thing of little value; a small amount (*wouldn't give tuppence for his chances*).

**twopenny** /tup-uh-nee/ *attrib. adj.* cheap, worthless, insignificant.

**two-piece** — *adj.* (of a suit etc.) consisting of two matching items. — *n.* two-piece suit etc.

**two-ply** — *adj.* of two strands or layers etc. — *n.* **1** two-ply wool. **2** two-ply wood.

**two-pot screamer** *n. colloq.* person who is easily or quickly affected by alcoholic liquor.

**twosome** *n.* two persons together.

**two-step** *n.* dance with a sliding step in march or polka time.

**two-stroke** — *attrib. adj.* (of an internal-combustion engine) having its power cycle completed in one up-and-down movement of the piston. — *n.* two-stroke engine.

**two-time** *v. colloq.* **1** be unfaithful to (a lover). **2** swindle. □ **two-timer** *n.*

**two-tone** *adj.* having two colours or sounds.

**two-tooth** *n.* (meat from) a sheep from one to two years old, having two full-grown permanent teeth.

**'twould** /twuud/ *archaic* it would. [contraction]

**two-up** *n.* gambling game, institutionalised in Australia, in which two coins are tossed in the air and bets placed on a showing of two heads or two tails (also *attrib.*) (*Aussie Rules and two-up are dinkum Australian sports*).

**two-up ring** *n.* the site of a two-up game.

**two-up school** *n.* **1** group of people who have assembled to play two-up. **2** place where such an assemblage is regularly held.

**two-way** *adj.* **1** involving two directions or participants. **2** (in Aboriginal English) involving both Aboriginal and European culture (*two-way medicine*; *two-way school*). **3** (of a radio) capable of transmitting and receiving signals.

**-ty¹** *suffix* forming nouns denoting quality or condition (*cruelty*; *plenty*). [French from Latin *-tas -tatis*]

**-ty²** *suffix* denoting tens (*ninety*). [Old English *-tig*]

**tycoon** /tuy-**koon**/ *n.* business magnate. [Japanese, = great lord]

**tying** *pres. part.* of TIE.

**tyke** /tuyk/ *n.* (also **tike**) **1** a dog. **2** a small child. **3** a Roman Catholic. [Old Norse; sense 3 probably an alteration of *Teague* nickname for an Irishman]

**tympani** var. of TIMPANI.

**tympanum** /**tim**-puh-nuhm/ *n.* (*pl.* **-s** or **-na**) **1** middle ear. **2** eardrum. **3** *Archit.* **a** vertical triangular space forming the centre of a pediment. **b** similar space over a door between the lintel and the arch. [Greek *tumpanon* drum]

**type** /tuyp/ — *n.* **1 a** class of things or persons having common characteristics (*there are two types of politician — honest and dishonest*). **b** kind or sort (*would like a different type of car*). **2** person, thing, or event exemplifying a class or group (*he's the perfect type of the modern yuppie*; *he's not the marrying type*). **3** (in *comb.*) made of, resembling, or functioning as (*ceramic-type material*; *cheddar-type cheese*). **4** *colloq.* person, esp. of a specified character (*a quiet type*; *not my type*). **5** object, conception, or work of art, serving as a model for subsequent artists. **6** *Printing* **a** piece of metal etc. with a raised letter or character on its upper surface for printing. **b** kind or size of such pieces (*printed in large type*). **c** set or supply of these (*ran short of type*). **7** *Theol.* a foreshadowing in the Old Testament of a thing, person, or event in the New Testament (*Jonah in the whale's belly is a type of Christ in the tomb*). **8** *Biol.* organism having, or chosen as having, the essential characteristics of its group and giving its name to the next highest group. — *v.* (**-ping**) **1** write with a typewriter. **2** typecast. **3** esp. *Biol.* &

*Med.* assign to a type; classify. [Greek *tupos* impression]

**typecast** *v.* (*past* and *past part.* **-cast**) assign (an actor) repeatedly to the same type of role.

**typeface** *n. Printing* **1** inked surface of type. **2** set of characters in one design.

**typescript** *n.* typewritten document.

**typesetter** *n. Printing* **1** person who composes type. **2** composing machine. □ **typeset** *v.* **typesetting** *n.*

**typewriter** *n.* machine with keys for producing printlike characters one at a time on paper inserted round a roller.

**typhoid** /**tuy**-foid/ *n.* (in full **typhoid fever**) infectious bacterial fever attacking the intestines.

**typhoon** /tuy-**foon**/ *n.* violent hurricane in E. Asian seas. [Chinese, = great wind, and Arabic]

**typhus** /**tuy**-fuhs/ *n.* infectious fever with a purple rash, headaches, and usu. delirium. [Greek, = stupor]

**typical** /**tip**-i-kuhl/ *adj.* **1** serving as a characteristic example; representative (*a typical outback pub*). **2** (often foll. by *of*) characteristic of a particular person, thing, or type (*typical of him to refuse*). □ **typicality** /-**kal**-uh-tee/ *n.* **typically** *adv.* [medieval Latin: related to TYPE]

**typify** /**tip**-uh-,fuy/ *v.* (**-ies**, **-ied**) **1** be typical of. **2** represent by or as a type or symbol. □ **typification** /-fi-**kay**-shuhn/ *n.* [Latin: related to TYPE]

**typist** /**tuy**-puhst/ *n.* person who types, esp. for a living.

**typo** /**tuy**-poh/ *n.* (*pl.* **-s**) *colloq.* typographical error. [abbreviation]

**typography** /tuy-**pog**-ruh-fee/ *n.* **1** printing as an art. **2** style and appearance of printed matter. □ **typographer** *n.* **typographical** /-puh-**graf**-i-kuhl/ *adj.* **typographically** /-puh-**graf**-i-kuh-lee, -klee/ *adv.* [French: related to TYPE]

**tyrannical** /tuh-**ran**-i-kuhl/ *adj.* despotic; unjustly severe. □ **tyrannically** *adv.* [Greek: related to TYRANT]

**tyrannise** /**ti**-ruh-,nuyz/ *v.* (also **-ize**) (**-sing** or **-zing**) (often foll. by *over*) treat despotically or cruelly. [French: related to TYRANT]

**tyrannosaurus** /tuh-,ran-uh-**saw**-ruhs/ *n.* (*pl.* **-ruses**)(also **tyrannosaur**) dinosaur with very short front legs and a long well-developed tail. [from TYRANT, after *dinosaur*]

**tyranny** /**ti**-ruh-nee/ *n.* (*pl.* **-ies**) **1** cruel and arbitrary use of authority. **2 a** rule by a tyrant. **b** period of this. **c** nation ruled by a tyrant. □ **tyrannous** *adj.* [Greek: related to TYRANT]

**tyrant** /**tuy**-ruhnt/ *n.* **1** oppressive or cruel ruler. **2** person exercising power arbitrarily or cruelly. [Greek *turannos*]

**tyre** /tuyuh/ *n.* rubber covering, usu. inflated, placed round a wheel to form a soft contact with the road. [perhaps = archaic *tire* headdress]

**Tyrian** /**ti**-ree-uhn/ — *adj.* of ancient Tyre in Phoenicia. — *n.* native or citizen of Tyre. [Latin *Tyrus* Tyre]

**Tyrian purple** see PURPLE *n.* 2.

**tyro** /**tuy**-roh/ *n.* (also **tiro**) (*pl.* **-os**) beginner or novice. [Latin, = recruit]

**tzatziki** /tsat-**see**-kee/ *n.* Greek side dish of yoghurt with cucumber. [modern Greek]

# U

**U**[1] /yoo/ *n.* (also **u**) (*pl.* **Us** or **U's**) **1** twenty-first letter of the alphabet. **2** U-shaped object or curve.

**U**[2] /yoo/ *adj. colloq.* upper class or supposedly upper class. [abbreviation]

**U**[3] /oo/ *n.* Burmese title of respect before a man's name. [Burmese]

**U**[4] *symb.* uranium.

**ubiquitous** /yoo-**bik**-wuh-tuhs/ *adj.* **1** (seemingly) present everywhere simultaneously. **2** often encountered. □ **ubiquity** *n.* [Latin *ubique* everywhere]

**U-boat** /**yoo**-boht/ *n. hist.* German submarine. [German *Untersee* undersea]

**u.c.** *abbr.* upper case.

**udder** *n.* baglike mammary organ of cattle etc., with several teats. [Old English]

**uey** /**yoo**-ee/ *n.* (also **u-ie**, **uy**, **youee**) *colloq.* U-turn (*did an illegal uey and was nabbed*).

**ufella** /**yoo**-fel-uh/ *pron.* (in Aboriginal English) = YOU. [representing pronunciation of YOU, FELLA]

**UFO** /**yoo**-foh, yoo-ef-**oh**/ *n.* (also **ufo**) (*pl.* **-s**) unidentified flying object.

**ugari** /**yoo**-guh-ree/ *n.* (also **yugari**) Queensland name for the PIPI. [Yagara *yugari*]

**ugh** /uhx, ug, ux/ *int.* **1** expressing disgust etc. (*she punctuated my story with expressive ughs*). **2** sound of a cough or grunt. [imitative]

**ugh boot** *n. propr.* boot made of sheepskin with the wool on the inside.

**uglify** /**ug**-luh-,fuy/ *v.* (**-ies**, **-ied**) make ugly.

**ugly** /**ug**-lee/ *adj.* (**-lier**, **-liest**) **1** unpleasant to the eye, ear, or mind etc. (*ugly scar*; *ugly snarl*). **2** unpleasantly suggestive; discreditable (*ugly rumours*). **3** threatening, dangerous (*an ugly look*). **4** morally repulsive (*ugly vices*). □ **ugliness** *n.* [Old Norse]

**ugly customer** *n.* threatening or violent person.

**ugly duckling** *n.* person lacking early promise but blossoming later.

**UHF** *abbr.* ultra-high frequency.

**u-ie** var. of UEY.

**UK** *abbr.* United Kingdom.

**Ukrainian** /yoo-**kray**-nee-uhn/ — *n.* **1** native or language of Ukraine. **2** person of Ukrainian descent. — *adj.* of Ukraine, its people, or language. [*Ukraine* in eastern Europe]

**ukulele** /,yoo-kuh-**lay**-lee/ *n.* small four-stringed Hawaiian guitar. [Hawaiian]

**ulcer** *n.* **1** open sore on or in the body, often forming pus. **2** corrupting influence etc. □ **ulcerous** *adj.* [Latin *ulcus -cer-*]

**ulcerate** /**ul**-suh-,rayt/ *v.* (**-ting**) form into or affect with an ulcer. □ **ulceration** /-**ray**-shuhn/ *n.*

**-ule** *suffix* forming diminutive nouns (*globule*). [Latin *-ulus*]

**ulna** /**ul**-nuh/ *n.* (*pl.* **ulnae** /-nee/ ) **1** thinner and longer bone in the forearm, opposite to the thumb. **2** corresponding bone in an animal's foreleg or a bird's wing. □ **ulnar** *adj.* [Latin]

**-ulous** *suffix* forming adjectives (*fabulous; populous*).

**ult.** *abbr.* ultimo.

**ulterior** /ul-**teer**-ree-uh/ *adj.* **1** not evident or admitted; hidden, secret (esp. *ulterior motive*). **2** situated beyond. [Latin, = further]

**ultimate** /**ul**-tuh-muht/ — *adj.* **1** last or last possible, final (*ultimate offer; ultimate analysis*). **2** fundamental, primary, basic (*ultimate truths*). **3** difficult to better; being the 'last word' in its class (the *'Oxford English Dictionary' is the ultimate dictionary*). — *n.* **1** (prec. by *the*) best achievable or imaginable (*the ultimate in dictionaries*). **2** final or fundamental fact or principle. □ **ultimately** *adv.* [Latin *ultimus* last]

**ultimatum** /,ul-tuh-**may**-tuhm/ *n.* (*pl.* **-s**) final statement of terms, the rejection of which could cause hostility etc. [Latin: related to ULTIMATE]

**ultimo** /**ul**-tuh-,moh/ *adj. Commerce* of last month (*the 28th ultimo*). [Latin, = in the last (*mense* month)]

**ultra** /**ul**-truh/ *adj.* extreme, esp. in religion or politics. [see ULTRA-]

**ultra-** *comb. form* **1** extreme(ly), excessive(ly) (*ultra-modern*). **2** beyond; on the other side of (*ultrasonic*). [Latin *ultra* beyond]

**ultra-high** /,ul-truh-**huy**/ *adj.* (of a frequency) in the range 300 to 3000 megahertz.

**ultramarine** /,ul-truh-muh-**reen**/ — *n.* **1** brilliant blue pigment orig. from lapis lazuli. **2** colour of this. — *adj.* of this colour. [Italian and medieval Latin, =

beyond the sea, from where lapis lazuli was brought]

**ultramicroscopic** /ˌul-truh-ˌmuy-kruh-**skop**-ik/ *adj.* too small to be seen by an ordinary optical microscope.

**ultrasonic** /ˌul-truh-**son**-ik/ *adj.* of or using sound waves pitched above the range of human hearing. □ **ultrasonically** *adv.*

**ultrasonics** *n.pl.* (usu. treated as *sing.*) science of ultrasonic waves.

**ultrasound** /**ul**-truh-ˌsownd/ *n.* **1** ultrasonic waves. **2** (also *attrib.*) use of such waves as a diagnostic medical procedure.

**ultraviolet** /ˌul-truh-**vuy**-uh-luht, -**vuy**-luht/ *adj.* **1** having a wavelength (just) beyond the violet end of the visible spectrum. **2** of or using such radiation.

**ultra vires** /ˌul-truh **vuy**-ˌreez, ˌuul-trah **veer**-rayz/ *adv. & predic.adj.* beyond one's legal power or authority. [Latin]

**ululate** /**yoo**-luh-ˌlayt/ *v.* (**-ting**) howl, wail. □ **ululation** /-**lay**-shuhn/ *n.* [Latin]

**Uluru** /ˌoo-luh-**roo**/ *n.* Western Desert Language name, now the official Australian name, for what was formerly called 'Ayers Rock' in central Australia.

**Ulysses butterfly** /yoo-**lis**-eez, **yoo**-luh-seez/ *n.* large swallowtail butterfly of northern Queensland and elsewhere, having brilliant blue, black-bordered wings. [*Ulysses* Latin form of Odysseus, the wide-travelling hero of Greek legend]

**umbel** /**um**-buhl/ *n.* flower-cluster with stalks springing from a common centre and forming a flat or curved surface. □ **umbellate** *adj.* [Latin *umbella* sunshade]

**umbelliferous** /um-buh-**lif**-uh-ruhs/ *adj.* (of a plant) bearing umbels, such as parsley and carrot.

**umber** /**um**-buh/ — *n.* **1** natural pigment like ochre but darker and browner. **2** colour of this. — *adj.* of this colour. [Latin *umbra* shadow]

**umbilical** /um-bil-uh-kuhl, ˌum-buh-**luy**-kuhl/ *adj.* of the navel. [from UMBILICUS]

**umbilical cord** *n.* cordlike structure attaching a foetus to the placenta.

**umbilicus** /um-**bil**-uh-kuhs, ˌum-buh-**luy**-kuhs/ *n.* (*pl.* **-bilici** /-**bil**-uh-suy, -buh-**luy**-suy/ or **-cuses**) navel. [Latin]

**umbra** /**um**-bruh/ *n.* (*pl.* **-s** or **-brae** /-bree/ ) total shadow, esp. that cast on the earth by the moon during a solar eclipse. [Latin, = shadow]

**umbrage** /**um**-brij/ *n.* offence taken (esp. *take umbrage at*). [Latin: related to UMBRA]

**umbrella** /um-**brel**-uh/ *n.* **1** collapsible cloth canopy on a central stick, used against rain, strong sun, etc. **2** protection, patronage. **3** (often *attrib.*) coordinating agency (*umbrella organisation*). [Italian diminutive: related to UMBRA]

**umbrella fern** *n.* any of several ferns of eastern Australia and elsewhere, the fronds of which produce an umbrella-like appearance.

**umbrella grass** *n.* any of several Australian grasses, useful as fodder, having an umbrella-like flowering panicle.

**umbrella tree** *n.* tree of Queensland and the NT, having jade-green leaflets radiating umbrella-like from a single point, red leaf-stalks, and scarlet flowers; often cultivated as an ornamental and as an indoor plant.

**umlaut** /**uum**-lowt/ *n.* **1** mark (¨) used over a vowel, esp. in Germanic languages, to indicate a vowel change. **2** such a vowel change, e.g. German *Mann*, *Männer* /**men**-uh/, English *man, men*. [German]

**umpire** /**um**-puyuh/ — *n.* **1** person enforcing rules and settling disputes in various sports. **2** person chosen to arbitrate between disputants, or to see fair play. — *v.* (**-ring**) (often foll. by *for, in*, etc.) act as umpire (in). [French *nonper* not equal: related to PEER²]

**umpteen** /ump-**teen**, **ump**-teen/ *colloq.* — *adj.* indefinitely many; a lot of. — *pron.* indefinitely many. □ **for the umpteenth time** for the latest in a very long list of times (*I'm telling you for the umpteenth time — I'm not interested*). [jocular formation on -TEEN]

**umpy** /**um**-pee/ *n.* (also **umpie, ump**) *colloq.* umpire. [abbreviation]

**UN** *abbr.* United Nations.

**un-¹** *prefix* **1** added to adjectives and participles and their derivative nouns and adverbs, meaning: **a** not: denoting the absence of a quality or state (*uneducated; unusable*). **b** reverse of, usu. with an implication of approval or disapproval, or with some other special connotation (*unselfish; unsociable; unscientific*). **2** (less often) added to nouns, meaning 'a lack of', 'the reverse of' (*unrest; untruth*). [Old English]

■ **Usage** The number of words that can be formed with this prefix (and with *un-²*) is virtually unlimited; consequently only a selection can be given here.

**un-²** *prefix* added to verbs and (less often) nouns, forming verbs denoting: **1** reversal or cancellation of an action or state (*undress; unsettle*). **2** deprivation or separation (*unmask*). **3** release from (*unburden*; *uncage*). **4** causing to be no longer (*unman*). [Old English]

■ **Usage** See note at *un* -¹.

**un-³** *prefix Chem.* denoting 'one', combined with other numerical roots *nil* (= 0), *un* (= 1), *bi* (= 2), etc., to form the names of elements based on the atomic number, and terminated with *-ium*, e.g. *unnilquadium* = 104, *ununbium* = 112. [Latin *unus* one]

**unabashed** /ˌun-uh-**basht**/ *adj.* not abashed. ☐ **unabashedly** *adv.*

**unabated** /ˌun-uh-**bay**-tuhd/ *adj.* not abated; undiminished.

**unable** /un-**ay**-buhl/ *predic. adj.* (usu. foll. by *to* + infin.) not able; lacking ability.

**unabridged** /ˌun-uh-**brijd**/ *adj.* complete; not abridged.

**unaccompanied** /ˌun-uh-**kum**-puh-need/ *adj.* **1** not accompanied. **2** *Mus.* without accompaniment.

**unaccomplished** /ˌun-uh-**kum**-plisht, -**kom**-plisht/ *adj.* **1** not accomplished; uncompleted (*all these unaccomplished tasks*). **2** lacking accomplishment, skill, expertise (*some quite unaccomplished singing*).

**unaccountable** /ˌun-uh-**kown**-tuh-buhl/ *adj.* **1** unable to be explained. **2** unpredictable or strange in behaviour. **3** not answerable for one's actions. ☐ **unaccountably** *adv.*

**unaccounted** /ˌun-uh-**kown**-tuhd/ *adj.* (often foll. by *for*) unexplained; not included in an account.

**unaccustomed** /ˌun-uh-**kus**-tuhmd/ *adj.* **1** (usu. foll. by *to*) not accustomed. **2** unusual (*unaccustomed silence*).

**unadorned** /ˌun-uh-**dawnd**/ *adj.* plain.

**unadulterated** /un-uh-**dul**-tuh-ˌray-tuhd/ *adj.* **1** pure. **2** complete, utter (*unadulterated nonsense*).

**unadvised** /ˌun-uh-**vuyzd**/ *adj.* **1** indiscreet; rash. **2** without advice. ☐ **unadvisedly** /-**vuy**-zuhd-lee/ *adv.*

**unaffected** /ˌun-uh-**fek**-tuhd/ *adj.* **1** (usu. foll. by *by*) not affected. **2** free from affectation. ☐ **unaffectedly** *adv.*

**unalike** /ˌun-uh-**luyk**/ *adj.* not alike; different.

**unalloyed** /ˌun-uh-**loid**, un-**al**-oid/ *adj.* **1** complete; utter (*unalloyed joy*). **2** pure.

**unambiguous** /ˌun-am-**big**-yoo-uhs/ *adj.* not ambiguous; clear or definite in meaning. ☐ **unambiguously** *adv.*

**unanimous** /yoo-**nan**-uh-muhs/ *adj.* **1** all in agreement (*committee was unanimous*). **2** (of an opinion, vote, etc.) by all without exception (*unanimous choice*). ☐ **unanimity** /-nuh-**nim**-uh-tee/ *n.*

**unanimously** *adv.* [Latin *unus* one, *animus* mind]

**unannounced** /ˌun-uh-**nownst**/ *adj.* not announced; without warning (of arrival etc.).

**unanswerable** /un-**ahn**-suh-ruh-buhl, -**an**-suh-/ *adj.* **1** irrefutable (*unanswerable case*). **2** unable to be answered (*unanswerable question*).

**unappealing** /ˌun-uh-**pee**-ling/ *adj.* unattractive.

**unapproachable** /ˌun-uh-**proh**-chuh-buhl/ *adj.* **1** not approachable; remote, inaccessible. **2** (of a person) unfriendly.

**unarmed** /un-**ahmd**/ *adj.* not armed; without weapons.

**unashamed** /ˌun-uh-**shaymd**/ *adj.* **1** feeling no guilt. **2** blatant; bold. ☐ **unashamedly** /-**muhd**-lee/ *adv.*

**unassailable** /ˌun-uh-**say**-luh-buhl/ *adj.* unable to be attacked; impregnable.

**unassuming** /ˌun-uh-**syoo**-ming/ *adj.* not pretentious; modest.

**unattached** /ˌun-uh-**tacht**/ *adj.* **1** not engaged, married, etc. **2** (often foll. by *to*) not attached, esp. to a particular organisation etc.

**unattended** /ˌun-uh-**ten**-duhd/ *adj.* **1** (usu. foll. by *to*) not attended. **2** (of a person, vehicle, etc.) alone.

**unattributable** /ˌun-uh-**trib**-yuh-tuh-buhl/ *adj.* (esp. of published information) that cannot be or is not allowed to be attributed to a source etc.

**unavailing** /ˌun-uh-**vay**-ling/ *adj.* achieving nothing; ineffectual. ☐ **unavailingly** *adv.*

**unavoidable** /ˌun-uh-**voi**-duh-buhl/ *adj.* inevitable. ☐ **unavoidably** *adv.*

**unaware** /ˌun-uh-**wair**/ — *adj.* **1** (usu. foll. by *of* or *that*) not aware (*unaware of his presence*). **2** unperceptive. — *adv.* = UNAWARES. ☐ **unawareness** *n.*

**unawares** *adv.* **1** unexpectedly (*met them unawares*). **2** inadvertently (*dropped it unawares*).

**unbalanced** /un-**bal**-uhnst/ *adj.* **1** (of wheels, a mechanism, etc.) not in proper balance. **2** emotionally unstable. **3** biased (*unbalanced report*).

**unbar** /un-**bah**/ *v.* (**-rr-**) **1** unlock, open. **2** remove a bar from (a gate etc.).

**unbearable** /un-**bair**-ruh-buhl/ *adj.* unendurable. ☐ **unbearably** *adv.*

**unbeatable** /un-**bee**-tuh-buhl/ *adj.* not beatable; excelling.

**unbeaten** /un-**bee**-tuhn/ *adj.* **1** not beaten. **2** (of a record etc.) not surpassed.

**unbecoming** /ˌun-bee-**kum**-ing, ˌun-buh-/ *adj.* **1** unflattering (*unbecoming hat*). **2** (usu. foll. by *to*, *for*) not fitting;

indecorous (*it's quite unbecoming for you to visit him so often*). □ **unbecomingly** *adv.*

**unbeknown** /ˌun-buh-**nohn**/ *adj.* (also **unbeknownst** /-**nohnst**/ ) (foll. by *to*) without the knowledge of (*unbeknown to us*).

**unbelief** /ˌun-bee-**leef**, ˌun-buh-/ *n.* lack of esp. religious belief. □ **unbeliever** *n.* **unbelieving** *adj.*

**unbelievable** /ˌun-bee-**lee**-vuh-buhl, ˌun-buh-/ *adj.* not believable; incredible. □ **unbelievably** *adv.*

**unbend** /un-**bend**/ *v.* (*past* and *past part.* **unbent**) **1** straighten. **2** relax; become affable.

**unbending** *adj.* **1** inflexible. **2** firm; austere. **3** relaxing from strain, activity, or formality.

**unbiased** /un-**buy**-uhst/ *adj.* (also **unbiassed**) impartial.

**unbidden** /un-**bid**-uhn/ *adj.* not commanded or invited (*arrived unbidden*).

**unbind** /un-**buynd**/ *v.* (*past* and *past part.* **unbound**) release; unfasten, untie.

**unblinking** /un-**bling**-king/ *adj.* **1** not blinking. **2** steadfast; not hesitating (*an unblinking determination*). **3** stolid; cool, unemotional (*an unblinking response to the charges*). □ **unblinkingly** *adv.*

**unblushing** /un-**blush**-ing/ *adj.* **1** shameless. **2** frank.

**unbolt** /un-**bohlt**/ *v.* release the bolt of (a door etc.).

**unborn** /un-**bawn**/ *adj.* not yet, or never to be, born (*unborn child; unborn hopes*).

**unbosom** /un-**buuz**-uhm/ *v.* (often *refl.*) disclose (thoughts etc.); unburden oneself.

**unbound¹** /un-**bownd**/ *adj.* **1** not bound. **2 a** (of a book) without a binding. **b** having paper covers.

**unbound²** *past* and *past part.* of UNBIND.

**unbounded** /un-**bown**-duhd/ *adj.* infinite, limitless (*unbounded optimism*).

**unbridle** /un-**bruy**-duhl/ *v.* (**-ling**) **1** remove a bridle from (a horse). **2** remove constraints from (one's tongue, a person, etc.). **3** (as **unbridled**) *adj.*) unconstrained (*unbridled insolence*).

**unbroken** /un-**broh**-kuhn/ *adj.* **1** not broken. **2** untamed (*unbroken horse*). **3** uninterrupted (*unbroken sleep*). **4** unsurpassed (*unbroken record*).

**unbuckle** /un-**buk**-uhl/ *v.* (**-ling**) release the buckle of (a strap, shoe, etc.).

**unburden** /un-**ber**-duhn/ *v.* **1** relieve of a burden. **2** (often *refl.*; often foll. by *to*) relieve (oneself, one's conscience, etc.) by confession etc. (*unburdened himself to her*).

**unbutton** /un-**but**-uhn/ *v.* **1** unfasten (a shirt etc.) by taking the buttons out of the buttonholes. **2** unbutton the clothes of (a person). **3** (*absol.*) *colloq.* relax from tension or formality; become communicative (*had a drink and began to unbutton*).

**uncalled-for** /un-**kawld**-faw/ *adj.* (of a remark, action, etc.) rude, unnecessary.

**uncanny** /un-**kan**-ee/ *adj.* (**-ier, -iest**) seemingly supernatural; mysterious. □ **uncannily** *adv.* **uncanniness** *n.*

**unceasing** /un-**see**-sing/ *adj.* not ceasing; continuous (*unceasing effort*).

**unceremonious** /ˌun-se-ruh-**moh**-nee-uhs/ *adj.* **1** abrupt; discourteous (*unceremonious dismissal*). **2** lacking ceremony or formality; informal (*a warm and unceremonious welcome of his workers to his house*). □ **unceremoniously** *adv.*

**uncertain** /un-**ser**-tuhn/ *adj.* **1** not certainly knowing or known; subject to doubt (*result is uncertain*). **2** unreliable (*his staying power is uncertain*). **3** changeable, erratic (*uncertain weather*). **4** not fully confident or assured, tentative (*his approach was uncertain*). □ **in no uncertain terms** clearly and forcefully. □ **uncertainly** *adv.* **uncertainty** *n.* (*pl.* **-ies**)

**uncertainty principle** *n.* *Physics* principle that the momentum and position of a particle cannot both be precisely determined at the same time.

**unchallengeable** /un-**chal**-uhn-juh-buhl/ *adj.* not challengeable; unassailable.

**uncharitable** /un-**cha**-ruh-tuh-buhl/ *adj.* **1** censorious, severe in judgment. **2** not generous. □ **uncharitably** *adv.*

**uncharted** /un-**chah**-tuhd/ *adj.* not mapped or surveyed.

**unchecked** /un-**chekt**/ *adj.* **1** not checked. **2** unrestrained (*unchecked violence*).

**unchristian** /un-**kris**-chuhn/ *adj.* contrary to Christian principles, esp. uncaring or selfish.

**uncial** /**un**-see-uhl/ — *adj.* of or written in rounded unjoined letters similar to capitals, found in manuscripts of the 4th–8th c. — *n.* uncial letter, style, or MS. [Latin *uncia* inch]

**uncircumcised** /un-**ser**-kuhm-ˌsuyzd/ *adj.* not circumcised.

**uncivil** /un-**siv**-uhl/ *adj.* ill-mannered; impolite. □ **uncivilly** *adv.*

**uncivilised** /un-**siv**-uh-ˌluyzd/ *adj.* (also **-ized**) **1** not civilised. **2** rough; uncultured.

**unclasp** /un-**klahsp**, -**klasp**/ *v.* **1** loosen the clasp(s) of. **2** release the grip of (a hand etc.).

**unclassified** /un-**klas**-uh-,fuyd/ *adj.* **1** not classified. **2** (of government information) not secret.

**uncle** /**ung**-kuhl/ *n.* **1 a** brother of one's father or mother. **b** aunt's husband. **2** (in Aboriginal English) male of one's parents' generation; community elder. [Latin *avunculus*]

**-uncle** *suffix* forming nouns, usu. diminutives (*carbuncle*). [Latin *-unculus*]

**unclean** /un-**kleen**/ *adj.* **1** not clean. **2** unchaste. **3** religiously impure; forbidden.

**unclear** /un-**kleer**/ *adj.* **1** not clear or easy to understand. **2** (of a person) uncertain (*I'm unclear as to what you mean*).

**unclench** /un-**klench**/ *v.* **1** release (clenched hands etc.). **2** (of hands etc.) become relaxed or open.

**Uncle Sam** *n. colloq.* the federal government or citizens of the US.

**unclothe** /un-**kloh**th/ *v.* (**-thing**) **1** remove clothes, leaves, etc. from. **2** expose, reveal.

**unclouded** /un-**klow**-duhd/ *adj.* **1** clear; bright. **2** untroubled (*unclouded serenity*).

**uncluttered** /un-**klut**-uhd/ *adj.* not cluttered; austere, simple.

**uncoloured** /un-**kul**-uhd/ *adj.* **1** having no colour. **2** not influenced; impartial. **3** not exaggerated.

**uncomfortable** /un-**kumf**-tuh-buhl/ *adj.* **1** not comfortable. **2** uneasy; disquieting (*uncomfortable silence*). □ **uncomfortably** *adv.*

**uncommitted** /,un-kuh-**mit**-uhd/ *adj.* **1** not committed. **2** not attached to any specific political cause or group.

**uncommon** /un-**kom**-uhn/ *adj.* **1** not common; unusual. **2** remarkably great etc. (*uncommon appetite*). □ **uncommonly** *adv.*

**uncommunicative** /,un-kuh-**myoo**-ni-kuh-tiv/ *adj.* not wanting to communicate; taciturn.

**uncomplaining** /,un-kuhm-**play**-ning/ *adj.* not complaining; resigned. □ **uncomplainingly** *adv.*

**uncomplimentary** /,un-kom-pluh-**men**-tuh-ree/ *adj.* insulting.

**uncompromising** /un-**kom**-pruh-,muy-zing/ *adj.* stubborn; unyielding. □ **uncompromisingly** *adv.*

**unconcern** /,un-kuhn-**sern**/ *n.* **1** calmness. **2** indifference; apathy. □ **unconcerned** *adj.* **unconcernedly** /-uhd-lee/ *adv.*

**unconditional** /,un-kuhn-**dish**-uh-nuhl/ *adj.* not subject to conditions; complete

(*unconditional surrender*). □ **unconditionally** *adv.*

**unconditioned reflex** *n.* instinctive response to a stimulus.

**unconfined** /,un-kuhn-**fuynd**/ *adj.* not confined; boundless.

**unconnected** /,un-kuhn-**nek**-tuhd/ *adj.* **1** not physically joined. **2** not connected or associated. **3** (of speech etc.) disconnected; not joined in order or sequence (*unconnected ideas*). **4** not related by family ties.

**unconscionable** /un-**kon**-shuh-nuh-buhl/ *adj.* **1** without or contrary to conscience. **2** unreasonably excessive (*unconscionable waste*). [from UN-[1], CONSCIENCE]

**unconscious** /un-**kon**-shuhs/ — *adj.* not conscious (*unconscious of any change; fell unconscious; unconscious prejudice*). — *n.* that part of the mind which is inaccessible to the conscious mind but which affects behaviour, emotions, etc. □ **unconsciously** *adv.* **unconsciousness** *n.*

**unconsidered** /,un-kuhn-**sid**-uhd/ *adj.* **1** not considered; disregarded. **2** (of a response etc.) immediate; not premeditated.

**unconstitutional** /,un-kon-stuh-**tyoo**-shuh-nuhl/ *adj.* in breach of a political constitution or procedural rules. □ **unconstitutionally** *adv.*

**uncontrolled** /,un-kuhn-**trohld**/ *adj.* not controlled; unrestrained; unchecked.

**unconventional** /,un-kuhn-**ven**-shuh-nuhl/ *adj.* not bound by convention or custom; unusual; unorthodox. □ **unconventionally** *adv.*

**uncoordinated** /,un-koh-**aw**-duh-,nay-tuhd/ *adj.* **1** not coordinated. **2** (of a person's movements etc.) clumsy.

**uncork** /un-**kawk**/ *v.* **1** draw the cork from (a bottle). **2** vent (feelings etc.).

**uncorroborated** /,un-kuh-**rob**-uh-,ray-tuhd/ *adj.* (esp. of evidence etc.) not corroborated.

**uncountable** /un-**kown**-tuh-buhl/ *adj.* **1** inestimable, immense (*uncountable wealth*). **2** (of a noun) not used in the plural or with the indefinite article (e.g. *happiness, milk*).

**uncounted** /un-**kown**-tuhd/ *adj.* **1** not counted. **2** very many; innumerable.

**uncouth** /un-**kooth**/ *adj.* (of a person, manners, appearance, etc.) lacking in ease and polish; uncultured, rough. [Old English, = unknown]

**uncover** /un-**kuv**-uh/ *v.* **1** remove a cover or covering from. **2** make known; disclose (*uncovered the truth*).

**uncritical** /un-**krit**-i-kuhl/ *adj.* **1** not critical; complacently accepting. **2** not in accordance with the principles of criticism. □ **uncritically** *adv.*

**uncrown** /un-**krown**/ *v.* **1** deprive of a crown, a position, etc. **2** (as **uncrowned** *adj.*) **a** not crowned. **b** having the status but not the name of (*uncrowned king of boxing*).

**unction** /**ungk**-shuhn/ *n.* **1 a** anointing with oil etc. as a religious rite or medical treatment (*extreme unction*). **b** oil, ointment, etc. so used. **2 a** soothing words or thought. **b** excessive or insincere flattery. **3 a** emotional fervency. **b** pretence of this. [Latin *ungo unct-* anoint]

**unctuous** /**ungk**-choo-uhs/ *adj.* **1** (of behaviour, speech, etc.) unpleasantly flattering; oily. **2** (esp. of minerals) having a greasy or soapy feel. □ **unctuously** *adv.* [medieval Latin: related to UNCTION]

**uncured** /un-**kyoord**/ *adj.* **1** not cured. **2** (of pork etc.) not salted or smoked.

**uncut** /un-**kut**/ *adj.* **1** not cut. **2** (of a book) with the pages sealed or untrimmed. **3** (of a book, film, etc.) complete; uncensored. **4** (of esp. a diamond) not shaped. **5** (of fabric) with a looped pile. **6** *colloq.* (of the penis, or of a male) uncircumcised. **7** *colloq.* (of drugs, esp. heroin) undiluted, unadulterated.

**undeceive** /un-duh-**seev**/ *v.* (**-ving**) (often foll. by *of*) free (a person) from a misconception, deception, or error.

**undecided** /un-duh-**suy**-duhd/ *adj.* **1** not settled or certain (*the question is undecided*). **2** hesitating; irresolute (*undecided about their relative merits*).

**undefined** /un-duh-**fuynd**/ *adj.* **1** not defined. **2** not clearly marked; vague, indefinite.

**undemanding** /un-duh-**mahn**-ding, -**man**-ding/ *adj.* not demanding; easily done or satisfied (*undemanding reading*).

**undemonstrative** /un-duh-**mon**-struh-tiv/ *adj.* not emotionally expressive; reserved.

**undeniable** /un-duh-**nuy**-uh-buhl/ *adj.* unable to be denied or disputed; certain. □ **undeniably** *adv.*

**under** — *prep.* **1 a** in or to a position lower than; below; beneath (*under the table*). **b** on the inside of (*vest under his shirt*). **2** inferior to; less than (*no-one under a major*; *is under 18*; *was under $20*). **3 a** subject to; controlled by (*under constraint*; *born under Saturn*; *prospered under him*). **b** undergoing (*is under repair*). **c** classified or subsumed in (*you'll find that book under biology*; *goes under many names*). **4** at the foot of or sheltered

by (*under the cliff*). **5** planted with (a crop). **6** powered by (sail, steam, etc.). — *adv.* **1** in or to a lower position or condition (*kept him under*). **2** *colloq.* in or into unconsciousness (*put him under for the operation*). — *adj.* lower (*under jaw*). □ **under arms** see ARM². **under one's belt** see BELT. **under one's breath** see BREATH. **under a cloud** see CLOUD. **under control** see CONTROL. **under the counter** see COUNTER¹. **under fire** see FIRE. **under a person's nose** see NOSE. **under the sun** anywhere in the world. **under the table** see TABLE. **under a person's thumb** see THUMB. **under way** in motion; in progress. **under the weather** see WEATHER. □ **undermost** *adj.* [Old English]

**under-** *prefix* in senses of UNDER: **1** below, beneath (*underground*). **2** lower; subordinate (*undergraduate*). **3** insufficiently, incompletely (*undercook*; *underdeveloped*).

**underachieve** *v.* (**-ving**) do less well than might be expected (esp. academically). □ **underachiever** *n.*

**under-age** *adj.* (also **under age**) carried on by a person below the legal age (for an activity) (*under-age drinking*).

**underarm** — *adj.* & *adv. Sport*, esp. *Cricket* with the arm below shoulder-level. — *attrib. adj.* **1** under the arm (*underarm seam*). **2** in the armpit.

**underbelly** *n.* (*pl.* **-ies**) undersurface of an animal, vehicle, etc., esp. as vulnerable to attack.

**underbid** — *v.* /un-duh-**bid**/ (**-dd-**; *past* and *past part.* **-bid**) **1** make a lower bid than. **2** (also *absol.*) *Bridge* etc. bid less on (one's hand) than warranted. — *n.* /**un**-duh-bid/ such a bid.

**undercarriage** *n.* **1** wheeled retractable structure beneath an aircraft, used for landing etc. **2** supporting frame of a vehicle.

**undercharge** /un-duh-**chahj**/ *v.* (**-ging**) **1** charge too little to (a person). **2** give too little charge to (a gun, electric battery, etc.).

**underclothes** *n.pl.* clothes worn under others, esp. next to the skin.

**underclothing** *n.* underclothes collectively.

**undercoat** — *n.* **1** preliminary layer of paint under a finishing coat. **2** paint for this. — *v.* apply such a layer of paint.

**undercook** /un-duh-**kuuk**/ *v.* cook insufficiently.

**undercover** /un-duh-**kuv**-uh, **un**-/ *adj.* (usu. *attrib.*) **1** surreptitious. **2** spying incognito, esp. by infiltration (*undercover agent*).

**undercurrent** n. **1** current below the surface. **2** underlying often contrary feeling, influence, etc. (*undercurrent of protest*).

**undercut** — v. /ˌun-duh-**kut**/ (**-tt-**; *past and past part.* **-cut**) **1** sell or work at a lower price than. **2** strike (a ball) to make it rise high. **3** cut away the part below. **4** render unstable or less firm; undermine. — n. /**un**-duh-ˌkut/ **1** underside of sirloin. **2** hairstyle in which the hair is cut very short from the nape of the neck upwards to a certain extent at the back and sides and the rest is left long; not tapered.

**underdaks** n.pl. colloq. briefs, underpants.

**underdeveloped** /ˌun-duh-duh-**vel**-uhpt/ adj. **1** not fully developed; immature. **2** (of a country etc.) below its potential economic level. □ **underdevelopment** n.

**underdog** n. **1** oppressed person. **2** loser or expected loser in a fight, sporting competition, etc.

**underdone** /ˌun-duh-**dun**, **un**-/ adj. **1** undercooked. **2** colloq. (of a sportsperson etc.) not at the peak of fitness or preparedness.

**underestimate** — v. /ˌun-duhr-**es**-tuh-ˌmayt/ (**-ting**) form too low an estimate of. — n. /ˌun-duhr-**es**-tuh-muht/ estimate that is too low. □ **underestimation** /-may-shuhn/ n.

**underexpose** /ˌun-duh-rek-**spohz**/ v. (**-sing**) expose (film) for too short a time or with insufficient light. □ **underexposure** n.

**underfelt** n. felt laid under a carpet.

**underfoot** /ˌun-duh-**fuut**/ adv. (also **under foot**) **1** under one's feet. **2** on the ground. **3** so as to obstruct or inconvenience.

**undergarment** n. item of underclothing.

**undergo** /ˌun-duh-**goh**/ v. (3rd sing. present **-goes**; past **-went**; past part. **-gone**) be subjected to; suffer; endure.

**undergraduate** /ˌun-duh-**graj**-oo-uht, -**grad**-yoo-/ n. person studying for a first degree.

**underground** — adv. /ˌun-duh-**grownd**/ **1** beneath the surface of the ground. **2** in or into secrecy or hiding. — adj. /**un**-duh-ˌgrownd/ **1** situated underground. **2** secret, hidden, esp. working secretly to subvert a ruling power. **3** unconventional, experimental. (*underground literature*). — n. /**un**-duh-ˌgrownd/ **1** underground railway. **2** secret subversive group or activity.

**underground mutton** n. joc. rabbit.

**underground orchid** n. either of two completely subterranean orchids (the only such in the world), having dark-coloured flowers and living on decayed vegetable matter, one endemic in south-western WA, the other in eastern Australia.

**undergrowth** n. dense shrubs etc., esp. in a forest.

**underhand** adj. **1** deceitful; crafty; secret. **2** Sport, esp. Cricket underarm.

**underlay**[1] — v. /ˌun-duh-**lay**/ (past and past part. **-laid**) lay something under (a thing) to support or raise it. — n. /**un**-duh-ˌluy/ thing so laid (esp. under a carpet).

**underlay**[2] past of UNDERLIE.

**underlie** /ˌun-duh-**luy**/ v. (**-lying**; past **-lay**; past part. **-lain**) **1** (also absol.) lie under (a stratum etc.). **2** (also absol.) (esp. as **underlying** adj.) be the basis of (a doctrine, conduct, etc.). **3** exist beneath the superficial aspect of.

**underline** /ˌun-duh-**luyn**/ v. (**-ning**) **1** draw a line under (a word etc.) to give emphasis, indicate italic type, etc. **2** emphasise, stress.

**underling** /**un**-duh-ling/ n. usu. derog. subordinate.

**underlying** pres. part. of UNDERLIE.

**undermanned** /ˌun-duh-**mand**/ adj. having an insufficient crew or staff.

**undermentioned** /ˌun-duh-**men**-shuhnd, **un**-/ adj. mentioned later in a book etc.

**undermine** /ˌun-duh-**muyn**/ v. (**-ning**) **1** injure (a person, reputation, health, etc.) secretly or insidiously. **2** weaken, injure, or wear out (health, confidence, etc.) imperceptibly or insidiously. **3** wear away the base of (*banks were undermined*). **4** make an excavation under.

**underneath** /ˌun-duh-**neeth**/ — prep. **1** at or to a lower place than, below. **2** on the inside of. — adv. **1** at or to a lower place. **2** inside. — n. lower surface or part. — adj. lower. [Old English: related to NETHER]

**undernourished** /ˌun-duh-**nu**-risht/ adj. insufficiently nourished. □ **undernourishment** n.

**underpaid** past and past part. of UNDERPAY.

**underpants** n.pl. undergarment, esp. men's, covering the genitals and buttocks.

**underpart** n. lower or subordinate part.

**underpass** n. **1** road etc. passing under another. **2** subway.

**underpay** /ˌun-duh-**pay**/ v. (past and past part. **-paid**) pay too little to (a person) or for (a thing). □ **underpayment** n.

**underpin** /ˌun-duh-**pin**/ v. (**-nn-**) **1** support from below with masonry etc. **2** support, strengthen.

**underplay** /ˌun-duh-**play**/ v. **1** make little of. **2** *Theatr.* perform with deliberate restraint.

**underprivileged** /ˌun-duh-**priv**-uh-lijd/ adj. less privileged than others; having below average income, rights, etc.

**underproof** adj. containing less alcohol than proof spirit does.

**underrate** /ˌun-duh-**rayt**/ v. (**-ting**) have too low an opinion of.

**underscore** /ˌun-duh-**skaw**/ v. (**-ring**) = UNDERLINE.

**undersell** /ˌun-duh-**sel**/ v. (*past* and *past part.* **-sold**) **1** sell at a lower price than (another seller). **2** *refl.* sell (oneself etc.) short or underplay one's abilities through a lack of confidence in self.

**undersexed** /ˌun-duh-**sekst**/ adj. having unusually weak sexual desires.

**undershot** adj. **1** (of a water-wheel) turned by water flowing under it. **2** (of a lower jaw) projecting beyond the upper jaw.

**undersigned** /un-duh-ˌsuynd, -**suynd**/ adj. (usu. *absol.*) whose signature is appended (*we, the undersigned*).

**undersized** /un-duh-ˌsuyzd, -**suyzd**/ adj. smaller than average.

**underslung** /un-duh-ˌslung/ adj. **1** supported from above. **2** (of a vehicle chassis) hanging lower than the axles.

**undersold** *past* and *past part.* of UNDERSELL.

**underspend** /ˌun-duh-**spend**/ v. (*past* and *past part.* **-spent**) (usu. *absol.*) spend less than (the expected amount), or too little.

**understaffed** /ˌun-duh-**stahft**/ adj. having too few staff.

**understand** /ˌun-duh-**stand**/ v. (*past* and *past part.* **-stood**) **1** perceive the meaning of (words, a person, a language, a subject, etc.) (*understood you perfectly*; *cannot understand algebra*). **2** perceive the significance or explanation or cause of (*do not understand why he came*). **3** (often *absol.*) sympathise with, know how to deal with (*quite understand your difficulty*; *ask her, she understands*). **4 a** (often foll. by *that*) infer, esp. from information received; take as implied; take for granted (*I understand him to be a distant relation*; *am I to understand that you refuse?*). **b** *absol.* believe or assume from knowledge or inference (*he is coming tomorrow, I understand*). **5** supply (an implied missing word) mentally (*the verb may be either expressed or understood*). □ **understand each other 1** know each other's views. **2** agree or collude. □ **understandable** adj.

**understandably** adv. [Old English: related to STAND]

**understanding** — n. **1 a** ability to understand or think; intelligence. **b** power of apprehension or abstract thought. **2** individual's perception or judgment of a situation etc. **3** agreement, esp. informal (*had an understanding with the rival company*). **4** harmony in opinion or feeling (*disturbed the good understanding between them*). **5** sympathetic awareness or tolerance. — adj. **1** having understanding or insight or good judgment. **2** sympathetic to others' feelings. □ **understandingly** adv.

**understate** /ˌun-duh-**stayt**/ v. (**-ting**) **1** express mildly or in a restrained way. **2** represent as less than it actually is. □ **understatement** n.

**understood** *past* and *past part.* of UNDERSTAND.

**understudy** esp. *Theatr.* — n. (pl. **-ies**) person ready to take on another's role etc. when required. — v. (**-ies, -ied**) **1** study (a role etc.) thus. **2** act as an understudy to.

**undersubscribed** /ˌun-duh-suhb-**skruybd**/ adj. without sufficient subscribers, participants, etc.

**undertake** /ˌun-duh-**tayk**/ v. (**-king**; *past* **-took**; *past part.* **-taken**) **1** agree to perform or be responsible for; engage in, enter upon (work, a responsibility, etc.). **2** (usu. foll. by *to* + infin.) promise. **3** guarantee, affirm (*undertake that he is innocent*).

**undertaker** /un-duh-ˌtay-kuh/ n. professional funeral organiser.

**undertaking** /ˌund-uh-**tay**-king/ n. **1** work etc. undertaken, enterprise (*serious undertaking*). **2** pledge or promise.

**under the counter** see COUNTER.

**undertone** n. **1** subdued tone or sound or colour. **2** underlying quality. **3** undercurrent of feeling.

**undertook** *past* of UNDERTAKE.

**undertow** n. current below the surface of the sea moving in the opposite direction to the surface current.

**undervalue** /ˌun-duh-**val**-yoo/ v. (**-ues, -ued, -uing**) **1** value insufficiently. **2** underestimate.

**underwater** /ˌun-duh-**waw**-tuh/ — adj. situated or done under water. — adv. under water.

**underwear** n. underclothes.

**underweight** — adj. /ˌun-duh-**wayt**/ below normal weight. — n. /**un**-duh-ˌwayt/ insufficient weight.

**underwent** *past* of UNDERGO.

**underwhelm** /ˌun-duh-**welm**/ v. *joc.* fail to impress. [alteration of OVERWHELM]

**underworld** n. **1** those who live by organised crime and vice. **2** mythical abode of the dead under the earth.

**underwrite** /ˌun-duh-**ruyt**, **un**-/ v. (**-ting**; past **-wrote**; past part. **-written**) **1 a** sign and accept liability under (an insurance policy, esp. on shipping etc.). **b** accept (liability) in this way. **2** undertake to finance or support. **3** engage to buy all the unsold stock in (a company etc.). □ **underwriter** /**un**-/ n.

**undescended** /ˌun-duh-**sen**-duhd/ adj. (of a testicle) remaining in the abdomen instead of descending normally into the scrotum.

**undeserved** /ˌun-duh-**zervd**/ adj. not deserved (as a reward or punishment). □ **undeservedly** /-vuhd-lee/ adv.

**undesirable** /ˌun-duh-**zuy**-ruh-buhl/ — adj. not desirable; objectionable, unpleasant. — n. undesirable person. □ **undesirability** /-**bil**-uh-tee/ n.

**undetermined** /ˌun-duh-**ter**-muhnd/ adj. = UNDECIDED.

**undid** past of UNDO.

**undies** /**un**-deez/ n.pl. colloq. underwear; underpants. [abbreviation]

**undifferentiated** /ˌun-dif-uh-**ren**-shee-ˌay-tuhd/ adj. not differentiated; amorphous.

**undigested** /ˌun-duy-**jes**-tuhd, ˌun-duh-/ adj. **1** not digested. **2** (of facts etc.) not properly arranged or considered.

**undiminished** /ˌun-duh-**min**-isht/ adj. not diminished or lessened.

**undiplomatic** /ˌun-dip-luh-**mat**-ik/ adj. tactless.

**undisciplined** /un-**dis**-uh-pluhnd/ adj. lacking discipline; not disciplined.

**undisclosed** /ˌun-dis-**klohzd**/ adj. not revealed or made known.

**undiscriminating** /ˌun-duh-**skrim**-uh-ˌnay-ting/ adj. lacking good judgment.

**undisguised** /ˌun-dis-**guyzd**/ adj. not disguised; open.

**undisputed** /ˌun-dis-**pyoo**-tuhd/ adj. not disputed or called in question.

**undistinguished** /ˌun-dis-**ting**-gwisht/ adj. not distinguished; mediocre.

**undisturbed** /ˌun-dis-**terbd**/ adj. not disturbed or interfered with.

**undivided** /ˌun-duh-**vuy**-duhd/ adj. not divided or shared; whole, entire (undivided attention).

**undo** /un-**doo**/ v. (3rd sing. present **-does**; past **-did**; past part. **-done**; partic. **-doing**) **1** unfasten (a coat, button, parcel, etc.), or the clothing of (a person). **2** annul, cancel (cannot undo the past). **3** ruin the prospects, reputation, or morals of.

**undoing** n. **1** ruin or cause of ruin. **2** process of reversing what had been done. **3** action of opening or unfastening.

**undone** /un-**dun**/ adj. **1** not done (left the job undone). **2** not fastened (your fly is undone). **3** archaic ruined (I am undone, alas!).

**undoubted** /un-**dow**-tuhd/ adj. certain, not questioned, not regarded as doubtful. □ **undoubtedly** adv.

**undreamed** /un-**dreemd**, un-**dremt**/ adj. (also **undreamt** /un-**dremt**/ ) (often foll. by of) not dreamed, thought, or imagined (an undreamed of coincidence).

**undress** /un-**dres**/ — v. **1** take off one's clothes. **2** take the clothes off (a person). **3** joc. shear (a sheep). — n. **1** ordinary or casual dress, esp. as opposed to full dress or uniform. **2** being naked or scantily clad (in a state of undress).

**undressed** /un-**drest**/ adj. **1** not, or no longer, dressed. **2** (of food) without a dressing. **3** (of leather etc.) not treated.

**undue** /un-**dyoo**/ adj. **1** excessive, disproportionate (undue severity). **2** not suitable or proper (undue influence on an impressionable mind). □ **unduly** adv.

**undulate** /**un**-dyoo-ˌlayt/ v. (**-ting**) (cause to) have a wavy motion or look. □ **undulation** /ˌun-dyuh-**lay**-shuhn/ n. [Latin unda wave]

**undying** /un-**duy**-ing/ adj. **1** immortal. **2** never-ending; lifelong (undying love).

**unearned** /un-**ernd**/ adj. not earned.

**unearned income** n. income from investments etc. rather than from working.

**unearth** /un-**erth**/ v. discover by searching, digging, or rummaging.

**unearthly** /un-**erth**-lee/ adj. **1** supernatural, mysterious. **2** colloq. absurdly early or inconvenient (unearthly hour). □ **unearthliness** n.

**unease** /un-**eez**/ n. nervousness, anxiety.

**uneasy** /un-**ee**-zee/ adj. (**-ier**, **-iest**) **1** nervous, anxious. **2** disturbing (uneasy suspicion). □ **uneasily** adv. **uneasiness** n.

**uneconomic** /ˌun-ee-kuh-**nom**-ik, ˌun-ek-uh-/ adj. not economic; unprofitable.

**uneconomical** adj. not economical; wasteful.

**unedifying** /un-**ed**-uh-ˌfuy-ing/ adj. distasteful, degrading.

**unemployable** /ˌun-em-**ploi**-uh-buhl/ adj. unfit for paid employment. □ **unemployability** /-**bil**-uh-tee/ n.

**unemployed** /ˌun-em-**ploid**, ˌun-uhm-/ — adj. **1** not having paid work; out of work. **2** not in use (while the machines are unemployed). — n. (prec. by the) those who are unemployed.

**unemployment** /ˌun-em-**ploi**-muhnt, ˌun-uhm-/ *n.* **1** state of being unemployed. **2** condition or extent of this in a country or region.

**unemployment benefit** *n.* government payment made to an unemployed person.

**unencumbered** /ˌun-en-**kum**-buhd, ˌun-uhn-/ *adj.* **1 a** (of an estate) not having liabilities (e.g. a mortgage). **b** (of a motor vehicle) not subject to financial interest by a lending institution. **2** free; not burdened.

**unendurable** /ˌun-en-**dyoor**-ruh-buhl, ˌun-uhn-/ *adj.* too bad to be borne.

**unequal** /un-ee-kwuhl/ *adj.* **1** not equal. **2** (of work or achievements etc.) not of the same quality throughout. **3** not with equal advantage to both sides; not well matched (*an unequal contest*). **4** (foll. by *to*) unable to deal with the demands of a particular job or task. □ **unequally** *adv.*

**unequalled** *adj.* superior to all others.

**unequivocal** /ˌun-ee-**kwiv**-uh-kuhl, ˌun-uh-/ *adj.* not ambiguous, plain, unmistakable. □ **unequivocally** *adv.*

**unerring** /un-**er**-ring/ *adj.* not erring; true, certain. □ **unerringly** *adv.*

**UNESCO** /yoo-**nes**-koh/ *abbr.* (also **Unesco**) United Nations Educational, Scientific, and Cultural Organisation.

**unethical** /un-**eth**-i-kuhl/ *adj.* not ethical, esp. unscrupulous in business or professional conduct. □ **unethically** *adv.*

**uneven** /un-ee-vuhn/ *adj.* **1** not level or smooth. **2** of variable quality etc. **3** (of a contest) unequal. □ **unevenly** *adv.* **unevenness** *n.*

**unexampled** /ˌun-eg-**zahm**-puhld, -**zam**-, ˌun-uhg-/ *adj.* having no precedent or parallel.

**unexceptionable** /ˌun-ek-**sep**-shuh-nuh-buhl, ˌun-uhk-/ *adj.* with which no fault can be found; entirely satisfactory (*unexceptionable behaviour*).

■ **Usage** See note at *exceptionable*.

**unexceptional** /ˌun-ek-**sep**-shuh-nuhl, ˌun-uhk-/ *adj.* not out of the ordinary; usual, normal.

**unexpected** /ˌun-ek-**spek**-tuhd, ˌun-uhk-/ *adj.* not expected; surprising. □ **unexpectedly** *adv.* **unexpectedness** *n.*

**unexpressed** /ˌun-ek-**sprest**, ˌun-uhk-/ *adj.* not expressed or made known (*unexpressed fears*).

**unexpurgated** /un-**ek**-spuh-ˌgay-tuhd/ *adj.* (esp. of a text etc.) not expurgated; complete.

**unfailing** /un-**fay**-ling/ *adj.* not failing or dwindling; constant; reliable (*unfailing support; unfailing resources*). □ **unfailingly** *adv.*

**unfair** /un-**fair**/ *adj.* **1** not equitable or honest (*obtained by unfair means; unfair business practices*). **2** not impartial or according to the rules (*unfair decision; unfair play*). □ **unfairly** *adv.* **unfairness** *n.*

**unfaithful** /un-**fayth**-fuhl/ *adj.* **1** not faithful, esp. adulterous. **2** treacherous; disloyal. □ **unfaithfully** *adv.* **unfaithfulness** *n.*

**unfamiliar** /ˌun-fuh-**mil**-yuh/ *adj.* **1** not familiar, strange (*unfamiliar territory*). **2** not part of one's everyday (or expert) knowledge (*being a pom, I'm unfamiliar with many Australian customs*). □ **unfamiliarity** /-ee-a-ruh-tee/ *n.*

**unfasten** /un-**fah**-suhn/ *v.* **1** make or become loose. **2** open the fastening(s) of (*unfasten your seat-belts*). **3** detach (*unfasten the lifeboats*).

**unfathomable** /un-**fath**-uh-muh-buhl/ *adj.* incapable of being fathomed or fully understood (*the Trinity is an unfathomable mystery to me*).

**unfavourable** /un-**fay**-vuh-ruh-buhl/ *adj.* (also **unfavorable**) not favourable; adverse, hostile. □ **unfavourably** *adv.*

**unfazed** *adj. colloq.* untroubled; not disconcerted.

**unfeasible** /un-**fee**-zuh-buhl/ *adj.* not feasible; impractical.

**unfeeling** /un-**fee**-ling/ *adj.* unsympathetic, harsh.

**unfeigned** /un-**faynd**/ *adj.* genuine, sincere.

**unfetter** /un-**fet**-uh/ *v.* **1** release from fetters. **2** not subject to the usual controls or limitations; let loose (*unfettered passions; unfettered corporate greed*).

**unfinancial** /ˌun-fuy-**nan**-shuhl/ *adj.* **1** insolvent. **2** not having paid a subscription (*some members are unfinancial*).

**unfit** /un-**fit**/ — *adj.* **1** not physically fit. **2** (often foll. by *for*, or *to* + infin.) not fit or suitable (*unfit for the job*). — *v.* (**-tt-**) (often foll. by *for*) make unsuitable (*his known belief that women must be subservient to their husbands unfits him to try this case of rape in marriage; this will unfit him for active service*).

**unfitted** /un-**fit**-uhd/ *adj.* **1** not fit. **2** not fitted or suited. **3** having no fittings.

**unfitting** /un-**fit**-ing/ *adj.* not suitable, unbecoming.

**unflagging** /un-**flag**-ing/ *adj.* tireless, persistent.

**unflappable** /un-**flap**-uh-buhl/ *adj. colloq.* not subject to nervous excitement or anxiety; imperturbable; calm. □ **unflappability** /-**bil**-uh-tee/ *n.*

**unfledged** /un-**flejd**/ *adj.* **1** (of a person) inexperienced. **2** (of a bird) not yet fledged.

**unfold** /un-**fohld**/ *v.* **1** open the fold or folds of, spread out (*unfolded the map*). **2** reveal (thoughts etc.) (*unfolded his desire for me*). **3** become opened out (*watch the bud unfold in slow motion*). **4** develop (*as the story unfolded*).

**unforced** /un-**fawst**/ *adj.* **1** easy, natural. **2** not compelled or constrained.

**unforeseen** /ˌun-faw-**seen**/ *adj.* not foreseen; unexpected.

**unforgettable** /ˌun-fuh-**get**-uh-buhl/ *adj.* that cannot be forgotten; memorable, wonderful.

**unformed** /un-**fawmd**/ *adj.* **1** not formed. **2** shapeless. **3** not developed.

**unfortunate** /un-**faw**-chuh-nuht/ — *adj.* **1** having bad fortune; unlucky. **2** unhappy. **3** regrettable. **4** disastrous. — *n.* unfortunate person.

**unfortunately** *adv.* **1** (qualifying a sentence) it is unfortunate that. **2** in an unfortunate manner.

**unfounded** /un-**fown**-duhd/ *adj.* without foundation (*unfounded rumour*).

**unfreeze** /un-**freez**/ *v.* (**-zing**; *past un-froze*; *past part.* **unfrozen**) **1** (cause to) thaw. **2** derestrict (assets, credits, etc.).

**unfrock** /un-**frok**/ *v.* = DEFROCK.

**unfroze** *past* of UNFREEZE.

**unfrozen** *past part.* of UNFREEZE.

**unfurl** /un-**ferl**/ *v.* **1** unroll, spread out (a sail, umbrella, etc.). **2** become unrolled.

**unfurnished** /un-**fer**-nisht/ *adj.* **1** (usu. foll. by *with*) not supplied. **2** without furniture.

**ungainly** /un-**gayn**-lee/ *adj.* (of a person, animal, or movement) awkward, clumsy. □ **ungainliness** *n.* [obsolete *gain* straight, from Old Norse]

**Ungarinyin** /uun-gah-ˌrin-yin/ *n.* Aboriginal language spoken by the Ngarinyin people in the north Kimberley region of WA.

**unget-at-able** /ˌun-get-**at**-uh-buhl/ *adj.* *colloq.* inaccessible.

**ungodly** /un-**god**-lee/ *adj.* **1** impious, wicked. **2** *colloq.* outrageous (*ungodly hour*).

**ungovernable** /un-**guv**-uh-nuh-buhl/ *adj.* uncontrollable, violent (*an ungovernable temper*).

**ungracious** /un-**gray**-shuhs/ *adj.* discourteous; grudging (*an ungracious apology*). □ **ungraciously** *adv.*

**ungrammatical** /ˌun-gruh-**mat**-i-kuhl/ *adj.* contrary to the rules of grammar. □ **ungrammatically** *adv.*

**ungrateful** /un-**grayt**-fuhl/ *adj.* not feeling or showing gratitude. □ **ungratefully** *adv.*

**ungreen** /un-**green**/ *adj.* not concerned with the protection of the environment; harmful to the environment (*ungreen attitudes of some loggers; ungreen practices of some industries*).

**unguarded** /un-**gah**-duhd/ *adj.* **1** incautious, thoughtless (*unguarded remark*). **2** not guarded; without a guard (*unguarded premises*).

**unguent** /ung-gwuhnt/ *n.* soft ointment or lubricant. [Latin *unguo* anoint]

**ungulate** /**ung**-gyuh-luht, -ˌlayt/ — *adj.* hoofed. — *n.* hoofed mammal. [Latin *ungula* hoof, claw]

**unhallowed** /un-**hal**-ohd/ *adj.* **1** not consecrated. **2** not sacred; unholy, wicked.

**unhand** /un-**hand**/ *v. rhet.* or *joc.* take one's hands off (a person); release (*unhand me, villain!*).

**unhappy** /un-**hap**-ee/ *adj.* (**-ier, -iest**) **1** miserable. **2** unfortunate (*as things turned out, our decision to merge was an unhappy one*). □ **unhappily** *adv.* **unhappiness** *n.*

**unhealthy** /un-**hel**-thee/ *adj.* (**-ier, -iest**) **1** in poor health. **2 a** harmful to health (*smoking is utterly unhealthy*). **b** unwholesome (*unhealthy fumes from the factory*). **c** morally dangerous (*he has an unhealthy influence over them*). **d** psychologically unwholesome (*he has an unhealthy interest in instruments of torture*). **e** *colloq.* dangerous (*this place is going to be unhealthy for you, mate, if you're still here in five minutes*). □ **unhealthily** *adv.* **unhealthiness** *n.*

**unheard** /un-**herd**/ *adj.* **1** not heard. **2** (usu. **unheard-of**) unprecedented.

**unhinge** /un-**hinj**/ *v.* (**-ging**) **1** take (a door etc.) off its hinges. **2** (esp. as **unhinged** *adj.*) make mad or crazy.

**unholy** /un-**hoh**-lee/ *adj.* (**-ier, -iest**) **1** impious, wicked. **2** *colloq.* dreadful (*unholy row*).

**unhorse** /un-**haws**/ *v.* (**-sing**) throw (a rider) from a horse.

**uni** /**yoo**-nee/ *n.* (*pl.* **-s**) *colloq.* university (*Melbourne Uni; I'm at uni*; also *attrib.*: *uni courses*). [abbreviation]

**uni-** *comb. form* one; having or consisting of one. [Latin *unus* one]

**Uniat** /**yoo**-nee-ˌat, -uht/ (also **Uniate** /-ˌayt/ ) — *adj.* of the Church in E. Europe, N. Africa, or SW Asia, acknowledging papal supremacy but retaining its own liturgy etc. — *n.* member of such a Church. [Latin *unio* UNION]

**unicameral** /ˌyoo-nee-**kam**-uh-ruhl/ *adj.* with a single legislative chamber. [related to CHAMBER]

**UNICEF** /**yoo**-nuh-ˌsef/ *abbr.* United Nations Children's (orig. International Children's Emergency) Fund.

**unicellular** /ˌyoo-nee-**sel**-yuh-luh/ *adj.* (of an organism etc.) consisting of a single cell.

**unicorn** /**yoo**-nuh-ˌkawn/ *n.* mythical white horse with a single long straight (and usu. spiralled) horn in the middle of its forehead. [Latin *cornu* horn]

**unicycle** /**yoo**-nee-ˌsuy-kuhl/ *n.* single-wheeled cycle, esp. as used by acrobats. □ **unicyclist** *n.*

**unification** /ˌyoo-nuh-fuh-**kay**-shuhn/ *n.* act or instance of unifying or state of being unified. □ **unificatory** *adj.*

**uniform** /**yoo**-nuh-ˌfawm/ — *adj.* **1** not changing in form or character; the same, unvarying (*uniform appearance*). **2** conforming to the same standard, rules, etc. **3** constant over a period (*uniform acceleration*). — *n.* distinctive clothing worn by soldiers, police, schoolchildren, etc. — *v.* clothe in a uniform (*a uniformed officer*). □ **uniformity** /ˌyoo-nuh-**faw**-muh-tee/ *n.* **uniformly** *adv.* [Latin: related to FORM]

**unify** /**yoo**-nuh-ˌfuy/ *v.* (**-ies**, **-ied**) make or become united or uniform. [Latin: related to UNI-]

**unilateral** /ˌyoo-nee-**lat**-uh-ruhl/ *adj.* done by or affecting only one person or party (*unilateral disarmament*). □ **unilaterally** *adv.*

**unimaginable** /ˌun-i-**maj**-uh-nuh-buhl/ *adj.* impossible to imagine.

**unimaginative** /ˌun-i-**maj**-uh-nuh-tiv/ *adj.* lacking imagination; stolid, dull. □ **unimaginatively** *adv.*

**unimpeachable** /ˌun-im-**pee**-chuh-buhl/ *adj.* giving no opportunity for censure; beyond reproach or question.

**unimproved** /ˌun-im-**proovd**/ *adj.* **1** not made better. **2** (of land) not used for agriculture or building; not developed.

**uninformed** /ˌun-in-**fawmd**/ *adj.* not informed; ignorant.

**uninitiated** /ˌun-i-**nish**-ee-ˌay-tuhd/ *adj.* not initiated; not admitted or instructed.

**uninspired** /ˌun-in-**spuy**-uhd/ *adj.* not inspired; commonplace, pedestrian. □ **uninspiring** *adj.*

**uninterested** /un-**in**-truh-stuhd/ *adj.* not interested; indifferent.

■ **Usage** See note at DISINTERESTED.

**uninviting** /ˌun-in-**vuy**-ting/ *adj.* unattractive, repellent.

**union** /**yoon**-yuhn/ *n.* **1** act or instance of uniting or state of being united. **2 a** whole formed from parts or members. **b** political unit so formed. **3** = TRADE UNION. **4** marriage. **5** concord (*perfect union*). **6** (**Union**) **a** club offering dining and sporting facilities, social activities, etc., at some universities. **b** buildings of this. **c** = RUGBY UNION. **7** *Math.* totality of the members of two or more sets. [Latin *unus* one]

**union-bashing** *n.* *colloq.* media or government campaign against trade unions.

**unionise** *v.* (also **-ize**) (**-sing** or **-zing**) organise in or into a trade union. □ **unionisation** /-zay-shuhn/ *n.*

**unionist** *n.* **1** member of a trade union. **2** advocate of trade unions. □ **unionism** *n.*

**Union Jack** *n.* **1** national ensign of the United Kingdom. **2** = DOUBLE DRUMMER.

**unique** /yoo-**neek**/ *adj.* **1** being the only one of its kind; having no like, equal, or parallel. **2** unusual, remarkable (*unique opportunity*). □ **uniquely** *adv.* [Latin *unicus* from *unus* one]

■ **Usage** In sense 1, *unique* cannot be qualified by adverbs such as *absolutely*, *most*, and *quite*. The use of *unique* in sense 2 is regarded as incorrect by some people.

**unisex** /**yoo**-nee-ˌseks/ *adj.* **1** (of clothing, hairstyles, etc.) designed for both sexes. **2** catering to both sexes (*unisex hair salon; unisex toilet*).

**unisexual** /ˌyoo-nee-**sek**-shoo-uhl/ *adj.* *Bot.* having stamens or pistils but not both.

**unison** /**yoo**-nuh-suhn/ — *n.* **1** concord (*acted in perfect unison*). **2** *Mus.* **a** coincidence in pitch of sounds or notes. **b** this regarded as an interval. **3** *Mus.* combination of voices or instruments at the same pitch or at pitches differing by one or more octaves (*sung in unison*). — *adj.* *Mus.* coinciding in pitch. [Latin *sonus* SOUND¹]

**unit** /**yoo**-nuht/ *n.* **1 a** individual thing, person, or group, esp. for calculation. **b** smallest component of a complex whole (*the family as the unit of society*). **2** quantity as a standard of measurement (*unit of heat; SI unit*). **3 a** smallest share in a unit trust. **b** smallest wager on a totalisator. **4 a** measure of educational attainment credited to a student for successfully completing one section of an academic course (*has six units towards the degree*). **b** such a section of an academic course (*enrolled in three units this year*). **5** part of a mechanism with a specified function. **6** fitted item of furniture, esp. as part of a set. **7** subgroup with a special function. **8** group of buildings, wards, etc., in a hospital. **9 a** accommodation unit in a larger building or group of buildings, esp. in a block of flats or a motel. **b** = HOME UNIT. **10 a** single-digit number. **b** the number 'one'. [Latin *unus* one]

**Unitarian** /ˌyoo-nuh-**tair**-ree-uhn/ — *n.* **1** person who believes that God is one, not a Trinity. **2** member of a religious body so believing. — *adj.* of Unitarians. □ **Unitarianism** *n.* [Latin *unitas* UNITY]

**unitary** /**yoo**-nuh-tuh-ree, -tree/ *adj.* **1** of a unit or units. **2** marked by unity or uniformity. [from UNIT or UNITY]

**unit cost** *n.* cost of producing one item.

**unite** /yoo-**nuyt**/ *v.* (**-ting**) **1 a** join together; combine. **b** join together for a common purpose or action (*united in their struggle*). **2** join in marriage. **3** (cause to) form a physical or chemical whole (*oil will not unite with water*). [Latin *unio -it-* from *unus* one]

**United Kingdom** *n.* Great Britain and Northern Ireland.

**United Nations** *n.pl.* (as *sing.* or *pl.*) supranational peace-seeking organisation.

**United States** *n.* (in full **United States of America**) federal republic of 50 States, mostly in N. America and including Alaska and Hawaii.

**Uniting Church** *n.* (also **Uniting Church in Australia**) Australian Church, formed in 1977 from the Methodist Church of Australasia, part of the Presbyterian Church of Australia, and part of the Congregational Union of Australia.

**unit price** *n.* price charged for each unit of goods supplied.

**unit trust** *n.* company investing contributions from many persons in various securities and paying proportional dividends.

**unity** /**yoo**-nuh-tee/ *n.* (*pl.* **-ies**) **1** oneness; being one; interconnected parts constituting a whole (*disturbs the unity of the idea*; *the picture lacks unity*; *national unity*). **2** thing forming a complex whole (*person regarded as a unity*). **3** harmony (*lived together in unity*). **4** *Math.* the number 'one', the factor that leaves unchanged the quantity on which it operates. **5** *Theatr.* each of the three dramatic principles requiring limitation of the supposed time of a drama to that occupied in acting it or to a single day (*unity of time*), use of one scene throughout (*unity of place*), and a single plot (*unity of action*). [Latin *unus* one]

**unity ticket** *n.* (in a trade-union election) alliance of candidates, of differing political or ideological persuasion, united for electoral advantage.

**univalent** /ˌyoo-nee-**vay**-luhnt/ *adj.* having a valency of one. [from UNI-, VALENCE¹]

**univalve** /**yoo**-nee-ˌvalv/ *Zool.* — *adj.* having one valve. — *n.* univalve mollusc.

**universal** /ˌyoo-nuh-**ver**-suhl/ — *adj.* of, belonging to, or done etc. by all persons or things in the world or in the class concerned; applicable to all cases (*the feeling was universal*; *met with universal approval*). — *n.* **1** term, characteristic, or concept of general application. **2** = UNIVERSAL JOINT. □ **universality** / -sal-uh-tee/ *n.* **universally** *adv.* [Latin: related to UNIVERSE]

**universal joint** *n.* (also **universal coupling**) joint or coupling which can transmit rotary power by a shaft at any angle.

**universal suffrage** *n.* right of voting in a political election extending to all adults.

**universe** /**yoo**-nuh-ˌvers/ *n.* **1** all existing things; the whole creation; the cosmos. **2** all human beings. **3** *Statistics & Logic* all the objects under consideration. [Latin *universus* combined into one]

**university** /ˌyoo-nuh-**ver**-suh-tee/ *n.* (*pl.* **-ies**) **1** educational institution of advanced learning and research, conferring degrees. **2** members of this. [Latin: related to UNIVERSE]

**UNIX** /**yoo**-niks/ *n. propr. Computing* operating system developed in the early 1970s with the aim of improving communication between different brands of computers.

**unkempt** /un-**kempt**/ *adj.* untidy, dishevelled. [= *uncombed*]

**unkind** /un-**kuynd**/ *adj.* not kind; harsh, cruel. □ **unkindly** *adv.* **unkindness** *n.*

**unknowable** /un-**noh**-uh-buhl/ — *adj.* that cannot be known. — *n.* **1** unknowable thing. **2** (**the Unknowable**) the postulated absolute or ultimate reality.

**unknowing** /un-**noh**-ing/ *adj.* (often foll. by *of*) not knowing; ignorant, unconscious. □ **unknowingly** *adv.*

**unknown** /un-**nohn**/ — *adj.* (often foll. by *to*) not known, unfamiliar. — *n.* unknown thing, person, or quantity. □ **unknown to** without the knowledge of (*did it unknown to me*).

**unknown quantity** *n.* mysterious or obscure person or thing.

**Unknown Soldier** *n.* unidentified soldier etc. symbolising a nation's dead in war.

**unlace** /un-**lays**/ *v.* (**-cing**) **1** undo the lace(s) of. **2** unfasten or loosen in this way.

**unladen weight** *n.* weight of a vehicle etc. when not loaded.

**unlawful** /un-**law**-fuhl/ *adj.* not lawful, illegal; not permissible. □ **unlawfully** *adv.*

**unleaded** /un-**led**-uhd/ *adj.* (of petrol etc.) without added lead.

**unlearn** /un-**lern**/ *v.* (*past* and *past part.* **unlearned** or **unlearnt**) **1** forget deliberately. **2** rid oneself of (a habit, false information, etc.).

**unlearned**[1] /un-**ler**-nuhd/ *adj.* not well educated; ignorant.

**unlearned**[2] /un-**lernd**/ *adj.* (also **unlearnt** /un-**lernt**/ ) not learnt; not acquired by learning.

**unleash** /un-**leesh**/ *v.* **1** release from a leash or restraint. **2** set free to engage in pursuit or attack.

**unleavened** /un-**lev**-uhnd/ *adj.* not leavened; made without yeast etc.

**unless** /un-**les**, uhn-**les**/ *conj.* if not; except when (*shall go unless I hear from you*). [= *on less*]

**unlettered** /un-**let**-uhd/ *adj.* illiterate; not well educated.

**unlicensed** /un-**luy**-suhnst/ *adj.* not licensed, esp. to sell alcohol or drive a motor vehicle.

**unlike** /un-**luyk**/ — *adj.* **1** not like; different from. **2** uncharacteristic of (*greed is unlike her*). **3** dissimilar, different. — *prep.* differently from (*acts quite unlike anyone else*).

**unlikely** /un-**luyk**-lee/ *adj.* (**-ier, -iest**) **1** improbable (*unlikely tale*). **2** (foll. by *to* + infin.) not expected (*unlikely to die*). **3** unpromising (*unlikely candidate*). □ **unlikeliness** *n.*

**unlike signs** *n.pl. Math.* plus and minus.

**unlimited** /un-**lim**-uh-tuhd/ *adj.* **1** without limit; unrestricted; very great in number or quantity (*unlimited expanse*). **2** (of the members of a company) having complete liability for the company debts.

**unlined**[1] /un-**luynd**/ *adj.* **1** (of paper etc.) without lines. **2** (of a face etc.) without wrinkles.

**unlined**[2] /un-**luynd**/ *adj.* without a lining.

**unlisted** /un-**lis**-tuhd/ *adj.* **1** not in a published list of telephone numbers. **2** (of a company) not listed on a stock exchange.

**unload** /un-**lohd**/ *v.* **1** (also *absol.*) remove a load from (a vehicle etc.) (*unloaded the van; the van is unloading*). **2** remove (a load) from a vehicle etc. (*unloaded the crates from the van*). **3** remove the ammunition from (a gun etc.). **4** dispose of stocks, shares, etc., by selling off. **5** *colloq.* (often foll. by *on*; also *absol.*) **a** give vent to feelings etc; unburden oneself (*unloaded his grief; unloaded his problems on me*). **b** divulge information etc. (*threatened to unload it all on the police*). **c** get rid of a thing that is unwanted or an embarrassment, esp. by sale (*unloaded the stolen towels on a clergyman's wife at a dollar a pop*). **d** get rid of an unwanted person, esp. by dumping on someone else (*tried to unload some of his visiting rellies on me*). **6** *colloq.* get rid of.

**unlock** /un-**lok**/ *v.* **1 a** release the lock of (a door, box, etc.). **b** release or disclose by unlocking. **2** release thoughts, feelings, etc. from (one's mind etc.). □ **unlock the land** *hist.* release Crown land for occupation by small farmers.

**unlooked-for** /un-**luukt**-faw/ *adj.* unexpected, unforeseen.

**unloose** /un-**loos**/ *v.* (**-sing**) (also **unloosen**) loose; set free.

**unlucky** /un-**luk**-ee/ *adj.* (**-ier, -iest**) **1** not fortunate or successful. **2** bringing bad luck. □ **unluckily** *adv.*

**unmade** /un-**mayd**/ *adj.* **1** (esp. of a bed) not made. **2** existing without having been made, uncreated.

**unmade road** *n.* vehicular way which has been cleared of vegetation but not formed, sealed, etc.

**unmake** /un-**mayk**/ *v.* (**-king**; *past* and *past part.* **unmade**) **1** undo the making of. **2** deprive of a particular rank or station; depose.

**unman** /un-**man**/ *v.* (**-nn-**) **1** deprive of supposedly manly qualities (e.g. self-control, courage). **2** deprive (a ship) of men.

**unmanageable** /un-**man**-uh-juh-buhl/ *adj.* not easily managed or controlled.

**unmanned** /un-**mand**/ *adj.* (esp. of aircraft, spacecraft) without a crew.

**unmannerly** /un-**man**-uh-lee/ *adj.* ill-mannered. □ **unmannerliness** *n.*

**unmarked** /un-**mahkt**/ *adj.* **1** not marked. **2** having no distinguishing or identifying mark (*unmarked grave; unmarked police car*). **3** not noticed.

**unmarried** /un-**ma**-reed/ *adj.* not married, single.

**unmask** /un-**mahsk**/ *v.* **1 a** remove the mask from. **b** expose the true character of. **2** remove one's mask.

**unmatched** /un-**macht**/ *adj.* not matched or equalled.

**unmentionable** /un-**men**-shuh-nuh-buhl/ — *adj.* unsuitable for polite conversation. — *n.* (in *pl.*) *joc.* undergarments.

**unmerciful** /un-**mer**-suh-ˌfuhl/ *adj.* merciless. □ **unmercifully** *adv.*

**unmet** /un-**met**/ *adj.* (of a demand, goal, etc.) not achieved or fulfilled.

**unmindful** /un-**muynd**-fuhl/ *adj.* (often foll. by *of*) not mindful.

**unmistakable** /,un-muh-**stay**-kuh-buhl/ *adj.* clear, obvious, plain. □ **unmistakably** *adv.*

**unmitigated** /un-**mit**-uh-,gay-tuhd/ *adj.* not mitigated; absolute (*unmitigated disaster*).

**unmoral** /un-**mo**-ruhl/ *adj.* not concerned with morality (cf. IMMORAL). □ **unmorality** /,un-muh-**ral**-uh-tee/ *n.*

**unmoved** /un-**moovd**/ *adj.* **1** not moved. **2** constant in purpose. **3** not affected by emotion.

**unmusical** /un-**myoo**-zi-kuhl/ *adj.* **1** not pleasing to the ear. **2** unskilled in or indifferent to music.

**unnameable** /un-**nay**-muh-buhl/ *adj.* that cannot be named, esp. too bad to be named or mentioned.

**unnamed** /un-**naymd**/ *adj.* not named.

**unnatural** /un-**nach**-uh-ruhl/ *adj.* **1** contrary to nature; not normal. **2 a** lacking natural feelings. **b** extremely cruel or wicked. **3** artificial. **4** affected. □ **unnaturally** *adv.*

**unnecessary** /un-**nes**-uh-suh-ree, -uh-sree/ *adj.* **1** not necessary. **2** more than is necessary; superfluous. □ **unnecessarily** *adv.*

**unnerve** /un-**nerv**/ *v.* (**-ving**) deprive of confidence, strength, resolution, etc.

**unnumbered** /un-**num**-buhd/ *adj.* **1** not marked with a number. **2** not counted. **3** countless.

**unobjectionable** /,un-uhb-**jek**-shuh-nuh-buhl/ *adj.* not objectionable; acceptable.

**unobtrusive** /,un-uhb-**troo**-siv/ *adj.* not making oneself or itself noticed. □ **unobtrusively** *adv.*

**unofficial** /,un-uh-**fish**-uhl/ *adj.* not officially authorised or confirmed. □ **unofficially** *adv.*

**unorganised** /un-**aw**-guh-,nuyzd/ *adj.* (also **-ized**) **1** not organised; not formed into an orderly and regulated whole. **2** (of workers) not members of, or organised into, a trade union.

**unoriginal** /,un-uh-**rij**-uh-nuhl/ *adj.* lacking originality; derivative.

**unpaired** /un-**paird**/ *adj.* **1** not being one of a pair. **2** not united or arranged in pairs.

**unpalatable** /un-**pal**-uh-tuh-buhl/ *adj.* **1** not pleasant to the taste. **2** (of an idea, suggestion, etc.) disagreeable, distasteful.

**unparalleled** /un-**pa**-ruh-,leld/ *adj.* having no parallel or equal.

**unparliamentary language** *n.* oaths, insults, abuse, etc. which are not allowed in parliamentary debate.

**unperson** /**un**-,per-suhn/ *n.* person whose name or existence is denied or ignored, esp. by a government.

**unpick** /un-**pik**/ *v.* undo the sewing of (stitches, a garment, etc.).

**unplaced** /un-**playst**/ *adj.* not placed, esp. not one of the first three in a race etc.

**unplayable** /un-**play**-uh-buhl/ *adj.* **1** *Sport* (of a ball) too fast etc. to be returned. **2** that cannot be played.

**unpleasant** /un-**plez**-uhnt/ *adj.* not pleasant, disagreeable. □ **unpleasantly** *adv.* **unpleasantness** *n.*

**unplug** /un-**plug**/ *v.* (**-gg-**) **1** disconnect (an electrical device) by removing its plug from the socket. **2** unstop.

**unplumbed** /un-**plumd**/ *adj.* **1** not plumbed. **2** not fully explored or understood.

**unpointed** /un-**poin**-tuhd/ *adj.* **1** having no point or points. **2** not punctuated. **3** (of brickwork etc.) not pointed.

**unpolished** /un-**pol**-isht/ *adj.* **1** not made smooth or bright by polishing; rough. **2** without refinement; crude.

**unpopular** /un-**pop**-yuh-luh/ *adj.* not popular; disliked. □ **unpopularity** /-la-ruh-tee/ *n.*

**unpractical** /un-**prak**-tuh-kuhl/ *adj.* **1** not practical. **2** (of a person) without practical skill.

**unpractised** /un-**prak**-tuhst/ *adj.* **1** not experienced or skilled. **2** not put into practice.

**unprecedented** /un-**pres**-uh-,den-tuhd, -**pree**-suh-/ *adj.* having no precedent; unparalleled. □ **unprecedentedly** *adv.*

**unprepossessing** /,un-pree-puh-**zes**-ing/ *adj.* unattractive.

**unpretentious** /,un-pruh-**ten**-shuhs/ *adj.* simple, modest, unassuming.

**unprincipled** /un-**prin**-suh-puhld/ *adj.* lacking or not based on moral principles.

**unprintable** /un-**prin**-tuh-buhl/ *adj.* too offensive or indecent to be printed.

**unprofessional** /,un-pruh-**fesh**-uh-nuhl/ *adj.* **1** contrary to professional standards. **2** unskilled, amateurish. □ **unprofessionally** *adv.*

**unpromising** /un-**prom**-uh-sing/ *adj.* not likely to turn out well.

**unprompted** /un-**promp**-tuhd/ *adj.* spontaneous.

**unprovoked** /,un-pruh-**vohkt**/ *adj.* without provocation.

**unputdownable** /,un-puut-**dow**-nuh-buhl/ *adj. colloq.* (of a book) compulsively readable.

**unqualified** /un-**kwol**-uh-,fuyd/ adj. **1** not legally or officially qualified (an unqualified practitioner). **2** not modified or restricted; complete (unqualified success). **3** not competent (unqualified to say).

**unquestionable** /un-**kwes**-chuh-nuh-buhl/ adj. that cannot be disputed or doubted. □ **unquestionably** adv.

**unquestioned** /un-**kwes**-chuhnd/ adj. not disputed or doubted; definite, certain.

**unquestioning** /un-**kwes**-chuh-ning/ adj. **1** asking no questions. **2** (of obedience etc.) absolute. □ **unquestioningly** adv.

**unquiet** /un-**kwuy**-uht/ adj. **1** restless, agitated. **2** anxious.

**unquote** /un-**kwoht**/ v. (as int.) verbal formula indicating closing quotation marks.

**unravel** /un-**rav**-uhl/ v. (-ll-) **1** make or become disentangled, unknitted, unknotted, etc. **2** probe and solve (a mystery etc.). **3** undo (esp. knitted fabric).

**unread** /un-**red**/ adj. **1** (of a book etc.) not read. **2** (of a person) not well-read.

**unreadable** /un-**ree**-duh-buhl/ adj. **1** too dull, bad, or difficult to read. **2** illegible. **3** not able to be interpreted (an unreadable expression on his face).

**unreal** /un-**reerl**/ adj. **1** not real. **2** imaginary; illusory. **3** colloq. **a** incredibly good. **b** incredibly bad. □ **unreality** /-ree-al-uh-tee/ n.

**unrealistic** /un-ree-uh-**lis**-tik/ adj. **1** not realistic. **2** not practical or realisable; far-fetched (his plans for the future are quite unrealistic). □ **unrealistically** adv.

**unreason** /un-**ree**-zuhn/ n. madness; chaos; disorder.

**unreasonable** /un-**ree**-zuh-nuh-buhl/ adj. **1** going beyond the bounds of what is reasonable or equitable; excessive (unreasonable demands). **2** not guided by or listening to reason. □ **unreasonably** adv.

**unrecognised** /un-**rek**-uhg-,nuyzd/ adj. (also **-ized**) not recognised; not given sufficient acknowledgment.

**unreel** /un-**reel**/ v. unwind from a reel.

**unreflecting** /un-ruh-**flek**-ting/ adj. not thoughtful.

**unregenerate** /un-ree-**jen**-uh-ruht, un-ruh-/ adj. obstinately wrong or bad.

**unrelated** /un-ruh-**lay**-tuhd/ adj. **1** not connected by blood (he and I are quite unrelated). **2** not standing in relationship or connection (these three murders are quite unrelated).

**unrelenting** /un-ruh-**len**-ting/ adj. **1** not relenting or yielding. **2** unmerciful. **3** not

abating or relaxing (unrelenting pursuit of the fugitives). □ **unrelentingly** adv.

**unreliable** /un-ruh-**luy**-uh-buhl/ adj. not reliable; erratic. □ **unreliability** /-bil-uh-tee/ n.

**unrelieved** /un-ruh-**leevd**/ adj. **1** lacking the relief given by contrast or variation; monotonously uniform (unrelieved expanses of scrub). **2** not aided or assisted.

**unremarkable** /un-ruh-**mah**-kuh-buhl/ adj. not remarkable; uninteresting, ordinary.

**unremitting** /un-ruh-**mit**-ing/ adj. never relaxing or slackening; incessant. □ **unremittingly** adv.

**unremunerative** /un-ruh-**myoo**-nuh-ruh-tiv/ adj. not, or not very, profitable.

**unrepeatable** /un-ruh-**pee**-tuh-buhl/ adj. **1** that cannot be done, made, or said again. **2** too indecent to be said again.

**unrequited** /un-ruh-**kwuy**-tuhd/ adj. (of love etc.) not returned.

**unreserved** /un-ruh-**zervd**/ adj. **1** not reserved (unreserved seats). **2** total; without reservation; absolute (has my unreserved support). □ **unreservedly** /-zer-vuhd-lee/ adv.

**unresolved** /un-ruh-**zolvd**/ adj. **1** uncertain how to act, irresolute, undecided. **2** (of questions etc.) undetermined, undecided, unsolved.

**unrest** /un-**rest**/ n. **1** lack of rest. **2** restlessness, disturbance, agitation (industrial unrest).

**unrighteous** /un-**ruy**-chuhs/ adj. not righteous; unjust, wicked, dishonest.

**unrivalled** /un-**ruy**-vuhld/ adj. having no equal; peerless.

**unroll** /un-**rohl**/ v. **1** open out from a rolled-up state. **2** display or be displayed like this.

**unruffled** /un-**ruf**-uhld/ adj. **1** not agitated or disturbed; calm. **2** not physically ruffled (the sea was as calm and unruffled as a pond).

**unruly** /un-**roo**-lee/ adj. (**-ier, -iest**) not easily controlled or disciplined, disorderly. □ **unruliness** n. [related to RULE]

**unsaddle** /un-**sad**-uhl/ v. (-ling) **1** remove the saddle from (a horse etc.). **2** dislodge from a saddle.

**unsafe** /un-**sayf**/ adj. **1** not safe. **2** not to be trusted to; unreliable. **3** Law (of a verdict, conviction, etc.) likely to constitute a miscarriage of justice.

**unsafe sex** — n. sexual intercourse entered into without proper precaution (esp. the use of a condom) against contracting AIDS and other sexually transmitted diseases (cf. SAFE SEX).

— *attrib. adj.* (**unsafe-sex**) of or pertaining to unsafe sex (*too many, especially the young, still use unsafe-sex practices*).

**unsaid** /un-**sed**/ *adj.* not uttered or expressed (*left it unsaid*).

**unsatisfactory** /ˌun-sat-uhs-**fak**-tuh-ree, -tree/ *adj.* not satisfactory; poor, unacceptable.

**unsaturated** /un-**sach**-uh-ˌray-tuhd/ *adj. Chem.* (of esp. a fat or oil) having double or triple bonds in its molecule and therefore capable of further reaction.

**unsavoury** /un-**say**-vuh-ree/ *adj.* (also **unsavory**) **1** disagreeable to the taste, smell, or feelings; disgusting. **2** disagreeable, unpleasant (*an unsavoury character lurking by those trees*). **3** morally offensive (*went into unsavoury details*).

**unscathed** /un-**skaythd**/ *adj.* without suffering any injury.

**unschooled** /un-**skoold**/ *adj.* **1** uneducated, untaught. **2** untrained, undisciplined. **3** not made artificial by education or training; natural, spontaneous.

**unscientific** /ˌun-suy-uhn-**tif**-ik/ *adj.* **1** not in accordance with scientific principles or methods. **2** not familiar with science. □ **unscientifically** *adv.*

**unscramble** /un-**skram**-buhl/ *v.* (**-ling**) make plain, decode, interpret (a scrambled transmission etc.).

**unscreened** /un-**skreend**/ *adj.* **1 a** not passed through a screen or sieve. **b** not checked, esp. for security or medical problems. **2** not having a screen. **3** not shown on a screen.

**unscrew** /un-**skroo**/ *v.* **1** unfasten by removing a screw or screws or by twisting like a screw. **2** loosen (a screw or screwtop).

**unscripted** /un-**skrip**-tuhd/ *adj.* (of a speech etc.) delivered without a prepared script.

**unscrupulous** /un-**skroo**-pyuh-luhs/ *adj.* having no scruples, unprincipled. □ **unscrupulously** *adv.* **unscrupulousness** *n.*

**unseasonable** /un-**see**-zuh-nuh-buhl/ *adj.* **1** not appropriate to the time or occasion. **2** untimely, inopportune. □ **unseasonably** *adv.*

**unseasonal** /un-**see**-zuh-nuhl/ *adj.* not typical of or appropriate to the time or season. □ **unseasonally** *adv.*

**unseat** /un-**seet**/ *v.* **1** remove from a (esp. parliamentary) seat. **2** dislodge from a seat, esp. on horseback.

**unseeded** /un-**see**-duhd/ *adj. Sport* (of a player) not seeded.

**unseeing** /un-**see**-ing/ *adj.* **1** unobservant. **2** blind. □ **unseeingly** *adv.*

**unseemly** /un-**seem**-lee/ *adj.* (**-ier, -iest**) **1** indecent. **2** unbecoming. □ **unseemliness** *n.*

**unseen** /un-**seen**/ — *adj.* **1** not seen. **2** invisible. **3** (of a translation or a piece of music) to be done or performed without preparation. — *n.* unseen translation.

**unselfish** /un-**sel**-fish/ *adj.* mindful of others' interests; sharing. □ **unselfishly** *adv.* **unselfishness** *n.*

**unsettle** /un-**set**-uhl/ *v.* (**-ling**) **1** disturb the settled state or arrangement of; discompose. **2** derange (*the shock unsettled his mind*).

**unsettled** /un-**set**-uhld/ *adj.* **1** not peaceful or orderly; disturbed; restless (*dangerous and unsettled times*). **2** (of weather etc.) changeable; variable. **3** still in a state of flux, not yet come to rest (*the dust was still unsettled, eddying about in thick swirls*). **4** open to change or further discussion; not determined or decided (*a few unsettled matters remain on the agenda*). **5** (of a bill etc.) unpaid. **6** not settled or stable in character (*had an unsettled childhood because of constant shifts of school*). **7** unpopulated or sparsely populated by settlers (*unsettled regions of Australia*). **8** unbalanced, mentally disturbed.

**unshakeable** /un-**shay**-kuh-buhl/ *adj.* firm; obstinate. □ **unshakeably** *adv.*

**unshrinking** /un-**shring**-king/ *adj.* unhesitating, fearless.

**unsighted** /un-**suy**-tuhd/ *adj.* **1** not sighted or seen. **2** prevented from seeing, esp. by an obstruction.

**unsightly** /un-**suyt**-lee/ *adj.* unpleasant to look at, ugly (*unsightly sores all over his hands*). □ **unsightliness** *n.*

**unskilled** /un-**skild**/ *adj.* **1** not needing special skill or training (*unskilled work does not pay good wages*). **2** lacking special skill or training (*it is difficult for unskilled young people to get a job*).

**unsociable** /un-**soh**-shuh-buhl/ *adj.* not sociable, disliking the company of others.

**unsocial** /un-**soh**-shuhl/ *adj.* **1** not social; not suitable for or seeking society. **2** outside the normal working day (*unsocial hours*). **3** antisocial.

**unsolicited** /ˌun-suh-**lis**-uh-tuhd/ *adj.* not asked for; voluntary (*as publishers we receive hundreds of unsolicited manuscripts*).

**unsophisticated** /ˌun-suh-**fis**-tuh-ˌkay-tuhd/ *adj.* artless, simple, natural.

**unsought** /un-**sawt**/ *adj.* **1** not searched out or sought for. **2** unasked; without being requested.

**unsound** /un-**sownd**/ *adj.* **1 a** not physically healthy; diseased; weak. **b** not mentally healthy; not sane. **2** (of fruit, timber, goods, etc.) not in sound or good condition; rotten. **3** lacking in firmness or solidity (*the foundations of this building are unsound*). **4** not soundly based on reason; ill-founded (*your conclusion is unsound*). **5** of doubtful financial viability (*an unsound business*). **6** (of sleep) broken or disturbed. □ **of unsound mind** insane. □ **unsoundness** *n.*

**unsparing** /un-**spair**-ring/ *adj.* **1** lavish, profuse (*unsparing in his generosity*). **2** merciless (*unsparing in his revenge*).

**unspeakable** /un-**spee**-kuh-buhl/ *adj.* **1** that cannot be expressed in words (*unspeakable terror*). **2** indescribably bad or objectionable (*whispered something unspeakable in my ear*). □ **unspeakably** *adv.*

**unspectacular** /ˌun-spek-**tak**-yuh-luh/ *adj.* not spectacular; dull.

**unsporting** /un-**spaw**-ting/ *adj.* not fair or generous.

**unsportsmanlike** /un-**spawts**-muhn-ˌluyk/ *adj.* unsporting.

**unstable** /un-**stay**-buhl/ *adj.* **1** not stable; likely to fall. **2** showing a tendency to sudden mental or emotional changes. **3** changeable. **4** *Chem.* (of a compound) likely to decompose. **5** *Physics* (of an isotope) subject to spontaneous radioactive decay. □ **unstably** *adv.*

**unsteady** /un-**sted**-ee/ *adj.* (**-ier, -iest**) **1** not steady or firm. **2** changeable. **3** not uniform or regular. □ **unsteadily** *adv.* **unsteadiness** *n.*

**unstick** /un-**stik**/ *v.* (*past* and *past part.* **unstuck**) separate (a thing stuck to another). □ **come unstuck** *colloq.* come to grief, fail.

**unstinting** /un-**stin**-ting/ *adj.* ungrudging, lavish. □ **unstintingly** *adv.*

**unstressed** /un-**strest**/ *adj.* **1** (of a word, syllable, etc.) not pronounced with stress. **2** not subjected to stress.

**unstring** /un-**string**/ *v.* (*past* and *past part.* **unstrung**) **1** remove or relax the string(s) of (a bow, harp, etc.). **2** remove (beads etc.) from a string. **3** (esp. as **unstrung** *adj.*) unnerve.

**unstructured** /un-**struk**-chuhd/ *adj.* **1** not structured. **2** informal.

**unstuck** *past* and *past part.* of UNSTICK.

**unstudied** /un-**stud**-eed/ *adj.* easy, natural, spontaneous.

**unsubstantial** /ˌun-suhb-**stan**-shuhl/ *adj.* = INSUBSTANTIAL.

**unsubtle** /un-**sut**-uhl/ *adj.* not subtle; obvious; clumsy.

**unsuited** /un-**soo**-tuhd/ *adj.* **1** (usu. foll. by *for*) not fit (*unsuited for the job*). **2** (usu. foll. by *to*) not adapted (*said that his hands were unsuited to such rough work*).

**unsung** /un-**sung**/ *adj.* not celebrated, unrecognised (*unsung heroes*).

**unsure** /un-**shaw**/ *adj.* **1** not sure. **2** unsafe; liable to yield or give way (*the ground is unsure; unsure foundations*). **3** dependent on chance or accident; uncertain, precarious (*all I am sure of is that life is unsure*). **4** lacking in confidence, uncertain, subject to doubt (*feeling quite unsure of himself*). **5** unreliable; untested (*an unsure scheme for beating the odds in gambling*).

**unswerving** /un-**swer**-ving/ *adj.* **1** steady, constant. **2** not turning aside. □ **unswervingly** *adv.*

**unsworn** /un-**swawn**/ *adj.* **1** (of a person) not subjected to or bound by an oath or affirmation. **2** not confirmed by an oath or affirmation (*unsworn statement by the accused*).

**untangle** /un-**tang**-guhl/ *v.* (**-ling**) disentangle (*untangle the string; I'll leave you to untangle this mess*).

**untapped** /un-**tapt**/ *adj.* not (yet) tapped or used (*untapped resources*).

**untenable** /un-**ten**-uh-buhl/ *adj.* (of a theory etc.) not tenable; that cannot be defended.

**untenanted** /un-**ten**-uhn-tuhd/ *adj.* not occupied by a tenant or tenants; vacant.

**unthinkable** /un-**thing**-kuh-buhl/ *adj.* **1** unimaginable, inconceivable. **2** too unlikely or undesirable to be considered. □ **unthinkably** *adv.*

**unthinking** /un-**thing**-king/ *adj.* **1** thoughtless. **2** unintentional, inadvertent. □ **unthinkingly** *adv.*

**unthrone** /un-**throhn**/ *v.* (**-ning**) dethrone.

**untidy** /un-**tuy**-dee/ *adj.* (**-ier, -iest**) not neat or orderly. □ **untidily** *adv.* **untidiness** *n.*

**untie** /un-**tuy**/ *v.* (**untying**) **1** undo (a knot, package, etc.). **2** release from bonds or attachment.

**until** /un-**til**, uhn-/ *prep.* & *conj.* = TILL¹. [earlier *untill: un* from Old Norse *und* as far as]

---

■ **Usage** *Until*, as opposed to *till*, is used esp. at the beginning of a sentence and in formal style, e.g. *until you told me, I had no idea; he resided there until his decease.*

---

**untimely** /un-**tuym**-lee/ *adj.* **1** inopportune. **2** (of death) premature. □ **untimeliness** *n.*

**untiring** /un-**tuyuh**-ring/ *adj.* tireless. □ **untiringly** *adv.*

**unto** *prep. archaic* = TO (in all uses except signalling the infinitive). [from UNTIL, with *to* replacing *til*]

**untold** *adj.* **1** not told. **2** not (able to be) counted or measured; immeasurable (*untold misery*).

**untouchable** /un-**tuch**-uh-buhl/ — *adj.* that may not or cannot be touched. — *n.* member of a hereditary Hindu group held to defile members of higher castes on contact. □ **untouchability** /-bil-uh-tee/ *n.*

■ **Usage** The use of this term, and social restrictions accompanying it, were declared illegal under the Indian constitution in 1949.

**untouched** /un-**tucht**/ *adj.* **1** not touched. **2** not affected physically; not harmed, modified, used, or tasted. **3** not affected by emotion. **4** not discussed.

**untoward** /ˌun-tuh-**wawd**, un-**toh**-uhd/ *adj.* **1** inconvenient, unlucky (*untoward circumstances forced his resignation*). **2** at variance with good conduct or propriety; unseemly (*untoward behaviour*). **3** difficult to control, manage, etc. (*untoward material to work with*).

**untranslatable** /ˌun-trans-**lay**-tuh-buhl, -tranz-/ *adj.* that cannot be translated satisfactorily.

**untried** /un-**truyd**/ *adj.* **1** not tried or tested. **2** inexperienced.

**untroubled** *adj.* calm, tranquil.

**untrue** /un-**troo**/ *adj.* **1** not true; contrary to what is the fact. **2** (often foll. by *to*) not faithful or loyal (*untrue to his wife and to his principles*). **3** deviating from an accepted standard (*your aim's untrue*; *your scales are untrue*).

**untruth** /un-**trooth**/ *n.* **1** the state of being untrue; falsehood. **2** false statement; lie.

**untuck** /un-**tuk**/ *v.* free (bedclothes etc.) from being tucked in or up.

**untutored** /un-**tyoo**-tuhd/ *adj.* uneducated, untaught.

**unused** *adj.* **1** /un-**yoozd**/ **a** not in use. **b** never having been used. **2** /un-**yoost**/ (foll. by *to*) not accustomed (*unused as I am to public speaking . . .*).

**unusual** *adj.* **1** not usual. **2** exceptional; remarkable. □ **unusually** *adv.*

**unutterable** *adj.* **1** inexpressible; beyond description (*unutterable torment*; *an unutterable idiot*). **2** incapable of being uttered; unpronounceable. □ **unutterably** *adv.*

**unvarnished** /un-**vah**-nisht/ *adj.* **1** not varnished. **2** (of a statement or a person) plain and straightforward (*the unvarnished truth*; *an unvarnished liar*).

**unveil** /un-**vayl**/ *v.* **1** remove a covering from (a statue, plaque, etc.) as part of the ceremony of the first public display. **2** disclose, reveal, make publicly known. **3** remove a veil from; remove one's veil.

**unversed** /un-**verst**/ *adj.* (usu. foll. by *in*) not experienced or skilled (*I'm quite unversed in these matters — you'll have to show me what to do*).

**unvoiced** /un-**voist**/ *adj.* **1** not spoken. **2** *Phonet.* (of a consonant etc.) not voiced (e.g. *t, p, k*).

**unwaged** /un-**wayjd**/ — *adj.* not receiving a wage; unemployed (*are we supposed to do unwaged work?*). — *n.* (prec. by *the*) the unemployed (*the waged have no idea what we the unwaged go through day after day*).

**unwanted** *adj.* not wanted.

**unwarrantable** /un-**wo**-ruhn-tuh-buhl/ *adj.* indefensible; unjustifiable. □ **unwarrantably** *adv.*

**unwarranted** /un-**wo**-ruhn-tuhd/ *adj.* **1** unauthorised. **2** unjustified.

**unwary** /un-**wair**-ree/ *adj.* **1** not cautious. **2** (often foll. by *of*) not aware of possible danger etc. □ **unwarily** *adv.* **unwariness** *n.*

**unwearying** /un-**weer**-ree-ing/ *adj.* **1** persistent. **2** not causing or producing weariness.

**unwelcome** *adj.* not welcome or acceptable; unpleasing (*an unwelcome guest*; *unwelcome news*; *his admiration of me is most unwelcome*).

**unwell** /un-**wel**/ *adj.* ill.

**unwholesome** *adj.* **1** not promoting, or detrimental to, physical or moral health. **2** unhealthy, insalubrious. **3** unhealthy-looking.

**unwieldy** /un-**weel**-dee/ *adj.* (**-ier, -iest**) cumbersome, clumsy, or hard to manage, owing to size, shape, or weight. □ **unwieldily** *adv.* **unwieldiness** *n.* [*wieldy* active, from WIELD]

**unwilling** *adj.* not willing or inclined; reluctant. □ **unwillingly** *adv.* **unwillingness** *n.*

**unwind** /un-**wuynd**/ *v.* (*past and past part.* **unwound**) **1** draw out or become drawn out after having been wound. **2** relax (*unwinding after a hard day's work*).

**unwitting** *adj.* **1** not knowing or aware (*an unwitting offender*). **2** unintentional. □ **unwittingly** *adv.* [Old English: related to WIT]

**unwonted** /un-**wohn**-tuhd/ *adj.* not customary or usual.

**unworkable** *adj.* not workable; impracticable.

**unworldly** *adj.* **1** not motivated by or concerned with the things of this earth; spiritually-minded; not materialistic. **2** not experienced in the things of this earth; unsophisticated; naïve. **3** not of this earth; other-worldly. □ **unworldliness** *n.*

**unworthy** *adj.* (**-ier, -iest**) **1** (often foll. by *of*) not worthy of, or befitting the character of, a person etc. (*that was unworthy of you*). **2** (of things) lacking in worth or value (*withheld the prize for best Australorp as all the exhibits were unworthy*). **3** (of words, actions, etc.) hurtful or injurious to reputation; unseemly; offensive (*an unworthy suggestion*). **4** (of persons) lacking worth or merit; despicable. **5** conventionally used (esp. in church etc.) as an expression of humility (*Lord, we thy unworthy servants . . . etc.*). □ **unworthily** *adv.* **unworthiness** *n.*

**unwound** *past* and *past part.* of UNWIND.

**unwritten** *adj.* **1** not written. **2** (of a law etc.) based on custom or judicial decision, not on statute.

**unyielding** *adj.* **1** not yielding to pressure etc. **2** firm, obstinate.

**unzip** /un-**zip**/ *v.* (**-pp-**) unfasten the zip of.

**up** — *adv.* **1 a** at, in, or towards a higher place or position (*jumped up in the air*). **b** to or in a place regarded as higher, e.g. the north or a capital city (*up in Queensland; went up to Sydney; up the country*). **2 a** to or in an erect or required position or condition (*stood it up; wound up the watch*). **b** in or into a condition of efficiency, activity, or progress (*stirred up trouble; the hunt is up*). **3 a** in a stronger or leading position (*three goals up; am $10 up; is well up in class*). **b** *colloq.* ahead etc. as indicated (*went up in front*). **4** to a specified place, person, or time (*a child came up to me; fine up till now*). **5** higher in price or value (*our costs are up; shares are up*). **6 a** completely (*burn up; eat up*). **b** more loudly or clearly (*speak up*). **7** completed (*time is up*). **8** into a compact, accumulated, or secure state (*pack up; save up; tie up*). **9** out of bed, having risen (*are you up yet?; sun is up*). **10** happening, esp. unusually (*something is up*). **11** (usu. foll. by *before*) appearing for trial etc. (*up before the magistrate; up for drink driving*). — *prep.* **1** upwards and along, through, or into (*climbed up the ladder; went up the road*). **2** from the bottom to the top of. **3 a** at or in a higher part of (*is up the street*). **b** towards the source of (a river). — *adj.* **1** directed upwards (*up stroke*). **2** of travel towards a particular place (*pressed the 'up' button*). — *n.* spell of good fortune (*he has his ups and downs; I'm on an up at the moment*). — *v.* (**-pp-**) **1** *colloq.* start, esp. abruptly, to speak or act (*upped and hit him*). **2** raise (*upped their prices*). □ **be all up with** be hopeless for (a person). **be up oneself** *colloq.* have an inflated opinion of oneself. **on the up** (or **up and up**) *colloq.* steadily improving. **up against 1** close to. **2** in or into contact with. **3** *colloq.* confronted with (a problem etc.). **up against it** *colloq.* in great difficulties. **up and about** (or **doing**) having risen from bed; active. **up and down 1** to and fro (along). **2** *colloq.* in varying health or spirits. **up for 1** available for or standing for (office etc.) (*up for sale; up for election*). **2** under consideration for (*up for a medal*). **up there Cazaly** see CAZALY. **up to 1** until (*up to the present moment*). **2** not more than (*you can have up to five*). **3** less than or equal to (*sums up to $10*). **4** incumbent on (*it is up to you to say*). **5** capable of (*I'm not up to a long walk*). **6** occupied or busy with (*what have you been up to?*). **up to date** see DATE[1]. [Old English]

**up-** *prefix* (in senses of UP) added: **1** as an adverb to verbs and verbal derivations, = 'upwards' (*upcurved; update*). **2** as a preposition to nouns forming adverbs and adjectives (*up-country; uphill*). **3** as an adjective to nouns (*upland; up-stroke*).

**up-and-coming** *adj. colloq.* (of a person) promising; progressing.

**upbeat** — *n.* unaccented beat in music. — *adj. colloq.* optimistic, cheerful.

**upbraid** /up-**brayd**/ *v.* (often foll. by *with, for*) chide, reproach. [Old English: related to *braid* brandish]

**upbringing** *n.* rearing of a child. [obsolete *upbring* to rear]

**upcoming** *adj.* forthcoming; about to happen.

**up-country** — *n.* country which is inland and away from a major centre of population. — *adj.* situated in, belonging or related to, such country (*jackerooing on an up-country station; up-country town*). — *adv.* in or to such country.

**update** — *v.* /up-**dayt**/ (**-ting**) bring up to date. — *n.* /**up**-dayt/ **1** updating. **2** updated information etc.

**up-end** /up-**end**/ *v.* set or rise up on end.

**upfront** /up-**frunt**, **up-**/ *colloq.* — *adv.* (usu. **up front**) **1** at the front; in front. **2** (of payments) in advance. — *adj.* **1** honest, frank, direct. **2** (of payments) made in advance.

**upgrade** — v. /**up**-grayd/ (**-ding**) **1** raise in rank etc. **2** improve (equipment etc.). — n. /**up**-grayd/ **1** act or instance of upgrading. **2** an upgraded piece of equipment etc.

**upheaval** /up-**hee**-vuhl/ n. violent or sudden change or disruption. [from *upheave,* = heave or lift up]

**uphill** — adv. /up-**hil**/ up a slope. — adj. /**up**-hil/ **1** sloping up; ascending. **2** arduous, difficult (*an uphill task*; *an uphill battle to win the election*).

**uphold** /up-**hohld**/ v. (*past* and *past part.* **upheld**) **1** confirm (a decision etc.). **2** support, maintain (a custom etc.). □ **upholder** n.

**upholster** /up-**hohl**-stuh/ v. provide (furniture) with upholstery. [back formation from UPHOLSTERER]

**upholsterer** n. person who upholsters, esp. for a living. [obsolete *upholster* from UPHOLD in sense 'keep in repair']

**upholstery** n. **1** covering, padding, springs, etc. for furniture, car-seats, etc. **2** upholsterer's work.

**upkeep** n. **1** maintenance in good condition. **2** cost or means of this.

**upland** /**up**-luhnd/ — n. (usu. in *pl.*) higher or inland parts of a country. — adj. of these parts.

**uplift** — v. /up-**lift**/ **1** raise. **2** (esp. as **uplifting** adj.) elevate morally or emotionally. — n. /**up**-lift/ colloq. morally or spiritually elevating influence.

**up-market** adj. & adv. of or directed at the upper end of the market; classy.

**upmost** var. of UPPERMOST.

**upon** /uh-**pon**/ prep. = ON. [from *up on*]

■ **Usage** *Upon* is sometimes more formal than *on*, but is standard in *once upon a time* and *upon my word.*

**upper**[1] — attrib. adj. **1** higher in place; situated above another part (*the upper atmosphere*; *the upper lip*). **2** higher in rank etc. (*upper class*). — n. part of a boot or shoe above the sole. □ **on one's uppers** colloq. very short of money.

**upper**[2] n. colloq. amphetamine or other stimulant.

**upper case** n. capital letters.

**upper crust** n. colloq. (prec. by *the*) those on the upper levels of society.

**uppercut** — n. upwards blow delivered with the arm bent. — v. hit upwards with the arm bent.

**upper hand** n. (prec. by *the*) dominance, control.

**Upper House** n. one of the houses of a legislature consisting of two houses, usu. the smaller and less representative, e.g.

the Senate in the Federal Parliament of Australia.

**uppermost** — adj. (also **upmost**) **1** highest. **2** predominant. — adv. at or to the uppermost position.

**uppity** /**up**-uh-tee/ adj. colloq. arrogant, snobbish.

**upright** — adj. **1** erect, vertical. **2** (of a piano) with vertical strings. **3** strictly honourable or honest. — n. **1** upright post or rod, esp. as a structural support. **2** (in *pl.*) *Aust. Rules* goalposts. **3** upright piano. [Old English]

**uprising** n. rebellion or revolt.

**uproar** n. tumult; violent disturbance. [Dutch, = commotion]

**uproarious** /up-**raw**-ree-uhs/ adj. **1** very noisy. **2** provoking loud laughter; very funny. □ **uproariously** adv.

**uproot** /up-**root**/ v. **1** pull (a plant etc.) up from the ground. **2** displace (a person) from an accustomed location. **3** eradicate.

**uprush** n. upward rush (*an uprush of blood to the head*).

**ups-a-daisy** var. of UPSY-DAISY.

**ups and downs** n.pl. **1** rises and falls. **2** mixed fortune.

**upset** — v. /up-**set**/ (**-tt-**; *past* and *past part.* **upset**) **1** overturn. **2** disturb the composure or digestion of (*was very upset by the news*; *ate something that upset me*). **3** disrupt (*this will upset their plans*). — n. /**up**-set/ **1** emotional or physical disturbance. **2** surprising result (in a game etc.). — adj. /up-**set**, **up-**/ disturbed (*upset stomach*).

**upshot** n. outcome, conclusion.

**upside down** adv. & adj. **1** with the upper and lower parts reversed; inverted. **2** in or into total disorder. [from *up so down*, perhaps = 'up as if down']

**upsilon** /**uup**-suh-,lon/ n. twentieth letter of the Greek alphabet (Υ, υ). [Greek, = slender U, from *psilos* slender, with ref. to its later coincidence in sound with Greek *oi*]

**upstage** /up-**stayj**/ — adj. & adv. nearer the back of a theatre stage. — v. (**-ging**) **1** move upstage to make (another actor) face away from the audience. **2** divert attention from (a person) to oneself; outshine.

**upstairs** — adv. /up-**stairz**/ to or on an upper floor. — attrib. adj. /**up**-stairz/ (also **upstair**) situated upstairs. — n. /up-**stairz**/ upper floor.

**upstanding** /up-**stan**-ding/ adj. **1** standing up. **2** strong and healthy. **3** honest.

**upstart** — n. person who has risen suddenly to prominence, esp. one who behaves arrogantly. — *adj.* **1** that is an upstart. **2** of or characteristic of an upstart.

**upstream** *adv. & adj.* in the direction contrary to the flow of a stream etc.

**upsurge** *n.* upward surge; rise (esp. in feelings etc.).

**upswing** *n.* upward movement or trend.

**upsy-daisy** /**up**-see-,day-zee/ *int.* (also **ups-a-daisy**) expressing encouragement to a child who is being lifted or has fallen. [earlier *up-a-daisy*]

**uptake** *n.* **1** understanding (esp. *quick* or *slow on the uptake*). **2** taking up (of an offer etc.).

**upthrust** *n.* **1** upward thrust. **2** upward displacement of part of the earth's crust.

**uptight** /up-**tuyt**, **up**-tuyt/ *adj. colloq.* nervously tense or angry.

**uptime** /**up**-tuym/ *n.* time, or percentage of time, that a computer system etc. is available for productive use.

**up-to-date** see DATE[1].

**up to putty** see PUTTY.

**upturn** — *n.* /**up**-tern/ upward trend; improvement. — *v.* /up-**tern**/ turn up or upside down.

**upward** /**up**-wuhd/ — *adv.* (also **upwards**) towards what is higher, superior, larger in amount, more important, etc. — *adj.* moving or extending upwards. □ **upwards of** more than (*upwards of forty*).

**upwardly** *adv.* in an upward direction.

**upwardly mobile** — *adj.* able to, or aspiring to, advance socially or professionally. — *n.* a person or people in this position.

**upwind** /**up**-wind/ *adj. & adv.* in the direction from which the wind is blowing.

**uranium** /yoo-**ray**-nee-uhm, yuh-/ *n.* radioactive grey dense metallic element, capable of nuclear fission and used as a source of nuclear energy. [*Uranus*, name of a planet]

**urban** /**er**-buhn/ *adj.* of, living in, or situated in a town or city. [Latin *urbs* city]

**urbane** /er-**bayn**/ *adj.* suave; elegant and refined in manner. □ **urbanity** /er-**ban**-uh-tee/ *n.* [Latin: related to URBAN]

**urchin** /**er**-chuhn/ *n.* **1** mischievous child, esp. one who is young and (seemingly) not looked after or cared for (*street urchin*). **2** = SEA URCHIN. [Latin *ericius* hedgehog]

**Urdu** /**er**-doo/ *n.* language related to Hindi but with many Persian words, used esp. in Pakistan. [Hindustani]

**-ure** *suffix* forming: **1** nouns of action or process (*seizure*). **2** nouns of result (*creature*). **3** collective nouns (*nature*). [Latin *-ura*]

**urea** /yoo-**ree**-uh/ *n.* soluble nitrogenous compound contained esp. in urine. [French *urée* from Greek *ouron* urine]

**ureter** /yoo-**ree**-tuh/ *n.* duct conveying urine from the kidney to the bladder. [Greek *oureō* urinate]

**urethra** /yoo-**ree**-thruh/ *n.* (*pl.* **-s**) duct conveying urine, leading from the bladder to the extremity of the penis (in males) or to the vulva (in females). □ **urethral** *adj.* [Greek: related to URETER]

**urge** /erj/ — *v.* (**-ging**) **1** (often foll. by *on*) drive forcibly; impel; hasten (*urged them on*; *urged the horses to gallop*). **2** encourage or entreat earnestly or persistently (*urged him to stay*; *urged that they should go*). **3** (often foll. by *on*, *upon*) advocate (an action or argument etc.) emphatically (to a person) (*urged on him the need for a meeting*). **4** adduce forcefully as a reason or justification (*urged the seriousness of the problem*). — *n.* **1** urging impulse or tendency. **2** strong desire. [Latin *urgeo*]

**urgent** *adj.* **1** requiring immediate action or attention. **2** importunate. □ **urgency** *n.*

**urgently** *adv.* [French: related to URGE]

**urger** /**er**-juh/ *n.* **1** person who urges. **2** *colloq.* person who gives (unsolicited) tips at a race-meeting (for a consideration); tout. **3** *colloq.* person who takes advantage of others; petty racketeer.

**uric** /**yoo**-rik/ *adj.* of urine. [French *urique*: related to URINE]

**uric acid** *n.* crystalline acid forming a constituent of urine.

**urinal** /**yoo**-ruh-nuhl, yoo-**ruy**-/ *n.* **1** sanitary fitting, usu. against a wall, for men to urinate into. **2** place or receptacle for urination. [Latin: related to URINE]

**urinary** /**yoo**-ruh-nuh-ree/ *adj.* of or relating to urine.

**urinate** /**yoo**-ruh-,nayt/ *v.* (**-ting**) discharge urine. □ **urination** /-**nay**-shuhn/ *n.*

**urine** /**yoo**-ruhn, -ruyn/ *n.* waste fluid secreted by the kidneys, stored in the bladder, and discharged through the urethra. [Latin *urina*]

**urn** *n.* **1** vase with a foot and usu. a rounded body, used esp. for the ashes of the dead. **2** large vessel with a tap, in which tea or coffee etc. is made or kept hot. [Latin *urna*]

**urogenital** /,yoo-roh-**jen**-uh-tuhl/ *adj.* of the urinary and reproductive systems. [Greek *ouron* urine]

**urology** /yoo-**rol**-uh-jee/ *n.* the study of the urinary system. □ **urological** /-ruh-**loj**-i-kuhl/ *adj.* **urologist** *n.*

**Ursa Major** /,er-suh **may**-juh/ *n.* = *Great Bear* (see BEAR[2]). [Latin]

**Ursa Minor** n. = *Little Bear* (see BEAR²). [Latin]

**ursine** /er-suyn/ adj. of or like a bear. [Latin *ursus* bear]

**urticaria** /er-tuh-**kair**-ree-uh/ n. nettle-rash. [Latin *urtica* nettle, from *uro* burn]

**US** abbr. United States.

**us** /us, uhs/ pron. **1** objective case of WE (*they saw us*). **2** colloq. = WE (*it's us again*). **3** colloq. = ME¹ (*give us a kiss*). [Old English]

**USA** abbr. United States of America.

**usable** /**yoo**-zuh-buhl/ adj. that can be used.

**usage** /**yoo**-sij/ n. **1** use, treatment (*damaged by rough usage*). **2** customary practice, esp. in the use of a language or as creating a precedent in law.

**use** — v. /yooz/ (**using**) **1 a** cause to act or serve for a purpose; bring into service; avail oneself of (*rarely uses the car; use your discretion*). **b** consume; expend (*my car uses too much oil*). **2** treat in a specified manner (*used him shamefully*). **3** exploit for one's own ends (*they are just using you*). **4** (in past /yoost/; foll. by *to* + infin.) did or had in the past (but no longer) as a customary practice or state (*I used to drink; it used not to rain so often*). **5** (as **used** adj.) second-hand. **6** (as **used** /yoost/ predic. adj.) (foll. by *to*) familiar by habit; accustomed (*used to hard work*). — n. /yoos/ **1** act of using or state of being used; application to a purpose (*put it to good use; is in daily use; worn with use*). **2** right or power of using (*lost the use of his legs*). **3** benefit, advantage (*a torch would be of use; it's no use talking*). **4** custom or usage (*established by long use*). □ **could use** colloq. **1** would be glad to have (*I could use a drink*). **2** would be improved by having (*the house could use a lick of paint*). **have no use for 1** not need. **2** dislike, be contemptuous of. **in use** being used. **make use of 1** use. **2** benefit from (*make use of this good weather while it lasts*). **out of use** not being used. **use up 1** consume completely. **2** find a use for (leftovers etc.). **3** exhaust or wear out, e.g. with overwork. [French *us, user*, ultimately from Latin *utor us-*]

**use-by date** n. latest recommended date for consumption marked on the packing of, esp. perishable, food.

**useful** adj. **1** that can be used to advantage; helpful; beneficial. **2** colloq. creditable, efficient (*useful footballer*). □ **make oneself useful** help. □ **usefully** adv. **usefulness** n.

**useless** adj. **1** serving no purpose; unavailing. **2** colloq. feeble or ineffectual

(*useless at swimming*). □ **uselessly** adv. **uselessness** n.

**user** n. **1** person who uses a thing. **2** person who takes illegal drugs (cf. PUSHER).

**user-friendly** adj. (of a computer etc.) designed to be easy to use.

**usher** — n. **1** person who shows people to their seats in a cinema, church, etc. **2** officer walking before a person of rank (e.g., in the Senate of the Parliament of Australia, *the Usher of the Black Rod*). **3** doorkeeper at a court etc. — v. **1** act as usher to. **2** (usu. foll. by *in*) announce, herald, or show in. [Latin *ostium* door]

**usherette** /,ush-uh-**ret**/ n. female usher, esp. in a cinema.

**us mob** pron. (in Aboriginal English) us; we (*that's us mob there; us mob are not really happy*).

**USSR** abbr. hist. Union of Soviet Socialist Republics.

**usual** /**yoo**-zhoo-uhl/ adj. **1** customary, habitual (*went as usual*). **2** (absol.; prec. by *the, my,* etc.) colloq. person's usual drink etc. □ **usually** adv. [Latin: related to USE]

**usurer** /**yoo**-zh-uh-ruh/ n. person who practises usury.

**usurp** /yoo-**zerp**/ v. seize (a throne or power etc.) wrongfully. □ **usurpation** /,yoo-zuh-**pay**-shuhn/ n. **usurper** n. [French from Latin]

**usury** /**yoo**-zhuh-ree/ n. **1** lending of money at interest, esp. at an exorbitant or illegal rate. **2** interest at this rate. □ **usurious** /yoo-**zhoor**-ree-uhs/ adj. [Anglo-French or medieval Latin: related to USE]

**ute** /yoot/ n. colloq. utility (sense 4). [abbreviation]

**utensil** /yoo-**ten**-suhl/ n. implement or vessel, esp. for kitchen use. [medieval Latin: related to USE]

**uterine** /**yoo**-tuh-,ruyn/ adj. of the uterus.

**uterus** /**yoo**-tuh-ruhs/ n. (pl. **uteri** /-,ruy/) womb. [Latin]

**utilise** /**yoo**-tuh-,luyz/ v. (also **-ize**) (**-sing** or **-zing**) use; turn to account. □ **utilisation** /-,**zay**-shuhn/ n. [Italian: related to UTILITY]

**utilitarian** /,yoo-til-uh-**tair**-ree-uhn/ — adj. **1** designed to be useful rather than attractive; severely practical. **2** of utilitarianism. — n. adherent of utilitarianism.

**utilitarianism** n. **1** doctrine that actions are right if they are useful or benefit a majority. **2** doctrine that the greatest happiness of the greatest number should be the guiding principle of conduct.

**utility** /yoo-**til**-uh-tee/ n. (pl. **-ies**) **1** usefulness. **2** useful thing. **3** = PUBLIC

UTILITY. **4** (also **utility truck**) small truck, having a cabin and a tray in the rear used for carrying light loads. **5** (in full **utility player**) esp. *Australian Rules* person who is able to perform well in a number of positions. **6** (*attrib.*) basic and standardised (*utility furniture*). [Latin *utilis* useful: related to USE]

**utmost** /**ut**-mohst/ — *attrib. adj.* furthest, extreme, greatest. — *n.* utmost point or degree etc. □ **do one's utmost** do all that one can. [Old English, = *outmost*]

**Utopia** /yoo-**toh**-pee-uh/ *n.* imagined perfect place or state of things. □ **Utopian** *adj.* (also **utopian**). [title of a book by Thomas More, from Greek *ou* not, *topos* place]

**utter**[1] *attrib. adj.* complete, absolute (*utter misery*; *saw the utter absurdity of it*). □ **utterly** *adv.* [Old English, comparative of OUT[1]]

**utter**[2] *v.* **1** emit audibly (*uttered a startled cry*). **2** express in words (*uttered his contempt in speech as well as in writing*). **3** *Law* put (esp. forged money) into circulation. [Dutch]

**utterance** *n.* **1** act or instance of uttering. **2** thing spoken. **3** power or manner of speaking.

**utterly** *adv.* entirely, completely.

**uttermost** *attrib. adj.* utmost.

**U-turn** /**yoo**-tern/ *n.* **1** U-shaped turn of a vehicle so as to face in the opposite direction. **2** abrupt reversal of policy.

**UV** *abbr.* ultraviolet.

**uvula** /**yoo**-vyuh-luh/ *n.* (*pl.* **uvulae** /-‚lee/ ) fleshy part of the soft palate hanging above the throat. □ **uvular** *adj.* [Latin diminutive of *uva* grape]

**uxorious** /uk-**saw**-ree-uhs/ *adj.* greatly or excessively fond of one's wife. [Latin *uxor* wife]

**uy** var. of UEY.

# V

**V¹** /vee/ *n.* (also **v**) (*pl.* **Vs** or **V's**) **1** twenty-second letter of the alphabet. **2** V-shaped thing. **3** (as a Roman numeral) 5.

**V²** *abbr.* volt(s).

**V³** *symb.* vanadium.

**v.** *abbr.* **1** verb. **2** verse. **3** versus. **4** very. **5** *vide.*

**vac¹** *n. colloq.* vacation. [abbreviation]

**vac²** — *n. colloq.* vacuum cleaner. — *v.* use a vacuum cleaner on (*need to vac the carpets*). [abbreviation]

**vacancy** /**vay**-kuhn-see/ *n.* (*pl.* **-ies**) **1** state of being vacant. **2** unoccupied job. **3** available room in a motel etc. **4** emptiness of mind.

**vacant** *adj.* **1** not filled or occupied. **2** not mentally active; showing no interest. □ **vacantly** *adv.* [Latin: related to VACATE]

**vacant possession** *n.* ownership of a house etc. with any previous occupant having moved out.

**vacate** /vuh-**kayt**, vay-/ *v.* (**-ting**) leave vacant, cease to occupy (a house, post, etc.). [Latin *vaco* be empty]

**vacation** /vuh-**kay**-shuhn, vay-/ *n.* **1** fixed holiday period, esp. in universities and lawcourts. **2** holiday. **3** vacating or being vacated. [Latin: related to VACATE]

**vaccinate** /**vak**-suh-ˌnayt/ *v.* (**-ting**) inoculate with a vaccine to immunise against a disease. □ **vaccination** /-**nay**-shuhn/ *n.* **vaccinator** *n.*

**vaccine** /**vak**-seen, vak-**seen**/ *n.* preparation, orig. cowpox virus, used to stimulate the production of antibodies and procure immunity from one or several diseases. [Latin *vacca* cow]

**vacillate** /**vas**-uh-ˌlayt/ *v.* (**-ting**) **1** be irresolute; fluctuate in opinion. **2** move from side to side; waver. □ **vacillation** /-**lay**-shuhn/ *n.* **vacillator** *n.* [Latin]

**vacuole** /**vak**-yoo-ˌohl/ *n.* tiny space in an organ or cell, containing air, fluid, etc. [Latin *vacuus* empty]

**vacuous** /**vak**-yoo-uhs/ *adj.* **1** expressionless (*vacuous stare*). **2** showing absence of thought or intelligence, inane. □ **vacuity** /vuh-**kyoo**-uh-tee/ *n.* **vacuously** *adv.* [Latin *vacuus* empty]

**vacuum** /**vak**-yoom/ — *n.* (*pl.* **-s** or **-cua**) **1** space entirely devoid of matter. **2** space or vessel from which all or some of the air has been pumped out. **3** absence of the normal or previous content, activities, etc. (*your absence has left a vacuum; the end of the footy season creates a vast vacuum for many Aussies*). **4** (*pl.* **-s**) *colloq.* vacuum cleaner. — *v. colloq.* clean with a vacuum cleaner. [Latin *vacuus* empty]

**vacuum brake** *n.* brake worked by the exhaustion of air.

**vacuum cleaner** *n.* machine for removing dust etc. by suction. □ **vacuum-clean** *v.*

**vacuum flask** *n.* vessel with a double wall enclosing a vacuum, ensuring that the contents remain hot or cold.

**vacuum-packed** *adj.* sealed after the partial removal of air.

**vacuum tube** *n.* tube with a near-vacuum for the free passage of electric current.

**vade-mecum** /ˌvah-day-**may**-kuhm/ *n.* handbook etc. carried constantly for use. [Latin, = go with me]

**vag** /vag/ *colloq.* — *n.* **1** a vagrant. **2** vagrancy. — *v.* (**-gg**) arrest for vagrancy (*walked into this small town and immediately got vagged*). □ **on** (or **under**) **the vag** on a charge of vagrancy. [abbreviation of VAGRANT or *vagrancy*]

**vagabond** /**vag**-uh-ˌbond/ — *n.* wanderer or vagrant, esp. an idle one. — *attrib. adj.* **1** having no fixed habitation; wandering. **2** *colloq.* shiftless, idle, good-for-nothing (*your vagabond mates have cleaned out the fridge*). [Latin *vagor* wander]

**vagary** /**vay**-guh-ree/ *n.* (*pl.* **-ies**) caprice; eccentric idea or act (*the vagaries of Fortune*). [Latin *vagor* wander]

**vagina** /vuh-**juy**-nuh/ *n.* (*pl.* **-s** or **-nae** /-nee/) canal from the uterus to the vulva in female mammals. □ **vaginal** *adj.* [Latin, = sheath]

**vagrant** /**vay**-gruhnt/ — *n.* person without a settled home or regular work. — *adj.* wandering, roving. □ **vagrancy** *n.* [Anglo-French]

**vague** /vayg/ *adj.* **1** uncertain or ill-defined (*a vague answer*). **2** (of a person or mind) imprecise; inexact in thought, expression, or understanding. □ **vaguely** *adv.* **vagueness** *n.* [Latin *vagus* wandering]

**vain** *adj.* **1** having too high an opinion of one's looks, abilities, etc. **2** empty, trivial, unsubstantial (*vain boasts; vain triumphs*). **3** useless; futile (*in the vain hope* *of finding it).* □ **in vain 1** without success. **2** lightly or profanely (*take his name in vain*). □ **vainly** *adv.* [Latin *vanus*]

**vainglory** /ˌvayn-**glaw**-ree/ *n.* boastfulness; extreme vanity. □ **vainglorious** *adj.* [French *vaine gloire*]

**valance** /**val**-uhns/ *n.* (also **valence**) short curtain round the frame or canopy of a bedstead, above a window, etc. [Anglo-French *valer* descend]

**vale** *n.* (*archaic* except in place-names) valley. [Latin *vallis*]

**valediction** /ˌval-uh-**dik**-shuhn/ *n. formal* **1** bidding farewell. **2** words used in this. □ **valedictory** *adj.* & *n.* (*pl.* **-ies**). [Latin *vale* farewell]

**valence¹** /**vay**-luhns/ *n.* = VALENCY.

**valence²** var. of VALANCE.

**valency** /**vay**-luhn-see/ *n.* (*pl.* **-ies**) combining power of an atom measured by the number of hydrogen atoms it can displace or combine with. [Latin *valentia* power]

**valentine** /**val**-uhn-ˌtuyn/ *n.* **1** card or gift sent, or a message placed in a newspaper, chosen anonymously, as a mark of love on St Valentine's Day (14 February). **2** sweetheart chosen on this day. [*Valentine*, name of two saints]

**valet** /**val**-ay, **val**-uht/ — *n.* man's personal servant. — *v.* (**-t-**) **1** work as a valet (for). **2** clean or clean out (a car). [French *va(s)let*, related to VARLET, VASSAL]

**valet parking** *n.* parking (of one's car) by an attendant as a service provided at an airport, hotel, etc.

**valetudinarian** /ˌval-uh-ˌtyoo-duh-**nair**-ree-uhn/ — *n.* person of poor health or who is unduly anxious about health. — *adj.* of a valetudinarian. □ **valetudinarianism** *n.* [Latin *valetudo* health]

**valiant** /**val**-yuhnt, **val**-ee-uhnt/ *adj.* brave. □ **valiantly** *adv.* [Latin *valeo* be strong]

**valid** /**val**-uhd/ *adj.* **1** (of a reason, objection, etc.) sound, defensible. **2 a** executed with the proper formalities, legally acceptable (*valid contract*; *valid passport*). **b** not yet expired. □ **validity** /vuh-**lid**-uh-tee/ *n.* [Latin *validus* strong: related to VALIANT]

**validate** /**val**-uh-ˌdayt/ *v.* (**-ting**) make valid; ratify. □ **validation** /-**day**-shuhn/ *n.*

**valise** /vuh-**leez**, -**lees**/ *n.* small travelling bag. [French from Italian]

**Valium** /**val**-ee-uhm, **vay**-lee-uhm/ *n. propr.* drug diazepam used as a tranquilliser. [origin uncertain]

**valley** /**val**-ee/ *n.* (*pl.* **-s**) **1** long low area between hills. **2** region drained by a river (*the Nile Valley*). [French: related to VALE]

**valour** /**val**-uh/ *n.* (also **valor**) courage, esp. in battle. □ **valorous** *adj.* [Latin *valeo* be strong]

**valuable** /**val**-yoo-buhl/ — *adj.* of great value, price, or worth. — *n.* (usu. in *pl.*) valuable thing, esp. a small article of personal property. □ **valuably** *adv.*

**valuation** /ˌval-yoo-**ay**-shuhn/ *n.* **1** estimation (esp. professional) of a thing's worth. **2** worth so estimated. □ **valuate** /**val**-yoo-ˌayt/ *v.*

**value** /**val**-yoo/ — *n.* **1** worth, desirability, or utility, or the qualities on which these depend (*the value of regular exercise*). **2** worth as estimated (*set a high value on my time*). **3** amount for which a thing can be exchanged in the open market. **4** equivalent of a thing (*paid them the value of their stolen property*). **5** (in full **value for money**) something well worth the money spent. **6** ability of a thing to serve a purpose or cause an effect (*news value*; *nuisance value*). **7** (in *pl.*) one's principles, priorities, or standards. **8** *Mus.* duration of a note. **9** *Math.* amount denoted by an algebraic term. — *v.* (**-ues**, **-ued**, **-uing**) **1** estimate the value of, esp. professionally. **2** have a high or specified opinion of; attach importance to (*I value your advice*). □ **valueless** *adj.* **valuer** *n.* [French past part. of *valoir* be worth, from Latin *valeo*]

**value judgment** *n.* subjective estimate of worth etc.

**Valuer General** *n.* State official who assesses properties for rating purposes etc.

**valve** *n.* **1** device controlling flow through a pipe etc., esp. allowing movement in one direction only. **2** structure in an organ etc. allowing a flow of blood etc. in one direction only. **3** = THERMIONIC VALVE. **4** device to vary the effective length of the tube in a trumpet etc. **5** half-shell of an oyster, mussel, etc. □ **valvular** /**val**-vyuh-luh/ *adj.* [Latin *valva* leaf of a folding door]

**vamoose** /vuh-**moos**/ *v.* chiefly *US colloq.* depart hurriedly. [Spanish *vamos* let us go]

**vamp¹** — *n.* upper front part of a boot or shoe. — *v.* **1** (often foll. by *up*) repair or furbish. **2** (foll. by *up*) make by patching or from odds and ends. **3** improvise a musical accompaniment. [French *avantpié* front of the foot]

**vamp²** *colloq.* — *n.* woman who uses sexual attraction to exploit men. — *v.* act as a vamp. [abbreviation of VAMPIRE]

**vampire** /**vam**-puyuh/ *n.* **1** supposed ghost or reanimated corpse sucking the blood of sleeping persons. **2** person who preys ruthlessly on others. **3** (in full **vampire bat**) tropical (esp. South American) bloodsucking bat. [French or German from Magyar]

**van¹** *n.* **1** covered vehicle for conveying goods etc. **2** railway carriage for luggage and for the guard. [abbreviation of CARAVAN]

**van²** *n.* vanguard, forefront. [abbreviation]

**vanadium** /vuh-**nay**-dee-uhm/ *n.* hard grey metallic element used to strengthen steel. [Old Norse *Vanadís* name of the Scandinavian goddess Freyja]

**vandal** /**van**-duhl/ *n.* person who wilfully or maliciously damages property. □ **vandalism** *n.* [*Vandals*, name of a Germanic people that sacked Rome and destroyed works of art in the 5th c.: Latin from Germanic]

**vandalise** /**van**-duh-,luyz/ *v.* (also **-ize**) (**-sing** or **-zing**) wilfully or maliciously destroy or damage (esp. public property).

**Vandemonia** /van-duh-**moh**-nee-uh/ *n. hist.* name for Tasmania, esp. as a penal colony. [from *Van Diemen's Land*, former name of Tasmania]

**Vandemonian** /van-duh-**moh**-nee-uhn/ *hist.* — *n.* **1** person native to or resident in Tasmania. **2** convict who has served a sentence in Tasmania. — *adj.* **1** of, belonging to, or inhabiting Tasmania. **2** of or pertaining to Tasmania as a penal colony. [VANDEMONIA]

**Van Diemen's Land** /van-**dee**-muhnz/ *n. hist.* name given to Tasmania by its discoverer, Abel Tasman, in 1642. [Anthony *Van Diemen* (d. 1645) governor of the Dutch East Indies]

**vane** *n.* **1** weather-vane. **2** blade of a screw propeller or windmill etc. [British dial. var. of obsolete *fane* banner]

**vanguard** /**van**-gahd/ *n.* **1** foremost part of an advancing army etc. **2** leaders of a movement etc. [French *avan(t)garde* from *avant* before: related to GUARD]

**vanilla** /vuh-**nil**-uh/ *n.* **1 a** tropical fragrant climbing orchid. **b** (in full **vanilla-pod**) fruit of this. **2** extract from the vanilla-pod, or a synthetic substance, used as flavouring. [Spanish diminutive of *vaina* pod]

**vanilla lily** *n.* small Australian plant of the lily family bearing umbels of purple flowers strongly scented of vanilla.

**vanish** /**van**-ish/ *v.* **1** disappear. **2** cease to exist. **3** *Math.* become zero. [Latin: related to VAIN]

**vanishing point** *n.* **1** point at which receding parallel lines appear to meet. **2** stage of complete disappearance of something.

**vanity** /**van**-uh-tee/ *n.* (*pl.* **-ies**) **1** conceit about one's appearance or attainments. **2** thing concerning which a person is very vain (*his muscles are his abiding vanity and obsession*). **3** futility, unsubstantiality, unreal thing (*the vanity of human achievement*). [Latin: related to VAIN]

**vanity publishing** *n.* getting one's own work published by paying a commercial publisher for the production costs etc. (cf. SELF-PUBLISHING).

**vanity unit** *n.* wash-basin set into a unit with cupboards beneath.

**vanquish** /**vang**-kwish/ *v. literary* conquer, overcome. [Latin *vinco*]

**vantage** /**van**-tij, **vahn**-/ *n.* (also **vantage point**) place giving a good view or prospect. [French: related to ADVANTAGE]

**vapid** /**vap**-uhd/ *adj.* insipid; dull; flat. □ **vapidity** /vuh-**pid**-uh-tee/ *n.* [Latin *vapidus*]

**vapor** var. of VAPOUR.

**vaporise** /**vay**-puh-,ruyz/ *v.* (also **-ize**) (**-sing** or **-zing**) change into vapour. □ **vaporisation** /-**zay**-shuhn/ *n.*

**vapour** /**vay**-puh/ *n.* (also **vapor**) **1** moisture or other substance diffused or suspended in air, e.g. mist, smoke. **2** gaseous form of a substance. **3** medicinal inhalant. □ **vaporous** *adj.* **vapoury** *adj.* [Latin *vapor* steam]

**vapour trail** *n.* trail of condensed water from an aircraft etc.

**variable** /**vair**-ree-uh-buhl/ — *adj.* **1** that can be varied or adapted (*a rod of variable length; the pressure is variable*). **2** apt to vary; not constant (*a variable mood; variable fortunes*). **3** *Math.* (of a quantity) indeterminate; able to assume different numerical values. **4** (of wind or currents) tending to change direction. **5** *Bot.* & *Zool.* (of a species) including individuals or groups that depart from the type. — *n.* variable thing or quantity. □ **variability** /-**bil**-uh-tee/ *n.* **variably** *adv.*

**variance** /**vair**-ree-uhns/ *n.* **1** (usu. prec. by *at*) difference of opinion; dispute; lack of agreement (*we were at variance; a theory at variance with all known facts*). **2** *Statistics* quantity equal to the square of the standard deviation.

**variant** — *adj.* **1** differing in form or details from a standard (*variant spelling*). **2** having different forms (*forty variant types*). — *n.* variant form, spelling, type, etc.

**variation** /,vair-ree-**ay**-shuhn/ *n.* **1** act or instance of varying. **2** departure from the normal kind, amount, a standard, etc. (*prices are subject to variation*). **3** extent of this. **4** variant thing (*this pattern is a variation of the one in the knitting-book*).

**5** *Mus.* repetition of a theme in a changed or elaborated form.

**varicoloured** /ˈvair-ree-ˌkul-uhd/ *adj.* (also **varicolored**) **1** variegated in colour. **2** of various colours. [Latin *varius* VARIOUS]

**varicose** /ˈva-ruh-ˌkohs, -kuhs/ *adj.* (esp. of a vein etc.) permanently and abnormally dilated and swollen. [Latin *varix* varicose vein]

**varied** /ˈvair-reed/ *adj.* showing variety.

**variegated** /ˈvair-ree-uh-ˌgay-tuhd/ *adj.* **1** with irregular patches of different colours. **2** having leaves of two or more colours. □ **variegate** *v.* **variegation** /-ˈgay-shuhn/ *n.* [Latin: related to VARIOUS]

**varietal** /vuh-ˈruy-uh-tuhl/ *adj.* **1** esp. *Bot.* & *Zool.* of, forming, or designating a variety. **2** (of wine) made from a single designated variety of grape.

**variety** /vuh-ˈruy-uh-tee/ *n.* (*pl.* **-ies**) **1** diversity; absence of uniformity; many-sidedness (*not enough variety in our lives*). **2** quantity or collection of different things (*for a variety of reasons*). **3 a** class of things that differ from the rest in the same general class. **b** member of such a class. **4** (foll. by *of*) different form of a thing, quality, etc. **5** *Biol.* subdivision of a species. **6** series of dances, songs, comedy acts, etc. (*variety show*). [Latin: related to VARIOUS]

**variorum** /ˌvair-ree-ˈaw-ruhm/ — *adj.* **1** (of an edition of a text) having notes by various editors or commentators. **2** (of an edition of an author's works) including variant readings. — *n.* a variorum edition. [Latin: related to VARIOUS]

**various** /ˈvair-ree-uhs/ *adj.* **1** different, diverse (*from various backgrounds*). **2** several (*for various reasons*). □ **variously** *adv.* [Latin *varius*]

■ **Usage** *Various* (unlike *several*) cannot be used with *of*, as (wrongly) in *various of the guests arrived late.*

**varlet** /ˈvah-luht/ *n.* **1** *archaic* menial; rascal. **2** *hist.* knight's attendant. [French var. of *vaslet* VALET]

**varnish** /ˈvah-nish/ — *n.* **1** resinous solution used to give a hard shiny transparent coating. **2** similar preparation (*nail varnish*). **3** deceptive outward appearance or show. — *v.* **1** apply varnish to. **2** give a deceptively attractive appearance to. [French *vernis*, probably ultimately from *Berenice* in Cyrenaica]

**varnish wattle** *n.* wattle of all States except WA and the NT, having golden ball flowers and extremely shiny young growth, seemingly lacquered or varnished.

**vary** /ˈvair-ree/ *v.* (**-ies, -ied**) **1** make different; modify, diversify (*seldom varies the routine*). **2 a** undergo change; become or be different (*the temperature varies from 30°C to 70°C*). **b** be of different kinds (*his mood varies*; *the garden varies as season follows season*). [Latin *vario*: related to VARIOUS]

**vas** /vas/ *n.* (*pl.* **vasa** /ˈvay-suh/) vessel or duct. [Latin, = vessel]

**vascular** /ˈvas-kyuh-luh/ *adj.* of or containing vessels for conveying blood, sap, etc. [Latin *vasculum* diminutive of VAS]

**vas deferens** /ˌvas ˈdef-uh-ˌrenz/ *n.* (*pl.* **vasa deferentia** /ˌdef-uh-ˈren-shee-uh/) duct which conveys the sperm from the testicle to the urethra. [Latin, = vessel bearing away]

**vase** /vahz/ *n.* vessel used as an ornament or container for flowers. [Latin: related to VAS]

**vasectomy** /vuh-ˈsek-tuh-mee/ *n.* (*pl.* **-ies**) removal of part of each vas deferens, esp. for sterilisation.

**vaseline** /ˈvas-uh-ˌleen, -leen/ *n. propr.* type of petroleum jelly used as an ointment, lubricant, etc. [German *Wasser* water, Greek *elaion* oil]

**vassal** /ˈvas-uhl/ *n.* **1** *hist.* feudal tenant of land. **2** humble dependant. □ **vassalage** *n.* [medieval Latin *vassallus* retainer]

**vast** /vahst/ *adj.* **1** immense, huge (*vast expanse of water*; *vast crowds*). **2** great, considerable (*makes a vast difference*). □ **vastly** *adv.* **vastness** *n.* [Latin]

**vat** *n.* tank, esp. for holding liquids in brewing, distilling, food manufacture, dyeing, and tanning. [British dial. var. of *fat*, from Old English]

**Vatican** /ˈvat-i-kuhn/ *n.* **1** palace and official residence of the Pope in Rome. **2** papal government or authority (*the Vatican has decreed that . . .*). **3** (in full **Vatican City**) sovereign, independent State in Rome which includes the Vatican and St. Peter's Basilica in its territory. [name of a hill in Rome]

**vaudeville** /ˈvaw-duh-vil/ *n.* **1** variety entertainment. **2** light stage play with interspersed songs. □ **vaudevillian** /-ˈvil-yuhn/ *adj.* & *n.* [French]

**vault** /vawlt, volt/ — *n.* **1** arched roof. **2** vaultlike covering (*vault of heaven*). **3** underground chamber: **a** as a place of storage (*bank vault*). **b** as a place of interment beneath a church or in a cemetery etc. **4** act of vaulting. **5** = VAULTING-HORSE. — *v.* **1** leap, esp. using the hands or a pole. **2** spring over in this way. **3** (esp. as **vaulted**) **a** make in the form of a vault. **b** provide with a vault or vaults. [Latin *volvo volut-* roll]

**vaulting-horse** *n.* wooden box for vaulting over.

**vaunt** /vawnt/ — *v. literary* boast; boast of; extol boastfully. — *n.* a boast. [Latin: related to VAIN]

**VC** *abbr.* **1** Victoria Cross. **2** Vice-Chancellor.

**VCR** *abbr.* video cassette recorder.

**VD** *abbr.* venereal disease.

**VDU** *abbr.* visual display unit.

**'ve** *abbr.* (usu. after pronouns) have (*I've, they've*).

**veal** *n.* calf's flesh as food. [French from Latin *vitulus* calf]

**vector** /vek-tuh/ *n.* **1** *Math. & Physics* quantity having direction as well as magnitude. **2** carrier of disease. [Latin *veho vect-* convey]

**Veda** /vay-duh, vee-/ *n.* (in *sing.* or *pl.*) oldest Hindu scriptures. □ **Vedic** *adj.* [Sanskrit, = knowledge]

**veer** /veer/ — *v.* **1** change direction, esp. (of the wind) clockwise. **2** change in course or opinion etc. — *n.* change of direction. [French *virer*]

**veg**[1] /vej/ *n. colloq.* vegetable(s). [abbreviation]

**veg**[2] /vej/ *v.* (also **veg out**) *colloq.* relax, do nothing (*veging out in front of the telly*). [VEG(ETATE)]

**vegan** /vee-guhn/ — *n.* person who does not eat animals or animal products. — *adj.* using or containing no animal products. [shortening of VEGETARIAN]

**vegemite** /vej-uh-muyt/ *n. propr.* **1** concentrated yeast extract used as a spread. **2** *colloq.* an Australian child (*happy little vegemites*).

**vegetable** /vej-uh-tuh-buhl, vej-tuh-buhl/ — *n.* **1** plant, esp. a herbaceous plant used for food, e.g. a cabbage, potato, or bean. **2** *colloq. derog.* **a** *offens.* person who is severely mentally incapacitated, esp. through brain injury etc. **b** dull or inactive person. — *adj.* **1** of, derived from, or relating to plant life or vegetables as food. **2** dull, monotonous (*a vegetable existence*). [Latin: related to VEGETATE]

**vegetal** /vej-uh-tuhl/ *adj.* of or like plants. [medieval Latin: related to VEGETATE]

**vegetarian** /ˌvej-uh-**tair**-ree-uhn/ — *n.* person who does not eat meat or fish. — *adj.* excluding animal food, esp. meat (*vegetarian diet*). □ **vegetarianism** *n.* [from VEGETABLE]

**vegetate** /vej-uh-ˌtayt/ *v.* (**-ting**) **1** live an uneventful or monotonous life. **2** grow as plants do. [Latin *vegeto* animate]

**vegetation** /ˌvej-uh-**tay**-shuhn/ *n.* plants collectively; plant life. [medieval Latin: related to VEGETATE]

**vegetative** /**vej**-uh-tuh-tiv, -ˌtay-tiv/ *adj.* **1** concerned with growth and development as distinct from sexual reproduction. **2** of vegetation. [French or medieval Latin: related to VEGETATE]

**vegie** /**vej**-ee/ *n.* (usu. in *pl.*) *colloq.* vegetable.

**vehement** /**vee**-uh-muhnt/ *adj.* showing or caused by strong feeling; ardent (*vehement protest*). □ **vehemence** *n.* **vehemently** *adv.* [Latin]

**vehicle** /**vee**-uh-kuhl, **veer**-kuhl/ *n.* **1** any conveyance used on land or in space for transporting people, goods, etc. **2** thing or person as a medium for expression or action (*the stage is the best vehicle for her talents*). **3** liquid etc. as a medium for suspending pigments, drugs, etc. □ **vehicular** /vuh-**hik**-yuh-luh/ *adj.* [Latin *veho* carry]

**veil** /vayl/ — *n.* **1** piece of usu. transparent fabric attached to a woman's hat etc., esp. to conceal or protect the face. **2** piece of linen etc. as part of a nun's headdress, resting on the head and shoulders. **3** thing that hides or disguises (*a veil of silence*). **4** a curtain, esp. that separating the sanctuary in a Jewish temple or that screening the door of the altar tabernacle in e.g. a Catholic church. — *v.* **1** cover with a veil. **2** (esp. as **veiled** *adj.*) partly conceal (*veiled threats*). □ **draw a veil over** avoid discussing; hush up. **take the veil** become a nun. [Latin *velum*]

**vein** /vayn/ — *n.* **1 a** any of the tubes conveying blood to the heart. **b** (in general use) any blood-vessel. **2** rib of an insect's wing or leaf. **3** streak of a different colour in wood, marble, cheese, etc. **4** fissure in rock filled with ore. **5** specified character or tendency; mood (*spoke in a sarcastic vein*). — *v.* fill or cover with or as with veins. □ **veined** *adj.* **veiny** *adj.* (**-ier, -iest**). [Latin *vena*]

**velar** /**vee**-luh/ *adj. Phonet.* (of a sound) pronounced with the back of the tongue near the soft palate. [Latin *velaris* from *velum* curtain, covering]

**Velcro** /**vel**-kroh/ *n.* (also **velcro**) *propr.* fastener consisting of two strips of fabric which cling when pressed together. [French *velours croché* hooked velvet]

**veld** /velt/ *n.* (also **veldt**) *S.Afr.* open country. [Afrikaans: related to FIELD]

**vellum** /**vel**-uhm/ *n.* **1 a** fine parchment, orig. calfskin. **b** manuscript on this. **2** smooth writing-paper imitating vellum. [French *velin*: related to VEAL]

**velocity** /vuh-**los**-uh-tee/ *n.* (*pl.* **-ies**) speed, esp. of inanimate things (*wind velocity*; *velocity of light*). [Latin *velox* swift]

**velodrome** /**vel**-uh-,drohm/ *n.* place or building with a track for cycle-racing. [French *vélo* bicycle]

**velour** /vuh-**loor**/ *n.* (also **velours** pronunc. same) plushlike fabric. [French]

**velvet** /**vel**-vuht/ — *n.* **1** soft fabric with a thick short pile on one side. **2** furry skin on a growing antler. — *adj.* of, like, or soft as velvet. □ **on velvet** in an advantageous or prosperous position. □ **velvety** *adj.* [Latin *villus* tuft, down]

**velveteen** /,vel-vuh-**teen**/ *n.* cotton fabric with a pile like velvet.

**velvet glove** *n.* outward gentleness, esp. cloaking firmness.

**Ven.** *abbr.* Venerable (as the title of a high-ranking Buddhist monk or an archdeacon or *RC Ch.* a dead person proclaimed such as a first step towards possible canonisation).

**venal** /**vee**-nuhl/ *adj.* corrupt; able to be bribed; involving bribery. □ **venality** /-**nal**-uh-tee/ *n.* **venally** *adv.* [Latin *venum* thing for sale]

■ **Usage** *Venal* is sometimes confused with *venial*, which means 'pardonable' or 'not causing a state of spiritual death'.

**vend** *v.* offer (small wares) for sale. □ **vendible** *adj.* [Latin *vendo* sell]

**vendetta** /ven-**det**-uh/ *n.* **1** blood feud. **2** prolonged bitter quarrel. [Latin: related to VINDICTIVE]

**vending machine** *n.* slot machine selling small items.

**vendor** *n. Law* seller, esp. of property. [Anglo-French: related to VEND]

**veneer** /vuh-**neer**/ — *n.* **1** thin covering of fine wood etc. applied to a coarser wood. **2** a layer in plywood. **3** (often foll. by *of*) deceptively pleasing appearance (*his friendliness is only a veneer*). — *v.* **1** apply a veneer to (wood etc.). **2** disguise (an unattractive character etc.) with a more attractive manner etc. [German *furnieren* to furnish]

**venerable** /**ven**-uh-ruh-buhl/ *adj.* **1** entitled to deep respect on account of character, age, associations, etc. (*venerable old man*; *venerable relics*). **2** (of a high-ranking Buddhist monk or an archdeacon in the Anglican Church. **b** title of a deceased person proclaimed as having attained a certain degree of sanctity: the first stage in a process which may lead to beatification or eventual canonisation (*the Venerable Bede*). [Latin: related to VENERATE]

**venerate** /**ven**-uh-,rayt/ *v.* (**-ting**) respect deeply. □ **veneration** /-**ray**-shuhn/ *n.* **venerator** *n.* [Latin *veneror* revere]

**venereal** /vuh-**neer**-ee-uhl/ *adj.* **1** of or relating to sexual desire or intercourse. **2** of or relating to venereal disease. [Latin *venus veneris* sexual love]

**venereal disease** *n.* disease contracted by sexual intercourse with an infected person or congenitally.

**Venetian** /vuh-**nee**-shuhn/ — *n.* native, citizen, or dialect of Venice. — *adj.* of Venice. [from French or medieval Latin *Venetia* Venice]

**venetian blind** *n.* window-blind of adjustable horizontal slats.

**vengeance** /**ven**-juhns/ *n.* punishment inflicted for wrong to oneself or one's cause. □ **with a vengeance** to a high or excessive degree (*punctuality with a vengeance*). [French *venger* from Latin *vindico* avenge]

**vengeful** *adj.* vindictive; seeking vengeance. □ **vengefully** *adv.* [obsolete *venge* avenge: related to VENGEANCE]

**venial** /**vee**-nee-uhl/ *adj.* (of a sin or fault) pardonable; not mortal. □ **veniality** /-nee-**al**-uh-tee/ *n.* **venially** *adv.* [Latin *venia* forgiveness]

■ **Usage** *Venial* is sometimes confused with *venal*, which means 'corrupt'.

**venial sin** *n. Theol.* a sin not grave enough to bring about a state of spiritual death (opp. MORTAL SIN).

**venison** /**ven**-uh-suhn, -zuhn/ *n.* deer's flesh as food. [Latin *venatio* hunting]

**Venn diagram** *n.* diagram using overlapping and intersecting circles etc. to show the relationships between mathematical sets. [*Venn*, name of a logician]

**venom** /**ven**-uhm/ *n.* **1** poisonous fluid of esp. snakes. **2** malignity; spite. [Latin *venenum*]

**venomous** /**ven**-uh-muhs/ *adj.* **1 a** containing, secreting, or injecting venom. **b** (of a snake etc.) inflicting poisonous wounds by this means. **2** (of a person etc.) spiteful, malignant. □ **venomously** *adv.*

**venous** /**vee**-nuhs/ *adj.* of, full of, or contained in, veins. [Latin: related to VEIN]

**vent¹** — *n.* **1** opening allowing the passage of air etc. **2** outlet; free expression (*gave vent to my anger*). **3** anus, esp. of a lower animal. — *v.* **1** make a vent in (a cask etc.). **2** give free expression to. □ **vent one's spleen on** scold or ill-treat without cause. [Latin *ventus* wind]

**vent²** *n.* slit in a garment, esp. in the lower edge of the back of a jacket. [French *fente* from Latin *findo* cleave]

**ventilate** /ven-tuh-,layt/ v. (**-ting**) **1** cause air to circulate freely in (a room etc.). **2** air (a question, grievance, etc.). **3** Med. **a** oxygenate (the blood). **b** admit or force air into (the lungs). □ **ventilation** /-lay-shuhn/ n. [Latin ventilo blow, winnow: related to VENT[1]]

**ventilator** n. **1** appliance or aperture for ventilating a room etc. **2** Med. = RESPIRATOR 2.

**ventral** /ven-truhl/ adj. **1** Anat. & Zool. of or on the abdomen (cf. DORSAL). **2** Bot. of the front or lower surface. [venter abdomen, from Latin]

**ventricle** /ven-tri-kuhl/ n. **1** cavity in the body. **2** hollow part of an organ, esp. the brain or heart. □ **ventricular** /-trik-yuh-luh/ adj. [Latin ventriculus diminutive of venter belly]

**ventriloquism** /ven-tril-uh-,kwiz-uhm/ n. (also **ventriloquy**) skill of speaking or uttering sounds without moving the lips, so that the sounds seem to come from a source other than the speaker, e.g. a dummy. □ **ventriloquist** n. [Latin venter belly, loquor speak]

**venture** /ven-chuh/ — n. **1** the undertaking of a risk; a risky undertaking. **2** a commercial speculation. — v. (**-ring**) **1** dare; not be afraid (ventured to stop them). **2** dare to go, make, or put forward (venture out; venture an opinion). **3 a** expose to risk; stake (a bet etc.) (ventured all he had on one last fling). **b** take risks (nothing ventured, nothing gained). **4** (foll. by on, upon) dare to engage in etc. (ventured on a longer journey). [from ADVENTURE]

**venturesome** adj. **1** disposed to take risks. **2** risky.

**venue** /ven-yoo/ n. **1** place at which something occurs; meeting place. **2** place for a sporting match, meeting, concert, etc. [French, from venir come]

**Venus flytrap** /vee-nuhs/ n. flesh-consuming plant with leaves that spring shut on insects etc. [Latin Venus goddess of love]

**veracious** /vuh-ray-shuhs/ adj. formal **1** truthful by nature. **2** (of a statement etc.) true. □ **veracity** /vuh-ras-uh-tee/ n. [Latin verax from verus true]

**verandah** /vuh-ran-duh/ n. (also **veranda**) **1** open-sided roofed structure along one or more sides of a house or commercial building, the main purpose

---

## Verb

A verb says what a person or thing does, and can describe:

an action, e.g. run, hit
an event, e.g. rain, happen
a state, e.g. be, have, seem, appear
a change, e.g. become, grow

Verbs occur in different forms, usually in one or other of their tenses. The most common tenses are:

| | |
|---|---|
| the simple present tense: | The boy walks down the road. |
| the continuous present tense: | The boy is walking down the road. |
| the simple past tense: | The boy walked down the road. |
| the continuous past tense: | The boy was walking down the road. |
| the perfect tense: | The boy has walked down the road. |
| the past perfect tense: | The boy had walked down the road. |
| the future tense: | The boy will walk down the road. |

Each of these forms is a finite verb, which means that it is in a particular tense and that it changes according to the number and person of the subject, as in

I am          you walk
we are        he walks

An infinitive is the form of a verb that usually appears with 'to', e.g.

to wander, to look, to sleep.

In this dictionary the designation absol. (= absolute) refers to uses of transitive verbs (i.e. verbs which take an object) with an object implied but not stated, e.g. smoking kills, let me explain.

In this dictionary the designation refl. (= reflexive) refers to a verb which has a reflexive pronoun as its object, e.g. she acquitted herself well.

In this dictionary the designation pass. (= passive) refers to the passive voice. Verbs can be in the active voice or the passive voice. 'Voice' shows the relation of the subject to the action. In he kicked the cat the verb is in the active voice because the subject ('he') is the doer of the action of the verb. In the cat was kicked by him the verb is in the passive voice because the subject 'the cat' is the recipient of the action of the verb.

of which is the provision of shelter. **2** such a structure that is enclosed or partially enclosed and used for relaxation or as additional living space. **3** (*attrib.*) (of a person) inclined to direct from afar and to take no active part, 'armchair' (*he's a verandah gardener — it's his wife who does the digging*). [Hindi from Portuguese *varanda*]

**verb** *n.* word used to indicate action, a state, or an occurrence (see panel). [Latin *verbum* word]

**verbal** — *adj.* **1** of or relating to words. **2** oral, not written (*gave a verbal statement*). **3** *Gram.* of, deriving from, or in the nature of a verb (*verbal noun*). — *n. colloq.* verbal statement to the police. — *v.* (**-ll-**) *colloq.* attribute a damaging statement to (a suspect) (*swore he had been verballed*). □ **verballing** *n.* (in sense of verb). **verbally** *adv.* [Latin: related to VERB]

---

■ **Usage** Some people reject sense 2 of *verbal* as illogical, and prefer *oral*. However, *verbal* is the usual term in expressions such as *verbal communication*, *verbal contract*, and *verbal evidence*.

---

**verbalise** *v.* (also **-ize**) (**-sing** or **-zing**) put into words.

**verbal noun** *n.* noun derived from a verb (e.g. *smoking* in *smoking is forbidden*: see -ING[1]).

**verbatim** /ver-**bay**-tuhm/ *adv. & adj.* in exactly the same words. [medieval Latin: related to VERB]

**verbena** /ver-**bee**-nuh/ *n.* (*pl.* same) plant of a genus of usu. annual or biennial plants with clusters of fragrant flowers. [Latin]

**verbiage** /**ver**-bee-ij/ *n. derog.* too many words or unnecessarily difficult words. [French: related to VERB]

**verbose** /ver-**bohs**/ *adj.* using more words than are needed. □ **verbosity** /-**bos**-uh-tee/ *n.* [Latin *verbosus* from *verbum* word]

**verdant** /**ver**-duhnt/ *adj.* (of grass, a field, etc.) green, lush. □ **verdancy** *n.* [perhaps from French *verdeant* from Latin *viridis* green]

**verdict** /**ver**-dikt/ *n.* **1** decision of a jury in a civil or criminal case. **2** decision; judgment. [Anglo-French *verdit* from *ver* true, *dit* saying]

**verdigris** /**ver**-duh-gree, -grees/ *n.* greenish-blue substance that forms on copper or brass. [French, = green of Greece]

**verdure** /**ver**-joor/ *n. literary* green vegetation or its colour. [French *verd* green]

**verge[1]** *n.* **1** edge or border. **2** brink (*on the verge of tears*). **3** grass edging of a road etc. [Latin *virga* rod]

**verge[2]** *v.* (**-ging**) **1** (foll. by *on*) border on (*verging on the ridiculous*). **2** incline downwards or in a specified direction. [Latin *vergo* bend]

**verger** *n.* **1** church caretaker and attendant. **2** officer preceding a bishop etc. with a staff. [Anglo-French: related to VERGE[1]]

**verify** /**ve**-ruh-,fuy/ *v.* (**-ies**, **-ied**) **1** establish the truth, correctness, or validity of by examination etc. (*verified my figures*). **2** (of an event etc.) bear out (a prediction or promise). □ **verifiable** *adj.* **verification** /-fuh-**kay**-shuhn/ *n.* [medieval Latin: related to VERY]

**verily** /**ve**-ruh-lee/ *adv. archaic* really, truly. [from VERY]

**verisimilitude** /,ve-ree-suh-**mil**-uh-,tyood/ *n.* appearance of being true or real. [Latin *verus* true, *similis* like]

**veritable** /**ve**-ruh-tuh-buhl/ *adj.* real; rightly so called (*a veritable feast*). □ **veritably** *adv.* [French: related to VERITY]

**verity** /**ve**-ruh-tee/ *n.* (*pl.* **-ies**) **1** a fundamental truth. **2** *archaic* truth. [Latin *veritas* truth]

**vermicelli** /,ver-muh-**chel**-ee, -**sel**-ee/ *n.* pasta in long slender threads. [Latin *vermis* worm]

**vermicide** /**ver**-muh-,suyd/ *n.* drug that kills intestinal worms. [Latin *vermis* worm]

**vermiculite** /ver-**mik**-yuh-,luyt/ *n.* a hydrous silicate mineral used esp. as a moisture-holding medium for plant growth. [Latin *vermiculatus* worm-eaten, from *vermis* worm]

**vermiform** /**ver**-muh-,fawm/ *adj.* worm-shaped. [medieval Latin: related to VERMICIDE]

**vermiform appendix** *n.* small blind tube extending from the caecum in man and some other mammals.

**vermilion** /vuh-**mil**-yuhn/ — *n.* **1** cinnabar. **2 a** brilliant red pigment made esp. from this or artificially. **b** colour of this. — *adj.* of this colour. [Latin *vermiculus* diminutive of *vermis* worm]

**vermin** /**ver**-muhn/ *n.* (usu. treated as *pl.*) **1** animals harmful to crops, native wildlife, etc., e.g. introduced species such as rabbits and foxes; disease-carrying species such as rats. **2** parasitic worms or insects, e.g. hookworm, ticks, fleas. **3** vile people. □ **verminous** *adj.* [Latin *vermis* worm]

**vermouth** /**ver**-muhth, vuh-**mooth**/ *n.* wine flavoured with aromatic herbs. [German: related to WORMWOOD]

**vernacular** /vuh-**nak**-yuh-luh/ — n. **1** language or dialect of a particular country (*the Mass is now said or sung in the vernacular, not in Latin*). **2** language of a particular class or group (*shearers' vernacular; in ultra-feminist vernacular, would a manhole mutate into a person-hole?*). **3** everyday, colloquial speech. — adj. (of language) native; not of foreign origin or of learned formation. [Latin *vernaculus* native]

**vernal** /**ver**-nuhl/ adj. of or in spring. [Latin *ver* spring]

**vernal equinox** n. spring equinox (see EQUINOX).

**vernier** /**ver**-nee-uh/ n. small movable graduated scale for obtaining fractional parts of subdivisions on a fixed scale of a barometer, sextant, etc. [*Vernier*, name of a mathematician]

**vernier engine** n. auxiliary engine for slight changes in the motion of a space rocket etc.

**verruca** /vuh-**roo**-kuh/ n. (pl. **verrucae** /-see/ or **-s**) wart or similar growth, esp. on the foot. [Latin]

**versatile** /**ver**-suh-,tuyl/ adj. **1** adapting easily to different subjects or occupations; skilled in many subjects or occupations. **2** having many uses. □ **versatility** /-**til**-uh-tee/ n. [Latin *verto vers-* turn]

**verse** n. **1** poetry in general (opp. PROSE). **2 a** metrical line in accordance with the rules of prosody. **b** stanza of a poem or song. **3** each of the short numbered divisions of the Bible. **4** poem. [Latin *versus*: related to VERSATILE]

**versed** /verst/ adj. (foll. by *in*) experienced or skilled in (*well versed in the Western Desert language*). [Latin *versor* be engaged in]

**versicle** /**ver**-suh-kuhl/ n. each of a priest's short sentences in a liturgy, answered by the congregation. [Latin diminutive: related to VERSE]

**versify** /**ver**-suh-,fuy/ v. (**-ies**, **-ied**) **1** turn into or express in verse. **2** compose verses. □ **versification** /-fuh-**kay**-shuhn/ n. **versifier** n.

**version** /**ver**-*zh*uhn/ n. **1** account of a matter from a particular point of view (*told them my version of the incident*). **2** book etc. in a particular edition or translation (*Douay Version of the Bible; Authorised Version*). **3** form or variant of a thing as performed, adapted, etc. (*performed an Aboriginal version of the arrival of the First Fleet*). [Latin *verto vers-* turn]

**vers libre** /vair leebr, lee-bruh/ n. verse with no regular metrical pattern. [French, = free verse]

**verso** /**ver**-soh/ n. (pl. **-s**) **1 a** left-hand page of an open book. **b** back of a printed leaf of paper or manuscript (opp. RECTO). **2** reverse of a coin. [Latin *verso* (*folio*) on the turned (leaf)]

**versus** /**ver**-suhs/ prep. against (esp. in law and sport) (*the Cats versus the Sydney Swans; the case of Smith versus Jones*). [Latin: related to VERSE]

**vertebra** /**ver**-tuh-bruh/ n. (pl. **-brae** /-,bree/ ) each segment of a backbone. □ **vertebral** adj. [Latin *verto* turn]

**vertebrate** /**ver**-tuh-bruht, -,brayt/ — adj. (of an animal) having a backbone or spinal column. — n. vertebrate animal. [Latin *vertebratus* jointed: related to VERTEBRA]

**vertex** /**ver**-teks/ n. (pl. **-tices** /-tuh-,seez/ or **-texes**) **1** highest point; top, apex. **2 a** each angular point of a triangle, polygon, etc. **b** meeting-point of lines that form an angle. [Latin, = whirlpool, crown of a head, from *verto* turn]

**vertical** /**ver**-ti-kuhl/ — adj. **1** at right angles to a horizontal plane; perpendicular. **2** in a direction from top to bottom of a picture etc. **3** of or at the vertex. — n. vertical line or plane. □ **vertically** adv. [Latin: related to VERTEX]

**vertical blind** n. window-blind of adjustable vertical strips of fabric.

**vertical take-off** n. take-off of an aircraft directly upwards.

**Verticordia** /,ver-tuh-**kaw**-dee-uh/ n. (also **feather flowers**) highly ornamental genus of plants, containing about 50 species mostly confined to south-western WA, with profuse feathery flowers in brilliant hues (red, gold, mauve, purple, cream). [Latin *verto* turn, *cor cordis* heart]

**vertiginous** /ver-**tij**-uh-nuhs/ adj. of or causing vertigo. [Latin: related to VERTIGO]

**vertigo** /**ver**-tuh-,goh/ n. dizziness caused esp. by heights. [Latin, = whirling, from *verto* turn]

**verve** n. enthusiasm, vigour, spirit. [French]

**very** /**ve**-ree/ — adv. **1** in a high degree (*did it very easily*). **2** in the fullest sense (foll. by *own* or superl. adj.: *do your very best; my very own room*). — adj. real, true, actual; truly such (usu. prec. by *the, this, his,* etc. emphasising identity, significance, or extreme degree: *the very thing we need; his very words; the very same*). □ **not very** in a low degree, far from being. **very good** (or **well**) formula of consent or approval. [Latin *verus* true]

**very high frequency** n. (in radio) 30-300 megahertz.

**vesicle** /ves-i-kuhl/ n. **1** small bladder, bubble, or blister. **2** small cavity in volcanic rock produced by gas bubbles. [Latin]

**vespers** n.pl. **1** RC Ch. **a** sixth of the seven canonical hours of the breviary. **b** service for this, said or chanted in the evening. **2** (in the Anglican Church etc.) evensong. [Latin *vesper* evening]

**vessel** /ves-uhl/ n. **1** hollow receptacle, esp. for liquid. **2** ship or boat, esp. a large one. **3** duct or canal etc. holding or conveying blood or sap etc., esp. = BLOOD-VESSEL. [Latin diminutive: related to VAS]

**vest** — n. **1** waistcoat. **2** chiefly *Brit.* undergarment worn on the trunk (cf. SINGLET). — v. **1** (foll. by *with*) bestow (powers, authority, etc.) on. **2** (foll. by *in*) confer (property or power) on (a person) with an immediate fixed right of future possession. **3** clothe (oneself), esp. in vestments. [Latin *vestis* garment]

**vestal** /ves-tuhl/ — adj. **1** chaste, pure. **2** of or relating to the goddess Vesta. — n. **1** chaste or virginal woman, esp. a nun. **2** *Rom. Antiq.* = VESTAL VIRGIN. [*Vesta*, Roman goddess of the hearth and home]

**vestal virgin** n. *Rom. Antiq.* virgin consecrated to Vesta and vowed to chastity. [*Vesta*, Roman goddess of the hearth and home]

**vested interest** n. **1** personal interest in a state of affairs, usu. with an expectation of gain. **2** *Law* interest (usu. in land or money held in trust) recognised as belonging to a person.

**vestibule** /ves-tuh-byool/ n. hall or lobby of a building. [Latin]

**vestige** /ves-tij/ n. **1** trace or piece of evidence; sign (*vestiges of an earlier civilisation*). **2** slight amount; particle (*without a vestige of clothing*). **3** part or organ of an animal or plant that is reduced or functionless but was well developed in its ancestors. □ **vestigial** /ves-**tij**-uhl/ adj. [Latin *vestigium* footprint]

**vestment** /vest-muhnt/ n. ceremonial garment, esp. a chasuble as worn by a priest etc. at Mass etc., or an official or state robe as worn by a lay person. [Latin: related to VEST]

**vestry** /ves-tree/ n. (pl. **-ies**) = SACRISTY.

**vet¹** — n. colloq. veterinary surgeon. — v. (**-tt-**) make a careful and critical examination of (a scheme, work, candidate, etc.). [abbreviation]

**vet²** n. veteran. [abbreviation]

**vetch** n. plant of the pea family used largely for fodder. [Latin *vicia*]

**veteran** /vet-uh-ruhn, vet-ruhn/ n. **1** (often *attrib.*) old soldier or long-serving member of any group (*war veteran*; *veteran actor*). **2** ex-serviceman or servicewoman. [Latin *vetus -er-* old]

**veteran car** n. car made before 1916, or (strictly) before 1905.

**veterinarian** /,vet-uh-ruh-**nair**-ree-uhn/ n. formal veterinary surgeon.

**veterinary** /vet-ruhn-ree, vet-uh-ruhn-uh-ree/ — adj. of or for the diseases and injuries of esp. farm and domestic animals. — n. (pl. **-ies**) veterinary surgeon. [Latin *veterinae* cattle]

**veterinary surgeon** n. person qualified to treat diseased or injured animals.

**veto** /vee-toh/ — n. (pl. **-es**) **1** right to reject a measure, resolution, etc. unilaterally. **2** rejection, prohibition. — v. (**-oes**, **-oed**) **1** reject (a measure etc.). **2** forbid, prohibit. [Latin, = I forbid]

**vex** v. **1** anger, irritate. **2** archaic grieve, afflict. [Latin *vexo* afflict]

**vexation** /vek-**say**-shuhn/ n. **1** act or instance of vexing or state of being vexed. **2** annoying or distressing thing.

**vexatious** /vek-**say**-shuhs/ adj. **1** causing vexation. **2** *Law* (of litigation) lacking sufficient grounds and seeking only to annoy the defendant.

**vexed** adj. (of a question) much discussed; problematic.

**VHF** abbr. very high frequency.

**VHS** abbr. propr. format for recording and playing video tape. [Video Home System]

**via** /vuy-uh/ prep. by way of; through; by means of (*Canberra to Adelaide via Melbourne*; *send it via your son*). [Latin, ablative of *via* way]

**viable** /vuy-uh-buhl/ adj. **1** (of a plan etc.) feasible, esp. economically. **2 a** (of a plant, animal, etc.) capable of living or existing in a particular climate etc. **b** (esp. of a foetus) capable of developing and surviving independently. □ **viability** /-bil-uh-tee/ n. [French *vie* life]

**viaduct** /vuy-uh-,dukt/ n. long bridge, esp. a series of arches, carrying a road or railway across a valley or hollow. [Latin *via* way, after AQUEDUCT]

**vial** /vuy-uhl/ n. small (usu. cylindrical glass) vessel, esp. for holding medicines. [related to PHIAL]

**viand** /vuy-uhnd, vee-uhnd/ n. formal (usu. in pl.) article of food. [Latin *vivo* live]

**viaticum** /vuy-**at**-i-kuhm/ n. (pl. **-ca**) the Eucharist as given to a person near, or in danger of, death. [Latin, = 'food for the road or journey']

**vibes** n.pl. colloq. **1** vibrations, esp. feelings or atmosphere communicated (*I don't like the vibes of this place*). **2** = VIBRAPHONE. [abbreviation]

**vibrant** /**vuy**-bruhnt/ *adj.* **1** vibrating. **2** (often foll. by *with*) thrilling, lively (*vibrant with emotion*). **3** (of sound) resonant. **4** (of colours) bright and striking. □ **vibrancy** *n.* **vibrantly** *adv.* [Latin: related to VIBRATE]

**vibraphone** /**vuy**-bruh-fohn/ *n.* instrument like a xylophone but with motor-driven resonators under the metal bars giving a vibrato effect. [from VIBRATO]

**vibrate** /vuy-**brayt**/ *v.* (**-ting**) **1** move rapidly to and fro. **2** (of a sound) throb; resonate. **3** (foll. by *with*) quiver, thrill (*vibrating with passion*). **4** swing to and fro, oscillate. [Latin *vibro* shake]

**vibration** /vuy-**bray**-shuhn/ *n.* **1** act or instance of vibrating. **2** (in *pl.*) **a** mental, esp. occult, influence. **b** atmosphere or feeling in a place, regarded as communicable to people present in it. **3** *Physics* (esp. rapid) motion to and fro esp. of the parts of a fluid or an elastic solid whose equilibrium has been disturbed or of an electromagnetic wave.

**vibrato** /vuh-**brah**-toh/ *n.* rapid slight variation in musical pitch producing a tremulous effect. [Italian: related to VIBRATE]

**vibrator** /vuy-**bray**-tuh/ *n.* device that vibrates, esp. an instrument for massage etc. □ **vibratory** *adj.*

**viburnum** /vuy-**ber**-nuhm, vuh-/ *n.* a shrub, usu. with white flowers. [Latin, = wayfaring-tree]

**vicar** /**vik**-uh/ *n.* **1** (in the Anglican Church) incumbent of a parish. **2** *RC Ch.* representative or deputy of a bishop. □ **Vicar of Christ** the Pope as Christ's representative on earth. [Latin *vicarius* substitute: related to VICE³]

**vicarage** *n.* vicar's house.

**vicarious** /vuh-**kair**-ree-uhs, vuy-/ *adj.* **1** experienced indirectly or second-hand (*received vicarious pleasure as he listened to his friend's account*). **2** acting or done for another (*vicarious suffering*). □ **vicariously** *adv.* [Latin: related to VICAR]

**vice**¹ /vuys/ *n.* **1 a** grossly immoral conduct, great wickedness. **b** form of this, esp. involving prostitution, drugs, etc. **2 a** depravity, evil. **b** evil habit; a particular form of depravity (*the vice of gluttony*). **3** weakness; indulgence (*brandy is my one vice*). [Latin *vitium*]

**vice**² /vuys/ *n.* clamp with two jaws holding an object so as to leave the hands free to work on it. [*vis* screw, from Latin *vitis* vine]

**vice**³ /vuy-see/ *prep.* in the place of; succeeding. [Latin, ablative of (*vix*) *vicis* change]

**vice-** *comb. form* forming nouns meaning: **1** substitute, deputy (*vice-president*). **2** next in rank to (*vice admiral*). [related to VICE³]

**vice-chancellor** /vuys-**chahn**-suh-luh, -**chan**-/ *n.* deputy chancellor; chief executive officer of a university.

**vicegerent** /vuys-**je**-ruhnt/ — *adj.* exercising delegated power. — *n.* vicegerent person; deputy. [Latin *gero* carry on]

**viceregal** /vuys-**ree**-guhl/ *adj.* **1** of a viceroy. **2** of or relating to the governor general or a State governor.

**vice ring** *n.* group of criminals organising prostitution etc.

**viceroy** /**vuys**-roi/ *n.* sovereign's deputy ruler in a colony, province, etc. [French: related to VICE-, *roy* king]

**vice squad** *n.* police department concerned with prostitution, drugs, gambling, etc.

**vice versa** /ˌvuy-see **ver**-suh, ˌvuys/ *adj.* with the order of the terms changed; the other way round (*could go from right to left or vice versa*). [Latin, = the position being reversed]

**vichyssoise** /ˌvish-ee-**swahz**/ *n.* (usu. chilled) creamy soup of leeks and potatoes. [French, = of Vichy]

**vicinity** /vuh-**sin**-uh-tee/ *n.* (*pl.* **-ies**) **1** surrounding district. **2** (foll. by *to*) nearness. □ **in the vicinity** (often foll. by *of*) near (to). [Latin *vicinus* neighbour]

**vicious** /**vish**-uhs/ *adj.* **1** bad-tempered, spiteful (*vicious dog; vicious remark*). **2** violent (*vicious attack*). **3** (of reasoning etc.) faulty, unsound. □ **viciously** *adv.* **viciousness** *n.* [Latin: related to VICE¹]

**vicious circle** *n.* self-perpetuating, harmful sequence of cause and effect.

**vicissitude** /vuh-**sis**-uh-tyood, vuy-/ *n. literary* change of circumstances, esp. a variation of fortune. [Latin: related to VICE³]

**victim** /**vik**-tuhm/ *n.* **1** person or thing injured or destroyed (*road victim; victim of greed*). **2** prey; dupe (*fell victim to his charm*). **3** creature sacrificed to a deity or in a religious rite. [Latin]

**victimise** *v.* (also **-ize**) (**-sing** or **-zing**) **1** single out for punishment or discrimination. **2** make (a person etc.) a victim. □ **victimisation** /-zay-shuhn/ *n.*

**victor** /**vik**-tuh/ *n.* winner in a battle or contest. [Latin *vinco vict-* conquer]

**Victoria Cross** /vik-**taw**-ree-uh/ *n.* highest British decoration for conspicuous bravery in the armed services. [Queen *Victoria*]

**Victorian**¹ — *n.* native or resident of the State of Victoria. — *adj.* of or relating to the State of Victoria or to its inhabitants. [British queen *Victoria* (d. 1901)]

**Victorian²** — *adj.* **1** of the time of Queen Victoria. **2** prudish; strict. — *n.* person of this time.

**Victoriana** / vik-ˌtaw-ree-**ah**-nuh/ *n.pl.* articles, esp. collectors' items, of the Victorian period.

**Victorian Christmas bush** *n.* a prostanthera (mint bush) of Victoria and other southern and eastern regions, bearing profuse sprays of white (or mauve or pink) flowers in summer, usu. at Christmas time.

**Victoria rifle-bird** *n.* (also **Queen Victoria rifle-bird**) bird of paradise of rainforest in north-eastern Queensland (see also RIFLE-BIRD).

**victorious** / vik-**taw**-ree-uhs/ *adj.* **1** conquering, triumphant. **2** marked by victory (*this victorious day*). □ **victoriously** *adv.* [Latin: related to VICTOR]

**victory** / **vik**-tuh-ree/ *n.* (*pl.* **-ies**) defeat of an enemy or opponent.

**victual** / **vit**-uhl/ — *n.* (usu. in *pl.*) food, provisions. — *v.* (**-ll-**) **1** supply with victuals. **2** obtain stores. [Latin *victus* food]

**victualler** / **vit**-luh/ *n.* **1** person etc. who supplies victuals. **2** (in full **licensed victualler**) publican etc. licensed to sell alcohol.

**vid** *n.* = VIDEO *n.* 3. [abbreviation]

**vide** / **vee**-day, **vuy**-dee/ *v.* (in *imper.*) see, consult (a passage in a book etc.). [Latin *video* see]

**videlicet** / vee-**del**-uh-ˌset/ *adv.* = VIZ. [Latin *video* see, *licet* allowed]

**video** / **vid**-ee-oh/ — *adj.* **1** of the recording (or reproduction) of moving pictures on magnetic tape. **2** of the broadcasting of television pictures. — *n.* (*pl.* **-s**) **1** such recording or broadcasting. **2** = VIDEO RECORDER. **3** a film on videotape. — *v.* (**-oes**, **-oed**) record on videotape. [Latin, = I see]

**video cassette** *n.* cassette of videotape.

**video clip** *n.* short film usu. of a pop star or group performing a song.

**videodisc** *n.* disc for recording moving pictures and sound.

**video game** *n.* computer game played on a television screen.

**video nasty** *n. colloq.* video film depicting scenes of explicit and gratuitous violence, cruelty, etc.

**video recorder** *n.* (also **video cassette recorder**) apparatus for recording and playing videotapes.

**videotape** — *n.* magnetic tape for recording moving pictures and sound. — *v.* (**-ping**) record on this.

**videotape recorder** *n.* = VIDEO RECORDER.

**videotext** / **vid**-ee-oh-ˌtekst/ *n.* (also **videotex**) system that links a television receiver etc. to an electronic news and information service.

**vie** / vuy/ *v.* (**vies**; **vied**; **vying**) (often foll. by *with*) compete; strive for superiority. [probably French: related to ENVY]

**Vietnamese** / ˌvee-et-nuh-**meez**, ˌvyet-nuh-/ — *adj.* of Vietnam. — *n.* (*pl.* same) native or language of Vietnam.

**view** / vyoo/ — *n.* **1** range of vision; extent of visibility (*came into view; in full view of the crowd*). **2 a** what is seen; prospect, scene, etc. (*fine view of the town; a room with a view*). **b** picture etc. representing this. **3 a** opinion. **b** manner of considering a thing (*took a long-term view*). **4** inspection by the eye or mind; visual or mental survey. **5** opportunity for visual inspection; a viewing (*private view of the exhibition*). **6** expectation; prospect (*there's little view of an immediate decrease in unemployment*). — *v.* **1 a** look at; inspect with the idea of purchasing (*we are to view the house at 3*). **b** survey visually or mentally (*different ways of viewing the subject*). **2** form a mental impression or opinion of; consider (*does not view the matter in the same light*). **3** watch television. □ **have in view 1** have as one's object. **2** bear (a circumstance) in mind. **in view of** considering. **on view** being shown or exhibited. **with a view to** with the hope or intention of. [Latin *video* see]

**viewer** *n.* **1** person who views, esp. television. **2** device for looking at film transparencies etc.

**viewfinder** *n.* device on a camera showing the borders of the proposed photograph.

**viewpoint** *n.* point of view; standpoint.

**vigil** / **vij**-uhl/ *n.* **1** keeping awake during the night etc., esp. to keep watch at a sickbed etc. or pray. **2** eve of a festival or holy day (*the vigil of Christmas; vigil of the Assumption*). [Latin *vigilia*]

**vigilance** *n.* watchfulness, caution. □ **vigilant** *adj.* [Latin: related to VIGIL]

**vigilante** / ˌvij-uh-**lan**-tee/ *n.* member of a self-appointed group maintaining order etc. [Spanish, = vigilant]

**vigneron** / **vee**-nyuh-ˌron, **vin**-yuh-ron/ *n.* grower of vines for wine. [from French *vigne* vine]

**vignette** / vee-**nyet**/ *n.* **1** short description, character sketch. **2** illustration, esp.

on the title-page of a book, not in a definite border. **3** photograph or portrait showing only the head and shoulders, with the background gradually shaded off. [French, diminutive: related to VINE]

**vigoro** /**vig**-uh-roh/ *n.* team game combining elements of baseball and cricket. [probably from VIGOUR]

**vigour** /**vig**-uh/ *n.* (also **vigor**) **1** physical or mental strength or energy. **2** healthy growth. **3** forcefulness; animation. □ **vigorous** *adj.* **vigorously** *adv.* [French from Latin *vigeo* be lively]

**Viking** /**vuy**-king/ *n.* Scandinavian pirate and raider of the 8th–11th c. [Old Norse]

**vile** *adj.* **1** disgusting (*used some vile words*). **2** depraved (*performed some vile acts*). **3** *colloq.* abominable (*vile weather*). □ **vilely** *adv.* **vileness** *n.* [Latin *vilis* cheap, base]

**vilify** /**vil**-uh-,fuy/ *v.* (**-ies**, **-ied**) defame; malign. □ **vilification** /-fuh-**kay**-shuhn/ *n.* [Latin: related to VILE]

**villa** /**vil**-uh/ *n.* **1** (in ancient Rome etc.) large country house with an estate. **2** (esp. in Mediterranean countries) country house; mansion. **3** (in full (**villa unit**) = HOME UNIT. [Italian and Latin]

**village** /**vil**-ij/ *n.* **1** small country settlement. **2** shopping centre in a suburb (*Corio village*). □ **villager** *n.* [Latin: related to VILLA]

**villain** /**vil**-uhn/ *n.* **1** wicked person. **2** chief evil character in a play, story, etc. **3** *colloq.* rascal. [Latin: related to VILLA]

**villainous** *adj.* wicked.

**villainy** *n.* (*pl.* **-ies**) wicked behaviour or act. [French: related to VILLAIN]

**villein** /**vil**-uhn/ *n. hist.* feudal tenant entirely subject to a lord or attached to a manor. □ **villeinage** *n.* [var. of VILLAIN]

**vim** *n. colloq.* vigour. [perhaps from Latin, accusative of *vis* energy]

**vinaigrette** /,vin-uh-**gret**/ *n.* **1** salad dressing of oil, wine vinegar, and seasoning. **2** small bottle for smelling-salts. [French, diminutive: related to VINEGAR]

**vindaloo** /vin-duh-**loo**/ *n.* (also *attrib.*) highly spiced hot Indian curry made with meat, fish, or poultry (originating in the Portuguese cuisine of Goa in India). [Portuguese *vin d'alho* wine and garlic sauce]

**vindicate** /**vin**-duh-,kayt/ *v.* (**-ting**) **1** clear of blame or suspicion. **2** establish the existence, merits, or justice of (something disputed etc.). **3** justify by evidence or argument. □ **vindication** /-**kay**-shuhn/ *n.* **vindicator** *n.* **vindicatory** *adj.* [Latin *vindico* claim]

**vindictive** /vin-**dik**-tiv/ *adj.* **1** tending to seek revenge. **2** spiteful (*a vindictive remark*). □ **vindictively** *adv.* **vindictiveness** *n.* [Latin *vindicta* vengeance: related to VINDICATE]

**vine** *n.* **1** climbing or trailing plant with a woody stem, esp. bearing grapes. **2** stem of this. [Latin *vinea* vineyard]

**vinegar** /**vin**-uh-guh/ *n.* sour liquid (got from malt, wine, cider, etc., by fermentation) used as a condiment or for pickling. □ **vinegary** *adj.* [French, = sour wine: related to EAGER]

**vine scrub** *n.* seasonally dry tropical or sub-tropical rainforest in Australia.

**vineyard** /**vin**-yahd, -yuhd/ *n.* plantation of grapevines, esp. for wine-making.

**vino** /**vee**-noh/ *n. colloq.* wine, esp. of an inferior kind. [Italian, = wine]

**vinous** /**vuy**-nuhs/ *adj.* **1** of, like, or due to wine. **2** addicted to wine. [Latin *vinum* wine]

**vintage** /**vin**-tij/ *— n.* **1 a** season's produce of grapes. **b** wine from this. **2 a** gathering of grapes for wine-making. **b** season of this. **3** wine of high quality from a particular year and district. **4 a** year etc. when a thing was made etc. **b** thing made etc. in a particular year etc. (*searched the op shops for clothes of the 60s vintage*). *— adj.* **1** of high or peak quality, esp. from the past or characteristic of the best period of a person's work (*a CD of vintage Joan Sutherland*). **2** of a past season. [Latin *vinum* wine]

**vintage car** *n.* car made 1917–1930.

**vintner** *n.* wine-merchant. [Anglo-Latin from French, ultimately from Latin *vinetum* vineyard, from *vinum* wine]

**vinyl** /**vuy**-nuhl/ *n.* plastic made by polymerisation, esp. polyvinyl chloride. [Latin *vinum* wine]

**viol** /**vuy**-ohl/ *n.* medieval stringed instrument of various sizes, like a violin but held vertically. [French from Provençal]

**viola**[1] /vee-**oh**-luh/ *n.* **1** instrument larger than the violin and of lower pitch. **2** a viola-player. [Italian and Spanish: related to VIOL]

**viola**[2] /vuy-**oh**-luh/ *n.* any plant of the genus including the pansy and violet, esp. a cultivated hybrid. [Latin, = violet]

**viola da gamba** /vee-,oh-luh duh **gam**-buh/ *n.* viol held between the player's legs. [Italian, = viola for the legs]

**violate** /**vuy**-uh-,layt/ *v.* (**-ting**) **1** disregard; break (an oath, treaty, law, etc.). **2** treat (a sanctuary etc.) profanely; disrespect. **3** disturb (a person's privacy etc.). **4** assault sexually; rape. □ **violable** *adj.* **violation** /-**lay**-shuhn/ *n.* **violator** *n.* [Latin *violo*]

**violence** /**vuy**-uh-luhns/ n. **1** quality of being violent. **2** violent conduct or treatment. **3** unlawful use of force. □ **do violence to** act contrary to; outrage. [Latin: related to VIOLENT]

**violent** /**vuy**-uh-luhnt/ adj. **1** involving or using great physical force (*violent person*; *violent storm*). **2 a** intense, vehement (*violent pain*; *violent dislike*). **b** lurid (*violent colours*). **3** (of death) resulting from violence or poison. □ **violently** adv. [French from Latin]

**violet** /**vuy**-uh-luht/ — n. **1** plant with usu. purple, blue, or white, sweet-scented flowers. **2** bluish-purple colour at the end of the spectrum opposite red. — adj. of this colour. [French diminutive of *viole* VIOLA²]

**violin** /ˌvuy-oh-**lin**/ n. **1** high-pitched stringed instrument played with a bow. **2** a violin-player (*spoke to the violins about their playing*). □ **violinist** n. [Italian diminutive of VIOLA¹]

**violist** /**vuy**-uh-luhst, vee-**oh**-luhst/ n. viol- or viola-player.

**violoncello** /ˌvuy-uh-luhn-**chel**-oh/ n. (pl. **-s**) formal = CELLO. [Italian, diminutive of *violone* bass viol]

**VIP** abbr. very important person.

**viper** /**vuy**-puh/ n. **1** small venomous snake of Europe etc.. **2** malignant or treacherous person. [Latin]

**virago** /vuh-**rah**-goh/ n. (pl. **-s**) fierce or abusive woman. [Latin, = female warrior]

**viral** /**vuy**-ruhl/ adj. of or caused by a virus.

**virgin** /**ver**-juhn/ — n. **1** person who has never had sexual intercourse. **2** (**the Virgin**) Christ's mother Mary. **3** (**the Virgin**) sign or constellation Virgo. — adj. **1** not yet used, processed, explored, etc. (*virgin soil*; *virgin wool*; *virgin bush*). **2** (of olive oil etc.) obtained from the first pressing of olives etc. **3 a** virginal (*virgin modesty*). **b** undefiled, spotless, pure (*virgin snow*). [Latin *virgo -gin-*]

**virginal** — adj. of or befitting a virgin. — n. (also **virginals** or **pair of virginals**) Mus. early form of spinet in a box, used in the 16th and 17th centuries. [Latin: related to VIRGIN; name of the instrument perhaps from its use by young women]

**virgin birth** n. **1** (usu. preceded by *the*) doctrine of Christ's birth from a virgin mother (cf. IMMACULATE CONCEPTION). **2** parthenogenesis.

**virginity** /vuh-**jin**-uh-tee/ n. state of being a virgin.

**Virgo** /**ver**-goh/ n. (pl. **-s**) **1** constellation and sixth sign of the zodiac (the Virgin).

**2** person born when the sun is in this sign. [Latin: related to VIRGIN]

**virile** /**vi**-ruyl/ adj. **1 a** (of a man) vigorous or strong. **b** marked by strength, force, energy, etc. (*virile poetry*). **2** sexually potent. **3** of a man as distinct from a woman or child. □ **virility** /vuh-**ril**-uh-tee/ n. [Latin *vir* man]

**virology** /vuy-**rol**-uh-jee/ n. the study of viruses. □ **virologist** n.

**virtual** /**ver**-choo-uhl/ adj. being so in practice though not strictly or in name (*the virtual manager*; *a virtual promise*). [medieval Latin: related to VIRTUE]

**virtually** adv. in effect, nearly, almost.

**virtual reality** n. simulation of the real world by a computer.

**virtue** /**ver**-choo/ n. **1** moral excellence; goodness. **2** particular form of this (*patience is a virtue*). **3** (esp. female) chastity. **4** good quality (*has the virtue of speed*). **5** efficacy; inherent power (*no virtue in such drugs*). □ **by** (or **in**) **virtue of** on account of, because of. [Latin: related to VIRILE]

**virtuoso** /ˌver-choo-**oh**-soh, -zoh/ n. (pl. **-si** /-see/ or **-s**) (often attrib.) highly skilled artist, esp. a musician (*a virtuoso on the organ*; *a virtuoso performance*). □ **virtuosic** /-os-ik/ adj. **virtuosity** /-os-uh-tee/ n. [Italian: related to VIRTUOUS]

**virtuous** /**ver**-choo-uhs/ adj. **1** morally good. **2** archaic chaste. □ **virtuously** adv. [Latin: related to VIRTUE]

**virulent** /**vi**-ruh-luhnt/ adj. **1** strongly poisonous. **2** (of a disease) violent or malignant. **3** bitterly hostile (*virulent abuse*). □ **virulence** n. **virulently** adv. [Latin: related to VIRUS]

**virus** /**vuy**-ruhs/ n. **1** microscopic organism, multiplying in living cells, and often causing diseases. **2** such a disease. **3** = COMPUTER VIRUS. [Latin, = poison]

**visa** /**vee**-zuh/ n. endorsement on a passport etc., esp. allowing entrance to or exit from a country. [Latin, = seen]

**visage** /**viz**-ij/ n. literary face. [Latin *visus* sight]

**vis-à-vis** /ˌvee-zah-**vee**/ (also **vis-a-vis**) — prep. in relation to (*vis-à-vis the proposed extension*). — adv. facing one another; opposite. — n. person occupying a corresponding position in another group etc. (*my vis-à-vis in the Indonesian Embassy*). [French, = face to face: related to VISAGE]

**viscera** /**vis**-uh-ruh/ n.pl. interior organs of the body in the great cavities (e.g. brain, heart, liver), esp. in the abdomen (e.g. the intestines). [Latin]

**visceral** adj. **1** of the viscera. **2** of inward feelings rather than reason.

**viscid** /**vis**-uhd/ *adj.* glutinous, sticky. [Latin: related to VISCOUS]

**viscose** /**vis**-kohz, -kohs/ *n.* **1** cellulose in a highly viscous state, used for making rayon etc. **2** fabric made from this. [Latin: related to VISCOUS]

**viscosity** /vis-**kos**-uh-tee/ *n.* (*pl.* **-ies**) **1** quality or degree of being viscous. **2** *Physics* **a** (of a fluid) internal friction, the resistance to flow. **b** quantity expressing this. [French or medieval Latin: related to VISCOUS]

**viscount** /**vuy**-kownt/ *n.* nobleman ranking between an earl or count and a baron. □ **viscountcy** *n.* (*pl.* **-ies**). [Anglo-French: related to VICE-, COUNT²]

**viscountess** *n.* **1** viscount's wife or widow. **2** woman holding the rank of viscount.

**viscous** /**vis**-kuhs/ *adj.* **1** glutinous, sticky. **2** semifluid. **3** *Physics* having a high viscosity; not flowing freely. [Latin *viscum* birdlime]

**visibility** /viz-uh-**bil**-uh-tee/ *n.* **1** state of being visible. **2** range or possibility of vision as determined by the light and weather (*visibility was down to 50 metres*).

**visible** /**viz**-uh-buhl/ *adj.* **1** able to be seen by the eye. **2** able to be perceived or ascertained; apparent; open (*has no visible means of support; spoke with visible impatience*). **3** (of exports etc.) consisting of actual goods. □ **visibly** *adv.* [Latin: related to VISION]

**vision** /**vizh**-uhn/ *n.* **1** act or faculty of seeing, sight. **2 a** thing or person seen in a dream or trance. **b** supernatural or prophetic apparition (*vision of the Virgin Mary at Fatima*). **3** thing or idea perceived vividly in the imagination (*romantic visions of youth; had visions of a tropical paradise*). **4** imaginative insight (*his work shows vision and flair*). **5** statesmanlike foresight; imaginative planning for the future (*a political party devoid of vision*). **6** person or thing (e.g. a scene etc.) of extraordinary beauty. **7** television or cinema picture, esp. of specified quality (*poor vision*). [Latin *video vis-* see]

**visionary** — *adj.* **1** given to seeing visions or to indulging in fanciful theories. **2** having vision or foresight (*a visionary plan for urban restructuring*). **3** not real, imaginary (*these threats to Australia are merely visionary*). **4** not practicable (*wildly visionary schemes*). — *n.* (*pl.* **-ies**) visionary person.

**visit** /**viz**-uht/ — *v.* (**-t-**) **1** (also *absol.*) go or come to see or inspect (a person, place, etc.). **2** stay temporarily with (a person) or at (a place). **3** (of a disease, calamity, etc.) attack (*visited by floods and then by disease*). **4** *archaic* **a** (foll. by *with*) punish (a person). **b** (often foll. by *upon*) inflict punishment for (a sin) (*the sins of the fathers need not be visited upon the children*). — *n.* **1 a** act of visiting. **b** temporary stay, esp. as a guest. **2** (foll. by *to*) occasion of going to a doctor etc. **3** formal or official call. [Latin: related to VISION]

**visitant** /**viz**-uh-tuhnt/ *n.* **1** visitor, esp. a ghost etc. **2** migratory bird resting temporarily in an area.

**visitation** /viz-uh-**tay**-shuhn/ *n.* **1** official visit of inspection. **2** trouble or difficulty etc. seen as divine punishment. **3** (**Visitation**) **a** visit of the Virgin Mary to Elizabeth. **b** festival of this.

**visitor** *n.* **1** person who visits. **2** migrant bird staying for part of the year (*spring visitor*).

**visor** /**vuy**-zuh/ *n.* (also **vizor**) **1** movable part of a helmet covering the face. **2** shield for the eyes, esp. one at the top of a vehicle windscreen. [Anglo-French *viser*: related to VISAGE]

**vista** /**vis**-tuh/ *n.* **1** long narrow view as between rows of trees. **2** mental view of a long series of remembered or anticipated events (*opened up new vistas to his ambition*). [Italian]

**visual** /**vizh**-yoo-uhl/ — *adj.* of, concerned with, or used in, seeing. — *n.* (usu. in *pl.*) visual image or display; picture. □ **visually** *adv.* [Latin *visus* sight]

**visual aid** *n.* film etc. as a teaching aid.

**visual display unit** *n.* *Computing* device displaying data on a screen.

**visualise** *v.* (also **-ize**) (**-sing** or **-zing**) make visible esp. to one's mind (a thing not visible to the eye) (*visualised their reactions when he turned up at the family conference*). □ **visualisation** *n.*

**vital** /**vuy**-tuhl/ — *adj.* **1** of or essential to organic life (*vital functions*). **2** essential, indispensable (*of vital importance*). **3** full of life or activity. **4** fatal to life or to success etc. (*vital error*). — *n.* (in *pl.*) the body's vital organs, e.g. the heart and brain. □ **vitally** *adv.* [Latin *vita* life]

**vitalise** /**vuy**-tuh-luyz/ *v.* (also **-ize**) (**-sing** or **-zing**) **1** endow with life. **2** make lively or vigorous. □ **vitalisation** /-zay-shuhn/ *n.*

**vitality** /vuy-**tal**-uh-tee/ *n.* **1** liveliness, animation. **2** ability to survive or endure. [Latin: related to VITAL]

**vitamin** /**vit**-uh-min, **vuy**-tuh-/ *n.* any of various substances present in many foods and essential to health and growth (*vitamin A, B, C,* etc.). [Latin *vita* life, AMINE]

**vitiate** /vish-ee-,ayt/ v. (**-ting**) **1** impair the quality or efficiency of; debase. **2** make invalid or ineffectual. □ **vitiation** /-ay-shuhn/ n. [Latin: related to VICE¹]

**viticulture** /vit-ee-,kul-chuh/ n. cultivation of grapes. [Latin vitis vine]

**vitreous** /vit-ree-uhs/ adj. **1** of, or of the nature of, glass. **2** like glass in hardness, brittleness, transparency, etc. (vitreous enamel). [Latin vitrum glass]

**vitreous humour** n. transparent jelly-like tissue in the eye between the lens and the retina.

**vitrify** /vit-ruh-,fuy/ v. (**-ies**, **-ied**) change into glass or a glasslike substance, esp. by heat. □ **vitrifaction** /-fak-shuhn/ n. **vitrification** /-fuh-kay-shuhn/ n. [French or medieval Latin: related to VITREOUS]

**vitriol** /vit-ree-ol/ n. **1** sulphuric acid or a sulphate. **2** caustic or hostile speech, criticism, or feeling. [Latin vitrum]

**vitriolic** /,vit-ree-ol-ik/ adj. (of speech or criticism) caustic, hostile.

**vituperate** /vuh-tyoo-puh-,rayt, vuy-/ v. (**-ting**) criticise abusively. □ **vituperation** /-ray-shuhn/ n. **vituperative** /-ruh-tiv/ adj. [Latin]

**viva¹** /vuy-vuh/ colloq. — n. (pl. **-s**) = VIVA VOCE. — v. (**vivas**, **vivaed**, **vivaing**) = VIVA-VOCE. [abbreviation]

**viva²** /vee-vuh/ — int. long live. — n. cry of this as a salute etc. [Italian, = let live]

**vivace** /vuh-vah-chay/ adv. Mus. in a lively manner. [Latin: related to VIVA-CIOUS]

**vivacious** /vuh-vay-shuhs/ adj. lively, animated. □ **vivacity** /vuh-vas-uh-tee/ n. [Latin vivax from vivo live]

**vivarium** /vuy-vair-ree-uhm, vuh-/ n. (pl. **-ria** or **-s**) **1** glass bowl etc. for keeping animals for scientific study. **2** enclosure for keeping animals in (nearly) their natural state. [Latin]

**viva voce** /,vuy-vuh voh-chee/ — adj. oral. — adv. orally. — n. oral examination esp. for an academic qualification. — v. (**viva-voce**) (**-vocees**, **-voceed**, **-voceing**) examine orally. [medieval Latin, = with the living voice]

**vivid** /viv-uhd/ adj. **1** (of light or colour) strong, intense. **2** (of a memory, description, the imagination, etc.) clear, lively, graphic. **3** (of a person) lively, vigorous. □ **vividly** adv. **vividness** n. [Latin]

**vivify** /viv-uh-,fuy/ v. (**-ies**, **-ied**) enliven, animate, give life to. [French from Latin]

**viviparous** /vuh-vip-uh-ruhs, vuy-/ adj. Zool. bringing forth young alive, not hatching them by means of eggs (cf. OVIPAROUS). [Latin vivus alive, pario produce]

**vivisect** /viv-uh-,sekt/ v. perform vivisection on.

**vivisection** /,viv-uh-sek-shuhn/ n. surgical experimentation on living animals for scientific research. □ **vivisectional** adj.

**vivisectionist** n. & adj. **vivisector** /viv-uh-,sek-tuh/ n. [Latin vivus living, DIS-SECTION]

**vixen** /vik-suhn/ n. **1** female fox. **2** spiteful or quarrelsome woman. [Old English: related to FOX]

**viz.** /viz/ adv. namely; that is to say; in other words. [abbreviation of VIDELICET, z = medieval Latin symbol for abbreviation of -et]

**vizier** /vuh-zeer/ n. hist. high official in some Muslim countries. [ultimately from Arabic]

**vizor** var. of VISOR.

**V-neck** n. (often attrib.) V-shaped neckline on a pullover etc.

**vocab** /voh-kab/ n. colloq. vocabulary [abbreviation]

**vocabulary** /vuh-kab-yuh-luh-ree/ n. (pl. **-ies**) **1 a** words used by a particular language. **b** words used by a particular book, branch of science, author, etc. (scientific vocabulary; the vocabulary of Shakespeare). **2** list of these, in alphabetical order with definitions or translations. **3** individual's stock of words (limited vocabulary). [medieval Latin]

**vocal** /voh-kuhl/ — adj. **1** of or uttered by the voice. **2** expressing one's feelings freely in speech (very vocal about his rights). — n. **1** (in sing. or pl.) (esp. in pop, rock, etc.) sung part or piece of music. **2** (in pl.) (esp. in pop, rock, etc.) the words of such a sung part. □ **vocally** adv. [Latin: related to VOICE]

**vocal cords** n. folds of the lining membrane of the larynx with edges vibrating in the air-stream to produce the voice.

**vocalise** — v. /voh-kuh-luyz/ (also **-ize**) (**-sing** or **-zing**) **1** form (a sound) or utter (a word) with the voice. **2** articulate, express (vocalised his indignation). **3** Mus. sing with several notes to one vowel. — n. /voh-kuh-leez/ Mus. a sung passage consisting of music without words. □ **vocalisation** /voh-kuh-luy-zay-shuhn/ n.

**vocalist** n. singer.

**vocation** /voh-kay-shuhn/ n. **1 a** strong feeling of suitability for a particular career. **b** this regarded as a divine call to a career in the Church. **2** employment, trade, profession. □ **vocational** adj. [Latin voco call]

**vocative** /vok-uh-tiv/ Gram. — n. case of a noun etc. used in addressing a person or thing. — adj. of or in this case.

**vociferate** /vuh-sif-uh-,rayt/ v. (**-ting**) **1** utter noisily. **2** shout, bawl. □ **vociferation** /-ray-shuhn/ n. **vociferator** n. [Latin: related to VOICE, *fero* bear]

**vociferous** /vuh-sif-uh-ruhs/ adj. **1** noisy, clamorous. **2** insistently and forcibly expressing one's views. □ **vociferously** adv.

**vodka** /vod-kuh/ n. alcoholic spirit distilled esp. in Russia from rye etc. [Russian]

**vogue** /vohg/ n. **1** (prec. by *the*) prevailing fashion. **2** (often *attrib.*) popular use or currency (*had a great vogue*). □ **in vogue** in fashion. □ **voguish** adj. [French from Italian]

**voice** — n. **1 a** sound formed in the larynx and uttered by the mouth, esp. by a person speaking, singing, etc. **b** power of this (*lost her voice*). **2 a** use of the voice; spoken or written expression (esp. *give voice*). **b** opinion so expressed (*most voices were in favour of the idea*). **c** right to express an opinion (*I have no voice in this matter*). **d** medium for expression (*Shakespeare is the voice of emotions common to all human beings*). **3** sound or sounds produced by something inanimate (*the voice of thunder*; *the voice of conscience*). **4** *Gram.* set of verbal forms showing whether a verb is active or passive. — v. (**-cing**) **1** express (*voiced his concern*). **2** (esp. as **voiced** adj.) utter with vibration of the vocal cords (e.g. *b*, *d*). □ **in good voice** singing or speaking well or easily. **with one voice** unanimously. [Latin *vox voc-*]

**voice box** n. larynx.

**voiceless** adj. **1** dumb, speechless. **2** uttered without vibration of the vocal cords (e.g. *f*, *p*).

**voice-over** n. commentary in a film etc. by an unseen narrator.

**void** — adj. **1 a** empty, vacant (*the void deeps of space*; *the position has been void since the sacking of the last incumbent*). **b** (foll. by *of*) lacking; free from (a bad quality or a good) (*a style void of affectation*; *he is void of pity and remorse*). **2** esp. *Law* (of a contract etc.) invalid, not legally binding (*null and void*). — n. empty space, vacuum (*vanished into the void*; *cannot fill the void made by her death*). — v. **1** render void. **2** excrete; empty (the bowels etc.). [French]

**voile** /voil/ n. fine semi-transparent fabric. [French, = VEIL]

**vol.** *abbr.* volume.

**volatile** /vol-uh-,tuyl/ adj. **1** changeable in mood; fickle (*his affections are volatile, to say the least*). **2** (of trading conditions etc.) unstable. **3** (of a political situation etc.) **a** likely to erupt in violence. **b** unstable, apt to change (*the electorate seems remarkably volatile this time round*). **4** *Chem.* evaporating rapidly. □ **volatility** /-til-uh-tee/ n. [Latin *volo* fly]

**vol-au-vent** /vol-oh-,von/ n. small puff pastry case with a savoury filling. [French, literally 'flight in the wind']

**volcanic** /vol-kan-ik/ adj. of, like, or from a volcano. □ **volcanically** adv.

**volcano** /vol-kay-noh/ n. (*pl.* **-es**) **1** mountain or hill from which lava, steam, etc., escape through openings in the earth's crust. **2 a** state of things likely to cause a violent outburst (*we're sitting on a political volcano*). **b** violent, esp. suppressed, feeling. [Latin *Volcanus* Vulcan, Roman god of fire]

**volition** /vuh-lish-uhn/ n. act or power of willing. □ **of one's own volition** voluntarily. □ **volitional** adj. [Latin *volo* wish]

**volley** /vol-ee/ — n. (*pl.* **-s**) **1 a** simultaneous firing of a number of weapons. **b** bullets etc. so fired. **2** (usu. foll. by *of*) torrent (of abuse etc.). **3** playing of a ball in tennis, football, etc., before it touches the ground. — v. (**-eys, -eyed**) return or send by or in a volley. [French *volée* from Latin *volo* fly]

**volleyball** n. game for two teams hitting a large ball by hand over a high net.

**volt** n. SI unit of electromotive force, the difference of potential that would carry one ampere of current against one ohm resistance. [*Volta*, name of a physicist]

**voltage** n. electromotive force expressed in volts.

**volte-face** /volt-fahs/ n. sudden reversal of one's attitude or opinion (*the government's remarkable volte-face on the issue of...*). [French from Italian]

**voltmeter** n. instrument measuring electric potential in volts.

**voluble** /vol-yuh-buhl/ adj. speaking or spoken fluently or at length. □ **volubility** /-bil-uh-tee/ n. **volubly** adv. [Latin *volvo* roll]

**volume** /vol-yoom/ n. **1** single book forming part or all of a work. **2 a** solid content, bulk. **b** space occupied by a gas or liquid. **c** (foll. by *of*) amount or quantity (*large volume of business*). **3** strength of sound, loudness (*turn down the volume!*). **4** (foll. by *of*) **a** moving mass of water etc. **b** (usu. in *pl.*) mass of smoke etc. □ **speak volumes** be highly significant (*a look that speaks volumes*; *this one action by the company speaks volumes about its real attitude to trade unions*). [Latin *volumen*: related to VOLUBLE, ancient books being in roll form]

**volumetric** /,vol-yuh-**met**-rik/ *adj.* of measurement by volume. □ **volumetrically** *adv.* [from VOLUME, METRIC]

**voluminous** /vuh-**loo**-muh-nuhs/ *adj.* **1** large in volume. **2** (of drapery etc.) loose and ample. **3** written, or writing, at great length; producing a large output (of books etc.) (*a voluminous novel*; *a voluminous writer of cheap romances*; *a voluminous correspondent*). [Latin: related to VOLUME]

**voluntary** /**vol**-uhn-tree, -tuh-ree/ — *adj.* **1** acting, done, or given willingly; not compulsory (*asked for voluntary contributions*; *a voluntary psychiatric patient*). **2** unpaid (*voluntary work*). **3** brought about by voluntary action. **4** (of a movement, muscle, or limb) controlled by the will. — *n.* (*pl.* **-ies**) organ solo played before or after a church service. □ **voluntarily** *adv.* **voluntariness** *n.* [Latin *voluntas* will]

**volunteer** /,vol-uhn-**teer**/ — *n.* person who voluntarily undertakes a task or enters military etc. service. — *v.* **1** (often foll. by *to* + infin.) undertake or offer (one's services, a remark, etc.) voluntarily. **2** (often foll. by *for*) be a volunteer. [French: related to VOLUNTARY]

**voluptuary** /vuh-**lup**-choo-uh-ree, -tyoo-/ *n.* (*pl.* **-ies**) person who seeks luxury and sensual pleasure. [Latin: related to VOLUPTUOUS]

**voluptuous** /vuh-**lup**-choo-uhs, -tyoo-/ *adj.* **1** of, tending to, occupied with, or derived from, sensuous or sensual or sexual pleasure (*a voluptuous feast*; *voluptuous satin sheets*; *a long, voluptuous embrace*). **2** (of a woman) having a full and curvaceous figure (*voluptuous Rubens nudes*). □ **voluptuously** *adv.* [Latin *voluptas* pleasure]

**volute** /vuh-**lyoot**/ — *n.* **1** spiral stonework scroll as an ornament of esp. Ionic capitals. **2** convolution, twist, or turn of a spiral shell. — *adj.* esp. *Bot.* rolled up. □ **voluted** *adj.* **volution** *n.* [Latin *volvo volut-* roll]

**vomer** /**voh**-muh/ *n.* the small thin bone separating the nostrils in man and most vertebrates. [Latin = ploughshare]

**vomit** /**vom**-uht/ — *v.* (**-t-**) **1** eject (contents of the stomach) through the mouth; be sick. **2** (of a volcano, chimney, etc.) eject violently, belch forth. — *n.* matter vomited from the stomach. [Latin]

**voodoo** /**voo**-doo/ — *n.* religious witchcraft as practised esp. in the W. Indies. — *v.* (**-doos, -dooed**) affect by voodoo; bewitch. □ **voodooist** *n.* [Dahomey]

**-vora** /vuh-ruh/ *comb. form* forming names of groups meaning 'feeding on' (*carnivora*).

**voracious** /vuh-**ray**-shuhs/ *adj.* **1** gluttonous, ravenous. **2** very eager (*voracious reader*). □ **voraciously** *adv.* **voraciousness** *n.* **voracity** /vuh-**ras**-uh-tee/ *n.* [Latin *vorax* from *voro* devour]

**-vore** /vaw/ *comb. form* forming names of individuals meaning 'feeding on' (*a herbivore*).

**-vorous** /vuh-ruhs/ *comb. form* forming adjectives meaning 'feeding on' (*carnivorous*; *herbivorous*; *omnivorous*).

**vortex** /**vaw**-teks/ *n.* (*pl.* **-texes** or **-tices** /-tuh-,seez/ ) **1** whirlpool, whirlwind. **2** any whirling motion or mass. **3** thing viewed as destructive or devouring (*the vortex of society*). □ **vortical** *adj.* [Latin: related to VERTEX]

**votary** /**voh**-tuh-ree/ *n.* (*pl.* **-ies**; *fem.* **votaress**) (usu. foll. by *of*) **1** person dedicated to the service of God or a god or cult. **2** devotee of a person, occupation, etc. [Latin: related to VOTE]

**vote** — *n.* **1** formal expression of choice or opinion by a ballot, show of hands, etc., in an election etc. **2** (usu. prec. by *the*) right to vote, esp. in a parliamentary election. **3** opinion expressed by a vote (*vote of no confidence*). **4** votes given by or for a particular group (*the Labor vote*). **5** ticket etc. used for recording a vote. — *v.* (**-ting**) **1** (often foll. by *for, against*) give a vote. **2 a** enact or resolve by a majority of votes. **b** grant (a sum of money) by vote. **3** pronounce by general consent (*it was voted a failure*). **4** (often foll. by *that*) suggest, urge (*I vote we call it a day and go home*). □ **vote down** defeat (a proposal etc.) in a vote. **vote in** elect by voting. **vote with one's feet** *colloq.* indicate an opinion by one's presence or absence. [Latin *votum* from *voveo vot-* vow]

**voter** *n.* person voting or with the right to vote at an election.

**votive** /**voh**-tiv/ *adj.* offered or consecrated in fulfilment of a vow (*votive offering*). [Latin: related to VOTE]

**vouch** *v.* (foll. by *for*) answer for, be surety for (*will vouch for the truth of this*; *can vouch for him*). [French *vo(u)cher* summon, invoke]

**voucher** *n.* **1** document exchangeable for goods or services. **2** receipt. [from Anglo-French, or from VOUCH]

**vouchsafe** /vowch-**sayf**/ *v.* (**-fing**) *formal* **1** condescend to give or grant (*vouchsafed me no answer*). **2** (foll. by *to* + infin.) condescend (*vouchsafed to bid us good morning as she passed*).

**vow** — *n.* **1** solemn promise esp. in the form of an oath to God, a saint, etc. **2** (in *pl.*) the solemn promises to God by which a monk, nun, or priest, is bound to poverty, chastity, and obedience. **3** promise of fidelity (*marriage vows*). — *v.* **1** promise solemnly (*vowed obedience*). **2** declare solemnly (*vowed that he would do it whatever the cost*). [French *vou(er)*: related to VOTE]

**vowel** /vow-uhl/ *n.* **1** speech-sound made with vibration of the vocal cords but without audible friction. **2** letter(s) representing this, as *a, e, i, o, u, aw, ah*. [Latin: related to VOCAL]

**vox pop** *n.* (often *attrib.*) *colloq.* popular opinion as represented by informal comments from the public. [abbreviation of VOX POPULI]

***vox populi*** /,voks pop-yuh-,lee, -,luy/ *n.* public opinion, popular belief. [Latin, = the people's voice]

**voyage** /voi-ij/ — *n.* journey, esp. a long one by sea or in space. — *v.* (**-ging**) make a voyage. □ **voyager** *n.* [Latin VIATICUM]

**voyeur** /vwah-**yer**, voi-**er**/ *n.* **1** person who derives sexual pleasure from secretly observing others' sexual activity or organs. **2** (esp. covert) spectator. □ **voyeurism** *n.* **voyeuristic** /-ris-tik/ *adj.* [French *voir* see]

**vs.** *abbr.* versus.

**V-sign** /vee-suyn/ *n.* **1** sign of the letter V made with the first two fingers pointing up and the back of the hand facing outwards, as a gesture of abuse etc. **2** similar sign made with the palm of the hand facing outwards, as a symbol of victory.

**VTR** *abbr.* videotape recorder.

**vulcanise** /vul-kuh-,nuyz/ *v.* (also **-ize**) (**-sing** or **-zing**) treat (rubber etc.) with sulphur at a high temperature to strengthen it. □ **vulcanisation** /-zay-shuhn/ *n.* [*Vulcan*: related to VOLCANO]

**vulcanite** /vul-kuh-,nuyt/ *n.* hard black vulcanised rubber. [related to VULCANISE]

**vulcanology** /,vul-kuh-**nol**-uh-jee/ *n.* the study of volcanoes. □ **vulcanological** /-nuh-**loj**-i-kuhl/ *adj.* **vulcanologist** *n.*

**vulgar** /vul-guh/ *adj.* **1 a** coarse; indecent; tasteless. **b** of or characteristic of the common people. **2** in common use; prevalent (*vulgar errors*). □ **vulgarly** *adv.* [Latin *vulgus* common people]

**vulgar fraction** *n.* fraction expressed by numerator and denominator, not decimally.

**vulgarian** /vul-**gair**-ree-uhn/ *n.* vulgar (esp. rich) person.

**vulgarise** /vul-guh-,ruyz/ *v.* (also **-ize**) (**-sing** or **-zing**) **1** make vulgar. **2** spoil by popularising. □ **vulgarisation** /-zay-shuhn/ *n.*

**vulgarism** *n.* vulgar word, expression, action, or habit.

**vulgarity** /vul-ga-ruh-tee/ *n.* (*pl.* **-ies**) vulgar act, expression, or state.

**vulgar tongue** *n.* (prec. by *the*) national or vernacular language.

**Vulgate** /vul-gayt, -guht/ *n.* Latin version of the Bible prepared mainly by St. Jerome in the late fourth century; the official Roman Catholic Latin text as revised in 1592. [Latin: related to VULGAR]

**vulnerable** /vul-nuh-ruh-buhl/ *adj.* **1** easily wounded or harmed. **2** (foll. by *to*) exposed to damage, temptation, criticism, etc. □ **vulnerability** /-bil-uh-tee/ *n.* **vulnerably** *adv.* [Latin *vulnus vulner-* wound]

**vulpine** /vul-puyn/ *adj.* **1** of or like a fox. **2** crafty, cunning. [Latin *vulpes* fox]

**vulture** /vul-chuh/ *n.* **1** large carrion-eating bird of prey, reputed to gather with others in anticipation of a death. **2** rapacious person. [Anglo-French from Latin]

**vulva** /vul-vuh/ *n.* (*pl.* **-s**) external female genitals, esp. the external opening of the vagina consisting of the two pairs of labia and the cleft between these. [Latin]

**vv.** *abbr.* **1** verses. **2** volumes.

**vying** *pres. part.* of VIE.

# W

**W¹** /dub-uhl-ˌyoo/ *n.* (also **w**) (*pl.* **Ws** or **W's**) twenty-third letter of the alphabet.

**W²** *abbr.* (also **W.**) **1** watt(s). **2** West; Western.

**W³** *symb.* tungsten. [*wolframium*, Latinised name]

**WA** *abbr.* **1** Western Australia. **2** Western Australian.

**WACA** /wak-uh/ *n.* **1** Western Australian Cricket Association. **2** cricket ground of this Association in Perth (*played at the WACA*) (also *attrib.*). [abbreviation]

**wacker** var. of WHACKER.

**wacko** /wak-oh/ *colloq.* — *adj.* crazy; weird. — *n.* (*pl.* **-os** or **-oes**) weird or crazy person. [WACKY, -O]

**wacky** *adj.* (**-ier**, **-iest**) *colloq.* crazy; weird. □ **wackiness** *n.* [originally British dial., = left-handed]

**wad** /wod/ — *n.* **1** lump of soft material used esp. to keep things apart or in place or to block a hole. **2** bundle of banknotes or documents. **3** (in *sing.* or *pl.*) large quantity (esp. of money). — *v.* (**-dd-**) **1** stop up or keep in place with a wad. **2** line, stuff, or protect with wadding. [origin uncertain]

**wadding** *n.* soft fibrous material used in quilt-making etc., or to pack fragile articles.

**waddle** /wod-uhl/ — *v.* (**-ling**) walk with short steps and a swaying motion (e.g. like a duck or goose). — *n.* waddling gait. [from WADE]

**waddy¹** /wod-ee/ — *n.* (*pl.* **-ies**) (also **waddie**) **1** Aboriginal war-club made of wood. **2** club, cudgel, stick, etc., used as a weapon by a person other than an Aborigine (*the gatecrashers smashed some chairs and using the legs as waddies waded into us*). — *v.* strike, beat, or kill (an animal or person) with a waddy; bludgeon (*surrounded the beast and waddied it to death*). [Dharuk *wadi* tree, stick, club]

**waddy²** /wod-ee/ *n.* an Aboriginal male. [Western Desert language *wadi* initiated man]

**waddy tree** *n.* = WADDYWOOD 1.

**waddywood** /wod-ee-ˌwuud/ *n.* **1** (also **waddy tree**) any of several Australian trees yielding a hard wood used by Aborigines for making waddies, esp. the rare wattle *Acacia peuce* of southwestern Queensland and the NT. **2** =

WHALEBONE TREE. [probably Midhaga *wadi*]

**wade** — *v.* (**-ding**) **1** walk through water, mud, etc., esp. with difficulty. **2** (foll. by *through*) go through (a tedious task, book, etc.). **3** (foll. by *into*) *colloq.* attack (a person or task) vigorously. — *n.* spell of wading. □ **wade in** *colloq.* make a vigorous attack or intervention. [Old English]

**wader** *n.* **1** long-legged water-bird that wades. **2** (in *pl.*) high waterproof boots.

**wadgula** /wah-dyoo-lah/ *n.* (in Aboriginal English) a white person. [alteration of *white fellow*]

**wadi** /wod-ee/ *n.* (*pl.* **-s**) rocky watercourse in N. Africa etc., dry except in the rainy season. [Arabic]

**wafer** /way-fuh/ *n.* **1** very thin light crisp sweet biscuit. **2** thin disc of unleavened bread used in the Eucharist, host. **3** disc of red paper stuck on a legal document instead of a seal. □ **wafery** *adj.* [Anglo-French *wafre* from Germanic]

**wafer-thin** *adj.* very thin.

**waffle¹** /wof-uhl/ *colloq.* — *n.* verbose but aimless or ignorant talk or writing; nonsense. — *v.* (**-ling**) indulge in waffle. □ **waffler** *n.* **waffly** *adj.* [British dial., = yelp]

**waffle²** /wof-uhl/ *n.* small crisp batter cake. [Dutch]

**waffle-iron** *n.* utensil, usu. of two shallow metal pans hinged together, for baking waffles.

**waft** /woft/ — *v.* convey or travel easily and smoothly as through air or over water (*clouds wafting gently past in the wind*). — *n.* (usu. foll. by *of*) whiff or scent (*wafts of boronia in the evening air*). [originally 'convoy (ship etc.)' from Dutch or Low German *wachter* from *wachten* to guard]

**wag¹** — *v.* (**-gg-**) **1** shake or wave to and fro (*wagged its tail*; *heads wagging in denial*). **2** play truant; be absent from (school etc.). — *n.* single wagging motion (*with a wag of his tail*). □ **tongues wag** there is talk. [Old English]

**wag²** *n.* facetious person. [Old English]

**Waga-waga** /wah-gu ˌwah-gu/ *n.* an Aboriginal language spoken in southeastern Queensland in a vast area roughly bounded by Toowoomba, Biloela, and Condamine: now extinct.

**wage** /wayj/ — n. **1** (in sing. or pl.) fixed regular payment to an employee, esp. a manual worker (cf. SALARY). **2** (in sing. or pl., with the pl. sometimes treated as sing.) requital (the wages of sin is death). — v. (**-ging**) carry on (a war etc.). [Anglo-French from Germanic]

**waged** — adj. receiving a wage; in regular paid employment. — n. (prec. by the) the employed.

**wager** n. & v. = BET. [Anglo-French: related to WAGE]

**wagga** /wog-uh/ n. (in full **wagga blanket**) improvised covering, usu. of lengths of sacking etc. sewn together, often padded with whatever scraps etc. come to hand. [abbreviation of Wagga Wagga a town in NSW]

**waggish** adj. playful, facetious. □ **waggishly** adv. **waggishness** n.

**waggle** /wag-uhl/ — v. (**-ling**) colloq. wag (waggled his behind as he addressed the ball with his club). — n. a waggling motion.

**waggly** adj. unsteady; waggling.

**wagon** /wag-uhn/ n. (also **waggon**) **1** four-wheeled vehicle for heavy loads. **2** railway vehicle, esp. an open truck. **3** colloq. station wagon. □ **on the wagon** colloq. teetotal. [Dutch: related to WAIN]

**wagoner** n. (also **waggoner**) driver of a wagon.

**wagtail** n. **1** = WILLY WAGTAIL. **2** any of several migrant birds which constantly wag their tails from side to side (yellow wagtail; white wagtail).

**wagyl** /wog-uhl/ n. **1** (in Aboriginal myth) creator of waterways in Australia; the rainbow serpent. **2** carpet snake. [Nyungar waagul]

**wahlenbergia** /wah-luhn-**ber**-jee-uh/ n. (also **bluebell**, **royal bluebell**) any of several Australian herbs of the genus of the same name, esp.: **1** W. gloriosa (also the **Austral bluebell**) bearing large, dark blue flowers held erect over the dark green foliage, the floral emblem of the ACT. **2** W. stricta of all States except the NT, bearing a profusion of light blue flowers which often carpet large areas of the landscape in blue. [G. Wahlenberg Swedish botanist (d. 1851)]

**waif** /wayf/ n. **1** homeless and helpless person, esp. an abandoned child. **2** ownerless object or animal. [Anglo-French, probably from Scandinavian]

**wail** — n. **1** prolonged plaintive high-pitched cry of pain, grief, etc. **2** sound like this. — v. **1** utter a wail. **2** lament or complain persistently or bitterly. □ **wailer** n. **wailingly** adv. [Old Norse]

**wain** n. archaic wagon. [Old English]

**wainscot** /wayn-skuht/ — n. boarding or wooden panelling on the lower part of a room-wall. — v. (**-t-**) line with wainscot. [Low German wagenschot from wagen WAGON]

**wainscoting** n. **1** wainscot. **2** material for this.

**wainwright** /wayn-ruyt/ n. person who builds and repairs wagons.

**waist** n. **1 a** part of the human body below the ribs and above the hips; narrower middle part of the normal human figure. **b** circumference of this. **2** narrow middle of a violin, wasp, etc. **3** part of a garment encircling the waist. **4** part of a ship between the forecastle and the quarter-deck. □ **waisted** adj. (also in comb.). [Old English: related to WAX²]

**waistcoat** n. close-fitting waist-length garment without sleeves or collar, buttoning down the front, and worn usu. over a shirt and under a jacket.

**waist-deep** adj. & adv. (also **waist-high**) up to the waist.

**waistline** n. outline or size of a person's body at the waist.

**wait** — v. **1 a** defer action or departure for a specified time or until some event occurs (wait a minute; wait till I come; wait for a fine day). **b** be expectant (waited to see what would happen). **c** (foll. by for) refrain from going so fast that (a person) is left behind (wait for me!). **2** await (an opportunity, one's turn, etc.). **3 a** defer (a meal etc.) until a person's arrival (waited dinner for them). **b** be postponed (this business can't wait). **4** act as a waiter or attendant. **5** (foll. by on, upon) **a** await the convenience of. **b** serve as an attendant to. — n. **1** period of waiting. **2** (usu. foll. by for) watching for an enemy (lie in wait). □ **wait and see** await the progress of events. **wait on** colloq. be patient; wait; hang on. **wait up** (often foll. by for) not go to bed until a person arrives or an event happens. **you wait!** used to imply a threat, warning, etc. [Germanic: related to WAKE¹]

**wait-a-while** n. any of several Australian plants which may impede passage with their barbed leaves or prickles, esp. the lawyer palm.

**waiter** n. man who serves at table in a hotel or restaurant etc.

**waiting game** n. the delaying of action in order to have a greater effect later.

**waiting list** n. list of people waiting for a thing not immediately available.

**waiting room** n. room for people to wait in, esp. to see a doctor etc.

**waitress** *n.* woman who serves at table in a hotel or restaurant etc.

**waive** *v.* (**-ving**) refrain from insisting on or using (a right, claim, opportunity, etc.) (*waived his right to be paid compensation*). [Anglo-French *weyver*: related to WAIF]

**waiver** *n. Law* **1** waiving of a legal right etc. **2** document recording this.

**wake¹** — *v.* (**-king;** *past* **woke** or **waked;** *past part.* **woken** or **waked**) **1** (often foll. by *up*) (cause to) cease to sleep. **2** (often foll. by *up*) (cause to) become alert or attentive (*someone needs to wake him up to the risk he's running*). **3** *archaic* (except as **waking** *adj. & n.*) be awake (*waking hours*). **4** disturb (silence or a place) with noise (*screams woke the stillness of the night*). **5** evoke (an echo). — *n.* **1** watch kept beside a corpse before burial; attendant lamentation and (less often) merrymaking. **2** gathering of mourners after a funeral. □ **be a wake-up** (often foll. by *to*) *colloq.* be alert or aware. **wake up to** (**oneself**) *colloq.* take a good look at (oneself) and be more responsible, realistic, etc. [Old English]

**wake²** *n.* **1** track left on the water's surface by a moving ship. **2** turbulent air left behind a moving aircraft etc. □ **in the wake of** following, as a result of. [Low German from Old Norse]

**wakeful** *adj.* **1** unable to sleep. **2** (of a night etc.) sleepless. **3** vigilant. □ **wakefully** *adv.* **wakefulness** *n.*

**waken** *v.* make or become awake. [Old Norse]

**wale** *n.* **1** ridge on corduroy etc. **2** *Naut.* a broad thick timber along a ship's side. [Old English]

**waler** /**way**-luh/ *n.* **1** horse bred in NSW and imported into India. **2** light, Australian-bred horse. [abbreviation of New South *Wales*]

**walk** /wawk/ — *v.* **1 a** progress by lifting and setting down each foot in turn, never having both feet off the ground at once. **b** (of a quadruped) go with the slowest gait. **2 a** travel or go on foot. **b** take exercise in this way. **3** traverse on foot at walking speed, tread the floor or surface of (*walked the streets*). **4** cause to walk with one (*walk the dog*). **5** (of a ghost) appear. — *n.* **1 a** act of walking, the ordinary human gait. **b** slowest gait of an animal. **c** person's manner of walking (*know him by his walk*). **2 a** distance which can be walked in a (usu. specified) time (*ten minutes' walk from here*). **b** excursion on foot (*went for a walk*). **3** place or track intended or suitable for walking (*nature walk*). □ **in a walk** without effort (*won in a*

*walk*). **walk all over** *colloq.* **1** defeat easily. **2** take advantage of. **walk away from 1** easily outdistance. **2** refuse to become involved with. **3** survive (an accident etc.) without serious injury. **walk away with** *colloq.* = *walk off with*. **walk into** *colloq.* **1** encounter through unwariness (*walked into the trap*). **2** get (a job) easily. **walk matilda** = *waltz matilda* (see MATILDA). **walk off 1** depart (esp. abruptly). **2** get rid of the effects of (a meal, ailment, etc.) by walking (*walked off his anger*). **walk off with** *colloq.* **1** steal. **2** win easily. **walk on air** feel elated. **walk out 1** depart suddenly or angrily. **2** stop work in protest. **walk out on** desert, abandon. **walk the streets** be a prostitute. □ **walkable** *adj.* [Old English]

**walkabout** *n.* **1** *hist.* person who travels on foot; a swagman or traveller. **2** journey on foot as undertaken by an Aborigine in order to live in the traditional manner (esp. one undertaken as a temporary withdrawal from white society). **3** informal stroll among a crowd by a visiting dignitary. □ **go walkabout** see GO.

**walkathon** /**waw**-kuh-ˌthon/ *n.* organised fund-raising walk. [WALK, (MAR)ATHON]

**walker** *n.* **1** person or animal that walks. **2 a** framework in which a baby can walk unaided. **b** = WALKING FRAME.

**walkie-talkie** /ˌwaw-kee-**taw**-kee/ *n.* two-way radio carried on the person.

**walk-in** *attrib. adj.* (of a storage area) large enough to walk into (*a walk-in clothes-cupboard*).

**walking frame** *n.* metal frame used as a support by people who have difficulty walking.

**walking stick** *n.* stick carried for support when walking.

**walking-stick palm** *n.* small palm of south-eastern Queensland and north-eastern NSW, having a slender trunk with a knob on the end (used frequently as a walking stick).

**walkman** *n.* (*pl.* **-s**) *propr.* type of personal stereo.

**walk of life** *n.* occupation, profession.

**walk-on** *n.* **1** (in full **walk-on part**) non-speaking dramatic role. **2** player of this.

**walkout** *n.* sudden angry departure, esp. as a protest or strike.

**walkover** *n.* easy victory or achievement.

**walkway** *n.* passage or path (esp. raised) for walking along.

**wall** /wawl/ — *n.* **1 a** continuous vertical structure of usu. brick, stone, or wood, esp. enclosing or dividing a space or supporting a roof. **b** the surface of a wall, esp. inside a room (*hung the picture on the wall*). **2** thing like a wall, esp.: **a** a steep side of a mountain. **b** a protection or obstacle (*a wall of steel bayonets; a wall of indifference*). **c** *Anat.* the outermost layer or enclosing membrane etc. of an organ etc. (*stomach wall*). — *v.* **1** (esp. as **walled** *adj.*) surround with a wall (*a walled garden*). **2 a** (usu. foll. by *up, off*) block (a space etc.) with a wall. **b** (foll. by *up*) enclose within a sealed space (*walled them up in the dungeon*). □ **go to the wall** be defeated or pushed aside; fail, be ruined. **up against the wall** in dire difficulty, with no resources or avenues of escape left. **up the wall** *colloq.* crazy or furious (*it's driving me up the wall*). **walls have ears** beware of eavesdroppers. □ **wall-less** *adj.* [Latin *vallum* rampart]

**wallaby** /wol-uh-bee/ *n.* (*pl.* **-ies**) **1** any of various marsupials similar to but smaller than a kangaroo (often with descriptive epithet: *nail-tailed wallaby; parma wallaby; red-necked wallaby; rock wallaby;* etc.). **2** itinerant rural worker; swagman. **3 a** (**the Wallabies**) Australian international Rugby Union team. **b** member of this team. □ **on the wallaby** = *on the wallaby track*. [Dharuk *walabi* or *waliba*]

**wallaby grass** *n.* any of many perennial Australian grasses valued as winter fodder.

**wallaby rat** *n.* (in Tasmania) the long-nosed potoroo.

**wallaby track** *n.* route followed by a person who journeys through the country in search of seasonal work. □ **on the wallaby track** (or **on the wallaby**) **1** vagrant; unemployed. **2** on the move, not settling down in one place.

**wallaroo** /wol-uh-**roo**/ *n.* (also **euro, hill kangaroo, rock kangaroo**) any of several large, stocky kangaroos of rocky or hilly country, esp. the dark, shaggy-haired kangaroo of NSW and southern Queensland. [Dharuk *walaru*]

**wall bar** *n.* one of a set of parallel bars, attached to the wall of a gymnasium, on which exercises are performed.

**wallet** /wol-uht/ *n.* small flat esp. leather case for holding banknotes etc. [Anglo-French]

**wall-eye** *n.* **1** eye with a streaked or opaque white iris. **2** eye squinting outwards. □ **wall-eyed** *adj.* [Old Norse]

**wallflower** *n.* **1** European wild or garden plant, having brown, yellow, or red fragrant flowers, often found clinging to walls etc. **2** *colloq.* person sitting (against the wall) on a dance-floor for lack of partners.

**wallop** /**wol**-uhp/ *colloq.* — *v.* (**-p-**) **1** thrash; beat. **2** defeat convincingly (*walloped him at tennis*). — *n.* heavy blow. [earlier senses 'gallop', 'boil', from French *waloper* from Germanic: cf. GALLOP]

**walloper** *n. colloq.* **1** person or thing that wallops. **2** police officer.

**walloping** *colloq.* — *n.* **1** a thrashing. **2** a decisive defeat. — *adj.* **1** huge (*made a walloping profit*). **2** severe (*came down with a walloping cold*).

**wallow** /**wol**-oh/ — *v.* **1** (esp. of an animal) roll about in mud etc. **2** (usu. foll. by *in*) indulge in unrestrained pleasure, misery, etc. (*wallowing in nostalgia*). — *n.* **1** act or instance of wallowing. **2** place used by buffalo etc. for wallowing. [Old English]

**wallpaper** — *n.* paper for pasting on to interior walls as decoration. — *v.* decorate with wallpaper.

**wall-to-wall** *adj.* **1** (of a carpet) fitted to cover a whole room etc. **2** *colloq.* ubiquitous (*wall-to-wall pop music*).

**wallum** /**wol**-uhm/ *n.* **1** small, gnarled banksia of south-eastern Queensland and eastern NSW. **2** (also **wallum country**) **a** a sandy coastal heathland in which this plant is the predominant species. **b** any area of coastal lowland. [Gabi-gabi *walum* or *walam*]

**wally** /**wol**-ee/ *n.* (*pl.* **-ies**) *colloq.* foolish or inept person. [origin uncertain]

**wally grout** /,wol-ee **growt**/ *n. colloq.* shout; turn to buy a round of drinks. [rhyming slang; *Wally Grout* Australian test cricketer]

**Walmatjari** /wahl-mah-,jah-ree/ *n.* an Aboriginal language spoken in north-central WA.

**walnut** /**wawl**-nut/ *n.* **1 a** Northern hemisphere tree with aromatic leaves and drooping catkins. **b** nut of this tree containing an edible kernel. **c** (also *attrib.*) its timber. **2 a** any of several Australian forest trees of the laurel family, logged for their attractively patterned wood supposed to resemble that of the northern hemisphere walnut. **b** (also *attrib.*) the wood of these trees (*people sitting at their Australian walnut tables don't consider the fact that animals which can't survive in logged areas do not migrate to unlogged areas: they perish*). [Old English, = foreign nut]

**walrus** /**wawl**-ruhs, **wol**-/ *n.* (*pl.* same or **-es**) large amphibious long-tusked arctic mammal. [Dutch]

**waltz** /wolts, wawlts/ — *n.* **1** ballroom dance in triple time performed by couples revolving with sliding steps. **2** music for this. — *v.* **1** dance a waltz. **2** move (a person) in, or as if in, a waltz, with ease (*waltzed him off to Paris*). **3** (often foll. by *in*, *out*, *round*, etc.) *colloq.* move easily, lightly, casually, etc. □ **waltz off with** *colloq.* **1** steal (*waltzed off with the day's takings*). **2** win easily (*waltzed off with the first prize*). [German *Walzer* from *walzen* revolve]

**waltz matilda** see MATILDA.

**wambenger** /**wom**-ben-juh/ *n.* = PHASCOGALE. [possibly from Nyungar *wambanang*]

**wan** /won/ *adj.* (**wanner**, **wannest**) pale; exhausted-looking; unhappy (*wan features; a wan smile*). □ **wanly** *adv.* **wanness** *n.* [Old English, = dark]

**WAN** /wan/ *abbr. Computing* wide area network.

**wand** /wond/ *n.* **1** supposedly magic stick used by a fairy, wizard, magician, etc. **2** staff as a symbol of office. [Old Norse]

**wander** /**won**-duh/ — *v.* **1** (often foll. by *in*, *off*, etc.) go about from place to place aimlessly. **2 a** (of a river, road, etc.) wind about; meander. **b** (esp. of a person) get lost; leave home; stray from a path etc. **3** talk or think incoherently; be inattentive or delirious (*his mind is wandering*). **4** cover by wandering (*he wanders the world*). — *n.* act or instance of wandering (*went for a wander round the garden*). □ **wanderer** *n.* [Old English: related to WEND]

**wanderer** *n.* migratory, predominantly reddish brown and black butterfly of Australia and elsewhere.

**wandering Jew** *n.* **1 a** legendary person who, because he mocked Christ at the time of the crucifixion, was condemned to wander the world until the second advent. **b** person who never settles down. **2** creeping Australian plant with bright blue flowers.

**wanderlust** *n.* eagerness for travelling or wandering; restlessness. [German]

**wanderoo** /ˌwon-duh-**roo**/ *n.* Sri Lankan langur. [Sinhalese *wanderu* monkey]

**Wandjina** /**won**-jee-nuh/ *n.* (also **Wondjina**) Aboriginal ancestral spirit of fertility and rain, found in rock-paintings of the Kimberley ranges in WA. [Ungarinyin *wanjina* of uncertain meaning]

**wandoo** /won-**doo**/ *n.* **1** the gum *Eucalyptus wandoo* of south-western WA having a smooth mottled white trunk. **2** the very hard, strong, durable wood of this tree. [Nyungar *wandu*]

**wane** — *v.* (**-ning**) **1** (of the moon) decrease in apparent size after the full moon (cf. WAX²). **2** decrease in power, vigour, importance, size, etc. — *n.* pro-

cess of waning. □ **on the wane** waning; declining. [Old English]

**Wangganguru** /ˌwung-gu-**ngoo**-roo/ *n.* an Aboriginal language once spoken over a vast area of northern SA and extending into the NT: now extinct.

**Wangka-Yutjuru** /ˌwahng-ku **yuu**-chuu-roo/ *n.* an Aboriginal language spoken in western Queensland: now extinct.

**wangle** /**wang**-guhl/ *colloq.* — *v.* (**-ling**) obtain or arrange by using trickery, improper influence, persuasion, etc. — *n.* act of wangling. [origin unknown]

**wank** *colloq.* — *n.* **1** (usu. applied to a male) person who deludes himself as to his importance etc.; fool. **2 a** rubbish, nonsense (*I've heard the rumour — it's an utter wank*). **b** self-indulgent posturing (*what a wank his farewell speech turned out to be!*). **4** *coarse colloq.* act or instance of masturbating. — *v. coarse colloq.* (usu. foll. by *off*) masturbate. [origin unknown]

**wanker** *n. colloq.* (usually applied to a male) person who deludes himself, thinks highly of himself and shows it in his behaviour etc.; contemptible person.

**wanna** /**won**-uh/ *n.* (also **wonna**) Aboriginal woman's digging stick. [Nyungar *wana*]

**wannabe** /**won**-uh-bee/ *n. colloq.* **1** avid fan who tries to emulate the person he or she admires. **2** anybody who would like to be someone else. [corruption of *want to be*]

**want** /wont/ — *v.* **1 a** (often foll. by *to* + infin.) desire; wish for possession of; need (*wants a drink; wants it done immediately; wanted to leave; wanted him to leave*). **b** need or desire (a person). **c** require to be attended to; need (*garden wants weeding*). **d** (foll. by *to* + infin.) *colloq.* ought; should (*you want to be careful; you don't want to overdo it*). **2** (usu. foll. by *for*) lack; be deficient (*he wants for nothing*). **3** be without or fall short by (*the drawer wants a handle*). **4** (foll. by *in* or *out*) *colloq.* desire to be in or out etc. (*wants in on the deal; wanted out of the contract*). **5** (as **wanted** *adj.*) (of a suspected criminal etc.) sought by the police. — *n.* **1** (often foll. by *of*) lack, absence, or deficiency (*could not go for want of time; shows a great want of judgment*). **2** poverty; need (*is in great want*). **3 a** desire for a thing etc. (*meets a long-felt want*). **b** thing so desired (*can supply your wants*). □ **want ad** *colloq* classified newspaper advertisement for something sought. [Old Norse]

**wanting** *adj.* **1** lacking (in quality or quantity); not equal to requirements (*wanting in judgment*). **2** absent, not supplied or provided. □ **be found wanting** fail to meet requirements.

**wanton** /won-tuhn/ — *adj.* **1** licentious; sexually promiscuous. **2** capricious; arbitrary; motiveless (*wanton destruction*). **3** luxuriant; unrestrained (*wanton profusion*). — *n. literary* licentious person. □ **wantonly** *adv.* [from obsolete *wantowen*, = undisciplined]

**war** /waw/ — *n.* **1 a** armed hostilities between esp. nations; conflict. **b** specific instance or period of this. **c** suspension of international law etc. during this. **2** hostility or contention between people, groups, etc. **3** (often foll. by *on*) sustained campaign against crime, poverty, etc. — *v.* (**-rr-**) **1** (as **warring** *adj.*) a rival; fighting (*warring factions in the Labor Party*). **b** conflicting (*warring principles*). **2** make war. □ **at war** (often foll. by *with*) engaged in a war. **go to war** declare or begin a war. **have been in the wars** *colloq.* appear injured, bruised, unkempt, etc. [Anglo-French from Germanic]

**warabi** /wo-ruh-bee/ *n.* the smallest rock wallaby, restricted to rugged, inhospitable parts of the Kimberley region, WA. [Wunambal *warabi*]

**waratah** /wo-ruh-tah/ *n.* **1** any of four species of the Australian genus *Telopea*, all highly ornamental shrubs with very large red flowers (*Gippsland waratah*; *Tasmanian waratah*). **2** (also **New South Wales waratah**) tall shrub, *Telopea speciosissima*, bearing huge (15 cm in diameter) crimson flowerheads surrounded by large red bracts: this flower is the floral emblem of New South Wales. [Dharuk *warrada*]

**Waray** /wah-ruy/ *n.* an Aboriginal language spoken in the northern region of the NT.

**warb** /wawb/ *n.* (also **waub**) *colloq.* idle, unkempt, or disreputable person. [origin unknown]

**warble** /waw-buhl/ — *v.* (**-ling**) **1** sing in a gentle trilling manner. **2** speak in a warbling manner. — *n.* warbled song or utterance. [French *werble* (r)]

**warbler** *n.* **1** bird that warbles. **2** any of many small Australian birds usu. having a very melodic call (*brown warbler*; *reed warbler*; *white-throated warbler*).

**warby** /waw-bee/ *adj. colloq.* shabby; decrepit. [from WARB]

**war crime** *n.* crime violating the international laws of war. □ **war criminal** *n.*

**war cry** *n.* **1** phrase or name shouted to rally one's troops. **2** party slogan etc.

**ward** /wawd/ *n.* **1** separate part of a hospital or room for a particular group of patients (*men's surgical ward*). **2** administrative division of a constituency, usu. electing a councillor or councillors etc. **3 a** minor under the care of a guardian or court. **b** (in full **ward of court**) minor or mentally deficient person placed under the protection of a court. **4** (in *pl.*) the corresponding notches and projections in a key and a lock. □ **ward off 1** parry (a blow). **2** avert (danger etc.). [Old English]

**-ward** *suffix* (also **-wards**) added to nouns of place or destination and to adverbs of direction, and forming: **1** adverbs (usu. **-wards**) meaning 'towards' (*backwards*; *homewards*). **2** adjectives (usu. **-ward**) meaning 'turned or tending towards' (*downward*; *onward*). **3** (less commonly) nouns meaning 'the region towards or about' (*look to the eastward*). [Old English]

**war dance** *n.* dance performed by primitive peoples etc. before a battle or to celebrate victory.

**warden** /waw-duhn/ *n.* **1** (often in *comb.*) supervising official (*traffic warden*). **2** president or governor of a college, school, hospital, youth hostel, etc. [Anglo-French and French: related to GUARDIAN]

**warder** /waw-duh/ *n.* (*fem.* **wardress**) prison officer. [French: related to GUARD]

**wardrobe** /waw-drohb/ *n.* **1** large cupboard for storing clothes. **2** person's stock of clothes. **3** costume department or costumes of a theatre, film company, etc. [French]

**wardrobe mistress** *n.* (*masc.* **wardrobe master**) person in charge of a theatrical or film wardrobe.

**wardroom** *n.* mess in a warship for commissioned officers.

**-wards** var. of -WARD.

**wardship** *n.* **1** guardian's care or tutelage. **2** condition of being a ward.

**ware** *n.* **1** (esp. in *comb.*) things of a specified kind made usu. for sale (*chinaware*; *hardware*). **2** (usu. in *pl.*) articles for sale. **3** ceramics etc. of a specified kind (*Delft ware*). [Old English]

**warehouse** /wair-hows/ — *n.* building in which goods are stored, esp. the wares of a wholesale dealer. — *v.* also /-howz/ (**-sing**) store temporarily in a repository.

**warfare** *n.* waging war, campaigning.

**warfarin** /waw-fuh-rin/ *n.* water-soluble anti-coagulant used in the treatment of stroke victims etc. and also as a rat poison. [Wisconsin Alumni Research Foundation, - *arin*]

**war game** *n.* **1** military training exercise. **2** battle etc. conducted with toy soldiers.

**warhead** *n.* explosive head of a missile.

**warhorse** *n.* **1** *hist.* trooper's powerful horse. **2** *colloq.* veteran soldier, politician, etc.

**warlike** *adj.* **1** hostile. **2** soldierly. **3** military.

**warlock** /waw-lok/ *n.* wizard; sorcerer. [Old English, = traitor]

**warlord** *n.* regional military ruler with his own army.

**Warlpiri** /wahl-bree/ *n.* an Aboriginal language spoken in the central regions of the NT.

**warm** /wawm/ — *adj.* **1** of or at a fairly or comfortably high temperature. **2** (of clothes etc.) affording warmth (*wear a warm pullover*). **3 a** sympathetic, friendly, loving (*a warm welcome*; *has a warm heart*). **b** hearty, enthusiastic (*was warm in her praise*). **4** animated, heated (*the dispute grew warm*). **5** *iron.* dangerous, difficult, hostile (*a warm reception from his opponents in the crowd*). **6** *colloq.* **a** (in a game) close to the object etc. sought. **b** near to guessing. **7** (of a colour etc.) reddish or yellowish; suggestive of warmth. — *v.* **1** make warm. **2 a** (often foll. by *up*) warm oneself. **b** (often foll. by *to*) become animated or sympathetic (*warmed to his subject*). — *n.* act of warming or state of being warmed (*had a nice warm by the fire*). □ **warm up 1** make or become warm. **2** prepare for a performance etc. by practising. **3** reach a temperature for efficient working. **4** reheat (food). □ **warmly** *adv.* **warmth** *n.* [Old English]

**warm-blooded** *adj.* **1** having blood temperature well above that of the environment. **2** ardent; passionate.

**warm-hearted** *adj.* kind, friendly. □ **warm-heartedness** *n.*

**warmonger** *n.* person who promotes war. □ **warmongering** *n.* & *adj.*

**warm-up** *n.* period of preparatory exercise.

**warm work** *n.* **1** work etc. that makes one warm through exertion. **2** dangerous conflict etc.

**warn** /wawn/ *v.* **1** (also *absol.*) **a** (often foll. by *of* or *that*) inform of danger, unknown circumstances, etc. (*warned him of the danger*; *warned her that she was being watched*). **b** (foll. by *to* + infin.) advise or admonish (a person) to take certain action (*warned him to have the tree cut*; *warned him not to go*). **c** (often foll. by *against*) inform (a person etc.) about a specific danger (*warned her against trusting him*). **2** give a person cautionary notice regarding conduct etc. (*shall not warn you again*). □ **warn off** tell

(a person) to keep away (from). [Old English]

**warning** *n.* **1** in senses of WARN. **2** thing that warns (*the pain in his chest was a warning of something seriously wrong*). **3** (*attrib.*) serving as or relating to warning (*a warning frown*; *warning bell*). [Old English]

**war of nerves** *n.* attempt to wear down an opponent psychologically.

**warp** /wawp/ — *v.* **1** make or become distorted, esp. through heat, damp, etc. **2** make or become perverted, bitter, or strange (*a mind warped by malice*; *warped sense of humour*). — *n.* **1 a** warped state, esp. of timber. **b** perversion, bitterness, etc., of the mind. **2** lengthwise threads in a loom. [Old English]

**warpath** *n.* □ **on the warpath 1** (of N. American Indians) going to war. **2** *colloq.* any hostile course or attitude (*he's on the warpath again*).

**warrant** /wo-ruhnt/ — *n.* **1 a** thing that authorises a person or an action; a sanction. **b** justifying reason or ground for an action, belief, or feeling (*I have some warrant for my fear of spiders*; *you've no warrant for thinking him a crook*). **2 a** written authorisation, money voucher, etc. **b** written authorisation allowing police to search premises, arrest a suspect, etc. **3** certificate of service rank held by a warrant-officer. — *v.* **1** serve as a warrant for; justify (*nothing can warrant his behaviour*). **2** guarantee or attest to esp. the genuineness of. □ **I** (or **I'll**) **warrant** I am certain; no doubt. [French *warant*, from Germanic]

**warrant officer** *n.* officer ranking between commissioned officers and NCOs.

**warranty** *n.* (*pl.* **-ies**) **1** undertaking as to the ownership or quality of a thing sold etc., often accepting responsibility for defects or repairs over a specified period. **2** (usu. foll. by *for* + verbal noun) authority or justification. [Anglo-French *warantie*: related to WARRANT]

**warren** /wo-ruhn/ *n.* **1** network of rabbit burrows. **2** densely populated or labyrinthine building or district. [Anglo-French *warenne* from Germanic]

**Warrgamay** /wahr-gu-muy/ *n.* an Aboriginal language once spoken in a wide region of north-eastern Queensland south of Cairns: now extinct.

**warrigal** /wo-ruh-guhl/ — *n.* **1** = DINGO. **2** = MYALL[1] *n.* 1. **3** (in full **warrigal cabbage**) plant occurring in Australia and New Zealand, having fleshy leaves used as a vegetable. **4** wild or untamed horse.

— *adj.* wild; untamed. [Dharuk *warrigal* wild dingo]

**warring** see WAR *v.*

**warrior** /**wo**-ree-uh/ *n.* **1** person experienced or distinguished in fighting. **2** fighting man, esp. of primitive peoples. **3** (*attrib.*) martial (*warrior nation*). [French *werreior*: related to WAR]

**wart** /wawt/ *n.* **1** small hard round growth on the skin caused by a virus. **2** protuberance on the skin of an animal, surface of a plant, etc. □ **warts and all** *colloq.* with no attempt to conceal blemishes. □ **warty** *adj.* [Old English]

**warthog** *n.* African wild pig with large curved tusks and warty lumps on its face.

**Warumungu** /wah-roo-,muung-oo/ *n.* an Aboriginal language spoken in the central region of the NT.

**Warungu** /wah-roong-oo/ *n.* an Aboriginal language spoken in north-eastern Queensland: now extinct.

**wary** /**wair**-ree/ *adj.* (**-ier, -iest**) **1** on one's guard; circumspect. **2** (foll. by *of*) cautious; suspicious (*my kids are wary of strangers*). **3** showing or done with caution or suspicion (*a wary expression on his face*). □ **warily** *adv.* **wariness** *n.* [*ware* look out for, avoid]

**was** *1st & 3rd sing. past of* BE.

**wash** /wosh/ — *v.* **1** cleanse with liquid, esp. water. **2** (foll. by *out, off, away*, etc.) **a** remove (a stain or dirt) in this way. **b** (of a stain etc.) be removed by washing. **3** wash oneself or one's hands and face. **4** wash clothes, dishes, etc. **5** (of fabric or dye) bear washing without damage (*this garment washes well*). **6** (of an argument, explanation, etc.) stand scrutiny; be believed or acceptable (*that excuse just won't wash*). **7** (of a river, sea, etc.) touch (a country, coast, etc.) with its waters (*rocky promontory washed by the Southern Ocean*). **8** (of liquid) carry along in a specified direction (*a wave washed him overboard; was washed up on the shore*). **9 a** scoop out (*the water has washed a channel*). **b** erode, denude (*sea-washed cliffs*). **10** (foll. by *over, along*, etc.) sweep, move, or splash (*the flood washed over the bridge*). **11** (foll. by *over*) occur all around without greatly affecting (a person) (*the family squabbles washed right over her*). **12** sift (ore) by the action of water. **13** brush watery paint or ink over (paper in a water-colour painting etc.). **14** *poet.* moisten, water (*roses washed with dew*). — *n.* **1** act or instance of washing or the process of being washed (*needed only one wash*). **2** clothes etc. for washing or just washed (*hang out the wash*). **3** motion of agitated water or air, esp. from the pas-

sage of a ship etc. or aircraft. **4** liquid to spread over a surface to cleanse, heal, or colour. **5** thin coating of water-colour, wall-colouring, etc. **6** lotion or cosmetic (*mouth-wash*). **7 a** soil swept off by water; alluvium. **b** sandbank exposed only at low tide. □ **come out in the wash** *colloq.* be resolved in the course of time. **wash one's dirty linen in public** let private quarrels or difficulties become generally known. **wash down 1** wash completely (esp. a large surface or object). **2** (usu. foll. by *with*) accompany or follow (food) with a drink. **wash one's hands of** renounce responsibility for. **wash out 1** clean the inside of by washing (*wash out the toilet bowl*). **2** cause (an event) to be cancelled because of rain. **3** (of a flood, downpour, etc.) make a breach in (a road etc.). **4** = sense 2 of *v.* **wash up 1** (also *absol.*) wash (dishes etc.) after use. **2** carry on to a shore (*it's amazing what the sea washes up*). □ **washable** *adj.* [Old English]

**washaway** /**wosh**-uh-way/ *n.* **1** removal of earth, a portion of a road or railway line, etc., by flood. **2** hole or gap or channel caused by this.

**washboard** *n.* **1** (formerly) ribbed board on which clothes are scrubbed. **2** this as a percussion instrument.

**washed out** *adj.* (also **washed-out**) **1** faded; pale. **2** *colloq.* pale, exhausted.

**washed up** *adj.* (also **washed-up**) *colloq.* defeated, having failed (*he's all washed-up*).

**washer** *n.* **1** person or machine that washes. **2** flat ring inserted at a joint to tighten it and prevent leakage or under the head of a screw etc., or under a nut, to disperse its pressure. **3** cloth for washing the face.

**washing** *n.* clothes etc. for washing or just washed.

**washing machine** *n.* machine for washing clothes.

**washing soda** *n.* sodium carbonate, used dissolved in water for washing and cleaning.

**washing-up** *n.* **1** process of washing dishes etc. **2** used dishes etc. for washing.

**wash-out** *n.* *colloq.* complete failure, non-event.

**washup** *n.* **1** end or outcome of a process (*you'll find, in the washup, that my predictions were correct*). **2** discussion and analysis of course and result of game, contest, etc.

**wasn't** /woz-uhnt/ *contr.* was not.

**Wasp** /wosp/ — *n.* (also **WASP**) *derog.* middle-class White Protestant (*the WASPS believe they have a god-given* *right to dominate*). — *adj.* of or pertaining to WASPS (*WASP values*). [White Anglo- Saxon Protestant]

**wasp** /wosp/ *n.* stinging insect with black and yellow stripes. [Old English]

**waspish** *adj.* irritable, snappish; sharp in retort.

**wasp-waist** *n.* very slender waist.

**wassail** /wos-ayl, wos-uhl/ *archaic* — *n.* festive occasion; drinking-bout. — *v.* make merry. □ **wassailer** *n.* [Old Norse *ves heill* be in health: related to WHOLE]

**wastage** /ways-tij/ *n.* **1** amount wasted. **2** loss by use, wear, or leakage. **3** (also **natural wastage**) loss of employees other than by redundancy.

**waste** — *v.* (**-ting**) **1** use to no purpose or with inadequate result or extravagantly (*waste time; wasting water*). **2** fail to use (esp. an opportunity) (*wasted his chance*). **3** (often foll. by *on*) **a** give (advice etc.) or utter (words etc.) without effect (*your pleas are wasted on him*). **b** (often in *passive*) fail to be appreciated or used properly (*she was wasted on him; feel wasted in this job*). **4** wear gradually away; make or become weak (*wasting with hunger; his body wasted by AIDS*). **5 a** ravage, devastate (*cities wasted by repeated bombing*). **b** *colloq.* kill, murder (a person); kill ruthlessly in war (*wasted entire villages*). **6** be expended without useful effect (*his efforts were wasted*). — *adj.* **1** superfluous; no longer needed (*waste products*). **2** not inhabited or cultivated; desolate (*waste ground*). — *n.* **1** act or instance of wasting; extravagant or ineffectual use of an asset, of time, etc. (*waste of resources*). **2** waste material; refuse; useless by-products. **3** waste region; WASTELAND. **4** state of being used up; diminution by wear and tear (*the body is subject to waste*). □ **go** (or **run**) **to waste** be wasted. **waste one's breath** talk or give advice to no effect. [Latin: related to VAST]

**wasted** *adj. colloq.* intoxicated (from alcoholic drinks or drugs).

**wasteful** *adj.* **1** extravagant. **2** causing or showing waste. □ **wastefully** *adv.*

**wasteland** *n.* **1** unproductive or useless area of land. **2** place or time considered spiritually or intellectually barren.

**waste paper** *n.* used or valueless paper.

**waste product** *n.* useless by-product of manufacture or of an organism.

**waster** *n.* **1** wasteful person. **2** *colloq.* wastrel.

**wastrel** /way-struhl/ *n.* wasteful or good-for-nothing person.

**watch** /woch/ — *v.* **1** keep the eyes fixed on; look at attentively (*watched the*

*mating antics of the magpies*). **2 a** keep under observation; follow observantly (*watched the suspect's house; watched the strategies of the two chess players*). **b** monitor or consider carefully (*have to watch my weight*). **3** (often foll. by *for*) be in an alert state; be vigilant (*watch for the holes in the road; watch for an opportunity*). **4** (foll. by *over*) look after; take care of (*I'll watch over them while you're away*). **5** keep vigil (at a sickbed, at church, etc.) (*get some sleep — I'll watch by grandpa's bed tonight*). — *n.* **1** small portable timepiece for carrying on the wrist or in a pocket. **2** state of alert or constant observation or attention (*keep watch; I've had a watch put on the house*). **3** *Naut.* **a** usu. four-hour spell of duty. **b** (in full **starboard** or **port watch**) each of the halves into which a ship's crew is divided to take alternate watches. **4** *hist.* watchman or watchmen. □ **on the watch for** waiting for (an anticipated or feared occurrence). **watch it!** *colloq.* **1** be careful (*watch it! — it's about to spill*). **2** exclamation of hostile warning, = 'stop, or I'll deal with you!' **watch out 1** (often foll. by *for*) be on one's guard. **2** as a warning of immediate danger. □ **watcher** *n.* (also in *comb.*). [Old English: related to WAKE[1]]

**watchdog** *n.* **1** dog guarding property etc. **2** person or body monitoring others' rights, behaviour, etc.

**watchful** *adj.* **1** accustomed to watching, alert. **2** on the watch. □ **watchfully** *adv.* **watchfulness** *n.*

**watch-house** *n.* building, now usu. attached to a police station, in which suspected law-breakers are held under temporary arrest.

**watching brief** *n.* brief of a barrister who follows a case for a client not directly concerned.

**watchman** *n.* man employed to look after an empty building etc. at night.

**watchword** *n.* **1** phrase summarising a guiding principle (*the watchword is vigilance*). **2** *hist.* military password.

**water** /waw-tuh/ — *n.* **1** colourless transparent liquid compound of oxygen and hydrogen. **2** liquid consisting chiefly of this and found in seas and rivers, in rain, and in secretions of organisms (e.g. tears, urine — *water in his eyes; pass water*). **3** expanse of water; a sea, lake, river, etc. **4** (in *pl.*) part of a sea or river (*in southern Australian waters*). **5** (often as **the waters**) mineral water at a spa etc. **6** state of a tide (*high water*). **7** solution of a specified substance in water (*lavender-water*). **8** transparency and brilliance of a gem, esp. a diamond. **9**

(*attrib.*) **a** found in or near water (esp. in names of Australian fauna and flora: *water goanna*; *water rat*; *water bush*; *water gum*; etc.). **b** of, for, or worked by water (*water trough*; *water meter*; *water wheel*). **c** involving, using, or yielding water (*water polo*; *water vine*). **10** (usu. in *pl.*) amniotic fluid, released during labour. — *v.* **1** sprinkle or soak with water (*vehicle that waters the road*). **2** supply (a plant) with water (*watered the lawn*). **3** give water to (an animal) (*water the horses*). **4** secrete water (*his eyes were watering*; *my mouth watered*). **5** (as **watered** *adj.*) (of silk etc.) having irregular wavy glossy markings. **6** adulterate with water (*watered the milk*). **7** (of a river etc.) supply (a place) with water (*regions watered by the Murrumbidgee*). **8** (of an animal) go to a pool etc. to drink (*emus and kangaroos watering at this billabong*). **9** (of a ship etc.) take in a supply of water (*the vessel will water at Geelong*). □ **by water** using a ship etc. for transport. **cast one's bread upon the waters** see BREAD. **in deep water** see DEEP. **like water** in great quantity, profusely (*spends money like water*). **like water off a duck's back** see DUCK. **make one's mouth water** cause one's saliva to flow, stimulate one's appetite or anticipation. **of the first water 1** (of a diamond) of the greatest brilliance and transparency. **2** of the finest quality or extreme degree (*a performance of the first water*). **throw** (or **pour**) **cold water on** see COLD. **water down 1** dilute. **2** make less forceful or horrifying (*watered down his account of the massacre*). **water under the bridge** past events accepted as irrevocable. [Old English]

**water-bag** *n.* canvas bag used to carry water while travelling.

**Water-bearer** var. of WATER-CARRIER.

**waterbed** *n.* mattress of rubber, plastic, etc., filled with water and held in a supporting frame.

**water buffalo** *n.* common domestic Indian buffalo, introduced to Australia and now naturalised in the NT.

**water-burner** *n.* (also **water-scorcher**) *colloq.* highly inferior cook.

**water-cannon** *n.* device using a jet of water to disperse a crowd etc.

**Water-carrier** *n.* (also **Water-bearer**) (prec. by *the*) zodiacal sign or constellation Aquarius.

**water chestnut** *n.* edible corm from a sedge, used in Chinese cookery.

**water closet** *n.* **1** toilet that can be flushed. **2** room containing this.

**watercolour** *n.* (also **water-color**) **1** artists' paint made of pigment to be diluted with water and not oil. **2** picture painted with this. **3** art of painting with watercolours. □ **watercolourist** *n.*

**water core** *n.* disease of apples.

**watercourse** *n.* **1** brook, stream, or artificial water-channel. **2** bed of this.

**watercress** *n.* pungent cress growing in running water and used in salad.

**water-diviner** *n.* person who searches for underground water by holding a rod supposed to dip when over the right spot.

**water dragon** *n.* large green or brown black-barred lizard with a spiny crest on head and back, occurring widely in eastern mainland Australia in or near water.

**waterfall** *n.* stream or river flowing over a precipice or down a steep hillside.

**waterfowl** *n.* (usu. collect. as *pl.*) birds frequenting water, esp. swimming birds.

**waterfront** *n.* part of a town adjoining a river, lake, harbour, etc.

**Watergate** see -GATE.

**water gum** *n.* = KANOOKA.

**water hammer** *n.* knocking noise in a water-pipe when a tap is suddenly turned off.

**water-holding frog** *n.* any of several burrowing frogs of drier inland Australia having the ability, when pools etc. begin to dry up, to take in water until its body swells greatly, and also to store water in its burrow.

**waterhole** *n.* **1** shallow depression in which water collects; a pond or pool which may be very large. **2** cavity in the bed of a watercourse, esp. one that retains water when the main stream dries up. **3** = WATERING-HOLE.

**watering can** *n.* portable container with a long spout, for watering plants.

**watering hole** *n.* **1** waterhole from which animals regularly drink. **2** *colloq.* hotel or bar, esp. one frequented by a regular group.

**water-joey** /**joh**-ee/ *n.* person who is employed to carry water and to supply the needs of a group, esp. in the bush etc.

**water jump** *n.* jump over water in a steeplechase etc.

**water level** *n.* **1 a** surface of the water in a reservoir etc. **b** height of this. **2** level below which the ground is saturated with water. **3** level using water to determine the horizontal.

**water lily** *n.* aquatic plant with floating leaves and large usu. cup-shaped flowers, often fragrant.

**waterline** *n.* line along which the surface of water touches a ship's side (marked on a ship for use in loading).

**waterlogged** *adj.* (of the ground, a boat, etc.) saturated or filled with water.

**waterloo** /ˌwaw-tuh-**loo**/ *n.* decisive defeat or contest (*met his waterloo*). [*Waterloo* in Belgium, where Napoleon was defeated]

**water main** *n.* main pipe in a water-supply system.

**water mallee** *n.* any of several mallee eucalypts the roots of which when cut yield a considerable quantity of drinkable water.

**watermark** — *n.* faint design made in some paper during manufacture, visible when held against the light, identifying the maker etc. — *v.* mark with this.

**watermelon** *n.* large dark green melon with red pulp and watery juice.

**water polo** *n.* game played by two teams each with seven swimmers, with a ball like a football.

**waterproof** — *adj.* impervious to water. — *n.* waterproof garment or material. — *v.* make waterproof.

**water rat** *n.* (also **beaver rat**) large aquatic rodent, widespread near water in Australia, having dense, soft fur and webbed hind feet.

**water-scorcher** *n.* = WATER-BURNER.

**watershed** *n.* **1** line of separation between waters flowing to different rivers, basins, or seas. **2** turning-point in affairs (*reached a watershed in his life when his wife died*). [from *shed* ridge]

**waterside** *n.* edge of a sea, lake, or river.

**watersider** *n.* = WATERSIDE WORKER.

**waterside worker** *n.* person employed to load and unload a ship's cargo; wharf-labourer.

**water-ski** — *n.* each of a pair of skis for skimming the surface of the water when towed by a motor boat. — *v.* travel on water-skis. □ **water-skier** *n.*

**water softener** *n.* apparatus for softening hard water.

**waterspout** *n.* gyrating column of water and spray formed by a whirlwind between sea and cloud.

**water-table** *n.* = WATER-LEVEL 2.

**watertight** *adj.* **1** closely fastened or fitted so as to prevent the passage of water. **2** (of an argument etc.) unassailable.

**water tower** *n.* tower with an elevated tank to give pressure for distributing water.

**water vine** *n.* any of several climbing plants, esp. of eastern Australian rainforests, yielding drinkable water when cut.

**waterway** *n.* navigable channel.

**waterwheel** *n.* wheel driven by water to work machinery, or to raise water.

**water wings** *n.pl.* = FLOATIES.

**waterworks** *n.* **1** establishment for managing a water-supply. **2** *colloq.* shedding of tears. **3** *colloq.* urinary system.

**watery** *adj.* **1** containing too much water. **2** too thin in consistency. **3** of or consisting of water. **4** (of a writer's style etc.) vapid, uninteresting (*watery prose*). **5** (of colour) pale. **6** (of the sun, moon, or sky) rainy-looking. **7** (of eyes) moist; tearful. □ **wateriness** *n.*

**Wathawurung** /ˈwut-u-wu-rung/ *n.* an Aboriginal language once spoken on the west side of Port Phillip Bay, including the present city of Geelong and the town of Bacchus Marsh and extending inland probably as far as the city of Ballarat: now extinct.

**Watjari** /ˈwuch-u-ree/ *n.* an Aboriginal language spoken in west-central WA.

**watjin** /ˈwahd-jin/ *n.* (also **waatgin**, **wijen**, **wodgin**) (in Aboriginal English) a white woman. [alteration of *white gin*: see GIN²]

**watt** /wot/ *n.* SI unit of power, equivalent to one joule per second, corresponding to the rate of energy in an electric circuit where the potential difference is one volt and the current one ampere. [*Watt*, name of an engineer]

**wattage** *n.* amount of electrical power expressed in watts.

**watt-hour** *n.* energy used when one watt is applied for one hour.

**wattle¹** /ˈwot-uhl/ — *n.* **1** any plant of the largest Australian plant genus *Acacia* (of which there are in Australia nearly 800 described species), having long pliant branches used by early settlers for building wattle-and-daub huts (see sense 2): wattles vary in size from prostrate plants to trees over 30 m tall, have foliage consisting of true leaves or phyllodes or both, and bear densely profuse often perfumed ball- or rod-flowers in colours ranging from cream through yellow to deepest gold. **2 a** interlaced rods and split rods as a material for making fences, walls, etc. **b** (in *sing.* or *pl.*) rods or twigs for this use. — *v.* **1** make (a fence, hut, etc.) of wattle. **2** enclose or fill up with wattles. [Old English *watul*, of unknown origin]

**wattle²** /ˈwot-uhl/ *n.* fleshy appendage on the head or throat of a wattle bird, turkey, or other birds. [origin unknown]

**wattle and daub** *n.* network of rods and twigs plastered with clay or mud as a building material.

**wattle bark** *n.* the bark of any of several species of wattle, some of which are cultivated commercially for the high tannin content of their bark.

**wattle bird** *n.* any of several large Australian honeyeaters with loud harsh calls and sometimes conspicuous facial wattles (*brush wattle bird*; *red wattle bird*; *yellow wattle bird*).

**Wattle Day** *n.* annual celebration (the date of which varies locally in Australia) of the blossoming of the wattle.

**wattle flower** *n.* the floral emblem of Australia (see GOLDEN WATTLE; FLORAL EMBLEM).

**wattle goat-moth** *n.* spectacular Australian moth, the female having a wing-span of about 18 cm and a body the size of a mouse, which lays its eggs on wattles, the larvae being among the insects which are known as witchetty grubs.

**waul** /wawl/ (also **wawl**) — *v.* give a loud plaintive cry like a cat or a new-born infant. — *n.* such a cry.

**wave** — *v.* (**-ving**) **1 a** (often foll. by *to*) move a hand etc. to and fro in greeting or as a signal (*waved to me from across the street*). **b** move (a hand etc.) in this way (*waved her hand in farewell*). **2 a** show a sinuous or sweeping motion as of a flag, tree, tall grass, etc., in the wind (*trees waving in the wind*). **b** impart a waving motion to (*waved the flag to and fro*). **3** direct (a person) by waving (*waved them away*; *waved them to follow*). **4** express (a greeting etc.) by waving (*waved goodbye to them*). **5 a** give an undulating form to (hair etc.). **b** (of hair etc.) have such a form. — *n.* **1** ridge of water between two depressions. **2** long body of water curling into an arch and breaking on the shore. **3** thing compared to this, e.g. a body of persons in one of successive advancing groups (*wave after wave of invaders scrambling ashore under fire*). **4** gesture of waving. **5 a** process of waving the hair. **b** undulating form produced by this. **6** temporary occurrence or increase of a condition or influence (*wave of enthusiasm*; *heat wave*). **7** *Physics* **a** disturbance of the particles of a fluid medium to form ridges and troughs for the propagation or direction of motion, heat, light, sound, etc. **b** single curve in this motion. **8** undulating line or outline. □ **make waves** *colloq.* cause trouble. **wave aside** dismiss as intrusive or irrelevant. **wave down** wave to (a vehicle or driver) to stop. [Old English]

**waveband** *n.* range of radio wavelengths between certain limits.

**waveform** *n. Physics* curve showing the shape of a wave at a given time.

**wavelength** *n.* **1** distance between successive crests of a wave. **2** this as a distinctive feature of radio waves from a transmitter. **3** *colloq.* particular mode or range of thought (*we don't seem to be on the same wavelength*).

**wavelet** *n.* small wave on water (as on e.g. a lake).

**waver** *v.* **1** be or become unsteady; falter; begin to give way (*the rioters wavered when they saw the tanks*; *her courage never wavered*). **2** be irresolute or undecided between different courses or opinions (*he wavered between faith and agonising doubt*). **3** (of a light) flicker. [Old Norse: related to WAVE]

**wavy** *adj.* (**-ier**, **-iest**) having waves or alternate contrary curves (*wavy hair*). □ **waviness** *n.*

**wawl** var. of WAUL.

**wax¹** — *n.* **1** sticky plastic yellowish substance secreted by bees as the material of honeycomb cells; beeswax. **2** this bleached and purified, used for candles, modelling, etc. **3** any similar substance, e.g. the yellow substance secreted by the ear. **4** (*attrib.*) made of wax. **5** = WAX PLANT. — *v.* **1** cover or treat with wax. **2** remove unwanted hair from (legs etc.) using wax; depilate. □ **be wax in a person's hands** be entirely subservient to a person. □ **waxy** *adj.* (**-ier**, **-iest**). [Old English]

**wax²** *v.* **1** (of the moon between new and full) have a progressively larger part of its visible surface illuminated, increasing in apparent size (opp. WANE). **2** become larger or stronger (*their anger waxed with every hour*). **3** pass into a specified state or mood (*wax lyrical*). □ **wax and wane** undergo alternate increases and decreases. [Old English]

**waxen** *adj.* **1** having a smooth pale translucent surface as of wax. **2** *archaic* made of wax.

**wax flower** *n.* any of several Australian plants having very waxy flowers, esp. several species of eriostemon cultivated as ornamentals.

**waxhead** *n. colloq.* surfer.

**wax plant** *n.* **1** (also **wax**) a genus of twelve small to medium-sized shrubs endemic to WA, having showy, often highly waxy, white, pink, rose, or purple flowers, esp. the Geraldton wax and the Esperance wax. **2** (occasionally) = HOYA.

**waxwork** *n.* **1** object, esp. a lifelike dummy, modelled in wax. **2** (in *pl.*) exhibition of wax dummies.

**way** — *n.* **1** road, track, path, etc., for passing along. **2** course or route for reaching a place (*asked the way to Queanbeyan*; *couldn't find the way out*).

**3 a** method or plan for attaining an object (*that is not the way to do it*). **b** ability to obtain one's object (*has a way with him*). **4** style, manner (*I like the way you dress*). **5 a** person's chosen or habitual course of action (*I did it my way*). **b** custom or manner of behaving; personal peculiarity (*he has a way of forgetting things*). **6** specific manner of life or procedure (*refused to amend his ways; soon got into the way of working with the computer*). **7** normal course of events (*that is always the way*). **8** travelling distance; length traversed or to be traversed (*is a long way away*). **9 a** unimpeded opportunity or space to advance (*make way*). **b** space free of obstacles (*the way is clear*). **10** advance in some direction; impetus, progress (*pushed my way through; the project is under way*). **11** being engaged in movement from place to place; time spent in this (*met them on the way home; songs to cheer the way*). **12** specified direction (*step this way*). **13** *colloq.* scope or range (*want a few things in the stationery way*). **14** specified condition or state (*things are in a bad way*). **15** particular or respect (*is useful in some ways*). **16** (in *pl.*) part into which a thing is divided (*split it three ways*). — *adv. colloq.* to a considerable extent; far (*you are way off the mark*). □ **by the way** incidentally (*by the way, whatever happened to the novel you were writing?*). **by way of 1** by means of (*got to where he is by way of bribery and corruption*). **2** as a form of (*did it by way of apology*). **3** passing through, via (*went to Ballarat by way of Geelong*). **come one's way** become available to one (*luck never seems to come my way*). **every which way** *colloq.* in all ways imaginable (*tried every which way to avoid the confrontation*). **2** all over the place (*the sudden gust blew his notes every which way*). **get** (or **have**) **one's way** = *have it one's own way.* **get out of the** (or **my** etc.) **way** stop obstructing a person. **give way 1 a** make concessions (*gave way on all the lesser issues*). **b** yield; fail to resist. **2** (often foll. by *to*) concede precedence (to) (*gave way to the car on his right*). **3** (of a structure etc.) be dislodged or broken under a load; collapse (*the scaffolding gave way under their weight*). **4** (foll. by *to*) be superseded by (*this outdated method must give way to the new*). **5** (foll. by *to*) be overcome by (an emotion etc.) (*he gave way at last to his grief*). **go out of one's way** make a special effort (*went out of his way to help*). **have it one's own way** get what one wants; ensure that one's wishes are met. **have a way with** have a flair for dealing with (*he*

*has a way with animals*). **in a way** to some extent. **in the** (or **one's**) **way** forming an obstruction or hindrance. **lead the way 1** act as guide or leader. **2** show how to do something. **look the other way 1** pretend not to see what one should notice. **2** disregard an acquaintance etc. whom one sees. **no way** *colloq.* under no circumstances; never (*no way will I let you use the car*). **one way and another** taking various considerations into account (*one way and another, he hasn't done such a bad job*). **one way or another** by some means (*one way or another I'll get him out of the house*). **on the** (or **one's**) **way 1** in the course of a journey etc. **2** having progressed (*is well on the way to completion*). **3** *colloq.* (of a child) conceived but not yet born. **on the way out** *colloq.* going out of fashion or favour; heading towards retirement etc. **out of the way 1** no longer an obstacle or hindrance. **2** disposed of; settled. **3** unusual. **4** (of a place) remote. [Old English]

**wayback** — *n.* **1** the Australian outback (*jackerooing in the wayback*). **2** person inhabiting or coming from the outback (*gave a lift to a dinkum wayback*). — *adj.* of or pertaining to the outback (*a wealthy wayback grazier*). — *adv.* far away in the outback; in or from a remote area of Australia (*lives way wayback, between the Black Stump and Bullamakanka*).

**way back** *adv. colloq.* long ago.

**waybill** *n.* list of passengers or parcels on a vehicle.

**wayfarer** *n.* traveller, esp. on foot. □ **wayfaring** *n.* & *adj.*

**way gone** *adj. colloq.* completely drunk.

**waylay** *v.* (*past* and *past part.* **waylaid**) **1** lie in wait for. **2** stop to talk to or rob.

**Way of the Cross** *n.* **1** devotional religious exercise conducted progressively at each STATION OF THE CROSS. **2** the fourteen stations of the cross.

**way-out** *adj. colloq.* **1** unusual; eccentric. **2** progressive; avant-garde (*can't stand this way-out art*).

**-ways** *suffix* forming adjectives and adverbs of direction or manner (*sideways*).

**ways and means** *n.pl.* **1** methods of achieving something. **2** methods of raising government revenue.

**wayside** *n.* **1** side of a road. **2** land at the side of a road.

**wayward** *adj.* **1** childishly self-willed or perverse (*a wayward child; wayward behaviour*). **2** capricious (*a wayward whim*). **3** unaccountable or freakish (*a wayward wind*). □ **waywardness** *n.* [from AWAY, -WARD]

**Wb** *abbr.* weber(s).

**WC** *abbr.* (also **wc**) water-closet.

**we** /wee, wuh/ *pron.* (*obj.* **us**; *poss.* **our**, **ours**) **1** *pl.* of I[2], denoting the speaker and one or more other persons associated with him or her. **2** used by a royal person in a proclamation etc. or by an editor etc. in a formal context (*Queen Victoria is reputed to have been addicted to saying 'We are not amused'*). **3** people in general, rather than the speaker and another (or others) in particular (*in ordinary life we use words very loosely*). **4** *colloq.* = I[2] (*give us a chance — I'm doing the best I can*). **5** *colloq.* (often implying condescension) (*and how are we feeling today, Mrs Smith?*). [Old English]

**weak** *adj.* **1** deficient in strength, power, or number; fragile (*weak link in the chain*). **2** deficient in vigour; sickly; feeble (*weak health; a weak imagination*). **3 a** deficient in resolution; easily led (*a weak character*). **b** (of an action etc.) indicating a lack of resolution (*a weak surrender*). **c** (of a person's features etc.) indicating weakness of character or intention (*a weak chin; a weak smile*). **4** unconvincing or logically deficient (*a weak argument*). **5** (of a mixed liquid) watery, dilute (*weak tea*). **6** (of a syllable etc.) unstressed. **7** *Gram.* (of a verb) forming inflections by the addition of a suffix to the stem, as in *starve, starved* (opp. STRONG *adj.* 13). □ **weakish** *adj.* [Old Norse]

**weaken** *v.* make or become weak or weaker.

**weakie** *n.* (also **weaky**) *colloq.* **1** = WEAKLING. **2** coward.

**weak-kneed** *adj. colloq.* lacking resolution or moral courage.

**weakling** *n.* feeble person or animal.

**weakly** — *adv.* in a weak manner. — *adj.* (**-ier**, **-iest**) sickly, not robust.

**weak-minded** *adj.* **1** mentally deficient. **2** lacking in resolution or moral courage.

**weak moment** *n.* time when one is unusually compliant or susceptible to temptation etc.

**weakness** *n.* **1** state or condition of being weak; defect. **2** weak point. **3** (foll. by *for*) self-indulgent liking (*weakness for chocolate*).

**weak point** *n.* (also **weak spot**) **1** place where defences are assailable. **2** flaw in an argument or character or in resistance to temptation.

**weal**[1] /weel/ — *n.* ridge raised on the flesh by a stroke of a rod or whip. — *v.* mark with a weal. [var. of WALE]

**weal**[2] /weel/ *n. literary* welfare. [Old English]

**wealth** /welth/ *n.* **1** riches; abundant possessions. **2** state of being rich. **3** (foll. by *of*) abundance or profusion (*a wealth of new material*). [Old English]

**wealthy** *adj.* (**-ier**, **-iest**) having an abundance, esp. of money.

**wean** /ween/ *v.* **1** accustom (an infant or other young mammal) to food other than (esp. its mother's) milk. **2** (often foll. by *from, away from*) disengage (from a habit etc.) by enforced discontinuance (*I'm being weaned from smoking*). [Old English, = accustom]

**weaner** *n.* animal, usu. a lamb or calf, weaned during the current year.

**weapon** /wep-uhn/ *n.* **1** thing designed, used, or usable for inflicting bodily harm (e.g. a gun, a guided missile, a stick). **2** means employed for trying to gain the advantage in a conflict etc. (*irony is a double-edged weapon; his tears were a devastating weapon*). □ **weaponed** *adj.* (also in *comb.*). **weaponless** *adj.* [Old English]

**weaponry** *n.* weapons collectively.

**wear** /wair/ — *v.* (*past* **wore**; *past part.* **worn**) **1** have on one's person as clothing or an ornament etc. (*he's wearing shorts; he wears an earring*). **2** be dressed habitually in (*they wear black*). **3** exhibit or present (a facial expression or appearance) (*she wore a frown; the day wore a different aspect*). **4** *colloq.* (usu. with *neg.*) tolerate, accept (*they won't wear that excuse*). **5** (often foll. by *away, down*) **a** injure the surface of, or partly obliterate or alter, by rubbing, stress, or use (*rocks worn down to weird shapes by time and weather*). **b** undergo such injury or change (*the soles of my shoes wear away too quickly for my liking*). **6** make (a hole etc.) by constant rubbing or dripping etc. **7** (often foll. by *out*) exhaust; tire or be tired (*the children have worn me out; I'm utterly worn*). **8** (foll. by *down*) overcome by persistence (*wore down their resistance with a relentless flow of talk*). **9** remain for a specified time in working order or a presentable state; last long (*this upholstery fabric is tough — it will wear for ever*). **10** (foll. by *well, badly,* etc.) endure continued use or life (*a colour that wears well and does not fade*). **11** (of time) pass, esp. tediously (*the day wore on*). **12** (of a ship) fly (a flag). — *n.* **1** act of wearing or state of being worn (*suitable for informal wear*). **2** things worn; fashionable or suitable clothing (*sportswear; footwear*). **3** (in full **wear and tear**) damage from continuous use. **4** capacity for resisting wear and tear (*still a great deal of wear left in it*). □ **wear one's heart**

**on one's sleeve** show one's feelings openly. **wear off** lose effectiveness or intensity (*my headache's beginning to wear off*). **wear out 1** use or be used until useless. **2** tire or be tired out (*the mental effort wore him out*). **wear thin** (of patience, excuses, etc.) begin to fail. □ **wearer** *n*. [Old English]

**wearisome** /weer-ree-suhm/ *adj.* tedious; tiring by monotony or length.

**weary** /weer-ree/ — *adj.* (**-ier, -iest**) **1** very tired after exertion or endurance. **2** (foll. by *of*) no longer interested in; tired of (*weary of your constant bickering*). **3** tiring, tedious (*a weary wait for the bus*). — *v.* (**-ies, -ied**) make or grow weary (*the walk wearied her*; *I weary of your endless complaining*). □ **wearily** *adv.* **weariness** *n.* [Old English]

**weasel** /wee-zuhl/ *n.* small flesh-eating mammal of Europe etc., related to the stoat and ferret. □ **weasel out** (often foll. by *on, of*) default on an obligation, commitment, etc. (*he weaselled out; he weaselled out on her; weaselled out of his promise*). [Old English]

**weather** /weth-uh/ — *n.* **1** state of the atmosphere at a place and time as regards heat, cloudiness, dryness, sunshine, wind, and rain, etc. **2** (*attrib.*) *Naut.* windward (*on the weather side*). — *v.* **1** expose to or affect by atmospheric changes, esp. deliberately to dry, season, etc. (*weathered timber*). **2 a** (usu. in *passive*) discolour or partly disintegrate (rock or stones) by exposure to air. **b** be discoloured or worn in this way (*the nose of the statue has weathered away*). **3 a** come safely through (a storm) (*will we weather this tempest?*). **b** survive (a difficult period etc.) (*trying to weather the trauma of divorce*). □ **keep a weather eye open** be watchful. **make heavy weather of** *colloq.* exaggerate the difficulty presented by (a problem, course of action, etc.). **under the weather** *colloq.* indisposed; out of sorts. [Old English]

**weather-beaten** *adj.* affected by exposure to the weather (*a weather-beaten face*).

**weatherboard** — *n.* **1** each of a series of overlapping horizontal boards on a wall. **2** weatherboarded building, usu. a dwelling. — *adj.* (also **weatherboarded**) (of a building) having external walls with overlapping horizontal boards. — *v.* clad (external walls) with weatherboards. □ **weatherboarding** *n.* (in sense 1 of *n.*).

**weathercock** *n.* **1** weather-vane in the form of a cock. **2** inconstant person.

**weathering** *n.* **1** action of the weather on materials etc. exposed to it. **2** exposure to

adverse weather conditions (see WEATHER *v.* 1).

**weatherproof** *adj.* resistant to the effects of bad weather, esp. rain.

**weather-vane** *n.* **1** revolving pointer on a church spire etc. to show the direction of the wind. **2** inconstant person.

**weave**[1] — *v.* (**-ving**; *past* **wove**; *past part.* **woven** or **wove**) **1 a** form (fabric) by interlacing long threads in two directions. **b** form (thread) into fabric in this way (*wove the yarn into a skirt-length*). **2 a** make fabric in this way (*he knows how to weave*). **b** work at a loom. **3 a** (foll. by *into*) make (facts etc.) into a story or connected whole (*wove the incidents into his novel*). **b** make (a story) in this way (*wove an intricate plot*). — *n.* style of weaving (*plain weave*). [Old English]

**weave**[2] *v.* (**-ving**) move repeatedly from side to side; take an intricate course to avoid obstructions (*weaving in and out of the traffic*). □ **get weaving** *colloq.* begin action; hurry. [Old Norse: related to WAVE]

**weaver** *n.* person who weaves fabric.

**web** *n.* **1 a** woven fabric. **b** amount woven in one piece. **2** complex series (*web of lies*; *web of intrigue*). **3** cobweb, gossamer, or a similar product of a spinning creature. **4** membrane between the toes of a swimming animal or bird. □ **webbed** *adj.* [Old English]

**webbing** *n.* strong narrow closely woven fabric used for supporting upholstery, for belts, etc.

**weber** /vay-buh/ *n.* the SI unit of magnetic flux. [*Weber*, name of a physicist]

**web-footed** *adj.* having the toes connected by webs.

**wed** *v.* (**-dd-**; *past* and *past part.* **wedded** or **wed**) **1** usu. *formal* or *literary* marry. **2** unite (*wed efficiency to economy*). **3** (as **wedded** *adj.*) of or in marriage (*wedded bliss*). **4** (as **wedded** *adj.*) (foll. by *to*) obstinately attached or devoted to (a pursuit etc.) (*wedded to his work*). [Old English, = pledge]

**we'd** /weed/ *contr.* **1** we had. **2** we should; we would.

**wedding** /wed-ing/ *n.* marriage ceremony. [Old English: related to WED]

**wedding breakfast** *n.* meal etc. between a wedding and departure for the honeymoon.

**wedding bush** *n.* rounded shrub of NSW, Queensland, Tasmania, and Victoria, bearing profuse snow-white flowers like those traditionally associated with weddings.

**wedge** — *n.* **1** piece of tapering wood or metal etc. driven between two objects or parts to secure or separate them. **2** anything resembling a wedge (*a wedge of cheese*). **3** anything causing division, separation, etc. (of persons) (*the issue of ordaining women drove a wedge into the faithful*). **4** golf club with a wedge-shaped head. — *v.* (**-ging**) **1** secure or fasten with a wedge (*wedged the door open*). **2** force open or apart with a wedge. **3** (foll. by *in*, *into*) pack or thrust (a thing or oneself) tightly in or into (*had somehow got his head wedged in between the railings*). □ **thin end of the wedge** *colloq.* thing of little importance in itself, but likely to lead to more serious developments. □ **wedgelike** *adj.* [Old English]

**wedgebill** *n.* either of two conspicuously-crested brown and grey songbirds of drier eastern Australia (*chirruping wedgebill*) and drier western Australia (*chiming wedgebill*).

**wedge-tailed eagle** *n.* large eagle, widespread in Australia, having dark brown plumage and a wedge-shaped tail.

**wedgie** *n.* = WEDGE-TAILED EAGLE.

**wedlock** /wed-lok/ *n.* the married state. □ **born in** (or **out of**) **wedlock** born of married (or unmarried) parents. [Old English; = marriage vow]

**Wednesday** /wenz-day/ — *n.* day of the week following Tuesday. — *adv. colloq.* **1** on Wednesday. **2** (**Wednesdays**) on Wednesdays; each Wednesday. [Old English]

**wee**[1] *adj.* (**weer** /wee-uh/ ) little, tiny. [Old English]

**wee**[2] *n. & v. colloq.* = WEE-WEE.

**weebill** /wee-bil/ *n.* olive-brown to yellowish bird widespread in mainland Australia, Australia's smallest bird.

**weed** — *n.* **1** wild (or any) plant growing where it is not wanted. **2** thin weak-looking person or horse. **3** (prec. by *the*) *colloq.* **a** marijuana. **b** tobacco. — *v.* **1** clear (an area) of weeds (*weeding the garden*). **2** (often foll. by *out*) **a** sort out and remove (inferior or unwanted parts etc.) (*these files need weeding; weed out the books you will never read again*). **b** rid (a quantity or company) of unwanted members etc. (*weed the herd by at least a quarter; weed out all but the fittest from the squad*). **3** cut off or uproot weeds (*he's busy weeding*). [Old English]

**weeds** /weedz/ *n.pl.* (in full **widow's weeds**) *archaic* deep mourning worn by a widow. [Old English; = garment]

**weedy** *adj.* (**-ier**, **-iest**) **1** (esp. of a person) weak, feeble. **2** having many weeds.

**weei** /wee-uy/ *n.* (also **weeai**, **weeay**, **wei**) an Aboriginal boy. [Aranda *aweye* young male person or animal]

**wee juggler** /wee jug-luh/ *n.* = MAJOR MITCHELL COCKATOO. [Wiradhuri *wijagala*]

**week** *n.* **1** period of seven days reckoned usu. from midnight on Saturday. **2** any period of seven days. **3** the six days between Sundays. **4 a** the five days Monday to Friday. **b** time spent working in this period (*35-hour week; three-day week*). **5** (in *pl.*) a long time (*did it weeks ago*). **6** (prec. by a specified day) a week after (that day) (*Tuesday week; tomorrow week*). [Old English]

**weekday** *n.* day other than Saturday and Sunday (often *attrib.*: *weekday afternoons*).

**weekend** — *n.* **1** Sunday and Saturday or part of Saturday. **2** this period extended slightly esp. for a holiday or visit etc. (*going away for the weekend*) (also *attrib.*: *weekend activities*). — *v.* spend a weekend (*decided to weekend at Hall's Gap*).

**weekender** *n.* a house used only for holidaying in or at weekends.

**weekly** — *adj.* done, produced, or occurring once a week. — *adv.* once a week. — *n.* (*pl.* **-ies**) weekly newspaper or periodical.

**weelo** /wee-loh/ *n.* (also **curlew**, **stone curlew**, **stone plover**) either of two ground-nesting birds formerly widespread in Australia but no longer found in closely settled areas. [Nhanta *wirlu*]

**weeny** /wee-nee/ *adj.* (**-ier**, **-iest**) *colloq.* tiny. [from WEE[1]]

**weep** — *v.* (*past* and *past part.* **wept**) **1** shed tears. **2 a** (often foll. by *for*) bewail, lament over (*wept for his lost innocence*). **b** utter or express with tears (*'Don't go,' he wept; wept her thanks*). **3 a** be covered with or send forth drops (*water weeping from the faulty joint*). **b** come or send forth in drops; exude liquid (*if you prune the vine now, it will weep badly; grass-tree weeping a yellowish gum; a weeping sore*). **4** (as **weeping** *adj.*) (of a tree etc.) having drooping branches (*weeping gum; weeping myall; weeping Polly grass*). — *n.* spell of weeping (*had a good weep and a cup of tea*). [Old English]

**weepie** *n. colloq.* sentimental or emotional film, play, etc.

**weeping fig** *n.* large, spreading tree (*Ficus benjamina*) of northern Queensland and elsewhere, cultivated as an ornamental.

**weepy** *adj.* (**-ier**, **-iest**) *colloq.* inclined to weep; tearful.

**weero** /wee-roh/ *n.* = COCKATIEL. [Yindjibarndi *wiru*]

**weet-weet** /weet-weet/ n. Aboriginal throwing weapon and toy, consisting of a flexible handle with a wooden or bone knob at the end. [Wuywurung *wij-wij*]

**weevil** /wee-vuhl/ n. destructive beetle feeding esp. on grain. [Low German]

**wee-wee** /wee-wee/ (also **wee**) colloq. (esp. in use by or to small children) — n. **1** act or instance of urinating. **2** urine. — v. (-**wees**, -**weed**) urinate. [origin unknown]

**weft** n. **1** threads woven across a warp to make fabric. **2** yarn for these. **3** thing woven. [Old English: related to WEAVE[1]]

**weigh** /way/ v. **1** find the weight of. **2** balance in the hands to guess or as if to guess the weight of. **3** (often foll. by *out*) take a definite weight of (a substance); measure out (a specified weight) (*weigh out the flour*; *weigh out 300 grams*). **4 a** estimate the relative value, importance, or desirability of (*weighed the consequences*; *weigh the merits of the candidates*). **b** (foll. by *with, against*) compare (one consideration with another) (*weighed the extent of his support against that of his opponent*). **5** be equal to (a specified weight) (*weighs 3 kilos*; *weighs very little*). **6 a** have (esp. a specified) importance; exert an influence (*unemployment will weigh heavily in the minds of the voters*). **b** (foll. by *with*) be regarded as important by (*the point that weighs with me*). **7** (often foll. by *on*) be heavy or burdensome (to); be depressing (to) (*it weighs heavily on his mind*). □ **weigh anchor** take the anchor up, begin the (ship's) voyage. **weigh down 1** bring or keep down by exerting weight. **2** be oppressive to (*weighed down with worries*). **weigh in 1** (of a boxer before a contest, or a jockey after a race) be weighed. **2** weigh (an air passenger's luggage) before departure. **3** (often foll. by *with*) bring one's influence etc. to bear, make a strong contribution (to a discussion etc.) (*she weighed in to stop the argument before they came to blows*; *he weighed in with a handy 72 runs*). **weigh into** colloq. attack (physically or verbally) (*weighed into his opponents*). **weigh out** (of a jockey) be weighed before a race. **weigh up** colloq. form an estimate of; consider carefully (*weighed up his chances*). **weigh one's words** carefully choose the way one expresses something. [Old English, = carry]

**weighbridge** n. weighing machine for vehicles.

**weigh-in** n. weighing of a boxer before a fight.

**weight** /wayt/ — n. **1** force experienced by a body as a result of the earth's gravitation. **2** heaviness of a body regarded as a property of it (*is twice your weight*; *kept in position by its weight*). **3 a** quantitative expression of a body's weight (*has a weight of 3 kilos*). **b** scale of such weights (*troy weight*). **4** body of a known weight for use in weighing or weight training (*100 gram weight*). **5** heavy body, esp. as used in a mechanism etc. (*a clock worked by weights*). **6** load or burden (*a weight off my mind*). **7 a** influence, importance (*carried weight with the public*). **b** preponderance (*the weight of evidence was against them*). **8** Athletics = SHOT[1] 7. — v. **1 a** attach a weight to. **b** hold down with a weight. **2** (foll. by *with*) impede or burden (*weighted with cares*). □ **pull one's weight** do one's fair share (of work etc.). **throw one's weight about** (or **around**) be unpleasantly self-assertive. **worth one's weight in gold** very useful or helpful. [Old English]

**weighting** n. extra allowance paid in special cases.

**weightless** adj. (of a body, esp. in an orbiting spacecraft etc.) not apparently acted on by gravity. □ **weightlessness** n.

**weightlifting** n. sport of lifting heavy weights. □ **weightlifter** n.

**weight training** n. physical training using weights.

**weighty** adj. (-**ier**, -**iest**) **1** heavy. **2** momentous, important. **3** (of utterances etc.) deserving consideration; serious. **4** influential, authoritative. □ **weightily** adv. **weightiness** n.

**weir** /weer/ n. dam across a river to raise the level of water upstream or regulate its flow. [Old English]

**weird** adj. **1** uncanny, supernatural. **2** colloq. strange, queer, incomprehensible (*weird hair-do*; *weird behaviour*). □ **weirdly** adv. **weirdness** n. [Old English *wyrd* destiny]

**weirdo** /weer-doh/ n. (pl. -**s**) colloq. odd or eccentric person.

**welch** var. of WELSH.

**welcome** /wel-kuhm/ — n. act or instance of greeting or receiving gladly; kind or glad reception (*gave them a warm welcome*). — int. expressing such a greeting (*welcome home!*). — v. (-**ming**) receive with a welcome (*welcomed them home*; *would welcome the opportunity*). — adj. **1** that one receives with pleasure (*welcome guest*; *welcome news*; *welcome swallow*). **2** (foll. by *to*, or *to* + infin.) cordially allowed or invited (*you are welcome to use my car*). □ **make welcome** receive hospitably. **outstay one's**

**welcome** stay too long as a visitor etc. **you are welcome** there is no need for thanks. □ **welcomer** n. **welcoming** adj. **welcomingly** adv. [Old English]

**welcome swallow** n. swallow which migrates to Australia and, recently, New Zealand.

**weld** — v. **1 a** hammer or press (pieces of iron or other metal usu. heated but not melted) into one piece. **b** join by fusion with an electric arc etc. **c** form by welding into some article. **2** fashion (arguments, members of a group, etc.) into an effectual or homogeneous whole. — n. welded joint. □ **weldable** adj. **welder** n. [alteration of WELL², probably influenced by the form welled]

**welfare** /wel-fair/ n. **1** well-being, happiness; health and prosperity (of a person or community etc.). **2** financial support given by the government to those in need. [from WELL¹, FARE]

**welfare state** n. **1** system whereby the nation undertakes to protect the health and well-being of its citizens, esp. those in financial or social need, by means of grants, pensions, etc. **2** country practising this system.

**welfare work** n. organised effort for the welfare of the poor, the sick, etc., in the community.

**welkin** n. poet. sky. [Old English, = cloud]

**well¹** — adv. (**better**, **best**) **1** in a satisfactory way (works well). **2** in the right way (you did well to tell me). **3** with some distinction (plays the piano well). **4** in a kind way (treated me well). **5** thoroughly, carefully (polish it well; think well before you act). **6** with heartiness or approval; favourably (speak well of; the book was well reviewed). **7** probably, reasonably (you may well be right; I couldn't well refuse). **8** to a considerable extent (is well over forty). **9** successfully; fortunately (it turned out well). **10** luckily; opportunely (well met!). **11** with a fortunate outcome (were well rid of them). **12** profitably (did well for themselves). **13** comfortably; liberally (we live well here; the job pays well). — adj. (**better**, **best**) **1** (usu. predic.) in good health (are you well?; is not a well person). **2** (predic.) **a** in a satisfactory state or position (all is well). **b** advisable (it would be well to enquire). — int. expressing surprise, resignation, etc., or continuation of talk after a pause (well, I suppose so; well, who was it?). □ **as well** see AS. **as well as** see AS. **leave** (or **let**) **well alone** avoid needless change or disturbance. **well and truly** decisively, completely. **well done!** expressing praise for something done. **well worth** certainly worth. [Old English]

**well²** — n. **1** shaft sunk into the ground to obtain water, oil, etc. **2** enclosed space like a well-shaft, e.g. in the middle of a building for stairs or a lift, or for light or ventilation. **3** (foll. by of) a source, esp. a plentiful one (she's a well of information). — v. (often foll. by out, up) spring as from a fountain; flow copiously (his eyes welled with tears; tears welled up in his eyes). [Old English]

**we'll** /weel/ contr. we shall; we will.

**well-** (in comb.) = WELL¹ adv.

■ **Usage** A hyphen is normally used in combinations of well- when used attributively, but not when used predicatively (e.g. a well-adjusted person but he is well adjusted).

**well-adjusted** adj. **1** mentally and emotionally stable. **2** in a good state of adjustment.

**well-advised** adj. (usu. foll. by to + infin.) prudent (you'd be well-advised to wait).

**well-appointed** adj. (of a home, motel, etc.), having all the necessary equipment, furnishings, comforts, etc.

**well-balanced** adj. **1** sane, sensible. **2** equally matched.

**well-being** n. state of being well, contented, healthy, etc.

**well-bred** adj. having or showing good breeding or manners.

**well-built** adj. (of a person) big, strong, and well-proportioned.

**well-connected** adj. associated with influential relatives or persons in positions of power etc.

**well-disposed** adj. (often foll. by towards) friendly or sympathetic.

**well-endowed** adj. well provided with talent etc.

**well-founded** adj. (of suspicions etc.) based on good evidence.

**well-grounded** adj. **1** = WELL-FOUNDED. **2** having a good training in or knowledge of the groundwork of a subject.

**well-heeled** adj. colloq. wealthy.

**wellies** /wel-eez/ n.pl. colloq. wellingtons. [abbreviation]

**well-in** adj. colloq. **1** affluent, well-to-do. **2** = WELL-CONNECTED.

**well-informed** adj. **1** having much knowledge or information about a subject. **2** having a very good general knowledge.

**wellington** /wel-ing-tuhn/ n. (in full **wellington boot**) waterproof boot usu. reaching the knee. [Duke of Wellington]

**well-meaning** adj. (also **well-meant**) having or showing good intentions (but ineffective or unwise) (*made a well-meaning attempt to reconcile husband and wife and made matters worse*).

**wellnigh** *adv.* almost (*wellnigh impossible*).

**well off** *adj.* (also **well-off**) **1** having plenty of money. **2** in a fortunate situation or favourable circumstances.

**well-oiled** *adj. colloq.* very drunk.

**well-preserved** *adj.* **1** in good condition. **2** (of an elderly person) showing little sign of age, looking much younger than his or her years.

**well-read** *adj.* **1** knowledgable through much reading. **2** learned in a subject (*well-read in Aboriginal mythology*).

**well-rounded** *adj.* **1** complete and symmetrical. **2** (of a phrase etc.) complete and well expressed. **3** (of a person) having or showing a fully developed personality, ability, etc.

**well-spoken** *adj.* articulate or refined in speech.

**wellspring** *n.* **1** source of a stream etc., fountainhead. **2** source of abundant supply (*he's a wellspring of wisdom*).

**well-to-do** *adj.* prosperous.

**well-worn** *adj.* **1** much worn by use. **2** (of a phrase etc.) trite.

**Welsh** — *adj.* of or relating to Wales or its people or language. — *n.* **1** the Celtic language of Wales. **2** (prec. by *the*; treated as *pl.*) the people of Wales. [Old English, ultimately from Latin *Volcae*, name of a Celtic people]

**welsh** *v.* (also **welch**) **1** (of a loser of a bet, esp. a bookmaker) decamp without paying. **2** evade an obligation. **3** (foll. by *on*) **a** fail to carry out a promise to (a person). **b** fail to honour (an obligation). **4** (foll. by *on*) inform on, tell tales on; betray (a mate etc.). □ **welsher** *n.* (also **welcher**). [origin unknown]

**Welsh rabbit** *n.* (also, by folk etymology, **Welsh rarebit**) dish of melted cheese etc. on toast.

**welt** — *n.* **1** leather rim sewn round the edge of a shoe-upper for the sole to be attached to. **2** = WEAL¹. **3** ribbed or reinforced border of a garment. **4** heavy blow. — *v.* **1** provide with a welt. **2** raise weals on; thrash. [origin unknown]

**welter**¹ — *v.* **1** roll, wallow; be washed about (*the little vessel weltering in the wild waves*). **2** (foll. by *in*) lie prostrate or be soaked in (*the corpse weltering in its own blood*). — *n.* **1** general confusion, upheaval, turmoil (*the welter of politics in Victoria*). **2** rolling, tossing, tumbling (of the sea or waves) (*clinging to a plank in the welter of the sea*). **3** (foll. by *of*) dis-

orderly mixture or contrast (of things, beliefs, etc.) (*a welter of miscellaneous exhibits; a welter of inconsistencies*). [Low German or Dutch]

**welter**² *n.* **1** heavy rider or boxer. **2** horse race in which the minimum weight for riders is 51 kg. □ **make a welter of it** *colloq.* engage in (an activity etc.) to excess (*partying every night — you're making a welter of it*). [origin unknown]

**welterweight** *n.* **1** weight in certain sports intermediate between lightweight and middleweight, in the amateur boxing scale 63.5–67 kg. **2** sportsman of this weight.

**Wemba-wemba** / wem-bu-ˌwem-bu/ *n.* generic term (though a dialect in itself) for the dialects of an Aboriginal language spoken by peoples in Western Victoria and an adjoining portion of NSW: from Bendigo and Ballarat in the east to the SA border in the west, from Balranald and Mildura in the north to Hamilton and Chatsworth in the south: now extinct.

**wen** *n.* benign tumour on the skin, esp. on the scalp. [Old English]

**wench** *n. joc.* girl or young woman. [abbreviation of *wenchel*, from Old English, = child]

**wend** *v.* □ **wend one's way** make one's way, go. [Old English, = turn]

**went** *past* of GO.

**wept** *past* of WEEP.

**were** *2nd sing. past, pl. past,* and *past subjunctive* of BE.

**we're** /weer/ *contr.* we are.

**weren't** /wernt/ *contr.* were not.

**werewolf** /weer-wuulf, wair-/ *n.* (also **werwolf** /wer-wuulf/) (*pl.* **-wolves**) mythical being who at times changes from a person to a wolf. [Old English, = man-wolf]

**west** — *n.* **1 a** point of the horizon where the sun sets at the equinoxes. **b** compass point corresponding to this. **c** direction in which this lies. **2** (usu. **the West**) **a** European civilisation. **b** States of western Europe and N. America. **c** western part of a country, State, town, etc. — *adj.* **1** towards, at, near, or facing the west. **2** coming from the west (*west wind*). — *adv.* **1** towards, at, or near the west. **2** (foll. by *of*) further west than. □ **go west** *colloq.* be killed or destroyed etc. **to the west** (often followed by *of*) in a westerly direction. [Old English]

**westbound** *adj.* travelling or leading westwards.

**westering** *adj.* (of the sun) nearing the west.

**westerly** — *adj. & adv.* **1** in a western position or direction. **2** (of a wind) blowing from the west. — *n.* (*pl.* **-ies**) such a wind.

**western** — *adj.* **1** of or in the west. **2** used as a distinguishing epithet in the names of Australian fauna (*western black cockatoo*; *western brown snake*; *western rosella*; *western whipbird*; etc.). — *n.* film or novel about cowboys in western North America. □ **westernmost** *adj.*

**Western Australian** — *adj.* of or pertaining to the State of Western Australia. — *n.* person native to or resident in the State of Western Australia.

**Western Australian Christmas tree** see NUYTSIA.

**western bristlebird** *n.* rare, ground-dwelling, brownish bird of south-western WA.

**Western Church** *n.* major part of Christendom continuing to derive its authority, doctrine, and ritual from the popes in Rome (cf. EASTERN CHURCH).

**Western Desert language** *n.* name for a single Aboriginal language (with many dialects) spoken over about one and a quarter million square kilometres of central and western Australia (about one sixth of the total area of Australia) including large areas of WA, SA, and the NT.

**westerner** *n.* native or inhabitant of the west.

**western grey** *n.* (in full **western grey kangaroo**) kangaroo of south-western and central southern Australia (distinguished as a species from the eastern grey in 1966).

**Western hemisphere** *n.* that half of the earth containing the Americas.

**westernise** *v.* (also **-ize**) (**-sing** or **-zing**) influence with, or convert to, the ideas and customs etc. of the West.

**western myall** *n.* tall wattle of SA and WA, bearing slender drooping silvery phyllodes and masses of bright yellow ball-flowers in spring (see also MYALL[2]).

**westie** /wes-tee/ *colloq. derog.* — *n.* **1** resident of the western suburbs of Sydney. **2** person who is regarded as uncultured, lacking style, etc. — *adj.* of, pertaining to, or belonging to a westie.

**West Indian** *n.* **1** native or national of the West Indies. **2** person of West Indian descent.

**west-north-west** *n.* point or direction midway between west and north-west.

**Westralia** /wes-**tray**-lyuh/ *n. colloq.* Western Australia. [abbreviation]

**Westralian** *colloq.* — *adj.* of or pertaining to Western Australia. — *n.* person native to or resident in Western Australia.

**westringia** /wes-**trin**-jee-uh/ *n.* any of over 20 species of shrub of the genus *Westringia* endemic to temperate Australia, having white, blue, or bluey-mauve flowers and whorled leaves. [J.P. *Westring* Swedish physician]

**west-south-west** *n.* point or direction midway between west and south-west.

**westward** /west-wuhd/ — *adj. & adv.* (also **westwards**) towards the west. — *n.* westward direction or region.

**wet** — *adj.* (**wetter**, **wettest**) **1** soaked or covered with water or other liquid. **2** (of the weather etc.) rainy. **3** (of paint etc.) not yet dried. **4** (of sheep) having a fleece which is too damp to be shorn. **5** *colloq.* feeble, inept; lacking spunk or zest (*how wet can a guy get*; *the wettest party I've ever been to*). **6** (of a member of a political party) having liberal tendencies, esp. as regarded by the right wing (opp. DRY *adj.* 11). — *v.* (**-tt-**; *past* and *past part.* **wet** or **wetted**) **1** make wet. **2 a** urinate in or on (*wet the bed*). **b** *refl.* urinate involuntarily. — *n.* **1** moisture; liquid that wets something (*floor covered in wet and slime*). **2 a** rainy weather. **b** (prec. by *the*) = WET SEASON (opp. the DRY). **3** *colloq.* feeble and inept person; person lacking spunk etc. **4** political conservative with liberal tendencies, esp. as regarded by the right wing (opp. DRY *n.* 2). □ **get wet** *colloq.* become extremely irritable, exasperated, etc. **wet behind the ears** *colloq.* immature, inexperienced. **wet through** (or **to the skin**) with one's clothes soaked. **wet one's whistle** *colloq.* have a drink. □ **wetly** *adv.* **wetness** *n.* **wettable** *adj.* **wetting** *n.* **wettish** *adj.* [Old English]

**wet blanket** *n. colloq.* gloomy person who dampens the enjoyment of others.

**wet dream** *n.* erotic dream with the involuntary ejaculation of semen.

**wether** /we*th*-uh/ *n.* castrated ram. [Old English]

**wetlands** *n.pl.* swamps and other damp areas of land.

**wet-nurse** — *n.* woman employed to suckle another's child. — *v.* **1** act as a wet-nurse to. **2** *colloq.* treat as if helpless.

**wet season** *n.* period of substantial rainfall, rainy season (esp. in central and northern Australia) (opp. DRY SEASON).

**wetsuit** *n.* rubber garment worn by skin-divers etc. to keep warm.

**wetting agent** *n.* substance that helps water etc. to penetrate (soils etc.) or adhere to (leaves etc.).

**wet weekend** n. colloq. thing regarded as the epitome of boredom, misery, gloom, or which seems never-ending (his speech dragged on longer than a wet weekend). □ **face as long as a wet weekend** glum, gloomy expression.

**we've** /weev/ contr. we have.

**whack** /wak/ colloq. — v. **1** strike or beat forcefully with a sharp blow. **2** put (whack a few more steaks on the barbie; whack your things down over there). **3** (as **whacked** adj.) **a** tired out. **b** drunk. — n. **1** sharp or resounding blow. **2** share (coming for his whack). □ **have a whack at** attempt. [imitative]

**whacker** /wak-uh/ n. (also **wacker**) colloq. fool; generalised term of abuse. [WACKY]

**whacking** colloq. — adj. very large. — adv. very (a whacking great semi).

**whacko** /wak-oh/ colloq. — int. (also **whacko the diddle oh**) exclamation of delight or enjoyment. — adj. (also **whacko-the-chook**, or **-the-diddle-oh**, or **-the-goose**) absolutely splendid (had a whacko-the-chook time at Surfers').

**whale**[1] — n. (pl. same or **-s**) **1** very large marine mammal with a streamlined body and horizontal tail, and breathing through a blowhole on the head. **2** colloq. = MURRAY COD. — v. (**-ling**) **1** hunt whales. **2** travel the course of a river as a swagman. □ **a whale of a** colloq. an exceedingly good or fine etc. **a whale in the bay** colloq. person with money to spend. [Old English]

**whale**[2] v. colloq. beat, thrash. □ **whale into** colloq. **1** attack (physically or verbally). **2** begin (working, doing, eating, etc.) energetically (whaled into the piles of homework).

**whalebird** n. = PRION.

**whalebone** n. elastic horny substance in the upper jaw of some whales, used as a stiffening material in garments etc.

**whalebone tree** n. (also **waddywood**) medium-sized tree of rainforests in eastern NSW and eastern Queensland, having very springy whalebone-like branches and yielding a hard yellowish timber used by Aborigines for making waddies (see WADDY[1]) and later by whites for making tool-handles etc.

**whaler** n. **1** whaling ship or seaman. **2** any of several sharks of Australian waters (probably so called because they were seen near whales), esp. the large bronze whaler (blue whaler; bronze whaler; Swan River whaler). **3** swagman whose route follows the course of a river which provides food in the form of whales

(see WHALE[1] n. 2) (Darling whaler; Murray whaler; Murrumbidgee whaler).

**wham** colloq. — int. expressing forcible impact. — n. forceful hit, stroke, etc. (give it a wham). — v. (often foll. by into) hit with forcible impact (my car whammed into the tree). [imitative]

**whammy** n. colloq. evil or unlucky influence; blow; stroke of extreme misfortune (the crash was a real whammy to them both).

**wharf** /wawf/ — n. (pl. **wharves** /wawvz/ or **-s**) quayside area to which a ship may be moored to load and unload. — v. **1** moor (a ship) at a wharf. **2** store (goods) on a wharf. [Old English]

**wharfage** n. **1** accommodation at a wharf. **2** fee for this.

**wharfie** n. colloq. waterside worker; wharf-labourer.

**what** /wot/ — interrog. adj. **1** asking for a choice from an indefinite number or for a statement of amount, number, or kind (what books have you read?; what news have you?). **2** colloq. = WHICH interrog. adj. (what book have you chosen?). — adj. (usu. in exclam.) how great or remarkable (what luck!). — rel. adj. the or any . . . that (will give you what help I can). — pron. (corresponding to the functions of the adj.) **1** what thing or things? (what is your name?; I don't know what you mean). **2** (asking for a remark to be repeated) = what did you say? **3** asking for confirmation of something (you did what?; what, you really mean it?). **4** how much (what you must have suffered!). **5** (as rel. pron.) that or those which; a or the or any thing which (what followed was worse; tell me what you think). — adv. to what extent (what does it matter?). □ **so what?** see SO[1]. **what about** what is the news or position or your opinion of (what about the wife — was she injured as well?; what about a game of tennis?). **what-d'you-call-it** (or **what's-it** etc.) colloq. substitute for a name not recalled or not known (try using the what's-it). **what ever** what at all or in any way (what ever do you mean?) (see also WHATEVER). **what for** colloq. **1** for what reason? **2** severe reprimand (esp. give a person what for). **what have you** (prec. by or or and) colloq. anything else similar (get all the magazines, papers, and what have you, into this crate). **what is more** moreover. **what next?** colloq. what more absurd, shocking, or surprising thing is possible? **what of?** what is the news concerning? **what of it?** why should that be considered significant? **what's-his** (or **-her** or **-its**) **-name** colloq. substitute for a name not recalled (*saw what's-his-name the other day*). **what's what** *colloq.* **1** what is useful or important etc. **2** the true state of affairs (*he knows what's what*). **what with** *colloq.* because of (usu. several things) (*what with the rain and the car playing up, I haven't been able to do the shopping*). [Old English]

**whatever** /wot-ev-uh/ *adj. & pron.* **1** = WHAT (in relative uses) with the emphasis on indefiniteness (*lend me whatever you can; whatever money you have*). **2** though anything (*we are safe whatever happens*). **3** (with *neg.* or *interrog.*) at all; of any kind (*there is no doubt whatever*). **4** *colloq.* = *what ever*. □ **or whatever** *colloq.* or anything similar.

**whatnot** /wot-not/ *n.* **1** stand with shelves for small objects. **2 a** *colloq.* indefinite or trivial thing. **b** suchlike things (*he's brought a pav, some sweets, and whatnot*).

**whatsoever** /ˌwot-soh-ev-uh/ *adj. & pron.* = WHATEVER.

**wheat** *n.* **1** cereal plant bearing dense four-sided seed-spikes. **2** its grain, used in making flour etc. [Old English]

**wheat cocky** *n.* wheat farmer.

**wheaten** *adj.* made of wheat.

**wheatgerm** *n.* embryo of the wheat grain, extracted as a source of vitamins.

**wheat lumper** *n.* person employed to load or unload sacks of wheat. □ **wheat lumping** *n.*

**wheatmeal** *n.* flour made from wheat with some of the bran and germ removed.

**wheedle** /wee-duhl/ *v.* (**-ling**) **1** coax by flattery or endearments. **2** (foll. by *out*) get (a thing) out of a person or cheat (a person) out of a thing by wheedling. [origin uncertain]

**wheel** — *n.* **1** circular frame or disc which revolves on an axle and is used for vehicular or other mechanical motion. **2** wheel-like thing (*potter's wheel; steering wheel*). **3** motion as of a wheel, esp. the movement of a line of soldiers with one end as a pivot. □ (in *pl.*) *colloq.* car (*getting my wheels next week*). **5** steering-wheel. **6** = BIG WHEEL 2. — *v.* **1 a** turn on an axis or pivot. **b** swing round in line with one end as a pivot (*the marching squad wheeled right*). **2 a** (often foll. by *about*, *round*) change direction or face another way (*he wheeled round when he heard my footsteps*). **b** cause to do this. **3** push or pull (a wheeled thing, or its load or occupant) (*helped me wheel the trolley in the supermarket*). **4** go in circles or curves (*gulls wheeling in the sky*). □ **at the wheel 1** driving a vehicle. **2** directing a ship. **3** in control of affairs (*in this company she*

*is at the wheel*). **on wheels** (or **oiled wheels**) smoothly (*the project went ahead on oiled wheels*). **silly as a wheel** *colloq.* very silly. **wheel and deal** engage in political or commercial scheming. **wheels within wheels 1** intricate machinery. **2** indirect or secret agencies; intricate behind-the-scenes plots. □ **wheeled** *adj.* (also in *comb.*). [Old English]

**wheelbarrow** *n.* small handcart with one wheel and two shafts for carrying garden loads etc.

**wheelbase** *n.* distance between the axles of a vehicle.

**wheelchair** *n.* chair on wheels for an invalid or disabled person.

**wheel-clamp** see CLAMP *n.* 2.

**-wheeler** *comb. form* vehicle with a specified number of wheels (*three-wheeler*).

**wheeler-dealer** *n.* person who *wheels and deals* (see WHEEL).

**wheelhouse** *n.* steersman's shelter.

**wheelie** *n. colloq.* **1** stunt of riding a bicycle or motor cycle for a short distance with the front wheel off the ground. **2 a** stunt of violently accelerating a car so as to cause the drive wheels to spin. **b** such spinning caused by accelerating sharply round a corner etc.

**wheelspin** *n.* rotation of a vehicle's wheels without traction.

**wheelwright** *n.* person who makes or repairs wooden wheels.

**wheeze** — *v.* (**-zing**) **1** breathe with an audible chesty whistling sound. **2** (often foll. by *out*) utter with this sound. — *n.* **1** sound of wheezing. **2** *colloq.* clever scheme. □ **wheezy** *adj.* (**-ier, -iest**). **wheezily** *adv.* **wheeziness** *n.* [probably from Old Norse, = hiss]

**whelk** *n.* marine mollusc with a spiral shell. [Old English]

**whelm** *v. poet.* **1** engulf, submerge. **2** crush with weight; overwhelm. [Old English]

**whelp** — *n.* **1** young dog; puppy. **2** *archaic* cub. **3** ill-mannered child or youth. — *v.* (also *absol.*) give birth to (a whelp or whelps or (*derog.*) a child). [Old English]

**when** — *interrog. adv.* **1** at what time? **2** on what occasion? **3** how soon? **4** how long ago? — *rel. adv.* (prec. by *time* etc.) at or on which (*there are times when I could cry*). — *conj.* **1** at the or any time that; as soon as (*come when you like; come when ready; when I was your age*). **2** although; considering that (*why stand when you could sit?*). **3** after which; and then; but just then (*was nearly asleep when the bell rang*). — *pron.* what time?; which time (*till when can you stay?; since when it has improved*). — *n.* time, occasion, date (*fixed the where and when*). [Old English]

**whence** *formal — interrog. adv.* from what place? (*whence did they come?*). — *conj.* **1** to the place from which (*return whence you came*). **2** (often prec. by *place* etc.) from which (*the source whence these errors arise*). **3** and thence (*whence it follows that*). [Old English: related to WHEN]

■ **Usage** The use of *from whence* rather than simply *whence* (as in *the place from whence they came*), though common, is generally considered incorrect.

**whenever** /wen-ev-uh/ *conj. & adv.* **1** at whatever time; on whatever occasion (*do it whenever you like*). **2** every time that (*whenever he opens his mouth he puts his foot in it*).

**whensoever** /ˌwen-soh-ev-uh/ *conj. & adv. formal* = WHENEVER.

**where** /wair/ — *interrog. adv.* **1** in or to what place or position? (*where is the milk?*; *where are you going?*). **2** in what direction or respect? (*where does that argument lead?*; *where does it concern us?*). **3** in what book etc.?; from whom? (*where did you read that?*; *where did you hear that?*). **4** in what situation or condition? (*where does that leave us?*). — *rel. adv.* (prec. by *place* etc.) in or to which (*places where they meet*). — *conj.* **1** in or to the or any place, direction, or respect in which (*go where you like*; *that's where you're wrong*; *tick where applicable*). **2** and there (*reached Pimbaacla, where the car broke down*). — *pron.* what place? (*where do you come from?*). — *n.* place; scene of something (see WHEN *n.*). [Old English]

**whereabouts** — *interrog. adv.* /ˌwair-ruh-**bowts**/ approximately where? (*whereabouts are they?*). — *n.* /**wair**-ruh-ˌbowts/ (as *sing.* or *pl.*) person's or thing's location (*his whereabouts are a mystery*).

**whereas** *conj.* **1** in contrast or comparison with the fact that (*Labor did well, whereas the Coalition suffered heavy losses*). **2** (esp. in legal preambles) taking into consideration the fact that.

**whereby** *conj.* by what or which means.

**wherefore** — *adv. archaic* **1** for what reason? **2** for which reason. — *n.* see WHY.

**wherein** *conj. formal* in what or which place or respect.

**whereof** *conj. formal* of what or which.

**whereupon** *conj.* immediately after which.

**wherever** — *adv.* in or to whatever place. — *conj.* in every place that. □ **or wherever**

*colloq.* or in any similar place (*it's in the top drawer — or wherever*).

**wherewithal** /ˈwair-with-ˌawl, -with-/ *n. colloq.* money etc. needed for a purpose (*hasn't the wherewithal to buy new shoes*).

**whet** *v.* (**-tt-**) **1** sharpen (a tool) by grinding. **2** stimulate (the appetite or a desire etc.) (*whetted his greed*). [Old English]

**whether** /**weth**-uh/ *conj.* introducing the first or both of alternative possibilities (*I doubt whether it matters*; *I do not know whether they have arrived or not*). □ **whether or no** whether it is so or not. [Old English]

**whetstone** *n.* tapered stone used with water to sharpen tools.

**whew** /fyoo/ *int.* expressing surprise, consternation, or relief. [imitative]

**whey** /way/ *n.* watery liquid left when milk forms curds. □ **whey-faced** pallid or pale, esp. with fear. [Old English]

**which** — *interrog. adj.* asking for choice from a definite set of alternatives (*which John do you mean?*; *say which book you prefer*). — *rel. adj.* being the one just referred to; and this or these (*ten years, during which time they admitted nothing*; *give warning — which action is within your power — and they will benefit*). — *interrog. pron.* **1** which person or persons? (*which of you is responsible?*). **2** which thing or things? (*say which you prefer*). — *rel. pron.* (poss. **of which**, **whose** /hooz/) **1** which thing or things, usu. introducing a clause not essential for identification (*the house, which is empty, has been damaged*). **2** used in place of *that* after *in* or *that* (*there is the house in which I was born*; *that which you have just seen*). [Old English]

**whichever** *pron. & adj.* **1** any which (*take whichever you like*; *take whichever book you fancy*). **2** no matter which (*whichever one wins, they both get a prize*).

**whiff** — *n.* **1** puff or breath of air, smoke, etc. (*went out for a whiff of air*). **2** slight smell (*caught the whiff of a cigar*). **3** (foll. by *of*) trace of scandal etc. — *v.* blow or puff lightly. [imitative]

**whiffle** /**wif**-uhl/ *v.* (of the wind) blow lightly; shift about (*wind whiffling through the gum-trees*).

**whiffy** *adj. colloq.* (**whiffier**, **whiffiest**) having an unpleasant smell.

**while** — *n.* period of time (*a long while ago*; *waited a while*; *all this while*). — *conj.* **1** during the time that; for as long as; at the same time as (*while I was away, the house was burgled*; *fell asleep while reading*). **2** in spite of the fact that; although; whereas (*while I want to believe it, I cannot*). — *v.* (**-ling**) (foll. by *away*) pass (time etc.) in a leisurely or interesting way (*whiled away the afternoon browsing in bookshops*). — *rel. adv.* (prec. by *time* etc.) during which (*the summer while I was abroad*). □ **between whiles** in the intervals. **for a while** for some time. **in a while** soon. **once in a while** see ONCE. **the while** in the meantime. **worth while** (or **one's while**) worth the time or effort spent. [Old English]

■ **Usage** *Worth while* (two words) is used only predicatively, as in *thought it worth while to ring the police*, whereas *worthwhile* is used both predicatively and attributively.

**whilst** /wuylst/ *adv. & conj.* while. [from WHILE]

**whim** *n.* **1** sudden fancy; caprice. **2** capriciousness. [origin unknown]

**whimbrel** /wim-bruhl/ *n.* small curlew of Australian coastal areas, a migrant usu. from eastern Asia. [WHIMPER imitative]

**whimp** var. of WIMP.

**whimper** — *v.* make feeble, querulous, or frightened sounds; cry and whine softly. — *n.* such a sound. [imitative]

**whimsical** /wim-zi-kuhl/ *adj.* **1** capricious. **2** fantastic. **3** odd or quaint; fanciful, humorous. □ **whimsicality** /-kal-uh-tee/ *n.* **whimsically** *adv.*

**whimsy** /wim-zee/ *n.* (*pl.* **-ies**) **1** whim; capricious notion or fancy. **2** capricious or quaint humour. [origin uncertain]

**whine** — *n.* **1** complaining long-drawn wail as of a dog. **2** similar shrill prolonged sound (*the whine of the dentist's drill*). **3 a** querulous tone (*had a whine in his voice*). **b** instance of feeble or monotonous complaining (*his life is one long whine*). — *v.* (**-ning**) **1** emit or utter a whine. **2** complain monotonously and annoyingly. **3** utter in a whining tone ('*Nobody loves me,*' *he whined*). □ **whiner** *n.* **whiningly** *adv.* **whiny** *adj.* (**whinier, whiniest**) [Old English]

**whinge** /winj/ — *v.* (**-geing** or **-ging**) *colloq.* whine; grumble peevishly. — *n.* a whining complaint; an act or instance of whingeing (*having a whinge*). [Old English]

**whingeing pom** *n.* (also **whingeing pommy**) *colloq. derog.* person from Britain (esp. England), esp. a migrant, who complains about life in Australia (see POM).

**whinny** /win-ee/ — *n.* (*pl.* **-ies**) gentle or joyful neigh. — *v.* (**-ies, -ied**) give a whinny. [imitative]

**whip** — *n.* **1** lash attached to a stick for urging on animals or punishing etc. **2** (in

parliament) member of a political party appointed to control its discipline and tactics, esp. ensuring attendance and voting in debates. **3** action of beating cream, eggs, etc., into a froth. — *v.* (**-pp-**) **1** beat or urge on with a whip. **2** beat (cream or eggs etc.) into a froth. **3** take or move suddenly, unexpectedly, or rapidly (*whipped out a knife; whipped behind the door*). **4** *colloq.* (foll. by *off*) steal. **5** *colloq.* defeat soundly (*whipped them at tennis*). **6** bind with spirally wound twine. **7** sew with overcast stitches. □ **fair crack of the whip** *colloq.* (also **fair suck of the sauce bottle**) **1** equitable opportunity; reasonable chance. **2** (as *int.*) give someone a chance! **when the whips are cracking** *colloq.* when the action starts. **whip on** urge into action. **whip the cat** suffer remorse. **whips of** *colloq.* an abundance of; plenty of (*has whips of cash*). **whip up 1** excite or stir up. **2** make quickly (*whipped up a dress for the party*). [Low German or Dutch]

**whipbird** *n.* **1** (in full **eastern whipbird**) predominantly olive-green bird of eastern mainland Australia, having a crest and a long tail, and uttering a cry like the crack of a stockwhip (also called *stockwhip bird* and, formerly, *coachman* or *coach-whip*). **2** (in full **western whipbird**) predominantly olive-green bird of coastal heaths and mallee scrubs in parts of southern Australia, lacking the startling whip-crack call of the eastern species.

**whipcord** *n.* **1** tightly twisted cord such as is used for making whiplashes. **2** a close-woven worsted fabric.

**whip hand** *n.* **1** hand that holds the whip (in riding etc.). **2** (usu. prec. by *the*) advantage or control in a situation.

**whiplash** *n.* **1** flexible end of a whip. **2** blow with a whip. **3** = WHIPLASH INJURY.

**whiplash injury** *n.* injury to the neck caused by a sudden severe jerk of the head, esp. as in a motor accident.

**whippersnapper** /wip-uh-ˌsnap-uh/ *n.* **1** small child. **2** insignificant but presumptuous person.

**whippet** /wip-uht/ *n.* cross-bred dog of the greyhound type used for racing. [probably from obsolete *whippet* move briskly, from *whip it*]

**whipping** *n.* beating or flogging, usu. with a whip.

**whipping boy** *n.* scapegoat.

**whipping side** *n.* the last side (of the sheep) to be shorn.

**whippoorwill** /wip-uh-ˌwil/ *n.* American nightjar. [imitative]

**whippy** n. **1** the base in a game of hide-and-seek. **2** place in which money is kept, hiding-place for cash. [origin unknown]

**whip-round** n. colloq. informal collection of money among a group of people.

**whip snake** n. any of several slender whip-like snakes of mainland Australia, esp. the widespread, venomous, yellow-faced whip snake.

**whipstick** n. **1** form of growth (usu. of mallee eucalypts) characterised by a number of slim, even stems; a tree of this habit. **2** area of vegetation dominated by such trees (*surveying wildlife out in the whipstick*). **3** (in full **whipstick mallee**, **whipstick scrub**) area dominated by whipsticks.

**whipstock** n. handle of a whip.

**whiptail wallaby** n. light to brownish-grey wallaby of eastern Queensland and eastern NSW, having a long, slender, dark-tipped tail.

**whirl** — v. **1** swing round and round; revolve rapidly. **2** (foll. by *away*) convey or go rapidly in a vehicle etc. **3** send or travel swiftly in an orbit or a curve (*whirling the bullroarer round and round above his head*). **4 a** (of the brain, senses, etc.) seem to spin round (*my head's whirling*). **b** (of thoughts etc.) be confused; follow each other in bewildering succession (*dozens of excuses whirled in his mind*). — n. **1** whirling movement (*vanished in a whirl of dust*). **2** state of intense activity (*the social whirl*). **3** state of confusion (*in a whirl*). □ **give it a whirl** colloq. attempt it. [Old Norse, and Low German or Dutch]

**whirligig** /**wer**-lee-gig/ n. **1** spinning or whirling toy. **2** revolving motion. **3** anything regarded as hectic or constantly changing (*the whirligig of time*).

**whirlpool** n. powerful circular eddy of water.

**whirlwind** n. **1** rapidly whirling funnel-shaped mass or column of air moving over land or water. **2** confused, hectic process (*a whirlwind of activity*). **3** (*attrib.*) very rapid (*a whirlwind romance*).

**whirly** n. (also **whirly-whirly**) = WILLY WILLY. [abbreviation of WHIRLWIND]

**whirr** — n. continuous rapid buzz or soft clicking sound (*the whirr of wings*). — v. (**-rr-**) make this sound. [Scandinavian]

**whisk** — v. **1** (foll. by *away*, *off*) **a** brush with a sweeping movement. **b** take suddenly (*whisked the plate away*). **2** whip (cream, eggs, etc.). **3** convey or go (esp. out of sight) lightly or quickly (*whisked me off to the doctor*). **4** wave or lightly brandish (*whisking flies away in the great Australian salute*). — n. **1** whisking

action or motion. **2** utensil for whisking eggs or cream etc. **3** bunch of grass, twigs, bristles, etc., for removing dust or flies. [Scandinavian]

**whisker** n. **1** (usu. in *pl.*) hair growing on a man's face, esp. on the cheek. **2** each of the bristles on the face of a cat etc. **3** colloq. small distance (*within a whisker of*; *won by a whisker*). □ **have whiskers on it** (of news, a subject, etc.) be no longer novel or fresh. □ **whiskered** adj. **whiskery** adj. [from WHISK]

**whisky** /**wis**-kee/ n. (*pl.* **-ies**) spirit distilled esp. from malted grain, esp. barley or rye. [abbreviation of *usquebaugh* from Gaelic, = water of life]

**whisky drinker** n. colloq. = CHERRY NOSE.

**whisper** — v. **1 a** speak very softly without vibration of the vocal cords. **b** talk or say in a barely audible tone or in a secret or confidential way. **2** (of leaves, wind, or water) rustle or murmur. — n. **1** whispering speech (*talking in whispers*). **2** soft, rustling or murmuring sound. **3** thing whispered. **4** rumour or piece of gossip (*have you heard the whisper that . . .*). □ **it is whispered** there is a rumour. □ **whisperer** n. **whispering** n. & adj. [Old English]

**whist** n. card-game usu. for two pairs of players. [earlier *whisk*, perhaps from WHISK (with ref. to whisking away the tricks): perhaps associated with *whist*! (= silence)]

**whistle** /**wis**-uhl/ — n. **1** clear shrill sound made by forcing breath through a small hole between nearly closed lips. **2** similar sound made by a bird, the wind, a missile, etc. **3** instrument used to produce such a sound. **4** colloq. penis. — v. (**-ling**) **1** emit a whistle. **2 a** give a signal or express surprise or derision by whistling. **b** (often foll. by *up*) summon or give a signal to (a dog etc.) by whistling. **c** (foll. by *up*) summon by, or as if by, whistling (*I'll whistle up some help*). **3** (also *absol.*) produce (a tune) by whistling. **4** (foll. by *for*) vainly seek or desire (*she rode off telling him he could whistle for his money*). □ **as clean** (or **clear** or **dry**) **as a whistle** very clean (or clear or dry). **blow the whistle on** colloq. inform on. **wet one's whistle** see WET. **whistle in the dark** pretend to be unafraid. **whistle in** (or **against**) **the wind** make a futile protest. [Old English]

**whistle-blower** n. person who exposes or brings to public attention an irregularity or a crime, esp. from within an organisation.

**whistler** n. **1** any of many small insect-eating Australian birds, typically having a rich whistled song (*golden whistler*; *rufous whistler*). **2** = WHISTLING DUCK.

**whistle-stop** *n.* **1** small unimportant town on a railway. **2** politician's brief pause for an electioneering speech on tour.

**whistling dick** *n.* (esp. in Tasmania) = GREY THRUSH.

**whistling duck** *n.* **1** (also **plumed tree-duck, whistling tree-duck, whistle-duck, whistler**) **a** a perching duck of northern and eastern Australia having a loud whistling call. **b** (also **wandering whistling duck**) closely related duck of northern and eastern Australia and elsewhere in the Indo-Pacific region. **2** (also **whistle-duck, whistler**) = PINK-EARED DUCK.

**whistling eagle** *n.* (also **whistling kite**) dark and light brown bird of prey of Australia and elsewhere, having a loud whistling call.

**whistling tree-frog** *n.* either of two frogs of south-eastern mainland Australia having loud, melodious, whistle-like calls.

**Whit** — *n.* = WHITSUNTIDE. — *attrib. adj.* of Whitsuntide or Whit Sunday. [Old English, = white]

**whit** *n.* particle; least possible amount (*not a whit better*). [apparently = WIGHT]

**white** — *adj.* **1** resembling a surface reflecting sunlight without absorbing any of the visible rays; of the colour of milk or snow. **2** nearly this colour; pale, esp. in the face (*he turned as white as a sheet*). **3** (also **White**) **a** of the human group having light-coloured skin. **b** of or relating to white people. **4** albino (*white mouse*). **5** (of hair) having lost its colour, esp. in old age. **6** (of coffee or tea) with milk or cream. **7** used as a distinguishing epithet in the names of Australian fauna, esp. birds (*white-backed magpie*; *white-breasted robin*; *white-quilled goose*; *white-tailed kingfisher*; etc.). **8** used as a distinguishing epithet in the names of Australian flora to indicate colour of bark, wood, flowers, etc. (*white apple*; *white cedar*; *white gum*; *white pine*; *white stringybark*; *white waratah*; etc.). **9** (of wine) made from white grapes or dark grapes with the skins removed. — *n.* **1** white colour or pigment. **2 a** white clothes or material. **b** (in *pl.*) white garments as wcrn in cricket, tennis, etc. **3 a** (in a game or sport) white piece, ball, etc. **b** player using these. **4** = EGG WHITE. **5** whitish part of the eyeball round the iris. **6** (also **White**) member of a light-skinned race. □ **bleed white** drain (a person,

country, etc.) of wealth etc. □ **whiteness** *n.* **whitish** *adj.* [Old English]

**white ant** — *n.* **1** termite. **2** *colloq.* saboteur; person who undermines (a political party, policy, etc.). — *v.* (**white-ant**) **1** destroy (a wooden structure). **2** undermine or sabotage (an enterprise, organisation, etc.). □ **white-anter** *n.* **white-anting** *n.*

**White Australia Policy** *n. hist.* policy of restricting immigration into Australia to white persons only.

**whitebait** *n.* (*pl.* same) (usu. in *pl.*) any of several Australian fish caught small and eaten whole (e.g. the young of the JOLLYTAIL).

**white beech** *n.* large tree of Queensland and NSW, having white tube-flowers streaked with purple and yellow followed by globe-shaped blue fruits; has been subjected to intensive logging.

**whiteboard** *n.* kind of 'blackboard' made of white plastic, and written on with a felt pen rather than with chalk.

**white-breasted sea eagle** *n.* (also **white-bellied sea eagle**) very large grey and white bird of prey of Australia and elsewhere.

**white cedar** *n.* (also **melia** /mee-lee-uh/) **1** tree of Queensland and NSW, deciduous, having a furrowed bark, highly scented lilac flowers, and oval fruits favoured by parrots. **2** the attractively figured wood of this tree.

**white cell** *n.* leucocyte.

**white cockatoo** *n.* (also **sulphur-crested cockatoo, yellow-crested cockatoo**) very large, predominantly white cockatoo of northern and eastern Australia, with a curling yellow crest and extremely raucous call.

**white-collar** *attrib. adj.* (of a worker or work) clerical or professional rather than manual.

**white corpuscle** *n.* = WHITE CELL.

**white death** *n.* = WHITE POINTER.

**white elephant** *n.* useless possession.

**white-eye** *n.* = SILVER-EYE.

**whiteface** *n.* any of three small brownish birds of drier southern and central mainland Australia (*banded whiteface*; *chestnut-breasted whiteface*; *southern whiteface*).

**white feather** *n.* symbol of cowardice.

**white fellow** (in Aboriginal English) — *n.* (also **white fella, white feller**) non-Aboriginal inhabitant of Australia, usu. with reference to one of British descent. — *adj.* (**whitefellow, white-fella, white-feller**) non-Aboriginal; alien (to the Aborigines) (*whitefellow names like 'Ayers Rock' for Uluru*).

**white flag** n. symbol of surrender.

**White Friar** n. Carmelite.

**whitegoods** n.pl. large domestic electrical appliances such as fridges.

**whitehead** n. colloq. white or white-topped skin-pustule.

**white heat** n. **1** temperature at which metal emits white light. **2** state of intense passion or activity (worked at white heat to get it done in time). □ **white-hot** adj.

**white hope** n. person expected to achieve much.

**white lead** n. mixture of lead carbonate and hydrated lead oxide used as pigment.

**white leghorn** n. **1** breed of hardy, egg-laying, domestic fowl. **2** colloq. female player of lawn bowls (who wears a mandatory white uniform).

**white lie** n. harmless or trivial untruth.

**white light** n. colourless light, e.g. ordinary daylight.

**white magic** n. magic used for beneficent purposes (opp. BLACK MAGIC).

**white meat** n. poultry, veal, rabbit, and pork.

**white monk** n. Cistercian.

**white myrtle** n. tall rainforest tree (family Myrtaceae) of NSW and Queensland, having beautiful foliage, shiny green above and silver below, white flowers, and black fruit.

**whiten** v. make or become white. □ **whitener** n.

**white noise** n. noise containing many frequencies with equal intensities.

**White Paper** n. Government report giving information on a particular issue.

**white pepper** n. pepper made by grinding a ripe or husked berry.

**white pointer** n. (also **white shark, white death**) largest of man-eating sharks, of southern Australia including Tasmania, and worldwide in temperate and tropical seas.

**white slave** n. woman tricked or forced into prostitution.

**white spirit** n. light petroleum as a solvent.

**white sugar** n. purified sugar.

**whitewash** — n. **1** solution of quicklime or whiting for whitening walls etc. **2** means employed to conceal mistakes or faults. **3** sporting match in which an opponent does not score. — v. **1** cover with whitewash. **2** attempt to clear the reputation of by concealing facts. **3** defeat (an opponent) without allowing any opposing score.

**white water** n. shallow or foamy stretch of water.

**white-winged chough** see CHOUGH.

**whitewood** n. any of many Australian trees yielding a very pale wood, esp. the small tree Atalaya hemiglauca of drier inland Australia, having waxy grey-green leaves and winged fruits.

**whither** / with-uh / archaic — adv. **1** to what place or state? **2** (prec. by place etc.) to which. — conj. **1** to the or any place to which (go whither you will). **2** and thither. [Old English]

**whiting**[1] n. (pl. same) **1** any of several silvery marine fish of Australian waters valued as food, esp. the spotted whiting. **2** unrelated small European fish with white flesh, used as food. [Dutch: related to WHITE]

**whiting**[2] n. ground chalk used in white-washing etc.

**whitlow** / wit-loh / n. inflammation near a fingernail or toenail. [originally white FLAW]

**Whitsun** / wit-suhn / — n. = WHIT-SUNTIDE. — adj. = WHIT. [Whitsun Day = Whit Sunday]

**Whit Sunday** n. seventh Sunday after Easter, commemorating Pentecost.

**Whitsuntide** n. weekend or week including Whit Sunday.

**whittle** / wit-uhl / v. (**-ling**) **1** (often foll. by at) pare (wood etc.) with repeated slicing with a knife. **2** (often foll. by away, down) reduce by repeated subtractions (our few remaining native forests are being whittled away; need to whittle down expenditure). [British dial. thwittle]

**whiz** (also **whizz**) — n. **1** sound made by a body moving through the air at great speed. **2** (also **wiz**) colloq. person who is remarkable or highly skilful in some respect (she's a wiz at chess). — v. (**-zz-**) move with or make a whiz. [imitative: in sense 2 influenced by WIZARD]

**whiz-bang** adj. (also **whizz-bang**) colloq. excellent; spectacular.

**whiz-kid** n. colloq. brilliant or highly successful young person.

**WHO** abbr. World Health Organisation.

**who** / hoo / pron. (obj. **whom** / hoom / or colloq. **who**; poss. **whose** / hooz / ) **1 a** what or which person or persons? (who called?; you know who it was; whom did you see?). **b** what sort of person or persons? (who am I to object?). **2** (a person) that (anyone who wishes can come; the woman whom you met; the man who you saw). **3** and (or but) he, they, etc. (gave it to Tom, who sold it to Jim). [Old English]

■ **Usage** In the last example of sense 1a and the last two examples of sense 2 whom is correct, but who is common in less formal contexts.

**whoa** /woh/ *int.* used to stop or slow a horse etc. [var. of HO]

**who'd** /hood/ *contr.* **1** who had. **2** who would.

**whodunit** /hoo-**dun**-uht/ *n.* (also **whodunnit**) *colloq.* detective story, play, or film. [= *who done* (illiterate for *did*) *it?*]

**whoever** /hoo-**ev**-uh/ *pron.* (*obj.* **whomever** /hoom-/ or *colloq.* **whoever**; *poss.* **whosever** /hooz-/) **1** the or any person or persons who (*whoever comes is welcome*). **2** though anyone (*whoever else objects, I do not; whosever it is, I want it*). **3** *colloq.* (as an intensive) who ever; who at all (*whoever heard of such a thing?*)

**whole** /hohl/ — *adj.* **1** uninjured, unbroken, intact, or undiminished (*swallowed it whole; there's not a plate left whole*). **2** not less than; all there is of; entire, complete (*waited a whole year; the whole school knows; tell the whole truth*). **3** (of blood or milk etc.) with no part removed. — *n.* **1** thing complete in itself. **2** all there is of a thing (*spent the whole of the summer holidays at Hall's Gap*). **3** (foll. by *of*) all members etc. of (*the whole of Orroroo knows it*). □ **as a whole** as a unity; not as separate parts. **on the whole** taking everything relevant into account; in general. **whole box and dice** *colloq.* everything. **whole lot** see LOT. □ **wholeness** *n.* [Old English]

**wholegrain** *attrib. adj.* made with or containing whole grains (*wholegrain bread*).

**wholehearted** *adj.* **1** (of a person) completely devoted or committed. **2** (of an action etc.) done with all possible effort or sincerity. □ **wholeheartedly** *adv.* **wholeheartedness** *n.*

**wholemeal** *n.* (usu. *attrib.*) meal or flour with none of the bran or germ removed.

**whole number** *n.* number without fractions; integer.

**wholesale** — *n.* selling of goods in large quantities to be retailed by others (cf. RETAIL). — *adj. & adv.* **1** by wholesale; at a wholesale price (*can get it for you wholesale*). **2** on a large scale (*wholesale destruction occurred*). — *v.* (**-ling**) sell wholesale. □ **wholesaler** *n.* [originally *by whole sale*]

**wholesome** *adj.* **1 a** promoting physical, mental, or moral health (*wholesome pursuits; wholesome meals*). **b** indicating physical, mental, or moral health (*a wholesome appearance; wholesome behaviour*). **2** prudent (*wholesome respect*). [Old English: related to WHOLE]

**wholism** var. of HOLISM.

**wholly** /**hoh**-lee/ *adv.* **1** entirely; without limitation (*he's wholly responsible*). **2**

purely, exclusively (*a wholly bad example*).

**whom** *objective case* of WHO.

**whomever** *objective case* of WHOEVER.

**whomsoever** *objective case* of WHOSOEVER.

**whoop** /hoop, woop/ — *n.* **1** loud cry of (or as of) excitement etc. **2** long rasping indrawn breath in whooping cough. — *v.* utter a whoop. □ **whoop it up** *colloq.* **1** engage in revelry. **2** make a stir. [imitative]

**whoopee** /wuu-**pee**/ *int.* expressing exuberant joy. □ **make whoopee** /**wuup**-ee/ *colloq.* **1** have fun, make merry. **2** make love. [imitative]

**whooping cough** /**hoo**-ping/ *n.* infectious bacterial disease, esp. of children, with a series of short violent coughs followed by a whoop.

**whoops** /wuups/ *int. colloq.* expressing surprise or apology, esp. on losing balance or making an obvious mistake. [var. of OOPS]

**whoosh** /wuush/ — *v.* move or cause to move with a rushing sound (*the skier whooshed past me*). — *n.* sudden movement accompanied by a rushing sound. — *int.* an exclamation imitating this. [imitative]

**whop** *v.* (**-pp-**) *colloq.* **1** thrash. **2** defeat decisively. [origin unknown]

**whopper** *n. colloq.* **1** something big of its kind. **2** great lie.

**whopping** *adj. & adv. colloq.* (esp. as an intensifier) huge (*a whopping success; a whopping great lie*).

**whore** /haw/ — *n.* **1** prostitute. **2** *derog.* promiscuous woman. — *v.* **1** (of a man) resort to whores for sex. **2** (usu. foll. by *around*) (of a man or woman) be sexually promiscuous; act in a whorish manner. □ **whorer** *n.* [Old English]

**whorehouse** *n.* brothel.

**whorish** /**haw**-rish/ *adj.* of or like a whore. □ **whorishly** *adv.* **whorishness** *n.*

**whorl** /wawl, werl/ *n.* **1** ring of leaves etc. round a stem. **2** one turn of a spiral, esp. on a shell. **3** complete circular line in a fingerprint. □ **whorled** *adj.* [apparently var. of WHIRL]

**whose** /hooz/ — *pron.* of or belonging to which person (*whose is this book?*). — *adj.* of whom or which (*whose book is this?; the man, whose name was Fred; the house whose roof was damaged*).

**whosoever** /,hoo-soh-ev-uh/ *pron.* (*obj.* **whomsoever** /,hoom-/; *poss.* **whosoever** /,hooz-/) *archaic* = WHOEVER.

**who's who** *n.* **1** who or what each person is (*know who's who*). **2** list or directory with facts about notable persons.

**why** /wuy/ — adv. **1 a** for what reason or purpose (*why did you do it?*; *I do not know why you came*). **b** on what grounds (*why do you say that?*). **2** (prec. by *reason* etc.) for which (*the reasons why I did it*). — *int.* expressing: **1** surprised discovery or recognition (*why, it's you!*). **2** impatience (*why, of course I do!*). **3** reflection (*why, yes, I think so*). **4** objection (*why, what is wrong with it?*). — *n.* (*pl.* **whys**) reason or explanation (*I need to know the why of it*). □ **whys and wherefores** reasons; explanation. **why so?** on what grounds?; for what reason or purpose? [Old English: related to WHAT]

**wick** *n.* **1** strip or twist of thread feeding a flame with fuel in a candle, lamp, etc. **2** *colloq.* penis. □ **get on a person's wick** *colloq.* annoy a person. [Old English]

**wicked** /wik-uhd/ *adj.* (**-er, -est**) **1** sinful, iniquitous, immoral. **2** spiteful; intending or intended to give pain (*a wicked lie*). **3** playfully malicious (*has a wonderfully wicked wit*). **4** *colloq.* very bad; formidable (*wicked weather*; *a wicked cough*). □ **wickedly** *adv.* **wickedness** *n.* [origin uncertain]

**wicker** *n.* plaited osiers etc. as material for baskets etc. [Scandinavian]

**wickerwork** *n.* **1** wicker. **2** things made of wicker.

**wicket** /wik-uht/ *n.* **1** *Cricket* **a** three stumps with the bails in position defended by a batsman. **b** ground between two wickets. **c** state of this as indicated (*a slow wicket*). **d** instance of a batsman being got out (*bowler has taken four wickets*). **e** the pair of batsmen batting at any one time (*the third-wicket partnership*). **2** (in full **wicket-door** or **-gate**) small door or gate, esp. beside or in a larger one or closing the lower part only of a doorway. □ **on a good** (or **sticky**) **wicket** *colloq.* in a favourable (or unfavourable) position (*he's on a good wicket having married the boss's daughter*). [Anglo-French *wiket* = French *guichet*]

**wicket-keeper** *n.* fieldsman stationed close behind a batsman's wicket.

**widdershins** /wid-uh-shinz/ *adv.* (also **withershins** /with-/ ) esp. *Scot.* **1** in a direction contrary to the sun's course (considered unlucky). **2** anticlockwise. [German, = contrary]

**wide** — *adj.* **1** having sides far apart, broad, not narrow (*wide river*; *wide sleeve*; *wide angle*). **2** (following a measurement) in width (*a metre wide*). **3 a** extending far (*wide range*; *wide experience*). **b** considerable (*won by a wide margin*). **4** not restricted (*a wide public*). **5 a** liberal; unprejudiced (*takes wide views*). **b** not specialised; general (*has wide interests*). **6** open to the full extent (*staring with wide eyes*). **7** (foll. by *of*) not within a reasonable distance of, far from (*wide shot*; *wide of the target*). **8** (in *comb.*) extending over the whole of (*nationwide*). — *adv.* **1** widely. **2** to the full extent (*wide awake*). **3** far from the target etc. (*I'm shooting wide*). — *n.* = WIDE BALL. □ **give a wide berth to** see BERTH. **wide brown land** Australia. **wide of the mark** see MARK.

**wide open 1** (often foll. by *to*) exposed or vulnerable (to attack etc.). **2** (of a contest) with no contestant who can be predicted as a certain winner. **the wide world** all the world, great as it is. [Old English]

**wide-angle** *adj.* (of a lens) having a short focal length and hence a field covering a wide angle.

**wide area network** *n.* *Computing* (also **WAN**) communication network over a broad geographic region and possibly including some local area networks.

**wide awake** *adj.* **1** fully awake. **2** *colloq.* wary, knowing.

**wide ball** *n.* *Cricket* ball judged to be beyond the batsman's reach, so scoring a run.

**wide comb** see COMB.

**wide-eyed** *adj.* surprised; naïve.

**widely** *adv.* **1** to a wide extent; far apart. **2** extensively (*widely read*; *widely distributed*). **3** by many people (*it is widely thought that . . .*). **4** considerably; to a large degree (*holds a widely different view*).

**widen** *v.* make or become wider.

**widespread** *adj.* widely distributed or disseminated (*widespread rumours*).

**wide worker** *n.* Australian sheep dog which controls the movement of sheep while remaining at some distance from them.

**widgeon** /wij-uhn/ *n.* (also **wigeon**) any of several wild Australian ducks, esp. the pink-eared duck. [origin uncertain]

**widow** /wid-oh/ — *n.* **1** woman who has lost her husband by death and not married again. **2** woman whose husband is often away on a specified activity (*golf widow*). — *v.* **1** make into a widow or widower. **2** (as **widowed** *adj.*) bereft by the death of a spouse. □ **widowhood** *n.* [Old English]

**widower** *n.* man who has lost his wife by death and not married again.

**widow's peak** *n.* V-shaped growth of hair towards the centre of the forehead.

**width** *n.* **1** measurement of distance from side to side. **2** large extent. **3** breadth or liberality of thought, views, etc. **4** strip of material of full width as woven. □ **width-ways** adv. **widthwise** adv. [from WIDE]

**wield** v. **1** hold and use (a weapon or tool). **2** command or exert (power or authority etc.). □ **wielder** n. [Old English]

**wieldy** adj. (**-ier, -iest**) easily wielded, controlled, or handled.

**Wiener schnitzel** /**vee**-nuh ˌshnit-suhl/ n. veal cutlet breaded, fried, and garnished. [German]

**wife** n. (pl. **wives**) **1** married woman, esp. in relation to her husband. **2** a archaic woman (the Wife of Bath). **b** (in comb.) a woman engaged in a specified activity (housewife; midwife). □ **wifely** adj. [Old English, = woman]

**wig** — n. **1** artificial head of hair (esp. to conceal baldness or as a disguise, or worn by a judge or barrister). **2** the wool which grows above and around the eyes of a sheep. — v. **1** provide with a wig. **2** clip the wool from around the eyes of (a sheep). [abbreviation of periwig]

**wiggle** /**wig**-uhl/ — v. (**-ling**) move or cause to move quickly from side to side etc. (see if you can wiggle your toes). — n. act of wiggling; kink in a line etc. □ **wiggly** adj. (**-ier, -iest**). [Low German or Dutch wiggelen]

**wight** /wuyt/ n. archaic person. [Old English, = thing, creature]

**wig tree-fern** n. tree-fern (a cyathea) of the far north of Queensland, having curious, curly, wig-like growths at the base of each frond.

**wigwam** /**wig**-wawm, -wom, -wam/ n. N. American Indian's hut or tent. □ **a wigwam for a goose's bridle** used as a snubbing reply to an unwanted question. [Ojibwa. Wigwam in the idiom a wigwam for a goose's bridle is an alteration of earlier whim-wham 'a trifle, ornament' by the process of folk etymology.]

**wijen** var. of WATJIN.

**Wik-Mungkan** /ˌwik-**muung**-kuhn/ n. an Aboriginal language of the far north of Queensland, Cape York Peninsula.

**wilco** /**wil**-koh/ int. colloq. expressing compliance or agreement. [abbreviation of will comply]

**wild** /wuyld/ — adj. **1** a in its original natural state; not domesticated, cultivated, or civilised (wild pig; wild strawberry). **b** (in comb.) designating Australian flora which, the early settlers felt, resembled European plants, or which acted as substitutes for them (wild ginger; wild grape; wild hop; wild lemon; wild nutmeg; wild parsnip; wild violet; etc.). **2** unrestrained, disorderly, uncontrolled (wild youth; wild hair). **3** tempestuous, violent (a wild and stormy

night; wild fighting in the streets). **4** intensely eager, frantic (wild excitement; wild delight). **5** (foll. by about) colloq. enthusiastically devoted to (is wild about him). **6** colloq. infuriated (makes me wild). **7** haphazard, ill-aimed, rash (wild guess; wild venture). **8** colloq. exciting, delightful (a wild party). — adv. in a wild manner; wildly (shooting wild). — n. (often in pl.) **1** wild tract of land. **2** desert. □ **in the wild** in an uncultivated etc. state. **in the wilds** colloq. far from towns etc. **run wild 1** grow or stray unchecked or undisciplined (this creeper is running wild; cats running wild). **2** behave in a riotous, undisciplined way (allows his children to run wild). □ **wild and woolly** uncouth, lacking refinement; rough and ready. □ **wildly** adv. **wildness** n. [Old English]

**wild card** n. **1** card having any rank chosen by the player holding it. **2** Computing character that will match any character or sequence of characters in a file name etc. **3** person or thing that can be used in several different ways; person whose behaviour cannot be predicted (he's the wild card when it comes to the vote).

**wildcat** — n. **1 a** = NATIVE CAT. **b** European or American wild cat. **2** hot-tempered or violent person. **3** exploratory oil well. — adj. (attrib.) **1** (of a strike) sudden and unofficial. **2** reckless; financially unsound (wildcat business ventures).

**wild cauliflower** n. spectacular WA verticordia, having creamy flowers (said to resemble the florets of a cauliflower) completely covering the shrub in spring.

**wild colonial boy** n. **1** bushranger. **2** larrikin.

**wilderness** /**wil**-duh-nuhs/ n. **1** uncultivated and still wild region of forest, scrub, bush, desert, etc., WILDERNESS AREA. **2** part of a garden left with an uncultivated appearance. **3** (foll. by of) confused assemblage of things. □ **in the (political) wilderness** out of office; out of a former position of political influence and power. [Old English: related to WILD, DEER]

**wilderness area** n. tract of land that is largely undisturbed by humans and where indigenous plants and animals flourish in their natural environment.

**wildfire** n. hist. combustible liquid used in war. □ **spread like wildfire** spread with great speed.

**wildflower** n. **1** flower of an indigenous plant growing in e.g. a wilderness area (Western Australian wildflowers; wildflowers of the Little Desert in Victoria). **2** such a plant as introduced into garden etc. cultivation (*a raised bed of wild-flowers putting pansies and petunias to shame*).

**wildfowl** *n.* (*pl.* same) game-bird.

**wild-goose chase** *n.* foolish or hopeless quest.

**wild horse** *n.* **1** = BRUMBY. **2** (in *pl.*) *colloq.* even the most powerful influence etc. (*wild horses would not drag the secret from me*).

**wildlife** *n.* wild animals collectively, esp. as inhabiting a wilderness area.

**wild pineapple** see MACROZAMIA.

**wild turkey** *n.* = PLAIN TURKEY.

**wile** /wuyl/ — *n.* (usu. in *pl.*) stratagem; trick or cunning procedure. — *v.* (**-ling**) (foll. by *away, into,* etc.) lure, entice (*wiled him into some dubious practices*). [perhaps from Scandinavian]

**wilful** /wil-fuhl/ *adj.* **1** intentional, deliberate (*wilful murder; wilful neglect*). **2** (of a person) headstrong, obstinate. ▢ **wilfully** *adv.* **wilfulness** *n.* [from WILL²]

**wilga** /wil-guh/ *n.* (also **sheep bush**) small drought-resistant tree of inland Australia, having a spreading crown and pendulous foliage (a favourite fodder for sheep), and bearing creamy flowers. [Wiradhuri *wilgarr*]

**wilgie** /wil-gee/ *n.* red ochre used by Aborigines to paint the body on ceremonial occasions. [Nyungar *wilgi*]

**will¹** *v.aux.* (*3rd sing. present* **will**; *past* **would** /wuud/) **1** (strictly only in the 2nd and 3rd persons: see SHALL) expressing the future tense in statements, commands, or questions (*you will regret this; they will leave at once; will you go to the party?*). **2** (in the 1st person) expressing the speaker's determination or intention (*I will return soon; we will do it, whatever you may say*). **3** expressing desire, consent, or inclination (*will you have a drink?; come when you will; the door will not open*). **4** expressing a request as a question (*will you please open the window?*). **5** be able to (*the jar will hold a kilo*). **6** have a habit or tendency to (*accidents will happen; will sit there for hours*). **7** expressing probability or expectation (*that will be my wife at the door*). ▢ **will do** *colloq.* expressing willingness to carry out a request. [Old English]

**will²** — *n.* **1** faculty by which a person decides what to do (*the mind consists of the understanding and the will*). **2** strong desire or intention (*will to live*). **3** self-control; determination, will-power (*has a strong will; overcame his shyness by force of will*). **4** legal written directions for the disposal of one's property after death (*make one's will*). **5** disposition (good or

bad) towards others (*good will; ill will*). **6** *archaic* what one desires or ordains (*thy will be done*). — *v.* **1** try to cause by will-power (*willed her to win; willed his hand to stop shaking*). **2** intend; desire (*what God wills*). **3** bequeath by a will (*willed all his money to charity*). ▢ **at will** as or whenever or wherever one wishes (*did it at will; travelled at will*). **a will of one's own** obstinacy; wilfulness of character. **with a will** energetically or resolutely. [Old English]

**willies** /wil-eez/ *n.pl. colloq.* nervous discomfort (*gives me the willies*). [origin unknown]

**willie wagtail** var. of WILLY WAGTAIL.

**willing** *adj.* **1** ready to consent or undertake (*willing ally; I'm willing to do it*). **2** given or done etc. by a willing person (*willing help*). ▢ **willingly** *adv.* **willingness** *n.*

**will-o'-the-wisp** /wil-uh-*th*uh-wisp/ *n.* **1** phosphorescent light seen on marshy ground, perhaps resulting from the combustion of gases. **2** elusive person. **3** delusive hope or plan (*his great scheme turned out to be a will-o'-the-wisp*). [originally *Will with the wisp*: *wisp* = handful of (lighted) hay]

**willow** /wil-oh/ *n.* **1** tree with pliant branches yielding osiers and timber for cricket-bats etc., usu. growing near water. **2** any of several Australian trees resembling the willow, including some species of wattle. **3** cricket bat. [Old English]

**willow myrtle** *n.* small Australian tree *Agonis flexuosa* (see PEPPERMINT 4).

**willow wattle** *n.* any of several Australian wattles having pendulous foliage and occurring along watercourses, esp. COOBA.

**willowy** *adj.* **1** (esp. of a person) lithe and slender (*a willowy lad*). **2 a** having or bordered by willows. **b** bendable, pliable.

**will-power** *n.* control by deliberate purpose over impulse.

**willy** /wil-ee/ *n.* = WILLY WILLY. [abbreviation]

**willy-nilly** /wil-ee-**nil**-ee/ — *adv.* whether one likes it or not (*you will do it willy-nilly*). — *adj.* existing or occurring willy-nilly. [later spelling of *will I, nill I* I am willing, I am unwilling]

**willy wagtail** *n.* (also **willie wagtail**) black and white bird, a fantail, widespread in Australia.

**willy willy** *n.* (*pl.* **-ies**) (also **willy**) whirlwind or dust-storm. [either from Yindjibarndi *wili-wili* or from Wemba-wemba *wilang-wilang*]

**wilt** — v. **1** (of a plant, leaf, or flower) wither, droop. **2** (of a person or a person's spirits, confidence, etc.) lose energy, flag, tire, droop (*I'm wilting in this heat; his resolution wilted in the face of all the opposition*). **3** cause to wilt (*this heatwave is wilting all my plants*). — n. plant-disease causing wilting. [originally British dial.]

**wiltja** /wil-chuh/ n. Aboriginal shelter. [Western Desert language *wilja* shelter, shade, or shadow]

**wily** /wuy-lee/ adj. (**-ier**, **-iest**) crafty, cunning. □ **wiliness** n.

**Wimmera rye** /wim-uh-ruh/ n. (in full **Wimmera ryegrass**) Mediterranean annual grass, widely sown as pasture grass, and also naturalised and sometimes regarded as a weed. [*Wimmera* region of western Victoria]

**wimp¹** n. colloq. feeble or ineffectual person. □ **wimp out** colloq. fail to carry out (an undertaking etc.) through weakness of will, lack of nerve, etc. (*wimped out on his commitment to investigate the allegations*). □ **wimpish** adj. **wimpy** adj. [origin uncertain]

**wimp²** n. Computing user-friendly computer system having windows, a mouse, pull-down menus, etc. [*w*indows, *i*cons, *m*ouse, *p*ull-down menus]

**wimple** /wim-puhl/ n. headdress also covering the neck and the sides of the face, worn by some nuns. [Old English]

**wimp-out** n. colloq. failure to carry out (an undertaking etc.) through weakness of will etc.

**win** — v. (**-nn-**; *past* and *past part.* **won** /wun/) **1** acquire or secure as a result of a fight, contest, bet, litigation, or some other effort (*won first prize; he won my admiration*). **2** be victorious in (a fight, game, race, etc.) (*won the election; won the Stawell Gift*). **3 a** be the victor (*who won?; persevere and you will win*). **b** (foll. by *through*, *free*, etc.) make one's way, or become, as a result of successful effort (*won through to the further shore; won free of all the red-tape*). **4** reach by effort (*win the summit; won the shore at last*). — n. victory in a game etc. □ **win the day** be victorious in battle, argument, etc. **win over** persuade, gain the support of. **win one's spurs** colloq. gain distinction or fame. **win through** (or **out**) overcome obstacles. **you can't win** colloq. there is no way to succeed or to please. **you can't win 'em all** colloq. resigned expression of consolation on failure. □ **winnable** adj. [Old English, = toil]

**wince** — n. a start or an involuntary shrinking movement of the face, showing pain or distress. — v. (**-cing**) give a wince. □ **wincingly** adv. [Germanic: related to WINK]

**winch** — n. **1** crank of a wheel or axle. **2** windlass. — v. lift with a winch. [Old English]

**wind¹** — n. **1** air in natural motion, esp. a current of this. **2 a** breath, esp. as needed in exercise or playing a wind instrument. **b** power of breathing easily (*let me get my wind back*). **3** empty talk (*his speech was mostly wind*). **4** gas generated in the bowels etc.; flatulence. **5** artificially produced current of air (as from a fan, or for sounding an organ, etc.). **6** wind instruments of an orchestra etc. (*poor balance between wind and strings*). **7** scent carried by the wind. — v. **1** cause to be out of breath by exertion or a blow (*the run winded me*). **2** make (a baby) bring up wind after feeding. **3** detect the presence of by a scent (*the wallabies have winded us*). **4** renew the wind of by rest (*let's stop and wind the horses*). **5** /wuynd/ (*past* and *past part.* **winded** or **wound** /wownd/) poet. sound (a bugle etc.) by blowing. □ **between wind and water** at a vulnerable point. **break wind** see BREAK. **close to** (or **near**) **the wind 1** sailing as nearly against the wind as is consistent with using its force. **2** verging on indecency or dishonesty. **get wind of** begin to suspect; hear a rumour of. **get** (or **have**) **the wind up** colloq. be alarmed or frightened. **in the wind** about to happen (*I suspect a separation is in the wind*). **like the wind** swiftly. **put the wind up** colloq. alarm, frighten. **take the wind out of a person's sails** frustrate a person by anticipating an action or remark etc. □ **windless** adj. [Old English]

**wind²** /wuynd/ — v. (*past* and *past part.* **wound** /wownd/) **1** (often as **winding** adj.) go in a spiral, curved, or crooked course (*winding staircase; the path winds up the hill*). **2** make (one's way) thus (*wound his way into our affections*). **3** wrap closely; coil (*wound the blanket round her; I wound my arms round the child*). **4 a** coil; provide with a coiled thread etc. (*wind the ribbon on to the card; wound the thread onto a reel*). **b** surround with or as with a coil (*the creeper winds round the tree-trunk*). **5** wind up (a clock etc.). — n. **1** bend or turn in a course. **2** single turn when winding (*give it three winds*). □ **wind down 1** lower by winding. **2** (of a mechanism) unwind. **3** draw gradually to a close (*the party is beginning to wind down*). **4** (of a person) relax. **wind off** unwind. **wind round one's finger** (or **little finger**) persuade (a person) without difficulty; dominate (a person) completely. **wind up 1** coil the whole of (a piece of string etc.). **2** tighten the coiling or coiled spring of (esp. a clock). **3** *colloq.* **a** increase the intensity of (feelings etc.), excite (*wound myself up to fever pitch*). **b** provoke (a person) to anger etc. **4** bring to a conclusion; end (*wound up his speech*). **5 a** arrange the affairs of and dissolve (a company). **b** cease business and go into liquidation. **6** *colloq.* arrive finally; end in a specified state or circumstance (*wound up at Woolloomooloo; you'll wind up in prison; wound up owing $100*). [Old English]

**windbag** /wind-bag/ *n. colloq.* person who talks a lot but says little of any value.

**windbreak** *n.* thing (esp. a row of trees or shrubs) serving to break the force of the wind.

**windburn** *n.* inflammation of the skin caused by exposure to the wind.

**windcheater** *n.* wind-resistant jacket.

**wind-down** *n. colloq.* gradual lessening of excitement or activity.

**winder** /wuyn-duh/ *n.* winding mechanism, esp. of a clock or watch.

**windfall** /wind-fawl/ *n.* **1** fruit, esp. an apple, blown to the ground by the wind. **2** unexpected good fortune, esp. a legacy.

**Windies** /win-deez/ *colloq. n.pl.* **1** (nickname for) the West Indies cricket team. **2** (**Windie**) *sing.* member of this team. [contraction of *West Indies*]

**winding-sheet** /wuyn-ding/ *n.* sheet in which a corpse is wrapped for burial.

**wind instrument** /wind/ *n.* musical instrument sounded by an air-current, esp. the breath.

**windjammer** *n.* merchant sailing-ship.

**windlass** /wind-luhs/ — *n.* machine with a horizontal axle for hauling or hoisting. — *v.* hoist or haul with a windlass. [Old Norse, = winding-pole]

**windmill** *n.* mill worked by the wind acting on its sails. □ **tilt at windmills** attack an imaginary enemy.

**windmill grass** *n.* any of several Australian grasses with windmill-like flowerheads.

**window** /win-doh/ *n.* **1 a** opening in a wall or vehicle etc., usu. with glass to admit light. **b** the glass filling this opening (*have broken the window*). **2** space for display behind the front window of a shop. **3** aperture in a wall etc. through which customers are served in a bank, ticket office, etc. **4** opportunity to learn from observation. **5** transparent part in an envelope showing an address. **6** *Computing* rectangular area on a computer screen, usu. with graphics

capability, that allows the user to view and control a number of different tasks. □ **windowless** *adj.* [Old Norse, = windeye]

**window dressing** *n.* **1** art of arranging a display in a shop-window etc. **2** adroit presentation of facts etc. to give a deceptively favourable impression.

**window-seat** *n.* **1** seat below a window, esp. in an alcove. **2** seat next to a window in an aircraft, train, etc.

**window-shop** *v.* look at goods displayed in shop-windows, without buying anything.

**windpipe** *n.* air-passage from the throat to the lungs.

**windscreen** *n.* screen of glass at the front of a motor vehicle.

**wind-sock** *n.* canvas cylinder or cone on a mast to show the direction of the wind at an airfield etc.

**windsurfing** *n.* sport of riding on water on a sailboard. □ **windsurf** *v.* **windsurfer** *n.*

**windswept** *adj.* exposed to or swept back by the wind.

**wind-tunnel** *n.* tunnel-like device producing an air-stream past models of aircraft etc. for the study of aerodynamics.

**wind-up** — *n.* conclusion; finish. — *attrib. adj.* (of a mechanism) operating by being wound up.

**windward** /wind-wuhd/ — *adj. & adv.* on the side from which the wind is blowing (opp. LEEWARD). — *n.* windward direction (*on the windward of*). □ **get to windward of 1** place oneself there to avoid the smell of. **2** gain an advantage over.

**windy** *adj.* (**-ier, -iest**) **1** stormy with wind (*a windy night*). **2** exposed to the wind; windswept (*a windy plain*). **3** generating or characterised by flatulence. **4** wordy; lacking substance (*a windy speech*). **5** *colloq.* nervous, frightened. □ **windily** *adv.* **windiness** *n.* [Old English: related to WIND[1]]

**wine** — *n.* **1** fermented grape juice as an alcoholic drink. **2** fermented drink resembling this made from other fruits etc. as specified (*elderberry wine; ginger wine*). **3** dark red colour of red wine (*a blouse of wine silk*). — *v.* (**-ning**) **1** drink wine. **2** (esp. in phr. **wine and dine**) entertain with wine. [Old English]

**wine bar** *n.* bar or small restaurant where wine is the main drink available.

**wine cask** *n.* Australian invention of a plastic or foil-lined container filled with wine, enclosed within a cardboard box, and having a spigot so that wine not drawn off remains under a vacuum.

**wine cellar** *n.* **1** cellar for storing wine. **2** its contents.

**wineglass** n. glass for wine, usu. with a stem and foot.

**winepress** n. press in which grapes are squeezed in making wine.

**wine vinegar** n. vinegar made from wine as distinct from malt etc.

**wing** — n. **1** each of the limbs or organs by which a bird, bat, or insect is able to fly. **2** winglike structure supporting an aircraft. **3 a** part of a building etc. extended in a certain direction (*lived in the north wing*). **b** fence, usu. one of a pair, built out from a stockyard and serving to guide stock towards its entrance. **4 a** forward player at either end of a line in football, hockey, etc. **b** side part of a playing-area. **5** (in pl.) sides of a theatre stage out of view of the audience (*watched from the wings*). **6** polarised section of a political party in terms of its views (*right wing*; *left wing*; *centre-left wing*; etc.). **7 a** flank of a battle array. **3** flank of a travelling mob of sheep, cattle, etc. **8 a** air-force unit of several squadrons or groups. **b** (in pl.) pilot's badge in the air force (*get one's wings*). — v. **1** travel or traverse on wings or in an aircraft (*birds winging westward*; *I'm winging my way back to Oz*). **2** wound in a wing or an arm (*the bullet winged me*). **3** equip with wings. **4** enable to fly; send in flight (*fear winged my feet*; *winged an arrow towards them*). □ **on the wing** flying, in flight. **on a wing and a prayer** with only the slightest chance of success. **take under one's wing** treat as a protégé. **take wing** fly away. **waiting in the wings** holding oneself in readiness. □ **winged** adj. **winglike** adj. [Old Norse]

**wing-case** n. horny cover of an insect's wing.

**wing commander** n. RAAF officer next below group captain.

**winger** n. **1** (in football etc.) wing player. **2** (in comb.) member of a specified political wing (*left-winger*).

**wingman** n. Aust. Rules player in the wing position.

**wing nut** n. nut with projections for the fingers to turn it.

**wing-span** n. (also **wing-spread**) measurement right across the wings.

**wink** — v. **1** (often foll. by at) close and open one eye quickly, esp. as a signal (*he winked at me*). **2** close and open (one or both eyes) quickly; blink. **3** (of a light etc.) twinkle; (of an indicator) flash on and off. — n. **1** act or instance of winking. **2** colloq. brief moment of sleep (*didn't sleep a wink*). □ **in a wink** very quickly (*it was all over in a wink*). **wink at 1** purposely avoid seeing; pretend not to notice (*the boss kindly winked at my blunder*). **2** connive at (a wrongdoing etc.) (*I will not wink at theft*). □ **winker** n. (in sense 3 of v.). [Old English]

**winkle** /wing-kuhl/ — n. small edible sea snail. — v. (**-ling**) (foll. by out) extract with difficulty (*winkled the secret out of him*). [abbreviation of periwinkle]

**winner** n. **1** person etc. that wins. **2** colloq. successful or highly promising idea etc. (*the new scheme seemed a winner*).

**winning** — adj. **1** having or bringing victory or an advantage (*the winning entry*; *a winning stroke*). **2** attractive, persuasive (*winning smile*; *winning ways*). — n. (in pl.) money won. □ **winningly** adv.

**winning-post** n. post marking the end of a race.

**winnow** /win-oh/ v. **1** blow (grain) free of chaff etc. by an air-current. **2** (foll. by out, away, from, etc.) get rid of (chaff etc.) from grain. **3 a** sift, examine (evidence etc.). **b** clear, sort, or separate out (rubbish etc.). □ **winnower** n. [Old English: related to WIND[1]]

**wino** /wuy-noh/ n. (pl. **-s**) colloq. alcoholic.

**winsome** adj. winning, attractive, engaging (*a winsome smile*). □ **winsomely** adv. **winsomeness** n. [Old English, = joyous]

**winter** — n. **1** coldest and last season of the year, in Australia June, July, August. **2** (attrib.) characteristic of or fit for winter (*winter winds*; *winter wear*). **3** bleak or lifeless period (*nuclear winter*). **4** poet. a year (esp. of a person's age) (*a man of fifty winters*). — v. (usu. foll. by at, in) pass the winter (*we Melburnians like to winter in places like Darwin*). [Old English]

**winter solstice** n. about 21 June (see SOLSTICE).

**wintertime** n. season or period of winter.

**wintry** adj. (**-ier, -iest**) **1** characteristic of winter. **2** lacking warmth; unfriendly. □ **wintriness** n.

**win-win** attrib. adj. of or designating a situation in which both sides in a dispute or negotiated settlement etc. (esp. industrial) can be seen as gaining and neither side as being defeated (opp. NO-WIN).

**wipe** — v. (**-ping**) **1** clean or dry the surface of by rubbing with hand or cloth etc. (*wiped his face*). **2** rub (a cloth) over a surface. **3** (often foll. by away, off, etc.) **a** clear or remove by wiping (*wiped the mess off the table*; *wiped away a tear*). **b** erase or eliminate completely (*the village* *was wiped off the map*). **4** erase a magnetic medium (of data); erase data (from such a medium) (*wiped the tape; wiped the recording from the video*). **5** *colloq.* reject or dismiss (a person or idea) (*my girlfriend wiped me; you can wipe that idea*). — *n.* **1** act of wiping (*give the floor a wipe*). **2** piece of specially treated material for wiping (*antiseptic wipes*). ◻ **wipe down** clean (a wall etc.) by wiping. **wipe the floor with** *colloq.* inflict a humiliating defeat on. **wipe off** annul (a debt etc.). **wipe** (an expression, esp. a smile) **off a person's** (or **one's**) **face** (cause him or her to) cease showing it (*wipe that smile off your face!*). **wipe out 1** destroy, annihilate, obliterate (*thousands were wiped out by the bombing; wiped it out of my mind*). **2** clean the inside of. **wipe up 1** dry (dishes etc.). **2** take up (a liquid etc.) by wiping. [Old English]

**wipe-out** *n.* **1** *Surfing* fall from a surfboard. **2 a** instance of destruction etc. **b** failure; defeat. **3** obliteration of one radio signal by another.

**wiper** *n.* windscreen wiper.

**Wiradhuri** /wu-**raj**-u-ree/ *n.* an Aboriginal language spoken over a vast area from southern NSW to northern Victoria: now extinct.

**wire** — *n.* **1 a** metal drawn out into a thread or thin flexible rod. **b** piece of this. **c** (*attrib.*) made of wire. **2** length of this for fencing or to carry an electric current etc. **3** *colloq.* telegram. — *v.* (**-ring**) **1** provide, fasten, strengthen, etc., with wire. **2** (often foll. by *up*) install electrical circuits in (a building, equipment, etc.). **3** *colloq.* telegraph (*wired me that they were coming*). ◻ **down to the wire** all the way (to the finishing line). **get one's wires crossed** become confused and misunderstood. **straight wire** *colloq.* the complete truth. [Old English]

**wire door** *n.* = SCREEN DOOR.

**wire grass** *n.* any of many perennial Australian grasses having a tufted or tussocky habit and stiff, wiry stems.

**wireless** *n.* radio; radio receiving set.

---

■ **Usage** Now old-fashioned, esp. with ref. to broadcasting, and superseded by *radio*.

---

**wire netting** *n.* netting of meshed wire.

**wire-tapping** *n.* tapping of telephone lines to eavesdrop.

**wirilda** /wuh-**ril**-duh/ *n.* (in full **wirilda wattle**) shrub or small tree of southern Australia, having long, narrow grey-green phyllodes and creamy yellow ball-flowers, often cultivated as an ornamental. [Yaralde, probably *wurrulde*]

**wiring** *n.* system or installation of wires providing electrical circuits.

**wirra**[1] /**wi**-ruh/ *n.* small cup-like digging scoop of the Aborigines, traditionally made of hardwood. [Western Desert language]

**wirra**[2] /**wi**-ruh/ *n.* (also **cooba, willow wattle**) tall willow-like wattle occurring near watercourses in drier Australia and bearing gold ball-flowers in winter and spring. [Diyari]

**wirrah** /**wi**-ruh/ *n.* either of two marine fish of rocky reefs of south-eastern and south-western Australia, often also called 'boot' in reference to its tough and tasteless flesh. [possibly from an Aboriginal language]

**wirrang** /**wi**-rang/ *n.* = ROCK WALLABY. [Wiradhuri *wirang*]

**wirri** /**wi**-ree/ *n. hist.* Aboriginal weapon used either as a club or as a missile in both fighting and hunting. [Gaurna]

**wiry** *adj.* (**-ier, -iest**) **1** (of a person) sinewy, untiring. **2** like wire; tough, coarse. ◻ **wiriness** *n.*

**wisdom** /**wiz**-duhm/ *n.* **1** experience and knowledge together with the power of applying them critically or practically. **2** prudence; common sense. **3** wise sayings etc. regarded collectively. ◻ **in his** (or **her** etc.) **wisdom** usu. *iron.* thinking it would be best (*the committee in its wisdom decided to abandon the project*). [Old English: related to WISE[1]]

**wisdom tooth** *n.* hindmost molar usu. cut at about 20 years of age.

**wise**[1] /wuyz/ *adj.* **1** having, showing, or dictated by wisdom. **2** prudent, sensible. **3** having knowledge (esp. as specified) (*wise in linguistics*; often in *comb.*: *streetwise; worldly-wise*). **4** suggestive of wisdom (*with a wise nod of his head*). **5** *colloq.* (often foll. by *to*) having (usu. confidential) information (about) (*I'm wise to what is going on*). ◻ **be** (or **get**) **wise to** *colloq.* be (or become) aware of. **none the wiser** knowing no more than before. **put wise** (often foll. by *to*) *colloq.* inform (of). **wise up** *colloq.* put or get wise. ◻ **wisely** *adv.* [Old English]

**wise**[2] /wuyz/ *n. archaic* way, manner, or degree. ◻ **in no wise** not at all. [Old English]

**-wise** *suffix* forming adjectives and adverbs of manner (*clockwise*; *lengthwise*) or respect (*moneywise*).

---

■ **Usage** Fanciful phrase-based combinations, such as *employment-wise* (= as regards employment) should be restricted to informal contexts or avoided.

---

**wiseacre** /**wuyz**-,ay-kuh/ n. person who affects a wise manner. [Dutch *wijsseggher* soothsayer]

**wisecrack** *colloq.* — n. smart pithy remark. — v. make a wisecrack.

**wise guy** n. *colloq.* know-all.

**wish** — v. 1 (often foll. by *for*) have or express a desire or aspiration for (*wish for happiness*). 2 have as a desire or aspiration (*I wish I could sing*). 3 want or demand, usu. so as to bring about what is wanted (*I wish to go now; I wish you to do it; I wish it done at once*). 4 express one's hopes for (*wish you success; she wished him dead*). 5 (foll. by *on, upon*) *colloq.* foist on (*wished an impossible task on me*). — n. 1 a desire, request, or aspiration. b expression of this. 2 thing desired. □ **best** (or **good**) **wishes** hopes felt or expressed for another's happiness etc. [Old English]

**wishbone** n. forked bone between the neck and breast of a fowl often broken between two people, the longer portion entitling the holder to make a wish.

**wishful** *adj.* (often foll. by *to* + infin.) desiring. □ **wishfulness** n. **wishfully** *adv.*

**wish-fulfilment** n. tendency for subconscious desires to be satisfied in fantasy.

**wishful thinking** n. belief founded on wishes rather than facts.

**wishy-washy** /**wish**-ee-,wosh-ee/ *adj.* 1 feeble in quality or character. 2 (of soup, tea, etc.) weak, watery. [from WASH]

**wisp** n. 1 small bundle or twist of straw etc. 2 small separate quantity of smoke, hair, etc. 3 small thin person etc. □ **wispy** *adj.* (**-ier, -iest**) **wispily** *adv.* **wispiness** n. [origin uncertain]

**wisteria** /wis-**teer**-ree-uh/ n. (also **wistaria**) climbing plant with blue, purple, or white hanging flowers. [*Wistar*, name of an anatomist]

**wistful** *adj.* yearning, mournfully expectant or wishful. □ **wistfully** *adv.* **wistfulness** n. [apparently an assimilation of obsolete *wistly* 'intently' to *wishful*]

**wit** n. 1 (in *sing.* or *pl.*) intelligence; quick understanding (*has quick wits; hasn't the wit to come in out of the rain*). 2 a unexpected and humorous combining or contrasting of ideas or expressions (*conversation sparkling with wit*). b power of giving pleasure by this. 3 person possessing such power. □ **at one's wit's** (or **wits'**) **end** utterly at a loss or in despair. **have** (or **keep**) **one's wits about one** be alert. **live by one's wits** live by ingenious or crafty expedients, without a settled occupation. **out of one's wits** mad. **to wit** that is to say, namely. [Old English]

**witch** — n. 1 sorceress, woman supposed to have dealings with the Devil or evil spirits. 2 old hag. 3 fascinating girl or woman. — v. *archaic* bewitch. [Old English]

**witchcraft** n. 1 use of magic. 2 bewitching charm.

**witch-doctor** n. tribal magician of primitive people.

**witchery** n. = WITCHCRAFT.

**witchetty** /**wich**-uh-tee/ n. (in full **witchetty grub**; also **witchety, margoo**) large, edible, wood-eating larva or pupa of any of several Australian moths and beetles (see also BARDI). [probably Adnyamathanha *wityu* hooked stick used to extract such grubs from holes etc. in wood, *varti* grub or insect]

**witchetty bush** n. any of several wattles of drier Australia, esp. *Acacia kempeana*, so named because witchetty grubs are commonly to be found in plenty in its trunk and branches and at its roots.

**witch-hazel** n. (also **wych-hazel**) 1 American shrub with bark yielding an astringent lotion. 2 this lotion.

**witch-hunt** n. 1 *hist.* search for and persecution (usu. by burning alive) of supposed witches. 2 campaign against persons suspected of unpopular or unorthodox views, or of disloyalty etc., followed by 'modern' persecution (e.g. the witch-hunts against supposed Communists in America — see MCCARTHYISM).

**witching hour** n. (prec. by *the*) midnight.

**with** /with, with/ *prep.* expressing: 1 instrument or means used (*cut with a knife; can walk with assistance*). 2 a association or company (*lives with his mother; works with the Railways*). b parting of company (*dispense with*). 3 cause or origin (*shiver with fear; in bed with measles*). 4 possession (*man with dark hair*). 5 circumstances (*sleep with the window open*). 6 manner (*behaved with dignity; handle with care; won with ease*). 7 agreement (*sympathise with*). 8 disagreement, antagonism (*incompatible with; quarrel with*). 9 understanding (*are you with me?*). 10 responsibility or care for (*the decision rests with you; leave the child with me*). 11 reference or regard (*be patient with them; how are things with you?*). 12 material (*inlaid with gold*). 13 addition or supply; possession of as a material, attribute, circumstance, etc. (*fill it with water; threaten with dismissal; decorate with holly*). 14 relation or causative association (*changes with the weather; keep pace with the cost of living*). 15 an accepted circumstance (*with all your* *faults, we like you).* □ **away** (or **in** or **out** etc.) **with** (as *int.*) take, send, or put (a person or thing) away (or in or out etc.). **get with it** *colloq.* **1** become realistic, aware; awake to (oneself, a situation, etc.). **2** become up to date. **3** cope, concentrate. **with it** *colloq.* **1** fashionable, trendy (*he's really with it when it comes to clothes*). **2 a** expert, well-informed (*she's very with it on car engines*). **b** alert, intelligent, dynamic (*Bill's a live wire — really with it*). **with that** thereupon. [Old English]

**withdraw** /wi*th*-draw, with-/ *v.* (*past* **withdrew**; *past part.* **withdrawn**) **1** pull or take aside or back (*withdrew my hand*). **2** discontinue, cancel, retract (*withdrew my support*). **3** remove; take away (*withdrew my child from that school*). **4** take (money) out of an account. **5** retire or move apart (*withdrew to the bedroom*). **6** (as **withdrawn** *adj.*) abnormally shy and unsociable; mentally detached. [from *with-* = away]

**withdrawal** *n.* **1** act or instance of withdrawing or being withdrawn. **2** process of ceasing to take an addictive drug etc., often with an unpleasant reaction (*withdrawal symptoms*). **3** = COITUS INTERRUPTUS.

**withe** /with, wi*th*, wuy*th*/ *n.* (also **withy** /with-ee/) (*pl.* **withes** or **withies**) tough flexible shoot, esp. of willow, used for binding, basketwork, etc. [Old English]

**wither** /wi*th*-uh/ *v.* **1** (often foll. by *up*) make or become dry and shrivelled. **2** (often foll. by *away*) deprive of or lose vigour or freshness. **3** (esp. as **withering** *adj.*) blight with scorn etc. (*withered me with a glance; a withering look*). □ **witheringly** *adv.* [apparently var. of WEATHER]

**withers** /wi*th*-uhz/ *n.pl.* ridge between a horse's shoulder-blades. [obsolete *wither* against (the collar)]

**withershins** var. of WIDDERSHINS.

**withhold** /wi*th*-hohld, with-/ *v.* (*past* and *past part.* **-held**) **1** (often foll. by *from*) hold back; restrain (*withheld the facts from the shareholders*). **2** refuse to give, grant, or allow (*withhold one's consent*). □ **withholder** *n.* [from *with-* = away]

**within** /wi-*th*in, -*th*in/ — *adv.* **1** inside; to, at, or on the inside. **2** indoors (*he's not within*). **3** in spirit (*pure within*). — *prep.* **1** inside (*within the walls*). **2 a** not beyond or out of (*within one's means*). **b** not transgressing or exceeding (*within the law; within the speed limit*). **3** not further off than (*within three kilometres; within ten days; not within cooee*). □ **within one's grasp** close enough to be obtained. **within reach** (or **sight**) **of** near enough to be reached or seen. [Old English: related to WITH, IN]

**without** /wi-*th*owt, -*th*owt/ — *prep.* **1** not having or feeling or showing (*came without any money; without hesitation; without any emotion*). **2** with freedom from (*without fear; without embarrassment*). **3** in the absence of (*cannot live without you; train left without us*). **4** with neglect or avoidance of (*do not leave without telling me*). **5** *archaic* outside (*without the convent wall*). — *adv.* *archaic* or *literary* **1** outside (*seen from without*). **2** out of doors (*he is without*). **3** in outward appearance (*rough without but kind within*). [Old English: related to WITH, OUT¹]

**withstand** /wi*th*-stand, with-/ *v.* (*past* and *past part.* **-stood**) **1** oppose, hold out against (a person, a force, etc.) (*withstood the onslaught*). **2** make opposition; offer resistance (*come what may, I shall withstand*). □ **withstander** *n.* [Old English: related to WITH, STAND]

**withy** var. of WITHE.

**witless** *adj.* foolish, stupid; crazy. [Old English: related to WIT]

**witness** /wit-nuhs/ — *n.* **1** = EYEWITNESS. **2 a** person giving sworn testimony. **b** person attesting another's signature to a document. **3** (foll. by *to, of*) person or thing whose existence etc. attests or proves something (*is a living witness to her generosity*). **4** testimony, evidence, confirmation (*this is witness of the truth*). — *v.* **1** be an eye-witness of (*did you witness the accident?*). **2** be witness to the authenticity of (a signature etc.). **3** serve as evidence or an indication of. **4** (foll. by *against, for, to*) give or serve as evidence (*witnessed against me*). **5** be the scene or setting of (*this stretch of scrub has witnessed the massacre of Aborigines by the whites*). □ **bear witness to** (or **of**) **1** attest the truth of. **2** state one's belief in. **call to witness** appeal to for confirmation etc. [Old English: related to WIT]

**witticism** /wit-uh-,siz-uhm/ *n.* witty remark. [from WITTY]

**wittingly** /wit-ing-lee/ *adv.* aware of what one is doing; intentionally. [from WIT]

**witty** *adj.* (**-ier, -iest**) showing esp. verbal wit. □ **wittily** *adv.* **wittiness** *n.* [Old English: related to WIT]

**wives** *pl.* of WIFE.

**wizard** /wiz-uhd/ — *n.* **1** sorcerer; magician. **2** person of remarkable powers or skill, genius (*a wizard in mathematics*). — *adj.* *colloq.* wonderful. □ **wizardly** *adj.* **wizardry** *n.* [from WISE¹]

**wizened** /**wiz**-uhnd/ *adj.* (of a person or face etc.) shrivelled-looking. [Old English]

**WNW** *abbr.* west-north-west.

**WO** *abbr.* Warrant-Officer.

**woad** *n.* **1** plant yielding a blue dye. **2** dye from this. [Old English]

**wobbegong** /**wob**-ee-₊gong/ *n.* = CARPET SHARK. [perhaps from a NSW Aboriginal language]

**wobble** /**wob**-uhl/ — *v.* (**-ling**) **1 a** sway or vibrate unsteadily from side to side. **b** cause to do this (*stop wobbling the table — I'm trying to write*). **c** quiver (*his huge belly wobbled as he laughed*). **2** stand or go unsteadily; stagger. **3** waver, vacillate; act inconsistently. **4** (of the voice or sound) quaver, pulsate (*the boy's voice wobbled between gruff and falsetto*). — *n.* state or instance of wobbling. [cf. Low German *wabbeln*]

**wobble-board** *n.* piece of fibreboard, used as a musical instrument, which, when held in both hands and wobbled, produces a low, rhythmic, booming sound.

**wobbles** *n.pl.* affliction, esp. of cattle, brought about by eating the leaves of certain Australian plants (esp. macrozamia) and characterised by irreversible loss of coordination of the hind limbs.

**wobbly** *adj.* (**-ier, -iest**) **1** wobbling or tending to wobble. **2** wavy (*wobbly line*). **3** weak after illness (*feeling a bit wobbly still*). **4** wavering, insecure (*the economy was wobbly*). □ **throw a wobbly** see THROW.

**wodgil** /**woj**-uhl/ *n.* (in full **wodgil scrub**) vegetation community of tall, shrubby growth dominated by wattles. [probably from a WA Aboriginal language]

**woe** /woh/ *n.* **1** affliction; bitter grief. **2** (in *pl.*) calamities. **3** (in *pl.*) *joc.* problems (*went on and on about his woes*). □ **woe betide** see BETIDE. **woe is me** *archaic* alas. [Old English]

**woebegone** /**woh**-buh-₊gon/ *adj.* dismal-looking. [from WOE, *begone* = surrounded]

**woeful** *adj.* **1** sorrowful (*a woeful expression*). **2** causing or feeling affliction. **3** very bad (*woeful ignorance*; *the house is in a woeful condition*). □ **woefully** *adv.*

**wog**[1] *n.* *colloq.* *offens.* foreigner or migrant, esp. a southern European one. [origin unknown]

**wog**[2] *n. colloq.* **1 a** illness or infection, usu. minor (e.g. flu, an upset stomach). **b** germ etc. causing this (*think I've caught a wog*). **2** name applied to various predatory or disagreeable insects and grubs. [origin unknown]

**woggle** /**wog**-uhl/ *n.* leather etc. ring through which the ends of a boy scout's neckerchief are passed at the neck (often, in Australia, the gumnut of the flowering gum being used for this purpose). [origin unknown]

**wogoit** /**wog**-oit/ *n.* ring-tailed rock possum of northern Australia. [Waray, probably *wogoj*]

**wok** *n.* bowl-shaped frying-pan used in esp. Chinese cookery. [Chinese]

**woke** *past* of WAKE[1].

**woken** *past part.* of WAKE[1].

**wolf** /wuulf/ — *n.* (*pl.* **wolves** /wuulvz/) **1** wild animal of Europe, North America, and Asia, related to the dog, usu. hunting in packs. **2** *colloq.* man given to seducing women. **3** rapacious or greedy person. — *v.* (often foll. by *down*) devour (food) greedily. □ **cry wolf** raise repeated false alarms (so that a genuine one is disregarded). **keep the wolf from the door** avert hunger or starvation. **throw to the wolves** sacrifice without compunction. □ **wolfish** *adj.* [Old English]

**wolf in sheep's clothing** *n.* hostile person who pretends friendship.

**wolfram** /**wuul**-fruhm/ *n.* **1** tungsten. **2** (also **wolframite**) tungsten ore. [German]

**wolfsbane** *n.* aconite.

**wolf-whistle** *n.* whistle (sliding rapidly up and down the scale) made to a sexually attractive person.

**wollamai** /**wol**-uh-muy/ *n.* = SNAPPER. [Dharuk *walamay*]

**Wollemi pine** /**wol**-uh-muy/ *n.* ancient conifer, formerly known only from fossils, discovered growing in the Wollemi National Park, NSW, in 1994.

**wolves** *pl.* of WOLF.

**woman** /**wuum**-uhn/ *n.* (*pl.* **women** /**wim**-uhn/) **1** adult human female. **2** the female sex (*how does woman differ from man?*). **3** *colloq.* wife or girlfriend. **4** (prec. by *the*) feminine characteristics (*every man needs to bring out the woman in him*). **5** (*attrib.*) female (*woman doctor*; *women friends*). **6** (in *comb.*) woman of a specified nationality, skill, etc. (*Englishwoman*; *horsewoman*). □ **womanish** *adj.* **womanly** *adj.* [Old English]

**womanhood** *n.* **1** female maturity. **2** womanly instinct. **3** womankind.

**womanise** *v.* (also **-ize**) (**-sing** or **-zing**) chase after women; philander. □ **womaniser** *n.*

**womankind** *n.* (also **womenkind**) women in general.

**womb** /woom/ *n.* **1** organ of conception and gestation in a woman and other female mammals; uterus. **2** place of origination and development (*the womb of Time*). □ **womblike** *adj*. [Old English]

**wombat** /**wom**-bat/ *n*. **1** any of several thickset, burrowing, plant-eating marsupials of southern and eastern Australia, the commonest and most widespread of which is the hairy-nosed wombat. **2** *colloq*. slow or stupid person. [Dharuk *wambad*, *wambaj*, or *wambag*]

**wombat berry** *n*. Australian climber of the lily family having tubers favoured by wombats, shiny lance-shaped leaves, white or pink flowers, and globular orange berries, often cultivated as an ornamental.

**women** *pl*. of WOMAN.

**womenfolk** *n*. **1** women in general. **2** the women in a family.

**womenkind** var. of WOMANKIND.

**women's business** *n*. Aboriginal rituals open only to women.

**women's camp** *n*. (also **women's country**) (in Aboriginal English) a place open only to women.

**women's lib** *n*. *colloq*. = WOMEN'S LIBERATION.

**women's libber** *n*. *colloq*. supporter of women's liberation.

**women's liberation** *n*. the liberation of women from inequalities and subservient status in relation to men, and from attitudes causing or prolonging these.

**Women's Liberation** *n*. (also **Women's Liberation Movement**) movement campaigning for women's liberation.

**women's refuge** *n*. usu. temporary accommodation for women in danger as a result of domestic violence inflicted on or threatened to them, domestic disputes, etc.

**women's rights** *n.pl*. rights that promote a position of legal and social equality of women with men.

**womma¹** /**wom**-uh/ *n*. = HONEY-ANT. [Yankunytjatjara *wama* any sweet substance or delicacy]

**womma²** /**wom**-uh/ *n*. (also **woma**) python of arid Australia. [Diyari *wama*]

**wompoo pigeon** /**wom**-poo/ *n*. large green fruit-pigeon with purple breast, yellow belly, and grey head, inhabiting near-coastal rainforest in north-eastern Australia. [imitative of its far-reaching booming call; perhaps a borrowing from an Aboriginal language]

**won** past and past part. of WIN.

**wonder** /**wun**-duh/ — *n*. **1** emotion, esp. admiration, excited by what is unexpected, unfamiliar, or inexplicable. **2** strange or remarkable thing, specimen, event, etc. **3** (*attrib*.) having marvellous or amazing properties etc. (*wonder drug*; *wonder woman*). **4** surprising thing (*it's a wonder you weren't hurt*). — *v*. **1** (often foll. by *at*) be filled with wonder or great surprise. **2** (foll. by *that*) be surprised to find (*I wonder that you didn't discover it sooner*). **3** desire or be curious to know (*I wonder what the time is*). **4** expressing a tentative enquiry (*I wonder whether you'd mind*). □ **I shouldn't wonder** *colloq*. I think it likely. **I wonder** (as a response to something said) I very much doubt it. **no** (or **small**) **wonder** one cannot be surprised. **work** (or **do**) **wonders 1** do miracles. **2** be remarkably effective. [Old English]

**wonderful** *adj*. **1** very remarkable or admirable. **2** arousing wonder. □ **wonderfully** *adv*. [Old English]

**wonderment** *n*. surprise, awe.

**wondrous** /**wun**-druhs/ *poet*. — *adj*. wonderful. — *adv*. wonderfully (*wondrous kind*). □ **wondrously** *adv*.

**wonga¹** /**wong**-guh/ *n*. = CUMBUNGI. [Wemba-wemba *wanggal*]

**wonga²** /**wong**-guh/ *n*. = CORROBOREE. [Pajamal *wangga*]

**wongai** /**wong**-guy/ *n*. seashore tree occurring in Cape York Peninsula and on the islands of north-eastern Australia, bearing bright red, sticky, edible fruits. [Kala Lagaw Ya *wongay*]

**wonga-wonga** /**wong**-guh-, wong-guh/ *n*. (also **wonga pigeon**, **wonga wonga pigeon**) large, ground-feeding grey and white pigeon of eastern mainland Australia. [probably Dharuk *wanga-wanga*]

**wonga-wonga vine** /**wong**-guh-, wong-guh/ *n*. (also **pandorea**) vigorous twining climber *Pandorea pandorana* of eastern Australia, having glossy leaves and numerous clusters of showy creamy tubular flowers spotted with red, purple, or orange; often cultivated as an ornamental. [possibly associated with *wonga-wonga* the pigeon]

**Wongi** /**wong**-guy/ *n*. an Aborigine. [Western Desert language *wanggayi*].

■ **Usage** See KOORI¹.

**wongi** /**wong**-gee/ — *n*. conversation; a chat (*invited me over for a wongi*). — *v*. talk; tell (*wongied till late at night*). [*wangga* (speak, talk; language) is common to most western Australian Aboriginal languages]

**wonguim** /**wong**-gwuhm/ *n*. boomerang which can be made to return to its thrower. [Wathawurung and Wuywurung *wanggim*]

**wonky** /**wong**-kee/ adj. (**-ier**, **-iest**) colloq.
**1** unwell (still feeling a bit wonky). **2**
crooked, askew. **3** loose, unsteady (ladder's a bit wonky, but). **4** broken, not
working; unreliable. [fanciful formation]

**wont** /wohnt/ — predic. adj. archaic or
literary (foll. by to + infin.) accustomed
(as he is wont to say). — n. formal or joc.
what is customary, one's habit (as is my
wont). [Old English]

**won't** /wohnt/ contr. will not.

**wonted** /**wohn**-tuhd/ attrib. adj. habitual, usual.

**woo** v. (**woos**, **wooed**) **1** court; seek the
hand or love of. **2** try to win (fame,
fortune, etc.). **3** seek the favour or
support of (he is wooing the voters). **4** coax
or importune. □ **wooer** n. [Old English]

**wood** /wuud/ n. **1 a** hard fibrous substance of the trunk or branches of a tree
or shrub. **b** this for timber or fuel etc. **2**
(in sing. or pl.) (mainly Brit. & US)
growing trees densely occupying a tract
of land. **3** wooden cask for wine etc.
(matured in wood). **4** wooden-headed golf
club. □ **have the wood on** (a person) colloq.
have an advantage over (a person). **not
see the wood for the trees** fail to grasp the
main issue from over-attention to details.
**out of the wood** (or **woods**) out of danger
or difficulty. **take to the woods** hist.
become a bushranger. [Old English]

■ **Usage** In Australia wood or woods
(sense 2) has been superseded by bush or
forest.

**wood-and-water joey** n. **1** unskilled
labourer who performs the menial tasks
of an establishment; general rouseabout.
**2** servile employee.

**woodblock** n. block from which woodcuts
are made.

**woodchip** — n. **1** (in pl.) fragments of
wood. **2** (attrib.) of or pertaining to the
production or deployment of woodchips
(woodchip industry). — v. reduce felled
trees to woodchips for use in paper-
making etc. (native Australian forests
being felled and woodchipped to feed
foreign demand).

**wood chop** n. wood-chopping contest.

**woodcraft** n. **1** bushmanship. **2** skill in
woodwork.

**woodcut** n. **1** relief cut on a block of wood.
**2** print made from this.

**wood duck** n. **1** (also **maned duck, maned
goose**) mainly grey perching duck,
having a brown, prominently maned
head and a somewhat goose-like stance,
occurring in lightly-treed country near
water in Australia. **2** colloq. customer
who is easily duped (e.g. by a salesman).

**wooded** adj. having many trees.

**wooden** /**wuu**-duhn/ — adj. **1** made of
wood. **2** like wood. **3 a** stiff, clumsy or
stilted; without animation (wooden
movements; wooden performance). **b** expressionless (wooden stare). — v. strike,
knock down (woodened him with her
handbag). □ **woodenly** adv. **woodenness**
n.

**wooden pear** var. of WOODY PEAR.

**wooden spoon** n. (imaginary) prize for
a person or team that comes last in a
sporting competition etc.; booby prize.

**woodheap** n. (also **woodpile**) pile or stack
of wood, esp. firewood.

**woodland** n. (often attrib.) open forest,
usu. dominated by eucalypts, without
dense canopy.

**woodpecker** n. **1** bird that taps tree-
trunks in search of insects. **2** either of two
Australian birds (unrelated to the
woodpecker, there being no true wood-
peckers in Australia): **a** = TREECREEPER. **b**
= SITTELLA. **3** colloq. a machine-gun.

**woodpile** n. = WOODHEAP.

**wood pulp** n. wood-fibre prepared for
paper-making.

**woodser** n. colloq. = JIMMY WOODSER.

**woodshed** n. shed where wood for fuel is
stored. □ **something nasty in the woodshed** colloq. shocking thing kept secret.

**woodswallow** n. any of several predominantly grey insect-eating birds of
Australia, having bluish bills tipped in
black (little woodswallow; dusky woodswallow; white-browed woodswallow).

**woodwind** n. **1** wind instruments that
were (mostly) orig. made of wood, e.g. the
flute, clarinet, oboe, and saxophone. **2**
one such instrument.

**woodwork** n. **1** making of things in wood.
**2** things made of wood, esp. the wooden
parts of a building. □ **crawl** (or **come**) **out
of the woodwork** colloq. (of something
distasteful) appear; become known.

**woody** adj. (**-ier**, **-iest**) **1** (of a region)
wooded. **2** like or of wood (woody tissue).
□ **woodiness** n.

**woody pear** n. (also **wooden pear**) any of
four tall Australian shrubs (or small
trees) related to the waratah, having
showy sprays of creamy white flowers
followed by large, pear-like, woody fruits.

**woof**[1] /wuuf/ — n. gruff bark of a dog.
— v. give a woof. [imitative]

**woof**[2] /woof, wuuf/ n. = WEFT 1. [Old
English: related to WEB]

**woofer** /**wuu**-fuh/ n. loudspeaker designed to reproduce low frequencies.
[from WOOF[1]]

**wool** /wuul/ *n.* **1** fine soft wavy hair from the fleece of sheep etc. **2** woollen yarn or cloth or clothing. **3** wool-like substance (*steel wool*). □ **keep** (or **lose**) **one's wool** *colloq.* keep (or lose) one's temper. **pull the wool over a person's eyes** deceive a person. [Old English]

**wool bin** *n.* any of several compartments into which a wool-classer directs graded fleeces.

**wool blind** *adj.* (of a sheep) having wool growing over the eyes.

**wool cheque** *n.* amount received from the sale of a season's wool.

**wool-classer** *n.* person who grades fleeces. □ **wool-classing** *n.*

**wool clip** *n.* (also **clip**) annual wool production of a sheep-farmer or of a district etc.

**wool-gathering** *n.* absent-mindedness.

**wool-grower** *n.* sheep-farmer. □ **wool-growing** *adj.*

**woollen** — *adj.* made wholly or partly of wool. — *n.* **1** woollen fabric. **2** (in *pl.*) knitted woollen garments. [Old English]

**woolloomooloo** /ˌwuu-luh-muh-**loo**/ *n. colloq.* a fight or quarrel. [*Woolloomooloo* wharf-side suburb in Sydney]

**woolly** — *adj.* (**-ier**, **-iest**) **1** bearing or naturally covered with wool or wool-like hair. **2** like wool (*woolly clouds*). **3** woollen (*a woolly cardigan*). **4** (of a sound) indistinct. **5** (of thought) vague or confused (*woolly thinking*). **6** *Bot.* downy. — *n.* (*pl.* **-ies**) *colloq.* **1** woollen garment, esp. a pullover. **2** a sheep. **3** sheep-farmer. □ **woolliness** *n.*

**woolly bush** *n.* any of several Australian plants related to the banksias, having silky hairs on the leaves.

**woolly butt** *n.* any of several eucalypts having a thick fibrous bark on all (or esp. the lower part) of the trunk.

**wool man** *n.* sheep-farmer.

**wool press** *n.* machine which compresses a bale of wool. □ **wool pressing** *n.*

**wool presser** *n.* person who operates a wool press.

**wool scour** *n.* shed where wool is washed.

**woolshed** *n.* shearing shed.

**woolstore** *n.* warehouse in which wool is stored.

**woomera** /**wuum**-uh-ruh/ *n.* Aboriginal implement used to propel a spear; spear-thrower, throwing-stick. [Dharuk *wamara*]

**woop woop** /**wuup**-wuup/ *n.* **1** jocular name for any remote outback region of Australia. **2** (**Woop Woop**) an imaginary remote town, the epitome of remoteness (see also BULLAMAKANKA; OODNAGALAHBI). [jocular use of reduplication in Aboriginal languages to indicate intensity or plurality]

**woozy** *adj.* (**-ier**, **-iest**) *colloq.* **1** dizzy or unsteady. **2** slightly drunk. □ **woozily** *adv.* **wooziness** *n.* [origin unknown]

**wop** *n. colloq. offens.* **1** Italian or other S. European. **2** (*attrib.*) of or pertaining to these peoples. [origin uncertain]

**word** /werd/ — *n.* **1** sound or combination of sounds forming a meaningful element of speech, usu. shown with a space on either side of it when written or printed. **2** speech, esp. as distinct from action (*bold in word but not in deed*). **3** one's promise or assurance (*gave me his word*). **4** (in *sing.* or *pl.*) thing said, remark, conversation (*can I have a word with you?*; *said a few words*). **5** (in *pl.*) text of a song or an actor's part. **6** (in *pl.*) angry talk (*have words*). **7** news, message (*send word*). **8** command (*gave the word to begin*). **9** rumour (*the word is that he's about to quit*). **10** basic unit of the expression of data in a computer. — *v.* **1** put into words; select words to express (*how shall we word that?*). **2** (foll. by *up*) *colloq.* inform (*worded me up about the situation at home*). □ **be as good as** (or **better than**) **one's word** fulfil (or exceed) what one has promised. **have no words for** be unable to express. **have a word** (often foll. by *with*) speak briefly (to). **in other words** expressing the same thing differently. **in so many words** in those very words; explicitly. **in a** (or **one**) **word** briefly. **my word** expression of emphatic agreement (*This place is going to the dogs.* — *My word!*). **of one's word** reliable in keeping promises (*a woman of her word*). **put in a** (**good**) **word for** speak favourably (of a person). **take a person at his** or **her word** interpret a person's words literally. **take a person's word for it** believe a person's statement without investigation etc. **word for word** in exactly the same or (of translation) corresponding words. □ **wordage** *n.* **wordless** *adj.* **wordlessly** *adv.* **wordlessness** *n.* [Old English]

**word-blindness** *n.* = DYSLEXIA.

**wording** *n.* form of words used.

**word of mouth** *n.* speech (only), not writing.

**word-perfect** *adj.* knowing one's part etc. by heart.

**wordplay** *n.* witty use of words, esp. punning.

**word processor** *n.* computer program, or device incorporating a computer, used for storing text entered from a keyboard, making corrections, and providing a printout. □ **word-process** v. **word processing** n.

**wordy** adj. (**-ier, -iest**) using or expressed in too many words. □ **wordily** adv. **wordiness** n.

**wore** past of WEAR.

**work** /werk/ — n. **1** application of mental or physical effort to a purpose; use of energy (did some strenuous work). **2 a** task to be undertaken. **b** (prec. by the; foll. by of) task occupying (no more than) a specified time (the work of a moment). **3** thing done or made by work; result of an action; thing made (this is her best work; work of art). **4** employment or occupation etc., esp. as a means of earning income (out of work). **5** literary or musical composition (the works of Shakespeare). **6** actions or experiences of a specified kind (nice work!). **7** (in comb.) things made of a specified material or with specified tools etc. (ironwork; needlework). **8** (in pl.) operative part of a clock or machine. **9** Physics the exertion of force overcoming resistance or producing molecular change. **10** (in full **the works**) colloq. **a** all that is available or needed. **b** full, esp. harsh, treatment. **11** (in pl.) operations of building or repair (road works). **12** (in pl.; often treated as sing.) factory etc. (cement works; repair works). **13** (usu. in pl.) Theol. meritorious act. **14** (usu. in pl. or in comb.) defensive structure (earthworks). — v. **1** (often foll. by at, on) do work; be engaged in bodily or mental activity. **2 a** be employed in certain work (works in industry). **b** (foll. by with) be the workmate of (a person). **3** make efforts (works for peace). **4** (foll. by in) be a craftsman in (a material). **5** operate or function, esp. effectively (how does this machine work?; your idea will not work). **6** operate, manage, control (cannot work the machine). **7 a** put or keep in operation or at work; cause to toil (this mine is no longer worked; works the staff hard). **b** cultivate (land). **8 a** bring about; produce as a result (worked miracles). **b** colloq. arrange (matters) (worked it so that we could go; can you work things for us?). **9** knead, hammer; bring to a desired shape or consistency (work the dough). **10** do, or make by, needlework etc. **11** (cause to) progress or penetrate, or make (one's way), gradually or with difficulty in a specified way (worked the peg into the hole; worked our way through the crowd). **12** (foll. by loose etc.) gradually become (loose etc.) by constant movement. **13** artificially excite (worked themselves into a rage). **14 a**

purchase with one's labour instead of money (work one's passage). **b** obtain by labour the money for (worked my way through university). **15** (foll. by on, upon) have influence (it worked on his imagination; worked on him to get him to agree). **16** be in motion or agitated; ferment (his features worked violently; the yeast began to work). **17** solve a sum by mathematics. □ **at work** in action, engaged in work. **get worked up** become angry, excited, or tense. **give a person the works** colloq. **1** give or tell a person everything. **2** treat a person harshly. **have one's work cut out** be faced with a hard task. **work back** work overtime. **work in** find a place for. **work off** get rid of by work or activity. **work out 1 a** solve (a sum) or find (an amount) by calculation. **b** solve, understand (a problem, person, etc.). **2** (foll. by at) be calculated. **3** give a definite result (this sum will not work out). **4** have a result (the plan worked out well). **5** provide for the details of (has worked out a scheme). **6** engage in physical exercise or training. **work over 1** examine thoroughly. **2** colloq. treat with violence. **work a point** colloq. take an unfair advantage. **work through** arrive at an understanding of (a problem) etc. **work up 1** bring gradually to an efficient or (of a painting etc.) advanced state. **2** (foll. by to) advance gradually to a climax etc. (the skirmish worked up to a violent battle; my argument was working up to that very conclusion). **3** elaborate or excite by degrees (worked up a ravenous appetite; worked up her resentment). **4** mingle (ingredients). **5** learn (a subject) by study (worked up my French). **work wonders** see WONDER. [Old English]

**workable** adj. that can be worked, will work, or is worth working (a workable quarry; a workable scheme). □ **workability** n.

**workaday** adj. **1** ordinary, everyday, practical. **2** dull, unimaginative, commonplace; pedestrian.

**workaholic** /,wer-kuh-**hol**-ik/ n. colloq. person addicted to working. [-HOLIC]

**workbench** n. bench for manual work, esp. carpentry.

**worker** n. **1** person who works, esp. for an employer. **2** neuter bee or ant. **3** person who works hard. **4** draught bullock or horse.

**workers' compensation** n. **1** legislation that provides for the compensation of an employee injured in the course of employment. **2** payment made under this legislation.

**work experience** *n*. scheme intended to give young people temporary experience of employment.

**workforce** *n*. **1** workers engaged or available. **2** number of these.

**workhorse** *n*. hard and willing worker.

**working** — *attrib. adj.* **1 a** engaged in work (*working mother*; *working man*). **b** while so engaged (*all his working life*; *in working hours*). **2** functioning or able to function (*working model*). — *n*. **1** activity of work. **2** act or manner of functioning of a thing (*its working is erratic*). **3** mine or quarry. **4** (usu. in *pl*.) machinery, mechanism.

**working bee** *n*. gathering of volunteers to perform a (communal) task.

**working capital** *n*. capital actually used in a business.

**working class** *n*. social class employed, esp. in manual or industrial work, for wages. □ **working-class** *adj*.

**working hypothesis** *n*. hypothesis used as a basis for action.

**working knowledge** *n*. knowledge adequate to work with.

**working order** *n*. condition in which a machine works.

**working party** *n*. group of people appointed to study and advise on a particular problem.

**workload** *n*. amount of work to be done.

**workman** *n*. **1** man employed to do manual labour. **2** person with regard to skill in a job (*a good workman*).

**workmanlike** *adj*. competent, showing practised skill.

**workmanship** *n*. degree of skill in doing a task or of finish in the product made.

**workmate** *n*. person working alongside another.

**workout** *n*. session of physical exercise or training.

**worksheet** *n*. **1** paper for recording work done or in progress. **2** paper listing questions or activities for students etc. to work through.

**workshop** — *n*. **1** room or building in which goods are manufactured. **2** place or meeting for concerted discussion or activity (*dance workshop*). — *v*. put to test or trial in a practical way (esp. of a hitherto unperformed play etc.) in a non-public context (*I learned a lot from seeing parts of my play workshopped by actors*). □ **workshopping** *n*.

**work-shy** *adj*. disinclined to work.

**workstation** *n*. (also **work station**) **1** location of a stage in a manufacturing process. **2** desk with a computer (or computer terminal); the computer itself.

**work to rule** — *v*. (esp. in the context of an industrial dispute) follow official working rules exactly in order to reduce output. — *n*. (**work-to-rule**) act or instance of working to rule. — *adj*. (**work-to-rule**) of or pertaining to this form of industrial action.

**world** /werld/ *n*. **1 a** the earth, or a planetary body like it. **b** its countries and people. **2** particular division, section, or generation of the earth's inhabitants or human society: **a** with ref. to the place or time of their existence (*the ancient world*; *the medieval world*; *the New World*; *the Third World*). **b** with ref. to their interests or pursuits (*the world of art*; *the world of high finance*; *the world of sport*; *the fashionable world*; *the academic world*). **3 a** each of the three primary divisions of natural objects (*the animal world*; *the vegetable world*; *the mineral world*). **b** particular class of physical or mental etc. things (*the reptile world*; *the world of fantasy*). **4** society at large, the public (often with ref. to its judgment or opinion) (*the whole world knows the truth of the matter*). **5 a** the universe or all that exists; everything. **b** everything that exists outside oneself (*dead to the world*). **c** that which exists within oneself, one's private mental life (*he's withdrawn into his own inner world*). **d** (prec. by *the, this*) mortal life (opp. the afterlife) (*must do what we can in this world*). **e** secular interests and affairs (opp. the spiritual life) (*withdrew from the world into a monastery*). **6** human affairs; their course and conditions (*how goes the world with you?*). **7** any complex unity viewed as being an epitome of the universe (*a drop of water is a world in itself*). **8** (foll. by *of*) a vast amount (*that makes a world of difference*; *he thinks the world of you*). **9** (*attrib.*) affecting many nations, of all nations (*world politics*; *world champion*). □ **bring** (or **come**) **into the world** give birth (or be born). **for all the world** (foll. by *like, as if*) precisely (*looked for all the world as if they were real*). **in the world** of all; at all (*what in the world is it?*). **man** (or **woman**) **of the world** person experienced and practical in human affairs. **out of this world** *colloq*. extremely good etc. (*the food was out of this world*). **think the world of** have a very high regard for. [Old English]

**world-class** *adj*. of a quality or standard fit to be regarded as high throughout the world.

**World Heritage list** *n*. list kept by UNESCO of sites designated by a government for conservation and protection under the World Heritage Convention.

**World Heritage listing** *n.* process of entering (an area etc.) on the World Heritage list.

**worldly** *adj.* (**-ier, -iest**) **1** of the affairs of the world, temporal, earthly, secular (opp. spiritual, religious, etc.) (*worldly goods*; *worldly pleasures*). **2** experienced in life, sophisticated, practical. □ **worldliness** *n.*

**worldly-wise** *adj.* prudent or shrewd in one's dealings with the world.

**world music** *n.* rock music that incorporates local or ethnic elements (esp. from the developing world).

**world war** *n.* war involving many major nations.

**world-weary** *adj.* bored with human affairs. □ **world-weariness** *n.*

**worldwide** — *adj.* occurring in or known in all parts of the world. — *adv.* throughout the world.

**WORM** /werm/ *n.* (also **worm**) class of storage device in which data, once written, cannot be erased or overwritten. [abbreviation: *write once read many times*]

**worm** /werm/ — *n.* **1** any of various types of creeping or burrowing invertebrate animals with long slender bodies and no limbs. **2** larva of an insect, esp. in fruit or wood. **3** (in *pl.*) intestinal or other internal parasites. **4** maggot supposed to eat dead bodies in the grave. **5** insignificant or contemptible person. **6 a** spiral part of a screw. **b** short screw working in a worm-gear. **7 a** = COMPUTER VIRUS. **b** rogue software package which, when entered into a computer, replicates itself until all available space in the system is used up. — *v.* **1** (often *refl.*) move with a crawling motion (*wormed through the bushes*; *wormed his way through the shrubbery*). **2** *refl.* (foll. by *into*) insinuate oneself into favour etc. (*wormed himself into her affections*). **3** (foll. by *out*) obtain (a secret etc.) by cunning persistence (*wormed the information out of me*). **4** rid (a dog etc.) of worms. [Old English]

**worm-cast** *n.* convoluted mass of earth left on the surface by a burrowing earthworm.

**wormeaten** *adj.* **1** eaten into by worms; decayed. **2** old and dilapidated.

**worm-gear** *n.* arrangement of a toothed gear worked by a revolving spiral.

**worm-hole** *n.* hole left by the passage of a worm.

**worm's-eye view** *n.* view from below or from a humble position.

**worm-wheel** *n.* wheel of a worm-gear.

**wormwood** /werm-wuud/ *n.* **1** plant with a bitter aromatic taste, used in vermouth and absinthe. **2** bitter mortification; source of this. [Old English: cf. VERMOUTH]

**wormy** *adj.* (**-ier, -iest**) **1** full of worms. **2** wormeaten. □ **worminess** *n.*

**worn** /wawn/ *past part.* of WEAR. — *adj.* **1** damaged by use or wear. **2** looking tired and exhausted. **3** (in full **well-worn**) (of a joke etc.) stale; often heard.

**worrisome** /wu-ree-suhm/ *adj.* causing worry or distress.

**worry** /wu-ree/ — *v.* (**-ies, -ied**) **1** give way to anxiety; fret (*you worry too much*). **2** harass, importune; be a trouble or anxiety to (*worries his parents continually*). **3** (of a dog etc.) shake or pull about with the teeth; harass (*dog worrying a sock*; *dog worrying sheep*). **4** (as **worried** *adj.*) **a** uneasy; troubled in the mind. **b** suggesting worry (*a worried look*). — *n.* (*pl.* **-ies**) **1** thing that causes anxiety or disturbs tranquillity. **2** disturbed state of mind; anxiety. □ **not to worry** *colloq.* there is no need to worry. **no worries** *colloq.* no bother, no trouble; fine; okay (*Can I borrow the car? — No worries*). **worry for** (in Aboriginal English) be concerned about or preoccupied with (*he worries for his country*). **worry out** obtain (the solution to a problem etc.) by dogged effort. □ **worriedly** *adv.* **worrier** *n.* **worryingly** *adv.* [Old English, = strangle]

**worse** /wers/ — *adj.* **1** bad to a greater degree. **2** (*predic.*) in or into worse health or a worse condition (*is getting worse*; *none the worse for it*). — *adv.* more badly; more ill. — *n.* **1** worse thing or things (*you might do worse than accept*). **2** (*prec.* by *the*) worse condition (*a change for the worse*). □ **none the worse** (often foll. by *for*) not adversely affected (by). **the worse for wear 1** damaged by use. **2** injured. **3** *colloq.* drunk. **worse luck** unfortunately. **worse off** in a worse (esp. financial) position. [Old English]

**worsen** *v.* make or become worse.

**worship** /wer-shuhp/ — *n.* **1 a** homage or service to a deity. **b** acts, rites, or ceremonies, of this. **2** adoration or devotion shown towards a person or principle (*the worship of wealth*; *regarded him with worship in their eyes*; *hero worship*). — *v.* (**-pp-**) **1** adore as divine; honour with religious rites. **2** idolise or regard with adoration (*worships the ground she walks on*). **3** attend public worship. **4** be full of adoration. □ **worshipper** *n.* [Old English: related to WORTH, -SHIP]

**worst** /werst/ — *adj.* bad in the greatest degree. — *adv.* most badly. — *n.* worst part or possibility (*the worst of the storm is over*; *prepare for the worst*). — *v.* get the better of; defeat (*worsted him thrice running*). □ **at its** etc. **worst** in the worst state. **at worst** (or **the worst**) in the worst possible case. **do your worst** expression of defiance. **get the worst of it** be defeated. **if the worst comes to the worst** if the worst happens. [Old English: related to WORSE]

**worsted** /wuus-tuhd/ *n.* **1** fine woollen yarn. **2** fabric made from this. [*Worste(a)d* in Norfolk]

**wort** /wert/ *n.* **1** archaic (except in names) plant (*liverwort*). **2** infusion of malt before it is fermented into beer. [Old English]

**worth** /werth/ — *predic. adj.* (used like a preposition) **1** of a value equivalent to (*is worth $50*; *is worth very little*). **2** such as to justify or repay (*worth doing*; *not worth the trouble*). **3** possessing or having property amounting to (*is worth a million dollars*). — *n.* **1** what a person or thing is worth; the (usu. specified) merit of (*of great worth*; *of very little worth*). **2** equivalent of money in a commodity (*ten dollars' worth of petrol*). □ **for all one is worth** *colloq.* with one's utmost efforts. **for what it is worth** without a guarantee of its truth or value. **worth it** *colloq.* worth while. **worth one's salt** see SALT. **worth one's weight in gold** see WEIGHT. **worth while** (or **one's while**) see WHILE. [Old English]

**worthless** *adj.* without value or merit. □ **worthlessness** *n.*

**worthwhile** *adj.* that is worth the time, effort, or money spent.

---

■ **Usage** See note at *while.*

---

**worthy** /wer-*th*ee/ — *adj.* (**-ier, -iest**) **1** deserving respect, estimable (*lived a worthy life*). **2** entitled to (esp. condescending) recognition (*a worthy old couple*). **3 a** (foll. by *of* or *to* + infin.) deserving (*worthy of a mention*). **b** (foll. by *of*) adequate or suitable to the dignity etc. of (*words worthy of the occasion*). — *n.* (*pl.* **-ies**) **1** worthy person. **2** person of some distinction. □ **worthily** *adv.* **worthiness** *n.*

**-worthy** *comb. form* forming adjectives meaning: **1** deserving of (*noteworthy*). **2** suitable or fit for (*newsworthy*; *roadworthy*).

**would** /wuud, wuhd/ *v.aux.* (*3rd sing.* **would**) *past* of WILL[1], used esp.: **1** in reported speech (*he said he would be home by evening*). **2** to express a condition (*they would have been killed if they had gone*). **3** to express habitual action (*would wait every evening*). **4** to express a

question or polite request (*would they like it?*; *would you come in, please?*). **5** to express probability (*she would be over fifty by now*). **6** to express consent (*they would not help*).

**would-be** *attrib. adj.* desiring or aspiring to be (*a would-be politician*).

**wouldn't** *contr.* would not. □ **I wouldn't know** (as is to be expected) I do not know.

**wouldn't it!** *colloq.* expressing dismay, exasperation, or disgust (*My raffle ticket blew out of the train-window and it had the winning number. Wouldn't it! — Wouldn't it!*).

**wound[1]** /woond/ — *n.* **1** injury done to living tissue by a deep cut or heavy blow etc. **2** pain inflicted on one's feelings; injury to one's reputation. — *v.* inflict a wound on (*wounded soldiers*; *wounded his feelings*). □ **woundingly** *adv.* [Old English]

**wound[2]** /wownd/ *past* and *past part.* of WIND[2].

**wound-up** *adj.* excited; tense; angry.

**wove** *past* of WEAVE[1].

**woven** *past part.* of WEAVE[1].

**wow[1]** /wow/ — *int.* expressing astonishment or admiration. — *n. colloq.* a sensational success. — *v. colloq.* impress greatly. [imitative]

**wow[2]** /wow/ *n.* slow pitch-fluctuation in sound-reproduction, perceptible in long notes. [imitative]

**wowse** /wowz/ *v.* (esp. as **wowsing**) preach at, moralise; behave puritanically (*wowsing on at me because I went to the party*). [back-formation from WOWSER *n.*]

**wowser** /wow-zuh/ — *n.* **1** puritanical fanatic; person who tries to inflict his or her rigid or narrow morality on others or would have it inflicted on all society; kill-joy. **2** teetotaller. — *v.* preach at, moralise; behave puritanically. — *adj.* of or pertaining to a wowser; publicly censorious of others and the pleasures they seek. □ **wowserish** *adj.* **wowserly** *adv.* [origin uncertain]

**woylie** /woi-lee/ *n.* = KANGAROO RAT. [Nyungar *walyu*]

**WP** *abbr.* word processor or processing.

**w.p.m.** *abbr.* words per minute.

**wrack** *n.* **1** seaweed cast up or growing on the shore. **2** destruction; ruin. **3** wreck or wreckage. [Low German or Dutch *wrak*: cf. WRECK]

**wraith** /rayth/ *n.* **1** ghost. **2** spectral appearance of a living person supposed to portend that person's death. [origin unknown]

**wrangle** /rang-guhl/ — *n.* noisy argument or dispute. — *v.* (**-ling**) engage in a wrangle. [Low German or Dutch]

**wrap** /rap/ — v. (-**pp**-) **1** (often foll. by *up*) envelop in folded or soft encircling material (*wrap it in tissue*; *wrap up a parcel*). **2** (foll. by *round*, *about*) arrange or draw (a pliant covering) round (a person) (*wrapped the shawl closer round me*). — n. **1** shawl, scarf, etc. **2** wrapping material (*Christmas wrap*). □ **take the wraps off** disclose. **under wraps** in secrecy. **wrapped up** in engrossed or absorbed in. **wrap up 1** *colloq.* finish off (a matter) (*that about wraps it up for the day*; *wrapped up the deal in under an hour*). **2** put on warm clothes (*wrap up well*). [origin unknown]

**wraparound** n. *Computing* facility on a screen where long text is displayed as two or more successive lines.

**wrapped** adj. (also **rapt**) entranced; overjoyed. □ **wrapped in** infatuated by (*he's wrapped in her*).

**wrapper** n. **1** cover for a sweet, book, posted newspaper, etc. **2** loose enveloping robe or gown.

**wrapping** n. (esp. in *pl.*) material used to wrap; wraps, wrappers.

**wrapping paper** n. strong or decorative paper for wrapping parcels.

**wrasse** /ras/ n. any of various bright-coloured marine fish with thick lips and strong teeth, some being good food-fish (as the species found on the Great Barrier Reef). [Cornish *wrach*]

**wrath** /roth/ n. *literary* extreme anger. [Old English: related to WROTH]

**wrathful** adj. *literary* extremely angry. □ **wrathfully** adv.

**wreak** /reek/ v. **1** (usu. foll. by *on*, *upon*) give rein to (vengeance or one's anger etc.) (*wreaked vengeance on them both*). **2** cause (damage etc.) (*wreak havoc*). [Old English, = avenge]

**wreath** /reeth/ n. (pl. **-s** /reethz/) **1** flowers or leaves fastened in a ring, esp. as an ornament for the head or for laying on a grave etc. **2** curl or ring of smoke, cloud, or soft fabric. [Old English: related to WRITHE]

**wreathe** /reeth/ v. (-**thing**) **1** encircle or cover as, with, or like a wreath. **2** (foll. by *round*) wind (one's arms etc.) round (a person etc.). **3** (of smoke etc.) move in wreaths. **4 a** form (flowers etc.) into a wreath. **b** make a garland.

**wreck** — n. **1** the sinking or running aground of a ship. **2** ship that has suffered a wreck. **3** greatly damaged building, thing, or person (*had become a physical and mental wreck*). **4 a** (foll. by *of*) wretched remnant (*tried to survive on the wrecks of his fortune*). **b** ruin (*the wreck of all his hopes*). — v. **1 a** seriously damage (a vehicle etc.). **b** ruin (hopes, a

life, etc.). **2 a** cause the wreck of (a ship). **b** suffer a wreck (*they were wrecked on the Australian shore*). **3** (as **wrecked**) *adj.* **a** involved in a shipwreck (*wrecked sailors*). **b** *colloq.* exhausted or ill, esp. after eating, drinking, merrymaking to excess. [Anglo-French *wrec* from Germanic]

**wreckage** n. **1** wrecked material. **2** remnants of a wreck. **3** act or process of wrecking.

**wrecker** n. **1** person or thing that wrecks or destroys. **2** person employed in demolition or breaking up damaged vehicles. **3** firm etc., the business of which is the demolition of houses, buildings, etc.

**wreckers** n. business which sells products from demolished buildings, damaged vehicles, etc. (*you can get some good stuff cheap at the wreckers*).

**wren** n. **1** small usu. brown short-winged songbird of Europe etc. with an erect tail. **2** (also **fairy wren**) any of many small, ground-frequenting insectivorous Australian birds, unrelated to the European bird, the males having brightly coloured (esp. blue) plumage (*splendid wren*), and sometimes chestnut shoulder patches (*variegated wren*). [Old English]

**wrench** — n. **1** violent twist or oblique pull or act of tearing off. **2** adjustable tool like a spanner for gripping and turning nuts etc. **3** instance of painful uprooting or parting (*leaving home was a great wrench*). — v. **1** twist or pull violently round or sideways. **2** twist (the ankle etc.) (*stumbled and wrenched his ankle*). **3** (often foll. by *off*, *away*, etc.) pull off with a wrench. **4** distort (facts etc.) to suit a theory etc. (*wrenched the evidence to suit his argument*). [Old English]

**wrest** v. **1** wrench away from a person's grasp (*wrested the pistol from him*; *wrested the presidency from the incumbent*). **2** (foll. by *from*) obtain by effort or with difficulty (*wresting a meagre living from almost barren soil*). [Old English]

**wrestle** /res-uhl/ — n. **1** contest in which two opponents grapple and try to throw each other to the ground, esp. as an athletic sport. **2** hard struggle. — v. (-**ling**) **1** (often foll. by *with*) take part or fight (a person) in a wrestle (*wrestled his opponent to the ground*). **2 a** (foll. by *with*, *against*) struggle (*wrestled against poverty*). **b** (foll. by *with*) do one's utmost to deal with (a task, difficulty, etc.) (*wrestled with his problems*). □ **wrestler** n. **wrestling** n. [Old English]

**wretch** n. **1** unfortunate or pitiable person. **2** (often as a playful term of depreciation) reprehensible person. [Old English, = outcast]

**wretched** /rech-uhd/ adj. (**wretcheder**, **wretchedest**) **1** unhappy, miserable; unwell. **2** of bad quality; contemptible. **3** displeasing, hateful. □ **feel wretched 1** be unwell. **2** be much embarrassed. □ **wretchedly** adv. **wretchedness** n.

**wrick** var. of RICK².

**wriggle** /rig-uhl/ — v. (**-ling**) **1** (of a worm etc.) twist or turn its body with short writhing movements. **2** (of a person or animal) make wriggling motions. **3** (foll. by along, through, etc.) go thus (wriggled through the gap). **4** be evasive; squirm out of (a difficult situation etc.) (wriggled out of the embarrassing spot he was in). — n. act of wriggling. □ **get a wriggle on** hurry up, 'get a move on' (get a wriggle on, mate, we're way behind). □ **wriggly** adj. [Low German wriggelen]

**wriggler** n. the larva of a mosquito.

**wright** /ruyt/ n. maker or builder (usu. in comb.: playwright; shipwright). [Old English: related to WORK]

**wring** — v. (past and past part. **wrung**) **1 a** squeeze tightly; press (the hand) with emotion (wrung his hand). **b** (often foll. by out) squeeze and twist, esp. to remove liquid (wrung out the wet cloth). **2** break by twisting (wrung the bird's neck). **3** distress, torture (wrung him with repeated accusations). **4** extract by squeezing. **5** (foll. by out, from) obtain by pressure or importunity; extort (wrung a confession from him). — n. act of wringing. □ **wring one's hands** clasp them as a gesture of great distress. **wring the neck of** kill (a chicken etc.) by twisting its neck. [Old English]

**wringer** n. device for wringing water from washed clothes etc.

**wringing** adj. (in full **wringing wet**) so wet that water can be wrung out.

**wrinkle** /ring-kuhl/ — n. **1** crease in the skin, esp. caused by age. **2** similar mark in another flexible surface. — v. (**-ling**) **1** make wrinkles in. **2** form wrinkles. [probably related to Old English gewrinclod sinuous]

**wrinkly** — adj. (**-ier**, **-iest**) having wrinkles. — n. colloq. offens. old or middle-aged person.

**wrist** n. **1** joint connecting the hand with the arm. **2** part of a garment covering this. [Old English]

**wristlet** n. band or ring to strengthen, guard, or adorn the wrist.

**wristwatch** n. small watch worn on a strap etc. round the wrist.

**writ** n. **1** form of written command to act or abstain from acting in some way. **2** document ordering the election of a member or members of parliament. **3** archaic written matter (Holy Writ). [Old English: related to WRITE]

**write** v. (**-ting**; past **wrote**; past part. **written**) **1** mark paper or some other surface with symbols, letters, or words (he's in his room writing). **2** form or mark (such symbols etc.) (write the letter Q). **3** form or mark the symbols of (a word or sentence, or document etc.) (wrote the paragraph on the blackboard). **4** fill or complete (a sheet, cheque, etc.) with writing. **5** transfer (data) into a computer store. **6** (esp. in passive) indicate (a quality or condition) by one's or its appearance (guilt was written on his face). **7** compose (a text, novel, etc.) for written or printed reproduction or publication (is writing a fantasy trilogy). **8** be engaged in composing a text, article, etc. (she writes for the local newspaper). **9** (usu. foll. by to) write and send a letter (to a person) (wrote to her last week). **10** colloq. write and send a letter to (a person) (wrote her last week). **11** convey (news etc.) by letter (wrote that they would arrive next Friday). **12** state in a book etc. (it is written that). **13** (foll. by into, out of) include or exclude (a character or episode) in a story by changing the text (wrote the nun out of the plot). □ **write down 1** record in writing. **2** write as if for those considered inferior (the best writers for teenagers never write down to their readers). **write in** send a suggestion, query, etc., in writing to e.g. a broadcasting station. **write off 1** (foll. by for) = send away for (see SEND). **2** cancel the record of (a bad debt etc.); acknowledge the loss of (an asset). **3** completely destroy (a vehicle etc.). **4** dismiss as insignificant. **write once read many times** see WORM. **write oneself off** colloq. get completely drunk. **write out** write in full or in finished form. **write up 1** write a full account of; bring (a diary etc.) up to date. **2** praise in writing. [Old English]

**write-off** n. **1** thing written off, esp. a vehicle too badly damaged to be repaired. **2** colloq. drunk person. **3** something or someone dismissed as worthless or ineffectual; a failure.

**writer** n. **1** person who writes or has written something. **2** person who writes books, author.

**writer's block** n. periodic lack of inspiration affecting creative writers.

**writer's cramp** n. muscular spasm due to excessive writing.

**write-up** n. written or published account, review.

**writhe** /ruyth/ v. (**-thing**) **1** twist or roll oneself about in or as in acute pain. **2** suffer mental torture or embarrassment (*writhed with shame*; *writhed at the thought*). **3** twist (one's body etc.) about. [Old English]

**writing** n. **1** written words etc. (*couldn't decipher the writing on the old tombstone*). **2** handwriting. **3** (usu. in *pl.*) author's works (*the writings of Banjo Paterson*). □ **in writing** in written form. **the writing on the wall** ominously significant event etc.

**written** *past part.* of WRITE.

**wrong** — *adj.* **1** mistaken; not true; in error (*gave a wrong answer*; *I was wrong*). **2** unsuitable; incorrect; less or least desirable (*the wrong road*; *wrong way to hold the racquet*; *a wrong decision*; *wrong way to end a business letter*). **3 a** contrary to law or morality (*it is wrong to steal*). **b** (in Aboriginal English) not according to law, esp. marriage laws (*he is wrong for her*; *wrong marriages*). **4** amiss; out of order, in a bad or abnormal condition (*something wrong with my heart*; *has gone wrong*). — *adv.* (usually placed last) in a wrong manner or direction; with an incorrect result (*guessed wrong*). — *n.* **1** what is morally wrong. **2** injustice; unjust action or treatment (*suffer a wrong*). — *v.* **1** treat unjustly; do wrong to. **2** mistakenly attribute bad motives to. □ **do wrong** sin. **do wrong to** malign or mistreat (a person). **get in wrong with** incur the dislike or disapproval of (a person). **get wrong 1** misunderstand (a person, statement, etc.). **2** obtain an incorrect answer to. (**get**) **the wrong end of the pineapple** see PINEAPPLE. **get** (or **get hold of**) **the wrong end of the stick** misunderstand completely. **go wrong 1** take the wrong path. **2** stop functioning properly. **3** depart from virtuous or suitable behaviour. **in the wrong** responsible for a quarrel, mistake, or offence. **on the wrong side of 1** out of favour with (a person). **2** (of a person's age) closer to the next decade. **wrong side out** inside out. **wrong way round** in the opposite or reverse of the normal or desirable orientation or sequence etc. □ **wrongly** *adv.* **wrongness** n. [Old English]

**wrongdoer** n. person who behaves immorally or illegally. □ **wrongdoing** n.

**wrong-foot** v. *colloq.* **1** (in tennis, football, etc.) play so as to catch (an opponent) off balance. **2** disconcert; catch unprepared.

**wrongful** *adj.* unwarranted, unjustified (*wrongful arrest*). □ **wrongfully** *adv.*

**wrong-headed** *adj.* perverse and obstinate.

**wrong side** n. worse or undesirable or unusable side of esp. fabric.

**wrong'un** /rong-uhn/ n. *colloq.* **1** person of bad character. **2** *Cricket* = GOOGLY.

**wrote** *past* of WRITE.

**wroth** /rohth, roth/ *predic. adj. archaic* angry. [Old English]

**wrought** /rawt/ *archaic past* and *past part.* of WORK. — *adj.* (of metals) beaten out or shaped by hammering.

**wrought iron** n. tough malleable form of iron suitable for forging or rolling, not cast.

**wrung** *past* and *past part.* of WRING.

**wry** /ruy/ *adj.* (**wryer, wryest** or **wrier, wriest**) **1** distorted or turned to one side. **2** (of a face, smile, etc.) contorted in disgust, disappointment, or mockery. **3** (of humour) dry and mocking. □ **wryly** *adv.* **wryness** n. [Old English]

**WSW** *abbr.* west-south-west.

**wt.** *abbr.* weight.

**WTO** *abbr.* World Trade Organisation, the successor to GATT.

**Wuna** /wuur-nu/ n. an Aboriginal language spoken in the NT east of Darwin.

**Wunambal** /wuu-nahm-bahl/ n. an Aboriginal language spoken in the far north of WA.

**wurley** /wer-lee/ n. **1** = GUNYAH. **2** any temporary shelter. [Gaurna *warli*]

**wurrung** /wu-rung/ n. (also **crescent nail-tailed wallaby**) nail-tailed wallaby having a crescent-shaped white marking on the shoulder: now presumed extinct. [probably Nyungar *warang*]

**wuss** /wuus/ n. *colloq.* timid, un-macho male; a wimp (e.g. a surfie who tests the water temperature before venturing in); a weak or ineffectual person. □ **wussy** /wuus-ee/ *adj.* [origin uncertain: perhaps an abbreviation of *pussy-wussy* kitten]

**Wuywurung** /wuy-wu-rung/ n. an Aboriginal language spoken in the region now occupied by Melbourne and up to as far north as Seymour, and to the north of Westernport, and from the Goulburn River across to Bendigo: now extinct, the last few speakers being recorded in the 1960s.

**wych-hazel** var. of WITCH-HAZEL.

**WYSIWYG** /wiz-ee-wig/ *adj.* (also **wysiwyg**) *Computing* denoting a form of text onscreen exactly corresponding to its appearance on a printed version. [acronym of *what you see is what you get*]

**wyvern** /wuy-vuhn/ n. winged two-legged dragon with a barbed tail. [from Latin *vipera* viper]

# X

**X** /eks/ *n.* (also **x**) (*pl.* **Xs** or **X's**) **1** twenty-fourth letter of the alphabet. **2** (as a Roman numeral) ten. **3** (usu. **x**) *Algebra* first unknown quantity. **4** unknown or unspecified number or person etc. **5** cross-shaped symbol used esp. to indicate position (*X marks the spot*) or incorrectness, or to symbolise a kiss or a vote, or as the signature of a person who cannot write.

**xanthic** /zan-thik/ *adj.* usu. *Bot.* yellowish. [Greek *xanthos* yellow]

**Xanthippe** /zan-**thip**-ee/ *n.* (also **Xantippe** /-**tip**-ee/ ) shrewish or ill-tempered woman. [name of Socrates' wife]

**xanthophyll** /zan-thuh-fil, -thoh-/ *n.* any of various oxygen-containing carotenoids associated with chlorophyll, some of which cause the yellow colour of leaves in autumn. [Greek *xanthos* yellow, *phullon* leaf]

**xanthorrhoea** /zan-thuh-**ree**-uh/ *n.* (also **blackboy**, **grass-tree**, **yacca**) any of 17 species of the Australian genus of the same name, varying in form from herb-like plants to small trees of all States, the most typical being *Xanthorrhoea australis*, having a tall trunk surmounted by a crown of grass-like leaves from which arises a flowering spike 4 to 5m tall. [Greek *xanthos* yellow, *rhoia* flowing, referring to the aromatic yellow resin exuded by some species]

**X chromosome** *n.* (in humans and some other mammals) sex chromosome of which the number in female cells is twice that in male cells. [*X* as an arbitrary label]

**Xe** *symb.* xenon.

**xeno-** /zen-oh/ *comb. form* **1 a** foreign. **b** a foreigner. **2** other. [Greek *xenos* strange, foreign; stranger]

**xenon** /zen-on, zee-non/ *n.* heavy inert gaseous element. [Greek, neuter of *xenos* strange]

**xenophobe** /zen-uh-,fohb/ *n.* person suffering from xenophobia.

**xenophobia** /,zen-uh-**foh**-bee-uh/ *n.* hatred or fear of foreigners or strangers. □ **xenophobic** *adj.* [Greek *xenos* strange, stranger]

**xerography** /zeer-**rog**-ruh-fee, ze-/ *n.* dry copying process in which powder adheres to areas remaining electrically charged after exposure of the surface to light from an image of the document to be copied. □ **xerograph** /zeer-ruh-,grahf, -graf, **ze-**/ *n.* [Greek *xēros* dry]

**xerox** /zeer-roks, ze-/ — *n. propr.* **1** machine for copying by xerography. **2** copy thus made. — *v.* reproduce by this process.

**xi** /suy, gzuy/ *n.* fourteenth letter of the Greek alphabet (Ξ, ξ). [Greek]

**-xion** see -ION.

**Xmas** /kris-muhs, eks-muhs/ *n. colloq.* = CHRISTMAS. [abbreviation, with X for the initial chi of Greek *Khristos* Christ]

**X-rated** *adj.* (of a videotape) classified as non-violent erotica for viewing by persons over 18 years of age only.

**X-ray** /eks-ray/ — *n.* **1** (in *pl.*) electro-magnetic radiation of short wavelength, able to pass through opaque bodies. **2** photograph made by X-rays, esp. showing the position of bones etc. by their greater absorption of the rays. — *adj.* (of traditional Aboriginal painting) characterised by the depiction of the internal organs (spinal column, heart, lungs, etc.) as well as by the external form, this being a convention to indicate that a living being is more than mere outer appearance. — *v.* photograph, examine, or treat with X-rays. [*X*, originally with ref. to the unknown nature of the rays]

**xylem** /zuy-luhm/ *n. Bot.* woody tissue (cf. PHLOEM). [Greek]

**xylo-** /zuy-loh/ *comb. form* wood. [Greek *xulon* wood]

**xylograph** /zuy-luh-,grahf, -,graf/ *n.* wood-cut or wood-engraving (esp. an early one). □ **xylography** /-log-ruh-fee/ *n.*

**xylophone** /zuy-luh-,fohn/ *n.* musical instrument of graduated wooden or metal bars struck with small wooden hammers. □ **xylophonist** *n.*

# Y

**Y¹** /wuy/ *n.* (also **y**) (*pl.* **Ys** or **Y's**) **1** twenty-fifth letter of the alphabet. **2** (usu. **y**) *Algebra* second unknown quantity. **3** Y-shaped thing.

**Y²** *symb.* yttrium.

**-y¹** *suffix* forming adjectives: **1** from nouns and adjectives, meaning: **a** full of; having the quality of (*messy*). **b** addicted to (*boozy*). **2** from verbs, meaning 'inclined to', 'apt to' (*sticky*). [Old English]

**-y²** *suffix* (also **-ey, -ie**) **1** forming diminutive nouns, pet names, etc. (*granny; Stewie; nightie*). **2** widespread in Australia as a mark of familiarity, added to: **a** usu. monosyllabic forms (*bluey; chalkie; littley; tinny*; etc.). **b** shortened forms of words or collocations (*Aussie; blowey; ocky; tilly*; etc.). [originally Scottish]

**-y³** *suffix* forming nouns denoting: **1** state, condition, or quality (*orthodoxy; modesty*). **2** an action or its result (*colloquy; remedy*). [Latin *-ia*, Greek *-eia*]

**yabber** /yab-uh/ *colloq.* — *n.* (also **yabber-yabber**) talk, conversation; discussion; language (*had a good yabber with the blokes*). — *v.* talk, converse (*those Brits hadn't a clue when we yabbered in Strine*). □ **yabbering** *n.* [probably from an Aboriginal language]

**yabber-stick** *n.* = MESSAGE-STICK.

**yabby** /yab-ee/ — *n.* (also **yabbie**) (*pl.* **-ies**) any of several Australian freshwater crayfish valued as food. — *v.* fish for yabbies. □ **yabbying** *n.* [Wemba-wemba *yabij*]

**yacca** /yak-uh/ *n.* (also **yacka, yakka**) = BLACKBOY; GRASS-TREE (see also XANTHORRHOEA). □ **yacca gum** resin exuded by this tree. [possibly from Gaurna *yakko* a kind of gum obtained from a grass-tree etc.]

**yacht** /yot/ — *n.* **1** light sailing-vessel. **2** larger usu. power-driven vessel for cruising. — *v.* race or cruise in a yacht. [Dutch *jaghtschip*, literally 'pursuit-ship']

**yachtie** /yot-ee/ *n. colloq.* a yachting enthusiast.

**yachtsman** *n.* (*fem.* **yachtswoman**) person who sails yachts.

**yack** var. of YAK².

**yacka** var. of YACCA; YAKKA¹.

**yackai** /yak-uy/ — *n.* call used by an Aborigine (and also later by whites) to command attention (cf. COOEE) or express emotion such as pain or surprise. — *v.*

utter such a call (*yackaied to the others who were some distance away; yackaied with delight*). [Wiradhuri *yagaay*]

**yacker** var. of YAKKA; YAKKER.

**Yadhaykenu** /yah-*th*uy-,kay-noo/ *n.* an Aboriginal language spoken in the north of Cape York Peninsula, Queensland.

**Yagara** /yah-gu-ru/ *n.* an Aboriginal language of the Brisbane region of Queensland and covering a vast surrounding area: now extinct.

**yahoo¹** /yah-hoo/ *n.* **1** name given by Aborigines to: **a** an evil spirit. **b** monster in the form of a huge, hairy man. **2** bird of northern and eastern Australia (*grey-crowned babbler*) having a loud call sounding like 'ya-hoo'. [probably from a NSW Aboriginal language, or perhaps from YAHOO²]

**yahoo²** /yah-hoo/ — *n.* bestial person. — *v.* behave roughly or like a yahoo (*told them to quit yahooing and settle down*). [name of a race of hairy, man-like brutes in Swift's *Gulliver's Travels*]

**Yahweh** /yah-way/ *n.* (also **Yahveh** /-vay/) the Hebrew name of God in the Old Testament. [Hebrew *YHVH* with added vowels; often mistakenly written out as *Jehovah*]

**yak¹** *n.* long-haired humped Tibetan ox. [Tibetan]

**yak²** *colloq. derog.* (also **yakker, yakkety-yak, yackety-yack**) — *n.* trivial or unduly persistent conversation. — *v.* engage in this (*yakking to the neighbours; yakkety-yakking all afternoon*). □ **yak-yak-yak!** derisive exclamation intended to indicate that ongoing conversation etc. is trivial or long-winded. [imitative]

**yakka¹** /yak-uh/ *n.* (also **yacka, yacker, yakker**) *colloq.* work. □ **hard yakka** strenuous labour. [Yagara *yaga*]

**yakka²** /yak-uh/ var. of YACCA.

**yakker** *n. colloq.* **1** *derog.* = YAK². **2** = YAKKA¹.

**Yale lock** *n. propr.* type of lock with a revolving barrel, used for doors etc. [*Yale*, name of its inventor]

**yam** *n.* **1 a** tropical or subtropical climbing plant. **b** edible starchy tuber of this. **2 a** any of several Australian plants (e.g. MURNONG) having an edible tuberous root. **b** the tuber of these plants. [Portuguese or Spanish]

**yam daisy** *n.* small plant of temperate Australia with slender leaves and bright yellow daisy-flowers on tall stems, the tuberous rootstock of which was valued by the Aborigines as food.

**Yammagi** /**yam**-uh-jee/ *n.* an Aborigine. [Watjari *yamaji* person, man]

■ **Usage** See Koori¹.

**yammer** /**yam**-uh/ *colloq.* — *n.* **1** lament, wail, whinge. **2** voluble talk. — *v.* utter a yammer. [Old English]

**yam-stick** *n.* (also **digging-stick**) Aboriginal tool made from a rod of wood pointed at each end and used to excavate yams etc.

**Yandruwandha** /**yahn**-droo-,wahnd-hu/ *n.* an Aboriginal language spoken over a vast area of north-eastern SA and south-western Queensland: now extinct.

**yandy** /**yan**-dee/ (also **yandi**, **yandie**) — *n.* (also **yandy dish**) shallow (wooden) winnowing dish used to separate edible seeds from refuse, or particles of mineral from alluvial material. — *v.* winnow (*showed us the alluvial gold he'd yandied*). [Yindjibarndi and neighbouring languages *yandi* winnowing dish]

**yang** *n.* (in Chinese philosophy) the active male principle of the universe (cf. YIN).

**yang-yang** *adj.* (of a horse) high-spirited. [origin unknown]

**Yank** *n. colloq.* often *derog.* American. [abbreviation of YANKEE]

**yank** *v. & n. colloq.* pull with a jerk. [origin unknown]

**Yankee** /**yang**-kee/ *n. colloq.* often *derog.* = YANK. [origin uncertain: perhaps from Dutch *Janke*, diminutive of *Jan* John, as a nickname]

**Yankunytjatjara** /**yahn**-kuun-ju-, jah-ru/ *n.* a dialect of the Western Desert language.

**yap** — *v.* (**-pp-**) **1** bark shrilly or fussily. **2** *colloq.* talk noisily, foolishly, or complainingly. — *n.* act, instance, or sound of yapping. □ **yappy** *adj.* (**-ier, -iest**) in sense 1 of *v.* [imitative]

**yapunyah** /yuh-**pun**-yuh/ *n.* (also **napunyah**) either of two species of eucalypt occurring along watercourses in Queensland, NSW, and the NT. [Gunya *yapany*]

**Yaralde** /**yu**-ruhl-dee/ *n.* a single Aboriginal language with dialectal variants spoken over a vast area of south-eastern SA: now extinct.

**yard¹** *n.* **1** unit of linear measure in the imperial system equal to 3 feet (0.9144 metre). **2** spar slung across a mast for a sail to hang from. [Old English, = stick]

**yard²** — *n.* **1** the garden of a house (*playing cricket in the back yard*). **2** enclosure in which sheep, cattle, etc. are confined for a particular purpose. **3** enclosed area in which business or work is carried out (*timber yard; shipyard*). — *v.* confine (livestock) in an enclosure. [Old English, = enclosure]

**yard-arm** *n.* either end of a ship's yard.

**yarding** *n.* **1** confining of animals in an enclosure. **2** the animals so confined (*a yarding of 1,000 cattle*).

**yardstick** *n.* **1** any standard of comparison. **2** (formerly) measuring rod a yard long, usu. divided into inches etc.

**yarmulke** /**yah**-muhl-kuh, -muul-/ *n.* (also **yarmulka**) skullcap worn by Jewish men. [Yiddish]

**yarn** — *n.* **1** spun thread, esp. for knitting, weaving, etc. **2 a** *colloq.* a chat; a talk. **b** long or rambling story, traveller's tale, anecdote. — *v.* **1** *colloq.* talk, have a chat. **2** tell yarns. [Old English]

**yarra** /**ya**-ruh/ *adj. colloq.* insane; stupid (*their racket nearly drove me yarra*). [from the name of a psychiatric hospital at *Yarra* Bend, Victoria (cf. *round the bend* at BEND¹)]

**yarraman** /**ya**-ruh-muhn/ *n.* horse. [the word is probably from an Aboriginal language, although its exact meaning in that language is unknown: the word was taken into the early pidgin used by white settlers and Aborigines to communicate with each other; each believed that *yarraman* was the word for 'horse' in the other's language]

**yarran** /**ya**-ruhn/ *n.* **1** small to medium wattle of inland eastern Australia, having a rough bark, smooth foliage, and an unpleasant odour. **2** the dark brown, durable wood of this tree. [Kamilaroi *yarraan*]

**yashmak** /**yash**-mak/ *n.* veil concealing the face except the eyes, worn by some Muslim women. [Arabic]

**yate** /yayt/ *n.* **1** any of several eucalypts of southern WA yielding a remarkably hard, strong timber. **2** the wood of these trees. [perhaps from a WA Aboriginal language]

**yaw** — *v.* (of a ship or aircraft etc.) fail to hold a straight course; go unsteadily. — *n.* yawing of a ship etc. from its course. [origin unknown]

**yawl** *n.* a kind of ship's boat or sailing- or fishing-boat. [Low German *jolle* or Dutch *jol*]

**yawn** — *v.* **1** open the mouth wide and inhale, esp. when sleepy or bored. **2** (of a chasm etc.) gape, be wide open. — *n.* **1** act of yawning. **2** *colloq.* boring idea, activity, etc. (*playing cricket with the kids is a real yawn*). [Old English]

**Yawor** /**yah**-wuur/ *n.* an Aboriginal language spoken in the north of WA.

**yaws** /yawz/ *n.pl.* (usu. treated as *sing.*) contagious tropical skin-disease with large red swellings. [origin unknown]

**Yb** *symb.* ytterbium.

**Y chromosome** *n.* (in humans and some other mammals) sex chromosome occurring only in male cells. [*Y* as an arbitrary label]

**ye¹** /yee/ *pron. archaic pl.* of THOU¹ (*ye gods!*).

**ye²** /yee/ *adj. pseudo-archaic* = THE (*ye olde tea-shoppe*). [from the obsolete *y*- shaped letter for *th*]

**yea** /yay/ *archaic* — *adv.* **1** yes. **2** indeed (*ready, yea eager*). — *n.* utterance of 'yea'; 'yes' vote. [Old English]

**yeah** /yair/ *adv. colloq.* yes. [a casual pronunciation of YES]

**year** /yeer/ *n.* **1** time occupied by the earth in one revolution round the sun, approx. 365¼ days. **2** = CALENDAR YEAR. **3** period of twelve months, starting at any point (*four years ago; tax year*). **4** (in *pl.*) age, time of life (*young for his years*). **5** (usu. in *pl.*) *colloq.* very long time (*it took us years to get served*). **6 a** academic level or grade (*doing 4th year medicine; she's in year 11 at high school*). **b** group of students entering college etc. in the same academic year (*she was in my year*). □ **of the year** chosen as outstanding in a particular year (*sportsman of the year*). **year in, year out** continually over a period of years. [Old English]

**yearling** *n.* animal between one and two years old.

**yearly** — *adj.* **1** done, produced, or occurring once a year. **2** of or lasting a year. — *adv.* once a year.

**yearn** /yern/ *v.* be filled with longing, compassion, or tenderness. □ **yearning** *n. & adj.* [Old English]

**yeast** *n.* greyish-yellow fungus obtained esp. from fermenting malt liquors and used as a fermenting agent, to raise bread, etc. [Old English]

**yeasty** *adj.* (**-ier, -iest**) **1** of, like, or tasting of yeast; frothy. **2** in a ferment. **3** working like yeast.

**yelka** /yel-kuh/ *n.* (also **yulka**) any of several Australian sedges yielding a small edible tuber; the tuber itself. [Aranda *yalge*]

**yell** — *n.* loud sharp cry of fright, anger, pain, encouragement, delight, etc.; a shout. — *v.* cry, shout. [Old English]

**yellow** /yel-oh/ — *adj.* **1** of the colour of buttercups, lemons, egg yolks, etc. **2** used as a distinguishing epithet in the names of Australian fauna and flora (*yellow-plumed honeyeater; yellow-bellied glider; yellow-faced rock wallaby; yellow-eye mullet; yellow bloodwood*). **3** having an almost yellow skin or complexion. **4** *colloq.* cowardly. — *n.* **1** yellow colour or pigment. **2** yellow clothes or material (*can't wear yellow*). — *v.* turn yellow (*the leaves are yellowing now*). □ **yellowish** *adj.* **yellow-**

**ness** *n.* **yellowy** *adj.* [Old English: related to GOLD]

**yellow-belly** *n. colloq.* coward.

**yellowbelly** *n.* (also **callop, golden perch**) large freshwater food-fish with yellowish underparts, native to south-eastern Australia and probably introduced into WA and the NT.

**yellow box** *n.* medium to tall eucalypt of Queensland, NSW, the ACT, and Victoria, having an often twisted trunk with yellow tints beneath the bark, and profuse nectar-rich flowers highly valued by apiarists.

**yellow-box honey** *n.* valued Australian honey, rich in flavour, derived from the nectar of the yellow box.

**yellow fever** *n.* tropical virus disease with fever and jaundice.

**yellow flag** *n.* flag displayed by a ship in quarantine.

**yellow gum** *n.* any of several eucalypts of south-eastern mainland Australia, having a very smooth, mottled, yellowish trunk.

**yellow jacket** *n.* (also **yellow jack**) any of several eucalypts of Queensland and WA having a yellowish bark.

**yellow monday** *n.* (also **yellow munday; mundy**) cicada of south-eastern Australia when yellow (see GREENGROCER).

**yellow oriole** see ORIOLE.

**yellow spot** *n.* point of acutest vision in the retina.

**yellow streak** *n. colloq.* trait of cowardice.

**yellow stringybark** *n.* any of several very rough-barked eucalypts of eastern Victoria and south-eastern NSW, having a yellow timber.

**yellowtail** *n.* any of several southern Australian marine food-fish having a yellow caudal fin, esp. the jack mackerel and the kingfish.

**yelp** — *n.* sharp shrill cry of, or as of, a dog in pain or excitement. — *v.* utter a yelp. [Old English]

**yen¹** *n.* (*pl.* same) chief monetary unit of Japan. [Japanese from Chinese]

**yen²** — *n.* longing or yearning (*I've a yen for some Sri Lankan curry*). — *v.* (**-nn-**) feel a longing. [Chinese]

**yeo** /yoh/ *var.* of YOE.

**yeoman** /yoh-muhn/ *n. Brit. hist.* man holding and cultivating a small landed estate, or acting as a servant in a royal or noble household. □ **yeomanly** *adj.* [from earlier *yoman, yeman*, etc., probably = young man]

**yeoman service** *n.* (also **yeoman's service**) efficient or useful help in need (*she did yeoman service in helping us stump-grub the paddock*).

**yes** — *adv.* **1** indicating that the answer to the question is affirmative, the statement etc. made is correct, the request or command will be complied with, or the person summoned or addressed is present. **2 (yes?) a** indeed? is that so? **b** what do you want? — *n.* **1** an utterance of the word *yes*. **2** affirmation or assent. **3** 'yes' vote. □ **say yes** grant a request, confirm a statement. [Old English, = *yea let it be*]

**yes-man** *n. colloq.* weakly acquiescent person.

**yesterday** /yes-tuh-ˌday/ — *adv.* **1** on the day before today. **2** in the recent past. — *n.* **1** the day before today. **2** the recent past. [Old English]

**yesteryear** /yes-tuh-ˌyeer/ *n. archaic* or *rhet.* **1** last year. **2** the recent past. [Old English *yester-* that is last past, YEAR]

**yet** — *adv.* **1** as late as, or until, now or then (*there is yet time; your best work yet*). **2** (with *neg.* or *interrog.*) so soon as, or by, now or then (*it is not time yet; have you finished yet?*). **3** again; in addition (*more and yet more*). **4** in the remaining time available (*I will do it yet*). **5** (foll. by *compar.*) even (*a yet more difficult task*). **6** nevertheless; and (or but) in spite of that (*it is strange, yet it is true*). — *conj.* but at the same time; but nevertheless (*I won, yet what good has it done?*). □ **nor yet** and also not (*won't listen to me nor yet to you*). [Old English]

**yeti** /yet-ee/ *n.* = ABOMINABLE SNOWMAN. [Tibetan]

**yew** *n.* **1** dark-leaved evergreen tree of Europe etc. bearing berry-like cones. **2** its springy wood, used formerly as the material for archers' bows. [Old English]

**Y-fronts** /wuy-frunts/ *n. propr.* men's or boys' briefs with a Y-shaped seam of overlapping folds at the front.

**Yiddish** /yid-ish/ — *n.* language used by Jews in or from Europe, orig. a German dialect with words from Hebrew and several modern languages. — *adj.* of or relating to this language. [German *jüdisch* Jewish]

**Yidiny** /yi-di-nee/ *n.* an Aboriginal language spoken in the Cairns region of northern Queensland.

**yield** — *v.* **1** (also *absol.*) produce or return as a fruit, profit, or result (*the land yields crops; the land yields poorly; the investment yields 15%*). **2** give up; surrender, concede (*yielded the fortress; yielded themselves prisoners*). **3 a** (often foll. by *to*) surrender; submit; defer to (*yielded to the enemy; do you yield?; I yield to your greater knowledge; yielded to persuasion*). **b** (as **yielding** *adj.*) compliant; submissive; (of a substance) soft and pliable. **4** (foll. by *to*) give right of way to (other

traffic). **5** (foll. by *to*) be inferior or confess inferiority to (*I yield to none in this matter*). — *n.* amount yielded or produced. [Old English, = pay]

**yike** /yuyk/ *n. colloq.* **1** quarrel; fight (*watched the yike on telly between the Prime Minister and the Leader of the Opposition*). **2** complaint; gripe (*his constant yike is that no one takes him seriously*). [origin unknown]

**yin** *n.* (in Chinese philosophy) the passive female principle of the universe (cf. YANG).

**Yindjibarndi** /yin-jee-**bun**-dee/ *n.* an Aboriginal language still actively spoken on the Lower Hamersley Range and the Fortescue River of WA.

**Yingkarta** /ying-gah-du/ *n.* an Aboriginal language spoken in western WA.

**Yitha-yitha** /yith-u ˌyith-u/ *n.* an Aboriginal language spoken in south-western NSW and north-western Victoria: now extinct.

**yob** /yob/ *n.* (also **yobbo**) *colloq.* lout, hooligan. □ **yobbish** *adj.* [back slang for BOY]

**yobbo** /yob-oh/ *n.* (*pl.* **-s**) *colloq.* = YOB.

**yodel** /**yoh**-duhl/ — *v.* (**-ll-**) **1** sing with melodious inarticulate sounds and frequent changes between falsetto and normal voice in the manner of Swiss mountain-dwellers. **2** *colloq.* vomit. — *n.* **1** yodelling cry. **2** *colloq.* act or instance of vomiting. □ **yodeller** *n.* [German]

**yoe** /yoh/ *n.* (also **yeo**) ewe (*curses the old snagger with the bare-bellied yeo*). [British dial.]

**yoga** /yoh-guh/ *n.* **1** Hindu system of meditation and asceticism designed to effect reunion with the universal spirit. **2** system of physical exercises and breathing control used in yoga. □ **yogic** /yoh-gik/ *adj.* [Sanskrit, = union]

**yoghurt** /yoh-guht, yog-uht/ *n.* (also **yogurt**) semi-solid sourish food made from milk fermented by added bacteria. [Turkish]

**yogi** /yoh-gee/ *n.* (*pl.* **-s**) master of yoga; devotee of yoga. [Hindustani: related to YOGA]

**yohi** /yoh-wuy/ *adv.* (also **youi, youai**) (in Aboriginal English) an affirmative reply, 'yes'. [Yagara *yaway*]

**yoke** — *n.* **1** wooden crosspiece fastened over the necks of two oxen etc. and attached to the plough or wagon to be pulled. **2** (*pl.* same or **-s**) pair (of oxen etc.). **3** object like a yoke in form or function, e.g. a wooden shoulder-piece for carrying a pair of pails, the top section of a garment from which the rest hangs. **4** sway, dominion, or servitude (*under the tyrant's yoke; the weary yoke of household chores*). **5** bond of union, esp. of marriage (*the yoke* *of wedlock is no joke).* — *v.* (**-king**) **1** put a yoke on. **2** couple or unite (a pair). **3** (foll. by *to*) link (one thing) to (another) (*I am yoked to my desk*). **4** match or work together. [Old English]

**yokel** /yoh-kuhl/ *n.* rustic; country bumpkin. [perhaps British dial.]

**yolk** /yohk/ *n.* yellow inner part of an egg. [Old English: related to YELLOW]

**Yolngu**[1] /yol-nyoo/ *n.* (also **Yolnu**) an Aborigine. [Yolngu language *yuulngu*]

■ **Usage** See KOORI[1].

**Yolngu**[2] /yol-ngoo/ *n.* an Aboriginal language still actively spoken in the northeastern sections of Arnhem Land, the NT.

**Yom Kippur** /yom ki-poor/ *n.* most solemn religious fast day of the Jewish year, Day of Atonement. [Hebrew]

**yon** *adj. & adv. literary* yonder. [Old English]

**yonder** — *adv.* over there; at some distance in that direction; in the place indicated. — *adj.* situated yonder.

**yoni** /yoh-nee/ *n.* symbol of the female genitals venerated by Hindus etc. (see also LINGAM). [Sanskrit, = source, womb, female genitals]

**yonks** *n.pl.* (also **yonkers**) *colloq.* a long time (*yonks ago; haven't seen him in yonkers*). [origin unknown]

**yore** *n.* □ **of yore** a long time ago. [Old English, = long ago]

**yorga** /yaw-guh/ *n.* a woman, esp. an Aboriginal woman. [Nyungar]

**york** *v. Cricket* bowl out with a yorker. [back-formation from YORKER]

**yorker** *n. Cricket* ball that pitches immediately under the bat. [probably with ref. to the practice of Yorkshire cricketers]

**you** /yoo/ *pron.* (*obj.* **you**; *poss.* **your**, **yours**) **1** the person or persons addressed. **2** (as *int.* with a noun) in an exclamatory statement (*you fools!*). **3** (in general statements) one, a person, people (*you get used to it*). **4** (of a thing) suitable to or characteristic of the person addressed (*that hat just isn't you; intolerance is you to a T*). □ **you and yours** you and your family, property, etc. **you-know-what** (or **- who**) something (or someone) unspecified but understood (*don't let the kids see the you-know-what*). [Old English, originally objective case of YE[1]]

**youai** var. of YOHI.

**you'd** /yood, yuhd/ *contr.* **1** you had. **2** you would.

**youee** var. of UEY.

**youi** var. of YOHI.

**you'll** /yool, yuhl/ *contr.* you will; you shall.

**young** /yung/ — *adj.* (**younger** /yung-guh/) **1** not far advanced in life, development, or existence; not yet old (*he's too young to be up this late; a young koala; the night's still young*). **2 a** immature; inexperienced (*young in the ways of the world*). **b** (in Aboriginal English) newly initiated. **3** of or characteristic of youth (*young love; young ambition*). **4** representing young people (*Young Farmers*). **5 a** distinguishing a son from his father (*young George*). **b** as a familiar or condescending form of address (*listen, young lady*). **6** (**younger**) distinguishing one person from another of the same name (*the younger Pitt*). — *n.* (*collect.*) **1** offspring, esp. of animals before or soon after birth. **2** young people (*the young aren't interested in politics*). □ **with young** (of an animal) pregnant. □ **youngish** *adj.* [Old English]

**youngie** /yung-ee/ *n. colloq.* young person (opp. OLDIE).

**youngster** *n.* child, young person.

**your** /yaw/ *poss. pron.* **1** of or belonging to you. **2** *colloq.* often *derog.* much talked of; well known (*your typical professor*). [Old English]

**you're** /yaw, yuh/ *contr.* you are.

**yours** /yawz/ *poss. pron.* **1** the one or ones belonging to you (*it is yours; yours are over there*). **2** your letter (*yours of the 10th*). **3** introducing a formula ending a letter (*yours ever; yours truly*). □ **of yours** of or belonging to you (*friend of yours*).

**yourself** /yaw-self/ *pron.* (*pl.* **yourselves**) **1 a** *emphat. form* of YOU. **b** *refl. form* of YOU. **2** in your normal state of body or mind (*are quite yourself again*). □ **be yourself** see ONESELF.

**youse** /yooz/ *pron. colloq.* used when addressing more than one person; you (*pl.*) (*we were told not to have anything to do with youse; are youse guys coming or not?*). [origin uncertain; perhaps a pluralisation of YOU]

■ **Usage** This pronoun is often heard in colloquial speech, but its use is regarded as unacceptable in speech and it should not be used in formal writing.

**youth** /yooth/ *n.* (*pl.* **-s** /yoothz/) **1** state of being young; period between childhood and adult age. **2** vigour, enthusiasm, inexperience, or other characteristic of this period. **3** young man. **4** (as *pl.*) young people collectively (*the youth of the country*). [Old English: related to YOUNG]

**youthful** *adj.* young or still having the characteristics of youth. □ **youthfully** *adv.* **youthfulness** *n.*

**youth hostel** *n.* any of a chain of cheap lodgings for (esp. young) holiday-makers, esp. walkers and cyclists. □ **youth hosteller** *n.*

**you've** /yoov, yuhv/ *contr.* you have.

**yowie**[1] /**yoh**-ee/ *n.* ewe. [diminutive of YOE]

**yowie**[2] /**yow**-ee/ *n.* ape-like or humanoid monster supposed to inhabit parts of eastern Australia. [Yuwaalaraay *yuwi* dream spirit]

**yowl** — *n.* loud wailing cry of, or as of, a cat or dog in distress. — *v.* utter a yowl. [imitative]

**yo-yo** /**yoh**-yoh/ — *n.* (*pl.* **yo-yos**) **1** toy consisting of a pair of discs with a deep groove between them in which string is attached and wound, and which can be made to fall and rise. **2** thing that repeatedly falls and rises. **3** *colloq.* idiot, fool. — *v.* (**-es, -ed**) **1** play with a yo-yo. **2** move up and down; fluctuate (*the dollar's yo-yoing badly*). [origin unknown]

**ytterbium** /i-**ter**-bee-uhm/ *n.* metallic element of the lanthanide series. [*Ytterby* in Sweden]

**yttrium** /**it**-ree-uhm/ *n.* metallic element resembling the lanthanides. [related to YTTERBIUM]

**yu** /yoo/ *n.* Aboriginal shelter, esp. from the wind. [Western Desert language *yuu* wind-break]

**yuan** /yoo-**ahn**/ *n.* (*pl.* same) chief monetary unit of China. [Chinese]

**yuck** /yuk/ *int.* (also **yuk**) *colloq.* expression of strong distaste. [imitative]

**yucky** *adj.* (also **yukky**) (**-ier, -iest**) *colloq.* **1** messy; repellent; disgusting. **2** sickly, sentimental.

**yugari** var. of UGARI.

**Yugoslav** /**yoo**-guh-ˌslahv/ (also **Jugoslav**) — *n.* **1** native or national of Yugoslavia. **2** person of Yugoslav descent. — *adj.* of Yugoslavia. ◻ **Yugoslavian** /-**slah**-vee-uhn/ *adj. & n.* [Serbo-Croat *jug* south: related to SLAV]

**Yuin** /yoo-uhn/ *n.* an Aborigine. [Dharawal and Dhurga *yuwiny*]

■ **Usage** See KOORI[1].

**yuk** var. of YUCK.

**yukky** var. of YUCKY.

**yule** *n.* (in full **yule-tide**) *archaic* the Christmas festival. [Old English]

**yulka** var. of YELKA.

**yumcha** /ˌyum-**chah**/ *n.* Chinese meal in which diners select from a wide range of dishes served from a trolley. [Cantonese, from Mandarin *yin ch'a* drink tea]

**yuppie** /**yup**-ee/ *n.* (also **yuppy**) (*pl.* **-ies**) (often *attrib.*) *colloq.*, usu. *derog.* young ambitious professional person working in a city. [from young *u*rban *p*rofessional]

**Yura** /yoo-ruh/ *n.* an Aborigine; Aboriginal people, esp. of SA. [Adnyamathanha]

■ **Usage** See KOORI[1].

**Yuwaalaraay** /yoo-wah-lu-ruy/ *n.* an Aboriginal language of northern NSW (between Walgett and Lightning Ridge): no longer actively spoken.

**Yuwaaliyaay** /yoo-wah-lu-yuy/ *n.* an Aboriginal language of northern New South Wales (between Lightning Ridge and Mungindi): no longer actively spoken.

# Z

**Z** /zed/ *n.* (also **z**)(*pl.* **Zs** or **Z's**) **1** twenty-sixth letter of the alphabet. **2** (usu. **z**) *Algebra* third unknown quantity.

**zabaglione** /zah-buh-**lyoh**-nay/ *n.* Italian dessert of whipped and heated egg yolks, sugar, and wine. [Italian]

**zac** *n.* (also **zack**) *colloq.* **1** *hist.* Australian sixpenny coin. **2** five-cent coin. **3** trifling sum of money (*I won't contribute another zac until I know where my money is going*). **4** prison term of six months or six years. [probably from Scottish dial.]

**zambuk** /**zam**-buk/ *n.* (also **zambuck**) member of the St John's Ambulance Brigade, esp. one in attendance at a sporting fixture. [*Zambuk* proprietary name of an antiseptic ointment]

**zamia** /**zay**-mee-uh/ *n.* (in full **zamia palm**) = MACROZAMIA.

**zany** /**zay**-nee/ — *adj.* (**-ier, -iest**) comically idiotic; crazily ridiculous. — *n.* fool, idiot; jester. [French or Italian]

**zap** *colloq.* — *v.* (**-pp-**) **1 a** kill or destroy; attack (*zapped the enemy; zapped the blowie*). **b** 'destroy' a television commercial by using the remote control device as a gun to kill the sound or (while watching a videotaped film etc.) to fast-forward the tape. **c** hit hard (*zapped the ball over the net*). **2** move quickly (*I'll zap over to the milk-bar and get some*). **3** exhaust (*all this digging has zapped me*). **4** (foll. by *up*) **a** enliven (*this party needs to be zapped up*). **b** make quickly, whip up (*I'll zap up some more sangers in a jiff*). — *int.* expressing the sound or impact of a bullet, ray gun, etc., or any sudden event. — *n.* liveliness, energy (*he's lost his zap*). [imitative]

**zapped** /zapt/ *adj. colloq.* exhausted.

**zappy** *adj.* (**-ier, -iest**) *colloq.* lively, energetic.

**Zarathustrian** var. of ZOROASTRIAN.

**zeal** *n.* earnestness or fervour; hearty persistent endeavour. [Greek *zēlos*]

**zealot** /**zel**-uht/ *n.* extreme partisan; fanatic. □ **zealotry** *n.*

**zealous** /**zel**-uhs/ *adj.* full of zeal; enthusiastic. □ **zealously** *adv.*

**zebra** /**zeb**-ruh, **zee**-bruh/ *n.* (*pl.* same or **-s**) black-and-white striped African animal of the family including the ass and horse. [Italian or Portuguese from Congolese]

**zebra crossing** *n.* striped street-crossing where pedestrians have precedence.

**zebra duck** *n.* = PINK-EARED DUCK. [from its zebra-like markings]

**zebra finch** *n.* small bird widespread in much of mainland Australia, having black and white tail-bars.

**zebu** /**zee**-boo/ *n.* (*pl.* same or **-s**) humped ox of India, E. Asia and Africa, used in Australia for cross-breeding. [French]

**zed** — *n.* **1** the letter Z. **2** *colloq.* a nap, sleep (*go away — I'm having a zed*). — *v. colloq.* nap, sleep (*he's been zedding all arvo*). □ **push up zeds** *colloq.* sleep, nap (*he's pushing up zeds on the sofa*). [Greek ZETA]

**Zeitgeist** /**tsuyt**-guyst/ *n.* the spirit of the times. [German]

**Zen** *n.* form of Buddhism emphasising meditation and intuition. [Japanese, = meditation]

**zenith** /**zen**-uhth/ *n.* **1** point of the heavens directly above an observer (opp. NADIR). **2** highest point (of power or prosperity etc.). □ **zenithal** *adj.* [Latin from Arabic]

**zephyr** /**zef**-uh/ *n. literary* mild gentle breeze. [Greek, = west wind]

**zero** /**zeer**-roh/ *n.* (*pl.* **-s**) **1** figure 0; nought; nil. **2** point on the scale of a thermometer etc. from which a positive or negative quantity is reckoned. **3** (*attrib.*) no, not any (*zero growth*). **4** (in full **zero hour**) **a** hour at which a planned, esp. military, operation is timed to begin. **b** crucial moment. **5** lowest or earliest point (*down to zero; the year zero*). **6** *colloq.* nonentity; dull or boring person. □ **zero in on** (**-oes, -oed**) **1** take aim at. **2** focus one's attention on. [Arabic: related to CIPHER]

**zero option** *n.* disarmament proposal for the total removal of certain types of weapons on both sides.

**zest** *n.* **1** piquancy; stimulating flavour or quality. **2 a** keen enjoyment or interest. **b** (often foll. by *for*) relish (*has no zest for partying these days*). **c** gusto. **3** scraping of orange or lemon peel as flavouring. □ **zestful** *adj.* **zestfully** *adv.* **zesty** *adj.* (**zestier, -iest**). [French]

**zeta** /**zee**-tuh/ *n.* sixth letter of the Greek alphabet (Z, ζ). [Greek]

**zeugma** /**zyoog**-muh/ *n.* figure of speech using a verb or adjective with two nouns, to one of which it is strictly applicable while the word appropriate to the other is not used (e.g. *with weeping eyes and* [sc. *grieving* ] *hearts*) (cf. SYLLEPSIS). [Greek, = a yoking, from *zugon* yoke]

**zidovudine** /ˌzuy-doh-**vyoo**-deen/ *n.* = AZT.

**ziff** *n. colloq.* beard (*ziffs are going out of fashion*). □ **ziffed** *adj.* [origin unknown]

**ziggurat** /ˈzig-uh-ˌrat/ *n.* rectangular stepped tower in ancient Mesopotamia, surmounted by a temple. [Assyrian]

**zigzag** /ˈzig-zag/ — *adj.* with abrupt alternate right and left turns (*zigzag line*). — *n.* zigzag line; thing having the form of a zigzag or having sharp turns. — *adv.* with a zigzag course. — *v.* (**-gg-**) move in a zigzag course. □ **to zig when** (**one**) **should have zagged** do the wrong thing; move in the wrong direction; make a mess of things; etc. [French from German]

**zigzag wattle** *n.* large wattle of arid Queensland, having lance-like leaves, cream flowers, and branches which zigzag from leaf-node to leaf-node.

**zilch** *n. colloq.* nothing. [origin uncertain]

**zillion** /ˈzil-yuhn/ *n. colloq.* indefinite large number. [probably after *million*]

**zinc** *n.* greyish-white metallic element used as a component of brass and in galvanising sheet iron. [German *Zink*]

**zing** *colloq.* — *n.* vigour, energy. — *v.* move swiftly, or with a high-pitched sound (*mossies zinging past my ears*). [imitative]

**Zion** /ˈzuy-uhn, ˈzuy-on/ *n.* (also **Sion**) **1** ancient Jerusalem; its holy hill. **2 a** the Jewish people or religion. **b** the Christian Church. **3** the Kingdom of Heaven. [Hebrew *ṣīyôn*]

**Zionism** *n.* movement (orig.) for the re-establishment and (now) the development of a Jewish nation in what is now Israel. □ **Zionist** *n. & adj.*

**zip** — *n.* **1** light fast sound as of a bullet passing through air. **2** energy, vigour. **3 a** (in full **zip fastener**) fastening device of two flexible strips with interlocking projections, closed or opened by sliding a clip along them. **b** (*attrib.*) having a zip fastener (*zip bag*). — *v.* (**-pp-**) **1** (often foll. by *up*) fasten with a zip-fastener. **2** move with zip or at high speed (*the car zipped past us at what seemed the speed of light*). [imitative]

**zipper** *n.* = ZIP 3a.

**zippy** *adj.* (**-ier, -iest**) *colloq.* lively, speedy.

**zircon** /ˈzer-kuhn, ˈzer-kon/ *n.* zirconium silicate of which some translucent varieties are cut into gems. [German *Zirkon*]

**zirconium** /zuh-ˈkoh-nee-uhm/ *n.* grey metallic element occurring naturally in zircon and used in various industrial applications.

**zit** *n. colloq.* pimple. [origin unknown]

**zither** /ˈzith-uh/ *n.* stringed instrument with a flat soundbox, placed horizontally and played with the fingers and a plectrum. [Latin: related to GUITAR]

**Zn** *symb.* zinc.

**zodiac** /ˈzoh-dee-ˌak/ *n.* **1** belt of the heavens including all apparent positions of the sun, moon, and planets as known to ancient astronomers, and divided into twelve equal parts (**signs of the zodiac**). **2** diagram of these signs. □ **zodiacal** /zuh-ˈduy-uh-kuhl, zoh-/ *adj.* [Greek *zōion* animal]

**zombie** /ˈzom-bee/ *n.* **1** *colloq.* person who acts mechanically or lifelessly. **2** corpse said to have been revived by witchcraft. [West African]

**zone** — *n.* **1** area having particular features, properties, purpose, or use (*danger zone; erogenous zone; smokeless zone*). **2** well-defined region of more or less belt-like form. **3** area between two concentric circles. **4** (in full **time zone**) range of longitudes where a common standard time is used. **5** *Geol. etc.* a range between specified limits of depth, height, etc., esp. a section of strata distinguished by characteristic fossils. **6** *Geog.* any of five divisions of the earth bounded by circles parallel to the equator (see FRIGID ZONES, TEMPERATE ZONE, TORRID ZONE). **7** encircling band of colour etc. — *v.* (**-ning**) **1** encircle as or with a zone. **2** arrange or distribute by zones. **3** assign as or to a particular area. □ **zonal** *adj.* **zoning** *n.* (in sense 3 of *v.*). [Greek *zōnē* girdle]

**zonk** *colloq.* — *v.* **1** hit or strike. **2** (foll. by *out*) **a** overcome with sleep; intoxicate (*the injection zonked him out in seconds*). **b** fall heavily asleep (*he zonked out in my bed*). — *n.* **1** sound of a blow or heavy impact. **2** fool; moron; dill. [imitative]

**zonked** /zongkt/ *adj. colloq.* (often foll. by *out*) exhausted; intoxicated. [ZONK]

**zoo** *n.* zoological garden. [abbreviation]

**zoological** /ˌzoh-uh-ˈloj-i-kuhl, ˌzoo-uh-/ *adj.* of zoology.

■ **Usage** See note at *zoology*.

**zoological garden** *n.* (also **zoological gardens** *n.pl.*) public garden or park with a collection of animals for exhibition and study.

**zoology** /zoh-ˈol-uh-jee, ˌzoo-/ *n.* the study of animals. □ **zoologist** *n.* [Greek *zōion* animal]

■ **Usage** The second pronunciation given for *zoology*, *zoological*, and *zoologist*, with the first syllable pronounced as in *zoo*, although extremely common, is considered incorrect by some people.

**zoom** — *v.* **1** move quickly, esp. with a buzzing sound. **2** cause an aeroplane to mount at high speed and a steep angle.

**3** (often foll. by *in* or *in on*) (of a camera) change rapidly from a long shot to a close-up (of). **4** (of prices etc.) rise sharply. — *n.* **1** aeroplane's steep climb. **2** zooming camera shot. [imitative]

**zoom lens** *n.* lens allowing a camera to zoom by varying the focal length.

**zoomorphic** /zoh-uh-**maw**-fik/ *adj.* **1** dealing with, or represented in, animal forms. **2** having gods of animal form. □ **zoomorphism** *n.*

**zoophyte** /**zoh**-uh-,fuyt/ *n.* plantlike animal, esp. a coral, sea anemone, or sponge. [Greek *zōion* animal, *phuton* plant]

**Zoroastrian** /,zo-roh-**as**-tree-uhn/ — *adj.* of Zoroaster (or Zarathustra) or the dualistic religious system taught by him. — *n.* follower of Zoroaster. □ **Zoroastrianism** *n.* [*Zoroaster*, Persian founder of the religion]

**zot** *v. colloq.* **1** kill, swat (*zotted the blowie with my magazine*). **2** (foll. by *off*) leave or go quickly.

**Zr** *symb.* zirconium.

**zucchetto** /tsuu-**ket**-oh, zuu-/ *n.* ecclesiastical skullcap, black for a priest, purple for a bishop, red for a cardinal, white for the Pope. [Italian]

**zucchini** /zoo-**kee**-nee, zuh-/ *n.* (*pl.* same or -**s**) small, usu. green, variety of vegetable marrow; courgette. [Italian, pl. of *zucchino*, diminutive of *zucca* gourd]

**Zulu** /**zoo**-loo/ — *n.* (*pl.* -**s**) **1** member of a S. African Bantu people. **2** their language. — *adj.* of this people or language. [native name]

**zygomaturus** /,zuy-goh-muh-**tyoo**-ruhs/ *n.* large extinct Australian marsupial of the genus of the same name.

**zygote** /**zuy**-goht, **zig**-oht/ *n. Biol.* cell formed by the union of two gametes. [Greek *zugōtos* yoked: related to ZEUGMA]

**zymotic** /zuy-**mot**-ik/ *adj.* of fermentation. [Greek *zumē* leaven]

**zzz** /zuhz/ *colloq.* — *n.* a sleep. — *v.* (foll. by *out*) sleep. [from the convention used in comics etc. in which a sleeping person is shown as having a stream of zeds issuing from the mouth]

## Appendix 1   Military Ranks of the Armed Forces of Australia

Appendix 1 is a list of Australian military ranks, since many of these ranks are better understood in tabular rather than descriptive form.

| Army | Navy | Air Force |
|---|---|---|
| **Commissioned officers** | | |
| General | Admiral | Air Chief Marshal |
| Lieutenant General | Vice Admiral | Air Marshal |
| Major General | Rear Admiral | Air Vice Marshal |
| Brigadier | Commodore | Air Commodore |
| Colonel | Captain | Group Captain |
| Lieutenant Colonel | Commander | Wing Commander |
| Major | Lieutenant Commander | Squadron Leader |
| Captain | | Flight Lieutenant |
| Lieutenant | Lieutenant | Flying Officer |
| Second Lieutenant | Sub Lieutenant | Pilot Officer |
| **Warrant and non-commissioned officers** | | |
| Warrant Officer Class 1 | Warrant Officer | Warrant Officer |
| Warrant Officer Class 2 | | |
| Staff Sergeant | Chief Petty Officer | Flight Sergeant |
| Sergeant | Petty Officer | Sergeant |
| Corporal or Bombardier | Leading Seaman | Corporal |
| Lance Corporal or Lance Bombardier | | Leading Aircraftman |
| Private, including Craftsman, Gunner, Sapper, Signalman, Trooper | Able Seaman | Aircraftman |

# Appendix 2    **Punctuation Marks**

Appendix 2 explains and illustrates the usage of punctuation marks in standard Australian English.

## 1 Comma (,)
This is used:

1.1    To separate main clauses when the second is not closely identified with the first, e.g. *Cars will turn here, and buses will go straight on*.

1.2    To avoid momentary misunderstanding, e.g. *In the valley below, the houses looked very small*.

1.3    In a sentence which would mean something different without the comma, e.g. *She did not leave, because he asked her to stay*.

1.4    Between adjectives qualifying a noun, except when the last adjective is more closely related to the noun, e.g. *a cautious, eloquent man* but *a distinguished foreign author*.

1.5    To separate items in a list of more than two items, e.g. *potatoes, peas, and carrots*.

1.6    Before or after a salutation or vocative, e.g. *Come here, boy; Dear Madam, Thank you for your letter*.

1.7    To mark the beginning and end of a parenthetical word or phrase, e.g. *It appears, however, that they were wrong*.

1.8    Before a quotation, e.g. *I boldly cried out, 'Woe to this city!'* (Compare this usage with 3.3 below.)

## 2 Semicolon (;)
This is used:

2.1    To separate two or more clauses which are of more or less equal importance and are linked as a pair or series, e.g. *To err is human; to forgive, divine*.

2.2    To separate lengthy or complicated items in lists (especially those entries requiring commas).

## 3 Colon (:)
This is used:

3.1    To separate main clauses when there is a step forward from the first to the second, as from introduction to main theme, from cause to effect, or from premise to conclusion e.g. *Country life is the natural life: it is there that you will find real friendship*.

3.2    To introduce a list of items (a dash should not be added), and after expressions such as *namely, for example, to resume, to sum up, the following*.

3.3    Before a quotation, especially when the break before the quotation requires emphasis (compare with 1.8 above), e.g. *Then he wrote these words: 'I have named none to their disadvantage.'*

## 4 Full Stop, Full Point, Period (.)
This is used:

4.1    At the end of all sentences which are not questions or exclamations.

4.2 After many abbreviations and initials. If such a point closes a sentence, it also serves as the sentence's full point, e.g. *. . . cats etc.* but *(. . . cats etc.)*.

## 5 Question Mark (?)
This is used:
5.1 After any sentence which asks a question, but not after an indirect question, e.g. *What is it?* but *I asked what it was*.
5.2 Before a word etc. whose accuracy is doubted, e.g. *Julius Caesar, born ?100 BC*.

## 6 Exclamation Mark (!)
This is used after an exclamatory word, phrase, or sentence expressing absurdity, command, disgust, emotion, enthusiasm, pain, sorrow, a wish, or wonder.

## 7 Apostrophe (')
This is used:
7.1 To show the possessive case, e.g. *Maria's book*.
7.2 To show an omission, e.g. *Maria's angry*.
7.3 At the end of a quotation: see following section.

## 8 Quotation Marks (' ')
8.1 A quotation is normally preceded by a turned comma (') and followed by an apostrophe. Double marks are used for a quotation within a quotation. The apostrophe should come after any punctuation mark which is part of the quotation, but before any mark which is not, e.g. *'She asked "Were are we?"'* but *'Did she say "Here we are"?'* Quotation marks are only used when the exact words of the original are quoted.
8.2 Quotation marks are used when citing titles of articles, series, chapters, essays, poems, and songs, but not for titles of books of the Bible.
8.3 They may be used to enclose slang and technical terms.

## 9 Parentheses ( )
These enclose:
9.1 Interpolations and remarks made by the writer of the text, e.g. *He is (as he always was) a rebel*.
9.2 An authority, definition, explanation, reference, or translation.
9.3 In a report of a speech, interruptions by the audience.
9.4 Reference letters or figures, e.g. (1), (*a*).

## 10 Square Brackets [ ]
These enclose material added by someone other than the author, often by way of explanation, e.g. *He [Bloggs] fell down*.

## 11 Dash (—)
This is used:
11.1 Instead of the parentheses in 9.1 above.
11.2 Instead of the colon in 3.1 above.
11.3 To indicate pauses in hesitant speech, or the ending and resumption of a sentence interrupted by another speaker.
11.4 To replace an omitted word.

## 12 Hyphen (-)

This is used:

12.1 In compounds used attributively, e.g. *She is a well-known artist* but *The artist is well known*.

12.2 In compounds formed from words which have a syntactical relationship, e.g. *weight-carrying*, *punch-drunk*.

12.3 To join a prefix to a proper name, e.g. *anti-Darwinian*.

12.4 To prevent misconceptions by linking words, e.g. *twenty-odd people*.

12.5 To prevent misconceptions by separating a prefix from the main word, e.g. *One player resigned, but later he re-signed*.

12.6 To separate letters representing similar sounds, e.g. *sword-dance*, *pre-eminent*.

12.7 To represent a common second element in all but the last word of a list, e.g. *two-, three-, or fourfold*.

12.8 At the end of a line in printing, to indicate that the last word has been divided.

## 13 Ellipsis, Marks of Omission (. . .)

These are used to show an omission. If the omission follows a complete sentence, the three points are preceded by the full point of the sentence, but if it follows an incomplete sentence a fourth point should not be added.

# Appendix 3   The Australian Language

Appendix 3 contains eleven categories of terms that are either distinctively Australian or interesting because of their relative newness to the language. The words in the lists are random samples of headwords in the dictionary relating to these categories.

## A  Aboriginal English

The words in this list are mainly English (or of English derivation) but are used by Aborigines in a special way.

auntie 2
balander
big mob
Big Sunday
blackfellow
business 5
cheeky 2
country 6
countryman 3
cousin 1b
cut v. 15
finger talk
go through the Rules
  (see RULE)
grow up (see GROW)
humbug n. 1b
jump up
knock 'em down
language 2b
law 11
lawman

longa
meat 4
milli-milli
old people
Old Rule (see RULE n. 9)
one 7
own v. 1b
paint-up
poison adj.
rubbish adj.
Rules (see RULE)
run v. 30, 31, n. 14
shame job
sickness country
silly 2b
sing 7
sister 1b
smoke out (see SMOKE)
sorry 4
sorry business
sorry camp

sorry cut
story 1b
sugar bag 1
sulky 2
Sunday business
sundown way
sunrise way
two-way 2
uncle 2
us mob
wadgula
watjin
women's camp
wrong 3b

## B  Aboriginal Life and Culture

The words in this list relate to Aboriginal life and culture. They are a mixture of words of Aboriginal and English provenance.

Alcheringa
avoidance relationship
bone n. 6, v. 3
bora
boylya
bucklee
bugeen
churinga
customary law

dowak
Dreaming
Dreamtime
emu dance
firestick farming
fringe-dweller
kangaroo dance
kipper[2]
Koori

kopi
koradji
kurdaitcha
leangle
letter-stick
lil-lil
makarrata
make[2]
men's business

mimi
mission 2
moiety
munjon
music stick
myall[1]
nulla-nulla
outstation movement
pecked (see PECK)
pipeclay

pirri
pitchi
rainbow serpent
red hand
remove 2c
sacred site
skin 7
songman
toa
totem 2

towri
traditional 2
traditional owner
tula
wagyl 1
walkabout 2
Wandjina
wilgie
wonga[2]
X-ray adj.

## C  Borrowings from Aboriginal Languages

The words in this list are of Aboriginal provenance and are now part
of Australian English. (See also sections relating to fauna, flora, and
landscape for further words derived from Aboriginal languages.)

billabong
bingy
bogey[3]
boggi
bombora
bondi[2]
boomalli
boomerang
borak
cooee
coolamon
coolibah
corroboree
dingo
galah
gang-gang
gibber[2]
gin[2]
gunyah
humpy

kangaroo
koala
kookaburra
kurrajong
kylie
lerp
lubra
maluka
Moomba
mulga
mulloway
myall[1,2]
pink-eye[3]
quamby
quandong
Quinkan
quokka
quoll
tally-walka
waddy

wallaby
wallaroo
waratah
warrigal
weei
willy willy
witchetty
wombat
wongi
woomera
wurley
yabber
yabby
yackai
yandy
yarraman
yate
yowie[2]

## D  Colloquialisms and Idiomatic Phrases

The words in this list are a sample of the vast range of colourful
Australian colloquialisms.

aerial ping-pong
Alf
amber fluid

anotherie
apples
artist 4

arvo
as Australian as meat
   pie (see MEAT PIE)

banana bender
bandicoot *v.*
barbie
Barcoo
bastard 2
Bedourie
begger on (the) coals
bewdy (see BEAUTY *n.*
2a; *adj.*; *int.*)
black stump
blind Freddy
bogan
Bullamakanka
but *adv.* 3
come in spinner (see
SPINNER)
come the raw prawn
(see PRAWN)
corroboree *n.* 3, 4, *v.* 2
cossie
cow[1] 4
croweater
Darwin stubby
dingo on a person (see
DINGO)
dinkum
drover's dog
dry as a mallee cow
(see MALLEE)
duff
flying the Australian
flag (see FLAG[1])
furph
galah
game as a meat-ant
(see MEAT-ANT)
get the rough end of the
pineapple (see
PINEAPPLE)
got Buckley's (see GOT
and BUCKLEY'S)
gumleaf band
have a joey in the
pouch (see JOEY)
have kangaroos in the
top paddock (see
KANGAROO)
hooroo
Hughie
illywhacker
jarrah-jerker

kanga cricket
kangaroo-hop
lagerphone
lamington drive
larrikin
mad as a cut snake
(see MAD)
mad as a gum-tree full
of galahs (see
GALAH)
motser
mozzie
mulga Bill
mullygrubber
Norm
no worries (see
WORRY)
-o
ocker
oil 4, 5
on one's pat (see PAT[4])
on the wallaby (see
WALLABY TRACK)
onya!
Orstralia
othersider
overlander
overland fish
oyster *adj.* 1
perish *n.*
picnic races
pig's (see PIG)
pike[2]
pissant
poddy-dodge
point the bone 2
poon[1, 2]
possie
post-and-rail tea
purler
quid
Rafferty's rules
red steer
rellie
Richard
ridge[2]
roll one's swag (or
bluey) (see ROLL)
roo bar
rort
rouse[2]
rubbity

sambo
Sandgroper
sanger
scale[4]
screamer
seppo
she 2
she's right (see RIGHT)
shiralee
shivoo
short of a sheet of bark
(see SHORT)
shouse
show bag
skerrick
slanguage
sling the billy (see
BILLY)
snag[2]
snig
Speewah
starve the bardies! (or
crows! or lizards! or
roan bullock! etc.)
(see STARVE)
stir the possum (see
POSSUM)
stringybark cockatoo
stubby short of a
six-pack (see
STUBBY)
sundowner
tall poppy
Tantanoola tiger
tarpaulin muster
taw
Territory rig
tide is out (see TIDE)
tin arse
tothersider
touch the sides (see
TOUCH)
triantelope
troppo
turn-up for the books
(see TURN-UP)
two-pot screamer
uey
underground mutton
wacker
warrigal *n.* 4, *adj.*
water-scorcher

| | | |
|---|---|---|
| westie | (see WOULDN'T) | youse |
| woodser | wowse | you wouldn't read about |
| woop woop | yakka[1] | it (see READ) |
| wouldn't it! | yarra | ziff |

## E Computing

The words in this list, although not distinctively Australian, are a
sample of the words relating to computing that are contained in the
body of this dictionary. Some of them have developed purely from the
world of computing, whereas others are words that computing has
taken from standard English and provided with specific computing-
related meaning.

| | | |
|---|---|---|
| AIDS[2] | hack | random-access memory |
| Algol | handshake 2 | real time |
| BASIC | hard disk | reboot |
| binary code | housekeeping 4 | ROM |
| bit[4] | intelligent 3 | semiconductor memory |
| boot[1] v. 3 | job-control language | speech recognition |
| byte | kill v. 6 | supercomputer |
| CD-ROM | kilobyte | systems analysis |
| check digit | LAN | touch screen |
| COBOL | language 4 | transputer |
| configuration 5 | logic 4 | Trojan Horse |
| cps 1 | mainframe | UNIX |
| database | megabyte | wide area network |
| data bus | MIDI | wild card |
| DOS | mips | wimp[2] |
| download | modem | wraparound |
| dynamic 4 | node 6 | WYSIWYG |
| echo n. 5 | null 3 | |
| field n. 13 | output | |
| Fortran | Postscript | |
| global 3 | programming language | |

## F Fauna

Names derived wholly or partly from Aboriginal languages are
indicated by an asterisk.

| | | |
|---|---|---|
| animated stick | barramundi* | bogong* |
| anvil bird | bearded dragon | boobook* |
| apostle[2] | bettong* | brain-fever bird |
| archer-fish | bicycle lizard | bridled nail-tailed |
| bandy-bandy* | bilby* | wallaby |
| barking lizard | bird-eating spider | bristlebird |
| barking spider | bobuck* | brolga* |

brumby*
budgerigar*
butcherbird
callop*
catbird
channel-billed cuckoo
cherry nose
chowchilla*
chuditch*
cobra[2]*
congolli*
corella*
corroboree frog*
cranky fan
cunjevoi[1]*
currawong*
dalgite*
desert chat
dibbler*
dingo*
dugite*
dunnart*
elegant parrot
elephant beetle
fiddler 3
firetail
floury baker
flying possum
fortescue
friar-bird
frogmouth
galah*
gang-gang*
gastric brooding frog
gibber bird*
gnow*
godwit
greengrocer 2
green leek
hairy-nosed wombat
happy family
happy jack
hard-gut
holy cross toad
honey-bag
itchy grub
jabiru
jacky winter
jelly blubber
jewel beetle
kakka
kangaroo*

kangaroo mouse*
koala*
kookaburra*
land mullet
laughing owl
lavender bug
leaden flycatcher
leaf-cutting bee
letter-winged kite
lily-trotter
lobby[2]
log-runner
long tom 2
lousy jack
lowan*
luderick*
mado*
magnetic termite
marron*
marsupial lion
megapode
metallic starling
mickey[3]
mopoke 1, 2
morwong*
mountain devil 1
mouse spider
mudskipper
muk-muk*
mulgara*
mulloway*
mullygrub
musk duck
mutton-fish
nabarlek*
nankeen kestrel
nannygai*
native companion
noisy pitta
noolbenger*
norne*
numbat*
old wife
orange horseshoe bat
owlet nightjar
paddymelon[1]*
pardalote
perentie*
phalanger
phascogale

pheasant coucal
pie-dish beetle
pilot bird
pinky* 1
pipi
platypus frog
pobblebonk
poddy mullet*
policeman bird
policeman fly
potoroo*
pouched mouse
powerful owl
pratincole
pretty face
prion
procession caterpillar
quarrion*
quokka*
quoll*
racehorse goanna
rain bird
rajah shieldrake
rat-kangaroo
razor-grinder
restless flycatcher
rhinoceros beetle
rifle fish
St Andrew's Cross
  spider
Samson fish
sand goanna
satin bowerbird
scissors-grinder
screaming-woman
  bird
semaphore crab
sergeant baker
settler's clock
sleepy lizard
smoker 1
soapie 1
soldier ant
soldier crab
spangled drongo
squatter pigeon
squeaker
squirrel glider
stick-nest rat
stinkbird

storm bird
stripey
sugar ant
sweetlip
tailor-bird
taipan*
tallegalane*
tammar*
tarwhine*
Tasmanian devil
Tasmanian tiger
tattler
teraglin*
thickhead 2
thorny devil
thresher shark
thunderbird
thylacine

tillywurti*
tommy rough
toolache*
tooth-billed cat bird
topknot pigeon
tree duck
tree-kangaroo
triller
trumpeter 2
tuan*
twenty-eight
Ulysses butterfly
Union Jack 2
wallaby 1*
wallaroo*
wambenger*
wanderer
warrigal 1*

water dragon
water-holding frog
wattle goat-moth
wee juggler*
whalebird
whimbrel
whipbird
whisky drinker
whistling dick
whistling tree-frog
white death
witchetty*
wobbegong*
wombat*
yabby*
yellow monday
zebra duck
zygomaturus

## G Flora

Names derived wholly or partly from Aboriginal languages are
indicated by an asterisk.

adjigo*
alunqua*
anthouse plant
apple dumpling
Austral ladies' tresses
bacon-and-eggs
ballart*
bangalay*
bangalow
batswing coral tree
beaked hakea
beefwood
belah*
bendee*
biddy bush
billy buttons
bimble*
bindi-eye*
birdlime tree
bird orchid
bitter bark
bladder saltbush
blind-your-eye

bloodwood
bluebeard
blue devil
blue fairies
boab
bolwarra*
bombax
boobialla*
boonaree*
booyong*
boronia
bottle tree
brigalow*
cabbage tree
caladenia
camel poison
canagong*
candlebark
carbeen*
caterpillar flower
cat head
cheese tree
chef's hat correa

chocolate lily
cider gum
coachwood
colane*
compass bush
conesticks
conkerberry*
cooba*
coolibah*
cooloolah*
copper cups
corkbark
corkscrew grass
cotton tree
cudgerie*
cumbungi*
cunjevoi*
curl flower
curly wigs
dancing orchid
dead finish 1
desert lime

digger's delight
dillon bush*
donkey orchid
early Nancy
false sarsaparilla
fan-flower
feather flower
fern root
fever bark
finger cherry
finger lime
firewheel tree
flannel flower
flying duck orchid
foam bark
geebung*
ghost gum
giant lily
gidgee* 1
gimlet 2
golden moths
greenhood
gruie*
gungurru*
gunyang*
gympie*
heartleaf
honey flower
horizontal[2]
horseradish tree
hyacinth orchid
Illawarra flame-tree
illyari*
jarrah*
jitta*
joonda*
kangaroo thorn*
kapok tree
karara*
karkalla*
karpe*
karri*
kerosene bush
kurrajong*
lady's finger
lambs' tails
lapunyah*
lawyer palm
leschenaultia
lignum

mallee*
mallet[2]*
man fern
marara*
marlock*
marri*
minnerichi*
Moreton Bay fig
morrel*
mosquito orchid
mottlecah
mountain devil 2
mugga*
mulga*
mulla mulla*
mungite*
muntry*
munyeroo*
murnong*
muskwood
muzzlewood
myall[2]*
nardoo*
native bread
native cherry
native cranberry
native cumquat
native grape
native mulberry
native orange
nelia*
nepenthes
New South Wales
    Christmas bush
niggerhead 2
nonda*
nutmeg 2
nuytsia
old man saltbush
old man's beard
pandanny
paper daisy
parakeeliya*
parson's bands
penda*
pepper 5
pindan*
pisonia
pituri*
poached egg daisy

porcupine
portulaca
possum banksia
poverty bush
prickly moses
punty*
quandong*
rabbit-ears
raspberry jam
red heart 2,3
Rhododendron lochae
robin redbreast 3
roly-poly 2
rosella[2]
rose of the west
royal bluebell
sago grass
sarsaparilla
sassafras 3
scarlet running
    postman
scribbly gum
sea-urchin hakea
shatterwood
smokebush
snake flower
snake orchid
snappy gum
sneezewood
snottygobble
snow-in-summer
soap tree
soursob
spider orchid
spinning gum
stagger-weed
sticky wattle
stinging tree
stinking Roger
Sturt's desert rose
sugar gum
sundew
sun orchid
sunshine wattle
supplejack
tallow-wood
tanglefoot
tar tree
tassel fern
three-cornered jack

tinsel lily
trigger plant
tuart*
tuckeroo*
turpentine 2
umbrella fern
underground orchid
vanilla lily
varnish wattle
waddy tree*
waddywood*
wait-a-while
walking-stick palm

wallum*
wandoo*
waratah*
warrigal 3*
wax flower
whalebone tree
whipstick
wig tree-fern
wild cauliflower
wild pineapple
wilga*
windmill grass
wirilda*

wirra[2]*
wombat berry
wonga[1]*
wongai*
woody pear
yacca*
yam daisy
yapunyah*
yarran*
yate*
yelka*
zigzag wattle

## H  Historical

This list contains words relating to Australian history.

assignment 4
bark hut
birthstain
blackbird[2]
blackbirding
black crow
black game
black line
box[1] n. 4b
brickfielder
cabbage-tree hat
cabbage-tree mob
canary 2
certificate 2
chain-gang
chief 1c
colonial experience
colonial youth
colony 2
conditional
   emancipation
contact 5
convict n. 2,3
convict boy
convict colony
cornstalk 1
crimean shirt
croppy
currency 2
currency lad
dispersal
dog-licence

dump[2]
eight, ten, two, and a
   quarter
First Fleeter
free adj. 1b, c
free-selection
fuzzy wuzzy
gentleman convict
gumsucker
holey dollar
horse duffer
hut n. 3, v.
ironed gang
joe[2]
Kanaka
king[4]
knight of the road
lag[3]
larrikin
legitimate n.
lime-juicer
Mechanics' Institute
mob n. 5a
moratorium 3
nasho
native 2,3
new chum
old chum
original adj. 2
penal colony
pomegranate 3
Protector

public servant 1
pure merino
reffo
remittance man
reward claim
robbery under arms
rush-oh
savage n. 1b
School of Arts
select v. 2
servant 3
settle 12c
sevener
shanty[1] 3a
shepherd n. 3, v. 3a
snipe-shooting
squat v. 3
station 7a,b
sterling adj. 4, n. 2
suss[2]
swy 1
ticket-of-leave
transport v. 2, n. 4
triangle 5
Vandemonia
walkabout 1
White Australia Policy
wirri
yoolahng
zac 1

## I Landscape

Names derived wholly or partly from Aboriginal languages are indicated by an asterisk.

backblocks
back country
billabong*
bombora*
brigalow country*
  (see BRIGALOW)
brush²
channel country
cowal*
crabhole 2
Darling shower
dead men's graves
debil debil
Deep North
doctor 4
down country
dry heart
dry track
fern gully
Fremantle doctor
gibber country*
gibber plain*
gilgai*
gnamma*
grazing country
green ban
green drought
gully 2

homeland centre
hot wind
inside country
jingera*
Kelly country
mainlander
mallee country*
  (see MALLEE)
malee desert*
  (see MALLEE)
mallee district*
  (see MALLEE)
mallee land*
  (see MALLEE)
mallee scrub*
  (see MALLEE)
mickery*
morning glory 2
mound spring
mud spring
mulga*
mulga country, flats,
  scrub, etc. (see
  MULGA)
mutton-bird gales
never-never
niggerhead 1
outback

pindan*
pound³ 2
rainforest
razor-back
red centre
red heart 1
rock-hole
scrub²
scrub plain
soak n. 3
spinifex country
stone-country
sub-artesian
tally-walka*
tier 2
tiger country
turkey-bush scrub
up-country
vine scrub
wallum 2*
whipstick
wilderness area
willy willy*
wodgil*

## J Multicultural

This list of words relating mainly to food shows the extensive contribution of non-Anglo-Celtic cultures to Australian society.

antipasto
ashram
Asianisation
bagel
baklava
bean curd
bean shoot
biriani
Bombay duck
brinjal
cabana²

cabanossi
calamari
candlenut
cannelloni
cappuccino
cardamom
cassata
Ceylon moss
chapati
chèvre
chick-pea

chilli
chilli con carne
chillied
chow-chow
coconut milk
coriander
cumin
curry¹
curry-powder
dhal
dim sum

doona
felafel
fenugreek
feta
filo pastry
French stick
futon
garam masala
gazpacho
gelato
green gram
halva
jaggery
karaoke
kebab
kedgeree
kibble
lambada
lasagne
lentil
lychee
mantra
moussaka
mozzarella
mung
nacho
nashi
noodle[1]
okra
oregano
ouzo
paella
pancetta
pappadam
paprika

parmesan
pasta
pastrami
pâté
patisserie
patty
pepperoni
pilau
pimento
pimiento
pine nut
pita
pitta[2]
pizza
pizzeria
plantain
pocket bread
pumpernickel
quiche
ratatouille
ravioli
red pepper
retsina
rice-paper
risotto
rollmop
saffron
sake[2]
salami
salsa
samosa
satay
sauerkraut
saveloy
schnitzel

sesame
shiatsu
shish kebab
souvlaki
spring roll
taco
tagliatelle
t'ai chi
tamarillo
tamarind
tandoor
tandoori
tantra
taramasalata
taro
tarragon
temper *v.* 4
tempura
tequila
terrine
tofu
tortilla
trattoria
turkey lolly
turkish delight
turmeric
water chestnut
wok
yoga
yoghurt
yumcha
zabaglione
zucchini

## K New Words

This list is a sampling of recent additions to our language.

abled
Aboriginalisation
acca
AC/DC
advertorial
ageist
agro-politician
AID
AIDS[1]
AIDS[2]
animalist

animal libber
antibody negative
antibody positive
antique *v.*
antivenom
ARC
aromatherapy
artist 4
-athon
buy back the farm (see FARM)

cellular telephone
deconstruction
detailing
dietary fibre
dink[3]
direct billing
drivetime
econocrat
EEO
electronic mail
enterprise bargaining

fantasy 4
fanzine
-fest
gap insurance
-gate
gender gap
grey power
-holic
in vitro fertilisation
irradiation
kidult
Mabo
medifraud
Mexican wave
mickey mouse
microwave proof
Mondayitis
mortgage belt
nappy valley
negative gearing
neo-mort
New Right
-nik
nimby
orc
out$^1$ $v$. 4
out$^2$
-out
overservicing
palimony
paparazzo
passive smoking
people meter
positive
    discrimination
post-structuralism

post-traumatic stress
    disorder
power dressing
premenstrual
    syndrome
productivity
    bargaining
PWA
reflexology
RSI
safe sex
scheduled fee
scientism
sci-fi
self-publishing
sell off the farm (see
    FARM)
semiotics
sexual harassment
sex worker
s/he
shuttle diplomacy
SIDS
ska
sledge$^2$
smoke-free
spontaneous
    generation
STD 2
sunrise industry
talk down 2 (see TALK)
talkfest
talking book
talk show
talk up 2 (see TALK)
tall-poppy syndrome

telegenic
telemarketing
televangelist
teno
terra nullius
thanatology
think-tank
-thon
thrash $n$.
thrill $adj$.
time-share
tisk-tisk (see TSK-TSK!)
toxic shock syndrome
toy boy
transfer fee
transsexual
triple antigen
ungreen
unputdownable
unsafe sex
unwaged
up-market
upwardly mobile
vanity publishing
vegan
vibrator
virtual reality
voice-over
waged
wall-to-wall 2
win-win
workshop $v$.
wuss
yuppie
zidovudine

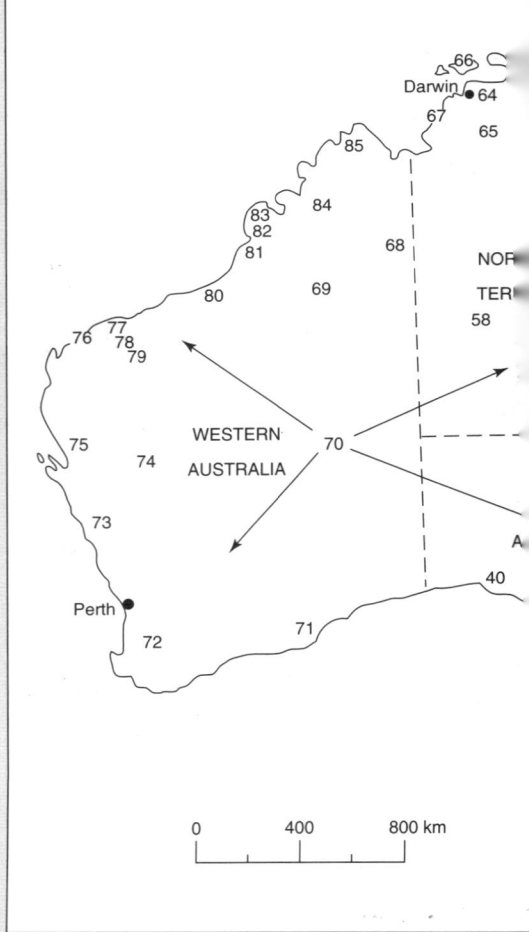

Darwin

WESTERN AUSTRALIA

Perth

NOR

TER

58

A

0   400   800 km